THE
MACMILLAN
ENCYCLOPEDIA

List of Contributors

MILLENNIUM AND SUBSEQUENT EDITIONS

Editors
Alan Isaacs BSc, PhD, DIC, ACGI
Elizabeth Martin MA
Jonathan Law BA

Computerization
John Daintith BSc, PhD
Anne Stibbs BA

Illustrations and Picture Research
Linda Wells
Catherine Whitaker

Design
Wilf Dickie

Artwork
Hardlines Charlbury, Oxfordshire
Lynn Williams

FIRST EDITION

Editor
Alan Isaacs BSc, PhD, DIC, ACGI

Subject Editors
Barbara Barrett BA
John Daintith BSc, PhD
Thomas Hill Long MA
Elizabeth Martin MA
David Pickering MA
Judith Ravenscroft BA, MPhil
Michael Scott Rohan BA
Jennifer Speake MA, MPhil
Edmund Wright MA, DPhil

Assistant Editors
Hazel Egerton BA
Robert Hine BSc, MSc
Jonathan Hunt MA
Susan O'Neill BSc
Carol Russell BSc
Mary Shields BA, PhD
Jacqueline Smith BA
Anne Stibbs BA
Elizabeth Tootill BSc
Maurice Waite BA
Rosalind Fergusson BA

Illustration and Design
Barbara Barrett BA
Jennifer Speake MA, MPhil
Robert Updegraff (colour section design)

Picture Research
Juliet Brightmore (consultant)
Jacqueline Smith BA
Valerie Walker

Artwork (black and white)
Oxford Illustrators Ltd

Contributors
J. E. Abbott BA
Francis Absalom BSc
Joan Ashley BA, LRAM
Howard H. R. Bailes BA, PhD
Jill Bailey MSc
Helen Banks BSc
Antoinette Bates BA
Alison Bideleux MA
T. J. Boardman BA
Charles Boyle BA, BLitt
O. M. C. Buchan BA, MA
W. P. Cass MA
Kathleen Clarke BA
P. B. Clarke MA, MPhil
J. A. Cudden MA, BLitt
S. R. Elliot BComm
Martin Elliott BSc, ARCS
Jane A. Freeman BA
B. J. Golding BA, PhD
Chris Gray BA
M. B. Hamilton BSc, MPhil
P. W. Hanks MA
Stephen G. Harris, Attorney at Law
G. R. Hawting BA, PhD
Vincent Hetreed MA
Anne Holloway BA
Glyn Alyn Hughes BA
Valerie Illingworth BSc, MPhil
Yvonne Jacobs MA
J. B. Katz MA
Helen Kearsley BA
Susan Laker BA
N. R. M. de Lange MA, DPhil
David Langford MA
Marise Larkin MA
Richard Latham Barrister at Law
Bridget Loney MA
Michael MacCarthy-Morrogh BA
Iseabail Macleod MA
Martin Meggs BA, MSc
Denise Mitchell BA
J. S. Morris BA
Said Mosteshar-Gharai BSc, MSc, PhD, ACA
Jocelyn Murray BA, PhD
H. M. Nahmad MLitt
Ruth D. Newell MSc, DIC

Pastor Stuart Olyott BD, MTheol, ALBC
John Oram MSc
Stephanie L. Pain BSc
Ann Palmer MA, MPhil
Christopher D. Parker BA, DipLib
Kathleen A. Pavelko BA, MA
I. G. Pears BA
Volodimir Pechenuk MA
David A. Ramsay BSc, MB, ChB
Brian Russell Davis MA, LLB, Barrister at Law
Elfrida Savigear BSc
Michael Scherk BA
Kenneth Scholes
Nigel Seller MA
J. H. Shaw
N. Shiel BA, MPhil, FRNS
Adrian Shubert BA, MA
Laurel Thomas Silantien AB, MM
R. L. Sims BA, PhD
Richard Smith BSc, MB, ChB
Jane Southern BSc, MSc
Stella Stiegeler BSc
B. R. Stratton BSc, PhD
Stephanie Stuart BA
Eric A. Taylor MA, MB, BChir, MRCP, MRCPsych
Ivan Vince BSc, MSc, PhD
Margaret Wallis MA
C. S. P. Wolstenholme MA
Rebecca Woodell BA, MS
R. Wrigley BA

Advisers
Stephen Brooks MA
Jacqueline Bruce
Richard Elms
Clive Farahar
A. M. Genton MD
Lawrence Hills BSc
Michael Naish
Sally Naish
Michael D. Robson
J. T. R. Sharrock PhD
Margaret Spencer
Mike Torbe BA
Basil Wright MA

Keyboarders
Jessica Scholes
Elizabeth Bonham
Gwyneth Shaw
Sandra McQueen
Brenda Tomkins
Linda Wells

THE MACMILLAN ENCYCLOPEDIA

MACMILLAN

First published 1981 by Macmillan, London

This revised edition
published 2002 by Macmillan
an imprint of Pan Macmillan Ltd
Pan Macmillan, 20 New Wharf Road, London N1 9RR
Basingstoke and Oxford
Associated companies throughout the world
www.panmacmillan.com

ISBN 0 333 908139

A CIP catalogue record for this book is available from
the British Library.

Typeset by Market House Books Limited
Printed and bound in Great Britain by The Bath Press, Bath

Picture Credits

Black and White
The following copyrighted photographs appear in this Encyclopedia: Alfred Gregory/Camera Press London 948; Angela Silvertop/Hutchison Picture Library 663; Anthony Kersting, London 29, 36, 47, 196, 227, 361, 508, 517, 636, 650, 681, 762, 768, 837, 864, 896, 966, 1096, 1215; Arthur Christiansen/FLPA-Images of Nature 393; B. Borrell/FLPA-Images of Nature 826; B. Castillo/Camera Press London 166; Barnaby's Picture Library 843, 1237 (top right); Barnaby's Picture Library/Brian Gibbs 1081; Barnaby's Picture Library/Juliette Soester 562; Barnaby's Picture Library/Mario Frova 347; Barnaby's Picture Library/Mrs. E. Preston 317; Barnaby's Picture Library/Peter Murphy 1002; Barnaby's Picture Library/Ray Roberts 1298; Barnaby's Picture Library/Rod Dallas-Smith 438; Barnaby's Picture Library/W.F. Meadows 1317; Bernard Régent/The Hutchison Picture Library 1292; Bob Penn/Camera Press London 916; C. Carvalho/FLPA-Images of Nature 28; Camera Press London 89, 143, 408, 696, 789, 815, 931, 975, 1294; Carl R. Sams II/Still Pictures 222; Charles Ira Sachs/Camera Press London 1249; Chris Duffy/Camera Press London 670; Clare Hume/Camera Press London 1301; Cyril Maitland/Camera Press London 884; D. Haigh/FLPA-Images of Nature 44; Dave Watts/Still Pictures 673; David Hosking/FLPA-Images of Nature 1328; Department of Clinical Radiology, Salisbury District Hospital/Science Photo Library 1360; Derek Bayes/Camera Press London 757; Ed Reschke/Still Pictures 1302; Eye of Science/Science Photo Library 994; Francis Starner/Camera Press London 1307; Frank W. Lane/FLPA-Images of Nature 1193; Fritz Siedel/FLPA-Images of Nature 1183; Godfrey Argent 203; Gregory Sams/Science Photo Library 475; Herbert Giradet/Still Pictures 184; Horace Bristol/Camera Press London 268; Horst Tappe/Camera Press London 327; ILN/Camera Press London 340; Irene Vandermolen/L. Lee Rue/FLPA-Images of Nature 614; J. Horner/The Hutchison Picture Library 183; J.C. Allen/FLPA-Images of Nature 441; Jacques Delacour/Still Pictures 1116; Jeremy Horner/The Hutchison Picture Library 675, 1108; Jitendra Arya/Camera Press London 876; John Hatt/The Hutchison Picture Library 1211; Jorgen Schytte/Still Pictures 365; JS Library International 415, 945, 1236; Klaus Francke/Camera Press London 213; Klein Hubert/Still Pictures 693; L. Lee Rue/FLPA-Images of Nature 211, 606, 1371; Linda Lewis/FLPA-Images of Nature 1119; Lynwood M. Chace/FLPA-Images of Nature 920; M. & C. Denis-Huot/Still Pictures 199; M. MacIntyre/The Hutchison Picture Library 173, 1065; M. Rock/The Hutchison Picture Library 1182; Mark Carwardine/Still Pictures 685; Mark Edwards/Still Pictures 204, 215, 1163, 1168; Martin B. Withers/FLPA-Images of Nature 566, 1024, 1175; Martin Smith/FLPA-Images of Nature 899; Martin Wright/Still Pictures 1105; Mary Evans Picture Library 37, 96, 105, 131, 136, 154, 192, 206, 209, 219, 244, 261, 263, 333, 352, 383, 387, 552, 563, 719, 725, 737, 738, 751, 798, 954, 1036, 1040, 1041, 1053, 1061, 1095, 1237 (top left), 1322, 1340, 1352, 1363; Mary Evans Picture Library/Explorer 125; Mary Evans Picture Library/Ida Kar Collection 579; Melanie Friend/The Hutchison Picture Library 677, 732; Michael Clark/FLPA-Images of Nature 929; Michel Gunther/Still Pictures 1060; N. Dennis–Wildlife Pictures/Still Pictures 810; Nancy Durrell McKenna/The Hutchison Picture Library 537; NASA/Science Photo Library 1173; Nick de Morgoli/Camera Press London 976; Nigel Sitwell/The Hutchison Picture Library 101; P. Moszynski/The Hutchison Picture Library 849; Peter Yates/Science Photo Library 1310; Philippe Plailly/Science Photo Library 1113; Photo AKG London/Burgerbibliothek, Bern 1062; Photo AKG London/Städelsches Kunstinstitut, Frankfurt 1302 (bottom); Photo AKG London 110, 144, 158 (bottom), 165 (top), 195, 205, 241, 281, 285, 289, 394, 449, 575, 588, 590, 591, 598, 724, 793, 875, 886, 889, 891, 926, 937, 983, 1149, 1221, 1269, 1277, 1332, 1341, 1349, 1361, 1374; Photo AKG London/Erich Lessing/Musée du Louvre, Paris 52; Photo AKG London/AP 963, 1010, 1085; Photo AKG London/Archives Nationales, Paris 659; Photo AKG London/Biblioteca Ambrosiana, Milan 727; Photo AKG London/Biblioteca Marucelliana, Florence 493; Photo AKG London/Bibliothèque Nationale, Paris 10, 1208; Photo AKG London/British Museum, London 141; Photo AKG London/Camerphoto/Galleria dell'Accademia, Venice 63; Photo AKG London/Erich Lessing 234, 938; Photo AKG London/Erich Lessing/Musée du Louvre, Paris 176; Photo AKG London/Erich Lessing/Beethoven-Haus, Bonn 133; Photo AKG London/Erich Lessing/Galleria degli Uffizi, Florence 787; Photo AKG London/Erich Lessing/Gesellschaft der Musikfreunde, Vienna 856; Photo AKG London/Erich Lessing/Kunsthistorisches Museum, Vienna 764; Photo AKG London/Erich Lessing/Musée du Louvre, Paris 66, 303, 425, 1281; Photo AKG London/Erich Lessing/National Archaeological Museum, Athens 832; Photo AKG London/Erich Lessing/National Museum of Archaeology, Naples 32; Photo AKG London/Erich Lessing/private collection, France 252; Photo AKG London/Erich Lessing/Vojvodjanski Muzej, Novi Sad 817; Photo AKG London/Galleria Nazionale, Palazzo Barberini, Rome 577; Photo AKG London/Gert Schütz 829; Photo AKG London/Heiner Heine 1045; Photo AKG London/Heinrich Hoffmann 445; Photo AKG London/Institute of Directors, London 507; Photo AKG London/Jean-Louis Nou/Government Museum, Mathura 866; Photo AKG London/Keith Collie 72; Photo AKG London/Kestner-Museum, Hannover 336; Photo AKG London/NASA 64; Photo AKG London/Paul Almasy 295, 513, 1094; Photo AKG London/private collection, Frankfurt am Main 1190; Photo AKG London/Pushkin Museum, Moscow 1257; Photo AKG London/Schlöss Charlottenburg 869; Photo AKG London/Städelsches Kunstinstitut, Frankfurt 523; Photo AKG London/State Hermitage, St. Petersburg 1083; Photo AKG London/Stefan Diller/San Francesco Museo, Assisi 619; Photo AKG London/Stefan Drechsel 722; Photo AKG London/University Library, Heidelberg 274; Photo AKG London/Vatican Museum, Rome 712; Photo AKG London/Victoria and Albert Museum, London 586; Photo AKG London/Walter Grunwald 35; Photo AKG/European Parliament 1195; Popperfoto 74, 79, 90, 180, 191, 253, 258, 271, 313, 359, 390, 459, 461, 498, 530, 546, 547, 602, 654, 666, 709, 745, 765, 769, 950, 1004, 1043, 1117, 1133, 1158, 1250; Popperfoto/AFP/Gerard Julien 661; Popperfoto/Donald McLeish 969; Popperfoto/Duncan Willetts 807; Popperfoto/Jarche 375 (bottom); Popperfoto/Langrish 1020; Popperfoto/Paul McFegan/Sportsphoto 277; Popperfoto/Reuters 369, 1237 (bottom right), 1297; Popperfoto/Reuters/Bob Collier 1157; Popperfoto/Reuters/Corine Dufka 1088; Popperfoto/Reuters/Jose Manuel Ribeiro 443; Popperfoto/Reuters/Nathalie Koulischer 1367; Popperfoto/Reuters/Pascal Volery 1067; Putao/Still Pictures 941; R. Van Nostrand/FLPA-Images of Nature 914; Ray Roberts/Camera Press London 1074; Richard Harrington/Camera Press London 399; Richard Open/Camera Press London 1321; Robert Valarcher/Still Pictures 255; Roger Clark/Camera Press London 846; Roger Tidman/FLPA-Images of Nature 728; Roland Seitre/Still Pictures 229, 492, 512; Ronald Thompson/FLPA-Images of Nature 1350; S. Errington/The Hutchison Picture Library 373, 428; S. McCutcheon/FLPA-Images of Nature 454; Serge Dumont/Still Pictures 1191; Shehzad Noorani/Still Pictures 115; Sheila Terry/Science Photo Library 1068; Silvestris/FLPA-Images of Nature 1; Stephen Pern/The Hutchison Picture Library 521; Stewart Mark/Camera Press London 158 (top), 784; Still Pictures/EIA 1335; T. Domico/Still Pictures 785 (middle right); The Fotomas Index UK 20, 160, 165 (bottom), 235, 236, 246, 259, 370, 375 (top), 642, 651, 688, 877, 959, 990, 1030, 1121, 1132, 1237 (bottom left), 1247, 1333, 1370; Theodore Wood/Camera Press London 470; Thomas D. Mangelsen/Still Pictures 993; Thomas Raupach/Still Pictures 773; Tony Souter/The Hutchison Picture Library 1144; Ulrich Baumgarten/Vario Press/Camera Press London 1070, 1154; Werner Forman Archive 198, 653, 697, 799, 927, 998, 1137; Werner Forman Archive/British Museum, London 102, 1289; Werner Forman Archive/Cairo Museum 1278; Werner Forman Archive/Field Museum of Natural History, Chicago 1151; Werner Forman Archive/Gulistan Imperial Library, Teheran 699; Werner Forman Archive/Museum Fur Volkerkunde, Berlin 621; Werner Forman Archive/National Museum of Anthropology, Mexico 805; Werner Forman Archive/National Museum, Delhi 297; Werner Forman Archive/private collection 4, 1025; Xavier Eichaker/Still Pictures 842

Colour
Plate I Oxford Scientific Films Ltd.; Plate II Paul Cooper/Tony Lodge.; Plate III Artwork: Hilary Burn. Photograph: H. Schrempp/Frank Lane Picture Agency.; Flags Barclays Bank International Ltd.; Maps Jon Beck; Endpapers Artwork: Barry/Fallon Design.

Every endeavour has been made to obtain permission to use copyright material. The publishers would appreciate errors or omissions being brought to their attention.

Foreword to the First Edition by the Rt Hon Harold Macmillan (later Lord Stockton)

In 1877 my great-uncle Alexander Macmillan published Autenrieth's *Homeric Dictionary*. This standard work of reference is still available (though no longer, alas, at its original price of six shillings). In the course of a hundred years many dictionaries and encyclopedias have appeared over the imprint of Macmillan. They have dealt, for instance, with Quotations, with Music and Musicians, and with many more specialised subjects such as Educational Media, Labour Biography and even Diseased English. But the present work is our first attempt to produce a comprehensive general encyclopedia covering the whole field of human knowledge within the compass of a single volume. This is indeed a formidable task, for in these hundred years progress in science and technology has been vast and all too often bewildering. It is my hope and belief—and I speak as one whose Fellowship of the Royal Society is more a mark of his respect for the Sciences than of any personal proficiency in them—that the articles in these pages upon such matters, clearly written in precise and reasonably simple terms, will serve to alleviate that bewilderment. Nor is it only upon scientific questions that this work should provide instant answers. The team of editors has drawn upon a wide range of authoritative skills in compiling succinct entries upon many other aspects of the physical world, upon men and women, upon the arts, upon the ideas which we need to understand in order to appreciate the intellectual currents of our time. More than usual care has been taken to ensure that the hundreds of illustrations, many of them in colour, should enlighten the mind as well as please the eye. Moreover this encyclopedia, taking advantage of the technology which it is one of its functions to elucidate, has been compiled with the aid of a computer, which vastly simplifies the task of revising subsequent editions and keeping them up to date. Accordingly, I have every hope that this new encyclopedia will have a fair chance of following Autenrieth's precedent and being on sale in a hundred years' time. Be that as it may, there is no doubt in my mind that it will help to provide thousands of readers with those many rudiments of knowledge without which even the greatest wisdom is powerless to act.

Preface to the First Edition

'I have taken all knowledge to be my province.'
(Francis Bacon in a letter to Lord Burleigh)

Following Bacon, we have tried in this entirely new encyclopedia to cover, in some 25 000 articles and almost 1.5 million words, the whole range of human activity—arts, sciences, ideas, beliefs, history, biography, and geography, as well as sports, hobbies, and pastimes. To accomplish this somewhat daunting undertaking we have made extensive use of our own computerized system, designed to assist in the compilation and typesetting of large reference books. This system has enabled us to create an easily and quickly updatable data base with automatic checking of cross references. It has also enabled us to compile the book by subject, rather than alphabetically, thus ensuring an even and consistent treatment within each subject. Automatic alphabetization meant that the rules of alphabetization could be laid down and followed without fear of human error.

To cover such a wide range of subjects in a relatively compact volume we have also been obliged to discipline our contributors and editors to provide the maximum amount of information in the space allotted to them and to confine themselves to facts rather than opinions. We were also faced with the problem of making complex and sometimes sophisticated concepts intelligible in a lim-ited space to readers with no specialized knowledge of a subject. Our solution to this problem has been guided by three principles. The first is not to distort the facts by oversimplification; the second is to avoid all forms of jargon and to write in simple nontechnical language comprehensible to the general reader; and the last is to ensure that the articles are sufficiently informative to be of value to students. It should however, be said that a one-volume general encyclopedia containing 25 000 articles cannot provide the depth of knowledge possible in a multivolume set. Each kind of encyclopedia fulfils its own purpose. This book is essentially for quick, easy, and accurate reference. Who was *Gurdjieff* and what did he believe? What is a *capybara* and what does it look like? When did *Martin Luther King* die and who killed him? Where is *Samarkand* and how many people live there? What is the theory of *relativity* about and what are its practical applications? How does Australian Rules *football* differ from Rugby football and what size ball is used in each? What is the *Theatre of the Absurd* and who are its chief exponents? It is to this kind of question that we have sought to provide precise and intelligible answers.

Finally, I would like to take this opportunity of thanking all the editors, contributors, and advisers whose industry enables me to claim the accuracy, wide scope, and comprehensibility essential to a reference book of this kind.

A.I. (1981)

Preface to this Edition

The Macmillan Encyclopedia was first published in 1981. It was revised in 1983 and every year from 1986 to 1998. Over these 17 years the encyclopedia established itself as a highly regarded standard reference work. To celebrate the new millennium the publishers decided that an entirely new edition should be produced by the same team that compiled it originally. In this new edition the page was redesigned and all the photographs were replaced. Editorially, we increased the text by over 100 000 words—adding over 700 new entries and expanding and updating many of the existing entries. A number of the new entries were longer articles on topics of general interest, such as *ethnic identity*, *medical ethics*, and *single-parent families*. The purpose of adding these broader topics was to complement the value of the book as a source of factual information by enhancing its interest for the browser.

In the editions for 2001, 2002, and 2003 we have updated the book by making the appropriate changes to existing entries and by adding new entries for topics that have been of particular interest during the year. In all these new editions, as in earlier versions, we have paid particular attention to the National Curriculum. Feedback from both teachers and pupils enables us to claim that *The Macmillan Encyclopedia* is unrivalled as a resource for school homework and projects. For the Millennium Edition, we also compiled a 19-page chronology covering the thousand years from 1000 to 1999. Since then we have made yearly additions to this chronology. The chronology does not attempt to provide a detailed history of the world. It is intended to pinpoint key events and to highlight human achievements in science and technology and the arts that have taken place during that period. Clearly in a fairly compressed space it is not possible to list every work of art by every artist and writer. For example, Shakespeare's 36 plays are not listed individually; instead, the dates of several representative plays and the First Folio of the 36 plays are given. In general, only the best-known one or two of the principal works of an artist, writer, etc., are listed. The history time line provides a context within which scientists and artists were excelling themselves.

A.I. (2002)

Notes

1. Cross references
The extensive use of cross references has made the book virtually self-indexing. The symbol ▷ preceding a word tells the reader that further information on the entry will be found at the article on the word indicated; a raised square (▫) tells the reader that an illustration relevant to the article will be found at or near the word so marked; the article itself at that word may also contain pertinent information. The colour plates, to which the reader may also be directed (e.g. *see* Plate I), are collected at the centre of the book, with the maps.

2. Chinese transliterations
This encyclopedia follows official Chinese practice in using the pinyin system of transliterating Chinese names. The Wade-Giles equivalent (formerly the system most commonly used in the English-speaking world) and, when it exists, the conventional Western name is given in brackets following the pinyin name. However, a small number of names are so well known in their Wade-Giles or conventional Western forms that it has become usual to retain these very familiar spellings. They are Canton, Chaing Kai-shek, China, Chou En-lai, Inner Mongolia, Mao Tse-tung, Sun Yat-sen, Tibet, Yangtze River, Yellow River.

3. Population figures
For towns and cities the population figures given refer, wherever possible, to the town or city proper rather than the urban agglomeration of which it forms part.

Kings and Queens of England (1066–1910) and of Scotland (1603–1910)

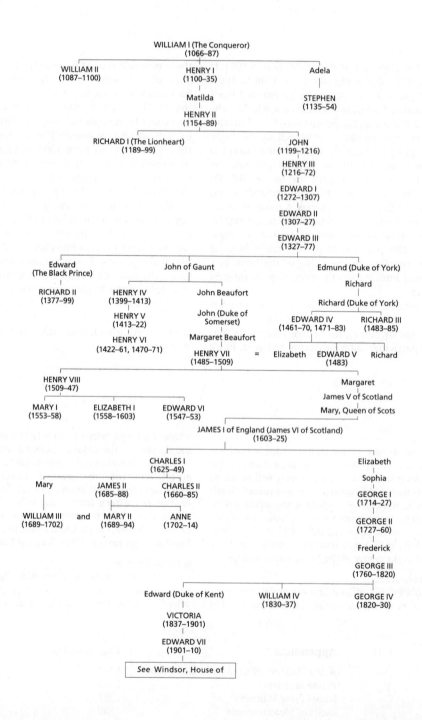

A

● **Aachen** ▶ (French name: Aix-la-Chapelle) 50 46N 06 06E A spa city in W Germany, in North Rhine-Westphalia near the Belgian and Dutch borders. It is an important industrial centre with iron and steel and textile industries. Its technical university was established in 1870.

History: it was the N capital of Charlemagne's empire and many Holy Roman Emperors were crowned in the cathedral (founded in 796 AD). It was annexed by France in 1801 and passed to Prussia (1815). Extensively damaged during World War II, it was the first major German city captured by the Allies (1944). Population (1996 est): 247 923.

● **Aalborg** ▷*See* Ålborg.

● **Aalesund** ▷*See* Ålesund.

● **Aalst** ▶ (French name: Alost) 50 47N 05 12E A town in N central Belgium, on the River Dender. It possesses the country's oldest town hall (begun 1200). Industries include textiles and brewing. Population (1991): 76 364.

● **Aalto, Alvar** ▶ (1898–1976) Finnish architect and furniture designer. Aalto established a distinctive "Finnish" style, with his use of timber and high pitched roofs. He established his reputation with the tuberculosis sanatorium (1923–33) at Paimio and founded his own furniture-making firm. After World War II he became increasingly individualistic and his hall of residence (1947–48) at the Massachusetts Institute of Technology (USA), the town hall at Säynätsalo (1949–52), and the Helsinki Hall of Culture (1958) are among his best work.

● **Aaltonen, Wäinö** ▶ (1894–1966) Finnish sculptor. He is known for the portrait sculptures of the Finnish Olympic runner Paavo Nurmi (1924) and of Sibelius (1928).

● **aardvark** ▶ (Afrikaans: earth pig) A nocturnal African mammal, *Orycteropus afer*, also called ant bear. It is about 1.5 m long, lives in grassland, and has a long snout, large ears, and a thick tail. Its strong claws are used to dig burrows and tear open the mounds of termites, which are picked up with its long sticky tongue. The aardvark is the only member of its order (*Tubulidentata*).

● **aardwolf** ▶ A nocturnal mammal, *Proteles cristatus*, that lives in open and bushy regions of southern and eastern Africa. It resembles a small striped hyena, about 50 cm high at the shoulder, but has small simple teeth suitable for feeding on termites (which form the main part of its diet). It spends the day in burrows, often those deserted by other animals. Family: *Hyaenidae* (hyenas); order: *Carnivora*.

● **Aarhus** ▷*See* Århus.

● **Aaron** ▶ In the Old Testament, the elder brother of Moses, whom he assisted as leader of the Israelites in their journey from Egypt to the Promised Land (Canaan). Although he yielded to demands to build the ▷golden calf, he and his descendants were confirmed by Jehovah as priests of the Hebrew nation.

● **abaca** ▶ (*or* Manila hemp) A fibre obtained from the leafstalks of a palmlike plant, *Musa textilis* of the Philippines, related to the banana. It is used for ships' ropes and similar objects as it is buoyant and resistant to the action of sea water.

● **abacus** ▶ A calculating device consisting of balls strung on wires or rods set in a frame. It is probably of Babylonian origin but its use declined in Europe with the introduction of ▷Arabic numerals in about the 10th century AD. It is still in use in the Middle East and Japan.

● **Abadan** ▶ 30 20N 48 15E A city in SW Iran, on an island in the Shatt (river) al-Arab. Much of Iran's oil is brought here by pipeline for refining or exporting, although its oil installations were heavily damaged during the Gulf War. Population (1991): 87 774.

● **Abakan** ▶ 53 43N 91 25E A city in S central Russia. It is in a coal-mining district and has metal, footwear, and food processing industries. Population (1995 est): 161 000.

● **abalone** ▶ A marine ▷gastropod mollusc belonging to the widely distributed family *Haliotidae*, of rocky coasts, also called ear shell or ormer. Up to 30 cm long, their dishlike ⬚shells have a row of holes along the outer edge through which deoxygenated water and waste products are expelled from the body. The large foot is considered a delicacy and the shells are used as mother-of-pearl for ornaments.

● **abandonment** ▶ In law, the voluntary relinquishment of property or rights without passing them on to another. For example, when a ship is left crewless and adrift, notice of abandonment can be issued to the insurers and a claim made for a constructive total loss (as opposed to an actual total loss if it sinks).

● **Abbadids** ▶ A Muslim dynasty in Andalusia (1023–91). Abbad I (reigned 1023–42) declared Seville's independence from Córdoba (1023) and by war and intrigue enlarged his territory. Abbad II (reigned 1042–69) continued this expansion, but failed to capture Córdoba. He is remembered for his delight in a flower garden planted over his enemies' skulls. Abbad III (d. 1095; reigned 1069–91), poet and king, made Seville an important cultural centre. The hostility of Spanish Christians forced him into an alliance with the ▷Almoravids, who later deposed him (1091) and exiled him to N Africa, where he died.

● **Abbado, Claudio** ▶ (1933–) Italian conductor. Associated with ▷La Scala, Milan, since 1971, he was also director of the London Sym-

aardvark ▶ This strange animal feeds entirely on termites and ants. It has very few teeth, which are weak and peg-shaped and specialized to cope with its diet.

phony Orchestra (1983–86) and of the Vienna State Opera (1986–91). In 1989 he succeeded von Karajan as conductor of the Berlin Philharmonic.

● **Abbas, Ferhat** ▷*See* Front de Libération nationale.

● **'Abbasids** ▶ A powerful dynasty of ▷caliphs, which ruled Islam from 750 AD to 1258. They were descended from Mohammed's uncle al-Abbas (566–652). In 750 they seized power from the Umayyads in Damascus and moved their capital to Baghdad. The 'Abbasids were known for their imposition of strict religious orthodoxy and their patronage of scholarship. Under ▷Harun ar-Rashid (786–809) the dynasty was at its peak. By the 10th century its powers were declining as provincial governors asserted their independence of Baghdad, which was still, however, an important commercial, cultural, and intellectual centre. Baghdad fell to the Mongols in 1258 and a branch of the 'Abbasids was installed in Cairo until that city fell to the Ottomans in 1517. The last of the line died in 1538.

● **Abbas (I) the Great** ▶ (1557–1628) Shah of Persia (1588–1628) of the Safavid dynasty, who greatly extended Persian territory by defeating the Uzbeks (1598) and the Ottomans (1605, 1618). He created a standing army, established the Persian capital of Isfahan, and patronized the arts.

● **Abbas II** ▶ (1874–1944) The last Khedive of Egypt (1892–1914), who supported nationalist opposition to British influence and was deposed when Britain declared a protectorate over Egypt in 1914.

● **Abbeville** ▶ 50 06N 1 57E A town in N France, in the Somme department situated near the mouth of the River Somme. It was here that Louis XII married Mary, sister of Henry VIII of England. Notable buildings include a gothic church (15th–17th centuries) and there are brewing, sugar-refining, and carpet industries. Population (latest est): 25 998.

● **Abbevillian** ▶ A culture of the Lower ▷Palaeolithic in Europe. It is characterized by crude stone hand axes made by hammering flakes off a flint with another stone. Named after ▷Abbeville in France, the Abbevillian also appears in Britain but in Africa similar early hand axes are designated ▷Acheulian.

● **Abbey Theatre** ▶ A Dublin theatre opened in 1904 and closely associated with the ▷Irish Literary Renaissance. Annie Horniman (1860–1937), a friend of W. B. Yeats, initiated the building of the theatre as a home for the Irish National Dramatic Society, a company founded by the actors Frank Fay (1870–1931) and his brother W. G. Fay (1872–1947). The Abbey produced plays by Yeats, Lady Gregory, Synge, George Russell (pseudonym AE; 1867–1935), Shaw, and O'Casey and gained an international reputation as a repertory theatre dedicated to performing mainly plays by Irish playwrights on Irish subjects. The original playhouse burnt down in 1951, but a new theatre was built and opened in 1966.

● **Abd Allah** ▶ (1846–99) Sudanese leader, known as the Khalifa (caliph). In 1885 he succeeded Muhammad Ahmad (*see* Mahdi, al-) as leader of the uprising against the Egyptian government of the Sudan. He was defeated by ▷Kitchener in 1898 and was killed in subsequent mopping-up operations.

● **'Abd al-Malik ibn Marwan** ▶ (c. 646–705 AD) Fifth ▷caliph (685–705) of the Umayyad dynasty, who subdued opposition to Umayyad rule of Islam. He defeated the northern Arab tribes in 691 and, with the help of his general al-Hajjaj, overcame resistance in Iraq (692). In 697 he captured Carthage. During his reign, Arabic became the administrative language of the empire and a new Muslim currency was coined.

● **'Abd ar-Rahman III an-Nasir** ▶ (891–961 AD) Emir (912–29) and first caliph (929–61) of the Umayyad Arab dynasty of Córdoba. He conquered Muslim Spain and campaigned against the Christian north: in 924 he took Pampalona, in Navarre, but was defeated by the King of León in 939. Under his rule, Córdoba became a noted centre of learning and the arts.

● **Abdelkader** ▶ (c. 1807–83) Algerian nationalist, who resisted the French invasion. He became Emir of Mascara in 1832 and gained control of the Oran region. Victories against the French (1835–37) facili-

tated a further extension of his territories. Defeated in 1841, he withdrew to Morocco and finally surrendered to the French in 1847.

● **abdication crisis** ▷*See* Edward VIII.

● **abdomen** ▶ In mammals (including humans), the region of the body extending from the lower surface of the diaphragm to the pelvis. The abdomen contains the intestines, liver, pancreas, kidneys, gall bladder, and—in females—the ovaries and womb. In arthropods, the abdomen is the posterior section of the body, which is usually segmented.

● **Abdulhamid II** ▶ (1842–1918) Sultan of the Ottoman Empire (1876–1909), notorious for the Armenian massacres (1894–96). Following defeat by Russia (1877), he dismissed parliament and suspended the constitution. Thereafter he ruled autocratically, instituting many administrative reforms, especially in education, and opposing Western interference in Ottoman affairs. The revolt of the ▷Young Turks in 1908 brought about his deposition.

● **Abdullah I** ▶ (1882–1951) Emir of Transjordan (1921–46) and first King of Jordan (1946–51). He was a leader of the Arab revolt against Turkish rule during World War I. He was assassinated.

● **Abdullah II** ▶ (1962–) King of Jordan (1999–). He is the eldest son of King ▷Hussein by his second wife, the English-born Princess Muna. He was named as heir to the throne (in place of his uncle, Prince Hassan) in the last days of Hussein's life. He is married to the Palestinian-born Queen Rania (1970–). The Crown Prince is Abdullah's half-brother, Prince Hamzah (1981–).

● **Abdul Rahman, Tunku** ▶ (1903–90) Malaysian statesman. He was the first prime minister of independent Malaya (1957–63) and of Malaysia (1963–70). He led the Alliance Party to electoral victory in 1955, becoming chief minister and negotiating Malayan independence from Britain (1957) and the formation of Malaysia (1963).

● **Abel** ▷*See* Cain.

● **Abel, Sir Frederick Augustus** ▶ (1827–1902) British chemist. He improved guncotton manufacture and helped Sir James Dewar (1842–1923) to invent cordite. Abel also invented an apparatus to determine the flashpoint of petroleum. He received the Bessemer medal (1897) for research into steel manufacture.

● **Abel, Niels Henrik** ▶ (1802–29) Norwegian mathematician. One of the great mathematical problems of Abel's day was to find a general solution for a class of equations called quintics. Abel proved that such a solution was impossible, but died before his achievement could be recognized.

● **Abelard, Peter** ▶ (1079–1142) French philosopher. His ill-fated marriage with Heloïse, niece of a canon of Paris, ended when Abelard was castrated by thugs hired by the canon (1118). He retired to a monastery and she became a nun. Abelard turned his powers as a logician to establishing a coherent relationship between faith and reason (*see* scholasticism). A fierce disputant, he was perpetually in trouble with the church authorities; his *Sic et Non* (*For and Against*) outraged opponents by listing points on which acknowledged authorities differed.

● **abelmosk** ▶ A flowering plant, *Hibiscus moschatus* (*H. abelmoschus*), native to India. It has large flowers with yellow petals and red centres and grows to a height of 60–180 cm. Abelmosk is cultivated for its seeds, which yield musk used in perfumes, and for its young fruits, which are used as vegetables. Family: *Malvaceae* (mallow family).

● **Abeokuta** ▶ 7 10N 3 26E A city in SW Nigeria. It is an important quarrying and agricultural centre but manufacturing is limited. Population (1996 est): 427 400.

● **Abercrombie, Sir (Leslie) Patrick** ▶ (1879–1957) British town planner and architect. His first venture was the replanning of Dublin (1913) but he is best known for his detailed schemes for London, *The County of London Plan* (1943) and *The Greater London Plan* (1944). Later plans include those for Edinburgh, Hull, and the West Midlands. He was professor at Liverpool University (1915–35) and London University (1935–46).

● **Abercromby, Sir Ralph** ▶ (1734–1801) British general, whose successes against the French in the Netherlands and the West Indies during the French Revolutionary Wars helped to restore the morale of the British army. He brilliantly organized the landing at Aboukir of the Anglo-Turkish force that drove the French out of Egypt but was killed in battle a few days later.

● **Aberdare** ► 51 43N 3 27W A town in South Wales, in the county borough of Rhondda, Cynon, Taff. Light industries, including the manufacture of electrical cables, have replaced coalmining as the principal economic activities. Population (1991): 29 040.

● **Aberdeen** ► **1.** 57 10N 2 04W A city and port in NE Scotland, in City of Aberdeen council area on the North Sea coast between the mouths of the Rivers Don and Dee. Aberdeen is a cathedral city with a university dating from 1494 (King's College). Fishing has always been important, as has the working of local granite; the "Granite City" provided stone for London's cobbled streets in the 18th century. Other industries include shipbuilding, paper making, textiles, chemicals, and engineering. Aberdeen's proximity to North Sea oil has transformed it into an important service centre for the oil industry. Aberdeen has well-known research institutes for fisheries, soils, and animal nutrition. Population (1996 est): 217 260. **2. City of Aberdeen** A council area in NE Scotland, established in 1996. Area: 186 sq km (72 sq mi). Population (1999 est): 213 070.

● **Aberdeen, George Hamilton-Gordon, 4th Earl of** ► (1784–1860) British statesman; prime minister (1852–55). He was foreign secretary in Sir Robert ▷Peel's Conservative government (1841–46) and supported the repeal of the ▷Corn Laws (1846), which led Peel's supporters to break away from the Conservative Party. Aberdeen succeeded Peel as leader of the "Peelites" (1850) and led a coalition government of Whigs and Peelites. He was forced to resign because of his mismanagement of the ▷Crimean War.

● **Aberdeen Angus** ► A breed of polled (naturally hornless) beef cattle, originating from NE Scotland. Short, stocky, and usually black (some have red coats), they are hardy and adapt well to different climates. Angus bulls are commonly mated with dairy breeds to produce a polled beef cross.

● **Aberdeenshire** ► A council area of NE Scotland, bordering on the North Sea. Under local government reorganization in 1975 the historic county of Aberdeenshire became part of Grampian Region. It was restored as an independent ▷unitary authority (with adjusted borders) in 1996. The City of Aberdeen forms a separate council area. Aberdeenshire consists of fertile lowlands in the NE rising to the Cairngorm and Grampian Mountains in the SW. Agriculture is important, especially sheep farming and stock raising. Fishing is a major source of income. Industries include fish processing, tourism, whisky distilling, and those associated with North Sea oil. Area: 6318 sq km (2439 sq mi). Population (1999 est): 226 260. Administrative centre: Aberdeen.

● **Aberdeen terrier** ▷See Scottish terrier.

● **Aberfan** ► 51 42N 3 21W A coalmining village in South Wales, in Merthyr Tydfil county borough. In 1966 mining waste from a giant slag heap engulfed part of the village (including the school), with the loss of 144 lives, including 116 children.

● **aberration** ► **1.** A defect in a lens or mirror that causes blurring or distortion of the image. The three most important types are spherical aberration, chromatic aberration, and ▷astigmatism. Spherical aberration is caused by rays from the outside of the lens or mirror being brought to a focus at a different point from those nearer to the centre. In chromatic aberration, different colours are focused at different points, since the refractive index of glass varies with the wavelength (see achromatic lens). **2.** An apparent displacement in the position of a heavenly body due to the motion of the observer with the earth in its orbit round the sun.

● **Aberystwyth** ► 52 25N 4 05W A resort in Wales, in Ceredigion on Cardigan Bay. A college of the University of Wales was established in 1872 and the National Library of Wales in 1911. Population (1991): 11 154.

● **Abidjan** ► 5 19N 4 00W The former capital of Côte d'Ivoire, off the Gulf of Guinea. Developed by the French in the 1920s, it became the capital in 1934. It is now an important port, linked to the sea by the Vridi Canal. The National University was founded in 1964. Population (1995 est): 2 797 000.

● **Abilene** ► 32 27N 99 45W A city in the USA, in Texas. It has two universities and an air force base. A trading centre for agricultural products and livestock, it has electronic and food-processing industries. Population (1996 est): 108 476.

● **Abingdon** ► 51 41N 1 17W A market town in S England, in Oxfordshire on the River Thames. Its many historical buildings include the remains of a Benedictine abbey dissolved by Henry VIII. Among its varied industries are brewing and the manufacture of leather goods. Population (1991): 35 234.

● **Abjuration, Act of** ► (1581) The declaration of independence by the United Provinces. The Dutch thus renounced their allegiance to Spain. ▷See also Revolt of the Netherlands.

● **Abkhazia** ► (or Abkhaz Republic) An administrative division of Georgia between the Black Sea and the Caucasus Mountains. Most of the population is Abkhazian or Georgian and lives along the narrow subtropical coastal lowland. The region is predominantly agricultural, producing tobacco, tea, and citrus fruits, and the chief mineral is coal. There are several health resorts.
History: invaded by the Romans, it later gained independence before coming under the Ottoman Turks in the 16th century. It became a Russian protectorate in 1810 and an autonomous republic of the Soviet Union in 1921. In 1992 it declared independence, leading to a conflict (1993–94) in which Georgian troops unsuccessfully attempted to regain control. The political situation remains unresolved. Area: 8600 sq km (3320 sq mi). Population (1993 est): 516 600. Capital: Sukhumi.

● **Åbo** ▷See Turku.

● **Abolition Movement** ► The campaign to abolish ▷slavery in the USA. Opponents of slavery formed an antislavery society in 1833. They helped runaway slaves escape to Canada via their secret ▷Underground Railroad route; such publications as *Uncle Tom's Cabin* by Harriet ▷Beecher Stowe unveiled the slavery issue, which was settled by the ▷Civil War.

● **Abomey** ► 7 14N 2 00E A town in S Benin. It was the capital of the Yoruba kingdom of Dahomey until captured by the French (1893). Population (1992): 125 565.

● **Abominable Snowman** ► A creature, also called Yeti (Tibetan: Snowman), that is believed to live at high altitudes in the Himalayas. There have been no authenticated sightings, but gigantic footprints in the snow have been photographed (which may have other natural causes).

● **Aborigines** ► **1.** The dark-skinned hunters and gatherers who inhabited Australia before European settlement. There were about 500 Aboriginal tribes, which were linguistic groups having no social or political unity. The main social units were seminomadic bands. They were a diverse people culturally but, in general, material culture was rudimentary, while kinship organization and terminology were complex. Political affairs were conducted by older men. Male initiation and circumcision were commonly practised. Aboriginal mythology was generally rich and elaborate and included accounts of creation during the primordial dawn, which they call "Dream Time." There are roughly 136 000 people of Aboriginal descent in Australia. The small proportion who maintain a nomadic way of life are threatened by encroachments upon their lands as these are opened up for mineral exploitation. A movement to protect Aborigines' rights has gathered momentum; in 1993 Aborigines were granted permission to reclaim land formerly held under native title but this was curtailed by further legislation in 1998. **2.** Any indigenous people, especially as contrasted with invaders or colonizers. □ p. 4.

● **abortion** ► The expulsion or removal of a fetus from the womb before it is capable of independent survival. In the UK a fetus is not legally viable until 24 weeks old. Expulsion of a dead fetus at any later time is called a stillbirth. Abortion may be spontaneous (a miscarriage) or induced for therapeutic or social reasons (termination of the pregnancy). In the UK (excluding Northern Ireland) induced abortion is legal if it is carried out under the terms of the Abortion Act (1967) and

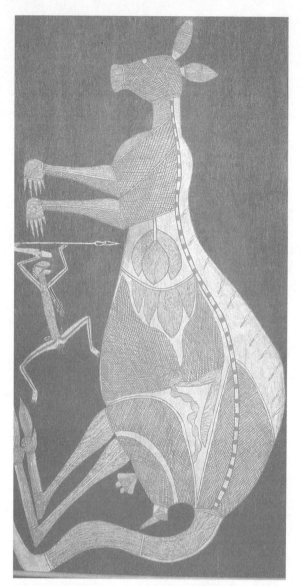

Aborigines ► A 20th-century bark painting of a kangaroo and a hunter.

the Abortion Regulations (1991): two doctors must agree that termination of the pregnancy is necessary for one of the reasons specified in the Regulations and the operation must be performed in approved premises. Under certain circumstances a pregnancy may be terminated after the 24th week; for example if there is a substantial risk that the child will be born with a serious mental or physical handicap. Methods used include ▷dilatation and curettage, suction of the womb using an aspirator, and the administration of certain drugs (e.g. mifepristone).

● **Aboukir, Battle of ►** (25 July, 1799) The land battle in which Napoleon defeated the Ottoman Turks during his occupation of Egypt. The 7000-strong French army defeated the unruly Turkish force of 18 000.

● **Aboukir Bay, Battle of** ▷*See* Nile, Battle of the.

● **Abraham ►** In the Old Testament, patriarch and founder of the Hebrew nation (Genesis 11–25). Born Abram at Ur in Chaldaea proba-

bly about 2000 BC, he followed a divine command and went first to Haran in N Mesopotamia and then to Canaan, accompanied by Sarah, his wife, and his nephew Lot. After withdrawing to Egypt because of famine, he returned to Canaan, where God established a covenant with him in which Abram, now called Abraham by God, agreed to circumcise himself and to have all his male descendants circumcised. In return Abraham (then aged 100) and Sarah (then 90) were promised a son, who would be the father of a people that would have the land of Canaan as an everlasting possession. After the birth of their son, Isaac, God tested Abraham's obedience by commanding him to sacrifice Isaac; when he was about to obey, a ram was substituted and God reaffirmed his promises. Isaac's son ▷Jacob had 12 sons, traditionally the ancestors of the 12 ▷tribes of Israel. ▷*See also* Esau; Ishmael.

● **Abraham, Plains of ►** A plateau in E Canada, on the W edge of Quebec citadel. Here Gen James Wolfe defeated the French under Gen Montcalm (13 September, 1759), leading to British control over Canada. Both commanders were killed.

● **abrasives ►** Hard rough substances used to wear down the surfaces of less resistant materials. They are widely used in both industry and the home for polishing, cleaning, and shaping. Abrasives are either natural, such as sandpaper, emery, and pumice, or synthetic, such as silicon carbide and carborundum.

● **abraxas ►** A mystic word, the Greek letters of which make 365 when read as numbers. Such words are found engraved and sometimes personified as a half-animal half-human deity on gemstones used as charms until the 13th century AD. It is particularly associated with ▷Gnosticism.

● **Abruzzi ►** (*or* Abruzzo) A region in E central Italy. It consists of the Apennines in the W and a coastal region in the E. Agriculture is limited, producing mainly cereals. Manufacturing industry is primarily for local needs but there is a large fishing fleet. Area: 10 794 sq km (4167 sq mi). Population (1994 est): 1 262 948. Capital: L'Aquila.

● **Absalom** ▷*See* David.

● **Absalon ►** (*or* Axel; c. 1128–1201) Danish ecclesiastic and statesman, who was chief adviser to Valdemar I and Canute VI (1163–1202; reigned 1182–1202) successively and the founder of Copenhagen. His campaign against the Wends in 1169 and on the S Baltic coast extended Danish territories. As Archbishop of Lund from 1177, he contributed to the systematization of Danish ecclesiastical law.

● **abscess ►** A pus-filled cavity surrounded by inflamed tissue, usually caused by bacterial infection. Abscesses may form anywhere in the body, including the skin, gums, and internal organs. They usually require draining and sometimes also antibiotics.

● **abscission ►** The separation of a plant organ, such as a fruit or a leaf, from its stem. Individual cells at the base of the organ weaken by losing calcium from their cell walls and a sealant layer of cells protects the newly exposed surface. Abscission is controlled by plant hormones (see auxin).

● **absinthe ►** A highly alcoholic drink made from spirits infused with herbs, including aniseed and wormwood. Absinthe has been banned in many countries because of the harmful effects of wormwood, and substitutes, known by different names (e.g. anis, pastis), are drunk instead. Absinthe is pale green and becomes cloudy when diluted with water.

● **absolute magnitude** ▷*See* magnitude.

● **absolute zero ►** The lowest temperature that can theoretically be attained. It is equal to −273.15°C or 0 K. In practice, absolute zero can never be reached, although temperatures of a few thousandths of a degree above absolute zero have been achieved. ▷*See* cryogenics; zero-point energy.

● **absolution** ▷*See* confession.

● **absolutism ►** A political system, characteristic of European monarchies between the 16th and 18th centuries, in which the sovereign attempted to centralize power in his own person (see monarchy). ▷Louis XIV of France is often regarded as the typical absolute monarch. Justified by the theory of the ▷divine right of kings, absolutism was associated in the 18th century with enlightened despotism (see

Enlightenment) but was challenged by the ideals of the ▷American and ▷French Revolutions.

● **absorbed dose** ▷*See* gray.

● **absorption** ▶ The assimilation of a substance by a solid or liquid, with or without chemical reaction. Moisture, for instance, can be absorbed from air by dehydrating agents, such as sulphuric acid. Certain porous solids, such as charcoal and zeolites, are able to absorb large quantities of gas. The process is distinguished from ▷adsorption in that the absorbed substance is held in the bulk of the solid rather than on a surface.

● **abstract art** ▶ Any nonrepresentational form of art. Tendencies to abstraction can be found in almost any age or school of art, particularly oriental and decorative art. However, the widespread use of ▷photography in the 20th century to create a visual record of people, places, events, etc., made the representational function of painting less important. This shift of emphasis released artists from the confines of realism, enabling them to explore various forms of abstraction. The first purely abstract painting in the modern tradition is usually held to be a watercolour produced by ▷Kandinsky in about 1910. Since then two main tendencies of abstract painting have developed: the hard-edged geometric style exemplified by the work of ▷Mondrian, ▷Malevich, and the constructivists (*see* constructivism) and the freer more subjective and spontaneous style of the abstract expressionists (*see* abstract expressionism), such as Jackson ▷Pollock. Another major division is between those artists and sculptors who attempt to reduce natural objects to their essential forms, such as ▷Brancusi and the cubists (*see* cubism), and those who maintain that shape, line, and colour have an aesthetic and emotional value independent of any reference to the natural world. A characteristic of abstract sculpture is the use of new materials, such as plastic, glass, and steel. ▷*See also* action painting; minimal art; Op art; orphism; Stijl, de; suprematism.

● **abstract expressionism** ▶ An art movement that developed in New York in the years after World War II, characterized by the rejection of realism and an emphasis on spontaneous subjective expression. It is associated with the development of experimental improvisational techniques, notably the ▷action painting of Jackson ▷Pollock. By the 1950s the work of Pollock, ▷de Kooning, ▷Rothko, and others had made abstract expressionism the dominant trend in modern art. The first major art movement to develop in the USA independently of European influence, it had the effect of making New York, rather than Paris, the centre of the modern art world. ▷*See also* abstract art.

● **Abstraction-Création** ▶ An international group of abstract geometric artists, active from 1931 to 1936 and based in France under Georges Vantongerloo (1886–1965) and Auguste Herbin (1882–1960). It was also the name of their annual journal and exhibition.

● **abstract music** ▷*See* programme music.

● **Absurd, Theatre of the** ▷*See* Theatre of the Absurd.

● **Abu al-Wafa** ▶ (940–98 AD) Persian mathematician and astronomer, who made notable contributions to ▷trigonometry. He invented the secant and cosecant functions (the inverse of the sine and cosine), drawing up accurate tables for them and for the sine and tangent functions.

● **Abu Bakar** ▶ (c. 1843–95) Sultan of Johore (now in Malaysia) from 1885 to 1895. He became ruler of Johore in 1862, a year after Britain gained control of the state's foreign affairs, and contributed greatly to the maintenance of internal stability, fostering trade and agricultural development.

● **Abu Bakr** ▶ (c. 573–634 AD) The first ▷caliph (632–34), known as as-Siddiq (the righteous). One of the earliest Muslims, Abu Bakr accompanied Mohammed to Medina and became caliph on his death. As caliph he defeated the rebellious tribes and began the invasion of Syria and Iraq.

● **Abu Dhabi** ▷*See* United Arab Emirates.

● **Abu Hanifah** ▶ (700–67 AD) Influential Muslim theologian and teacher of jurisprudence. Of Persian origin, he lived in Kufa (now in Iraq), where he died, perhaps in prison, after refusing to accept a post under the ruling dynasty. He left virtually no writings, but was known as a champion of the use of reason and analogy in law. His teachings form the basis of one of the two orthodox schools of the ▷Sunnites.

● **Abuja** ▶ 9 10N 7 06E The federal capital of Nigeria, in the centre of the country. In December 1991 the seat of government moved here. Population (1996 est): 350 100.

● **Abu Nuwas** ▶ (c. 762–c. 813 AD) Arab poet. Although he learned his craft from older poets and from the Bedouins, he abandoned traditional poetic forms for sophisticated lyrics celebrating the pleasures of wine and erotic affairs with women and boys. A favourite at the Abbasid court of ▷Harun ar-Rashid at Baghdad, he is portrayed in the *Arabian Nights* as a free-thinking pleasure-seeker.

● **Abu Simbel** ▶ A monumental rock-cut temple complex constructed about 1250 BC by Pharaoh Ramses II in the Nile valley near modern Kurusku. The entrance to the main temple features four colossal statues of Ramses, each 20 m (66 ft) high. In 1968 the entire complex was disassembled and rebuilt on higher ground nearby to escape inundation resulting from the building of the ▷Aswan High Dam.

● **Abutilon** ▶ A genus of tropical and subtropical perennial herbs and shrubs (over 100 species). The plants reach a height of 30–150 cm and have drooping stems with bell-shaped flowers. Some species are grown as ornamental plants. *A. avicennae* is cultivated in China for fibre (China jute). Family: *Malvaceae* (mallow family).

● **Abydos** ▶ 1. An ancient city in Upper Egypt, founded before 3000 BC and continuously occupied until Roman times. It was a principal centre of ▷Osiris worship. The most impressive remaining structure is Seti I's Great Temple (c. 1300 BC), with shrines for six deities and the god pharaoh. The Table of Abydos, a king list carved on its walls, provides information about earlier pharaohs. 2. An ancient town in ▷Asia Minor overlooking the Hellespont (*see* Dardanelles) just NE of the modern Turkish town of Canakkale. Here ▷Xerxes crossed the Hellespont in 480 BC using a bridge of boats on his way to invade Greece. It was also from Abydos that the legendary Leander swam the Hellespont each night to be with his lover Hero at Sestos (*see* Hero and Leander). Abydos has a more historical claim to fame in its fierce resistance to Philip of Madedon in 200 BC; it survived as the toll station of the Hellespont well into the Byzantine Empire.

● **abyssal zone** ▶ The ocean depths lying below 1000 m. It is the zone of greatest ocean depth, lying seawards of the continental slope (*see* continental shelf). Since no light penetrates to these depths, they contain relatively little marine life and the temperature never rises above 4°C. The ocean depths below 6000 m are sometimes classified as the **hadal zone**.

● **Abyssinia** ▷*See* Ethiopia, Federal Democratic Republic of.

● **Abyssinian cat** ▶ A breed of short-haired cat, many individuals of which are descendants of one exported to the UK from Abyssinia in the 19th century. They have slender bodies and wedge-shaped heads with large ears. The reddish-brown coat has black or brown markings and the eyes are green, yellow, or hazel. The Red Abyssinian is a rich copper-red.

● **Acacia** ▶ A genus of tropical and subtropical trees and shrubs (over 700 species), particularly abundant in Australia (*see* wattle). Acacias have clusters of yellow or white flowers, produce long flattened pods, and usually have compound leaves consisting of many small leaflets. In some species the leaflets do not develop and the leafstalks assume their function, being broad and flattened. These species are often very spiny. Acacias yield a number of useful products: ▷gums (including gum arabic), tannins, dyes, and woods suitable for furniture. Many are grown as ornamental plants. Family: ▷*Leguminosae*.

● **Académie Française** ▶ The French literary academy founded by Cardinal de Richelieu in 1634 (incorporated 1635) to preserve the French literary heritage. Its membership is limited at any one time to 40 "immortals," who have included Corneille, Racine, and Voltaire. It is continuously engaged in the revision of the official French dictionary.

● **Academy, Greek** ▸ The college founded (c. 385 BC) near Athens by Plato, which continued in various guises until its dissolution by Justinian in 529 AD. It is famed mainly for contributions to philosophy and science. At first metaphysics and mathematics predominated but in the mid-3rd century BC philosophical scepticism took precedence.

● **Academy of Motion Picture Arts and Sciences** ▸ An organization founded in Hollywood in 1927 to raise the artistic and technical standards of the film industry. It is responsible for the annual presentation of the **Academy Awards**, popularly known as Oscars, for excellence in acting, writing, directing, and other aspects of film production.

● **Acadia** ▸ A former French colony in E Canada centred on present-day Novia Scotia. The original French settlement was destroyed by the British in 1613. Conflict over Acadia between French and British continued until 1763, when it fell finally to the British. Many Acadians were deported by the British and resettled in Louisiana, where their descendants, called Cajuns, still live. Longfellow's poem *Evangeline* tells their story.

● **Acanthus** ▸ A genus of perennial herbaceous plants (about 50 species), mostly native to the Mediterranean region: *A. mollis* and *A. spinosus* are the species most commonly planted in temperate gardens. Growing to a height of 1–1.5 m, they have tough leaves, often spiny and with deeply cut margins, and spikes of purple and white flowers. The fruit—a capsule—explodes to disperse the seeds. Family: *Acanthaceae*.

acanthus ▸ The decorative architectural motif used on Corinthian and Composite columns was inspired by the spiky leaf of *Acanthus spinosus*.

● **acanthus** ▸ A decorative element of classical architecture. It is mainly found on the capitals of Corinthian and Composite columns, comprising heavy carvings of stylized leaves.

● **a cappella** ▸ (Italian: in the church style) A marking on a piece of music for several voices, indicating that it is to be sung unaccompanied.

● **Acapulco** ▸ 16 51N 99 56W A seaside resort in S Mexico, on the Pacific Ocean. Known as the Riviera of Mexico, it has fine sandy beaches and many hotels. Population (1995): 592 528.

● **ACAS** ▸ (advisory, conciliation and arbitration service) A public body set up by parliament in 1975 to work with trade unions and employers to settle disputes and promote methods of collective bargaining.

● **Accademia** ▸ The principal art gallery in Venice, opened in 1756 to display work by Venetian artists. Formerly a monastery, it houses masterpieces by such painters as Bellini, Titian, and Canaletto in a collection with items dating from the 13th century.

● **acceleration** ▸ The rate of change of a body's velocity. Linear acceleration is the rate of change of linear velocity. It is measured in such units as metres per second per second. Angular acceleration is the rate of change of angular velocity and is measured in such units as radians per second per second.

● **acceleration of free fall** ▸ (g) Formerly called acceleration due to gravity; the acceleration of a falling body when air resistance is neglected. Caused by gravitational attraction between the body and the earth, it varies slightly at different points on the earth's surface. Its standard value is 9.806 metres per second per second.

● **accelerator principle** ▸ The economic principle that investment will accentuate economic booms and ▷depressions. As income rises, businesses gain confidence in the expected future level of demand and increase their investment in plant and equipment; this pushes up employment in the capital-goods industries and heightens the boom. The converse applies to a slump.

● **accelerators** ▸ Large machines that are used for accelerating beams of charged particles (electrons, protons, etc.) to very high speeds primarily for research in ▷particle physics. The particles are accelerated by electric fields either in a straight line, as in the ▷linear accelerator, or in a circle, as in the ▷cyclotron, ▷synchrotron, and ▷synchrocyclotron. The beam is confined to its path by magnetic fields. The energies of the particles are measured in millions of electronvolts, some modern accelerators attaining 10^{12} eV. Particle accelerators are used by directing a beam of particles at a stationary target or, for greater energy, by colliding two beams of particles together. Accelerators are also used to create artificial isotopes and in ▷radiotherapy. The first accelerator was a linear accelerator, produced in 1932 by ▷Cockcroft and ▷Walton. ▷*See also* CERN.

● **accent** ▸ The characteristic pronunciation used by a person or group, especially when speaking their native language. This is distinct from ▷dialect, which may contain different grammatical structures and vocabulary as well as a different accent. The most distinctive feature of a person's accent tends to be the way in which they pronounce ▷vowel sounds, although initial and final consonants may be omitted in some accents. For example, in the mode of English speech known as Estuary English (because it originated in Essex and north Kent along the Thames Estuary), *'im* (for 'him') and *lookin'* (for 'looking') accompany a broadening of vowels.

In English, as in other languages, accents can identify a person's cultural and educational background as well as their geographical area of origin. In Britain the standard accent is that spoken in southern England by people educated at public schools and universities. This used to be called the King's (or Queen's) English. However, as the House of Windsor have adopted upper-class vowel sounds (*hice* for 'house', *Undergrind* for 'Underground', etc.), which are not regarded as standard, an English phonetician, Daniel ▷Jones, coined the term ▷Received Pronunciation (RP) to act as the standard for pronunciation guides given in dictionaries. In the 1930s and 1940s, RP was often called BBC English, because such newscasters as Alvar Liddell (who was of Swedish extraction) provided a widely emulated model for native English speakers.

In more recent decades it has been argued that the enforcement of RP in schools and the broadcast media has had the effect of stigmatizing those with nonstandard accents, however carefully and articulately they may speak. As a result many BBC and other broadcasters now have regional accents that sacrifice universal intelligibility for the principle that such accents reflect the way people actually speak, rather than the way in which some people think they ought to speak. However, despite the ▷politically correct view that all accents are equal, surveys show that the British public continue to have strong if irrational preferences: for example, rural Scottish and Yorkshire accents are associated with such qualities as honesty and dependability.

An interesting aspect of accent was revealed in 1990 when the first successful larynx transplant was carried out. Although the recipient's own larynx had been destroyed in an accident, he was able to speak again when a donor's larynx was inserted in his throat. His new voice had some of the characteristics of the donor's voice, but his basic accent, controlled by his brain, remained unchanged.

● **accentor** ▶ A small sparrow-like songbird belonging to an Old World family (*Prunellidae*; 12 species), usually restricted to northern and mountain regions. It has a red or brownish-grey plumage with grey underparts, often streaked or striped. Accentors feed on insects or—in winter—seeds and berries. The family includes the ▷dunnock (hedge sparrow).

● **acceptance house** ▶ A financial institution (usually a merchant bank) that deals in ▷bills of exchange. It buys them at a discount, the value of which depends on the standing of the drawer, and either holds them to maturity or endorses them and resells them at a smaller discount. An **acceptance credit** is a bill of exchange made payable to an exporter by his foreign customer and drawn on an acceptance house. The exporter can discount the bill to receive payment before the bill falls due.

● **accessory** ▶ In law, a person who incites another to commit a crime but is not present when the crime is committed (i.e. counsels or procures) or one who provides assistance (e.g. tools) either before or during commission of the crime (i.e. aids and abets). A person who assists another whom he knows has committed a crime may be guilty of impeding apprehension or prosecution.

● **Accius, Lucius** ▶ (170–c. 85 BC) Roman tragic dramatist, admired for his melodramatic plots and lively rhetorical style. About 700 lines survive from over 40 of his plays, mainly on Greek mythological themes. He also wrote treatises on poetry and grammar.

● **accomplice** ▶ In law, a person concerned with one or more other persons in committing a crime, either as its actual perpetrator or as an ▷accessory.

● **Accoramboni, Vittoria** ▶ (1557–85) Italian woman, whose life story was portrayed by John ▷Webster in *The White Devil* (1612) and by Ludwig Tieck in his novel *Vittoria Accoramboni* (1840). She married the Duke of Bracchiano (d. 1585) after the murder of her first husband by her brother in 1581. She was killed by Ludovico Orsini, a relative of Bracchiano.

● **accordion** ▶ A portable musical instrument invented in Berlin in 1822. A member of the reed-organ family, the accordion is a boxlike instrument in which bellows operated by the left arm force air through reeds mounted in end panels. In the modern **piano accordion** a small piano-like keyboard played by the right hand supplies the melody, while buttons operated by the left hand produce chords. The instrument is supported in front of the player's body by straps.

● **accountancy** ▶ The profession of preparing, verifying, and interpreting the accounts of a business. The main branches are bookkeeping, auditing, financial accounting, and cost accounting. Bookkeeping is concerned with the preparation of records of all the financial transactions undertaken by a firm or a self-employed person, usually on a day-to-day basis. The books of account kept by a firm usually include a cash book to record all payments and receipts, a nominal ledger in which all transactions with named clients, suppliers, etc., are recorded, a purchase and a sales ledger, and sometimes purchase and sales day books. Auditing is the process of verifying that the bookkeeping and the preparation of accounts have been carried out accurately and truthfully. In most countries, including the UK and the USA, auditing is carried out by an independent firm of accountants, which is required to certify that a company's accounts are a true record of its transactions during the past year. Financial accounting consists of analysing a firm's transactions and summarizing them in the firm's annual accounts. These will normally consist of a profit and loss account and a balance sheet. The former lists the total sales, total purchases, opening and closing value of the stock (or work in progress), and the expenses, enabling the profit or loss in the period to be calculated. The balance sheet lists the firm's assets and liabilities. Cost accounting identifies the costs of production at all stages of a manufacturing process. Unlike financial accounting it can be used to measure economic performance and the relative efficiency of the constituent parts of a business.

In the UK, members of the Institute of Chartered Accountants (founded 1880) specialize in financial accounting and auditing and have been trained with a professional partnership. Members of the Association of Certified Accountants (1904), who train in commerce, industry, or the public services, are also empowered to audit accounts. Members of the Institute of Cost and Management Accountants (1919) specialize in cost accounting and are not authorized auditors.

● **Accra** ▶ 5 32N 0 12W The capital of Ghana, a port on the Gulf of Guinea. It is built on the site of three 17th-century trading fortresses founded by the English, Dutch, and Danish. It became the capital of the Gold Coast in 1877. Following the opening of a railway to the agricultural hinterland (1923) it developed rapidly into the commercial centre of Ghana. The University of Ghana was founded in 1948 at Legon, just outside Accra. Population (1990 est): 1 781 100 (metropolitan area).

● **Accrington** ▶ 53 46N 2 21W An industrial town in NW England, in Lancashire. It specializes in textiles, textile and general engineering, and brick manufacturing. Population (1991): 36 466.

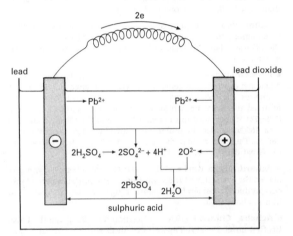

accumulator ▶ A single cell of a lead (Pb) sulphuric acid (H_2SO_4) accumulator. The reactions shown are those taking place during discharge. During charging the lead sulphate ($PbSO_4$) is converted back to lead dioxide (PbO_2) and sulphuric acid, the density of which rises.

● **accumulator** ▶ A cell or battery that can be recharged by passing a current through it in the direction opposite to that of the discharge current, thus reversing the chemical changes occurring during discharge at the electrodes. The most common example is the lead-acid accumulator used in motor vehicles. This consists, when charged, of a positive lead dioxide electrode and a negative spongy lead electrode, both immersed in sulphuric acid with a relative density of 1.20–1.28. During discharge lead sulphate forms on the electrodes and the acid density falls.

Nickel-iron (NiFe) accumulators with an electrolyte of 20% potassium hydroxide are also used. The rechargeable batteries used in cordless devices are usually nickel-cadmium cells in which a nickel hydroxide cathode and a cadmium anode are immersed in a potassium hydroxide electrolyte. These are light in weight and can be sealed. ▷*See also* electric car.

● **ACE inhibitors** ▶ (*or* angiotensin-converting enzyme inhibitors) A class of drugs used to treat raised blood pressure and heart failure. Drugs of this class interfere with the action of the enzyme that converts the inactive form of angiotensin to the form in which it becomes a strong artery constrictor. ACE inhibitors therefore prevent constriction of the arteries and reduce blood pressure and the workload on the heart. They are often used in combination with a ▷diuretic. Captopril and enalapril are widely used examples.

● **Acer** ▷*See* maple.

● **acetaldehyde** ▷*See* ethanal.

● **acetic acid** ▷*See* ethanoic acid.

● **acetone** ▷*See* propanone.

● **acetylcholine** ▶ A chemical that transmits impulses between the ends of two adjacent nerves and is confined largely to the parasympathetic nervous system. Acetylcholine is released on stimulation of the nerve and diffuses across the gap of the ▷synapse to stimulate the adjacent nerve. It is rapidly converted to an inactive form by the enzyme cholinesterase, permitting the passage of a further impulse.

● **acetylene** ▷*See* ethyne.

● **acetylenes** ▷*See* alkynes.

● **acetylsalicylic acid** ▷*See* aspirin.

● **Achaea** ▶ A region of ancient Greece occupying the N coast of the Peloponnesus and SE Thessaly. The 12 towns of the region formed the **Achaean League** in the 4th century BC. Dissolved in the late 4th century, it was revived by the ten surviving cities in 280 BC and included non-Achaean cities, such as Sicyon. The League finally disintegrated when Achaea was annexed by Rome in 146 BC. Its NW part approximates the modern department of Achaea.

● **Achaeans** ▶ An ancient Greek people mentioned by Homer as being among the besiegers of ▷Troy. They were probably related to the ▷Dorians but also seem to have had associations with ▷Mycenaean civilization.

● **Achaemenians** ▶ An ancient Persian dynasty founded by Achaemenes in the 7th century BC. Cyrus I (reigned c. 645–602 BC), Cambyses I (c. 602–559 BC), ▷Cyrus the Great (559–530 BC), who founded the Achaemenian (or Persian) Empire, and ▷Cambyses II (529–521 BC) belonged to the senior branch of the family. ▷Darius I (522–486 BC) headed the junior line, which included ▷Xerxes I (486–465 BC). The Achaemenian dynasty ended in 330 BC, when Alexander the Great defeated Darius III (336–330 BC).

● **Achard, Franz Karl** ▶ (1753–1821) German chemist, who pioneered the extraction of the sugar from beetroot. His imperfect process produced considerable amounts of sugar on an estate granted to him in about 1800.

● **Achebe, Chinua** ▶ (1930–) Nigerian novelist of the Ibo tribe. His first novel, *Things Fall Apart* (1958), deals with the arrival of missionaries and colonial government in the Ibo homeland. The conflict between traditional African society and Western values is a central theme in all his work. His other works include the novels *A Man of the People* (1966) and *Anthills of the Savannah* (1987), as well as short stories, poems, and essays.

● **achene** ▶ A small dry ▷fruit having a single seed that is attached to the fruit wall at one point only. The fruit does not open at maturity (i.e. the fruit is indehiscent) and the seed is thus retained until germination. Lettuce fruits are examples.

● **Achernar** ▶ A conspicuous blue star, apparent magnitude 0.5 and 114 light years distant, that is the brightest star in the constellation Eridanus.

● **Acheron** ▶ A river in N Greece, in Greek mythology the chief river of the underworld. In Dante, it is the river across which the souls of the dead are ferried to hell by ▷Charon.

● **Acheson, Dean (Gooderham)** ▶ (1893–1971) US lawyer and statesman. As secretary of state in ▷Truman's cabinet (1949–53), his foreign policy aimed at the containment of Soviet communism. This led him to play a leading role in developing the Truman Doctrine, the Marshall Plan (*see* Marshall, George), and the ▷North Atlantic Treaty Organization. After 1953 he continued advising American presidents.

● **Acheulian** ▶ A culture of the Lower ▷Palaeolithic. It is characterized by hand axes made by hammering flakes off a flint with a hammer of wood, antler, or bone, thus producing a more regular and effective tool than the ▷Abbevillian hand axe. Named after St Acheul near Amiens (N France) the Acheulian occurs in Eurasia and Africa where it apparently originated and survived longest (until about 58 000 years ago). Acheulian sites provide the earliest evidence of man's use of fire and are associated with *Homo erectus* remains (*see* Homo).

● **Achilles** ▶ In Greek mythology, the greatest Greek warrior in the Trojan War. The son of Peleus, King of Thessaly, and Thetis, a sea nymph, he was dipped by his mother in the River Styx as a child,

which made his whole body invulnerable except for the heel by which she had held him. After a quarrel with ▷Agamemnon he ceased fighting until the death of his friend ▷Patroclus at the hand of ▷Hector. Achilles then slew Hector and was himself later killed by Paris, who shot a poisoned arrow into his heel. The tendon connecting the heelbone to the calf muscles is called the **Achilles tendon**.

● **Achill Island** ▶ 54 00N 10 00W A mountainous island in the Republic of Ireland, off the W coast of Co Mayo. The chief occupations are farming and fishing. Area: 148 sq km (57 sq mi). Population (1991): 2853.

● **achromatic lens** ▶ A combination of lenses used to eliminate chromatic ▷aberration in an optical system. The simplest type has two lenses of different powers made from different kinds of glass. The chromatic aberration of one lens is cancelled by the chromatic aberration of the other lens.

● **acid house** ▷*See* pop music.

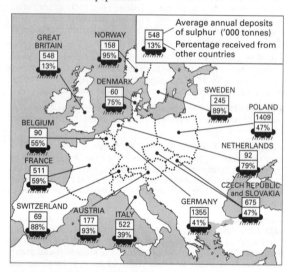

acid rain ▶ Sulphur deposits in Europe.

● **acid rain** ▶ Rain that contains sulphuric and nitric acids as a result of the absorption of sulphur dioxide and nitrogen oxides, mostly from industrial and vehicle emissions, in the atmosphere. It is contended that the effects of acid rain can include destruction of fish, crops, and trees, as well as damage to buildings. In 1985 19 countries agreed to make substantial reductions in the emission of sulphur dioxide by 1993.

● **acids and bases** ▶ Acids are chemical compounds containing hydrogen that can be replaced by a metal atom to produce a ▷salt. They have a sour taste and turn litmus red. When dissolved in water they dissociate into ions. Hydrochloric acid (HCl), for instance, gives chloride ions and hydrogen ions: $HCl + H_2O \rightarrow Cl^- + H^+ + H_2O$. The hydrogen ion is associated with a water molecule, a combination referred to as a hydroxonium ion (H_3O^+).

    Strong acids dissociate completely in water; hydrochloric acid, sulphuric acid, and nitric acid are common examples. Such compounds are extremely corrosive, sulphuric and nitric acids being particularly so because they are also powerful oxidizing agents. **Weak acids** do not dissociate completely. Many are organic compounds, usually carboxylic acids, containing the carboxylate group –CO.OH, and occur naturally: for example, acetic acid in vinegar, citric acid in citrus fruits, and lactic acid in milk.

    Bases are compounds that react with acids to form salts and water. Bases that dissolve in water, known as **alkalis**, produce hydroxide ions (OH^-). Many are metal hydroxides, such as sodium hydroxide (NaOH) and potassium hydroxide (KOH). Ammonia (NH_3) is also a base, reacting with water molecules to form ammonium ions and hydroxide ions: $NH_3 + H_2O \rightarrow NH_4^+ + OH^-$. The neutralization of an acid by a base in solution is a reaction in which hydrogen and hydroxide ions combine to give water. In chemistry the simple concept of acids and bases has been extended to include the concept of an acid as any compound that can donate a proton and a base as a proton acceptor. This (the Brønsted-Lowry theory) can be applied to reactions in nonaqueous solvents. A further extension of the terms (Lewis theory) defines an acid as an acceptor of an unshared electron pair and a base as a pair donor. ▷*See also* pH.

● **acmeism** ▶ A movement in Russian poetry in the 1910s and 1920s that asserted the value of precision against what was seen as the abstract vagueness of the symbolist movement. Because it was apolitical it met with official hostility, and several of its members, including ▷Akhmatova and ▷Mandelstam, were persecuted.

● **acne** ▶ A skin condition, common in adolescence, affecting the face, chest, and back. Acne is caused by overactivity and inflammation of the sebaceous glands: oily sebum accumulates in the hair follicles, producing pustules and blackheads. Severe cases can be treated with antibiotics, retinoids (e.g. isotretinoin), or other drugs.

● **Aconcagua, Mount** ▶ (Spanish name: Cerro Aconcagua) 32 40S 70 02W A mountain in W Argentina, in the Andes, regarded as being the highest point in the W hemisphere. It is of volcanic origin. Height: 6960 m (22 835 ft).

● **aconite** ▶ A European herbaceous plant, *Aconitum napellus*, also known as monkshood. Growing to a height of 1 m, its flowers are usually purplish-blue and hood-shaped; the bulbous roots yield poisonous ▷alkaloids, including aconitine, which have been used in medicine as ▷narcotics and analgesics. The genus, which is restricted to N temperate regions, also includes wolfsbane (*A. lycotonum*). Family: *Ranunculaceae* (buttercup family).

● **acornworm** ▶ A wormlike marine invertebrate animal, 5–180 cm long, that burrows in soft sand or mud. Its front end is acorn-shaped, with the mouth at the base. It filters food particles from sea water, which enters the mouth and passes out through gill slits along the length of the body. Chief genera: *Balanoglossus, Saccoglossus*; phylum: ▷*Hemichordata*.

● **acouchi** ▶ (*or* acushi) A small long-legged ▷rodent belonging to the genus *Myoprocta* (about 5 species). Acouchis have the same habits and lifestyle as the closely related agoutis but are smaller, measuring up to 45 cm long. They have a thin white-tipped tail and lack the coloured rump hairs of agoutis.

● **acoustics** ▶ The branch of physics concerned with the production, propagation, reception, properties, and uses of sound. It has several subdivisions. The most important, architectural acoustics, is concerned with the design of public auditoriums so that sounds can be heard in all parts of them with the maximum clarity and the minimum distortion. ▷Ultrasonics is the study of very high frequency sound. The structure and function of sound sources, such as loudspeakers, and sound receptors, such as microphones, also form part of acoustics. Other fields include speech communication and the design of machines that can understand spoken instructions.

● **acquired character** ▷*See* Lamarckism.

● **acquittal** ▶ In law, the clearing of an accused person of the charge against him, usually by court verdict. In England there must be a verdict of "not guilty"; in Scotland the verdict may be either "not guilty" or "not proven." Acquittal prevents a person from being prosecuted for the same offence again. Anyone charged as an ▷accessory to a crime is automatically acquitted if the principal is acquitted.

● **Acre** ▶ (Arabic name: 'Akko) 32 58N 35 06E A town in N Israel, on the Mediterranean coast. Acre was held by the Crusaders for many years and was in Turkish hands for several centuries. Allocated to the Arabs under the UN plan for ▷Palestine, it fell to the Jews in May, 1948, and became part of Israel. It contains walls and a mosque from the 18th century, and caravanserais. It is a fishing port and a centre for light industry. Population (1989 est): 40 500.

● **acrolith** ▶ A statue made, especially in ancient Greece, of marble for the flesh and gilded wood for the clothing. This method was a cheaper substitute for chryselephantine (gold and ivory) statuary.

● **acromegaly** ▶ A rare disease in which a noncancerous tumour of the pituitary gland secretes abnormally large amounts of ▷growth hormone. This causes enlargement of the face, hands, feet, and heart. The tumour can be destroyed by X-rays, surgically removed, or treated with drugs (e.g. bromocriptine).

● **acropolis** ▶ (Greek: high town) In ancient Greek towns, the isolated rocky plateau on which stood the religious and administrative nucleus of the town and which served as a citadel in time of war. The most famous is the Acropolis of Athens, which is still adorned by remains of buildings erected by ▷Cimon, ▷Themistocles, and ▷Pericles after the sack of Athens by the Persians (480 BC). These buildings include the ▷Propylaea, ▷Parthenon, and the reconstructed Erectheum (completed 1987) and temple of Athena Nike.

● **acrylic painting** ▶ A method of painting using acrylic paint. An opaque bright smooth easily applied mixture, it has been used by many pop artists, notably David ▷Hockney.

● **acrylics** ▶ Synthetic materials produced by ▷polymerization of acrylonitrile (vinyl cyanide; $CH_2{:}CHCN$). Acrylic resins are used in paints and plastics, the most common being ▷Perspex. Acrylic fibre is widely used in textiles, mainly for knitwear, furnishing fabrics, and carpets. The fibres are strong, absorb little water, and resist most substances encountered in use, although they become plastic in hot water or steam. Modacrylic is acrylic fabric or yarn with more than 15% of other fibres added.

● **Acta** ▶ The ancient Roman *Acta Senatus* (*Senate Business*) were official records of ▷Senate proceedings compiled by a senator chosen by the emperor. The *Acta Diurna* (*Daily News*) constituted a popular gazette of political and social news, instituted by Julius Caesar in 59 BC and continuing until 300 AD. The emperor's official enactments were also known as *Acta*.

● **Actaeon** ▶ A mythological Greek hunter, son of the god Aristaeus and Autonoe, daughter of Cadmus, King of Thebes. Ovid, in his *Metamorphoses*, relates how Actaeon accidentally caught sight of the goddess Artemis bathing naked and was turned by her into a stag and killed by his own hounds.

● **ACTH** ▶ (adrenocorticotrophic hormone) A peptide hormone, secreted by the anterior lobe of the pituitary gland, that stimulates the cortex of the adrenal glands to produce three types of ▷corticosteroid hormones. Secretion of ACTH is stimulated by physical stress and is regulated by secretions of the ▷hypothalamus of the brain.

● **actinides** ▶ A group of related chemical elements in the periodic table ranging from actinium (atomic number 89) to lawrencium (atomic number 103). They are all radioactive and include a number of ▷transuranic elements. Chemically, actinides resemble the ▷lanthanides, having unfilled inner electron shells.

● **actinium** ▶ (Ac) A highly radioactive metal that occurs naturally in uranium minerals. It is the first of the actinide series of elements and is chemically similar to the lanthanide elements. It was discovered in 1899 by A. L. Debierne (1874–1949). At no 89; at wt (227); mp 1051°C; bp 3200 ± 300°C; half-life of ^{227}Ac 21.6 yrs.

● **actinium series** ▶ One of three naturally occurring series of radioactive decays. The actinium series is headed by uranium-235 (known as actino-uranium), which undergoes a series of alpha and beta decays ending with the stable isotope lead-207. ▷*See also* thorium series; uranium series.

● **actinomycetes** ▶ Bacteria belonging to the phylum *Actinobacteria*. They have rigid cell walls and often form branching filamentous mouldlike colonies. Some may cause diseases in plants and animals, particularly *Mycobacterium tuberculosis*, which causes tuberculosis, and *M. leprae*, which causes leprosy; others are relatively harmless parasites inhabiting the gastrointestinal tract. Many are found in soil, where they decompose organic matter. Certain actinomycetes (e.g. *Streptomyces*) produce valuable ▷antibiotics (such as streptomycin).

● **Action Française** ▶ A right-wing French movement and its daily newspaper of the same name. The movement arose at the end of the 19th century on a platform of strongly nationalist, antisemitic, and antidemocratic views in the wake of the ▷Dreyfus case. Its leader Charles ▷Maurras sought to restore the monarchy, a policy for which he obtained much Roman Catholic support, despite his own atheism. Reaching the peak of its influence after World War I, it lost ground after being criticized by the pope in 1926. It failed to survive World War II because of its association with the collaborationist Vichy government of Marshal ▷Pétain, and Maurras was condemned to life imprisonment.

● **action painting** ▶ A 20th-century art technique in which paint is sprayed, splashed, or dribbled over a large canvas to form an unpremeditated and usually abstract design. Associated mainly with the US abstract impressionist painters of the 1950s and 1960s (*see* abstract expressionism), it was invented by Jackson ▷Pollock in 1947 to give free rein to his own emotions. It was later also used by Willem ▷de Kooning to produce figurative pictures.

● **action potential** ▶ The change in electric potential on the surface of a nerve cell that occurs when the cell is stimulated. It results from sodium and potassium ions moving across the cell membrane. The electrochemical impulse travels along the nerve fibre, and in this way information is transmitted through the ▷nervous system. ▷*See also* neurone; synapse.

● **Actium, Battle of** ▶ (31 BC) The decisive land and sea battle that ended the civil war in ancient Rome. Octavian, later ▷Augustus (the first Roman emperor), defeated the forces of ▷Mark Antony and ▷Cleopatra.

● **activated charcoal** ▶ Charcoal that has been processed to increase its power of absorption by heating it to drive off absorbed gas. It then has a high capacity for further absorption of gas. Its uses include removing impurities from gases and liquids and as filters in gas masks.

● **activation energy** ▶ The energy required for a chemical reaction to take place. In some reactions the activation energy is zero and the reactants will react spontaneously. In others, energy is required to stretch and break the existing bonds between the reactant atoms before they can react to form the new bonds of the products. During a reaction, the energy of a system increases to a maximum before decreasing to the energy of the products. The activation energy is the difference between this maximum and the energy of the reactants. It is thus the energy barrier that has to be overcome to enable a reaction to proceed.

● **active galaxy** ▶ A galaxy that emits an unusually large amount of energy from a very compact central source. ▷Quasars, ▷Seyfert galaxies, and ▷radio galaxies are examples. The energy is thought to arise as a result of gas spiralling into a supermassive ▷black hole at the centre of the galaxy.

● **act of God** ▶ In law, an occurrence due to a sudden violent natural cause, such as a storm, which could not reasonably have been guarded against and loss from which could not have been avoided or predicted.

● **Act of Parliament** ▷*See* parliament.

● **Acton, John Emerich Edward Dalberg-Acton, 1st Baron** ▶ (1834–1902) British historian, born in Naples. As a Whig MP (1859–66) he formed a close friendship with Gladstone. Acton mobilized liberal Roman Catholic opinion against the doctrine of papal infallibility promulgated in 1870. Appointed professor of modern history at Cambridge (1895) he planned the *Cambridge Modern History*.

● **Actors' Studio** ▶ An actors' workshop founded in New York in 1947 by Elia ▷Kazan and others. Under its director Lee ▷Strasberg, it became famous for teaching "method" acting, a psychological approach to acting developed from the theories of ▷Stanislavsky. Film actors influenced by it include Marlon ▷Brando, Rod Steiger (1925–), and James ▷Dean.

● **Acts of the Apostles** ▶ The fifth book of the New Testament, written by Luke about 63 AD as a sequel to his Gospel. Starting with the ascension of Christ, it deals with the spread of the Christian Church from a single congregation at Jerusalem, where Peter is prominent, to Paul's first missionary journey and his eventual imprisonment at Rome.

● **actuary** ▶ A mathematician employed by an ▷insurance company to calculate the premiums payable on policies. The calculations are based on statistically determined risks and eventualities (e.g. sickness, life expectancy). In the UK qualifications are awarded by the Institute of Actuaries through examination.

● **actus reus** ▷*See* criminal law.

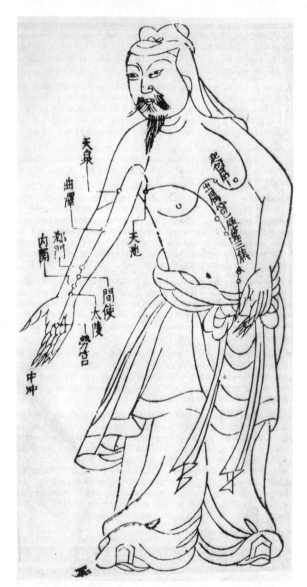

acupuncture ▶ A Ming dynasty ink drawing of the puncture points.

● **acupuncture** ▶ A traditional Chinese system of healing in which thin metal needles are inserted into selected points in the body. The needles are stimulated by manual rotation or electrically. Acupuncture is used in the Far East to relieve pain and in China as an anaesthetic. The traditional explanation of its effectiveness, dating back to 2500 BC, relates to balancing the opposing life forces ▷yin and yang. Research in the West suggests that the needles activate deep sensory nerves, which causes the release of endorphins (natural pain killers; *see* encephalins).

● **acyclovir** ▶ A drug that inhibits viral DNA synthesis in cells infected with herpes. It is used for treating herpes infections, including shingles and genital herpes, and is especially useful in patients with compromised immune systems (e.g. those on chemotherapy or with AIDS).

● **Adad** ▶ A Babylonian and Assyrian weather god. He was worshipped as both creator and destroyer of life: his summer rains ensured a good harvest but his storms and floods brought death. His father was Anu, god of the heavens.

● **Adalbert** ▶ (c. 1000–72) German churchman, Archbishop of Bremen. From a noble Saxon family, he became a trusted and powerful adviser to Emperor Henry III. He was active in the evangelization of Scandinavia, the Orkneys, Iceland, and Greenland until his exile from Henry IV's court in 1066.

● **Adam, Adolphe-Charles** ▶ (1803–56) French composer. He composed over 60 operas but is primarily remembered for his romantic ballet *Giselle* (1841), the earliest full-length ballet in the traditional repertoire.

● **Adam, Robert** ▶ (1728–92) British architect and interior designer, born in Kirkcaldy, Fifeshire, the son of the Palladian architect **William Adam** (1689–1748). He evolved a unique style that blended the ▷rococo and ▷neoclassicism, although he occasionally used ▷gothic forms. After visiting Italy (1755–58), Robert, often in collaboration with his brother **James Adam** (1732–94), built many country houses, notably Kenwood House (1768), the interior of Syon House (1769), and Osterley Park (1780). His building of town houses in London, such as Apsley House (1775), led him into financial difficulties. His last years were spent in Edinburgh, where he built Charlotte Square (1791).

● **Adam and Eve** ▶ In the Old Testament, the first human beings. According to Genesis (2.7–3.24), Jehovah (*or* Yahweh) created Adam from dust in his own image and put him in the Garden of Eden. His wife Eve was created from one of his ribs. Tempted by the serpent (the devil) to eat the forbidden fruit of the Tree of Knowledge of Good and Evil, Eve succumbed to the temptation and induced Adam to eat the fruit also. They became aware of their guilt and were expelled from Eden. Their sons included ▷Cain and Abel.

● **Adam de la Halle** ▶ (c. 1240–1290) French poet and musician. He travelled with his patron Robert II of Artois and became famous at the court of Charles of Anjou in Naples, where he died. His *Jeu de la feuillée* and *Jeu de Robin et Marion*, the first comic opera, combined popular songs with a sequence of realistic narrative scenes.

● **adamellite** ▶ A variety of ▷granite consisting of roughly equal proportions of potassium feldspar and sodic plagioclase feldspar, with one or more ferromagnesian minerals.

● **Adamnan, St** ▶ (c. 625–704 AD) Abbot of ▷Iona, born in Co Donegal, Ireland. He is remembered for championing the Roman system of dating Easter, which differed from the system used by the Celtic Churches, and for his biography of his predecessor, St ▷Columba. Feast day: 23 Sept.

● **Adamov, Arthur** ▶ (1908–70) French dramatist of the ▷Theatre of the Absurd. Born in Russia, Adamov went to Paris in 1924 and edited a surrealist journal, *Discontinuité*. The experimental forms of his plays owe much to the logic of dreams: *La Parodie* (1947) features a handless clock and in *Le Ping Pong* (1955) men are dominated by the futile relentless action of a pinball machine. His later, more political, work included anti-Gaullist sketches. He committed suicide.

● **Adams, Charles Francis** ▶ (1807–86) US diplomat; ambassador to Britain (1861–68). He was influential in keeping Britain neutral during the US Civil War and attempted to prevent British-built ships from joining the Confederate fleet, protesting against the dispatch of the *Alabama* (1862). He represented the USA in the subsequent *Alabama* claims for compensation against Britain (1871).

● **Adams, Gerry** ▶ (Gerard A.; 1948–) Northern Irish politician, president of Sinn Féin (1983–). He announced a complete IRA ceasefire (1994–96; renewed 1997) and was a leading participant in the talks that produced the Good Friday Agreement of 1998. In 1983 and 1997 he was elected to the British parliament but declined to take his seat.

● **Adams, Henry** ▶ (1838–1918) US historian. After working as a radical political journalist, he became disillusioned with active politics and turned to fiction and history, writing a long history of early democracy in America (1889–91). His most influential works were *Mont Saint Michel and Chartres* (1913), a study of art and religion in the middle ages, and his autobiography, *The Education of Henry Adams* (1918).

● **Adams, John** ▶ (1735–1826) US statesman; first vice president (1789–97) and second president of the USA (1797–1801). Adams was prominent in the development of North American revolutionary thought. During the American Revolution he successfully mobilized European support for the North American cause, which he represented in the peace negotiations. His term as president was troubled by disputes with his vice president, Thomas ▷Jefferson, over US policy towards Revolutionary France. Adams was defeated by Jefferson in the election of 1800. His son **John Quincy Adams** (1767–1848) was sixth president of the USA (1825–29). As a young man Adams practised law, wrote political articles and pamphlets, and began his successful career as a diplomat. From 1803 to 1808 he was a member of the Senate and from 1809 to 1817 he was US minister to several European countries, including Russia and Great Britain. As secretary of state (1817–25) he was largely responsible for the ▷Monroe Doctrine (1823). As president he was opposed by Andrew ▷Jackson, who defeated Adams in the presidential election in 1828. From 1831 Adams served in the House of Representatives, where he campaigned against slavery.

● **Adams, John Couch** ▶ (1819–92) English astronomer, who became professor at Cambridge University (1858). He predicted (1845) to within 2° the position of the then undiscovered planet ▷Neptune, which was confirmed in 1846. Adams later worked on lunar parallax, the earth's magnetism, and the Leonid meteors.

● **Adams, Richard** ▶ (1920–) British novelist. He worked in the civil service from 1948 to 1974. His *Watership Down* (1972), an epic treatment of the adventures of a community of rabbits, became an international bestseller. His later novels include *Shardik* (1974), *The Plague Dogs* (1977), *The Girl in a Swing* (1980), and *Traveller* (1989).

● **Adams, Samuel** ▶ (1722–1803) US politician. A propagandist of revolution against Britain, he led the ▷Stamp Act agitation of 1765. His protests against British troops in Boston led to the Boston Massacre (1770) and he helped to plan the ▷Boston Tea Party (1773). He signed the Declaration of Independence (1776), served in the ▷Continental Congress until 1781, and was governor of Massachusetts (1794–97).

● **Adamson, Robert** ▷*See* Hill, David Octavius.

● **Adana** ▶ 37 00N 35 19E A city in S Turkey, the fourth largest in the country. Its prosperity comes from the surrounding fertile valleys, where much cotton is grown, and its position on the Anatolian-Arabian trade routes. It has a university (1973). Population (1995 est): 1 066 544.

● **adaptation** ▶ In biology, a change in a physical characteristic of an animal or plant that makes it better suited to survive in a particular environment. For example, cacti have adapted to desert environments by evolving swollen water-storing stems. ▷*See also* adaptive radiation.

● **adaptive radiation** ▶ The process by which a uniform population of animals or plants evolves into a number of different forms over a period of time. The original population increases in size and spreads to occupy different habitats. It forms several subpopulations, each adapted to the particular conditions of its habitat. In time—and if the subpopulations differ sufficiently—a number of new species will be formed from the original stock. The Australian marsupials evolved in this way into burrowers, fliers, carnivores, herbivores, and many other different forms.

● **addax** ▶ A rare African antelope, *Addax nasomaculatus*, about 1 m high at the shoulder, that lives in small herds in the Sahara Desert. It has a greyish hide with a white patch on the face, long spirally twisted horns, and broad hooves suitable for running over loose sand. □mammal.

● **adder** ► A European ▷viper, *Vipera berus*, about 80 cm long, common in heathland areas. It is usually greyish with a broad black zigzag line along its back and black spots on its sides. Although venomous, its bite is rarely fatal. It is one of the three species of snakes found in Britain. The name adder is also given to a highly venomous Australian snake (death adder) of the cobra family and to some harmless North American snakes. ⌐reptile. ▷*See also* puff adder.

● **addiction** ▷*See* drug dependence.

● **Addington, Henry, 1st Viscount Sidmouth** ► (1757–1844) British statesman; prime minister (1801–04), replacing Pitt the Younger. Addington was attacked for his management of the Napoleonic Wars and resigned. As home secretary (1812–21) he introduced stern measures against radical and working-class movements and he has been held responsible for the ▷Peterloo Massacre.

● **Addis Ababa** ► 9 02N 38 43E The capital of Ethiopia, on a central plateau 2440 m (8000 ft) above sea level. It became the new capital of Ethiopia in 1889 and was capital of Italian East Africa (1936–41). Growth in the 20th century has been rapid. It is the country's administrative centre and chief market place. Its major industries produce cement, tobacco, textiles, and shoes. A railway line links the city with the port of Djibouti on the Gulf of Aden. It is also an important pan-African centre with the headquarters of the Organization of African Unity and the UN Economic Commission for Africa. The National University was established in 1961. Population (1994 est): 2 316 400.

● **Addison, Joseph** ► (1672–1719) British essayist, poet, and Whig statesman. He studied and taught at Oxford until 1699. On his return from a European tour in 1703 he published "The Campaign" (1705), a poem commissioned by the government to celebrate Marlborough's victory at Blenheim, and in 1706 became an undersecretary in the Whig administration. He was elected to parliament in 1708. He began to contribute to Richard ▷Steele's journal, the *Tatler*, and in 1711 Addison and Steele founded the *Spectator*, for which Addison wrote essays famous for their clarity, wit, and elegance. He is also remembered for the tragedy *Cato* (1713).

● **Addison, Thomas** ► (1793–1860) British physician, who was the first person to ascribe correctly the symptoms of what is now called ▷Addison's disease to a functional deficiency of the adrenal glands. He also described pernicious (Addison's) ▷anaemia and made a study of poisons.

● **Addison's disease** ► A rare disease of the adrenal glands, first described by Thomas ▷Addison, characterized by a reduced secretion of corticosteroid hormones. This leads to weakness, intestinal upsets, darkening of the skin, low blood pressure, and collapse. Formerly fatal, Addison's disease can now be readily treated with synthetic steroids.

● **addition reaction** ► A chemical reaction in which atoms or molecules combine to form a single molecule. It is frequently encountered in organic ▷chemistry, since many substances readily add to the double or triple bonds in alkenes, alkynes, aldehydes, etc. ▷Aromatic compounds are less susceptible, while ▷alkanes do not undergo addition. ▷*See also* polymerization; substitution reaction.

● **additive process** ▷*See* colour.

● **additives** ▷*See* food additives.

● **Adelaide** ► 34 56S 138 36E The capital of South Australia, on the Torrens River. Founded in 1837, the city was laid out in wide straight streets according to plans by Col William Light (South Australia's first surveyor general). Extensive parklands remain, separating the city from its suburbs. The University of Adelaide was founded in 1874; other notable buildings include the Anglican cathedral of St Peter and the Roman Catholic cathedral. It is an important commercial centre with harbour facilities at ▷Port Adelaide. Industries include the manufacture of cars and textiles, oil refining, and electronics. Population (1995 est): 1 081 000.

● **Adélie Land** ▷*See* Terre Adélie.

● **Aden** ► 12 50N 45 03E The main port and commercial centre of Yemen, on the **Gulf of Aden**, an arm of the Indian Ocean connecting with the Red Sea. Taken by the British in 1839, Aden was an impor-

tant coaling station on the route to India through the Suez Canal (opened 1869). It became part of the Federation of South Arabia in 1963 and was the scene of fighting between rival nationalist groups until 1968, when it became the capital of the independent republic of South Yemen, now part of Yemen. Economic activity centres on the port, which suffered from the closure of the Suez Canal (1967–75), and an oil refinery. Population (1995 est): 562 000.

● **Adenauer, Konrad** ► (1876–1967) German statesman. He was a successful Rhineland politician until the Nazi government forced him out of public life (1934) and imprisoned him (1934, 1944). In 1946 Adenauer re-emerged as chairman of the Christian Democratic Union (CDU) and became the first chancellor (1949–63) of the Federal Republic of Germany. He presided over the German economic miracle but was personally more concerned with foreign policy. He established that West Germany was part of W Europe, did much to restore its international prestige, and built up Franco-German friendship.

● **adenoids** ► Two masses of tissue situated at the back of the nose. They consist of lymphatic tissue, which destroys disease-causing microbes in the throat. In children they are normally large, and when associated with recurrent throat infections or persistent breathing through the mouth are usually removed surgically. This operation is often combined with tonsillectomy (removal of the tonsils) as the tonsils tend to be infected at the same time.

● **adenosine triphosphate** ▷*See* ATP.

● **Ader, Clément** ► (1841–1926) French engineer, inventor, and an early enthusiast of air travel. In 1890 he constructed a steam-powered aircraft with bat-shaped wings. The craft, which could not be steered, made the first heavier-than-air flight (of 50 m).

● **ADH** ► (antidiuretic hormone) ▷*See* diabetes (insipidus).

● **adhesives** ► Substances used for bonding materials together. Adhesives are usually colloidal solutions that set to a hard film adhering to the surfaces of the materials. There are many different types. Animal glues are forms of collagen (a protein) produced by boiling bones, hides, horns, etc., and drying the resulting jelly. They are water soluble and usually contain additives to preserve them. Vegetable glues (mucilages) are also water-soluble substances, such as starch, or gums, such as gum arabic or tragacanth. Other natural adhesives include waterglass, pitch, and rubber latex. In addition many synthetic resins are used as adhesives. **Thermoplastic adhesives** (polymers, such as polystyrene, asphalt, and polyvinyl compounds) remain soluble after setting and melt when heated; these are used where flexible bonding is needed, for example in attaching the soles of shoes, safety glass, sticky tape, etc. **Thermosetting adhesives** (condensation polymers, such as ▷epoxy resins) are insoluble, chemically inert, and will not melt. They are set by heat or by an added catalyst (hardener). They are used for bonding wood, paper, textiles, plastics, etc.

● **adiabatic process** ► Any process in which heat neither enters nor leaves a system. Usually, such a process changes the temperature of the system. An example is the sudden compression of a gas, causing its temperature to rise. The compression is assumed to take place so quickly that the gas loses none of its acquired heat.

● **Adige, River** ► A river in N Italy, rising in the Alps and flowing S and SE through Verona to enter the Adriatic Sea near the Po delta. The Adige valley forms a major communications route through the Italian Alps, but river navigation is difficult because of its rapid current. Length: 354 km (220 mi).

● **Ádi Granth** ► The sacred canonical scriptures of ▷Sikhism, compiled in 1604 by Arjun Mal (1581–1606). It consists of about 6000 hymns, mostly the work of the first five ▷gurus, together with the writings of some Bhakta saints and Muslim Sufis (*see* Sufism). The Sikhs do not venerate images but the *Ádi Granth* has itself become the object of worship.

● **Adirondack Mountains** ► A mountain range in the USA, in N New York state. It consists of a glaciated plateau rising to 1629 m (5344 ft) at Mount Marcy. Its scenic gorges, waterfalls, and many lakes make it a popular tourist area.

● **adjutant stork** ► A large carrion-eating ▷stork, *Leptotilos dubius*, occurring in Asia and similar to the related ▷marabou. It has a white plumage with grey back, wings, and tail, and a heavy pointed bill. Its head and neck are bald. Order: *Ciconiiformes*.

● **Adler, Alfred ►** (1870–1937) Austrian psychiatrist, who introduced the concept of the inferiority complex. Initially an associate of Sigmund ▷Freud, Adler's views diverged from Freud's and by 1911 he had founded his own school of thought. Adler viewed each individual as a unique entity striving to compensate for feelings of inferiority resulting from physical or social disabilities (*The Neurotic Constitution*, 1912) and regarded sex as simply an opportunity to express dominance. Adler emphasized the importance of education and, in 1921, opened the first of his child-guidance clinics in Vienna.

● **Adler, Felix ►** (1851–1933) German-born US educationalist, who founded the Society for Ethical Culture (1876). Through the resulting ethical movement and in books, such as *An Ethical Philosophy of Life* (1918), he advanced the view that moral considerations arose independently of any religious creeds. He instigated many educational and social reforms.

● **Adler, Larry ►** (1914–2001) US harmonica player and entertainer, who lived in the UK. His virtuosity inspired Vaughan Williams, Darius Milhaud, Malcolm Arnold, and others to write serious music for the harmonica.

● **administrative law ►** The law regulating the organization, responsibilities, and powers of a country's administrative bodies, such as the civil service, customs and excise, and social services. Many countries enforce this law through special courts, but in ▷common law countries, such as England, it is dealt with in the ordinary courts.

● **Admiral's Cup ►** A biennial sailing competition held by the Royal Ocean Racing Club since 1957. The competition comprises three races in the Solent and two longer offshore races—from Cherbourg to the Isle of Wight and from Plymouth to the Fastnet Rock off the SW coast of Ireland and back (the Fastnet Cup). Three yachts represent each nation.

● **Admiralty, Board of ►** The government department that from 1832 to 1964 administered the British navy. It succeeded the Navy Board, which was established in 1546 and developed out of the office of the Keeper of the King's Ships, which evolved in the 13th century. In 1964 the Board was absorbed by the Ministry of Defence and the office of Lord High Admiral was invested in the person of the monarch.

● **Admiralty Court** ▷*See* maritime law.

● **Admiralty Islands ►** A group of about 40 islands in the SW Pacific Ocean, in Papua New Guinea in the Bismarck Archipelago. Copra and pearls are exported. The main island is Manus with the chief town, Lorengau. Area: about 2000 sq km (800 sq mi). Population (1995): 35 200.

● **adobe ►** Bricks consisting of sun-dried clay. The earliest known adobe buildings date from the 8th millennium BC in Jericho. However, it has also been used extensively in Africa, China, Latin America, and the SW of the USA. In Africa and the Middle East the technique is still in use.

● **Adonis ►** In Greek mythology, a youth from Cyprus, loved by ▷Aphrodite for his great beauty. ▷Zeus decreed that his time should be divided between Aphrodite on earth, Persephone, queen of the underworld, and himself. He was celebrated in many festivals as a vegetation god, his death and resurrection representing the seasonal decay and regeneration of nature.

● **adoption ►** In law, the process whereby the natural parent's legal rights and obligations towards an unmarried minor are transferred to another adult. The need for a male heir has traditionally been one of the prime motives for adoption and the welfare of the adopted child was not the main consideration. This was reflected in Roman Civil law, which subsequently influenced the adoption laws of a number of European and Latin-American countries. Adoption had no place in English law until 1926, much later than some Commonwealth countries (e.g. New Zealand; 1895). Later legislation, now consolidated in the Adoption Act (1976) as amended by the Children Act (1989), controls the work of adoption societies, rights of the natural

parents, and the adopted child's right to know his original name. The increased effectiveness of birth control, the legalization of abortion, and the social acceptance of one-parent families have decreased the number of children available for adoption in recent years. Greater emphasis is now given to finding adoptive homes for children with special needs, e.g. older children, children of mixed race, and those who are physically or mentally handicapped.

● **Adorno, Theodor (Wiesengrund) ►** (1903–69) German philosopher and musicologist of the ▷Frankfurt School. As a Jew, he left Germany for Britain in 1934, moving on to the USA in 1938. After the war he returned to Frankfurt, where he reopened the Institute of Social Research in 1950. In the *Dialectic of the Enlightenment* (with Max Horkheimer; 1947) and *Negative Dialectics* (1966) he attacked ▷Marxism, ▷existentialism, and scientific empiricism, claiming that all systematic thought distorts reality. His *The Philosophy of Modern Music* (1949) is less obscure.

● **Adowa ►** (Adwa *or* Aduwa) 14 02N 38 58E A town in N Ethiopia. Emperor Menelik II defeated the Italians nearby in 1896. It is a market centre for agricultural produce including grains, honey, and coffee. Population (latest est): 26 782.

● **adrenal glands ►** Two small pyramid-shaped ▷endocrine glands in man and other mammals, one at the upper end of each of the kidneys. Each gland has an outer cortex, controlled by hormones secreted by the pituitary gland, and an inner medulla, controlled directly by the nervous system. The cortex secretes three classes of steroid hormones that regulate the balance of salts and water, the use of carbohydrates, and the activity of the sex glands (*see* corticosteroids). The medulla produces the hormones ▷adrenaline and ▷noradrenaline.

● **adrenaline ►** (*or* epinephrine) A hormone secreted by the central core (medulla) of the adrenal glands. A ▷catecholamine derived from the amino acid tyrosine, adrenaline increases heart rate, raises blood pressure, and increases the level of blood glucose. Its release is triggered by stress in preparation by the body for "fight or flight." Adrenaline is also secreted by nerve endings of the sympathetic nervous system. ▷*See also* noradrenaline.

● **adrenocorticotrophic hormone** ▷*See* ACTH.

● **Adrian, Edgar Douglas, 1st Baron ►** (1889–1977) British physiologist, whose work was largely concerned with the electrical properties of the nervous system. He developed techniques for recording nerve impulses from single nerve fibres and later studied the electrical activity of the brain. He shared a Nobel Prize (1932) with Sir Charles ▷Sherrington and was awarded the OM (1942).

● **Adrian IV ►** (Nicholas Breakspear; c. 1100–59) Pope (1154–59). The only English pope, also known as Hadrian IV, he was unanimously elected after a career of papal service, leading the mission to the Scandinavian churches (1152). His claim that the Holy Roman Empire was held by papal grant occasioned a major quarrel with Emperor ▷Frederick Barbarossa, whom he refused to crown until Frederick had done homage for his office. Adrian also intervened in the internal politics of France and Sicily.

● **Adrianople, Battle of ►** (378 AD) The battle in which the Eastern Roman emperor ▷Valens was defeated and killed defending Adrianople (now Edirne, Turkey) against the Visigoths. The Huns had driven the Visigoths across the Danube in 376 AD, prompting them to attack the Romans at Adrianople.

● **Adriatic Sea ►** A northern arm of the Mediterranean Sea, extending between Italy and Croatia for about 750 km (466 mi). Its principal ports are Brindisi, Bari, Venice, Trieste, and Rijeka. The Italian and Croatian coasts are strikingly different: the one flat and sandy, the other rocky and irregular. In recent years pollution of the Adriatic and the resultant blooms of algae have adversely affected the tourist resorts, as has the fighting between Croatia and Serbia.

● **adsorption ►** The production of a layer of atoms or molecules of a substance on a solid or liquid surface. The adsorbed atoms or molecules may be strongly held by chemical bonds (**chemisorption**), in which case the adsorbed layer is usually only one molecule thick.

Adsorption may also occur through weaker physical forces (**physisorption**), often giving rise to several molecular layers.

● **Adullamites** ▶ A group of disaffected Liberal MPs, led by Robert Lowe (1811–92), who opposed parliamentary reform and defeated the Liberal reform bill of 1866 (*see* Reform Acts). The group's name comes from Adullam's cave of the discontented (I Samuel 22.1–2).

● **adult education** ▶ Education of all kinds for adults, but usually the various forms of education provided for adults once their formal education has ceased. Adult education may be specifically vocational or assist in general cultural development. Its origins in the UK date from the 19th century, when such establishments as the London Mechanics' Institute and the London Working Men's College were founded (1823, 1854). The modern university-extension provision evolved from work in Cambridge in 1873 and closely associated with this movement were Ruskin College (1899) and the Workers' Educational Association (WEA). The latter was founded in 1903 by Albert Mansbridge (1876–1952), who sought to involve the university-extension service with the cooperative and trades-union movements. Some 150 000 adult students now follow classes organized by more than 800 WEA branches. The Education Act (1944) made Local Education Authorities (LEAs) responsible for the provision of full-time and part-time education for adults. These now directly sponsor many of the colleges that offer part-time courses while the Further Education Funding Councils in England and Wales provide grants for some full-time courses for adults. The National Institute of Adult Continuing Education provides information on all aspects of adult education, including *Time to Learn*, a directory of learning holidays. Birkbeck College, in the University of London, offers part-time courses for students of all ages and the ▷Open University, in partnership with the BBC, provides distance teaching for adults leading to degrees. ▷*See also* distance learning; University of the Third Age.

● **adultery** ▶ Voluntary sexual intercourse between a married person and someone who is not that person's husband or wife. In many countries, including some US states, adultery is a crime; under some systems, such as Islamic law, it may carry the death penalty. Generally, however, it is only a ground for ▷divorce or judicial separation; in English law it may be evidence of the "irretrievable breakdown" of a marriage.

● **Aduwa** ▷*See* Adowa.

● **advaita** ▶ (Sanskrit: nondualism) The Hindu philosophical view, derived from the ▷Upanishads, that the individual soul and ultimate reality are indivisibly one; the apparent separation of subject and object, or spirit and matter, is only illusion. Realization of this truth leads to liberation. Some thinkers see all phenomena, including the self, as altogether unreal; others maintain that the existence of the soul is qualified by, or dependent upon, ▷Brahman, who alone is fully real. Chief among the proponents of *advaita* is the 8th-century philosopher ▷Sankara.

● **advanced gas-cooled reactor** ▶ (AGR) ▷*See* nuclear energy; thermal reactor.

● **Advent** ▶ (from Latin: *adventus*, coming) The first season of the ▷church year, leading up to ▷Christmas. It begins on the Sunday nearest St Andrew's Day (30 Nov). From the 6th century it has been observed as a solemn preparation for celebrating Christ's birth and for his Second Coming.

● **adventists** ▶ Several Protestant Christian denominations that stress a belief in the imminent Second Coming of Christ. In the USA adventism began in 1831 with the millenarian preaching of William Miller (1782–1849), who predicted the Second Coming for 1843–44, but postponed the date when his prediction proved false. In the UK a similar movement was founded in 1832 as the Catholic Apostolic Church. There have been many adventist movements, the Seventh-Day Adventists being the main church today.

● **advertising** ▶ The publicizing of a product or service, usually in order to increase sales. In some cases it is used to discourage sales (e.g. of cigarettes) or to promote noncommercial activities (e.g. road safety). Although some 2% of the ▷gross national product in the UK and some 3% in the USA is spent on advertising, there is no evidence to show that advertising actually persuades people to buy things they do not want. Consumer advertising seeks to sell one branded product at the expense of others (e.g. toothpaste), to publicize a manufacturer's name when his product is the same as everyone else's (e.g. petrol), or to persuade people that a category of products (e.g. wool) should be bought in preference to some other category (e.g. man-made fibres). Trade advertising is restricted to specific sections of the public (e.g. doctors or caterers). Advertisements may be informative, assisting purchasers to make a choice between products, or persuasive, in which case it may exaggerate some aspect of a product by appealing to the purchaser's image of himself, often in relation to his sexual fantasies. Advertising is carried by the press (about 70–75% of advertising expenditure in the UK), by television and radio (20–25%), and on hoardings and buses, in cinemas, and at the point of sale (making up the balance). Advertising in the UK is controlled by the industry's own Advertising Standards Authority (which issues its own code of practice), by the Trade Descriptions Act (1968), and by the Independent Broadcasting Authority (which vets all broadcast advertisements). The industry in the UK and the USA is largely in the hands of advertising agencies, which work closely with their clients researching, copywriting, and producing the advertisements as well as booking space in the press and time for broadcasting.

● **advocaat** ▶ A liqueur, originally Dutch, made from brandy and egg yolks flavoured with vanilla.

● **advocate** ▶ In Scotland and in some countries, such as France, having a legal system based on Roman law, a person whose profession is to plead the cases of others in a court of justice. The English equivalent is a ▷barrister. In Scotland, the **Lord Advocate** is the chief law officer of the Crown, generally equivalent to the ▷attorney general in England.

● **Adwa** ▷*See* Adowa.

● **Adygeya Republic** ▶ A constituent republic in SW Russia. It was formed in 1922 for the Muslim Adygei people and became a republic in 1991. It has valuable forests and oil and natural-gas deposits. Area: 7600 sq km (2934 sq mi). Population (1995 est): 450 000. Capital: Maikop.

● **Adzharia** ▶ (*or* Adzhar Republic) An administrative division in Georgia on the Black Sea. It is mainly mountainous with a subtropical coastal plain. A popular holiday region, it is also an important producer of tea and citrus fruits. Industries include shipyards and oil refining. Area: 3000 sq km (1160 sq mi). Population (1993 est): 386 700. Capital: Batumi.

● **Aechmea** ▶ A genus of herbaceous plants (over 140 species), native to South America, where they grow upon the branches of trees (but are not parasitic). From the centre of a rosette of spiny-toothed leaves, 30–60 cm long, grow showy red or yellow flowers, often with blue tips. Some species, for example *A. fulgens* and *A. fasciata*, are grown as greenhouse ornamentals. Family: *Bromeliaceae* (pineapples, etc.).

● **Aedes** ▶ A genus of mosquitoes, widespread in the tropics and subtropics, that transmit diseases of man and livestock including yellow fever and dengue (transmitted by *A. aegypti*) and Rift Valley fever (transmitted by *A. cabalus*).

● **Aegae** ▶ (modern name: Vergina) The capital, with ▷Pella, of ancient Macedon (*see* Macedonia). During the 1970s archaeological work on a nearby mound revealed tombs believed to be those of ▷Philip II of Macedon and his immediate family. Treasures found here include magnificent wall paintings, golden jewellery, and silver vases.

● **Aegean civilizations** ▶ The prehistoric settlements on the islands of the Aegean Sea (between mainland Greece and Asia Minor). At the beginning of the Bronze Age (c. 3000 BC) an influx of immigrants to the ▷Cyclades islands (S Aegean) brought a high level of sophistication and prosperity, which can be seen from the excavations on Thera (*or* Santorini). The subsequent ▷Minoan civilization was at its greatest between the 17th and 15th centuries BC. At the end of the 15th century the related ▷Mycenaean civilization of mainland Greece began to assert its supremacy, lasting until about 1200.

● **Aegean Sea** ▶ A section of the NE Mediterranean Sea, lying between Greece and Turkey and containing many islands, including the Cyclades, Dodecanese, and N Sporades.

● **Aegina** ▶ (Modern Greek name: Aíyina) A Greek island in the Aegean Sea, one of the largest in the Saronic group lying SSW of Piraeus. It achieved its greatest prosperity in the 5th century BC but fell to Athens (458), which later expelled all its inhabitants. Today it serves as a holiday resort for Athenians. Area: 85 sq km (33 sq mi).

● **Aegina, Gulf of** ▷*See* Saronic Gulf.

● **Aegis** ▶ In Greek mythology, a breastplate worn by Zeus and his daughter Athena. At its centre was an image of ▷Medusa, which petrified enemies.

● **Aelfric** ▶ (c. 955–c. 1020) Anglo-Saxon prose writer and Abbot of Eynsham from 1005. His *Catholic Homilies* (990–92), collections of sermons, and his *Lives of the Saints* (996–97) were important contributions to the spread of learning in the 10th century, directed at a wider audience than the monks at the monastery of Cernel (now Cerne Abbas, Dorset) where he was novice master. He also wrote a Latin grammar, thus acquiring his nickname, Grammaticus.

● **Aeneas** ▶ A legendary Trojan leader, son of ▷Anchises and ▷Aphrodite, and hero of Virgil's *Aeneid*. After the Greek victory in the Trojan War, he sailed away from burning Troy with his family and other survivors and was shipwrecked near Carthage. He fell in love with ▷Dido but abandoned her to continue his divinely ordained voyage to Italy, where he founded what was to become Rome.

● **Aeneas Silvius** ▷*See* Pius II.

● **aeolian harp** ▶ A musical instrument named after the Greek wind god ▷Aeolus, consisting of a wooden resonating box strung with gut strings of varying thicknesses. When hung in the open air it produces chordal sounds that vary according to the wind pressure.

● **Aeolus** ▶ The Greek god of the winds and ruler of Aeolia. In Homer's *Odyssey* he gave Odysseus a bag containing contrary winds; Odysseus' companions untied it, causing his ship to be blown back to Aeolia.

● **Aepyornis** ▶ A genus of extinct flightless birds, also called elephant birds because of their huge size. They are known only from fossil bones and eggs found in Madagascar.

● **aerial** ▶ (*or* antenna) An electrical conductor that transmits and receives □radio or other electromagnetic waves. An oscillating ▷electromagnetic field, caused by waves from a distant source, induces an oscillating current in the receiving aerial. A transmitting aerial works by the same process in reverse, creating waves from an electrical signal. A modern aerial for UHF (ultra-high frequency) and VHF (very high frequency) consists of a dipole formed from two metal rods, each approximately one-quarter of the operating wavelength. In the Yagi aerial named after H. Yagi (1886–1976), a reflector rod is set behind the dipole and several director rods are placed in front of it. This provides a more directional array than the simple dipole and is widely used as a receiving and transmitting aerial for television.

● **aerobe** ▶ An organism that requires free oxygen for oxidation of foodstuffs to release chemical energy in the process of ▷respiration. Most living organisms are aerobes; exceptions include certain yeasts and bacteria. These organisms, called **anaerobes**, produce chemical energy by a series of reactions in which free oxygen is not required. **Obligate anaerobes**, which include a few bacteria, never use oxygen for respiration, while **facultative anaerobes** normally use oxygen but are able to switch to anaerobic respiration when free oxygen is deficient.

● **aerobics** ▶ A method of keeping fit by exercising to stimulate the heart and lungs to work faster, thereby increasing the volume of oxygen available to the body. It involves repetitive and sustained use of the muscles and claims to reduce the resting pulse rate and increase the efficiency of the heart. The system was started in the USA by Dr Ken Cooper for the US forces in the 1970s and subsequently adapted by Jackie Sorensen as a dance and exercise form.

● **aerodynamics** ▶ The study of the behaviour and flow of air around objects. As air is a viscous fluid any object moving through it experiences a drag. Aerodynamics is important in the design of vehicles travelling at more than 50 km per hour (31 mph), buildings and bridges, engines, furnaces, as well as aircraft (*see* aeronautics) and missiles. Proposed cross-sections of models of such objects are often tested in wind tunnels or in water, smoke or coloured dyes being used to trace the flow of the fluid around the surface and to measure the lift and drag forces. This enables the best streamlined shapes to be found in order to avoid ▷turbulence.

● **aerofoil** ▷*See* aeronautics.

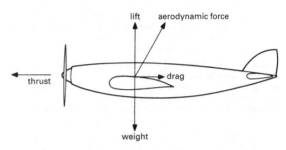

forces acting on aircraft

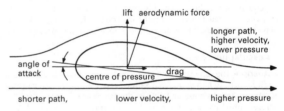

aeronautics ▶The forces acting on an aircraft. The aerofoil cross-section shows how the lift, which keeps it in the air, results from the passage of the aerofoil through the air, causing a lower pressure above it and a higher pressure below it.

● **aeronautics** ▶ The science and history (*see also* aircraft) of manned flight. An object flying through air is subject to four basic forces: its own weight (vertically downwards as a result of gravity), lift (to counterbalance its weight and keep it in the air), thrust (to force it through the air), and drag (resulting from friction between the body and the air). Birds and insects use their wings to provide both lift and thrust; man, in his heavier-than-air fixed-wing craft, uses an aerofoil to provide the lift and an ▷internal-combustion engine (propeller or jet) to provide the thrust (*see also* gliders). ▷Helicopters use rotating aerofoils to provide lift, while ▷rockets use no lift surfaces, the jet of expanding gas providing both lift and thrust. Man's lighter-than-air craft (*see* airships; balloons) use helium or hydrogen to reduce the craft's weight in relation to the volume of air it displaces to such an extent that the lift is provided by buoyancy. The use of aerofoils as lift surfaces depends on Bernoulli's principle, according to which the total energy of a flowing fluid remains constant; thus, if the velocity of the fluid increases, its pressure decreases in proportion. An aerofoil is a wing so shaped that (at subsonic speeds) air is accelerated over its rounded leading edge and curved upper surface, causing a reduced pressure above it. A smaller reduction in air velocity on its underside causes a slightly increased pressure below it. The combination of these pressure differences provides the lift. The design of practical aircraft wings has to take into account a number of complex factors, including suitable streamlining to avoid ▷turbulence in the airflow, stability over different angles of attack, the provision of suitable control surfaces (flaps, ailerons, etc.), and adequate strength and rigidity. At supersonic speeds these forces are somewhat altered (*see* sound barrier) and the aerofoil has to be more sweptback and more streamlined. At hypersonic speeds (i.e. in excess of five times the speed of sound) the ▷aerodynamics changes again and blunter noses and even smaller wings are needed.

● **aerosol** ▶ A colloidal suspension of particles of liquid or solid in a gaseous medium. Fog, mist, and smoke are common natural examples. By means of pressurized packages, aerosols can be produced from a huge range of substances, including insecticides, paints, hairsprays, etc. In these, the substance is mixed with an easily liquefied gas (often a fluorinated or chlorinated hydrocarbon), which acts as a propellant when the pressure is released. Fears have been expressed that fluorinated hydrocarbons, being lighter than air, could cause chain reactions in the upper atmosphere, which could destroy the ▷ozone layer. As this layer protects life on earth from the sun's ultraviolet radiation, measures have been encouraged to ban the use of fluorinated hydrocarbons in aerosols. ▷See colloid.

● **Aeschines** ▶ (c. 397–c. 322 BC) Athenian orator, who was an opponent of ▷Demosthenes. He was part of the Greek embassy to Philip of Macedon that in 350 negotiated peace, for which Demosthenes tried unsuccessfully in 343 to convict him of treason. In 330 Aeschines was defeated in his attempt to prevent Demosthenes being awarded a crown for his services to Athens and he retired to Rhodes.

● **Aeschylus** ▶ (c. 525–456 BC) Greek tragic dramatist, the first of the great trio of Athenian tragedians that included Sophocles and Euripides. He wrote over 80 plays, of which only 7 survive: *The Persians* (472), *Seven against Thebes* (467), the *Oresteia* trilogy (*Agamemnon, Libation Bearers*, and *Eumenides*; 458), *Suppliant Women* and *Prometheus Bound*. His introduction of a second actor, allowing dialogue and action independent of the chorus, and his innovations in costume and scenery, transformed the conventions of drama. His deeply religious plays dramatize the perpetual conflict between human passions and divine will.

● **Aesculapius** ▷See Asclepius.

● **Aesop** ▶ The supposed author of a collection of Greek fables, said by Herodotus to be a slave from Samos who lived in the 6th century BC. Originating in popular folklore, the fables are anecdotal stories whose animal characters are used to illustrate a moral point. The Roman poet Phaedrus popularized them in the 1st century AD, and the French poet La Fontaine wrote more sophisticated versions in the 17th century.

● **Aesthetic movement** ▶ A British literary and artistic movement of the late 19th century, summarized in the slogan "art for art's sake." Reacting against the ugliness of industrialism and against contemporary utilitarian social philosophies, its followers sought to create beauty for its own sake, self-consciously divorcing art from life. Their artistic precursors were the ▷Pre-Raphaelite Brotherhood, formed in 1848, whose emphasis on pure aesthetics was continued by Swinburne, William Morris, and others, culminating in the work of Oscar Wilde, Aubrey Beardsley, and the other contributors to the periodical *The Yellow Book* (1894–97).

● **aesthetics** ▶ The philosophical study of art and critical judgments about art. It includes questions concerning the nature of beauty and general questions about ascribing value—what we mean when we say that a work of art is good and how we arrive at standards of judgment. Objective views hold that beauty or value is in the object and that aesthetic judgments are true or false. Subjective views see value as something an observer brings to the work of art—it may be purely a matter of personal preference or, as ▷Kant held, something that can be universally agreed on.

● **aestivation** ▶ **1.** A state of ▷dormancy experienced by certain animals as a means of surviving a hot dry season. ▷Lungfish, for example, are adapted for aestivation. **2.** The way in which petals and sepals are folded in the flower bud before opening.

● **Aeth–** ▶ For names beginning Aeth *see* Eth–.

● **Aetius, Flavius** ▶ (d. 454 AD) Roman general. After a chequered early career, he became virtual ruler of the western Empire, dominating the emperor, Valentian III (reigned 425–55). Aetius defeated the Huns under Attila at the ▷Catalaunian Plains (451) but was powerless to halt their invasion of Italy. He was subsequently murdered by Valentian.

● **Aetolia** ▶ A region of ancient Greece N of the Gulf of Corinth. In 326 BC the tribes of Aetolia formed the **Aetolian League**, a federation that became a leading military power in Greece. In 27 BC Aetolia was included in the Roman province of Achaea. It is now part of the department of Aetolia and Acarnania.

● **Afars** ▶ A Cushitic-speaking people of the Horn of Africa, also known as Danakils. They are mainly nomads, herding goats and camels. Their social organization is complicated, with patrilineal kinship groups, age sets each under the authority of a chief, and a class division between the Asaimara (red men) nobles and the Adoimara (white men) lower class. Afars are nominally Muslim but earlier Cushitic beliefs persist.

● **Afars and the Issas, French territory of the** ▷See Djibouti, Republic of.

● **Affenpinscher** ▶ A breed of toy dog, also called monkey terrier. Small but sturdy, it has small erect ears, a short tail, and a short usually black coat with long hair on the legs and face. Height: 23.5–28 cm.

● **affidavit** ▷See oath.

● **affirmative action** ▶ In the USA, a government policy that aims to remedy the long-standing discrimination against women and members of certain ethnic groups by a degree of positive discrimination in their favour in such fields as employment, education, etc. The Equal Opportunities Act (1972) provides legal powers to enforce affirmative action in businesses or organizations that receive federal funding. Similar policies, sometimes extended to cover such minority groups as homosexuals and the disabled, have been adopted by some European countries (including Sweden and the Netherlands). Many public and commercial organizations have accepted the principles of affirmative action, although in the USA it has remained subject to frequent legal challenge, and the Republican Party is now opposed to it.

● **affluent society** ▶ The concept of a society in which people have more disposable income than they require for their basic needs; it was introduced by J. K. ▷Galbraith in his 1958 book of that name. Galbraith advocated that in the affluent societies of the USA and western Europe, governments should curb the excesses of consumerism and do more to reduce poverty. He predicted that private affluence could lead to public squalor when advertising enticed people to make unnecessary use of scarce resources and to cause excessive pollution, while unfair distribution of wealth created a disaffected underclass that threatened the stability of society.

● **Afghan hound** ▶ A breed of large dog having long legs, large drooping ears, and a very long silky coat, which may be of any colour. The Afghan probably originated in ancient Egypt and was later used in Afghanistan to hunt leopards and gazelles. Height: 68–73 cm (dogs); 61–66 cm (bitches).

● **Afghani, Jamal ad-Din al-** ▶ (1838–97) Muslim religious and political reformer. Of obscure origins, al-Afghani lived at various times in Istanbul, Egypt, Paris, India, and Persia. He argued for the unity of all Muslims and resistance to European interference in the Muslim countries.

● **Afghanistan, Islamic State of** ▶ A state in central Asia. The country is mountainous, the Hindu Kush range rising over 6000 m (20 000 ft). The only lower-lying areas are along the River Amu Darya (ancient name: Oxus) in the N and the delta of the River Helmand in the SW. The population consists of mixed ethnic groups, the largest being the ▷Pathans and the Tadzhiks.
Economy: virtually all forms of economic activity have been devastated by 20 years of civil war. The only notable exception is the cultivation of opium poppies and the production and sale of narcotics; although officially discouraged, this is now the country's main source of revenue. Stock raising was formerly important but agriculture is now mainly at subsistence level. Textiles were also important, especially carpet making. During the 1970s there were attempts to develop industry, to exploit mineral and natural gas resources, and to improve communications, but all such development has halted.

Exports formerly included Persian lambskins, fruit, cotton, wool, carpets, and natural gas.

History: before the opening up of international sea routes in the 15th century Afghanistan was an important centre on the overland routes across central Asia. For centuries under the rule of different powers, including the Arabs from the 7th century and the Mongols in the 13th century, it first became an independent kingdom in 1747. During the 19th century Afghanistan became involved in the struggle between Britain and Russia for influence in central Asia (*see* Anglo-Afghan Wars). After two wars with Britain it became a buffer state between British India and Russia, with Britain controlling its foreign policy. In 1919, under the leadership of ▷Amanollah Khan, Afghanistan attempted to free itself of British influence, which led to the third Anglo-Afghan War and independence by the Treaty of Rawalpindi (1919). In 1926 Amanollah declared himself king. He was deposed in 1929 by a brigand chief, Habibullah, who was in turn defeated by Nader Khan. When the latter was assassinated in 1933 he was succeeded by his son, King Zahir. Since World War II there has been friction with Pakistan over the question of an independent Pathan state in Pakistan. In 1973 the monarchy was overthrown by the former prime minister Mohammed Daud and a republic was established. A new constitution was adopted in 1977, with Daud as president. In 1978 he was killed in a military coup and a government was set up by the Marxist People's Democratic Party. Two further coups occurred in 1979; in the second Babrak Karmal came to power with Soviet aid. Soviet military occupation of Afghanistan provoked worldwide condemnation and Afghan rebels (Mujahidin) waged a fierce guerrilla war against government and Soviet forces. This resulted in the evacuation of Soviet troops by 1989 and the overthrow of the pro-Soviet government of Mohammad Najibullah in 1992. The Mujahidin then proclaimed an Islamic state, but fighting continued between rival factions. In 1995 the ▷Taleban militia took control of S Afghanistan and in 1996 they ousted the Kabul government and imposed strict Islamic law. By late 1998 they had defeated rival forces in the N (the Northern Alliance) to take control of virtually the whole country. In October–November 2001 Afghan cities suffered massive US airstrikes after the Taleban refused to hand over Osama ▷Bin Laden, whose Afghan-based ▷al-Qaida organization was widely held responsible for the events of ▷September 11 (*see* war on terrorism). As the Taleban regime collapsed, the Northern Alliance reoccupied Kabul and other major cities. In December 2001 the Alliance set up an interim administration under Hamid Karzai. Fierce fighting between US-led forces and Taleban-al-Qaida fighters has continued in the S. The conflict has greatly exacerbated Afghanistan's already severe refugee problem.

Islamic State of Afghanistan

Official languages	Pushtu and Dari Persian
Official currency	afghani of 100 puls
Area	657 500 sq km (250 000 sq mi)
Population (2000 est)	25 889 000
Capital	Kabul

● **AFL-CLO** ▷*See* American Federation of Labor-Congress of Industrial Organizations.

● **aflatoxin** ▷*See* Aspergillus.

● **Africa** ▶ The second largest continent in the world. Linked to SW Asia by the Isthmus of Suez, it is of irregular triangular shape with more than two-thirds of its area lying to the N of the equator, which runs across the centre of the continent. Except for Australia, its relief is the most uniform of all the continents, consisting principally of two well-defined physical regions: a S tableland and a lower but still elevated plain in the N. A notable feature of the NE is the ▷Great Rift Valley, which contains the most extensive system of freshwater lakes in the world after North America, as well as the continent's highest point, Mount ▷Kilimanjaro. Madagascar, the fourth largest island in the world, lies off the SE coast but there are few island groups. The principal rivers are the Nile, Niger, Congo, and Zambezi. Africa's climate and vegetation vary considerably from the arid desert of the Sahara to the tropical rainforest of the Congo basin. The inhabitants of Africa are principally of Negroid origin, although the originators

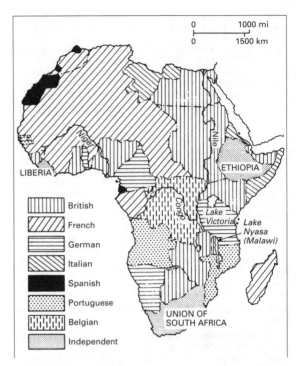

Africa ▶ In the so-called "scramble for Africa" (1880–1912) the European powers annexed most of the continent. The map shows the position in 1914.

of the Berber language group remain dominant in N Africa and the Sahara and there are a few Cushite-speaking peoples in the NE.

History: Africa's long history has been substantiated by Louis ▷Leakey's finds of hominoid man at Olduvai Gorge. The earliest African civilization was established in Egypt in about 3400 BC. Also in N Africa the Phoenicians founded Carthage (9th century BC), later conquered by the Romans (146 BC). From the 7th century AD Arab influence was strong and Islam spread with the trans-Saharan and East African coastal trade. Several African kingdoms and empires emerged during this period, notably the Sudanese empires of Ghana, Mali, and Songhai. From the 15th century European exploration and exploitation began, initiated by the Portuguese. Slaves, ivory, and gold were exported from Africa from the 17th to the late 19th centuries, during which time the Atlantic slave trade was active, over 10 million slaves being shipped to the plantations of America and the West Indies. This enforced migration considerably changed the composition of the American and West Indian populations. From 1880 to 1912 most of Africa was partitioned by the European powers, which imposed political boundaries upon the continent that bore no relationship to former political and social organizations; this resulted in long-standing problems. From the 1950s onwards there was a general movement towards self-determination and Africa now consists of independent nations. Nevertheless, large areas of the continent have remained politically unstable and economically undeveloped, as well as being prey to natural disasters, such as the droughts that afflicted E and S Africa in the 1980s and 1990s. The 1990s saw a trend away from dictatorship and one-party rule in favour of multiparty democracy, as well as the disappearance of the last White-dominated regimes (in Namibia and South Africa). Area: about 30 300 000 sq km (11 700 000 sq mi). Population (1996 est): 720 363 000.

● **African Adam and Eve** ▷*See* mitochondrial Eve.

● **African art** ▶ The traditional art of the peoples of sub-Saharan or Black Africa. Among these peoples the visual or plastic arts were not distinguished one from another or from the religious and cultural life of the community. Artists, however, were professionals who enjoyed a respected and sometimes priestly and hereditary status, working on commission or with royal patronage. They produced ceremonial masks, figures for use in the ancestor cults, weapons, furnishings, and everyday utensils. Carving and sculpture in wood, ivory, copper alloys, terracotta, and clay were the dominant forms, but artistic skills extended to textiles, basketry, leatherwork, and wall and body painting; they also included the mastery of sophisticated techniques, such as the ▷cire perdue process of bronze-casting. Most of the extant examples of traditional art are less than 200 years old, but these are often representative of much earlier developments. Art flourished in the area of W Africa roughly extending from Senegal and Mali in the N, through the countries bordering the Atlantic, to N Angola and Zambia and E to the chain of great lakes. Within this area a large number of styles are evident. The Dogon of Mali are noted for their stylized rectangular wooden masks. The Yoruba of Nigeria and Dahomey (now Benin) made naturalistic human heads and figures, and similar figures in brass and terracotta were produced at the Yoruba centre, Ife, in Nigeria, as early as the 12th century. The skill in casting metal passed from Ife to Dahomey, where the Edo people produced brass reliefs and sculpture. The Baule of Côte d'Ivoire made finely polished masks and figures; they and the Ashanti of Ghana are the only African people to have used gold leaf to cover sculptures and other carved wooden objects. In the Congo region, ancestral figures, masks, fetishes, and other decorated objects were made in great profusion. Human and animal forms were rendered not naturalistically but symbolically, as part of a magical or religious view of reality. It was this quality in African art that appealed to and influenced such 20th-century Western artists as Picasso, Modigliani, and Epstein.

● **African Charter on Human and People's Rights** ▷See human rights.

● **African languages** ▶ A geographical classification of the heterogeneous languages spoken in the African continent. The ▷Hamito-Semitic group extends across N Africa from Mauritania to Somalia. The ▷Nilo-Saharan group is spoken in many dialects in central Africa, and the ▷Niger-Congo languages, many of them ▷Bantu languages, cover most of the area S of the Sahara. In S Africa the ▷Khoisan languages survive. There are up to a thousand indigenous languages of the continent as well as the European languages (English, Afrikaans, French, Portuguese) imported by colonizers. ▷Malagasy, a language of ▷Austronesian origin, is spoken in Madagascar. ▷Swahili is an important lingua franca in East Africa. Certain African languages are unique in using click sounds in their phonology; predominance of certain consonantal groups (kp, gb, mb, nd) is also common in Africa.

● **African lily** ▷See Agapanthus.

● **African National Congress** ▶ (ANC) A Black nationalist movement in S Africa. Founded in 1912 as the South African Native National Congress, the ANC fought ▷apartheid from its introduction in 1948. The ANC was outlawed by the South African government in 1960 and turned to sabotage and guerrilla activity. Nelson ▷Mandela, for many years its symbolic head, became president after his release from long imprisonment in 1990, succeeding Oliver ▷Tambo. The ANC was legalized (1990) and subsequently played a major role in constitutional negotiations. In 1994 the ANC won South Africa's first multiracial elections and Mandela became president of South Africa. In 1998 Mandela was succeeded as president of the ANC by Thabo ▷Mbeki, who became president of South Africa in 1999.

● **African Union** ▷See Organization of African Unity.

● **African violet** ▶ A flowering plant, *Saintpaulia ionantha*, native to tropical E Africa and widely grown as a house plant. 10–15 cm high, it has hairy leaves and clusters of pink, blue, purple, or white flowers. Family: *Gesneriaceae*.

● **Afrikaans** ▷See Afrikaner.

● **Afrikaner** ▶ A South African of Dutch or ▷Huguenot descent. The Afrikaners comprise about 60% of the Republic's White population. Formerly called "Boers" (farmers), they have undergone considerable urbanization since the 1930s. In the 18th and 19th centuries they led a seminomadic life, resisting governmental control from Cape Town. Their two independent states, the South African Republic and the Orange Free State, came under British rule after the second ▷Boer War. Their language, Afrikaans, derives, but is distinct, from Dutch. ▷See also Great Trek.

● **Afro-Asiatic languages** ▷See Hamito-Semitic languages.

● **afterlife** ▶ The belief, common to many religions, philosophies, and cultures, that some aspect of a human being, often called a soul or spirit, survives physical death. In ancient Greece, ▷Plato and other philosophers taught that the soul, being rational, must of necessity be immortal. In Judaism, Christianity, and Islam doctrines of the afterlife reflect belief in a God of justice who will right earthly wrongs: traditionally, ▷heaven is the destination of those who have pleased the Deity, while the wicked can expect to suffer in ▷hell or some intermediate state, such as ▷purgatory. In Hinduism the atman (soul) is subject to rebirth until moksha (enlightenment) frees the individual from the cycle. ▷Nirvana presents a similar end to the cycle of reincarnation in Buddhism.

By its very nature, the concept of an afterlife is beyond the reach of any form of evidence and it can only be accepted as an act of faith. Atheists are content to accept that no part of an individual endures beyond the grave, except in the memories of the living and in the works they leave behind. Many others retain a vague hope in some form of afterlife without accepting orthodox religious doctrine.

● **Agade** ▷See Akkad.

● **Agadir** ▶ 30 30N 9 40W A port in SW Morocco, on the Atlantic coast, trading centre of the Sous Plain. An earthquake in 1960 destroyed much of the town and killed about 12 000 people. Population (1994 est): 155 244.

● **Aga Khan III** ▶ (1877–1957) Imam (leader) of the ▷Ismaili sect of Muslims (1885–1957). He was an early president of the All-India Muslim League and represented India at the League of Nations in 1932 and from 1934 to 1937.

● **Aga Khan IV** ▶ (1936–   ) Imam (leader) of the ▷Ismaili sect of Muslims (1957–   ), succeeding his grandfather ▷Aga Khan III.

● **agama** ▶ A common African broad-headed lizard belonging to the family *Agamidae* (50 species). 30–45 cm long, agamas have a thick body and a tapering tail and feed on insects. The common agama (*Agama agama*) is variously coloured: dominant males have a brick-red head, blue body and legs, and banded tail; other males are duller coloured, like the females.

● **Agamemnon** ▶ King of Mycenae and commander of the Greek army in the Trojan War. His quarrel with Achilles is the main theme of Homer's *Iliad*. After his return from Troy he was murdered by his wife Clytemnestra and her lover Aegisthus. The subsequent vengeance of his son Orestes is the theme of ▷Aeschylus' *Oresteia* trilogy.

● **Agaña** ▶ 13 28N 144 45E The capital of Guam in the W Pacific Ocean, in the Mariana Islands. The city was largely destroyed in World War II. The University of Guam was established here in 1952. Population (1995 est): 2000.

● **Agapanthus** ▶ A genus of herbaceous plants native to South Africa and cultivated for ornament in greenhouses and tropical gardens. *A. africanus* (African lily) has long strap-shaped leaves and large clusters of blue funnel-shaped flowers borne on a tall stalk. There are many cultivated varieties and hybrids. Family: *Amaryllidaceae*.

● **agar-agar** ▶ A gelatinous substance obtained from seaweed. A solution in water sets to a firm jelly, which is used for growing bacteria.

● **agaric** ▶ A fungus belonging to a large worldwide order (*Agaricales*). The group includes many edible ▷mushrooms, such as the white mushroom (*Agaricus bisporus*) and field mushroom (*A. campestris*), as well as the poisonous death cap (*see* Amanita). The visible part of the fungus consists of a stipe (stalk) bearing a cap with gills on the undersurface. Phylum: ▷*Basidiomycota*. ▷*See also* fly agaric.

● **Agartala** ▶ 23 49N 91 15E A city in NE India, the capital of Tripura. It is a commercial centre. Population (1991): 157 636.

● **Agassi, Andre** ▶ (1970–   ) US tennis player, who won the Wimbledon men's singles in 1992, the US Open in 1994 and 1999, the Australian Open in 1995 and 2000, and the French Open in 1999. He married Steffi ▷Graff in 2001.

● **Agassiz, Jean Louis Rodolphe** ▶ (1807–73) Swiss natural historian. Agassiz's early work centred on the study of extinct species, fossilization, and glaciation. His later theories on animal species were contrary to those of Charles Darwin. In his *Essay on Classification* (1859) he argued that organisms were immutable and could not have evolved from one source. As professor of zoology at Harvard University, his innovative teaching methods revolutionized the study of natural science in the USA. His son **Alexander Agassiz** (1835–1910) was a marine zoologist and mining engineer. His copper mine became noted for its enlightened management. He founded his own research station, from which he mounted expeditions to study marine fauna and the sea bed.

● **agate** ▶ A banded or concentrically patterned form of ▷chalcedony. The banding is due to intermittent deposition in rock cavities and the colours, ranging from white, milky blue, yellow, and brown to red, are due to traces of mineral or organic colouring matter. Being hard, it is used for mortars for grinding. It is also used for ornamental purposes, for which the stone may be artificially dyed.

● **Agathocles** ▶ (361–289 BC) Tyrant (317–304) and King (304–289) of Syracuse. After seizing power he gained control of E Sicily but fled to Africa after his defeat (311) by the Carthaginians. By 304 he had brutally pacified the Sicilian opposition and took the title of king.

● **Agave** ▶ A genus of plants (about 300 species) of the S USA and tropical America, many of which are grown for ornament. Agaves have a basal tuft of thick fleshy, sometimes toothed, leaves and a cluster of flowers that—in some species—grows on a tall stalk (up to 12 m high). Growth is slow—it may be 60 or more years before flowers are produced; after flowering the plant dies. Several species are important as a source of fibre, especially ▷sisal; the fermented juice of others is used as an alcoholic drink (pulque) or distilled to produce spirits (*see* tequila). Family: *Agavaceae* (or *Amaryllidaceae*). ▷*See also* century plant.

● **Agee, James** ▶ (1909–55) US poet, novelist, and film critic. After graduating from Harvard he published a book of poems, *Permit Me Voyage* (1934), and wrote influential film reviews for various magazines. *Let Us Now Praise Famous Men* (1941), in collaboration with the photographer Walker Evans, is a bitter account of the lives of Alabama sharecroppers. He also produced two autobiographical novels, *The Morning Watch* (1951) and *A Death in the Family* (1957, Pulitzer Prize), and several filmscripts.

● **ageing** ▶ (*or* senescence) The degenerative process in an organism that precedes death. In man ageing is characterized by a gradual decline in the efficiency of the repair mechanisms of the body tissues, leading to increased susceptibility to disease; it is also associated with a reduction and then loss of fertility. Sometimes there is marked mental deterioration (senility). There are several theories to account for the ageing process. Some maintain that it is due to the accumulation of errors in metabolism brought about by errors in DNA replication as well as faulty protein synthesis; others that ageing—particularly in plants after flowering and some animals after reproduction—is genetically programmed.

● **Agence France-Presse** ▷*See* news agency.

● **agent orange** ▶ (2,4,5,-trichlorophenoxyethanoic acid) A toxic herbicide used in jungle warfare as a defoliant. Its name derives from the orange rings painted on its containers when used by the US forces in Vietnam. Many US troops who handled it later developed cancer.

● **Age of Reason** ▷*See* Enlightenment.

● **age set** ▶ A recognized group of persons, usually males initiated at the same time, found in many primitive societies. Each age set may pass through a series of stages (age grades) having various functions requiring abilities dependent upon age, such as physical strength, experience, and wisdom. Typically there will be one or more grades of warriors and of elders who exercise political and often ritual authority. ▷*See also* initiation rites.

● **Agesilaus II** ▶ (444–360 BC) King of Sparta (c. 399–360). A noted general, he achieved some success against the Persians in Asia Minor (396–395) and against the Boeotians at Coronea (394). His subsequent diplomatic activities contributed to Sparta's disastrous defeat by the Thebans at Leuctra (371). Xenophon wrote a memoir of Agesilaus.

● **aggadah** ▷*See* haggadah.

● **Aggiornamento** ▷*See* Roman Catholic Church.

● **agglomerate** ▶ A rock composed of a mixture of coarse angular fragments and finer-grained material formed by volcanic explosions; it is usually found in or near the volcanic vent.

● **aggression** ▶ In biology, behaviour intended to injure or intimidate another animal that is usually competing for food, a mate, ▷territory, or social dominance. Aggressive attitudes are often intended to exaggerate the aggressor's size or ferocity; for example fish erect their fins, some mammals erect their hairs, and dogs bare their teeth. Aggression between individuals of the same species often involves ritualized ▷displays that usually avoid the dangers of actual combat, with one or the other contestants conceding dominance. Indeed, in much animal behaviour aggression is more often a substitute for combat than a prelude to it.

In human psychology, many theories have been advanced for both individual aggression and mob aggression. Unlike similar behaviour in animals, personal aggression is unlikely to be a purely instinctive response to threat. In ▷Freud's psychoanalytical theory, it is seen as a projection of the death wish, in ▷Adler's view it is a manifestation of the will to power, while in early social learning theory it was seen as a response to frustration when the individual's objectives are obstructed. In more recent social learning theory aggression is regarded as no more than an element in the repertoire of human behaviour that is effective in certain situations. While an aggressive response to some situations may still be partially instinctive, human behaviour is more likely to be determined by rational rather than purely emotional or instinctive criteria. Individuals often make a conscious choice between coercion and aggression. This choice will depend on how confident people are in their social skills and how they perceive their chances if aggression culminates in violence.

For crowds, many of the inhibitions that restrain the individual from aggression disappear. In mob violence, because the individual alone is not responsible either for making the decision to respond aggressively or for the consequences of the aggression, aggression is more spontaneous and more gratuitous (*see* football hooliganism). Individuals often refrain from aggression out of cowardice. In a sense, the aggressive crowd is composed of cowards, hiding behind each other's valour.

In politics, aggression may be a means by which a minority asserts its right to independence, or the response to such an assertion. On the other hand, it may be the way in which a power seeks to extend its area of dominance to achieve its military, economic, or ideological ends. Unlike animal behaviour, aggression is only effective as a political policy if it is backed by sufficient resources to give the aggressor a likelihood of victory if it leads to combat.

● **Agha Mohammad Khan** ▶ (1742–97) Shah of Persia (1796–97), who founded the Qajar dynasty (1796–1925). The chief (1758) of one of the clans of the Qajar tribe, he made himself ruler of the whole of Persia and was crowned in 1796. He was the first ruler to make Tehran his capital.

● **Agincourt, Battle of** ▶ (25 October, 1415) The battle that took place during the ▷Hundred Years' War at Agincourt (now in the Pas-de-Calais), in which the French were defeated by an English army led by Henry V. The decisive English victory, which owed much to their outstanding archers, was achieved with not more than 1600 dead; the French may have lost as many as 6000 men.

● **Agnes, St** ▶ (4th century AD) Roman virgin and martyr. Nothing certain is known about her life, but according to legend she was martyred under Diocletian for refusing to marry and subsequently resisting plans to make her a prostitute. Feast day: 21 Jan. Emblem: a lamb.

● **Agnesi, Maria Gaetana** ▶ (1718–99) Italian mathematician and philosopher. A child prodigy, Agnesi became the first woman to occupy a chair of mathematics when she was appointed to that at Bologna University in 1750. On the death of her father in 1752, she devoted herself to religion and charitable work. The curve $x^2 y = a^2 (a - y)$ is known as the "Witch of Agnesi" because she called it a *versiera* (Latin: turning), a word also meaning witch in colloquial Italian. □ p. 20.

● **Agnew, Spiro T(heodore)** ▶ (1918–96) US Republican politician; vice president (1969–73), who gained notoriety for his attacks on the critics of President Nixon. In 1973 a federal tax case forced him to resign his office. He was given a suspended prison sentence and fined $10,000.

Maria Agnesi ▶ A child prodigy, Agnesi delivered an hour-long Latin oration demanding education for women at the age of nine. Her groundbreaking work in algebra, geometry, and calculus was completed in her twenties.

● **Agni ▶** The Hindu god of fire, whose other attributes include the protection of mankind against evil, guarding the home, bringing rain, cleansing human beings from sin after death, and bestowing immortality.

● **Agnon, Shmuel Yosef ▶** (Samuel Josef Czaczkes; 1888–1970) Jewish novelist, born in Galicia, who settled in Palestine in 1907. His treatment of contemporary Jewish themes in *The Day Before Yesterday* (1945) and other works was influenced by folklore and traditional religious literature. In 1966 he shared the Nobel Prize.

● **agnosticism ▶** The philosophical view that doubts the existence of God and other spiritual phenomena and claims that even if they do exist it is impossible to know anything about them. Although this position occurs sporadically throughout history, the term was apparently coined by T. H. ▷Huxley in 1869. Agnosticism was subsequently enthusiastically embraced by rationalists, who hesitated on philosophical or social grounds to adopt outright ▷atheism.

● **agora ▶** A central feature of ancient Greek town planning. Similar to the Roman ▷forum, the primary function of the agora was as the town market. It also became the main social and political meeting place. With the acropolis, it contained the most important buildings of the town.

● **agoraphobia ▶** *▷See* phobia.

● **Agostini, Giacomo ▶** (1944–) Italian racing motorcyclist, winner of a record 15 world championship titles: 350 cc in 1968–74 and 500 cc in 1966–72 and 1975. He is the only man to have won two world championships in five consecutive years.

● **agouti ▶** A rabbit-sized rodent belonging to a genus (*Dasyprocta*; 13 species) of Central and South American forests. Agoutis have long legs, small ears, and a very short hairless tail. The hair on the rump is often long and brightly coloured and can be erected when the animal is alarmed. Agoutis feed on leaves, roots, and berries and are commonly eaten by the Indians. Family: *Dasyproctidae* (agoutis and pacas); suborder: *Hystricomorpha*.

● **AGR ▶** (advanced gas-cooled reactor) *▷See* nuclear energy; thermal reactor.

● **Agra ▶** 27 09N 78 00E A city in India, in Uttar Pradesh on the River Jumna. Former capital of the Mogul Empire (1566–69 and 1601–58), it fell to the British in 1803 and from 1835 until 1862 was capital of the North-West Provinces. Notable buildings include the celebrated ▷Taj Mahal and a fine 16th-century fort. Its university was established in 1927. A major commercial, industrial, and communications centre, it produces carpets. Population (1991): 899 195.

● **agranulocytosis ▶** The condition resulting from a deficiency or absence of certain white blood cells (called granulocytes). Agranulocytosis may be caused by an allergic reaction to drugs, ▷cytotoxic drugs (which damage the bone marrow), and severe infection. Symptoms include weakness, fever, and a sore throat; treatment includes withdrawal of the suspect drug, fresh-blood transfusions, and antibiotics.

● **agribusiness ▶** The businesses associated with supplying farmers and the processing and distribution of their products. In many countries agribusiness is the largest employer of labour in the economy. On the supply side it includes suppliers of agricultural equipment, fertilizers, pest controls, and other chemicals; stock breeders; seed suppliers; and finance houses and banks. On the sales side it includes food processors; merchants; feedstuff suppliers; and the distributors and retailers of these products.

● **Agricola, Georgius ▶** (George Bauer; 1494–1555) German physician and mineralogist. Working as a physician in several mining towns, he carried out a systematic study of mining and minerals; this study consistently discounted the traditional "magical" attributes of minerals, describing instead their observable physical properties. His *De re metallica* (1556) was the standard text on mining and metallurgy for two centuries.

● **Agricola, Gnaeus Julius ▶** (40–93 AD) Roman governor of Britain and father-in-law of his biographer Tacitus. Sent to govern Britain in 78, he followed a policy of romanization, exploration, and expansion. He advanced the Roman frontiers in annual campaigns, reaching the Scottish Highlands before his recall in 84.

● **Agricola, Johann ▶** (Johannes Schnitter; c. 1494–1566) German Protestant reformer. A pupil of ▷Luther at Wittenberg, he later worked as a reformer in Frankfurt and Eisleben. From 1536 he taught at Wittenberg but quarrelled with Luther over doctrine and in 1540 moved to Berlin, where he became court preacher to the Elector of Brandenburg.

● **agricultural revolution ▶** The major changes in agriculture in Britain that took place mainly in the 18th century. The open-field system of strip farming was replaced by larger enclosed fields, hedged and ditched, in which improved agricultural methods and new implements could be used (*see* Tull, Jethro; Townshend, Charles, 2nd Viscount); the quality of cattle and sheep was improved by scientific stock breeding (*see* Bakewell, Robert). This resulted in a greater production of food for the growing industrial population (*see* industrial revolution), although it meant hardship for those farmers who were displaced by ▷enclosure or by the ▷Highland Clearances.

● **agriculture ▶** The practice or study of farming. Settled farming probably dates back to the 10th millennium BC, when it began to replace man's activities as a hunter and gatherer of food. The domestication of cattle, goats, sheep, and pigs together with the cropping of wheat, barley, rice, etc., enabled primitive civilizations to flourish in such regions as the fertile river basins of the Tigris, Euphrates, and Nile.

Farming has developed in various ways in different parts of the world, depending largely on climatic conditions, the type of land, and the local system of land tenure. Many areas are suitable only for ▷livestock farming whereas in many others large-scale ▷arable farming is possible. In some cases the most economically successful farms are mixed arable and livestock. Until the end of the 19th century farming was based on energy derived from man and his draught animals. Some parts of the world still use such traditional methods; however, during the 20th century, especially in developed countries, the ▷tractor became the primary energy source. The 20th century also saw great success in improving breeds of plants and animals and soil fertility (*see* fertilizers), increasing mechanization, and control of plant and animal pests. These measures are now being applied in the developing world, where they are bringing about the Green Revolution that is needed to feed the world's growing population.

However, misuse of modern intensive farming methods can cause such problems as soil erosion, while ▷pollution by excessive use of fertilizers, weedkillers, insecticides, etc., can seriously damage the environment. Consequently there has been a reaction in favour of so-called organic farming in parts of the Western world. The reconciliation of optimum food production with conservation of the environment is one of the principal tasks of the UN ▷Food and Agriculture Organization.

● **Agrigento** ▶ 37 19N 13 35E A seaport in Italy, in S Sicily. Founded about 580 BC, it has famous ancient temples and is the birthplace of the philosopher Empedocles. Sulphur mining is the main occupation. Population (1990): 56 372.

● **agrimony** ▶ A herbaceous perennial plant of the genus *Agrimonia* (especially *A. eupatoria*), native to Europe but grown in most temperate regions. Up to 1 m tall, it has a spike of small yellow flowers and toothed oval leaves that yield a yellow dye. Family: *Rosaceae*.

● **Agrippa, Marcus Vipsanius** ▶ (?63–12 BC) Roman general and close associate of Emperor ▷Augustus, whose daughter Julia was his third wife. After military successes in Gaul (38 BC) Agrippa became consul (37 BC). He played an important part in the defeat of Mark Antony at ▷Actium (31 BC) and contributed to the military successes of Augustus.

● **Agrippina the Elder** ▶ (?13 BC–33 AD) The daughter of ▷Agrippa, wife of ▷Germanicus Julius Caesar, and mother of Emperor ▷Caligula. A courageous and high-minded woman, she accompanied her husband on his campaigns. After his death she incurred the hostility of Tiberius, who exiled her to Pandataria, where she died in suspicious circumstances. Her daughter, **Agrippina the Younger** (15–59 AD), was notorious for her political intrigues. She probably murdered her uncle, Emperor Claudius, who was also her third husband, to make way for the succession of her son, Nero. She exerted considerable political influence early in Nero's reign, but after they had quarrelled he had her murdered.

● **agrochemical** ▶ A chemical substance used in farming. Agrochemicals may be ▷fertilizers or they may be ▷pesticides to control organisms that damage agricultural plants (*see also* herbicide; insecticides).

● **agronomy** ▶ The management of land, especially for the production of arable crops. Agronomy involves determining the nature of a soil and how its fertility may be improved by such processes as drainage, irrigation, the application of natural and artificial fertilizers, and husbandry techniques (e.g. ▷crop rotation). Equally important is the breeding of crop plants that are suited to a particular soil.

● **Aguascalientes** ▶ 21 51N 102 18W A city in central Mexico. The commercial centre for a region producing fruit and vegetables, its industries include ceramics production, tanning, and railway engineering. There are medicinal hot springs nearby. Population (1990): 440 425.

● **Agulhas, Cape** ▶ 34 50S 20 00E A cape in South Africa, in Western Cape. It is the most southerly point of the African continent and has a lighthouse (1849).

● **Ahab** ▶ (*or* Achab; d. 854 BC) King of Israel (c. 875–854). Through an alliance with Judah he successfully resisted the Assyrians but became unpopular through the influence of his wife Jezebel, who persuaded him to introduce the worship of ▷Baal. He died in battle against the Assyrians.

● **Ahad Ha'am** ▶ (Asher Ginsberg; 1856–1927) Hebrew essayist and an influential Zionist thinker. Born in Russia, he moved to London in 1908 and participated in negotiations leading to the ▷Balfour Declaration. In 1922 he settled in Palestine. Critical of political ▷Zionism, he looked to nationalism to achieve a Jewish moral and cultural regeneration.

● **Ahaggar Mountains** ▶ (*or* Hoggar Mts) A plateau area in S Algeria, in the central Sahara. It averages about 900 m (2950 ft) but reaches 2918 m (9573 ft) at Mount Tahat.

● **Ahern, Bertie** ▶ (1951–) Irish statesman. Leader of Fianna Fáil (1994–), he became prime minister of Ireland in 1997 and was an architect of the Good Friday Agreement for Northern ▷Ireland of April 1998.

● **ahimsa** ▶ (Sanskrit: noninjury) The ethical practice, strictly observed in ▷Jainism but also of fundamental importance in ▷Hinduism and ▷Buddhism, of not causing harm to any living thing. Because of the belief in reincarnation, these religions respect all forms of life

as being parts of the cycle of rebirth. Vegetarianism is consequently widespread in Asia. ▷Gandhi's doctrine of nonviolent resistance (*satyagraha*) was derived from the principle of ahimsa.

● **Ahmadabad** ▶ (*or* Ahmedabad) 23 03N 72 40E An industrial city in central India, in Gujarat. Founded in 1411, it is a major rail centre and its textile industry (established 1859–61) is one of the largest in the country. Its university was established in 1949. Population (1991): 2 872 865.

● **Ahmadiya** ▶ A religious sect founded in the Punjab by Mirza Ghulam Ahmad of Qadiyan (1839–1908), who was of Muslim background. His teaching combined elements of Islam, Christianity, and Hinduism. He taught that Jesus was buried in Srinigar and that he himself was the messiah and ▷Mahdi. In 1918 the Ahmadiya split into two groups, the larger regarding Mirza Ahmad as a prophet, the smaller regarding him only as a reformer. Both groups are based in Pakistan, but have communities elsewhere.

● **Ahmadnagar** ▶ (*or* Ahmednagar) 19 08N 74 48E A town in W India, in Maharashtra. It was conquered in 1490 by Ahmad Nizam Shah, founder of the Ahmadnagar dynasty. A commercial centre, its industries include cotton and leather processing. Population (1991): 181 015.

● **Ahmad Shah Durrani** ▶ (c. 1723–73) Afghan ruler (1747–73), who founded the Durrani dynasty. Ahmad was commander in India for the Persian ▷Nader Shah. When Nader died (1747), Ahmad became shah and built an empire that was bordered by the River Oxus, Tibet, the River Indus, and Persia. After his death, the empire collapsed.

● **Ahmed III** ▶ (1673–1736) Sultan of the Ottoman Empire (1703–30). After a successful war against Russia (1711–13) Ahmed was defeated by Austria; by the Peace of Passarowitz (1718) the Ottomans lost their last possessions in Hungary and parts of Serbia. He was deposed and died in captivity. His reign is known as the Tulip Age because of the flower's contemporary popularity.

● **Ahmose I** ▶ King of Egypt (c. 1570–1546 BC), who founded the 18th dynasty. He liberated Egypt from the ▷Hyksos, retaking Memphis, and reasserted Egyptian power in Nubia and Palestine. After many years of alien domination, he reorganized his reunited country and encouraged trade.

● **Ahmose II** ▶ King of Egypt (570–526 BC) of the 26th dynasty. He came to power in a military coup but ruled for 44 years in peace and prosperity.

● **Ahriman** ▷*See* Ahura Mazda.

● **Ahura Mazda** ▶ The supreme deity of ▷Zoroastrianism, creator of all things good and just. He represents the creative principle, living in eternal light, opposed to Ahriman, the destructive principle of greed, anger, etc., living in darkness.

● **Ahvaz** ▶ 31 17N 48 43E A town in SW Iran, the capital of Khuzestan province. On the site of an ancient city it is a centre for the nearby oilfields. Population (1994 est): 828 380.

● **Ahvenanmaa Islands** ▷*See* Åland Islands.

● **ai** ▷*See* sloth.

● **AI** ▷*See* artificial intelligence.

● **Aidan, St** ▶ (c. 600–51 AD) Irish monk at ▷Iona who became bishop of Northumbria in 635. He founded the monastery at Lindisfarne (*see* Holy Island), the centre of his missionary activity in N England. His life is described by ▷Bede in his *Ecclesiastical History*. Feast day: 31 Aug.

● **AIDS** ▶ (acquired immune deficiency syndrome) A viral disease characterized by a decrease of certain T-lymphocytes, resulting in a breakdown of the immune system and increased susceptibility to other diseases. First described in 1981, it originated in central Africa, probably by the mutation of a virus carried by chimpanzees. The causative agent is thought to be HIV (human immunodeficiency virus); it is transmitted in blood, semen, or vaginal fluid. It is possible that a very high proportion of virus carriers will develop the disease but the exact percentage is uncertain and carriers can remain free of symptoms for up to ten years after the initial infection. There is as yet no cure, but zidovudine (called AZT in the USA) combined with other antiviral drugs, including the recently developed protease inhibitors, delays the progress of the disease.

In the Western world AIDS occurs most frequently in homosexual and bisexual males and intravenous drug users who share needles, but it can also be transmitted to heterosexuals by any penetrative intercourse with an AIDS carrier, to a fetus from an infected mother across the placenta, and to those who receive transfusions of infected blood (all of which is now tested). By the end of 2000, AIDS had resulted in an estimated 18.8 million deaths worldwide (including over 10 000 in Britain), while those suffering from AIDS or HIV were estimated at over 36 million. The governments of many countries are attempting to limit the spread of AIDS by campaigns discouraging casual sexual relationships and encouraging the use of condoms. Owing in part to such campaigns, the disease has not spread through the heterosexual population of the Western world to the extent predicted by some early forecasts. In large parts of sub-Saharan Africa, however, HIV is now carried by an estimated one in five of the adult population (although among males who have been circumcised the incidence of infection is much lower; *see* circumcision). In 2000 about 80% of all deaths from AIDS and nearly 80% of new cases of HIV infection occurred in central and southern Africa.

● **Aiken, Howard Hathaway** ▶ (1900–73) US mathematician, who pioneered the construction of electronic computers. His Mark I, built in 1944 and later used by the US navy, anticipated the modern digital computer.

● **aikido** ▶ A Japanese form of unarmed combat, primarily for self-defence by means of dodging an attacker and leading him in the direction in which his momentum takes him before subduing him without injury. Like other ▷martial arts it emphasizes the need for a calm frame of mind and total physical control. In sporting competitions two people fight in one or two one-minute rounds. ▷*See also* judo; jujitsu.

● **Ailanthus** ▷*See* tree of heaven.

● **Ailred of Rievaulx, St** ▶ (1109–67) Abbot (from 1147) of the Cistercian monastery of Rievaulx in Yorkshire, known as the English St Bernard. Part of his youth was spent at the court of David I of Scotland. His influential theological writings contain an element of mysticism and include *De spirituali amicitia*, a treatise on friendship considered in spiritual terms and based on Cicero's *De amicitia*. He also wrote a life of Edward the Confessor. Feast day: 12 Jan or 3 March.

● **Ailsa Craig** ▶ 55 16N 5 07W A granite cone-shaped island in Scotland, rising abruptly out of the sea at the mouth of the Firth of Clyde. Its rock is quarried to produce ▷curling stones. Area: about 2.6 sq km (1 sq mi).

● **AIM** ▶ (Alternative Investment Market) ▷*See* stock exchange; stocks and shares.

● **Ain, River** ▶ A river in E France, flowing SSW from the Jura Mountains to join the River Rhône 29 km (18 mi) above Lyons. Length: 190 km (118 mi).

● **Ainsworth, W(illiam) Harrison** ▶ (1805–82) British historical novelist. He followed the success of his first novel, *Rookwood* (1834), about the highwayman Dick Turpin, with 38 others, the best known of which are *The Tower of London* (1840), *Old St Paul's* (1841), *Windsor Castle* (1843), and *The Lancashire Witches* (1848). He also edited three popular magazines.

● **Aintree** ▶ 53 29N 2 57W A suburb of Liverpool, NW England, with a famous racecourse where the Grand National steeplechase has been held annually since 1839. It also has a motor-racing circuit.

● **Ainu** ▶ A Mongoloid people living on certain islands of Japan and Russia (Hokkaido, Sakhalin, Kurile Islands). Traditionally a hunting and food-gathering people, they are now few in number and much changed in both appearance and culture. They were once noted for their profusion of body hair, but intermixture has made them resemble the Japanese and their traditional culture has largely disappeared. Their language is not related to any other known language.

● **air** ▷*See* atmosphere.

● **air conditioning** ▶ A system for controlling the temperature, humidity, and purity of the air in a confined space, such as an office, building, or vehicle. An air-conditioning installation will usually include a cooler (consisting of a refrigerator), a condenser to control the humidity of the air, and filters to cleanse the air. It may also include a heater to warm the air in winter and a humidifier to increase humidity, if required. In many modern office buildings windows do not open and fresh air of appropriate temperature and humidity is circulated throughout by means of air ducts. In older buildings, single-room air conditioning can be achieved by window units or portable air conditioners. All air-conditioning units must have access to a condenser outside the building to dispose of waste heat and moisture. Built-in compact air-conditioning units in cars, coaches, and lorries are already widespread in the USA and are becoming increasingly popular in Europe.

● **aircraft** ▶ Any machine capable of flying. Man's attempts to fly fall into two categories: those using lighter-than-air machines (*see* airships; balloons) and those using heavier-than-air machines. The latter include wing-flapping birdlike devices, rotating wing machines (*see* helicopter), and fixed-wing aircraft, first ▷gliders and then powered aeroplanes. By the end of the 19th century it was clear to all but the most eccentric that man was both too weak and too heavy to emulate birds. Flapping wings combine both thrust and lift (*see* aeronautics) in one device; man needs to separate these two components, obtaining lift from a fixed wing and thrust from an engine. 19th-century experience of gliding, especially by Otto ▷Lilienthal, provided the Wright Brothers with the information they needed to build their first powered aircraft. The power source was provided by the Otto-Daimler ▷internal-combustion engine. By 1907 the Wrights were able to remain airborne for 45 minutes; in 1909 the Frenchman Louis ▷Blériot flew across the English Channel, and in the same year the French rotary Gnome engine revolutionized aircraft-engine design (this engine and its derivatives powered many early aircraft, including several used in World War I). By the beginning of the war aircraft were sufficiently advanced to be used for reconnaissance and their usefulness as bombers soon became evident. Fast manoeuvrable fighters to shoot down the slower heavily laden bombers were an obvious subsequent development. By the end of the war aerial combat was established as an integral part of modern warfare, both sides being equipped with a range of fighters, bombers, and reconnaissance aircraft.

After the war and during the 1920s, air circuses and flying clubs run by ex-wartime pilots using World War I aircraft sprang up all over the world, popularizing the concept of flying and heralding the age of civil aviation. In 1924 Imperial Airways was formed in the UK, using Handley ▷Page airliners, and during the 1930s a worldwide network of commercial routes developed. The Atlantic was first flown nonstop solo (from New York to Paris) in 1927 by Charles ▷Lindbergh and by 1939 there was a transatlantic service using Class C Short flying boats with in-flight refuelling (*see also* seaplane).

Between the wars all the main countries of the world were also building up their air forces. By the outbreak of World War II aircraft of all kinds were poised for aerial combat. The first RAF bombing raid of the war was carried out by Vickers Wellingtons and Bristol Blenheims (of which over 6000 were built). During the course of the war these bombers were augmented by some 6000 Handley Page Halifaxes (which entered service in 1940) and 7400 Avro Lancasters (1942). The USA's main bombing force consisted of 12 700 Boeing B17s, 18 000 Consolidated B24 Liberators, and towards the end of the war, a fleet of Boeing B29 Superfortresses. Germany entered the war with 370 Dornier Do 17s and the Heinkel He 111, some 7300 of which had been made by the end of the war. The Junkers 88 entered service in 1940 and at the end of the war (1945) the Arado Ar 234 jet bomber was used for the first time. Dominant British fighters were the Supermarine Spitfire and the Hawker Hurricane, the latter being slightly slower than the main German fighter, the Messerschmitt Me Bf109. Later British fighters included the Bristol Beaufighter and the De Havilland Mosquito. The US fighter pilots had some 10 000 Lockheed P38 Lightnings and 15 000 P51 Mustangs. The British jet-powered Gloster Meteor entered service in 1944, as did the German Messerschmitt Me 262 jet.

By the end of the war the practicality of the ▷jet engine had been established and it has dominated aircraft design ever since. However, the first postwar generation of civil aircraft used the jet engine to drive propellers (e.g. the Vickers Viscount), the first true jet to carry passengers being the ill-fated British Comet. The Boeing 707 (with its four engines in pods suspended below the wings) followed in 1954 and the French Caravelle (with two rear-mounted engines) in 1959.

The first aircraft to break the ▷sound barrier were military and nearly all modern warplanes are supersonic and armed with missiles. Examples include the English Electric Lightning and Avro Vulcan; the US McDonnell Douglas Phantom, Convair Hustler, and General Dynamics Swingwing F111; the French Mirage; and the Soviet MiGs (see also VTOL; STOL). The latest generation of warplanes includes the US SR-71A and B2 Stealth bomber; unmanned bomber planes are also in an advanced state of development. The first propeller-driven fighter plane to be developed since the advent of the supersonic jet fighter was the 'heliplane' P1233-1 (1987), which is designed for manoeuvrability in low-level dogfights. The first supersonic passenger aircraft (SST) to fly was the Soviet Tupolev Tu-144 in 1968. This was followed by the Anglo-French ▷Concorde, which—despite opposition from conservationists—went into transatlantic service in 1976. However, by the start of the 21st century the fleets owned by British Airways and Air France were coming to the end of their lives with no further SSTs in development. It therefore seems that long- and medium-range passenger services are likely to be dominated for the foreseeable future by the wide-bodied (jumbo) jets, such as the Boeing 747 and the European Airbus. □ pp. 24–25.

● **aircraft carrier** ► A naval vessel with a large flat deck for launching and landing warplanes. The first flight from the deck of a ship was made in 1910, and the first true aircraft carrier, HMS Argus, was completed for the Royal Navy in 1918, too late for action in World War I. Carriers played a dominant role in World War II, despite early predictions that ▷battleships would be the most important warships. Carriers were especially effective in the war against the Japanese, where they were employed in combined UK and US operations and were instrumental in destroying the Japanese fleet. After World War II carriers came to be regarded chiefly as tactical units, although they saw considerable action in the Korean and Vietnam Wars. The USS Enterprise, the first nuclear-powered carrier (1961), displaced 76 000 tonnes and steamed more than 432 000 km (270 000 mi) before requiring refuelling. The introduction of larger and heavier aircraft required the refitting of carriers. Because of the increased range of aircraft, the enormous cost of carriers, and the development of sophisticated missiles, there have been few aircraft carriers built in the 1970s. However, there was a revival of interest in aircraft carriers in the 1980s; the UK has three: the Invincible, the Illustrious, and a new Ark Royal.

● **air-cushion vehicle** ▷See hovercraft.

● **Airdrie** ► 55 52N 3 59W A town in Scotland, in North Lanarkshire. Industries include the manufacture of metal goods and drugs, engineering, electronics, and whisky distilling. Population (1991): 36 998.

● **Airedale terrier** ► The largest breed of terrier, originating in Yorkshire. It has a long squarish muzzle, a short tail, and a tan-coloured wiry coat with a black saddle region. A powerful and intelligent dog, the Airedale has been used as a guard dog, for hunting, and as a police dog. Height: 58–61 cm (dogs); 56–58 cm (bitches). ⁻dog.

● **air pollution** ► (or atmospheric pollution) The release into the atmosphere of gases, liquid droplets, or solid particles that have undesirable effects on people, wildlife, buildings, etc. The main culprits are vehicle emissions, power stations, and other large combustion plants. The pollutants consist of carbon dioxide (see greenhouse effect) and a small quantity of carbon monoxide, the oxides of sulphur and nitrogen (see acid rain), and particles of liquids (e.g. diesel oil) or solids (e.g. coal dust). The UK government aims to bring pollutants within strict limits by 2005, with the limits set for particulate matter at 50 micrograms per cubic metre of air (see also pollution; radioactive waste). Natural causes of atmospheric pollution include volcanos, forest fires, and dust storms.

● **air raid** ► The aerial bombardment of military or civilian targets. The tactic was introduced in World War I by the Germans, who first

used their Zeppelins (see airships) to bomb England in 1915 and subsequently (1917) used powered aircraft for the same purpose. Between the wars, the Italians in Abyssinia and the Germans on the side of the Nationalists in the ▷Spanish Civil War bombed cities (see Guernica). In World War II, air raids became established tactical operations: the Germans bombed London, Coventry (both 1940), and other cities, while the British and Americans bombed Berlin, Hamburg (1943), Dresden (1945), Tokyo (1945), and other cities. The saturation bombing of German cities as a strategic manoeuvre to terrify their populations into submission, advocated by "Bomber" ▷Harris, was subsequently regarded as being an inefficient use of air power, as well as morally questionable. Nearly 600 000 Germans were killed by RAF bombs, while only 60 000 Britons died from Luftwaffe bombs.

In the ▷Gulf War aircraft and guided missiles were used by the US-led coalition forces to destroy military targets in Iraq. In 1999 NATO carried out air raids against targets in Yugoslavia during the ▷Kosovo crisis; heavy air raids against targets in Afghanistan also featured in the US-led ▷war on terrorism in late 2001.

● **air sac** ► In zoology, a thin-walled air-filled sac that functions in the breathing mechanism of birds, some insects, and some lizards. In birds there are five pairs in the spaces between the internal organs and around or in some bones. They are connected with the air passages and enable a constant supply of air to the lungs during flight.

● **airships** ► Dirigible ▷balloons that obtain their thrust from a propeller. The first airship to fly was a French steam-powered machine, designed in 1852 by H. Giffard; however, the first practical airship was the electrically powered La France (1884), built by Renard and Krebs. By 1900 the initiative in airships had passed to Germany, with the machines of Count Ferdinand von Zeppelin (1838–1917) leading the field. Between 1910 and 1914 Zeppelins were in extensive passenger service, carrying some 35 000 passengers, without mishap. In World War I these machines were used by the Germans to bomb England—the first effective use of aerial bombardment. From then onwards the history of airships is one of disaster followed by disaster. The British R101 caught fire at Beauvais in 1930, the US Shenandoah and the Akron were lost in 1933, and the German Hindenberg was destroyed in 1937. These disasters with hydrogen-filled airships cost many lives and gave them a reputation from which they have never recovered. However, the availability of the nonflammable gas helium has created a mild revival in recent years.

● **air space** ► In international law, the space above a country over which that country is sovereign. Under the Outer Space Treaty (1967), outer space is not subject to national appropriation.

● **Airy, Sir George Biddell** ► (1801–92) British astronomer, who was astronomer royal from 1835 to 1881. He uncovered errors in current planetary theory, showing that the motions of the earth and Venus are not in simple ratio. He is noted for his estimate (1826) of the earth's density from gravity measurements in mines.

● **Aisne, River** ► A river in N France. Rising in the Argonne Forest, it flows mainly NW joining the River Oise near Compiègne. It was a major battleground of ▷World War I. Length: 282 km (175 mi).

● **Aistulf** ► (d. 756) King of the Lombards (749–56). Aistulf captured Ravenna (751) and then threatened Rome. The pope sought the aid of ▷Pepin the Short, King of the Franks, who twice defeated Aistulf at Pavia (755, 756).

● **Aix-en-Provence** ► (Latin name: Aquae Sextiae) 43 31N 5 27E A city in S France, in the Bouches-du-Rhône department. The capital of Provence in the middle ages, it has a gothic cathedral and a university (1409). The artist Cézanne was born here. An agricultural centre, it trades in olive oil and fruit. Population (1999): 134 222.

● **Aix-la-Chapelle** ▷See Aachen.

● **Aix-la-Chapelle, Congress of** ► (1818) Meeting of the Quadruple Alliance (Great Britain, Austria, Prussia, and Russia) and France at Aix-la-Chapelle (now Aachen). The Alliance reaffirmed the political reorganization of Europe established by the Congress of ▷Vienna (1814–15) and restored France's status as an independent power: it

civil aircraft

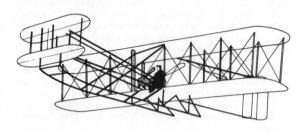

Wright Brothers' Flyer The first powered flight at Kitty Hawk, North Carolina, USA, on 17 December, 1903 lasted 12 seconds.

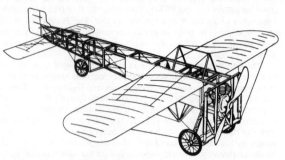

Blériot XI Louis Blériot's 30-minute flight from Calais to Dover on 25 July, 1909 was the first cross-channel flight.

Handley Page 42E Hannibal In 1928 the British airline, Imperial Airways, brought eight HP42 aircraft. The 24-seater Hannibal had a top speed of 100 mph (160 km/hr).

Douglas DC3 Introduced in 1936, it was widely used in World War II as the Dakota transport. Its Pratt and Whitney 1200 hp engines gave it a maximum speed of 200 mph (320 km/hr).

Vickers Viscount Introduced into service in 1950, it was the first successful turboprop airliner. Powered by four Rolls-Royce Dart engines, it carried 60 passengers.

De Havilland Comet I The first jet airliner, it went into service in 1952. Crashes due to metal fatigue caused its withdrawal and in 1958 it was replaced by the Comet IV.

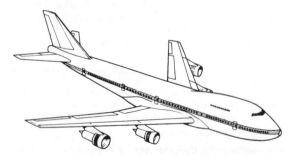

Boeing 747 Nicknamed the "jumbo jet" this wide-bodied jetliner, which can carry up to 500 passengers, has been in service with many airlines since 1970.

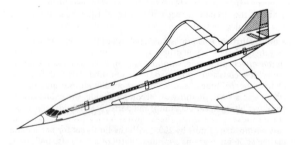

Concorde The first supersonic airliner, it was built by the French and British in cooperation. Powered by four Rolls-Royce Olympus engines, it came into service in 1976.

military aircraft

Sopwith Camel   A highly manoeuvrable fighter, first delivered in 1917. Its 130 hp Clerget engine gave it a top speed of 113 mph (181 km/hr).

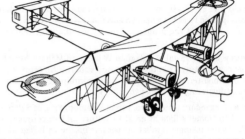

Handley Page 0/400   The largest World War I bomber. Its twin 360 hp engines enabled it to carry 2000 lbs (907 kg) of bombs.

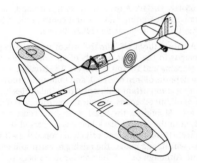

Supermarine Spitfire   British fighter. Originally powered by a Rolls-Royce Merlin engine, it later had the Griffon engine, giving it a top speed of 450 mph (724 km/hr).

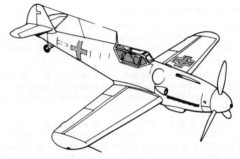

Messerschmitt 109   German fighter, designed in 1935. The latest version (109G) had an 1800 hp engine enabling it to fly at 430 mph (692 km/hr).

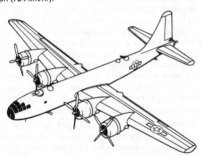

Boeing B-29 Superfortress   This enormous US bomber entered the war in 1943 and was used to drop the atom bombs on Japan.

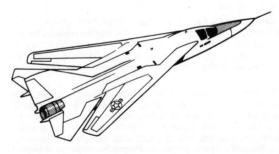

General Dynamics F-111   US fighter and fighter-bomber, the first warplane to have swing wings (1967). It was powered by a Pratt and Whitney TF30 turbo fan.

Hawker Siddeley Harrier   British VTOL aircraft developed in 1969. Two movable nozzles direct the thrust of its engine downwards for vertical take-off.

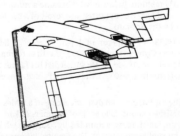

Northrop B2 stealth bomber   US bomber, publicly revealed in 1989. The most expensive warplane ever developed, costing £350 million each, its revolutionary 'flying wing' design is alleged to make it invisible to enemy radar.

withdrew its occupying forces and admitted France into what thus became the Quintuple Alliance.

● **Aix-les-Bains** ► (Latin name: Aquae Gratianae) 45 41N 5 55E A spa and resort in E France, in the Savoie department. Situated in a picturesque valley, it is noted for its hot sulphurous springs. Population (1990): 24 830.

● **Ajaccio** ► 41 51N 8 43E The capital of Corsica, a port on the Gulf of Ajaccio. Napoleon I was born here and his home is now preserved as a museum. Tourism is the principal industry. Population (1990 est): 55 279.

● **Ajanta** ► 20 30N 75 48E A village in W India, in Maharashtra. Its Buddhist caves, dating from the 1st century BC to the 7th century AD, consist of monasteries and temples, some containing remarkable paintings illustrating the life of the times.

● **Ajax** ► A legendary Greek hero, son of Telamon, King of Salamis. Described in Homer's *Iliad* as great in stature and in courage, he fought ▷Hector in single combat. He became insane with rage after being defeated by Odysseus in the contest for the armour of the dead ▷Achilles. ▷Sophocles' play *Ajax* depicts the hero recovering his sanity, only to be driven by shame to suicide.

● **Ajman** ▷*See* United Arab Emirates.

● **Ajmer** ► (Ajmere *or* Ajmir) 26 29N 74 40E A city in India, in Rajasthan. It contains the white marble tomb of a Muslim saint and a Mogul palace. It is a commercial and industrial centre. Population (1991 est): 401 930.

● **Akashic records** ► The "pictures" of all past events, emotions, and thoughts, believed by occultists to be retained in supersensory fluid called Akasha. Clairvoyants and mediums claim to have access to these records.

● **Akbar (I) the Great** ► (1542–1605) The third Mogul emperor (1556–1605). Akbar embarked on the extension of his rule over all N India by a series of military campaigns in Punjab, Rajput, Gujarat, Bengal, Kashmir, and Sind. Late in his reign he conquered the Deccan, further to the south. He was noted for his able administration, the development of trade, reforms of taxation, the abolition of extortion, and his tolerance towards non-Muslims. ▷*See also* Mogul art and architecture.

● **Akhenaton** ► (*or* Ikhnaton) King of Egypt (1379–1362 BC) of the 18th dynasty, one of whose wives was ▷Nefertiti. He replaced the traditional ▷Amon cult with the monotheistic worship of the sun god, ▷Aton, and built a new capital Akhetaton (*see* Tell el-Amarna). Internal disorder during his reign enabled the Hittite king, ▷Suppiluliumas, to remove N Syria from Egyptian control.

● **Akhmatova, Anna** ► (Anna Andreevna Gorenko; 1889–1966) Russian poet. Her first books, *Evening* (1912) and *Beads* (1914), consisting chiefly of short, intensely lyrical, love poems, were immediately successful. She was married to Nikolai Gumiliov (1886–1921), founder of ▷acmeism, from 1910 until 1918. After the Revolution she wrote on public as well as personal themes. Her works were banned (1922–40) but in the 1960s were restored to favour.

● **Akiba ben Joseph** ► (died c. 135 AD) One of the outstanding teachers of early rabbinic Judaism, who became a master of biblical interpretation and law. He supported the revolt of ▷Bar Kokhba and was martyred by the Romans.

● **Akihito** ► (1933–) Emperor of Japan (1989–). Educated in Tokyo, he became Crown Prince in 1952, the first to marry a commoner, Michido Shoda (1934–). He succeeded his father ▷Hirohito. His eldest son, Naruhito (1960–), the Crown Prince, was educated at Oxford.

● **Akkad** ► The capital city and dynastic name of a S Mesopotamian kingdom established about 2300 BC, N of ▷Sumer. Akkad, the site of which is still unidentified, was founded by ▷Sargon, who extended his rule over most of Mesopotamia. The Semitic language of Akkad, Old Akkadian, spread to much of the Middle East, developing later into the languages of both Babylonia and Assyria. About 2150 BC, barbarian invasions brought about Akkad's decline and the short-lived reascendancy of ▷Ur.

● **Akmola** ▷*See* Astana.

● **Akola** ► 20 40N 77 05E A town in W India, in Maharashtra. It is a commercial centre. Population (1991): 327 946.

● **Akron** ► 41 04N 81 31W A city in the USA, in Ohio. It is the main centre of the US rubber industry, specializing in tyres; other industries include plastics and chemicals. Its university was established in 1870. Population (1996 est): 216 882.

● **aksak** ► A type of musical metre, found in the vigorous asymmetrical dance rhythms of the E Mediterranean, deriving from Turkish sources. ▷Bartók recorded examples of these rhythms in Bulgaria and named them Bulgarian rhythms.

● **Aksum** ► (*or* Axum) 14 05N 38 40E An ancient town in N Ethiopia. It was capital of the Christian Aksumite Empire (1st–6th centuries AD). According to tradition, the ▷Ark of the Covenant was brought here from Jerusalem. The old town is now a popular tourist attraction.

● **Aktyubinsk** ► 53 43N 91 25E A city in W Kazakhstan on the River Ilek. Founded (1869) as a Russian fort, it is now an important industrial centre. Population (1991): 266 600.

● **Akureyri** ► 65 41N 18 04W A town in N central Iceland, on Eyja Fjord. It is an important trading and cultural centre; industries include fishing and textiles. Population (1992): 14 665.

● **Alabama** ► A state in the SE USA, on the Gulf of Mexico. Except for the forested uplands in the NE it consists of an undulating plain, drained by the Alabama and Tombigbee Rivers. The iron and steel industry, based on deposits of iron ore, coal, and limestone around Birmingham, is the most important industry. Other industries include the production of oil, metal goods, chemicals, plastics, and defence and space projects. Mobile on the coast is an important seaport. Cotton production in the central Black Belt has decreased since the boll weevil blight (1915) but remains a principal crop along with peanuts, soya beans, wheat, and maize; the raising of cattle and poultry is also important. Although one of the poorest states because of its depressed agriculture, it has a rich rural culture particularly among its large Black community.

History: first explored by the Spanish in the 16th century, it passed to the British (1763) following disputes with the Spanish and French. In 1783 it came under US control and with an area to the S added in the Louisiana Purchase (1803) became a state in 1819. New settlers established large cotton plantations based on slave labour and following secession from the Union (1861), the state sent most of its White male population to fight againt the N. Since its readmittance (1868) relations between the White and Black communities have been troubled: there have been many civil-rights protests, including the ▷Montgomery bus boycott (1955–56). Area: 135 776 sq km (52 423 sq mi). Population (1996 est): 4 273 084. Capital: Montgomery.

● **Alabama claims** ► Compensation claimed by the US Government from Britain for damage caused by the *Alabama* and other warships of the ▷Confederate States in the Civil War (1861–65). Britain was accused of violating its neutrality by allowing these ships to be built or equipped in its shipyards. In 1871 the dispute was referred to arbitration by Italy, Switzerland, and Brazil. Britain was found liable and ordered to pay £3 million. This was the first major settlement of an international dispute by arbitration.

● **alabaster** ► A pure fine-grained form of ▷gypsum. It is white or delicately shaded and often translucent and attractively veined. It has long been worked ornamentally, for carvings, etc., but weathers too easily for external use. The alabaster of Volterra, Tuscany, is well known.

● **Alain-Fournier** ► (Henri-Alban Fournier; 1886–1914) French novelist. The son of a country schoolmaster, he became a literary journalist in Paris and was killed in World War I. The mood of his one completed novel, *Le Grand Meaulnes* (1913), is nostalgic and almost mystical; set in the French countryside of his childhood, it describes a young man's search for a girl he has glimpsed only briefly.

● **Alamo, the** ► A mission in the USA, in San Antonio, Texas. During the Texas revolution it was defended from 24 Feb until 6 March, 1836, by less than 200 Texan volunteers (including the legendary Davy Crockett), who were all massacred during the onslaught of 4000 Mexican troops led by Santa Anna. Six weeks later a victory at San Jacinto secured Texan independence.

● **Alamogordo** ▶ 32 54N 105 57W A town in the USA, in S New Mexico. The first atom bomb was exploded in a test near here on 16 July, 1945. Population (1990): 27 596.

● **Alanbrooke, Alan Francis Brooke, 1st Viscount** ▶ (1883–1963) British field marshal. He joined the Royal Field Artillery in 1902, serving as a staff officer in World War I. In World War II, after service in France, he became commander in chief of the home forces. Appointed Chief of the Imperial General Staff in 1941, he advised Churchill at all his conferences with Roosevelt and Stalin.

● **Åland Islands** ▶ (Finnish name: Ahvenanmaa Islands) A group of over 6000 islands and islets, under Finnish administration but semiautonomous, at the entrance to the Gulf of Bothnia. Population (1998 est): 25 392. Capital: Mariehamn.

● **Alarcón, Pedro Antonio de** ▶ (1833–91) Spanish novelist. He began his career as a poet and journalist, but his literary reputation is based on his novels, especially *The Three-Cornered Hat* (1874), which was used by Manuel de ▷Falla as the basis for a ballet.

● **Alarcón y Mendoza, Juan Ruiz de** ▶ (1581–1639) Spanish dramatist. Born in Mexico, he became one of the leading dramatists of the Golden Age of Spanish drama. His best-known play is *La verdad sospechosa* (?1619), a satirical comedy. He apparently ceased to write after being appointed to the Council for the Indies in 1626.

● **Alaric I** ▶ (c. 370–410 AD) King of the ▷Visigoths. Alaric served in the Roman army as the commander of the Gothic auxiliary forces before his election as King of the Visigoths. After failing to reach a peaceful agreement with the Roman imperial administration, he invaded Greece and Italy. Alaric died shortly after his forces sacked Rome (410).

● **Alaska** ▶ The largest state in the USA, occupying the extreme NW corner of the North American continent. It is a mountainous volcanic area, rising over 6000 m (20 000 ft) to Mount McKinley, the highest peak in North America. There are numerous rivers, chief of which is the Yukon flowing W into the Bering Sea. It has an indented coastline with many islands. One third of the state lies within the Arctic Circle. The economy is based principally on the state's rich mineral wealth. The discovery of oil (1950) and subsequent finds (1968) have made oil production the major industry (*see* Trans-Alaska Pipeline) and there are rich supplies of natural gas. Coal, gold, and copper are mined. Fishing, especially salmon, and forestry are also major industries. Agricultural development is hindered by the short growing season and severe climate. Fur trapping has declined in importance although sealskins (from the offshore Pribilof Islands) remain an important export. Conflict between further development and the preservation of the natural landscape has become a major problem. In 1989 oil spillage from the *Exxon Valdez* in Prince William Sound caused massive environmental damage. *History*: first settled by Russians following voyages by the Dane, Vitus Bering (1728, 1741), it was under the trade control of the Russian American company until 1867 when it was purchased by the USA. A number of gold rushes in the late 19th century helped to swell the sparse population. It became the 49th state in 1959. Area: 1 700 138 sq km (656 424 sq mi). Population (1997 est): 609 311. Capital: Juneau.

● **Alaska Highway** ▶ A road from Dawson Creek, Canada to Fairbanks, Alaska, built for defence against Japan (1942). Open throughout the year, it now serves tourism and economic development. Length: 2437 km (1523 mi).

● **Alaskan malamute** ▷See husky.

● **Alastor** ▶ In Greek legend, the son of Neleus and brother of Nestor, killed by Heracles on the island of Pylos. The name was also applied to the personified spirit of vengeance that could possess a man.

● **Alba, Fernando Alvarez de Toledo, Duke of** ▶ (*or* Alva; 1507–83) Spanish general, who successfully commanded Habsburg forces against Protestants in Germany and the French in Italy. Philip

II of Spain placed him in command of the Netherlands (1567–73), where his ruthless attempts to subdue the Dutch Protestants made him very unpopular and led to his recall. He led the successful expedition against Portugal (1580–81). ▷*See also* Revolt of the Netherlands.

● **Albacete** ▶ 39 00N 1 52W A city in SE central Spain, in Murcia. A market centre, it is famous for the manufacture of cutlery and daggers. Its notable buildings include the 16th-century cathedral. Population (1995 est): 143 177.

● **albacore** ▶ A fast-swimming ▷tuna fish, *Thunnus alalunga*, found in warm seas. Up to 1 m long, it has very long pectoral fins. It is the chief source of tuna for canning.

● **Alba-Iulia** ▶ (German name: Karlsburg) 46 04N 23 33E A town in W central Romania, on the River Mureş. A former capital of Transylvania, its manufactures include leather goods and wine. Population (latest est): 64 369.

● **Alban, St** ▶ (3rd century AD) The first English martyr. A pagan soldier, he protected a Christian priest and was converted by him. The Roman authorities had him scourged and beheaded on a site subsequently dedicated to him as the Abbey of St Albans. Feast day: 22 or 17 June. Emblem: a stag.

● **Albania, Republic of** ▶ (Albanian name: Shqiperia) A country in SE Europe, occupying part of the Balkan Peninsula on the Adriatic Sea. It consists of a mountainous interior, rising to over 2700 m (9000 ft), with extensive forests and fertile coastal lowlands. The people, of whose origins little is known, belong to two main groups, the ▷Ghegs (N of the River Shkumbi) and the ▷Tosks (S).

Economy: mainly agricultural, although industry is increasing (the main industries being agricultural processing, textiles, oil products, and cement). There have been attempts to develop the rich mineral resources, especially oil, lignite, copper, chromium, limestone, salt, and bauxite, and also rich natural-gas deposits. Exports include crude oil, bitumen, chrome ore, copper wire, tobacco, fruit, and vegetables. Under communism, the centrally controlled economy was badly mismanaged and Albania became one of the poorest countries in Europe. Despite liberalization in the 1990s the economy remains desperately weak, owing in part to the prevalence of smuggling, corruption, and fraudulent financial schemes. Albania is now heavily dependent on Western aid.

History: became independent in 1912 after more than four centuries of Turkish rule. Following a civil war, in which Italy intervened, Albania became a republic in 1925 and a monarchy in 1928, when its president, Ahmed Beg Zogu (1895–1961), was proclaimed as King Zog. After occupation by Italy and Germany during World War II, another republic was set up in 1946, with a communist-controlled assembly. It aligned itself with the Soviet Union but after the death of Stalin relations between the two countries weakened and diplomatic relations were broken off from 1961 to 1990. Albania maintained close relations with China. As first party secretary, the authoritarian Enver ▷Hoxha was executive leader from 1946 to 1985. Pressure for liberal reform led to free multi-party elections in 1991 (in which the Communists—renamed Socialists—were returned to power) and limited economic reorganization. The country's economic weakness continued with severe food shortages. Elections in 1992 resulted in victory for the Democratic Party, whose leader, Sali Berisha, became president. In 1993 a new constitution declared Albania a parliamentary republic. Although the Democratic Party was re-elected in 1996, the elections were widely regarded as irregular. In early 1997 the collapse of several fraudulent savings schemes prompted massive street protests, leading to the resignation of the government. Repressive measures by President Berisha were met with fierce armed resistance in the S. Elections in 1997 resulted in victory for the Socialists under Fatos Nano: Berisha was succeeded as president by Rexhep Mejdani. In September 1998 violent protests in Tirana, apparently orchestrated by Berisha, forced the prime minister and government to flee the capital. Pandeli Majko subsequently became prime minister, resigning in favour of Ilir Meta in 1999. In November 1998 a new Western-style constitution was approved in a referendum. In 1999 the country's fragile economy was further destabilized by the arrival of thousands of ethnic Albanians fleeing Serb repression in ▷Kosovo.

Republic of Albania

Head of state	President Rexhep Mejdani
Official language	Albanian
Currency	lek of 100 qindars
Area	28 748 sq km (11 101 sq mi)
Population (1997 est)	3 293 000
Capital	Tirana
Main port	Durrës

● **Albanian** ▶ An Indo-European language, the only modern representative of a distinct branch of this linguistic group, spoken by two million Albanians and known by them as Shqiptar. It has two main dialects, those of the ▷Ghegs and the ▷Tosks.

● **Albany** ▶ 42 40N 73 49W A city in the USA, the capital of New York state on the Hudson River. Founded in 1614 by the Dutch, it is one of North America's oldest cities and has several notable public buildings, including the state capitol (1879). Economic growth accelerated with the building of the Erie Canal (1825) and today its main manufactures are electrical goods, textiles, dental goods, chemicals, and building materials. Population (1996 est): 103 564.

● **Albany** ▶ 34 57S 117 54E A port in SW Western Australia, on King George Sound. Industries include fish and meat canning. Population (latest est): 13 990.

albatross ▶ A pair of royal albatrosses (*Diomedea epomophora*) with their chick.

● **albatross** ▶ A large seabird belonging to a family (*Diomedeidae*; 14 species) that occurs mainly in southern oceans. It has a stout hooked bill; usually a white or brown plumage, often with darker markings on the back, wings, or tail; and very long narrow wings (the wandering albatross, *Diomedea exulans*, has the largest wingspan of any bird, reaching up to 3.5 m). Albatrosses can glide for hours over the open sea, feeding on squids and cuttlefish; they come ashore only to breed. Order: *Procellariiformes* (see petrel).

● **albedo** ▶ A measure of the reflecting power of a nonluminous object, such as a planet or natural satellite or a surface feature on such a body. It is the ratio of the amount of light reflected in all directions from the object to the amount of incident light. Clouds, snow, and ice have high albedos while volcanic rocks have very low albedos.

● **Albee, Edward** ▶ (1928–   ) US dramatist. His early one-act plays, notably *Zoo Story* (1958) and *The Death of Bessie Smith* (1960), analyse contemporary social tensions using techniques of the ▷Theatre of the Absurd. His first three-act play, *Who's Afraid of Virginia Woolf?* (1962), which dramatizes the love-hate relationship of an academic couple, was very successful. Later plays include *A Delicate Balance* (1967, Pulitzer Prize), *Seascape* (1975), *Marriage Play* (1986), *Three Tall Women* (1991, Pulitzer Prize), and *The Play About the Baby* (1998).

● **Albemarle, 1st Duke of** ▷*See* Monck, George, 1st Duke of Albemarle.

● **Albéniz, Isaac Manuel Francisco** ▶ (1860–1909) Spanish composer and pianist. A child prodigy, he frequently ran away from home, giving recitals in North and South America and Europe. He began serious composition after studying with d'Indy and Dukas in Paris. His works include operas, songs, and *Iberia* (1906–09), a collection of 12 piano pieces.

● **Alberoni, Giulio** ▶ (1664–1752) Spanish-Italian cardinal and statesman, who rose to prominence during the War of the Spanish succession. In 1713 he was appointed consular agent for Parma at the court of Philip V of Spain and in 1715 became prime minister of Spain and a cardinal. An ambitious foreign policy, which angered England, France, and Holland, resulted in his banishment to Italy (1719).

● **Albers, Josef** ▶ (1888–1976) German abstract painter, designer, and poet. His successful career as an influential art teacher and theoretician began at the ▷Bauhaus school of design and after 1933 continued in the USA, where he painted a famous series of abstract paintings entitled *Homage to the Square*.

● **Albert I** ▶ (1875–1934) King of the Belgians (1909–34). As commander in chief of the Belgian army, Albert led his country's heroic but unsuccessful resistance to the German invasion (1914) and contributed to the Allied victory in World War I. After the war he did much to encourage industrial reconstruction and currency reform.

● **Albert (I) the Bear** ▶ (?1100–70) The first Margrave of Brandenburg (1150–70), who took the title following conquests that brought him Havelland in E Europe. Further campaigns extended his territories, in which he sponsored land-reclamation schemes and missionary work.

● **Albert II Alcibiades** ▶ (1522–57) Margrave of Brandenburg, prominent in the conflict between Emperor Charles V and the German Protestants. A Protestant, he nevertheless supported Charles until 1551, when he turned his coat and joined Maurice of Saxony and the French. Defeated by Charles' brother Ferdinand, in 1553, he was outlawed and fled to France.

● **Albert III** ▶ (1443–1500) Duke of Saxony jointly with his brother Ernest (1441–86) from 1464 until 1485, when the Saxon lands were divided between them. He campaigned for the Holy Roman Emperor and in 1488–89 restored imperial authority in Holland, Flanders, and Brabant. He died while repressing a rebellion in Friesland, where he was governor (1498–1500).

● **Albert, Lake** ▶ (name from 1970 to 1997: Lake Mobutu) A lake in Uganda and the Democratic Republic of Congo. Discovered for Europeans by Baker in 1864, it is some 160 km (100 mi) long and is drained by the Albert Nile River. Area: about 5346 sq km (2064 sq mi).

● **Albert, Prince** ▶ (1819–61) Prince Consort of the United Kingdom and the younger son of Ernest I, Duke of Saxe-Coburg-Gotha. In 1840 he married his cousin Queen Victoria and became her chief adviser. Although he was initially unpopular, his devotion to duty and his active patronage of the arts, science, and industry eventually won him respect. He is perhaps best remembered for his organization of the ▷Great Exhibition (1851). He died of typhoid. The **Albert Memorial** in Hyde Park, by Sir George Gilbert Scott, completed in 1872 and extensively restored in 1997–98, was built in his memory and the **Royal Albert Hall** in Kensington was named after him by Victoria, who never fully recovered from his death.

● **Alberta** ▶ A province of W Canada, mostly on the Great Plains. It consists mainly of a plateau, rising to the foothills of the ▷Rocky Mountains in the SW. The undulating S prairie and parkland further N support profitable ranches and grain farms. Alberta is Canada's largest oil and gas producer, possesses vast coalfields, and includes the Athabasca tar sands, one of the world's largest oil reserves. Manufacturing is based on agriculture and mineral resources. Lumbering, construction, and tourism are also important.
History: first explored in the 18th century, Alberta became Canadian territory in 1869. The arrival of the railway from E Canada (1883) facilitated agricultural settlement, and Alberta grew rapidly (especially 1900–14), becoming a province in 1905. Alberta's government tends to be controlled by one party for long periods, notably by the

Social Credit Party (1935–71). Area: 644 389 sq km (248 799 sq mi). Population (1997 est): 2 847 000. Capital: Edmonton.

● **Albert Canal** ▶ A canal in Belgium, completed in 1939. It links the River Meuse at Liège with the River Scheldt at Antwerp. Length: 130 km (80 mi).

Leon Battista Alberti ▶ The west front of Sta Maria Novella (Florence).

● **Alberti, Leon Battista** ▶ (1404–72) Italian Renaissance architect. Alberti, who was also a painter, writer, musician, and scientist, is known mainly for being among the first Renaissancè architects fully to grasp the principles of classical architecture. As his innovative façade of Sta Maria Novella in Florence demonstrates, he adapted these rules to 15th-century requirements. He built relatively little, his most significant buildings being the churches of S Sebastiano and S Andrea in Mantua and the incomplete Tempio Malatestiano in Rimini. His abiding influence upon architecture was through his treatise *De re aedificatoria* (*On Architecture*; 1452), which was translated into several European languages in the 16th century.

● **Alberti, Raphael** ▶ (1902–99) Spanish poet. Born into a poor branch of a respectable Catholic family, he rebelled against his family and his Jesuit education. His first collection of poems, *Marineo en tierra* (1924), won the National Prize for Literature. In 1927 he suffered a mental breakdown, an experience analysed in *Sobre los ángeles* (1929). In 1931 he became a communist and after the Civil War exiled himself to Argentina, returning in 1977.

● **Albert of Brandenburg** ▶ (1490–1545) German churchman, Cardinal Archbishop and Elector of Mainz. Although a religious liberal, a patron of the arts, and a friend of ▷Erasmus, he is chiefly remembered as the object of Luther's attacks for his sale of indulgences. In later life he supported the ▷Counter-Reformation.

● **Albertsville** ▷*See* Kalemie.

● **Albertus Magnus, St** ▶ (c. 1200–80) German bishop, philosopher, and Doctor of the Church. Provincial of the German Dominicans (1254–57) and for a short time Bishop of Regensburg, he taught constantly throughout his life. His best-known pupil was ▷Aquinas. An outstanding scholar, he wrote extensively on logic, natural and moral sciences, scripture, and theology. Feast day: 15 Nov.

● **Albi** ▶ 43 56N 2 08E A town in S France, the capital of the Tarn de-

partment on the River Tarn. A centre of Catharism, it gave its name to the Albigensian heresy (*see* Albigenses). Notable buildings include the gothic cathedral and the 13th-century archbishop's palace, which is now a museum housing works by Toulouse-Lautrec (a native of Albi). An agricultural market, it has textile, glass, and cement industries. Population (1990): 48 700.

● **Albigenses** ▶ Followers of the Christian heresy of Catharism (*see* Cathari), who flourished in southern France in the 12th and 13th centuries. The Albigenses, named after the town of Albi in Languedoc, were the object of the Albigensian Crusade, launched in 1208 and led by the father of Simon de ▷Montfort. They were finally suppressed by the Inquisition, which operated in the area from 1233.

● **albinism** ▶ An inherited disorder in which tyrosinase, one of the enzymes required for the formation of the pigment ▷melanin, is absent. Albinos have abnormally pale skin, fair hair, and pink or light-blue irises. The condition can be eased by the use of spectacles to treat the lens abnormalities common in albinos and by protection of the skin and eyes from direct sunlight. Albinism, which can affect all human races, is also seen in wild and domestic animals.

● **Albino horse** ▶ A horse exhibiting the characteristics of albinism and bred to maintain the colour type. Albinos have pinkish skin, pure-white hair, and blue eyes. Defective eyesight is common, lessening its usefulness as a riding horse.

● **Albinoni, Tomaso** ▶ (1671–1750) Italian composer and court musician to the Duke of Mantua. His works, which influenced J. S. Bach, include 50 operas, a violin concerto, and two oboe concertos. The *Adagio* for organ and strings often attributed to Albinoni was in fact composed by his Italian biographer Remo Giazotto (1910–   ) and incorporates a fragment of a bass part by Albinoni.

● **Alboin** ▶ (died c. 573) King of the Lombards (c. 565–c. 573). He succeeded to lands in central Europe and then conquered N Italy, establishing the kingdom of Lombardy (572), with his capital at Pavia.

● **Ålborg** ▶ (*or* Aalborg) 57 03N 09 56E A city and seaport in Denmark, in N Jutland. Founded in 1342 AD, it has a gothic cathedral and a 16th-century castle. A university was established in 1974. Its industries include shipbuilding and textiles. Population (1996 est): 159 980.

● **Albright, Madeleine (Korbel)** ▶ (1937–   ) Czech-born US politician. After spending World War II in London she emigrated to the USA in 1948. A Democrat, she served in various posts during the ▷Carter administration before becoming resident professor of international affairs at Georgetown University (1982). Under Bill ▷Clinton she became US representative to the UN (1992) and in 1996 the first woman secretary of state.

● **albumins** ▶ A class of proteins that are soluble in both water and dilute aqueous salt solutions. Serum albumins are constituents of blood; α-lactalbumin is found in milk; and ovalbumin is part of egg white. Preparations of albumins are used in therapeutic transfusions.

● **Albuquerque** ▶ 35 05N 106 38W A city in the USA, in New Mexico on the Rio Grande. The state's largest city, it is situated in a rich agricultural area and food canning and the manufacture of livestock products are its principal industries. It is the home of the University of New Mexico (1892). Population (1996 est): 419 681.

● **Albuquerque, Alfonso de** ▶ (1453–1515) Portuguese governor in India (1509–15). He led his first expedition to India in 1503. By a series of conquests he established Portuguese influence in the Indian Ocean based on three strongholds—Goa, Ceylon, and Malacca. He led the first European fleet to sail into the Red Sea and took Hormuz in 1515. Enemies at the Portuguese court sought to discredit him and he was recalled, dying at sea.

● **Albury-Wodonga** ▶ 36 03S 146 53E An area of urban growth in SE Australia, in New South Wales on the Murray River. It is an important trading centre with engineering, clothing, and food-processing industries. Population (1991 est): 63 610.

● **Al Bu Sa'id** ▶ The ruling dynasty of Oman since 1749 and of Zanzibar from 1749 to 1964. In 1749 Ahmad ibn Sa'id, the dynasty's founder, seized power over Oman and Zanzibar. In 1856 Oman and Zanzibar were divided. Zanzibar continued under Bu Sa'idi rule under the British protectorate (1890–1963) but the dynasty was overthrown when Zanzibar was incorporated into Tanzania (1964). The present ruler of Oman is Qaboos ibn Sa'id.

● **Alcaeus** ▸ (6th century BC) Greek lyric poet. A member of the aristocracy of the island of Lesbos and a friend of ▷Sappho, he went into exile when the tyrant Pittacus gained power. His work, only fragments of which survive, was greatly admired by ▷Horace.

● **Alcántara** ▸ 39 44N 6 53W A town in W Spain in Estremadura. A magnificent Roman bridge (105 AD) spans the River Tagus here. Population (1981): 2317.

● **Alcatraz** ▸ An island in the USA, in W California in San Francisco Bay. It was the site of a notorious maximum security prison from 1934 until 1962.

● **alcázar** ▸ (Arabic al-qasr: castle, palace) A Spanish fortress built during the conflicts between Moors and Christians in the 14th and 15th centuries. The most renowned is the Alcázar of ▷Seville, built by King ▷Pedro the Cruel. The word remains an element in certain placenames.

● **Alcázar de San Juan** ▸ 39 42N 3 12W A town in S central Spain, in New Castile on La Mancha plain. It is associated with Cervantes' *Don Quixote*. Population (1991): 25 679.

● **alchemy** ▸ A pseudoscience combining practical ▷chemistry with magical or mystical views of man and his relationship to the universe. Originating independently in China and Egypt, probably before the 3rd century BC, alchemy remained a legitimate branch of science and philosophy in Asia, Europe, and the Islamic lands for over 1500 years and is the ancestor of modern chemistry. It had three principal goals, the emphasis on which varied from place to place: the elixir of life (to ensure immortality), the panacea (or universal medicine), and the means of transmuting base metals into gold (*see* philosopher's stone). In China, ▷Taoism, which highly esteemed long life, fostered alchemical experimentation in search of the elixir. In Europe, concentration upon gold-making brought alchemy into disrepute.

● **Alcibiades** ▸ (c. 450–404 BC) Athenian general and politician. Brought up by ▷Pericles, he was the pupil and lover of ▷Socrates. Alcibiades encouraged Athenian imperialism during the ▷Peloponnesian War (431–404) until, accused of desecrating monuments in Athens, he defected to Sparta (415). He regained Athenian favour (410) and was a successful commander until defeat, the fault of a subordinate forced him into exile (406). He was murdered in Phrygia.

● **Alcmaeon** ▸ (c. 500 BC) Greek pioneer in medical science, from Croton (S Italy). Following ▷Pythagoras' experimental tradition, Alcmaeon used dissection and vivisection to investigate human sense organs. He discovered the optic nerve and located the centre of sensation in the brain.

● **Alcmaeon** ▸ In Greek mythology, the son of Amphiarus, one of the ▷Seven Against Thebes, and Eriphyle. He killed his mother to avenge the death of Amphiarus, and was pursued by the Furies. His first wife was Arsinoë, daughter of King Pegeus of Psophis, but on his wanderings he married the daughter of the river god Achelous, and was pursued and killed by Pegeus and his sons. His own sons later avenged his death by killing Pegeus.

● **Alcmaeonids** ▸ An aristocratic family prominent in virtually all ancient Athenian political crises, usually on the radical side. In 632 BC Megacles (an Alcmaeonid) violated the sanctuary of Athena by having a political opponent treacherously murdered there. The oracle of Delphi placed a hereditary curse on the family, banishing it from Athens. The Alcmaeonids returned under Solon, withdrew under Pisistratus, and returned again after the expulsion of Hippias (511/510 BC). ▷Cleisthenes was an Alcmaeonid; ▷Pericles and ▷Alcibiades had Alcmaeonid mothers.

● **Alcock, Sir John (William)** ▸ (1892–1919) British aviator. He served with the Royal Naval Air Service in World War I and in 1919, accompanied by **(Sir) Arthur Brown** (1886–1948), was the first to fly the Atlantic Ocean. They flew a Vickers-Vimy from St John's, Newfoundland, to Clifden, Co Galway, in 16 hours 27 minutes. A few months later Alcock was killed in a flying accident.

● **Alcock Convention** ▸ (1869) A treaty between Britain and China, drawn up by Sir Rutherford Alcock (1809–1907) but not ratified owing largely to the objections of British merchants. It intended that Britain would lose its most-favoured-nation relationship with China, gained after the second ▷Opium War, in return for tax concessions and freedom to navigate China's waterways.

● **Alcoforado, Marianna** ▸ (1640–1723) Portuguese nun. She was long mistakenly believed to be the author of a famous series of five love letters written to a French officer who had deserted the author and who was also wrongly identified as Noël Bouton (1636–1715), Comte de Chamilly and Marshal of France. The letters, published as *Lettres portugaises* (1669), were in fact the work of the Vicomte de Guilleragues (d. 1685), who until recently was believed to have been only its translator. The title of the book was referred to in that of the feminist *New Portuguese Letters* (1972) by the so-called Three Marias (Maria Isabel Barreno, Maria Teresa Horta, and Maria Velho da Costa), who were then imprisoned until the revolution of 1974.

● **Alcoholics Anonymous** ▸ A voluntary organization started in the USA in 1934 to help alcoholics to help themselves. Members, who must have an honest desire to stop drinking, help one another on the basis of group therapy by sharing their experiences of alcoholism. There are local autonomous groups in over 90 countries, including the UK, which has more than 950 groups. An associated organization, called **ALANON**, provides support for the close relatives of alcoholics.

● **alcoholism** ▸ An illness caused by physical and psychological dependence on alcohol (*see also* drug dependence). The incidence of alcoholism varies between different societies: it is most common in countries where alcohol is readily available and where heavy drinking is socially acceptable. Alcoholism causes mood changes, deterioration in personal standards and habits, and periods of memory loss. Continued heavy consumption will eventually lead to cirrhosis of the liver, heart disease, and damage to the nerves. Sudden withdrawal may produce specific symptoms: tremor, delusions, and hallucinations. Treatment, which is lengthy and difficult, includes initial alcohol withdrawal (with appropriate sedation) accompanied and followed by adequate psychological support. Drugs such as disulfiram (Antabuse), which cause vomiting after drinking alcohol, may assist the treatment. Nonmedical solutions to problems of alcoholism include group therapy in the company of other alcoholics (*see* Alcoholics Anonymous).

● **alcohols** ▸ The class of organic compounds that includes ▷ethanol (ethyl alcohol; C_2H_5OH) and ▷methanol (methyl alcohol; CH_3OH). Ethanol is the common alcohol found in intoxicating drinks and is often called simply "alcohol." Alcohols contain at least one hydroxyl group and have the general formula ROH, where R is a ▷hydrocarbon group. They react with ▷acids to give ▷esters and water. Primary alcohols oxidize to form ▷aldehydes and secondary alcohols to form ▷ketones.

● **alcohol strength** ▸ The measurement of the percentage volume of ▷ethanol (ethyl alcohol) in alcoholic drinks in order to calculate government duty on them. In the USA, 100° proof is 50% alcohol by volume. Until January, 1980, the UK used a similar system for spirits, but with 57.06%, measured at 15°C, as the standard (100° proof), pure alcohol being 175° proof. France and Italy formerly used the Gay-Lussac scale, which simply states the percentage volume of alcohol, measured at 15°C. The **OMIL** (International Organization of Legal Metrology) system, now used throughout the EU, is based on percentage volume of alcohol at 20°C. Thus a bottle of spirits labelled in the EU "35% vol" is approximately equivalent to 61° proof in the former UK system or 70° proof in the US system.

In most taxation systems distilled spirits and fermented liquors containing more than 23% alcohol are taxed on the volume of alcohol present. Beers and wines, on the other hand, are taxed on the volume of drink, the rate of duty depending on the alcohol content—progressively higher strength bands commanding a higher rate.

● **Alcott, Louisa May** ▸ (1832–88) US novelist. Daughter of the social theorist Bronson Alcott, her education was supplemented by instruction from ▷Thoreau, ▷Emerson, and her neighbour Nathaniel ▷Hawthorne. Her first book, *Flower Fables* (1854), was written when she was 16 to raise money for her family. *Hospital Sketches* (1863) recounted her experiences as a nurse in the Civil War. *Little Women* (1868–69), her most famous book, was largely autobiographical. Other works include *An Old-Fashioned Girl* (1870), *Little Men* (1871), and *Jo's Boys* (1886).

● **Alcuin** ▸ (c. 735–804 AD) English theologian and educator, who inspired the Carolingian renaissance. Born at York and educated at the cathedral school, he became the religious and educational adviser to Charlemagne after meeting him in 781. He established important libraries and developed a method of teaching based on ▷Boethius, St ▷Augustine of Hippo, and the study of grammar. Among his pupils was Rabanus Maurus (c. 780–856). He compiled numerous educational manuals and was also a poet. His letters are important sources for the study of Carolingian society.

● **Aldabra Islands** ▸ 9 45S 46 22E An atoll in the W Indian Ocean. Formerly administered from the Seychelles, they were part of the British Indian Ocean Territory from 1965 to 1976. There are no permanent inhabitants and the wildlife, notably the giant tortoise, is protected.

● **Aldanov, Mark** ▸ (M. Aleksandrovich Landau; 1886–1957) Russian novelist. He emigrated to France in 1919 and to the USA in 1941. His best-known work is a trilogy about Revolutionary France, comprising *Saint Helena* (1924), *The Ninth Thermidor* (1926), and *The Devil's Bridge* (1928). *The Fifth Seal* (1936) was an anti-Soviet satire and *The Tenth Symphony* (1931), a portrait of Beethoven's Vienna.

● **Aldebaran** ▸ A conspicuous ▷red giant, apparent magnitude 0.9 and 68 light years distant, that is the brightest star in the constellation Taurus. It is both a visual ▷binary star and an irregular ▷variable star.

● **Aldeburgh** ▸ 52 9N 1 35E A small resort in SE England in Suffolk. Once an important port, it is now famous for its annual music festival established in 1948 by Benjamin ▷Britten and Peter ▷Pears, who lived here. The festival, which is attended by musicians from all over the world, takes place both in Aldeburgh itself and in a concert hall built at the Maltings in nearby Snape. Aldeburgh is also the birthplace of the poet George ▷Crabbe, and Dr Elizabeth Garrett ▷Anderson was elected the first woman mayor in England here in 1908. Population (1991): 2654.

● **aldehydes** ▸ A class of organic chemicals that contain the –CHO group. They are prepared by the oxidation of alcohols and are themselves oxidized to form carboxylic acids. Common aldehydes are ▷methanal (formaldehyde) and ▷ethanal (acetaldehyde).

● **alder** ▸ A tree or shrub belonging to a genus (*Alnus*; about 30 species) of the N hemisphere. The leaves are roundish and toothed; the flowers grow as separate male and female catkins on the same tree. The fruit is a woody cone containing small winged nuts. The black alder (*A. glutinosa*), about 20 m high, is found in wet places throughout Europe and Asia and in N Africa. Its timber is used in general turnery. Family: *Betulaceae* (birch family).

● **alderfly** ▸ An insect, also known as a fish fly, having two pairs of delicate finely veined wings and long antennae. Up to 50 mm long (including the wings), alderflies live near fresh water, feeding on smaller insects and laying their eggs on reeds. The larvae, which are also carnivorous, live in the water and crawl out to pupate in burrows in the soil. Family: *Sialidae*; order: *Neuroptera* (lacewings, etc.).

● **alderman** ▸ In the UK, senior members of the major local authorities, normally elected by the directly elected members, until the Local Government Act (1972) abolished the office as an active rank except in the ▷City of London. The term derives from the Anglo-Saxon local official—the ealdorman. In the USA, many cities call their local-government officers aldermen but their powers vary from city to city.

● **Aldermaston** ▸ 51 23N 1 09W A village in S England, in West Berkshire unitary authority, Berkshire. It is associated with protest marches (1958–63) organized by the ▷Campaign for Nuclear Disar-

mament and is the site of the Atomic Weapons Research Establishment. Population (1987 est): 2157.

● **Alderney** ▸ (French name: Aurigny) 49 43N 2 12W The third largest of the Channel Islands, separated from France by the dangerous Race of Alderney channel. Its economy is based on dairy farming and tourism. Area: 8 sq km (3 sq mi). Population (1991): 2297. Chief town: St Anne.

● **Aldershot** ▸ 51 15N 0 47W A town in S England, in Hampshire. It is the chief garrison town and army training centre in the UK. Population (1991): 51 536.

● **Aldhelm, St** ▸ (c. 640–709 AD) English abbot and bishop. Abbot of Malmesbury from about 675, he became Bishop of Sherborne about 705. He founded several churches and monasteries. His Latin writings include various treatises, a work on saints, and religious poems. Feast day: 25 May.

● **Aldington, Richard** ▸ (1892–1962) British poet, novelist, and biographer. In 1913 he married his fellow Imagist poet Hilda ▷Doolittle. He suffered shell shock in World War I; *Death of a Hero* (1929), *The Colonel's Daughter* (1931), and other novels mirrored postwar anger and disillusion. Among his frequently controversial biographies are studies of D. H. Lawrence (1950) and T. E. Lawrence (1955).

● **Aldiss, Brian W(ilson)** ▸ (1925–) British novelist, best known for his science fiction. He has written a history of the genre, *Trillion Year Spree* (1986), and edited many science-fiction anthologies. His own books include *The Saliva Tree* (1966), *Last Orders* (1977), *Forgotten Life* (1988), *Dracula Unbound* (1991), and *Remembrance Day* (1993).

● **aldol** ▸ An organic compound that contains a hydroxyl group (OH) and an aldehyde group (CHO) bound to adjacent carbon atoms. **Acetaldol** ($CH_3CHOHCH_2CHO$) is used as a sedative and hypnotic drug.

● **aldosterone** ▸ A steroid hormone that acts on the kidney tubules to regulate the content of salts and water in the body. Derived from cholesterol, aldosterone is produced by the cortex of the adrenal glands in response to changing blood volume, changing levels of sodium and potassium, and the presence of the pituitary hormone ▷ACTH.

● **Aldrich, Thomas Bailey** ▸ (1836–1907) US short story writer and poet. He left school at 13 and began writing for magazines while working in New York as a clerk. He is also known for his autobiography, *The Story of a Bad Boy* (1870).

● **Aldridge, Ira Frederick** ▸ (1804–67) US actor. The first great Black tragedian, he made his debut as Othello in London in 1826 and toured Europe in Shakespearean roles. He became a naturalized British citizen in 1863.

● **Aldridge-Brownhills** ▸ A town in central England, in Walsall unitary authority, West Midlands. Formed by the amalgamation of neighbouring towns in 1966, it is a developing industrial centre. Population (1991): 37 444.

● **Aldrin, Jr, Edwin Eugene** ▸ (1930–) US astronaut, the second man to walk on the moon. Known as "Buzz," he was an air force pilot during the Korean War before becoming an astronaut in 1963. He undertook a 5½-hour spacewalk in 1966 and was lunar module pilot (under Neil ▷Armstrong) in Apollo 11 when it made the first moon landing in 1969.

● **ale** ▷*See* beer and brewing.

● **aleatoric music** ▸ Music that incorporates elements of chance in its structure. The term from Latin *alea*, a game of dice, was first used in the 1950s to describe John ▷Cage's experiments in determining pitch, rhythm, structure, and dynamics by the use of the ▷I Ching. ▷Boulez, ▷Stockhausen and others have experimented with this type of music. Computers have also been used to generate aleatoric music.

● **Alegría, Ciro** ▸ (1909–61) Peruvian novelist, imprisoned and finally exiled to Chile and the USA from 1934 until 1948 for his political activities. His works embody his deep knowledge of, and sympathy for, the Peruvian Indians: his best-known novel is *Broad and Alien Is the World* (1941).

● **Aleichem, Sholem** ► (Sholem Yakov Rabinowitz; 1859–1916) Russian Jewish writer, the author of many stories, plays, and novels in Yiddish. His works deal humorously and sympathetically with Jewish life in Ukraine. The musical *Fiddler on the Roof* (1964) was adapted from his stories.

● **Alekhine, Alexander** ► (1892–1946) French chess player, born in Russia. He became world champion by defeating ▷Capablanca (1927), losing the championship in 1935, but holding it again from 1937 until his death. The aesthetic merits of chess were more important to him than winning.

● **Alemán, Mateo** ► (1547–?1614) Spanish writer, famous for his picaresque novel *Guzman de Alfarache* (1599–1604), the scurrilous adventures of a youth who runs away from home and is finally condemned to the galleys, where he repents. The book became popular throughout Europe. Often imprisoned for debt, Alemán emigrated to Mexico in 1607.

● **Alençon** ► 48 25N 0 05E A town in NW France, the capital of the Orne department situated at the confluence of the Rivers Sarthe and Briant. The former capital of the duchy of Alençon, the town is famed for its lace (especially point d'Alençon). It serves an agricultural area. Population (1990): 31 140.

● **Aleppo** ► (Arabic name: Halab) 36 14N 37 10E A town in NW Syria. The Crusaders tried in vain to capture it, and from 1516 to 1919 Aleppo was part of the Ottoman Empire. After World War II, it was incorporated into independent Syria. It is now an industrial centre; its university was founded in 1960. Population (1994 est): 1 591 400.

● **Alessandria** ► 44 55N 8 37E A town in N Italy, in Piedmont on the River Tanaro. It is a railway centre and has an important engineering industry. The surrounding district is agricultural. Population (1990): 93 866.

● **Ålesund** ► (*or* Aalesund) 62 28N 6 11E A seaport in W Norway. Founded in the 9th century AD, it is an important trading centre, especially for fishing in northern waters. Population (1990): 35 888.

● **Aletsch Glacier** ► The largest glacier in Europe, in Switzerland in the Bernese Oberland lying SE of the Aletschhorn mountain. Length: 26 km (16 mi).

● **Aleut** ► A native of the Aleutian Islands and W Alaska, similar to the ▷Inuit in culture. Aleuts hunted seals, whales, and walrus, using skin-covered boats called bidarkas, which were like ▷kayaks but often two-manned. They also fished for salmon and in some areas hunted caribou and bear. They produced fine basketry and worked stone, bone, and ivory. Their population was considerably reduced during the Russian administration of the area and today their culture has been much changed by the impact of the modern world. Their language is closely related to Inuit. The principal dialects are Attuan and Unalaskan.

● **Aleutian Islands** ► A chain of volcanic Alaskan islands lying between the Bering Sea and the Pacific Ocean, divided politically between Russia and the USA. The chief settlements are on Unalaska. Russian exploitation of supplies after 1741 greatly reduced the population, but fishing and seal, otter, and fox hunting are now regulated. There are strategic US military stations on the islands and underground nuclear tests have been made (since 1971).

● **A level** ▷*See* public examinations.

● **alewife** ► A small silvery fish, *Pandopus pseudoharengus*, up to 30 cm long. It occurs chiefly in the Atlantic coastal waters of North America but has recently become established in the Great Lakes. It is an important food fish and is also used in the manufacture of fertilizers. Family: *Clupeidae* (herrings).

● **Alexander** ► (1876–1903) King of Serbia (1889–1903); the last of the ▷Obrenović dynasty. Alexander's arbitrary rule, including the abolition of the liberal constitution in 1894, and his unpopular marriage in 1900 led to his assassination, and that of his wife, by a group of army officers.

● **Alexander I** ► (c. 1077–1124) King of the Scots (1107–24), who ruled the highlands while his brother and successor David ruled the lowlands. He was noted for his reform of the Scottish church and his foundation of the monastery of Scone (1114). He aided Henry I of England's campaign against Wales (1114).

● **Alexander I** ► (1777–1825) Emperor of Russia (1801–25), succeeding his unstable father Paul I. Alexander made some educational and administrative reforms but was more concerned with foreign policy. France's defeat of Russia at ▷Friedland in 1807 forced Alexander to agree to the Treaty of ▷Tilsit, which lasted until Napoleon's unsuccessful invasion of Russia in 1812. After Napoleon's defeat, Russia controlled the ▷Congress Kingdom of Poland. Alexander turned to religious mysticism, hoping to establish a new Christian order in Europe by means of the Holy Alliance (1815) with Austria and Prussia. Towards the end of his life he withdrew into seclusion.

● **Alexander II** ► (1198–1249) King of the Scots (1214–49). Hoping to regain the northern counties of England, he supported the unsuccessful ▷Barons' War (1215–17) against King John. In 1221 he married Joan, the sister of Henry III of England, and gave up his claims to English territory in 1237, when the present border between England and Scotland was fixed.

● **Alexander II** ► (1818–81) Emperor of Russia (1855–81). After the conclusion of the ▷Crimean War (1856) Alexander embarked upon a programme of modernization. He emancipated the serfs (1861) and reorganized administration, the army, the judicial system, local government, and education. These reforms were not wholly successful because Alexander lacked personnel able to implement them. He presided over Russian expansion into Central Asia and the victorious war against Turkey (1877–78). The end of his reign saw the growth of radical opposition and he was killed by a bomb thrown into his coach.

Alexander (III) the Great ► A detail of a mosaic at Pompeii, which shows Alexander on his horse Bucephalus pursuing the fleeing Darius III of Persia. Alexander's decisive victory was achieved at Gaugamela in 331.

● **Alexander (III) the Great** ► (356–323 BC) King of Macedon (336–323), who between 334 and his death conquered most of the world known to antiquity. Alexander, who was a pupil of Aristotle, inherited a plan to invade Persia from his father Philip II; having secured his position in Macedon and Greece, he put this plan into action. In 333 he defeated the Persian king Darius III (d. 330) at Issus; in 332 he reduced Tyre in his greatest victory. Alexander then proceeded to conquer Egypt and Babylon (331). Moving on to Media and then east into central Asia, he finally embarked on the Indian expedition (327–325). He crossed the River Indus and conquered the Punjab. Forced to turn back by his reluctant army, he died at Babylon shortly after the marathon return journey. In the administration of his empire Alexander adopted a novel policy of appointing subject races to posts of responsibility, which some historians have called idealism and others, opportunism. His outstanding gifts as a general, however, are indisputable.

● **Alexander III** ► (Rolando Randinelli; c. 1105–81) Italian pope. Elected in 1159, he was immediately challenged by the antipope Victor IV, who was supported by ▷Frederick Barbarossa. He eventually forced Frederick to reconcile himself with the Church at the Peace of Venice in 1177. He imposed penance on ▷Henry II of England for the murder of Thomas ▷Becket. He called and presided at the third ▷Lateran Council, which conferred the exclusive right of papal elections on the cardinals.

● **Alexander III** ► (1241–86) King of the Scots (1249–86). He married (1251) Margaret, daughter of Henry III of England. Under his leadership, the Scots defeated the Norwegians at the battle of Largs (1263) and by the Treaty of Perth (1266) gained the Isle of Man and the Hebrides from Norway.

● **Alexander III** ► (1845–94) Emperor of Russia (1881–94). Owing to the assassination of his father Alexander II and the influence of the lawyer K. P. Pobedonostsev (1827–1907), Alexander's reign showed extreme conservatism. He increased police powers, persecuted revolutionaries, permitted education to decline, and encouraged the russification of subject races. Under him, Russia made its last conquests in Central Asia.

● **Alexander VI** ► (Rodrigo Borgia; c. 1431–1503) Pope (1492–1503), notorious for his immorality, nepotism, and extravagance. Father of four illegitimate children, he used papal wealth to further the career of his son, Cesare ▷Borgia, who pursued Alexander's territorial ambitions in Italy. He was a generous patron of artists and was responsible for demarcating the respective areas of influence of Spain and Portugal in the New World.

● **Alexander, Harold, 1st Earl Alexander of Tunis** ► (1891–1969) British field marshal. After distinguished service in World War I, Alexander held command in India. In World War II he commanded the evacuation of British forces from Dunkirk and was the last man to leave France. He became commander in chief in the Middle East (1942) and then, as Eisenhower's deputy, directed the offensive that defeated the Germans in N Africa (1943). He ended the war as Allied supreme commander in the Mediterranean and was subsequently governor general of Canada (1946–52) and Conservative minister of defence (1952–54).

● **Alexander, Sir William, 1st Earl of Stirling** ► (c. 1576–1640) Scottish poet and colonist, who founded Nova Scotia (New Scotland). In 1604 he published a collection of sonnets, *Aurora*, and, in 1614, *Doomesday, or the Great Day of the Lord's Judgement*. In 1621 he was granted territory in Newfoundland but subsequently abandoned it for Nova Scotia. His attempts to find colonists for the region had little success and he was forced to relinquish it by war with the French in 1629.

● **Alexander Archipelago** ► A chain of islands in the USA, off the SE coast of Alaska. They consist of the summits of a submerged mountain chain and their rugged densely forested terrain supports an abundance of wildlife.

● **Alexander Nevsky** ► (c. 1220–63) Prince of Novgorod (1236–63) and Grand Prince of Vladimir (1252–63). Alexander's fame rests on his defeat of the Swedes (1240) near the Neva River (thus acquiring his name Nevsky) and of the Teutonic Knights (1242) on Lake Peipus. Despite the opposition of many Russians, he accepted the overlordship of the invading Mongols, thereby saving N Russia from certain devastation.

● **Alexander of Hales** ► (c. 1170–1245) English scholastic philosopher, born at Hales (Gloucestershire). He became professor of theology in Paris and in 1236 a Franciscan. He is renowned for his efforts to combine the newly rediscovered ▷Aristotelianism, as mediated by the Arabic thinkers, such as ▷Averroes, with the Platonist tradition mediated by St ▷Augustine of Hippo.

● **Alexander Severus** ▷*See* Severus Alexander.

● **Alexandra** ► (1844–1925) A Danish princess who married (1863) Edward VII of the United Kingdom, when he was the Prince of Wales. In 1902 she founded Queen Alexandra's Imperial (now Royal) Army Nursing Corps and in 1912 she instituted the Alexandra Rose Day in aid of hospitals.

● **Alexandra** ► (1872–1918) The wife from 1894 of ▷Nicholas II of Russia. A German princess and granddaughter of Queen Victoria, Alexandra fell under the evil influence of ▷Rasputin. His disastrous domination of her government while Nicholas was supreme commander of the Russian forces in World War I precipitated the Russian Revolution and the execution of Alexandra and her family by the Bolsheviks.

● **Alexandria** ► (Arabic name: al-Iskandariyah) 31 13N 22 55E The chief seaport and second largest city in Egypt, between Lake Mareotis and the Mediterranean Sea. It handles most of Egypt's trade and the chief export is cotton; industries include oil refining and cotton ginning. The University of Alexandria was established in 1942.

History: founded in 332 BC by Alexander the Great, partly on the island of Pharos, which was linked to the mainland by a mole, it remained the Egyptian capital for over a thousand years. It was a Greek and Jewish cultural centre with a famous library (*see* Alexandria, Library of) and in 30 BC fell to the Romans, becoming their most important regional capital. It declined following the discovery of the Cape of Good Hope passage and the removal of the capital to Cairo. It was bombarded by the British in 1882, Pompey's Pillar being one of the few ancient monuments to escape destruction. Two obelisks that also survived, ▷Cleopatra's Needles, were removed and one is now in London, the other in New York. During World War II the city suffered many air raids but since then has seen rapid expansion. Population (1994 est): 3 382 000.

● **Alexandria, Catechetical School of** ► A Christian theological school at Alexandria from the late 2nd to the 4th century AD. Its early teachers, ▷Clement of Alexandria and ▷Origen, dominated the School's approach, which was a Platonic mystical philosophy that stressed divine transcendence, the deity of Christ, and a Trinitarianism that was almost tritheism. Athanasius was typically Alexandrian in opposing the Arian and related heresies.

● **Alexandria, Library of** ► The greatest library of the ancient world, which in its heyday may have contained more than 700 000 items. A composite library, museum, and school, it was founded in the 3rd century BC by Ptolemy I Soter and his son, Ptolemy II Philadelphus. Large parts were destroyed in fires, notably in 97 BC, and it was gradually dispersed over the centuries. The survival of much of classical Greek literature is due to the work of its scholars.

● **alexandrine** ► A verse metre consisting of a line of 12 syllables usually with major stresses on the sixth and final syllables. The name is derived from 12th-century French poems about Alexander the Great. It was the dominant verse form in 17th-century French poetry and was used by ▷Racine and ▷Corneille.

● **Alexis** ► (1690–1718) The son and heir of ▷Peter the Great of Russia. Alexis' unhappy relations with his father progressively worsened and in 1716 Alexis fled to Vienna. Peter lured him back and condemned him to death for treason. He died before his execution.

● **Alexius I Comnenus** ► (1048–1118) Byzantine emperor (1081–1118), who founded the Comnenian dynasty. Seizing the throne in a coup, Alexius revived the weakened Byzantine state, defeating the Normans and Seljuq Turks, who were encroaching on Byzantine territory, and introducing administrative reforms. However, in the second half of his reign, the Empire was threatened by the advance of the Crusaders. His achievements were celebrated in the *Alexiad* of his daughter ▷Anna Comnena.

● **alfalfa** ► A perennial flowering plant, *Medicago sativa*, also called lucerne. Growing to a height of 1 m, it resembles clover, having clusters of small purple flowers. Native to Europe, it is widely grown as forage for cattle and because of its ability to fix nitrogen. Family: *Leguminosae*.

● **al-Farabi, Mohammed ibn Tarkhan** ▶ (d. 950) Muslim philosopher, physician, mathematician, and musician, of Central Asian origin. He is acknowledged to be one of the greatest Muslim thinkers and his works on medicine and music became standard treatises. But it was his contribution to Arabic philosophy that earned him renown. A staunch believer in the truth of Islam, Al-Farabi strove to bring Greek philosophy into conformity with its doctrines.

● **al-Fatah** ▷See Fatah, al-.

● **Alfieri, Vittorio, Count** ▶ (1749–1803) Italian poet and dramatist. He abandoned a military career in order to travel widely throughout Europe (1767–72). After the success of his first play, *Cleopatra* (1775), he devoted himself entirely to literature. He wrote 28 plays, of which his 19 tragedies, among them *Saul* and *Mirra*, depict romantic heroes struggling against tyranny and oppression. He also wrote poetry and an autobiography, *La vita* (1804).

● **Alfonso (V) the Magnanimous** ▶ (1385–1458) King of Aragon (1416–58) and, as Alfonso I, of Sicily (1416–58) and Naples (1443–58). During the 1420s he helped Queen Joanna II of Naples (1371–1435; reigned 1414–35) to resist the claims of Louis III of Anjou (1403–34) to the Neapolitan throne. After her death he seized the throne himself and his court at Naples became a brilliant centre of Renaissance culture.

● **Alfonso VI** ▶ (d. 1109) King of León (1065–1109) and of Castile (1072–1109). In 1085 Alfonso took Toledo from the Muslims but in the following year suffered defeat by the Almoravids of N Africa, with whom conflict continued until 1108. Alfonso's marriage to Constance of Burgundy brought cultural ties with France and he supported the introduction of Cluniac monasticism to León. His reign is also notable for the exploits of El Cid.

● **Alfonso VIII** ▶ (d. 1214) King of Castile (1158–1214), famous for his defeat of the Moors at Navas de Tolosa (1212). He married Eleanor, a daughter of Henry II of England; their daughter was ▷Blanche of Castile.

● **Alfonso (X) the Wise** ▶ (c. 1221–84) King of Castile and León (1252–84). He made his court at Toledo a centre of learning and a haven for Arab and Jewish, as well as Christian, scholars. He compiled a legal code, the *Seven Divisions of the Law*, but it never came into effective use. He also failed in an attempt (1257) to become the first Spanish Holy Roman Emperor.

● **Alfonso XIII** ▶ (1886–1941) King of Spain from birth until 1931. Alfonso, who came of age in 1902, ruled during a turbulent period of social unrest and political instability and several attempts were made on his life. The dictatorship (1923–30) of Miguel ▷Primo de Rivera undermined his reign and he abdicated in 1931 following Republican victories in municipal elections.

● **Alfred the Great** ▶ (849–99) King of Wessex (871–99). He prevented the Danish conquest of England, defeating the invaders at Edington (878) after a campaign of guerrilla warfare based at ▷Athelney. The legend of the king travelling incognito and burning the peasant housewife's cakes, possibly refers to this unsettled period of his life. After his victory he allowed the Danes to keep their conquests in Mercia and East Anglia provided that Guthrum, their king, was converted to Christianity. Alfred built a navy to defend the south coast against further Danish invasions (885–86; 892–96) and protected Wessex with a chain of fortifications. He took London (886), thus gaining control of all England save the Danish areas. Alfred did much to revive learning, translating important Latin works into English. He also devised a legal code.

● **Alfvén, Hannes Olof Gösta** ▶ (1908–95) Swedish astrophysicist. A specialist in ▷plasma physics, his original work includes studies of sunspots, cosmic rays, and the aurora. His work on the interaction of plasma with magnetic fields (magnetohydrodynamics) forms the basis of several proposed systems for harnessing nuclear fusion power; he shared the 1970 Nobel Prize for this work.

● **algae** ▶ A vast group of simple organisms (about 25 000 species) traditionally regarded as plants but placed in the kingdom ▷*Protoctista* in modern classifications (*see* taxonomy). Algae contain the green pigment chlorophyll (and can therefore carry out photosynthesis) but have no true stems, roots, or leaves. They range from single-celled organisms to the giant seaweeds. Most algae are aquatic, although some live in damp places on land—on rocks, trees, or in soils. A few are parasitic or associate with other organisms (*see* lichens). Reproduction is extremely variable and may involve asexual means, such as cell division, fragmentation, or spore production, and/or sexual means by gamete production. The more advanced algae often alternate between sexual and asexual phases. Algae provide a valuable food source for aquatic herbivorous animals and many are used as fertilizers and in industry. They include the ▷green, ▷yellow-green, ▷brown, and ▷red algae; the organisms formerly known as blue-green algae are now classified as bacteria (*see* blue-green bacteria).

● **Algarve** ▶ A region in S Portugal, bordering on Spain and the Atlantic Ocean and corresponding approximately to the modern administrative district of Faro. It became a Moorish kingdom in 1140 and was the last stronghold of the Moors in Portugal, being reconquered in 1249. Sparsely populated inland, its fertile coastal belt is densely populated and produces chiefly maize, figs, almonds, and olives; fishing is also important. Tourism is a flourishing industry.

● **algebra** ▶ The branch of mathematics that uses symbols to represent unknown quantities. The first treatise on the subject was written by Diophantus of Alexandria in the 3rd century AD and the name derives from the Arabic *al-jabr*, a term used by the mathematician al-Khwarizmi to denote the addition of equal quantities to both sides of an equation and later adopted as the name for the whole subject. Algebra was used in ancient Babylon, Egypt, and India and brought to Europe by the Arabs. In classical algebra symbols, such as x and y, represent ordinary numbers and the central part of the subject is the study of algebraic equations. Modern, or abstract, algebra is concerned with any system of quantities that obey a particular set of general rules and relationships. Such systems may or may not obey the ▷commutative laws or even the ▷associative laws that hold in arithmetic.

● **Algeciras** ▶ 36 08N 5 27W A port in S Spain, in Andalusia on the Bay of Gibraltar. Founded in 713 AD, it was destroyed by Alfonso XI of Castile (1311–50; reigned 1312–50) in 1344. The present town was rebuilt in 1760. In 1906 it was the site of the Algeciras Conference, a meeting of European powers to solve their dispute over Morocco. Its exports include oranges and cork. Population (1995 est): 104 216.

● **Algeria, Democratic and Popular Republic of** ▶ A country in N Africa, on the Mediterranean Sea. It consists chiefly of the N Sahara Desert, with the Atlas Mountains in the N and small fertile areas near the coast. The inhabitants, who live almost entirely in the N, are mainly Arabs and Berbers.
Economy: mainly agricultural although industrialization has proceeded rapidly since independence, financed by the discovery of oil (the main export) and natural gas in the desert areas. Since 1996 gas has been piped directly to Spain, resulting in a huge increase of gas exports to Europe. Most industry was state controlled until the mid-1990s, when Algeria agreed a liberalization programme with the IMF.
History: a former province of the Roman Empire, Algeria was subjugated in the 7th century by the Arabs, who introduced Islam. Overrun by Turks in the 16th century, it became a pirate state in the 18th century under the domination of *deys*, independent rulers who preyed on Mediterranean shipping. Algeria was annexed by the French in the 19th century and in 1881 the N section became part of Metropolitan France. A fierce war of independence, waged by the ▷Front de Libération nationale (FLN), lasted from 1954 to 1962 when independence was granted by de Gaulle, following referendums held in both Algeria and France. A republic was set up under Ahmed ▷Ben Bella but was overthrown in 1965 by a Council of Revolution. Col Houari ▷Boumédienne became president and in 1976 a new constitution was adopted in which the FLN became the only permitted political party. Following Boumédienne's death in 1978, Col Benjedid Chadli became the new president. Riots in 1988 prompted promises of constitutional reform. A multiparty system was restored in 1989, but when the fundamentalist Islamic Salvation Front were poised to win a general election in 1992 the elections were cancelled and a

transitional government installed. Some 100 000 people have died in the subsequent guerrilla war. Islamic extremists were responsible for the shooting of President Mohamed Boudiaf (1992) and former prime minister Kasdi Merbah (1993). In 1996 a new constitution, designed to exclude religious parties from politics, was endorsed in a referendum. Elections in 1997 resulted in victory for the government but led to intensified violence. The country's first free presidential elections, held in 1999, were marred by the withdrawal of all the opposition candidates. A peace plan unveiled by the new president, Abdelaziz Bouteflika, was overwhelmingly backed in a referendum and by January 2000 the main insurgent group had agreed to disband.

Democratic and Popular Republic of Algeria

Head of state	President Abdelaziz Bouteflika
Official language	Arabic; French is widely spoken
Official religion	Islam
Currency	dinar of 100 centimes
Area	2 381 745 sq km (919 595 sq mi)
Population (1998 est)	30 045 000
Capital and main port	Algiers.

● **Algiers** ▶ (Arabic name: al-Jaza'ir; French name: Alger) 36 45N 3 05E The capital of Algeria, an important Mediterranean port. Its main exports include wine, citrus fruits, and iron ore. The University of Algiers was founded in 1879 and the University of Science and Technology in 1974.

History: originally founded by the Phoenicians, it was re-established by the Arabs in the 10th century. Overrun by Turks in the 16th century, it became a base for Barbary pirates until taken by the French in 1830. During World War II it was the headquarters of the Allied forces in N Africa and for a time the seat of the French government-in-exile. It was the scene of uprisings during the Algerian struggle for independence from France (1954–62). Population (1995 est): 2 168 000.

● **algin** ▶ (sodium alginate) A slimy substance extracted from seaweed. It is used as a thickener in such foods as ice cream and in industrial compounds.

● **Algirdas** ▶ (*or* Olgierd; d. 1377) Grand Duke of Lithuania (1345–77). A pagan ruler, Algirdas was nevertheless tolerant of the Orthodox Church. He fought the Poles, Mongols, and Teutonic Knights and extended Lithuania eastwards.

● **Algol** ▶ (*or* Winking Demon) A white 2nd-magnitude star in the constellation Perseus. Its regular variations in brightness have been long known. The prototype of the **Algol variables**, a class of eclipsing ▷binary stars, Algol and its fainter companion revolve around one another in 2.87 days.

● **Algol** ▶ (*al*gorithmic language) A computer-programming language. It is used to express mathematical and scientific problems for processing by computer. Algol is a high-level language, i.e. statements made in it resemble English rather than a computer notation. ▷*See* program, computer.

● **Algonquian** ▶ A group of North American Indian languages, including ▷Cree, ▷Cheyenne, ▷Blackfoot, and others, spoken by tribes living to the S and E of Hudson Bay and in the eastern woodland zone. The Algonquian tribes lived by hunting and fishing and roamed widely in small family groups and bands. They moved possessions by means of toboggans and dressed in clothes made from the skins of animals, such as caribou and moose, decorated with bright quillwork and beadwork. Religion was little developed, involving belief in a single creator god, fear of spirits and witches, and reliance on the protective and curative powers of medicine men, the only persons with authority.

● **Algonquin** ▶ The language and name of a North American Indian people of Quebec and Ottawa in Canada. The ▷Algonquian language group was named after it. Algonquin culture was similar to that of other Algonquian-speaking tribes of the area.

● **Algonquin Round Table** ▶ A circle of US writers who met regularly at the Algonquin Hotel in New York in the 1920s and 1930s. Members included Robert ▷Benchley, George ▷Kaufman, Dorothy ▷Parker, James ▷Thurber, and Alexander ▷Woollcott. They wined and dined well, leaving for posterity many humorous anecdotes of their times together.

● **Algren, Nelson** ▶ (1909–81) US novelist. He trained as a journalist in Chicago, where most of his fiction is set, and briefly became a migrant worker during the Depression. In his novels, such as *Never Come Morning* (1942), he portrayed the underworld of American city life in an intense naturalistic style. *The Man with the Golden Arm* (1949), about drug addiction, brought him international fame.

● **Alhambra** ▶ A castle on a hilly terrace outside ▷Granada (Spain), built between 1238 and 1358. It was the last stronghold of the Muslim kings of Granada. Combining citadel and palace, it is an outstanding example of Moorish architecture, with magnificent courts and gardens. The name derives from Arabic *al-hamra*, the red, an allusion to the red stucco used on the walls. □ p. 36.

● **Al Hudaydah** ▷*See* Hodeida.

● **Ali** ▶ (c. 600–61) The cousin of ▷Mohammed and his son-in-law by marriage to ▷Fatimah. Born at Mecca, he was the second, or perhaps the first, person to embrace Islam. He became the fourth caliph in 656, but was murdered in 661 at Kufa, Iraq. His tomb is venerated at Najaf. According to ▷Shiite Muslims, Ali was the only legitimate successor of Mohammed and only his descendants can be ▷imams.

● **Ali, Muhammad** ▶ (Cassius Marcellus Clay; 1942–) US boxer. A gold medallist in the 1960 Olympic Games, he became professional world heavyweight champion (1964). On becoming a Black Muslim he changed his name and was soon afterwards stripped of his title for three years because of his refusal to join the US army. Defeated (1971) by Joe ▷Frazier, he again became champion in 1974 by defeating George Foreman (1949–), losing the title briefly in 1978 to Leon Spinks. His defeat of Spinks later that year made him the only boxer to become world champion three times. In 1980 he was defeated by Larry Holmes in his bid to regain the world title. He now suffers from Parkinson's disease as a result of blows to the brain.

● **Alia, Ramiz** ▶ (1925–) Albanian politician; head of state (1982–92). He succeeded Enver Hoxha as first secretary of the Party of Labour in 1985.

● **Alicante** ▶ 38 21N 0 29W A port in SE Spain, in Valencia on the Mediterranean. Exports include wine, olive oil, and fruits. Industries include oil refining, textiles, chemicals, soap, and tobacco. It is a tourist resort. Population (1995 est): 276 526.

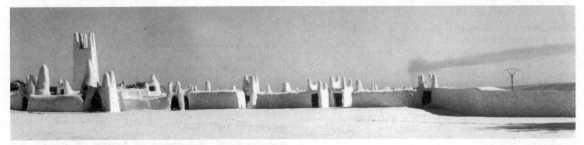

Algeria ▶ Taghit, often regarded as the most beautiful oasis town in the Algerian desert.

Alhambra ► The arcade round the Court of the Lions features the horseshoe arches characteristic of Moorish architecture.

● **Alice Springs ►** 23 42S 133 52E A town in central Australia, in S Northern Territory. It is a major centre for beef cattle and mineral transportation, linked by air, road, and rail with Adelaide and by air and the Stuart Highway with Darwin. It is also a base for tourism. Population (1994): 24 852.

● **alien ►** A person who, according to the law of a state, is not a citizen of that state. According to the British Nationality Act (1981), an alien is someone who is neither a commonwealth citizen (*see* British citizenship), nor a British-protected person, nor a citizen of the Republic of Ireland. Aliens may own property in the UK (but not a British ship) but may not vote or hold public office. ▷*See also* migration, human; naturalization.

● **Alien and Sedition Acts ►** (1798) Four laws enacted in the USA ostensibly to prevent domestic subversion but actually to check the threat posed to the ▷Federalist Party by Thomas Jefferson's Republican Party. The Naturalization Act delayed voting rights for the immigrants upon whom the Republicans depended for support. The Alien Act and Alien Enemies Act authorized deportation of aliens suspected of threatening the government and the Sedition Act prohibited criticism of the government, thereby nullifying the First Amendment. When Jefferson became president (1800) three of the laws were allowed to lapse; the Naturalization Act was repealed in 1802.

● **alienation ►** A pathological feeling of self-estrangement and loss of moral purpose. Hegel used the term to refer to a condition in which an individual's freedom of choice and action appears to him to have become an independent force constraining him. Marx made special use of the concept of alienated labour, believing that when men are forced to sell their labour to employers they are alienated from their own productive abilities. In contemporary common usage the term is applied loosely to situations in which people feel alienated from society, considering themselves to be "outsiders" with no sense of belonging to a community. In this meaning it overlaps the concept of ▷anomie.

● **Aligarh ►** 27 42N 78 25E A city in N India, in Uttar Pradesh. An ag-

ricultural trading centre, it is the site of the notable Aligarh Muslim University (founded as a college in 1875). Population (1991): 479 978.

● **alimentary canal** ▷*See* digestion.

● **Ali Pasa, Mehmed Emin ►** (1815–71) Grand Vizier (chief minister) of the Ottoman Empire five times between 1852 and 1871. He represented the Ottomans at the Congress of Paris (1856) following the Crimean War and was an advocate of Ottoman friendship with France and Britain. He was one of the architects of the period (1839–76) of Ottoman reform known as the Tanzimat (Reorganization).

● **aliphatic compounds ►** Organic chemical compounds that are not ▷aromatic. They include the ▷alkanes, ▷alkenes, and ▷alkynes as well as some cyclic compounds (cycloalkanes).

● **Aliutor** ▷*See* Palaeo-Siberian languages.

● **alizarin ►** (1,2 dihydroxy-anthraquinone; $C_{14}H_6O_2(OH)_2$) An orange-red crystalline solid, formerly extracted from madder root and used in dyeing. It is almost insoluble in water but dissolves in alcohol. Alizarin is now made from ▷anthracene and yields a wide variety of dyes.

● **alkali** ▷*See* acids and bases.

● **alkali metals ►** The elements forming group 1 of the ▷periodic table: lithium, sodium, potassium, rubidium, caesium, and francium. All are soft, silvery-white ▷metals with low densities, melting points, and boiling points. In chemical reactions they tend to form positive ions and have a valence of 1. They are highly reactive, form soluble salts with nonmetals, generally release hydrogen on contact with water, and react with air to form oxides. The oxides and hydroxides are alkalis.

● **alkaline-earth metals ►** The elements forming group 2 of the ▷periodic table: beryllium, magnesium, calcium, strontium, barium, and radium. They are similar to the ▷alkali metals in appearance and chemistry, but are harder, have higher melting and boiling points, and are somewhat less reactive. They have a valence of 2. The **alkaline earths** are the oxides of these metals.

● **alkaloids ►** A group of nitrogen-containing basic compounds that are produced by plants and have diverse effects on the body. Many alkaloids are used as medicinal drugs, including quinine, morphine, hyoscine (*or* scopolamine), and atropine. Others, such as strychnine and coniine (from hemlock), are poisons. Caffeine, nicotine, and LSD are also alkaloids.

● **Alkan, Charles Henri Valentin ►** (C. H. V. Morhange; 1813–88) French pianist and composer. By his teens he was a brilliant performer but became a recluse early in life. His many compositions, chiefly for the piano, are always original and difficult, and frequently very large scale. He was killed by a falling bookcase.

● **alkanes ►** (*or* paraffins) A series of hydrocarbons, which contain only single bonds between the carbon atoms. They have the general formula C_nH_{2n+2}. The first four members of the series methane (CH_4), ethane (C_2H_6), propane (C_3H_8), and butane (C_4H_{10}) are gases, higher members are liquids or waxes. They are obtained from natural gas or oil and they and their substitution products have many uses.

● **alkanet ►** A herbaceous plant of the genus *Anchusa*, native to Eurasia but widely grown for ornament (*A. azurea* is a common garden plant). It may reach a height of 50–120 cm, with clusters of small blue or white flowers and narrow or oval leaves. Family: *Boraginaceae*.
     A similar and related plant, *Pentaglottis sempervirens*, is also called alkanet.

● **alkenes ►** (*or* olefins) Hydrocarbons that contain at least one carbon–carbon double bond in their molecules. The simplest types, with one double bond, have the general formula C_nH_{2n}; ethylene (*or* ethene, C_2H_4) is the first member of this series. The alkenes are more reactive than the ▷alkanes, undergoing addition and polymerization reactions. They are obtained by cracking petroleum and their main use is as starting materials in industrial chemistry.

● **Al Khalil** ▷*See* Hebron.

● **al-Khwarizmi, Muhammed ibn Musa ►** (c. 780–c. 850 AD) Arabic mathematician, who introduced the Hindu decimal system and the use of zero into Arabic mathematics. He also extended the work of Diophantus on algebraic equations in a book the title of which included the word *al-jabr* ("transposition"), from which the modern word "algebra" is derived.

● **Al-Kindi, Abu Yusuf Ya'qub ibn Ishaq** ► (died c. 870) Muslim Arab philosopher, born in al-Kufa (now in Iraq). He was dubbed "philosopher of the Arabs" as he was the only Arabic philosopher of pure Arab stock. He made the whole field of Greek science his own and was among the first Arabic scholars to interest himself in philosophy from a scientific rather than a theological viewpoint.

● **Alkmaar** ► 52 38W 4 44E A town in the NW Netherlands, in North Holland province. A commercial centre, it holds a famous cheese market between May and Oct. Population (1994): 92 962.

● **Al Kut** ► 32 30N 45 51E A town in E Iraq, on the River Tigris to the SE of Baghdad. It was the scene of heavy fighting between the British and the Turks in World War I. The Kut barrage (completed 1939) diverts water into irrigation channels.

● **alkynes** ► (*or* acetylenes) Hydrocarbons that contain at least one carbon–carbon triple bond in their molecules. The simplest types, with one triple bond, have the general formula C_nH_{2n-2}; ▷ethyne (*or* acetylene, C_2H_2) is the first member of this series. The alkynes, like the ▷alkenes, undergo addition and polymerization reactions. They are extremely reactive, tending to explode under pressure, and are difficult to use in large quantities.

● **Allah** ► (Arabic, probably from *al-ilah*: the god) The Islamic name of God. Allah was worshipped in pre-Islamic Arabia as early as the 3rd century BC. In Mecca he was given special rank as "the god," but lesser tribal gods continued to be worshipped alongside him until ▷Mohammed proclaimed the rigorous monotheism of Islam. As formulated by Mohammed, Allah is the one omnipotent and omniscient God, the same God as worshipped by Jews and Christians. He is eternal, the creator of the universe, the judge of men, merciful and compassionate. His word is embodied in the ▷Koran.

● **Allahabad** ► 25 57N 81 50E A city in N India, in Uttar Pradesh at the confluence of the Rivers Ganges and Jumna. It is principally an administrative and educational centre; its university was established in 1887. The Maha Kumbh Mela religious festival, the biggest such event in the world, is held here every 12 years. A former centre of the independence movement, it was the home of the Nehru family. Population (1991): 806 447.

● **Allbutt, Sir Thomas Clifford** ► (1836–1925) British physician, who (in 1866) introduced the modern clinical thermometer. Allbutt also made valuable contributions to the study of syphilis and heart disease, most notably angina pectoris.

● **Allegheny Mountains** ► A mountain range in the USA, extending from North Carolina to Pennsylvania. Part of the Appalachian Mountains, it consists of well-rounded uplands rising to 1480 m (4860 ft) at Spruce Knob. It forms the watershed between the Atlantic Ocean and the Mississippi River and was for many years a frontier zone between French settlers in the Mississippi Basin and English colonists along the coast.

● **allegory** ► A verse or prose narrative in which characters and events in the plot refer to a deeper, usually moral, meaning. It is an ancient and universal form, similar to but usually longer than the ▷fable and the parable. Examples of allegory include the French *Roman de la rose* (13th century), Bunyan's *The Pilgrim's Progress* (1678), Swift's *Gulliver's Travels* (1726), and Orwell's *Animal Farm* (1945).

● **Allegri, Gregorio** ► (1582–1652) Italian composer. He was appointed a singer in Pope ▷Urban VIII's chapel in 1629. An important composer of church music, he wrote a famous *Miserere* for nine voices, two volumes of concertinos, and two volumes of motets.

● **allele** ► Any one of the various alternative forms of a ▷gene that can occur at the same site on a ▷chromosome. In *Drosophila* fruit flies, for example, several alternative eye colours are possible depending on which of the various alleles of the gene for eye colour is present in the individual.

● **allelopathy** ► The release by a plant of a chemical that inhibits the growth of nearby plants, to reduce competition. For example, in dry habitats volatile terpenes are released from the leaves of some plants to inhibit the germination of nearby herbaceous plants. Some plants also produce alkaloids (called allelochemicals) to discourage herbivorous animals from consuming them.

allemande ► A late 18th century engraving satirizing the vogue for this elaborate dance.

● **allemande** ► A 16th-century processional dance in 4/4 time originating in Germany. Popular in France and in England under the name almand or almain, it reappeared in the 18th century as an elaborate figure dance for couples, in 2/4 time. A stylized version of the early dance was frequently used by Bach, Couperin, and other contemporary composers to open a suite. The name is also applied to a lively German-Swiss folk dance resembling the *Ländler*.

● **Allen, Bog of** ► (Irish name: Moin Almkaine) An area of peat bogs in the Republic of Ireland, covering much of the central plain. The peat is used for fuelling power stations and for domestic use. Area: 958 sq km (370 sq mi).

● **Allen, Ethan** ► (1739–89) American soldier, who pursued the independence from New York and New Hampshire of the Green Mountain region (now Vermont). Between 1770 and 1775 he commanded the ▷Green Mountain Boys, which with Benedict ▷Arnold's forces captured Fort Ticonderoga (1775), the first American victory in the American Revolution. He was imprisoned by the British (1775–78) and died shortly before Vermont achieved statehood in 1789.

● **Allen, William, Cardinal** ► (1532–94) English churchman. He was principal of St Mary's Hall, Oxford. With the accession of Elizabeth I, he went into exile rather than take the oath of supremacy. He founded the Roman Catholic seminary at Douai (1568), where priests were trained for mission work in England and where the ▷Douai Bible was begun with his encouragement. He was made cardinal in 1587 and supported the Spanish Armada in 1588, a decision that adversely affected his influence among many English Roman Catholics. He spent his last years at the English college at Rome, which he had founded.

● **Allen, Woody** ► (Allen Stewart Konigsberg; 1935–) US film actor, director, and screenwriter. His performances are witty portrayals of social inadequacy and embarrassment. His films include *Play It Again, Sam* (1972), the Oscar-winning *Annie Hall* (1977), *Manhattan* (1979), *Hannah and Her Sisters* (1986), *Crimes and Misdemeanours* (1990), *Bullets over Broadway* (1994), *Deconstructing Harry* (1997), and *Sweet and Lowdown* (2000).

● **Allenby, Edmund Henry Hynman, 1st Viscount** ► (1861–1936) British field marshal. After experience in the Boer War, he commanded the Third Army in France in World War I. In 1917, appointed commander in chief of the Egyptian Expeditionary Force against the Turks in Palestine, he captured (9 Dec) Jerusalem (as a "Christmas present" for the British people) and then devastated the Turks at Megiddo (1918). He ended his career as high commissioner in Egypt (1919–25).

● **Allende (Gossens), Salvador** ▶ (1908–73) Chilean statesman; president of Chile (1970–73), the first Marxist to come to power through free elections. A founder of the Chilean Socialist Party, Allende governed a coalition of left-wing parties. His nationalization policies created much opposition and he was overthrown and killed by a military coup.

● **Allentown** ▶ 40 37N 75 30W A town in the USA, in Pennsylvania. It has important steel and machinery industries. Population (1996 est): 102 211.

● **allergy** ▶ An abnormal reaction by the body that is provoked by certain substances, including pollen, dust, car exhaust fumes, certain foods and drugs, fur, moulds, etc. Normally all foreign substances (antigens) entering the body are destroyed by ▷antibodies without further trouble. Allergic people, however, become hypersensitive to certain antigens (called allergens), so that whenever they are subsequently encountered they stimulate not only the normal antibody reaction but also the specific symptoms of the allergy. Allergic conditions include ▷hay fever, some forms of ▷asthma and ▷dermatitis, and ▷urticaria. Treatment includes the use of ▷antihistamines, corticosteroids, and ▷desensitization.

● **Alleyn, Edward** ▶ (1566–1626) English actor. He acted in many of the plays of Christopher Marlowe and was the main rival of Richard ▷Burbage in the Elizabethan theatre. He became a prosperous theatre owner and founded Dulwich College in 1619.

● **Allied Powers** ▶ The nations united in opposition to the ▷Central Powers in World War I and to the ▷Axis Powers in World War II. In World War I the Allies were initially the UK, France, and Russia, bound by the Treaty of London (1914), and later included Italy, Japan, and Portugal; the USA was an associated power from 1917. In World War II the chief Allies were the UK, France (1939–40, 1944–45), the Soviet Union (from June, 1941), the USA (from December, 1941), and China.

● **Allier, River** ▶ A river in central France. Rising in the Cévennes, it flows NNW through the fertile Limagne area, joining the River Loire near Nevers. Length: 403 km (250 mi).

● **alligator** ▶ A large broad-snouted ▢reptile belonging to the genus *Alligator* (2 species). Each side of the jaw contains 17–22 teeth, which are all covered when the mouth is closed. The American alligator (*A. mississippiensis*) is mainly black and lives in rivers of the SE USA, reaching a length of 5–6 m; the rare Chinese alligator (*A. sinensis*) of the Yangtze River is smaller. They dig burrows in which they hibernate during cold weather. Order: *Crocodilia* (*see* crocodile).

● **Allingham, Margery** ▶ (1904–66) British detective-story writer. Her mild-mannered likeable detective Albert Campion appeared in a popular series of novels begun in the 1920s and ending with *Cargo of Eagles* (1968). *Tiger in the Smoke* (1952), *The China Governess* (1963), and *The Mind Readers* (1965) are among her most acclaimed books.

● **Allium** ▶ A genus of herbaceous plants (about 450 species), including the ▷onion, ▷shallot, ▷garlic, ▷leek, ▷chive, etc. They have bulbs, those of several species being widely used in temperate regions for food and flavouring, and in many the flowers are replaced by small bulbs (bulbils), by means of which the plants can be propagated. Family: *Liliaceae* (or *Alliaceae* according to some authorities).

● **Alloa** ▶ 56 07N 3 49W A town in Scotland, the administrative centre of Clackmannanshire at the head of the Forth estuary. Industries include brewing, engineering, textiles, and agricultural implements. Population (1991): 18 842

● **allopathy** ▶ Literally, the use of drugs or other means to induce a reaction in the body that will counteract—and therefore relieve—the symptoms of a disease. The term is used by practitioners of ▷homeopathy to describe the orthodox system of medicine.

● **Allosaurus** ▶ A large bipedal dinosaur of the Jurassic and Cretaceous periods (200–65 million years ago). Up to 11 m long, it had large strong hind limbs, a well-developed tail, small forelegs, and thick protective knobs of bone over the eyes. Although fairly slow, it hunted prey, possibly in groups, and was equipped with sharp claws, powerful jaws, and sharp pointed teeth. Order: ▷*Saurischia*.

● **allotropes** ▶ Two or more different physical forms of the same element or compound. Allotropes have different arrangements of atoms in their crystals or molecules and occasionally quite different chemical behaviour. Diamond and graphite, for example, are allotropes of carbon.

● **Alloway** ▶ 55 26N 4 38W A village in SW Scotland, in South Ayrshire on the River Doon. The birthplace of Robert Burns, it has many associations with his poems.

● **alloy** ▶ A blend of a metal with other metals or nonmetals, formed by mixing the molten substances and allowing the mixture to cool and solidify. An alloy is usually harder than any of its constituents. The first alloy was probably ▷bronze, which was used in Europe in about 2000 BC. ▷Steel and ▷brass are the most widely used alloys. Alloys of aluminium are also widely used, especially in the aircraft industry. Some metals, such as lead and aluminium, will not mix when they are melted together because their different densities make them separate into two layers. However, many metals do combine to form alloys, which may consist of intermetallic compounds, solid solutions, heterogenous mixtures, or any combination of these forms. In general, intermetallic compounds tend to be hard and brittle: iron carbide, which strengthens iron to form ▷steel is an example. Solid solutions, on the other hand, are usually soft and ductile: cartridge-case ▷brass is a typical example.

Most alloys melt over a range of temperatures unlike a pure metal, which has a specific melting point. **Eutectic alloys** are an exception to this rule, they consist of solid solutions having the lowest melting point of all the possible mixtures of the components. They are used in fuses and other safety mechanisms.

● **All Saints' Day** ▶ A Christian feast commemorating all saints, whether known or unknown. In the Eastern Churches it has always been observed on the first Sunday after Pentecost. In the West its date varied until fixed as 1 Nov by Gregory III. ▷*See also* Hallowe'en.

● **All Souls' Day** ▶ A Christian feast in the Western Church commemorating all Christians who have died (the "faithful departed"). It is observed on 2 Nov. Requiem masses, containing the *Dies Irae*, are celebrated.

● **allspice** ▶ (*or* pimento) A widely used aromatic spice, so named because it combines the flavours of several different spices. It is derived from the powdered dried unripe berries of an evergreen tree, *Pimenta dioca*, which is native to Central America and the West Indies and grows to a height of 9 m. Family: *Myrtaceae*.

● **Allston, Washington** ▶ (1779–1843) The earliest US Romantic painter. He studied at Harvard University before training at the Royal Academy (1801–03) in England. He finally settled in Boston in 1818. The drama of his early landscapes and biblical subjects was replaced by a quieter mood in such later works as *Moonlight Landscape* (Boston). He also wrote poetry and one novel.

● **Alma Ata** ▶ 43 19N 76 55E (name until 1921: Verny) The former capital of Kazakhstan. Situated in the foothills of the Trans-Alay Alatau (mountains), it is one of Asia's most beautiful cities. Industries include food and tobacco processing, and it has a thriving film industry. Its Russian Orthodox cathedral is the world's second highest wooden building. It has many educational institutions.

History: founded in 1854 as a fort, it soon became a trade centre. The completion of the Turkistan-Siberian railway in 1930, on which it is situated, resulted in rapid growth of the city. The capital transferred to Astana (formerly Akmola) in 1997. Population (1995 est): 1 150 500.

● **Almada** ▶ 38 40N 9 09W A town in S central Portugal, on the Tagus estuary opposite Lisbon. A statue of Christ, 110 m (360 ft) high, was erected here in 1959. Population (1991): 153 189.

● **Almadén** ▶ 38 47N 4 50W A town in W central Spain in New Castile. It possesses rich mercury mines, which have been worked since Roman times. Population (1991): 7723.

● **Almagest** ▶ *See* Ptolemy.

● **almanac** ▶ A calendar of the months and days of the year containing astronomical and other miscellaneous data. It usually includes information about eclipses, phases of the moon, positions of the planets, times of sunset and sunrise and of high and low tides, as well as religious and secular holidays. A well-known example is *Old Moore's Almanac*, founded in 1699 by Francis Moore (1675–1715) to promote sales of his medicines. Modern almanacs include official government publications listing national statistics.

● **al-Mansurah** ▷*See* Mansura, El.

● **Alma-Tadema, Sir Lawrence** ▶ (1836–1912) Painter of Dutch birth, whose successful career began in Antwerp and continued from about 1870 in England, where he took British nationality. A visit to Italy (1863) developed his interest in Egyptian and classical antiquity, which thereafter became almost his sole subject matter.

● **Almeida, Francisco de** ▶ (c. 1450–1510) Portuguese colonialist. The first viceroy of Portuguese India (1505–09), Almeida consolidated Portuguese rule there and expanded its power in the Indian Ocean. He organized further voyages that reached Madagascar and fought the Arabs on the African coast.

● **Almelo** ▶ 52 21N 6 40E A town in the E Netherlands, in Overijssel province on the Overijssel Canal. An industrial centre, it produces furniture and textiles. Population (1993): 63 998.

● **Almería** ▶ 36 50N 2 26W A port in S Spain, in Andalusia on the Gulf of Almería. It was a thriving town under the Moors (8th–15th centuries) and has a fine 16th-century cathedral. Its exports include grapes and oranges. Population (1996 est): 112 704.

● **Almodóvar, Pedro** ▶ (1949–   ) Spanish film director, noted for his provocative black comedies, often on sexual themes. His films include *Women on the Verge of a Nervous Breakdown* (1988), *The Flower of My Secret* (1995), and *All About My Mother* (1999).

● **Almohads** ▶ A fundamentalist reforming Muslim movement that ruled much of N Africa and Spain (1130–1269). Comprising the Masmudah Berber tribe, the Almohads recognized Ibn Tumart (d. 1130) as their leader in 1121 and he directed them against the ruling ▷Almoravids, taking the title of mahdi. On his death he was succeeded by Abd al-Mu'min (d. 1163), who completed the conquest of N Africa and Spain from the Almoravids. The Almohads regarded Muslims who did not follow them as unbelievers and Abd al-Mu'min became their ▷caliph. His descendants ruled the state until the fall of Marrakech to the Marinid Berber dynasty in 1269.

● **almond** ▶ A tree, *Prunus amygdalus*, native to SW Asia but widely grown in warm regions for its nuts. The edible nuts are produced by a variety called sweet almond; the nuts of the bitter almond yield aromatic almond oil, used as a flavouring. Almond trees grow to an average height of 7 m; they have attractive pink flowers and are grown for ornament in cooler regions. Family: *Rosaceae*. ▷*See also* Prunus.

● **Almoravids** ▶ A military Muslim missionary movement that ruled much of N Africa and Spain in the 11th and 12th centuries. The Almoravids were founded by Ibn Yasin (d. 1059) and after his death Yusuf ibn Tashufin (d. 1107) conquered NW Africa and invaded Spain. At the battle of Zallaqah (1086) he defeated the rising Christian power of León and Castile and Muslim Spain now came under Almoravid control. After Yusuf's death in Marrakech, the Almoravid capital that he had founded, his state was ruled by his descendants until 1147, when it fell to the ▷Almohads.

● **Alnico** ▶ An ▷alloy of aluminium, nickel, and cobalt. It is a ferromagnetic material and is used to make permanent magnets.

● **Aloe** ▶ A genus of succulent herbaceous plants (about 200 species), all native to Africa. A stem is usually absent, the toothed fleshy leaves forming a basal rosette, up to 40 cm in diameter. The flowers are red or yellow and some species are ornamental (e.g. *A. variegata*); the juice of some species, especially *A. vera*, is used as a purgative (bitter aloes). Family: *Liliaceae*.

● **alopecia** ▶ (*or* baldness) An absence of hair from areas of the skin on which it normally grows. The loss of hair with ageing in men is largely hereditary. In women, acute loss of hair, which usually starts to regrow at once, can occur after pregnancy or serious illness, especially if ▷cytotoxic drugs have been taken. Alopecia areata is an autoimmune disease causing bald patches, on which the hair may regrow. Alopecia totalis is also an autoimmune disease causing loss of all hair, which regrows in 70% of cases within several years. In scarring alopecias the hair lost is not replaced.

● **Aloysius, St** ▶ (Luigi Gonzaga; 1568–91) Italian patron saint of youth. A noble, he entered the Society of Jesus against his father's wishes in 1585 and studied philosophy and theology. Famous for his simple piety and charity, he died while tending plague victims in Rome. Feast day: 21 June.

● **alpaca** ▶ A shaggy-coated hoofed mammal, *Lama pacos*, traditionally domesticated and bred in the South American Andes. Its dark fine high-quality fleece reaches nearly to the ground from its shoulder height of 90 cm and is shorn every two years, each animal yielding about 3 kg. Alpacas thrive at high altitudes, keeping to damp grassy plateaus. Family: *Camelidae* (camels).

● **Alp Arslan** ▶ (c. 1029–1072) Sultan of Turkey (1063–72) of the Seljuq dynasty. He succeeded his uncle ▷Toghril Beg. His victory over the Byzantines at Manzikert in 1071 opened Asia Minor to Muslim penetration for the first time.

● **alphabets** ▶ Writing systems in which each symbol represents a speech sound (*see* phonetics). Many ▷pictographic writing systems developed as far as ideography and even ▷syllabaries, but the breakthrough to true alphabetic phonetic writing took place, it seems, only on the E shores of the Mediterranean around 2000 BC. From this ▷Semitic alphabet all the major alphabets in use today—Roman,

Phoenician	Early Hebrew	Early Aramaic	Early Greek	Classical Greek	Etruscan	Early Latin	Classical Latin	Russian-Cyrillic	Modern Roman
								А	A
								Б	B
								Г	C
								Д	D
								Е	E
								Ф	F
								Г	G
								И	H
								I	I
									J
								К	K
								Л	L
								М	M
								Н	N
								О	O
								П	P
									Q
								Р	R
								С	S
								Т	T
								У	U
									V
									W
								Х	X
								Ц	Y
								З	Z

alphabets ▶ The letters of the modern Roman alphabet have developed from the ancient Phoenician syllabary. This script in its Aramaic form was also the ultimate source of the Arabic alphabet and probably of the Brahmi alphabet, from which the many scripts of modern India are derived. The Cyrillic alphabet was derived directly from the Greek, whereas the Roman came through Etruscan and Latin.

Greek, ▷Cyrillic, Hebrew, Arabic, and ▷Devanagari—are ultimately derived.

It is hard now to appreciate the achievement of identifying speech sounds separately from meaning and of analysing syllables into vowels and consonants. It meant that the number of symbols required to record a language was reduced from many thousands to between 20 and 40. Moreover, it became possible to write down unfamiliar or foreign words without reference to their sense.

Correspondence between conventional ▷spelling and speech sounds is rarely exact. Speech sounds change continually over the centuries, while spelling forms tend to become conventionalized and static. In Greek, for example, where the alphabet has been used to represent the language for almost 3000 years, the letters ι, η, υ, ει, and οι, which originally represented different sounds, now all represent the sound /i:/; by contrast, γ, which used to represent a single sound, now represents four quite distinct sounds, depending on the letters adjoining it. On the other hand, Czech and Turkish, both of which have adopted or revised a modified version of the Roman alphabet within the last hundred years, display great regularity between sound and spelling. These two and many other languages that have taken over the Roman alphabet use accents and other diacritics to indicate sounds for which there is no standard Roman alphabet symbol. With the passage of time, however, the use of diacritics itself becomes conventionalized and unsystematic.

Attempts have been made to develop alphabets that record speech sounds regularly and systematically. The most important of these is the ▷International Phonetic Alphabet.

● **Alpha Centauri** ▶ A conspicuous nearby ▷multiple star in the constellation Centaurus. The two brightest components form a yellow visual ▷binary star that is seen as the third brightest star in the sky, magnitude –0.27. The much fainter third component, **Proxima Centauri**, is the nearest known star, lying 4.3 light years away.

● **alpha decay** ▶ A spontaneous radioactive disintegration in which a nucleus ejects an ▷alpha particle. This process reduces the mass number of the nucleus by four and its atomic number by two. An example is the decay of uranium-238 into thorium-234.

● **alpha-fetoprotein** ▶ (afp) ▷See prenatal diagnosis.

● **alpha particle** ▶ The nucleus of a helium-4 atom, consisting of two protons and two neutrons. It is extremely stable and is emitted by some radioactive nuclei in the process known as ▷alpha decay.

● **Alphege, St** ▶ (954–1012) Archbishop of Canterbury and martyr. He became Bishop of Winchester in 984 and Archbishop of Canterbury in 1006. He was captured by the Danes in 1011 and murdered because he refused to save himself at the expense of his tenants. Feast day: 19 April.

● **Alpher, Ralph Asher** ▶ (1921–) US physicist. His major work was in cosmology. With George ▷Gamow and Hans ▷Bethe he produced the so-called Alpher-Bethe-Gamow (αβγ) theory of the origin of the elements, which Gamow incorporated into the ▷big-bang theory. In 1948 Alpher predicted (with Robert C. Herman) that the big bang would have produced a microwave background radiation, first detected in 1965.

● **alphorn** ▶ A musical instrument used in Switzerland for calling cattle. Made of wood, it is commonly 2 m long or more. Its mouthpiece is similar to that of a cornet. Being valveless, it plays only harmonics.

● **Alpine orogeny** ▶ The period of mountain building that occurred mainly during the Tertiary period, beginning about 65 million years ago. The region most affected extends from S Europe and N Africa across S Asia to Indonesia, resulting in the formation of the Alps, Atlas Mountains, and Himalayas. It is the most recent ▷orogeny and is probably still continuing in some parts of the world.

● **Alps** ▶ The highest mountain range in Europe. It extends some 800 km (497 mi) in an arc roughly E-W through France, Switzerland, Italy, and Austria, and rises to 4807 m (15.771 ft) at Mont Blanc near the W end. Several major rivers rise here, including the Rhône, Rhine, Drava, and Po. The snowline varies between 2400 m and 3000

m (7874 ft and 9843 ft) and many of the lower slopes are used as pasture in summer, while in winter the Alps are a skiing area. ▷See also Maritime Alps.

● **al-Qaida** ▶ (Arabic: the base) The international terrorist organization created by Osama ▷Bin Laden that is presumed to have carried out the attacks on America on ▷September 11, 2001. The seeds of al-Qaida were sown during Bin Laden's guerrilla campaign against the Soviets in Afghanistan (1979–89), but the organization took definitive shape when he moved to Sudan in 1991 and began training operatives for a holy war against the USA. Bomb attacks on US servicemen in Yemen (1992), Somalia (1993), and Saudi Arabia (1995) followed and in 1998 al-Qaida blew up the US embassies in Kenya and Tanzania, killing over 200. From 1996 al-Qaida had its command centre in S Afghanistan, where it forged links with the ▷Taleban. Following September 11, al-Qaida's headquarters and training camps became the prime targets in the US-led ▷war on terrorism, which effectively smashed its nerve centre. However, al-Qaida cells are still thought to be active in many countries.

● **Alsace** ▶ (German name: Elsass) A planning region and former province in NE France, separated from Germany by the River Rhine. It is an agricultural area and has potassium deposits.

History: under Roman occupation from the 1st century AD, it became a Frankish duchy in the 5th century and was part of the Holy Roman Empire from the 10th to the 17th centuries. Its cities, effectively independent in the middle ages, were important centres of the Reformation in the 16th century. The French gained control of Alsace in 1648, after the Thirty Years' War, but it was lost to Germany in 1871, after the Franco-Prussian War, and linked with ▷Lorraine to form the German territory of **Alsace-Lorraine**. This existed until it reverted to France in 1919. Under German control again in World War II, it was restored to France in 1945. Area: 8310 sq km (3208 sq mi). Population (1999): 1 734 145.

● **Alsatian dog** ▷See German shepherd dog.

● **alsike** ▶ A perennial Eurasian ▷clover, *Trifolium hybridum*, also called Swedish or Alsatian clover, with typically three-lobed leaves and pink flowers. Capable of fixing nitrogen, it is often used to improve the nitrate level in soil.

● **Altaic languages** ▶ A family of languages comprising languages of the ▷Turkic, ▷Mongolian, and ▷Manchu-Tungus groups. Named after the Central Asian Altai Mountains, languages of this family are spoken in N China, Mongolia, Russia and neighbouring states, Afghanistan, Iran, and Turkey. The genetic relationship between the various Altaic languages is debatable, but certain common features are discernible, notably sound harmony. The connection of ▷Japanese and ▷Korean with this family is questionable.

● **Altai Mountains** ▶ A mountain system in Asia, extending from Siberia, Russia, into China and Mongolia. It rises to 4506 m (14 783 ft) at Belukha in Russia and has important lead, silver, and zinc reserves.

● **Altair** ▶ A conspicuous white star, apparent magnitude 0.77 and 16.5 light years distant, that is the brightest star in the constellation Aquila.

● **Altai Republic** ▶ A constituent republic of Russia. Formed in 1922 as the Oirot Autonomous Region, it formed the Gorno-Altai Autonomous Region (1948–91). It was renamed in 1992 having acquired republican status. Gold and mercury are mined and livestock breeding is important. Area: 92 600 sq km (35 740 sq mi). Population (1996 est): 202 000. Capital: Gorno-Altaisk.

● **Altamira** ▶ Upper ▷Palaeolithic cave site in N Spain, recognized in 1879. Doubts as to the authenticity of the 150 magnificent polychrome paintings of animals on the cave's ceiling were settled by Henri ▷Breuil in 1901. Bison, painted in red ochre with black manganese manes, tails, and hooves, are the chief species depicted. ▷See also Magdalenian.

● **Altdorf** ▶ 46 53N 8 38E The town in central Switzerland where William Tell engaged in his legendary exploits. Population (latest est): 8230.

● **Altdorfer, Albrecht** ▶ (c. 1480–1538) German artist, who was one of the first European painters to paint landscapes for their own sake. His masterpieces, few of which survive, show his love of forested mountains, depicted in minute detail, and include *The Battle of Issus* and *St George* (both Alte Pinakothek, Munich). He became city architect of Regensburg.

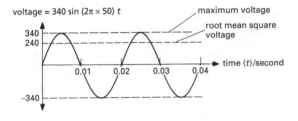

voltage = 340 sin $(2\pi \times 50)$ *t*

maximum voltage

root mean square voltage

340
240

−340

time (*t*)/second

0.01 0.02 0.03 0.04

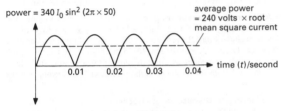

power = 340 I_0 sin^2 $(2\pi \times 50)$

average power = 240 volts × root mean square current

time (*t*)/second

0.01 0.02 0.03 0.04

alternating current ▶ The voltage and power waveforms in a 240-volt, 50-hertz domestic mains supply. The current ($I = I_0$ sin $(2\pi \times 50)t$) has a similar waveform to the voltage.

● **alternating current ▶** (ac) Electrical current that periodically reverses its direction. This form of current is produced when a coil of wire rotates in a magnetic field and, as this is the way in which current is produced in ▷power stations by ▷electric generators, it is the form of current most widely used. The electromotive force (emf), *E*, produced by a generator is equal to E^1sin ωt, where E^1 is the maximum emf, ω is the angular velocity of rotation, and *t* is the time. Thus the current has the form of a sine wave, with a frequency $\omega/2\pi$.

The chief advantage of ac is that the voltage can be stepped up with a transformer before transmission to minimize energy losses in the lines and then reduced to a safer level by another transformer for domestic use. In the UK the ac supply has a frequency of 50 hertz, is transmitted at several hundreds of kilovolts, and is used at 240 volts. In the USA the supply frequency is 60 hertz.

● **alternation of generations ▶** A phenomenon occurring in the ▷life cycles of many organisms, including plants and some animals (particularly ▷cnidarians), in which there is an alternation between two distinct forms (generations), which differ from each other in structure, reproduction, and also often in habit. In plants the generation reproducing sexually is the gametophyte and the asexual generation is the sporophyte. Either phase may be predominant in a particular species; for example, the gametophyte is dominant in mosses and the sporophyte in flowering plants. In cnidarians sedentary asexual polyps alternate with free-living sexual medusae.

● **alternative energy ▶** Power based on natural energy flows in the environment and **renewable sources** (i.e. those that do not use up finite mineral resources). Most countries at present rely heavily on fossil fuels (oil, coal, and natural gas) and ▷nuclear power for their energy needs. However, reserves of fossil fuels are declining and they also contribute to the ▷greenhouse effect by emitting carbon dioxide into the atmosphere on combustion. Estimates of reserves of recoverable uranium are also uncertain and there is opposition to the development of nuclear reactors, mainly on the grounds of safety and environmental hazard from radioactive waste disposal. Fusion reactors are still very much in the experimental stage. Although nuclear power is still regarded as an option in some countries, it is being run down in the UK. In the late 1990s in the UK over 2.3 million tonnes of oil equivalent was provided by renewable sources. Some 80% of this was ▷biomass energy, 17% ▷hydroelectric power, 2.5% ▷wind power,

and only 0.5% ▷solar power. However, in 2002 the UK government imposed a **renewables obligation** on all energy suppliers as a result of which they will have to take 3% of their energy from renewable sources. This will rise to 10% in 2010 and is likely to be 20% in 2020. This development is part of the UK's obligation to cut CO_2 emissions according to the ▷Kyoto agreement. Most of the investment being made to comply with these regulations is going into wind power and the extensive development of wind farms, together with intensified research into ▷wave-power machinery. ▷Geothermal energy and ▷tidal power are also being explored.

● **Alternative Investment Market ▶** (AIM) ▷*See* stock exchange; stocks and shares.

● **alternative medicine ▶** Systems of treatment of physical and mental illness used as alternatives to those of orthodox ▷medicine. Known also as fringe, natural, and unorthodox medicine, its recent growth is undoubtedly due to the fact that many diseases, such as allergies, arthritis, cancer, and depression, often fail to respond to conventional treatment. It includes such specialties as ▷osteopathy, ▷homeopathy, ▷acupuncture, ▷aromatherapy, and ▷hypnosis, which are recognized and practised by some qualified doctors, as well as many others, including ▷chiropractic, ▷naturopathy, ▷herbalism, dietary treatments, ▷reflexology, ▷Ayurvedic medicine, the laying on of hands, and self-healing (e.g. by yoga, biofeedback, etc.). ▷*See also* holistic medicine.

● **alternative technology ▶** Any means of applying scientific knowledge to industry or agriculture that avoids capital-intensive high technology, usually with the aim of restricting both costs and damage to the environment. In developed countries advocates of alternative technology often make use of organic farming techniques, recommend greater utilization of ▷alternative energy sources, and make determined (but sometimes implausible) attempts to conserve raw materials by ▷recycling and to conserve energy by insulation. In less developed countries alternative technology is seen as a third (intermediate) alternative to high technology on the one hand and traditional technology on the other. It aims to provide access to Western techniques at much lower cost than would be required for high-tech solutions. Very often it is based on cooperation between groups of indigenous farmers, enabling them to acquire equipment that they could not afford on their own.

● **alternator** ▷*See* electric generator.

● **Althing ▶** The parliament of Iceland, the oldest in the world, founded in about 930 AD. Since independence in 1944 it has been the country's sovereign legislature. It has 60 members in two houses of equal power.

● **Althorp House ▶** A country house in Northamptonshire (England), the ancestral home and burial place of ▷Diana, Princess of Wales: it has been the seat of the Spencer family since 1508. The original medieval house was given its present neoclassical form by Henry Holland in 1787. It contains important collections and works of art, including portraits by Reynolds and Gainsborough. The grave of Diana, Princess of Wales, is situated on Round Oval Island in Althorp Park. A museum dedicated to her life opened in 1998.

● **Althusser, Louis ▶** (1918–90) Algerian-born French philosopher. A Marxist, he sought to reinterpret Marxism in the context of ▷structuralism in such works as *For Marx* (1965), *Lenin and Philosophy* (1969), and *Essays in Self-Criticism* (1976). His work was regarded as highly influential in the 1970s, but after murdering his wife in 1980 he spent the rest of his life in a psychiatric hospital.

● **Altichiero ▶** (c. 1330–c. 1390) Italian painter. Influenced by ▷Giotto, Altichiero is credited with founding the Veronese school. His only surviving works in Verona are frescoes in S Anastasia but there are also cycles in the Basilica of S Antonio and the Oratorio di S Giorgio in Padua.

● **altimeter ▶** A device for measuring altitude in one of two ways. A **pressure altimeter** consists of an aneroid ▷barometer calibrated in metres (or feet) above sea level. A **radio altimeter** consists of a device that measures the time taken for a radio or radar signal to reach the ground and return.

● **altitude** ▶ The angular distance of an astronomical body above or below an observer's horizon. It reaches a maximum of 90° when the body is directly overhead. It is used with the angular distance **azimuth**, measured eastwards along the horizon from the direction of N, to specify the position of an astronomical body on the ▷celestial sphere.

● **Altman, Robert** ▶ (1922–   ) US film director, screenwriter, and producer, noted for his idiosyncratic black comedies and satires. His films include *M·A·S·H* (1970), *Nashville* (1975), *The Player* (1992), *Short Cuts* (1994), *Kansas City* (1996), and *The Gingerbread Man* (1998).

● **alto** ▶ A high adult male singing voice produced by falsetto. Range: that of the ▷countertenor and ▷contralto.

● **altocumulus cloud** ▶ (Ac) A medium type of ▷cloud appearing as globular masses in bands across the sky.

● **altostratus cloud** ▶ (As) A medium type of ▷cloud appearing as a greyish sheet, sometimes thin enough for the sun to be seen through it. It usually heralds rain.

● **Altrincham** ▶ 53 24N 2 21W A town in NW England, in Trafford unitary authority, Greater Manchester. Originally a market town, it is now a residential suburb of Manchester. Population (1991): 40 042.

● **altruism** ▷*See* egoism.

● **aluminium** ▶ (Al) A light silvery-white metal first isolated by Wöhler in 1827. It is the most abundant metal in the earth's crust and the main source is ▷bauxite, an impure hydrated oxide. The metal is extracted by electrolysis of the oxide dissolved in a flux of low melting point with the mineral cryolite. Its most important uses depend on its lightness (relative density 2.70), ductility, and good electrical conductivity. It is used in electrical power cables, kitchen utensils, and many industrial applications. Pure aluminium is soft, but its alloys with copper, magnesium, and other elements have considerable strength. This combined with their low densities makes such alloys important in aircraft construction. Compounds include alum ($K_2SO_4Al_2(SO_4)_3.24H_2O$) and the oxide alumina (Al_2O_3), which occurs naturally as corundum and ▷ruby and is used as an abrasive, a gem, and in ▷lasers. The hydroxide ($Al(OH)_3$) is used in glass manufacture and as an antacid in medicine. At no 13; at wt 26.9815; mp 660.4°C; bp 2520°C.

● **alums** ▶ Crystalline hydrated double sulphates of monovalent and trivalent metals. The typical example is potash alum (often called simply alum; $K_2SO_4.Al_2(SO_4)_3.24H_2O$), which is used as a mordant, size for paper, styptic, and astringent. In other alums the potassium and aluminium ions are replaced by other monovalent or trivalent ions respectively. For example, **chrome alum** ($K_2SO_4.Cr_2(SO_4)_3$) is a dark-purple substance used in dyes, printing, and tanning.

● **alunite** ▶ (*or* alumstone) A mineral consisting of potassium and aluminium sulphate and aluminium hydroxide, $K_2SO_4.Al_2(SO_4)_3.4Al(OH)_3$. A source of alum, it is usually associated with volcanic rocks altered by sulphurous gases.

● **Alvarado, Pedro de** ▶ (c. 1485–1541) Spanish conquistador, who accompanied Hernán Cortés in his conquest of Mexico, becoming governor of Tenochtitlán (Mexico City). He conquered parts of Guatemala (1523–24) and El Salvador (1524). In 1534 he embarked on an expedition to take Ecuador but was bought off by a rival.

● **Alvarez, Luis Walter** ▶ (1911–88) US physicist, who worked at the University of California. With F. ▷Bloch he made the first measurement of the neutron's magnetic moment and won the Nobel Prize (1968) for research on short-lived fundamental particles. During World War II, he worked on the development of the atom bomb.

● **Álvarez Quintero brothers** ▶ Spanish dramatists, Serafin (1871–1938) and Joaquín (1873–1944) Álvarez Quintero. In collaboration, they wrote nearly 200 popular plays, set mainly in their native Andalusia. *El Amor que pasa* (1904) and *Malvaloca* (1912) were more serious works.

● **Alvars** ▶ A group of wandering poets and mystics, fervently devoted to Vishnu, which flourished in S India in the 7th–10th centuries AD. Almost exclusively male, they worshipped ecstatically, with song and dance. Their 4000 hymns in the Tamil language, collected in the 10th century, sing the praises of Vishnu and his various incarnations.

● **alveolus** ▷*See* lungs.

● **Alyattes** ▶ (d. 560 BC) Fourth King of Lydia (c. 617–560), which he made a major power. Alyattes extended his kingdom as far as the River Halys (585) following a war against Media that was ended by the combatants' fear at the sight of the sun's eclipse. Alyattes, who was buried in a huge round tomb near Sardis, was succeeded by his son Croesus.

● **Alypius** ▶ (4th century AD) Greek writer, from Alexandria in Egypt. His *Introduction to Music* is the chief surviving guide to classical Greek music, preserving its notation and complex scale system.

● **Alyssum** ▶ A genus of low-growing herbaceous plants (about 150 species), mostly native to S Europe but widely grown in gardens. Alyssums have small flowers grouped in terminal clusters. Varieties of sweet alyssum (*A. maritimum*), 10–15 cm high, have white or pink flowers and are grown as annuals. Perennial alyssums include *A. saxatile*, which grows to 30 cm high and has yellow flowers. Family: *Cruciferae*.

● **Alzheimer's disease** ▶ A degenerative disease that affects nerve cells of the brain. It causes speech disturbances, loss of mental faculties, and other symptoms of senile dementia though it may occur in middle age. Its cause is uncertain but it appears to be associated with the presence of large amounts of a protein, β-amyloid, in the brain. Some forms of Alzheimer's are thought to be inherited. Named after the German neurologist Alois Alzheimer (1864–1915).

● **Amadeus, Lake** ▶ A salt lake in Australia, in SW Northern Territory. It normally consists of a salt flat but intermittently contains water. Area: 880 sq km (340 sq mi).

● **Amadeus (VIII) the Peaceful** ▶ (1383–1451) Count of Savoy (1391–1434). Amadeus became duke in 1416, when Savoy was made a duchy by Emperor Sigismund. Amadeus abdicated in 1434 and in 1439 was elected antipope as Felix V by the schismatic Council of ▷Basle. He resigned in 1449.

● **Amagasaki** ▶ 34 42N 135 23E A port in Japan, in S Honshu on Osaka Bay. An industrial centre, it has metal, chemical, and textile industries. Population (1995): 488 574.

● **Amalasuntha** ▶ (*or* Amalasuentha; 498–535 AD) The daughter of Theodoric, King of the Ostrogoths, and regent (526–34) for her son Athalaric (516–34). After Athalaric's death she shared the throne with her cousin and second husband, Theodahad (d. 536), who was party to her murder.

● **Amalekites** ▶ In the Old Testament, a nomadic tribe living in SW Palestine and the Sinai, who were descended from Esau. They attacked the Israelites on their journey out of Egypt and remained their enemies until finally suppressed during the reign of Hezekiah.

● **Amalfi** ▶ 40 37N 14 36E A seaport and resort in Italy in Campania on the Gulf of Salerno. A major port in the 10th century, its maritime code of law was recognized in the Mediterranean area until the latter half of the 18th century.

● **amalgam** ▶ An alloy of ▷mercury with various other metals, including silver, gold, and palladium. Amalgams of mercury with silver and tin are used in dentistry to fill tooth cavities, setting hard within a few minutes.

● **Amalia, Anna** ▶ (1739–1807) Duchess of Saxe-Weimar after her marriage (1756) to Ernst August, Duke of Saxe-Weimar; (ruled 1748–58). After her husband's death, she was regent (1758–75) for her son Carl August (1757–1828; ruled 1758–1828). She is remembered for her patronage of such writers as ▷Goethe and ▷Herder.

● **Amanita** ▶ A genus of widely distributed mushroom fungi (about 100 species). Several species are extremely poisonous, including the deadly destroying angels (*A. vena* and *A. virosa*), the ▷death cap, and the ▷fly agaric. Some species are harmless and sometimes eaten, for example panther cap (*A. pantherina*). Order: *Agaricales* (*see* agaric).

● **Amanollah Khan** ▶ (1892–1960) Emir (1919–26) and King (1926–29) of Afghanistan. Amanollah obtained Afghan independence from Britain in 1919. He introduced a policy of Westernization and declared Afghanistan a kingdom in 1926. In 1929 a revolt forced him into exile in Switzerland.

● **Amaranthus** ▶ A genus of herbaceous plants (50–60 species) native to tropical and subtropical regions but now widely distributed (*see* pigweed). The small petal-less flowers grow in long drooping spikes. Several species are grown for ornament, including *A. caudatus* (love-lies-bleeding), 60–100 cm tall with dark-red flowers, *A. tricolor* (Joseph's coat), with purple flowers and red, yellow, and green leaves. Family: *Amaranthaceae*.

● **Amaravati school** ▶ A style of Indian religious sculpture that originated in Amaravati in S India in the 2nd century BC and flourished until the 3rd century AD. A series of bas-reliefs of the life of Buddha have survived from Amaravati, showing the school's fusion of naturalism with elegance. The style spread through Ceylon to SE Asia.

● **Amarillo** ▶ 35 14N 101 50W A city in the USA, in N Texas. Expansion followed the arrival of the railway (1887) and the discovery of gas (1918) and oil (1921). Today Amarillo has meat-packing, metal-refining, clothing, and fibreglass industries. Population (1996 est): 169 588.

● **Amarna Tablets** ▶ ▷Cuneiform inscriptions found at Tell el-Amarna (Middle Egypt) in 1887. Most of the tablets were written about 1350 BC. They record administrative correspondence between the pharaoh and his vassal kings in Palestine and Syria.

● **Amaryllis** ▶ A perennial herbaceous plant, *Amaryllis belladonna*, also called belladonna lily, native to South Africa but widely cultivated for ornament. Growing from bulbs, it has strap-shaped leaves and a 45 cm long stem bearing a cluster of 5–12 funnel-shaped sweet-scented flowers, usually rose-pink and often veined. Family: *Amaryllidaceae*.

● **Amaterasu** ▶ In Japanese mythology, the sun goddess, supreme among the *kami* (spirits). She was the daughter of ▷Izanagi, born either from his eye or from a mirror held by him. She was symbolized by a mirror, which she gave to her grandson Ninigi, forerunner of the Japanese emperors, as part of the imperial regalia. It is still preserved at the Shinto shrine at Ise (S Honshu).

● **Amateur Athletic Association** ▶ The governing body for men's athletics in England and Wales, founded in Oxford (1880). It holds annual championships, which are given the status of unofficial British championships.

● **Amati** ▶ A family of violin makers in Cremona, Italy. **Andrea Amati** (c. 1520–c. 1578) developed the design that became the standard modern violin. His sons **Antonio Amati** (?1550–1638) and **Girolamo Amati** (1551–1635) worked as a team. Girolamo's son **Nicolò Amati** (1596–1684) was the family's greatest craftsman and taught Andrea ▷Guarneri and ▷Stradivari. They also made violas and cellos.

● **amatol** ▶ An explosive mixture of ammonium nitrate and ▷TNT often in the proportions 40:60, but other proportions are also in use. It was extensively used as a filling for bombs and shells in World War II.

● **Amazon, River** ▶ (Portuguese name: Rio Amazônas) The largest river system and the second longest river in the world, it is the chief river of South America. Rising as the Río Marañón in the Andes, in Peru, it flows generally W–E to enter the Atlantic Ocean in NE Brazil. Its drainage basin extends over much of Brazil, and parts of Venezuela, Colombia, Ecuador, Peru, and Bolivia. It is covered by a mantle of tropical rain forest (selva) and provides valuable forest products including rubber, quinine, and nuts. Navigable to oceangoing vessels as far as Iquitos, 3700 km (2300 mi) upstream, the river and its tributaries provide an essential communications system. Destruction of the rain forest in recent years has caused concern within ecological circles. Length: 6440 km (4000 mi). Drainage basin area: about 5 827 500 sq km (2 250 000 sq mi).

● **Amazon ant** ▶ A ▷slave-making ant of the genus *Polyergus* (especially *P. rufescens* or *P. lucidus*). Amazon ants, which have long sharp sickle-shaped mandibles, raid nests of *Formica* ants to steal eggs and larvae that hatch to become workers in their own colony. Amazon ants cannot feed or brood without slave workers.

● **Amazons** ▶ (Greek: breastless ones) A mythical nation of female warriors who were believed by the ancient Greeks to live in Pontus, near the Black Sea. Trained for war and hunting, the Amazons got their name from their habit of removing the right breast to facilitate the drawing of bows. They intervened in the ▷Trojan War against the Greeks, but Achilles killed their queen, Penthesilea. The Athenians said that at one time they invaded Attica but were defeated by ▷Theseus, who took their queen Hippolyte captive.

● **Ambartsumian, Viktor A(mazaspovich)** ▶ (1908–96) Armenian astrophysicist, who taught at the University of Leningrad before becoming director of the Byurakan Observatory. He wrote the first classic Russian textbook of theoretical astrophysics. His most notable work was the description of radio sources as explosions in the core of galaxies.

● **amber** ▶ A translucent or opaque yellow fossil resin exuded by coniferous trees; insects and leaves are often preserved in the mineral, having been trapped on the sticky surface prior to hardening. It is found predominantly in Tertiary deposits around the S Baltic coast. It is used for beads, ornaments, and amber varnish.

● **ambergris** ▶ A waxy substance found in the intestines of sperm whales. Mainly cholesterol, with fatty oils and steroids, it has a musky scent. It is used in making perfumes.

● **Ambler, Eric** ▶ (1909–98) British novelist. He began writing suspense novels in the 1930s, skilfully creating an atmosphere of fear and tension appropriate to the times. These novels, which include *The Dark Frontier* (1936), *The Mask of Dimitrios* (1939), and *Journey into Fear* (1940), were set mostly in W Europe; in later novels, such as *A Passage of Arms* (1959), he used more exotic settings. Other works are *The Nightcomers* (1956) and *In Case of Time* (1981).

● **Ambleside** ▶ 54 26N 2 58W A small town in the English Lake District, in Cumbria at the N end of Lake Windermere. It is a centre for tourism and outdoor pursuits. Population (1991): 2905.

● **ambo** ▶ A raised platform in early churches with a reading stand for the reading of the Bible during services. It was most popular in Italy, although even there it began to be replaced by the pulpit during the 14th century.

● **Amboise** ▶ 47 25N 1 00E A town in France, in the Indre-et-Loire department on the River Loire. Its fine gothic chateau was damaged during World War II but has since been restored. Population (latest est): 11 415.

● **amboyna** ▶ A tropical Asian tree, *Pterocarpus indicus*, that reaches a height of about 9 m and yields reddish beautifully grained wood used for furniture. Family: *Leguminosae*.

● **Ambrose, St** ▶ (c. 339–97 AD) Italian bishop of Milan and Doctor of the Church. Born at Trier, he was appointed a provincial governor in 370 with his headquarters at Milan. After becoming a priest, he was made Bishop of Milan in 374 and was famous as a preacher and for his breadth of scholarship. He championed orthodoxy and the rights of the church against the civil power. Feast day: 7 Dec.

● **ambrosia** ▶ The food of the gods in Greek mythology. Bestowing eternal life on those who ate it, ambrosia was (according to Homer and others) taken with the drink **nectar**; it was also described as a perfume.

● **ambrosia beetle** ▶ A wood-boring beetle, *Trypodendron lineatum*, that tunnels into the wood of dying and fallen trees. It carries its food supply—a type of fungus—with it and this produces black spores that colour infected wood distinctively. Family: *Scolytidae* (bark beetles).

● **Amenemhet III** ▶ King of Egypt (c. 1842–1797 BC) of the 12th dynasty. He regulated the lake of El ▷Faiyum to irrigate S Egypt, and built the Labyrinth (later described by the Greek historian Herodotus) nearby as an administrative centre.

● **Amenhotep III** ▶ King of Egypt (c. 1417–1379 BC) of the 18th dynasty. He controlled Palestine and Syria through vassal kings and maintained good relations with ▷Babylon. Many of the monumental buildings at ▷Karnak, ▷Luxor, and elsewhere in Egypt were erected by him. He was the father of ▷Akhenaton.

● **America** ▷*See* United States of America.

● **American eagle** ▷*See* bald eagle.

● **American Federation of Labor-Congress of Industrial Organizations** ▶ (AFL-CIO) A federation of US trade unions formed by the amalgamation in 1955 of the two major US unions—the AFL and CIO. It is currently composed of about 110 national and international unions giving a US membership of about 13.5 million and an affiliated membership of 55 000. Delegates from the member unions attend a biennial convention to decide policy. Committees contribute recommendations on subjects ranging from civil rights to safety and occupational health. Affiliated members must conform to requirements laid down by the AFL-CIO but remain autonomous within these limits.

● **American football** ▷*See* football.

● **American Import Duties Act** ▷*See* Townshend Acts.

American Indians ▶ A Peruvian woman and her child.

● **American Indians** ▶ A diverse group of peoples of North, Central, and South America and the Caribbean Islands. In many respects they resemble the Mongoloid peoples of Asia, which has led to their classification as a subtype of the ▷Mongoloid race. However, their physical diversity, and the possession of certain features not common among Mongoloids, suggests other origins. Their ancestors probably migrated to the Americas from Asia via Alaska between 10 000 and 20 000 years ago (or earlier). They have coarse dark and usually straight hair, a skin coloration ranging from copper-brown to a yellowish-brown, dark eyes, and sparse body hair. They speak a great variety of languages and their traditional cultures range from that of primitive hunters and gatherers to the elaborate and complex civilizations of the ▷Aztecs, ▷Mayas, and ▷Incas. ▷*See* North American Indians.

● **American literature** ▶ The literature in English of the British colonies of North America and, after 1776, of the United States. The earliest colonial literature consisted mainly of religious and political tracts. The first notable poets were Anne Bradstreet (1612–72) and Edward Taylor (1642–1729), both of Massachusetts. The intellectual dominance of New England was continued into the early 18th century by the theologian and metaphysician Jonathan Edwards (1703–

58). The period of the American Revolution was dominated by political writers, such as Benjamin Franklin and Thomas Paine. Influential writers of the early 19th century included Washington Irving, James Fenimore Cooper, and Edgar Allan Poe and American literature came to its full maturity in the works of the New England writers Nathaniel Hawthorne, Ralph Waldo Emerson, and Herman Melville, the poets Walt Whitman and Emily Dickinson, and the humorist Mark Twain. The influence of English literature on the early development of American literature was now reciprocated, notably in the works of the novelist Henry James and the poets T. S. Eliot and Ezra Pound, all of whom went to live in Europe. They were followed in the 1920s by Ernest Hemingway and F. Scott Fitzgerald. Other writers who achieved a transatlantic reputation include the dramatists Eugene O'Neill, Tennessee Williams, and Arthur Miller and the poets Robert Frost, Robert Lowell, and John Berryman. The vitality of 20th-century American literature is most evident in the novel, practitioners of which include William Faulkner, John Steinbeck, Vladimir Nabokov, Thomas Wolfe, Norman Mailer, Saul Bellow, Gore Vidal, Kurt Vonnegut, John Updike, and Thomas Pynchon.

● **American Revolution** ▶ (or American War of Independence; 1775–83) The conflict in which the 13 colonies of North America gained independence from Britain. American resentment at Britain's authoritarian rule focused in the mid-18th century on taxation. Protests against such legislation as the ▷Stamp Act (1765) and ▷Townshend Acts (1767) culminated in the ▷Boston Tea Party (1773), to which Britain responded with the punitive ▷Intolerable Acts (1774). The first ▷Continental Congress was summoned at Philadelphia and, after attempts by both sides at negotiation had failed, the first shots of the war were fired at ▷Lexington and Concord (April, 1775). In the autumn the Americans invaded Canada, taking Montreal and besieging Quebec until forced to withdraw to Ticonderoga in Spring, 1776. On 4 July the second Continental Congress issued the ▷Declaration of Independence. Gen Howe landed on Long Island in August and defeated the newly appointed American commander in chief, Washington, near White Plains. At the beginning of January, 1777, however, Washington dealt a counterblow at Princeton before settling in winter quarters. Britain's strategy in 1777 was based on a plan for Burgoyne to march S from Canada and join forces with Howe at the Hudson River. Burgoyne duly arrived at the Hudson (Aug) but Howe had left New York by sea, landed at Chesapeake Bay, and defeated Washington at the Brandywine, taking Philadelphia (Sept). Burgoyne, meanwhile, was forced to surrender his army at ▷Saratoga, a defeat that proved a turning point by bringing France into the war on the American side. In 1778 the British began an offensive in the S. Howe's successor, Clinton, took Charleston, South Carolina, and Cornwallis defeated Gates at Camden (1780). In early 1781 the British lost badly at Cowpens (17 Jan) but won, with heavy casualties, the battle of Guilford Court House (15 March). Cornwallis now moved into Virginia, establishing a base at Yorktown. There besieged by a Franco-American force under the Comte de Rochambeau (1725–1807) and Washington, on 19 October Cornwallis surrendered. Ultimate American victory was now assured although conflict continued, chiefly at sea. The British navy had been threatened throughout by American privateers and the activities of such commanders as John Paul ▷Jones, but the main threat at sea came from America's European allies—the French, Spanish (from 1779), and Dutch (from 1780), who gained control of the English Channel and threatened invasion. Rodney's success (1782) in the West Indies was not sufficient to reverse the effect of Yorktown but enabled Britain to regain control of the Atlantic. In 1783 Britain acknowledged American independence in the Treaty of ▷Paris.

The American Revolution was a major issue in British politics and the administration of Lord ▷North, dominated by George III, came under violent attack. However, the loss of the colonies can only in part be attributed to the incompetence of British direction; the leadership of Washington and French aid were also significant factors.

● **American Samoa** ▷*See* Samoa, American.

● **America's Cup** ▶ A cup offered in a yacht race at Cowes in 1851 and won by the US schooner *America*. Since 1857 it has been the prize in a periodic sailing competition. The New York Yacht Club retained it until 1983, when it was won by an Australian syndicate. The result of the 1987 race was contested in the courts, which in 1989 awarded the cup to the USA. It was won by the USA in 1992 and by New Zealand in 1995.

● **americium** ▶ (Am) The fourth transuranic element, synthesized (1944) by G. T. Seaborg and others by addition of neutrons to plutonium followed by β-decay. It forms the oxide (AmO_2) and such trihalides as $AmCl_3$; it is strongly radioactive. At no 95; at wt (243); mp 1176°C.

● **Amersfoort** ▶ 52 09N 5 23E A town in the central Netherlands, in Utrecht province. Its medieval buildings include a 14th-century watergate. Industries include chemicals, machinery, and carpets. Population (1996 est): 114 884.

● **amethyst** ▶ A gemstone comprising a purple variety of ▷quartz. Its colour is due to impurities, particularly iron oxide. The best crystals are found in Brazil and the Urals. It is used for jewellery. Birthstone for February.

● **Amhara** ▶ A descendant of the Semitic conquerors of the Cushitic peoples of Ethiopia. They occupy the S area of the central highlands of Ethiopia which, with the Tigré, they have dominated politically until the present day. Their society is hierarchical and largely feudal. The emperors were believed to be descended from ▷Solomon. They are a Christian people, who belong to the Coptic Church. Amharic is the language of the Amharas and the official language of Ethiopia. It is derived from a language related to Ethiopic or Ge'ez, the liturgical language of the Ethiopian Church, and is written in Ge'ez characters. It is similar to ▷Semitic languages in grammar but its vocabulary is largely ▷Cushitic.

● **Amherst, Jeffrey, Baron** ▶ (1717–97) British soldier in the ▷Seven Years' War in North America. In 1758 he took the fortress of Louisburg and became commander in chief in America. By 1760 he had conquered Montreal. He was governor general of British North America from 1760 to 1763.

● **Amici, Giovanni Battista** ▶ (1786–1863) Italian astronomer, microscopist, and optical instrument maker. He is best known as the inventor of the ▷achromatic lens. He discovered many details of orchid pollination and seed development; in astronomy, he studied double stars and Jupiter's moons, as well as designing improved mirrors for reflecting telescopes.

● **Amiel, Henri Frédéric** ▶ (1821–81) Swiss philosopher and writer. Amiel's principal work is his diary (kept 1847–81), *Fragments d'un journal intime* (1883). Profoundly introspective, it contains some fine descriptive writing and penetrating observations.

● **Amiens** ▶ 49 54N 2 18E A city in NE France, the capital of the Somme department situated on the River Somme. Known as Samarobriva in pre-Roman times, it was the ancient capital of Picardy. The Peace of Amiens (1802), which marked a respite in the Revolutionary and Napoleonic Wars, was signed here. Its fine gothic cathedral survived both World Wars. An important railway junction, Amiens' industries include textiles, tyres, and chemicals. Population (1990): 136 234.

● **Amies, Sir (Edwin) Hardy** ▶ (1909–) British fashion designer. Famous for his tailored clothes for both women and (from 1959) for men, he was appointed official dressmaker to Queen Elizabeth II. He was knighted in 1989.

● **Amin Dada, Idi** ▶ (c. 1925–) Ugandan politician; president (1971–79). He rose rapidly in the army, becoming commander in 1966. He overthrew Milton ▷Obote to become president and in 1972 ordered the expulsion of 80 000 non-Ugandan Asians. In 1975 he became president of the Organization of African Unity. A flamboyant and unpredictable personality, he and his government were notorious for their brutality; Amin was overthrown in a Tanzanian-backed coup after which he went into exile.

● **Amindivi Islands** ▷*See* Lakshadweep.

● **amines** ▶ A class of basic organic compounds derived from ammonia (NH_3), in which one (primary amines), two (secondary amines), or three (tertiary amines) of the hydrogen atoms are replaced by organic radicals or groups. ▷*See also* amino acids.

● **amino acids** ▶ A group of organic acids that are characterized by having at least one carboxyl group (–COOH) and at least one amino group (–NH_2). About 20 different amino acids comprise the basic constituents of ▷proteins, the arrangement and types of amino acids determining the structure and hence the function of the protein molecule. Certain essential amino acids cannot be manufactured by the body and must be supplied in the diet. In man these are: arginine, histidine, isoleucine, leucine, lysine, methionine, phenylalanine, threonine, tryptophan, and valine.

● **Amirante Islands** ▶ An archipelago of coral islands in the W Indian Ocean, belonging to the Seychelles. They are leased to private companies, usually for coconut plantations.

● **Amis, Sir Kingsley** ▶ (1922–95) British novelist and poet, one of the ▷Angry Young Men of the 1950s. Educated at Oxford, he taught at Swansea and Cambridge universities and in the USA. His first novel, *Lucky Jim* (1954), a comic satire on middle-class academic life, was a popular success. In later novels, such as *I Want It Now* (1968), *Ending Up* (1974), *Jake's Thing* (1978), *Stanley and the Women* (1984), *Difficulties With Girls* (1988), and *The Folks that Live on the Hill* (1990), his humour became progressively darker; in 1986 he won the Booker Prize for *The Old Devils*. He published poetry and contributed to the important verse anthology *New Lines* (1956). His memoirs appeared in 1991. His son **Martin Amis** (1949–) is also a writer. His novels include *The Rachel Papers* (1974), the highly successful *Money* (1984), *London Fields* (1989), *Time's Arrow* (1991), and *The Information* (1995). His other books include *The Moronic Inferno* (1986), a collection of essays on the US way of life; and *Heavy Water* (1998), a collection of short stories.

● **Amish** ▶ US and Canadian Protestant sect, a conservative faction of the ▷Mennonites from whom they broke away. Jakob Ammann, a Mennonite bishop in Switzerland, made the break in the 1690s, and by 1727 his followers had begun to settle in Pennsylvania. The Amish dress uniformly and are self-sufficient, depending on farming.

● **Amman** ▶ 31 57N 35 56E The capital of Jordan. Amman was the capital of the biblical Ammonites; there are Greek and Roman remains. Under the British mandate in Palestine, the town grew from a village, becoming (1946) the capital of independent Jordan. The city has had large influxes of refugees following the Arab-Israeli Wars (1948, 1967, and 1973); in 1970 tension resulting from the refugee presence led to fighting on the streets of Amman between Jordanian forces and Palestinians. The university was founded in 1962. Amman is an important communications centre, with some manufacturing. Population (1994 est): 963 490.

● **Ammanati, Bartolommeo** ▶ (1511–92) Florentine mannerist architect and sculptor. Beginning as an assistant of ▷Sansovino in Venice, Ammanati later worked with ▷Vasari in Rome. In Florence he was responsible for the Ponte Sta Trinità and the garden façade of the Palazzo Pitti; as a sculptor he is best known for the Neptune fountain in the Piazza della Signoria.

● **ammeter** ▶ An instrument for measuring electric current. The two most common types are the moving-coil and the moving-iron ammeters. The moving-coil ammeter is more sensitive but will only measure alternating current. The moving-iron ammeter will measure both alternating and direct current but is less sensitive and its scale is nonlinear. Some instruments are electronic and have a digital display.

● **ammonia** ▶ (NH_3) A colourless toxic gas used for the manufacture of fertilizers, nitric acid, explosives, and synthetic fibres. When dissolved in water, ammonia produces an alkaline solution of ammonium hydroxide (NH_4OH), an unstable compound that cannot be isolated from solution.

● **ammonite** ▶ A ▷cephalopod mollusc belonging to the subclass *Ammonoidea* (over 600 genera), abundant during the late Palaeozoic and Mesozoic eras, becoming extinct 100 million years ago. Their fossilized remains have either straight or coiled shells, up to 200 cm in diameter, containing chambers that provided buoyancy for the swimming animal. □fossil.

● **Ammonites** ► An ancient Semitic tribe who were descended from Ben-ammi, the son of Lot, and lived E of Jordan. They worshipped the god Moloch and often fought the Israelites.

● **amnesia** ► Loss of memory resulting from such causes as head injuries, drugs, hysteria, senility, or psychological illness. The memory loss may be for events before the injury or disease (retrograde amnesia) or for events after it (anterograde amnesia). In some cases specific areas of the brain show pathological changes. Treatment is related to the cause.

● **Amnesty International** ► An organization, founded by Peter Benenson in the UK in 1961, aiming to defend freedom of speech, opinion, and religion in all parts of the world. It campaigns for the release of "prisoners of conscience," against torture, and for human rights and aids refugees. It has some 1 100 000 members in 150 countries and is funded by voluntary contributions. It won the Nobel Peace Prize in 1977.

● **amniocentesis** ► The removal for examination of a small quantity of the fluid (amniotic fluid) that surrounds an unborn baby in the mother's womb. The specimen may be taken by needle through the abdominal wall or, later in pregnancy, the opening of the womb. Tests on the amniotic fluid may reveal the presence of certain diseases or congenital disorders in the baby (e.g. Down's syndrome or spina bifida). If serious abnormality is detected, abortion can be considered. Amniocentesis is routinely offered when there is a family history of congenital disease and to pregnant women over 35 years of age. ▷*See also* prenatal diagnosis.

● **Amoeba** ► A genus of free-living microscopic organisms (⌐protozoa). They occur widely in soil, fresh water, and salt water and their flexible cells assume various shapes. The common amoeba (*A. proteus*) may be up to 0.5 mm long. Amoebas move by extending their cytoplasm into broad lobes (pseudopodia), which are also used to engulf food particles (e.g. bacteria and other protozoans) and liquids. They reproduce by binary ▷fission and under adverse conditions form cysts with a thick protective wall surrounding the cell. Some related forms are parasitic, including *Entamoeba histolytica*, which causes amoebic dysentery in man. Phylum: *Rhizopoda*.

● **Amon** ► The supreme Egyptian deity. Originally a local god of Thebes, he acquired major status in the ascendancy of the 18th (Theban) dynasty in about 1570 BC. He became associated with the rival god ▷Ra and as Amon-Ra became the national god. Great temples were built to him at Luxor and Karnak (c. 1400 BC). Except during the brief reign of ▷Akhenaton, Amon-Ra remained supreme god until 663 BC.

● **Amorites** ► Semitic nomads of Palestine and Syria, who invaded the centres of civilization of Mesopotamia during the late 3rd millennium and 2nd millennium BC. They occupied ▷Babylonia, assimilated its culture and established numerous small kingdoms. Many Babylonian kings, including ▷Hammurabi, were of Amorite stock. ▷Mari and ▷Aleppo were important centres under Amorite control.

● **amortization** ► **1.** The discharging of a debt (e.g. a mortgage) through (usually equal) periodic payments of principal and interest. **2.** The depreciation of an asset through wear or obsolescence. The value of a fixed asset purchased by a company is not charged in full to its profit and loss account in the year in which it is purchased. Instead it is amortized over its useful life in the accounts, i.e. only a certain portion of its cost is charged to the profit and loss account each year.

● **Amos** ► (early 8th century BC) An Old Testament prophet of Judah. **The Book of Amos** contains his prophecies delivered in Israel. He denounces the luxury and injustice of the privileged nation and predicts God's judgment by means of an Assyrian invasion and natural calamities.

● **amount of substance** ► A quantity proportional to the number of particles, such as atoms or ions, in a substance. The constant of proportionality is the ▷Avogadro number. Amount of substance is measured in ▷moles.

● **Amoy** ▷*See* Xiamen.

● **ampere** ► (A) The ▷SI unit of electric current equal to the current that when passed through two parallel infinitely long conductors placed 1 metre apart in a vacuum produces a force between them of 2×10^{-7} newton per metre. This 1948 definition replaced all former definitions. Named after A. M. ▷Ampère.

● **Ampère, André Marie** ► (1775–1836) French physicist, who was a professor at Bourg and later in Paris. He introduced the distinctions between electrostatics and electric currents and between current and voltage, demonstrated that current-carrying wires exert a force on each other, and gave an explanation of magnetism in terms of electric currents. The unit of electric current is named after him.

● **Ampère's law** ► The strength of the magnetic field at any point produced by a current (I) flowing through a conductor of length l is proportional to Il/d^2 where d is the distance between the point and the conductor. Named after A. M. ▷Ampère.

● **amphetamine** ► A stimulant drug that produces a feeling of alertness and wellbeing, increases muscular activity, and reduces fatigue and appetite. Because of the risk of addiction, amphetamine is now rarely prescribed (in the form of dexamphetamine sulphate; trade name Dexedrine) and is a controlled drug (*see* drugs). It is occasionally used to treat attention deficit disorder in children. ▷*See also* drug dependence.

● **amphibian** ► An animal belonging to the class *Amphibia*, which contains about 200 species of frogs, toads, newts, salamanders, and caecilians. Adult amphibians breathe through lungs but require damp surroundings to minimize loss of body fluids through their thin moist skin. Generally amphibians lay their eggs in ponds or rivers. The eggs hatch into aquatic tadpole larvae that breathe using gills and develop into adults by complete ▷metamorphosis.

● **amphiboles** ► A group of rock-forming minerals, mostly complex hydrous ferromagnesian silicates. The anthophyllite-cummingtonite subgroup contains anthophyllite, gedrite, cummingtonite, and grunerite; the hornblende subgroup contains tremolite, actinolite, hornblende, edenite, hastingsite, and kaersutite; the alkali amphibole subgroup contains glaucophane, nebeckite, richterite, and katophorite. Amphiboles are common in igneous and metamorphic rocks and often occur in fibrous or acicular forms, including some forms of ▷asbestos.

● **amphioxus** ▷*See* lancelet.

● **amphisbaena** ► A wormlike lizard, also called worm lizard, belonging to the family *Amphisbaenidae* (120 species) occurring in tropical and subtropical America and Africa and the Mediterranean region. Up to 60 cm long, amphisbaenas are specialized for burrowing having reduced eyes, a small head with thick skull bones, and, except for one genus (*Bipes*), no legs. They feed on insects and larvae.

● **amphitheatre** ► An elliptical or circular building with tiers of seats surrounding an arena, designed by the Romans as a setting for gladiatorial shows, mock sea battles, etc. Small wooden amphitheatres were built throughout the Roman world. The earliest stone amphitheatre is that at Pompeii (c. 70 BC); others include the ▷Colosseum in Rome, that in Verona, and remains in Arles, Nîmes, Capua, and in Sicily and N Africa.

● **Amphitrite** ► The Greek goddess of the sea. Poseidon chose her to be his wife when he saw her dancing with her sister Nereids. She rejected him and fled to the island of Naxos, but he sent a dolphin to reclaim her. She bore him three sons, Triton, Rhodos, and Benthesicyma.

● **Amphitryon** ► In Greek mythology, a grandson of Perseus who was betrothed to Alcmene, daughter of the King of Mycenae. While he was at war, Zeus assumed his appearance and seduced Alcmene, who conceived ▷Heracles.

● **amphora** ► An ancient Greek two-handled vase used as a container for liquids and fruit, and sometimes as an urn for holding ashes of the dead or for prize awards. The most important are the Black Figure vases (600–480 BC) of black-painted red earthenware, depicting mythological scenes. Other undecorated types, sometimes ta-

amphora ▶ A Greek form of the 6th century BC.

pering to a pointed base, were in general use for transporting oil and wine until Roman times.

● **amphoteric compounds ▶ 1.** Compounds that behave as both ▷acids and bases. For example, with strong acids aluminium hydroxide acts as a base, $Al(OH)_3$, forming aluminium salts. With strong bases it behaves as an acid, H_3AlO_3, forming salts containing the ion AlO_3^{3-}. The formation of amphoteric hydroxides is a characteristic of ▷metalloids. **2.** Compounds that contain both basic and acidic functional groups. For example, the amino acid glycine, H_2NCH_2COOH, has both the amine group ($-NH_2$, basic) and the carboxylate group ($-COOH$, acidic). In acidic solutions it behaves as a base to form the $^+H_3NCH_2COOH$ ion; in basic solutions it acts as an acid to form the $H_2NCH_2COO^-$ ion. In neutral solutions, the ion $^+H_3NCH_2COO^-$ can exist (see zwitterion).

● **amplifier ▶** A device for increasing the magnitude of some quantity by using power from an external source, especially an electronic device for intensifying a signal in an alternating-current circuit, with an external steady voltage. Amplifiers are designed to multiply the input (current, voltage, or power) by a specific factor, known as the gain and often consist of several stages, the output from one stage becoming the input to the next stage. This method is used in the specialized type of amplifier used in sound-reproduction systems.

● **amplitude modulation** ▷See modulation.

● **Amr ibn al-As ▶** (d. 663 AD) Arab soldier, who led the Muslim conquest of Egypt. Following the conquest of Syria he led the invasion of Egypt; Alexandria fell in 642. Having helped ▷Mu'awiyah I secure the caliphate (661), he governed Egypt until his death.

● **Amritsar ▶** 31 35N 74 56E A city in NW India, in Punjab. Founded in 1577 by the fourth guru of the Sikhs, Ram Das, it has become the centre of the Sikh faith. It was the scene of a massacre (1919), in which hundreds of Indian nationalists were killed when fired upon by troops under British control. In 1984 about 1000 people died when the Sikh shrine, the Golden Temple, was fortified by Sikh extremists and stormed by the Indian army. The assassination of Mrs ▷Gandhi later in the year was a reprisal for this event. A commercial, cultural, and communications centre, it manufactures textiles and silk. Population (1991): 709 456.

● **Amsterdam ▶** 52 21N 4 54E The official capital of the Netherlands, in North Holland province on the Rivers Amstel and IJ. The government seat is at The Hague. Linked to the North Sea by canal (1876), it is a major seaport. It is also an important financial and industrial centre, possessing a renowned diamond cutting and polishing trade. Industries include shipbuilding, dairy produce, tobacco, and brewing. The city is mostly built on piles and linked with a radial system of canals and approximately 1000 bridges. Notable buildings include the 13th-century Oude Kerk (Old Church), the 15th-century Nieuwe Kerk (New Church), and a royal palace (1665). It possesses two universities, the Rijksmuseum, containing a superb collection of Dutch and Flemish paintings, and the Stedelijk Museum with its leading modern-art collection.

History: chartered in 1300, it joined the Hanseatic League in 1369. During the 17th century it prospered as a seaport; it gained significantly through Antwerp's loss of trade following the closure of the River Scheldt under the Treaty of Westphalia (1648). It became the capital in 1808. Population (1996 est): 718 119.

● **Amu Darya, River ▶** A river in central Asia. Rising in the Pamirs, it flows mainly NW through the Hindu Kush, Turkmenistan, and Uzbekistan to join the Aral Sea through a large delta. It forms part of the N border of Afghanistan and is important for irrigation. It is navigable for over 1450 km (800 mi). Length: 2400 km (1500 mi).

● **Amundsen, Roald ▶** (1872–1928) Norwegian explorer, the first person to reach the South Pole. In 1897 he became first mate on the *Belgica*, which was engaged in Antarctic exploration. After sailing the ▷Northwest Passage in the *Gjöa* (1903–06) he abandoned his plan to reach the North Pole on hearing of ▷Peary's success (1909). He himself beat ▷Scott to the South Pole, which he reached on 14 December, 1911. In 1926 he flew a dirigible over the North Pole with Umberto ▷Nobile. Amundsen died while searching for Nobile following the latter's dirigible crash in the Arctic Ocean.

● **Amundsen Sea ▶** A small section of the S Pacific Ocean, bordering on Ellsworth Land in Antarctica.

● **Amur, River ▶** (Chinese name: Heilong Jiang *or* Hei-Lung Chiang) A river in NE Asia. Rising in N Mongolia, it flows generally SE and NE through Mongolia, Russia, and China, to the Sea of Okhotsk. Forming the border between Russia and Manchuria, it was the scene of much Sino-Soviet friction. Length: 4350 km (2700 mi).

● **amyl alcohol ▶** ($C_5H_{11}OH$) A colourless oily liquid ▷alcohol that has eight ▷isomers: pentan-1-ol, pentan-2-ol, etc. It is obtained from ▷fusel oil and is used as a solvent.

● **amylase ▶** An enzyme that breaks down starch and glycogen into maltose and glucose. In animals it is present in saliva (as ptyalin) and in pancreatic juice.

● **Amyot, Jacques ▶** (1513–93) French bishop and scholar. He was in turn tutor to ▷Henry II's sons, grand chaplain of France, and Bishop of Auxerre. His writings are mainly translations of classical works, the most famous being his version of Plutarch's *Lives*, *Les Vies des hommes illustres Grecs et Romains* (1559), which greatly influenced Renaissance humanism in France and England.

Amritsar ▶ The Golden Temple, centre of the Sikh religion; it is built on an island on a small lake called the "Pool of Immortality."

● **Anabaptists** ▶ (from Greek: rebaptizers) Any of various radical religious groups originating in several continental countries during the ▷Reformation. They were called Anabaptists because they rejected infant baptism in favour of baptizing adults when they professed their faith. Persecuted by Roman Catholics and Protestants, they were accused of fanaticism, heresy, and immorality. They believed in pacifism, common ownership of goods, millenarianism, and held radical political views. Prominent leaders were the German Thomas Münzer (c. 1490–1525), killed after the Peasants' Revolt, and ▷John of Leiden. Their modern descendants, such as the ▷Mennonites, number more than 500 000.

● **anabolic steroids** ▷*See* androgens.

● **anabolism** ▷*See* metabolism.

● **anaconda** ▶ A nonvenomous South American ▷constrictor snake, *Eunectes murinus*. Up to 10 m long, it is typically dark green with oval black spots and lives in swamps and rivers, feeding on fish and small caymans and also hunting deer, peccaries, and birds along the water's edge.

● **Anacreon** ▶ (6th century BC) Greek lyric poet. He fled from his native island of Teos before the Persian invasion, and lived at Samos and then Athens, under the patronage of Hipparchus. His work, only fragments of which survive, consisted chiefly of love lyrics and drinking songs, written in a formal and restrained style.

● **anaemia** ▶ A reduction in the number of red cells or the quantity of red pigment (*see* haemoglobin) in the blood. It may be due to loss of blood, for example after an accident or operation or from chronic bleeding of a peptic ulcer, or lack of iron, which is necessary for the production of haemoglobin. **Haemolytic anaemias** are caused by increased destruction of the red blood cells, as may occur in certain blood diseases (e.g. ▷sickle-cell disease and ▷thalassaemia) and malaria or because of the presence of toxic chemicals. Anaemia can also result from the defective production of red cells, such as occurs in **pernicious anaemia** (when it is due to deficiency of ▷vitamin B$_{12}$).

The main symptoms of anaemia are extreme tiredness and fatiguability, breathlessness, pallor, palpitations, and poor resistance to infection. The treatment depends on the cause.

● **anaerobe** ▷*See* aerobe.

● **anaesthesia** ▶ A state of insensitivity to pain. Anaesthesia occurs in certain diseases of the nervous system, but the term usually refers to the state induced artificially for surgical operations. It may be produced by anaesthetic drugs or other means, including ▷hypnosis and ▷acupuncture. Alcohol and opium derivatives have been used as anaesthetics for centuries, but it was not until the 1840s that the first anaesthetic gases—ether, nitrous oxide, and chloroform—were used to induce **general anaesthesia** (total unconsciousness). This procedure now involves premedication (including administration of sedatives) to prepare the patient for surgery, followed by induction of anaesthesia by injecting a short-acting barbiturate (usually sodium thiopentone). Anaesthesia is maintained by inhalation of an anaesthetic gas (e.g. halothane). **Local anaesthesia** is usually used for dental surgery and also for other operations when the medical state of the patient makes general anaesthesia unadvisable. Bupivacaine and lignocaine are widely used local anaesthetics. **Spinal anaesthesia** (epidural or subarachnoid) produces loss of sensation in a particular part of the body by injecting a local anaesthetic into the space round the spinal cord. It may be used, for example, during a difficult childbirth.

● **anagnoresis** ▶ (Greek: recognition) A literary term referring to the moment of recognition of a previously unsuspected truth. The concept was defined in Aristotle's *Poetics*. It is considered an essential part of the plot of tragedy, in which the protagonist's recognition of his tragic flaw occurs at the climax and leads to his downfall. The best-known example occurs in Sophocles' *Oedipus Rex* when Oedipus discovers that he has unknowingly killed his father and married his mother.

● **Anaheim** ▶ 33 50N 117 56W A city in the USA, in S California near Los Angeles. It is a major tourist centre, containing the famous Disneyland opened in 1955. Population (1996 est): 288 945.

● **analgesics** ▶ A class of drugs that relieve pain. **Narcotic analgesics**, such as ▷morphine, are powerful pain killers that act directly on the brain. Some anaesthetics also have analgesic properties. ▷Aspirin and paracetamol are examples of **antipyretic analgesics**, which also reduce fever. These drugs are not addictive but are less potent than the narcotics. ▷*See also* drug dependence; narcotics.

● **analog computer** ▷*See* computer.

● **analytic geometry** ▶ The study of geometrical relations by algebraic methods. Geometrical figures are placed in a ▷coordinate system, each point in the figure being represented by its coordinates, which satisfy an algebraic equation. Also known as coordinate geometry or Cartesian geometry, after its inventor René ▷Descartes.

● **analytic philosophy** ▶ The type of philosophy dominant in Anglo-American universities in the 20th century, as opposed to the European traditions of existentialism and phenomenology. Analytic philosophy, which was developed in the early years of the century by ▷Frege, ▷Moore, ▷Russell, and ▷Wittgenstein, does not seek to create theories that add to our knowledge but to elucidate the knowledge we already possess, especially by logical and linguistic analysis. ▷*See* logical positivism; linguistic philosophy.

● **anamorphosis** ▶ A perspective technique used in painting and drawing to distort an image or object seen from a normal viewpoint. The image's true form is only recreated when viewed from an angle or through a special device, such as a peephole. A famous example is the elongated skull in Hans Holbein's *Ambassadors* (1533; National Gallery, London).

● **Ananda** ▶ (5th century BC) The first cousin, favourite disciple, and personal attendant of the Buddha. At his insistence a Buddhist order was founded to admit women.

● **anapaest** ▷*See* metre (poetry).

● **anaphylaxis** ▶ A form of ▷allergy that follows the interaction of the foreign substance (allergen) with antibody that is bound to the surface of certain cells (mast cells). This leads to the release of bradykinin, ▷histamine, and other chemicals, which cause the symptoms. Symptoms are either local (such as asthma) or general (shock and collapse). The latter usually follows injection of the allergen (such as penicillin) and is a medical emergency; it is treated with injections of corticosteroids and adrenaline.

● **anarchism** ▶ A political theory advocating abolition of the state and all governmental authority. Most anarchists believe that voluntary cooperation between individuals and groups is not only a fairer and more moral way of organizing society but is also more effective and orderly. Anarchism aims at maximizing personal freedom and holds that societies in which freedom is limited by coercion and authority are inherently unstable. ▷Proudhon thought that anarchism could be achieved by peaceful change, but ▷Bakunin believed that violent means were necessary. As an influential political force, anarchism was defeated in Russia by communism but persisted in Europe, especially in Spain until the end of the Civil War (1939).

● **Anastasia** ▶ (1901–?1918) The youngest daughter of □Nicholas II of Russia. Although she was believed to have been executed after the Russian Revolution, a Mrs Anna Anderson (d. 1984) claimed from 1920 that she was Anastasia. In 1961 her claim was officially rejected.

● **Anastasius I** ▶ (c. 430–518 AD) Byzantine emperor (491–518). Anastasius instituted thorough financial and administrative reforms and built a defensive wall to protect Constantinople. His adherence to the heretical ▷Monophysite doctrine was unpopular.

● **Anatolia** ▷*See* Asia Minor.

● **Anatolian languages** ▶ An extinct subgroup of the ▷Indo-European language family, which included Palaic, Luwian, Lydian, and Lycian. Originally spoken in Asia Minor, some date back to 2000 BC. The classification is sometimes used in a geographical sense to include all the languages of ancient Asia Minor, some of non-Indo-European origin. There is some confusion about the relation of the Anatolian languages to Hittite and a precise classification of the relations between these and Indo-European has not been achieved. ▷*See also* Indo-Hittite languages.

● **anatomy** ► The study of the structure of living organisms. Early studies of human anatomy were made by the Greek physician Galen, in the 2nd century AD, but it was not until the 16th century that the prejudice against dissecting human cadavers was overcome and anatomists—notably ▷Vesalius—made valuable contributions to the science. In the 17th century William ▷Harvey discovered the circulation of blood and the development of the microscope enabled advances in the detailed structure of the body to be made by such microscopists as ▷Malpighi, ▷Leeuwenhoek, and ▷Swammerdam. In the 20th century anatomy received a valuable tool with the development of the electron microscope, which greatly extended the investigation of microscopic structure. Today anatomy explores structure within the context of function (*see* physiology). Specialized branches of anatomy include embryology (the study of development), ▷histology (tissues), and ▷cytology (cells).

● **Anaxagoras** ► (c. 500–428 BC) Greek philosopher, born at Clazomenae (Asia Minor). In about 480 he moved to Athens, but because of his influence on ▷Pericles, he was eventually (450) banished on a trumped-up charge of impiety. He diverged from some other early Greek philosophers by stating that the physical universe was made up of an infinite number of substances and that matter was infinitely divisible. He was also the first to explain solar eclipses.

● **Anaximander** ► (c. 610–c. 546 BC) Greek philosopher, born in Miletus (Asia Minor). He was one of the earliest thinkers to develop a systematic philosophical view of the physical universe. He held that it came from something unlimited, not just one particular kind of matter, and maintained that the earth lay unsupported at the centre of the universe. He also had an evolutionary view of the origin of life, holding that it arose in the sea, and that man evolved from some more primitive species.

● **Anaximenes** ► (died c. 528 BC) Greek philosopher, who lived in Miletus (Asia Minor). He believed that the universe fundamentally consisted of air or vapour; different degrees of condensation corresponded to different degrees of density in matter. He held that air possessed life and that its motion accounted for changes in physical objects.

● **ANC** ▷*See* African National Congress.

● **ancestor worship** ► In many primitive societies, the propitiation of the spirits of dead forebears, usually with the object of persuading them to exert their powers on behalf of their descendants in hunting, warfare, etc. Ancestor cults can also be socially important in reinforcing the authority of living elders, who, as guardians of the ancestral shrines, are the spirits' mouthpieces. Festivals for the dead involving visits to the tombs, food offerings, and sacrifices were features of ancient Greek and Roman religion. An ancestor cult formed an important part of traditional Chinese religion and also survives in the Buddhist family altar (*butsudan*) in Japanese households.

● **Anchieta, José de** ► (1534–97) Portuguese poet and scholar. He became a Jesuit in 1551, and in 1553 joined a mission in Brazil. He helped protect the Indians from slavery and was a founder of the city of São Paulo. As well as his chiefly religious poetry and historical works he wrote a grammar of the Indian language, Tupí, and descriptions of the Indian culture.

● **Anchises** ► In Greek mythology, a Trojan nobleman, father of ▷Aeneas by ▷Aphrodite. He was blinded for boasting of his relationship with the goddess. Carried from burning ▷Troy on Aeneas' back, he died in Sicily.

● **anchor** ► Any device used for mooring a vessel to the bottom of a body of water. In ancient times a heavy stone was used, attached to the vessel by a rope. Today various patent anchors are in use. They are designed for different kinds of bottom—sandy, rocky, muddy, etc.— and usually dig into the bottom with their bladelike flukes. Depending on the size of the vessel, the anchor rode, or attachment to the vessel, may be entirely of heavy chain, as in the case of larger boats and ships, or of a short length of chain to which a rope, usually of nylon, is attached.

● **Anchorage** ► 61 10N 150 00E A city and major port in the USA, in S Alaska at the head of Cook Inlet. Founded in 1914 as the terminus of the Alaska Railroad, its main industries are defence projects and the development of natural resources, especially coal and gold. Population (1994 est): 253 649.

● **anchovy** ► A small herring-like fish belonging to the tropical and warm-temperate family *Engraulidae* (100 species). 10–25 cm long, anchovies have a large mouth extending behind the eye, a small lower jaw, and a pointed snout. They live in large shoals, chiefly in coastal waters, and are widely fished for food, bait, and animal feeds. □oceans.

● **Anchusa** ▷*See* alkanet.

● **ancien régime** ► The social and political system of France prior to the ▷French Revolution.

● **ancient lights** ► In English law, the right of an owner of a building to have uninterrupted light through a window. The passage of light through a window is protected against obstruction if it has been enjoyed without interruption for at least 20 years.

● **Ancona** ► 43 37N 13 31E A seaport in central Italy, the capital of Marche on the Adriatic Sea. It dates from 1500 BC, when it was founded by the Dorians. Its industries are connected with shipbuilding, engineering, and sugar refining. Population (1994 est): 100 597.

● **Andalusia** ► (Spanish name: Andalucía) The southernmost region of Spain, bordering on the Atlantic Ocean and Mediterranean Sea. It occupies chiefly the river basin of the Guadalquivir and is one of Spain's most fertile regions producing citrus fruit, olives, and wine. Under Roman control after the 2nd century BC, the region was named Andalusia (after its 5th-century Vandal settlers) by the Muslims, who invaded the region in the early 8th century; much evidence of the Muslim occupation remains. In the 15th century Castile finally recovered Andalusia from the Muslims. After the ▷Moriscos (Christians of Moorish descent) were expelled in 1609 the region's prosperity diminished. It is now popular with tourists, who are attracted by the great Moorish buildings found especially in Córdoba, Seville, and Granada. It became an autonomous region in 1981. Population (1994 est): 7 053 043.

● **Andalusian horse** ► A breed of large strong horse developed in Spain in the 15th century. Andalusian horses are usually grey (but sometimes bay or black), with a long silky mane and tail and a high stepping movement. Docile and attractive, they are often used in parades and bullfighting. Height: 1.60–1.70 m (15¾–16¾ hands).

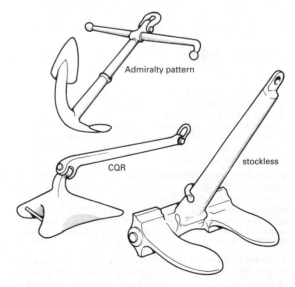

Admiralty pattern

CQR

stockless

anchor ► Three common forms of anchor.

● **Andaman and Nicobar Islands** ► A Union Territory of India, comprising two island groups in the E Bay of Bengal. The Andaman forests support plywood and match industries. Coconuts, rubber, and coffee are also important. The Nicobar Islands 120 km (75 mi) S of the Andaman Islands, produce coconuts, arecanuts, and fish.

History: the Andaman Islands were an Indian penal colony until 1945. Both groups were occupied by Japan (1942–45) and transferred to India (1947). Area: 8293 sq km (3215 sq mi). Population (1994 est): 322 000. Capital: Port Blair.

● **Andamanese** ▶ The indigenous inhabitants of the Andaman and Nicobar Islands in the Bay of Bengal. They are of negrito racial type. Their traditional culture, surviving only in southern areas among the Jarawa and Onge tribes, was based upon gathering shellfish, fishing, and hunting, using single outrigger canoes, nets, lines, and bows and arrows. Tools and weapons were often made from large shells. There was no method known to them of making fire. Social organization was simple. Tribes were divided into hunting bands, several of which might acknowledge a common chief. Trading between coastal and inland bands was extensive. Ritual initiation was important and various taboos were a prominent feature of their ritual life. Their language, Andamanese, is almost extinct and has no known relations.

● **Andersen, Hans Christian** ▶ (1805–75) Danish author, famous for his fairy tales. The son of a shoemaker, he attempted to become an actor in Copenhagen. A benefactor enabled him to attend the university there in 1828; he subsequently travelled widely in Europe and wrote novels, plays, and travel books. His international reputation, however, was earned by the 168 fairy tales that he wrote between 1835 and 1872. These include such classics as "The Snow Queen," "The Little Mermaid," and "The Ugly Duckling."

● **Anderson, Carl David** ▶ (1905–91) US physicist, who worked at the California Institute of Technology. He shared the 1936 Nobel Prize for showing (1932) that cloud-chamber tracks were made by ▷positrons, whose existence had been predicted by Dirac. In 1935 Anderson discovered the first ▷meson, thinking it was the particle predicted by ▷Yukawa. In fact Anderson's meson is now known as the muon, whereas Yukawa's particle is known as the pion (discovered by ▷Powell).

● **Anderson, Elizabeth Garrett** ▶ (1836–1917) British physician, who pioneered the admission of women into the medical profession. Refused admission to medical schools, she studied privately and in 1865 was granted a licence to practise. She helped establish a hospital for women in London, now named after her.

● **Anderson, John, 1st Viscount Waverley** ▶ (1882–1958) British civil servant and politician. In World War II he was home secretary and minister of home security (1939–40), when the Anderson air raid shelter was named after him; he was chancellor of the exchequer (1943–45).

● **Anderson, Lindsay** ▶ (1923–94) British film director. His films include *This Sporting Life* (1963), *If* (1968), *O Lucky Man* (1972), and *The Whales of August* (1987).

● **Anderson, Marian** ▶ (1897–1993) US singer. Born into a poor Black family in Philadelphia, she raised money to study in New York by singing in her Baptist Church. In 1935 she became the first Black singer to perform in opera at the Metropolitan; she also appeared at the White House. A civil-rights activist, she was a delegate to the UN General Assembly in 1958. Her autobiography, *My Lord, What a Morning*, was published in 1956.

● **Anderson, Philip Warren** ▶ (1923–   ) US physicist. After obtaining his PhD at Harvard, Anderson joined Bell Telephone Laboratories, where he remained until retiring in 1984. A solid-state physicist, he conceived a model (known as the Anderson model) to describe what happens when an impurity atom is present in a metal. He worked extensively on superconductivity and superfluidity, receiving a share of the 1977 Nobel Prize for his work.

● **Anderson, Sherwood** ▶ (1876–1941) US author. Born in a small town in Ohio, he held a variety of jobs before abandoning job and family in 1906 to become a writer. He was encouraged by Theodore ▷Dreiser, Carl ▷Sandburg, and other Chicago writers and by Gertrude ▷Stein in Paris. He finally settled in Virginia as a newspaper owner; there he in turn encouraged ▷Faulkner and ▷Hemingway. *Winesburg, Ohio* (1919), his best-known book, is a series of tales about the stunted lives of a small-town community. His novels included *Poor White* (1920) and *Dark Laughter* (1925).

● **Andes** ▶ (Spanish name: Cordillera de los Andes) A mountain system in W South America. It extends N for about 7250 km (4500 mi) from Cape Horn to the Isthmus of Panama, reaching 6960 m (22 835 ft) at Mount Aconcagua and separating a narrow coastal belt from the rest of the continent. Comprising a series of parallel mountain ranges, it is chiefly of volcanic origin and contains several active volcanoes, including ▷Cotopaxi; earthquakes are common phenomena. It is rich in minerals; the metals extracted include gold, silver, platinum, mercury, copper, and lead.

● **andesite** ▶ A group of volcanic rocks comprising the fine-grained equivalent of ▷diorite. They consist mainly of plagioclase-feldspar and one or more ferromagnesian minerals, and many andesites are porphyritic. They are found associated with basalts and rhyolites in island arcs and orogenic regions. The Andesite Line is the geographic boundary between continental andesitic rocks and oceanic basalts, traced through the Pacific.

● **Andhra Pradesh** ▶ A state in E central India, on the Bay of Bengal. The coastal plain rises westwards over the Eastern ▷Ghats into the ▷Deccan plateau. Rice, sugar cane, cotton, tobacco, and pulses are farmed. Large forests provide teak, bamboo, and fruit trees. Manganese, iron ore, mica, and coal are mined. Industries include textiles, machinery, and shipbuilding (developed with cheap hydroelectricity).

History: the Andhra people and culture have flourished since the 1st century BC. From 1700 local rulers gradually lost control to France and Britain. A centre of 20th-century Indian nationalism, the Telegu-speaking area of ▷Madras became Andhra Pradesh state in 1953. Further boundary adjustments were made in 1956 and 1960. The region suffered an earthquake in 1993, which killed 10 000 people. Area: 275 068 sq km (106 204 sq mi). Population (1994 est): 71 800 000. Capital: Hyderabad. Chief seaport: Vishakhapatnam.

● **Andizhan** ▶ 40 40N 72 12E A city in Uzbekistan on the River Andizhan-Say. Situated in the fertile ▷Fergana Valley, Andizhan has always been the region's main trade centre. Its industries include engineering. Population (1996 est): 319 900.

● **Andong** ▶ (or An-tung) 40 06N 124 25E A port in NE China, in Liaoning province on the Yalu estuary and on the border with North Korea. It was opened to foreign trade in 1907. Its industries, developed under the Japanese occupation (1931–45), include paper, silk, cotton, and chemicals. Population (1995): 188 452.

● **Andorra, Principality of** ▶ (Catalan name: Valls d'Andorra; French name: Les Vallées d'Andorre) A small principality in the E Pyrenees, between France and Spain. It is mountainous with peaks reaching heights of almost 3000 m (about 9500 ft).

Economy: tourism is an important source of revenue supplementing the primarily agrarian economy (wheat, potatoes, livestock raising, tobacco, and forestry). Banking and offshore financial services are also important.

History: records of Andorra's existence as a state date from 1278, when it was placed under the joint overlordship of the Bishop of Urgel in Spain and the Comte de Foix in France. The latter's rights passed in the 16th century to the French Crown and are now held by the president. Until the mid-1990s executive and legislative powers lay with the co-princes' permanent delegates in Andorra while a Council General of the Valleys held responsiblity for administration. However, in 1993 Andorra voted to adopt a democratic constitution, reducing the powers of the co-princes. The first sovereign government of Andorra took office in 1994, under President Marc Forné Molné. Andorra is a tax haven and immigration has been substantial in recent years.

Principality of Andorra

Heads of state	the President of the French Republic and the Bishop of Urgel, represented by their permanent delegates
Official language	Catalan; French and Spanish are also spoken
Official currency	euro of 100 cents
Area	465 sq km (179 sq mi)
Population (2000 est)	66 700
Capital	Andorra la Vella

● **Andrássy, Gyula, Count** ▶ (1823–90) Hungarian revolutionary and statesman. In the ▷Revolution of 1848 Andrássy supported Lajos ▷Kossuth. With Ferenc ▷Deák he negotiated the Dual Monarchy of ▷Austria-Hungary (1867) and was Hungary's first constitutional prime minister (1867–71). From 1871 to 1879 he was the Austro-Hungarian foreign minister and strove to halt Russian expansion into the Balkans.

● **André, John** ▶ (1751–80) British soldier. While adjutant to the commander of British troops in the American Revolution, he negotiated with the treacherous Benedict ▷Arnold, the commander of West Point, for its surrender. He was captured by Washington's army and tried and executed as a spy.

● **Andrea del Sarto** ▶ (Andrea d'Agnolo; 1486–1530) A leading Florentine Renaissance painter, whose work, through its influence on his pupils ▷Pontormo, Giovanni Battista Rosso (1494–1540), and ▷Vasari, became a starting point for Tuscan ▷mannerism. He combined Florentine draughtsmanship with a Venetian feeling for colour and atmosphere and his compositions resemble relief sculpture. Andrea spent most of his life in Florence, producing frescoes in the cloister of the Scalzi and the SS Annunziata. Among his most important paintings are several representing the Holy Family, some portraits, and the *Madonna of the Harpies* (1517; Uffizi).

● **Andreotti, Giulio** ▶ (1919–   ) Italian politician; prime minister of Italy (1972–73; 1976–79; 1989–92). A Christian Democrat, he was minister of foreign affairs (1983–89). In 1995 he went on trial for Mafia involvement and in 1996 for conspiracy to murder a journalist, being eventually acquitted of both charges in 1999.

● **Andrew, St** ▶ In the New Testament, one of the 12 Apostles. Originally a fisherman in partnership with his brother Simon Peter, he was a disciple of John the Baptist before following Jesus. Apparently crucified, he is the patron saint of Scotland and Russia. Feast day: 30 Nov.

● **Andrewes, Lancelot** ▶ (1555–1626) Anglican bishop and writer. A fellow of Pembroke College, Cambridge, he became Bishop of Winchester in 1619 and acted as adviser to James I. He was renowned as a preacher but is best remembered for his *Private Prayers* (published posthumously).

● **Andrews, Dame Julie** ▶ (Julia Elizabeth Wells; 1935–   ) British-born US actress. A child actress at 12, she later appeared in the stage musicals *The Boy Friend* (1954) and *My Fair Lady* (1956) on Broadway. However, she is best remembered for her starring roles in the films *Mary Poppins* (1964) and *The Sound of Music* (1965). She was created DBE in 2000.

● **Andrić, Ivo** ▶ (1892–1975) Bosnian writer. He wrote his first major book, *Ex Ponto* (1918), while imprisoned by the Austrians during World War I. He later served abroad in the Yugoslav diplomatic service, but his native Bosnia provided the settings for his novels, notably *Bosnian Story* (1945) and *The Bridge on the Drina* (1945). He was awarded the Nobel Prize in 1961.

● **Androcles** ▶ The hero of a story by Aulus Gellius (?125–?165 AD). Androcles was an escaped slave who removed a thorn from the paw of a lion. The lion later recognized the recaptured slave in the arena and spared him; both were freed. The story was satirized in *Androcles and the Lion* by G. B. ▷Shaw.

● **androgens** ▶ A group of steroid hormones that influence the development and function of the male reproductive system and determine male secondary sexual characteristics, such as the growth of body hair and deepening of the voice at puberty. The major androgens are ▷testosterone and androsterone, produced by the testes in higher animals and man and also in small amounts by the adrenal glands and ovaries in mammals. Natural and synthetic androgens are used in medicine to treat conditions caused by androgen deficiency. Some synthetic androgens (anabolic steroids) promote the growth of muscle and bone and are administered to debilitated patients. Prolonged use can cause liver damage, and their use by athletes is banned by most athletic authorities.

● **Andromache** ▶ In Greek mythology, the wife of Hector, the chief Trojan warrior. She appears in Homer's *Iliad*. After the fall of Troy she became the slave of Neoptolemus, son of Achilles, and bore him three sons. After his death she married Helenus, brother of Hector.

● **Andromeda** ▶ (astronomy) A constellation in the N sky near Cassiopeia. The brightest star is the 2nd-magnitude Alpheratz. The constellation contains the spiral **Andromeda galaxy**, the largest of the nearby galaxies in the ▷Local Group.

● **Andromeda** ▶ (mythology) The daughter of Cepheus, king of Ethiopia, and Cassiopeia, who boasted that Andromeda was more beautiful than the ▷nereids. In retaliation the nereids persuaded Poseidon to send a sea monster to devastate the kingdom: the gods would be appeased only by Andromeda's sacrifice to the monster. Chained to a rock to await her fate, she was rescued by ▷Perseus, who married her.

● **Andropov** ▷*See* Rybinsk.

● **Andropov, Yuri Vladimirovich** ▶ (1914–84) Soviet statesman; general secretary of the Soviet Communist Party (1982–84) and president of the Soviet Union (1983–84). He headed the KGB (1967–82).

● **androsterone** ▷*See* androgens.

● **anechoic chamber** ▶ A room used in acoustical experiments that is designed to absorb nearly all the sounds produced in it. Its walls, floor, and ceiling are constructed from insulating and absorbent materials.

● **Aneirin** ▶ (6th century AD) Welsh poet. His poem "Y Gododdin," preserved in the manuscript *Book of Aneirin* (c. 1250), celebrates the heroes of an expedition sent from Edinburgh to recapture Catterick from the Saxons. Out of 300 warriors only one survived.

● **anemometer** ▶ An instrument for measuring the velocity of a fluid, often the velocity of the wind. In one type, the fluid drives a small windmill or set of cups, the rate of rotation of which is a measure of the fluid velocity. Other types of anemometer are the ▷pitot tube and the ▷Venturi tube.

● **Anemone** ▶ A genus of herbaceous perennial plants (about 150 species) mostly native to N temperate regions. The leaves are segmented and the flowers lack true petals (the sepals function as petals). The Eurasian wood anemone (*A. nemorosa*), 10–15 cm high, has white flowers. Many species are cultivated as ornamentals for their brightly coloured flowers, including the poppy and Japanese anemones (*A. coronaria* and *A. japonica*). Family: *Ranunculaceae*.

● **aneroid barometer** ▷*See* barometer.

● **aneurysm** ▶ A swelling in the wall of an artery, due to a weakness in the wall. This may be caused by disease or may be the result of a congenital deficiency in the wall. Aneurysms may rupture, causing fatal haemorrhage. Treatment consists of surgical removal of the aneurysm and its replacement with a graft.

● **Angara, River** ▶ A river in Russia, in SE Siberia. It flows mainly NNW from Lake Baikal to the River Yenisei. Length: 1840 km (1150 mi).

● **Angarsk** ▶ 52 31N 103 55E A city in SE central Russia on the Trans-Siberian Railway. An oil-refining centre, it is connected by pipeline to the Volga-Urals field. Population (1995 est): 267 000.

● **Angel Falls** ▶ (Spanish name: Salto Angel) The highest cataract in the world, in SE Venezuela on a tributary of the Río Caroní. Height: 979 m (3211 ft).

● **angelfish** ▶ **1.** A fish of the tropical marine family *Chaetodontidae*, having a narrow oval laterally compressed body, a small mouth, and often an elongated snout. Up to 70 cm long, angelfish are solitary, living around coral reefs and feeding on small invertebrates. They are usually patterned in a variety of brilliant colours. **2.** A South American ▷cichlid fish of the genus *Pterophyllum*, especially *P. scalare*, which is valued as an aquarium fish.

● **Angelica** ▶ A genus of tall perennial herbs (about 70 species) distributed in the N hemisphere and New Zealand. They grow up to 2 m tall and have umbrella-like clusters of white or greenish flowers. The Eurasian species *A. archangelica* yields an oil used in liqueur and perfume making, and its stems are candied to make the confectionary angelica. *A. sylvestris* (wild angelica) is native to Eurasia. Family: *Umbelliferae*.

● **Angelico, Fra ▶** (Guido di Pietro; c. 1400–55) Italian painter of the early ▷Renaissance, born in Vicchio (Tuscany). In the early 1420s he became a Dominican monk in Fiesole. His order transferred in 1436 to St Mark's Convent, Florence, where he painted several frescoes, including a famous *Annunciation*. From 1445 to about 1450 he painted fresco cycles in the Vatican but only the *Scenes from the Lives of SS Stephen and Lawrence* has survived. His other major work is *The Coronation of the Virgin* (Uffizi). He was an exclusively religious painter, whose spiritual serenity is reflected both in his art and his "angelic" nature (hence his popular name).

Fra Angelico ▶ Detail from *The Coronation of the Virgin* (1430–36; Louvre).

● **Angell, Sir Norman ▶** (1874–1967) British author, economist, and Labour politician. He received the Nobel Peace Prize in 1933 for his opposition to totalitarianism and his influential antiwar book *The Great Illusion* (1910).

● **Angelou, Maya ▶** (Marguerite Johnson; 1928–   ) US Black novelist, poet, and dramatist. She established her reputation with the autobiographical novel *I Know Why the Caged Bird Sings* (1970); various sequels similarly portray life in the southern USA.

● **angels ▶** (Greek: messengers) In Christianity, Judaism, and Islam, supernatural beings who were created at the same time as the material universe and whose primary role was to praise and serve God. Many, however, followed Lucifer in his rebellion (*see* Devil), becoming devils in ▷hell. In both Old and New Testaments angels appear as emissaries from God to man. ▷Dionysius the Areopagite systematized angelology into nine orders in the celestial hierarchy, the rank of angel being the lowest. Later medieval theologians debated such questions as the nature of angels' bodies; angels are usually depicted as winged human figures. ▷*See also* archangels.

● **Angers ▶** 47 29N 0 32W A city in W France, the capital of the Maine-et-Loire department on the River Maine. The former capital of Anjou, it has many fine buildings, including a 13th-century moated chateau, a cathedral (12th–13th centuries), and the 15th-century Logis Barrault (Barrault House). Its varied manufactures include wine, textiles, and agricultural machinery. Population (1990): 146 163.

● **Angevins ▶** Two dynasties descended from the rulers of the medieval French duchy of ▷Anjou. Founded by Fulk I (d. 938), his succes-

sors as Counts of Anjou, notably Fulk III Nerra (972–1040) and ▷Geoffrey Martel, expanded the county in France during the 10th and 11th centuries. The marriage in 1128 of Geoffrey Plantagenet, Count of Anjou, to ▷Matilda, daughter of Henry I of England, gave rise to the accession to the English throne in 1154 of their son as Henry II, the first ▷Plantagenet King of England. The so-called Angevin empire, which stretched from the River Tweed to the Pyrenees, was broken up by ▷Philip II Augustus of France in the early 13th century and in 1246 Louis VIII's brother Charles became Count of Anjou. Charles conquered Naples and Sicily, where as ▷Charles I he founded a second Angevin dynasty. The Angevin claim to Naples and Sicily passed to the French Crown in 1486.

● **angina pectoris ▶** Chest pain caused by a reduction in the supply of blood to the heart due to narrowing of the coronary blood vessels supplying the heart. It is usually associated with ▷atherosclerosis, is brought on by exercise, and can herald a heart attack. Treatment includes rest and administration of glyceryl trinitrate and drugs to reduce blood pressure.

● **angiography** ▷*See* arteriography.

● **angioplasty** ▷*See* coronary heart disease.

● **angiosperm ▶** Any flowering plant. Angiosperms comprise a vast phylum (or division) of diverse leafy green plants (*Anthophyta* or *Angiospermophyta*; about 240 000 species) in which the seeds are formed within an ovary, which becomes the ▷fruit. They are thought to have evolved from the cone-bearing ▷gymnosperms at the end of the Jurassic period (about 135 million years ago), rapidly radiating and becoming the dominant plants in the mid-Cretaceous (about 100 million years ago). They include many trees and shrubs but most are herbaceous. The 300 families are grouped into two classes: the ▷monocotyledons and ▷dicotyledons.

● **Angkor ▶** A ruined city in Cambodia, founded about 880 AD as capital of the ▷Khmer empire. It was rediscovered, covered by jungle, in 1860. Angkor was the centre of a sophisticated irrigation system, with huge reservoirs (barays). Its temples, decorated with relief sculptures, were intended to emulate mountains in dressed stone; chief of these are the Angkor Wat (early 12th century) and Bayon (c. 1200).

● **anglerfish ▶** A marine fish, also called goosefish, belonging to the order *Lophiiformes*. Anglerfish are generally small and have flat bodies, large heads, and wide mouths. The first ray of the spiny dorsal fin is modified to form a "fishing line" ending with a fleshy flap of skin—the "bait," which is often luminous in deepsea species. Fish, invertebrates, and even seabirds are lured and snapped up by the huge mouth. In some deepsea species, the male is parasitic on the female, becoming permanently anchored by the mouth and dependent upon her for nourishment. □oceans.

● **Angles ▶** A Germanic tribe originating from the Angeln district of Schleswig, which together with the ▷Saxons and ▷Jutes invaded and conquered most of England during the 5th century AD. They settled in ▷Northumbria, ▷Mercia, and ▷East Anglia. England is named after them.

● **Anglesey ▶** (Welsh name: Ynys Môn; Latin name: Mona) A low-lying island off the NW coast of Wales, linked to the mainland by road and rail bridges over the Menai Strait. Part of Gwynedd from 1974 until 1996, it has now been reinstated as a separate county. The chief agricultural activity is sheep rearing. Tourism is important. The terminus of the Irish ferry from Dublin is at Holyhead on an adjoining island in the NW. Recent industrial developments include the building of an aluminium smelter. Area: 705 sq km (272 sq mi). Population (1994 est): 68 400. Administrative centre: Llangefni.

● **Anglesey, Henry William Paget, 1st Marquess of ▶** (1768–1854) British field marshal. He served with distinction in command of the cavalry at Waterloo, where he lost a leg. He later became lord lieutenant of Ireland, where he became an advocate of ▷Catholic emancipation.

● **Anglican Communion ▶** The fellowship of episcopal Churches in communion with the see of Canterbury. Until 1786, when the consecration of bishops for foreign sees was legalized, it consisted of the Churches of England, Ireland, and Wales and the Episcopal Church of

Scotland. In 1787 the Protestant Episcopal Church of the USA was founded and thereafter Anglican dioceses were formed in all parts of the British Empire and elsewhere. The member churches are fully autonomous, comprising about 350 dioceses; they meet for consultation at the ▷Lambeth Conferences. ▷See also Church of England.

● **angling** ▶ Fishing with a baited hook, line, and usually a rod. There are four main categories. Game fishing, for salmon and trout, takes place in fast streams and rivers. Coarse fishing for members of the carp family, such as roach and bream, is a sport in which the fish are returned to the water. Sea fishing for mackerel, flatfish, etc., is popular in shallow waters round the UK. Big-game fishing for shark, tuna, and swordfish requires specially equipped motorboats. Competitions were common in Britain by the 18th century. The National Angling Championship was instituted in 1906 and in 1957 the first world championship was staged.

● **Anglo-Afghan Wars** ▶ Three wars between the British in India and Afghan rulers. In the first war (1838–42) the British, concerned about Russian influence in Afghanistan, sent a small army to Kabul to instal a pro-British king. The British forces were destroyed. In the second war (1878–80) the British were more successful, capturing Kabul and, by the Treaty of Gandamak, establishing the right to maintain a Resident in Kabul. However, after the Resident was murdered, the British withdrew. In the third war (1919) the Emir of Afghanistan, ▷Amanollah Khan, attacked the British in India; although defeated, he managed to establish Afghani independence by the Treaty of Rawalpindi (1919).

● **Anglo-Burmese Wars** ▶ The wars that resulted in the British annexation of Burma (now Myanmar). In the first Anglo-Burmese War (1824–26) Burmese forces provoked the British-Indian forces into war by crossing into Bengal to attack Arakanese refugees and Britain captured, and kept, Rangoon. The aggressive action of a British naval officer provoked the second war (1852), which resulted in the annexation of Lower Burma. In the third war (1885), which occurred when the French, encouraged by the Burmese king, threatened British interests in Burma, Britain gained Upper Burma.

● **Anglo-Catholicism** ▶ A movement within the Anglican Communion that stresses the continuity of the Church of England with Catholic Christianity. The main impetus of modern Anglo-Catholicism was provided by the ▷Oxford Movement, which sought to revive the High Church ideals of earlier, especially 17th-century, Anglican churchmen. Anglo-Catholics emphasize the historic episcopate, the sacramental life of the Church, and traditional Catholic practices with regard to the celebration of the Eucharist, vestments, etc. At present Anglo-Catholicism is a major influence in most Churches of the Anglican Communion. Some Anglo-Catholics left the Church of England following the decision (1992) to ordain women.

● **Anglo-Dutch Wars** ▷See Dutch Wars.

● **Anglo-Egyptian Treaty** ▶ (1936) The treaty between Britain and Egypt whereby Britain gained independence after 50 years of British occupation. Britain maintained a military alliance with Egypt and a naval base at Alexandria.

● **Anglo-Japanese Alliance** ▶ (1902–23) The alliance between Britain and Japan contracted to maintain their interests in China and Korea respectively against Russian encroachment. The alliance brought Japan into World War I but subsequently lapsed as Britain sought friendship with the USA, Japan's rival in the Pacific.

● **Anglo-Maori Wars** ▷See Maori Wars.

● **Anglo-Saxon Chronicle** ▷See English literature.

● **Anglo-Saxons** ▶ The Germanic conquerors of Britain during the 5th century AD (see Angles; Saxons; Jutes). They first established a number of separate kingdoms, principally ▷Northumbria, ▷Mercia, and ▷Wessex, but eventually England was unified under an Anglo-Saxon dynasty. Kings ruled with the assistance of a ▷witan or council of wise men, and local government and justice took the form of ▷hundred courts. They were converted to Christianity following the mission of St ▷Augustine of Canterbury. The Anglo-Saxons developed a rich art and literature. Their language is known as Old English. ▷See also English.

● **Angola, Republic of** ▶ A country in SW Africa, on the Atlantic Ocean situated mainly to the S of the River Congo. The Cabinda district, however, lies to the N of the Congo and is separated from the rest of the country by a section of the Democratic Republic of Congo. The country consists of a narrow coastal plain and a broad dissected plateau that reaches heights of over 2000 m (6500 ft). The inhabitants are almost all Negroes (mainly of Bantu origin) with small numbers of mixed race and a rapidly decreasing White population.

Economy: agriculture is organized on a state-run and cooperative basis and the main crops are sugar cane and coffee. Angola is rich in mineral resources and diamonds have long been an important source of revenue. There is considerable oil production, especially offshore from Cabinda, and this has opened up new possibilities for industrial development. Hydroelectricity is being harnessed from the short steep river systems descending to the coastal plains and these schemes will provide irrigation as well as power. Main exports include oil, coffee, diamonds, and iron ore. Although potentially one of Africa's wealthiest countries, Angola's economy has been severely disturbed by the civil wars of the last 27 years; reforms intended to encourage free enterprise were introduced in the late 1980s.

History: discovered and settled by the Portuguese in the late 15th century, the area remained a Portuguese colony (apart from a brief period of Dutch occupation from 1641 to 1648) until 1951 when it became an overseas province of Portugal. During the 1950s and 1960s there was a rise in nationalism and three main independence movements emerged: the MPLA (Popular Movement for the Liberation of Angola), the FNLA (National Front for the Liberation of Angola), and UNITA (National Union for the Total Independence of Angola). In 1974 Portugal agreed in principle to independence for Angola but lack of internal unity led to civil war. The various groups took over different parts of the country and in November, 1975, Portugal granted independence to the "Angolan people" rather than to any one group. The People's Republic of Angola was declared by the MPLA, with its capital in Luanda, and a coalition of the FNLA and UNITA, led by Dr Jonas ▷Savimbi, formed a People's Democratic Republic of Angola, based on Huambo. The MPLA was supported by the Soviet Union and Cuba and the FNLA by the USA and certain W European countries. Eventually, the MPLA gained control in 1976 but opposition continued with increased South African involvement until South African forces withdrew in 1988; a Cuban withdrawal was also agreed in 1988. A ceasefire to the 16-year-old civil war was agreed in 1991. Following the MPLA's victory in multiparty elections held in 1992, renewed fighting broke out. In 1996 the MPLA and UNITA agreed to form a unity government but negotiations broke down in 1999 and UNITA launched a major offensive. The death of the veteran rebel leader Savimbi in early 2002 raised new hopes of peace; a ceasefire was agreed in April.

Republic of Angola

Head of state	President Dr José Eduardo dos Santos
Official language	Portuguese
Official currency	kwanza of 100 lwei
Area	1 246 700 sq km (481 351 sq mi)
Population (2000 est)	10 145 000
Capital and main port	Luanda

● **Angora goat** ▶ A breed of goat, originating in Turkey, whose long silky hair is regularly sheared and used commercially to make ▷mohair. Mohair is now also obtained from several other goat breeds derived from the Angora.

● **Angora rabbit** ▶ A breed of domesticated rabbit, originating in France in the 17th century, of which there are now both English and French varieties. The long wool, which is usually white but can be black or blue, is periodically shorn and spun for use in clothing manufacture (**Angora wool**).

● **angostura** ▶ A bitters made from distilled herbs and plants. Angostura bitters originated in Ciudad Bolívar (formerly Angostura) in Venezuela as a tonic and febrifuge but its manufacture was transferred to Trinidad in 1975. A few drops are added to gin to make a pink gin.

● **Angoulême** ► 45 40N 0 10E A town in SW France, the capital of the Charente department on the River Charente. It is the site of a 12th-century cathedral; its manufactures include paper, felt, and iron. Population (latest est): 50 151.

● **Angoulême, Charles de Valois, Duc d'** ► (1573–1650) French soldier. An illegitimate son of Charles IX, he was imprisoned (1605–16) for conspiring against Henry IV. He subsequently rose through the influence of Richelieu and Mazarin to important military commands, including that of the siege of Huguenot-held La Rochelle (1627).

● **Angry Young Men** ► A group of British novelists and dramatists in the 1950s whose attitudes included dissatisfaction with postwar British society and disrespect for the so-called "Establishment" and its traditional institutions. Many of them came from working-class or lower-middle-class backgrounds. The phrase "angry young man" was first applied to the dramatist John ▷Osborne. Among other writers associated with this group were the novelists Kingsley ▷Amis, John ▷Wain, and John ▷Braine, the dramatist Arnold ▷Wesker, and the critic Colin ▷Wilson.

● **Ångström, Anders Jonas** ► (1814–74) Swedish physicist and astronomer. He was a founder of spectroscopy, his work on solar spectra leading to the discovery (1862) of hydrogen in the sun. He also studied geomagnetism. The **angstrom**, a unit of wavelength equal to 10^{-10} m (one tenth of a nanometre), is named after him.

● **Anguilla** ► 18 14N 63 05W A West Indian island in the E Caribbean Sea, in the Leeward Islands. Formerly part of the UK Associated State of St Kitts-Nevis-Anguilla, it became a separate British dependency in December, 1980. Its economy is based chiefly on stock raising, salt production, boatbuilding, and fishing. Area: 90 sq km (35 sq mi). Population (1992): 8800. ▷See also St Kitts-Nevis, Federation of.

● **angular momentum** ► The product of the ▷moment of inertia of a body and its angular velocity about an axis. It is an important quantity in physics since the total angular momentum of a closed system is conserved.

● **angular velocity** ▷See velocity.

● **Angus** ► A council area of E Scotland, on the North Sea. Under local government reorganization in 1975 the historic county of Angus (once known as Forfarshire) was incorporated into Tayside Region. In 1996 it was restored as an independent ▷unitary authority with slightly adjusted borders; the city of Dundee now forms a separate authority. Angus consists of hills and plains to the S and E, rising to the Grampian Mountains in the NW. Agriculture is important, with cereals and root crops in the arable coastal plains. Other sources of income include fishing, textiles, and engineering. Area 2181 sq km (842 sq mi). Population (1996 est) 111 020. Administrative centre: Forfar.

● **angwantibo** ► A rare nocturnal arboreal prosimian primate, *Arctocebus calabarensis*, also called golden potto, found in West African forests. 23–30 cm long, it has brown fur and large eyes and feeds on insects. Family: *Lorisidae*.

● **Anhui** ► (or Anhwei) A province in E China. The Yangtze River in the S and the Huai River in the N are linked by ancient waterways, which provide transport and irrigation. Main products are tea, rice, soya beans, silk, and steel. Area: 13 986 sq km (54 000 sq mi). Population (1995 est): 59 550 000. Capital: Hefei.

● **anil** ► A small shrub, *Indigofera anil*, native to India and the original source of the blue dye ▷indigo, which is now produced synthetically. Family: *Leguminosae*.

● **aniline** ► (or phenylamine; $C_6H_5NH_2$) A colourless oily nonflammable liquid ▷amine. It is used to make dyes, plastics, and drugs and is made by the reduction of nitrobenzene obtained from coal tar.

● **animal** ► A living organism belonging to the kingdom *Animalia*. Animals are typically mobile and feed on ▷plants, other animals, or their remains. Their body ▷cells lack the rigid cellulose wall of plant cells and they require specialized tissues, such as bone, for protection and support. Because of their activity, animals have specialized organs for sensing the nature of their environment; information from the sense organs is transmitted and coordinated by means of a nervous system. Individuals of the same species have a consistent body form; growth occurs in all regions of the body and ceases at a certain stage of development, usually when sexual maturity has been attained. There are over one million species of animals, grouped into over 30 phyla. ▷See also life; taxonomy.

A simplified classification of the animal kingdom (major phyla only)

phylum (approx. no. species)	important classes	representative members
Porifera (5000)		sponges
Cnidaria (9000)	Hydrozoa	*Hydra*, Portuguese man-of-war
	Scyphozoa	jellyfish
	Anthozoa	sea anemones, corals
Platyhelminthes (18 500)	Turbellaria	planarians
	Trematoda	flukes
	Cestoda	tapeworms
Nematoda (12 000)		roundworms
Mollusca (50 000)	Gastropoda	snails, slugs
	Bivalvia	mussels, oysters, cockles
	Cephalopoda	squids, octopus
Annelida (12 000)	Oligochaeta	earthworms
	Polychaeta	lugworms
	Hirudinea	leeches
Arthropoda (>1 000 000)	Arachnida	spiders, scorpions
	Crustacea	lobsters, crabs, woodlice
	Insecta	beetles, wasps, ants, flies, bugs
	Chilopoda	centipedes
	Diplopoda	millipedes
Echinodermata (6500)	Asteroidea	starfish
	Ophiuroidia	brittle stars
	Echinoidea	sea urchins
	Holothuroidea	sea cucumbers
Chordata (55 000)	Chondrichthyes	sharks, rays
	Osteichthyes	bony fish (salmon, carp, eels, perch, etc.)
	Amphibia	frogs, toads, newts, salamanders
	Reptilia	lizards, snakes, crocodiles,turtles
	Aves	birds
	Mammalia	mammals, including humans

● **animal behaviour** ▷See ethology.

● **animal rights movement** ► A campaign conducted by several organizations in protest against cruelty to and exploitation of animals. Targets of the movement, which developed in the 1970s, include zoos, animal research centres, ▷foxhunting, and the export of farm animals. Some groups, such as the League Against Cruel Sports, favour parliamentary action, while others, such as the Animal Liberation Front, condone criminal acts, including the release of research animals and bombing campaigns.

● **animal husbandry** ▷See livestock farming.

● **animal worship** ▷See totemism.

● **animation** ► The process of photographing drawings, models, or other inanimate objects so that they are given the illusion of movement when the film is projected. The most familiar technique involves photographing a series of gradually changing cartoon drawings; other methods include photographing models that are moved slightly between exposures, drawing directly onto film, or, increasingly, the manipulation of images by computer (*see* computer graphics).

Many precinematic devices of the magic-lantern type exploited the optical phenomenon known as persistence of vision to produce "moving" drawings. The earliest known animated film dates from about 1898, while the first cartoon film is generally thought to be *Humorous Phases of Funny Faces* (1907). Animated versions of newspaper comic strips became a popular attraction in US cinemas from about 1910. From the late 1920s film animation worldwide was dominated by Walt ▷Disney, who enjoyed huge success with cartoon shorts featuring such characters as Mickey Mouse before going on to create a series of increasingly sophisticated feature-length cartoons, beginning with *Snow White and the Seven Dwarfs* (1938). In recent decades the main development has been the growing use of computer-aided techniques. In 1996 the Disney company released *Toy Story*, the first feature-length animation to have been generated entirely by computer.

● **animism** ▶ 1. The belief that the physical world is permeated by a spirit sometimes called the *anima mundi*. Georg Ernst ▷Stahl was its chief proponent. 2. In anthropology, all forms of belief in spiritual agencies. ▷Tylor, who coined this use of the word, distinguished two classes of such beings: the souls of the dead (*see* ancestor worship) and other personalized supernatural entities.

● **anise** ▶ An annual Egyptian herb, *Pimpinella anisum*, growing to a height of up to 75 cm and having umbrella-like clusters of small yellow-white flowers. It is cultivated in subtropical areas for the liquorice-flavoured oil (principally anthole) extracted from its small seeds, which is used in certain foods, beverages, and liqueurs. Family: *Umbelliferae*.

● **Anjou** ▶ A former province in W central France, approximating to the present-day Maine-et-Loire department. Anjou was inherited by the future Henry II of England in 1151 and remained under the same ruler as England until the early 13th century. Permanently annexed to the French Crown in 1480, it ceased to exist as a province in 1790. ▷*See also* Angevins.

● **Ankara** ▶ 39 55N 32 50E The capital of Turkey, in the W central region of the country. There is evidence of human settlement from very early times, and it has long been an important trading town. Conquered by Alexander the Great in the 4th century BC, it later came within the Roman and Byzantine Empires. It was attacked by Persians and Arabs, and in the 11th century it was defeated by the Turks. It became the capital of modern Turkey in 1923 and since then has expanded considerably; it has three universities. Population (1997): 2 984 099.

● **ankh** ▷*See* crosses.

● **Ankhesenamen** ▶ (born c. 1373 BC) The wife of ▷Tutankhamen, portrayed on several objects discovered in his tomb. After his death she offered to marry a son of ▷Suppiluliumas I, thus making him King of Egypt, but he was murdered en route to Egypt. She became the consort of Tutankhamen's adviser Ay, who became king.

● **ankylosaur** ▶ A heavily armoured dinosaur of the late Cretaceous period. Ankylosaurs were low and flat and their backs were covered with protective bony plates. *Euoplocephalus* (or *Ankylosaurus*) up to 5 m long, weighed 3 tonnes, and its plated tail ended in a large bony knob. Order: ▷*Ornithischia*.

● **ankylosing spondylitis** ▶ A rheumatic disease in which inflammation of the joints of the backbone may result in fusion of the vertebrae and rigidity of the spine, which becomes fixed in a hunched position. The pain and stiffness are relieved by analgesics and exercises.

● **An Lu Shan** ▶ (703–57 AD) Chinese military governor, who in 756 declared himself emperor of a new Yan dynasty. Tang imperial troops opposed him but An Lu Shan seized the capital Chang An and the emperor was forced to flee. An Lu Shan was murdered shortly afterwards but only in 763 did the imperial army succeed in putting down the rebellion.

● **Annaba** ▶ (former name: Bône) 36 57N 7 39E A large port in E Algeria, on the Mediterranean Sea. An early centre of Christianity, it held the bishopric of St Augustine (396–430 AD). In 1832 it was captured by the French. Mineral exports are important, particularly phosphates and iron ore. Industries include flour milling and iron and steel processing. Population (1998): 348 554.

● **Anna Comnena** ▶ (1083–?1148 AD) Byzantine historian. The daughter of Emperor ▷Alexius I Comnenus, Anna married (1097) Nicephorus Bryennius (?1062–1137) and conspired (1118) to depose her brother John II (1088–1143; reigned 1118–43) in favour of her husband. She was banished to a convent, where she wrote the *Alexiad*, an account of her father's achievements and of the early Crusades.

● **Anna Ivanovna** ▶ (1693–1740) Empress of Russia (1730–40). A niece of ▷Peter the Great, Anna married (1710) Frederick William, Duke of Courland (d. 1710). She was elected empress by the Supreme Privy Council on the condition that she accepted provisions curtailing her powers. In practice, however, she became an autocrat, whose administration was run by her German advisers. In the Russo-Turkish War (1736–39) she regained Azov.

● **Annam** ▶ A region in central Vietnam, long ruled from Hue. The Chinese, who had occupied it in 111 BC, were driven out in 939 AD, and it was a powerful independent state until becoming a French protectorate in 1884. In 1949 it became part of independent Vietnam.

● **Annan, Kofi** ▶ (1938–) Ghanaian international civil servant; secretary general of the United Nations (1996–). He previously held UN posts in Geneva and New York. Annan and the UN were jointly awarded the Nobel Peace Prize in 2001.

● **Annapolis** ▶ 38 59N 76 30W A city in the USA, the capital of Maryland on the Severn River. Founded in 1648, it was here that Congress received George Washington's resignation as commander in chief of the Continental Army and ratified the peace treaty ending the American Revolution (1783). The US Naval Academy was established here in 1845 and the many historic buildings and riverside setting make it a popular tourist resort. It is also a minor seaport and has seafood industries. Population (latest est): 33 187.

● **Annapolis Royal** ▶ 44 44N 65 32W A port in E Canada, in Nova Scotia. One of the first settlements in Canada (1632), it was Nova Scotia's capital until 1749. A market town, it attracts many tourists. Population (1991): 633.

● **Annapurna, Mount** ▶ 28 34N 83 50E A massif in NW central Nepal, in the Himalayas. Its highest peak **Annapurna I**, at 8078 m (26 504 ft), was first climbed in 1950 by a French team.

● **Ann Arbor** ▶ 42 18N 83 43W A city in the USA, in Michigan. An educational centre, it is the site of the University of Michigan (1817) and its manufactures include chemicals and precision instruments. Population (1996 est): 108 758.

● **Anne** ▶ (1665–1714) Queen of England and Scotland (Great Britain from 1707) and Ireland (1702–14). Anne, the last Stuart monarch, was the daughter of the Roman Catholic James II but was herself brought up as a Protestant. Following the overthrow (1688) of James, she supported the accession of her Protestant brother-in-law, William III, whose heiress she became. She married (1683) Prince George of Denmark (1653–1708) and was pregnant 18 times by him; none of her five children born alive survived childhood. Anne therefore agreed to the Act of ▷Settlement (1701), which provided for the Hanoverian succession after her death. Anne was greatly influenced by the Duke and Duchess of ▷Marlborough. This friendship led her to abandon her Tory and Anglican loyalties and follow the Marlboroughs in supporting the rival Whigs (*see* Whigs; Tories), especially in their aggressive stategy in the War of the ▷Spanish Succession. In 1710, however, having quarrelled with the Marlboroughs and being faced with a country dissatisfied with the Whig leadership, Anne appointed a Tory ministry.

● **Anne (Elizabeth Alice Louise)** ▶ (1950–) Princess of the United Kingdom, who was granted the title Princess Royal in 1987. The only daughter of Elizabeth II and Prince Philip, she is eighth in line of succession to the throne. An accomplished horsewoman, in 1973 she married Lieut Mark Phillips (1948–), having a son Peter (1977–) and a daughter Zara (1981–); they separated in 1989 and divorced in 1992. In 1992 she married Cmdr Timothy Laurence. She has gained worldwide admiration for her work as president of the Save the Children Fund.

● **annealing** ▷*See* heat treatment.

● **Annecy** ▶ 45 54N 6 07E A town in SE France, the capital of the Haute-Savoie department. Its situation on Lake Annecy and pleasant climate have made it a popular tourist centre. Population (latest est): 51 593.

• **annelid worm** ▶ An invertebrate animal belonging to a phylum (*Annelida*) of about 12 000 species, widely distributed in salt water, fresh water, and on land. The body is characteristically a muscular cylinder divided into many fluid-filled segments. Annelids vary greatly in form and habit and are divided into three classes: the Polychaeta, or bristleworms (*see* ragworm; lugworm; fanworm); the Oligochaeta (*see* earthworm; tubifex), and the Hirudinea (*see* leech).

• **Anne of Austria** ▶ (1601–66) The wife (1615–43) of Louis XIII of France, whose antipathy towards her was aggravated by that of his chief minister Cardinal de Richelieu. After her husband's death she was regent (1643–51) for her son Louis XIV and chose her lover ▷Mazarin to succeed Richelieu.

• **Anne of Bohemia** ▶ (1366–94) The first wife (from 1382) of Richard II of England and daughter of Emperor Charles IV. Her household extravagance was a cause of dissension between Richard and parliament. She died of the plague.

• **Anne of Brittany** ▶ (1477–1514) Duchess of Brittany (1488–1514), succeeding her father Francis I (1435–88; ruled 1458–88). Her marriages to Charles VIII of France (1491) and to his successor Louis XII (1499) initiated the union of Brittany with France, in spite of Anne's desire to preserve Breton autonomy.

• **Anne of Cleves** ▶ (1515–57) The fourth wife of Henry VIII of England. The marriage (January, 1540) was arranged to effect an alliance with German Protestant rulers but Henry found Anne unattractive and quickly divorced her (July, 1540).

• **Anne of Denmark** ▶ (1574–1619) The wife (from 1589) of James I of England and VI of Scotland. She spent heavily on building and court entertainments (appearing herself in Ben Jonson's masques) and was suspected of Roman Catholic sympathies.

• **Annigoni, Pietro** ▶ (1910–88) Italian painter. One of the few famous 20th-century artists to use the techniques of the Old Masters, Annigoni worked chiefly in ▷tempera and ▷fresco. He is best known for his portraits of President Kennedy (1961) and Queen Elizabeth II (1955 and 1970). In later years he painted a fresco cycle of the life of Christ in the Church of S Michele Arcangelo, in Ponte Buggianese, near Florence.

• **annihilation** ▶ The conversion of a particle and its antiparticle into electromagnetic radiation (annihilation radiation) as a result of a collision. The energy of the radiation is equivalent to the combined mass of the two particles. ▷*See also* antimatter.

• **annual percentage rate** ▶ (APR) ▷*See* interest.

• **annual rings** ▶ (or growth rings) A pattern of rings visible in a cross section of a tree trunk, produced by different rates of wood growth corresponding to the seasonal fluctuations in climate in temperate regions. Each year the wood produced in spring consists of large cells corresponding to vigorous growth; autumn wood has small cells as growth slows down, and in winter growth ceases. The number of rings gives an estimate of the age of the tree. ▷*See also* dendrochronology.

• **annuals** ▶ Plants that complete their life cycle—from germination, flowering, and seed production to death—within one year. Many annuals are used for bedding plants and flower extensively in the summer. *Compare* perennials.

• **annuity** ▶ A form of pension in which an ▷insurance company makes a series of periodic payments to a person (annuitant) or his or her dependents over a number of years (term), in return for money paid to the insurance company either in a lump sum or in instalments. An immediate annuity begins at once and a deferred annuity after a fixed period. An annuity certain is for a specific number of years. A life annuity is paid from a certain age until death. A perpetuity continues indefinitely.

• **annulment** ▶ The process establishing that a marriage is not legally valid, as opposed to ▷divorce, which ends a valid marriage. An invalid marriage is considered void, never to have existed. A marriage is void from the beginning if there is a serious defect, for example if the husband or wife is insane, too young, or already married. In less serious cases, for example when the husband or wife is unable or unwilling to consummate the marriage, the marriage may be declared void if either partner wishes it.

• **Annunciation** ▶ In the Bible, the announcement by the angel Gabriel to the Virgin Mary of her conception of Christ (Luke 1.26–38). The feast, the Annunciation of the Blessed Virgin Mary, or Lady Day, is celebrated on 25 March.

• **anode** ▶ The positive electrode of an electrolytic cell, valve, etc. It is the electrode by which the electrons leave the system. *Compare* cathode.

• **anodizing** ▶ A process in which aluminium or an alloy, is covered with a protective layer by oxidation in an electrolytic cell. Usually the cell contains chromic acid; the metal treated is the anode of the cell. The porous oxide layer formed, can be dyed to give a coloured finish.

• **anointing of the sick** ▶ The ▷sacrament in the Orthodox Church and the Roman Catholic Church in which a priest anoints with oil the eyes, ears, nostrils, lips, hands, and feet of a person while he recites absolution for this person's sins. It is performed on the seriously ill and as a last rite for the dying (it used to be called extreme unction). It is based on James 5.14: "Is there any sick among you? Let him call for the elders of the church; and let them pray over him, anointing him with oil, in the name of the Lord."

• **anole** ▶ A small arboreal New World lizard belonging to the genus *Anolis* (165 species). 12–45 cm long, anoles have a triangular head and pads on their fingers and toes covered with minute hooks for grip. Their skin changes colour from brown to green in response to changes in temperature, light, or danger. Males have an expansible red or yellow throat fan (dewlap). Family: *Iguanidae*.

• **anomie** ▶ A condition of a society or of individuals in which social standards or goals are unclear, in conflict, or absent. Anomic individuals reject or are unable to find meaningful social norms by which to interpret or organize their lives. Losing their sense of social belonging, they may turn to crime, the selfish pursuit of power, or even suicide. The term was first introduced into sociology in a systematic form by ▷Durkheim in his *Suicide* (1897).

• **Anopheles** ▶ A widespread genus of ▷mosquitoes (about 350 species), the females of which are important as vectors of the malarial parasite ▷*Plasmodium*. The best-known malaria carrier is *A. maculipennis*. Some species transmit filariasis and encephalitis. Unlike other mosquitoes the larvae lack a siphon and lie flat on the surface of the water.

• **anorexia nervosa** ▶ A psychological illness in which the patient, usually an adolescent girl, refuses food over a long period. It often starts with dieting to lose weight, which becomes obsessional: the patient becomes emaciated and may—without treatment—starve to death. The psychological causes are complex, often involving disturbances in family relationships. Hospitalization may be required for the treatment, which involves intensive nursing, sedation, and ▷psychotherapy. ▷*See also* bulimia nervosa.

• **Anouilh, Jean** ▶ (1910–87) French dramatist. His commitment to the theatre was early and total; his first play, *The Ermine*, was performed in 1932. He achieved his first success in 1937 with *Traveller without Luggage*. His plays include reworkings of Greek myths (*Antigone*, 1944), social comedies (*Ring Round the Moon*, 1950), and historical dramas (*Becket*, 1959). A skilled craftsman, he exploited the most basic dramatic conventions, such as coincidences and flashbacks. His work, although often considered old-fashioned, remains popular both in France and abroad.

• **Anschluss** ▶ (German: union; 1938) The union of Austria with Germany. Following the forced resignation of the Austrian chancellor ▷Schuschnigg, Nazi forces entered Austria and Schuschnigg was imprisoned. *Anschluss* was declared and ratified by a plebiscite.

• **Anselm of Canterbury, St** ▶ (c. 1033–1109) Italian theologian and philosopher, Archbishop of Canterbury, and Doctor of the Church. Appointed to the see of Canterbury in 1093, Anselm defended church rights against William II Rufus until he went into exile to Rome in 1097. Recalled by ▷Henry I in 1100, he eventually reached an uneasy compromise with him. He is the leading early scholastic philosopher and is perhaps best known for his formulation of the **ontological argument** for the existence of God, which states that if God is "that than which nothing greater can be conceived," then the existence of God is necessary, for to argue that God does not exist involves one in a contradiction since it is possible to conceive of a greater entity than a nonexistent God. Feast day: 21 April. Emblem: a ship.

● **Ansermet, Ernest** ► (1883–1969) Swiss conductor. Briefly a mathematics teacher, he studied composition with Ernest ▷Bloch and conducting with ▷Nikisch. After touring with ▷Diaghilev's ballet company he founded the Suisse Romande Orchestra in 1918, remaining its director until 1967. He was famous for his interpretations of ▷Stravinsky and other 20th-century composers.

● **Ansgar, St** ► (or Anskar; c. 801–65) A native of Picardy; missionary to and patron saint of Scandinavia. Appointed in 832 as papal legate to the Scandinavians, Ansgar preached in Denmark and Sweden, building the first church in Sweden. Despite his extensive activity, Scandinavia lapsed into paganism after his death. Feast day: 3 Feb.

● **Anshan** ► (or An-shan) 41 05N 122 58E A city in NE China, in Liaoning province. Its steel complex, the largest in China, was developed under Japanese occupation (1931–45), when its population grew rapidly. It also has engineering, chemical, and cement industries. Population (1991 est): 1 390 000.

● **Anson, George Anson, Baron** ► (1697–1762) British admiral. During the War of the Austrian Succession, he commanded six ships in attacks on Spanish possessions in South America (1740). He went on to circumnavigate the world in a voyage lasting four years, returning to Britain with only one surviving vessel but with Spanish treasure worth £500,000. He related his adventures in *A Voyage round the World* (1748).

● **ant** ► An insect belonging to the family *Formicidae* (over 10 000 species). Ants occur in almost all terrestrial habitats, are 0.05–25 cm long, and show a high degree of social organization. A colony consists of wingless sterile female workers and a smaller number of fertile males and females that are generally the progeny of a single queen. The young males and females fly from the nest to mate, after which the males die and the young queens found new colonies. Ant societies range from simple groups of a few individuals to large complex nests comprising millions of ants and sometimes involving a second species taken as slaves to work in the colony (*see* slave-making ant).

Some ants have stings; others secrete burning acids (such as formic acid) as a defence. Feeding habits vary from rapacious predators (*see* army ant) to harmless scavengers; others milk honeydew from aphids and certain species cultivate fungi as a food supply within the nest. Order: ▷*Hymenoptera*. □insect.

● **Antakya** ▷*See* Antioch.

● **Antalya** ► 36 53N 30 42E A city in SW Turkey, on the Gulf of Antalya. Founded in the 2nd century BC, it flourished particularly under the Seljuqs in the 13th century, and it is now an important coastal resort. Nearby are two Roman amphitheatres and the ruins of Perga. Population (1995 est): 502 269.

● **Antananarivo** ► (former name: Tananarive) 18 52S 47 30E The capital of Madagascar. It was occupied by the French in 1895. A cultural centre, it has a university (1961) and two cathedrals. Industries include tobacco and leather goods. Population (1993): 1 052 835.

● **Antar** ► (6th century AD) Arab poet and warrior, celebrated in the 10th-century *Romance of Antar* as the model of desert chivalry. The son of a Bedouin chieftain and a slave girl, Antar was said to have proved his courage in numerous battles and adventures before being allowed to marry his beloved Abla.

● **Antarctica** ► The most southerly continent, surrounding the South Pole. Almost circular in shape, most of it lies within the **Antarctic Circle**, an imaginary circle at latitude 66° 30'S that is the most southerly point at which the sun is visible at the summer solstice. The continent consists chiefly of a vast ice-covered plateau and contains about 90% of the world's ice. Calculations suggest that should

this ice melt sea levels would rise by about 60 m (200 ft). The continent's climate is the severest in the world; in 1960 the world's lowest recorded temperature–of −87.8°C (−126°F)–was made at the Soviet station of Vostok. Although lacking in vegetation it has abundant wildlife including whales, seals, and penguins. Scientific stations were established during the International Geophysical Year (1957–58). Some nations (*see* Australian Antarctic Territory; British Antarctic Territory; Norwegian Antarctic Territory; Ross Dependency; Terre Adélie) have political claims to territory in Antarctica. Argentina and Chile have also laid claims, as yet unrecognized, to portions of British Antarctic Territory (*see also* Antarctic Treaty).

History: in his voyage of 1772–75 Capt James Cook reached 71° 10'S. Many explorations took place during the 19th century. The South Pole was reached first by Roald ▷Amundsen of the Norwegian Antarctic Expedition on 14 December, 1911, and a month later by ▷Scott of the British Antarctic Expedition. Scott and his team perished on the return journey. Area: about 14 200 000 sq km (5 500 000 sq mi).

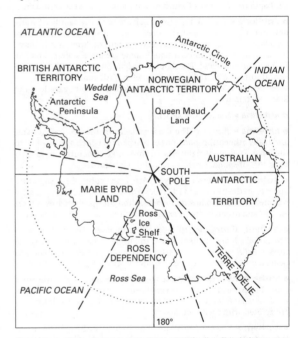

Antarctica ► Under the Antarctic Treaty (1959) all political claims were halted and freedom of scientific research in the continent was ensured.

● **Antarctic Ocean** ▷*See* Southern Ocean.

● **Antarctic Peninsula** ► A peninsula extending 1930 km (1200 mi) N from Antarctica towards South America, claimed by the UK. The first part of Antarctica to be sighted (1820), it has volcanic mountains in the S.

● **Antarctic Treaty** ► (1959) An agreement, signed by Argentina, Australia, Belgium, Chile, France, Japan, New Zealand, Norway, South Africa, the Soviet Union, the UK, and the USA, to maintain the Antarctic as a demilitarized zone for 30 years.

● **Antares** ► An immense remote yet conspicuous red ▷supergiant, apparent magnitude 0.94 and about 400 light years distant, that is the brightest star in the constellation Scorpius. It is a visual ▷binary star.

● **ant bear** ▷*See* aardvark.

● **antbird** ► A passerine bird belonging to a large family (*Formicariidae*; 223 species) occurring in the forest undergrowth of Central and South America. About 8–35 cm long, antbirds have shrill voices and hooked bills and feed chiefly on insects (although the larger species may eat small lizards, snakes, and young birds). The female is dull brown but the male usually has a brightly patterned plumage.

● **anteater** ► A long-tailed animal belonging to a family (*Myrmecophagidae*; 3 species) occurring in tropical South America. It is toothless and has a narrow snout with a long sticky tongue used to pick up ants and termites after tearing open their nests with its powerful claws. The giant anteater (*Myrmecophaga tridactyla*) reaches 1.8 m in length and has grey and black fur and a bushy tail (▷mammal). The other species are smaller arboreal animals with prehensile tails (*see* tamandua). Order: *Edentata*.

The name anteater is given to several other unrelated animals that feed on ants or termites: the ▷pangolins (scaly anteaters), ▷echidnas (spiny anteaters), and ▷aardvark.

● **Antelami, Benedetto** ► (active 1177–1233) Italian sculptor. The most famous Italian sculptor of the medieval period, Antelami developed a style that marked the transition between the ▷romanesque and the ▷gothic. His best-known works are the reliefs on the doors of the baptistry at Parma, of which he was probably also the architect.

● **antelope** ► A hoofed mammal belonging to the family ▷Bovidae and occurring chiefly in Africa but occasionally in Asia. Antelopes are typically fast-running and graceful, grazing or browsing in large herds on open grasslands, although some are more solitary and live in bush and woodland. The shoulder height varies from 25 cm in the ▷royal antelope to 180 cm in the ▷eland. All male antelopes and some females have horns. ▷*See also* dik-dik; duiker; gazelle; gnu; kudu; waterbuck.

● **antenna** ► (radio) ▷*See* aerial.

● **antenna** ► (zoology) The sensory feeler of insects, crustaceans, and many other arthropods, one or two pairs of which are attached to the head. They are usually jointed threadlike structures containing receptors of sound, smell, touch, and temperature.

● **Antenor** ► (late 6th century BC) Athenian sculptor. His signature appears on the base of a marble ▷kore on the Athenian Acropolis. He sculpted the Harmodios and Aristogeiton group, looted by Xerxes (480 BC) and restored after Alexander the Great's Persian expedition.

● **Antheil, George** ► (1900–59) US composer. He studied with Ernest ▷Bloch and in 1922 moved to Europe, where his avantgarde work *Le Ballet mécanique* (1924) for bells, motor horns, aeroplane propellers, etc., caused a furore. His later works are more traditional.

● **anthelminthics** ► Drugs used to treat infections of the intestines caused by parasitic worms. Piperazine or mebendazole is commonly used to expel roundworms and threadworms. Tapeworm infections are treated with niclosamide.

● **anthem** ► A piece of music for church choir, authorized for use in the Anglican service but not a part of the liturgy; it developed from the Latin ▷motet. In Tudor and early Stuart times "full anthems," by composers, such as ▷Tallis and ▷Byrd, were written for unaccompanied choir, although in practice the vocal parts were often strengthened instrumentally. After the Restoration ▷Purcell, ▷Blow, and others inserted solos between the choral sections, accompanying these "verse anthems" with independent organ or orchestral parts. ▷*See also* national anthem.

● **anther** ▷*See* stamen.

● **antheridium** ► The reproductive organ producing the male cells (gametes) in ferns, mosses, algae, and fungi. It is usually a club-shaped structure, the rounded head containing the gametes.

● **Anthony of Egypt, St** ► (c. 251–356 AD) Egyptian hermit and founder of Christian monasticism. An ascetic from the age of 20, he withdrew until 305 into complete isolation, emerging to organize followers into a monastic community. His combat with temptation in the desert is described in Athanasius' *Life of Saint Anthony*; it became a frequent subject in Christian art. Feast day: 17 Jan.

● **Anthony of Padua, St** ► (1195–1231) Portuguese friar and Doctor of the Church. He devoted his efforts to converting heretics in N Italy and the Albigenses in S France until his appointment as professor of theology to the Franciscan Order in 1223. He is often invoked as a finder of lost property. Feast day: 13 June.

● **anthracene** ► ($C_{14}H_{10}$) A colourless crystalline ▷aromatic compound. It is obtained from coal tar and is used in making dyes.

● **anthracite** ▷*See* coal.

● **anthrax** ► A contagious disease of many animals, including farm livestock, that can be transmitted to man. Caused by the bacterium *Bacillus anthracis*, it is usually contracted by eating contaminated food. Onset is often sudden with a rise in body temperature, staggering, respiratory distress, convulsions, and death. In horses and pigs a subacute form may occur, with progressive swelling of the throat and neck resulting in laboured breathing and choking. In many countries the authorities must be notified of any outbreaks. Treatment is with antibiotics and prevention is by vaccination of herds in areas where the disease is endemic. Humans may develop localized swellings after handling infected carcasses or acquire a pneumonia from inhaling the bacterial spores (woolsorters' disease).

Although several governments and terrorist groups are believed to have developed anthrax as a biological weapon, it has never been used in conflict. In late 2001 five people died when parcels containing anthrax spores were sent to government and media targets in the USA: no clear suspect has emerged.

● **anthropoid ape** ► A tailless ▷primate belonging to the family *Pongidae*, which includes the gibbons, chimpanzees, orang-utans, and gorillas. ▷*See* ape.

● **anthropology** ► The scientific study of man in his physical and social aspects. In the widest meaning of the term it includes ▷archaeology, ▷linguistics, cultural or social anthropology, and physical anthropology. It is particularly concerned with the systematic and comparative study of human diversity. Physical anthropology is concerned with the origins and evolution of man through the examination of his fossil remains, and the study and classification of the races of man through comparison of anatomical and physiological characteristics (*see also* anthropometry). Cultural anthropology is concerned with the evolution of human society and culture, including language, and with the systematic comparison of social, linguistic, technical, and behavioural diversity. Social anthropology is the comparative study of social behaviour, social organization, social forms and institutions, custom, culture, and belief, and has traditionally confined itself to the study of "primitive" societies.

● **anthropometry** ► The science concerned with the measurement of the human body, particularly with respect to the variation that exists between different populations and races. Anthropometry ranges from the measurement of structural characteristics, such as height, cranial capacity, etc., to the analysis of chemical constituents of the body, such as blood groups. By comparing fossil and present-day measurements anthropometry has also helped to reveal the sequence of events that has occurred during the evolution of man.

● **anthropomorphism** ► Mankind's tendency to ascribe to non-human creatures the motives, feelings, etc., of human beings. This is particularly evident in the concept of God. The anthropomorphism of ancient Greek religion was ridiculed by ▷Xenophanes of Colophon (6th century BC) but Christian discussions of the divine personality, will, etc., have still not escaped from an implicit anthropomorphism. Religious art can scarcely avoid being anthropomorphic.

● **anthroposophy** ► A philosophy propounded by Rudolf ▷Steiner, which holds that the key to an understanding of the cosmos exists in man himself and that man should therefore find means to develop his latent spiritual powers.

● **Anthurium** ► A genus of tropical American plants (550 species), some of which are cultivated as greenhouse or pot plants for their ornamental flowers or foliage. The flower heads consist of a cylindrical cluster (spadix) of tiny flowers surrounded by a large petal-like part (spathe), which is often brightly coloured (e.g. in *A. scherzerianum* it is red). Family: *Araceae* (arum family).

● **anti-aircraft gun** ► Any gun capable of rapid fire, high elevation, and speedy adjustment. Calibres are 20 mm to 140 mm (0.8–5.5 in) but most common pieces are 87 mm to 100 mm. Upper range limit is about 12 000 m (40 000 ft) and targets may be engaged at a few hundred feet. Guns are aimed visually or electronically so that the aircraft flies into the round or shellburst. The role of anti-aircraft guns has largely been replaced by ground-to-air guided missiles.

● **antiballistic missiles** ▶ High-speed nuclear weapons used to attack hostile ▷ballistic missiles. Operated by ground-based radar and computers, they rely for their final attack on their own guidance systems, destroying the target by radiation from their warheads. Short-range versions with low-yield warheads (e.g. US *Sprint*) are designed to seek and destroy targets within the earth's atmosphere; long-range missiles with high-yield warheads operate in space (e.g. US *Spartan*).

● **Antibes** ▶ 43 35N 7 07E A town in France, in the Alpes-Maritimes department. A tourist resort and a port for pleasure craft on the Côte d'Azur, it produces flowers, perfumes, and chocolates. Population (latest est): 60 000.

● **antibiotics** ▶ Drugs that are derived from microorganisms and are used to treat infections caused by bacteria or fungi. Synthetic drugs with similar properties are also known as antibiotics. Bactericidal antibiotics, such as ▷penicillin, actually kill bacteria, whereas bacteriostatic antibiotics, such as ▷tetracycline and ▷chloramphenicol, simply halt their growth. Examples of antifungal antibiotics are nystatin, griseofulvin, and the imidazoles (e.g. ketoconazole). Possible adverse effects of antibiotic treatment include allergic reactions, and the indiscriminate use of antibiotics has resulted in the appearance of some new life-threatening infections that do not respond to most existing drugs; efforts are under way to develop new antibiotics to combat these resistant strains of bacteria.

● **antibody** ▶ A protein produced by certain white blood cells (lymphocytes) that reacts specifically with and neutralizes a foreign protein (e.g. a bacterium), which is known as the **antigen**. Antibody production is stimulated by contact with the antigen: subsequent exposure to the antigen produces a greater antibody response, which provides the basis of ▷immunity. Antibodies contribute to the body's resistance to infection and are responsible for the rejection of foreign tissue or organ transplants. ▷*See also* monoclonal antibody.

● **Antichrist** ▶ In the New Testament, a person or institution opposed to Christ, whose appearance will precede His second coming (John 2.18–22). Some early Christians believed ▷Nero to be the Antichrist; many reformers, for example Wycliffe and Luther, saw the pope or the papacy in this role.

● **anticline** ▶ An arch-shaped ▷fold or upfold in folded rock strata, the oldest rocks occurring at the core. In areas of complex folding an upfold may have its youngest rocks at the core, the resulting structure being termed an antiform. *Compare* syncline.

● **anticoagulants** ▶ Drugs, such as ▷heparin and ▷warfarin, that interfere with blood clotting. They are used when there has been, or there is a risk of, clots forming in the blood vessels, as after ▷thrombosis of the leg veins.

● **Anti-Comintern Pact** ▶ An agreement among the Axis powers in opposition to the Comintern (or Third ▷International). Germany and Japan signed the Pact in 1936 to protect themselves against communism and they were later joined by Italy (1937) and Spain (1939).

● **Anti-Corn Law League** ▶ An organization formed in 1839 to work for the repeal of the ▷Corn Laws. Under the able leadership of Richard ▷Cobden and John ▷Bright, the League gained widespread support from manufacturers as well as workers and achieved its objective in 1846.

● **anticyclone** ▶ (*or* high) An area of atmospheric pressure higher than the surrounding air with one or more isobars of approximately circular form around its centre. Winds, generally light, circulate around the high pressure centre in a clockwise direction in the N hemisphere and anticlockwise in the S hemisphere. Calm settled weather is usually synonymous with anticyclones in temperate latitudes.

● **antidepressants** ▶ A class of drugs used to relieve depression. The most widely used are the tricyclic antidepressants, which include amitriptyline and imipramine. They provide a wide range of drugs to treat a variety of depressive symptoms, but can also have side effects, including dryness of the mouth and sedation. The SSRIs

(selective serotonin reuptake inhibitors), such as fluoxetine (Prozac), act by preventing the reabsorption in the brain of the neurotransmitter ▷serotonin. They are less sedative than the tricyclics. The MAO inhibitors prevent the action of the enzyme monoamine oxidase in breaking down adrenaline and related compounds that affect mood. These antidepressants may have serious side effects and are therefore restricted to the treatment of severe psychological disorders.

● **antidiuretic hormone** ▶ (ADH) ▷*See* diabetes (insipidus).

● **Antietam, Battle of** ▶ (17 September, 1862) A decisive engagement in the US Civil War, which prevented the Confederate capture of Washington, DC. In the last of a series of battles, the advance of the Confederate general Robert E. ▷Lee, was checked at Antietam by the Federal general George B. ▷McClellan. The South lost about 10 000 men but McClellan allowed Lee to withdraw into Virginia.

● **antiferromagnetism** ▶ The magnetic property of a material that has its microscopic magnetic ▷moments lined up in domains, as in ▷ferromagnetism, except that in these materials the antiparallel arrays oppose each other. The lower the temperature, the greater this alignment; up to a certain temperature, known as the Néel temperature, the relative magnetic ▷permeability is slightly greater than one and increases with temperature. Above this temperature the material is paramagnetic (*see* paramagnetism).

● **antifreeze** ▶ A substance added to water in cooling systems to lower the freezing point and thus prevent damage in cold weather from freezing. Glycols and methanol, together with a corrosion inhibitor, are commonly used.

● **antigen** ▷*See* antibody.

● **Antigone** ▶ In Greek mythology, the daughter of ▷Oedipus and Jocasta, whose story forms the basis of Sophocles' tragedy *Antigone*. When her father was banished from Thebes she accompanied him into exile in Colonus. Her brothers Eteocles and ▷Polyneices had agreed to reign alternately in Thebes, but Eteocles' refusal to yield the crown led to their killing each other in single combat. Despite the Theban senate's decree prohibiting the burial of Polyneices, Antigone performed the funeral rites for her brother. She was consequently ordered to be buried alive by Creon, ruler of Thebes, and hanged herself.

● **Antigonus I** ▶ (c. 382–301 BC) Macedonian general, nicknamed Monophthalmus or Cyclops (One-eye). After the death of his patron ▷Antipater, Antigonus became ruler of Asia Minor. He declared himself king in 306 but his ambition to rule a reunited Macedonian empire was opposed. His rivals combined forces, after Antigonus' successes against them individually, and defeated and killed him in battle at Ipsus.

● **Antigonus II Gonatas** ▶ (c. 320–239 BC) King of Macedon (276–239), who re-established Macedonian hegemony in Greece. He defeated Athens and Sparta in the Chremonidean War (c. 267–c. 262) and Ptolemy II of Egypt in the naval battle of Cos. During his reign the Macedonian court became a centre of culture.

● **Antigua and Barbuda** ▶ A West Indian country in the E Caribbean Sea, comprising the islands of Antigua, Barbuda, and Redonda.

Economy: Tourism is the chief source of revenue; sugar and cotton production are also important. Offshore banking services are being developed.

History: Antigua was discovered by Columbus (1493) and colonized by British settlers in 1632. It formed an associated state within the British Commonwealth from 1967 until gaining independence in 1981. It is a member of CARICOM. Elections in 1994 resulted in victory for the ruling Labour Party led by Lester Bird.

Antigua and Barbuda

Head of state	Queen Elizabeth II, represented by the governor-general, Sir James Carlisle
Official currency	dollar of 100 cents
Area	440 sq km (170 sq mi)
Population (1997 est)	64 500
Capital	St John's

● **antihistamines** ► Drugs that interfere with the action of ▷hista-mine. There are two types. H_1-antagonists (e.g. chlorpheniramine, cyclizine) prevent histamine from causing allergic reactions and are used to treat hay fever, nettle rash, and other allergies; these drugs are also taken to prevent travel sickness. H_2-antagonists (e.g. cimetidine, ranitidine) prevent histamine from stimulating the se-cretion of gastric juice and are used to treat peptic ulcers.

● **Anti-Lebanon Mountains** ► A mountain range running NE–SW for 150 km (93 mi) along the Lebanese-Syrian border and rising to 2814 m (9232 ft) at Mount Hermon.

● **Antilles** ► The islands of the West Indies, excluding the Bahamas. The group is divided into the ▷Greater Antilles and the ▷Lesser Antil-les.

● **Anti-Masonic Party** ► A minority US political party that arose after the disappearance of a former freemason in 1826. The widely held belief that the man had been murdered by freemasons for re-vealing their secrets led to the formation of the party to oppose Masonic candidates for office in the New York Assembly. Effective on the state level, the party held the first national nominating conven-tion in US politics (1831), a system later adopted by the major parties. The Anti-Masons merged with the Whigs (who opposed the policies of Andrew Jackson) in 1838.

● **antimatter** ► Matter in which the constituent atoms consist of antiparticles. For every elementary particle (*see* particle physics) there exists an antiparticle that is identical except for certain of its properties, such as electric charge and isospin number, which are of equal magnitude but opposite in sign. The photon and the neutral pion are their own antiparticles. An atom of antimatter would con-tain a nucleus of antiprotons and antineutrons surrounded by posi-trons (antielectrons). If matter were to meet antimatter, they would annihilate each other in a burst of radiation. In 1995 physicists at ▷CERN successfully created antimatter for one 30-millionth of a second. ▷*See also* annihilation.

● **antimony** ► (Sb) A metallic element, probably known in antiq-uity. It occurs in nature as the element and more commonly in the sulphide ▷stibnite (Sb_2S_3). The element exists in two forms: the normal metallic form, which is brittle bluish-white, and an amor-phous grey form. It is a poor conductor of heat and electricity. It forms the oxide (Sb_2O_3) by burning in air and the volatile hydride, stibine (SbH_3), which like many antimony compounds is toxic. Pure antimony is used in making ▷semiconductors; other uses include ad-dition to lead to increase its hardness in battery plates, in type metal, and as oxides or sulphides in paints, glasses, and ceramics. At no 51; at wt 121.75; mp 630.7°C; bp 1587°C.

● **anti-novel** ▷*See* nouveau roman.

● **Antioch** ► (modern Turkish name: Antakya) 36 12N 36 10E A town in central S Turkey, near the coast and the Syrian border. Founded in 301 BC, it had a large early Christian community, and there are no-table Roman mosaics in the Archaeological Museum. Population (1990): 123 871.

● **Antiochus I Soter** ► (324–261 BC) King of Syria (281–261) of the Seleucid dynasty. Antiochus lost some Seleucid territory to Egypt but achieved peace with Macedon (278) and repulsed a Gallic invasion, which earned him the title Soter (Saviour). He founded many cities.

● **Antiochus II** ► (c. 287–246 BC) King of Syria (261–246) of the Seleucid dynasty. Little is known of his reign apart from his reconquest (260–253) of some of the territory in Asia Minor lost by his father ▷Antiochus I Soter and his political marriage (252) to the Egyp-tian princess Berenice.

● **Antiochus (III) the Great** ► (c. 242–187 BC) King of Syria (223–187) of the Seleucid dynasty. After crushing separatist revolts at home, Antiochus initiated a policy of expansion. His incursions on Egyptian territory were temporarily halted by his defeat at Raphia (217) but his great campaign (212–206) through Armenia, Parthia, and Bactria to the River Indus paralleled that of Alexander the Great. He finally defeated the Egyptians in 198. Antiochus then became in-volved in hostile diplomacy with Rome and in 192 invaded Greece.

Driven out by the Romans (190), his defeat destroyed Seleucid power in the Mediterranean.

● **Antiochus IV Epiphanes** ► (c. 215–163 BC) King of Syria (175–163) of the Seleucid dynasty. Antiochus maintained the empire, cam-paigning successfully against the Egyptians until forced by the Romans to withdraw (168). He promoted Greek culture throughout the empire but met with resistance from the ▷Maccabees (167–160) when he ruthlessly imposed Greek religion on the Jews.

● **Antiochus VII Sidetes** ► (c. 159–129 BC) The last Seleucid King of Syria (139–129). Following early military successes, including the reconquest of Jerusalem (134), he attempted to postpone the Parthian conquest of the Seleucid empire and died in battle.

● **antioxidants** ► Substances that inhibit oxidation of such prod-ucts as foods, paints, plastics, fuels, etc. Natural antioxidants, includ-ing ascorbic acid (vitamin C), vitamin E, and beta carotene, reduce damage to cells caused by free ▷radicals.

● **antiparticle** ▷*See* antimatter.

● **Antipater** ► (397–319 BC) Macedonian general. Antipater was chief military and diplomatic aide to Philip of Macedon and then to Alexander the Great, becoming regent after Alexander's departure for the East. To maintain this position after Alexander's death, he suppressed internal rebellions and crushed the imperial ambitions of Alexander's second-in-command Perdiccas (d. 321). After Antip-ater's death Alexander's empire began to disintegrate.

● **Antipater** ► (d. 4 BC) The son of ▷Herod the Great. Disowned in in-fancy, but restored to favour in about 17 BC, he struggled ruthlessly to succeed his father. He had his half-brothers executed in about 7 BC but was himself executed shortly before Herod's own death.

● **Antipater the Idumaean** ► (d. 43 BC) Procurator (governor) of Judaea (47–43). His adroit manipulation of successive Roman back-ers, including ▷Caesar, who appointed him procurator, brought priv-ileges for Judaea and financial advantages for himself. He was assassinated and his son ▷Herod the Great subsequently succeeded to his position.

● **Antiphon** ► (c. 480–411 BC) Athenian orator, important in the de-velopment of a vigorous and precise Greek prose style. Antiphon con-spired to establish oligarchic rule at Athens (411) but a more moderate democratic government prevailed and he was tried and ex-ecuted despite a brilliant self-defence.

● **Antipodes Islands** ► 49 42S 178 50E A small group of rocky un-inhabited islands in the S Pacific Ocean, belonging to New Zealand. Their fur seal population has been greatly reduced by hunting. Area: 62 sq km (24 sq mi).

● **antipope** ► Those raised to the papacy in opposition to a lawfully elected pope. There have been about 40 antipopes. The first, Hippolitus, was created in the early 3rd century. During the later Roman Empire and during the middle ages most antipopes repre-sented rival factions supporting different political or doctrinal claims. In the 11th and 12th centuries some 14 antipopes were chosen by the Holy Roman Emperors, who had had until 1059 a con-siderable voice in papal elections and who resented the Church's growing independence from lay control. From 1378 another group of antipopes was elected following the ▷Great Schism, when a group of cardinals left Avignon (*see* Avignon papacy) to return to Rome; the popes remaining at Avignon and under French control were styled antipopes thereafter. The Council of Pisa (1409) elected a new pope to end the Schism, but he too was regarded as an antipope until unity was restored at the Council of ▷Constance (1515). There have been no antipopes since the mid-14th century.

● **antipsychotics** ► A group of drugs used to relieve agitation and other symptoms in patients suffering from schizophrenia or other se-rious mental disorders. Formerly known as major tranquillizers, antipsychotics are used in smaller doses to treat anxiety. Traditional antipsychotics, including the ▷phenothiazines and the butyro-phenones (e.g. haloperidol), can have severe side effects, including in-voluntary writhing movements. More recently developed drugs, such as clozapine and risperidone (the so-called atypical antipsychotics), have fewer side effects and are used to treat patients who do not respond to conventional treatment.

● **antique** ▶ An artefact of aesthetic and historical or sociological significance, now not in general use or manufacture. The term does not include painting and sculpture. Until recently an antique was required to predate about 1830, when factory production increased, but now import and export laws of most countries require an age of a hundred years for antiques. Antique collecting was a pastime of the wealthy aristocracy until the 20th century, when its increasing popularity has widened the scope of collectable items to include all kinds of domestic ephemera.

● **Antirrhinum** ▶ A genus of chiefly Mediterranean and W North American herbaceous plants (about 40 species). The most widely cultivated species is the ornamental snapdragon (*A. majus*), 30–80 cm high with brightly coloured two-lipped tubular flowers adapted to pollination by large bees. It grows naturally as a perennial but is usually treated as an annual and grown from seed. Family: *Scrophulariaceae*.

● **antisemitism** ▶ Hostility towards the ▷Jews, which has characterized their existence since the ▷diaspora (6th century BC). Its origins perhaps go back to the distrust invariably felt for a coherent minority held together by strong religious and cultural ties, which are themselves strengthened as the hostility intensifies. The early history of the Jews did nothing to dispel this inherent mistrust: represented as God's chosen people in the Old Testament and the betrayers of Christ in the New Testament, their unpopularity in medieval Europe was reflected in totally unfounded beliefs that they used Christian children as human sacrifices. Encouraged and, in some cases, forced to become moneylenders (an activity forbidden to Christians by canon law; *see* usury), they were by the 13th century persecuted throughout Europe. Expulsion (England, 1290; France, 1306; Spain, 1492), massacre (Germany, 1348; Spain, 1391), the Inquisition (1478), and papal bull (1555) deprived medieval Europe of large numbers of its Jews, many of whom enriched the Muslim countries of N Africa and Turkey. It was not until the 18th-century ▷Enlightenment had introduced a degree of religious freedom that they came back in any numbers. However, in the 19th century the earlier church-led antisemitism was replaced by a spurious nationalism, especially in Germany. In France, it became public in the ▷Dreyfus affair. In Russia, government-tolerated (and sometimes inspired) ▷pogroms were common in the late 19th and early 20th centuries but antisemitism reached its peak in Hitler's final solution, which cost the Jews six million lives (*see* holocaust). In the postwar years, since the establishment of the state of Israel, antisemitism has to some extent been replaced by Arab anti-Zionism. It does, however, persist, especially in E Europe.

● **antiseptic** ▶ A substance that kills bacteria and other dangerous microorganisms and can be applied to the skin (to cleanse wounds, before surgery, etc.) or taken internally. Antiseptics are generally distinguished from ▷disinfectants, which are too toxic to be used on or within the body.

● **Antisthenes** ▶ (c. 445–c. 360 BC) Greek philosopher and disciple of ▷Socrates. Antisthenes was a critic of society and is regarded as a formative influence on cynicism (*see* Cynics). Principally a moral philosopher, he argued for a simple and virtuous way of life that would lead to happiness.

● **antitank gun** ▶ Any flat-trajectory gun using ammunition suitable for destroying ▷tanks. Guns in tanks themselves are the most common examples. Artillery weapons are light low-silhouette easily deployed pieces. Short-range specialized missiles are replacing the lighter antitank guns.

● **antitoxin** ▶ An ▷antibody produced against a toxin. Antitoxins can be isolated from inoculated healthy animals and used to treat or prevent specific infections; for example, an antitoxin against tetanus is obtained from the plasma of animals inoculated against tetanus.

● **antitrust acts** ▶ US legislation to control ▷monopolies and preserve a freely competitive market. In the 19th century some businessmen fixed prices and destroyed rival businesses by manipulating raw materials and access to transport. The Sherman Antitrust Act (1890),

the first of several measures, prohibited contracts "in restraint of trade." Interpreted narrowly at first, these laws were strengthened by successive legislation (including the Clayton Act 1914 and the Antimerger Act 1950) prohibiting or restricting interlocking directorships, price fixing, and takeovers. In the UK, the less stringent Fair Trading Act (1973) performs similar functions.

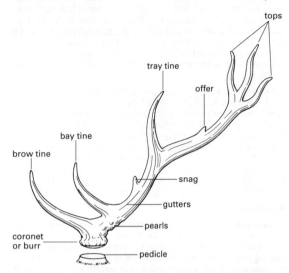

antlers ▶ The number of branches increases with the age of the stag. This antler has 6 branches; a stag with a head of 12 branches is called a royal.

● **antlers** ▶ The paired bony structures growing from the heads of deer, generally confined to males. In temperate regions the antlers begin to grow in early summer: they are at first covered with velvety skin, which is later shed. Used for fighting and display, the antlers are shed each year at the end of the mating season. Deer grow their first set of antlers, which are usually straight spikes, at the age of 1–2 years. The number of points is increased in successive years.

● **antlion** ▶ An insect belonging to a family (*Myrmeleontidae*) in which the adults resemble dragonflies and live only long enough to mate and lay eggs. The predatory larva lives 1–3 years, generally at the bottom of a conical pit in loose sand: any insect that falls into the pit is snapped up with its large jaws, which protrude from the sand. Order: ▷Neuroptera.

● **Antofagasta** ▶ 21 51S 102 18W A city in NW Chile, a port on the Pacific Ocean. It is a commercial and industrial centre. The chief industries are metal refining and founding; exports include nitrates and copper. The University of the North was established here in 1956. Population (1995 est): 236 730.

● **Antonello da Messina** ▶ (c. 1430–c. 1479) Italian painter, born in Messina (Sicily). He trained in Naples, where he probably learned the Flemish technique of oil painting; this he introduced to Venice during a visit in 1475. The realism of Flemish art also deeply influenced his style, particularly in *St Jerome in His Study* and *Portrait of a Man* (both National Gallery, London).

● **Antonescu, Ion** ▶ (1882–1946) Romanian general and politician. A pro-Nazi, he became prime minister (1940), replacing ▷Carol II's government with a totalitarian regime. In 1941 he commanded the army in Bessarabia. He was executed for war crimes.

● **Antonine Wall** ▶ A Roman frontier defence work 58.5 km (36.5 mi) long, linking the Firths of Forth and Clyde in S Scotland and still surviving in places. It was built about 142 AD by Lollius Urbicus, governor of Britain, for the emperor ▷Antoninus Pius, and abandoned in 196 AD. A military road linked 29 small forts along a turf wall 3 m (10 ft) high and 4.3 m (14 ft) wide, behind a substantial ditch. ▷See also Hadrian's Wall.

● **Antoninus Pius** ▶ (86–161 AD) Roman emperor (138–61).

Antoninus was admitted by Emperor Hadrian to his advisory council and adopted as his successor in 138. His reign was peaceful and generally prosperous. Only minor campaigns were fought abroad and noted legal reforms were introduced; the ▷Antonine Wall was built during his reign. He was deified after his death.

● **Antonioni, Michelangelo** ▶ (1912–) Italian film maker. Born into a bourgeois provincial family, in 1939 he moved to Rome to work for the magazine *Cinema*. His first films were *Gente del Po* (1943–47) and *Cronaca di un amore* (1950). Later films include *L'avventura* (1959), *La notte* (1961), *Blow-Up* (1966), *Zabriskie Point* (1970), and *The Passenger* (1975). Despite having lost the power of speech owing to a stroke, he returned to directing after a long interval with *Beyond the Clouds* (1995).

● **Antrim** ▶ **1.** A historic county of NE Northern Ireland, bordering on the Atlantic Ocean and the Irish Sea. Its administrative powers were devolved to the new district councils in 1973. It consists mainly of a basalt plateau sloping inland to Lough Neagh in the SW. There are many peat bogs in the interior. On the N coast is the famous ▷Giant's Causeway. Outside Belfast the county is agricultural, producing oats, potatoes, flax, and livestock. Industry includes the manufacture of man-made fibres, which has largely replaced linen production. Area: 3100 sq km (1200 sq mi). **2.** A district in Northern Ireland, in Co Antrim. Area: 415 sq km (160 sq mi). Population (1991): 45 400.

● **An-tung** ▷*See* Andong.

● **Antwerp** ▶ (Flemish name: Antwerpen; French name: Anvers) 51 13N 4 25E A city in Belgium, on the River Scheldt. It is one of the largest seaports in the world and has important shipbuilding and ship-repairing industries. Other industries include oil refining, diamond cutting, textiles, and electronics. It possesses many fine buildings, including the 14th-century gothic cathedral, the printer Christopher Plantin's house (now a museum), and the 16th-century Butchers' Hall. It is the birthplace of Rubens and Van Dyck; some of their paintings form part of the collection in the Royal Gallery of Fine Arts. There is a large Flemish-speaking population.

History: it was the leading commercial centre of western Europe in the 16th century but religious strife and its sacking by Spaniards (1576) led to its decline, further hastened by the closure of the River Scheldt (1648). Its economy revived when Belgium bought the shipping rights of the river from the Netherlands. Antwerp was occupied and damaged in both World Wars. Population (1996 est): 455 852.

● **Anu** ▶ The Mesopotamian god of the heavens and father of all the gods. He represented the infinite and all-embracing sky and was worshipped as the source of all order and rule.

● **Anubis** ▶ Egyptian god of the dead, usually represented as a crouching jackal or a jackal-headed man. He supervised the weighing of the souls of the dead, and also the embalming of the body. He was reputed to have invented this process to preserve the body of ▷Osiris.

● **Anura** ▶ An order of amphibians (over 2000 species) comprising the ▷frogs and ▷toads. Anurans are specialized for jumping, having a short backbone, no tail, and large muscular hind legs. The eggs hatch into tadpoles, which undergo ▷metamorphosis. This order is also called the *Salientia*.

● **Anuradhapura** ▶ 8 20N 80 25E A town in Sri Lanka. The ancient capital of the island (5th century BC to 8th century AD), it is the site of the sacred bo tree descended from the original at ▷Buddh Gaya and the first Buddhist temple in Ceylon. Population (1995 est): 42 600.

● **anus** ▷*See* intestine.

● **Anvers** ▷*See* Antwerp.

● **Anville, Jean-Baptiste Bourguignon d'** ▶ (1697–1782) French geographer and cartographer, specializing in ancient and medieval geography. As geographer to the French king from 1719, he improved maps of Italy, Asia, and Africa.

● **anxiety** ▶ Generalized pervasive fear. Anxiety is partly the feeling of apprehension, partly the behaviour of avoiding frightening situations, and partly the associated bodily changes, such as sweating, a fast pulse, and tense muscles. It is normal to feel anxiety when some danger is present or expected. Severe anxiety out of all proportion to

any real threats can be treated by tranquillizing drugs, ▷psychotherapy, ▷behaviour therapy, and ▷autosuggestion. Neuroses are now more usually known as **anxiety disorders**. ▷*See also* neurosis; obsession; panic disorder; phobia; post-traumatic stress disorder.

● **Anyang** ▶ 36 04N 114 20E A city in E China, in Henan province. The last capital (1384–1111 BC) of the Shang dynasty, it has many archaeological remains. Industries include cotton and steel. Population (1995 est): 590 996.

● **ANZAC** ▶ The Australian and New Zealand Army Corps, which served in World War I in Europe and the Middle East. On ANZAC Day, 25 April (the day of the ANZAC landing in Gallipoli in 1915), in Australia and New Zealand the dead of both World Wars are remembered.

● **Anzengruber, Ludwig** ▶ (1839–89) Austrian dramatist and novelist. Originally an actor, he wrote successful realistic plays about rural life, including the tragedy *Der Meineidbauer* (1871) and the comedy *Die Kreuzelschreiber* (1872).

● **Anzio** ▶ 41 27N 12 38E A seaport and resort in Italy, in Lazio on the Tyrrhenian Sea. The birthplace of Nero, it was the scene of Allied landings in World War II. Population (1991 est): 32 383.

● **ANZUS** ▶ A security treaty concluded in 1951 by Australia, New Zealand, and the USA, requiring members to provide mutual aid in the event of aggression by foreign powers.

● **Aomori** ▶ 40 50N 140 43E A city in Japan, in N Honshu on Mutsu Bay. One of Japan's major ports, it exports rice, fish, and timber. Population (1993 est): 288 291.

● **aorta** ▷*See* artery; heart.

● **Aosta** ▶ 45 43N 7 19E A town in Italy, capital of Valle d'Aosta on the River Dora Baltea. Situated amidst impressive mountain scenery, it has important Roman remains and a cathedral (12th–19th centuries). Population (1990): 36 339.

● **aoudad** ▶ A tawny-coloured sheep, *Ammotragus lervia*, also called Barbary sheep, that is the only wild sheep in Africa. Aoudads live in dry rocky northern regions. They stand 102 cm at the shoulder and have outward-curving horns.

● **Aouita, Saïd** ▶ (1960–) Moroccan middle-distance runner. He was the world record holder in the 2000 m event from 1987 to 1995. He also held the world record for the 1500 m (1987–93) and 5000 m (1987–94) events.

● **Apache** ▶ A North American Indian people with six major divisions: the Jicarillos, Mescaleros, Chiricahuas, and Western Apache of the S Plains and SW region of the USA; and the Lipan and Kiowa-Apache living further to the east. Their language is of ▷Athabascan type. They frequently raided the villages of Pueblo Indians and Spanish settlements to steal cattle and horses. In addition to hunting, some groups practised farming. Normally tribal unity was slight but occasionally independent local groups of matrilineal kin would form alliances under the leadership of chiefs, such as Cochise, Geronimo, and Victorio, who led guerrilla campaigns against the Americans during the late 19th century. There are today about 10 000 Apaches on reservations.

● **apartheid** ▶ (Afrikaans: apartness) The policy of separate development of the White and non-White populations in South Africa, in force from 1948 until 1994. Apartheid, which was introduced by the Afrikaner National Party, aimed to divide South Africa into separate regions for Whites and Blacks. As a result of this policy, in 1961 South Africa was forced to withdraw from the British Commonwealth. In 1985 non-Whites won limited constitutional rights and interracial marriage was allowed. Increased internal unrest, combined with pressure from outside, led to the declaration of a state of emergency in 1986, sanctioning restrictions on press coverage and detention of Black activists. Continuing pressure forced the resignation of President P. W. ▷Botha in 1989. In 1990 ▷de Klerk began dismantling apartheid. By the end of June 1991 all apartheid laws had been repealed, but Blacks did not have the vote and segregation persisted. In 1992 68.6% of Whites voted in a referendum to continue the reform process and a new constitution enfranchising all South African adults was adopted in 1993.

● **apatite** ▶ The commonest phosphorous mineral, of composition $Ca_5(PO_4)_3(OH,F,Cl)$. It is found as an accessory mineral in many igneous rocks, especially pegmatites, as well as metamorphosed limestones. It is used in the production of fertilizers. The enamel of teeth is composed almost entirely of apatite (*see also* fluoridation) and the chief inorganic constituent of bone is hydroxyapatite, $Ca_{10}(PO_4)_6$-$(OH)_2$.

● **Apatosaurus** ▶ A herbivorous dinosaur, which has also been called *Brontosaurus*, of the late Jurassic period, which ended about 135 million years ago. Up to 21 m long and weighing up to 30 tonnes, it had massive pillar-like legs, a long neck and tail, and spent most of its time in swamps, coming ashore to lay eggs. With its nostrils placed high on its head, it was able to stand almost fully submerged. Order: ▷*Saurischia*. □fossil.

● **ape** ▶ A highly intelligent tailless ▷primate belonging to the family *Pongidae* (11 species), found in central Africa and S Asia. There are two subfamilies: the arboreal *Hylobatinae* (*see* gibbon; siamang) and the ground-dwelling *Ponginae* (*see* chimpanzee; orang-utan; gorilla), also called great apes. Forest apes are often solitary but ground-dwelling apes live in complex societies and all have highly developed means of communication.

Some tailless primates of other families are also called apes.

● **Apeldoorn** ▶ 52 13N 5 57E A city in the E central Netherlands, in Gelderland province. The 17th-century Castle Loo, a royal summer residence, is nearby. Its industries include electronics, blanket, cloth, and paper production. Population (1996 est): 150 915.

● **Apelles** ▶ (4th century BC) The court painter of Alexander the Great. He seems to have specialized in portraits and allegories aiming, like many contemporary artists, at *trompe l'oeil* realism. His most famous pictures included *Aphrodite Rising from the Waves* and *Alexander as Zeus*. His style of portraiture influenced fashions in painting for more than two centuries.

● **Apennines** ▶ (Italian name: Appennini) A mountain range in Italy. It extends about 1050 km (652 mi) down the Italian peninsula from the Maritime Alps in the NW to the Strait of Messina in the S. The range is not generally very high but it affords few easy crossing points; the highest peak is Monte Corno at 2914 m (9560 ft). The Apennines are volcanic in the S (*see* Vesuvius).

● **aperture synthesis** ▷*See* radio telescope.

● **aphelion** ▶ The point in the orbit of a body around the sun at which the body is furthest from the sun. The earth is at aphelion on 3 July. *Compare* perihelion.

● **aphid** ▶ An □insect, also called a plant louse, belonging to a family (*Aphidae*) of important plant pests. Small, soft, and often wingless, aphids have long thin antennae and weak legs and are usually green (greenfly), red, or brown. There are two thin tubes projecting from the abdomen from which honeydew is secreted. Aphids feed on plant sap, piercing plant tissues with sharp beaklike mouthparts, causing leaf curl, retardation of growth, and often forming galls. The aphid's great fecundity and the ability of the female to reproduce by ▷parthenogenesis results in frequent outbreaks of the pest. Order: ▷*Hemiptera*.

● **Aphraates** ▶ (4th century AD) The first Father of the Syrian Church. He lived a monastic life and may also have been a bishop. He wrote numerous tractates summarizing the Christian faith.

● **aphrodisiac** ▶ A drug that increases sexual desire or sexual performance. No true aphrodiasic has yet been discovered and most preparations act (if at all) by suggestion. Some drugs (such as alcohol and morphine) produce a general euphoria and reduce inhibitions but usually have an adverse effect on sexual performance. Local irritants, such as cantharides (Spanish fly), can prolong an erection at the cost of considerable discomfort.

● **Aphrodite** ▶ In Greek mythology, the goddess of love, called ▷Venus by the Romans. According to Homer she was the daughter of Dione and Zeus; Hesiod says that she was born from the foam after

▷Uranus had been castrated and his genitals thrown into the sea. She was said to have emerged from the sea at Paphos in Cyprus or at the island of Cythera. She was the wife of Hephaestus but was unfaithful to him and had an affair with Ares. She is portrayed by later writers as the mother of Eros. Paris' choice of her as the most beautiful of the three goddesses at the wedding feast of Peleus and Thetis (the others were Hera and Athena) caused the ▷Trojan War. She was revered throughout Greece as the personification of spiritual love but she also embodied sensual lust.

● **Apia** ▶ 13 48S 171 45W The capital and chief port of Samoa, in N Upolu on the S Pacific Ocean. The head of state's residence was formerly the home of Robert Louis Stevenson. Copra, bananas, and cocoa are exported. Population (1991): 32 859.

● **Apiaceae** ▷*See* Umbelliferae.

● **apiculture** ▷*See* beekeeping.

● **Apis** ▶ The Egyptian bull god. Originally a minor fertility god, he became associated with ▷Ptah and later ▷Osiris, at which point he became known as Serapis. A bull sacred to him was kept until another with appropriate markings was found; it was then ritually drowned in the Nile and its body mummified in the Serapeum vault at Saqqarah.

apocalypse ▶ Detail from the *Apocalypse* polyptych by Jacopo Alberegno (d. 1397), showing "The woman clothed with the sun and the seven-headed dragon."

● **apocalypse** ▶ (Greek: revelation) In the New Testament, the Revelation of St John the Divine (*see* Revelation, Book of). The term is also used of various noncanonical writings, such as the *Book of Enoch*, and of parts of the Old Testament books of *Isaiah*, *Ezekiel*, and *Daniel*. These are all examples of "apocalyptic literature." Full of symbolism and imagery, they describe visions of a great new era that will suddenly supersede the present age of suffering.

● **Apocrypha** ▶ (Greek: hidden things) Twelve books taken over by the early Christian Church from the Greek version of the Old Testament but not forming part of the Hebrew Bible. They originated in the Hellenistic Judaism of Alexandria but were not accepted as canonical by orthodox Jews and were treated in various ways in Christian Bibles. In the ▷Vulgate, most of them are printed with the Old Testament but they are omitted or printed as a separate section in Protestant versions of the Bible. They are: I Esdras, Tobit, Judith, the Rest of Esther, the Wisdom of Solomon, Ecclesiasticus, Baruch with the Epistle of Jeremy, the Song of the Three Holy Children, the History of Susanna, Bel and the Dragon, the Prayer of Manasses, and I and II Maccabees.

● **apogee** ▶ The point in the orbit of the moon or of an artificial satellite around the earth at which the body is furthest from the earth. *Compare* perigee.

● **Apollinaire, Guillaume** ▶ (Wilhelm de Kostrowitzky; 1880–1918) French poet. Born in Italy, he settled in Paris in 1900. A champion of ▷cubism and other avantgarde movements, he blended lyricism with experiment in his poetry, first collected in *Alcools* (1913). While recovering from a head wound sustained in World War I, he wrote a surrealist play, *Les Mamelles de Tirésias* (1917), and a modernist manifesto, *L'Esprit nouveau et les poètes*. The poems in *Calligrammes* (1918) included daring typographical experiments. He died in the 1918 flu epidemic.

● **Apollo** ▶ A Greek god symbolic of light, reason, and male beauty. He is also associated with medicine, prophecy, music and poetry, the care of animals and crops, morality, and the maintenance of society. He and his sister ▷Artemis were the children of ▷Zeus by ▷Leto. He established his oracle at Delphi after killing Python, its guardian dragon.

● **Apollo moon programme** ▶ The US programme to land men on the moon by 1970, announced by President Kennedy in 1961. The programme was directed by ▷NASA. The preliminary manned Mercury (1961–63) and Gemini (1965–66) projects provided valuable experience. A Saturn V rocket launched the Apollo spacecraft towards the moon and, once the craft was in lunar orbit, a capsule—the lunar module—descended to the moon's surface carrying two astronauts. The third astronaut remained in the orbiting craft. At the end of the surface mission the lunar module's descent stage was left on the moon while its ascent stage was shot into lunar orbit and docked with the orbiting craft. Following the transfer of the two astronauts, the ascent stage was jettisoned and the spacecraft returned to earth. The astronauts travelled to and from the moon in the command module, the rocket engines for in-flight manoeuvres, fuel cells, etc., being carried in the separate service module. The latter was jettisoned prior to re-entering the earth's atmosphere; the command module finally splashed down in the ocean. The first six Apollo missions were unmanned test flights, the next four being manned. Apollo 11 made the first manned lunar landing in July, 1969. Of the six ensuing missions, all, except Apollo 13, were highly successful, the scientific information obtained increasing with each lunar landing.

● **Apollonius** ▶ (2nd century AD) Greek grammarian, nicknamed Dyskolos (Bad-tempered). Of his 29 works on grammar, 4 survive. He introduced critical methods, seeking explanations rather than descriptions of sentence structure.

● **Apollonius of Perga** ▶ (c. 261–c. 190 BC) Greek mathematician, who studied under ▷Archimedes. In a series of eight books, he described the curves known as ▷conic sections, comprising the circle, ellipse, parabola, and hyperbola.

● **Apollonius of Rhodes** ▶ (3rd century BC) Greek epic poet. He was sometime head of the Library of Alexandria and was the chief rival of the poet ▷Callimachus. His four-volume *Argonautica*, in the

style of ▷Homer, tells the story of the quest for the ▷Golden Fleece and is notable for its sympathetic treatment of Medea's love for Jason. He also wrote epigrams, and commentaries on other Greek poets.

● **Apollonius of Tyana** ▶ (1st century AD) Pythagorean philosopher and reputed miracle worker, from Tyana in Cappadocia. His biography (c. 200 AD) by the Roman Flavius Philostratus was possibly commissioned as anti-Christian propaganda by the empress Julia Domna.

● **apologetics** ▶ In Christianity, the defence of the faith by theologians using intellectual and philosophical arguments. The name apologists refers especially to 2nd-century writers, such as ▷Justin Martyr and ▷Tertullian, who argued for Christianity against paganism. Later apologists defended orthodox Christian doctrines against heresies. In the 20th century apologists have attempted to explain Christian belief in a scientific age.

● **apomixis** ▶ The formation and development of an embryo without the fusion of male and female sex cells. This can occur in both plants and animals but is more common in plants. The embryo is usually formed from the unfertilized egg (*see* parthenogenesis).

Apollo moon programme ▶ Edwin Aldrin on the upper north surface of the moon.

Apollo moon programme

craft	astronauts	launch date	comments
Apollo 7	W. Schirra W. Cunningham D. Eisele	11 October, 1968	first manned flight of Apollo spacecraft
Apollo 8	F. Borman J. Lovell W. Anders	21 December, 1968	first manned flight around moon
Apollo 9	J. McDivitt D. Scott R. Schweickart	3 March, 1969	complete Apollo craft tested in earth orbit
Apollo 10	T. Stafford J. Young E. Cernan	18 May, 1969	rehearsal of moon landing
Apollo 11	N. Armstrong E. Aldrin M. Collins	16 July, 1969	first manned moon landing, 20 July
Apollo 12	C. Conrad A. Bean R. Gordon	14 November, 1969	second moon landing
Apollo 13	J. Lovell F. Haise J. Swigert	11 April, 1970	mission aborted after in-flight explosion in service module
Apollo 14	A. Shepard E. Mitchell S. Roosa	31 January, 1971	third moon landing
Apollo 15	D. Scott J. Irwin A. Worden	26 July, 1971	fourth moon landing
Apollo 16	J. Young C. Duke T. Mattingly	16 April, 1972	fifth moon landing
Apollo 17	E. Cernan H. Schmitt R. Evans	7 December, 1972	last moon landing

● **apoplexy** ▷See stroke.

● **apoptosis** ▶ Programmed cell death, which occurs naturally during the development and maintenance of animal tissues and organs. During these processes more cells are produced than are required for building tissues and organs. The embryonic hand, for example, is a spadelike structure on which fingers develop as the cells between them undergo apoptosis. The unwanted cells are programmed to die, either because the chemical signals that direct them to go on living are suppressed or because they receive a specific signal to die. It is thought that failure of apoptosis is associated with the uncontrolled cell growth in leukaemia and other cancers.

● **aposematic coloration** ▷See mimicry.

● **a positiori knowledge** ▷See a priori knowledge.

● **apostasy** ▷See heresy.

● **Apostles** ▶ In the New Testament, the 12 men chosen by Jesus as his disciples who, after his death, were to spread his teaching throughout the Roman world. Originally they were: Andrew, Bartholomew (*or* Nathaniel), James son of Alphaeus, James son of Zebedee, John, Jude (*or* Thaddeus), Judas Iscariot, Matthew (*or* Levi), Philip, Simon Peter, Simon the Zealot, and Thomas. After his suicide Judas Iscariot was replaced by Matthias. St Paul is also included among the Apostles because of his claim to having seen Jesus after the resurrection. ▷See also Acts of the Apostles.

● **Apostles' Creed** ▶ A Christian profession of faith in three sections concerning God the Father, Jesus Christ, and the Holy Spirit. Widely used in the Western Churches, it is of uncertain date but its present title first occurs in a letter of St Ambrose of about 390 AD.

● **Apostolic Constitutions** ▶ Eight books of Christian ecclesiastical administrative regulations and instructions for worship. Although its full title is "Ordinances of the Holy Apostles through Clement," and it ends with the 85 "Apostolic Canons," it probably originated in late 4th-century Syria and not from the Apostles. Much of it is derived from the 3rd-century *Didascalia Apostolorum* and the 2nd-century *Didache*, significant sources of information about the early Church.

● **apostolic succession** ▶ A Christian doctrine held by the Roman Catholic and Orthodox Churches and by some Anglicans. It claims that as the Apostles appointed the first bishops there is a continuous succession from the Apostles to the present ministries; the authority given by Christ to the Apostles has thus passed to the ministries of these Churches.

● **Appalachian Mountains** ▶ A mountain range in North America extending NE–SW from the Gaspé Peninsula, in Canada, to Alabama and separating the Mississippi-Missouri lowlands from the Atlantic coastal plain. It consists of a series of mountain ranges and plateaus, including the ▷Allegheny Mountains, the ▷Catskill Mountains, the Blue Ridge Mountains of Virginia, and the White Mountains of New Hampshire. Its highest point is Mount Mitchell, at 2038 m (6684 ft). Coalmining is important, providing anthracite and bitumen; iron ore is also extracted. Poor communications and lack of employment have contributed to a regional assistance programme in the area. It also contains the **Appalachian Trail**, the longest continuous footpath in the world.

● **Appaloosa** ▶ An American breed of spotted riding horse with a wispy mane and tail. The white Appaloosa is completely white with dark spots over the whole body but other types may be of any colour as long as the hindquarters are white with spots of the colour of the rest of the coat. Height: 1.47–1.60 m (14½–15¾ hands).

● **apparent magnitude** ▷See magnitude.

● **appeal** ▶ In law, the review of a court decision by a higher court, usually at the request of one of the parties to the case. The decisions of some administrative or professional bodies may also be appealed against in the courts. Appeals in ▷common law systems are usually based on alleged errors of law in the original trial, but may sometimes also be based on errors of fact. ▷See also courts of law.

● **appeasement** ▶ The policy implemented by the British prime minister, Neville ▷Chamberlain, and his French counterpart, Édouard ▷Daladier, of giving way to the demands of Hitler and Mussolini in the hope of maintaining peace. It culminated in the ▷Munich Agreement (1938) and was finally shown to be futile in 1939, when Hitler seized Czechoslovakia (March) and then precipitated World War II by marching into Poland (September). Strongly opposed by Winston Churchill, appeasement has been seen by some apologists as an attempt on the part of Britain and France to buy the time required to be able to confront the Germans with the necessary military strength.

● **Appel, Karel** ▶ (1921–) Dutch painter and sculptor, who cofounded the COBRA group of northern European expressionists in 1948. Appel paints in a turbulent semiabstract style that shows the influence of primitive art. He moved to Paris in 1950 and since 1957 has lived mainly in New York.

● **appendicitis** ▶ Inflammation of the ▷appendix. Appendicitis is most common in childhood and adolescence. It usually starts with a vague pain around the navel that becomes localized in the right lower region of the abdomen. Diarrhoea may also occur. Surgical removal to prevent rupture of the appendix and subsequent ▷peritonitis is usually required.

● **appendix** ▶ (*or* vermiform appendix) A thin blind-ended tube, 7–10 cm long, that opens from the end of the large intestine. It has no known function in man and is prone to infection (*see* appendicitis). In herbivorous animals (e.g. rabbits and cows) the appendix is large and functions in the digestion of vegetable matter. ▷See Plate II.

● **Appert, Nicolas** ▶ (1750–1841) French inventor, who discovered that food can be preserved by boiling it in sealed containers. In 1812 he opened the world's first commercial canning factory.

● **Appian Way** ▶ The road, built about 312 BC by the statesman Appius Claudius, between Rome and Capua. It was the first in the strategic network of Roman roads. A short stretch is still visible near Rome.

● **apple** ▶ A deciduous tree or shrub of the genus *Malus* (about 35 species), native to N temperate regions and widely cultivated for their rounded fleshy ⁰fruits (pomes). Several species have been cultivated, especially *M. pumila* of W Asia, with the development of numerous varieties of dessert, cooking, and ▷cider apples. Shoots of the required variety are grafted onto selected rootstocks. Some varieties are ornamental. Apples are also used for soft drinks and as a source of pectin. Family: *Rosaceae*. ▷See also crab apple.

● **Appleby** ▶ 54 36N 2 29W An ancient market town in NW England, in Cumbria on the River Eden. Appleby has a castle, a bullring, and holds an annual horse fair. Population (1991): 2570.

● **Appleton layer** ▷See ionosphere.

● **Appomattox** ▶ 37 21N 78 51W A town in the USA, in central Virginia. The Confederate leader, Robert E. Lee, surrendered here to Ulysses Grant on 9 April, 1865, effectively ending the US Civil War.

● **APR** ▶ (annual percentage rate) ▷See interest.

● **apricot** ▶ A tree, *Prunus armenica*, native to China and widely grown in warm temperate countries, especially Spain, for its fruits. It is 6–9 m tall and has white five-petalled flowers and heart-shaped leaves. The orange-yellow fruits have sweet flesh and smooth stones. Family: *Rosaceae*.

● **April Theses** ▶ The ▷Bolshevik party programme devised by ▷Lenin during the ▷Russian Revolution (1917). Its demands included the cessation of Bolshevik support for the Provisional Government, Russia's withdrawal from World War I, and the redistribution of land among the peasants.

● **a priori knowledge** ▶ Any kind of knowledge that is in no way derived from sense experience, observation, or experiment. Many philosophers therefore hold that a priori knowledge is impossible. However, those attracted to ▷intuitionism have defended its possibility, especially with regard to theological problems. Kant insisted on the reality of a priori knowledge in the form of the necessary conditions of our having any experience at all, e.g. the notions of causality, space, and time. Knowledge derived from experience is called **a postiori knowledge.**

● **apse** ▶ A semicircular or polygonal eastern end of a church, characteristic of the ▷basilica and ▷romanesque and ▷Norman architecture. Seats for the clergy ran round the apse walls behind the centrally placed altar.

● **Apuleius, Lucius** ▶ (2nd century AD) Roman writer and rhetorician. Educated at Carthage and Athens, he travelled in the East before returning to Africa to marry Pudentilla, a rich widow. His *Apologia* is his defence against a charge that he had won her by magic. *The Golden Ass*, the only surviving complete Latin novel, describes the misadventures of one Lucius, who is accidentally turned into an ass; he is finally restored to human form by Isis.

● **Apulia** ▶ (or Puglia) A region in SE Italy, on the Adriatic Sea. It consists of lowlands in the N and S (the "heel" of Italy) and a hilly central area. Wheat is the main agricultural crop; tobacco, vegetables, olives, figs, vines, and almonds are also produced. Manufacturing industry is mainly related to agriculture although modern industries are being developed. Area: 19 347 sq km (7470 sq mi). Population (1994 est): 4 065 603. Capital: Bari.

● **Aqaba** ▶ 29 32N 35 00E A port in Jordan, on the **Gulf of Aqaba**, a narrow inlet at the NE end of the Red Sea. Aqaba was the Roman stronghold of Aelana. Being Jordan's only port, it has been considerably expanded, despite difficult navigation and an exposed site, to handle the export of phosphates. Population (1990 est): 46 090.

● **Aquae Sulis** ▷*See* Bath.

● **aquamarine** ▶ A pale blue or green variety of ▷beryl. Many fine specimens of this gemstone come from Brazil, Madagascar, and California.

● **aqua regia** ▶ A fuming yellow corrosive mixture of one part ▷nitric acid to three or four parts ▷hydrochloric acid. It dissolves all metals, even gold, and is used in ▷metallurgy.

● **aquarium** ▶ A receptacle containing fresh or salt water for maintaining aquatic plants or animals (particularly fish) or a building in which such receptacles are kept or displayed. To duplicate natural conditions, modifications including the use of a water heater (for tropical species), aerator, and filter may be necessary. The first public aquarium was opened at the London Zoo in Regent's Park, London, in 1853.

● **Aquarius** ▶ (Latin: Water Bearer) A large constellation in the S sky, lying on the ▷zodiac between Pisces and Capricornus.

● **aquatint** ▶ An etching technique that produces a tonal effect similar to that of wash drawing. A satisfactory method was invented in the 1760s by a Frenchman, Jean Baptiste Le Prince (1733–81). Sharply defined areas of tone are employed, usually in conjunction with etched lines. A printing plate is sprinkled with powdered asphaltum or resin, which is then fixed to the plate by heating. Stopping-out varnish is used to mask different areas as the plate is immersed for varying lengths of time in an acid bath. ▷Goya, ▷Picasso, and ▷Miró have used the technique with outstanding effect.

● **aquavit** ▶ A ▷spirit distilled from grains and flavoured with caraway seeds. It is best served ice cold. Aquavit is drunk predominantly in Scandinavia.

● **Aquaviva, Claudio** ▶ (1543–1615) Italian churchman, the fifth general of the Society of Jesus, elected in 1581. The son of a nobleman, he saw Jesuit numbers increase from 5000 to 13 000 during his office and laid down definitive educational guidelines for the order in *Ratio studiorum* (1599).

● **aqueduct** ▶ A narrow bridge, channel, or conduit designed to enable water to flow at a steady rate over an irregular natural terrain, such as a valley. Aqueducts were built by the Greeks, but the technique was developed to its highest level of sophistication by the Romans. Impressive Roman examples still survive at Nîmes, Segovia, and Rome. Much the same principles are still used in modern irrigation systems throughout the world.

● **Aquila** ▶ (Latin: Eagle) An equatorial constellation lying in the Milky Way near Cygnus. The brightest star is ▷Altair.

● **Aquilegia** ▶ A genus of perennial herbaceous plants (100 species) of temperate regions, commonly known as columbines. Their showy flowers have petals with long honey-secreting spurs. A favourite garden flower, aquilegias have been cultivated since the 16th century. Many modern garden hybrids, which have large long-spurred flowers, are derived from the European columbine (*A. vulgaris*), 40–100 cm high with purple to white flowers. Family: *Ranunculaceae*.

● **Aquilèia** ▶ 45 47N 13 22E A town in N Italy, at the head of the Adriatic Sea. Founded by the Romans in 181 BC, it was of great strategic and military importance but failed to regain its former prominence following its destruction by Attila in 452 AD. Population (1990): 67 820.

St Thomas Aquinas ▶ A portrait painted c. 1476 by Justus van Gent (Louvre, Paris).

● **Aquinas, St Thomas** ▶ (c. 1225–74) Italian Dominican theologian, scholastic philosopher, and Doctor of the Church, known as *Doctor Angelicus*. Born near Naples, the son of Count Landulf of Aquino, he was educated at the Benedictine school at Monte Cassino and at the University of Naples. Joining the Dominican Order in 1244 in spite of parental opposition, he became a pupil of ▷Albertus Magnus in Paris (1245) and followed him to Cologne in 1248. He returned to Paris as a lecturer in 1252, becoming a leading defender of the Dominicans against their critics at the University of Paris. He was a lecturer and theological adviser to the papal Curia between 1259 and 1269 and then taught at Paris until 1272, when he was appointed a professor at Naples. He died at Fossanova on his way to the Council of Lyons and was canonized in 1323. His prolific writings include commentaries on the Scriptures, on Aristotle and other philosophers, and academic disputations. His two most influential works are the *Summa contra gentiles* (1259–64), written for the use of missionaries, and the uncompleted *Summa theologica* (1266–73), the first systematic work on Latin theology. In opposition to the Averroists (*see* Averroes) and Augustinians he attempted to reconcile Christian faith and human reason. The Roman Catholic Church recognizes him as one of its most important theologians. Feast day: 7 March.

● **Aquino, Cory** ► (Maria Corazón Aquino; 1933–) Philippine stateswoman; president (1986–92). She succeeded her assassinated husband **Benigno S. Aquino** (1933–83) as leader of the opposition to the corrupt Marcos regime, becoming head of state following the overthrow of Marcos. Her government survived a number of attempted coups by the military.

● **Aquitaine** ► (Latin name: Aquitania) A planning region in SW France, bordering on the Bay of Biscay. Formerly an administrative region in Roman Gaul, it extended from the Pyrenees N to the River Loire. It became an independent duchy under the Merovingians (7th century). The marriages of Eleanor of Aquitaine to Louis VII of France and then to Henry II of England resulted in rival French-English claims to the territory (*see* Hundred Years' War). Area: 41 408 sq km (15 984 sq mi). Population (1995 est): 2 866 300.

● **arabesque** ► A type of decorative design employing intricate geometrical patterns on a flat surface. The term (meaning "Arabian") was first used in England in the mid-17th century to describe panels of scrollwork ornamentation that were thought to resemble the Arab style. Historically, however, arabesque decoration is Greco-Roman in origin.

● **Arab horse** ► An ancient breed of horse originally bred by the Bedouins in Arabia. It is usually grey, chestnut, or bay with a long silky mane and tail and an arched neck. The Arab is prized as a riding horse because of its speed, hardiness, and docility. Height: 1.42–1.52 m (14–15 hands).

● **Arabia** ► A peninsula in the Middle East, forming the SW tip of Asia and bordered by the Red Sea, the Gulf of Aden, the Gulf of Oman, and the Persian Gulf. It consists of Saudi Arabia, Yemen, Oman, the United Arab Emirates, Qatar, Bahrain, and Kuwait. Mountains in the W (most fertile in the S) slope downwards to steppe and desert in the E. Agriculture is still the main occupation, despite flourishing modern oil industries.
  History: as remains of irrigation systems show, S Arabia was the site of technologically advanced ancient civilizations. Arabia was often conquered in part, but its total conquest was long prevented by its deserts. It was conquered briefly by the Persians in 575 AD and later unified from Mecca by Islam in the 7th century. Arabia quickly became disunited again, however. From the 16th century until World War I the Ottoman Turks held nominal control over much of the peninsula, challenged chiefly by the ▷Wahhabiyah, a Muslim sect that was led by the Saud family, which conquered Arabia (except for the SW) and finally established Saudi Arabia (1932). From the mid-19th century until the late 1960s the UK was the chief foreign presence.

● **Arabian Desert** ► **1.** A desert chiefly in Saudi Arabia, covering most of ▷Arabia. Area: about 2 300 000 sq km (887 844 sq mi). **2.** A desert in E Egypt between the River Nile and the Red Sea.

● **Arabian Sea** ► A section of the NW Indian Ocean between Arabia and India. Connected to the Mediterranean Sea by the Red Sea and the Suez Canal, it forms a major shipping route.

● **Arabic** ► A member of the ▷Semitic group of languages. It is written from right to left. Arabic is the mother-tongue of some 110 million people inhabiting SW Asia (the Middle East) and the countries of N Africa. Arabic can be roughly classified into three parts: (a) Classical Arabic, the language of the ▷Koran and the great Arab writers and poets; (b) Modern Literary, or Standard, Arabic, the language of the press and broadcasting; and (c) the colloquial dialects (vernaculars), which differ from country to country. Categories (a) and (b) are known as "Written Arabic," the vernaculars are almost entirely spoken forms.

● **Arabic literature** ► The literature of the Arabic-speaking peoples, the majority of whom live in N Africa and the Middle East. Most Arabic writing is scholarly, consisting of works on religion, philosophy, grammar, history, translations from the Greek, etc. Literature strictly speaking may be divided into two periods, the classical (6th–16th centuries) and the modern literary revival in the Middle East,

which started in the 19th century and reflected a heavy indebtedness to the West. The earliest example of classical literature was a pre-Islamic poetic form, the *qasidah* (6th century), which continued to dominate Arabic verse for generations. An ode of 60 to 100 lines, it was written in praise of the poet himself, his tribe, or his patron. Its main interest for modern readers lies in the dramatic descriptions of early Bedouin desert life; the most important collection is the *Mu'allaqat* (8th century). During the Umayyad period (661–750) there arose a second important poetic genre, the *ghazal*, a short love poem. The golden age of classical Arabic literature developed during the 'Abbasid period (750–1055) with the assimilation of many Greek and Roman authors and the growth of a cosmopolitan urban culture, of which ▷Abu Nuwas was the outstanding poet. The traditional verse continued to flourish, however, its most famous practitioner being al-▷Mutanabbi. Literary prose also developed during the 'Abbasid period; among the most influential writers were the essayist al-Jahiz (d. 869) and the critic and philologist Ibn Qutaybah (d. 899). The best-known prose romance is the collection of stories called *The Arabian Nights* (or *The Thousand and One Nights*), current among Arab storytellers by the 10th century. Arabic declined as a literary medium under the ▷Mamelukes (1250–1517) and in the Ottoman Empire (16th–19th centuries). Nationalist movements especially in Egypt and Syria beginning in the late 19th century largely account for the modern literary renaissance in these countries, where writers have adopted such Western forms as the novel and drama.

● **Arabic numerals** ► The number symbols 0, 1, 2, 3, 4, 5, 6, 7, 8, 9. They are believed to have originated in India and were introduced into Europe by the Arabs in about the 10th century AD. *Compare* Roman numerals.

● **Arab-Israeli Wars** ▷*See* Israel, State of.

● **Arab League** ► An organization formed to promote Arab unity and cooperation. Formed in Cairo in 1945, it consisted of those Arab countries that were then independent; others joined on attaining independence. Palestine, represented by the PLO, is a member. The League, which established a secretariat in Cairo, has had some success in the scientific and cultural field but in politics has been often split. In 1979, following the Egyptian-Israeli peace treaty, Egypt was expelled from the League, which was relocated in Tunis. It returned to Cairo following Egypt's readmission in 1989.

● **arable farming** ► The cultivation of plants for food, fibres, vegetable oils, etc., especially on a field scale. Fruit and vegetable production is usually considered as a specialized farming activity (*see* horticulture). The methods employed in arable farming depend on the crop being grown, the climate and soil type of the region, farming traditions, and the economic state of the farmer and his market. Arable farming is often carried out in conjunction with livestock farming, enabling the farmer to grow his own animal feeds and to make use of animal manures as ▷fertilizers. Grass is the chief feed for ▷ruminant livestock and a major arable crop. Special seed mixtures are sown to produce either permanent pasture or a temporary grass ley, often as part of a system of ▷crop rotation. Apart from grazing, grass is cut and conserved for winter food as hay (dried grass) or ▷silage.
  Cereal crops are a principal source of food for man and are important animal feedstuffs. The major cereals are wheat, barley, rice, and maize with oats, millet, sorghum, and rye cultivated to a lesser extent. Wheat may be sown either in autumn or spring, according to the variety, and is harvested in late summer when the grain is hard, yielding between 1.5 and 4 tonnes of grain per hectare. Cereals are harvested using a ▷combine harvester and the grain is often dried to ensure safe storage.
  Beans are grown as a major source of vegetable protein, the most important being ▷soya bean, produced chiefly in China and the USA. They are harvested mechanically using a specially adapted combine harvester that separates the beans from the rest of the crop. Harvesting root crops, such as potatoes and sugar beet, requires specialized machines that excavate the crop and remove soil. Turnips and swedes are root crops grown mainly for animal fodder. Crops grown for their oil content include sunflower, groundnut, linseed, cottonseed, and rape; cotton, flax, and jute are important sources of textile

fibres. Many other crops, including tea, coffee, and tobacco, are of major economic importance and each requires specialized husbandry techniques to give maximum yields. Modern scientific investigation of arable crops (*see* agronomy) together with innovations in mechanization, fertilizers, pesticides, ▷irrigation, and plant breeding have increased crop yields and productivity, bringing about a Green Revolution in many countries.

● **Arabs** ► A Semitic people originally inhabiting the Arabian peninsula. They are roughly divided into two cultural groups: the nomadic ▷Bedouin tribes and the settled communities of the towns and oases. Wealth from oil has recently led to industrialization and Westernization in the towns, but Islam remains a strong conservative force in social customs, particularly in the restrictions it places upon women's role in society. The Arabs were known in antiquity to the Greeks, Romans, and Jews and are mentioned by name in the later Old Testament books. They appeared as a power in world history early in the 7th century AD, with the rise of Islam, and they carried their language (*see* Arabic), religion, and culture as far as Spain in the W and Indonesia in the E. In modern usage "Arab" designates Arabic-speaking peoples of SW Asia, Egypt, N Africa, and parts of sub-Saharan Africa, whether or not they are of Arab descent.

● **Aracajú** ► 10 54S 37 07W A city and port in NE Brazil, the capital of Sergipe state near the mouth of the Rio Continguiba. It is a commercial and industrial centre with sugar refining, cotton milling, and tanning. Its university was founded in 1967. Population (1996): 428 194.

● **Arachne** ► In Greek mythology, a girl from Lydia who defeated Athena in a tapestry-weaving contest. The jealous goddess destroyed all Arachne's work; she attempted to hang herself, but Athena changed her into a spider.

● **arachnid** ► An invertebrate animal belonging to a class (*Arachnida*; 65 000 species) of chiefly terrestrial ▷arthropods, including the ▷spiders, ▷scorpions, ▷harvestmen, ▷ticks, and ▷mites. An arachnid's body is divided into two parts: a combined head and thorax (cephalothorax) and an abdomen. The cephalothorax bears four pairs of legs and two pairs of head appendages, one of which consists of strong pincer-like claws. Arachnids are mostly carnivorous, feeding on the body juices of insects and other small animals; many secrete poison from specialized glands to kill prey or enemies. Others are parasites, some of which are carriers of disease. Arachnids usually lay eggs, which hatch into immature adults.

● **Arad** ► 46 10N 21 19E An industrial city in W Romania, on the River Mureş. It was Austro-Hungarian until 1919 and has a large Hungarian community. Population (1997 est): 184 619.

● **Arafat, Yassir** ► (1929–) Palestinian leader. In the 1950s he was one of the founders of al-▷Fatah and in 1968 became president of the ▷Palestine Liberation Organization. Since 1983 his leadership has been rejected by some factions within the PLO. In 1988 he recognized the state of Israel and renounced terrorism; in 1993 he signed a peace agreement between the PLO and Israel, leading to the award of the 1994 Nobel Peace Prize (jointly with ▷Rabin and ▷Peres). Following Israel's partial withdrawal from the ▷West Bank and ▷Gaza Strip he was elected first president of the new Palestinian National Authority in 1996. He signed a further land-for-peace deal with Israel in 1998 but subsequent talks (2000) ended in impasse, leading to renewed violence. From late 2001 until May 2002 Israeli military operations in the West Bank kept Arafat a virtual prisoner in his Ramallah base.

● **Arafura Sea** ► A shallow section of the W Pacific Ocean between Australia and New Guinea. It contains uncharted rocks, which make navigation dangerous.

● **Arago, (Dominique) François (Jean)** ► (1786–1853) French astronomer and physicist, who was professor of physics at the École Polytechnique in Paris. He did important work in astronomy, electricity, magnetism, meteorology, and optics (particularly polarized light). An advocate of the wave theory of light, he worked with ▷Fresnel to obtain evidence to support it.

● **Aragon** ► An autonomous region and medieval kingdom in NE Spain, of which Ramoir I (d. 1063) was the first king (1035–63). A series of conquests during the 11th and 12th centuries brought the Aragonese rule over much of N Spain. Union with Catalonia was secured by marriage in 1140. Later expansion gave the Aragonese Sicily (1282) and Sardinia (1320) and culminated in the conquest by ▷Alfonso the Magnanimous of the kingdom of Naples (1442). In 1469 ▷Ferdinand the Catholic, heir to the Aragonese throne, married ▷Isabella the Catholic of Castile and on his accession in 1479 the two kingdoms were united. Area: 47 609 sq km (18 382 sq mi). Population (1998 est): 1 183 234.

● **Aragon, Louis** ► (1897–1982) French poet, novelist, and journalist. In 1919 he and André ▷Breton founded the surrealist journal *Littérature*; his first books of poetry, *Feu de joie* (1920) and *Le Mouvement perpétuel* (1925), and his prose work *Le Paysan de Paris* (1926) are vigorously surrealist. He became a communist after a visit to the Soviet Union in 1930 and turned to social realism, especially in novels such as *Holy Week* (1958) and the series entitled *Le Monde reél* (1933–51). He was editor of the left-wing weekly *Les Lettres françaises*.

● **aragonite** ► A whitish mineral calcium carbonate, usually with sharp orthorhombic crystals (often twinned). With age, heat, or pressure aragonite changes into calcite and is therefore generally found in relatively young rocks. Many shells consist of aragonite.

● **Araguaia, Rio** ► A river in central Brazil, rising in the Brazilian Highlands and flowing generally NE to join the Rio Tocantins. Length: over 1771 km (1100 mi).

● **Arakan** ► (official name: Rakhine) A state in W Myanmar (Burma), extending along the Bay of Bengal and flanked by the Arakan Yoma, a mountain range rising over 3000 m (1000 ft). The principal economic activity is the cultivation of rice. The majority of the inhabitants are of Burmese descent but there is a large minority of Bengali Muslims in the N.

History: a powerful kingdom in the 15th century, it was absorbed into Burma (1783) before passing to Britain (1826–1948). The activities of various secessionist movements led to its change of status (from a division to a state) in 1975. Area: 36 762 sq km (14 191 sq mi). Population (1994 est): 2 482 000. Capital: Sittwe.

● **Arakcheev, Aleksei Andreevich, Count** ► (1769–1834) Russian soldier and statesman. From 1796 to 1798 Arakcheev reorganized the Russian army but his brutality led to his dismissal. He was recalled by Alexander I in 1808 and became war minister. After Napoleon's defeat (1815) he served as minister of internal affairs, establishing many military-agricultural communities, in which Russia's army lived in times of peace. He resigned in 1826, after the accession of Nicholas I.

● **Aral Sea** ► A salt-water lake in W Asia in Kazakhstan and Uzbekistan, now considered one of the worst ecological disasters in the world. Although it was once the fourth largest lake in the world, excessive use of its source rivers (the Amu Darya and Syr Darya) for irrigation has reduced its water volume by more than half and caused the waterline to recede by over 40 miles in the last 20 years. It is also heavily polluted by agricultural chemicals. Area (including salt flats): about 66 000 sq km (25 477 sq mi).

● **Aram, Eugene** ► (1704–59) British philologist. Aram's extensive knowledge of etymology led him to compile a *Comparative Lexicon of the English, Latin, Greek, Hebrew, and Celtic Languages*. His career was curtailed when he was hanged for murdering (1745) a former friend, Daniel Clark.

● **Aramaic** ► A western branch of the Semitic group of languages. Its 22-character alphabet is the ancestor of both Hebrew and Arabic alphabets. Aramaic became extensively used during the late Babylonian empire and was the official language of the Persian Empire under ▷Darius I. It replaced Hebrew as the language of the Jews from about the time of the Exile in 605 BC until after the rise of Islam.

● **Aran Islands** ► (Irish name: Arainn) A group of islands in Galway Bay, off the W coast of the Republic of Ireland, comprising Inishmore (the largest), Inishmaan, and Inisheer. Area: 46 sq km (18 sq mi). Chief town: Kilronan.

● **Aranjuez** ► 40 02N 3 37W A town in central Spain, in New Castile on the River Tagus. Its fine palace (1778) was used by the Spanish court until 1890. It is a tourist resort and market town. Population (latest est): 37 079.

● **Arany, János** ▶ (1817–82) Hungarian poet. Born into a poor peasant family, he became a teacher, editor, and notary. His poem *Toldi* (1847), the adventures of a peasant youth at the 14th-century Hungarian court, was acclaimed as a national epic; he added two sequels, the romantic *Toldi szerelme* (1848) and the comic *Toldi estége* (1854). He took part in the Revolution of 1848, and in 1858 became a member of the Hungarian Academy of Sciences. His powerful but melancholy ballads are perhaps his finest works.

● **Ararat, Mount** ▶ (Turkish name: Ağri Daği) 39 44N 44 15E A mountain in E Turkey, near the Armenian and Iranian borders. It is volcanic in origin and isolated but for a secondary peak 12 km (7 mi) away. Traditionally, Noah's ark came to rest here after the flood (Genesis 8.4). Height: 5165 m (16 946 ft).

● **Araucanians** ▶ Indians of central Chile, divided into three major groups, the Picunche, Mapuche, and Huilliche. They were farmers and herders of llamas, living in small autonomous hamlets of patrilineal kin. They could build in stone but lacked the elaborate culture of other Andean peoples, such as the ▷Inca. The Mapuche resisted Chilean rule until late in the 19th century. There are now about 200 000 living on reservations.

● **Araucaria** ▶ A genus of coniferous trees (about 15 species), native to Australasia and South America (it is named after a district of Chile). They have whorled horizontal branches covered with scale leaves, and male and female flowers usually grow on separate trees. The genus includes the ornamental ▷monkey puzzle and several trees yielding useful timber, including the Norfolk Island pine (*A. heterophylla*); the hoop pine (*A. cunninghamii*) and the bunya bunya (*A. bidwillii*), both from E Australia; and the parana pine (*A. angustifolia*), of Brazil. Family: *Araucariaceae*.

● **Arawak** ▶ Indians of the Greater Antilles and northern and western areas of the Amazon basin. Their languages are the most widespread of the South American Indian languages and include Goajiro in Colombia, Campa and Machiguenga in Peru, and Mojo and Bauré in Bolivia. They are sedentary farmers growing manioc and maize. Prior to the Spanish conquests they were divided into numerous hereditary chiefdoms. They were never a warlike people and in the Caribbean area ▷Carib tribes frequently raided Arawak groups and enslaved Arawak women. Their religion involved belief in personal guardian spirits. The tribal gods were the spirits of chiefs represented by a hierarchy of idols called zemis, which were housed in temples.

● **Arbil** ▷See Irbil.

● **arbitrage** ▶ Nonspeculative dealing in exchange rates, commodities, interest rates, etc., between different markets. The arbitrageur knows what rates or prices prevail in the different markets across the world and will only trade if the profit of buying in one market and selling in another exceeds the costs of doing so. For example, a large stock of a commodity in a producer country may force the price well below that in a user country, where it is temporarily in short supply. The arbitrageur takes advantage of this difference, dealing simultaneously in both markets.

● **arbitration** ▶ **1.** A method of settling a commercial dispute in which each party presents his case to one or more disinterested parties (arbitrators), who are often appointed by a trade association. Arbitration awards can be appealed against in the courts on questions of law. This method of settling disputes is widely used in commerce because it is quicker and cheaper than litigation. In the UK, arbitrations are governed by the Arbitration Act (1979). **2.** An attempt to settle an industrial dispute by submitting the case to an arbitrator, such as a government conciliation service (*see* ACAS). In this case the award is usually accepted as binding on both sides, but usually it is an issue, such as wage rates, that cannot be settled by law.

● **arbor vitae** ▶ A coniferous tree of the genus *Thuja* (6 species), native to North America and E Asia. They have scalelike leaves, which densely cover the flattened stems, and small scaly cones, 1–1.8 cm long. The Chinese arbor vitae or cedar (*T. orientalis*), which grows to a height of 30 m, is a popular ornamental tree; the giant arbor vitae, or

western red cedar (*T. plicata*), of W North America, grows to a height of 40 m and yields a valuable timber. Family: *Cupressaceae*.

● **Arbroath** ▶ 56 34N 2 35W A town and fishing port in E Scotland, in Angus. It has a ruined abbey, where Scotland declared its independence in 1320. Population (1991): 23 474.

● **Arbus, Diane** ▶ (Diane Nemerov; 1923–71) US photographer. She married the photographer Allan Arbus when she was 18; together they worked as fashion photographers until 1957, when Diane began to pursue a separate career photographing people on the fringe of society, as well as children and ordinary people. The compelling honesty of her work, which appeared in many magazines, resulted in an exhibition at the Museum of Modern Art in New York. She also taught photography. She committed suicide.

● **Arbuthnot, John** ▶ (1667–1735) Scottish writer and physician. He became one of Queen Anne's physicians in 1705 and a Fellow of the College of Physicians in 1710. He wrote about many scientific subjects but is best known as a friend of ▷Pope and ▷Swift and a leading member of the ▷Scriblerus Club. His *History of John Bull* (1712), a political satire, was the first appearance of that famous character.

● **Arbutus** ▶ A genus of evergreen trees and shrubs (about 20 species) distributed in Central and North America and W Europe. The small white or pinkish flowers are borne in terminal clusters and the berries are fleshy and reddish. The leaves are tough, dark green, toothed, and shiny above. The strawberry tree (*A. unedo*) of SW Europe is widely grown as an ornamental, reaching a height of 9 m. Family: *Ericaceae*.

● **Arcadia** ▶ A mountainous region of ancient Greece, in the central Peloponnesus, that was identified in the literature of Greece, Rome, and the Renaissance (e.g. in Sidney's *Arcadia*) as an earthly paradise. It is a modern department.

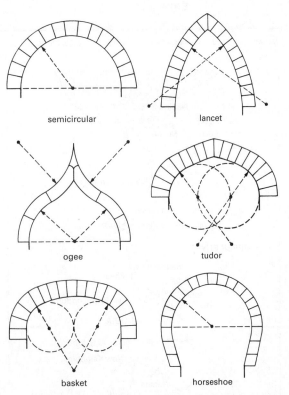

semicircular

lancet

ogee

tudor

basket

horseshoe

arch ▶ The semicircular arch characterized Roman, Romanesque, and Norman architecture; the lancet, ogee, Tudor, and basket arches were gothic and later medieval developments; the horseshoe arch is typical of Islamic architecture.

archaeology

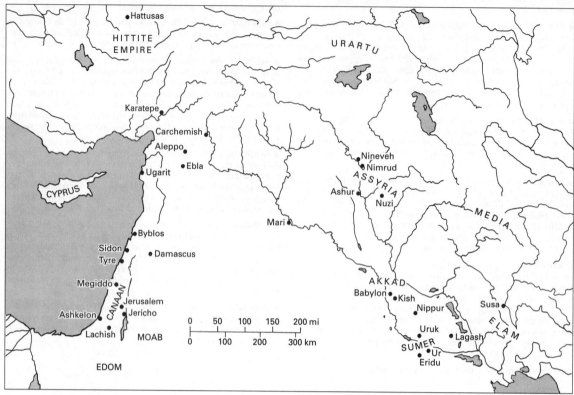

Mesopotamia and the Levant Kingdoms and towns (c. 2000–700 BC).

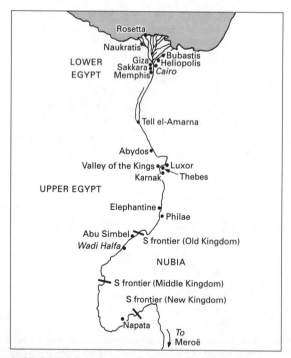

Ancient Egypt Civilization grew up in the fertile narrow strip along the banks of the Nile (c. 4500).

Pre-Columban Mesomerica The homelands of the principal ancient Mesoamerican peoples and the sites of their towns (c. 1000 BC–1500 AD).

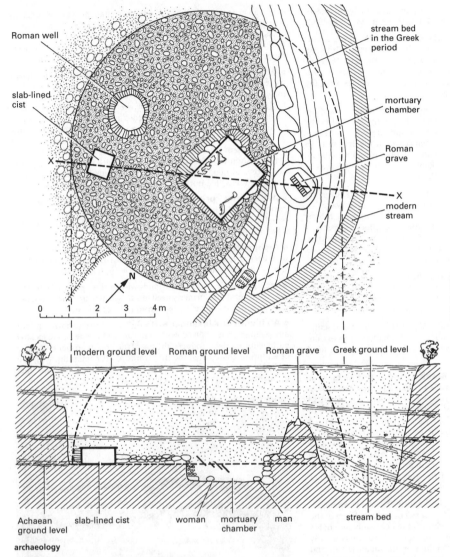

Roman well

slab-lined cist

X

N

0 1 2 3 4 m

stream bed in the Greek period

mortuary chamber

Roman grave

X
modern stream

(a) A plan of an ancient Greek burial mound showing the relative positions of the original mortuary chamber and other burials in the mound.

modern ground level   Roman ground level   Roman grave   Greek ground level

Achaean ground level   slab-lined cist   woman   mortuary chamber   man   stream bed

(b) A stratigraphic section (through XX) of the same mound showing the comparative levels of the ground at various periods.

archaeology

● **Arc de Triomphe** ▶ A ceremonial arch standing at the centre of the Étoile at the top of the Champs Elysées in Paris. It was commissioned to celebrate the victories of ▷Napoleon I and built between 1806 and 1836 to the designs of Jean Chalgrin (1739–1811).

● **arch** ▶ In architecture, a structure spanning a horizontal space. The development of the arch was one of the greatest Roman contributions to building technology. By using interlocking and mutually supporting pieces of stone it is possible to span greater distances than can be achieved with single megaliths; also arches can be employed to provide a more even distribution of pressure throughout the building. The basic forms of arch are the pointed, or gothic, arch, and the rounded, or classical, arch. □ p. 69.

● **archaebacteria** ▶ A group of ▷bacteria that thrive in such unlikely environments as sulphurous hot springs, boiling muds, volcanic vents, and very salty sediments. Many are found in conditions similar to those existing on earth more than 300 million years ago and are probably direct descendants of the earliest living organisms. Archaebacteria are classified as a separate subkingdom or kingdom (*Archaea*) of bacteria. They differ from the so-called "true bacteria" in the structure of the RNA making up their ribosomes and in lacking a rigid cell wall.

● **archaeology** ▶ The scientific study that is concerned with the recovery and interpretation of the material remains of man's past. Archaeology may be supplemented by written records, where they exist, but its techniques are principally concerned with nonliterary evidence for man's social and cultural development. Modern archaeology has numerous specialized branches—classical, industrial, underwater, etc. Before the 19th century, digging was carried out to plunder precious objects from ruins. Scientific excavation followed the realization that often more could be learnt from the surroundings in which objects are discovered than from the objects themselves. Essential techniques include stratigraphy, based on the principle that in any sequence of deposits the uppermost is latest and the lowest earliest, and typology, the study of changes in forms (e.g. of pottery). New methods of dating constantly evolve: ▷radiometric dating, ▷palaeomagnetism, ▷thermoluminescence, ▷varve dating, and ▷dendrochronology are all valuable techniques with different types of material.

● **Archaeopteryx** ▶ A genus of extinct primitive birds, fossils of which date from the Jurassic period (160–120 million years ago). It had many reptilian features, such as numerous teeth, a long bony tail, and claws on the hand, but was fully feathered and is believed to be the ancestor of modern birds. *Archaeopteryx* lived in dense forests, climbing trees using its claws and gliding down in search of food.

● **Archangel** ▶ (Russian name: Arkhangelsk) 64 32N 40 40E A port in NW Russia, on the River Dvina, 50 km (30 mi) from the White Sea. Founded in 1584, it was Russia's leading port until the early 18th century. The country's largest timber-exporting port, it has timber-processing and shipbuilding industries and also supports a fishing fleet. Population (1997 est): 371 000.

● **archangels** ▶ In Christian belief, supernatural beings ranked immediately above ▷angels in the celestial hierarchy. Michael is the only archangel mentioned in the New Testament (Jude); in Revelation 12 he is the leader of the angels who cast out the dragon from heaven. Gabriel, as the angel of the annunciation, is traditionally included among the archangels, as is Raphael, the helper of Tobias in the apocryphal Book of Tobit, and Uriel.

● **archbishop** ▶ A chief bishop who has some jurisdiction over the other bishops in an ecclesiastical province, i.e. a group of dioceses, as well as in his own diocese. Until the 8th or 9th century such men were called "metropolitans," a title still used by Orthodox Christians whose archbishops are of lower rank. Some Roman Catholic archbishops have no provincial authority. The Church of England has only the Archbishops of Canterbury and of York.

● **archegonium** ▶ The reproductive organ producing the female cells (gametes) in ferns, mosses, algae, fungi, and some gymnosperms. It is flask-shaped, the swollen base containing the egg cell and the neck providing an entrance for the male gametes.

● **Archer, Frederick Scott** ▶ (1813–57) British inventor and sculptor. In 1851 he developed the wet collodion photographic process, enabling multiple copies of pictures to be made. This system was used for several decades.

● **Archer, Jeffrey (Howard), Baron** ▶ (1940–) British novelist and politician. His bestselling novels include *Kane and Abel* (1979), *First Among Equals* (1984), and *The Fourth Estate* (1996). A Conservative MP from 1969 to 1974, he resigned as deputy chairman (1985–86) of the party following sexual allegations. Although he successfully sued the newspaper concerned, in 1999 he was obliged to withdraw as Conservative candidate for mayor of London after it was revealed that he had asked a friend to lie for him in this trial. He was subsequently (2000) sentenced to four years in prison for perjury and attempting to pervert the course of justice. He was created Lord Archer of Weston-super-Mare in 1992.

● **Archer, Thomas** ▶ (1668–1743) English baroque architect. Having studied abroad, Archer had a considerable knowledge of the work of ▷Bernini and ▷Borromini, whose influence is apparent in his own buildings, for example at Heythrop House (1710). He is mainly known for two London churches, St John's, Smith Square (1714), and St Paul's, Deptford (1712), and his work at Chatsworth (Derbyshire).

● **Archer, William** ▶ (1856–1924) British drama critic. He worked as a theatre critic in London from 1879. *Pillars of Society* (1880) was the first of his translations of Ibsen's plays, culminating in the *Collected Works* (12 vols, 1906–12). He encouraged G. B. Shaw during his early career.

● **archer fish** ▶ A small fish of the genus *Toxotes*, especially *T. jaculatrix*, which occurs in coastal and estuarine waters of SE Asia and Australia. Up to 18 cm long, archer fish capture insects by firing a stream of water droplets through the mouth. Family: *Toxotidae*.

● **archery** ▶ A sport in which (generally) arrows are shot at a target over a prescribed distance. The modern bow developed from the medieval longbow, but archery dates back 30 millenniums. **Target archery** consists of shooting at a target of standard size marked with five or ten scoring zones. **Field archery** consists of shooting at large animal figures with superimposed scoring rings. In **clout shooting** arrows are shot into the air to fall on a target marked on the ground, while in **flight shooting** the purpose is to achieve the maximum distance. Archery is an amateur sport, governed internationally by the Fédération internationale de Tir à l'Arc (founded 1931).

● **Archilochus** ▶ (c. 680–c. 640 BC) Greek poet. Probably the bastard son of an aristocrat of Paros and a slave woman, he was forbidden to marry Neobule by her father Lycambes, who became the target of viciously satirical poems. Archilochus became a mercenary soldier and probably died in battle. His poems, only fragments of which survive, range from the lyrical to the biting, often colloquial in style.

● **Archimedes** ▶ (c. 287–c. 212 BC) Greek mathematician and inventor, regarded as the greatest scientist of classical times. He was born in Syracuse, Sicily, and studied in Alexandria, afterwards returning to Syracuse, where he remained for the rest of his life. He is best known for his discovery of ▷Archimedes' principle, supposedly in response to the King of Syracuse asking him to determine whether a gold crown had been adulterated with silver. Legend has it that he made his discovery while taking a bath and ran through the streets of Syracuse shouting "Eureka!" He is credited with inventing ▷Archimedes' screw, although this was probably already known to the Egyptians. He was killed during the Roman invasion of Syracuse.

● **Archimedes' principle** ▶ The principle that when a body is partly or wholly immersed in a fluid its apparent loss of weight is equal to the weight of the liquid displaced. It is named after ▷Archimedes.

● **Archimedes' screw** ▶ A device for raising water, reputed to have been invented by ▷Archimedes. It consists of an inclined helical screw rotated about a central axis in a trough of water.

● **archipelago** ▶ A group of islands within close proximity to each other. The term was formerly used for the sea in which the islands are scattered, originally being applied to the Aegean Sea.

● **Archipenko, Alexander** ▶ (1887–1964) Russian-born sculptor and painter. From 1908 he worked in Paris, where he was associated with ▷cubism. He introduced the use of the hole as an elemental part of sculpture and created the first works of art combining sculpture and painting. His geometrical sculptures of moving figures declined in quality after his move to New York (1923).

architecture ▶ Frank Lloyd Wright's Guggenheim Museum (1956–59) in New York City.

● **architecture** ▶ The art of designing and constructing buildings that are both functionally and aesthetically satisfying. Factors principally influencing an architect are: the use to which the building will be put; the materials obtainable; the resources available in money and labour; and contemporary artistic taste. The earliest civilizations built on a monumental scale for their gods or the deified dead (*see* pagoda; pyramids; ziggurat). Secular architecture reflected the needs of local rulers for security, comfort, and—very important—display. The Greeks (*see* Greek art and architecture) were the first to develop the concepts of proportion and harmony that still influence Western architecture. Roman engineers greatly extended flexibility of design by their use of ▷arches and domes (*see* Roman art and architecture). Western European medieval architecture (*see* Norman art and archi-

architecture

The orders of classical architecture

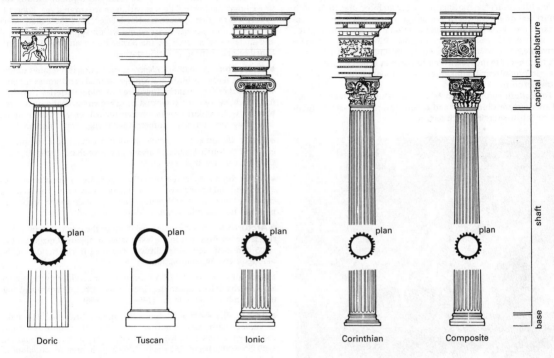

Doric   Tuscan   Ionic   Corinthian   Composite

plan (×5)

entablature · capital · shaft · base

Some terms in classical architecture

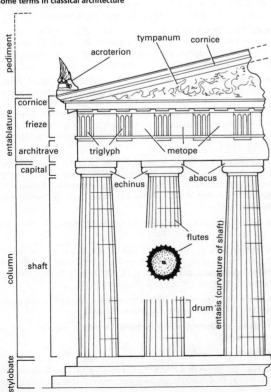

pediment · cornice · tympanum · acroterion · cornice · frieze · architrave · capital · column · shaft · stylobate · triglyph · echinus · metope · abacus · flutes · entasis (curvature of shaft) · drum

Some terms in gothic architecture

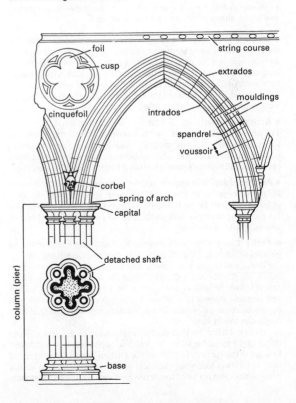

foil · cusp · cinquefoil · string course · extrados · mouldings · intrados · spandrel · voussoir · corbel · spring of arch · capital · detached shaft · column (pier) · base

tecture; Romanesque art and architecture) reached its zenith in the gothic ▷cathedral (*see also* gothic art and architecture). The ▷Renaissance (*see also* baroque) brought a resurgence of interest in all types of building; the rediscovered principles of classical architecture dominated theory and practice until the ▷gothic revival at the beginning of the 19th century (*see also* English art and architecture). In the 20th century technical advances in the use of concrete, steel, and glass encouraged architects to design buildings that have been criticized for their severity and unadorned functionalism. However, the best architects of the 20th century have shown that inspiration does not always have to give way to the restrictions imposed by economics and function. ▷*See* brutalism; functionalism; international style; modernism; postmodernism.

For Eastern European and Asian architecture, *see* Byzantine art and architecture; Chinese art and architecture; Indian art and architecture; Japanese art and architecture.

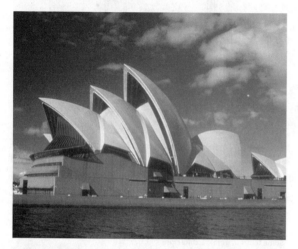

architecture ▶ The innovative Sydney Opera House (1957–73) designed by Jørn Utzon, although not completed to his design.

● **archons** ▶ The supreme magistrates in most ancient Greek city states. At Athens there were nine archons, including an eponymous archon, who was the chief archon and gave his name to the year, a king-archon (responsible for religion), and a polemarch (responsible for military affairs). In origin the Athenian archons were a ruling aristocracy, which had replaced the earlier monarchy. After 487 BC they were chosen by lot and their role became chiefly judicial.

● **Archytas** ▶ (early 4th century BC) Greek mathematician, from Tarentum (S Italy). Famous as an innovator, he distinguished between geometrical, arithmetical, and harmonic progressions, worked out the numerical relations between notes of different musical scales, and found a geometrical construction to double the cube.

● **Arcimboldo, Giuseppe** ▶ (1527–93) Mannerist painter, born in Milan. He moved to Prague in 1562, becoming painter and designer of court pageants to the Habsburg emperors. He is remembered for his grotesque portraits, such as the head of a cook composed of pots and pans, fish, and meat.

● **Arctic Circle** ▶ The area around the North Pole enclosed by the parallel of latitude 66°32N. It includes parts of Greenland, Russia, the USA, Canada, and Scandinavia and extensive areas of ice-covered ocean, notably the Arctic Ocean. Within the Arctic Circle the sun remains below the level of the horizon for a period of time in winter and remains above it in summer; the length of time for which this occurs increases polewards. The population consists mainly of Eskimos, who live by hunting.

History: during the 16th century exploration of the Arctic by the Dutch and English began in the search for a Northeast or Northwest Passage to the Far East. In 1725–42 the Russian Imperial Navy carried out exploration following the ideas of Peter the Great and Russia became the most active of the Arctic explorers. In 1879 a US expedi-

tion under G. W. De Long (1844–81) became trapped in the ice while attempting to reach the North Pole and its ship was crushed. Wreckage found off the coast of Greenland suggested that a sea route through the ice was possible. The Norwegian Fridtjof ▷Nansen in the *Fram* drifted for nearly two years (1893–95) through the ice and proved that the North Pole was within an ice-covered sea. Robert E. ▷Peary was the first to reach the North Pole (1909). Since then extensive exploration has been carried out with mapping and geological and meteorological studies; the Soviet Union and the USA established several drifting scientific stations.

● **Arctic fox** ▶ A small fox, *Alopex lagopus*, found throughout tundra regions. It feeds on birds and small mammals and grows a dense woolly coat of fur in winter. There are two colour varieties: the white fox, which has a white winter coat and a brown summer coat; and the blue fox, which is dark grey in summer and pale grey in winter. Arctic foxes have been farmed commercially for their fur. □mammal.

● **Arctic Ocean** ▶ The world's smallest ocean, almost completely enclosed by North America, Eurasia, and Greenland. Explored since the 17th century, it is covered by ice.

● **Arctic tern** ▶ A slender red-billed ▷tern, *Sterna paradisaea*, up to 38 cm long and having a white plumage with grey wings and a black crown. It breeds in coastal regions from N Britain to the Arctic and migrates to Antarctic seas in winter.

● **Arcturus** ▶ A conspicuous ▷red giant in the constellation Boötes that is the brightest star in the N sky. It has an apparent magnitude of –0.05 and is 36 light years distant. The stars in the handle of the ▷Plough curve in its direction.

● **Ardebil** ▶ 38 15N 48 18E A town in NW Iran, close to the border with Azerbaidzhan and to the Caspian Sea. It has a carpet- and rug-making industry. Population (1994 est): 329 869.

● **Arden, Elizabeth** ▶ (Florence Nightingale Graham; 1884–1966) Canadian beautician and businesswoman. After training as a nurse she moved to New York where she opened her own beauty salon in 1909. From this beginning she built up a chain of over 100 salons in the USA and Europe and used these salons to supply a range of over 300 of her own cosmetics. She was also a racehorse owner and a well-known social figure, who invariably dressed in pink.

● **Arden, Forest of** ▶ An area in the Midlands of England, in Warwickshire. Formerly part of an extensive forest, it is the apparent setting for Shakespeare's *As You Like It* (although the Ardennes region of France and Belgium may be intended).

● **Arden, John** ▶ (1930–) British dramatist and novelist. Associated with London's Royal Court Theatre in the 1950s, Arden was acclaimed for such Brechtian plays as *Serjeant Musgrave's Dance* (1959) and *Armstrong's Last Goodnight* (1964). Later works include plays written with his wife Margaretta (Ruth) D'Arcy and such historical novels as *Silence Among the Weapons* (1982) and *Jack Juggler and the Emperor's Whore* (1995).

● **Ardennes** ▶ A chain of wooded hills in W Europe. It extends through N Luxembourg, S Belgium, and NE France at an average height of about 500 m (1640 ft), forming the watershed between the Rivers Meuse and Moselle. There was heavy fighting here in both World Wars.

● **Ards** ▶ A district in Northern Ireland, in Co Down. Area: 368 sq km (142 sq mi). Population (1993): 66 200.

● **Arduin** ▶ (*or* Ardoin; d. 1015) Marquess of Ivrea, who seized the Italian throne (1002). Forced by Emperor Henry II to withdraw (1004), Arduin continued to harass Henry's authority in N Italy until defeated in 1014. He retired to a monastery.

● **are** ▶ (a) A unit of area in the ▷metric system equal to 100 square metres. The ▷hectare is more frequently used.

● **Areas of Outstanding Natural Beauty** ▶ (AONBs) ▷*See* National Parks.

● **Areca** ▷*See* betel.

● **Arendt, Hannah** ▶ (1906–75) German-born US political philosopher. After studying at Heidelberg she moved first to Paris (1933) and then to the USA (1940). *The Origins of Totalitarianism* (1951) established her reputation; other works include *On Revolution* (1963) and *The Life of the Mind* (1978).

● **Arequipa** ▶ 16 25S 71 32W A city in S Peru. Originally Inca, it was refounded by the Spanish (1540). Buildings include the cathedral (1612) and two universities. It is a commercial and wool-processing centre. Population (1998): 710 103.

● **Ares** ▶ The Greek god of war, identified by the Romans with ▷Mars. Son of Zeus and Hera, his popularity never rivalled that of the other Olympian gods. He loved ▷Aphrodite, by whom he fathered Deimos, Phobos, and Harmonia.

● **Aretino, Pietro** ▶ (1492–1556) Italian satirist. Son of a shoemaker, he claimed to be the bastard son of a nobleman. In Rome (1517–27) he was patronized by Pope Leo X and became famous for his satires and bawdy lyrics. He then settled in Venice, where he made a fortune by writing scurrilous satires on people or by being bribed not to do so. His letters, published in six volumes (1537–57), provide a vivid portrait both of Aretino and of his times. The earthy *Ragionamenti* (1534–36) portrayed the underworld of prostitutes. He also wrote five comedies.

● **Arezzo** ▶ 43 28N 11 53E A city in central Italy, in Tuscany. Originally an Etruscan settlement, it has many fine medieval buildings. Petrarch was born here. A market town, it has various industries. Population (latest est): 91 527.

● **argali** ▶ A race of mountain-dwelling sheep, *Ovis ammon ammon*, of central Asia. Argalis are the largest Eurasian wild sheep, reaching a weight of 170 kg and having massive curved horns. They live in herds and graze at very high altitudes during the summer.

● **Argenteuil** ▶ 48 52N 2 20E An industrial town in France, a NW suburb of Paris on the River Seine. It developed around the 7th-century convent of which Héloïse was abbess. Population (latest est): 93 096.

● **Argentina, Republic of** ▶ The second largest country in South America, occupying almost all the land S of the Tropic of Capricorn and E of the Andes. It includes the E part of the island of Tierra del Fuego and has claims to the ▷Falkland Islands and ▷South Georgia. It consists chiefly of subtropical plains and forests (the Gran Chaco) in the N, the fertile temperate pampas in the centre, the Andes in the W, and the semidesert Patagonian plateau in the S. The inhabitants are almost entirely European in origin, mainly Italian and Spanish, with a very small and dwindling Indian population.
Economy: chiefly agricultural with stock rearing, especially cattle, having overwhelming importance. The main industries have traditionally been meat processing and packing but there has been growth in a variety of areas, including oil refining, plastics, textiles, engineering, and chemicals. Natural-gas deposits have been developed and Argentina is practically self-sufficient in oil, the main oilfields being around Comodoro Rivadavia. There are plans to increase the use of hydroelectric power and nuclear energy is being developed. Main exports include meat and meat products, wool, cereals, minerals, and metals. Policies of privatization and deregulation were followed by the Menem government in the 1990s. The economy has been in a state of severe crisis since early 2001.
History: colonized by the Spanish from 1515 onwards. During this period the native Indian inhabitants, who had previously had to defend themselves against the Incas, put up a fierce resistance but by the 19th century they had almost been wiped out. The country gained its independence in 1816, under José de San Martín, and a new constitution in 1853 marked the end of a period of civil war and unrest. Since the late 19th century Argentina has been ruled for most of the time by a series of military dictatorships. Most prominent among the rulers since World War II has been Lt Gen Juán ▷Perón, who came to power in 1946. Following the death (1952) of his very popular wife, Eva, his power was weakened and in 1955 he was overthrown in a military revolution. The Perónist movement, however, continued to attract strong popular support; he returned to power in 1973 but died the following year. He was succeeded by his third wife, Isabel, but as the economic situation continued to deteriorate and political violence and industrial unrest increased, many allegations of corruption were made against her government. In 1976 Lt Gen

Jorge Rafael Videla came to power at the head of a three-man junta and severe measures, including widespread political murder, were used to suppress opposition groups. Lt Gen Roberto Viola succeeded Videla as president in 1981 but was later removed from office by the military junta, led by Gen Leopoldo Galtieri, who became president in December, 1981. On 2 April, 1982, Argentina launched an invasion of the Falkland Islands but following armed conflict with a UK task force was forced to surrender on 14 June, 1982; a defeat that forced Galtieri's resignation. Raúl Alfonsín was elected president in October 1983, ending seven years of military rule. The Perónist Carlos Saúl Menem was president from 1989 until 1999, when he was succeeded by Fernando de la Rua. In December 2001 Rua's attempts to arrest the deepening economic and financial crisis provoked riots and a general strike, leading to his resignation. Three other people served very briefly as president before Eduardo Duhalde took office in January 2002.

Republic of Argentina

Head of state	President Eduardo Duhalde
Official language	Spanish
Official religion	Roman Catholic
Official currency	peso of 100 centavos
Area	2 777 815 sq km (1 072 515 sq mi)
Population (2000 est)	37 032 000
Capital and main port	Buenos Aires

● **argentite** ▶ An important ore of silver, sometimes called silver glance. It is a sulphide of silver, found in association with other sulphide ores, such as lead, zinc, and copper.

● **argon** ▶ (Ar) A noble gas that occurs in the atmosphere (0.94%). Although previously observed in the solar spectrum, it was first isolated in 1894 by Rayleigh and Ramsay, by the distillation of liquid air. Chemically inert, it is used to fill fluorescent lamps and as an inert gas blanket for welding reactive metals. At no 18; at wt 39.948; mp −189.2°C; bp −185.7°C.

● **Argonauts** ▶ In Greek mythology, the 50-man crew of ▷Jason's ship *Argo*, on the quest of the ▷Golden Fleece. Accounts vary, but most agree that it included the shipbuilder Argo, the tireless helmsman Tiphys, the keen-sighted Lynceus, ▷Heracles and his follower Hylas, and even ▷Orpheus and the Dioscuri, ▷Castor and Pollux. During the voyage the Argonauts encountered such perils as the ▷Sirens, the ▷Harpies, the Symplegades (moving rocks that crushed ships) and the bronze giant Talos.

● **Argonne** ▶ A hilly forested area in NE France. It was the scene of heavy fighting during both World Wars.

● **Argos** ▶ 37 38N 22 43E A town in the NE Peloponnese (S Greece). Belonging in Homeric times to a follower of ▷Agamemnon, Argos gave its name to the surrounding district (the Argolid). Eclipsed by nearby Sparta after the 6th century BC, Argos remained neutral or the ineffective ally of Athens during the 5th-century struggles between Sparta and Athens. Considerable remains of the city survive.

● **Argus** ▶ In Greek mythology, a giant with 100 eyes who was beheaded by Hermes. He was (at the command of Hera) the guardian of Io, who was desired by Zeus; when he was killed Hera set his eyes in the tail of the peacock.

● **Argyll, Archibald Campbell, 1st Marquess of** ▶ (1607–61) Scottish statesman. He became a member of Charles I's privy council in 1626 but relinquished his post after becoming a ▷Covenanter in support of Presbyterianism. In the English Civil War he defeated the royalist ▷Montrose (1645) and ruled Scotland until the Scots' defeat by Cromwell (1651). He was executed after the Restoration of Charles II.

● **Argyll and Bute** ▶ A council area of W Scotland, bordering on the Atlantic Ocean and the North Channel. Under local government reorganization in 1975 the historic county of Argyll and the county and island of Bute became a single district within the new Strathclyde Region. This district became an independent ▷unitary authority in 1996 (with slightly adjusted borders). Chiefly mountainous, it includes the islands of Mull, Islay, and Jura among many others.

Fishing (including large-scale salmon farming) and livestock are important. Other economic activities include tourism, whisky distilling, and textiles. Area: 6930 sq km (2676 sq mi). Population (1996 est): 90 550. Administrative centre: Lochgilphead.

● **Århus** ► (*or* Aarhus) 56 10N 10 13E A seaport in Denmark, in E Jutland. One of the oldest cities in Denmark, it has a gothic cathedral and a university (1928). Its industries include oil refining, electronics, machinery, and textiles. Population (1996 est): 279 759.

● **aria** ► (Italian: air) A solo song with instrumental accompaniment, usually in an opera or oratorio. The name was originally also used of separate instrumental pieces but its meaning became restricted with the development of the three part *aria da capo* in the works of Monteverdi, Scarlatti, and Handel. Attacked as undramatic by reformers, such as Gluck and Wagner, the form is little used in modern opera.

● **Ariadne** ► In Greek legend, the daughter of ▷Minos, King of Crete, and Pasiphaë. She helped ▷Theseus to kill the Minotaur and escape from its labyrinth. After he abandoned her she married ▷Dionysus.

● **Ariane** ▷*See* European Space Agency.

● **Arianism** ► A Christian heresy started by ▷Arius, which held that the Son of God, Jesus Christ, was not truly divine. In 325 AD the Council of Nicaea banished the Arians, who included some influential bishops, and affirmed that the Father and the Son were coequal, coeternal, and "of one substance." Although the Arians were soon restored and a version of the heresy was officially accepted for a time, Arianism was finally defeated at the Council of Constantinople in 381 AD.

● **Arias Sánchez, Oscar** ► (1941–) Costa Rican statesman; president (1986–90). His plan to establish peace between Nicaragua, Guatemala, El Salvador, Honduras, and Costa Rica failed to bring regional conflicts to an end by 1988. However, in 1990 the five countries reaffirmed their commitment to the plan. He won the Nobel Peace Prize in 1987.

● **Arica** ► 18 30S 70 20W An oasis town and port in N Chile, on the Pacific Ocean. A railway line connects it with La Paz in Bolivia and it handles about half Bolivia's trade. Population (1995 est): 173 336.

● **Aries** ► (Latin: Ram) A constellation in the N sky, lying on the ▷zodiac between Taurus and Pisces. The brightest star, Hamal, is of 2nd magnitude.

● **Arikara** ► An Indian people of North America who lived along the Missouri River in what are now North and South Dakota. They were related to the ▷Pawnee in their language, which belongs to the Caddoan group, and in culture, which was of Plains Indian type. They were expert corn growers and their farming villages were often trade centres visited by the nomadic hunting tribes. They practised the sun-dance cult involving self-torture. There are today approximately 700 living on the Fort Berthold Reservation.

● **Ariosto, Ludovico** ► (1474–1533) Italian poet. He spent most of his life in the active service of the Este, the ducal family of Ferrara. He wrote plays and much lyric verse but is best known for his epic poem, *Orlando furioso* (1516). One of the greatest works of the Italian Renaissance, it recounts the adventures of the paladin Roland (*see* Charlemagne) and the wars between the Franks and Saracens. It was published in its revised form in 1532. Its precursor was the *Orlando innamorato* (1483) of ▷Boiardo.

● **Aristaeus** ► In Greek legend, the son of ▷Apollo and the nymph Cyrene. He was the patron of bee keepers, and was credited with the introduction of the vine and the olive. According to Virgil, he caused the death of ▷Eurydice.

● **Aristagoras** ► (5th century BC) Tyrant of ▷Miletus (Asia Minor). He persuaded the Greek cities of ▷Ionia to rebel against Persian rule (499) but despite Athenian assistance the rebellion failed (494). He died fighting in Thrace.

● **Aristarchus of Samos** ► (c. 310–230 BC) Greek astronomer, who maintained that the earth rotates upon its axis and orbits the sun. He made the first attempts to estimate trigonometrically the size and distance from the earth of the sun and the moon.

● **Aristarchus of Samothrace** ► (c. 217–145 BC) Greek critic and grammarian, head of the Library of Alexandria (c. 180–145). He edited editions of ▷Homer and wrote commentaries on ▷Aeschylus, ▷Sophocles, and ▷Herodotus.

● **Aristide, Jean Bertrand** ► (1953–) Haitian politician; president of Haiti (1991, 1994–96). Aristide was a Catholic priest who was expelled from the Church (1988) for revolutionary teachings. He was elected president in 1991 but overthrown in a military coup shortly afterwards. In 1994, supported by US forces, he returned to power.

● **Aristides the Just** ► (c. 520–c. 468 BC) Athenian statesman and noted commander in the ▷Greek-Persian Wars. Ostracized (c. 485) because of his opposition to Themistocles' naval policy, Artistides returned in 480 and offered his services against the Persians, commanding land forces at Salamis. In 477 he was chosen to assess the tribute required from each member of the ▷Delian League.

● **Aristippus** ► (c. 435–c. 356 BC) Greek philosopher, a pupil of ▷Socrates. He founded the Cyrenaic school of ▷hedonism and was concerned with practical morality (*see* Cyrenaics). Seeing pleasure as the highest good, he equated virtue with the rationally controlled pursuit of enjoyment.

● **Aristophanes** ► (c. 450–c. 385 BC) Greek comic dramatist. He wrote about 40 plays, of which 11 survive: *The Acharnians* (425), *The Knights* (424), *The Clouds* (423), *The Wasps* (422), *The Peace* (421), *The Birds* (414), *Lysistrata* (411), *Thesmophoriazusae* (410), *The Frogs* (405), *Women in Parliament* (393), and *Plutus* (388). His plots were satirical fantasies on contemporary topics, such as literature, ▷Socrates, social manners, and militaristic Athenian foreign policy; this led to his unsuccessful prosecution by the politician ▷Cleon.

● **Aristotelianism** ► Tendencies in philosophical thought that originated with ▷Aristotle. Interpretations of his work appeared until the eclipse of ancient philosophy in the 6th century AD. Texts were preserved by Arab scholars, their work culminating in the 12th-century commentaries of ▷Averroes. ▷Aquinas in the 13th century made Aristotle the metaphysical basis of Christian theology but the Latin Averroists produced their own conflicting theories, holding, for instance, that a proposition can be philosophically true although theologically false. In the Renaissance the term Aristotelianism became synonymous with obscurantist opposition to new learning and science.

● **Aristotle** ► (384–322 BC) Greek philosopher and scientist. His father was court physician in Macedonia. Aristotle joined ▷Plato's Academy at Athens (367–347) but, failing to become head of the Academy at Plato's death, he accepted the protection of Hermeias, ruler of Atarneus in Asia Minor, and married his patron's niece. About 343 ▷Philip of Macedon appointed Aristotle tutor to his son ▷Alexander, then aged 13. After Alexander's accession in 336, Aristotle founded, with generous assistance from Alexander, a research community complete with library and museum at Athens (the ▷Lyceum). There ▷Theophrastus studied botany and Aristoxenus (born c. 370) music, and Aristotle, among other projects, organized a comparative study of 158 constitutions of Greek states. When Alexander died in 323 BC, anti-Macedonian reaction at Athens forced Aristotle to withdraw to ▷Chalcis, where he died. Aristotle wrote over 400 books on every branch of learning, including logic, ethics, politics, metaphysics, biology, physics, psychology, poetry, and rhetoric. Ironically, those that survive (about one-quarter), edited by Andronicus of Rhodes about 40 BC, are apparently memoranda for his students' use, not intended for general publication. ▷*See also* Aristotelianism.

● **arithmetic** ► The branch of mathematics that deals with elementary theories of numbers, measurement, and computation. The fundamental operations of arithmetic are addition, subtraction, multiplication, and division. Addition and multiplication are assumed to obey the ▷associative law, the ▷commutative law, and the ▷distributive law. Other operations in arithmetic include extracting roots, raising a number to a power, and taking ▷logarithms. Arithmetic is also concerned with fractions and the various number systems, such as the ▷decimal system and the ▷binary system.

● **arithmetic progression** ► (*or* arithmetic sequence) A sequence of numbers in which successive terms have a constant difference, for example, 1, 4, 7, 10, 13....

● **Arius** ▶ (c. 250–336) Libyan theologian, who initiated the heresy ▷Arianism. He was a priest at Alexandria until excommunicated for his views in 321. However, by enlisting the support of such prominent churchmen as ▷Eusebius, Arius developed his cause into a major controversy. At the first Council of ▷Nicaea (325) he was condemned through the influence of ▷Athanasius. Recalled from exile (c. 334), he died a few days before he was to be received back into the Church.

● **Arizona** ▶ A state in the SW USA. It falls into two natural regions: in the NE lies part of the Colorado Plateau, an area of dry plains and escarpments, and in the S and W is an area of desert basins and gentle valleys, drained by the Gila and Salt Rivers. The Colorado River flows through the Grand Canyon in the NW of the state. In such an arid region inadequate water supplies have long been a problem and a number of major irrigation projects have been built since the beginning of 20th century. Most of the population lives in urban settlements in the S and W. Manufacturing (electrical, communications, aeronautical, and aluminium products) is the major industry. The state produces over half of the USA's copper as well as gold, silver, oil, and timber. Tourism is an important source of revenue. The main crops are cotton, vegetables, and citrus fruits; livestock is also important. It is traditionally a centre for Indian folk arts and crafts, having the largest Indian population in the USA; the main tribes are the Navajo, Hopi, and Apache.
History: inhabited by Indians as early as 25 000 BC, the area was explored by the Spanish in the 16th century. Following the Mexican War, Arizona, then part of New Mexico, was ceded to the USA (1848). It was swept by Apache wars until 1877 and became a state in 1912. Area: 295 023 sq km (113 909 sq mi). Population (1997 est): 4 554 966. Capital: Phoenix.

● **Arkansas** ▶ A state in the S central USA, lying W of the Mississippi River. It consists chiefly of the largely forested uplands of the N and W, descending to the Mississippi alluvial plain in the E and the West Gulf coastal plain in the S. The Arkansas River bisects the state from W to E. The state is no longer primarily agricultural although the Mississippi Plain provides rich fertile agricultural land; soya beans and rice have replaced cotton as the major crop. Oil production began in 1921; there are major lumbering, petroleum, and gas developments around Smackover and El Dorado and coal deposits in the Arkansas River Valley. The state produces 90% of US bauxite from an area to the S and SW of Little Rock. Manufactures include electronic equipment and wood products. Arkansas remains, however, one of the poorest US states.
History: explored by the Spanish and French in the 16th and 17th centuries, it formed part of the ▷Louisiana Purchase by the USA in 1803. It became a state in 1836, seceded from the Union in 1861, and was readmitted in 1868. Area: 137 539 sq km (53 104 sq mi). Population (1997 est): 2 522 819. Capital: Little Rock.

● **Arkansas River** ▶ A river in the S central USA, rising in central Colorado and flowing E and SE to join the Mississippi in Arkansas. Length: 2335 km (1450 mi).

● **Arkhangelsk** ▷*See* Archangel.

● **Ark of the Covenant** ▶ In the Old Testament, the sacred chest of the Israelites that contained the tablets of the law (*see* Ten Commandments) and was symbolic of God's presence and the ▷covenant made between God and Israel. Made of acacia wood, inlaid, and covered with gold, it was eventually placed in the Temple of Jerusalem. It probably disappeared during the ▷Babylonian exile. The shrine in a synagogue where the encased scrolls of the ▷Torah are kept is also called an ark or "holy ark" (*aron kodesh*).

● **ark shell** ▶ A ▷bivalve mollusc belonging to a chiefly tropical family (*Arcidae*). Ark shells are boat-shaped and are attached to rocks by means of strong threads. The Noah's ark shell (*Arca tetragona*) occurs in rock crevices along the S coast of Britain and is about 4.5 cm long.

● **Arkwright, Sir Richard** ▶ (1732–92) British inventor and industrialist, who invented a spinning frame powered by water, the so-called water frame (patented in 1769). Arkwright subsequently mechanized other spinning processes and his mills were vandalized by spinners put out of work by the incipient factory system.

● **Arlen, Michael** ▶ (Dikran Kuyumjian; 1895–1956) British novelist, born in Bulgaria of Armenian parents, who wrote several novels about London society. His most popular work was *The Green Hat* (1924).

● **Arles** ▶ 43 41N 4 38E A town in SE France, in the Bouches-du-Rhône department on the Rhône delta. An important Roman settlement, it became the capital of Gaul in the 4th century AD and the capital of the kingdom of Arles (formed from the kingdoms of Burgundy and Provence) in the 10th century. It has many Roman remains, including an amphitheatre. Other notable buildings include the 11th-century cathedral and the museum of arts and crafts founded by the poet Mistral. Several painters have lived and worked here, including Van Gogh and Gauguin. An agricultural market, it manufactures chemicals, machinery, and food products. Population (1990): 52 590.

● **Arlington, Henry Bennet, 1st Earl of** ▶ (1618–85) English statesman, who was a leading member of the faction called the ▷Cabal. As secretary of state (1662–74) he negotiated (1668) the Triple Alliance of England, the Netherlands, and Sweden against France but was involved in Charles II's secret Treaty of Dover (1670) with the French king, Louis XIV. In 1674 Arlington was impeached for embezzlement and, although cleared, resigned and became Lord Chamberlain.

● **Arlington National Cemetery** ▶ The largest cemetery in the USA, in Arlington, Virginia, just outside Washington DC; it comprises 170 hectares (420 acres). Since 1864 it has been the burial ground of Americans killed in action and of eminent public servants.

● **arm** ▶ In human anatomy, the upper limb, which extends from the shoulder to the wrist. The bone of the upper arm (the humerus) is connected by a ball-and-socket joint to the shoulder bone, permitting a wide range of movements. It forms a hinge joint at the elbow with the bones of the forearm (the ulna and radius), permitting movement in one plane only. The radius can be twisted across the ulna, enabling the palm of the hand to be turned upwards. ▷*See* Plate II.

● **Armada, Spanish** ▶ The fleet of 130 ships sent by Philip II of Spain in 1588 to invade England. After indecisive encounters with the English fleet led by Howard of Effingham, under whom Sir John Hawkins held command, the Armada anchored off Calais only to be dispersed by English fireships during the night of 28 July. A major engagement off Gravelines followed, in which the Armada was defeated. It suffered further losses in storms as it escaped round Scotland and Ireland, arriving in Spain with 86 ships. The defeat was a major psychological blow to Spain, which had claimed divine authority for its crusade against Protestant England. ▷*See also* Drake, Sir Francis.

● **armadillo** ▶ A mammal belonging to the family *Dasypodidae* (12 species), widespread in the southern USA and South America. Armadillos have jointed bands or horny plates that enable them to roll themselves into a ball for protection. They have long-clawed toes for burrowing, simple peglike teeth, and feed on insects and other invertebrates. They range from the giant armadillo (*Priodontes giganteus*), about 120 cm long, to the rare pink fairy armadillo (*Chlamyphorus truncatus*), 12 cm long. Order: *Edentata*.

● **Armageddon** ▷*See* Megiddo.

● **Armagh** ▶ 1. A historic county in S Northern Ireland, bordering on the Republic of Ireland. Its administrative powers were devolved to the new district councils in 1973. It consists of lowlands with bogs in the N, adjoining Lough Neagh, and low hills in the S. Armagh is predominantly agricultural; produce includes potatoes, flax, and apples. Area: 1326 sq km (512 sq mi). 2. A district in Northern Ireland, in Co Armagh. Area: 667 sq km (258 sq mi). Population (1998): 53 200. 3. 54 21N 6 39W A cathedral city in Northern Ireland, in Co Armagh. Centre of the ancient kingdom of Ulster, it is now the seat of both Protestant and Catholic archbishops. Industries include textiles, chemicals, optical equipment, and food processing. Population (1991): 14 640.

● **Armani, Giorgio** ► (1934–) Italian fashion designer. He co-founded the Armani fashion house in 1975 and became famous for the understated elegance of his menswear: he later produced clothes in a similar style for women.

● **Armenia, Republic of** ► A republic in W Asia. It is a densely populated and mountainous region, with no navigable rivers.

Economy: industry includes food processing, metallurgy, and chemicals. The rich mineral deposits include copper, lead, and zinc. The raising of livestock is the chief agricultural activity, although grains and fruit are grown in the more fertile areas. Wine production is expanding. The economy has suffered from embargoes imposed by Turkey and Azerbaidzhan because of the ▷Nagorno-Karabakh dispute and there has been large-scale emigration. An IMF-sponsored programme of liberalizing the economy was agreed in 1994.

History: the country forms the E part of the historic area inhabited by the ▷Armenians, also known as Armenia. After centuries of Mongol, Ottoman, and Persian rule, it was acquired by Russia in 1828. The Russian province declared its independence in 1918 but was invaded by Soviet and Turkish forces in 1920; it subsequently formed part of the Transcaucasian Soviet Federated Republic (*see* Transcaucasia). It became a separate Soviet republic in 1936. In 1988 a severe earthquake caused 25 000 deaths and much damage. Demands for the return of the disputed Nagorno-Karabakh area from Azerbaidzhan led to civil conflict in the late 1980s. Armenian forces became involved in the fighting in 1991; a ceasefire was agreed in 1994. Armenia declared independence in 1991 and elections were held the same year. A new constitution was promulgated following a referendum in 1995. Presidential elections in 1998 resulted in victory for the hardline nationalist Robert Kocharyan. In October 1999 prime minister Vazgen Sarkissian and several officials were shot dead in parliament by maverick extremists.

Republic of Armenia

Head of state	President Robert Kocharyan
Official language	Armenian
Official currency	dram of 100 luma
Area	29 800 sq km (11 490 sq mi)
Population (1998 est)	3 000 000
Capital	Yerevan

● **Armenian Church** ► The Church founded by St Gregory the Illuminator (c. 240–332) about 300 AD. Armenia was the first nation to adopt Christianity as a state religion. Its Church is the second largest of the Eastern Christian Churches and has much in common with the others, although it has also absorbed some Western influences. The head of the Church is the Patriarch of Etchmiadzin, called the Catholicos. There are Armenian churches in several parts of the world, including London and Manchester.

● **Armenians** ► A people of NE Turkey and Armenia. Approximately 1.5 million live in Turkey, Europe, and America and 3 million in Armenia, with smaller numbers in Georgia and Azerbaidzhan. Their culture is ancient and highly developed, with a literature written in an alphabet derived from Greek and Syriac script. Their language is the only representative of a distinct branch of the Indo-European family. Herodotus claimed they were related to the ancient Phrygians. They call themselves Hay and their land Hayastan. They are mainly Monophysite Christians and belong to the ▷Armenian Church. During the 19th and 20th centuries they suffered massacres by the Ottoman Turks, their rulers since the 16th century, who feared their growing nationalism.

● **Armentières** ► 50 41N 2 53E An industrial town in N France, in the Nord department on the River Lys. It was razed to the ground in World War I, when it also inspired the song "Mademoiselle from Armentières." Its manufactures include linen and hosiery. Population (1990): 26 240.

● **Armero** ► 4 59N 74 55W A town in Colombia, completely destroyed during the eruption of the Nevado del Ruiz volcano in November 1985. An estimated 25 000 people died.

● **Armidale** ► 30 42S 151 40E A town in Australia, in NE New South Wales. Often regarded as ▷New England's "capital," it is a tourist resort. It is the site of the University of New England (1954). Population (latest est): 21 500.

● **armillary sphere** ► A model of the universe, devised by the astronomers of Greece in the 3rd century BC, consisting of a small sphere representing the earth surrounded by a set of graduated metal rings representing circles on the celestial sphere, including the ecliptic, celestial equator, and the orbits of the moon, planets, etc. It was used by astronomers to teach navigation by the stars and for measuring star positions.

● **Arminius** ► (c. 18 BC–17 AD) Leader of the Germanic tribe of the Cherusci, famous as a master of the surprise attack. He led a revolt against the Romans (9 AD), destroying three legions. Defeated (16 AD) by Germanicus, Arminius nevertheless thwarted the Roman conquest of Germany. He was killed by a pro-Roman German tribesman.

● **Arminius, Jacobus** ► (1560–1609) Dutch Protestant theologian and reformer. A pupil of ▷Beza, he was a professor of theology at Leiden. Current Calvinist theology taught that God preordained some men to salvation and others to destruction. Arminius, however, emphasized God's grace and man's freedom to accept or reject salvation. This controversial doctrine later came to be known as Arminianism.

● **Armory show** ► The first exhibition of European avantgarde art organized in the USA. It was held in the 69th regiment armory in New York in 1913. ▷Picasso, ▷Braque, ▷Matisse, and the cubist school were given great prominence.

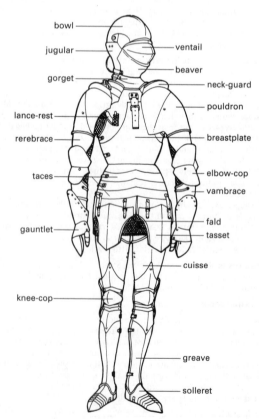

armour ► The skill of the European armourer reached its height in the late 15th and early 16th centuries, when suits of plate armour were made to cover the entire body.

● **armour** ► Defensive equipment used as a protection in warfare. Body armour (helmet, breastplate, greaves) was used in Bronze Age

Greece. The Romans evolved heavier armour for both men and horses. In the early Middle Ages ▷chainmail was widely used but after about 1300 plate armour, often sumptuously decorated and encasing the whole body, was worn by knights on horseback. Gunpowder gradually rendered body armour obsolete, although in World War I metal helmets were revived as a means of protection from shrapnel.

Armour is also used to protect modern war vehicles and their occupants against projectiles or fragments. Armour plate includes hardened metal alloys cast in varying thicknesses and designed to be mounted with sloping surfaces to give protection against armour-piercing projectiles. Its considerable weight has prompted experiments in light alloys and plastics, using multiple skins to inhibit projectile penetration. Most recent is the "Chobham" armour, produced by the Military Vehicle and Engineering Establishment at Chobham, Surrey.

● **armoured car** ▶ A wheeled armoured patrol vehicle, first used in combat in Libya (1912). Early types included converted lorries with poor protection, armament, and cross-country performance. They now have independent suspension, all-wheel drive, better armour, carry machine guns or a light gun, and may be amphibious.

● **arms control** ▷*See* disarmament.

● **Armstrong, Edwin Howard** ▶ (1890–1954) US electrical engineer, who in 1939 introduced frequency ▷modulation as a method of broadcasting radio signals to reduce the static associated with amplitude modulation. He had earlier invented the ▷superheterodyne receiver, which improved radio reception and greatly increased the popularity of radio sets. A contentious and litigious man, he committed suicide.

Louis Armstrong ▶ A charismatic figure, he was much loved by jazz fans for his warm and humourous personality as well as his trumpet playing.

● **Armstrong, Louis** ▶ (1900–71) US Black jazz trumpeter and singer, known as "Satchmo." Born in New Orleans, he learned to play the cornet in his youth. His career took him to Chicago, where he made many recordings (some of them with Earl Hines), which earned him a worldwide reputation. He played with several large orchestras as a soloist and toured Europe in 1932. His gravelly singing voice and superb trumpet playing were featured in many films.

● **Armstrong, Neil Alden** ▶ (1930–   ) US astronaut, the first man to walk on the moon. A navy pilot during the Korean War, he worked for the National Aeronautics and Space Administration (NASA) (1955–71) and became an astronaut in 1962. He flew Gemini 7 (1966) and was commander of Apollo 11 (1969). As he stepped onto the moon he said "That's one small step for a man, one giant leap for mankind."

● **Armstrong, William George, Baron** ▶ (1810–1900) British engineer and industrialist, who pioneered the design and construction of hydraulic machinery. His hydroelectric generator utilized high-pressure steam issuing through nozzles from a boiler. He also

invented a breech-loading gun, a landmark in the development of artillery.

● **army** ▶ An organized force of soldiers, which may be composed of full-time professionals, ▷militia reserves, conscripts, or mercenaries or of a combination of these. Armies exist for combat and to enhance a nation's prestige; they may also exert domestic political power and provide manpower for such activities as roadbuilding and land development.

Armies were raised throughout the ancient world, where mercenaries were usually relied upon to supplement a militia (as in the Greek city states) or a standing army (as in Rome). The medieval armies of Europe depended upon the mounted feudal knight, who was obliged to undertake short-term military service for his lord. As campaigns became longer, mercenaries were increasingly relied upon and with the introduction of firearms in the 15th century the foot soldier became important. Early modern standing armies reached their zenith with those of the 17th- and 18th-century absolute monarchs, especially Louis XIV of France and Frederick the Great of Prussia. By comparison the standing army maintained since 1661 in England was small, Cromwell's ▷New Model Army having left a lasting distrust of militarism. The 19th century saw a growing emphasis on the mass armies that resulted from ▷conscription—a measure widely adopted in Continental Europe. The British army, which had declined from the brilliance attained under ▷Wellington, was reorganized between 1871 and 1907, especially by ▷Cardwell and ▷Haldane, and a highly trained reserve (*see* Territorial Army) replaced the volunteer militia. With the adoption of conscription in World War I Britain was able to field 5 585 000 imperial troops by 1918. Its numbers declined between the wars and again after World War II. Postwar trends have included the combination of national armies into such allied forces as those of NATO and the UN, and the growing specialization of armies in response to technological advances.

● **army ant** ▶ A New World ▷ant of the genus *Eciton* or related genera that does not build a permanent nest but has alternating nomadic and static phases synchronized to the egg-laying of the wingless queen. The wasplike males are large and winged and the soldier ants have large hooked jaws and hunt in vast "armies," killing other insects and small animals. Subfamily: *Dorylinae*. ▷*See also* driver ant.

● **army worm** ▶ The ▷caterpillar of a widely distributed moth, *Leucania unipunctata*. Army worms periodically swarm in large numbers, eating crops in their path and causing severe damage, especially in North America.

● **Arnauld, Antoine** ▶ (1612–94) French theologian, philosopher, and logician; member of a prominent Jansenist family connected with the Abbey of Port-Royal. His attacks on the Jesuits, especially *De la fréquente communion* (1643), forced him into exile in Brussels. He raised important objections to ▷Descartes' *Meditations* and, with ▷Pascal and Pierre Nicole (1625–95), wrote the influential *La Logique ou l'art de penser* (1662), known as the *Port-Royal Logic*.

● **Arne, Thomas Augustine** ▶ (1710–78) British composer of great popularity in his lifetime. His most famous work is probably the song "Rule Britannia!" from the masque *Alfred* (1740). He wrote at least 50 operas and stage works, including music for Shakespeare's plays and Milton's *Comus*.

● **Arnhem** ▶ 52 00N 5 53E A city in the E Netherlands, the capital of Gelderland province. In World War II a large airborne landing of British troops attempted to secure a bridgehead over the River Rhine here to facilitate an Allied invasion of Germany. The attempt failed with heavy casualties in the ensuing battle (17–27 September, 1944). A railway junction, its industries include engineering and pharmaceuticals. Population (1996 est): 135 026.

● **Arnhem Land** ▶ A plateau in Australia, in N Northern Territory. It is primarily an Aboriginal reserve. Bauxite deposits are worked at Gove. Area: about 150 000 sq km (60 000 sq mi).

● **Arno, River** ▶ A river in central Italy. Rising in the Apennines, it flows mainly W through Florence and Pisa to the Ligurian Sea. It burst its banks in 1966 causing disastrous floods in Florence. Length: 240 km (150 mi).

● **Arnold, Benedict** ► (1741–1801) American general in the American Revolution. Brilliant but erratic, he served with distinction at Fort Ticonderoga and Quebec (1775), commanded a fleet on Lake Champlain (1776), and fought in Connecticut, the Mohawk Valley, and Saratoga (1777). In 1780 he treacherously planned to surrender the vital West Point position. The plot miscarried and he fled to the British for whom he led raids in Virginia and Connecticut. From 1781 he lived in England.

● **Arnold, Sir Malcolm** ► (1921–) British composer. He began his career as trumpeter with the London Philharmonic Orchestra. His compositions include nine symphonies, concertos for guitar, harmonica, and trumpet, overtures, and ballet and film music.

● **Arnold, Thomas** ► (1795–1842) British educator. Appointed headmaster of Rugby (1828), Arnold reformed the school and instituted the form and prefectorial systems, which came to characterize English public schools. Arnold's piety was infectious, and Rugby became noted for "muscular Christianity." *Tom Brown's Schooldays* (see Hughes, Thomas) provides a eulogistic record of Arnold's achievement. His son **Matthew Arnold** (1822–88) was a poet and critic. He worked as a government inspector of schools from 1851 to 1886. His critical works include *Essays in Criticism* (1865; 1888) and *Culture and Anarchy* (1869), in which he advocated literary and cultural values as an antidote to the progressive materialism of Victorian society. His moral beliefs and doubts were given more personal expression in his poetry, which included "Dover Beach" (1867) and the narrative poems "The Scholar Gypsy" (1853) and "Sohrab and Rustum" (1853).

● **Arnold of Brescia** ► (d. 1155) Italian religious reformer. He studied at Paris, perhaps under ▷Abelard, and became an Augustinian canon after returning to Italy, where he immediately condemned the worldliness prevalent in the Church. He argued, among other things, that the papacy should not have secular power. He was excommunicated in 1148 and was eventually captured by Emperor Frederick Barbarossa, condemned, and hanged at Rome.

● **aromatherapy** ► A form of ▷alternative medicine that uses essential oils of plant origin, either combined with massage or taken internally, to enhance physiological functions or for the bactericidal properties attributed to them. Cosmetic aromatherapy is also given by many beauty salons to improve the health and appearance of the skin. The art was practised in classical Greece and was revived in the 1930s, when it was noticed that certain plant oils improved healing and left no scar. It became popular in the 1990s as more practitioners became available.

● **aromatic compound** ► A type of cyclic organic chemical compound that includes ▷benzene and its derivatives. On conventional theories of valence these compounds appear to be unsaturated (i.e. contain double bonds). However, benzene and similar compounds are much less reactive than the ▷alkenes, tending to undergo substitution reactions rather than addition reactions. The explanation for the stability of the benzene ring lies in a model in which the carbon atoms are joined by single bonds and the extra six valence electrons are free to move around the ring in a delocalized orbital. The phenomenon also occurs in some other compounds having an unsaturated ring, for example ferrocene ($Fe(C_5H_5)_2$). Aromatic compounds were originally distinguished from ▷aliphatic compounds because of the distinctive properties of benzene compounds, many of which have a fragrant odour.

● **Arp, Jean (Hans)** ► (1887–1966) French sculptor and poet. He was one of the founders of the ▷dada movement (1916) and later associated with the surrealist movement in Paris. Arp experimented with collages of torn coloured papers, designed according to chance, and produced numerous painted wood reliefs. In about 1930 he began his abstract sculptures suggesting organic rather than geometric forms. His wife and occasional collaborator was the artist Sophie Tauber (1889–1943).

● **Árpád** ► (died c. 907 AD) Magyar chieftain. In 875 Árpád led the Magyars from the Caucasus region into present-day Hungary in search of a new homeland after their defeat by the Pechenegs. He founded the first Hungarian royal dynasty, the Árpád, which ruled Hungary until 1301.

● **arquebus** ▷*See* musket.

● **Arrabal, Fernando** ► (1932–) Spanish playwright, novelist, and poet who writes in French and lives in France. His plays, which have some of the characteristics of the ▷Theatre of the Absurd, deal chiefly with themes of terror and violence; they include *Le Cimetière des voitures* (1958), *Le Grand Cérémonial* (1966), and *And They Put Handcuffs on the Flowers* (1973).

● **Arran** ► 55 35N 5 15W A Scottish island in the Firth of Clyde, off the Kintyre peninsula. Chiefly mountainous, its picturesque scenery contributes to its popularity as a tourist centre. Area: 427 sq km (165 sq mi). Population (latest est): 4000.

● **Arras** ► 50 17N 2 46E A town in N France, the capital of the Pas-de-Calais department on the River Scarpe. The former capital of Artois, it passed to France in 1640. It had a famous medieval tapestry trade and the tapestry called "arras" is named after it. Robespierre was born here. The 18th-century cathedral and fine 16th-century town hall were badly damaged during World War I. An agricultural market, its industries include agricultural machinery and hosiery. Population (1990): 42 715.

● **Arrau, Claudio** ► (1903–91) Chilean pianist. He gave his first recital at the age of five and studied in Berlin under Martin Krause (1853–1918), a pupil of Liszt. He returned to Chile in 1940 to found a piano school. He was famous particularly for his interpretations of Beethoven and Brahms.

The conventional formula of benzene devised by F. A. Kekulé von Stradonitz (1829–96). With alternating double bonds it would be unsaturated and have properties similar to the alkenes.

In the benzene molecule the bonds are actually intermediate between single and double bonds. This is often represented as a resonance hybrid between the two conventional structures.

The modern explanation of the bonding involves a delocalized orbital above and below the ring. The six valence electrons (one from each carbon atom) are free to move in this orbital. This explains the properties of benzene and the fact that all C-C bonds are equal.

aromatic compound

● **arrest** ► The forcible detention of a person to compel obedience to the law. In England, a person may be arrested on a magistrate's warrant to answer to a criminal charge, or for a civil offence, such as contempt of court. He may also be arrested if he commits, or is clearly about to commit, a crime. In theory any citizen can make an arrest and is bound to do so if a felony or breach of the peace is committed in his presence, but in practice most valid arrests are made by the police or other law-enforcement officers. A warrant is not required for the arrest of those who commit murder, theft, and certain other offences (the so-called "arrestable offences").

● **Arrhenius, Svante August** ▶ (1859–1927) Swedish physicist and chemist, who became professor of the University of Stockholm in 1895. He won the 1903 Nobel Prize for Chemistry for his theory of electrolytic dissociation. He later worked on the application of physical chemistry to living processes. His theory of universal life-diffusion involved "spores" emitted by habitable worlds and driven by light-pressure across space.

● **arrhythmia** ▶ An abnormal rhythm of the heart beat. Sometimes this may produce symptoms, such as palpitation, breathlessness, and chest pain. Arrhythmias may be associated with heart disease but may occur without any obvious cause.

● **Arrian** ▶ (Flavius Arrianus; 2nd century AD) Roman historian. As governor of ▷Cappadocia, he defeated a barbarian invasion (134 AD). He wrote several works on Asian history; his *Anabasis* is our most important source of information about ▷Alexander the Great.

● **Arromanches-les-Bains** ▶ 49 20N 0 38W A village in NW France, in the Calvados department. The main supply centre for the Allied Normandy invasion of 1944, it is the site of one of the two prefabricated Mulberry harbours.

● **arrow-poison frog** ▶ A small generally brightly coloured terrestrial frog belonging to a family (*Dendrobatidae*) occurring in Central and South American forests. Poisons produced by skin glands protect the frogs from predators and were used by Indians to poison arrow tips. In many species the young are incubated on the back of the male. Chief genera: *Dendrobates, Phyllobates*.

● **arrowroot** ▶ A herbaceous perennial plant, *Maranta arundinacea*, native to Guyana but widely cultivated in the West Indies for the edible and very pure fine starch that is extracted from its underground fleshy tubers and used in cooking. The plant is about 1.5 m high and has short-stalked white flowers and broad-bladed leaves with long narrow sheaths. Several other species yield a similar starch. Family: *Marantaceae*.

● **Arrowsmith, Aaron** ▶ (1750–1823) British cartographer, who founded a map-making firm (1790) that produced maps of exceptional quality. The business was carried on by his sons and by his nephew **John Arrowsmith** (1790–1873), who produced the *London Atlas* (1834) and was a founder of the Royal Geographical Society.

● **Arrow War** ▷*See* Opium Wars.

● **arrow worm** ▶ A small planktonic invertebrate animal belonging to a phylum (*Chaetognatha*; 50 species) occurring chiefly in tropical seas. Arrow worms have an elongated arrow-shaped body divided into a head, trunk, and tail, with fins on the sides and tail. They feed on crustaceans, larvae, etc.

● **ars antiqua** ▶ (Latin: old art) A style of European music of the 13th century. It was particularly associated with composers of the Parisian school, such as ▷Pérotin and Léonin (late 12th century), and characterized by the use of complex forms of ▷organum. It was succeeded by ▷*ars nova*.

● **arsenic** ▶ (As) A brittle semimetal that occurs in nature in a variety of forms: native, as the sulphides realgar (As_2S_2) and orpiment (As_2S_3), as sulpharsenides, such as arsenopyrite (FeSAs), and as arsenates. The element occurs in several forms and was known to the ancients. Pure arsenic has important uses as a dopant in the semiconductor industry. Arsenic and its common compounds are extremely poisonous; tests for its presence need to be accurate and reliable. Compounds include the white oxide (As_2O_3), the gaseous hydride arsine (AsH_3), and arsenates, some of which are used as insecticides. At no 33; at wt 74.9216; mp 817°C (28 atm); sublimes 613°C.

● **arsine** ▶ (*or* hydrogen arsenide; AsH_3) A colourless poisonous gas that smells like garlic. It is an unstable compound and decomposes into ▷arsenic and hydrogen.

● **Arsinoe II** ▶ (c. 316–270 BC) The daughter of ▷Ptolemy I Soter of Egypt. After two dynastic marriages she became the wife of and coruler with her brother ▷Ptolemy II Philadelphus (c. 276). Ambitious, forceful, and capable, she was an active participant in war, politics, and administration.

● **Arsinoe III** ▶ (c. 235–c. 204 BC) The sister and wife of Ptolemy IV Philopator (reigned 221–203 BC) of Egypt. She participated energetically in the power politics surrounding her lethargic husband. News of her murder, suppressed until Ptolemy's death, caused rioting, which overthrew her former rivals.

● **ars nova** ▶ (Latin: new art) A style of European music of the 14th century, which succeeded ▷*ars antiqua*. The name was taken from the title of a treatise by Philippe de Vitry (1291–1361), which set out new principles for the composition of ▷motets and for the notation of complex rhythms. Its greatest French exponents were ▷Machaut and ▷Dufay.

● **arson** ▶ At common law, maliciously setting fire to something, originally someone else's house or building, but later including other substantial objects, such as bridges and vehicles. As a distinct offence, arson was abolished in English law by the Criminal Damage Act (1971), which is the statute covering all types of criminal damage (the destruction or damage of property belonging to another). Criminal damage committed by fire is still, however, charged as arson.

● **Artaud, Antonin** ▶ (1896–1948) French actor, poet, producer, and theoretician of the theatre. In the 1920s he was involved with ▷surrealism and cofounded, with the poet and playwright Roger Vitrac (1899–1952), the Théâtre Alfred Jarry, where surrealist-inspired plays were produced that were forerunners of the ▷Theatre of the Absurd. Impressed by the symbolism, gesture, and other nonlinguistic elements of oriental theatre, he developed the theory of a ▷Theatre of Cruelty in essays later collected in *Le Théâtre et son double* (1938).

● **Artaxerxes II** ▶ (c. 436–358 BC) King of Persia (404–358). He defended his position against his brother ▷Cyrus the Younger, who was defeated and killed at ▷Cunaxa (401), and against a revolt of the provincial governors, the Satraps (366–358). Persia nevertheless declined under his rule.

● **Art Deco** ▶ The style of design predominant in the decorative arts of the 1920s and 1930s. The name derives from the 1925 Exposition Internationale des Arts Décoratifs et Industriels Modernes in Paris. In deliberate contrast to ▷Art Nouveau, Art Deco was characterized by emphatic geometrical lines and shapes, vibrant colour schemes, and the use of modern man-made substances, such as plastic. Influenced by the ▷Bauhaus, Art Deco included among its practitioners ▷Lalique and ▷Erté. It was debased by shoddy mass production, but interest in the style rekindled late in the 1960s.

● **Artemis** ▶ In Greek mythology, the daughter of Zeus and Leto and twin sister of Apollo. Settled in ▷Arcadia, she and her band of Oceanids and nymphs spent their time hunting. Love was banned, and Artemis rigorously punished all transgressors. ▷Actaeon was killed for watching her bathe and ▷Orion for touching her. Despite this severity, her help was invoked during childbirth, and she was protectress of both animal and human young. Ephesus was the most famous centre of her worship. She was associated with the moon and identified by the Romans with ▷Diana. *Compare* Hecate.

● **Artemis, Temple of** ▶ One of the Seven Wonders of the World, built at ▷Ephesus in 356 BC. The deity worshipped here was the many-breasted fertility goddess called Diana of the Ephesians in Acts 19.28, rather than the classical ▷Artemis.

● **Artemisia** ▶ (5th century BC) Queen of Halicarnassus. She accompanied Xerxes I on his invasion of Greece, despite her prophecy that the mission would fail, and fought bravely at Salamis (480).

● **Artemisia** ▶ (botany) ▷*See* wormwood.

● **arteriography** ▶ The radiological examination of arteries (*see* radiology). It is particularly useful for identifying coronary arteries clogged by ▷atherosclerosis (coronary arteriography *or* angiography).

● **arteriosclerosis** ▶ The loss of elasticity in the walls of arteries. It covers various conditions of the arteries and arterioles (small arteries) associated with the ageing process. It is also used as a synonym for ▷atherosclerosis.

● **artery** ▶ A thick-walled blood vessel that carries oxygen-rich blood away from the ▷heart to supply all the tissues and organs of the body. The largest is the aorta, which leads directly from the heart and descends into the abdomen, giving rise to all the other arteries (*see* Plate II). In middle age the lining of the arteries commonly becomes thickened by ▷atherosclerosis, which may lead to various diseases caused by obstruction of blood flow (e.g. strokes, heart attacks). ▷*See also* blood pressure.

● **artesian well** ▶ A well sunk into an aquifer (a water-saturated rock stratum) that is confined between two layers of impermeable rock and through which water flows upwards under pressure. The aquifer reaches the surface and receives rainfall where the water table is higher than the site of the well, resulting in a head of pressure.

● **Artevelde, Jacob van** ▶ (c. 1290–1345) Flemish statesman. In the 1330s he established the alliance of Flemish towns with those of Brabant, Hainault, and Holland to protect the Low Countries from the economic repercussions of the war between France and England. His dictatorial policies in Ghent, his home town, led to his assassination in 1345.

● **arthritis** ▶ Inflammation of one or more joints, causing pain, swelling, and restriction of movement. Many different diseases can cause arthritis, the most important of which are ▷osteoarthritis, rheumatoid arthritis, and ▷gout. **Rheumatoid arthritis**, which is more common in women, usually affects the hands and feet and often also the hips, knees, and shoulders. The synovial membrane lining the joint becomes inflamed, resulting in damage to the cartilage over the joint with consequent pain and deformity. An autoimmune disease (*see* autoimmunity), it is diagnosed by a blood test (the blood contains the rheumatoid factor) and X-rays. Treatment is usually based on analgesic and anti-inflammatory drugs; some patients benefit from gold salts and steroids, while severe cases may require surgical replacement of the affected joint(s).

● **arthropod** ▶ An invertebrate animal belonging to the largest and most diverse phylum (*Arthropoda*) of the animal kingdom, containing about a million species. These are grouped into three superclasses or subphyla (elevated to the status of phyla in some classification systems), based on the structure of their jointed appendages: *Chelicerata* (▷arachnids, ▷horseshoe crabs, sea spiders), *Uniramia* (or *Mandibulata*; ▷insects, ▷centipedes, ▷millipedes), and *Crustacea* (▷crustaceans). An arthropod has a segmented body with a hard outer skeleton (cuticle) made of ▷chitin, which is shed periodically to allow the body to grow. The appendages are modified for swimming, walking, feeding, respiration, reproduction, etc. Young arthropods often go through ▷metamorphosis to reach the adult form. Arthropods are found in fresh and salt water, air, and land and have exploited every food source. Many are harmful—as pests, parasites, or vectors of disease—but others are beneficial to man, as pollinators, food sources, predators of pests, and decomposers of organic wastes.

● **Arthur, Chester A(lan)** ▶ (1830–86) US statesman; Republican president (1881–84). Arthur came to power through the New York City Republican patronage system. As president he ran a surprisingly honest administration, which tried to reform the spoils system of appointments based on party service.

● **Arthur I** ▶ (1187–1203) Duke of Brittany, who claimed the English throne after the death (1199) of his uncle Richard I. Captured by Richard's successor John, Arthur was murdered, perhaps at John's command.

● **Arthurian legend** ▶ The body of medieval ▷romances concerning the legendary British king Arthur and his knights. Arthur first emerges as a figure of romance in the *Historia Regum Britanniae* of ▷Geoffrey of Monmouth, although a 6th-century military leader of the Welsh may have been a historical model. In the legend, he is the son of Uther Pendragon, was born at Tintagel in Cornwall, became king of Britain at 15, and won a number of famous victories. He married Guinevere and held court at Caerleon in Wales (or, in some versions, at □Camelot, which may have been near South Cadbury, Somerset). Involved in a war at Rome, he left his kingdom in the charge of his nephew Modred, who betrayed him and abducted Guinevere. Arthur returned to Britain and defeated Modred but was himself mortally wounded. He was taken away to the Isle of Avalon (the Celtic paradise, associated with Glastonbury) to be healed. Succeeding writers added new characters, themes, and episodes. ▷Wace

introduced the knightly fellowship of the Round Table and also mentioned the ancient tradition that one day Arthur would return from Avalon to rule Britain again. ▷Layamon added magical elements to the story, and French and other writers from the 12th century onwards, starting with ▷Chrétien de Troyes, took up the exploits of individual knights, such as Lancelot, Perceval, Gawain, and Galahad, and focused on the quest of the ▷Holy Grail, the adulterous affair of Guinevere and Lancelot, and other episodes. Other well-known characters were the magician Merlin and the sorceress Morgan le Fay (Arthur's sister). Sir Thomas ▷Malory's *Morte d'Arthur* (c. 1470) was the culmination of the medieval tradition, although the material has continued to inspire such versions as Tennyson's *Idylls of the King* (from 1842) and T. H. White's *The Once and Future King* (1958).

● **Arthur's Pass** ▶ 42 55S 171 34E A pass in the Southern Alps, New Zealand, linking the W coast by road and rail with Christchurch in the E. Height: 926 m (3038 ft).

● **artichoke** ▶ A perennial thistle-like herbaceous plant, *Cynara scolemus*, also known as globe artichoke, native to central and W Mediterranean regions and widely grown in warm temperate areas for its nutty-tasting immature flower heads, which are considered a great delicacy. The hairy indented straplike leaves, 1 m long, arise each year from the base of the short annual stems, which carry branched flower stalks bearing purplish flowers. Family: ▷*Compositae*. ▷*See also* Jerusalem artichoke.

● **Articles of Confederation** ▶ The first constitution of the USA (written 1776–77, adopted 1781), which was replaced by the Constitution of 1789. The leaders of the American Revolution feared the abuses of a centralized government and adopted a federal system that guaranteed each state its "sovereignty, freedom, and independence." The ▷Continental Congress could not levy taxes but could wage war and borrow and issue money.

● **artificial insemination** ▶ The artificial introduction of semen into the vagina of a female at a stage in the menstrual or oestrous cycle when the chances of conception are high (i.e. at ovulation). Although practised as early as the 14th century by Arab horse breeders, the techniques of artificial insemination used in the livestock industry were developed largely in the Soviet Union during the early 20th century. Semen collected from a single well-bred male can be stored at low temperatures for months before being used to fertilize many females. This has resulted in dramatic breed improvements and the control of venereal disease. Artificial insemination is occasionally used in human medicine; stores of human semen are kept frozen in sperm banks. In cases when the husband is infertile semen is obtained from an anonymous donor (artificial insemination donor—AID). Semen may be provided by the husband in cases of impotence (artificial insemination husband—AIH). When the wife is infertile the husband's semen may be used to artificially inseminate a surrogate mother. This woman gives birth to the child, usually for money, and must then be prepared to relinquish all claims on it to the natural father and his wife. Commercial surrogacy is growing in the USA, but in the UK the Surrogacy Arrangements Act (1985) prohibited commercial agencies from engaging women as surrogate mothers. ▷*See also* GIFT; test-tube baby.

● **artificial intelligence** ▶ (AI) The design of computer programs to perform tasks that involve intelligence when carried out by human beings. Tasks performed by AI include playing games, learning, using natural language and speech, formulating plans, proving theorems, and visual perception. Perceptual tasks involve unconscious processes in humans, which are hard to simulate. AI programs sometimes simulate human behaviour by building computer models of cognitive processes, but in most cases they adopt any technique that will do the task set or do it better than it has been done before.

● **artificial kidney** ▷*See* dialysis.

● **artificial respiration** ▶ The restoration of the flow of air into and out of the lungs when the patient's own breathing movements have ceased, for example after drowning, poisoning, etc. Mouth-to-mouth respiration—the "kiss of life"—involves a person breathing out into the patient's mouth: carbon dioxide in this exhaled air acts as a stimulus for the natural breathing reflexes. In hospitals artificial respiration by a ▷respirator is sometimes provided during surgery etc.

● **Artigas, José Gervasio** ► (1764–1850) The national hero of Uruguay. He fought for his country's independence from Argentina until he was driven into exile in Paraguay in 1820.

● **artillery** ► ▷Firearms with a calibre in excess of 20 mm, used to bombard enemy positions, disrupt communications, destroy enemy artillery, and provide cover and support for friendly troop deployments. Early guns were classed by projectile weight, e.g. 12-pounder. Modern weapons are identified by calibre: light (below 120 mm), medium (121–160 mm), heavy (161–210 mm), and super or very heavy (above 211 mm). Projectiles of ▷guns have flat trajectories, while ▷mortars and ▷howitzers have high trajectories, with correspondingly short ranges. Artillery rockets (excluding antitank missiles) deliver more explosive further, without needing heavy launchers. Some artillery projectiles have nuclear warheads, but most are high explosive. Modern electronic equipment enables artillery fire to score a direct hit with near certainty on any visible target; some modern artillery can be fired by remote control. The development of very long-range weapons (popularly called "superguns") in the 1980s caused some disquiet; in the aftermath of the Gulf War of 1991 Iraq was discovered to have been assembling such guns.

● **Artiodactyla** ► An order of hoofed mammals (150 species), distributed worldwide except for Australasia and Antarctica. Artiodactyls are terrestrial herbivores having two or four toes on each foot and often bearing horns. The group is divided into three suborders: *Suiformes* (pigs, peccaries, and hippopotamuses); *Tylopoda* (camels and llamas); and *Ruminantia* (*see* ruminant), which comprises deer, cattle, sheep, goats, antelopes, giraffes, pronghorns, and chevrotains. *Compare* Perissodactyla.

● **Art Nouveau** ► A decorative style pervading all visual art forms in Britain, France, Germany (*see* Jugendstil), Austria (Sezessionstil), Belgium, Spain, and the USA in the 1890s and early 1900s. It is characterized by designs of naturalistic foliage and biomorphic shapes linked by undulating lines. In Britain it is associated with the ▷Arts and Crafts movement of William ▷Morris, the designs of C. R. ▷Mackintosh, and the graphic work of Aubrey ▷Beardsley. On the Continent leading examples of Art Nouveau are the Parisian metro designs of Hector Guimard (1867–1942), the extravagant Barcelona flats and hotels of Antonio ▷Gaudí, and the Belgian stores and houses of Victor ▷Horta. A parallel effect in glassware of tinted glass and lead solder was achieved by René ▷Lalique and Emile Gallé (1846–1904).

● **Artois** ► A former province of NW France, approximating to the present-day Pas-de-Calais. It belonged until 1180 to the Counts of ▷Flanders, after which it passed to ▷Philip II Augustus of France. Acquired by the Counts of ▷Burgundy in 1329, it passed to the ▷Habsburgs in 1500 until regained by France during the ▷Thirty Years' War (1618–48).

● **Arts and Crafts movement** ► An English 19th-century aesthetic movement derived from William ▷Morris and his Pre-Raphaelite associates, whose firm was founded (1861) to produce handmade furnishings. The movement revived the principles of medieval craftsmanship and respect for materials; it also promoted the ideal of the artist as craftsman-designer. It culminated in the establishment of the Century Guild for Craftsmen (1882) and the Arts and Crafts Exhibition Society (1888). The preference for curvilinear patterns helped to create the emerging ▷Art Nouveau style.

● **Arts Councils** ► Four bodies, the Arts Councils of England, Scotland, Wales, and Northern Ireland, which act as the main channels for government support of the arts in the UK. In 1946 the Arts Council of Great Britain was established by royal charter to make the arts more accessible to the public and to encourage higher standards of artistic performance. The Scottish and Welsh Arts Councils became autonomous bodies in 1994 (that for Northern Ireland always having been separate). The Arts Council of England is funded by the Department of Culture, Media, and Sports and funds such national arts institutions as the Royal National Theatre as well as the ten regional Arts Boards. Since 1995 it has been responsible for allocating a large

portion of the funds from the National Lottery. Chairman of the Arts Council of England: Gerry Robinson.

● **Aruba** ► 12 30N 70 00W A West Indian island, formerly (until 1986) part of the Netherlands Antilles, but now a separate Dutch overseas territory. Oil refining is important. Official currency: florin of 100 cents. Area: 193 sq km (75 sq mi). Population (1994 est): 71 000. Chief town: Oranjestad.

● **arum** ► (*or* arum lily) A plant of the tropical African genus *Zantedeschia* (8 species), especially *Z. aethiopica*, widely grown as an ornamental. It has arrow-shaped leaves and a flower head of tiny yellow flowers surrounded by a white funnel-shaped spathe. Family: *Araceae*. The European genus *Arum*, of the same family, contains the ▷cuckoo-pint. The related bog arum, or wild calla (*Calla palustris*), grows in swamps of N temperate and subarctic regions. It has heart-shaped leaves and small flowers enveloped in a white spathe.

● **Arunachal Pradesh** ► (name until 1972: North-East Frontier Agency) A state in NE India, stretching N from the Brahmaputra Valley to the Himalayas. There it shares a disputed border with Tibet, from which Chinese troops have invaded twice since 1945. It became the 24th state of India in 1987. Over 60% is rainforest and most of the population is tribal. Area: 83 743 sq km (32 648 sq mi). Population (1994): 965 000. Capital: Itanagar.

● **Arundel** ► 50 51N 0 34W A market town in SE England, in West Sussex on the River Arun. Its 11th-century castle (mainly rebuilt in the 19th century) is the seat of the Dukes of Norfolk. Other notable buildings include the 19th-century Roman Catholic cathedral. Population (1991): 3033.

● **Arundel, Thomas** ► (1353–1414) English churchman, Archbishop of Canterbury (1396–97, 1399–1414). Impeached for opposing Richard II in 1397, he returned from banishment with Bolingbroke in 1399 and crowned him Henry IV. He actively suppressed the ▷Lollards.

● **Arval Brethren** ► (Latin: *Fratres Arvales*, Brothers of the Field) In ancient Rome, a college of 12 priests, who organized a festival every May dedicated to the corn goddess Dea Dia. The priests were chosen from high-ranking officials and included the emperor.

● **Aryans** ► Peoples speaking ▷Indo-European, ▷Indo-Iranian, or ▷Indo-Aryan languages. It has been claimed that all the Indo-European peoples originated from an Aryan people who dispersed from a common homeland into Europe and N India. Indo-Aryan-speaking peoples certainly invaded and settled in N India in the second millennium BC. They were tribal herdsmen who later became farmers. The earliest literature of India, the Vedas, written in ▷Sanskrit, contains hymns, spells, and details of Aryan ritual practices.

● **Arya Samaj** ► A controversial Hindu theosophical movement, founded in 1875 at Bombay by Swami Dayananda Saraswali (1824–83). It denounced popular idolatry and advocated a return to the oldest Vedic authorities. It also supported the emancipation of women and untouchables, because the old authorities neither justified nor assumed their lower status. Unlike many contemporary movements, Arya Samaj made no attempt to convert non-Indians.

● **ASA rating** ► The American Standards Association measure of the sensitivity or speed of photographic ▷film. A film rated at 200 is twice as fast (i.e. needs half the exposure time) as 100 ASA film. General-purpose films have speeds between 50 and 160 ASA. High-speed films for indoor photography and poor light are rated between 200 and 500 ASA.

● **asbestos** ► A fibrous form of certain silicate minerals, particularly the ▷amphiboles anthophyllite, tremolite, riebeckite, and actinolite, or a fibrous form of ▷serpentine, called chrysotile. Blue asbestos is crocidolite, a fibrous riebeckite. Asbestos is heat-resistant, chemically inert, and has a high electrical resistance; it has therefore a wide industrial application. The fibres are spun and woven or made into blocks. The main producer is Canada. ▷*See also* asbestosis.

● **asbestosis** ► A lung disease caused by the inhalation of asbestos fibres. It is an ▷occupational disease to which those exposed to large amounts of the mineral are particularly prone: tighter factory health controls have greatly reduced its incidence. It affects the air sacs of the lungs, which become thickened and scarred, causing breathlessness: patients are liable to develop lung cancer.

● **Ascaris** ▶ A genus of ▷nematode worms with a worldwide distribution, important as parasites of livestocks and man. Adult worms are smooth and cylindrical, 15-30 cm in length, and can live in the intestines of their hosts for up to a year. After mating, eggs pass out in the host's faeces and infection occurs when food contaminated with eggs is eaten.

● **Ascension** ▶ 7 57S 14 22W A rocky island in the S Atlantic Ocean, a dependency of St Helena. It has little vegetation and was uninhabited until 1815. A British telecommunications centre, it is also a US air base and space research station. Area: 88 sq km (35 sq mi). Population (1993): 1117. Chief settlement: Georgetown.

● **Ascension** ▶ In the Christian calendar, the day on which it is believed Christ ascended into Heaven (Acts 1.4-11). Since the 4th century it has been celebrated 40 days after Easter.

● **asceticism** ▶ Systematic self-discipline for spiritual ends, usually involving fasting, vigils, sexual abstinence, and renunciation of worldly goods and pleasures. ▷Stoicism advocated ascetic practices in order to subdue unruly passions. Christian asceticism is based on the theory of identifying with Christ's sufferings and is viewed not as an end in itself but as a means to contemplation of and spiritual union with the divine. It became an important element in certain monastic orders and in Christian ▷mysticism. In Islam, asceticism is particularly associated with ▷sufism and there is also a strong tradition of asceticism in Buddhism and Hinduism (*see* fakir).

● **Asch, Sholem** ▶ (1880–1957) Jewish novelist, born in Poland, who wrote chiefly in Yiddish. He travelled in Europe, Israel, and the USA, becoming a US citizen in 1920. In his controversial later novels, which include *The Nazarene* (1929) and *The Apostle* (1943), he expressed his belief in the essential unity of Judaism and Christianity.

● **Aschaffenburg** ▶ 49 58N 9 10E A town in central Germany, in Bavaria on the River Main. It contains the 17th-century Johannisburg Castle, a former residence of the Archbishops of Mainz. Its varied manufactures include clothing and precision instruments. Population (latest est): 62 050.

● **Ascham, Roger** ▶ (1515–68) English scholar and writer. His humanist scholarship was founded on his classical studies at Cambridge University. He served as Latin secretary to Edward VI, Mary, and Elizabeth I. His major works were *Toxophilus* (1545), a treatise on archery, and *The Scholemaster* (1570), a practical treatise on education.

● **Asclepius** ▶ (*or* Aesculapius) In Greek mythology, the god of medicine; a son of ▷Apollo. He was instructed by the centaur ▷Chiron in hunting and medicine and learned many miraculous cures. When he restored ▷Hippolytus to life as a favour to Artemis, Zeus became angry and struck him dead with a thunderbolt. The sick, believing in Asclepius' power to cure them through dreams, came to sleep in his temples at Epidaurus and on the island of Cos. His snake-entwined staff is the original medical symbol. *Compare* caduceus.

● **Ascoli Piceno** ▶ 42 52N 13 35E A town in central Italy, in Marche. An ancient settlement, it has many Roman and medieval remains. Its manufactures include glass, chemicals, and textiles. Population (latest est): 54 193.

● **Ascomycota** ▶ (*or* Ascomycetes) A large phylum of fungi (over 30 000 species), known as sac fungi because their spores are formed in a saclike structure (called an ascus). The nonreproductive part of these fungi is often a microscopical meshwork of cells. The group includes the ▷truffles, ▷yeasts, ▷Penicillium, and ▷Aspergillus.

● **ascorbic acid** ▷*See* vitamin C.

● **Ascot** ▶ 51 25N 0 41W A village in S England, in Bracknell Forest unitary authority, Berkshire. The construction of its famous racecourse was ordered by Queen Anne in 1711. Traditionally the sovereign opens the Royal Ascot meeting in June, driving in an open carriage round the course from nearby Windsor Castle. Population (latest est): 13 500, with Sunningdale.

● **ASCII** ▷*See* character set.

● **ASDIC** ▷*See* echo sounding.

● **ASEAN** ▷*See* Association of South-East Asian Nations.

● **asepsis** ▶ The condition in which material is uncontaminated by bacteria, fungi, and other disease-causing microorganisms. Surgical operations, the packaging of surgical supplies, and the preparation of intravenous drugs are carried out under aseptic conditions, which are produced by using ▷antiseptics, heat, or radiation.

● **Asgard** ▶ In Norse mythology, the home of the gods and of heroes killed in battle, comprising over 12 kingdoms and palaces, as well as ▷Valhalla. From earth it was reached by the bridge Bifrost (the rainbow).

● **ash** ▶ A tree of the genus *Fraxinus* (about 50 species), native to the N hemisphere. Many species yield a pale-yellow wood of commercial importance and others are widely grown as ornamentals. Reaching a height of 30 m, ashes have compound leaves made up of pairs of oval or lance-shaped leaflets, small inconspicuous flowers, and winged fruits ("ash keys"). Most species are deciduous, including the European ash (*F. excelsior*). Family: *Oleaceae* (olive family). ▷*See also* mountain ash.

● **Ashanti** ▶ A people of the S part of Ghana, who speak the Twi language. They are an agricultural people producing crops for local markets and cocoa for export. Their social organization is based upon matrilineal kin groups living in villages governed by headmen. The Ashanti established an empire in S Ghana during the 18th and 19th centuries, ruled by a paramount chief with military and religious functions. They worship a pantheon of gods and practise an ancestor cult.

● **Ashanti** ▶ A former kingdom in W Africa, now comprising S Ghana. During the 18th century it was active in the slave trade, supplying slaves to British and Dutch traders. Following several wars it became a British colony in 1902. The modern region of Ashanti occupies part of its area.

● **Ashby-de-la-Zouch** ▶ 52 46N 1 28W A market town in central England, in Leicestershire. Mary, Queen of Scots, was imprisoned in its castle in 1569. Population (1991): 10 595.

● **Ashcan School** ▶ A group of realist US painters active in the years before World War I. Although they painted urban outcasts and street life in New York, their preoccupation was with the visual rather than the social aspects of their subjects. Robert Henri (1865–1929), John Sloan (1871–1951), and George Bellow (1882–1925) were leading members of the group.

● **Ashcroft, Dame Peggy** ▶ (1907–91) British actress. She made her debut at the Birmingham Repertory Theatre in 1926. Her most notable performances included Juliet in 1935, Hedda Gabler in 1954, and roles in plays by Pinter and Beckett. She won an Oscar for her performance in the film *A Passage to India* (1984).

● **Ashdod** ▶ 31 48N 34 38S A town in central Israel, on the Mediterranean coast. It was an important city in the ancient Philistine Empire, and an artificial harbour (started 1961) has now made it into one of Israel's major ports. There is also textile manufacturing. Population (1997 est): 137 100.

● **Ashdown, Paddy, Baron** ▶ (Jeremy John Durham A.; 1941–) British politician, leader of the Liberal Democrats (1988–99). He entered parliament in 1983 after service in the Commandos and the Special Boat Section. He was knighted in 2000 and raised to the peerage in 2001.

● **Asher, tribe of** ▶ One of the 12 ▷tribes of Israel. It claimed descent from Asher, the son of Jacob and Jacob's concubine Zilpah. Its original territory was to the W and NW of the Sea of Galilee, adjoining Phoenicia.

● **Ashes** ▶ A mock trophy awarded to the winning team in cricket Test matches between England and Australia. It originated with the first Australian victory (1882), when an obituary for English cricket in the *Sporting Times* ended with words: "The body will be cremated and the ashes taken to Australia." In 1883 the victorious English captain was presented with an urn (now kept in the pavilion at ▷Lord's cricket ground) containing the ashes of the stumps used in the match.

● **Ashford** ▶ 51 09N 0 53E A market town in SE England, in Kent. It has light industries, including food and cosmetics, and is a centre for warehousing and distribution. Ashford is situated near the high-speed rail link to the Channel Tunnel and has the only international passenger station between London and the Continent. Population (1991): 52 002.

● **Ashkelon** ▶ (or Ashqelon) 31 40N 34 35E A seaport 19 km (12 mi) N of Gaza (Israel), known from the biblical story of Samson as a ▷Philistine stronghold. In Hellenistic times it was a cultural centre. The Arabs captured it in 636 AD. During the Crusades it changed hands several times before being destroyed by Sultan ▷Baybars I (1270). The modern Israeli settlement was established in 1948.

● **Ashkenazim** ▶ Jews of German or Eastern European origin, as opposed to ▷Sephardim. They have a distinct tradition of pronouncing Hebrew, as well as other customs, and until the 20th century they mostly spoke ▷Yiddish. The first Ashkenazy synagogue in London was founded in 1690. Ashkenazim now form some 85% of world Jewry.

● **Ashkenazy, Vladimir** ▶ (1937–) Russian-born pianist and conductor, famous for his interpretations of Mozart and Chopin, among others. He was joint winner of the 1962 Tchaikovsky Competition. He settled in Iceland in 1973 and was music director of the Royal Philharmonic Orchestra (1987–94).

● **Ashkhabad** ▶ 37 58N 58 24E The capital of Turkmenistan. It is near the Iranian border in an oasis in the ▷Kara Kum desert. Although virtually destroyed in 1948 by an earthquake, it has been rebuilt and is now an administrative, industrial, and transportation centre, producing food, carpets, glass, and machinery. Population (1995 est): 536 000.

● **Ashley Cooper, Anthony** ▷See Shaftesbury, Anthony Ashley Cooper, 1st Earl of.

● **Ashley, Laura** ▶ (born Laura Mountrey; 1925–85) British clothes designer and businesswoman. Born in Wales, she worked in London until her marriage to Bernard Ashley in 1949. During her first pregnancy she printed a floral fabric in her home, which she made into scarves. The success of this venture encouraged the Ashleys to expand into making dresses, skirts, and blouses, based on Victorian and Edwardian floral styles. Her first boutique in London, which opened in 1967, became a model for an international chain, developed in the 1970s and 1980s. After her death, her husband and children continued to run the company.

● **Ashmolean Museum** ▶ A museum in Oxford, housing paintings and archaeological collections. The collection was donated to Oxford University in 1675 by Elias Ashmole (1617–92) and put on public display in 1683. Now in C. R. ▷Cockerell's neoclassical building (1845), its highlights include Italian Renaissance paintings and English 19th-century works.

● **Ashmore and Cartier Islands** ▶ An external territory of Australia, situated in the Indian Ocean about 320 km (200 mi) NW of Cape Londonderry in Western Australia. The uninhabited territory consists of Cartier Island and the three Ashmore Islands, a group of tiny coral islets within a reef. The Ashmore Islands have an automated weather station and the reef is a national nature reserve. Area: 3 sq km (1.5 sq mi).

● **ashrama** ▶ In ▷Brahmanism, the *ashramas* are the four ideal stages of life through which Hindus of the upper three castes should pass. First comes the celibate student of religion, then the married householder, the forest hermit, and finally the wandering ascetic. Only in later life, therefore, can spiritual release be sought.

● **Ashton, Sir Frederick (William Mallandaine)** ▶ (1904–88) British ballet dancer and choreographer, born in Ecuador. He joined the Sadler's Wells Ballet in 1935, became an associate director in 1952, and was director of the Royal Ballet from 1963 to 1970. His works include *Cinderella* (1948), *Ondine* (1958), *La Fille mal gardée* (1960), and many ballets choreographed for Margot Fonteyn.

● **Ashton-under-Lyne** ▶ 53 29N 2 06W A town in N England, in Tameside unitary authority, Greater Manchester. It has plastics, engineering, and leather-goods industries. Population (1991): 43 906.

● **Ashur** ▶ The oldest Assyrian capital (modern Qalat Sharqat) on the River Tigris 96 km (60 mi) S of Mosul in Iraq. Ashur was already an important trading city in the heyday of ▷Sumer and ▷Akkad. Named after its guardian sun-god, Ashur became capital of the rising ▷Assyrian Empire (14th century BC) to which it gave its name. With its later cocapitals ▷Nimrud and ▷Nineveh it was destroyed in 612 BC. First excavated in 1903, Ashur's ruins include major temples and a ▷ziggurat.

● **Ashurbanipal** ▶ King of Assyria (668–?627 BC), son of Esarhaddon. He suppressed two serious revolts during his reign and conquered the city of Tyre, but is best known as the founder of a remarkable library at Nineveh, some of the items in which are now in the British Museum.

● **Ashurnasirpal II** ▶ King of Assyria (883–859 BC), who continued the restoration of the ▷Assyrian Empire by efficient administration, an invincible army, and brutality in punishing rebellion. He used deported captives to rebuild Kalhu (now ▷Nimrud, Iraq).

● **Ash Wednesday** ▶ In the Christian calendar, the first day of ▷Lent, which is so named from the custom, probably dating from the 8th century, of marking the foreheads of the congregation with ashes as a sign of penitence.

● **Asia** ▶ The largest continent in the world, it occupies about one-third of the dry land in the world. Asia is generally accepted as extending W to the Ural Mountains in Russia, although physically Europe is a peninsula of Asia. It is separated from the continent of Africa by the Red Sea and bounded on the N by the Arctic Ocean. Its S and E limits are less distinct and it includes the islands of Indonesia, Japan, the Philippines, and Taiwan. Asia is a continent of great diversity. Topographically it is the highest of the continents and has the greatest relief. It contains the world's highest point (Mount ▷Everest) and also its lowest (the ▷Dead Sea). Its great central mass of mountains and plateaus, which include the Himalayas, has historically formed a major barrier between N and S Asia. Vast alluvial plains border the major rivers, including the Rivers Ganges, Mekong, and Ob and the Yangtze and Yellow Rivers. Containing about half of the world's total population, it is the most populous continent, the highest concentrations being in the SE (China, India, and Japan). There are three main population groups: Negroid (in the Philippines), Mongoloid (including the Chinese, Japanese, and Koreans), and Caucasoid (including the Arabs, Afghans, and Pakistanis). Other groups, including the Malays, are a mixture of these main races. All the world's major religions originated in Asia, only Judaism and Christianity spreading W to any great extent. Others include Hinduism (with the largest following), Buddhism, Islam, Confucianism (in China), and Shintoism (in Japan). Agriculture is the chief occupation, employing about two-thirds of the total population. Asia also has important mineral resources, notably the oil and natural-gas deposits of the Arab states. Area: 44 391 162 sq km (17 139 445 sq mi). Population (1996 est): 3 499 626 000.

● **Asia Minor** ▶ (or Anatolia) The westernmost part of Asia between the Black Sea in the N, the Mediterranean Sea in the S, and the Aegean Sea in the W; it approximates present-day Turkey in Asia. For much of the second millennium BC, Asia Minor was the centre of the ▷Hittite empire. After the Hittites' collapse (12th century BC) central and W Asia Minor were dominated by ▷Phrygia until the 8th century, when the Assyrian Empire conquered SE Asia Minor. Phrygia fell to ▷Lydia in the 6th century but in 546 Cyrus the Great established Achaemenian control over Asia Minor. In 333 it was conquered by Alexander the Great: during the ▷Hellenistic age, the S was contested by the ▷Seleucids and the ▷Ptolemies, while small kingdoms, such as ▷Pergamum, ▷Cappadocia, ▷Bithynia, and ▷Pontus, were established elsewhere. Asia Minor came under Roman control in the 2nd and 1st centuries BC, forming part of the ▷Roman Empire and then the ▷Eastern Roman (subsequently Byzantine) Empire. Conquered by the Seljuq Turks in the 11th century AD and by the Mongols in the 13th, it was part of the Ottoman Empire during the 14th and 15th centuries.

● **Asian Games** ► An athletics meeting for all Asian countries affiliated to the International Amateur Athletic Federation. Quadrennial from 1954, they began in New Delhi in 1951.

● **asiento de negros** ► A contract between the Spanish Crown and a private contractor, in which the Crown sold the exclusive rights to import slaves into its American colonies. The *asiento* began in 1595 and was held successively by Portuguese, Genoese, French, English, and Spanish contractors before it was suppressed in 1778.

● **Asimov, Isaac** ► (1920–92) US science fiction writer and biochemist, born in Russia. He began writing science fiction in 1939. His many books include the *Foundation Trilogy* (1951–53; sequel 1982) and collections of short stories, notably *I, Robot* (1950), *Nightfall* (1969), and *The Edge of Tomorrow* (1986). His books popularizing scientific topics include *Inside the Atom* (1956) and *The Stars in their Courses* (1971).

● **Aske, Robert** ▷*See* Pilgrimage of Grace.

● **Askey, Arthur** ► (1900–82) British comedian. He became famous as 'Big-Hearted Arthur' in music hall and in radio shows, especially the wartime *Bandwagon*; his films included *The Ghost Train* (1941).

● **Asmara** ► (*or* Asmera) 15 20N 38 49E The capital of Eritrea, in the central highlands. The population still includes many Italians, Eritrea having been an Italian colony from 1890 until Allied occupation (1941). Notable buildings include the cathedral (1922) and Grand Mosque (1937); it has a university (1958). Industries include meat processing, distilling, and clothing. Population (1995 est): 431 000.

● **Aso, Mount** ► 32 55N 131 02E A volcano in Japan, on central Kyushu. It has five cones, one with the longest active crater in the world, 114 km (71 mi) in circumference. Height: 1592 m (5223 ft).

● **Asoka** ► (died c. 232 BC) Emperor of India (c. 270–c. 232 BC) of the Maurya dynasty (c. 321–c. 185 BC). His dominion extended over the whole of N India and most of the S. After his conquests he adopted the Buddhist faith and had his edicts carved on rock and stone pillars throughout the empire, telling the story of his conversion and issuing orders to comply with the morality of the new faith.

● **asp** ► An aggressive European ▷viper, *Vipera aspis*, that lives in dry habitats. About 60 cm long, it is grey-brown to coppery brown with dark bars or zigzags, grey, yellowish, or blackish underparts, and a yellow patch under the tail tip. The snout is upturned into a small spike. The 'asp' that killed Cleopatra was probably the Egyptian cobra (*Naja haje*).

● **Asparagus** ► A genus of herbaceous plants (about 300 species), with creeping underground stems (rhizomes), found throughout the Old World. *A. officinalis* is widely cultivated in temperate and subtropical regions for its young edible shoots, which are considered a delicacy. Several African species are ornamental: *A. plumosus*, known as **asparagus fern**, produces attractive feathery sprays of branchlets. Family: *Liliaceae*.

● **aspen** ► One of several ▷poplar trees having slender flattened leafstalks, so that the leaves tremble in the faintest breeze. The European aspen (*Populus tremula*), which grows to a height of 25 m has rounded toothed leaves. Its soft white wood is used for matches and paper pulp.

● **Asperger's syndrome** ► A mild form of ▷autism in which sufferers (nearly always male) are typically isolated and friendless. Those affected are often highly intelligent but lack emotional empathy. Preoccupation with detail and obsessive interest in specialized subjects are characteristic. Named after an Austrian paediatrician Hans Asperger (1906–80).

● **Aspergillus** ► A genus of fungi that includes many common moulds, often found on rotting food. Some species, especially *A. fumigatus*, can cause disease in man (aspergillosis), the most severe form of which affects the lungs producing tuberculosis-like symptoms. *A. flavus*, a mould that infects peanuts, produces the poison aflatoxin, which may be responsible for certain cancers. Phylum: ▷*Ascomycota*.

● **asphalt** ► A black highly viscous or solid hydrocarbon compound, used in road construction and the manufacture of roofing materials. It is obtained from the distillation of certain crude oils and from surface deposits (asphalt lakes), which occur naturally after the lighter fractions of a crude oil reservoir have evaporated.

● **asphodel** ► A white- or yellow-flowered lily-like plant of the mostly Mediterranean genera *Asphodelus* and *Asphodeline*. In Greek mythology, the asphodel associated with the dead and said to grow in the Elysian fields was *Asphodeline lutea*, which has yellow flowers. The asphodel of the early English and French poets was probably the daffodil. The bog asphodel (*Narthecium ossifragum*), of NW Europe, grows in swampy regions. It grows to a height of 30 cm and has a head of small yellow flowers. Family: *Liliaceae*.

● **asphyxia** ► Suffocation: obstruction to the supply of oxygen to the tissues. This is a life-threatening condition since the brain cannot survive for longer than about four minutes without oxygen. It can result from any condition that prevents air from reaching the lungs, including drowning and choking. Breathing poisonous gas (e.g. carbon monoxide) also causes asphyxia.

● **Aspidistra** ► A genus of herbaceous plants (8 species) native to E Asia. *A. elatior* is grown as a hardy pot plant in Western countries for its ornamental leaves, which are long, stiff, dark green (sometimes striped), and grow in sheaves from the reduced stem. It may occasionally produce small purple bell-shaped flowers. Family: *Liliaceae*.

● **aspirin** ► Acetylsalicylic acid: an ▷analgesic widely used in the form of tablets to treat mild pain, such as headache. It also relieves inflammation and is therefore helpful in the treatment of rheumatoid arthritis, and it reduces fever. Daily doses are also now used in the prevention of coronary thrombosis and strokes. In some people aspirin may cause bleeding from the stomach and it should not be given to children under 12.

● **Asplund, Erik Gunnar** ► (1885–1940) Swedish architect. A pioneer of the modern movement, Asplund combined elements of Swedish traditional styles and classical motifs in his work. He is best known for the Stockholm Public Library (1924–28) and the Woodland Chapel at the Stockholm Cemetery (1935–40). He planned the 1930 Stockholm Exposition, for which he designed a number of buildings.

● **Asquith, Herbert Henry, 1st Earl of Oxford and** ► (1852–1928) British statesman and Liberal prime minister (1908–16). Asquith's government introduced important social reforms, including noncontributory old-age pensions (1908 budget) and the National Insurance Act (1911); it ended the veto of the House of Lords with the 1911 Parliament Act. After the outbreak of World War I Asquith headed a coalition government (1915–16). He remained leader of the Liberal Party until 1926. His second wife **Margot Asquith** (1865–1945) wrote an outspoken *Autobiography* (1922). His children by his first marriage included **Lady Violet Bonham-Carter, Baroness Asquith** (1887–1969), who was president of the Liberal Party Organization (1944–45). His children by his second marriage included **Anthony Asquith** (1902–68), director of such films as *The Winslow Boy* (1948).

● **ass** ► A small fast-running mammal belonging to the genus *Equus* (horses), native to Africa and Asia. Asses are about 200 cm long, weigh up to 250 kg, and have long ears. The Asiatic wild ass (*E. hemionus*) has a grey or tan hide, a dark mane, and a dark stripe along the back. The African wild ass (*E. asinus*) is the ancestor of the domestic donkey. Asses have long been used as pack animals. ▷*See also* mule.

● **Assad, Hafiz al-** ► (1928–2000) Syrian statesman; president (1971–2000). In 1966, following a coup by radical Ba'athists, he became minister of defence. In 1970 he led a coup by the military wing of the Ba'ath party. His long period of rule saw economic progress based on oil wealth but severe repression of political opponents. In foreign affairs he remained deeply hostile to Israel and the West until the early 1990s, after which he tentatively mended relations. He was succeeded by his son, Bashar al-Assad (1965–   ).

● **Assam** ► A state in NE India, mostly in the Brahmaputra Valley beyond Bangladesh. High rainfall supports tea, Assam's economic mainstay. Rice, jute, sugar cane, and cotton are also grown. Other than forest products and crafts there is little manufacturing. Assam produces half of India's oil, as well as coal.
History: a flourishing region by 1000 BC, Assam received later migrants from China and Burma (now Myanmar). Burmese invasions

led Britain to assume control (1826). In World War II Assam played a strategic role in the Allied advance into Burma. In recent years the region has been troubled by ethnic unrest. Area: 78 523 sq km (30 310 sq mi). Population (1991): 22 294 562. Capital: Dispur.

● **assassin bug** ▶ An insect belonging to a widely distributed family (*Reduviidae*; 4000 species), usually black or brown with a long beak used to pierce the skin and suck blood or body fluids from its prey. Assassin bugs generally prey on other insects but some attack mammals, including man. As well as inflicting a painful bite, they may transmit diseases, such as kala-azar and Chagas' disease. Suborder: *Heteroptera*; order: ▷Hemiptera.

● **Assassins** ▶ (Arabic: hashish eaters) A sect of the Ismaili. In Persia and Syria in the 12th and 13th centuries they were notorious for their practice of stabbing opponents to further their political and religious aims. It was commonly believed that the stabbings were carried out while they were under the influence of hashish, hence their name. They killed mainly Muslims, but also some Crusaders.

● **assault and battery** ▶ In law, battery is the unlawful use of any physical force on someone else. Assault is an attempt to commit a battery or any other unlawful act that makes someone reasonably fear battery, whether or not there is any real intention to harm him. The offender is likely to face criminal charges and may also be sued for damages by his victim. Some "aggravated" assaults, as for example with a deadly weapon, carry higher penalties.

● **assemblage** ▶ A work of art in which random objects and materials are integrated on a panel or in a free-standing construction, often to produce a satirical or surrealist effect. Early examples, from around 1915, include the ▷ready-mades of ▷Duchamp and the collages of Picasso. More recent assemblages are those of the ▷pop art movement, using everyday objects, such as clothing, furniture, and household utensils.

● **assembler** ▶ A computer ▷program that makes up part of the ▷software of a computer. It converts instructions in a programming language into a form that the machine can follow directly.

● **Asser** ▶ (died c. 909) Welsh monk and Bishop of Sherborne. Known for his learning, he was invited to the court of Alfred the Great. Although his biography of Alfred, *De rebus gestis Alfredi Magni*, ends in 887, it is the chief source of historical information about Alfred's reign.

● **assignats** ▶ Paper money issued (1789–96) during the ▷French Revolution in order to pay off the government's debts. Initially they stimulated the economy and solved the problem of money shortage but ultimately they caused inflation, which reached a peak in 1795, when assignats with a face value of 45,500 million francs but virtually no real value were in circulation.

● **Assiniboine River** ▶ A river in W Canada, rising in SE Saskatchewan and flowing generally SE through wheat-growing country to join the Red River at Winnipeg. Length: 950 km (590 mi).

● **Assisi** ▶ 43 04N 12 37E A town in central Italy, in Umbria. It is the birthplace of St ▷Francis of Assisi, who founded the Franciscan Order in 1209. The Franciscan convent has two gothic churches containing frescoes by Giotto (badly damaged by earthquake in 1997). Population (1990): 24 790.

● **Assiut** ▷*See* Asyut.

● **Associated Press** ▷*See* news agency.

● **association** ▶ In psychology, the linking of one idea to another. Similarity of meaning, physical similarity, and contrast can all cause an idea to call forth several others. When two mental events occur together an association forms between them: this is the basis of one kind of learning. According to the associationist school of psychology, the association of ideas is the basic process underlying human behaviour. **Free association** is the chief method of ▷psychoanalysis: a patient speaks aloud his stream of consciousness, from which the analyst obtains clues to the underlying unconscious thought processes.

● **Association football** ▷*See* football.

● **Association of Caribbean States** ▶ A trading group embracing all 25 countries that border the Caribbean Sea, established in 1994 under the sponsorship of the ▷Caribbean Community (CARICOM). In addition to the 15 members of CARICOM it includes Belize, Colombia, Costa Rica, Cuba, the Dominican Republic, Honduras, Mexico, Nicaragua, Panama, and Venezuela.

● **Association of South-East Asian Nations** ▶ (ASEAN) An international organization, founded in 1967, to assist the development of its member states (now Brunei, Indonesia, Laos, Malaysia, Myanmar (Burma), the Philippines, Singapore, Thailand, and Vietnam). It aims to eliminate trade barriers, promote cultural exchanges, facilitate communications, and improve technology, commerce, and industry.

● **associative law** ▶ The mathematical rule, obeyed by addition and multiplication in ordinary ▷arithmetic, that the order in which successive identical operations are performed does not affect the result: for addition $a + (b + c) = (a + b) + c$; for multiplication $a(bc) = (ab)c$.

● **assurance** ▶ A form of ▷insurance against an event, such as death, that must occur. There are four main types: term assurance, whole-life assurance, endowment assurance, and an ▷annuity. Term assurance is a form of life assurance that only pays out if the assured dies within a stipulated period (e.g. while a businessman is on a specific journey). Whole-life assurance pays out on the death of the assured whenever it occurs. Premiums may continue to be paid throughout the assured's life or may cease at a stipulated age (e.g. 65). Endowment assurance pays out either on the death of the assured, whenever it occurs, or after a fixed number of years (e.g. when the assured reaches the age of 60). Most assurers require the assured to submit to a medical examination before granting whole-life or endowment assurance. Policies may be "with profits," entitling the assured to a share in the assurer's profits (which is added to the sum assured when it is paid out), or, for a lower premium, "without profits," in which case only the sum assured is paid out (which in times of inflation may have considerably less purchasing power than the assured intended).

● **Assyrian Empire** ▶ An ancient kingdom on the Upper Tigris (now N Iraq), where the Assyrians (named after their god Ashur) settled in about 2500 BC, forming a dependency of Babylon. Ashur-uballit I (c. 1365–c. 1330) laid the foundations of the Empire, which after a period of decline was extended by ▷Tiglath-pileser I (1120–1074), who conquered the city of Babylon. A new era of aggressive expansion was initiated by ▷Ashurnasirpal II (883–859). The Assyrian domain was extended to Syria and Palestine under Shalmaneser III (858–824) and Assyrian ascendancy reached its zenith under ▷Tiglath-pileser III (745–727). ▷Sargon II (722–705), ▷Sennacherib (704–681), and ▷Esarhaddon (680–669) maintained the Empire but ▷Nineveh, the capital, fell to Media and Babylon in 612. The Assyrians built magnificent palaces with friezes that reflected their warlike character.

● **Astaire, Fred** ▶ (Frederick Austerlitz; 1899–1987) US dancer and film star. He began his career as a music-hall dancer. His best-known films are the 1930s musicals in which he partnered Ginger Rogers. These include *Top Hat* (1935), *Follow the Fleet* (1936), and *Shall We Dance* (1937). His later costars included Judy Garland, Leslie Caron, and Audrey Hepburn.

● **Astana** ▶ (name until 1961 and from 1994 until 1998: Akmola; name from 1961 until 1994: Tselinograd) 51 10N 71 25E A city in N Kazakhstan; it replaced Alma Ata as the capital of Kazakhstan in 1998, when it was given its present name. Population (1995 est): 280 200.

● **Astarte** ▶ The Phoenician goddess of love and fertility, equivalent to the Babylonian ▷Ishtar and sometimes regarded as the counterpart of ▷Aphrodite. She was associated with the moon and often represented by a crescent.

● **astatine** ▶ (At) A short-lived radioactive ▷halogen. Its longest-lived isotope, ^{210}At, has a half-life of 8.1 hours. Small amounts exist in nature as a result of uranium and thorium decay. At no 85; at wt (210); mp 302°C; bp 337°C.

● **Astbury, John** ▶ (1688–1743) English potter, to whom are attributed some of the earliest Staffordshire figures in red clay decorated with white. He also made tableware and it is possible that he originated the groups of figures known as pew groups. Astburyware, produced also by his son Thomas Astbury (1719–60), is of a very fine quality and is now extremely valuable.

● **Aster** ▶ A genus of perennial herbaceous plants (about 500 species), many species of which are commonly known as Michaelmas daisies. Native to N temperate regions, they are widely grown as garden plants. Usually 60–100 cm tall, they have flowers with blue, red, or white rays and a central yellow disc. *A. amellus* and *A. aeris* are common ornamental species. Family: ▷*Compositae*.

● **Asteraceae** ▷*See* Compositae.

● **asteroid** ▷*See* minor planet.

● **asthma** ▶ A disorder in which breathlessness and wheezing are aggravated by certain stimuli, which cause the bronchi (which conduct air to the lungs) to become constricted. Bronchial asthma may be stimulated by a wide range of conditions and substances: it may be an allergic reaction (*see* allergy), it may occur secondarily to respiratory infection, or it may be brought on by exertion, certain drugs, or strong emotion. The most common treatment is by means of bronchodilator drugs (which dilate the bronchi), with or without corticosteroids, which are usually administered in the form of aerosol inhalers; severe asthmatic attacks require oral corticosteroids. Cardiac asthma is associated with some forms of heart disease and requires a different treatment.

● **Asti** ▶ 44 54N 8 13E A town in NW Italy, in Piedmont. It is famous for its sparkling wine (Asti Spumante). Population (1990): 74 649.

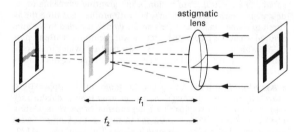

astigmatic
lens

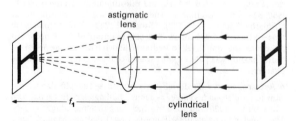

astigmatic
lens

cylindrical
lens

astigmatism ▶ An astigmatic lens cannot focus vertical and horizontal lines at the same time. Here the vertical focal length f_1 is shorter than the horizontal focal length f_2. In the human eye this would be corrected by spectacles with cylindrical lenses, reducing the overall focal length in the horizontal plane only, so that both vertical and horizontal lines are in sharp focus at distance f_1.

● **astigmatism** ▶ A form of ▷aberration that can occur in mirrors and lenses (including the eye). It results when the curvature is different in two mutually perpendicular planes; rays in one plane may then be in focus while rays in the other are out of focus. It is corrected in the eye by the use of cylindrical lenses.

● **Astilbe** ▶ A genus of perennial herbaceous flowering plants (about 25 species), native to E Asia and North America and commonly cultivated for ornament in temperate regions. The flowers (usually pink or red) grow in branching plumelike clusters; the plants may reach a height of 1.5 m. Family: *Saxifragaceae*.

● **Aston, Francis William** ▶ (1877–1945) British chemist, who worked in the Cavendish Laboratory, Cambridge. He developed the mass spectrometer for separating ions according to their atomic weight. His discovery of the isotopes of many nonradioactive elements, and of the whole-number rule governing their masses, won him the 1922 Nobel Prize for Chemistry.

● **Astor, John Jacob** ▶ (1763–1848) US businessman; founder of the well-known family of financiers. A German emigrant, he made a fortune with his monopolistic American Fur Company. He then invested so extensively in New York property that the Astor family became known as the landlords of New York. He died reputedly the richest man in the USA.

● **Astor, Nancy Witcher, Viscountess** ▶ (1879–1964) British politician, who was the first woman MP to sit in the House of Commons (1919–45). An American by birth, she championed the causes of women's rights and education, representing the constituency that was formerly that of her husband **Waldorf, 2nd Viscount Astor** (1879–1952). An MP from 1910 to 1919, Astor (the great-great-grandson of John Jacob ▷Astor) was proprietor (1919–45) of the *Observer* newspaper.

● **Astrakhan** ▶ 46 22N 48 04E A port in SE Russia, on the River Volga. The city was an important trading centre with the East until the Russian Revolution, after which its importance declined. Astrakhan fur, from the Karakul lamb of central Asia, was first brought to Russia by Astrakhan traders. More than half the population is employed in fishing or allied occupations. Population (1995 est): 486 000.

● **astrobiology** ▶ (*or* exobiology) The branch of biology that investigates the possibility of life on other planets. Astrobiologists monitor the electromagnetic spectrum, including light and radio waves, emitted by the stars for evidence of the organic molecules that are a prerequisite of life on earth. They are also involved in designing life-detecting experiments carried to planets in our own solar system by space probes.

● **astrolabe** ▶ An instrument, invented in about 200 BC, used primarily in navigation and astronomy until the 18th century, when it was superseded by the ▷sextant. A disc of wood or metal calibrated round its circumference in degrees, it was fitted with a sighting pointer (alidade), the angle of which when aligned with the sun or certain stars enabled the time of day as well as latitude and longitude to be calculated.

● **astrology** ▶ The study of the movements and positions of the heavenly bodies in relation to their presumed influence upon human affairs. Astrology originated in ▷Babylonia and then passed to Greece, India, China, and the Islamic lands. In medieval Europe astrologers had a respected role in public and personal life. Astrology is based upon an elaborate system of putative correspondences between celestial and mundane phenomena: each "house" (*see* zodiac), for instance, imparts a particular character to those born under its influence and the sun, moon, and principal planets in various positions relative to the houses and to each other predispose people to good or ill. The two branches of astrology are "natural" (concerned mainly with observations and theory) and "judicial" (foretelling events in individual lives by means of a horoscope, or natal chart). ▷*See also* birthstone.

● **astrometry** ▶ The measurement of the positions of stars and other celestial objects using optical or radio astronomy techniques.

● **astronomer royal** ▶ An eminent British astronomer appointed by the sovereign on the advice of the prime minister. Until 1971 the astronomer royal was also head of the Royal Greenwich Observatory. The first holder was John Flamsteed, appointed in 1675 when the Observatory was founded. The present holder is Sir Martin Rees.

● **astronomical clock** ▷*See* time.

● **astronomical unit** ▶ (AU) A unit of length equal to the mean distance between the earth and the sun (1.495×10^{11} metres, 92.9×10^6 miles).

● **astronomy** ▶ The study of celestial bodies and the universe of which they form part. One of the most ancient of the sciences, naked-eye astronomy flourished in China, Babylonia, Egypt, and classical Greece (*see* Aristarchus of Samos; Hipparchus; Ptolemaic system). After the decline of ancient Greek culture, interest in astronomy was the preserve of the Arabs for many centuries. European interest in the heavens, transmitted from the Arabs through Spain, reawakened in the 16th century with the work of ▷Copernicus and Tycho ▷Brahe, who were able to separate the science of astronomy from ▷astrology. But it was not until 1609 that Galileo's refracting ▷telescope (invented in Holland in 1608) enabled the sky to be investigated in any detail; in 1671 Newton devised the more effective reflecting telescope. These devices provided the means for the development of ▷astrometry and ▷celestial mechanics. In the 19th century, the use of spectroscopy (*see* spectrum) to study the physical and chemical composition of celestial bodies provided the basis for the new sciences of ▷astrophysics and astrochemistry.

Until the 1930s all observations of the heavens were made by observing the light that passed through the "optical window" in the atmosphere. ▷Jansky's discovery (1932) that radio waves are emitted by celestial bodies, enabled the "radio window" in the earth's atmosphere: light, near-ultraviolet, and near-infrared radiation, spanning wavelengths from about 300–900 nanometres, can pass through the atmosphere without significant absorption by atoms and molecules. There is also a "radio window" allowing radio waves with wavelengths of about 30 metres to less than a millimetre to be transmitted to the earth's surface. Jansky's discovery (1932) of the first cosmic radio source marked the beginnings of ▷radio astronomy. The optical and radio windows, together with several narrow-band infrared windows are the only wavelength ranges at which ground-based astronomical observations are possible.

The advent of high-altitude balloons and rockets and then artificial satellites orbiting above the atmosphere has revolutionized astronomy: the radiation from space that is absorbed by the atmosphere—gamma rays, X-rays, ultraviolet, and most wavelengths of infrared radiation—can now be studied in ever-increasing detail by equipment carried on these platforms. Investigations of cosmic sources of X-rays, gamma rays, and ultraviolet radiation are providing information on the more violent phenomena occurring in the universe. Observations of infrared sources, by satellite-based and high-altitude ground-based telescopes, are yielding information on, for example, the birth of stars. Planetary probes, such as the Voyager craft, have greatly increased our knowledge of the solar system.

Highly sensitive electronic devices are now available to detect the various forms of radiation from celestial bodies, while computer systems are used to control the major telescopes and to process the information they gather. The advances in observational astronomy produce results that in turn develop the theoretical branches of astronomy, such as ▷cosmology.

● **astrophysics** ▶ The study of the physical and chemical processes and characteristics associated with celestial objects. It is based on theories developed in astronomy, physics, and chemistry and on observations of the radiation emitted by the objects. Originally only studies at optical and then at radio and infrared wavelengths were made, but sources of X-rays, gamma rays, and ultraviolet radiation can now also be observed. ▷*See also* cosmology.

● **Asturias** ▶ An autonomous region in NW Spain on the Bay of Biscay. When the Muslims invaded Spain in 718, the Visigoths withdrew to Asturias, where, protected by the Cantabrian Mountains in the S, they established a new kingdom, preserving Visigothic and Christian traditions. During the next two centuries, Asturias, the sole surviving Christian Spanish kingdom and the centre of resistance to the Muslim advance, expanded into León and Galicia, especially under Alfonso III (reigned 866–c. 910). After his death the kingdom was divided between León, Castile, and Navarre. Population (1992 est): 1 118 610. Capital: Oviedo.

● **Asturias, Miguel Ángel** ▶ (1899–1974) Guatemalan novelist and poet. His novel *El Señor Presidente* (1946) is a study of political dictatorship; other works, such as *Hombres de Maíz* (1949) and *Mulata de tal* (1960), reflect his interest in Mayan culture. He was awarded the Nobel Prize in 1967.

● **Asunción** ▶ 25 15S 57 40W The capital of Paraguay, an important port in the S on the River Paraguay. Founded in 1536, it was for a time

the centre of the Spanish settlements in the area. The National University was founded in 1890 and the Catholic University in 1960. Industries include flour milling, food processing, and textiles. Population (1992): 502 426.

● **Aswan** ▶ (or Assuan; Greek name: Syene) 24 05N 32 56E A city in S Egypt, on the River Nile. Some ruins of the ancient city of Syene remain. The city is a popular tourist centre and winter resort. Nearby quarries supplied granite for many Egyptian monuments. The ▷Aswan High Dam and earlier Aswan Dam are nearby. Population (1992 est): 220 000.

Aswan High Dam ▶ Spanning the Nile at one of its narrowest points, this dam controls the annual flooding of the Nile and has provided irrigation water and hydroelectric power.

● **Aswan High Dam** ▶ A major dam in Egypt, on the River Nile near Aswan. Begun in 1960 and financed by the Soviet Union, it was completed in 1970. It is about 5 km (3 mi) long and 100 m (328 ft) high; its reservoir, **Lake Nasser**, extends for about 560 km (350 mi) behind the dam. Since its construction the famous annual Nile floods have been controlled and water is available for irrigation, for domestic and industrial purposes, and for hydroelectric power. Ancient Nubian monuments (notably the ▷Abu Simbel and ⌐Philae temples) that were threatened with permanent flooding were moved to new sites. About 7 km (4 mi) downstream is the earlier **Aswan Dam** (completed 1902); 2 km (1.2 mi) long and 54 m (177 ft) high, this provides irrigation water.

● **asymptote** ▶ A straight line that a two-dimensional curve approaches but never meets as the curve is extended infinitely.

● **Asyut** ▶ (or Assiut; ancient name: Lycopolis) 27 14N 31 07S The largest city in Upper Egypt, on the River Nile. It is an important commercial centre and is renowned for its handicrafts, such as ivory carvings and tulle shawls, and its textile industries. Below the city the Asyut barrage provides water for irrigation. It has a university (1957). Population (1986 est): 291 300.

● **Atacama Desert** ▶ (Spanish name: Desierto de Atacama) A cool arid area in N central Chile, extending for about 1100 km (700 mi) S from the Peruvian border. It consists chiefly of a series of salt basins and is one of the driest areas in the world; in some parts no rain has ever been recorded. There are valuable deposits of copper and it is a major source of nitrates. Area: about 80 290 sq km (31 000 sq mi).

● **Atahuallpa** ▶ (or Atahualpa; d. 1533) The last King of the Inca Empire (1532–33). On the death of his father Huayna Capac (1525) the Empire was divided between Atahuallpa and his brother Huascar. Atahuallpa overthrew his brother and declared himself king but was then captured by the Spanish conquistador Pizarro and, in spite of paying a huge ransom, was executed.

● **Atalanta** ▶ A swift-footed huntress of Greek mythology. Hippomenes (or Meilanion), on her promise to marry any man who could outrun her, raced with her. Furnished with three of the Hesperides' golden apples by ▷Aphrodite, which he dropped to distract her, he won the race and married her.

Kemal Atatürk ▶ A photograph taken during World War I. A great Westernizer, Atatürk abolished the traditional fez, gave women the vote, and replaced the Arabic alphabet with the Roman alphabet.

● **Atatürk, Kemal** ▶ (Mustafa Kemal; 1881-1938) Turkish statesman, who was the chief founder of modern Turkey; president (1923-38). Born in Salonika, he entered the army and distinguished himself in World War I. After the war he opposed the humiliating Treaty of Sèvres and as president of the provisional government organized the defeat of the Greek invasion of Asia Minor (1920). In 1922 the Ottoman sultan was deposed and Mustafa Kemal became the first president of Turkey. From then until his death he worked to make Turkey a modern secular state. He took the surname Atatürk (Father of the Turks) in 1934.

● **ataxia** ▶ Loss of muscular coordination, often caused by disease of the part of the brain (the cerebellum) that controls movement. Ataxia may accompany severe vitamin B_{12} and folic acid deficiencies or follow a brain haemorrhage.

● **Atget, (Jean) Eugène (Auguste)** ▶ (1856-1927) French photographer. He turned to photography in 1898 after a career first at sea and later on the stage. He specialized in scenes of Parisian life, including a notable series on brothels (commissioned 1921). Apart from Man ▷Ray's interest in the surrealist effect of his shop-window series, he received recognition only after his death.

● **Athabasca, Lake** ▶ A lake in W Canada, in NW Saskatchewan and NE Alberta, drained by the Slave River. Uranium ores were discovered on the N shore (1950s). Area: 8080 sq km (3120 sq mi).

● **Athabascan** ▶ A group of North American Indian languages spoken by tribes living to the west of Hudson Bay in Alaska and Canada, and by some tribes of the SW USA. The northern group includes Koyukon, Tanana, ▷Ojibwa, Slave, and Yellowknife, and the southern group includes ▷Apache and ▷Navajo.

● **Athabasca River** ▶ A river in W Canada, in N Alberta flowing from the Rocky Mountains to Lake Athabasca through tar sands estimated to contain half the world's known oil reserves. Length: 1230 km (765 mi).

● **Athanasian Creed** ▶ A Christian profession of faith traditionally attributed to St ▷Athanasius but probably dating from the 5th century. Its central statements concern the doctrines of the ▷Trinity and of the ▷Incarnation. Once popular in the Western Churches, it is now little used.

● **Athanasius, St** ▶ (296-373 AD) Egyptian churchman, Bishop of Alexandria. After attending the Council of ▷Nicaea in 325, he was appointed Bishop of Alexandria in 328 and remained primate of Egypt for 43 years. During this time he led the opposition to the powerful ▷Arianism that flourished in the East under the emperors Constantine and Constantius. He was expelled from his see four times, but his orthodox teaching regarding the divinity of Jesus Christ was ultimately affirmed by the Council of Constantinople (381). Feast day: 2 May.

● **atheism** ▶ The denial of the existence of God (or gods). Historically atheism has taken many different forms. In theocratic societies charges of atheism were frequently made against individuals or groups suspected of antisocial behaviour or of dissent from the prevailing orthodoxy. Philosophical materialists, such as ▷Hobbes, were also attacked as atheists but the spread of ▷rationalism in the 18th century created a climate sympathetic to atheism. In the 19th century, scientific advances challenged the old arguments for the existence of God, making atheism respectable philosophically, if not socially. Today rigorous atheists hold either that the concept of God, being untestable, is simply meaningless (*see* logical positivism) or that all we know by scientific means about the universe suggests that God is a false notion (*see* humanism). *Compare* agnosticism.

● **Athelney, Isle of** ▶ A small area in Somerset, near the confluence of the Rivers Tone and Parrett. It was formerly an island, isolated by marshes. Alfred the Great built a small fortification here in 878 as a base for his campaign against the Danes.

● **Athelstan** ▶ (d. 939) King of England (925-39), succeeding his father Edward the Elder; he was crowned King of Mercia in 924. He defeated a Scottish invasion force in 937 and is also known for six extant legal codes.

● **Athena** ▶ (or Pallas Athena) The Greek goddess of war and of wisdom, the protectress of Athens. Born from the head of Zeus, fully armed with a javelin, she was his favourite child. In the Trojan War she constantly aided the Greeks. She also helped Heracles in his labours and guided Perseus on his expedition against the Gorgons. Odysseus voyaged home from Troy under her protection. A virgin goddess, in peacetime she was a patroness of the arts and industry. Athens is named after her, and the Parthenon was the centre of her worship. She is identified with the Roman ▷Minerva.

● **Athenagoras** ▶ (2nd century AD) Greek Christian apologist, who taught in Athens and Alexandria. His *Apology* or *Legatio pro Christianis* (177) addressed to ▷Marcus Aurelius, defended Christianity against charges of cannibalism and licentiousness arising from misunderstandings of the doctrines of the Eucharist and universal love.

● **Athens** ▶ (Modern Greek name: Athínai) 37 59N 23 42E The capital of Greece, situated on a plain in the SE of the country near the Saronic Gulf. It is the administrative, cultural, and economic centre of the country and is administratively joined to its port and main industrial sector, ▷Piraeus. Tourism is an important source of revenue. Athens combines the ancient and the modern, with only one or two small Byzantine and neo-Byzantine churches surviving to testify to the period between Roman times and the early 19th century. The many remains of ancient Athens are focused on the Acropolis. Crowned by the ▷Parthenon, it contains the Ionic Erechtheum, the Propylaea (a gateway), and the tiny temple of Athena Nike. To the NW, the recently restored Agora (market), contains the Theseum (5th century BC), probably the best-preserved ancient temple. To the N and E lies modern Athens, which includes the university, founded in 1837.

History: there is evidence of settlements dating back to the 3rd millennium BC. Athens probably enjoyed its first rise to fame under Pisistratus and his sons in the 6th century BC. Around 506 Cleisthenes established a democracy for the free men of Athens. During the following century it became the leading Greek city state, defeating the Persians with the aid of its navy (*see* Greek-Persian Wars). The Long Walls, connecting the city to Piraeus, and the Parthenon date from this period. Under Pericles, it reached a peak of intellectual brilliance with the philosophy of Socrates and the drama of Aeschylus, Sophocles, and Euripides. Defeated by Sparta in the ▷Peloponnesian War (431-404), it recovered slowly, regaining its intellectual supremacy with such figures as Plato, Aristotle, and Aristophanes. Its role as a political power, however, was finally lost when defeated by Philip of Macedon in 338 BC; in the 2nd century BC it came under the rule of Rome. Owing to the influence of Hellenic culture on the Romans it continued to prosper and, despite being overrun by Germanic tribes in the 4th century AD, maintained its academic standing until the closure of the schools of philosophy by Justinian in 529. The city fell to the Crusaders in 1204 and was under Turkish occupation from 1456 until 1833, when it became the capital of the newly independent kingdom of Greece. It has been the scene of frequent revolts and civil wars and was occupied by the Germans in World War II. Population (1991): 748 110.

● **atherosclerosis** ▶ (*or* atheroma) Patchy thickening of the lining of arteries caused by the deposition of fatty material and fibrous tissue. This tends to obstruct the blood flow and predisposes to ▷thrombosis, which may lead to a heart attack or a stroke. In the Western world atherosclerosis is common in adults: its cause is believed to be associated with a diet high in animal fats (*see* cholesterol) and refined sugar, cigarette smoking, and obesity. Its incidence increases with age and it is exacerbated by high blood pressure. Its extent can be reduced by treatment of any underlying illness.

● **Atherton, Michael** ▶ (1968–) British cricketer. A batsman, he plays for Lancashire (1987–) and England (1989–). He was captain of the England side from 1993 to 1998.

● **athlete's foot** ▷*See* ringworm.

● **athletics** ▶ Sports that involve running, walking, throwing, and jumping competitions. They are divided into track and field events. At international level the track events include races over 100 m, 200 m, 400 m, 800 m, 1500 m, 5000 m, and 10 000 m; the 110 m and 400 m hurdles (*see* hurdling); the 4 × 100 and 4 × 400 m relay races; the 3000 m steeplechase; the ▷marathon; and the 20 km walk (*see* walking). The standard field events are ▷high jump, ▷long jump, ▷triple jump, ▷pole vault, ▷shot put, ▷discus throw, ▷hammer throw, and ▷javelin throw. In addition there are the ▷decathlon (for men), the modern pentathlon, and the ▷pentathlon (for women). The governing body is the International Amateur Athletic Federation.

● **Athlone, Alexander Cambridge, 1st Earl of** ▶ (1874–1957) British soldier and administrator, who was the brother of George V's consort Queen Mary and married Princess Alice (1883–1981), a granddaughter of Queen Victoria. After service in the Boer War and World War I, he was governor general of South Africa (1925–31) and of Canada (1940–45).

● **Athos, Mount** ▶ **1.** 40 10N 24 19E A mountain in NE Greece, at the end of Aktí, the easternmost promontory of Chalcidice. Height: 2033 m (6670 ft). **2.** An autonomous Greek Orthodox monastic republic occupying the mountain. Area: 80 sq km (31 sq mi). Population (1991): 1557.

● **Atlanta** ▶ 33 45N 84 23W A city in the USA, the capital of Georgia, situated at the foot of the Appalachian Mountains. Founded in 1837 and partly destroyed by Gen Sherman in 1864, it is now the industrial, administrative, transportation, and cultural centre of the SE USA. Its major industries include aircraft, machinery, cottonseed oil, textiles, clothing, and chemicals. Population (1996 est): 401 907.

● **Atlantic, Battle of the** ▷*See* World War II.

● **Atlantic Charter** ▶ (1941) A declaration made by Franklin D. Roosevelt and Winston Churchill that stated common national policies. These included freedom of choice of government, improved economic and social conditions, freedom of the seas, and the abolition of Nazism.

● **Atlantic City** ▶ 39 23N 74 27W A city in the USA, in New Jersey on Absecon Beach (an island on the Atlantic coast). A major pleasure resort, it has five piers and a multitude of amusements, shops, hotels, and parks; gambling casinos were introduced in the late 1970s. A popular conference centre, it is the site of the annual Miss America Pageant (first held in 1921). Its industries include glassware, china, and confectionery. Population (1990): 37 986.

● **Atlantic Intracoastal Waterway** ▶ A shipping route along the Atlantic coast of the USA. It serves the ports between Cape Cod and Florida Bay. Length: 2495 km (1550 mi).

● **Atlantic Ocean** ▶ The world's second largest ocean, extending between Antarctica, America, Europe, and Africa, and most heavily travelled seaway. Its major currents include the ▷Gulf Stream crossing it W–E. Its floor is rich in minerals, oil and gas now being exploited. The Mid-Atlantic Ridge rises above sea level as islands, such as the Azores. The youngest ocean, it was formed when the continents now surrounding it split apart 200 million years ago.

● **Atlantic Wall** ▶ The extensive fortifications built by the Germans in ▷World War II along the Atlantic coast. They failed to prevent ▷D-Day Normandy landings by US and British troops (6 June, 1944).

● **Atlantis** ▶ In Greek legend, a large island civilization in the Atlantic beyond the Pillars of Hercules (Straits of Gibraltar), which, according to Plato's dialogues the *Timaeus* and *Critias*, was destroyed by earthquake. The story, transmitted to the Greeks by the Egyptians, may refer to a cataclysmic volcanic eruption (c. 1450 BC) on the island of ▷Thera in the Cyclades N of Crete.

● **Atlas** ▶ In Greek mythology, the brother of Prometheus and son of the Titan Iapetus and the nymph Clymene. As a punishment for his part in the revolt of the Titans against the Olympians he was forced to hold up the pillars separating heaven from earth. From the 16th century this was commonly depicted in the frontispieces of books of maps, which thus came to be called atlases.

● **Atlas Mountains** ▶ A mountain system in NW Africa, extending generally NE from the Atlantic coast of Morocco to Tunisia. It consists of several mountain chains and plateaus and rises to 4165 m (13 664 ft) at Mount Toubkal in the Moroccan Great Atlas range.

● **ATM** ▷*See* automated teller machine.

● **atman** ▶ (Sanskrit: breath, soul) A fundamental concept of Hinduism, signifying the individual soul or the eternal essential self. When the body dies the *atman* is continuously reincarnated until final spiritual release is achieved. In the later ▷Upanishads, and in the Hindu philosophical schools of Samkhya and orthodox Vedanta, the function of *atman* and its relation to ▷Brahman is the central issue. Some thinkers regard these two as analogous principles only; for others they are essentially identical.

● **atmosphere** ▶ (meteorology) The gaseous envelope surrounding the earth or any other celestial body. The earth's atmosphere is composed of nitrogen (78.08%), oxygen (20.95%), argon (0.93%), and carbon dioxide (0.03%), together with small proportions of other gases and variable amounts of water vapour. In the lowest layer of the

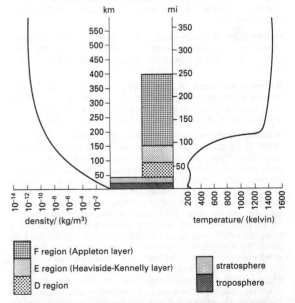

atmosphere ▶ The density of the atmosphere falls off sharply with height above the earth's surface. The more complicated temperature variation is shown in the graph, which also illustrates the regions of the ionosphere.

earth's atmosphere, the **troposphere**, air temperature decreases as height increases. The thickness of this layer varies from about 7 km (4.5 mi) to about 28 km (17.5 mi) at the equator. It is here that most meteorological phenomena occur. In the **stratosphere**, which goes up to about 50 km (31 mi), temperature is fairly constant because the sun's radiation counteracts the effect of decreasing density. Above this is the ▷ionosphere. The outermost layer is called the **exosphere**. From 100 km (62 mi) upwards the oxygen dissociates into atoms. There is little nitrogen above 150 km (93 mi). ▷*See also* ozone layer.

● **atmosphere** ▶ (unit) A unit of pressure equal to 101 325 pascals or 760 millimetres of mercury.

● **atmospheric pressure** ▶ The pressure exerted by the atmosphere. It decreases with altitude and, at ground level, varies around 760 millimetres of mercury, 101 325 pascals, or 1013.25 millibars.

● **atom** ▷*See* atomic theory.

● **atomic bomb** ▷*See* nuclear weapons.

● **atomic clock** ▶ A highly accurate clock based on the frequency at which certain atoms or molecules vibrate between two states. For example, the nitrogen atom in the ammonia molecule vibrates through the plane of the three hydrogen atoms and back again with a frequency of 23 870 hertz. In the ammonia clock, a quartz-crystal oscillator feeds energy into ammonia gas at this frequency. The ammonia only absorbs energy at this frequency, enabling a feedback circuit to control the frequency of the oscillator. ▷*See also* caesium clock.

● **atomic energy** ▷*See* nuclear energy.

● **Atomic Energy Authority** ▶ A UK body established in 1954 to research into and develop nuclear energy. Its principal research establishments are situated at Harwell and Culham, both in Oxfordshire.

● **Atomic Energy Commission** ▶ A US agency established in 1946 to control the production of nuclear weapons and atomic energy.

● **atomic force microscope** ▶ (AFM) A type of high-resolution microscope in which a small diamond probe held on a spring-loaded arm is scanned slowly across a specimen. The tracking force between the tip and the surface is continuously measured and the height of the probe is adjusted to keep this force constant. A computer-generated contour map of the surface can be produced, with resolution of individual atoms. The technique is useful for nonconducting samples, such as biochemical molecules. ▷*See also* scanning tunnelling microscope.

● **atomic mass unit** ▶ (amu) A unit of mass equal to one-twelfth of the mass of an atom of carbon-12 ($1.660\ 33 \times 10^{-27}$ kg). The unit is also called the dalton (after John ▷Dalton). ▷*See also* relative atomic mass.

● **atomic number** ▶ (Z) The number of protons in a nucleus of an atom. It determines the position of the element in the ▷periodic table and, in a neutral atom, is equal to the number of electrons surrounding the nucleus. It is also known as proton number.

● **atomic theory** ▶ The theory that an atom is the smallest particle of an element that can take part in a chemical reaction. ▷Democritus is credited with first conceiving the idea, which was, however, vigorously attacked by ▷Aristotle since Democritus's atoms existed in a vacuum, an idea repugnant to Aristotle. The atomic concept fell from favour until the early 19th century, when John ▷Dalton used the idea to explain the fact that elements combined together in simple proportions. The structure of the atom was first investigated by Lord ▷Rutherford, who discovered that it consisted of a heavy positively charged core (the ▷nucleus) surrounded by ▷electrons (*see also* Bohr atom), but the modern concept of the atom was not finally elucidated until the advent of Schrödinger's ▷wave mechanics.

Almost all of the atom's mass is concentrated in the nucleus, which consists of positively charged ▷protons and neutral ▷neutrons of almost equal mass (the mass of the electron is only 1/1836 that of the proton). The number of electrons in a neutral atom is equal to the number of protons in the nucleus, as the charge on the proton is equal but opposite to that of the electron. The electrons can be thought of as existing in a series of shells around the nucleus, each shell corresponding to a particular energy level. According to the ▷Pauli exclusion principle each shell may only hold a certain number of electrons. The chemical behaviour of an atom is largely determined by the number of electrons in its outermost shell, as atoms are most stable when they have no partly filled shells, a state often achieved by chemical combination. In combining, atoms may either share electrons to form covalent bonds or gain (or lose) electrons to form electrovalent (ionic) bonds (*see* chemical bond).

All the nuclei of an element contain the same number of protons (p) but not always the same number of neutrons (n). Atoms with the same value of p but a different value of n are called isotopes of that element. The value of ($n + p$) is called the mass number. Isotopes are referred to in several ways, e.g. uranium-235, U-235, ^{235}U, $^{235}_{92}$U (92 in this case being the ▷atomic number, and 235 being the mass number). ▷*See also* particle physics.

● **atomic weight** ▷*See* relative atomic mass.

● **atomism** ▶ The philosophical attitude that seeks irreducible elements, whether of matter or thought, to account for the (compound) phenomena that we actually experience. The Greek ▷Democritus believed that the world is composed of qualitatively similar atoms of different shapes. In this view, atoms may be either completely independent of one another or related in contingent or necessary ways. ▷Lucretius was an influential proponent of atomism, and ▷Gassendi, ▷Boyle, and John ▷Locke revived it in the 17th century. Logical atomism, held temporarily by both ▷Russell and ▷Wittgenstein, assumed that there were unanalysable specks of meaning that could be articulated in atomic propositions, from which no subordinate proposition could be derived.

● **Aton** ▶ In Egyptian religion, the one supreme god proclaimed by ▷Akhenaton and symbolized by a solar disc with arms.

● **atonality** ▶ The use in music of all 12 notes of the scale in such a way as to avoid ▷tonality. Atonality arose from the increasing ▷chromaticism of the music of the late 19th century. Schoenberg's second string quartet (1907–08), for example, begins in the key of F sharp minor but has an atonal final movement. ▷*See also* serialism.

● **atonement** ▶ In religious belief, the idea of reconciliation between God and man or, literally, at-one-ment with God. It implies that the relationship between God and mankind has been damaged by human failing or ▷sin. In Judaism, ▷Yom Kippur or the Day of Atonement is the holiest day of the year. In Christianity, the crucifixion of Christ is interpreted as a sacrifice that effects a reconciliation with God, ending the estrangement resulting from the human sinfulness that started with Adam.

● **ATP** ▶ (adenosine triphosphate) An energy-rich compound (a ▷nucleotide) with an important role in the metabolism of living organisms. On its formation from ADP (adenosine diphosphate) in the mitochondria of cells, ATP incorporates a large amount of energy that, on release, is used by cells to manufacture proteins, carbohydrates, etc., and to provide energy for muscle contraction and other dynamic processes.

● **Atreus** ▶ In Greek mythology, King of Mycenae, the son of Pelops and father of Agamemnon and Menelaus. His house was cursed as a result of a feud between him and his brother Thyestes over the throne of Mycenae. After Thyestes had seduced his wife, Atreus killed Thyestes' sons and served them at a feast. Another son of Thyestes, Aegisthus, later killed Atreus.

● **atrium** ▶ (architecture) **1.** Originally an important part of a Roman house, a central, partly covered court, frequently colonnaded, which often contained the shrine to the household god. Around it were the entrances to the main rooms. Later it became the main reception room of the house. **2.** An open area or courtyard in front of early Christian churches.

● **atropine** ▶ An alkaloid, extracted from deadly nightshade, that acts on certain nerves of the autonomic nervous system. It is used during anaesthesia to decrease lung secretions, which lowers the risk of postoperative chest infections. It also dilates the pupil and speeds up the heart rate.

There is no simple way to illustrate an atom:

 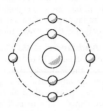 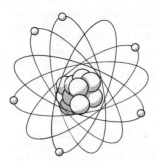 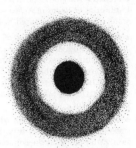

by the 19th century it was regarded as a minute solid billiard ball;	with the work of Rutherford between 1906 and 1914 and Bohr in 1913 it was depicted as a miniature solar system with a central nucleus and orbiting electron;	Sommerfeld's refinements of quantum theory in 1916 led to a model with precessing elliptical orbits and spinning electrons;	by 1926 Schrödinger's wave mechanics had been published, based on de Broglie's dual wave–particle concept of electrons. The atom is now regarded as a nucleus surrounded by a "haze" of probabilities that electrons will occur in certain positions.

The main characteristic of an atom, as the smallest particle of matter, is not what our models of it look like but the way it absorbs and emits energy.

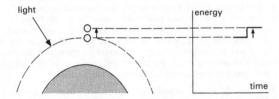 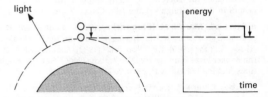

When an atom absorbs energy (e.g. when light of the right wavelength falls on it) its electrons jump to a higher energy level.

When these electrons fall back to their original (ground) state they emit energy (as light, ultraviolet, etc.).

All matter and therefore all atoms, according to modern physics, consists of two kinds of particles: leptons and quarks. Electrons are leptons; the particles of the nucleus (protons and neutrons) are each made up of different arrangements of three quarks.

The simplest atomic nucleus is the hydrogen nucleus consisting of one proton.

An isotope of hydrogen, deuterium, has a nucleus consisting of one proton and one neutron.

All other nuclei consist of arrangements of protons and neutrons. The carbon nucleus consists of six protons and six neutrons.

atomic theory

● **Atropos** ▷See Fates.

● **Attalus I Soter** ▶ (269–197 BC) Ruler of ▷Pergamum (241–197), who took the title of king after a victory over the Galatians (before 230). By his conquests in Asia Minor and his support of Rome against Philip V of Macedon (237–179; reigned 220–179), he made Pergamum a significant power.

● **attar of roses** ▶ (otto of rose or essence of rose) A fragrant colourless or pale-yellow oil distilled from fresh rose petals. It is produced in Bulgaria, S France, Morocco, and Turkey. About 1 gram of attar is extracted from 4 kilograms of roses. Rosewater is a by-product of the distillation. It is used to make perfumes and in flavourings.

● **Attenborough, Richard, Baron** ▶ (1923–　) British film actor, director, and producer. After numerous appearances in British war films and comedies he developed into a versatile character actor in such films as *Loot* (1969) and *10 Rillington Place* (1971). As director, his films include *Young Winston* (1974), *A Bridge Too Far* (1977), *Gandhi* (1982), *A Chorus Line* (1985), *Cry Freedom* (1987), *Shadowlands* (1994), and *In Love and War* (1996). His brother **Sir David Attenborough** (1926–　) is a naturalist and broadcaster, whose television series include *Zoo Quest* (1954), *Life on Earth* (1978), *The Living Planet* (1983), *The Trials of Life* (1990), and *The Life of Birds* (1998). In 1991 he was appointed president of the British Association.

● **attention deficit disorder** ▶ (or hyperactivity disorder) A psychiatric disorder, especially of young children, associated with learning difficulties, hyperactivity, and disruptive, defiant, or aggressive behaviour. The disorder is more frequent in the epileptic, intellectually impaired, and the brain damaged. Family therapy and such drugs as dexamphetamine (Dexedrine) and methylphenidate (Ritalin) are used to manage the disorder.

● **attenuation** ▶ The reduction in amplitude of an electromagnetic wave or an electric current during transmission. In electric circuits attenuation is often introduced to reduce unwanted components of a signal. Broadcast electromagnetic radiation is attenuated as it passes through buildings, etc., and to a lesser extent by the atmosphere. In space attenuation is negligible.

● **Attica** ▶ A region of ancient E central Greece. According to Greek legend the 12 towns of Attica were united by Theseus into a single state, which was dominated by Athens by the 5th century BC.

● **Attila** ▶ (c. 406–53) King of the Huns (434–53), known as the Scourge of God. After murdering his brother and coruler, Bleda, he extended his possessions in central Europe and attacked (441–43) the eastern frontier of the Roman Empire. In 451 he invaded Gaul and suffered his only defeat, at the battle of the ▷Catalaunian Plains. His campaigns in Italy (452) caused much destruction; the pope paid him to spare Rome.

● **Attlee, Clement (Richard), 1st Earl** ▶ (1883–1967) British statesman; Labour prime minister (1945–51). A barrister by profession, Attlee taught at the London School of Economics (1913–23) and became mayor of Stepney (1919). He was elected MP for Limehouse in 1922 and was leader of the Labour Party (1935–55) and deputy prime minister of the wartime coalition government (1942–45). As the first postwar prime minister he presided over the establishment of the welfare state, nationalizing major industries and introducing the ▷National Health Service. His government also granted independence within the Commonwealth to India.

● **attorney general** ▶ The chief law officer of the Crown in England and Wales and its representative in the courts. He is legal adviser to the government and the House of Commons, of which he is always a member and to which he is answerable, and is head of the English bar. He advises on the drafting of Acts of Parliament. With his subordinate, the Director of Public Prosecutions, he prosecutes crimes in the sovereign's name. ▷See Crown Prosecution Service.

● **Atwood, Margaret (Eleanor)** ▶ (1939–) Canadian novelist, poet, and short-story writer. Her novels include *The Handmaid's Tale* (1986), *Cat's Eye* (1989), *The Robber Bride* (1993), *Alias Grace* (1996), and the Booker-Prize-winning *The Blind Assassin* (2000). Her other publications include *Wilderness Tips and Other Stories* (1991).

● **Aube, River** ▶ A river in N central France, rising on the Plateau de Langres and flowing NW to the River Seine. Length: 225 km (140 mi).

● **Auber, Daniel François Esprit** ▶ (1782–1871) French composer. He is remembered for his 48 operas, chiefly light works to librettos by the playwright A. E. Scribe (1791–1861), written for the Paris Opéra-Comique. Of these only *La Muette de Portici* (1828) and *Fra Diavolo* (1830) are still performed.

● **aubergine** ▶ A spiny herbaceous plant, *Solanum melongena*, native to S Asia and also known as eggplant. It is commonly grown in warmer regions for its fruit, a large white, yellow, or purple berry that is eaten as a vegetable. The plant grows to a height of 60–100 cm. Family: *Solanaceae*.

● **Aubrey, John** ▶ (1626–97) English antiquary. *Miscellanies* (1696), a collection of folklore, was his only work published during his lifetime, but he is best known for the biographical material he collected, which was published during the 19th century as *Lives of Eminent Men* (1813) and *Brief Lives* (1898). A one-man play based on his *Brief Lives* was produced in 1967.

● **Aubrietia** ▶ (*or* Aubrieta) A genus of trailing herbaceous perennial flowering plants (about 15 species), native to mountainous areas of E Europe and W Asia. *A. deltoidea* is commonly grown in rock gardens, bearing small purple, red, or pink flowers. Family: *Cruciferae*.

● **Aubusson** ▶ 45 58N 2 10E A town in central France, in the Creuse department on the River Creuse. It has been renowned for its carpets and tapestries since the 16th century. Population (latest est): 6153.

● **Aubusson, Pierre d'** ▶ (1423–1503) French cardinal and grand master of the Knights ▷Hospitallers. Remembered chiefly for his defence of Rhodes against the Turks in 1480, he secured a long-term truce in 1481 by agreeing to imprison the Ottoman sultan's enemy and brother.

● **Auch** ▶ 43 40N 0 36E A market town in SW France, the capital of the Gers department on the River Gers. The former capital of Armagnac and Gascony, it has a gothic cathedral with a magnificent 17th-century organ. Population (latest est): 25 600.

● **Auchinleck, Sir Claude** ▶ (1884–1981) British field marshal. He served his apprenticeship in the Middle East in World War I. In World War II, after a brief period in Norway and then as commander in chief in India, he succeeded Wavell in N Africa (1941). He reached Cyrenaica, only to be pushed back by Rommel. Blamed, probably unjustly, for the retreat, he was replaced by Alexander.

● **Auckland** ▶ 36 55S 174 47E The largest city and port in New Zealand, on North Island occupying an isthmus between Waitemata Harbour and Manukau Harbour. Founded in 1840, it was the capital of New Zealand until 1865. The university was established in 1882 and there are two cathedrals (Roman Catholic and Anglican). The city is connected with the mainly residential North Shore by the Auckland Harbour Bridge (1959). There are engineering, food processing, ship-building, and chemical industries. The chief exports are iron and steel, dairy products, and meat. Population (1996 est): 353 670.

● **Auckland, George Eden, Earl of** ▶ (1784–1849) British statesman; governor general of India (1836–42). He attempted to control Afghanistan against Russian and Persian expansion in central Asia. Following Afghan attacks on British forces, he was recalled.

● **Auckland Islands** ▶ 50 35S 166 00E A group of six uninhabited islands in the S Pacific Ocean, belonging to New Zealand. An attempt to introduce cattle and sheep was unsuccessful (1852). Area: 611 sq km (234 sq mi).

● **auction** ▶ A method of selling goods publicly, in which many prospective buyers compete with each other, the sale being made to the highest bidder. If bidding does not reach a reserve price specified by the vendor, then the auctioneer withdraws the goods. Rules vary from trade to trade, but the auctioneer usually acts as the seller's agent, charging him a commission on goods sold. Antiques, works of art, houses, and some commercial commodities are sold by auction. In a **Dutch auction**, the sale is offered first at an unrealistically high price, which is lowered gradually until a bid is made.

● **Auden, W(ystan) H(ugh)** ▶ (1907–73) British poet. His early volumes, beginning with *Poems* (1930) and *Look, Stranger!* (1936), established him as the leading figure of a group of left-wing poets of the 1930s, the other members of which were Stephen ▷Spender, Louis ▷MacNeice, and C. ▷Day Lewis. He also wrote verse dramas in collaboration with Christopher ▷Isherwood, with whom he went to the USA in 1939. He became a US citizen in 1946, returning to England while he was professor of poetry at Oxford (1956–61). He wrote several opera libretti, notably for Stravinsky's *The Rake's Progress* (1951). His later poetry was characterized by a form of Christian existentialism that replaced his earlier Marxism.

● **audio frequency** ▶ A frequency in the range 20 to 20 000 hertz, i.e. the range of frequencies to which the human ear is sensitive.

● **audiometry** ▶ The study of hearing measurement, especially with a view to assessing the extent to which a person's hearing is impaired. Measurements are usually made using an **audiometer**, which consists of a device capable of producing a range of audio-frequency sounds over a range of volumes. This enables subjects being examined to indicate the lowest intensity at which they can detect sounds over the whole audio range.

● **audiovisual education** ▶ Education carried out with the help of audio (sound) or visual techniques. There are a whole range of audiovisual aids, including television, tape and video recorders, teaching machines, overhead projectors, and the long-established wallcharts and blackboards. Although audiovisual education has been used throughout history, its systematic application developed in the 20th century. Research has shown that, when properly used, it increases both the student's interest and his recall of the material presented. Since 1958 the US Congress has provided aid for educational broadcasting. In the UK, the BBC and the independent television companies run an extensive educational service. ▷*See also* Open University.

● **auditing** ▷*See* accountancy.

● **auditory nerve** ▷*See* □ear.

● **Audubon, John James** ▶ (1785–1851) US naturalist and artist noted for his lifelike drawings and paintings of birds. Educated in France, Audubon emigrated to the USA, where he developed an interest in bird migration and began painting birds and other animals. *The Birds of America* (4 vols, 1827–38) established his reputation as an illustrator. The National Audubon Society, founded in his honour in 1886, is dedicted to the conservation of birds throughout the USA.

● **Augean stables ▶** The stables of the legendary Greek King Augeas in which he kept 3000 oxen. One of the 12 labours of ▷Heracles was to clean the stables in one day, even though they had not been cleaned for 30 years. Heracles succeeded by diverting the River Alpheus through them. However, Augeas broke his promise to give Heracles a tenth of the herd, provoking Heracles to lead an army against him, killing him and his sons.

● **Augereau, Pierre François Charles, Duc de Castiglione ▶** (1757–1816) French marshal. He rose rapidly in the French army, serving under Napoleon in Italy. In 1797 he directed the coup d'état that overthrew the ▷Directory. He subsequently opposed Napoleon but his uncertain loyalties forced his retirement after the restoration of the monarchy.

● **Auger effect ▶** The spontaneous ejection of an electron from an excited, singly charged, positive ion to form a doubly charged ion. The ion may be excited by a gamma ray from its nucleus or by bombarding it with particles, such as photons or electrons. It is named after the French physicist Pierre Auger (1899–1994).

● **Aughrim, Battle of ▶** (12 July, 1691) The final defeat of the main army of the former King James II of England by the army of William III in Ireland. It was the most disastrous battle in Irish history, with 7000 Jacobite dead. It is still celebrated by Ulster Unionists on its anniversary.

● **Augsburg ▶** 48 21N 10 54E A city in S Germany (formerly in West Germany), in Bavaria at the confluence of the Rivers Wertach and Lech. It is a major industrial centre; its manufactures include textiles, chemicals, cars, aircraft, and printing machinery. Many of its historic buildings, including the 10th-century cathedral, survived the bombardment of World War II.

History: founded by the Romans in 15 BC, it became an important banking and commercial centre in the 15th and 16th centuries mainly with the aid of the Fugger and Welsen merchant families. An imperial free city from 1276, it was the seat of the notable diets of 1530 (*see* Augsburg Confession) and 1555 (*see* Augsburg, Peace of). It is the birthplace of Holbein and Brecht. Population (1996 est): 259 699.

● **Augsburg, League of ▶** (1686) An alliance originally consisting of the Holy Roman Empire, Spain, Sweden, and several German states. In 1689 they were joined by England, Holland, and Savoy, thus forming the ▷Grand Alliance, which waged war on Louis XIV of France from 1689 to 1697.

● **Augsburg, Peace of ▶** (1555) A religious compromise issued by an imperial diet at Augsburg, over which the future Emperor ▷Ferdinand I presided, which established the coexistence of Roman Catholicism and Lutheranism in Germany. Each prince was to determine whether his territory was to be Catholic or Lutheran. In order to safeguard Catholic property, any prince who became a Protestant was to renounce his land and revenues. The settlement gave Germany 50 years of peace.

● **Augsburg Confession ▶** The main and distinctive confession of faith of the Lutheran Churches. Drawn up in its original form by Melancthon and approved by Luther, it was presented to the imperial diet that Emperor Charles V summoned at Augsburg in 1530 to judge Luther's controversial preaching.

● **augury ▶** Ritual divination practised in ancient Rome by augurs, priests skilled in the auspices, or interpretation of certain natural occurrences. The word "auspice" derives from the Latin for "bird" + "observation"; the commonest means of augury were the flight and song of birds, but thunder, lightning, movements of animals, and the appetites of tame chickens were also studied. Signs on the augur's left were propitious, those on his right unpropitious. Augury accompanied every major undertaking, to ascertain through the auspices whether the gods were favourably inclined.

● **Augusta ▶** 33 29N 82 00W A town in the USA, in Georgia on the Savannah River. It is a medical and service centre for the many government installations nearby. Population (1990): 44 639.

● **Augusta ▶** 44 17N 69 50W A city in the USA, the capital of Maine on the Kennebec River. Established as a trading post in 1628, it has a large timber industry. Population (1990): 21 325.

● **Augustine of Canterbury, St ▶** (died c. 604) Italian churchman, the first Archbishop of Canterbury. Chosen by Pope ▷Gregory I to evangelize England in 596, he converted Ethelbert I of Kent and successfully established Canterbury as the primatial see. He was less successful in persuading the already existing Welsh ▷Celtic Church to acknowledge him as primate. Feast day: 26 or 27 May.

● **Augustine of Hippo, St ▶** (354–430 AD) North African theologian; Father and Doctor of the Church, born at Tagaste. His mother was a Christian but, after studying at Carthage, he became a Manichaean. He taught rhetoric in Rome and in Milan, where he was attracted to ▷Neoplatonism. However, under the influence of St ▷Ambrose, Bishop of Milan, he was finally converted to Christianity in 386. On his return to Africa, he lived as a monk until he was ordained at Hippo in 391. He became Bishop of Hippo in 396 and died there during a Vandal siege. His works are the most important and influential of those written by the early Fathers, especially *The City of God*, a defence of Christianity in 22 books, and his spiritual autobiography, *The Confessions*. His other writings include commentaries on the scriptures, sermons, letters, and treatises against the heresies ▷Manichaeism, Donatism (*see* Donatists), and Pelagianism (*see* Pelagius). He was most actively involved in the Pelagian controversy, in which he upheld the doctrines of original sin and divine grace. Feast day: 28 Aug.

● **Augustinians ▶** A term sometimes used generally to refer to all the Roman Catholic religious orders that follow the Rule of St Augustine, a programme for the religious life drawn up by ▷Augustine of Hippo. More specifically it refers to the orders of the Augustinian (*or* Austin) Canons, founded in the 11th century, and the Augustinian Hermits (*or* Austin Friars), founded in the 13th century, both of which have corresponding orders for women.

● **Augustus ▶** (*or* Octavian; 63 BC–14 AD) The first Roman emperor, who restored the greatness of the Roman world following the disintegration of the Republic. Augustus, who was born Gaius Octavius, was the great-nephew and adopted son of Julius Caesar. After Caesar's assassination in 44, Augustus (now Gaius Julius Caesar Octavianus; *or* Octavian) came to an agreement with ▷Mark Antony and in 43 they formed the second ▷Triumvirate with ▷Lepidus. Lepidus was forced to retire in 36 and Augustus' relations with Mark Antony failed to withstand Antony's abandonment of his wife Octavia (Augustus' sister) for ▷Cleopatra. Antony's defeat at Actium in 31 allowed Augustus to establish his personal supremacy at the head of an autocratic government known as the principate. In 27 he was proclaimed Augustus (sacred).

Augustus was an outstanding administrator and consolidated the so-called Pax Romana (Roman Peace) that he had established with a durable administrative and financial system. The patronage of his close adviser ▷Maecenas fostered a literary renaissance and with the military assistance of ▷Agrippa, and later of his own stepson ▷Tiberius, he secured and then expanded the Empire. In 4 AD he named Tiberius, the son of his third wife ▷Livia Drusilla, his heir. Augustus was deified after his death.

● **Augustus I ▶** (1526–86) Elector of Saxony (1553–86). A moderate Protestant, he was a follower of Lutheranism and a harsh opponent of Calvinism. His economic, administrative, and social reforms made Saxony one of the most prosperous German states.

● **Augustus (II) the Strong ▶** (1670–1733) King of Poland (1697–1706, 1710–33). Augustus' invasion of Livonia (1700) began the Great ▷Northern War, in which he was defeated by Charles XII of Sweden (1702). Augustus was deposed by the Polish diet (1704), formally abdicating in 1706, but was restored by Russia in 1710. His malgovernment precipitated Poland's decline.

● **auk ▶** A stout-bodied seabird belonging to a family (*Alcidae*; 22 species) occurring in the N hemisphere and having a black and white plumage and short pointed wings. The family includes ▷puffins, ▷razorbills, ▷guillemots, the little auk (*Plautus alle*), and the extinct flightless great auk (*Pinguinus impennis*). Order: *Charadriiformes* (gulls, plovers, etc.).

● **Aung San** ▶ (c. 1914–47) Burmese statesman; leader of the independence movement. Committed to radical politics from his student days at Rangoon University, Aung San founded the Anti-Fascist People's Freedom League in 1944. He played a crucial role in the negotiations that led to Burmese independence from Britain but was assassinated before it was fully attained. His daughter, **Aung San Suu Kyi** (1945–   ), cofounded the National League for Democracy and led protests against martial law. Placed under house arrest in 1989, she became a symbol of opposition to military rule. Her supporters won free elections in 1990 but the military held on to power by force. She was awarded the Nobel Peace Prize in 1991 and released in 1995. Her attempts to tour the country by car (from 1998) led to repeated confrontations with the military and she was placed under renewed house arrest in 2000. She entered into talks with the government in 2000 and was released in May 2002.

● **Aurangzeb** ▶ (1618–1707) The last Mogul emperor of India (1658–1707); the youngest son of ▷Shah Jahan. When Shah Jahan fell ill in 1657 Aurangzeb fought a war of succession against his older brother Dara Shikoh. Easily winning, he ascended the throne of Delhi with the title Alamgir ("world-seizer"). A ruthless ruler, he augmented the empire to its greatest extent but in his fervent Muslim orthodoxy he made enemies of his Hindu subjects and in effect weakened Mogul power.

● **Aurelian(us), Lucius Domitius** ▶ (c. 215–275 AD) Roman emperor (270–75). Aurelian was of humble birth and owed his accession to the army. He restored imperial unity by his victories over the Vandals, ▷Zenobia of Palmyra, and the Gallic Empire at Châlons. He was murdered near Byzantium.

● **Auric, Georges** ▶ (1899–1983) French composer. Initially influenced by ▷Ravel and ▷Debussy, he later became a member of the avantgarde group Les ▷Six. He is best known for his scores for films, such as *À nous la liberté* (1932), *The Lavender Hill Mob* (1951), and *Moulin Rouge* (1952).

● **auricula** ▶ A species of ▷Primula, *P. auricula*, or any of the hybrids derived from it. Native to the Alps, it is widely grown as a garden plant, having showy yellow flowers.

● **Auriga** ▶ (Latin: Charioteer) A conspicuous constellation in the N sky near Orion, lying in the Milky Way. The brightest star is ▷Capella.

● **Aurignacian** ▶ A culture of the Upper ▷Palaeolithic marked by the use of thick scrapers and heavy blades of stone and flint, flat bone points, and polished bone or antler pins. First recognized at Aurignac (SW France) in 1860 the industry dates back to about 34 000 BC. Since it differs, especially in bonework, from earlier and later (▷Gravettian) toolkits, Aurignacian culture may have come from outside Europe. These people hunted mammoth and horse; they also engraved symbols and pictures on rocks (*see* Lascaux).

● **aurochs** ▶ An extinct European wild ox, *Bos primigenius*, that survived in Poland until the early 17th century. Standing 1.8 m at the shoulder, aurochs were black with long curved horns and are believed to be ancestors of modern domestic cattle.

● **aurora** ▶ A display of diffuse changing coloured light seen high in the earth's atmosphere, often taking the form of streamers or drapery and usually green or red. Aurorae occur predominantly in polar regions when energetic charged particles from the sun become trapped in the earth's magnetic field. The rapidly moving particles interact with atoms and molecules in the upper atmosphere and cause them to emit light. In the N hemisphere they are called the Northern Lights.

● **Aurora** ▶ In Roman mythology, the goddess of the dawn. She was called Eos by the Greeks.

● **Auschwitz** ▷*See* Oświęcim.

● **auscultation** ▶ The use of a ▷stethoscope to listen to sounds produced by movements of liquid or gas within the body, which forms an essential part of a medical examination. Auscultation of lungs, heart, and intestines are the most useful for reaching a diagnosis.

● **Ausgleich** ▶ (German: compromise; 1867) The constitutional settlement that established the Dual Monarchy of ▷Austria-Hungary (1867–1918).

● **Ausonius, Decimus Magnus** ▶ (died c. 395 AD) Roman poet, born at Burdigala (Bordeaux). The tutor of ▷Gratian, Emperor Valentinian's son, Ausonius became governor of Gaul. *Mosella*, his most famous poem, described the River Moselle and its surrounding countryside.

Jane Austen ▶ An engraving based on a sketch by her elder sister Cassandra, who produced the only known life portrait of the novelist. Jane, who never married, maintained a lively correspondence with Cassandra throughout her life.

● **Austen, Jane** ▶ (1775–1817) British novelist. She was the daughter of a clergyman and lived an outwardly uneventful life with her family in the south of England, settling in Chawton in Hampshire in 1809. Her six major novels are *Sense and Sensibility* (1811), *Pride and Prejudice* (1813), *Mansfield Park* (1814), *Emma* (1815–16), *Northanger Abbey* (1818), and *Persuasion* (1818). Their heroines are drawn from the rural landed gentry, and their plots trace the development of relationships that generally culminate in marriage. Her novels are distinguished by her delicate and often ironic wit and her sensitive insight into personal and social tensions.

● **austenite** ▶ A form of ▷steel that exists when the metal is heated to about 1000°C, in which the carbon exists as a solid solution in the iron. Austenitic steels retain this structure at room temperature because of the presence of an alloying element, such as manganese. Austenite is nonmagnetic and has a high ductility. Named after Sir William C. Roberts-Austen (1843–1902).

● **Austerlitz, Battle of** ▶ (2 December, 1805) The battle in which Napoleon's 68 000-strong army outmanoeuvred and defeated almost 90 000 Russians and Austrians led by ▷Kutuzov. It took place near Austerlitz (now Slavkov u Brna, in the Czech Republic). Napoleon's victory forced the Austrians to make peace with France by the Treaty of Pressburg and the Russian army to return to Russia.

● **Austin** ▶ 30 18N 97 47W A city in the USA, the capital of Texas on the Colorado River. The site of the University of Texas (1883), its industries include tourism and some manufacturing. Population (2000 est): 656 562.

● **Austin, Herbert, 1st Baron** ▶ (1866–1941) British engineer, who founded the Austin Motor Company. He designed his first car, a three-wheeler named the Wolseley, in 1895. Production of Austin motor cars began in 1906 and the famous Austin Seven was first produced in 1921.

● **Austin, John** ▶ (1790–1859) British jurist, famous for his work in jurisprudence. He was called to the Bar in 1818 and was later a professor at London University (1826–32), his lectures there providing the basis for his best-known book, *The Province of Jurisprudence Determined* (1832). In this he clarified the distinctions between the laws of the sovereign authority and the moral laws of God and man. Although unsupported in his own lifetime, Austin's ideas later became very influential in legal education.

● **Austin, John Langshaw** ▶ (1911–60) British philosopher, who lived and worked in Oxford. Austin was an influential proponent of ▷linguistic philosophy, holding that philosophical and conceptual difficulties can be elucidated and often dissolved by examining the language ordinarily used to talk about such concepts. He used this approach in his lectures, published posthumously in 1962 as *Sense and Sensibilia* and *How to Do Things with Words*. In the former he criticized certain philosophical views on perception and in the latter analysed the nature of "speech acts", i.e. those utterances that constitute acts executed in and by speech (apology, prayer, oaths, etc.).

● **Australasia** ▶ A term applied loosely to encompass the islands of the S Pacific: Australia, New Zealand, New Guinea, and their associated islands. The Malay Archipelago and the Philippines are also sometimes included. ▷*See also* Oceania.

● **Australia, Commonwealth of** ▶ A country in the S Pacific, comprising the whole of the smallest continent and the island of Tasmania to the SE. External territories include ▷Norfolk Island, ▷Christmas Island, the ▷Cocos (Keeling) Islands, and the ▷Australian Antarctic Territory. Much of the country has a hot dry climate and a large part of the vast central plains are desert or semidesert. The most fertile areas are in the E, along the coastal plains, and in the extreme SW. The Great Barrier Reef lies off the tropical NE coast and the highest mountains, rising over 2000 m (7000 ft), are in the Great Dividing Range, which runs parallel to the E coast. The Murray River and its tributaries in the SE form the main river system. The inhabitants are very largely of European, especially British, origin but there are about 100 000 Aborigines and people of mixed race living in the interior. Since World War II the population has increased dramatically, largely as a result of immigration.

Economy: agriculture continues to make a substantial contribution to the economy, the main crops being wheat and other cereals, sugar cane, and fruit. Livestock, particularly sheep and cattle, is also important. Since the 1960s, however, growth in the industrial sector has been especially marked, the leading manufactures being iron and steel products, transportation equipment, and machinery. Mining is now of vital importance, especially the extraction of coal, iron, bauxite, uranium, copper, lead, and zinc. There have been significant discoveries of oil and natural gas and over 70% of oil for home consumption is now produced in Australia. The main exports are coal and gas, iron and iron ore, nonferrous ores, and cereals.

History: the country was inhabited by the Aborigines, immigrants from SE Asia, for approximately 20 000 years before the arrival of the Europeans, beginning with the Portuguese in the 16th century and the Dutch in the early 17th century. In 1770 Captain Cook claimed the fertile E coast for Britain and the area, known as New South Wales, was at first used mainly as a penal colony, the American colonies no longer being available for this purpose. After the introduction of the merino sheep, however, civilian settlements were established further to the N and W towards the interior, eventually reaching the far side of the Blue Mountains in 1813. Colonies were developed in Tasmania, Western Australia, Victoria, South Australia, and Queensland. By 1829 the whole continent was a British dependency. Notable among the explorations carried out were those of Hamilton ▷Hume, Charles ▷Sturt, John McDouall ▷Stuart, and Robert ▷Burke and William John Wills (1834–61). The discovery of gold in Victoria in 1851 attracted large numbers of immigrants. In 1901 the six colonies were federated to form the Commonwealth of Australia, becoming an independent dominion of the British Empire. In 1911 the site for the federal capital, under the title of the Australian Capital Territory, and the Northern Territory were transferred to Commonwealth administration (from New South Wales and South Australia respectively). Strong measures were introduced in the late 19th century to prevent immigration by non-Whites and these had a continuing influence on immigration policy. In 1974, however, Gough ▷Whitlam abolished the "white Australia" policy and a new immigration scheme was introduced in 1979, which was aimed at extending the country's nondiscriminatory image. Australia played a significant part in both World Wars, taking an important role in the

Gallipoli campaign in World War I and cooperating closely with the USA in World War II. Since the war closer ties have been developed with Asia, especially with Japan, which now takes a third of Australia's exports. The Northern Territory achieved self-government in 1978 although the federal government retained control over its uranium resources. Australia is a member of the Commonwealth. In 1986 Elizabeth II signed legislation formally ending constitutional links between Australia and the UK. The 1980s and 1990s saw growing support for Australia becoming a republic: a people's Constitutional Convention was elected in 1997 and voted to sever links with the Crown. However, a referendum motion to replace the Queen with an appointed president was defeated in 1999. The Conservative coalition led by John Howard was re-elected in 1998 and again in 2001.

Commonwealth of Australia

Head of state	Queen Elizabeth II, represented by the governor-general, Sir William Deane
Official language	English
Official currency	Australian dollar of 100 cents
Area	7 686 884 sq km (2 967 283 sq mi)
Population (2000 est)	19 165 000
Capital	Canberra
Main port	Sydney

● **Australia Day** ▶ A holiday in Australia that commemorates the founding of the first colony (Sydney) on 26 Jan 1788.

● **Australian Alps** ▶ A mountain range in SE Australia. Part of the ▷Great Dividing Range, it extends from E Victoria into SE New South Wales and contains the ▷Snowy Mountains and Mount ▷Kosciusko, Australia's highest mountain. It is a popular winter-sports area.

● **Australian Antarctic Territory** ▶ The area of Antarctica claimed by Australia. It includes all the land lying S of latitude 60°S and between longitudes 45°E and 160°E, excluding ▷Terre Adélie. Several research stations are sited here.

● **Australian Capital Territory** ▶ An administrative division of SE Australia. It was created in 1911 from the Limestone Plains region of New South Wales as a site for ▷Canberra, the capital of Australia. Jervis Bay was transferred to the territory in 1915 for development as a seaport. It is the site of several important institutions, including the Australian Academy of Science, the Royal Military College, and the Royal Australian Naval College (at Jervis Bay). Area: 2432 sq km (939 sq mi). Population (2000 est): 308 400.

● **Australian Rules** ▷*See* football.

● **Austral Islands** ▷*See* Tubuai Islands.

● **Australopithecus** ▶ A genus of fossil manlike higher primates of the late Pliocene and Pleistocene epochs of S and E Africa (the name derives from Latin: literally, "southern ape"). Although small in brain size, their cranial and skeletal structures were more like those of modern man than of apes and—unlike apes—they walked erect. They ate fruit, seeds, and meat, but there is no evidence that they used tools. A number of species have been identified. The earliest known australopithecines include *A. anamensis*, which lived nearly 4 million years ago, and *A. afarensis*, living between 3.6 and 3 million years ago. The best-known representative of the latter species is the skeleton named "Lucy", discovered in Ethiopia in 1974 and no taller than 1.07 m (3¼ ft). These early australopithecines probably evolved into a number of other species, some of which were the ancestors of modern man, while others became extinct. One branch of the latter group were the so-called robust (heavy-jawed) australopithecines, such as *A. boisei* and *A. robustus*, which lived 2.5–1 million years ago. The creature discovered by Louis ▷Leakey at ▷Olduvai Gorge in 1959 and named by him *Zinjanthropus* has now been included with the other australopithecines as a representative of *A. boisei*.

● **Austrasia** ▶ The eastern Frankish kingdom created together with ▷Neustria by the partition in 511 of the Merovingian kingdom by ▷Clovis. Occupying an area that is now NE France and West Germany, its capital from 629 was at Metz. Austrasia was increasingly dominated by the mayors of the palace (viceroys), the last of which, ▷Pepin the Short, deposed the Merovingians in 751 and reunited the territories of the ▷Franks into what became the Carolingian empire.

● **Austria, Republic of** ▶ (German name: Österreich) A country in central Europe, on the N side of the Alps. A large part of the country is mountainous but the E area consists of lower hills and plains, with the River Danube flowing through the NE. Most of the inhabitants are German but there are minorities of Croats, Slovenes, and others.

Economy: although agriculture and forestry are important, there is considerable heavy industry, based particularly on iron and steel. Hydroelectric power is a valuable source of energy. Tourism (both summer and winter) makes an important contribution to the economy. Main exports include iron and steel, machinery, textiles, paper and paper products, and wood.

History: Austria has a long history of human habitation, going back to the Celtic settlements of the early Iron Age. The area was part of the Roman Empire from 15 BC until the 5th century AD when it was overrun by Germanic tribes. In succeeding centuries it was occupied in turn by Slavs and Magyars from whom it was taken in 955 by the Holy Roman Emperor ▷Otto I. He conferred it upon Leopold of Babenberg, who founded the first Austrian dynasty. In 1282 the ▷Habsburgs acquired Austria, which was to become the core of their vast empire. In 1526 Bohemia and Hungary were united under the Austrian Crown. The Austrian Empire continued to hold a predominant position in Europe until the middle of the 19th century when its power was lessened by successive defeats, especially in the ▷Austro-Prussian War. In 1867 the Habsburgs were forced to acknowledge the nationalist aspirations of Hungary and formed the Dual Monarchy of ▷Austria-Hungary, under the Emperor ▷Francis Joseph. During his reign there was considerable unrest, especially among the Slav peoples of the very diverse Empire; the assassination of the Archduke Francis Ferdinand by Serbian nationalists in 1914 was the immediate cause of World War I. Following military defeat in 1918 Austria lost its remaining Empire and became a republic. In spite of efforts on the part of the chancellor ▷Schuschnigg to maintain independence, it was annexed by Nazi Germany in 1938 (*see* Anschluss). After World War II it was occupied jointly by the Allies, regaining its independence as a republic in 1955. Chancellor Bruno ▷Kreisky, who came to power in 1970 as head of Austria's first all-socialist government, resigned in 1983. The socialists then formed a series of coalition governments, with Franz Vranitsky as chancellor from 1986 until 1997. Following elections in 1999 a new coalition was formed (2000) that included members of the extreme right-wing Freedom Party: this led EU and other countries to impose diplomatic sanctions on Austria. Austria became a member of the EU in 1995 and adopted the single European currency in 1999–2002.

Republic of Austria

Head of state	President Thomas Klestil
Official language	German
Currency	euro of 100 cents
Area	85 853 sq km (32 375 sq mi)
Population (2000 est)	8 091 000
Capital	Vienna

● **Austria-Hungary, Dual Monarchy of** ▶ The Habsburg monarchy from 1867 to 1918. It was established by the ▷Ausgleich (compromise) in response to the militant demands of Hungarian nationalism. The empire of Austria and the kingdom of Hungary each had its own laws, parliament, and ministries but were united by the monarch (Emperors ▷Francis Joseph and then ▷Charles), minister for foreign affairs and minister for war, and by the biannual meetings of delegations of each parliament. The Dual Monarchy disappeared in 1918 with the proclamation of an Austrian republic.

● **Austrian Succession, War of the** ▶ (1740–48) The war between Austria and Prussia, in which Britain supported Austria and France and Spain were allied to Prussia. It was brought about by the disputed succession of ▷Maria Theresa to the Austrian lands and began when ▷Frederick the Great of Prussia annexed the Austrian province of Silesia. Unstable alliances were formed between European powers and hostilities overseas, especially between France and Britain, were exacerbated. The war was ended by the Treaty of Aix-la-Chapelle, at which Prussia obtained most of Silesia.

● **Austro-Asiatic languages** ▶ A family of about 150 languages and dialects spoken in SE Asia. They include Vietnamese, ▷Khmer, Nicobarese in the Nicobar Islands, and the ▷Munda languages of India. In fact there is little superficial resemblance among languages of the family, and their common ancestors and date of separation are difficult to establish. There have, accordingly, been attempts to link them to other language families, as was done in the Austro-Tai hypothesis (first proposed in 1906), which postulated a super-family to include the Austro-Asiatic languages, the ▷Austronesian languages, and certain languages of Indochina.

● **Austronesian languages** ▶ A large language family, also called Malayo-Polynesian, spoken in the Malay peninsula, Taiwan, Madagascar, and the islands of the Pacific Ocean. There are two subgroups: the Western branch, which has up to 200 member languages and includes Malay, Indonesian, Malagasy, Javanese, and Tagalog; and the Eastern or Oceanic branch, which has up to 300 members and includes the languages of the islands in the S and central Pacific, such as Samoa, Tahiti, Tonga, Fiji, New Guinea, and Hawaii. There is some doubt as to whether the languages of Taiwan form a separate group or are to be included in the Western branch.

● **Austro-Prussian War** ▶ (or Seven Weeks' War; 1866) A war between German states led respectively by Austria and Prussia. The Prussian victory was a landmark in Bismarck's strategy for uniting Germany under Prussian leadership.

● **auteur theory** ▶ In film criticism, emphasis on the role of the director. It was developed in the 1950s by several writers for the French magazine *Cahiers du Cinéma* who later became directors themselves, notably Truffaut, Godard, and Chabrol.

● **Authorized Version** ▷*See* King James Version.

● **autism** ▶ A rare and severe mental illness that starts in early childhood. Autistic children are aloof and do not form normal personal relationships but they can become emotionally attached to things. They do not communicate normally, often cannot form abstract concepts, and they are very upset by tiny changes in their familiar surroundings. Many have learning disabilities, but some may have highly developed intellectual abilities in specific areas. The cause is unknown, but some cases can be caused by brain damage and others may be inherited. Lengthy specialized education is usually necessary for autistic children. ▷*See also* Asperger's syndrome.

● **auto-da-fé** ▶ (Portuguese: act of faith) The public ceremony at which persons convicted of crimes by the ▷Inquisition in Portugal, Spain, and their colonies were sentenced. Punishment of victims, including the burning of heretics, was the responsibility of the secular authorities. The first *auto-da-fé* was held in Seville in 1481 and the last in Mexico in 1815.

● **autogiro** ▶ An aircraft with large horizontal freely rotating blades to obtain lift. It differs from the ▷helicopter in that a propeller provides forward motion, which in turn causes the rotation of the unmotorized horizontal blades.

● **autoimmunity** ▶ A condition in which the body produces antibodies (called autoantibodies) that damage or destroy its own tissues. This produces symptoms of various **autoimmune diseases**, the majority of which are poorly understood. Rheumatoid ▷arthritis is caused by the production of autoantibodies against joint tissue; the disease can be diagnosed by the detection of these antibodies in the serum. A more general production of autoantibodies causes systemic ▷lupus erythematosis, which can affect most tissues in the body.

● **Autolycus** ▶ In Greek mythology, the son of ▷Hermes and the grandfather of the hero ▷Odysseus. He was renowned as a thief and trickster and possessed the gift of invisibility.

● **automated teller machine** ▶ (ATM) A computerized device that enables bank and building society customers to withdraw cash outside banking hours. ATMs also accept cash and cheques, provide statements, and effect transfers. Operated by cash cards and a personal identification number (PIN), they are placed on the outside walls of banks and building societies.

● **automatic pilot** ▶ A device utilizing a gyroscope for keeping an aircraft on course. When the aircraft goes off course, the gyro axis rotates, operating electrical contacts, which make the necessary adjustments to the control surfaces.

● **automation** ▶ The use of electronic devices controlled by a computer in mechanical processes that would otherwise be controlled by human operators. It has made considerable impact on production engineering in such fields as steel and chemical manufacture. Telecommunications, transport, and mining also employ automated systems.

● **autonomic nervous system** ▷*See* nervous system.

● **autopsy** ▶ (necropsy *or* postmortem) The dissection and examination of a dead body. An autopsy is performed when the cause of death is uncertain: it may provide further information on a poorly understood disease or evidence of criminal involvement. Except for sudden or mysterious death, permission for autopsy must be granted by the relatives.

● **autoradiography** ▶ The use of photography to examine the distribution of a ▷radioisotope in a thin specimen. The specimen is placed on a photographic plate, which after development shows the distribution of the radioisotope.

● **autosuggestion** ▶ A way of changing one's behaviour by firmly repeating ideas to oneself. It can be used to control undesirable habits or to cope with anxiety and is sometimes taught to psychiatric patients. ▷*See also* hypnosis.

● **autotroph** ▶ A living organism that can manufacture the substances it requires for its life and growth from inorganic compounds, such as carbon dioxide, mineral nitrates, and other salts. Most plants are autotrophic, making their own proteins, carbohydrates, etc., from these simple compounds using the sun's energy by the process of ▷photosynthesis. Organisms, such as animals, fungi, and some bacteria, that lack this ability, and must ingest organic matter in the form of other organisms or their products, are called **heterotrophs**. ▷*See also* nutrition.

● **autumnal equinox** ▷*See* equinox.

● **autumn crocus** ▶ A herbaceous perennial European plant, *Colchicum autumnale*, also called meadow saffron. It has narrow leaves, up to 30 cm long, and a single purple crocus-like flower, which appears in autumn after the leaves have died. The drug colchicine, extracted from the corms, is used to treat gout and in genetic research. Family: *Liliaceae. Compare* Crocus.

● **Autun** ▶ 46 58N 4 18E A town in central France, in the Saône-et-Loire department on the River Arroux. Famous for its Roman school of rhetoric, it has several Roman remains. Its manufactures include furniture and leather. Population (latest est): 19 129.

● **Auvergne** ▶ A planning region and former province in S central France. Its name derives from the Averni, who strongly resisted Roman control of the area. Crossed by the volcanic Auvergne Mountains that rise to over 1800 m (6000 ft), it has many mineral springs and some level fertile districts. It is predominantly agricultural and is noted for the growing of wheat and grapes and the rearing of cattle; cheese and wine are also produced. Area: 25 988 sq km (10 032 sq mi). Population (1995 est): 1 315 400.

● **Auxerre** ▶ 47 48N 3 35W A town in central France, the capital of the Yonne department on the River Yonne. Its gothic cathedral has exceptional 13th-century stained glass windows. Wine and metal goods are produced here. Population (1990): 40 600.

● **auxin** ▶ An organic substance, produced within a plant, that stimulates, inhibits, or modifies growth of the plant. Auxins are sometimes known as plant hormones. The main auxin is indoleacetic acid (IAA). Auxins are responsible for a variety of effects, for example shoot curvature, leaf fall, and fruit growth. Synthetic auxins, such as 2,4-dichlorophenoxyacetic acid (2,4-D), are used as weedkillers for broad-leaved weeds (*see* herbicide).

● **Ava** ▶ The former Burmese capital (1364–1783, 1823–37), 9.5 km (6 mi) S of ▷Mandalay, formerly famous for its Buddhist temples.

● **avadavat** ▶ A small plump songbird, *Estrilda amandava*, also called red munia. Occurring in meadows and marshes of Asia, it is the only ▷waxbill found outside Africa. In the breeding season the male plumage is bright red with mottled brown patches and white speckling.

● **avalanche** ▶ A rapid movement of snow and ice, and sometimes rock debris, down steep slopes. They may occur in winter, when fresh snow slides off an older compacted snow surface, and in spring, when thaws cause the mass to slip. Avalanches can cause severe damage with loss of life and property and in populous mountain areas steel avalanche-sheds are used to protect roads and railways.

● **Avalon** ▶ The paradise of Celtic mythology to which King Arthur (*see* Arthurian legend) was taken after his final battle. It was ruled by ▷Morgan le Fay, famous for her magical powers, and has been identified with Glastonbury in Somerset.

● **avatar** ▶ (Sanskrit: descent) In Hinduism, a manifestation on earth of a divine being. Born independently of the cycle of life and death, an avatar enables the divine to intervene in the affairs of men and women. The most important are the ten avatars of ▷Vishnu, which include ▷Krishna and ▷Buddha, as well as Katki, who has still to appear.

● **Avebury** ▶ 51 27N 1 51W A village in S England, in Wiltshire, on the site of a large complex of Neolithic and early Bronze Age stone circles, banks, and ditches. The principal circle, with its ditch and outer bank, encloses over 12 hectares (30 acres); within it are two smaller ones. Nearby is ▷Silbury Hill.

● **Aveiro** ▶ 40 38N 8 40W A port in NW Portugal, on an inlet of the Atlantic Ocean. Its museum contains art treasures. It has agricultural industries. Population (1981 est): 28 625.

● **Avellaneda** ▶ 34 40S 58 20W A city in Argentina, a suburb of Buenos Aires on the Río de la Plata. It is highly industrialized with meat processing, oil refining, and tanning. Population (1991): 346 620.

● **avens** ▶ A perennial herbaceous plant of the genus *Geum* (about 40 species), native to temperate and Arctic regions. Most plants rarely exceed 60 cm in height. Their flowers, 2–3 cm long, are white, yellow, orange, or red, either solitary or in clusters. *G. coccineum* is a common ornamental plant. Family: *Rosaceae*.

● **average** ▶ **1.** (mathematics) A representative or middle value of a set of quantities. The arithmetical average (*or* arithmetical mean) is found by adding the quantities in a set and dividing the total by the number of quantities: the arithmetical average of 7, 8, 13, and 20 is 12 (48 divided by 4). The geometric average (*or* geometric mean) is found by multiplying together the numbers in a set and extracting a root equal to the number of quantities: the geometric average of 2, 9, and 12 is 6 ($^3\sqrt{216}$). **2.** (insurance) Loss or damage to property. In ▷marine insurance it refers to a partial loss. A **particular average** affects only one interest, whereas a **general average** is shared among all the parties concerned (e.g. if a deck cargo has to be jettisoned to save a ship in a storm, all the cargo owners have to contribute to the loss). In fire insurance, average is used to combat underinsurance. For example, if an insurer has only insured his goods for a proportion of their total value, he will only be paid that proportion of any claim for a partial loss.

● **Avernus, Lake** ▶ A small crater lake near Naples and Cumae (the earliest Greek colony in Italy). In ancient times it was believed to be the entrance to the infernal regions, and *Avernus* was often used by writers as a synonym for the underworld. In Virgil's *Aeneid*, Aeneas descends to the underworld through a cave near the lake.

● **Averroes** ▶ (Ibn Rushd; 1126–98) Muslim philosopher and a judge in Córdoba and Seville. Averroes' main works were his commentaries on Aristotle, which greatly influenced the philosophy of medieval Christianity. He defended philosophy as the highest form of enquiry, holding that faith and reason are not necessarily in conflict but are separate ways of arriving at the truth.

● **aversion therapy** ▶ A form of ▷conditioning used to treat some kinds of undesirable behaviour, such as sexual deviation, alcoholism, and drug addiction. An unpleasant stimulus (e.g. an electric shock) is associated with a stimulus related to the problem behaviour (e.g. the taste of alcohol). ▷*See also* behaviour therapy.

● **Avery, Oswald Theodore** ▶ (1877–1955) Canadian bacteriologist, whose work demonstrated the importance of ▷DNA and led Watson and Crick to investigate its structure and method of replication. It was known that an extract (nonliving) of smooth-coated (S) bacteria contained a substance capable of converting living rough-coated bacteria into the S strain. In 1944, Avery identified this substance as DNA.

● **Avesta** ▶ The sacred scriptures of ▷Zoroastrianism. Written in Old Iranian, the five books of the *Avesta* contain prayers (probably by Zoroaster himself) hymns, ritual and liturgical instruction, and the main body of Zoroastrian law. Its surviving form dates from about the 6th century AD.

● **Avicenna** ▶ (980–1037) Persian philosopher and physician. Avicenna received extensive education in science and philosophy and served various rulers during his life, as government official and physician. His encyclopedia of philosophy, *Ash-Shifa* (*The Recovery*), encompasses logic, psychology, metaphysics, and natural sciences and parts were subsequently translated into Latin. Avicenna's *Canon of Medicine*, based on Roman and Arabic medicine and his own medical knowledge, became a popular text throughout the Middle East and Europe.

● **Aviemore** ▶ 57 12N 3 50W A winter sports resort in Scotland, in Moray on the River Spey, between the Monadhliath and Cairngorm Mountains. Population (1991): 2214.

● **Avignon** ▶ 43 56N 4 48E A town in SE France, the capital of the Vaucluse department on the River Rhône. The papacy, under French control, was removed to Avignon (1309–77; *see* Avignon papacy) and there were subsequently rival popes at Rome and Avignon until 1417 (*see* Great Schism). Famous landmarks include the 14th-century papal palace and the 12th-century bridge, of which only four arches remain. A popular tourist centre, Avignon trades in wine and has chemical, soap, and cement industries. Population (1990): 89 440.

● **Avignon papacy** ▶ (1309–77) The period during which the popes resided in Avignon (France) rather than Rome. It is sometimes called the Babylonian Captivity (in reference to the ▷Babylonian exile in Jewish history). The papal court was established in Avignon, a papal fief, by ▷Clement V, who, like his six successors in Avignon, was French. English and German criticism of French dominance over the papacy eventually forced its return to Rome under Gregory XI. Shortly afterwards the division in the Church known as the ▷Great Schism occurred, largely in response to the increased power acquired by the cardinals during the Avignon papacy.

● **Avignon school** ▶ A school of painting established when Clement V moved the papal court from Rome to Avignon in 1309 and imported Italian 14th-century masters, notably Simone ▷Martini, to decorate the papal palace. After the pope's return to Rome (1377) painters remaining in Avignon developed a unique style, fusing Italian and Flemish influences. The artists of the school include Nicholas Froment (active 1450–90) and its most celebrated work is the anonymous *Villeneuve Pietà* (c. 1460; Louvre).

● **Avila** ▶ 40 39N 4 42W A town in central Spain, in Old Castile on the River Adaja. A popular tourist centre, the old part of the town is enclosed by 12th-century walls and has a notable gothic cathedral (11th–15th centuries). St Teresa was born here. Population (latest est): 45 100.

● **avocado** ▶ A tree, *Persea americana*, up to 18 m tall, native to Mexico and Central America but now extensively cultivated in Florida, California, and South Africa for its fruit. These fruits—**avocado pears**—may reach a weight of 2 kg: they have a green to dark-purple skin, a fatty flesh rich in fat, protein, and vitamins A and B, and a single hard seed.

● **avocet** ▶ A wading bird of the genus *Recurvirostra*, having long slender legs and a long thin upcurved bill used to skim the surface of mud or water in search of small invertebrates. The Eurasian avocet (*R. avosetta*), 50 cm long, has a black-and-white plumage and grey-blue legs and is protected in Britain. Family: *Recurvirostridae*; order: *Charadriiformes* (gulls, plovers, etc.). ▷*See* Plate III.

● **Avogadro, Amedeo, Conte di Quaregna e Ceretto** ▶ (1776–

1856) Italian physicist, who became professor of physics at the University of Turin. He developed ▷Gay-Lussac's hypothesis that equal volumes of gases contain equal numbers of particles, establishing the difference between atoms and molecules. Because he made this vital distinction the theory is now known as **Avogadro's hypothesis**. His name is also commemorated in the **Avogadro number** (*or* the Avogadro constant), the number of molecules in one mole of substance (it has the value $6.022\,52 \times 10^{23}$ mol^{-1}). Avogadro's work was largely neglected during his life and was not acknowledged until ▷Cannizzaro brought it to public notice in 1854.

● **avoirdupois units** ▷*See* units of measurement.

● **Avon** ▶ A former county of SW England, formed in 1974 from parts of NE Somerset and S Gloucestershire surrounding the main urban areas of Bristol and Bath. In 1996 it was abolished and administrative powers were devolved to four ▷unitary authorities: North Somerset, Bath and North East Somerset, Bristol, and South Gloucestershire. The historic county boundaries of Somerset and Gloucestershire were restored for ceremonial and related purposes.

● **Avon, (Robert) Anthony Eden, 1st Earl of** ▶ (1897–1977) British statesman; Conservative prime minister (1955–57). Foreign secretary from 1935 to 1938, he resigned in opposition to Neville Chamberlain's policy of ▷appeasement. During World War II he was secretary for war and then (1940–45) foreign secretary. From 1951 to 1955 he was again foreign secretary, playing an important part in the 1954 ▷Geneva Conference and in the establishment of the ▷European Defence Community. He succeeded Churchill as prime minister and in 1956, following Nasser's nationalization of the ▷Suez Canal and an Israeli attack on Egypt, joined France in an offensive against Egypt. Egypt retained control of Suez and, despite Eden's claim that the Anglo-French initiative had ended the war between Egypt and Israel, he was much criticized and resigned shortly afterwards. He became Earl of Avon in 1961.

● **Avon, River** ▶ The name of several rivers in the UK, including: **1.** A river in central England, flowing SW from Northamptonshire to the River Severn at Tewkesbury. Length: 154 km (96 mi). **2.** A river in SW England, flowing E then S and W from Gloucestershire to the Severn estuary at Avonmouth. Length: 120 km (75 mi). **3.** A river in S England, flowing S from Wiltshire to the English Channel. Length: 96 km (60 mi).

● **AWACS** ▶ (Airborne Warning and Control System) A US ▷radar system mounted on an aircraft to give early warning of the movements of enemy aircraft and, if appropriate, to direct intervention measures against them.

● **Axel** ▷*See* Absalon.

● **Axholme, Isle of** ▶ A low-lying area in E England, in NW Lincolnshire between the Rivers Don, Idle, and Trent. Once waterlogged, it was drained in the early 17th century as part of the ▷Fens.

● **axiology** ▶ The theory of values in ethics and aesthetics, particularly the search for the good and its nature. Axiology investigates basic principles governing moral judgment and the place of values (or norms) within the frameworks of philosophical systems. ▷Plato held to an absolute theory of the Idea of the Good, while ▷Hume and others believed that values were relative, depending on persons making value judgments. ▷Kant found the source of value in practical reason, while in ▷utilitarianism it lay in the principle of the greatest happiness for the greatest number.

● **axiom** ▶ An assumption or principle, used to prove a theorem, that is itself accepted as true without proof. Some mathematicians reserve the term for an assumption in logic, using postulate for an assumption made in other fields.

● **axis deer** ▶ A slender deer, *Axis axis*, also called chital, that usually lives in small herds near rivers in India and Sri Lanka. Axis deer measure up to 100 cm at the shoulder and are reddish with white spots and pale underparts.

● **Axis Powers** ▶ The coalition of Germany, Italy, and Japan that opposed the ▷Allied Powers in ▷World War II. It originated in agreements going back to 1936 and it culminated in the Tripartite Pact (1940).

● **Axminster carpet** ▶ A type of carpet developed at a factory in Axminster, England (1755–1835). It was handmade in Axminster and elsewhere until the 19th-century mechanization of the carpet industry. Although the industry was only revived in Axminster in 1937, Axminster carpets had been in continuous production in other towns, a special loom having been invented in 1876. Their distinguishing features were a long soft pile and tufts individually coloured to produce patterns of unlimited complexity.

● **axolotl** ▶ A salamander, *Ambystoma mexicanum*, occurring in Mexican lakes. It reaches a length of 25 cm, has a long tail and weak limbs, and is typically dark brown. Axolotls retain their larval characteristics permanently, reproducing in this state, although under certain conditions they may develop into adults. Family: *Ambystomatidae*.

● **axon** ▷*See* neurone.

● **Axum** ▷*See* Aksum.

● **Ayacucho** ▶ 13 10S 74 15W A city in S central Peru. The battle of Ayacucho (1824) was fought nearby, resulting in Peru gaining independence from Spain. An agricultural centre, tourism is also important. It has a university (founded 1677 and reopened 1957). Population (1993): 114 809.

● **Ayatollah Ruholla Khomeini** ▷*See* Khomeini, Ayatollah Ruholla.

● **Ayckbourn, Sir Alan** ▶ (1939–　) British dramatist. After working in provincial repertory theatre, he gained his first London success with *Relatively Speaking* (1967). His comedies include *Absurd Person Singular* (1973), the trilogy *The Norman Conquests* (1974), *A Chorus of Disapproval* (1985), *Body Language* (1990), *Haunting Julia* (1994), and *Things We Do For Love* (1998) all characterized by ingenious construction and detailed observation of middle-class life. He directs a repertory theatre in Scarborough. He was knighted in 1997.

● **aye-aye** ▶ A rare arboreal ▷prosimian primate, *Daubentonia madagascariensis*, occurring only in the coastal forests of N Madagascar. It is 86–104 cm long including the tail (50–60 cm) and has dark shaggy fur and large ears used to detect wood-boring insects, extracting them with its incisor teeth and narrow elongated third finger. Family: *Daubentoniidae*.

● **Ayer, Sir Alfred (Jules)** ▶ (1910–89) British philosopher; Wykeham Professor of Logic at Oxford (1959–78). Ayer's major contribution to British philosophy was his bringing to England the teachings of the ▷Vienna Circle, in particular the doctrine of ▷logical positivism. This he expounded in *Language, Truth and Logic* (1936), which taught that if a proposition is neither verifiable by sense experience, nor a tautology, then it can contain no meaning. His later books include *The Foundations of Empirical Knowledge* (1940), *The Problem of Knowledge* (1956), and the autobiographical volumes *Part of My Life* (1977) and *More of My Life* (1984).

● **Ayers Rock** ▶ (Aboriginal name: Uluru) The largest monolith in the world, in Australia, in SW Northern Territory. It consists of a vast red rock rising 335 m (1099 ft) above the surrounding plain with a circumference of 10 km (6.25 mi). Its colour varies according to atmospheric changes and the position of the sun. Named after Sir Henry Ayers (1821–97), South Australian premier.

● **Ayesha** ▶ (c. 613–78) The third and favourite wife of ▷Mohammed and daughter of ▷Abu Bakr. She married at the age of nine. She led a revolt against ▷Ali but was defeated (656) and ended her life in exile in Medina. She is known as "the mother of believers."

● **Aylesbury** ▶ 51 50N 0 50W A market town in S central England, the administrative centre for Buckinghamshire. Lying in an agricultural area, it has food-processing industries as well as insurance and various light industries. Population (1991): 58 058.

● **Aylward, Gladys** ▶ (1903–70) British missionary. From 1930 she worked as an independent missionary in China. Her life story was the subject of a popular film, *The Inn of the Sixth Happiness* (1958), in which she was played by Ingrid Bergman.

● **Aymara** ▶ A people of the Peruvian and Bolivian highlands. They grow potatoes and other crops and herd llamas and alpacas. Their costume is characterized by the woollen poncho and conical headwear with earflaps. They live in small extended-family settlements in which elders, who are also ritual shamans (*see* shamanism), have authority. In the 15th century the Aymara were incorporated into the Inca empire under Viracocha. Later Spanish influence made them nominally Catholic but earlier beliefs persist. Today there are approximately 1 360 000 Aymaras and their language, Aymaran, is one of the strongest surviving native Indian languages.

● **Ayr** ▶ 55 28N 4 38W A port and resort in SW Scotland, in South Ayrshire where the River Ayr enters the Firth of Clyde. Many of its historic buildings are associated with Robert Burns. It exports coal, iron, and agricultural produce. Population (1991): 47 962.

● **ayre** ▶ A type of song of the Elizabethan period, consisting of a principal voice part accompanied by instruments or other voices, each verse being sung to the same music. In 1597 John Dowland published his *First Book of Songs and Ayres of Four Parts*; other composers of ayres include Morley and Campion.

● **Ayrshire** ▶ A historic county of SW Scotland, bordered on the W by the Firth of Clyde and including the island of Arran. Under local government reorganization in 1975 it became part of Strathclyde Region. Further reorganization in 1996 led to the creation of three new council areas, ▷East Ayrshire, ▷North Ayrshire, and ▷South Ayrshire.

● **Ayrshire cattle** ▶ A breed of red or brown and white cattle originating in Ayrshire, SW Scotland. A hardy breed, Ayrshires are primarily producers of good quality milk, used especially in cheese making. Many herds have been replaced by the higher yielding ▷Friesian cattle.

Ayers Rock ▶ An aerial view showing the effects of erosion, which has produced gullies and basins on top and deep fluting lower down. Caves at the base of the rock, which contain carvings and paintings, are sacred to several Aboriginal tribes. Ayers Rock is within Uluru National Park.

Aztecs ► This pectoral ornament, which was worn by a high priest, takes the form of a double-headed serpent, one of the symbols of the rain god Tlaloc. It probably formed part of the treasure sent to Cortés by the last Aztec emperor, Montezuma II, who believed Cortés to be the god Quetzalcoatl.

● **Ayub Khan, Mohammad** ► (1907–74) Pakistani statesman; president (1958–69). After a distinguished military career he became defence minister in 1954. Following President Iskander Mirza's coup d'état in 1958 Ayub Khan became chief martial law administrator and then ousted Mirza to become president. He negotiated (1966) the ceasefire agreement with ▷Shastri following the India-Pakistan war of 1965. He was forced to resign following civil unrest in East Pakistan.

● **Ayurvedic medicine** ► (Sanskrit: life knowledge) A traditional form of Indian ▷holistic medicine that includes religious and social aspects. It derives from the Hindu sacred texts (*see* Vedas) and later Hindu works. Diagnosis involves both a medical case history and an astrological assessment, while treatment may include massage, prayer, breathing exercises, and herbal remedies. In 1970 the Indian parliament instituted a register of qualified Ayurvedic practitioners. ▷*See also* alternative medicine.

● **Ayutthaya** ► (*or* Ayuthi) 14 20N 100 35E A city in central Thailand. The former capital of the country (1350–1767), it is noted for its exceptional architecture, which survived a sacking by the Burmese. Population (latest est): 60 000.

● **azalea** ► A deciduous shrub of the genus ▷*Rhododendron*. (Most horticulturalists prefer to restrict the term rhododendron to the large evergreen species.) Growing to a height of up to 2 m, azaleas are all native to the uplands of North America and S Asia but are now widely cultivated as ornamentals. The attractive flowers are large, fragrant, and funnel-shaped (about 6 cm in diameter) and of various colours. Family: *Ericaceae*.

● **Azaña, Manuel** ► (1880–1940) Spanish statesman, who was prominent in the Second Republic (1931–39). His premiership (1931–33) introduced internal reforms but was unpopular for its repression of opposition. He was president (1936–39) during the Spanish Civil War and fled to France after Gen Franco's Nationalist victory.

● **Azande** ► An African people speaking a Sudanic language who live in areas of the Sudan, the Democratic Republic of Congo, and the Central African Republic. They are an ethnically mixed people, who practise agriculture, hunting, and various crafts, including ironwork. They were traditionally divided into a number of warring kingdoms. They live in scattered homesteads and are organized into a number of dispersed patrilineal clans. Their religion takes the form of an ancestor cult. Belief in witchcraft is a central aspect of their lives, most misfortunes being attributed to it.

● **azeotrope** ► A mixture of liquids that boils at a constant temperature, the composition of the vapour produced at a given pressure being the same as that of the liquid. The components of an azeotrope cannot therefore be separated by distillation. Ethanol and water form an azeotrope which boils at 78.2°C.

● **Azerbaidzhan, Republic of** ► A republic in W Asia, on the Caspian Sea. It consists mainly of the hot dry plain of the Rivers Kura and Araks, surrounded by the Caucasus Mountains. The Azerbaidzhani, who comprise most of the population, are a Turkic-speaking Shiite Muslim people renowned for their carpet weaving.
Economy: Azerbaidzhan is one of the oldest oil-producing areas of the world and its most important industries are oil and gas, with a developing chemical industry. Agriculture is diversified and expansion is planned. The main crops are cotton, tobacco, and fruit, including grapes for wine.
History: Islam was introduced by the region's Arab conquerors in the 7th century. After some 300 years of Persian rule, the region was acquired by Russia in the early 19th century. It proclaimed its independence in 1918, but was subsequently absorbed into the Transcaucasian Soviet Federated Socialist Republic (*see* Transcaucasia), becoming a separate Soviet republic in 1936. In 1988–90 riots over Armenian claims to the disputed ▷Nagorno-Karabakh area escalated into a state of virtual civil war. Azerbaidzhani troops fought with Armenian forces in the region from 1991 until 1994, when a ceasefire was declared to allow peace negotiations to continue. Presidential elections were held in 1991 and the new leadership declared independence from the disintegrating Soviet Union. In 1993 a military coup ousted President Abulfaz Elchibey and the former communist leader Heidar Aliyev became head of state. Aliyev was re-elected in 1998, amidst widespread allegations of fraud; protests by opposition parties led to violent clashes in Baku.

Republic of Azerbaidzhan

Head of state	President Heidar Ali Riza Aliyev
Official language	Azeri
Official currency	manat of 100 gopik
Area	86 600 sq km (33 430 sq mi)
Population (1997 est)	7 617 000
Capital	Baku

● **Azhar, al-** ► A mosque and centre of traditional Muslim studies in Cairo. Inaugurated in 972 AD following the Fatimid conquest of Egypt, al-Azhar was originally controlled by the ▷Ismaili. It became a ▷Sunnite institution under Saladin but it was not until after the Ottoman conquest (1517) that it gained its present pre-eminence. It is now regarded as the most authoritative centre of Islam. In Egypt it has university status.

● **Azikiwe, (Benjamin) Nnamdi** ► (1904–96) A prominent figure in the struggle for independence in Nigeria. Popularly known as Zik, in 1944 he founded the National Council of Nigeria and the Cameroons to fight colonial rule. At independence (1960) he was appointed governor general and when Nigeria became a republic became its first president (1963–66).

● **azimuth** ▷*See* altitude.

● **azo dyes** ▶ A class of synthetic dyes containing the **azo group** (–N=N–). First produced in 1858, they now outsell all other dyes combined. This success is due to exceptional colour-fastness and versatility in application, including the ability to dye natural and synthetic fibres direct, i.e. without a mordant. Virtually any colour may be obtained; examples are methyl orange, Bismarck brown, and Congo red.

● **Azores** ▶ (Portuguese name: Açôres) 38 30N 28 00W Three groups of volcanic islands in the N Atlantic Ocean, in Portugal. The chief islands include São Miguel, Terceira, Faial, and Flores. Settled by the Portuguese in the 15th century, they were previously uninhabited. Naval fighting between the English and Spanish took place here in the 16th and 17th centuries. The site of US air bases, they produce fruit, tobacco, and wine. Area: 2300 sq km (888 sq mi). Population (1992 est): 236 500. Capital: Ponta Delgada, on São Miguel.

● **Azorín** ▶ (José Martinéz Ruíz; 1874–1967) Spanish novelist, essayist, and critic. His works include the autobiographical novels *La voluntad* (1902) and *Antonio Azorín* (1903), as well as the collection of essays *Los pueblos* (1905), inspired by the history and landscape of Castile.

● **Azov, Sea of** ▶ A NE arm of the Black Sea, to the main body of which it is connected by the narrow Kerch Strait. Area: 38 000 sq km (14 668 sq mi).

● **AZT** ▷See AIDS.

● **Aztecs** ▶ A ▷Nahuatl-speaking people who ruled an empire in central and S Mexico before their defeat by Hernán Cortés in the 16th century. They had an advanced, elaborate, and rich civilization centred on their capital Tenochtitlán and other cities. They were expert builders and constructed large palaces and temples in which they worshipped many gods, especially Huitzilopochtli to whom they sacrificed human victims, captives of warfare, by ripping out their hearts while they still lived. Their social organization was hierarchical with authority and influence vested in a class of chiefs and priests and in the kings, the last of whom was ▷Montezuma II.

● **Aztec-Tanoan languages** ▶ An American Indian language group, spoken in the SW USA and central America. It has two branches: Uto-Aztecan and Kiowa-Tanoan. Uto-Aztecan is the larger; its most widely used language, Nahua, is spoken by the ▷Nahuatl people of central and W Mexico. Other Uto-Aztecan languages include those of the Paiute Indians in California and Utah, the ▷Hopi in Arizona, and the ▷Comanche in Texas. The Kiowa-Tanoan branch has only four members and is spoken in New Mexico and by the ▷Kiowa of Oklahoma.

● **Azuela, Mariano** ▶ (1873–1952) Mexican novelist. He practised medicine in Mexico City before joining Pancho Villa's forces during the Mexican revolution. *The Underdogs* (1916) described the suffering it caused. Later novels, such as *Los caciques* (1917) and the posthumous *Esa sangre*, express disgust with Mexican society both before and after the revolution.

B

● **Baader-Meinhof Gang** ▶ A group of terrorists, calling themselves the Rote Armee Faktion (Red Army Faction), who aimed at the violent overthrow of capitalist society in West Germany. The gang was named after two of its leading members, Andreas Baader (1943–77) and Ulrike Meinhof (1934–76), both of whom died in prison. By mid-1984 most of the gang had been arrested. Sporadic terrorist activities continued until 1998, when the group formally disbanded.

● **Baal** ▶ An ancient fertility god worshipped throughout the Near East, especially in Canaan. As champion of the divine order against chaos he defeated the sea god Yamm. The myth of his conflict with Mot, god of death and sterility, is closely linked to the natural processes of vegetation: his defeat and descent into the underworld represents famine and drought, and his resurrection and victory over Mot symbolizes rain and fertility.

● **Baalbek** ▶ 34 00N 36 12E A town in E Lebanon, originally commanding Phoenician trade routes. The Roman colony here, called Heliopolis, has left extensive and imposing remains, including temples dedicated to Jupiter and Venus (1st–3rd centuries AD). In recent years it has become a centre for Muslim Shiite activity and a haven for terrorist groups. Population (1995 est): 15 600.

● **Ba'al Shem Tov** ▶ (Israel ben Eliezer; c. 1700–60) Charismatic Jewish leader and mystic, the founder of ▷Hasidism. He lived in Podolia (then part of Poland) and attracted an enormous following by his powerful personality and his teaching, a blend of popular pietism and mystical Judaism. He is the subject of many legends. His name means "Master of the Good Name."

● **Ba'athism** ▶ An Arab political movement, influential in many Middle Eastern countries, notably Syria and Iraq, that urges the creation of a united socialist Arab nation. The Ba'athists supported the formation of the ▷United Arab Republic (1958–61) and rose to power in Syria in 1963 and in Iraq (where Saddam ▷Hussein became its leader) in 1968. The Syrian and Iraqi wings of the movement have been deeply divided since the 1970s.

● **Babbage, Charles** ▶ (1792–1871) British mathematician and inventor. In an attempt to produce more accurate mathematical tables, Babbage conceived the idea of a mechanical computer that could store information. Although he never completed the machine, it was the forerunner of the modern computer. He was an outspoken critic of the Royal Society for its complacency and of British mathematics in general for languishing in the shadow of Newton.

● **Babbitt, Irving** ▶ (1865–1933) US scholar and critic. While professor of French at Harvard (1894–1933), he wrote extensive works on literature and social questions, including *Rousseau and Romanticism* (1919) and *Democracy and Leadership* (1924). He was a leader of the "neohumanist" thinkers, who opposed Romanticism and advocated the classical values of restraint and moderation.

● **Babbitt, Milton** ▶ (1916–) US composer. He taught music and mathematics at Princeton University. His compositions employ ▷serialism and include music for synthesizers; they include *Philomel* (1963–64) and *Soli e Duettini* (1989–90).

● **babbler** ▶ A small songbird belonging to a family (Timaliidae; 280 species) occurring in Old World regions, particularly in SE Asia. Babblers have short rounded wings, a long tail, strong legs and bill, and a noisy babbling cry. The plumage is often brightly coloured, although some species are plain brown. Babblers live in wooded regions, searching the undergrowth in groups for insects and berries.

● **Babel, Isaac Emmanuilovich** ▶ (1894–1941) Russian short-story writer. Of Jewish descent, he served in the imperial army, but fought for the Bolsheviks in 1917. His *Odessa Tales* were published in 1916 in a journal edited by ▷Gorki. *Red Cavalry* (1926) was a series of sketches based on his experience in the war against Poland. He died in a Siberian prison camp, a victim of Stalin's purges, but was posthumously rehabilitated in the 1950s.

● **Babel, Tower of** ▶ In the Bible (Genesis 11.1–9), a tower intended to reach heaven. Angered by the presumption of the building, Jehovah caused the builders to speak different languages, so that they were incomprehensible to each other and were forced to abandon the work. The legend attempts to account for the diversification of languages. It also probably alludes to the Babylonian ziggurats, which for the Israelites were examples of Gentile pride.

● **Bab el-Mandeb** ▶ A strait between Africa and the SW Arabian Peninsula, connecting the Red Sea with the Gulf of Aden. It is 32 km (20 mi) wide and at one point is divided by Perim Island.

● **Babeuf, François-Noël** ▶ (1760–97) French revolutionary. Propagator of extreme egalitarian ideas, he plotted to overthrow the ▷Directory. His "conspiracy of equals" was exposed and Babeuf was executed. Secret societies perpetuated his doctrines, known as Babouvism.

● **Babi faith** ▶ A religion founded in 1844 by the Persian Mirza 'Ali Mohammed (1819–50), who became known as the Bab (the Gate). He proclaimed himself the 12th and last imam of certain ▷Shiite sects, which had prophesied his reappearance. He was imprisoned and later shot on government orders, and his followers were subsequently persecuted. Babism centred on the belief that God reveals himself to man through prophets who would continue to appear until the end of the world. It was the immediate precursor of the ▷Baha'i faith.

● **Babington, Anthony** ▶ (1561–86) English conspirator, who with John Ballard plotted to kill Elizabeth I and place the Roman Catholic Mary, Queen of Scots, on the throne. The conspiracy failed: Babington, Ballard, and subsequently Mary were executed.

● **babirusa** ▶ A hairless wild pig, *Babyrousa babyrussa*, of Sulawesi (Indonesia). About 100 cm long, babirusas live in damp forests and are good swimmers, feeding on water plants, fruit, and tubers. Males have two pairs of curved tusks; the tuskless females have only one pair of teats.

● **Babi Yar** ▶ A ravine in Ukraine, near Kiev, in which the Germans massacred some 100 000 people in 1941. Most of the victims were Jews, but others were Russians and Poles. The Russian poet Yevgenii ▷Yevtushenko commemorated the atrocity in his poem *Babi Yar* (1961), and the Russian novelist ▷Kuznetsov wrote a novel with the same title in 1966.

● **baboon** ▶ A large ▷Old World monkey belonging to the genus *Papio* (5 species), of African and Asian grassland. Baboons are 95–185 cm long including the tail (45–70 cm) and have a shaggy mane and a long doglike face with large teeth. They feed on insects, small vertebrates, and vegetable matter. They live in well-organized troops containing 40–150 individuals arranged in a social hierarchy according to age and sex. ▷*See also* hamadryas. ⌐mammal.

● **Babur** ▶ (Zahir-ud-din Muhammad; 1483–1530) Emperor of India (1526–30), who founded the ▷Mogul dynasty. Descended from Genghis Khan and Timur, Babur became ruler of Fergana (1495) in Uzbekistan but failed to reconquer his ancestors' kingdom of Samarkand. Capturing Kabul, he invaded India from Afghanistan in 1525. In 1526 he defeated and killed Ibrahim Lodhi, Sultan of Delhi (1517–26), and rapidly subjugated all of N India. His story is told in his memoirs, the *Babur-Nameh*.

● **Babylon** ▶ The capital of ancient Babylonia, strategically positioned on the River ▷Euphrates S of modern Baghdad. Its first period of prominence was about 2150 to 1740 BC, under a dynasty of which ▷Hammurabi was the most illustrious member. Subsequently, rising ▷Assyrian power threatened Babylonian independence, though some Babylonians, such as Nebuchadnezzar I (reigned c. 1146–1123), temporarily reversed the trend. Sacked by ▷Sennacherib (689 BC), Babylon was rebuilt from 625 BC onwards, especially during the reign (c. 605–562) of ▷Nebuchadnezzar II. It was the remains of this city that were excavated by ▷Koldewey and from which the famous Ishtar Gate was recovered. In 539 BC Babylon surrendered to ▷Cyrus the Great of Persia. By 275 BC it was virtually depopulated. Under Saddam ▷Hussein there have been attempts to reconstruct the city, which have destroyed much of the authentic remains. ▷*See also* Babel, Tower of; Hanging Gardens of Babylon; ziggurat.

● **Babylonia** ▶ The area of ▷Mesopotamia on the alluvial plain along the lower reaches of the River Euphrates, which was controlled by ancient ▷Babylon. Before about 2000 BC approximately the same area was known as ▷Sumer. The Babylonians were a blend of Semitic peoples, like their rivals, the ▷Assyrians, to the NW. Apart from Babylon, the former Sumerian capital of ▷Ur and the port of ▷Eridu were major cities.

● **Babylonian exile** ▶ The period from the destruction of the ▷Temple of Jerusalem by ▷Nebuchadnezzar (586 BC) to the Jews' return under ▷Cyrus the Great (538 BC), during which time most of the Jews lived in exile in ▷Babylonia. It was here that parts of the Hebrew Bible were written, and that certain characteristic Jewish attitudes and institutions (e.g. the ▷synagogue) developed. This exile established the beginnings of the ▷diaspora; many Jews remained in Babylonia, and in late antiquity and the middle ages it had one of the most important Jewish communities in the world.

● **Bacall, Lauren** ▶ (Betty Jean Perske; 1924–　) US film actress. Her films with Humphrey ▷Bogart, who became her husband in 1945, include *To Have and Have Not* (1944), *The Big Sleep* (1946), and *Key Largo* (1948). Her other films include *How to Marry a Millionaire* (1953), *The Shootist* (1976), and *The Mirror has Two Faces* (1996).

● **Bacău** ▶ 46 32N 26 59E A city in E Romania, on the River Bistriła. An important road and rail junction, its industries include oil refining, textiles, and paper manufacture. Population (1994 est): 207 730.

● **baccarat games** ▶ Various related card games, the object of which is to hold cards totalling nine, counting only the final digit of a total of ten or over (thus 10 equals 0). **Chemin de fer** was formerly popular in casinos. In this game the punters take turns to be banker, against whom the other punters make their bets. The banker then deals two cards to another punter and two to himself. If the cards of either total nine, or failing that eight, this total wins and bets are settled accordingly. Otherwise a third card is taken or refused as necessary (taken if the total is four or under, refused if six or over). The highest total wins. **Punto banco,** the form now most widely played in UK casinos, is identical to chemin de fer except that bets are placed against the casino on either the banker or his opponent.

● **Bacchanalia** ▶ The Roman form of the Hellenistic mystery rites in honour of Bacchus (*see* Dionysus). The cult reached Rome from S Italy in the 2nd century BC. Originally involving only women, Bacchic worship included ecstatic rituals and secret orgies. In 186 BC a decree of the Senate prohibited Bacchanalia in Rome.

● **Bacchus** ▷*See* Dionysus.

● **Bacchylides** ▶ (c. 516–c. 450 BC) Greek lyric poet, nephew of

Simonides and a rival of Pindar. Born on the island of Ceos, he lived at the court of Syracuse until the death of his patron Hiero in 467. Egyptian papyrus fragments discovered in 1896 contain parts of 14 odes and 6 ▷dithyrambs.

Johann Sebastian Bach ▶ The composer holding the manuscript of his three-part canon.

● **Bach, Johann Sebastian** ▶ (1685–1750) German composer and keyboard player, the greatest member of a large musical family. An orphan from the age of nine, he was brought up and taught by his brother Johann Christoph Bach (1671–1721). He subsequently became a chorister in Lüneburg and in 1703 a violinist at the Weimar court. In 1707 he married his cousin Maria Barbara Bach (1684–1720); after her death he married Anna Magdalena Wilcken (1701–60). In 1708 he rejoined the Weimar court as organist, remaining there for nine years. He became kapellmeister at the court of Prince Leopold of Anhalt at Köthen in 1717 and finally cantor of St Thomas' Church, Leipzig, in 1723. During his lifetime Bach achieved greater recognition as an organist than as a composer; he composed much organ music and was a skilled improviser on keyboard instruments. Among his greatest works are the *St John Passion* (1723), the *St Matthew Passion* (1729), and the *Mass in B minor* (1733–38), as well as over 200 cantatas. His compositions for orchestra include violin and harpsichord concertos and the *Brandenburg Concertos* (1721). For the harpsichord and clavichord he composed *The Well-Tempered Clavier* (Part I, 1722; Part II, 1744), a collection of 48 preludes and fugues, and the *Goldberg Variations* (1742); he also wrote music for the violin, cello, and lute. Bach's music did not become widely known until Mendelssohn revived it, giving the first performance of the *St Matthew Passion* since Bach's time in 1829.

Of Bach's 20 children, 3 sons became famous musicians. His eldest son **Wilhelm Friedemann Bach** (1710–84) studied in Leipzig and became church organist in Dresden (1733–46) and subsequently in Halle (1746–64). He ended his life in poverty, leaving cantatas, concertos, and symphonies.

His third son **Carl Philipp Emanuel Bach** (1714–88) studied law and philosophy but later turned to music, becoming musician to Frederick the Great in Berlin and subsequently becoming director of the principal church in Hamburg in succession to Telemann. In his works, which were highly regarded by Haydn and Mozart, he developed a new monophonic style of composition that became the basis of the classical style. His works include symphonies, concertos, and much keyboard music.

J. S. Bach's 11th son **Johann Christian Bach** (1735–82), called the English (or London) Bach, studied in Berlin and after holding posts in Italy became music master to the British royal family. He composed 13 operas, as well as concertos, church music, and piano pieces.

● **Bach flower remedies** ▶ A series of liquid extracts from the flowers of 38 species of plants, including agrimony, clematis, elm, gorse, holly, pine, and willow, used by some homeopaths and herbalists to treat mental and emotional problems associated with illness. The extracts do not cure the physical illness but are intended to calm fraught patients. The Bach Rescue Remedy, containing extracts of cherry plum, clematis, impatiens, rockrose, and star of Bethlehem, is used to calm patients in shock, who have had an accident or received bad news. The system was devised by a British doctor, Edward Bach (1880–1936), in the 1920s.

● **bacille Calmette Guérin** ▷See BCG.

● **bacillus** ► Any rod-shaped bacterium. The term is used specifically for bacteria of the genus *Bacillus*: spore-forming species including parasites of plants and animals. *B. anthracis* was first shown to cause anthrax in livestock by Robert ▷Koch.

● **backcross** ► The mating of an organism with one of its parents. Backcrosses are used in animal and plant breeding to select individuals that will be pure-breeding for a particular desirable characteristic.

● **backgammon** ► A board game for two players that was known in ancient Mesopotamia, Greece, and Rome and in medieval England (as "the tables"). Each player has 15 pieces, which are moved round the 24 chevrons (points) marked on the board, the number of points moved being indicated by the throws of two dice. From their prescribed starting positions the players move in opposite directions. Each tries to bring all his pieces into the last quarter (his home board or inner table), after which he can remove them from the board (bear them off). Simultaneously he must block his opponent's moves. A chevron is occupied (point is made) when a player has two or more pieces on it, i.e. his opponent cannot land on it. A single piece on a point is a blot, i.e. vulnerable to the opponent's taking it and forcing it to travel round the board again.

● **background radiation** ► Low-intensity radiation naturally present on the earth. It results either from the bombardment of the earth by ▷cosmic rays or from naturally occurring radioactive substances in the earth's crust.

● **backswimmer** ► A ▷water bug, belonging to the worldwide family *Notonectidae* (nearly 200 species), that swims on its back, using a pair of oarlike legs for propulsion. Backswimmers can fly but are normally found in fresh water, preying voraciously on insects, tadpoles, and small fish. They must return to the surface periodically to replenish their air store.

● **Bacolod** ► 10 38N 122 58E A port in the central Philippines, in NW Negros. It is a sugar-refining centre serving the Philippines' most important sugar-growing area. Population (1994 est): 343 048.

● **Bacon, Francis** ► (1909–92) British painter, born in Dublin of English parentage. He was self-taught and began painting in the 1930s but his characteristic style did not become evident until 1945, when his nightmarish *Three Studies for Figures at the Base of a Crucifixion* ensured him an undeniable place in modern British art. Another of his well-known paintings is *Study after Velázquez* (1951), a version of Velázquez's portrait of Pope Innocent X. His paintings are characterized by strong rich colours, a sinister blurring or erasure of human features, and an often violent dramatic quality.

● **Bacon, Francis, 1st Baron Verulam, Viscount St Albans** ► (1561–1626) English lawyer and philosopher. He was called to the Bar in 1582 and became an MP in 1584. During the 1590s, in the hope of political advancement, he cultivated the friendship of the 2nd Earl of ▷Essex but in 1601 assisted the prosecution for treason of his former patron. Under James I (reigned 1603–25) Bacon's career advanced more smoothly: he became a commissioner for the union of Scotland and England (1604), attorney general (1613), and Lord Chancellor (1618). In 1621, however, he was found guilty of bribery and corruption; he was fined £40,000 and banished from office and parliament.

Bacon's fame rests more securely on his philosophical and literary output and his influence on scientific thought in the later 17th century was considerable. In 1597 he published his first group of *Essays* on truth, death, friendship, etc.; further such discourses appeared in 1625. *The Advancement of Learning* (1605) presented a new classification of sciences and was expanded in the *De augmentis scientiarum* of 1623. In *Novum organum scientiarum* (1620) he argued

that knowledge can be derived only from experience, advocating the scientific method of ▷induction. His other works include a *History of Henry VII* (1622) and the *New Atlantis* (1626), which describes his ideal state.

● **Bacon, John** ► (1740–99) British neoclassical sculptor. He trained as a porcelain modeller, but is noted for tombs, such as the Chatham monument in Westminster Abbey (1779). He also improved the pointing machine, a device for reproducing a plaster cast in stone or marble.

● **Bacon, Roger** ► (c. 1214–c. 1292) English monk, scholar, and scientist, called Doctor Mirabilis for his diverse skills and learning. In three books written for Pope Clement IV he attempted to systematize the current state of knowledge; other works prophesied aeroplanes, microscopes, round-the-world voyages, steam engines, and telescopes. His astronomical knowledge enabled him to detect errors in the Julian ▷calendar. He has also been credited with the invention of ▷gunpowder and of the magnifying glass.

● **bacteria** ► Microscopic single-celled organisms found wherever life is possible. Bacteria are distinguished from all other organisms by the structures of their cells, in which the genetic material is not enclosed in a nucleus; they are placed in the kingdom *Bacteria* (or *Prokaryotae*). The recent discovery of bacteria in environments apparently unlikely to support life, such as hot springs and very salty muds, has led to the division of the kingdom into the *Archaea* (see archaebacteria) and *Eubacteria* (the majority of bacteria); these two groups are regarded by some taxonomists as separate kingdoms. The *Eubacteria* ("true bacteria") are generally 0.0001–0.005 mm long; they may be spherical (see coccus), rodlike (see bacillus), spiral-shaped (spirillum), or filamentous and often occur in chains or clusters of cells. Most have a rigid cell wall, which may be surrounded by a slimy capsule, and they often have long whiplike flagella for locomotion and short hairlike pili used in a form of sexual reproduction. A few bacteria are autotrophic, i.e. they can grow on simple inorganic substrates using carbon dioxide gas from the atmosphere to manufacture their own nutrients, but the majority are heterotrophic, requiring a source of organic carbon and a variety of other nutrients for growth. A single bacterium reproduces by dividing into two new cells; some species can do so every 15 minutes leading to rapid population growth. Some form resistant spores, which can survive for several years in adverse conditions.

The most important role of bacteria is in decomposing dead plant and animal tissues and releasing their constituents to the soil (see carbon cycle). Nitrogen-fixing bacteria in the soil or sea convert atmospheric nitrogen gas to nitrites and nitrates, which can then be used by plants (see nitrogen cycle). Many industrial processes are dependent on bacteria, including cheese making and ▷fermentation reactions. Bacteria inhabit the digestive systems of animals and play an important part in digestion, especially in ▷ruminants. However, certain (pathogenic) species may infect body tissues and cause disease while others, such as *Salmonella*, can cause ▷food poisoning.

● **bacteriophage** ► (or phage) A ▷virus that infects a bacterium. 25–800 nanometres in size, phages may be spherical, filamentous, or tadpole-shaped with a head and tail. They consist of a protein coat surrounding a core of nucleic acid (either DNA or RNA) that is inserted into the bacterium. The viral genes then use the protein-synthesis apparatus of the bacterium to produce new phages, which are released from the cell, usually causing its destruction. Phages are used in ▷genetic engineering to transfer foreign DNA into bacterial hosts.

● **Bactria** ► An ancient region of central Asia, SE of the Aral Sea. An Achaemenian province from about 600 BC, it was conquered, despite fierce resistance, by Alexander the Great and subsequently passed to the Seleucids. In the mid-3rd century BC Diodotus I (died c. 239) established an independent Bactrian-Greek kingdom that later encompassed Afghanistan, Pakistan, and the central Asian republics of the former Soviet Union. From the 1st century AD the nomadic Kushan tribe occupied Bactria, introducing Buddhism and artistic styles influenced by Buddhist, Iranian, and Greek-Roman sources. Until about 600 AD Bactria was the hub of overland trade between east and west and a centre for the interchange of religious and artistic ideas.

● **Bactrian camel** ▷See camel.

● **Badajoz** ▶ 38 53N 6 58W A city in SW Spain, in Estremadura on the River Guadiana. Attacked on numerous occasions, it was pillaged by Wellington's troops (1812) during the Peninsular War. It has a 13th-century cathedral. Population (1995 est): 131 154.

● **Badakhshan** ▷*See* ▶ Gorno-Badakhshan.

● **Badalona** ▶ 41 27N 2 15E A port in NE Spain, in Catalonia, forming an industrial suburb of Barcelona. Industries include glass, shipbuilding, and textiles. Population (1995 est): 217 983.

● **Baden** ▶ 47 28N 8 19E A spa town in N Switzerland. The diet (assembly) of the Swiss Confederation met here (1424-1712). Its hot sulphur springs have been visited since Roman times. Population (1981): 23 140.

● **Baden-Baden** ▶ 48 45N 8 15E A spa in SW Germany, in Baden-Württemberg in the Black Forest. The hot springs have been used since Roman times. Population (1991): 52 520.

● **Baden-Powell, Robert Stephenson Smyth, 1st Baron** ▶ (1857-1941) British general and founder of the Boy Scouts. After service in India and various parts of Africa, he achieved fame through his defence of Mafeking in the ▷Boer War (1899-1900). Utilizing the experience of character training he had gained overseas, he founded the Boy Scouts in 1908 and, with his sister Agnes, the Girl ▷Guides Association in 1910. ▷*See also* Scout Association.

● **Baden-Württemberg** ▶ A *Land* in SW Germany, bordering on France and Switzerland, formed by an amalgamation of three former *Länder* (1952). It contains the Black Forest, several spas, and fertile agricultural land. Its population and economy have expanded greatly since World War II, when many refugees from further E settled here. A large proportion of Germany's watches, jewellery, leather goods, and musical and medical instruments are made in Baden-Württemberg and there are also textile, chemical, and car industries. Area: 35 751 sq km (13 800 sq mi). Population (1995 est): 10 272 100. Capital: Stuttgart.

● **Bader, Sir Douglas** ▶ (1910-82) British fighter pilot. After losing his legs in a flying accident (1931), Bader argued himself back into the RAF at the start of World War II. Becoming a national hero, he was finally shot down and imprisoned by the Germans, who only prevented his escape by depriving him of his artificial legs. In 1976 he was knighted for his work for the disabled.

● **badger** ▶ A nocturnal burrowing mammal of the ▷weasel family (*Mustelidae*). The largest of the eight species is the gregarious Eurasian badger (*Meles meles*), about 90 cm long, with short strong legs, long coarse greyish hair on the body, and a black and white striped head. It lives in a complex of burrows (a set) and feeds on insects, rodents, worms, berries, etc. The American badger (*Taxidea taxus*) is smaller and lives alone when not breeding. The remaining badgers are found in S and SE Asia and include the smallest species—the ferret badgers (genus *Melogale*), about 60 cm long.

● **Bad Godesberg** ▷*See* Godesberg.

● **badlands** ▶ An elevated area dissected by gullies and deep valleys. This type of landscape is typical of arid and semiarid areas, where rainfall is intermittent and an adequate vegetation cover is prevented from forming or is destroyed through, for example, overgrazing; severe soil erosion may occur. The name was originally applied to the Bad lands of S Dakota (USA).

● **badminton** ▶ An indoor court game for two or four players, played with rackets and a shuttlecock of nylon or cork and feathers. It originated in about 1870, probably from battledore and shuttlecock and may have first been played in the park of ▷Badminton House. It is a volleying game (the shuttles do not bounce) and points are scored only by the serving side. If the serving side fails to make a good return the service changes (in doubles games both partners serve before their opponents). A game is usually played to 15 points (women's singles go to 11 points).

● **Badminton** ▶ 51 33N 2 17W A village in England, in South Gloucestershire unitary authority, Gloucestershire. In the park of Badminton House (1682), the home of the Duke of Beaufort, annual horse trials are held. The game of ▷badminton probably originated here.

● **Badoglio, Pietro** ▶ (1871-1956) Italian general, who rose to prominence during World War I. He directed Mussolini's conquest of Ethiopia (1935-36) but in 1940 resigned during the disastrous Italian campaign in Greece. After Mussolini's fall (1943), he became prime minister and negotiated the armistice with the Allies. He resigned in 1944.

● **Baeck, Leo** ▶ (1873-1956) German Jewish theologian. Under the ▷Nazis, he became the spiritual leader of German Jewry, continuing to teach in Theresienstadt concentration camp (1943-45). After the war he settled in London. In his major work, *The Essence of Judaism* (1905), Baeck argued for the superiority of Judaism to Christianity.

● **Baedeker, Karl** ▶ (1801-59) German publisher of guidebooks. His first guide, to Coblenz (1829), was followed by a series that became internationally famous.

● **Baekeland, Leo Hendrik** ▶ (1863-1944) US industrial chemist, born in Belgium. He invented Bakelite (*see* plastics), the first synthetic thermosetting plastic. The discovery was made while Baekeland was searching for a synthetic substitute for ▷shellac.

● **Baer, Karl Ernest von** ▶ (1792-1876) Russian embryologist. He showed that mammalian eggs were not the follicles of the ovary but microscopic particles inside the follicles. He described the development of the embryo from layers of tissue, which he called *germ layers*, and demonstrated similarities in the embryos of different species of vertebrates.

● **Baeyer, (Johann Friedrich Wilhelm) Adolf von** ▶ (1835-1917) German chemist, who became professor at the University of Strassburg and then at Munich. He discovered barbituric acid (1865), synthesized indigo (1878), and developed several organic dyes. Baeyer also calculated the angles between the carbon atoms in organic compounds, showing (1885) how strained bonds affect chemical reactivity in closed carbon chains. He was awarded the 1905 Nobel Prize for his synthesis of indigo.

● **Baez, Joan** ▶ (1941-   ) US folksinger, whose performance at the 1959 Newport Festival led to a series of successful recordings of folksongs and later of contemporary protest songs. An active pacifist, she opposed the Vietnam War.

● **Baffin, William** ▶ (c. 1584-1622) English navigator. In two voyages (1615, 1616) with Capt Robert Bylot he attempted in the *Discovery* to find the ▷Northwest Passage. He eventually despaired of its existence but explored the Hudson Strait, giving his name to Baffin Bay and Baffin Island.

● **Baffin Island** ▶ The largest island of the Canadian Arctic, lying N of Hudson Strait. It is separated from Greenland by a Strait forming **Baffin Bay** (in the N) and Davis Strait. Mountainous with many glaciers and snowfields, its sparse population is concentrated in Frobisher Bay. Since April 1999 it has formed part of the new Inuit territory of Nunavut. Area: 476 068 sq km (183 810 sq mi).

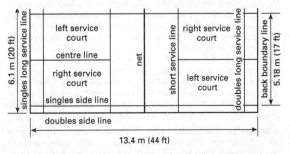

badminton ▶ The dimensions of the court. The top of the net at the centre is 1.5 m (5 ft) above the floor.

● **Bagehot, Walter** ▶ (1826-77) British economist, political theorist, literary critic, and journalist. He first worked as a banker, his interest in banking theories being reflected in his *Lombard Street* (1873).

While editor of the *Economist* magazine (1860–77), he wrote his major political works, *The English Constitution* (1867), which analyses the comparative powers of the British organs of government, and *Physics and Politics* (1872), applying Darwin's principles of natural selection to political society.

● **Baghdad** ▶ 33 20N 44 26E The capital of Iraq, on the River Tigris near the centre of the country. Built by the caliph Mansur in the 8th century, it was a centre of commerce, learning, and religion until sacked by the Mongols in 1258. Modern Baghdad grew after becoming the capital of independent Iraq (1927) and is now an important administrative, communications, and manufacturing centre with three universities (1947, 1957, and 1963). Population (1995 est): 4 478 000.

● **Baghdad Pact** ▶ A treaty between Turkey, Iraq, Iran, Pakistan, and the UK. Signed in 1955, its goals were military, economic, and social cooperation in the Middle East. When Iraq withdrew from it in 1959, its headquarters moved to Ankara from Baghdad and it was renamed the ▷Central Treaty Organization.

● **Baghdad Railway** ▶ A rail link between Europe and Asia Minor, running from Turkey to Iraq. Its construction, begun in the late 19th century with German finance, was seen by the British as a threat to their position in India and was a point of contention in World War I.

● **Baglioni** ▶ A family that dominated Perugia (Italy) from 1425 until 1534. Its leading members were **Malatesta Baglioni** (1389–1437), who established the family's position in Perugia; **Giampaolo Baglioni** (c. 1470–1520), who came to power in 1500 following a family feud that resulted in the assassination of many of his relatives; and **Malatesta Baglioni** (1491–1531), a ▷condottiere who served both Venice and Florence, betraying the latter to the pope in 1530. The Baglioni were banished from Perugia in 1534.

● **bagpipes** ▶ A reed-pipe instrument of ancient origin, found in many countries. Air is forced into a windbag either by the mouth (Scottish bagpipes) or by a bellows (Northumbrian pipes). By pressing the bag under his arm the player pushes air into the sounding pipes, which consist of one to three drones and a single chanter pipe. Drone pipes each sound one continuous note. The chanter pipe is fitted with holes, which are covered by the player's fingers. Bagpipes are regarded as the national instrument of Scotland, having been introduced to the British Isles in the 13th century.

● **Baguio** ▶ 16 25N 120 37E A city in the N Philippines, in W Luzon. It is a popular summer resort and the site of the national military academy. Gold and copper are mined. Population (1994 est): 169 565.

● **bagworm moth** ▶ A moth belonging to the widely distributed family *Psychidae* (800 species). The larvae live in cases made of silk covered with leaves, twigs, grass, etc., with only the head and forelegs projecting. Males emerge after pupation, flying in search of the wingless females, which remain in their cases.

● **Baha'i faith** ▶ A religion founded in Persia in 1863 by Mirza Husain 'Ali (1817–92), who was known as Baha' Allah (Glory of God). He proclaimed himself to be the Promised One whose coming was foretold by the Bab (*see* Babi faith). His eldest son and then his great-grandson led the Baha'is after his death until 1957. Since 1963 the faith has been governed by the Universal House of Justice, a council at Haifa, Israel, elected by national spiritual assemblies. The basic tenet of the faith is that God reveals himself to man through prophets who appear at various stages in history and the most recent of these is Baha' Allah. Baha'is advocate a universal faith, world peace, an international language, the equality of men and women, and the abolition of all prejudices. The faith has now spread to the West despite persecution in Iran and prohibition in Indonesia.

● **Bahamas, Commonwealth of the** ▶ A state consisting of about 700 islands and innumerable cays in the West Indies, off the SE coast of Florida. The principal islands, which are mainly low lying, include New Providence (with the capital Nassau), Grand Bahama, Abaco, Eleuthera, Andros, and Watling Island (San Salvador). The majority of the population is of African descent.
Economy: with its mild subtropical climate and beautiful beaches, the main industry of the Bahamas is tourism, which accounts for

over 50% of revenue and employment. The country has also developed as an offshore financial centre. Foreign investment is encouraged by the lack of direct taxation, 90% of companies being foreign-owned. Efforts have been made to develop agriculture, fisheries, and industry (especially oil refining and chemicals). Main exports include cement, petroleum and petroleum products, chemicals, and fish.
History: in 1492 Columbus made his first landing in the W hemisphere on the island of San Salvador. The first European occupation comprised an English religious settlement in the mid-17th century, and the islands became a British crown colony in 1717. From 1964 the country had increasing control over its own affairs and in 1973 it attained full independence within the Commonwealth. The 1997 general election was won by the Free National Party under Hubert Ingraham (1947–   ).

Commonwealth of the Bahamas

Head of state	Queen Elizabeth II, represented by the governor-general, Sir Orville Turnquest
Official language	English
Official currency	Bahamian dollar of 100 cents
Area	13 864 sq km (5353 sq mi)
Population (1999 est)	297 000
Capital	Nassau

● **Bahawalpur** ▶ 29 24N 71 47E A city in Pakistan, on the railway between Karachi and Lahore. It is a growing industrial centre producing cotton and soap. Population (latest est): 178 000.

● **Bahia** ▷*See* Salvador.

● **Bahía Blanca** ▶ 38 45S 62 15W A port in Argentina. It is a major distribution centre; exports include grain, meat, and wool. The National University of the South was founded here in 1956. Population (1991): 271 467.

● **Bahrain, State of** ▶ A country in the Arabian Gulf, occupying a low-lying archipelago between Saudi Arabia and the Qatar Peninsula. The main islands, Bahrain and Al-Muharraq, are connected by a causeway; there are also plans for a causeway to Saudi Arabia. The inhabitants are mainly Arabs; the majority are Shiite Muslims but the ruling family and most of the economic elite are Sunnites.
Economy: almost totally dependent upon oil. A large refinery on Bahrain Island processes not only the relatively small amounts of local oil, first discovered in 1931, but also much larger amounts coming from Saudi Arabia by pipeline. Efforts to develop other industry have shown some success. An aluminium smelter on Bahrain is the largest non-oil industrial plant in the Gulf. The formerly important pearl-fishing industry has declined. Bahrain is important as a transport centre in the Gulf and the modern harbour of Mina Salman has extensive shipping facilities and a free transport area. In 1975 the government licensed the setting up of Offshore Banking Units, a move that gave Bahrain increased commercial importance in the Gulf.
History: the islands were under Portuguese rule from 1521 until 1602, when Iran gained control. In 1783 the Iranians were expelled by the Khalifa family, who have ruled the area for most of the time since. Bahrain was a British protected state from 1861 until 1971 when full independence was declared by the emir, Sheikh Isa ibn Sulman al-Khalifa (1933–99). Bahrain became a member of OPEC in 1970. In 1975 political unrest led to the dissolution of the National Assembly. Growing opposition to the regime in the mid-1990s led the emir to set up an appointed consultative council, but protests by Shiite opposition groups continued. In a referendum in 2001 Bahrainis voted overwhelmingly to make the country a parliamentary democracy.

State of Bahrain

Head of state	Sheikh Hamad Ibn Isa al-Khalifa
Official language	Arabic; English is also widely spoken
Official religion	Islam
Official currency	Bahrain dinar of 1000 fils
Area	660 sq km (255 sq mi)
Population (1999 est)	646 000
Capital and main port	Manama

● **Baikal, Lake** ▶ A lake in SE Russia. It is the largest freshwater lake in Asia and at 1620 m (5316 ft) the deepest in the world. It is fed by over 300 streams but drained by only one, the River Angara. Area: 31 500 sq km (12 160 sq mi).

● **Baikonur** ▶ 62 30W 45 40N A launching site for spacecraft in Kazakhstan, situated in desert plains about 200 km (124 mi) E of the Aral Sea. Formerly the centre for the Soviet Union's space programme, it saw the launching of the world's first satellite (1957) and first manned space flight (1961). The supporting town of **Tyuratum** (formerly Leninsk) grew up in the 1950s and has an estimated population of about 50 000. Following the break-up of the Soviet Union, Russia agreed to rent the site from Kazakhstan until 2114.

● **bail** ▶ The release by a court of an imprisoned person, usually while awaiting trial, into the keeping of people who agree to ensure his reappearance at a particular date and time. If these people, called "sureties," then fail to produce him, they forfeit whatever sum of money the court has set for bail. The person bailed must also stand as surety for himself; if thought trustworthy, he may be bailed without other sureties, "in his own recognizance."

● **Bailey, David** ▶ (1938–) British photographer and film director. His photographic publications include *Warhol* (1974), *Mixed Moments* (1976), *Nudes 1981–84* (1984), and *If We Shadows* (1992).

● **Bailey bridge** ▶ A type of military bridge invented by Sir Donald Bailey (1901–85) during World War II. Consisting of light strong standardized interlocking truss sections, it can be easily assembled in the field. Pontoons can be provided for longer spans, the longest of which was that of the 1200 m (4000 ft) bridge built across the River Maas in Holland.

● **Baily, Francis** ▶ (1774–1844) British amateur astronomer, who gave his name to "Baily's beads," the broken line of sunlight shining through lunar valleys close to total eclipse. He revised current star catalogues and calculated accurate values for the earth's density and ellipticity.

● **Bainbridge, Dame Beryl** ▶ (1934–) British novelist and playwright. She worked as an actress before writing such novels as *The Dressmaker* (1973), *An Awfully Big Adventure* (1989), *Every Man for Himself* (1996), and *Master Georgie* (1998). Her plays include *Somewhere More Central* (1981) and *Evensong* (1986). She was appointed DBE in 2000.

● **Baird, John Logie** ▶ (1888–1946) British electrical engineer, who invented an early television system. In 1924 he succeeded in transmitting the outline of shapes; in 1925 he could transmit features and by 1926, moving objects; he produced colour-television pictures in 1928. However, his 240-line television system was not adopted by the BBC. Baird also pioneered the use of radar and fibre optics.

● **Bairnsfather, (Charles) Bruce** ▶ (1888–1959) British cartoonist and author. He became famous in World War I for his war cartoons featuring the character Old Bill and during World War II he was an official war cartoonist.

● **Baja California** ▷*See* Lower California.

● **Bakelite** ▷*See* Baekeland, Leo Hendrik; plastics.

● **Baker, Sir Benjamin** ▶ (1840–1907) British civil engineer, who worked with Sir John Fowler (1817–1918) on the construction of the first underground railway, the London District line from Westminster to the City (1869), and on the Forth railway bridge. Baker also designed Avonmouth docks.

● **Baker, Dame Janet (Abbott)** ▶ (1933–) British mezzo-soprano. After studying at the Royal College of Music, she made a brilliant career singing lieder and in oratorio. Her appearances in Mozart's *Così fan tutte* and Berlioz's *The Trojans* launched her successful operatic career. She was awarded the DBE in 1976 and retired from opera in 1982.

● **Baker, Sir Samuel White** ▶ (1821–93) British explorer. In 1861, accompanied by his wife, he set off from Cairo to locate the source of the Nile. Informed by ▷Speke and J. A. Grant (1827–92) of an unexplored great lake, he found (1864) and named Lake Albert. He led an Egyptian expedition to annex the S Nile basin, where as Egypt's governor general (1869–74) he abolished slavery.

● **Bakewell** ▶ 53 13N 1 40W A market town in N England, in Derbyshire in the Peak District National Park. A tart filled with almond-flavoured sponge on a layer of jam (Bakewell tart) originated here. Nearby are two stately homes, Chatsworth House and Haddon Hall. Population (1991): 3818.

● **Bakewell, Robert** ▶ (1725–95) British agriculturalist, whose breeding techniques transformed livestock farming. By rigorous selection and culling he improved several breeds of cattle and sheep as meat producers.

● **Bakhtaran** ▶ (name until 1987: Kermanshar) 34 19N 47 04E A town in W Iran, with a largely Kurdish population. It has a university (1974) and an oil refinery. Population (1994 est): 665 636.

● **Bakhtyari** ▶ A major tribe of W Iran of some 400 000 Muslims speaking the Luri dialect of Persian. About one-third are still nomadic herdsman living in tents. They make a gruelling annual migration of 150 miles from their winter pastures on the plains to the summer pastures in the mountains. Their hereditary chiefs have often played an influential role in Iranian politics. Their women have a greater degree of freedom than is usual among Muslims.

● **baking powder** ▶ A mixture of ▷sodium bicarbonate and ▷tartaric acid or ▷cream of tartar, used in baking. It generates carbon dioxide on heating or wetting, making dough rise.

● **Bakst, Léon** ▶ (Lev Samoilovich Rosenberg; 1866–1924) Russian artist, who modernized theatre design. He was born in St Petersburg, where he trained in the Imperial Academy of Arts and became court painter, before turning to scenery design in 1900. His greatest achievements were for ballets produced by Sergei ▷Diaghilev in Paris, where he later settled.

● **Baku** ▶ 40 22N 49 53E The capital of Azerbaidzhan, a port on the Caspian Sea. The old town is a maze of narrow streets and ancient buildings. In 1990 it was a focus for violent ethnic unrest. It has been a centre of oil production since the 19th century. Population (1995 est): 1 739 900.

● **Bakunin, Mikhail Aleksandrovich** ▶ (1814–76) Russian anarchist. He studied at Berlin University, where he became exposed to socialist philosophy. He participated in the Revolutions of 1848 and in 1849 he was arrested in Dresden, handed over to Russian officials, and exiled to Siberia. In 1861 he escaped to London. He participated in the First ▷International but came into conflict with Marx and was expelled.

● **Bakwanga** ▷*See* Mbuji-Mayi.

● **Bala, Lake** ▶ (Welsh name: Llyn Tegid) The largest natural lake in Wales, in Gwynedd. It is used for angling and sailing. The town of Bala lies at its N end. Length: 6 km (4 mi).

● **Balaclava, Battle of** ▶ (25 October, 1854) An indecisive battle between Russian and British-Turkish forces in the ▷Crimean War. It is notorious for the heavy British casualties caused by misunderstanding between Lord ▷Raglan, the British commander in chief, and Lord ▷Lucan, the cavalry commander. The courageous Light Brigade charged Russian artillery at the end of a narrow valley and of its 673 men, 113 were killed and 134 wounded. The battle was made famous by Tennyson's poem "Charge of the Light Brigade." □ p. 110.

● **Balaguer, Joaquín** ▶ (1907–) Dominican politician, president of the Dominican Republic (1961–62; 1966–78; 1986–96). Vice-president under ▷Trujillo (1957–61), he became president for the first time on the latter's assassination. Although exiled between 1962 and 1965, he returned to dominate his country's politics for the next 30 years. In 1994 he was re-elected for the last time at the age of 87 but evidence of fraud led parliament to curtail his term of office and he retired in 1996.

● **Balakirev, Mili Alekseevich** ▶ (1837–1910) Russian composer, one of the ▷Five and founder of the Free School of Music in St Petersburg (1862). His works, such as the tone poem *Tamara* (1867–82) and the piano fantasy *Islamey* (1869), reflect his romanticism and Russian nationalism.

Battle of Balaclava ▶ Glorified by Tennyson's poem the "Charge of the Light Brigade," the battle in all its brutal reality is depicted in this unsigned engraving.

● balalaika ▶ A Russian plucked instrument of the guitar family, played singly or in a balalaika orchestra. It has a long fretted fingerboard, a triangular body, and three wire strings that are plucked with a plectrum. The smaller size is held like a guitar and the larger balanced on the floor like a double bass.

● balance ▶ A sensitive device for comparing two masses, consisting of a beam pivoted at its centre (usually on an agate knife edge) with pans hanging from each of its ends. The material of unknown mass is placed in one pan and standard weights are placed in the other. A pointer indicates when the beam is horizontal and the whole device is enclosed in a glass case to avoid draughts and temperature changes. The accuracy of a balance is increased by using a rider—a small weight hung on a calibrated scale on the balance arm itself. A standard balance will weigh to the nearest 0.0001 g, while sensitive **microbalances** can weigh objects of 1 microgram. ▷See also spring balance.

● balance of nature ▶ The state of equilibrium said to exist in natural ▷communities and ▷ecosystems of plants and animals, resulting in diversity of species and overall stability. Changes occur gradually in the process of ecological ▷succession and there is a natural regulation of populations: a sharp increase in the population of a particular species is normally compensated for by a proportional increase in the mortality of that species (for example through increased activity of its natural predators), so that its numbers remain fairly constant. This ecological balance can be adversely affected by such human activities as ▷pollution of the environment, destruction of habitats by overgrazing, deforestation, etc., and excessive exploitation of economically important species by overfishing, whaling, etc.

● balance of payments ▶ The difference between a country's income and its expenditure abroad. It is usually divided into a current account and a capital account. The current account records the country's ▷balance-of-trade earnings or deficit on visible goods and its invisible earnings or deficit on such items as insurance, transport, tourism, and some kinds of government spending. The capital account records all long- and short-term capital flows, both in the public and private sectors. If the sum of the current and capital accounts shows a deficit there will be a net loss of foreign exchange, which the government must take steps to remedy. Measures include deflation by ▷monetary or ▷fiscal policy to reduce imports, the imposition of ▷tariffs or import ▷quotas, incentives to increase exports, the introduction of stringent ▷exchange control regulations, and ultimately ▷devaluation of the currency. If the balance of payments shows a persistent surplus a revaluation of the currency may be required.

● balance of power ▶ The principle seeking to ensure that no nation or group of nations becomes too dominant. Practised by Greek city states, which formed intercity alliances, the principle was adopted in Europe in the alliance system of 15th-century Italy. In 1815 at the Congress of ▷Vienna, Prussia, Russia, Britain, France, and Austria realigned European frontiers to establish themselves as equal powers and to ensure peace. Tensions remained, however, and rival alliances led to further wars to prevent or restore national dominance. In the 20th century the League of Nations and the UN have both tried to establish international harmony, but the development of nuclear weapons acts as the greatest deterrent to any state sufficiently ambitious to threaten international equilibrium.

● balance of trade ▶ The difference in money between the value of a country's imports and its exports. The balance of trade is sometimes known as the visibles account because it refers only to actual goods. Together with the invisibles account and capital transfers it makes up the ▷balance of payments. The invisibles account includes such earnings as selling insurance abroad and spending by foreign tourists. Thus the balance of trade can be in deficit without necessarily meaning that the balance of payments will also be in deficit.

● balance sheet ▶ A statement that provides a quantified summary of the assets and liabilities of an organization at a specified date; it is usually produced annually, giving figures relating to the last day of its annual accounting period. The first part of the statement lists the fixed and current assets and liabilities of the organization; the second shows the source of funds (i.e. shareholding, loans, etc.). The balance sheet does not necessarily show the value of an organization because some assets may be over- or undervalued. Under the UK Companies Act, the balance sheet is a document that an organization must produce, at least annually, as part of its financial accounts. The other essential document is the **profit and loss account**, which shows the total income and the total expenditure of the organization in a specified period, the difference being its profit or loss, taking into account the difference in the value of its stock in this period.

● Balanchine, George ▶ (Georgy Melitonovich Balanchivadze; 1904–83) US ballet dancer and choreographer, born in Russia. He worked for Diaghilev's Ballets Russes in Europe from 1924 and went to the USA in 1933. In 1948 he became first artistic director of the New York City Ballet. His ballets include *Firebird* (1950) and *Don Quixote* (1965), and he also choreographed for films and stage musicals.

● Balaton, Lake ▶ A lake in W Hungary, the largest in central Europe. There are vineyards and holiday resorts on its shore and its outlet is a canal leading to a tributary of the River Danube. Area: 598 sq km (231 sq mi).

● **Balboa** ▶ 8 57N 79 33W A port in Panama, at the Pacific end of the Panama Canal. It was named after the explorer, Vasco Núñez de ▷Balboa. It has extensive harbour facilities. Population (latest est): 2750.

● **Balboa, Vasco Núñez de** ▶ (c. 1475–1517) Spanish explorer. Having settled in Hispaniola, he became a stowaway on an expedition to present-day Colombia (1510), moved on to Panama, and founded a settlement at Darién (1511). In 1513 he set off across the Isthmus in search of gold. Sighting the Pacific, which he called the South Sea, after 25 gruelling days, he claimed it for Spain. He was subsequently accused, unjustly, of treason and beheaded by the governor of Darién, Pedrarias (d. 1531).

● **Balchin, Nigel** ▶ (1908–70) British novelist. He studied natural science at Cambridge and later worked as an industrial psychologist. *The Small Back Room* (1943) is based on his experience as a scientific adviser to the Army Council during World War II. *Mine Own Executioner* (1945) and *The Fall of the Sparrow* (1955) are brilliant psychological character studies.

● **Balcon, Sir Michael** ▶ (1896–1977) British film producer. As executive producer of Ealing Studios from 1938 to 1959 he was responsible for many successful comedies such as *Kind Hearts and Coronets* (1949) and *The Lavender Hill Mob* (1951). His later films included *Tom Jones* (1963).

● **bald eagle** ▶ A large ▷eagle, *Haliaetus leucocephalus*, also called the American eagle; it is the national emblem of the USA and an endangered species. It is dark brown with a white head and tail and has a prominent curved beak and unfeathered legs. It feeds on carrion and fish.

● **Balder** ▶ The Norse god of light and beauty, the son of ▷Odin and ▷Frigga. The most beloved of the gods, he was killed with an arrow made of mistletoe on the orders of ▷Loki.

● **baldness** ▷*See* alopecia.

● **Baldwin, James Arthur** ▶ (1924–87) US Black writer. His first novel, *Go Tell It on the Mountain* (1953), is based on his experience of poverty and religion in Harlem, where he was born. He lived in Paris from 1948 to 1957, when he returned to the USA as an active civil-rights campaigner. His works include novels, such as *Giovanni's Room* (1956) and *Just Above My Head* (1979), two plays, and essays, notably *The Fire Next Time* (1963) and *Evidence of Things not Seen* (1986).

● **Baldwin, Stanley, 1st Earl Baldwin of Bewdley** ▶ (1867–1947) British statesman and Conservative politician, who was prime minister (1923–24, 1924–29, 1935–37). As chancellor of the exchequer (1922–23), Baldwin negotiated the British World War I debt to the USA. He dealt as prime minister with the ▷General Strike (1926), to which his government responded with the anti-union Trade Disputes Act (1927). Baldwin was much criticized for condoning Italy's conquest of Ethiopia and his apparent reluctance to rearm in the face of Germany's military build-up. His management of the events leading to ▷Edward VIII's abdication (1936) reflected public opinion.

● **Baldwin I** ▶ (c. 1058–1118) King of Jerusalem (1100–18). Baldwin succeeded his brother Godfrey of Bouillon, whom he had accompanied on the first Crusade, taking Edessa in 1098. Baldwin considerably expanded the territory of Jerusalem.

● **Balearic Islands** ▶ An archipelago in the W Mediterranean Sea comprising an autonomous region of Spain. It includes the chief islands of ▷Majorca, ▷Minorca, ▷Ibiza, and Formentera, together with several islets. The islands were conquered by Aragon from the Moors in the 14th century. Area: 5014 sq km (1936 sq mi). Population (2000 est): 845 630. Capital: Palma, on Majorca.

● **baleen** ▶ (or whalebone) The horny material that forms the food-sieving plates in whalebone ▷whales. Baleen was formerly used to manufacture stays in corsets, but has now largely been replaced by synthetic materials.

● **Balenciaga, Cristóbal** ▶ (1895–1972) Spanish fashion designer. Cutting, fitting, and sewing his own designs, he opened fashion houses in Barcelona, Madrid, and Paris; his simple but elegant suits and evening dresses were popular in the 1950s, but he retired in the 1960s when new styles took over.

● **Balfour, Arthur James, 1st Earl of** ▶ (1848–1930) British statesman and Conservative prime minister (1902–05). As secretary for Ireland (1887–92) he incurred the nickname Bloody Balfour, failing in his policy of "killing Home Rule by kindness." His government passed an Education Act (1902), the Irish Land Purchase Act (1903; *see* Land Acts, Irish), and concluded the Anglo-French entente (1904). In World War I Balfour was foreign secretary (1916–19), issuing his famous ▷Balfour Declaration.

● **Balfour Declaration** ▶ (1917) The decision of the British Government, stated in a letter of 2 Nov from Arthur ▷Balfour to Lionel Walter, 2nd Baron Rothschild (1868–1937), chairman of the British Zionist Federation, to support the establishment of a national Jewish home in Palestine. The letter promised British aid to this end, providing that the interests of existing non-Jewish communities in Palestine be maintained as well as the rights and political status of Jews in any other country. Although Arab aspirations in Palestine prevented the British government from fulfilling the promise of the Declaration, which was abandoned in 1939, it helped to form a basis for the partition of Palestine and the creation of the State of ▷Israel in 1948.

● **Bali** ▶ An Indonesian island off E Java. Mountainous and volcanic, it has southern fertile plains that produce chiefly rice. The Balinese are famed for their arts and handicrafts, and it is a popular tourist resort.
  History: Hindu since the 7th century AD, Bali resisted the 16th–17th century spread of Islam through Indonesia and became an enclave of Hindu culture. Dutch rule became complete only in 1908, although trade began in the 17th century. Bali was occupied by the Japanese in World War II and became part of Indonesia in 1945. In the 1965–67 Indonesian purge of communists 40 000 people were killed. Area: 5558 sq km (2146 sq mi). Population (1995 est): 2 902 200. Chief town: Denpasar.

● **Balikpapan** ▶ 1 15S 116 50E A port in Indonesia, in SE Kalimantan on the Makassar Strait. Its refinery processes local and imported oil. Population (1995 est): 416 200.

● **Balkan Mountains** ▶ (Bulgarian name: Stara Planina) A mountain range extending 500 km (311 mi) E–W across central Bulgaria. It rises to 2376 m (7795 ft) at Botev Peak.

● **Balkans** ▶ An area in SE Europe consisting of present-day Greece, Albania, Croatia, Bosnia-Hercegovina, the Former Yugoslav Republic of Macedonia, the Union of Serbia and Montenegro, Bulgaria, part of Romania, and the European part of Turkey. Part of the Roman empire from the 2nd century BC and of the Eastern Roman (Byzantine) Empire from the 5th century AD, the Balkans were ruled by the Ottoman Turks from the 15th century until independence was granted to Greece (1829), Serbia (1878), Romania (1878), Bulgaria (1908), and Albania (1912). The competition between European powers for control of the Balkans contributed to the outbreak of World War I, after which Yugoslavia was created out of Serbia. All the Balkan states, except Greece, became communist after ▷World War II. In the 1990s the region was plunged into turmoil once more with the disintegration of Yugoslavia, the civil war in Bosnia-Hercegovina, and the ▷Kosovo war between NATO and Serbia.

● **Balkan Wars** ▶ (1912–13) Two military confrontations that preceded World War I. In the first (1912–13) the Balkan League (Bulgaria, Serbia, Greece, and Montenegro) defeated Turkey. In the concluding Treaty of London, Turkey lost all its European possessions except E Thrace. In the second Balkan War (1913) the victors fought over their acquisitions in Macedonia, from most of which Bulgaria was excluded by the Treaty of ▷Bucharest; Turkey regained Thrace.

● **Balkhash, Lake** ▶ A lake in E Kazakhstan. Since it has no outlet, it fluctuates in size. Area: about 20 000 sq km (7720 sq mi).

● **Ball, John** ▶ (d. 1381) English rebel, a leader of the ▷Peasants' Revolt (1381). An unbeneficed priest, he was noted for his sermons and became the ideological spokesman for the peasants. He was executed after the rising's failure.

● **Balla, Giacomo** ▶ (1871–1958) Italian futurist painter. He was in-

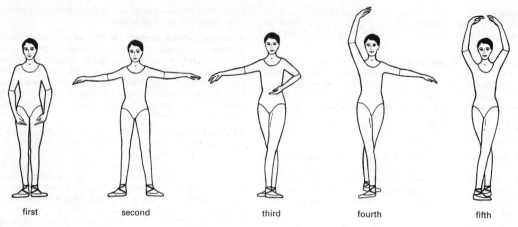

first   second   third   fourth   fifth

The five ballet positions

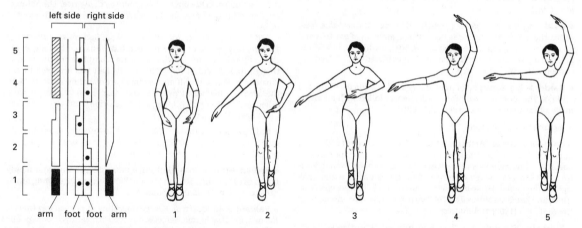

ballet ► Rudolph Laban (1879–1958) published his system for recording dance movements (labanotation) in 1928, since when it has gained widespread acceptance. In this simple example, the initial positions of the legs and arms are indicated at (1). Subsequent positions (2–5) are seen by reading upwards from the bottom. The dancer, starting with feet together and arms at her sides, takes four even steps forward, beginning with the right foot, and moves her arms upwards and outwards (the different shadings representing low, middle, and high positions).

fluenced by ▷pointillism before he became associated with ▷futurism (1910) and painted many dynamic studies of light and movement, notably birds in flight.

● **ballad** ► A form of popular narrative poetry. Originally intended for singing or recitation, ballads have a simple basic stanza form (four lines rhyming *abcb*); repetition and direct speech are characteristic devices. Subject matter includes love, family feuds, war, magic, biblical tales, and the deeds of Robin Hood and the knights of the Round Table (*see* Arthurian legend). Many fine ballads were composed in the 15th century in N England and Scotland; debased versions were later printed on single sheets of paper (broadside ballads) for sale by pedlars. Later still a tradition of literary ballads grew up (e.g. Kipling's "Danny Deever"). Notable ballad collections are Bishop ▷Percy's *Reliques* (1765) and F. J. Child's *English and Scottish Popular Ballads* (1883–98).

● **ballade** ► A form of medieval French lyric poetry or song. It consists of three stanzas and a final *envoi* (address); each stanza has the same rhyme scheme and final line, which serves as a refrain. It was used for formal and commemorative songs. Guillaume de ▷Machaut pioneered this form in the 14th century, and in the 15th century it was used by Charles d'▷Orléans and François ▷Villon, among others.

● **Ballantyne, R(obert) M(ichael)** ► (1825–94) British novelist

and writer. A prolific and successful author of adventure stories for boys, he is best known for *The Coral Island* (1857). The settings of his books reflect his wide travels in Canada, Africa, Scandinavia, and elsewhere.

● **Ballard, J(ames) G(raham)** ► (1930–) British writer born in Shanghai. His science fiction and futuristic writings culminated in *Crash* (1973) and *High Rise* (1975). In later novels, such as *Empire of the Sun* (1984), relating his experiences in China during World War II, *The Day of Creation* (1987), and *The Kindness of Women* (1991), he moved away from science fiction.

● **Ballesteros, Severiano** ► (1957–) Spanish golfer. His first major win was the Dutch Open Championship (1976). Other victories have included three British Open Championships (1979, 1984, and 1988). In 1997 he was nonplaying captain of the victorious European team in the Ryder Cup.

● **ballet** ► A dramatic art in which dancing and mime, accompanied by music, combine to tell a story or evoke a mood. Ballet originated in the formal dances of French court entertainments, notably under Louis XIV (*see* Lully, Jean Baptiste). In the 18th century ballet established itself in the public theatre but still as an adjunct to ▷opera or other forms of drama. Idolized ballerinas such as Sallé (1707–56) and Carmargo (1710–70) introduced less constricting dress and Jean-

Georges Noverre (1727–1810) extended ballet's dramatic range. Dancing on the tips of the toes (*sur les pointes*) was introduced early in the 19th century, possibly by Taglioni (1804–84). This period saw the heyday of romantic ballet, epitomized in Coralli's *Giselle* (1841). Modern ballet arose in the early 20th century when ▷Fokine and ▷Diaghilev (*see also* Ballets Russes) combined the polished technique of the imperial Russian dancers with the naturalism advocated by the American Isadora ▷Duncan. This gave scope to the talents of such dancers as ▷Nijinsky and ▷Pavlova, the composers ▷Stravinsky and ▷Ravel, the choreographers ▷Massine and ▷Balanchine, and the designer ▷Bakst. Independent ballet companies grew up all over Europe and the USA during the 1930s. England had two such groups, one led by Marie ▷Rambert (subsequently the Ballet Rambert, now the Rambert Dance Company) and the other by Ninette de ▷Valois and Frederick ▷Ashton (now the ▷Royal Ballet). Other notable companies are the ▷Bolshoi Ballet and ▷Kirov Ballet from Russia and the American New York City Ballet. Since World War II innovative choreographers such as ▷Cranko, ▷Béjart, and Twyla ▷Tharp have created new ballets inspired by folk dance, jazz, and even gymnastics. ▷*See also* modern dance.

● **Ballets Russes** ► A Russian ballet company (1909–29) founded in Paris by ▷Diaghilev. It gave the West its first opportunity to see Russian imperial dancers. In attempting to fuse dance, mime, music, and scenery into a harmonious unity, it fostered the most avantgarde talents of the period and greatly influenced the subsequent development of ballet. Its choreographers included ▷Fokine, ▷Massine, ▷Balanchine, and ▷Nijinsky, who was also one of its principal dancers. ▷Ravel and ▷Stravinsky composed music for several of its ballets. Among its scene designers were ▷Bakst and the painters ▷Picasso, ▷Matisse, and ▷Miró.

● **Balliol, John** ► (c. 1250–1314) King of the Scots (1292–96), chosen by Edward I of England, arbitrator in the contest for the throne. In 1295 he rebelled against English domination and was defeated by Edward at Dunbar (1296) and deposed. He ended his life in exile in France. His son **Edward Balliol** (d. 1364) became King of the Scots in 1332, after invading Scotland, supported by Edward III of England. An uprising against Balliol was put down by Edward (1333), who retained the Scottish lowlands, but internal opposition forced Balliol's abdication in 1356.

● **ballistic missiles** ► Rocket-powered nuclear missiles without wings or other lift surfaces that are propelled to desired altitudes and velocities and then follow an unpowered trajectory similar to that of a projectile fired from a gun. Their accuracy requires careful thrust calculations and on-board preset or inertial guidance systems and is calculated as a probability (e.g. 45–60%) of landing within a stated radius about their target (Circular Error of Probability or CEP). Intercontinental ballistic missiles (ICBMs) are capable of reaching any point on the surface of the earth. Both the USA and the former Soviet republics possess large numbers of these, some of which (MIRVs—multiple independently targeted re-entry vehicles) have up to ten separate warheads. ▷*See also* antiballistic missiles; V-2.

● **ballistics** ► The study of projectiles and the extent to which their trajectories are affected by shape, propulsion s systems, gravity, temperature, wind, etc. There are three branches: interior, dealing with all aspects of propulsion within a gun barrel or at launch; exterior, concerned with the trajectory of the projectile in flight; and terminal, relating to the effects of the missile on the target.

● **ball lightning** ► A luminous moving sphere, several centimetres in diameter, occurring just above the ground on rare occasions during thunderstorms. It hisses, has a distinct odour, and may be either red, orange, or yellow. It lasts for only a few seconds and then either dies away or explodes. One theory suggests that it consists of ▷plasma.

● **balloons** ► Lighter-than-air craft, consisting of a bag of gas that displaces a volume of air of greater mass than the total mass of the balloon and its contents. The first successful balloon flight, indeed man's first aerial voyage, was made in 1783 by the ▷Montgolfier brothers' hot-air balloon; it flew 9 km across Paris. Two years later a *Charlière* hydrogen balloon (designed by J. A. C. Charles, the formulator of ▷Charles's law) flew across the English Channel. In 1821 coal gas was used for the first time as a cheap alternative to hydrogen.

This opened the way for many exploits by showmen, scientists, and explorers. Balloons must be tethered (for parachuting, scientific experiments, etc.) or they will fly where the wind blows them; dirigible balloons (*see* airships) first appeared in the middle of the 19th century. However, by the end of the century interest in flying was centred on heavier-than-air machines (*see* aircraft).

The use of balloons in war began with Napoleon's observation balloons in 1794, after which they continued to play a sporadic but largely ineffectual part, until their extensive use in both World Wars in the form of barrage balloons.

The sport of **ballooning** has enjoyed a revival in recent years, the preferred vehicle being a hot-air balloon carrying its own propane air heater. The height record for a manned balloon is 30 480 m (D. Simons, US Air Force, 1957). The first Atlantic crossing by a helium balloon was achieved in 1978. Richard Branson made the first Atlantic crossing by hot-air balloon in 1987 and the first Pacific crossing in 1991. In 1999 Brian Jones of the UK and Bertrand Piccard of Switzerland achieved the first circumnavigation of the globe in a hot-air balloon.

● **Ballymena** ► A district in central Northern Ireland, in Co Antrim. Area: 634 sq km (247 sq mi). Population (1991): 56 641.

● **Ballymoney** ► A district in N Northern Ireland, in Co Antrim. Area: 417 sq km (161 sq mi). Population (1991): 24 198.

● **balm** ► A fragrant-leaved herbaceous plant of, or related to, the genus *Melissa*, native to the Old World. Lemon balm, or balm gentle (*M. officinalis*), is widely grown in temperate regions and used for flavouring foods or beverages and scenting perfumes. The European bastard balm (*Melittis melissophyllum*) is more strongly scented. Family: ▷*Labiatae*.

● **Balmaceda, José Manuel** ► (1840–91) Chilean statesman; president (1886–91). A liberal, he was first elected to the Chilean congress in 1864. As a cabinet minister under President Santa Maria (1881–86) he became known for his anticlerical reforms. His presidency saw economic growth but was impaired by a power struggle with congress, leading to civil war in 1891. Following the defeat of his forces, he committed suicide rather than stand trial.

● **Balmoral Castle** ► The principal country residence of the British monarch in Scotland, situated in SW Aberdeenshire by the River Dee. It was bought by the royal family in 1848 and rebuilt in the 1850s in the revived Scottish baronial style. It is also noted for its extensive and carefully landscaped gardens.

● **balsa** ► An evergreen tree, *Ochroma pyramidale*, native to Central and South America, also called corkwood. About 12 m tall, it is the source of an extremely light pale-coloured wood, which is widely used for corks, canoes, floats, etc. Although easily crushed, it is technically a hardwood. Family: *Bombacaceae*.

● **balsam** ► An aromatic resinous substance of plant origin, used in medicine for its soothing and healing properties and in perfumery. Balsam of Peru is derived from the Central American leguminous tree *Myroxylon peneirae*, grown in El Salvador.

The name is also given to many plants of the family *Balsaminaceae*. The garden balsam (*Impatiens balsamina*), native to India, is widely cultivated for its showy red flowers, which have a tubular spur and five unequal petals. The balsam apple (*Momardica balsamina*) is an ornamental vine.

● **Balthazar** ▷*See* Magi.

● **Balthus** ► (Count Balthasar Klossowski de Rola; 1908–2001) French painter of Polish aristocratic descent. Best known for his paintings of adolescent girls, often seminaked and in mysterious dimly lit settings, he also painted landscapes and street scenes.

● **Baltic Exchange** ► A freight-chartering exchange in the City of London. It originated in the Baltic coffee house in the 18th century. The Baltic formerly dealt in some commodities (grain, potatoes, and meat) but these activities moved to the London Commodity Exchange after the building was severely damaged by an IRA bomb in 1992. Freight futures are still dealt in the Baltic Exchange by the Baltic International Freight Futures Exchange (BIFFEX).

● **Baltic languages** ► A group of Indo-European languages closely related to the Slavonic languages and spoken on the E shores of the Baltic Sea. ▷Lithuanian and ▷Latvian (Lettish) are still extant: Old Prussian has been extinct since the 17th century. Deriving from northern Proto-Indo-European, the Baltic, Slavonic, and Germanic languages share morphological and word-formation features.

● **Baltic Sea** ▶ A section of the Atlantic Ocean in N Europe, bounded by Denmark, Sweden, Finland, Latvia, Lithuania, Estonia, Russia, Poland, and Germany. To the W, it leads into the Little Belt, the Great Belt, and the Sound, and to the E, the Gulfs of Bothnia, Finland, and Riga. Receiving rivers draining almost one-fifth of Europe, it has low salinity, and can freeze.

● **Baltic Shield** ▷See shield.

● **Baltic states** ▶ The republics of Latvia, Lithuania, and Estonia on the SE coast of the Baltic Sea. The Danes conquered N Estonia in the 13th century while S Estonia with Latvia (then comprising Livonia) fell to the Teutonic Knights. Lithuania formed an independent state until united with Poland in 1569 in the Union of ▷Lublin. The region came under Russian rule in the 18th century but briefly, between World Wars I and II, formed the independent states of Latvia, Lithuania, and Estonia. These became constituent republics of the Soviet Union in 1940, regaining their independence in 1991.

● **Baltimore** ▶ 39 25N 76 40W A city in the USA, the largest in Maryland at the mouth of the Patapsco River. Established in 1729, it was named after the Barons Baltimore, the first of whom, George Calvert (c. 1580–1632), founded Maryland. It was the starting point of the USA's first railway (1827). It is the site of many historical buildings, including the USA's first Roman Catholic cathedral (1806–21) and the Edgar Allan Poe House (1830). Baltimore is a major educational and cultural centre and contains a number of universities. It has been a busy seaport and shipbuilding centre since the late 18th century (Baltimore clippers were renowned throughout the world); other important industries include the manufacture of steel, sugar and food processing, oil refining, and chemicals. Population (1996 est): 675 401.

● **Baltimore oriole** ▶ An American ▷oriole, *Icterus galbula*, of North America, so named because the black and orange plumage of the male resembles the colours of the Barons Baltimore (*see* Baltimore). It feeds on insects, has an attractive song, and builds a woven pouchlike nest.

● **Baluchistan** ▶ A province in W Pakistan, on the Arabian Sea and the Iranian and Afghani borders. Mostly arid highlands, it is inhabited by pastoral Pathans, Baluchs, and other peoples. The NW deserts are practically uninhabited but the coastal plain and E lowlands support cereals and herbs. There is little industry other than crafts, textiles, and food processing. It has extensive mineral resources. *History*: on trade routes from India to the Middle East, Baluchistan has flourished since ancient times. Nominally part of larger empires, it usually enjoyed autonomy until Britain won control (19th century). In 1947 it became part of Pakistan. Area: 347 190 sq km (134 050 sq mi). Population (1995 est): 6 341 000. Capital: Quetta.

● **Baluchitherium** ▶ An extinct hornless rhinoceros that lived in the Oligocene epoch (between 30 million and 20 million years ago). Fossilized remains found in central Asia show that it was over 5 m high, with a heavy giraffe-like body, and was probably the largest terrestrial mammal ever.

● **Balzac, Honoré de** ▶ (1799–1850) French novelist. Educated at Vendôme, he became a lawyer's clerk in Paris. He wrote popular novels under pseudonyms, and then attempted to become a businessman; in 1828, however, bankruptcy forced him to turn to writing again. *Les Chouans* (1829), a historical novel about Breton peasants, was his first successful novel, and in the next 20 years he added over 40 novels to his life's work, the cycle *La Comédie humaine*. In these novels, which included *Eugénie Grandet* (1833), *Le Père Goriot* (1834), and *La Cousine Bette* (1846), he developed new techniques of realism to explore human behaviour. Balzac lived extravagantly in Parisian society, constantly in debt and in love, and married his last mistress, Eveline Hanska, during his fatal illness in 1850.

● **Bamako** ▶ 12 40N 7 59W The capital of Mali, a port in the S on the River Niger. A centre of Muslim learning under the medieval Mali Empire, it had dwindled to a small village by the end of the 19th century when it was occupied by the French. It became the capital of the French Sudan in 1905. Population (1995 est): 800 000.

● **Bamberg** ▶ 49 54N 10 54E A town in SE central Germany, in Bavaria on the River Regnitz. The romanesque cathedral was founded in 1004 and its bishops were princes of the Holy Roman Empire until 1803. Its varied industries include engineering and textiles. Population (1991): 70 690.

● **bamboo** ▶ A treelike plant of the tribe *Bambuseae*, native to tropical and subtropical regions, particularly SE Asia. From an underground stem (rhizome) arise hollow woody jointed stems, which may reach a height of 40 m in some species. These are used for building and a variety of other purposes, while the young shoots are eaten as a vegetable. Some bamboos are cultivated in temperate gardens for their graceful foliage. Family: *Gramineae* (grasses).

● **Bana** ▶ (7th century AD) Sanskrit writer. He travelled widely in India before becoming court poet of the Buddhist emperor ▷Harsa. The *Harsacarita* is a prose chronicle written to celebrate his patron's accession to the throne. The prose romance *Kadambari* exploits sophisticated narrative techniques to describe a complex love intrigue.

● **Banaba** ▷See Ocean Island.

● **banana** ▶ A palmlike plant of the Old World tropical genus *Musa*, especially *M. paradisiaca sapientum*, cultivated throughout the tropics from prehistoric times for its edible fruit. The "trunk," up to 9 m high, is composed of the overlapping bases of the leaves, which are often 3 m or more long. The tip of the flowering stem bears male flowers and hangs down; clusters of female flowers, further up the stem, develop into seedless fruits, up to 30 cm long, without being fertilized. (All cultivated bananas are sterile hybrids: the plants are propagated from suckers arising from the underground rhizome.) Most bananas are eaten fresh, but varieties called plantains are cooked and eaten when still green, forming a staple food in East and West Africa and the Caribbean. Family: *Musaceae*.

● **Banbridge** ▶ A district in S Northern Ireland, in Co Down. Area: 442 sq km (170 sq mi). Population (1998): 37 700.

● **Banbury** ▶ 52 04N 1 20W A market town in central England, in Oxfordshire on the River Cherwell. The original Banbury Cross of the nursery rhyme was destroyed in 1602 by Puritans but replaced in the 19th century. It has various light industries, including high-tech and telecommunications. Population (1991): 39 906.

● **Banda, Hastings Kamuzu** ▶ (c. 1905–97) Malawi statesman; president (1964–94). A physician, he worked in the UK and the USA before returning home (then Nyasaland) in 1958 to lead the fight against federation with Rhodesia and for independence. On independence (1964) he was elected president, becoming president for life in 1971. His rule was eccentric and authoritarian. Defeated in elections in 1994, he was put on trial (1995) for alleged conspiracy to murder four opposition politicians in 1983 but was acquitted.

● **Bandar Abbas** ▶ 27 12N 56 15E A town in S Iran, on the Strait of Hormuz. It is a naval base important to the security of the Persian Gulf. Population (1994 est): 383 515.

● **Bandaranaike, S(olomon) W(est) R(idgeway) D(ias)** ▶ (1899–1959) Sri Lankan statesman; prime minister (1956–59). In 1951 he founded the Sri Lanka Freedom Party (SLFP) and became prime minister as head of an alliance of socialist and nationalist parties— the People's United Front, which pursued a neutral foreign policy and nationalist domestic policies (including the replacement of English by Sinhalese as the official language). Following his assassination by a Buddhist monk, he was succeeded as head of the SLFP by his wife **Sirimavo Ratwatte Dias Bandaranaike** (1916–2000), who became the world's first woman prime minister (1960–65, 1970–77, 1994–2000). Her socialist coalition with the Marxist party was defeated in 1965 but returned to power from 1970 until 1977. In 1980 she was charged with misuse of power and expelled from Parliament. Their daughter **Chandrika Bandaranaike Kumaratunga** (1945–   ) became prime minister in August 1994 but was elected president in November. Sirimavo Bandaranaike then became prime minister for the third time. Kumaratunga was re-elected as president in 1999.

● **Bandar-e Bushehr** ▷*See* Bushire.

● **Bandar Seri Begawan** ▶ (former name: Brunei Town) 4 56N 114 58E The capital of Brunei, a port in the NE near the mouth of the Brunei River. Population (1994): 49 902.

● **Bandeira, Manuel Carneiró de Sousa** ▶ (1886–1968) Brazilian poet. He was forced by tuberculosis to give up his architectural studies in São Paulo. After meeting the French poet Paul ▷Éluard while in a Swiss sanatorium, he decided to try a literary career. The originality of his first book, *A cinza das horas* (1917), was immediately recognized; his modernist style developed more fully in *Libertinagem* (1930) and *Estrêla da Manhã* (1936).

● **bandicoot** ▶ A ratlike ▷marsupial mammal of a family (*Peramelidae*; 20 species) occurring in Australia (including Tasmania) and New Guinea. About the size of rabbits, bandicoots are mainly carnivorous, eating insects, worms, and grubs. They are shy creatures and build nests of grass and leaves among thick vegetation.

● **Bandjermasin** ▷*See* Banjarmasin.

● **Bandung** ▶ 6 57S 107 34E A city in Indonesia, in W Java. A cultural and industrial centre and tourist resort, it was formerly the administrative centre of the Netherlands East Indies. Its chief industries are chemicals, quinine, plastics, metal processing, and textiles. It has two universities, established in 1957 and 1959, and a nuclear research centre (1964). At the **Bandung Conference** of 1955 representatives of 29 African and Asian countries met to oppose colonialism. Population (1995 est): 2 368 200.

● **bandwidth** ▶ The range of frequencies over which a signal of a particular frequency spreads. For example, in radio modulation it is the range of frequencies occupied by the modulating signal on either side of the carrier wave. A television picture transmitted at 625 lines per frame requires a bandwidth of 5.5 megahertz, whereas a much simpler telephone signal requires only 4 kilohertz. In computers, the bandwidth is the number of bits per second transmitted between two digital devices.

● **Banff** ▶ 57 40N 2 31W A town in NE Scotland, in Aberdeenshire on the Moray Firth, at the mouth of the River Deveron. It is a resort with fishing and distilling industries, and was the county town of the former county of Banff, covering 1632 sq km (630 sq mi) from the Moray Firth to the Cairngorm Mountains. Population (1991): 4110.

● **Banff** ▶ 51 10N 115 34W A town in W Canada, in Alberta in the Rocky Mountains. The headquarters of Banff National Park, it is a mountain resort and conference centre and has a School of Fine Arts. Population (1991): 5688.

● **Bangalore** ▶ 12 58N 77 35E A city in S India, the capital of Karnataka. Founded in the 16th century, it fell to the British in 1791. The Institute of Science was established in 1909 and Bangalore University in 1964. An expanding industrial centre, Bangalore's industries include machine tools, aircraft assembly, and electronics. Population (1991): 2 650 659.

● **Bangka** ▶ (*or* Banka) An Indonesian island in the Java Sea, off SE Sumatra. Its tinmines are among the world's most productive; other mineral deposits include gold, manganese, and iron. The population is largely Chinese. Area: 11 914 sq km (4600 sq mi). Chief town: Pangkalpinang.

● **Bangkok** ▶ (Thai name: Krung Threp) 13 44N 100 30E The capital and main port of Thailand, in the SW near the mouth of the River Chao Phraya. It became a royal city and the capital in 1782. Distinctive features of the city are its canal system and the many Buddhist temples. There has been considerable expansion since World War II. Most of the country's industry and commerce is centred on Bangkok and it has eight universities. Population (1999 est): 5 647 799.

● **Bangladesh, People's Republic of** ▶ A country in the Indian subcontinent, lying between the Himalayas and the Bay of Bengal, in the delta of the Rivers Ganges and Brahmaputra. The land, which is generally low lying, is on the whole fertile but it has to support a very large population, most of whom are Bengalis. The country is subject to disastrous floods and cyclones.

Economy: about three-quarters of the inhabitants are occupied in

Bangladesh ▶ Flooding is a frequent hazard in this low-lying country. Because the wells are submerged, this woman, sitting on a banana-tree raft, is seeking clean water.

agriculture, rice being by far the most important food crop. Bangladesh produces 70% of the world's raw jute, its main export. Fishing, both freshwater and saltwater, is important not only as a valuable food source, but also for oil and other fish products. Traditional industries include jute milling and textile manufacture but industrial development is hindered by the lack of mineral resources. Reserves of oil and natural gas remain largely undeveloped. Although private enterprise is now encouraged, Bangladesh remains one of the poorest countries in the world and is heavily dependent on foreign aid. Communications are greatly aided by the many natural shipping channels that the country's rivers provide.

History: the area formed part of the kingdom of Bengal, and its conquest by the Afghans in the 12th century led to the growth of the Islamic religion. It was part of British India from 1857 until 1947 when it became independent as a province of Pakistan (East Pakistan). Discontentment under a government centred in West Pakistan, aggravated by the disparity in allocation of development funds to each province, led to the outbreak of civil war in 1971. Indian forces coming to the aid of the Bengalis. In 1972 East Pakistan achieved independence as Bangladesh, with Sheikh ▷Mujibur Rahman as its first prime minister, and became a member of the Commonwealth. In 1974 floods and famine led to political unrest and terrorism and in 1975 Mujibur assumed absolute power; shortly afterwards he and most of his family were assassinated in a military coup. After several more coups, Gen ▷Ziaur Rahman assumed power in 1976. In 1977 amendments to the constitution established Bangladesh as an Islamic state. Gen Ziaur was elected president in 1978; he was assassinated in 1981. The military, led by Lt Gen Hussain Mohammed ▷Ershad, took power in March, 1982, and in 1983 Ershad became president. Martial law was lifted in 1986, but demonstrations led to Ershad's resignation in 1990. In 1991 Gen Ziaur's widow, Begum Khaleda Zia, won free elections to become prime minister and Abdur Rahman Biswas was elected president under a new constitution. In 1996 the general election was boycotted by the opposition amidst riots and protests. Continuing crisis led Begum Zia to step down and a second election was won by the centrist Awami League under Mujibur's daughter, Sheikha Hasina Wajded. In 1998 floods left about two-thirds of the land area under water and some 25 million people without homes. Begum Zia's Bangladesh Nationalist Party was returned to power with a large majority in 2001.

People's Republic of Bangladesh

Head of state	President Shahabuddin Ahmed
Official language	Bengali
Official religion	Islam
Official currency	taka of 100 paise
Area	142 797 sq km (55 126 sq mi)
Population (2000 est)	129 194 000
Capital	Dhaka
Main port	Chittagong

● **Bangor** ▶ 54 40N 5 40W A resort in Northern Ireland, in North Down district, Co Down, lying on Belfast Lough. Its abbey was founded by St Comgall in 558 AD. Population (1991): 52 437.

● **Bangor** ▶ 53 13N 4 08W A city in North Wales, in Gwynedd on the Menai Strait. A college of the University of Wales was established in 1884. The 6th-century cathedral was founded by St Deiniol and holds the tombs of Welsh princes. Population (1991): 12 330.

● **Bangui** ▶ 4 23N 19 20E The capital of the Central African Republic, a port in the SW on the Ubangi River. Founded in 1889, it handles goods for both the Central African Republic and Chad; its main exports are cotton and coffee. A university was established in 1969. Population (1995 est): 553 000.

● **Bangweulu, Lake** ▶ 11 15S 29 45E A lake in E Zambia. Livingstone, the first European to visit the lake (1868), died nearby. It is shallow and bordered by swamps. During the rainy season its waters cover an area of up to 9800 sq km (3783 sq mi).

● **Banja Luka** ▶ 44 47N 17 11E A town in NW Bosnia-Hercegovina, on the River Vrbas. It has several mosques, a university (1975), and diverse industries. It was occupied by Bosnian Serb forces during the civil war (1992–95). Population (1991): 195 139.

● **Banjarmasin** ▶ (*or* Bandjermasin) 3 22S 114 33E A port in Indonesia, in S Kalimantan on the Barito delta. Its exports include rubber and timber. Its university was established in 1960. Population (1995 est): 534 600.

● **banjo** ▶ A plucked string instrument of US origin, originally played by plantation slaves. The banjo became popular in minstrel shows, vaudeville, jazz, and folk music. The body of the banjo is a round metal hoop covered with parchment on one side; the fretted fingerboard has five or six strings, which are plucked with the fingers or with a plectrum.

● **Banjul** ▶ (name until 1973: Bathurst) 13 20N 16 38W The capital of The Gambia, a port in the W at the mouth of the River Gambia, founded by the British in 1816. Population (1993): 42 407.

● **Banka** ▷*See* Bangka.

● **Bank for International Settlements** ▶ (BIS) A bank in Basle, Switzerland, which acts as a bank for ▷central banks (mostly European and American) and is governed by representatives of several of them. It was set up in 1930 to coordinate reparations after World War I. Although most of its functions are now performed by the ▷International Monetary Fund, it has important duties as a trustee.

● **Bankhead, Tallulah** ▶ (1903–68) US actress. She won acclaim in such plays as Lillian Hellman's *Little Foxes* (1939) but her popularity as a film star owed more to her extravagant lifestyle than to the quality of her performances.

● **bank holidays** ▶ The days designated as holidays in the UK, so called because they were originally the days on which the Bank of England was closed. The bank holidays common to the UK are New Year's Day, Good Friday, Easter Monday, May Day, Spring holiday, Summer holiday, Christmas Day, and Boxing Day. Scotland also enjoys 2 January, while Northern Ireland also has St Patrick's Day (17 March) and the Battle of the Boyne (12 July).

● **Bank of England** ▶ The British ▷central bank, which was nationalized in 1946. It was originally incorporated in 1694, being set up by a group of London merchants to lend money to William III. Since the mid-19th century it has been the only bank authorized to issue banknotes. The Bank conducts ▷monetary policy through ▷open-market operations (acting as lender-of-the-last-resort to the ▷discount houses), and through regulation of the supply of credit by charging a high interest rate on special deposits called from the ▷commercial banks. Operational responsibility for setting interest rates was restored to the Bank in 1997. The Bank is responsible for financing the national debt and for holding the country's gold reserves.

● **Bank of the United States** ▶ One of two consecutive US banks set up to act as banker to the Federal Government. The first, based in Philadelphia, was established by Alexander Hamilton in 1791 and closed down in 1811. The second was established in 1816 with a 20-year charter to reorganize government finances after the War of 1812 with Britain. President Andrew Jackson would not renew the charter and in 1833 put the government's money into state banks. ▷*See also* Federal Reserve System.

● **bank rate** ▷*See* interest.

● **bankruptcy** ▶ The legal process by which the property of a person who cannot pay his debts is distributed among his creditors. In England bankruptcy was originally a branch of the criminal law aimed at preventing fraudulent traders evading their creditors, but since the reign of Queen Anne the law has also sought to protect the bankrupt by ending his obligation to repay most of his past debts. Modern bankruptcy law, almost entirely contained in the Bankruptcy Act (1914) and the Insolvency Acts (1976, 1986), stipulates the circumstances in which a person may be made bankrupt, what portion of his property is to be distributed, and the creditors who are to be paid in priority to others. Liquidation is the equivalent process applicable to a company.

● **banks** ▷*See* Bank for International Settlements; Bank of England; Bank of the United States; central bank; commercial banks; International Bank for Reconstruction and Development; merchant banks.

● **Banks, Sir Joseph** ▶ (1743–1820) British botanist and explorer. During his most famous expedition, around the world with James ▷Cook (1768–71), he showed that the marsupial mammals of Australia were more primitive than the placental mammals of other continents and discovered many new species of plants. He promoted the introduction of economic plants from their native regions to other countries and was known as a patron of young scientists. He was president of the Royal Society from 1778 until his death.

● **Banksia** ▶ A genus of shrubs and trees (about 50 species) all native to dry areas of Australia; some are known as Australian honeysuckles. The flowers are borne in dense spikes and give rise to hard winged seeds. Family: *Proteaceae*.

● **Banks Island** ▶ The westernmost island of Canada's Arctic Archipelago, in the Northwest Territories. Mostly hilly plateau, it supports numerous Arctic animals. Area: 60 166 sq km (23 230 sq mi).

● **Bann, River** ▶ The longest river in Northern Ireland. Rising in the Mourne Mountains, it flows N through Banbridge, Portadown, and Lough Neagh to enter the Atlantic Ocean near Coleraine. Length: 50 km (80 mi).

● **Banner System** ▶ A system of military organization adopted by the Manchu tribes and used by the ▷Qing dynasty to rule China. It was initiated in 1601 by ▷Nurhachi, who enrolled his warriors under yellow, white, blue, or red banners. Later four bordered banners were added and all tribesmen were enrolled. Each banner formed an administrative unit, which contributed a quota of men when it became necessary to raise an army and also facilitated taxation. In return bannermen were allocated land. After the Manchu conquest of China and the establishment of the Qing, eight Chinese and eight Mongol banners were added.

● **Bannister, Sir Roger (Gilbert)** ▶ (1929–   ) British doctor and middle-distance runner, who on 6 May, 1954, was the first man to run a mile in under 4 minutes (3 minutes 59.4 seconds).

● **Bannockburn** ▶ 56 06N 3 55W A village in Scotland, near Stirling on the Bannock Burn (a tributary of the River Forth). 1.5 km (1 mi) NW is the battlefield where, in 1314, Robert the Bruce, King of the Scots, routed the English under Edward II, who had come to relieve the besieged Stirling Castle. Population (1991): 2675.

● **banshee** ▶ (Irish *bean-sidhe*: woman of the fairies) In Irish folklore, a female spectre whose weeping announced the imminent death of a person.

● **bantam** ▶ One of many breeds of dwarf fowl, possibly named after the district of Bantam in Indonesia, from where they were formerly exported to the West. Bantams generally weigh about 500 g or less.

● **Banten** ▶ A region in W Java (Indonesia), which was the centre of a Muslim sultanate until 1683 when it became part of the Dutch East Indies. The town of Banten was a flourishing port for the European spice trade from the 16th to the 18th centuries, after which the harbour silted up.

● **banteng** ▶ A wild ox, *Bos banteng*, of forests in SE Asia. About 150 cm high at the shoulder, bantengs are brown with white socks and a white rump patch and have relatively small horns. They feed on young grass and bamboo shoots.

● **Banting, Sir Frederick Grant** ▶ (1891–1941) Canadian physiologist, who, with C. H. ▷Best, discovered a technique for isolating the hormone ▷insulin from pancreatic tissue in 1921. This enabled the successful treatment of patients suffering from ▷diabetes (caused by lack of insulin). Banting was awarded a Nobel Prize (1923) with J. J. R. ▷Macleod but he divided his share with Best in recognition of his colleague's achievement.

● **Bantock, Sir Granville** ▶ (1868–1946) British composer, who was professor of music at Birmingham University (1908–34). His compositions include the oratorio *Omar Khayyám* (1909), the *Hebridean Symphony* (1915), and five ballets.

● **Bantu** ▶ A large subgroup of African languages of the ▷Niger-Congo group spoken across the S half of Africa by about 60 million people. It includes Zulu, Xhosa, and Kongo; perhaps the most widely known is ▷Swahili, the language of Tanzania and lingua franca of E Africa. The Bantu languages are tonal, with the exception of Swahili, and make extensive use of suffixes and prefixes. Many use a number of click sounds. The Bantu people have a tradition of diverse culture and social organization and have included herdsmen, farmers, hunter-gatherers, and fishers. They probably migrated southwards from an area near the Cameroon-Nigeria border, displacing small pygmy and Bushmen tribes, approximately 2000 years ago.

● **Bantu Homelands** ▶ (*or* Bantustans) The areas of South Africa, comprising just over 13% of the land area, that were designated for the Black populations from 1950 until 1994. Acts of parliament in 1913 and 1936 controlled the extent of African lands and prohibited Blacks from holding land in White areas. The Bantu Authorities Act (1951) gave limited administrative and legislative powers to the Bantu authorities, and the Bantu Self-Government Act (1959) divided the Black populations into national units, most of them with Homelands in several separate areas. Limited self-government was granted to these areas; the ▷Transkei was the first to receive this (1963). The Bantu Homelands Constitution Act (1971) aimed at similar self-government for other areas. Full independence was granted to Transkei (1976), ▷Bophuthatswana (1977), ▷Venda (1979), and Ciskei (1981), but this was not recognized outside South Africa. Self-government without full independence was granted to Gazankulu, KaNgwane, KwaNdbele, KwaZulu, Lebowa, and Qwaqwa. In April 1994 the Homelands were reintegrated into South Africa.

● **banyan** ▶ A tropical Asian tree, *Ficus benghalensis*, related to the fig and reaching a height of 30 m. Individual trees commonly grow into impenetrable thickets as the branches produce supporting aerial roots, which grow down to penetrate the soil and subsequently give rise to thorny branches of their own. Family: *Moraceae*.

● **baobab** ▶ A tropical African tree, *Adansonia digitata*, with a tapering conical trunk (the base of which may exceed 10 m in diameter) reaching a height of 18 m and bearing branches at its apex. The drab bat-pollinated flowers give rise to fruits that contain a succulent edible pulp surrounded by a tough woody capsule. The bark yields a fibre of local importance, and the trees are grown as ornamentals in some subtropical areas. Family: *Bombacaceae*.

● **Baotou** ▶ (*or* Pao-t'ou) 40 38N 109 59E A city in N China, in the Inner Mongolia AR on the Yellow River. It is an industrial centre, with a nuclear power station, iron and steel, sugar, and textile industries. Population (1991 est): 1 200 000.

● **baptism** ▶ A ceremony of initiation, occurring in many religions, involving the use of water as a symbol of purification from sin. In the Christian Church, where it is a ▷sacrament and is done in the name of the Father, the Son, and the Holy Spirit, it involves the candidate's immersion in water or the mere wetting of his or her head. Both the ▷Baptists and the modern descendants of the ▷Anabaptists practise adult baptism, but most other Churches prefer infant baptism.

● **Baptists** ▶ Protestant Christians who baptize, by immersion, only those old enough consciously to accept the Christian faith. Each Baptist Church is autonomous, but in the UK there used to be two main types, "General Baptist" Churches, owing their origin in 1612 to John Smyth (c. 1554–1612) and Thomas Helwys (c. 1550–c. 1616), and "Particular Baptist" Churches, founded in 1633 by Calvinists who believed that salvation was only for a particular few. The latter had modified its doctrines by 1891, when both movements merged into the Baptist Union. The first Baptist Church in America was established at Providence, Rhode Island, by Roger Williams in 1639. The majority of Baptists, of whom there are over 30 million worldwide, live in the USA and are associated with the Baptist World Alliance.

● **Baqqarah** ▶ A cattle-herding Arab people of Chad and the Sudan. They have dark skins and speak a distinct dialect of Arabic. They migrate seasonally between northern wet-season grazing lands and southern dry-season river areas.

● **bar** ▶ A unit of pressure equal to 10^5 pascals (0.987 atmosphere). The commonly used unit is the millibar (one-thousandth of a bar).

● **Barabbas** ▶ In the New Testament, the criminal who was released instead of ▷Jesus at Passover. The fourth Gospel states that he was a robber, whereas Mark and Luke describe his offence as insurrection and murder.

● **Barak, Ehud** ▶ (1942–   ) Israeli politician and soldier of Polish-Lithuanian descent; prime minister (1999–2001). A former chief of staff of the Israeli army (1991–94), he served briefly (1995) in the cabinet of ▷Rabin, whom he succeeded as Labour leader. He won a landslide victory over ▷Netanyahu in the election of 1999, but his attempts to make a further peace deal with the Palestinians ended in failure and he was heavily defeated by ▷Sharon in elections in 2001.

● **Barbados, State of** ▶ An island state in the West Indies, E of the Windward Islands. It is generally low lying except for a district in the NE and is subject to hurricanes. Most of the population is of African descent.

Economy: tourism is now the chief economic activity, although high-density agriculture, with sugar cane as the main crop, remains important. The policy of encouraging industry has been helped by the discovery of offshore oil and natural gas. Main exports include sugar and sugar products (including rum), petroleum and petroleum products, clothing, and electrical goods.

History: occupied by the British in 1627, it remained a British colony until 1966, when it became a fully independent state within the Commonwealth. The 1994 general election was won by the Barbados Labour Party led by Owen Arthur. In 1998 a constitutional commission recommended that Barbados should become a republic but remain inside the Commonwealth.

State of Barbados

Head of state	Queen Elizabeth II, represented by the governor-general, Sir Clifford Husbands
Official language	English
Official currency	Barbados dollar of 100 cents
Area	430 sq km (166 sq mi)
Population (1999 est)	266 000
Capital and main port	Bridgetown

● **Barbarossa** ▶ (Khayr ad-Din; d. 1546) Turkish pirate. Barbarossa (Italian: Redbeard) entered the service of the Ottoman Sultan of Turkey to protect his possessions on the Barbary coast of N Africa against Spanish and Portuguese attack. He captured Algiers in 1529 and Tunisia in 1534 and his defeat of Emperor Charles V's fleet in 1538 gave the Turks control of the E Mediterranean.

● **Barbary** ▶ A region in N Africa stretching from Egypt to the Atlantic Ocean and from the Mediterranean Sea to the Sahara. It is named after its oldest inhabitants, the ▷Berbers. In antiquity it consisted of Mauritania, Numidia, Africa, Propria, and Cyrenaica. It was successively conquered by the Romans, Vandals, Arabs, Turks, Spaniards (parts of Morocco), French (Algeria, Tunisia, and Morocco), and Italians (Tripoli). Between the 16th and 18th centuries, Barbary was notorious for its pirates.

● **Barbary ape** ▶ A large monkey, *Macaca sylvana*, also called magot, the only ▷macaque found in N Africa. Barbary apes are tailless and roam in bands over the forest floor, feeding on seeds, leaves, insects, and small animals. The colony of Barbary apes in Gibraltar was probably introduced by man.

● **barbastelle** ▶ A large-eared insect-eating bat, *Barbastella barbastella*, of Europe, S Asia, and NE Africa. About 5 cm long, slender, and long-legged, barbastelles fly early in the evening. Family: *Vespertilionidae*.

● **barbel** ▶ A long slender freshwater fish, belonging to the genus *Barbus*, that is related to ▷carp and occurs in clear fresh waters of Asia, Africa, and Europe. It has four fleshy threadlike appendages (barbels) near its mouth, which detect prey, mainly invertebrates, while exploring the river bed. *B. barbus* of Europe is usually 30–50 cm long.

● **Barber, Samuel** ▶ (1910–81) US composer. Two of his works, the opera *Vanessa* (1958) and the piano concerto (1963), won Pulitzer Prizes. His style, although basically lyrical, became increasingly dissonant in his later works. His output include a chamber music, choral works, symphonies, and concertos. His best-known work is the *Adagio for Strings*, an arrangement of the slow movement of his string quartet (1936).

● **barberry** ▷*See* Berberis.

● **barber's shop** ▶ Unaccompanied close-harmony singing that originated in barber shops in the USA during the late 19th century. Linked to an older European tradition, the genre has enjoyed revivals in the 20th century.

● **barbet** ▶ A small brightly coloured forest bird belonging to a tropical family (*Capitonidae*; 76 species) most commonly found in Africa. 8–30 cm long, barbets have large heavy bills with bristles around the chin and beak and a monotonously repeated call. They feed mainly on fruit but also take insects, lizards, and birds' eggs. Order: *Piciformes* (woodpeckers, etc.).

● **Barbican** ▶ A street and area near the ancient walls of the City of London, NE of St Paul's Cathedral. Named after an old watch tower forming part of the City's outer fortifications (from French *barbacane*), the area was devastated by bombing in World War II. In 1958 the site was compulsorily purchased to build a residential area around an arts centre, now known as the Barbican Arts Centre (1982), containing an art gallery, three cinemas, two theatres, and a concert hall. The surrounding residential area has flats to accommodate some 6500 people (some in tower blocks) as well as shops, schools, and open spaces. The complex also contains the Museum of London (1976), depicting the history of the capital and housing Roman and other early remains uncovered during excavation of this and other sites in London.

● **Barbirolli, Sir John** ▶ (1899–1970) British conductor of Franco-Italian parents. Originally a cellist, he organized his own string orchestra, and subsequently became conductor of several major opera companies and orchestras in Britain and the USA. From 1949 until his death he was principal conductor of the Hallé Orchestra, Manchester.

● **barbiturates** ▶ A class of drugs that act by depressing the activity of the brain. The short-acting barbiturate thiopentone is used for inducing ▷anaesthesia, while the long-acting phenobarbitone is used to control some forms of epilepsy. Barbiturates were formerly widely used as sleeping tablets and sedatives, but because they are habit-forming, have toxic side-effects, and can be fatal in overdosage their use is now severely limited.

● **Barbizon school** ▶ A group of French landscape painters who worked in the village of Barbizon, near the Forest of Fontainebleau, in the 1840s. Truth to nature combined with romantic settings typify the works of the school's founder Theodore ▷Rousseau, ▷Daubigny, Narcisse-Virgile Diaz de la Pena (c. 1807–76), and others. Dark trees and ponds betray their debt to Dutch landscape painting but their practice of open-air oil sketching to capture light effects inspired the impressionists to paint finished works outside. Fringe members of the school included ▷Corot and ▷Millet.

● **Barbour, John** ▶ (1316–95) Scottish poet. He became archdeacon of Aberdeen in 1357, studied at Oxford and Paris, and received a royal pension in 1388. In *The Bruce*, a Scottish epic, he celebrated Scotland's fight for independence under ▷Robert (I) the Bruce and James Douglas.

● **Barbuda** ▷*See* Antigua and Barbuda.

● **Barbusse, Henri** ▶ (1873–1935) French novelist. His novel *Under Fire* (1916), based on his experiences in World War I, expresses the disillusion that led him to pacifism and later to communism. His socialist novel *Clarté* (1919) lent its name to a short-lived international movement. He died in the Soviet Union.

● **barcarolle** ▶ A piece of music imitating the songs of Venetian gondoliers. It is usually in 6/8 or 12/8 time and has a gentle rocking movement. Examples include Offenbach's *Barcarolle* from *The Tales of Hoffman* and Chopin's piano *Barcarolle*.

● **Barcelona** ▶ 41 25N 2 10E A city in NE Spain, in Catalonia on the Mediterranean Sea. It is Spain's second largest city, its largest port and commercial and industrial centre. Manufactures include locomotives, textiles, and electrical equipment. The country's cultural centre and the focus of Catalan art and literature, it has many educational establishments, libraries, and museums; the University of Barcelona was founded in 1430. The city's buildings include the palace of the Aragón kings, a cathedral (14th–15th centuries), and a 14th-century monastery. It has several Art Nouveau buildings designed by Antonio Gaudí, notably the Sagrada Familia church (1903–26).

History: founded by the Carthaginians, it was taken by the Moors in 713 and by Charlemagne in 801. In 1137 Catalonia and Aragón united and Barcelona became the capital, rivalling Genoa and Venice as a leading European port. During the 19th century it became important industrially through its cotton industry. The centre of the Catalan separatist government, it was the seat of the Catalan autonomous government and later of the Republican government, during the Spanish Civil War (1936–39). In 1939 Barcelona fell to Gen Franco and the Republican government surrendered. The 1992 Olympics were held here. Population (1995 est): 1 614 571.

● **Barclay de Tolly, Mikhail Bogdanovich, Prince** ▶ (1761–1818) Russian field marshal. In 1810, after brilliant campaigns against Napoleon, he became minister of war. Promoted field marshal (1814), he commanded the army that invaded France in 1815.

● **Bar Cochba** ▷*See* Bar Kokhba.

● **bar code** ▶ An array of parallel bars of different widths printed on the packaging of an item for sale in a retail shop. When scanned by a laser beam at a checkout, the price and description of the goods are shown on the till screen and the stock record is reduced accordingly. Developed in the 1970s, the system is also used in libraries for identifying books.

● **Barcoo River** ▷*See* Cooper Creek.

● **bard** ▶ In ancient Celtic societies, a poet whose duty was to eulogize heroes and to celebrate victories and the laws and traditions of the community. Bards constituted a distinct social class with hereditary rights and privileges. The class was at one time subdivided according to functions. In 10th-century Wales the three bardic ranks were *pencerdd* (chief of song), *bardd teulu* (household bard), and *cerddor* (minstrel); an earlier Irish classification was *druid*, *filid*, and *baird*. Bards ceased to exist in Gaul at an early date, but they survived in Scotland and Ireland to the 18th century; in a somewhat artificial and diminished role, they continue to exist in Wales. ▷*See also* eisteddfod; Welsh literature.

● **Bardeen, John** ▶ (1908–91) US physicist, who became professor at the University of Illinois in 1951. He shared the 1956 Nobel Prize for his part in the invention of the transistor (with W. B. ▷Shockley and W. H. ▷Brattain) while working at the Bell Telephone Laboratories in 1948. He also shared the 1972 Nobel Prize for his work on the theory of ▷superconductivity (with L. N. Cooper and J. R. Schrieffer), known as the BCS theory after the initials of its authors.

● **Bardot, Brigitte** ▶ (1934–) French film actress. Her first major film, *And God Created Woman* (1956), was directed by Roger Vadim, to whom she was married from 1952 to 1957. Subsequent films included *Vie privée* (1961), *Viva Maria* (1965), and *Shalako* (1968). She became probably the best-known sex symbol of the 1960s but after two further unsuccessful marriages she turned her back on the cinema, banished the popular press from her life, and devoted herself to animal welfare.

● **Bar-do Thödol** ▷*See* Book of the Dead.

● **Bardsey** ▶ 52 46N 4 48W A Welsh island in St Georges Channel, off the SW coast of the Lleyn Peninsula. It contains the ruins of a 6th-century abbey and was a place of pilgrimage in the middle ages.

● **Barebones Parliament** ▶ The assembly, also known as the parliament of saints, called by Oliver ▷Cromwell in July, 1653. It consisted mainly of merchants and lesser gentry, "godly men" nominated by the congregations, and was named after one of them, Praisegod Barebone (c. 1596-1679). In December the moderates among them resigned their power to Cromwell.

● **Bareilly** ▶ 28 20N 79 24E A city in India, in Uttar Pradesh. Founded in 1537, it was a centre of the Indian Mutiny. The Indian Veterinary Research Institute was established nearby in 1889. Manufactures include sugar, rope, and furniture. Population (1991): 587 211.

● **Barenboim, Daniel** ▶ (1942–) Israeli pianist and conductor, who studied in Salzburg, Paris, and Rome. He made his debut in London in 1955. In 1967 he married the cellist Jacqueline ▷du Pré, with whom he gave recitals. Barenboim conducted the Orchestre de Paris from 1975 to 1989 and became music director of the Chicago Symphony Orchestra in 1991.

● **Barents, Willem** ▶ (c. 1550-97) Dutch navigator. He led three expeditions (1594, 1595, 1596) to discover a ▷Northeast Passage, reaching the Novaya Zemlya islands and discovering Spitsbergen (1596). On his last voyage he was forced to winter at Icehaven, where his camp was found in 1871. He died at sea on his return journey. The Barents Sea is named after him.

● **Barents Sea** ▶ A section of the Arctic Ocean between Eurasia and Svalbard, Franz Josef Land, and Novaya Zemlya. It covers part of the Eurasian continental shelf, which before the Pleistocene Ice Age was land. It is rich in fish.

● **Barère, Bertrand** ▶ (1755-1841) French revolutionary. Initially a moderate in the National Convention, he subsequently became a member of the Committee of ▷Public Safety during the ▷Reign of Terror. Imprisoned after the fall of Robespierre (July, 1794), he escaped into exile, returning to France in 1830.

● **Barghest** ▶ (*or* Barguest) In English superstition, a terrifying enormous dog whose appearance varied in different parts of the country. In Manchester it was headless and in E Anglia one-eyed. Those who saw it were supposed to die.

● **Barham, Richard Harris** ▶ (1788-1845) British humorous writer. He became a clergyman in 1813 after studying at Oxford and began writing while recovering from serious illness. He is best known for the verse narratives of *The Ingoldsby Legends*, comic treatments of largely supernatural themes. Written for magazines, they were collected in three volumes (1840, 1842, 1847).

● **Bar Hebraeus** ▶ (1226-86) Syrian bishop and scholar. Bar Hebraeus studied medicine at Antioch and Tripoli. He was consecrated bishop in 1246 and became Primate of the East in 1264. His writings, in Syriac and Arabic, include the *Granary of Mysteries* and the *Chronicle*.

● **Bari** ▶ 41 07N 16 52E A seaport in Italy, the capital of Apulia on the Adriatic Sea. It has a cathedral (12th-15th centuries) and a university (1924). Industries include chemicals, textiles, and oil refining. Population (1996 est): 336 560.

● **Baring, Evelyn** ▷*See* Cromer, Evelyn Baring, 1st Earl of.

● **barite** ▶ (*or* barytes) A barium ore consisting of barium sulphate, sometimes called heavy spar. It is colourless when pure, but often white, yellow, or brown, due to impurities. It is used in the manufacture of paint and heavy paper, as a mineral filler in rubber and linoleum manufacture, and in concrete and glassmaking. The chief producers are the USA, Germany, and Ireland.

● **baritone** ▶ A deep adult male singing voice, lower than tenor and higher than bass. Range: G at the bottom of the bass stave to G two octaves above.

● **barium** ▶ (Ba) A silvery reactive metal that resembles calcium in its behaviour. It was discovered in 1808 by Sir Humphry Davy and occurs naturally as barytes ($BaSO_4$) and witherite ($BaCO_3$). The sulphate is used as a white pigment in paint and, because of its opacity to X-rays, is used in X-ray diagnosis. All soluble barium compounds are toxic, the carbonate being used as rat poison. At no 56; at wt 137.327; mp 729°C; bp 1805°C.

● **bark** ▶ The dead outer layer of the stems and roots of woody plants, which protects the inner tissues from desiccation, extremes of temperature, pests and diseases, and physical damage. Antiseptic deposits, such as tannins, give the colour. Bark may include layers of insulating ▷cork, which is responsible for the characteristic ridges and patterns on some tree trunks. Small breathing pores (called lenticels) in the bark are conspicuous in many of the smooth-barked trees (such as *Prunus* species) but are hidden in the cracks of rough-barked species. The bark of some trees is of commercial importance, being a source of cinnamon, quinine, and various other products.

● **bark beetle** ▶ A hard cylindrical beetle, also called an engraver beetle, belonging to a family (*Scolytidae*; 7000 species) of wood borers. It is usually less than 6 mm long, coloured red-brown or black, and causes considerable damage to trees. It burrows underneath the bark to lay eggs that develop into burrowing larvae: the elaborate patterns of tunnels produced are generally characteristic of the species. Certain species also transmit diseases (*see* elm bark beetle) and can be serious economic pests.

● **Barker, George** ▶ (1913-91) British poet. He left school at 14 but taught in universities in England, Japan, America, and Italy. His poetry is noted for its passionate vigorous lyricism; it first achieved wide popularity in the 1940s. His many books include *The True Confession of George Barker* (1950), *Dialogues, Etc.* (1976), and *Collected Poems* (1989).

● **Barker, Harley Granville** ▷*See* Granville-Barker, Harley.

● **Barkhausen, Heinrich** ▶ (1881-1956) German physicist, who became professor of electrical engineering at the University of Dresden. He discovered (1919) the effect in which ferromagnetic materials placed in an increasing magnetic field become magnetized in small jumps (Barkhausen effect).

● **Barking and Dagenham** ▶ A borough of E Greater London, created in 1965 from most of the former boroughs of Barking and Dagenham. Industries include a power station and motor vehicle manufacture. Area: 34 sq km (13 sq mi). Population (1991): 145 200.

● **barking deer** ▷*See* muntjac.

● **Barkly Tableland** ▶ An area of Australia, extending SE of the Gulf of Carpentaria, in Northern Territory, into Queensland. It consists of undulating uplands on which beef cattle are raised. Area: about 130 000 sq km (50 000 sq mi).

● **Bar Kokhba** ▶ (Bar Cochba *or* Simeon bar Kosiba; d. 135 AD) Jewish freedom fighter. In 132 he launched a revolt against Roman rule and attempted to set up an independent Jewish state. He was hailed as Messiah by ▷Akiba, but did not enjoy widespread support and was killed when his last stronghold, Betar, fell. Some of his correspondence has been recovered from caves in the Judaean desert.

● **Barlach, Ernst** ▶ (1870-1938) German expressionist sculptor and playwright. First influenced by ▷*Jugendstil*, he only found his mature style after visiting Russia (1906). His bulky figures, usually in wood, with their expressive faces and angular and rigid outlines were inspired both by his studies of Russian peasants and by ▷gothic sculpture. The Nazis destroyed much of his work.

● **Bar-le-Duc** ▶ 48 46N 5 10E A town in NE France, the capital of the Meuse department on the River Ornain. Its manufactures include metal goods, textiles, and jams; it is also a centre of the cheese industry. Population (latest est): 20 029.

• Barletta ▶ 41 20N 16 17E A seaport in Italy, in Apulia on the Adriatic coast. It possesses a romanesque cathedral and a castle. An agricultural centre, it has an important wine trade; chemicals and cement are also manufactured. Population (1990): 88 750.

• barley ▶ A ▷cereal grass of the genus *Hordeum*, especially *H. vulgare*, which produces its grain in four rows and can be grown as far north as N Norway; *H. distichon* (two-rowed barley); and *H. hexadistichon* (six-rowed barley). Over 165 million tonnes of grain are harvested annually in temperate, subtropical, and subarctic regions from the various strains of barley. It is malted and used in the brewing industry, made into food for cattle and pigs, milled to produce pearl and pot barley (used in soups and stews), and used in breadmaking.

• Bar Mitzvah ▶ (Hebrew: son of the commandment) The ceremony marking the initiation of a Jewish boy into the adult community at the age of 13. At this age he assumes his full religious responsibilities and it is customary for him to read publicly from the ▷Torah in the synagogue for the first time. In some communities a parallel ceremony (Bat Mitzvah) exists for girls.

• Barnabas, St ▶ In the New Testament (Acts), a Christian Apostle of the 1st century. After going with St Paul to evangelize Cyprus (his birthplace) and the European mainland, he clashed with him and they parted company. He is traditionally regarded as the founder of the Cypriot Church. Feast day: 11 June.

• barnacle ▶ A marine ▷crustacean belonging to the class *Cirripedia* (1000 species). Some members of the group are parasites, but the typical (nonparasitic) barnacles live attached—head downwards—to rocks, ships' hulls, etc., and filter food particles from the water with long feathery appendages, which protrude from the calcareous shell. Goose barnacles (e.g. *Lepas anatifera*)—so called because they were believed in the middle ages to be an immature form of the barnacle goose—are attached by means of a stalk; others, including the acorn barnacle (*Balanus*), are unstalked. Barnacles are hermaphrodite; their larvae are free-swimming, but later settle and become fixed to a surface by means of a cement-like substance secreted by their antennae.

• barnacle goose ▶ A European ▷goose, *Branta leucopsis*, which is a regular winter visitor to Britain. It has a distinctive cream face, dark crown and breast, and a white chevron on the tail and grazes on coastal meadows and salt marshes. They were once believed to hatch from barnacles!

• Barnard, Christiaan Neethling ▶ (1922–) South African surgeon, who (in 1967 at the Groote Schuur Hospital in Cape Town) performed the world's first successful heart transplant operation. His patient, Louis Washkansky, received the heart of a road-accident victim but died 18 days later from pneumonia. Barnard retired in 1983 and subsequently entered politics.

• Barnard, Edward Emerson ▶ (1857–1923) US astronomer, who became professor at the University of Chicago (1895). He discovered Jupiter's fifth satellite (1892), a total of 16 comets, and **Barnard's Star** (1916) in the constellation Ophiuchus, the star with the most rapid proper motion.

• Barnardo, Thomas John ▶ (1845–1905) British doctor and philanthropist. In 1867 Barnardo founded the first of his famous homes at Stepney, London, to care for destitute children by taking them from a damaging environment and providing a home, education, and training. Over a hundred homes exist in the UK, with others in Australia and New Zealand.

• Barnaul ▶ 53 21N 83 45E A city in S Russia, on the River Ob. The centre of an industrial and mining area, its industries include engineering, textiles, chemicals, and timber. Population (1995 est): 596 000.

• Barnave, Antoine Pierre ▶ (1761–93) French revolutionary. A chief spokesman of the ▷Jacobins, he developed royalist sympathies in 1791 through personal contact with Louis XVI. Advocating a constitutional monarchy, he became leader of the ▷Feuillants and was executed.

• Barnes, William ▶ (1801–86) British poet. His *Poems of Rural Life in the Dorset Dialect* (1879) expressed his deep feeling for the landscape and traditional customs of Dorset, where he worked as a schoolteacher and clergyman. He also wrote philological works.

• Barnet ▶ A residential borough of NW Greater London, created in 1965 from parts of Hertfordshire and Middlesex, including ▷Finchley and ▷Hendon. It was the site of a Yorkist victory (1471) in the Wars of the Roses, when the Earl of Warwick was killed. Area: 89 sq km (34 sq mi). Population (1991): 305 900.

• barn owl ▶ An ▷owl belonging to a family (*Tytonidae*; 9 species) with a worldwide distribution. Barn owls have heart-shaped faces, long feathered legs, and usually a reddish plumage with pale underparts. The common barn owl (*Tyto alba*), 30–45 cm long, nests in old barns and belfries and hunts for small rodents.

• Barnsley ▶ 1. 53 34N 1 28W A town in N England, in Barnsley unitary authority, South Yorkshire, on the River Dearne. Formerly a centre for coalmining and heavy industry, it now has varied industries, including electronics, new technology, glass manufacture, and textiles. It is the site of a famous market (founded 1249) and a large college of further education. Population (1991): 75 120. **2.** A unitary authority in N England, in South Yorkshire. Area: 329 sq km (127 sq mi). Population (1995 est): 226 700.

• Barnstaple ▶ 51 5N 4 04W A town and resort in SW England, in N Devon on the estuary of the River Taw. Formerly a port, it is now the regional administrative and agricultural centre for N Devon. Population (1991): 27 691.

• Barnum, Phineas Taylor ▶ (1810–91) US showman. His presentation of such novel exhibits as human freaks and natural curiosities at the American Museum from 1842 attracted unprecedented crowds. In 1850 he organized the successful US tour of the Swedish singer Jenny Lind. His circus, established in 1871, merged with that of his rival, J. A. Bailey (1847–1906), to become the Barnum and Bailey Circus in 1881.

• Baroda ▷*See* Vadodara.

• Baroja, Pío ▶ (1872–1956) Spanish novelist. He abandoned a career as a doctor to manage a family bakery in Madrid. His first book of short stories, *Vida sombrías* (1900), was followed by nearly a hundred novels. His early heroes were rebels or reformers embodying his own desire to inspire political action, but the tone of later books—especially *Laura, o la soledad sin remedio* (1939)—was more sceptical and pessimistic.

• barometer ▶ An instrument for measuring atmospheric pressure. There are two main types: the mercury barometer and the aneroid barometer. In the mercury barometer, atmospheric pressure forces mercury from a reservoir into a vertical evacuated glass tube marked with a scale. The height of the mercury column is directly proportional to the atmospheric pressure. In the aneroid barometer, variations in the atmospheric pressure on the lid of an evacuated metal box cause a pointer to move round a dial. The aneroid barometer is less sensitive than the mercury barometer but it is smaller, more portable, and more convenient to use.

• baron ▷*See* peerage.

• baronet ▶ A hereditary honour introduced by James I in 1611 to raise money to suppress rebellion in Ulster. Baronets, who had to show that they had a clear income of £1000 p.a., had to pay £1080 (roughly the cost of maintaining 30 soldiers for 3 days, at 8d per day, in Ulster) to the Crown. A baronet ranks between a knight and a baron (*see* peerage), has no seat in the House of Lords, has the title "Sir" (followed by Bart. or Bt. after his name), and usually cannot pass his title to females. Sales of baronetcies ceased in 1937.

• Barons' Wars ▶ 1. (1215–17) The civil war between King John of England and his barons. John's failure to honour the ▷Magna Carta led the barons to offer the English Crown to the future Louis VIII of France, who invaded England. John's death and the reissue of Magna Carta (1216) removed many baronial grievances but war continued until the barons' defeat at Lincoln and Sandwich (1217). Peace was established and the Magna Carta again reissued. **2.** (1264–67) The civil war between Henry III of England and his barons led by Simon de ▷Montfort. War broke out following Henry's repudiation of the Provisions of ▷Oxford. He was captured at the battle of ▷Lewes (1264) and England was controlled by de Montfort until his death at Evesham (1265). Hostilities continued (*see* Kenilworth) until the royalist capture of the Isle of Ely in 1267.

● **baroque** ► In architecture, a style dominant in European Roman Catholic countries during the 17th and early 18th centuries. The name probably derives from the Spanish *barrueco*, an irregularly shaped pearl. The baroque began in Italy as a reaction against ▷classicism. It was characterized by curved and broken lines, ornate decoration (which led to the ▷rococo), and elaborate spatial effects. English architects, such as ▷Wren and ▷Vanbrugh, were influenced by it.

In art, the baroque was a style that developed from Italian ▷mannerism, complementing baroque architecture. Both art and architecture were used to popularize Catholic beliefs during the ▷Counter-Reformation. Baroque art was characterized by the vivid presentation of stories of saints, miracles, and the crucifixion. Leading exponents of the baroque were the sculptor and architect ▷Bernini, the architect ▷Borromini, and the painters ▷Caravaggio and ▷Rubens.

In music, the compositions of the 17th and early 18th centuries, from Monteverdi to Bach, are frequently called baroque music. A variety of styles and forms flourished during this period, the use of the term referring to the period rather than a particular style. This period saw the development of ▷opera, ▷oratorio, the concerto grosso (*see* Corelli, Arcangelo), and the trio sonata.

● **Barossa Valley** ▷*See* South Australia.

● **Barotse** ▷*See* Lozi.

● **Barotseland** ► A former kingdom in central Africa, now comprising Western Province in Zambia. Inhabited by the ▷Lozi people, it was put under British protection through two treaties (1890, 1900) by the Lozi chief, Lewanika (d. 1916). The area attempted to break away as a separate kingdom on Zambian independence (1964).

● **barque** ► A sailing vessel with three or more masts. Square sails are set on all masts except the aftermast, which carries fore-and-aft sails. In a **barquentine** only the foremast has square-rigged sails.

● **Barquisimeto** ► 10 03N 69 18W A city in NW Venezuela. It is the commercial centre of a coffee-growing area and has a university (1963). Population (1990): 625 450.

● **Barra** ► An island in NW Scotland, in the Outer Hebrides separated from South Uist by the Sound of Barra. Its economy is based on fishing, crofting, and tourism. Area: 91 sq km (35 sq mi). Population (latest est): 1200. Chief settlement: Castlebay.

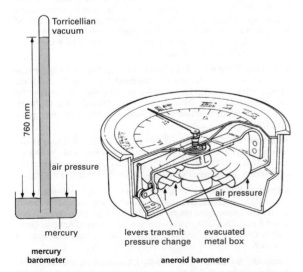

mercury barometer

aneroid barometer

barometer ► In the mercury barometer the height of the mercury column is directly proportional to the air pressure and is independent of the diameter of the tube. In the aneroid barometer movements of the lid of the evacuated metal box are transmitted to the pointer by the levers.

● **barracuda** ► A shoaling fish of the family *Sphyraenidae* (about 20 species), found in all tropical seas and caught for food and sport. Its body is up to 1.8 m long and bears two dorsal fins. Barracudas feed voraciously on other fish and the larger species are considered dangerous to man. Order: *Perciformes*.

● **Barranquilla** ► 11 00N 74 50W An important port in NW Colombia, on the Río Magdalena near its mouth on the Caribbean Sea. Its manufactures include textiles, vegetable oils, and chemicals. It has two universities (1941, 1967). Population (1997 est): 1 157 826.

● **Barras, Paul François Jean Nicolas, Vicomte de** ► (1755–1829) French revolutionary. Although he joined the National Convention as a Jacobin, Barras turned against Robespierre and helped to secure his downfall in 1794. As commander of Paris, Barras suppressed a royalist uprising in 1795 by allowing Napoleon Bonaparte to turn his guns on the agitators. A member of the Directory from 1795 to 1799, Barras resigned during Napoleon's coup d'état (1799).

● **Barrault, Jean-Louis** ► (1910–94) French actor and director. He directed influential productions of both classical and avantgarde plays and was director of the Théâtre de France from 1959 to 1968. Barrault was also renowned for his mime, especially in the film *Les Enfants du paradis* (1944).

● **barrel organ** ► **1.** A musical instrument popular in the 18th and 19th centuries, much used in churches. It consists of a simple organ mechanism operated by a wooden cylinder (or barrel) set with brass pins and turned by a handle, which also works a bellows. **2.** A musical instrument of the 19th century more properly called **barrel piano** and often confused with the barrel organ. A popular street instrument, its barrel and pin mechanism causes leather-covered hammers to strike strings.

● **Barren Grounds** ► (or Lands) The largely uninhabited permafrost plain of N Canada, stretching from about 59°N to the Arctic Ocean and from Hudson Bay to the Mackenzie Valley. Caribou and other animals live on the short grasses and other flowering plants.

● **Barrès, Maurice** ► (1862–1923) French writer and politician. In the trilogy *La Culte de moi* (1888–91) he described a searching period of self-analysis resulting in his entry into politics. His rigid nationalism was expounded in another trilogy, *Le Roman de l'énergie nationale* (1897–1902), and linked with Catholicism in *La Colline inspirée* (1913). His memoirs, *Mes cahiers* (14 vols, 1929–57), were published posthumously.

● **Barrie, Sir James (Matthew)** ► (1860–1937) British dramatist. The son of a Scots weaver, he came to London to write in 1885. After two successful novels about Scottish rural life he wrote mostly for the theatre. His best-known plays are *The Admirable Crichton* (1902), *Peter Pan* (1904), also a popular children's book, and *Dear Brutus* (1917).

● **barrier reef** ▷*See* reef.

● **Barrington, Jonah** ► (1940–　) British squash player. Responsible for attracting a much wider audience to the game, he won the Open Championship in 1966, 1967, and 1969–72; he turned professional in 1969.

● **barrister** ► A member of the legal profession in England and Wales or Northern Ireland who has been "called to the Bar." Barristers argue cases in court and also act as specialist advisers to clients through their solicitors. Until 1990 they had the exclusive right to argue cases in the higher courts (solicitors are now eligible to perform this role in some circumstances). In Scotland barristers are known as advocates, and abroad as advocates or attorneys. The right to confer the title of barrister-at-law is restricted to the ▷Inns of Court. In order to qualify, students must "keep" 12 terms by dining a set number of times per term at their Inn and must pass the examinations set by the Council of Legal Education. On the payment of fees, they are then called to the Bar. They must also spend one year as a pupil in the chambers of a practising barrister. A barrister is usually instructed by a ▷solicitor before conducting a case in court. Since 1989 barristers may appear in court without their instructing solicitors in certain cases. Other changes to cut litigation costs were introduced in 1990. A barrister cannot be sued for negligence in presenting a case and cannot sue a client for unpaid fees. ▷*See also* Queen's Counsel.

● **barrow** ▶ A prehistoric burial mound, also called a tumulus or cairn. From about 2000 BC earth barrows, concealing stone or timber passages and burial chambers, were built all over Europe for the interment of warrior chiefs. Long (i.e. rectangular or trapezoidal) barrows, such as at West Kennet (S England), were used for Neolithic multiple burials. Round barrows were more usual in Bronze Age cultures. Barrows continued in use in Iron Age Europe, for example the ▷Hallstatt barrow cemetery at Hohmichele (Germany) on the Upper Danube (6th century BC), and as late as the 7th century AD, for example the ▷Sutton Hoo ship burial.

● **Barrow-in-Furness** ▶ 54 07N 3 14W A town in NW England, on the S coast of Cumbria. Rich local iron ore (now exhausted) gave rise to iron and steel industries, and shipbuilding followed. The first British nuclear submarine was built here. Population (1991): 48 947.

● **Barry** ▶ 51 24N 3 18W A port in South Wales, in Vale of Glamorgan county borough on the Bristol Channel. It exports coal, steel products, and cement. Barry Island, to the SW, is a holiday resort. Population (1991): 49 887.

● **Barry, Sir Charles** ▶ (1795–1860) British architect. Barry worked in both classical and gothic styles. In 1836 he won the competition to rebuild the Houses of Parliament (*see* Palace of Westminster), which, assisted by ▷Pugin, he designed in the gothic manner. He also designed the Travellers' Club (1829–31) and Reform Club (1837) in London.

● **Barrymore, Lionel** ▶ (1878–1954) US actor. After studying art in Paris and achieving success as a stage actor he became known primarily as a film actor. He is remembered for his performances in the first series of *Dr Kildare* films. His sister **Ethel Barrymore** (1879–1959) acted with Sir Henry Irving in London, and later became a leading stage actress in the USA. A theatre in New York was named after her in 1928. Their brother **John Barrymore** (1882–1942) was also an actor. His greatest stage success was his performance of Hamlet in 1922. As a film star during his later career he was famous for such films as *Grand Hotel* (1932) and *Moby Dick* (1930). He was also renowned for his heavy drinking and stormy private life. His granddaughter **Drew Barrymore** (1975–) became a child star in *E.T.* (1982) and later found adult success in *Bad Girls* (1993) and *The Wedding Singer* (1998).

● **Bart, Jean** ▶ (1650–1702) French admiral, whose early successes against pirates earned him swift promotion under Louis XIV. He fought in the Dutch War of 1672–78 and in the War of the ▷Grand Alliance (1689–97), when he was captured by the English; escaping from Plymouth, he was received as a hero by Louis at Versailles.

● **Bart, Lionel** ▶ (1930–99) British composer and playwright, who wrote the music and lyrics for *Lock Up Your Daughters* (1954), *Fings Ain't Wot They Used T'Be* (1959), and *Oliver!* (1960), which had an enormous success and is frequently revived.

● **barter** ▶ A method of trading in which goods and services are paid for by other goods or services rather than by money. This is clearly a cumbersome system that does not have the benefit of enabling intermediaries to take part in trade (a benefit that is only possible if money is used as the medium of exchange). However, in international trade the modern version of barter, known as **countertrading**, is sometimes used. For example, a country rich in a particular commodity may pay for its armaments by providing the supplier with a specified quantity of this commodity. The armament supplier then has the task of selling the commodity.

● **Barth, Heinrich** ▶ (1821–65) German explorer and geographer. He travelled widely in the Mediterranean (1845–47) and in 1850 joined, as scientific observer, an expedition to West Africa sponsored by the British Government. Setting out from Tripoli he crossed the Sahara and, in spite of the death of his two companions, covered 19 200 km (12 000 mi). He recorded this expedition in *Travels and Discoveries in North and Central Africa* (5 vols, 1857–58).

● **Barth, John** ▶ (1930–) US novelist and academic. His novels, which combine philosophical seriousness with bawdy humour, include *The Sotweed Factor* (1960), *Giles Goat-Boy* (1966), *Chimera* (1974), *Sabbatical* (1982), *The Last Voyage of Somebody the Sailor* (1991), and *Once Upon a Time* (1994). He often emphasizes the artificiality of fiction by parodying literary conventions.

● **Barth, Karl** ▶ (1886–1968) Swiss Protestant theologian. As a pastor during World War I, he became disillusioned with modern liberal theology in the face of extreme suffering. In such influential works as *Epistle to the Romans* (1919) and the four-volume *Church Dogmatics* (1932–67) he returned to the principles of the Reformation and the teachings of the Bible, emphasizing God's sovereignty and man's sinfulness, which necessitates grace. He held professorships at several German universities (1921–35) and at Basle (1935–62).

● **Barthes, Roland** ▶ (1915–80) French literary critic and writer. Barthes's earlier works, such as *Writing Degree Zero* (1953) and *On Racine* (1963), made him a major figure in the structuralist movement (*see* structuralism) of the 1960s and 1970s. In *Mythologies* (1957) he pioneered a semiotic approach to popular culture that has proved widely influential. Later works include *The Pleasure of the Text* (1975). He died following a car crash.

● **Bartholdi, Frédéric August** ▶ (1834–1904) French sculptor, famous for his patriotic monuments. Best known are the Lion of Belfort, commemorating the gallant defence of Belfort during the Franco-Prussian War (1870–71), and the ▷Statue of Liberty.

● **Bartholomew, St** ▶ Christian Apostle. Although mentioned in lists of the Apostles, his name is never connected with any incident from the New Testament. He is sometimes identified with the Nathanael mentioned by John (1.45–51; 21.2). The historian Eusebius tells of his taking the Gospel to India. Feast day: 24 Aug.

● **Bartók, Béla** ▶ (1881–1945) Hungarian composer. Bartók studied and taught at the Budapest Academy of Music, where he and ▷Kodály undertook research into Hungarian folksong. In 1940 he went to live in the USA, where he died in poverty. His music blends elements of E European folk music with dissonant harmonies into an astringent and often percussive style. A virtuoso pianist, he composed three piano concertos, a set of progressive pieces for students, entitled *Mikrokosmos* (1926–37), and other piano works. His stage works include the opera *Duke Bluebeard's Castle* (1911) and the ballet *The Miraculous Mandarin* (1919). In his six string quartets and *Music for Strings, Percussion, and Celesta* (1936) he explored unusual sonorities. His most popular work is the *Concerto for Orchestra* (1943).

● **Bartolommeo, Fra** ▶ (Baccio della Porta; c. 1472–1517) Florentine Renaissance painter. After training under Cosimo Rosselli (1439–1507), he became a supporter of ▷Savonarola, whose death moved him to join the Dominican monastery of S Marco (1500) and abandon painting until 1504. His exclusively religious works were close to ▷Raphael and ▷Leonardo da Vinci in style; they include *St Mark* and the *Pietà* (both Palazzo Pitti, Florence).

● **Barton, Clara** ▶ (1821–1912) US schoolteacher, who founded the American Red Cross. During the American Civil War (1861–65) she helped obtain supplies for wounded soldiers. She later worked for the International Red Cross in the Franco-Prussian War (1870–71) and then established its American branch, serving as its first president (1881–1904).

● **Barton, Sir Edmund** ▶ (1849–1920) Australian statesman; Australia's first prime minister (1901–03). He was leader of the Federal Convention in 1897 that drafted the bill to unite the separate states of Australia. He resigned in 1903 to become a High Court judge.

● **Barton, Elizabeth** ▶ (c. 1506–34) English nun, known as the Maid of Kent. A servant girl, she was subject to trances and claimed to foretell the future. After she became a nun, her pronouncements criticized Henry VIII's intention to divorce Catherine of Aragon. Examined by Cranmer, she confessed that her trances were false and was executed.

● **Baruch, Bernard** ▶ (1870–1965) US economist and adviser to Presidents Wilson, F. D. Roosevelt, and Truman. He helped to coordinate US industries during World War I and to draft the economic items of the Treaty of Versailles. He served on the UN ▷Atomic Energy Commission.

● **baryon** ▶ A collective term for ▷nucleons and other elementary particles that have a proton or neutron in their decay products. All baryons have a ▷quantum number called the baryon number of +1 (or –1 for antiparticles), which is conserved in interactions. ▷*See* particle physics.

● **Baryshnikov, Mikhail (Nikolayevich)** ▶ (1948–) Soviet-born ballet dancer. A leading dancer with the Kirov Ballet (1967–74), he defected to the West in 1974, while on tour in Canada. He then danced with the American Ballet Theatre (ABT) (1974–78) and the New York City Ballet (1978–79) before becoming artistic director of the ABT (1980–90). In 1986 he appeared in the film *White Nights*.

● **barytes** ▷*See* barite.

● **baryton** ▶ A musical instrument of the ▷viol family popular in the 18th century. Held between the knees, it had six gut strings and a number of sympathetic wire strings, which could be plucked. Haydn, whose patron Prince Esterhazy was a keen player, wrote many pieces for it.

● **basal metabolic rate** ▷*See* metabolism.

● **basalt** ▶ A volcanic rock of basic composition, typically dark, heavy, and fine textured. It consists essentially of calcic plagioclase feldspar and pyroxene, with magnetite, apatite, and often olivine as accessory minerals. Three broad groups of basalt are recognized: alkali basalt, high-alumina basalt, and tholeiite. The basalts constituting the ocean floor, generated at midocean ridges, are tholeiites. Many volcanoes and huge lava plateaus consist of basalt, which constitutes over 90% of volcanic rocks.

● **bascule** ▷*See* bridge.

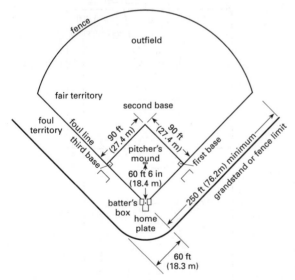

baseball ▶ The dimensions of the field.

● **baseball** ▶ A nine-a-side bat-and-ball game that evolved from ▷rounders, played mainly in the USA, Japan, and Latin America. The object for each team while batting is to score as many runs as possible and while fielding to prevent the other team from doing so; the team with the highest score wins. A team bats until three players are out; one turn at bat for both teams constitutes an inning, of which there are usually nine in a game. The pitcher, standing at the pitcher's mound, throws the ball to the batter, standing at home plate, who tries to strike it into fair territory and run. He scores a home run by making a complete circuit of the bases (first, second, third, and home). A player may be struck out (if he misses the ball or hits it into foul territory in each of three attempts), caught attempts), caught out, tagged out (if he or the base he is running towards is touched by a player with the ball), or put out by being hit by a batted ball while running.

● **Basel** ▷*See* Basle.

● **basenji** ▶ A breed of dog originating in central Africa. It is lightly built, has a wrinkled forehead, pricked ears, and tightly curled tail, and does not bark. The short coat is usually chestnut or black with white markings. Height: 40–43 cm.

● **base rate** ▷*See* interest.

● **bases** ▷*See* acids and bases.

● **Bashkir** ▶ A Turkic language and people of E central Russia. The language is related to Tatar and Kazakh. The Bashkirs, originally nomads herding horses and sheep, settled in their present territory under Mongol rule (13th–15th centuries). Russian domination after 1551 led to settled agriculture. Soviet collectivization obliterated the clan organization. Bashkirs are Muslims or Orthodox Christians.

● **Bashkir Republic** ▶ (Bashkiria *or* Bashkortostan) A constituent republic of Russia in the E central part. The ▷Bashkirs comprise some 22% of the population. The republic has large oil and natural-gas deposits, as well as coal, iron ore, and copper and has expanding chemical, coal, steel, and timber industries. Bashkiria was annexed by Russia in 1557. In 1919 it became the first autonomous Soviet republic and in 1992 became a constituent republic of Russia. Area: 143 600 sq km (55 430 sq mi). Population (1995 est): 4 008 000. Capital: Ufa.

● **Basic** ▶ (beginner's *all*-purpose symbolic *i*nstruction *c*ode) A computer language developed in the USA in the 1960s. Originally intended as an educational language, suitable for teaching programmers, it later became widely used on early personal computers. More recently it has been extended into **Visual Basic** and **Visual Basic for Applications** (VBA), which are used in developing interfaces and applications in Microsoft Windows.

● **Basic English** ▶ A simplified form of English using a vocabulary of 850 words. It was developed in the late 1920s by C. K. ▷Ogden as a simply learnt method of international communication and a rival to ▷Esperanto. The vocabulary has 600 nouns, 150 adjectives, and 100 operations, which include verbs. These building blocks are used to form complex ideas; for instance "prepare" would be expressed as "get ready," and such combinations can replace 4000 standard English verbs.

● **basic-oxygen process** ▶ (BOP) A modern method of steelmaking that originated as the Linnz-Donnewitz (L-D) process; molten pig iron and scrap are placed in a furnace similar to the ▷Bessemer converter, which it has largely replaced. High-pressure oxygen blown onto the metal through a water-cooled lance converts the charge to steel, the excess heat produced enabling up to 30% scrap to be incorporated.

● **Basidiomycota** ▶ (*or* Basidiomycetes) A large phylum of fungi (22 000–25 000 species) that includes many ▷mushrooms, the ▷bracket fungi, ▷puffballs, etc., as well as important microscopic forms, such as the parasitic ▷rust fungi and ▷smuts of crops. They reproduce by basidia, which are typically club-shaped and produce spores at the tips of stalklike projections.

● **Basie, Count** ▶ (William B.; 1904–84) US Black jazz pianist and "big band" leader. He was influenced by Harlem ragtime pianists, played in vaudeville shows, and formed his own band in 1935. His albums include *Atomic Mr Basie* and *Straight Ahead*.

● **basil** ▶ An annual herbaceous plant of the Indian genus *Ocimum*, cultivated as a pot herb. Sweet basil (*O. basilicum*), up to 30 cm high, has toothed leaves and small white or bluish flowers. The dried clove-scented leaves are used to flavour various dishes. Family: ▷Labiatae.

● **Basil (I) the Macedonian** ▶ (d. 886 AD) Byzantine emperor (876–86), who founded the Macedonian dynasty. Of humble origin, Basil became coemperor (867) with Michael III (reigned 842–68) but murdered him in 868. He strengthened Byzantine power in Asia Minor and in S Italy and revived Roman law in a legal text known as the Basilica.

● **Basil II Bulgaroctonus** ▶ (c. 958–1025 AD) Byzantine emperor (976–1025). He secured Byzantine conquests in Syria and conquered new territory in Georgia and Armenia. He was named Bulgaroctonus (slayer of the Bulgars) after defeating the Bulgarians at Ochrida

(1014): he blinded their entire army except for every 100th man, who was left with one eye with which to lead his comrades back; the Bulgarian khan died of shock.

● **Basildon ►** 51 34N 0 25E A town in SE England, in Essex, created as a new town in 1949 from several townships. Its industries include engineering (including automobile research), printing, and other light and service industries. Population (1991): 100 924.

● **basilica ► 1.** A Roman public meeting hall. In imperial times, many had a layout similar to the Basilica of Maxentius in Rome: rectangular ground plan, colonnaded aisles, entrance porch (narthex), and windows in the upper storey (clerestory). **2.** A Christian church based on a similar plan (e.g. S Giovanni in Laterano in Rome). The influence of the plan can still be seen in western church architecture.

● **Basilicata ►** A mountainous region in S Italy. A poor region, it produces wheat, olives, vines, potatoes, sheep, and goats. Area: 9987 sq km (3856 sq mi). Population (1996 est): 609 238. Capital: Potenza.

● **basilisk ► 1.** An arboreal lizard belonging to the tropical American genus *Basiliscus*. Up to 60 cm long, it has a narrow body, a long whiplike tail, and a flat lobe protruding from the back of its head. It has long hind legs with lobed toes fringed with scales, enabling it to run over the surface of water. Family: *Iguanidae*. **2.** A legendary snakelike serpent of ancient Greece and Rome whose glance was believed to be fatal to all living things except the weasel, and later the cock.

● **Basil the Great, St ►** (c. 330–79 AD) Bishop of Caesarea in Cappadocia. With St ▷Gregory of Nazianzus and St ▷Gregory of Nyssa (his brother), known as the Cappadocian Fathers, he was a leading defender of orthodox Christian philosophy against ▷Arianism in the 4th century. Educated in pagan and Christian culture, he adopted a monastic life and then lived as a hermit before becoming Bishop of Caesarea in 370. His rule formed the basis of monasticism in the Eastern Church. He is the traditional author of the liturgy of St Basil, still used on certain days in the Orthodox Church. He wrote many theological works. Feast day: 14 June.

● **Basingstoke ►** 51 16N 1 05W A town in S England, in Hampshire. Considerable industrial and residential development has been carried out in recent decades. It is the headquarters of the Civil Service Commission and the Automobile Association. Its manufactures include agricultural machinery, scientific instruments, and leather goods. It has also developed as a warehousing and distribution centre for southern England. Population (1991): 77 837.

● **Baskerville, John ►** (1706–75) British printer, who designed the typeface that bears his name. His first work, a Virgil, was printed in 1757 and, while printer to Cambridge University (1758–68), he produced a masterly edition of the Bible (1763). His work was distinguished by the use of original high-gloss paper and black ink.

● **basketball ►** A five-a-side court game invented in the USA (1891) by James Naismith (1861–1939). The object is to toss or put an inflated ball into the opponents' basket, a net mounted 3.05 m (10 ft) above the floor on a backboard. Players use only their hands, passing the ball or dribbling it by bouncing, and they may not run with it. A professional game has 4 12-minute quarters. Five substitutes are allowed to each side. The premier professional basketball league is the National Basketball Association in the USA. ▷*See also* Harlem Globetrotters.

● **basking shark ►** A large ▷shark belonging to the family *Cetorhinidae*. Up to 15 m long, they are grey-brown or blackish and inhabit cold and temperate regions of the Atlantic, Pacific, and Indian Oceans. Basking sharks usually occur in shoals near the surface and float or swim slowly, feeding on plankton.

● **Basle ►** (French name: Bâle; German name: Basel) 47 33N 7 36E The second largest city in Switzerland, on the River Rhine where the French, German, and Swiss borders meet. A Roman fort originally occupied the site. During the Reformation it became a major literary centre and the scholar Erasmus taught at the university (founded 1460). Its notable features include the medieval city gates and the cathedral. Basle is a major commercial and industrial centre, strategically positioned in the European railway system and the chief riverport in Switzerland. Industries include chemicals, pharma-

ceuticals, and engineering. The Bank for International Settlements was established here in 1929. Population (1996 est): 174 007.

● **Basle, Council of ►** A general council of the Roman Catholic Church summoned by Pope Martin V in 1431 to consider the heretical ▷Hussites and the nature of papal power. The council, having reaffirmed the principle that general councils are answerable only to God, grew increasingly antipapal and in 1437 Eugenius IV, Martin's successor, moved it to Ferrara. However, a minority of councillors remained at Basle, electing the antipope, Felix V, in 1439. He resigned in 1449 and the council was brought to an end.

● **Basque ►** A non-Indo-European language spoken by the Basque people of the W Pyrenean areas of Spain and France. Basque is a very ancient language, apparently unrelated to any other and called Euskara by the Basques themselves. It is still spoken by about 500 000 people. The Basques, predominantly farmers and seafarers, are descended from a people known to the Romans as the Vascones. Today there are about 750 000 Basques in Spain and 170 000 in France. They are strongly Roman Catholic and traditionally enjoyed a degree of regional autonomy, forming an independent government (1936–37) at the time of the Spanish Civil War. The **Basque Provinces** became an autonomous region of Spain in 1978. Nationalism remains a significant force and there is a strong Basque Separatist movement. From 1968 guerrilla tactics were adopted by the ETA (*Euskadi ta Azkatasuna*) and the French-based *Enbata* groups. ETA declared a "total and indefinite ceasefire" in 1998, leading to direct contacts with the Spanish government, but returned to violence in 2000.

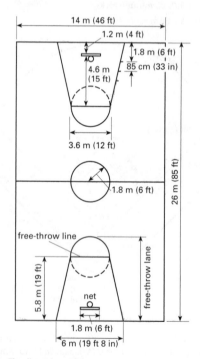

basketball ► The dimensions of the court.

● **Basra ►** 30 30N 47 50E A town in SE Iraq, on the Shatt (river) al-Arab. It is linked by rail and river steamer to Baghdad; the modern port (Al Ma'qil) was built by the British during World War I. Population (latest est): 406 296.

● **bas-relief** ▷*See* relief sculpture.

● **bass ►** (fish) One of several perchlike ▷bony fish of the order *Perciformes*, often valued as food and game fish. The majority belong to the family *Serranidae* (*see* sea bass), which includes the common European bass (*Dicentrarchus labrax*). This can grow up to 1 m long and has a grey or blue back with a white or yellowish belly and silvery flanks. North American freshwater bass belong to the family *Centrarchidae*.

● **bass** ▶ (music) **1.** The deepest adult male singing voice. Range: E below the bass stave to E two octaves above. **2.** The lowest voice or instrumental part of a piece of music.

● **Bassano, Jacopo** ▶ (Jacopo *or* Giacomo da Ponte; c. 1517–92) Italian painter of the Venetian school, born in Bassano, the son of a painter. In Venice he was influenced by Titian before adopting the elongated figure style of ▷Parmigianino. He was one of the earliest painters of rustic life, in both secular, e.g. *Pastoral* (Lugano), and religious scenes, e.g. *Adoration of the Kings* (National Gallery, Edinburgh).

● **Bassein** ▶ 16 46N 94 45E A port in S Myanmar (Burma) on the River Bassein, a distributary of the Irrawaddy delta. Situated at the terminus of a railway to Rangoon, it is the country's second port exporting chiefly rice, coal, and salt. Population (1983): 144 092.

● **Basseterre** ▶ 17 18N 62 43W A town on the island of St Kitts, capital of St Kitts-Nevis. Founded in 1627, it is the island's only port. Population (1994 est): 12 605.

● **basset horn** ▶ A woodwind instrument, the tenor member of the ▷clarinet family. It has a rich velvety tone but lacks the brilliance of the upper range of the A or B flat clarinet.

● **basset hound** ▶ A breed of ▯dog originating in France. It has a long body with very short legs and a narrow face with drooping ears and a mournful expression. The short smooth coat ranges from black to light brown in colour with white patches. Basset hounds have a keen sense of smell and were formerly popular hunting dogs. Height: 33–38 cm.

● **bassoon** ▶ A musical instrument of the woodwind family. Its conically bored tube is about 2.5 m (8 ft) long and is bent back on itself. It has a metal crook into which a double reed is inserted. Its wide compass (three and a half octaves above B flat below the bass stave) allows it a melodic as well as a bass role.

● **Bass Rock** ▶ 56 05N 2 38W A Scottish islet at the mouth of the Firth of Forth. It consists of a circular volcanic plug 1.6 km (1 mi) in circumference and is noted for its colonies of seabirds.

● **Bass Strait** ▶ A channel separating the mainland of Australia from Tasmania. It has valuable oil and natural-gas deposits. Length: 290 km (180 mi). Maximum width: 240 km (150 mi).

● **basswood** ▶ A ▷lime tree, *Tilia americana*, also called American lime or linden, sometimes exceeding 25 m in height. It yields commercially important timber that is especially prized for carving, and a tough fibre derived from the bark is of local importance.

● **bast fibres** ▶ Fibres, such as ▷flax, ▷hemp, and ▷jute, that are obtained from the stems of certain plants. The fibres are freed from the stalk by retting (soaking) or mechanical peeling and are used for textiles, sacking, twines, and ropes.

● **Bastia** ▶ 42 41N 9 26E A port in Corsica, on the NE coast. Founded by the Genoese in the 14th century, it was the former capital of Corsica and is the island's largest city. Fishing and the manufacture of tobacco and wine are the principal economic activities. Population (1990): 45 081.

● **Bastille** ▶ A fortress in Paris, which was a state prison in the 17th and 18th centuries and a symbol of the corrupt and despotic Bourbon monarchy. It was built in about 1370 to protect the wall around Paris against English attack and became a state prison under Cardinal de ▷Richelieu. The storming of the Bastille on 14 July, 1789, is regarded as the beginning of the ▷French Revolution.

● **Basutoland** ▷*See* Lesotho, Kingdom of.

● **bat** ▶ A flying mammal belonging to the order *Chiroptera* (981 species), distributed in most temperate and tropical regions. There are two suborders: the ▷fruit bats (*Megachiroptera*; 150 species) and the insect-eating bats (*Microchiroptera*; 831 species). Bats may also feed on pollen, nectar, blood, and small animals. The wings are extensions of skin that are supported between the forelimb, with its very long fingers, the hind limbs, and the tail. Insectivorous bats use ▷echolocation for navigation and catching prey on the wing whereas

fruit bats have large eyes adapted for night vision. Bats roost in caves and buildings during daytime.

● **Bataan** ▶ A mountainous forested peninsula in the Philippines, in W Luzon W of Manila Bay. In a famous action during World War II, US-Filipino forces resisted the Japanese invasion for almost three months here (1942); after their capture, thousands died on a forced Death March. Length: about 48 km (30 mi).

● **Batavia** ▷*See* Jakarta.

● **bateleur** ▶ An African snake ▷eagle, *Terathopius ecaudatus*, having very long wings and a short tail. It is highly manoeuvrable and flies vast distances, preying on snakes, other reptiles, mammals, and carrion, which it seizes with its short rough powerful toes.

● **Bates, H(erbert) E(rnest)** ▶ (1905–74) British writer. After working as a solicitor's clerk and provincial journalist he began to write novels about English rural life. His service in the Royal Air Force in World War II yielded many short stories—as "Flying Officer X"—and three novels under his own name, of which the best known is *Fair Stood the Wind for France* (1944). In *The Darling Buds of May* (1958) he created the famous Larkin family.

● **Bates, Henry Walter** ▶ (1825–92) British naturalist and explorer, who demonstrated the phenomenon of ▷mimicry in animals. In the Amazon valley he observed that many animals resembled their natural backgrounds and that certain species of butterfly mimicked the coloration of others, distasteful to predators. This latter phenomenon is now called Batesian mimicry.

● **Bateson, William** ▶ (1861–1926) British biologist, whose experiments on inheritance helped found the science of genetics, a term that he first proposed. Bateson investigated the way in which certain traits, such as comb shape in fowl, are transmitted from one generation to the next. His results (1905–08) corroborated the findings of Gregor ▷Mendel published in 1865. He also found that certain characteristics were inherited together (a phenomenon now known as linkage, due to the occurrence of the controlling genes on the same chromosome), but he refused to accept the chromosome theory proposed by T. H. ▷Morgan to account for this.

● **batfish** ▶ A carnivorous fish, belonging to a family (*Ogcocephalidae*; about 60 species) of ▷anglerfish, found in tropical and temperate seas. It has a slender lumpy-skinned body up to 36 cm long and a broad flat head with an elongated upturned snout. Using thickened limblike pectoral and pelvic fins, it crawls on the bottom searching for prey.

Bastille ▶ A contemporary illustration of the storming of the fortress.

● **Bath** ▶ 51 23N 2 22W A city in SW England, in Bath and North East Somerset unitary authority, Somerset, on the River Avon. A spa town of great architectural interest, it was an early Roman centre known as Aquae Sulis because of its hot natural springs, at a temperature of around 49°C (120°F). The Roman baths have survived and are considered the best Roman remains in the UK. Bath became fashionable as a spa town in the 18th century when many of the finest buildings were built, including the Royal Crescent and the Assembly Rooms. Restoration of the spa is due for completion in 2001. Bath Abbey, mainly 16th-century, lies in the town centre. Bath University dates from 1966. Apart from tourism, economic activities now include public and defence administration, education, and printing and publishing. Population (1991): 85 202. □Georgian style.

● **Bath, Order of the** ► A British order of knighthood, formed by George I in 1725 as a successor to the Knights of the Bath, traditionally founded by Henry IV in 1399. It comprises the sovereign and three classes of knights companions: knights and dames grand cross (GCB), knights and dames commanders (KCB), and companions (CB). Women have been admitted since 1971. Its name is derived from the bathing ceremony that formed the principal rite of admission to the original order.

● **Bath and North East Somerset** ► A unitary authority in SW England, in Somerset; it was formerly (1974–96) part of the county of Avon. Area: 351 sq km (136 sq mi). Population (1996): 158 692.

● **batholith** ► A large mass of intrusive igneous rock of unknown depth and often occupying many thousands of square kilometres. They are composed mainly of granite and occur in association with mountain belts. They are often surrounded by a zone of mineralized rocks (metamorphic aureole).

● **Bathsheba** ► In the Old Testament, the wife of King David and mother of King Solomon. Originally the wife of Uriah the Hittite, Bathsheba committed adultery with David, who got rid of Uriah by sending him to his death "in the forefront of the hottest battle" (2 Samuel. 11–12). David then married her and, having repented after being confronted with God's displeasure at his duplicity, became the father of the future King Solomon.

● **Bathurst** ► 33 27S 149 35E A city in Australia, in E central New South Wales, on the Macquarie River. Founded in 1815, it is Australia's oldest inland city. Population (1989 est): 26 500.

● **Bathurst** ▷See Banjul.

● **bathyscaphe** ▷See Piccard.

● **batik** ► Cloth, traditionally cotton, dyed by a special method. An ancient Indonesian craft, developed especially in Java, batik work involves the application of melted wax, later removed, to protect parts of the material from the dye; repeating the process using different wax patterns and several dyeings produces intricate multicoloured geometric patterns, symbolic motifs, or stylized pictures of birds, animals, or flowers. Some designs have been passed on in families for a thousand years.

● **Batista y Zaldívar, Fulgencio** ► (1901–73) Cuban statesman, who was president from 1940 to 1944 and, after returning to power in 1952 by means of a military coup, from 1954 to 1958. His authoritarian government generated opposition, notably from Castro's guerrilla movement, by which Batista was ousted.

● **Batley** ► 53 44N 1 37W A town in N England, in Kirklees unitary authority, West Yorkshire. It has long been associated with wool textiles; shoddy (woollen material made from reclaimed fibres) was invented here. Population (1991): 48 030.

● **Baton Rouge** ► 30 30N 91 10W A city in the USA, the capital of Louisiana situated on the Mississippi River at the head of oceangoing navigation. It is a major deepwater port with oil and sugar refineries. Its state institutions include the Louisiana State University (1860). Population (1996 est): 215 882.

● **Battambang** ► (or Batdambang) 12 55N 102 55E A city in W Cambodia, the second largest in the country, on the Sangke river. An ancient cultural and trading centre, it has 10th-century Khmer remains and several notable Buddhist temples. During the 18th century (and again from 1941 to 1946) it was under Thai rule. The main industries are textiles and the processing of rice and other foods. Population (latest est): 551 860.

● **Battani, al-** ► (Latin name: Albatenius; c. 858–929) Islamic astronomer, born in Haran (Turkey) and noted for his book on stellar motions. Using trigonometric methods, he improved the accuracy of many astronomical measurements, including the length of the year, the precession of the equinoxes, and the inclination of the ecliptic.

● **Batten, Jean** ► (1909–82) New Zealand aviator. In 1935 she became the first woman to fly solo from Australia to Britain. She later established records for the fastest flights between these countries.

● **Battenberg** ▷See Mountbatten, Louis, 1st Earl Mountbatten of Burma.

● **battered baby syndrome** ► Injuries inflicted on babies or young children by their parents. Battering usually occurs in the first six months of life and commonly takes the form of facial bruises, cigarette burns, head injuries (often with brain damage), and fractured bones. The parents are often emotionally disturbed or have themselves suffered from physical abuse in infancy or early childhood. Two-thirds of battered children suffer from further injury if discharged from hospital without the support of a social worker and surveillance of family doctor and health visitor; a court order is often necessary to safeguard a child from further abuse.

● **Battersea** ► A district in the Greater London borough of Wandsworth, on the River Thames. It is noted for its power station, built in 1937 by Sir Giles Scott (now disused and being redeveloped), its Dogs' Home (1860), and its 198-acre park, which during the 1951 ▷Festival of Britain became the Festival Gardens.

● **battery** ► **1.** A number of ▷electric cells joined together in parallel. The common dry battery consists of one or more ▷Leclanché cells. The alkaline dry battery has a negative electrode of zinc, a positive electrode of manganese dioxide, and an electrolyte of potassium hydroxide. A mercury dry cell is the same except that the negative electrode is mercury(II) oxide mixed with graphite. ▷See also accumulator. **2.** See livestock farming.

● **Battle** ► 50 55N 0 29E A town in S England, in East Sussex. It was the scene of the Battle of Hastings (1066) in which Harold II was defeated by William the Conqueror, who built Battle Abbey to commemorate his victory. Population (1991): 5234.

● **battleship** ► A heavily armoured naval vessel designed to combine large size, manoeuvrability, and extensive cruising range with the most powerful armament. Larger than a ▷cruiser and smaller than an ▷aircraft carrier, the battleship was the flagship of a fleet. No new battleships have been built since World War II.

● **Batumi** ► 41 37N 41 36E A port in Georgia, on the Black Sea. It has an oil refinery, shipping oil piped from Baku, light industries, and tea plantations on the city's outskirts. Population (1994 est): 137 100.

● **baud** ► A unit used to measure the speed of transmission of data in computing, usually taken as 1 bit per second. It is named after J. M. E. Baud (1845–1903), a French engineer.

● **Baudelaire, Charles** ► (1821–67) French poet. He inherited his father's fortune in 1842 and lived extravagantly until what was left of the capital was placed in trust by his family (1844). Forced to earn a living, he began to publish art criticism and wrote the autobiographical novel La Fanfarlo (1847). In 1852 he discovered Edgar Allan ▷Poe, publishing translations of his works (1856–65). His only volume of poetry, Les Fleurs du mal (1857, revised 1861), contained erotic poems, which led to his being convicted for obscenity. He became increasingly disillusioned; while in Belgium in 1866 he became paralysed as a result of venereal disease and died in Paris soon after.

● **Baudot code** ▷See character set.

● **Baudouin I** ► (1930–93) King of the Belgians (1951–93), succeeding his father Leopold III. He was interned by the Nazis in World War II. In 1960 he married Fabiola de Mora y Aragón (1928–). A devout Catholic, he abdicated for two days in 1990 to avoid signing an act legalizing abortion.

● **Bauhaus** ► A German school of design. One of the most important influences on 20th-century art, the Bauhaus enjoyed a short life. Founded in 1919 at Weimar it was closed by the Nazis in 1933. From 1925 to 1932 it was housed at Dessau in a building designed by ▷Gropius (its director until 1928), itself a work of great influence.

Connected with some of the best designers of the age, the Bauhaus sought to produce a practical synthesis of all the arts, from furniture design to architecture, and to develop a coherent style appropriate for the industrial 20th century. The functional style the Bauhaus helped to evolve still has considerable influence in the arts, from the international style of architecture to tubular steel furniture. ▷*See also* Kandinsky, Wassily; Klee, Paul; Mies van der Rohe, Ludwig; Moholy-Nagy, László.

● **Baum, L(yman) Frank** ▶ (1856–1919) US novelist. After working as a journalist, he created in *The Wonderful Wizard of Oz* (1900) a classic children's fantasy land with 13 sequels; in all, he wrote about 60 books, mostly for children.

● **Baumgarten, Alexander Gottlieb** ▶ (1714–62) German philosopher, a follower of Christian Wolff (1679–1754) and ▷Leibniz. In 1740, he became professor of philosophy at Frankfurt-am-Oder. He invented the term ▷aesthetics and his *Aesthetica* (1750) is a pioneering work on that subject.

● **Baur, Ferdinand Christian** ▶ (1792–1860) German Protestant theologian. Baur's early work was concerned with the gnostic background of Christianity. He was much influenced by ▷Hegel. In 1826, he became professor of theology at Tübingen University, and his later work on St Paul marked the beginnings of radical biblical criticism.

● **Bausch, Pina** ▶ (Philippine B.; 1940–　) German dancer, choreographer, and ballet director. After training and working as a dancer in the USA, she returned to Germany and established the Wuppertal Dance Theatre in 1973. Her innovative and acclaimed works for the company, many of which incorporate elements of theatre as well as dance, include *Bluebeard* (1977), *Nelken* (1982), and *Nur Du* (1996).

● **Bautzen** ▶ 51 14N 14 23E A town in E Germany, on the River Spree. A battle was fought here in 1813, in which Napoleon's army defeated an allied army of Russians and Prussians. Its industries include the manufacture of vehicles and machinery. Population (1989 est): 52 390.

● **bauxite** ▶ The chief ore of aluminium. It is a residual deposit formed by the weathering of aluminium-rich rocks (mainly syenites) under tropical conditions and consists mainly of hydrated aluminium oxide. The main producers are Australia, Jamaica, Suriname, Guyana, Guinea, and Sierra Leone.

● **Bavaria** ▶ (German name: Bayern) The largest *Land* of Germany, bordering on Austria and the Czech Republic. A third is forested, providing valuable timber resources. It is mainly agricultural, the chief crops being rye, wheat, and barley; hops are grown around Munich. It is a popular tourist area.
History: an independent duchy ruled by the Wittelsbachs from 1180, it was proclaimed a kingdom in 1805. The last Wittelsbach king was deposed in 1918 and Bavaria became a socialist republic. From the ensuing political unrest Hitler drew much of his early support. Bavaria became a state of the Federal Republic of Germany in 1948. Area: 70 547 sq km (29 232 sq mi). Population (1995 est): 11 921 900. Capital: Munich.

● **Bax, Sir Arnold Edward Trevor** ▶ (1883–1953) British composer. Of his large output his tone poems, such as *Tintagel* (1917) and *The Garden of Fand* (1916), and his seven symphonies remain the most popular. Knighted in 1937, he was Master of the King's Music from 1941.

● **Baxter, Richard** ▶ (1615–91) English Puritan minister and author. A noted clergyman during the Commonwealth period, after the Restoration he was offered a bishopric, but was forced to leave the Church because of the Act of Uniformity (1662). In about 1673 he took out a licence as a Nonconformist minister. His best-remembered work, *The Saints' Everlasting Rest* (1650), is devotional.

● **bay** ▶ A Mediterranean evergreen tree, *Laurus nobilis*, also known as sweet bay and bay laurel, widely grown as an ornamental shrub or pot plant. It can reach a height of 20 m, has aromatic dark-green lance-shaped leaves, small yellowish flowers, and blackish berries. The leaves are used to season food. Family: *Lauraceae* (*see* laurel).

● **Bayar, Mahmud Celal** ▶ (1884–1986) Turkish statesman; president (1950–60). He became involved in politics after an early career in banking. As minister of the economy (1932–37) under ▷Atatürk, he

encouraged state direction of the economy (etatism), a policy he abandoned as president. He was a founder (1946) of the Democratic Party. In 1960 an army coup deposed him and he was sentenced to death but later reprieved.

● **Bayard, Pierre Terrail, Seigneur de** ▶ (c. 1473–1524) French soldier, known as "le bon chevalier sans peur et sans reproche" (the good knight without fear and without reproach). He served in the Italian wars of Charles VIII, Louis XII, and Francis I, gaining particular distinction at Fornovo (1495) and Marignano (1515). Pope Julius II sought unsuccessfully to hire him.

● **Baybars I** ▶ (1223–77) Sultan of Egypt and Syria (1260–77) of the ▷Mameluke dynasty. Brought to Egypt as a slave, he rose in the army and in 1260 he was prominent at the decisive victory over the Mongols at Ayn Jalut. Between 1263 and 1271 he severely reduced the power of the Crusaders in Syria.

● **bayberry** ▶ A deciduous shrub, *Myrica pensilvanica*, rarely exceeding 3 m in height, bearing flowers in catkins and oblong 10-cm-long leaves. It is native to E North America and sometimes cultivated in other temperate areas. Family: *Myricaceae*. The name is also given to the purple-blue berries of the ▷bay tree.

● **Bayeux** ▶ 49 16N 0 42W A town in NW France, in the Calvados department on the River Aure. The ▷Bayeux tapestry originally hung in the nave of the fine 13th-century cathedral but is now exhibited in a former seminary nearby. It was the first French town to be liberated by the Allies in World War II (7 June, 1944). Industries include dairy foods and plastics. Population (1990): 14 704.

● **Bayeux tapestry** ▶ An 11th-century embroidered linen strip, 69 m (231 ft) long, which depicts the Norman conquest of England (1066). The tapestry, which starts with King Harold's visit to Normandy and ends with the battle of Hastings, is of great historical value. It was reputedly commissioned for Bayeux cathedral by its bishop, Odo, the half-brother of William the Conqueror, whose wife Matilda is traditionally credited with its making (it is sometimes called **Queen Matilda's tapestry**), although some experts believe it was made in England in a Saxon monastery. It is now exhibited in a seminary near Bayeux cathedral.

● **Bayezid II** ▶ (c. 1447–1512) Ottoman Sultan of Turkey (1481–1512). During his reign Turkish dominions in the Balkans and the Crimea were extended; war with Venice (1499–1503) brought territory in Greece and the Adriatic. Warfare with Egypt and the Safavid dynasty of Persia occupied the last decade of his reign. In 1512 Bayezid abdicated, dying soon afterwards.

● **Bay Islands** ▶ (Spanish name: Islas de la Bahía) A group of islands in Honduras, lying about 56 km (35 mi) off its N coast in the Caribbean Sea. The group consists of the three main islands of Roatán, Guanaja, and Utila, and various islets. Sighted by Columbus in 1502, they were settled by English pirates in the 17th century and annexed by Britain in 1852 before being ceded to Honduras in 1859. The inhabitants are mainly English-speaking Protestants of mixed British and Carib Indian descent, who live by farming and fishing. Chief town: Roatán. Area: 260 sq km (100 sq mi). Population (1991 est): 24 000

● **Bayle, Pierre** ▶ (1647–1706) French Protestant critic and controversialist. He taught philosophy at Sedan from 1675 until forced into exile in Rotterdam. There he was professor of philosophy from 1781 to 1793, when his contentious religious tracts and determined opponents lost him the chair. Undeterred, he began publication of his masterwork, the *Dictionnaire historique et critique* (1796), a model of scholarship, style, and philosophical scepticism, which was both influential and successful.

● **Baylis, Lilian** ▶ (1874–1937) British theatre manager. She founded the first ▷Old Vic company at the Victoria Theatre, a music hall, in 1912, and supervised the production of all of Shakespeare's plays between 1914 and 1923. In 1931 she founded the Sadler's Wells company for opera and ballet.

● **Bayliss, Sir William Maddock** ▶ (1860–1924) British physiologist, who, with Ernest Starling (1866–1927), made the first discovery of a hormone. Working with dogs they showed how food stimulated the secretion of a messenger chemical by the duodenum. This chemical—secretin, which they called a hormone—circulated in the blood to activate the secretion of digestive juice by the pancreas.

● **Bay of Pigs** ► (Spanish name: Bahia de los Cochinos) A bay on the SW coast of Cuba where on 17 April, 1961, about 1200 Cuban exiles attempted to invade the country. Hoping to overthrow the Marxist regime of Fidel ▷Castro, and supported by the US ▷Central Intelligence Agency, the invasion was unsuccessful largely because it lacked sufficient US military backing.

● **bayonet** ► A blade that may be attached to the muzzle of a firearm. The bayonet, which is thought to have originated in the early 17th century in Bayonne (France), replaced the pike. Early bayonets were inserted into the gun, which could not then be fired, a drawback resolved in the 1680s by the development of the socket bayonet. This was attached to a tube that was placed over the muzzle. Bayonets were used in both World Wars.

● **Bayonne** ► 43 30N 1 28W A town in SW France, in the Pyrénées-Atlantiques department at the confluence of the Rivers Adour and Nive. The chief port of the Basque country, it was formerly famous for its swords and knives; the bayonet was developed here in the early 17th century. Its varied industries include aircraft, distilling, and leather. Population (1990): 41 846.

● **Bay Psalm Book** ► Probably the first book printed in America, which contained the Psalms in metrical form. It was published in 1640 in Cambridge, Massachusetts, by a group of Congregationalists.

● **Bayreuth** ► 49 27N 11 35E A town in S Germany, in Bavaria. It is famous as the home and burial place of Richard Wagner, who designed its Festival Theatre (1872–76), where his operas are performed annually. Its industries include the manufacture of textiles and machinery. Population (1991): 72 780.

● **Bayswater** ► A district in the Greater London borough of the City of Westminster. Named after Bayard's Watering, a natural spring in one of the district's main streets, Queensway, it was a fashionable residential area in Victorian times. Many of the large houses and elegant terraces are now hotels.

● **Bazaine, Achille François** ► (1811–88) French marshal, who served in the Crimean War (1854–56), in Italy against Austria (1859), and in Mexico (1863). He was commander in chief in the Franco-Prussian War (1870–71), when he surrendered after being besieged at Metz. For this he was condemned for treason but escaped to exile in Spain.

● **bazooka** ► Originally a 2.36 inch (60 mm) antitank rocket launcher fired from the shoulder and used by the US army in World War II. It consisted of a 54 inch (1.4 m) breech-loaded tube, open at both ends, firing a 3½ lb (1.6 kg) rocket to an effective range of about 135 m (150 yd). The term was later applied to all similar weapons. The name came from a tubular wind instrument made famous by Bob Burns, an American comedian.

● **BBC** ▷See British Broadcasting Corporation.

● **BCG** ► (bacille Calmette Guérin) A vaccine consisting of a weakened form of the tuberculosis bacterium, which is injected to give partial protection against tuberculosis. It acts by stimulating the body's defence system without causing the disease. A successful vaccination produces a lump at the injection site.

● **BCS theory** ▷See Bardeen, John; superconductivity.

● **Beachy Head** ► 50 44N 0 16E A headland in SE England, on the East Sussex coast. It consists of vertical chalk cliffs 171 m (570 ft) high and forms the E end of the South Downs. In January 1999 some 120 000 cu m (4.24 million cu ft) of the cliff collapsed into the English Channel—the biggest alteration to Britain's coastline in living memory.

● **Beaconsfield** ► 51 37N 0 39W A town in SE England, in Buckinghamshire. It has associations with the statesmen Edmund ▷Burke and Benjamin ▷Disraeli (Earl of Beaconsfield). Population (1991): 12 292.

● **Beaconsfield, Benjamin Disraeli, 1st Earl of.** ▷See Disraeli, Benjamin, 1st Earl of Beaconsfield.

● **Beadle, George Wells** ► (1903–89) US geneticist, who provided fundamental evidence for the nature of gene function. Working with moulds, he proposed the theory that each gene was responsible for the production of a single enzyme, which itself controlled a particular chemical reaction in the cell. He shared a Nobel Prize (1958) with ▷Tatum and ▷Lederberg.

● **beagle** ► A long-established breed of dog originating in the UK. It has a deep chest, strong shoulders, and drooping ears. The short smooth coat is usually dark brown to light tan with white patches. With their keen sense of smell, beagles have long been used as hunting hounds; more recently, they have become popular household pets. Height: 33–40 cm.

● **Beagle Channel** ► A strait south of Tierra del Fuego, at the southernmost tip of South America. About 240 km (150 mi) long, it was named after the ship in which Charles Darwin explored the area (1831–36). In recent years it has become the focus of a territorial dispute between Argentina and Chile.

● **beaked whale** ► A toothed ▷whale of the family Ziphiidae (18 species), found in oceans worldwide. Beaked whales are characterized by their snout, which is drawn into a beak continuous with the forehead (unlike the beak of dolphins), and their tail fluke, which lacks a central notch. Ranging in length from 4.5 to 13 m, they feed on fish and cephalopod molluscs, obtained in deep dives during which they may remain submerged for 10–20 minutes. The family includes the bottle-nosed whales (Hyperoodon ampullata and H. planifrons), up to 9 m long.

● **Beaker people** ► An early-Bronze Age people who inhabited Europe c. 4000 BC. Originating in Spain, they spread through Europe in search of usable metals. Sites associated with them have produced distinctive decorated earthenware beakers. They were also responsible for the first work at Stonehenge.

● **Beale, Dorothea** ► (1831–1906) British schoolmistress. A pioneer of women's education and suffrage, Dorothea Beale became principal of Cheltenham Ladies' College in 1858. Her introduction of a curriculum similar to that followed in the male public schools revolutionized women's education.

● **beam engine** ▷See ▯steam engine.

● **bean** ► The seed or fruit of certain herbs, shrubs, or trees of the family ▷Leguminosae. They are widely cultivated and not only form a good source of protein for man and livestock but also provide raw material for a wide range of derived products. ▷See broad bean; carob; French bean; haricot bean; Lima bean; mung bean; runner bean; soya; tonka bean.

● **bear** ► A large heavy mammal belonging to a family (Ursidae; 8 species) found in Europe, Asia, and America. Bears have a shaggy coat and a short tail and walk flat on the soles of their broad feet. They can stand erect and make good use of their powerful limbs and long curved claws. Eyesight and hearing are poor but bears have an excellent sense of smell; they can exist on any food but most of them are vegetarian. Newborn bears are very small (about the size of rats), blind, and toothless. Order: ▷Carnivora. ▷See black bear; brown bear; panda; polar bear; sloth bear; spectacled bear; sun bear.

● **bearbaiting** ► A ▷blood sport formerly popular in Britain and Europe. A bear, sometimes blinded, was chained to a stake in a bear pit or bear garden and dogs were let loose to attack it, many being killed. As dogs were expendable but bears were valuable the bears were not generally allowed to die. **Bullbaiting** used bulls in a similar way. Both bearbaiting and bullbaiting were made illegal in the UK in 1835.

● **bearberry** ► A prostrate evergreen shrub of the genus Arctostaphylos, native to North and Central America, especially A. uva-ursi, which is also widespread in Europe and Asia. The woody stems may reach 2 m in length, sending out roots at intervals. The flowers are white to pink and bell-shaped, and the berries are red. Family: Ericaceae.

● **bearded lizard** ► An Australian lizard, Amphibolurus barbatus, occurring in scrub and desert regions. Up to 60 cm long, it has a long head, a whiplike tail, a grey to yellowish spiny skin, and a bright-yellow mouth; a throat pouch swells to resemble a spiny beard during aggressive or courtship displays. It feeds on insects, small lizards, and snakes.

● **bearded tit** ▷See reedling.

● **bearded vulture** ▷See lammergeier.

● **Beardsley, Aubrey Vincent** ▶ (1872–98) British illustrator. Virtually self-taught, he was encouraged by ▷Burne-Jones. As illustrator of the periodicals *The Yellow Book* and *The Savoy* and of several books, including Wilde's *Salome* and Pope's *Rape of the Lock*, he achieved notoriety with his grotesque and erotic imagery. His designs are composed of curved lines, characteristic of ▷Art Nouveau, which contrast with dense areas of black ink. He died of tuberculosis in France.

● **beardworms** ▷See Pogonophora.

deep groove   taper roller
ball bearing   bearing

bearings ▶ Common examples of ball bearings and roller bearings.

● **bearings** ▶ A support for a rotating shaft or the interface between a crank and a reciprocating part. Bearings are designed to reduce friction and wear to a minimum and to dissipate the heat generated. In plain bearings, lubrication is achieved by maintaining a film of lubricant between the faces either as a result of their relative motion or by pumping it through channels into the interface. Some small bearings, made of powdered copper or bronze impregnated with oil or graphite, are self-lubricating, while some low-friction plastics (e.g. polytetrafluoroethylene) do not require lubrication. Bearing surfaces or shells are usually made of softer materials (e.g. brass or white metal) than is the shaft. In **ball and roller bearings** friction between the faces is reduced by replacing the sliding action of a plain bearing by a rolling action. The balls or rollers are usually made from chromium (0.5–2.0%) steels.

● **bear market** ▶ A stock and share market or commodity market in which there is a continuing downward movement in prices. An initial fall in prices, caused by adverse economic factors, is often magnified by consequent selling by investors. *Compare* bull market.

● **Beas, River** ▶ A river in NW India, flowing mainly W from the Himalayas to the River Sutlej. It forms part of the Punjab irrigation scheme. Length: 470 km (290 mi).

● **beatification** ▷See canonization.

● **beating the bounds** ▶ A traditional ceremony that takes place in several English towns and villages on Ascension Day. Primarily a religious event, it evolved during the reign of Elizabeth I, and is derived from the earlier ceremonies of Rogationtide. A priest leads those present round the ▷parish boundaries offering prayers for the harvest while young boys beat the boundary stones with sticks. An equivalent Scottish ceremony is called riding the marches.

● **Beatitudes** ▶ In the New Testatment, the eight blessings with which ▷Jesus opened the Sermon on the Mount (Matthew 5.3–12). They describe such Christian virtues as meekness, mercy, and purity of heart (e.g. "Blessed are the meek: for they shall inherit the earth."). The word derives from the Latin of the ▷Vulgate, *beati sunt* (blessed are).

● **Beatles** ▶ A British rock group that achieved worldwide popularity during the 1960s. The Beatles appeared at the Cavern Club in Liverpool in 1962 and recorded "Love Me Do" and "She Loves You," which became a British number one in 1963. By this time the group consisted of George ▷Harrison, John ▷Lennon, Paul ▷McCartney, and Ringo ▷Starr; they toured the USA successfully, made two films, and were awarded MBEs in 1965. The most original of the group's albums were *Sergeant Pepper's Lonely Hearts Club Band* (1967), reflecting their experience of drugs and mysticism, and the double *White Album* (1968). In 1970 they disbanded. Several new Beatles' recordings featuring the voice of Lennon (shot dead in 1980) and backing by the surviving members appeared in 1995–96.

● **Beat movement** ▶ US movement of the 1950s that opposed conventional society by seeking liberation through art, drugs, sex, and any other "consciousness-expanding" means. The movement centred on the artistic communities of Greenwich Village in New York and of San Francisco and Los Angeles. Among its prominent writers were William ▷Burroughs, Allen ▷Ginsberg, and Jack ▷Kerouac, and later the poets Lawrence ▷Ferlinghetti and Gregory Corso (1930–).

● **Beaton, Sir Cecil (Walter Hardy)** ▶ (1904–80) British photographer. From the 1920s onwards he became famous for his society portraits, many taken for *Vanity Fair* and *Vogue* magazines. After World War II, in which he produced many photographs used for propaganda, he turned also to set and costume designs for ballet, theatre, and films, notably *My Fair Lady*. His photographic books include *The Book of Beauty* (1930).

● **Beaton, David** ▶ (1494–1546) Scottish cardinal, who led the pro-French anti-Protestant faction at the Scottish court under ▷James V and ▷Mary, Queen of Scots. He became Archbishop of St Andrews in 1539. A vigorous persecutor of the Protestants, he was murdered by Protestant nobles at St Andrews.

● **Beatrix** ▶ (1938–) Queen of the Netherlands since the abdication (1980) of her mother Queen Juliana. Her marriage (1966) to the German-born Claus von Amsberg (1926–) caused some controversy, owing to his service with German forces during World War II.

● **beats** ▶ Variations in the intensity of sound when two tones of nearly equal frequency are heard simultaneously. The effect is similar to that of ▷interference. At certain times, the amplitudes of the waves reinforce each other and, at intermediate times, they tend to cancel each other out. The frequency of the beats is equal to the difference in the frequencies of the two notes.

● **Beatty, David, 1st Earl** ▶ (1871–1936) British admiral. As commander of a cruiser squadron in World War I, Beatty took part in the destruction of three German cruisers in Heligoland Bight (1914) and the sinking of the *Blücher* near Dogger Bank (1915). He also fought in the battle of Jutland (1916). As commander of the Grand Fleet, he received the German naval surrender in 1918. He was first sea lord from 1919 to 1927.

● **Beauce** ▶ An area in central France, in the Paris Basin. Consisting of a fertile plain, it is an important wheat-growing area and is known as the "granary of France."

● **Beaufort, Henry** ▶ (c. 1374–1447) English cardinal; half-brother of Henry IV. He became Bishop of Winchester in 1404 and was chancellor three times (1403–04, 1413–17, 1424–26). In 1427 he was appointed papal legate to oppose the Hussites. An influential figure in the minority and early government of Henry VI, he overcame the attempts of his nephew Humphrey, Duke of ▷Gloucester, to demote him.

● **Beaufort, Margaret** ▶ (1443–1509) Countess of Richmond. In 1455 she married Edmund Tudor (d. 1456). Their son Henry VII traced his Lancastrian claim to the English throne through Margaret to ▷John of Gaunt. During the Wars of the ▷Roses, she was imprisoned (1461) by the Yorkists. She was a patron of ▷Caxton and supported foundations at Oxford and Cambridge.

● **Beaufort scale** ▶ A scale of wind speed. It is based on easily observable indicators, such as smoke, tree movement, and damage incurred, and was devised in 1805 by Admiral Sir Francis Beaufort (1774–1857). □ p. 130.

Beaufort scale

Beaufort number	description of wind	wind speed	
		knots	metres per second
0	calm	<1	0.0– 0.2
1	light air	1– 3	0.3– 1.5
2	light breeze	4– 6	1.6– 3.3
3	gentle breeze	7–10	3.4– 5.4
4	moderate breeze	11–16	5.5– 7.9
5	fresh breeze	17–21	8.0–10.7
6	strong breeze	22–27	10.8–13.8
7	near gale	28–33	13.9–17.1
8	gale	34–40	17.2–20.7
9	strong gale	41–47	20.8–24.4
10	storm	48–55	24.5–28.4
11	violent storm	56–63	28.5–32.6
12	hurricane	≥64	≥32.7

● **Beaufort Sea** ▶ The section of the Arctic Ocean N of North America, between the Chukchi Sea and the Canadian archipelago. It is often covered by floating ice.

● **Beauharnais, Alexandre, Vicomte de** ▶ (1760–94) French general, who served in the American Revolution and then became involved in French Revolutionary politics. He commanded in the Rhine (1793) but was guillotined (1794) for failing to relieve Metz. His widow ▷Joséphine married Napoleon, whom his son **Eugène de Beauharnais** (1781–1824) served in Italy and Egypt. In 1805 he became viceroy of Italy and in 1812 commanded in Napoleon's Russian campaign. He lived in exile after Napoleon's fall. His sister **Hortense de Beauharnais** (1783–1837) married (1802) Napoleon's brother Louis ▷Bonaparte, King of Holland. Their son was the future Napoleon III.

● **Beaujolais** ▶ An area of east central France in the departments of Rhône and Loire, which is known for its light red ▷wine. The centre of the wine trade is Villefranche; the northern part of the area is known as Beaujolais Villages.

● **Beaulieu** ▶ 50 49N 1 27W A village in S England, in Hampshire. The parish church was formerly the refectory of a Cistercian abbey founded here in 1204 by King John. In the grounds of the Palace House, home of Lord Montague, is the National Motor Museum. Population (latest est): 1200.

● **Beaumarchais, Pierre-Augustin Caron de** ▶ (1732–99) French dramatist. Son of a watchmaker, he became rich and famous with *The Barber of Seville* (1775) and *The Marriage of Figaro* (1778), his comedies about the intrigues of a cunning valet; they inspired operas by ▷Rossini and ▷Mozart. He undertook secret missions abroad for Louis XV and Louis XVI, supplied arms to the American revolutionaries, and sponsored the first complete edition of ▷Voltaire's works. Constantly involved in lawsuits, he wrote *Mémoires* (1773–75) in self-defence.

● **Beaumaris** ▶ 53 16N 4 05W A resort in North Wales, situated on the island of Anglesey at the N end of the Menai Strait. It is a yachting centre with a moated castle (1295). Population (1991): 1561.

● **Beaumont** ▶ 30 04N 94 06W A city and port in the USA, in Texas on the canal from Port Arthur. Following the first Texan oil strike (1901) at nearby Spindletop, Beaumont developed into a major oil city. Population (1996 est): 111 224.

● **Beaumont, Sir Francis** ▶ (1584–1616) British dramatist. From about 1607, he collaborated with John ▷Fletcher in writing about 12 plays, including *Philaster* (1610) and *The Maides Tragedy* (1611). He was probably sole author of *The Knight of the Burning Pestle* (1607). In 1613 he retired from the theatre.

● **Beaumont, William** ▶ (1785–1853) US physician, who investigated digestion in the human stomach. As an army surgeon in 1822, he treated a trapper named Alexis St Martin for shotgun injuries. These left a permanent opening in his patient's stomach wall and abdomen through which Beaumont sampled the stomach contents. He recognized the chemical nature of digestion, including the importance of hydrochloric acid. His patient lived to the age of 82.

● **Beaune** ▶ 47 02N 4 50E A town in E central France, in the Côte-d'Or department. The centre for the wine trade of Burgundy, it has a wine museum and its manufactures include casks, oil, and mustard. Population (latest est): 21 127.

● **Beauregard, Pierre (Gustave Toutant)** ▶ (1818–93) US Confederate general in the American Civil War. As commander of Charleston, South Carolina, he ordered the first shots to be fired in the conflict when his forces bombarded the Federal Fort Sumter (April 1861). He was victorious at the first battle of ▷Bull Run (1861) and at Shiloh (1862), and commanded the Tennessee Army until the Confederate surrender.

● **Beauvais** ▶ 49 26N 2 05E A town in N France, in the Oise department. Its fine cathedral (begun 1227) was damaged during World War II and the factory in which the famous Gobelin tapestries had been made since the 17th century was completely destroyed (the industry was subsequently moved to Paris). Beauvais is a market town, trading in dairy produce, fruit, and cereals. Population (1990): 56 280.

● **Beauvais tapestry** ▶ Tapestry produced by the state-subsidized Beauvais factory, in France, established in 1664. François ▷Boucher designed pastoral, Italian, and Chinese scenes for the workshops, which specialized in furniture and screen tapestries. Production declined in the 19th century.

● **Beauvoir, Simone de** ▶ (1908–86) French novelist and essayist. The constant companion of Jean-Paul ▷Sartre, whom she met at the Sorbonne in 1929, her writings explored the implications of ▷existentialism. Her novels include *The Blood of Others* (1948), *The Mandarins* (1956), and *The Woman Destroyed* (1968). *The Second Sex* (1953) argued for the liberation of women from their traditional roles. She also published five volumes of autobiography (1958–81).

● **Beaux-Arts** ▶ A French classical-revival style of architecture that flourished at the École des Beaux Arts, Paris, in the late 19th century. J.L.C. Garnier (1825–98) built the Paris Opéra (1861) and the Monte Carlo Casino (1878) in this style.

● **beaver** ▶ A large aquatic ▷rodent, *Castor fiber*, of Europe, Asia, and North America. Over 1 m long and weighing up to 40 kg, beavers have a dark sleek waterproof coat and a broad flat tail used for balance and swimming. They live in family groups, building a "lodge" of sticks and mud with underwater entrances and dams above and below. They use their large incisor teeth to cut wood for building and bark for a winter food. During the summer they feed on vegetation. Family: *Castoridae*. □mammal.

● **Beaverbrook, Max(well) Aitken, 1st Baron** ▶ (1879–1964) British newspaper proprietor and politician, born in Canada. In 1919 he bought a majority interest in the *Daily Express*, which became the most widely read daily in Britain. In 1921 he founded the *Sunday Express* and in 1929 bought the *Evening Standard* (London). In World War I he served in Lloyd George's War Cabinet as minister of information (1918). His posts in Churchill's World War II Cabinet included that of minister of aircraft production (1940–41).

● **Bebel, August** ▶ (1840–1913) German socialist leader. Bebel became interested in the labour movement while living in Leipzig, where in 1865 he came under the influence of Wilhelm ▷Liebknecht. In 1869 he helped to found the German Social Democratic Party, for which he became a leading spokesman in the Reichstag.

● **Bebington** ▶ 53 25N 3 01W A town in NW England, in Wirral unitary authority, Merseyside. It contains Port Sunlight, a model village built in 1888 for workers at the Lever Brothers (now Unilever) factory. Other industries include oil and chemicals. Population (1991): 60 148.

● **bebop** ▷*See* bop.

● **Beccaria, Cesare Bonesana, Marchese de** ▶ (1738–94) Italian legal theorist and political economist. He achieved international fame with the publication of his *Crimes and Punishments* (1764), the first comprehensive account of the principles behind criminal law.

In attacking legal corruption, torture, capital punishment, etc., it was responsible for the reform of penal codes in many countries. Beccaria became a professor of political philosophy at Milan in 1768 and held several important public offices in Austria.

● **bêche-de-mer** ▷*See* trepang.

● **Bechet, Sidney** ▶ (1897–1959) US Black jazz clarinetist and soprano saxophone player. He achieved wide recognition after a tour of Europe in 1919, subsequently worked with Duke Ellington, and after World War II lived in Paris.

● **Bechstein, Wilhelm Carl** ▶ (1826–1900) German piano maker and businessman. In 1853 he founded the Bechstein firm of piano makers in Berlin. During the late 19th century the company achieved great success by combining mechanization and large-scale production with maintenance of the highest standards. Bechstein pianos are still regarded as among the finest in the world.

● **Bechuanaland** ▷*See* Botswana, Republic of.

● **Becker, Boris** ▶ (1967–) German tennis player. In 1985, aged 17, he became the youngest player to win the men's singles at Wimbledon. He was also the first unseeded player to win the event. He won the title again in 1986 and 1989. He also won the US Open in 1989 and the Australian Open two years later.

● **Becket, St Thomas** ▶ (c. 1118–70) English churchman. The son of a London merchant, Becket entered the household of Theobald (d. 1161), Archbishop of Canterbury, and in 1154 became ▷Henry II's chancellor. Succeeding Theobald as archbishop in 1162, Becket resigned the chancellorship and quarrelled with Henry on the issues of criminous clerks (*see* benefit of clergy), freedom of ecclesiastical elections, and the right of appeals to Rome. Becket's refusal to swear allegiance to the Constitutions of ▷Clarendon forced his exile in France (1164–70). Attempts to resolve the quarrel failed and on 29 December, 1170, he was murdered in Canterbury Cathedral by four courtiers at Henry's instigation. Canonized in 1173, his shrine at Canterbury became one of the most important pilgrimage centres in medieval Europe.

● **Beckett, Samuel** ▶ (1906–89) Irish novelist, dramatist, and poet. After studying and teaching at Trinity College, Dublin, he lived mainly in Paris from 1933. He wrote in both French and English. His plays, which include *Waiting for Godot* (1954), and his prose works, such as the trilogy *Molloy* (1951), *Malone Dies* (1951), and *The Unnamable* (1953), treat human existence with a nihilism tempered by desperate humour. His later works, such as *Not I* (1973), are notably brief and concentrated. He won the Nobel Prize in 1969.

● **Beckford, William** ▶ (?1760–1844) British writer. He inherited his father's vast fortune at the age of 11 and used the rest of his life to spend it. He commissioned James ▷Wyatt to build ▷Fonthill Abbey (a short-lived masterpiece of the gothic architectural revival), collected art, travelled in Europe, and became an MP. He wrote the classic gothic novel *Vathek* (1782), two travel books, and a journal.

● **Beckham, David** ▶ (1975–) British Association footballer. A midfielder, he plays for Manchester United (1995–) and England (1996–), becoming England captain in 2000. His wife, Victoria, is a member of the Spice Girls pop group ('Posh Spice').

● **Beckmann, Max** ▶ (1884–1950) German expressionist painter, born in Leipzig. His experiences of World War I inspired his grotesque paintings of distorted sometimes mutilated bodies, often indicting German social evils, as in *Night* (1919; Düsseldorf). In later years in Amsterdam and the USA he painted a series of triptychs influenced partly by Hieronymus ▷Bosch.

● **becquerel** ▶ (Bq) The ▷SI unit of activity (radioactivity) equal to the number of atoms of a radioactive substance that disintegrate in one second. Named after Antoine Henri ▷Becquerel.

● **Becquerel, (Antoine) Henri** ▶ (1852–1908) French physicist, who was professor at the Conservatoire des Arts et Métiers in Paris. He discovered radioactivity (1896) by chance, on finding that invisible rays from uranium salts could affect a photographic plate even through a light-proof wrapper. For his fundamental research on these radiations, Becquerel shared the Nobel Prize (1903) with his associates Pierre and Marie ▷Curie. He also performed research in mag-

netism and in optics, particularly polarization and absorption in crystals. His grandfather **Antoine César Becquerel** (1788–1878) left the army to join ▷Ampère in his study of electricity, becoming one of the founders of electrochemistry.

St Thomas Becket ▶ When Henry II raged over the intransigence of his archbishop, four of his knights took literally his words: "Will no one rid me of this turbulent priest?" Becket is seen in this 13th-century manuscript being assassinated by them at the altar in Canterbury Cathedral.

● **bedbug** ▶ A flat wingless insect, about 5 mm long, belonging to a family (Cimicidae; 30 species) of blood-sucking parasites. In temperate regions *Cimex lectularius* is the species that most commonly attacks man, hiding by day in bedding, furniture, etc., and becoming active at night. It inflicts a painful bite but does not transmit disease. Bedbugs can be easily eradicated by insecticide sprays or fumigation. Order: *Hemiptera* (bugs).

● **Bedchamber Crisis** ▶ (1839) A constitutional dispute that arose over Queen Victoria's ladies of the bedchamber. After the resignation of the Whig prime minister, Lord Melbourne, Sir Robert Peel attempted to form a Tory ministry and requested that Victoria dismiss her Whig ladies. The queen, at that time a passionate Whig, stubbornly refused, with the result that Peel felt unable to take office. Melbourne remained as prime minister until his government fell in 1841, when Victoria, influenced by Prince ▷Albert, consented to the dismissal of three ladies.

● **Beddoes, Thomas Lovell** ▶ (1803–49) British poet. After 1825 he lived mostly in Europe, where he studied medicine and became involved in revolutionary politics. His obsessive interest in death dominates all his works, especially *Death's Jest-Book, or the Fool's Tragedy* (1850). He committed suicide.

● **Bede, St** ▶ (c. 673–735 AD) English historian, known as the Venerable Bede. After 682 he lived at the monastery of Jarrow in Northumberland. His *Ecclesiastical History of the English People* (c. 731), written in Latin and later translated into English under King Alfred, is a great historical work and remains an important source for British history, especially the early Anglo-Saxon period (5th–8th centuries). He also wrote poems in English, but only one is extant, his "Death Song." He was the author of many grammatical, scientific, and historical works. Feast day: 27 May.

● **Bedford** ▶ 52 08N 0 29W A town in S England, the administrative centre of Bedfordshire on the Great Ouse. John ▷Bunyan was born nearby and spent 12 years in Bedford gaol. The business sector includes manufacturing, distribution, and call centres. Population (1991): 73 917.

● **Bedford, John, Duke of** ▶ (1389–1435) The third son of Henry IV; known as John of Lancaster. He was protector of England and regent of France (1422–35) during the minority of his nephew Henry VI. He pursued the ▷Hundred Years' War and procured the execution of Joan of Arc (1431).

● **Bedford Level** ▷See Fens, the.

● **Bedfordshire** ▶ A county in the S Midlands of England. It is chiefly low lying, rising to the Chiltern Hills in the SW, and drained by the Great Ouse River. Agricultural products include wheat and vegetables. The chief industries, centred on Luton, Dunstable, and Bedford, are motor vehicles, agricultural engineering, and electrical goods. Luton became an independent ▷unitary authority in 1997. Area (excluding Luton): 1192 sq km (460 sq mi). Population (1997 est, excluding Luton): 362 300. Administrative centre: Bedford.

● **Bedlam** ▶ The popular name for the Bethlehem Royal Hospital, a mental hospital located from 1815 until 1931 at what is now the Imperial War Museum in Lambeth, S London. Founded in Bishopsgate as a priory (1247), it moved to Moorfields in 1676 and then to Lambeth; in 1931 it was transferred to Beckenham, in Kent. Bethlehem Hospital now forms part of the Kings College Hospital group. "Bedlam" has passed into the English language as a synonym for "madhouse."

● **Bedlington terrier** ▶ A breed of dog originating in Bedlington, N England, in the early 19th century. It has long legs and a long narrow face and is a popular sporting dog locally. The thick coat may be blue, blue and tan, liver, or sandy. Height: about 40 cm.

● **Bednorz, Johannes Georg** ▶ (1950–) German-born physicist, who worked at the IBM Research Laboratory in Zürich, Switzerland, on ▷superconductivity. With K. A. Müller he was awarded the Nobel Prize in 1987 for developing a range of mixed-phase oxides that exhibited superconductivity at temperatures up to 90 K. This development has opened the possibility of using superconducting electronic circuits in practical devices.

● **Bedouin** ▶ The nomadic ▷Arab tribes of the Syrian and Arabian deserts and other desert regions of the Arab world. Their economy is based on camels, sheep, and goats. At present they are found within the political boundaries of Saudi Arabia, Yemen, the United Arab Emirates, Kuwait, Iraq, Jordan, Israel, Egypt, and the ▷Maghrib states. The policies of these countries are to restrict the movements of the nomadic population and induce them to take up a settled existence. Courageous fighters, the Bedouin played an active role in the early Arab conquests.

● **bedsore** ▶ An ulcer that develops in areas of skin subject to continuous pressure, such as may occur in elderly or other bedridden patients who are unable to change their position frequently. The pressure reduces the blood supply to the affected part. Patients at risk require careful nursing, with frequent changes of position and massage to prevent bedsores from developing.

● **bedstraw** ▶ A weak, often climbing, plant of the widely distributed genus *Galium* (300 species), common in damp places. Lady's bedstraw (*G. verum*), native to Europe, is a weedy perennial, up to 75 cm tall, with small yellow flowers. Its name derives from the legend that Mary rested on a bed of these plants while giving birth to Christ. Family: *Rubiaceae* (madder family). ▷See also cleavers.

● **Bedworth** ▶ 52 28N 1 29W A market town in central England, in Warwickshire. It has coalmining, brick-making, and light engineering industries. Population (1991): 31 932.

● **bee** ▶ A four-winged insect (10–30 mm long) belonging to the superfamily *Apoidea* (about 12 000 species), of worldwide distribution. Bees feed on pollen and nectar from flowering plants using well-developed tongues and are important pollinators, transferring pollen on their hairy bodies and broad back legs. The ovipositor is used to sting attackers and in some species is barbed, remaining in the wound.

Most solitary bees nest in soil, hollow trees, or wall cavities. Some, however, tunnel into wood (*see* carpenter bee) or construct nests using earth (*see* mason bee) or leaves (*see* leafcutter bee). The female lays one or more eggs in a nest that is then sealed, leaving the larvae to develop. The social bees (families *Apidae* and *Halictidae*) live in communities organized into castes—workers (infertile females), drones (males, developed from unfertilized eggs), and a queen (a fertile female). Colonies are established in trees, walls, or cliffs (*see also* honeybee). Order: *Hymenoptera*.

● **Beebe, Charles William** ▶ (1877–1962) US explorer and naturalist. He led many expeditions and, in 1934, made a record undersea descent of 923 m (3028 ft) in a bathysphere. He wrote many books describing his observations and adventures.

● **beech** ▶ A tree of the genus *Fagus* (10 species), native to N temperate regions. Beeches have smooth grey bark and a broad dense crown, occasionally reaching a height of 40 m. The leaves are oval, pointed, and toothed, the flowers are unisexual and inconspicuous, and the fruits are nutlike seeds enclosed in husks (beechnuts or mast). The common beech of Europe and Asia is *Fagus sylvatica*, the timber of which is used for furniture and flooring, while that of North America is *F. grandiflora*. Family: *Fagaceae*.

In the S hemisphere beeches are represented by a related genus (*Notofagus*; 14 species) and differ in being evergreen and having separate trees bearing male or female flowers. Some are of importance for their durable timber, edible nuts, or ornamental value.

● **Beecham, Sir Thomas** ▶ (1879–1961) British conductor. He used his inherited fortune for the advancement of English musical life. He was a memorable interpreter of Haydn and Mozart and championed the works of Richard Strauss, Sibelius, and particularly Delius, whose friend and biographer he became. He founded the London Philharmonic Orchestra (1932) and the Royal Philharmonic Orchestra (1947).

● **Beecher, Lyman** ▶ (1775–1863) US Presbyterian minister and temperance campaigner. After studying at Yale University he preached in New York and New England until he went to Cincinnati, Ohio, in 1832 as the principal of the new Lane Theological College. He is remembered as a powerful Puritan preacher with an evangelical zeal that inspired his five sons to become ministers. Of these, **Henry Ward Beecher** (1813–87) was a pastor first in Indianapolis and then for 40 years in Brooklyn, New York, where his sermons and antislavery writings were widely influential. Of Lyman's eight daughters the eldest, **Catharine Esther Beecher** (1800–78), became a tireless advocate of women's education and the principal of schools for young ladies in Hartford, Connecticut and later in Cincinnati. She was nevertheless strongly opposed to feminism, campaigning instead for domesticity and family values for women. Catharine's younger sister, **Harriet Beecher Stowe** (1811–96), joined her as a teacher in Cincinnati before marrying the Rev Calvin Ellis Stowe in 1836. Living close to the border with Kentucky, a slave-holding state, she had frequent contact with escaping slaves. After the passing of the Fugitive Slave Law (1850), which she strongly opposed, she wrote the best-selling *Uncle Tom's Cabin* (first published serially in 1851–52). The book did much to consolidate antislavery feeling in the North and was deeply offensive to the South; it was therefore a powerful factor in bringing about the US ▷Civil War. After the success of this book she became a full-time writer, producing a further 11 works of fiction, only one of which was concerned with slavery.

● **Beeching, Richard, Baron** ▶ (1913–85) British administrator and engineer. As chairman of the British Railways Board (1963–65), he produced the controversial *Beeching Report* (1963), which proposed closing many rural and branch lines in order to concentrate on intercity services. The plan was largely, but not wholly, implemented in the mid-1960s effectively forcing many country dwellers onto the roads, either in buses or cars. In 1965 Beeching became deputy chairman of ICI and was created a life peer.

● **bee-eater** ▶ A brightly coloured bird belonging to a family (*Meropidae*; 24 species) occurring mainly in tropical Old World regions. Bee-eaters have pointed wings, long central tail feathers, a slender curved bill, and, commonly, a black eye stripe. They nest in burrows and feed in flight, chiefly on bees and wasps. Order: *Coraciiformes* (hornbills, kingfishers, etc.).

● **beekeeping** ▶ (*or* apiculture) The rearing of colonies of ▷honeybees in hives either for their ▷honey or ▷beeswax or for pollinating flowers. Sheets of wax in wooden frames (starter combs) are hung vertically inside the hive. Onto these the bees build wax cells that they fill with honey and seal. When a frame is full it is removed, the honey is extracted, and the comb is reused. A colony makes about 32 kg of honey in a summer, but 14 kg of this is needed by the bees for food during the winter; following a bad summer they must be fed sugar syrup. About 10 000–20 000 bees survive the winter; during the spring, when a colony has increased to over 50 000, a large group is likely to leave the hive (i.e. it swarms). The beekeeper collects the swarm and puts it into an empty hive.

● **Beelzebub** ▷*See* Devil.

● **beer and brewing** ▶ Beer is an alcoholic drink made from fermented malt flavoured with hops. Brewing is the process of making beer. Barley, or other grain, is first malted by being allowed to germinate, the resulting malt being dried (kilned), ground, and heated with water (mashed). Starch in the grain is converted into soluble carbohydrates by enzymes in the malt. The resulting liquid wort is boiled with hops to concentrate the wort and utilize the bitter flavour of the hops. The wort is then filtered and cooled ready for fermentation. Yeast is added and the carbohydrates in the wort are converted into alchohol. The liquid is drained and stored. Different brewing methods and types of ingredients produce different varieties of beer. Beer was drunk in ancient Egypt and has been enjoyed in a great many countries ever since. **Ale** was originally a stronger drink than beer, brewed without hops. The terms are now interchangeable, although ale is sometimes reserved for stronger brews fermented at higher temperatures. **Mild** beer is made with fewer hops than **bitter** and a darker malt is used to impart colour. **Lager** is traditionally a light beer matured over a long period at low temperature. **Stout** is made from a blend of roasted barley and malts.

● **Beerbohm, Sir Max** ▶ (1872–1956) British caricaturist and writer. He published several collections of essays, caricatures, and brillant parodies during the 1890s. His only novel, *Zuleika Dobson* (1911), is an ironic romance set at Oxford University. From 1911 to his death he lived in Rapallo (Italy), returning to England only during World War II.

● **Beersheba** ▶ 31 15N 34 47E A town in S Israel, the largest in the Negev. In World War I it was the scene of a British victory over the Turks. Beersheba has a university (1965) and manufactures chemicals and glass. Population (1997 est): 156 500.

● **beeswax** ▶ A substance produced by bees to build honeycombs. It is collected by heating the honeycomb in water (after removing the honey) so that the floating wax can be separated after solidification on cooling. Beeswax (melting point 61–69°C) is used in high-quality polishes, etc.

● **beet** ▶ A herbaceous plant, *Beta vulgaris*, native to Europe and the Mediterranean region, stemless but sometimes exceeding 1 m in height. Several varieties are widely cultivated in temperate areas, the most important of which is the ▷sugar beet. The taproot of the red or garden beet yields beetroot, while the mangel-wurzel (*B. vulgaris vulgaris*) is an important fodder variety. The spinach beet is grown for its leaves, used as a vegetable. Family: *Chenopodiaceae*.

● **Beethoven, Ludwig van** ▶ (1770–1827) German composer, born in Bonn. His father, a court musician, attempted to exploit him as a child prodigy. Often boorish and temperamental, he nevertheless won a considerable following for his piano playing and compositions in Vienna, where he settled in 1792 after studying there with Haydn. At the age of 30 he began to go deaf, an experience that increased his loneliness and eccentricity, but did not stop him compos-

Ludwig van Beethoven
▶ A portrait (1819) by Joseph Stieler (1781–1858).

ing. His later years were plagued by illness and by his adoption of his troublesome nephew Karl. About 600 of Beethoven's works survive, among them 9 symphonies, 5 piano concertos, 1 violin concerto, 16 string quartets, 10 violin and piano sonatas, 32 piano sonatas, 2 ballets, 2 masses, 1 opera, and about 200 song settings. His early masterpieces, influenced by Mozart and Haydn, include much chamber music, piano works, and the first and second symphonies. During his middle years he produced the *Emperor* piano concerto (1809), the *Kreutzer* sonata (1803), the opera *Fidelio* (1805–14), and the rest of the symphonies, up to the eighth. His last most intense works include the *Missa Solemnis* (1818–23), the ninth symphony (1817–23), and the innovative late string quartets.

● **beetle** ▶ An insect belonging to the largest order (*Coleoptera*; about 278 000 species) of the animal kingdom. The forewings are specialized as hard structures (called elytra), which cover the functional hindwings when these are not in use. The elytra and the thick cuticle provide protection against predation and desiccation and enable aquatic species to trap a store of air. Beetles occupy a wide range of habitats and have exploited all possible food sources—many feed on plants or animals or scavenge their remains and a few are parasitic.

Many beetles are economically important: some species are pests of crops, timber, textiles, and stored grains and cereals; others are useful by preying on insect pests or by speeding up ▷decomposition. ▷*See also* weevil.

● **Beeton, Isabella Mary** ▶ (1836–65) British writer, author of one of the most famous English cookery books, *The Book of Household Management* (1861), first published serially in a women's magazine founded by her husband. This book contains over 3000 recipes as well as a wealth of legal and medical advice, a considerable achievement for a woman who died at the age of 29.

● **beetroot** ▷*See* beet.

● **Begin, Menachem** ▶ (1913–92) Israeli statesman; prime minister (1977–83). Born in Russia, he led the Zionist Youth Movement in Poland at the outset of World War II and from 1942 commanded Jewish forces in Palestine. In 1948 he founded the Freedom (Herut) Movement and was joint chairman of the Unity Party (1973–84). In 1978, under the instigation of the US president Jimmy Carter, he negotiated the Camp David peace treaty with President ▷Sadat of Egypt (signed 1979), for which Begin and Sadat were jointly awarded the Nobel Peace Prize (1978).

● **Begonia** ▶ A genus of generally succulent herbaceous plants (about 1000 species) native to the tropics. They are widely grown as pot or garden plants for their brightly coloured flowers with pink, yellow, or white "petals" in two unequal pairs (as in *B. semperflorens*) or for their variegated leaves (as in *B. rex*). The underground parts are long lived and may be tuberous, fibrous, or rhizomatous. Family: *Begoniaceae*.

● **Behan, Brendan** ► (1923–64) Irish playwright. His first play, *The Quare Fellow* (1954), and his autobiography, *Borstal Boy* (1958), were based on his years of detention and imprisonment for Irish Republican Army (IRA) activities. His best-known play, *The Hostage* (1957), treated a tragic situation with characteristic liveliness and boisterous comedy.

● **behaviourism** ► A school of psychology, founded in the USA by J. B. ▷Watson in the early 20th century, in which observable behaviour is studied but ideas, feelings, thoughts, etc., are deemed insignificant. The behaviourist aims to understand the laws relating a stimulus to a response, how responses are built up into complex behaviours, and how ▷conditioning affects behaviour. The approach was successful in describing how animals learnt tasks in the laboratory but cannot fully account for such complex processes as emotion, language, and interpersonal relationships. ▷*See* cognitive psychology.

● **behaviour therapy** ► A method of treating mental disorders, developed by ▷Eysenck, that is based on ▷behaviourism and the view that psychological problems are the result of faulty learning. ▷Conditioning is used to teach new behaviour or to eliminate undesirable behaviour, such as excessive drinking (*see* aversion therapy). ▷Phobias are treated by repeated exposure to the feared object or situation, which gradually reduces the subject's fear of it.

● **Behn, Aphra** ► (1640–89) British novelist and dramatist. The details of her colourful life are uncertain, but she is known to have spent some time as a British government agent in Holland. She later attracted much attention (and scandal) in London by her Bohemian lifestyle. She wrote many popular plays, notably *The Rover* (1678), but is chiefly remembered for her exotic novel, *Oroonoko* (1688), about an enslaved Negro prince. She is generally considered to be Britain's first professional woman author.

● **Behrens, Peter** ► (1868–1940) German architect. Coming to architecture from the ▷Arts and Crafts movement, he erected his most influential buildings before World War I. He evolved a modernistic style notable for its lack of ornamentation. His most important building was the AEG turbine works in Berlin (1909–11), which was one of the first industrial buildings to be evaluated as a work of architecture.

● **Behring, Emil Adolf von** ► (1854–1917) German bacteriologist, who produced an antitoxin that conferred passive immunity against tetanus. By 1882 Behring and Paul ▷Ehrlich had developed a serum that provided effective immunity against diphtheria. He was awarded a Nobel Prize in 1901.

● **Behzad** ► (c. 1455–c. 1536) Persian painter, one of the finest Islamic miniaturists. As director of the academy at Herat he was an influential teacher and inspired many imitators of his richly coloured dramatic style.

● **Beibu Gulf** ▷*See* Tonkin, Gulf of.

● **Beida** ▷*See* Zawiyat al-Bayda'.

● **Beiderbecke, Bix** ► (Leon Bismarck B.; 1903–31) US jazz musician. A legendary cornetist, he recorded with Frankie Trumbauer (1900–57), Louis ▷Armstrong, and Paul Whiteman (1890–1967) before his death from alcohol and drugs. A recording of *In a Mist* (1927) displays his skill as a pianist.

● **Beijing** ► (Peking *or* Pei-ching) 39 55N 116 25E The capital of the People's Republic of China, an administratively autonomous city in the NE of the country in Hobei province. The city has expanded since 1949 and there has been rapid development of industries, including iron and steel, machinery, and textiles. It is symmetrically laid out around two walled cities, the N inner city and the S outer city; the old Imperial City lies within the inner city and at its centre the moated "Forbidden City" contains the Imperial Palaces (now museums). There are three universities, the oldest being Beijing University (1898).
History: the site has a long history of human habitation. As Ta-tu, it became the capital (of N China) under the Yuan dynasty in 1272. Later, when the capital was moved to Nanjing, it became known as Pei-p'ing (*or* Beibing). As Beijing (1420), it again became capital under

the third Ming emperor. In 1928 the Nationalist (Guomindang) government moved the capital to Nanjing and from 1937 until 1945 Beijing was occupied by the Japanese. It became the capital of the People's Republic of China in 1949. In 1989 Tiananmen Square in Beijing was the site of demonstrations for liberal reform; they ended in a massacre of about 2600 protesters by government forces, causing worldwide condemnation. Population (1991 est): 7 000 000.

● **Beira** ► 19 49S 34 52E A port in E Mozambique, on the Mozambique Channel. Founded in 1891 by the Portuguese, it became a major port serving central S Africa. It was the main export outlet of Rhodesia (now Zimbabwe) until Mozambique's independence (1975). It revived in the late 1980s when the 'Beira Corridor' trade route across Mozambique to Zimbabwe was established. Exports include ores, cotton, and food products. Population (1991 est): 298 847.

● **Beirut** ► 33 52N 35 30E The capital of Lebanon, on the E Mediterranean Sea. Originally a Phoenician city, it was captured by the Arabs in 635. It was part of the Ottoman Empire from 1517 until 1918, when the French took control. In 1941 it became the capital of independent Lebanon and the financial centre of the Arab world. Civil war between Muslims and Christians (1975–76), invasion (1982) by Israeli forces to flush out the PLO, and occupation by Syrian forces to restrain the Israelis led to intervention by a UN peace-keeping force (UNIFIL) and the end of Beirut's prosperity. Divided by a "green line" between a Muslim western sector and a Christian eastern sector, it became a battlefield of street warfare and hostage taking between Christian, Muslim, Druze, and Palestinian factions. In 1990 peace talks led to the withdrawal of all private militias from the city. Population (1996 est): 1 900 000.

● **Béjart, Maurice** ► (Maurice-Jean de Berger; 1927–) French ballet dancer and choreographer. He founded his first company in 1954 and the Ballet of the Twentieth Century in 1960, in Brussels; it transferred to Lausanne in 1987 and is now known as the Béjart Ballet Lausanne. The company has carried out many tours, takings its expressionist modern style to all parts of the world.

● **Bejaïa** ► (French name: Bougie) 38 40N 4 50W A city and port in Algeria, on the Mediterranean Sea at the mouth of the Soummam stream. The site of several ancient settlements, it has Roman and Berber remains. During the middle ages it was a centre for trade with Europe and a notorious haunt of pirates. The modern port was developed during the French occupation and is now significant as the terminus of one of the Sahara's chief oil pipelines. Population (latest est): 114 534.

● **Bekaa Valley** ► (El Beqa'a *or* al-Biqa) A wide fertile valley in central Lebanon, running for about 125 km (78 mi) between the Lebanon Mountains to the W and the Anti-Lebanon Mountains to the E. Watered by the River Litani in the S and the Orontes in the N, it contains almost half Lebanon's cultivable land. Crops include grains, fruits, and root vegetables; wine and arrack are produced. The main towns include Baalbek and Zahlé. Of strategic importance to both Israel and Syria, the Bekaa valley became a stronghold for the ▷Hizbollah Shiite Muslims in the 1980s.

● **bel** ▷*See* decibel.

● **Belarus, Republic of** ► (Belorussia *or* Byelorussia *or* White Russia) A republic in E Europe. Its inhabitants are Belarussians, a ▷Slav people, with minorities of Russians and Poles.
Economy: as mineral resources are scarce, industry became dependent on the supply of cheap raw materials from other parts of the Soviet Union: this situation led to severe recession in the early years after independence. In 1994 Belarus entered a monetary and economic union with Russia in an attempt to solve this problem. Domestic peat is now an important fuel; meat and dairy farming on the country's rich steppe lands support the economy. Policies of privatization and structural reform were introduced in the 1990s.
History: part of Lithuania (13th–14th centuries) and then Poland (16th–18th centuries), Belarus was conquered by Russia during the reign of Catherine the Great. The scene of heavy fighting in both World Wars, Belarus was a Soviet republic from 1919 until it became independent in 1991. Although a multiparty constitution was adopted, the former communists have continued to dominate poli-

tics. In 1996, 1997, and 1999 President Aleksandr Lukashenko signed controversial treaties with Russia establishing joint economic, defence, and foreign policies. In 1996 Lukashenko's plans to assume near-dictatorial powers were opposed by parliament but backed by a referendum. He was re-elected by a landslide in 2001 but foreign observers condemned the poll as unfair.

Republic of Belarus

Head of state	President Aleksandr Lukashenko
Official languages	Belarussian and Russian
Official currency	rouble of 100 kopeks
Area	207 600 sq km (80 134 sq mi)
Population (2000 est)	9 989 000
Capital	Minsk

● **Belau, Republic of** ▶ (name until 1981: Palau *or* Pelew) A country in the W Pacific Ocean comprising 8 inhabited islands and about 332 islets.

Economy: fishing, including the sale of fishing licenses to foreign tuna fleets, is the main source of income. Tourism is developing.

History: formerly part of the Spanish Empire, the islands were sold to Germany in 1899. They were then administered by Japan from 1914 until their occupation by US forces in World War II. The islands became part of the UN Trust Territory of the Pacific Islands in 1947. The islanders voted against becoming part of Micronesia in 1978 and became autonomous in 1981 (with the USA retaining control of foreign and defence policy). Disputes over US plans to base nuclear weapons in Belau led to the suicide of President Lazarus Salii in 1988 and delayed full independence until 1994.

Republic of Belau

Head of state	President Tommy Remengesau
Official languages	Palauan and English
Official currency	US dollar
Area	488 sq km (188 sq mi)
Population (2000 est)	18 800
Capital	Koror

● **Belaúnde Terry, Fernando** ▶ (1912–2002) Peruvian statesman; president (1963–68; 1980–85). A cofounder (1956) of the centrist Popular Action Party, he pursued policies of land reform and a major road construction programme during his first term as president. In 1968 he was deposed in a military coup and fled to the USA, returning in 1976. His second term was marked by soaring inflation, terrorist outrages, and human-rights abuses by the military.

● **bel canto** ▶ (Italian: fine singing) A delicate and lyrical style of singing that was developed in Italian opera during the 17th and 18th centuries and reached its peak in the 19th century. Notable singers included Jenny ▷Lind.

● **Belém** ▶ **1.** 1 27S 48 29W A port in N Brazil, the capital of Pará state on the Rio do Pará. It exports products from the Amazon basin including nuts, jute, and rubber. Its university was founded in 1957. Population (1996): 851 705. **2.** A western suburb of ▷Lisbon in Portugal on the right bank of the River Tagus. It is known for the Jerónimos monastry, founded by Manuel I in 1499 to commemorate the discovery by Vasco da Gama of a sea route to India and built on the site of a chapel in which he worshipped. It is a notable example of Manueline architecture. Here, also, is the Tower of Belém (1515), built as a fort to guard the Tagus estuary. The Paço de Belém (1770) is the official residence of the president of Portugal.

● **belemnite** ▶ The fossilized shell of an extinct ▷cuttlefish, sometimes called a thunderbolt. Cylindrical and pointed at one end, they are most commonly found in deposits of the Jurassic and Cretaceous periods (150–65 million years ago).

● **Belfast** ▶ **1.** 54 40N 5 50W The capital of Northern Ireland, a seaport situated where the River Lagan enters Belfast Lough, in Belfast district, Co Antrim and Co Down. It is the province's commercial and administrative centre and its industries include shipbuilding, electronics, and engineering. The principal buildings, including the City

Hall (1906) and Parliament Buildings (1932) at Stormont, were built in the late 19th and early 20th centuries. Queen's University received a royal charter in 1909.

History: large-scale growth of Belfast came with the expansion of the linen-making and shipbuilding industries in the 19th century; it became a city in 1888. The Parliament of Northern Ireland sat in the city from 1921 to 1972. Its recent history has been marked by conflict between Protestant and Roman Catholic communities, each being concentrated in ghettoes. The British army has maintained a presence on the streets since August 1969 (much reduced since the terrorist ceasefires of the mid-1990s). Population (1991): 279 237. **2.** A district of W Northern Ireland, in Co Antrim and Co Down. Area: 115 sq km (44 sq mi). Population (1998 est) 297 200.

● **Belfort** ▶ 44 17N 1 32E A town in E France, the capital of the Territoire de Belfort. Strategically situated between the Vosges and Jura mountains, it has been besieged many times. Industries include wine. Population (1990): 51 913.

● **Belgae** ▶ The Germanic tribes occupying NE ▷Gaul in ancient Roman times. Julius Caesar named them and considered them the most warlike of the Gauls. He defeated them in 57 BC but they then fought the Romans from SE Britain, to which they had been migrating from about 100 BC.

● **Belgaum** ▶ 15 54N 74 36E A city in India, in Karnataka. Manufactures include cotton, furniture, and leather. Population (1991): 325 639.

● **Belgian Congo** ▷*See* Congo, Democratic Republic of.

● **Belgium, Kingdom of** ▶ (French name: Belgique; Flemish name: België) A country in NW Europe, on the North Sea. It is generally low lying except for the Ardennes in the SE. The main rivers are the Scheldt and the Meuse and these and others are linked by canals to form an extensive network of inland waterways. The population is divided between the French and the Flemish, with small minorities of Germans and others.

Economy: highly industrialized; engineering, food processing, textiles and chemicals continue to dominate the economy, although the service sector has grown in recent decades. Apart from coal, which is no longer mined, Belgium has no natural resources. Agriculture is highly intensive but produces only for the home market; the main cash crop is sugar beet. Belgium has been an important centre for trade since the middle ages. It still has one of the highest proportions of export revenue to total income in the world. In 1921 a customs union was formed with Luxembourg and in 1948 both joined with the Netherlands to form the ▷Benelux economic union. Belgium is also a member of the EU and almost two-thirds of its trade is with other members. Main exports include iron and steel, chemicals, machinery, and motor vehicles.

History: the name Belgium comes from the ▷Belgae, a Celtic tribe named by Caesar, and the area was part of the Roman Empire until about the end of the 2nd century AD, when it was invaded by Germanic tribes. In medieval times it was divided into several counties, duchies, and the bishopric of Liège, during which time the cities of Ghent, Bruges, and Ypres rose to virtual independence and economic prosperity through the wool industry. In view of its strategic position, Belgium had considerable importance in the balance of power in Europe over the centuries and from the middle ages onwards it was ruled by several European nations in turn, including Austria, Spain, and France. After being occupied by France during the Napoleonic Wars, it was joined to the Netherlands in 1815. Following an uprising, it became independent in 1830, and the National Congress elected Prince Leopold of Saxe-Coburg as King of the Belgians (*see* Leopold I) in 1831. The country was recognized by all of Europe in 1839. In spite of efforts to remain neutral it was attacked and occupied by Germany in both World Wars. When the Germans invaded in 1940, King ▷Leopold III surrendered immediately but the government struggled on in exile in London. In 1950, after a political crisis, the king was persuaded to abdicate in favour of his son, ▷Baudouin, who was succeeded in 1993 by his brother Albert II (1934–). Since World War II there has been tension between the French-speaking Walloons in the S and the Flemish-speaking community in the N. In 1977 an agreement was reached dividing Belgium into the semiautonomous regions of French-speaking Wallonia, Flemish-speaking Flanders, and bilingual Brussels. The three regions were given greater autonomy under a new federal constitution adopted in 1993. The loss in 1960 of the Belgian Congo (which became Zaïre and is now the Democratic Republic of Congo) weakened Belgium's economy. Dr Wilfried Martens (1936–   ) led a series of coalition governments from 1979 to 1992, when he was succeeded by Jean-Luc Dehaene. Following elections in 1999 Guy Verhofstadt became prime minister. Belgium adopted the European single currency in 1999–2002.

Kingdom of Belgium

Head of state	King Albert II
Official languages	French, Flemish, Dutch, and German
Official currency	euro of 100 cents
Area	30 513 sq km (11 781 sq mi)
Population (2000 est)	10 249 000
Capital	Brussels
Main port	Antwerp

● **Belgorod-Dnestrovski** ▸ (Romanian name: Cetatea Alba) 46 10N 30 19E A port in Ukraine, on the Dnestr estuary. A commercial centre, it has fishing, fish-processing, and winemaking industries.

History: founded by Greek colonists in the 6th century BC, it passed to the Romans and then the Byzantines. Turkish from 1484, it was acquired by Russia in the 19th century. It was then under Romanian (1918–40) and Soviet (1940–91) rule. Population (1991 est): 56 800.

● **Belgrade** ▸ (Serbo-Croat name: Beograd) 44 50N 20 30E The capital of the Union of Serbia and Montenegro and of Serbia, situated at the confluence of the Rivers Danube and Sava. A settlement from very early times, it became the Serbian capital in the early 15th century. It later suffered Turkish and Austrian occupations but again became capital of Serbia in the late 19th century and of Yugoslavia after World War I. It was occupied by the Germans in World War II and has expanded considerably in the years since then. The University of Belgrade was founded in 1863 and the Arts University in 1973. Population (2000 est): 1 194 878.

● **Belgravia** ▸ A fashionable and expensive district, mainly in the Greater London borough of the City of Westminster. It contains residential squares, including Belgrave and Eaton Squares, planned by Thomas Cubitt and built on reclaimed marshland (1825–30). Many foreign embassies are situated in Belgravia.

● **Belinsky, Vissarion** ▸ (1811–48) Russian literary critic, an influential advocate of social realism and naturalism. He championed ▷Pushkin, ▷Lermontov, and ▷Gogol, whom he later denounced as a betrayer of naturalism.

● **Belisarius** ▸ (c. 505–65 AD) Byzantine general of ▷Justinian I's reign. After successfully checking Persian invasions on the empire's eastern frontier and overthrowing the African Vandal kingdom (534), Belisarius began his conquest of the Ostrogoths of Italy, and captured Rome, Naples, and Ravenna (540) before being recalled to Constantinople. In 546 he returned to Italy to quell the resurgent Ostrogoths but was again recalled, his command being given to ▷Narses.

● **Belitung** ▸ (or Billiton) An Indonesian island in the Java Sea. Its tin-mines, now government owned, have attracted a large Chinese community. Area: 4833 sq km (1866 sq mi). Chief town: Tanjungpandan.

● **Belize** ▸ (name until 1973: British Honduras) A country in Central America, on the Caribbean Sea between Mexico and Guatemala. The country is generally low lying, rising to the Maya Mountains in the SW. It is subject to hurricanes. The population is of African, Spanish-American, and Mayan Indian descent, with small minorities of E Indians, Syrians, and Chinese.

Economy: mainly agricultural; although almost half the country is forested, the combined value of sugar and citrus exports have exceeded that of timber since the early 1960s. In late 1998 agriculture was devastated by Hurricane Mitch and consequent flooding. Fish (especially lobsters) are exported to the USA. Revenue from tourism increased by around 50% in the early 2000s.

History: archaeological evidence suggests that the area was once an important Mayan settlement. The coast was sighted by Columbus in 1502 but the first European occupation was an independent settlement of British woodcutters, which held out against the Spanish throughout the 17th century. From the late 18th century more control was exercised by the British Government and in 1862 it became a colony under Jamaica. It became an independent colony in 1884 and attained internal self-government in 1964. Despite claims, based on early Spanish treaties, made to it by Guatemala, Belize became an independent state within the Commonwealth in 1981. The 1999 elections were won by the People's United Democratic Party led by Said Musa.

Belize

Head of state	Queen Elizabeth II, represented by the governor-general, Sir Colville Young
Official language	English; Spanish is also spoken
Official currency	Belize dollar of 100 cents
Area	22 963 sq km (8867 sq mi)
Population (2000 est)	253 000
Capital	Belmopan

● **Belize City** ▸ 17 29N 88 10W The chief port of Belize, on the Caribbean coast. It was formerly capital of Belize but following a severe hurricane (1961), Belmopan, which became capital in 1970, was constructed inland. The main exports are timber, coconuts, and maize. Population (1994): 48 655.

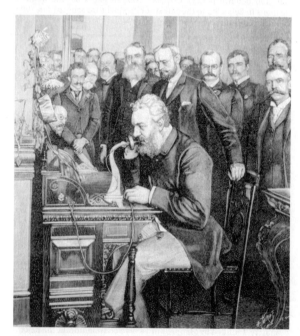

Alexander Graham Bell ▸ Inaugurating the New York–Chicago telephone line in 1892.

● **Bell, Alexander Graham** ▸ (1847–1922) Scottish-born US scientist and inventor. He went to Canada in 1870 and to the USA in 1873, where he became professor of vocal physiology at Boston University. Bell's work in telegraphy and telephony led to the invention of the telephone, which he patented in 1876, demonstrated at American exhibitions, and had in commercial use by 1877. He also did work in sound recording, electro-optical communication, and aerodynamics.

● **Bell, Currer, Ellis, and Acton** ▷*See* Brontë sisters.

● **Bell, Gertrude** ▸ (Gertrude Margaret Lowthian Bell; 1868–1926)

British traveller, scholar, and diplomat. She travelled widely in the Middle East and was political secretary in Baghdad from 1917. She translated the Persian poet ▷Hafiz, wrote several travel books, and founded the national archaeological museum in Baghdad.

● **belladonna** ▷*See* deadly nightshade.

● **belladonna lily** ▷*See* Amaryllis.

● **Bellarmine, St Robert** ▶ (1542–1621) Italian Jesuit theologian, cardinal (from 1599), and archbishop of Capua (1602–05): canonized in 1930. An influential counter-Reformation theologian, he held Galileo in high esteem and privately advised him to regard the Copernican system as hypothetical, although he formally pronounced the system "false and erroneous". His writings include *Disputationes de controversiis Christianae fidei* (1586–93), a statement of Catholic doctrine, and he played an important part in the revised edition of the Vulgate published in 1592. The stoneware wine jugs with a bearded face that were popular in the Rhineland between about 1550 and 1700 became known as Bellarmines, on the grounds that they originated as Protestant caricatures of the cardinal.

● **Bellay, Joachim de** ▶ (1522–60) French poet. In 1549 he published *Défense et illustration de la langue française*, the manifesto of the ▷Pléiade, and *Olive*, the first book of love sonnets in French. While accompanying his cousin Cardinal Jean du Bellay on a mission to Rome, he wrote *Antiquités de Rome* (1558) and *Regrets* (1558).

● **Bell Bay** ▶ 41 8S 146 53E A port in Australia, in N Tasmania on the River Tamar estuary. It is the site of a large aluminium plant using bauxite from Queensland.

● **bellbird** ▷*See* cotinga.

● **Bellerophon** ▶ In Greek mythology, the grandson of Sisyphus and son of Glaucus, King of Corinth. Sent by Iobates, King of Lycia, to kill the ▷Chimera, he was able to carry out his task by flying above the dragon on Pegasus, a winged horse he had previously captured and tamed with the aid of Athena.

● **Bellingshausen, Fabian Gottlieb, Baron von** ▶ (1778–1852) Russian explorer. In 1819 he led an expedition to the Antarctic, surveying the South Georgia and South Sandwich Islands and discovering the islands Peter I and Alexander I. The Bellingshausen Sea was named after him.

● **Bellingshausen Sea** ▶ A section of the S Pacific Ocean bordering on Antarctica, extending between the Antarctic Peninsula and Ellsworth Land. It always contains pack ice.

● **Bellini, Jacopo** ▶ (c. 1400–c. 1470) Venetian painter, who was a pupil of ▷Gentile da Fabriano. In the early 1420s he probably visited Florence. Although his few surviving paintings retain the decorative conventions of Byzantine and Gothic art, his two sketchbooks (British Museum and Louvre) reveal a remarkable understanding of perspective. They influenced his son-in-law Andrea ▷Mantegna and his two sons, who both trained under him. The eldest, **Gentile Bellini** (c. 1429–1507), is best known for his portraits and procession scenes. *The Procession in St Mark's Square* (Accademia, Venice) depicts his native city with a realism that anticipates Canaletto. In 1479 he accompanied the Doge to Constantinople, where he painted Sultan Mehmed II (National Gallery, London). Gentile's brother **Giovanni Bellini** (c. 1430–1516) was an important influence on Venetian art, especially through his pupils ▷Titian and ▷Giorgione. His early work is indebted to Mantegna. From about 1475 his use of the Flemish technique of oil painting, introduced to him by ▷Antonello da Messina, led to his richer use of colour and softer treatment of form. His paintings included several altarpieces, such as *Madonna and Saints* (S Zaccaria, Venice), and portraits, such as *Doge Loredano* (National Gallery, London).

● **Bellini, Vincenzo** ▶ (1801–35) Italian opera composer. Of his 11 operas, *La somnambula* and *Norma* (both 1831) and *I Puritani* (1835) remain popular, although they require outstanding singers to meet the demands of the ▷coloratura style.

● **Bellinzona** ▶ 46 12N 9 02E A town in S Switzerland, on the River Ticino. It is dominated by three 15th-century castles. A tourist centre, it also has small industries. Population (1990): 35 860.

● **Bello, Andrés** ▶ (1781–1865) Venezuelan scholar and poet. He accompanied Simón Bolívar on a revolutionary mission to London in 1810 and stayed there until 1829. The pastoral poems of *Silvas americanas* (1826–27) are influenced by Virgil. He founded the University of Chile (1843), drafted the country's legal code, and wrote a definitive Spanish grammar (1847).

● **Belloc, (Joseph-Pierre) Hilaire** ▶ (1870–1953) British poet and essayist. Born in France, he was educated at Oxford and served as a Liberal MP from 1906 to 1910. His works include essays, historical biographies, and satirical novels, often illustrated by his friend G. K. ▷Chesterton. An energetic Roman Catholic apologist, he vigorously opposed the socialism of G. B. ▷Shaw and H. G. ▷Wells. His most popular works are light verse, such as *Cautionary Tales* (1907).

● **Bellotto, Bernardo** ▶ (1720–80) Venetian painter, mainly of cityscapes. His early works are virtually indistinguishable from those of his uncle and tutor, ▷Canaletto. In 1747 he left Venice, becoming court painter in Dresden (1747–58; 1761–67) and then Warsaw (1768–80). His paintings are noted for their meticulous detail.

● **Bellow, Saul** ▶ (1915–) Canadian-born US novelist, the son of poor Russian Jewish immigrants. His first novel, *Dangling Man* (1944), was influenced by ▷existentialism. His later novels, such as *Mr Sammler's Planet* (1970), *Humboldt's Gift* (1975), and *The Dean's December* (1982), are ironic studies of urban Jewish intellectuals. Other publications include *Him with his Foot in his Mouth* (1986), *More Die of Heartbreak* (1987), and *The Actual* (1997); in 1976 he won the Nobel Prize.

● **bell ringing** ▷*See* bells; change ringing.

● **Bell Rock** ▶ (or Inchcape Rock) 56 26N 2 24W A reef off the NE coast of Scotland, in the North Sea. A lighthouse designed by Robert Stevenson, grandfather of Robert Louis Stevenson, was built here (1807–11).

● **bells** ▶ Hollow metal cup-shaped structures that when struck emit either pure tones or an acceptable mixture of tones. Bells vary in size from small hand bells to the 220-tonne "Tsar Kolokol" in the grounds of the Kremlin, Moscow. Large bells, especially church bells, are cast in bronze in an insulated mould, which is allowed to cool slowly (up to two weeks) to prevent the formation of cracks. After sand-blasting and polishing, the bells may be machined internally so that they resonate at a desired pitch. Most church bells have an internal clapper but some large Buddhist-temple bells are struck externally. ▷*See also* carillon.

● **Bell's palsy** ▶ Paralysis of the muscles on one side of the face, causing weakness and inability to close the eye. First described by the Scottish physiologist Sir Charles Bell (1774–1842), it usually resolves spontaneously; the cause is not known.

● **Bell's theorem** ▶ A theorem proposed in 1964 by the British theoretical physicist John S. Bell (1928–90). It concerns the notion that quantum mechanics is not a complete description of reality and that some more satisfactory explanation involving undiscovered "hidden variables" exists. Such an alternative could account for certain unusual features of quantum mechanics, such as the ▷EPR paradox. Bell considered a system in which two photons are created; each will have values of ▷spin directed along three mutually perpendicular axes X, Y, Z. The spin components may be in one of two opposite directions: X^+ or X^-, Y^+ or Y^-, Z^+ or Z^-. If simultaneous measurements are made on one photon in one direction and on the other photon in a different direction, Bell showed that a set of inequalities, called **Bell's inequalities**, would hold between probabilities of measurements. These inequalities can be proved to be true only if hidden variables are involved. If quantum mechanics is valid, the inequalities are violated.

The inequalities provided a means of investigating the hidden variables experimentally. A number of tests have been carried out, the best known of which was **Aspect's experiment**, performed in 1982 by Alain Aspect in Paris, using pairs of photons emitted in opposite directions to a separation of 12 metres. The results showed that Bell's inequalities were, in fact, violated; they are therefore generally accepted as supporting the principles of quantum mechanics and demonstrating that the particles in the EPR paradox form part of a **quantum entanglement** system, even though widely separated.

● **Belmonte y García, Juan** ▶ (1892–1962) Spanish matador, who was active from 1913 until 1934. His technique of working very close to bulls revolutionized bullfighting.

● **Belmopan** ▶ 17 12N 88 00W The capital of Belize, on the River Belize about 80 km (50 mi) inland from Belize City, which it succeeded as capital in 1970 after the latter was damaged by a hurricane in 1961. Population (1996 est): 6490.

● **Belo Horizonte** ▶ 19 54S 43 54W A city in SE Brazil, in Minas Gerais state. Founded in 1897, it was Brazil's first planned city. Distinctive architecture includes Oscar Niemeyer's Chapel of São Francisco. The chief industries include cotton textiles, meat processing, and iron and steel. It is the site of two universities. Population (1997): 1 529 566.

● **Belorussia** ▷*See* Belarus, Republic of.

● **Belsen** ▷*See* concentration camps.

● **Belshazzar** ▶ In the Old Testament, the son of ▷Nebuchadnezzar and the last King of Babylon. At a feast given by him, the prophet Daniel interpreted the supernatural handwriting that appeared on the wall—*Mene, Mene, Tekel, Upharsin*—as foretelling the destruction of Babylon and Belshazzar's downfall (Daniel 5.25).

● **beluga** ▶ **1.** A giant ▷sturgeon, *Huso huso*, up to 8.4 m long, that occurs in the Caspian and Black Seas and the River Volga of E Europe. It is a highly prolific egg producer and the source of the best caviar. **2.** ▷*See* white whale.

● **Belyi, Andrei** ▶ (Boris Nikolaevich Bugaev; 1880–1934) Russian symbolist poet and critic. He studied mathematics and philosophy at Moscow University, but his interest in mysticism led him into symbolism. In 1901 he published *Simfoniya*, an attempted synthesis of all the arts around a prose poem, and several volumes of poetry and criticism. Disillusioned with the aftermath of the Revolution, he lived abroad from 1921 to 1923.

● **Bemba** ▶ A Central ▷Bantu people of NE Zambia and neighbouring areas of the Democratic Republic of Congo and Rhodesia whose language has become widely spoken in Zambia. They were traditionally ruled by members of the matrilineal royal clan from which the supreme chief, or Chitimukulu, came.

● **Bembo, Pietro** ▶ (1470–1547) Italian scholar. He was secretary to Pope Leo X from 1513 to 1521 and was made cardinal in 1539. His most important work, *Prose della volgar lingua* (1525), set out to develop Italian into a literary language equal to Latin. *Rime* (1530) is a collection of his Italian poetry.

● **Benares** ▷*See* Varanasi.

● **Ben Bella, Ahmed** ▶ (1916–) Algerian statesman; president (1963–65). After service in the French army during World War II he helped to form the ▷Front de Libération nationale (FLN) in 1954. Imprisoned by the French for six years, he was released at independence in 1962 and elected prime minister (1962–63) and then president. He was overthrown in 1965 by ▷Boumédienne and imprisoned until 1979. In 1990 he returned to active politics in Algeria after nine years in exile.

● **Benbow, John** ▶ (1653–1702) English naval officer. During the War of the Spanish Succession, Benbow fought a superior French force off Santa Marta for four days, unsupported by his fellow captains, who disobeyed his orders. Although he was wounded, he continued to direct the battle from the deck, but was compelled to withdraw and died in Jamaica.

● **Benchley, Robert Charles** ▶ (1889–1945) US humorist and leading wit of the ▷Algonquin Round Table. He edited *Vanity Fair* and worked as drama critic for *Life* and the *New Yorker*. He published 15 volumes of his collected humorous essays, including *My Ten Years in a Quandary* (1936). He acted in several films and himself made 46 short comic films.

● **Benda, Julien** ▶ (1867–1956) French novelist and philosopher. An advocate of the classical ideals of reason and order, he wrote several books attacking the philosophy of ▷Bergson. His most famous work, *La Trahison des clercs* (1927), demanded that the intellectual's commitment to truth should not be compromised by political or emotional involvements.

● **Bendigo** ▶ 36 48S 144 21E A city in Australia, in central Victoria. It grew rapidly following a gold discovery in 1851 and is now a commercial centre with the third largest livestock market in Australia. Population (1991 est): 70 360.

● **bends** ▷*See* decompression sickness.

● **Benedict XV** ▶ (Giacomo della Chiesa; 1854–1922) Pope (1914–22). A former papal diplomat, he was elected shortly after the outbreak of World War I, in which he maintained a strict neutrality while attempting to negotiate peace and to curb atrocities. Thereafter he reformed papal administration and diplomacy and was a notable supporter of missionary activity.

● **Benedictines** ▶ The monks and nuns belonging to the Roman Catholic Order of St Benedict (OSB), a union of independent abbeys all of which follow the Rule of St ▷Benedict of Nursia. They have always acted as scholars and educators and were important in preserving the learning of antiquity after the fall of the Roman Empire. They have also exercised a great influence in maintaining high standards for the sacred art and music used in the liturgy. The liqueur Bénédictine is named after the order and is made at Fécamp, France.

● **Benedict of Nursia, St** ▶ (c. 480–c. 550) Italian saint, the father of western monasticism. Educated at Rome, he withdrew from society about 500 and lived for a time as a hermit near Rome. He eventually established 12 monasteries with 12 monks each. About 525 he and a few monks established themselves at Monte Cassino, where he drew up his monastic rule, which provided for government by an elected abbot, residence in one place, obedience, observance of prayers at fixed hours (the Divine Office), common ownership of property, and a life of work, prayer, and study. The Rule was originally intended for laymen, and Benedict himself was apparently not ordained. He was buried at Monte Cassino. Feast day: 21 March. Emblems: a broken cup and a raven.

● **benefit of clergy** ▶ The development in England of the 12th-century canon law that criminous clerks (criminal clerics) should not be tried by both ecclesiastical and secular courts. Henry II's acceptance of this principle gave all clerics the right to be tried solely in ecclesiastical courts. These could not inflict capital punishment, from which clergy were thus immune. Much abused in the later middle ages, the privilege was increasingly limited during and after the Reformation although it was not finally abolished until the early 19th century.

● **Bene Israel** ▶ (Hebrew: Children of Israel) Indian Jewish community of uncertain origin, now concentrated mainly in Bombay.

● **Benelux** ▶ The customs union formed by Belgium, the Netherlands, and Luxembourg in 1948. It was the first free-trade market in Europe. The three countries standardized prices, welfare benefits, wages, and taxes and allowed free immigration and movement of labour and capital between them. All three countries are now members of the ▷European Union, which has similar aims.

● **Beneš, Edvard** ▶ (1884–1948) Czechoslovak statesman. In 1918 Beneš helped Tomáš ▷Masaryk to found Czechoslovakia and became foreign minister, playing an important role in the League of Nations. In 1935 he became president but went into exile when he was forced to cede the ▷Sudetenland to Germany (1938). He spent World War II as president of a provisional government in London, returning to Czechoslovakia in 1945. He resigned the presidency in 1948, when Czechoslovakia became a communist state.

● **Benét, Stephen Vincent** ▶ (1898–1943) US poet and novelist. Son of an army officer, he wrote chiefly on themes of American history and myth. His best-known work is *John Brown's Body* (1928), an epic poem about the Civil War.

● **Benevento** ▶ 41 08N 14 46E A town in S Italy, in Campania. It has Roman remains, including Trajan's Arch (114–17 AD), and a 9th-century cathedral. Its manufactures include leather goods, agricultural machinery, confectionery, and Strega liqueur. Population (1990): 64 842.

● **Bengal** ► A region of the Indian subcontinent, in the NE on the Bay of Bengal around the vast Ganges and Brahmaputra deltas. Divided between India and Bangladesh, it has a flourishing culture.

History: on the fringe of early Indian civilization, Bengal became the centre of Buddhist (8th–12th centuries), Hindu (11th–13th centuries), and finally Islamic dynasties. The base for British expansion through India, it was partitioned between India and Pakistan at independence (1947). ▷*See also* West Bengal.

● **Bengal, Bay of** ► The shallow NE limb of the Indian Ocean, between the Indian subcontinent on the W and Myanmar (Burma) and the Andaman and Nicobar Islands on the E. Shipping and coastal life are dominated by the NE winter monsoon and the SW summer monsoon.

● **Bengali** ► An Indo-Aryan language spoken by 80 million people in Bangladesh and West Bengal (India). The literary form of the language uses many ▷Sanskrit words. It was the first Indian language to imitate Western literary modes in fiction, drama, and poetry. There is a distinct colloquial form.

● **Benghazi** ► (or Banghazi; Italian name: Bengasi) 32 07N 20 05E The second largest city in Libya, on the Gulf of Sidra. Severely damaged during World War II, it has experienced recent growth with the development of local oilfields; other industries include light engineering. Population (1991): 500 000.

● **Benguela** ► (or Benguella) 12 34S 13 24E A town in W Angola, on the Atlantic Ocean. It is overshadowed as a port by Lobito; industries include fish drying and soap production. Population (latest est): 155 000.

● **Ben-Gurion, David** ► (1886–1973) Israeli statesman, known as the Father of the Nation. He was Israel's first prime minister (1948–53, 1955–63). Born David Gruen in Poland, he adopted the Hebrew name Ben-Gurion after arriving in Palestine in 1906. In 1917 he joined the British Army's Jewish Legion to free Palestine from Ottoman control (achieved in 1918) and after the establishment of British rule worked to establish a Jewish home in Palestine, promised in the ▷Balfour Declaration. In 1920 he founded the General Federation of Labour (the Histadrut) and in 1930, the Israeli Workers' Party (Mapai). Becoming chairman of the Zionist Executive in 1935, he led the Zionist effort to establish a Jewish state, finally achieved in 1948. As prime minister he formed an Israeli army from the various guerrilla groups and adopted a tough line against Arab attack. After resigning the prime ministership in 1963, he was leader of the opposition party, the Rafi, until his retirement in 1970.

● **Beni, Río** ► A river in Bolivia. Rising near La Paz, it flows NE to join the Río Mamoré. Length: over 1600 km (1000 mi).

● **Benin, Republic of** ► (name until 1975: Dahomey) A country in West Africa, on the Gulf of Guinea. Flat forests and swamps in the S rise to plateaus in the centre and to mountains in the N. The population is mainly Fon and Yoruba in the N and Somba and Bariba in the S.

Economy: chiefly agricultural, the main crops being maize, cassava, rice, and vegetables. Cotton has been introduced in the N and coffee in the S, and these provide the main exports. Forests produce palm oil and kernels, and there is some freshwater fishing. Offshore oil has been found but production, which began in the 1980s, has so far proved disappointing. The country has a massive external debt.

History: the powerful Aja kingdom of Dahomey was a centre of the slave trade in the 17th century but was conquered by the French in 1893 and became part of French West Africa. Dahomey attained self-government in 1958 and became an independent republic within the French Community in 1960. After that the country was shaken by a series of military coups, in the last of which (1972) Brig Gen Mathieu Kérékou (1933–) seized power; in 1974 he established a Marxist-Leninist state. Increasing unrest led to the approval of a new pluralistic constitution in 1990; the following year parliamentary elections were held and Nicéphore Soglo was elected president. In 1996 the former military leader Kérékou was voted back into power as president.

Republic of Benin

Head of state	President Mathieu Kérékou
Official language	French
Official currency	CFA (Communauté financière africaine) franc of 100 centimes
Area	112 600 sq km (43 464 sq mi)
Population (1997 est)	5 902 000
Capital	Porto Novo
Main port	Cotonou

● **Benin City** ► 6 19N 5 41E A city in Nigeria. It is an important centre for the rubber industry and also exports palm oil. Population (1996 est): 229 400.

● **Benjamin** ► In the Old Testament, the youngest son of Jacob by Rachel, who died during childbirth. He was named Ben-oni (son of ill luck) by Rachel before she died but called Benjamin (son of good luck) by Jacob. He became his father's favourite after Joseph was sold into slavery in Egypt. Figuratively he represents the especially loved younger son. His descendants formed one of the 12 ▷tribes of Israel and later, with the tribe of Judah, formed the southern kingdom of Judah.

● **Benjamin, Arthur** ► (1893–1960) Australian pianist and composer, who became a professor at the Royal College of Music in London in 1926. As well as the popular *Jamaican Rumba* (1938), he wrote five operas and a harmonica concerto (1953).

● **Benn, Tony** ► (Anthony Neil Wedgwood B.) (1925–) British Labour politician. The 2nd Viscount Stansgate from 1960, he renounced his peerage in 1963, the first person to do so under the Peerage Act (1963). He was minister of technology (1966–70), for industry (1974–75), and for energy (1975–79). In the 1980s he emerged as the leader of the party's left wing, standing unsuccessfully for the deputy leadership of the party in 1981 and the leadership in 1988. He is also known for his voluminous political *Diaries* (from 1987).

● **Bennett, Alan** ► (1934–) British actor and dramatist, noted for his depiction of the lower middle classes and "respectable" working classes in the North of England. He first attracted attention as a Cambridge undergraduate in the Cambridge Footlights revue *Beyond the Fringe* (1959), which he cowrote with Jonathan ▷Miller. His plays include *Forty Years On* (1968), *Habeas Corpus* (1973), *Single Spies* (1988), and *The Madness of George III* (1991; filmed 1995). His numerous works for television include two series of monologues entitled *Talking Heads* (1988, 1998), which demonstrate his ear for linguistic idiosyncracies. *Writing Home* (1994) was a bestselling collection of essays and diaries.

● **Bennett, (Enoch) Arnold** ► (1837–1931) British novelist. The son of a solicitor in Newcastle-under-Lyme, he published his first novel, *A Man from the North*, in 1898 and lived in Paris from 1902 to 1912. His best-known novels are about life in the Potteries area of Staffordshire, where he grew up. They include *Anna of the Five Towns* (1902), *The Old Wives' Tale* (1908), and *Clayhanger* (1910).

● **Bennett, James Gordon** ► (1795–1872) US newspaper editor, born in Scotland. He founded the *New York Herald* (1835), in which he pioneered many of the techniques of modern journalism. His son **James Gordon Bennett** (1841–1918) became editor of the *Herald* in 1867. He financed several explorers, including Stanley in his quest for Livingstone.

● **Bennett, Richard Bedford, Viscount** ► (1870–1947) Canadian statesman; Conservative prime minister (1930–35). A lawyer and businessman, he was a champion of protective tariffs. In 1932 he presided over the Imperial Economic Conference in Ottawa, which established bilateral trade agreements between countries in the British Commonwealth.

● **Bennett, Sir Richard Rodney** ► (1936–) British composer known primarily for his scores for such films as *Far from the Madding Crowd* (1967), *Murder on the Orient Express* (1974), *Yanks* (1980), and *Four Weddings and a Funeral* (1994) and for his five major operas, including *The Mines of Sulphur* (1963) and *Victory* (1970). Also active as a pianist in jazz and classical music, he has written an opera for children, *All the King's Men* (1969), and many varied instrumental works.

● **Bennett, Sir William Sterndale** ► (1816–75) British pianist, conductor, and composer. A child prodigy, his first piano concerto (1832) impressed Mendelssohn, who introduced him to Schumann. Bennett was a prolific composer of opera and instrumental works; his works are little known today.

● **Ben Nevis** ▶ 56 48N 5 00W The highest mountain in the British Isles, in Highland, Scotland, in the Grampians. Height: 1343 m (4406 ft).

● **Benny, Jack** ▶ (Benjamin Kubelsky; 1894–1974) US comedian. In vaudeville from an early age, he began making films in 1929. His act featured meanness, joke playing of the violin, and, from 1933, always being 39 years old. His film *To be or Not To Be* (1942) was outstanding and he had his own radio (1932–55) and television (1950–65) shows.

● **Benoit de Sainte-Maure** ▶ (12th century AD) French poet. His long epic poem, *Roman de Troie*, is loosely based on the legends of ▷Troy. He is possibly also the author of a verse history of the Dukes of Normandy, commissioned by Henry II in 1174.

● **Benoni** ▶ 26 12S 28 18E A city in South Africa, in Gauteng on the Witwatersrand. Founded in 1903 as a gold-mining centre, it is an important industrial city, especially for engineering. Population (1991): 113 501.

● **Benson, Sir Frank** ▶ (1858–1939) British actor-manager. In 1883 he founded his own company, which toured Britain with productions of Shakespeare. He trained many actors and was knighted on stage in 1916.

● **Bentham, Jeremy** ▶ (1748–1832) British philosopher, pioneer of ▷utilitarianism. From a wealthy middle-class background, he went to Oxford and then, aged only 15, to Lincoln's Inn. He preferred legal theory to practice and in 1776 published *A Fragment on Government*. In 1789 *Principles of Morals and Legislation* presented utilitarianism to the world. He travelled widely, championing prison reform and the French Revolution. He retired to the country in 1814, a republican hero, and wrote copiously on politics and ethics until his death. He founded the *Westminster Review* (1823) to promote philosophical radicalism.

● **benthos** ▶ An ecological division of aquatic life comprising all those organisms that live on the sea bed. The benthos includes bacteria, seaweeds and other algae, and a variety of crawling, burrowing, or sedentary animals, such as corals, sponges, polychaete worms, bivalve molluscs, crustaceans, starfish and other echinoderms, and bottom-dwelling fish. *Compare* nekton; plankton.

● **Bentinck, Lord William (Henry Cavendish)** ▷*See* Portland, William Henry Cavendish Bentinck, 3rd Duke of.

● **Bentivoglio** ▶ An aristocratic family that ruled Bologna (Italy) from 1447 until 1506. **Sante Bentivoglio** (1424–63) established his family's supremacy in Bologna. He and his son **Giovanni Bentivoglio** (1443–1508) were notable patrons of the arts. Increasingly autocratic, and unpopular, Giovanni and his family were expelled from Bologna in 1506 with the support of Pope ▷Julius II. Subsequent members of the family, notably **Guido Bentivoglio** (1579–1644), were famous diplomats and authors.

● **Bentley, Edmund Clerihew** ▶ (1875–1956) British writer. A close friend of G. K. ▷Chesterton, he wrote a classic detective novel, *Trent's Last Case* (1913). He invented the clerihew, a humorous verse form consisting of two rhyming couplets, the first rhyme being provided by the subject's name: Sir Christopher Wren Said, "I am going to dine with some men. If anybody calls Say I am designing St Paul's."

● **Bentley, Richard** ▶ (1662–1742) English scholar. Bentley was appointed Keeper of the Royal Libraries in 1694 and in 1700 Master of Trinity College, Cambridge. His critical works on the scriptures and the classics, in particular his famous *Dissertation on the Letters of Phalaris* (1699), combined the philological and historical approaches, paving the way for modern textual criticism.

● **Benton, Thomas Hart** ▶ (1889–1975) US painter of rural life. As the leader and spokesman of the American Regionalist painters of the 1930s, Benton advocated the need to free US painting from the overwhelming influence of French abstract art and to create an indigenous artistic tradition. He is also known for his murals for such

public institutions as the New School of Social Research, New York, and the Missouri State Capitol in Jefferson City.

● **bentwood furniture** ▶ Furniture constructed by a mass-production process invented by a Viennese designer Michael Thonet (1796–1871). It involved steaming beechwood rods and laminated board until they could be bent into the desired shapes. The shaped sections were transported unassembled and screwed together at the destination. Typical chairs, coat stands, etc., are curved in rococo style. The technique has been exploited by modern designers, such as Marcel ▷Breuer and many Scandinavian designers.

● **Benue, River** ▶ A river in West Africa. Rising in N Cameroon, it flows W across Nigeria to join the River Niger at Lokoja. Length: 1400 km (870 mi).

● **Benxi** ▶ (or Pen-ki) 41 21N 123 45E A city in NE China, in Liaoning province. It is a centre of iron and steel production. Population (1993 est): 768 778.

● **Benz, Karl (Friedrich)** ▶ (1844–1929) German engineer and ▢car manufacturer. In 1885 he built the first car to be driven by an internal-combustion engine. By 1895 he was offering for sale a range of four-wheeled cars in competition with those produced by Gottlieb ▷Daimler. The Benz Company merged with Daimler in 1926 to form Daimler-Benz, the makers of Mercedes-Benz cars.

● **benzene** ▶ (or benzol; C_6H_6) A colourless highly flammable liquid. It is the simplest ▢aromatic compound, its molecules consisting of a ring of six carbon atoms each with a hydrogen atom attached. Benzene is obtained from ▷oil and from ▷coal tar. It is widely used in the chemical industry, for example in making ▷detergents, ▷nylon, and ▷insecticides.

● **benzodiazepines** ▶ A class of tranquillizing drugs that act by depressing specific areas of the brain. Benzodiazepines, such as diazepam (Valium) and chlordiazepoxide (Librium), are used as ▷sedatives in the treatment of anxiety. Diazepam is also used to control epileptic fits and chlordiazepoxide is helpful in the treatment of alcohol-withdrawal symptoms. Nitrazepam (Mogadon) is used as a sleeping pill (see hypnotics). Recent years have seen mounting concern about the effects of long-term usage, which may include depression and memory loss. Prolonged use can also result in dependence, and abuse of benzodiazepines, particularly temazepam (Normison), has increased; temazepam is now a controlled drug (see drugs).

● **benzoic acid** ▶ (C_6H_5COOH) A white crystalline powder, the simplest of the aromatic ▷fatty acids. It occurs naturally in many plants and is used in preserving food.

● **benzoin** ▶ 1. ($C_6H_5CHOHCOC_6H_5$) A white or yellowish crystalline substance used to make other organic compounds. 2. (or gum benjamin) A fragrant gum resin obtained from the trunk of a SE Asian tree, *Styrax benzoin*. It is used in medicine (as a constituent of friar's balsam), in cosmetics, and in perfumery.

● **Ben-Zvi, Itzhak** ▶ (1884–1963) Israeli statesman; president (1952–63). Born in Russia, where he was an active Zionist, he went to Palestine in 1907. With David ▷Ben-Gurion, Ben-Zvi helped to found the state of Israel (1947). He was also a noted archaeologist.

● **Beowulf** ▶ An Anglo-Saxon epic poem preserved in a late 10th-century manuscript. Probably composed or at least reworked in the 8th century by a Christian poet sympathetic to pagan ideals of honour and courage, it alludes to historical events of early 6th-century Scandinavia. In the first part the hero, Beowulf, kills the marauding monster, Grendel; when Grendel's mother retaliates he kills her in her underwater cave. In the second part, Beowulf, now king of the Swedish tribe of Geats, slays a dragon and seizes its hoard of treasure, but is mortally wounded.

● **Bérain the Elder, Jean** ▶ (1637–1711) French designer, engraver, and painter; royal designer to Louis XIV of France. He designed festival decorations, furniture, tapestries, and opera costumes for the court, often decorated with immense detail, which influenced the later rococo style. He used many Chinese motifs in his designs to satisfy the king's fondness for oriental art.

● **Beranger, Pierre Jean de** ▶ (1780–1857) French poet and songwriter. His satirical verse and republican sentiments led to his imprisonment under the Bourbon monarchy.

● **Berbera** ▶ 10 30N 45 25E A port in N Somalia, on the Gulf of Aden. It has a deepwater harbour and exports sheep, leather, ghee, frankincense, and myrrh. Population (latest est): 70 000.

● **Berberis** ▶ A genus of deciduous or evergreen spiny shrubs (over 400 species), commonly known as barberry, mostly native to Central and E Asia and South America but also occurring in parts of Europe, Africa, and North America. The small yellow or orange flowers usually grow in clusters and the fruits are bright-red berries. Several species are widely grown as ornamentals for their flowers, fruits, or attractive autumn foliage. Berberis is implicated in a rust disease of wheat and is therefore outlawed in some areas. Family: *Berberidaceae*.

● **Berbers** ▶ A Muslim people occupying parts of N Africa (Morocco, Algeria, Tunisia, and adjacent regions) and speaking a non-Semitic language. Prior to the Arab conquests of the 7th century AD and the establishment of Arabic speech, Berber languages were spoken over the whole of the area from Egypt to the Atlantic. Though Arabic has long been the dominant language it has not entirely ousted Berber, which is spoken by an estimated ten million people, and Morocco is still predominantly Berber in population. The Berbers played an important role in the Islamic conquest of the Iberian peninsula in the 8th century and in the subsequent occupation of Spain. The Berbers are largely agriculturalists, although some still follow a nomadic way of life.

● **Berchtesgaden** ▶ 47 38N 13 00E A resort in SE Germany, in the Bavarian Alps. It is the site of Hitler's fortified mountain retreat, the Berghof. Salt has been mined here since the 12th century. Population (1992): 7865.

● **Berdyaev, Nikolai** ▶ (1874–1948) Russian mystical philosopher. He was expelled from Russia (1922) for teaching religion and until World War II his academy near Paris and his journal *The Path* spread his ideas in Europe. He saw communism as an ungodly manifestation of Russia's messianic destiny. *Dreams and Reality* (1950) summarizes his ideas.

● **Berdyansk** ▶ (name from 1939 until 1958: Osipenko) 46 45N 36 47E A port in Ukraine, on the Sea of Azov. It is a seaside resort and its most important economic activities relate to fishing. Flour milling and oil refining are also carried out. Population (1991 est): 135 000.

Beowulf ▶ Facsimile of a page from the only preserved 10th-century manuscript.

● **Berenson, Bernard** ▶ (1865–1959) US art historian, whose works set new standards of criticism. Inspired by the beauty of Italy, where he spent much time, he wrote the definitive *Italian Painters of the Renaissance* (1894–1907). His aesthetic delight is captured in *Drawings of the Florentine Painters* (1903).

● **Berezniki** ▶ 59 26N 56 49E A port in E Russia on the River Kama.

Founded in 1883, it became one of the largest centres for the chemical industry in the Soviet Union. Population (1995 est): 184 000.

● **Berg, Alban** ▶ (1885–1935) Austrian composer. A friend and pupil of ▷Schoenberg, he adopted ▷atonality and used ▷serialism, though in a highly personal and original fashion. His greatest works are the operas *Wozzeck* (1915–21) from the play by ▷Büchner and *Lulu* (1928–35) from plays by ▷Wedekind, the intensely personal *Lyric Suite* (for string quartet; 1925–26), and a violin concerto (1935).

● **Bergamo** ▶ 45 42N 9 40E A city in Italy, in Lombardy in the foothills of the Alps. It has a 12th-century romanesque cathedral. Machinery, textiles, and cement are manufactured. Population (1996 est): 116 990.

● **bergamot** ▶ A tree, *Citrus bergamia*, closely related to the orange. An essence (oil of bergamot) extracted from the rind of its fruit is used in perfumery, for which the tree is cultivated in S Italy and Sicily. ▷*See* Citrus. The name is also given to two plants of the mint family (*Labiatae*): *Mentha citrata*, which yields an extract similar to oil of bergamot, and *Monarda citriodora* (lemon bergamot) sometimes used in a tealike beverage.

● **Bergen** ▶ 60 23N 5 20E A seaport and second largest city in Norway, situated in the SW. Founded about 1070 AD, it became the chief commercial city and the country's capital (12th–13th centuries). It had important connections with Hanseatic merchants (14th–18th centuries). It was rebuilt after damage by fire in 1702, 1855, and 1916 and by bombing during World War II. It is a cultural centre with a university (1948), several museums, and an art gallery. Other notable buildings include the 12th-century Mariakirke (a stone-built church) and the 13th-century Håkonshall (a royal palace). Its industries include shipbuilding and oil refining. It exports fish products and base metals. Population (1997 est): 224 130.

● **Bergenia** ▶ A genus of herbaceous perennial plants (6 species), native to central and E Asia but often cultivated as ornamentals for their attractive foliage and early-blooming pink or white flowers. Family: *Saxifragaceae*.

● **Bergen op Zoom** ▶ 51 30N 4 17E A port in the SW Netherlands, in North Brabant province. An important 15th-century cloth and fishing centre, its industries now include oyster fisheries and iron and steel processing. Population (1991): 46 900.

● **Bergius, Friedrich** ▶ (1884–1949) German chemist, who shared the 1931 Nobel Prize with C. Bosch for research in high-pressure chemical techniques. He manufactured light motor fuels from either coal or heavy petroleum residues by treating them with hydrogen under high pressure and temperature (1913). This process was used extensively by Germany in World War II. After Germany's defeat he emigrated to Spain and then to Argentina.

● **Bergman, Hjalmar (Fredrik Elgérus)** ▶ (1883–1931) Swedish novelist and dramatist. His two novels of provincial life, *Markurells i Wadköping* (*God's Orchid*; 1919) and *Farmor och vår Herre* (*Thy Rod and Thy Staff*; 1921), drew upon his early life in the town of Örebro. He wrote a number of film and radio scripts as well as such plays as *Swedenhielms* (1925).

● **Bergman, Ingmar** ▶ (1918–   ) Swedish film and stage director and screenwriter. His films, which express his austere human vision with great intensity, include *The Seventh Seal* (1956), *Wild Strawberries* (1957), *Persona* (1966), *Scenes from a Marriage* (1974), *Autumn Sonata* (1978), and *Fanny and Alexander* (1982). He was director of the Royal Dramatic Theatre, Stockholm, from 1963 to 1966.

● **Bergman, Ingrid** ▶ (1915–82) Swedish actress. She went to Hollywood in 1939 and became an international film star in the film *Intermezzo* (1939). She later appeared in such films as *Casablanca* (1942), *For Whom the Bell Tolls* (1943), and *Gaslight* (1944). After leaving her Swedish husband to have a child by the Italian film director Roberto ▷Rossellini she was ostracized by Hollywood. However, she returned to America to make her Oscar-winning film *Anastasia* (1956), as well as *Murder on the Orient Express* (1974), and her last film *Autumn Sonata* (1978). She also played in several stage productions. □Bogart, Humphrey.

● **Bergson, Henri** ► (1859–1941) French philosopher and psychologist, one of the most influential thinkers of his time. To reconcile free will and ▷determinism, Bergson distinguished between consciousness, an indivisible flow of cumulative states in which (free) will operates, and the external physical world where causality reigns and objects and events are fixed and discrete. He championed creative against analytic thinking in stylish and penetrating works that include *Matière et mémoire* (1896) and *L'Évolution créatrice* (1907). He won the Nobel Prize for Literature in 1927.

● **Beria, Lavrenti Pavlovich** ► (1899–1953) Soviet politician. A Georgian, he became head of the Soviet secret police in 1938, and a member of the politburo in 1946. During the 1930s and 1940s he took a leading role in the Stalinist purges in which millions were executed or deported to labour camps. After Stalin's death in March, 1953, he was involved in a power struggle with Malenkov and Khrushchev. He was accused of conspiracy in July, tried secretly, and executed in December 1953.

● **beriberi** ► A disease caused by deficiency of ▷vitamin B$_1$ (thiamine), common in areas where the staple diet is polished rice (thiamine occurs mainly in the rice husks). Dry beriberi affects the peripheral nerves, causing muscular weakness and pain. Wet beriberi is probably the result of combined protein malnutrition and thiamine deficiency: it causes accumulation of fluid and swelling of the limbs, leading eventually to heart failure. Treatment consists of providing a diet with adequate thiamine and vitamin supplements.

● **Bering, Vitus Jonassen** ► (*or* V. J. Behring; 1681–1741) Danish navigator. In 1724 he was commissioned by the Russians to explore the area between Siberia and America. He made several voyages from Kamchatka on the last of which (1741) he sighted Alaska from the strait named after him. On his way back, suffering from scurvy, he was wrecked off Bering Island, where he died. The Bering Sea is also named after him.

● **Bering Sea** ► A section of the N Pacific Ocean between Russia, Alaska, and the Aleutian Islands. Navigation is difficult, with storms and a partial ice covering in winter. The NE continental shelf contains oil and gas, as yet unexploited.

● **Bering Strait** ► A narrow shallow channel between Asia and North America, connecting the Bering Sea with the Arctic Ocean. During the Ice Age it bridged the continents when the sea level fell.

● **Berio, Luciano** ► (1925–) Italian composer, a pupil of Dallapiccola. He has lived in the USA since 1962 and was married (1950–65) to the soprano Cathy Berberian (1925–83). A leading composer of the avantgarde, Berio has used serialism, electronic effects, taped sounds, and unusual instrumental techniques in his works. These include a number of *Sequenzas*, each for a different solo instrument, *Omaggio a Joyce* (for taped voice; 1958), *Sinfonia* (1968), partly based on music by Debussy and Mahler, *Un re in ascolto* (1984), and *Continuo* (1991).

● **Beriosova, Svetlana** ► (1932–98) British ballet dancer, born in Lithuania. In 1952 she joined the British Sadler's Wells company, becoming prima ballerina in 1955. She danced both classical and modern roles, and was noted for her *Giselle* (1956).

● **Berkeley** ► 37 53N 122 17W A city in the USA, in California on San Francisco Bay. It is the headquarters of the University of California, where ▷berkelium was discovered. Its manufactures include soap, paint, and chemicals. Population (2000): 102 743.

● **Berkeley, Busby** ► (William Berkeley Enos; 1895–1976) US dance director. He is best known for his elaborate choreography for such Hollywood film musicals as *42nd Street* (1933), the *Gold Diggers* series (1933–37), and *Babes in Arms* (1939).

● **Berkeley, George** ► (1685–1753) Irish bishop and idealist philosopher. In *A New Theory of Vision* (1709), *Principles of Human Knowledge* (1710), and *Three Dialogues between Hylas and Philonous* (1713), he argued that the material world exists only in being perceived by the mind, a view that influenced ▷Hume and, indirectly, ▷Kant. Berkeley's later works, such as *Siris* (1744) are interesting but increasingly eccentric.

● **Berkeley, Sir Lennox Randal Francis** ► (1903–89) British

composer. He studied under Nadia Boulanger and taught at the Royal Academy of Music from 1946 to 1968. Berkeley's compositions include the *Serenade for Strings* (1939), *Four Poems of St Teresa* for contralto and strings (1947), and the fourth symphony (1978).

● **Berkeley, Sir William** ► (1606–77) English colonist; governor of Virginia (1641–49, 1660–77). His attempts to foster trade relations with the Indians were thwarted by Nathaniel Bacon (1647–76), who led a force against the Indians that was defeated by Berkeley's troops (Bacon's Rebellion). He was also the author of a play, *The Lost Lady* (1638).

● **berkelium** ► (Bk) A synthetic transuranic element synthesized by Seaborg and others in 1949 by bombarding americium with helium ions. The longest-lived isotope (^{249}Bk) has a half-life of 314 days; visible amounts of the chloride (BkCl$_3$) have been produced. At no 97; at wt (247).

● **Berkshire** ► A historic county of S England. Under local government reorganization in 1974 it lost a substantial part of the NW to Oxfordshire, while gaining part of SW Buckinghamshire. In 1998 Berkshire county council was abolished, with administrative powers being devolved to six ▷unitary authorities: Bracknell Forest, Reading, Slough, West Berkshire, Windsor and Maidenhead, and Wokingham. The county consists mainly of lowlands rising to the Berkshire Downs in the W. It is bordered by the River Thames in the NE and crossed by the River Kennet. It is predominantly agricultural; chief products are barley, dairy produce, pigs, and poultry. Industries include paints, plastics, and pharmaceutical goods at Slough and light engineering and horticulture at Reading. Area: 1256 sq km (485 sq mi).

● **Berlichingen, Götz von** ► (1480–1562) German knight and mercenary. A professional adventurer, he was already famous for his exploits, in which he lost his right hand, when he became a rebel leader in the ▷Peasants' War (1525). After imprisonment he served Emperor Charles V against the Turks in the 1540s. He inspired Goethe's *Götz von Berlichingen* (1773).

● **Berlin** ► 52 31N 13 20E The capital city and a *Land* of Germany, in the NE of the country on the River Spree. Its numerous industries include the manufacture of electrical equipment, machinery, clothing, and chemicals, as well as publishing and printing. It is a major cultural centre. In the middle of the city, on the former border of East and West Berlin, stands the ▷Brandenburg Gate, E of which runs the Unter den Linden (the famous tree-lined avenue), carefully restored in the 1960s. The former government district, including the restored Reichstag building, was redeveloped for the transfer of the federal government from Bonn in 1999. Humboldt University, formerly Frederick William University (1810), is associated with famous scholars such as Humboldt, Fichte, Hegel, and Ranke. The Free University of Berlin was established in 1948. A major landmark is the Kaiser Wilhelm Church, the ruins of which have been preserved as a reminder of the World Wars.
    History: founded in the 13th century, it was an important strategic and commercial centre and a member of the Hanseatic League. Its independence was reduced by the ▷Hohenzollern Electors of Brandenburg from the 15th century, but it became their capital and grew in importance with their increasing power, becoming the capital of Prussia in the 18th century and of the German Empire in 1871. Badly damaged in World War II, it was occupied by the four major powers after the defeat of Germany. In 1948 Berlin became two separate administrative units: Soviet-controlled East Berlin and West Berlin, formed from the US, UK, and French zones. The Soviet Union blockaded the city for almost a year (1948–49) but it failed to extend its influence to West Berlin (*see* Berlin airlift). From 1949–90 East Berlin was the capital of East Germany. West Berlin remained an enclave within East Germany, administratively associated with but not officially part of West Germany. Despite difficulties in communications it became an active industrial and commercial centre, subsidized by West Germany. In 1961 a dividing wall was built by the East Germans to curb the flow of refugees from E to W; in 1989 pressures for liberalization in East Germany led to easier passage through the partly demolished wall. Full reunification was achieved in 1990,

Berlin ▶ The Brandenburg Gate with crowds of East and West Germans standing on the Wall after it was breached in 1989.

when Berlin became capital of the reunited Germany. Population (1996 est): 3 471 418.

● Berlin, Congress of ▶ (1878) A meeting of European powers, which revised the Treaty of ▷San Stefano that had ended the 1877–78 Russo-Turkish War. The Congress, which was dominated by the German chancellor, ▷Bismarck, limited Russian naval expansion, permitted Austria-Hungary to occupy Bosnia-Hercegovina, and gained Turkish recognition of the independence of Serbia, Romania, and Montenegro and of Bulgarian autonomy under Turkish suzerainty.

● Berlin, Irving ▶ (Israel Baline; 1888–1989) US composer of songs, musical comedies, and film scores, born in Russia. He emigrated with his family to the USA in 1893. He wrote "Alexander's Ragtime Band" while working as a singing waiter and subsequently composed the music, and often the lyrics, for many musicals, including *Top Hat* (1935), *Annie Get Your Gun* (1946), and *Call Me Madam* (1953). His two best-known hits were "God Bless America" (1917) and "White Christmas" (1942).

● Berlin, Sir Isaiah ▶ (1909–97) Latvian-born British philosopher and historian. Although based in Oxford, he was also a diplomat in Washington and Moscow. His works, which defend liberal pluralism and attack the idea of historical determinism, include *The Inevitability of History* (1954), *The Age of Enlightenment* (1956), *Two Concepts of Liberty* (1959), and *The Magus of the North* (1993).

● Berlin airlift ▶ (1948–49) An operation by the Allies after World War II to supply isolated West Berlin with the necessities of life. In 1948 the Soviet Union cut off all rail, road, and water links with the city in an attempt to force the Allies to abandon their rights there. The airlift continued until the blockade was lifted as a result of an embargo on exports from the E European states.

● Berliner Ensemble ▶ A theatre company founded by Bertolt ▷Brecht in East Berlin in 1949. It became fully independent after its move to the Theatre am Schiffbauerdamm in 1945 and was directed after Brecht's death in 1956 by his widow, Helene Weigel (1900–71). The company devoted itself exclusively to works written or adapted by Brecht, and its several European tours won international acclaim for his work.

● Berlinguer, Enrico ▶ (1922–84) Italian politician; leader of the

Italian Communist Party (1958–84). He was noted for his willingness to work through parliamentary channels and was instrumental in March, 1978, in establishing Communist support for the coalition government of Giulio ▷Andreotti.

● Berlin West Africa Conference ▶ (1884–85) A series of meetings held at Berlin under the chairmanship of ▷Bismarck to settle the dispute over possession of the Congo Basin (Central Africa). Among the powers that attended were France, Germany, the UK, Belgium, and Portugal. The Conference declared that the Congo Basin should be neutral with free trade and shipping and that an independent Congo Free State be established; it forbade slave trading.

● Berlioz, (Louis) Hector ▶ (1803–69) French Romantic composer and conductor. Against family opposition he abandoned medicine for music. His first successful work, the *Symphonie Fantastique* (1830–31), was influenced by his love for an Irish actress, Harriet Smithson (1800–54). As winner of the Prix de Rome he went to Italy to study; on his return in 1833 he married Harriet. His dramatic symphony *Harold in Italy* (1834) and choral symphony *Romeo and Juliet* (1839) were popular successes, but the cantata *The Damnation of Faust* (1846) and the opera *Benvenuto Cellini* (1834–38) failed. The oratorio *The Childhood of Christ* (1850–54) was his last major success, for his two-part opera *The Trojans* (1856–59) was not performed complete in his lifetime. Other orchestral works include the overture *Le Corsaire* (1851–52) and *Le Carnaval romain* (1844). He was the author of a treatise on orchestration and memoirs.

● Bermejo, Río ▶ A river of S central South America. Rising in S Bolivia, it flows SE into Argentina to join the River Paraguay. Length: 1046 km (650 mi).

● Bermuda ▶ A United Kingdom overseas territory, comprising some 300 coral islands (of which 20 are inhabited), in the W Atlantic Ocean. The largest island is Bermuda (or Great Bermuda), while smaller ones include Somerset, Ireland, and St George. Approximately three-quarters of the population is Black.
Economy: the subtropical climate has contributed to tourism, which forms the basis of the islands' economy. Low taxation has attracted international finance and insurance. Agricultural products include vegetables and bananas; onions, potatoes, and lily bulbs are exported to the USA.
History: visited by the Spanish navigator Juan de Bermudez in 1515, the islands were first settled in 1609 by English colonists shipwrecked there on the way to Virginia. They became the responsibility of the English Crown in 1684 and self-governing in 1968. Demands for independence led to serious unrest in the 1970s, but in 1995 islanders voted against independence in a referendum. In 1998 the United Bermuda Party lost power for the first time since independence and the Labour Party formed a government under Jennifer Smith.

Bermuda

Head of state	Queen Elizabeth II, represented by the governor-general, Thorold Masefield
Official language	English
Official currency	Bermuda dollar of 100 cents
Area	53 sq km (20 sq mi)
Population (1994)	60 075
Capital	Hamilton

● Bermuda Triangle ▶ The most notorious of several geographic regions, all lying roughly between 30° and 40° of latitude, in which numerous ships and aircraft have vanished without trace. The Triangle covers about 3 900 000 sq km (1 500 000 sq mi) between Bermuda, Florida, and Puerto Rico. No generally satisfactory explanation of these disappearances has been advanced, but the great depth of the sea and powerful currents may explain the lack of wreckage.

● Bern ▶ (French name: Berne) 46 57N 95 58W The capital of Switzerland, on the River Aare. Founded as a military post in the 12th century, it joined the Swiss Confederation in 1353 and became the capital in 1848. Its many notable buildings include the gothic cathedral (15th century). Since the 16th century it has had a bear pit, now maintained as a tourist attraction. The university was founded in 1834. It has considerable industry and contains the headquarters of several international organizations. Population (1995 est): 128 422.

● **Bernadette of Lourdes, St** ► (1844–79) French peasant girl, who in 1858 claimed to have had 18 visions of the Virgin Mary at a grotto near Lourdes. At 20 she became a nun. She was canonized in 1933. The shrine built at the spot is a place of international pilgrimage where miraculous cures are claimed to have occurred. Feast day: 18 Feb or 16 April.

● **Bernadotte, Folke, Count** ► (1895–1948) The nephew of Gustavus V of Sweden (1858–1950; reigned 1907–50). He became president of the Swedish Red Cross in 1946. In 1948 he was appointed mediator in Palestine but was assassinated by Jewish terrorists.

● **Bernadotte, Jean Baptiste Jules** ► (c. 1763–1844) French marshal, who was King of Sweden (1818–44) as Charles XIV John, founding the present Swedish royal house. Rising from the ranks, he became famous under Napoleon with whose support in 1810 Bernadotte was adopted as heir by the dying Charles XIII of Sweden. Turning against Napoleon, Bernadotte contributed to his defeat at Leipzig (1813). In 1814 he forced Denmark to cede Norway to the Swedish monarchy.

● **Bernanos, Georges** ► (1888–1948) French novelist and Catholic polemicist. His constant theme was the war between good and evil, characteristically portrayed in his best-known book, *The Diary of a Country Priest* (1936). Disturbed by European political trends, he lived in exile in Brazil from 1938 to 1945.

● **Bernard, Claude** ► (1813–78) French physiologist, who helped establish the experimental principles used in modern research. A student of François ▷Magendie, Bernard discovered that a secretion of the pancreas breaks down fat into its constituents and that the liver is able to synthesize glucose from glycogen. He also showed how blood flow through capillaries is regulated by contraction of their walls, controlled by vasoconstrictor nerves. Bernard developed the concept of the internal environment (*milieu intérieur*) of the body, the regulation of which is a basic physiological function.

● **Bernardin de Saint-Pierre, Jacques Henri** ► (1737–1814) French writer. He was a disciple of Rousseau, whose ideas about nature influenced the didactic romance for which he is chiefly remembered, *Paul et Virginie* (1787), which is set on the island of Mauritius.

● **Bernard of Chartres** ► (died c. 1130) French scholastic philosopher, who taught at Chartres (1114–24). A Platonist, he held a realist theory of universals (*see* realism) but tried to reconcile Platonic and Aristotelian metaphysics. His only extant work is a treatise on Neoplatonism.

● **Bernard of Clairvaux, St** ► (1090–1153) French theologian and Doctor of the Church. A Cistercian, he established in 1115 a monastery at Clairvaux that became a model of reform and influenced other monasteries in France and elsewhere. He was chosen by Pope Eugenius III to preach the second Crusade in 1146. His faith was based on an exalted mysticism, which is the subject of many of his Latin writings. Feast day: 20 Aug. Emblem: a beehive.

● **Bernard of Menthon, St** ► (923–1008) Italian churchman and vicar general of the diocese of Aosta. A native of Savoy, he established hospices on two Alpine passes, which are named after him, as are the dogs that were kept by the monks and trained to aid travellers. Feast day: 28 May.

● **Berne Convention** ► An international ▷copyright agreement of 1866. Its main provision guarantees copyright in all signatory countries of any work copyrighted in any one of them. The USA is still not a signatory.

● **Bernese Oberland** ► (*or* Bernese Alps) A section of the Alps in SW Switzerland, 105 km (65 mi) long, between the Rivers Rhône and Aare. Its mountain peaks include the Eiger and the Finsteraarhorn; it is popular with climbers.

● **Bernhard, Prince** ▷*See* Juliana.

● **Bernhard of Saxe-Weimar, Duke** ► (1604–39) German general, who fought for the Protestants in the ▷Thirty Years' War. He took command of the forces of Gustavus Adolphus on Gustavus' death in 1632 and campaigned successfully in S Germany. After losing at Nördlingen (1634) he held command for the French in SW Germany.

Sarah Bernhardt ► On her appointment to the Legion of Honour (16 March, 1914).

● **Bernhardt, Sarah** ► (Sarah Henriette Rosine Bernard; 1844–1923) French actress. Her voice and emotional power were especially suited to tragic roles. Plays in which she gave notable performances include *Phèdre* (1879), *La Dame aux camélias*, and *L'Aiglon* by Edmond Rostand. Her worldwide tours gained her international acclaim. She was also manager of several theatres in Paris and opened the old Théâtre des Nations as the Théâtre Sarah Bernhardt.

● **Bernina, Piz** ► 46 23N 9 54E A mountain in SE Switzerland, in the Alps near St Moritz. Height: 4049 m (13 284 ft).

● **Bernini, Gian Lorenzo** ► (1598–1680) Italian ▷baroque sculptor and architect, born in Naples, the son of a sculptor. Precociously talented, he worked chiefly in Rome under papal patronage. His first major sculptures were for Cardinal Scipione Borghese and included *Apollo and Daphne* (1622–24; Borghese Gallery, Rome). Encouraged by Urban VIII, he extended his talents into the fields of painting and, more successfully, architecture, major works being the baldachin over the tomb of St Peter (1624–33) and the piazza and colonnade (1656–67) of St Peter's, Rome. Later sculptures included fountains for Roman piazzas, *The Ecstasy of St Teresa* (1645–52; Cornaro Chapel, Sta Maria della Vittoria, Rome), and such portrait busts as *Louis XIV* (1665; Versailles).

● **Bernoulli** ► A family of notable Swiss mathematicians and physicists, who, as Flemish Protestants, were driven out of the Netherlands in the 1580s. The most famous was **Daniel Bernoulli** (1700–82), who made important contributions to fluid dynamics, especially his discovery in 1738 of ▷Bernoulli's principle concerning the speed and pressure of fluid flow. He also attempted to explain the properties of gases at varying temperatures and pressures by regarding the gas as consisting of many tiny particles. His father **Jean Bernoulli** (1667–1748) and uncle **Jacques Bernoulli** (1654–1705) were both eminent mathematicians, who often worked together and jointly developed the calculus of variations. Jean also made discoveries in ▷probability theory and Jacques in ▷complex numbers. Daniel's brother **Nicolas Bernoulli** (1695–1726) also contributed to the theory of probability.

● **Bernoulli's principle** ► The principle of conservation of energy applied to fluid flow. If the effects of friction are neglected the total energy of the flow at any point in a pipe is equal to the sum of the kinetic energy due to the flow velocity, the gravitational potential energy due to height, and the energy of pressure in the fluid itself. Bernoulli's theorem states that the sum of these three components is constant throughout a flow system. Named after Daniel ▷Bernoulli.

● **Bernstein, Eduard** ► (1850–1932) German politician. A journalist, Bernstein joined the Socialist Democratic Party in 1872. In 1878 he was exiled from Germany on account of his political beliefs. He returned to Berlin in 1901, becoming the leader of the revisionist movement. He was elected to the Reichstag in 1902. As a protest against his party's support of World War I, he joined the Independent Social Democrats. His most important book, *Evolutionary Socialism* (1898), contains his criticisms of Marxist theory.

● **Bernstein, Leonard** ▶ (1918–90) US conductor, composer, and pianist. From 1958 to 1969 he was musical director and conductor of the New York Philharmonic Orchestra and became famous for his concerts and recordings. His compositions, including symphonies, choral works, and songs, often contain jazz and folk elements. His musicals, such as *On the Town* (1944) and *West Side Story* (1957), have been widely popular.

● **Berre, Étang de** ▶ 43 27N 5 05E A saltwater lagoon in S France, in the Bouches-du-Rhône department. Connected by canal to the Mediterranean Sea (through the Rove tunnel) and the Gulf of Fos, it has important oil refineries and saltworks situated around its shores. Area: 155 sq km (60 sq mi).

● **Berruguete, Pedro** ▶ (c. 1450–c. 1504) Castillian Renaissance painter. In the 1470s he worked in Italy at the court of Urbino, where he painted *Federigo da Montefeltro and his Son* (Urbino). On returning to Spain (1482), he painted frescoes for Toledo cathedral and altarpieces for the Dominican order, in Avila. His son **Alonso Berruguete** (c. 1489–1561) was a mannerist painter and sculptor, who worked in Italy (c. 1504–c. 1517) and became court painter to Emperor Charles V (1518). He combined his talents in his masterpiece the San Benito altarpiece (now dismantled) in Valladolid.

● **berry** ▶ Loosely, any small succulent ▷fruit. Botanically, a berry is a simple fruit with a thin skin and pulpy flesh containing many loose seeds: the tomato and grape are examples. Blackberries and raspberries are not strictly berries, but collections of small ▷drupes.

● **Berry** ▶ A French province that was sold to the Crown by the Viscount of Bourges in 1101 and was absorbed by the departments of Cher and Indre in 1790.

● **Berry, Chuck** ▶ (Charles Edward B.; 1926–　) US singer and songwriter, who was one of the first musicians to popularize rock and roll. His songs, such as "Maybellene," "Johnny B. Goode," and "Roll Over, Beethoven" influenced the Beatles, the Rolling Stones, and others.

● **Berry, Jean de France, Duc de** ▶ (1340–1416) The third son of John II of France, who was appointed (1358) governor of Auvergne, Languedoc, Périgord, and Poitou, where his repressive policies caused a peasants' revolt (1381–84). He was coregent during the minority (1380–88) of his nephew Charles VI.

● **Berry, Marie-Caroline de Bourbon-Sicile, Duchesse de** ▶ (1798–1870) The wife of Charles, Duc de Berry (1778–1820), the son of Charles X of France. After Charles X's death, she conspired to obtain the French throne for her son Henri, Comte de Chambord (1820–83), instigating an unsuccessful revolt in the Vendée (1832).

● **Bersaglieri** ▶ A corps of light infantry sharpshooters raised in 1836 by Charles Albert of Sardinia-Piedmont as part of his reorganization of the Sardinian army. They served with distinction in the Crimean War and in both World Wars.

● **berserkers** ▶ (Old Norse: bear-shirts) In Scandinavian mythology, savage warriors whose frenzy in battle transformed them from men into wolves or bears and made them immune from being harmed by the sword or fire. In the frenzy of battle they would howl and foam at the mouth—hence the phrase "to go berserk." They were devotees of ▷Odin and, in early Scandinavian history, warriors called berserkers were often employed as bodyguards to nobles.

● **Berthelot, (Pierre Eugène) Marcelin** ▶ (1827–1907) French chemist and politician, who became professor at the Collège de France (1865). A pioneer of organic chemical synthesis, he demolished the theory that organic compounds contained a "vital force." As a student of chemical thermodynamics he distinguished between endothermic and exothermic reactions, but wrongly concluded that the heat of a reaction was its driving force. He became a senator in 1881 and foreign secretary in 1895.

● **Berthollet, Claude Louis, Comte** ▶ (1748–1822) French chemist and physician. He discovered potassium chlorate and introduced bleaching by chlorine; he also showed that ammonia consists of hydrogen and nitrogen. Berthollet helped to clarify the concept of chemical affinity and, working with ▷Lavoisier, developed a new chemical nomenclature. He travelled to Egypt as scientific adviser to Napoleon, who made him a senator and a count.

● **Bertillon, Alphonse** ▶ (1853–1914) French criminal investigator, who developed a system for identifying criminals based on the description and measurement of physical characteristics. The system, also known as anthropometry, was eventually superseded by fingerprinting techniques. His brother **Jacques Bertillon** (1851–1922) was a statistician. As head of the Paris bureau of social statistics, he developed new systems of data analysis. He was particularly interested in the high incidence of alcoholism in France and the decline of the French population in comparison with rates in other countries.

● **Bertolucci, Bernardo** ▶ (1940–　) Italian film director. Most of his earlier films were strongly influenced by Marxist ideology, notably *Before the Revolution* (1965) and the epic *1900* (1977). He achieved his greatest commercial successes with *Last Tango in Paris* (1972) and *The Last Emperor* (1988). More recent films include *Little Buddha* (1994), *Stealing Beauty* (1996), and *Besieged* (1999).

● **Bertrand, Henri Gratien, Comte** ▶ (1773–1844) French marshal, who in 1804 became an aide de camp to Napoleon, whose complete trust he won. He accompanied Napoleon into exile, both to Elba and St Helena, where he kept a diary that is an important historical source.

● **Bertran de Born** ▶ (?1140–?1215) French knight and troubadour poet. He composed lyrics glorifying love, ambition, and especially war. His castle at Hautefort was besieged and captured by Richard Lionheart, whose loyal officer he became.

● **Berwick, James Fitzjames, Duke of** ▶ (1670–1734) Marshal of France, who was the illegitimate son of James II of England. He was educated in France and gained military experience in Europe. On the deposition of James (1688), Berwick supported his attempts to regain the throne and played a prominent part in the battle of the ▷Boyne. His victory in the employ of France at Almansa (1707) established Philip V on the Spanish throne. He was killed besieging Philippsburg in the War of the Polish Succession.

● **Berwickshire** ▶ A former county of SE Scotland. Under local government reorganization in 1975 its boundaries were adjusted to form a district of the same name, in the Borders Region. The district was abolished in 1996, when it became part of the new ▷unitary authority ▷Scottish Borders.

● **Berwick-upon-Tweed** ▶ 55 46N 2 00W A town in NE England, in Northumberland at the mouth of the River Tweed. A border town long disputed between England and Scotland, Berwick changed hands 14 times. The Battle of ▷Flodden (1513) was fought some 16 km (10 mi) to the SW. Three **Treaties of Berwick** have also been signed here; the first (1357) allowed David II of Scotland to be released for a ransom; the second (1560) committed the English to giving Scottish Protestants military aid against the Catholics; and the third (1639) ended the first ▷Bishops' War. Industries include engineering, fertilizers, food processing, and salmon fishing. Population (1991): 13 544.

● **beryl** ▶ A mineral consisting of beryllium alumino-silicate, found principally in granites and granite pegmatites. It occurs as crystals up to one metre in length and is white, pale blue, or green. It is the chief source of beryllium. ▷Aquamarine and ▷emerald are gem varieties.

● **beryllium** ▶ (Be) A light (relative density 1.85) alkaline-earth metal that was discovered in 1828 by F. Wöhler and A. Bussy (1794–1882) independently. Its salts are highly toxic and require careful handling. It occurs in nature in such minerals as ▷beryl and phenacite (Be_2SiO_4). It is transparent to X-rays and is used as windows on X-ray tubes. Alloys with copper are extensively used and the oxide (BeO), having a high melting point (2530°C), is used as a ceramic. At no 4; at wt 9.0122; mp 1289°C; bp 2472°C.

● **Berzelius, Jöns Jakob, Baron** ► (1779–1848) Swedish chemist, whose main work was the discovery of atomic compositions of chemical compounds. He discovered the elements selenium (1817), silicon (1824), and thorium (1828) and determined the atomic and molecular weights of more than 2000 elements and compounds. He introduced the current notation for chemical formulae and the use of oxygen as a reference standard for atomic weights. Following the invention of electric cells, Berzelius experimented on electrolysis and developed a theory of electrostatic bonding in compounds. He published a standard textbook of chemistry in 1830.

● **Bes** ► The Egyptian god of recreation, also associated with children and childbirth. Images of the god, represented as a grotesque dwarf with a tail, were kept in homes as protection against evil.

● **Besançon** ► 47 14N 6 02E A town in E France, the capital of the Doubs department on the River Doubs. It has a cathedral (11th–13th centuries) and a university (1691). Victor Hugo was born here. It is the French watchmaking centre and produces cars and textiles. Population (1990): 119 194.

● **Besant, Annie** ► (1847–1933) British theosophist and political campaigner. A friend of Charles ▷Bradlaugh, Annie Besant promoted the causes of atheism, birth control, and trades unionism until her conversion (1889) to ▷theosophy by Madame ▷Blavatsky. Visiting (1893) India, she founded a Hindu university and worked for Indian home rule.

● **Besant, Sir Walter** ► (1836–1901) British novelist and social reformer. His novels *All Sorts and Conditions of Men* (1882) and *Children of Gibeon* (1886) describe the slums of E London, where (in 1887) he helped to found the People's Palace. He was a founder of the Society of Authors (1884).

● **Bessarabia** ► A region in E Europe, largely in Moldova and Ukraine, with a predominantly Moldavian population. The main crops are wine grapes, fruit, wheat, and tobacco; cattle and sheep are raised. The chief industry is agricultural processing.

History: the region was colonized by the Greeks and later fell successively to the Romans, Huns, Magyars, Mongols, and Turks, passing to Russia in 1812. In 1918 Bessarabia declared its independence, later voting for union with Romania, who ceded it (1940) to the Soviet Union; it remained under Soviet control until 1991. Area: 44 300 sq km (17 100 sq mi).

● **Bessarion, John** ► (c. 1400–72) Greek scholar and cardinal. As Archbishop of Nicaea, he attempted to unite the Byzantine and Western Churches, eventually joining the latter and settling in Italy, where he became a cardinal in 1439. He was an outstanding scholar and exercised an important influence in introducing the study of Greek in the Renaissance. His large library of Greek manuscripts is preserved in Venice.

● **Bessel, Friedrich Wilhelm** ► (1784–1846) German astronomer, who used his measurements of parallax to calculate a star's distance and who suggested that irregularities he had observed in Uranus's orbit were due to an unknown planet (Neptune was discovered shortly after his death). The **Bessel function**, developed in his calculations, still has wide use in physics.

● **Bessemer, Sir Henry** ► (1813–98) British engineer and inventor, who patented (1855) a process for manufacturing cheap steel (*see* Bessemer process). His Sheffield steelworks, built in 1859, are still producing steel. Bessemer was a prolific inventor, patenting some 114 inventions.

● **Bessemer process** ► A steelmaking process invented by Sir Henry ▷Bessemer in 1855. A long cylindrical vessel (Bessemer converter) is charged with molten pig iron; air, introduced through holes in the bottom of the converter, is blown through the iron to oxidize the carbon, silicon, and manganese impurities. Phosphorus is removed by reaction with the converter's basic refractory lining. Carbon, in the form of spiegel, is then added to give steel of the required carbon content. It has now been largely replaced by the ▷basic-oxygen process.

● **Best, Charles Herbert** ► (1899–1978) US physiologist, who, as an undergraduate assistant to ▷Banting, helped discover the technique for isolating the hormone insulin from pancreatic tissue in 1921. Best also discovered choline, a B vitamin.

● **Best, George** ► (1946–) Northern Ireland Association football player. A flamboyant striker, he made his professional debut for Manchester United at the age of 17 and went on to make 37 international appearances for Northern Ireland. He was named British and European footballer of the year in 1969. Although regarded as one of the most talented British footballers of all time, he suffered from personal problems (including alcoholism) and his career ended prematurely.

● **bestiary** ► A medieval treatise containing accounts of animal species, both real and imaginary. They were based on ancient Greek and Latin sources and often fancifully illustrated. Wildly inaccurate in their natural history, bestiaries attempted to draw morals from each beast's attributes.

● **Bestuzhev-Riumin, Aleksei Petrovich, Count** ► (1693–1766) Russian statesman. Bestuzhev served as a diplomat abroad until 1740. In the reign of the empress ▷Elizabeth he directed foreign policy and was Russia's chancellor from 1744 to 1758. He allied Russia with Austria and Britain against France and Prussia, a policy made obsolete by the realignment of European alliances on the eve of the ▷Seven Years' War. He was dismissed in 1758.

● **beta blocker** ► A drug, such as propranolol, atenolol, or oxprenolol, that prevents certain nerve endings (known as beta receptors) of the sympathetic ▷nervous system from being stimulated, thus reducing heart activity. Developed by Sir James ▷Black, beta blockers are used to treat ▷angina, ▷arrhythmia, and ▷hypertension.

● **Beta Centauri** ► A remote yet conspicuous blue ▷giant star, apparent magnitude 0.63 and about 390 light years distant, that is the second brightest star in the constellation Centaurus.

● **beta decay** ► A radioactive process in which a neutron within a nucleus decays by the ▷weak interaction into a proton, an electron (**beta particle**), and an antineutrino; alternatively, a proton may decay into a neutron, a positron, and a neutrino. Since the nuclear charge changes by one in both cases, the nucleus is converted into the nucleus of another element.

● **betatron** ► A type of particle ▷accelerator used for producing very high energy electrons. The electrons are accelerated round a circular path in an evacuated torus-shaped chamber, by means of a large pulsed magnetic field. Electron energies up to 300 MeV have been produced.

● **betel** ► A mixture of the boiled dried seeds (**betel nuts**) of the areca, or betel palm (*Areca catechu*), and the leaves of the betel pepper (*Piper betle*), which produces copious salivation when chewed with lime—a practice common among the populations of S Asia and the East Indies. Betel nuts contain an alkaloid of some value in expelling intestinal worms, and the mild stimulation resulting from chewing the mixture has led to its use in some religious ceremonies.

● **Betelgeuse** ► An immense remote yet conspicuous red ▷supergiant, over 500 light years distant, that is the second brightest star in the constellation ▷Orion. It is a ▷variable star with its magnitude ranging, usually, from 0.3 to 0.9 over a period of about 5.8 years.

● **Bethany** ► (present-day name: Al-'Ayzariyah) 31 46N 35 15E A village on the ▷West Bank of the River Jordan, near Jerusalem. It is now named after Lazarus, whom Christ resurrected here (John 11.1–44).

● **Bethe, Hans Albrecht** ► (1906–) US physicist, born in Germany. After studying under ▷Rutherford he returned to Germany but left when Hitler came to power. After two years in England he finally settled in the USA, working on the atom bomb during World War II. His earlier researches in quantum electrodynamics proved valuable in working out the details of the nuclear fusion process that occurs in stars, which is sometimes called the **Bethe cycle** – *see* carbon cycle (physics). For this work he received the 1967 Nobel Prize. ▷*See also* Alpher, Ralph Asher.

● **Bethlehem** ► 31 42N 35 12E A town on the ▷West Bank of the River Jordan, near Jerusalem. The Church of the Nativity was built in

326 over the grotto that is the presumed birthplace of Jesus Christ. A university was founded here in 1973. Population (latest est): 91 010.

● **Bethlehem** ► 40 36N 75 22W A city in the USA, in Pennsylvania. A major steel centre, it also has cement, textile, and electrical-equipment industries. Population (1994 est): 72 821.

● **Bethlen, Gábor** ► (1580–1629) Prince of Transylvania (1613–29), a Protestant, who opposed Emperor Ferdinand II during the Thirty Years' War. Bethlen, after seizing northern Hungary, was elected King in 1620 but renounced the Crown (1621) in exchange for Ferdinand's agreement to allow Hungarian Protestants to worship freely. Bethlen again took up arms against Ferdinand in 1623 and 1626 but then withdrew from the war.

● **Bethmann-Hollweg, Theobald von** ► (1856–1921) German statesman. As minister of the interior, secretary of state, and chancellor (1909–17) successively, he instituted a number of electoral and legal reforms. In 1914, attempting to justify aggressive German foreign policy, he described the treaty guaranteeing Belgian neutrality as a "scrap of paper." In 1917 his efforts to secure a negotiated peace led to his overthrow by ▷Ludendorff and ▷Hindenburg.

● **Béthune** ► 50 32N 2 38E A town in France, in the Pas-de-Calais department. A coalmining centre, it also produces beet sugar and textiles. Population (latest est): 26 105.

● **Betjeman, Sir John** ► (1906–84) British poet. Educated at Marlborough and Oxford, he published his first book of poetry in 1933. His verse autobiography, *Summoned by Bells* (1960), reflected the nostalgia and gentle social satire characteristic of his other poems. He also revived and fostered interest in Victorian and Edwardian architecture. He was poet laureate from 1972.

● **betony** ► A perennial herb, *Stachys officinalis* (or *Betonica officinalis*), up to 30 cm high. It has round-toothed leaves and a dense head of reddish-purple tubular flowers. Betony is found on open grassland, heaths, and hedgerows from Eurasia to N Africa. The leaves may be used for tea and for herbal tobacco. Family: ▷*Labiatae*.

● **Betterton, Thomas** ► (?1635–1710) English actor. The leading actor of the Restoration stage, he acted in many contemporary and Shakespearean plays. He became a theatre manager and adapted several Elizabethan and Jacobean plays to suit contemporary taste.

● **Betti, Ugo** ► (1892–1953) Italian dramatist. He studied law and became a magistrate and, after 1944, librarian at the Ministry of Justice. The themes of many of his 26 plays, notably *Corruption in the Palace of Justice* (1944) and *The Fugitive* (1953), concern justice and social responsibility.

● **Betty Trask Award** ► An annual prize of £12,500 for authors under 35 awarded for a first novel "of a romantic or traditional, rather than experimental, nature." Set up in 1984 by a legacy of the writer Betty Trask and administered by the Society of Authors, it was at its inception Britain's largest literary prize.

● **Betws-y-Coed** ► 53 05N 3 48W A village and resort in North Wales, in Conwy county borough in Snowdonia at the confluence of the Rivers Llugwy and Conwy. It is renowned for its scenery, especially its waterfalls. Population (1991): 2860.

● **Beust, Friedrich Ferdinand, Count von** ► (1809–86) German statesman; the chief opponent of ▷Bismarck. As prime minister of Saxony (1853–66) he allied Saxony with Austria in the Austro-Prussian War of 1866. He became chancellor of the Austrian Empire in 1867 and negotiated the *Augsleich* that established the Dual Monarchy of ▷Austria-Hungary.

● **Bevan, Aneurin** ► (1897–1960) British Labour politician, who was the son of a Welsh miner and himself a miner at the age of 13. By 1929, however, he had been elected to parliament for Ebbw Vale, a seat that he held until his death. A brilliant orator, Nye Bevan clashed with the Labour Party in 1939 over what he considered to be its ambivalence towards Hitler. He edited the socialist *Tribune* from 1940 to 1945. As minister of health (1945–51), he was the architect of the ▷National Health Service (NHS). He was minister of labour in 1951, but during that year resigned from the government, with Harold ▷Wilson, in protest against ▷Attlee's proposal to introduce charges

into the NHS. Bevan's subsequent attempt (1955) to become leader of the Labour Party was defeated by Hugh ▷Gaitskell. His wife **Jennie, Baroness Lee** (1904–88), a Labour MP (1929–31, 1945–70), was minister for the arts (1967–70).

● **bevatron** ► A type of ▷synchrotron used for accelerating protons at Berkeley, California (USA). It can produce protons with energies up to 6 GeV.

● **Beveridge, William Henry Beveridge, 1st Baron** ► (1879–1963) British economist, writer, and academic. Beveridge joined the Board of Trade in 1908 and became an authority on unemployment. His best-known work was the *Report on Social Insurance and Allied Services* (1942), the so-called **Beveridge Report**, which became the basis of much of the social legislation introduced by the postwar Labour government in creating Britain's welfare state.

● **Beverley** ► 53 51N 0 26W A market town in NE England, the administrative centre of the East Riding of Yorkshire. Beverley Minster dates from the 13th century. The principal industries are tanning, car accessories, and industrial plastics. Population (1991): 23 632.

● **Beverly Hills** ► A city in the USA, in California. A residential suburb of Los Angeles, it is the home of many film and television celebrities. Population (1990): 31 971.

● **Bevin, Ernest** ► (1881–1951) British politician and trade-union leader. Bevin formed, and was general secretary (1921–40) of, the Transport and General Workers' Union and in 1937 became chairman of the TUC. In 1940 he became minister of labour, serving in Churchill's war cabinet. In this capacity he introduced the "Bevin Boys", young men chosen by ballot to do their national service in the coalmines rather than the services. He was foreign secretary (1945–51) in the postwar Labour Government, when he helped to form NATO. However, his intransigent attitude to a shipload of Jewish refugees from the holocaust who were attempting to reach Palestine brought Britain's attempt to administer the territory into disrepute. It was also a powerful factor in persuading the UN to sanction the state of Israel, after Bevin agreed to relinquish Britain's Palestine Mandate (1947–48).

● **Bewick, Thomas** ► (1753–1828) British wood engraver, born near Newcastle upon Tyne, where he spent most of his life. Although trained under a local metal engraver, whose partner he later became, he specialized in ▷wood engraving, which he revived as an art form and raised to a new level of technical virtuosity. He was an amateur naturalist and his best works are his animal studies, particularly in *The History of British Birds* (*Land Birds*, 1797; *Water Birds*, 1804).

● **Bexhill-on-Sea** ► 50 50N 0 29E A resort in SE England, on the East Sussex coast. Population (1991 est): 38 905.

● **Bexley** ► A borough of SE Greater London, bordering on the River Thames in the N. Created in 1965 from part of Kent, it is an industrial as well as a residential area. Population (1991): 218 100.

● **Beza, Theodore** ► (1519–1605) French Calvinist theologian. Trained as a lawyer, he went to Geneva in 1548, having formally renounced the Roman Catholic faith. He became professor of Greek at Lausanne University and first rector of the Geneva Academy (1559), which Calvin had just founded for the education of Protestant theologians. He is remembered both as a Bible translator and a defender of Protestantism. After Calvin's death (1564) Beza succeeded to his leadership of the Swiss Calvinists.

● **Béziers** ► 43 21N 3 13E A town in S France, in the Hérault department. In 1209 many of the inhabitants were massacred by Simon de Montfort during the crusade against the Albigenses. It is a commercial centre for wines and spirits and its manufactures include chemicals and textiles. Population (1990 est): 72 362.

● **bezique** ► A card game, usually for two players, that became popular in France about 1860. Two packs of 32 cards are used (standard packs with the cards from two to six removed). Each player is dealt eight cards; the next card indicates the trump suit and the rest form the stockpile. The object is to score points by collecting melds (certain combinations of cards) and to take tricks containing brisques (aces and tens). Play continues until one player's score reaches 1000 or 1500.

● **Bhagalpur** ▶ 25 14N 86 59E A city in India, in Bihar. An agricultural trading centre, its manufactures include textiles (especially silk). Its university was established in 1960. Population (1991): 254 993.

● **Bhagavadgita** ▶ (Sanskrit: Song of the Lord) Hindu poem probably composed about 300 BC, forming part of the epic ▷*Mahabharata*. It blends and reconciles a number of Hindu philosophies. Arjuna, one of the five Pandava brothers, is compelled to battle with his kinsmen, the Kauravas; he is persuaded by ▷Krishna, acting as his charioteer, of the virtue of selflessly performing the duties of caste. Krishna enumerates the ways by which one can attain liberation from the limitations of matter: by virtuous actions, by devotion to God, by philosophical speculation, by asceticism, or by meditation.

● **Bhakti** ▶ (Sanskrit; to revere) A movement in Hinduism that emphasizes personal devotion and love towards a chosen god rather than ritualistic worship. Claimed by its adherents to be the most important means to salvation, it is available to all irrespective of sex or caste. A Bhakti literature extolling the virtues of a personal emotional attachment to one's god arose in southern India in the 7th century. Most of the literature relates to Vishnu's incarnations as Rama or Krishna, although some devotees, such as the Sikh Guru ▷Nanak, did not personalize the god.

● **Bhamo** ▶ 24 15N 97 15E A town in Myanmar (Burma), on the Irrawaddy River near the border with China. Principally a trading centre, it has a government sugar factory.

● **Bharat** ▷*See* India, Republic of.

● **Bharhut** ▶ A Buddhist stupa (shrine) complex in Nagod state (N India), excavated in 1874. It provided evidence for the earliest phases of Buddhist architecture; carvings on the stone railings are the earliest representational reliefs from India (2nd century BC). Nothing now remains at the site.

● **Bhaskhara II** ▶ (1114–c. 1185) Indian mathematician, who was the first to use the decimal system in a written work, invented the + and – convention, and used letters to represent unknown quantities as in modern algebra.

● **Bhatpara** ▶ 22 51N 88 31E A city in India, in West Bengal. It is an ancient seat of Sanskrit learning. Jute processing is the principal industry. Population (1991): 304 298.

● **Bhavachakra** ▶ (Sanskrit: wheel of becoming) In Buddhism, an image of the cyclical nature of earthly existence, in the form of a wheel held by the demon of impermanence. Its segments represent the six possible states into which beings are reborn: the realms of gods, titans, hungry ghosts, humans, animals, and demons. At the centre, turning the wheel, are greed, hatred, and delusion, depicted as a cockerel, snake, and pig, biting each other's tails. Around the rim, the 12 stages in the cycle of life are symbolically expressed.

● **Bhavnagar** ▶ 21 59N 72 19E A port in India, in Gujarat on the Gulf of Cambay. An important industrial and commercial centre, its manufactures include textiles, bricks, and tiles. Population (1991): 400 306.

● **Bhopal** ▶ 23 17N 77 28E A city in India, the capital of Madhya Pradesh. Notable buildings include the unfinished Taj-ul-Masjid, the largest mosque in India. Its university was established in 1970. Bhopal's varied manufactures include vehicle parts and cotton textiles. In 1984 over 2000 people died after poisonous isocyanate gas escaped from the US-owned Union Carbide factory in the city. Population (1991): 1 063 662.

● **Bhubaneswar** ▶ 20 13N 85 50E A city in India, the capital of Orissa. An ancient city dating back to 500 AD, it is famous for its many temples. Utkal University (founded in 1943) was moved here in 1962. Population (1991): 411 542.

● **Bhutan, Kingdom of** ▶ (Bhutanese name: Druk-yul) A small country in the E Himalayas, strategically positioned between India and Tibet. It is entirely mountainous, rising over 7300 m (21 900 ft) in the N. Over half the population are of Tibetan origin, known as Bhutias, with minorities of Nepalese in the S and Indians in the E. *Economy*: mainly agricultural; forests cover some 60% of the land

and there are plans for further planting. As well as traditional industries, such as bamboo and lacquer woodwork, other small industries are being encouraged and hydroelectricity is being developed. Almost all foreign trade is with India. A new postal system was inaugurated in 1972 and since then postage stamps have been a valuable source of foreign currency, together with tourism, which has developed significantly in recent decades.

History: although the early history of Bhutan is obscure it does appear to have existed as a political entity for many centuries under a spiritual figurehead known as the Dharma Raja. In 1865 part of S Bhutan was annexed by the British, following various border disputes, and a treaty was concluded in which Britain agreed to pay an annual subsidy. By a further treaty in 1910 Britain agreed not to interfere in Bhutan's internal affairs and in 1949 this was replaced by a similar treaty concluded with India. In 1910 Sir Ugyen Wangchuk was elected the first hereditary maharaja (now referred to as king). In 1969 the absolute monarchy was replaced by a "democratic monarchy" and power is now divided between the king, the Council of Ministers, the National Assembly, and the monastic head of Bhutan's lamas. The 1990s saw ethnic tensions between Bhutias and Nepalese immigrants, many of whom fled to Nepal to escape increasing discrimination.

Kingdom of Bhutan

Head of state	King Jigme Singye Wangchuk
Official language	Dzongkha Bhutanese
Official currency	ngultrum of 100 chetrums
Area	46 600 sq km (18 000 sq mi)
Population (1999 est)	658 000
Capital	Thimphu

● **Bhutto, Benazir** ▶ (1953–) Pakistani politician; prime minister (1988–90, 1993–96). As leader of the party founded by her father, she became the first female leader of a Muslim country. In 1990 she was dismissed by the president on grounds of incompetence and corruption but was re-elected in 1993. She was again dismissed for alleged corruption in 1996 and defeated in the subsequent elections (1997). In 1999 she was found guilty (in absentia) of corruption and sentenced to five years' imprisonment; however, in 2001 Pakistan's Supreme Court set aside the conviction and ordered a retrial. Her father, **Zulfikar Ali Bhutto** (1928–79), formed the Pakistan People's Party in 1967; after the secession of East Pakistan (Bangladesh) he became president (1971–73) and prime minister (1973–77). He was ousted by a military coup, defeated in the subsequent election, and executed for conspiracy to murder an opponent.

● **Biafra** ▶ The secessionist eastern region of Nigeria (1967–70). In an attempt to protect the ▷Ibo people against the dominant ▷Hausa, a unilateral declaration of independence was made under the leadership of Lieut Col Odumegwu Ojukwu (1933–). The federal government under Gen Yakubu Gowon (1934–) refused to recognize the new state and took up arms against it. The decimated Ibo surrendered on 15 January, 1970.

● **Biafra, Bight of** ▷*See* Bonny, Bight of.

● **Bialik, Chaim Nachman** ▶ (1873–1934) Jewish poet and translator, born in the Ukraine. His major poem *The Talmud Student* (1894) established his reputation. His poetry is often visionary but also condemns Jewish passivity in the face of oppression. He settled in Palestine in 1924.

● **Białystok** ▶ 53 09N 23 10E A city in NE Poland. It grew mainly under the Branicki family in the 18th century. In World War II the Germans killed half the population and destroyed the industry but cloth manufacture has been revived. Population (1996 est): 277 800.

● **Biarritz** ▶ 43 29N 1 33W A town in SW France, in the Pyrénées-Atlantiques department on the Bay of Biscay. It became a fashionable resort under the patronage of the Empress Eugénie in the 1850s. Population (1990): 28 890.

● **biathlon** ▶ 1. An athletic event consisting of combined shooting and cross-country ▷skiing, first included in the Winter Olympic Games in 1960; competitors ski 20 km (12.5 mi) with rifles and ammunition and at each of four points along the course take five shots at 150 m (164 yd). **2.** An athletic event consisting of running 4000 m (2.5 mi) and swimming 300 m (328 yd), introduced in 1968 by the Modern Pentathlon Association of Great Britain in preparation for the ▷pentathlon.

● **Bible** ▶ (Greek *biblia*, books) The sacred book of Christianity, comprising the collected books of the ▷Old Testament, the ▷New Testament, and in, some versions, additional Old Testament writings known as the ▷Apocrypha. *Canon*: the canon of the Hebrew scriptures was definitively established by the rabbinical council of Jamnia (90–100 AD), although most of the books had acquired authority much earlier. The council rejected a number of books that formed part of the Greek version of the Jewish scriptures, the ▷Septuagint: these constitute most of the Apocrypha, accepted in varying degrees as sacred scripture by some Christian Churches and rejected by others. The New Testament canon was also established gradually but had essentially its present form by the 3rd century AD. To Christians it represented the complete fulfilment of the prophecies of the Old Testament. *Divine inspiration and biblical criticism*: both Jews and Christians have traditionally regarded their scriptures as divinely inspired, leading to the assumption that they must be correct in every particular. Although Roman Catholics and Protestants differed as to whether the Bible was the sole source of revealed truth, almost all Christians agreed, until relatively recently, on the literal truth of the contents, a belief slowly eroded by the development of science from the 17th century onwards. Despite the attempts to condemn scientific findings when these appeared to conflict with scripture, as in the case of ▷Galileo, scientific method was increasingly applied to the study of the Bible itself and during the 19th century the procedures of historical scholarship, textual criticism, archaeology, etc., were brought to bear on all aspects of the text. As a result, many traditional assumptions (such as the ascription of the ▷Pentateuch to Moses or the Gospel of St ▷John to an eyewitness) have been rendered untenable. Almost all forms of modern biblical criticism set out from the understanding that these ancient writings must be interpreted within their historical and cultural contexts, with particular attention to the meanings that the original authors sought to convey. *Texts*: the oldest extant complete manuscript of the Old Testament dates from the 11th century AD, but there are much earlier versions of parts of the text, for example the Pentateuch (*see also* Dead Sea Scrolls). The fact that there is almost no variation among the many manuscripts of the Old Testament attests to the care with which the Jewish scribes, known as the Masoretes, preserved the text from the 6th century AD onwards. The earliest fragments of the New Testament date from the 2nd century AD; thereafter there are an extremely large number of manuscripts of quite early date. *Translations*: the first translation of the Bible is the Latin ▷Vulgate of St Jerome. In England translations were made in Old English and Norman French. Major English versions are: the version prefaced by ▷Wycliffe (1382–88), the last manuscript Bible written before the introduction of printing; the New Testament (1525) and other sections by ▷Tyndale; the Bible of Miles ▷Coverdale; the Great Bible (1539), supervised by Coverdale under the patronage of Thomas Cromwell; the ▷Geneva (*or* Breeches) Bible; the Bishops' Bible (1568); the ▷Douai Bible; the ▷King James (*or* Authorized) Version; the *Revised Version* (1881–95); the *Revised Standard Version* (1946–57), a modernization of the King James Version; and *The New English Bible* (1961–70).

● **Bible Societies** ▶ Various Protestant organizations formed to promote and distribute Bibles to all peoples. One of the first societies, the Society for Promoting Christian Knowledge, was founded in England in 1698. The large interdenominational British and Foreign Bible Society was founded in 1804. The American Bible Society distributes several million Bibles annually. In 1946 some 20 international societies combined to form the United Bible Societies.

● **Bibliothèque Nationale** ▶ The national ▷library of France in Paris, containing around seven million volumes. It is based on the royal libraries of Charles the Wise (1364–80) and his successors, notably those of Louis XI, Charles VIII, and Francis I. From 1537 it received a copy of every book published in France. It was given its present name in 1795.

● **bicycles** ▶ Light two-wheeled vehicles, moved by cranks attached to pedals operated by the rider. Bicycles developed in the 19th century from a two-wheeled hobby-horse, known as the dandy-horse or celeripede. Around 1840 a Scotsman, Kirkpatrick Macmillan, applied the dandy-horse principle to models with pedals. The first true bicycles, with cranks on their front wheels, went into production in Paris in 1865. Known as velocipedes, or boneshakers, these wooden-wheeled devices nevertheless popularized cycling. To increase efficiency the front wheel was gradually made larger, resulting in the 20-year vogue of the ordinary (or pennyfarthing) bicycle. This was superseded by the safety bicycle, which had a chain and sprocket drive to the rear wheel and was essentially the same as the modern bicycle; it went into production in 1885. Pneumatic rubber tyres (1889), a freewheeling mechanism (1894), and variable gears (1899) were later refinements. The 1980s saw the introduction of wide-tyred machines, called mountain bikes or all-terrain bikes (ATBs), with numerous gears; this is now perhaps the most common form of bicycle.

An inexpensive means of transport and recreation, bicycles have enjoyed a revival in developed countries owing to the environmental concerns of the 1980s and 1990s. Cycling is also a form of competitive sport. Racing first became popular in France, where the earliest race was held (1868) and now has a wide following throughout Europe (*see* Tour de France). Road races take place on public roads, sometimes through normal traffic, using lightweight bicycles with sophisticated gears. Track races are run on special steeply banked tracks and cyclo-cross races are held across country.

● **Bidault, Georges** ▶ (1899–1983) French statesman; prime minister (1946, 1949–50). A leader of the French resistance during World War II, Bidault served as president of the Resistance Council in 1944 and foreign minister and president in de Gaulle's first (provisional) government. He broke with the Gaullists over their policy towards Algerian independence, becoming head of the Organisation de l'Armée secrète, and from 1962 to 1968 lived in exile.

● **Biddle, John** ▶ (1615–62) English religious leader, founder of Unitarianism (*see* Unitarians). While a schoolmaster he wrote his *Twelve Arguments* against the deity of the Holy Ghost, for which he was imprisoned in 1645. Although his adherents began to meet openly from 1652, he was arrested and banished under Cromwell and finally died in prison in London.

● **Bideford** ▶ 51 01N 4 13W A town in SW England, in N Devon on the Torridge estuary. Once a busy port (used by ▷Drake, ▷Raleigh, and ▷Grenville), it is now mainly a resort and market town. Population (1991): 14 326.

● **Biedermeier style** ▶ A style of furniture and painting that flourished under bourgeois patronage in Austria, Germany, and Scandinavia from about 1816 to about 1848. It was satirically named after the fictional character Gottlieb Biedermeier, who was created by the poet Ludwig Eichrocht (1827–92) to characterize bourgeois bad taste. Biedermeier furniture, which was the first to be mass produced, utilized French ▷Empire style design for modern functional purposes. Biedermeier paintings aimed at extreme naturalism in outdoor scenes and intimacy in interiors and portraits.

● **Biel** ▶ (French name: Bienne) 47 09N 7 16E A town in NW Switzerland, on Lake Biel. It is the only official bilingual Swiss town (French and German). A watchmaking centre, it also manufactures machinery. Population (1990 est): 52 020.

● **Biela's comet** ▶ A comet, period 6.6 years, that was discovered in 1826 and was observed on its 1846 return to split in two. Although seen in 1852 the portions subsequently disintegrated. The resulting stream of meteoroids (*see* meteor) produced spectacular meteor storms in 1872 and 1885. It was named after the astronomer Wilhelm von Biela (1782–1856).

● **Bielefeld** ▶ 52 02N 8 32E A city in NW Germany, in North Rhine-Westphalia. Its linen mills were the first in Germany to be mechanized (1851). Silks, clothing, and machinery are also manufactured here. Population (1996 est): 324 066.

● **Bielsko-Biała** ▶ 49 50N 19 00E A town in S Poland. It was formed in 1951 from two towns on the River Biała. It has an important textile industry. Population (1996 est): 180 700.

● **Bien Hoa** ► 10 58N 106 50E An ancient city in S Vietnam, on the River Dong Nai. Known for its pottery, it also has paper, steel, and chemical industries. Population (1992 est): 273 879.

● **Bienne** ▷See Biel.

● **Bierce, Ambrose Gwinnett** ► (1842–?1914) US writer. After service in the Civil War, he became a journalist in California and London (1872–75). His story collections, *In the Midst of Life* (1891) and *Can Such Things Be?* (1893), and *The Devil's Dictionary* (1906), reflect his preoccupation with death and its aftermath. He disappeared in Mexico during ▷Villa's revolt.

● **bigamy** ► The offence of marrying a person while being married to another. Defences to a charge of bigamy include an honest and reasonable belief in the death of the original marriage partner, especially if absent for seven years or more, and an honest and reasonable belief that the first marriage was invalid or has been dissolved. Although a person would not be guilty of bigamy if he can prove these defences, the second marriage will still be invalid in such cases.

● **Big Bang** ▷See stock exchange.

● **big-bang theory** ► A cosmological theory (*see* cosmology), first proposed in the 1920s, that all the matter and radiation in the universe originated in an immense explosion that began the expansion of the universe, which still continues. In its present form the theory was revived by Ralph ▷Alpher, Hans ▷Bethe, and George ▷Gamow (known as the αβγ theory). In this theory the cosmic explosion is thought to have occurred about 10 to 20 thousand million years ago. As the initially high temperature of the early constituents decreased, hydrogen and helium were able to form: the observed cosmic abundance of helium agrees well with the predicted value. This matter eventually interacted to form galaxies. The theory also predicts that the radiation formed shortly after the explosion should by now have cooled to about three kelvin. This is the temperature of the isotropic microwave background, detected in 1965 and considered strong evidence for the theory.

● **Big Ben** ► The 14-ton 9ft-diameter bell in the clock tower of the ▷Palace of Westminster (London), named after Sir Benjamin Hall (1802–67), commissioner of works when the clock was installed (1859). The sound of Big Ben striking the hour, first broadcast in 1923, has become a British institution. Both the clock and the tower itself are also known by this name. A light in the lantern above the clock faces indicates that the House of Commons is in session.

● **bighorn** ► A mountain sheep, *Ovis canadensis*, of North America. The species ranges from the small Nelson's bighorn to the Rocky Mountain bighorns, which stand 100 cm at the shoulder. Bighorns have ribbed horns that grow in a spiral up to 100 cm long.

● **Bihar** ► A state in N India, bordering on Nepal. The densely populated rural Ganges plain in the N produces rice, other grains, sugar cane, pulses, and vegetables. The S Chota Nagpur plateau yields minerals, including mica, and supports iron and steel and engineering works. Nevertheless, Bihar remains India's poorest state.
History: the centre of N Indian civilization from 1500 BC, Bihar was part of various empires and saw the early development of Buddhism and Jainism. It was a centre of 19th-century Indian nationalism. More recently Bihar has seen rising political violence from Maoist insurgents and right-wing militias. Area: 173 876 sq km (67 116 sq mi). Population (1994 est): 93 080 000. Capital: Patna.

● **Bihari** ► An Indo-Aryan language spoken in Bihar (India) and in Nepal by about 40 million people. It is related to ▷Bengali and less closely to ▷Hindi. There are three main dialects; only one, Maithili, has any significant literature.

● **Bijapur** ► 16 52N 75 47E A city in India, in Karnataka. The ancient capital of a powerful Islamic kingdom (1489–1686), it has many fine Islamic buildings. Population (1991): 186 846.

● **Bikaner** ► 28 01N 73 22E A city in India, in Rajasthan. The former centre of a princely state, its fort (1571–1611) houses a fine collection of Sanskrit and Persian manuscripts. Bikaner is famous for the manufacture of carpets, shawls, and blankets. Population (1991): 415 000.

● **Bikini Atoll** ► 11 35N 165 20E An atoll in the central Pacific Ocean in the ▷Marshall Islands. It was the site of US atomic and hydrogen bomb tests from 1946 to 1958.

● **Biko, Steve(n Bantu)** ► (1946–77) Black South African medical student who formed the South African Student Organization (SASO) in 1968. In 1972 he cofounded ▷Black Consciousness (also known as the Black People's Convention), which actively opposed ▷apartheid and aimed to encourage pride in Black culture. His arrest and death in police custody caused international disquiet, making him a symbol of the struggle against apartheid.

● **Bilbao** ► 43 15N 2 56W A port in N Spain, the largest city in the Basque Provinces on the River Nervión. One of Spain's chief ports, its exports include iron ore, lead, and wine. Metallurgical industries are especially important; others include chemicals, fishing, and shipbuilding. Its university was founded in 1968. The city's most famous modern building, Frank Gehry's Guggenheim Art Museum, was opened in 1997. Population (1998 est): 358 467.

● **bilberry** ► A deciduous shrub, *Vaccinium myrtillus*, 30–60 cm high, also known as blaeberry, huckleberry, and whortleberry. It is found on acid moors and mountains in N Europe and N Asia. The green angular stems bear small pointed leaves that turn red in autumn. The globular pink flowers, which droop like tiny bells, develop into blue berries. These may be eaten raw or cooked, used in preserves, or used to make wine and spirits. Family: *Ericaceae* (heath family).

● **Bilderdijk, Willem** ► (1756–1831) Dutch poet and dramatist, a precursor of Romanticism in Dutch literature. He is best known for an unfinished epic poem on biblical themes entitled *De ondergang der eerste wareld* (*The Destruction of the First World*; 1810).

● **Bildungsroman** ► (German: education novel) A novel that describes the emotional and psychological development of its young hero or heroine from childhood or adolescence to maturity. Often semiautobiographical, such novels tend to focus on the protagonist's troubled quest for identity and self-expression. The genre was established by Goethe's *Wilhelm Meister's Apprentice Years* (1795–96) and has remained a largely German form, with such later examples as Mann's *The Magic Mountain* (1924). English-language examples include Joyce's *A Portrait of the Artist as a Young Man* (1914).

● **bile** ► A yellow, green, or brown alkaline fluid secreted by the liver and stored in the ▷gall bladder. Contraction of the gall bladder, which is triggered by a hormone that is released from the duodenum in the presence of food, causes the bile to be expelled through the common bile duct into the intestine. Bile is composed of a mixture of bile salts (which emulsifies fatty foods for digestion) and bilirubin (a breakdown product of the blood pigment ▷haemoglobin).

● **bilharziasis** ▷See schistosomiasis.

● **billiards** ► A game for two players, using cues and balls on a table. In **English billiards** the table measures 12 × 6 ft (3.6 × 1.8 m) and has six pockets (holes round the edges of the table); points are scored using two white cue balls 2 in (5.2 cm) in diameter (one for each player), and a red ball. A cannon, in which the cue ball strikes both the other balls, scores two points; a winning hazard, in which the cue ball pockets another ball, scores two points (white) or three (red); a losing hazard, in which the cue ball is pocketed after striking another ball, scores two points (off white) or three (off red). A break lasts until the player fails to score. **Carom billiards** is played on a smaller table with no pockets and scoring is by cannons (*or* caroms). **Bar billiards** is played on a small table with a timing device and holes in the surface, into which balls are potted off each other until the time runs out. ▷*See also* pool; snooker.

● **Billingsgate** ► The oldest market in London, dating from the 10th century. It was originally situated close to London Bridge but in 1982 was moved to the Isle of Dogs. It became a fish market in the 16th century. The market porters were formerly known for their heavy leather hats on which they balanced boxes of fish.

● **Billiton** ▷See Belitung.

● **bill of exchange** ► (*or* monetary draft) A written order signed by one person (drawer) requiring a second person (drawee) to pay on demand or at a stated date an amount of money to, or to the order of, a specified person or the bearer (payee). A cheque is a bill of exchange payable on demand and drawn on a banker. Bills of exchange are used in foreign trade and can be discounted (sold for cash before their maturity date at less than their face value) with an ▷acceptance house, bank, etc.

● **Bill of Rights ▶ 1.** An act of parliament that incorporated the Declaration of Rights, the conditions on which the English throne was offered to William and Mary in 1689 (*see* Glorious Revolution). It curtailed the royal prerogative. MPs were to be freely elected and guaranteed freedom of speech. Roman Catholics were barred from the throne. **2.** (1791) The first ten amendments to the US Constitution, described by Jefferson as "what the people are entitled to against every government on earth." They are (1) freedom of press, speech, and religion; (2) the right to bear arms; (3) prohibition of quartering of troops; (4) protection against unlawful search and seizure; (5) the right of due process of law; (6) the right to a fair and public trial; (7) the right to a trial by jury; (8) prohibition of cruel punishments; (9) protection of nonenumerated rights; and (10) reservation of powers, i.e. powers not reserved for the federal government reside in the states.

● **Billroth, Christian Albert Theodor ▶** (1829–94) Prussian-born surgeon. At Vienna University from 1867, he pioneered several important operations on the stomach and intestine.

● **Billy the Kid ▶** (William Bonney; 1859–81) US outlaw. Born in New York, he was raised in the west and is said to have killed his first man at the age of 12. He took part in the New Mexico cattle war (1878), in which he killed a sheriff. When he was shot by Sheriff Pat Garrett, 21 deaths had been attributed to him.

● **bimetallism ▶** A monetary system in which currency was convertible into either of two metals (usually gold and silver) in a fixed ratio. Widely adopted in the early 19th century, it proved unstable, as one metal was always undervalued and one overvalued. *Compare* gold standard.

● **binary star ▶** Two stars moving around each other under mutual gravitational attraction. Possibly 50% of stars are members of binary or other multiple systems. The components of a **visual binary** can be distinguished by telescope whereas a **spectroscopic binary** can only be detected by spectroscope measurements, the components usually being very close. In an **eclipsing binary** the orbital plane is so orientated that one component passes alternately in front of and then behind the other, causing the combined brightness to fluctuate. In a **close binary** the two components are close enough to exchange gaseous matter and can even share gas. This greatly affects their evolution and can lead to violent phenomena, such as ▷nova explosions or intense X-ray emission, if one component is a ▷white dwarf, a ▷neutron star, or a ▷black hole.

● **binary system ▶** A number system that uses only two digits 0 and 1. Numbers are expressed in powers of 2 instead of powers of 10, as in the decimal system. In binary notation, 2 is written as 10, 3 as 11, 4 as 100, 5 as 101, and so on. ▷Computers calculate in binary notation, the two digits corresponding to two switching positions (e.g. on or off) in the individual electronic devices in the logic circuits.

● **binding energy ▶** The energy released when protons and neutrons bind together to form an atomic nucleus. The mass of a nucleus is always less than the sum of the masses of the constituent protons and neutrons. The missing mass is converted into the binding energy according to ▷Einstein's law $E = mc^2$.

● **bindweed ▶** A widely distributed climbing plant of the temperate and subtropical genera ▷*Convolvulus* and *Calystegia*. Bindweeds twine their stems around other plants for support and can be persistent weeds. The leaves are large and arrow-shaped and the conspicuous white, pink, or yellow flowers are funnel-shaped. Family: *Convolvulaceae*. Black bindweed and copse bindweed (genus *Bilderdykia*; 3 species) lack the conspicuous flowers of the other bindweeds. Family: *Polygonaceae* (dock family).

● **Binet, Alfred ▶** (1857–1911) French psychologist, who pioneered intelligence tests. Binet observed how his two young daughters responded to his tests using simple objects and pictures (*Experimental Study of Intelligence*, 1903). He later applied his techniques to measure the educational achievements of schoolchildren.

● **Bingen ▶** 49 58N 7 55E A town in W Germany, in Rhineland-Palatinate at the confluence of the Rivers Rhine and Nahe. According to legend Archbishop Hatto II was devoured (c. 970) by mice on a nearby rock in the Rhine for maltreating his subjects. It is a centre of the wine and tourist trades. Population (latest est): 23 141.

● **bingo ▶** (former names: tombola; housy-housy) A gambling game that developed in the 1880s from the children's game of lotto. Each player buys a card containing lines of random numbers (from 1 to 75 in the USA and usually from 1 to 90 in the UK). As numbers are called out, the players cover corresponding squares on their cards with counters; the first person to complete a line or the card wins. The stake money is pooled. It became particularly popular in the UK following a relaxation of the gaming laws during the 1960s.

● **Bin Laden, Osama ▶** (1957–) Saudi-born leader of the ▷al-Qaida terrorist movement. The heir to a vast fortune from his father's construction business, Bin Laden trained as a civil engineer before dedicating himself to militant Islamic activities in the late 1970s. His role in organizing guerrilla resistance to the Soviet invaders in Afghanistan (1979–89) made him a hero to many Muslims. However, his opposition to the stationing of US troops on Saudi soil (in 1990) led him to organize a series of attacks on US military and diplomatic targets from Sudan (from 1992). In 1996 Bin Laden transferred these operations to Afghanistan, where he forged links with the ▷Taleban. In 2001 he achieved worldwide notoriety as the presumed orchestrator of the devastating terrorist attacks on New York and Washington on ▷September 11. Although the USA's subsequent ▷war on terrorism destroyed al-Qaida's Afghan bases, Bin Laden is thought to have survived; his whereabouts are unknown.

● **binoculars ▶** A portable optical instrument used for magnifying distant objects. It consists of two telescopes fixed side by side, one for each eye, inside which there are a number of lenses for magnifying and focusing the image and usually prisms for altering the direction of the light and thus increasing the effective length of the telescope.

● **binomial nomenclature ▶** A system devised by ▷Linnaeus in the 18th century for the scientific naming of plants and animals, each species being identified by two internationally recognized Latin names—the name of the genus (written with an initial capital letter) followed by the name of the species. The names are usually written in italics and the specific name may be followed by the author's name, usually abbreviated. Thus the wolf is *Canis lupus* L (for Linnaeus).

● **binomial theorem ▶** The theorem, discovered by Isaac ▷Newton in 1676, that the quantity $(a + n)^n$, where n is an integer, can be expanded in a series: $(a + b)^n = an + na^{n-1}b + [n(n-1) a^{n-2}b^2] / 2! + [n(n-1)(n-2) a^{n-3}b^3] / 3! + ... + b^n$ where, for example, 3! (called factorial three) is $3 \times 2 \times 1$.

● **binturong ▶** A mammal, *Arctictis binturong*, of SE Asia, closely related to the ▷palm civets. Measuring up to 1.5 m long, it has a dark-grey shaggy coat, tufted ears, short legs, and a bushy prehensile tail (60 cm long). Binturongs live in trees and feed on fruit and vegetation; they are more vocal than civets, often growling or hissing.

● **Binyon, Laurence ▶** (1869–1943) British poet, also known for his influential studies of Far Eastern art. Among his works are the World War I elegy, "For the Fallen" (1914), and a translation of Dante's *Divine Comedy* (1933–43).

● **bioassay ▶** A test of the strength or quantity of a biologically active substance by a comparison of its effect upon animals, isolated tissues, or microorganisms with that of a standard preparation.

● **Bío-Bío, River ▶** A river in Chile. Rising in the Andes, it flows generally NW to enter the Pacific Ocean and forms the S boundary of middle Chile. Length: about 390 km (240 mi).

● **biochemical oxygen demand ▶** (BOD) A measure of the amount of oxygen required by microorganisms to break down the organic material in a given sample of water. BOD is determined under standard conditions and used as an index of water pollution. A high BOD indicates that a greater proportion of oxygen is used by microorganisms in degrading the pollutants, hence there is less available for fishes, etc.

● **biochemistry ▶** The scientific study of the chemical composition and reactions of living organisms. Central to biochemistry is ▷metabolism and the determination of the complex sequence of reactions involved in the digestion of food, the utilization of energy, the manufacture of new tissues, the breakdown of old tissues, and the formation of excretory products. Biochemists are also concerned with the role of ▷genes, ▷hormones, and ▷enzymes in initiating and controlling metabolic reactions.

● **biodegradable substances** ▶ Materials that can be broken down by biological processes—such as decomposition by fungi and bacteria—and can therefore be reused by living organisms (*see* recycling). Substances that are **nonbiodegradable**, such as plastics, can pollute the environment.

● **bioengineering** ▶ (*or* biomechanics) The application of biological and engineering principles to the design and manufacture of equipment for use in conjunction with biological systems (e.g. artificial limbs, pacemakers, life-support systems).

● **bioethics** ▶ The branch of ▷ethics concerned with moral problems arising from advances in medical genetics and ▷biotechnology. These relate to the use and consequences of genetic screening for inherited diseases, ▷gene therapy, ▷prenatal diagnosis, and assisted reproduction. ▷*See also* eugenics; medical ethics.

● **biofuels** ▷*See* biomass energy.

● **biogas** ▷*See* biomass energy.

● **biogenetic law** ▶ (*or* recapitulation theory) A theory postulated by Ernst ▷Haeckel in 1866 stating that the development of an animal in its lifetime tends to recapitulate the evolutionary development of its ancestors (*see* phylogeny).

● **biogeography** ▶ The study of the geographical distribution of animals (*see* zoogeography) and plants (plant geography *or* phytogeography) at the local, regional, or global level, with emphasis on the factors responsible for their present distribution. Movements of land masses in the geological past (*see* continental drift), creating barriers to dispersal, were major influences on distribution at the global level. Other factors include climate, interactions between species (such as competition), and human influence on habitats.

● **Bioko** ▷*See* Equatorial Guinea, Republic of.

● **biological clock** ▶ An internal timing mechanism that regulates the ▷biorhythms of an organism. The clock operates even in an artifically controlled environment in the absence of external cues, such as daylength or temperatures changes, but under these conditions it may speed up or slow down. The physiological processes involved are poorly understood; in certain mammals the ▷pineal gland is thought to play a role.

● **biological control** ▶ The control of pests by the use of living organisms. The controlling agent is usually a predator, parasite, or disease of the pest. For example, the virus disease myxomatosis was introduced to Australia and Britain to control the rabbit population. Other methods of controlling insect pests include the release of sterile males to mate among the population, so reducing the numbers of eggs laid. Biological control avoids the indiscriminate action and environmental pollution of chemical ▷pesticides.

● **biological sciences** ▶ The scientific disciplines concerned with the study of life. The earliest recorded biological observations come from ancient Egypt but it was Greek and Roman scholars, such as ▷Aristotle, ▷Hippocrates, and ▷Galen, who made the first detailed anatomical descriptions of living things. Not until the 16th and 17th centuries were further advances made by such anatomists as ▷Vesalius and William ▷Harvey. The introduction of the microscope in the 17th century enabled microorganisms, tissues, and individual cells (*see* cytology) to be observed for the first time. By the 18th century a wealth of descriptions of individual organisms had been produced and attempts were made to arrange them into related groups (*see* taxonomy), notably by ▷Linnaeus and Georges ▷Cuvier, who founded the science of palaeontology. Various theories of ▷evolution culminated in Charles ▷Darwin's theory of the origin of species (1858). Six years later, Gregor ▷Mendel reported his findings on the principles of inheritance, which are fundamental to ▷genetics, although it was not until 1953 that James ▷Watson and Francis ▷Crick determined the molecular structure of ▷DNA. During the 20th century progress in ▷biochemistry, ▷physiology, cytology, and ▷bio-

physics has been made possible by such innovations as electron microscopy, chromatography, and ▷radioactive tracers. Advances in genetics and ▷microbiology have revolutionized industry, medicine, and agriculture. ▷*See also* botany; ecology; ethology; zoology.

● **biological warfare** ▶ The use of disease-causing microorganisms as weapons. In World War I, the Germans infected Allied cavalry horses with bacteria causing ▷glanders. Although biological warfare is now officially banned by the major powers, research continues in developing new strains of such organisms. They are required to be highly virulent (but not necessarily lethal) and could be deployed by bombs or delivered in the warhead of a missile. Alternatively, they could be added to water or food supplies. A more recent concern is so-called **bioterrorism**, such as the ▷anthrax attacks on US and Pakistani targets in late 2001.

● **bioluminescence** ▶ The production of light by living organisms, including certain bacteria, fungi, and various animals (e.g. fireflies and glowworms, protozoans, and bony fishes). In some the ▷luminescence is due to symbiotic light-producing bacteria. The light is emitted by the compound luciferin when it is oxidized: the reaction is catalysed by an enzyme, luciferase. The emission of light may be continuous, as in bacteria, or intermittent, as in the flash of fireflies. Bioluminescence can attract mates or lure prey.

● **biomass** ▶ The total weight (mass) of all living organisms (or of all members of a particular species) found in a given area. Biomass is expressed as mass per unit area.

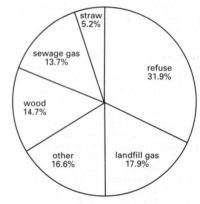

biomass energy ▶ In the UK in 1996, biofuels provided 80.3% of the 2.3 million tonnes of oil equivalent supplied by alternative energy sources. The pie chart shows the composition of these biofuels.

● **biomass energy** ▶ Energy obtained from the methane (biogas) generated by sewage or farm, industrial, and household organic waste (*see* waste disposal), from specially cultivated organisms, or from crops, such as trees (in so-called energy forests) and sugar cane, grown for their energy potential. Known collectively as **biofuels**, these ▷alternative energy sources already supply some 4% of USA's primary fuel requirements. Some claim that up to 85% of the waste collected by UK local authorities could be turned into biofuels with an energy content 60% that of coal.

● **biome** ▶ A geographical region that is characterized by a predominant type of vegetation and associated fauna. Examples include grassland, desert, tropical forest, etc.

● **bionics** ▶ The study of living systems in order to design man-made systems based on similar principles. It assumes that most living creatures have adapted in the best possible way to their environments. The applications of bionics include the design of a ship's propeller modelled on a fish's tail and the use of knowledge of nerve physiology in data-processing systems.

● **bionomics** ▷*See* ecology.

● **biophysics** ▶ The scientific discipline concerned with the explanation of biological phenomena in terms of the laws of physics. Biophysics emerged in the 1940s with the work of such scientists as Max

▷Perutz and John ▷Kendrew, who used ▷X-ray diffraction to determine the structure of biological molecules; this was followed by Maurice ▷Wilkins' work on DNA. More recent topics include the nature of the nervous impulse, the properties of biological membranes, the mechanism of muscle contraction, and the operation of sense organs.

● **biopsy** ▶ The removal of a sample of living tissue from the body for microscopic examination. Biopsies are used to assist in the diagnosis of diseases, including cancer (from biopsies of tumours), jaundice (from a liver biopsy), and anaemia (from a bone-marrow biopsy).

● **biorhythm** ▶ A periodic pattern of behaviour or metabolic activity occurring in a wide range of animals and plants. Many bodily functions, for example waking and sleeping, have a 24-hour **circadian rhythm**; other biorhythms may cycle once every 28 days (lunar rhythms) or once a year (circannual rhythms, such as hibernation and migration). Biorhythms are often regulated by the organism's ▷biological clock in conjunction with environmental stimuli, such as daylength or tidal flow.

● **biosphere** ▶ The zone of the earth and its atmosphere that is occupied by living organisms. The most heavily populated regions of the biosphere are the surfaces of land and sea.

● **biosynthesis** ▶ The manufacture of biological molecules by a living cell in the process of anabolism (see metabolism). Biosynthesis is catalysed by enzymes, production of which is directed by the cell's genes. This enables biosynthesis to be switched on and off, and allows different types of cell to manufacture different materials.

● **biotechnology** ▶ Technology based on biological processes. This traditionally includes such processes as the manufacture of beer, cheese, yogurt, etc., involving fermentation, and the production of antibiotics from moulds. Since the advent of ▷genetic engineering, which enables the isolation of a desired gene sequence and the large-scale growth of its product, the scope of biotechnology has widened to include the manufacture of hormones (e.g. insulin), vaccines, ▷monoclonal antibodies, and other medically useful products.

● **biotin** ▷See vitamin B complex.

● **biotite** ▷See micas.

● **bipolar disorder** ▷See manic-depressive psychosis.

● **birch** ▶ A deciduous tree or shrub of the genus Betula (40 species), of the N hemisphere. Birches grow to a height of up to 25 m and have thin smooth bark, pale grey or yellowish-brown, that peels off in strips. The glossy leaves are usually triangular, with toothed edges. The flowers are male and female catkins producing tiny winged nuts. Birch wood, especially that of the Eurasian silver birch (B. pendula), is used for turned articles. Birch bark is used for tanning and roofing, and the bark of the paper birch (B. papyrifera) was used by American Indians to make birch-bark canoes. Family: Betulaceae.

● **bird** ▶ A warm-blooded animal belonging to the class Aves (about 8600 species), adapted for flight by having fore limbs modified as wings and a body covering of ▷feathers. Other adaptations include a light skeleton with hollow bones and a large keel-shaped breastbone providing attachment for the powerful flight muscles. The jaws are elongated into a horny bill (teeth are absent or reduced). Birds have good eyesight and colour vision and most are active by day. Through flight, they have managed to colonize almost every available terrestrial, freshwater, and marine habitat.

Social behaviour plays an important part in the life of birds, which show complex patterns of behaviour in territorial and courtship displays, ▷nest building, egg incubation, and care of the young. Many communicate by means of song (see songbird) and some undergo long seasonal ▷migrations.

Birds are of great economic importance to man. The eggs and flesh of many provide food, several species being domesticated and bred for this purpose (see poultry), and wildfowl and game birds are hunted for sport. Other species are pests, damaging crops (particularly cereals) or fouling buildings in cities. Certain diseases, notably psittacosis, are transmitted to man by birds. Modern birds include both flying and flightless species (see ratite); the largest of the 28 orders is the Passeriformes (see passerine bird). ▷See also ornithology.

● **bird of paradise** ▶ A bird, 30–65 cm long, belonging to a family (Paradisaeidae; 40 species) occurring in New Guinea and neighbouring islands. The male is usually brightly coloured, with long tail feathers and ornamental plumes, and performs an acrobatic display to attract the dull-coloured female. Their feathers are much prized and were formerly exported for use in ladies' hats. ▷See Plate III.

● **bird-of-paradise flower** ▶ A herbaceous perennial plant, Strelitzia reginae, native to South Africa and cultivated for ornament. The flower cluster, 20 cm long, is orange, scarlet, and blue and resembles a bird's head. The oblong leaves rise to a height of 90 cm from the rootstock. Family: Musaceae (banana family).

● **bird of prey** ▶ A bird that hunts other animals for food, also called raptor. Birds of prey are divided into the nocturnal hunters, comprising the owls (order Strigiformes), and those that hunt by day, comprising the eagles, falcons, hawks, secretary bird, and the vultures (order Falconiformes). Live prey is normally taken but the vultures specialize in feeding on carrion. Birds of prey are characterized by their strong hooked bills for tearing flesh, clawed talons, and powerful flight with a high-speed dive onto prey.

● **bird's nest fern** ▶ An Old World tropical ▷fern, Asplenium nidus, that has a dense rosette of leaves, 60–120 cm long, with a central hollow forming a nest in which humus collects. The roots branch into this to obtain water and nutrients. Family: Aspleniaceae.

● **bird's nest orchid** ▶ A widely distributed saprophytic ▷orchid, Neottia nidus-avis, most commonly growing in beech woodlands. Named from the dense round cluster of roots at the stem base, it reaches a height of 25–40 cm and produces spikes of brown flowers.

● **bird song** ▶ The call notes produced by birds by means of a unique vocal organ, the ▷syrinx. These calls are elaborated in the ▷songbirds, which have highly developed syrinxes, into songs of great complexity and often beauty. However, both the songs of these birds and the simpler call notes of other birds serve the same functions. Bird song is used mainly by males to advertise their ▷territories and to attract a mate. It is also important in communication, especially between parent birds and their chicks. Each species has its own pattern of bird song.

● **bird spider** ▶ Any of the large ▷tarantula spiders that may catch and eat small birds.

● **bird-wing butterfly** ▶ A ▷papilionid butterfly characterized by its wings, which—in the males—are black and typically marked with patches of iridescent blue, green, or gold. The front wings are longer than the hindwings and can reach a span of over 40 cm. Females are larger, with a wingspan of up to 60 cm, but lack the iridescent colours of the males. Bird-wings are restricted to SE Asia and Australasia; there are about 30 species in three genera (Troides, Ornithoptera, and Trogonoptera).

● **bireme** ▷See ships.

● **Birendra Bir Bikram Shah Dev** ▶ (1945–) King of Nepal (1972–2001). He succeeded his father Mahendra. In 1990 pressure for reform led him to lift a 30-year ban on political parties. In June 2001 Birendra, his queen Aishwarya, and six other members of the royal family were shot dead by his son, Crown Prince Dipendra, who then shot himself. On Dipendra's death two days later Birendra's brother Gyanendra became king.

● **Birkbeck, George** ▶ (1776–1841) British educationalist. As professor of natural philosophy at the Andersonian Institute, Glasgow, Birkbeck lectured unpaid to working men. With Brougham, ▷Bentham, ▷Cobbett, and others, he founded the London Mechanics' Institute (1824). This became affiliated to London University and is now Birkbeck College.

● **Birkeland, K. O. B.** ▷See nitrogen fixation.

● **Birkenhead** ▶ 53 24N 3 02W A port in NW England, in Wirral unitary authority, Merseyside. It is linked with Liverpool across the River Mersey by road and rail tunnels and ferry. Population (1991): 93 087.

● **Birkenhead, F(rederick) E(dwin) Smith, 1st Earl of** ▶ (1872–1930) British Conservative politician. A barrister, Birkenhead entered parliament in 1906. As attorney general (1915–19) he prosecuted Sir

Roger ▷Casement and while lord chancellor (1919–22) he introduced major land-law reforms. He was secretary for India (1924–28).

● **Birkhoff, George David ▶** (1864–1944) US mathematician, who gave the Maxwell-Boltzmann theory of gases a mathematical basis. He produced mathematical theories of aesthetics and gravitation. ▷*See also* statistical mechanics.

● **Birmingham ▶** 1. 52 30N 1 50W A city in central England, in Birmingham unitary authority, West Midlands. Britain's second largest city, it is a centre of the motor-vehicles industry and besides general engineering and metalworking also produces chemicals, plastics, tyres, chocolate, and jewellery. A cultural centre, it possesses three universities—Aston University (1966), Birmingham University (1900), and the University of Central England in Birmingham (formerly Birmingham Polytechnic)—an art gallery (1874–81), a symphony orchestra, a repertory theatre founded in 1913 by Sir Barry Jackson (1879–1961), and several museums; the Sadler's Wells Royal Ballet moved there in 1990 and Symphony Hall, a major orchestral venue, opened in 1991. It has an 18th-century cathedral and a Roman Catholic cathedral (1839–41) designed by Pugin. Among postwar developments are a modern shopping complex centred on the Bull Ring, the National Exhibition Centre (1976) at Bickenhill, Solihull, and Gravelly Hill Interchange (or Spaghetti Junction), where several motorways meet.
  History: originally an Anglo-Saxon settlement, its development dates largely from the industrial revolution. It was severely damaged by bombing during World War II. Population (1994 est): 965 928. 2. A unitary authority in central England, in West Midlands. Area: 283 sq km (109 sq mi). Population (1995 est): 1 017 500.

● **Birmingham ▶** 33 30N 86 55W A city in the USA, in Alabama. Settled in 1813, it is the state's largest city and the main industrial centre of the South. Industries include iron and steel (which use local iron ore deposits), engineering, construction, and paint. Population (1996 est): 258 543.

● **Biró, Laszlo ▶** (1900–85) Hungarian inventor, who in 1938 patented the ballpoint pen containing quick-drying ink. Such pens are now commonly known as biros.

● **Birobidzhan** ▷*See* Jewish autonomous region.

● **birth control** ▷*See* contraception.

● **birthmark ▶** A blemish that is present on the skin at birth. Known medically as a naevus, it is usually harmless and may disappear with age. Birthmarks are caused by a defect in the skin cells or underlying blood vessels.

● **birthstone ▶** In ▷astrology, a gemstone associated with a birth month. The belief that gems had supernatural powers led to them being worn for luck. The modern list of birthstones is:

January—garnet;	July—ruby;
February—amethyst;	August—sardonyx;
March—bloodstone;	September—sapphire;
April—diamond;	October—opal;
May—emerald;	November—topaz;
June—pearl;	December—turquoise.

● **Birtwistle, Sir Harrison ▶** (1934–) British composer, noted for his savagely dissonant works. His compositions include the operas *Punch and Judy* (1966–67), *The Mask of Orpheus* (1984), *Yan Tan Tethera* (1986), *Gawain* (1991), and *The Last Supper* (2000); *An Imaginary Landscape* (for orchestra; 1971); *Endless Parade* (for trumpet and orchestra; 1987); and the large-scale orchestral work *Exody* (1998). He was knighted in 1988 and appointed CH in 2000.

● **Biscay, Bay of ▶** (French name: Golfe de Gascogne; Spanish name: Golfo de Vizcaya) An inlet of the Atlantic Ocean, off the coast of W France and N Spain. It is subject to gales and rough seas. The fish caught here include anchovies, cod, sardines, and tuna. Width: about 320 km (199 mi).

● **bisexuality** ▷*See* homosexuality.

● **Bishkek ▶** (or Pishpek; name 1925–91: Frunze) 42 53N 74 46E The capital city of Kirgizstan, on the River Chu. Industries include the manufacture of agricultural machinery, textiles, food, and tobacco products. Population (1996 est): 589 800.

● **Bishop Auckland ▶** 54 40N 1 40W A town in NE England, in Durham on the River Wear. Its palace is the traditional seat of the bishops of Durham. It has engineering, electrical, and various light industries. Population (1991): 23 154.

● **Bishops' Wars ▶** (1639, 1640) The wars fought between the Scots and Charles I of Great Britain following his attempts to enforce the Anglican Prayer Book and government of the Church by bishops on the Presbyterian Scots. The first war was ended by the Treaty of Berwick; after his defeat in the second war, Charles was forced to summon the ▷Long Parliament.

● **Biskra ▶** 34 50N 5 45E An oasis town in N Algeria, on the N edge of the Sahara. It is an important centre for the date trade. Population (latest est): 128 280.

● **Bisley ▶** 51 20N 0 39W A village in SE England, in Surrey. Rifle ranges were constructed on Bisley Common in 1890 by the National Rifle Association, which still meets here annually.

● **Bismarck ▶** 46 50N 100 48W A city in the USA, the capital of North Dakota on the Missouri River. Named after Otto von Bismarck (1873) to entice German investment, it is an agricultural market centre. Population (1990): 49 256.

Bismarck ▶ A *Punch* cartoon (1890) captioned "Dropping the Pilot," satirizing Bismarck's resignation following disagreement with the emperor.

● **Bismarck, Otto Eduard Leopold, Prince von ▶** (1815–98) Prussian statesman; first chancellor of the German Empire (1871–90). A conservative, known as the Iron Chancellor, Bismarck came to prominence after the collapse of the ▷Revolution of 1848. As Prussian prime minister (1862–90) he was determined to establish Prussian hegemony in Germany and to undermine Austrian dominance there. He embroiled Austria in war over Schleswig-Holstein and following its defeat in the Austro-Prussian War of 1866 ▷William I of Prussia became president of the North German Confederation. After victory in the ▷Franco-Prussian War (1870–71) William accepted the imperial crown and Bismarck became chancellor of the new German Empire. Bismarck's domestic policy in succeeding years was concerned chiefly with keeping liberalism at bay. He also came into conflict with the Roman Catholic Church (*see* Kulturkampf) and, abroad, presided over the Congress of ▷Berlin (1878) and formed the ▷Triple

Alliance with Austria and Italy. Losing the support of William II, Bismarck resigned in 1890 over the abolition of antisocialist laws.

● **Bismarck Archipelago** ▶ A group of volcanic islands in the SW Pacific Ocean, in Papua New Guinea. It includes New Britain, New Ireland, and the Admiralty Islands. Area: 49 658 sq km (19 173 sq mi). Population (1995 est): 424 000.

● **bismuth** ▶ (Bi) A dense white brittle metal, similar in properties to tin and lead. It was first distinguished by C. Geoffroy in 1753. It is obtained as a by-product of lead, copper, tin, silver, and gold refining and also occurs naturally as the pure metal, the sulphide (Bi_2S_3), and the oxide (Bi_2O_3). It has unusual properties for a metal, having low thermal and electrical conductivity, and decreasing in volume on melting. With tin and cadmium it is used to make low-melting alloys in ▷fire prevention systems. At no 83; at wt 208.98037; mp 271.4°C; bp 1564°C.

● **bison** ▶ A massive hoofed □mammal belonging to the genus *Bison* (2 species). The North American bison (*B. bison*) was once abundant on the plains but is now found only on reserves. Once numbering about 30 million, they were reduced to a mere 500 specimens by 1900. Over 150 cm at the shoulder and weighing up to 1000 kg, it has a shaggy mane and low-slung head with incurved horns. The smaller European bison (*B. bonasus*), also called wisent, is now found only in zoos. Family: ▷*Bovidae*.

● **Bissau** ▶ 11 50N 15 37N The capital and chief port of Guinea-Bissau, on the Geba estuary. Founded by the Portuguese in 1687, it became capital of Portuguese Guinea in 1941. Population (1995 est): 233 000.

● **bistort** ▶ A perennial herb, *Polygonum bistorta*, of temperate Europe, also called snake-root or Easter-ledges. The upper leaves are triangular, with sheathing bases, and there is a dense terminal spike of tiny pink flowers. Family: *Polygonaceae* (dock family).

● **bit** ▶ A binary digit. The basic unit of information in information theory and computer memory stores. It is the amount of information needed to specify one of two alternatives, i.e. to distinguish between 1 and 0 in the ▷binary system of notation.

● **Bithynia** ▶ An ancient region of Asia Minor, S of the Black Sea. Of Thracian origin, the Bithynians long remained independent, resisting the aggression of the Achaemenians, Alexander the Great, and the Seleucids. By the 3rd century BC it had become a kingdom and expanded territorially and commercially. Conflict with Pergamum and later Pontus brought Roman involvement. Bequeathed by Nicomedes IV (reigned 91–74 BC) to Rome, Bithynia became an increasingly important province as Rome's frontiers expanded E.

● **Bitola** ▶ (Turkish name: Monastir) 41 01N 21 21E A town in S Macedonia. After five centuries of Turkish rule, it was taken by the Serbs in 1912. Its products include sugar, carpets, and textiles. Population (1994): 75 386.

● **bittern** ▶ A bird belonging to the subfamily *Botaurinae*, occurring throughout the world in swamps and reedbeds. The European bittern (*Botaurus stellaris*) is a solitary bird, about 70 cm long, with a yellow-brown dark-streaked plumage that provides excellent camouflage. The male produces a "booming" call. The little bittern (*Ixobrychus minutus*) is only 34 cm long with buffish-white wing patches. Family: *Ardeidae* (herons, etc.).

● **bittersweet** ▶ A perennial plant, the woody ▷nightshade.

● **bitumen** ▶ The tarry residue left after ▷distillation of oil, lignite, or coal, consisting almost entirely of a mixture of carbon with large ▷hydrocarbon molecules. Its principal uses are in roadmaking, waterproofing buildings, and binding cement. Bitumen sometimes occurs naturally in asphalt lakes.

● **bivalve** ▶ A ▷mollusc belonging to the class *Bivalvia* (also called *Pelecypoda* or *Lamellibranchia*; about 10 000 species). Bivalves are characterized by having two hinged shell plates (valves) and include ▷clams, ▷mussels, ▷oysters, and ▷scallops. Bivalves inhabit both salt and fresh water: some are free swimming; others burrow in sand, mud, or rock. They draw water between the shell valves using their ciliated gills and inner surfaces (mantle) to extract oxygen and food

particles from it. Most bivalves are of separate sexes but some are hermaphrodite. Some hermaphrodite bivalves, including *Ostrea* oysters, incubate the fertilized eggs.

● **Bizerte** ▶ (or Bizerta) 37 18N 9 52E A port in N Tunisia, on the Mediterranean Sea. It dates back to Phoenician times as a port and was known as Hippo Zarytus or Diarrhytus. France retained it as a naval base following Tunisian independence (1956) but surrendered it after fighting in 1963. Population (1994): 98 900.

● **Bizet, Georges** ▶ (Alexandre César Léopold B.; 1838–75) French composer. He studied under ▷Gounod and ▷Halévy and in 1855 produced his first major work, the symphony in C major (not discovered until 1935). He won the Prix de Rome in 1857. Among his best-known works are the incidental music to ▷Daudet's play *L'Arlésienne* (1872) and the opera *Carmen* (1873–74), which was at first disliked by the public and attacked by the critics. This censure hastened Bizet's death, three months after the premiere; it is now one of the world's most popular operas.

● **Bjerknes, Vilhelm Friman Koren** ▶ (1862–1951) Norwegian meteorologist and physicist. A pioneer of weather forecasting, his 1897 mathematical models of atmospheric and oceanic motions led to his full-scale meteorological predictions (1904). His son **Jakob Bjerknes** (1897–1975), also a meteorologist, initiated the use of high-altitude photography in weather surveys and forecasting (1952).

● **Bjørnson, Bjørnstjerne (Martinius)** ▶ (1832–1910) Norwegian novelist, poet, and playwright, who was also active in politics and worked as a theatre director and newspaper editor. His works, based on the sagas and his knowledge of rural life, include the novel *På Guds veje* (*In God's Way*; 1889) and the plays *En fallit* (*The Bankrupt*; 1875) and *Det ny system* (*The New System*; 1879). He is also remembered as the author of the Norwegian national anthem. He was awarded the Nobel Prize in 1903.

● **Black, Sir James (Whyte)** ▶ (1924–　) British biochemist. His discovery of ▷beta blockers in the late 1950s and his work on drugs for peptic ulcers and other uses won him a Nobel Prize (1988). He was appointed to the OM in 2000.

● **Black, Joseph** ▶ (1728–99) Scottish physician and chemist, born in Bordeaux, who became professor at Glasgow University and later at Edinburgh University. He independently discovered carbon dioxide, deduced its presence in air, and discovered the bicarbonate compounds. His work on heat led him to introduce the concepts caloric, heat of fusion, latent heat, specific heat, and thermal capacity. He was also the first to distinguish between heat and temperature.

● **Black and Tans** ▶ The irregular forces recruited by the British Government to fight the IRA in Ireland in 1920–21. Their name derives from their uniform, khaki with black caps and belts. Their brutal methods, which included indiscriminate reprisals against those thought to be Republican sympathizers, made them hated by the Irish.

● **black bear** ▶ The native bear of North American forests, *Ursus* (or *Euarctos*) *americanus*. American black bears grow to a weight of 150 kg; they climb well and eat berries, pine cones, and grass as well as small animals.
　　The name is also used for the Himalayan black, or moon, bear, *Selenarctos thibetanus*, which inhabits forests of central and E Asia and has a white V-shaped mark on its chest.

● **Blackbeard** ▷*See* Teach, Edward.

● **black beetle** ▷*See* cockroach.

● **blackberry** ▶ (or bramble) A prickly shrub, *Rubus fruticosus* (an aggregate species), occurring throughout Europe. The stems, up to 5 m long, root wherever they touch the ground. The leaves consist of five oval toothed leaflets and the pinkish-white flowers are borne in terminal clusters. The fruits consist of an aggregate of several small berries and are eaten raw or made into pies, jellies, preserves, etc. Family: *Rosaceae*.

● **blackbird** ▶ A songbird, *Turdus merula*, that is one of the commonest European birds, particularly in urban areas. The male, about 25 cm long, is black with a bright-yellow bill and eye ring; the larger female is dark brown with a dark bill. Blackbirds feed chiefly on worms and other invertebrates but will also eat scraps. Family: *Turdidae* (thrushes).

● **blackbirding** ▶ The kidnapping of Polynesians to provide slave labour for the sugar and cotton plantations of Australia and the South Pacific islands. Legislation against it was passed in Australia (1868) but was not effective, although blackbirding among British subjects was reduced by British government legislation, and it was not until the beginning of the 20th century that the practice died out.

● **black body** ▶ A theoretical body that absorbs all the electromagnetic radiation falling upon it. When heated it emits radiation (blackbody radiation) having a continuous distribution of wavelengths with a maximum at a particular wavelength, which depends only on the temperature of the body. ▷*See* Stefan-Boltzmann law.

● **black box** ▷*See* flight recorder.

● **blackbuck** ▶ A common antelope, *Antilope cervicapra*, of Indian grasslands. Blackbucks are about 80 cm high; females are yellowish brown and males darker, both with white underparts. Males have ridged spiral horns up to 65 cm long. They live in herds of 10–30 animals, grazing at dawn and dusk.

● **Blackburn** ▶ 53 45N 2 29W A town in NW England, in Blackburn with Darwen unitary authority, Lancashire, on the Leeds-Liverpool Canal. Historically associated with the textile industry (especially cotton), the town now has a mixture of modern and traditional industries, including engineering and electronics. Blackburn has a modern Anglican cathedral and is surrounded by the Pennine moorlands. Population (1991): 105 994.

● **Blackburn with Darwen** ▶ A unitary authority in NW England, in Lancashire. Area: 137 sq km (53 sq mi). Population (1999 est): 136 612.

● **blackcap** ▶ A European ▷warbler, *Sylvia atricapillus*. About 14 cm long, it has an olive-brown plumage with paler underparts and a darker cap (black in the male and reddish-brown in the female). Blackcaps feed chiefly on insects but—before migrating—they eat fruit to build up energy reserves.

● **Black Consciousness** ▶ The recognition by minority Black communities of their identity, history, and culture, as distinct from that of Whites. Movements contributing to the development of Black Consciousness in the USA have included the Universal Negro Improvement Association in the 1920s, the National Association for the Advancement of Coloured People, and the ▷Black Muslims. In South Africa the Black Consciousness Movement was led by Steven ▷Biko, whose death (1977) from injuries while in police detention provoked worldwide concern.

● **Black Country, the** ▶ An industrial area of central England. Situated NW of Birmingham, it grew up around the coalfield of what was then S Staffordshire. It gained its name from the grime produced by intense industrialization in the 19th century. Although mining is no longer practised there are numerous metal-processing and manufacturing industries in the area.

● **blackcurrant** ▶ A shrub, *Ribes nigrum*, native to most of Europe and N Asia and widely cultivated. The stems and three-lobed leaves emit a characteristic smell. The drooping clusters of greenish bell-shaped flowers develop into edible black berries, used in preserves, wine, beverages, and as a source of vitamin C. Family: *Grossulariaceae* (gooseberry family).

● **Black Death** ▶ The worst outbreak of ▷plague, principally bubonic but also pneumonic and septicaemic, of the medieval period. Originating in the Far East, it spread through Europe and England in May, 1348. Estimates of mortality rates vary from 20% to more than 50%. The outbreak had a profound effect not only on demographic trends but also upon rural society and the economy as a whole. Further outbreaks followed in the 1350s and 1370s.

● **black earth** ▷*See* chernozem.

● **black economy** ▶ Earnings that do not appear in national income statistics, because they are undeclared for tax purposes (e.g.

moonlighting, company perks, cash payments, etc.). In industrial countries they can amount to as much as 10% of the ▷gross national product.

● **Blackett, Patrick Maynard Stuart, Baron** ▶ (1897–1974) British physicist, who was professor at Birkbeck College, London (1933–37), Manchester University (1937–63), and Imperial College, London (1963–74). Working at the Cavendish Laboratory in Cambridge he made the first cloud-chamber photographs showing nuclear disintegrations (1925) and identified the distintegration products. He improved the Wilson cloud-chamber and used it to study cosmic radiation, for which work he received the Nobel Prize (1948). He was awarded the OM in 1967 and made a life peer in 1969.

● **black-eyed Susan** ▶ A North American perennial herb of the genus *Rudbeckia* (19 species) whose showy flower heads have yellow rays and blackish centres. The plants grow to a height of 60 cm and have rough narrow leaves. Also called coneflowers, many species (e.g. *R. fulgida* var *speciosa*) are cultivated in gardens. Family: ▷*Compositae*.

● **blackfly** ▶ Any black ▷aphid, especially the bean aphid (*Aphis fabae*). Bean aphids occur in masses on beans, spinach, dock, etc., in summer months. They overwinter as fertilized eggs in *Euonymus*, *Viburnum*, and *Philadelphus* trees.

● **black fly** ▶ A small humpbacked fly, also called buffalo gnat and turkey gnat, belonging to a family (*Simuliidae*; about 300 species) of worldwide distribution. The bloodsucking females attack man and domestic animals and some are vectors of disease. In Africa, for example, *Simulium damnosum* and *S. neavei* transmit a filarial worm that causes ▷onchocerciasis (river blindness).

● **Blackfoot** ▶ An Algonquian language and confederacy of three North American Indian peoples of the Plains: the Siksikas, Piegans, and Bloods. They were nomadic buffalo hunters and fierce warriors, who resisted the white man's encroachments in Alberta and Montana for many years.

● **Black Forest** ▶ (German name: Schwarzwald) A forested mountainous area in SW Germany, in Baden-Württemberg E of the Rhine Valley. Owing to the mainly coniferous forests the timber industry is important, with associated woodcrafts; it is also a popular tourist area.

● **black grouse** ▶ A Eurasian ▷grouse, *Lyrurus tetrix*, of moorlands. The male (also called blackcock), 50 cm long, has a glossy black plumage and a lyre-shaped tail; the female is reddish brown. Both have conspicuous red wattles above the eyes. In the breeding season the males perform an elaborate courtship display (lek) on a communal display ground.

● **Black Hand** ▶ A Serbian secret society pledged to the liberation of Serbs from Habsburg and Ottoman rule. On 28 June, 1914, they assassinated the Austrian archduke, Francis Ferdinand, contributing to the outbreak of World War I.

● **Black Hawk War** ▶ (1832) A conflict between the USA and the Sauk and Fox Indians. The Indian chief Black Hawk (1767–1838) resisted attempts to force his people W of the Mississippi River and near La Crosse, Wisconsin, nearly a thousand Indians were massacred by the US army despite a flag of surrender.

● **Blackheath** ▶ 51 28N 0 01E A residential district mainly in the Greater London boroughs of Lewisham and Greenwich. Originally an extensive heath, it was the rallying point of two rebellions led by Wat Tyler (1381) and Jack Cade (1450) and was notorious as a haunt of highwaymen.

● **Black Hills** ▶ A mountain range in the USA, in SW South Dakota and NE Wyoming. The densely forested hills rise to 1890 m (6200 ft) at Harney Peak and contain the ▷Mount Rushmore National Memorial. Minerals, including gold, have been mined since the 1870s and the hills are now a major recreational area.

● **black hole** ▶ A celestial "object" that has undergone such total ▷gravitational collapse that no light can escape from it: its ▷escape velocity exceeds the speed of ▷light. Once a collapsing object's radius has shrunk below a critical value (the Schwarzschild radius) it becomes a black hole; for a star, this radius is about 10 km or less. The surface having this radius is called the **event horizon** of the black hole. The object will contract until compressed to an infinite density at a single central point—a ▷singularity. A black hole is thus a region of greatly distorted space (and time) the size of which increases with the mass of the contracting material.

No black hole has as yet been unambiguously detected. The collapsed cores remaining from the ▷supernova explosions of massive stars are, however, promising candidates, especially if they are components of a ▷binary star and thus more easy to detect. The X-ray binary Cygnus X-1 has a probable black-hole component. Black holes of immense mass (10^6 to 10^9 solar masses) are now thought to exist at the centres of certain galaxies, possibly including our own, and to be the powerful sources of energy in ▷active galaxies such as ▷quasars.

● **Black Hole of Calcutta** ▶ A small cell (5.5 m × 4.5 m) in which over one hundred British soldiers were allegedly confined overnight in 1756. According to their commander John Holwell less than 25 men survived. The outrage was perpetrated by the Nawab of Bengal, who, objecting to the fortification of Calcutta by the East India Company, attacked and defeated the British garrison.

● **blackjack** ▶ A card game based on ▷pontoon (or vingt-et-un) played by a croupier and six punters in casinos. Using four standard packs, the objective is for the punters to score exactly 21, counting court cards as 10 and the ace as 1 or 11. The croupier deals two cards face up to each punter and 1 to himself; blackjack consists of a 10 and an ace, and pays 3 to 2, unless the dealer also makes blackjack on his second card (a "standoff", in which case no money changes hands).

● **blackmail** ▶ In law, the criminal offence of making any unwarranted demand with a view to gain, backed up by a threat of violence or injury to the person involved or to his property or by a threat of exposing his immorality or misconduct.

● **black mass** ▶ An obscene and blasphemous parody of the Roman Catholic mass, celebrated by satanists in honour of the devil. A naked woman is usually present at or on the altar and participants take hallucinatory drugs or other potions. ▷*See* satanism.

● **Blackmore, R(ichard) D(oddridge)** ▶ (1825–1900) British historical novelist, famous chiefly for *Lorna Doone* (1869), a romance set on Exmoor during the reign of James II.

● **Black Mountain** ▶ A ridge in South Wales, in E Carmarthenshire and W Powys, rising to 802 m (2632 ft) at Carmarthen Van.

● **Black Mountains** ▶ A mountain range in SE Wales and W central England, in Monmouthshire, Powys, and Herefordshire, mainly in the ▷Brecon Beacons National Park. It rises to 811 m (2660 ft) at Wann Fach.

● **Black Muslims** ▶ Members of the Nation of Islam movement founded in Detroit (USA) in 1930 by W. D. Fard, known variously as Walli Farrad, Wallace Fard Muhammad, etc., and believed by Black Muslims to be the Mahdi or Saviour. After the disappearance of Fard in 1933, the movement was led by Elijah Muhammad (1897–1975) and expanded greatly. Restricted to Blacks, it aimed to establish a new Islamic state. ▷Malcolm X was a leading member until 1964. In the 1970s the movement split into two strands, one of which abandoned racist and other unorthodox doctrines. The other group, which did not, is now led by Louis Farrakhan.

● **Blackpool** ▶ **1.** 53 50N 3 03W A coastal resort in NW England, in Blackpool unitary authority, Lancashire. It is an entertainments centre famous for its 160-m (520-ft) Tower (modelled on the Eiffel Tower), Pleasure Beach, and illuminations; it is also a conference centre. Population (1991): 146 262. **2.** A unitary authority in NW England, in Lancashire. Area: 35 sq km (13 sq mi). Population (1997 est): 151 200.

● **Black Prince, Edward the** ▷*See* Edward, the Black Prince.

● **Black Rod** ▶ In the UK, an official of the House of Lords, first appointed in 1522, having been called usher of the Order of the ▷Garter since 1350. He maintains order in the House, and when the monarch delivers a speech there, summons members of the Commons by knocking on their door with his staff of office (the black rod).

● **Black Sea** ▶ An inland sea bounded by Bulgaria, Romania, Moldova, Ukraine, Russia, Georgia, and Turkey; it is connected to the Mediterranean Sea via the Bosporus in the SW and to the sea of Azov in the N. The principal towns on its coast are Burgas and Varna in Bulgaria, Constanța in Romania, Odessa in Moldavia, Sevastopol in Ukraine, and Trabzon in Turkey. Its salinity is kept low principally by the influx of fresh water from the Rivers Danube and Dnepr.

● **Blackshirts** ▶ The colloquial name for the Fasci di Combattimento, founded by Mussolini in 1919 and forming the backbone of Italian ▷fascism. They wore distinctive black shirts; their name is also used in reference to the ▷SS.

● **black snake** ▶ A small-headed venomous snake, *Pseudeschis porphyriacus*, of Australian wetlands. About 1.5 m long, it is blue-black with a red belly. Family: *Elapidae* (cobras, mambas, coral snakes). In North America the name is given to a nonvenomous snake, *Zamenis constrictor*.

● **Blackstone, Sir William** ▶ (1723–80) British jurist. His fame rests largely on his *Commentaries on the Laws of England* (1765–69), a series of lectures that he had earlier delivered to his students at Oxford. Highly influential in legal education, they presented the first comprehensive account of English law. Blackstone became an MP in 1791 and a judge of the Court of Common Pleas in 1770.

● **black swan** ▶ The only Australian ▷swan, *Cygnus atratus*. Almost 1 m in length, both sexes have a pure black plumage, red bill, and a trumpeting call.

● **blackthorn** ▶ (or sloe) A thorny shrub, *Prunus spinos*, forming dense thickets, up to 4 m high, in many parts of Europe and Asia. The clusters of white flowers usually appear before the leaves, which are oval and toothed. The bitter-tasting blue-black stone fruits are used to flavour sloe gin; the hard wood is used for walking sticks and tool handles. Family: *Rosaceae*.

● **Blackwall Tunnel** ▶ A road tunnel under the Thames in E London. The northbound tunnel, 7 km (4410 ft) long, was built in 1891–97 by Sir Alexander Binnie. The 4.6-km (2870-ft) south-bound tunnel was built in 1960–67 by Mott, Hay, and Anderson.

● **blackwater fever** ▶ A serious complication of malaria in which the malarial parasite causes widespread destruction of red blood cells, leading to the excretion of blood pigments in the urine (which becomes dark brown—hence the name). The patient has a high fever and jaundice and requires careful nursing, with blood transfusions if necessary.

● **Blackwell, Elizabeth** ▶ (1821–1910) British-born US physician, the first woman to qualify as a doctor in modern times. In 1832 she emigrated with her family to the USA, where she began a course of private medical study. Although initially barred from formal training, she later (1847) gained her MD from a medical school in New York state and took hospital posts in London and Paris. After returning to the USA, she founded the New York Infirmary (1853) and its associated Women's Medical College (1868) with her sister, **Emily Blackwell** (1826–1910). She spent her later years in England, where she established (1875) the London School of Medicine for Women.

● **black widow** ▶ A venomous ▷spider, also called button or redback spider, that belongs to a genus (*Latrodectus*; about 6 species) found in tropical and subtropical regions. The female of *L. mactans*, the most common North American species, has a shiny black body, 25 mm long, with red markings on the abdomen. (The male is about 6 mm long and usually killed and eaten by the female after mating.) The bite of this spider—although serious—is rarely fatal. Family: *Theridiidae*.

● **Blackwood, Algernon Henry** ▶ (1869–1951) British novelist and short-story writer. He worked in Canada and the USA before returning to England in 1899. *The Empty House* (1906), a collection of ghost stories, was followed by many works concerning the supernatural, including *Tales of the Uncanny and Supernatural* (1949).

● **bladder** ▶ In anatomy, any hollow organ containing fluid, especially the urinary bladder situated in the pelvis, into which urine drains from the ▷kidneys (via the ureters). Urine is stored in the bladder and released at intervals by relaxation of a circular (sphincter) muscle at its opening into the urethra (which leads to the exterior; *see* Plate II). Bladder emptying is normally under voluntary control.

● **bladderwort** ► A plant of the widely distributed genus *Utricularia* (about 200 species, many tropical). Most bladderworts are submerged aquatic plants with finely divided leaves bearing small bladders, which trap tiny aquatic animals by a trapdoor mechanism triggered by sensitive hairs. The two-lipped tubular flowers protrude above the water. Some bladderworts are troublesome weeds of ricefields. Family: *Lentibulariaceae*.

● **Blaenau Gwent** ► A county borough in SE Wales, created in 1996 from part of N Gwent. Area: 109 sq km (42 sq mi). Population (1998 est): 72 000. Administrative centre: Ebbw Vale.

Tony Blair

● **Blair, Tony** ► (Anthony Charles Lynton B.; 1953–) British Labour politician: prime minister (1997–). He entered parliament in 1983 and was shadow home secretary (1992–94) before becoming party leader in 1994. Having reformed the party's constitution and modernized its image, he led it to a landslide victory in the general election of 1997. In government he promoted major constitutional changes, including ▷devolution in Scotland and Wales, a new settlement in Northern Ireland, and reform of the House of Lords. His government was re-elected with a large majority in 2001. Following the events of ▷September 11, Blair pledged full support for the USA's ▷war on terrorism in Afghanistan and elsewhere.

● **Blake, Peter** ► (1932–) British painter, born in Dartford. In the late 1950s he became one of the leading British exponents of ▷pop art with his half-painted half-collage pinup girls, pop singers, wrestlers, and advertisements.

● **Blake, Sir Peter James** ► (1948–2001) New Zealand yachtsman. An experienced round-the-world sailor, he led the New Zealand team that won the America's Cup in 1995. In 1997 he was nominated to carry on the work of Jacques ▷Cousteau as captain of *Calypso II*. He was killed by river pirates during an expedition to the Amazon.

● **Blake, Robert** ► (1599–1657) English admiral. A Parliamentarian in the Civil War, Blake was one of ▷Cromwell's most successful commanders and in 1650 destroyed Prince Rupert's Royalist fleet. In the first ▷Dutch War, he was largely responsible for the English victory and defeated ▷Tromp at the battle of Portland (1653). He destroyed a pirate fleet off Tunis (1655) and sank 16 Spanish ships at Santa Cruz off Tenerife (1657). He died while returning to Plymouth.

● **Blake, William** ► (1757–1827) British visionary poet, painter, and engraver. Born in London, he trained under the engraver James Basire between about 1772 and 1779, when he entered the Royal Academy schools. His books of poems, the texts of which he engraved and illustrated, include *Songs of Innocence* (1789), *Songs of Experience* (1794), various "Prophetic Books," *Milton* (1808), and *Jerusalem* (1820). All were influenced by his unorthodox Christian and political beliefs. As an artist he was inspired by his visions, gothic sculpture, and engravings after Michelangelo. Although unrecognized by his generation, except by his patron John Linnell (1792–1882) and artist friends such as ▷Fuseli and ▷Palmer, he was a precursor of Romanticism.

● **Blanc, Louis** ► (1811–82) French socialist. A utopian revolutionary, Blanc propagated his doctrines of economic equality in his journal *Revue du progrès* from 1839. A member of the provisional government in the ▷Revolution of 1848, he found little support from his colleagues and fled to England. He returned to Paris in 1870 and remained politically active until his death. His books include *Organisation du travail* (1840).

● **Blanchard, Jean Pierre François** ► (1753–1809) French balloonist. With **John Jeffries** (1744–1819), an American, he made the first Channel crossing in a balloon, from Dover to Calais (1785). He invented a parachute and was killed using it to jump from a balloon.

● **Blanche of Castile** ► (c. 1188–1252) The daughter of Alfonso VIII of Castile, she married (1200) ▷Louis VIII of France. She was Queen of France (1223–26) and regent for her son ▷Louis IX during his minority (1226–36) and during his Crusade (1248–52). She ruled firmly, suppressing a revolt of the nobility and effecting peace with England.

● **blank verse** ► Unrhymed iambic pentameter lines, the distinctive form of English narrative and dramatic verse since its introduction from Italy in the early 16th century by Henry Howard, Earl of ▷Surrey. It was used in the plays of ▷Marlowe and ▷Shakespeare. The form has been used by most major English poets to suit their different ends: in ▷Milton's *Paradise Lost* (1667) it is formal and grand, in ▷Wordsworth's *Prelude* (1805) it is intimate and casual.

● **Blanqui, Louis Auguste** ► (1805–81) French revolutionary. Interested in the practice of revolution rather than in abstract ideas, Blanqui introduced the notion, later taken up by Marx, that revolutions must begin with the temporary dictatorship of a revolutionary elite. From 1830 he built up a network of secret societies. In 1871, although in prison, he was elected president of the ▷Commune of Paris. His followers, the Blanquists, joined with the Marxists in 1881.

● **Blantyre** ► (or Blantyre-Limbe) 15 46S 35 00E The largest city in Malawi, in the Shire Highlands. In 1956 it was linked with Limbe, a railway centre. Blantyre is Malawi's chief industrial centre and its executive and judicial capital. Industries include distilling, textiles, and cigarette production. Population (1994 est): 446 800.

● **Blantyre** ► 55 47N 4 06W A town in Scotland, in South Lanarkshire near Glasgow. It is the birthplace of David Livingstone. Formerly the centre of a coalmining area, it now has engineering industries. Population (1991): 18 484.

William Blake ► A relief etching illustrating his *Jerusalem*.

● **Blarney** ► 51 56N 8 34W A village in the Republic of Ireland, in Co Cork. Blarney Castle contains the famous Blarney Stone, which is kissed in order to receive the gift of "blarney" or smooth talk. Population (latest est): 1500.

● **Blasco Ibáñez, Vicente** ► (1867–1928) Spanish novelist. He wrote many novels set in Valencia but is best known for his World War I novels, especially *The Four Horsemen of the Apocalypse* (1916), three times filmed. He was frequently penalized for his political activities and in 1923 exiled himself to France.

● **Blasis, Carlo** ► (1803–78) Italian dance teacher. In 1837 he became director of the dance academy at La Scala, Milan. His books on the theory of classical ballet, especially *Treatise on the Dance* (1820) and *The Code of Terpsichore* (1828), had an international influence.

● **blasphemy** ► Any written or spoken insult to God or to any person, institution, or thing regarded by a community as sacred. Societies and religions have taken different views of what constitutes blasphemy and how it should be punished. In Judaism, the ▷Ten Commandments specifically forbid "taking the name of God in vain", for which the Mosaic punishment was death by stoning. Although Jesus himself was accused of blasphemy for claiming to be God, both Catholic and Protestant countries punished blasphemy with death or other severe penalties until the ▷Enlightenment. Subsequently it was redefined in most jurisdictions as an offence against the social order, rather than against God, and punishments were reduced accordingly. In English law any blasphemous attack on the Church of England or its doctrines is treated as an attack on the state. It is, therefore, still regarded as a crime at ▷common law. In Calvinist Scotland it was punishable by death until the 18th century. However, prosecutions for blasphemy are now rare and it has been suggested that its criminal status be abolished. On the other hand, UK laws only treat insults to Anglican belief as blasphemy, and there have been suggestions that these laws should be extended to other religions as Britain is now a multiracial society. In the USA, many states still retain laws against blasphemy. Blasphemy is still a crime in some non-Christian countries, being punishable by death in some Islamic states. The ▷fatwa issued in 1989 by Ayatollah ▷Khomeini against Salman Rushdie, the author of *Satanic Verses* (1988), is an extreme example of a religious reaction to a book regarded by a minority as blasphemous.

● **blast furnace** ► A furnace heated by solid fuel, usually coke, through which a blast of air is blown to aid combustion. Blast furnaces are used in the ▷smelting of ore. In steel making, iron ore, coke, and limestone are poured in at the top of a vertical furnace and hot air is blown in at the bottom to burn the coke. Molten iron is drawn off at the bottom. A glassy waste, called slag, is also produced.

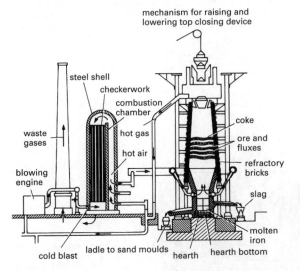

blast furnace

Labels on figure:
mechanism for raising and lowering top closing device
steel shell
checkerwork
combustion chamber
waste gases
hot gas
hot air
blowing engine
cold blast
ladle to sand moulds
hearth
coke
ore and fluxes
refractory bricks
slag
molten iron
hearth bottom

● **blastula** ► A hollow sphere of cells (blastomeres) produced by repeated ▷cleavage of a fertilized egg cell (zygote). It is an early stage in embryonic development, before differentiation into tissues and organs has begun. A blastula consists of an outer layer (the blastoderm) surrounding a cavity (the blastocoel).

● **Blaue Reiter, Der** ► (German: The Blue Rider) A group of artists formed in Munich in 1911 by ▷Marc and ▷Kandinsky when the latter's work was rejected by the exhibition committee of ▷Neue Künstlervereinigung. Their manifesto *Der Blaue Reiter Almanac* (1911) and their exhibitions illustrated their diverse influences: primitive and naive art, children's pictures, religious paintings on glass, and their modern favourites ▷Cézanne and ▷Delaunay. Their aim was to unite in an expressionist style (*see* expressionism) the symbolic and spiritual elements manifest in the art of all ages. The group, which also included Paul ▷Klee and August ▷Macke, disbanded during World War I.

● **Blavatsky, Helen Petrovna** ► (1831–91) Russian theosophist, who founded the Theosophical Society in New York in 1875. She later established a following in India, but her claims to supernatural powers were discredited by scientific investigations during the 1880s and 1890s. Her best-known book is *Isis Unveiled* (1877). ▷*See also* theosophy.

● **Blaydon** ► 54 58N 1 42W A town in NE England, in Gateshead unitary authority, Tyne and Wear, on the River Tyne. It is concerned chiefly with the manufacture of coal by-products, chemicals, and engineering. Population (1991): 15 510.

● **bleaching** ► The whitening, lightening, or removing of colour by chemical treatment, exposure to sunlight, air, or moisture. Most bleaching agents are oxidizing agents, which convert a pigment into an oxidized colourless form. Examples are hydrogen peroxide, ▷bleaching powder, and hypochlorites. In some processes reducing agents, such as sulphur dioxide, are used. Bleaching is an important part of textile and paper manufacture.

● **bleaching powder** ► (*or* chloride of lime) A whitish powder containing calcium hypochlorite ($Ca(OCl)_2$), calcium chloride ($CaCl_2$), calcium hydroxide ($Ca(OH)_2$), and water. It reacts with dilute acids to produce chlorine, which acts as a bleaching agent.

● **bleak** ► A fish, *Alburnus alburnus*, related to the ▷carp, with a slender silvery-green body, about 20 cm long. It lives in schools near the surface of fresh waters in N Europe and feeds on invertebrates. The scales are used in the manufacture of artificial pearls.

● **bleeding** ▷*See* haemorrhage.

● **bleeding heart** ► An ornamental plant of the genus ▷*Dicentra*, especially *D. spectabilis* from Siberia and Japan and *D. eximia* from North America. They are perennials with arching stems, up to 90 cm long, bearing strings of large rose-red heart-shaped flowers with whitish tips, which glisten when the blooms are fresh. Some species have attractive fernlike foliage. Family: *Fumariaceae*.

● **Blenheim, Battle of** ► (13 August, 1704) The battle won by the Duke of ▷Marlborough and ▷Eugène of Savoy against the French army in the War of the ▷Spanish Succession. It was fought at Blenheim (now Blindheim) on the Danube River and ▷Blenheim Palace was built for Marlborough by a grateful parliament.

● **Blenheim Palace** ► The baroque palace built between 1705 and 1725 at Woodstock, Oxfordshire (England). Designed by ▷Vanbrugh, it was a gift from Queen Anne to the Duke of ▷Marlborough as a monument to his victories over the French. The gardens were laid out by Capability ▷Brown. Sir Winston ▷Churchill was born at Blenheim.

● **Blenkinsop, John** ► (1783–1831) British engineer, who built the first practical steam locomotive (1812), a twin-cylinder engine driving cogs that engaged with rack rails. It was used for transporting coal from Middleton to Leeds.

● **blenny** ► A small fish belonging to a family (Blenniidae; about 300 species) found among rocks in shallow waters of tropical and temperate seas. Blennies have an elongated scaleless body with a blunt nose, a long dorsal fin, and one- to three-rayed pelvic fins located in front of the larger pectoral fins. Many have small tentacles on their heads. The name is also used for several other fish of the order *Perciformes*.

● **Blériot, Louis** ► (1872–1936) French aviator. Beginning his career as a motorcar engineer he was the first to fly the English Channel (1909), from Calais to Dover, in a monoplane. He later became a manufacturer of □aircraft.

● **blesbok** ► A small fast-running South African antelope, *Damaliscus dorcas*. About 110 cm high at the shoulder, blesboks are red with a white muzzle, rump, and shanks and have lyre-shaped ridged horns. Bonteboks (*D. dorcas dorcas*) are a subspecies with a larger rump patch and more white on the legs.

● **Bletchley Park** ► A house in Milton Keynes unitary authority, Buckinghamshire, that served as the headquarters of the Allied codebreakers in World War II. Artur Scherbius had invented a coding machine for the Germans, known as the **Enigma Machine**, which consisted of a keyboard, a plugboard, and a number of rotors. A machine was obtained by the British in 1939 and taken to Bletchley Park, where the experts were able to use it to decipher German messages, having developed one of the first electronic computers to keep pace with German modifications of Enigma. Bletchley was able to give the RAF details of German plans in the Battle of Britain and the Royal Navy information that led to victory in the Battle of the Atlantic.

● **blewits** ► An edible ▷mushroom, *Tricholoma* (or *Lepista*) *saevum*, occurring mainly in open pastures. It has a bluish-grey stalk and a flat clay-coloured cap, 6–12 cm in diameter, producing pale-pink spores. The wood blewits (*T. nudum*) has a lilac or purple cap and is usually found beneath trees. It also is edible. Family: *Tricholomataceae*.

● **Bligh, William** ► (1754–1817) British admiral. He accompanied Captain ▷Cook on his second voyage round the world and in 1787 sailed to Tahiti on the *Bounty*. While setting sail for home, his crew mutinied under Fletcher ▷Christian, leaving Bligh and 18 officers aboard a small boat without maps. Owing to Bligh's skills as a navigator they reached safety after sailing some 5800 km (3604 mi). Although Bligh was widely regarded as having provoked the mutiny by his harsh manner, he was exonerated by a court martial. In 1805 he was made governor of New South Wales but again fell foul of his subordinates (*see* Rum Rebellion).

● **blight** ► A severe disease of plants caused by pests, fungi, or other agents or by a mineral deficiency. Symptoms commonly include spotting followed by wilting, and the plant eventually withers and dies. The notorious potato blight that devastated Ireland in the mid-19th century was caused by the fungus *Phytophthora infestans*. Control measures against blights vary according to the cause of the disease.

● **blindness** ► Partial or complete loss of sight (visual impairment less severe than total loss of sight is classified as blindness for administrative purposes). Sudden blindness may be caused by direct injury to the eye or to the part of the brain that receives the visual signals.

Gradual blindness is caused by a wide variety of diseases, including ▷trachoma, ▷glaucoma, ▷cataracts, macular degeneration (an age-related condition causing progressive loss of central vision), diabetes mellitus, and tumours (especially of the pituitary gland), that compress the optic nerve. Aids available for the visually handicapped include books in ▷Braille or on tape and specially trained ▷guide dogs. In many countries the blind are entitled to special education and financial benefits. *See also* colour blindness.

● **blindworm** ▷*See* slowworm.

● **Bliss, Sir Arthur Edward Drummond** ► (1891–1975) British composer. He studied under Stanford and Vaughan Williams. Director of music at the BBC (1942–44), Bliss was knighted in 1950 and was Master of the Queen's Music from 1953. His works include *A Colour Symphony* (1922), a piano concerto (1938), the opera *The Olympians* (1948–49), and a cello concerto (1970).

● **blister** ► An accumulation of fluid (usually colourless serum) within the skin. Blisters can be caused by friction, sensitivity to chemicals, and ▷burns. They may also develop in certain diseases, including chickenpox. Blisters usually heal spontaneously, but some (especially severe burns or those on the feet) require dressings. They should not be burst intentionally as this may lead to infection.

● **blister beetle** ► A brightly coloured beetle, about 10–15 mm long, belonging to a widely distributed family (*Meloidae*; about 2000 species), which also includes the ▷oil beetles. The larvae are parasitic upon other insects, while the adults generally feed on plants—often causing severe damage. Their secretion of cantharidin, a powerful blistering agent, has led to the medicinal use of various European and Asian species, especially ▷Spanish fly.

● **Blitzkrieg** ► (German: lightning war) A military tactic aiming to shock and disorganize enemy forces by swift suprise attacks using tanks and aerial bombardment. It was extensively used by the Germans in ▷World War II in Poland, Belgium, the Netherlands, France, and Africa. It was also used by the US general, Patton, in Europe in 1944. The **Blitz** refers to the intensive German air raids on London during the Battle of ▷Britain in World War II. Between July and December, 1940, 23 000 civilians died.

● **Blixen, Karen** ▷*See* Dinesen, Isak.

● **Bloch, Ernest** ► (1880–1959) Swiss-born composer of Jewish descent. He lived in various countries before taking up residence in the USA in 1916. His opera *Macbeth* (1903–09), the rhapsody *Schelomo* (1916), *Concerto Grosso* (1925), and *Sacred Service* (1930–33) incorporate Jewish musical elements into a cosmopolitan 20th-century style.

● **Bloch, Felix** ► (1905–83) US physicist, born in Zurich. After working in Germany he left Europe when Hitler came to power and emigrated to the USA, becoming a US citizen in 1939. He developed the ▷nuclear magnetic resonance technique for magnetic field measure-

William Bligh ► A contemporary engraving by Robert Dodd shows Bligh and his officers being set adrift by the *Bounty* mutineers.

ments in atomic nuclei, for which he shared the Nobel Prize (1952) with the independent discoverer, E. M. ▷Purcell. Bloch's concept of magnetic neutron polarization (1934) enabled him, in conjunction with L. ▷Alvarez, to measure the neutron's magnetic moment. During World War II he worked on the atomic bomb. In 1954 he became the first director of CERN.

● **Bloch, Marc** ► (1886–1944) French historian, of French-Alsatian Jewish parents, who was born in Lyons. His works included reviews for the magazine *Annales*, *French Rural History* (1931), and *Strange Defeat* (1940). A hero of World War I, he was captured, tortured, and executed by the Germans in World War II.

● **Bloemfontein** ► 29 07S 26 14E The judicial capital of South Africa and the capital of Free State. Founded in 1846, it is an important transportation and agricultural centre. Industrial development is being encouraged with the opening of new gold mines nearby. It has the University of the Orange Free State (1855) and the US universities of Harvard and Michigan have observatories here. Population (1991): 126 867.

● **Bloemfontein Convention** ▷*See* Sand River Convention.

● **Blois** ► 47 36N 1 20E A town in France, the capital of the Loir-et-Cher department on the River Loire. It has a famous chateau, begun in the 13th century, and trades in wine, brandy, and grain. Population (1990): 51 550.

● **Blok, Aleksandr Aleksandrovich** ► (1880–1921) The leading Russian symbolist poet. His early poetry, notably *Verses about the Beautiful Lady* (1901–02), celebrated his love for Liubov Mendeleyeva, whom he married in 1903. But his love for Russia was the deeper theme, and in *Scythians* (1918) and *The Twelve* (1918) he expressed a revolutionary optimism that soon turned to deep disillusion.

● **Blondel, Maurice** ► (1861–1949) French philosopher. He invented a philosophy of action, seeking a compromise between intellectualism and pragmatism. His chief works are *Action* (1893), *The Process of Intelligence* (1922), and *Being and Beings* (1935).

● **Blondin, Charles** ► (Jean-François Gravelet; 1824–97) French acrobat and tightrope walker. In 1859 he walked across a tightrope suspended over Niagara Falls and later repeated the feat with various acrobatic variations.

● **blood** ► The red fluid contained within the arteries and veins and pumped around the body by the ▷heart. Blood consists of a watery fluid (*see* plasma) in which are suspended various blood cells—the red cells (*see* erythrocyte), containing the red oxygen-carrying pigment haemoglobin, and several kinds of white cells (*see* leucocyte), concerned with the body's defence mechanisms. The ▷platelets are small particles involved in blood clotting. Blood acts as a medium for transporting oxygen, carbon dioxide, digested food, hormones, waste materials, salts, and many other substances to and from the tissues. An average adult has about 70 millilitres of blood per kilogram of body weight (i.e. about 5 litres in an average man). Blood is present in all animals with a circulatory system: its functions are similar to that of human blood although its composition varies. ▷*See also* blood clotting; blood groups; circulation of the blood.

● **blood bank** ▷*See* blood transfusion.

● **Blood, Colonel Thomas** ► (c. 1618–80) Irish adventurer, best known for his attempt in 1671 to steal the crown jewels. Visited in prison by Charles II, Blood ingratiated himself with the king and was released.

● **Blood, Council of** ► (*or* Council of Troubles; 1567–74) A court established in the Low Countries during the ▷Revolt of the Netherlands by the Spanish governor, the Duke of ▷Alba, to suppress Protestantism and particularism. Thousands were imprisoned or executed without proper trial and, following the arrest of two prominent magnates, ▷Egmont and ▷Horn, many others fled abroad. Alba used the threat of the council to impose the tenth penny, an unpopular tax that united Catholics and Calvinists against Spain. After Alba's departure (1573), the council was abolished.

● **blood clotting** ► The mechanism by which blood is converted from a liquid to a solid state, which normally occurs after injury to

blood vessels and prevents loss of blood. The process involves a number of chemical reactions between certain soluble proteins (clotting factors) in the blood, resulting in the formation of the enzyme thrombin, which converts a soluble protein (fibrinogen) to a fibrous protein (fibrin), which forms the basis of the blood clot. ▷Platelets accumulate at the site of the injury, their presence being essential for the reactions to occur. ▷*See also* thrombosis.

● **blood fluke** ► A parasitic flatworm of the genus *Schistosoma* (3 species), which causes the disease ▷schistosomiasis among human populations in many parts of the world. The flukes are carried by freshwater snails and enter their human hosts to inhabit blood vessels, feeding on blood and causing severe debilitation. ▷*See also* fluke.

● **blood groups** ► The different types into which blood can be classified on the basis of the presence or absence of certain proteins (*see* antibody) on the surface of the red cells, which is genetically determined. The major grouping is the ABO system, which was the first human blood system to be discovered—in 1900, by Karl Landsteiner (1868–1943). It consists of four groups: A, B, AB, and O. Group A cells carry the A antigen and the plasma contains antibodies against B antigen (anti-B antibodies); the converse applies to group B blood. Transfusion of blood between these groups will cause destruction of the donor blood cells (*see* blood transfusion). Group O blood contains neither antigen and can therefore be used in transfusions to people of groups A and B. Group AB blood contains neither anti-A nor anti-B antibody: people of this blood group can accept both A and B blood during transfusion. There are numerous other minor blood-group systems of which the rhesus system is the most important (*see* rhesus factor).

● **bloodhound** ► An ancient breed of dog with a keen sense of smell, originating round the Mediterranean and widely used for tracking purposes. It has a sturdy frame and a large head with long drooping ears and wrinkled skin around the eyes. Bloodhounds are black and tan, liver and tan, or red in colour. Height: 63–69 cm (dogs); 58–64 cm (bitches).

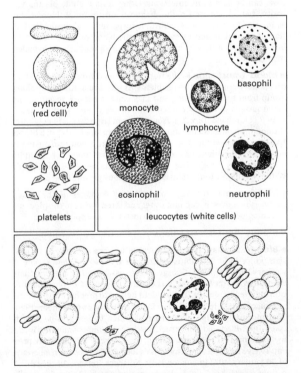

blood ► Blood cells and platelets, showing surface and side views of a red cell and five types of white cell (above). Human blood, magnified about 1500 times (below), containing a single white cell, a mass of red cells, and two clusters of platelets.

● **blood poisoning** ▸ (*or* septicaemia) The presence of bacteria or bacterial toxins in the blood. The symptoms include fever, rigors, and various aches and pains. The bacteria may come from any infected region (such as an abscess) and they may be carried to other parts of the body, including the brain and kidneys. Treatment consists of the injection of large doses of antibiotics.

● **blood pressure** ▸ The pressure that blood exerts on the walls of the arteries, due to the pumping action of the heart. Blood pressure is at its lowest between heartbeats (i.e. at diastole) and at its highest when the ventricles of the heart are contracting (i.e. systole). It is recorded, using an instrument called a ▷sphygmomanometer, as the height in millimetres of a column of mercury (mmHg). Blood pressure varies with age and individual variations are common within each age group depending on such external factors as stress, but a healthy adult might have a systolic pressure of about 120 mmHg and a diastolic pressure of 80 mmHg. This is normally expressed as 120/80. Abnormally high blood pressure (*see* hypertension) may be associated with various diseases or it may arise without any obvious cause. Abnormally low blood pressure occurs in ▷shock.

● **blood sports** ▸ Sports in which a quarry is hunted and killed or a spectacle is made of an animal being killed. In the UK most of the blood sports in the latter category have been made illegal—bullbaiting and ▷bearbaiting since 1835, ▷cockfighting since 1849, and badger baiting since 1973. ▷Bullfighting, however, continues in Spain and several other countries. In the former category, ▷foxhunting, staghunting, beagling, and ▷coursing still continue in the UK, although MPs have recently (2001) voted to make them illegal.

● **bloodstone** ▸ A mineral of a green colour speckled with red. It is a variety of ▷chalcedony. Birthstone for March.

● **blood test** ▸ An analysis of a blood sample. Such tests may be useful in the diagnosis of disease. A common test is the measurement of the erythrocyte sedimentation rate (ESR)—the rate at which red blood cells settle out of plasma, which increases in rheumatic disease, cancer, and some infections. Other tests include plasma viscosity, red-cell counts (in the diagnosis of anaemia), blood-sugar estimation (when diabetes mellitus is suspected), and the determination of alcohol, drugs, or bacteria in the blood or the individual's blood group. The blood is usually taken from a vein using a hypodermic needle.

● **blood transfusion** ▸ The transfer of blood from one individual (the donor) to another (the recipient). As blood of a different ▷blood group from that of the recipient may cause a serious reaction, the blood groups of both the donor and the recipient must be determined beforehand. Direct person-to-person transfusion is now rare; the donor blood is usually stored, at a temperature of 4°C, in a **blood bank** and used within 3–4 weeks of collection. Blood transfusion is performed when there has been extensive loss of blood; for example, during surgery or following an accident. Some people (e.g. Jehovah's Witnesses) object to transfusion on religious grounds.

● **bloodworm** ▸ The larva of nonbiting ▷midges of the genus *Chironomus*. It lives in stagnant water and is red owing to the pigment ▷haemoglobin, which it uses to help increase its supply of oxygen.

● **Bloody Assizes** ▷*See* Jeffreys of Wem, George, 1st Baron.

● **Bloody Sunday** **1.** The massacre of unarmed protestors by Russian police in St Petersburg on 22 January, 1905. A deputation of workers led by a priest, Georgy Gapon, assembled to present their grievances to Tsar Nicholas II. The police responded by opening fire, causing over 100 deaths. The incident helped to precipitate the ▷Revolution of 1905. **2.** In Ireland, the violent events of 21 November, 1920. That morning the IRA assassinated 11 men believed to be British spies. The ▷Black and Tans struck back by firing indiscriminately into a football crowd at Croke Park, Dublin, where several IRA men were present. Twelve innocent spectators were killed. **3.** The controversial events of 30 January, 1972 in Londonderry, Northern Ireland. An illegal but mainly peaceful civil-rights demonstration was held that day in the Catholic Bogside area; when minor disturbances broke out, British paratroops fired live rounds into the crowd, killing 13 innocent people. The result was increased Catholic support for the IRA and an escalation of violence throughout the province. A new inquiry into these much-disputed events began in January 1998.

● **Bloomfield, Leonard** ▸ (1887–1949) US linguist, whose book *Language* (1933) outlines a strictly scientific behaviourist framework for the description of language, on which modern American structural ▷linguistics is based.

● **Bloomsbury** ▸ A district in the London borough of Camden, noted for its literary, artistic, and educational associations. Named after the manor ("bury") of William Blemond (13th century), it is now dominated by the University of London, many hospitals, and the British Museum; there are many fine Georgian buildings.

● **Bloomsbury group** ▸ A group of English writers and artists active in the 1910s and 1920s who initially met in private houses in Bloomsbury, London, for aesthetic and philosophic discussions. The group eventually included the writers Virginia ▷Woolf, E. M. ▷Forster, and Lytton ▷Strachey, the art critics Clive Bell (1881–1964) and Roger ▷Fry, the painter Vanessa Bell (1879–1961; Virginia Woolf's sister and Clive Bell's wife), and the economist J. M. ▷Keynes. Most of them had studied at Cambridge University and were influenced by G. E. ▷Moore's *Principia Ethica* (1903) in their belief in the importance of personal relationships and aesthetic experience.

● **Blow, John** ▸ (1649–1708) English composer. Blow was organist of the Chapel Royal and Westminster Abbey, where he taught Henry Purcell. The first Composer for the Chapel Royal (1699), he wrote Church services, anthems, and organ pieces, and the masque *Venus and Adonis* (1680–85).

● **blowfly** ▸ A large buzzing fly belonging to the family *Calliphoridae*. Some blowflies lay their eggs in human food, but more commonly the larvae develop in dung or decaying organic material. The larvae of certain species (e.g. of the American genus *Cochliomyia*)—known as screwworms—are serious pests of sheep and cattle. Chief genera: *Calliphora* (bluebottles), *Lucilia* (greenbottles).

● **Blücher, Gebhard Leberecht von, Prince of Wahlstatt** ▸ (1742–1819) Prussian general, known as Marshal Forward. He fought against Revolutionary France and later held command in the War of Liberation against Napoleon, whom he helped to defeat at Leipzig (1813). In 1814 he crossed the Rhine and marched to Paris. His pursuit of Napoleon's forces at Waterloo contributed to the allied victory.

● **blue** ▸ A butterfly belonging to the family *Lycaenidae*, characteristically small and having blue or violet wings in the male; the females are usually brownish, and the undersurface of the wings in both sexes is typically greyish and marked with darker spots. In some species the hindwings have "tails," like the related ▷hairstreaks. Unusually, the caterpillars are short and broad, resembling slugs or woodlice, and often secrete honeydew, which attracts ants; the larvae are protected by the ants and in some species are taken to their nests, where they feed on ant grubs. Blues are widely distributed; European species include the common blue (*Polyommatus icarus*).

● **Bluebeard** ▸ A European folktale character who murders successive wives and locks their bodies in a forbidden room. His new wife discovers the bodies and is rescued by her brothers. The story may have been based on the crimes of Gilles de ▷Rais.

● **bluebell** ▸ One of several plants having bell-shaped blue flowers. In England the bluebell is *Endymion non-scriptus*, a perennial herb, up to 50 cm high, very common in woods and shady places. It overwinters as a bulb and produces blue (sometimes white or pink) flowers in spring. Family: *Liliaceae*. In Scotland the name is applied to the ▷harebell.

● **blueberry** ▸ A North American shrub of the genus *Vaccinium*, such as *V. corymbosum* (high-bush blueberry) or *V. pennsylvanicum* (low-bush blueberry). It is similar to the ▷bilberry, except that the sweet blue berries, eaten raw or cooked, are borne in clusters rather than singly. Family: *Ericaceae* (heath family).

● **bluebird** ▸ A songbird of the New World genus *Sialia* (3 species). The eastern bluebird (*S. sialis*) of E North America is about 17 cm long and has a blue back and red-brown breast. Family: *Turdidae* (thrushes). *Compare* fairy bluebird.

● **bluebottle** ▷*See* blowfly.

● **Bluefields** ▶ 12 00N 83 49W The chief Caribbean port of Nicaragua, in the SE near the River Escondido. A 17th-century base (as Blewfeldt) of Dutch pirates, it was the capital of the British Mosquito Coast until 1850. Population (latest est): 18 000.

● **bluefish** ▶ A food fish, *Pomatomus saltator* (or *P. saltatrix*), also called tailor or snapper. The only member of the family *Pomatomidae*, it is found in all warm seas. It has a blue-green elongated body, up to 1.2 m long, with a whitish belly, a large mouth, and two dorsal fins. It lives in large schools and preys on other fish. Order: *Perciformes*.

● **blue fox** ▷*See* Arctic fox.

● **bluegrass** ▶ A perennial grass, *Poa pratensis*, also called meadow grass, native to Europe, Asia, and North America. It has erect stems, 30–90 cm high, smooth leaves (which may be blue-tinged or green), and flower clusters 5–20 cm long.

● **blue-green bacteria** ▶ Bacteria belonging to the phylum *Cyanobacteria*; they were formerly classified as algae (blue-green algae; division *Cyanophyta*). They contain a blue pigment (phycocyanin) in addition to the green chlorophyll. Reproduction is asexual. Blue-green bacteria occur on moist surfaces and in the soil, where they contribute to ▷nitrogen fixation. Some live in symbiotic association with fungi to form ▷lichens. Aquatic blue-green bacteria are a constituent of plankton, sometimes forming dense masses (blooms), which contribute to ▷eutrophication.

● **blue gum** ▶ A fast-growing evergreen Australian ⬚tree, *Eucalyptus globulus*, up to 40 m high with patchy grey and fawn bark. It has blue-green leaves up to 25 cm long. The timber is used for construction and pulp, and eucalyptus oil is distilled from the leaves. Family: *Myrtaceae*. ▷*See also* Eucalyptus.

● **Blue Mountains** ▶ A mountain range in Australia, in New South Wales. Part of the ▷Great Dividing Range, it reaches 1180 m (3871 ft) at Bird Rock and contains the Blue Mountains National Park. It is a popular tourist area.

● **Blue Riband of the Atlantic** ▶ An award given for the fastest crossing of the Atlantic by a recognized shipping route, excluding powerboats or purpose-built vessels. First awarded in 1838, the title has been held by many famous passenger liners, notably the *Queen Mary* (1938–52) and the *United States* (1952–   ), which won it with a time of 3 days, 10 hours, and 40 minutes. Since 1933 the Hales Trophy has been awarded to holders of the Riband. In 1990 a British catamaran ferry, *Hoverspeed Great Britain*, reduced the record to 3 days, 7 hours, and 54 minutes; it was awarded the Hales Trophy but denied the Blue Riband on the grounds that the vessel was not in regular Atlantic service. Similar objections were raised when the record was further reduced by the Australian-built ferry *Catalonia* in 1998.

● **Blue Ridge Mountains** ▷*See* Appalachian Mountains.

● **blues** ▶ A type of US folk music that evolved from the Negro spirituals and work songs of the 1860s and became a song form used in jazz, rhythm and blues, and rock. The blues is a slow bitter-sweet song, the syncopated melodic line and harmonies of which contain "blue" notes, which are flattened versions of certain notes in the major or minor scale. In origin it always consisted of three sets of four bars, in which the second set is a repetition of the first. The final line is improvised. The first published blues were "Memphis Blues" (1912) by W. C. Handy (1873–1958) and Jelly Roll Morton's "Jelly Roll Blues" (1915). The blues influenced the development of jazz and rock music and stimulated classical composers such as George Gershwin, who wrote the orchestral *Rhapsody in Blue* (1924).

● **blue shark** ▶ A ▷shark, *Prionace glauca*, that is abundant in warm-temperate and tropical seas. It has a slender dark-blue body, up to 4 m long, with a white belly and long sickle shaped pectoral fins. It is found usually near the surface and feeds voraciously on shoaling fish, squid, and other sharks. Family: *Carcharhinidae*.

● **Bluestockings** ▶ A group of intellectual society hostesses in 18th-century England. They included Elizabeth Montagu (1720–1800) and the novelist Fanny ▷Burney; their guests were accustomed to wearing ordinary blue, rather than formal dress, stockings to the meetings. The term is still used to describe intellectual women.

● **bluetit** ▶ A European tit, *Parus caeruleus*, formerly a woodland species but now common in towns and gardens. It has a blue crown and wings, a yellow breast, white face and wing bars, and a black collar and eyestripe. Bluetits feed chiefly on insect larvae.

● **bluets** ▶ A tufted herb of the genus *Houstonia* (about 25 species), native to North America and widely grown in rock gardens. The small white, blue, or purple funnel-shaped flowers are borne singly or in clusters. Some species form mats, providing a close ground cover in shade. Family: *Rubiaceae* (madder family).

● **blue whale** ▶ The largest living ▷whale, *Balaenoptera musculus*, probably the largest animal ever. It grows to over 30 m and weighs over 150 tonnes. Widely distributed, the blue whale is nearing extinction due to overhunting; it has now been designated an ▷endangered species. Family: *Balaenopteridae* (*see* rorqual). ⬚mammal.

● **Blum, Léon** ▶ (1872–1950) French socialist, statesman, and writer; prime minister (1936–37, 1938, 1946–47). His ▷popular front government of 1936–37 brought about radical reforms in labour organizations and nationalized the Bank of France. After the fall of France to the Germans in 1940 Blum was arrested by the Vichy government and spent the remainder of the war in prison. From 1946 until his death he led the moderate socialist wing in France.

● **Blunden, Edmund Charles** ▶ (1896–1974) British poet and critic. Educated at Oxford, he lived and taught in Japan in the 1920s and late 1940s and at Hong Kong University from 1953 to 1964. *Undertones of War* (1928) is an account of his experiences in World War I. His love of the English countryside is a constant theme of his work.

● **blunderbuss** ▶ A short-range smoothbore gun with a bell-shaped muzzle, firing many balls. In use from the 17th to 19th centuries, its name is derived from the Dutch word *donderbus*, thunder gun. It ranged in size from the pistol to the small artillery piece.

● **Blunkett, David** ▶ (1947–   ) British Labour politician; home secretary (2001–   ). Blind from childhood, he was leader of Sheffield council from 1980 to 1987, when he entered parliament. He was secretary of state for education from 1997 to 2001.

● **Blunt, Anthony** ▶ (1907–83) British art historian and spy. As an academic at Cambridge in the 1930s he helped the Soviet agents ▷Burgess and ▷Maclean to recruit. During World War II he joined the British Secret Service, which enabled him to pass information to the Soviets. After Burgess and Maclean were exposed, he arranged their defection to the Soviet Union in 1951. In 1964 he confessed to British Intelligence in return for secrecy and nonprosecution: he was unmasked in 1979 and stripped of his knighthood (awarded in 1956). Blunt served as director of the Courtauld Institute (1947–74) and Surveyor of the Queen's Pictures (1945–72).

● **B-lymphocytes** ▷*See* immunity.

● **Blyth** ▶ 55 07N 1 30W A port in NE England, in Northumberland at the mouth of the River Blyth. Fishing is important and there are dry docks. Population (1991): 35 327.

● **Blyth, Sir Chay** ▶ (Charles Blyth; 1940–   ) British yachtsman. In the 1970s he embarked on a series of voyages, circumnavigating the world: westwards in 1970–71 (solo) and eastwards in 1973–74 (with a crew). He has also won a number of races, including the Observer double-handed transatlantic race (1981). He was knighted in 1997.

● **Blyton, Enid** ▶ (1897–1968) British writer of children's books. After training as a kindergarten teacher and working in educational journalism, she published her first book in 1923 and introduced her famous character Noddy in 1949. She wrote over 600 books for children of all ages. In recent decades her work has been condemned by educators and librarians on both literary and political grounds; nevertheless, her books remain highly popular with children.

● **boa** ▶ A snake belonging to the subfamily *Boinae* (40–60 species) of the ▷constrictor family and occurring in Old and New World regions. 20–760 cm long, boas may be terrestrial, semiaquatic, or arboreal and are usually green, brown, or yellowish with a camouflaging pattern of blotches and diamonds. They kill their prey by biting and then constricting. The boa constrictor (*Boa constrictor*), occurring from Mexico to Argentina, is about 3.5 m long, hunts birds and small mammals at night, and bears live young.

● **Boadicea** ▶ (Latin name: Boudicca; d. 61 AD) Queen of the ▷Iceni. Her husband Prasutagus ruled in what is now Norfolk (England). At his death in 60, Roman officials attempted to seize his wealth and maltreated Boadicea and her daughters. She led the Iceni into open rebellion, sacking Colchester, London, and St Albans. The Roman governor Suetonius Paulinus defeated the rebels at or near Fenny Stratford on Watling Street. Boadicea committed suicide.

● **boar, wild** ▶ A Eurasian wild ▷pig, *Sus scrofa*, once common in forests throughout Europe. Up to 1.5 m long and 1 m high at the shoulder, wild boars have a rough bristly coat coloured greyish brown. The ancestors of domestic pigs, they are still hunted for sport in some regions. Males have four tusks.

● **Boas, Franz** ▶ (1858–1942) German-born US anthropologist. In 1886 Boas left his post at the Berlin Royal Ethnological Museum and embarked upon extensive research among the Indians of the NW American coast. In 1899 he became the first professor of anthropology at Columbia University. His most famous books are *The Mind of Primitive Man* (1911), *Primitive Art* (1927), and *Race, Language and Culture* (1940). Boas was concerned not only with the physical features of ethnic groups, but also with cultural and psychological aspects. He strongly opposed the racial theories of the Nazis.

● **boatbill** ▶ A nocturnal heron, *Cochlearius cochlearius*, occurring in tropical American swamps. It is about 50 cm tall and has a grey plumage with black markings on the head and neck. It resembles the ▷night heron but has a broad flattened hook-tipped bill. ▷*See* Plate III.

● **Boat Race** ▶ An annual ▷rowing race on the River Thames between Oxford and Cambridge Universities, first held in 1829 at Henley. The present course of 6.8 km (4.25 mi) from Putney to Mortlake was established in 1845. By 2002 Cambridge had won 77 races and Oxford 70, with one dead heat (1877). Record: 16 minutes 45 seconds by Oxford (1984). The first woman to participate was Susan Brown, the Oxford cox, in 1981; there is also a Women's Boat Race.

● **Boa Vista** ▶ 2 51N 60 43W A town in N Brazil, the capital of Roraima territory on the Rio Branco. Mineral resources include diamonds, gold, bauxite, and cassiterite. Population (1996): 150 442.

● **bobcat** ▶ A short-tailed cat *Felis rufa*, resembling a lynx, found in North America from S Canada to Mexico. About 90 cm long, it is brown with grey or white markings and has large ears tipped with a tuft of hairs. Bobcats feed at night on small birds, rodents, and deer.

● **Bobo-Dioulasso** ▶ 11 11N 1 18W A city in SW Burkina Faso, the country's main trade and communications centre. Industries include food processing and handicrafts. Population (1993 est): 300 000.

● **bobolink** ▶ An American ▷oriole, *Dolichonyx oryzivorus*, that nests in Canada and the northern USA and migrates to South America in winter. It is black below and white above and nests on the ground, foraging for insects and seeds.

● **Bobruisk** ▶ (*or* Bobruysk) 53 08N 29 10E A port in Belarus, on the River Berezina. It has an 18th-century fortress and its industries include engineering, machine building, timber, and tyre manufacturing. Population (1998 est): 227 000.

● **bobsledding** ▶ The sport of racing bobsleds (also called bobsleighs or bobs), which was developed by British sportsmen at St Moritz (Switzerland) in the late 19th century. A bobsled is a steel-bodied toboggan with two pairs of runners, the front pair steerable, and a rear brake, holding two or four people. In a race, the bobsleds slide one at a time down a narrow icy chute some 1500 m (1640 yd) long with high walls and banked turns, reaching speeds of over 130 km per hour (81 mph).

● **Boccaccio, Giovanni** ▶ (1313–75) Italian writer and poet. Son of a merchant of Florence, he was sent to Naples about 1328 to learn business. Literature interested him more, however; between then and 1341, when he returned to Florence, he wrote *Filocolo*, a prose romance, *Filostrato*, which supplied the plot of Chaucer's *Troilus and Criseyde*, and *Teseida*, the source of Chaucer's *Knight's Tale*. Between

1348 and 1353 he composed the *Decameron*, a collection of a hundred stories told by a party of young people escaping from plague-stricken Florence in 1348. He met ▷Petrarch in 1350 and was much influenced by him. In later life he chiefly wrote scholarly works in Latin and lectured on Dante's *Divine Comedy*. He also founded the first chair of Greek in W Europe, at the University of Florence.

● **Boccherini, Luigi** ▶ (1743–1805) Italian violoncellist and composer. He became famous in Rome while still a boy. Boccherini produced his first opera *La confederazione* (1765) in Lucca. His large output includes cello concertos and sonatas, symphonies, choral works, and string quintets and quartets.

● **Boccioni, Umberto** ▶ (1882–1916) Italian futurist painter and sculptor. He trained under ▷Balla before settling in Milan (1907), where, influenced by the poet ▷Marinetti, he aimed to express the violence and speed of modern life in such paintings as *The City Rises* (1910; New York). His manifesto of futurist sculpture (1912) advocated the use of materials such as glass, cement, lightbulbs, etc.

● **Bochum** ▶ 51 28N 7 11E A city in NW Germany, in North Rhine-Westphalia. It is the site of the Ruhr University (1965). The manufacture of cars, textiles, and chemicals has replaced coalmining and iron and steel production. Population (1998 est): 395 837.

● **Bodawpaya** ▶ (d. 1819) King of Burma (1789–1819). His aggressive policies ensured considerable expansion of Burmese territory during his reign. He annexed Arakan (1785), Manipur (1813), and Assam (1816) and almost caused an Anglo-Burmese war by demanding the surrender of Chittagong, Dacca, and Murshidabad from the British Indian government. His sudden death averted a confrontation. A major survey of Burma was compiled during his reign (1784).

● **Bodensee** ▷*See* Constance, Lake.

● **Bode's law** ▶ (*or* Titius-Bode law) A relationship between the distances of the planets from the sun. Take the number sequence 0, 3, 6, 12, 24, ..., add 4 to each number, and divide each sum by 10. The resulting sequence is in good agreement with observed planetary distances (in astronomical units) out to Uranus, provided the belt of ▷minor planets is considered a single entity. Formulated by Johann Titius (1729–96) and popularized in 1772 by Johann Bode (1747–1826), it is still unexplained by theory.

● **Bodhidharma** ▶ (6th century AD) Indian Buddhist patriarch from Conjeeveram, near Madras. He entered China about 520. Teaching a form of meditation called *dhyana* (Chinese *ch'an*, Japanese *zen*), he is credited with founding ▷Zen Buddhism.

● **Bodhisattva** ▶ In Mahayana Buddhism, the title of a person who is to become a Buddha. The term is also used to describe the Buddha (Gautama) before his enlightenment. The Bodhisattva ideal is that of the individual who seeks enlightenment not for himself alone but for all beings. In Indian art the Bodhisattvas are depicted as youthful and represent various aspects of the nature of Buddha.

● **Bodin, Jean** ▶ (1530–96) French philosopher and jurist. Although a Protestant, he was a successful lawyer and became parliamentary representative of Vermandois (1576). He visited Britain in 1581 where his belief in witchcraft, propounded in *Démonomanie des sorciers* (1580), later influenced James I. His greatest work, *La République* (1576), is a comprehensive political philosophy.

● **Bodleian Library** ▶ The major ▷library of Oxford University, first established in 1409 and restored and enlarged by Sir Thomas Bodley (1545–1613) from 1598 to 1602. Since 1610 it has been entitled to receive a free copy of every book published in Britain; it contains well over 2.5 million volumes.

● **Bodmin** ▶ 50 29N 4 43W A market town in SW England, in Cornwall; formerly important for trade in tin. Nearby is **Bodmin Moor**, a granite upland reaching 420 m (1375 ft) at Brown Willy. Population (1991): 12 553.

● **Bodoni, Giambattista** ▶ (1740–1813) Italian printer. In 1768 he became the Duke of Parma's printer and, influenced by François-Ambroise Didot (1730–1804), began to design his own typefaces. The best known, designed in 1790 and named after him, is still in use.

● **body language** ▷*See* nonverbal communication.

● **body temperature** ▷*See* temperature.

● **Boehm, Theobald** ▶ (1794–1881) German flautist. He invented the **Boehm System**, a keyed mechanism for the flute that is still in use today and has been applied successfully to the clarinet and the oboe.

● **Boehme, Jakob** ▷*See* Böhme, Jakob.

● **Boeotia** ▶ A region of central Greece, N and W of ▷Attica. Its main geographical features are rich central plains, surrounded by hills and mountains, and Lake Copaïs (now drained). The dozen or so city states that shared the territory formed a federal state dominated by ▷Thebes in 446 BC. The Boeotians had a reputation for good living and stupidity, belied by the military success of Thebes and the poetry of ▷Hesiod and ▷Pindar, among others. Boeotians took no part in Greek colonization overseas.

● **Boer** ▷*See* Afrikaner.

● **Boer Wars** ▶ (or South African Wars) The wars fought against the British by the Boers or ▷Afrikaners of South Africa. In the first (1880–81) the Boers of the Transvaal under ▷Kruger rebelled against British rule. After inflicting a massive defeat on the British garrison at ▷Majuba Hill, the Transvaal regained its independence under the ▷Pretoria Convention. In the second Boer War (1899–1902) the Boer forces of the South African Republic (previously the Transvaal) and Orange Free State were initially successful, besieging Ladysmith, Mafeking (held courageously by ▷Baden-Powell from October, 1899, until his relief in February, 1900), and Kimberley. They suffered reverses during 1900 but, using guerrilla tactics, were able to hold off the British under ▷Kitchener and F. S. ▷Roberts. The British devastated the countryside, rounded up Boer women and children, of whom some 20 000 died in concentration camps, and finally defeated the Boers, who lost their independence in the Peace of Vereeniging (1902).

● **Boethius, Anicius Manlius Severinus** ▶ (c. 480–524 AD) Roman statesman and philosopher. A patrician by birth, Boethius was consul in 510 during the Gothic occupation of Rome under ▷Theodoric, to whom he became chief minister. His championing of Roman traditions and institutions earned Theoderic's displeasure, and Boethius was imprisoned, tortured, and eventually executed. His translations of Aristotle and treatises on music and mathematics were standard texts in medieval Europe but his most famous work is *The Consolation of Philosophy*, written while he was in prison. A dialogue between the author and the personification of philosophy, the

Consolation seeks to prove that virtue alone remains constant and the knowledge of God is the only true wisdom.

● **Bogarde, Sir Dirk** ▶ (Derek van den Bogaerde; 1921–99) British film actor of Dutch descent. He acted in many British films in the 1950s and 1960s, including *Doctor in the House* (1953) and *The Servant* (1963), but his major performances were in later films of international stature, such as *The Damned* (1969), *Death in Venice* (1970), and *Providence* (1978). Also a writer, he was the author of the autobiographical *A Postilion Struck by Lightning* (1977), *Backcloth* (1986), *A Short Walk from Harrods* (1993), and *Cleared for Take Off* (1995) as well as the novels *Voices in the Garden* (1981), *Jericho* (1992), and *Closing Ranks* (1997).

Humphrey Bogart ▶ With Ingrid Bergman in their movie classic *Casablanca* (1942).

● **Bogart, Humphrey** ▶ (1899–1957) US film actor. He achieved international success in the 1930s in such films as *Dead End* (1937) and *Angels with Dirty Faces* (1938), usually playing tough gangster parts. His first starring role was in *High Sierra* (1941). The mixture of cynicism and chivalry that he portrayed in *The Maltese Falcon* (1941) and *Casablanca* (1942) became his trademark. In 1944 he made *To Have and Have Not*, which saw the screen debut of Lauren ▷Bacall, to whom he was subsequently married. His last films were *The African Queen* (1951), with Katharine Hepburn, and *The Caine Mutiny* (1954), which he made while suffering from the cancer from which he died.

Boer Wars ▶ A contemporary drawing of an attack by British troops, under Col de Lisle, on a Boer convoy led by Christian de Wet, commander of the Orange Free State forces in the second Boer War.

• **Boğazköy** ▶ (or Boğazkale) ▷*See* Hattusas.

• **Bognor Regis** ▶ 50 47N 0 41W A resort on the S coast of England, in West Sussex. George V convalesced here in 1929 and granted Bognor its title. Population (1991): 56 744.

• **Bogomils** ▷*See* Cathari.

• **Bogor** ▶ (former name: Buitenzorg) 6 34S 106 45E A city in Indonesia, on W Java. It is famed for its botanical garden (1817) and former Dutch governor general's residence (1745). It is an agricultural centre with an agricultural university (founded 1963) and an important research institute. Population (1995 est): 285 000.

Bogotá ▶ The baroque cathedral is a fine example of Spanish colonial architecture.

• **Bogotá, Santa Fé de** ▶ 4 38N 74 15W The capital of Colombia, on a fertile central plateau of the E Andes at an altitude of 2640 m (8600 ft). Founded by the Spanish in the early 16th century on the site of the conquered Indian settlement of Bacatá, it became capital of the viceroyalty of New Grenada and an important cultural centre. Today it possesses a university (1867), a number of colleges, and several notable technical schools. Regular airlines have helped to improve its rather isolated position from the rest of the country. Population (1995 est): 5 237 635.

• **Bohai** ▷*See* Chihli, Gulf of.

• **Bohemia** ▶ (Czech name: Čechy; German name: Böhmen) The western part of the Czech Republic. It consists chiefly of a plateau enclosed by mountains. The most industrialized part of the Czech Republic, Bohemia possesses important mineral resources, including uranium, coal, and iron ore. Agriculture is well developed. It is renowned for its many mineral springs.
History: Bohemia derives its name from the Boii (the first known inhabitants), who were displaced by the Czechs (1st–5th centuries AD). Bohemia became part of the greater Moravian empire in the 9th century, during which period Christianity was introduced. St Wenceslas was the first great Bohemian ruler but his brother, Boleslav I (d. 967; reigned 929–67), was forced to acknowledge the rule of Emperor Otto I and for many centuries thereafter Bohemia was linked with the Holy Roman Empire. During the 11th century there was a successful expedition into Moravia, which was linked from then on with Bohemia. It achieved the height of its power following the acquisitions of the Přemyslid Otakar II (1230–78; reigned 1253–78). The Přemyslid dynasty came to an end with the assassination of Wencelas III (1289–1306; reigned 1305–06) and John of Luxembourg was subsequently elected king (1310). The golden age of Bohemia was established by his son Charles I (Emperor ▷Charles IV), who founded the university at Prague in 1348. The reigns of his successors were marked by religious upheavals inspired by Jan Hus (*see* Hussites). The accession (1526) of Archduke Ferdinand began the long Habsburg domination of Bohemia. It was laid waste during the Thirty Years' War and after the Peace of Westphalia (1648) forcible Germanization and oppressive taxation reduced most Czechs to

misery. There was a rebirth of Czech nationalism during the 19th century but full independence was only attained at the end of World War I, when Bohemia became a province (1918–49) of the Republic of Czechoslovakia. When this broke up in 1991, Bohemia and Moravia together formed the Czech Republic.

• **Bohemond I** ▶ (or Bohemund; c. 1056–1111) Prince of Antioch (1099–1111). He fought (1080–85) with his father Robert Guiscard against Alexius I Comnenus and was a leader of the first Crusade, during which he took Antioch (1098). He was captured by the Turks (1100–03) and after renewed warfare with Alexius became his vassal (1108).

• **Böhm, Karl** ▶ (1894–1981) Austrian conductor, who was noted particularly for his performances of operas by Mozart and Richard Strauss. He was conductor of the Dresden State Opera (1934–43) and the Vienna State Opera (1943–45).

• **Böhme, Jakob** ▶ (or Boehme; 1575–1624) German Lutheran theosophist, who lived most of his life as a shoemaker in Silesia. His first work, the *Aurora* (1612), was condemned by the local authorities. Although forbidden to write, he later published such works as *Der Weg zu Christo* and *Mysterium magnum* (both 1623). He was influenced by ▷Paracelsus, alchemy, and astrology but also claimed divine inspiration for his writings. His central belief was that God was the source of everything, including evil, since he had two wills, one good and the other evil. He has influenced many thinkers, notably ▷Hegel and ▷Schelling.

• **Bohr, Niels Henrik David** ▶ (1885–1962) Danish physicist, who worked with J. J. ▷Thomson at Cambridge and ▷Rutherford at Manchester. He made an immense contribution to atomic theory by combining Rutherford's nuclear model with Planck's quantum theory. The model of the atom he proposed (the ▷Bohr atom) was modified by ▷Sommerfeld but is essentially the basis for modern atomic theory. Bohr also invented the concept of complementarity to combine the particle and wave aspects of subatomic particles. In 1916 he returned to Copenhagen as professor of physics and was awarded a Nobel Prize in 1922. During the 1930s his Institute of Theoretical Physics in Copenhagen became a haven for many Jewish and other physicists expelled by Hitler. In 1939 he took news of Lise ▷Meitner's and Otto ▷Hahn's uranium fission work to the USA and started the process that culminated in the manufacture of the atomic bomb. Bohr himself later worked at Los Alamos on the bomb, after escaping from German-occupied Denmark. A fervent advocate of atomic energy for peaceful uses, he organized the first Atoms for Peace Conference in 1955. His son **Aage Bohr** (1922–   ) shared the 1975 Nobel Prize for Physics for his work on atomic theory.

• **Bohr atom** ▶ A model of the atom, put forward by Niels ▷Bohr in 1913. His model assumes that electrons move around a central nucleus in circular orbits. The electrons are confined to fixed orbits at fixed distances from the nucleus, each orbit corresponding to a specific energy level. If the electron gains or loses the right amount of energy, in the form of a photon of electromagnetic radiation, it jumps or falls into another orbit. The jumps are quantized (*see* quantum theory), the energy associated with each jump being equal to hf, where h is the Planck constant and f is the frequency of the radiation. The model gives a good explanation of the spectral emission of the hydrogen atom and was later modified by ▷Sommerfeld to explain the fine structure of the hydrogen lines, by assuming that the electrons move in precessing elliptical orbits.

• **Boiardo, Matteo Maria, Conte di Scandiano** ▶ (1441–94) Italian poet. He served the Dukes of Ferrara as governor of Modena (1480–82) and Reggio (1487–94). His chief work was the unfinished *Orlando innamorato* (1483), a chivalrous epic about Roland (*see* Charlemagne) and the precursor of the more famous *Orlando furioso* by ▷Ariosto.

• **boil** ▶ An inflamed pus-filled swelling on the skin, usually caused by infection of a hair follicle with the bacterium *Staphylococcus aureus*. Boils are more likely to develop when constitutional resistance is low or when the diet is inadequate. The application of a warm poultice will bring the boil to a head and allow the pus to drain. A **carbuncle** is a collection of boils situated close together; it is slightly more difficult to treat and may require the use of antibiotics.

• **Boileau(-Despréaux), Nicolas** ▶ (1636–1711) French poet and critic. After the publication of his satires in 1666 he became friendly with ▷Molière, ▷Racine, and other leading writers. *L'Art poétique* (1674) was received as a definitive guide to the classical principles in literature and had a powerful contemporary influence in France and England. He also wrote a mock epic, *Le Lutrin* (1674), and translated ▷Longinus' treatise *On the Sublime*.

• **boiling point** ▶ The temperature at which the ▷vapour pressure of a liquid is equal to the atmospheric pressure. The boiling point of a liquid is usually given at standard atmospheric pressure (101 325 pascals).

• **Bois de Boulogne** ▶ A park in W Paris, France, bordering on the River Seine. It was presented to the city in 1852 by Napoleon III and contains the Auteuil and Longchamp racecourses. Area: 860 ha (2125 acres).

• **Boise** ▶ 43 38N 116 12W A city in the USA, the capital and largest city of Idaho. The centre of a gold rush in 1862, it has timber, food-processing, and agricultural industries. Population (1998 est): 157 452.

• **Boito, Arrigo** ▶ (1842–1918) Italian composer, librettist, and poet. He wrote the librettos for Verdi's operas *Otello* (1887) and *Falstaff* (1893) and adapted the libretto of his own opera *Mefistofele* (1868) and from ▷Goethe's *Faust*.

• **Bokassa I** ▶ (Jean Bedel B.; 1921–96) Emperor of the Central African Empire from 1977 until his overthrow in 1979. He seized power in the Central African Republic in 1966, becoming president and later proclaiming himself emperor. After returning from exile (1986), he was sentenced to forced labour for life for atrocities committed during his reign but was released in 1993.

• **Bokhara** ▷*See* Bukhara.

• **Bolden, Buddy** ▶ (Charles B.; 1868–1931) US Black jazz cornettist, originally a barber. He frequently worked with several bands in the course of one evening. He became insane in 1907 and died in hospital.

• **Bolesław (I) the Brave** ▶ (c. 966–1025) The first King of Poland, who extended the territory of the Polish principality, which he inherited in 992, and was crowned king (1000) by Emperor Otto III. He reorganized the Polish church, making it responsible directly to the pope and independent of the German church.

• **Bolesław (II) the Generous** ▶ (1039–81) King of Poland (1058–79), recognized as such by the pope in 1076. Bolesław successfully pursued Polish interests at the expense of German influence until a revolt of the clergy and nobility led to his excommunication and deposition.

• **Bolesław (III) the Wry-Mouthed** ▶ (1086–1138) Ruler of Poland (1102–38). Bolesław never took the title of king. Between 1113 and 1135 he reconquered and christianized Pomerania.

• **Boletus** ▶ A genus of mushrooms (about 50 species). The undersurface of the cap bears a series of vertical tubes (instead of gills), in which the spores are formed. Most grow near trees and they are generally edible or harmless (*see* cep). An exception is Satan's boletus (*B. satanas*), which is poisonous but not deadly. It has a short stalk and a grey or greyish-green cap 10–20 cm in diameter. Family: *Boletaceae*; phylum: ▷*Basidiomycota*.

• **Boleyn, Anne** ▶ (c. 1507–36) The second wife (from 1533) of Henry VIII of England. The daughter of Sir Thomas Boleyn (1477–1539), she was forcefully wooed by Henry while he was still seeking to get his marriage to Catherine of Aragon annulled. Anne became his second wife in 1533 but disappointed him by failing to produce a son: her only live birth, a daughter, became Elizabeth I. Henry soon tired of Anne, who was accused of treason by committing adultery and executed.

• **Bolger, James Brendan** ▶ (1935–) New Zealand politician; prime minister (1990–97). He led the National Party to victory in the elections of 1990 and 1993. After further elections in 1996 he formed a coalition government but resigned the following year.

• **Bolingbroke, Henry St John, 1st Viscount** ▶ (1678–1751) English statesman and philosopher. A Tory, he became an MP in 1701 and was secretary of war (1704–08) before becoming secretary of state for the north in 1710. A supporter of the ▷Jacobites, he fled to France on the accession of George I (1714), where he helped to organize the Fifteen Rebellion. In France he encountered the major thinkers of the ▷Enlightenment and wrote *Reflections upon Exile* and *Reflections Concerning Innate Moral Principles*. He returned to England in 1725. In contributions to the journal, *The Craftsman*, he outlined his aim, which he never achieved, to create a Country Party of Whigs and Tories united by their opposition to ▷Walpole. In 1735 he returned to France. He also wrote *The Idea of a Patriot King* (1749).

• **Bolívar, Simón** ▶ (1783–1830) South American soldier and statesman, known as the Liberator. The son of a wealthy Venezuelan creole family, his childhood tutor and subsequent travels in Europe instilled in Bolívar an admiration for the ideas of the Enlightenment. He returned to Latin America in 1807 and devoted the rest of his life to its liberation from Spain. In 1813 he seized Caracas but after defeat in 1814 went into exile until 1817. His victory at the battle of ▷Boyacá (1819) achieved the liberation of New Granada, which was renamed Colombia. Bolívar became its president and, after liberating Venezuela and Quito (Ecuador) in 1821, organized a federation of the three newly independent states. Latin America was finally freed of the Spanish by campaigns in Peru, and Upper Peru took the name Bolivia in honour of Bolívar. His dream of a united Andean republic was never realized and he died disillusioned by the political bickering that thwarted this goal.

• **Bolivia, Republic of** ▶ An inland country in central South America consisting of low plains in the N and E, crossed by the Madre de Dios, Bené, and Mamoré river systems; in the W, ranges of the Andes rise to over 6400 m (21 000 ft) and the Altiplano, a plateau averaging about 3900 m (13 000 ft), contains Lakes Titicaca and Poopó. Bolivia has some of the world's highest inhabited regions, most of the population, which is of mixed Indian and Spanish descent, living at altitudes of over 3000 m (10 000 ft).
Economy: despite abundant natural resources, Bolivia's economy has remained weak, partly owing to falls in world commodity prices and the country's endemic political instability. Hyperinflation was rampant in the late 1970s and 1980s but has since been stabilized. Mining, gas, and petroleum are the main industries. Mineral resources include tin, zinc, lead, antimony, and copper; silver is still mined but has declined in importance. Agriculture is being improved in the E part and the main crops are sugar cane, potatoes, maize, rice, and wheat. Livestock, including llamas, is raised and forestry is being developed. Main exports include minerals, oil (through a pipeline to Arica on the Chilean coast; a pipeline to Brazil is being constructed), natural gas (to Argentina), hides and skins, and vicuña wool. The illegal trade in coca, which is smuggled to Colombia for processing into cocaine, has created large profits for drugs barons and continues to cause social problems. The country suffers from a massive external debt.
History: ruins near ▷Tiahuanaco indicate the existence of a pre-Inca civilization (the Aymaras) going back to the 10th century. The area later became part of the Inca Empire and was conquered by the Spanish in the 16th century, when it became known as Upper Peru. The discovery of tin and silver at Potosí soon after the Spanish conquest led to great prosperity. In 1776 it became part of the viceroyalty of Buenos Aires. After a long war it gained its independence with the help of Simón Bolívar in 1825 and became a republic with Antonio José de ▷Sucre as first president. During the remainder of the century as a result of civil wars and struggles with neighbouring countries Bolivia lost much territory, including access to the Pacific coast. Political unrest and violent changes of government continued for most of the 20th century. In 1952 the ruling military junta was overthrown by a popular revolution and the reformer Victor Paz Estenssoro became president. He was overthrown in a coup in 1964. In 1971 a further coup brought Gen Hugo Banzer to power: he achieved a measure of political stability, remaining in office until overthrown in 1978. After two decades that saw frequent political upheavals (including the return of the veteran Paz Estenssoro in 1985–89), the former dictator Banzer was elected president in 1997. He was

succeeded by his deputy, Jorge Quiroga, in 2001. Disputes with Peru and Chile continue over access to the Pacific coast.

Republic of Bolivia

Head of state	President Jorge Quiroga
Official languages	Spanish, Quechua, and Aymara
Official currency	boliviano of 100 centavos
Area	1 098 580 sq km (424 160 sq mi)
Population (2000 est)	8 329 000
Capital	La Paz (legal capital: Sucre)

● **Böll, Heinrich** ▶ (1917–85) German novelist. After infantry service in World War II, he became a full-time writer in 1951. His novels and stories include *The Train Was on Time* (1949), *The Clown* (1963), *The Lost Honour of Katharina Blum* (1975), and *The Safety Net* (1982). He won the Nobel Prize in 1972.

● **Bollandists** ▶ The ▷Jesuit scholars who continued the work on the *Acta Sanctorum*, an authoritative edition of the lives of the saints, begun by the founder and first editor of the project, John van Bolland (1596–1665). The first two volumes of the work were published in Antwerp in 1643, and the most recent one appeared in 1940.

● **boll weevil** ▶ A stout brownish ▷weevil, *Anthonomus grandis*, also called cotton boll weevil. Originally a native of the New World tropics, it is now a major insect pest of cotton crops in the W hemisphere. The female lays a single egg within each cotton boll, which thus fails to develop.

● **Bologna** ▶ 44 30N 11 20E A city in N Italy, the capital of Emilia-Romagna. The history of the site of Bologna dates from Etruscan times. It became a free city in the middle ages and the Emperor Charles V was crowned here in 1530. It has an ancient university (1088) and a 14th-century gothic church. Its industries include engineering and food processing. Population (1996 est): 386 491.

● **Bologna, Giovanni da** ▷*See* Giambologna.

● **Bolsheviks** ▶ One of the two factions into which the Russian Social Democratic Workers' Party split in 1903 in London (the other was the ▷Mensheviks). The Bolsheviks, which means those in the majority, were led by ▷Lenin, who believed that the revolution must be guided by a single centralized party of professional revolutionaries (*see also* Leninism). The Bolsheviks came to power in the ▷Russian Revolution (1917) and from 1918 until 1952 the Soviet Communist Party was termed Communist Party (Bolsheviks).

● **Bolshoi Ballet** ▶ The principal Russian ballet company, based at the Bolshoi Theatre in Moscow. It originated from a dancing class established by the Moscow orphanage in the late 18th century and moved into its present premises in 1856 after fire had destroyed the first Bolshoi Theatre. Known for its dramatic style and its realistic and elaborate scenery, it first appeared in the West in 1956 in London. From 1964 to 1998 it was directed by the choreographer Yuri Grigorovich (1927–).

● **Bolt, Robert Oxton** ▶ (1924–95) British dramatist, famous for the play and film *A Man for All Seasons* (1960), a study of Sir Thomas ▷More. He also wrote screenplays for such films as *Lawrence of Arabia* (1962) and *The Mission* (1986). He was married (twice) to the actress Sarah Miles (1941–).

● **Bolton** ▶ **1.** 53 35W 2 26W A town in NW England, in Bolton unitary authority, Greater Manchester. Traditionally a cotton-spinning town (Samuel Crompton, inventor of the spinning mule, was born here), Bolton also manufactures textile machinery and chemicals and is involved in engineering. Population (1991): 139 020. **2.** A unitary authority in NW England, in Greater Manchester. Area: 140 sq km (54 sq mi). Population (1999 est): 258 584.

● **Boltzmann, Ludwig Eduard** ▶ (1844–1906) Austrian physicist, who developed statistical mechanics with J. C. ▷Maxwell and J. W. ▷Gibbs, notably the Maxwell-Boltzmann statistics of particle systems obeying classical laws. He also linked thermodynamics with molecular physics by showing that increasing entropy is related to increasing disorder among particles. Working with his teacher Josef Stefan (1835–93), he showed that Stefan's law could be derived thermody-

namically and it is now usually known as the ▷Stefan-Boltzmann law.

● **Boltzmann constant** ▶ (k) A constant, obtained by dividing the ▷gas constant by the ▷Avogadro number, equal to 1.3806×10^{-23} joule per kelvin. Named after Ludwig ▷Boltzmann.

● **Bolyai, János** ▶ (1802–60) Hungarian mathematician, who (with ▷Lobachevski) was the first to study the properties of spaces with ▷non-Euclidean geometry.

● **Bolzano** ▶ 46 30N 11 22E A city in Italy, in Trentino-Alto Adige. It has a 14th-century gothic cathedral. Bolzano is a centre for tourism and trades in fruit and wine. There are steel and textile industries. Population (1998 est): 97 073.

● **Boma** ▶ 5 50S 13 03E A port in SW Democratic Republic of Congo on the Congo River. It was formerly the capital of the Congo Free State, later the Belgian Congo (1886–1926). Forest products, such as palm oil, are exported. Population (1994 est): 135 284.

● **bombardier beetle** ▶ A blue-grey and orange beetle, about 9 mm long, belonging to a widely distributed genus (*Brachinus*) of ▷ground beetles. It has an efficient means of chemical defence, emitting puffs of an irritant secretion from the anal glands. Similar beetles of the genus *Pherosophus* occur in Africa, Asia, and the East Indies.

● **Bombay** ▶ (official name from 1995: Mumbai) 18 56N 72 51E A city in India, the capital of Maharashtra and the country's main seaport on the W coast. The city proper occupies a group of islands that are united by a system of causeways and breakwaters; the site, known as Bombay Island, is linked with Salsette Island in the N. Its natural harbour, 11 km (7 mi) wide, is the focus of most of India's international trade. Bombay is also the financial and commercial centre of the country. The Tata hydroelectric system powers much of Bombay's industry, which includes cotton textiles, food processing, and oil refining. The city is also the site of the country's first nuclear reactor. The harbour is dominated by the Gateway of India, a monumental arch that was built to commemorate the visit of George V of the UK in 1911. The University of Bombay (1857) and numerous government buildings are situated in the centre of the city and the many temples (dating from the 8th century AD and earlier) reflect the cultural and religious diversity to be found in the city. The population is mainly Hindu but there are large Muslim, Christian, and Jewish minorities. The city's island location has led to problems of overcrowding and a twin city on the mainland is planned.

History: ceded to the Portuguese in 1534, it passed to Charles II of England in 1661 and to the British East India Company in 1668. The arrival of the railways, the opening of the Suez Canal, and land reclamation led to considerable expansion in the 19th century. Population (1991): 9 909 547.

● **Bombay duck** ▶ A fish, *Harpodon nehereus*, found in the estuaries of N India, where it is widely used for food. It has a grey or brown body, about 40 cm long, with speckles and large pectoral and pelvic fins. Order: *Myctophiformes*.

● **Bon** ▶ The pre-Buddhist religion of Tibet, characterized by the belief in a supreme sky god and a hierarchy of good and evil spirits, gods, demons, and ghosts. Elaborate ritual, including animal or even human sacrifice, abounded; religious practice was presided over by a class of shamans (*see* shamanism), priest-magicians who could influence the spirits by means of white or black magic, even being able to open the gate between earth and heaven. It was absorbed into Tibetan Buddhism, to which it lent a very individual character.

● **Bon, Cape** ▶ 37 05N 11 02E A peninsula in NE Tunisia, extending into the Mediterranean Sea. Its fertile plains produce oranges, olives, and market-garden produce. Length: about 75 km (46 mi). Width: 35 km (22 mi).

● **Bonaparte** ▶ (*or* Buonaparte) A Corsican family that included the French emperors, ▷Napoleon I and ▷Napoleon III, and the nominal emperor, ▷Napoleon II. **Carlo Bonaparte** (1746–85), a lawyer, had four sons. **Joseph Bonaparte** (1768–1844) was a diplomat of indifferent qualities who rose to high office by virtue of the position of his brother Napoleon I, from whom he received the thrones of Naples (1806) and Spain (1808). After Napoleon's defeat at Waterloo (1815)

Joseph lived in exile. **Lucien Bonaparte** (1775–1840) was president of the Council of Five Hundred under the Directory and became a critic of Napoleon's policies. The brothers were reconciled, however, on the eve of Waterloo and after Napoleon's defeat Lucien lived in exile in Italy. **Louis Bonaparte** (1778–1846) was created King of Holland by Napoleon in 1806 but, exasperated by Louis' inability to enforce the ▷Continental System, Napoleon obliged him to relinquish the Crown in 1810. He too died in exile. His son by Hortense de ▷Beauharnais became Napoleon III. **Jérôme Bonaparte** (1784–1860) was created King of Westphalia in 1807 and was a commander in Napoleon's Russian invasion and at Waterloo. He survived to become a dignitary in the Second Empire (1852–70), established by his nephew Napoleon III.

The exploits of these and other members of the Bonaparte family formed the iconography of **Bonapartism**, a movement that sought to recreate the Napoleonic empire and to establish the dynasty in France. Louis Napoleon's *Des idées napoléoniennes* (1839) typified the romantic and conservative nature of Bonapartism.

● **Bonaventure, St** ▶ (Giovanni di Fidanza; c. 1221–74) Italian Franciscan theologian, known as Doctor Seraphicus. He studied and lectured at Paris, in 1257 receiving the degree of doctor and becoming minister general of the Franciscan Order. He wrote the official biography of St Francis. As a theologian, he supported the traditional teachings of St Augustine, as opposed to the new Aristotelian thought that influenced his contemporary St Thomas ▷Aquinas. Feast day: 14 July. Emblem: a cardinal's hat.

● **bond** ▶ (finance) A security issued by a government, local authority, or public company as a means of raising capital. Most bonds pay a fixed rate of interest and are redeemable on a stated day. ▷*See also* gilt-edged security; junk bond.

● **bond** ▶ (chemistry) ▷*See* chemical bond.

● **Bond, Edward** ▶ (1934–) British dramatist. A Marxist, he has used techniques of both realism and epic theatre to express his bleak vision of the cruelty of society. His portrayal of a violent infanticide in *Saved* (1965) aroused controversy. His other plays include *Lear* (1971), *Restoration* (1981), and *In the Company of Men* (1996).

● **Bondi, Sir Hermann** ▶ (1919–) British cosmologist and mathematician, born in Vienna. With Fred ▷Hoyle and T. ▷Gold he developed the steady-state theory of the universe. Formerly director of ESRO, he was chairman of the Natural Environment Research Council (1980–84).

● **bone** ▶ A rigid tissue that forms most of the skeleton of higher animals and man. The shape of individual bones is governed by their function (*see* skeleton). Most bones have a central cavity filled with ▷marrow. Bone is composed of a matrix of fibres of the protein collagen, responsible for the strength of bones, and bone salts, chiefly calcium salts (*see* apatite). This tissue is formed by activity of bone cells (osteoblasts), which become enclosed in the matrix when they have ceased to function. Bone formation starts during embryonic life. Most bones (including the long bones) develop from cartilage and the process is complete at birth. Membrane bones (e.g. the skull bones) are formed directly in connective tissue, the process being completed after birth (hence the gap (called a fontanelle) in a newborn baby's skull). The branch of medicine concerned with the diagnosis and treatment of diseases of bones is called **osteology**. ▷*See* Plate II.

● **Bône** ▷*See* Annaba.

● **bone-black** ▶ (or *animal charcoal*) ▷Charcoal obtained by heating bones. It is about one-tenth carbon, the rest being calcium and magnesium phosphates and other salts. Bone-black is used as an absorbent, for example in removing colouring, refining sugar, and removing ▷fusel oil from whisky.

● **boneset** ▶ A plant of the genus *Eupatorium*, also called thoroughwort, found in tropical South America, Mexico, and the West Indies but grown elsewhere as greenhouse or border plants. Boneset is a perennial herb, shrub, or small tree. The flat-topped flower heads consist of disc florets, usually rose or white, with protruding styles. Family: ▷*Compositae*. ▷*See also* comfrey.

● **bongo** ▶ An antelope, *Boocerus euryceros*, of dense tropical central African forests. About 120 cm high at the shoulder, bongos are red-brown with vertical white body stripes and white markings on the head and legs. The male has spiralled horns up to 100 cm long. Bulls are solitary; cows and calves live in small herds. They feed on leaves and shoots. ◻mammal.

● **Bonhoeffer, Dietrich** ▶ (1906–45) German pastor and theologian. As a young theological lecturer and pastor, Bonhoeffer identified himself with the German ▷Confessing Church, which opposed the pro-Nazi part of the Lutheran church, and during the war became involved with anti-Hitler conspirators. He was arrested in 1943, sent to Buchenwald concentration camp, and finally hanged. His posthumous *Letters and Papers from Prison* (1953) and radical theological writings continue to be influential.

● **Boniface, St** ▶ (or *St Wynfrith*; c. 680–754 AD) English missionary, known as the Apostle of Germany. He was born in Crediton, Devon, and entered the Benedictine Order. He visited Frisia in 716 and in 718 was granted papal authority to evangelize the Germans. He successfully established Christianity in several German states and instituted church reforms elsewhere, culminating in his appointment as Archbishop of Mainz in 751. He was martyred with 53 companions in Frisia. Feast day: 5 June.

● **Boniface VIII** ▶ (Benedict Caetani; c. 1234–1303) Pope (1294–1303). He was elected after a long career in papal administration. An expert in canon law, he repeatedly clashed with ▷Philip IV of France over the royal claim to judge and tax the clergy (which he also disputed with ▷Edward I of England). The bull *Unam Sanctam* (*One Holy*; 1302) proclaimed papal supremacy over temporal powers. In 1303 he was captured in Italy by Philip's forces and although soon released died shortly after.

● **Bonington, Sir Chris** ▶ (Christian John Storey B.; 1934–) British mountaineer, author, and photographer. He is famous especially for the first British ascent of the N face of the Eiger (1962) as well as his leadership of the 1970 Annapurna I and the 1975 Everest expeditions. He finally reached the summit of Everest in 1985.

● **Bonington, Richard Parkes** ▶ (1801–28) British landscape painter. He was born near Nottingham but lived in France after 1817. In Paris he studied under Baron ▷Gros and became friendly with ▷Delacroix. Together they studied Rubens and Constable and their visit to England (1825) inspired Bonington to devote more time to history painting.

● **Bonin Islands** ▶ A Japanese group of about 30 forested volcanic islands in the central Pacific Ocean, the most important being Chichi-jima. Strategically important during World War II, they were captured by the USA in 1945 (returned 1968). Sugar cane, cocoa, and bananas are produced, timber is exported, and there is offshore whaling. Area: 103 sq km (40 sq mi). Population (latest est): 2010. Chief settlement: Omura.

● **bonito** ▶ A swift marine food and game fish, of the worldwide genus *Sarda*, which is related to ▷mackerel and ▷tuna. About 75 cm long, bonitos are greenish blue above, with dark longitudinal stripes, and silvery below. Other related fish called bonito include the leaping bonito (*Cybiosarda elegans*), plain bonito (*Orcynopsis unicolor*), and ▷skipjack tuna. ◻oceans.

● **Bonn** ▶ 50 43N 7 07E A city in NW Germany, in North Rhine-Westphalia on the River Rhine. The old part of the town contains the cathedral (12th–13th centuries) and Beethoven's birthplace (now a museum). The university was founded in 1786.

History: originally settled by the Romans, it was destroyed by the Normans in the 9th century AD, and was the seat of the Electors of Cologne from the 13th to the 16th centuries. It passed from France to Prussia in 1815 and was the capital of West Germany from 1949 to 1990; although Berlin became the official capital of the reunited Germany in 1990, Bonn remained the seat of government until 2000. Population (1999 est): 304 100.

● **Bonnard, Pierre** ▶ (1867–1947) French painter. He took up art in Paris in the 1880s, after studying law, and as a member of the ▷Nabis, he painted decorative domestic scenes, influenced by Japanese prints. More original works of this period were his lithographs, *As-*

pects of the Life of Paris (1895), and illustrations for Verlaine's book *Parallèlement* (1900). After 1900 his paintings of interiors, landscapes, and bathing women were treated with dazzling colour and light.

● **Bonnet, Charles** ► (1720–93) Swiss naturalist, noted for his speculations about evolution. He demonstrated that aphid eggs could develop without fertilization (*see* parthenogenesis). This led him to propose that every organism contained a sequence of preformed individuals corresponding to successive generations. His theory of evolution argued that periodic destruction of most life forms was followed by evolutionary advancement of the survivors.

● **Bonneville Salt Flats** ► (*or* Bonneville Flats) A barren salt plain in the USA, in NW Utah. The flats form part of the Great Salt Lake Desert and are a relict feature of an ancient lake. Several world land speed records have been established here since 1935.

● **Bonnie Prince Charlie** ▷*See* Charles Edward Stuart, the Young Pretender.

● **Bonny, Bight of** ► (name until 1975: Bight of Biafra) An inlet of the Atlantic Ocean, bordering on Nigeria and Cameroon. It is the innermost bay of the Gulf of Guinea.

● **bonsai** ► An ordinary shrub or tree, such as a conifer or flowering cherry, that is developed as a miniature (up to about 60 cm high). The technique was first practised as an art form in China over 700 years ago, probably using weather-beaten trees, which were considered aesthetically pleasing. It was later perfected by the Japanese (who treat good specimens as heirlooms) and has now spread to the W hemisphere. Bonsais grow from seeds or cuttings planted usually in earthenware pots with one or more drainage holes and containing a compost with a limited nutrient and water supply. Both branches and roots are trained and pruned. The trees may take ten years or more to acquire an aged appearance, and some live 300–400 years. Good hardy species may be kept outdoors for most of the year.

● **bontebok** ▷*See* blesbok.

● **bony fish** ► Any fish belonging to the class *Osteichthyes*, which includes the majority of food and game fishes (*see* teleost). They have bony skeletons and their gills are covered by a structure called an operculum. Many species use a ▷swim bladder for buoyancy control and even for breathing air (*see* lungfish). Fertilization of the eggs occurs outside the body. Subclasses: *Actinopterygii*; *Sarcopterygii*.

● **booby** ► A large tropical seabird belonging to the family *Sulidae* (gannets, etc.; 9 species) characterized by a large head, a large stout tapering bill, large webbed feet, and a wedge-shaped tail. Boobies are 65–85 cm long and typically have a white plumage with brown markings. Boobies soar high over the sea, diving to catch fish and squids.

● **boogie-woogie** ► A piano blues in which the left hand establishes a driving repetitive pattern with eight beats to the bar, while the right provides a variety of syncopation. Originating in the SW USA, it was popular in the 1930s.

● **book** ► A set of sheets of paper or similar material, usually bearing printed or handwritten words, folded and bound together between protective covers. The handwritten book (the codex), combining compactness, strength, and ease of use began to oust its predecseeor, the papyrus scroll, during the 2nd century AD. Vellum, being more durable than papyrus, became the preferred writing surface until the use of ▷paper spread slowly across Europe from 11th-century Byzantium. Printing at first brought no radical changes in book production, the sheets still being folded and bound by hand. Development of more efficient presses and cheaper paper production in the late 18th and early 19th centuries gradually brought the price of books within reach of the general public. During the 20th century paper binding, pioneered in the UK by Penguin Books Ltd, brought about a revolution in publishing so that in the UK alone over 35 000 new titles are published each year. In response libraries have evolved new methods of data storage, using microfiche and microfilm (*see* microcopy) as well as the various forms of electronic publishing.

● **bookbinding** ► The practice of sewing or gluing together the pages of a ▷book along one edge and securing them between protective covers (boards) joined across the back (spine) by a flexible hinge. Although utilitarian in purpose, bookbinding has long been prac-

tised as a decorative art. In the middle ages wooden boards were common. The advent of printing encouraged diversification in the materials used, with leather and vellum becoming paramount. Gold tooling, the commonest form of decoration, reached a peak of elaboration in the 17th and 18th centuries. The spread of literacy caused a demand for cheaper binding materials, such as cloth bindings (1822) and paper and plastics (20th century). Nowadays books are bound by machinery, first invented in the late 19th century. The bindings are similar to hand bindings except in paperbacks, which are glued together. Hand binding is now used only to produce luxury books.

● **Booker Prize** ► An annual prize of £50,000 for a work of British, Irish, or Commonwealth fiction in the English language. It has been awarded since 1969 by the British food trading company Booker International, in conjunction with the Publishers' Association; it is administered by the ▷Book Trust. From 2002 it will be known as the Man Booker Prize, under a new sponsorship agreement by the Man Group. The first International Booker Prize was awarded in 1992.

Booker Prize

Year	Winner	Title
1969	P H Newby	*Something to Answer For*
1970	Bernice Rubens	*The Elected Member*
1971	V S Naipaul	*In a Free State*
1972	John Berger	*G*
1973	J G Farrell	*The Siege of Krishnapur*
1974	Nadine Gordimer	*The Conservationist*
	Stanley Middleton	*Holiday*
1975	Ruth Prawer Jhabvala	*Heat and Dust*
1976	David Storey	*Saville*
1977	Paul Scott	*Staying On*
1978	Iris Murdoch	*The Sea, The Sea*
1979	Penelope Fitzgerald	*Offshore*
1980	William Golding	*Rites of Passage*
1981	Salman Rushdie	*Midnight's Children*
1982	Thomas Keneally	*Schindler's Ark*
1983	J M Coetzee	*Life and Times of Michael K*
1984	Anita Brookner	*Hotel du Lac*
1985	Keri Hulme	*The Bone People*
1986	Kingsley Amis	*The Old Devils*
1987	Penelope Lively	*Moon Tiger*
1988	Peter Carey	*Oscar and Lucinda*
1989	Kazuo Ishiguro	*The Remains of the Day*
1990	A S Byatt	*Possession*
1991	Ben Okri	*The Famished Road*
1992	Michael Ondaatje	*The English Patient*
	Barry Unsworth	*Sacred Hunger*
1993	Roddy Doyle	*Paddy Clarke Ha Ha Ha*
1994	James Kelman	*How Late It Was, How Late*
1995	Pat Barker	*The Ghost Road*
1996	Graham Swift	*Last Orders*
1997	Arundhati Roy	*The God of Small Things*
1998	Ian McEwan	*Amsterdam*
1999	J M Coetzee	*Disgrace*
2000	Margaret Atwood	*The Blind Assassin*
2001	Peter Carey	*The True History of the Kelly Gang*

● **bookkeeping** ▷*See* accountancy.

● **booklouse** ► A soft-bodied wingless insect (1–7 mm long), also called dustlouse, of the order *Psocoptera* (about 1600 species). Booklice inhabit buildings, often feeding on old books, papers, and entomological collections. ▷*See also* bookworm.

● **Book of Changes** ▷*See* I Ching.

● **Book of Common Prayer** ▷*See* Common Prayer, Book of.

● **Book of the Dead** ► 1. A collection of ancient Egyptian texts dating from the 16th century BC. They consist of charms, formulas, and spells written on papyrus and placed inside mummy cases for use by the dead in the afterlife. □Osiris. 2. (*or* Bar-do Thödol) The Tibetan Book of the Dead, an ancient Buddhist text that purports to describe the experiences of the soul after death. Recited by lamas over a dying or recently deceased person (or sometimes over an effigy of the corpse), it describes the various, mainly terrifying, apparitions that the spirit is believed to encounter in the interval between death and rebirth. It is thought to show the influence of shamanic practices (*see* shamanism) on Tibetan Buddhism.

● **Book Trust** ▶ A British society founded in 1925 (as the National Book League) to promote general interest in books. As well as providing library and information facilities, it publishes book lists, organizes exhibitions, and administers literary prizes, notably the annual Booker Prize for fiction.

● **bookworm** ▶ Any insect that damages books by gnawing the bindings and boring holes in the paper. Bookworms therefore include ▷silverfish, booklice, moth and beetle larvae, etc.

● **Boole, George** ▶ (1815–64) British mathematician, who applied the methods of algebra to logic. By replacing logical operations by symbols, Boole showed that the operations could be manipulated to give logically consistent results. His method, known as Boolean algebra or symbolic logic, led to mathematics being given a logically consistent foundation. The subject was further developed by G. ▷Frege, B. A. W. ▷Russell, and A. N. ▷Whitehead.

● **boom** ▶ The phase in the ▷trade cycle in which output reaches a peak. Booms are characterized by full employment, rising prices, high profits, and high investment that goes with business confidence. *Compare* depression; recession.

● **boomerang** ▶ A curved hand-thrown wooden missile used by Australian Aborigines to kill game, as a weapon of war, or in play. The angled shape and the spin given to the missile when thrown enables the light types to return to the thrower if they miss their target. Up to 75 cm (30 in) long, they can be effective to a distance of 45 m (50 yd).

● **boomslang** ▶ A venomous green snake, *Dispholidus typus*, occurring in African savanna and reaching 1.8 m in length. It feeds on birds and chameleons, often holding its body erect before striking. Small amounts of its venom can cause fatal haemorrhaging in man. Family: *Colubridae*.

● **Boone, Daniel** ▶ (1734–1820) American pioneer. Between 1767 and 1773 he explored Kentucky and in 1775 led an expedition to establish a colony there for the Transylvania Company. He formed the first settlement in Kentucky at Boonesborough, which he courageously defended against Indian attack. Boonville was named after him.

● **Boot, Sir Jesse, 1st Baron Trent** ▶ (1850–1931) British pharmacist and retailer, who opened his first shop in 1877. By introducing mass retailing at low prices, he pioneered the modern chain store and expanded to over 1000 branches.

● **Boötes** ▶ (Latin: herdsman) A large constellation in the N sky near Ursa Major. The brightest star is ▷Arcturus.

● **Booth, Charles** ▶ (1840–1916) British sociologist. Booth's *Life and Labour of the People in London* (1891–1903) was the first accurate sociological analysis of poverty to be published in England. He also devised the old-age pension.

● **Booth, Edwin** ▶ (1833–93) US actor. He was best known for his performances in Shakespearean tragic roles, especially Hamlet. His brother **John Wilkes Booth** (1839–65), also an actor, shot President Abraham □Lincoln on 14 April, 1865. The president died next morning and Booth was killed two weeks later, while attempting to evade capture.

● **Booth, William** ▶ (1829–1912) British preacher and founder of the ▷Salvation Army. He was born in Nottingham and became an itinerant Methodist preacher, but left the Methodists in order to do evangelistic work among the poor. He established a mission in Whitechapel in 1865. The reluctance of established churches to accept his slum converts led to the foundation of the Salvation Army, with Booth as General (1877). He was greatly aided in his work by his wife **Catherine Booth** (1829–90); a fervent preacher and social campaigner, she was also one of the first advocates of women's ministry in the Church. Their eldest son, **William Bramwell Booth** (1856–1929), was chief of staff of the Salvation Army from 1880 and later

General (1912–29). His daughter **Evangeline Booth** (1865–1950) was also a leading officer and then General (1934–39).

● **Boothia Peninsula** ▶ A peninsula of N Canada projecting into the Arctic Ocean, in Nunavut. The northernmost part of the North American mainland, it is sparsely populated, with a police post and trading post. Area: 32 375 sq km (12 500 sq mi).

● **Bootle** ▶ 53 28N 3 00W A town in NW England, in Sefton unitary authority, Merseyside. Bootle's docks are extensive and modern and its industries include engineering, tanning, tin smelting, and flour milling. Population (1991): 65 454.

● **bootlegging** ▶ The illegal distribution or production of highly taxed goods, especially liquor or cigarettes. During ▷Prohibition (1920–33) in the USA, when the manufacture, sale, and transportation of alcohol was banned, a well-organized illegal industry developed. Gangsters, such as Al ▷Capone, controlled both speakeasies (illegal bars) and private distribution systems. Other illegal activities (graft, extortion, protection rackets, prostitution) accompanied bootlegging and became the basis of the organized crime empires active in the USA today. Bootlegging, including the use of illegal stills, continues in certain areas of the USA, especially "dry" areas (where alcoholic spirits are not sold).

● **bootstrap theory** ▶ The theory in which no elementary particle is regarded as being more fundamental than any other. Each particle exists by virtue of the existence of all the others. Its name derives from the phrase "to pull oneself up by the bootstraps." The theory avoids the problem of a series of classes of particles, each more fundamental than the last. ▷*See also* particle physics.

● **bop** ▶ (*or* bebop) A type of ▷jazz that originated in the USA in the 1940s as a reaction against swing. Bop emphasized the art of melodic improvisation neglected during the swing era, but was also characterized by harmonic and rhythmic experimentation. In New York City, Dizzy Gillespie and Charlie "Bird" Parker established small bop bands that required the audience to listen rather than dance.

● **Bophuthatswana** ▶ Formerly, a ▷Bantu Homeland in South Africa, consisting of several separate landlocked areas. Bophuthatswana was created in the 1960s by the South African government as a "homeland" for the Tswana people who had lived in the area since the 17th century. However, some 65% of its modern citizens lived and worked in South Africa. In 1972 it became self-governing under the Bantu Homelands Constitution Act (1971). Bophuthatswana became fully independent in name in 1977, but this was recognized only by South Africa. The president, Chief Lucas Mangope (1923–), was deposed and rule from Pretoria imposed following riots in 1994 in the months preceding South Africa's first multiracial elections. Following these, Bophuthatswana was reintegrated into South Africa and full South African citizenship granted to its inhabitants. Capital: Mmabatho.

● **borage** ▶ A widely grown annual Mediterranean herb, *Borago officinalis*. Borage is a stiff hairy plant, up to 60 cm high, with terminal clusters of small blue flowers with backward-pointing petals. It is used in herbal remedies, pot-pourri, beverages, and salads and the flowers may be candied. Family: *Boraginaceae*.

● **boranes** ▶ Compounds of boron and hydrogen. The simplest is diborane B_2H_6, which is made by reacting sodium borohydride ($NaBH_4$) with ▷sulphuric acid. The formulas of boranes are not accounted for by classical theories of valence and their molecules contain electron-deficient bonds.

● **Borås** ▶ 57 44N 12 55E A town in S Sweden. It is a centre of the textile industry. Population (1994): 96 123.

● **borax** ▶ (*or* sodium tetraborate; $Na_2B_4O_7$) A natural substance, usually occurring in hydrated crystalline form. It is found in some salt lakes and in alkaline soils and is used in the manufacture of glass and enamel and as a water softener.

● **Bordeaux** ▶ (Latin name: Burdigala) 44 50N 0 34W A city in SW France, the capital of the Gironde department on the River Garonne. It is a major seaport and wine centre. Industries include shipbuilding, engineering, oil and sugar refining, and chemicals. There are many fine 18th-century buildings and squares, a cathedral (12th-15th centuries), and a university (1441).

History: an important commercial centre under the Romans, it became the capital of Aquitania (*see* Aquitaine) but declined following the collapse of the Roman Empire. It flourished once again under English rule (1154-1453). It became a centre of the Fronde in the 17th century and of the Girondins during the French Revolution. It was the seat of the French government for a brief period in 1914 and again in 1940. Population (1990): 213 274.

● **Borden, Sir Robert Laird** ▶ (1854-1937) Canadian statesman; Conservative prime minister (1911-20). An advocate of economic independence, he opposed a reciprocal trade agreement with the USA and came to power after defeating the Liberals on this issue. He formed a coalition government to introduce conscription in 1917 and gave women the vote in 1918. Borden supported British policies but claimed more independence for Canada in world affairs, winning separate Canadian representation at the League of Nations.

● **Borders Region** ▶ A former administrative region in SE Scotland, bordering on England. It was created under local government reorganization in 1975 from the counties of Berwick, Roxburgh, Peebles, Selkirk, and part of Midlothian. In 1996 it became a ▷unitary authority and was renamed ▷Scottish Borders.

● **border terrier** ▶ A breed of working dog originating in the border region of England and Scotland. It has a deep narrow body, triangular forward-falling ears, and a short strong muzzle. The coat is red, yellowish-brown, grey and tan, or blue and tan. Weight: 6-7 kg (dogs); 5-6 kg (bitches).

● **Bordet, Jules Jean Baptiste Vincent** ▶ (1870-1961) Belgian bacteriologist, who discovered (1895) the two factors (antibody and complement) in blood serum responsible for the rupture of bacterial cells. This fundamental discovery paved the way for diagnostic tests for many bacterial diseases, including syphilis. Bordet founded the Pasteur Institute, Brussels (1901), and was awarded the 1919 Nobel Prize for Medicine.

● **bore** ▶ In oceanography, a tidal flood wave with a steep front occurring in certain estuaries and travelling upstream at great speed, sometimes to a distance of several kilometres. It occurs when the spring flood tide brings sea water into an estuary more quickly than it can travel up the river, so that a ridge of water builds up.

● **Borelli, Giovanni Alfonso** ▶ (1608-79) Italian physicist and physiologist, who attempted to explain the workings of the body in purely mechanical terms (*De Motu Animalium*, 1680-81). A friend of ▷Galileo, Borelli made contributions to astronomy, including ideas concerning the attractive forces between planets, their orbits, and the path taken by comets through space.

● **Borg, Björn** ▶ (1956-) Swedish tennis player, the world's leading player in the late 1970s. In 1980 he won the men's singles at Wimbledon for the fifth consecutive year, having beaten Fred ▷Perry's record of three consecutive wins in 1979. He retired from world-class tennis in 1983, returned in 1991, but retired again in 1993.

● **Borgå** ▷*See* Porvoo.

● **Borges, Jorge Luis** ▶ (1899-1986) Argentinian writer and scholar. Educated in Europe, he joined the Spanish avantgarde Ultraist movement in 1920. In 1921 he returned to Argentina, where he founded three literary journals and published a book of poems in 1923. His best-known works are collections of intricate and paradoxical stories, especially *Fictions* (1944, 1966) and *The Aleph* (1949, 1970). His last book (with Maria Kodama) was *Atlas* (1986). He became director of the National Library (1955) after losing his sight.

● **Borghese** ▶ An Italian family that originated in Siena and rose to fame following its move to Rome in the 16th century and the election in 1605 of **Camillo Borghese** (1552-1621) as Pope Paul V. He advanced his family's fortunes, particularly those of his adopted nephew **Scipione Caffarelli** (1576-1633), a church politician and art patron, who sponsored ▷Bernini and built the Villa Borghese (now an art gallery) in Rome. In 1803 **Camillo Filippo Ludovico Borghese**

(1775-1832) married Napoleon's sister, Marie Pauline (1780-1825). The family split into two branches later in the 19th century.

● **Borgia, Cesare** ▶ (c. 1475-1507) Duke of the Romagna and captain general of the armies of the Church. The illegitimate son of Pope ▷Alexander VI, Borgia became Archbishop of Valencia and a cardinal following his father's election to the papacy (1492). He surrendered his cardinalship to marry the sister of the King of Navarre and to become captain general of the Church. He won the Romagna, with French help, in three campaigns (1499-1502), for which Machiavelli regarded him as the saviour of Italy. Borgia was forced to relinquish the Romagna after Alexander's death (1502) and was imprisoned. He escaped and died in the employ of the Navarrese king. His sister **Lucrezia Borgia**, unfairly notorious for immorality, was married three times by her father Alexander VI to further his political aims. Her third husband Alfonso (1486-1534) became Duke of Este and she presided over a distinguished court at Ferrara.

● **Borglum, Gutzon** ▶ (1867-1941) US sculptor, famous for his gigantic sculptured heads. Best known are those of US presidents carved on rocks of the ▷Mount Rushmore National Memorial, the head of Lincoln in the US Capitol Rotunda, and the 12 apostles in the Church of St John the Divine, New York.

● **Boris (I) of Bulgaria** ▶ (d. 907 AD) Khan of Bulgaria (852-89). Boris was converted to Orthodox Christianity in 865 and encouraged the spread of Christianity among the Bulgars. His reign gave birth to Slavonic-Bulgarian literature and civilization. In 889 he abdicated and entered a monastery.

● **Boris III** ▶ (1894-1943) King of Bulgaria (1918-1943). Boris ruled as a dictator from 1938 and supported the Axis Powers in World War II. He apparently died of a heart attack but may have been assassinated.

● **Borlaug, Norman** ▶ (1914-) US plant breeder, who developed new strains of wheat and rice for underdeveloped countries. Working in Mexico since 1944, he received the Nobel Peace Prize (1970) for his role in the "green revolution."

● **Bormann, Martin** ▶ (1900-45) German Nazi leader, who became Hitler's personal secretary in 1942. He was sentenced to death in absentia at Nuremberg. In 1998 DNA testing confirmed that a skeleton found in Berlin in 1973 was his. He is assumed to have committed suicide in May, 1945.

● **Born, Max** ▶ (1882-1970) British physicist, born in Germany. He shared the 1954 Nobel Prize with W. Bothe for his work in statistical mechanics. Born and ▷Heisenberg developed matrix mechanics, which ▷Schrödinger was able to show was equivalent to his own wave mechanics. Born was professor of natural philosophy at Edinburgh University from 1936 to 1953.

● **Borneo** ▶ An island SE of Peninsular Malaysia, in the Greater Sunda Islands, the third largest island in the world. During the 19th century Borneo was settled and virtually partitioned by the Dutch and British to protect their East India companies from piracy. It now consists politically of the Indonesian territory of ▷Kalimantan, the Malaysian states of ▷Sabah and ▷Sarawak, and the British-protected sultanate of ▷Brunei. It is mountainous with coastal swamps and dense jungle. The chief population groups are the coastal Malays and indigenous Dyaks. It possesses valuable resources of oil, coal, and gold. Area: 750 000 sq km (290 000 sq mi).

● **Bornholm** ▶ 55 02N 15 00E A Danish island in the Baltic Sea, SE of Sweden. Dairy farming is practised and industries include pottery, using locally worked clay, and watchmaking; tourism is important during summer. Area: 588 sq km (227 sq mi). Population (1995 est): 44 936. Chief town: Rønne.

● **Bornu** ▶ A former Muslim Negro kingdom in West Africa. It existed from the 11th century until the late 19th century, when it was divided between Britain, France, and Germany. Most of the area was incorporated into the protectorate of Northern Nigeria in 1900 and the modern Nigerian state of Bornu encompasses part of the former kingdom.

● **Borobudur** ▶ A huge Buddhist stupa (shrine) complex in central Java, built about 800 AD and abandoned, unfinished, about 1000. It

Borobudur ► The stupa complex in central Java.

has five square terraces of diminishing size, one on top of the other, on the vertical surfaces of which is carved a continuous relief depicting the Buddha's life and doctrine. On top, three circular terraces support 72 stupas around a crowning central stupa, all with a Buddha icon. Restored (1973–83) at a cost of £20 million, it was badly damaged by terrorists in 1985.

● **Borodin, Aleksandr Porfirevich** ► (1833–87) Russian composer, one of the ▷Five. A professor of chemistry and medicine, he had little formal training and lacked time to compose. Nevertheless, he produced two symphonies (1867 and 1876), the tone poem *In the Steppes of Central Asia* (1880), three string quartets, and the opera *Prince Igor* (completed by ▷Rimsky-Korsakov and Glazunov in 1890), which contains the famous *Polovtsian Dances*.

● **Borodino, Battle of** ► (7 Sept, 1812) A battle in the Napoleonic Wars in which the French under Napoleon defeated the Russians under Kutuzov 110 km (70 mi) W of Moscow. This narrow and bloody victory allowed the French to enter Moscow unopposed but failed to destroy the Russian army.

● **boron** ► (B) A nonmetallic element isolated (1808) by Sir Humphry Davy. It has two forms: an impure brownish amorphous powder and pure brown crystals. The main source, kernite ($Na_2B_4O_7.4H_2O$), is mined in California. Boron is used in semiconductors and in hardened steel, while Boron fibres are used in lightweight composite materials. The isotope boron-10 absorbs neutrons: boron carbide (B_4C) and boron alloys are used in the control rods and shielding of nuclear reactors. Other compounds include borax ($Na_2B_4O_7.10H_2O$), used in glass manufacture, and boric acid (H_3BO_3), used in ceramics and fire-proofing. At no 5; at wt 10.81; mp 2092°C; bp 4002°C.

● **borough** ► In England and Wales and some other countries, a town or urban area enjoying various legal privileges (usually including a degree of self-government) by special charter. Boroughs originated from the Anglo-Saxon *burhs*, towns specially designated as defensive settlements; during the middle ages they became identified as those towns incorporated by royal charter that sent representatives to Parliament. In England and Wales the Local Government Act (1888) designated many of the most populous boroughs as county boroughs, with full administrative independence from their surrounding counties. The boroughs and county boroughs were abolished for administrative purposes by the Local Government Act (1972), except in ▷London (outside the City), where boroughs remain the units of local government. A district council may now be granted the title borough (and the council chairman entitled ▷mayor) by royal charter but this is purely of ceremonial significance. During the 1990s county boroughs were reintroduced in Wales and many of the former English county boroughs were reinstated in the form of

▷unitary authorities. The Scottish equivalent of the borough is the burgh.

● **Borromeo, St Charles** ► (1538–84) Italian churchman, Cardinal and Archbishop of Milan. He was appointed to his offices in 1560 by his uncle, Pope Pius IV. He played a leading part in the third convocation of the Council of Trent (1562–63) and actively supported the evangelization of Switzerland. These activities and the capable reforms he carried out in his archdiocese made him an important Counter-Reformation figure. Feast day: 4 Nov.

● **Borromini, Francesco** ► (1599–1667) Italian baroque architect. Born in N Italy, he settled in Rome, where all his work was executed. With ▷Bernini, he brought the baroque style in Rome to its peak. His highly individual approach resulted in forms never before achieved. Although less successful than Bernini, in his main buildings, S Carlo (1641), S Ivo (1660), and the oratorio of S Filippo Neri (1650), he showed a virtuosity of decoration and a command of complex spatial effects that his rival never approached.

● **Borrow, George Henry** ► (1803–81) British writer. He spent most of his life wandering round rural England and on the Continent. These travels provided the material for his many books, such as *Lavengro* (1851) and *The Romany Rye* (1857), in which he gave a romantic account of gipsy life.

● **Borrowdale** ► A scenic valley in NW England, in Cumbria extending southwards from Derwentwater towards Scafell. Borrowdale gives its name to a series of volcanic rocks that cover the central Lake District.

● **Borstal system** ► An English penal system established by the Prevention of Crime Act (1908) for the rehabilitation of offenders aged between 15 and 21. They could be detained in an institution called a Borstal for up to two years. Following release, the offender remained under supervision for two years and could be recalled if he committed an offence. The name derives from the prison at Borstal near Rochester, Kent, where the system was introduced. Borstal sentences has been abolished by the Criminal Justice Act (1982): offenders under 21 are now detained in a young offender institution.

● **borzoi** ► A breed of large ▢dog originating in Russia, also called Russian wolfhound and used originally for hunting wolves and for hare coursing. The borzoi is a lightly built swift runner with a long silky coat, which is usually white with black to light-brown patches. Height: about 70 cm.

● **Bosanquet, Bernard** ► (1848–1923) British philosopher. His early neo-Hegelian philosophy saw the individuality of persons, institutions, and works of art as a combination of abstract general concepts (universals). His *Philosophical Theory of the State* (1899) presents a solution to the problem of communal will and individual liberty.

● **Bosch, Carl** ► (1874–1940) German chemist, who developed the Haber process for the conversion of atmospheric nitrogen into ammonia, so that it could be used industrially. This ▷Haber-Bosch process has been used to manufacture enormous quantities of nitrates for both explosives and fertilizers. He shared the 1931 Nobel Prize for Chemistry for his work on high-pressure reactions.

● **Bosch, Hieronymus** ► (Jerome van Aeken; c. 1450–c. 1516) Dutch painter. He was born in 's Hertogenbosch (hence his name), where from 1486 he belonged to the Roman Catholic Brotherhood of Our Lady. His allegories have been interpreted as forerunners of ▷surrealism or expressions of heretical beliefs but as his patrons, including Philip II of Spain, were devout Catholics, they were probably intended as sermons on the consequences of sin. The obscure symbolism and fantastic imagery of half-animal half-human creatures and devils was inspired by contemporary proverbs and writings. Among his major works are *The Haywain* (El Escorial) and *Garden of Earthly Delights* (Prado).

● **Bose, Sir Jagadis Chandra** ► (1858–1937) Indian plant physiologist and physicist. His research into plant behaviour showed how plants responded to external stimuli (such as injury) and revealed parallels between plant and animal tissues. He invented the crescograph, which measures plant growth, and founded the Bose Research Institute, Calcutta.

● **Bose, Subhas Chandra** ▶ (c. 1897–c. 1945) Indian nationalist leader. He joined Gandhi's movement of noncooperation with the British and became president of the ▷Indian National Congress in 1938. In 1939 he resigned because of disagreement with Gandhi. He left India in 1941 and in Singapore, with Japanese help, he organized the Indian National Army to free India from British rule (1943). He was said to have been killed in an air crash in 1945.

● **Bose-Einstein statistics** ▶ One of two statistical approaches to quantum mechanical problems (*see* statistical mechanics): it assumes that any number of identical particles may occupy the same energy level. The other statistical method is called ▷Fermi-Dirac statistics. Particles that obey Bose-Einstein statistics are called ▷bosons. Named after S. N. Bose (1894–1974) and A. ▷Einstein.

● **Bosnia-Hercegovina** ▶ A republic in SE Europe. It consists of a chiefly mountainous triangular-shaped area with karst topography in the SW.

Economy: always a poor region by European standards, Bosnia has suffered almost total economic disruption from the civil war of the early 1990s. It is primarily agricultural, with cereals, vegetables, fruit, and tobacco; sheep are also raised. There is some heavy industry, including mining and steel making.

History: part of ancient Illyria, the region was inhabited by Slavs from the 7th century AD onwards. Bosnia became a separate political entity in the 10th century but later came under the control of Hungary. It became an independent kingdom in the late 14th century. In 1463 it annexed Hercegovina but fell to the Turks, remaining under their control for four centuries. In 1908 it was annexed to Austria-Hungary; Serbian opposition to this led to the assassination of Archduke Francis Ferdinand at Sarajevo, precipitating World War I. After the war Bosnia was incorporated into the new kingdom of Serbs, Croats, and Slovenes, subsequently renamed ▷Yugoslavia. Following World War II it became a constituent republic of communist Yugoslavia. In 1992 Bosnians, the majority of whom are Muslims and Croats, voted for independence in a referendum; this was opposed by the Bosnian Serbs, leading to civil war. Although Bosnia's independence was recognized by most states in 1992, Serbian militias took control of the N of the country and besieged Sarajevo. The conflict involved the brutal "ethnic cleansing" of Muslims by Serbs (and later Croats) with the aim of establishing their own separate territories. In 1995 Croatia invaded W Bosnia and repulsed Serb forces; NATO also carried out air strikes against Serb positions. A US-brokered peace deal signed in Dec 1995 stated that Bosnia would remain a single state within its present borders but would henceforth consist of two entities, a Muslim–Croat Federation in the W and a Bosnian Serb Republic in the N and E. Following elections in 1996, the sitting president, Alija ▷Izetbegović, became chairman of a new joint presidency comprising a representative of each of the three communities. The chair passed to Bozidar Matic in 2001.

Bosnia-Hercegovina

Head of state	Chairman of the presidency Bozidar Matic
Official language	Serbo-Croat
Official currency	euro of 100 cents
Area	51 129 sq km (19 737 sq mi)
Population (2001 est)	3 922 000
Capital	Sarajevo

● **boson** ▶ A class of elementary particles with integral spin. Bosons always obey ▷Bose-Einstein statistics and include all the ▷mesons and the ▷photon. ▷*See* particle physics.

● **Bosporus** ▶ (Turkish name: Karadeniz Boğazi) A strait separating Europe and Asia and connecting the Black Sea with the Sea of Marmara. It has Istanbul at its S end and is spanned by a suspension bridge. Length: about 30 km (19 mi). Width: about 0.6–4 km (0.4–2.5 mi).

● **boss** ▶ In architecture, a small projection in a roof vault, covering the crossing of the supporting ribs. Although sometimes plain, medieval bosses were frequently carved into decorative shapes. ▷*See also* gothic art and architecture.

● **Bossuet, Jacques Bénigne** ▶ (1627–1704) French Roman Catholic bishop and preacher. He became famous for several funeral orations on prominent persons, such as that on ▷Henrietta Maria delivered in 1669. He became Bishop of Meaux in 1681, having first been tutor to the dauphin, and later attempted to bring about a compromise between Louis XIV and the pope on the issue of ▷Gallicanism. He wrote a number of devotional and apologetic works.

● **Boston** ▶ 42 20N 71 05W A city in the USA, the capital of Massachusetts on Massachusetts Bay. It is an important port and market for fish and a major financial centre. Its industries include publishing, food processing, and the manufacture of machinery. An architecturally exceptional city, its most notable buildings are the old State House (1748), Faneuil Hall (1762), and the State Capitol (1798). Boston is a major cultural and educational centre. It is the site of Boston University (1869), Northeastern University (1898), and Boston Latin School (established in 1635 and one of the country's first free secondary schools). Harvard Medical School is also situated here. Notable residents have included Nathaniel Hawthorne, Henry Thoreau, Ralph Emerson, and Longfellow.

History: founded in 1630 by Puritan Englishmen, it prospered as the main colony of the Massachusetts Bay Company. It became a centre of opposition to the British prior to the American Revolution (*see* Boston Tea Party). Boston flourished as the commercial, industrial, and financial centre of the New England states during the early 19th century. It was a leading force in the antislavery movement during the 1830s. Population (2000): 589 141.

● **Boston** ▶ 52 59N 0 01W A market town and small port in E England, in Lincolnshire on the River Witham. St Botolph's church (known as "the Stump") is a famous landmark. Industries include canning. Population (1991): 34 606.

● **Boston Tea Party** ▶ (1773) An expression of colonial hostility towards Britain before the ▷American Revolution. A group of American radicals objecting to the import of cheap tea, enforced by the Tea Act to rid the East India Company of its surplus stocks, threw a cargo of tea into Boston harbour. Britain retaliated with the ▷Intolerable Acts. ▷*See also* Stamp Act.

● **Boston terrier** ▶ A breed of □dog originating in the USA from crosses between bulldogs and terriers. It is compactly built with a short square muzzle and a short tail. The short smooth coat is brown to brownish-yellow with white markings. Height: about 38 cm.

● **Boswell, James** ▶ (1740–95) Scottish writer, the biographer of Samuel ▷Johnson. Son of an Edinburgh advocate, he came to London in 1760 and first met Johnson in 1763. He travelled widely on the Continent from 1764 to 1766, meeting other famous men, such as Voltaire and Rousseau. Although he practised law in Edinburgh from 1766 to 1788 he maintained a close relationship with Johnson. The biography, published in 1791, was widely acclaimed but in later years he suffered from severe depression and alcoholism.

● **Bosworth Field, Battle of** ▶ (22 August, 1485) The battle fought near Market Bosworth, Leicestershire, in which Henry Tudor defeated Richard III, thereby ending the Wars of the ▷Roses. Richard was killed in the battle and Henry became the first ▷Tudor monarch, as Henry VII.

● **botanic gardens** ▶ Collections of growing plants designed to display both familiar native plants and more unusual alien species, particularly ornamentals. Often the plants are grouped to demonstrate their evolutionary and geographical relationships or their similar ecological requirements. Some gardens concentrate on certain types of plants: an arboretum is one specializing in trees and shrubs. Botanic gardens originated in ancient China, as collections of fruit, vegetables, and medicinal plants, but it was not until the 16th and 17th centuries that they became popular in Europe, the first being established in Italy at Pisa (1543) and Padua (1545). Today the larger botanic gardens have extensive herbaria, where dried labelled specimens are kept for reference. Many have their own laboratories and libraries, providing facilities for research scientists, and often hold courses in horticultural techniques for trainee gardeners. Most gardens preserve and propagate rare species, with elaborate greenhouses and culture techniques for those with specialized needs. ▷*See also* Kew Gardens.

● **botany** ► The scientific study of plants. From ancient times plants have figured prominently in human cultures as man is dependent on them for food, shelter, drugs, and many other purposes. Scientific botany dates from the 4th century BC, with the studies of the ancient Greeks—notably ▷Theophrastus, who is said to have founded the science, and ▷Dioscorides Pedanius, who published one of the first herbals. Until the 17th century botany was almost entirely restricted to the description and properties of medicinal plants. The basic principles of modern plant classification were laid down by John ▷Ray at the end of the 17th century, and by the middle of the 18th century ▷Linnaeus had published his works on the naming and classification of plants, which established the principles of ▷taxonomy still used today for both plants and animals. The invention of the microscope in the 16th century enabled detailed studies of plant structure, culminating in ▷Schleiden's theory of the cellular nature of plants in the 1830s. The 18th century saw important advances in plant physiology with the discovery of ▷photosynthesis, the food-manufacturing process of green plants. During the 19th century the origin of plant species was elucidated in Charles ▷Darwin's theory of evolution and Gregor ▷Mendel—working with plants—established the mechanisms of inheritance. Botany in the 20th century has been revolutionized by advances in physiology, biochemistry, breeding techniques, and genetic engineering, which have greatly increased the economic importance of plants and enabled a scientific approach to the related disciplines of ▷horticulture, ▷agriculture, and forestry. ▷*See also* biological sciences.

● **Botany Bay** ► An inlet of the Tasman Sea, in SE Australia. It was the site of Capt Cook's first landing in Australia (1770). A convict settlement that Capt Arthur Phillip planned to establish here (1788) was moved to Port Jackson 9 km (5 mi) to the N. The bay is now surrounded by the suburbs of Sydney. Industries, located chiefly on the N shore, include chemicals, plastics, and fibreglass, with an oil refinery on the SE shore. Area: about 42 sq km (16 sq mi).

● **bot fly** ► A hairy beelike fly belonging to the families *Gasterophilidae* (horsebot flies), *Calliphoridae* (e.g. the deer bot fly), or *Oestridae* (e.g. the sheep bot fly). The larvae are parasitic in mammals, often living within nasal and sinus cavities or in the digestive tract to cause irritation, weakening, and vertigo. When mature the larvae pass out with the faeces. *Compare* warble fly.

● **Botha, Louis** ► (1862–1919) South African statesman; the first prime minister of the Union of South Africa (1910–19). He commanded the Transvaal's forces during the second ▷Boer War and became prime minister of the Transvaal in 1907. In World War I he suppressed a revolt of Afrikaner nationalists led by ▷de Wet and conquered German South West Africa.

● **Botha, Pieter Willem** ► (1916–) South African statesman; prime minister (1978–84) and president (1984–89). As defence minister (1966–78) he involved South Africa in the Angolan civil war (1975). Although a firm supporter of ▷apartheid, he presided over the new constitution of 1984, which allowed some non-Whites limited political power. He resigned after attempting to resist further reform. In 1998 he was prosecuted for refusing to appear before the post-apartheid Truth and Reconciliation Commission.

● **Botham, Ian Terence** ► (1955–) British cricketer. A brilliant all-rounder, he played for Somerset (1973–86), Worcestershire (1987–91), Durham (1991–93), Queensland (1987–88), and England (1977–93), captaining the side (1980–81). He held a record number of test wickets (1986–88) and scored over 3000 runs in Test matches. He retired in 1993.

● **Bothe, Walther Wilhelm Georg Franz** ► (1891–1957) German experimental physicist, who (with H. ▷Geiger) developed the coincidence method for particle counting. The use of this technique in cosmic radiation research brought him a share (with Max ▷Born) in the Nobel Prize for 1954. During World War II he built Germany's first cyclotron. He was responsible for discovering the particle later identified by James ▷Chadwick as the neutron.

● **Bothnia, Gulf of** ► A shallow section of the Baltic Sea, between

Sweden and Finland. It remains frozen for about five months of the year because of its low salinity. Its many small islands restrict navigation. Area: about 117 000 sq km (45 200 sq mi).

● **Bothwell, James Hepburn, 4th Earl of** ► (c. 1535–78) The third husband of Mary, Queen of Scots. He was almost certainly responsible for the murder of her second husband ▷Darnley in 1567, after which he allegedly abducted Mary and married her; they may already have been lovers. Following their defeat at Carberry Hill, Bothwell escaped to Denmark, where he died, insane, in captivity.

● **bo tree** ► An Indian tree, *Ficus religiosa*, up to 30 m high, also called the peepul or pipal. It has heart-shaped leaves with long narrow tips and globular fleshy purple fruits. Related to the fig, the bo tree is sacred to Buddhists, as it was the tree under which Buddha sat when he attained enlightenment. Family: *Moraceae* (mulberry family).

● **Botswana, Republic of** ► (former name until 1966: Bechuanaland) A country in the centre of S Africa, lying between the Rivers Zambezi and Molopo. It is largely an arid plateau, with the Kalahari Desert in the S and W and some hills in the E. The River Okavango in the N, with its marshy basin, is important for irrigation. The majority of the population, consisting mainly of the Bantu-speaking Tswana group, lives along the E border. The original inhabitants, the Bushmen, now comprise only a small minority.

Economy: formerly chiefly agricultural, with beef cattle predominating; traditional agriculture is still the most important occupation. Large quantities of minerals, including diamonds, nickel, copper, and coal, were discovered in the 1960s, and by the late 1990s diamonds provided over three-quarters of export revenue. These developments, together with foreign aid, have financed a policy of government-directed economic and structural development, and Botswana's economy is currently one of the fastest growing in Africa.

History: the area became the British Protectorate of Bechuanaland in 1885 and was annexed to the Cape Colony in 1895. It later became a British High Commission Territory, gaining internal self-government in 1965 and full independence in 1966 as the Republic of Botswana within the Commonwealth. Until 1980 it was under the democratic rule of Sir Seretse ▷Khama, who maintained a delicate balance in opposing the policies of neighbouring South Africa and Rhodesia, while being dependent on them for trade. He was succeeded by Quett Masire, who in 1998 retired in favour of Festus Mogae.

Republic of Botswana

Head of state	President Festus Mogae
Official language	English; the main African language is Tswana
Official currency	pula of 100 thebe
Area	575 000 sq km (222 000 sq mi)
Population (1997 est)	1 501 000
Capital	Gabarone

● **Botticelli, Sandro** ► (Alessandro di Mariano Filipepi; c. 1445–1510) Florentine ▷Renaissance painter, named after his brother's nickname, meaning "little barrel." He trained under Filippo ▷Lippi. His chief patrons were the Medici, for whom he produced illustrations for Dante's *Divine Comedy* and allegorical paintings, influenced by humanist writers, such as *Primavera*, *Birth of Venus* (both Uffizi), and *Mars and Venus* (National Gallery, London). They are notable for their graceful draughtsmanship. In 1481–82 he worked on frescoes for the Sistine Chapel, in the Vatican. Probably under the influence of the religious leader ▷Savonarola, his later works, e.g. *Mystic Nativity* (1501; National Gallery, London), became more religious and emotional.

● **bottlebrush** ► An evergreen Australian shrub or tree of the genus *Callistemon* (25 species). Growing to a height of about 6 m, it has stiff narrow leaves, 5 cm long. The flower heads consist mainly of bunches of fluffy red or yellow stamens, resembling bottle brushes. The fruits are woody. Bottlebrushes may be grown as ornamental hedges and shrubs. Family: *Myrtaceae*.

● **bottlenose** ► A ▷dolphin, *Tursiops truncatus*, with a short beak.

Grey-blue and growing to 4 m, bottlenose dolphins are a shallow-water species and have become popular in dolphinariums. They have been the subject of research into the social behaviour and language of whales. □mammal.

● **bottle-nosed whale** ▷*See* beaked whale.

● **Bottrop** ▸ 51 31N 6 55E A city in NW Germany, in North Rhine-Westphalia in the ▷Ruhr. Its main industries are coalmining and the manufacture of by-products. Population (1996 est): 120 642.

● **botulism** ▸ A rare and serious form of ▷food poisoning from foods containing the toxin produced by the bacterium *Clostridium botulinum*. The toxin can affect the cardiac and respiratory centres of the brain and may result in death by heart or lung failure. The bacterium thrives in improperly preserved foods, such as tinned raw meats. The toxin is invariably destroyed in cooking.

● **Botvinnik, Mikhail Moiseivich** ▸ (1911–95) Russian chess player, who was world champion (1948–57, 1958–60, 1961–63), losing the title to ▷Petrosian (1963).

● **Bouaké** ▸ 7 42N 5 00W A city in central Côte d'Ivoire. It is an important trade centre, linked by rail and road to Abidjan, with a trade in coffee, cocoa, and rice. Population (1995 est): 330 000.

● **Boucher, François** ▸ (1703–70) French ▷rococo painter, born in Paris, the son of a lacemaker. He studied in Italy (1727–31) but was chiefly influenced by ▷Watteau, many of whose drawings he engraved. He worked for Louis XV, and Madame de Pompadour, whom he painted (National Gallery of Scotland), and to whom he gave art lessons. He became director of both the Gobelins tapestry factory (1755), for which he produced designs, and of the French Academy (1765). His paintings are mainly mythological and pastoral scenes and nudes.

● **Boucher de Perthes, Jacques** ▸ (1788–1868) French antiquary. In the Somme valley he discovered stone implements together with extinct animal remains; these made him challenge contemporary theories about human origins. His *De la création* (1838–41) and *Antiquités celtiques et antédiluviennes* (1847) argue for the human race's great antiquity.

● **Boudicca** ▷*See* Boadicea.

● **Boudin, Eugène** ▸ (1824–98) French painter and forerunner of ▷impressionism, born in Honfleur. He painted his coastal scenes in the open air instead of the studio and encouraged ▷Monet in this practice.

● **Bougainville** ▸ A volcanic forested island in the SW Pacific Ocean, the largest in the ▷Solomon Islands and a part of Papua New Guinea. Copra, cocoa, timber, and tortoise shell are exported. It has one of the world's largest open-cast copper mines. Secessionist rebels took over the island and declared independence in 1990; it was reoccupied by government troops in 1992 and a peace treaty was signed in 1998. Area: about 10 360 sq km (4000 sq mi). Population (1990 est): 159 500. Chief town: Kieta.

● **Bougainville, Louis Antoine de** ▸ (1729–1811) French navigator. After service in the Seven Years' War in Canada he joined the navy. Between 1766 and 1769 he circumnavigated the world and wrote an account of the journey in *A Voyage round the World* (1771). He was later a successful commander in the American Revolution. The island Bougainville and the plant genus *Bougainvillea* are named after him.

● **Bougainvillea** ▸ A genus of tropical South American shrubs (18 species) climbing by means of hooked thorns. The shrubs bear numerous showy "flowers," usually reddish-purple, for most of the year. The coloured parts are actually large bracts, which surround the small inconspicuous flowers. *Bougainvillea* is grown as an ornamental throughout the tropics and subtropics. Family: *Nyctaginaceae*.

● **Boulanger, Nadia (Juliette)** ▸ (1887–1979) French composer, teacher, and conductor. Lennox ▷Berkeley and Aaron ▷Copland were among her pupils. Her works include the cantata *La Sirène* (1908; awarded the Prix de Rome), the opera *La Ville morte* (1911), choral works, and instrumental pieces.

● **Boulder** ▷*See* Kalgoorlie.

● **boulder clay** ▷*See* till.

● **boules** ▸ A French game similar to ▷bowls, often played on rough ground. The players aim small metal bowls at a target ball (*cochonnet*).

● **Boulez, Pierre** ▸ (1925–) French composer and conductor. A pupil of Messiaen, Boulez' work reflects the influence of Schoenberg, Webern, and Cage. He has used ▷serialism in such works as *Structures I and II* (two pianos; 1951–52 and 1956–61) and has set poems by René Char in *Le Marteau sans maître* (contralto and 6 instruments; 1953–55) as well as poems by Mallarmé in *Pli selon pli* (soprano and orchestra; 1957–60). His more recent works include *Le Visage nuptial* (1989) and *Dérive 2* (1993).

● **Boulle, André Charles** ▸ (or Buhl; 1642–1732) French cabinet-maker in the service of Louis XIV. He gave his name to the technique of boullework (or buhlwork), a style of marquetry using brass, tortoiseshell, mother of pearl, etc., inlaid on ebony.

● **Boulogne-sur-Mer** ▸ 50 43N 1 37E A port and resort in N France, in the Pas-de-Calais department on the English Channel. It was severely damaged in World War II. It is the country's main fishing port and has a ferry service to England. Industries include boatbuilding, textiles, and steel. Population (1990): 44 244.

● **Boult, Sir Adrian (Cedric)** ▸ (1889–1983) British conductor. A pupil of Arthur Nikisch (1855–1922), he was conductor of the BBC Symphony Orchestra (1930–49) and the London Philharmonic Orchestra (1949–57). Knighted in 1937, he was associated with the works of Elgar, Holst, and Vaughan Williams.

François Boucher A typical mythological and erotic subject for this master of the rococo style, *La Toilette de Venus* (1749; Louvre).

● **Boulter, Hugh** ▶ (1672–1742) English churchman; Anglican Archbishop of Armagh (1724–42). Lord Justice as well as head of the Church of Ireland, he intensified the penal laws against Roman Catholics (1728).

● **Boulton, Matthew** ▷*See* Watt, James.

● **Boumédienne, Houari** ▶ (Mohammed Boukharouba; 1925–78) Algerian statesman; president (1965–78). In 1960 he became chief of staff of the nationalist forces fighting the French. After independence in 1962 he became minister of defence and then vice president under ▷Ben Bella. In 1965 he overthrew Ben Bella to become president.

● **Bounty, HMS** ▷*See* Bligh, William; Christian, Fletcher.

● **Bourbaki, Nicolas** ▶ A pseudonym for a group of French mathematicians who, since 1939, have been producing, from a few basic premisses, a rigorous development of mathematics, often at variance with conventional mathematics.

● **bourbon** ▶ (whiskey) ▷*See* whisky.

● **Bourbons** ▶ A European ruling dynasty that originated in Bourbonnais (now Allier, central France). It acquired ducal status in 1272, when Agnès Bourbon married the sixth son of Louis IX. The first Bourbon king of France was ▷Henry IV (reigned 1589–1610) after whom the house continued to rule until the ▷French Revolution (1792). The Bourbons were restored after the defeat of Napoleon (1814), but were again expelled (1830) in favour of a cadet branch, which ruled until the ▷Revolutions of 1848 (*see* Louis Philippe). The present pretender to the French throne is Henry, Count of Clermont (1933–).

The Bourbon Louis XIV's grandson became (1700) ▷Philip V of Spain, where the Bourbons ruled almost continuously until the abdication of ▷Alfonso XIII in 1931. His grandson ▷Juan Carlos was restored to the Spanish throne in 1975. In Naples and Sicily Bourbons ruled between 1734 and 1860.

● **Bourdelle, Émile** ▶ (1861–1929) French sculptor. Influenced by his teacher ▷Rodin, Bourdelle initially relied on vigorous surface carving but after 1910 his work, inspired by classical Greek sculpture, became more popular.

● **Bourdon gauge** ▶ A pressure gauge consisting of a C-shaped closed tube that tends to straighten as the pressure of fluid inside it rises; this movement is transferred to a pointer or a digital display. Invented by E. Bourdon (1808–84).

● **Bourgeois, Léon** ▶ (1851–1925) French statesman; prime minister (1895–96). He was the chief theorist of solidarism, the concept that an individual's rights in society must be balanced by his responsibility to it. Prominent in the League of Nations, he won the Nobel Peace Prize in 1920.

● **bourgeoisie** ▶ Originally, the urban merchants who developed trade at the end of the middle ages and who led the struggle against the feudal aristocracy for the rights of citizenship. The meaning was later extended to include the whole middle class. In the 19th century, ▷Marx used the concept within his theory of class struggle to describe the propertied entrepreneurs who created industrial capitalism and liberal democracy; conflict between the bourgeoisie and the ▷proletariat would ultimately lead to revolution. ▷*See* Marxism.

● **Bourges** ▶ (Latin name: Avaricum) 47 05N 2 23E A city in central France, the capital of Cher department. An important town of Aquitaine, it became the capital of Berry (12th century) and the French centre of power following the battle of Agincourt (1415). It has a gothic cathedral. Industries include aircraft, textiles, and armaments. Population (1990): 75 609.

● **Bourguiba, Habib** ▶ (1903–2000) Tunisian statesman; president (1957–87). A leading figure in the struggle for independence, he formed the Neo-Destour Party in 1934. He spent ten years between 1934 and 1955 in French prisons. After independence in 1956 he became president and was re-elected three times before becoming life president in 1975. He was deposed in a coup and thereafter remained under house arrest.

● **Bourke-White, Margaret** ▶ (Margaret White; 1906–71) US photographer. During the 1930s she recorded the effects of the Great Depression for *Life* magazine and travelled to the Soviet Union. An official Army Air Force photographer in World War II, she later made photographic expeditions to Korea, India (where she photographed Gandhi), and South Africa.

● **Bourmont, Louis Auguste Victor de Ghaisnes, Comte de** ▶ (1773–1846) French marshal, who served Napoleon but deserted him for the allies shortly before Waterloo. In 1829 he became minister of war but went into exile after the July Revolution (1830).

● **Bournemouth** ▶ 1. 50 43N 1 54W A resort in S England, in Bournemouth unitary authority, Dorset, on Poole Bay. It has 10 km (6 mi) of sands, famous gardens, and a famous symphony orchestra. Apart from tourism, the main economic activities are conferencing and financial services. Population (1991): 155 488. 2. A unitary authority in S England, in E Dorset. Area: 46 sq km (17 sq mi). Population (1999) 160 700.

● **Bournville** ▶ A suburb of Birmingham, in England. It was founded as a model factory (1879) and village (1894) by George Cadbury and was a forerunner of the garden cities.

● **Boutros Ghali, Boutros** ▶ (1922–) Egyptian politician and lawyer; secretary general of the United Nations (1992–96). He was previously the Egyptian minister of state for foreign affairs (1977–91) and deputy prime minister (1991–92). Owing to disagreements over UN policy and funding, the USA vetoed his reappointment for a second term.

● **Bouts, Dierick** ▶ (c. 1400–75) Netherlandish painter, born in Haarlem, who lived and worked in Louvain. His paintings, strongly influenced by van der ▷Weyden, are notable for their treatment of landscape. *The Last Supper* (S Pierre, Louvain) and *The Justice of Emperor Otto* (Brussels) are his major works.

● **Bouvet** ▶ 54 26S 3 24E An uninhabited Norwegian island in the S Atlantic Ocean. Area: 48 sq km (19 sq mi).

● **Bouvines, Battle of** ▶ (27 July, 1214) The battle in which ▷Philip II Augustus of France defeated the Holy Roman Emperor ▷Otto IV. The failure of the planned diversionary attack by King John of England facilitated Philip's victory, which increased the baronial opposition to John in England (*see* Barons' Wars).

● **Boveri, Theodor Heinrich** ▶ (1862–1915) German cell biologist, noted for his studies of chromosomes. Boveri showed that the egg nucleus and the sperm nucleus both contribute hereditary material during the formation of a new cell (zygote) and that irregular distribution of chromosomes leads to abnormal development. These findings led ▷Sutton to propose his chromosome theory of inheritance in 1903.

● **Bovet, Daniel** ▶ (1907–92) Swiss pharmacologist, who discovered pyrilamine, the first of the allergy-relieving antihistamine drugs (1944). He also made various synthetic substitutes for the muscle-relaxing drug curare (1947). He received the Nobel Prize for Physiology in 1957.

● **Bovidae** ▶ A family of hoofed ▷ruminant mammals (about 128 species), comprising antelopes, cattle, sheep, and goats. Most live in herds and graze on the plains, although some inhabit mountainous regions. Several species have been domesticated by man for meat, milk, hides, and wool. Order: ▷*Artiodactyla*.

● **bovine spongiform encephalopathy** ▷*See* BSE.

● **bow** ▶ 1. ▷*See* archery. 2. (in music) A long stick between the ends of which strands of horsehair are attached, used for sounding the strings of such musical instruments as the violin and cello. Early bows were curved like an archer's bow, to keep the horsehair taut. However, modern bows are much straighter and use an adjustable screw frog for this purpose. the horsehair is rubbed with ▷rosin to make it stick to the instrument's strings, enabling a better sound to be produced.

● **Bow, Clara** ▶ (1905–65) US film actress. She personified the vivacious "flapper" of the 1920s in such films as *Mantrap* (1926) and *It* (1927), after which she became known as the "It" girl. She retired after being unsuccessful in sound films and spent much of her later life in mental hospitals.

● **Bowdler, Thomas** ► (1754–1825) British doctor and editor. His *Family Shakespeare* (1818) expurgated all words, expressions (and even plots) "which cannot with propriety be read aloud in a family." He also "bowdlerized" Gibbon's *History of the Decline and Fall of the Roman Empire* (1826).

● **Bowen, Elizabeth** ► (1899–1973) British novelist. Born in Dublin, daughter of an Anglo-Irish landowner, she was brought to England as a child. Her novels, in which themes of loneliness and personal relationships are delicately explored, include *The Death of the Heart* (1938) and *The Heat of the Day* (1949).

● **Bowen, Norman Levi** ► (1887–1956) Canadian experimental petrologist, who was professor at Queens University, Kingston (1919–21), and Chicago University (1937–47) and worked at the Geophysical Laboratory, Washington. His important work on the role of silicates in igneous rocks is summarized in *The Evolution of Igneous Rocks* (1928).

● **Bower, Frederick Orpen** ► (1855–1948) British botanist, who elucidated the evolution of primitive land plants. Many years studying liverworts, mosses, and ferns led him to conclude that they had evolved from algal ancestors.

● **bowerbird** ► A songbird belonging to a family (*Ptilonorhynchidae*; 18 species) found in Australasian forests. 22-35 cm long, it is closely related to the bird of paradise but has a duller plumage, often grey or black. Male bowerbirds court females by building typically dome-shaped bowers with twigs, moss, and stones, often decorating them with feathers, flowers, and shells.

● **bowfin** ► A ▷bony fish, *Amia calva*, also called grundle or mudfish, found in fresh waters of E North America. It has a mottled green body, up to 60 cm long, a long dorsal fin, and feeds on fish and invertebrates. Family: *Amiidae*; order: *Amiiformes*.

● **Bowie, David** ► (David Jones; 1947–) British pop singer and songwriter. Both his musical style and his theatrical public image have undergone several changes during the course of his career. His albums include *Ziggy Stardust* (1972), *Heroes* (1977), *Let's Dance* (1983), and *Outside* (1997). He has also acted in films, notably *The Man Who Fell to Earth* (1976), and starred on stage in *The Elephant Man* (1979).

● **Bowie, James** ► (1796–1836) US frontiersman. Inventor of the heavy-bladed Bowie knife, he was a commander in the Texas Revolution and died at the ▷Alamo.

● **bowling** ► (or tenpin bowling) A game in which two players or teams compete by attempting to knock down standing pins with rolling balls. The ten pins, 38.1 cm (15 in) high and each weighing about 1.5 kg (3.5 lb), are placed in a triangle 18.29 m (20 yd) distant at the end of a wooden lane. The balls, which have a thumb hole and two finger holes, have a maximum circumference of 68.5 cm (27 in) and a maximum weight of 7.26 kg (16 lb). Each player has two tries to knock the pins down, points being awarded accordingly. The pins are then reset for the next frame. Ten frames comprise a game.

● **bowls** ► A game in which biased bowls ("woods") are rolled towards a smaller one (the "jack"). **Flat green bowls** is played on a level grass surface 40–44 yd (36.6–40.2 m) square (for championship greens). Matches are usually played between two sides of four, each player using two bowls; a contest consists of three to six simultaneous matches. The jack is rolled onto the green by the first player and is followed by the other bowls in turn, the object being to position them as near the jack as possible. Playing all the bowls constitutes one "end." A score is agreed and the bowls are then delivered in the other direction for the next end. Matches between fours are played to 21 ends. **Crown green bowls** is played, mainly in N England, on a green 30–60 yd (27.4–54.9 m) square and sloping up to a central area raised 6–12 in (15–30 cm). Matches are usually singles, each player using two bowls; they last until one player reaches a score of 21. Bowls are also played indoors. ▷*See also* boules.

● **Bow porcelain** ► A mid-18th-century English soft-paste ▷porcelain made at or near Bow (London). The makers were two London merchants using a patent of Thomas Frye, first registered in 1744.

The factory closed about 1776. Wares included portrait and fictional figures, copies of Chinese porcelains (particularly blue and white), and ▷Meissen derivatives.

● **Bow Street Runners** ▷*See* Fielding, Henry; police.

● **box** ► A small evergreen tree, *Buxus sempervirens*, up to 9 m high, native to S Europe, Africa, and S England. The leaves are small and glossy and the flowers and seedpods inconspicuous. Being slow growing, box is widely grown as hedges for topiary or screening. The hard wood is used for decorative inlay work and engravings. Family: *Buxaceae*.

● **box elder** ► A ▷maple tree, *Acer negundo*, up to 20 m high, native to North America but widely planted in Europe as a street ornamental. Also called ash-leafed maple, it has compound pale-green leaves with five toothed leaflets.

● **boxer** ► A breed of working dog originating in Germany. It has a powerful frame with long straight legs and a broad muzzle. The short glossy coat is fawn to yellowish-brown or brindle, sometimes with white markings, and the mask is black. Height: 56–61 cm (dogs); 53–58 cm (bitches).

● **Boxer Rising** ► (1900) A rebellion in China so called because the rebels belonged to a secret society named the Fists of Righteous Harmony. They opposed the Western presence in China and engaged in violence against foreign missionaries and Chinese Christians. Wearing yellow sashes and believing themselves invulnerable to foreign weapons, they marched on Beijing, killing and pillaging as they went. The rebellion was suppressed by an international force of troops.

● **boxing** ► Fist-fighting between men wearing gloves in a roped-off ring. Organized boxing in modern times began in 18th-century England, where it became an aristocratic pastime. The basis of modern boxing rules are the **Queensberry Rules**, drawn up under the patronage of the Marquess of Queensberry (1844–1900), published in 1867, and first used in 1892. They established the use of gloves as opposed to fighting with bare fists, which was the custom in the prize fights of the time. In professional boxing the ring is 14 × 20 ft (4 × 6 m) square. The weight limits for professional boxers are: flyweight, 112 lb (50.8 kg); bantamweight, 118 lb (53.5 kg); featherweight, 126 lb (57.2 kg); lightweight, 135 lb (61.2 kg); light welterweight, 140 lb (63.5 kg); welterweight, 147 lb (66.7 kg); light middleweight, 154 lb (69.8 kg); middleweight, 160 lb (72.6 kg); light heavyweight, 175 lb (79.4 kg); heavyweight, unlimited. A bout consists of up to 15 3-minute rounds, separated by 1-minute intervals, and is presided over by a referee. A boxer is assisted by two or four seconds. A fight may be decided on points (marks awarded by the referee or judges after each round), by disqualification, or by knockout (inability to rise within ten seconds). Concern has been expressed regarding the danger to health of this sport. World titles are currently offered by the World Boxing Council, the World Boxing Association, the International Boxing Federation, and the World Boxing Organization.

● **box turtle** ► A terrestrial turtle belonging to the North American genus *Terrapene* (6 species). Up to 18 cm long, box turtles have a high-domed rounded carapace patterned with brown and yellow and a hinged plastron, which allows tight closure of the shell, forming a protective box. They feed on worms, insects, and berries. Family: *Emydidae*.

● **Boyacá, Battle of** ► (7 August, 1819) The victory, after a heroic crossing of the Andes, of Simón ▷Bolívar's army over a Spanish force. It assured the liberation of Venezuela and Colombia.

● **boyar** ► A member of the highest rank of the feudal Russian aristocracy. As the leaders of the retinues of the princes, boyars wielded considerable power: they received extensive grants of land and, as members of the Boyars' Duma (council), were the major legislators of medieval Russia. ▷Ivan (IV) the Terrible severely restricted their powers during the 16th century and the Boyars' Duma was finally abolished by ▷Peter (I) the Great in 1711 in his extensive reforms of government and administration.

● **Boyce, William** ► (c. 1710–79) British composer. Boyce was composer to the Chapel Royal, director of the Three Choirs Festival, and

Master of the King's Music. He wrote choral anthems, sonatas, overtures, songs, and symphonies; he also collected and edited *Cathedral Music* (1760–78).

● **Boycott, Charles Cunningham** ▶ (1832–97) British estate manager in Ireland. Boycott clashed with the ▷Land League over its request for rent reductions and as a result the local community refused to associate with, or "boycotted," him.

● **Boycott, Geoffrey** ▶ (1940–) British cricketer who played for Yorkshire (1962–86; captain 1970–78) and England (1964–74, 1977–81). An outstanding opening batsman, he made 150 centuries in first-class cricket.

● **Boyd-Orr, John, 1st Baron Boyd-Orr of Brechin Mearns** ▶ (1880–1971) Scottish scientist and expert on nutrition. In the 1930s he identified nutritional problems among the British population. First director general of the United Nations Food and Agriculture Organization (1945–48), he was awarded the Nobel Peace Prize (1949).

● **Boyer, Charles** ▶ (1899–1978) French film actor. He went to Hollywood in 1929 and specialized in the roles of romantic lovers in such films as *Mayerling* (1937) and *Love Affair* (1939).

● **Boyle, Robert** ▶ (1627–91) Irish physicist and chemist. Boyle showed that air possesses weight, it is necessary for sound propagation, and its pressure affects the boiling point of water. His chemical work, summarized in *The Skeptical Chymist* (1661), distinguished between elements, compounds, and mixtures and dismissed the Aristotelian concept of the four elements. His work on gases, with Robert ▷Hooke, led to the law that bears his name. Boyle published his law in 1663, but in France it is named after Edmé Marriotte (1620–84), who did not publish it until 1676.

● **Boyle's law** ▶ At constant temperature, the pressure of unit mass of a gas is inversely proportional to its volume. This law is only approximately true for real gases. A gas that obeys Boyle's law exactly is called an ▷ideal gas. Named after Robert ▷Boyle.

● **Boyne, Battle of the** ▶ (1 July, 1690) The victory of William III of England over the former King James II in Ireland. The battle was fought at the River Boyne, N of Dublin, where James hoped to halt the Williamites' advance southwards. It was not an overwhelming victory, but the spectacle of two kings fighting in Ireland for an English throne ensured its fame. The battles of the Boyne and of ▷Aughrim are still celebrated by ▷Orange Order lodges with provocative marches on the latter's anniversary, 12 July.

● **Boyoma Falls** ▶ (former name: Stanley Falls) A series of seven cataracts in the NE central Democratic Republic of Congo, on the River Lualuba, where it becomes the Congo River, close to Kisangani.

● **Boys' Brigade** ▶ An organization founded in Glasgow in 1883 by Sir William Alexander Smith to promote Christian values among boys aged 6 to 18. With about 3000 companies attached to local churches, the Brigade's activities range from first aid to the Duke of Edinburgh's Award Scheme. The Brigade's motto is "Sure and Steadfast". There are also branches in the USA and the Commonwealth.

● **Boy Scouts** ▷*See* Scout Association.

● **Boz** ▷*See* Dickens, Charles.

● **Bo Zhu Yi** ▶ (or Po Chü-i; 772–846) Chinese poet and imperial official, he became a governor in the provinces and eventually president of the imperial board of war (841). His many poems and ballads deal with the social problems of his age. Their lasting popularity rests on their lucid language, which, according to tradition, he achieved by reading his work to a peasant woman and deleting anything she did not understand.

● **Brabant** ▶ 1. A former duchy in the Low Countries, between the Rivers Meuse and Scheldt. On Belgian independence (1830) it was divided, forming the Belgian provinces of Antwerp and Brabant and the Dutch province of ▷North Brabant. 2. A former province in central Belgium. The region is densely populated with large industrial areas, including Brussels. Agriculture is also highly developed. In 1995 it was divided into two provinces, **Flemish Brabant**, with its capital at Leuven, and **Walloon Brabant**, with its capital at Wavre.

● **Brabham, Jack** ▶ (John Arthur B.; 1926–) Australian motor-racing driver, who won 14 Grand Prix races between 1955 and 1970 and was world champion in 1959, 1960, and 1966.

● **Bracegirdle, Anne** ▶ (c. 1673–1748) English actress. She was trained by Thomas ▷Betterton and achieved her greatest successes in the plays of Congreve, whose mistress she was for some years. She retired in 1707.

● **Brachiopoda** ▶ A phylum of primitive marine invertebrate animals (about 250 species) called lamp shells because of their resemblance to ancient Roman oil lamps. The body is protected by two shell valves, usually attached to the sea bed by a fleshy stalk (peduncle). Ciliated tentacles filter food particles from the water into the mouth. Eggs and sperm are discharged into the sea and produce free-swimming ciliated larvae.

● **bracken** ▶ (or brake) A ▷fern, *Pteridium aquilinum*, that is abundant almost throughout the world. Its black underground rhizome creeps extensively, producing aerial fronds, up to 5 m high, with stout erect stalks bearing triangular blades made up of branches of paired leaflets. Spore capsules occur in brownish clusters (sori) around the margins on the underside of the leaflets. Bracken is sometimes considered a pest by farmers; the roots have been used in tanning and the fronds in thatching and as fodder. Family: *Dennstaedtiaceae*.

● **bracket fungus** ▶ A fungus that forms a fruiting body resembling a shelf or bracket, usually on trees or timber. The spores are produced in fine tubes that open at pores on the surface. A common species is *Coriolus versicolor*, producing semicircular brackets, 3–5 cm across, which are marked with concentric coloured zones of brown, yellow, grey, or green. Family: *Polyporaceae*; phylum: ▷*Basidiomycota*.

● **Bracknell** ▶ 51 26N 0 46W A town in SE England, in Bracknell Forest unitary authority, Berkshire. A former new town (designated in 1949), it is now a location for high-tech electronic industries and services. The Meteorological Office has its headquarters here. Population (1991): 60 895.

● **Bracknell Forest** ▶ A unitary authority in SE England, in SE Berkshire. Area: 109 sq km (42 sq mi). Population (1999 est): 110 000.

● **bract** ▶ A modified leaf, often small and scalelike, found at the base of a flower or flower cluster. Occasionally bracts are large and coloured, resembling petals, as in the poinsettias. Smaller bracts (bracteoles) may be found on the flower stalk.

● **Bracton, Henry de** ▶ (or Bratton; d. 1268) English jurist. He was a justice of assize in SW England from 1248 until his death and a judge in the king's court until 1257. He is best known for his treatise, *De legibus et consuetudinibus Angliae*, which is the most comprehensive work on English medieval law.

● **Bradbury, Sir Malcolm Stanley** ▶ (1932–2000) British novelist, academic, and critic, who established his reputation with *The History Man* (1975). His other works include the comic novels *Eating People is Wrong* (1959), *Rates of Exchange* (1983), and *To the Hermitage* (2000) and the critical work *The Modern British Novel* (1993). He also wrote numerous adaptations for television. He was knighted in 2000.

● **Bradbury, Ray** ▶ (1920–) US science-fiction writer. Many of his works of fantasy and science fiction deal essentially with the themes of conventional fiction, and his literary style has been much admired. His novels include *The Illustrated Man* (1951), *Fahrenheit 451* (1953), *Death is a Lonely Business* (1986), and *A Graveyard for Lunatics* (1990).

● **Bradford** ▶ 1. 53 48N 1 45W A city in N England, in Bradford unitary authority, West Yorkshire. Situated on the edge of the Pennine moors, it is the foremost wool textile town in the UK and a world centre for the raw-wool market. Besides woollens and worsteds, many other fabrics are manufactured and engineering and microelectronics are important. Financial services are of growing importance, as is tourism. Bradford has a 15th-century cathedral and a university (1966). Population (1991): 289 376. 2. A unitary authority in N England, in West Yorkshire. Area: 370 sq km (143 sq mi). Population (1999 est): 457 344.

● **Bradford, William** ▶ (1663–1752) British printer, who emigrated to Pennsylvania in 1682. In 1725 he founded the *New York Gazette*, the first New York newspaper.

● **Bradlaugh, Charles** ▶ (1833–91) British radical reformer. An atheist, Bradlaugh pressed for greater freedom for the individual and in 1877 he was unsuccessfully prosecuted with Annie ▷Besant for republishing *Fruits of Philosophy*, which advocated birth control. He became an MP in 1880 but refused to take the parliamentary oath and was not permitted to take his seat until 1886.

● **Bradley, Andrew Cecil** ▶ (1851–1935) British literary critic. Educated at Oxford, he held professorships at the Universities of Liverpool (1882–89), Glasgow (1889–1900), and Oxford (1901–06). His *Shakespearean Tragedy* (1904) has had a lasting influence on Shakespeare criticism.

● **Bradley, Francis Herbert** ▶ (1846–1924) British philosopher. He lived as a semi-invalid, holding a sinecural fellowship at Oxford. Indebted to ▷Hegel, his idealist metaphysics are often brilliant in detail and grandiose in conception, but unwieldy in overall effect. In his greatest work, *Appearance and Reality* (1893), he argues against the acceptance of any general categories as absolutely real. Truth is relative and reality is unknowable and transcendent.

● **Bradley, Omar Nelson** ▶ (1893–1981) US general. In World War II, he commanded in North Africa and Sicily (1945) and the First US Army in the invasion of France (1944). In 1948 he became army chief of staff and was then the first chairman of the joint chiefs of staff (1949–53).

● **Bradman, Sir Donald George** ▶ (1908–2001) Australian cricketer, who played for New South Wales, South Australia, and Australia (1928–48) and was the most outstanding batsman of his or any subsequent era. He scored 117 centuries in 338 first-class innings and in Test matches averaged 99.94 runs. His best score was 452 not out (1929–30). As Australian captain (1936–48) he never lost a series and on retirement (1949) he became an administrator of the game.

Braemar ▶ Throwing the hammer at the most prestigious of the Highland Games.

● **Braemar** ▶ 57 01N 2 34W A village in NE Scotland, in Aberdeenshire on Clunie Water (a tributary of the River Dee). It is a resort and the scene of the annual Highland Games.

● **Braga** ▶ 41 32N 8 26W A city in N Portugal. It has a cathedral (12th–17th centuries) and is the seat of the primate of Portugal. A nearby holy sanctuary is visited by many pilgrims. Industries include jewellery and cutlery. Population (1991): 90 535.

● **Bragança** ▶ (or Braganza) The ruling dynasty of Portugal from 1640 to 1910 and of Brazil from 1822 to 1889. The family was descended from Alfonso, illegitimate son of ▷John I and 1st Duke of Bragança. The first Bragança king was ▷John (IV) the Fortunate (1640–56) and the last was Manuel II (1889–1932; reigned 1908–10), after whose deposition Portugal became a republic. When Brazil became independent (1822), it was ruled by two members of the family, ▷Pedro I (1822–31) and ▷Pedro II (1831–89), before becoming a republic (1889).

● **Bragg, Sir William Henry** ▶ (1862–1942) British physicist, who worked in Australia from 1886 to 1908. His early research, described in *Studies in Radioactivity* (1912), concerned the passage of alpha and beta particle and gamma rays through matter. He invented the Bragg diffractometer for measurement of X-ray wavelengths (1912) and with his son **Sir (William) Lawrence Bragg** (1890–1971) discovered the law of X-ray diffraction that bears their name. Together they wrote *X-rays and Crystal Structure* (1915) and were jointly awarded the Nobel Prize for 1915.

● **Bragg's law** ▶ A law stating that, if two parallel X-rays of wavelength λ are reflected by adjacent planes, distance d apart, in a crystal lattice and the rays then constructively interfere, then $2d\sin\theta = n\lambda$, where n is an integer and θ the angle between the X-rays and the planes. θ is called the Bragg angle. If n is half-integral, then destructive ▷interference is observed. Named after Sir William and Sir Lawrence ▷Bragg.

● **Brahe, Tycho** ▶ (1546–1601) Danish astronomer, who made accurate astronomical instruments and used them to make observations enabling him to revise the existing, often inaccurate, astronomical tables. He first attracted attention by observing a nova in 1572. As a result King Frederick II had two observatories built for him on the island of Hveen, where he worked from 1580 to 1597. During this period he made extensive observations, which led him to support ▷Copernicus' theory that the planets revolve round the sun. However, he believed the earth to be immovable, with the sun and planets revolving round it. After Frederick's death, he quarrelled with his successor and moved to Prague: there he met ▷Kepler, who became his student. After Tycho's death, Kepler used his teacher's observations to test his laws of planetary motion.

● **Brahma** ▶ The creator god of later Vedic religion. Arising from the cosmic Golden Egg, he brings into existence the cyclical process of the creation and destruction of the world. His four heads and arms represent the four ▷Vedas, castes, and yugas (ages of the world). Brahma represents the creative aspect of supreme deity in the ▷Trimurti triad but since the 7th century his worship has been superseded by that of ▷Shiva and ▷Vishnu, the other members of the triad.

● **Brahman** ▶ (Hinduism) In the ▷Upanishads, the absolute unmanifest changeless source of the phenomenal universe, seen as self-existent, extra-temporal Being, all-pervading and infinite. Brahman is both the basis of existence and the state of one who has achieved release (*see* atman). Brahman originally meant "the sacred Word," and as such was the exclusive domain of the literate priestly caste. In its extended significance it therefore came to be considered the proper spiritual object of that class alone. ▷*See* Brahmanism.

● **Brahman** ▶ (cattle) ▷*See* zebu.

● **Brahmanas** ▶ Commentaries on the ▷Vedas, written in Sanskrit between about 1000 and 600 BC. They systematically explore Aryan legends and folklore in order to account for traditional rituals and are major sources of Indian philosophy, theology, and myth.

● **Brahmanism** ▶ An early speculative rather than devotional form of ▷Hinduism, derived from the ▷Vedas and characterized by the veneration of an elite priestly caste, who, as the privileged keepers of religious knowledge, were seen as actually embodying the sacred word. ▷*See also* Brahman.

● **Brahmaputra River** ▶ A river in S Asia. Rising in SW Tibet as the Tsangpo, it flows generally E across the Himalayas before turning S into the Assam Valley of NE India as the Dihang. From here, as the Brahmaputra, it flows WSW across NE India to join the River ▷Ganges N of Gaolundo Ghat. Together they enter the Bay of Bengal in a large delta. The floodplains are highly cultivated. Length: 2900 km (1800 mi).

● **brahmin** ▶ (*or* brahman) The first of the four major Hindu castes, that of the priests. Observing many social taboos and being innately more ritually pure than the warrior, merchant, or peasant classes, brahmins alone are able to perform the most important religious tasks, to study and recite the scriptures. Since in India spiritual and secular knowledge are virtually inseparable, brahmins frequently hold considerable intellectual and political power. After India achieved independence in 1947, opposition to brahminical elitism strengthened, but this has not yet significantly weakened their sacerdotal role.

● **Brahmo Samaj** ▶ A Hindu revivalist movement, arising in response to contact with Christianity. Founded by Rammohan Ray (1772–1833), it intended to restore monotheistic Hinduism and the authority of the ▷Upanishads. Unlike the ▷Arya Samaj, it set out to be a universal religion. Disagreements between advocates of devotion or asceticism, rather than rational theism, led to schisms and the incorporation of Christian elements and in some cases to wholly new philosophical formulations.

● **Brahms, Johannes** ▶ (1833–97) German composer, born in Hamburg. Brahms' precociousness was demonstrated by his youthful piano compositions; as a young man he became a friend of the violinist Joseph Joachim (1831–1907), Liszt, and the Schumanns. Brahms moved to Vienna in 1863 and later became musical director of the Gesellschaft der Musikfreunde (Society of Friends of Music; 1872–75). Musically conservative, Brahms composed in traditional forms and was unsympathetic to the progressive ideas espoused by Wagner and Liszt, although his compositions abound in lyrical melodies and rich harmonies. His main orchestral works comprise four symphonies, two piano concertos, a violin concerto, and a concerto for violin and cello. His choral works include *A German Requiem* (1868) and the *Alto Rhapsody* (1869). He wrote a large quantity of chamber music, including a piano quintet, three piano quartets, and three piano trios; string sextets, quintets, and quartets; a clarinet quintet and trio; and sonatas for violin, cello, and clarinet. He also composed much piano music and many songs.

● **Brăila** ▶ 46 82N 27 58E A port in E Romania, situated at the limit for oceangoing ships on the River Danube. Following the Turkish occupation of the city (1544–1828), it was rebuilt with radiating and concentric streets. It is a major grain centre. Population (1994 est): 235 763.

● **Braille, Louis** ▶ (1809–52) French teacher, who, blinded by an accident at the age of three, published a system of writing that allows the blind to read by touch. He later applied the Braille system to the reading of music. Modern Braille consists of 63 characters, each of which is made up of one to six embossed dots.

Braille ▶ The alphabet.

● **brain** ▶ The mass of nervous tissue that lies within the skull and is ensheathed by three membranes (meninges). It is the organ of the mind and it controls many bodily activities. The hindmost part of the brain, joining the ▷spinal cord, is the medulla oblongata: this ascends to the pons, which joins the midbrain. These parts are together called the brainstem, which contains the vital centres controlling breathing and heartbeat and also regulates the level of consciousness and conveys information to and from the cerebrum. The cerebellum is connected to the brainstem and is important in the coordination of movements. The upper end of the brainstem is connected to the largest and most highly developed part of the brain—the cerebrum. This consists of two cerebral hemispheres connected to each other by a tract of nerve fibres. Its surface is intricately folded and is made up of an outer layer of nerve cell bodies (grey matter) and an inner mass of nerve fibres (white matter). The cerebrum is largely responsible for understanding the environment, language, rational thought, and the voluntary control of movements. The hemispheres differ in function: one hemisphere controls the dominant side of the body (normally the left hemisphere in right-handed people) and that hemisphere controls speech. The nondominant hemisphere specializes in analysing how things are arranged in space. Deep within the cerebrum and brainstem lie cavities (ventricles) filled with ▷cerebrospinal fluid. The brain of vertebrate animals is similar but less highly developed than the human brain; in lower animals a collection of ganglia (nerve cell bodies) functions as the brain. □ p. 182. ▷*See also* death; electroencephalography; hypothalamus; nervous system; neurone.

● **Braine, John** ▶ (1922–86) British novelist, born in Bradford. The radical views expressed in *Room at the Top* (1957) established him as one of the ▷Angry Young Men. Later works include *Life at the Top* (1962).

● **brake** ▶ **1.** A device used to slow down or stop the rotation of a shaft or wheel. An essential component of all vehicles, modern braking systems depend either on the friction between a pair of expanding shoes and the inside of a drum attached to the wheel (**drum brakes**) or between two calliper-operated pads and the two sides of a disc (**disc brakes**) attached to the wheel or shaft. Disc brakes, because they are open to the atmosphere, dissipate the heat generated by braking more effectively than drum brakes, which are liable to brake fade as the drums heat up. On modern road vehicles the brakes are operated by hydraulic pressure (using oil as the brake fluid) and are often power-assisted by a servo-mechanism. More sophisticated vehicles have electronically controlled antilock devices known as ABS (antilock braking systems) **2.** A device that absorbs and measures the power developed by an engine or motor. Brake horsepower is the power so measured. 1 brake HP = 746 watts.

● **Bramah, Joseph** ▶ (1748–1814) British engineer and inventor, who in 1784 designed a lock that remained pick-proof until 1851. Bramah went into partnership with Henry ▷Maudslay and their innovations in manufacturing the parts of the lock to the required accuracy greatly advanced the precision of machine tools. Bramah also invented (1795) a hydraulic press.

● **Bramante, Donato** ▶ (1444–1514) Italian Renaissance architect. Bramante started his career as a painter and later executed his first building projects in Milan. However, he spent his last 16 years in Rome, where most of the buildings for which he is remembered were erected, showing as they do a much more sophisticated handling of classical forms. His earlier buildings, such as S Maria delle Grazie (1480s) in Milan, do not show the same assurance that he exhibited in, for example, the Tempietto di S Pietro in Montorio (1502). The Palazzo Caprini (1514) influenced secular architects and Bramante's designs for St Peter's are reflected in the later designs of ▷Michelangelo.

● **bramble** ▷*See* blackberry.

● **brambling** ▶ A finch, *Fringilla montifringilla*, 14.5 cm long, that breeds in Asia and N Europe and migrates south in winter. It has a brown-speckled plumage with white wing bars and orange underparts but in winter the male has a black head and back.

● **Bran** ▶ A legendary Celtic god-king of Britain, whose story is told in the ▷*Mabinogion*. A giant, he once waded across the sea between

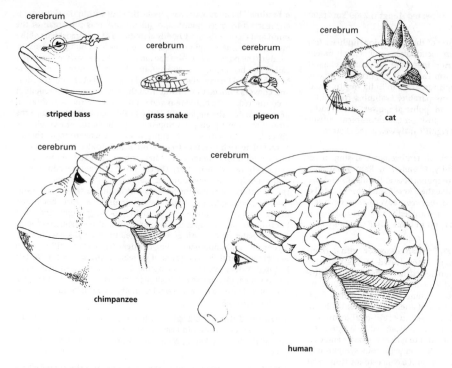

striped bass

grass snake

pigeon

cat

chimpanzee

human

brain ▶ The brains of these representative vertebrates (drawn to the same scale) show a progressive increase in the size and complexity of the cerebrum. In humans this development is such that the cerebrum covers or encloses all the other parts of the brain.

Britain and Ireland. His severed head lived on for some 80 years, renowned for the good advice and entertainment it gave his followers. In accordance with his wish, Bran's head was buried in London to protect Britain from invasion. It was dug up by King Arthur, who believed that the country was better protected by the valour of individuals.

● **Branagh, Kenneth ▶** (1961–) British actor and director, born in Ireland. Founder (1986) of the Renaissance Theatre Company, he has been admired in both Shakespearean and contemporary plays. His films include *Henry V* (1989), *Much Ado About Nothing* (1993), *Mary Shelley's Frankenstein* (1994), and *The Gingerbread Man* (1998; as actor only). He separated from his wife, the actress Emma ▷Thompson, in 1995.

● **Branchiopoda ▶** A class of small ▷crustaceans (over 800 species) that, except for the brine shrimp, occur in fresh water. They include the ▷fairy shrimps, ▷tadpole shrimps, ▷water fleas, and clam shrimps, all bearing flat fringed appendages used for locomotion, respiration, and filter feeding. ▷Parthenogenesis is common.

● **Brancusi, Constantin ▶** (1876–1957) Romanian sculptor. At first locally trained, he moved to Paris in 1904, where he developed a highly individual style based on radical simplification of form. His stone and metal sculptures include the *Sleeping Muse* series beginning in 1906 and the *Birds* variations (1912–40). His wood sculptures, such as the *Prodigal Son* (1915), are often mythological or religious in theme. He is considered one of the most influential sculptors of the 20th century.

● **Brandenburg ▶** 52 24N 12 31E A city in E Germany, on the River Havel. It was the former capital of the Prussian province of Brandenburg. The city was severely damaged during World War II. Its industries include steelworks and machinery and textile manufacturing. Population (1989 est): 93 660.

● **Brandenburg ▶** A *Land* and former electorate of E Germany. The region was conquered by the Germans between the 10th and 12th centuries and in 1157 ▷Albert (I) the Bear became margrave, and then ▷elector, of Brandenburg. Under ▷Frederick William, the Great Elector (1640–88), Brandenburg gained suzerainty of Prussia and became a leading German power. In 1701 the Elector of Brandenburg became ▷Frederick I of Prussia. After World War II some eastern parts of

Brandenburg became Polish. It was reinstated as a *Land* in 1990. Population (1995 est): 2 536 700.

● **Brandenburg Gate ▶** A ceremonial gateway in □Berlin. The Brandenburg Gate was built (1789) in the neoclassical style by C. G. Langhans (1732–1808). Situated at the W end of Unter den Linden, it became the symbol of the city. In 1989 it witnessed celebrations marking the opening of the Berlin Wall.

● **Brandes, Georg Morris Cohen ▶** (1842–1927) Danish literary critic. Because of his radical and atheistic tendencies he was denied a professorship at Copenhagen University until 1902. *Mainstreams in the Literature of the Nineteenth Century* (1872–75) established his reputation. There followed monographs on *Kierkegaard* (1871), *Ibsen* (1899), and *Anatole France* (1905), and a study of Shakespeare (1897–98).

● **Brando, Marlon ▶** (1924–) US film actor. His acting was influenced by the "method" style developed by the New York Actors' Studio in the 1950s from the theories of ▷Stanislavsky. His films include *A Streetcar Named Desire* (1951), *On the Waterfront* (1954), *The Godfather* (1972), *Apocalypse Now* (1979), and *Don Juan de Marco* (1995).

● **Brandt, Bill ▶** (1905–83) British photographer. He is best known for his photographs of British life in the 1930s, particularly the working classes, and for photographic books, such as *The English at Home* (1936) and *Perspective of Nudes* (1961).

● **Brandt, Willy ▶** (1913–92) German statesman; chancellor of West Germany (1969–74). In Norway from 1933, he was a leader of the resistance movement against the Nazis throughout World War II. A member of the Social Democratic Party from 1931, he was its chairman from 1964 to 1987. As chancellor he negotiated treaties with Russia, Poland, and East Germany and in 1971 was awarded the Nobel Peace Prize. He resigned the chancellorship when it was revealed that one of his aides was an East German spy. He subsequently chaired an international commission on the state of the world economy (the Brandt Commission), which published its report in 1980.

● **brandy ▶** A ▷spirit distilled from fermented grape juice (wine); the term also denotes drinks distilled from the fermented juices of other fruits. The best types of wine brandy are matured in oak casks and named after the Cognac and Armagnac districts of France where they are made. Marc (French) or grappa (Italian) brandy is made from the refermented grape pips, skins, and stems left after pressing for wine. VSOP—very superior old pale—brandy is usually 20–25 years old.

● **Brandywine, Battle of the** ▶ (11 September, 1777) A battle fought in SE Pennsylvania during the ▷American Revolution. Sir William ▷Howe, advancing on Philadelphia, encircled ▷Washington's troops in an attempt to cut off the city. Howe crossed the Brandywine Creek, defeated Washington's troops, and subsequently occupied Philadelphia.

● **Branson, Sir Richard** ▶ (1950–) British entrepreneur and founder of the Virgin Group, including Virgin Records (sold in 1992), Virgin Atlantic Airways, and Virgin Rail Group. His *Atlantic Challenger II* achieved a record time for an Atlantic crossing in 1986 but he was denied the ▷Blue Riband on a technicality. He was the first to cross both the Atlantic (1987) and the Pacific (1991) in a hot-air balloon, but his attempts (1997, 1998) to circle the world in a balloon proved unsuccessful. He was knighted in 2000.

● **Brant, Joseph** ▶ (1742–1807) Mohawk Indian chief. He went to a mission school, where he became an Anglican, and commanded the Mohawks on the British side in the American Revolution. He subsequently settled them in Canada and in 1785 visited England to claim compensation for war losses. He later resisted the taking of Mohawk lands by speculators.

● **Brant, Sebastian** ▶ (?1458–1521) German poet. He studied and taught law at Basle, and was made an imperial councillor by Maximilian I. His most important work was *The Ship of Fools* (1494); a series of satires on contemporary vices (with illustrations ascribed to Dürer). It became popular throughout Europe.

● **Branting, Karl Hjalmar** ▶ (1860–1925) Swedish statesman; prime minister (1920, 1921–23, 1924–25). His domestic policy pioneered welfare state legislation in Sweden. An enthusiastic supporter of the League of Nations, he was awarded, with the Norwegian pacifist, Christian Lange (1869–1938), the Nobel Peace Prize in 1921.

● **Brantôme, Pierre, Abbé and Seigneur de Bourdeille** ▶ (c. 1540–1614) French chronicler. Only nominally a priest, he was a courtier under Marguerite de Valois and Henry II and travelled throughout Europe as a soldier. He began writing when crippled in a riding accident. His *Mémoires* (1665–66) chronicle the lives of illustrious men and women of his time.

● **Braque, Georges** ▶ (1882–1963) French painter, who with ▷Picasso developed ▷cubism. He was initially influenced by impressionism and later fauvism before painting his earliest cubist landscapes (1908–09) at L'Estaque and Guyon, inspired by ▷Cézanne. His favourite subjects were still lifes, which during their period of close collaboration, sometimes looked identical to those of Picasso. Notable among Braque's innovations were the use of lettering in compositions, e.g. *The Portuguese* (1911; Basle), mixing paint with sand to produce interesting textures, and papiers collés (paper pasted on canvases). After World War II he painted independently in large flat planes instead of small fragmented cubes. In his later years he produced sculpture and eight paintings of studio interiors (1948–55).

● **Brasília** ▶ 16 0S 48 10W The capital and a federal district of Brazil, situated on the central plateau. The idea of a capital in the interior was first suggested in 1789, but it was not until 1956 that the present site was chosen. It was inaugurated in 1960, the chief designer being Lúcio Costa and the principal architect, Oscar ▷Niemeyer. Its fine modern buildings include the National Congress Building and the cathedral. The university was founded in 1962. Population (1995 est): 1 778 000.

● **Brașov** ▶ (German name: Kronstadt) 45 39N 25 35E A city in E central Romania, surrounded by the Transylvanian Alps. It has many historic buildings and the first book printed in Romanian appeared here in the 16th century. Its varied industries include motor vehicles, chemicals, and textiles. Population (1994 est): 324 210.

● **brass** ▶ An ▷alloy of copper and zinc. Brasses containing less than 36% zinc are ductile when cold and can be easily worked into complex shapes. Those with more than 36% zinc are harder and stronger. Brass is easy to machine and stamp into shape and is used for screws,

hinges, and a wide variety of articles. It does not rust but exposure to sea water causes dezincification (leaching out of the zinc). This is partially prevented by the addition of tin (1%) in Naval Brass, sometimes with about 0.05% of arsenic. ▷*See also* Muntz metal.

● **Brassica** ▶ A genus of mainly annual or biennial herbs (about 40 species, especially in the Mediterranean region), with erect clusters of four-petalled yellow flowers. Many species have basal rosettes of large simple leaves, but in others the leaves are spaced out up the main stem. The genus includes many important vegetables, mostly cultivated varieties of native species; the leaves, buds, stems, or roots may be eaten. Family: ▷*Cruciferae* (or *Brassicaceae*). ▷*See also* broccoli; Brussels sprout; cabbage; cauliflower; kale; rape; swede; turnip.

● **brass instruments** ▶ Wind instruments made of brass. The ▷French horn, ▷trumpet, ▷trombone, and ▷tuba are commonly used in the symphony orchestra; brass bands use a greater variety, including ▷bugles and ▷cornets. Brass instruments have either a cup-shaped or cone-shaped mouthpiece, the shape of which influences the tone quality, as does the type of bore, which may be conical (horn) or cylindrical (trumpet). A brass instrument plays the harmonic series natural to its length; additional series are made available by the use of crooks, slides, or valves.

● **Bratby, John** ▶ (1928–92) British painter and writer. He studied at the Royal College of Art and from 1955 exhibited annually at the Royal Academy. He became known for his domestic interiors in the "kitchen sink" style and later for his numerous portraits. His paintings for the film (1958) of Joyce Carey's novel *The Horse's Mouth* (1944) became widely known.

● **Bratislava** ▶ (German name: Pressburg; Hungarian name: Pozsony) 48 10N 17 10E The capital of Slovakia, on the River Danube; until 1993 the capital of the Slovak Republic of Czechoslovakia. It was the capital of Hungary (1526–1784). Notable buildings include the gothic cathedral (13th century), where many of the kings of Hungary were crowned, and its castle. The university was founded in 1919. It is an important industrial centre and river port, producing textiles, chemicals, and electrical goods. Population (1996 est): 452 053.

● **Brattain, Walter Houser** ▶ (1902–87) US physicist, who shared the 1956 Nobel Prize for his part in the invention of the transistor (with W. B. ▷Shockley and John ▷Bardeen) while working at the Bell Telephone Laboratories in 1948.

● **Brauchitsch, Walther von** ▶ (1881–1948) German general. He became commander in chief of the German army in 1938 but was dismissed (1941) by Hitler after the failure of the Moscow campaign. He died awaiting trial for alleged war crimes.

● **Braun, Eva** ▶ (1910–45) The mistress and finally the wife of Adolf Hitler. Their relationship probably began in 1933 and they were married shortly before their suicides on 30 April, 1945.

● **Braun, Wernher von** ▷*See* von Braun, Wernher.

● **Braunau am Inn** ▶ 48 16N 13 03E A city in N Austria, in Upper Austria. It has numerous 16th–17th-century houses and several nota-

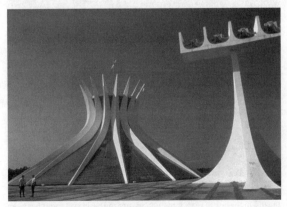

Brasília ▶ Oscar Niemeyer's cathedral (1964).

ble gothic churches. Adolf Hitler was born here. It has Austria's largest aluminium plant. Population (1991): 16 457.

● **Braunschweig** ▷*See* Brunswick.

● **Brazil, Federative Republic of** ▶ (Portuguese name: Brasil) A country comprising almost half the area of South America, situated in the NE. The N of the country is dominated by the Amazon basin with its tropical rain forests. The land rises to the Guiana Highlands in the N and the Brazilian Highlands in the S, with large tracts of grassland in between. The Mato Grosso Plateau in the SW is arid savanna. The population is largely of European descent, with some African and Asian minorities and a very small and dwindling Indian minority. Most of the inhabitants live along the coast, especially in the S and SE, although the government has launched ambitious road and regional plans in an attempt to open up and develop the interior; the ecological consequences of these plans upon Brazil's rainforests have caused an international outcry. The building of ▷Brasília was the most impressive single attempt to draw the population away from the overcrowded coastal areas.

Economy: following large-scale industrialization in the 1960s and 1970s, Brazil enjoyed a remarkable annual growth rate and now has the eighth largest economy in the world. Agriculture remains important, the chief crops being sugar cane, manioc, maize, rice, and beans. Brazil is the world's largest producer of coffee. Cocoa, bananas, and oranges are also important. Numbers of livestock have increased and Brazil is now ahead of Argentina as a cattle producer. The fishing industry is nationalized with territorial waters extending to 320 km (200 mi). Brazil is exceptionally rich in mineral resources, many of them as yet untapped, although more mines have been opened up in the interior. The iron-ore reserves are estimated to be the largest in the world. There are gold deposits in most parts of the country and the large mine at Minas Gerais dates back to the late 17th century. More recently large deposits of phosphates have been

discovered there, as well as uranium, manganese, and copper. The country's many other minerals include high-grade quartz crystal. The most important manufacturing industries are textiles, and the production of motor vehicles and machinery. 90% of power comes from hydroelectricity. There is now an agreement with Germany, based on Brazil's rich uranium deposits, to build eight nuclear power stations. Oil production only provides a fraction of Brazil's domestic needs although new offshore fields have been found near Campos. Main exports now include industrial goods as well as sugar, coffee, cotton, and minerals, especially iron ore. Since the return to civilian rule in the mid-1980s governments have struggled, with some success, to curb high inflation and to stabilize the economy. A privatization programme has gained pace since the early 1990s. In late 1997 the economy suffered badly as a result of the financial crisis in Asia, leading to the imposition of harsh austerity measures; there was a further financial and currency crisis in 1999.

History: claimed by the Portuguese in 1494, it became a Portuguese settlement from the 16th century. During the Napoleonic Wars the Portuguese court was transferred to Brazil and in 1815 it was made a kingdom. In 1822 independence was declared by ▷Pedro I, son of John VI of Portugal, with a constitution that proclaimed him emperor. In 1889 his son ▷Pedro II was deposed and Brazil became a republic. From 1930 to 1945 it was ruled under the benevolent dictatorship of Getúlio ▷Vargas. Less stable governments followed, including a further period under Vargas (1950–54). In 1964 Gen Humberto Castelo Branco (1900–67) came to power in a military coup. In 1967 Marshal Artur da Costa e Silva (1902–69) was elected president and in 1968 he assumed absolute powers. He resigned in 1969 and was replaced by a military junta. Elections were held in 1985, ending 20 years of military rule; when president elect Tancredo Neves died before taking office, vice-president José Sarne (1930–) assumed power. In 1990 Sarne was succeeded by Fernando Collor de Mello (1949–), who resigned following accusations of corruption, and Itamar Franco (1931–) took over the presidency (1992–95). He was succeeded by the social democrat F. H. Cardoso, who was re-elected in 1998.

Federative Republic of Brazil

Head of state	President Fernando Henrique Cardoso
Official language	Portuguese
Official currency	cruzeiro real of 100 centavos
Area	8 511 965 sq km (3 286 000 sq mi)
Population (1998 est)	161 766 000
Capital	Brasília
Main port	Rio de Janeiro

● **Brazil nut** ▶ The seed of a tall forest tree, *Bertholletia excelsa*, up to 45 m high, native to tropical South America. The tree produces showy fluffy flowers that develop into hard woody fruits, up to 15 cm in diameter, each containing 12–24 seeds (the nuts). Commercial supplies come entirely from wild trees. Family: *Lecythidaceae*.

● **brazilwood** ▶ An evergreen tree, *Caesalpinia brasiliensis*, of tropical South America. The leaves are bipinnate—each leaflet is divided into smaller leaflets—and the irregular orange flowers develop into seed pods. The tree yields a very hard wood from which a red dye is extracted; the wood is also used for cabinetwork. Family: *Leguminosae*.

● **brazing** ▷*See* solder.

● **Brazza, Pierre Paul François Camille Savorgnan de** ▶ (1852–1905) French explorer of Italian descent. In 1878 he colonized French Equatorial Africa, founding Brazzaville. He was the first governor of the French Congo (1886–97).

● **Brazzaville** ▶ 4 07W 15 15E The capital of Congo-Brazzaville, situated in the S on the Congo River opposite Kinshasa (in the Democratic Republic of Congo, formerly Zaïre). Founded in the 1880s, Brazzaville developed as a European centre and an important riverport, and became capital of French Equatorial Africa in 1910. During World War II it was the centre of the Free French forces in Africa. It became capital of the newly independent Republic of Congo (now Congo-Brazzaville) in 1960. The Marien-Ngouabi University was founded in 1972. Population (1995 est): 937 579.

Brazil ▶ In the last 10 years some 10% of Amazon basin rain forest has been burnt to make room for cattle ranches.

● **bread** ▶ A staple food made basically by baking a mixture of ▷flour and water. Ordinary leavened bread is made by mixing a dough of flour, water, yeast, sugar, salt, and sometimes other ingredients. The dough is kneaded and left to rise twice, a process that can take several hours, before being baked. White loaves, rolls, French sticks, and brown bread are made from different types of wheat flour. Rye bread is another variety, which has a stronger more bitter flavour and can be black, brown, or white.

Bread has been baked since the earliest times, evidence of barley cakes having been found in Neolithic dwellings.

● **breadfruit** ▶ The starchy fruit of a tropical tree, *Artocarpus communis*. Roasted, it forms a staple part of the diet in the Pacific islands, to which it is native; it is widely cultivated elsewhere. The tree grows to a height of 30 m and has thick shiny divided leaves. The large round fruits, up to 30 cm across, have a thick warty rind and develop from long female catkins. Family: *Moraceae*.

● **bread mould** ▶ A fungus that grows on bread, especially one of the genera *Rhizopus* or *Mucor*. Black bread mould (*R. stolonifer*) forms a filamentous branching structure from which arise erect stalks bearing black spore cases resembling pinheads. It also grows on fruit, manure, and other decaying organic matter. Phylum: *Zygomycota*.

● **bream** ▶ One of several ▷teleost fishes, especially *Abramis brama*, a food and game fish related to ▷carp that occurs in European lakes and slow-moving rivers. Its deep body, 30–70 cm long, is bluish grey or brown above and silvery below. It lives in schools in deep water and feeds on invertebrates or small fish. ▷*See also* sea bream.

● **Bream, Julian Alexander** ▶ (1933–) British guitarist and lutenist. Taught by his father, Bream gave his first public performance at the age of 12. His outstanding talent attracted Andrés Segovia's attention. His repertoire includes arrangements of baroque and Renaissance pieces as well as works written for him by Britten and Henze.

● **breast** ▶ The milk-producing (mammary) gland of women. Each of the two breasts consists of a mass of fatty tissue in which are embedded milk-secreting lobes, which drain through a series of ducts to the nipple. **Breast cancer** is the commonest form of cancer in women. Treatment typically involves surgery (*see* mastectomy), sometimes with radiotherapy, followed by chemotherapy (usually using ▷tamoxifen). The activity of the gland is controlled by the hormone prolactin, secreted by the pituitary gland (*see* lactation).

● **breathalyzer** ▶ A device used by the police in a roadside test to estimate the amount of alcohol in the breath. In the UK a suspected driver blows through a tube into the device, which indicates when enough breath has been delivered and records the level of alcohol in the breath. If the level is above the legal limit (35 micrograms of alcohol per 100 millilitres of breath; equivalent to 80 milligrams per 100 millilitres of blood), the suspect is arrested and taken to a police station, where a further specimen of breath (or alternatively a specimen of blood or urine) is taken for analysis. It is this specimen that provides evidence for prosecution for drunken driving offences.

● **breathing** ▷*See* respiration.

● **Brébeuf, St Jean de** ▶ (1593–1649) French Jesuit missionary and patron saint of Canada. Ordained in 1623, he evangelized the Huron Indians in New France until he was tortured to death by the Hurons' enemies, the Iroquois. Feast day: 26 Sept.

● **breccia** ▶ A sedimentary rock consisting of relatively large (over 2 mm in diameter) angular fragments of pre-existing rocks. These fragments have usually undergone little transport from their source and are poorly sorted. Scree material cemented together forms one kind of breccia.

● **Brecht, Bertolt** ▶ (1898–1956) German dramatist and poet. He first studied medicine, serving briefly as a medical orderly in 1918. He abandoned the exuberant expressionism of his early plays after his conversion to Marxism in 1928, producing his best-known work the next year, *Die Dreigroschenoper*, an adaptation of John Gay's *The Beggar's Opera* with music by Kurt Weil. In 1933 he left Germany and lived in Scandinavia and the USA (1941–47). During these years he wrote his most powerful plays, notably *Galileo* (1938), *Mother Courage*

(1939) and *The Caucasian Chalk Circle* (1949). These exploit his "distancing" technique, in which by emphasizing the unreality of the play he increases its didactic impact. In 1949 he returned to East Berlin and founded his famous ▷Berliner Ensemble Company.

● **Brecon Beacons** ▶ A mountainous area of S Wales, in S Powys near Brecon, consisting of the three main peaks of Corn Du, Cribyn, and Pen y Fan (886 m, 2906 ft) and surrounding hills. The Brecon Beacons National Park covers a large area (1351 sq km, 522 sq mi) of S Wales, extending from the Black Mountains on the English border in the E to the Black Mountain in Carmarthenshire in the W.

● **Breconshire** ▶ A former county of SE Wales. Under local government reorganization in 1974 it was mainly absorbed into ▷Powys.

● **Breda** ▶ 51 35N 4 46E A town in the SW Netherlands, in North Brabant province. Occupied several times, its capture by the Spanish in 1625 is depicted in Velázquez' famous painting, *The Surrender of Breda*. Its industries include engineering and chemicals. Population (1996 est): 130 033.

● **Breda, Treaty of** ▶ (1667) A treaty, signed at Breda in the Netherlands, between England, France, Denmark, and the Netherlands at the end of the second ▷Dutch War. Under its terms England acquired New Amsterdam (subsequently New York).

● **Breeches Bible** ▷*See* Geneva Bible.

● **breeder reactor** ▷*See* fast reactor.

● **breeding** ▶ The controlled mating of selected animals or plants, usually in order to produce offspring with improved performance, such as a higher milk yield in dairy cattle, or certain desirable characteristics, such as a particular flower colour in garden plants. Based on careful selection of parents (often over many generations) and a knowledge of genetics, modern plant and animal breeding is aimed at improving yield, resistance to disease, hardiness to climate, consumer appeal of the product, etc., and has helped meet increased world demand for food.

● **Bregenz** ▶ 47 31N 9 46E A town in W Austria, the capital of Vorarlberg on Lake Constance. A tourist resort, it manufactures textiles and machinery. Population (1991): 26 743.

● **Brehon Laws** ▶ A collection of ancient Irish laws, dating back to the 8th century, which constitute one of the most important sources for the history of contemporary Irish society. The Brehon was an official who pronounced upon the law. The Laws describe conditions of tenure and transfer of land and the legal status and responsibilities of clan members, besides fixing penalties and fines for criminal acts.

● **Breitenfeld, Battles of** ▶ Two battles fought in Germany during the ▷Thirty Years' War and won by Sweden. ▷Gustavus II Adolphus led the Swedish-Saxon army to victory against the Catholic and imperial forces under ▷Tilly in 1631. The second battle (1642) was part of a campaign to win Saxony.

● **Bremen** ▶ 53 05N 8 48E The second largest port in Germany, capital of the *Land* of Bremen on the River Weser. Its cathedral (founded 1043) was restored following damage during World War II. Its industries include shipbuilding, oil refining, and food processing. Population (1996 est): 549 357.

● **Bremen** ▶ The smallest *Land* of Germany, comprising the cities of ▷Bremen and ▷Bremerhaven enclosed by the *Land* of Lower Saxony. Area: 404 sq km (156 sq mi). Population (1996 est): 679 757.

● **Bremerhaven** ▶ 53 33N 8 35E A city in NW Germany, in Bremen on the Weser estuary. A major fishing, freight, and passenger port, its industries include fish processing and shipbuilding. Population (1996 est): 130 400.

● **bremmstrahlung** ▶ Electromagnetic radiation emitted by a charged particle when it is decelerated on passing close to a nucleus. The effect is most often observed with electrons since they are light and therefore easily decelerated. The radiation from one particle is emitted as a single photon. It is an important method by which ▷cosmic rays dissipate their energy on entering the earth's atmosphere.

● **Brendan, St** ▶ (484–c. 578 AD) Irish abbot, the traditional founder of the monastery at Clonfert (Cluain Fearta), Co Galway. The Latin *Navigation of St Brendan* (c. 1050) recounts his legendary voyage to "northern and western islands" (perhaps the Orkneys and Hebrides). Feast day: 16 May.

● **Brendel, Alfred** ► (1931–   ) Austrian pianist. He has toured worldwide and is famous as an interpreter of Beethoven, Mozart, and Schubert.

● **Bren gun** ► A gas-operated light machine gun with interchangeable barrels first built at *Brno*, Czechoslovakia (1933), and later manufactured at *Enfield*, UK (1935). Widely used in World War II, it was accurate, reliable, and easily maintained.

● **Brenner Pass** ► (German name: Brenner Sattel; Italian name: Passo del Brennero) 47 02N 11 32E The lowest of the chief passes in the Alps, on the Austrian-Italian border. Important since Roman times, it links Innsbruck (Austria) with Verona (Italy) by road and rail.

● **Brent** ► A borough of NW Greater London, created in 1965 from the former municipal boroughs of ▷Wembley and Willesden. Area: 44 sq km (17 sq mi). Population (1994 est): 244 500.

● **Brentano, Clemens** ► (1778–1842) German writer, one of the Heidelberg School of Romantic writers. With Achim von Arnim he published the influential folksong collection, *Des Knaben Wunderhorn* (1805–08). Emotionally unstable in early life, he became a Catholic in 1817 and for six years was a monk.

● **Brentano, Franz** ► (1838–1916) German psychologist and philosopher. He trained as a priest but resigned over the doctrine of papal infallibility. Thinking psychology a necessary foundation for philosophy, he suggested distinguishing marks for psychic phenomena, chief among which was intentionality ("directedness-to-an-object") adopted by ▷Russell and ▷Moore. His main works are *Psychology from an Empirical Standpoint* (1874) and *The Origin of Ethical Knowledge* (1889).

● **brent goose** ► A dark-coloured ▷goose, *Branta bernicla*. 53–58 cm long, it breeds in the Arctic and winters in temperate N Atlantic coastal regions, feeding chiefly on eelgrass on mudflats. The pale-bellied form occurring in Canada and the eastern USA and the dark-bellied form of Arctic Russia and European coasts are both geographic races.

● **Brescia** ► 45 33N 10 13E A city in Italy, in Lombardy. It has Roman remains, 9th-century and 17th-century cathedrals, and a 12th-century palace. A railway junction, its manufactures include metal goods, firearms, machinery, and textiles. Population (1996 est): 190 208.

● **Breslau** ▷*See* Wrocław.

● **Bresson, Robert** ► (1907–99) French film director and screenwriter. In most of his austere films concerning moral and religious dilemmas he used unknown actors. His films include *Le Journal d'un curé de campagne* (1950), *Mouchette* (1967), *Lancelot du lac* (1974), and *L'Argent* (1983).

● **Brest** ► (name until 1921: Brest-Litovsk; Polish name: Brześć nad Bu-giem) 52 08N 23 40E A port in Belarus on the Rivers Bug and Mukhavets near the Polish border. The Treaties of ▷Brest-Litovsk were negotiated here in World War I. It is a major industrial, commercial, and transportation centre. Population (1996 est): 293 000.

● **Brest** ► 48 23N 4 30W A port and naval base in NW France, in the Finistère department on the Atlantic Ocean. A German U-boat base in World War II, it was almost entirely destroyed by Allied bombing. It is the site of the University of Brittany. Industries include fishing, chemicals, and clothing. Population (1990): 153 099.

● **Brest-Litovsk, Treaties of** ► (1918) The peace treaties between the Central Powers and, respectively, Ukraine and Soviet Russia towards the end of World War I. An independent Ukraine was recognized by the first treaty. By the second, Russia acknowledged Ukrainian independence and also lost its Polish and Baltic possessions. The treaties were annulled following the ultimate defeat of the Central Powers.

● **Brethren** ► Members of the Protestant Brethren Churches. The largest, called the Church of the Brethren, was founded in Germany

in the early 18th century. Persecution forced its members to emigrate to America, where they became known as "Tunkers," "Dunkers," or "German Baptists." They believe in temperance and pacifism and practise adult baptism by triple immersion.

● **Brétigny, Treaty of** ► (1360) The treaty that concluded the first phase of the ▷Hundred Years' War. Never fully effective, it promised a ransom of £500,000 for ▷John (II) the Good of France (captured at Poitiers in 1356) and granted territories, including Aquitaine, to Edward III of England. In return, Edward was to renounce his claim to the French throne.

● **Breton** ► A ▷Celtic language with four distinct dialects spoken in Brittany by about one million people. It was originally introduced to this area by immigrants from SW England, who had been displaced by invading Anglo-Saxon tribes. It is related to ▷Cornish and ▷Welsh but has been strongly influenced by French. It has a literature that dates from the 15th century. Official encouragement of French has tended to decrease the number of Breton speakers.

● **Breton, André** ► (1896–1966) French poet. After involvement with ▷dada, he became the leader of French ▷surrealism in 1922 and wrote three manifestos (1924, 1930, 1942) defining its aims. His many essays explore surrealist themes, such as the relationship between dreams and reality. His novel *Nadja* (1928) freely blends real and surreal; *Poèmes* (1948) seeks to express the unconscious mind. Briefly a Communist Party member, he lived in the USA from 1938 to 1946.

● **Bretton Woods Conference** ► (1944) A conference held at Bretton Woods, New Hampshire (USA), at which the USA, UK, and Canada established a system of international financial rules, which led to the setting up of the ▷International Monetary Fund (IMF) and the ▷International Bank for Reconstruction and Development (World Bank). The chief features of the system were, first, an obligation for each country to maintain the exchange value of its currency within 1% of a value fixed in terms of gold; and, secondly, the provision by the IMF of finance to bridge temporary payments imbalances. The system eventually collapsed in 1971, following the US Government's suspension of convertibility from dollars to gold.

● **Breuer, Josef** ► (1842–1925) Austrian physiologist and pioneer of psychoanalysis. After successfully treating hysteria in one of his patients, Breuer collaborated with Sigmund ▷Freud in writing *Studies in Hysteria* (1895). Earlier, working with Ewald Hering (1834–1918), Breuer described the Hering-Breuer reflex involved in the nervous control of breathing movements.

● **Breuer, Marcel Lajos** ► (1902–81) US architect, furniture designer, and teacher, born in Hungary. In the 1920s he taught at the ▷Bauhaus, designing the first tubular steel chair (1925). After 1937 he practised in the USA as an architect. One of the best-known buildings on which he worked is the UNESCO headquarters in Paris (1958).

● **Breuil, Henri** ► (1877–1961) French archaeologist, famous for his work on ▷Palaeolithic art. Although ordained an abbé (1900), Breuil devoted his outstanding talents as a draughtsman to copying cave paintings all over Europe (*see also* Altamira) and in N Africa, China, and S Africa. He was professor at the Collège de France (1929–47) and published over 600 books and articles.

● **brewing** ▷*See* beer and brewing.

● **Brewster, Sir David** ► (1781–1868) Scottish physicist, who studied the polarization of light, double refraction in crystals, and relations between crystalline forms and optical properties (*see* Brewster's law). He also invented and patented the kaleidoscope. In 1831 he helped to found the British Association for the Advancement of Science.

● **Brewster's law** ► Light reflected from a solid surface is plane polarized, with maximum polarization occurring when the tangent of the angle of incidence is equal to the refractive index. Named after Sir David ▷Brewster.

● **Brezhnev, Leonid Ilich** ► (1906–82) Soviet statesman; secretary of the Soviet Communist Party (1964–82) and president of the Soviet Union (1977–82). Brezhnev, a metallurgist, was a political leader in the Red Army during World War II. He became a member of the presidium in 1957 and its chairman in 1960. He and ▷Kosygin forced

Khrushchev to resign in 1964 and Brezhnev became first secretary of the Communist Party. By the late 1960s he had became the most powerful Soviet leader and in 1977 became president. He pursued a policy of detente with the West while insisting on the right to intervene in the affairs of other Warsaw Pact countries. Soviet denunciation of his leadership began in 1987 during the more liberal administration of Gorbachov.

● **Brian, Havergal** ▶ (1876–1972) British composer. He was self-taught and his work was largely neglected until shortly before his death. His 32 symphonies form the core of a large output of music of all kinds; the *Gothic Symphony* (1919–22) is one of the longest symphonies in existence and requires a huge number of performers.

● **Brian Boru** ▶ (926–1014) High King of Ireland (1001–14) after victories over the Danes and the other Irish. He was murdered after his victory at the battle of Clontarf. Brian was the last high king with effective jurisdiction over most of Ireland.

● **Briand, Aristide** ▶ (1862–1932) French socialist statesman; prime minister (1909–11, 1913, 1915–17, 1921–22, 1925–26, 1929) and foreign minister (1925–32). The crisis of Verdun in ▷World War I precipitated the fall of his government in March, 1917, when Clemenceau's attacks upon Briand for his attempt to negotiate peace forced him to retire. From 1919 he was a leading advocate of international cooperation and was instrumental in securing the ▷Locarno Pact (1925) and the ▷Kellogg-Briand Pact (1928). With Gustav ▷Stresemann, he shared the Nobel Peace Prize in 1926.

● **briar** ▶ A shrubby rambling ▷rose with arching prickly stems, found in hedgerows and scrub in many parts of Europe. The principal species are *Rosa rubiginosa*, *R. micrantha*, *R. agrestis*, and *R. elliptica*. ▷*See also* sweet briar.

Briar is also the name of a shrubby white ▷heath (*Erica arborea*), the roots and knotted stems of which are used for making briar pipes.

● **bribery and corruption** ▶ The giving of a gift to a person in a position of trust, to induce him to act contrary to his duty. If such a gift is secretly given and received it is presumed to be corrupt. If an agent acting on behalf of another (his principal) accepts a bribe from the other side of the negotiations (third party), the principal is not bound by any ▷contract that may result. Both the agent and the third party may be punished by a fine or imprisonment according to the Prevention of Corruption Acts (1906, 1916). Bribery of public servants is illegal according to the Public Bodies Corrupt Practices Act (1889; amended by the 1916 Act). Obtaining a title or similar honour by bribery is a crime according to the Honours (Prevention of Abuses) Act (1925). Bribery in connection with parliamentary and other elections is a corrupt practice forbidden by the Parliamentary Elections Act (1868) and the Representation of the People Act (1949).

● **bricks** ▶ A traditional building material in the form of a rectangular block usually measuring $225 \times 112 \times 75$ mm. They are normally made from clay and baked or fired in a kiln at about 900°C. Water is driven off, organic matter becomes oxidized, and some of the clay minerals fuse and fill the gaps between the clay particles. Iron oxide gives the brick its reddish colour. London stock bricks are yellowish on account of the sand and alumina they contain. Bricks are laid in various patterns, known as bonds. Refractory bricks made from fireclay are used to line furnaces.

● **Bride, St** ▷*See* Bridget, St.

● **bridge** ▶ A card game deriving from ▷whist. **Straight bridge** was first played in Britain about 1880; having overtaken whist in popularity, about 1911 it was displaced by its descendant, **auction bridge**, in which the opposing pairs of partners competed to decide the trump suit. By 1929 **contract bridge**, which had developed in the USA, was popularized by Ely ▷Culbertson, and put greater emphasis on skill, supplanted other forms of bridge. Two pairs of partners (referred to as North-South and East-West in bridge notation) bid to name the trump suit (or to play without a trump suit, i.e. in "no trumps") and "contract" to win a specified number of tricks (e.g. "four spades") above the six tricks of the "book." A game consists of 100 points, with each spade or heart trick counting 30, each diamond or club 20, and for a bid in no trumps 40 for the first trick and 30 for subsequent tricks. Only the tricks contracted for in the bidding are counted to-

wards game; extra points are awarded separately for "honours" (ace to ten of trumps), overtricks, and for slams (when the partners have bid for and won all the tricks or all but one trick in a hand). Penalty points are awarded to the opponents for undertricks (when the partners who have declared trumps fail to win the number of tricks they contracted for in the bidding). The side winning two games consecutively or two games out of three wins the rubber, which counts as either 500 or 700 extra points. The playing of the hand after the bidding is similar to whist, except that the declarer's partner, called the dummy, puts his entire hand face upwards on the table to be played by the declarer.

● **Bridge, Frank** ▶ (1879–1941) British composer. Bridge studied composition with Stanford and played the viola in the English String Quartet. The orchestral suite *The Sea* (1910–11) earned him early popularity. His later works, such as the third string quartet (1926) and *Oration* (for cello and orchestra; 1930), are in a highly individual modern idiom. He was the teacher of Benjamin ▷Britten.

● **Bridgend** ▶ A county borough of S Wales, created in 1996 from part of Mid Glamorgan. Area: 264 sq km (102 sq mi). Population (1996 est): 130 874.

● **Bridge of Sighs** ▶ (Italian name: Ponte dei Sospiri) A covered bridge in □Venice (Italy) linking the Doge's Palace with the state prison. Its name derives from the sighs of the prisoners who were conducted over it.

● **Bridgeport** ▶ 41 12N 73 12W A city in the USA, in SW Connecticut on Long Island Sound. The showman P. T. Barnum lived here and the main attraction of his circus, the midget ▷Tom Thumb, was born here. An industrial city, its manufactures include electrical equipment and aircraft. Population (1996 est): 137 990.

● **bridges** ▶ Structures that provide a means of crossing a river,

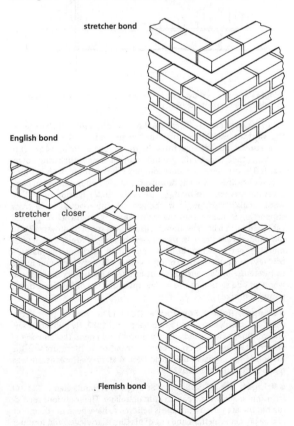

stretcher bond

English bond

header

stretcher   closer

Flemish bond

bricks ▶ The factors of cost, strength, and decorative effect influence a bricklayer's choice of bond for a particular task.

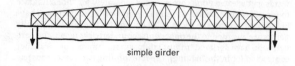

simple girder

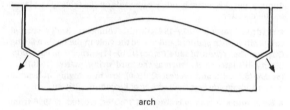

arch

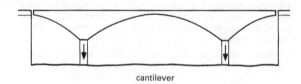

cantilever

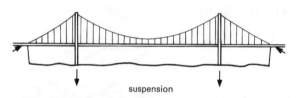

suspension

bridges ► The arrows show how forces are exerted onto or away from the foundations in each of the basic structural types.

valley, road, or railway. There are three basic designs, which differ in the way they bear the weight of the bridge and its load; some bridges consist of composite structures. **Beam** (or girder) **bridges** are supported at their ends by the ground, with the weight thrusting downwards. The cantilever is a more complex form of girder. **Arch bridges** thrust outwards as well as downwards at their ends and are in compression. **Suspension bridges** use cables under tension to pull inwards against anchorages in the ground. The roadway, or a truss supporting it, hangs from the main cables by a network of vertical cables. In certain bridges, there is insufficient room to allow traffic to pass underneath them. In these cases the bridges are designed with movable parts. Swing bridges can rotate horizontally. Bascule bridges are cantilever-type bridges with a counterweight and hinge to rotate the bridge vertically. Lift bridges have towers that lift the whole of one section of the bridge upwards. ▷See also Bailey bridge; pontoon bridge.

● **Bridges, Robert Seymour ►** (1844–1930) British poet. Educated at Oxford, he worked as a doctor until 1882. He published several volumes of lyrics and a long philosophical poem, *The Testament of Beauty* (1929), but an even greater contribution to literature was his edition of the poems of his friend Gerard Manley ▷Hopkins. He was made poet laureate in 1913.

● **Bridget, St ► 1.** (St Bride or St Brigit of Ireland; died c. 523 AD) Irish abbess and second patron saint of Ireland. The traditions regarding her life are various, but she is believed to have been the daughter of a pagan clan chieftain and one of his Christian slaves, and founder of the first Irish convent, at Kildare. Feast day: 1 Feb. ▷See also Brigit. **2.** (St Bridget of Sweden; 1303–73) Swedish religious visionary. She was

married to a rich nobleman and acted as a tutor to the royal family before renouncing the world in 1345. In 1346 she founded her own religious order, the Brigittines. From 1349 she lived in Rome, where she became famous for her charitable acts and attacks on religious abuses. Her *Revelations*, an account of her visions, was published after her death. Canonized in 1391, she is the patron saint of Sweden. Feast day: 23 July.

● **Bridgetown ►** 14 05N 59 35W The capital of Barbados, a port in the SW on Carlisle Bay, founded in 1628. The main industries are sugar, rum, and tourism. The University of the West Indies was founded in 1963. Population (1990): 6070.

● **Bridgewater Canal ►** A waterway constructed in 1759–61 by James ▷Brindley (1716–72) from Worsley to Manchester (later extended to Liverpool) for transporting coal. It is a gravity-flow canal constructed on an aqueduct across the Irwell Valley and is a masterpiece of 18th-century engineering. It was the first British canal.

● **Bridgman, Percy Williams ►** (1882–1961) US physicist, whose experiments with high pressures led to the invention of a seal the efficiency of which increased with pressure, enabling him to attain pressures of up to 20 000 atmospheres. Bridgman studied the effects of such pressures on solids and, in 1955, his methods were used by the General Electric Company to synthesize diamonds. For this work he was awarded the Nobel Prize in 1946. In *The Logic of Modern Physics* (1927) he made an important contribution to the (operational) concept of scientific meaning.

● **Bridgwater ►** 51 08N 3 00W A market town in SW England, in Somerset on the River Parrett. The Battle of Sedgemoor (1685) was fought nearby. Its varied industries include the manufacture of bricks, furniture, and plastics. Population (1991): 34 610.

● **Bridie, James ►** (Osborne Henry Mavor; 1888–1951) British dramatist. For many of his popular comedies of the 1930s and 1940s he drew on his Glaswegian background and his interest in medicine. His plays, which were never popular outside the UK, include *Tobias and the Angel* (1930) and *The Anatomist* (1931). He was the founder of the Glasgow Citizens' Theatre.

● **Brie ►** An area in N France, between the Rivers Seine and Marne. Predominantly agricultural, it produces wheat and sugar beet and is noted for its cheese. Area: 6500 sq km (2510 sq mi).

● **brig ►** A sailing vessel with two masts, both carrying square sails.

● **Brigantes ►** A large Celtic tribe that inhabited N Britain between the Humber and the Tyne at the time of the Roman conquest. Named after the Celtic goddess Brigantia, they initially had friendly relations with the Romans under their queen ▷Cartimandua. However, after Cartimandua left her anti-Roman husband King Venutius, he was defeated (71 AD) by the Romans, who annexed the Brigantes' territory and established a permanent military base at Eboracum (York).

● **brigantine ►** A sailing vessel with two masts, square-rigged on the foremast, with a fore-and-aft topsail.

● **Briggs, Henry ►** (1561–1630) English mathematician. On hearing of John ▷Napier's use of ▷logarithms, which have a base of e, Briggs realized that logarithms to the base ten, known as common or Briggsian logarithms, would make calculations simpler. Common logarithms are now widely used although Napierian logarithms are used for some purposes.

● **Bright, John ►** (1811–89) British radical politician. Bright, a Quaker, was a leader with ▷Cobden of the ▷Anti-Corn Law League, which successfully achieved the repeal of the Corn Laws in 1846. One of the Manchester School of middle-class liberal reformers, and an outstanding orator, he became an MP in 1843. He bitterly opposed the ▷Crimean War and led the campaign for an extension of the franchise, achieved in the 1867 Reform Act.

● **Bright, Richard ►** (1789–1858) British physician, who described many disorders, particularly the group of symptoms, including oedema (retention of body fluid), that he showed to be due to kidney disease. This is sometimes called **Bright's disease** (see nephritis).

● **Brighton ►** 50 50N 0 10W A coastal resort in S England, in Brighton and Hove unitary authority, East Sussex. Originally a fishing village, its growth began with the development of sea bathing in the 1750s and the patronage of the Prince Regent (later George IV), who had the Royal Pavilion redesigned by John ▷Nash in oriental style. Other notable features include the Lanes (famous for their antique shops) and the boating marina (completed in 1979). Brighton is also a conference centre and site of the University of Sussex (1961) and the University of Brighton (1992). Brighton and Hove achieved city status in 2000. Population (1991 est): 133 400.

● **Brighton and Hove** ▶ A unitary authority and city in S England, in East Sussex. Area: 72 sq km (28 sq mi). Population (1996 est): 249 500.

● **Brigit** ▶ A Celtic goddess of fire, fertility, learning, culture, and crafts. Elements of her cult were passed into the traditions surrounding St ▷Bridget, notably the burning of a sacred fire by her shrine.

● **brill** ▶ An edible ▷flatfish, *Scophthalmus rhombus*, related to ▷turbot, that occurs in European coastal waters, down to depths of 70 m. Its smooth body, up to 70 cm long, is sandy to grey or dark-brown with light and dark spots above and white with darker blotches below.

● **Brillat-Savarin, Anthelme** ▶ (1755–1826) French lawyer and writer. His *Physiologie du goût* (1825) is a collection of gastronomical anecdotes and aphorisms. After the Revolution he became a judge of the French supreme court.

● **brilliant cut** ▶ A method of cutting diamonds and other gems to impart maximum brilliance. The upper and lower halves of the stone are cut into 33 and 25 polished facets respectively. These facets meet around the girdle or perimeter of the circular stone.

● **brimstone** ▶ A lemon-yellow butterfly, *Gonopteryx rhamni*, found in Europe, N Africa, and parts of Asia. Adults hibernate, flying early in spring. The next generation emerges in June or later, the caterpillars feeding on buckthorn. Family: *Pieridae*.

● **Brindisi** ▶ (Latin name: Brundisium) 40 37N 17 57E A seaport in SE Italy, in Apulia. It was an important Roman naval base and a centre of the Crusades in the middle ages. It has a 12th-century cathedral and a castle. Population (1991): 93 290.

● **Brindley, James** ▶ (1716–72) British canal builder. He built his first canal (*see* Bridgewater Canal) for the Duke of Bridgewater in 1759–61. He designed and built some 588 km of canals, without ever using diagrams or calculations.

● **brine shrimp** ▶ A crustacean belonging to a genus (*Artemia*) of ▷fairy shrimps that lives in salty pools and lakes. The widely distributed species *A. salina*, 10 mm long, is often cultivated for fish food.

● **briquette** ▶ A block of compressed coal dust bound with pitch or a similar substance. Briquetting converts fuel of little use into one of higher quality that can be sold for domestic heating.

● **Brisbane** ▶ 27 30S 153 00E The third largest city in Australia, the capital and chief port of Queensland on the Brisbane River. The chief industries are engineering, shipbuilding, oil refining, food processing, and wool scouring. Exports include wool, meat, mineral sands, and wheat. The University of Queensland was established in 1910 and Griffith University in 1975; other notable buildings include Parliament House (1869), two cathedrals, the Observatory (1829) built by convicts, and the Queen Elizabeth II Stadium built for the 1982 Commonwealth Games.

History: founded in 1824 as a penal settlement, it was opened to colonists in 1842. It is named after the Scottish soldier, Sir Thomas Brisbane (1773–1860), a governor of New South Wales and a noted astronomer. Population (1995 est): 1 489 100.

● **brisling** ▷*See* sprat.

● **Brissot, Jacques-Pierre** ▶ (1754–93) French journalist and revolutionary. A legal reformer and humanitarian before the French Revolution, he became leader of the Brissotins, later called the ▷Girondins, in 1789. A proponent of revolutionary war, his policies led to the French declaration of war on Austria in 1792. Internal rivalries and disputes over the war produced a power struggle with the ▷Jacobins. After the defeat of the Girondins, Brissot was executed.

● **bristlecone pine** ▶ A ▷pine tree, *Pinus aristata*, native to mountainous regions of Colorado, Arizona, and New Mexico. Up to 15 m tall, it has cones about 7.5 cm long with bristles on each scale. Some bristlecone pines have reached an age of 5000 years and have been used in ▷dendrochronology.

● **bristletail** ▶ A slender wingless insect, 5–20 mm long, that has two or three long tail bristles and belongs to the orders *Thysanura* (three-pronged bristletails) or *Diplura* (two-pronged bristletails). Most bristletails live in damp sheltered places, e.g. under stones and logs, and feed on plant detritus. However, a few species feed on books and papers or anything containing starch (*see* silverfish; firebrat).

● **bristle worm** ▷*See* annelid worm.

● **Bristol** ▶ **1.** 51 27N 2 35W A port and industrial city in SW England, mainly in Bristol unitary authority; it is situated on the River Avon, 11 km (7 mi) from the Bristol Channel. Bristol developed as a major port in the 17th and 18th centuries, trading mostly with the Americas (and prospering greatly from the slave trade). Its docks at Avonmouth and Portishead (including the modern Portbury dock) on the Bristol Channel now handle much import and export trade. The historic dock area in Bristol itself has been redeveloped as a cultural and recreational area. Notable buildings include the 12th-century cathedral, the 14th-century Church of St Mary Redcliffe, and the circular Roman Catholic cathedral (1973). Nearby is the Avon Gorge, spanned by Brunel's Clifton Suspension Bridge (1832–64). Bristol University dates from 1909. Bristol's industries include engineering (particularly aircraft manufacture), chemicals, tobacco, soap, paper manufacture, chocolate, printing, and nonferrous metal refining. Population (1991): 407 992. **2.** A unitary authority in SW England, created in 1996 from part of Avon. Area: 110 sq km (42 sq mi). Population 1996 est): 374 300.

● **Bristol Channel** ▶ An inlet of the Atlantic Ocean in the UK, between South Wales and SW England. It forms an extension of the Severn Estuary and has the greatest tidal range in England. Length: about 137 km (85 mi).

● **Britain, Battle of** ▶ The ▷World War II air battle in which ▷Goering's Luftwaffe attempted to destroy the RAF in the late summer of 1940, as a prelude to the planned German invasion of Britain. Dismissed by some postwar historians as an inconsequential series of events in the on-going air war, the battle is seen by many others as the turning point in Britain's fortunes after the fall of France. Winston Churchill was in no doubt: "Never in the field of human conflict was so much owed by so many to so few", he reported to the House of Commons in August 1940. The "few" were the RAF pilots who, heavily outnumbered by German fighters and bombers, managed to destroy some 1700 aircraft for a loss of 900 RAF planes. Finding this loss unacceptable and having failed to achieve air supremacy, Hitler abandoned his invasion plans in October and turned instead to bombing London and other cities. Air Marshal ▷Dowding, who commanded Fighter Command during the battle, later revealed that the Luftwaffe's bombing of airfields in southern England had so weakened the RAF that by the end of September their reserves of aircraft and pilots were virtually exhausted. Hitler's policy change gave Fighter Command a breathing space in which to recover.

The dogfights between the rival fighters, 600 Spitfires (*see* Mitchell, R. J.) and Hurricanes of the RAF and 800 Messerschmitt 109s of the Luftwaffe, failed to reveal significant differences in the performance of the machines. It seems likely that it was the early use of ▷radar and Dowding's tactics that won the battle.

● **Britannia coins** ▶ A range of four British gold coins (£100, £50, £25, and £10 denominations). They were introduced in October 1987 for investment purposes, in competition with the ▷krugerrand. Although all sales of gold coins attract VAT, Britannia coins are widely dealt in as bullion coins.

● **Britannia metal** ▶ An ▷alloy of tin (80–90%) with variable amounts of antimony and copper. It resembles silver and was formerly used for tableware instead of ▷pewter.

● **British Academy** ▶ A learned society formed in 1901 to provide British representation of the humanities at the International Association of Academies. Incorporated in 1902, it promotes the study of languages and literatures, history, archaeology, philosophy, religion, law, economics, and the visual arts.

● **British Antarctic Territory** ▸ A United Kingdom overseas territory, established in 1962, that consists of the South Orkney and South Shetland islands and a large part of the Antarctic extending to the South Pole. It is used as a base for the British Antarctic Survey stations. Area: 1 709 340 sq km (600 000 sq mi).

● **British Association for the Advancement of Science** ▸ An organization formed in 1831 by scientists disillusioned with the conservatism of the ▷Royal Society. It received a royal charter in 1928. Its major event is its annual conference at which the social implications of scientific advances are discussed.

● **British Broadcasting Corporation** ▸ (BBC) A broadcasting authority in the UK. The BBC was set up as a private company in 1922 and incorporated as a public body under royal charter in 1927; it is responsible to parliament and is politically neutral and independent. It runs two national television stations, five national radio stations, and a number of local radio stations. It relies on revenue from television licences as it is not permitted to carry advertising. The BBC provides external services in 38 languages, for which it receives a subsidy from the government. Director General: Greg Dyke.

● **British citizenship** ▸ A form of citizenship introduced on 1 January, 1983 by the British Nationality Act (1981). With British Dependent Territories citizenship and British Overseas citizenship, it replaced the composite citizenship of the UK and Colonies created by the British Nationality Act (1948). From 1983 until 1999 full British citizenship could be acquired only by birth in the UK, the Channel Islands, the Isle of Man, Gibraltar, or the Falkland Islands (from 1985) to a parent who was either a British citizen or a settled resident there, by descent, by registration, or by ▷naturalization. In 1999 the government restored full British citizenship to UK Overseas (formerly Dependent) Territories and Overseas citizens. The expression Commonwealth citizen covers all forms of British citizenship and citizenship of any country of the Commonwealth. British citizens have automatic citizenship of the European Union.

● **British Columbia** ▸ The westernmost province of Canada, on the Pacific Ocean. Mostly in the mountainous Cordilleran region, it is bounded by the ▷Rocky Mountains in the E and the ▷Coast Mountains, including islands, in the W. The main rivers are the Fraser, Kootenay, Thompson, and Columbia. Forests cover over 55% of the surface and provide the basis for most manufacturing. Fishing, hydroelectricity, and tourism are also economically important. There are rich mineral resources; gold, silver, lead, zinc, copper, coal, and oil are all produced. Although only a small area is farmed, dairy produce, mixed farming, and fruit are valuable. Prosperous and urbanized, British Columbia is Canada's fastest-growing province; half the population lives in the Lower Mainland.

History: visited by Captain Cook (1778), British Columbia also attracted Russians, Spaniards, and Canadians. A British colony established on Vancouver Island (1849) spread to the mainland when gold was discovered (1858). Entry into Canada (1871) and the transcontinental railway (1885) provided the basis for economic development. Area: 930 528 sq km (359 277 sq mi). Population (1999 est): 4 029 000. Capital: Victoria.

● **British Council** ▸ An institution set up in 1934 and incorporated by royal charter in 1940. The Council's chief aims are to promote a knowledge of the UK abroad, to promote the teaching of English, and to foster educational cooperation between the developing countries and the UK.

● **British Council of Churches** ▸ A body, set up in 1947, of representatives of the major Churches in Britain and Ireland except the Roman Catholic Church (although this sends observers to meetings). The recommendations it makes to member Churches are designed to effect unity and joint action. It founded Christian Aid and is an Associate Council of the ▷World Council of Churches.

● **British Dependent Territories** ▷*See* United Kingdom Overseas Territories.

● **British Empire** ▷*See* Empire, British.

● **British Expeditionary Force** ▸ (BEF) Army formations that helped France counter German invasions in World Wars I and II. In World War I, its 6 divisions had increased to 65 by 1918 and it suffered almost 3 million casualties, of which 900 000 were fatal. In World War II it consisted of 10 divisions until its evacuation from Dunkirk (1940).

● **British Film Institute** ▸ (BFI) An organization founded in 1933 to encourage the development, study, and appreciation of cinema in Britain: its remit now includes television and video. The BFI runs the National Film Theatre on London's South Bank and maintains Britain's National Film Archive. It also provides publishing, research, and information services. Since 1999 it has been a subsidiary of the Film Council, a new umbrella body set up to promote Britain's film industry.

● **British Guiana** ▷*See* Guyana, Cooperative Republic of.

● **British Honduras** ▷*See* Belize.

● **British Indian Ocean Territory** ▸ A United Kingdom overseas territory, established in 1965, consisting of the Chagos Archipelago, largest island of which is **Diego Garcia** (claimed by Mauritius). Aldabra, Farquhar, and Desroches were returned to the Seychelles in 1976. The islands, which are spread over some 54 390 sq km (21 000 sq mi) of ocean, were retained for strategic purposes when the UK withdrew from its other possessions in the region in the 1960s. Under an agreement of 1966 the islands were made available to the US military. Construction of a major US naval and air base on Diego Garcia was accompanied by the expulsion of all 2000 inhabitants from the islands. In 2000 the British High Court ruled that this action had been illegal and that the islanders had the right to return. The Diego Garcia base has played a key role in US actions in the Middle East.

● **British Isles** ▸ An archipelago separated from the mainland of NW Europe by the North Sea and the English Channel. It consists of ▷Great Britain, Ireland, the Isle of Man, and the Channel Islands. Area: about 314 950 sq km (121 577 sq mi).

● **British Legion** ▷*See* Royal British Legion.

● **British Library** ▸ The national ▷library of the UK, formed in 1973 from the British Museum library, founded in 1753, and other collections. Until 1997, the library's 18 million volumes were stored in 18 London buildings and one in West Yorkshire. The first reading room of a purpose-built library in St Pancras (London) opened to the public in November 1997. It will eventually accommodate 1200 readers.

● **British Medical Association** ▸ (BMA) The major UK body representing the interests of members of the medical profession (including GPs, hospital doctors, community health workers, and university teaching staff). Founded as the Provincial Medical and Surgical Association by Charles Hastings (1794–1866) in 1832, it adopted its present name in 1855. As a result of the BMA's campaign the Medical Act (1858) established the General Medical Council, which maintains a register of medically qualified practitioners. The formation of the National Health Service in 1946 involved the government in discussions with the BMA, which was concerned to maintain the traditional independence of doctors. Listed as a trade union, the BMA campaigns for better pay and conditions for its members, but is also concerned to uphold standards of practice in the profession. Its main publication is the *British Medical Journal* (BMJ).

● **British Museum** ▸ The national museum of the UK containing probably the finest collection of antiquities in the world. Founded in 1753 to house the private collection of Sir Hans ▷Sloane, it now occupies Sir Robert ▷Smirke's neoclassical building (1847) in Bloomsbury, London. Its Egyptian, Assyrian, Greek, Roman, Chinese, and Cambodian collections are unique and include a number of Egyptian mummies, the Elgin Marbles, and the Rosetta Stone. Its reading room (*see also* British Library) is available only to ticket holders. The natural history exhibits were transferred to the Natural History Museum (designed by ▷Waterhouse and built 1873–80) in South Kensington.

● **British North America Act** ▸ (1867) An act passed by the British parliament uniting the colonies of Novia Scotia, New Brunswick, Canada West (now Ontario), and Canada East (now Quebec) as the Dominion of Canada.

● **British Raj** ▶ (Hindi: rule) The period during which the Indian subcontinent was under British rule. It began in 1858, when as a result of the ▷Indian Mutiny, the administrative powers of the East India Company were transferred to the British government; it ended in 1947 when Britain gave way to Indian nationalism and granted independence to India and the newly created Pakistan. During the Raj, the ten provinces of British India were administered by the British-run Indian Civil Service, which introduced the rule of law, land reform, railways, communications, and Western education. The British also restructured the army and the police. When the Raj finally departed from the subcontinent, India and Pakistan were left with parliamentary government, an efficient British-style administration, some industry, and English as a second language.

The families of the British officers, engineers, and civil servants who operated the Raj lived what would now be regarded as racist, snobbish, pampered, and privileged lives. Politically and economically, India provided the UK with a dominant presence in Asia and a source of great material wealth. Both sides, therefore, made substantial gains from the 90 years of the Raj.

● **British Standards Institution** ▶ (BSI) An institution founded in 1901 (renamed in 1931). Its function is to approve standards for various products, especially in engineering, building, textiles, and chemicals, to establish minimum standards of quality and avoid duplication of design, sizes, and patterns. Products that conform to BSI standards bear the Kite mark. ▷*See also* International Organization for Standardization.

● **British Technology Group** ▶ A UK body set up in 1981 to promote development of new scientific and engineering products and processes. Formed when the National Enterprise Board merged with the National Research and Development Corporation, it provides finance for further research into projects initiated at British universities and other institutions.

● **British thermal unit** ▶ (btu) A former unit of energy equal to the amount of heat required to raise the temperature of 1 lb of water through 1°F. It equals 1055.06 joules (251.997 calories).

● **British Union of Fascists** ▷*See* Mosley, Sir Oswald Ernald.

● **British Virgin Islands** ▷*See* Virgin Islands.

● **Britons** ▶ The indigenous inhabitants of Britain before the Anglo-Saxon settlements. They spoke languages of the Brythonic branch of the ▷Celtic language family. At the Roman conquest (1st century AD) Britain was divided into tribal kingdoms with a common Celtic culture (*see* La Tène). Religious affairs were conducted by ▷Druids. ▷*See also* Belgae.

● **Brittain, Vera (Mary)** ▶ (1893–1970) British writer and pacifist. She is best known for the memoir *Testament of Youth* (1933), which describes her experiences during World War I, and its sequels *Testament of Friendship* (1940) and *Testament of Experience* (1957). She also wrote novels, journalism, and poetry. Her daughter became the politician Shirley ▷Williams.

● **Brittany** ▶ (Breton name: Breiz; French name: Bretagne) A planning region and former province in NW France. It consists of a peninsula between the Bay of Biscay and English Channel. It was part of ancient Armorica and in 56 BC was conquered by Julius Caesar. During the 5th–6th centuries AD Celts from Britain migrated here to escape the Anglo-Saxon invasion. Finally incorporated into France in 1532, it has retained its own distinctive culture. It is an important area for tourism. Area: 27 184 sq km (10 494 sq mi). Population (1995 est): 2 846 900.

● **Britten, (Edward) Benjamin, Baron** ▶ (1913–76) British composer and pianist, a pupil of Frank ▷Bridge. He spent the years 1939–42 in the USA and subsequently founded the English Opera Group (1947) and the Aldeburgh Festival (1948). He wrote many works, as well as leading roles in his operas, for his lifelong partner, the tenor Peter ▷Pears. Among Britten's best-known compositions are the operas *Peter Grimes* (1945), *Billy Budd* (1951), and *Death in Venice* (1973); the orchestral works *Variations on a Theme by Frank Bridge* (1937) and the *Cello Symphony* (1964); choral works, such as the *Spring Symphony*

Benjamin Britten

(1949) and *A War Requiem* (1962); and many chamber and instrumental works.

● **brittle star** ▶ A marine invertebrate animal, also called sand star or serpent star, belonging to a subclass (*Ophiuroidea*) of ▷echinoderms. It has a small disclike body bearing five long fragile arms, used for locomotion. Brittle stars occur on soft muddy sea beds and are active at night, feeding on small crustaceans, molluscs, and bottom debris. Class: *Stelleroidea* (starfish and brittlestars). □oceans.

● **Brixham** ▶ 50 02N 3 30W A small resort and fishing port in SW England, in S Devon. It was the landing place of William of Orange (1688) and there are several notable palaeolithic remains nearby. Population (1991): 15 865.

● **Brno** ▶ (German name: Brünn) 49 12N 16 40E The second largest city in the Czech Republic, in S Moravia, formerly (1918–49) the capital of the Czechoslovakian province of Moravia. A fortified town in the middle ages, it contains the Spilberk fortress, an Austrian political prison (1621–1857). Other notable buildings include the 15th-century cathedral; its university was founded in 1919. The botanist Gregor Mendel devised his fundamental principles of heredity here (1865). Brno is now an important industrial centre specializing in engineering and textiles; the ▷Bren gun was originally developed here. Population (1995 est): 389 576.

● **broad bean** ▶ A stiff upright annual plant, *Vicia faba*, 60–150 cm tall, with a ribbed stem and compound grey-green leaves composed of a few large leaflets. The flowers have white petals and dark-purple blotches on the wings. The large pod has a woolly lining surrounding large flat edible beans, for which the plant is cultivated throughout Europe, both as a vegetable and as an animal feed. ▷*See also* bean.

● **broadbill** ▶ A brightly coloured passerine bird belonging to a family (*Eurylaimidae*; 14 species) of tropical African and Asian forests. It is about 12 cm long with a large head, partly joined toes, and a very broad short bill. Most species are insectivorous, feeding in trees or on the wing.

● **Broadmoor** ▶ A high-security hospital for mentally ill criminals in S England, at Crowthorne in Bracknell Forest, Berkshire, capable of housing 775 patients. It was opened in 1863.

● **Broads, the** ▶ A low-lying area in E England, mainly in Norfolk but extending into Suffolk. It consists of a system of shallow lakes, believed to have originated as medieval peat diggings, linked to the Rivers Bure and Yare and their tributaries. They are now of major recreational importance providing boating and fishing facilities. The profusion of vegetation and wildlife also makes the Broads an area of interest to naturalists. The area was given a special legal status, equivalent to that of the National Parks, in 1989.

● **Broadway** ▶ A major street in New York City along and near which are sited most of the leading commercial theatres. The word is used to refer to commercial theatre in the USA in general. ▷*See also* Off-Broadway theatres.

● **Broadwood, John** ▶ (1732–1812) Scottish manufacturer of pianos and harpsichords. Broadwood worked for Burkhard Tschudi (1702–73), the Swiss-born harpsichord maker, became his partner (1770), and took sole control of the company in 1782. He produced his first piano in 1773.

● **broccoli** ▶ A cultivated variety of wild ▷cabbage (*Brassica oleracea*) with a stout upright stem and a loose cluster of flower heads at the top. It is grown in temperate and cool regions. The leaves are narrow and curly; the lower ones are shed as the plant grows, leaving a scarred stem. Sprouting broccoli has purple or white flowers. Calabrese or green sprouting broccoli is an Italian variety, often with fused parallel stems. Both are eaten as vegetables while the flowers are in bud.

● **broch** ▶ A circular dry-stone defensive structure built in N Scotland and adjacent islands, probably in the period 100 BC to 100 AD. The six-storey-high broch at Mousa (Shetland) is a famous example.

● **Broch, Hermann** ▶ (1886–1951) Austrian novelist. His trilogy *The Sleepwalkers* (1931–32) is a historical study of Europe in a variety of literary forms. Briefly imprisoned by the Nazis, he emigrated to the USA in 1940. There he continued to experiment with innovative literary techniques, most notably in *The Death of Virgil* (1945).

● **Brocken** ▶ 51 48N 10 37E A mountain in central Germany, the highest of the Harz Mountains. According to legend, this bare granite peak is the scene of the witches' sabbath (*see* witchcraft) on Walpurgis Night (1 May). The **Brocken spectre** (*or* Brocken bow), first observed here, is a magnified shadow of the observer cast against mist or cloud below the level of the summit and surrounded by coloured fringes resulting from the diffraction of light.

● **Brodsky, Joseph** ▶ (1940–95) Soviet-born Jewish poet and critic, who was forced into exile and became a US citizen in 1977. He subsequently wrote in both Russian and English and was awarded the Nobel prize for literature in 1987. His works include the long poem *Gorbunov and Gorchakov* (1965–68).

● **Broglie, Louis Victor, 7th Duc de** ▷*See* de Broglie, Louis Victor, 7th Duc de.

● **Broken Hill** ▶ 31 57S 141 30E A mining city in Australia, in W central New South Wales. The rich silver, lead, and zinc deposits were discovered in 1883. The city helped to establish the trades union movement and the Barrier Industrial Council (representing the unions) plays an important role in the city's affairs. Population (latest est): 24 550.

● **Broken Hill** ▶ (Zambia) ▷*See* Kabwe.

● **bromine** ▶ (Br) A dense reddish-brown liquid element, discovered by A. J. Balard (1802–76) in 1826. It is extracted from sea water and other natural brines by electrolysis or by displacement with chlorine. The liquid element is volatile and its vapour has a pungent smell reminiscent of chlorine with severe irritating effects on the eyes and throat. Compounds include silver bromide (AgBr), used in photography, and ethylene dibromide ($C_2H_4Br_2$), used to scavenge lead in making additives for motor fuel. Other compounds are used as fumigants, dyes, flame-proofing agents, and in medicine. At no 35; at wt 79.904; mp −7.2°C; bp 58.78°C.

● **Bromley** ▶ The largest borough of Greater London, situated in the SE. A mainly residential area, it was created in 1965 from land that was formerly part of Kent, including Orpington and Penge, and parts of Chislehurst and Sidcup. Area: 153 sq km (59 sq mi). Population: (1994 est): 293 000.

● **bronchial tubes** ▷*See* lungs.

● **bronchitis** ▶ Inflammation of the bronchi—the tubes conducting air to the lungs. Acute bronchitis is often due to a virus infection, particularly a cold or influenza. Chronic bronchitis is common in middle-aged and elderly men in the UK, being aggravated by cigarette smoking and air pollution. Irritation of the mucus-secreting glands in the bronchi results in a persistent cough, with the production of large amounts of sputum. The patient is breathless and liable to chest infections. Treatment consists of stopping smoking (and reduc-

ing exposure to other irritants) and the prompt management of any chest infection.

● **Bronowski, Jacob** ▶ (1908–74) British mathematician, science writer, and broadcaster, born in Poland. He became widely known for his television series *The Ascent of Man* (1973), a history of the development of science and technology. He also wrote on poetry and on the importance of the scientific method, especially in *The Commonsense of Science* (1951).

Brontë sisters ▶ From a rough painting by their brother Branwell, showing (left to right) Charlotte, Emily, Branwell, and Anne.

● **Brontë sisters** ▶ Three British novelists, daughters of the rector of Haworth, an isolated village in Yorkshire. After briefly attending a local boarding school, **Charlotte Brontë** (1816–55) and **Emily Brontë** (1818–48) rejoined their sister **Anne Brontë** (1820–49) at home. Their early writings chronicled the imaginary kingdoms of Angria and Gondal. All the sisters worked for brief periods as governesses and teachers to help pay off the debts of their artist brother, **(Patrick) Branwell Brontë** (1817–48), an alcoholic and opium addict who died of tuberculosis. In 1846 the sisters published *Poems by Currer, Ellis, and Acton Bell* and in 1847, under the same pseudonyms, the novels *Jane Eyre* (by Charlotte), *Wuthering Heights* (by Emily), and *Agnes Grey* (by Anne). In 1848 Emily died of tuberculosis, as did Anne in 1849. Charlotte published *Shirley* (1849) and *Villette* (1853). She married her father's curate in 1854 and died in pregnancy a year later.

● **Brontosaurus** ▷*See* Apatosaurus.

● **Brontotherium** ▶ A genus of extinct North American hoofed mammals—▷titanotheres—that lived during the Oligocene epoch (between 38 and 26 million years ago). Standing 2.5 m at the shoulder, *Brontotherium* had a large skull with a pair of bony horns.

● **Bronx, the** ▶ 40 50N 73 52W One of the five boroughs of New York City, USA, situated NE of the Harlem River. It is mainly residential but has an industrialized waterfront. Overcrowding and poor housing conditions have made it the object of local and federal urbanization programmes. Area: 107 sq km (41 sq mi). Population (1990): 1 203 789.

● **bronze** ▶ An ▷alloy of copper and (4–11%) tin. Because it melts between 900°C and 1000°C, about the temperature of an ordinary wood fire, it was one of the first metals to be used for making weapons and utensils, being known around 2000 BC in Britain. It is harder than pure copper and "copper" coins are usually made of bronze containing 95% copper, 4% tin, 1% zinc, and occasionally other metals. Phosphor bronze contains 0.5% phosphorus. ▷*See also* gun metal.

● **Bronze Age** ▶ The cultural phase during which metallurgical technology, based first on copper (in the Chalcolithic period) and then on bronze (copper alloyed with tin), replaced the stone technology (*see* Stone Age) of the ▷Neolithic period. In Eurasia the development of international trade, literacy, the plough, and the wheel took place during this phase, which began at varying dates according to locality (the earliest being about 6500 BC in Anatolia); it gave way to the ▷Iron Age in about 1000 BC. In Africa, iron, discovered about 800 BC, replaced stone without an intervening Bronze Age. In the Americas, copper, discovered about 100 AD, was followed rapidly by iron, while in Australasia, the introduction of metallurgy occurred in the colonial period.

● **Bronzino, Il** ► (Agnolo di Cosimo; 1503–72) Florentine mannerist painter (*see* mannerism). His religious and allegorical works, such as *Venus, Cupid, and Folly* (National Gallery, London), were influenced by ▷Michelangelo and Bronzino's teacher ▷Pontormo. As court painter to Cosimo I de' Medici he painted many portraits, including *Eleanor of Toledo and Her Son Giovanni* (Uffizi).

● **Brook, Peter** ► (1925–   ) British theatre director. His work for the Royal Shakespeare Company, of which he became a director in 1962, included experimental productions of Shakespeare and of such plays as Peter Weiss' *The Marat/Sade* (1962). Since 1970 he has worked with the International Centre for Theatre Research in Paris, where he has developed acting techniques evolved during a tour of Africa and Asia; his work with the company includes a nine-hour staging of the Indian epic the *Mahabharata* (1985). He has also directed films, including *Lord of the Flies* (1962) and *King Lear* (1969). He was appointed a Companion of Honour in 1998.

● **Brooke, Sir James** ► (1803–68) British explorer. Born in India, he bought an armed yacht—the *Royalist*—in England and departed on a voyage of exploration. He helped to suppress a rebellion in Sarawak for which he was made raja by the Sultan of Brunei. He formed a native council and strove to abolish head hunting, piracy, and opium smuggling. In 1847 he became British consul general for Borneo.

● **Brooke, Rupert (Chawner)** ► (1887–1915) British poet and critic. His scholarship, charm, and good looks gained him influential friends in literary and political circles. He received a naval commission in 1914 but died of blood poisoning on a hospital ship in the Aegean, without having seen action. His romantic image and the patriotism of his wartime poetry, *1914 and Other Poems* (1915), made him a national hero.

● **Brookeborough, Basil Stanlake Brooke, 1st Viscount** ► (1888–1973) Northern Irish statesman; prime minister of Northern Ireland (1943–63). A Unionist MP from 1929, he was minister of agriculture (1933–41) and of commerce (1941–43). He was committed to union with Great Britain.

● **Brooklyn** ► 40 40N 73 58W One of the five boroughs of New York City, USA, situated at the SW end of Long Island. Settled by Dutch farmers in 1636, it has many colonial buildings and is the site of Pratt Institute (1887), Brooklyn Institute of Arts and Sciences (1823; comprising Brooklyn Museum, Brooklyn Children's Museum, and Brooklyn Botanic Garden and Arboretum), and branches of four New York universities. The New York Naval Shipyard, established here in 1801, was converted to civilian use in the 1960s. Three bridges, including the famous Brooklyn Bridge (1869–83), span the East River connecting Brooklyn with Manhattan. A major port, it handles a vast amount of shipping; its waterfront is 53 km (33 mi) long. Area: 210 sq km (81 sq mi). Population (1990): 2 291 664.

● **Brookner, Anita** ► (1928–   ) British writer and art historian. A teacher at the Courtauld Institute of Art, London, she has written several books on art but is better known for her novels, including the Booker prizewinner *Hotel du Lac* (1984), *Latecomers* (1988), *Brief Lives* (1990), *Fraud* (1992), and *Falling Slowly* (1998).

● **Brooks, Mel** ► (Melvyn Kaminsky; 1926–   ) US comedy writer, actor, and film director, known for his offbeat humour. His films include *The Producers* (1968), *Blazing Saddles* (1974), *Young Frankenstein* (1974), *High Anxiety* (1977), and *Robin Hood: Men in Tights* (1993). In 2001 his stage version of *The Producers* triumphed on Broadway.

● **broom** ► A bushy deciduous shrub, *Sarothamnus scoparius* (or *Cytisus scoparius*), 60–200 cm high, with shiny green stems, small pointed compound leaves, and yellow flowers. Broom is found in heaths and woodland glades in Europe and is often grown as an ornamental. The branches are used for brooms and thatching. Family: ▷Leguminosae.

● **Broome, David** ► (1940–   ) British show jumper. He won the European championships in 1961, 1967, and 1969, Olympic bronze medals in 1960 and 1968, and the world championship in 1970. Professional from 1973, he continued as a leading British rider during the 1980s.

● **broomrape** ► A parasitic plant of the worldwide genus *Orobanche* (about 100 species), lacking chlorophyll but having underground tubers attached to the roots of the host plant. The flowering shoots rise 5–70 cm above ground on scaly stems topped by spikes of tubular two-lipped flowers, which may be white, yellow, or purple. Family: *Orobanchaceae*.

● **brotulid** ► A fish, also called brotula, belonging to the family *Brotulidae* (it is sometimes placed with the cusk eels in the family *Ophidiidae*). Brotulids have an eel-like body, up to about 90 cm in length, and most live in deep marine waters. Order: *Perciformes*.

● **Brough, Louise** ► (1923–   ) US tennis player, who in 1948 and 1950 won all three titles at Wimbledon (singles, doubles, and mixed doubles). She also won all 22 of her ▷Wightman Cup rubbers (1946–57).

● **Brougham, Henry Peter, 1st Baron Brougham and Vaux** ► (1778–1868) British statesman and lawyer who became Lord Chancellor (1830–34). In this capacity he set up the Central Criminal Court and, in the House of Lords, helped to pass the Reform Bill (1832) and the act abolishing slavery in the British Empire. He also designed a compact four-wheeled carriage (1838), known as a **brougham**, which was light enough to be drawn by one horse.

● **Brouwer, Adriaen** ► (c. 1605–38) Flemish painter, who worked in Holland, initially as a pupil of ▷Hals, and later in Antwerp. He excelled in small paintings of brawling and drunken peasants, the sombre colouring of which was increasingly influenced by Dutch art.

● **Brouwer, L(uitzen) E(gbertus) J(an)** ► (1881–1966) Dutch mathematician, who made important contributions to the development of ▷topology. He is often regarded as the founder of the subject in its modern form. He is also the founder of a school of mathematics known as intuitional mathematics, which holds that mathematics is a mental construction in which laws should be self-evident and derived by intuition.

● **Brown, Sir Arthur** ▷*See* Alcock, Sir John.

● **Brown, Capability** ► (Lancelot B.; 1716–83) British landscape gardener. Brown, carrying on the work of William ▷Kent, abandoned the formal continental style, seeking to create a stylized imitation of nature (as at Blenheim Palace). He was also an architect, designing houses and garden buildings. His nickname arose because he frequently told his patrons that their grounds had "capabilities" for landscaping.

● **Brown, Ford Madox** ► (1821–93) British painter, born in Calais. After studying in Belgium, Paris, and Rome, he returned to England, where he was influenced by the Pre-Raphaelites. He painted chiefly historical themes, although his most famous paintings, *Work* (Manchester) and *The Last of England* (Birmingham), are contemporary subjects. He also decorated Manchester town hall.

● **Brown, George** ▷*See* George-Brown, Baron.

● **Brown, (James) Gordon** ► (1951–   ) British Labour politician; chancellor of the exchequer (1997–   ). He entered parliament in 1983 and was shadow secretary of state and industry (1989–92) and shadow chancellor (1992–97). As chancellor he cut the lower rates of income tax, introduced tax credits for low-income families, and presided over a period of economic stability and growth.

● **Brown, John** ► (1800–59) US abolitionist, who believed slaves must be freed by force. He raided the Federal Arsenal at Harpers Ferry, Virginia, in an attempt to establish a slave refuge and a base for promoting slave uprisings. He was captured and executed for treason, becoming an abolitionist martyr; he is the hero of the song "John Brown's Body."

● **Brown, Robert** ► (1773–1858) Scottish botanist, who in 1831 first recognized the ▷nucleus as a fundamental constituent of cells. Four years earlier, while observing a solution of pollen grains in water under a microscope, he discovered the effect now known as the ▷Brownian movement.

● **brown algae** ► ▷Algae of the phylum *Phaeophyta* (1500 species), which contain a brown pigment (fucoxanthin) in addition to and sometimes masking the green chlorophyll. Brown algae include the larger ▷seaweeds, such as wracks and kelps. Mainly marine, they are abundant along coasts in colder regions. Many show ▷alternation of generations.

● **brown bear** ► A large bear, *Ursus arctos*, of the N hemisphere. Brown bears have a thick shaggy coat, humped on the shoulders and varying in colour from blackish-brown to grey, and they take a wide variety of food including fish, fruit, and cattle. There are many local races and subspecies, including the North American grizzly and Kodiac bears. The reputedly ferocious grizzly bear (*U. arctos horribilis*), mostly restricted to N Canada and Alaska, reaches a length of 2.5 m and a weight of 550 kg; the Alaskan Kodiac bear—a giant race of grizzly—is the largest living land carnivore, reaching a length of 2.8 m and a weight of 760 kg.

● **Browne, Hablot Knight** ► (1815–82) British artist, better known as Phiz. He is renowned mainly for his illustrations of books by Charles Dickens, notably *The Pickwick Papers*. He also produced cartoons for *Punch* and watercolours.

● **Browne, Robert** ► (c. 1550–1633) Puritan separatist, whose followers, known as Brownists, were the spiritual ancestors of Congregationalists. After founding self-governing congregations in Norwich and preaching against the discipline of the Established Church, he was imprisoned and forced into exile in Holland (1581–84). He was later reconciled with the Church of England.

● **Browne, Sir Thomas** ► (1605–82) English physician and writer. He studied medicine at Oxford and in Europe and settled in Norwich in 1637. *Religio Medici* (1643) is a book of philosophic and religious reflections, written in elaborate prose. In *Pseudodoxia Epidemica* (1646, also known as *Vulgar Errors*) he critically surveyed many popular superstitions. He also wrote two antiquarian treatises, *Hydriotaphia: Urn Burial* (1658) and *The Garden of Cyrus* (1658).

● **Brownian movement** ► The continuous random movement of very small particles (less than about one-thousandth of a millimetre in diameter) when suspended in a fluid. It is caused by collisions between the particles and the atoms or molecules of the fluid. Brownian movement can be observed in smoke suspended in air and in a suspension of pollen grains in a liquid. Named after Robert ▷Brown.

● **Browning, Robert** ► (1812–89) British poet. The son of a bank clerk, his early education consisted chiefly of wide reading in his father's library. After the failure of his autobiographical poem *Pauline* (1833) he wrote several verse dramas and numerous dramatic monologues, including the famous "My Last Duchess" (1842). His work found little recognition until the publication of his *Dramatis Personae* in 1864. The epic but uneven poem cycle *The Ring and the Book* (1868–69) was his last major work. His wife **Elizabeth Barrett Browning** (1806–61) was also a poet. A spinal injury when she was 15 made her a lifelong semi-invalid. She met Robert Browning in 1845 and in 1846 she defied her domineering father and eloped with Browning to Italy. Here she wrote her most famous work, *Sonnets from the Portuguese* (1850), and the verse novel *Aurora Leigh* (1856). In later years she became involved in Italian politics, the campaign for the abolition of slavery, and spiritualism.

● **Browning Automatic Rifle** ► (BAR) A gas-operated shoulder-fired automatic ▷rifle designed in 1917 by John Moses Browning (1855–1926). The standard automatic weapon in the US army until the Korean War, it weighed over 8.6 kg (19 lbs), including its 20-round magazine.

● **Brownshirts** ► The colloquial name for the Nazi Sturmabteilung (SA; stormtroopers). Their name refers to their brown uniforms. They were founded in 1921 and reorganized by Ernst ▷Röhm in 1930. Squads of thugs, who molested and murdered the Nazis' opponents, they numbered two million by 1933. In 1934 Hitler eliminated Röhm and greatly reduced the power of the Brownshirts. ▷*See also* SS.

● **Broz, Josip** ▷*See* Tito.

● **Brubeck, Dave** ► (1920–   ) US jazz pianist and composer, who studied composition with Darius Milhaud and Arnold Schoenberg. Brubeck introduced complex rhythms into jazz and formed a quartet in 1951. Among his most famous pieces are "Take Five," and "Blue Rondo à la Turque."

● **Bruce, James** ► (1730–94) British explorer, who in the course of an arduous expedition that set out from Cairo in 1768 reached Lake Tana, source of the Blue Nile (1770). He described his experiences in *Travels to Discover the Source of the Nile* (1790).

● **Bruce, Lenny** ► (Leonard Alfred Schneider; 1925–66) US comedian and satirist. Performing in nightclubs from the mid-1950s, Bruce became notorious for his iconoclastic approach to such taboo subjects as sex and religion. He was imprisoned for obscenity in 1961 and banned from Britain and Australia. He died of an accidental drugs overdose.

● **Bruce, Robert** ▷*See* Robert (I) the Bruce.

● **Bruce, Stanley Melbourne, 1st Viscount Bruce of Melbourne** ►(1883–1967) Australian statesman; prime minister (1923–29). He fought with the British Army in World War I and entered politics as a member of the National Party in 1918. His coalition government of National and Country Parties implemented social and welfare legislation in the areas of public health and devised a scheme of national insurance against unemployment. From 1933 to 1945 he was high commissioner in London and represented Australia in the British war cabinet (1942–45).

● **brucellosis** ► (or undulant fever) An infectious disease of cattle and other farm animals that is caused by the bacterium *Brucella abortus* and can be contracted by man through drinking unpasteurized contaminated milk. Symptoms include fever (which may be intermittent), sweating, weakness, cough, joint pain, and sometimes swelling of the lymph nodes. Tetracycline usually cures the disease. The slaughter of infected animals has reduced the incidence of brucellosis in Europe.

● **Bruch, Max** ► (1838–1920) German composer. He wrote in a romantic but conservative style. He is best known for his first violin concerto (1868) and *Kol Nidrei* (1880) for cello and orchestra, based on a Jewish hymn.

● **Brücke, Die** ► (German: The Bridge) An organization of German artists founded in 1905. Its members, notably ▷Kirchner, were influenced, like their French contemporaries, the fauves (*see* fauvism), by ▷Van Gogh, ▷Gauguin, ▷Munch, and primitive art. However, their crudely painted and vibrantly coloured figure studies and landscapes expressed an underlying anxiety more typical of such early German artists as ▷Grünewald. Although the group broke up in 1913, it has had a lasting influence on the graphic arts, particularly the ▷woodcut. ▷*See also* expressionism.

● **Bruckner, Anton** ► (1824–96) Austrian composer and organist. He was a professor at the Vienna conservatoire (1871–91). In 1891 he was granted a pension and apartments in the Belvedere palace in Vienna, where he worked on his ninth symphony (1887–96), which remained unfinished. His 11 symphonies (which include the F minor work known as Symphony 00 and the D minor work known as Symphony 0) exhibit the influence of Wagner and Schubert. They had a mixed reception during his lifetime and were frequently performed in shortened versions. Bruckner also composed choral music, chamber music, organ music, and a *Te Deum* (1881–84) for orchestra, soloists, and chorus.

● **Brudenell, James Thomas** ▷*See* Cardigan, James Thomas Brudenell, 7th Earl of.

● **Brueghel the Elder, Pieter** ► (or Bruegel; 1525–69) Flemish painter, noted for his often satirical scenes of peasant life and his landscapes. Although popularly called Peasant Brueghel, he was a learned man, whose patrons included Cardinal de Granvelle (1517–86). He studied under Pieter Coecke van Aelst (1502–50), whose daughter he later married, but he was chiefly influenced by Hieronymus ▷Bosch in such works as the macabre *Triumph of Death* (Prado). He visited Italy (c. 1551–53) but Italian art influenced his style only in his last years. In 1563 he settled in Brussels, where he executed his best-known works, e.g. *Peasant Wedding* (Kunsthistorisches

Pieter Brueghel the Elder ▶ "The Beekeepers," a copper plate engraving.

Museum, Vienna), and a landscape series entitled the *Labours of the Months*. Many of his paintings were copied by his eldest son **Pieter Brueghel the Younger** (?1564–?1638). His younger son **Jan Brueghel the Elder** (1568–1625), popularly called Velvet Brueghel, is noted for his flower and landscape paintings. He was a friend of Rubens.

● **Bruges** ▶ (Flemish name: Brugge) 51 13N 3 14E A town in NW Belgium. It was the capital of Flanders in the 12th century and during the 13th and 14th centuries it became the centre of the Hanseatic League in Europe. It has many fine gothic buildings, including the 14th-century cathedral, the Church of Notre Dame (containing Michelangelo's marble statue, the Virgin and Child) and the Market Hall (13th–15th centuries) with its famous belfry and 47-bell carillon. It is linked by canal to many European ports. The traditional industry is lace; newer industrial developments include the manufacture of ships and electronic equipment. Population (1996 est): 115 815.

● **bruise** ▶ An area of discoloured skin caused by the leakage of blood from damaged blood vessels beneath the skin. Bruises are usually caused by a blow to the skin and are always more pronounced where the blood vessels are loosely suspended in the tissue (e.g. around the eye). They change from bluish to greenish yellow, as the blood pigment is chemically broken down and absorbed.

● **Brummel, George Bryan** ▶ (1778–1840) British dandy, known as Beau Brummel. He was a prominent member of fashionable society and a close friend of the Prince Regent, later George IV. He fled to France to evade his creditors in 1816 and died in an asylum.

● **Brunei, State of** ▶ A small sultanate in NW Borneo, on the South China Sea. It consists of two separate areas, entirely bounded (except for its coast) by the Malaysian state of Sarawak. It is low lying with some hills in the S; the interior is largely forest. The people are mainly Malays; about a quarter of the population are Chinese or other minorities.
  Economy: dominated by oil (the main export) since the discovery of the Seria oilfield in 1929; production is being kept up by the addition of offshore oilfields. Recent efforts to diversify the economy include the construction of a deepwater port and a natural-gas liquefaction plant. Agriculture is being encouraged in an attempt to make Brunei more self-sufficient in food production. The economy has suffered from the Asian financial crisis of 1997 and recent falls in oil prices.
  History: a powerful state in the 16th century controlling the whole of Borneo, as well as parts of the Philippines, it became a British protected state in 1888. In 1962 there was a revolt, mainly in protest against the proposal to join the Federation of Malaysia, and since then the sultan has ruled by decree. In 1967 Hassanal Bolkia Mu'izuddin Waddaulah (1946–) succeeded his father as sultan. Self-government was achieved in 1971 and de facto independence in

1983; it became officially independent in 1984. Unemployment and social unrest rose during the 1990s.

State of Brunei

Head of state	Sultan Hassanal Bolkia Mu'izuddin Waddaulah
Official language	Malay; Chinese and English are also widely spoken
Official religion	Islam
Official currency	Brunei dollar of 100 cents
Area	5800 sq km (2226 sq mi)
Population (1997 est)	308 000
Capital and main port	Bandar Seri Begawan

● **Brunel, Isambard Kingdom** ▶ (1806–59) British engineer, who was one of the most original inventors of the 19th century. His most famous works were the Clifton suspension bridge, which spanned the Avon Gorge, completed in 1864, and his ships the *Great Western* (1837), the *Great Britain* (1843; ⬜ships), the first large ship to be driven by screw propellers and now preserved in Bristol, and the *Great Eastern* (1858). Much of his work was done for the Great Western Railway, for which he built over 1600 km of track, using the broad (7 ft) gauge rather than the standard (4 ft 8½ in) gauge. His father **Sir Marc Isambard Brunel** (1769–1849) was also an engineer. Born in France, he worked in New York after fleeing the French Revolution in 1793. He moved to England in 1799, where he became famous for his work on tunnelling. In 1818 he patented the tunnelling shield, which allowed tunnels to be dug below water. In 1825 he began tunnelling beneath the River Thames from ▷Rotherhithe to Wapping, a project fraught with difficulties that was not completed until 1842. The tunnel, which was 460 metres long, 11 metres wide, and 7 metres high, was opened in 1843 but not used for transportation until 1865.

● **Brunelleschi, Filippo** ▶ (1377–1446) Italian architect. The founder of Renaissance architecture, Brunelleschi began his career as a goldsmith, only taking up architecture in his thirties, after spending some time studying Roman remains. His taste for classical architecture probably arose from a desire to understand Roman building techniques. This is demonstrated by his most famous construction, the dome of Florence cathedral (1430s), which used classical methods of construction. The Ospedale degli Innocenti (1419–26) is often regarded as the first architectural expression of the Renaissance. ⬜ p. 196.

● **Brunhild** ▶ (or Brynhild) A heroine of Norse and Germanic legend. In the *Volsungasaga* she is Odin's daughter, doomed to sleep on a fire-encircled rock until wakened by a mortal (*see* Siegfried). In the ▷*Nibelungenlied* she is queen of Issland.

● **Brünn** ▷*See* Brno.

● **Brunner, Emil** ▶ (1889–1965) Swiss Protestant theologian. A professor at the University of Zurich from 1924 to 1953, he became a supporter of the theological views of Karl ▷Barth. However, he differed from Barth in allowing that God's image in mankind survived the Fall, despite man's sinfulness.

● **Bruno, Frank(lin Roy)** ▶ (1961–) British boxer. He became European heavyweight champion in 1985 and WBC heavyweight champion of the world in 1995. He lost the latter title to Mike ▷Tyson in 1996 and retired.

● **Bruno, Giordano** ▶ (1548–1600) Italian philosopher. He became a Dominican (1563) but in 1576 his heretical opinions forced him to flee, first to Geneva, then to France, England, and Germany. Returning to Italy (1592) he was tried by the Inquisition, refused to recant, and was burned. His pantheistic philosophy, viewing all creation as one life, animated by God as "world-soul," influenced ▷Spinoza, ▷Descartes, and ▷Leibniz.

● **Bruno of Cologne, St** ▶ (c. 1032–1101) German founder of the Carthusian order. He was educated at Cologne and Rheims, where he later taught at the cathedral school. He eventually withdrew with six companions to the mountainous region near Grenoble and built a monastery, which became the mother house of the Carthusians. Called to Italy by Pope Urban II, his former pupil, he founded the monastery of La Torre in Calabria, where he died. Feast day: 6 Oct.

● **Brunswick** ▶ (German name: Braunschweig) 52 15N 10 30E A city in N Germany, in Lower Saxony on the River Oker. It was the capital of the former duchy of Brunswick. Notable buildings include the castle and the cathedral (both 12th-century), the old town hall (14th–15th centuries), and the ducal palace (1768–69). It has the oldest technical university in Germany (1745). Manufactures include electronic goods, motor vehicles, and pianos. Population (1996 est): 252 544.

● **brush turkey** ▷See megapode.

● **Brussels** ▶ (Flemish name: Brussel; French name: Bruxelles) 50 51N 4 22E The capital of Belgium, situated in the centre of the country on the River Senne. As headquarters of the EU and NATO, it is an important international centre. Its varied industries include the manufacture of machinery, chemicals, and lace. Fine buildings include the 15th-century gothic town hall, the 13th-century Maison du Roi, the church of St Gudule, the 18th-century Palais de la Nation (parliament building), and the Royal Palace. The Free University was founded in 1834 and a Flemish-speaking counterpart became independent in 1970.

History: settled by the French in the 7th century AD, it developed into a centre of the wool industry in the 13th century. It became the capital of the Spanish Netherlands in the 15th century and later of the Austrian S Netherlands. In 1830 it was chosen as capital of the new kingdom of Belgium. It was occupied by the Germans in both World Wars. Population (1995 est): 951 980.

● **Brussels, Treaty of** ▷See European Economic Community; North Atlantic Treaty Organization.

● **Brussels sprout** ▶ A variety of wild cabbage, *Brassica oleracea* var. *gemmifera*, cultivated for its large edible buds in Europe and the USA. The stout erect shoots, up to 80 cm high, have long-stalked curly leaves arranged spirally up the stem; in the angle between the leaf bases and the stem are large buds, like miniature cabbages up to 5 cm in diameter. ▷See also Brassica.

● **brutalism** ▶ (or new brutalism) An aspect of the ▷international style of architecture; the word was originally used to describe the work of such postwar British architects as Peter and Alison ▷Smithson, who were much influenced by ▷Le Corbusier. Brutalist architecture is characterized by the use of monumental untreated concrete structures, exposed services, and adherence to the principles of ▷functionalism.

● **Bruton, John Gerard** ▶ (1947–) Irish statesman; prime minister of Ireland (1994–97). Leader of Fine Gael (1990–), he was first elected to the Dáil Éireann in 1969.

● **Brutus, Marcus Junius** ▶ (?85–42 BC) Roman soldier and one of the assassins of Julius Caesar. Brutus, who supported Pompey against Caesar in the civil war, was pardoned by Caesar and made governor of Cisalpine Gaul (46) but later joined the conspiracy to murder Caesar (44). He committed suicide after his defeat by Antony and Octavian at Philippi (42).

● **Bryansk** ▶ 53 15N 34 09E A city in W Russia. Dating from at least the 12th century, it held an important position on the trade route between Moscow and the Ukraine; it is now a communications centre with varied industries. Population (1995 est): 462 000.

● **Bryant, William Cullen** ▶ (1794–1878) US poet, journalist, and critic. He wrote his most famous poem, "Thanatopsis," when he was 17. The success of his *Poems* (1821) enabled him to abandon his law practice and move to New York. From 1829 he was editor of the liberal *Evening Post*.

● **Bryce, James, 1st Viscount** ▶ (1838–1922) British Liberal politician, historian, and ambassador to the USA (1907–13). An MP (1880–1907), Bryce headed the Bryce Commission (1894–95), which recommended the establishment of a ministry of education. He co-founded the *English Historical Review (1885) and wrote The American Commonwealth* (1888).

● **bryony** ▶ Either of two unrelated Eurasian plants. **Black bryony** (*Tamus communis*) is a herbaceous climber with heart-shaped leaves and bell-shaped yellow flowers in separate male and female spikes. The fruits are scarlet berries. Family: *Dioscoreaceae* (yam family). **White bryony** (*Bryonia dioica*) is a perennial climbing herb with a hairy stem and palmately lobed leaves. Greenish male and female

Brunelleschi ▶ Florence cathedral showing Brunelleschi's spectacular dome (1430s).

flowers occur on separate plants and produce poisonous scarlet berries. Family: *Cucurbitaceae* (gourd family).

● **bryophytes** ▶ A group of flowerless plants comprising the ▷hornworts, ▷liverworts, and ▷mosses. The plant body is either differentiated into stems and leaves or is a flat branching structure (thallus). Bryophytes range in size from microscopic to over 1 m long; they lack true vascular (conducting) tissues and the rootlike rhizoids serve mainly for anchorage. Bryophytes show ▷alternation of generations: the plant itself is the sexual (gametophyte) phase, which bears male and female sex organs (antheridia and archegonia, respectively). A fertilized egg cell develops into a spore capsule—the asexual (sporophyte) phase—attached to the gametophyte. The spores are dispersed and germinate to form new plants.

● **Bryozoa** ▶ (or Ectoprocta) A phylum of aquatic (mainly marine) colonial invertebrate animals (about 6000 species), called moss animals, found as matlike encrustations on rocks. Each individual, up to 3 mm long, has a chitinous or gelatinous case and a ring of ciliated tentacles around the mouth. These waft food particles into the U-shaped digestive tract. Ciliated larvae establish new colonies by ▷budding.

● **Brythonic languages** ▷*See* Celtic languages.

● **Brześć nad Bugiem** ▷*See* Brest.

● **BSE** ▶ (or bovine spongiform encephalopathy) A fatal disease of cattle causing degeneration of brain tissue and popularly known as "mad cow disease." Now believed to be caused by an abnormal protein in the brain (*see* prion) and having a very long incubation period, it was apparently transmitted to cattle in feed containing brains of sheep infected with scrapie, which is also caused by prions; it can also pass from infected cows to their calves. The first cases were recorded in the UK in 1986; subsequently, the disease appeared in cats and other animals that had eaten food containing infected beef offal. Concern that BSE might spread to humans led the British government to impose a ban (1989) on the use of beef offal in human foods, but it was not strictly enforced. In 1996 several people died from a new strain of ▷Creutzfeldt-Jakob disease, which scientists declared most probably resulted from eating BSE-infected beef products. This led the EU to impose a worldwide ban on British beef exports until an agreed programme of cattle slaughter had been completed (the ban was lifted in 1999). From 1997 until late 1999 the British government, on scientific advice, banned the sale of beef on the bone. In 2000 the official inquiry into the origin and spread of BSE blamed intensive farming practices, the animal feed industry, and lack of openness by British government departments. By 2001 fears were also growing about the safety of beef from Ireland, France, Portugal, and other European countries.

● **Bubastis** ▶ (modern name: Tall Bastah) A ruined temple city in Lower Egypt. Bubastis was the capital of the 18th nome (province) and attained importance when the pharaohs of the 19th dynasty (1320–1200 BC) moved their capital to the Nile Delta. It became a royal residence when Sheshonk I was pharaoh (952 BC). After the Persian conquest (525 BC) the city declined. Bubastis was sacred to the cat goddess Bast.

● **bubble chamber** ▶ An instrument used for observing particle decays and interactions. It contains a liquid, usually hydrogen, helium, or deuterium, under pressure and at a temperature slightly above its normal boiling point. The particle induces boiling along its path and the bubbles are photographed to record the particle's track and those of any charged decay or reaction products.

● **Buber, Martin** ▶ (1878–1965) Austrian-born Jewish religious philosopher. He produced, with Franz Rosenzweig (1886–1929), a German translation of the Bible. His best-known work was *I and Thou* (1923). A Zionist, he settled in Palestine in 1938 and advocated a joint Arab-Jewish state.

● **bubonic plague** ▷*See* plague.

● **Bucaramanga** ▶ 7 08N 73 10W A city in N Colombia. It is the commercial centre for an area producing coffee and tobacco; manufactures include cigarettes and textiles. The Industrial University of Santander was founded here in 1947. Population (1997 est): 508 240.

● **buccaneers** ▶ Bands of pirates who lived by plunder in the Caribbean in the second half of the 17th century. Most were English or French and they preyed primarily on Spanish shipping and settlements. They were often hired by the French governors of Tortuga and the English of Jamaica. By 1670, under Henry ▷Morgan, they were a major hazard. In 1685 the English navy began hunting them and after 1697 no European country employed them.

● **Bucer, Martin** ▶ (1491–1551) German Protestant reformer. A Dominican friar, Bucer abandoned his vows and married in 1522, settling in Strasbourg. He advised Henry VIII on his divorce from Catherine of Aragon and tried to mediate between ▷Luther and ▷Zwingli in their debate concerning the Eucharist. In 1549 he became Regius Professor of Divinity at Cambridge. His views on the Eucharist had some influence on the Prayer Book of 1552.

● **Buchan, John, 1st Baron Tweedsmuir** ▶ (1875–1940) British novelist. *Prester John* (1910) was the first of his adventure novels that included *The Thirty-Nine Steps* (1915), in which Richard Hannay first appeared, and *The Three Hostages* (1924). Director of Information during World War I, he was made governor general of Canada in 1935.

● **Buchanan, George** ▶ (1506–82) Scottish historian and scholar. He held academic posts in France, Portugal, and Scotland besides tutoring Mary, Queen of Scots, and James VI. As well as political works and his *History of Scotland* (1582) he wrote powerful satires and plays, all in Latin.

● **Buchanan, James** ▶ (1791–1868) US statesman; Democratic president (1857–61). Buchanan tried to avert civil war by compromise, dividing his cabinet between representatives of slave-holding and free states. However, he split the Democrats by recommending a proslavery constitution for Kansas and lost the 1860 election to Abraham Lincoln.

● **Bucharest** ▶ (Romanian name: Bucureşti) 44 25N 26 07E The capital of Romania, in the SE on a tributary of the Danube. Its many industries include flour milling, textiles, chemicals, and oil refining.
History: human settlement dates from prehistoric times. A fortress was built against Turkish invasion in the 15th century and it became capital of Walachia in 1659. During the 19th century Bucharest played an important role in revolutionary movements, becoming capital of Romania in 1862. The university was founded in 1864. It was badly damaged by German bombing in World War II. In the uprising of 1989 many died in Bucharest when troops fired on demonstrators. Population (1996): 2 037 278.

● **Bucharest, Treaties of** ▶ 1. (1812) The treaty ending the Russo-Turkish war of 1806–12. It assigned Bessarabia to Russia and Walachia and Moldavia to Turkey; the Serbs were to receive autonomy. 2. (1886) The treaty ending the Serbian-Bulgarian war (1885–86) over Eastern ▷Rumelia, which was kept by Bulgaria. 3. (1913) The treaty ending the second ▷Balkan War, which partitioned Macedonia between Serbia, Greece, Romania, and the defeated Bulgaria. 4. (1918) The treaty in which Romania acknowledged its defeat by the Central Powers in World War I. It was annulled after their defeat by the Allies.

● **Buchenwald** ▷*See* concentration camps.

● **Buchman, Frank Nathan Daniel** ▶ (1878–1961) US Lutheran pastor who became a well-known evangelist. At Oxford University, he founded the Oxford Group, later the ▷Moral Rearmament movement.

● **Büchner, Georg** ▶ (1813–37) German dramatist. A medical student, he fled to Zürich after publishing a revolutionary pamphlet in 1834. He wrote the tragedies *Danton's Death* (1835) and *Woyzeck* (1836) and the comedy *Leonce und Lena* (1836), and a fragment of a novel, *Lenz* (1836).

● **Buck, Pearl S(ydenstricker)** ▶ (1892–1973) US novelist. The daughter of missionaries, she grew up in China and later returned there as a teacher. Her novels about China include *The Good Earth* (1931) and *The Three Daughters of Madame Liang* (1969). She won the Nobel Prize in 1938.

● **Buckingham** ▶ 52 00N 1 00W A market town in S central England, in N Buckinghamshire on the River Ouse. Nearby is Stowe House, a public school since 1923 but formerly the seat of the dukes of Buckingham. The University College at Buckingham, the only independent university in the UK, was established here in 1975. Industries include light engineering. Population (1991): 10 168.

• **Buckingham, George Villiers, 1st Duke of** ► (1592–1628) A favourite of James I of England. He replaced Robert Carr, Earl of ▷Somerset, in the king's favour (1615), becoming Earl of Buckingham (1617), Lord High Admiral (1619), and Duke of Buckingham (1623). His attempt to negotiate the marriage of Prince Charles to the daughter of the Spanish king failed (1623), as did his planned expedition to Cádiz (1625) in the subsequent hostilities. Charles I resisted parliament's attempts to impeach Buckingham, who was assassinated after his unsuccessful expedition to relieve the Huguenots at La Rochelle (1627). His son **George Villiers, 2nd Duke of Buckingham** (1628–87) was a member of the ▷Cabal under Charles II. After his father's death he was brought up in the royal family, with whom he went into exile after the final royalist defeat in the Civil War (1651). Becoming a privy councillor at the Restoration, he helped oust ▷Clarendon (1667) but was overshadowed by ▷Arlington when the Cabal came to power. Also a playwright, he wrote the satirical *The Rehearsal* (1671); he is portrayed as Zimri in Dryden's *Absalom and Achitophel*.

• **Buckingham Palace** ► The London residence of the British monarch. It was built about 1705 for the Duke of Buckingham, becoming a royal residence in 1761. It was completely redesigned by Nash for George IV, but its main façade was not added until 1913. It opened to the public in 1993.

• **Buckinghamshire** ► A county in the south Midlands of England, bordering on Greater London. Under local government reorganization in 1974 it lost part of the S, including Slough, to Berkshire. Milton Keynes became an independent ▷unitary authority in 1997. Known appropriately as Leafy Bucks because of the many trees throughout the county, the land rises gently N from the River Thames to the Chiltern Hills before descending to the fertile Vale of Aylesbury in the N. It is mainly agricultural, the chief crops being barley, wheat, and oats; sheep, cattle, poultry, and pig farming are also significant. Industry includes the manufacture of furniture at High Wycombe, based on the extensive beech woods. Area (excluding Milton Keynes): 1568 sq km (605 sq mi). Population (1997 est, excluding Milton Keynes): 473 000. Administrative centre: Aylesbury.

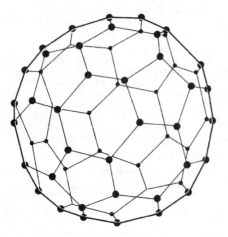

buckminsterfullerene ► This allotrope of carbon has a structure consisting of 60 carbon atoms arranged at the corners of polyhedrons with faces that are hexagons or pentagons.

• **buckminsterfullerene** ► A form of carbon molecule that contains 60 carbon atoms arranged in a ball-like structure, known informally as **buckyball**, resembling the geodesic dome designed by R. Buckminster ▷Fuller, after whom it is named. A similar form of carbon is the **bucky tube**, the atoms of which are linked in a tubular arrangement.

• **buckthorn** ► A small thorny deciduous tree or shrub of the genus *Rhamnus* (about 13 species), widespread in the N hemisphere. The leaves are oval, with attractive autumn colours. The small green flowers produce blue-black berries. The wood is used for charcoal and slow fuses, and the bark for dyes. The alder buckthorn (*Frangula alnus*) is a similar and related shrub that lacks thorns. Family: *Rhamnaceae*.

• **buckwheat** ► A herbaceous plant of the genus *Fagopyrum*, especially *F. esculentum*. Up to 60 cm tall, they have arrow-shaped leaves and clusters of densely packed small pink or white flowers. Buckwheats are native to Asia but widely cultivated for their seed, used as a cereal substitute, or as green fodder. Family: *Polygonaceae* (dock family).

• **Budapest** ► 47 33N 19 03E The capital of Hungary, situated in the N of the country on the River Danube. Most of Hungary's industry is sited here and includes machinery, iron and steel, and chemicals. The university was founded in 1635.

History: from the 14th century the fortress of Buda, on the W bank of the Danube, was the seat of the Magyar kings. After occupation by the Turks, it came under Habsburg rule in the 17th century. In 1872 it united with Pest to form the city that became the capital of Hungary in 1918. In 1956 it was the scene of a popular rising, suppressed by Soviet troops. A further rising in 1989 ended Communist rule. Population (1997 est): 1 885 000.

Buddha ► A 5th-century carving in the rock at Yunkang, Shanxi province, in China.

• **Buddha** ► Title of **Gautama Siddhartha** (c. 563–c. 483 BC), Indian prince, whose teachings formed the basis of Buddhism. The son of Suddhodana and his queen, Maya, in Kapilavastu (Nepal), Gautama was reputed to have been a child of exceptional intelligence and beauty about whom many stories and legends have been told. At the age of 16 he married his cousin Princess Yasodhara, who some 13 years later bore him a son, Rahula. Soon after this event Gautama, renouncing his life of indolence and luxury, abandoned his family and set out to seek solutions to the problems of the transcience and suffering of human existence. He was then about 29. After six years of emaciating asceticism he reluctantly concluded that austerity was as unlikely as triviality to provide the solution he sought. Abandoned now by his five companions for his rejection of mortification, he determined to seek enlightenment, alone, within himself. According to tradition, this he achieved while seated beneath a bo tree, in what is now called Buddh Gaya, in Bihar (his title, *Buddha*, is Sanskrit for the Awakened One). Probably 35 years old at this time, he devoted the rest of his life to teaching the principles (*see* dharma) of this enlightenment, first moving to Benares, where he founded the Buddhist order of monks, and thereafter teaching in various places in N India. He died at Kusinagara in Uttar Pradesh. ▷*See also* Buddhism.

● **Buddhaghosa** ▶ (5th century AD) Buddhist scholar. A Brahman convert from Buddh Gaya, he wrote the *Visuddhi-magga* (*Path of Purity*), a collation of Sinhalese Buddhist commentaries that he collected in Ceylon and translated into Pali.

● **Buddh Gaya** ▶ (*or* Bodh Gaya) 24 42N 85 00E A village in India, in Bihar. It was here that Gautama Siddhartha (the ▷Buddha) attained enlightenment under the sacred bo (*or* bodhi) tree. Population (1991 est): 21 686.

● **Buddhism** ▶ The nontheistic religion and philosophical system founded in NE India in the 6th century BC by Gautama Siddhartha (the ▷Buddha). His followers seek to emulate his example of perfect morality, wisdom, and compassion, culminating in a transformation of consciousness known as enlightenment. Buddhism teaches that greed, hatred, and delusion separate the individual from the true preception of the nature of things, causing him to remain tied to the ▷Bhavachakra. The apparent substantiality of all objects, including the self, is illusion; everything mundane is impermanent and ultimately unsatisfying. The central beliefs of Buddhism are based on the Buddha's ▷Four Noble Truths, the last of which is the ▷Eightfold Path by which enlightenment may be attained and the individual self annihilated in ▷nirvana. Buddhism is not dogmatic, but through its long history has developed into many schools (*see* Mahayana; Theravada; Zen Buddhism). With more than 500 million followers in Sri Lanka, Nepal, Japan, and elsewhere in the Far East, Buddhism is currently gaining adherents in the West.

● **budding** ▶ In biology, a method of asexual reproduction in lower plants and animals, for example liverworts and coelenterates, in which new individuals develop from outgrowths of cells (buds) on the parent. The process also occurs in single-celled fungi, for example yeasts. In horticulture the term is used for the ▷grafting of a bud onto a stock.

● **Buddleia** ▶ A genus of trees and shrubs (about 100 species), mostly native to tropical or warm temperate regions but widely introduced. The small four-petalled flowers are usually clustered in dense heads; the fruit is a capsule or berry. Many species are grown as ornamentals, especially *B. davidii* (butterfly bush), 4–5 m high; and *B. globosa*, which has round orange flower heads. Family: *Buddleiaceae*.

● **Budé, Guillaume** ▶ (1467–1540) French Renaissance scholar. Budé wrote many important Greek commentaries and philological works. He founded the Collège de France (1530) and as royal librarian built the library that formed the nucleus of the Bibliothèque Nationale.

● **Budge, (John) Don(ald)** ▶ (1915–2000) US tennis player, the first to win all four major singles titles (Australian, French, US, and Wimbledon) in one year (1938). He was also an outstanding doubles player.

● **budgerigar** ▶ A small ▷parakeet, *Melopsitticus undulatus*, occurring in large flocks in arid regions of Australia. It is 19 cm long and has a green and yellow plumage with barred upper parts. Since its introduction to Britain in 1840 it has become a popular cagebird; white, violet, yellow, blue, and grey forms have been produced by selective breeding.

● **budget** ▶ A prediction of the financial behaviour of a firm, government, etc., over a specified period. Careful budgeting enables any deviation from a plan to be noted early and the appropriate action to be taken.

In the UK, the government's budget is presented to parliament by the chancellor of the exchequer, traditionally (but not invariably) on a Tuesday in March; in times of crisis supplementary budgets may be introduced at other times of the year. The chief components of the budget are the ▷taxation rates (which become incorporated in the Finance Act) and the planned public expenditure (incorporated in the Appropriations Act), which together determine the impact the government will have on the economy. In the 19th and early 20th centuries, governments attempted to run balanced budgets (i.e. neither in surplus nor in deficit) by analogy with good individual housekeeping. Since World War II governments have used the budget in attempts to counter the effects of the ▷trade cycle (*see* deficit financing;

fiscal policy), evoking controversy (*see* Keynes, John Maynard, 1st Baron; monetarism).

● **Buenaventura** ▶ 3 54N 77 02W A port in W Colombia, on the Pacific Ocean. Exports include coffee and sugar from the Cauca Valley and gold and platinum from the Chocó district. Population (1995 est): 266 988.

● **Bueno, Maria (Esther)** ▶ (1939–) Brazilian tennis player, who was Wimbledon singles champion in 1959, 1960, and 1964. She also won the US singles title four times, the Wimbledon doubles five times, and the US doubles four times.

● **Buenos Aires** ▶ 34 50S 58 37W The capital of Argentina and one of the world's largest ports, situated on the Río de la Plata estuary. It is the financial, commercial, and industrial centre of the country. Its chief exports are beef and wool. A cultural centre, Buenos Aires possesses many universities (including the University of Buenos Aires, 1821), the national library, and a famous opera house (the Teatro Colón). There are several fine avenues, including the Avenida de Mayo and the Avenida de Julio. Notable buildings include the cathedral (completed in 1804).

History: founded in 1580, after Indian attacks on earlier settlements, it became capital of the newly created viceroyalty of the Río de la Plata in 1776 and of the new Republic of Argentina in 1880. In the late 19th and early 20th centuries its population was greatly swelled by European immigrants, especially Spanish and Italian. Population (1995 est): 2 998 006.

buffalo ▶ A buffalo in Tanzania with oxpeckers, which remove parasites from the animal.

● **buffalo** ▶ A large African hoofed mammal, *Syncerus caffer*, also called Cape buffalo. Weighing over 700 kg and measuring 110–150 cm at the shoulder, buffaloes have massive curved horns and a smooth black coat. They live in large herds in grassy areas where both tree cover and water are available. Once numerous, their numbers have been reduced by hunting and disease. Family: ▷*Bovidae*. *Compare* bison; water buffalo.

● **Buffalo** ▶ 42 52N 78 55W A city in the USA, in New York state on Lake Erie and the Niagara River. The state's second largest city, it is linked to New York City by the New York State Barge Canal (formerly Erie Canal). A major port, its industries include iron and steel, motor vehicles, and electrical equipment. Population (1996 est): 310 548.

● **Buffalo Bill** ▷*See* Cody, William F(rederick).

● **buffalo gnat** ▷*See* black fly.

● **buffer solution** ▶ A solution the ▷pH of which is insensitive to dilution or the addition of moderate amounts of acid or base. Generally it consists of a mixture of a weak acid or base and its salt. If, for example, acid is added to an acetic acid-acetate mixture, the hydrogen ions will combine with acetate ions to form acetic acid molecules, thus lowering the acidity. Buffers are present in many living organisms, as fluctuations in pH would destroy the enzymes, etc.

● **Buffet, Bernard** ▶ (1928–99) French painter. Precociously talented, he established his reputation by 1948. His figurative paintings are notable for their strong black lines, melancholy colours, and elongated human forms.

● **Buffon, Georges Louis Leclerc, Comte de** ▶ (1707–88) French naturalist, who formulated a crude theory of evolution and was the first to suggest that the earth might be older than suggested by the Bible. He estimated the age of the earth to be 75 000 years, with life emerging some 40 000 years ago.

● **bug** ▶ A common name for any insect-like animal. Specifically, the term refers to insects of the order ▷*Hemiptera* (the true bugs), especially the ▷bedbug and insects of the suborder *Heteroptera* (plant bugs, water bugs, etc.).

● **Bug, River** ▶ 1. (*or* Western Bug) A river in E central Europe, rising in SW Ukraine and flowing NW as part of the border between Ukraine and Poland to the River Vistula. Length: 724 km (450 mi). 2. (*or* Southern Bug) A river in Ukraine, rising in the W and flowing SE to the Dnieper estuary on the Black Sea. Length: 853 km (530 mi).

● **Buganda** ▶ A former kingdom in East Africa, now comprising an administrative region of Uganda bordering on Lake Victoria. The UK Government assumed responsibility for Buganda in 1893. When Uganda became a republic (1963) the kabaka (king) of Buganda became president of Uganda. His arrest (1966) by the former prime minister Dr Milton Obote caused widespread rioting in Buganda.

● **Bugatti, Ettore (Arco Isidoro)** ▶ (1881–1947) Italian car manufacturer. In 1909 he founded a factory in Molsheim, Alsace, to produce cars to race at Le Mans. His finest car was probably the Type 41—the Golden Bugatti.

● **bugle** ▶ A high-pitched brass (or copper) instrument with a wide conical tube, a cup-shaped mouthpiece, and a small bell. It lacks valves and so can only play a single harmonic series (usually having the fundamental of C). Formerly much used for military signalling, it is also used on ceremonial occasions and in the brass band.

● **bugloss** ▶ A biennial herb of the Eurasian genus *Echium* (about 30 species), e.g. viper's bugloss (*E. vulgare*). Up to 90 cm high, the plants are covered in bristly hairs and produce spikes of funnel-shaped flowers, about 2 cm long, usually bluish with several protruding stamens. Another plant called bugloss is *Lycopsis arvensis*, an annual similar to *Echium* species but with smaller flowers. Family: *Boraginaceae*.

● **Buhl, André Charles** ▷*See* Boulle, André Charles.

● **building society** ▶ An association in the UK that accepts savings from the public, paying a specified rate of interest, and uses these funds to provide ▷mortgages to home buyers. Over 400 such societies belong to the Building Societies Association, which agrees the rates of ▷interest to be paid on deposits and the rate to be charged for mortgages. Building-society interest rates move in line with other interest rates to enable them to attract sufficient funds. Many societies now provide cheque accounts for investors, on which interest is paid, and a wide variety of other banking services. The distinction between banks and building societies is rapidly disappearing and some building societies have now become public limited companies.

● **Bujumbura** ▶ (former name: Usumbura) 3 30S 29 20E The capital of Burundi, a port on the NE shore of Lake Tanganyika. Founded in the 19th century, it became the capital of Ruanda-Urundi after World War I. The university was founded in 1960. Population (1994 est): 300 000.

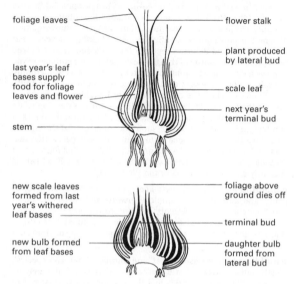

foliage leaves

flower stalk

plant produced by lateral bud

last year's leaf bases supply food for foliage leaves and flower

scale leaf

next year's terminal bud

stem

new scale leaves formed from last year's withered leaf bases

foliage above ground dies off

terminal bud

new bulb formed from leaf bases

daughter bulb formed from lateral bud

bulb ▶ A section through a daffodil bulb in spring (above) and summer (below) to show growth cycle.

● **Bukavu** ▶ (name until 1966: Costermansville) 2 20S 28 52E A port in E Democratic Republic of Congo, on Lake Kivu. A commercial centre, it has local agricultural and brewing industries. Population (1994 est): 201 569.

● **Bukhara** ▶ (*or* Bokhara) 39 47N 64 26E A city in S Uzbekistan. The Bukhara province of which it is the capital was the centre of a powerful kingdom, which was ceded to Russia in 1868. The city grew rapidly in the 1950s after the discovery of natural gas. It has textile industries, and the traditional crafts of gold embroidery and metalworking are still practised. Population (1993 est): 236 000.

● **Bukhari, al-** ▶ (810–70 AD) Muslim scholar and historian. After extensive travels, he collected more than 600 000 traditional records (*see* Hadith) of the words and deeds of the prophet Mohammed. He published a selection of these, arranged by subject, which he considered authentic teachings. The resulting collection is revered by orthodox Muslims as second in authority only to the Koran.

● **Bukharin, Nikolai Ivanovich** ▶ (1888–1938) Soviet politician and communist theoretician. In exile after 1911, Bukharin edited the socialist newspaper *Novy Mir*, in New York. He returned to Russia during the Revolution and became editor of the newspaper *Pravda*. He believed that Russia should achieve socialism slowly and therefore supported Lenin's New Economic Policy (1924). He was chairman of the Comintern until dismissed by Stalin in 1929. He helped draft the 1936 constitution but was expelled from the Communist Party shortly afterwards and died in Stalin's purges.

● **Bukovina** ▶ (*or* Bucovina) An area in E Europe, in the NE Carpathian Mountains. As part of the principality of Moldavia, it fell to the Turks in 1512 and was ceded to Austria in 1775. Occupied by the Romanians in 1918, the N part was ceded to the Soviet Union (1940) and is now part of independent Ukraine. S Bukovina remained a Romanian province until it was abolished in 1952.

● **Bulawayo** ▶ 20 10S 28 43E The second largest city in Zimbabwe. It was founded on its present site in 1894 by the British, near to its original site of the kraal of Lobengula, the centre of the Ndebele tribe. Nearby are the popular tourist attractions of Rhodes Matapos National Park and the Khami Ruins. The city is the country's chief industrial centre with metal, motor-tyre, and cement industries. Population (1992): 620 936.

● **bulb** ▶ A modified underground stem of certain perennial herbaceous plants, for example onions, daffodils, and tulips, that serves as an overwintering organ. Food is stored in overlapping fleshy leaves or leaf bases, borne on a very short stem, and is used to produce one or more plants the following season. When a bulb produces two or more plants it acts as an organ of vegetative reproduction. East Anglia (UK) and the Netherlands are centres for the commercial production of spring-flowering bulbs.

● **bulbul** ▶ A gregarious forest-dwelling songbird belonging to an Old World family (*Pycnonotidae*; 120 species). 12–22 cm long, bulbuls are yellow, green, or brown, sometimes with bright patches on the head and beneath the tail. They have a slender bill surrounded by stiff bristles and feed largely on fruit and berries.

● **Bulganin, Nikolai Aleksandrovich** ▶ (1895–1975) Soviet statesman; prime minister (1955–58). Bulganin joined ▷CHEKA in 1918; in World War II he became (1944) a member of Stalin's war cabinet and in 1947, defence minister. As prime minister, Bulganin participated in the attempt to oust Khrushchev in 1957 and was subsequently dismissed.

● **Bulgaria, Republic of** ▶ A country in SE Europe, in the E Balkans on the Black Sea. The low-lying Danube basin in the N rises to the Balkan Mountains in the centre of the country; further S, beyond the valley of the River Maritsa, the Rhodope Mountains reach heights of almost 3000 m (10 000 ft). The inhabitants are mainly Bulgars, with minorities of Macedonians, Turks, and Gipsies.

Economy: industrialization proceeded rapidly under the communist regime installed after World War II. Particular emphasis was given to heavy manufacturing, engineering, and petrochemical industries. Coal, iron, and other minerals are mined and hydroelectricity and nuclear energy contribute to power supplies. Oil has been found offshore in the Black Sea and natural gas is also being produced. Agricultural production, the traditional mainstay of the economy prior to 1945, was mechanized and organized on a cooperative basis, the main crops being wheat, maize, beet, and barley. In 1991 legislation permitted the return of collectivized land and privatization of state companies. The country suffered a severe financial crisis when the national currency collapsed in 1996. Although the government responded with a package of radical economic reforms, inflation has soared. Main exports include machinery, chemicals, food products, wine and spirits, textiles, tobacco, and nonferrous metals.

History: following the invasion of the Bulgars in the 7th century AD and their gradual adoption of the culture and language of the conquered Slavs, Bulgaria became a significant power in SE Europe. Despite coming under Turkish rule in 1396, the Bulgars succeeded in retaining their national identity over the centuries. Growing nationalism led to a series of insurrections against Ottoman rule in the 19th century, and Bulgaria had achieved virtual independence by 1878. The country became fully independent in 1908 under the Saxe-Coburg ruler ▷Ferdinand, who took the title of tsar. Bulgaria aligned itself with Germany in both World Wars. In 1944 it was occupied by the Soviet Union and power was seized by the Fatherland Front, a left-wing alliance, which formed a pro-Soviet government that declared war on Germany. In 1946 a People's Republic was proclaimed and Bulgaria became one of the Soviet Union's satellite states. Under a new constitution in 1971 Todor ▷Zhivkov became head of state. Democratic multiparty elections were held in 1990, resulting in victory for the former Communists, now styled Socialists. Further elections in 1991 resulted in victory for an anti-Communist coalition; a broader coalition took over in 1992. The Socialists returned to power in 1994 but a nonsocialist president, Peter Stoyanov, was elected in 1996. In 1997 economic crisis led to mass protests against the government and parliamentary elections were won by a centre-right coalition. A new centrist party led by the former King Simeon II was victorious in the elections of 2001.

Republic of Bulgaria

Head of state	President Georgi Parvanov
Official language	Bulgarian
Official currency	lev of 100 stotinki
Area	110 912 sq km (42 823 sq mi)
Population (2000 est)	8 172 000
Capital	Sofia
Main port	Varna

● **Bulgarian** ▶ A language belonging to the South ▷Slavonic group spoken by eight million people in Bulgaria, Greece, Romania, Moldova, and Ukraine. It differs from other Slavonic languages as it lacks case declensions for nouns and shares grammatical features and vocabulary elements with other non-Slavonic Balkan languages. The literature written in Bulgarian dates from the 9th century.

● **Bulgars** ▶ A people that settled N of the Black Sea in the 5th century. One group migrated across the Danube in the 7th century, forming the state of Moesia; they gradually merged with the local Slavs, their name surviving in modern Bulgaria. By the 9th century the other group had migrated N to the Volga, become Muslim, and established themselves as fur traders. They were subjected by the Mongols in the 13th century and absorbed by the Muscovite state in the 15th century.

● **Bulge, Battle of the** ▷*See* World War II.

● **bulimia nervosa** ▶ A psychological illness in which the sufferer eats excessively and then induces vomiting in order to lose weight. Closely related to ▷anorexia nervosa, it is most common in young women obsessed with slimming. The frequent vomiting exposes the gullet, throat, and mouth to stomach acids, which can cause ulceration, infection, or even perforation. Treatment involves psychotherapy.

● **bulk modulus** ▷*See* elastic modulus.

● **bull** ▶ (from Latin: *bulla*, seal) Originally, the seal attached to papal edicts. The term was later used for the documents themselves, but now refers only to the most important missives. Named by their opening word or phrase, for example *Pastor Aeternus* (Eternal Father; 1870), they assert doctrine.

● **Bull, John** ▶ (c. 1562–1628) English composer and organist at the Chapel Royal (1591–92). He left England in 1613 and became organist of Antwerp Cathedral (1617). He wrote church music, fantasies for viols, and keyboard music.

● **Bull, John** ▶ (caricature) ▷*See* John Bull.

● **bullace** ▶ A type of ▷plum, *Prunus insititia*, probably originating in SW Asia. The young branches are hairy and have few thorns. It bears blue-black fruits.

● **bullbaiting** ▷*See* bearbaiting.

● **bulldog** ▶ A breed of dog originating in England, where it was used in bull- and bear-baiting. It has a compact rounded body with short sturdy legs and a short tail. The large head has an undershot jaw and loose folds of skin. The fine short coat can be any colour except black. Weight: 25 kg (dogs); 23 kg (bitches).

● **bullfighting** ▶ Subduing and killing bulls. The national spectator sport of Spain, it is also popular in parts of France and Latin America, and mounted bullfighting, in which the bulls are not killed, is practised in Portugal. The bulls are specially bred. At a normal Spanish *corrida de toros* (bullfight) three matadors kill two bulls each. Following the initial ceremonial procession the first bull enters the ring. Preliminary passes are made by the *banderilleros* (assistants) with their capes to attract the bull's attention and allow the matador to assess the bull's reactions. The matador then makes his first series of passes with his cape, controlling the direction and extent of the bull's charge. During the next stage, the matadors make the bull charge at a mounted picador, who uses a form of lance to stab the bull's neck, weakening the muscle so that it lowers its head. This procedure is repeated up to three times, each of the three matadors taking turns to draw the bull away from the horse and continue the capework. During the following stage the neck muscle is further weakened by pairs of barbed sticks (*banderillas*) thrust into it by the *banderilleros*. In the final stage the matador performs a series of passes with his *muleta* (a small red cape folded over a stick) to weaken the bull further until he can reach over its head to thrust his sword in at the right angle to sever its aorta.

● **bullfinch** ▶ A plump woodland ▷finch, *Pyrrhula pyrrhula*, of N Eurasia. It is about 14 cm long and has a grey back, a pinkish breast, and black head, wings, and tail. Bullfinches have strong stout bills and strip buds and flowers from trees, for which they are often regarded as pests.

● **bullfrog** ▶ A large frog, *Rana catesbiana*, of North America. Dull green with a slightly warty skin, bullfrogs grow to about 20 cm and can jump up to 2 m. Females are larger than males. They are the only common American frogs large enough to be used as food.

Other large frogs—*Pyxicephalus adspersus* in Africa and *Rana tigrina* in India—are also called bullfrogs.

● **bullhead** ▶ One of several predatory bottom-dwelling fish, also called sculpin, belonging to the family *Cottidae*, including the Eurasian miller's thumb (*Cottus gobio*). Bullheads have a conical body, up to 30 cm long and often covered with bony plates, a broad head, and two dorsal fins. They are found in fresh water and shallow seas of the N hemisphere. Order: *Perciformes*. ▷*See also* catfish.

● **bull market** ▶ A security or commodity market in which there is a continuing upward movement in prices. An initial rise in prices is often magnified by consequent buying by investors. *Compare* bear market.

● **bull mastiff** ▶ A breed of dog resulting from crosses between bulldogs and mastiffs. It is sturdily built with a short broad muzzle and folds of skin surrounding the face. The short coat is red, fawn, or streaked brown. Height: 63–68 cm (dogs); 61–66 cm (bitches).

● **Bull Run, Battles of** ▶ (*or* Battles of Manassas) Two battles in the US ▷Civil War fought in NE Virginia. Both were Confederate victories. In the first (21 July, 1861), Federal forces failed to prevent the unification of Confederate forces under Gen P. G. T. Beauregard (1818–93) and Gen Joseph E. Johnstone (1807–91) at Manassas Junction near a stream named Bull Run. The untried Federal troops were repulsed after an unsuccessful attack. The second battle (29–30 August, 1862) followed an unsuccessful Federal attempt to capture Gordonsville, a rail junction near Richmond, the Confederate capital. The 70 000 Federal troops had withdrawn to await reinforcements when Stonewall ▷Jackson attacked and forced their retreat to Washington.

● **bull terrier** ▶ A breed of dog originating in the UK from crosses between bulldogs and terriers. It is strongly built with a courageous temperament. The coat is either pure white (with darker head markings) or coloured. Height: 48–56 cm. (Miniature bull terriers must not exceed 36 cm.) **Pit bull terriers** resemble ▷Staffordshire bull terriers but are larger and originally bred for dog fighting. Under a 1991 amendment to Dangerous Dogs Act (1989) they must be registered with the police and muzzled in public.

● **Bülow, Bernhard Heinrich, Fürst von** ▶ (1849–1929) German statesman and diplomat; chancellor (1900–09). He pursued aggressive foreign policies that contributed to German isolation in Europe. He resigned after losing the confidence of Emperor William II and of the Reichstag and served from 1914 to 1915 as ambassador to Italy.

● **Bülow, Hans Guido, Freiherr von** ▶ (1830–94) German pianist and conductor. Bülow championed Wagner until his wife Cosima (Liszt's daughter) eloped with Wagner in 1866. From that time he championed the works of Brahms.

● **bulrush** ▶ A widely distributed perennial herbaceous plant, *Scirpus lacustris*, growing in ponds, lakes, and rivers. 1–3 m high, it has cylindrical leafless stems bearing branched clusters of small reddish-brown flowers. Family: *Cyperaceae* (sedges, etc.). The name is also applied to the ▷reedmace, and the biblical bulrush is the ▷papyrus.

● **Bultmann, Rudolf (Karl)** ▶ (1884–1976) German New Testament scholar. A professor at Marburg University (1921–51), he allied himself with the anti-Nazi ▷Confessing Church during the Third Reich. In his writings he argued that the New Testament message

must be "demythologized" (stripped of its mythical concepts) if it was to have any modern relevance.

● **Bulwer-Lytton, Edward George Earle** ▷*See* Lytton, Edward George Earle Bulwer-Lytton, 1st Baron.

● **bumblebee** ▶ A social ▷bee, also called humblebee, belonging to a genus (*Bombus*) found in temperate regions. Bumblebees, 15–25 mm long, are black with yellow or orange bands. They live in colonies, on or below the ground, containing 100–400 workers in the summer. Their life cycle is like that of the ▷honeybee, although only young fertilized queens survive the winter. Solitary parasitic bumblebees belong to the genus *Psithyrus*. Family: *Apidae*. ⃞insect.

● **Bunbury** ▶ 33 20S 115 34E A port in SW Western Australia, at the junction of the Collie and Preston Rivers. It is protected by a breakwater 1.5 km (1 mi) long. The main exports are wheat, timber, and fruit. Population (latest est): 27 000.

● **Bunche, Ralph** ▶ (1904–71) US political scientist and UN official. Bunche specialized in colonial areas during World War II and became the first Black American to hold an important position in the State Department. He was a founder of the UN and director of its trusteeship division. Bunche won the Nobel Peace Prize for negotiating the 1949 Arab-Israeli truce and supervised the UN Congo peace force in 1960.

● **Bundaberg** ▶ 24 50S 152 21E A port in Australia, in E Queensland on the Burnett River. It is a commercial centre for an important sugar-producing region; associated industries include rum distilling. Population (1993): 52 267.

● **Bundelkhand** ▶ A region in present-day Madhya Pradesh state, in N central India, taking its name from the Bundela Rajputs, a dynasty that ruled here from the 14th to the 18th centuries. The area is rich in architectural history; in the 10th and 11th centuries the Candella kings built many beautiful temples at Khajuraho and a fine fortress was erected later at Jhansi.

● **Bunin, Ivan Alekseevich** ▶ (1879–1953) Russian poet and novelist. He published his first book of poems in 1891, and translated works by ▷Byron and ▷Longfellow. His prose works include novels (*The Village*, 1910), short stories (*The Gentleman from San Francisco*, 1916), and autobiographical works (*The Well of Days*, 1910). In 1920 he emigrated to Finland. He won the Nobel Prize in 1933.

● **bunion** ▶ A deformity and swelling at the joint at the base of the big toe. It is usually caused by pressure from ill-fitting shoes: the toe becomes bent towards the others and a fibrous fluid-filled sac (bursa) develops over the affected joint. Bunions may require surgical treatment.

● **Bunker Hill, Battle of** ▶ (17 June, 1775) A battle of the ▷American Revolution actually fought on Breed's Hill (next to Bunker Hill) in Charlestown, near Boston. The Americans defended the strategic hill from two British attacks but Sir William ▷Howe displaced the Americans at the third attempt. The American defence helped raise support for the Revolutionary cause.

● **Bunsen, Robert Wilhelm** ▶ (1811–99) German chemist, after whom the Bunsen burner is named. He did not, however, invent the Bunsen burner although he did popularize it. In collaboration with ▷Kirchhoff, Bunsen developed the technique of spectroscopy, using a Bunsen burner to heat the substance. In 1860 they used the technique to discover the elements ▷rubidium and ▷caesium. He also invented a carbon-zinc electric cell (1841).

● **Bunsen burner** ▶ A gas burner for laboratory use, popularized by R. ▷Bunsen. It consists of a vertical metal tube with a variable air inlet at the bottom. Gas is led into the bottom of the tube and the gas–air mixture burnt at the top. Adjustment of the air inlet allows control of combustion intensity, temperature, sooting, and other flame properties.

● **bunting** ▶ A sparrow-like bird belonging to a subfamily (*Emberizinae*) of the ▷finches. Buntings are 12–20 cm long and usually have a brownish or greyish plumage. They live on the ground or in bushes and thickets and scratch for seeds with their characteristically large feet. The subfamily includes the ▷yellowhammer and the ▷snow bunting. ▷See Plate III.

● **Buñuel, Luis** ► (1900–83) Spanish film director. He worked mainly in France and Mexico. His films are characterized by surrealist techniques and by their anticlericalism and satire on social hypocrisy. They include *Un Chien andalou* (1928; scripted with Salvador Dali), *Viridiana* (1961), *The Discreet Charm of the Bourgeoisie* (1972), and *That Obscure Object of Desire* (1977).

● **bunya bunya** ▷See Araucaria.

● **Bunyan, John** ► (1628–88) British writer. Son of a tinker, he fought in the parliamentary army during the Civil War. From 1650 to 1656 he underwent a spiritual crisis, finally resolved by his conversion to religion. He became the leader of a group of Baptists in Bedford and in 1660 he was imprisoned for preaching without a licence. During his 12 years in prison he wrote his spiritual autobiography, *Grace Abounding* (1666), and began his major work, *The Pilgrim's Progress* (1678). An imaginative allegory written in plain but majestic prose, it has been widely read and admired for centuries.

● **Burbage, Richard** ► (c. 1567–1619) English actor. The son of the actor-manager James Burbage (c. 1530–97), he is usually considered Britain's first great actor. He played the leading roles in the first productions of many of Shakespeare's plays, including *Richard III*, *Hamlet*, and *King Lear*. He also acted in plays by Kyd, Webster, and Ben Jonson, and was a shareholder in the Blackfriars and the Globe theatres.

● **Burbank, Luther** ► (1849–1926) US plant breeder, who developed many new varieties of agricultural importance. His first commercial success, the Burbank potato, enabled him to settle in California, where—by skilful selection and breeding techniques—he originated more than 800 new strains and varieties of fruit, vegetables, and flowers.

Margaret Burbidge ► Having worked at the Yerkes Observatory in America, she found the Royal Greenwich Observatory at Herstmonceux in Sussex limited her opportunities for observational astronomy and she resigned after one year.

● **Burbidge, (Eleanor) Margaret** ► (1925–) British astronomer, who became director of the ▷Royal Greenwich Observatory (1972–73) and president of the American Association for the Advancement of Science. With her husband, British physicist **Geoffrey Burbidge** (1925–), ▷Hoyle, and William Fowler, she published an important paper on the synthesis of elements in stars and has done much work on quasars.

● **burbot** ► A food fish, *Lota lota*, that is similar and related to the ▷ling. Up to 1.1 m long, it lives on the bottom in cold fresh waters of Europe, Asia, and North America and feeds voraciously on other fish.

● **Burckhardt, Jacob Christoph** ► (1818–97) Swiss art and cultural historian. The son of a Protestant clergyman, he studied in Berlin and Bonn. From 1843 he lectured at Basle University, becoming professor of history there in 1858, after three years at Zürich. His

most important work, *The Civilization of the Renaissance in Italy* (1860), was a model for later cultural histories.

● **burdock** ► A tall stiff biennial plant of the genus *Arctium* (about 5 species), 60–130 cm high, found in Europe and Asia. They have broad heart-shaped leaves and reddish-purple thistle-like flower heads, surrounded by many large stiff hooked bracts, which are retained by the fruits. Family: ▷Compositae.

● **Burgas** ► 42 30N 29 29E A city in E Bulgaria, on the Black Sea. Bulgaria's second largest port, its industries include fishing, mining, and oil refining. Population (1996 est): 199 470.

● **Bürge, Joost** ► (1552–1632) Swiss mathematician, who invented ▷logarithms independently of, and probably before, John ▷Napier. He also contributed to the exponential notation (i.e. y^x to indicate y multiplied by itself x times).

● **Burgenland** ► A federal state in E Austria, bordering on Hungary. It was ceded to Austria by Hungary following World War I. Predominantly agricultural, it produces cereals, root crops, and fruit and vegetables; livestock are also extensively raised. Area: 3965 sq km (1531 sq mi). Population (1994 est): 273 613. Capital: Eisenstadt.

● **Bürger, Gottfried** ► (1747–94) German poet. At Göttingen University he studied law and eventually became professor of aesthetics. His ballad *Lenore* (1773) influenced writers of the early Romantic period throughout Europe. He also translated many traditional English and Scots ballads.

● **Burgess, Anthony** ► (John Anthony Burgess Wilson; 1917–93) British novelist and critic. A teacher and lecturer in English literature and phonetics, he became a full-time writer in 1959. His novels include the sinister tragicomedy *A Clockwork Orange* (1962), which was filmed by Stanley ▷Kubrick, *Inside Mr Enderby* (1963), *Earthly Powers* (1980), *Any Old Iron* (1989), and *A Dead Man in Deptford* (1993). *Little Wilson and Big God* (1988) and *You've Had Your Time* (1990) are autobiographical.

● **Burgess, Guy** ▷See Maclean, Donald.

● **Burgh, Hubert de** ► (d. 1243) Justiciar of England (1215–32) under John and then Henry III. He supported John against the baronial rebels (*see* Barons' Wars) and became one of the most important members of the minority council of Henry III. He was created justiciar for life in 1227 but fell from favour in 1232 and was outlawed. Restored to grace in 1234, he never again regained his former ascendancy.

● **Burghley, William Cecil, Lord** ► (1520–98) English statesman; close adviser to Elizabeth I from her accession (1558). He served both Somerset and Northumberland under Edward VI and outwardly espoused Roman Catholicism under Mary I. A moderating influence on Elizabeth, his pragmatism is evident in her religious settlement (*see* Reformation). He helped to bring about the Treaty of Edinburgh (1660) with Scotland, which undermined French influence there. He influenced Elizabeth's pro-Protestant foreign policy, aiding the Revolt of the Netherlands against Spain, and helped to prepare England for the threatened Spanish invasion (*see* Armada, Spanish). He helped to secure the execution of Mary, Queen of Scots, in 1587. He was succeeded as royal adviser by his son **Robert Cecil, 1st Earl of Salisbury** (c. 1563–1612), who negotiated the accession of James VI of Scotland to the English throne as James I (1603). As lord treasurer (1608–12), he was James' chief adviser.

● **burglary** ► In law, the crime of entering a building, ship, or other inhabited vehicle as a trespasser, intending to commit theft, rape, grievous bodily harm, or unlawful damage, or entering as a trespasser only but subsequently stealing or inflicting grievous bodily harm. The possession of weapons, such as firearms or explosives, in these circumstances is the more serious crime of aggravated burglary.

● **Burgos** ► 42 21N 3 41W A city in N Spain, in Old Castile. Its cathedral (13th–16th centuries) contains the remains of the legendary hero El Cid. Population (1995 est): 166 732.

● **Burgoyne, John** ► (1722–92) British general and dramatist. In the American Revolution he commanded the British force in the N, ordered in conjunction with a column under Sir William ▷Howe to divide the Americans along the Hudson River. Howe's progress was blocked and Burgoyne was defeated by ▷Gates at Saratoga (1777). His plays include *The Heiress* (1786).

● **Burgundian school** ▶ A group of musicians working at the court of the Dukes of Burgundy in the 15th century. Under Philip the Good, who reigned from 1419 to 1467, there was a great flowering of the arts. Two composers are outstanding: Guillaume ▷Dufay and Gilles Binchois (c. 1400–60). Their compositions include chansons with French texts, motets, masses, and magnificats.

● **Burgundy** ▶ A planning region and former province of France, E of the Rivers Rhône and Saône. It is a major ▷wine-producing area. The Burgundians were a Scandinavian people who occupied the region in the 4th century AD, establishing a powerful kingdom that was conquered by the Franks in 534. The NW part of the former kingdom became a duchy in the 9th century and passed to the French Crown in the mid-14th century. John the Good transferred it to his fourth son, Philip the Bold, and after the death (1477) of his descendant Charles the Bold it was annexed by the Crown. Area: 31 582 sq km (12 191 sq mi). Population (1999 est): 1 610 067.

● **Buridan, Jean** ▶ (c. 1297–c. 1358) French scholastic philosopher. He became professor of philosophy at Paris. He is associated with "Buridan's ass," an illustration of a position in arguments about free will; the animal starves through being unable to choose between equally attractive piles of hay.

● **Burke, Edmund** ▶ (1729–97) British political philosopher and politician. An MP from 1765, he became a Rockingham Whig. He attacked George III's exalted view of the monarch's political role in the pamphlet *Thoughts on the Cause of the Present Discontents* (1770) and in two famous speeches, "On American Taxation" (1774) and "On Moving His Resolutions for Conciliation with the Colonies" (1777), blamed the unrest in the American colonies on British misgovernment. He also campaigned against the corrupt Indian administration of the ▷East India Company, bringing about the impeachment of Warren ▷Hastings (1788). An opponent of democracy on the grounds that it brought demagogues to the fore, he believed that the common good was best secured by responsible aristocratic government. He thus condemned the French Revolution (*Reflections on the Revolution in France*, 1790). He has been regarded as the foremost Conservative philosopher. He also wrote a widely read work on aesthetics, *A Philosophical Enquiry into the Origin of Our Ideas of the Sublime and Beautiful* (1757).

● **Burke, Robert O'Hara** ▶ (1820–61) Irish explorer of Australia. Educated in Belgium, he served in the Austrian army and later joined the Irish police. In 1853 he emigrated to Australia and organized an expedition (which included W. J. Wills) to cross Australia from S to N (1860). Burke and Wills, and two others, reached the mouth of the Flinders in 1861 but on the return journey both died of starvation.

● **Burke, William** ▶ (1792–1829) Irish criminal. In company with William Hare, his landlord in Edinburgh and a fellow Irishman, he murdered at least 15 people and also dug up corpses to sell them to medical schools. After their arrest, Hare turned king's evidence and Burke was hanged.

● **Burkina Faso** ▶ (name until 1984: Upper Volta) A landlocked country in West Africa. It consists mainly of a low-lying plateau, crossed by the headwaters of the River Volta: the Black, Red, and White Voltas. The population is almost entirely African, the largest groups being the Mossi and Fulani.
Economy: chiefly agricultural, with most of the population living by subsistence farming. The main food crops are millet and sorghum; livestock is important and is the main export. Production of rice, groundnuts, cotton, and sugar is being increased by schemes to improve water supplies. Some minerals, including manganese, have been found but lack of communications makes their exploitation difficult. Industry remains very limited and is mainly state owned. The country is heavily dependent on Western aid and has a massive external debt.
History: the area was occupied by powerful Mossi states from the 14th century. It became part of the French protectorate of Soudan in 1898 and from 1919 formed the separate protectorate of Upper Volta.

Burkina Faso ▶ Fuel wood is still an important energy source for these women.

In 1932 it was divided between Niger, Ivory Coast, and Soudan but was reconstituted in 1947. In 1958 Upper Volta became an autonomous republic, gaining full independence outside the French Community in 1960. A military coup in 1966 brought Lt Col (later Gen) Sangoulé Lamizana (1916–) to power; he was elected president in 1978 but was overthrown in 1980. In 1983, after another military coup, Capt Thomas Sankara assumed power. A further coup in 1987, led by Capt Blaise Compaoré (1951–), resulted in Sankara's death and a return to democracy. Compaoré was elected president in 1991 (re-elected 1998) and his Popular Front party won legislative elections in 1992 (re-elected 1997); all these contests were boycotted by the opposition.

Burkina Faso

Head of state	President Blaise Compaoré
Official language	French
Official currency	CFA (Communauté financière africaine) franc of 100 centimes
Area	274 002 sq km (105 764 sq mi)
Population (2000 est)	11 946 000
Capital	Ouagadougou

● **burlesque** ▶ A dramatic genre that developed in England in the late 17th century. It consisted of comic parodies of serious drama and opera, the most celebrated examples including Buckingham's *The Rehearsal* (1671), Sheridan's *The Critic* (1779), and Gay's *The Beggar's Opera* (1728). In the USA the term was used for variety performances involving striptease and slapstick comedy.

● **Burlington, Richard Boyle, 3rd Earl of** ▶ (1694–1753) English connoisseur and architect. Famous for his devotion to Palladianism, Burlington was a notable patron of the arts and launched the career of William ▷Kent. He was also a competent architect, building his own villa at Chiswick (1725), and the Assembly Rooms at York (1731).

● **Burma, Socialist Republic of the Union of** ▷*See* Myanmar, Union of.

● **Burmese** ▶ A language of the Tibeto-Burman branch of the ▷Sino-Tibetan language family spoken by 20 million people in Myanmar (Burma), where it is the official language. Written in an alphabet derived from the ▷Pali script of India, Burmese literature dates from the 11th century AD.

● **Burmese cat** ▶ A breed of short-haired cat originating from an Asian hybrid imported into the USA in 1933. The Burmese has a long slender body, large ears, greenish-yellow eyes, and usually a dark-brown coat. Other colours include silvery-grey (the Blue Burmese), red, and cream.

● **Burne-Jones, Sir Edward Coley** ▶ (1833–98) British Pre-Raphaelite painter and designer. After meeting ▷Rossetti (1856) he began his art career but only established his reputation in an exhibition in 1877. Typical of his dreamy romantic paintings, inspired by Botticelli's style, is *King Cophetua and the Beggar Maid* (Tate Gallery). More influential for the 20th century were his designs for stained glass and tapestries, often for the firm of William ▷Morris, for whose Kelmscott Press he also illustrated the works of Chaucer (1896).

● **burnet** ▶ A slender perennial herb of the genera *Sanguisorba* (about 3 species) and *Poterium* (about 25 species), of N temperate regions. 500–1000 cm high, they have pinnate toothed leaves and oval heads of crimson or greenish petal-less flowers borne on long stems. The leaves are used to flavour salads and soups. Family: *Rosaceae*.

● **Burnet, Sir Frank Macfarlane** ▶ (1899–1985) Australian physician, who advanced understanding of virus diseases and immunology. Burnet discovered the phenomenon of acquired immunological tolerance to foreign tissue transplants, for which he shared a Nobel Prize (1960) with Sir Peter ▷Medawar. He did work in the identification of bacteria and in the culture of viruses. He received the OM in 1957.

● **Burnet, Gilbert** ▶ (1643–1715) English bishop and historian, born in Edinburgh. While abroad during James II's reign, he became a friend of William of Orange, who appointed him Bishop of Salisbury in 1689. His books include *History of My Own Time* (1723–34).

● **Burnett, Frances Eliza Hodgson** ▶ (1849–1924) British novelist. The daughter of a Manchester manufacturer, she moved to the USA in 1865. Her best-known works are the children's books *Little Lord Fauntleroy* (1885), *The Little Princess* (1905), and *The Secret Garden* (1909).

● **Burney, Fanny** ▶ (Mrs Frances Burney D'Arblay; 1752–1840) British novelist, daughter of the music historian Charles Burney (1726–1814). After the success of her first novel, *Evelina* (1778), she became a close friend of Dr ▷Johnson. She held a court position under Queen Charlotte from 1786 until 1791. In 1793 she married a French emigré, Alexandre D'Arblay. Her letters and journals provide a lively record of her period.

● **Burnley** ▶ 53 48N 2 14W A town in N England, in Lancashire in the Calder Valley. Traditionally a cotton-weaving town (with some spinning and dyeing), it has seen some diversification of industry in recent decades (aerospace, motor vehicles, engineering, services). Population (1991): 74 661.

● **burns** ▶ Damage to the skin caused by heat, electricity, chemicals, or radiation. In order of increasing severity, burns may cause reddening of the skin, as in sunburn (first-degree burn), blistering (second-degree burn), and finally damage to the tissues beneath the skin (third-degree burn). The extent rather than the thickness of the burn determines its effect. Both second- and third-degree burns cause fluid loss, which may be extensive enough to lead to ▷shock. Treatment consists of the application of wet dressings and later the administration of intravenous fluids and transfer of the patient to clean surroundings, where the burns are exposed and allowed to heal. The danger of infection can be prevented by the use of antibiotics. Skin grafting may be necessary to replace the skin destroyed by severe burns.

● **Burns, John Elliot** ▶ (1858–1943) British socialist and trade-union leader. A member of the Amalgamated Society of Engineers, Burns was a leader of the dockers' strike in 1889. In 1892 he entered parliament and in 1905 became the first working-class cabinet minister as president of the Local Government Board. He was appointed president of the Board of Trade in 1914 but resigned on the outbreak of World War I.

● **Burns, Robert** ▶ (1759–96) Scottish poet. Son of a poor farmer in Ayrshire, in 1783 he began writing poems in traditional styles. *Poems, Chiefly in the Scottish Dialect* (1786), published in Kilmarnock, won him immediate fame; from 1786 until 1788 he was lionized by Edinburgh society, which was little to his taste (he was a lifelong radical) or his profit. His return to farming was a failure and from 1789 he worked

Robert Burns ▶ An unsigned painting of about 1870. The farmer poet has for over 200 years remained an inspiration to his fellow Scots.

for the excise service. His poems range from sentimental love lyrics, often patterned on traditional songs, to broad humour, as in "Tam o'Shanter" (1788), and scathing satire, as in "The Twa Dogs" (1786) and "Holy Willie's Prayer" (1785). He collected and wrote numerous songs for inclusion in *The Scots Musical Museum* (1787–1803) and *Select Scottish Airs* (1793–1818). **Burns Night** (25 Jan) is celebrated by Scots all over the world to commemorate his birth. The Burns supper includes haggis and recitations of his poetry.

● **Burr, Aaron** ▶ (1756–1836) US statesman; Republican vice president (1801–05) after tying with Jefferson in the election of 1800. In 1804, after killing his political rival Alexander ▷Hamilton in a duel, Burr fled to Philadelphia and plotted to establish an empire in the West. He was arrested for treason but acquitted. After further intrigues, including a scheme for Napoleon to conquer Florida, Burr gave up politics for law.

● **Burra, Edward** ▶ (1905–76) British painter. His early watercolours were chiefly scenes of Mediterranean low life. Later, in response to the horrors of the Spanish Civil War and World War II, he began to paint sinister subjects in a realistic style. His works include *Soldiers* (1942; Tate Gallery).

● **Burroughs, Edgar Rice** ▶ (1875–1950) US novelist. After a variety of unsuccessful jobs he gained wealth and international fame from his fantasy fiction. *Tarzan of the Apes* (1914) introduced his most famous character, an English nobleman's child, abandoned in the African jungle and reared by apes.

● **Burroughs, William S(eward)** ▶ (1914–97) US novelist. He graduated from Harvard in 1936 and wandered in the USA and Europe. In 1944 he became a drug addict and in 1951 he killed his wife in a shooting accident. *Junkie* (1953) and *The Naked Lunch* (1959) were influential novels of the ▷Beat movement. He lived mostly in Paris, London, and Tangiers, continuing his literary experiments in such novels as *Nova Express* (1964) and *The Western Lands* (1988).

● **burrowing owl** ▶ A long-legged ground-dwelling ▷owl, *Speotyto cunicularia*, of grasslands from Florida and the western USA to Argentina. 22 cm long, it nests in colonies, often in disused rodent burrows, and feeds at night on frogs, lizards, mice, and insects.

● **Bursa** ▶ 40 12N 29 04E A town in NW Turkey. It was the capital of the Ottoman Turks for most of the 14th century and contains notable mosques and sultans' tombs and a university (1975). Population (1995 est): 1 016 760.

● **bursitis** ▶ Inflammation of a bursa, the fibrous fluid-filled sac surrounding a joint, causing pain. Causes include injury, overuse of the joint, and infection; housemaid's knee is a type of bursitis producing swelling in front of the kneecap. Treatment includes corticosteroid injections.

● **Burton, Sir Richard** ▶ (1821–90) British explorer, diplomat, and

Sir Richard Burton ► The flamboyant Victorian diplomat and explorer earned a second reputation as the translator of such erotic works as the *Kama Sutra*, some of which had to be published privately.

translator. After military service in India he travelled in Arabia and Somaliland. He made two attempts (1855, 1857–58) to find the source of the Nile and on the second, with ▷Speke, came upon Lake Tanganyika. Burton served as consul in Fernando Po (1861), Santos (1865), Damascus (1869), and Trieste (1872). He published many travel books and translations of oriental erotica, including *Kama Sutra* (1883), *The Perfumed Garden* (1886), and the *Arabian Nights* (1885–88).

● **Burton, Richard ►** (Richard Jenkins; 1925–84) British actor, born in Wales. Originally a stage actor, especially of Shakespearean roles, from the 1950s he acted mostly in films. These included *Look Back in Anger* (1959), *Becket* (1964), and *Who's Afraid of Virginia Woolf?* (1966). His two marriages to Elizabeth Taylor were highly publicized.

● **Burton, Robert ►** (1577–1640) British scholar. He was educated at Oxford and spent his life there as a don. *The Anatomy of Melancholy* (1621, revised five times) is a vast, witty, and erudite miscellany of Jacobean knowledge on what is now called depression; it includes folklore, superstitions, and the learning of the ancient Greeks and Arabs.

● **Burton-upon-Trent ►** 52 49N 1 36W A town in central England, in E Staffordshire on the River Trent. Its main industries are brewing, engineering, the manufacture of tyres and rubber products, and food processing. Burton's brewing tradition dates back to brewing by the Benedictine monks of Burton Abbey (founded 1002). Population (1991): 60 525.

● **Burundi, Republic of ►** A small inland country in central Africa, bordering on Lake Tanganyika in the SW. It consists chiefly of high plateau along the main Nile-Congo dividing range, descending rapidly to the Great Rift Valley in the W. Most of the people belong to the ▷Hutu, a Bantu tribe, but the Tutsi have dominated politics; there are other tribal minorities.

Economy: mainly subsistence agriculture; coffee accounts for 80% of exports and cotton and tea are also important. Gold, nickel, and vanadium have been found, but mining and industry still provide minimal revenue. In the 1990s the economy was devastated by the civil war and the imposition of a trading blockade by many African countries (from 1996). There is a huge external debt.

History: the area (with present-day Rwanda) became part of German East Africa in 1890. From 1919, as the S part of Ruanda-Urundi, it was administered by Belgium, first under League of Nations mandate and then as a UN trust territory. It became independent in 1962 and in 1964 a monetary and customs union with Rwanda was dissolved. In 1966 the hereditary ruler Mwami Mwambutsa IV was deposed by his son, who was enthroned as Mwami Ntare V. In the same year, following a military coup, Capt (later Lt Gen) Michel Micombero (1940–83) set up a republic with himself as president. In 1972 he assumed absolute powers and ethnic fighting broke out in which thousands were killed. In 1976 Micombero lost power in a coup and Jean-Baptiste Bagaza became president; in 1987 Bagaza himself was overthrown and Maj Pierre Buyoya assumed power. In 1993 the first democratic elections were held but the new government was overthrown in a coup and the country's first Hutu president, Melchior Ndadaye, was killed. Senior army officials opposed

the coup and reinstated the surviving ministers. Cyprien Ntaryamira, also a Hutu, was elected president in 1994 but killed three months later. During this period violence intensified, with wholesale massacres of both Hutus and Tutsis, and some 500 000 refugees fled to neighbouring countries. A power-sharing government was then established, with Sylvestre Ntibantunganya as president. Despite this, ethnic violence continued, reaching a new peak in mid-1996. In July 1996 a Tutsi-led coup overthrew the government and reinstated Buyoya as president; despite the formation of another multiethnic administration, fighting continued. A peace agreement was signed in 2001 but rejected by the main Hutu rebel groups.

Republic of Burundi

Head of state	President Pierre Buyoya
Official languages	French and Kirundi; Swahili is also used
Official currency	Burundi franc of 100 centimes
Area	27 834 sq km (10 759 sq mi)
Population (2000 est)	6 055 000
Capital	Bujumbura

● **Bury ►** 1. 53 36N 2 17N A town in NW England, in Bury unitary authority, Greater Manchester, on the River Irwell. Cotton spinning and weaving are important, as are the woollen and felt industries and paper making. Population (1991): 62 633. 2. A unitary authority in NW England, in Greater Manchester. Area: 99 sq km (38 sq mi). Population (1999 est) 176 760.

● **Buryat Republic ►** (*or* Buryatia) A constituent republic of SE central Russia. Over half its area is forested. The Buryats, who comprise about 24% of the population, are traditionally nomads and speak a Mongolian language. The region has deposits of coal, molybdenum, and gold. The main industries are mining and timber; wheat and fodder crops are grown and stock breeding is also important. Area: 351 300 sq km (135 650 sq mi). Population (1996 est): 1 053 000. Capital: Ulan Ude.

● **burying beetle ►** A beetle, also called a sexton beetle, belonging to a genus (*Necrophorus*) found chiefly in N temperate regions. They are 1.5–35 mm long and many have black and orange markings. They feed and lay their eggs on the dead bodies of small animals, which they first bury: the larvae use the same food source. Family: *Silphidae* (carrion beetles).

● **Bury St Edmunds ►** 52 15N 0 43E A town in E England, in Suffolk. Its ruined abbey, which was built to house the shrine of St Edmund, last King of East Anglia (martyred in 870 AD), became a famous place of pilgrimage. Bury St Edmunds is a market town with brewing, sugar-refining, and agricultural machinery industries. Population (1991): 31 237.

● **Busby, Matt ►** (Sir Matthew B.; 1909–94) British Association footballer, who played for Manchester City (1926–36), Liverpool (1936–39), and Scotland. He later managed Manchester United (1945–71), which under his control won the FA Cup twice and the League championship five times. He rebuilt the team after eight players died in an aircrash (1958) that he himself survived.

● **Bush, George (Herbert Walker) ►** (1924–) US statesman; Republican president (1989–93). Ambassador to the UN (1971–72), he was director of the CIA (1976–77). He was vice president (1981–88) under Ronald ▷Reagan and won the presidency in 1988. In 1989 he authorized military action against Panama. Following Iraq's invasion of Kuwait in 1990 he ordered US-led forces into action in the ▷Gulf War. In the 1992 presidential elections he was defeated by Bill ▷Clinton. He was awarded an honorary knighthood in 1993.

His son **George W(alker) Bush** (1946–) also became Republican president (2001–), having previously been governor of Texas (1995–2001). Following a legal battle that ended in the Supreme Court, he emerged victorious over his Democrat opponent, Al ▷Gore, in the bitterly disputed election of 2000. In office Bush was accused of isolationism after pulling the USA out of several international treaties, including the ▷Kyoto agreement. Following the events of ▷September 11, 2001, he authorized a massive US attack on targets in Afghanistan (*see* war on terrorism).

● **bushbaby ►** A small nocturnal ▷prosimian primate belonging to the genus *Galago* (4 species), of African forests and bush. They are 27–80 cm long including the tail (15–40 cm). Common bushbabies (*G. senegalensis*) have soft dense greyish fur and a long bushy tail. They live in small groups and climb acrobatically among the trees in search of large insects; they also eat fruit and leaves. Family: *Lorisidae*.

● **bushbuck** ▶ A small antelope, *Tragelaphus scriptus*, of tropical African bush and forest, also called harnessed antelope. 66–109 cm high at the shoulder, bushbucks are red with white spots and stripes on the flanks and legs. Males have black-tipped horns with a single spiral turn. They are shy and nocturnal, living in pairs.

● **bush cricket** ▶ A ▷cricket belonging to the family *Tettigoniidae* (over 4000 species), having a green or brown body and short tail appendages (cerci). Bush crickets rarely fly or jump, but crawl among bushes and trees in fields and meadows. The swordlike ovipositor with which the female inserts eggs into plant tissues can cause considerable damage. Many species are carnivorous, usually eating small insects. □insect.

● **bushel** ▶ A unit of capacity (dry or liquid) equal to 8 gallons or 2219.36 cubic inches in the UK and 2150.42 cubic inches in the USA.

● **Bushido** ▶ The military and ethical code of the Japanese ▷samurai class. It originated in about the 13th century, although the term was not used until the 17th. Obedience to one's lord and fearlessness were its main virtues, along with austerity, honesty, and kindness. In the 13th–14th centuries it was influenced by Zen Buddhism and in the 17th–19th centuries, by Confucianism. In the mid-19th century it became the basis of Japanese emperor worship and nationalism. ▷*See also* martial arts.

● **Bushire** ▶ (*or* Bandar-e Bushehr) 28 59N 50 50E A town in SW Iran, on the N shore of the Persian Gulf. The port serves inland Iran but has lost trade to Abadan. Population (1994 est): 140 615.

● **Bushman** ▷*See* Khoisan.

● **bushmaster** ▶ A ▷pit viper, *Lachesis muta*, occurring in scrub and forests of Central and South America. The longest venomous snake of the New World, it reaches a length of 1.8 m and is brownish pink with dark diamond-shaped blotches. Its venom can prove fatal to man.

● **Bushnell, David** ▶ (1742–1824) US inventor, who in 1776 built the first submarine, nicknamed the Turtle. It was intended to be a combat vessel, laying mines on the hulls of enemy ships, but it lacked the necessary manoeuvrability.

● **bushrangers** ▶ Outlaws in the Australian outback in the late-18th and 19th centuries. They robbed farmsteads and stagecoaches, murdered, and plundered, but while some were ruthless and cruel, others shared their gains with the poor. The most famous of the Australian bushrangers is probably Ned ▷Kelly.

● **Busoni, Ferruccio** ▶ (1866–1924) Italian virtuoso pianist and composer. An admirer of Liszt, he exploited the extreme possibilities of the piano in both his playing and in his transcriptions and compositions for the instrument. Among his works are a piano concerto (1903–04), the *Fantasia contrappuntistica* (for piano; 1910), and the opera *Doktor Faust* (1916–24).

● **Buss, Frances Mary** ▶ (1827–94) English educationalist. As teacher and later headmistress at the North London Collegiate School she set new standards for girls' secondary education and campaigned for the admission of women to universities.

● **Bustamante, Sir (William) Alexander** ▶ (William Alexander Clarke; 1884–1977) Jamaican statesman; first prime minister of Jamaica (1962–67). A trade unionist, he oversaw the country's transition to independence in 1962.

● **Bustamante y Sirvén, Antonio Sánchez de** ▶ (1865–1951) Cuban lawyer. He is best known for the Bustamante Code, a system of international law regarding the security of people and property. It was ratified by the sixth Pan-American Congress in 1928.

● **bustard** ▶ A large omnivorous bird of a family (*Otididae*; 22 species) occurring in grassland regions of the Old World and having long legs adapted for running. Bustards have a long stout neck, broad wings, and a grey or brown mottled plumage, often with ornamental plumes. The great bustard (*Otis tarda*), 120 cm long and weighing 14 kg, is the largest European land bird. Order: *Gruiformes* (cranes, rails, etc.).

● **butadiene** ▶ (H₂C:CHHC:CH₂) A colourless flammable gas made from ▷butanes and butenes. It is used in making synthetic rubbers.

● **butane** ▶ (C₄H₁₀) A colourless flammable gaseous ▷alkane found in crude oil. It is used in the manufacture of synthetic rubber and, in its pressurized liquefied form, as a fuel.

● **butcherbird** ▷*See* shrike.

● **butcher's broom** ▶ A small evergreen European shrub, *Ruscus aculeatus*, up to 80 cm high. The leaves are reduced to small brown scales, but the plant has oval flattened branches that function as leaves. There are separate male and female flowers, which are small and greenish and grow on separate plants. The fruit is a red berry. Family: *Liliaceae*.

● **Bute** ▶ A Scottish island in the Firth of Clyde, in Argyll and Bute council area, separated from the mainland by the Kyles of Bute. Agriculture consists of sheep and cattle rearing, dairy farming, and the production of oats. The island serves Glasgow as a popular holiday resort. Area: 121 sq km (47 sq mi). Population (latest est): 8000. Chief town: Rothesay.

● **Bute, John Stuart, 3rd Earl of** ▶ (1713–92) British statesman; prime minister (1762–63). A close friend of George III and extremely unpopular, he was forced to resign after securing the passage of a cider tax.

● **Buthelezi, Mangosouthu Gatsha** ▶ (1928–) South African politician; chief minister of the former KwaZulu homeland of South Africa (1970–94); minister of home affairs (1994–). A Zulu, the great-grandson of ▷Cetshwayo, he is the founder of ▷Inkatha. He is in favour of autonomy for the Zulu people.

● **Butler, Benjamin Franklin** ▶ (1838–93) US statesman; Republican congressman (1867–75, 1877–79). Butler was hated by southerners for his military governorship of New Orleans during the Civil War. As a Radical Republican congressman, he advocated the impeachment of Andrew ▷Johnson and harsh Reconstruction policies. He ran unsuccessfully for the presidency on a populist ticket in 1884.

● **Butler, Joseph** ▶ (1692–1752) English theologian. He was successively Bishop of Bristol (1738), Dean of St Paul's (1740), and Bishop of Durham (1750). He is best known for his *Analogy of Religion* (1736), defending the reasonableness of the Christian conception of the world against ▷deism.

● **Butler, Josephine Elizabeth** ▶ (1828–1906) British social reformer. She was a staunch defender of women's rights, advocating education for women and opposing prostitution, notably in her campaign (1869) against the Contagious Diseases Act, which implied official toleration of it.

● **Butler, Reg(inald) Cotterell** ▶ (1913–81) British sculptor. Butler trained as an architect and practised as an engineer before devoting himself to sculpture. Influenced by Henry ▷Moore and Alexander ▷Calder, he produced iron and stainless steel constructions suggestive of plant and insect forms.

● **Butler, R(ichard) A(usten), Baron** ▶ (1902–82) British Conservative politician. An MP from 1929, he became minister of education in 1941 and was responsible for the 1944 Education Act. He was chancellor of the exchequer from 1951 to 1955 and then Lord Privy Seal and leader of the House of Commons. He was twice defeated in the bid for the Conservative Party leadership—by Macmillan in 1957 and by Douglas-Home in 1963, under whom he was home secretary (1957–62) and then foreign secretary (1963–64). He was Master of Trinity College, Cambridge (1965–78), and was the author of *The Art of the Possible* (1971).

● **Butler, Samuel** ▶ (1612–80) British satirical poet. The son of a farmer, he was made steward of Ludlow Castle after the Restoration and later became secretary to George Villiers, 2nd Duke of ▷Buckingham. In the mock romance *Hudibras* (3 parts, 1663, 1664, 1678) he satirized the fanaticism and intellectual hypocrisy of the Puritans. The newly founded Royal Society was among the targets of his other works.

● **Butler, Samuel** ► (1835–1902) British novelist. Son of a village rector and grandson of a bishop, he rejected his family, religion, and prospects, emigrating to New Zealand from 1859 to 1864, when he returned wealthy. After failing as an artist, he turned to literature and engaged in the Darwinian controversy. *Erewhon* (1872), which made him famous, satirizes Victorian utopian ideals. The autobiographical *The Way of All Flesh* (1903) recounts his painful liberation from his claustrophobic family background.

● **Butor, Michel** ► (1926–) French experimental novelist, essayist, and critic. He studied philosophy at the Sorbonne and has taught in Egypt, Thessalonika, Geneva, and Manchester. His early novels, employing the techniques of the anti-novel (*see* nouveau roman), include *Passing Time* (1956) and *Second Thoughts* (1957). Later works, such as *Mobile* (1962), *Third Below* (1977), and *Boomerang* (1978), combine elements of fiction, travel writing, and the essay.

● **Butt, Dame Clara** ► (1873–1936) British contralto singer, noted for her deep resonant voice. Elgar wrote his song cycle *Sea Pictures* for her and she frequently sang with her husband, the baritone Kennerley Rumford (1870–1957). She was made a DBE in 1920.

● **butte** ► A small steep-sided mass of rock left upstanding after the erosion of a ▷mesa. It usually consists of a resistant rock capping that protects the underlying rock from erosion.

● **buttercup** ► An annual or perennial herbaceous plant of the worldwide genus *Ranunculus* (about 300 species), usually with much divided leaves. The flowers are usually yellow, with spirally arranged petals and stamens. The fruit is a head of small nutlets (achenes). A common Eurasian species, widely introduced, is the perennial meadow buttercup (*R. acris*), up to 70 cm high. The genus, which is poisonous to livestock, also includes the ▷crowfoots. Family: *Ranunculaceae*.

● **Butterfield, William** ► (1814–1900) British architect of the ▷gothic revival. Although predominantly a builder of churches, Butterfield is probably best known for his design of Keble College, Oxford (1870). This epitomizes his style, with the use of brick, often multicoloured and arranged in patterns, in an idiosyncratic interpretation of the gothic form.

● **butterflies and moths** ► Insects belonging to the order *Lepidoptera* (about 100 000 species), distributed worldwide. The adults have two pairs of scale-covered wings, which are often highly coloured and patterned. They range in size from the smallest moths, with a wingspan of only 4 mm, to butterflies with wingspans of up to 300 mm. They all undergo a complete metamorphosis comprising a four-stage life cycle: egg, larva (*see* caterpillar), ▷pupa (chrysalis), and adult (imago). The caterpillars feed mainly on plants, eating leaves or boring into stems and roots, in some cases becoming serious crop pests (e.g. the cabbage white butterfly and the spruce budworm). Some species pupate by spinning silken cocoons (*see* silkworm). The adults are often strong fliers, seeking out a mate and migrating long distances. They feed mainly on nectar and other plant juices using a long tubular proboscis and may aid plant pollination in the process (*see* Yucca). The forewings and hindwings of moths are locked together by a "bristle-and-catch" device (frenulum). Butterflies generally are active by day and rest with their wings held together vertically; moths, which are mainly nocturnal, generally rest with their wings flat. Another differentiating feature is the antennae, which are smooth and club-shaped in butterflies and plumed or feathery in moths. ▷*See* Plate I.

● **butterfly bush** ▷*See* Buddleia.

● **Buttermere** ► A lake in NW England, in Cumbria in the Lake District. Set amid picturesque scenery, it is popular with tourists. Length: 2 km (1.25 mi).

● **butterwort** ► A ▷carnivorous plant of the genus *Pinguicula* (about 30 species), found in the N hemisphere and South America. These perennial herbs, 12–15 cm high, have a rosette of yellow-green leaves covered with sticky glands on which insects are trapped. The single

spurred funnel-shaped violet or pink flower arises on a slender stalk. Family: *Lentibulariaceae*.

● **button quail** ► A small ground-dwelling bird of a family (*Turnicidae*; 15 species) found in warm Old World grassland regions. Button quails are 13–19 cm long with a brown streaked plumage, short wings, and a small slender bill. The female courts the male and leaves him to incubate the eggs and tend the young. Order: *Gruiformes* (cranes, rails, etc.).

● **buttress** ► A projecting mass of masonry strengthening a wall. The huge vaults of Roman and Byzantine public buildings caused buttresses to be built to counteract the outward thrust of the roof. In ▷gothic architecture, the graceful but highly functional **flying buttress** developed to support the upper walls of large churches.

● **butyl rubber** ► A synthetic ▷rubber made by copolymerization of isobutylene with ▷isoprene. It is less permeable to gas than natural rubbers and is used in tyre inner tubes.

● **Buxtehude, Dietrich** ► (1637–1707) Danish organist and composer. He settled in Germany in 1668 as organist at the Marienkirche, Lübeck. In 1673 he started his famous *Abendmusiken* ("evening concerts"); J. S. Bach walked 200 miles to Lübeck to hear Buxtehude's music. He composed much influential organ music and sacred music.

● **Buxton** ► 53 17N 1 55W A spa and resort in N central England, in the Peak District of Derbyshire on the River Wye. Its famous mineral waters were first used by the Romans. Notable buildings include the Crescent and the Devonshire Royal Hospital. During the 1970s Buxton Opera House, built in 1903 and formerly used only as a theatre and cinema, was restored to its original condition. Population (1991): 19 854.

● **buzzard** ► A ▷hawk belonging to a widespread genus (*Buteo*) characterized by broad wings, a large rounded tail, and a brown plumage. Buzzards hunt in open country for small mammals, reptiles, insects, and carrion and soar gracefully at great heights. The common Eurasian buzzard (*B. buteo*), 55 cm long, occurs in a number of races; the migratory rough-legged buzzard (*B. lagopus*) is distinguished by its feathered legs.

● **buzz bomb** ▷*See* V-1.

● **Byatt, A(ntonia) S(usan), Dame** ► (1936–) British novelist and writer. Her novels include the linked works *The Virgin in the Garden* (1978), *Still Life* (1985), and *Babel Tower* (1996) and the Booker-prizewinning *Possession* (1990); her shorter fiction includes *The Matisse Stories* (1993) and *Elementals* (1998). The sister of Margaret ▷Drabble, she was appointed DBE in 1999.

● **Byblos** ► 34 08N 35 38E A ▷Phoenician city state on the E Mediterranean coast, now Jubeil (Lebanon). Egyptian records from the 14th to the 10th centuries BC attest a thriving trade with Byblos; excavations here have revealed strong cultural links with Egypt. Under Greek and Roman rule Byblos dwindled in relative commercial importance but remained famous as the centre of orgiastic worship of Astarte (*see* Aphrodite) and her lover ▷Adonis. ▷*See also* Sidon; Tyre.

● **Bydgoszcz** ► (German name: Bromberg) 53 16N 17 33E A city in N Poland. It is an important inland port on a canal linking the Rivers Vistula and Oder. Industries include engineering, printing, and the processing of forest products. Population (1996 est): 386 100.

● **Bylot, Robert** ▷*See* Baffin, William.

● **Byng, George, Viscount Torrington** ► (1663–1733) English admiral. An ardent supporter of William III he gained rapid promotion and in the War of the Spanish Succession captured Gibraltar (1704). He defeated the fleet of ▷James Edward Stuart, the Old Pretender, off Scotland (1708) and crowned his career by destroying a Spanish fleet off Messina (1717). His son **John Byng** (1704–57) was also an admiral, owing his rapid promotion to his father's influence. In 1756, however, he failed ignominiously to relieve Minorca, then under attack by the French, and retreated to Gibraltar. He was shot for failing to do his duty—or, in Voltaire's satirical view, as a warning to his colleagues ("pour encourager les autres").

● **Byng of Vimy, Julian, 1st Viscount** ► (1862–1935) British field marshal. He won distinction in World War I first at ▷Gallipoli, then as commander of the successful Canadian troops at Vimy Ridge. After the war he was governor general of Canada (1921–26) and then commissioner of the Metropolitan Police (1928–31).

● **Byrd, Richard E(velyn)** ► (1888–1957) US explorer. A naval pilot, he served in World War I and in 1926 began a series of record-breaking flights over the two Poles and the Atlantic Ocean. In 1928 he set out on the first of several expeditions to explore Antarctica from the air. In 1934–35, he spent five months alone in a hut at Bolling Advance Base, describing his experience in *Alone* (1938).

● **Byrd, William** ► (?1543–1623) English composer. Despite being a Roman Catholic he retained the regard of Queen Elizabeth and was made organist of Lincoln Cathedral and subsequently of the Chapel Royal (1572). His compositions include Catholic masses and motets, Anglican services, psalm settings and anthems, pieces for the virginals (he is known as the father of keyboard music), solo songs, and music for viols. With ▷Tallis (his teacher) he held a music printing monopoly.

● **Byrd Land** ▷*See* Marie Byrd Land.

● **Byron, George Gordon, 6th Baron** ► (1788–1824) British poet. Born with a clubfoot, he grew up in Aberdeen until he inherited (1798) the title of his great-uncle. Thereafter he went to Harrow School and Cambridge. His first book, *Hours of Idleness* (1807), was followed in 1809 by a satire aimed at its ungenerous reviewers. After two years travelling in Europe he published the first two cantos of *Childe Harolde's Pilgrimage* (1812) to immediate acclaim and was lionized by London society. His many lovers probably included his half-sister Augusta Leigh (whose daughter, Medora, came to believe that

Lord Byron ► Byron's romantic looks and adventurous spirit are captured in this 19th-century engraving, from a portrait painted just before his first departure for Greece in 1809. Byron's mother considered this an excellent likeness.

Byron was her father), as well as Lady Caroline Lamb, wife of the future Lord ▷Melbourne, and Claire Clairmont (Shelley's step-sister-in-law, by whom he had a daughter, Allegra). He married Annabella Milbanke in 1815 but she left him the following year. Byron then left England for ever. He stayed near Geneva with ▷Shelley and then went to Italy. In 1818 he began writing the witty verse satire *Don Juan*. In 1823 he became involved in the Greek struggle for independence and he died while training troops at Missolonghi. Byron's legitimate daughter, **Augusta Ada Byron** (1815–51), who became Countess of Lovelace, was a mathematician who assisted Charles ▷Babbage in his work on mechanical computers. The programming language ADA is named after her.

● **byte** ► A unit of information in a computer consisting of a group of ▷bits (8 in most small computers, 16 in larger ones). For some purposes a byte is equal to a character, e.g. a disk holding 250 000 bytes will hold this number of characters.

● **Bytom** ► (German name: Beuthen) 50 21N 18 51E A town in SW Poland. It is a major heavy-industry centre in a coal, zinc, and lead mining area. Population (1996 est): 227 600.

● **Byzantine art and architecture** ► The painting, architecture, and decoration that developed in the ancient city of Constantinople (formerly Byzantium; modern Istanbul) after 330 AD, when it became the new Roman imperial capital, until 1453, when Constantinople fell to the Turks. Primarily religious and often symbolic or didactic, Byzantine art suppressed both realistic portrayal and opportunities for individual artistic expression. Owing to Constantinople's position as a meeting point of Asia and Europe, the bright colours and intricacy of oriental design mingle in Byzantine mosaics and ▷icons with Christian symbolism. Three main phases of Byzantine art succeeded one another between 330 and 1453 AD. The first phase (330–726) came to an end with the Iconoclastic controversy (726–843), which resulted in the destruction of many works of art (*see* iconoclasm). During the second golden age (843–1204) and the final phase (1204–1453) a complicated iconography of religious pictures was evolved, wherein each divine person, prophet, saint, angel, and apostle was allocated their strict position on the wall, apse, or dome of the church. This was possible because of the design of the Byzantine ▷basilica with its characteristic dome rising from a square base—an innovation that greatly extended the versatility of the Roman dome, which was restricted to circular buildings. The Church of Holy Wisdom (Hagia Sophia) in Constantinople, built between 532 and 537, is the outstanding example of a Byzantine basilica with a central dome (in this case buttressed by semidomes). The characteristic brickwork, pillars, and internal mosaics of Byzantine buildings also had a profound effect on Western architecture from the spectacular St Mark's (11th century) in Venice to Westminster Cathedral in London in the 20th century.

● **Byzantine Empire** ▷*See* Eastern Roman Empire.

● **Byzantium** ▷*See* Istanbul.

C

● **cab** ▶ A horse-drawn passenger vehicle introduced into London streets from Paris early in the 19th century. The name is an abbreviation of the French *cabriolet*, a two-wheeled carriage invented in the 17th century as a private vehicle for two people. London cabs, painted yellow, were first licensed for hire in 1823, the fare being fixed at two thirds of the ▷hackney-coach fare. Their popularity led to the invention in 1834 of the lighter and faster **hansom cab** by the architect Joseph Aloysius Hansom (1803–82). The name cab was extended to include the four-wheeled "growler," a descendant of the hackney coach, and both types were controlled by a series of acts, including the Hackney Carriage Act (1831) and the London Cab Act (1934). By the end of the 19th century, when taximeters were introduced to record the fare automatically, there were over 7000 hansoms and 4000 four wheelers plying the London streets. Motorized cabs, introduced in 1907 and widely known as taxis, had completely replaced the horse-drawn vehicles by 1918. The design of the modern London taxi was influenced by the Model T Ford, many characteristics of which it retains.

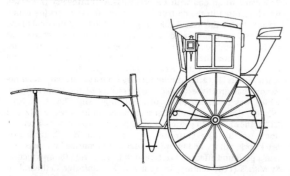

cab ▶ A 19th-century hansom cab with its characteristic elevated driver's seat at the rear.

● **Cabal** ▶ Five ministers of Charles II of England who dominated politics from 1667 to about 1674. They were Sir Thomas Clifford (1630–73), Lord Ashley (later 1st Earl of ▷Shaftesbury), the 2nd Duke of ▷Buckingham, the Earl of ▷Arlington, and the Earl of ▷Lauderdale. It was not a united body: the king played one minister off against another to retain control of policy. Clifford and Arlington supported a secret pro-Catholic policy of friendship with France, which cost them their offices in 1673–74.

● **Caballé, Montserrat** ▶ (1933–   ) Spanish soprano. She sang at La Scala, Milan, and in 1965 made her debut in New York. A member of the Metropolitan Opera, she specializes in bel canto roles, such as the title role in Bellini's *Norma*, and in Spanish music.

● **cabbage** ▶ A flowering plant, ▷*Brassica oleracea* var. *capitata*, widely cultivated as a vegetable. The short stem bears a round heart, up to 25 cm in diameter, of tightly compressed leaves. Many varieties have been developed for cooking, salads, and pickling. For example, the Savoy cabbage is a cooking variety with dark-green wrinkled leaves. All cabbages and many other brassicas—including cauliflower, broccoli, kale, and Brussels sprouts—are derived from the wild cabbage (*B. oleracea*), a perennial herb native to coastal regions of W Europe. 30–60 cm high, its straggling stem bears a spike of yellow flowers. Family: *Cruciferae*.

● **cabbage palm** ▶ A West Indian palm tree, *Roystonea oleracea*, that may grow to a height of 30 m but is often cut when young for its cabbage-like head of leaves, which is eaten as a vegetable. An oil and a type of sago is obtained from the fruit. The name is given to several other palms, including *Livistona australis*, of E Australia.

● **cabbage root fly** ▶ A plant-eating fly, *Erioischia brassicae*, whose larva is a serious economic pest. The larvae feed on the roots of cabbages, radishes, etc., having developed from eggs laid around the stems. Family: *Muscidae*.

● **cabbage white butterfly** ▶ A white butterfly belonging to the genus *Pieris*, whose caterpillars eat cabbages and related vegetables. The species are the large white (*P. brassicae*), the green-veined white (*P. napi*), and the small white (*P. rapae*). Family: *Pieridae*.

● **caber tossing** ▶ An event in Scottish athletics. A competitor carries the caber, a tapering tree trunk 4–5 m (13–17 ft) long, vertically in his cradled hands and then tosses it forwards. As the top end hits the ground, the other end should continue over it so that the tossed caber should lie in the direction in which it was thrown; a toss more than 90° askew is invalid. Each competitor has three tosses, followed by more if there is a tie in the number of perfect tosses. If no competitor achieves a toss, the caber is either shortened or replaced by a lighter one. The Braemar caber, which weighs 54.5 kg (120 lb) and is 5.8 m (19 ft) long, was tossed in 1951 by George Clark, after remaining untossed since 1891.

● **Cabimas** ▶ 10 26N 71 27W A city in NW Venezuela, on the NE shore of Lake Maracaibo. It is an important centre within the Ambrosio oilfields. Population (1994 est): 165 755.

● **Cabinda** ▶ (or Kabinda) A district of Angola, forming an enclave between the Congo and the Democratic Republic of Congo (formerly Zaïre) on the Atlantic coast. Extensive oil deposits were discovered offshore in 1968 and led to the expansion of the chief town, Cabinda. The area also produces coffee, palm oil, timber, and cocoa. Area: 7270 sq km (2806 sq mi). Population (1993 est): 174 000.

● **cabinet** ▶ A committee of the executive heads of government. In the UK the cabinet originated in the 16th-century cabinet council, a committee of the ▷Privy Council the growing size of which led to the monarch's reliance on a small inner group of advisers. Cabinet power was enhanced by William III's recognition that his ministers should be selected from the political group prominent in parliament and by the emergence in the 18th century of the ▷prime minister, who chaired cabinet meetings in the customary absence from them of George I and George II. By the end of the 19th century the principle of collective cabinet responsibility to parliament, and not to the Crown, had been established. Cabinets now consist of some 20 leading ministers, from either house of parliament, whom the prime minister has appointed to head executive departments. Cabinet meetings are secret and minutes may not be made publicly available until 30 years have elapsed. However, the principle of cabinet secrecy was undermined in 1975 by the failure of the attorney general to gain an injunction to prevent publication of the ▷Crossman diaries.

In the USA the cabinet comprises the heads of the 13 executive departments and the attorney general, who are not members of ▷Congress and are responsible only to the ▷president. The extent of its role depends on the extent to which the president chooses to consult it.

● **cable TV** ▶ A system of television broadcasting in which signals are transmitted by cables instead of by radio waves. Developed in 1949 to improve reception in areas in which aerials were unsatisfactory, cable TV was first widely adopted in the USA in the 1970s with the easing of government controls and increased access to communications satellites. The first cable TV systems in the UK were installed in selected areas in the 1980s, offering possibilities of home banking, shopping, and information.

● **Cabora Bassa Dam** ▶ 15 34S 33 00E A dam in Mozambique, on the Zambezi River. It is the largest dam in S Africa.

● **Cabot, John** ▶ (Italian name: Giovanni Caboto; c. 1450–c. 1499) Italian explorer. He settled in England in about 1484 and under Henry VII's patronage discovered Cape Breton Island (which he thought to be Asia) in 1497. He set out again in 1498 and appears to have died at sea. His son **Sebastian Cabot** (c. 1476–1557) was a cartographer to Henry VIII. For Spain he explored the coast of South America (1525–28).

● **Cabral, Pedro Álvares** ▶ (?1467–1520) Portuguese navigator. In 1500, on his way to India with 13 ships, he landed in Brazil, which he claimed for Portugal. Resuming his voyage E, he landed at Mozambique and thence reached Calicut, where he established the first commercial treaty between Portugal and India. He returned to Portugal in 1501 with only four ships.

● **Cabrini, St Frances Xavier** ▶ (1850–1917) Italian founder of the Missionary Sisters of the Sacred Heart, known as Mother Cabrini. She sailed in 1889 to the USA and established 67 houses there and in Buenos Aires, Paris, and Madrid. She worked mainly among poor Italian immigrants and was the first US citizen to be canonized. Feast day: 13 Nov.

● **cacao** ▷See cocoa and chocolate.

● **Caccini, Giulio** ▶ (c. 1545–c. 1618) Italian singer and composer. He developed the monodic style (a single vocal line supported by a chordal bass), which led to the earliest operas; his opera *Euridice* was performed in 1602.

● **Cáceres** ▶ 39 29N 6 23W A market town in W Spain, in Estremadura. It produces textiles and cork. The old part lies within Roman and Moorish walls. Population (1991): 71 745.

● **cachalot** ▷See sperm whale.

● **cacomistle** ▶ An arboreal nocturnal mammal of the American genus *Bassariscus* (2 species). Cacomistles are greyish brown with small faces, long ears, and pointed snouts; the long bushy tail, patterned with black and white rings, accounts for about half the total body length (60–100 cm). They feed on small animals and fruit. The North American cacomistle, or ring-tailed cat (*B. astutus*) occurs from the SW USA to S Mexico. Family: *Procyonidae* (raccoons, etc.); order: *Carnivora*.

● **Cactoblastis** ▷See cactus moth.

● **cactus** ▶ A flowering plant belonging to the family *Cactaceae* (over 2000 species). These perennial herbs and shrubs grow chiefly in the drier regions of tropical America and the West Indies. Plant size and shape varies widely; the larger species may grow to a height of 10 m or more. Cacti show pronounced modifications to prevent water loss—their leaves or shoots are reduced to spines, they have thick waxy outer layers, and many possess succulent water-storing stems. The flowers, borne singly, are large and brightly coloured. Some genera are cultivated as ornamentals or for their soft timber or alkaloid content, and the fruits of many species are edible (*see* prickly pear).

● **cactus moth** ▶ A South American cactus-boring ▷pyralid moth, *Cactoblastis cactorum*, that was introduced into Australia in 1925 as a means of biologically controlling the prickly pear cactus, which had ruined large areas.

● **CAD** ▶ (computer-aided design) The use of computers in the design of products, buildings, electronic circuits, etc. The programs take basic design criteria together with data about component sizes, tolerances, etc. Usually they display plans or three-dimensional views of the product, and these may be modified by the designer. Systems used for CAD can also list analyses of the design (e.g. safety factors, or electrical characteristics of circuits). Often, the output can be transferred directly to a computer-aided manufacturing system (▷CAM).

● **Cadbury, George** ▶ (1839–1922) British businessman and Quaker, who in 1861 took over, with his brother **Richard Cadbury** (1835–99), his father's cocoa and chocolate business and established Cadbury Brothers. The Cadburys greatly improved working conditions and George founded (1894) a garden village at Bournville, near Birmingham, which influenced subsequent town planning.

● **caddis fly** ▶ A mothlike insect, also called sedge fly, belonging to the worldwide order *Trichoptera* (about 5000 species). Caddis flies—1.5–40 mm long, with long antennae—are found in cool damp places and feed on nectar. The omnivorous larvae (caddis worms) live in flowing fresh water, often in portable cases constructed from sand, stones, pieces of leaf, etc.

● **Caddo** ▶ A North American Indian language and people of the SE USA. The Caddoan group of languages is named after the Caddo, a semisedentary agricultural people. Their villages of conical huts were built around a central temple mound. Their kinship organization was matrilineal; political and ritual affairs were conducted by a hereditary elite.

● **cade** ▶ A ▷juniper tree or shrub, *Juniperus oxycedrus*, native to Mediterranean coastal regions and growing to a height of 8 m. Also called prickly juniper, it has needles and rounded reddish berry-like fruits, 6–10 mm in diameter. Oil of cade is distilled from the wood and used in medicine.

● **Cade, Jack** ▶ (d. 1450) English rebel, who led a Kentish rebellion in 1450 against Henry VI. The rebels, who were chiefly opposing high taxes and court corruption, demanded the recall of Richard Plantagenet, Duke of York, from Ireland. In spite of initial successes in Kent and London the rebellion was soon quelled and Cade was killed.

cactus ▶ The giant saguaro cactus, *Carnegiea gigantea* (or *Cereus giganteus*) of Arizona, can reach a height of 21 m.

● **Cader Idris** ► A mountain ridge in NW Wales, in Gwynedd, in Snowdonia National Park. It rises to 892 m (2927 ft) at Pen-y-Gader.

● **Cádiz** ► 36 32N 6 18W A city and seaport in SW Spain, in Andalusia on the Gulf of Cádiz. Founded by Phoenician merchants (c. 1100 BC), it was taken from the Moors by Alfonso the Wise of Castile in 1262. Following the discovery of America it prospered as a base for the Spanish treasure fleet; the harbour was burned by Sir Francis Drake in 1587. It has two cathedrals and a notable collection of works by the artist Murillo. An important port and naval base, it has tuna fisheries and shipbuilding industries. Population (1995 est): 154 511.

● **cadmium** ► (Cd) A soft dense metal, discovered in 1817 by Friedrich Strohmeyer (1776–1835). Cadmium occurs naturally as the mineral greenockite (CdS) and in zinc, copper, and lead sulphide ores. It is chemically similar to lead and is a component of low-melting-point alloys. It is used in the control rods of nuclear reactors, in light meters, television-tube phosphors, batteries, solders, and low-friction alloys. Cadmium and its compounds are poisonous and care should be taken in working with solders that contain cadmium. Compounds include several salts, the yellow sulphide (CdS) and the oxide (CdO). At no 48; at wt 112.411; mp 321.1°C; bp 767°C.

● **Cadmus** ► Legendary Greek hero. Obeying the oracle of Delphi, he followed a cow into Boeotia and founded the city of Thebes where it lay down. When he sowed in the ground the teeth of a dragon he had killed, a race of warriors emerged. He married Harmonia, daughter of Ares and Aphrodite, and introduced the alphabet into Greece.

● **caduceus** ► A snake-entwined winged staff carried by ▷Hermes and other heralds in Greek mythology. It was used in ancient Rome as a symbol of neutrality and since medieval times as a symbol of medicine, because of its similarity to the staff of ▷Asclepius.

● **Cadwalader** ► (Catgualart; d. 682 AD) Legendary king of the Britons, according to ▷Geoffrey of Monmouth. Probably a confusion of the historical kings Caedwalla and Ceadwalla, Cadwalader—the son of the Welsh king Cadwallon (d. 633)—reputedly led his people to Brittany to escape the plague and then went on to Rome to pursue a religious life. He was later considered a saint.

● **caecilian** ► A limbless burrowing ▷amphibian of the order *Apoda*, or *Gymnophiona* (over 150 species), found in tropical and warm temperate regions. Caecilians are 11–140 cm long and feed on termites and earthworms, which they detect by means of a pair of sensory tentacles on the head (eyes are reduced or absent).

● **Caedmon** ► (died c. 680 AD) English poet, known only from the account given by ▷Bede in his *Ecclesiastical History*. He was an illiterate herdsman who in his old age was suddenly divinely inspired to compose a hymn on the Creation. The *Hymn* is a typical example of Old English oral verse. Caedmon later entered the monastery of Whitby.

● **Caen** ► 49 11N 0 22W A city and port in NW France, the capital of the Calvados department on the River Orne. Situated at the centre of an agricultural and horse-breeding area, Caen has iron, silk, and leather industries. Stone from nearby quarries was used to build several cathedrals and churches in England. A cultural centre, its university was established in 1432. It has many fine churches. *History*: captured by the English in 1346 and again in 1417, it became a Huguenot stronghold in the 17th century. The construction of a ship canal in the 19th century made it an important port. Caen was badly damaged (1944) during World War II. Population (1990): 115 624.

● **Caerleon** ► 51 37N 2 57W A town in South Wales, in Newport county borough on the River Usk. A Roman legionary fortress was built here (c. 75 AD) to control a British tribe, the Silures. There was accommodation for 5000 troops and an ▷amphitheatre, the best preserved in Britain. Before 300 the garrison was withdrawn. Caerleon is also linked with ▷Arthurian legend. Population (1991): 8931.

● **Caernarfon** ► 53 08N 4 16W A town in North Wales, on the Menai Strait, the administrative centre of Gwynedd. It is a tourist centre, market town, and small port. The castle (built by Edward I in 1284) is the likely birthplace of Edward II, the first Prince of Wales; Prince ▷Charles was invested here as Prince of Wales in 1969. Population (1991): 9695.

● **Caernarfonshire** ► A former county of NW Wales, bordering on the Irish Sea. Under local government reorganization in 1974 it was absorbed into the new authority of ▷Gwynedd.

● **Caerphilly** ► 1. 51 35N 3 14W A market town in SE Wales, in Caerphilly county borough. In a former coalmining area, it is known for Caerphilly cheese (originally made here) and its castle, the largest in Wales. Population (1991): 28 481. 2. A county borough in SE Wales, created in 1996 from parts of Mid Glamorgan and Gwent. Area: 275 sq km (106 sq mi). Population (1999 est): 169 100.

● **Caesar, (Gaius) Julius** ► (100–44 BC) Roman general and statesman, whose career marked the end of the Roman Republic. A patrician, Caesar allied himself with the popular party by his marriage in 84 to ▷Cinna's daughter Cornelia. After her death in 68, he married Pompeia, whom he divorced in 62, and in 59 he married Calpurnia.

During the 60s Caesar ascended the political ladder, joining ▷Pompey and ▷Crassus in the first ▷Triumvirate (60) and becoming consul (59) and then governor of Gaul. Caesar's subjugation of Gaul (58–50), and his brief campaigns in Britain (55, 54), confirmed his military reputation and made him a popular hero. Crassus's death (53) and Pompey's developing association with Caesar's opponents in the Senate brought the Triumvirate to an end (50) and the Senate, with Pompey's support, asked Caesar to resign his armies. He refused and, crossing the River Rubicon into Italy (49), initiated the civil war. Caesar defeated Pompey at ▷Pharsalus (48) and spent the following winter in Alexandria with ▷Cleopatra, who became his lover. She is reputed to have had a son, Caesarion, by him. Caesar then campaigned in NE Anatolia, defeating Pharnaces II at Zela (47), the victory provoking his comment "veni, vidi, vici" ("I came, I saw, I conquered"). He went on to defeat the remnants of Pompey's party at ▷Thapsus (46) and Munda (45), after which he returned to Rome as dictator. There, he introduced a revised (Julian) ▷calendar and other reforms, but on the Ides of March (15 March, 44), he was assassinated in the Senate House by republicans, including ▷Brutus and ▷Cassius Longinus, who feared his monarchical aspirations.

Caesar wrote outstanding accounts of his campaigns in Gaul (*De bello gallico*) and the civil war (*De bello civili*).

● **Caesarea** ► 32 30N 34 54E An ancient town in Israel, on the Mediterranean coast between Tel Aviv-Yafo and Haifa. Built by Herod the Great, it had a large early Christian community and was for a time the capital of Roman Palestine. Caesarea was twice held by the Crusaders and finally destroyed by Muslims in 1265. Many Roman remains have been excavated.

● **Caesarean section** ► A surgical operation in which a baby is delivered through an incision made in the abdominal wall and the womb, so called because traditionally Julius Caesar was believed to have been born in this way, although Roman law only permitted this operation if the mother was dead and it is known that Caesar's mother survived his birth. More plausibly, the term derives from the Latin *caedere* to cut (past participle *caesus*). According to ▷Pliny the Elder, the ancient Roman family Julii took the name Caesar when an early member was delivered by cutting the mother. Caesarean section is employed when a baby cannot be delivered through the vagina; for instance, because it is abnormally positioned or is too large. It may also be performed to deliver preterm babies who are at risk if the pregnancy continues to term. Because obstetricians and midwives are now sometimes sued for negligence if a birth goes wrong, and because many women are now choosing to have a Caesarean to avoid the injuries that can occur during a natural birth, the number of Caesareans has greatly increased in recent decades—to 17% of births in the UK and up to 30% in some parts of the USA.

● **caesium** ► (Cs) The most reactive and electropositive alkali metal. It was discovered by Bunsen and Kirchhoff in 1860 and occurs naturally in the mica lepidolite and as pollucite, $(Cs,K)AlSi_2O_6.nH_2O$. Caesium reacts explosively with water to give the hydroxide (CsOH) and is used in ▷caesium clocks and in photoelectric cells. Chief compounds are the nitrate ($CsNO_3$) and chloride (CsCl). At no 55; at wt 132.905; mp 28.39°C; bp 671°C.

● **caesium clock** ► An ▷atomic clock that depends on the energy difference between two states of the caesium nucleus in a magnetic field. A nonuniform magnetic field is used to split a beam of caesium atoms into two components. Nuclei in the lower energy state are irradiated by radio-frequency radiation at the difference frequency between the two states, so that some are excited to the higher state. By reanalysing the mixture, the radio-frequency oscillator can be locked to the difference frequency of 9 192 631 770 hertz with an accuracy of one part in 10^{13}. This extremely accurate clock is now used in the definition of the ▷second.

● **Caffaggiolo maiolica** ▶ An important category of Italian pottery mainly produced from about 1504 to 1540 under Medici patronage. Its main characteristic is bold bright decoration in orange, yellow, red, and green, on a cobalt-blue background. ▷*See* maiolica.

● **caffeine** ▶ (*or* theine; $C_8H_{10}O_2N_4$) A white crystalline substance (in its pure form) that occurs in ▷coffee, ▷tea, ▷cocoa, and some other natural products. It acts as a heart and central-nervous-system stimulant and as a diuretic, which are the main reasons for the popularity of tea and coffee beverages. Coffee as a drink contains some 70 mg/100 ml and tea contains 50–60 mg/100 ml. However, an excess of caffeine can be harmful to health.

● **Cage, John** ▶ (1912–92) Avantgarde US composer, who studied with Schoenberg and Varèse. His works include *Sonatas and Interludes* (1946–48) for prepared piano (with pieces of wood, metal, etc., fixed across its strings); *Imaginary Landscape No 4* (1951) for 12 randomly tuned radio sets; *4 minutes 33 seconds* (1954), silence in three movements for any instrument(s); and *Europeras 3 and 4* (1990). His books, including *Silence* (1961), reflect his philosophy of indeterminism.

● **Cagliari** ▶ 39 13N 9 08E A seaport in Italy, in Sardinia. It has Roman remains, a 14th-century cathedral, and a university (1606). There are milling, tanning, and fishing industries. Lead, salt, and zinc are exported. Population (1996 est): 174 543.

● **Cagliostro, Alessandro, Conte di** ▶ (Giuseppe Balsamo; 1743–95) Italian adventurer. His pretended skills in alchemy and magic gained him fame throughout Europe, especially in Paris. He was arrested for promoting freemasonry and died in prison in Italy.

● **Cagney, James** ▶ (1899–1986) US actor. He began making films in the 1930s, after working as a vaudeville singer and dancer, and became famous for his portrayals of tough gangsters. His films include *Public Enemy* (1931) and *The Roaring Twenties* (1939).

● **Caicos Islands** ▷*See* Turks and Caicos Islands.

● **Caillaux, Joseph** ▶ (1863–1944) French statesman; prime minister (1911–12). He was finance minister three times before World War I and introduced direct income tax into France. In 1914 his wife shot and killed Gaston Calmette (1858–1914), the editor of *Le Figaro*, who had cast aspersions on his financial dealings while in office. An advocate of a negotiated peace during World War I, Caillaux was arrested in 1917 on a charge of dealing with the enemy. His civil rights were restored in 1925.

● **Cain** ▶ In the Old Testament, the elder son of Adam and Eve. He became jealous of his younger brother Abel, a shepherd whose burnt offerings were accepted by God in preference to his own. He murdered Abel and was banished, marked as the world's first murderer.

● **Caine, Sir Michael** ▶ (Maurice Micklewhite; 1933–) British film actor. His films include *The Ipcress File* (1965), *Alfie* (1966), *Sleuth* (1973), *Educating Rita* (1983), *Noises Off* (1991), and *Little Voice* (1999). He won an Oscar for his performance in *Hannah and Her Sisters* (1986) and was knighted in 2000.

● **Cainozoic era** ▷*See* Cenozoic era.

● **cairn** ▷*See* barrow.

● **Cairngorm Mountains** ▶ A mountain range in NE Scotland, in Aberdeenshire and Highland, forming a N extension of the Grampians. Its highest peaks include Ben Macdhui at 1309 m (4296 ft) and Braeriach at 1296 m (4252 ft). The area is popular for winter sports, centred on Aviemore.

● **Cairns** ▶ 16 51S 145 43E A port in Australia, in NE Queensland on Trinity Bay. It is the commercial centre for an agricultural, mining, and timber region; sugar is exported. Population (1995 est): 100 900.

● **cairn terrier** ▶ A breed of small □dog originating in the Scottish

Highlands, where it was used to flush game from cover (such as stone cairns). It has a long outer coat and a short soft undercoat; the colour varies from red, sandy, or mottled grey to almost black. Height: about 25 cm.

Cairo ▶ The mosque of El Azhar was founded in 970 AD. It is the earliest surviving Fatimid building.

● **Cairo** ▶ (Arabic name: El Qahira) 30 01N 31 14E The capital of Egypt, situated in the N of the country on the E bank of the River Nile. It is the largest city in Africa and the cultural and commercial centre of Egypt. Industry has developed dramatically since the 1920s and in particular since the revolution of 1952, with traditional textile manufacturing and food processing retaining importance alongside newer industries, such as metallurgy and plastics. Its many mosques include the Mosque of Omar (643 AD), Cairo's earliest remaining Arabic building, and the Mohammed Ali Mosque, housed in the 12th-century citadel. The Mosque and University of El Azhar was founded in 970 AD; three other universities were established in the 20th century.

History: the Arabic city of El Fustat was founded in 641 AD, and from the 9th century, as El Qahira, it was successively the capital of the Fatimid, Ayyubite, and Mameluke dynasties. It was under the Mamelukes that the city enjoyed the period of its greatest prosperity. Following its conquest by the Turks in the 16th century, it declined in power, but in the 19th century its prosperity was restored under Mehemet ▷Ali and his successors. During World War II it was the seat of the Allied headquarters in the Middle East. Population (1996 est): 9 900 000. ▷*See also* Giza, El.

● **caisson** ▶ A large cylindrical or box-shaped structure sunk into the ground during excavation work. Caissons aid construction of underwater foundations, for example in the construction of piers for bridges, and may become part of the permanent structure.

● **caisson disease** ▷*See* decompression sickness.

● **Caithness** ▶ A former county of NE Scotland. Under local government reorganization in 1975 its boundaries were adjusted to form a district of the same name, in the Highland Region. This district was abolished in 1996.

● **Cajun** ▷*See* Acadia.

● **cakewalk** ▶ A ballroom dance of the early 1900s, originally performed by Black slaves satirizing the elegance of plantation society. Couples walked round in a square, being judged for the grace and inventiveness of their movements. The winners received a cake, whence the expression "to take the cake."

● **Calabar** ▶ (former name: Old Calabar) 4 56N 8 22E A port in SE Nigeria. It was a centre of the slave trade in the 18th and 19th centuries; exports now include palm oil, rubber, timber, and cocoa. Population (1996 est): 174 400.

● **calabash** ▶ A tree, *Crescentia cujete*, 7.5–15 m tall, native to tropical

America (particularly Brazil). Funnel-shaped flowers are borne on the old stems and produce gourdlike fruits, up to 50 cm long. These fruits have woody outer layers and, after removal of the inner pulp, are used as pots, cooking utensils, etc. Family: *Bignoniaceae*.

● **Calabria** ▶ A mountainous region occupying the southern "toe" of Italy. It is basically a poor agricultural region (producing olives, citrus fruits, vines, and cereals) with the lowest per capita income of any Italian region. Crotone is the main industrial centre. Area: 15 080 sq km (5822 sq mi). Population (1994 est): 2 079 588. Capital: Catanzaro.

● **Calais** ▶ 50 57N 1 52E A port in N France, in the Pas-de-Calais department. Its prosperity lies in being on the shortest sea route to England. It produces lace, tulle, and other textiles.
    History: besieged and captured by the English under Edward III in 1346 (commemorated in Rodin's statue *The Burghers of Calais*), Calais remained in English hands until 1558. In World War I it was a British base; in World War II it was the target of savage bombardment and was heroically defended in support of the withdrawal from ▷Dunkirk. Population (1995 est): 75 309.

● **calamine** ▶ An ore of zinc. In English usage it refers to zinc carbonate (smithsonite) and in the USA it refers to zinc silicate (hemimorphite). A skin lotion of the same name contains zinc oxide.

● **Calamites** ▶ An extinct genus of treelike vascular plants, prominent during the Carboniferous period, 345–280 million years ago. Their fossilized remains form a major constituent of the Carboniferous coal seams (*see also* Lepidodendron). Phylum: *Sphenophyta* (*see* horsetail).

● **Calamity Jane** ▶ (Martha Canary; c. 1852–1903) US frontierswoman, who featured in many stories and legends of the Wild West. She worked in frontier towns and camps, frequently dressed as a man, and was skilled in riding and shooting. She later appeared in Wild West Shows.

● **Calas, Jean** ▶ (1698–1762) French Huguenot, who was accused of the murder of his son in 1761 in order to prevent his becoming a Roman Catholic. He protested his innocence but was tried and executed. His conviction was reversed after ▷Voltaire, at the request of his widow, led a campaign for religious toleration and legal reform.

● **Calceolaria** ▶ A genus of perennial herbs and shrubs (300–400 species) native to temperate South America. The plants grow to a height of 30–70 cm and bear brightly coloured slipper-shaped flowers. Some species and hybrids are grown as ornamentals. Family: *Scrophulariaceae*.

● **Calchas** ▶ A legendary Greek prophet who foretold the length of the ▷Trojan War and advised the Greeks to build the wooden horse by which they gained entry to Troy. He died after being defeated by Mopsus in a trial of prophecy.

● **calcite** ▶ A common rock-forming mineral consisting of crystalline calcium carbonate. It is usually colourless or white. It occurs in igneous, metamorphic, and sedimentary rocks. Most ▷limestones consist largely of calcite, sometimes in the form of fossil shells, and calcite is a common cementing material in coarse-grained sedimentary rocks. Calcite is very soluble in slightly acidic water.

● **calcitonin** ▶ A polypeptide hormone, secreted by the thyroid gland in mammals, that reduces the level of calcium in the blood when this rises above normal. A hormone from the ▷parathyroid gland raises blood calcium levels and therefore acts antagonistically.

● **calcium** ▶ (Ca) A reactive metal, first isolated by Sir Humphry Davy in 1808. It occurs in nature as ▷calcite ($CaCO_3$), ▷fluorite (CaF_2), and ▷gypsum ($CaSO_4.2H_2O$) and is an essential constituent of shells, bones, and teeth. The element is extracted by electrolysis of the molten chloride ($CaCl_2$). It forms many compounds. These include quicklime (CaO), which has many industrial uses as a base in addition to its role in ▷cement, the nitrate ($Ca(NO_3)_2$), chloride ($CaCl_2$), and carbide (CaC_2), from which acetylene is produced by the addition of water. The metal is reactive. It is used to clear residual gases from vacuum systems and as a reducing agent in the production of uranium. At no 20; at wt 40.08; mp 842 ± 2°C; bp 1494°C.

● **calculator** ▶ Any device for carrying out mathematical functions (+,−,×,÷). Originally mechanical, they were later electrically operated; purely electronic calculators, based on the digital ▷computer, have now replaced all others. Electronic calculators use a silicon chip ▷integrated-circuit package, often smaller than a 2p piece, that contains the equivalent of hundreds of ▷transistors built into complex logic circuits, which perform the basic functions using binary arithmetic (*see* binary system). Multiplication and division are performed by repeated additions or subtractions. The high speed of a modern calculator enables the solution to a problem to appear on the digital display apparently instantaneously. Many electronic calculators have more complex functions available (percentages, square roots, trigonometric functions, etc.) by pressing a single key and some provide a memory in which the intermediate results of a chain of calculations can be stored. Advanced types enable the user to program a sequence of functions for the calculator to perform automatically.

● **calculus** ▶ The mathematical techniques, developed by ▷Newton and ▷Leibniz, based on the concept of infinitely small changes in continuously varying quantities. For example, calculus is used to define

1. The derivative dx/dt at P gives the slope of the curve at P. When the function has a stationary (e.g. a maximum as at A or a minimum as at B) value, $dx/dt = 0$.

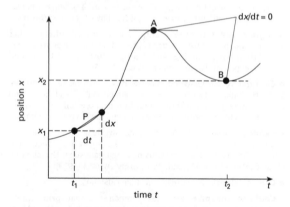

2. The integral $\int_{t_1}^{t_2} v.dt$ $(= x_2 - x_1)$ is the shaded area, i.e. it is the sum of all the areas $v.dt$ of the infinitely thin slices. The area between A and B is subtracted since v is negative.

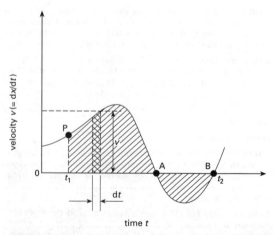

calculus ▶ The two basic techniques are 1. differentiation and 2. integration.

the velocity of a moving body as the rate of change of its position at any instant. Velocity (v) is said to be the derivative of position (x) with respect to time (t); in calculus it is written $v = dx/dt$. In this notation dt is a vanishingly small time interval and dx is the distance the body travels in this time. If x is a known function of t, values for v at any time can be obtained by calculating the derivative of (differentiating) this function with respect to time. Similarly, the derivative of the velocity (or the second derivative of position) at any instant gives its acceleration (a), i.e.

$$d^2x/dt^2 = dv/dt = a.$$

The **differential calculus** is the system of rules for making such calculations. On a graph, the derivative of a function is the gradient of the curve at any point. A maximum or minimum value of the function can be found, as they occur when the gradient is zero. The **integral calculus** is concerned with the same process in reverse. If velocity is a continuously varying function of time, the change in position over a measurable time interval is calculated by summing the products of v and dt for each of the infinitely small intervals of time (dt) that make up the interval. The extraction of integrals follows general rules, each type of function having a corresponding integral. The integral of v between time t_1 and t_2, written

$$\int_{t_1}^{t_2} v.dt,$$

gives the change in position in this interval. On a graph, the area between the curve of a function and the horizontal axis is the integral of the function over the specified interval.

Equations that contain derivatives are called **differential equations**. They are solved by guessing at a general form of solution and trying it in the equation, using the rules of differential calculus.

● **Calcutta** ▶ (official name from 1999: Kolkata) 22 35N 88 21E A city

Calcutta ▶ A mother and child living in extreme poverty.

in India, the capital of West Bengal on the River Hooghly. It is an industrial centre and the most important seaport on the E coast of India. Jute manufacturing, engineering, cotton, and chemicals are important. Calcutta is the focal point of rail, road, and air routes and its port is a major outlet for iron, coal, manganese, mica, and jute goods. The city is part of a conurbation that has a combined population of over nine million, many of whom live in appalling conditions; less than one-third of the conurbation is sewered, water supplies are inadequate, and many thousands sleep on the streets. By way of contrast, the city centre contains many imposing buildings, situated around Fort William (a British building dating from 1758). There are three universities, including Calcutta University (1857).

History: founded in 1692 as a trading post for the British East India Company, it was the scene of fighting (1756–57) between the British under Clive and the forces of Siraj-ud-Dawlah, Nawab of Bengal (*see* Black Hole of Calcutta). Population (1991 est): 10 916 272.

● **Calder, Alexander** ▶ (1898–1976) US sculptor, who invented the mobile. Calder produced his first mobiles in Paris (c. 1931). Originally motorized, the abstract shapes of these flat metal discs suspended from wires were influenced by ▷Miró. Calder later turned to monumental free-standing constructions.

● **Calderdale** ▶ A unitary authority in N England, in West Yorkshire. Area: 364 sq km (140 sq mi). Population (1999): 191 585.

● **caldera** ▷*See* volcanoes.

● **Calderón de la Barca, Pedro** ▶ (1600–81) Spanish dramatist. He studied law and theology but rejected a career in the Church; in 1623 he began writing plays at the court of Philip IV. After the death of Lope de ▷Vega he became the leading Spanish dramatist. His many plays include *The Constant Prince* (1629), *Life Is a Dream* (1635), and *The Mayor of Zalamea* (1640). He was ordained in 1651.

● **Caldwell, Erskine** ▶ (1903–87) US novelist. He gained international fame with his novels *Tobacco Road* (1932) and *God's Little Acre* (1933). His social criticism is most forcefully expressed in his journalism, notably in *You Have Seen Their Faces* (1937) and *In Search of Bisco* (1965).

● **Caldy** ▶ (Welsh name: Ynys Byr) 51 38N 4 42W A Welsh island, off the Pembrokeshire coast. Historically a religious retreat, it has been the property of a Cistercian community since 1929.

● **Caledonia** ▶ The name given by ancient Roman writers to Scotland. Remote and rugged, Caledonia was scarcely known in antiquity. The Roman governor in Britain, Gnaeus Julius ▷Agricola, defeated the Caledonians in 83 AD near present-day Inverness, as did the emperor Lucius Septimius Severus in 209, but the clans and their chieftains remained independent until united under Kenneth I MacAlpine in the 9th century.

● **Caledonian Canal** ▶ A system of lochs and canals in Scotland, linking the North Sea with the Irish Sea, via the Great Glen. Engineered by Thomas Telford, it was opened to navigation in 1822. Length: about 100 km (60 mi).

● **Caledonian orogeny** ▷*See* orogeny.

● **calendar** ▶ Any of a variety of systems for the reckoning of time over an extended period. Calendars are usually based on the earth's orbital period around the sun (a year), although in some systems the moon's orbital period around the earth (a month) is taken as the basis. Since the seasons recur after each tropical ▷year (which contains 365.2422 days), the length of the calendar year, averaged over many years, should correspond as closely as possible to that of the tropical year. This is achieved by using leap years, which contain one more day than the usual calendar year.

In 46 BC, Julius Caesar established the so-called **Julian calendar** in which a period of three years, each of 365 days, was followed by a leap year of 366 days. The average length of the year was therefore 365.25 days. Since this was over 11 minutes longer than the tropical year, an extra day appeared about every 128 years. This discrepancy was amended by the **Gregorian calendar**, which was introduced in Roman Catholic countries in 1582 by Pope Gregory XIII, was made law in Britain and its colonies in 1752, and is now in almost worldwide use. Leap years are restricted to century years divisible by 400

Calendars still in use				
Gregorian calendar	Hebrew calendar	Islamic calendar	Chinese calendar	
solar year of 365.2425 days	lunar year; the year 5750 started on 18 September, 1990	lunar year; the year 1410 started on 1 January, 1990	lunar and solar cycles; 24 fortnightly periods	
January (31 d)	Shevat (30 d) (Jan/Feb)	Muharram (30 d)	Xiao Han Da Han	Jan Jan/Feb
February (28 d; 29 days in leap year)	Adar (29 d) (Feb/Mar)	Safar (29 d)	Li Chun Yu Shui	Feb Feb/Mar
March (31 d)	Nisan (30 d) (Mar/Apr)	Rabī' I (30 d)	Jing Zhe Chun Fen	Mar Mar/Apr
April (30 d)	Iyar (29 d) (Apr/May)	Rabī' II (29 d)	Qing Ming Gu Yu	Apr Apr/May
May (31 d)	Sivan (30 d) (May/June)	Jumādā I (30 d)	Li Xia Xiao Man	May May/June
June (30 d)	Tammuz (29 d) (June/July)	Jumādā II (29 d)	Mang Zhong Xia Zhi	June June/July
July (31 d)	Av (30 d) (July/Aug)	Rajab (30 d)	Xiao Shu Da Shu	July July/Aug
August (31 d)	Elul (29 d) (Aug/Sept)	Sha'ban (29 d)	Li Qiu Chu Shu	Aug Aug/Sept
September (30 d)	Tishri (30 d) (Sept/Oct)	Ramadān (30 d)	Bai Lu Qui Fen	Sept Sept/Oct
October (31 d)	Heshvan (29 or 30 d) (Oct/Nov)	Shawwāl (29 d)	Han Lu Shuang Jiang	Oct Oct/Nov
November (30 d)	Kislev (29 or 30 d) (Nov/Dec)	Dhūal-Qa'dah (30 d)	Li Dong Xiao Xue	Nov Nov/Dec
December (31 d)	Tevet (29 d) (Dec/Jan)	Dhūal-Hijjah (20 or 30 d)	Da Xue Dong Zhi	Dec Dec/Jan

(e.g. 1600 and 2000) and any other year divisible by four. This reduces the average length of the calendar year to a much more acceptable 365.2425 days. ▷See also French Republican calendar.

● **Calgary** ▶ 51 05N 114 05W A city in W Canada, in Alberta. It developed with the arrival of the railway (1884) and local oil discoveries, becoming the centre of Canada's petroleum industry. Calgary is the distribution and farming centre of S Alberta and is the site of the University of Calgary (1945). The Calgary Stampede, a famous rodeo, is celebrated annually. Population (1991): 710 677.

● **Calhoun, John C(aldwell)** ▶ (1782–1850) US statesman; vice president (1824–32), a champion of the southern states and a defender of slavery. His famous Nullification theory claimed the rights of states to nullify congressional laws that they considered unconstitutional. He encouraged the annexation of Texas to provide another slaveholding state and to strengthen the power of the South.

● **Cali** ▶ 3 24N 76 30W The third largest city in Colombia. It is the industrial and commercial centre for a rich agricultural area producing coffee, sugar, and cotton. Its university was founded in 1945. Population (1997 est): 1 985 906.

● **calico** ▶ A simple woven cotton fabric that originated as a printed fabric from Calicut, India. Strong and serviceable with a wide range of textures, it is used mainly for dresses and domestic purposes. British calico is now usually bleached or plain white; US calico is generally printed.

● **Calicut** ▷See Kozhikode.

● **California** ▶ The third largest state in the USA, on the W coast. It consists of a narrow coastal plain rising to the Coast Range, with the fertile central valleys of the Sacramento and San Joaquin Rivers, deserts in the S, and the Sierra Nevada Mountains in the E. It is the most populous state in the USA and the predominantly urban population is concentrated along the coast. It is the most prosperous state and has a varied economy. Oil is exploited along with natural gas, cement, sand and gravel, and borate. Aircraft and ship construction are important industries, as well as general construction and food processing; wine production is especially important. Since the 1980s the area S of San Francisco has become known as Silicon Valley owing to the concentration of high-tech industry. Employment is also provided by the many military bases and the film industry. Tourism is important in the many national parks throughout the state. California's agriculture is famous and the state produces grapes, tomatoes, cotton, sugar beet, strawberries, citrus fruits, hay, beef cattle, and turkeys. The state has a large number of cultural and educational institutions, many supported by public finance like the University of California.
History: first discovered by the Spanish (1542) it remained under their control until it was ceded to the USA (1848). In the same year gold was discovered, leading to a rapid increase in the number of immigrants. California became a state in 1850. Area: 411 013 sq km (158 693 sq mi). Population (1990): 29 760 021. Capital: Sacramento.

● **California, Gulf of** ▶ An inlet of the Pacific Ocean, in Mexico between the state of Sonora and the peninsula of Lower California. Length: 1223 km (760 mi).

● **californium** ▶ (Cf) A synthetic transuranic element first isolated in 1950. Californium-252 is an intense neutron emitter. It is used as a neutron source in instruments for determining moisture contents and discovering precious metals. At no 98; at wt (251).

● **Caligula** ▶ (Gaius Caesar; 12–41 AD) Roman emperor (37–41), son of Germanicus Caesar and Agrippina the Elder. Succeeding Tiberius, he initially enjoyed great popularity but his subsequent tyrannical and extravagant behaviour brought allegations of madness, from both contemporaries and historians, and he was assassinated.

● **caliph** ▶ The title borne by the leaders of Islam. The first caliph was ▷Abu Bakr, who succeeded Mohammed in 632. The ▷Umayyads ruled from 661 to 750 and were overthrown by the ▷'Abbasids, who ruled in Baghdad until 1258 and then in Egypt, until ousted by the Ottomans in 1517. The title was then borne by the Ottoman sultans until 1922 and was abolished in 1924. Rival Muslim dynasties, such as the Egyptian ▷Fatimids (909–1171), also claimed the title.

● **calisaya** ▷*See* Cinchona.

● **calisthenics** ▷*See* gymnastics.

● **calla** ▷*See* arum.

● **Callaghan, (Leonard) James, Baron** ▶ (1912–) British statesman; Labour prime minister (1976–79). He was chancellor of the exchequer (1964–67), resigning in protest against Harold ▷Wilson's devaluation of the pound, and then home secretary (1967–70) and foreign secretary (1974–76). He became prime minister when Wilson resigned. Although a popular premier, he presided over severe industrial unrest and was defeated in the 1979 election by Margaret ▷Thatcher. He stood down as leader of the Labour Party in 1980 and was made a life peer in 1987.

● **Callao** ▶ 12 05S 77 08W A major port in W Peru, on the Pacific Ocean. It was the site of the first railway in South America (1851) connecting with Lima. Exports include minerals, metals, and fishmeal. Population (1995): 684 135.

● **Callas, Maria** ▶ (Maria Anna Kalageropoulos; 1923–77) US-born soprano of Greek parentage. She possessed a brilliant coloratura voice and fine acting ability. From 1950 she was prima donna of La Scala, Milan, where she was famous for her interpretations of Bellini, Donizetti, Verdi, and Puccini.

● **Calles, Plutarco Elías** ▶ (1877–1945) Mexican soldier and statesman. As president (1924–28) his anticlerical policies caused the rebellion of the Church's supporters (the *cristeros*) and his attempts to control oil rights brought conflict with the USA. He wielded dictatorial power from 1928 to 1934, when he was succeeded by Lázaro ▷Cárdenas, who forced Calles into exile in 1936.

● **Callias** ▶ (5th century BC) Athenian diplomat. He may have negotiated the so-called peace of Callias with Persia (c. 450), which established Persian and Athenian spheres of influence. He probably also helped negotiate the Thirty Years' Peace with Sparta (c. 446).

● **Callicrates** ▶ (5th century BC) Athenian architect, chiefly famous for his collaboration with ▷Ictinus over the design of the ▷Parthenon. The temple of Athena Nike (450 BC) on the Athenian Acropolis was also his work.

● **calligraphy** ▶ The art of handwriting. The term derives from the Greek words meaning beautiful writing. The aim of the calligrapher is to produce a script of intrinsic beauty appropriate to the subject matter, using the type of paper, ink, and writing instrument most suited to his purpose. In Europe, monks practised calligraphy from the 6th century, at first using Roman capital letters called majuscules, but scripts using minuscules were soon developed. From these arose the beautiful ▷italic and 19th-century copperplate scripts suitable for formal and commercial documents. In England calligraphy was revived in the 20th century by Edward Johnston (1872–1944). In China, Japan, and Islamic countries calligraphy has a long history as a pure art form in which the artist combines the medium, the sentiment, and the format into an artistic composition.

● **Callimachus** ▶ (c. 305–c. 240 BC) Greek poet and scholar. His many works, of which only fragments remain, include a catalogue of the Library of Alexandria, some fine epigrams, of which 64 survive in the *Greek Anthology*, and the *Aetia*.

● **Callimachus** ▶ (late 5th century BC) Greek sculptor, reputedly the inventor of the Corinthian ▷capital and an innovator in using drills in sculpture. Little is known of his work; ancient critics accused him of overelaboration.

● **Calliope** ▶ In Greek legend, goddess of epic poetry and the chief of the nine ▷Muses. She was loved by Apollo; her children included Hymen, Ialemus, and ▷Orpheus.

● **Callisto** ▷*See* Galilean satellites.

● **Callot, Jacques** ▶ (c. 1592–1635) French graphic artist, born in Nancy. In Italy (c. 1609–21) he worked for the Medici, principally on etchings of pageants. After returning to Nancy he made many etchings of beggars, hunchbacks, etc., but his best work is the *Miseries of War* series (1632–33) evoked by the Thirty Years' War.

● **callus** ▶ A region of thickened hardened skin produced by constant friction or pressure. Skin calluses occur most commonly on the palms of the hands and soles of the feet. A bone callus is the mass of tissue that forms around the broken ends of a fractured bone, enabling normal healing and union. A similar tissue is produced by plants at the site of an injury.

● **Calmette, Albert Léon Charles** ▶ (1863–1933) French bacteriologist. A pupil of Louis ▷Pasteur, he developed the vaccine bacille Calmette-Guérin (*see* BCG) with Camille Guérin. He founded the Pasteur Institute at Lille (1896).

● **calorie** ▶ A former unit of heat replaced by the joule. Formerly defined as the amount of heat required to raise the temperature of 1 gram of water through 1°C, the calorie is now defined as 4.1868 joules. The kilocalorie or Calorie (1000 calories) is still used to express the energy value of foods.

● **Caltanissetta** ▶ 37 29N 14 04E A town in Italy, in Sicily. It has a 17th-century cathedral. It has an important sulphur industry. Population (1990): 62 588.

● **Calvary** ▶ A hill beyond the walls of Jerusalem where Christ was crucified. The Hebrew name is Golgotha (a skull). Its location is unknown. Traditionally it is taken as the spot, now within the Church of the Holy Sepulchre, where St Helena found a supposed relic of the Cross in 327 AD.

● **Calvin, John** ▶ (1509–64) French Protestant reformer, founder of ▷Calvinism. He studied law and theology and in the early 1530s openly sided with Protestantism. Settling in Basle in 1536, he published the first edition of his influential *Institutes*. During a visit to Geneva in 1536 he met the Protestant reformer, Guillaume ▷Farel; their efforts to organize the Reformation in the city resulted in their exile (1538). Calvin then preached in Strasbourg, where he met other reformers, notably ▷Bucer. He was invited back to Geneva in 1541, remaining there as its virtual dictator until his death. He sought to shape Geneva as a model community where every citizen came under the legal discipline of the Church.

● **Calvin, Melvin** ▶ (1911–97) US biochemist, who determined the series of reactions by which green plants use carbon dioxide to manufacture starch during ▷photosynthesis. Calvin was awarded a Nobel Prize in 1961.

● **Calvinism** ▶ The Christian teaching of John ▷Calvin, much of it published in his work *The Institutes*. On it are based the doctrines of most of the reformed Churches that are not Lutheran, including the state Churches of Holland and Scotland (*see* Presbyterianism), various Nonconformist Churches, and some Churches in North America and Germany. Calvin's systematic writings stress the transcendent power of God and man's total depravity outside God's redeeming grace. Like Luther, Calvin believed that faith must be based on Scripture alone, that righteousness in God's eyes could only be achieved through faith, and that men lacked free will. Unlike Luther, he believed that some people, the elect, were predestined for salvation and everybody else for damnation, and that the Church should control the state.

● **Calvino, Italo** ▶ (1923–85) Italian novelist and short-story writer, noted for his witty and erudite fantasies. His novels include the trilogy *Our Forefathers* (1952–60), *Invisible Cities* (1972), and *Mr Palomar* (1983). He is also known for his collection of *Italian Folktales* (1956). In 1993 *The Road to San Giovanni*, a collection of his essays, was published.

● **calx** ▷*See* phlogiston theory.

● **calypso** ▶ A type of popular song that originated in Trinidad. The words are sung rapidly and without regard for natural word stress. Accompanied by guitars and percussion, the calypso usually satirizes local events.

● **Calypso** ▶ A Greek nymph, the daughter of ▷Atlas, who kept ▷Odysseus with her on the island of Ogygia for several years, until she was persuaded by his yearning and the intervention of Hermes to let him return home.

● **calypso orchid** ► A rare and highly prized perennial orchid, *Calypso bulbosa*, also known as the fairy slipper orchid, native to cold N temperate regions. 8–10 cm high, it has a solitary pink flower with brown, purple, and yellow markings and a single crinkled dark-green leaf.

● **cam** ▷*See* camshaft.

● **CAM** ► (computer-aided manufacture) The use of computers in the organization and control of such manufacturing processes as the control of throughput in a continuous chemical production plant, or the control of machine tools in the mass-production of components (*see* robotics). ▷*See also* CAD.

● **Camagüey** ► 21 25N 77 55W A city in E central Cuba. Founded in the 16th century, it has many old buildings, including the cathedral (1617). It is the centre of a cattle-raising and sugar region. Population (1994 est): 293 961.

● **Camargue, la** ► The Rhône delta area in S France, between the river channels of the Grand Rhône and the Petit Rhône. Once marshy, much land has been reclaimed and cattle, especially bulls for the bullring, and horses are reared. Rice is also grown here. Area: about 560 sq km (215 sq mi).

● **Camberwell beauty** ► A ▷nymphalid butterfly, *Nymphalis antiopa*, occurring in temperate Eurasia and in North America, where it is called mourning cloak because of its sombre coloration: purple wings with cream edges. The adults hibernate and the caterpillars feed on various trees.

● **cambium** ► A layer of cells in woody plants that is responsible for producing additional ▷xylem and ▷phloem tissue, bringing about an increase in girth. The cambium also produces bark and callus tissue after injury. ▷*See also* meristem.

● **Cambodia** ► A country in SE Asia, in the Indochina Peninsula on the Gulf of Thailand. It consists mainly of an alluvial plain drained by the River Mekong and enclosed by mountains. Most of the inhabitants are Khmers, with small minorities of Vietnamese and Chinese.
Economy: mainly agricultural, the staple crop being rice. Production was severely reduced during the ▷Khmer Rouge regime but is now recovering well. Cambodia's small industrial sector, which includes textiles and metals, was suspended entirely during the Khmer Rouge era but has since been revived; garment-making has become important and now accounts for 70% of exports. Cambodia is rich in forests, and phosphates, gemstones, and gold are produced; iron ore and manganese deposits remain largely unexploited. Freshwater fish are abundant. Tourism is a new and growing industry.
History: the kingdom of Funan (1st–6th centuries AD) was conquered by the Buddhist ▷Khmers. Following the collapse of their empire in the 15th century, Cambodia was prey to attack from the Thais and Vietnamese until 1863, when it became a French protectorate. In 1887 it became part of the Union of ▷Indochina. In 1949 it achieved self-government as a member of the French Union, gaining full independence in 1953. Under Prince ▷Sihanouk Cambodia was used as a base by North Vietnamese forces (*see* Vietnam War); following his failure to negotiate their withdrawal, he was deposed (1970) by Gen Lon Nol (1913–85), who was supported by the USA. Shortly afterwards US and South Vietnamese troops invaded the renamed Khmer Republic to support Lon Nol against the communist Khmer Rouge guerrillas. In the ensuing civil war the Khmer Rouge was finally victorious in 1974 and, in 1975, the Khmer Republic became Democratic Kampuchea under a new constitution. The Khmer Rouge government, led by ▷Pol Pot, attempted to reshape the country's economy on cooperative lines by driving the Cambodians out of the towns, depriving them of their property, and killing many thousands of the aged, sick, or dissenting: altogether some two million people are believed to have perished as a result of these policies. The Vietnamese invaded in Dec 1978; Pol Pot was overthrown and a government was set up under the pro-Vietnamese Heng Samrin. The retreating Khmer Rouge devastated the land. In 1982 three exiled Cambodian factions (including the Khmer Rouge) formed the Coalition Government of Democratic Kampuchea (CGDK). With a seat at the UN, it obtained Western aid for its forces in their attempts to force Vietnamese withdrawal. The Vietnamese finally left in Sept 1989, but fighting continued between the government forces of Hun Sen, the prime minister, and CGDK guerrillas. In 1991 UN peace talks led to the formation of a new governing coalition including elements of the Khmer Rouge. Sihanouk returned to become head of state. A democratic monarchist constitution was adopted in 1993. Following multiparty elections, Hun Sen shared the premiership with Prince Norodom Ranariddh. However, the Khmer Rouge refused to take part in the elections and continued fighting: in the later 1990s some elements sought peace with the government, leading to a violent split in the movement, further defections among the leadership, and—following the death of Pol Pot—its effective demise by 1999. In 1997 troops loyal to Hun Sen seized Phnom Penh and forced Prince Ranariddh into exile. Elections held the following year (which Prince Ranariddh was permitted to contest) resulted in victory for Hun Sen's party.

Cambodia

Head of state	King Norodom Sihanouk
Official language	Khmer; French is widely spoken
Official currency	riel of 100 sen
Area	181 000 sq km (71 000 sq mi)
Population (2001 est)	12 720 000
Capital and main port	Phnom Penh

● **camboge** ▷*See* gamboge.

● **Cambrai** ► (ancient name: Camaracum) 50 10N 3 14E A town in NE France, in the Nord department. Industries include textiles (cambric was first made here in the 16th century) and sugar refining. The town suffered damage in both World Wars. Population (latest est): 36 618.

● **Cambrian Mountains** ► A mountain system in Wales, extending N–S from Gwynedd through Powys to Carmarthenshire. The name is sometimes used generally for all the Welsh mountains and sometimes reserved for the central range, i.e. excluding Snowdon in the NW and the Brecon Beacons and Black Mountains in the SE.

● **Cambrian period** ► The earliest geological period of the ▷Palaeozoic era. It began about 590 million years ago and lasted at least 70 million years, succeeding the Precambrian and preceding the Ordovician period. Rocks of this period are the first to contain an abundance of fossils, including trilobites, brachiopods, and gastropods.

● **Cambridge** ► 52 12N 0 07E A city in E England, the administrative centre of Cambridgeshire on the River Cam (*or* Granta), a tributary of the Great Ouse. The city is dominated by its university (*see* Cambridge, University of). Industries include electronics, high-tech research and development, biotechnology, and the manufacture of scientific instruments. It is an important market centre for East Anglia. Its many historic university buildings, its famous Backs (lawns sloping down to the river), and Bridge of Sighs make it a tourist centre. Population (1999 est): 91 933.

● **Cambridge** ► 42 22N 71 06W A city in the USA, in Massachusetts on the Charles River opposite Boston. It is the site of Harvard University (1636) and the Massachusetts Institute of Technology (MIT). The first printing press in America was set up here (1639) and at the start of the American Revolution, George Washington established his headquarters (1775–76) in Craigie House, later the home of Longfellow. Industries include printing and publishing. Population (2000): 101 355.

● **Cambridge, University of** ► One of the oldest universities in Europe. It is organized as a federation of colleges (*see* Oxford, University of), the oldest of which, Peterhouse, dates from 1284. King's College was founded in 1441 and its chapel (built 1446–1515 in the perpendicular gothic style) is a distinctive landmark. The largest college, Trinity, was founded by Henry VIII in 1546. Written examinations were first introduced in 1772, and in the 19th century other reforms were made in an attempt to improve academic standards. The first college for women, Girton, opened in 1869 (although it was not initially located at Cambridge); all but three of the colleges now take students of both sexes. In 1998–99 there were 17 350 undergraduates in residence.

Colleges and halls of Cambridge University with dates of foundation

Peterhouse	1284	Emmanuel	1584
Clare	1326	Sidney Sussex	1596
Pembroke	1347	Downing	1800
Gonville and Caius	1348	Girton	1869
Trinity Hall	1350	Newnham	1871
Corpus Christi	1352	Selwyn	1882
King's	1441	St Edmund's	1896
Queens	1448	New Hall	1954
St Catharine's	1473	Churchill	1960
Jesus	1496	Darwin	1964
Christ's	1505	Wolfson	1965
St John's	1511	Clare Hall	1966
Magdalene	1542	Fitzwilliam	1966
Trinity	1546	Robinson	1977

● **Cambridge Platonists** ▶ A group of 17th-century English philosophers and theologians under the leadership of Benjamin Whichcote (1609–83). Philosophically they took their ideas from ▷Platonism and ▷Neoplatonism and opposed the rationalism of ▷Hobbes. In religion they favoured mysticism and religious tolerance and attempted to reconcile Christianity with the scientific advances made in their time. They believed in an absolute standard of morality based on reason that is independent of the divine will of God.

● **Cambridgeshire** ▶ A county of E England. In 1965 it was combined with the Isle of ▷Ely and in 1974 it absorbed Huntingdon and Peterborough as well as parts of W Suffolk. Peterborough became an independent ▷unitary authority in 1998. It consists chiefly of low-lying fenland, crossed by the Rivers Ouse and Nene. It is mainly agricultural, products being cereals, fruit, and vegetables. Area (excluding Peterborough): 3068 sq km (1184 sq mi). Population (1996 est, excluding Peterborough): 544 600. Administrative centre: Cambridge.

● **Cambyses II** ▶ King of Persia (529–522 BC) of the Achaemenian dynasty; the son of ▷Cyrus the Great. He conquered Egypt (525), where, according to the Greek historian, Herodotus, his tyrannical disrespect for native religion caused resentment. He campaigned unsuccessfully against Carthage and Ethiopia. Cambyses died, perhaps a suicide, during a revolt against his rule.

● **camcorder** ▷See video camera.

● **Camden** ▶ A borough of NW Greater London, created in 1965 from the former metropolitan boroughs of ▷Hampstead, Holborn, and St Pancras. Area: 21 sq km (8 sq mi). Population (1996 est): 184 100.

● **Camden** ▶ 39 52N 75 07W A city in the USA, in New Jersey on the Delaware River. The former home of Walt Whitman, it manufactures textiles and radio and television appliances. Population (1996 est): 84 844.

● **Camden, Battle of** ▶ (16 August, 1780) A battle of the ▷American Revolution. In an attempt to take the British stronghold at Camden, South Carolina, after the fall of ▷Charleston, the Americans were routed by ▷Cornwallis.

● **Camden, William** ▶ (1551–1623) English historian and antiquarian. A dedicated scholar, he wrote *Britannia* (published in Latin 1586; English translation 1610), a topographical study of Britain. He taught at Westminster School (1575–97) and endowed a chair of ancient history at Oxford (1622). The Camden Society (founded 1838) for the promotion of historical publications is named after him.

● **Camden Town group** ▶ An association of London painters founded in 1911 by Walter ▷Sickert and his circle, including Spencer Gore (1878–1914), Harold Gilman (1876–1919), and Charles Ginner (1879–1952). A breakaway group from the ▷New English Art Club, its members specialized in contemporary London scenes, particularly theatre and café scenes and dully lit and depressing domestic interiors. They were largely responsible for introducing ▷postimpressionism into the UK. In 1913 the Camden Town group became part of the London group, an amalgam of several art societies.

● **camel** ▶ A hoofed ▢mammal belonging to the genus *Camelus* (2 species). Camels are now almost entirely domesticated and are used for riding, as pack animals, and as a source of milk, meat, wool, and hides. The one-humped Arabian camel (*C. dromedarius*) is about 2 m high at the shoulder and generally brown in colour. The dromedary is a long-legged breed of Arabian camel, developed for racing and riding. The heavier two-humped Bactrian camel (*C. bactrianus*) is native to central Asian steppes, where wild herds still exist. Adapted to living in sandy deserts, camels can close their nostrils, have heavy protective eyelashes, hairy ear openings, and horny knee pads for kneeling. Although unable to store water, camels can replace rapidly that lost from the body, drinking up to 60 litres at a time. Fat is stored in the hump, which shrinks when food is scarce. Family: *Camelidae*; order: *Artiodactyla*.

● **Camellia** ▶ A genus of evergreen shrubs and trees (80–100 species) native to India, China, and Japan. The best known, *C. japonica*, grows to a height of 9 m and has attractive glossy oval leaves. The popular double-flowered varieties have overlapping petals ranging from white to pink and red. The genus also includes the ▷tea plant. Family: *Theaceae*.

● **Camelot** ▶ The legendary capital of King Arthur's kingdom (*see* Arthurian legend). Cadbury Camp, near Yeovil, and Winchester are among the places identified with it.

● **Camembert** ▶ 48 52N 0 10E A village in NW France, in the Orne department. Camembert is famous for the creamy cheese named after it.

● **cameo** ▶ A semiprecious stone ornamented with a portrait or figures carved in relief. Cameo makers achieved brilliant skills during the Renaissance, when collectors paid high prices for modern gems, as well as for the earliest Hellenistic and Roman examples.

● **camera, photographic** ▶ A device for producing a photographic image. Basically, a camera consists of a light-tight box containing a lens and light-sensitive ▷film or plate. The light image coming through the lens is brought into focus on the film by adjusting the distance between the film and the lens. A picture is taken by opening the shutter over the lens for a certain period to expose the film. The exposure time is determined by the shutter speed. The diameter of the opening (aperture) in front of the lens is measured by its ▷f-number. Shutter speed and lens aperture determine the light available to record the image. In the simplest cameras they are fixed, but sophisticated cameras have variable settings. Sometimes the aperture or the shutter speed can be controlled automatically by an ▷exposure meter. Many high-quality cameras used by professionals are **single-lens reflex** (SLR), in which the image seen by the photographer is actually formed by the lens that will take the photograph,

Camelot ▶ A romantic 19th-century rendering of Arthur's capital by Gustave Doré, in his illustrations for Tennyson's *Idylls of the King*.

rather than through a separate viewfinder lens. This is achieved by using a pivoted mirror to deflect the light entering the main lens to the viewfinder. Before the film is exposed, the mirror swings aside to allow the light to reach the film. ▷*See also* digital photography; video camera; cinematography.

● **camera, television** ▶ A camera for the instantaneous transmission of ▷television pictures. The scene to be televised is focused onto a screen in the electronic camera tube. This optical image is scanned in horizontal lines, fast enough to appear as a continuous moving picture to the human eye; in most cameras, the image is scanned 25 to 30 times per second. The intensity of light at each point of the image is converted to an electrical signal, which is amplified before being transmitted together with the sound and synchronization signals.

● **Cameron, James** ▶ (1954–) Canadian film director and screenwriter, noted for his spectacular action movies. His films, which include *The Terminator* (1984) and *Terminator 2* (1991), are remarkable for their computer-generated special effects. His *Titanic* (1997), the most expensive and subsequently the highest grossing film in cinema history, collected 11 Academy Awards.

● **Cameron, (Mark) James (Walter)** ▶ (1911–85) British journalist, author, and broadcaster. He probably won more awards than any other international reporter. His books included *Witness in Vietnam* (1966) and *Point of Departure* (1967); his radio play *The Pump* (1973) won the Prix Italia.

● **Cameron, Julia Margaret** ▶ (1815–79) British photographer, born in Calcutta. In England, she devoted herself chiefly to portrait photographs, notably of her friends Tennyson, Longfellow, Darwin, and Ellen Terry. She died in Ceylon.

● **Cameroon, Republic of** ▶ (French name: République du Cameroun) A country in W Africa, on the Gulf of Guinea. Hot swampy coastal plains rise to forested plateaus in the centre and to the Adamwa Highlands in the N. The main river is the Sanaga. The population consists of many different ethnic groups, the most numerous being the Bamileke.
Economy: chiefly subsistence agriculture; the main cash crops are cocoa and coffee. Aluminium smelting is the chief industry. Oil was discovered in 1973 and exports of crude oil now provide about half the country's revenue. Other mineral deposits, and the country's extensive forests, remain largely unexploited.
History: the area was largely uninhabited when the coast was explored by the Portuguese and others in the 15th and 16th centuries. In 1884 the German protectorate of Kamerun was established. After World War I it was divided into the French and British Cameroons, which were governed from 1922 under League of Nations mandate and from 1946 as UN trust territories. The French Cameroons attained self-government in 1957 and became independent as the Federal Republic of the Cameroon in 1960 with Ahmadou Ahidjo (1924–) as president (1960–82). After a plebiscite in the British Cameroons in 1961, the N joined Nigeria and the S joined Cameroon, declared a united republic in 1972. In 1990–91 the one-party rule of the Cameroon National Union met with mounting opposition. Free elections to the legislature were held in 1992 but boycotted by opposition parties. In 1992 President Paul Biya (1933–) won presidential elections amid allegations of electoral fraud. Riots led to the imposition of a state of emergency. Legislative elections in 1997 resulted in victory for the ruling party but were marred by allegations of fraud and intimidation. Cameroon joined the Commonwealth in 1995.

Republic of Cameroon

Head of state	President Paul Biya
Official languages	French and English
Official currency	CFA (Communauté financière africaine) franc of 100 centimes
Area	475 442 sq km (183 530 sq mi)
Population (1997 est)	14 678 000
Capital	Yaoundé
Main port	Douala

● **Camisards** ▶ Protestants in the Bas-Languedoc and Cévennes re-

gions of S France who in 1702 rebelled against persecution by Louis XIV. They sacked churches and killed priests. The government responded with executions and the burning of villages. By 1705 the revolt was over.

● **Camões, Luís de** ▶ (c. 1524–80) Portuguese poet and soldier. After 17 years wandering in the Portuguese colonies in India and China and suffering shipwreck, he returned destitute to Lisbon. In 1572 he published *The Lusiads*, an epic celebrating the 1497 voyage of Vasco da Gama. His lyrical poetry, published posthumously in 1595, is greatly admired.

● **camomile** ▶ (*or* chamomile) A perennial scented European herb, *Anthemis nobilis* (or *Chamaemelum nobile*). The spreading much-branched stems (10–30 cm in length) carry long-stalked daisy-like flowers. An infusion of the flowers (camomile tea) is used as a tonic. Family: ▷*Compositae.*

● **Camorra** ▶ A criminal secret society, at its height in 19th-century Naples. The Bourbon kings used its members in the police, army, and civil service but after Naples became part of a united Italy (1861) the society was suppressed and its members fled to the USA, where they joined the ▷Mafia.

● **camouflage** ▶ Means by which animals can blend into their surroundings for concealment and protection. The commonest forms of camouflage are colouring and patterning of the body either to match the colour of the background or to disguise the shape of the animal. The former type is common in birds' eggs and larvae (e.g. caterpillars); the latter is seen in the zebra and many antelopes. Body form and posture can also be adapted for camouflage; stick insects, with their twiglike bodies, are a well-known example. ▷*See also* mimicry.
Camouflage also has an important military role. British troops in India adopted earth-coloured uniforms (khaki) for the first time in the 19th century. Similar techniques are now used to conceal aeroplanes, ships, and other weapons from the enemy.

● **Campaign for Nuclear Disarmament** ▶ (CND) An organization formed in 1958 to campaign for Britain's nuclear disarmament. In the late 1950s and early 1960s, led by Canon John Collins (1905–82) and Bertrand ▷Russell, it organized large demonstrations, including the Aldermaston marches. It revived in the early 1980s amid new fears of nuclear war under the chairmanship of Bruce Kent, a former Catholic priest, who resigned in 1990 after a sharp decline in membership due to lessening East–West tensions. Chairman: Ms J. Bloomfield.

● **Campagna di Roma** ▶ A plain in W central Italy, surrounding Rome. Fertile during classical times, it subsequently deteriorated into marshes. Recently drained, it now produces fruit and vegetables. Area: about 2000 sq km (800 sq mi).

● **Campanella, Tommaso** ▶ (1568–1639) Italian philosopher and Dominican friar. He opposed ▷Aristotelianism, believing that the foundations of philosophy should be empirical. From 1599 to 1626 he was imprisoned by the Spaniards ostensibly for political reasons but probably because of his religious heterodoxy. After 1634 he lived under ▷Richelieu's protection in Paris. His *City of the Sun* (1623) describes a Platonic-Christian utopia (*see* utopianism).

● **Campania** ▶ A region in S Italy. It consists of a coastal plain along the Tyrrhenian Sea and mountains in the interior and the Sorrento Peninsula. The region produces fruits, vines, olives, and grains. An industrial belt stretches from Caserta along the Bay of Naples. Area: 13 595 sq km (5249 sq mi). Population (1994 est): 5 708 657. Capital: Naples.

● **Campanula** ▶ A genus of annual and perennial herbaceous plants (about 300 species), often known as bellflowers, native to N temperate zones (particularly the Mediterranean region) and tropical mountains. 15–120 cm high, they bear spikes of blue, pink, or white bell-shaped flowers. The fruit is a capsule. Some species (including the ▷Canterbury bell) are grown as ornamentals. Family: *Campanulaceae.*

● **Campbell, Colin, Baron Clyde** ▶ (1792–1863) British field marshal. Campbell had a varied career, serving outstandingly in the ▷Peninsular War against Napoleon, the second Sikh War (1848–49), and the ▷Crimean War; as commander in chief in India he suppressed the ▷Indian Mutiny (1858).

● **Campbell, Sir Malcolm** ▶ (1885–1948) British motor engineer, who broke the land-speed record nine times between 1924 and 1935 and the water-speed record three times between 1937 and 1939. He was the first man to exceed 483 km per hour (300 mph; 1935). His son **Donald Malcolm Campbell** (1921–67) also set land- and water-speed records, including 648.7 km per hour (403.1 mph) for a wheel-driven car at Lake Eyre (1964). He was killed in an attempt to break his own water-speed record on Coniston Water. The speed at which he crashed, 527.9 km per hour (328 mph), is still the unofficial record. His daughter **Gina Campbell** (1948–) broke the women's water-speed record in 1984.

● **Campbell, Mrs Patrick** ▶ (Beatrice Stella Tanner; 1865–1940) British actress. Her stage successes included plays by Shakespeare and Ibsen. Famed for her wit as well as her passionate acting, she created the role of Eliza Doolittle in *Pygmalion* (1914) by her friend George Bernard Shaw.

● **Campbell, Roy (Dunnachie)** ▶ (1901–57) South African poet. His active life, mostly in France, Spain, and Portugal, is chronicled in *Light on a Dark Horse* (1951). His first book, *The Flaming Terrapin* (1924), is characteristic of all his work, which includes satires, romantic lyrics, and translations.

● **Campbell, Thomas** ▶ (1777–1844) British poet, remembered primarily for "The Pleasures of Hope" (1799), a conventional quasi-philosophic poem in the manner of Alexander ▷Pope, and patriotic poems, such as "Hohenlinden."

● **Campbell-Bannerman, Sir Henry** ▶ (1836–1908) British statesman; Liberal prime minister (1905–08), whose cabinet included ▷Lloyd George, ▷Asquith, ▷Churchill, and ▷Haldane. His government granted the Transvaal and Orange River Colony responsible government and passed the Trades Disputes Act (1906), which gave trades unionists greater freedom to strike. Resigning shortly before his death, he left his successor Asquith a strong and united Liberal Party.

● **Camp David** ▶ The retreat in the Appalachian Mountains, Maryland, of the US president. It was here that Anwar Sadat and Menachem Begin agreed in September, 1978, to a framework for establishing peace in the Middle East. Mediated by President Carter, and known as the **Camp David Accord**, this laid the foundations for the treaty between Israel and Egypt signed in March, 1979. It did not, as hoped, form the basis for a peaceful settlement of the Arab-Israeli dispute but caused the isolation of Egypt from its former Arab allies.

● **Campeche** ▶ 19 50N 90 30W A port in SE Mexico, on the Gulf of Mexico. Founded in 1540, its importance as a port has declined and the shallow waters hinder further development. The chief exports include timber, fish, and sugar cane and it has a university (1954). Population (1990): 172 208.

● **Camperdown** ▶ A village in the NW Netherlands, in North Holland province, on the North Sea. The British defeated the Dutch in a naval battle off the coast here (1797).

● **camphor** ▶ ($C_{10}H_{16}O$) A colourless crystalline ▷ketone. Obtained from the wood of the SE Asian camphor tree (*Cinnamomum camphora*) and also made synthetically, it is used in the manufacture of celluloid and as an insect repellent.

● **Campi, Giulio** ▶ (1502–72) Italian Renaissance architect and the founder of the Cremonese school of painting, which was influenced by such painters as Titian and Correggio. His followers included his brothers **Vincenzo Campi** (1539–91) and **Antonio Campi** (1536–c. 1591).

● **Campina Grande** ▶ 7 15S 35 53W A city in NE Brazil, in Paraíba state. It is a commercial and industrial centre and has a university (1966). Population (1991): 298 331.

● **Campinas** ▶ 22 54S 47 06W A city in S Brazil, in São Paulo state. It is a trading centre for coffee and serves an extensive agricultural area. Population (1991): 748 076.

● **campion** ▶ An annual or perennial flowering plant of the genus *Silene*. Campions are native to N temperate (particularly the Mediterranean) and cold regions, grow to a height of 30–100 cm, and bear pink, red, or white flowers. The fruit is a capsule. Species include moss campion (*S. acaulis*) and bladder campion (*S. vulgaris*). Family: Caryophyllaceae.

● **Campion, St Edmund** ▶ (1540–81) English Jesuit martyr. He was educated at St John's College, Oxford, and ordained an Anglican deacon. Uneasy about his commitment, he visited Dublin and then Douai and was received into the Catholic Church (1571). He became a Jesuit and returned to England in 1580 as a secret missionary. After distributing copies of an anti-Anglican pamphlet in Oxford in 1581, he was arrested, tortured, convicted of treason, and hanged, refusing to deny his faith. He was beatified in 1886 and canonized in 1970. Feast Day: 25 Oct.

● **Campion, Jane** ▶ (1954–) New Zealand film director and screenwriter. Her films include *Sweetie* (1987), *An Angel at My Table* (1990), the award-winning *The Piano* (1993), *The Portrait of a Lady* (1997), and *Holy Smoke* (2000).

● **Campion, Thomas** ▶ (or Campian; 1567–1620) English composer, poet, and physician. He composed songs with lute accompaniment, publishing several collections in conjunction with his friend Philip Rosseter (1568–1623), masques, and theoretical works on composing and on the art of writing poetry.

● **Campo Formio, Treaty of** ▶ (1797) The settlement between France and Austria signed at present-day Campoformido, NE Italy, following Austria's defeat by Napoleon during his first Italian campaign. Austria gained Venice, thus ending Venetian independence, and ceded its Belgian provinces to France.

● **Campo Grande** ▶ 20 24S 54 35W A city in SW Brazil, the capital of Mato Grosso do Sul state situated on the São Paulo-Corumbá railway. Its university was founded in 1970. Population (1991): 516 403.

● **Campos** ▶ 21 40S 41 21W A city in E Brazil, in Rio de Janeiro state. The chief products are cacao, sugar cane, and *aguardiente* (a form of brandy). Population (1991): 275 508.

● **Campylobacter** ▷*See* food poisoning.

● **Cam Ranh Bay** ▶ 11 53N 109 10E An inlet of the South China Sea, on the coast of central S Vietnam. About 20 km (12 mi) wide and almost enclosed by two peninsulas, it is an excellent harbour: the bay and the northern peninsula were used as a US military, naval, and air base during the Vietnam War.

● **camshaft** ▶ A rotating shaft equipped with a series of eccentric circular or pear-shaped discs (cams). These enable irregular or intermittent motion to be transferred to "followers" set perpendicularly to the camshaft, which move up and down as the cams rotate. Camshafts are used to control the valves in a four-stroke ▷internal-combustion engine. An **overhead camshaft** is set in the cylinder head and operates the valves directly, but in many older engines the camshaft is at the base of the engine and operates the valves through pushrods.

● **Camus, Albert** ▶ (1913–60) French novelist, an exponent of ▷existentialism. Born in poverty in Algiers, he won a school scholarship and studied philosophy at university. During World War II he edited *Combat*, a journal of the French Resistance. He published essays, plays, and novels, notably *The Plague* (1947) and *The Rebel* (1953); *The Rebel* provoked a fierce controversy with Jean-Paul ▷Sartre. In 1957 he won the Nobel Prize. He was killed in a car accident.

● **Canaan** ▶ An area roughly corresponding to modern Israel, W Jordan, and S Syria, known from the Bible as the land promised by God to the Israelites before the Exodus. As early as the 18th century BC Canaan was mentioned in a document from ▷Mari as a political entity, probably comprising loosely allied city states. Excavations at ▷Jericho, Hazor, and elsewhere have revealed sophisticated Bronze Age cultures prior to the Hebrew settlement (c. 1200 BC).

● **Canada** ▶ A country occupying the entire northern half of the North American continent (except for Alaska). More than half of Canada consists of the Canadian Shield, at the centre of which lie the Hudson Bay lowlands. The Western Cordillera, which includes the

Coast Mountains and the Rocky Mountains, runs parallel to the Pacific coast and contains Mount ▷Logan, Canada's highest peak. Between the Rocky Mountains and the Canadian Shield lie the Interior Lowlands (consisting of prairies, plains, and the Mackenzie Lowlands). The SE is dominated by the St Lawrence River and the ▷Great Lakes and is the most densely populated area in the country. The N end of the Appalachian Mountains lies in the extreme SE. The N Arctic region of lakes and islands is one of the world's least populated areas. The population is mainly of British and French descent but there are several substantial minorities, including Germans, Italians, Ukrainians, and Dutch as well as the original inhabitants, the Indians and Inuit.

Economy: agriculture and industry are highly developed. The numerous manufacturing industries (concentrated mainly in Ontario and Quebec) include paper, iron and steel, motor vehicles, telecommunications equipment, and food processing. Canada is the world's largest producer of zinc, potash, and uranium; the rich mineral resources also include asbestos, nickel, cadmium, sulphur, molybdenum, silver, and gold. Oil production has increased considerably since the discovery of large oilfields in Alberta; an extensive pipeline system includes the Interprovincial Pipeline from Edmonton (Alberta) to Port Credit (Ontario) and the Trans-Mountain pipeline from Edmonton to Vancouver. Natural gas is also produced and the Trans-Canada pipeline from the prairies to Montreal is the longest in the world. Although only about 7% of the land is farmed, agriculture, most of it highly mechanized, is important; cereals are grown in the Prairie Provinces and fruit in British Columbia and Ontario. There is a valuable fishing industry; salmon, lobster, and cod are the most important catches. Forests cover over 40% of the land and forestry has long been important to the economy. The other traditional industry, the fur trade, continues, especially with mink farms and the trapping of beaver. Tourism is important, the majority of visitors coming from the USA, with whom Canada has very close links. Almost 80% of its trade is with the USA. Exports include motor vehicles and parts, wood, wood pulp, and paper, oil, gas, and petroleum products.

History: there is evidence of Viking settlement in the NE of Canada around 1000 AD. In 1497 John Cabot reached the coasts of Newfoundland and Nova Scotia, the first of which was claimed for England in 1583. In 1534 Jacques Cartier explored the Gulf of St Lawrence and in 1608 Champlain established the first permanent settlement at Quebec. Known as New France, this became a royal province in 1663. In the course of his explorations Champlain supported the ▷Huron Indians in their alliance with the northern tribes against the ▷Iroquois; later in the 17th century, when the Iroquois defeated the Huron, the French colony was almost completely destroyed. The fur trade was of extreme importance to all settlers and in 1670 the English set up the Hudson's Bay Company. By 1696 the French and English were in open conflict: in 1713 the Treaty of Utrecht gave ▷Acadia, Newfoundland, and Hudson Bay to Britain and after the Seven Years' War, during which Gen Wolfe defeated the French under Gen Montcalm (1759), Canada was ceded to Britain by the Treaty of Paris (1763). In the late 18th century the United Empire Loyalists, fleeing from the American Revolution, settled in Canada. The ensuing racial tension led to the division of Quebec into French-speaking Lower Canada and English-speaking Upper Canada (1791), which were reunited in 1841. By the British North America Act (1867) a confederation of Lower Canada (Quebec), Upper Canada (Ontario), Nova Scotia, and New Brunswick was established. In 1869 Rupert's Land was bought from the Hudson's Bay Company; the province of Manitoba

was created from it in the following year. In 1871 British Columbia and in 1873 Prince Edward Island joined the confederation. Alberta and Saskatchewan were created from the NW Territories in 1905. Canada's position as an independent constitutional monarchy in the British Commonwealth was defined by the Statute of Westminster in 1931. It played an important part in both World Wars. The main political problem in recent decades has been French-Canadian separatist agitation, led by the Quebec Liberation Front (Parti québecois). Since 1982 Quebec has acted outside the constitution, despite attempts to achieve reconciliation via the so-called "Meech Lake Accord" (1985). Proposals to give Quebec greater autonomy were rejected in a national referendum in 1992. In 1995 voters in Quebec rejected by 1% a proposal that the province should become a sovereign state. In 1979 the Liberal Party, which had held office for 36 out of the previous 43 years (the last 11 under Pierre ▷Trudeau), lost power to the Progressive Conservatives under Joseph Clark. In 1980 Trudeau was returned to power. In 1982 a new constitution severing all remaining links with the UK except those to the Crown was signed by Elizabeth II. In 1984 Trudeau retired and the Progressive Conservatives under Brian Mulroney won the ensuing general election, being re-elected in 1988. The Liberal Party regained power with a landslide victory in 1993 and Jean Chrétien became prime minister; the Liberals were re-elected in 1997 and 2000. In 1992 a free-trade agreement with the USA and Mexico was completed (*see* North American Free Trade Agreement). In 1999 a vast area of the Arctic NE was designated as an autonomous Inuit territory to be known as ▷Nunavut.

Canada

Head of state	Queen Elizabeth II, represented by the governor-general, Roméo Le Blanc
Official languages	English and French
Official currency	Canadian dollar of 100 cents
Area	9 976 169 sq km (3 851 809 sq mi)
Population (1999 est)	30 626 000
Capital	Ottawa
Main port	Montreal

● **Canada balsam** ▶ A transparent resin obtained from fir trees. It is used as an adhesive in optical instruments because its refractive index is similar to that of glass.

● **Canada goose** ▶ A large ▷goose, *Branta canadensis*, that breeds in Canada and Alaska, migrating in flocks to the southern USA for the winter. It is 60–100 cm long and has a black head and neck, white throat, dark-brown back, and pale underparts. The Canada goose has been introduced to parts of Europe.

● **Canadian railways** ▶ Canada has two great transcontinental systems: the Canadian Pacific Limited (CP Rail) and the Canadian National Railway (CN). The CP, running from Halifax on the Atlantic Ocean to Vancouver on the Pacific Ocean was the first to be completed in 1885.

● **Canadian River** ▶ A river in the S central USA, flowing generally E from NE New Mexico to the Arkansas River in Oklahoma. Length: 1458 km (906 mi).

● **Canadian Shield** ▷*See* shield.

● **Canaletto** ▶ (Antonio Canal; 1697–1768) Venetian painter, famous for his views of Venice. He trained under his father, a theatri-

Canada goose ▶ A family of Canada geese. Introduced into England in the 17th century, these birds are now commonly found in parks. They pair for life.

cal-scenery painter, before visiting Rome (1719–20), where he designed opera sets. His popularity with English collectors led to a stay in England (1746–55), where he painted views of London. His early work, which was painted in the open air, was considerably freer than his later much more architectural painting, for which he used mechanical drawing instruments.

● **canals** ▶ Man-made open water channels. They are divided into two categories: conveyance canals and navigation canals. The former carry water for irrigation, power, or drainage; the latter, to facilitate transportation, often connect two natural waterways. Canals have been dug from ancient times. The Grand Canal in China, started in 109 BC, was 1000 km (620 mi) long by the 8th century and carried 1.8 million tonnes of freight per annum. Some modern ship canals achieve spectacular reductions in voyage distances, especially the ▷Suez Canal (completed in 1869) and the ▷Panama Canal (1914). Others of considerable local importance include the Corinth Canal (1893), the Kiel Canal (1895), and the St Lawrence Seaway (1959) connecting the Great Lakes. In canal construction, the availability of water is the primary concern. Conveyance canals are often narrow, have a high water velocity, and are earth lined and consequently are subject to erosion. Barge or ship canals are often completely lined with concrete or have concrete edges to prevent wave erosion. Variations in land or water level are common and ▷locks must be installed to conserve water and allow for the passage of vessels.

● **canary** ▶ A small songbird, *Serinus canarius*, native to the Canary Islands, Madeira, and the Azores. Wild canaries have an olive-green plumage with yellow to grey underparts streaked with black. Popular as cagebirds since the 15th century, they have been selectively bred both for their musical song and attractive plumage—usually pure yellow but sometimes white or striped and occasionally with ornamental plumes. Subfamily: *Carduelinae*; family: *Fringillidae* (finches).

● **canary grass** ▶ An annual grass, *Phalaris canariensis*, 20–60 cm high, native to the Canary Islands and N Africa and cultivated commercially in Europe for birdseed. The related reed canary grass (*P. arundinaceae*), which is widely distributed, is an important forage grass and grows 61–183 cm high.

● **Canary Islands** ▶ (Spanish name: Islas Canarias) A group of islands in the Atlantic Ocean, close to NW Africa; an autonomous region of Spain. Since 1927 they have constituted two provinces named after their capitals of Las Palmas (including the islands of Fuerteventura, Gran Canaria, and Lanzarote) and Santa Cruz de Tenerife (including the islands of Ferro, Gomera, La Palma, and ▷Tenerife). The islands became Spanish possessions in the 15th century; the earliest inhabitants, the Guanches, are now extinct. The islands are of volcanic formation and, with the help of irrigation, fruit such as bananas and tomatoes are grown for export. Tourism is also important. Total area: 7270 sq km (2807 sq mi). Population (1994 est): 1 534 897.

● **Canary Wharf** ▷*See* Docklands; London.

● **canasta** ▷*See* rummy games.

● **Canaveral, Cape** ▶ (name from 1963 until 1973: Cape Kennedy) A barrier island in the USA, in E central Florida separated from the mainland by lagoons. It is the site of operations by NASA at the Kennedy Space Center. The first flight to land on the moon was launched here in 1969. In 1973 Skylab, the first orbiting laboratory, was launched from here.

● **Canberra** ▶ 35 15S 149 10E The capital of Australia, in the Australian Capital Territory on the Molonglo River. As a result of a competition in 1911, it was planned by the American architect Walter Burley Griffin, as the new federal capital, being formally inaugurated in 1927. The establishment of the National University in 1946 and the growth of government departments have led to sizeable increases in population. Population (1995 est): 303 700.

● **cancan** ▶ A boisterous dance originally performed in Parisian dance halls around 1830 as a solo or by groups of women. Tourists flocked to see its spectacular and indecorous high kicking. Famous cancan music includes the galop from Offenbach's *Orpheus in the Underworld*.

● **cancer** ▶ A group of diseases caused by the abnormal and uncontrolled division of cells to form tumours that invade and destroy the tissues in which they arise. Such tumours are described as malignant: their cells spread through the bloodstream or lymphatic system or across body cavities to set up secondary tumours at other sites in the body (this spread is called metastasis). The cause of cancer remains uncertain, although it is known that exposure to certain substances (*see* carcinogen) will produce it; a genetic element, diet, and certain viruses have also been implicated in certain cancers. Although only a few cancers are inherited, the importance of genetic factors in the development of many others is being increasingly recognized, with the identification of specific genes associated with certain cancers. It seems likely that most cancers arise when an inherited susceptibility to the disease is triggered by carcinogenic, dietary, or other environmental factors.

In the UK, cancer accounted for about a quarter of all deaths in 1996 (27% in males; 23% in females). Cancer can arise in almost any tissue: in the Western world the breasts, colon, lungs, bronchi, prostate gland, and stomach are common sites. In the UK, the most common cancer in males is lung cancer, followed by prostate and colorectal cancers; in females the three most common cancers are (in order) breast cancer, colorectal cancer, and lung cancer. **Carcinomas** are cancers arising in ▷epithelium; less common but more malignant are **sarcomas**—cancers of connective tissue (bone, cartilage, muscle, etc.). ▷Leukaemia, affecting the bone marrow and other blood-forming tissues, and ▷lymphoma, cancer of the lymph nodes, are forms of sarcoma. Treatment of cancer includes ▷cytotoxic drugs, radiotherapy, and surgery.

● **Cancer** ▶ (Latin: Crab) An inconspicuous constellation in the N sky, lying on the ▷zodiac between Leo and Gemini. It contains the star cluster ▷Praesepe.

● **candela** ▶ (cd) The ▷SI unit of luminous intensity defined since 1979 as the intensity in a given direction of a source emitting monochromatically at 540×10^{12} hertz with a radiant intensity in that direction of 1/683 watt per steradian.

● **Candela, Felix** ▶ (1910–) Mexican architect and engineer, born in Spain. Employing a naturalistic modern style, his work is characterized by use of thin, prestressed concrete roofs, often spanning large distances, e.g. the Church of the Miraculous Virgin, Mexico City (1953).

● **Candia** ▷*See* Iráklion.

● **Candida** ▶ A genus of fungi. They are yeasts with typically spherical, ovoid, or elongated cells that reproduce by budding and spore formation; they do not undergo sexual reproduction. Several species, especially *C. albicans*, cause ▷candidiasis.

● **candidiasis** ▶ An infection caused by a species of yeast (*Candida albicans*). Popularly known as thrush, it affects the mouth and the genital and anal areas most frequently; it may develop after treatment with certain antibiotics and with diseases (e.g. leukaemia, AIDS) and drugs (e.g. steroids) that reduce the natural immunity of the body. The infection is cleared by such fungicides as nystatin.

● **Candlemas** ▶ The Christian feast of the Purification of the Virgin Mary and the Presentation of Christ in the Temple (Luke 2.22–38), which is observed on 2 Feb. It is so called because of the distribution of candles, symbolizing Christ's appearance as the "light of the world."

● **candytuft** ▶ An annual or perennial flowering plant of the genus *Iberis* (about 30 species), native to S Europe and Asia and growing well in dry chalky soils. The stems (up to 15–50 cm in height) bear white, pink, red, or blue flowers in flat-topped clusters. The fruits are pods containing winged seeds. Some species are grown as garden plants. Family: *Cruciferae*.

● **cane** ▶ The stem of certain large grasses and of some palms. In some species it is hollow and jointed, e.g. ▷reeds (*Phragmites* species), ▷bamboo (*Bambusa* species), and ▷sugar cane; in others it is solid, e.g. ▷rattan and Malacca (*Calamus* species) used for making furniture, walking sticks, etc.

● **Canea** ▶ (Greek name: Khaniá) 35 31N 24 01E The capital of Crete, on the Gulf of Khaniá. Founded by Venetians in 1252, it is surrounded by massive Venetian walls. The island's main port, it exports leather, olives, olive oil, and fruit. Population (1991 est): 133 060.

● **cane rat** ▶ An African ▷rodent belonging to the genus *Thryonomys* (2 species) common in reed beds. About 40 cm long, cane rats have bright-orange incisor teeth, feeding on reeds, roots, bulbs, grasses, and sugar cane and can become a pest in plantations. Family: *Thryonomyidae*.

● **Canetti, Elias** ▶ (1905–94) Bulgarian writer, who lived in the UK. He usually wrote in German and is known for his studies of the psychology of power and crowd behaviour as well as such novels as *Auto da Fé* (1946) and his autobiographical writings. He won a Nobel Prize in 1981.

● **Canidae** ▶ The dog family: a family of mammals belonging to the order ▷*Carnivora*. It includes the dogs, wolves, jackals, coyote, and foxes.

● **Canis Major** ▶ (Latin: Great Dog) A constellation in the S sky near Orion. The brightest stars are ▷Sirius, the ▷giant stars Adhara and Mirzam, and the ▷supergiant Wezen.

● **Canis Minor** ▶ (Latin: Little Dog) A small constellation in the S sky, lying near Canis Major and Orion. The brightest star is ▷Procyon.

● **canker** ▶ 1. A disease of plants, especially fruit trees, caused by various fungi and bacteria. Cankers can be seen as dead, discoloured, irregular, or cracked areas on the stem and branches; mechanical or climatic injury and attack by insect pests often predispose to infection. Treatment is by removal of the diseased parts. 2. A chronic disease of horses' hooves, caused by continually wet conditions underfoot. The affected hooves become soft and swollen and eventually infected, causing inflammation and discharge. Treatment is by removing affected tissue and dressing with antibiotics. Prevention is by ensuring a dry stable floor. 3. Inflammation of the outer ear affecting dogs, cats, and rabbits and causing irritation. Treatment is by antiseptic lotion or powder.

● **canna** ▶ A genus of ornamental herbaceous plants (about 155 species), native to tropical and subtropical America. Up to 3 m high, they have spirally arranged leaves, which may be green, bronze, or purple, and clusters of showy flowers, 15 cm across and ranging from pale yellow to scarlet. They are popular bedding plants. Family: *Cannaceae*.

● **cannabis** ▶ The resin (hashish) or crushed leaves and flowers (marihuana, "grass," or "pot") obtained from certain species of ▷hemp. The drug is eaten or inhaled and produces euphoria, distortion of time sense, and increased awareness of sight, sound, and memory. Occasionally anxiety may also be experienced. Although moderate use of the drug is not considered very harmful, cannabis can cause dependence and a small minority of users progress to "hard" drugs. For these reasons a legal ban on its sale and use has been maintained in most countries, despite a persistent and growing campaign for decriminalization. In 2001 the UK government announced that possession of small quantities of cannabis for one's personal use would no longer be an arrestable offence.

● **Cannae, Battle of** ▶ (216 BC) The battle, fought at the village of Cannae in Apulia (SE Italy), in which ▷Hannibal and the Carthaginians killed almost 50 000 Romans. It is the worst Roman defeat on record.

● **Cannes** ▶ 43 33N 7 00E A resort in S France, in the Alpes-Maritimes department on the French Riviera. Its development as a fashionable resort dates from 1834, when the British statesman Lord Brougham (1778–1868) built a villa here. It has numerous hotels, sports facilities, boulevards, and casinos. The Île St Honorat contains the oldest monastery in W Europe. There are aircraft and textile industries and fruit and flowers are grown. Since 1947 the annual Cannes International Film Festival has been held here, the main award being the Palme d'Or. Population (1990): 69 363.

● **cannibalism** ▶ The practice of eating human flesh, either as food or for ritual or magical purposes. Extreme hunger has prompted modern occurrences among concentration-camp prisoners and aircrash survivors. In ritual cannibalism certain parts of a defeated enemy may be eaten in order to absorb his strength and courage or to prevent his spirit taking revenge. In other cases (endocannibalism) it forms part of rituals performed at the death of a kinsman. The word is derived from the ▷Arawak term for the ▷Carib Indians among whom it was common. Ritual cannibalism was practised also by the New Zealand Maoris, the Fijian islanders, in Polynesia, in parts of Africa, in New Guinea, and by some North American Indian peoples.

● **canning** ▶ The preservation of meat, fish, or fruit in vacuum-sealed airtight metal containers, which have been sterilized by heating followed by rapid cooling. Fruit keeps safely for at least one year, meat and vegetables for two, although in practice they may stay fresh for much longer, especially if kept cool. Canning was introduced in the 18th century and originally used pure ▷tin cans. Now cans are made of ▷tinplate. Canned foods may be reheated but do not need further cooking. ▷*See also* food preservation.

● **Canning, George** ▶ (1770–1827) British statesman; foreign secretary (1807–09, 1822–27) and Tory prime minister (1827). An MP from 1793, he held office under Pitt and contributed (1797–98) to the weekly *Anti-Jacobin*, which opposed the French Revolution. He became foreign secretary in 1807 but resigned in 1809 in opposition to the management of the Napoleonic Wars by the secretary for war, Castlereagh. Castlereagh challenged Canning to a duel in which Canning was slightly hurt. He again became foreign secretary after Castlereagh's suicide and was responsible, with William Huskisson (1770–1830), for the liberalization of Tory policies in the 1820s. He supported the revolt of Spain's American Colonies (1823) and the War of ▷Greek Independence (1825–27), before briefly becoming prime minister. His son **Charles John, Earl Canning** (1812–62) was governor general of India (1856–62), where he became known as Clemency Canning because of his mild handling of the Indian Mutiny.

● **Canning Basin** ▶ (former name: Desert Artesian Basin) An arid and largely unexplored sedimentary basin of NW Western Australia. It forms part of the ▷Great Sandy Desert and is covered by active longitudinal sand dunes. Area: about 400 000 sq km (150 000 sq mi).

● **Cannizzaro, Stanislao** ▶ (1826–1910) Italian chemist, who resurrected ▷Avogadro's hypothesis, which had been neglected for 50 years, and used it to clarify the problem of representing compounds by formulas. He also discovered a method, called Cannizzaro's reaction, of converting an aldehyde into an acid and an alcohol.

● **Cannock** ▶ 52 42N 2 01W A town in W central England, in Staffordshire. Cannock is a commuter town for the West Midlands conurbation; local industries include coalmining, brick making, and light industries. To the E lies **Cannock Chase**, a wooded plateau that was once a royal hunting ground. It is now a recreational area for the West Midland towns. Population (1991): 60 106.

● **cannon** ▶ An early form of ▷artillery firearm used primarily until 1670 as a siege gun. A 14th-century invention (by the German monk, Berthold Schwarz), early cannon were made of wrought-iron rods welded together, covered in lead, and wrapped with iron bands. Some had a removable breech. Cast guns were made in England after 1500. They fired stones, cast-iron and wrought-iron balls. Modern cannons include ▷guns, ▷mortars, and ▷howitzers.

● **Cannon, Annie** ▷*See* Harvard classification system.

● **Cannon, Walter Bradford** ▶ (1871–1945) US physiologist, who pioneered the use of X-rays in physiological studies. By administering a suspension, or meal, of radio-opaque bismuth, the intestine could be revealed on X-rays. Cannon also investigated the body's reaction to stress, particularly the role of the sympathetic nervous system, and he identified a chemical transmitter secreted by sympathetic nerve endings, which he termed "sympathin" (now known to be adrenaline or noradrenaline).

● **Cano, Juan Sebastián del** ▶ (c. 1460–1526) Spanish navigator. He accompanied Magellan's expedition, taking command after Magellan's death. He successfully completed the voyage—the first round the world—in 1522. He died on a second expedition.

● **canoe** ▶ A double-ended vessel designed mainly for propulsion by paddles, although certain kinds are equipped with sails (sailing canoe). The modern canoe is, typically, about 3–7 m (10–20 ft) long, and they are usually single or two seaters although Canadian canoes can accommodate up to four people. It is made of waterproofed canvas stretched over a ribbed frame or of aluminium, wood, or fibreglass. The modern canoe is modelled on native craft that have been in use in the Americas and in the Pacific for thousands of years. Some Pacific native war canoes, equipped with outriggers, could accommodate as many as 40 people. Other large canoes served, until the 20th century, as the chief means of transport among the islands of the Pacific. Depending on their age and provenance, native canoes were made by hollowing out logs or by stretching animal skins or birchbark over a ribbed frame. Canoes are much favoured for sport on lakes and rivers, being easy to manoeuvre and readily portable. ▷See also kayak.

● **canonization** ▶ In the Christian Church, the conferring of the status of ▷saint on a dead person. In the Roman Catholic Church this is done by a formal declaration of the pope after a long investigation of the person's suitability. **Beatification,** by which the Church permits the veneration of a person, with the title "Blessed," within a particular diocese, order, or other limited area, precedes canonization and depends on evidence of the person's exceptional virtue and authentic miracles. The Church then puts the case for the canonization and appoints someone, the *Promotor Fidei* (Latin: promoter of the faith, popularly known as the devil's advocate), to oppose it, and completes the process after proof of further miracles. In the early days of Christianity each area recognized its own saints, who were usually local martyrs. Ulrich of Augsburg (c. 890–973) is the first person known to have been canonized by a pope (in 993 AD). About 1170 Pope Alexander III decreed that only the Roman Catholic Church could add new names to the list of saints.

● **canon law** ▶ The laws of Christian Churches, particularly the Roman Catholic, Anglican, and Orthodox Churches. They include regulations governing the clergy, the ▷ecclesiastical courts, matters of worship and doctrine, and so on. The origins of canon law lie in the decrees of the various councils of bishops in the early Church, in authoritative pronouncements of important bishops, and in the Decretals, or letters having the force of law, of the Popes. In the 12th century many laws from these sources were included by Gratian (died c. 1179) in his *Decretum*, a collection of rules that the Roman Catholic Church recognized as authoritative. The *Decretum* in turn formed part of a later collection, the ▷Corpus Juris Canonici, which in 1917 was revised to form the Codex Juris Canonici, the present Roman Catholic code of law. The ecclesiastical law of the Church of England was mainly contained in the early-17th-century *Book of Canons*, but new laws were introduced in the 1960s.

● **Canopic jars** ▶ Earthenware jars used in ancient Egypt in sets of four as containers for the internal organs removed from mummified bodies. Their lids, originally plain, were later modelled as the human, falcon, dog, and jackal heads of the four sons of the god ▷Horus.

● **Canopus** ▶ A conspicuous luminous white ▷supergiant, apparent magnitude –0.7 and 200 light years distant, that is the brightest star in the constellation Carina and the second brightest star in the sky.

● **Canossa** ▶ A 10th-century castle near Reggio nel Emilia, in Italy. It is famous as the place in which Emperor Henry IV received absolution from Gregory VII in 1077 to end the ▷investiture controversy.

● **Canova, Antonio** ▶ (1757–1822) Italian sculptor. One of the finest interpreters of the style of ▷neoclassicism, Canova worked first in Venice, in Rome after 1781, in Vienna, and in Paris, where he was employed by Napoleon. He achieved a wide reputation with his idealized marbles. His best-known works are *The Tomb of Clement XIII* (1783–87; SS Apostoli, Rome) and *Pauline Borghese as Venus Victrix* (1805–07; Borghese Gallery, Rome). Another work, *The Three Graces*, was the focus of a controversy in 1990 when attempts were made to export it from the UK, where it is kept at Woburn Abbey.

● **Cánovas del Castillo, Antonio** ▶ (1828–97) Spanish statesman and writer. Following the overthrow of the First Republic in 1874 and the restoration of the monarchy he created a system of government by two parties in rotation, which remained in force until 1923. He led the conservative party and was many times prime minister. He was assassinated by an anarchist.

● **Cantabrian Mountains** ▶ (Spanish name: Cordillera Cantábrica) A mountain range in N Spain extending E–W along the Atlantic coast and rising to 2648 m (8868 ft).

● **Cantacuzino** ▶ A family prominent in Romania from the 17th century. Descended from an imperial Byzantine family, the Cantacuzino settled in Moldavia and Walachia (present-day Romania) in the 16th century. Its members included **Şerban Cantacuzino** (d. 1688), who ruled Walachia from 1679 to 1688, and his nephew **Ştefan Cantacuzino**, who ruled from 1714 until ousted and executed in 1716. Şerban's cousin **Dumitraşcu Cantacuzino** (1648–85) was an unpopular ruler of Moldavia (1673–75, 1684–85). A descendant, **Constantin Cantacuzino** (1793–1877), governed Walachia (1848–49, 1854).

● **Canterbury** ▶ 51 17N 1 05E A city in SE England, in Kent on the River Stour. The cathedral (11th–15th centuries, but built on the site of an Anglo-Saxon church), where Thomas ▷Becket was martyred in 1170, is the seat of the Archbishop and Primate of the Anglican Church. Canterbury is a tourist, market, and educational centre; the University of Kent (1960) overlooks the city. Population (1991): 36 464.

● **Canterbury, Archbishop of** ▶ The chief bishop of the ▷Anglican Communion of churches, called Primate of All England. The first of the line was St ▷Augustine of Canterbury. He takes precedence after the royal princes and before the Lord Chancellor and the other peers and signs himself with his Christian name and the Latin abbreviation of Canterbury, for example "George Cantuar." Archbishops of the 20th century, beginning with the 96th, are listed in the table.

Archbishops of Canterbury in the 20th century

Archbishop of Canterbury	term of office
Randall Thomas Davidson (1848–1930)	1903–28
Cosmo Gordon Lang (1864–1945)	1928–42
William Temple (1881–1944)	1942–44
Geoffrey Francis Fisher (1887–1972)	1945–61
Arthur Michael Ramsey (1904–88)	1961–74
Frederick Donald Coggan (1909–2000)	1974–80
Robert Alexander Kennedy Runcie (1921–2000)	1980–91
George Leonard Carey (1935–)	1991–2002

● **Canterbury bell** ▶ An annual or biennial flowering plant, *Campanula medium*, native to S Europe and frequently grown as a garden ornamental. The plant grows to a height of 75 cm and bears spikes of pink, blue, or white bell-shaped flowers, each 5 cm or more long. Family: *Campanulaceae*.

● **Canterbury Plains** ▶ A low-lying area of New Zealand, on E central South Island bordering on the Pacific Ocean. It is the most densely populated area of South Island and is important for fat-lamb raising and the production of cereals, fodder crops, and vegetables. Area: about 10 000 sq km (4000 sq mi). Chief town: Christchurch.

● **cantharidin** ▷See Spanish fly.

● **Can Tho** ▶ 10 03N 105 46E A port in S Vietnam, on the Mekong delta. It is the industrial centre of an important rice-growing area, with a university (1956). Population (1992 est): 215 587.

● **Canton** ▶ (Chinese names: Guangzhou or Kuang-chou) 23 08N 113 20E A port in S China, the capital of Guangdong province on the Zhu Jiang (Pearl River) delta. Densely populated, it is the commercial and industrial centre of S China and attracts much of the country's foreign trade through its biannual trade fair. It has a university and various colleges. Its industries include steel, shipbuilding, paper, textiles, and the manufacture of machinery and chemicals.
    History: Chinese since the 3rd century BC, it was the first Chinese city to trade regularly with Europeans (from the 16th century), having long traded with Hindus and Arabs, and was the focus of the first Opium War (1839–42). The birthplace of ▷Sun Yat-sen, it was the starting point of the revolution against the Qing (1911). His Guomindang (Nationalist) government was based here in the early

1920s. Canton was occupied by Japan (1938–45). Population (1991 est): 3 580 000.

• **Canton** ► 40 48N 81 23W A city in the USA, in NE Ohio. An important industrial centre, it has a large iron and steel industry. It was the home of President McKinley. Population (1996 est): 81 079.

• **Cantona, Eric** ► (1966–) French soccer player. A forward, he played for the French national side from 1987 but became known for controversy. He later played for Leeds United (1992–93) and Manchester United (1993–97).

• **Canton and Enderbury** ► Two uninhabited coral atolls in the S Pacific Ocean, in the Phoenix Islands. Claims between the USA and the UK were settled in 1939, when they agreed to exercise joint control over the islands for 50 years. Canton was used as an international airport for transpacific flights until the advent of long-range jets.

• **Cantonese** ▷*See* Chinese.

• **Cantor, Georg** ► (1845–1918) Russian mathematician, born in St Petersburg. Cantor's family moved in 1856 to Germany, where he spent the rest of his life. He was the first mathematician to set the concept of infinity on a rigorous mathematical foundation. He defined different types of infinity for the set of integers, the set of real numbers, etc., each type being represented by a number known as a transfinite number. His ideas created great controversy and were viciously attacked, by Leopold Kronecker (1823–91) in particular. Cantor broke down in 1884 under the strain and died in a mental asylum.

• **Canute II** ► (or Cnut; c. 994–1035) Danish King of England after defeating ▷Edmund Ironside (1016). He became King of Denmark (1019) and of Norway (1028). He defended England from Viking attacks (1017, 1026, 1028) and subjected Malcolm II of Scotland (1028). He went on a pilgrimage to Rome in 1027 to attend the coronation of ▷Conrad II. According to legend, he responded to flatterers by demonstrating his inability to induce the waves to recede.

• **canyon** ► A deep steep-sided gorge found mainly in arid and semiarid areas, the depth of which considerably exceeds its width. Canyons are often formed by rapidly eroding rivers down-cutting into soft rock. The lack of rainfall hinders weathering and maintains the steep slopes; where hard- and soft-rock bands occur, a stepped formation results. The largest and best-known canyon is the ▷Grand Canyon (USA).

• **Cao Chan** ► (or Zao Zhan; ?1715–63) Chinese novelist, famous for the semiautobiographical *Dream of the Red Chamber*, a novel written in the last years of his life. It combines a tragic love story with a description of the downfall of a great Chinese family. It mirrors the fortunes of Cao Chan's own family, which held the hereditary office of commissioner of imperial textiles in Nanking.

• **Capablanca y Graupera, José Raúl** ► (1888–1942) Cuban chess player, who was world champion from 1921 to 1927. Extraordinarily gifted, he played at speed and with exceptional insight. He worked as a diplomat and wrote books on chess, including *Chess Fundamentals* (1922).

• **capacitance** ► The ability of an electrical component to store charge. It is measured in ▷farads and defined as the ratio of the stored charge in coulombs to the voltage drop across the component. Capacitance is one of the factors that control the frequency response of circuits and components to alternating currents.

• **capacitor** ► An electrical component (formerly called a condenser), with an appreciable ▷capacitance. It consists of two conductor or semiconductor plates separated by a ▷dielectric. The value of the capacitance is a function of the geometry and the electrical properties of the dielectric and often also of the operating voltage and the frequency. Variable capacitors are used for tuning electronic circuits.

• **Cape Breton Island** ► An island in SE Canada, in Nova Scotia, separated from the mainland by the Strait of Canso. Hilly and forested, it encloses tidal salt lakes. Coal, steel, fishing, and tourism are important. It was ceded to Britain by the French (1763). Area: 10 280 sq km (3975 sq mi). Population (1991): 120 098.

• **Cape Coast** ► 5 10N 1 13W A town in central Ghana, on the Gulf of Guinea. It was the capital of the British colony of the Gold Coast until 1874. It has a cathedral and a university (1962). Fishing is important. Population (latest est): 57 224.

• **Cape Cod** ► A sandy peninsula in the USA, in Massachusetts between Cape Cod Bay and the Atlantic Ocean. The ▷Pilgrim Fathers landed here in December 1620. A popular summer resort area, it also produces cranberries and asparagus. Length: 105 km (65 mi).

• **Cape Frontier Wars** ► (1779–1878) The wars fought intermittently in S Africa between the White settlers moving E from the Cape and the ▷Xhosa people. Conflict between the two groups arose mainly over land and cattle. The Xhosa had been driven back along the coast by the colonists beyond the Keiskamma River by 1819 and in 1846 the land between the Fish and the Keiskamma Rivers was annexed as British Kaffraria. The final war was in 1877–78 in which the Xhosa were defeated and their lands absorbed into the Cape Colony.

• **Cape gooseberry** ▷*See* Chinese lantern plant.

• **Cape Horn** ► (Spanish name: Cabo de Hornes) The most southerly point in South America, at the S end of Horn Island, Chile. It is notorious for its stormy weather.

• **Čapek, Karel Matelj** ► (1890–1938) Czech dramatist, novelist, and travel-writer. His early plays included *RUR* (1921), in which he coined the word "robot," but he is best known for *The Insect Play* (1921), written with his brother **Josef Čapek** (1887–1945), who died in Belsen.

• **Capella** ► A yellow ▷giant star, apparent magnitude 0.1 and 45 light years distant, that is the brightest star in the constellation Auriga. It is a ▷multiple star, having three components.

• **Cape of Good Hope** ► A headland in the extreme SW of South Africa. It was discovered (1488) by Bartolomeu ▷Dias, who named it the Cape of Storms.

• **Cape Province** ► (official name: Cape of Good Hope Province; Afrikaans name: Kaapprovinsie) A former province in South Africa, in the extreme S. In 1994 it was replaced by the new regions **Northern Cape**, **Western Cape**, **Eastern Cape**, and part of **North West**. The area consists chiefly of plateaus separated by mountain ranges. Western Cape produces most of South Africa's fruit and vegetables for export and has many vineyards. Sheep and cattle rearing is extensive and wheat and alfalfa are grown throughout the area. Diamonds and copper are the chief minerals, others being asbestos, manganese, and iron ore. Industries include food processing and canning, textiles, and motor-vehicle production.

History: first settled by the Dutch (1652), the area was ceded to Britain in 1814, becoming known as the Cape Colony. The discovery of diamonds in Griqualand West led to its annexation to the Cape Colony (1871). In 1910 the colony became a province in the Union of South Africa.

• **caper** ► A spiny shrub, *Capparis spinosa*, native to S Europe. The pickled flower buds are the capers used in flavouring. The fruit is a berry. Family: *Capparidaceae*.

• **capercaillie** ► The largest European ▷grouse, *Tetrao urogallus*, of Eurasian coniferous forests, where it feeds on pine buds and pine needles. The male, almost 100 cm long, is glossy black with red wattles above the eyes. The smaller female is brown with black and white markings.

• **Capernaum** ► 32 53N 35 34E An ancient town in N Israel, on the N shore of the Sea of Galilee. It is the site of many biblical events, and a synagogue dating from about 200 AD has been excavated.

• **Capetians** ► The ruling dynasty of France from 987 to 1328. It was founded by ▷Hugh Capet, who became King of France in 987, replacing the Carolingians. Successive kings, notably ▷Philip II Augustus and ▷Louis IX, expanded their own authority and the territory under their control (originally comprising little more than the Île-de-France). The Capetians established a royal bureaucracy, from which the ▷parlements developed, and were the first kings to summon the ▷States General.

• **Cape Town** ► (Afrikaans name: Kaapstad) 33 56S 18 28E The legislative capital of South Africa, on the S shore of Table Bay, an inlet of the Atlantic Ocean. Founded by Jan van Riebeeck in 1652 as a supply post for the Dutch East India Company, it is the oldest White settlement in South Africa. The famous National Botanical Gardens at Kirstenbosch were part of the Groot Schuur estate, the home of Cecil Rhodes. Cape Town castle (17th century) is the oldest building in South Africa; the university was established in 1918 and has an observatory. Cape Town is a major port, with dockyard facilities, and is an important commercial and industrial city besides being a popular holiday centre. Its industries include oil refining, chemicals, motor vehicles, and textiles. Population (1991): 854 616.

● **Cape Verde** ▶ (French name: Cap Vert) 14 43N 17 33W The westernmost point of Africa, in Senegal, consisting of a promontory extending into the Atlantic Ocean.

● **Cape Verde, Republic of** ▶ (Portuguese name: Cabo Verde) A country occupying an archipelago in the N Atlantic Ocean, off the coast of West Africa. It consists of ten islands and five islets, most of which are mountainous. The majority of the population is of mixed African and European descent.
Economy: mainly subsistence agriculture, although the arid climate means that cultivation is limited. Coffee and bananas are grown for export. Ship refuelling and fishing are important; fish and fish products are the main exports. Volcanic rock and salt are also exported. Privatization and other free-market reforms were introduced in the mid-1990s.
History: the Cape Verde Islands were settled by the Portuguese in the mid-15th century, becoming a Portuguese colony in the 19th century and gaining full independence in 1975. Plans to federate with Guinea-Bissau were abandoned in 1980. Multiparty elections held in 1991 ended 15 years of one-party rule when the ruling PAICV (African Party for the Independence of Cape Verde) was defeated by the opposition Movement for Democracy (MPD). The PAICV returned to power in 2001, when Jose Maria Neves became prime minister.

Republic of Cape Verde

Head of state	President Pedro Pires
Official language	Portuguese
Official currency	Cape Verdean escudo of 100 centavos
Area	4033 sq km (1557 sq mi)
Population (1999 est)	406 000
Capital	Praia
Main port	Mindelo

● **Cape York Peninsula** ▶ The most northerly part of Australia, in Queensland, situated between the Gulf of Carpentaria and the Coral Sea. It is mainly low-lying grass and scrubland in the W, rising to the Great Dividing Range in the E and contains large areas that are uninhabited although bauxite mining is important.

● **Cap Haïtien** ▶ (*or* Le Cap) 19 47N 72 17W A port in N Haiti, on the Atlantic Ocean. The chief exports are coffee and sugar and it is the site of one of the world's largest sisal plantations. Population (1995): 100 638.

● **capillary** ▶ Any tube of very small diameter, especially in anat-

omy, a minute thin-walled blood vessel (0.005–0.02 mm diameter), networks of which connect the smallest ▷arteries with the smallest ▷veins. Nutrients and oxygen diffuse across the capillary walls to nourish the tissues. Waste products and carbon dioxide return from the tissues to the capillary blood.
The process by which liquids spontaneously rise or fall in capillary tubes is called **capillarity**. It results from attractive forces between the molecules of the liquid and those on the surface of the capillaries.

● **capital** ▶ An element of architecture used to join a column to the part of the building it supports. In classical architecture there are five orders of columns with strictly defined types of capital for each (*see* orders of architecture). In romanesque and gothic architecture, the rules became less strict and the type of capital used depended mainly on the skill and taste of the masons involved. Thus the capital could vary from the plain (called a cushion capital) to the highly ornate, decorated with carvings of foliage, people, and animals (grotesque and historiated types).

● **capital-gains tax** ▶ (CGT) A UK tax, introduced in 1965, on the profit arising from the disposal of an asset by sale or gift (and until 1971 by death). It applies to stocks and shares (except some government stocks), to dwellings that are not the owner's only residence, and to all other saleable assets with some exceptions (e.g. cars, assets sold for less than £6,000, the first £250,000 of assets disposed of on retirement). It does not apply to gains from betting or life assurance policies. The rate of tax is the taxpayer's marginal rate of income tax on the gain; however, the first £7,500 (from 2001) of a person's gains in any year are exempt and certain reductions apply to shares in a company held by employees for more than four years. Similar taxes are levied in other countries.

● **capitalism** ▶ An economic and political system that developed following the industrial revolution. Essential features of the system are uncontrolled free markets, based on the profit motive, and unrestricted ownership of the means of production (capital). If the system is allowed to develop without restriction it has certain undesirable attributes (*see* laissez-faire). This has led Western countries to restrict capitalism by substantial government regulation. Communist countries have followed the doctrines of Karl Marx (*see* Marxism), who maintained that capitalism contains the seeds of its own destruction, replacing the free-market system with central direction of the economy and state ownership of all the means of production. The 1980s saw a move away from government regulation of the economy in most Western countries. Most previously communist countries have now adopted free-market policies, as have many countries in the developing world.

● **capital punishment** ▶ The punishment of a convicted criminal by execution, in Britain formerly by beheading or hanging. In 18th-century Britain over 200 offences carried the death penalty, including such crimes as petty theft and forgery. It was, in fact, imposed for only a few offences. In 1868 public executions were abolished and by the Homicide Act (1957) only certain kinds of ▷murder remained punishable by death (murder committed in the course or furtherance of theft, in resisting arrest, etc.). In 1965 the death penalty was

Cape Town ▶ The Table Mountain seen from Blouberg.

abolished for all forms of murder, leaving treason, violent piracy, and (until 1971) arson in royal dockyards as the only capital crimes. The death penalty was formally abolished for all peacetime offences in 1999. In 1979, 1983, 1988, 1990, and 1994 motions that it be reintroduced for certain murders were defeated in a free vote in the House of Commons.

In many other countries the death penalty has been retained although its effectiveness as a deterrent is still an open question; opponents point to the macabre and uncivilized procedure of execution, the reluctance of juries to convict, and the inability to repair a miscarriage of justice. Nevertheless several US states revived the death penalty in 1976 and others have followed suit; since then over 500 offenders have been executed, while a further 3500 wait on "death row." In 1999 it was calculated that 85% of all executions worldwide are now carried out by four countries – China, Iraq, Saudi Arabia, and the USA. ▷See also electrocution; guillotine.

● **capital-transfer tax** ▷See inheritance tax.

● **Capitol** ► **1.** (or Capitoline Temple) A temple built on the Capitoline Hill (one of the seven hills of Rome) by Tarquinius Priscus (d. 578 BC) but not dedicated until 509 BC. Destroyed by lightning in 183 BC, burnt during the civil wars in 83 BC, and subsequently burnt and rebuilt several times, it was finally plundered by the Vandals in 455 AD. ▷Michelangelo's Piazza del Campidoglio now stands on the site. **2.** The meeting place of the US Congress in Washington, DC. It was designed by William Thornton, a West Indian doctor with no previous architectural experience. The cornerstone was laid by George Washington in 1793.

● **capitulary** ► Legal and administrative instruments of the ▷Carolingian kings, arranged in *capitula* (articles). These documents are concerned with many topics, both secular and ecclesiastical, including law and order, the regulation of trade, and the administration of royal estates. Although originals do not survive, copies amply illustrate the scope and power of early Carolingian administration.

● **Capodimonte porcelain** ► A valuable soft-paste ▷porcelain made (1743–59) near Naples at a factory started by Charles IV of Naples. Typical pieces were peasant figures and vessels and services modelled like local sea shells and seaweeds.

● **Capone, Al** ► (1899–1947) US gangster, probably born in Italy. He dominated the Chicago underworld of organized crime in the late 1920s. In the St Valentine's Day Massacre of 1929, his men killed seven members of a rival gang. He was imprisoned in 1931 for income-tax evasion.

● **Caporetto** ▷See Kobarid.

● **Capote, Truman** ► (1924–84) US novelist. In his early novels and stories, such as *Other Voices, Other Rooms* (1948), he explored traditional southern literary themes of loneliness and the macabre. Later he turned to journalism, an interest reflected in *In Cold Blood* (1966), a novel about an actual multiple murder. Other works include *Breakfast at Tiffany's* (1958) and *Music for Chameleons* (1980).

● **Capp, Al** ► (Alfred Caplin; 1909–79) US cartoonist, born in New Haven, Connecticut. He is famous for his comic strip *Li'l Abner* depicting the hillbillies of Dogpatch, Kentucky, which first appeared in the *New York Mirror* in 1934 and which he continued to produce until 1977.

● **Cappadocia** ► The eastern region of Asia Minor. After early colonization by Semitic merchants, subjection to the Hittites, and invasions from the east, Cappadocia was conquered by the Persians in 584 BC but became an independent kingdom in the 3rd century BC. Feudal and isolated, Cappadocia resisted the hellenizing efforts of its ruling dynasty, which was largely pro-Roman; as the Roman Empire expanded eastwards Cappadocia became strategically important and was a Roman province by 17 AD.

● **Capra, Frank** ► (1897–1991) US film director, born in Italy. His best-known films include several popular sentimental comedies, notably *It Happened One Night* (1934), *Arsenic and Old Lace* (1942), and *It's a Wonderful Life* (1946). During World War II he directed propaganda films for the US War Department.

● **Capri, Island of** ► (Latin name: Capreae) An Italian island at the

SW entrance to the Bay of Naples. Its mild climate, fine scenery, and beaches have made it a popular resort since Roman times. The Blue Grotto, a cavern accessible only by sea, is a notable feature. Area: about 13 sq km (5 sq mi). Population (latest est): 8000.

● **capriccio** ▷See veduta.

● **Capricorn** ► (astrology) ▷See zodiac.

● **Capricornus** ► (Latin: Goat) A constellation in the S sky, lying on the ▷zodiac between Aquarius and Sagittarius.

● **Caprivi Strip** ► A narrow extension of NE Namibia giving the country access to the Zambezi River. Length: about 450 km (280 mi). It was ceded by Britain to German South West Africa in 1893 and named after Graf von Caprivi, the German chancellor at that time.

● **Capsicum** ► A genus of annual and perennial flowering plants (about 50 species), native to Central and South America. The fruits (berries) of some species, particularly the various cultivated varieties of *C. annuum* and *C. frutescens*, are the ▷chillies and peppers used in cookery. Large fruits (up to about 10 cm long) are the sweet peppers, which have a mild taste and are used in salads or cooked as a vegetable. They are usually green but may be yellow or red (the red varieties—paprika—can be ground to produce a spice). Smaller berries (about 2 cm long) are the hot-tasting red peppers (or chillies); when dried and ground these form cayenne pepper. Dwarf varieties are grown for ornament. Family: ▷*Solanaceae*.

● **capsid** ► A delicate ▷plant bug belonging to the family *Miridae* (about 8000 species). Capsids are 2.5–6 mm long and usually green or brown. They are found among all types of vegetation, feeding on plant juices, and are often serious crop pests. A few species prey on small arthropods.

● **capsule** ► In botany, a type of dry ▷fruit that releases its seeds at maturity through pores, teeth, or slits: an example is the poppy capsule. The term also refers to the spore-producing structures of mosses and liverworts and the slimy envelope surrounding some bacterial cells. In zoology, it is the layer of connective tissue surrounding some organs, for example the kidney.

● **Capua** ► 41 06N 14 12E A market town in S Italy, in Campania on the River Volturno. It has Roman remains and a 9th-century cathedral. Population (1990): 19 520.

● **capuchin monkey** ► A long-tailed ▷monkey belonging to the genus *Cebus* (4 species), of South America. Capuchins are 70–90 cm long including the tail (40–50 cm) and live in large troops in the treetops, feeding chiefly on fruit but also eating insects, birds, and eggs. They became familiar as organ-grinders' monkeys. Family: *Cebidae*.

● **Capuchins** ► A Roman Catholic order of friars founded in 1525. They are reformed ▷Franciscans, named after the pointed cowl (capuche) they wear in emulation of St Francis. Opposed by the established Franciscans, they were almost suppressed in 1542, but survived to become an important force during the Counter-Reformation, being recognized in 1619 as one of the three independent branches of the Franciscan order. From their foundation they were noted for their works of charity and their asceticism.

● **capybara** ► The largest living rodent, *Hydrochoerus hydrochaeris*. Resembling giant guinea-pigs, up to 1.25 m long and 50 cm high, capybaras graze on river banks in Central and South America, living in groups of up to 20 individuals. They have short coarse yellowish-brown hair and partially webbed feet (they are expert swimmers). The capybara is the only member of its family (*Hydrochoeridae*).

● **car** ► A self-propelled road vehicle. The search for a means of replacing the horse as a means of transport began seriously at the beginning of the 18th century, when ▷Newcomen and ▷Watt had shown that steam could be harnessed to produce power. Nicolas-Joseph ▷Cugnot in 1769 used a steam engine to drive a gun tractor and a steam-powered tricycle; in 1808 Richard ▷Trevithick built a working steam carriage. But none of these vehicles nor the many other steam carriages of the first half of the 19th century were more than cumbersome novelties. An effective horseless carriage needed a smaller more efficient power source. This was eventually provided by two German engineers, Nikolaus ▷Otto and Gottlieb ▷Daimler, who in 1876 patented the Otto-cycle ▷internal-combustion engine. In 1885, another German, Karl ▷Benz, used a 3 hp version of this engine to power a tricycle capable of 15 mph (20 km per hour). By 1890 both Daimler and Benz were selling the motorized dog carts that were the forerunners of the modern car. In France, during the closing decade of the 19th century, Panhard, Comte Albert de Dion, Georges Bouton, and Peugeot were all producing and selling cars. In the USA, Henry Ford built his first car in 1896 and during the next decade introduced the mass-production techniques that eventually enabled popular motoring to become a possibility. In the UK, however, the development of the motor car from the early steam carriages was hampered by nervous legislation introduced in 1865, which insisted that they must be preceded on the roads by a man carrying a red flag. This law was not repealed until 1896. Some ten years later Henry ▷Royce, dissatisfied with imported cars, decided to build his own. In partnership with C. S. ▷Rolls, he sold his first Rolls-Royce Silver Ghost in 1907.

At the start of World War I, some 130 000 cars were registered in the UK; by this time they were much the same in basic shape and design as they are today. Propeller shafts had replaced chains and belts, pneumatic tyres had ousted solid tyres, and open carriage bodies had given way to saloons. Although World War I was the last of the "horse" wars, by 1918 more and more motorized vehicles (including ▷tanks) were in military use. Nevertheless, motoring was still the preserve of the affluent. In the early 1920s a family Ford, Austin, Citroën, Morris, or Renault cost about £500. It was not until 1925, when Ford brought the price of his Model T down to $290 in the USA and £185 in the UK, that motoring became more widely accessible. During the 1930s the price of cars steadily declined until at the beginning of World War II a British-made Ford 8 or Austin 7 could be bought for about £100. But the real mass market did not develop until after World War II. Before the war it was rare for a model to sell a million vehicles, now a popular car has to do so to be a commercial success.

Since the 1950s competition throughout the world has been fierce. The UK used to be the most prolific manufacturer of cars, but as a result of amalgamations, sales to large foreign concerns, and intransigent trade-union pressures the industry has declined. Although cars are still manufactured in the UK, most of the companies making them are foreign-owned. In 1994 Rover, the last UK volume manufacturer, was bought by the German company BMW, and in 1998 the jewel in the crown of British motoring, Rolls-Royce, was also sold to the Germans. Over half the cars sold in the UK are imported, mostly from France, Germany, Italy, and Japan. The cars themselves are not greatly changed from the prewar vehicles. They are slightly faster (most family saloons are capable of 100 mph, although laws in many countries do not allow them to exceed 70 mph), somewhat more economical (small family cars can do 50 miles per gallon), and considerably more reliable than they used to be. They are also more comfortable and have been made safer by the use of seat belts and in-

flatable air bags. More recent innovations include engines with four valves per cylinder (instead of two), ▷fuel injection (replacing the ▷carburettor), electronic ignition (replacing the distributor), ▷turbochargers with an exhaust-powered turbine driving a supercharger, and anti-lock disc ▷brakes. Air conditioning, for many years available for American cars, is now frequently available in European cars. As a mass producer of carbon dioxide (see greenhouse effect), toxic gases (see catalytic converter), and lead (see tetraethyl lead), the modern car is the enemy of conservationists and with 355 cars per 1000 of UK population (562 in the USA) the congestion it creates makes it the enemy of town planners. ▷See electric car. □ p. 230.

● **caracal** ▶ A long-legged short-tailed ▷cat, *Felis caracal*, of African and Asian deserts, bush, and mountains. Caracals are about 70 cm long with a reddish-brown coat, and feed mainly on birds but also catch small mammals.

● **Caracalla** ▶ (Marcus Aurelius Antoninus; 188–217 AD) Roman emperor (211–17). Rivalry between Caracalla and his brother and coemperor Geta (189–212) threatened to divide the Empire until Caracalla procured Geta's murder. Caracalla extended Roman citizenship to all free inhabitants of the Empire—probably for financial reasons (212). In 214 he embarked on war against the Parthians, claiming to be following Alexander the Great's ambition to unite East and West, but was assassinated during the campaign.

● **caracara** ▶ A long-legged ▷falcon belonging to the subfamily *Daptriinae*, of Central and South America. Caracaras can run swiftly and spend much time on the ground. They are omnivorous and frequently feed on carrion.

● **Caracas** ▶ 10 35N 66 56W The capital of Venezuela, situated near the N coast and linked by road to its port, La Guaira. Founded by the Spanish as Santiago de León de Caracas in the 16th century, it suffered damage and destruction from the English and the French in the 16th and 18th centuries and later from severe earthquakes. In the 20th century it has grown considerably, especially since the oil boom of the 1950s. The Central University of Venezuela was founded in 1725, and there are three other universities. It is the birthplace of Simón Bolívar. Population (1990 est): 1 824 892.

● **carat** ▶ 1. A unit of weight for precious stones, formerly defined as 4 grains (Troy), but now equal to 0.200 grams. 2. A measure of the fineness of gold equal to the number of parts of gold by weight in 24 parts of the alloy. Thus 18-carat gold contains 18/24ths pure gold.

● **Caratacus** ▶ (or Caractacus; 1st century AD) King of the ▷Catuvellauni; son of ▷Cunobelinus (Cymbeline). Caratacus organized resistance to the Roman invasion of 43 AD. Defeated, he fled first to Wales then to the north British queen, ▷Cartimandua, who betrayed him. He was pardoned by Emperor Claudius but died in exile.

● **Caravaggio** ▶ (Michelangelo Merisi; 1573–1610) An influential Italian ▷baroque painter, whose nickname derives from his birthplace. In Rome his chief patron was Cardinal Francesco del Monte, for whom he painted scenes of the life of St Matthew in S Luigi dei Francesi. He executed numerous altarpieces, some of which, e.g. *Death of the Virgin* (Louvre), were condemned for depicting sacred personages as coarse peasants. He is also noted for his dramatic contrasts of light and shade in such paintings as *Supper at Emmaus* (National Gallery, London), which were extremely influential, particularly in N Europe. His violent temper led him to kill a man after a disputed tennis match in 1606. He spent his last years in exile in Naples, Malta, and Sicily.

● **caravel** ▶ A sailing vessel used by the Spanish and Portuguese from the middle ages onwards. It was usually rigged with a lateen sail on two or more masts.

● **caraway** ▶ A perennial flowering plant, *Carum carvi*, native to N temperate regions from Europe to the Himalayas. The much-branched stem grows to a height of 25–60 cm and terminates in clusters of small white flowers. The fruit is an oblong capsule containing the familiar caraway seeds, used in cookery. Family: ▷Umbelliferae.

capybara ▶ These rodents are semiaquatic; they can swim underwater using their partly webbed feet.

● **carbohydrate** ▶ One of a large group of chemical compounds containing the elements carbon, hydrogen, and oxygen and having the general formula $C_x(H_2O)_y$. Green plants manufacture carbohy-

car

Benz 8hp   1600 of these "horseless carriages" were sold between 1898 and 1900. Described as the first reliable car offered to the public, its twin-cylinder 1570 cc engine gave it a top speed of 18 mph (29 km/hr).

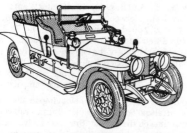

Rolls-Royce Silver Ghost   First built in 1907 (and continuing in production until 1927) it quickly established itself as "the best car in the world." Its 7-litre 6-cylinder engine gave it a top speed of 65 mph (105 km/hr).

Ford Model T   15 million of this first mass-produced car (nicknamed the "Tin Lizzie") were made between 1908 and 1927. Its 4-cylinder, 2898 cc engine gave it a top speed of 40 mph (64 km/hr).

Bugatti Royale   Made to compete with the Rolls-Royce, this 13-litre 8-cylinder car cost over £5000 in 1927 – too much for even its intended royal customers. Six were sold. In 1987 one survivor was sold for £5.5 M.

Volkswagen   Nicknamed "the Beetle," this 1937 German design by Ferdinand Porsche was still selling in the 1970s, making it the best selling car ever made. Its air-cooled slow-revving rear engine increased from 1131 to 1600 cc over the years.

MG TC   This post-war British sports car (1946-55) was little changed from the TA model first built in 1937. The TC had a 1250 cc engine.

Buick   This 1949 US car represented a release from wartime restrictions and set the trend for a generation of large American cars.

Mini   The best selling British car ever made. Designed by Alec Issigonis, the mini was introduced in 1959 and is still selling. Its frontwheel drive, transverse engine, and 10-inch wheels make it an extremely roomy car for its size.

Chrysler Voyager   A US people carrier for the 1990s with up to seven seats. Engine options include a 3.3 litre V-6 petrol engine and a 2.5 litre 4-cylinder turbocharged diesel.

drates—such as ▷sugars and ▷starch—during ▷photosynthesis and their cell walls consist largely of carbohydrates—predominantly ▷cellulose. Hence plant carbohydrates are the primary source of food energy for animals. ▷Glycogen is a carbohydrate energy reserve found in animals, while chitin is a structural carbohydrate occurring in arthropods (and also in fungi). Chemically, carbohydrates can be classified according to the number of sugar units they contain—one (*see* monosaccharide), several (oligosaccharides), or many (*see* polysaccharide).

● **carbolic acid** ▷*See* phenols.

● **carbon** ▶ (C) A chemical element that is unique in terms of the huge number and variety of its compounds. Carbon is the basis of organic ▷chemistry and of all living systems. The element occurs naturally in two main forms: ▷graphite, which is a soft greyish-black mineral, and ▷diamond, the hardest substance known. A third form, ▷buckminsterfullerene, contains ball-shaped carbon structures. ▷Charcoal and ▷coke are also composed of carbon. Large amounts of carbon are fixed as calcium carbonate ($CaCO_3$) in ▷calcite. The extensive and varied chemistry of carbon results from its ability to form single, double, and triple bonds with itself and other elements. Simple compounds of carbon may join together to form polymers; for example polyethene, $(C_2H_4)_n$, from ethene. At no 6; at wt 12.011; sublimes at $3367 \pm 25°C$.

● **Carbonari** ▶ Members of a secret society in early 19th-century Italy that advocated constitutional government. The Carbonari emerged as opponents of Joachim ▷Murat, who ruled Naples for Napoleon. The movement spread to N Italy and was supported by those dissatisfied with the conservative regimes imposed on Italy after the fall of Napoleon. Support for the Carbonari dwindled following the formation of ▷Young Italy by Mazzini but the society had helped pave the way for the unification of Italy (*see* Risorgimento).

● **carbon cycle** ▶ (biology) The process by which carbon (in the form of carbon dioxide) in the atmosphere is taken up by plants during photosynthesis and transferred from one organism to the next in a ▷food chain, i.e. the plants are eaten by herbivorous animals that are themselves eaten by carnivores. At various stages carbon is returned to the environment with the release of carbon dioxide at ▷respiration and through decay.

● **carbon cycle** ▶ (physics; *or* Bethe cycle) A cycle of thermonuclear reactions in which a nucleus of carbon-12 acts as a catalyst in converting four hydrogen nuclei into a helium nucleus. The cycle produces energy and is believed to be a major source of energy in some stars. The reactions are:

$$^{1}_{1}H + {}^{12}_{6}C \rightarrow {}^{13}_{7}N \rightarrow {}^{13}_{6}C + {}^{0}_{1}e$$
$$^{1}_{1}H + {}^{13}_{6}C \rightarrow {}^{14}_{7}N$$
$$^{1}_{1}H + {}^{14}_{7}N \rightarrow {}^{15}_{8}O \rightarrow {}^{15}_{7}N + {}^{0}_{1}e$$
$$^{1}_{1}H + {}^{15}_{7}N \rightarrow {}^{12}_{6}C + {}^{4}_{2}He.$$

● **carbon dioxide** ▶ (CO_2) A colourless odourless noncombustible gas. It is present (about 0.03% by volume) in air, being produced by combustion of carbon compounds and by respiration (*see also* greenhouse effect). Industrially, CO_2 is made from chalk or limestone and is used as a coolant in nuclear reactors, as a refrigerant, in fire extinguishers, and in "fizzy" drinks.

● **carbon fibres** ▶ Black silky threads of pure carbon, made by the heat treatment of organic textile fibres (such as Courtelle) so that the side chains of the molecules are removed. They are some eight times stronger than steel and are used to reinforce resinous, ceramic, or metallic substances (with up to 600 000 fibres per square centimetre) to make components for jet engines, rockets, etc., where strength at high temperature is required.

● **Carboniferous period** ▶ A geological period of the ▷Palaeozoic era occurring about 370–280 million years ago between the Devonian and Permian periods. During the period land plants increased prolifically and led to the formation of the world's major coal deposits. Amphibians became more common and by the end of the period some reptiles had evolved. The Carboniferous is divided into Lower and Upper (Mississippian and Pennsylvanian). Limestone deposits were widespread in the Lower Carboniferous; millstone grits and the Coal Measures (alternating beds of coal, sandstone, shale, and clay), in the Upper.

● **carbon monoxide** ▶ (CO) A colourless odourless flammable gas. It is produced by the incomplete combustion of carbon compounds (e.g. coke or natural gas) and is used as a fuel (*see* water gas). CO is highly toxic, combining with red blood cells and preventing them from carrying oxygen. It is present in the exhaust fumes of internal-combustion engines.

● **carbon tetrachloride** ▷*See* tetrachloromethane.

● **carborundum** ▶ A dark crystalline compound (silicon carbide) manufactured by heating silica (sand) with carbon (coke). It is used as an abrasive and as a refractory material.

● **carboxylic acids** ▷*See* fatty acid.

● **carbuncle** ▷*See* boil.

● **carburettor** ▶ The device in a petrol engine that vaporizes the fuel and mixes it with air in the correct proportions. The float-chamber carburettor was invented in 1892 by Wilhelm Maybach, who was a partner of Gottlieb ▷Daimler. Vaporization is carried out by sucking the liquid petrol from the float chamber through a fine jet situated in (or near to) the throat of a tube through which the combustion air enters the engine. The carburettor also contains a choke to make the petrol-air mixture richer (i.e. contain more petrol and less air) for cold starting, a throttle valve (which controls the speed of the engine by admitting more or less of the mixture), and an air filter. In most modern petrol engines the carburettor is replaced by a ▷fuel-injection system.

● **Carcassonne** ▶ 43 13N 2 21E A town in SW France, the capital of the Aude department. It comprises a medieval fortified town, surrounded by towers and ramparts crowning a hill on the right bank of the River Aude, and a largely modern town, where there is a 13th-century cathedral (restored), on the left bank. A tourist centre, it is situated in a wine-producing region. Population (1990): 44 990.

● **Carchemish** ▶ A ▷Hittite stronghold on the Upper Euphrates in E Turkey. After the Hittite empire's collapse (12th century BC), Carchemish survived as an independent kingdom until conquered by ▷Sargon II of Assyria (717 BC). In 605 BC it was the scene of a battle in which the Babylonians defeated an Egyptian army. ▷Woolley and T. E. ▷Lawrence excavated fine Hittite reliefs there (1912–14, 1919).

● **carcinogen** ▶ An agent that causes cancer. Carcinogens can be chemicals, radiation, and some viruses. Chemical carcinogens include tar (e.g. from cigarette smoking), aniline, and azo dyes. Large doses of radiation and several viruses (including some ▷retroviruses and papilloma viruses) can also cause cancer.

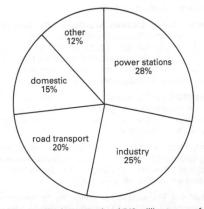

carbon dioxide ▶ In 1995 the UK produced 542 million tonnes of CO_2, the main greenhouse gas, by combustion of fossil fuels. The pie chart shows the main sources. Over the preceding 25 years the weight of CO_2 from road transport almost doubled, but the emission from power stations fell by some 25% due to the replacement of coal-burning stations by nuclear and gas-fired stations.

• **carcinoma** ▷*See* cancer.

• **cardamom** ► (*or* cardamum *or* cardanon) A perennial herb, *Elettaria cardamomum*, native to India. 1.5–3 m tall, it has large leaves, green and purple veined flowers, and small capsules filled with hard angular seeds. The spice cardamom consists of whole or ground dried fruit or seeds. It is cultivated in India, Sri Lanka, and Guatemala. Family: *Zingiberaceae* (ginger family).

• **Cardano, Girolamo** ► (1501–76) Italian mathematician, who contributed to the development of negative and imaginary ▷numbers and, being an inveterate gambler, constructed a mathematical theory of chance. He also published a method of solving cubic equations known as Cardano's rule, although it was first derived by Niccolò Tartaglia (1500–57). His main works were *De subtilitate rerum* (1551) and *De varietate rerum* (1557).

• **Cárdenas, Lázaro** ► (1895–1970) Mexican statesman. As president (1934–40) Cárdenas strove to realize many of the promises of the post-1910 revolutionary movement. He redistributed land, promoted mass education, and supported organized labour. His most famous achievement was the nationalization of the oil industry in 1938.

• **Cardiff** ► (Welsh name: Caerdydd) **1.** 51 30N 3 13W The capital of Wales (since 1955), a city situated in the SE of the principality at the mouth of the River Taff. Its port still handles general cargo but employment is now largely dependent on service occupations (especially financial services). At the centre of the city lies the Norman castle, rebuilt by the 3rd Marquess of Bute in the 1870s. University College, Cardiff (founded 1883), the University of Wales Registry (1893), the University of Wales Institute of Science and Technology (UWIST), the Welsh National School of Medicine, and the National Museum of Wales are all located in the city. Since May 1999 Cardiff has been home to the Welsh Assembly; the Assembly Building is the work of Richard ▷Rogers. In addition to Cardiff Arms Park, the traditional home of Welsh rugby, a Millennium Stadium was constructed for the 1999 rugby World Cup. The cathedral at ▷Llandaff and the Welsh Folk Museum at St Fagans are situated on the city's outskirts.

History: originally a small Roman fort, the site was reoccupied by the Normans, who built the stone castle keep. It received its first royal charter in 1581, at which time it was a favourite haunt of pirates. It was not until 1881, however, that Cardiff expanded from a small market town to become the largest town in Wales. Its prosperity was based on coal from the valleys to the N of the city and by 1913 it was the largest coal-exporting port in the world. Trade declined rapidly, however, after World War I. The import of iron ore was switched to other ports and in 1978 the East Moors steelworks were closed down. The Cardiff Bay area, including the port and quayside, was redeveloped as a commercial, residential, and leisure area in the 1990s. Population (1992): 295 600. **2.** A county borough in SE Wales, created in 1996 from part of South Glamorgan. Area: 139 sq km (54 sq mi). Population (1999 est): 315 040.

• **Cardigan, James Thomas Brudenell, 7th Earl of** ► (1797–1868) British cavalry officer. In 1824 Cardigan bought himself a command in the Hussars, where his arrogant behaviour led to a notorious duel. In 1854, during the Crimean War, he led the fatal charge of the Light Brigade at ▷Balaclava, made famous by Tennyson. The woollen garment known as a cardigan was named after him.

• **Cardiganshire** ► A former county of W Wales, on Cardigan Bay. Under local government reorganization in 1974 it became part of Dyfed; in 1996 it became an independent ▷unitary authority under its Welsh name, ▷Ceredigion.

• **Cardin, Pierre** ► (1922–) French fashion designer, who opened a fashion house in Paris (1949) and made his reputation with his oriental styles and slim coats with huge collars. He was the first couturier to show a collection for men (1960).

• **cardinal** ► A North American ▷bunting, *Pyrrhuloxia cardinalis*, having a strong stout bill and a crested head. The male, about 20 cm long, has a bright scarlet plumage with a black bib; the female is yellowish brown with a red crest. They have a distinctive whistling song.

• **cardinals, college of** ► (*or* Sacred College) The body of the highest dignitaries next to the pope in the ▷Roman Catholic Church. Orig-inating in the advisory roles played by the parish priests and deacons of the city of Rome, the body was later extended to include six cardinal bishops responsible for the election of the pope. This function was invested in the college as a whole by the Third ▷Lateran Council (1179). Since then the number of cardinal bishops, priests, and deacons has increased from 70 under Sixtus V (1586) to the present membership of 125 established under John XXIII and Paul VI. Cardinals are nominated and elected by the pope, who invests them with the flat broad-brimmed red hat symbolic of their rank. They assist the pope as a privy council, conducting the temporal affairs of the Church, advising on doctrine, etc.; they elect the pope from among their own number.

• **Carducci, Giosuè** ► (1835–1907) Italian poet and critic. The son of a country doctor, he became professor of Italian literature at Bologna University in 1860 and won the Nobel Prize in 1906. He was elected senator in 1890. He wrote vigorous patriotic and anticlerical poetry but *Rime nuove* (1861–87) and *Odi Barbare* (1877–89) also contain more lyrical verse.

• **Cardwell, Edward, Viscount** ► (1813–86) British politician best known for his work in reforming the army. As secretary of state for war (1868–74), Cardwell, in spite of bitter opposition, abolished peacetime flogging in the army, shortened the period of service, abolished the purchase of commissions, and reorganized the war office.

• **Carême, Marie Antonin** ► (1784–1833) French chef, known as the "architect of French cuisine." Of humble origins, he became head chef for Talleyrand, George IV of Britain, and Alexander I of Russia. He was particularly noted for his extravagant pastry designs imitating classical architecture.

• **Carew, Thomas** ► (c. 1595–1640) British poet. He served in the diplomatic service in Venice, The Hague, and Paris before receiving a court appointment in 1628. His love lyrics and his elegy on John Donne were widely circulated. He also wrote a masque, *Coelum Britannicum* (1634).

• **Carey, George Leonard** ► (1935–) British churchman; Archbishop of Canterbury (1991–2002). He was formerly Bishop of Bath and Wells (1987–91). In 1992 the Synod's vote to allow women to be ordained priests left Carey with the task of holding the Church together.

• **Carey, William** ► (1761–1834) British Baptist missionary. A shoemaker, Carey helped to found the Baptist Missionary Society in 1792. In 1793 he sailed for Bengal, where he lived until his death, translating the Bible into various Indian dialects and compiling Indian grammars and dictionaries.

• **cargo cults** ► Religious cults found chiefly in Melanesia since the late 19th century. Their adherents believe that a new paradise will be heralded by the arrival of a supernatural cargo of goods brought by spirits, gods, ancestors, or White foreigners. The cults probably evolved from Christian millennial teachings and native jealousy of European wealth.

• **Caria** ► A mountainous area in SW Asia Minor under the rule of ▷Lydia until 546 BC, when it passed to the Persians. The Carians joined the Ionian Greeks' unsuccessful revolt against the Persians (499–493 BC). Under the Hecatomnid dynasty (395–334 BC), Caria joined the Greek world.

• **Carib** ► An American Indian people of the Lesser Antilles and northern South America, after whom the Caribbean was named. The maritime island Caribs were warriors and cannibals, who before the advent of the Spaniards expelled the ▷Arawak Indians from the Lesser Antilles, enslaving the women and killing and eating the men. As a consequence, in these islands men spoke Carib and women spoke Arawak. The mainland Caribs were less aggressive; they cultivated manioc and hunted with the blowpipe.

• **Caribbean Community** ► (CARICOM) An association of 15 states in the Caribbean region (Antigua and Barbuda, Bahamas, Barbados, Belize, Dominica, Grenada, Guyana, Haiti, Jamaica, Montserrat, St Kitts-Nevis, St Lucia, St Vincent and the Grenadines, Suriname, and Trinidad and Tobago). It was established in 1973 and aims to coordinate the economic policies of member states through the Caribbean Common Market (which replaced the Caribbean Free Trade Area (CARIFTA) formed in 1968); to coordinate foreign policies; and to foster cooperation. In 1988 members agreed to abolish nearly all trade barriers. Its headquarters are in Georgetown (Guyana). ▷*See also* Association of Caribbean States.

● **Caribbean Sea** ▶ A section of the Atlantic Ocean, between the West Indies, E Central America, and N South America. With the opening of the Panama Canal (1914) it became an important shipping route. Its tropical climate and warm waters attract many tourists. Area: 2 718 200 sq km (1 049 500 sq mi). Maximum depth: 7686 m (25 216 ft).

● **caribou** ▷*See* reindeer.

● **caricature** ▷*See* cartoon.

● **CARICOM** ▷*See* Caribbean Community.

● **caries** ▶ (*or* dental caries) Cavities in the teeth caused by bacterial erosion of the enamel and dentine. The bacteria feed on sugar from the diet: the sugar and bacteria become attached to the teeth to form a layer called plaque, and acid formed by bacterial breakdown of the sugar causes the damage of caries. Caries is particularly common in children and adolescents; a high-sugar diet is a major contributory factor. Treatment consists of drilling away the damaged part of the tooth and replacing it with filling. The absorption of fluoride by growing teeth strengthens them against bacterial attack (*see* fluoridation).

● **carillon** ▶ 1. A set of church bells hung in a tower, activated from a manual and pedal console similar to that of an organ. It is a popular instrument in Belgium and Holland. Carillons vary in size from two to four octaves. The wooden keys are depressed with the closed hand. 2. A set of tuned tubular bells set in a frame and used in the percussion section of the orchestra. Usually consisting of 18 bells, they are struck at the top and are fitted with a foot-operated damper to enable the player to silence them.

● **Carina** ▶ (Latin: Keel) A constellation in the S sky near Crux. The brightest star is ▷Canopus.

● **Carinthia** ▶ (German name: Kärnten) A federal state in S Austria. It first came into Austrian possession in 1335; following World War I parts were ceded to Italy and Yugoslavia. Chiefly mountainous, it has picturesque alpine scenery and many lakes. The main occupations are livestock rearing, forestry, mining, and tourism. Area: 9537 sq km (3681 sq mi). Population (1994 est): 559 696. Capital: Klagenfurt.

● **Carisbrooke** ▶ 51 41N 1 19W A village in S England, near Newport on the Isle of Wight. Charles I was imprisoned in its 11th-century castle.

● **Carl August** ▶ (1757–1828) Duke (1758–1815) and Grand Duke (1815–28) of Saxe-Weimar-Eisenach, who was the first German ruler to grant his state a liberal constitution. Carl August opposed Napoleon and made territorial gains at the Congress of Vienna (1815). He was a patron of ▷Goethe.

●**Carl XVI Gustaf** ▶ (1946–) King of Sweden (1973–), succeeding his grandfather Gustaf VI (1882–1973). The monarch became little more than a figurehead under a new constitution effective from Carl's succession. In 1976 the king married Silvia Sommerlath (1943–). They have three children.

● **Carling, Will(iam)** ▶ (1965–) British Rugby Union player. As captain of England (1988–96) he led the team to Grand Slam victories in 1991 and 1992. He retired from international rugby in 1997.

● **Carlisle** ▶ 54 54N 2 55W A city in NW England, the administrative centre of Cumbria on the River Eden. Once a Roman military centre (Luguvallum) and important fortress in the border wars with the Scots, it has a 12th-century cathedral and a castle (11th–13th centuries). Industries include metal goods, food processing, and textiles but most employment is now in the services sector. Population (1991): 72 439.

● **Carlism** ▶ A Spanish conservative movement, initiated by those who supported as ▷Ferdinand VII's successor in 1833 his brother Don ▷Carlos, rather than Ferdinand's daughter ▷Isabella II. The Carlists

wanted a severe repression of liberals, the restoration of the Spanish Inquisition, and the maintenance of traditional regional liberties (*fueros*). In the first Carlist War (1833–39) they were supported by small landowners in the NE but were defeated. Carlism survived in Navarre and Aragon but in the second Carlist War (1872–76) was again defeated. During the Spanish Civil War Carlist regiments fought with Franco's armies. The present Carlist pretender is Carlos Hugo de Bourbon-Parma (1930–).

● **Carlos, Don** ▶ (1788–1855) Spanish pretender. The brother of ▷Ferdinand VII and an ultra-Catholic reactionary, he contested the succession of his niece ▷Isabella II in 1833. His followers, who became known as Carlists, opposed Isabella's government in a series of Carlist wars (*see* Carlism).

● **Carlos I** ▶ (1863–1908) King of Portugal (1889–1908). His calm handling of foreign affairs resolved colonial disputes with Britain but his reign saw considerable unrest at home. He was assassinated with his son Luis in Lisbon and succeeded by another son, Manuel II.

● **Carlow** ▶ (Irish name: Ceatharlach) A county in the E Republic of Ireland, in Leinster. Chiefly low lying, it rises to mountains in the E. Agriculture is intensive producing barley, wheat, and sugar beet. Area: 896 sq km (346 sq mi). Population (1996 est): 42 000. County town: Carlow.

● **Carlsbad** ▶ 32 25N 104 14W A city in the USA, in SE New Mexico on the Pecos River. Founded in 1887, the nearby Carlsbad Caverns National Park makes it a popular tourist centre. Potash, discovered in 1931, is extensively mined and it is a major shipping point. Population (1994 est): 65 461.

● **Carlson, Chester** ▶ (1906–68) US physicist who invented xerography (*see* photocopying machine). Originally an employee of the Bell Telephone Company, he invented the Xerox process in 1938 and became a multimillionaire.

● **Carlyle, Thomas** ▶ (1795–1881) Scottish historian and essayist. In 1826 he married Jane Baillie Welsh and moved to London in 1834. *Sartor Resartus* (1836), a blend of fiction, philosophy, and autobiography, was published in 1836 and was followed by his major work, *The French Revolution*, in 1837. This and later works express his view of history as shaped by the "Hero," or inspired individual. After his wife's death in 1866 he became grief-stricken at his neglect of her and retired from public life.

● **Carmarthen** ▶ (Welsh name: Caerfyrddin) A town in SW Wales, the administrative centre of Carmarthenshire on the River Towy. It is an agricultural centre, manufacturing dairy products and pharmaceuticals. Population (1991): 13 524.

● **Carmarthenshire** ▶ (Welsh name: Sir Caerfyrddin) A county of SW Wales, on Carmarthen Bay. Under local government reorganization in 1974 it became part of Dyfed but it was reinstated as a county in 1996. It is generally hilly, with lower land along the coast of Carmarthen Bay to the S. The county is predominantly agricultural, with dairy farming the main activity. New industries have been introduced to the former coalmining and steel-working area in the SE. Tourism is important. Area: 2380 sq km (919 sq mi). Population (1996 est): 169 000. Administrative centre: Carmarthen.

● **Carmel, Mount** ▶ 32 45N 35 02E A mountain in N Israel, extending in a ridge for 25 km (16 mi) SE from Haifa. The Carmelite religious order was founded here. Height: 546 m (1791 ft).

● **Carmelites** ▶ A Roman Catholic religious order founded in the mid-12th century by St Berthold (died c. 1195), who claimed direct inspiration from Elijah and established a monastery at Mount Carmel. With the collapse of the Crusader kingdoms, the order moved to Europe. In 1452 an order of Carmelite nuns was instituted. In the 16th century the order was reformed by St ▷Teresa of Avila and emphasized the cultivation of the contemplative life.

● **Carmichael, Hoagy** ▶ (Howard Hoagland Carmichael: 1899–1981) US jazz pianist, singer, actor, and composer. His songs include "Stardust" (1929) and "Two Sleepy People" (1938).

● **Carmina Burana** ▶ A miscellany of lyrics, mainly in Latin, preserved together with six religious dramas in a 13th-century manuscript from Benediktbeuern, Bavaria. The work of earlier medieval wandering scholars, they encompass religious, pastoral, and erotic themes. ▷*See also* Orff, Carl.

● **Carnac** ► 47 35N 3 05W A village in Brittany (NW France). It is famous for the megalithic monuments in its vicinity (*see* megalith). Chief of these, and unique of their kind, are the avenues (alignments) of monoliths, set upright in parallel rows that run continuously for hundreds of metres. The three main groups, called Ménec, Kermario, and Kerlescan, may have had both ritual and astronomical significance.

Carnac ► Nearly 3000 menhirs still stand in the Carnac alignments.

● **Carnap, Rudolf** ► (1891–1970) German-born logical positivist philosopher. A founder of the ▷Vienna Circle, he was professor of philosophy successively at Vienna, Prague, Chicago, and the University of California at Los Angeles. He worked on formal logic and its applications to science and ▷epistemology. By developing logical syntax and ▷semantics, he tried to construct a formal language for the empirical sciences to eliminate confusion, ambiguity, and similar obstacles to knowledge.

● **Carnarvon Range** ► A plateau in Australia, in SE Queensland. Part of the Great Dividing Range, it lies within a nature reserve and is being developed as a tourist area. It includes the Carnarvon Gorge, which is 32 km (20 mi) long.

● **Carnatic music** ► The music of S India as opposed to that of N India. Not having been subjected to the influences of invading cultures, the S has kept an unbroken tradition that lays stress on complex rhythmic patterns. The scale is subdivided into 12 sections similar to those of the European chromatic scale. Primarily vocal, it also employs instruments, especially drums.

● **carnation** ► A large-flowered cultivated form of the clove pink (*Dianthus caryophyllus*). These perennials grow to heights of 40–60 cm, have tufts of dense grasslike foliage, and double flowers in white,

yellow, orange, pink, red, or lavender. Hardy border carnations are suitable for outdoor cultivation, while the perpetual flowering varieties should be grown under glass. Flowers of carnations (and pinks) are noted for their clovelike fragrance. Family: *Caryophyllaceae*. ▷*See also* Dianthus.

● **carnauba wax** ► A hard high-quality wax gathered from the leaves of the Brazilian carnauba palm (*Copernica cerifera*) and used for making high-gloss polishes. The tree secretes the wax to prevent excess evaporation from its leaves.

● **Carné, Marcel** ► (1903–96) French film director. He collaborated with the scriptwriter Jacques ▷Prévert on several films noted for their fatalistic treatment of social themes and their powerful evocation of atmosphere. These include *Le Jour se lève* (1939) and *Les Enfants du Paradis* (1945).

● **Carnegie, Andrew** ► (1835–1919) US industrialist, born in Scotland. He founded the Keystone Bridge Company (1865) to manufacture iron and, increasingly, steel. By 1888 he owned auxiliary coal- and iron-fields, railways, and steamships and in 1901 his companies merged with the US Steel Corporation. A noted philanthropist, he believed that a rich man should distribute his wealth for the benefit of society and donated over £70 million to causes in the USA and the UK. He founded the Carnegie Institute of Technology in Pittsburgh in 1900, the Carnegie Institution in Washington in 1902, and many libraries. He also contributed substantially to the building of Carnegie Hall.

● **Carnera, Primo** ► (1906–67) Italian boxer, who was idolized during the 1930s although he was heavyweight champion only briefly (1933–34). 6.5 ft (1.98 m) tall, he was known for his knockout victories. He later took up wrestling and acted in the film *On the Waterfront* (1954).

● **Carnivora** ► An order of mammals adapted for hunting and eating flesh. **Carnivores** have strong jaws, with sharp incisor teeth and pointed canine teeth; some of the cheek (molar) teeth, called carnassials, act as shears to chop up meat. They are the major predators and most species are terrestrial, stalking or pouncing on their prey. The 252 species are divided into seven families: ▷*Canidae* (dogs); *Ursidae* (*see* bear); *Procyonidae* (*see* raccoon); ▷*Mustelidae* (weasels, skunks, etc.); ▷*Viverridae* (genets, mongooses, etc.); and ▷*Felidae* (cats).

In a wider sense the term "carnivore" is used for any meat-eating animal, including birds, reptiles, insects, etc., as well as mammals of other orders (e.g. toothed whales). In a □food chain, carnivores function as secondary and tertiary (top) consumers.

● **carnivorous plant** ► A plant that obtains at least some of its nutrients by the digestion of insects and other small animals. Carnivorous, or insectivorous, plants show remarkable structural adaptations for their mode of life. ▷Butterworts and ▷sundews trap and digest insects by means of the sticky secretions produced by glands in the leaves. The ▷Venus flytrap traps its prey between bilobed hinged leaves with marginal teeth. Another common method of capture and digestion is by means of liquid-filled "pitchers" into which the insects fall (*see* pitcher plant).

● **Carnot, (Nicolas Léonard) Sadi** ► (1796–1832) French scientist and soldier, whose investigations of the efficiency of steam engines led him to the concept of ideal reversible cycles, a fundamental idea in the study of ▷thermodynamics. His *Réflexions sur la puissance motrice du feu* (1824) describes what are now known as the ▷Carnot cycle and Carnot's theorem (no engine can be more efficient than a reversible engine working between the same temperatures). His father **Lazare Nicolas Marguerite Carnot** (1753–1823) was a statesman and military engineer, known as the "organizer of victory" in the French Revolutionary Wars. He was a member of the Legislative Assembly (1791), the National Convention (1792), and the Committee of ▷Public Safety. Carnot was exiled in 1815 and settled in Magdeburg. His *De la défense de places fortes* (1810) became a classic work on fortifications.

● **Carnot cycle** ► A reversible thermodynamic cycle of changes of pressure and ▷temperature in the gas in an ideal heat engine. The gas is compressed adiabatically (at constant heat content), thus raising its temperature, say from T_1 to T_2. It is then expanded isothermally (at constant temperature). The gas is then expanded adiabatically, lowering its temperature from T_2 back to T_1, and finally compressed isothermally at T_1, thus completing the cycle. The efficiency of this cycle depends not on the nature of the gas but only on the temperature range, i.e. it is equal to $(T_1 - T_2)/T_1$, where T_1 and T_2 are thermodynamic temperatures. Named after Sadi ▷Carnot.

● **Caro, Sir Anthony (Alfred)** ▶ (1924–) British metal sculptor. A former assistant to Henry ▷Moore, he developed his distinctive style of abstract sculpture using industrial metals in the early 1960s. He was knighted in 1987 and appointed to the OM in 2000. With Norman ▷Foster and others he designed the Millennium footbridge, London (2000).

● **Caro, Joseph** ▶ (1488–1575) Jewish legal scholar and mystic. A refugee from Spain (1492), he settled in Safed (Galilee), an important centre of the ▷kabbalah. His most enduring work is the legal code *Shulhan Arukh* (*The Prepared Table*; 1564–65), which is still regarded as authoritative by orthodox Jews.

● **carob** ▶ The horn-shaped edible fruit pod of the carob tree, *Ceratonia siliqua*, an evergreen native to the Mediterranean region. The pods, sometimes known as algaroba or St John's bread, contain a sugary pulp and are used for fodder. The seeds are believed to have been the original carats of jewellers. Carob is also widely used as a substitute for chocolate. Family: ▷*Leguminosae*.

● **carol** ▶ A song of a joyful nature, originally accompanied by dancing. During the middle ages the word was applied to a variety of different types of song. Generally written in a simple verse-plus-refrain form, carols became associated with Christmas or Easter, but often had roots in pre-Christian beliefs. The first printed carol was the *Boar's Head Carol* (1521), one of many associated with the feast of the winter solstice. Others derive from miracle and mystery plays; the few that survive in manuscripts of the 15th century celebrate the events of the first Christmas. Many of the best-known Christmas carols were written in the late 18th century.

● **Carol I** ▶ (1839–1914) The first King of Romania (1881–1914). Elected to the Romanian princedom in 1866, he became king when Romania gained independence from the Ottoman Empire. He introduced reforms and exploited Romania's oilfields but his economic programme did not help the peasants, who rebelled in 1907.

● **Carol II** ▶ (1893–1953) King of Romania (1930–40). In 1925 Carol renounced his right of succession to the throne to live in Paris with his mistress Magda Lupescu and his son ▷Michael succeeded in 1927. Carol returned to Romania in 1930 and was proclaimed king but was forced to abdicate in 1940 by the pro-German ▷Antonescu. He settled finally in Mexico, where in 1947 he married Mme Lupescu.

● **Carolina** ▷*See* North Carolina; South Carolina.

● **Caroline Islands** ▶ An archipelago in the W Pacific Ocean, consisting of ▷Belau and the Federated States of ▷Micronesia. Spain claimed the islands in 1899 but sold them to Germany. They were controlled by Japan (1914–44) and the USA (1944–47) before becoming part of the UN Trust Territory of the ▷Pacific Islands. Tourism is important and copra is the main export. Area: 1183 sq km (457 sq mi). Population (1991 est): 115 208.

● **Caroline of Ansbach** ▶ (1683–1737) The wife of George II of Great Britain and a strong supporter of Sir Robert ▷Walpole. She was appointed regent during George's absences abroad.

● **Caroline of Brunswick** ▶ (1768–1821) The wife of George IV of the United Kingdom. After their separation (1796), he forbade her to see their child Charlotte. When George became king (1820), his attempt to divorce Caroline failed owing to popular support for her but she was excluded from the coronation (1821).

● **Carolingians** ▶ The second Frankish ruling dynasty. It was founded by ▷Pepin the Short, who deposed the last ▷Merovingian king in 751, and it was named after Pepin's son ▷Charlemagne, who greatly expanded the Frankish territories. Crowned Emperor of the West in 800 by Pope Leo III, Charlemagne and his son ▷Louis the Pious were great patrons of learning and art, fostering the Carolingian renaissance (*see* Alcuin; Einhard). **Carolingian art** consists of characteristic architecture (the Palatine Chapel in Aachen,

built 792–805, survives), sculpture (only small works survive), metalwork, and illuminated manuscripts. After the death of Louis the Carolingian empire was split into three kingdoms (843). The middle Frankish kingdom was divided into Italy, Lotharingia (Lorraine), and Provence; in the eastern Frankish kingdom (Germany) the dynasty survived until 911; and the western Frankish kingdom (France) was ruled by Carolingians until the failure of the line in 987.

● **Carossa, Hans** ▶ (1878–1956) German novelist. A practising doctor, he was influenced by Goethe's scientific theories as well as his literary works. Among his best-known novels are the autobiographical sequence *Eine Kindheit* (1922), *Rumänisches Tagebuch* (1924), and *Verwandlungen einer Jugend* (1928) and the anti-Nazi *Ungleiche Welten* (1951).

● **carotenoids** ▶ A group of yellow, orange, or red pigments manufactured by bacteria, fungi, and plants and essential in the diet of animals. There are two groups—carotenes (including beta-carotene, a precursor of ▷vitamin A) and xanthophylls. Carotenoid pigments are important for display and camouflage colouring in both plants and animals and also as eye pigments.

● **carp** ▶ An omnivorous freshwater fish, *Cyprinus carpio*, native to Asia but widely introduced elsewhere and raised for food. It has an elongated body, usually about 35 cm long, with large scales, greenish or brownish above and paler below, four barbels on the upper lip, and a long dorsal fin. It hibernates in the bottom mud. Related fish include the Crucian carp and golden carp (*see* goldfish). Family: *Cyprinidae* (about 2000 species); order: *Cypriniformes*.

● **Carpaccio, Vittore** ▶ (c. 1460–c. 1525) Venetian painter, noted for his paintings of his native city and his narrative cycles. His works, influenced by Gentile and Giovanni ▷Bellini, include a cycle of *Scenes from the Life of St Ursula* and *The Miracle of the Cross* (Accademia, Venice).

● **Carpathian Mountains** ▶ A mountain range in Slovakia, Poland, Hungary, Ukraine, Moldova, and Romania. They form a rough semicircle about 1450 km (900 mi) long (including the Transylvanian Alps, also known as the **Southern Carpathians**) between Bratislava and the Iron Gate, both on the River Danube. The highest peak is Mount Gerlachovka, at 2663 m (8737 ft), in N Slovakia.

● **carpel** ▶ The female organ of a flower, consisting of the stigma, style, and ovary (⁰plant). After fertilization, each carpel may ripen to produce a fruit containing one or more seeds. ▷*See also* pistil.

● **Carpentaria, Gulf of** ▶ A shallow inlet of the Arafura Sea, in N Australia situated between Arnhem Land and Cape York Peninsula. It contains many islands, including ▷Groote Eylandt and Wellesley. There are important bauxite and manganese deposits. Area: about 287 500 sq km (110 000 sq mi).

● **carpenter bee** ▶ A large black solitary ▷bee belonging to the European genus *Xylocopa*. *X. violacea* (25 mm long) excavates galleries in

Caroline of Brunswick ▶ Her eccentric behaviour on the continent, after her separation from George IV, led to an enquiry by the Privy Council (1806) into her private life. No charges against her were made, however.

wood or large plant stems to make its nest. The lesser carpenter bees (genus *Ceratina*) are found mainly in Africa. Family: *Apidae*.

● **Carpentier, Georges** ▶ (1894–1975) French boxer, who was world light-heavyweight champion from 1920 to 1922. His unsuccessful fight against Jack ▷Dempsey (1921) drew the first million-dollar gate. He also fought at several other weights.

Ghiordes

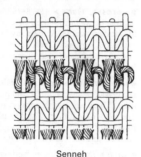
Senneh

carpet ▶ The two varieties of knot used in oriental handknotted carpets are the Ghiordes (Turkish) and Senneh (Persian) knots.

● **carpet** ▶ A floor covering of fabric. Although tapestries were sometimes used as floor coverings in the middle ages, knotted carpets originated in Asia and date back to about the 3rd century BC. They are woven with tufts of wool, or sometimes silk, knotted round the warp threads as the carpet is woven or round a jute or hessian backing to form a pile. Oriental carpets traditionally have symbolic designs and colours, which distinguish them as Persian, Turkish, Indian, etc. From the 12th century onwards, these designs have been used and adapted by European carpet manufacturers, the Savonnier carpets of 17th-century France being a typical example. Modern machine-made carpets, such as Wilton, have the pile formed by cut loops instead of knots, while Brussels carpet has uncut loops. In the type of carpet now called "tufted" the tufts are held in place by a foam-rubber backing. Synthetic fibre is replacing wool, especially for fitted carpet, which is made in rolls instead of the traditional squares or rectangles and cut to meet individual requirements.

● **carpetbaggers** ▶ Northern profiteers during the ▷Reconstruction of the South (1865–77) after the US Civil War, who often carried their possessions in a heavy cloth satchel (carpetbag). By manipulating the uneducated newly enfranchised Black voters, the carpetbaggers helped the Republicans gain local and state control. A few carpetbaggers, however, were sincere advocates of equal rights for Blacks.

● **carpet beetle** ▶ A small oval beetle, up to 10 mm long, belonging to a genus (*Anthrenus*) of worldwide pests. It is the hairy red-brown or golden-brown larvae that cause the damage, by feeding on virtually all materials of animal origin, especially furs and fabrics. *A. musaeorum* is a major pest of museum collections. Family: *Dermestidae*.

● **Carpini, Giovanni da Pian del** ▶ (c. 1180–c. 1252) Italian traveller in Mongolia. A Franciscan friar, at Pope Innocent IV's behest he led a remarkable mission to the Mongols, whose incursions into Christian lands were causing alarm. He departed from Lyon in 1245, reached Karakoram, where he was presented to the khan, in 1246, and then made the return trip largely in winter (1246–47).

● **Carr, Robert** ▷*See* Somerset, Robert Carr, Earl of.

● **Carracci** ▶ A family of Bolognese painters, who were instrumental in reviving the Renaissance art of Raphael, Titian, and Correggio after the heyday of ▷mannerism. They founded an influential teaching academy (1582) and collaborated on decorations for Bolognese palaces. **Ludovico Carracci** (1555–1619) devoted his life to art instruction and painting altarpieces. His cousin **Agostino Carracci** (1557–1602) was a noted engraver and assisted his brother **Annibale Carracci** (1560–1609), the most famous of the three, on decorations in the gallery of the Farnese Palace, Rome.

● **carrageen** ▶ (or carageen) An edible brownish-red ▷seaweed,

Chondrus crispus, also called Irish or sea moss, that grows abundantly on rocky coasts of W Britain and Ireland, N Europe, and North America. A red alga, it has thin, usually flat, branching fronds, about 5–30 cm long, and contains a gelatinous substance (carrageenin) used in jellies, lotions, cosmetics, food products, shoe polishes, etc.

● **Carrantuohill** ▶ 52 00N 9 45W The highest mountain in Ireland, in Co Kerry, in Macgillicuddy's Reeks. Height: 1041 m (3414 ft).

● **Carranza, Venustiano** ▶ (1859–1920) Mexican statesman and soldier in the post-1910 revolutionary movement. He was the first president (1917–20) under the 1917 constitution and his nationalist policies brought him into conflict with the USA. He was deposed and killed in a coup in 1920.

● **Carrara** ▶ 44 04N 10 06E A town in central Italy, in Tuscany. It is famous for its white marble, which was used by the sculptor Michelangelo. Population (1990): 68 480.

● **Carrel, Alexis** ▶ (1873–1944) French surgeon, who pioneered the technique for sewing (suturing) blood vessels together. He perfected this after moving to the USA, where he also worked on techniques for keeping organs alive outside the body. He was awarded a Nobel Prize (1912).

● **Carreras, José** ▶ (1946–) Spanish tenor. He made his operatic debut in his native Barcelona in 1970 and has since appeared in opera houses throughout the world, mainly in productions of Verdi, Puccini, and Donizetti. In the 1990s he found a huge international audience for his performances with the tenors Placido ▷Domingo and Luciano ▷Pavarotti.

● **Carrhae, Battle of** ▶ (53 BC) The battle near Carrhae (now Haran, Turkey) in which the Roman forces under Marcus Licinius ▷Crassus were defeated by the Parthians.

● **Carrickfergus** ▶ **1.** 54 43N 5 49W A town in E Northern Ireland, in Co Antrim; sited on Belfast Lough, it has an impressive Norman castle. It is a fishing port with a textile industry. Population (1991): 22 885. **2.** A district in E Northern Ireland, in Co Antrim. Area: 85 sq km (33 sq mi). Population (1991): 32 750.

● **carrion crow** ▶ An omnivorous Eurasian crow, *Corvus corone corone*, about 46 cm long with a pure-black plumage and a harsh croaking call. It is a notorious egg thief, unpopular with gamekeepers. ▷*See also* hooded crow.

● **carrion flower** ▶ A cactus-like succulent plant belonging to the genus *Stapelia* (60 species), native to arid parts of Africa. Several are grown for their showy purplish flowers, although they have a foetid odour. *S. gigantea* has a leafless square stem, 5–30 cm high, bearing a flower with a diameter of 30 cm. Family: *Asclepiadaceae*.

The name is also given to a species of ▷greenbrier, *Smilax herbacea*, which has small green evil-smelling flowers.

● **Carroll, Lewis** ▶ (Charles Lutwidge Dodgson; 1832–98) British writer and mathematician. He lectured in mathematics at Oxford

Lewis Carroll ▶ A page from his original manuscript for *Alice in Wonderland* (British Museum).

University from 1855 to 1881, and took holy orders in 1861 but never held a benefice. The children's classic, *Alice's Adventures in Wonderland* (1865), was written for the young Alice Liddell, the daughter of the head of his Oxford College. It and the sequel, *Through the Looking-Glass* (1872), are sophisticated books that combine elements of fantasy, logic, and nonsense and have had a lasting appeal to adults as well as children. He also wrote nonsense verse, notably *The Hunting of the Snark* (1876), and was a pioneer of portrait photography.

● **carrot** ▶ A biennial flowering plant, *Daucus carota*, found in grassy places in temperate regions from Europe to India. The stem grows to a height of 30–100 cm and bears a head of small white flowers. *Daucus carota sativus* is the cultivated carrot. This is grown as an annual in many varieties, and produces an orange thick fleshy edible root. Family: ▷*Umbelliferae*.

● **Carson, Edward Henry, Baron** ▶ (1854–1935) Irish politician and barrister at both the Irish and English bars; solicitor general for Ireland (1892) and England (1900–06). In 1895 Carson successfully defended Lord Queensberry in the Oscar ▷Wilde libel case. As an MP in the English parliament (1892–1921), he led opposition to the Irish ▷Home Rule bill (1912) and raised the Ulster Volunteers to oppose its enactment. In World War I he served in Asquith's and Lloyd George's cabinets.

● **Carson, Kit** ▶ (Christopher C.; 1809–68) US frontiersman. A saddler in Missouri, stationed on the Santa Fe trail, he joined a wagon train in 1826 and made Taos, New Mexico, his headquarters for a career as a guide. Well-versed in Indian ways, he was a guide in ▷Frémont's expeditions to the West in the 1840s and after distinguished service in the Mexican War became US Indian agent at Taos (1853). He subsequently fought for the Federals in the Civil War. Illiterate, Carson dictated his memoirs (1856), published as *Dear Old Kit* (1968).

● **Carson, Rachel Louise** ▶ (1907–64) US science writer, who worked as a genetic biologist (1936–52) and later as editor for the US Fish and Wildlife Service. Her books, notably *The Sea around Us* (1951) and *Silent Spring* (1962), greatly increased public awareness of the natural environment and warned of the dangers of pollution.

● **Carson City** ▶ 39 10N 119 46W A city in the USA, the capital of Nevada. It is named after the famous frontiersman Kit Carson. Although silver and copper are mined, the main industry is gambling. Population (1996 est): 86 516.

● **Cartagena** ▶ 10 24N 75 33W A port in N Colombia, on the Caribbean Sea. It is important industrially, producing textiles, petrochemicals, and pharmaceuticals. It receives oil by pipeline from Berrancabermeja; exports include coffee and oil. The University of Cartagena was founded in 1827. Population (1997 est): 812 595.

● **Cartagena** ▶ (*or* Carthagena) 37 36N 0 59W A port in SE Spain, in Murcia on the Mediterranean Sea. Founded by the Carthaginian general, Hasdrubal, in the 3rd century BC, it was destroyed by Ferdinand II of Castile in 1243. In the 16th century, under Philip II of Spain, it became a great naval port and remains the country's chief Mediterranean naval base. It exports minerals, olive oil, and fruits and has boatbuilding industries. Population (1995 est): 180 553.

● **Cartago** ▶ 9 50N 83 52W A town in central Costa Rica, at the foot of the volcano Irazú. It serves an agricultural area. Population (latest est): 23 928.

● **Carte, Richard D'Oyly** ▷*See* D'Oyly Carte, Richard.

● **cartel** ▶ An association of producers who join together to secure a higher price for their products by restricting the supply. However, a cartel is inherently unstable; all the members have an interest in producing as much as they can at the new price, in defiance of the cartel agreement. The need to enrol all producers and to maintain strict discipline explains why the highly successful oil cartel OPEC has not been followed by other primary-product cartels. A successful cartel is, however, usually regarded as being against the public interest as it maintains prices at an artificially high level by excluding the laws of supply and demand. In some countries, therefore, cartels are illegal.

● **Carter, Angela** ▶ (1940–92) British writer. Her works, which blend fantasy, satire, and macabre humour, are much preoccupied with society's attitude to female sexuality. They include the novels *The Magic Toyshop* (1967), *The Infernal Desire Machine of Dr Hoffman* (1972), *Nights at the Circus* (1984), and *Wise Children* (1991), as well as short stories, collections of her journalism, and scripts for radio and the cinema.

● **Carter, Elliott (Cook)** ▶ (1908–) US composer. He studied with Walter Piston (1894–1976) at Harvard and Nadia Boulanger in Paris. Since 1950 he has evolved a contrapuntal style of great rhythmical complexity. His works include a *Double Concerto* (for piano, harpsichord, and two chamber orchestras; 1961) and *Symphony for Three Orchestras* (1978).

● **Carter, Howard** ▶ (1874–1939) British archaeologist. Carter worked in Egypt from 1892 and collaborated with Lord Carnarvon (1866–1923) after 1907. In 1922 they discovered the tomb of ▷Tutankhamen, work on which occupied Carter for the next ten years.

● **Carter, Jimmy** ▶ (James Earl C.; 1924–) US statesman; Democratic president (1977–81). Carter left his family peanut farming and warehousing business in Georgia for politics. He was governor of Georgia from 1970 to 1974 and in his presidential campaign promised ambitious social and economic reforms. He signed a treaty giving up US control of the Panama Canal by 2000 AD, attempted unsuccessfully to limit US energy consumption, but is best known for bringing about the peace treaty between Egypt and Israel (1979). The last year of his presidency was overshadowed by his humiliating failure to achieve the release of US hostages held in Iran following the Islamic revolution there: in the 1980 presidential elections he was heavily defeated by Ronald ▷Reagan. Subsequently he won respect as an international peacebroker in Ethiopia, Korea, Haiti, and elsewhere.

● **Carteret, John** ▷*See* Granville, John Carteret, 1st Earl.

● **Cartesian coordinates** ▷*See* coordinate systems.

● **Carthage** ▶ (Punic name: *Kart-Hadasht*, New City) An ancient city of N Africa, near modern Tunis. Traditionally founded 814 BC by ▷Dido and exiles from ▷Tyre, Carthage rapidly became leader of the ▷Phoenician trading cities of N Africa, waging intermittent war with the Greeks of Marseilles and Sicily. From 264 BC Carthage fought the three ▷Punic Wars with ▷Rome, her former ally, and was totally destroyed (146 BC). Refounded by Julius ▷Caesar (45 BC), Carthage became, in turn, the commercial, cultural, and administrative capital of Roman Africa, the capital of the ▷Vandal kingdom (439–533 AD), and a Byzantine outpost, until destroyed by the Muslims in 697 AD.

● **Carthusians** ▶ A contemplative Roman Catholic religious order founded in 1084 by St Bruno and taking its name from the location of the first community, La Grande Chartreuse, near Grenoble. Although originally without a written rule, the Carthusians observed a rigorous life of fasting and solitude and were vowed to silence. The order remained fairly small but disciplined. At the time of the dissolution of the monasteries there were nine Carthusian monasteries, or ▷Charterhouses, in England. At present the order's English headquarters is the Charterhouse, Parkminster, Sussex. The French monks are noted for the liqueur Chartreuse, which they make.

● **Cartier, Jacques** ▶ (1491–1557) French navigator. In 1534, under the patronage of Francis I, he sailed in search of the ▷Northwest Passage and explored the coast of N Canada and Newfoundland. The next year he sailed up the St Lawrence as far as what became Montreal but failed to found a colony there (1536). His discoveries were important to French claims in Canada in the 17th century.

● **Cartier-Bresson, Henri** ▶ (1908–) French photographer and pioneer of photojournalism. He studied painting before taking up photography in 1932. Although also providing a record of events on his worldwide travels, his often poignant photographs, collected in such books as *The Decisive Moment* (1952) and *Europeans* (1955), concentrate on ordinary people and their fleeting expressions and gestures. As a film maker, he collaborated with Jean ▷Renoir in the late 1930s and returned to this medium in the 1960s.

● **cartilage** ▶ A flexible supportive tissue consisting chiefly of a ▷polysaccharide—chondroitin sulphate—in which elastic or collagen fibres may be embedded. Cartilage lines the bone ends at joints and also provides the skeleton of the nose, external ear, and parts of the throat (larynx) and airways of the respiratory tract. A tough cartilage forms the intervertebral discs between the bones of the spine. During development a large amount of ▷bone is formed from pre-existing cartilage.

● **cartilaginous fish** ▶ Any ▷fish belonging to the class *Chondrichthyes*, comprising the ▷sharks, ▷rays, and ▷chimaeras. They have a cartilaginous skeleton, usually a ventrally situated mouth, and exposed gill slits. The males have pelvic fins modified to form copulatory organs (claspers) and fertilization occurs inside the female's body. Some species deposit their eggs on the sea bed while in others the eggs are retained and develop internally resulting in the birth of live young.

● **Cartimandua** ▶ (1st century AD) Queen of the ▷Brigantes. She concluded a treaty with the Roman invaders in 43 AD, but was faced with internal dissention, which was quelled by the Romans. In 51 AD she betrayed ▷Caratacus, the leader of British resistance, to the Romans to ensure their support. When her husband Venutius attempted to overthrow her (57 AD), the Romans put down his rebellion. Thereafter Cartimandua and Venutius were reconciled and ruled jointly until 69, when she left him for another man. In 71 the Romans defeated Venutius and annexed their territory.

● **Cartland, Dame Barbara** ▶ (1901–2000) British author of popular romantic fiction. Her prolific output (she wrote over 700 books) also included biography, memoirs, and books on health subjects. She was appointed DBE in 1991.

● **cartography** ▶ The science of map and chart making. Belief in the flatness of the world, the centrality of the Mediterranean lands (or Jerusalem in Christian maps), and an all-encircling Ocean dominated classical and medieval cartography. Maps and charts were individually hand drawn at first, but 15th- and 16th-century maps were printed by woodblock and coloured by hand. More elaborate maps and charts, richly decorated with lettering and illustrations were introduced by the Italians in the mid-16th century. The difficulty of accurately representing the curved surface of the earth on the plane surface of a map is dealt with by using different □map projections for different purposes. Modern map making is assisted by aerial surveying and satellite photography. ▷*See also* digital mapping.

● **cartoon** ▶ **1.** A full-sized preparatory drawing or painting for a mural, easel painting, tapestry, or mosaic. Among the most famous are Raphael's cartoons (Victoria and Albert Museum) for tapestries for the Sistine Chapel, in the Vatican. **2.** A nonrealistic portrait or figure drawing transferring a person's most readily recognizable features into a comic likeness. Beginning in Italy as a branch of high art with ▷Leonardo da Vinci's grotesque heads and ▷Bernini's political drawings, caricatures became a favourite genre in British popular and broadsheet art with the political satires of ▷Rowlandson and ▷Gillray. This tradition was developed in the Victorian period by such artists as Phiz (*see* Browne, Hablot Knight) and ▷Cruikshank and later produced the comic strip of modern newspapers. **3.** ▷*See* animation.

● **Cartwright, Edmund** ▶ (1743–1823) British inventor and industrialist, who contributed to the mechanization of weaving and spinning. In 1785 he invented a power loom and then set up a factory in Doncaster for weaving and spinning yarn. Four years later he invented a machine for combing wool. In 1793 his business failed but parliament recognized his achievements in 1809 with an award of £10,000.

● **Caruso, Enrico** ▶ (1873–1921) Italian tenor, born in Naples. The greatest lyric tenor of his time, he excelled in Verdi and Puccini and was acclaimed in Europe and the USA, where he sang at the Metropolitan Opera, New York.

● **Carver, George Washington** ▶ (1864–1943) US agriculturalist, born into a Black slave family. Carver demonstrated to southern farmers how fertility could be restored to their land by diversification, especially by planting peanuts and sweet potatoes. He also discovered a wide range of by-products that could be obtained from these crops.

● **Cary, (Arthur) Joyce (Lunel)** ▶ (1888–1957) British novelist. His early novels, notably *Mister Johnson* (1939), are mostly set in West Africa, where he worked before settling in Oxford in 1920. His best-known book, *The Horse's Mouth* (1944), is part of a trilogy about art; he also wrote a political trilogy.

● **caryatid** ▶ A carved column in the shape of a draped female figure that first appeared in Greek architecture around 500 BC. The most notable caryatids to have survived are on the Erechtheum on the ▷Acropolis of Athens. Caryatids enjoyed a limited revival in 19th-century classicism.

● **caryopsis** ▶ A grain: the small dry ▷fruit of grasses and cereals. It resembles an achene, being single-seeded and indehiscent, but differs in having the seed completely fused to the fruit wall.

● **Casablanca** ▶ (Arabic name: Dar-el-Beida) 33 39N 7 35W A port in Morocco, on the Atlantic coast. First established by the Portuguese (1515), it was taken by the French in 1907. During World War II it was the scene of the **Casablanca Conference** (1943), a summit meeting between Franklin D. Roosevelt and Sir Winston Churchill. The largest and most important city in Morocco, its port handles most of the country's trade, the chief export being phosphates. Its major industries include textiles, electronics, chemicals, cement, and food processing. Fishing and tourism are also important. It is the site of the magnificent King Hassan II Mosque, inaugurated in 1993. Population (1994 est): 523 279.

● **Casals, Pablo** ▶ (Pau C.; 1876–1973) Spanish cellist, conductor, and composer. He performed and conducted in every European country and in the USA. Casals revolutionized the style and technique of cello playing and excelled as an interpreter of Bach's six suites for unaccompanied cello and of the cello concertos of Dvořák, Elgar, and Schumann. An opponent of the Franco regime in Spain, Casals settled in Prades in France; he established a chamber-music festival there in 1950.

● **Casanova, Giovanni Giacomo, Chevalier de Seingalt** ▶ (1725–98) Italian adventurer. He lived in many European cities, working at different times as a violinist, a spy, and a librarian. His adventures, which included a dramatic escape from prison in Venice in 1756 and many romantic liaisons, are recorded in his memoirs, of which the first complete edition was published in 1960.

● **Cascade Range** ▶ A volcanic mountain range in North America. It extends N–S, nearly parallel to the Pacific coast, between the Fraser River in British Columbia (Canada) and N California (USA), where it becomes continuous with the ▷Sierra Nevada. It reaches 4392 m (14 408 ft) at Mount Rainier.

● **case hardening** ▶ A surface-hardening process in ▷steel manufacture, in which the metal is heated to over 900°C for several hours in the presence of carbon. The carbon is absorbed on the surface to a depth depending on the temperature and duration of the treatment. The steel is then cooled quickly (quenched) to complete the process. ▷*See also* heat treatment.

● **casein** ▶ The major protein present in milk. Casein is easily digested and contains a good balance of essential ▷amino acids, making it—in dietary terms—a high-quality protein. Cheese consists largely of insoluble para-casein, formed from casein by the action of enzymes. Casein is also used industrially to make thermoplastics (e.g. knife handles), paints, and adhesives.

● **case law** ▷*See* common law.

● **Casement, Sir Roger (David)** ▶ (1864–1916) British consular official and Irish nationalist, executed by the British for treason. Casement spent his consular career in Africa, where he disclosed the atrocities suffered by native labour in the Congo. He retired to Ireland in 1912. In World War I he tried unsuccessfully to raise German help for the Irish nationalists. After returning to Ireland in a German submarine, he was arrested, tried, and hanged. His diaries, which describe his homosexuality, were privately circulated by the government at the time of his conviction in order to quell international pressure for a reprieve: following widespread allegations that they had been forged by the British, they were released in 1959. The current view is that the diaries are probably genuine.

● **Caserta** ► 41 04N 14 20E A market town in S Italy, in Campania. The centre of Garibaldi's campaigns for the unification of Italy in the 19th century, it has a 12th-century cathedral and a palace. Population (1990): 69 350.

● **cashew** ► A tree, *Anacardium occidentale*, native to tropical America and cultivated widely in the tropics. It grows to 12 m and has sweet-scented red flowers. The fruit is a kidney-shaped nut that develops at the end of a hanging pear-shaped receptacle. The edible kernel—the cashew nut—is extracted after the fruit is roasted. Family: *Anacardiaceae*.

● **cashmere** ► A warm soft wool-like fabric made from the undercoat of the Kashmir goat, produced mainly in China, Mongolia, and Iran. Originally used in shawls from Kashmir, it is an expensive fabric as each goat produces only small quantities of fine soft hair and processing is costly. Imitations are common.

● **Casimir (III) the Great** ► (1310–70) King of Poland (1333–70). Casimir extended Polish territory, codified laws, and founded Cracow University (1364). He encouraged Polish culture and bettered the lot of the peasants.

● **Casimir IV** ► (1427–92) Grand Duke of Lithuania (1440–92) and King of Poland (1447–92), whose reign saw a flowering of Polish culture. Casimir greatly enhanced the prestige of the Jagiellon dynasty by his own and his children's political marriages. After a 13-year war with the ▷Teutonic Knights he won control of W Prussia (1466).

● **Caspar** ▷*See* Magi.

● **Caspian Sea** ► The largest inland sea in the world, bounded by Iran, Russia, Azerbaidzhan, Kazakhstan, and Turkmenistan and fed chiefly by the River Volga. Its surface is 28.5 m (93.5 ft) below sea level and is becoming lower due to irrigation and increased evaporation from the Volga. The chief ports are Astrakhan in Russia and Baku in Azerbaidzhan. Sturgeon and seals are caught here and oil and gas extracted. Area: about 370 000 sq km (142 827 sq mi).

● **Cassander** ► (c. 358–297 BC) King of Macedon (305–297). In the wars of succession that followed the death of Alexander the Great in 323, Cassander fought for control of parts of Alexander's empire and won most of Macedon and Greece. He murdered Alexander's mother, widow, and son to secure his position.

● **Cassandra** ► A legendary Trojan prophetess, daughter of King Priam of Troy. After she had refused to submit to Apollo's advances, he condemned her prophecies to eternal disbelief. When Troy fell she was taken by Agamemnon, with whom she was later murdered.

● **Cassatt, Mary** ► (1844–1926) US painter. She worked chiefly in Paris, where she exhibited with the impressionists (1879–81, 1886) and was influenced by her friend ▷Degas. Typical of her work are mother-and-child scenes.

● **cassava** ► A shrubby flowering plant, *Manihot esculentus* (or *M. utilissimus*), also known as manioc, native to tropical America. Many varieties of this species—divided into two groups, sweet and bitter cassavas—are cultivated in the tropics for their edible starchy tuberous roots. These can be processed into tapioca, ground to produce manioc or cassava meal (Brazilian arrowroot), used as animal fodder, or cooked and eaten as a vegetable. Family: *Euphorbiaceae* (spurge family).

● **cassette** ► A plastic case containing a length of magnetic sound recording tape wound onto two spools. Cassettes are easy to use but can hold only relatively short tapes, their length being limited by the minimum thickness of tape that can be used without breakage. Commercial cassettes are two-track, i.e. can be used to record in both directions, and are available with 30, 60, 90, or 120 minutes' playing time.

● **cassia** ► The aromatic bark of a Chinese tree, *Cinnamomum cassia*, used as a substitute for cinnamon. The dried unripe fruits (cassia buds) are also used as a spice. Family: *Lauraceae*.

● **Cassia** ► A genus of trees, shrubs, and herbs (500–600 species) of tropical and warm regions of Asia, Africa, and America. The laxative drug senna is extracted from the dried leaves and pods (fruits) of many cultivated species. The fruit of *C. fistula* (cassia pods or purging

cassia) is also a laxative. Some species are grown as ornamentals. Family: ▷*Leguminosae*.

● **Cassino** ► 41 29N 13 50E A town in central Italy, in Lazio. It was a key position during World War II and the town and Benedictine monastery (Monte Cassino) were destroyed in the fighting of 1944. Both the abbey and the town were rebuilt after the war, the latter on a wholly new plan. Population (1990): 34 590.

● **Cassiodorus, Flavius Magnus Aurelius** ► (c. 490–c. 583 AD) Christian writer, born in S Italy, who helped to preserve classical learning. After serving in the government of the Ostrogothic king, Theodoric I, Cassiodorus retired to found a monastery at Vivarium in Calabria (550); his most famous work, the *Institutiones*, was a guide to the education of monks.

● **Cassiopeia** ► A conspicuous constellation in the northern sky, lying partly in the Milky Way. The five brightest stars form a W-shape. It contains the remnants of two recent ▷supernovae—**Tycho's star** and the intense radio source **Cassiopeia A**. It is named after Cassiopeia, the mother of ▷Andromeda.

● **cassiopeium** ▷*See* lutetium.

● **Cassirer, Ernst** ► (1874–1945) German philosopher and historian. He taught in Hamburg (1919–34) until Nazism forced him into exile in the USA. Interested in people's formation of concepts, he added mythical, historical, and practical categories, based on analysis of language, to ▷Kant's scientific ones, seeing these as complementary views of one reality. His works include *Substance and Function* (1910) and *Philosophy of Symbolic Forms* (1923).

● **cassiterite** ► The only commercial ore of tin, consisting of stannic oxide. It is found in association with acid igneous rocks and as alluvial deposits. It is brown or black.

● **Cassius Longinus, Gaius** ► (d. 42 BC) Roman general. Having shown competence in eastern campaigns, Cassius supported ▷Pompey until Pompey's defeat by Julius Caesar at ▷Pharsalus. He was then pardoned by Caesar but joined the conspiracy to assassinate him in 44. Outlawed, Cassius committed suicide after defeat in the battle of ▷Philippi.

● **Cassivelaunus** ► King of the ▷Catuvellauni, who organized, with some success, resistance to Caesar's invasion of SE Britain in 54 BC. Only after his stronghold was captured did Cassivelaunus agree peace terms.

● **Casson, Sir Hugh (Maxwell)** ► (1910–99) British architect. A planning adviser to many war-damaged areas in England after World War II, he was director of architecture for the Festival of Britain (1951). His books include *Victorian Architecture* (1948) and several volumes of his watercolours and drawings. He was professor at the Royal College of Art (1953–75) and president of the Royal Academy of Arts (1976–84).

● **cassowary** ► A large flightless bird belonging to a family (*Casuariidae*; 3 species) occurring in rain forests of Australia and New Guinea. The largest cassowary (*Casuarius casuarius*) is 150 cm tall and has a black plumage, two red throat wattles, and a blue head with a protective bony helmet. Cassowaries have long powerful legs, each having a long sharp claw, and feed on seeds and berries. Order: *Casuariiformes*.

● **Castagno, Andrea del** ► (Andrea di Bartolo de Simone; c. 1421–57) Italian ▷Renaissance painter, who was born near Castagno but settled in Florence. His major frescoes depict the *Last Supper* and the *Passion* (Sta Apollonia, Florence). Later works, showing the influence of ▷Donatello, include the equestrian portrait of *Niccolò da Tolentino* (Duomo, Florence).

● **castanets** ► A percussion instrument used in Spain and Italy, consisting of two small cup-shaped pieces of wood (usually chestnut) attached to the finger and thumb of each hand. These are clapped together and dancers often accompany themselves with them. In the symphony orchestra the characteristic sound is produced by two wooden cups attached to a handle and shaken. □musical instruments.

● **Castel Gandolfo** ► (Latin name: Alba Longa) 41 45N 12 39E A village in central Italy, in Lazio on the shore of Lake Albano. The summer residence of the pope is situated here.

● **Castellammare di Stabia** ► 38 01N 12 52E A seaport and resort in Italy, in Campania on the Bay of Naples. It was the site of the Roman resort of Stabiae, which was destroyed by the eruption of Vesuvius in 79 AD. Industries include marine engineering and textiles. Population (1993 est): 67 974.

● **Castellón de la Plana** ► 39 59N 0 03W A city in E Spain. Its industries include textiles and paper and it exports oranges and almonds through its port, El Gráo. Population (1998 est): 137 741.

● **Castelo Branco, Camilo** ► (1825–95) Portuguese novelist. An illegitimate child with little formal education, he led an adventurous life that is reflected in his many popular novels and stories. His best-known work, *Amor de Perdição* (1862), was written while he was in prison for adultery. Suffering from blindness, he committed suicide.

● **castes** ► The elements of a system of social stratification in which social boundaries are very definite. A pure caste system consists of a hierarchy of hereditary endogamous occupational groups, in which positions are fixed and mobility from one caste to another is prevented by ritual systems. The classical Hindu caste system (Sanskrit word: varna) of India provides the cardinal example. Traditionally there are four main caste divisions: brahmins (priests), ksatriyas (warriors), vaisyas (merchants), and sundras (serfs). Outside these groups are the "outcastes" or "untouchables". Each stratum is elaborately subdivided; the 1901 census identified 2378 main castes, some of which had several hundred subcastes. Vigorous attempts have been made to abolish the system, especially by Mahatma Gandhi, but despite legislation (1947) abolishing "untouchability" and prohibiting discrimination on the basis of caste, prejudice remains strong. In 1997 India elected its first "untouchable" president, K. R. Narayanan.

● **Castiglione, Baldassare** ► (1478–1529) Italian courtier and writer. A member of an aristocratic family, he was born near Mantua and in 1503 entered the service of the Duke of Urbino, whose court was one of the most distinguished in Renaissance Italy. He performed important diplomatic missions for the Duke; he was later Mantuan ambassador in Rome and after 1524 in the service of Pope Clement VII as papal nuncio in Spain. His literary reputation rests on *Il Cortegiano* (1528), prose dialogues, set in the court of Urbino, which describe the qualities of the ideal courtier. The work was translated into English as *The Courtier* by Sir Thomas Hoby (1530–66) in 1561 and exercised a great influence on such writers as Surrey, Wyatt, and Sidney.

● **Castile** ► A former kingdom in central Spain. Originally a district at the foot of the Cantabrian Mountains, Castile expanded to the River Duero in the 9th and 10th centuries, becoming a united country. In 1035 it became a kingdom and in 1230 was united with the kingdom of ▷León, a union dominated by Castile. In 1479 Spain was virtually united following the marriage of ▷Isabella the Catholic to ▷Ferdinand the Catholic and Castile became the political, adminis-

trative, cultural, and linguistic centre of Spain. Today, opposition to Castilian dominance persists.

● **Castilho, Antonio Feliciano de** ► (1800–75) Portuguese poet. Blind from childhood, he achieved literary distinction after publishing several volumes of romantic poetry, notably *A Noite de Castelo* (1836). After 1840 he worked mainly on translations, and his advocacy of neoclassical doctrines provoked fierce controversy.

● **casting metals** ► The process of shaping molten metals in a mould. In casting individual items a sand mould is often used. A solid pattern of the shape, made of wood, plastic, or metal, is placed in a moulding box packed tightly with sand and bonded with oil or clay. The pattern is then carefully removed leaving a shaped cavity into which the molten metal is poured and allowed to solidify. If the casting is to be repeated, permanent metal moulds called dies are used. **Die casting** is faster and can make more complex shapes than foundry sand casting. **Centrifugal casting**, spinning the molten material at a high speed so that the centrifugal force flings it outwards into a surrounding mould, is used for pipes and similar shapes.

● **cast iron** ► A form of impure iron containing between 2.5% and 4.5% of carbon by weight. The high carbon content makes it relatively hard and brittle and it tends to crack under tension. Cast iron is made by casting ▷pig iron and adjusting its composition to improve the strength. It is used for complicated shapes.

● **castle** ► A fortified defensive building. Its name deriving from Latin *castellum*, a small fortified place, the castle underwent many changes in its history to counteract the development of increasingly powerful weapons. In the early middle ages a castle consisted of a simple building on a mound of earth surrounded by a wooden fence (the motte and bailey castle), a design later copied in stone. The simplest stone castle, such as the White Tower in London, is called a keep or donjon. Later designs became more complicated, involving extensive outworks of battlemented towers and walls (curtain walls), for example Caernarfon Castle in Wales. As they could not be built to withstand cannon fire castles lost their military usefulness; some, such as Windsor Castle, were converted into large houses. ▷*See also* chateau.

● **Castle, Barbara, Baroness** ► (1910–2002) British Labour politician. An outspoken socialist, she was first elected to parliament in 1945. Under Harold Wilson she served in several cabinet posts, including minister of transport (1965–68) and secretary of state for employment (1968–70). In the first position she introduced the ▷breathalyzer to curb drunken driving and in the second she unsuccessfully attempted to legislate for trade union reform. Following her departure from the cabinet in 1976, she became a member of the European Parliament (1979–86). Her publications include two volumes of diaries (1980, 1984).

● **Castleford** ► 43 44N 1 21W A town in N England, in Wakefield unitary authority, West Yorkshire, on the River Aire. Traditionally a coalmining town, it also produces glass, chemicals, and earthenware. Population (1991): 38 536.

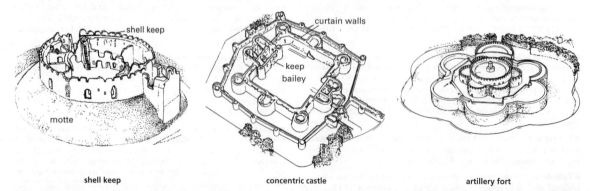

shell keep   concentric castle   artillery fort

castle ► The early medieval shell keep gave way to the massive fortifications of the 14th and 15th centuries, which were in turn superseded by the artillery fort with its low walls and sweeping lines of fire.

● **Castle Hill Rising** ► (1804) A rising in New South Wales (Australia) led by Irish convicts. The rebels seized the convict station at Parramatta but were defeated by government troops, who killed 15 convicts. Nine rebels were tried and hanged.

● **Castlemaine** ► 37 05S 144 19E A town in Australia, in central Victoria. It is the site of one of the oldest gold diggings in the country. Population (1986): 6603.

● **Castlereagh** ► A district of E Northern Ireland, in Co Down. Area: 84 sq km (32 sq mi). Population (1991): 60 799.

● **Castlereagh, Robert Stewart, Viscount** ► (1769–1822) British statesman, born in Ulster; foreign secretary (1812–22). An MP in the Irish parliament (1790), he became Viscount Castlereagh in 1796, when his father Robert Stewart (1739–1821) became 1st Marquess of Londonderry. Appointed chief secretary for Ireland in 1798, he resigned in 1801, when George III rejected Catholic Emancipation. His policies as secretary for war (1807–09) were attacked by Canning, with whom Castlereagh fought a duel. As foreign secretary he played an important role at the Congress of ▷Vienna (1814–15) and at subsequent congresses of European powers. He later opposed Metternich's interference in the internal affairs of other states. He was unfairly blamed for the reactionary policies of Lord Liverpool's government and his unpopularity was exacerbated by his austere personality. There was rejoicing in the streets of London after he committed suicide, believing himself to be being blackmailed for homosexual acts.

● **Castner process** ► The production of sodium cyanide from molten sodium, charcoal, and ammonia. Sodamide and sodium cyanamide are by-products. The extremely poisonous sodium cyanide finds use in the extraction of gold and silver, in hardening steel, and in dye manufacture. Named after Hamilton Young Castner (1859–99).

● **Castor** ► A white star, apparent magnitude 1.56 and 46 light years distant, that is the second brightest star in the constellation Gemini. It is a ▷multiple star. Castor and ▷Pollux are named after the twins of classical mythology.

● **Castor and Pollux** ► Twin heroes of classical mythology, also known as the Dioscuri. Pollux was immortal, the son of ▷Zeus and ▷Leda; Castor was mortal, the son of Tyndareus and Leda. When Castor died, Pollux asked Zeus to allow them to remain unseparated. Transformed into the Gemini constellation, they were the patrons of mariners.

● **castor oil** ► A pale yellow viscous oil extracted from the seeds of the ▷castor-oil plant. It is used as a laxative and is also a raw material for the manufacture of resins, plastics, and lubricants.

● **castor-oil plant** ► A flowering plant, *Ricinus communis*, up to 12 m high, native to tropical Africa and Asia. It is cultivated widely, in the tropics for its seeds, from which castor oil is extracted, and in temperate regions as an ornamental shrub (seldom taller than 2 m). Family: *Euphorbiaceae* (spurge family).

● **castration** ► Removal of the testes (orchidectomy) or ovaries (oophorectomy). In medicine, castration may be performed in cases of cancer of the testes: it always produces sterility but—unless done before puberty—need not cause impotence. Testicular castration is widely used in livestock management to increase meat production or docility. ▷See also eunuch.

● **castrato** ► A ▷eunuch singer, fashionable in Italian opera and in church choirs during the 17th and 18th centuries. Castration before puberty (a practice ended in 1878 by Leo XIII) ensured that the soprano (or sometimes alto) voice quality remained in adulthood. Among the most technically brilliant of the castrati was Giuseppe Farinelli (1705–1782). Composers of Italian opera, such as Handel, frequently wrote the leading male role in the soprano range for a eunuch.

● **Castres** ► 43 36N 2 14E A town in S France, in the Tarn department. A Huguenot stronghold in the 16th century, it has a major machine-tool industry. Population (latest est): 46 877.

● **Castries** ► 14 01N 60 59W The chief town and main port of St Lucia, in the Windward Islands. Founded by the French in 1650, it has a fine harbour. Population (1992 est): 13 615.

Fidel Castro ► A postcard from the Soviet Union.

● **Castro (Ruz), Fidel** ► (1926–) Cuban statesman; president (1976–). The son of a wealthy sugar planter, Castro became an opponent of the dictator Fulgencio ▷Batista. On 26 July, 1953, he led an unsuccessful attack on the Moncada barracks and was imprisoned until 1955. In 1956 he invaded Cuba from Mexico with a small armed band and after a long guerrilla war he defeated government troops. He entered Havana on 1 January, 1959. Castro established a socialist government, which the USA attempted to subvert (see Bay of Pigs) and continues to ostracize economically. As a result, Cuba became heavily dependent on the Soviet Union. During the 1970s Castro's defiance of the USA made him an admired and influential figure in much of the developing world. However, with the collapse of the Soviet Union, Cuba has faced serious economic problems and Castro has come to seem an increasingly isolated and outdated figure.

● **Castrop-Rauxel** ► 51 33N 07 18E A town in W Germany, in North Rhine-Westphalia in the ▷Ruhr. Its industries include coalmining and chemicals. Population (1989 est): 80 000.

● **Casuarina** ► A genus of shrubs and trees (about 45 species) native to Australia, tropical SE Asia, Malaysia, Polynesia, the Mascarene Islands, and Pacific islands. The young branches, which are slender, green, and drooping, function as leaves (the true leaves are reduced to scales). The she oak (*C. equisetifolia*), up to 45 m tall, is widely cultivated in warm regions for its very hard reddish-brown wood (beefwood or ironwood) and as an ornamental. Family: *Casuarinaceae*.

● **cat** ► A carnivorous mammal belonging to the family *Felidae* (36 species). Most cats have sheathed claws and sharp canine teeth to kill their prey, which consists of mammals, birds, and fish. Their acute vision (especially in poor light), sense of smell, and hearing are adaptations for hunting stealthily, often at night. With no natural enemies, the kittens (or cubs) are born blind and toothless and learn hunting techniques through play.

The wide range of different breeds of domestic cat (*Felis catus*), including ▷Persian, ▷Siamese, and ▷Abyssinian, are thought to have been developed from the African ▷wildcat, or cafer cat and possibly the European wildcat. Wild species range in size from the ▷tiger to the tiny South African black-footed cat (*F. nigripes*), which is smaller than the average domestic cat.

● **catabolism** ▷See metabolism.

● **catacombs** ► Subterranean cemeteries, especially those containing early Christian graves. The earliest and biggest catacombs are in Rome, particularly those of St Calixtus and St Sebastian along the ▷Appian Way. Most catacombs consist of narrow passages into the walls of which the burial niches were cut. With the acceptance of Christianity they fell into disuse, although some remained as centres of pilgrimage.

● **Catalan** ► A ▷Romance language spoken by about five million people in Catalonia and the Balearic Islands in Spain, Andorra, and the Roussillon region of France. It is closely related to Spanish and to the Occitan language of France. It was the official language of Aragon in the 12th century and has a literature dating from this period.

● **Catalaunian Plains, Battle of the** ▶ (451 AD) The battle on the Catalaunian Plains, probably near modern Châlons-sur-Marne in Champagne (E France), in which the Huns under ▷Attila were defeated by a combined force of Romans and Visigoths under ▷Aetius and Theodoric I.

● **catalepsy** ▶ A condition associated with certain abnormal mental states, including schizophrenia and hysteria, in which the patient, usually female, remains motionless, often with the limbs in fixed positions, for a variable length of time.

● **Catalhüyük** ▶ A Neolithic site SE of Konya (S Turkey), discovered in 1958. It was a settlement of cattle breeders and agriculturalists, dating from the late 7th and early 6th millenniums BC. Houses built to a standard pattern and luxury goods, such as obsidian mirrors, suggest advanced social organization. Notable finds include shrines with animal frescoes or plasterwork.

● **Catalonia** ▶ (Spanish name: Cataluña; Catalan name: Catalunya) A mainly mountainous region of NE Spain, on the Mediterranean Sea. Agriculture is important, the main crops being cereals, olives, and grapes. It is the most highly industrialized region in Spain, being well provided with hydroelectric power from the River Ebro (and its tributaries). Tourism is important, especially on the coast.
History: united with Aragon in 1137 and Castile in 1497, Catalonia has nevertheless maintained a strong separatist tradition. In 1932 an autonomous government was established and this lasted throughout the Civil War (1936–39), in which Catalonia played a prominent role on the Republican side. A centre of opposition throughout the Franco regime, the Catalan government was restored provisionally in 1978. Area: 31 932 sq km (12 329 sq mi). Population (1994 est): 6 090 107. Capital: Barcelona.

● **Catalpa** ▶ A genus of trees (11 species) native to E Asia, North America, and the West Indies. They were widely grown as ornamentals for their attractive heart-shaped leaves, 12–30 cm long, and trumpet-shaped flowers, which are white with yellow and purple markings. The fruit is a long pod. The genus includes the Indian bean tree (*C. bignonioides*), up to 15 m high, which yields a durable timber. Family: *Bignoniaceae*.

● **catalysis** ▶ The acceleration of a ▷chemical reaction by a substance (**catalyst**) that is not itself consumed in the reaction. Virtually every reaction must overcome an energy barrier as the molecules of the reactants rearrange to form the products. The catalyst allows the reaction to proceed via a different lower-energy pathway. Since the reverse reaction is also accelerated, catalysis does not shift the chemical equilibrium, merely speeds its attainment. Catalysis may be homogeneous (all in the same phase) or heterogeneous (at an interface) as in the ▷Haber-Bosch process. Catalysis by a reaction product is called autocatalysis. Catalysis is used extensively in chemical processes. In living organisms ▷enzymes catalyse biochemical reactions.

● **catalytic converter** ▶ A device, first developed in the 1950s, for removing carbon monoxide, oxides of nitrogen, and hydrocarbons from the exhaust gases of motor vehicles by passing them over catalysts in the exhaust system. Oxidation catalysts (platinum and palladium) ensure that carbon monoxide is oxidized to the dioxide and that hydrocarbons are also fully oxidized to carbon dioxide and water. Three-way catalysts (rhodium metals) also convert the oxides of nitrogen into nitrogen and oxygen. Catalytic converters typically reduce carbon monoxide and hydrocarbons by up to 87%, while the oxides of nitrogen can be reduced by 65%.

● **catalytic cracking** ▶ A chemical process used in ▷oil refining. Crude oil, which contains large molecules, is decomposed by heat and pressure in the presence of a catalyst, usually a clay-type substance containing alumina and silica. Without a catalyst the same process, known as thermal cracking, needs a pressure of between 20 and 40 atmospheres and a temperature of 540°C. Catalytic cracking is carried out at between two and three atmospheres at a slightly lower temperature.

● **catamaran** ▶ A modern boat or ship with two identical hulls, fastened parallel to one another. Sailing catamarans usually have a single mast with a triangular mainsail and jib. Because of their buoyancy, the twin hulls offer very little resistance to the water, making such vessels extremely fast. The same principle has been adopted for some modern high-speed car ferries. The original catamaran was a native canoe-like vessel of the SW Pacific. ▷*See also* trimaran.

● **Cat and Mouse Act** ▷*See* women's movement.

● **Catania** ▶ 37 31N 15 06E A port in Italy, in E Sicily near Mount Etna. Destroyed by an earthquake in 1693, it was rebuilt in a baroque style. The university was founded in 1434. Its industries include sulphur refining. Population (1996 est): 341 623.

● **Catanzaro** ▶ 38 54N 16 36E A market town in S Italy, the capital of Calabria. Citrus fruit is grown in the area. Population (1991): 103 802.

● **cataract** ▶ (geography) ▷*See* waterfall.

● **cataract** ▶ (ophthalmology) Opacities in the lens of the eye resulting in blurred vision and caused by the deposition of small crystals or changes in the composition of the lens substance. The former condition increases with age; such cataracts are a common cause of blindness in the elderly. Certain diseases, such as poorly controlled diabetes mellitus, can also lead to cataracts. Cataracts are usually treated by removal of the lens (by surgery or ultrasound) and the use of appropriate spectacles. In some cases a plastic lens may be implanted to replace the one removed.

● **catarrh** ▶ Inflammation of the mucous membranes lining the nose, nasal sinuses, throat, or air passages, causing the production of thick phlegm. Catarrh is commonly due to viral infections, particularly the common cold, and hay fever.

● **catastrophe theory** ▶ A theory of dynamic systems using methods of ▷topology. Originally, catastrophe theory was developed by the French mathematician René Thom (1923–), in 1972, as a theory of biological differentiation, in which gradual growth stimulates and is stimulated by "catastrophic" large-scale changes. It has since been applied to other fields, including optics, engineering, sociology, economics, and linguistics. The theory is based on analogy with topological form. For instance, if a system depends on three factors, a particular state of the system can be represented by a point in three-dimensional space and possible states are represented by a region (or shape). The behaviour of the system is investigated by considering the topological classification of these representations, in particular the theory shows how discontinuous catastrophic changes can occur. In engineering, a structure may be stable under a certain range of conditions and collapse if other conditions are applied.

● **catastrophism** ▶ A formerly held theory according to which geological changes have occurred as a result of sudden short-lived catastrophes. Such events do occur (e.g. floods), but they have temporary and local effects. *Compare* uniformitarianism.

● **catchment area** ▶ **1.** The area from which a river is fed with water; it is usually bounded by a ▷watershed or divide. **2.** The area served by a public facility, such as a hospital or school, or by the sales representative of a business.

● **catechism** ▶ A form of instruction in the essentials of Christian doctrine. Catechisms were originally for the instruction of converts preparing for ▷baptism, frequently taking the form of a set of responses. With the spread of infant baptism, from the 6th century their function became the basic education of children in the faith, often as preparation for ▷confirmation. After the Reformation, printed forms of catechisms were also used as an expression of particular Churches' beliefs, as, for example, that printed in the Book of ▷Common Prayer.

● **catechol** ▶ (pyrocatechol *or* 1,2 dihydroxy-benzene; $C_6H_4(OH)_2$) A colourless crystalline ▷aromatic compound used as a developer in photography. ▷*See also* catecholamines.

● **catecholamines** ▶ Amine derivatives of ▷catechol. They include ▷adrenaline, ▷noradrenaline, and dopamine, which act as neurotransmitters and hormones. Depletion of dopamine in the basal ganglia of the brain is associated with ▷Parkinson's disease.

● **catechu** ▶ A vegetable extract containing ▷tannin and used in tanning and dying. Black catechu is obtained mainly from wood. Pale catechu (gambier; terra japonica) is produced from leaves and is used in medicine as an astringent. Extract from betel or areca nuts is also called catechu.

● **categorical imperative** ▶ The fundamental moral law in ▷Kant's ethical theory: an act is moral only if the principle on which it is justified is universally applicable.

● **catenary** ▶ The curve obtained by suspending a string between two points. If the middle of the string, the lowest point, is at height a above a reference level, then the height, y, at distance x along the string from the middle is given by:

$$y = \tfrac{1}{2}a\,(e^{x/a} + e^{-x/a}).$$

● **caterpillar** ▶ The larva of ▷butterflies and moths. Soft-bodied and wingless, all caterpillars have a head and 13 body segments with 3 pairs of true thoracic legs and 5 pairs of abdominal prolegs, which aid in locomotion. The mouthparts are adapted for chewing leaves or feeding on sap. Some species are serious crop pests. Caterpillars exhibit a wide variety of camouflaging colours and shapes. Some produce irritating or poisonous secretions.

● **Catesby, Robert** ▷See Fawkes, Guy.

● **catfish** ▶ A ▷bony fish of the order *Siluriformes* (about 2500 species), with a stout scaleless body, 4–450 cm long, a broad flat head, and long whisker-like barbels. Freshwater catfish (family *Ictaluridae*), sometimes called bullheads, occur worldwide; marine catfish (family *Ariidae*) inhabit tropical and coastal waters and are generally bottom-dwelling scavengers used as food, game, and aquarium fish. ▷See also wels.

The name is also used for marine fish of the family *Anarhichadidae* (order *Perciformes*).

● **catgut** ▶ The tough cord made from the intestines of the sheep or sometimes the ox and the horse (but not the cat). It is used for stringing tennis rackets, violin strings, and for surgical stitching.

● **Cathari** ▶ (or Cathars) A heretical sect in medieval Europe. It spread from Bulgaria, where its adherents were called Bogomils, to W Europe in the 11th century. From the mid-12th century the Cathari flourished in S France (*see* Albigenses) and in Italy until they were wiped out in the 14th century by the Inquisition. Their doctrine, influenced by ▷Gnosticism and ▷Manichaeism, taught that the material world was irredeemably evil but that man's soul was good and could secure its reunion with God. They were sceptical about much biblical doctrine, holding, for instance, that Christ was only an angel. They were divided into two classes, the perfect and the believers. The perfect lived in celibacy, marriage being regarded, with all other fleshly indulgences, as evil. The believers could join the perfect immediately before death by receiving the Cathari's chief rite, a laying on of hands, called the *consolamentum*.

● **Cathay** ▶ The medieval European name for China, derived from Khitan, the name of a Mongol people who invaded N China in the 10th century. It was introduced to Europe by such early travellers as Marco Polo. China is still called Khitan by the Russians.

● **cathedral** ▶ The principal church of an ecclesiastical area (diocese), governed by a bishop or an archbishop. The name comes from Latin *cathedra*, bishop's seat. Generally larger and more magnificent than other churches, cathedrals, such as ▷St Peter's Basilica, Rome, ▷St Paul's Cathedral, London, and ▷Notre-Dame de Paris, contain some of their country's finest works of art. Of the 45 Anglican cathedrals in England, less than half are medieval. Only three have been built in the 20th century: Liverpool (begun 1904), Guildford (built between 1936 and 1965), and the rebuilt Coventry cathedral (consecrated 1962). The Roman Catholic cathedrals of Westminster (1895–1903) and Liverpool (opened 1967) are buildings of architectural interest.

● **Catherine I** ▶ (1684–1727) The second wife from 1712 of Peter the Great and Empress of Russia (1725–27). Of Lithuanian peasant origin, Catherine was captured in 1702 in the Great Northern War and became Peter's mistress. After Peter's death in 1725, his adviser Prince A. D. Menshikov (1672–1729), supported by the palace guards, secured the throne for Catherine.

● **Catherine (II) the Great** ▶ (1729–96) Empress of Russia (1762–96), who gained the throne in a coup in which her unpopular husband, Emperor Peter III (1728–62; reigned 1762), was murdered. Catherine's reign marked the expansion of Russian territory as a result of her successful wars against the Turks (1768–74, 1787–92) and the partition of Poland (1772, 1793, 1795). Influenced by the ideas of the Enlightenment, she had to abandon her scheme to emancipate the serfs in the face of opposition from their masters. Of her many lovers, only ▷Potemkin exerted a durable influence on government.

● **Catherine de' Medici** ▶ (1519–89) Regent of France (1560–63) during the minority of her second son, Charles IX, and virtual ruler until his death (1574). The daughter of Lorenzo de' Medici, Duke of Urbino, she married Henry II of France in 1533. Intent on upholding royal authority during the ▷Wars of Religion, she advocated tolerance for the ▷Huguenots but later supported the Catholics. She was largely responsible for the ▷St Bartholomew's Day Massacre. Her influence waned during the reign of her third son ▷Henry III.

● **Catherine of Alexandria, St** ▶ Legendary 4th-century Christian martyr, who protested to the emperor Maxentius at the persecution of Christians. The wheel on which she was being broken (after which the firework known as the Catherine wheel is named) was reputedly shattered by an angel and she was instead beheaded. Her feast day (25 Nov) was removed from the church calendar in 1969.

● **Catherine of Aragon** ▶ (1485–1536) The first wife (1509–33) of Henry VIII of England and the mother of Mary I. Failing to bear him a son, she was put aside by Henry, who argued that their marriage was invalid because Catherine was the widow of his brother Arthur. The pope's refusal to grant Henry an annulment provoked the English ▷Reformation.

● **Catherine of Braganza** ▶ (1638–1705) The wife (from 1662) of Charles II of England. A Portuguese princess and a devout Roman Catholic, her unpopularity was intensified by her failure to produce an heir to the throne.

● **Catherine of Genoa, St** ▶ (1447–1510) Italian mystic. From a noble family, she married at the age of 16 but underwent a religious conversion 10 years later and devoted herself to caring for the sick. She had a number of mystical experiences, which are recounted in *Vita e dottrina* (1551). Feast day: 15 Sept.

● **Catherine of Siena, St** ▶ (Caterina Benincasa; 1347–80) Italian nun and mystic. She joined the Dominican Tertiary Order at 16 and devoted herself to caring for the sick and poor and to contemplation. In 1376 she went to Avignon to persuade Pope Gregory IX to return to Rome. She was reported to have received the stigmata on her body in 1375. Her letters and a work on mysticism, the *Dialogue*, are extant. Feast day: 30 April.

● **Catherine of Valois** ▷See Tudors.

● **catheter** ▶ A tube inserted into a hollow organ of the body in order to drain or introduce fluids. A urinary catheter is inserted into the bladder through the urethra to relieve obstruction (commonly caused by enlargement of the prostate gland in elderly men) to the flow of urine. Cardiac catheters are used to measure blood pressure in the heart; similar catheters are used to inject radio-opaque substances into blood vessels for X-ray examination or to introduce tiny inflatable balloons into blocked arteries in the operation of angioplasty (*see* coronary heart disease).

● **cathode** ▶ The negative electrode of an electrolytic cell, valve, etc. It is the electrode by which the electrons enter the system. *Compare* anode.

● **cathode-ray oscilloscope** ▶ (CRO) An instrument that displays electrical quantities on the screen of a ▷cathode-ray tube. It can be used to show the variation of a signal strength with time or with another electrical quantity. The CRO is used extensively in scientific work.

● **cathode rays** ▶ A stream of electrons emitted by a ▷cathode, when a voltage is applied between a cathode and an ▷anode either in an evacuated glass tube or one containing gas at low pressure. The electron beam can be focused onto a fluorescent screen to produce a visual display. This effect is used in the ▷cathode-ray tube used in television receivers, radar screens, and oscilloscopes.

● **cathode-ray tube** ▶ (CRT) A vacuum tube that converts electrical signals into visible form by projecting a beam of electrons onto a fluorescent screen. It is an essential component of the television receiver and the ▷cathode-ray oscilloscope (CRO). The electron beam is produced by an electron gun, and deflected horizontally and vertically by an arrangement of plates and magnets, which move it back and forth across the screen and focus it by creating an ▷electromagnetic field, the strength of which varies according to input signals. In a television tube the beam intensity varies to form the light and dark regions of the picture.

● **Catholic emancipation** ▶ A campaign in Britain and Ireland to secure full civil and political rights for Roman Catholics. Since the Reformation, Catholics had been subject to a number of restrictions concerning property ownership, inheritance, and government employment and could not sit in parliament. In the late 18th century several relief acts were passed but parliamentary representation was still denied. The opposition of the Tory establishment and the monarchy continued until ▷O'Connell's efforts achieved the Catholic Emancipation Act of 1829.

● **Catiline** ▶ (Lucius Sergius Catilina; d. 62 BC) Roman politician, who plotted to seize power in 62. Thwarted by Cicero, Catiline fled to a rebel force in Etruria and his fellow conspirators were executed. He was defeated and killed in battle.

● **catkin** ▷*See* inflorescence.

George Catlin ▶ A painting by the artist depicting himself (left) in the tent of a Mandan Indian chief. Catlin made a number of drawings and paintings of this people in 1832.

● **Catlin, George** ▶ (1796–1872) Pennsylvanian artist and author. He is famous for his painted and written studies of the American Indians, among whom he lived (1832–40). His best-known book is *Manners, Customs, and Conditions of North American Indians* (1841).

● **catmint** ▶ A perennial flowering plant, *Nepeta cataria*, native to chalky regions of temperate Europe. The branching stem grows to a height of 40–100 cm and bears toothed heart-shaped leaves and small white flowers spotted with purple. The plant has a strong minty scent, attractive to cats. Family: ▷*Labiatae*.

● **Cato Street Conspiracy** ▶ (1820) A conspiracy against the British government led by Arthur Thistlewood (1770–1820). A fanatical idealist, Thistlewood and four others planned to murder all the ministers of the cabinet as a prelude to insurrection. The plan was revealed by government spies (who may have instigated the whole conspiracy) and the leaders, arrested in Cato Street, NW London, were hanged.

● **Cato the Elder** ▶ (Marcus Porcius C.; 234–149 BC) Roman states-

man, who wrote the first history of Rome. A moral and political conservative, Cato as censor (184) legislated against luxury and sponsored improvements in public works. His embassy to Carthage (153) led him to fear the resurgence of Rome's old enemy; "Carthage must be destroyed" was his repeated cry until the third ▷Punic War was declared (149). His simple writing style was influential and he is the first important Latin prose author.

● **Cato the Younger** ▶ (Marcus Porcius C.; 95–46 BC) Roman politician; the great-grandson of Cato the Elder and an opponent of Julius Caesar. Caesar, with ▷Pompey and ▷Crassus, created the first ▷Triumvirate (60) partly to neutralize Cato's opposition to their political ambitions. Forced to support Pompey in the civil war in an attempt to save the Republic, Cato escaped after Pompey's death to Utica, in Africa. On hearing of Caesar's victory at ▷Thapsus, he committed suicide after ensuring the evacuation of his supporters.

● **CAT scanner** ▷*See* tomography.

● **Catskill Mountains** ▶ A mountain range in the USA, in the N Appalachian Mountains. Consisting of forested steep-sided mountains, it rises to 1261 m (4204 ft) at Slide Mountain. The area supplies water to New York City and is a popular recreation area for New Yorkers. The mountains are associated with the fictional character Rip Van Winkle, created by Washington Irving.

● **cat's-tail** ▷*See* reedmace.

● **Catterick** ▶ 54 22N 1 38W A village in N England, in North Yorkshire on the River Swale. Nearby is an important army garrison; there is also a famous racecourse.

● **cattle** ▶ Ruminant mammals belonging to the genus *Bos* (7 species), also called oxen, native to Eurasia and Africa. Modern domestic cattle (*B. taurus*), which are probably descended from such ancestors as the ▷aurochs, vary in body shape, size, and colour according to breed but are generally 90–110 cm high at the shoulder and weigh 400–900 kg. ▷Zebus and ▷gayals are similarly now found only in the domestic state. Cattle are used for milk and meat production and for draught purposes (*see* livestock farming). Family: *Bovidae*. ▷*See also* banteng; gaur; yak.

● **Cattleya** ▶ A genus of tropical American epiphytic ▷orchids (about 65 species), grown commercially for ornament and the florist trade. They have large pseudobulbs, one or two leaves, and clusters of 1–30 large brightly coloured flowers. *C. labiata* has been crossed with other orchid genera to produce many showy hybrids.

● **Catullus, Valerius** ▶ (c. 84–c. 54 BC) Roman poet. Born in Verona, he became the leading member of a group of young innovatory poets in Rome. 116 poems survive, of which the most famous are the 25 lyrics addressed to a married woman named Lesbia, recording in passionate language the shifting moods of love from ecstasy to despair. The other poems include elegies and vicious satirical attacks on Julius Caesar and other politicians.

● **Catuvellauni** ▶ A powerful and prosperous Belgic tribe that occupied an area extending from the Thames into the Midlands. Led by Cassivelaunus, they resisted Julius Caesar's invasion of Britain in 54 BC; after being defeated, they moved their capital from near Wheathampstead, Hertfordshire, to Verulamium (St Albans). Their chief ▷Caratacus led British resistance to the Roman invasion of 43 AD.

● **Caucasian languages** ▷*See* Northeast Caucasian languages; Northwest Caucasian languages; South Caucasian languages.

● **Caucasoid** ▶ A race or group of races and peoples originally inhabiting Europe, North Africa, and the Near East. In modern times Caucasoids have spread to North and South America, Australia, New Zealand, parts of Africa, and elsewhere. They are characterized by skin pigmentation ranging from very pale to dark brown, straight to curly hair, narrow high-bridged noses, plentiful body hair, and a high frequency of Rh-negative blood type.

● **Caucasus Mountains** ▶ (Russian name: Kavkaz) Two mountain ranges in SE Europe and W Asia, extending NW–SE between the Black Sea and the Caspian Sea and separated by the River Kura: the **Great Caucasus**, some 1000 km (621 mi) long, to the N on the Russian borders with Georgia and Azerbaidzhan; and the **Little Caucasus**, about half that length, along the Turkish borders with Georgia, Armenia, and Azerbaidzhan. Their highest point is Mount ▷Elbrus. *▷See also* Ciscaucasia; Transcaucasia.

● **Cauchy, Augustin Louis, Baron** ▶ (1789–1857) French mathematician, who pioneered the study of functions of ▷complex numbers. He also derived a mathematical basis for the luminiferous ether. An outspoken and extreme conservative, Cauchy went into exile in Italy in 1830 on the accession of King Louis Philippe.

● **cauliflower** ▶ A variety of wild ▷cabbage, *Brassica oleracea* var. *botrytis*, cultivated as a vegetable in Europe and the USA. The short stem bears a round white heart, up to 25 cm in diameter, of tightly compressed flower buds surrounded by green leaves. *▷See also* Brassica.

● **causation** ▶ The relationship between two events in which the first (the cause) brings about the second (the effect). The law of cause and effect has long presented philosophers with a number of problems. Do all events have to have an antecedent cause? Can a cause be instantaneous with the effect? Can the effect precede the cause? ▷Hume argued that causal necessity is a concept produced only by the human brain, that in reality some regularities of non-necessary conjunctions do occur, but that they do not constitute an immutable law of nature. Bertrand ▷Russell later agreed that a scientific understanding of the universe does not require the concept. Indeed, subsequent quantum mechanics (*see* quantum theory) is based on the principle that events at the atomic level do not necessarily have causes; some occur at random. According to the ▷Heisenberg uncertainty principle, an electron, say, travelling at a known velocity cannot have a fully defined position at any particular instant. Its position can only be expressed as a ▷probability. This being the case, how can two consecutive observations of the same particle be distinguished from two obsevations of different particles? If a particle cannot be identified without this element of uncertainty, how can its destiny be known? If the particle's identity and destiny are in doubt, how can one say whether or not the law of cause and effect is being obeyed?

● **Cauvery, River** ▶ (*or* R. Kaveri) A river in S India. Rising in the Western Ghats, it flows mainly ENE to the Bay of Bengal. It has a wide delta, the principal channel being the Coleroon, and it irrigates the area by way of a system of canals. It is sacred to the Hindus. Length: 756 km (470 mi).

● **Cavafy, Constantine** ▶ (C. Kavafis; 1863–1933) Greek poet. He lived nearly all his life in Alexandria, where he worked as a civil servant. Many of his poems are ironic treatments of subjects from the ancient Hellenistic world; he also wrote erotic homosexual love poems. He spoke and read English and had a strong influence on E. M. ▷Forster and Lawrence ▷Durrell.

● **Cavalcanti, Guido** ▶ (c. 1255–1300) Italian poet. A friend of Dante, he wrote about 50 poems on themes of love and emotional suffering. He died of a disease contracted while exiled from Florence for his political activities.

● **Cavalier poets** ▶ A group of English poets connected with the court of Charles I (1625–49). They included Richard ▷Lovelace, Robert ▷Herrick, Thomas ▷Carew, Edmund ▷Waller, and Sir John ▷Suckling. Their love lyrics and poems about war and honour were characterized by a sophisticated elegance appropriate to their positions as courtiers and gentlemen.

● **Cavaliers** ▶ The royalist party during the English ▷Civil War. After the ▷Restoration of the monarchy (1660) the name was kept by the court party and was given to the parliament that sat from 1661 to 1679. The cavaliers were distinguished by their elaborate dress, with lace ruffles, feathers, and velvet, in contrast to the sober attire of the ▷Roundheads.

● **Cavalli, Francesco** ▶ (1602–76) Italian composer of opera and church music. A pupil of Monteverdi in Venice, he wrote over 40 dramatic works based on legends of gods and heroes. *Calisto* (1651), in an edition prepared by Raymond Leppard (1927–), was revived at Glyndebourne in 1970.

● **Cavallini, Pietro** ▶ (c. 1250–c. 1330) Roman fresco painter and mosaicist. He was the first to abandon the stylizations of ▷Byzantine

art and his chief works are the mosaics of the *Life of the Virgin* for Sta Maria in Trastevere and the frescoes in Sta Cecilia.

● **cavalry** ▶ A force of mounted soldiers. Employed throughout the ancient world for its speed and mobility, the invention of stirrups (c. 400 AD) increased its usefulness by enabling heavily armoured lancers and swordsmen to fight on horseback. The introduction of ▷small arms in the 15th century shifted the emphasis in warfare to infantry and the use of ▷machine guns from the late 19th century rendered the role of cavalry in battle suicidal. Modern armoured units have adopted the name and role of cavalry.

● **Cavan** ▶ (Irish name: Cabhán) A county in the NE Republic of Ireland, in Ulster. It is generally hilly, drained chiefly by the River Erne, with lakes and ▷drumlins. Although largely infertile, agriculture is the mainstay of the economy producing oats, potatoes, and dairy products. Some small industries exist in the towns. Area: 1890 sq km (730 sq mi). Population (1996 est): 53 000. County town: Cavan.

● **cave fish** ▶ One of several cave-dwelling ▷teleost fishes, especially members of the family *Amblyopsidae*, found in fresh water in dark limestone caves of North America. They have translucent colourless elongated bodies, about 10 cm long, reduced nonfunctional eyes, and numerous sensory papillae covering the body to compensate for blindness.

● **Cavell, Edith** ▶ (1865–1915) British nurse. From 1907 she worked at a training institute for nurses in Brussels. She was executed by the Germans in 1915 for helping Allied soldiers to escape from German-occupied Belgium. Before she died she is reputed to have said "I realize that patriotism is not enough. I must have no hatred or bitterness towards anyone."

● **Cavendish** ▶ (Henry Jones; 1831–99) British authority on card games. He is known chiefly for his treatise *The Principles of Whist, Stated and Explained by "Cavendish"* (1862).

● **Cavendish, Lord Frederick Charles** *▷See* Phoenix Park Murders.

● **Cavendish, Henry** ▶ (1731–1810) British physicist; grandson of the Duke of Devonshire, from whom he inherited a fortune. He discovered hydrogen and investigated its properties. He also identified the gases in the atmosphere and showed that water is a compound. The first to measure accurately the universal gravitational constant, he used it to calculate the mass of the earth. The Cavendish Laboratory at Cambridge University is named after him.

● **caves** ▶ Underground hollows, usually opening directly onto the ground surface or connected with it by a passage. In limestone regions, where most caves occur, many constitute part of a system of natural underground drainage and are connected by subterranean streams. These caves are excavated by the slow solution of limestone by slightly acidic rain water percolating through its joints. The other main type of cave is that eroded from the base of a cliff by the sea. Such caves are located at some point of weakness in an otherwise resistant rock, such as a fault plane or bed of softer material. ▷Fingal's Cave in the Scottish Hebrides is a spectacular cavern in columnar basalt, the sea forming its floor.

● **caviare** ▶ A delicacy, eaten as an hors d'oeuvre, which consists of sturgeon's roe, salted and freed from all fat. It is a Russian speciality. The roe of the beluga is considered the best, although caviare is also obtained from other types of sturgeon. Real caviare is extremely expensive, but a substitute made from lump fish roe is relatively inexpensive.

● **Cavite** ▶ 14 30N 120 54E A town in the N Philippines, in SW Luzon on Manila Bay. Formerly a centre of opposition to Spanish and US rule, it is the site of a major US naval base. Population (1994 est): 103 422.

● **Cavour, Camillo Benso di, Count** ▶ (1810–61) Italian statesman; the architect of Italian unification (*see* Risorgimento). Committed to liberal politics from boyhood, he helped to found the organ *Il risorgimento* in 1847. In 1852 he formed his first government under ▷Victor Emmanuel II of Sardinia-Piedmont. Cavour accepted an alliance with France and Britain during the Crimean War and negotiated a further alliance with France at Plombières in 1859 to oust

Austria from Italy. He resigned when France came to terms with Austria but became prime minister again in 1860, negotiating the union of Sardinia-Piedmont with Parma, Modena, Tuscany, and the Romagna, and by 1861 had achieved the establishment of a united Italy.

● **cavy** ► A small South American ▷rodent belonging to the genus *Cavia* (6 species); the ancestor of the domestic guinea pig. Cavies are mainly nocturnal and live in groups in scrub and grassland, digging burrows and feeding on vegetation and seeds. The adults generally breed twice a year and the young cavies are independent at three weeks. Family: *Caviidae*.

● **Cawdor** ► 57 32N 3 55W A village in Scotland, in the E Highland Region. Cawdor Castle is the traditional site of Macbeth's murder of Duncan (1040).

William Caxton ► Earl Rivers presents Caxton to Edward IV (from a manuscript in Lambeth Palace Library).

● **Caxton, William** ► (c. 1422–91) The first English printer. A cloth merchant, Caxton lived in Bruges from 1446 until 1470, when he moved to Cologne. There he learned the technique of printing and in 1474 set up a press that produced the first printed book in English, *Recuyell of the Historyes of Troye* (1475). On returning to England (1476), he set up a press at Westminster, where he printed a long and varied list, including Chaucer's *Canterbury Tales* (1478) and an encyclopedia that was the first illustrated English book, *The Myrrour of the Worlde* (1481).

● **Cayenne** ► 4 55N 52 18W The capital and main Atlantic port of French Guiana, in the NW of the Île de Cayenne. Founded by the French in 1643, it served as a French penal settlement (1854–1938). Cayenne pepper derives its name from a plant grown in the area. Population (1995 est): 45 000.

● **Cayley, Arthur** ► (1821–95) British mathematician, who invented ▷matrices, a branch of mathematics that remained a curiosity until Werner ▷Heisenberg used it in his theory of quantum mechanics. He also worked on analytical and ▷non-Euclidean geometry and was largely responsible for the resurgence of mathematics in Britain during his lifetime.

● **Cayley, Sir George** ► (1773–1857) British engineer and pioneer designer of flying machines. He studied the effects of streamlining, the properties of different shapes of wings, and the basic shape of heavier-than-air aircraft. He tested his theories with models and in 1853 built the first successful manned glider. He also invented the caterpillar tractor.

● **cayman** ► (or caiman) An amphibious reptile occurring in rivers of Central and South America. 1.2–4.5 m long, it feeds on fish, birds,

and insects. Genera: *Caiman* (2 species), *Melanosuchus* (1 species), *Paleosuchus* (2 species); subfamily: *Alligatorinae* (alligators and caimans); order: *Crocodilia* (*see* crocodile).

● **Cayman Islands** ► A United Kingdom overseas territory in the Caribbean Sea, consisting of three low-lying coral islands (Grand Cayman, Little Cayman, and Cayman Brac) lying about 320 km (200 mi) NW of Jamaica. The population is mainly of mixed African and European descent.
 Economy: since the 1970s the Cayman Islands have developed rapidly as an offshore financial centre owing to the complete lack of direct taxation (there are now some 650 banks and trust companies and 34 500 other companies registered on the islands). Tourism has also been successfully developed. As there is no industry or agriculture, nearly all goods are imported. The main exports are turtle shell, dried turtle meat, and tropical fish.
 History: discovered in 1503 by Columbus, who named them Las Tortugas because of the abundance of turtles. Formerly attached to Jamaica, they gained a certain measure of self-government in 1959 and became a separate British colony in 1962. Official language: English. Official currency: Cayman Islands dollar of 100 cents. Area: 260 sq km (100 sq mi). Population (1994): 31 930. Capital and main port: Georgetown.

● **CBE** ▷*See* Order of the British Empire.

● **CBI** ▷*See* Confederation of British Industry.

● **CB radio** ▷*See* citizens' band radio.

● **CD-ROM** ▷*See* compact disc.

● **Ceanannus Mór** ▷*See* Kells.

● **Ceanothus** ► A genus of North American shrubs (about 55 species) with small ovate usually evergreen leaves and dense clusters, about 6 cm long, of tiny blue or white flowers. Blue-flowered hybrids and varieties (California lilac) are widely grown in temperate gardens. Family: *Rhamnaceae* (buckthorn family).

● **Ceará** ▷*See* Fortaleza.

● **Ceauşescu, Nicolae** ► (1918–89) Romanian statesman; president (1974–89). Ceauşescu's rise in the Party hierarchy began in 1948. In 1965 he became the Party's general secretary and in 1967 president of the state council. He was noted for his opposition to Soviet interference in Romanian affairs. Resisting all pressures for liberal reform, he established his own personality cult. He was overthrown in the revolution of 1989 and executed (with his wife Elena) by firing squad.

● **Cebu** ► 10 17N 123 56E A port in the central Philippines, in E Cebu. The first Spanish settlement in the Philippines (founded 1565), it has a Roman Catholic cathedral and bishop's palace. Its four universities include the University of San Carlos (1595). A commercial centre, its industries include textiles and food processing. Population (1994 est): 688 196.

● **Cebu** ► An island in the central Philippines, in the Visayan Islands. Its populous coastal plains are cultivated chiefly with coconuts, maize, sugar cane, and hemp. Coal and copper are mined. Area: 5086 sq km (1964 sq mi). Population (latest est): 2 091 602. Chief town: Cebu.

● **Cecil, Lord David** ► (Lord Edward Christian David Gascoyne C.; 1902–86) British literary critic, professor of English literature at Oxford University from 1948 to 1970. His books include a study of William Cowper entitled *The Stricken Deer* (1929) and biographies of Jane Austen (1935), Hardy (1943), and Max Beerbohm (1964).

● **Cecil, Robert Gascoyne-Cecil, 1st Viscount** ► (1864–1958) British statesman. Cecil was minister of blockade and then deputy foreign secretary in World War I. He took part in the Paris Peace Conference (1919) and helped draft the charter of the League of Nations; he won the Nobel Peace Prize in 1937.

● **Cecil, William** ▷*See* Burghley, William Cecil, Lord.

● **Cecilia, St** ► (2nd or 3rd century AD) Roman Christian martyr. According to legend, she converted her pagan husband Valerian and his brother Tiburtius, who were martyred before her. Although there is doubt concerning her authenticity, she remains the patron saint of sacred music. Feast day: 22 Nov. Emblem: an organ.

● **cecropia moth** ▶ A large brown and reddish ▷saturniid moth, *Platysamia cecropia*. With a wingspan of 155 mm, it is the largest North American moth. The caterpillars are green and feed on a variety of trees.

● **cedar** ▶ A conifer of the genus *Cedrus* (4 species), native to the Mediterranean region and the Himalayas and widely planted for ornament and timber. Cedars usually grow to a height of 40 m. Their stiff needle-like leaves grow in tufts of 10–40 on short spurs and their cones are erect and barrel-shaped, 5–14 cm long. The best-known species are the ▷deodar; the Atlas cedar (*C. atlantica*), from the Atlas mountains; and the cedar of Lebanon (*C. libani*), of the E Mediterranean. Family: *Pinaceae*.

A number of unrelated trees are also known as cedars (*see* incense cedar; Japanese cedar; pencil cedar), and conifers of the genus *Thuja* (*see* arbor vitae) are sometimes called cedars.

● **Cedar Rapids** ▶ 41 59N 91 39W A city in the USA, in E central Iowa. Its industries include cereals and agricultural machinery. Population (2000 est): 120 758.

● **Ceefax** ▷*See* teletext.

● **Cela (y Trulock), Camilo José** ▶ (1916–2002) Spanish novelist and writer. His novels include *The Family of Pascal Duarte* (1942), *The Hive* (1951), and *Mazurka for Two Dead* (1983). He was awarded the Nobel Prize in 1989.

● **celandine** ▶ Either of two unrelated perennial herbaceous plants. **Greater celandine** (*Chelidonium majus*) is found in cool temperate and subarctic regions throughout Europe and Asia. The brittle branching stems, 30–90 cm long, bear deeply lobed leaves and bright-yellow flowers. The fruit is a narrow capsule, 3–5 cm long. Family: *Papaveraceae*.

Lesser celandine (*Ranunculus ficaria*), sometimes known as pilewort, is native to Europe. The branching stems, 5–25 cm long, bear long-stalked leaves and bright-yellow flowers, which fade to white. The roots form numerous tubers. Family: *Ranunculaceae*.

● **Celaya** ▶ 20 32N 100 48W A city in central Mexico. It is an agricultural trading centre. Population (2000 est): 270 000.

● **Celebes** ▷*See* Sulawesi.

● **celeriac** ▶ A variety of cultivated ▷celery, *Apium graveolens* var. *rapaceum*, also known as turnip-rooted or knob celery, grown for its globular edible root. The root, up to 15 cm in diameter, has a celery-like flavour.

● **celery** ▶ The cultivated form of wild celery, or smallage (*Apium graveolens*), a biennial herb native to grassy coastal areas from Europe to India and Africa. Many varieties of cultivated celery have been developed for their edible leafstalks (up to 30 cm in length), which may be pink, yellow, or green. Traditionally, the green varieties are blanched to tenderize the tissues. The wild plant has an erect grooved stem, 30–60 cm long, bearing whorls of clusters of small greenish-white flowers. Family: ▷*Umbelliferae*.

● **celesta** ▶ A small keyboard instrument the quiet bell-like tone of which is produced by hammers striking steel plates hung over wooden resonators. Invented about 1880, it was used by Tchaikovsky in his ballet *Casse-Noisette*.

● **celestial mechanics** ▶ The study of the motions of celestial bodies subject to mutual gravitational interaction through the application of the laws of ▷gravitation and of ▷mechanics.

● **celestial sphere** ▶ The imaginary sphere, of immense size, at the centre of which lies the earth and on the inner surface of which can be projected the stars and other celestial bodies. The directions of these bodies, as seen from earth, are measured in terms of their angular distances from certain points and circles on the celestial sphere. These circles include the ▷ecliptic, the observer's horizon, and the **celestial equator**, where the earth's equatorial plane meets the celestial sphere. The reference points include the ▷equinoxes, the ▷zenith, and the **celestial poles**, where the earth's axis meets the celestial sphere. The earth's daily rotation causes an apparent and opposite rotation of the celestial sphere.

● **celibacy** ▶ The state of being unmarried, especially after taking a religious vow. This is not the same as **chastity**, which is abstention from illicit sexual intercourse. A faithful married man is therefore chaste but not celibate. Celibacy has been regarded in many different ways; for some it is the most unnatural of the sexual perversions, while for others it is a unique source of spirituality. In Judaism and Islam celibacy is frowned upon as being in defiance of the first commandment "to be fruitful and multiply." In Christianity, largely owing to Christ's own example and a view that complete spiritual commitment requires an absence of worldly ties, celibacy has traditionally been regarded as a higher calling than marriage (a position endorsed by St Paul). In the early and medieval Church this view was reinforced by simple fear of sex and a good deal of misogyny.

Roman Catholic priests have been required to make a commitment to celibacy since 1139, when canon law stated (and continues to state) that matrimony and ordination are mutually exclusive. This replaced the earlier unenforceable rule that priests could be married as long as they did not have intercourse with their wives. In spite of the incomprehension of those outside the Church, and the dissent of some within it, celibacy remains the rule for Catholic clergy. In the Eastern Churches priests, but not bishops, are permitted to marry, while in those Protestant churches that retain an ordained priesthood celibacy is regarded as a matter of individual choice and conscience. Both Christian and non-Christian monastic orders have usually required complete sexual abstinence from their adherents.

● **Céline, Louis Ferdinand** ▶ (L. F. Destouches; 1884–1961) French novelist. The cynicism of his first book, *Journey to the End of the Night* (1932), also marks *Death on the Instalment Plan* (1936) and *North* (1960). A virulent antisemite, he was accused of collaboration with the Nazis and in 1945 fled to Denmark, where he was briefly imprisoned. Although condemned to death *in absentia* by a French court, he was later exonerated and returned to France.

● **cell** ▶ The basic unit of living matter, which performs the vital processes of producing energy, synthesizing new molecules from raw materials, division, and self-replication. All plants and animals are composed of cells, the average size of which ranges from 0.01 to 0.1

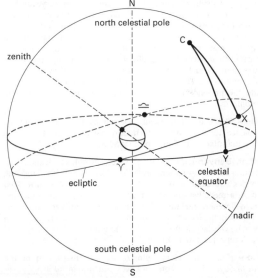

♈	first point of Aries; vernal equinox
♎	first point of Libra; autumnal equinox
C	celestial object
♈Y	right ascension of C (in hours anticlockwise from ♈)
♈X	celestial longitude of C (in degrees anticlockwise from ♈)
YC	declination of C
XC	celestial latitude of C

celestial sphere

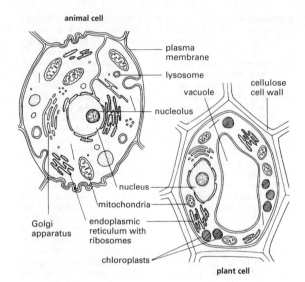

animal cell

plasma membrane
lysosome
vacuole
cellulose cell wall
nucleolus
nucleus
mitochondria
endoplasmic reticulum with ribosomes
Golgi apparatus
chloroplasts

plant cell

cell ► Plant and animal cells are basically similar but plant cells are supported by cellulose cell walls and contain the green pigment chlorophyll within chloroplasts. Plant cells often also have large fluid-filled vacuoles, which help to control turgidity of the cell.

mm; the simplest organisms (bacteria, protozoa, etc.) consist only of a single cell. The fundamental importance of cells was first recognized by ▷Schleiden and Schwann in 1838–39. A cell consists essentially of a mass of protoplasm bounded by a membrane. All cells except those of bacteria and mammalian red blood cells possess a ▷nucleus, containing the genetic material, and cytoplasm, within which are structures (organelles) specialized for different metabolic functions (*see* Golgi apparatus; lysosome; mitochondria; ribosome). Organisms consisting of cells of this type are called **eukaryotes**; bacteria, in which the genetic material is not enclosed in a nucleus, are called **prokaryotes** and classified in the kingdom *Prokaryotae* (or *Bacteria*). The cells of the body that are not involved in reproduction (called the somatic cells) divide by ▷mitosis to produce daughter cells identical to themselves. The reproductive cells divide by ▷meiosis to produce gametes, each containing half the number of chromosomes of the somatic cells. The differences between plant and animal cells include the presence in the former of a cellulose cell wall and ▷chloroplasts.

● Celle ► 52 37N 10 05E A town in N Germany, in Lower Saxony. Its ducal palace (1292) is famed for its theatre, used since 1674. Wax and dyes are manufactured. Population (1989 est); 71 050.

● Cellini, Benvenuto ► (1500–71) Florentine goldsmith and sculptor, famous for his autobiography (1558–62). First published in 1728, it provides a valuable account of his life and times. Cellini worked chiefly as a medallist and craftsman for the papacy in Rome, the Medici in Florence, and Francis I in France. The famous gold saltcellar (Kunsthistorisches Museum, Vienna) was made for Francis. As a sculptor he was largely unfulfilled, although his *Perseus* (Loggia dei Lanzi, Florence) attests to his skill in this medium.

● cello ► (full name: violoncello) A musical instrument of the ▷violin family, held between the knees and supported at its lower end by an adjustable pin. It has an extensive range above its lowest note (C two octaves below middle C). Its four strings are tuned C, G, D, A. Used to strengthen the bass line in baroque music, it emerged as a solo instrument in the 18th century.

● cellular network ► Any of the networks enabling ▷mobile phones to connect to the main telephone system. Established originally in the UK jointly by British Telecom and Securicor (as Cellnet), it consists of adjacent cells, each about 5 km across. In highly populated areas, such as cities, the cells are smaller and more numerous.

Each cell has a low-power transmitter and a receiving station connected to the main telephone network. All the transmitters work at the same frequency. The mobile telephone also has a battery-powered radio transmitter, which sends speech signals to the receiver in its cell. As subscribers move from one cell to another (e.g. by car), a computerized control system automatically allows them to send and receive signals in the new area. First-generation mobile phones used analogue signals; later phones employ digital signals, allowing more calls within a given frequency band.

● celluloid ► A highly flammable thermoplastic material made from cellulose nitrate and ▷camphor. It was the first commercially made plastic, introduced over a hundred years ago. There are many specialist uses for which it is still used because of its resistance to water, oils, and dilute acids. These include table-tennis balls and mortar-bomb capsules. The use of celluloid in photographic film has been superseded by that of nonflammable cellulose acetate.

● cellulose ► $(C_6H_{10}O_5)_n$ A ▷carbohydrate that is an important constituent of the cell walls of plants and many algae and consists of linked glucose units. Industrially, it is made from wood pulp and is used to manufacture ▷rayon and ▷cellulose-acetate plastics. Cellulose is important in the human diet since it—with other indigestible plant products—constitutes dietary ▷fibre.

● cellulose nitrate ► (*or* nitrocellulose) A range of compounds made by treating cellulose with a mixture of nitric acid and sulphuric acid. It is used as an explosive (gun cotton) and rocket propellant.

● Celsius scale ► A temperature scale devised by the Swedish astronomer Anders Celsius (1701–44), who originally designated zero as the boiling point of water and 100° as the freezing point. The scale was later reversed. Celsius temperature, t, is defined by the equation $t = T - 273.15$, where T is the thermodynamic temperature. Each degree Celsius is equal to one ▷kelvin. Until 1948 it was known as the centigrade scale.

● Celsus, Aulus Cornelius ► (1st century AD) Roman scholar, who wrote an encyclopedic work embracing agriculture, law, philosophy, and medicine, of which only the medical section has survived (*De medicina*). Popular during the Renaissance, it deals with hygiene, heart attacks, gallstones, and many other topics.

● Celtiberia ► A region of NE Spain, S of the River Ebro. From the 3rd century BC the area was inhabited by the warlike Celtiberians, who were descendants of the Celtic invaders of Spain and the Iberian natives. The Celtiberians were defeated by the Romans in 195 BC but their capital, Numantia, was not taken until 133 BC.

● Celtic art ► The style of ornamentation developed by ancient tribes in central Europe (*see* Celts). Primitive examples date from around 450 BC: masks and brooches in bronzework with increasingly sophisticated geometric patterns, animal and floral motifs, and, eventually, realistic human-head designs. The most elaborate jewellery, decorated swords, scabbards, and helmets belong to the ▷La Tène period (c. 350 BC). In Britain, Celtic craftsmanship flourished throughout the Roman occupation, producing work in gold and silver, shields inlaid with enamel, and bronze mirrors. Subsequently, Christian monks adapted traditional designs to adorn religious manuscripts, as in the 9th-century Book of ▷Kells.

● Celtic Church ► The Christian church established in Britain under the Roman Empire in the 2nd or 3rd century AD. It was extinguished in England by the Anglo-Saxon invasions, surviving in Wales and Ireland (which had been evangelized by St ▷Patrick) and spreading to S Scotland (c. 500). In 563 St ▷Columba founded a monastery on ▷Iona, from where missionaries led by St ▷Aidan re-established Christianity in ▷Northumbria from 635. However, this brought the Celtic Church into conflict with the Roman evangelization of England (*see* Augustine of Canterbury, St); in Northumbria these disputes were resolved in Rome's favour at the Synod of ▷Whitby (664) and by 768 the whole Celtic Church had submitted to Rome's authority.

● Celtic languages ► A branch of the Indo-European language family formerly widespread in W Europe. It is divided into two subgroups: Gaulish and Insular Celtic. The Gaulish languages are now extinct, being superseded in early medieval times by ▷Romance, ▷Germanic, and other languages. Insular Celtic can be further divided into a Goidelic branch (including ▷Manx and ▷Gaelic) and a Brythonic branch (including ▷Welsh, ▷Cornish, and ▷Breton).

● **Celtic League** ▶ An international organization, founded in Ireland in 1961, that aims to maintain links between the Celtic peoples of Scotland, Brittany, Wales, Ireland, Cornwall, and the Isle of Man. The League strongly favours cultural and political independence for all the Celtic peoples.

● **Celtic Sea** ▶ The part of the Atlantic Ocean between Ireland, Wales, and SW England explored for oil and gas during the 1970s.

● **Celts** ▶ A people who occupied a large part of Iron Age Europe. They were known to the Greeks as Keltoi and to the Romans as Gauls. There were numerous Celtic tribes and chiefdoms sharing a culture that can be traced back to the Bronze Age of central Europe (c. 1200 BC). Distinct stages in its development are represented by the ▷Urnfield and ▷Hallstatt cultures and it reached its highest level around the 5th century BC, a period represented by the ▷La Tène culture. The Celtic warrior aristocracy commanded considerable wealth and power. Burials (e.g. at Vix, France) were often rich and elaborate, containing objects of excellent craftsmanship and aesthetic quality. The Druidic priesthood conducted sacrifices and was responsible for the education of young nobles.

● **cement** ▶ A powdered mixture of calcium silicates and aluminates. On mixing with water it undergoes complex hydration processes and sets into a solid mass. **Portland cement** and similar materials are made by heating limestone with clay and grinding the product. Portland cement, invented by a British stonemason, Joseph Aspdin (1799–1855), was named after the stone quarried at Portland, Dorset, which it resembles. It is used in ▷mortars and ▷concrete.

● **cementation** ▶ The heating of ▷wrought iron with charcoal powder to form steel. The process was used to make swords and cutting tools before modern methods were developed. It is similar to ▷case hardening but the iron was often heated for days before quenching.

● **cementite** ▶ Iron carbide (Fe_3C), a constituent of ▷steel and ▷cast iron. It is a hard brittle white material that combines with ferrite (pure iron) in different ways depending on the type of steel. ▷See also pearlite.

● **Cennini, Cennino (di Drea)** ▶ (c. 1370–c. 1440) Florentine painter. His paintings have disappeared but he is famous for his *Il libro dell' arte*. Translated as *The Craftsman's Handbook* (1933), it is a valuable source of information about early artistic techniques, particularly ▷tempera painting.

● **cenotaph** ▶ Any memorial to the dead that does not contain a body, especially a war memorial. One of the most famous is that designed (1919–20) by ▷Lutyens in Whitehall, London, to commemorate the dead of World War I. ▷See also Remembrance Sunday.

● **Cenozoic era** ▶ (or Cainozoic era) The geological era beginning about 65 million years ago and following the ▷Mesozoic era. It is usually taken to include both the Tertiary and Quaternary periods. During this era (sometimes called the age of mammals) the mammals flourished, after the extinction of most of the reptiles dominant in the Mesozoic. Birds and flowering plants also flourished. The ▷Alpine orogeny took place in the earlier part of this era.

● **censors** ▶ Civil magistrates of ancient Rome responsible for the census, public morality, revision of the senatorial roll, and property investment. Two censors were elected every five years. They generally held office for 18 months. The censorship was instituted in about 443 BC and became the most prestigious magistracy until Sulla curtailed its authority in 81. It lasted until 22 BC.

● **censorship** ▶ The examination of printed matter, plays, films, broadcasts, etc., and the suppression of any material considered obscene, violent, irreligious, seditious, or otherwise socially damaging. In authoritarian societies censorship has been used as an instrument to curtail religious, political, and moral freedoms. It was practised throughout the ancient world and in the middle ages, but controlling the dissemination of texts and doctrines considered undesirable by the authorities only really became a problem when ▷printing enabled material to be widely distributed.

The most notorious instance of religious censorship was the Roman Catholic Church's ▷*Index Librorum Prohibitorum*. Instituted in 1564 in reaction to the spread of Protestantism and scientific inquiry, it only ceased publication in 1966.

Censorship on political grounds in the UK was at first operated through the Stationers' Company (incorporated 1557) and certain secular or spiritual dignitaries. Licensing was introduced in 1538 and legislation to enforce state control continued throughout the Tudor and Stuart periods. Although pre-publication censorship was finally dropped in 1695 the state continued to use the law to suppress seditious material until the 19th century. Licensing of plays was subject to similar restrictions, being carried out by the monarch's Master of the Revels from about 1574; the Lord Chamberlain took over in the early 18th century. Freedom from political censorship characterizes Western democracies but strict censorship is prevalent in China and most of the developing world. In 1993 the Calcutt Report made suggestions for curbing invasions of personal privacy by the UK press, which some editors regarded as censorship. ▷*See also* Defence Advisory Notice.

Legislation in the area of moral censorship is notoriously difficult to draft. In the UK the Obscene Publications Act (1857) prevented publication of unexpurgated editions of such works as D. H. Lawrence's *Lady Chatterley's Lover*. By the Obscene Publications Act (1959) the opinion of experts was allowed to be consulted as to the literary or artistic merits of a work, a relaxation tested in the celebrated *Lady Chatterley* trial (1960). The modified Act of 1964 further liberalized the law respecting material hitherto regarded as ▷pornography. In 1968 licensing of plays by the Lord Chamberlain was abolished. Subsequently (1980) an attempt to censor Howard Brenton's play *The Romans in Britain* by means of a private prosecution failed.

In the UK films and videos are censored by the British Board of Film Censors (BBFC), an unofficial body founded in 1912. Local authorities generally demand that films shown in their areas have been certified by the BBFC. Films are classed as 18 (for viewing only by adults over 18), 15 (filmgoers over 15), 12 (filmgoers over 12), PG (all ages admitted but parental guidance is advised), or U (all filmgoers). There is also an R18 rating for videos that may only be obtained from licensed sex shops. In 1994 new legislation increased the powers of the BBFC to refuse to certify films considered capable of causing psychological damage to children and increased the penalties for allowing children to rent or buy videos of unsuitable films.

The role of censorship in modern democratic societies committed to an ideal of free speech remains a controversial question. Although some are now prepared to argue for complete liberty of expression in all media, most others draw the line at, for example, child pornography or inflammatory racist material, for which there is existing legislation in the UK. Those who argue for continuing or increased restraints point to the vast influence of the modern mass media, and argue that society has a right—or duty—to make sure that these powers are not abused. Through the 1970s and 1980s such calls came not only from traditional moralists but also from many feminists, who argued that pornographic and sexist imagery has a destructive influence on women's lives. However, recent surveys in Britain and Europe seem to show a growing acceptance of sexual material (within certain constraints) by both men and women. Currently, the main focus of concern is violence in films, home videos, and computer games, and the psychological effect this may have on the immature or unstable. The ▷Internet, however, provides a worldwide medium entirely outside the control of governments or censors.

● **census** ▶ A survey ordered by a government to discover certain characteristics of the population, such as its size, occupations, distribution, and trends in fertility, emigration, and immigration. Censuses were taken in ancient China and ancient Rome but the earliest regular census was initiated in America in 1770. In the UK the first census of England and Scotland was taken by parish officials in 1801, since when a census has been taken every ten years. The census of England and Wales is now the responsibility of the Office for National Statistics, created in 1996 by a merger of the Office of Population Censuses and Surveys and the Central Statistical Office. Since 1971 the census form has included questions about ethnic origin.

● **centaur** ► In Greek legend, one of a race of wild creatures, half-human and half-horse, living in the mountains of Thessaly and descended from Ixion, King of the Lapiths. They were defeated by the Lapiths in a battle after their depravity at the wedding of Ixion's son. ▷*See also* Chiron.

● **Centaurus** ► (Latin: Centaur) A large conspicuous constellation in the S sky near Crux. The brightest stars are ▷Alpha and ▷Beta Centauri. It contains the intense radio source **Centaurus A** and the X-ray binary star **Centaurus X-3**.

● **centaury** ► An annual or perennial flowering plant belonging to the genus *Centaurium* (or *Erythraea*) (40–50 species), found in most regions except for tropical and S Africa. The common centaury (*C. erythraea*) is widely distributed in temperate regions. Growing to a height of up to 50 cm, the branching stems bear clusters of small pink flowers. Family: *Gentianaceae*. Certain plants closely related to *Centaurium* species are also called centaury, e.g. yellow centaury (*Cicendia filiformis*) and Guernsey centaury (*Exaculum pusillum*).

● **centigrade scale** ▷*See* Celsius scale.

● **centipede** ► An ▷arthropod belonging to the worldwide class (or subclass) *Chilopoda* (about 2800 species). It has long antennae and a slender flattened body of 15–181 segments. The first segment bears a pair of poison claws and nearly all the remaining segments bear a single pair of legs (*compare* millipede). The tropical order *Scolopendrida* contains the largest species, up to 280 mm long. Centipedes are found under stones, logs, and leaf litter during the day and at night prey on earthworms, insects, and sometimes small vertebrates. They lay eggs or produce live young.

● **CENTO** ▷*See* Central Treaty Organization.

● **Central African Federation** ▷*See* Rhodesia and Nyasaland, Federation of.

● **Central African Republic** ► (name from 1976 until 1979: Central African Empire) A country in central Africa, consisting mainly of a plateau lying at about 900 m (3000 ft). The dense forests in the S are drained by the River Ubangi, an important channel of communication. Most of the population belongs to the Banda and Baya tribes.
Economy: chiefly subsistence agriculture, which is often affected by drought. Diamonds have been successfully mined and are now the chief export. There is also a state uranium mine. Other exports are cotton, coffee, and timber. The country has a massive external debt. An IMF-backed programme of economic reforms began in 1994.
History: as Ubangi-Shari it was one of the four territories of French Equatorial Africa and from 1958 had internal self-government as a member of the French Community. It became independent in 1960 as the Central African Republic under the presidency of David Dacko (1930–). In a military coup in 1965, Jean Bédel ▷Bokassa came to power. A new constitution was adopted in 1976 in which the country became a parliamentary monarchy known as the Central African Empire, with Bokassa as Emperor Bokassa I. He was ousted in 1979 following allegations that he had ordered and personally committed massacres, exiled, and later imprisoned (1986–93). Dacko then returned to power but was overthrown in 1981 by Gen André Kolingba. In 1993 the delayed free presidential elections were won by Ange Félix Patasse. Following legislative elections in the same year a coalition government was formed. A military rebellion in 1996 was suppressed with the aid of French troops; there was a failed coup attempt in 2001.

Central African Republic

Head of state	President Ange Félix Patasse
Official language	French; Sango is the national language
Official currency	CFA (Communauté financière africaine) franc of 100 centimes
Area	625 000 sq km (241 250 sq mi)
Population (2000 est)	3 513 000
Capital	Bangui

● **Central America** ► An isthmus of S North America, extending from the Isthmus of Tehuantepec to the NW border of Colombia and comprising an area of 596 000 sq km (230 000 sq mi). It consists of Belize, Costa Rica, El Salvador, Guatemala, Honduras, Nicaragua, and Panama, together with four Mexican states. It is mountainous with many volcanoes, including Tajumulco, which rises to 4210 m (13 846 ft); its fertile volcanic regions yield many crops (especially bananas, coffee, and cocoa). The people are mainly of mixed European and Indian origin. Following the overthrow of Spanish rule Costa Rica, El Salvador, Guatemala, Honduras, and Nicaragua formed (1823–38) the **Central American Federation** (or United Provinces of Central America). In 1960 Costa Rica, El Salvador, Guatemala, Nicaragua, and Honduras (which withdrew in 1970) formed the **Central American Common Market** to coordinate their economic policies.

● **central bank** ► A bank that implements a government's ▷monetary policy, acting as banker to the government and to the commercial banks. Central banks are responsible for holding a country's gold reserves, conducting monetary relations with other countries, and financing the government debt. These objectives sometimes conflict: for example, the bank may wish to depress interest rates to stimulate investment at home, while wishing to raise interest rates to attract money into the country to aid the balance of payments. Most countries have a central bank; in the UK it is the ▷Bank of England. As part of its programme of monetary union, the EU established the European Central Bank in 1998 (▷*see* European Monetary System).

● **Central Criminal Court** ► The Crown Court having jurisdiction to try all offences committed in the City of London and Greater London. The recorder of London and common serjeant are permanent judges of the court and all judges of the Queen's Bench Division also officiate on a rota system. The court is known as the ▷Old Bailey.

● **Central Intelligence Agency** ► (CIA) A US government department established in 1947 to coordinate US intelligence operations. It is not permitted to operate within the USA and its involvement in the ▷Watergate affair raised considerable concern. There have also been criticisms of its interference in the internal affairs of foreign countries and it has been subjected in recent years to official inquiry.

● **central nervous system** ▷*See* nervous system.

● **Central Powers** ► The coalition, including Germany, Austria-Hungary, Turkey, and Bulgaria, that opposed the ▷Allied Powers during ▷World War I.

● **Central Region** ► A former administrative region in central Scotland, created under local government reorganization in 1975 from the counties of Clackmannanshire, most of Stirling, S Perth, and part of West Lothian. In 1996 it was abolished and replaced with the new council areas of ▷Stirling, ▷Clackmannanshire, and ▷Falkirk.

● **Central Treaty Organization** ► (CENTO) A mutual defence alliance between the UK, Iran, Pakistan, and Turkey. It succeeded the ▷Baghdad Pact. Its objective was military cooperation and the economic development of its Middle Eastern members. Because the UK and the USA, which was an associate member, saw CENTO primarily as an anti-Soviet military alliance and neglected the economic development of the organization's Middle Eastern members, Iran, Turkey, and Pakistan withdrew from the organization in 1979.

● **Central Valley** ► A valley in the USA, in California. About 720 km (450 mi) long and 80 km (50 mi) wide, it is a rich agricultural area, with fruit growing and wine making. The Central Valley Project is a series of dams and reservoirs used for irrigation, flood control, and hydroelectricity.

● **centre of gravity** ► A fixed point through which the resultant gravitational force on a body always passes no matter what its orientation.

● **centrifugal force** ▷*See* centripetal force.

● **centrifuge** ► A device for rotating mixtures of substances at high speed so that the heavier components can be separated from the lighter; the heavier components experience a greater centrifugal force, thus enabling components of different densities (e.g. milk and cream) to separate. The ultracentrifuge is a high-speed device used in the determination of molecular weights and in biochemistry. Large centrifuges are used in physiological research and in training programmes to obtain a high ▷acceleration of free fall (g).

● **centripetal force** ▶ A force that acts on a moving body causing it to move in a curved path. An object is constrained to move in a circle by a centripetal force directed towards the centre. It has an acceleration towards the centre of v^2/r, where v is the object's velocity and r the radius of the circle. The centripetal force is necessary to overcome the object's tendency to move in a straight line; it appears to be balanced by an equal **centrifugal force** directed radially outwards. However, this is a fictitious force. In the case of a satellite (mass m) orbiting the earth (mass M), the centripetal force is the gravitational force GmM/r^2, where G is the gravitational constant (*see* gravitation) and r is the height of the satellite above the centre of the earth. Thus $GmM/r^2 = mv^2/r$, which enables the height of the orbit to be calculated for a given value of v. It is sometimes said that the satellite stays in orbit when the centrifugal force balances the gravitational force, but as the centrifugal force is fictitious this causes confusion; the gravitational force is not balanced by the centrifugal force; it *is* the centripetal force.

● **century** ▶ The ancient Roman unit of a hundred. In the Roman army centuries were the 60 subdivisions, composed of about a hundred infantrymen, of a legion and were commanded by centurions. Centuries were also political divisions of Roman citizens, each of which had a group vote in the assembly of centuries (*see* comitia).

● **century plant** ▶ A perennial herbaceous plant, ▷*Agave americana*, native to SW North America. It is stemless but has spiny leaves, 1.5–1.8 m long, and after 10–15 years it produces a branched spike of yellow flowers, 7.5–12 m tall. After flowering it dies, leaving small plants growing around its base. Century plant is cultivated indoors and outdoors as an ornamental. Family: *Agavaceae*.

● **ceorl** ▶ The free peasant (as distinct from the slave) of Anglo-Saxon England. The economic pressures of the Danish invasions and the Norman conquest contributed to the ceorl's declining status and eventual absorption amongst the unfree ▷villeins. Thus "churl" has come to mean an uncouth person.

● **cep** ▶ (*or* cèpe) An edible mushroom, ▷*Boletus edulis*. Common in temperate woodlands from August to November, it has a stout whitish or brown stalk and a hemispherical cap, brown to white in colour and 6–20 cm in diameter.

● **Cephalonia** ▶ (Modern Greek name: Kefallinía) A Greek island in the E Ionian Sea, the largest of the Ionian group. It is mountainous, rising to 1628 m (5341 ft), but produces crops that include olives and grapes. Area: 935 sq km (360 sq mi). Population (1991): 32 374.

● **cephalopod** ▶ A ▷mollusc belonging to the class *Cephalopoda* (about 600 species), which includes ▷octopuses, ▷squids, and ▷cuttlefishes. The most advanced of the molluscs, cephalopods are carnivorous and mostly free swimming, with a ring of tentacles around the mouth, well-developed eyes, and shells that are reduced and often absent. They are found in both shallow and deepwater marine habitats. In cephalopods the sexes are usually separate and fertilization is internal, often preceded by courtship behaviour.

● **cephalosporins** ▶ A group of ▷antibiotics with a similar action and chemical structure to penicillin. They may be used to treat penicillin-resistant bacterial infections and infections of the urinary tract.

● **Cepheid variable** ▶ A highly luminous supergiant star the brightness of which varies very regularly in a period (1–70 days) that depends on the ▷luminosity of the star. By measuring the period and the average apparent ▷magnitude of a Cepheid, its distance can be determined. ▷*See also* variable star. Cepheids occur in ours and other galaxies and are a major means of measuring distances of galaxies up to about 20 million light years away.

● **Cepheus** ▶ (Latin: Whale) A constellation in the N sky near Cassiopeia. Named after Cepheus, the father of ▷Andromeda. The brightest star is the 2nd-magnitude Alderamin. ▷*See also* Cepheid variable.

● **Ceram** ▶ (*or* Serang) An Indonesian island in the Moluccas. Mountainous and forested, its exports include copra, dried fish, and birds of paradise. Area: 17 150 sq km (6622 sq mi). Chief town: Wahai.

● **ceramics** ▶ Any nonmetallic inorganic material that is made by heat treatment into useful articles. The main categories are heavy articles made of baked clay, such as bricks and tiles, refractories to withstand high temperatures, such as furnace linings, sintered articles, such as abrasives, and domestic products made from earthenware, stoneware, or ▷porcelain (*see also* pottery). Earthenware is made from clay, which when strongly heated fuses into a hard porous substance. The defect of porosity is overcome by glazing with a vitreous coating of silicate. Chinese examples date from about 3000 BC. Stoneware is made from a more silicaceous clay and fired at a higher temperature than earthenware. It is vitrified, resonant, and almost impervious. Porcelain, developed by the Chinese from stoneware, is vitrified, impervious, resonant, translucent, and white. It is usually glazed.

● **Cerberus** ▶ In Greek legend, the monstrous dog who guarded the entrance to the underworld, usually portrayed as having three heads and a dragon's neck and tail. The final task of ▷Heracles was to overpower this monster.

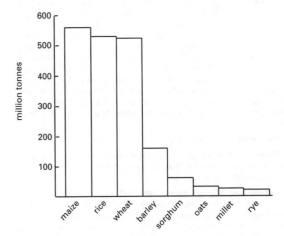

cereals ▶ World production of cereals (mid-1990s).

● **cereals** ▶ Cultivated ▷grasses selected for their high yields of grain, which is a major item in the diet of man and livestock. ▷Wheat, ▷rice, and ▷maize are the most important cereals, but ▷barley, ▷oats, ▷rye, and ▷millet are also widely cultivated. Cereals are usually sown annually and, under certain conditions (especially with rice), two or more harvests may be possible in one year. ▷*See also* arable farming.

● **cerebellum** ▷*See* brain.

● **cerebral haemorrhage** ▷*See* stroke.

● **cerebral palsy** ▶ Damage to the developing brain resulting in uncoordinated movements and muscular weakness and paralysis. The brain damage may be caused by injury during birth, insufficient oxygen (hypoxia) before, during, or immediately after birth, or a viral infection of the brain. Posture and speech are often impaired and in some cases intelligence is affected. Treatment includes appropriate physiotherapy (to improve movement and balance) and speech therapy; some children may also require special education.

● **cerebrospinal fluid** ▶ The fluid that surrounds the ▷brain and ▷spinal cord. It is produced by special blood vessels inside the cerebrum and is reabsorbed by special bunches of veins. It acts as a shock absorber and support for the central nervous system. A normal adult has 130 ml of clear fluid; samples of it are taken for diagnostic tests for diseases of the nervous system.

● **cerebrum** ▷*See* brain.

● **Ceredigion** ▶ A county of W Wales, on Cardigan Bay. Under local government reorganization in 1974 the historical county of Cardiganshire became part of Dyfed; in 1996 it was reinstated as a

▷unitary authority under its Welsh name, Ceredigion. It consists of a narrow coastal plain in the W rising to rolling uplands in the E and N. Agriculture and tourism are the chief economic activities, with some light industry. The county is one of the chief strongholds of the Welsh language. Area: 1793 sq km (692 sq mi). Population (1996 est): 63 700. Administrative centre: Aberaeron.

● **Ceres** ▶ (astronomy) The largest ▷minor planet, 1003 km in diameter, and the first to be discovered (in 1801 by Piazzi). It orbits at between 2.55 and 2.98 astronomical units from the sun, with a period of 4.6 years.

● **Ceres** ▶ (mythology) ▷*See* Demeter.

● **cerium** ▶ (Ce) The most abundant lanthanide element, discovered in 1803 by Berzelius and others. It occurs in minerals including monazite, (Ce,La,Th)PO$_4$, and allanite, a complex aluminosilicate. It is used as a catalyst in self-cleaning ovens, in gas mantles, as a polishing agent, and in volumetric analysis. At no 58; at wt 140.115; mp 798°C; bp 3443°C.

● **CERN** ▶ (European Laboratory for Particle Physics; formerly Organisation (previously Conseil) européenne pour la Recherche nucléaire) A W European organization founded in 1954 to carry out nuclear research. Its headquarters are in Geneva. It built and runs a 28GeV proton synchrotron ▷accelerator, with an intersecting storage ring system, which is 300 m (328 yd) in diameter. It also operates the Large Electron-Positron Collider (LEP), the world's largest accelerator, which was built in a 27 km (17 mi) long tunnel in the Jura mountains. In 1994 CERN decided to build a £2 billion accelerator called the large hadron collider (LHC), which is due to open in 2006, when it will be used to attempt to detect the ▷Higgs boson. ▷*See also* particle physics.

● **Cernauti** ▷*See* Chernovtsy.

● **Cerro de Pasco** ▶ 10 43S 76 15W A town in central Peru, in the Andes 4400 m (14 436 ft) above sea level. Copper, zinc, and lead are mined. Population (1993): 62 749.

● **Cervantes, Miguel de** ▶ (1547–1616) Spanish novelist. The son of a surgeon, he was largely self-educated. In 1569 he went to Italy and fought at the battle of Lepanto in 1571. Returning to Spain in 1575, he was captured by pirates and held in Algiers for five years. After 1580 he held minor jobs in the civil service while writing a pastoral novel, *La Galatea* (1585), and several plays. *Don Quixote* (Part I, 1605; Part II, 1615), his revolutionary picaresque novel about a self-deluding knight errant and his simple but cunning squire, Sancho Panza, won him fame throughout Europe but little financial reward.

● **cervical cancer** ▶ Cancer of the neck (cervix) of the womb, which affects about 2 in every 100 women. An increased risk has been associated with the presence of certain strains of human papillomavirus (HPV), the cause of ▷warts. Early detection can be achieved by a **cervical smear test** (the Papanicolaou test or Pap test), in which a few cells are scraped from the lining of the cervix and examined microscopically for signs of potential malignancy. At this stage the condition is treated by local surgery, often using a laser, and a complete cure is likely. Regular **cervical screening** tests can dramatically cut the mortality of this condition.

● **cervix** ▶ The lower part (neck) of the womb, leading into the vagina (the term is also used for any necklike part). Childbirth is dependent on the effective dilation of the cervix.

● **Cesenà** ▶ 44 09N 12 15E A town in N Italy, in Emilia-Romagna on the River Savio. It is the site of the Malatesta library (15th century), which contains many valuable manuscripts. Pope Pius VI and Pope Pius VII were born here. Pasta, wine, and beet sugar are produced. Population (1998): 88 487.

● **České Budjovice** ▶ (German name: Budweis) 49 00N 14 30E An industrial town situated in the S Czech Republic. Founded in 1265, it has an arcaded square. Manufactures include chemicals, machinery, and pencils. Population (1993): 175 000.

● **Cestoda** ▷*See* tapeworm.

● **Cetacea** ▶ An order of carnivorous marine mammals comprising ▷whales and ▷dolphins.

● **cetane number** ▶ A quality rating for Diesel fuel, similar to the ▷octane number for petrol. Two reference fuel compounds, cetane and alpha-methylnaphthalene, are given the numbers 100 and 0 respectively. Mixtures of these two have intermediate numbers and other Diesel fuels are compared with them in a standard engine. Most Diesel engines can run on fuel that has a cetane number of 40 or 50.

● **Cetatea Alba** ▷*See* Belgorod-Dnestrovski.

● **Cetinje** ▶ 42 23N 18 55E A town in Serbia and Montenegro, in N Montenegro. The former capital of the principality of Montenegro, it has a fortified monastery, which was the seat of the Montenegrin prince bishops. Population (1991): 15 924.

● **Cetshwayo** ▶ (c. 1826–84) King of the Zulus (1873–79), whose kingdom was conquered by the British. Cetshwayo inflicted a severe defeat on the British at Isandhlwana (1879) but was overwhelmed at Ulundi (1879). Captured, he was allowed to present his case in London and in 1883 was restored to central Zululand.

● **Ceuta** ▶ 35 53N 5 19W A Spanish military post and port, forming an enclave in NW Morocco. It has a fine 15th-century cathedral. Population (1994): 68 867.

● **Cévennes** ▶ A mountain range in SE France, constituting the SE edge of the Massif Central and rising to 1754 m (5755 ft).

● **Ceylon** ▷*See* Sri Lanka, Democratic Socialist Republic of.

Paul Cézanne ▶ This self-portrait in oils, dating from around 1875, is typical of Cézanne's middle period, showing his ambition to make something "solid and durable" of the impressionist style. It is one of about 20 self-portraits showing the artist in middle age.

● **Cézanne, Paul** ▶ (1839–1906) French postimpressionist painter, born in Aix-en-Provence, the son of a banker. After studying law for two years, he was encouraged by his childhood friend Emile ▷Zola to settle in Paris (1861). His crude and often erotic early paintings failed, however, to find favour. In 1872, while working with ▷Pissarro in Pontoise, he turned to ▷impressionism, a period represented by *The Suicide's House* (Louvre) but he soon rejected its flickering effects of light and movement in favour of more stability and solidity. His view that nature should be painted in the forms of the cone, cube, and cylinder and his distortion of perspective strongly influenced the development of ▷cubism. Living mainly in Provence, he painted portraits, e.g. *The Card Players* (Louvre), still lifes, landscapes, especially of Mont St Victoire and L'Éstaque, and a series of *Bathers*.

● **CFCs** ▶ (or chlorofluorocarbons) ▷*See* fluorocarbons.

● **c.g.s. system** ▶ A metric system of units based on the centimetre, gram, and second. It includes dynes, ergs, and both electrostatic and electromagnetic units. It has been replaced for scientific purposes by ▷SI units.

● **Chablis** ▶ 47 49N 3 48E A village in central France, in the Yonne department. Chablis is famous for its white wine.

● **Chabrier, Emmanuel** ▶ (1841–94) French composer. Prevented by his father from becoming a professional musician, he graduated in law and composed in his spare time. A performance of Wagner's *Tristan and Isolde* in 1880 made him decide to devote his life to music. His most famous composition is the rhapsody *España* (1883).

● **Chabrol, Claude** ▶ (1930–) French film director, a leading member of the ▷New Wave in the late 1950s. His films, many of which are influenced by Alfred Hitchcock and use murder plots to illuminate bourgeois social relationships, include *Les Biches* (1968), *Le Boucher* (1969), *Une Affaire des femmes* (1988), and *Au coeur du mensonge* (1999).

● **Chaco** ▷See Gran Chaco.

● **Chaco War** ▶ (1932–35) The war between Bolivia and Paraguay that resulted from a long-standing dispute over the vast Gran Chaco region. The dispute, which had arisen in the 19th century, flared up again in the 1920s when new Paraguayan settlements and word of oil deposits in Chaco upset the uneasy truce. Over 100 000 men died in this bloody war. The League of Nations failed to arbitrate a settlement but mediation by Argentina, Brazil, Chile, Peru, and the USA led to an armistice. The treaty, signed in 1938, favoured the military victor, Paraguay, which received most of the Chaco.

● **Chad, Lake** ▶ A lake in West Africa, between Chad, Niger, Nigeria, and Cameroon. It is shallow and has no apparent outlet. Although its area has always varied with rainfall, recent decades have seen it shrink from 10 000–25 000 sq km (3860–9650 sq mi) in the 1960s to a new low of 1350 sq km (520 sq mi) in 2001. The causes include global warming and increased use of the lake to supply drinking water.

● **Chad, Republic of** ▶ (French name: Tchad) A country covering an extensive area in N central Africa, consisting mainly of poor semidesert. The land rises from Lake Chad in the SW to the Tibesti Mountains in the N, reaching heights of about 3400 m (11 000 ft). The majority of the rather sparse population (concentrated in the S) is Sara, a Bantu people; most of the nomadic peoples of the N are Muslims.

Economy: mainly subsistence agriculture with livestock and fishing. Some oil and other minerals have been found but there is very little industry and Chad remains one of Africa's poorest countries, with a huge external debt. The main exports are cotton and meat.

History: from the 8th century onwards the area was settled by Berbers, who formed a series of empires and kingdoms, coming into frequent conflict with their Black African neighbours. French influence predominated from the 1890s and in 1908 Chad became one of the four territories of French Equatorial Africa. It had internal self-government as a member of the French Community from 1958, gaining independence in 1960. Since 1963 there has been considerable unrest in the N where the Muslim inhabitants have traditionally opposed the Black population of the S. The level of hostilities has increased in recent decades, causing deteriorations in Chad's international relations. In 1975 President Nagarta Tombalbaye was assassinated in a military coup and succeeded by Gen Félix Malloum. In 1979 a transitional government under President Goukouni Oueddei was formed. In 1982 the capital N'djamena was taken by rebel forces led by Hissene Habré, who became president. Renewed fighting broke out in 1983 between Libyan-backed forces led by Oueddei and the French-backed government forces; conflict halted in 1987 when both countries agreed to a ceasefire. In 1990 rebels overthrew Habré and Idriss Deby, head of the Patriotic Salvation Movement, became president. In 1993 a transitional legislature was appointed to establish multiparty democracy. A new constitution was approved by referendum in 1996; free elections that same year resulted in victory for Deby, who was re-elected in 2001.

Republic of Chad

Head of state	President Idriss Deby
Official language	French
Official currency	CFA (Communauté financière africaine) franc of 100 centimes
Area	1 284 000 sq km (495 624 sq mi)
Population (2000 est)	8 425 000
Capital	N'djamena

● **Chadwick, Sir Edwin** ▶ (1800–90) British social reformer, who was a disciple of Jeremy ▷Bentham. Chadwick was secretary to the poor-law commissioners (1834–46) and his famous *Report on the Sanitary Condition of the Labouring Population of Great Britain* (1842) prompted such reforming legislation as the Public Health Act of 1848. He was a member of the Board of Health from 1848 to 1854, when it was abolished largely because of the unpopularity that his tactlessness brought it.

● **Chadwick, Sir James** ▶ (1891–1974) British physicist, who worked at Cambridge with ▷Rutherford and went on to discover the ▷neutron in 1932. Physicists had previously suspected the existence of neutrons but could not detect them: by analysing the radiation emitted by beryllium when bombarded with alpha particles, Chadwick showed that it consisted of neutrons. For this work he was awarded the 1935 Nobel Prize.

● **Chadwick, Lynn** ▶ (1914–) British sculptor and designer. His first sculptures in the 1940s were chiefly mobiles in iron, bronze, glass, etc., influenced by Alexander ▷Calder, but he subsequently specialized in stable constructions in iron.

● **Chaeronea, Battles of** ▶ **1.** (338 BC) The battle in which ▷Philip II of Macedon, and his crack army, defeated Athenian and Theban forces at Chaeronea (on the River Cephisus in N Boeotia). It forced the Greek city states to acknowledge Philip's hegemony over Greece and the end of their autonomy. **2.** (86 BC) The battle won by the Roman general ▷Sulla over ▷Mithridates of Pontus at the same spot.

● **chafer** ▶ A herbivorous beetle belonging to the family *Scarabaeidae* (*see* scarab beetle). Chafers cause much damage to trees and crops by eating the foliage and flowers; the larvae, which live in the soil, attack the roots. Chief genera: *Melolontha* (*see* cockchafer), *Cetonia* (rose chafers), and *Phyllopertha* (garden chafers).

● **chaffinch** ▶ A ▷finch, *Fringilla coelebs*, about 15 cm long, that is common in woods and parks in Europe, W Asia, and N Africa. The male chaffinch has a chestnut back, pinkish breast, greyish-blue crown and nape, and two conspicuous white wing bars. The female has a duller plumage with an olive-green back. Chaffinches are often migratory and have a lively song.

Marc Chagall

● **Chagall, Marc** ▶ (1887–1985) Russian-born painter and printmaker of Jewish parentage. After studying in St Petersburg (1907–10) under ▷Bakst, he visited Paris (1910). There he painted some of his best-known works, recalling Russian village life, such as *Me and the Village* (1911; New York). His childlike figures and objects, distorted in scale and often floating upside down in space, influenced the surrealists. Moving to France (1922), he illustrated Gogol's *Dead Souls* and La Fontaine's *Fables*. During World War II he lived in the USA, where he designed ballet sets and costumes and subsequently worked on mosaics and tapestries for the Israeli Knesset building (1966). With ▷Picasso, he was the only painter to have an exhibition at the Louvre during his lifetime.

● **Chagas' disease** ▶ A South American disease caused by infection with a protozoan of the genus *Trypanosoma*. Named after a Brazilian physician, Carlos Chagas (1879–1934), it is a form of ▷trypanosomiasis transmitted by bugs. If untreated, it may result in serious damage to the heart and brain.

● **Chagos Islands** ▷See British Indian Ocean Territory.

● **chain** ▶ 1. A measure of length equal to 66 feet. 2. A measuring device used in surveying. A Gunter's chain is 66 feet long (consisting of 100 links), whereas an Engineer's chain is 100 feet long (also 100 links).

● **Chain, Sir Ernst Boris** ▶ (1906–79) British biochemist, born in Germany, who—with Lord ▷Florey—isolated and purified penicillin and performed the first clinical trials. Coming to England in 1933 as a refugee from Nazi Germany, Chain worked first at Cambridge under Sir Frederick ▷Hopkins and then at Oxford with Florey. For their work, Chain, Florey, and Sir Alexander ▷Fleming (the discoverer of penicillin) were awarded a Nobel Prize (1945).

● **chainmail** ▶ Body armour made by welding or rivetting interlaced iron rings. Light and providing adequate protection, it was popular from about 1100 to about 1400, when plate, first worn under and then over chainmail, began to replace it. Chainmail garments include coifs, mittens, and stockings and ultimately covered the entire body. Worn over felt or leather coats, examples from about 1200 weigh between 14 kg (30 lb) and 23 kg (50 lb).

● **chain reaction** ▶ A series of reactions in which the product of each reaction sets off further reactions. In a nuclear chain reaction each nuclear fission is induced by a neutron ejected by a previous fission. For example, the fission of a uranium-235 nucleus produces either two or three neutrons each of which can induce the fission of another uranium-235 nucleus. Chain reactions are used as a source of energy in nuclear reactors and ▷nuclear weapons. ▷See also nuclear energy; critical mass.

● **chaise** ▶ A light two- or four-wheeled carriage drawn by one, two, or four horses. A chaise usually had a collapsible hood (calash). "Chaise" could also apply to a ▷curricle or ▷phaeton.

● **Chaitanya movement** ▶ A Hindu ▷Bhakti school, named after its founder, the Bengali brahmin mystic Chaitanya (1485–1533). Through the ecstatic singing of hymns and mantras, devotees express their blissful surrender to ▷Krishna and Radha, who epitomize the quasi-erotic mutual love of God and the human soul; Chaitanya himself came to be worshipped as an incarnation of these divine lovers. The Sanskrit scriptures of the movement were subsequently evolved by a group of disciples, known as the six *gosvamins*. Most of the present sect leaders are their descendants and bear the same title.

● **Chakkri** ▶ The ruling dynasty of Thailand (formerly Siam). Its first king, Phraya Chakkri (1737–1809), styled himself Rama I after his accession in 1782. A capable military commander, he had put an end to the hostilities of the neighbouring Burmese by 1792 and then established the new capital of Bangkok. During the reigns of Rama II (1768–1824; reigned 1809–24) and Rama III (d. 1851; reigned 1824–51) Siam's relations with the West improved. Mongkut (posthumously styled Rama IV; 1804–68; reigned 1851–68) and ▷Chulalongkorn (Rama V; reigned 1868–1910) introduced various social and administrative reforms. A revolt against Prajadhipok (Rama VII; 1893–1941; reigned 1925–35) led to the establishment of a constitutional monarchy in 1932; he abdicated in 1935. The present king, Bhumibol Adulyadej (1927–   ), ascended the throne in 1946.

● **Chalcedon** ▶ (modern name: Kadiköy) A Megarian colony founded in the 7th century BC on the Asian side of the Bosporus. It was known as the city of the blind because it occupied a less strategic site than the opposite side of the Bosporus on which Byzantium (*see* Istanbul) was built. Absorbed first by Pergamum and later forming part of the Roman province of Asia, Chalcedon eventually became a suburb of Byzantium. It was the site in 451 AD of the Council of Chalcedon, the fourth ecumenical council of the Church. It condemned heresies relating to the dual (human and divine) nature of

Christ and reaffirmed the doctrines of the Council of ▷Nicaea and the first Council of ▷Constantinople.

● **chalcedony** ▶ A cryptocrystalline (submicroscopically grained) sometimes fibrous ▷silica mineral. The numerous varieties include carnelian (red); agate, onyx, and sardonyx (banded); jasper (red or brown); and chert and flint (opaque grey or black). The last two occur in limestones; others occur mainly in veins and amygdales.

● **Chalcidice** ▶ (Modern Greek name: Khalkidhikí) A peninsula in NE Greece. It ends in three promontories, the northernmost of which contains Mount ▷Athos. There are fertile low-lying areas but it is mostly wooded and mountainous. Area: 2945 sq km (1149 sq mi).

● **Chalcis** ▶ (modern name: Khalkís) 38 28N 23 36E The capital of the Greek island of ▷Euboea, famous as a trading and metalworking centre from the 8th to the 1st centuries BC; Aristotle died here in 322 BC. Chalcis established colonies in Italy, Sicily, and the peninsular region named after it, ▷Chalcidice. It joined Athens against the Persians in 480 BC but the two cities' traditional rivalry was successfully exploited by Philip of Macedon in the 4th century BC. It was partly destroyed in 146 BC by the Romans but was subsequently developed by the Venetians from the 13th century AD and was incorporated in the kingdom of Greece in 1830. Population (1995 est): 47 600.

● **chalcopyrite** ▶ The principal ore of copper, sometimes called copper pyrites, of composition $CuFeS_2$. It is brassy yellow with a greenish black streak and contains 34.5% copper. It occurs mainly in veins associated with the upper part of an acid igneous intrusion.

● **Chaldea** ▶ (*or* Chaldaea) The region of S Babylonia where the new Babylonian empire was established by Nabopolassar (d. 605 BC) in 625 in the last years of the Assyrian empire. At its height under ▷Nebuchadnezzar II (reigned 604–562), the Chaldean empire, centred on the rebuilt city of Babylon, dominated the Middle East for about 70 years until overthrown by the Achaemenians in 539. The Chaldeans' reputation as astronomers survived undiminished until Roman times.

● **Chaliapin, Feodor Ivanovich** ▶ (1873–1938) Russian bass. After a penurious youth, he was discovered as a singer and made his debut at La Scala, Milan, in 1901. He became world famous in the title role of Mussorgsky's *Boris Godunov*.

● **chalk** ▶ A sedimentary rock that is a pure-white fine-grained variety of ▷limestone (calcium carbonate). Coccoliths (the calcareous remains of extinct unicellular organisms) are the main constituents of chalk although other invertebrate remains are included. Chalk is very characteristic of the Upper Cretaceous period in W Europe and the Chalk is sometimes used synonymously with the Upper Cretaceous. Nodules of flint are often found in chalk; these are formed from the remains of siliceous organisms, dissolved and redeposited.

● **Challoner, Richard** ▶ (1691–1781) English Roman Catholic churchman and writer. Educated and ordained at Douai, from 1730 he led the Roman Catholic community in London, being consecrated a bishop in Hammersmith in 1741. He published a new translation of the Bible, and his prayer book for laymen, *Garden of the Soul* (1740), has remained very popular.

● **Chalmers, Thomas** ▶ (1780–1847) Scottish preacher and theologian. Ordained in the Church of Scotland in 1803, Chalmers was an influential minister in Glasgow, where he introduced important changes in parish structures. From 1823 he was a university professor at St Andrew's and then in Edinburgh. He was a leader in the Disruption of 1843, which led to the founding of the Free Church of Scotland.

● **Châlons-sur-Marne** ▶ 48 58N 4 22E A town in NE France, the capital of the Marne department. In 451 AD Attila and the Huns were defeated by the Romans on a nearby plain. The 13th-century cathedral suffered damage in World War II. It is the centre of the wine trade of Champagne. Population (1990): 51 530.

● **Chalon-sur-Saône** ▶ 46 47N 4 51E A town in E central France, in the Saône-et-Loire department on the River Saône. An important commercial centre, it has an engineering industry and a wine market. Population (1990): 54 575.

● **chamberlain** ▶ An officer appointed by a monarch, nobleman, or corporation to carry out ceremonial duties. The chamberlains of medieval England were financial officers and were figures of great political importance in the 12th century. The chamberlain was succeeded by the **Lord Chamberlain**, who is responsible for the administration of the royal household. Until 1968 he also licensed plays for public performance.

● **Chamberlain, Joseph** ▶ (1836–1914) British politician. As mayor of Birmingham (1873–76), Chamberlain effected a considerable improvement programme. He became a Liberal MP in 1876 and in 1885 presented the so-called unauthorized programme, which advocated such radical policies as free education and, with the phrase "three acres and a cow," the creation of smallholdings. In 1886 he split the Liberal Party because of Gladstone's support of Irish Home Rule. As leader of the anti-Gladstonian Liberal-Unionists, he supported the Conservatives and in 1895 became colonial secretary in the Conservative Government. His reputation was enhanced by his policies in the ▷Boer War but his commitment to imperial preference in tariff rates caused a rift in the Conservative ranks, which led to his resignation (1903). His eldest son **Sir (Joseph) Austen Chamberlain** (1863–1937) became a Liberal-Unionist MP in 1892. He was chancellor of the exchequer (1919–21) and then foreign secretary (1924–29), when he negotiated the ▷Locarno Pact and was awarded the Nobel Peace Prize (1925). Joseph's son by his second marriage **(Arthur) Neville Chamberlain** (1869–1940) was a Conservative MP and prime minister (1937–40) of the National Government, when he advocated a policy of appeasement towards the fascist powers. He recognized Italy's conquest of Ethiopia and kept out of the Spanish Civil War. To avoid a European war he visited Hitler three times in 1938, coming to the ▷Munich Agreement, which recognized Germany's possession of the Sudetenland. He returned to Britain claiming to have brought "peace for our time" but was forced by Hitler's invasion of Czechoslovakia to abandon appeasement. He declared war after Hitler's attack on Poland but his ineffective direction of the war led to his resignation in May, 1940, when he joined Churchill's war cabinet.

● **Chamberlain, Owen** ▶ (1920–) US physicist, who shared the 1959 Nobel Prize with Emilio ▷Segrè for their discovery of the antiproton (*see* antimatter) in 1955. They created the particle by bombarding a copper target with high-energy protons in the Berkeley ▷bevatron. During World War II he worked on the development of the atom bomb.

● **chamber music** ▶ Music written to be played in the intimacy of a room rather than in a large hall, church, or theatre. In the baroque period chamber sonatas were distinguished from church sonatas and in the late 18th century Haydn, Mozart, and Beethoven established the piano trio (violin, cello, and piano), the duo sonata (one instrument and piano), and the string quartet (two violins, viola, and cello) as the main chamber music forms. Chamber music has been written for other combinations of players, including the woodwind quintet (oboe, flute, clarinet, horn, and bassoon), the clarinet quintet (clarinet and string quartet), and the piano quintet (piano and string quartet). Haydn, Mozart, Beethoven, Schubert, Brahms, Dvořák, and Britten all wrote important chamber music compositions.

● **chamber of commerce** ▶ An organization that protects and promotes the interests of a town's manufacturers and merchants. Chambers of commerce occur in many countries, sometimes government sponsored and sometimes, as in the UK, as voluntary organizations. Many are authorized to issue certificates of origin and to certify commercial documents, some provide an ▷arbitration service for their members, and some (such as the London Chamber of Commerce) act as an examining board in commercial subjects. The Association of British Chambers of Commerce has some 90 members and is a member of the EC Permanent Conference of Chambers of Commerce and the International Chamber of Commerce.

● **Chambers, Sir William** ▶ (1723–96) British architect and interior designer. Trained in Paris and Rome, Chambers became the most reputable architect of his period, holding assorted official posts and practising a precise, sometimes dull, classicism. His major work was ▷Somerset House, London (1776). His *Treatise on Civil Architecture* (1759) became an influential text.

● **Chambéry** ▶ 45 34N 5 55E A town in E France, the capital of the Savoie department. It was the capital of Savoy (1232–1562) and has a 16th-century cathedral. Industries include tourism, aluminium, and vermouth production. Population (1990): 54 120.

● **Chambord** ▶ A chateau in the Loire Valley (France). Chambord was begun by Francis I in 1519 and was one of his most extravagant building projects. Elaborately decorated and much imitated, Chambord was never completed after work stopped in 1540.

● **chameleon** ▶ An arboreal lizard belonging to the Old World family *Chamaeleontidae* (84 species) and characterized by its ability to change its skin colour. 17–25 cm long, chameleons have a narrow body, an extensile tongue for capturing insects, and bulging eyes that can move independently. Some species have a helmet-shaped head or conspicuous horns. They may be green, yellow, cream, or dark brown, often with spots, and change colour by concentration or dispersion of pigment in skin cells. Genera: *Brookesia, Chamaeleo.* ▯reptile.

chamois ▶ The hide of this increasingly rare animal was formerly used for chamois (*or* shammy) leather, which is now made from the skins of sheep and goats.

● **chamois** ▶ An agile hoofed ▷mammal, *Rupicapra rupicapra*, of mountainous regions in Europe and SW Asia. Chamois grow to about 75 cm high at the shoulder and have distinctive narrow upright horns with backward-pointing hooked tips. Their tawny coat becomes darker and longer in winter, when they descend from the high slopes to the forests below. Family: ▷Bovidae.

● **chamomile** ▷*See* camomile.

● **Chamonix** ▶ 45 55N 6 52E A town in E France, in the Haute-Savoie department near the Swiss and Italian borders. Close to Mont Blanc, it is a mountaineering and winter-sports centre. Population (latest est): 9255.

● **Champa** ▶ An ancient Indochinese kingdom. The Chams were Indonesian in origin but when they established their kingdom on the coastal region of South Vietnam in 192 AD following the collapse of the Chinese Han dynasty their culture became predominantly Indian. Champa's prosperity was greatest between the 6th and 10th centuries, after the demise of Chinese domination and before the Vietnamese kingdom threatened its autonomy. Champa was finally absorbed by Vietnam in the 17th century.

● **champagne** ▶ A wine, usually sparkling, produced in the districts around Reims and Épernay, NE France. It is usually made from black (*pinot noir*) and white (*pinot chardonnay*) grapes. After fermentation sugar and yeast are added to the still wine, which, when bottled, undergoes a secondary fermentation, which produces the sparkle. A dosage of sugar syrup determines whether it will be sweet (*sec*) or dry (*brut*) champagne.

● **Champagne** ▶ A former province in NE France, now incorporated in the planning region of **Champagne-Ardenne**. Ruled by counts during the middle ages, it became important for its trade fairs and at the end of the 17th century began to produce the sparkling ▷champagne for which it is famous.

● **Champaigne, Philippe de** ▶ (1602–74) Painter of portraits and historical and religious scenes, born in Brussels. In 1621 he moved to Paris, where he worked for Marie de' Medici and Richelieu. His association with the Jansenists at Port Royal influenced his later portraits, notably *Ex Voto de 1662* (Louvre), which shows his daughter, a nun, after her recovery from paralysis.

● **champignon** ▶ One of several edible mushrooms of the family *Agaricaceae* (*see* agaric). The fairy-ring champignon (*Marasmius oreades*), common on meadows and lawns, has a light-brown cap, 2–5 cm in diameter, and a slender stalk. They occur in rings of mushrooms marking the perimeter of the underground body of the fungus.

● **Champlain, Lake** ▶ A long narrow lake in North America. It extends S from the Richelieu River in Canada, forming the boundary between Vermont and New York state in the USA for much of its length. It is named after Samuel de Champlain. Length: 172 km (107 mi).

● **Champlain, Samuel de** ▶ (1567–1635) French explorer. In 1603 he followed in ▷Cartier's footsteps, exploring the St Lawrence and the coast from a base in Acadia. In 1608 he founded a colony at Quebec—New France—of which he became commandant (1612). When Quebec was captured by the English in 1629 he was taken prisoner. Lake Champlain, which he visited in 1609, is named after him.

● **champlevé** ▶ (French: raised field) A technique of decorating metal surfaces with polychrome ▷enamelwork. The enamel is held in depressions incised in the metal. Fine examples survive from Celtic England, medieval Europe, and India.

● **Champollion, Jean-François** ▶ (1790–1832) French Egyptologist. After studying ▷Coptic, he started deciphering Egyptian ▷hieroglyphics, building on the intuitions of Thomas ▷Young about royal names on the ▷Rosetta Stone. His *Lettre à M. Dacier* (1822) identified and assigned phonetic values to about 40 symbols. These results were confirmed and expanded in the *Précis du système hiéroglyphique* (1824).

● **chancellor** ▶ In the UK, the name of various state officials. The chancellor, dating from the 10th century, was the head of the Chancery, the secretarial department of the ▷Curia Regis (King's Court). The name derives from the screen (Latin *cancelli*) behind which the secretaries worked within call of the King. By the 12th century he was the monarch's chief minister but his political prominence subsequently declined as his judicial activities in the Court of ▷Chancery developed and since the 17th century the **Lord (High) Chancellor**, as he came to be called, has always been a lawyer. He is appointed by the Crown on the advice of the prime minister, is a member of the cabinet, and speaker of the House of Lords (where he sits on the ▷woolsack) as well as being head of the judiciary. His rank follows that of the royal family and the Archbishop of Canterbury. Current Lord Chancellor: Lord Irvine of Lairg. The **chancellor of the exchequer** is the name given in the 13th century to the clerk of the Exchequer. He is now the minister responsible for the national economy and the presentation of the annual ▷budget. Current chancellor: Gordon ▷Brown. ▷*See also* Lancaster, Duchy of.

● **Chancery, Court of** ▶ In English law, the court in which the system of ▷equity developed. It developed in the 15th century as the personal court of the king's chief law officer, the Lord Chancellor (*see* chancellor), in which he dealt with cases for which the ▷common law could not provide a remedy. It dealt with such matters as partnerships, the administration of estates, and the execution of ▷trusts. In 1875 it was merged with the Supreme Court of Judicature; it survives as the Chancery Division of the High Court.

● **Chan Chan** ▶ The capital city of the pre-Inca ▷Chimú Kingdom, near Trujillo (Peru). Its adobe (mud brick) ruins of temples, residential buildings, cemeteries, and storerooms are divided into nine compounds, covering 36 sq km (14 sq mi). The multiplicity of reservoirs and aqueducts indicate the importance of irrigation in this arid region.

● **Chandannagar** ▶ 22 52N 88 22E A port in India, in West Bengal on the River Hooghly. A former French settlement (1673–1950), its industries include jute and cotton. Population (1991): 122 351.

● **Chandigarh** ▶ 30 43N 76 47E A Union Territory and modern (1953) city in NW India, on the Haryana-Punjab border. The joint capital of both states, it was planned by ▷Le Corbusier in 30 rectangular sectors for housing, government, and industry. Punjab University was established here in 1947. Area: 114 sq km (44 sq mi). Population (1991): 640 725.

● **Chandler, Raymond** ▶ (1888–1959) US novelist. Educated at Dulwich College, England, he returned to the USA and worked in business before starting to write detective stories in the 1930s. The detective Philip Marlowe features in all his nine novels, which include *The Big Sleep* (1939), *Farewell My Lovely* (1940), and *The Long Goodbye* (1954).

● **Chandra Gupta I** ▶ Emperor of India (320–c. 330 AD), who founded the Gupta dynasty. Crowned at Pataliputra, he married the daughter of the king of the neighbouring Lichavi clan and established the beginnings of a large empire.

● **Chandra Gupta II** ▶ (c. 375–415 AD) Emperor of India (c. 380–c. 415) of the Gupta dynasty; the grandson of ▷Chandra Gupta I. He extended the imperial boundaries to the Arabian Sea and was a patron of the arts.

● **Chandragupta Maurya** ▶ Emperor of India (c. 321–c. 297 BC), who founded the Maurya dynasty (c. 321–185 BC). He ousted the previous Nanda dynasty. According to tradition, he destroyed the garrison left behind by Alexander the Great. He extended his empire over the whole of India. The Greek ambassador and historian, Megasthenes, left accounts of the splendour of his reign.

● **Chandrasekhar, Subrahmanyan** ▶ (1910–95) US astronomer, born in Lahore, India (now in Pakistan), whose theoretical work led to a greater understanding of the evolution of stars, especially white dwarfs. He won the Nobel Prize for physics in 1983.

● **Chanel, Coco** ▶ (Gabrielle C.; 1883–1971) French fashion designer, who revolutionized women's clothes, introducing a note of simplicity and comfort. She opened a fashion house in Paris in 1924, becoming known particularly for her jersey dresses and suits and for her perfumes, including Chanel No 5. She retired in 1939 but began designing again in 1954.

● **Chaney, Lon** ▶ (1883–1930) US film actor, whose use of elaborate make-up and disguises earned him the nickname "The Man of a Thousand Faces." Chaney specialized in playing grotesque characters in such silent films as *The Miracle Man* (1919), *The Hunchback of Notre Dame* (1923), and *The Phantom of the Opera* (1925). His son **Lon Chaney Jnr** (1906–73), also a film actor, appeared mainly in horror movies, notably *The Wolf Man* (1941) and its sequels.

● **Chang-chia-k'ou** ▷*See* Zhangjiakou.

● **Chang-chou** ▷*See* Changzhou.

● **Changchun** ▶ 43 50N 125 20E A city in NE China, the capital of Jilin province. Jilin University was established here in 1958. Its chief industry is the manufacture of motor vehicles. Population (1991 est): 2 110 000.

● **Chang E** ▶ In Chinese mythology, the moon goddess. She stole the drug of immortality from her consort and fled to the moon, where she lives in the form of a toad.

● **change ringing** ▶ The sounding of a peal of church bells (which contains from 5 to 12 bells) in a fixed order. Each bell is rung by one person. The changes are prescribed by numerical order, e.g. 12345, 21345, 23145, etc. Traditional variations have such names as "Bob Major" or "Grandsire Triple." Change ringing is practised in English-speaking countries; one of its early protagonists was the Englishman Fabian Stedman, the author of *Tintinnalogia* (1688). Bells operated by a keyboard are called a carillon.

● **Chang Jiang** ▷*See* Yangtze River.

● **Changsha** ▶ 28 10N 113 00E A port in S China, the capital of Hunan province on the Xiang River. A commercial and cultural centre, Hunan University was established here in 1959. Population (1991 est): 1 330 000.

● **Changzhou** ▶ (*or* Chang-chou) 31 45N 119 57E A city in E China, in Jiangsu province on the ▷Grand Canal. A commercial centre for agricultural produce, it has textile and engineering industries. Population (1990): 313 469.

● **Channel Country** ▶ An area of Australia, in SW Queensland. It consists of flat alluvial land dissected by numerous river channels cut during annual floods. Following these it provides excellent pasture for cattle grazing.

● **Channel Islands** ▶ (French name: Îles Anglo-Normandes *or* Îles de la Manche) A group of islands in the English Channel, off the coast of NW France. The chief islands comprise ▷Jersey (the largest), ▷Guernsey, ▷Alderney, and ▷Sark. Since the Norman conquest (1066) they have been a dependency of the British Crown. During World War II they were the only British territory to come under German occupation. Tourism is of major economic importance but the islands are also noted for their early agricultural and horticultural produce, most of which is exported to the UK. This includes flowers, fruit, potatoes, and tomatoes; the Jersey and Guernsey breeds of cattle are world famous. Area: 194 sq km (75 sq mi). Population (1991): 145 821.

● **Channel tunnel** ▶ (*or* Chunnel) A tunnel linking Britain with France. First suggested to Napoleon in 1802, digging was actually started by two private companies in each country in 1882 at Folkestone in England (about 1.8 km of tunnel) and Sangatte in France. A press outcry in Britain forced the government to intervene on security grounds and the scheme was abandoned in 1883. In 1964 the two governments revived the project, simultaneously considering plans for a Channel bridge. The tunnel was agreed upon and in the early 1970s work again started, to be abandoned on economic grounds in 1974. In 1987 Britain and France began work on a 49.4-km (30.7-mi) rail tunnel, which finally opened in 1994, at a cost, originally estimated as £2.3 billion, of £10 billion. In November 1996 a fire in a freight train caused some damage, but no deaths. The tunnel was temporarily closed for repairs.

● **cha-no-yu** ▶ The Japanese tea ceremony, which originated in China but was practised by Zen priests in Japan from the 14th century and later by other members of society. Taking place in a room of simple perfection, it is presided over by a tea master. Its object is to achieve a contemplative calm, in which attention is exclusively fixed on the ritual and utensils used. The kettle, tea bowls, bamboo whisk, and ladle are chosen for their artistic merit. □ p. 258.

● **chanson de geste** ▶ A type of epic poem in Old French. Versions survive from the early 12th century but the genre is probably a century older. Loyalty and valour are typical themes in the *chanson*, many of which relate the real or imaginary deeds of Charlemagne's knights. The famous *Chanson de Roland* is about the heroic last stand of some of these knights at Roncesvalles in the Pyrenees (778).

● **chant** ▶ The short melodies to which psalms and canticles are sung in the Anglican Church. They may be single (one tune adapted for each verse) or double (alternating tunes for alternating verses). "Triple" or "quadruple" chants are less common. Many are adaptations from Latin plainsong made by John Marbeck (died c. 1585) in his *Booke of Common Praier Noted* (1550).

● **chanterelle** ▶ An edible ▷mushroom, *Cantharellus cibarius*, occurring in temperate woodlands. It is funnel-shaped and yellow with the gills clearly visible and measures 3–10 cm across the cap. The flesh is

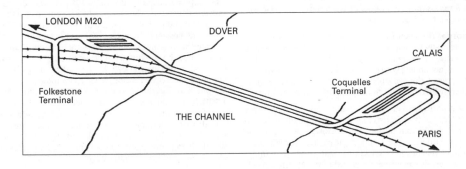

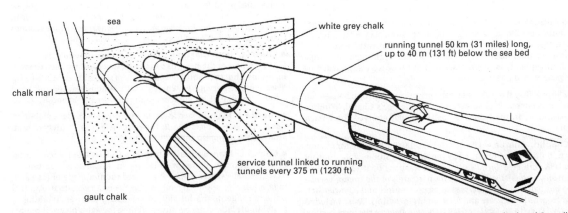

Channel tunnel ▶ A 100-mph (160 km/hr) rail shuttle ("Le Shuttle") ferrying motor vehicles between the terminals at Folkestone, England, and Coquelles, France (see map above) began to operate in 1994. The following year Eurostar began to provide a passenger service between London and Paris or Brussels. The tunnel consists of two running tunnels linked by a service tunnel.

regarded as a delicacy if cooked slowly. Family: *Cantharellaceae*; phylum: ▷*Basidiomycota*.

● **Chantilly** ▶ 49 12N 2 28E A town in France, in the Oise department near the Forest of Chantilly. Once renowned for its lace making, Chantilly is famous for its racecourse and the Grand Château's art collection. Population (1990): 11 341.

● **Chao K'uang Yin** ▷*See* Song.

cha-no-yu ▶ A lesson from the tea master in the Japanese tea ceremony.

● **Chao Phraya, River** ▶ The chief river in Thailand, rising in the N and flowing S through Bangkok to a delta on the Gulf of Thailand. Length: 1200 km (750 mi).

● **Chaos** ▶ In earliest Greek mythology, the goddess representing the primeval emptiness from which evolved Night, Erebus (darkness), Tartarus (the underworld), and Eros (desire). The concept of a confused and formless mass, out of which the ordered universe was created, dates from the time of Ovid.

● **chaos theory** ▶ The scientific study of systems that obey scientific laws but whose behaviour becomes unpredictable in the long term, either because there are too many variables or because the initial conditions are not known with sufficient accuracy. Chaos theory, which aims to predict the probable behaviour of these systems, is used in such diverse fields as biology, meteorology, and economics.

● **chaparral** ▶ A scrub form of vegetation occurring in S California (USA) and NW Mexico. It consists chiefly of sclerophyllous broad-leaved evergreen shrubs and bushes and is closely related to the maquis of lands bordering the Mediterranean. The climate with which this form of vegetation is associated, with mild wet winters and hot dry summers, is sometimes described as the Mediterranean type.

● **chapbook** ▶ A small cheap booklet or tract of a few stitched pages in multiples of four. Catering to popular tastes, they related heroic tales, legends, lessons, etc., and were often illustrated with woodcuts. From the 16th century chapmen sold them throughout Europe and subsequently in North America, until they were superseded by magazines in the 19th century.

● **Chapel Royal** ▶ A chapel for the private use of a royal household. The most famous English example is St George's Chapel, Windsor Castle. In Paris, the Sainte Chapelle originally served the French court.

● **Chaplin, Charlie** ▶ (Sir Charles C.; 1889–1977) US film actor, born in Britain and recruited by the Keystone Studio while touring the USA with Fred Karno's pantomime company in 1913. He gained immediate popular success with his portrayals of the tramp, a sensitive but pathetic figure dressed in baggy trousers and a bowler hat, and from 1918 he wrote and directed his own films. These included *The Gold Rush* (1924), *City Lights* (1931), and, following the introduction of sound, *Modern Times* (1936) and *The Great Dictator* (1940). Accused of having communist sympathies, he left the USA in 1952 to live in Swit-

zerland. Chaplin was married four times; Paulette Goddard (1911–90) was his third wife and Oona O'Neill (daughter of Eugene O'Neill) his fourth. He was awarded an honorary Oscar for his lifetime's achievement in 1973 and was knighted in 1976.

● **Chapman, George** ▶ (c. 1560–1634) British poet and dramatist, famous for his translations of Homer's *Iliad* (1598–1611) and *Odyssey* (1616). His epic poem *Euthymiae Raptus* (1609) expresses his complex philosophy. His plays include the comedy *Eastward Ho* (1605), for which he and his collaborators John ▷Marston and Ben ▷Jonson were imprisoned, and the tragedy *Bussy d'Ambois* (1604).

● **char** ▶ (*or* charr) A food and game fish belonging to the genus *Salvelinus*, related to ▷trout, especially *S. alpinus*, found in Arctic coastal waters and fresh waters of Europe and North America. Its torpedo-shaped body, about 30 cm long, is olive-green to moss-green with yellow spots above and silvery or bright red below.

● **charabanc** ▶ **1.** A large horsedrawn wagon with rows of bench seats, used to carry large groups of people. **2.** A motor coach, used for similar purposes.

● **characin** ▶ A predatory freshwater fish of the family *Characidae* (about 1000 species), found in tropical Africa and America. Characins have toothed jaws and two dorsal fins. Although they range from 2.5 to 152 cm long, most species are small and make colourful lively aquarium fish. Order: *Cypriniformes*. ▷*See also* piranha; tetra; tigerfish.

● **character set** ▶ A method of representing characters and certain operating instructions (control codes) by specific combinations of ▷bits in a computer system or in data transmission. Historically, the first binary-coded character set was patented in 1874 by the French inventor Jean-Maurice-Émile Baudot (1845–1903). Known as the **Baudot code**, it was based on 5 bits and, by use of a shift character, allowed representation of 26 upper-case letters, the numbers 0–9, punctuation symbols, and certain controls. This code is the basis of the present day ▷Telex system.

ASCII (American Standard Code for Information Interchange) was adopted in its present form in 1968. It uses 7 bits and allows 128 possible characters. The values 0–31 are control codes and values 32–127 are printable characters. The use of 8 bits rather than 7 creates an extra 128 possible characters. The characters higher than 127 are used for accented characters, drawing characters, and certain symbols. Although the 7-bit character set (0–127) is standard, the 8-bit set (128–255, sometimes known as "extended ASCII") has a number of variations. Moreover, although ASCII is standard on most computers, certain mainframe devices use a different 8-bit code known as **EBCDIC** (extended binary coded decimal interchange code).

More recently a 16-bit code, known as **Unicode**, has been introduced. This is designed as an international standard character set with unique values for all symbols and for all the characters in the world's living languages and many historic languages, including ancient runes and Egyptian hieroglyphics.

● **charcoal** ▶ The form of ▷carbon that is produced as a black porous residue from the partial burning of wood, bones, etc. It is a very clean smokeless fuel useful, for example, in barbecues and saunas. It is also extensively used in gas filters. ▷*See also* activated charcoal.

● **Charcot, Jean-Martin** ▶ (1825–93) French physiologist, noted for his studies of the nervous system. He described various diseases, including **Charcot's joint** degeneration of the joints associated with disease of the nervous system. He was a famous teacher—Sigmund ▷Freud was one of his students—and interested in hypnosis.

● **chard** ▶ **1.** The blanched leaves of a sucker growth of the globe ▷artichoke, used as a vegetable. **2.** The edible leaves of a variety of beet, *Beta vulgaris cicla*, also called Swiss chard.

● **Chardin, Jean-Baptiste-Siméon** ▶ (1699–1779) French painter of still lifes and domestic interiors in the Dutch tradition of ▷Vermeer. The writer ▷Diderot admired the simplicity of his paintings, e.g. *The Housewife* (Louvre) and *The Young Schoolmistress* (National Gallery, London), and his skill at rendering textures. Working in pastel in his later years because of failing eyesight, he produced his celebrated portraits of himself and his wife (both Louvre).

● **Charente, River** ▶ A river in W central France. Rising in the

Haute-Vienne department, it flows mainly W through Angoulême and Cognac to the Bay of Biscay. Length: 362 km (225 mi).

● **Chari, River** ▶ (*or* R. Shari) A river in N central Africa. Rising in the N Central African Republic, it flows N to Lake Chad, forming part of the Chad–Cameroon border. Length: 2250 km (1400 mi).

● **Charing Cross** ▶ A district in the Greater London borough of the city of Westminster at the W end of the Strand. The last of 12 crosses, marking the resting places of Queen Eleanor's coffin on its journey to Westminster Abbey, was erected here (1290) by Edward I; having decayed, the original cross was pulled down in 1647 and a replica set up in 1863.

● **chariot** ▶ **1.** A two-wheeled horsedrawn vehicle used for warfare in ancient Asian and European civilizations. Commonly drawn by two horses, a war chariot generally carried two men: the driver and an archer or spearman. **2.** A fashionable small travelling carriage of the 18th and early 19th centuries, drawn by two or four horses.

● **charismatic movement** ▶ A Christian movement that emphasizes the charismatic (divinely bestowed) gifts of speaking in tongues, laying on of hands, and baptism by the Holy Spirit. The practice began with the ▷Pentecostal Churches, but since the 1960s many charismatics have preferred to remain in their own Roman Catholic, Protestant, or Orthodox churches.

● **Charlemagne** ▶ (c. 742–814) King of the Franks (771–814) and the first postclassical western emperor (800–14). The son of Pepin the Short, he conquered the Saxon tribes (772–81) and became King of Lombardy (773). In 778 he campaigned in NE Spain, where at Roncesvalles his paladin Roland, the hero of the *Chanson de Roland*, was killed. In 800, having conquered most of western Christendom, he was crowned emperor of the West by Pope Leo III. Charlemagne did much to centralize the administration of the empire while maintaining the traditional customs of his conquered territories. His court at Aix-la-Chapelle became a great European centre, where Charlemagne, the patron of such scholars as ▷Alcuin and ▷Einhard, fostered the cultural revival known as the Carolingian renaissance.

● **Charlemagne Prize** ▶ Award made annually since 1950 by the city of Aachen, Germany, to a person who has contributed outstandingly to European cooperation. Recipients include Konrad Adenauer, Sir Winston Churchill, and Edward Heath.

● **Charleroi** ▶ 50 25N 4 27E A town in S central Belgium, on the River Sambre. The centre of a major coal-producing area, its industries include iron foundries and cutlery. Population (1997 est): 204 899.

● **Charles** ▶ (1887–1922) The last emperor of the Dual Monarchy of ▷Austria-Hungary (1916–18). Charles failed in his attempts to withdraw Austria-Hungary from World War I and following its defeat was exiled. He was formally deposed in 1919.

● **Charles (Philip Arthur George)** ▶ (1948–) Prince of Wales and heir-apparent to the throne of the United Kingdom as the eldest son of Elizabeth II. After studying at Gordonstoun School and Trinity College, Cambridge (1967–70), he served in the RAF and the Royal Navy before undertaking more public duties. He was married (1981–96) to ▷Diana, Princess of Wales, with whom he had two sons, Prince William (1982–) and Prince Henry ('Harry') (1984–), before their separation in 1992 and subsequent divorce. His critical views on modern architecture and ecological issues have aroused controversy. In 1990 he launched a scheme for youth volunteers to work on community projects under the control of the Prince's Trust. He became a leading advocate of modernizing the monarchy in response to public criticism of the royal family's apparent reluctance to join in the widespread expressions of grief on the death of his ex-wife.

● **Charles I** ▶ (1226–85) The first Angevin King of Naples and Sicily, after defeating Manfred (c. 1232–66; reigned 1258–66) at Benevento (1266) and Conradin (1252–68; reigned 1266–68) at Tagliacozzo (1268). Charles' rule gave rise (1282) to the revolt known as the ▷Sicilian Vespers and he was driven from his kingdom in 1284.

● **Charles I** ▶ (1600–49) King of England, Scotland, and Ireland (1625–49), succeeding his father James I. Charles' adherence to the ▷divine right of kings and consequent disputes with parliament led

Charles I ▶ Portrait (1634) by Van Dyck of Charles with his queen, Henrietta Maria.

ultimately to the ▷Civil War and his execution. His first three parliaments (1625; 1626; 1628–29) were dominated by Puritan members, who distrusted Charles' Roman Catholic queen ▷Henrietta Maria, and his own High Church loyalties. Parliament also disliked Charles' reliance on his favourite adviser, the Duke of ▷Buckingham, and attempted to make its award of financial grants to the king dependent on his agreement to its demands. Charles resorted to levying taxes without parliamentary consent and ruled without parliament from 1629 to 1640. His government, largely in the hands of ▷Strafford and ▷Laud, became increasingly unpopular and his attempt to impose Laud's Anglican prayer book on Presbyterian Scotland led to the ▷Bishops' Wars (1639–40). The financial demands of the Wars forced Charles to summon parliament again but the so-called Short Parliament (April–May 1640) proved so critical that he soon dissolved it. The ▷Long Parliament, summoned in November following Charles' defeat by the Scots, impeached Strafford (executed 1641) and Laud (executed 1645) and demanded far-reaching reforms (*see* Grand Remonstrance). Charles attempted unsuccessfully to arrest five members of the House of Commons for treason and in April 1642 the Civil War broke out. After his defeat at Naseby (1645), Charles' cause was lost and he surrendered to the Scots at Newark in 1646. He was handed to parliament (January 1647), seized by the army (June 1647), and escaped to the Isle of Wight, where he was held at Carisbrooke Castle. Charles negotiated secretly with the Scots but, after their defeat by Parliament at Preston (1648) brought the Civil War to an end, Charles was tried at Westminster Hall, found guilty of treason, and beheaded (30 January, 1649).

● **Charles (II) the Bald** ▶ (823–77) Holy Roman Emperor (875–77) and, as **Charles I**, King of France (843–77). After the death of his father Louis I, civil war broke out between Charles and his three older brothers. By 843 Charles had procured by the Treaty of Verdun the western Frankish territories, the nucleus of what was to become France.

● **Charles II** ▶ (1630–85) King of England, Scotland, and Ireland (1660–85). He fought with his father, Charles I, in the Civil War and, after his father's execution (1649), was crowned by the Scots. Defeated by Cromwell (1651), he was forced into exile. After the fall of the Protectorate (1659), George ▷Monck negotiated the ▷Restoration of the monarchy and Charles became king after promising a general pardon and liberty of conscience in the Declaration of Breda. In 1662 he married ▷Catherine of Braganza. At first dependent on the Earl of ▷Clarendon, Charles was forced to dismiss his adviser (1667) after the failure of the ▷Dutch War of 1665–67 and replaced him with a group of ministers known as the ▷Cabal. In 1670 he negotiated the Treaty of Dover with Louis XIV, promising to aid France against Holland and, in a secret clause, to declare himself a Roman Catholic, in return for annual French subsidies. His Roman Catholic sympathies became clear with his Declaration of Indulgence (1672), which annulled the penal laws against Dissenters and Roman Catholics. Parliament responded with the Test Act (1673) excluding Dissenters and Roman Catholics from office, which together with the unpopular Dutch War of 1672–74 served to destroy the Cabal. Fear of Roman Catholicism exacerbated by Catherine's childlessness, came to a head with the ▷Popish Plot (1678), which fabricated a Catholic plot to murder Charles and place his Roman Catholic brother and heir, later James II, on the throne. Charles resisted subsequent parliamentary attempts to exclude James from the succession and from 1681 ruled without parliament. On his deathbed he acknowledged his Roman Catholicism.

• **Charles II ►** (1661–1700) The last Habsburg King of Spain (1665–1700). Charles became effective ruler in 1675. His reign saw the recognition of Portuguese independence (1668) and the final eclipse of Spanish power in Europe. Charles' childlessness gave rise on his death to the War of the ▷Spanish Succession.

• **Charles (III) the Fat ►** (839–88) Holy Roman Emperor (881–87) and, as **Charles II**, King of France (884–87). Charles was the great-grandson of Charlemagne, whose empire he reunited after becoming King of Swabia (876), of Italy (879), and of the eastern Franks (882) and western Franks (France; 884). He was deposed in 887.

• **Charles III ►** (1716–88) King of Spain (1759–88). Charles ascended the Spanish throne after ruling (1734–59) Naples and Sicily. An enlightened despot (see Enlightenment), he encouraged efforts to modernize Spain, to develop its economy, and restore its international position. He sided with France in the Seven Years' War, losing Florida until 1783, when he regained it after the American Revolution.

• **Charles (IV) the Fair ►** (1294–1328) King of France (1322–28). Charles was the brother of ▷Isabella of France, with whom he conspired against her husband Edward II of England.

• **Charles IV ►** (1316–78) King of Bohemia (1346–78) and Holy Roman Emperor (1355–78). He made Prague his capital, where he founded (1348) Charles University. In 1356 he issued the Golden Bull, an imperial constitution, which confirmed the status of the seven imperial ▷electors.

• **Charles IV ►** (1748–1819) King of Spain (1788–1808), who was dominated by his wife María Luisa (1751–1819) and her favourite Manuel de ▷Godoy. Military defeat and Godoy's unpopularity led to aristocratic and popular opposition, which caused Charles to abdicate.

• **Charles (V) the Wise ►** (1337–80) King of France (1364–80) during the Hundred Years' War with England. As regent (1356–60) for his father John II, Charles suppressed the peasants' revolt known as the Jacquerie (1358). Between 1369 and 1375 he regained with the help of Bertrand du ▷Guesclin most of the territory lost to England by the disastrous Treaty of Brétigny (1360).

• **Charles V ►** (1500–58) Holy Roman Emperor (1519–56). Charles inherited Burgundy and the Netherlands (1506) from his father Philip of Burgundy (1478–1506); he became King of Spain and Naples (1516) on the death of his maternal grandfather Ferdinand II of Aragon and Holy Roman Emperor on the death of his paternal grandfather Maximilian I. Charles' vast possessions provoked intermittent warfare with ▷Francis I of France: in 1525, having defeated Francis at Pavia, Charles briefly took the French king prisoner and in 1527, in response to an alliance between France, the papacy, Venice, and Milan, Charles' troops sacked Rome. Their contest for European hegemony ended inconclusively with the Treaty of Crépy (1544). Charles also faced the aggression of the Ottoman Turks, who twice besieged Vienna (1529, 1532), but his commitments elsewhere in the Empire prevented a decisive confrontation and the Turks continued to threaten Christendom.
  Charles' reign saw the emergence of the ▷Reformation and in 1521 he presided over the Diet of Worms, which condemned ▷Luther. His subsequent attempts to conciliate the Protestants failed and in 1546 Charles took up arms against the Protestant Schmalkaldic League, defeating it at Mühlberg (1547). In 1551, however, two German Protestant rulers allied with Henry II of France and Charles was forced to accept Protestant demands (see Augsburg, Peace of). Ex-

hausted by the great and complex problems of his Empire, Charles retired to a Spanish monastery, dividing his possessions between his son, who became ▷Philip II of Spain, and his brother, Emperor ▷Ferdinand I.

• **Charles (VI) the Well-Beloved ►** (1368–1422) King of France (1380–1422). Charles suffered attacks of insanity from 1392 and the ensuing conflict for the regency led to civil war between the Armagnacs and the Burgundians. In 1415 Henry V of England invaded France and defeated the French at ▷Agincourt. After further campaigns, Henry married (1420) Charles' daughter Catherine of Valois (1401–37) and was named as regent of France and Charles' heir.

• **Charles VI ►** (1685–1740) Holy Roman Emperor (1711–40), who issued the Pragmatic Sanction (1713) to secure the succession of his daughter ▷Maria Theresa to his Austrian possessions. His claim (1700) to the Spanish throne gave rise to the War of the ▷Spanish Succession (1701–14), in which he was unsuccessful. In 1716–18 and 1736–39 he fought the Turks; he lost the War of the Polish Succession (1733–38).

• **Charles VII ►** (1403–61) King of France (1422–61). He suffered losses to the invading English and their Burgundian allies until 1429 when, with ▷Joan of Arc, he liberated Orleans. By 1453, he had driven the English from all of France, except Calais. He instituted reforms to strengthen the monarchy but his last years were troubled by the intrigues of the dauphin. ▷See also Hundred Years' War.

• **Charles VII ►** (1697–1745) Holy Roman Emperor (1742–45) during the War of the ▷Austrian Succession. The Elector of Bavaria (1726–45), Charles joined the alliance against Maria Theresa when she claimed the Austrian inheritance. He was elected emperor in opposition to Maria Theresa's husband Francis (subsequently Emperor Francis I).

• **Charles VIII ►** (1470–98) King of France (1483–98), who unsuccessfully claimed the throne of Naples. He entered Naples in 1495 but was forced to withdraw in the face of an alliance between Austria, Milan, Venice, and the papacy.

• **Charles IX ►** (1550–74) King of France (1560–74) during the ▷Wars of Religion. His mother ▷Catherine de' Medici dominated his reign and was largely responsible for the ▷St Bartholomew's Day Massacre of Huguenots that Charles ordered in 1572.

• **Charles IX ►** (1550–1611) King of Sweden (1607–11). During the absence of his nephew King Sigismund (1566–1632; reigned 1592–1604), who was also King of Poland (1587–1632), Charles virtually ruled Sweden, restoring Lutheranism (1593–99). He defeated Sigismund (1598) to become king.

• **Charles X Gustavus ►** (1622–60) King of Sweden (1654–60), who attempted to establish a united northern state. He invaded Poland in 1655 and declared war on Denmark in 1657, from which he regained lands in S Sweden by the Treaty of Roskilde (1658). He died during a second campaign against Denmark.

• **Charles X ►** (1757–1836) King of France (1824–30). Charles lived abroad after the French revolution, returning at the Bourbon restoration (1815), when he became leader of the ultraroyalist party. His reactionary rule led to his overthrow (1830) and he fled to England.

• **Charles XI ►** (1655–97) King of Sweden (1660–97), who reduced the power of the nobles to establish absolute rule. He was defeated (1675) by the Dutch alliance in the Dutch War of 1672–78 but was victorious (1678) against Denmark, marrying (1680) the sister of the Danish king. Thereafter he maintained Swedish neutrality.

• **Charles XII ►** (1682–1718) King of Sweden (1697–1718) during the Great ▷Northern War. In the face of an alliance between Denmark, Poland, and Russia, Charles invaded Denmark (1699) and attacked Russia, winning a victory on the Narva (1700). He dethroned the hostile Polish king (1704) and again invaded Russia (1707), where he suffered defeat and fled to Turkey. He died while invading Norway.

• **Charles XIV John ►** (King of Sweden) ▷See Bernadotte, Jean Baptiste Jules.

• **Charles, Ray ►** (1930–) US Black pianist, singer, and composer.

His style was influenced by gospel music and rhythm and blues; he recorded a number of songs, such as "Georgia On My Mind," in a modern jazz style.

● **Charles Albert** ▶ (1798–1849) King of Sardinia-Piedmont (1831–49) during the Risorgimento (the movement for Italian Unification). He introduced many administrative and economic reforms but reluctantly granted representative government to Sardinia in 1848. He joined Milan's revolt against its Austrian government but was defeated at Custoza (1848) and Novara (1849) and abdicated.

● **Charles Edward Stuart, the Young Pretender** ▶ (1720–88) The son of the Old Pretender, ▷James Edward Stuart. Romantically known as Bonnie Prince Charlie, in 1745 he landed in Scotland, rallied his ▷Jacobite supporters and marched S to claim the English throne. Lack of support forced his withdrawal again to Scotland. Defeated in battle at Culloden (1746), he escaped to exile in Europe.

● **Charles Martel** ▶ (c. 689–741) Mayor of the palace of Austrasia (the eastern Frankish empire). After the death (714) of his father Pepin of Herstal, Charles, an illegitimate son, competed for the succession with Pepin's widow, Plectrude, who was regent for her grandsons. Successful by 719, Charles extended his rule over all the Franks. In 732 near Poitiers, he defeated the invading Muslims.

● **Charles's law** ▶ For a gas at constant pressure, its volume is directly proportional to its absolute temperature. The law is not strictly obeyed but is closely approximated in gases above their ▷critical state. An alternative statement of the law is that gases expand by 1/273 of their volume at 0°C for every 1°C rise in temperature. Named after Jacques Charles (1746–1823).

● **Charles the Bold** ▶ (1433–77) The last Duke of Burgundy (1467–77), who attempted to create a Burgundian kingdom. In 1465 Charles joined a revolt against Louis XI of France, with whom he clashed until 1477. He extended his territory to the Rhine, conquering Lorraine in 1475. He then invaded Switzerland (1476) but was defeated near Granson and at Morat and died in battle while besieging Nancy.

● **Charleston** ▶ 38 23N 81 40W A city in the USA, the capital of West Virginia. It was the home (1788–95) of Daniel Boone. Industries include chemicals, glass, and paints. Population (1992 est): 57 083.

● **Charleston** ▶ 32 48N 79 58W A city in the USA, in South Carolina near the Atlantic coast. Founded in 1670, the first military action of the US Civil War took place here with the bombardment of Fort Sumter by Confederate troops in 1861. Despite earthquake damage in 1866, many of its colonial buildings remain, making it a popular tourist centre, with famous gardens. A major port, its manufactures include fertilizer, paper, and steel. Population (1992 est): 81 301.

● **Charleston** ▶ A ballroom dance of the 1920s named after Charleston, South Carolina, where it had been a popular Black dance in the early 1900s. It became a national craze following the Black musical *Runnin' Wild* (1923) with its 4/4 time, syncopated rhythms, and twisting toe-in steps.

● **Charleston, Battles of** ▶ Two battles of the ▷American Revolution fought at Charleston, South Carolina. In the first (1776) the Americans repulsed the British, whose invasion of the South was thus delayed. In the second the Americans surrendered (12 May, 1780) Charleston after a 45-day siege.

● **charlock** ▶ An annual herb, *Sinapis arvensis*, also called wild mustard. 30–80 cm high, with bright-yellow flowers and hairy toothed leaves, it is found throughout Eurasia and N Africa and has been introduced elsewhere. It is a serious weed of spring-sown crops. Family: ▷Cruciferae.

● **Charlotte** ▶ 35 03N 80 50W A city in the USA, in North Carolina. The commercial and industrial centre of the Carolina manufacturing belt, its products include textiles, machinery, and chemicals. Population (1996 est): 444 297.

● **Charlotte Amalie** ▶ (name from 1921 until 1936: St Thomas) 18 21N 64 56W The capital of the US Virgin Islands, a port on St Thomas Island. Established by the Danes in 1672, it is now a tourist resort. Population (1990): 12 331.

● **Charlotte Sophia** ▷*See* George III.

● **Charlottenburg** ▶ 52 31N 13 15E A district of Berlin, Germany, on the River Spree. The 1936 Olympic Games were held here. Population (latest est): 150 000.

● **Charlottesville** ▶ 38 02N 78 29W A city in the USA, in central Virginia. It was the home of Thomas Jefferson, who established the University of Virginia here in 1819. Population (1990): 40 341.

● **Charlottetown** ▶ 46 14N 63 09W A city and port in E Canada, the capital of Prince Edward Island. Founded in 1790, it is the province's commercial, industrial, and educational centre. Population (1991): 15 396.

● **Charlton, Bobby** ▶ (Sir Robert C.; 1937–) British Association footballer, who played for Manchester United (1954–73). He also played for England 106 times and scored a record 49 goals; he was a member of the England team that won the 1966 World Cup. His brother **Jackie Charlton** (John C.; 1935–) was also a footballer, who played for Leeds United (1952–73) and England. He was manager of the Republic of Ireland team from 1986 to 1995.

● **charm** ▶ A property of matter, expressed as a ▷quantum number, postulated to account for the unusually long lifetime of the psi particle (discovered in 1974). According to this hypothesis a quark (see particle physics) exists having the property called charm. The psi particle itself is a meson having zero charm as it consists of a charmed quark and its antiquark. However, there is evidence that some charmed ▷hadrons exist. Charm is believed to be conserved in ▷strong interactions and in electromagnetic interactions.

Charleston ▶ A 1926 cartoon.

● **Charnley, Sir John** ▶ (1911–82) British orthopaedic surgeon, whose invention of an artificial hip joint has enabled thousands of arthritic patients to benefit from hip replacement surgery. He became a fellow of the Royal Society (1975) and was knighted in 1977.

● **Charon** ▶ In Greek legend, the ferryman who carried the souls of the dead over the Rivers Styx and Acheron to the underworld. Only the correctly buried dead were taken. A coin placed in the mouth of the corpse was his payment.

● **Charpentier, Gustave** ▶ (1860–1956) French composer and pupil of Massenet. He wrote one successful opera, *Louise* (1900), a naturalistic treatment of the life of a Parisian working girl.

● **Charpentier, Marc-Antoine** ▶ (c. 1645–1704) French composer. He wrote the music for Molière's *Le Malade Imaginaire* (1673), much church music (including 11 masses), and some 30 secular songs. His theatre music inclues *Médée* (1693).

● **Charron, Pierre** ▶ (1541–1603) French theologian and philosopher. An intimate of ▷Montaigne, Charron studied law but entered the Church, becoming a fashionable preacher with a court appointment. *Les Trois Vérités* (1594) is a defence of Roman Catholicism. *De la sagesse* (1601), contrasting sceptical and rationalistic, foreshadows ▷deism, and offers a moral philosophy divorced from Christian sanctions.

● **Charterhouse** ▶ The English part-translation of the French *maison chartreuse*, ▷Carthusian house or monastery. The term was especially applied to the most famous monastery of the order, which was founded in 1371 near Aldersgate in the City of London. The monastery was dissolved in 1535, and in 1611 Thomas Sutton (1532–1611), a rich businessman, endowed a chapel, hospital, and school on the site. The school was removed to its present location near Godalming, Surrey, in 1871.

● **chartering** ▶ The hiring of a tramp steamer to carry a specific cargo for a particular voyage (voyage charter) or for a particular period (time charter). Most of the world's chartering is arranged on the London ▷Baltic Exchange. Tramps now include large ships with ▷containerization facilities and some tankers.

● **Charteris, Leslie** ▶ (L. Charles Bowyer Yin; 1907–93) British novelist, born in Singapore. In *Enter the Saint* (1930) he created the character of Simon Templar, better known as The Saint, who featured in many subsequent popular adventure novels. He became a US citizen in 1941.

● **Chartier, Alain** ▶ (c. 1385–c. 1440) French poet and prose writer. He served as secretary to Charles VI and as foreign emissary for Charles VII. His works include the *Quadrilogue invectif* (1422), a debate on the state of France and a call for national unity, and the poem, *La Belle Dame sans merci* (1424).

● **Chartism** ▶ A British working-class movement for political reform, centring on William ▷Lovett's London Working Men's Association (LWMA). Founded in June, 1836, the LWMA drew up a People's Charter (1838) of six points: universal male suffrage, the secret ballot, equal electoral districts, abolition of the property qualifications for MPs, payment of MPs, and annual general elections. The Chartists quickly gained support throughout the country and presented their Charter with 1.2 million signatures to parliament (1839). It was rejected, as were their later petitions (1842, 1848). Chartism lost support in the 1840s because of lack of organization, rivalry between its leaders, Lovett and Feargus ▷O'Connor, and reviving trade. The movement was spent by the end of the decade.

● **Chartres** ▶ 48 27N 1 30E A town in N central France, the capital of the Eure-et-Loire department on the River Eure. The gothic cathedral (begun c. 1194) is famous, especially for its 13th-century stained glass, and there are several other noteworthy churches (particularly St Pierre). Chartres is the principal market town of the Beauce region. Population (1990): 41 850.

● **Chartreuse, La Grande** ▶ A ▷Carthusian monastery in a remote valley in SE France, in the Isère department. The buildings date mainly from the 17th century. The liqueur Chartreuse is made by the monks, the income from it being devoted to maintaining Carthusian monasteries and to several charities.

● **Charybdis** ▷*See* Scylla and Charybdis.

● **chastity** ▷*See* celibacy.

● **chat** ▶ A songbird belonging to the ▷thrush family. True chats include ▷stonechats, ▷whinchats, ▷wheatears, and ▷redstarts; the name is also given to certain Australian wrens (family *Muscicapidae*) and to American wood warblers (family *Parulidae*).

● **chateau** ▶ A French castle or large country house. In the middle ages it was the fortified stronghold of the local seigneur. By the 16th century, however, defence needs had decreased and chateaux became the lightly fortified country residences of the nobility. Among the most famous are the chateaux of ▷Blois (1498–1524), ▷Chambord (1519–40), and d'Azay-le-Rideau (1520) in the Loire Valley. Under Louis XIV chateau building declined with the aristocracy's increasing dependence on the Crown for its income and the resultant need to live in Paris.

An estate or plantation in Bordeaux that produces wine is also called a chateau, whether a large house is attached to the estate or not. These Bordeaux chateau wines are known as claret if they are red.

● **Chateaubriand, Vicomte de** ▶ (1768–1848) French writer and diplomat. Son of a minor nobleman, he sailed to America in 1791 but soon returned to fight in the royalist army. He lived in England from 1793 to 1800. On returning to France, he published *Atala* (1801), an unfinished epic based on his experiences with the American Indians, and *Le Génie du Christianisme* (1802). After the restoration of the monarchy in 1814 he served as ambassador and as minister for foreign affairs. He is best known for his *Mémoires d'outre-tombe* (1849–50).

● **Chateauroux** ▶ 46 49N 1 41E A town in central France, the capital of the Indre department on the River Indre. Named after its 10th-century chateau, it has textile, machinery, and tobacco industries. Population (1990): 52 950.

● **Château-Thierry** ▶ 49 03N 3 24E A town in N France, in the Aisne department on the River Marne on the slopes of a hill surmounted by the ruins of an 8th-century castle. The site of many battles throughout the centuries, it was badly damaged in both world wars. Population (1990): 15 830.

● **Chatham** ▶ 51 23N 0 32E A town in SE England, in Kent on the Medway estuary. A naval base dating from Tudor times, its dockyards closed in 1984. Population (1991): 71 691.

● **Chatham, 1st Earl of** ▷*See* Pitt the Elder, William, 1st Earl of Chatham.

● **Chatham Islands** ▶ 44 00S 176 30W A group of islands in the S Pacific Ocean, comprising part of New Zealand. The main occupation is sheep farming. Area: 963 sq km (372 sq mi). Population (1983): 770. Chief settlement: Waitangi.

● **Chatsworth** ▶ An impressive country house in Derbyshire (England) belonging to the Dukes of Devonshire. Originally a Tudor house, Chatsworth was extensively remodelled (1686–96) by William Talman (1650–1719). Building continued fitfully until completed (1820–30) by Sir Jeffrey Wyatville (1766–1840).

● **Chattanooga** ▶ 35 02N 85 18W A city in the USA, in SE Tennessee on the Tennessee River. It was settled in 1815 and was the site of a decisive battle in the US Civil War (1863). It grew rapidly following the provision of cheap hydroelectric power by the Tennessee Valley Authority in the 1930s. Its varied industries include the manufacture of textiles, boilers, nuclear reactors, furniture, and chemicals. Population (1996 est): 150 425.

● **Chatterjee, Bankim Chandra** ▶ (1838–94) Indian novelist. A pioneer of the novel in India, he wrote romances, such as *Anandamath* (1882), the heroes of which are usually champions of Hindu nationalism. Many of his books were first published serially in *Banga Darshan*, the journal he founded in 1872.

● **Chatterton, Thomas** ▶ (1752–70) British poet. A solitary and precocious boy, he wrote and published poems purporting to be the work of a 15th-century Bristol monk, Thomas Rowley. Despite the genuine talent he displayed, he was ostracized when his deception was uncovered and subsequently committed suicide. His tragic life made him a hero of Romanticism.

● **Chaucer, Geoffrey** ▶ (c. 1342–1400) English poet, whose works established the Southern English dialect as the literary language of England. Chaucer made various journeys to Europe as a soldier and diplomat, held positions in the customs service, and received pensions from Richard II and Henry IV. He translated part of the French poem *Le Roman de la rose* into English and his own poems *The Book of the Duchess* and *The Parliament of Fowls* derive from the French tradition of the allegorical dream poem. Chaucer was also influenced by Dante, Petrarch, and Boccaccio: he parodied Dante's *Divine Comedy* in *The House of Fame* and used Boccaccio's poem *Il filostrato* as the basis for *Troilus and Criseyde*, a long poem dealing with the transitoriness of earthly love, human free will, and divine foreknowledge. Chaucer's

Geoffrey Chaucer ▶ This engraving is based on an illumination in a manuscript of Chaucer's works.

best-known work is *The Canterbury Tales* (begun 1387), a collection of stories told by a group of pilgrims travelling from London to Canterbury. The tales range from the tragedy of *The Knight's Tale* to the bawdiness of *The Miller's Tale*. Colourful portraits of each pilgrim are contained in the famous Prologue.

● **chaulmoogra ▶** Either of two trees, *Hydnocarpus wightiana* of SW Asia or *Taraktogenos kurzii* of Myanmar (Burma), both of which yield a medicinal oil used in treating leprosy. Family: *Flacourtiaceae*.

● **Chausson, Ernest ▶** (1855–99) French composer. His compositions were influenced by his teacher Franck and by Wagner. His small output includes *Poème de l'amour et de la mer* (for voice and orchestra; 1882–92), *Poème* (for violin and orchestra; 1896), and a symphony (1890). He was killed in a cycling accident.

● **Cheapside ▶** A street in the City of London, between St Paul's Cathedral and Poultry. Once an important market place it became a centre for goldsmiths and silversmiths. It was badly damaged by bombing during World War II, but Sir Christopher Wren's church of St Mary-le-Bow (1680), famous for its Bow Bells, still stands here.

● **Cheb ▶** (German name: Eger) 50 04N 12 20E A town in the W Czech Republic. It was a major border fortress, with a 12th-century castle, guarding the NW approach to Bohemia. Wallenstein was murdered here (1634). Following World War I it was a centre of the Sudeten-German movement. Population (1991): 31 847.

● **Chebishev, Pafnuti Lvovich ▶** (1821–94) Russian mathematician, who made many discoveries in the field of ▷prime numbers, the most important of which was a method of determining the number of primes below a given number. He also contributed to probability theory and mechanics.

● **Cheboksary ▶** 56 08N 47 12E A port in W central Russia, the capital of the Chuvash Republic on the River Volga. Its manufactures include electrical equipment and it has a large hydroelectric station. Population (1995 est): 450 000.

● **Chechenia ▶** (Chechenya *or* Chechnya) A constituent republic of Russia in the N Caucasus. Chechenia has an oilfield and deposits of natural gas and minerals. Its main industries are engineering, chemicals, food canning, and wine and brandy making. The presence of mineral waters has resulted in the development of health resorts.
History: the Chechens and Ingushes, neighbouring Muslim peoples, were conquered by Russia in the late 1850s. Each nationality became (1922 and 1924 respectively) a separate autonomous *oblast* (region) before uniting in 1936 to become one autonomous republic, the Checheno-Ingush Autonomous Republic. Following collaboration with the Germans in World War II, many Chechens and Ingushes were deported to Central Asia, being returned in 1957. The republic was re-established in 1957. Following the break-up of the Soviet Union in 1991, the republic declared independence from Russia and then Chechenia and Ingushetia declared independence from each other (1992). In 1994 the Russian army was sent in to suppress Chechen secessionists and fierce fighting resulted in the virtual destruction of Grozny. Violence continued until late 1996, when Russia withdrew its troops, effectively ceding control to the rebels. A peace deal left the formal political status of the republic unresolved. In 1999 Russia launched a renewed assault on Grozny, causing many civilian casualties and a refugee problem. Chechen forces abandoned the city to Russian troops in early 2000 but vowed further resistance. Area (including Ingushetia): 19 300 sq km (7350 sq mi). Population (1996 est): 1 165 000 (including Ingushetia). Capital: Grozny.

● **Cheddar ▶** 51 17N 2 46W A village in SW England, in Somerset, famous for its cheese, soft fruit (especially strawberries), and the caverns (containing stalagmites and stalactites) and rare limestone flora of the **Cheddar Gorge**, a pass through the Mendip Hills. Population (1991): 4484.

● **cheese ▶** A dairy product made from separated milk solids (curd). Curd is made by coagulating milk with rennet or some other enzyme and removing the liquid (whey). It is then salted, pressed into blocks, and left to mature. Cheese is a rich source of protein and calcium. It contains fat but little carbohydrate since most of it is left in the whey. **Hard cheeses**, such as Emmental and Cheddar, are left to mature for some time—years in the case of Italian Parmesan. Cheshire, Port Salut, Edam, and Gouda are **semihard cheeses**. **Soft cheeses** may be eaten relatively fresh, after one day in the case of fresh cream cheese. Brie, Camembert, and Limburg are surface-ripened soft cheeses. Blue cheese, Stilton, Gorgonzola, and Roquefort are ripened by moulds inside the cheese.

● **cheetah ▶** A large ▷cat, *Acinonyx jubatus*, of Africa and SW Asia, also called hunting leopard. It has a reddish-yellow coat with black spots and grows to about 2 m in length. Cheetahs have nonretractable claws and rough pads and hunt by running down prey, such as antelope. They are the fastest mammals, sprinting at up to 110 kph (70 mph).

● **Chefoo** ▷*See* Yantai.

● **CHEKA ▶** The first Soviet secret police agency. Founded in 1917, its full name was the Extraordinary Commission to Combat Counter-revolution, Sabotage, and Speculation. It was headed by Feliks Dzerzhinskii (1877–1926) and fought all anti-Bolshevik groups. Owing to its extreme brutality, it came under severe criticism and was reorganized in 1922.

● **Chekhov, Anton Pavlovich ▶** (1860–1904) Russian dramatist and short-story writer. He began writing comic sketches while studying medicine at Moscow University and developed as a more serious writer after graduating in 1884. Suffering from tuberculosis, he bought a farm at Melikhovo in 1892 and, after a haemorrhage in 1897, lived at Yalta in the Crimea. His first play, *The Seagull* (1896), failed at first but succeeded triumphantly when revived in 1898 by Stanislavsky's Moscow Art Theatre. His major plays—*Uncle Vanya* (1897), *The Three Sisters* (1901), and *The Cherry Orchard* (1904)—were written for this company, and in 1901 he married one of the actresses, Olga Knipper.

● **Chekiang** ▷*See* Zhejiang.

● **chelate ▶** An inorganic chemical complex in which a closed ring of atoms is formed including a metallic ion. For example, two molecules of ethylenediamine form two chelate rings with a cupric ion. Chlorophyll (with a central magnesium ion) and haemoglobin (with a central iron ion) are chelates. Chelating agents are used for sequestering unwanted metal ions. For example, they are added to shampoos in order to soften the water used with them by "locking up" calcium and magnesium ions.

● **Chelmsford ▶** 51 44N 0 28E A city in SE England, the administrative centre of Essex. Manufactures include electronic equipment, soft drinks, and packaging; it is also a centre for retail, distribution, and financial services. The Marconi company was founded here in 1899. Anglia University was established in 1992. There is a 15th-century cathedral. Population (1997 est): 155 486.

● **Chelonia ▶** An order of reptiles (600 species) comprising the aquatic ▷turtles and ▷terrapins and the terrestrial ▷tortoises, widely distributed in warm and temperate regions. They have a protective shell consisting of an upper carapace and a lower plastron joined together at the sides with openings for the head, tail, and limbs. The neck is long and mobile and can be withdrawn into the shell.

● **Chelsea** ▶ A residential district in the Greater London borough of Kensington and Chelsea, on the N bank of the River Thames. It is noted for the Chelsea Royal Hospital for old soldiers (Chelsea Pensioners), designed by ▷Wren and completed in 1692. Chelsea has a long history of literary and artistic associations.

● **Chelsea porcelain** ▶ A pioneer soft-paste ▷porcelain made at Chelsea (London) between 1743 and 1785. From early sparsely decorated figures and small dishes the factory improved to become one of the most important in contemporary Europe. Products included octagonal table wares from Japanese models, copies of Chinese vases and figures, scent bottles in ▷Meissen style, and ▷rococo vases with sumptuous gilding on rich claret, green, and blue grounds in the Sèvres style. ▷See also Derby ware.

● **Cheltenham** ▶ 51 54N 2 04W A town in SW England, in Gloucestershire. A fashionable spa town in the 18th century, it is famous for its schools (Cheltenham College, a boys' public school, and Cheltenham Ladies' College), its racecourse, and its extensive architecture in the Regency style. Population (1997 est): 106 500.

● **Chelyabinsk** ▶ 55 12N 61 25E A city in SW Russia. It is one of the country's major industrial centres, whose products include steel, chemicals, and tractors. Population (1995 est): 1 086 000.

● **Chelyuskin, Cape** ▶ 77 44N 103 55E A headland in N central Russia, the most northerly point of any continent.

● **chemical bond** ▶ The force that holds the atoms together in a molecule or the ions together in a crystalline solid. In general, atoms combine to form molecules and ions combine to form crystals in order to increase their stability by sharing or transferring outer electrons in such a way that the stable noble-gas configuration results (*see* atomic theory). In **covalent bonds**, atoms are held together by sharing pairs of electrons in their outer shells. In methane (CH_4), for example, each hydrogen atom forms a bond by sharing its only electron with one of the four electrons in the outer shell of the carbon atom. Each hydrogen atom then has a pair of electrons, giving it the stable two-electron outer shell of helium. The carbon atom, with four pairs of electrons in its outer shell, has the stable eight-electron outer shell of argon. In the **electrovalent** (*or* ionic) **bond** an outer electron is transferred from one atom to another so that ions are formed. The electrostatic force between the ions holds the molecule or crystal together. For example, a molecule of sodium chloride (NaCl) is formed when the single electron in the outer shell of the sodium atom is transferred to the chlorine atom. As the chlorine atom has seven electrons, the additional electron gives it the eight-electron argon stability. **Coordinate** (*or* dative) **bonds** are covalent bonds in which both electrons are donated by the same atom. They thus combine the concepts of sharing and transferring. ▷See also hydrogen bond.

● **chemical energy** ▶ Energy released in a usable form by a chemical reaction. In molecules, energy is stored as the potential energy of the electrons. During a reaction, rearrangement of the electrons takes place and excess energy is converted to other forms. The energy is usually transformed into heat, as in combustion, acid-base neutralization, etc., but it can be made available as electrical energy in cells. Occasionally, it gives rise to ▷luminescence.

● **chemical engineering** ▶ The design, maintenance, and operation of equipment used in industrial chemical processes. Chemical engineers study both chemistry and engineering subjects. In the UK the profession is controlled by the Institution of Chemical Engineers.

● **chemical equation** ▷See chemical reaction.

● **chemical reaction** ▶ A process in which one or more chemical substances change to other substances, either spontaneously or as a result of heat, irradiation, etc. Chemical reaction involves partial or complete transfer of one or more electrons between reacting species and a rearrangement of atoms to form different molecules. For a reaction to occur, reactant atoms (or molecules, ions, etc.) must collide.

Most reactions are thus bimolecular (involving collision between two molecules); a few are termolecular (three molecules). Many apparently complicated reactions proceed in a sequence of simple steps.

A chemical reaction can be expressed quantitatively in a **chemical equation**. This shows all the atoms and molecules present in the reactants on the left-hand side of the equation and all the atoms and molecules present in the products of the reaction on the right-hand side. The equations must be made to balance so that no atoms are either created or destroyed by the reaction. For example, when water forms as a result of the combustion of hydrogen in oxygen, the equation is:

$$2H_2 + O_2 \rightarrow 2H_2O.$$

Thus, two molecules of hydrogen combine with one molecule of oxygen to form two molecules of water—each side of the equation has four atoms of hydrogen and two atoms of water—it therefore balances. Using the concept of ▷amount of substance, a chemical equation can be used quantitatively. As one mole of a compound has a mass equal to its relative molecular mass in grams, two moles of hydrogen (r.a.m. = 2) weigh 4 g and one mole of oxygen weighs 32 g. Together they produce two moles of water (r.a.m. = 18), i.e. 36 g.

Double arrows are used to indicate that a reaction is reversible:

$$aA + bB \leftrightarrow cC + dD$$

is a general equation for a bimolecular reversible reaction. The direction in which the reaction proceeds depends on the temperature and the ▷equilibrium constant. ▷See also catalysis.

● **chemical warfare** ▶ The use of toxic substances to kill or disable personnel, pollute food or water supplies, or make any other military use of chemicals, for example smoke screens, etc. (explosives are excluded). Toxic substances are generally fired in shells as liquids or solids that form aerosols on explosion. Chlorine, ▷phosgene, and ▷mustard gas were used in World War I but not in World War II. Similar weapons were used more recently in Vietnam and during the ▷Iran-Iraq War. Poisons have now been developed to penetrate the skin, circumventing gas masks. Chemical warfare permits great flexibility in the amount and type of injuries inflicted, ranging from the relatively humane ▷tear gas to the lethal ▷nerve gases. In 1993 100 nations agreed to ban the production, storage, and use of such weapons.

● **chemiluminescence** ▶ The emission of light without heat in the course of a chemical reaction; often known as cold light. It occurs when the reaction yields product molecules in an excited energy state; light is emitted as the molecules revert to their ground state. Under certain conditions, the oxidation of many organic compounds, including glucose and formaldehyde, results in chemiluminescence. ▷See also bioluminescence.

● **chemin de fer** ▷See baccarat games.

● **chemisorption** ▷See adsorption.

● **chemistry** ▶ The scientific study of matter, especially the changes and interactions it can undergo. Chemistry can be said to have originated with ▷Aristotle's four-element (earth, air, fire, water) analysis of matter. This totally incorrect view of the substance of the world persisted unchallenged, untested, and unrefuted from the 4th century BC, through some 2000 years of ▷alchemy, until it was finally demolished by Robert ▷Boyle in his *Skeptical Chymist* (1661). The modern concept of an element, as a substance incapable of further decomposition, was provided by Boyle, who also correctly distinguished between elements, compounds, and mixtures. The elucidation of the structure of compounds in terms of the elements they contain was developed by such 18th-century chemists as ▷Cavendish, Joseph ▷Priestley, and ▷Lavoisier. ▷Berzelius' law of constant proportions and ▷Dalton's atomic theory, produced at the beginning of the 19th century, established chemistry on a quantitative basis. However, it was not until the beginning of the 20th century that the work of J. J. Thomson and Rutherford (*see* atomic theory) had established the structure of the atom, enabling the electronic theory of ▷valence to emerge. This theory made sense of the work of Newlands and ▷Mendeleyev in ordering the elements into the structure of the ▷periodic table. **Inorganic chemistry** is concerned with the study of all these elements (except carbon) and their compounds and interactions. **Organic chemistry** is the study of the enormous number of compounds of carbon; it originated with ▷Wöhler's synthesis of urea in 1828. Organic chemicals fall broadly into two classes: ▷aliphatic compounds (*see also* alkanes; alkenes; alkynes) and ▷aromatic compounds. Many industries, including dyeing, explosives, plastics, and pharmaceuticals, depend very largely on organic chemistry. **Physical chemistry** is concerned with the application of physics to a quantitative assessment of the structures and properties of compounds and the laws that control chemical reactions. Electrochemistry and ▷electrolysis, reaction kinetics, photochemistry, chemical ▷thermodynamics, and colloid chemistry are some of its main branches.

● **Chemnitz** ▶ (name 1953–90: Karl-Marx-Stadt) 50 49N 12 50E A city in SE Germany, on the River Chemnitz. A textile centre since the 14th century, it became famous for machine construction in the 19th century, when the first German machine tools and the first German locomotive were made here. Population (1996 est): 266 737.

● **chemoreception** ▶ The reception by an organism of chemical stimuli. In humans and other air-breathing vertebrates, chemicals ingested in food, etc., are sensed by taste buds on the tongue and walls of the mouth, while airborne chemicals are detected by smell (olfactory) receptors in the lining of the nasal passages (*see also* pheromone). Both smell and taste organs are present in fish but worms and other lower animals have only a general sensitivity to chemicals over the body surface. Chemoreception is used by animals for locating and identifying other organisms, food sources, and scent marks and trails.

● **chemotherapy** ▶ The treatment of disease by means of drugs. The term was originally coined by Paul ▷Ehrlich, for the synthetic chemicals used to treat infectious diseases (e.g. salvarsan for syphilis), but it was later expanded to include antibiotics. Today chemotherapy commonly refers to the chemical treatment of cancer—by means of ▷cytotoxic and other drugs—as distinct from treatment with X-rays (*see* radiotherapy).

● **Chenab, River** ▶ A river in NW India and Pakistan, one of the five rivers of the Punjab. Rising in the Himalayas, it flows SW to join the River Sutlej in Pakistan. Length: 1087 km (675 mi).

● **Chen-chiang** ▷*See* Jinjiang.

● **Cheng Ch'eng-kung** ▷*See* Zheng Cheng Gong.

● **Cheng-chou** ▷*See* Zhengzhou.

● **Chengde** ▶ (or Ch'eng-te; English name: Jehol) 40 48N 118 06E A city in NE China, in Hebei province. During the 18th and 19th centuries the Qing emperors spent the summers here. It was the capital of the former province of Jehol (1928–56). Population (1990): 246 799.

● **Chengdu** ▶ (or Ch'eng-tu) 30 37N 104 06E A city in central China, the capital of Sichuan province and the site of its university. An ancient cultural, and now also an industrial, centre, it produces textiles, chemicals, and machinery. Population (1991 est): 2 810 000.

● **Cheng Ho** ▷*See* Zheng He.

● **Ch'eng-te** ▷*See* Chengde.

● **Ch'eng-tu** ▷*See* Chengdu.

● **Chénier, André de** ▶ (1762–94) French poet, born in Istanbul of Greek-French parentage. He studied in Paris and worked in London before returning to Revolutionary France in 1789. An outspoken political journalist, he was arrested and guillotined. His posthumously published poems, notably the *Iambes* and *Odes*, had a strong influence on later Romantic poets.

● **Chennai** ▷*See* Madras.

● **Cheops** ▷*See* Khufu.

● **Chephren** ▷*See* Khafre.

● **Chepstow** ▶ 51 39N 2 41W A town in South Wales, in Monmouthshire on the River Wye. It is a tourist centre with light industry; the remains of the 12th-century Cistercian Tintern Abbey (celebrated in Wordsworth's poem of this name) are nearby. Population (1991): 9461.

● **cheque card** ▶ A card issued by a bank or building society to approved customers that guarantees payment to the payees of that cus-

tomer's cheques regardless of the state of his balance. A cheque that has been supported by a cheque card cannot be stopped.

● **Chequers** ▶ (or Chequers Court) A country house in S England, in Buckinghamshire near Princes Risborough. Dating from 1565, it was given to the nation by Arthur Hamilton, 1st Viscount Lee of Fareham (1868–1947), and has been the official country residence of British prime ministers since 1921, when it was occupied by David Lloyd George.

● **Cher, River** ▶ A river in central France, rising in the Massif Central near Aubusson and flowing NW to join the River Loire near Tours. Length: 354 km (220 mi).

● **Cherbourg** ▶ 49 38N 1 37W A seaport in NW France, in the Manche department on the Cotentin Peninsula. Cherbourg has civil and military docks and large shipbuilding yards. In the heyday of ocean liners Cherbourg was an important transatlantic port; the cross-channel service to Southampton remains important. Population (1990): 30 112.

● **Cheremkhovo** ▶ 53 08N 103 01E A city in SE Russia. A coalmining centre, it also refines oil and produces chemicals. Population (1990 est): 75 000.

● **Cherenkov, Pavel Alekseievich** ▶ (1904–90) Russian physicist, who discovered **Cherenkov radiation** in 1934. This radiation consists of blue-white light emitted by the atoms of a medium through which a high-energy charged particle is passing at a speed in excess of the speed of light in that medium. Three years later the effect was explained by ▷Franck and Igor Tamm (1895–1971). The three physicists shared the 1958 Nobel Prize.

● **Cheribon** ▷*See* Tjirebon.

● **Chernenko, Konstantin Ustinovich** ▶ (1911–85) Soviet statesman; secretary of the Soviet Communist Party and president of the Soviet Union (1984–85). A protégé of Brezhnev, he made few reforms in his short period in office.

● **Chernigov** ▶ 51 30N 31 18E A city in N central Ukraine, on the River Desna. Chernigov was heavily bombed during World War II although several medieval buildings remain. It is an important railway junction and its manufactures include tyres, pianos, and consumer goods. Population (1996 est): 312 000.

● **Chernobyl** ▶ 51 17N 30 15E A town in N Ukraine. In 1986 the nuclear reactor exploded, causing the deaths of 31 people at the time and a further 270 deaths later and increasing levels of radioactivity in many parts of the world (*see* meltdown). Mass evacuation of those near the reactor followed; the reactor itself was subsequently entombed in concrete. The accident led to reviews of the safety of ▷nuclear power. ▷*See also* radiation sickness.

● **Chernovtsy** ▶ (Romanian name: Cernauti) 48 19N 25 52E A city in Ukraine on the River Prut. It was held by Romania between 1918 and 1940. It is an important rail junction, industrial, cultural, and scientific centre. Population (1996 est): 261 000.

● **chernozem** ▶ (or black earth) A type of soil that is characteristic of the grasslands of the continental interiors. There is a dark surface layer rich in alkaline humus, underlain by calcium carbonate concretions. Chernozems are agriculturally among the richest soils in the world.

● **Cherokee** ▶ A North American Indian people of the hill country of E Tennessee and North Carolina, speaking an Iroquoian language. They lived in farming towns of 30 to 60 log cabins. There were about 60 such towns organized into two groups, the red (or war) towns and the white (or peace) towns, each under the authority of a separate chief and each separately responsible for the performance of ceremonies associated with war or peace.

● **Cherrapunji** ▶ 25 16N 91 42E A village in India, in Meghalaya. It has the world's second highest mean annual rainfall: 11 430 mm (450 in). Population (latest est): 6097.

● **cherry** ▶ A tree or shrub of the genus ▷*Prunus*, of N temperate regions, having small rounded juicy fruits surrounding a hard stone containing a seed. Cherry trees produce clusters of white or pinkish flowers in spring, and some varieties are grown only for ornament. Cherries cultivated for their fruits are of two main types—sour and sweet. Sour cherries have been developed from *P. cerasus*, a widespread shrubby tree growing to 7 m. Morello—the best variety—has dark-red fruits used in jams and liqueurs. Sweet dessert cherries arose from the gean (*P. avium*), native to Eurasia and N Africa. Found in woods and hedges, it grows to 25 m. Fruits of cultivated forms vary from pale yellow to dark red. Hybrids between *P. cerasus* and *P. avium* are used for cooking.

● **cherry laurel** ▶ An evergreen shrub, *Prunus laurocerasus*, 2–6 m high, producing spikes of fragrant whitish flowers in spring. A native of SE Europe and SW Asia, it has been introduced and locally naturalized elsewhere in hedges and woodlands. Family: *Rosaceae*.

● **chert** ▶ A variety of chalcedony, occurring in a stratified form. It consists of minute crystals of silica, of either organic or inorganic origin, found in sedimentary rocks.

● **cherubim and seraphim** ▶ Supernatural beings who, according to ▷Dionysius the Areopagite, are the two highest orders of ▷angels in the celestial hierarchy. The seraphim are described by Isaiah (Isaiah 6.2–7) as six-winged attendants upon God's throne. The cherubim, who are traditionally depicted as winged heads, appear in the Bible as guardians of the divine presence; for instance, they bar the approaches to the Garden of Eden after the Fall (Genesis 3.24).

● **Cherubini, Maria Luigi** ▶ (1760–1842) Italian composer. After a brief appointment as court composer to George III in London (1784–88), he spent most of the rest of his life in France, becoming director of the Paris Conservatoire in 1822. He was primarily an operatic composer, writing over 30 operas, of which the best known is *Médée* (1797); his *Deux Journées* (*The Watercarrier*; 1800) influenced Beethoven. He also wrote two settings of the requiem mass and six string quartets in an original style.

● **chervil** ▶ An annual herb, *Anthriscus cerefolium*, 30–50 cm high, grown for its leaves, used for salads and seasonings. Its white flowers grow in umbrella-like clusters. A native of central, E, and S Europe, it now grows on hedgebanks and waste ground throughout Europe, the Americas, N Africa, and New Zealand. Family: ▷*Umbelliferae*.

● **Cherwell, Viscount** ▷*See* Lindemann, Frederick Alexander, 1st Viscount Cherwell.

● **Chesapeake Bay** ▶ The largest inlet on the USA's Atlantic coast, bordering on Virginia and Maryland. Length: approximately 320 km (200 mi).

● **Cheshire** ▶ A county in NW England, bordering on Wales. It consists chiefly of the low-lying Cheshire Plain rising to the Pennines in the E. It is predominantly agricultural, dairy farming being especially important. In 1974 the northern part of the Wirral Peninsula, including Birkenhead, became part of Merseyside and the areas in the NE, including Stockport, passed to Greater Manchester. Warrington and Halton (Widnes and Runcorn) became independent ▷unitary authorities in 1998. Industries include chemicals, based on the Cheshire salt fields, and textiles. Area (excluding unitary authorities): 2077 sq km (802 sq mi). Population (1996 est, excluding unitary authorities): 668 000. Administrative centre: Chester.

● **Cheshire, (Geoffrey) Leonard, Baron** ▶ (1917–92) British philanthropist. In the RAF during World War II, he won the Victoria Cross. His horror at the atomic bombing of Nagasaki, at which he was a British observer, led him to devote himself to the relief of suffering. He founded the Cheshire Foundation Homes for the incurably sick, of which there are now some 330 in 53 countries and (in 1989) launched the World War Memorial Fund for Disaster Relief. He was made a life peer in 1991. He married (1959) **Sue, Baroness Ryder** (1923–2000), who founded the Sue Ryder Foundation for the Sick and Disabled of All Age Groups. A chain of charity shops fund her philanthropic activities, which began with refugee relief work after World War II.

● **Chesil Beach** ▶ (*or* Chesil Bank) 50 36N 2 32W A shingle bank in S England, on the Dorset coast, joining the Isle of ▷Portland to the mainland at Abbotsbury and extending westwards to near Bridport. On the landward side it encloses a long narrow lagoon known as the

Fleet. Its full length is about 28 km (18 mi) and it reaches a height of nearly 14 m (45 ft) at the Portland end.

● **chess** ▶ A board game for two players, each of whom controls 16 pieces. The pieces are moved according to strict rules, the object of the game being to force the opponent's king into a position from which it cannot escape. A player attempts to weaken his opponent's position by capturing his pieces. This he does by moving his own pieces onto the squares occupied by his opponent's pieces. Only the kings cannot be captured in this way. After an initial lottery to choose the player who makes the first move, the game becomes one of pure skill with a vast literature devoted to its tactics and strategy. Chess has been variously described as a game, sport, art, science, vocation, and (with advertising) the greatest waste of human ingenuity. To the extent that it simulates war it has been regarded as a psychological sublimation of human aggression, although more lyrical writers have seen it as a source of Indian symbolism and allegory. Chess pieces dating back to the 2nd century demonstrate the game's antiquity. Well known to 5th-century Hindus, it seems to have reached Europe, via Persia and Arabia, in the 10th century. The rules of the game have hardly changed since the 16th century, although the identities of some of the pieces have. Since 1922 the rules have been controlled by the Fédération internationale des Échecs (FIDE), which has organized world championships since 1946. In 1985, because of the prolonged indecisive 1984 championship contest, it decreed a maximum of 24 matches to decide the title. Famous world champions include Emanuel ▷Lasker (1894–1921), José ▷Capablanca (1921–27), Alexander ▷Alekhine, (1927–35; 1937–46), Boris ▷Spassky (1969–72), Bobby ▷Fischer (1972–75), Anatoly ▷Karpov (1975–85), and Gary ▷Kasparov (1985–93). In 1993 Kasparov and the British player Nigel Short (1965–   ) left FIDE, set up a rival league, the Professional Chess Association (PCA), and declared Kasparov world champion, while FIDE declared Karpov champion. The situation remains unresolved.

● **chest** ▶ A large domestic storage box. Chests from ancient Egypt are among the earliest surviving furniture. In Europe they were essential pieces of portable furniture doubling as a bed, table, or seat. The simplest consist of six boards nailed together with one forming a lid, but between the 15th and the 18th centuries they were elaborated into decorative furniture. In Europe specimens were panelled and carved; 16th-century Italian chests (cassoni) might be carved and gilded.

● **Chester** ▶ 53 12N 2 54W A city in NW England, the administrative centre of Cheshire on the River Dee. It was a Roman fortress (Deva) and a medieval walled city and port (the walls remain intact and there are many half-timbered buildings). The Rows are two-tiered arcades of shops with covered balustrades. Its cathedral dates from the 11th century. Chester is a commercial and railway centre, with clothing and metallurgical industries. Population (1995): 120 100.

● **chesterfield** ▶ A kind of settee introduced in 19th-century England. It has a low back curving to form upright armrests and is comfortably upholstered with coil springs.

● **Chesterfield** ▶ 53 15N 1 25W A town in N central England, in Derbyshire. Its 14th-century parish church has a famous crooked spire. Chesterfield's industries include engineering, glass, plastics, and packaging. Population (1997 est): 100 300.

● **Chesterfield, Philip Dormer Stanhope, 4th Earl of** ▶ (1694–1773) British statesman, diplomat, and writer. He served as ambassador to The Hague (1728–36), lord lieutenant of Ireland (1745–46), and secretary of state (1746–48). A patron of many authors, he is best remembered for his worldly and sophisticated *Letters to His Son* (1774).

● **Chesterton, G(ilbert) K(eith)** ▶ (1874–1936) British essayist, novelist, and poet. His best work was done as literary journalism, although the detective stories featuring a Roman Catholic priest and beginning with *The Innocence of Father Brown* (1911) were also highly successful. He met Hilaire ▷Belloc in 1900. Their names were often linked as romantic opponents of the socialism of G. B. Shaw and H. G. Wells. Chesterton was converted to Roman Catholicism in 1922, and thereafter most of his work was devoted to religious subjects, for example *St Francis of Assisi* (1923). His published work amounts to

chess

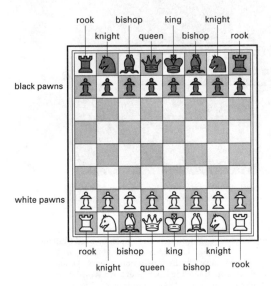

rook bishop king knight

knight queen bishop rook

black pawns

white pawns

rook bishop king knight

knight queen bishop rook

The chessboard ready for play. A white square is always on the player's right. The queen always starts on a square of her own colour.

	a	b	c	d	e	f	g	h	
8	QR1 QR8	QN1 QN8	QB1 QB8	Q1 Q8	K1 K8	KB1 KB8	KN1 KN8	KR1 KR8	**1**
7	QR2 QR7	QN2 QN7	QB2 QB7	Q2 Q7	K2 K7	KB2 KB7	KN2 KN7	KR2 KR7	**2**
6	QR3 QR6	QN3 QN6	QB3 QB6	Q3 Q6	K3 K6	KB3 KB6	KN3 KN6	KR3 KR6	**3**
5	QR4 QR5	QN4 QN5	QB4 QB5	Q4 Q5	K4 K5	KB4 KB5	KN4 KN5	KR4 KR5	**4**
4	QR5 QR4	QN5 QN4	QB5 QB4	Q5 Q4	K5 K4	KB5 KB4	KN5 KN4	KR5 KR4	**5**
3	QR6 QR3	QN6 QN3	QB6 QB3	Q6 Q3	K6 K3	KB6 KB3	KN6 KN3	KR6 KR3	**6**
2	QR7 QR2	QN7 QN2	QB7 QB2	Q7 Q2	K7 K2	KB7 KB2	KN7 KN2	KR7 KR2	**7**
1	QR8 QR1	QN8 QN1	QB8 QB1	Q8 Q1	K8 K1	KB8 KB1	KN8 KN1	KR8 KR1	**8**
	a	b	c	d	e	f	g	h	

BLACK *(top)*

WHITE *(bottom)*

Chess notations. In the algebraic notation each square is referred to by a file letter a–h and a rank number 1–8. In the descriptive notation the files bear the names of the piece on the first rank. The ranks are counted 1–8 away from the player.

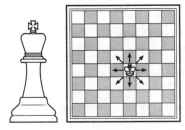

The king, weak and vulnerable, moves only one square at a time (in any direction). The name of the game is a corruption of the Persian word for king–shah.

The queen, the most powerful piece, moves any distance in any direction. Originally known as the counsellor, its present name and moves were adopted in the 15th century.

The rook or castle moves any distance vertically or horizontally. Originally represented as a chariot (Arabic: rukh), it is known in many languages as a castle or tower (French: tour).

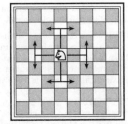

The knight, the only piece to jump over other pieces, moves one square horizontally and two vertically or two horizontally and one vertically. Usually represented by a horse's head, it is sometimes known as the horse (as it was in the Arabic version).

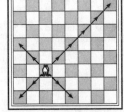

The bishop moves in any direction diagonally. In the Hindu and Arabic games the piece was called an elephant. In the European games the piece has acquired a variety of identities: a bishop in English, a jester (fou) in French, a runner (Laufer) in German, but still an elephant (slon) in Russian.

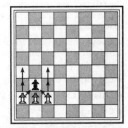

The pawn moves forward one square (or two on its first move). In Arabic it was called a foot-soldier, the English word deriving from the Latin pes, pedis. In some European languages the piece is called a peasant (e.g. German: Bauer).

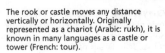

more than 100 volumes, among which are the critical studies *Dickens* (1906) and *The Victorian Age in Literature* (1913) and the fictional works *The Napoleon of Notting Hill* (1904), *The Club of Queer Trades*, (1905), and *The Man Who Was Thursday* (1908).

● **chestnut** ▶ A tree, *Castanea sativa*, also called sweet or Spanish chestnut, bearing large brown edible nuts inside prickly burs. Native to Europe and N Africa and widely introduced, it grows to a height of 30 m. The leaves—10–25 cm long—are toothed and pointed and the flowers grow in yellow catkins, 10–12 cm long. The North American chestnut (*C. dentata*)—once one of the largest common trees of eastern areas—has been largely destroyed by the chestnut blight fungus. Family: *Fagaceae* (beech family). *Compare* horse chestnut.

● **Chetniks** ▶ Members of a Yugoslav resistance movement in World War II. They were organized in groups by General Draža ▷Mihajlović in March, 1941, against the German invasion but were chiefly in conflict with the communist Partisans under ▷Tito. In 1944 the Allies transferred their support from the Chetniks to Tito. After the war the Chetniks were proscribed.

● **Chevalier, Maurice** ▶ (1888–1972) French singer and actor. Starting as an entertainer in Parisian revues, he went to Hollywood in the 1930s and starred in many successful musical films. These included *Love Me Tonight* (1932), *Love in the Afternoon* (1957), and *Gigi* (1958).

● **cheviot** ▶ A woollen fabric manufactured from the soft fine easily spun fleece of Cheviot sheep found in the English-Scottish border country. The cloth is much used as heavy suiting material; ▷worsted is sometimes added for greater firmness of texture.

● **Cheviot Hills** ▶ A range of hills in the UK. They extend along the border between Scotland and England, mainly in Northumberland, reaching 816 m (2677 ft) at The Cheviot.

● **chevrotain** ▶ A small hoofed mammal of the family *Tragulidae*. Asiatic chevrotains (genus *Tragulus*; 3–6 species), also called mouse deer, of SE Asia, measure 20–33 cm at the shoulder and resemble small deer. Their brownish coats have white underparts; some species have white stripes or spots on the body. They are not true deer, lacking antlers and having a three-chambered stomach; males have enlarged upper canine teeth that form tusks. The African water chevrotain (*Hyemoschus aquaticus*) is very similar.

● **chewing gum** ▶ A sweetened flavoured gum made from ▷chicle or a synthetic substitute, such as polyvinyl acetate, which is chewed to extract its flavour but not swallowed. It was first patented (1871) in the USA.

● **Cheyenne** ▶ An Algonquian-speaking North American Indian people of the Plains region. They orginally lived in what is now Minnesota but intertribal wars forced the abandonment of their agriculturalist life in favour of the nomadic buffalo-hunting culture of the Plains. After a period of wandering they eventually divided into a northern branch and a southern branch. They had an elaborate religious ritual, including the sun dance. They were governed by a council of 44 chiefs; an important feature of their social organization was the military or warrior societies. They frequently fought with White settlers and the northern branch was present at the Battle of the ▷Little Bighorn (1876).

● **Cheyenne** ▶ 41 08N 104 50W A city in the USA, the capital and largest city of Wyoming. It is an agricultural trading centre. Population (1990): 50 008.

● **Chiang Ch'ing** ▷*See* Jiang Qing.

● **Chiang Ching-kuo** ▷*See* Chiang Kai-shek.

● **Chiang-hsi** ▷*See* Jiangxi.

● **Chiang Kai-shek** ▶ (or Jiang Jie Shi; 1887–1975) Nationalist Chinese soldier and statesman. He took part in the overthrow of the ▷Qing dynasty in 1911, joined ▷Sun Yat-sen's ▷Guomindang (Nationalist People's Party) in 1918, and became commandant of the Whampoa military academy in 1923. After Sun's death (1925), Chiang became leader of the Guomindang and in 1926, in alliance with the communists (*see* United Fronts), launched the Northern Expedition to regain China from the ▷warlords. The Communist-

Chiang Kai-shek ▶ At his mountain home at Tsao Shan. On the wall behind are two poems, which he wrote during his imprisonment.

Guomindang coalition ended in 1927 and Chiang, with his capital at Nanjing, fought the communists until Japan invaded China in 1931. Chiang's own army (*see* Xi An incident) forced him to join forces with the communists against their common enemy, Japan (*see* Sino-Japanese Wars), but following Japan's defeat in World War II civil war again broke out in China (1946), ending with Guomindang defeat (1949). Chiang was forced to flee to ▷Taiwan, where he established the Republic of China. His son **Jiang Jing Guo** (*or* Chiang Ching-kuo; 1910–88), prime minister (1971–78) and president (1978–88), studied in the Soviet Union and married a Russian. On returning to China in 1937, he joined the Guomindang, fleeing with his father to Taiwan in 1949.

● **Chiang-su** ▷*See* Jiangsu.

● **Chianti** ▶ A region of hills in N central Italy, in Tuscany between Florence and Siena. Chianti wine is produced here.

● **chiaroscuro** ▶ (Italian: light-dark) The overall pattern of light and shade in a picture. Controlled chiaroscuro was an important element of ▷Renaissance composition, while strong contrasts of light and shade were a main feature of ▷baroque painting. Chiaroscuro is displayed to supreme effect in the etchings of ▷Rembrandt and ▷Whistler.

● **Chiba** ▶ 35 38N 140 07E A city and seaport in Japan, in central Honshu on Tokyo Bay. It is the site of an 8th-century Buddhist temple and a university (1949). Industries include steel, paper, and textiles. Population (1995 est): 856 882.

● **Chibcha** ▶ A South American Indian people of the central highlands of Colombia. At the time of the Spanish conquest they were more advanced socially and politically than any people in the area, except the ▷Inca. Chiefs, treated with great respect, inherited their position matrilineally. Their accession ceremonies, at which the new chief coated his body with gold dust before immersion in a sacred lake, are the probable origin of the ▷Eldorado legend.

● **Chicago** ▶ 41 50N 87 45W A city and major port in the USA, in Illinois on Lake Michigan. The third largest city in the country, it is the focal point of air, rail, and road routes and the commercial, financial, and industrial centre for a large region. Its manufactures include iron and steel, textiles, and chemicals; formerly it was also known for its stockyards, now closed. The first of its towering skyscrapers was built in 1887 and the Sears Tower (1974) was for many years the world's tallest office building, 443 m (1454 ft) high. It has several universities, including the University of Chicago (1892) and Northwestern University (1851); the Chicago Symphony Orchestra enjoys worldwide fame.

History: founded in 1803 near the site of Fort Dearborn, it became a city in 1837 and expanded rapidly with the construction of the railways. In 1871 it was almost completely destroyed by a disastrous fire, in which several hundred people were killed. Chicago was subsequently rebuilt in stone and steel. During the Prohibition years

(1919–33), Chicago was notorious for its gangster activities, especially those of Al ▷Capone. Population (1996 est): 2 721 547.

● **Chicago School** ► **1.** The group of architects who rebuilt Chicago after the fire of 1871. Most of the city's largely wooden buildings were completely destroyed, requiring their replacements to be built rapidly. The high price of land also encouraged the construction of tall closely packed buildings. In 1883 William Le Baron Jenney became the first to use an iron and steel skeleton to support multistorey buildings. His buildings, some of which used large expanses of glass, became a leading model for the later development of skyscrapers. However, it was Louis ▷Sullivan who chiefly developed the ▷functionalism for which the Chicago School became known. **2.** The group of economists led by Milton ▷Friedman at Chicago University between 1950 and 1978. Advocates of allowing market forces to determine the nature of the economy, the group believed that with the exception of monetary policy (*see* monetarism) government interference is liable to be harmful to an economy.

● **Chichén Itzá** ► A Maya city in N Yucatán (Mexico) that was the cultural centre of a wide area under Toltec influence from the late 10th to the 13th centuries. Remains include El Castillo (a pyramidal temple mound), an astronomical observatory, and a cenote (natural well), from which gold, jade, and other objects have been recovered.

● **Chicherin, Georgi Vasilievich** ► (1872–1936) Soviet statesman. Chicherin began his career in the Tsarist ministry of foreign affairs but in 1904, having become a revolutionary, moved to W Europe. In 1918 he returned to Russia and was entrusted by Lenin with Soviet diplomacy. Chicherin lost his position in 1928, following Stalin's rise to power.

● **Chichester** ► 50 50N 0 48W A market town in S England, the administrative centre of West Sussex. Chichester has Roman remains, including its street plan. Its cathedral dates from the 11th century. Other notable buildings include a 16th-century octagonal market cross and the Festival Theatre (1962). Population (1991): 26 572.

● **Chichester, Sir Francis (Charles)** ► (1901–72) British yachtsman. He won the first solo transatlantic race (in 40 days) in *Gipsy Moth III* (1960) and in 1966–67, in *Gipsy Moth IV*, was the first to sail round the world singlehanded making only one stop: he sailed from Plymouth, reaching Sydney in 107 days, and then back to Plymouth, in 119 days, going on to Greenwich, where he was knighted with Drake's sword.

● **chicken** ▷*See* fowl, domestic.

● **chickenpox** ► A common very infectious disease caused by the varicella-zoster virus (*see* herpes). It is usually contracted in childhood and one attack normally gives an immunity that lasts for life. At the end of the incubation period (about a fortnight) the patient develops a fever and an irritating rash. Small raised spots appear on the chest and spread—in the next few days—over the body, face, and limbs. The spots become sore reddened blisters, which then dry and flake off, usually in less than a week. The patient is infectious until the last blister has flaked off. ▷*See also* shingles.

● **chick pea** ► An annual plant, *Cicer arietinum*, up to 40 cm high, with whitish flowers and edible pealike seeds. It is the chief pulse crop of India, where the cooked seeds are called dhal. Probably native to W Asia, it has long been cultivated in S Europe and elsewhere. Family: ▷*Leguminosae*.

● **chickweed** ► A widely distributed annual or overwintering herb, *Stellaria media*, 5–40 cm high with small star-shaped white flowers. A weed, often eaten by birds, it was formerly used as a poultice for ulcers. Family: *Caryophyllaceae*.

● **Chiclayo** ► 6 47S 79 47W A city in N Peru, in the Lambayeque Valley. It is a trading centre for an area producing sugar cane, cotton, and rice. Population (1995): 668 066.

● **chicle** ► A gum formed from the coagulated milky substance obtained from the ▷sapodilla tree found in Central America. Chicle was formerly used in the manufacture of chewing gum, but it has now been replaced by synthetic substances.

● **chicory** ► A perennial herb, *Cichorium intybus*, 30–120 cm high,

with bright-blue flowers. The dried ground roots yield chicory, a coffee additive, while the blanched leaves are used in salads. A native of Eurasia and N Africa, it is widely cultivated elsewhere. Family: ▷*Compositae*. ▷*See also* endive.

● **Chiemsee** ► (*or* Bayrisches Meer) 47 53N 12 25E A lake in SE Germany. On one of its islands Louis II of Bavaria built a palace imitating Versailles. Area: 85 sq km (33 sq mi).

● **Chiengmai** ► (*or* Chiang Mai) 18 48N 98 59E A town in NW Thailand, near the Burmese border. A commercial and cultural centre, it has teak, silver, and silk industries. The university was established in 1964. Population (1993 est): 170 397.

● **Ch'ien-lung** ▷*See* Qian Long.

● **chiffchaff** ► A woodland ▷warbler, *Phylloscopus collybita*, about 10 cm long, with a grey-green plumage and whitish underparts. It occurs in Europe and W Asia during the summer and winters in S Europe and Africa. It resembles the ▷willow warbler but can be distinguished by its "chiff-chaff" call.

● **Chifley, Joseph Benedict** ► (1885–1951) Australian statesman; Labor prime minister (1945–49). Famous for seeing the "light on the hill" of socialism, he introduced welfare reforms and nationalization policies.

● **chigger** ▷*See* harvest mite.

● **chigoe** ► A ▷flea, *Tunga penetrans*, 1 mm long, also called jigger or sand flea, that spread to Africa and Asia from South America to become a pest of man. The female burrows beneath the skin, especially on the feet, to form itching sores that can become gangrenous. Family: *Pulicidae*.

● **Chihli, Gulf of** ► (Chinese name: Bohai *or* Po Hai) A large inlet of the Yellow Sea on the coast of NE China.

● **Chihuahua** ► 28 40N 106 06W A city in N Mexico. Miguel Hidalgo y Costillo, a leader in the Mexican independence movement, was executed here (1811). Its varied industries include smelting, timber, and meat packing and it has a university (1954). Population (1990): 530 487.

● **Chihuahua** ► A breed of ▯dog originating from an ancient Mexican breed and developed in the USA. Its coat is either smooth and glossy or long and soft. Height: about 13 cm.

● **Chikamatsu Monzaemon** ► (Sugimori Nobumori; 1653–1724) Japanese dramatist. His psychological insight and realistic techniques revolutionized puppet theatre. *The Battles of Coxingo* (1715) and *The Love Suicide at Amijima* (1720) are the best-known examples of his two main types of plays, historical romances and domestic tragedies.

● **chilblain** ► An itchy red swelling, usually on the fingers or toes, that develops in cold weather. Prevention, by wearing warm clothing, is the best form of treatment, but drugs that dilate the blood vessels may also be used.

● **child abuse** ► The physical or sexual abuse of children, usually by a relative (sometimes a parent). In the 1980s the extent of sexual abuse of minors became public knowledge, causing the medical and social services in the UK to pay special attention to the problem. Physical abuse of babies and young children is also a growing problem (*see* battered baby syndrome). In 1996 the child protection registers kept by local authority social services departments held the names of some 35 600 children considered to be at risk. In the same year the NSPCC received 5071 enquiries relating to sexual abuse, 3179 relating to physical abuse, and 1336 relating to emotional abuse. Several charities, including Childline and Kidscope, have been set up to attempt to alleviate these problems.

● **childbirth** ► (*or* labour) The series of events that lead to the birth of a baby. It usually starts spontaneously about 280 days (plus or minus 14 days) after conception but it may be induced by artificial means. The first stage of childbirth may last several hours: it is marked by rupture of the membranes surrounding the fetus and by regular contractions of the womb (uterus). This stage ends when the cervical canal is fully dilated. In the second stage continuing uterine contractions—assisted by conscious pushing by the mother—ease the baby through the cervix and out through the vagina. The ▷placenta (afterbirth) is delivered in the third stage of labour. The baby is normally born headfirst. ▷*See also* Caesarean section; infant mortality.

● **Childers, Robert Erskine** ▶ (1870–1922) Irish nationalist executed by the Irish Free State. In 1921 he became a Sinn Féin member of the Irish Assembly (Dáil Éireann) and minister of propaganda. He opposed the treaty that established the Irish Free State, joined the IRA, and was captured and shot. He also wrote the thriller *The Riddle of the Sands* (1903), made into a film in 1979. His son **Erskine Childers** (1905–74) was president of Ireland (1973–74).

● **Children's Crusade** ▶ (1212) A bizarre episode of the ▷Crusades, in which some 50 000 children set out from France and Germany to capture Jerusalem. None reached their destination and few returned home, most being sold into slavery. The enthusiasm aroused by the Children's Crusade encouraged Pope ▷Innocent III to summon the fifth Crusade.

● **Child Support Agency** ▶ (CSA) In the UK, a government agency established in 1993 to administer the Child Support Act (1991) by assessing and collecting child maintenance payments from absent parents (almost always fathers). The agency has caused a good deal of controversy, with its critics alleging that the CSA has found it more cost-efficient to increase payments from parents who were already contributing than to trace runaways or collect from those on very low incomes—thus punishing the more responsible parents. Plans to reform the agency's methods of assessment and collection were announced in 1998.

● **Chile, Republic of** ▶ A country in South America, extending in a narrow strip along the W coast of the S half of the continent. There are many islands off the coast, some of which (including ▷Easter Island) are well out into the Pacific Ocean. Chile also includes half of the island of Tierra del Fuego and has claims to part of Antarctica. The country is dominated by the Andes, which are separated from a lower coastal range by a central valley. The majority of the population is of mixed Spanish and Indian descent.

Economy: owing in part to the radical policies of privatization and deregulation imposed by the ▷Pinochet dictatorship in the 1970s and 1980s, Chile now has one of the most successful economies in South America. It is based chiefly on the export of minerals, found principally in the N. Chile is one of the world's largest producers and exporters of copper, while the production of iron ore now exceeds that of the traditional nitrates. Coal is also mined in quantity. Oil and natural gas are produced in the S but quantities are now declining. Major land reforms were introduced (1965–73) but much agricultural land was returned to its original owners after the fall of the ▷Allende government. The main crops are wheat, sugar beet, potatoes, and maize and there is an expanding wine industry. Fruit and forest production has grown in importance and there are government attempts to promote the dairy industry. Fishing is a major source of revenue.

History: when Magellan, the first European to set eyes on what became Chile, sailed through (1520) the strait named after him, S Chile was occupied by the Mapuche Indians, who continued to control the region until the 19th century. In the N the Atacama Indians had been subjugated in the 15th century by the Incas, who were themselves conquered by the Spaniards in 1532. A Spanish colony was founded at Santiago in 1541 and Chile was attached to the viceroyalty of Peru. It maintained, however, a certain independence and individuality throughout the colonial period, partly because of its inaccessibility. The revolt against Spain began in 1810, when a provisional republic was declared, but victory over the Spaniards was achieved only in 1817 with the military help of the Argentine liberator José de ▷San Martín. In 1818 the Republic of Chile was established under Bernardo ▷O'Higgins. Following the ratification of a constitution in 1833 Chile enjoyed political stability and prosperity, becoming the world's leading copper producer. Frontier disputes with Bolivia and Peru culminated in the War of the ▷Pacific (1879–83), in which Chile, with its superior navy, was victorious, gaining the provinces of Antofagasta from Bolivia and Tarapacà and Arica from Peru. The early 20th century witnessed economic decline, exacerbated by considerable European immigration and resistance from landlords to reform. The enlightened first presidency (1920–25) of Arturo

Alessandri Palma (1868–1952) was followed by a military dictatorship and his increasingly right-wing second term (1932–38) led to the election of a socialist Popular Front government. The postwar period saw a return to conservatism; in 1964 Eduardo ▷Frei, the first Christian Democratic president, was elected. In 1970 Salvador Allende became the world's first democratically elected Marxist head of state but was overthrown in 1973 by a military coup led by Gen Pinochet. Pinochet faced strong opposition to his brutal and repressive regime both at home and abroad, narrowly escaping assassination in 1986; in 1988 he accepted a plebiscite decision in favour of a return to democracy and, following elections, Patricio Aylwin succeeded him as president in 1990. In 1994 Frei's son, Eduardo Frei Ruíz-Tagle, became president. The ruling Coalition for Democracy (CPD) was re-elected in 1997. In 1998–2000 Chile's bitter political divisions were reopened by the arrest of Pinochet (firstly in London, then in Chile itself) for alleged human-rights violations. Presidential elections in 2000 were won by the socialist Ricardo Lagos. Chile is a member of the OAS, LAIA, and of Mercosur.

Republic of Chile

Head of state	President Ricardo Lagos
Official language	Spanish
Official currency	Chilean peso of 100 centavos
Area	741 767 sq km (286 397 sq mi)
Population (1999 est)	15 018 000
Capital	Santiago
Main port	Valparaiso

● **Chi-lin** ▷*See* Jilin.

● **Chillán** ▶ 36 37S 72 10W A city in central Chile, in the Central Valley. Prone to earthquake damage, Chillán serves an agricultural region producing chiefly grapes, fruit, cereals, and livestock. Population (1995 est): 157 083.

● **chilli** ▶ A tropical American shrubby plant, ▷*Capsicum frutescens*, also called red pepper, bearing elongated hot-tasting red fruits, 2–3 cm long. Sun-dried for storage, they are used in cooking and are also an essential ingredient of curry powder and tabasco sauce. Family: *Solanaceae*.

● **Chillon** ▶ A mainly 13th-century fortress at the E end of Lake Geneva (Switzerland). It was the prison (1530–36) of François Bonward (?1494–1570), the Genevan patriot made famous by Byron's poem *The Prisoner of Chillon* (1816).

● **Chiloé Island** ▶ An island administered by Chile, off the W coast of South America in the Pacific Ocean. The chief export is timber. Area: 8394 sq km (3241 sq mi). Chief town: Ancud. Population (latest est): 116 000.

● **Chiltern Hills** ▶ A chalk escarpment in S central England. It extends NE from the Goring Gap in the Thames Valley to near Luton, reaching 255 m (852 ft) at Coombe Hill. Many of its hills are covered with beech woods.

● **Chiltern Hundreds** ▶ In the UK, a nominal office of profit under the Crown, the holder of which is disqualified from membership of the House of Commons. It is one of the stewardships (the other is the Manor of Northstead, Yorks) for which an MP who wishes to resign (which he may not do directly) has been able to apply since the mid-18th century.

● **Chi-lung** ▷*See* Jilong.

● **chimaera** ▶ **1.** A ▷cartilaginous fish, also called ghost shark, ratfish, or rabbit fish, belonging to the order *Chimaeriformes* (about 28 species). It has a dark or silvery body, 60–200 cm long and a slender whiplike tail. It lives in cold ocean waters, down to 2500 m, and feeds on fish and invertebrates. Subclass: *Holocephali*. ◻fish. **2.** (or chimera) An organism that is composed of cells of two genetically different types. Plants with variegated leaves are chimaeras resulting from a mutation in a cell in the growing region (apical meristem). Plant chimaeras produced by ▷grafting are known as graft hybrids.

● **Chimborazo, Mount** ▶ 1 29S 78 52W An extinct volcano in the Andes, the highest point in Ecuador. Height: 6267 m (20 681 ft).

● **Chimbote** ▶ 9 04S 78 34W A port in NW Peru, on the Pacific Ocean. Steel processing and fishmeal production are the chief industries. Population (1993): 268 979.

● **Chimera** ▶ A legendary Greek fire-breathing monster with a lion's head, a goat's body, and a serpent's tail. After ravaging Lycia she was killed by Bellerophon. The name now applies to any fantastic imaginary creation.

● **Chimkent** ▶ 42 16N 69 05E A city in S Kazakhstan. It is an important railway junction and has chemical and textile industries. Population (1995 est): 397 600.

● **chimpanzee** ▶ An ape, *Pan troglodytes*, of West African forests. Chimpanzees are 100–170 cm tall when standing erect and live in small groups, mostly on the ground, feeding chiefly on fruit and leaves but occasionally eating meat. They communicate by facial expressions and a repertoire of calls and possess considerable intelligence, often using tools (such as branches). Bonobos are a race of smaller chimpanzees with black faces.

● **Chimú** ▶ A South American Indian people who established a large kingdom in Peru during the 14th century AD. Its capital was at ▷Chan Chan. They were conquered (c. 1470) by the ▷Incas, whose civilization was based on Chimú achievements in building, road construction, irrigation, and political organization. The Chimú produced pottery with moulded reliefs, fine textiles, and precious metalwork.

● **Ch'in** ▷*See* Qin.

● **China, People's Republic of** ▶ A country in E Asia, covering vast areas of land ranging from the low-lying and densely populated plains of the NE to the high peaks of the Tibetan Plateau in the W, rising well over 5000 m (16 500 ft). In the far NW much of the land is desert or semidesert. China proper falls into three natural regions, formed around the three main rivers: the Yellow River in the N, the Yangtze in the centre, and the Xi Jiang in the S. Over 90% of the inhabitants are Han Chinese.

Economy: despite the huge changes of recent decades, the economy is still mainly dependent upon agriculture, which is constantly threatened by drought and flood. There are however schemes to safeguard and increase production by means of irrigation, soil conservation, and fertilization. Agriculture was formerly socialized through a system of communes, but these have now fragmented into small private holdings. The emphasis is on foodcrops, rice in the S, wheat and millet in the N, as well as livestock, especially pigs. Cotton is grown in the N and tea in the S. The once vast forests have been largely cleared over the centuries but considerable reafforestation is now taking place. Coal is extensively mined in all parts of the country and is the major source of power. China has been self-sufficient in oil since 1973 and now exports crude oil to Kazakhstan and other neighbouring countries; small amounts of natural gas are also produced. The potential for hydroelectric energy is extensive and there are several projects throughout the country; the nuclear-power industry is also being developed. Iron ore is the most important mineral deposit and China is the main world producer of tungsten ore. Other minerals include antimony, lead, bauxite, and manganese. Although traditional small industries continue, the 1980s and 1990s saw rapid and large-scale development of more modern industries, especially textiles, steel, electronics, and chemicals. About 10% of the population is now employed in the manufacturing sector. The same period saw considerable liberalization of the economy: central planning and state control of industry have been loosened, stock markets have been set up, and several Special Economic Zones have been created to attract foreign investment. Foreign trade has increased enormously, with exports including farm produce, textiles, metals, and manufactured goods. A major trade deal with the USA was concluded in 1999.

History: China is one of the world's oldest civilizations, with a history of organized society going back over nearly four millenniums. The first important recorded dynasty was the Shang in the valley of the Yellow River (18th–12th centuries BC). From the 12th to the 3rd centuries BC the ▷Zhou spread S and E. Under the ▷Qin, in the 3rd century BC, a unified empire came into being and the first Great Wall was built. The rule of the ▷Han dynasty, from the 3rd century BC to the early 3rd century AD, saw spectacular advances in technology and manufacturing but its decline was followed by centuries of struggle

between different parts of the empire. With the ▷Tang dynasty (7th–10th centuries) China was once more reunited and reached the high point of its civilization. It was followed by the ▷Song (10th–13th centuries), the ▷Mongol (13th–14th centuries), the ▷Ming (14th–17th centuries), and the ▷Qing, which lasted until 1912. From the 16th century Europeans came to China and set up trading posts despite opposition from the Qing. British efforts to open up the country to free trade led to the Opium War in 1839 and to the opening of treaty ports (and also to the cession of Hong Kong). Later other trade concessions were made to several European countries and Chinese opposition to these moves included the Taiping Rebellion (1851–64) and the antiforeign Boxer Rebellion (1899–1900). In 1911 a revolution under the leadership of Sun Yat-sen ousted the Qing and a republic was set up. The 1920s saw the rise of the Guomindang (Nationalist People's Party) under Gen Chiang Kai-shek and the foundation of the Chinese Communist Party in 1921. In 1926 relations between them broke down and a struggle began that continued until after World War II. In the 1930s threats from Japan culminated in open attack and the occupation of parts of the country, which lasted until the end of World War II. This put a temporary halt to internal struggles, but in 1949 the Guomindang was defeated by the communists and a People's Republic was set up by ▷Mao Tse-tung. Chiang Kai-shek retreated to Taiwan, where he set up the Republic of China. During the early years of communism relations with the Soviet Union were close but they later deteriorated. In 1966 Mao launched the Great Proletarian ▷Cultural Revolution, designed to eradicate "revisionism" and to prevent the rise of a ruling class. From the late 1960s the question of a successor to Mao became important and first ▷Lin Biao and later ▷Deng Xiao Ping rose and fell. Both Mao and the prime minister, Chou En-lai, died in 1976 and were succeeded by the moderate ▷Hua Guo Feng. Attempts by the "radical" faction (known as the Gang of Four and including Mao's widow Jiang Qing) to gain power were thwarted by the arrest of its members. Deng Xiao Ping was reinstated in 1977 and became the dominant force in government until his death in 1997. His rule was characterized by economic liberalization,

China ▶ Part of the terracotta army found in the vicinity of the tomb of Qin Shi Huangdi (259–210 BC) in 1985.

leading to rising prosperity, but rejection of political reform. In 1989 a government crackdown on protestors demanding liberal reform involved a massacre of thousands of students in Tiananmen Square in Beijing. Following Deng's death, President Jiang Zemin emerged as China's new paramount leader. The former British crown colony of Hong Kong was returned to China in 1997, as was the Portuguese overseas territory of Macao in 1999. Since 1971 China has had a seat at the UN.

People's Republic of China

Head of state	President Jiang Zemin
Official language	Mandarin Chinese
Official currency	yuan of 10 chiao or 10 fen
Area	9 597 000 sq km (3 704 400 sq mi)
Population (1999 est)	1 251 238 000
Capital	Beijing
Main port	Shanghai

● **china clay** ► A mineral deposit consisting mainly of kaolin, a hydrous aluminium silicate. Kaolin is produced by weathering or by hydrothermal processes acting on the feldspars in granite. It is used for making high-grade ceramic products and in many industrial processes, including paper making.

● **Chi-nan** ▷See Jinan.

● **China Sea** ► A section of the W Pacific Ocean, lying mainly on the continental shelf to the SE of mainland Asia: it is separated from the open Pacific by the arc of islands extending from S Japan through Taiwan and the Philippines to Borneo. It has two major divisions, the **South China Sea** (or Nanhai) and the **East China Sea** (or Dong Hai), lying either side of Taiwan and connected by the Straits of Taiwan. The South China Sea lies SW of Taiwan and is bounded by China to the N, Vietnam and the Gulf of Thailand to the E, Borneo to the S, and the Philippine islands of Palawan and Luzon to the W. It has an area of about 2 197 300 sq km (848 400 sq mi). The smaller East China Sea lies NE of Taiwan and is bounded by China to the W, the Yellow Sea to the N, the Koreas and Japan to the NE, and the Ryukyu Islands to the E and S. Its area is about 751 080 sq km (290 000 sq mi). Both seas are relatively shallow with weak tides and a monsoon climate. They provide major NS and EW shipping routes and are very heavily fished.

● **chinch bug** ► A ▷ground bug, *Blissus leucopteris*, that has a black body (up to 5 mm long), red legs, and white wings. Native to tropical America, it has spread to North America to become a serious pest of cereal crops. The female lays eggs on the roots and stems and the larvae suck the sap.

● **chinchilla** ► A ▷rodent belonging to the genus *Chinchilla* (2 species), widely bred for its valuable long soft blue-grey fur. Measuring 30–50 cm long, wild chinchillas are found high in the Andes, living among rocks and feeding at night on vegetation. They faced extermination before the Chilean government banned hunting and established breeding farms. South American captive chinchillas are mostly short-tailed (*C. brevicaudata*) while in North America the long-tailed species (*C. laniger*) is bred. Family: *Chinchillidae*.

● **Chinchilla cat** ► A breed of long-haired cat. Chinchillas have a compact body with short legs and a broad head with a snub nose and small tufted ears. The white fur is tipped with black on the back, flanks, head, ears, and tail, giving it a silvery lustre. The eyes are emerald or blue-green.

● **Chinchilla rabbit** ► A breed of domesticated rabbit originating in France in the early 20th century. Although its thick bluish coat does not resemble that of the South American ▷chinchilla, it has been bred for its pelts.

● **Chindits** ► The 77th Indian Brigade, organized by Orde ▷Wingate in 1943 in Burma (now Myanmar) as a "long-range penetration" infantry division. A guerrilla force, the Chindits were so called after the mythological Burmese temple guardian, the *chinthe*, and because they operated beyond the River Chindwin. Initially successful in severing Japanese lines of communication they were later forced to return to India in small groups.

● **Chindwin, River** ► A river in N Myanmar (Burma), flowing S to join the Irrawaddy River near Myingyan. Length: 1046 km (650 mi).

● **Chinese** ► A language or group of languages of the Sino-Tibetan family spoken widely in E Asia. The many distinct forms or dialects of Chinese, which include Mandarin, Min, Kan, Hakka, Hsiang, Wu, and Cantonese (or Yüeh), are mutually unintelligible. In China there have been attempts recently to standardize the language, using Mandarin as a basis. Chinese is a tonal language, many words, otherwise identical, having quite distinct meanings according to intonation. Words are usually monosyllabic and do not change their form to indicate part of speech. The language is written in logographic characters or symbols of pictorial origin (*see* ideographic writing systems), which enables them to be understood by speakers of any Chinese dialect. There are as many as 40 000 of these of which 10 000 are in common use. Literacy requires knowledge of about 2000 of them. For transliteration purposes, Pinyin (phonetic spelling) is superseding the older Wade-Giles system, which does not attempt as close a phonetic description of the language. Pinyin is usually used in this book.

● **Chinese art and architecture** ► Early Chinese art (c. 1550–480 BC) consisted of magical, symbolic, and ritualistic objects of jade and bronze. These combine a few symbols to produce evocative nonrepresentational forms. During the Han dynasty (206 BC–220 AD) these forms were succeeded by sculptural art and painting, both influenced by the rise of Buddhism. Funerary ceramic art flourished and produced animal and human forms and copies of everyday artefacts. The Tang dynasty (618–906 AD) continued to make funerary objects, particularly realistic horsemen, warriors, and tomb guardians, but sculptures of Buddhist figures are dominant. The realistic outlook of the period was also reflected in landscape and figure painting.

The ensuing Song dynasty (960–1279 AD) was a golden age, when dreamlike landscape, animal, and bird painting flourished alongside ▷calligraphy, one of the most ancient and important Chinese arts. Monochrome ceramics of very refined form were made as objects of contemplation. This period saw the end of real creativity, the following Yuan dynasty being one of Mongol-inspired taste with a few exceptions, notably the four masters of the Yuan Dynasty. During the following Ming and Qing periods (14th–20th centuries) ceramic art excelled, the most famous example being the blue and white porcelain. At first it was restorative and of native origin and later innovatory, responding to European influence.

Chinese buildings before the Ming period were largely wooden and few have therefore survived. Paintings indicate that early Chinese architects used columns to support the roofs with walls as protective screens. The earliest Chinese buildings to survive are Tang dynasty stone ▷pagodas. Ming and post-Ming buildings are grand, with curving roofs and white marble balustrades, as in the Imperial City and the Forbidden City of ▷Beijing. These styles persisted through the 18th and 19th centuries. In the 20th century European styles appeared, with a Chinese Renaissance in the 1920s, in which Chinese features are superimposed on European buildings. In modern Beijing, nine storeys are the limit but within this restriction styles are mostly modern.

● **Chinese lantern plant** ► A hardy ornamental plant, *Physalis alkekengi*, also called bladder cherry or winter cherry. A native of S and central Europe, it grows to a height of 20–60 cm. The edible fruit is enclosed in a reddish inflated calyx resembling a lantern. A similar and related plant, the Cape gooseberry (*P. peruviana*), is native to S North America and N South America and cultivated for its edible yellow berries, which are used in sauces and preserves. Family: ▷Solanaceae.

● **Chinese literature** ► The oldest written records in Chinese date from about 1400 BC. The earliest major literary productions, however, were written mainly between about 200 BC and 200 AD. These were the Confucian classics, nine texts for instruction and discussion by ▷Confucius and his disciples. They are devoted to poetry, philosophy, history, ceremonies, and codes of protocol and have had a profound effect on Chinese thought and literary style to the present. The earliest is probably the manual of divination, the ▷*I Ching*. The *Shu Jing* (or *Shu Ching*; *Book of Documents*) covers political aspects of Confucian thought; the *Shih Jing* (or *Shih Ching*; Book of Songs) contains lyrics some of which are perhaps as early as the 10th century BC. Of the remaining classics, the best known are two books belonging to the historical work *Zuo Zhuan* (or *Tso Chuan*): the *Analects*, a collection of Confucius' sayings and discussions with his disciples, and *The Book of Mencius*. The work of China's first known poet, ▷Chu Yuan, is a long poem occupying the most prominent place in the *Chuchi* (or *Ch'u Tz'u*), an anthology that, together with the *Book of Songs*, had an enduring effect on verse forms. During the Qin and Han dynasties (221 BC–220 AD), the development of poetry was fostered by the creation in 133 BC of the Yuefu (Music Bureau) for the collection of folksongs. Under Buddhist influences poetry became increasingly individualistic and enjoyed a golden age during the Tang dynasty (618–906 AD). ▷Li Po, ▷Du Fu, and the Buddhist Wang Wei (699–759) were the leading poets, while Han Yu (768–824) pioneered new genres of prose. Musical drama was the major literary genre during the Yuan (Mongol) dynasty (1279–1368), and the novel, originating in printed versions of the tales of professional storytellers, flourished during the Ming dynasty (1368–1644). The two major novels of this period are the *Romance of the Three Kingdoms* and *The Water Margin*, both attributed to Luo Guan-zhong (*or* Luo Kuan-chung; 14th century). These works, dealing with heroic adventures, are skilfully shaped from episodic material and contrast with *The Dream of the Red Chamber* by ▷Cao Chan (*or* Zao Zhan), which is more realistic and partly autobiographical. The Qing (Manchu) dynasty (1644–1911) was unremarkable for literary work, but Western influences were introduced through translations during the 19th century, and in the 20th century there arose a number of writers indebted to Western ideas, for example to Romanticism and Symbolism. After the establishment of the republic in 1911, the outstanding poet was Hu Shi (1891–1962) and the leading writer was the satirist Lu Xun. Since the late 1930s literature has been generally subservient to political orthodoxy; although recent official patronage of the arts has encouraged many new writers, no single reputation has become well established outside China.

● **Chinese water deer** ▶ A very small ▷deer, *Hydropotes inermis*, most common along the banks of the Yangtze River in China. Only 50 cm high at the shoulder, with a pale-brown coat and short tail, it has no antlers; the male's upper canine teeth are elongated into tusks.

● **Ch'ing** ▷*See* Qing.

● **Ch'ing-hai** ▷*See* Qinghai.

● **Ching-te-chen** ▷*See* Fuliang.

● **Chinkiang** ▷*See* Jinjiang.

● **Chin-men** ▷*See* Jinmen.

● **chinoiserie** ▶ Decorative art and architecture that incorporated Chinese motifs into European fantasy designs and was popular in the late 17th and 18th centuries. The fashion was inspired by importation into Europe of Chinese porcelain, lacquer, etc., in the 17th century. French ▷rococo artists and architects enthusiastically adopted the style for interiors, furniture, silver, wallpaper, textiles, etc., as did ▷Meissen designers. English examples include the ▷willow pattern, combining Chinese elements into a new design; the interior of the Brighton Royal Pavilion is an architectural example.

● **Chinook** ▶ A North American Indian people of the NW Pacific coast of the USA. The Chinook language forms part of a division of the ▷Penutian language family. The Chinook were salmon fishers and traders, their location along the lower Columbia River being ideally suited for exchanging goods with peoples to the N and S and in the interior. Chinook Jargon, a combination of Chinook, ▷Nootka, and other Indian languages mixed with English and French words, became the trading language of the entire W coast of America. The Chinook practised the ▷potlatch and their religion emphasized the quest for a personal guiding spirit by undergoing various ordeals.

● **Chioggia** ▶ 45 13N 12 17E A fishing port in Italy, on an island in the Venetian lagoon. Population (latest est): 57 000.

● **chipmunk** ▶ A ▷ground squirrel belonging to the genus *Tamias* (18 species), of North America and Asian forests. Chipmunks are 15–30 cm long and have a black and white striped back and strong feet and claws for digging. They live in burrows and, in the winter, do not hibernate but feed on a store of nuts and dried fruit carried under ground in their large cheek pouches.

● **Chippendale, Thomas** ▶ (1718–79) British cabinetmaker, famous for his elegant furniture designs, especially his chairs. His il-

lustrated collection of rococo furniture designs, *The Gentleman and Cabinet Maker's Director* (1754), was the first comprehensive furniture catalogue and was influential in England and America, although his later neoclassical styles are considered the finest. His son, also **Thomas Chippendale** (died c. 1822), continued the business.

● **Chippewa** ▷*See* Ojibwa.

● **Chirac, Jacques** ▶ (1932–) French statesman; president (1995–), prime minister (1974–76; 1986–88). Having reorganized the Gaullists in the late 1970s, he became (1986) prime minister under ▷Mitterrand, whom he challenged unsuccessfully for the presidency in 1988. He was also mayor of Paris (1977–95). As president he introduced austerity measures to prepare France for the single European currency. Despite allegations of corruption and dishonesty, he was re-elected by a landslide in 2002, when his challenger was the right-wing extremist Jean-Marie Le Pen.

● **Chirico, Giorgio de** ▶ (1888–1978) Italian painter and forerunner of ▷surrealism, born in Greece. He trained in Munich and was influenced by Nietzsche's philosophy. In Paris (1911–15) he worked on scenes of eerie and deserted Italian squares. At Ferrara (1917) he established with Carlo Carrà (1881–1966) the school of ▷metaphysical painting, but reverted to a traditional style after 1919.

● **chiromancy** ▷*See* palmistry.

● **Chiron** ▶ (mythology) In Greek legend, a ▷centaur, son of Cronos and the sea nymph Philyra. He was revered for his wisdom and knowledge of medicine. After being accidentally wounded by Heracles he bequeathed his immortality to Prometheus and was transformed into the constellation ▷Sagittarius.

● **Chiron** ▶ (planet) A small planet between Saturn and Venus, which orbits the sun every 50.7 years at an average distance of 1.05×10^9 km. Discovered in 1977, it is 300–400 km in diameter and probably consists of ice and rock.

● **chiropody** ▶ The paramedical specialty that deals with the care of feet and the treatment of minor ailments of the feet, such as corns, calluses, and ingrowing toenails. In the UK the governing body is the Society of Chiropodists.

● **chiropractic** ▶ A fringe medical specialty based on the assumption that most diseases originate from disorders of the nervous system, particularly as a result of compression of the nerve roots as they emerge from the spine. A chiropractor attempts to relieve symptoms by manipulating the spine with his hands.

● **Chiroptera** ▷*See* bat.

● **chiru** ▶ An antelope, *Pantholops hodgsoni*, of Tibetan plateaus. About 80 cm high at the shoulder, chirus have a dense woolly pinkish-brown coat with white underparts; males have slender black horns up to 70 cm long. They live singly or in small groups and excavate shallow depressions for shelter.

● **Chita** ▶ 52 03N 113 35E A city in SE Russia. Founded by the ▷Cossacks (1653), it is a prosperous city with machine-building, textiles, and food-processing industries. Population (1999 est): 314 300.

● **chital** ▷*See* axis deer.

● **chitarrone** ▶ (Italian: big guitar) A large fretted instrument of the lute family, able to accommodate bass strings of over 1.5 metres (5 ft) in length. It was popular for accompanying singing in the early 17th century.

● **chitin** ▶ A complex carbohydrate that, in association with proteins, is the principal component of the outer cuticle of insects and other arthropods. Chitin occurs in several other animal groups and is a constituent of the cell walls of fungi.

● **chiton** ▶ A primitive ▷mollusc of the class *Amphineura* (about 600 species), also called sea cradle. Elliptical and measuring up to 30 × 15 cm, chitons live on rocky shores, clinging tightly and grazing on encrusted algae. They have eight shell plates with a fleshy girdle and curl up when detached.

● **Chittagong** ▶ 22 20N 91 48E A city and major port in Bangladesh, on the Indian Ocean. The focal point of road, rail, and air routes, it is the second most important industrial centre in the country. Its university was established in 1966. Population (1991): 1 599 000.

● **chivalry** ▸ The ideology and code of conduct of the knightly class of medieval Europe. The knightly ethic encompassed not only the military virtues of bravery and loyalty but also the concepts of honour and courtesy. The latter was related to the ideal of ▷courtly love, which found expression in such literature as the Arthurian romances. The chivalric ideal also enshrined a commitment to defend the Christian religion and as such was a major factor in the ▷Crusades. The earliest orders of chivalry were the ▷Hospitallers (1071) and ▷Templars (1120), both of which were founded to serve pilgrims to the Holy Land but came to play an important military role in the Crusades. Protecting pilgrims, giving aid to Christians in the East, halting the desecration of Christian shrines by Muslims, and liberating Jerusalem were among the reasons given by Pope Urban II in preaching for the First Crusade (1095–99). The knights responded with enthusiasm, seeing the prosecution of a Holy War as a means of serving God with devotion and sacrifice. Like many noble ideas inspired by religious beliefs, the chivalric ideal led in this case to widespread brutality and slaughter. All ties between the chivalric code and military conduct ended with the decline of cavalry and the invention of gunpowder, although elaborate jousts and tournaments kept its memory alive until the 16th century.

chivalry ▸ This 14th-century illustration shows Henry IV of Silesia-Breslau receiving the victor's wreath after a tournament.

● **chive** ▸ A small hardy perennial plant, ▷*Allium schoenoprasum*, native to Europe. It has small white elongated bulbs and produces clumps of thin tubular leaves and dense attractive spherical heads of bluish or lilac flowers on long stalks. The leaves are used for seasoning and garnishing foods. Family: *Liliaceae*.

● **chloral** ▸ (*or* trichlorethanal; CCl_3CHO) A colourless oily liquid made by treating acetaldehyde with chlorine. It is used in the manufacture of DDT.

● **chloramphenicol** ▸ An ▷antibiotic usually reserved for severe bacterial infections. It is particularly useful in the treatment of typhoid fever and some forms of pneumonia and meningitis. In rare cases chloramphenicol causes serious blood disorders. It is also used topically for treating eye infections. Tradename: Chloromycetin.

● **chlordiazepoxide** ▷*See* benzodiazepines.

● **Chlorella** ▸ A genus of unicellular ▷green algae found in fresh water or damp soil, some forming symbiotic relationships with fungi to give ▷lichens. Because they are rich in proteins, carbohydrates, and fats and reproduce rapidly by cell division, their use as a food source for man is now under study.

● **chlorine** ▸ (Cl) A greenish poisonous ▷halogen gas, discovered in 1774 by C. W. Scheele. It is found in nature only in compounds, especially common salt (NaCl), sylvite (KCl), and carnallite ($KMgCl_3.6H_2O$). Chlorine is liberated by the electrolysis of brine. It irritates the respiratory system and was used as a poisonous gas in World War I. Chlorine gas is reactive and combines directly with most elements. Its oxidizing properties make it a useful disinfectant for drinking-water supplies and swimming pools. It is used in the manufacture of ▷bromine, in bleach (NaOCl), hydrochloric acid (HCl), and carbon tetrachloride (CCl_4). Chlorinated organic chemicals are used in dyes, antiseptics, and insecticides. At no 17; at wt 35.453; mp –100.98°C; bp –34.6°C.

● **chlorofluorocarbons** ▸ (CFCs) ▷*See* fluorocarbons.

● **chloroform** ▸ (*or* trichloromethane; $CHCl_3$) A colourless volatile liquid. It is made by reacting ▷bleaching powder with acetone, acetaldehyde, or ethanol. Its main use is now in the manufacture of ▷fluorocarbons but it is also used as a solvent and as an anaesthetic.

● **chlorophyll** ▸ A green pigment present in organisms capable of ▷photosynthesis. Higher plants possess chlorophylls *a* and *b*, located in ▷chloroplasts; chlorophyll *c* is found in some primitive marine plants, and bacteriochlorophyll occurs in photosynthetic bacteria. The chlorophylls absorb red and blue light, trapping light energy for photosynthesis.

● **Chlorophyta** ▷*See* green algae.

● **chloroplast** ▸ A ▷plastid within a plant cell in which ▷photosynthesis takes place. It is bounded by a membrane and contains the green pigment ▷chlorophyll. The greatest concentration of chloroplasts occurs in the palisade mesophyll tissue of the leaves—the main photosynthesizing region.

● **chloroquine** ▸ A drug used to prevent and treat malaria. It acts by preventing the digestion of haemoglobin (the red pigment of blood) by the malaria parasite. It is also used in treating rheumatoid arthritis and related diseases.

● **chlorpromazine** ▷*See* phenothiazines.

● **chocolate** ▷*See* cocoa and chocolate.

● **Choctaw** ▸ A North American Indian people and language of the Muskogean group originally of SE Mississippi. They were skilled farmers, growing corn, maize, and beans. They practised the green corn (first-fruits) ceremony. They wore their hair long and practised head flattening through deformation during infancy. After supporting the French against the English during the 18th century, they were forced to move west, settling in Oklahoma during the 1830s.

● **Chodowiecki, Daniel Nikolaus** ▸ (1726–1801) German painter and engraver, who specialized in scenes of middle-class life. A noted book illustrator, he engraved editions of Cervantes' *Don Quixote* and Goldsmith's *Vicar of Wakefield*. His best-known painting is *The Parting of Jean Calas from his Family* (1767; Berlin-Dahlem Museum).

● **choir** ▸ 1. A group of trained singers. In the Christian Church the use of a choir was derived from Judaism and traditionally consisted of men and boys only. The choir leads the singing of the congregation as well as singing anthems. The most usual division of parts in a choir is into four: soprano, alto, tenor, and bass (SATB). In secular music the choir is often called a chorus. 2. The part of the chancel of a church, where the choir sits.

● **Choiseul, Étienne François, Duc de** ▸ (1719–85) French statesman; foreign minister (1758–70). As ambassador to Vienna in 1757 he negotiated the marriage of Marie Antoinette to the future Louis XVI. He secured good terms for France in the Treaty of ▷Paris after the Seven Years' War (1763). The influence of Louis XV's mistress, Mme ▷Du Barry, undermined his position and he was exiled in 1770.

● **cholera** ▶ An acute infection of the intestine caused by the bacterium *Vibrio cholerae*, which is transmitted in drinking water contaminated by faeces of a patient. Epidemics of cholera occur in regions where sanitation is poor. After an incubation period of 1–5 days, cholera causes severe vomiting and diarrhoea, which—untreated—leads to dehydration that can be fatal. Treatment consists of replacement of fluid and salts by mouth or intravenous infusion. Vaccinations against cholera provide only temporary immunity.

● **cholesterol** ▶ A compound derived from steroids and found in many animal tissues. Cholesterol is manufactured by the liver and other tissues and its derivatives form constituents of cell membranes, bile, blood, and gallstones. It is present in the bloodstream in the form of lipoproteins (*see* lipids), of which there are several types. Cholesterol and other lipids are transported from the liver to the tissues in the form of low-density lipoproteins (LDLs); they are conveyed from the tissues to the liver to be broken down as high-density lipoproteins (HDLs). High levels of LDL-cholesterol in the blood (over 4.4 mmol/l) are associated with an increased risk of heart disease, as a result of fatty deposits in the walls of arteries. ▷*See also* atherosclerosis.

● **Cholon** ▶ 10 45N 106 39E A port in S Vietnam, a part since 1932 of present-day ▷Ho Chi Minh City. It is the city's Chinese quarter (founded c. 1778). A trading centre for rice and fish, it has rice-milling, timber, and pottery industries. It suffered badly during the Vietnam War.

● **Cholula** ▶ (*or* Cholula de Rivadabia) 19 05N 98 20W A town in central Mexico. A major religious centre dedicated to the god Quetzalcoatl before the Spanish conquest, it is the site of a pyramid 53 m (177 ft) high, which was begun in the Teotihuacán period. Population (1990): 37 791.

● **Chomsky, Noam** ▶ (1928–) US linguist, under whose influence the aims and methods of general linguistic theory and especially of ▷grammar were radically revised. *Syntactic Structures* (1957) and *Aspects of the Theory of Syntax* (1965) work out implications of the observation that, although the number of grammatically well-formed sentences in a language is infinite, the rules according to which they are generated form a finite set. Chomsky's work draws on and develops that of his teacher Zellig Harris on the transformations by which a sentence may be generated from an underlying "deep structure." Chomsky has also undertaken studies of the theory of speech sounds and of semantic structures. A political radical, Chomsky was a leading opponent of US involvement in the Vietnam War and has continued his outspoken critique of US foreign policy in numerous books and newspaper articles.

● **Ch'ŏngjin** ▶ 41 50N 129 55E A city and seaport in North Korea, on the NE coast. Originally a small fishing village, it developed rapidly under Japanese occupation (1910–45). It is an important centre for the manufacture of iron and steel; other industries include shipbuilding, chemicals, and textiles. Population (latest est): 520 000.

● **Chongqing** ▶ (Ch'ung ch'ing *or* Chungking) 29 32N 106 45E A port in central China, in Sichuan province at the confluence of the Yangtze and Jialing (*or* Chia-ling) Rivers. A major commercial and industrial centre, it is a former capital of China (1937–46). Population (1993 est): 2 266 772.

● **Chopin, Frédéric (François)** ▶ (1810–49) Polish composer and pianist of French descent. He studied in Warsaw but later settled in Paris and never returned to Poland. In Paris he established himself as a celebrated virtuoso, much in demand as a teacher. He lived with the novelist George ▷Sand from 1838 to 1847, but never married her. During this period, with his health deteriorating as a result of tuberculosis, they spent a considerable time in Majorca. As a result of the ▷Revolution of 1848, Chopin left France for London, where he gave his last public performance in 1849. Later that year he returned to Paris, where at the age of 39 he finally succumbed to tuberculosis.
   A fervent nationalist, he was a student of Polish culture and much of his music was influenced by Polish folk music. He developed a highly characteristic style of writing for the piano, and much of his highly original romantic music has entered the repertoire of most professional and amateur pianists. He composed 2 concertos, 3 sonatas, 24 preludes, and many waltzes, nocturnes, polonaises, and studies. He also wrote a cello sonata, a piano trio, and songs.

● **Chopin, Kate** ▶ (1850–1904) US novelist and short-story writer. Of mixed Irish and French-Creole parentage, she married a New Orleans cotton merchant in 1870. Following the deaths of her husband and her mother, she began to write to support her family, publishing realistic tales of Cajun and Creole life in such collections as *Bayou Folk* (1894) and *A Night in Accidie* (1897). She is now best known for her novel *The Awakening* (1899), which deals with the sensuous awakening of a young married woman. Although the shocked reaction to this book ended her writing career, it is now regarded as a feminist classic.

● **chordate** ▶ Any animal that is distinguished by three features: a hollow dorsal nerve cord; a rodlike ▷notochord that forms the basis of the internal skeleton; and paired gill slits in the wall of the pharynx behind the head, although in higher chordates these are apparent only in early embryonic stages. Chordates comprise the ▷tunicates, ▷lancelets, and vertebrates. Some authorities place these three groups in a single phylum, *Chordata*, while others divide them into separate phyla: *Urochordata*, *Cephalochordata*, and *Craniata* (*see* Vertebrata), respectively.

● **chorea** ▶ Involuntary jerky movements caused by disease of the part of the brain controlling voluntary movement. It is a feature of **Huntington's disease** (*or* **chorea**), named after the US physician James Huntington (1850–1916). In this condition, which is hereditary, the jerky movements develop in early middle age and are later associated with mental deterioration. **Sydenham's chorea**, formerly known as ▷St Vitus's dance and named after the English physician George Sydenham (1624–89), is often associated with rheumatic fever in children. It can be treated with sedatives.

● **choreography** ▶ The art of composing ▷ballet and other theatrical dances. Choreography originally referred only to a dance notation, the lack of which has made precise reconstruction of many ballets difficult. The most comprehensive system for recording dance steps is that devised by the Hungarian dancer Rudolph Laban (1829–1958), known as Labanotation. The choreographer is usually a professional dancer, who selects, arranges into sequences, and teaches the dancers each step of the ballet. Often he works in close collaboration with composers, notable partnerships being between ▷Tchaikovsky and ▷Petipa and ▷Stravinsky and ▷Fokine. Famous contemporary choreographers have included ▷Cranko, ▷Robbins, ▷Béjart, ▷Ashton, ▷Balanchine, and ▷Bausch.

● **chorionic villus sampling** ▶ (CVS) ▷*See* prenatal diagnosis.

● **chorus** ▶ 1. In Greek drama, a group of actors who commented on the dramatic action through dance, song, and chanting. Greek tragedy originated in songs and dances performed by a chorus in honour of Dionysus. The dramas of Aeschylus required a chorus and only two actors, but its dramatic role declined in the plays of Sophocles (who introduced a third actor) and Euripides. The chorus, not directly involved in the main action, expressed the responses and judgments of average humanity. Its role has been revived in certain plays by ▷Brecht, Eugene ▷O'Neill, and T. S. ▷Eliot. 2. A body of singers or dancers who perform together.

● **Chorzów** ▶ 50 19N 18 56E A town in SW Poland. One of Silesia's first coalmining centres (1790), it remains a major mining town. Population (1996 est): 125 800.

● **Chota Nagpur** ▷*See* Bihar.

● **Chou** ▷*See* Zhou.

● **Chouans** ▶ Peasants in W France, including dealers in contraband salt, who revolted in 1793 against the government established by the French Revolution. They were provoked by such measures as the abolition of the salt tax (which ruined the contraband trade) and the enforcement of conscription. The revolt, led by Jean Cottereau (1757–94), was unsuccessful. It is the subject of Balzac's *Les Chouans* (1829).

● **Chou En-lai** ► (*or* Zhou En Lai; 1898–1976) Chinese communist statesman; prime minister (1949–76) and foreign minister (1949–58). Chou studied in Japan, France, and Germany. In 1924 he became a political instructor at the Whampoa Military Academy and secretary of the Canton provincial Communist Party. He led workers in the 1927 general strike in Shanghai, after which he escaped ▷Guomindang (Nationalist) assassins and fled to Nanchang, where he helped to organize an uprising. In 1932 he became political commissar to the Red Army and during the ▷Sino-Japanese War (1937–45) his reputation as a negotiator grew. After the establishment in 1949 of the People's Republic of China, he gained worldwide prominence as a diplomat and at home was largely responsible for establishing communist China's bureaucracy. Regarded as a moderate he exercised a stabilizing influence on his extremist colleagues.

● **chough** ► A large black songbird, *Pyrrhocorax pyrrhocorax*, about 37 cm long, with red legs and a long red down-curved bill. It occurs in the Alps, Spain, and a few sea cliffs around Britain where it can be seen giving displays of aerial acrobatics. The yellow-billed Alpine chough (*P. graculus*) occurs at high altitudes in European mountains. Family: *Corvidae* (crows).

● **chow chow** ► A breed of □dog originating in China more than 200 years ago. The chow has a compact body and—unusually—a blue-black tongue. The thick coat forms a mane around the neck and shoulders and the tail is held well over the back. Height: 46–51 cm.

● **Chrétien, (Joseph Jacques) Jean** ► (1934–) Canadian politician; prime minister (1993–). Liberal leader from 1990, he led the party to victory in 1993, 1997 (with a much reduced majority), and 2000.

● **Chrétien de Troyes** ► (12th century AD) French poet, author of the earliest romances dealing with the ▷Arthurian legend. He was a native of Champagne and a member of the court of Marie, countess of Champagne, to whom his romance *Lancelot* was dedicated. Little else is known of his life. His octosyllabic verse introduced a psychological subtlety in the treatment of ▷courtly love and chivalry that contrasts with the heroic themes of the ▷*chansons de geste*. His romances include *Erec, Cligés, Yvain,* and *Perceval* (or *Conte del Graal*), in which the ▷Holy Grail appears in a literary work for the first time.

● **Christadelphians** ► A religious movement founded in Brooklyn, New York, in 1848 by John Thomas (1805–71), an English immigrant. The sect rejects much orthodox Christian teaching, including the Trinity and the immortality of the soul. They are organized into autonomous democratic ecclesias (congregations). The sect is strongest in Britain and the USA.

● **Christchurch** ► 43 33S 172 40E A city in New Zealand, on E South Island. Founded in 1850, it has a gothic-style cathedral (completed in 1901) and many fine parks. The University of Canterbury was established in 1873. Industries, primarily associated with the rich agriculture of the Canterbury Plains, include meat processing, tanning, chemicals, and flour milling. Population (1996): 313 969.

● **Christchurch** ► 50 44N 1 54W A resort in S England, in Dorset on Christchurch Harbour. It has a famous priory church. Population (1991): 36 379.

● **Christian I** ► (1426–81) King of Denmark and Norway (1450–81) and Sweden (1457–64), who founded the Oldenburg ruling dynasty of Denmark (1450–1863). His claim to the Swedish Crown, which was disputed by Charles VIII of Sweden (d. 1470; reigned 1448–57, 1464–65, 1467–70), was finally ended by Christian's defeat at Brunkeberg (1471). In 1460 he gained Schleswig and Holstein but in 1469 the Norwegian islands of Orkney and Shetland were mortgaged to Scotland as part of his daughter Margaret's dowry on her marriage to the Scottish king James III.

● **Christian (II) the Cruel** ► (1481–1559) King of Denmark and Norway (1513–23) and of Sweden (1520–23). He acquired his nickname for his massacre of Swedish nobles in his conquest of Sweden. He was subsequently deposed and, after an attempt to regain Norway, imprisoned (1532–59).

● **Christian III** ► (1503–59) King of Denmark and Norway (1534–59), who established the state Lutheran Church in Denmark (1536) after

the ▷Count's War (1533–36). His administrative reforms laid the foundation for 17th-century Danish absolutism.

● **Christian IV** ► (1577–1648) King of Denmark and Norway (1588–1648). He entered the ▷Thirty Years' War in 1624 to defend the Protestant cause and Danish interests in the Baltic but was defeated by the Catholic League and withdrew (1629). At war with Sweden (1643–45), he was defeated with considerable loss of territory and domestic authority. He founded many towns, including Christiania (now Oslo).

● **Christian IX** ► (1818–1906) King of Denmark (1863–1906), who fought unsuccessfully with Germany over ▷Schleswig-Holstein. He succeeded to the throne through his marriage to the cousin of the childless Frederick VII of Denmark (1808–63; reigned 1848–63). He supported minority conservative governments until 1901, when he was forced to accept a liberal ministry.

● **Christian X** ► (1870–1947) King of Denmark (1912–47), whose courage and dignity during the German occupation of his country (1940–45) won him international respect; rejecting Nazi antisemitic legislation in 1942, he was imprisoned from 1943 to 1945.

● **Christian, Fletcher** ► (c. 1765–c. 1795) British seaman and mutineer. In 1787 he became an officer on the *Bounty* under Captain William ▷Bligh. Provoked by the alleged tyranny of Bligh, Christian led the famous mutiny of April 1789, which resulted in Bligh being set adrift in the South Pacific. Leaving most of his followers on Tahiti, Christian then led a small group of British and Tahitians to the uninhabited Pitcairn Island, where they settled. He apparently died there in a skirmish, although in some stories he makes a secret return to Britain.

● **Christian Aid** ► A British organization founded in 1949 by the ▷British Council of Churches to direct the use of donations made to assist the Third World. Christian Aid, which makes no distinctions as to race, religion, or politics, supports development programmes in agriculture, health, and education, giving relief aid in emergencies.

● **Christian Democrats** ► Political parties having programmes based on Christian principles and generally of a conservative nature. The German **Christlich-Demokratische Union** (Christian Democratic Union; CDU) was founded in West Germany in 1945 and held power, in alliance with the Christlich-Soziale Union (*see* Christian Social Union), from 1948 to 1969 under Konrad ▷Adenauer. From 1982 until 1998 it was the main party in the coalition government led by Helmut ▷Kohl. In Italy the **Democrazia Cristiana** (Christian Democratic Party; DC), founded in 1943 as the successor to the Partito Popolare Italiano (Italian Popular Party), dominated government from 1945 until the 1970s. In 1963 Aldo ▷Moro brought the Italian Socialist Party into a coalition government with the DC, which in the mid-1970s depended on the support of the Communist Party. Other Christian Democratic parties are found in Austria, Belgium, France, Norway, and Spain.

● **Christianity** ► The religious faith based on the person and teachings of ▷Jesus Christ, which had its origin in ▷Judaism. Its believers hold that Jesus is the ▷Messiah prophesied in the Old Testament. It began as a movement within Judaism, and one of the first disputes among the early Christians was the right of the Gentiles to be admitted to the faith. Chiefly through the missionary activities of St Paul, the Apostle of the Gentiles, Christianity spread rapidly through the Roman Empire, despite persecutions under Nero and later emperors. Christian belief was at first taught by the Apostles by word of mouth; however, the need for a written record of Jesus' life and teaching was soon fulfilled by the ▷Gospels. The definition of Christian belief and the authority of bishops and scriptures were well developed by the time Constantine, himself a convert, became emperor (312). A series of general councils, the first held in 325 at ▷Nicaea, defined orthodox Christian belief. Constantine's establishment of his new capital in the East, Constantinople, led to a growing polarization between the Eastern ▷Orthodox Church and the Western ▷Roman Catholic Church. Despite the collapse of the Western Empire, Western Christianity, under the Bishop of Rome who claimed authority as St Peter's successor, spread vigorously. The Orthodox Church, not so rigorously centralized, became increasingly isolated, and with the development of doctrinal differences the two Churches drifted apart. The date of the formal separation is generally regarded as 1054 (*see* East–West Schism). The Orthodox Church, under pressure from Islam to the east and often hostile Christians to the west, nevertheless established itself among the Slavs. The Western Church by the end of the first millennium was rapidly gaining power, the papacy reaching the zenith of its influence in the 13th century under Pope ▷Innocent III. In the later middle ages increasing nationalism and the assertion of power by temporal rulers weakened the united structure of the papacy and ▷Holy Roman Empire. At the same time dissident criticism of the Church, such as that of John ▷Wycliffe in England, increased.

By the 16th century the Church no longer had the power to override national interests; in this weakened state it was unable to resist the inevitable fragmentation caused by the ▷Reformation. Some reformers, such as the followers of Martin ▷Luther and the English Church, were comparatively conservative, while the ▷Calvinists, centred in Geneva, were considerably more radical. Coinciding with the exploration of the globe, the Reformation and the Roman Catholic response to it, the ▷Counter-Reformation, stimulated the spread of Christianity throughout the world, giving rise to many different Christian denominations and communions of the modern world.

Challenged in the 19th and 20th centuries by materialism, atheism, and agnosticism, the Christian Churches have come under severe pressure in many parts of the world. At the same time congregations have expanded rapidly in Africa, South America, and other parts of the developing world. The ecumenical movement of the 20th century has sought to unite Christendom and after centuries of hostility has had some success in healing its various schisms. The belief of Christianity is based on the New Testament and for most Christians is summarized in the traditional ▷creeds of the Church. The doctrines of the ▷Trinity, the ▷Incarnation of Christ, and the Resurrection are central, as is Christ's role as the redeemer of mankind. The total number of Christians has been estimated at over 1999 million (2000), or approximately 33% of the world population.

● **Christian Science** ► A religious movement founded by Mary Baker ▷Eddy. Having been influenced by P. P. Quimby (d. 1866), a spiritual leader, she formulated a set of principles of faith healing based on Christ's healing powers, which she claimed to have discovered and which she expounded in *Science and Health* (1875). The First Church of Christ, Scientist, opened in Boston, Massachusetts, in 1879. The movement spread throughout the world and by 1990 there were some 350 000–450 000 adherents organized in 2700 churches in over 60 countries. The emphasis of the movement on healing, primarily of sin and secondarily of disease, is based on the belief that matter is not an objective substance but a concept shaped by the limitations of the mind. There are no ordained clergy or ritual sacraments; services are simple, including hymns, Bible readings, and commentary from Mrs Eddy's works.

● **Christian Social Union** ► (German name: Christlich-Soziale Union; CSU) A German political party, the affiliate of the Christian Democratic Union (*see* Christian Democrats). The two parties held power from 1948 to 1969. In 1976, while in opposition, the CSU, led by Franz Josef Strauss (1915–88), staged a walkout on the Christian Democrats. However, the coalition soon re-formed and from 1982 the CSU played a part in the government of Helmut Kohl. Despite its name, the CSU forms the conservative wing in German politics.

● **Christians of St Thomas** ► The Christians of the Malabar Coast, in SW India. According to tradition, St Thomas the Apostle brought Christianity to the area. Their Church used a Syriac liturgy and originally held ▷Nestorian beliefs, but since the 16th century the Roman Catholic Church has been prominent in its development.

● **Christie, Dame Agatha** ► (1890–1976) British author of detective fiction and playwright. She introduced her most famous character, the Belgian detective Hercule Poirot, in *The Mysterious Affair at Styles* (1920); he met his end in *Curtain* (1975). Later detective novels include *The Murder of Roger Ackroyd* (1926), *Murder on the Orient Express* (1934), and *Death on the Nile* (1937); a number of these had locales with which she had become familiar after accompanying her second husband, the archaeologist Sir Max Mallowan (1904–78), on his expeditions. She wrote over 50 popular detective stories, creating other

fictional detectives, notably Miss Jane Marple. Several stories have been filmed, and her play *The Mousetrap* has had an unparalleled long run in London since its opening in 1952.

Linford Christie ► Setting a new world indoor record (20.25 seconds) for the 200 metres in June 1995, at the age of 35.

● **Christie, Linford** ► (1960–) British sprinter. He won gold medals for the 100 metres at the Commonwealth Games (1990, 1994), the Olympic Games (1992), and the World Athletics Championships (1993). In 1999–2000 he was suspended and then banned for alleged drug use, but maintained his innocence.

● **Christina** ► (1626–89) Queen of Sweden (1632–54). After reaching her majority (1644), she clashed repeatedly with her former regent ▷Oxenstierna. Her secret conversion to Roman Catholicism (then illegal in Sweden) led to her abdication, after which she lived in Rome. There, she became an outstanding patron of the arts, sponsoring the composers Scarlatti and Corelli and the architect and sculptor Bernini.

● **Christine de Pisan** ► (c. 1364–c. 1431) Venetian-born French writer. She grew up at the court of King Charles V of France, where she married an official. Following her husband's death in 1390, she supported her children by writing, thereby becoming one of the first professional women writers on record. Her works, which underwent a revival of interest in the late 20th century, argue against medieval ideas of women's moral and intellectual inferiority. They include the *Livres des trois vertus* (1402), *Le Livre de la cité des dames* (1405), and the autobiographical *La Vision* (1405).

● **Christmas** ► The Feast of the Nativity of Christ. In the West it has been celebrated on 25 Dec since 336 AD, partly in order to replace the pagan sun worship on the same date. In the East, both the Nativity and Epiphany were originally celebrated on 6 Jan, but by the end of the 4th century 25 Dec was almost universally accepted, although the Armenian Church still celebrates Christmas on 6 Jan. Many of the popular customs associated with Christmas can be traced back to pagan origins.

● **Christmas Island** ► An island in the Indian Ocean, SW of Java. It became a territory of the Commonwealth of Australia in 1958. The only commercial activity is phosphate mining. Area: 135 sq km (52 sq mi). Population (1991): 1275.

● **Christmas Island** ► (or Kiritimati) A large coral atoll in the W central Pacific Ocean, in Kiribati in the Line Islands. British and US nuclear tests were held here between 1957 and 1962. It has coconut plantations. Area: 359 sq km (139 sq mi). Population (latest est): 2537.

● **Christmas rose** ► A perennial herbaceous plant, *Helleborus niger*, about 35 cm tall, native to central and S Europe and Asia Minor. Grown in gardens for its attractive white or pink winter-flowering blossoms, it prefers rich moist shady sites. The poisonous rhizomes are irritant to the skin when fresh. Dried, they have been used medicinally. Family: ▷*Ranunculaceae*.

● **Christoff, Boris** ▶ (1919–93) Bulgarian singer. His powerful bass voice and skilful characterization made him a world-famous opera singer. He was particularly well known in the title role of Mussorgsky's opera *Boris Godunov*.

● **Christophe, Henri** ▶ (1767–1820) Haitian ruler. An ex-slave, Christophe served with ▷Toussaint L'Ouverture against the French and then joined ▷Dessalines' revolt. After Dessalines' assassination, in which Christophe took part, he ruled N Haiti (1808–20; as king from 1811). His cruelty caused a revolt and he shot himself.

● **Christopher, St** ▶ (3rd century AD) Christian martyr of Syria. According to legend, he carried a child across a river where he was working as a ferryman. The child grew heavier and he learned that it was Christ and he was thus carrying the weight of the world. He is the patron saint of travellers. Feast day: 25 July.

● **chromaticism** ▶ The use in music of notes that are not part of the normal diatonic ▷scale: the word comes from the Greek *chroma*, colour. Under the system of equal ▷temperament the octave is split into 12 equal parts, containing 7 diatonic and 5 chromatic notes. The practice of "colouring" music by the use of these chromatic notes dates from the 16th century and was widely used by Liszt and Wagner to effect frequent modulations from one key to another. In the early music of Schoenberg chromaticism became so heavy that the concept of key became meaningless and ▷atonality resulted.

● **chromatid** ▷*See* chromosome.

● **chromatography** ▶ A method of chemical analysis in which a mixture to be analysed constitutes a mobile phase, which moves in contact with an absorbent stationary phase. In **gas chromatography** (*or* gas-liquid chromatography) the mobile phase is a mixture of volatile substances diluted with an inert gas (e.g. argon). The stationary phase consists of a non-volatile liquid supported on an inert material of uniform particles (e.g. diatomaceous earth) in a tall column. The components of the mobile phase are selectively absorbed by the stationary phase. A detector measures the conductivity (or some other property) of the gas leaving the column, the resulting peaks on a strip chart of the detector output indicating the presence and concentration of the various components of the mixture. When the mobile phase is a liquid it can be introduced into a column of the solid stationary phase. The components of the mixture are selectively absorbed and form coloured bands down the length of the column. This method is known as **column chromatography**. In column chromatography, the stationary phase is an absorbent material such as alumina. **Thin-layer chromatography** is a similar technique used for analysis. The stationary phase is a thin layer of alumina on a glass plate, and a spot of sample is separated into spots of the constituents. More commonly, **paper chromatography** is used, in which the stationary phase is a sheet of absorbent paper. The solvent soaks along the paper carrying the constituents with it at different rates. Colourless compounds can be made visible by ultraviolet light or chemical developers. The rate at which a constituent moves relative to movement of the solvent can be used to identify it.

● **chromatophore** ▶ A granular cell containing pigment, found in great numbers in the skin of many animals. The distribution of the chromatophores accounts for the distinctive colours of these animals. Some animals (e.g. chameleons) have the ability to change the concentration and dispersion of pigment within the chromatophore very rapidly, effecting a change of skin colour that is of value in camouflage.

● **chrome dyes** ▶ Pigments consisting of chromium salts. **Chrome yellow** and **chrome orange** contain lead chromate ($PbCrO_4$), lead sulphate ($PbSO_4$), and lead monoxide (PbO). They display various shades, depending on the composition, and are used in paints. **Chrome green** contains chromic oxide (Cr_2O_3) and, unlike chrome yellow, is resistant to light and heat.

● **chromium** ▶ (Cr) A hard grey transition metal, discovered in 1798 by Louis Nicolas Vauquelin (1763–1829). It occurs in nature principally as chromite ($FeCr_2O_4$), which is mined in the former Soviet republics, Zimbabwe, and elsewhere. The metal is extracted by reducing the oxide (Cr_2O_3) with aluminium. The principal uses of chromium are in electroplating steel and in making alloys with iron. All chromium compounds are coloured and the most widely used, other than the oxide, are chromates (for example K_2CrO_4) and dichromates ($K_2Cr_2O_7$), which are used as oxidizing agents and in the dyeing industry. Lead chromate ($PbCrO_4$) is bright yellow and is used as a pigment. At no 24; at wt 51.996; mp 1863 ± 20°C; bp 2472°C.

● **chromophore** ▶ A group of atoms, generally in an organic compound, that absorbs light of characteristic wavelengths, thus imparting colour to the compound. Typical examples are the azo (−N=N−) and nitroso (−N=O) groups. In dyes, groups called auxochromes (colour enhancers) help to modify the colour conferred by the chromophore, as well as the solubility and related properties of the dye molecule. A group derived from sulphonic acid ($−SO_3H$) is a typical auxochrome. ▷*See also* azo dyes.

● **chromosome** ▶ One of the threadlike structures that carry the genetic information (*see* gene) of living organisms and are found in the nuclei of their cells. Chromosomes consist of a central axis of ▷DNA with associated ▷RNA and proteins. Before cell division, the long filamentous threads contract and thicken and each chromosome can be seen as two identical threads (chromatids) joined at the centromere. During cell division the chromatids separate to become the daughter chromosomes (*see* mitosis). Chromosome number is characteristic of a species. For example, a normal human body cell has 46 chromosomes comprising 22 matched pairs (called autosomes) and two ▷sex chromosomes. A human sperm or egg cell has half this number of chromosomes (*see* meiosis). Abnormal numbers or parts of chromosomes often lead to abnormalities in the individual concerned. ▷Down's syndrome is caused by the presence of an extra number 21 chromosome.

● **chromosphere** ▶ The layer of a star's atmosphere between the ▷photosphere and the ▷corona. It is much less dense than the photosphere. The sun's chromosphere is a few thousand kilometres thick; the temperature increases rapidly from about 4000°C near the photosphere to about 500 000°C at the base of the corona, with the atmosphere becoming increasingly rarefied with height. The solar chromosphere cannot be seen without special equipment, except at a total solar ▷eclipse.

● **chronic fatigue syndrome** ▶ (*or* postviral fatigue syndrome) A condition in which extreme fatigue can last for six months or more. Although it cannot be attributed to any other disease, it frequently follows serious viral diseases, especially glandular fever. The fatigue, which does not improve with bed rest and is made worse by exertion, is sometimes associated with a sore throat, slight fever, muscle pain, and depression (a consequence of the other symptoms and not a cause of the condition, as formerly thought). With no established cause, treatment is confined to relieving the symptoms and providing psychological support. The condition was formerly called myalgic encephalomyelitis (*or* ME) and also "yuppy flu." Some doctors formerly believed that no such physical disease existed and that those who claimed to have it were malingering or suffering from psychological problems. This view is no longer held and the medical establishment is interested in research into the causes.

● **chronicle plays** ▶ Plays that dramatize historical events in order to convey general moral lessons. The successors to the medieval ▷morality plays, they were popular in England during the Elizabethan era. Examples are Marlowe's *Edward II* (first produced in 1592) and Shakespeare's *King John* (c. 1596). Many of the plots were taken from Holinshed's *Chronicles* (1578).

● **Chronicles, Books of** ▶ Two Old Testament books covering the history of Judah from the Creation to the end of the ▷Babylonian exile (538 BC). They were probably written in the 4th century BC and originally formed a continuous history with the books of Ezra and Nehemiah. After opening with genealogies from Adam, they describe the reigns of David and Solomon and the succeeding Kings of Judah. Special emphasis is given to the building of the Temple at Jerusalem.

● **chronometer** ▷*See* clock.

● **chrysalis** ▶ The ▷pupa of most insects of the order Lepidoptera. ▷*See also* butterflies and moths.

● **Chrysanthemum** ▶ A genus of herbaceous plants and shrubs (about 200 species) native to Eurasia, Africa, and North America. The wild ancestors of the horticultural chrysanthemums are not known, but probably more than one species—almost certainly of Japanese and Chinese origin—was involved. The showy forms are widely cultivated, having colourful single or double flower heads. The different varieties may bloom at any time from early spring to autumn. Family: ▷*Compositae*. ▷*See also* pyrethrum.

● **Chrysoloras, Manuel** ▶ (c. 1365–1415) Greek scholar and envoy. Chrysoloras was sent on diplomatic missions by the Byzantine Emperor Manuel Palaeologus. In Florence he taught the humanists Bruni, Poggio, and Guarino. His work on grammar, *Erotemata*, introduced Greek to the West.

● **chrysoprase** ▶ An apple-green variety of ▷chalcedony, used as a gem.

● **Chrysostom, St John** ▶ (c. 347–407 AD) Bishop of Constantinople and Doctor of the Church. After a period as a hermit, he was ordained in 386 in Antioch and preached extensively there, soon gaining the epithet Chrysostom (Greek: golden-mouthed). As Patriarch of Constantinople from 398, he was a zealous reformer but alienated the Empress Eudoxia (d. 404) and other powerful persons. In 403 he was unjustifiably condemned on a number of charges, deposed from his see, and banished. He died while journeying to the Black Sea. His *Homilies* are important expositions of various biblical books. The liturgy in use in the Orthodox Churches is attributed to him, although in its present form it dates from a much later period. Feast day: 27 Jan.

● **chrysotile** ▷*See* asbestos; serpentine.

● **Chuang-tzu** ▷*See* Zhuangzi.

● **chub** ▶ One of several freshwater fish related to ▷carp, found in Europe and North America and used as food, game, or bait fish. The European chub (*Leucixus cephalus*) has a plump elongated body, usually 30–40 cm long, and is dark blue or green above and silvery below. Certain unrelated freshwater fish of the genus *Leucichthys* (order: *Salmoniformes*) are also called chub.

● **Chu Chiang** ▷*See* Zhu Jiang.

● **Ch'ü Ch'iu-pai** ▷*See* Qu Qiu Bai.

● **chuckwalla** ▶ A North American lizard, *Sauromalus obesus*, occurring in SW arid and rocky regions. 50 cm long, it is dark-grey with a red-banded and blotched tail. It feeds on vegetation, storing water in sacs beneath the skin, and shelters in crevices; it can inflate its lungs to increase its body size making it difficult to dislodge. Family: *Iguanidae*.

● **Chukchi** ▶ A people of the Chukchi peninsula in NE Siberia. One branch consists of nomadic reindeer herders; the other is a maritime fishing people whose members live in fixed villages. Their language is of Palaeo-Siberian type.

● **Chulalongkorn** ▶ (1853–1910) King of Siam (now Thailand) from 1868 to 1910. He built roads and railways, improved education, abolished slavery, and remodelled Siam's administration on Western lines. His diplomatic handling of France and Britain ensured Siam's continued independence.

● **Chungking** ▷*See* Chongqing.

● **Chur** ▶ (French name: Coire; Romansh name: Cuera) 46 52N 9 32E A town in E Switzerland. A tourist centre, it also trades in Valtelline wines. Population (1990): 30 236.

● **Church Army** ▶ A ▷Church of England organization founded in 1882 by Prebendary Wilson Carlyle (1847–1942). Consisting of trained lay evangelists, it fulfils a social role in work with prisoners, the homeless, and drug addicts.

● **Churchill** ▶ 58 45N 94 00W A town and port in central Canada, in Manitoba on Hudson Bay. Originally a trading post (1685), it exports prairie grain. Rocketry and weather research are conducted here. Population (latest est): 1003.

● **Churchill, Charles** ▶ (1731–64) British poet. The success of his satire on actors, *The Rosciad* (1761), allowed him to abandon a career in the church. A friend of John ▷Wilkes, he wrote several caustic attacks on the government, including *The Prophecy of Famine* (1763) and *The Candidate* (1764).

● **Churchill, Lord Randolph Henry Spencer** ▶ (1849–95) British Conservative politician; third son of the 7th Duke of Marlborough and the father of Sir Winston ▷Churchill. He entered parliament in 1874 and led the group of Tory Democrats known as the Fourth Party. After serving as secretary for India (1885–86), he was briefly chancellor of the exchequer, when his budget was not accepted by the prime minister, Lord ▷Salisbury, because Churchill wished to reduce funds allocated to the armed forces. He married (1874) Jeanette (Jennie) Jerome (1854–1921), an American.

● **Churchill, Sir Winston (Leonard Spencer)** ▶ (1874–1965) British statesman and author. The son of Lord Randolph ▷Churchill, he was a direct descendant of the 1st Duke of Marlborough. Churchill served in the army and as a war correspondent in the second Boer War before becoming a Conservative MP in 1900. In 1904 he joined the Liberals and subsequently served as president of the Board of Trade (1908–10), home secretary (1910–11), and first lord of the admiralty (1911–15). In 1915, during World War I, he rejoined the army and served in France. In 1917 he became minister of munitions, supporting the development of the ▷tank. Churchill lost his parliamentary seat in 1922 but was re-elected as a constitutionalist in 1924, becoming chancellor of the exchequer in Baldwin's government. From 1929 he was out of office until the outbreak of World War II, when he became first lord of the admiralty and then, in 1940, prime minister of a coalition government. During ▷World War II, his remarkable oratory and outstanding qualities as a leader made him a symbol of British resistance to tyranny throughout the free world. He was largely responsible for Britain's victorious alliance with the Soviet Union and the USA (1941) but came to view Soviet communism as a future threat, speaking later of an "iron curtain" drawn across Europe. Churchill's Conservative Party was defeated in 1945 but he returned as prime minister in 1951, serving until his resignation in 1955.

His writings include *The Second World War* (1948–54) and *A History of the English-Speaking Peoples* (1956–58); he won the 1953 Nobel Prize for Literature.

● **Churchill Falls** ▶ A waterfall in E Canada in W Labrador on the Churchill River. In 1967 work began on a huge hydroelectricity project expected to generate 5 222 000 kW. Height: 75 m (245 ft); 316 m (1038 ft) including rapids.

● **Churchill River** ▶ A river in W Canada, flowing from NW Saskatchewan E and NE through Manitoba to Hudson Bay. Length: 1610 km (1000 mi).

● **Church in Wales** ▶ The Welsh Anglican Church. From the 16th century until 1920 the Anglican Church was the Established Church of Wales. Since disestablishment in 1920 the Church in Wales has been an autonomous province of the ▷Anglican Communion consisting of six sees. One of the six diocesan bishops is elected Archbishop of Wales by an electoral college. Some 100 000 Welsh people belong to the church, which has 1142 parishes and 700 stipendary clergy.

● **Church of England** ▶ The Established Church in England, which embodies Protestant elements but also claims continuity with the English Church as established by St ▷Augustine, the first Archbishop of Canterbury. Christianity was probably introduced in Britain during the Roman occupation in the 2nd century AD. Prior to the mission of St Augustine (597), the native Church was dominated by Celtic missionaries from Ireland and Scotland. Conflicts between the indigenous Celtic Church and Rome were resolved in favour of Roman usage at the Synod of ▷Whitby (664), and thereafter the English Church remained under papal authority until the ▷Reformation. Under ▷Henry VIII, papal supremacy was rejected and the king was acknowledged Supreme Head of the Church. The two bases of Anglican doctrine and worship were formulated in the succeeding reigns:

the Book of ▷Common Prayer, introduced in the reign of ▷Edward VI, and the ▷Thirty-Nine Articles, published under Elizabeth I, whose excommunication (1570) by the pope completed the break with Rome. The Church was disestablished during the Commonwealth but re-established by Charles II. By the 19th century three parties had developed within the Church and these continue to the present: the Low Church or Evangelical group, which emphasizes the Protestant tradition; the High Church group (*see* Anglo-Catholicism); and a liberal group stressing adaptation to modern ideas. The two provinces of the Church are the archbishoprics of Canterbury (*see* Canterbury, Archbishop of) and York (*see* York, Archbishop of), each of which is further divided into bishoprics. Ecclesiastical affairs are supervised by the General Synod (established 1970 to replace the Church Assembly), composed of bishops, clergy, and laity; its decisions are subject to parliamentary approval. In 1992 the Synod voted to admit women to the priesthood; the first women were ordained as priests in 1994. Church property and endowments are administered by the Church Commissioners for England (established 1948). Although about 45% of the UK population remain affiliated to the Anglican Churches, in 1992 only about 2.5% regularly attended services. ▷*See also* Anglican Communion; charismatic movement; Evangelicalism; holy orders; Lambeth Conferences; latitudinarianism.

● **Church of Scotland** ▶ The Established Church in Scotland. The Scottish Church's secession from Rome was effected in 1560, largely under the influence of John ▷Knox. The argument over Church government between Episcopalians and Presbyterians continued until the reign of William of Orange, who established the Presbyterian Church in 1690. During the 18th century, disputes arose between traditional Evangelicals and Moderates, and this, together with the question of patronage, led to secessions. During the 19th and 20th centuries many of these divisions were healed, especially following abolition of patronage in 1874.

● **church year** ▶ The organization of the Christian churches' calendar around the great festivals of Christianity. In the Western Churches, the beginning of Advent (the Sunday nearest to the Feast of St Andrew, 30 Nov) marks the opening of the year. The Sundays of Advent are numbered one to four, leading to Christmas (25 Dec). Epiphany (6 Jan) follows after one or two intervening Sundays. The other major festivals are linked to the date of Easter, itself associated with the Jewish Passover. There are six Sundays in Lent and eight from Easter to Pentecost. The dates of Ash Wednesday, Good Friday, Whit Sunday (Pentecost), and Ascension Day depend on Easter. The Eastern Churches' year begins with Easter and ends with Lent.

● **Churriguera** ▶ A Spanish family of architects consisting of three brothers, José (1665–1725), Joaquín (1674–1724), and Alberto (1676–1750). The Churrigueras evolved a distinctive, highly decorative form of the ▷baroque later known as **Churrigueresque**. The characteristic ornamentation and twisted barley-sugar columns that adorn much of their work is particularly marked in José's church of S Estéban, Salamanca (1693).

● **Chu Teh** ▷*See* Zhu De.

● **Chuvash Republic** ▶ A constituent republic of W Russia. The region is a wooded steppe with peat bogs and mineral deposits. The Chuvash, who comprise about 70% of the population, are a Turkic-speaking people. Industries include engineering, oil and natural-gas refining, chemicals, and food processing, but the economy is predominantly agricultural, producing chiefly cereals and fodder crops; livestock is also important. Area: 18 300 sq km (7064 sq mi). Population (1995 est): 1 361 000. Capital: Cheboksary.

● **Chu Xi** ▶ (*or* Chu Hsi; 1130–1200) Chinese philosopher, born in Fujian province, the son of a government official. He was a precocious student and entered the government service, holding various important public posts for most of his life. His major work consists of four commentaries known as the *Ssu shu* or *Four Books*. These contain the formulation of ▷Confucianism that was adopted as the official philosophy of China until the communist revolution in the 20th century.

● **Chu Yuan** ▶ (c. 343 BC–c. 289 BC) Chinese poet, the earliest known by name. A nobleman of the state of Ch'u, he was banished to the S

after court intrigues and drowned himself in the River Mi-lo. His contribution to the anthology *Ch'u tz'u* greatly influenced the development of early Chinese poetry.

● **CIA** ▷*See* Central Intelligence Agency.

● **Ciano, Galeazzo** ▶ (1903–44) Italian fascist leader. The son-in-law of ▷Mussolini, Ciano was foreign minister from 1936 to 1943 and helped to form the military pact with Germany. In 1943 he voted against Mussolini in the Fascist Supreme Council and was shot by Mussolini's supporters in N Italy.

● **Cibber, Colley** ▶ (1671–1757) British actor, dramatist, and theatre manager. Son of a Danish sculptor, he wrote the sentimental comedy *Love's Last Shift* (1696) to supplement his earnings as an actor. His adaptation of Shakespeare's *Richard III* was the preferred acting version until the 19th century. His appointment as poet laureate in 1730 made him the target for satirical attacks by ▷Pope.

● **cicada** ▶ An insect belonging to the mainly tropical family *Cicadidae* (over 2000 species). Cicadas are 20–50 mm long and have large membranous wings. Males produce a variety of loud noises by vibrating two membranes at the base of the abdomen (this is called stridulation). Cicadas usually inhabit trees and the females lay eggs in the wood. The ▷nymphs (immature cicadas) drop to the ground and burrow underground to feed on plant juices from roots. After 1–17 years they emerge as adults. Order: ▷Hemiptera.

● **cicely** ▶ A perennial herbaceous plant, *Myrrhis odorata*, also called sweet cicely. 60–100 cm high, it has umbrella-like clusters of white flowers and a strong aromatic smell. Cicely is native to Europe and also occurs in Chile (where it was probably introduced). Formerly widely used as a vegetable, it is still used for seasoning. Family: ▷*Umbelliferae*.

● **Cicero** ▶ (Elyesa Bazna; 1904–70) Turkish secret agent who worked for Germany. He gained access to secret documents while a valet to the British ambassador in Turkey in 1943–44, but the German authorities did not completely trust the information he supplied. He ended his working life as a nightwatchman in Munich.

● **Cicero, Marcus Tullius** ▶ (106–43 BC) Roman orator and statesman. Established as a prominent lawyer by 70 BC, he was elected consul in 63 BC. His execution of the Catiline conspirators without trial lost him support and he was exiled in 58 BC for 18 months. During the civil war he supported Pompey against Caesar and lived privately in Rome during the latter's dictatorship. After the assassination of Caesar in 44 BC he made a series of attacks on Antony, the *Philippics*, for which he was later arrested and killed. The greatest of Roman orators, he also wrote treatises on rhetoric and philosophical works influenced by Greek political theory.

● **cichlid** ▶ A freshwater fish of the family *Cichlidae* (over 6000 species), found in tropical regions, especially Africa. Cichlids have a brightly coloured deep body, up to 30 cm long, and a single long dorsal fin; they feed on plants or animals. Most build nests for their eggs and guard the young but some species carry the eggs in their mouths (*see* mouthbrooder). Many are popular aquarium fish. Order: *Perciformes*.

● **CID** ▷*See* Criminal Investigation Department.

● **cider** ▶ An alcoholic drink made from fermented apple juice. In England cider is made predominantly in the West Country, from apples grown specifically for cider making. They are crushed to press out the juice, which ferments spontaneously. Fermentation lasts weeks or months, varying according to the apples used. The cider is then drawn off from the yeast deposit and stored in a cool place. Sweet cider has a large amount of unfermented sugar, dry cider little sugar, and rough cider is dry cider with some acetic acid. Cider is also made in France, especially in Normandy and Brittany, Spain, and the USA, where cider denotes unfermented apple juice and hard cider denotes cider.

● **Cienfuegos** ▶ 22 10N 80 27W A port in S Cuba, on the Caribbean Sea. A picturesque city with many fine buildings, it trades in tobacco, cattle products, and molasses and is the site of a naval base. Population (1994 est): 132 038.

● **cigar** ▶ A cylindrical roll of tobacco leaf, smoked originally by the Indians of the Americas and copied by sailors from Portugal and Spain; by the 19th century they became common in N Europe. The most expensive cigars are still made by hand in Cuba and Jamaica, machine-made cigars being made extensively in the USA, Europe, and the Far East. The cigar was replaced to some extent by the cigarette from the end of the 19th century, but small cigars have enjoyed some popularity in recent years.

● **cigarette** ▶ A cylindrical roll of fine-cut tobacco, rolled in thin paper. Cigarettes became popular in the late 19th century and are now the form in which most tobacco is smoked. The tobacco most commonly used is Virginia-cut, a type that originated in the USA and is now successfully grown in other countries. Since the 1960s there has been widespread concern over the association between smoking and lung ▷cancer, ▷bronchitis, and ▷heart disease. In the UK the government has imposed a ban on cigarette advertising on television and issued a health warning on all cigarette packets. Between 1972 and 1996–97 the percentage of smokers in the UK dropped from 52% (males) to 29% and 41% (females) to 28%.

● **Cilicia** ▶ The SE coastal region of Asia Minor. It was subject consecutively to the Hittites, the Assyrians, the Achaemenians, the Macedonians, and the Seleucids. From the 2nd century BC pirates based on Cilicia seriously threatened Mediterranean trade until suppressed by Pompey in 67, after which the region was incorporated into a series of Roman provinces.

● **Cilician Gates** ▶ (Turkish name: Külek Boğazi) 37 17N 34 46E A mountain pass in central S Turkey, in the Taurus Mountains. It lies on the route from Ankara to Adana and has been used for centuries.

● **Ciliophora** ▶ A phylum of microscopic single-celled organisms (see protozoa), the ciliates, having two nuclei and tracts of hairlike cilia over the cell surface, used for feeding and swimming. Most are free-swimming (see Paramecium) but some are attached to the substrate by a stalk (see Stentor; Vorticella). Most ciliates feed on organic detritus, other protozoans, etc., but some are parasitic, especially on fish and other aquatic animals.

● **Cimabue** ▶ (Cenni de Peppi; c. 1240–c. 1302) Florentine painter, who introduced a degree of naturalism into the stylized ▷Byzantine art of his period. His only certain work is a mosaic of St John (Duomo, Pisa) but the fresco cycle in the upper Church of St Francis, Assisi, and the *Santa Trinità Madonna* (Uffizi) are attributed to him. ▷Giotto was probably his pupil.

● **Cimarosa, Domenico** ▶ (1749–1801) Italian composer. He became court musician in St Petersburg and Vienna and was famous for his many operas. His best-known work is the ▷opera buffa *The Secret Marriage* (1792), which shows his flair for vocal ensemble writing and fine comic talent. He also wrote church music and chamber music.

● **cimbalom** ▶ The traditional musical instrument of Hungary; a type of dulcimer. The cimbalom has ten pairs of wire strings stretched over a shallow three-sided soundbox. The strings are struck with a small hammer. The Hungarian composer Kodály used it in the suite *Háry János* (1927).

● **Cimbri** ▶ A Germanic tribe from N Jutland. At the end of the 2nd century BC the Cimbri migrated southwards, defeating Roman armies in 113 BC (Noricum), 110 BC (Rhône valley), and 105 BC (Arausio, now Orange, France). In 101 BC Marius destroyed them; a remnant survived in Jutland.

● **Cimon** ▶ (died c. 450 BC) Athenian general and politician. The son of ▷Miltiades, Cimon opposed ▷Themistocles' policy of enmity towards the Spartans, believing Persia was the common Greek enemy, and in about 466 he scored a great victory against the Persians. His opponents, including ▷Pericles, caused him to be ostracized (461) but after his return to Athens, Cimon negotiated a truce with Sparta (c. 450) and died fighting the Persians in Cyprus.

● **Cinchona** ▶ A genus of trees (40 species) of the South American Andes, now cultivated elsewhere in the tropics, especially India. One of the most important species is calisaya (*C. calisaya*). The bark yields powerful medicinal drugs, including ▷quinine, used in the treatment of malaria, and quinidine, used to treat abnormal heart rhythms. Cultivation, which is generally by coppicing, has lost importance since the development of similar synthetic drugs lacking side-effects. Family: *Rubiaceae*.

● **Cincinnati** ▶ 39 10N 84 30W A city in the USA, in SW Ohio on the Ohio River. Founded in 1788, it developed as a meat-packing centre in the 19th century. Today it is an important inland port and major manufacturing centre best known as a producer of machine tools. The University of Cincinnati was established here in 1819. Population (1996 est): 345 818.

● **Cincinnatus, Lucius Quinctius** ▶ (5th century BC) Roman statesman. He was made dictator to rescue a Roman legion that was besieged by an Italian tribe. After his victory he returned to his farm, despite pleas that he remain dictator. His rejection of autocratic rule made him a symbol of traditional Roman values.

● **Cinderella** ▶ The heroine of a folktale, of which the first recorded version dates from 9th-century China. The story is of a girl treated cruelly by her stepfamily who receives help from a supernatural agent, in most versions an animal or her fairy godmother, and finally marries a prince. The story was introduced to England through Charles Perrault's *Tales of Mother Goose* (1697).

● **cinema** ▶ The art form and industry of films. The first motion picture exhibited to a public audience was made in 1895 by the French brothers Louis and Auguste ▷Lumière, whose equipment was developed from the inventions of Thomas ▷Edison, and the first commercial success was the American film *The Great Train Robbery* (1903). Influential pioneers of the silent cinema in the USA were D. W. ▷Griffith, Mack ▷Sennett, and Charlie ▷Chaplin. In Europe, technological developments were creatively exploited by such directors as F. W. Murnau (1889–1931) in Germany and ▷Eisenstein in Russia. The end of the era of silent films was signalled by the success of Al ▷Jolson's *The Jazz Singer* (1927), which had a synchronized musical score; colour film, introduced in the 1930s, added further popular appeal. The French directors René ▷Clair and Jean ▷Renoir made notable contributions to the early development of sound cinema. Between 1930 and 1945 (the so-called "Golden Age of Hollywood") the cinema industry in the USA became essentially an entertainment factory, controlled by such giant Hollywood studios as MGM and Paramount. From the early 1950s the decline in cinema audiences caused by the rival attraction of television, together with legal moves to curtail the studios' monopolistic powers, caused the break-up of the Hollywood system: subsequently many of the most significant developments in the cinema have been achieved by directors elsewhere. There was a postwar resurgence of the British film industry, which had developed in the 1930s as a result of the influence of the producer J. Arthur Rank. Prominent directors included Carol ▷Reed, David ▷Lean, and Alfred ▷Hitchcock; Michael ▷Balcon's Ealing comedies also added considerable prestige to British films. However, the

cinema ▶ The Mexican-born actor Ramon Novarro (1899–1968) became one of the first romantic idols of the cinema. He is seen here in the 1925 version of *Ben-Hur*, the most expensive and most spectacular film of the silent era.

most important postwar developments took place on the Continent, where many leading directors were in conscious reaction against the glossy conventions of prewar Hollywood. In Italy such neorealist directors (*see* neorealism) as ▷Rossellini and ▷De Sica employed documentary-style methods to explore social problems, while in France the ▷New Wave of the late 1950s, spearheaded by such directors as ▷Godard and ▷Truffaut, pioneered new techniques of shooting and editing. Other major directors to emerge in the 1950s and 1960s include such individualistic talents as Ingmar ▷Bergman in Sweden, ▷Fellini and ▷Antonioni in Italy, ▷Kurosawa in Japan, and Satyajit ▷Ray in India. By the late 1970s cinema had become a truly global medium, with thriving industries in Latin America, Australia and New Zealand, and many parts of Asia (the Indian film industry is now the largest in the world, with over 800 features released every year). Meanwhile, Hollywood has responded to these challenges in several different ways. In the 1970s the loosening of studio control enabled such US directors as ▷Coppola, ▷Scorsese, and ▷Altman to produce original and challenging films. Subsequently, however, the ever-increasing costs of film-making have led the studios to take fewer risks. The 1980s and 1990s saw the dominance of big-budget action spectaculars featuring the latest special effects—a tendency epitomized in the hugely successful work of ▷Spielberg. This trend has also received impetus from the most important technical development of recent years—the advent of increasingly sophisticated techniques for the computer manipulation of images.

● **cinematography** ▶ The recording of moving pictures. Essentially a motion film records a rapid sequence of still pictures (each slightly different from the previous one) fast enough to appear continuous to the human eye. The film moves through the camera in a series of jumps, as each frame must be held still for a split second as it is exposed. There are usually 24 frames (pictures) per second in sound film (the standard speed for silent films was 16 frames per second and some narrow-gauge films run at 18 fps). The sequence of transparencies produced by developing the film is passed through a projector in the same way. Sound can be carried as a magnetic or optical signal on a narrow strip at the side of the film, to synchronize with the picture. Various gauges (widths) of film are used: 8 mm for educational and amateur use (now almost entirely superseded by video); 16 mm with portable equipment for documentaries and low-budget productions; 35 mm for most commercial feature films.

● **cineraria** ▶ A herbaceous perennial pot plant developed from *Senecio cruentus* of the Canary Islands. There are numerous horticultural varieties, noted for their sometimes brilliantly coloured, daisy-like flowers. Useful for spring and winter flowering, they require a draught- and frost-free atmosphere. Family: ▷*Compositae*.

● **Cinna, Lucius Cornelius** ▶ (d. 84 BC) Roman politician. Expelled from Rome by his opponent Sulla (87), Cinna returned with ▷Marius and captured Rome. He tried to restrain Marius' brutal revenge on their opponents and as consul (86–84) restored order. He was killed in a mutiny shortly before Sulla's return to Italy.

● **cinnabar** ▶ (moth) A moth, *Callimorpha jacobaeae*, of Europe and Asia. Both the adults—scarlet and black—and the caterpillars—striped black and yellow—taste bad: their coloration discourages predators. The caterpillars feed on ragwort and have been used to control this weed. Superfamily: *Caradrinoidea* (noctuids, tiger moths, etc.).

● **cinnabar** ▶ (ore) A mineral consisting of mercury sulphide, the chief ore of mercury. It is bright red and occurs in veins and impregnations associated with volcanic rocks. Spain, the Soviet Union, Italy, and Mexico are the main producers.

● **cinnamon** ▶ An evergreen tree, *Cinnamomum zeylanicum*, 7–10 m high, native to Sri Lanka and cultivated widely in the tropics. Before 1776 only wild plants were used, owing to the belief that cultivation would destroy its flavour. It is coppiced, the bark of the twigs being peeled off and rolled up to form the spice. Family: *Lauraceae*.

● **cinquefoil** ▶ A shrub or herbaceous plant of the genus ▷*Potentilla*, having leaves with five divisions each. Creeping cinquefoil (*P. reptans*) has been used medicinally, and shrubby cinquefoil (*P. fruticosa*) is often grown in gardens. Family: *Rosaceae*.

● **Cinque Ports** ▶ An association of five English ports (Sandwich,

Dover, Hythe, New Romney, Hastings) in Kent and Sussex formed during the 11th century to defend the Channel coast. After the Norman conquest they were granted considerable privileges in return for providing the nucleus of the navy. Winchelsea and Rye were added to their number and many other towns in the southeast became associate members. In the later middle ages their power declined both because of competition from other ports and the silting-up of their harbours. The Lord Warden of the Cinque Ports survives as an honorary office. Holders have included Sir Winston Churchill (1941–65) and Elizabeth the Queen Mother (1978–).

● **Cintra** ▷*See* Sintra.

● **Ciompi, Revolt of the** ▶ (1378) A rising of the poorer wage-earners of Florence against the oligarchic rule of the major guilds. The Ciompi (wool workers) seized power together with the minor guilds, but a split in this alliance allowed the major guilds to destroy the revolt and to abolish the Ciompi's newly formed guild.

● **circadian rhythm** ▷*See* biorhythm.

● **Circassia** ▶ An area in S Russia, NW of the Great Caucasus. It is inhabited by the Circassian (*or* Cherkess) people, who, although Christian since the 6th century, adopted Islam under the influence of the Ottoman Empire in the 17th century and subsequently resisted Russian rule until the Ottoman Turks ceded Circassia to Russia in 1829.

● **Circe** ▶ Legendary Greek sorceress, who had the power to transform men into beasts. Odysseus, who visited her island of Aeaea on his voyage from Troy, was protected by the herb moly, and forced her to restore his men to human form.

● **circle** ▶ A curve defined as the locus of all the points lying in a plane at a certain distance, called the radius, from a fixed point, called the centre. Its diameter is any straight line joining two points on the circle and passing through the centre. The ratio of the distance around any circle (the circumference) to its diameter is equal to the number π (*see* pi). The area of a circle, radius r, is πr^2.

● **circuit breaker** ▶ A mechanism for breaking an electrical power circuit under load. Similar in function to a fuse, it has the advantage of being able to be reset immediately. It is used in power stations and high-voltage distribution lines and now often replaces fuses in low-voltage circuits.

● **circulation of the blood** ▶ The passage of blood through the ▯heart and the network of arteries and veins associated with it. By supplying the tissues with blood, the circulatory system effects the transport of oxygen, nutrients, etc., and the removal of waste products. Oxygen-rich blood is pumped out of the ▷heart into the aorta and then, via the arteries, to all the tissues of the body. Here oxygen is removed, and deoxygenated blood returns, through the veins, to the heart. This blood is then pumped to the lungs, where it is reoxygenated, and returned to the heart to repeat the circuit. The circulation of the blood was first discovered by William ▷Harvey in 1628. ▷*See* Plate II.

● **circumcision** ▶ The removal of all or part of the foreskin. In many primitive societies circumcision usually forms part of a ceremony initiating youths into adulthood. Among some Islamic peoples it is performed just before marriage; Jewish babies are circumcised in a religious ceremony when they are eight days old. In Judaism, the practice is required by the covenant made between Abraham and God (Genesis 17). Its historical origin is unknown but hygienic advantages have been claimed for it, especially in hot climates, and cancer of the penis is almost unknown among circumcised men. It has also been observed that the incidence of AIDS in African tribes that practise male circumcision is very much lower than in tribes that do not. Recent research to explain this observation has centred on the protective role of ▷keratin, which forms the outermost layer of the skin and cannot be penetrated by HIV. It has been found that, like the mucosa lining the vagina and the anus, the inside of the foreskin has no keratin layer and therefore provides a way for HIV to enter the body. Circumcision is sometimes carried out for medical reasons, usually to increase the flow of urine if the opening in the foreskin is too small (phimosis) or in cases in which the foreskin is too tight (paraphimosis). So-called female circumcision differs in different cultures. "Sunna" requires only removal of the clitoral prepuce, while excision involves removal of the clitoris and the labia minora; in infibulation all the external genitalia are removed and the two sides of the vulva are stitched to leave a tiny opening. These widely condemned mutilations, which became illegal in the UK in 1985, are a means of controlling the sexual behaviour of women and are still widely practised in Africa and Asian Arab states (WHO estimate that some 90 million circumcised women are currently alive).

● **Cirencester** ▶ 51 44N 1 59W A market town in SW England, in Gloucestershire. In Roman times it was the second largest town in Britain (Corinium) and it was an important wool centre in the middle ages. The Royal Agricultural College is situated here. Population (1991): 15 221.

● **cire perdue** ▶ (French: lost wax) A technique of metal casting used for small detailed castings, particularly statuary. A wax model is encased in a mould into which molten metal is poured: the wax then melts and is replaced by metal. The process was known in ▷Ur and was perfected in China about 500 BC.

● **cirque** ▶ (or corrie) A rounded rock basin with steep sides, often containing a lake or cirque glacier. Common in glaciated mountain ranges, cirques form through freeze–thaw action on the headwall and basin floor together with abrasion by slipping ice and debris.

● **cirrhosis** ▶ Destruction of the cells of the liver followed by their replacement with fibrous tissue, which eventually produces symptoms of liver failure (e.g. jaundice, swelling of the legs and abdomen, and vomiting of blood). Cirrhosis may be caused by ▷alcoholism, ▷hepatitis, obstruction of the bile duct, and heart failure, but often the cause is not known.

● **cirrocumulus cloud** ▶ (Cc) A high ▷cloud with a mottled appearance composed of ice crystals (sometimes known as "mackerel sky").

● **cirrostratus cloud** ▶ (Cs) A high thin veil of ▷cloud composed of ice crystals, visible as a halo around the sun or moon.

● **cirrus cloud** ▶ (Ci) A high detached wispy ▷cloud occurring in the troposphere above 6000 m (20 000 ft), composed of ice crystals. It is usually associated with fair weather.

● **CIS** ▷See Commonwealth of Independent States.

● **Cisalpine Republic** ▶ A state established in N Italy following Napoleon's successful Italian campaign of 1797. Extending from the Alps to the Apennines, it comprised Milan (the capital), Lombardy, the Venetian territories, and modern Emilia-Romagna. Although nominally independent, it was essentially a French puppet state. In 1802 it was renamed the Republic of Italy and in 1805 it became the basis of an enlarged kingdom of Italy. In 1815, following Napoleon's defeat, it was split up and returned to its hereditary rulers.

● **Ciscaucasia** ▶ (or North Caucasia) An oil-producing region in S Russia. Mainly steppe, it rises in the S to the Great ▷Caucasus range.

● **Ciskei** ▷See Bantu Homelands.

● **Cis-Sutlej states** ▶ Sikh principalities in India, so called by the British because they were on the British side (Latin cis, on this side of) of the River Sutlej. They were first united in 1785 under the Maratha, whose rule was broken by the rise of ▷Ranjit Singh and British power in the subcontinent. The majority of the Cis-Sutlej states came under British government in 1809, the remainder passing to Ranjit Singh. They continued to exist until Indian independence in 1947.

● **Cistercians** ▶ An order of Roman Catholic monks founded by St Robert of Molesme (c. 1027–1111) as a stricter offshoot of the ▷Benedictine order. The mother house at Cîteaux, France, from whence the order took its name, was founded in 1098. St ▷Bernard of Clairvaux contributed to the order and communities were established throughout W Europe in the 12th century. In the 17th century the order split into two: the monks of the Strict Observance (see Trappists) and the Common Observance.

● **CITES** ▷See endangered species.

● **Citizens Advice Bureaux, National Association of** ▶ (CAB) A British organization with over 1000 branches that provide free confidential advice to anyone on any subject. Their staff (mostly volunteers) is trained to advise on such matters as housing, state benefits, debt problems, and employment law. Chief Executive: Ann Abraham.

● **citizens' band radio** ▶ (CB) A short-distance two-way radio link, commonly installed in motor vehicles. These systems became popular in Britain in the 1970s although they were illegal and interfered with the emergency services. Many CB clubs were formed and a special CB language evolved. A CB channel was authorized in 1981.

● **Citlaltépetl** ▶ (Spanish name: Volcan Citlaltépetl) 19 00N 97 18W A dormant volcano in S central Mexico, the highest point in the country. Height: 5699 m (18 697 ft).

● **citric acid** ▶ An organic compound that occurs in plant and animal tissues and is involved in the series of metabolic reactions called the ▷Krebs cycle. A commercial preparation of citric acid is used as a flavouring agent in foods.

● **citron** ▶ A citrus tree, *Citrus medica*, 2–3 m high. Originally from the Far East, it is now cultivated in the Mediterranean. The rough yellowish sour fruits are used to make candied peel, produced by soaking in brine and preserving in sugar. ▷See Citrus.

● **citronella** ▶ A ▷grass, *Cymbopogon nardus*, cultivated in tropical regions of Africa and Asia and introduced into tropical America. It forms dense tufts and contains geraniol or citronella oil, used in cosmetics and insect repellents.

● **Citrus** ▶ The largest and most important genus of tropical and subtropical fruits (10 species), originating in SE Asia. All the species are small evergreen trees or shrubs with simple glossy leaves and five-petalled, usually white, flowers. The juicy fruits are rich in vitamin C, citric acid, and pectin (used in jam making). The most important are the ▷orange, ▷lemon, ▷lime, ▷grapefruit, ▷citron, and ▷tangerine. All contain essential oils used in perfumery and soap making (▷bergamot is grown especially for this). Family: *Rutaceae*.

● **cittern** ▶ A small instrument of the guitar family with a pear-shaped body, a fretted fingerboard, a flat back, and four pairs of wire strings. It was popular between the early 16th and mid-18th centuries.

● **City Hall** ▶ The headquarters of the ▷mayor of London and the Greater London Assembly. Opened in 2002 and standing opposite the Tower of London on the River Thames, it is an asymmetrical egg-shaped glass-fronted structure housing a circular debating chamber with a public gallery. Using London groundwater as a coolant, it is highly energy efficient. The architect was Norman ▷Foster.

● **City of London** ▶ A square mile in central London, on the north bank of the Thames between Tower Bridge and Blackfriars Bridge, nominally in which many of the country's financial institutions have their head offices. The ▷Bank of England is in Threadneedle Street, with the ▷Stock Exchange nearby, while ▷Lloyd's is in Lime Street. The London International Financial Futures and Options Exchange (LIFFE) is in Canon Bridge, and the associated LIFFE Commodity Products is at St Katherine Docks. An important source of invisible earnings, the City is the financial centre of the EU, rivalled by Frankfurt, and of international commerce, rivalled by Wall St in New York. The Corporation (governing body) of the City of London comprises three courts: the Court of Aldermen (see alderman), which elects the Lord Mayor (see mayor); the Court of Common Hall, which elects the ▷sheriffs and comprises the Lord Mayor, the 25 other aldermen, and the freemen and liverymen of the 84 City ▷livery companies; and the Court of Common Council, which is responsible for local government and comprises the Lord Mayor, the 25 other aldermen, and 155 councilmen.

● **city states** ▶ Independent municipalities, each comprising a town and its surrounding countryside, characteristic of ancient Greece. Of several hundreds of city states, Athens was the largest. Each enjoyed autonomy, its own laws and constitution (democratic, as at Athens, or oligarchic, as at Sparta), and its own presiding deity.

● **City Technology Colleges** ▶ (CTC) UK secondary schools financed jointly by industry and government and independent of the LEAs (see education). Introduced in 1988, they widen the choice for families in disadvantaged urban areas and specialize in technology and business. The first City College for the Technology of the Arts (CCTA) was opened in 1991. In 1998 there were 15 CTCs and CCTAs.

● **Ciudad Bolívar** ▶ 8 06N 63 36W A port in E Venezuela, on the

River Orinoco. Accessible to oceangoing vessels, its chief exports include gold, diamonds, and chicle. Population (1990 est): 225 846.

● **Ciudad Guayana** ▶ (former name: Santo Tomé de Guayana) 8 22N 62 37W An industrial complex in E Venezuela, on the River Orinoco. Founded in 1961, it amalgamated several industrial centres; industries include iron and steel processing and gold mining. Population (1990): 536 506.

● **Ciudad Juárez** ▶ 31 42N 106 29W A city in N Mexico, on the Rio Grande. Its importance is due to its location on the US border and as a marketing centre for cotton. Its university was founded in 1973. Population (1990): 797 679.

● **Ciudad Real** ▶ 38 59N 3 55W A town in S central Spain, in New Castile. It has a 13th-century gothic cathedral. An agricultural centre, it produces flour and brandy. Population (1991): 59 400.

● **civet** ▶ A solitary nocturnal mammal belonging to the family ▷*Viverridae*. The African civet (*Viverra civetta*) is cat-like, about 1.2 m long with coarse greyish spotted fur. Mainly carnivorous, civets also eat fruit and roots. The secretion of their anal glands is used in perfumes as a fixative, making other scents last longer. ▷*See also* palm civet.

● **Civic Trust** ▶ A charity, founded in 1957 and supported by voluntary contributions, aiming to improve the quality of the environment in the UK. It supports local amenity groups, advises on town planning, and encourages the construction and preservation of fine buildings.

● **civil defence** ▶ Arrangements for the defence of a civilian population, especially against air raids. In the UK, during World War II, the Air Raid Precautions (ARP), planned by the ministry of home security, included training air-raid wardens and firewatchers, gasmask distribution, building shelters, and organizing rescue services in conjunction with the police, fire, and ambulance services. Since World War II the UK has reduced its civil defence commitment on the grounds of economy and the difficulty of providing protection against nuclear attack. This view is not shared by the USA, where an extensive system of ▷fallout shelters is capable of protecting 160 million people.

● **civil disobedience** ▶ Passive (i.e. nonviolent) resistance to state power, usually involving mass defiance of unpopular laws or passive noncooperation with the authorities. Such methods can cause considerable difficulties for the state, which may be reluctant to use force against nonviolent protestors for fear of inflaming the situation or alienating world opinion. Civil disobedience was first developed as a concerted strategy by ▷Gandhi, who pioneered his techniques of ▷satyagraha first in South Africa and then in British India. Similar methods were subsequently adopted by supporters of the ▷Campaign for Nuclear Disarmament in the 1950s, by Martin Luther ▷King and the US ▷civil-rights movement of the 1960s, and by large crowds demanding reform in Czechoslovakia and other countries in the weeks before the collapse of communism in 1989. History suggests that such techniques are most likely to succeed when the regime is relatively liberal, when its authority is already crumbling, or when peaceful protests are backed by the implicit threat of mass violence should their demands not be met.

● **civil engineering** ▶ The branch of ▷engineering that deals with the design and construction of buildings and structures, such as roads, bridges, tunnels, railways, dams, canals, etc. The term was first used in 1750 by John Smeaton (1724–92) to distinguish himself from military engineers, although the practice went back to ancient times. It has diversified into numerous branches calling on specialized knowledge and developing such new materials as prestressed concrete. The professional body in the UK is the Institution of Civil Engineers (granted a royal charter in 1828).

● **civil law** ▶ The law governing the rights of individuals and their relationships with each other rather than the state. It is also called private law, as distinguished from public and ▷criminal law. The term is also used of the European systems derived from ▷Roman law, which differ from ▷common law systems. For example, in civil law court decisions have no force in the decision of similar cases. Roman law was revived in Europe from the 11th and 12th centuries and formed the basis of the ▷*Code Napoléon* (1804), on which some European, Latin American, and Asian states modelled their legal systems. English-speaking countries use common law, although Scottish law is related to civil law.

● **civil list** ▶ In the UK, the sum given annually from the Consolidated Fund to the monarch, her consort, and her mother to meet their expenses. Until 1993 her children (except the Prince of Wales, who receives the revenues of the Duchy of Cornwall) were also on the list. The list was introduced in 1689, became law in 1697, and in 1830 all government expenses were removed from it. Originally parliament voted at the monarch's accession the sum to be paid annually but because of inflation Parliament increased the amount fixed in 1952 both in 1972 and 1975; it is now reviewed every ten years. Civil list payments are not taxed but since 1993 the Queen's personal income is taxed. **Civil list pensions**, charged to the Consolidated Fund but not forming part of the civil list, are awarded by the monarch on the advice of the prime minister to distinguished persons.

● **civil rights** ▶ The individual's rights to liberty, equality of treatment, education, etc., under the law and safeguarded by the state. They form a part of the wider ranging ▷human rights. In countries with a written constitution, such as the USA, civil rights form part of the constitution. In England there have been a number of unsuccessful attempts to codify these rights, which are still only protected by the general law. ▷*See also* Bill of Rights.

● **civil-rights movement** ▶ In the USA, the political struggle for racial equality in the 1950s and 1960s led chiefly by Martin Luther ▷King, Jr. The movement's goals were equal rights for US Blacks. Its first success was in the campaign (1955–56) in Montgomery, Alabama, to desegregate the city's buses and the Civil Rights Acts of 1957, 1960, and 1964 prohibited racial discrimination in every important aspect of life.

● **civil service** ▶ The bureaucracy that implements government policies. In the UK civil servants were recruited by patronage until 1855, when the Civil Service Commission was established and initiated the recruitment of candidates by examination. As a result of the report of the Fulton Committee (1968), the Civil Service Commission came under a new Civil Service Department headed by the prime minister. This was subsequently disbanded but the prime minister remains minister for the Civil Service. The civil service has been criticized for the power of its permanent staff in comparison to that of relatively short-term ministers. The secretariats of the UN are regarded as forming an international civil service.

● **Civil War, English** ▶ (1642–51) The war between Charles I and parliament, which led to the execution of the king (1649) and the establishment of Oliver Cromwell's ▷Protectorate (1653). The Civil War was the outcome of a conflict between king and parliament that had steadily worsened during the reigns of James I (1603–25) and Charles. The struggle for power culminated in the events of the ▷Long Parliament (summoned in 1640). War was precipitated by Charles' rejection of parliament's Nineteen Propositions in June, 1642, and on 22 Aug he raised his standard at Nottingham. The first battle, at Edgehill, ended indecisively but during 1643 the royalists (or ▷Cavaliers) gained ground in the N and W. The parliamentarian (*see* Roundheads) negotiation of the ▷Solemn League and Covenant with the Scots led to its victory at ▷Marston Moor (1644); the formation of the ▷New Model Army brought about the decisive defeat of Charles at ▷Naseby (1645). In 1646 Charles surrendered to the Scots at Newark and the first Civil War was brought to an end. He was handed over to parliament in January, 1647, but was seized by the army in June. He escaped to the Isle of Wight and in December reopened negotiations with the Scots. The second Civil War ensued (1648), with royalist uprisings in Wales and Kent, ending with Cromwell's defeat of the Scots at Preston in August. In the following year, Charles was tried and executed and the ▷Commonwealth was established by the Rump Parliament. The Civil War was concluded by Cromwell's subjection of Ireland (1649–50), his defeat of Charles' heir (later Charles II) at Dunbar (1650), and his victory against the Scots at Worcester in 1651. In 1653 he dismissed the Rump and established the ▷Protectorate, which governed England until 1659 (*see* Restoration).

● **Civil War, US** ▶ (1861–65) The struggle between the Federal government of the USA and the 11 ▷Confederate States in the South. The war arose from the conflict of interest between the predominantly agricultural slave-owning South and the industrialized North. The election of a president, Abraham Lincoln, opposed to slavery precipitated the secession of the southern states under Jefferson Davis, and war broke out when the Confederates opened fire on Fort Sumter, South Carolina, which the Federal government had refused to evacuate. The opening campaigns in Virginia culminated in the Confederate victory at the first battle of ▷Bull Run (July). Early in 1862 the Confederate Stonewall Jackson conducted a brilliant campaign in the Shenandoah Valley but on 4 May the Federal Army of the Potomac under George B. McClellan captured Yorktown and defeated Robert E. Lee's force in the Seven Days' battles (25 June–1 July). The Confederates retaliated in August with a victory at the second battle of Bull Run and Lee pushed N into Maryland. Defeated at ▷Antietam (Sept), the Confederates were then victorious at Fredericksburg (Dec). In Tennessee the Confederate success at Shiloh (6–7 April) was followed by a reverse at Stones River (31 Dec–2 Jan). In 1863, following his victory at Chancellorsville, Virginia (1–5 May), Lee began his second invasion of the N, only to be defeated at ▷Gettysburg (July). In the W, Federal troops under Ulysses S. Grant besieged Vicksburg, Mississippi, which fell on 4 July, and, after defeat at Chickamauga (19–20 Sept), won the victory of Chatanooga (23–25 Nov). In 1864 Grant, by now the Federal general in chief, advanced against Lee, whom he fought inconclusively at ▷Cold Harbor (June). Sherman, who held the Federal command in the W, took Atlanta (Sept) before making his March to the Sea. After capturing Savannah in September, Sherman moved N through the Carolinas and on 9 April, 1865, Lee surrendered at Appomatox Court House. By 2 June the Federal victory was complete and the task of ▷Reconstruction lay ahead.

● **civitas** ▶ Citizenship in ancient Rome acquired either by birth or by grant from the people or emperor. It was a much coveted privilege, entailing voting rights and facilitating an administrative or military career. As Rome expanded *civitas* was gradually extended to its Italian allies (89 BC) and to subjects of some Roman provinces (from 43 BC). In 212 AD all free inhabitants of the Empire were made citizens. An autonomous provincial city was also known as a *civitas*.

● **Civitavecchia** ▶ 42 05N 11 47E A seaport in central Italy, in Lazio. It has Etruscan and Roman remains and a citadel designed by Michelangelo. There is a fishing industry. Population (1987): 50 800.

● **Clackmannanshire** ▶ A council area of central Scotland, lying N of the Firth of Forth. Under local government reorganization in 1975 the small county of Clackmannanshire was absorbed into Central Region; it became an independent ▷unitary authority in 1996. Comprising level plains rising to the Ochill Hills in the N, it is chiefly agricultural, with distilling and some light industry. Area: 157 sq km (60 sq mi). Population (1996 est): 48 700. Administrative centre: Alloa.

● **Clacton-on-Sea** ▶ 51 48N 1 9E A resort in SE England, on the Essex coast. Population (1991): 49 437.

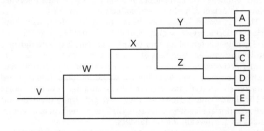

cladistics ▶ A cladogram showing the relationships of six species (A–F), which can be grouped into five clades each containing all the descendants of a common ancestor. For example, A–D form a clade sharing the ancestor X and A–F form a different clade, with the common ancestor V.

● **cladistics** ▶ A system of classification of living organisms in which species are allocated to groups (called clades) on the basis of shared characteristics that are thought to indicate common ancestry. For example, all organisms with mammary glands would form the clade "mammals." The relationship of the various clades is represented on a diagram (cladogram; see diagram). The cladogram can be taken as reflecting the evolutionary relationships of the clades. This assumes that new species are formed by the sudden splitting of two new forms from the ancestral form, in opposition to neo-Darwinism (*see* Darwinism). The so-called "transformed" cladists minimize the evolutionary significance of cladograms.

● **Clair, René** ▶ (René Chomette; 1898–1981) French film director. Both his silent comedies and his pioneering sound films, such as *Sous les toits de Paris* (1930), were distinguished by humour and fantasy. During World War II he worked in Hollywood. Later films included *Les Belles de nuit* (1952).

● **Clairvaux** ▶ (Latin: *clara vallis*, beautiful valley) The ▷Cistercian monastery founded (1115) by St ▷Bernard of Clairvaux in the Aube Valley (NE France), which remained the most influential Cistercian house until its suppression (1790) during the French Revolution.

● **clairvoyance** ▷*See* extrasensory perception.

● **clam** ▶ A ▷bivalve mollusc with two equal shells and a muscular burrowing foot. Burrowing clams live buried in sand and mud, mainly in shallow coastal waters; they feed by taking in water through a tube (siphon). The largest burrowing clam is the geoduck (*Panopea generosa*), weighing up to 5 kg, while the giant clam (*Tridacna gigas*) can exceed 250 kg.

● **clan** ▶ A group tracing actual or putative descent from a common ancestor. Clans are frequently important divisions in primitive soci-

US Civil War ▶ This was the first major conflict to be recorded by photography. The photograph shows Union troops in the trenches near Petersburg, Virginia (1864–65).

eties, as in the pre-18th-century Scottish Highlands. They are often exogamous (prohibiting marriage between members). Many have a totemic emblem, often an animal or plant from which members are believed to descend, and perform collective ceremonies.

The clan system in Scotland began to replace ▷feudalism from the late 14th century. Most clan members were not blood relations of the clan chief but feudal tenants, bound to provide him with fighting men when required. Members of a clan often bore the name of its founder preceded by Mac (son of), e.g. MacGregor. The clans all had much in common: they were Roman Catholic, spoke Gaelic, wore characteristic clothing (*see* Highland dress), and had common sports (*see* Highland Games). However, they were politically divided—and feuds, territorial disputes, and cattle rustling gained them a reputation for lawlessness among Lowlanders.

Most clans supported Charles I during the Engish Civil War. After the ▷Glorious Revolution (1689) many chiefs were reluctant to sign a declaration of loyalty to the Protestant William of Orange (William III), a factor that contributed to the massacre of the MacDonalds of ▷Glencoe in 1692. The clans came out in support of the Stuart Pretenders in the ▷Jacobite rebellions of 1715 and 1745, and the crushing of the Jacobites at ▷Culloden Moor in 1746 was followed by a government campaign to destroy the clan system. Highland dress was proscribed and the communal ownership of land used by the clans declared to have no legal basis. The demise of the Scottish clans was completed by the ▷Highland Clearances.

A similar system, consisting of chiefdoms and kingdoms, existed in Ireland. Members of an Irish clan often used the name of its founder preceded by O' (son of), e.g. O'Neill. The clans were largely autonomous until Henry II of England secured their submission in 1171–72. By the 16th century the clans had reasserted control of all but the English Pale (a small area around Dublin). However, by 1603 the English had again subdued the clans, confiscated much land, and were beginning to make a success of the ▷Plantation of Ireland (begun in 1556). Further military suppression and land appropriation during and after the Cromwellian and Williamite wars of the 17th century completed the destruction of the Irish clans. The clan chiefs are still officially recognized, both in Scotland and Ireland.

● **Clapham** ► A residential district in the London borough of ▷Wandsworth. Originally spelled Clopeham (meaning village on the hill), it remained a small village until many Londoners settled there after the ▷Fire of London in 1666. The adjacent marshland, now known as Clapham Common, was drained in 1760. Clapham Junction became a major railway interchange with the development of south London commuter lines in the 19th century.

● **Clapham Sect** ► (c. 1790–1830) A group of well-to-do Evangelicals, most of whom lived in ▷Clapham, who supported the missionary movement, the abolition of the slave trade, and domestic social reform. Members included William ▷Wilberforce, Henry Thornton (1760–1815), James Stephen (1758–1832), and John Venn (1759–1813), the rector of Clapham.

● **Clapton, Eric** ► (1945–) British blues and rock guitarist, singer, and songwriter. During the 1960s he played with the Yardbirds and John Mayall's Bluesbreakers before forming the trio Cream (1966–68), who became famous for their virtuoso improvisations. He recorded his best-known song, "Layla," in 1970, but subsequently declined into heroin addition and alcholism. His later mellower recordings include *August* (1986), *Unplugged* (1992), and *Pilgrim* (1998).

● **Clare** ► (Irish name: Chláir) A county in the W Republic of Ireland, in Munster situated between Galway Bay and the Shannon estuary. It consists of a low-lying central plain rising E to mountains and W to the limestone area of the Burren. Agriculture is the chief occupation. The salmon fisheries are important. Area: 3188 sq km (1231 sq mi). Population (1996 est): 94 000. County town: Ennis.

● **Clare, John** ► (1793–1864) British poet, the self-educated son of a labourer in Northamptonshire. His first book, *Poems Descriptive of Rural Life and Scenery* (1820), brought him fame and patronage in London. Three further volumes, including *The Shepherd's Calendar* (1827), were less successful, and he lived in great poverty. In 1837 he became insane and in 1841 was confined to an asylum in Northampton.

● **Clarendon, Constitutions of** ► (1164) Regulations concerning the relations between church and state issued by Henry II of England. They aimed to limit the power of the church, especially of the ecclesiastical courts, bringing it more firmly under royal authority. Thomas ▷Becket, Archbishop of Canterbury, repudiated his allegiance to the Constitutions, leading eventually to his murder.

● **Clarendon, Edward Hyde, 1st Earl of** ► (1609–74) English statesman and historian. In the lead-up to the English ▷Civil War he tried to influence Charles I towards moderation. He served as the king's chancellor of the exchequer during the war and went into exile in 1646, settling in France. At the Restoration (1660) he became Lord Chancellor and gave his name to the ▷Clarendon Code. His daughter Anne married the future James II. He fell from power after criticism of his sale of Dunkirk to France (1662) and his handling of the second ▷Dutch War (1664–67). Forced again into exile, he completed his *History of the Rebellion and Civil Wars in England* (1702–04).

● **Clarendon Code** ► (1661–65) A series of Acts, passed by Charles II's government, that were directed against ▷Nonconformists (*or* Dissenters). The Corporation Act (1661) excluded Nonconformists from municipal office, the Act of Uniformity (1662) enforced the use of the Church of England's Book of Common Prayer, the Conventicle Act (1664) prohibited Nonconformist services, and the Five Mile Act (1665) outlawed former Nonconformist ministers from the towns. The Code is named after the Earl of ▷Clarendon.

● **Clare of Assisi, St** ► (1194–1253) Italian nun, founder of the "Poor Clares." Influenced by the teaching of St ▷Francis of Assisi, she gave up all her possessions and followed him. St Francis established a community of women with Clare as abbess in 1215. They lived in absolute poverty without even communal property. She was canonized in 1255. Because she once saw mass celebrated at a distance, she was proclaimed patron saint of television in 1958. Feast day: 12 Aug.

● **claret** ▷*See* wine.

● **clarinet** ► A woodwind instrument with a single reed and a cylindrical bore. It is a transposing instrument existing in several sizes and generally has a fundamental of A or B flat; it has a range of three and a half octaves. The clarinet did not become a regular member of the orchestra until the late 18th century. Mozart popularized it, using it in several symphonies. The **bass clarinet** is pitched an octave lower than the B flat clarinet. ⬚musical instruments.

● **Clark, Helen** ► (1950–) New Zealand politician; prime minister (1999–). A Labour MP from 1981, she was deputy prime minister in 1989–90 before becoming Labour leader in 1993. She formed a government following Labour's victory in the 1999 general election.

● **Clark, Kenneth (Mackenzie), Baron** ► (1903–83) British art historian. As a young man, Clark worked with ▷Berenson in Florence. He was director of the National Gallery (1934–45), Slade Professor of Fine Art at Oxford (1946–50, 1961–62), and professor of art history at the Royal Academy (1977–83). His books and particularly his television series *Civilization* (1969) stimulated public appreciation of art. He became a life peer (1969) and a member of the OM (1976). His son **Alan Clark** (1928–99) was Conservative minister of defence (1989–92): he caused controversy over breaches of the ban on arms sales to Iraq and with his indiscreet *Diaries* (1993). His other books include *The Fall of Crete* (1963) and *Aces High* (1973).

● **Clarke, Sir Arthur C(harles)** ► (1917–) British science fiction writer and scientist. Having helped to develop the first communications satellites, he became famous with such novels as *2001, A Space Odyssey* (1968) and its sequels (1982 and 1988). He was knighted in 1998.

● **Clarke, Jeremiah** ► (?1673–1707) English composer and organist, a pupil of John Blow. He shot himself as the result of an unhappy love affair. The "Trumpet Voluntary" often attributed to Purcell is an arrangement of "The Prince of Denmark's March," one of Clarke's harpsichord pieces.

● **Clarke, Kenneth Harry** ► (1940–) British Conservative politician; chancellor of the exchequer (1993–97). His previous posts included secretary of state for health (1988–90) and for education

(1990–92) and home secretary (1992–93). His attempt to become leader of the Conservative Party in 1997 failed.

● **Clarke, Marcus (Andrew Hislop)** ▶ (1846–81) Australian novelist. Born in London, he emigrated to Australia in 1863 and became a journalist. His best-known novel, *For the Term of His Natural Life* (1874), is about a penal settlement.

● **Clarkia** ▶ A genus of herbaceous plants (36 species) found naturally in semiarid environments in California and Chile. Horticultural varieties are grown as summer annuals. About 30 cm tall, they are slender, showy, and most have pink flowers. Family: *Onagraceae* (willowherb family).

● **Clarkson, Thomas** ▶ (1760–1846) British campaigner for the abolition of slavery. With ▷Wilberforce and Granville Sharp (1735–1813) he formed an antislavery society in 1787, when he also wrote *A Summary View of the Slave Trade and of the Probable Consequences of Its Abolition.*

● **class** ▶ 1. ▷*See* social class. 2. ▷*See* taxonomy.

● **classical art and architecture** ▷*See* Greek art and architecture; Roman art and architecture.

● **classical literature** ▷*See* Greek literature; Latin literature.

● **classical physics** ▶ Theoretical physics until approximately the end of the 19th century, i.e. before the advent of Planck's ▷quantum theory (1900) and Einstein's special theory of ▷relativity (1905). Classical physics was largely based on ▷Newtonian mechanics and Maxwell's equations, which unified electricity, magnetism, and light (*see* Maxwell, James Clerk). The laws of classical physics can still be used with large-scale systems in which there is no very rapid relative motion, but for events at the subatomic level and in space, relativity and quantum theory must be taken into account.

● **classical revival** ▷*See* classicism; neoclassicism; Palladianism.

● **classicism** ▶ The aesthetic qualities that were embodied in the visual arts and literature of ancient Greece and Rome and served as ideals for various later European artistic movements. Its qualities include harmony and balance of form, clarity of expression, and emotional restraint.

The Italian Renaissance of the 15th and 16th centuries was the first attempt at a **classical revival** in the arts. Major productions of this period included the sculpture of ▷Michelangelo, the paintings of ▷Raphael and ▷Titian, and the architecture of ▷Palladio. These achievements provided the goals of artists throughout Europe during the next two centuries. The art of the French 17th-century painters ▷Poussin and ▷Claude Lorraine was greatly influenced by their study of Renaissance and classical models. Examples of the neoclassical movement (*see* neoclassicism) in the 18th century include the paintings of ▷David and ▷Ingres in France and the sculpture of ▷Canova in Italy, while in England the lectures of Sir Joshua ▷Reynolds at the Royal Academy were based on classical and Renaissance doctrines.

In literature, Renaissance interpretations of Aristotle's *Poetics* influenced writers throughout Europe in the 17th and 18th centuries, notably in France and England. The tragedies of ▷Racine and ▷Corneille represent classicism in literature at its height. Towards the end of the 18th century there was a reaction against neoclassicist doctrines, but the influences of classicism can still be seen in, for example, the art of ▷Picasso, the sculpture of ▷Rodin, and the poetry of T. S. ▷Eliot.

● **Classics** ▶ In ▷flat racing in England, five annual races (*see* Derby; Oaks; One Thousand Guineas; St Leger; Two Thousand Guineas) for three-year-old horses only.

● **classification** ▶ (biology) ▷*See* taxonomy.

● **clathrate** ▶ A compound formed by the physical trapping of molecules of one substance in the crystal lattice of another. No chemical bonds are formed between the host compound and the trapped molecule. Zeolites form clathrates with many simple compounds by virtue of their cagelike crystal structure. Ice can form clathrate compounds with some of the ▷noble gases.

● **Claudel, Paul** ▶ (1868–1955) French dramatist and poet. A diplomat who was converted to Roman Catholicism at the age of 18, he wrote plays dominated by religious themes, especially the relationship between human and divine love, as in the autobiographical *Partage de midi* (1906) and his best-known play, *The Satin Slipper* (1924). In *Cinq grandes odes* (1910) and other books he developed a lyrical free-verse style.

● **Claude Lorraine** ▶ (Claude Gellée; 1600–82) French landscape painter. He was born in Lorraine but settled in Rome (1626), where he had received his training. His paintings of the Roman countryside include biblical or classical figures and his seascapes are remarkable for their sunlight. Both were esteemed by such patrons as Pope Urban VIII. His *Liber veritatis* (British Museum), dating from 1635, documents his career through drawings and notes to prevent later forgeries.

● **Claudian** ▶ (c. 370–404 AD) Roman poet. Born in Alexandria, he went to Rome in 395. His praise for Stilicho, elected consul in 400, gained him high civil status. His works include panegyrics, satires, epigrams, and the epic poem *The Rape of Proserpine.*

● **Claudius I** ▶ (10 BC–54 AD) Roman emperor (41–54). Claudius owed his accession to the chaos that followed the murder of his nephew ▷Caligula. His rule was generally efficient: he extended the Empire, taking part in the invasion of Britain (43), but his susceptibility to the influence of freed men and his third wife Valeria ▷Messalina alienated the Senate. ▷Agrippina the Younger, his niece and fourth wife, was suspected of his murder. Claudius had been taught by Livy and himself wrote histories.

● **Clausewitz, Karl von** ▶ (1780–1831) Prussian general and military theorist. In 1812 Clausewitz negotiated the Treaty of Tauroggen, initiating the Prussian, Russian, and British war effort against Napoleon. In 1818 Clausewitz became director of the German War Academy. Of his many military works the posthumously published *Vom Kriege* is the most famous. Rejecting old systems of war in favour of total warfare backed by the people, *Vom Kriege* became a classic and had a profound influence up to World War I.

● **Clausius, Rudolf Julius Emanuel** ▶ (1822–88) German physicist, who in 1854 formulated the concept of ▷entropy and used it in a statement of the second law of thermodynamics. He also contributed to the development of the ▷kinetic theory of gases and suggested that electrolysis involved the dissociation of molecules into charged particles.

● **claustrophobia** ▷*See* phobia.

● **clavichord** ▶ A keyboard instrument, popular from the 15th to the 18th centuries and revived in the mid-20th century. Its delicate tone is produced by small brass plates (called tangents) fixed to the end of each key, which strike the strings. Its body consists of a portable rectangular wooden box. It is strung lengthways and has a range of about four octaves. It is said to have been J. S. Bach's favourite instrument.

● **clavicle** ▶ The collar bone. There are two clavicles, each running from the upper end of the breastbone to form a joint with the shoulder blade. They brace the shoulders and help to support the arms. Fractures of the clavicle are fairly common, caused by any fall involving the upper arm. ▷*See* Plate II.

● **clawed frog** ▶ A South African aquatic frog, *Xenopus laevis*, also called platanna. Up to 12 cm long, with a flattened head and body, it has three short black claws on its hind feet, probably used for stirring up mud to confuse enemies.

● **clay** ▶ A sedimentary deposit that has plastic properties when wet and hardens and cracks when dry. It consists of fine rock particles (less than 0.004 mm in diameter), formed from the decomposition of other rocks. The principal minerals present in clays (the **clay minerals**) are hydrous silicates, mainly of aluminium and magnesium, which occur as crystals with a layered structure, capable of absorbing and losing water. The main groups of clay minerals are kaolinite, montmorillonite-smectite, illite, and vermiculite.

● **Clay, Cassius** ▷*See* Ali, Muhammad.

● **Clay, Henry** ▶ (1777–1852) US politician; secretary of state (1825–29). He was a leader of the War Hawks, who advocated the ▷War of

1812 with Britain. As secretary of state he helped to establish Pan-Americanism. Called "The Great Compromiser," he is best known for his attempts at compromise (e.g. the Missouri Compromise of 1820) to hold the Union together on the issue of slavery.

● **clay-pigeon shooting** ▷See shooting.

● **Cleanthes** ▶ (c. 310–230 BC) Greek philosopher and follower of ▷Zeno of Citium. Cleanthes taught that reason is inherent in the nature of living things and virtue is voluntary assent to natural reason. ▷See also Stoicism.

● **clearances** ▷See Highland Clearances.

● **clearing house** ▶ **1.** An association of UK banks through which all the cheques from their branches are exchanged and the net amount owed by each bank to any other is calculated. The City of London clearing house exchanges cheques for £5,000 or more drawn on banks less than half a mile away in the "town clearing"; all others are dealt with in the "general clearing." The resulting debts and credits are entered as book transactions at the ▷Bank of England. **2.** Any institution that settles debts between members. For example, ▷commodity trading markets use a clearing house to avoid passing cheques between strings of brokers, dealers, etc., debts being settled by difference accounts through the clearing house.

● **clearwing moth** ▶ A moth of the widely distributed family *Sesiidae* (about 700 species), also called wasp moth. Many have clear wings and dark slender bodies with red or yellow markings, resembling bees and wasps. The larvae bore into roots and stems and are often serious pests.

● **cleavage** ▶ (biology) The repeated division of a fertilized egg cell (zygote) to produce a ball of cells that forms the ▷blastula. In egg cells with little yolk, such as those of frogs and mammals, the entire cell divides—called holoblastic cleavage. Meroblastic cleavage occurs in yolky egg cells, such as those of birds, when only the yolk-free region divides.

● **cleavers** ▶ A worldwide annual herb, *Galium aparine*, also called goosegrass, native to Eurasia. 15–120 cm high, this weed is named because it clings by tiny hooks on its stems and leaves. Its hooked fruits are dispersed by humans and animals. Family: *Rubiaceae* (madder family).

● **Cleese, John** ▶ (1939–) British comic actor and writer, best known for his TV series *Monty Python's Flying Circus* (1969–74) and *Fawlty Towers* (1974, 1978). Films include *Life of Brian* (1979), *A Fish called Wanda* (1988), and *Fierce Creatures* (1997). With the psychiatrist Robin Skynner (1922–) he wrote *Families and How to Survive Them* (1983), a psychological study.

● **Cleethorpes** ▶ 53 34N 0 02W A coastal resort in E England, at the mouth of the River Humber, in North East Lincolnshire unitary authority, Lincolnshire. Population (1991): 32 719.

● **clef** ▶ (French: key) The symbol placed at the beginning of a musical stave to indicate the pitch of the notes. The treble clef, a decorative G, indicates that the second line up of the stave is the G above middle C; the bass clef, an archaic F, indicates that the fourth line up is the F below middle C. The C clef can be set on any of the lines of the stave to establish it as middle C; the alto clef (used for viola music) has the C on the middle line; the tenor clef (used for cello music) has the C on the fourth line up.

● **cleft palate** ▶ An abnormality caused by failure of the left and right halves of the palate to fuse during embryonic development. It leaves the nasal and oral cavities in continuity and is often associated with a cleft in the upper lip (cleft lip or harelip). Both defects interfere with speech and feeding but can be repaired surgically at 16 to 18 months of age.

● **Cleisthenes** ▶ (d. 508 BC) Athenian politician, regarded as the architect of Athenian democracy. Cleisthenes, a member of the ▷Alcmaeonid family, achieved political power by appealing to the people for support and his democratic reforms (508) broadened the basis of political power in Athens. He is reputed to have introduced ▷ostracism.

● **Cleland, John** ▶ (1709–89) English novelist. He served as consul in Turkey and as an agent for the East India Company, but was later several times imprisoned for debt. His best-known book is the pornographic novel *Fanny Hill* (1748–49).

● **Clematis** ▶ A genus of herbaceous or woody plants (about 250 species), mainly climbing perennials, widely distributed in temperate regions. The fruits are often covered with persistent silky hairs, conspicuous and attractive in winter, as in traveller's joy, or old man's beard (*C. vitalba*) of Europe. There are many horticultural varieties, grown for their showy flowers, usually purple, pink, or white. Some species from which popular garden varieties have been developed are *C. alpina*, *C. montana*, and *C. patens*. Family: ▷Ranunculaceae.

● **Clemenceau, Georges** ▶ (1841–1929) French statesman; prime minister (1906–09, 1917–20). A member of the chamber of deputies from 1876 to 1893, when he became known as the Tiger for his attacks on other politicians, he subsequently devoted much of his energies to polemical journalism. During his first premiership he strengthened ties with Britain and broke irrevocably with the socialists at home. During the prewar years he urged military preparation against Germany and then attacked the World War I government for defeatism until again becoming prime minister, when he led France to victory. He condemned the failure of the Treaty of Versailles to provide for French security.

● **Clement I, St** ▶ (late 1st century AD) The fourth bishop of Rome. He was the supposed author of several patristic texts, including a letter to the church of Corinth and the *Apostolic Constitutions*, which suggest that he was highly esteemed by the Church as a mediator and legislator. He probably suffered martyrdom. Feast day: 23 Nov.

● **Clement V** ▶ (Bertrand de Got; 1264–1314) Pope (1305–14), first of the Avignon popes (*see* Avignon papacy). Clement was appointed by the influence of ▷Philip (IV) the Fair. Although he was a patron of learning, his pontificate was marked by venality, nepotism, and high taxation.

● **Clement VII** ▶ (Giulio de' Medici; 1478–1534) Pope (1523–34). A cousin of ▷Leo X, as pope he attempted to follow a middle course between the conflicting policies of Emperor ▷Charles V and ▷Francis I of France. This affected his ability to deal effectively with ▷Henry VIII's divorce from Catherine of Aragon and explains his failure to curb Protestantism. Like other early Renaissance popes, he was a patron of the arts and learning.

● **Clement IX** ▶ (Giulio Rospigliosi; 1600–69) Pope (1667–69). His pontificate was marked by disputes with Louis XIV concerning control of the French Church and Louis' harsh policy towards the Jansenists, whose persecution was stopped by the Peace of Clement IX (1669). Clement wrote opera libretti besides sacred poetry and drama.

● **Clement XI** ▶ (Giovanni Albani; 1649–1721) Pope (1700–21). Although austere and pious, he largely failed in the exercise of papal diplomacy, especially in the War of the ▷Spanish Succession, in the latter stages of which he reluctantly supported the Habsburg candidate. He also met with little success in attempts to defeat ▷Jansenism.

● **Clementi, Muzio** ▶ (1752–1832) Italian pianist and composer. After settling in England in 1766, he became famous as a virtuoso, a composer of piano music, a teacher, a music publisher, and a piano manufacturer.

● **clementine** ▶ A small ▷Citrus tree bearing edible fruits, regarded by some as a hybrid between the tangerine and sweet orange; by others as a variety of tangerine. It is grown mainly in N Africa.

● **Clement of Alexandria** ▶ (c. 150–c. 215 AD) Greek Christian theologian. He was probably born in Athens and is known to have studied Christianity at the school at Alexandria, of which he became head in 190. He was succeeded by his pupil ▷Origen after he had been forced to flee from Alexandria in 202 because of persecutions. Clement's writings are much influenced by ▷Gnosticism and his importance lies in bringing Greek philosophical ideas in to supplement Christian belief.

● **Cleon** ▶ (c. 422 BC) Athenian politician and demagogue. An artisan by birth, Cleon opposed the moderate imperialism of the aristocrats in the Peloponnesian War. He persuaded the Athenians to execute the rebellious citizens of Mytilene (427) but the decision was eventually reversed. Cleon opposed peace with Sparta (425) and was killed fighting at Amphipolis.

Cleopatra ▶ This Egyptian chalkstone relief shows Cleopatra as the Egyptian goddess Isis.

● **Cleopatra VII ▶** (69–30 BC) Queen of Egypt (51–48, 47–30), famous as the mistress of Julius Caesar and then of Mark Antony. Cleopatra was coruler with her brother Ptolemy XIII (61–48), who ousted her in 48. Restored by Caesar, she accompanied him to Rome and gave birth to (allegedly) his son Caesarion. After Caesar's murder, Cleopatra returned to Egypt and in 41 she met Antony. In 37 he abandoned his wife Octavia and lived with Cleopatra, who bore him three sons. Antony and Cleopatra's aspirations to expand Egypt led to conflict with Rome; as a result, in 31 Antony's brother-in-law Octavian defeated them at ▷Actium and in 30 they both committed suicide. Cleopatra is said to have done so by allowing an asp to bite her. Shakespeare's reconstruction of their story follows Plutarch's romantic account.

● **Cleopatra's Needles ▶** A pair of ancient Egyptian ▷obelisks carved in the reign of Thutmose III (c. 1475 BC) at Heliopolis. They were moved by ▷Augustus Caesar to Alexandria in 12 BC. They were moved again in 1878, one being set up on the Victoria Embankment, London, the other in Central Park, New York.

● **clerihew** ▷*See* Bentley, Edmund Clerihew.

● **Clermont-Ferrand ▶** 45 47N 3 05E A city in central France, the capital of the Puy-de-Dôme department. Founded by the Romans, it was the ancient capital of Auvergne in the 16th century. It has a fine gothic cathedral and its university was established in 1810. Clermont-Ferrand has France's largest rubber industry and manufactures textiles, chemicals, food products, and metal goods. Population (1990): 140 167.

● **Cleveland ▶** 41 30N 81 41W A city in the USA, in Ohio on Lake Erie. It is a major Great Lakes port and the largest city in Ohio. One of the country's leading iron and steel centres, its other industries include oil refining, food processing, and the manufacture of motor vehicles. Population (1996 est): 498 246.

● **Cleveland ▶** A former county in NE England, created in 1974 from parts of SE Durham and NE Yorkshire, including the industrial towns of Middlesbrough and Stockton-on-Tees. It was abolished in 1996. Administrative functions were devolved to four ▷unitary authorities (Hartlepool, Stockton-on-Tees, Middlesbrough, and Redcar and Cleveland), while the historic boundaries of Yorkshire and Durham were restored for ceremonial and related purposes.

● **Cleveland, Stephen Grover ▶** (1837–1908) US statesman; Democratic president (1885–89, 1893–97). His independence and honesty made the Democrats of ▷Tammany Hall his enemies. In his first term he tried to stamp out graft and excessive tariff protection. His second term was troubled by a financial crisis. He was repudiated by the Democrats and the Republicans won the 1896 election.

● **Cleveland Bay ▶** A breed of horse developed in the Cleveland region of N Yorkshire, England, and always reddish brown (bay) with black mane, tail, and legs. With a muscular body with short legs, Clevelands were used as pack and coach horses. They are crossed with Thoroughbreds to produce showjumpers. Height: 1.57–1.68 m (15½–16½ hands).

● **Clianthus ▶** A genus of shrubs (4 species) found in Australia, New Zealand, Indochina, and the Philippines. Several are cultivated for their attractive flowers. The glory pea (*C. formosis*) is an evergreen semiprocumbent shrub, 100 cm high, with red and purple flowers. Family: ▷*Leguminosae*.

● **click beetle ▶** A long flat beetle, also called skipjack beetle, belonging to a worldwide family (*Elateridae*; 8000 species). If upturned it rights itself by springing into the air with a clicking sound. The larvae, known as wireworms, are serious pests of root crops. Species of the genus *Pyrophorus* are luminous, resembling ▷firefly beetles.

● **cliffbrake ▶** A ▷fern of the genus *Pellaea* (about 80 species), found worldwide on rocks, mainly limestone. It has small elongated blue-green branched fronds, which overlap at the leaf margins to protect the spore capsules. Family: *Sinopteridaceae*.

● **climate ▶** The long-term weather conditions prevalent in an area. Climate is determined by three main factors. The first is latitude and the tilt of the earth's axis, which determines the amount of solar radiation received by an area. Second, the distribution of land and sea will affect climate as the land heats and cools far more rapidly than the sea. Ocean currents will also modify a region's climate, for example, the warm Gulf Stream is responsible for keeping the NW coast of Europe ice free. The third factor is the altitude and topography of an area; temperature will fall with increased altitude and hills and mountain barriers force clouds to rise and produce rainfall. Over long periods major changes in climate may occur, as in the ▷Ice Age. The study of the climate is called **climatology**.

● **climax ▶** In ecology, the final stage in the process of ecological ▷succession, in which a stable community of plants and animals becomes established. In Europe, a typical climax community would be a deciduous woodland.

● **climbing perch ▶** A ▷labyrinth fish, *Anabas testudineus*, also called climbing or walking fish, that occurs in ponds and ditches of Asia. Its brownish- or greenish-grey body is about 25 cm long. It can travel short distances overland using its tail, fins, and gill covers; during the dry season it lies dormant in mud.

● **clingfish ▶** A ▷bony fish, also called sucker, belonging to the family *Gobiesocidae* (about 100 species), found mainly in salt water. Clingfish have an elongated body, up to 7.5 cm long, a flattened head, and a suction disc formed from the pelvic fins to attach itself to the bottom. Order: *Gobiesociformes*.

● **Clinton, Bill ▶** (William Jefferson C.; 1946–) US statesman; Democratic president (1993–2001). Formerly state governor of Arkansas (1979–81, 1983–92), he defeated George ▷Bush in the presidential election of 1992. His first term saw US-brokered peace deals in ▷Bosnia-Hercegovina and the Middle East and an economic boom. A popular president, he was comfortably re-elected in 1996, despite mounting allegations of financial and personal impropriety. In 1998 he was obliged to confess to a sexual affair with a young White House trainee, despite his apparent denial on oath of any such relationship.

As a result the House of Representatives voted for his impeachment on counts of perjury and obstruction of justice, leading to a formal trial (1999) in the Senate, which found him not guilty of all charges. He ordered US airstrikes against Iraq (1996 and 1998) and military action by NATO against Yugoslavia (1999; ▷Kosovo). He was also active in the continuing peace processes in Israel and Northern Ireland. His wife **Hillary Rodham Clinton** (1947–   ) took a high profile during his presidency and was elected to the Senate in 2000.

● **Clinton, De Witt ▶** (1769–1828) US statesman; governor of New York (1817–23, 1825–28). He became famous for his scheme to build the Erie Canal—"Clinton's Ditch," which was finished in 1825. It opened up the West and made New York the most important US port.

● **Clio ▶** In Greek legend, goddess of history and one of the nine ▷Muses. She loved Pierus, King of Macedonia, and bore him a son, Hyacinthus.

● **clipper ship ▶** A fast sailing vessel developed in the 19th century for international commerce, so called because it clipped short the time required for a given passage. Clipper ships were designed more for speed than for their cargo capacity, which was relatively limited.

● **clitellum ▶** An external glandular beltlike swelling around the bodies of earthworms and leeches. It secretes the cocoon that contains the fertilized eggs.

● **clitoris** ▷*See* penis.

● **Clive, Robert, Baron Clive of Plassey ▶** (1725–74) British soldier and colonial administrator, who established British supremacy in India. He joined the East India Company in 1743, went to Madras, and made his name by capturing Arcot (1751) and holding it against a French-Indian force for 53 days. In 1757 he recaptured Calcutta from the Nawab of Bengal, Siraj-ud-Dawlah, whom he then defeated at ▷Plassey. This victory assured the East India Company control of Bengal, of which Clive was virtual ruler until 1760, when he returned to England. He was appointed governor and commander in chief of Bengal in 1764, remaining in office until 1767. He instituted many reforms but was subsequently named in an inquiry into the East India Company's affairs. He defended himself in parliament and was vindicated (1773) but later committed suicide.

● **Cliveden ▶** A country house in Buckinghamshire, near Maidenhead, owned for many years by the ▷Astor family. It was the scene of many houseparties for politicians and others (known as the **Cliveden set**) in the 1930s; it was sold as a hotel in 1985.

● **cloaca ▶** The posterior chamber of the body in all vertebrate animals except the placental mammals, into which the digestive, urinary, and genital tracts open. Faeces, urine, and eggs or sperm are discharged through its vent.

● **clock ▶** A mechanical device for measuring the passage of time. Clockwork has two essential components: an energy store (a raised weight or a coiled spring) and an escapement that regulates the release of energy from the store. The earliest recorded escapement was in a giant Chinese astronomical clock (c. 1090 AD). Early European clocks (called turret clocks from their usual position in church towers) were crude ironwork with verge escapements, driven by falling weights and recording time by striking on the hour, but the 14th-century Italian family of Dondi introduced dials on their sophisticated astronomical mechanisms. Late medieval clocks, such as the one (1392) in Wells Cathedral, England, were often embellished with ingenious automata. The innovation of mainsprings about 1500 enabled portable clocks (*see also* watch) to be made. Refinements in the 17th century were the anchor escapement (1671) and the application of pendulums to clockwork (*see* Huygens, Christiaan). Both resulted in greatly increased accuracy and during the next 150 years clocks successfully challenged ▷sundials as the principal domestic timekeepers. Long-case (grandfather) and bracket clocks assumed their modern forms. Carriage clocks were introduced in 1810 by the French firm of Breguet. An important advance in the 18th century was the development of an accurate marine chronometer, used by navigators to determine position.

Electricity was first used to provide the power to operate a clock in the 19th century. In the late 1920s the quartz-crystal clock was in-

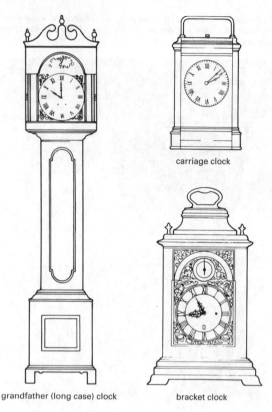

carriage clock

grandfather (long case) clock   bracket clock

clock ▶ Three traditional forms of domestic clock.

troduced. In this a quartz crystal is stimulated electrically to vibrate at a constant frequency by the ▷piezoelectric effect, producing a constant frequency electric signal that is fed to an integrated circuit to produce a pulse that drives the clock mechanism. Scientific advances in the 20th century have led to the development of clocks powered by the natural vibrations of atoms (*see* atomic clock). The ▷caesium clock, first made in 1955, is so accurate that one specific line in the spectrum of caesium is now the standard by which time is defined (*see* second), replacing the period of the earth's rotation.

● **Clodion ▶** (Claude Michel; 1738–1814) French ▷rococo sculptor. Working in Rome (1762–71) and Paris, he enjoyed a wide reputation until the French Revolution, when the rococo style was superseded by ▷neoclassicism. Although he specialized in small terracotta sculptures of nymphs, satyrs, etc., he also produced more sober works, notably the lifesize marble sculpture of Montesquieu (1783; Versailles).

● **cloisonné ▶** (French: partitioned) A technique of decorating metal surfaces with polychrome ▷enamelwork. Thin metal strips are soldered edgewise to the surface following the outlines of the design and the resulting compartments filled with coloured enamels. The work is then fired, fusion of the colours being prevented by the strips, and the surface ground smooth and polished. Beautiful cloisonné vases, brooches, etc., were produced in medieval Europe, while China and Japan perfected the technique in the 17th, 18th, and 19th centuries.

● **clone ▶** A population of organisms produced from a single parent cell by asexual division—for example by vegetative reproduction in plants or parthenogenesis in animals. The individuals of a clone are genetically identical. Thus cloning, if it could be achieved in humans, would provide the means of producing a whole generation of identical siblings—a concept regarded with horror by most people. The first successful cloning of a higher animal took place in Scotland in 1996, when the nucleus of a somatic (body) cell taken from the udder of an adult sheep was fused with an egg cell from another sheep that had had its own nucleus removed. The resulting embryo was inserted

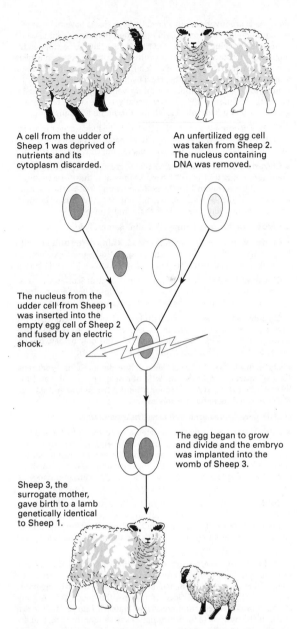

A cell from the udder of Sheep 1 was deprived of nutrients and its cytoplasm discarded.

An unfertilized egg cell was taken from Sheep 2. The nucleus containing DNA was removed.

The nucleus from the udder cell from Sheep 1 was inserted into the empty egg cell of Sheep 2 and fused by an electric shock.

The egg began to grow and divide and the embryo was implanted into the womb of Sheep 3.

Sheep 3, the surrogate mother, gave birth to a lamb genetically identical to Sheep 1.

clone ▶ The stages involved in producing the first clone of a higher animal.

into the womb of a third sheep, leading to the birth of a lamb genetically identical to the first sheep. The announcement of this achievement in 1997 raised fears about the prospects of human cloning. However, although now potentially possible, the production of human clones is at present regarded as ethically unacceptable: in the UK all experiments on human embryos are subject to strict controls by the Human Fertilization and Embryology Authority. In 1998 the Authority ruled that research into the creation of cloned human tissues for surgical transplant should be allowed to proceed but that reproductive human cloning should not be attempted. The first cloned human embryos were created by US scientists in 2001 but not allowed to develop. ▷*See also* stem cells.

● **Clonmel** ▶ 52 21N 7 42W A market town in the Republic of Ireland, the county town of Co Tipperary. Population (1991): 14 500.

● **Clontarf** ▶ The site of a battle (1014), near Dublin, in which ▷Brian Boru, high king of Ireland, defeated a large force of Danes. Boru was killed in the aftermath of battle, but Viking influence in Ireland was limited to seaports thereafter.

● **closed shop** ▶ A place of work in which all employees are required to be members of one or more specified trade unions. Closed shops are usually sanctioned by the employer, whose ▷collective bargaining position may be made simpler if the union (or unions) can speak for the whole workforce. The disadvantage of closed shops is that they exclude from employment those who object to belonging to a trade union. In the UK a series of trade-union and employment-law reforms passed in the 1980s had the effect of making closed-shop agreements unenforceable.

● **Clostridium** ▶ A genus of rod-shaped spore-forming bacteria that occur widely in soil and the gastrointestinal tract of animals and humans. Some produce powerful toxins, particularly *C. tetani*, which causes ▷tetanus, and *C. botulinum*, which causes ▷botulism.

● **clothes moth** ▶ A small ▷tineid moth whose larvae feed on clothes, carpets, blankets, etc. There are a number of widely distributed species. Adults generally have a wingspan of 12–25 mm and are pale grey-brown in colour. They prefer dark places. Pesticides, dry cleaning, and man-made fibres have reduced their damaging effects.

● **Clotho** ▷*See* Fates.

● **Clotilda** ▷*See* Clovis.

● **cloud** ▶ A mass of minute water droplets or ice crystals, or a combination of both, produced by the condensation of water vapour in the atmosphere. When conditions are favourable the droplets grow and precipitation may occur. Various classifications of clouds exist but the one internationally agreed upon and most extensively used by meteorologists is based on cloud appearance and height and comprises ten principal forms. The high clouds, normally above 5000 m (16 000 ft) are ▷cirrus (Ci), ▷cirrostratus (Cs), and ▷cirrocumulus (Cc). The medium clouds at 2000–5000 m (6500–16 000 ft) comprise ▷altocumulus (Ac) and ▷altostratus (As). Below this level the low clouds are ▷stratus (St), ▷stratocumulus (Sc), and ▷nimbostratus (Ns). Some clouds grow vertically and cannot be classified solely by height; these are chiefly ▷cumulus (Cu) and cumulonimbus.

● **cloud chamber** ▶ A device, invented by C. T. R. ▷Wilson, used to study the properties of ionizing particles. It contains a chamber filled with a saturated vapour. The vapour is expanded adiabatically (usually using a piston) to cool it and so make it supersaturated. When an ionizing particle passes through the chamber drops of liquid condense along its trail, thus making the trail visible.

● **clouded leopard** ▶ A large nocturnal forest ▷cat, *Neofelis nebulosa*, of SE Asia, Borneo, Sumatra, and Java. It is 120–190 cm long including its tail (60–90 cm) and has a greyish or yellowish coat with black markings. It is an expert climber, using its heavy tail for balance, and feeds on birds and small mammals. □mammal.

● **Clouet, Jean** ▶ (c. 1485–1540) Portrait painter, probably of Flemish origin. He worked in France as court painter to Francis I. The influence of Italian ▷Renaissance portraiture was stronger on his son **François Clouet** (c. 1515–72), who succeeded to his father's post in about 1540. François introduced informal poses, as in his portrait of ▷Diane de Poitiers (Washington), which shows her in her bath.

● **Clough, Arthur Hugh** ▶ (1819–61) British poet. His religious doubts led him to resign his position at Oriel College, Oxford, in 1848. He subsequently worked as a government education official. His early death from malaria inspired his friend Matthew ▷Arnold to write the elegy *Thyrsis* (1861). During his lifetime Clough published the lengthy poems *The Bothie of Tober-na-Vuolich* (1848) and *Amours de voyage* (1858). Much of his best-known work, including the unfinished *Dipsychus* (1865), appeared posthumously. Clough's colloquial style and concern for contemporary themes make his work unusual among the Victorian poets.

● **clove** ▶ An evergreen Indonesian tree, *Eugenia caryophyllata*, growing to a height of 12 m. The dried flower buds are used as spice. The whole tree is aromatic, clove oil being distilled from the buds, stalks, and leaves for use in medicine and as artificial vanilla. Clove production was once a Dutch Indonesian monopoly but the trees are now grown in many regions. Family: *Myrtaceae*.

● **Clovelly** ▶ 51 0N 4 24W A small resort and fishing village in SW England, in Devon, famous for its narrow stepped streets. Population (1989 est): 500.

● **clover** ▶ An annual or perennial plant of the genus *Trifolium* (about 290 species), which also includes the ▷trefoils. Clovers, which occur mainly in N temperate regions, have leaves divided into three leaflets and dense heads of flowers. They are valuable as fodder plants and for their nitrogen-fixing ability. ▷Alsike, red clover (*T. pratense*), and crimson clover (*T. incarnatum*) are three widely grown and naturalized species. Family: ▷Leguminosae.

● **Clovis** ▶ (c. 466–511) King of the Salian ▷Franks (481–511), of the Merovingian dynasty, who conquered N Gaul (494), founding a kingdom that dominated western Europe. He married (c. 493) Clotilda (c. 475–c. 545), a fervent Christian, whose efforts to convert him succeeded after an important victory over the Alamanni (496), when he was baptized with some 3000 warriors. He was regarded as defender of the faith against ▷Arianism. After defeating the Visigoths near Poitiers (507), he established his capital at Paris. Clovis sponsored the promulgation of the ▷Salic Law.

● **Clovis point** ▶ A fluted stone weapon point found in sites in many parts of North America after about 10 000 BC. They vary in length from 2.5 cm (1 in) to 19 cm (7½ in). *Compare* Folsom point.

● **clubfoot** ▶ A deformity in which the foot is abnormally twisted at the ankle joint, so that the sole cannot rest flat on the ground when the person is standing (usually the foot is twisted downwards and inwards). Its medical name is talipes. When the defect is present at birth it can often be corrected by strapping the foot in the correct position. Surgical correction may be necessary for severe deformities.

● **clubmoss** ▶ A perennial mosslike plant, also called ground pine, belonging to a genus (*Lycopodium*; about 200 species) of flowerless vascular plants, found mainly in tropical and subtropical forests and mountainous regions. It has a creeping stem with wiry branches, densely covered with green, yellowish, or greyish scalelike or needle-like leaves. The spore capsules occur at the base of special leaves (sporophylls), which are often arranged in conelike clusters (strobili). Order: *Lycopodiales*; phylum: *Lycophyta*. ▷*See also* Selaginella.

● **clubroot** ▶ A disease, caused by the slime mould *Plasmodiophora brassicae*, that affects the roots of plants of the family *Cruciferae*, especially brassicas (cabbages, etc.). The infected cells become greatly enlarged, resulting in the deformed nodular roots characteristic of the disease. Control measures include liming, growing in clean soil, and using fungicides.

● **clubs** ▷*See* London clubs; Working Men's Club and Institute Union.

● **Cluj** ▶ (German name: Klausenburg, Hungarian name: Koloszvár) 46 47N 23 37E A city in NW Romania, on the River Someşul. A former capital of Transylvania, it possesses several educational institutions, including a university (1872). Its manufactures include metal products, chemicals, and textiles. Population (1994 est): 326 017.

● **Cluny** ▶ 46 25N 4 39E A town in E France, in the Saône-et-Loire department. Its famous Benedictine abbey (founded 910 AD) became the centre of the Cluniac order, a reformed Benedictine order that was widely influential in Europe (c. 950–c. 1130). Population (1990): 4724.

● **cluster of galaxies** ▶ A group of ▷galaxies that are physically associated by mutual gravitational effects. Most galaxies are members of a cluster: our own Galaxy belongs to the ▷Local Group. The densest clusters contain a thousand or more galaxies. Adjacent clusters are loosely grouped into **superclusters**. Almost all the matter in the universe is concentrated in clusters and superclusters, which occupy only a few percent of the volume of space. ▷*See also* star cluster.

● **clutch** ▶ A device enabling two rotating shafts to be coupled and uncoupled. Positive clutches have square or spiral jaws to transmit torque without slipping. They can be used where slow speeds and light loads are involved, but normally both shafts have to be at rest for engagement. Friction clutches provide a period of slipping while the shafts are being engaged, and they do not have to be stopped for engagement. The torque is transmitted by friction between attachments to each shaft: in a plate clutch the attachments are flat discs, which press against each other; in a hydraulic clutch they are radial vanes immersed in a fluid. In a motor vehicle a clutch is used between the engine and the gearbox, usually a plate clutch for manual gearboxes and a hydraulic clutch for automatic transmissions.

● **Clutha River** ▶ A river in New Zealand, the longest river in South Island. It flows generally S from Lake Wanaka, in the Southern Alps, to enter the Pacific Ocean near Kaitangata. Length: 340 km (210 mi).

● **Clwyd** ▶ A former county of NE Wales, created under local government reorganization in 1974 from ▷Flintshire, most of ▷Denbighshire, and E Merionethshire. In 1996 it was replaced by the counties of Flintshire and Denbighshire (both reinstated with new borders) and the county boroughs of Wrexham and Conwy.

● **Clyde, Baron** ▷*See* Campbell, Colin, Baron Clyde.

● **Clyde, River** ▶ A river in W Scotland. Rising in the hills of South Lanarkshire, it flows NW through Glasgow and S of ▷Clydebank to enter the Atlantic Ocean at the Firth of Clyde. Length: 170 km (106 mi).

● **Clydebank** ▶ 55 54N 4 24W A town in W central Scotland, in West Dunbartonshire on the River Clyde. Shipbuilding has been replaced by more varied industrial activities. Population (1991): 29 171.

● **Clydesdale** ▶ A breed of draught horse that was developed in the Clydesdale region of Scotland in the 18th century. The Clydesdale has a compact body with strong legs and feet and may be bay, brown, black, or chestnut. Height: about 1.75 m (17 hands).

● **Clytemnestra** ▶ In Greek legend, the daughter of Tyndareus, King of Sparta, and Leda, and wife of ▷Agamemnon. She and her lover Aegisthus killed Agamemnon after the Trojan War and she herself was killed by her son ▷Orestes.

● **CND** ▷*See* Campaign for Nuclear Disarmament.

● **cnidarian** ▶ An aquatic invertebrate animal of the phylum *Cnidaria* (about 9000 species), including ▷*Hydra*, ▷jellyfish, ▷sea anemones, ▷corals, etc. There are two different generations of the life cycle (*see* polyp; medusa) and either or both may occur. The body cavity has a single opening (mouth) and stinging cells (nematocysts) are used for defence or catching prey. ▷*See also* coelenterate.

● **Cnidos** ▶ An ancient Greek city at the SW extremity of Asia Minor. Never politically important, Cnidos was known for its wine, ▷Praxiteles' statue of Aphrodite, and its medical school. The rebuilt city's rectangular street plan (c. 350 BC) is an outstanding example of Greek town planning.

● **coal** ▶ A carbonaceous mineral deposit used as a fuel and raw material for the plastics and chemical industries. Coal results from the compaction and heating of partially decomposed fossil vegetable matter. During the coalification process the plant remains are changed progressively from a peatlike material into lignite (brown coal), sub-bituminous and bituminous coal, semianthracite, and anthracite. During this process the percentage of carbon present increases and the moisture and volatile content decreases; anthracite is about 90% carbon. These coals are known as the humic coals. The sapropelic coals (cannel coal and boghead coal) are derived from finely divided vegetable matter (algae, spores, and fungal material). Most coal was formed in the Carboniferous period, although some of the younger coals, for example lignite, date from Mesozoic and Tertiary times.

Coal has been mined (*see* coalmining) in Britain since Roman times but on a small scale until the industrial revolution. In about 1800 coal was being carbonized on a commercial scale for the first time, the resulting ▷coal gas being used for gas lighting and the coke for smelting iron ore. By the middle of the 19th century, interest in the by-products, especially **coal tar**, was awakening. The chemistry of the constituents of coal tar developed into the study of organic chemistry, and the use of aromatic compounds from coal tar led to the development of the dyestuffs and explosives industries. In the 20th century these products also became the foundation of the plastics industry. During the 1920s and 1930s processes were also developed (mainly in Germany) for converting coal into oil—providing Germany with valuable quantities of oil during World War II. Subsequently, ▷natural gas has largely replaced coal gas and petrochemicals (*see* oil) have to a considerable extent replaced coal tar as sources of organic raw materials. In the UK, in 1993 and 1994 the government decided to close many mines due to the use of gas and cheaper foreign coal in power stations. Recent world consumption is slightly in excess of 3000 million tonnes per annum and known reserves are capable of supplying this quantity for several centuries. In the UK coal mines were privately owned until 1947, when they were nationalized under the National Coal Board (later the British Coal Corporation). The 1994 Coal Industry Act set up the Coal Authority, with the power to issue licences to private companies. Coal mining in the UK is now again in private hands. In 1999–2000 there were 15 deep mines still in operation.

Decline in the consumption of coal (millions of tonnes) in the UK

usage	1986	1996
Electricity supply	82.7	54.9
Coke ovens	11.1	8.6
Industry	8.2	3.6
Domestic	8.5	2.7
Miscellaneous	3.7	1.6
Total	114.2	71.4

● **coal gas** ► A gas consisting mainly of hydrogen (50%) and methane (30%), with some carbon monoxide (8%) and other gases. It is made by destructive distillation of coal, a process that involves heating it to 1000°C. Coal gas was formerly supplied to homes for heating and cooking, but it has now been largely replaced, in the UK, by ▷natural gas.

● **Coal Measures** ▷*See* Carboniferous period.

● **coalmining** ► The extraction of coal from below the ground. First, economically viable deposits of coal have to be located, and the necessary shafts sunk. Most mining in the UK has been carried out by the **longwall advancing** method, in which a long straight wall of coal is exposed and gradually cut away, advancing from the shaft to the boundary of the mine. The **longwall retreating** method, in which roadways are cut through the coal and then worked back from the boundary to the shaft, is used to a lesser extent. Belt conveyors or railways convey the coal from the face to the shaft; it is then wound mechanically to the surface in cages or skips. To provide for safety and efficiency, strict attention is paid to mine supports, explosive gases in the mine atmosphere, as well as ventilation, lighting, and drainage of the mine. Coalface activity was originally carried out with pick and shovel but in modern mines is now largely mechanized, some machinery being operated by remote control. The coal mined from the coalface contains stone and shale, which is removed before grading and sizing for the market.

● **Coalport porcelain** ► A style of porcelain first produced at Coalport, Shropshire, in 1795. Beginning with glazed bone china, the Coalport factory later produced porcelain decorated with a Willow pattern and transfer prints, often against a maroon background; after 1820 many of its designs were based on ▷Sèvres porcelain. The factory is now a museum.

● **coal tit** ► A Eurasian ▷tit, *Parus ater*. It is about 11 cm long with a grey back, buff underparts, a black crown and bib, and distinctive white cheeks and nape. It occurs in coniferous woodland, using its slender bill to extract insects from cones and beneath bark.

● **coastguard** ► A paranaval force formed by some countries during the 19th century to hinder smuggling. In Britain it now deals principally with lifesaving and maritime safety through a network of coastwatching stations and provides a meteorological service. The US Coast Guard provides, in addition, navigational aids, including lighthouses, ice patrols, and ice breaking and is responsible for customs, immigration, oil-pollution control, and the enforcement of maritime law; it can also serve in war.

● **Coast Mountains** ► A mountain range of W Canada, extending from the US border 1600 km (1000 mi) N into Alaska. Very rugged, it rises steeply from the Pacific coast. It includes a long glacier belt. Mount Waddington at 3978 m (13 260 ft) is the highest point.

● **Coastwatchers** ► Civilian volunteers working for Australian naval intelligence. First enlisted in 1919 to observe potential attacks off the Australian coast, in World War II they worked in the Japanese-occupied Pacific Islands (1942–44).

● **Coatbridge** ► 55 52N 4 01W A town in central Scotland, in North Lanarkshire. It has important metallurgical industries. Population (1991): 43 617.

● **Coates, Joseph Gordon** ► (1878–1943) New Zealand statesman; Reform Party prime minister (1925–28) after W. F. Massey's death. He is best known for his stringent policies while minister of public works (1931–33) and of finance (1931–35) under G. Forbes, when he devalued the New Zealand pound, lowered interest rates, and encouraged trade within the British Commonwealth.

● **coati** ► A carnivorous mammal, belonging to the genus *Nasua* (3 species), related to the ▷raccoons and occurring in Central and South American forests. About 1 m long including a 50-cm tapering tail, coatis have long snouts and greyish, reddish, or brown fur; they are good climbers, foraging in groups for seeds, eggs, and small mammals.

● **coaxial cable** ► A type of cable used in electrical wiring carrying weak or high-frequency signals (such as the lead from an aerial to a TV set). It consists of a central conductor coaxial with an insulator, a braided conductor, and a further insulator. The central conductor carries the signal, which is protected from interference by the coaxial braiding.

● **cob** ► A type of horse common in the UK. It has a deep short body with relatively short strong legs, a small well-shaped head, and a powerful neck. Usually calm and steady, cobs are particularly useful for elderly or inexperienced riders. Height: usually under 1.6 m (15¾ hands).

● **cobalt** ► (Co) A transition metal similar to iron and noted for its deep-blue colour when reacted in ceramics. It was discovered by G. Brandt (1694–1768) in 1735 and occurs naturally as cobaltite (CoAsS) and in copper, nickel, iron, silver, and lead ores. Cobalt is mined chiefly in the Democratic Republic of Congo and Canada. It is used as an alloy in the manufacture of cutting steels and magnets. The chloride ($CoCl_2$) and oxides (CoO and Co_3O_4) are used in the glass and ceramics industry. The isotope ^{60}Co is a strong gamma-emitter produced in nuclear reactors and used in radiotherapy (the **cobalt bomb**) and in industry. At no 27; at wt 58.9332; mp 1495°C; bp 2928°C.

● **Cobbett, William** ► (1763–1835) British journalist, who championed the cause of the underprivileged, especially agricultural workers. After army service in Canada he accused his officers of corruption and was forced to flee Britain for the USA (1792), returning in 1800. In 1802 he began to publish his weekly *Political Register*. He was imprisoned (1810–12) for attacking the flogging of militiamen and in 1817 was again forced to flee to the USA. Returning to Britain in 1819, he began in 1821 the country tours described in his *Rural Rides* (1830). In 1831 he was prosecuted for encouraging a riot of agricultural labourers but escaped conviction.

● **Cobden, Richard** ► (1804–65) British politician and economist, who was a leading advocate of free trade. A Manchester manufacturer, with John ▷Bright he formed the ▷Anti-Corn Law League (1839), which successfully fought for the repeal of the ▷Corn Laws (1846). An MP from 1843, he opposed Palmerston's foreign policy, negotiated an Anglo-French commercial treaty for the reduction of tariffs (1860), and campaigned for the 1867 Reform Act. In common with Bright, he was a leading member of the Manchester school of reformers and an outstanding orator.

● **Cóbh** ► (name from 1849 until 1922: Queenstown) 51 51N 8 17W A port in the Republic of Ireland, in Co Cork on Cork Harbour. A port of call for Atlantic liners, it is also a resort and yachting centre. Population (1991): 6200.

● **Coblenz** ▷*See* Koblenz.

● **cob nut** ▷*See* hazel.

● **Cobol** ▶ (*common business oriented language*) An international computer-programming language, developed in the USA and used to express problems in commerce. A high-level language, it can describe business procedures in the form of readable English statements that are sufficiently standardized for use in a computer. ▷*See also* program, computer.

● **cobra** ▶ A highly venomous snake found in warm regions of Africa and Asia and able to expand its neck ribs to form a hood. The king cobra *or* hamadryad (*Ophiophagus hannah*) of S Asia is over 3.6 m long, making it the largest venomous snake; it preys chiefly on other snakes. The common Indian cobra (*Naja naja*), used by snake charmers, is 1.7 m long and enters houses at night in search of rats. The spitting cobra or ringhals (*Hemachatus hemachatus*) and the black-necked cobra (*Naja nigricollis*) spit their venom into the eyes of attackers, causing blindness. Family: *Elapidae* (cobras, mambas, coral snakes). □reptile.

● **coca** ▶ A Peruvian tree, *Erythroxylon coca*, cultivated in Java, South America, and Sri Lanka for its leaves, which—when dried—yield cocaine. Coca leaves have been chewed for centuries in South America for their effect in relieving fatigue and hunger; prolonged use can cause addiction and mental and physical damage. Family: *Erythroxylaceae*.

● **cocaine** ▶ An alkaloid ($C_{17}H_{21}O_4N$) derived from ▷coca leaves and also made synthetically. The first drug to be used as a local anaesthetic, it has largely been replaced by safer drugs for this purpose (e.g. procaine) although it is still used in pain-killing mixtures for terminal illnesses (e.g. cancer). Cocaine is an addictive stimulant: it is taken for the euphoria produced by its action on the brain. **Crack**, a derivative of cocaine, is extremely addictive, reaching the brain within minutes of being inhaled by smoking. It can induce violence in habitual users. ▷*See* drug dependence.

● **coccus** ▶ Any spherical bacterium. Cocci may occur singly, in clusters, or in chains. Examples are *Neisseria gonorrhoeae* (the gonococcus, which causes gonorrhoea), *N. meningitidis* (the meningococcus, which causes septicaemia and meningitis), ▷*Staphylococcus*, and ▷*Streptococcus*.

● **coccyx** ▷*See* spine.

● **Cochabamba** ▶ 17 26S 66 10W A city in Bolivia, situated in the E Andes. It is an important agricultural trading centre (especially for grain). Industries include oil refining and it is the site of a university (1832). Population (1993 est): 188 756.

● **Cochin** ▶ 9 56N 76 15E A major port in India, in Kerala on the Malabar Coast. Founded by the Portuguese in the 16th century, it achieved its greatest prosperity under Dutch rule (1663–1795). It is the Indian Navy's major training centre. Population (1991): 564 038.

● **Cochinchina** ▶ A region in S Vietnam, long ruled from Saigon (now Ho Chi Minh City). It was divided for centuries before being annexed by ▷Annam in the 18th century. Following the dissolution of the Vietnamese empire it was a French colony (1867–1945) and then an overseas territory before becoming part of independent Vietnam (1949).

● **cochineal** ▶ A natural red dye obtained from the dried bodies of certain female scale insects, especially *Dactylopius coccus* of Mexico. It has now been largely replaced by aniline dyes, but continues to be used for colouring foodstuffs and cosmetics.

● **Cochise** ▶ (d. 1874) Apache Indian chief, who terrorized the SW USA during the 1860s trying to prevent White settlement on his homeland. He surrendered in 1871. His people were given a reservation on their own land but after his death were ordered to more distant country.

● **cochlea** ▷*See* □ear.

● **cochlear implant** ▷*See* hearing aid.

● **Cochrane, Thomas, 10th Earl of Dundonald** ▶ (1775–1860) British admiral. Cochrane was knighted after his flamboyant exploits in the Napoleonic Wars. As an MP (from 1806) he attacked naval corruption but in 1814 he was accused of fraud, and lost his knighthood, his parliamentary seat, and his commission. He was reinstated in 1832.

● **Cockaigne** ▶ An imaginary land of wealth and luxury, celebrated in medieval folklore. There are houses of barley sugar, roast pigs running in the streets with knives and forks in their backs, and a mountain of cheese. It features in some of the fairytales of the brothers Grimm.

● **cockatiel** ▶ A small Australian ▷cockatoo, *Nymphicus hollandicus*, of interior grasslands. It is 32 cm long and has a grey plumage with white wing patches, a yellow head and crest, and reddish ear patches.

● **cockatoo** ▶ A ▷parrot belonging to a genus (*Cacatua*; 17 species) ranging throughout Australia, Malaysia, and the Philippines. Cockatoos are usually white, often with a pink or yellow blush, although some species are black; all have a long erectile crest and a large hooked bill used to crack open nuts and extract grubs from wood.

● **cockchafer** ▶ A European beetle, *Melolontha melolontha*, also called maybug, that is very destructive to plants (*see* chafer). Up to 35 mm long, it is black with reddish-brown legs and wing cases and has a loud buzzing flight. The larvae—which cause the most damage, particularly to cereals and grasses—are also called white grubs or rookworms.

● **Cockcroft, Sir John Douglas** ▶ (1897–1967) British physicist, who shared the 1951 Nobel Prize with Ernest ▷Walton for their development of the first particle ▷accelerator. Their machine, built in 1932, was used for accelerating protons to split an atomic nucleus (of lithium) for the first time. In World War II he worked on the atom bomb and in 1946 became director of the Atomic Energy Research Establishment at Harwell. He was appointed OM in 1957.

● **Cockerell, Charles Robert** ▶ (1788–1863) British architect. Son of the architect Samuel Pepys Cockerell (1754–1827), he spent seven years abroad, developing a passion for Greek architecture that strongly influenced his work. His most notable buildings were Cambridge University Library (1836–42) and the Ashmolean Museum, Oxford (1841–45).

● **Cockerell, Sir Christopher Sydney** ▶ (1910–99) British engineer and inventor of the ▷hovercraft. After working on radar in World War II, he concentrated upon hydrodynamics. He filed his first patent for an air-cushion vehicle in 1955. The first practical hovercraft, the SR.NI, was launched in 1959, since when hovercraft have been built and used in many countries.

● **cocker spaniel** ▶ A breed of gundog, thought to be of Spanish origin. It is compact with short legs, a short tail, and a square muzzle. The long flat silky coat is usually black, red, or cream, either plain or in mottled combinations. Height: 39–41 cm (dogs); 38 cm (bitches). □dog.

● **cockfighting** ▶ A ▷blood sport in which gamecocks fight against each other, often to the death. Illegal in Britain since 1849, it is still widespread in certain parts of the world. The cocks are carefully bred and trained, equipped with steel or bone spurs on their legs, and set against each other in a cockpit. Being very aggressive the cocks peck and gouge each other with intense fury. Heavy wagering is a feature of the sport.

● **cockle** ▶ A ▷bivalve mollusc of the family *Cardiidae* (about 250 species). The ribbed shell valves, 1–23 cm in diameter, are rounded, producing a relatively globular bivalve. Cockles burrow in sand or mud, straining food particles from water drawn in through their protruding siphons. The European cockle (*Cardium* (or *Cerastoderma*) *edule*) is edible.

● **cocklebur** ▶ An annual plant, *Xanthium strumarium*, 20–75 cm high, the fruiting heads of which are densely covered with hooked spines, which catch onto fur and clothing. It has been so widely and unintentionally dispersed by man and animals in warm and temperate regions that its place of origin is uncertain. Family: ▷*Compositae*.

● **cock-of-the-rock** ▶ A passerine bird of the genus *Rupicola* (2 species) of tropical American forests. Males have brilliant reddish-orange plumage and an erectile crest and perform elaborate courtship displays (leks). Family: *Cotingidae* (▷cotingas).

● **cockroach** ► A nocturnal ⬚insect belonging to the mainly tropical family *Blattidae* (3500 species). It has a black or brown flat body, 12–50 mm long, with long antennae and leathery forewings. Cockroaches seldom fly; they feed on plant and animal materials and can be household pests. A widely distributed species is the common cockroach, or black beetle (*Blatta orientalis*). Order: *Dictyoptera*.

● **cocksfoot** ► A perennial ▷grass, *Dactylis glomerata*, also known as orchard grass, cultivated throughout North America, Eurasia, and Africa as a pasture grass. It grows in dense tussocks, up to 1 m tall.

● **cocoa and chocolate** ► Foods derived from the seeds of the cacao ⬚tree (*Theobroma cacao*), native to tropical America and cultivated mainly in West Africa. The tree is pruned to a height of 5–6 m and woody pods, 23–30 cm long, grow directly from its trunk. The pods contain 25–50 seeds (cocoa, or cacao, beans) embedded in a whitish pulp, which are scraped out, fermented, and dried before export. Manufacturing is carried out mainly in the importing countries, where the beans are shelled, roasted, and ground. From them cocoa powder and chocolate are made. Cocoa butter, a fat retained in chocolate but removed from cocoa powder, is a rich source of food energy. Moulded chocolate is run into moulds, which sometimes contain dried fruit, nuts, etc., to make blocks and bars of chocolate. Couverture (or confectionery) chocolate is used for covering biscuits, preserves, etc. Family: *Sterculiaceae*.

● **cocodemer** ► A ▷palm tree, *Lodoicea maldivica*, also known as double coconut, native to the Seychelles Islands. It grows 30 m tall and bears fleshy male and female flower spikes on separate plants. The female flowers produce the largest known fruit, up to 9 kg in weight, which takes ten years to ripen. It consists of a fleshy fibrous envelope surrounding a hard two-lobed nutlike portion, containing edible flesh.

● **coconut** ► The fruit of the coconut ▷palm, *Cocos nucifera*; one of the most important tropical crops. The tree has a slender trunk, up to 25 m high, which bears a crown of giant feather-like leaves. The coconuts, 30–45 cm long and 15–20 cm in diameter, take a year to ripen and have a thick fibrous husk surrounding a single-seeded nut. The hollow core contains coconut milk; the white kernel is eaten raw or dried to yield copra, from which coconut oil is extracted for use in soaps, synthetic rubbers, and edible oils. The residual coconut cake is used as a livestock feed and the coarse husk fibre (coir) is used for matting, etc.

● **coconut crab** ▷*See* robber crab.

● **Cocos Islands** ► (*or* Keeling Islands) Two Australian coral atolls in the E Indian Ocean. They were visited by Charles Darwin (1836). First settled in 1826, they were controlled by the family of a Scottish settler, John Clunies-Ross, from 1827 to 1972, although under Australian administration after 1955. Following a referendum, they became part of Northern Territory in 1984. Copra is produced and there is an important meteorological station. Area: 13 sq km (5 sq mi). Population (1993): 593.

● **Cocteau, Jean** ► (1889–1963) Immensely versatile French poet, artist, and film maker. He made his name with the novel *Les Enfants terribles* (1929) and sketches written for ▷Diaghilev's ballet company, such as *Parade* (1917). In World War I he served as an ambulance driver and became acquainted with ▷Picasso, ▷Modigliani, ▷Apollinaire, and other leading painters and writers. His creative work includes poetry (*L'Ange Heurtebise*, 1925), plays (*Orphée*, 1926), novels, films (*Le Sang d'un poète*, 1929; and *Orphée*, 1949), and graphic work in various media.

● **cod** ► A carnivorous fish, *Gadus morhua*, that lives near the bottom in temperate N Atlantic waters and is commercially fished for food and liver oil (*see* Cod Wars). Its elongated body, up to 1.8 m long, is generally dark grey with spots and has three dorsal fins, two anal fins, and a whisker-like barbel on its lower jaw. *G. macrocephalus* is a similar N Pacific species. Family: *Gadidae* (haddock, ling, pollack, whiting, etc.); order: *Gadiformes*.

● **codeine** ► An ▷analgesic drug used to relieve mild pain. It is a de-

rivative of morphine but less toxic and less likely to become addictive. The combination of aspirin and codeine is a stronger pain killer than either of the two drugs used separately. Codeine has a constipating action and is therefore an effective treatment for some forms of diarrhoea. It depresses the cough centre of the brain and is therefore often added to cough mixtures.

● **Code Napoléon** ► The systematic collection of the ▷civil law of France. Drafted by a commission set up by ▷Napoleon I when he was first consul, the code—properly called the *Code Civil* was brought into force in 1804. Representing the progressive legal thought of the time, it set out to be as clear and easily accessible as possible. It and the other codes subsequently produced under Napoleon's administration remain the basis of present French law and served as a model for civil law codes throughout Europe and the rest of the world.

● **codling moth** ► A small European moth, *Cydia pomonella* (wingspan about 18 mm), whose caterpillars eat apples and similar fruit. A serious economic pest, it has spread worldwide wherever apples are cultivated.

● **cod-liver oil** ► A pale yellow fatty oil obtained from the liver of the cod. It is a rich source of vitamins A and D and is used in medicine to correct the effects of such diseases as rickets.

● **Cod Wars** ► An intermittent dispute between Iceland and, chiefly, the UK over Iceland's extension of its fishing limits in response to depleted stocks of fish (notably ▷cod). In 1953 Iceland extended its fishing limit from 5 km (3 mi) to 6 km (4 mi) and in 1958, to 19 km (12 mi), thus seriously undermining the UK fishing industry. In retaliation the UK, on both occasions, temporarily closed its ports to Icelandic fish imports, and the dispute was only settled in 1961, when the UK agreed to the new limit in return for certain concessions. In 1973, however, Iceland extended the limit to 80.5 km (50 mi) but a temporary settlement was soon agreed with the UK. When this ran out in 1975, Iceland again extended the fishing limit, to 322 km (200 mi), which was not recognized by the International Court of Justice. British trawlers continued to fish within the 80.5-km limit and, coming into conflict with Icelandic coastguard vessels, were given the protection of British frigates. In February, 1976, the Icelandic Government broke diplomatic relations with the UK until a temporary settlement was agreed in June.

● **Cody, William F(rederick)** ► (1846–1917) US showman, known as Buffalo Bill. An army scout and Pony Express rider, he gained his nickname from his success in supplying the men working on the Union (later Kansas) Pacific Railway with buffalo—killing 4280 in eight months (1867–68). In 1883 he began touring the USA and Europe with his Wild West Show. .

Jean Cocteau

● **Coe, Sebastian** ► (1956–) British middle-distance runner. A gold medallist in the 1500 m race at the 1980 and 1984 Olympics, he has held the 1000 m world record (2 mins 12.18 secs) since 1981. He was Conservative MP for Falmouth and Camborne from 1992 to 1997.

● **coeducation** ► The education of both sexes together. Although support for the idea dates back to Plato, it has only recently been practised to any extent. Coeducation could be found in some elementary schools in the USA in the 17th century but it did not become widespread at all levels until the 20th century. Coeducation is also the norm in Scandinavia and in the former communist countries, and following World War II all Japanese schools became in principle coeducational. National attitudes still vary enormously, however, and many Muslim and Roman Catholic countries still favour the separate education of the sexes. In the UK mixed schools were slow to gain in popularity; coeducational primary schools are now the rule but until recently girls and boys frequently sat on different sides of the classroom and had separate playgrounds. The move towards comprehensive education has led to the widespread establishment of mixed secondary schools and girls are now admitted to many boys' public schools (especially in the sixth form). Nearly all universities are now coeducational.

● **coelacanth** ▶ A ▷bony fish of the suborder *Coelacanthini*. Once thought to have been extinct for 60 million years, several have been found living since the discovery, in 1938, of *Latimeria chalumnae* off SE Africa. It has a heavy body, up to 1.5 m long, with a short head and limblike fins, and crawls on the bottom, feeding on other fish. Order: ▷*Crossopterygii*.

● **coelenterate** ▶ An aquatic invertebrate animal of either of the phyla *Cnidaria* (see cnidarian) or *Ctenophora* (see ctenophore), which were formerly grouped in a single phylum, *Coelenterata*.

● **coeliac disease** ▶ A disease in which the small intestine is abnormally sensitive to gliadin (a component of the protein ▷gluten, found in wheat). It results in abnormalities in the cells of the intestine, which cannot digest or absorb food. The symptoms include diarrhoea, stunted growth, and general malaise, the condition is treated by a gluten-free diet.

● **coelom** ▶ The body cavity of many animals. In mammals (including humans) the embryonic coelom is divided into three cavities, which become occupied by the lung, heart, and intestines. In the fully developed mammal the coelom is reduced to the virtually nonexistent spaces between the membranes lining the heart (the pericardium), the lungs (the pleura), and the intestines (the peritoneum).

● **Coen, Jan Pieterszoon** ▶ (1587–1629) Dutch colonial administrator; governor general of the Dutch East Indies (1618–23, 1627–29). He first visited the East Indies in 1607, in the employ of the Dutch East India Company, which in 1614 appointed him to direct the Company's commerce in Asia. He instigated the conquest of the Banda Islands and the first Dutch settlement in Formosa (now Taiwan).

● **coenzyme** ▶ A nonprotein substance that forms a complex with certain enzymes and is essential for the proper functioning of these enzymes. Coenzymes include nucleotide derivatives, such as ▷ATP and NAD, coenzyme A (important in the ▷Krebs cycle), and ▷vitamins of the B complex.

● **Coetzee, J(ohn) M(axwell)** ▶ (1940–) South African novelist and writer. In such novels as *In the Heart of the Country* (1977) and the Booker-Prize-winning *Life and Times of Michael K* (1983) he explores issues of colonialism and racial inequality. More recent work includes the novels *Age of Iron* (1990), *The Master of Petersburg* (1994), and *Disgrace* (1999), another Booker Prize winner.

● **Coeur, Jacques** ▶ (c. 1395–1456) French merchant, who became *argentier* (court banker) to Charles VII of France around 1440. He helped to finance Charles' recapture of Normandy from the English (1450) but, disliked and envied for his wealth and power, he was arrested (1451) on a false charge of having murdered the king's mistress, Agnès Sorel. He escaped from prison and fled to Rome.

● **coffee** ▶ The seeds (called beans) of certain tropical evergreen trees of the genus *Coffea*, which—when roasted, ground, and brewed in hot water—yield a stimulating drink. *C. arabica*, which was first cultivated by Arabs in Yemen, is the most widely grown coffee tree, now mostly in Central and South America; it also produces the best quality beans. It is pruned to a height of 3–5 m for easy harvesting. *C. canephora*, which produces robusta coffee, is more disease resistant,

longer living, and can be grown at lower altitudes. *C. liberica*, of still lower quality, is grown in Malaysia and Guyana. The coffee beans are usually fermented, then sun dried before export. The main coffee-producing areas are South and Central America, Jamaica, East Africa, and Mysore in India. Family: *Rubiaceae*.

The drinking of coffee as a beverage began in the 14th century in Arab countries. Its spread was slow, however, until the 17th century, by the end of which many European and North American cities had **coffee houses**. Many of these, such as ▷Lloyd's coffee house in London, were meeting places for businessmen. In America, coffee became a substitute for tea when the British introduced a tea tax. The main attraction of coffee as a beverage is its bitter taste and the stimulant effect of the ▷caffeine it contains. The best coffee is brewed from a blend of freshly roasted, freshly ground, coffee beans. However, in recent years **instant coffee** has been produced to simplify the brewing of the beverage. This consists of granules of spray-dried or freeze-dried concentrated brewed coffee to which hot water is added. **Decaffeinated coffee** consists of coffee beans or instant coffee from which the caffeine has been removed using a solvent (e.g. methylene), carbon dioxide under pressure, or water.

● **cofferdam** ▶ A temporary walled structure to hold back water or earth while excavation or construction work is carried out. Thus they may be used during the construction of a permanent ▷dam or bridge piers. They are made by driving sheets of sectional steel vertically into the ground and bolt-ing or welding the sheets together. Occasionally concrete is used.

● **Cognac** ▶ 45 42N 0 19W A town in W France, in the Charente department. The name Cognac may only be applied to brandy produced around Cognac. Associated manufactures include bottles, corks, and barrels. Population (latest est): 20 995.

● **cognitive psychology** ▶ The branch of psychology concerned with all human activities relating to the acquisition and use of knowledge (perception, attention, memory, speech and language, and reasoning). In cognitive psychology the brain is regarded as an information-processing system that operates on and stores the information derived from the senses. A largely postwar development, it was required to compensate for the weakness of ▷behaviourism in those areas. Some cognitive psychologists make use of the computer metaphor to understand the way in which the brain works, although most would not suggest that computers actually parallel the physiological processes that underlie mental activity. More recently some cognitive psychologists have claimed that the computer metaphor is misleading, preferring instead a model based on large networks of ▷neurones.

● **cognitive therapy** ▶ A form of psychotherapy for depression and anxiety that attempts to change the patients' attitudes by altering their cognitive processes, so that they challenge the negative thoughts associated with depression and seek evidence to build their self-esteem. It was developed in the USA by A. T. Beck (1921–).

● **coherent radiation** ▶ Electromagnetic radiation in which different waves have a constant ▷phase difference. Light from most sources is not coherent because it is emitted in random bursts. However, light from a ▷laser is coherent.

● **Cohn, Ferdinand Julius** ▶ (1839–1884) German botanist, considered to be one of the founders of modern bacteriology. Following his early studies of algae and fungi, Cohn became interested in the identification of bacteria and established the basic elements of modern classifications. He also encouraged ▷Koch to publish his findings on anthrax.

● **Coimbatore** ▶ 11 00N 76 57E A city in India, in Tamil Nadu. It is a processing centre for hides, cotton, and oilseeds and has expanding industry. Population (1991): 816 321.

● **Coimbra** ▶ 40 12N 8 25W A city in central Portugal. It was formerly the capital of Portugal (1139–1260). It has two cathedrals and Portugal's oldest university, founded in Lis-bon (1290) and transferred in 1537. Industries include the pro-duction of beer, wine, and pottery. Population (1991): 96 140.

● **coke** ▶ A fuel consisting mainly of carbon. It is made by heating coal in the absence of air and is produced as a by-product of ▷coal gas. Coke is used in ▷blast furnaces and other industrial processes as well as for domestic heating.

● **Coke, Sir Edward** ▶ (1552–1634) English lawyer and politician. Initially a staunch supporter of the Crown, Coke became speaker of the House of Commons in 1593 and attorney general in 1594. Under James I he was appointed chief justice of the King's Bench (1613) but was dismissed in 1616 because of his defence of the common law against the royal prerogative. Reviving his political career in 1620, he became a leading spokesman for the protection of parliament's liberties and was largely responsible for the Petition of Right.

● **Coke of Holkham, Thomas William, Earl of Leicester** ▶ (1752–1842) British agriculturalist, who introduced new farming systems. By using new crops and replacing cattle with sheep, he was able to improve the productivity of his estates at Holkham in Norfolk.

● **cola** ▷See kola.

Cola ▶ A representation of the goddess Parvati of the late Cola period. Parvati is the female counterpart and benevolent aspect of Shiva, god of death; she is also an opponent of demons and goddess of the mountains.

● **Cola** ▶ A dynasty that ruled S India from the 10th to the 14th centuries. The empire of the Cola kings centred on Kanci and Tanjore and was marked by cultural and artistic distinction and social stability. In the early 11th century Cola power spread to Ceylon and Indonesia.

● **Colbert, Claudette** ▶ (Lily Claudette Chauchoin; 1905–96) US film actress, born in France. She is best known for her performances in Hollywood light comedies during the 1930s and 1940s. These include *Three-Cornered Moon* (1933), *It Happened One Night* (1934), and *Midnight* (1939).

● **Colbert, Jean-Baptiste** ▶ (1619–83) French statesman; an outstanding financial reformer. Rising to power through the influence of Cardinal Mazarin, Colbert became comptroller general of finance in 1665 and strove to make France under ▷Louis XIV the dominant power in Europe. An advocate of ▷mercantilism, he reformed taxation, tariffs, and financial administration, built roads and canals, and largely created a French navy. He was a lavish patron of the arts and sciences but his cold personality won him the nickname *le Nord* ("the North").

● **Colchester** ▶ 51 54N 0 54E A market town in SE England, in Essex on the River Colne. Founded by Cymbeline (Cunobelinus) in about 10 AD, Colchester was an important Roman town (Camulodunum); the Roman walls remain in part and there is a Norman castle. Essex University (1961) is nearby. Colchester's industries include engineering and printing. Population (1993 est): 149 100.

● **colchicine** ▷See autumn crocus.

● **cold** ▶ (or common cold) A mild but widespread viral disease affecting the mucous membranes of the nose and throat. Symptoms include a sore throat, running nose, sneezing, headache, a slight fever, and general aches and pains. The disease, which is transmitted by coughing and sneezing, usually lasts about a week: rest and mild ▷analgesics (such as aspirin) provide the only treatment required.

● **cold-bloodedness** ▷See poikilothermy.

● **Cold Harbor, Battles of** ▶ Two battles in the US ▷Civil War fought near Richmond, Virginia, the Confederate capital. In the first (27 June, 1862) the Confederate general, Robert E. ▷Lee defeated the Federal forces under George B. ▷McClellan, both sides suffering heavy losses. In the second (3–12 June, 1864), the Federal advance on Richmond under Ulysses S. ▷Grant was temporarily halted when he encountered Lee's entrenched forces. Despite his losses (7000 of his 100 000 men), Grant resumed his advance.

● **Colditz** ▶ 51 08N 12 49E A town in E Germany, on the River Mulde. It is famous for its castle, built by ▷Augustus II on a cliff above the town, which was used as a top-security prisoner-of-war camp during World War II. Many escapes were attempted, some of which were successful.

● **cold storage** ▶ A method of storing food or other perishables, such as photographic film, at a low temperature to prevent deterioration. ▷Refrigeration is used on a domestic scale in ▷freezing and also on an industrial scale in refrigerated warehouses, lorries, railway wagons, and ships' holds, etc.

● **Coldstream** ▶ 55 39N 2 15W A town in SE Scotland, on the English border. The Coldstream Guards were formed here in 1660. Like Gretna Green, it was a refuge for eloping couples. Population (1991): 1746.

● **Cold War** ▶ The hostility between the USA and the Soviet Union, and their respective allies, in the decades following World War II. The term was first used in 1947 by the US politician Bernard ▷Baruch. Fear of nuclear war prevented direct military confrontation, and the Cold War was fought on economic, political, and ideological fronts, as well as in numerous proxy conflicts in the developing world. At its most virulent in the 1950s and 1960s, which saw US action in the ▷Korean War and the ▷Vietnam War, it reached a peak of tension with the ▷Cuban Missile Crisis of 1963. A period of more relaxed relations, known as detente, began in the 1970s but was followed by renewed tension in the early 1980s (a period sometimes known as the Second Cold War). The later 1980s witnessed the reforms and international initiatives of Mikhail ▷Gorbachov, leading to the joint declaration in 1989 by Gorbachov and President ▷Bush in Malta that the Cold War had officially ended. After the fall of communist regimes in Eastern Europe in 1989, the break-up of the Soviet Union in 1991, and the radical political and economic reforms that followed, the West claimed to have won the Cold War.

● **Cole, Nat King** ▶ (Nathaniel Adams Coles; 1919–65) US popular singer and pianist. Beginning his career as a jazz pianist, he formed the King Cole Trio in 1939. However, he soon found greater success with his relaxed style of ballad singing, enjoying hits with such songs as "Mona Lisa" and "Unforgettable." He toured internationally and became the first US Black to host his own radio (1948) and television (1956) shows.

● **Coleoptera** ▷See beetle.

● **Coleraine** ▸ A district in N Northern Ireland, in Co Londonderry. Area: 477 sq km (184 sq mi). Population (1991): 50 438.

● **Coleridge, Samuel Taylor** ▸ (1772–1834) British poet and critic. His involvement in the 1790s in Robert ▷Southey's plan to start a utopian community in America resulted only in his unhappy marriage to Sara Fricker. In 1795 he met William ▷Wordsworth and their joint publication of *Lyrical Ballads* (first edition 1798) marked a decisive break with 18th-century poetry. His finest poems, such as *Kubla Khan* (1797; published 1816) and *The Rime of the Ancient Mariner* (1797–98), were written at this time, but his personal life was troubled by his marriage, his poverty, and his increasing opium addiction. His subsequent creative energies were committed to journalism, lectures, and the writing of the critical and metaphysical *Biographia Literaria* (1817). His voluminous *Notebooks*, publication of which is still in progress, constitute a major work of autobiography and self-analysis.

● **Coleridge-Taylor, Samuel** ▸ (1875–1912) British composer, the son of a doctor from Sierra Leone and a British mother. Educated at the Royal College of Music, he is best known for the trilogy *Song of Hiawatha* (1898–1900).

● **Colet, John** ▸ (c. 1466–1519) English theologian and humanist. After his ordination, he lectured at Oxford, collaborating with Thomas More and Erasmus, prior to his appointment as dean of St Paul's Cathedral. He founded St Paul's School in 1509. He was a fierce opponent of Church corruption and published numerous theological works.

● **Colette** ▸ (Sidonie-Gabrielle C.; 1873–1954) French novelist. After her divorce from her first husband, who had published her early novels (the *Claudine* series) under his own name, she became a music-hall performer in Paris. With *Chéri* (1920) and *La Fin de Chéri* (1926) she became an established writer, celebrated especially for her treatments of childhood and of the natural world, especially animals. Her long writing career was crowned with many honours.

● **Coleus** ▸ A genus of herbaceous or shrubby plants (150 species) originating in the Old World tropics. Many cultivated varieties of the species *C. blumei* are grown for their variegated leaves of a diversity of colours, including red, purple, yellow, and green. They can easily be grown from cuttings at almost any time of year. Family: ▷*Labiatae*.

● **colic** ▸ A severe fluctuating abdominal pain, usually due to contraction of the wall of the intestines and caused by such conditions as constipation or obstruction. Colic in babies is quite common and usually due to air in the intestines.

● **Coligny, Gaspard II de, Seigneur de Châtillon** ▸ (1519–72) French ▷Huguenot leader. He became an admiral of France in 1552 and was converted to Protestantism seven years later. He was chief commander of the Huguenots during the second and third ▷Wars of Religion but Catherine de' Medici, the mother of Charles IX, determined to end his influence over her son, arranged Coligny's murder in the ▷St Bartholomew's Day Massacre.

● **colitis** ▸ Inflammation of the large intestine (the colon), causing abdominal pain and diarrhoea (sometimes with the passage of blood). Colitis can be caused by bacterial infection (e.g. dysentery) or by ▷Crohn's disease. In ulcerative colitis the colon becomes ulcerated. The latter condition, which fluctuates in severity, is treated with corticosteroids or sulphasalazine (a sulphonamide drug). Surgery may be required for severe cases.

● **collage** ▸ A picture composed of a variety of glued-on scraps of materials, such as newspaper, wallpaper, cloth, string, wood veneer, etc. The first collage was made by ▷Picasso in 1912 with a piece of oilcloth. It was later followed by the collages of the ▷dada painters ▷Arp, ▷Ernst, and ▷Schwitters.

● **collagen** ▸ A structural protein that is the main component of the white fibres of connective tissue. Inelastic but with great tensile strength, it is found in tendons and ligaments and also in skin, bone, and cartilage.

● **collar bone** ▷See clavicle.

● **collards** ▸ A variety of white cabbage, also called colewort, that is cut for use before the hearts become solid. They are grown from July-sown seed, thinned, but not transplanted. In the USA collards are leaves of ▷kale.

● **collateral security** ▸ Property (e.g. shares, insurance policies, jewellery) pledged by a borrower as a safeguard for the repayment of a loan. On default the lender sells the collateral, deducts his debt and costs from the proceeds, and pays any balance to the borrower.

● **collective bargaining** ▸ Bargaining between trade unions and employers on all matters relating to conditions of employment, rates of pay, etc. If agreement cannot be reached by bargaining, the dispute may be referred to ▷arbitration, or either side may take action against the other (*see* strike; lockout).

● **collective farms** ▸ Agricultural cooperatives, especially those found formerly in communist countries. Collectivization was instituted in the Soviet Union, with considerable ruthlessness, by Stalin in the late 1920s; widespread resistance necessitated some modifications in the mid-1930s. The farms and farm equipment belonged to the state, which decided what was to be grown and in what quantities, but farmworkers, who lived in surrounding villages, paid rent for their homes and were permitted to have their own garden plots and livestock; profits were shared in collective farms while in state farms workers received wages. Since 1988, when President Gorbachov offered leases of up to 50 years on farmland, the system has been progressively abandoned. Collectivization was introduced into China in 1955 but responsibility for particular farms has since been returned to individual households. ▷*See also* kibbutz.

● **collective unconscious** ▸ In Jungian psychology, a body of images and ideas that are inherited and shared by all humans, rather than acquired by the individual. These ideas are called archetypes and ▷Jung believed them to be detected in the myths, dreams, and mental disturbances of mankind.

● **college** ▸ An educational establishment, especially one that specializes in a particular subject (College of Music) or in higher or further education, although some schools (e.g. Eton College, Stonyhurst College) use the name. The individual parts of a university are also referred to as colleges.

The more academic forms of ▷teacher training take place in **colleges of education**, **colleges of higher education**, and ▷universities. Colleges of higher education offer a wide range of first-degree courses and some also provide facilities for postgraduate studies. Since 1992 many have become universities, awarding their own degrees. **Colleges of further education** provide a wide range of vocational courses (*see* tertiary education) and some now offer courses of higher education as well. Indeed, there is no longer any formal distinction between colleges of further and higher education, although many institutions retain these names. ▷*See also* City Technology Colleges; polytechnics.

● **College of Arms** ▸ (*or* Heralds' College) An English heraldic society, comprising three kings of arms, six heralds, and four pursuivants of arms. Its origins lie in the royal officers of arms, who received a charter from Richard III in 1484. The College was reincorporated in 1555. Its functions include the settling of rights to bear arms, which the kings may grant by letters patent.

● **collie** ▸ A breed of □dog originating in Scotland and widely used as a sheepdog. It has a streamlined body and a pointed muzzle. The rough-coated collie has a long dense coat; the smooth-coated variety has a shorter smooth coat and the bearded collie has a long coat with a shaggy beard. Collies are grey, fawn, or sandy, with or without white markings. Height: 56–61 cm (dogs); 51–56 cm (bitches).

● **Collier, Jeremy** ▸ (1650–1726) English ▷Nonjuror. Imprisoned for refusing to take the oath of loyalty to William and Mary, Collier was later outlawed for giving absolution to two men who made an attempt on William's life. He became bishop of the Nonjurors in 1713. He is also known for his *Short View of the Immorality and Profaneness of the English Stage* (1698), an influential tract that effectively ended the bawdy era of the Restoration comedy.

● **collimator** ▸ **1.** A device used in conjunction with certain optical instruments for producing a beam of parallel light. A simple collimator consists of a slit placed at the focal point of a convex lens. **2.** A device used to produce a beam of radiation of the required dimensions in ▷radiotherapy.

● **Collingwood, Cuthbert, 1st Baron** ▶ (1750–1810) British admiral. He joined the navy at the age of 11 and fought outstandingly at the battles of the Glorious First of June (1794) and Cape St Vincent (1797) during the ▷Revolutionary and Napoleonic Wars. After Nelson's death at ▷Trafalgar (1805) he succeeded to his command and was eventually buried alongside him in St Paul's Cathedral.

● **Collingwood, R(obin) G(eorge)** ▶ (1889–1943) British philosopher, archaeologist, and historian, who taught philosophy at Oxford. His *New Leviathan* (1946) defends free institutions. *Essay on Philosophical Method* (1933), *Idea of Nature* (1945), and *Idea of History* (1946) present his own ▷idealism in relation to that of ▷Plato, ▷Hegel, and ▷Croce.

● **Collins, Michael** ▶ (1890–1922) Irish nationalist. A leading member of Sinn Féin, he was imprisoned for his part in the ▷Easter Rising (1916) and subsequently became finance minister in the republican government (1919). From 1919 to 1921 he masterminded the IRA's successful guerrilla campaign against the British forces in Ireland. Subsequently he played a major part in the negotiations that led to the establishment of the 26-county Irish Free State (1921). In the ensuing civil war he commanded the Free State army against republicans who opposed the Anglo-Irish treaty. He was assassinated ten days after becoming head of the Irish government.

● **Collins, (William) Wilkie** ▶ (1824–89) British novelist. He worked in commerce and practised law before publishing *Memoirs* (1848) of his father, a landscape painter. During the 1850s he enjoyed a mutually beneficial association with Dickens and in 1860 published his pioneering mystery novel, *The Woman in White*. His other novels include *No Name* (1862) and *The Moonstone* (1868).

● **Collins, William** ▶ (1721–59) British poet. He published *Persian Eclogues* (1742), influenced by Pope, while still studying at Oxford. His *Odes* (1747) were classical in form but foreshadowed Romanticism. After a breakdown in 1751 he was confined to an asylum in 1759.

● **colloid** ▶ A solution in which the solute (*or* disperse phase) is present in the solvent (dispersion medium) in the form of particles 10^{-9} to 10^{-6} m in length, rather than as single molecules or ions. If the disperse phase is solid and the dispersion medium is liquid the colloid is known as a **sol** (examples include milk, glue, and some drug preparations). If both are liquid the colloid is known as an **emulsion** (e.g. mayonnaise and most ointments). A colloidal suspension in which the particles of the disperse phase link together, with the dispersion medium circulating through the meshwork, is called a **gel** (e.g. a photographic emulsion). ▷*See also* aerosol.

Colloids consist of charged particles. In lyophilic (solvent-loving) colloids, stability is achieved by attraction between the particles and the molecules of the dispersion medium. Lyophilic colloids are reversible in the sense that when the particles are removed from the solution, they will re-form a solution by simply mixing with the dispersion medium. Lyophobic (solvent-hating) colloids usually consist of large inorganic particles (e.g. clays, metals, etc.). They maintain stability by repulsion between similarly charged aggregates. They often precipitate on the addition of a salt and are irreversible.

● **Colman, George** ▶ (1732–94) British dramatist and theatre manager. After studying law he became involved in the theatre through his friendship with the actor David ▷Garrick, with whom he collaborated on his best-known comedy, *The Clandestine Marriage* (1766). His son **George Colman, the Younger** (1762–1836) was a well-known writer of melodramas.

● **Colman, Ronald** ▶ (1891–1958) British actor. He went to the USA in 1920 after military service during World War I and played leading romantic roles in such films as *Lost Horizon* (1937) and *Random Harvest* (1943).

● **Colmar** ▶ 48 05N 7 21E A town in E France, the capital of the Haut-Rhin department. It was held by Germany from 1871 to 1919, and from 1940 until 1945. It has many notable buildings, including a Dominican monastery (13th–14th centuries). A trading centre for Alsatian wines, it has an important cotton industry. Population (1990): 64 889.

● **colobus** ▶ A leaf-eating ▷Old World monkey belonging to the genus *Colobus* (3 species), of African forests, also called guereza. 50–70 cm long, colobus monkeys have long hands with small thumbs and their long silky fur is brightly marked. They have been widely hunted for their skins. ▯mammal.

● **colocynth** ▶ The dried fruit of *Citrullus colocynthus*, a prostrate herbaceous perennial found in N Africa, the Middle East, and India and cultivated in Spain and Cyprus. It is a powerful laxative, used medicinally in very small amounts. It can cause poisoning. Family: *Cucurbitaceae*.

● **Cologne** ▶ (German name: Köln) 50 56N 06 57E A city in W Germany on the River Rhine, the largest in North Rhine-Westphalia. A port and major commercial centre, it is famed for its toilet water. Other industries include textiles, iron and steel, chemicals, and motor manufacture. It is the site of a university (1388) and the largest gothic cathedral in N Europe (founded 1248). The cathedral and the old gothic town hall were among the buildings reconstructed after World War II during which most of the city centre was destroyed.

History: founded by the Romans, it became the capital of the northern empire in 258 AD and later the seat of Frankish kings. During the middle ages its archbishops were powerful princes and it flourished as a mercantile and cultural centre, where Albertus Magnus, Thomas Aquinas, and John Duns Scotus taught. In 1798 it was annexed by France, passing to Prussia in 1815. Population (1996 est): 965 697.

● **Colombey-les-Deux-Eglises** ▶ 48 13N 4 54E A village in E central France, in the Haut-Marne department. It contains the former residence of Gen de Gaulle, who is buried here.

● **Colombia, Republic of** ▶ A country in NW South America, on the Pacific Ocean and the Caribbean Sea. It consists chiefly of a hot swampy coastal plain, separated by the Andes from the pampas and the equatorial forests of the upper Amazon basin. Most of the population is of mixed Spanish and Indian descent.

Economy: mainly agricultural. Coffee accounts for over half the total exports. Coca is grown illegally on a massive scale and there is also widespread trafficking in and processing of cocaine: it is estimated that about 80% of the world's supply of the drug originates in Colombia. Although industry is largely undeveloped, the manufacturing section has expanded in recent decades and the export of such products as textiles, paper products, and chemicals has risen. The country is rich in minerals; gold production is the highest in South America and silver, copper, lead, and mercury are also mined. Colombia is one of the world's richest sources of platinum and emeralds, and there are large reserves of coal and natural gas. The most valuable natural resource, however, is oil, which remains largely unexploited. There are plans to exploit the country's hydroelectric potential. Despite measures to liberalize the economy in the 1980s and 1990s, continuing political instability has deterred foreign investment.

History: inhabited by Chibchas and other Indians before the Spanish colonization of the 16th century. In 1819 Simón Bolívar secured the independence of Greater Colombia, which included what are now Panama, Venezuela, and Ecuador as well as Colombia. This lasted until 1830 when Venezuela and Ecuador broke away; Panama became independent following the so-called "War of the Thousand Days" (1899–1902). In the 1950s civil war, caused by struggles between the Liberal and Conservative Parties, led to the dictatorship of Gen Gustavo Rojas Pinilla (1900–75). He was overthrown in a military coup in 1957 and a more democratic government was re-established the following year. Since 1975 there has been almost continuous unrest, including strikes, student rioting, kidnappings, assassinations, and guerrilla activity, notably that involving the left-wing organization M-19 (disbanded as a guerrilla force in 1990). Despite government campaigns in the 1980s and 1990s, the cartels dealing in cocaine remain extremely powerful. In 1990 César Gaviria Trujillo (1947–) was elected president to succeed Virgilio Barco Vargas, who had held office since 1986. A new constitution was introduced in 1991 with the aim of ending government corruption and stemming unrest. Nevertheless, political and drug-related violence has contin-ued. Ernesto Samper (1951–   ) became president in 1994. A year later a political crisis arose when he was charged with accepting funds from the drug cartels. Presidential elections in 1998 resulted in vic-tory for the conservative Andres Pastrana. Although his swearing-in was met with the worst guerrilla violence in 25 years, substantive talks with the main left-wing guerrilla organizations began in January 1999. The peace process suffered frequent setbacks in 2000–01 and fi-nally collapsed in early 2002; government forces immediately moved against FARC-held territory in the S. Presidential elections in 2002 saw victory for Alvaro Uribe, who promised a hard line against FARC.

Republic of Colombia

Head of state	President Alvaro Uribe
Official language	Spanish
Official religion	Roman Catholic
Official currency	Colombian peso of 100 centavos
Area	1 138 914 sq km (456 535 sq mi)
Population (2000 est)	42 299 000
Capital	Bogotá
Main port	Barranquilla

● **Colombo** ► 6 55N 79 52E The capital and main port of Sri Lanka, on the W coast at the mouth of the River Kelani. Founded by the Arabs in the 8th century AD, it was later developed by the Portuguese, the Dutch, and the British. It has one of the largest artificial harbours in the world, from which tea, spices, and rubber are exported. The University of Sri Lanka was established here in 1972. Population (1997 est): 800 982.

● **Colombo, Matteo Realdo** ► (?1516–59) Italian physician, who first described the circulation of blood between the heart and lungs. From his dissections of human cadavers he described the membrane surrounding the lungs (pleura) and the membrane enclosing the ab-dominal organs (peritoneum).

● **Colombo Plan** ► An agreement, signed in Colombo (Ceylon) in 1951, designed to foster economic development in the countries of S and SE Asia. It now has 24 members—20 countries within the region and Australia, Japan, New Zealand, and the USA. There is an annual meeting of the Consultative Committee, and financial arrangements are made between individual governments.

● **colon** ▷See intestine.

● **Colón** ► (former name: Aspinwall) 9 21N 79 54W A port in central Panama, at the Caribbean end of the Panama Canal. It is a major com-mercial centre; industries include oil refining. Population (1994 est): 137 825.

● **colophony** ▷See rosin.

● **Colorado** ► One of the Mountain States in the W central USA. The flat grass-covered Great Plains of the E are cut by the South Platte and Arkansas Rivers flowing E from the Rocky Mountains which cover the W half of the state and contain the valley of the Colorado River. Most of the population lives in a transition zone, the Colorado Piedmont, which divides the two regions. Manufacturing is important, espe-cially the production of machinery, chemicals, and military equip-ment. Mining is declining, although Colorado still produces molybdenum, coal, oil, and sand and gravel. Tourism, especially winter sports, is of growing importance. The state's farmers are major producers of cattle along with pigs and lambs. As well as cul-tural and educational institutions the state has three important ob-servatories. *History*: explored by the Spanish, part of Colorado was acquired by the USA in the Louisiana Purchase (1803) and part from Mexico in 1848. Following the discovery of gold (1859), it became a territory in 1861 and a state in 1876. Area: 269 998 sq km (104 247 sq mi). Popula-tion (2000): 4 301 261. Capital: Denver.

● **Colorado potato beetle** ► A brown and yellow striped ▷leaf beetle, *Leptinotarsa decemlineata*, about 10 mm long. Both the adults and larvae eat potato leaves: the larvae also attack the tubers. It is native to W North America but has spread eastwards, throughout Europe, to become a serious pest of potato crops everywhere.

● **Colorado River** ► A river in the W USA, rising in the Rocky Mountains and flowing SW through Colorado, Utah, and Arizona (where it passes through the ▷Grand Canyon) to the Gulf of Califor-nia in Mexico. Its extensive use for irrigation and as a source of power (the many canyons providing ideal sites for dams, of which the Hoover Dam is one) is seen by conservationists as a serious threat to the natural landscape. Length: 2320 km (1440 mi).

● **Colorado Springs** ► 38 50N 104 50W A health resort in the USA, in Colorado situated at the foot of the Rocky Mountains. It is the site of the US Air Force Academy and the US Air Defence Command. Popu-lation (1998 est): 344 987.

● **coloratura** ► (Italian: colouring) A style of vocal music character-ized by elaborate and florid decorative passages. A **coloratura so-prano** is a soprano whose voice is suited to such music. Donizetti and Verdi made effective use of the coloratura style in many of their operas; the Russian composer Reinhold Glière (1876–1956) wrote a concerto for wordless coloratura soprano voice and orchestra.

● **Colosseum** ► An ▷amphitheatre in Rome. Now one of the most impressive of all Roman remains, the Colosseum was begun (c. 70 AD) by the emperor ▷Vespasian. It is an elliptical building, four storeys high, 188 m (617 ft) long, and 156 m (512 ft) wide. It could seat 47 000 people and was used mainly for gladiatorial and wild-beast fights, but could be flooded for mock naval battles.

● **Colossians, Epistle of Paul to the** ► A New Testament book written by the Apostle Paul about 60 AD to the church in Colossae in W Asia Minor. Its theme is that the Christian faith is sufficient and that speculative philosophy, specifically ideas that appear to be de-rived from ▷Gnosticism, diverts attention from this truth.

● **Colossus of Rhodes** ► A gigantic statue of the sun god ▷Helios by the harbour of Rhodes. Cast in bronze by Chares of Lindos about 280 BC and standing about 31 m (100 ft) tall, it was counted among the ▷Seven Wonders of the World. An earthquake destroyed it 50 years after its completion.

● **colostrum** ▷See lactation.

● **colour** ► The sensation produced when light of different wave-lengths falls on the human eye. Although it is actually continuous, the visible spectrum is usually split into seven major colours: red, orange, yellow, green, blue, indigo, and violet, in order of decreasing wavelength (from about 6.5×10^{-7} m for red light to 4.2×10^{-7} m for violet). A mixture of all these colours in equal proportions gives white light; other colours are produced by varying the proportions or omitting components. Coloured pigments, dyes, and filters selec-tively absorb certain wavelengths, transmitting or reflecting the rest. Thus a red book illuminated by white light absorbs all the compo-nents of white light except red, which is reflected. This is a subtractive process, since the final colour is that remaining after ab-sorption of the others. Combining coloured lights, on the other hand, is an additive process. A mixture of the whole spectrum gives white light, as will a mixture of lights of three ▷primary colours.

● **colour blindness** ► The inability to distinguish certain colours. There are various forms of colour blindness, the most common of which is red-green colour blindness (the inability to distinguish red and green). Colour blindness is an inherited condition: because it is a recessive trait carried on the X chromosome it is far more common in men than women (about 8% of males of Caucasian origin are colour blind). Very occasionally colour blindness may be due to disease of the retina (the light-sensitive layer of the eye). Diagnosis depends on the use of charts in which symbols made of colour dots are buried in a background of other dots. Inherited colour blindness cannot be cured, and sufferers must avoid activities in which the distinction of colour may be of importance.

● **colour photography** ► The recording of ▷colour images on pho-tographic ▷film that has three layers of light-sensitive emulsion, one for each of three ▷primary colours. Most colour film uses a subtractive reversal process. Coloured light entering the camera first falls on an emulsion sensitive only to blue light. On development of this layer, a black image is formed by deposition of silver where blue light has fallen. The unblackened areas are dyed yellow, the complementary colour of blue, and the silver deposit is removed. Since silver halide emulsions cannot be made insensitive to blue light, there is a yellow filter (to remove blue light) between the blue emulsion and the next layer, which is green-sensitive. This is developed to form a magenta image of the parts where no green light has fallen. The bottom layer is red-sensitive and gives a cyan (blue-green) negative image. When white light shines through the three superimposed images, the cyan dye subtracts red where it does not occur in the picture; the magenta subtracts green; and the yellow subtracts blue. The light emerging therefore reconstructs the original picture on a screen, in the case of a transparency, or onto printing paper. Positive colour paper prints directly from negatives that are not to be used for transparencies. These negatives incorporate dyes to correct for varying sensitivity in the printing-paper emulsion. For printing from transparencies, reversal colour paper is used and good colour reproduction is more difficult.

● **colour television** ▷*See* television.

● **colour vision** ▶ The ability of the human eye (and that of some other animals) to detect differences in the wavelength of light. The ability is due to the presence in the retina of the eye of cells known as cones (*see* retina), of which three types are believed to exist; one type being sensitive to red light, one to blue, and one to green. Light stimulates one or more of these types of cones in varying amounts depending on its colour. ▷*See also* colour blindness.

● **Colt revolver** ▶ A ▷revolver with a five-shot cylinder rotated and locked in line with the single barrel by cocking the weapon. Invented by the US engineer Samuel Colt (1814–62) in 1835, it became the .45 calibre Frontier Peacemaker (1873) and the standard .45 US army and navy revolver, remaining in service until 1945.

● **coltsfoot** ▶ A perennial early-flowering herb, *Tussilago farfara*, 5–15 cm high, bearing yellow single flower heads on scaly stems before the leaves appear. Found in Eurasia, N Africa, and North America (introduced), it can be a persistent weed. The dried leaves were previously smoked to cure coughs and asthma. Family: ▷*Compositae*.

● **colugo** ▶ An arboreal mammal belonging to the genus *Cyanocephalus* and order *Dermoptera* (2 species), also called flying lemur, found in Asia, Borneo, and the Philippines. About 60 cm long, colugos have a membrane of skin, extending from the chin via the fore and hind limbs to the tail, with which they can glide up to 70 m. Colugos feed on leaves and fruit.

● **Colum, Padraic** ▶ (Patrick Colm; 1881–1972) Irish poet and folklorist. Associated with ▷Yeats, ▷Synge, and other members of the Celtic literary revival, he founded *The Irish Review* in 1911. From 1914 he lived in the USA. His works include several volumes of lyrical poetry, plays, folklore anthologies, and a reminiscence of James ▷Joyce.

● **Columba, St** ▶ (c. 521–597 AD) Irish missionary and abbot. Ordained in 551, he founded churches and monasteries in Ireland before setting up a monastery on Iona. From here, Scotland was evangelized. Feast day: 9 June.

● **Columban, St** ▶ (*or* St Columbanus; c. 543–615 AD) Irish missionary and abbot. Establishing himself with 12 companions in Gaul in 590, he founded monasteries in the Vosges. Because of a conflict with the king, his monks went first to Switzerland and then to Italy in 612, where they founded a monastery at Bobbio in N Italy, which became an important centre of learning. Feast day: 23 Nov. Emblem: a bear.

● **Columbia** ▶ 34 00N 81 00W A city in the USA, the capital of South Carolina and an important commercial centre. Its industries include textiles, plastics, and machinery. Fort Jackson (a major US Army post) is adjacent to the city. The University of Carolina was established here in 1801. Population (1996 est): 112 773.

● **Columbia River** ▶ A river in North America, flowing SW from British Columbia, through Washington State, to the Pacific Ocean at Oregon. It is an important source of hydroelectric power and forms the only deepwater harbour N of San Francisco. Length: 1930 km (1200 mi).

● **columbine** ▷*See* Aquilegia.

● **columbium** ▷*See* niobium.

● **Columbus** ▶ 39 59N 83 03W A city in the USA, the capital of Ohio on the Scioto River. The industrial and commercial centre of a rich agricultural area, it manufactures aircraft, machinery, and footwear. It is the site of the Ohio State University (1872). Population (1996 est): 657 053.

● **Columbus** ▶ 32 28N 84 59W A city in the USA, in W Georgia on the Chattahoochee River. The state's second largest city, it has textile, food-processing, and chemical industries. Population (1996 est): 182 828.

● **Columbus, Christopher** ▶ (1451–1506) Italian navigator, who pioneered European contact with America. He was born in Genoa, became a pirate, and in 1476 was shipwrecked off the coast of Portugal, where he settled. He conceived the idea of reaching the East by sailing westwards but his plan was rejected by the Portuguese king (John the Perfect) and Columbus approached (1486) the Spanish monarchs Ferdinand and Isabella. He eventually won their patronage and on 3 August, 1492, set sail in the *Santa Maria*, accompanied by the *Pinta* and the *Niña*. On 12 Oct he landed on Samana Cay in the Bahamas (previously known as Watling Island, now San Salvador Island) and in November visited Hispaniola. On his return to Spain he was greatly honoured: Ferdinand and Isabella stood to receive him at court and offered him a seat. On his second voyage (1493–96) he visited Guadeloupe, Puerto Rico, and Jamaica and founded the first European town in the New World—named Isabella, after his patroness,

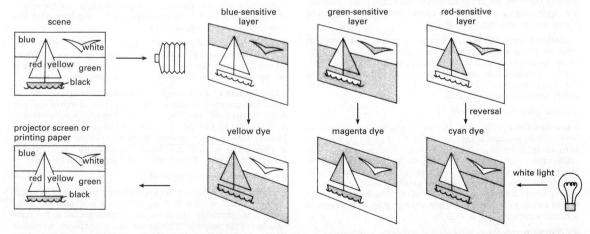

colour photography ▶ In colour reproduction with subtractive reversal film, light from the different coloured areas of the scene forms negatives for each primary colour. These are dyed to form filters that subtract colours from white light to reconstruct the original picture.

it is now a ruin in the Dominican Republic. On his third voyage (1498–1500) he reached Trinidad and the mainland of South America but the expedition ended in disaster: in 1499, following a revolt against his command, a Spanish governor was dispatched to relieve Columbus, who was sent back in chains to Spain. On his arrival, however, he was released and compensated and shortly afterwards set off on his last voyage (1502–04). From this he returned ill and disheartened, dying not long afterwards in Valladolid—still believing the lands he had visited were islands off the east coast of Asia. In 1542 his remains were taken to Hispaniola.

● **column** ▷*See* orders of architecture.

● **Colwyn Bay** ▶ 53 18N 3 43W A coastal resort in North Wales, in Conwy county borough. Population (1991): 29 883.

● **coly** ▶ A small grey or brown bird belonging to a family (*Coliidae*; 6 species) of Central and South Africa, also called mousebird because it creeps mouselike along branches. Colies are 30–35 cm long, including the long stiff tail feathers, and have a short crest, a short curved bill, and red legs with long claws. Order: *Coliiformes*.

● **coma** ▶ In medicine, a state of deep unconsciousness in which the subject is unrousable and does not respond to pain. Coma can be caused by a ▷stroke, drug overdosage, meningitis, or head injuries. Treatment is that of the underlying condition, with the maintenance of respiration.

● **Comanche** ▶ A North American Indian people of the southern Plains. They speak a language of the Uto-Aztecan group, closely related to ▷Shoshoni. They migrated to this area from Wyoming in the 18th century. Horse breeders and fierce warriors, they often attacked white settlers in Texas until they agreed to settle in Oklahoma in 1867.

● **Comaneci, Nadia** ▶ (1961–) Romanian gymnast, who in the 1976 Olympic Games won gold medals on the beam, the asymmetrical bars, and also in the individual all-round competition for women. She retired in 1984.

● **Combination Acts** ▶ (1799, 1800) The British laws that made illegal any combination of working men for the purpose of improving their working conditions. Provoked by the government's fear of revolutionary ideas spreading from France to England, they were unsuccessful in preventing the formation of trade unions and were repealed in 1824. An outbreak of strikes followed the repeal and another Act was passed (1825) allowing trade unions to exist but limiting their right to strike.

● **combined heat and power** ▶ (CHP) A method of generating electricity in which the waste heat produced in the generating process is used to heat water or raise steam for local district heating or industrial use. CHP generating stations are designed to produce heat of sufficiently high temperature to be useful, which usually involves a loss in the efficiency of the electricity-generating plant. However, the overall efficiency of the fuel to useful-energy conversion can be higher than an electricity-only station.

● **combine harvester** ▶ A machine for harvesting grain crops that combines the operations of cutting the crop (reaping) and separating the grain (threshing) from the rest of the plant. Horse-drawn models originated in the USA in the 1830s; in the 1940s, the predecessors of the modern self-propelled machines were introduced, replacing the earlier labour-intensive methods.

● **comb jelly** ▷*See* ctenophore.

● **combustion** ▶ A chemical reaction in which a substance combines with oxygen, producing heat and light. For a liquid or a solid to burn, the temperature must initially be high enough to release flammable vapour. To maintain combustion, the heat evolved must maintain this temperature to provide a constant supply of vapour. The oxidation reactions in combustion are generally chain reactions involving free radicals, the principal overall reactions being the oxidation of carbon to carbon dioxide and the oxidation of hydrogen to water ($C + 2H_2 + 2O_2 \rightarrow CO_2 + 2H_2O$).

● **COMECON** ▷*See* Council for Mutual Economic Assistance.

● **Comédie-Française** ▶ The French national theatre, founded by Louis XIV in 1680 and reconstituted in 1812 by Napoleon. The oldest state-subsidized theatre company in Europe, it is organized as a cooperative society, owned by its members. Probationary members are called *pensionnaires* and full members *sociétaires*; a pension is awarded on retirement after 20 years of service. Despite its strong emphasis on tradition, it has produced many of France's most original actors.

● **comedy** ▶ A type of ▷drama that evokes amusement and laughter. Traditionally, it deals with ordinary characters in everyday situations and ends happily, usually with a marriage. In ▷Shakespeare these elements blend with a more romantic narrative vein.

The earliest surviving comedies are those of the Greek dramatist ▷Aristophanes and his principal successor Menander in the 4th century BC: the latter's work was the main influence on the Romans ▷Plautus and ▷Terence (*see* Old Comedy; Middle Comedy; New Comedy; Roman Comedy). At the Renaissance comedy was revived by the Italian ▷commedia dell'arte, whose stock situations and characters influenced the work of many later dramatists, most notably ▷Molière. During the early 17th century the English dramatist Ben ▷Jonson pioneered the comedy of humours with characters who are gross caricatures of ruling passions. Examples of the satirical comedy of manners, in which more emphasis is placed on sophisticated witty dialogues, are the plays of ▷Congreve and ▷Wycherley in the late 17th century. The plays of Oscar ▷Wilde and Noel ▷Coward continued the tradition of the witty comedy of manners in England; otherwise comedy in the 20th century often reflects man's changed awareness of his own identity: the plays of ▷Ionesco and Samuel ▷Beckett, which often provoke laughter as a response to the meaninglessness of existence, are examples of what is sometimes labelled black comedy.

● **Comenius, John Amos** ▶ (1592–1671) Czech theologian and educationalist. Comenius wrote widely on education, advocating a broad curriculum incorporating science, handicrafts, economics, and languages. He was commissioned by ▷Oxenstierna to reform Swedish schools (1641–48). A virulent opponent of the papacy, he was drawn to the mysticism of Jacob ▷Böhme.

● **comet** ▶ A small body that moves, usually in a very elongated orbit, around the sun. A typical comet consists of a small nucleus of ice and dust surrounded by an immense tenuous luminous cloud of gas and dust, the coma. Tails of gas and of dust only appear when a comet is near the sun; they point away from the sun and may be millions of kilometres long. **Short-period comets** (such as ▷Halley's comet) have orbital periods of less than 150 years. The remainder have much longer periods, some exceeding 10 000 years, and move in approximately parabolic orbits. A comet eventually decays to produce a stream of meteoroids around its orbit. ▷*See also* Oort cloud.

● **comfrey** ▶ A perennial herbaceous plant, *Symphytum officinale*, also called boneset. Up to 100 cm high, it has drooping creamy or purplish flowers. Native to Europe and temperate Asia and formerly used medicinally, it is now grown as a garden flower, as are the related plants *S. grandiflorum* (yellow flowers) and *S. peregrinum* (blue and pink flowers). Family: *Boraginaceae*.

● **comic opera** ▶ An opera with a humorous or farcical plot. It is characterized by spoken dialogue and a comic or satirical libretto. Among the most famous comic operas are the Savoy Operas of ▷Gilbert and ▷Sullivan. *Compare* opéra comique; opera buffa.

● **Cominform** ▶ (Communist Information Bureau) An international communist organization. Founded in 1947, it united the Communist Parties of the Soviet Union, Bulgaria, Czechoslovakia, Hungary, Poland, Romania, Yugoslavia, France, and Italy. In 1948 Yugoslavia was expelled because of its refusal to follow the Soviet line. In 1956, partly in order to improve relations with Yugoslavia, the Soviet Union dissolved the Cominform. ▷*See also* International.

● **Comintern** ▷*See* International.

● **comitia** ▶ Assemblies of the Roman people summoned by magistrates and held at an official meeting place (*comitium*) on an appointed day (*comitialis*). The three *comitia* corresponded to the three divisions of the people into curiae (*see* curia), ▷centuries, and tribes. The Comitia Curiata was the earliest assembly but its legislative functions became largely formal. The Comitia Centuriata elected the chief magistrates and had some judicial powers. The Comitia Tributa was the assembly of the ▷plebeians; its enactments had authority after 287 BC.

● **Commandos** ▷*See* Royal Marines.

● **commedia dell'arte** ▶ An Italian form of popular theatre that flourished throughout Europe from the 16th to the 18th centuries. It was performed by professional actors whose comic and often vulgar improvisations were based on a set of stock situations, usually concerning romantic intrigues, and stereotyped characters. These included the valet Pedrolino (*see* Pierrot), the clown ▷Harlequin, the cuckold Pantaloon, and the lover Inamorato. Its influence can be seen in the works of such contemporary dramatists as Molière and in ▷pantomime and ▷farce. Its characters were popular subjects for 18th-century porcelain figures. ▷*See also* Punch and Judy.

commedia dell'arte ▶ A scene from the comedy *Le Tombeau de Maître André*, as depicted in a painting by Claude Gillot (1673–1723; Louvre).

● **commensalism** ▶ A relationship between two individuals of different species in which one (the commensal) lives in, on, or with the other (the host), from which it derives food, shelter, support, or transport. The association neither harms nor benefits the host. An example is provided by certain barnacles, which live attached to whales. ▷*See also* symbiosis.

● **commercial banks** ▶ Institutions that offer a deposit, transfer, and loan service to companies and private individuals. In the UK, the commercial banks (or high-street banks) are public limited companies (joint-stock banks), most of which amalgamated during the 19th century to emerge from World War I as the big five: Barclays Bank, Lloyds Bank (now Lloyds TSB), Midland Bank (now HSBC), National Provincial Bank, and Westminster Bank (in 1968 the last two merged to form the National Westminster Bank, now called NatWest and owned by the Royal Bank of Scotland). Others include the Abbey National, the Halifax, and the Woolwich, which were formerly building societies. The commercial banks make a profit by lending at a higher rate of interest than their borrowing rate. The ▷Bank of England controls the amount that they lend through ▷open-market operations. Many commercial banks own financial subsidiaries, including ▷merchant banks and life assurance companies.

● **commercial paper** ▶ A short-term unsecured way of borrowing money. The issuers of commercial paper are companies with a high credit rating (e.g. insurance companies, pension funds). In the USA commercial paper usually matures in 60 days or less, but the period is longer in the UK.

● **commesso** ▶ (*or* Florentine mosaic) A method of making mosaic pictures of flowers, landscapes, etc., with semiprecious stones, such as lapis lazuli, agate, and jasper. Commesso pictures, which were used chiefly as tabletops and small wall panels, have been made since 1588 at a special Florentine workshop, now state supported.

● **Committees of Correspondence** ▶ Liaison committees originally appointed by the American colonies for communication with England. As the American Revolution neared, the committees encouraged cooperation against the Crown and provided leadership for the coming war. First formed in Virginia, they organized the first ▷Continental Congress (1774).

● **commode** ▶ A low-level decorative chest of drawers or cupboard. As invented by André-Charles Boulle (1642–1732), the commode was an architectural piece of furniture, sarcophagus-shaped with heavy feet and fitted with drawers. It developed during the 18th century into an elegantly curved chest of drawers with ▷marquetry and ▷ormolu decoration. ▷Chippendale made important English examples.

● **commodity trading** ▶ The buying and selling of natural products, such as metals, coffee, rubber, and cocoa, conducted in commodity exchanges or markets (e.g. the London Commodity Exchange) by brokers on behalf of clients, who consist of producers, users, and speculators. The majority of dealings are in ▷futures (goods for delivery at a stipulated date in the future) and ▷options, although actuals (goods for immediate delivery) are also traded in some exchanges. Trading in futures rarely involves the exchange of goods, most transactions being closed out by equal sales or purchases on the same market using a ▷clearing house. Commodity exchanges enable producers and users to hedge their transactions in goods and help to stabilize prices by regulating supply and demand.

● **Commodus, Lucius Aelius Aurelius** ▶ (161–93 AD) Roman emperor (180–92). The son of Marcus Aurelius, Commodus showed increasing signs of mental imbalance, believing he was the incarnation of the demigod Hercules. He became increasingly unpopular and was finally assassinated.

● **Common Agricultural Policy** ▶ (CAP) The agricultural policy adopted by members of the EU. The aims of the policy are to ensure reasonable living standards for farmers and to secure regular supplies and reasonable prices for consumers. CAP involves the distribution of grants and a price-support system. Grants for such farm improvements as land drainage account for about one-third of CAP's cost and are uncontroversial. The price-support policy, however, has many critics. Target prices are agreed that make production in the EU profitable for farmers, but if market prices fall below these targets the EU engages in support buying to keep the price up to an intervention price level (a proportion of the target price). The system is criticized because it tends to produce embarrassing surpluses (the butter, beef, and wine "mountains" have been notorious) and because there is in principle no limit to the support that may be given. In the 1980s the imposition of production quotas on certain items, such as milk, and attempts by member governments to restrict the import of some foodstuffs caused widespread protest.

Another contentious factor of CAP is **green money**. The green pound is the exchange rate used by the UK when trading with EU partners in agricultural produce. Green money is criticized because there is no system for the automatic adjustment of green exchange rates. Also controversial is the 'set-aside' policy, under which (to reduce surpluses) farmers are paid not to use their land for food production.

● **common law** ▶ The part of the law of England and of most English-speaking countries that was originally unwritten and based on the common customs of the country. It developed with the rise of centralized government in England from the Norman Conquest (1066) to the 13th century, as the body of law common to all areas of the country. Its growth was the result of the principle of judicial precedent, by which an earlier judgment or decision was binding in deciding a similar case. Such decisions form the basis of **case law**, which can only be overruled by statute or by a higher court. Common law is not the result of legislation and is therefore distinguished from the statute law established by Acts of Parliament. It is also distinguished from ▷equity, administered by the Court of ▷Chancery, and from the ▷civil law of most European countries.

● **Common Market** ▷*See* European Economic Community.

● **Common Prayer, Book of** ▶ The official liturgy of the Church of England. After the Reformation, Thomas ▷Cranmer and others began to formulate an order of worship in English. The first Prayer Book was published under Edward VI in 1549, with parliament's approval. Criticism by reformers led to a more Protestant revision in 1552. The Roman Catholic Queen Mary abolished the Prayer Book, and from the accession of Elizabeth I to the end of the Civil War, it was reinstated, further revised, and again abolished, this time by the Puritans. The version of 1662, established by the Act of Uniformity, is still in use; a revised version was authorized in 1928. The 1980 *Alternative Service Book*, in modern English, was the preferred version of the Church of England until 2000–2001, when it was superseded by *Common Worship*, a book that includes both modern-language and traditional services.

● **commons** ▶ Unenclosed land for the common use of the inhabitants of a district. Originally, in every manor there was a tract of uncultivated land over which the inhabitants had **rights of common**, principally the rights to pasture animals, to fish (piscary), to cut wood, furze, etc. (estovers), and to dig turves (turbary). The Commons Registration Act (1965) provides for the maintenance of registers of all common land, village greens, and the rights of common.

● **Commons, Doctors'** ▷*See* Doctors' Commons.

● **Commons, House of** ▷*See* parliament.

● **common sense, philosophy of** ▶ A philosophical movement particularly associated with certain Scottish followers of Thomas ▷Reid and promoted in the 20th century by G. E. ▷Moore. It rejected the traditional philosophical ▷scepticism that had raised doubts about such questions as to whether material objects exist unperceived or whether other people exist. Common-sense philosophers base their case on the universal nonphilosophical consent on such subjects; while particular beliefs may be mistaken, there remains a broad base of common-sense views that must be certain.

● **Commonwealth** ▶ (1649–53) The period in English history between the execution of Charles I and the establishment of the ▷Protectorate; the term is sometimes used synonymously with Interregnum to refer to the entire period between the execution of Charles I and the ▷Restoration in 1660.

● **Commonwealth** ▶ A loose association of 54 independent nations, most of which were formerly subject to the imperial government of the UK (*see* Empire, British). The British Commonwealth of Nations was established by the Statute of Westminster (1931), which was based on the principles, enunciated at the 1926 ▷Imperial Conference, of member states' autonomy, equality, and common allegiance to the Crown. Membership was originally limited to the self-governing "White" states known as dominions, but as other colonies became independent after World War II they too joined the Commonwealth. The association changed its name to the Commonwealth of Nations in 1947. Its member states, the populations of which comprise nearly a quarter of the world's population, are currently Antigua and Barbuda, Australia, the Bahamas, Bangladesh, Barbados, Belize, Botswana, Brunei, Cameroon, Canada, Cyprus, Dominica, Fiji, The Gambia, Ghana, Grenada, Guyana, India, Jamaica, Kenya, Kiribati, Lesotho, Malawi, Malaysia, Maldives, Malta, Mauritius, Mozambique, Namibia, New Zealand, Nigeria, Pakistan, Papua New Guinea, St Kitts-Nevis, St Lucia, St Vincent and the Grenadines, Samoa, Seychelles, Sierra Leone, Singapore, Solomon Islands, South Africa, Sri Lanka, Swaziland, Tanzania, Tonga, Trinidad and Tobago, Uganda, the UK, Vanuatu, Zambia, and Zimbabwe. Nauru and Tuvalu are special members and are not represented at the meetings of Commonwealth heads; there are also a number of associated states and dependent territories. Myanmar (Burma) withdrew from the Commonwealth in 1947, Ireland in 1949, South Africa from 1961 to 1994, Pakistan from 1971 to 1989, and Fiji from 1987 to 1997. Nigeria was suspended from 1995 to 1999 and Zimbabwe from 2002; Pakistan was partially suspended from 1999, as was Fiji from 2000 to 2001. Commonwealth heads of government meet every two years but finance ministers meet annually. These meetings are supplemented by other ministerial contacts and such permanent organizations as the Agricultural Bureaux, the Education Liaison Committee, and the Science Council. The Commonwealth Secretariat headquarters are at Marl-borough House, Pall Mall, London, and its secretary general is the Nigerian Emeka Anyaoku. **Commonwealth Day** is celebrated on 12 March.

● **Commonwealth Institute** ▶ A centre of information about the British ▷Commonwealth. It moved from the Imperial Institute (founded in 1887) building in South Kensington, London, to a new building in Holland Park in 1962. It organizes exhibitions, conferences, and lectures.

● **Commonwealth of Independent States** ▶ (CIS) A community of nations founded in 1991 by Russia, Ukraine, and Belarus to replace the ▷Soviet Union in order to maintain unity in such areas as economic policy and international relations. Armenia, Azerbaidzhan, Kazakhstan, Kirgizstan, Tadzhikistan, Turkmenistan, and Uzbekistan subsequently joined. Georgia joined in 1993 and Moldova in 1994.

● **commune** ▶ An experimental community based on religious, social, political, or technological ideas, which are often incompatible with established social institutions. In the 19th century communes based upon the ideas of such men as Robert ▷Owen, Charles ▷Fourier, and William ▷Morris were established in Europe, the USA, and South America. They sought new physical environments, egalitarian principles of social organization, and the harmonious integration of family, work, and learning. During the 1960s and 1970s many communes, often influenced by Eastern mysticism, were established.

● **Commune of Paris** ▶ (1871) A revolt in Paris against the conservative provisional government established at Versailles following French defeat in the Franco-Prussian War and the collapse of the Second Empire. Fearing a restoration of the monarchy, republican Parisians formed a revolutionary government (March) that was reminiscent of the French Revolutionary Commune (1793). Defeated by government troops in May, the Communards lost some 20 000 supporters, 38 000 were arrested, and 7000 deported.

● **communications satellite** ▶ An unmanned artificial satellite by which long-distance television broadcasting, telephone communications, and computer data links are achieved. Radio signals, suitably modulated (*see* modulation), are sent from one transmitting station to the satellite, where they are amplified and retransmitted (at a different frequency) to one or more receiving stations. The orbits of communications satellites lie above the earth's atmosphere so that high-frequency radio waves (microwaves), which can penetrate the ▷ionosphere, must be used. The electronic equipment on board is powered primarily by solar cells (*see* solar power).

The first active satellite was the US Telstar 1, launched in 1962. Telstar and other early satellites were in relatively low elliptical orbits and were only visible for a short portion of their orbit. A communications satellite is now usually placed in a geostationary orbit. This is a circular orbit lying about 36 000 km above the earth's equator. The satellite completes such an orbit in the same time (24 hours) as the earth rotates on its axis and thus to a ground-based radio station appears to remain nearly stationary in the sky. Three or more satellites, suitably placed around the equatorial orbit, can provide worldwide communications links.

Various organizations, serving commercial, private, or government interests, have been set up to provide worldwide communications; notably **Intelsat** (International Telecommunications Satellite Organization), which was founded in 1964 and now has over 100 member countries. Communications satellites fall into four categories: domestic satellites of a country; international satellites in the fixed satellite service (FSS); satellites capable of direct broadcasting services (DBS), which are used for satellite broadcasting of ▷television programmes direct to people's homes; communications satellites not otherwise classified.

● **communism** ▶ A movement based on the principle of communal ownership of all property. It is associated with *The Communist Manifesto* (1848) of Marx and Engels according to which the capitalist profit-based system of private ownership is replaced by a communist society in which the means of production are communally owned. This process, initiated by the overthrow of the bourgeoisie (*see* Marxism), passes through a phase marked by the dictatorship of the proletariat (*see* Leninism) and the preparatory stage of ▷socialism.

In the later 19th century Marxist theories motivated several social democratic parties in Europe, although they later became committed to reforming capitalism rather than overthrowing it. The exception was the Russian Social Democratic Labour Party, which seized power in the Revolution of November, 1917. In 1918 this party changed its name to the Communist Party of the Soviet Union, thus establishing the modern distinction between communism and socialism.

After the Russian Revolution many socialist parties in other countries became communist parties, owing allegiance of varying degrees to the Soviet Communist Party (*see* International). In 1944–46 communist regimes were set up with the aid of the Soviet army in several E European countries. In 1949 the communists in China, with Soviet support, overthrew the Nationalists and inaugurated the People's Republic of China. The subsequent Sino-Soviet split, made public in 1961, was an important factor in world politics for the next 30 years. In 1989 mass unrest in E Europe led to the collapse of communist rule in Poland, Hungary, Czechoslovakia, Bulgaria, Romania, and East Germany. The Soviet Communist Party was suspended following the failed coup attempt by Communist hardliners in 1991. By the mid-1990s communist governments had been re-elected in several countries, including Poland, Hungary, and Romania, while in Russia the former communists have returned to dominate parliament since 1995.

In the 1970s the term **Eurocommunism** was introduced for the policies of communist parties in W Europe, which sought to break with the tradition of uncritical support of the Soviet Union. Communist parties have been electorally significant in France and Italy but not in the UK, where the Communist Party of Great Britain was founded in 1920: in 1991 it changed its name to the Democratic Left.

● **Communism Peak** ► (Russian name: Pik Kommunizma) 38 59N 72 01E The highest mountain in Tadzhikistan (formerly the highest in the Soviet Union), in the Pamirs. Height: 7495 m (24 589 ft).

● **community** ► In ecology, an interdependent group of living organisms that occupies a particular habitat. The plants and animals of a community are closely associated with each other in various ecological relationships: for example, they depend on one another for food (*see* food chain). The size and composition of the community depend on habitat and climate. During ecological ▷succession, the structure of a community constantly changes until the stable climax community is established. ▷*See also* ecology; ecosystem.

● **community charge** ▷*See* poll tax.

● **community service** ► A form of sentence originating in Scandinavia and introduced in the UK by the Criminal Justice Act (1972). The offender works for a prescribed number of hours on behalf of the community instead of being imprisoned or fined. In the UK the offender must consent, be aged 16 or over, and have committed no violence.

● **commutative law** ► The mathematical rule, obeyed by addition and multiplication but not division, that the result of an operation combining two quantities is independent of the order in which they are taken: for addition, $a + b = b + a$, and for multiplication, $ab = ba$.

● **Commynes, Philippe de** ► (c. 1445–1511) French statesman and chronicler. He served Charles the Bold, Duke of Burgundy, from 1464 and Louis XI from 1472. On the accession of Charles VIII in 1483 he was imprisoned but later returned to favour. His *Mémoires* (1524) are an important record of the reign of Louis XI and the Italian expedition of Charles VIII, and embody his advanced political theories.

● **Como** ► 45 48N 09 05E A city in N Italy, in Lombardy on Lake Como. Known as Comum in Roman times, it is the birthplace of the elder and younger Pliny. It fell to the Visconti in 1335 and in 1859 was liberated from Austrian occupation by Garibaldi. It has a 15th-century marble cathedral and a gothic town hall. Como is a tourist centre and its industries include the famous silk factories. Population (1998 est): 87 059.

● **Como, Lake** ► A lake in central N Italy, lying in a narrow forked valley at the S foot of the Alps. It is about 50 km (31 mi) long, dividing into two arms about halfway along, with a maximum depth of 410 m (1345 ft). There are many fashionable resorts on its shore such as Bellagio, Como, and Lecco. Area: 145 sq km (55 sq mi).

● **Comodoro Rivadavia** ► 45 50S 67 30W A port in SE Argentina,

on the Atlantic Ocean. It is Argentina's main oil-producing centre; a natural gas pipeline extends for 1770 km (1100 mi) to Buenos Aires. Population (1999): 144 074.

● **Comorin, Cape** ► 08 04N 77 35E A headland in India, the most southerly point of the subcontinent.

● **Comoros, Federal Islamic Republic of the** ► A country consisting of a group of islands in the Indian Ocean, between Madagascar and the African mainland. The main islands are Grand Comoro, Anjouan, and Mohéli; another island, Mayotte, has remained French. The population is of mixed African and Arab descent.

Economy: almost entirely agricultural. Sugar cane was formerly the main crop but others, such as vanilla and perfume plants, are now more important. Exports include vanilla, sisal, and essential oils such as ylang-ylang.

History: there were successive African, Malay, Malagasy, Arab, and other immigrations to the islands before they became a French colony in the 19th century. At first joined to Madagascar, the Comoros became a separate French overseas territory in 1947. In a referendum in 1974 the majority voted in favour of independence, except for the island of Mayotte, which voted to remain French. It has since been made an overseas department of France. Ahmed Abdallah became the first president in 1975 but later that year he was overthrown in a coup led by Ali Soilih. The government was taken over by a National Revolutionary Council. In 1976 the independence of the three islands was recognized by France and Soilih was elected president. He was overthrown (and later killed) in a military coup in 1978 and a Political-Military Directorate took over. The exiled Ahmed Abdallah was elected first president of the Federal Islamic Comoro Republic; effective control, however, lay with the mercenary leader Bob Denard. In 1989 Abdallah was assassinated; a French task force then forced Denard into exile. He returned to lead an abortive coup in 1995. In 1997 Anjouan and Mohéli declared independence from Comoros, seeking a resumption of French rule. The crisis led President Mohammed Taki Abdoulkarim to assume absolute powers. Following Taki's death in 1998, Col Azali Assoumani led a bloodless military coup (April 1999). In December 2001 voters backed a new federal constitution under which each of the three main islands will have financial and legislative autonomy.

Federal Islamic Republic of the Comoros

Head of state	President Azali Assoumani
Official languages	French and Arabic; Swahili is also used commercially
Official currency	Franc of 100 centimes
Area	1862 sq km (719 sq mi)
Population (2000 est)	578 000
Capital and main port	Moroni

● **compact disc** ► (CD) A 120 mm plastic disc used for recording digital information, especially the high-fidelity recording of music. A master disc is made by inscribing into a plastic disc minute pits of varying depth in an outward spiral track by means of a laser whose intensity is controlled by a digital recording instrument. The CD is made by impressing one of its sides with the master and covering the track made by a layer of reflective aluminium and another layer of plastic. In the CD player, laser light is alternately reflected and scattered by the pits; the varying light intensity produced is converted into digital signals, which a suitable amplifier converts into music. CDs are also used as high-capacity read-only memories (**CD-ROM**) for computers. Re-recordable CDs (CD-RW) are becoming increasingly popular for data storage. Digital versatile discs (**DVDs**) are similar to CDs but have a much higher capacity. They are used mainly for recording films. ▷*See also* interactive compact disc.

● **Companies Act** ► A series of UK Acts of Parliament, mostly consolidated in the Companies Act (1985), regulating the formation, management, and winding up of companies. The Act enables businesses to be incorporated by registration with the Registrar of Companies. Such companies have a legal identity and ▷limited liability. The Act prescribes the duties of directors, who manage the company and are responsible for protecting the interests of members (shareholders) and employees. Every company must have two or more members. Shares in a public company are transferable; those in a private company cannot be sold to the public.

● **Companions of Honour, Order of the** ► (CH) British order of chivalry, instituted in 1917. It comprises the sovereign and not more than 65 men and women who have made conspicuous contributions to the nation.

● **compass** ► A device for determining the direction of magnetic north. The **magnetic compass**, which has been in use as an aid to navigation probably since the 2nd century BC, consists of a magnetic needle balanced on a point, allowing it to pivot freely. The S end of the magnet indicates magnetic N, as shown on a card (called a compass card) marked with the points of the compass and fixed below it. In some magnetic compasses, the entire card pivots, indicating direction against a mark on the fixed housing. Such compasses are often filled with a fluid (usually alcohol) for damping. A more sophisticated kind of compass, used on larger vessels and in aircraft, is the **gyrocompass**, which employs the effect of the earth's rotation on the orientation of a spinning object's axis of rotation. Magnetic compasses are subject to interference from nearby ferrous metal objects and fittings, and compasses must be adjusted to compensate for distortion. Compensation must also be made, in the reading of a compass, for magnetic N not being in the same direction as geographic N in most longitudes. Up-to-date navigation charts mark on a compass rose the annual correction for position that must be allowed in various longitudes.

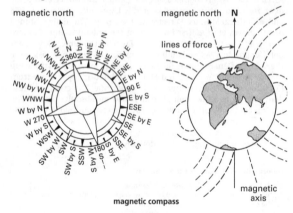

magnetic north

magnetic north **N**

lines of force

magnetic compass

magnetic axis

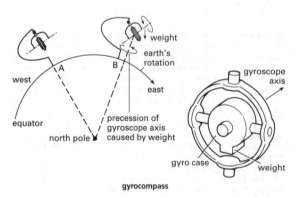

weight

earth's rotation

west

A B

east

equator

gyroscope axis

precession of gyroscope axis caused by weight

north pole

gyro case

weight

gyrocompass

compass ► In the magnetic compass, the magnetized needle lines up with the earth's magnetic field. In the gyrocompass a spinning gyroscope is suspended on three mutually perpendicular frames. The axis of spin of a free gyroscope shifts round as the earth rotates: as the axis of the gyrocompass moves from the horizontal at position A to position B, a weight pulls it downwards. As a result of the gyroscopic effect, the axis shifts round at right angles to the gravitational force (precesses) and describes a circle around the N–S direction. When the precession is damped, the gyroscope axis settles down pointing N.

● **Compiègne** ► 49 25N 2 50E A town and resort in N France, in the Oise department on the River Oise. Joan of Arc was captured here by the English in 1430. A railway coach in the forest of Compiègne was the scene of the signing of the Armistice (1918) ending World War I and of the agreement made between the Pétain government and Hitler in 1940. Industries include machinery, printing, and rubber. Population (1990): 44 703.

● **complementarity principle** ► The principle, proposed by Niels ▷Bohr, that an elementary particle may be regarded as either corpuscular or wavelike. Thus an experiment designed to detect a corpuscular property cannot, at the same time, detect a wave property, and vice versa. This wave-particle duality is a feature of ▷quantum theory and is implicit in the ▷Heisenberg uncertainty principle. ▷*See also* de Broglie wave.

● **complementary medicine** ▷*See* alternative medicine.

● **complex** ► In psychoanalysis, a group of associated ideas that are unacceptable to the conscious mind and have therefore been repressed into the ▷unconscious. Although the individual is no longer aware of these ideas they continue to influence his (or her) behaviour. ▷*See* inferiority complex; Oedipus complex.

● **complex numbers** ► Quantities that consist of a real number and an imaginary number. They may be written in the form $a + ib$, where a and b are real numbers and $i = \sqrt{-1}$. Two complex numbers can be added and subtracted: for example $(a + ib) + (c + id) = (a + c) + i(b + d)$. They may also be multiplied and divided into each other. A complex number $a + ib$ may be thought of as a pair of ordered numbers (a,b) similar to a pair of Cartesian coordinates (x,y). Then (a,b) can be regarded as a point on a plane called the complex plane or Argand diagram in which the real axis is taken as horizontal and the imaginary axis as vertical. Complex numbers are widely used in the physical sciences, particularly in electrical engineering in calculations concerning alternating current.

● **Compositae** ► (or Asteraceae) The largest family of flowering plants (about 900 genera and 14 000 species). They vary from small herbs to trees and are found worldwide. The tiny flowers are grouped into heads that resemble a single large flower. The individual florets may be similar, as in thistles, or of two types (disc and ray flowers), as in daisies. Many composites are cultivated as ornamentals (e.g. chrysanthemums, dahlias); others are weeds (daisies, dandelions, etc.) and some are edible (e.g. lettuce).

● **Composite order** ▷*See* orders of architecture.

● **comprehensive schools** ► Secondary schools attended by children of all abilities, without any entrance selection based on ability, known in the USA as a "one-track" school system. The extent to which comprehensives select internally for aptitude and ability varies considerably, some schools retaining mixed-ability classes at all levels. In the USA attempts to achieve a balanced "social mix" led to the controversial "bussing" of children from one area to another. In the UK the widespread introduction of comprehensive schools was initiated in 1965 by the Labour Government and by 1986 some 85% of the secondary-school population attended comprehensives. This resulted in many former ▷grammar schools becoming comprehensives. Proponents of this change argued that the former selective system was based on narrow and discredited ideas of ▷intelligence testing and condemned the vast majority of pupils to an inferior education. On the other hand critics of the comprehensive system argued that grammar schools, many of which were centres of excellence with long traditions of academic success, were lost forever and that, moreover, cleverer children would be held back by the less able children, who would be forced to follow a curriculum above their ability. In 1999 the government announced plans to provide gifted children with extra tuition in their own schools. Since 1979 Local Education Authorities (LEAs) have no longer been required to abolish selective schools; however, under proposals introduced in 1998 they will be obliged to do so if a ballot of local parents supports such a move.

● **compressor** ► A machine for delivering high-pressure gas. They have a wide variety of uses, from small garage machines for inflating tyres to large industrial machines for supplying compressed-air lines. The piston compressor resembles an internal-combustion engine in reverse and is driven by an electric motor or a diesel engine. The centrifugal compressor uses radial vanes to increase the momentum of the gas; they are extensively used in ▷gas turbines (driven by the turbine shaft) to supply pressurized air to the combustion chambers.

● **Compton, Arthur Holly** ▶ (1892–1962) US physicist, who discovered the ▷Compton effect (1923) while analysing the scattering of X-rays. He shared the 1927 Nobel Prize with C. T. R. ▷Wilson.

● **Compton, Denis (Charles Scott)** ▶ (1918–97) British cricketer, who played for Middlesex and England (1937–57). In 1947 he scored 18 centuries and a total of 3816 runs in one season. He also played Association football for Arsenal and England.

● **Compton-Burnett, Dame Ivy** ▶ (1892–1969) British novelist. *Pastors and Masters* (1925) was the first of a series of 17 novels set in a stylized Victorian-Edwardian upper-class world. The series includes *A House and Its Head* (1935) and *Manservant and Maidservant* (1947).

● **Compton effect** ▶ The increase in the wavelength of electromagnetic radiation when it is scattered by free electrons. The effect can only be explained by regarding the radiation as consisting of particles called photons. Part of the photon's energy is transferred to the electron, increasing its velocity. Named after Arthur ▷Compton.

● **computer** ▶ A device for processing information at high speeds, by electronic methods. The use of the binary system to represent numbers in calculations dates back to a suggestion by Gottfried ▷Leibnitz in 1679. It was not until the 18th century, however, that the concept of storing a sequence of instruction manually was introduced; Joseph-Marie ▷Jacquard's punched cards to drive weaving looms were in widespread use by 1801. Some 35 years later Charles ▷Babbage, with Ada ▷Byron as his assistant, combined a simple mechanical calculator with instructions on perforated paper to devise, but not to build, the first mechanical computer. No further progress occurred for a hundred years; in the 1930s research into electromechanical computers became of interest in both the USA and Germany. The use of thermionic valves to replace electromechanical devices was pioneered at ▷Bletchley Park, where the first mainframes, the Colossus computers, were involved in deciphering German codes in World War II. Alan Turing (*see* Turing machine), a member of this team, made considerable advances in the development of computer logic. Postwar developments in ▷information theory and the invention of the ▷transistor made possible the computer revolution of the next 20 years. Since the 1970s, advances in integrated circuits using silicon chips have led to the development of ▷minicomputers and then ▷microcomputers, commonly known as **personal computers** (PCs), and more recently of ▷laptop computers, palmtop computers, and personal digital assistants (PDAs). ▷*See also* character set.

A **digital computer** processes information in the form of groups of binary numbers (*see* bit), which are represented by the on and off positions of electronic switches. The sequence of operations it performs on this information is controlled by a ▷program; the suite of programs that enables a computer to perform useful functions is called its ▷software. The physical equipment, or **hardware**, of a computer generally has three main components: the central processing unit (CPU), main memory, and peripheral devices that enable information to be fed into the machine and displayed in a readable form, or act as auxiliary memory and data-storage devices. Input, formerly by punched tape or cards, is now by keyboard at a visual display unit (VDU) using a pointing device, such as a mouse or trackball; or with a joystick, stylus and graphics pad, or touch pad; or from digital video disk (DVD), digital camera, or television; or by methods of automatic data capture, such as optical character recognition (OCR). Output is by printout on paper, VDU, or magnetic disc or tape. Modern PCs and laptops are as powerful as, but much cheaper than, the mainframe computers of only a few years ago, and the **transputer**, which harnesses several microprocessors in parallel, now offers PC users the computing speed of a large mainframe. New ideas in chip manufacture and CPUs that work much faster by using optical, rather than electrical, impulses, together with sophisticated approaches to computing, including ▷artificial intelligence and true distributed processing, promise further increases in computing power. More speculative is the idea of **quantum computers**, which would exploit such quantum mechanical properties as superposition and quantum entanglement of states to enable parallel processing on a large scale.

An **analog computer** is a device that deals with continuously varying physical quantities, such as current or voltage. Analog computers are used mainly for simulation or monitoring and controlling continuous processes in industry or scientific research (*see* CAD; CAM). Sometimes they are used in combination with a digital computer (a configuration known as a **hybrid computer**).

● **computer-aided design** ▷*See* CAD.

● **computer-aided manufacture** ▷*See* CAM.

● **computer animation** ▷*See* animation; computer graphics.

● **computer graphics** ▶ The storage, manipulation, and reproduction of diagrams and pictures on a computer system. The illustrations in computer graphics range in complexity from simple line drawings, graphs, histograms, etc., through to full-colour high-quality photographs and three-dimensional images. The images can be output on a screen, paper, or film. In advanced printing processes pictures (and text) are directly transferred to a printing plate.

Data for computer graphics can be stored in a number of different file formats, but there are two main types. In **raster** (*or* bitmap) **graphics** the data represents lines of dots of different colours making up the picture much as the picture is formed on a television screen. Photographs and high-quality colour artwork are stored in this form. The picture can be originated using certain types of on-screen painting programs or may be scanned from an original hard copy. Images of this type can also be produced using ▷digital photography or can be captured as single frames from a video (vidcaps). Sophisticated picture-editing software exists enabling the user to change the colours and retouch photographs.

The other form of representation involves **vector graphics**. In this, lines, curves, etc., are represented by mathematical formulas rather than by individual dots. Vector illustrations can be created by a number of drawing programs. They are easy to edit and resize and are commonly used for diagrams that need clean crisp lines, as in scientific illustrations or computer-aided design.

Three-dimensional drawing and editing programs also exist. These typically produce a vector image of the framework of the shape in the form of a "wire frame." This may then be converted into a three-dimensional raster image with textured surfaces and different lighting effects—a process known as **rendering**. Three-dimensional graphics can be viewed from any direction. They are particularly useful in architectural and engineering design.

Computer animation is the use of computer graphics to obtain moving images, either by changing a picture with time or by sequentially displaying a series of separate images. Such techniques are extensively used in computer games and to create animated features or special effects for the cinema.

● **computerized tomography** ▷*See* tomography.

● **computer language** ▷*See* program, computer.

● **computer virus** ▶ An unauthorized computer program that exploits weaknesses in a computer's operating system to insert itself into the system; it then propagates itself to other machines via networks or disks. When activated it interferes with the machine's operation, and in some cases destroys data held on the machine. Computer viruses are a growing menace. ▷*See also* hacking.

● **Comte, Auguste** ▶ (1798–1857) French philosopher. Often said to be the founder of sociology, he coined the term, although work of a sociological nature had been done before his time. He is remembered for his positivism (the view that society could be studied scientifically by natural-science methods and was subject to general laws); his Law of the Three Stages of intellectual development (theological, metaphysical, and positive); and his view that the theoretical sciences formed a hierarchy, with sociology at the peak. His principal work is *Cours de philosophie positive* (6 vols, 1830–42).

● **Conakry** ▶ (*or* Konakry) 9 25N 13 56W The capital of Guinea, a port in the SW on Tombo Island, which is linked to the mainland by a causeway. It was founded by the French in 1884 and became capital in 1893. Population (1995 est): 1 508 000.

● **concentration camps** ▶ Prisons in which large numbers of people are held without trial, usually on account of their politics or race. During the second ▷Boer War, the British detained Afrikaners in such camps, with the loss of some 20 000 lives, mainly from disease. In Germany, camps were first established by the Nazis in 1933 to detain communists and Social Democrats; they were later used to imprison minority groups, such as Gipsies, homosexuals, and, above all, Jews. In 1940 the Nazis established extermination centres, the most notorious being Auschwitz (*see* Oświęcim) and ▷Treblinka in Poland and Belsen, Dachau, and Buchenwald in Germany. An estimated 20 million people were gassed or died of disease or starvation in German camps, of which some 6 million were Jews (*see* Wannsee conference). Notorious for their torture, medical experiments on living people, and general brutality, the German camps challenged the validity of European and especially German civilization. Although many of the perpetrators were brought to trial after 1945 as war criminals, many others escaped justice. ▷*See also* holocaust.

In the Soviet Union forced labour camps were first established in 1917 and expanded greatly during Stalin's purges in the 1930s. They were used to detain political dissidents until the early 1990s.

● **Concepción** ▶ 36 50S 73 03W A city in S Chile, on the River Bío-Bío. It suffered damage (1939 and 1960) from earthquakes. Industries include steel processing and oil refining. Its university was founded in 1919. Population (1999 est): 362 589.

● **conceptual art** ▶ A type of modern art in which the ideas of the artist are more important than the artefacts used to convey them, which are often deliberately banal or ephemeral. Conceptual artists tend to use ▷ready-mades, documentary materials (such as videos and texts), or live performances to illustrate their ideas. The genre has its roots in the ▷dada movement but took its current form in the 1960s and 1970s, when many radical artists came to view the creation of marketable art objects as in some way reprehensible.

● **concertina** ▶ A hexagonal musical instrument of the reed-organ family, invented in 1829 by Sir Charles Wheatstone. The concertina is hand held and notes are produced by pressing buttons on panels at either end of the bellows.

● **concerto** ▶ A musical composition for one or more solo instruments and orchestra, usually in three movements (a ▷sonata form movement, a slow movement, and a rondo finale). In the late 18th century Mozart perfected the form in his piano concertos; later composers treated it more freely. In the baroque period the word concerto was applied to a variety of other compositions.

● **concerto grosso** ▷*See* Corelli, Arcangelo.

● **conch** ▶ A heavy-shelled marine ▷snail of the family *Strombidae* (about 80 species). Conch shells have a roughly triangular outer whorl with a broad lip and can be 2–35 cm long. Indo-Pacific spider conchs (genus *Lambis*) have long horns around the shell's aperture.

● **Conchobar** ▷*See* Cuchulain.

● **conciliarism** ▶ The view of those Roman Catholics who regarded a general council of the Church as a superior authority to the pope. First proposed in the early 13th century, the theory gained support especially in the 15th century. Pius II refuted the doctrine in his bull *Execrabilis* (1460).

● **Concord** ▶ 43 13N 71 34W A city in the USA, the capital of New Hampshire. Founded in 1725, it was the home of Mary Baker Eddy (the founder of Christian Science). Industries include printing and publishing. Population (1992): 36 364.

● **Concord** ▶ 42 28N 71 17W A city in the USA, in Massachusetts on the Concord River. The first battle of the American Revolution occurred here on 19 April, 1775. Ralph Emerson, Nathaniel Hawthorne, Louisa May Alcott, and Henry Thoreau all lived in Concord. Population (latest est): 17 080.

● **concordance** ▶ An index of words used in a single book or all the works of an author, with accompanying citations. Originally used for study of the Bible, concordances are now used as a method of textual analysis of major literary authors.

● **Concorde** The supersonic passenger aircraft built by an Anglo-French consortium consisting of the British Aircraft Corporation and Aérospatiale, which went into service with British Airways and Air France in 1976. This exceptionally beautiful artefact carries up to 139 passengers at a cruising speed of Mach 2 (twice the speed of sound) flying at 18 000 m. Its 24 years of safe and fast (35 hours) transatlantic flights ended in July 2000, when a Concorde of the French fleet crashed on take-off from Paris, killing 115 people. All Concordes thereafter were grounded for modification, not returning to service until November 2001.

● **concrete** ▶ A building material that was used by the Romans but in its modern form came into use after the invention of Portland ▷cement in 1824. Concrete consists of a mixture of a cement, usually Portland cement, and an aggregate of sand, gravel, and broken stones. The strength of the concrete depends on the proportion of cement to the quantity and type of aggregate. Water is added, causing the cement to harden around the aggregate. The material can be reinforced with steel bars (usually up to 50 mm in diameter) to increase its tensile strength. **Reinforced concrete** was invented in France in about 1850. In **prestressed concrete** the concrete is maintained in a state of compression by stretching the steel reinforcing wires (usually 6 mm in diameter) and keeping them in a state of tension after the concrete has set around them. Prestressed concrete is now widely used as a structural material as it has a reduced tendency to bend under load. Concrete parts may be precast in a factory or poured wet on site to harden, usually inside wooden shuttering.

● **concussion** ▶ The sudden and temporary loss of consciousness that may follow a head injury. On recovering consciousness the patient may be disorientated and confused, possibly with some loss of memory. Headache and blurred vision are also possible.

● **Condé** ▶ A French princely family, a branch of the ▷Bourbon royal house. Its first prince **Louis I** (1530–60) was a Huguenot leader during the French ▷Wars of Religion and was shot after being taken prisoner in battle. He was succeeded as Huguenot leader by his son **Henri I** (1552–88), who fled to Germany followiong the ▷St Bartholomew's Day Massacre of Huguenots (1572). Henri's grandson was the general **Condé the Great** (Louis II; 1621–86). During the Thirty Years' War he won victories against Spain at Rocroi (1643) and Lens (1648), subsequently being recalled to suppress the first ▷Fronde (civil war). In the second Fronde he joined the rebels and fled to Spain. After defeat by ▷Turenne at the battle of the Dunes Condé was pardoned and became one of Louis XIV's outstanding generals.

● **condensation** ▶ **1.** A change of physical state from a gas or vapour to a liquid. Thus as a gas is cooled below a certain temperature it may (depending on the pressure) condense the liquid. Condensation occurs in buildings when warm moist air comes in contact with cold surfaces, such as windows and uninsulated walls. **2.** A type of organic chemical reaction in which two molecules combine to form a larger molecule with elimination of a smaller molecule, such as water or methanol. Condensation reactions are the basis of a type of ▷polymerization process.

● **Condillac, Étienne Bonnot de** ▶ (1715–80) French philosopher and psychologist. His ideas in *L'origine des connaissances humaines* (1746), *Traité des systèmes* (1749), and *Traité des animaux* (1755) resemble ▷Locke's; all knowledge springs from the senses and association of ideas. After 1800 his high reputation waned, but modern psychology largely vindicates his work.

● **condition** ▶ A statement in logic that determines the truth of another statement. A **sufficient condition** always ensures the truth of the second statement. A **necessary condition** must be true if the second statement is true.

● **conditioned reflex** ▶ A ▷reflex response that is evoked by a stimulus other than that which normally produces it. A classic example is provided by ▷Pavlov's experiments with dogs. The normal stimulus causing salivation (i.e. food) was paired with a different stimulus (a ringing bell) so often that eventually the bell by itself caused the dogs to salivate. A conditioned reflex gradually disappears if the stimulus is presented repeatedly; this process is called extinction. ▷*See also* conditioning.

● **conditioning** ▶ The process of modifying behaviour by changing the stimuli (and therefore responses) associated with it. Classical conditioning occurs when a response is associated with a stimulus by pairing the stimulus with an event that causes the response by reflex (*see* conditioned reflex). Operant conditioning is brought about by either rewarding or punishing an action by the subject, which thus either encourages or discourages the behaviour (*see also* aversion therapy). ▷Behaviourism uses both forms of conditioning to explain how people learn.

● **condom** ▷*See* contraception; sexually transmitted disease.

● **condominium** ▶ The joint exercise of sovereignty over a territory by two or more sovereign states, usually brought about by treaty to resolve a territorial dispute. The New Hebrides (now the Vanuatu Republic) was until 1980 the subject of a condominium created by Britain and France in 1906. In some countries, such as the USA, the term applies to multiple ownership of a building by the residents.

● **condor** ▶ A huge South American ▷vulture, *Vultur gryphus*, found high in the Andes. It is black with a white ruff, bare pink head and neck, and has a wingspan of 3 m. It feeds chiefly on carrion but also takes lambs and young deer. The very rare Californian condor (*Gymnogyps californianus*) is smaller with a bare yellow head and red neck.

● **Condorcet, Marie Jean Antoine de Caritat, Marquis de** ▶ (1743–94) French philosopher and politician. Distinguished as a mathematician and progressive man of letters in the 1770s and 1780s, he was elected to the Legislative Assembly (1791) after the French Revolution. As a moderate ▷Girondin he was arrested when the ▷Jacobins became dominant in 1793 and died, perhaps by his own hand, in prison. His most famous work, *Esquisse d'un tableau historique des progrès de l'esprit humain*, was published posthumously (1795).

● **condottiere** ▶ A leader of a mercenary army employed by an Italian city or lord between the 14th and 16th centuries. The earliest condottieri (from Italian *condotta*, contract) were foreign, one of the most famous being Sir John Hawkwood (d. 1394), the English adventurer, but by the end of the 14th century the Italians began to raise their own mercenary armies. Condottieri, among them Francesco ▷Sforza of Milan and Cesare ▷Borgia, began to conquer territories for themselves. The system disappeared with the foreign invasions and changed warfare of the late 15th century.

● **conductance** ▷*See* resistance.

● **conduction** ▶ **1.** (thermal) The transfer of heat from a region of high temperature to one of lower temperature, without the transfer of matter. It occurs as a result of the transfer of kinetic ▷energy by collisions between atoms and molecules in gases, liquids, and non-metallic solids. In metals, which are the best thermal and electrical conductors, the energy is transferred by collisions between the free electrons that move through the crystal lattice and the ions of the lattice. **2.** (electrical) The passage of an electric current through a substance. In metals, the best conductors, it results from the passage of free electrons moving in one direction under the influence of an electric field. In a liquid conductor it is due to the passage of positive ions in one direction and negative ions in the other. In gases it is due to positive ions flowing in one direction and electrons in the other. In ▷semiconductors it results from the passage of electrons in one direction and positive holes in the other.

● **conductor** ▶ (music) The director of an orchestra, choir, opera, or ballet during its performance. Until the 19th century some of the responsibility for controlling a performance rested with a keyboard player or the first violin (the leader of an orchestra). Their task was to ensure that all the players started and finished together, came in on cue, and played at the same tempo. As the orchestra grew in the 19th century and orchestration became more subtle, more control was needed over the balance between the different sections of the orchestra. Moreover, one single person was required to control the way in which the music was to be interpreted. The practice therefore developed of having a conductor to beat time, usually with a baton, and to make recognizable gestures to enable the musicians to play together and produce a coordinated interpretation of the music.

Opera and ballet companies usually employ a resident conductor to prepare and control during performance their entire repertoire. Orchestras and choirs often make use of high-profile conductors, who prepare a performance at a few rehearsals and then direct the orchestra at one particular concert or recording session.

● **cone** ▶ (botany) The structure, also called a strobilus, that bears the reproductive organs (sporophylls) in some flowerless vascular plants (e.g. club mosses, horsetails, and conifers). In conifers both male and female cones are produced: the cones of pines, larches, etc., are female strobili, made up of overlapping woody structures called bract scales, which bear the sporophylls in their axils.

● **coneflower** ▷*See* black-eyed Susan.

● **cone shell** ▶ A carnivorous marine ▷gastropod mollusc of the family *Conidae* (about 400 species), occurring in warm seas. 1–30 cm long and cone-shaped, the highly coloured and patterned shells are prized by collectors. The molluscs have a venomous sting and some can be dangerous to man.

● **Coney Island** ▶ 40 35N 73 59W A resort in the USA, in New York City on the S shore of Long Island. With its amusement parks, fine beach, and the New York Aquarium it attracts many tourists.

● **Confederate States** ▶ The 11 southern states of the USA that seceded from the Union (1860–61), precipitating the US ▷Civil War. A provisional government was established in February, 1861, before the outbreak of war (April, 1861) and was signed by South Carolina, Georgia, Texas, Virginia, Arkansas, Tennessee, North Carolina, Mississippi, Florida, Alabama, and Louisiana. Jefferson ▷Davis (Mississippi) was elected president and Alexander H. Stephens (1812–83; Georgia), vice president The Confederate States' decentralized government reflected the southern concern with ▷states' rights but its loose organization made efficient conduct of the war difficult. Unable to levy taxes, the government instead issued unguaranteed currency and created massive inflation. No foreign government ever recognized the legitimacy of the Confederacy.

● **Confederation of British Industry** ▶ (CBI) The employers' federation in the UK. The CBI formulates industry's views on economic matters and is consulted by the government. It was formed in 1965 from the Federation of British Industry, the National Association of British Manufacturers, and the Union of British Employers Confederation. President: Sir Clive Thompson.

● **Confederation of the Rhine** ▶ (1806–13) The union of the German states (except Austria and Prussia) under ▷Napoleon I. It facilitated the subsequent movement for German unification, which was achieved in 1871.

● **Confessing Church** ▶ A movement among German Evangelicals opposed to the rise of Nazism in the 1930s and to the pro-Nazi German Christian League. Developing from the Pastors' Emergency League of 1933, it was led by Martin ▷Niemöller and was openly active until World War II, when it was forced underground. It continued as a movement within the Evangelical Church after 1945.

● **confession** ▶ The admission of sins made by a penitent seeking forgiveness of them. As a religious practice it originated in Judaism and was taken over by the early Christian Church, in which public confession was customary. The fourth ▷Lateran Council (1215) made auricular confession (private confession to a priest, who is empowered to grant absolution) incumbent on all Christians once a year. In the Roman Catholic and Orthodox Churches auricular confession is part of the ▷sacrament of penance. Many Protestant Churches use a form of general confession, made by the whole congregation in public worship, although auricular confession is also practised in some Anglican and Lutheran Churches.

● **confirmation** ▶ A Christian rite generally held to complete the initiation of a member into the Church. Originally associated with ▷baptism, it became separated with the spread of infant baptism and in the middle ages came to be regarded as one of the seven ▷sacraments. In the Eastern Orthodox Church, it is administered by a priest immediately after baptism and followed by Holy Communion; in the West, it is usually conferred by a bishop—in the Roman Catholic Church not before the seventh birthday and in the Anglican Churches after the candidate has undergone instruction in the faith (traditionally at the age of 11 or 12 but now very often as an adult).

● **Confucianism** ▶ The traditional philosophy and, until recently, the state religion of China. It was founded in the 5th century BC by ▷Confucius, whose teaching is contained in five classical works or canonical books (not all of which were actually written by Confucius). While retaining the idea of a divine will (*ming*), Confuciansim emphasizes the moral duty of man to his fellows. Man is born good; the superior man follows his true nature and develops sincerity, fearlessness, compassion, and wisdom. Precise rules of conduct are recorded, regulating social intercourse and establishing the forms of ritual sacrifice to one's ancestors. The canonical books also include works on divination, poetry, and history. Although not sanctioned in China since the Cultural Revolution of 1966–68, Confucianism is still practised by expatriate Chinese and, as a fundamental ethical attitude, continues to influence Chinese culture.

● **Confucius** ▶ (Kong Zi *or* K'ung-fu-tzu; c. 551–479 BC) Chinese philosopher, the founder of ▷Confucianism. As a minor official in his native Lu, a small state situated in modern Shandong province, he gathered numerous disciples, mainly young gentlemen who wished to enter government service. Promoted to ministerial rank, he became famous for his just and effective policies, but on the ruler's refusing to heed his advice, he left Lu (c. 496) and spent many years wandering from court to court, seeking a prince receptive to his ideas. Most of the works attributed to him are later compilations but the *Analects* (*Lun Yu*) is probably an authentic collection of his sayings.

● **conga** ▶ A modern Cuban dance in march time in which the second beat in alternating measures is accompanied by a 16th note. Originally a parade dance performed by a line of people, it was popularized by the Spanish bandleader Xavier Cugat (c. 1900–90).

● **conger eel** ▶ A voracious ▷eel belonging to a family (*Congridae*; about 100 species) found in all oceans. 1–3 m long, conger eels have a greyish or blackish body with a paler belly, a large head, and a wide mouth with strong teeth.

● **conglomerates** ▶ Sedimentary rocks consisting of rounded fragments of former rocks cemented together, usually in sand. These fragments are over 2 mm in diameter and generally consist of hard material, such as quartzite or granite. Some conglomerates are used for crushed stone for road making and other purposes.

● **Congo, Democratic Republic of** ▶ (name from 1971 until 1997: Zaïre) A large country in central equatorial Africa, with a short coastline on the Atlantic Ocean. The central part is dominated by a vast plateau, rising to the Ruwenzori Mountains in the SE. It is drained by the Congo River and its many tributaries and fringed along its E border by a chain of lakes, including Lake Tanganyika, comprising part of the ▷Great Rift Valley. Most of the population is African, the largest groups being Luba, Mongo, and Kongo.

Economy: in the 1990s the economy suffered gravely from hyperinflation, government corruption, and reductions in foreign aid, followed by successive civil wars from 1997. Agricultural production has also fallen owing to drought. The chief cash crops are palm oil, coffee, cotton, and rubber; maize, rice, and cassava are grown extensively as the staple food crops. The country has rich mineral resources, principally copper (the chief export) from the Shaba mines, and is the world's chief producer of industrial diamonds and cobalt. Other minerals include manganese, zinc, gold, and uranium; offshore oil has been exploited since 1975. Hydroelectricity is a valuable source of power and the country is estimated to have 50% of Africa's potential capacity. The rivers, especially the Congo River, are also important for transport. The country has a very large external debt.

History: when the Portuguese penetrated the region in the late 15th century it was dominated by the kingdom of the Kongo. In the late 19th century it was explored by Livingstone and, under Belgian auspices, by Stanley. Leopold II of the Belgians established personal rule over the Congo Free State, which was recognized by the European powers at the Conference of Berlin (1884–85). In 1908 it was annexed by Belgium, becoming the colony of the Belgian Congo. Independence was obtained in 1960, as the Democratic Republic of the Congo. The almost immediate secession of Katanga province resulted in civil war in which the UN intervened (an international force remained in the country until 1964). In 1965 ▷Mobutu Sese Seko seized power and in 1971 the country was renamed Zaïre. In 1977–78 invasion forces twice entered Zaïre from Angola, in unsuccessful attempts to topple Mobutu; on the second occasion a massacre of Europeans brought French and Belgian forces to Zaïre. In 1978 Zaïre

became a one-party state: violent demonstrations in 1990 led to moves towards a multiparty system in 1991. However, Mobutu attempted to undermine the transitional government (elected in 1992), even setting up his own rival government (1993–94). The impasse led to economic collapse. In 1996 civil war erupted when Tutsi rebels in E Zaïre attacked Hutu militiamen who had taken refuge from Rwanda. By June 1997 the rebels held most of the country and Mobutu fled. The rebel leader, Laurent Kabila, became head of state and the country reverted to the name Democratic Republic of Congo. In August 1998 many of Kabila's former supporters rebelled against his rule and civil war erupted again. While the rebels found backing from Rwanda and Uganda, Angolan and Zimbabwean forces entered the country to support Kabila. Although the national governments signed a peace accord in 1999, fighting subsequently resumed. Laurent Kabila was killed during a coup attempt in January 2001 and succeeded by his son, Joseph Kabila.

Democratic Republic of Congo

Head of state	President Joseph Kabila
Official language	French
Official currency	Congolese franc
Area	2 345 409 sq km (895 348 sq mi)
Population (2000 est)	51 965 000
Capital	Kinshasa
Main port	Matadi

● **Congo-Brazzaville, Republic of** ▶ (name until 1960: Middle Congo; name from 1960 to 1999: Republic of Congo) A country in W central Africa, bordering on the Congo River. The narrow coastal plain rises to hills inland and lower valleys in the E provide fertile grasslands. The uplands give way to plains in the NE. The population is composed chiefly of Bantu tribes.

Economy: largely agricultural, the main cash crops being sugar cane, palm oil, cocoa, and tobacco. Minerals include lead, zinc, and gold, and oil was discovered in 1969. Forests cover about half the country and timber is one of the main exports; others include sugar and cassava. The country has a large external debt.

History: in the 15th century the Portuguese established trading relations with the Congo kingdom. In the 19th century the exploration of the Frenchman de ▷Brazza led to the establishment of the colony of Middle Congo, which in 1910 became one of the four territories of French Equatorial Africa. In 1958 it attained internal self-government as a member of the French Community and in 1960 became independent as the Republic of Congo. In 1968 Maj Marien Ngouabi came to power in a military coup and in 1970, under a new Marxist constitution, the country was renamed the People's Republic of the Congo. Ngouabi was assassinated in 1977 and the government was taken over by a military committee under Col Joachim Yhombi Opango until his resignation in 1979. Plans for a multiparty system were endorsed by a referendum in 1992 and elections were held in 1993. However, the result was disputed, leading to fighting between rival militias. In 1997 rebel troops ousted President Pascal Lissouba and reinstated the former military leader Denis Sassou Nguesso. Presidential elections in 2002 resulted in victory for Nguesso.

Republic of Congo-Brazzaville

Head of state	President Denis Sassou Nguesso
Official language	French
Official currency	CFA (Communauté financière africaine) franc of 100 centimes
Area	342 000 sq km (132 018 sq mi)
Population (2000 est)	2 831 000
Capital	Brazzaville
Main port	Pointe-Noire

● **congo eel** ▶ A large eel-like North American nocturnal ▷salamander of the genus *Amphiuma* and family *Amphiumidae* (2 species). The two-toed *A. means* grows to 85 cm and the three-toed *A. tridactylum* up to 115 cm. Both are grey-brown and feed on snails, crayfish, etc., in swamp habitats.

● **Congo River** ▶ (name from 1971 until 1997: Zaïre River) The second longest river in Africa. Its true source is disputed, one headstream being the River ▷Lualaba and the other the River Chambezi (later the River Luvua), which rises in a high plateau between Lakes Malawi and Tanganyika. Below the confluence of the two headstreams it flows N, being known as the Lualaba until the Boyoma Falls, where it becomes the Congo River. It flows W then SW, through Malebo Pool, to enter the Atlantic Ocean via a delta at Boma. The river is an important potential source of hydroelectric power with the construction of dams in the 1970s. Length: 4820 km (3000 mi).

● **Congregationalism** ▶ In Christianity, a form of church government in which centralized authority is rejected and each congregation is democratically autonomous. Congregationalist groups were active at the time of the Reformation, and in England the Independents, as they were known, were prominent during the Commonwealth, having played an important part in the opposition to Charles I. Congregationalism spread to America, where it flourished. In England and Wales, the ▷United Reformed Church was founded in 1972 by the union of most of the Congregationalists with the English Presbyterians.

● **Congress** ▶ The legislature of the USA instituted by the constitution (1789) and comprising the Senate, the upper house, and the House of Representatives, the lower house. The Senate serves as a check on the larger House of Representatives, with which it has equal legislative responsibility as well as further powers to ratify treaties and confirm appointments. Each state in the Union is equally represented by two senators, who must be at least 30 years old. There are 435 seats in the House of Representatives, which are allocated among the states according to population. Representatives, who must be at least 25 years old, are subject to re-election every two years. Only the House may originate revenue bills and initiate the impeachment of the ▷president.

● **Congress Kingdom of Poland** ▶ (1815–32) A Polish state, formed at the Congress of ▷Vienna, having administrative autonomy under the Russian Crown. Polish nationalists twice attempted to overthrow Russian dominance but were unsuccessful: after the November Insurrection (1830), Congress Poland lost its autonomy and following the January Insurrection (1863–64), it became a Russian province.

● **Congreve, William** ▶ (1670–1729) British dramatist. Born in Yorkshire and educated in Ireland, he returned to England in 1688 to study law but under the patronage of ▷Dryden entered the literary world instead. The comedies *Love for Love* (1695) and *The Way of the World* (1700) are his best-known plays, although his contemporaries most admired his tragedy *The Mourning Bride* (1697). He wrote little after 1700 and lived off various civil service sinecures.

● **conic section** ▶ Geometrical figures produced by the intersection of a plane and a cone. If the plane cuts the cone at right angles to its axis the figure is a ▷circle. If the plane is tilted slightly an ▷ellipse is formed. If the plane is tilted further, until it lies parallel to the side of the cone, the figure is a ▷parabola. Tilted more, the figure becomes

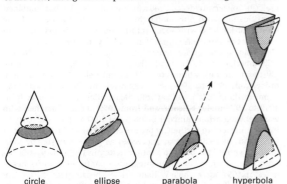

circle   ellipse   parabola   hyperbola

conic section ▶ The circle, ellipse, parabola, and hyperbola are produced by slicing through the cone as shown.

a ▷hyperbola. In the case of a hyperbola, the plane also intersects another cone the vertex of which touches the vertex of the first cone, the axes of the two cones being parallel. In this case two conic sections are produced. Therefore a hyperbola has two branches.

● **conifer** ▶ A ▷gymnosperm tree of the widely distributed phylum *Coniferophyta* (550 species), most abundant in the colder temperate zones, especially in the north; elsewhere they are usually found at high altitudes. Conifers are typically pyramidal in form, with a straight continuously growing stem that can reach great heights (*see* sequoia). Nearly all conifers are ▷evergreen (larches are exceptions), with simple needle-like or scalelike leaves. The reproductive organs are typically borne in separate male and female ▷cones, usually on the same tree, and produce winged seeds that are dispersed by wind (the yew and juniper are exceptions). The wood of conifers—called softwood—is economically important, being used for construction and as a source of paper pulp, etc. (*see* timber).

The principal families are the *Pinaceae* (pines, cedars, spruces, firs, larches, hemlocks, etc.); *Cupressaceae* (cypresses, junipers, arbor vitae, etc.); *Taxodiaceae* (sequoias, swamp cypress, etc.); *Taxaceae* (yews); and *Araucariaceae* (monkey puzzle, etc.).

● **Coniston Water** ▶ A lake in NW England, in Cumbria in the Lake District. World water-speed records were established here by Sir Malcolm Campbell (1939) and his son Donald Campbell (1959). Length: 8 km (5 mi).

● **conjugation** ▶ The process by which exchange of genetic material occurs in certain lower organisms by means of a connection between the cytoplasm of the two "mating" individuals. In ciliate protozoa and certain algae it is a type of sexual reproduction, the gametes (or gametic nuclei) passing through a cytoplasmic bridge (protozoa) or a conjugation tube (algae). In bacteria the connection between cells is by means of special hairs (pili) or cell-to-cell bridges.

● **conjunction** ▶ An alignment of two celestial bodies in the solar system, usually the sun and a planet, that occurs when the angular distance between them as seen from earth (i.e. the angle planet-earth-sun) becomes zero.

● **conjunctivitis** ▶ Inflammation of the conjunctiva—the membrane that covers the surface of the eye and lines the eyelids. Popularly known as pinkeye, it is marked by itching, redness, and watering of the eye. It may be caused by allergy, bacterial infection, or mechanical irritation.

● **Conn** ▶ (2nd century AD) King of Leinster and High King of Ireland. A tireless warrior, known as Conn of the hundred battles, he gained control over the whole of Ireland.

● **Connacht** ▶ (*or* Connaught) A province and ancient kingdom of NW Ireland. It consists of the counties of Galway, Leitrim, Mayo, Roscommon, and Sligo. Area: 17 122 sq km (6611 sq mi). Population (1996 est): 433 000.

● **Connaught** ▷*See* Connacht.

● **Connecticut** ▶ A state in the NE USA, in New England. Uplands in the E and W are separated by the central lowlands, which are drained by the Connecticut River. It is one of the most densely populated states in the USA. Manufacturing is important and traditionally produced goods are clocks, silverware, and brass products, as well as military equipment. Hartford is one of the principal insurance centres in the USA. Farming is only a minor activity producing dairy products, eggs, poultry, and vegetables for local markets with some tobacco for export. Yale University at New Haven is the most famous of its large number of universities and colleges.

History: one of the original 13 colonies in the USA, it was first explored by the Dutch in the early 17th century. The first settlement was by English colonists from the Massachusetts Bay Colony (1633–35). Area: 12 973 sq km (5009 sq mi). Population (1996 est): 3 274 238. Capital: Hartford.

● **connective tissue** ▶ The tissue that supports, binds, or separates the specialized tissues and organs of the body. Connective tissue consists of a semifluid ground substance of polysaccharide and protein in which are embedded white collagen fibres, yellow elastic fibres, and various cells (including fibroblasts, which produce the ground substance and the fibres). The amount of collagen determines the toughness of the tissue. Specialized connective tissue includes fatty tissue, blood, bone, and cartilage.

● **Connemara** ► An area in the W Republic of Ireland, in Co Galway bordering on the Atlantic Ocean. It contains many lakes, peat bogs, and the Twelve Bens, a group of quartzite mountains.

● **Connery, Sir Sean** ► (Thomas C.; 1929–) Scottish film actor who became famous as Ian Fleming's James Bond, a role he first played in *Doctor No* (1962). His other films include *The Hill* (1965), *The Man Who Would Be King* (1976), *The Name of the Rose* (1986), *Indiana Jones and the Last Crusade* (1989), *Rising Sun* (1993), *The Rock* (1996), and *Entrapment* (1999). He was knighted in 2000.

● **Connors, Jimmy** ► (1952–) US tennis player, who was Wimbledon singles champion in 1974 and 1982 and doubles champion in 1973. He also won the US singles title in 1974, 1976, 1978, 1982, and 1983 and the doubles title in 1975.

● **conquistador** ► (Spanish: conqueror) One of the men who conquered the Indians of Central and South America for Spain in the first half of the 16th century. Few in number, the conquistadores were driven by a fanatical desire to find fame and gold and to serve the Roman Catholic Church. The most famous were Hernán ▷Cortés and Francisco ▷Pizarro.

● **Conrad II** ► (c. 990–1039) German king (1024–39), who founded the Salian dynasty (1024–1125), and Holy Roman Emperor (1027–39). He conquered part of Poland (1028) and Burgundy (1033–34). While attempting to suppress a rebellion in N Italy (1036–38), he lost most of his army in an epidemic.

● **Conrad III** ► (1093–1152) The first Hohenstaufen German king (1138–52). He was proclaimed antiking (1127) in opposition to Lothair, after whose death (1137) he became king. His election was opposed by the Welf family and although peace was made in 1142 the conflict between the two families was renewed, giving rise to the ▷Guelf and Ghibelline struggle. In 1147 Conrad joined the second Crusade.

● **Conrad, Joseph** ► (Teodor Josef Konrad Watęcz Korzeniowski; 1857–1924) Polish-born British novelist, who knew no English before he was 20. Orphaned at the age of 11, he went to Marseilles in 1874, where he became a sailor, serving for 16 years in the British Merchant Navy. He became a naturalized British subject in 1886, and published his first novel, *Almayer's Folly*, in 1895. His seagoing experiences influenced both the themes of his fiction and his own moral outlook. His major novels include *Lord Jim* (1900), *Nostromo* (1904), *The Secret Agent* (1907), and *Under Western Eyes* (1911).

● **consanguinity** ► Relationship by blood, either real or putative. However, many societies do not consider everyone to whom they are genetically related to be blood kin. For example, some societies do not consider a father to be genetically related to his children and therefore they are not his consanguines. Consanguinity affects laws regarding property inheritance and prohibits marriage between close blood relatives. For instance, in the UK a man may not marry his grandmother, aunt, or niece and a woman may not marry her grandfather, uncle, or nephew, although sexual intercourse with the relation may not amount to ▷incest. Before 1986 it was illegal in the UK for a man to marry his mother-in-law, a prohibition based on an erroneous view of consanguinity; this form of marriage is now permitted provided that both the man's former wife and her father are dead.

● **Conscience, Hendrik** ► (1812–83) Flemish novelist. The author of over a hundred novels, he began writing sketches in Flemish in the late 1830s, and his historical romance *The Lion of Flanders* (1838) was the first major Flemish novel.

● **conscientious objection** ▷*See* pacifism.

● **conscription** ► The compulsory enlistment of recruits for military service. Conscription occurred in the ancient world and during the middle ages, when short-term ▷militia service was enforced for local defence. Universal male conscription was introduced in Revolutionary France in 1793 and in the early 1800s was adopted by Prussia. During the 19th century conscription was practised by most European powers and during the Civil War (1861–65) by the USA. Britain

did not adopt conscription in modern times until World War I, when in 1916 the compulsory recruitment of unmarried men, and shortly afterwards of married men, aged 18–41 was introduced. The first peacetime conscription was enforced in Britain in 1939 and after the outbreak of World War II women were compulsorily recruited for the first time (1941). The National Service Act of 1947 provided for a maximum annual conscription of 150 000 men. Conscription was abolished in Britain in 1962. In the USA, where it had also been adopted in both World Wars, conscription lasted until 1973. ▷*See also* pacifism.

● **Consejo Real** ► (Spanish: Royal Council) The central organ of government in Spain, created in 1386 in Castile by Juan I. It was dominated by the clergy and nobility until the reforms of Isabella I in 1480 replaced them with lawyers loyal to the Crown. It survived, with diminishing power, until the 19th century.

● **Consentes Dii** ► The 12 major Roman and Etruscan gods, six male and six female. They are Jupiter and Juno, Neptune and Minerva, Mars and Venus, Apollo and Diana, Vulcan and Vesta, Mercury and Ceres. They were first collectively mentioned in 217 BC.

● **conservation** ► The rational use of the earth's resources so that life can be sustained indefinitely. Pressure on both mineral and natural resources, resulting from increased agricultural and industrial activity, has required urgent examination of the consequent effects on the world ecosystem. The prudent use of fossil fuels (*see also* greenhouse effect) and minerals and the search for alternatives (*see* alternative energy) are becoming both political and economic necessities. The destruction of many natural habitats has led to the creation of nature reserves and national parks where wildlife can be protected. Legislation (*see* endangered species) can protect some rare species of animals and plants from extinction but international cooperation is needed to protect economically important species (including whales), to conserve fish stocks, and to prevent ▷pollution of the atmosphere and the oceans. In most cases the means to solve these problems are available but their high costs, or conflict with sectional interests, prevent their implementation. ▷*See also* forest.

● **conservation laws** ► A set of scientific laws stating that the total value of a specified physical quantity remains constant, in a closed system, for any changes that may take place in the system. An example is the **law of conservation of energy**, which says that, in a closed system, energy can neither be created nor destroyed—it can only be transformed from one form into another. Mass (or amount of substance) is another conserved quantity—the **law of conservation of mass**. According to the theory of ▷relativity, mass and energy are equivalent (related by Einstein's equation, $E = mc^2$, where E is energy, m mass, and c the speed of light). This leads to the **law of conservation of mass-energy**, in which the total of the mass and energy equivalents remains constant. Other conserved quantities include electric charge, linear momentum, and angular momentum.

● **Conservative Party** ► A UK political party that grew out of the ▷Tories in the 1830s under the leadership of Sir Robert ▷Peel. His repeal of the ▷Corn Laws (1846) caused a split in the party, with the Peelites later joining the Liberal Party. Under the leadership of ▷Disraeli the Conservatives acquired a distinct philosophy that combined identification with the monarchy, the British Empire, and the Church of England with social reform. Under ▷Salisbury and then ▷Balfour the party was almost continuously in power from 1886 to 1905 and again, under Bonar ▷Law, Stanley ▷Baldwin, Neville ▷Chamberlain, and ▷Churchill, from 1922 to 1945, being the dominant party in the coalitions of 1931–35 and 1940–45. It was again in office from 1951 to 1964, led successively by Churchill, Eden (*see* Avon, Anthony Eden, 1st Earl of), ▷Macmillan, and ▷Home, from 1970 to 1974 under ▷Heath, and from 1979 under ▷Thatcher, who was reelected prime minister in 1983 and 1987 and led the party in its commitment to furthering private enterprise and rewarding the successful. In 1990 she was succeeded as prime minister by John ▷Major, who led the party to another victory in 1992. The party's disunity over further European integration contributed to its heavy defeat in 1997, after which William ▷Hague became leader. The Conservatives suffered a second crushing defeat in 2001 and Hague was succeeded by Iain ▷Duncan Smith as leader.

● **consols** ▷*See* gilt-edged security.

John Constable ▶ Self-portrait in pencil and watercolour.

● **Constable, John** ▶ (1776–1837) British landscape painter, born in East Bergholt, Suffolk, the son of a miller. After working for his father, he trained in London at the Royal Academy schools, where he studied ▷Ruisdael and Claude. He painted the Suffolk countryside, Hampstead Heath, and Salisbury Cathedral with a particular concern for changing weather conditions, exemplified in *The Leaping Horse* (1825; Royal Academy) and *Dedham Vale* (1828; National Gallery, Edinburgh). Although he exhibited regularly at the Royal Academy, he was only elected a member in 1829. He achieved greater recognition in France, where his *Haywain* (National Gallery, London) won a gold medal and influenced ▷Delacroix. In his last years he assisted in the publication of mezzotints of his landscapes and painted in a gloomier more restless style after the death of his wife (1828).

● **Constance** ▶ (German name: Konstanz) 47 40N 09 10E A town in SW Germany, in Baden-Württemberg on Lake Constance. Its 11th-century church was formerly a cathedral. Manufactures include textiles, computers, and chemicals. Population (latest est): 69 510.

● **Constance, Council of** ▶ (1414–18) The 16th ecumenical council of the Roman Catholic Church, which ended the ▷Great Schism by electing Pope ▷Martin V (1417). It decreed that the authority of a general council was superior to that of the pope. The heretics ▷Wycliffe and ▷Hus were condemned, and Hus was burned at the stake.

● **Constance, Lake** ▶ (German name: Bodensee) A lake on the River Rhine in W Germany, Switzerland, and Austria. Area: 531 sq km (205 sq mi).

● **Constanţa** ▶ 44 10N 28 40E The chief seaport of Romania, situated on the Black Sea. Founded by the Greeks in the 7th century BC, it was rebuilt by Constantine the Great in the 4th century AD. Oil is pumped here from the Ploieşti fields to be refined and exported. Population (1994 est): 348 575.

● **constantan** ▶ An alloy of 55% copper and 45% nickel. It is used in electrical equipment, such as resistors and ▷thermocouples, because it has a high electrical resistance that does not change with temperature.

● **Constantine** ▶ (ancient name: Cirta) 36 23N 6 29E A town in N Algeria. It was destroyed in 311 AD but rebuilt by Constantine the Great in 313 and renamed after him. The old town is popular with tourists and noted for its handicrafts. Population (latest est): 438 000.

● **Constantine I** ▶ (1868–1923) King of Greece (1913–17, 1920–22). Constantine led Greece to victory in the ▷Balkan War (1912–13) but unpopularly maintained neutrality in World War I and was forced to abdicate (1917). Recalled in 1920, he again abdicated following a military revolt against his war with Turkey.

● **Constantine II** ▶ (1940–) King of Greece (1964–67). In 1967, following a military coup, Constantine went into exile, eventually moving to Britain. In 1973 he was officially deposed and Greece became a republic. He married (1964) Princess Anne-Marie of Denmark (1946–).

● **Constantine VII Porphyrogenitus** ▶ (905–59 AD) Byzantine emperor (913–59). Constantine reigned (919–45) with his father-in-law and coemperor, Romanus I Lecapenus (d. 948); while Romanus ruled, Constantine devoted himself to studying and writing. His works *On Imperial Administration* and *Ceremonies of the Byzantine Court* are invaluable sources for Byzantine social and economic history.

● **Constantine, Learie Nicholas, Baron** ▶ (1902–71) West Indian cricketer, who also played for Lancashire. A brilliant all-round cricketer renowned for his fast bowling, he was also a distinguished public figure. A barrister, he was high commissioner in London for Trinidad and Tobago (1962–64), a member of the British Race Relations Board (1966), and rector of the University of St Andrews (1968).

● **Constantine the Great** ▶ (?285–337 AD) Roman emperor in the West (312–24) and sole emperor (324–37). The son of Constantius (c. 250–306), Roman emperor in the West (305–06), Constantine was acclaimed as his father's successor by his troops at York but did not secure his position until he had defeated his rival Maxentius (d. 312). He became sole emperor after defeating the Eastern emperor Licinius (c. 270–325; reigned 311–24). Constantine was the first Roman emperor to adopt Christianity. During his campaign against Maxentius he was reputed to have had a vision of the Christian cross with the words "In this sign, conquer." In 313 Constantine issued the Edict of Milan, which established toleration of Christians, and in 325 summoned the Council of ▷Nicaea, the first general council of the Church. He was baptized on his deathbed. Constantine introduced administrative and military reforms and founded Constantinople (*see* Istanbul).

● **Constantinople** ▷*See* Istanbul.

● **Constantinople, Councils of** ▶ Three general councils of the Christian Church. **1.** (381) The council that was summoned to end the Arian dispute (*see* Arianism) and assert the doctrine of the Council of ▷Nicaea. **2.** (553) The council that attempted to resolve the conflict between the ▷Nestorians and ▷Monophysites. **3.** (680) The council that condemned the ▷Monothelite heresy and asserted the doctrines of the Council of ▷Chalcedon concerning the dual nature of Christ's will.

● **constellations** ▶ The 88 areas into which the N and S hemispheres of the sky are now divided, using established boundaries. Each star, galaxy, or other celestial body lies within, or sometimes overlaps, the boundaries of one of the constellations and is often named in terms of this constellation. The constellations all have Latin names. They originally had no fixed limits but were groups of stars forming a distinctive pattern outlining a mythological hero, animal, etc. The constellations that can be observed at night depend on the latitude of the observer and change with the time of night and the time of year.

● **constitution** ▶ The principles according to which a country is governed. Constitutions may be written or unwritten. The UK has an unwritten constitution comprising some statutes, much ▷common law, and a good deal of custom. The **US constitution** was drawn up in 1787, ratified in 1788, and came into effect in 1789. It contains 7 articles and 27 amendments of which 10 constitute the ▷Bill of Rights (1791). It defines the separation of powers, designed as a system of checks and balances, between the legislature (*see* Congress), the executive (*see* president), and the judiciary (*see* Supreme Court of the United States). Amendments subsequent to the Bill of Rights include the abolition of slavery (13), universal suffrage (15), and ▷Prohibition of liquor (18).

● **Constitutional Convention** ▶ (1787) An assembly of the delegates of 12 US states (Rhode Island alone abstained) that met in Philadelphia to draft the US constitution, which replaced the ▷Articles of Confederation. The Convention adopted a more centralized government and its "Great Compromise" was a bicameral congress with both proportional and equal representation. This allayed fears that large states would dominate a single-house legislature with proportional representation.

● **constrictor** ► A snake belonging to the family *Boidae* (70 species) occurring chiefly in tropical regions. Constrictors are nonvenomous and kill their prey by coiling their thick muscular body around it and squeezing until it suffocates. They often have claws, which are vestigial limbs. The family comprises two subfamilies, *Boinae* (*see* boa) and *Pythoninae* (*see* python).

● **constructivism** ► A movement in abstract sculpture, architecture, and design, which was launched in Russia by the *Realist Manifesto* (1920) of the brothers Naum ▷Gabo and Antoine ▷Pevsner with the aim of freeing contemporary art from political and social overtones. The chief principles were functionalism, the articulation of space, and the use of modern materials, such as plastic and steel. Many Russian constructivists left their country in 1922 because of state opposition. El ▷Lissitzky was influential at the ▷Bauhaus school, while Gabo spread the style to the UK and the USA.

● **consubstantiation** ► In Christian theology, a doctrine concerning the presence of Christ in the ▷Eucharist, especially associated with the teaching of Martin ▷Luther. Traditionally, the consecrated bread and wine were held to become, substantially, the body and blood of Christ (*see* transubstantiation). According to consubstantiation, the substances of the body and blood of Christ and of the bread and wine were held to coexist together in the consecrated Host.

● **consuls** ► The two magistrates who held supreme civil and military authority under the ▷Roman Republic. They were elected annually by the Comitia Centuriata (*see* comitia) and presided over the Senate. Under the Empire they were nominated by the emperor and held office for two to four months, the posts becoming honorary.

● **consumerism** ► The idea that consumers should influence the design, quality, service, and prices of goods and services provided by commercial enterprises. Movements based on this idea have developed in the USA (*see* Nader, Ralph) and in Europe as a response to the concentration of economic power in modern corporations and to the increased technical complexity of many contemporary consumer goods. Such organizations as the Consumers' Association in the UK, an independent non-profit-making body, established in 1957, which publishes its findings in its magazine *Which?*, carry out comparative tests on consumer goods and services and use their authority on consumers' behalf. Consumers' rights are protected in British law by such measures as the Trade Descriptions Act (1968), the Sale of Goods Act (1979), and the Consumer Protection Act (1987).

● **consumption** ► (economics) Expenditure on goods and services, excluding expenditure on capital goods (*see* investment). A country's national income is spent either on consumption or on investment. Public consumption consists of government spending on services, such as education, health, defence, etc. Private consumption is money spent by individuals on nondurables, such as food and drink, durables, such as cars and washing machines, and services, such as entertainment. There is some controversy as to whether private consumption is determined by an individual's lifetime prospects or his current income. This controversy has important consequences in economic planning: for example, whether or not tax cuts would reduce unemployment by increasing consumption.

● **contact lenses** ► A removable form of lens worn directly against the eye to replace spectacles for long or short sight, to protect the eye in some disorders of the cornea, or to apply drugs in the treatment of certain eye diseases. Invented in 1887 by Adolf Fick, they were originally made of glass. Modern lenses, developed by Kevin Tuohy in 1948, are made of plastic and can be hard (corneal), gas-permeable (allowing oxygen to permeate the cornea), or soft (hydrophilic).

● **Contadora Group** ► An organization of Central American countries created in 1983 to promote peace in the region. The original alliance was between Colombia, Mexico, Panama, and Venezuela; the ultimate aim is to establish a Central American parliament in imitation of the ▷European Community.

● **containerization** ► The use of large cuboid containers built to internationally accepted dimensions (usually $8 \times 8 \times 20$, 30, or 40 ft or $2.4 \times 2.4 \times 6.1$, 9.1, or 12.2 m) for the transport of goods. These containers are transported from the producing factory to the user, distributor, or export dock without being unpacked: thus they cut down on the cost and time involved in handling and reduce the chances of loss through pilferage or damage. Containerization has revolutionized international shipping, as specialized ships are needed.

● **conté crayon** ► A stick of soft crayon, named after its inventor, the French scientist Nicholas Jacques Conté (1755–1805). Unlike pastel, its colour is durable and nonsmudging, while its size makes it suitable both for line drawing and shading large areas.

● **contempt of court** ► An act or omission that tends to undermine the authority of a court or that is likely to prejudice the trial of an accused person. Examples are insulting a presiding judge or failing to comply with a court order; magistrates are not empowered to commit for contempt. The publication of matters *sub judice* (matters on which a court is to decide) is also a contempt. Contempt can be committed both inside and outside the court and in both civil and criminal proceedings. An offender may be fined or imprisoned.

● **continent** ► One of the following major land masses of the earth: Asia, Africa, North America, South America, Europe, Australia, and Antarctica. (These divisions do not correspond to the rigid plates into which the whole of the earth's crust is divided.) The continents occupy about 30% of the earth's surface area. The crust of which they are formed (mainly granitic) is less dense than the oceanic crust (basaltic). The constituents of the continental crust are called sial and those of the oceanic crust, sima. ▷*See also* continental drift.

● **Continental Congress** ► (1774–89) The body of representatives of the American colonies, which met in Philadelphia. The first Continental Congress (1774–75) was summoned to protest the ▷Intolerable Acts of the British parliament. With the outbreak of the ▷American Revolution, the second Continental Congress (1775–76) became the provisional government and proclaimed the ▷Declaration of Independence. In 1789 a permanent bicameral congress replaced the Continental Congress.

● **continental divide** ► A major ▷watershed separating the drainage basins of a continent. In North America a continental divide extends N–S along the Rocky Mountains dividing the rivers flowing E from those flowing W.

● **continental drift** ► The theory, first set out in 1912 by Alfred ▷Wegener and now widely accepted, that the continents drift slowly over the earth's surface (*see also* plate tectonics). Wegener's work was based on similarities in rock types, geological structures, flora and fauna, and the coastal outlines of the continents; in recent years geophysical data, particularly from geomagnetic studies, have provided firmer evidence for continental drift. It is believed that about 200 million years ago a supercontinent (termed Pangaea) began to break up (*see* Gondwanaland; Laurasia) and the fragments drifted apart until the continents reached their present positions. It is probable

continental drift ► The position of the continents (from left to right) 200 million years ago, 135 million years ago, and 65 million years ago.

that continents have been joining together and breaking up throughout the earth's history.

● **continental shelf** ▶ The area of sea floor adjacent to the continents, dipping gently from the shoreline to a depth of about 200 m. At this depth, the shelf edge, the continental slope begins, dipping more steeply to the ocean bottom. Shelves tend to be wider off low-lying regions; the average width is about 70 km.

● **Continental System** ▶ The trade blockade of Britain introduced by Napoleon in 1806 to ruin Britain's commerce and thus force peace on his own terms. Napoleon used his control of the coast from the Baltic to the Adriatic to forbid French allies or neutrals to trade with Britain or its colonies. Britain subjected all countries in alliance with France to counterblockade. The system failed because of the contraband trade and the new British markets in South America.

● **Contra** ▷See Nicaragua, Republic of.

● **contraception** ▶ The prevention of unwanted pregnancy, also known as birth control and family planning. Of the numerous methods available, the rhythm method and coitus interruptus are the simplest but least reliable. In the former sexual intercourse is avoided around the middle of the menstrual cycle, when ovulation is most likely to occur, estimated by monitoring body temperature, vaginal secretions, etc.; in the latter the penis is withdrawn from the vagina before ejaculation. Both the condom (or sheath), which is worn over the penis, and the diaphragm, which is fitted over the cervix of the uterus and should be used with a spermicidal jelly, are more effective since they prevent the sperm from entering the uterus. Condoms also protect against ▷sexually transmitted diseases and are recommended for "safe sex" in countering the spread of ▷AIDS and HIV infection. The female condom (e.g. Femidom), which is fitted into the vagina, offers similar protection. More reliable is the intra-uterine device (IUD)—a loop or coil, often impregnated with copper, that is inserted by a doctor into the uterus. Its method of action is not known. Some women, however, are unable to use an IUD as it causes side effects (such as heavy menstrual bleeding or recurrent infection). Since the 1960s, the most effective means of preventing pregnancy has been by taking hormonal pills (*see* oral contraceptive), but this, too, may produce side effects and is unsuitable for some women. Alternatively, hormonal contraceptives may be administered by means of skin patches. A long-term contraceptive method is the intramuscular injection, at two- or three-monthly intervals, of a synthetic hormone (progestogen). Permanent contraception is achieved by ▷sterilization, which includes vasectomy for men and cutting or blocking the Fallopian tubes for women. Recently developed methods for women include the hormonal "morning-after" pills, which must be taken within 72 hours of intercourse, only one course of which per cycle can be used; the administration of progestogen by means of a subcutaneous implant or a vaginal ring, which gradually release the hormone into the body; and hormonal IUDs (e.g. Mirena).

Family planning has had a long history, with early methods ranging from infanticide and abortion to the use of such preventive devices as sheep's bladders as condoms. The need for it, however, was not formally discussed until the beginning of the 19th century, when the writings of ▷Malthus drew attention to the problems of ▷overpopulation. Moral objections and the absence of an appropriate technology delayed the advent of the first family-planning clinics until the 1920s. In the UK they were pioneered by Marie ▷Stopes and in the USA by Margaret Sanger (1883–1966). Contraception is now an accepted means of controlling family size and population growth in most Western countries, even by Roman Catholics, who are forbidden to use mechanical or chemical means by their church, unless they have been, or are in danger of being, raped. However, in many parts of the developing world, where the combination of a rapidly expanding population with poverty and food shortages causes widespread distress, contraception has to be provided by governments and outside agencies, in the face of Catholic opposition.

● **contract** ▶ In law, an enforceable promise or bargain, usually written but sometimes oral. A simple promise for which nothing is given in exchange is not a contract and is only enforceable at law as a ▷deed. Something of value, called "consideration," must be exchanged in return for the promise; the value must be real but need

not be equivalent. Breach of contract, meaning failure to fulfil its conditions, may result in the offender being sued for damages.

● **contralto** ▶ The deepest female singing voice. Range: F below middle C to D an octave and a sixth above.

● **contrapposto** ▶ A technique in sculpture for resting a figure's weight on one leg to tilt the body in a realistic pose. Practised by ▷Polyclitus of Argos (5th century BC), it was revived during the Renaissance, notably in ▷Michelangelo's statue of David (Accademia, Florence).

● **Contreras, Battle of** ▶ (19–20 August, 1847) A battle of the ▷Mexican War fought near Mexico City. US forces under Gen Winfield Scott (1786–1866) routed the Mexican forces.

● **convection** ▶ The transfer of heat within a fluid by means of motion of the fluid. Convection may be natural or forced. In natural convection, the fluid flows by virtue of the warmer part being less dense than the cooler part. Thus the warmer fluid rises and the colder fluid sinks under the influence of gravity. In forced convection, some external cause, such as a fan, drives colder fluid into a warmer one, or vice versa.

● **Convention on International Trade in Endangered Species** ▷See endangered species.

● **convergence** ▶ (or convergent evolution) The development in unrelated animals of similarities resulting from adaption to the same way of life. Thus whales (mammals) and fish, both aquatic, have evolved similar features independently.

● **conversos** ▶ (Spanish: converts) The Spanish Jews who were forced to become Roman Catholics during the persecution of Jews in the late 14th and 15th centuries. The Spanish Inquisition was created to prevent the apostasy of *conversos* and the Muslim ▷Moriscos. ▷*See also* Marranos.

● **Convocations of Canterbury and York** ▶ The assemblies of the clergy of the two provinces of the Church of England. Dating from at least the 8th century, they were originally assemblies of bishops only. They later divided into two houses, an upper house composed of diocesan bishops and a lower house composed of certain lower clergy. The extent of their powers fluctuated, but essentially they exercised the right to tax themselves and managed to keep this prerogative until after the Restoration. From 1717 to 1852, however, they were prevented from dealing with questions of business and held only formal meetings. In 1969 many of their powers passed to the General Synod of the Church of England.

● **Convolvulus** ▶ A widely distributed genus of annual or perennial twining plants (about 250 species). The flowers are funnel or bell-shaped and attractive. The Eurasian ▷bindweed (*C. arvensis*) is a noxious weed with deep persistent roots and rapidly growing stems. Some species, such as *C. althaeoides*, are cultivated in gardens. Some have medicinal (purgative) properties. Family: *Convolvulaceae*.

● **Conwy** ▶ 53 18N 3 52W **1.** A market town and resort in North Wales, in Conwy county borough on the estuary of the River Conwy. A rare surviving example of a completely walled medieval town, it has a 13th-century castle. A tunnel under the estuary opened in 1991. Population (1991): 13 627. **2.** A county borough in N Wales created in 1996 from parts of Gwynedd and Clwyd. Area: 1130 sq km (436 sq mi). Population (1996 est): 70 200.

● **cony** ▷See hyrax; pika.

● **Coober Pedy** ▶ 28 56S 134 45E A town in central South Australia. It is an opal-mining centre producing over half the world's total output of opals. Many of the miners live underground to avoid the high temperatures, which often reach over 50°C (125°F). Population (latest est): 2078.

● **Cooch Behar** ▶ (or Kuch Bihar) 26 18N 89 32E A city in India, in West Bengal. It was the capital of the former state of Cooch Behar (until 1950). Population (latest est): 62 127.

● **Cook, Captain James** ▶ (1728–79) British navigator and cartographer. After working in ships engaged in the North Sea trade, he joined the Royal Navy (1755) and served in the Seven Years' War

(1756–63), during which he surveyed the St Lawrence River. His observations on the eclipse of the sun in 1766 were presented to the Royal Society, which gave him command of an expedition to Tahiti to observe the transit of the planet Venus across the sun and to search for Terra Australis, a presumed southern continent. The expedition set sail in the *Endeavour* in 1768 and, Venus observed, Cook went on to locate and chart New Zealand and the E coast of Australia, returning to England in 1771. The voyage was remarkable not least for the absence of scurvy among his crew–the result of a diet, devised by Cook, that was high in vitamin C. His second voyage (1772–75), in the *Resolution*, accompanied by the *Adventure*, achieved the circumnavigation of the Antarctic. He charted Easter Island and found New Caledonia, the South Sandwich Islands, and South Georgia Island. On his return he was made a captain and received the Royal Society's Copley Medal for his dietary work. On his third voyage (1776–79) he was killed in a quarrel with Hawaiians.

● **Cook, Sir Joseph** ▶ (1860–1947) Australian statesman, born in England; Liberal prime minister (1913–14). He was hampered by a majority of only one in the House of Representatives and a minority in the Senate.

● **Cook, Mount** ▶ (Maori name: Aorangi) 43 37S 170 08E The highest mountain in New Zealand, in South Island in the Southern Alps. It is permanently snow capped and flanked by glaciers. Height: 3764 m (12 349 ft).

● **Cook, Robin** ▶ (Robert Finlayson C.; 1946–   ) British Labour politician; foreign secretary (1997–2001) and leader of the house (2001–   ). He entered parliament in 1974 and held various front-bench posts from 1983, including opposition spokesman on foreign affairs (1994–97).

● **Cook, Thomas** ▶ (1808–92) British travel agent, who introduced conducted excursions and founded the travel agents Thomas Cook and Son. He organized his first excursion in 1841, a railway journey from Leicester to Loughborough for a temperance meeting.

● **Cookham-on-Thames** ▶ 51 34N 0 43W A village in SE England, in Maidenhead and Windsor unitary authority, Berkshire. A picturesque place on the River Thames, it was made famous by the paintings of Stanley ▷Spencer. Population (1991): 6096.

● **Cook Islands** ▶ A group of scattered islands in the SE Pacific Ocean, a New Zealand dependency. The chief islands are Rarotonga, Atiu, and Aitutaki. Fruit, copra, and mother-of-pearl are exported. Area: 241 sq km (93 sq mi). Population (1994): 18 500. Capital: Avarua.

● **Cookstown** ▶ A district in central Northern Ireland, in Co Tyrone. Area: 512 sq km (198 sq mi). Population (1996): 31 700.

● **coolabar** ▶ A tree, *Eucalyptus microtheca*, growing to 25 m, common inland in W Australia. The wood is grey near the outside, deep red within. Also called jinbul, moolar, blackbox, and dwarf box, it is used for building. Family: *Myrtaceae*. ▷See also Eucalyptus.

● **Coolidge, John Calvin** ▶ (1872–1933) US statesman; Republican president (1923–29). His presidency followed the scandals of the administration (1921–23) of Warren Harding (1865–1923) but Coolidge's own honesty was never questioned. He supported US business at home and abroad but did little to curb the speculation on the stock market that ended in the 1929 financial crash.

● **cool jazz** ▶ (or progressive jazz) A style of US ▷jazz developed on the W coast in the early 1950s. Cool jazz was characterized by subtle rhythms as well as by instruments and harmonies borrowed from European classical music. Less frenetic than ▷bop, cool jazz was also quieter and more economical. Important cool-jazz musicians include Stan Getz (1927–91), Miles ▷Davis, and Dave ▷Brubeck.

● **Cooper, Gary** ▶ (Frank James C.; 1901–61) US film actor. He is best known for his portrayals of tough but sensitive heroes in Hollywood westerns. These include *The Virginian* (1929), *The Westerner* (1940), and *High Noon* (1952).

● **Cooper, Sir Henry** ▶ (1934–   ) British boxer, European heavyweight champion (1964; 1968–71). Famous for his left, he is best remembered for knocking down Muhammed Ali in the fifth round of a non-title fight at Wembley. He was knighted in 2000.

● **Cooper, James Fenimore** ▶ (1789–1851) US novelist. Expelled from Yale, he served in the navy before his marriage in 1811. Financial need prompted him to start writing, and in *The Pioneers* (1823), his third novel, he portrayed for the first time the realities of frontier life. Sequels included *The Last of the Mohicans* (1826) and *The Pathfinder* (1840). A parallel series of novels about the sea included *The Red Rover* (1827) and *The Sea Lions* (1849). His democratic sympathies were strengthened during his stay in Europe from 1826 to 1833.

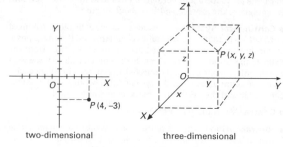

two-dimensional   three-dimensional

Cartesian coordinates

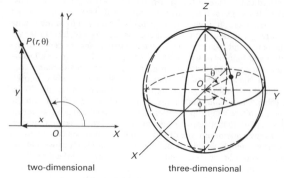

two-dimensional   three-dimensional

polar coordinates

● **coordinate systems** ▶ In two-dimensional Cartesian coordinates a point *P* is located by giving its *x*- and *y*-coordinates, in this case 4 and –3 (always given in this order, as shown). In three-dimensional Cartesian coordinates *P* is located in terms of three axes. In polar coordinates *P* is located by a radius *r* and an angle θ. In three dimensions a second angle, φ, is required. In the diagrams Cartesian coordinates are superimposed on the polar coordinates.

● **Cooper, Samuel** ▶ (1609–72) British miniaturist whose sitters included Cromwell, Charles II, and Cosimo III de' Medici. His bold sense of design and use of shadow, qualities usually associated with large-scale painting, are in marked contrast to Nicholas ▷Hilliard's miniature style. After his death he was often called "the Van Dyck in little."

● **cooperative societies** ▶ Societies set up to manufacture, buy, or sell produce, either without profit or with profits distributed to members or shareholders as dividends (i.e. a refund is made for every pound's worth of goods purchased from the cooperative). The cooperative movement was inspired by the British philanthropist Robert ▷Owen in the early 19th century and was seen as an alternative to the hardship that seemed to be caused by competition. Cooperative societies in agriculture, in which machinery is shared and produce is marketed jointly, are common in both the advanced and developing countries. In the UK the largest cooperative is the Cooperative Wholesale Society (CWS). The CWS distributes dividends to customers by way of stamps, issued in proportion to the value of purchases made, which are redeemable at a higher rate for shareholders than for ordinary customers.

● **Cooper Creek** ▶ (or Barcoo River) An intermittent river in E central Australia, in the ▷Channel Country. Rising in central Queensland it flows generally SW into Lake Eyre. Actual water flow in its lower reaches is irregular, occurring only in times of flood. The explorers Burke and Wills died here in 1861. Length: 1420 km (880 mi).

● **coordinated universal time** ▷*See* universal time.

● **coordinate systems** ▶ Geometrical systems that locate points in space by a set of numbers.

In **Cartesian coordinates**, devised by René ▷Descartes, a point is located by its distance from intersecting lines called axes. In a plane (two dimensions) there are two axes and in space (three dimensions) there are three. Usually the axes are at right angles to each other and are known as rectangular axes, but oblique axes are also used in exceptional circumstances.

Polar coordinates denote position by distance and direction. A fixed point, called the origin, and a fixed line, called the polar axis, are taken as the references. For any point, the polar coordinates are the length, r, of the radius of the circle centred at the origin and passing through the point, and the angle, q, between this radius and the polar axis. In three dimensions, spherical polar coordinates are used. The radius of a sphere centred at the origin and the two angles it makes with the polar axis define the point.

● **coot** ▶ An aquatic ▷rail of the genus *Fulica* (9 species). Coots have broadly lobed toes, diving deeply to feed on invertebrates and aquatic plants. The European coot (*F. atra*) occurs throughout the Old World and is 37 cm long with black plumage and a white bill and frontal shield.

● **copal** ▶ Any one of the many resins collected from living or fossilized tropical trees and used in the manufacture of varnishes and inks. Copals can vary from brownish-yellow to colourless.

● **Copán** ▶ 14 52N 89 10W A town in Honduras. Extensive ruins with temples, pyramids, astronomical stelae, and a ceremonial stairway remain from its heyday as a ▷Maya city (c. 300–900 AD). Population (1991): 21 200.

Copenhagen ▶ The statue of the Little Mermaid by the harbour in Copenhagen commemorates the city's association with the writer Hans Christian Andersen.

● **Copenhagen** ▶ (Danish name: København) 55 40N 12 35E The capital and chief port of Denmark, on the E coast of Sjælland. It is an industrial as well as a commercial and shipping centre, with engineering, food processing, and brewing. Notable buildings include the 17th-century Charlottenborg Palace (now the Royal Academy of Arts) and Christiansborg Palace (now the parliamentary and government buildings). An important centre of Scandinavian culture, Copenhagen possesses a university (1479) and several museums.
History: already a human settlement in the year 900 AD, it became capital of Denmark in 1443. Over the centuries it has been involved in many wars; it was attacked by the Hanseatic League in the middle ages and by Sweden in the 17th century. In 1801 the Danish fleet was destroyed by Nelson at the **Battle of Copenhagen**. In 1728, and again in 1795, it was badly destroyed by fire. Occupied by the Germans in World War II, it became the centre of a strong resistance movement. Population (1996 est): 1 362 264.

● **Copepoda** ▶ A class of ▷crustaceans (7500 species), mostly 0.5–2 mm long, that have long antennae, a single median eye, and no carapace. There are 11 pairs of appendages on the head and thorax and forked tail filaments (furca). Copepods occur in abundance in fresh and salt water, forming a constituent of plankton. Most feed on microscopic plants or animals but some are parasitic on fish, other crustaceans, etc. ▷*See also* Cyclops.

● **Copernicus, Nicolaus** ▶ (1473–1543) Polish astronomer, formulator of the modern heliocentric theory of the solar system. After studying mathematics and music at Cracow and Bologna, Copernicus became interested in the problem of calculating planetary positions, since existing tables were out of date. He noticed that by using a system in which the earth revolved round the sun, instead of ▷Ptolemy's geocentric system, these calculations would be much easier to make. He then realized that such a system could actually describe the solar system, rather than providing a simple working model of it, since it explained the occasional backward motion of the planets. Copernicus, realizing that these ideas were at variance with the Church's view that the earth was at the centre of the universe, only circulated them to a few friends. The full text of his book *De revolutionibus orbium coelestium* was not published until 1543: legend has it that Copernicus was presented with the first copy on his deathbed.

● **Copland, Aaron** ▶ (1900–90) US composer, a pupil of Nadia Boulanger. He was active as a teacher, pianist, and champion of contemporary music. He is best known for his compositions in a popular style, such as the ballets *Billy the Kid* (1938) and *Rodeo* (1942). His other works include a piano concerto (1927) in a jazz idiom, a *Piano Fantasy* (1950) using ▷serialism, and the tone poem *Inscape* (1967).

● **copper** ▶ (Cu) A reddish-brown metal, known from prehistoric times and named after the island of Cyprus, which was the principal source in Roman times. It occurs naturally as the native element, the sulphide chalcopyrite ($CuFeS_2$), the carbonate malachite ($CuCO_3.Cu(OH)_2$), and other minerals. It is mined in Zambia, the Democratic Republic of Congo, Chile, Australia, New Guinea, and elsewhere. Copper is extracted by smelting and electrolysis. It is malleable, ductile, and is important because of its good electrical (second only to silver) and thermal conductivity. Copper is widely used in the electrical industry and in the form of copper pipes in plumbing. It is contained in coins, and in the alloys ▷brass and ▷bronze. Common compounds are the oxides (Cu_2O, CuO) and copper sulphate ($CuSO_4$). At no 29; at wt 63.546; mp 1084.7°C; bp 2563°C.

● **Copperbelt** ▶ An area in central Africa, on the border between the Democratic Republic of Congo and Zambia. Rich in copper-ore deposits, it has the largest known deposits in the world, after the USA.

● **copperhead** ▶ A North American ▷pit viper, *Agkistrodon contortrix*, occurring in swampy or wooded regions. Up to 1 m long, it is reddish with a coppery head and brown bands on its back. A S Australian snake, *Denisonia superba*, about 1.5 m long and usually coppery-brown, is also called a copperhead.

● **Copperhead** ▶ A Northerner sympathetic to the South during the US ▷Civil War, especially one who opposed Lincoln's policies. Mostly midwestern Democrats, the Copperheads were accused of disloyalty to the northern cause and the Democratic Party suffered by association with them. The name derives from a newspaper reference comparing antiwar Democrats to copperhead snakes.

● **Coppermine River** ▶ A river in N Canada, in Mackenzie district. Rising in Lac de Gras, it flows NW past copper deposits into Coronation Gulf. Length: 845 km (525 mi).

● **coppicing** ▷*See* pollarding.

● **Coppola, Francis Ford** ▶ (1939–) US film director and writer. He is best known for *The Godfather* (1972) and *The Godfather, Part II* (1974), which depicted a Mafia family and together won nine Academy Awards; other films include *Apocalypse Now* (1979), *The Godfather, Part III* (1991), *Jack* (1996), and *The Rainmaker* (1998).

● **copra** ▷*See* coconut.

● **Coptic** ▶ A ▷Hamito-Semitic language spoken in Egypt from the early Christian period until the 8th century AD. It was the last stage of ancient Egyptian and was written in Greek characters with seven additional ▷demotic letters. There were six dialects of which Sahidic became the standard form in Upper Egypt after the 5th century. Bohairic of Lower Egypt was used for religious purposes by the Coptic Christians and has a literature of scriptural translations from Greek and original writings that reflect Gnostic and Manichaean tendencies.

● **Coptic Church** ▶ The largest Christian Church in Egypt. The Copts trace their history to St ▷Mark. As a result of its ▷Monophysite beliefs, which were condemned at the Council of Chalcedon (451), the Coptic Church became isolated from other Christian bodies. The Muslim conquest of Egypt in 642, together with language and cultural differences, widened the division. The Church suffered some persecution under Arab dominion. In 1741 a number of Copts entered the Roman Catholic communion, becoming the Uniat Coptic Church. Alexandria is the seat of the Coptic patriarch, who presides over the Church with 12 diocesan bishops. The Copts are in communion with the Armenian and Syrian (Orthodox) Churches.

● **copyright** ▶ A type of ▷intellectual property consisting of the rights of authors, composers, artists, photographers, publishers, and others who create or publish original works to reproduce or authorize others to reproduce their works. In the UK protection is given by the Copyright Act (1956), the Copyright, Designs, and Patents Act (1988), and the European Single Market Act (1992). The Copyright (Computer Software) Amendment Act (1985) extends copyright to computer programs. In EU countries copyright protection now lasts for 70 years after the death of the copyright holder (or the date of publication, if later). In the USA (since 1998) it lasts for 95 years after publication or until the death of the copyright holder, whichever is the later. In contrast to a ▷patent, copyright cannot exist in an idea, method, or scheme, but only in its expression. Infringement of copyright is known as piracy. Under the Universal Copyright Convention (1952, revised 1971), works must be marked with the symbol ©, the name of the copyright holder, and the date of first publication.

● **coracle** ▶ An ancient boat, usually round, made of wickerwork or laths over which a waterproofed animal skin has been stretched and fitted. Coracles were used in Ireland and in Wales and other parts of W Britain.

● **coral** ▶ A sedentary marine animal belonging to a class (*Anthozoa*) of ▷cnidarians. Individual corals—▷polyps—produce a protective skeleton that may be soft, horny, or stony. They usually occur in colonies and are found in all oceans, particularly warm shallow waters, feeding mainly on small animals. Reproduction can be asexual (by budding) or sexual, the eggs being fertilized in the water. The stony (*or* true) corals (order *Madreporaria*; about 1000 species) secrete a rigid external skeleton made of almost pure calcium carbonate. **Coral reefs** (*see* reef) are produced by succeeding generations of stony corals, occurring in colonies. Reef building occurs mostly at depths of less than 50 m and at temperatures above 20°C. Within this zone symbiotic algae (zooxanthellae) are present in coral tissues and stimulate the secretion of calcium carbonate, accelerating the growth of coral skeletons. The ▷Great Barrier Reef is the best-known example. In 1998 scientists warned that most of the world's coral reefs were dying, owing to the chemical effects of global warming.

● **Coralli, Jean** ▶ (J. C. Peracini; 1779–1854) Italian ballet dancer and choreographer. He trained in Paris and was choreographer at the Paris Academy from 1831 to 1845. He choreographed many of the most celebrated Romantic ballets, including *Giselle* (1841) and *La Peri* (1843).

● **Coral Sea** ▶ A section of the SW Pacific Ocean between NE Australia, New Guinea, and the New Hebrides. It contains many coral reefs, including the ▷Great Barrier Reef. In 1942 it was the scene of a US victory over the Japanese.

● **coral snake** ▶ A New World burrowing venomous snake having a patterned skin. They occur chiefly in the tropics and prey on other snakes. The main genus, *Micrurus* (40 species), ranges from the S USA to Argentina; most species are ringed with red, black, and yellow or white. Old World coral snakes are similar and found in SE Asia (genus *Calliophis*) and Africa (genus *Elaps*). Family: *Elapidae* (cobras, etc.). The rear-fanged false coral snakes have similar patterning but belong to the family *Colubridae* (grass snakes, etc.).

● **coral tree** ▶ A Brazilian tree, *Erythrina crista-galli*, 2–3 m high, with clusters of deep-scarlet flowers, for which it is often grown as an ornamental. Family: ▷*Leguminosae*.

● **cor anglais** ▶ A double-reeded musical instrument, the alto member of the oboe family. It is a transposing instrument, the notes sounding a fifth lower than written. It has a range of two and a half octaves from the E below middle C. Sibelius used its rich tone in *The Swan of Tuonela*.

● **Corbusier, Le** ▷*See* Le Corbusier.

● **Corby** ▶ 52 29N 0 40W A town in central England, in Northamptonshire. It was designated a new town in 1950. Since closure of Corby's iron and steel works (1979) the town has had a broad industrial base centred on light manufacturing. Population (1997 est): 51 600.

● **Cordaitales** ▶ An order of extinct ▷gymnosperm trees that—with ▷*Calamites* formed vast forests during the Carboniferous and Permian periods (370–240 million years ago); coal was formed from their fossilized remains. The trees probably grew up to 30 m high, with a tall columnar trunk and strap-shaped leaves, up to 1 m long.

● **Corday, Charlotte** ▶ (1768–93) French noblewoman, who assassinated Jean-Paul ▷Marat in his bath on 13 July, 1793. She was guillotined on 17 July. She sympathized with the Girondins, the revolutionary party that opposed the more radical Jacobins.

● **Cordeliers, Club of the** ▶ A French Revolutionary club founded in Paris in 1790 to defend the rights of man. It was temporarily disbanded following a demonstration against Louis XVI in 1791. After it was restored, it became more radical and was finally disbanded in 1794 following an unsuccessful insurrection.

● **cordgrass** ▷*See* Spartina.

● **Córdoba** ▶ 31 25S 64 11W A city in central Argentina. Founded in 1573, it has many notable old buildings, including the cathedral (1758) and the university (1613). A commercial and industrial centre, it manufactures cars, tractors, and textiles. Population (1991): 1 148 305.

● **Córdoba** ▶ 37 53N 4 46W A city in S Spain, in Andalusia on the River Guadalquivir. It became the capital of Moorish Spain in 756 AD and by the 10th century was Europe's largest city and a major cultural centre. Its immense Moorish cathedral (8th–10th centuries) was originally a mosque. Industries include silverware and textiles. Population (1995 est): 323 138.

● **Cordon Bleu** ▶ Originally, the blue ribbon of the knight's grand cross of the Order of the Holy Spirit, the first order of the Bourbon kings. The term is now used to describe food, or a chef, that achieves an (unspecified) degree of excellence.

● **Corelli, Arcangelo** ▶ (1653–1713) Italian violinist and composer. He rationalized contemporary violin technique and wrote sonatas for the instrument. He also established the concerto grosso, in which a small group of soloists (typically two violins and cello) is contrasted with the full orchestra, a form much used by baroque composers. His most famous work is the *Christmas Concerto* for strings and continuo.

● **Corelli, Marie** ▶ (1854–1924) British novelist. Of Scots-Italian parentage, she was educated in France as a musician. Her first book, the semiautobiographical *A Romance of Two Worlds* (1886), was followed by a series of popular romantic novels that included *Barabbas* (1893), *The Murder of Delicia* (1896), and *The Secret Power* (1921).

● **Coreopsis** ▶ A genus of North American, tropical African, and Hawaiian plants (120 species) commonly known as tick-seeds (because of the shape of their seedlike fruits). Annual or perennial herbs, they are often grown in gardens for their daisy-like flowers, which are usually yellow with a darker centre. Family: ▷Compositae.

● **Corfu** ▶ (Latin name: Corcyra; Modern Greek name: Kérkira *or* Kérkyra) A Greek island in the NE Ionian Sea, in the Ionian Islands. It has belonged to many powers, including Venice (1386–1797) and Britain (1815–64). The local produce includes olives, figs, and citrus fruit, and tourism is important. Area: 641 sq km (250 sq mi). Population (1991): 107 592. Chief town: Corfu.

● **corgi** ▶ One of two breeds of working ▯dog originating in SW Wales. Both are low-set: the Cardigan Welsh corgi has a long tail, rounded ears, and a shortish coat, which may be reddish brown, streaked brown, or black and tan; the Pembroke Welsh corgi has a short tail, pointed ears, and a finer coat of red, sable, fawn, or black and tan. Both breeds can have white markings. Height: 30 cm (Cardigan); 25–30 cm (Pembroke).

● **coriander** ▶ An annual plant, *Coriander sativum*, 20–70 cm high, with umbrella-like clusters of small pink or white flowers. Probably native to the Mediterranean, it is widespread in waste places and is also cultivated for its fruits, used in curries, alcoholic beverages, as a condiment, and medicinally for flatulence. Family: ▷Umbelliferae.

● **Corineus** ▶ A legendary Trojan hero after whom Cornwall is named. According to the medieval chronicler ▷Geoffrey of Monmouth he was a companion of Brutus, the grandson of Aeneas and legendary founder of Britain, and the killer of the giant Gogmagog (*see* Gog and Magog).

● **Corinth** ▶ (Greek name: Kórinthos) 37 56N 22 55E A port in S Greece, in the Peloponnese on the Isthmus of Corinth. The modern port was founded in 1858 near the site of the ancient city; its trade includes wine. A man-made canal 6.4 km (4 mi) long, built in 1881–93 and known as the **Corinth Canal**, runs across the Isthmus of Corinth.
    History: a settlement before 3000 BC, the ancient city of Corinth developed in commercial importance during the 8th century BC. It became the second largest and richest of the Greek city states after Athens, rivalry between the two culminating in the ▷Peloponnesian War. Corinth resisted Roman pressures but was destroyed by them in 146 BC, later to be revived as a Roman colony (44 BC). The city declined during the middle ages. Extensive excavations have taken place since 1896. Population (1981): 22 495.

● **Corinth, League of** ▶ (*or* Hellenic League) An alliance of Greek states formed in 338 BC at Corinth under the leadership of ▷Philip II of Macedon. The League was formed for a joint Greek and Macedonian campaign against Persia and contributed to the Asian campaign of ▷Alexander the Great, who succeeded Philip in 336. The League was disbanded after Alexander's death (323), being briefly revived in 303.

● **Corinthian order** ▷*See* orders of architecture.

● **Corinthians, Epistles of Paul to the** ▶ Two New Testament books written by the apostle Paul to the Christian Church at Corinth in about 57 AD. In the first he deals with problems that had arisen in the Church and answers questions on a number of practical and doctrinal issues, for example marriage and celibacy, the resurrection of the dead, and the Eucharist. In the second he explains the nature of his own apostolic ministry and defends himself against his opponents at Corinth.

● **Coriolanus, Gnaeus Marcius** ▶ Roman general, who defeated the Volsci and captured the town of Corioli. Exiled in 491 BC for his contempt for the common people during a famine, he led the Volsci against Rome but was dissuaded from sacking the city by his wife Virgilia and mother Volumnia. The story is the subject of Shakespeare's *Coriolanus* (1607).

● **Coriolis force** ▶ A ▷force required to account for the motion of a body as seen by an observer in a rotating frame of reference. It is often referred to as a fictitious force as it disappears on changing to a nonrotating frame. For example, a shell shot from a gun at the centre of a rotating table appears to an outside observer to travel in a straight line. To an observer on the table it appears to have a curved

path. The Coriolis force is required to account for this apparent tangential acceleration. The Coriolis force is responsible for the formation and direction of rotation of anticyclones and whirlpools. Named after the French physicist Gaspard de Coriolis (1792–1843).

● **cork** ▶ Tissue that forms the outer layer of ▷bark in woody plants. Cork provides extra insulation and physical protection to the internal cells of the plant. The cork oak (*Quercus suber*), an evergreen oak tree of S Europe and N Africa, is cultivated in Portugal and SW Spain as the source of commercial cork. The cork is stripped from the tree every 8–10 years and is used for shock absorbers, bungs, fishing floats, floor and wall coverings, shoe soles, etc.

● **Cork** ▶ (Irish name: Corcaigh) The largest county in the Republic of Ireland, in Munster bordering on the Atlantic Ocean. Mountains in the W extend eastwards intersected by valleys, notably that of the River Blackwater. Its many coastal inlets include Bantry Bay and Cork Harbour. Fishing is important; Ballycotton is noted for its game fishing. Agriculture is varied with dairy and arable farming. Its many castles include Blarney Castle, famous for the Blarney Stone. Area: 7459 sq km (2880 sq mi). Population (1996 est): 420 000. County town: Cork.

● **Cork** ▶ (Irish name: Corcaigh) 51 54N 8 28W The second largest city in the Republic of Ireland and county town of Co Cork, on Cork Harbour. The settlement grew up around St Finbarr's monastery (founded in about the 6th century AD) and it has remained important as a centre of learning with the presence of University College (founded 1845), part of the National University of Ireland. It has many notable buildings, especially its cathedrals and St Ann's Shaldon Church, famous for its bells. It is an important industrial and trading centre with a fine harbour. Exports include bacon, dairy produce, and livestock and it has bacon-curing, car assembly, and brewing and distilling industries. Population (1996): 127 092.

● **corkwood** ▷*See* balsa.

● **corm** ▶ A fleshy underground stem base of certain perennial herbaceous plants, such as the crocus and gladiolus, that acts as an overwintering structure. Growth the following season occurs by one or more buds: if two or more plants are produced the corm is acting as an organ of vegetative reproduction.

● **cormorant** ▶ A slender long-necked waterbird belonging to a family (*Phalacrocoracidae*; 30 species) and found on most coasts and some inland waters. 50–100 cm in length, cormorants are typically glossy black with white throat markings and have short legs, webbed feet, a long stiff tail, and a long slender hook-tipped bill; they feed mainly on fish caught underwater. Order: *Pelecaniformes* (gannets, pelicans, etc.). ▷*See also* shag.

● **corn** ▶ 1. ▷*See* maize. 2. The main cereal crop of a particular region; for example wheat in England.

● **Corn Belt** ▶ An area in the central USA, S and W of the Great Lakes, extending mainly through Indiana, Illinois, Iowa, and Nebraska. It possesses a distinctive agriculture with intensive maize and soya-bean production used in the raising of fat cattle and pigs.

● **corn borer** ▶ A small European ▷pyralid moth, *Pyrausta nubilalis*, accidentally introduced to North America. It is a serious economic pest, attacking over 200 plant species, including beans, celery, maize, and potatoes. The larvae burrow into plant stems near ground level, sometimes causing them to break off.

● **corncockle** ▶ An annual purple-flowered weed of arable land in most temperate regions, *Agrostemma githago*, growing to a height of 100 cm. Once abundant, it is now rare due to efficient seed clearing. Family: *Caryophyllaceae*.

● **corncrake** ▶ A migratory bird, *Crex crex*, also called landrail, that breeds in Eurasian grasslands, wintering in S Africa and Asia. It is 26 cm long with a streaked brown plumage and chestnut wing patches and is easily identified by its harsh rasping call. Family: *Rallidae* (rails).

● **cornea** ▶ The transparent outer layer at the front of the eyeball, through which light enters the ▯eye. Corneal grafts have been used successfully to replace diseased areas of cornea; since the cornea has no blood supply the graft cannot be rejected by blood-borne antibodies.

● **Corneille, Pierre** ▶ (1606–84) French dramatist. After a Jesuit education he worked in government service in his home town of Rouen from 1628 to 1650. His early comedies, beginning with *Mélite* (1629), were much admired by Cardinal Richelieu. *Le Cid* (1636), the seminal play of French classical tragedy, excited much controversy. Here and in *Horace* (1640), *Cinna* (1641), and *Polyeucte* (1643) he pioneered a dramatic genre the main emphasis of which was on moral conflicts expressed in majestic formal verse, a genre later perfected by his younger contemporary ▷Racine. In 1647 he moved to Paris and continued to write prolifically until his last play, *Suréna*, in 1674.

● **Cornelius, Peter von** ▶ (1783–1867) German painter, born in Düsseldorf. In Rome (1811–19) he was associated with a group of German artists, the Nazarenes, in the revival of fresco painting. He worked subsequently in Munich on frescoes for the museum of classical sculpture and in Berlin.

● **Corner Brook** ▶ 48 58N 57 58W A city in E Canada, in Newfoundland. It has one of the world's largest pulp mills. Population (1991): 22 410.

● **cornet** ▶ A valved brass instrument, with cup-shaped mouthpiece and conical bore. Pitched in B flat, it is similar to the trumpet but less brilliant. It has a range of two and a half octaves from the E below middle C and plays an important role in the brass band.

● **cornetfish** ▶ A tropical marine ▷bony fish, also called flutemouth, belonging to a family (*Fistulariidae*; about 4 species) related to ▷pipefish and ▷sea horses. It has a slender body, up to 1.8 m long, a long threadlike filament extending from the tail fin, and a long siphon-like snout. Order: *Gasterosteiformes*.

● **cornett** ▶ A woodwind instrument with a cup-shaped mouthpiece and finger holes. The brilliant tone of the treble cornett was much favoured by composers of the 16th and 17th centuries, such as Giovanni Gabrieli. ▷*See also* serpent.

● **cornflower** ▶ An annual, sometimes overwintering, herbaceous plant, *Centaurea cyanus*, growing to about 75 cm high. Flower heads are bright blue with a purplish centre. Probably native in most of Europe and the Near East, it is widely introduced as a cereal crop weed but is now becoming rare due to improved seed clearing. Horticultural garden varieties are popular. Family: ▷*Compositae*.

● **Cornforth, Sir John Warcup** ▶ (1917–) Australian chemist, who shared the 1975 Nobel Prize with Vladimir Prelog (1906–) for their work on stereochemistry. Cornforth showed the importance of stereoisomers in biological systems, using ▷radioactive tracers to follow the course of their reactions.

● **Cornish** ▶ A ▷Celtic language of the Brythonic group, formerly spoken in Cornwall and Devon, that became extinct in about 1800. It was closely related to Breton, which was introduced to Brittany from this area. A number of miracle and morality plays dating from the 15th century were written in Cornish.

● **Corn Laws** ▶ The British laws that regulated (1360–1846) the import and export of corn to guarantee farmers' incomes. The 1815 Corn Law prohibited the import of corn until home-grown corn had reached a price of 80 shillings a quarter (of a hundredweight). In 1828 a sliding scale of import duties was fixed and duties were levied on imported corn when the price of British corn was down to 73 shillings a quarter. These laws were bitterly resented by the working classes, because they kept the price of bread high, and by the manufacturers, who argued that little money was left for the purchase of manufactured goods. Opposition to the Corn Laws was led by the ▷Anti-Corn Law League and in 1846 Sir Robert ▷Peel's government repealed them. A nominal duty continued to be levied until 1869.

● **corn poppy** ▶ An annual, or sometimes biennial, poppy, *Papaver rhoeas*, with scarlet (occasionally pinkish) flowers. Also called field poppy, it grows to a height of 50 cm. It is a weed of arable and waste places, occurring throughout much of Eurasia and N Africa and introduced to North America, New Zealand, and Australia.

● **corn salad** ▶ A slender branching annual plant, *Valerianella lo-*

custa, also called lamb's lettuce. 7–40 cm high, with small pale-lilac flowers, it grows in dryish places and is sometimes cultivated for salads. It is native to Europe, N Africa, and W Asia and introduced to North America. Family: *Valerianaceae*.

● **cornucopia** ▶ A decorative motif from Greek antiquity denoting abundance and wealth. It consists of a goat's horn filled with fruit and flowers and was reputedly presented to the nymph Amalthaea by Zeus or vice versa.

● **Cornwall** ▶ (Celtic name: Kernow) The most southwesterly county of England, a rugged peninsula bordering on the Atlantic Ocean and the English Channel. It consists mainly of hills rising to Bodmin Moor in the E. Dairy farming and market gardening are important, the equable climate encouraging the growth of early fruit and vegetables. Tourism is a chief source of income. Tinmining, important since early times, was abandoned in the 1990s. Owing to the crises in farming and fishing and the end of the tin industry, Cornwall was in 1998 officially recognized as the poorest region of the UK (and one of the poorest in the EU). Since the 1970s an emergent Cornish nationalist movement has led to the unofficial revival (1974) of the Stannary or Tinners' Parliament and attempts to resurrect the Cornish language. Area: 3546 sq km (1369 sq mi). Population (1996): 483 300. Administrative centre: Truro.

● **Cornwall, Duchy of** ▶ A private estate of some 130 000 acres, mostly in Cornwall, Devon, and Somerset, belonging to the eldest son of the sovereign, who becomes Duke of Cornwall at birth or from the moment his parent is crowned. It was established in 1337 by Edward III to support his son, the Black Prince. If there is no Duke of Cornwall the revenue is paid to the Treasury. Although not required to pay tax, the present Prince of Wales donates 25% of the income to the Treasury.

● **Cornwallis, Charles, 1st Marquess** ▶ (1738–1805) British general in the ▷American Revolution. Although he opposed the taxation of the American colonies, he took a command when the revolution broke out and defeated Gates at ▷Camden (1780). In 1781, however, he was disastrously defeated at Yorktown. He then served twice as governor general of India (1786–93, 1805), where he promulgated the **Cornwallis Code** (1793), on which the government of India was based until 1833. The Code gave financial, judicial, and administrative control to the East India Company. Higher offices of state were reserved for Europeans.

● **Coromandel Coast** ▶ The SE coast of India between the Krishna Delta and Point Calimere.

● **Coromandel screens** ▶ Large 17th-century Chinese screens originally shipped from the ▷Coromandel Coast to Europe. They have up to 12 panels with brown or red lacquer grounds and incised polychromatic decoration.

● **corona** ▶ The outer layer of a star's atmosphere. It is very tenuous and extensive compared with the ▷chromosphere and has a temperature of over a million degrees Celsius. The sun's corona has two main components. The **inner corona** lies above the chromosphere and consists of rapidly moving electrons. Its temperature reaches about 2 000 000°C some 75 000 km above the visible solar surface (the ▷photosphere). The **outer corona** extends for millions of kilometres and consists of comparatively slow-moving dust particles. The solar corona cannot be seen without special equipment, except at a total solar ▷eclipse. It then appears as a pearly usually unsymmetrical halo around the darkened solar disc, the shape depending on the time of the ▷sunspot cycle. ▷*See also* solar wind.

● **coronary heart disease** ▶ The most common form of ▷heart disease in the Western world. It is caused by ▷atherosclerosis of the coronary arteries, which reduces the blood flow to the heart. This may precipitate the formation of a blood clot in these arteries—**coronary thrombosis**. The patient experiences sudden pain in the chest (*see* angina pectoris) and the result may be a heart attack, when the blood flow to the heart is suddenly stopped (*see* myocardial infarction). Associated with smoking, lack of exercise, high-fat diets, hypertension, and middle age, it is commoner in men. **Coronary bypass surgery** is a surgical procedure in which a piece of healthy saphenous vein (from the leg) or mammary artery is used as a graft to bypass a section of coronary artery blocked by atherosclerosis. The improved blood flow resulting relieves ▷angina and reduces the risk of coronary thrombosis. In **coronary angioplasty** a catheter is inserted into a narrowed coronary artery and a balloon at the tip of the catheter is inflated to dilate the blood vessel.

● **coroner** ▶ In England and Wales, an officer of the Crown appointed for life by a county council from among suitably qualified barristers, solicitors, or qualified medical practitioners. The main duty of a coroner (from Latin *corona*, crown) is to hold an **inquest** to inquire into the death of anyone who dies by an act of violence, in suspicious or unexplained circumstances, or in prison. The coroner is often assisted by a jury of 7 to 11 people. A jury verdict of manslaughter or murder is equivalent to an indictment, and the coroner can commit the accused for trial. A coroner also inquires into cases of ▷treasure trove. In Scotland, the coroner's duties are carried out by the procurator fiscal.

● **Corot, Jean Baptiste Camille** ▶ (1796–1875) French landscape painter. After training under two minor landscapists (1822–25), he visited Italy (1825–28), the subject of many of his landscapes. He exhibited at the Paris Salon from 1827, but did not achieve critical acclaim until the 1850s, with his misty landscapes populated by nymphs. More popular today are his open-air sketches, small landscapes, and figure studies. He influenced the impressionists.

● **corporate state** ▶ (*or* corporative state) A society in which the individual is represented in government by the economic group (corporation) to which he belongs rather than according to his geographical location. The ideas of ▷Guild Socialism were akin to corporatism, but it has only been adopted as a system of government by fascist dictators, such as Mussolini, Franco, and Salazar.

● **corporation tax** ▶ A tax levied on the profits of a company on an annual basis. In the UK, where the tax replaced profits tax in 1966, the rate of tax is announced by the chancellor of the exchequer. In 2002–03 it was 30% (19% for smaller companies and zero for very small companies). From 1973 until 1999 companies paid **advance corporation tax** (ACT) on their distributed profits, which was offset against their corporation tax liability. Since the abolition of ACT, large companies must pay the tax in instalments.

● **Corpus Christi** ▶ 27 47N 97 26W A city in the USA, in Texas on Corpus Christi Bay. A popular resort, its port exports cotton, petroleum, and sulphur. Industries include cement and chemicals as well as fishing. Population (1996 est): 280 260.

● **Corpus Christi, Feast of** ▶ (Latin: body of Christ) A Christian feast honouring the institution of the Eucharist, observed in the West on the second Thursday after ▷Whit Sunday. Originally a local festival in Liège, it was extended to the whole Catholic Church by Pope Urban IV in 1264. The chief rite is the procession of the Blessed Sacrament.

● **Corpus Juris Canonici** ▶ A collection of papal and conciliar decrees comprising the canon law of the Western Church. It is composed of six collections compiled between the 12th and 15th centuries. Pope Gregory XIII revised it in 1582. It was superseded in 1917 by the Codex Juris Canonici.

● **Corpus Juris Civilis** ▷*See* Roman law.

● **corpus luteum** ▷*See* ovary.

● **Correggio** ▶ (Antonio Allegri; c. 1494–1534) Italian Renaissance painter, born at Correggio, near Modena. Initially influenced by ▷Mantegna, he later studied ▷Leonardo and ▷Michelangelo. He worked chiefly in Parma, where he decorated the Camera di S Paolo, the domed vaulting of S Giovanni Evangelista, and the cathedral with frescoes that anticipate the ▷baroque. Using strong contrasts between light and shade, he painted religious subjects, e.g. *Adoration of the Shepherds* or *Night* (Dresden), and sensuous nudes, e.g. *Jupiter and Io* (Kunsthistorisches Museum, Vienna).

● **Corregidor** ▶ An island in the N Philippines, in the mouth of Manila Bay. It has been fortified since Spanish times. During World War II it held Manila harbour against the Japanese for five months although bombed continuously.

● **Correns, Carl Erich** ▶ (1864–1933) German botanist and geneticist, whose work on breeding garden peas confirmed the principles of heredity first established by ▷Mendel. In 1900, simultaneously with ▷de Vries, he rediscovered Mendel's original paper, which had been ignored since 1865.

● **Corrientes** ▶ 27 30S 58 48W A port in NE Argentina, on the Río Paraná. It is an important export centre for agricultural products, including cotton, rice, and tobacco. It has a university (1957). Population (1999 est): 325 628 (metropolitan area).

● **corsairs** ▷*See* buccaneers.

● **Corsica** ▶ (French name: Corse) An island in the Mediterranean Sea, separated from Sardinia by the Strait of Bonifacio. Together with 43 islets it comprises a region of France. It is mountainous with a rugged coastline and much of the island is covered with *maquis*, a dense thorny scrub type of vegetation. Agriculture is relatively undeveloped, producing citrus fruits, olives, vegetables, and tobacco; sheep and goats are extensively reared and tourism is a major source of income.
　History: under Genoese control from the 14th century, it was sold to France in 1768. During World War II it came under Italian occupation but was liberated by the French in 1943. Separatist protests led to France granting Corsica 'special status' in 1990. Area: 8680 sq km (3367 sq mi). Population (1999 est): 260 196. Capital: Ajaccio.

● **Cort, Henry** ▶ (1740–1800) British inventor and industrialist, who in 1784 invented the puddling process for producing wrought iron from pig iron. He also produced high-quality iron bars by passing iron through grooved rollers.

● **Cortes** ▶ The Spanish parliament, which first met in the kingdom of Léon in 1188. This was the first time that townsmen attended the king's court together with the clergy and nobility. The regional Cortes lost their influence during the 16th century. The first national Cortes met in 1810.

● **Cortés, Hernán** ▶ (1485–1547) Spanish conquistador. In Hispaniola and Cuba from 1504, he led a small expedition to Mexico in 1519 and reached Tenochtitlán, the capital of the Aztec Empire. In Cortés' absence, dealing with an attack from a Spanish force from Cuba, the Aztecs launched an attack on Tenochtitlán, forcing the Spaniards' retreat—the *noche triste* (night of sorrows). Cortés eventually rebuilt his forces and destroyed Tenochtitlán (1521) and the Aztec Empire, founding New Spain. After an expedition to Honduras (1524–26) Cortés returned to Spain (1528) but renewed his Pacific explorations in the 1530s. He died in poverty in Spain.

● **cortex** ▶ The outer tissues of an animal or plant organ. In plants the cortex is situated between the ▷epidermis and vascular (conducting) tissues of stems and roots. Its cell walls may contain corky and woody materials or silica, providing strength, and also stored food, usually starch. Resins, latex, tannins, and essential oils may also be present. In animals the outer tissue of the ▷adrenal gland, the cerebrum, and the ▷kidney is called the cortex.

● **corticosteroids** ▶ Steroid hormones secreted by the cortex of the adrenal glands (the term also includes synthetic drugs with similar properties). The glucocorticoids (e.g. cortisone) affect carbohydrate, fat, and protein metabolism. Synthetic glucocorticoids (e.g. prednisolone, dexamethasone) are used as anti-inflammatory drugs to treat allergic conditions (e.g. asthma), inflammatory disorders (e.g. ulcerative colitis and rheumatoid arthritis), autoimmune diseases, and some cancers. The mineralocorticoids (e.g. the hormone aldosterone and the drug fludrocortisone) control salt and water balance in the body.

● **Cortona** ▶ 43 17N 11 59E A town in Italy, in Tuscany. It is famous for its Etruscan and Roman remains and has a cathedral dating from the 15th century. Population (latest est): 22 700.

● **corundum** ▶ A mineral consisting mainly of aluminium oxide, the accessory minerals giving rise to a variety of colours. Sapphire is a blue variety containing iron and titanium; ruby contains chromium. It occurs in silica-poor igneous rocks, in metamorphosed shales, and in some metamorphosed limestone veins. The nongem varieties are used as abrasives (corundum is the second hardest mineral to diamond).

● **Corunna** ▷*See* La Coruña.

● **corvette** ▶ A small highly manoeuvrable lightly armed warship displacing approximately 1600 tonnes and carrying a complement of a hundred officers and men. They were used mainly for antisubmarine escort duty during World War II by the Royal Navy. In the days of sail, the corvette, smaller than a ▷frigate, was a sloop rigged as a ship. Those that remained after World War II were renamed antisubmarine frigates in 1959.

● **Corvo, Baron** ▷*See* Rolfe, Frederick William.

● **Corybant** ▶ One of the Corybantes, the eunuch priests or attendants of the goddess ▷Cybele, whose worship was accompanied by wild dancing and orgies. They castrated themselves in imitation of the self-mutilation of Cybele's lover, the fertility god Attis.

● **Corydalis** ▶ A genus of mainly N temperate herbs (320 species), mostly perennials with underground tubers. The flowers, usually yellow, grow in clusters and resemble those of peas. Garden varieties, 15–60 cm high, prefer shady cool positions. Family: *Fumariaceae*.

● **Cos** ▶ (Modern Greek name: Kos) A Greek island in the SE Aegean Sea, in the Dodecanese. It was a member of the Delian League and the home of the Greek physician, Hippocrates. It produces chiefly fruit but also silk and cotton. Cos lettuce originally came from here. Area: 282 sq km (109 sq mi). Population (latest est): 20 350.

● **Cosenza** ▶ 39 17N 16 16E A market town in Italy, in Calabria. Its manufactures include furniture and it has a 13th-century cathedral. Population (1991): 104 483.

● **Cosgrave, William Thomas** ▶ (1880–1965) Irish statesman. A member of ▷Sinn Féin, he took part in the ▷Easter Rising (1916) and was elected to the first Irish Assembly (1918). He was first president of the Irish Free State (1922–32) and then led the ▷Fine Gael opposition until 1944. His son **Liam Cosgrave** (1920–   ) became leader of Fine Gael in 1965 and was prime minister from 1973 until 1977, when he resigned the party leadership.

● **Cosmas and Damian, SS** ▶ (early 4th century AD) Christian martyrs. Nothing certain is known of their lives, but according to tradition they were twin brothers who practised as physicians in Asia Minor, refused to accept payment from their patients, and were martyred under Diocletian. They are patron saints of physicians. Feast day: 1 July or 26 Sept.

● **cosmetics** ▶ Beauty aids and preparations intended to improve the appearance of face, hair, or nails or the texture of the skin. Historically, among the most common cosmetics have been kohl, for shading around the eyes, and henna, for dyeing hair, fingertips, and toes; their use dates back at least to ancient Egypt. Rouge and face powders were used by the ancient Greeks and Romans. Although periodically cosmetics have met with public disapproval, as in Puritan and Victorian times, during the 20th century the manufacture of cosmetics has become an important industry, catering increasingly for men as well as women. Although modern Western cosmetics no longer contain such dangerous ingredients as the lead compounds found in ancient Greek face powders, some ingredients can nevertheless irritate sensitive skins. Many modern cosmetics, such as eyebrow pencils, are wax-based; lipsticks also contain nondrying oils. Petroleum jelly, liquid paraffin, and colouring are also widely used. Creams and lotions are emulsions of wax or oil in water, which evaporates on application; the oily film left prevents the skin from drying out. Face powder consists principally of zinc oxide, precipitated chalk, talc, and zinc stearate. Nail varnish consists of a nitrocellulose base, a plasticizer, and a modifying resin, all in a volatile solvent. Astringent lotions (including aftershave), which close the openings of the hair follicles, are based on alcohol solutions; antiperspirants are usually based on an aluminium salt, which prevents sweat from leaving the sweat ducts.

● **cosmic rays** ▶ A continuous stream of very high-energy particles that bombard the earth from space. The primary radiation consists of ▷protons and light nuclei with smaller numbers of neutral particles, such as ▷photons and ▷neutrinos. These particles collide with atomic nuclei in the earth's atmosphere producing large numbers of elementary particles, known as secondary radiation. One primary particle may produce a large number of secondary particles on colliding with a nucleus. This effect is called a shower. Some cosmic rays are believed to originate from the sun, others from outside the solar system.

● **cosmogony** ▶ The study of the origin and evolution of the universe and the astronomical objects it contains, especially in the solar system.

● **cosmology** ▶ The study of the origin, evolution, and structure of the universe. A great variety of cosmological models have been put forward through the ages. Two simple but incorrect common-sense models are the flat earth draped by a canopy of stars and the earth-centred (geocentric) universe, the ▷Ptolemaic system. More accurate theories emerged as instruments were developed to study the heavens (*see* astronomy). Current models are highly mathematical but are closely linked with observation. In every model the universe is expanding (*see* expanding universe). Most assume that there are no preferred places in the universe: all directions appear indistinguishable to an observer and this isotropy exists about every point in space (the cosmological principle). The standard cosmological model is the ▷big-bang theory. ▷*See also* steady-state theory.

● **Cossacks** ▶ A people of S and SW Russia descended from independent Tatar groups and escaped serfs from Poland, Lithuania, and Muscovy. They established a number of independent self-governing communities, which were given special privileges by Russian or Polish rulers in return for military service. Known for their horsemanship, each Cossack community provided a separate army. The Cossacks slowly lost their autonomy as Russia expanded in the 17th and 18th centuries and there were occasional rebellions. Many fled after the Revolution and collectivization subsumed remaining Cossack communities.

● **Costa Blanca** ▶ (Spanish: white coast) A coastal region of SE Spain, bordering on the Mediterannean Sea. It extends SW from Benidorm.

● **Costa Brava** ▶ (Spanish: wild coast) A coastal region in NE Spain, bordering on the Mediterranean Sea. It extends from Barcelona to the French border and is a popular tourist area with many resorts.

● **cost accounting** ▷*See* accountancy.

● **Costa del Sol** ▶ (Spanish: coast of the sun) A coastal region of S Spain, bordering on the Mediterranean Sea and extending from Malaga to Gibraltar. Torremolinos and Marbella are the principal resorts.

● **Costa Rica, Republic of** ▶ A country in the Central American isthmus between Nicaragua and Panama. It includes the island of Cocos, 483 km (186 mi) to the SW. The Caribbean lowlands rise to a central plateau area, with volcanic peaks reaching 3819 m (12 529 ft). The inhabitants are mainly of Spanish and mixed descent, with a dwindling Indian population.
Economy: chiefly agricultural, the main crops being coffee, bananas, and sugar. Livestock is important and crops, such as cocoa, have been introduced as part of a plan to diversify the economy. Almost 75% of the land is forested with valuable woods, such as mahogany, rosewood, and cedar. Mineral resources include gold, haematite ore, and sulphur. Manufacturing has grown in importance and now includes computer parts, processed foods, and textiles. Tourism has grown rapidly and is now the country's chief source of income, with ecological tourism in the rain forests proving a particular attraction. In late 1998 Hurricane Mitch and its aftermath caused huge damage to infrastructure and farming, setting back the country's development by an estimated 20 years.
History: after the arrival of Columbus in 1502, Costa Rica became a Spanish colony and the native Indian population was practically wiped out. It was part of the captaincy general of Guatemala until gaining independence in 1821. From 1824 until 1838 it formed part of the Central American Federation. In 1948 José Figueres Ferrer (1906–90), leader of the socialist National Liberation Party, came to power at the head of a junta. A new constitution brought more democratic rule—the army was abolished and banks nationalized. Since

then government has been relatively stable, although economic difficulties in the 1990s caused some unrest. Miguel Angel Rodriguez, a conservative economist, was elected president in 1998.

Republic of Costa Rica

Head of state	President Miguel Angel Rodriguez
Official language	Spanish
Official religion	Roman Catholic
Official currency	colon of 100 céntimos
Area	50 900 sq km (19 653 sq mi)
Population (1999 est)	3 594 000
Capital	San José
Main ports	Limón (on the Caribbean) and Puntarenas (on the Pacific)

● **cost-benefit analysis** ▶ An investigation to determine whether a certain investment project is of net benefit to the community or to decide between competing projects. This type of analysis is useful because a purely commercial assessment does not always take account of all the costs and benefits involved; for example, it would not show the benefit of reduced road congestion that might be entailed in building an underground railway. The weakness of cost-benefit analysis is that it is not always possible to quantify all the consequences.

● **Costermansville** ▷See Bukavu.

● **costmary** ▶ A perennial herb, *Chrysanthemum balsamita*, also called alecost. About 100 cm high, it is native to E Mediterranean regions and naturalized in S Europe. The spicy aromatic leaves were formerly used for flavouring ales and salads and to make an antiseptic tea. Family: ▷*Compositae*.

● **Costner, Kevin** ▶ (1955–) US film actor, director, and producer. He has appeared in *The Untouchables* (1987), *JFK* (1991), *Waterworld* (1995), and *Thirteen Days* (2001); he also directed and starred in the Oscar-winning *Dances with Wolves* (1990).

● **cost of living** ▶ A measure of the income required to purchase essential goods. Usually the Retail Price Index (formerly called the cost of living index), based on a standard "basket" of goods, is used as a guide to the cost of living (*see* price index). The cost of living can vary geographically and with time. Rates of ▷taxation also affect the cost of living. Index-linked pensions, social-security payment, gilts, and savings bonds are used to mitigate the effects of ▷inflation.

● **Cosway, Richard** ▶ (1742–1821) British portrait miniaturist. After studying with the portraitist Thomas Hudson (1701–79) he exhibited at the Royal Academy, becoming a member in 1771. He was patronized by the Prince of Wales (later George IV) and became extremely fashionable. His wife Maria Hadfield (1759–1838) was also a miniaturist.

● **cot death** ▶ (or sudden infant death syndrome; SIDS) The death of a baby, often occurring overnight in its cot, from an unidentifiable cause. In the UK in 1988, there were 2 cot deaths per 100 000 live births. In 1991–93 a campaign encouraging mothers to lie babies on their backs to sleep, not to overwrap them or smoke over them, and to call medical help if in doubt resulted in a 55% drop in deaths.

● **Côte d'Ivoire, Republic of** ▶ (name until 1986: Ivory Coast) A country in West Africa, on the Gulf of Guinea. Swamps and tropical forests give way to savanna on higher land to the N. The diverse African population includes Baule, Bete, Senufo, and Malinke.
　　Economy: chiefly agricultural, livestock being important as well as crops, including maize, yams, and other tropical plants. The main cash crop is coffee, of which, together with timber (particularly mahogany), Côte d'Ivoire is Africa's leading exporter. Other exports include cocoa, pineapples, and rubber. Mineral resources are on the whole sparse, although some manganese is mined, and diamond fields are being exploited. Oil was found in 1977 and began to be exploited in 1995. Industry is being developed, including tourism. The country has a very large external debt.
　　History: explored by the Portuguese in the late 15th century, the area was disputed by several European trading nations over the centuries, becoming a French colony in 1893. It became part of French West Africa in 1904 and an overseas territory in 1946. It possessed internal self-government as a member of the French Community from

1958 and became fully independent in 1960. Falls in world cocoa prices together with the high value of the CFA franc led to economic crisis in the 1980s. In the face of growing unrest President Félix ▷Houphouët-Boigny introduced multiparty democracy in 1990 and won the subsequent election; following his death in 1993 Henri Konan-Bédié became president. An IMF reform programme had some success in stabilizing the economy in the 1990s. In late 1999 President Bédié was deposed in a military coup and General Robert Guei became head of state. Presidential elections in 2000 resulted in victory for the opposition candidate Laurent Gbagbo and Guei fled amidst heavy fighting. Violent disorder has continued.

Republic of Côte d'Ivoire

Head of state	President Laurent Gbagbo
Official language	French
Official currency	CFA (Communauté financière africaine) franc of 100 centimes
Area	322 463 sq km (124 470 sq mi)
Population (1999 est)	15 818 000
Capital	Yamoussoukro
Main port	Abidjan

● **cotinga** ▶ A passerine bird of the family *Cotingidae* (90 species), native to the S USA, Central and N South America, and the West Indies. Typically living at the tops of forest trees and feeding on fruit and insects, they are 9–45 cm long with a broad and slightly hooked bill, short legs, and large feet. The males of some species have brightly coloured plumage, erectile crests, and fleshy wattles or other processes on their heads (*see* cock-of-the-rock; umbrella bird). Calls range from grunts and croaks to the penetrating bell-like notes of the bellbirds (genus *Procnias*).

● **Cotman, John Sell** ▶ (1782–1842) British watercolourist of the ▷Norwich school. He studied in London (c. 1798–1806), settling there in 1834. Typical of his compositions is *Greta Bridge* (British Museum). After 1831 he produced textured landscapes by mixing rice paste with watercolours.

● **Cotoneaster** ▶ A genus of shrubs and small trees (about 50 species) of N temperate regions of the Old World. Some species are evergreen. Many are grown in gardens for their attractive foliage and red or black berries. *C. horizontalis* is a popular ground and wall cover; *C. hybrida pendula* is a weeping standard. Family: *Rosaceae*.

● **Cotonou** ▶ 6 24N 2 31E The chief city in Benin, on the Gulf of Guinea. A deepwater port, it is the nation's commercial and financial centre; industries include textiles and brewing. Its university was founded in 1970. Population (1994 est): 750 000.

● **Cotopaxi** ▶ 0 40S 78 28W The world's highest active volcano, in N central Ecuador, in the Andes. Height: 5896 m (19 457 ft).

● **co-trimoxazole** ▶ A drug used especially in the treatment of urinary-tract infections. It is a combination of two antibacterial drugs—sulphamethoxazole (a ▷sulphonamide) and trimethoprim (an ▷antibiotic). Because side-effects may be severe, the drug is less widely prescribed now than formerly. Trade name: Septrin.

● **Cotswold Hills** ▶ A range of limestone hills in SW central England, mainly in Gloucestershire. It is noted for its picturesque towns and villages built in the local limestone. The steep W scarp reaches 333 m (1092 ft) at Cleeve Cloud near Cheltenham.

● **Cottbus** ▶ (or Kottbus) 51 45N 14 24E A town in E Germany, on the River Spree. It has several medieval churches and is a railway junction and industrial centre. Population (1996 est): 123 214.

● **cotton** ▶ A herbaceous plant of the genus *Gossypium* (20 or 67 species, according to the classification system), native to tropical and subtropical regions. Several species are cultivated for the whitish outer fibres of their seeds. Usually 1–2 m high, cotton plants bear whitish flowers and produce seed pods (bolls), which burst when filled with the soft masses of fibres. The bolls are harvested mechanically and the fibres separated from the seeds (ginning) and cleaned and aligned (carding), ready for spinning into yarn. The longest and most lustrous fibres are obtained from Sea Island or Egyptian cotton (*G. bardadense*). Cotton forms a light durable cloth used in garments, furnishings, and other products. The seeds are crushed to yield cottonseed oil, used in margarines, soaps, etc., and the residual meal is used as a livestock feed. Family: *Malvaceae*.

● **cottonmouth** ▷*See* water moccasin.

● **cotton stainer** ▶ A black and red ▷plant bug belonging to the genus *Dysdercus*, widely distributed in warm regions. They are serious pests of cotton plants in North America and India, staining the bolls with excrement and rendering them useless. Family: *Pyrrhocoridae*.

● **cottonwood** ▶ A North American poplar the seeds of which resemble cotton seeds, especially *Populus deltoides*, which grows in rich woods and river bottoms and reaches a height of 30 m. Its lightweight wood is used commercially.

● **cotyledon** ▶ The seed leaf of seed-bearing plants (conifers and flowering plants): a food store within seeds providing the embryo plant with sufficient energy to germinate. In some plants the cotyledons become the first leaves of the seedling and are often different in form from subsequent leaves. Flowering plants with one cotyledon are classified as ▷monocotyledons; those with two as ▷dicotyledons. ▷*See* germination.

● **coucal** ▷*See* cuckoo.

● **couch grass** ▶ A ▷grass, *Agropyron repens*, also known as quack grass or twitch, native to Europe and naturalized in other N temperate regions. 30–120 cm high, it spreads by underground rhizomes and is a serious weed of arable crops.

● **cougar** ▶ A red-brown ▷cat, *Felis concolor*, of North and South America, also called puma, mountain lion, and catamount. It is a slender muscular animal, 1.5–3 m long including its tail (50–80 cm), with long hind legs enabling a powerful leap. It feeds on deer and other animals.

● **coulomb** ▶ (C) The ▷SI unit of electric charge equal to the quantity of electricity transferred by a current of one ampere in one second. Named after Charles de ▷Coulomb.

● **Coulomb, Charles Augustin de** ▶ (1736–1806) French physicist, who invented the torsion balance and used it to establish ▷Coulomb's law. He developed a similar law for magnetic poles. The ▷coulomb is named after him.

● **Coulomb's law** ▶ The force between two electrically charged bodies is proportional to the product of their charges (q_1 and q_2) and inversely proportional to the square of the distance (d) between them. In free space $F = q_1 q_2/4\pi e_0 d^2$, where e_0 is the ▷electric constant. The law is named after Charles de ▷Coulomb. The force is known as the **Coulomb** (*or* electrostatic) **force. Coulomb scattering** is the scattering of a charged particle by a nucleus due to the Coulomb force.

● **council** ▷*See* local government.

● **Council for Mutual Economic Assistance** ▶ (COMECON) A former economic association of communist countries founded in 1949. Its members were the Soviet Union, Bulgaria, Czechoslovakia, East Germany, Hungary, Mongolia, Poland, Romania, and Cuba. East Germany withdrew on German reunification in 1990. In 1991 the remaining members voted to replace COMECOM with a looser organization designed to help their economies integrate with those of the West.

● **Council of Europe** ▶ An association of European states, founded in 1949, to uphold parliamentary democracy and promote the economic and social progress of its members. 44 European countries are currently members and special guest status is held by Bosnia-Hercegovina. Its seat is in Strasbourg. ▷*See also* European Court of Human Rights; human rights.

● **council area** ▷*See* unitary authority.

● **council tax** ▶ In the UK, a tax to finance ▷local government that replaced the ▷poll tax (community charge) in 1993. Adult residents of private households are liable to pay the tax, which is calculated by the local council according to the market value of the dwelling. There is a 25% discount for sole occupants of dwellings, and the amount payable by those on low incomes can be reduced by means of benefits. ▷*See also* rates.

● **counterfeiting** ▶ The illegal production of false money for gain. Counterfeiting is a form of forgery, distinguished because of the unique position of ▷money as a general medium of exchange. Most banknotes are produced with fine printing on watermarked paper, often with a strip of metal inserted, to make them hard to counterfeit. Many countries are signatories to an agreement of 1929 that allows extradition of counterfeiters.

counterpoint ▶ An example of counterpoint from J. S. Bach's *Fantasia in C minor*.

● **counterpoint** ▶ The art of combining two or more melodic lines simultaneously in music. The word derives from the Latin *punctus contra punctum*, point against point (i.e. note against note). As the melodic lines combine, harmonies are formed, which until the end of the 19th century were controlled by rules restricting any dissonances. Counterpoint was the principal technique of composition during the polyphonic period (*see* polyphony) and continued to be used throughout the harmonic period. In the 20th century contrapuntal techniques, with much freer use of dissonance, were used by Stravinsky, Hindemith, Tippett, and others.

● **Counter-Reformation** ▶ A movement within the ▷Roman Catholic Church dedicated to combating the effects of the Protestant ▷Reformation by reforming abuses within the Church and eradicating heresy by conversion, etc. Extending from the middle of the 16th to about the middle of the 17th century, it witnessed the emergence of the ▷Jesuits, the reforms instituted by the Council of ▷Trent, the extension of the ▷Inquisition from Spain to other countries, and a revival of Catholic spirituality. Although most of N Europe remained Protestant, Poland and S Germany were stabilized as Catholic during this period.

● **countertenor** ▶ A natural high male singing voice, higher than tenor, common in England in the 17th and 18th centuries. It is distinguished from the male ▷alto voice, which is produced by falsetto, but has the same range. Countertenor singing has been revived by Alfred Deller (1917–79) and James Bowman (1941–   ).

● **countertrading** ▷*See* barter.

● **country and western** ▶ A type of US popular music that evolved from the hillbilly ballads of the Appalachian Mountains and the cowboy songs of the West. The singer is usually accompanied by the guitar and other instruments, such as the banjo and fiddle. The lyrics are often tragic or sentimental, dealing with themes of rural poverty, divorce and separation, or death. The style was popularized by radio broadcasting in the 1920s and became increasingly commercialized in the years after World War II. Offshoots include the bluegrass style that emerged in the 1940s. Since the late 1960s there has been much mutual influence between country and western and mainstream pop and rock music. The commercial capital of country and western music is Nashville, Tennessee.

● **country house** ▶ In England, a large house on a country estate. The great country houses were mainly built between the reigns of Elizabeth I and Victoria; before about 1550 feudal conditions caused the aristocracy to live in ▷castles or fortified ▷manor houses and after 1860 political reform and industrialization shifted the major landowners' power base and attention to the towns. Country houses displayed their owners' wealth and status, enabling them to entertain their political allies in impressive style. Some country houses exhibit the architectural opulence of small palaces (e.g. Castle Howard, ▷Althorp House, and ▷Chatsworth), contain notable art collections, and are set in magnificent grounds (*see* Blenheim Palace). In the 20th century the incidence of taxation, especially death duties, and the decline in the influence of the aristocracy resulted in an inability by many of their owners to maintain these magnificent edifices. In the immediate postwar years, during the Labour government, many of these historic buildings had to be demolished. However, many of the architecturally most impressive were rescued by the ▷National Trust or ▷English Heritage and are now open to the public, often with their aristocratic former owners living in part of their family homes and showing visitors the splendours of their family possessions.

● **Countryside Council for Wales** ▷See nature conservation.

● **Count's War** ▶ (1533–36) The last war of succession in Denmark, constituting a revolt led by Count Christopher of Oldenberg (c. 1504–66) against Christian, heir to the throne. Oldenberg finally surrendered Copenhagen in July, 1536, after which Christian became king as ▷Christian III.

● **county** ▶ A geographical subdivision of a country, usually with powers of ▷local government. In the UK counties are long established: the name was applied by the Normans to the Anglo-Saxon ▷shire. The Local Government Act (1972; effective 1974) amalgamated some old counties and established new ones, dividing England into 45 (6 metropolitan and 39 nonmetropolitan) counties and Wales into 8. The Act placed various public services, such as transport planning and fire services, in the hands of elected county councils; the metropolitan county councils were abolished in 1986. The Local Government (Scotland) Act (1973) created nine new regions and three island areas. Although Northern Ireland has 6 historic counties, administration has been carried out by 26 district councils since 1973. In the 1990s Local Government Acts for Scotland and Wales (1994; effective 1996) replaced the Scottish system with 32 council areas and reorganized Wales into 10 counties and 12 county boroughs (all ▷unitary authorities). In England a comprehensive review of local government led to several counties being abolished and their powers devolved to the district councils (now unitary authorities). The USA does not have a comprehensive county system and the powers of counties differ widely between states. See map section (British Isles – Counties and Unitary Authorities).

● **county borough** ▷See borough.

● **county palatine** ▶ A county over which an earl palatine had jurisdiction in medieval England, in lieu of the king. After the ▷Norman conquest Cheshire, Shropshire, Durham, and Kent were so designated, Lancaster being added in 1351. Their jurisdictions are now vested in the sovereign.

● **Couperin, François** ▶ (1668–1733) French composer, called le Grand, the most famous member of a family that produced five generations of musicians. He was organist to Louis XIV and at St Gervais and is best known for his harpsichord music, a series of *ordres* consisting of pieces in dance forms with descriptive titles. He also wrote organ music, church music, and a book on the art of playing the harpsichord.

● **Courbet, Gustave** ▶ (1819–77) French painter, born in Ornans. Self-taught, he became leader of the school of realism. He painted portraits, including one of his friend Baudelaire, nudes, seascapes, hunting scenes, and everyday life, e.g. *Burial at Ornans* (Louvre) and *Bonjour Monsieur Courbet* (Montpellier). Reacting against academic criticism of his work, in 1855 he organized his first private exhibition. A political radical, he was imprisoned for his participation in the Commune of Paris (1871) and in 1873 he fled to Switzerland, where he died.

● **courgette** ▶ A variety of ▷marrow, also called zucchini, eaten when small and immature (up to 15 cm long). Mature courgettes resemble ordinary marrows.

● **Courrèges, André** ▶ (1923–   ) French fashion designer, who opened a fashion house in Paris in 1961. In 1964 he presented his "space-age" collection, which included close-fitting silver trousers, worn with short-sleeved jackets and calf-length boots. He helped to promote the unisex fashion.

● **courser** ▶ A brownish bird of the subfamily *Cursoriinae*, having long legs and a pointed curved bill. It occurs in arid regions of Africa, India, and Australia. The cream-coloured courser (*Cursorius cursor*) of Africa is 25 cm long with white underparts and eye stripes and feeds on insects and lizards. Family: *Glareolidae* (pratincoles and coursers).

● **coursing** ▶ A ▷blood sport dating back to at least 1500 BC, in which game (now usually hare) is pursued by hounds (usually greyhounds) that hunt by sight rather than scent. A meeting takes place on an open field and is presided over by a mounted umpire. Hounds compete in pairs in a knockout competition, chasing hares that have a start of at least 73 m (80 yd). They are judged on points for their speed up to the quarry, for overtaking each other, and for forcing the quarry to turn. The kill is less important, as most hares escape. The British coursing season is from September to March and its main event is the Waterloo Cup (first held in 1836), staged in February at Altcar, Lancashire. It lasts 3 days and 64 dogs take part. ▷Greyhound racing developed from coursing.

● **Courtauld Institute of Art** ▶ A gallery and college for the study of art history in London. The manufacturer and art collector Samuel Courtauld (1876–1947) donated his house in Portman Square with his collection of impressionist paintings to London University in 1931. In 1990 it moved into larger premises in the west wing of ▷Somerset House.

● **court cupboard** ▶ A set of three shelves supported by corner columns, often with a recessed cupboard between the top two. Popular throughout N Europe during the 16th century for displaying plate, they were usually made of oak.

● **courtly love** ▶ A literary convention describing passionate love, arising in 12th-century Provence in the poems of the ▷troubadours. (The term itself was coined in the 19th century.) It is not certain to what extent courtly love actually existed as a social phenomenon in feudal courts. In the literary convention both lover and beloved are of aristocratic rank. The lover is abjectly devoted to his chosen lady, whose virtues are idealized with quasi-religious fervour and who remains unobtainable because she is married to someone else. The lover is bound by rules of ▷chivalry and is ennobled by his attachment to the beloved. On the other hand, his love-sickness may be devastating and he can only be cured if his lady takes pity on him, that is, consents to an adulterous affair. Although the lover is supposed to be exalted by his love, he suffers enormously from fear of exposure, from the capricious behaviour of his lady, etc. The convention, which owes much to the influence of ▷Ovid, spread from Provence to Italy, influencing the ▷dolce stil nuovo; to N France, where it was important in the romances of ▷Chrétien de Troyes and in the 13th-century *Roman de la Rose*; to Germany in the work of the ▷Minnesingers; and to England, where it was treated in detail by Chaucer, especially in *Troilus and Criseyde*. It continued as an important element in the Elizabethan sonnet through the influence of ▷Petrarch.

● **court-martial** ▶ A court, consisting of commissioned officers in the army, navy, or air force, convened to try a member of any of these services for an offence against military discipline or against ordinary law. An appeal court was established in 1951 and is now governed by the Courts-Martial (Appeals) Act (1968). An offender is not immune from trial by ordinary courts, but they must take into account any punishment to which he was sentenced by the court-martial.

● **Courtrai** ▶ (Flemish name: Kortrijk) 50 50N 03 17E A town in Belgium, on the River Lys. It was the site of the battle of the Spurs (1297), in which the French army was defeated by the burghers of Bruges and Ghent. It is an important textile centre. Population (1995 est): 76 040.

● **courts of law** ▶ Assemblies in which the law is administered. In England and Wales ▷civil law (*see also* common law; equity) is administered by the County Courts and the High Court of Justice and ▷criminal law is administered by the Magistrates' Courts and the Crown Court. Appeals from the civil law courts lie to the civil division of the Court of Appeal and those from the criminal law courts lie from Magistrate's Courts to the Crown Court and from the Crown Court to the criminal division of the Court of Appeal. Two or more judges of the High Court, when sitting together, may constitute a Divisional Court, which hears appeals on points of law from Magistrates' Courts, Crown Courts, and certain tribunals. Normally, the appeal is by way of case stated (i.e. the lower court, at the request of one of the litigants, sets out in writing the point or points of law to be decided by the Divisional Court). The Divisional Court can either (1) order the lower court to continue its hearing of the case in point while directing how the law should be applied or (2) allow or dismiss the appeal itself, if all the facts of the case have already been heard and decided by the lower court. The House of Lords is the Supreme Court of

Appeal in both criminal and civil cases. The High Court of Justice and the Court of Appeal together with the Crown Court form the Supreme Court of Judicature.

The County Courts have jurisdiction over most civil law actions. All divorce petitions start in the County Courts but are transferred to the High Court if defended. The High Court of Justice comprises the ▷Chancery, Queen's Bench (including the Admiralty Court (see maritime law) and the Commercial Court), and Family Divisions.

A criminal case comes first before a Magistrates' Court (see magistrate), which has jurisdiction in less serious cases (e.g. traffic offences) but commits more serious cases for trial at the Crown Court. The Crown Court, which was created in 1971 to replace the Courts of Assize and Courts of Quarter Session, is organized in six circuits (Midland and Oxford, North Eastern, Northern, South Eastern, Wales and Chester, and Western). A Crown Court sits in London as the ▷Central Criminal Court (Old Bailey). ▷See also judge.

In Scotland the supreme court for civil cases is the Court of Session, established in 1532, and the supreme court for criminal cases is the High Court of Judiciary. Appeals from the former lie to the House of Lords and from the latter to a tribunal of three judges of the High Court of Justiciary. See also Crown Prosecution Service; ecclesiastical courts.

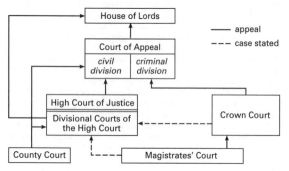

courts of law

● **Cousin, Victor** ▶ (1792–1867) French philosopher. He had a brilliant career, despite anti-establishment sympathies, and was a superb lecturer and prolific writer. As a minister under ▷Thiers (1840) he reformed French education. His talents were eclectic rather than analytic and his only original work is *Du vrai, du beau, et du bien* (1854).

● **Cousin the Elder, Jean** ▶ (1490–1560) French artist and craftsman, who designed tapestries and stained-glass windows. The nude study *Eva Prima Pandora* (Louvre) is attributed to him. His son **Jean Cousin the Younger** (c. 1522–c. 1594) was also a painter, engraver, and stained-glass designer, known for *The Last Judgment* (Louvre).

● **Cousteau, Jacques Yves** ▶ (1910–97) French naval officer and underwater explorer. He shared in the invention of the aqualung (1943) and invented a way of using television under water. In 1945 he founded the Undersea Research Group of the French navy at Marseilles and in 1950 became commander of the oceanographic research vessel *Calypso*. He is famous for such films as *The Silent World* (1953) and *The Living Sea* (1963). In 1985 he began a 2½-year voyage in a wind-powered vessel to support fuel saving and protest against nuclear weapons; in 1989 he led a campaign to protect Antarctica from commercial exploitation. His memoirs, *The Man, the Octopus, and the Orchid*, appeared shortly after his death.

● **couvade** ▶ A custom, common in many parts of the world among primitive peoples, in which the father retires to bed during his wife's confinement and simulates the pain of childbirth. Its intention is presumably to establish a role for the father and, by magical association, to lessen the pain of the mother. In the 20th century it has been reported among Basques and in Brazil.

● **covalent bond** ▷See chemical bond.

● **covenant** ▶ **1.** (law) A binding agreement between two parties whereby each promises to do something for the other (see deed). **2.** In the Old Testament, the agreement between God and Israel, which forms the basis of the Jewish religion. In return for obedience to God's will and the practice of ▷circumcision, God promised Abraham that his descendants would inherit the land that became Israel. Subsequently, when the Law (the ▷Ten Commandments) was delivered to Moses, the Israelites were promised a privileged relationship with God as the chosen people. The symbol of this agreement was the ▷Ark of the Covenant containing the tablets of the Law. In the New Testament, this belief is interpreted in Christian terms as including all men, who are redeemed by Christ.

● **Covenanters** ▶ Scottish Presbyterians who in the 16th and 17th centuries covenanted to defend their church. The National Covenant of 1638 was signed by thousands of Scottish Presbyterians after Charles I's attempt to introduce the English Prayer Book, this opposition culminating in the ▷Bishops' Wars. In the English ▷Civil War the Covenanters joined the parliamentarians in 1643 in return for the promise of church reform (see Solemn League and Covenant). After the Restoration (1660) they were persecuted and suppressed until the re-establishment of Presbyterianism in Scotland after the Glorious Revolution (1688).

● **Covent Garden** ▶ The principal English opera house, officially named the Royal Opera House. The first theatre on the site was opened in 1732, and the present building dates from the 1850s; it is currently the home of both the ▷Royal Opera and the ▷Royal Ballet Company. In 1997 it closed for two years to enable extensive rebuilding to be carried out. It takes its name from a square (originally a convent garden) onto which it backs, which was laid out in 1631 by Inigo ▷Jones. For many years London's fruit and vegetable market occupied the square but in 1973 it moved to Nine Elms (Wandsworth) and the square was redeveloped as a shopping precinct. The Old Flower Market has become the home of the London Transport Museum.

● **Coventry** ▶ **1.** 52 25N 1 30W A city in central England, in Coventry unitary authority, West Midlands. Heavily bombed during World War II, the city centre was almost entirely rebuilt. Its famous cathedral, designed by Sir Basil Spence, was opened in 1962 and retains the ruins of the old cathedral, which was bombed in 1940. Formerly a weaving town, Coventry is now an important centre for the motor-car industry and produces machinery, aerospace components, electrical and telecommunications equipment, and synthetic fabrics. It is also the site of the University of Warwick and Coventry University. Population (1991): 299 316. **2.** A unitary authority in central England, in West Midlands. Area: 97 sq km (37 sq mi). Population (1996 est): 306 500.

● **Coverdale, Miles** ▶ (1488–1568) English Protestant reformer. While an Augustinian friar at Cambridge, he was converted to Protestantism. In exile he published an English translation of the Bible (1535) and was largely responsible for the revisions resulting in the Great Bible of 1539. He was Bishop of Exeter from 1551 until exiled again under Queen Mary. After returning in 1559 he became a Puritan leader.

● **Covilhã, Pêro da** ▶ (c. 1460–c. 1526) Portuguese explorer. Sent by John II to find ▷Prester John and explore Africa and the East, he left Portugal in 1487 and travelled via Aden to India, visiting Cannanore, Calicut, and Goa. Later he set off from Cairo for Ethiopia. There he ended his days, honoured but forcibly detained.

● **Coward, Sir Noel** ▶ (1899–1973) British dramatist, composer, and actor. He first established his reputation with *The Vortex* (1924), an intense domestic drama, but his best-known plays are witty and elegant comedies of manners, such as *Hay Fever* (1925) and *Blithe Spirit* (1941). He also contributed as writer, director, composer, and performer to revues, musicals, and films, notably *In Which We Serve* (1942) and *Brief Encounter* (1946). His best-known songs include "Mad Dogs and Englishmen" and "Mad about the Boy."

● **cowboys** ▶ Mounted cattle herders and folk heroes of the US West, who from about 1820 worked in the open grassland W of the Mississippi River, from Canada to Mexico. Cowboys used horse, spur, rope, and branding iron to "round-up" the herds, i.e. drive them to market. The legendary cowboy of ▷westerns, drinking and fighting in a saloon, derives from his twice-yearly spree after the round-ups. Rail transport and barbed wire fences rendered the cowboy's jobs of herding and range riding obsolete. *Compare* gaucho.

● **Cowdrey, (Michael) Colin, Baron** ▶ (1932–2000) British cricketer, who played for Kent and was captain of England 27 times. He played in a record 114 Test matches and hit 107 centuries during his career (1950–76). His score of 7624 runs in Test cricket remained a British record for many years. He was raised to the peerage in 1997. His son **Christopher Cowdrey** (1957–) is also a cricketer; he captained Kent (1985–90) and England (1988).

● **Cowell, Henry** ▶ (1897–1965) US composer. He developed the technique of playing tone clusters on the piano by depressing adjacent notes with the forearm. He wrote over a thousand works and was active as a pianist and writer.

● **Cowes** ▶ 50 45N 1 18W A town in S England, situated on the Isle of Wight on the Medina estuary. It is a resort and internationally famous yachting centre. Cowes has boatbuilding, marine engineering, and radar industries; hovercraft are made here. Population (1991): 16 335.

● **Cowley, Abraham** ▶ (1618–67) English poet. During the Civil War he served as Queen Henrietta Maria's secretary in France and as a royalist secret agent in England. His best-known Metaphysical verse is contained in *The Mistress* (1647, 1656) and *Miscellanies* (1656). His *Pindaric Odes* (1656) introduced this poetic form to English.

● **cow parsley** ▶ A biennial herb, *Anthriscus sylvestris*, up to 100 cm high, with conspicuous umbrella-like clusters of white or pinkish flowers. It is found in hedgerows, wood edges, and waste places throughout much of Eurasia and N Africa and has been introduced to North America. Family: ▷*Umbelliferae*.

● **cowpea** ▶ An annual African plant, *Vigna unguiculata*, widely grown in tropical areas and the southern USA. Having a high protein content, cowpeas are an important food crop, especially in Africa. There are two forms: a short erect one grown in Africa and America, whose seeds are used dried, and a tall climbing one grown in SE Asia, whose long pods are eaten when young. Family: ▷*Leguminosae*.

● **Cowpens, Battle of** ▶ (17 January, 1781) A battle in the American Revolution in which the Americans defeated the British. Led by Gen Daniel Morgan (1736–1802), the Americans inflicted a surprise defeat on the larger British force, slowing down ▷Cornwallis' invasion of North Carolina.

Sir Noel Coward ▶ At Montreux, Switzerland (1967).

● **Cowper, William** ▶ (1731–1800) British poet. With John Newton, an evangelical curate, he published *Olney Hymns* in 1779. "John Gilpin's Ride" (1783), a comic ballad, and *The Task* (1785), a long discursive poem on rural themes, were both very successful. He was mentally unstable throughout his life, and frequently attempted suicide. After the death in 1796 of Mary Unwin, a widow with whom he had lived for many years, he expressed his despair in "The Castaway."

● **cowpox** ▶ A contagious virus disease of cattle that can be con-

tracted by man. Resembling a mild form of smallpox, it appears as blisters on the teats and udder. Animals should be isolated and recovery is usually complete. Edward ▷Jenner used fluid from cowpox blisters to produce the first effective smallpox vaccine.

● **cowrie** ▶ A ▷gastropod mollusc of the family *Cypraeidae* (about 160 species), mostly found in warm seas. 1–15 cm long, cowries have glossy □shells with inrolled lips that are covered by the mantle, which is withdrawn inside the shell when the animal is disturbed. Cowries feed at night on small animals. The shell of the tropical money cowrie (*Cypraea moneta*), about 3 cm long, is used as a form of currency in Africa and India.

● **cowslip** ▶ A perennial spring-flowering Eurasian herb, *Primula veris*, growing to a height of 20 cm. It has a rosette of crinkled leaves and hanging clusters of bright-yellow five-petalled flowers. It is found from lowland meadows to alpine pastures. Family: *Primulaceae* (primrose family).

● **coyote** ▶ A wild ▷dog, *Canis latrans*, of Central and North American grassland, also called prairie wolf. Coyotes are about 120 cm long, including the bushy tail (30 cm), and have yellowish fur. They hunt alone or in packs and take food ranging from insects to small deer.

● **coypu** ▶ A South American aquatic ▷rodent, *Myocaster coypus*. About 60 cm long (excluding a long hairless tail), it has thick brown fur and webbed hind feet. The underfur of the belly is known as nutria, and coypus are farmed for fur. In Britain escaped coypus caused extensive damage, especially in East Anglia, eating vegetation and undermining river banks until eradicated in the 1980s. Family: *Capromyidae*.

● **crab** ▶ A ▷crustacean belonging to the tribes *Brachyura* (true crabs; about 4500 species) or *Anomura* (about 1300 species, including the ▷hermit crab). True crabs have a wide flat body covered by a hard carapace, with the small abdomen tucked underneath. There is a large pair of pincers and four pairs of legs used for walking (typically in a sideways scuttle) or swimming. They are carnivores or scavengers and most species are marine (the ▷land crab is an exception). The European species *Cancer pagurus* is edible. Order: ▷*Decapoda*.

● **crab apple** ▶ A □tree, *Malus sylvestris*, 2–10 m high: one of the species from which cultivated ▷apples have been developed. It has pinkish-white five-petalled flowers that bloom in spring and small sour greenish fruits, used to make jelly. A native of Europe and Asia, it is sometimes grown as an ornamental. Family: *Rosaceae*.

● **Crabbe, George** ▶ (1754–1832) British poet, born in Aldeburgh, Suffolk, scene of many of his poems. In 1780 he left his doctor's practice there and went to London. Under the patronage of Edmund Burke he took orders, becoming chaplain to the Duke of Rutland and later vicar of Trowbridge, Wiltshire. *The Village* (1783) was a realistic portrayal of rural life, in contrast to conventional idealized treatments. This theme he took up again in the verse tales of *The Borough* (1810), source of ▷Britten's opera *Peter Grimes*, and *Tales of the Hall* (1819).

● **crabeater seal** ▶ A common Antarctic seal, *Lobodon carcinophagus*, that feeds entirely on krill. About 2.5 m long, crabeater seals are dark in winter and almost white in summer; they are slender and can travel fast over ice. □oceans.

● **Crab nebula** ▶ A turbulent expanding mass of gas, lying about 6000 light years distant in the constellation Taurus. It is the remnant of a ▷supernova that was observed in 1054. It emits radiation from all spectral regions and is an especially strong source of radio waves and X-rays. Within the nebula, and supplying energy to it, lies the **Crab pulsar**. This optical ▷pulsar was produced by the supernova and rotates extremely rapidly with a period of only 0.033 seconds.

● **crack** ▷*See* cocaine.

● **cracking** ▷*See* catalytic cracking; oil.

● **Cracow** ▷*See* Kraków.

● **Craig, Edward Henry Gordon** ▷*See* Terry, Dame Ellen.

● **Craigavon** ▶ A district in central Northern Ireland, in Co Armagh. Area: 279 sq km (108 sq mi). Population (1999): 79 100.

● **Craik, Dinah Maria Mulock** ▶ (1826–87) British novelist. Daughter of a clergyman, her best-known novels are *John Halifax: Gentleman* (1856) and *A Life for a Life* (1859).

● **Craiova** ▶ 44 18N 23 47E A city in S Romania, on the River Jiu. Industries include heavy engineering and food manufacture. Its university was established in 1966. Population (1994 est): 306 825.

● **crake** ▶ A small shy bird belonging to the ▷rail family. Crakes have a short conical bill and are commonly found in marshes and swamps. The Eurasian spotted crake (*Porzana porzana*) is 23 cm long and has a streaked olive back, a lightly spotted breast, and a red ring at the base of the bill.

● **Cram, Steve** ▶ (1960–) British middle-distance runner. He won the world championship 1500 m title in 1983; in 1985 he set new world records for the mile (which he held until 1993) and the 2000 m (which he held until 1987).

● **cramp** ▶ Painful spasmodic contraction of a muscle. Cramp is often caused by overexercise, often of the legs (in swimmers) or hands (writers' cramp). It may also be due to salt deficiency or poor circulation.

● **Cranach the Elder, Lucas** ▶ (Lucas Müller; 1472–1553) German artist. He studied painting under his father before moving to Wittenberg in 1505 to become court painter to Frederick the Wise, Elector of Saxony, and later to his two successors. Because of his portraits of Reformation leaders including his friend Luther, he is sometimes called the Reformation painter. He is also noted for his stylized but sensuous nudes, e.g. *Adam and Eve* (Courtauld Institute, London).

● **cranberry** ▶ A low evergreen shrub of the genus *Vaccinium*, bearing red edible berries and growing in acidic boggy areas. *V. oxycoccus* occurs in Europe, N Asia, and North America. *V. macrocarpon* of North America has larger fruits (about 1.5 cm across). The fruits of both are made into cranberry sauce. Family: *Ericaceae* (heath family).

● **crane** ▶ (bird) A large long-legged bird belonging to a family (*Gruidae*; 14 species) occurring in Old World regions and North America. Standing up to 140 cm tall with a wingspan of over 200 cm, cranes vary from grey to white with black wingtips; some species are crested. They have heavy bills, feeding in marshes and plains on grain, shoots, and small animals; northern species are migratory. Order: *Gruiformes* (rails, etc.). ▷*See also* demoiselle; whooping crane.

● **crane** ▶ (machinery) A machine for raising, lowering, or moving heavy objects. It is used in construction work, loading cargoes onto ships, etc. There are many types but most have an engine to wind cables supported by an inclined or horizontal jib or boom, which either has a pulley system at one end or, in the case of a travelling crane, a pulley system that can move along the whole length of the jib. In a gantry crane the jib is fixed on supports at both ends, which themselves travel along rails. Cranes are often mounted on lorries or locomotives.

● **Crane, Hart** ▶ (1899–1932) US poet. After an unhappy childhood in Ohio, he settled in New York in 1923 and began writing poems expressive of the personal conflicts caused by his homosexuality and alcoholism. *White Buildings* was published in 1926. *The Bridge* (1930), an epic poem in 15 parts, unites myth, history, and dream in a celebration of contemporary America. He went to Mexico to write another epic and drowned himself on the return voyage.

● **Crane, Stephen** ▶ (1871–1900) US novelist. His early work as a journalist in New York provided him with first-hand knowledge of the poverty and destitution portrayed in his novel *Maggie: A Girl of the Streets* (1893). He is best known for the war novel *The Red Badge of Courage* (1895) and his short stories, especially "The Open Boat." He worked as a war correspondent in Cuba and Greece, lived in England, and died in Germany of tuberculosis.

● **Crane, Walter** ▶ (1845–1915) British illustrator, painter, and designer of textiles and wallpaper. The son of a painter, he studied under a wood engraver in London, achieving fame for his illustra-

tions to children's books. He was later associated with the ▷Arts and Crafts movement.

● **cranefly** ▶ A harmless fly, also called daddy longlegs, belonging to the family *Tipulidae*. Craneflies are 6–75 mm long with long delicate legs and wings. They are found near water or vegetation and are attracted to light. The larvae generally occur in water or rotting vegetation. However some—the leatherjackets—live in the soil and are plant pests, feeding on the roots of cereals and grasses. ▯insect.

● **cranesbill** ▶ A herbaceous plant of the genus *Geranium* (about 400 species), widely distributed, especially in temperate regions, and usually having pink or purple flowers. They take their name from the long slender beaklike carpels. The meadow cranesbill (*G. pratense*), a perennial up to 60 cm high, has violet-blue flowers, and is widespread throughout Eurasia and North America. Family: *Geraniaceae*.

● **Craniata** ▷*See* Vertebrata.

● **Cranko, John** ▶ (1927–73) British choreographer, born in South Africa. He developed the Stuttgart Ballet into one of the leading European companies during the 1960s. His best-known works are full-length ballets such as *Romeo and Juliet* (1962) and *Onegin* (1965).

● **Cranmer, Thomas** ▶ (1489–1556) Anglican reformer and martyr. He was consecrated Archbishop of Canterbury in 1532, following his support of ▷Henry VIII in the king's divorce dispute with the pope. He is especially remembered for his contributions to the Prayer Books of 1549 and 1552. Under Queen Mary he was tried as a heretic and, after initially recanting, burned at the stake.

● **crannog** ▶ An artificial island of stone, timber, and peat, constructed as sites for houses in Ireland from the early Neolithic to the medieval eras. A notable example is the Lough Gara crannog.

● **Cranwell** ▶ 53 2N 0 30W A village in E England, in Lincolnshire. The Royal Air Force College (founded in 1919) is situated here.

● **craps** ▶ A dice game used for gambling, especially in the USA. It was developed in the 19th century by Black workers from the more complex game of ▷hazard. Two dice are used. Each player attempts to throw a "natural," a 7 or 11, which wins. 2, 3, or 12 ("craps") are losing combinations. If he throws a 4, 5, 6, 8, 9, or 10 he continues to throw until he wins by throwing the same number again or loses by throwing a 7. Bets are made by the other players against the thrower, among themselves, or (in a casino) against the house.

● **Crashaw, Richard** ▶ (c. 1613–49) British poet. He was ordained priest at Cambridge, where he published Greek and Latin verses. He became a Catholic in France in 1644 and obtained an ecclesiastical post in Italy. The baroque style of his religious poetry is illustrated in *Steps to the Temple* (1646).

● **Crassus, Marcus Licinius** ▶ (c. 115–53 BC) Roman politician and ally of Caesar, nicknamed *Dives* (wealthy). Crassus suppressed Spartacus' revolt (71), although Pompey took the credit. Failing to manipulate political affairs on his own, Crassus joined Pompey and Caesar in the first Triumvirate (60). He was killed during an invasion of Parthia.

● **crawfish** ▶ 1. ▷*See* spiny lobster. 2. ▷*See* crayfish.

● **Crawford, Joan** ▶ (Lucille le Sueur; 1908–77) US film actress. She began in musicals but became famous during the 1930s and 1940s for her portrayals of ambitious women in such films as *Grand Hotel* (1932) and *Mildred Pierce* (1945).

● **Crawley** ▶ 51 7N 0 12W A town in SE England, in West Sussex. Designated a new town in 1947, it has light engineering, electronics, plastics, and pharmaceuticals; financial services are also important. Gatwick airport is nearby. Population (1998 est): 95 000.

● **Craxi, Bettino** ▶ (1934–2000) Italian statesman; prime minister (1983–87). He became leader of the Italian Socialist Party in 1976 and in 1983 was elected the first socialist prime minister of Italy. His coalition was the longest government since World War II. In 1995 he was convicted in absentia on corruption charges. In 1999 he returned to Italy to serve his sentence under house arrest but died soon after.

● **crayfish** ▶ A freshwater ▷crustacean, also called crawfish and crawdad, belonging to the superfamily *Nephropidea*. It has a small lobster-like body, 25–75 mm long, and occurs under rocks or debris or in burrows in mud banks during the day. At night it feeds on plant and animal material. Some species are edible. Order: ▷Decapoda.

● **Crazy Horse** ▶ (?1849–77) Sioux Indian chief. Attempting to prevent White settlement in Sioux territory, he joined in the massacre of Gen ▷Custer's forces (1876). He surrendered in 1877 but was killed while resisting imprisonment.

● **cream of tartar** ▶ Potassium hydrogen tartrate that occurs in the later stages of the fermentation of grape juice as a deposit on the sides of the cask. After purification and crystallization it is used in baking powder and medicines.

● **creamware** ▶ A cream-coloured English earthenware that replaced ▷Delft and salt-glazed wares from about 1760. The universal adoption of creamware by English manufacturers was made possible by Josiah ▷Wedgwood, who perfected it and prevented restrictive patent rights being granted.

● **creationism** ▶ A pseudoscience developed in the USA by opponents of neo-▷Darwinism to explain evolutionary problems unresolved by Darwin's theory. Based on the biblical account of the Creation, it claims that each species is individually created in its present form, rather than evolving gradually. This view is without any scientific validity and is widely regarded as one of many creation myths.

● **Crécy, Battle of** ▶ (26 August, 1346) The first land battle of the ▷Hundred Years' War, fought in N France, in which the English, led by ▷Edward III, defeated the French under ▷Philip VI. It was a triumph for the English longbowmen over heavily armoured French knights; 1500 French soldiers were killed. The victory enabled Edward to move N and beseige Calais.

● **credit and credit ratings** ▶ The loan of money to an individual or company by a bank, credit-card organization, retailer, etc. Much consumer purchasing, especially of durables (see consumption), in industrial countries is on credit terms. The amount of credit that a person or company can command depends on his credit rating at the bank or on that given by an agency that specializes in listing the creditworthiness of companies. Credit ratings will depend on the applicants' known assets and liabilities, income (profitability for a company), and past record for trustworthiness. Influencing credit advances is a central part of a government's monetary policy.

● **credit card** ▶ A card that enables the holder to obtain goods or services on credit. They are issued by retail stores, banks, and credit-card companies to approved clients. The bank or credit-card company settles the client's bills, invoicing him monthly and charging interest on any outstanding debts. Their profit comes from the high rate of interest charged, the card-holders' subscriptions, and the fees paid by some organizations that accept cards. ▷See also cheque card; debit card.

● **credit insurance** ▶ A form of insurance that provides cover against bad trade debts. In the UK the government's Export Credits Guarantee Department (ECGD), set up in 1930, provides insurance for exporters, covering insolvency of the buyers, war risk, governmental interference, and exchange-control problems. This service for home traders is also provided by private-sector insurance companies, often in conjunction with ▷factoring.

● **Cree** ▶ An Algonquian-speaking North American Indian people of the region S of Hudson Bay, extending westwards to Lake Winnipeg. They lived by hunting and trapping in small wandering bands. One group, known as Plains Cree, moved into the Plains and, acquiring horses and guns, adopted the buffalo-hunting culture of this region. They were more aggressive than the northern groups, often raiding for horses. Among the Cree, belief in witchcraft and observance of taboos relating to animal spirits were common.

● **Creed, Frederick** ▶ (1871–1957) Canadian inventor, who moved to Scotland in 1897 and developed the Creed teleprinter (see Telex). The first such device was installed in Fleet Street in 1912 and was soon in widespread use.

● **creeds** ▶ In Christianity, formal summaries of the principal items of belief, often recited as part of the eucharistic service in many Churches. They originated as professions of faith said at baptism. The

two most widely used are the Apostles' Creed (probably 3rd century AD) and the Nicene Creed, probably a revision by the Council of Constantinople (381) of the creed promulgated at the Council of ▷Nicaea (325) and accepted by both Western and Eastern churches. The Athanasian Creed, probably dating from the 5th century, is a technical exposition of orthodox teaching on the Trinity and Incarnation, proclaiming the damnation of all who believe otherwise: it appears in the Book of Common Prayer but has been virtually abandoned in worship.

● **Creek** ▶ A Muskogean-speaking North American Indian people divided into the Muskogee of Georgia and the Hitchiti of Alabama. They were cultivators and hunters, practised the green corn (first-fruits) ceremony, and tattooed their bodies heavily. Their small towns of rectangular huts were built around a central square often containing a temple mound. Towns were grouped into red and white divisions, respectively concerned with matters of war and peace. A confederacy of Creek towns fought the encroaching whites in the 18th and early 19th centuries. On their defeat in the 1830s they were removed to the area of Oklahoma.

● **Creeley, Robert** ▶ (1926–   ) US poet. He travelled widely in India, Burma (now Myanmar), and Europe. As editor of the *Black Mountain Review* for seven years from 1955 he published a group of poets known for their linguistic economy and precision. His own volumes include *For Love* (1960), *Pieces* (1969), and *Collected Poems* (1983); he also wrote short stories and a novel, *The Island* (1963). In the 1980s and 1990s he published his correspondence and an *Autobiography* (1990).

● **cremation** ▶ The disposal of the dead by burning. Practised by many ancient European peoples, cremation was forbidden by the Christian Church on account of the doctrine of bodily resurrection of the dead. With 19th-century urban overcrowding in the West, cremation was revived. The first crematorium in England was founded at Woking in 1885 by the Cremation Society (established 1874), after legalization of the practice (which is now common). The Roman Catholic Church formerly disapproved of cremation but it is now accepted as it is among Jews (except for the most orthodox) and Muslims. In the East it has remained the most general method of corpse disposal among Hindus, Buddhists, and Sikhs.

● **Cremona** ▶ 45 08N 10 01E A town in N Italy, in Lombardy on the River Po. It has a 12th-century cathedral and a 13th-century palace. From the 16th to the 18th centuries it was famous for the manufacture of violins, including those of Stradivari. Population (1990): 75 160.

● **creodont** ▶ An extinct primitive carnivorous mammal of the early Tertiary period (55–45 million years ago). They were mostly short-legged and slow-moving, preying on herbivores.

● **creole** ▶ **1.** Originally a White person born in Spanish America during the colonial period (16th to 18th centuries). They suffered social and commercial disadvantages in comparison with the Spanish administrative class. **2.** A person of mixed blood living in the Caribbean area or in Latin America, extending to encompass a descendant of slaves in Suriname, a French-speaking descendant of French or Spanish settlers in Louisiana, and various other groups. More loosely, the term refers to people of Caribbean culture. **3.** A patois based on French, English, or Dutch and spoken especially in the West Indies as a mother tongue (*compare* pidgin).

● **creosote** ▶ A substance produced by distilling tar. The creosote used for preserving wood is obtained from coal tar and is a brownish mixture of aromatic hydrocarbons and ▷phenols. Creosote made from wood tar is a mixture of phenols and is used in pharmacy.

● **creosote bush** ▶ A shrub of the genus *Larrea* (5 species), of arid and semiarid areas of North and South America, where it is the dominant feature of the landscape. Up to 2 m high, these plants contain resinous phenolic substances that deter grazing animals. Family: *Zygophyllaceae*.

● **cresol** ▶ (or methylphenol; $CH_3C_6H_4OH$) A liquid ▷aromatic compound obtained from coal tar. It has three ▷isomers, a mixture of which is used as a disinfectant.

● **cress** ▶ A plant of the mustard family (*Cruciferae*) the sharp-tasting leaves of which are used in salads, especially garden cress, or peppergrass (*Lepidium sativum*), believed to be native to W Asia but widely naturalized in Europe. The seedlings are eaten, often with those of white mustard (*Sinapis alba*), with which it may be grown in containers. The European winter, or land, cress (*Barbarea verna*) grows to a height of 100 cm. Its leaves can be picked throughout winter.

● **Cressent, Charles** ▶ (1685-1768) French cabinetmaker. After working with ▷Boulle he became official cabinetmaker (1715) to the regent, the Duc d'Orléans. The leading designer of the period, he made popular the use of coloured-wood marquetry and ▷ormolu mountings.

● **Creswell Crags** ▶ A gorge near Creswell (Derbyshire, England) containing caves where ▷Mousterian flint tools and a ▷Magdalenian bone engraving of a horse's head were found.

● **Cretaceous period** ▶ A geological period of the Mesozoic era, between about 135 and 65 million years ago, following the Jurassic and preceding the Tertiary (when the Cenozoic era began). The period saw a widespread gradual marine transgression, Cretaceous rocks culminating in the thick chalk deposits of N Europe and the midwestern USA. The dinosaurs and other giant reptiles, as well as the ammonites and many other invertebrates, became extinct at the end of the Cretaceous.

● **Crete** ▶ (Modern Greek name: Kríti) The largest of the Greek islands, in the E Mediterranean Sea approximately 100 km (63 mi) SE of the mainland. It is generally mountainous, rising over 2400 m (7874 ft). The economy is based primarily on agriculture producing olives, wines, and citrus fruits; the raising of sheep and goats is also important. There is a thriving tourist industry, based on Iráklion.
History: colonized probably in the 6th millennium BC from Asia Minor, Crete achieved extensive maritime power during the Middle Minoan period (c. 2000–c. 1700 BC), from which many artefacts, inscriptions, and buildings have been discovered (*see* Minoan civilization). The most notable are the palace at ▷Knossos and clay tablets bearing two different scripts known as ▷Linear A and ▷Linear B. Politically insignificant in the history of classical Greece, it fell to Rome (67 BC), Byzantium (395 AD), and the Muslims (826). In 1204 it was sold to the Venetians, who gave both the island and Iráklion the name Candia. It fell to Turkey in 1669 and was officially incorporated into Greece in 1913. During World War II it was the scene (1941) of the first ever large-scale airborne invasion, in which the Germans took the island from British and Commonwealth troops, who had been evacuated here from the Greek mainland. Area: 8332 sq km (3217 sq mi). Population (1991): 540 054. Capital: Khaniá.

● **cretinism** ▶ The condition resulting from a deficiency of thyroid hormone, which is present from birth. It causes stunted growth and impairment of mental development. Cretinism is treated with injections of thyroxine, which must be started early and continued throughout life.

● **Creutzfeldt-Jakob disease** ▶ (CJD) A fatal neurological disease characterized by rapidly progressive dementia and involuntary jerking movements, first described by German psychiatrists H. G. Creutzfeldt (1885-1964) and A. M. Jakob (1884-1931) and now widely believed to be caused by deposits of abnormal ▷prion protein in the brain. Sporadic and inherited forms of CJD are rare and typically affect elderly people, but the disease can be transmitted accidentally (e.g. through injections of prion-infected growth hormone), appearing many years after the initial infection. In the mid-1990s a variant form of CJD arose in the UK, which was thought to be linked to the consumption of beef products from cattle infected with ▷BSE and affected mainly young people. Between 1995 and the end of March, 1999, 40 cases of new variant (nv) CJD were confirmed—by microscopical examination of brain tissue after death (the only way of making a positive diagnosis). In 1998 the possibility of diagnosing nv CJD during life—by examination of appendix and other tissue removed during surgery—was investigated.

● **Crewe** ▶ 53 05N 2 27W A town in NW England, in Cheshire. Crewe developed as an important railway junction with engineering and

workshops. Industry now consists of a mixture of engineering and high technology. Population (1991): 63 351.

● **cribbage** ▶ (or crib) A card game attributed to Sir John ▷Suckling. It is played by 2, 3, or 4 players with a standard pack of 52 cards. The rules vary in detail, but play basically consists of each player alternately playing a card until the total value of the cards played approaches 31. The last player able to play a card without exceeding 31 scores. Points are also scored for having certain combinations of cards in a hand or for playing during certain sequences of cards. The crib (consisting of cards discarded from each hand) scores for the dealer. The score is kept with small pegs on a cribbage board containing rows of holes.

● **Crichton, James** ▶ (1560-82) Scottish scholar and adventurer. After graduating from St Andrews University, Crichton toured Europe. Called "the Admirable Crichton," on account of his literary and athletic gifts, he was apparently killed by a jealous pupil in a brawl in Mantua.

● **Crick, Francis Harry Compton** ▶ (1916–) British biophysicist, who (with James D. ▷Watson) proposed a model for the molecular structure of ▷DNA (1953). Following this breakthrough, Crick continued to work on DNA, helping to determine the mechanism of protein synthesis. He shared a Nobel Prize (1962) with Watson and Maurice ▷Wilkins and was appointed to the OM in 1991.

● **cricket** ▶ (sport) An 11-a-side bat-and-ball team game, in which the object is to score the most runs. It originated in England among shepherds using their crooks as bats; its rules were laid down in 1744 and the game is played almost exclusively in the UK and its former empire. It is presided over by two umpires (from 1993 in test matches a third umpire can make decisions on stumpings and runnings out from the stand using video replays). It is played on a large field; the pitch is a strip of grass 22 yd (20.12 m) long having at each end a wicket of three stumps surmounted by two bails. The cork and twine ball, encased in leather, is 8.8–9 in (22.4–22.9 cm) in circumference and weighs 5.5–5.75 oz (155.9–163 g). The members of one team take

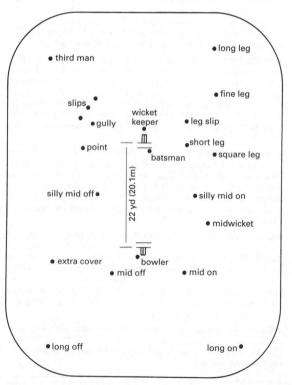

cricket ▶ The pitch, showing the usual fielding positions (for a right-handed batsman).

turns to bat in pairs, one defending each wicket; the batsmen's objective is to score runs by hitting the ball and exchanging ends before the ball is returned to the pitch. Each player bats until he is bowled, caught, stumped, run out, or judged lbw (leg before wicket). The members of the other team field, some taking turns to bowl the ball. After every over of six balls (sometimes eight in Australia) the bowler changes, the new bowler bowling from the other wicket. A match consists of one or two innings and may last for a few hours or up to six days. International cricket, governed by the International Cricket Conference, is played mainly in Test matches between England, Australia, the West Indies, New Zealand, India, Pakistan, Sri Lanka, and South Africa. The governing body in each country decides which teams are first class; in England first-class cricket chiefly involves the 18 professional first-class county teams (the 18th county, Durham, was added in 1990). ▷*See also* Ashes; Marylebone Cricket Club.

● **cricket** ▶ (zoology) An insect, resembling a grasshopper but with longer antennae, belonging to one of several families of the order ▷*Orthoptera*. The males stridulate (i.e. make a chirping noise) by rubbing the front wings together. True crickets (family *Gryllidae*; 2400 species) have black or brown flattened bodies, 3–50 mm long, with long tail appendages (cerci) and short forewings (they do not fly). The females have long needle-like ovipositors for depositing eggs in soil or crevices. True crickets are omnivorous and live in burrows or among vegetation; some, for example the widely distributed house cricket (*Acheta domesticus*), frequent buildings. ▷*See also* bush cricket; mole cricket.

● **Crimea** ▶ (Russian name: Krym) A peninsula and autonomous republic in Ukraine, almost totally surrounded by the Black Sea and the Sea of Azov and connected to the mainland in the N by the Perekop Isthmus. It is mainly flat but rises to 1545 m (5069 ft) in the S. Iron ore is mined here and wheat, tobacco, and wine are produced. The chief towns are Feodosia, Kerch, Sevastopol, Yalta, Yevpatoria, and Simferopol.
History: colonized by Greeks in the 6th century BC, the Crimea was continually invaded by Goths, Huns, and others and in 1239 was made a khanate by Tatars of the ▷Golden Horde. This was overthrown by Turks in 1475, and the area was annexed by Russia in 1783. Many Tatars emigrated then, and the remainder were deported in 1945 for alleged collaboration with the German forces of occupation (1941–43); they were allowed back in 1988. Following the breakup of the Soviet Union in 1991, many Crimeans now favour union with Russia or total independence. Area: about 27 000 sq km (10 423 sq mi). Population (1996 est): 2 205 600. Capital: Simferopol. ▷*See also* Crimean War.

● **Crimean War** ▶ (1853–56) The war between Russia, on one side, and Britain, France, the Ottoman (Turkish) Empire, and (from 1855) Sardinia-Piedmont, on the other. Caused by Russia's expansionist ambitions in the Balkans, the war was precipitated by Russia's desire to establish a protectorate over Orthodox Christians in the Ottoman Empire. In July, 1853, Russia occupied Moldavia and Walachia, in October, Turkey declared war, and in March, 1854, following the destruction of a Turkish fleet at Sinope, Britain and France entered the war. The major battles of the year-long siege of Sevastopol, in the Crimea, were of ▷Balaclava and ▷Inkerman, and the Russians eventually evacuated the port in September, 1855. Peace was formally concluded at Paris (1856). Over 250 000 men were lost by each side, many from disease in the appalling hospitals of the Crimea. The British Government dispatched Florence ▷Nightingale to inspect those at Scutari, where her work had a considerable effect in improving conditions.

● **Criminal Investigation Department** ▶ (CID) The investigative department of ▷police forces in the UK. A CID was created at ▷Scotland Yard in 1878, based on the detective branch that had been in existence since 1842. All UK police forces now have their own CIDs, all recruits to which must first have served as uniformed officers.

● **Criminal Justice (and Public Order) Act** ▶ (1994) A UK act of parliament that enacted a series of wide-ranging and controversial measures, mainly concerned with public order and police procedures. The act created a new offence of "aggravated trespass" (aimed at hunt saboteurs and other protestors) and gave police new powers

to prohibit unlicensed assemblies (e.g. rave parties). Police powers of stop-and-search were extended, as were powers to take fingerprints and samples for DNA analysis. Unauthorized camping in vehicles (as by Gipsies or ▷New Age Travellers) was made an offence. The historic right of an accused person to remain silent without prejudicing his or her case was ended. Other clauses dealt with bail procedures, young offenders, and ▷censorship of films and videos.

● **criminal law** ▶ The body of law determining the acts and circumstances that amount to a crime (a wrong against society prohibited by law) and the punishment for crimes. Criminal law, which is distinguished from ▷civil law, derives in England chiefly from ▷common law, although statute law has contributed significantly to its development. Most crimes entail both an act (actus reus) and a mental element (mens rea). However, there is a growing number of crimes in which no mental element is necessary (called crimes of strict liability), such as most motoring offences. ▷Insanity, infancy (children under the age of ten), or duress (an act committed under threat of death or serious personal injury) may excuse a crime, but ignorance of the law does not if, in cases involving a mental element, the offender intends the result of his acts.
In England all criminal cases appear first before a Magistrates' Court; minor offences are tried in the Magistrates' Court, while more serious offences are referred to the Crown Court for trial (see courts of law). Punishment of an offender depends on the nature of the crime and the offender's age. A juvenile offender (under 17 years old) is generally tried in a youth court (see juvenile delinquency). In criminal proceedings an offender aged between 10 and 14 who has committed a serious offence may be sentenced to custody under a secure training order for six months to two years. An offender between 15 and 21 may be sent to a ▷young offender institution for a minimum period of 21 days; the maximum detention period is 24 months. Young offender institutions replaced detention centres and youth custody centres. Offenders between 17 and 21 may alternatively be required to report periodically to attendance centres. A person under the age of 18 who is convicted of murder may not be sentenced to life imprisonment (mandatory for those of 18 and over) but instead must be ordered to be detained during Her Majesty's pleasure.
An adult (over 21) may be sentenced to death (see capital punishment), to life imprisonment, or to a specific term of imprisonment (statutes specify the maximum term that may be imposed for any statutory offence). Alternatively he may receive a suspended sentence of imprisonment of 2 years or less, which he will not serve unless convicted of another offence punishable with imprisonment during the period of suspension (1–2 years); or he may be placed in the charge of a probation officer for 6 months to 3 years. Other punishments include ▷community service, fines, and conditional discharges. ▷*See also* prisons.

● **criminology** ▶ The study of the cause, nature, and prevention of crime. Crime was generally equated with immorality until the 19th century, when the pioneer Italian criminologist Cesare ▷Lombroso suggested, in *L'uomo delinquente* (1876), that criminals are born and can be recognized by such physical attributes as a receding forehead. Although this view is no longer accepted, at various times evidence has been produced to suggest that such physiological abnormalities as an extra Y chromosome or an endocrine abnormality do predispose to criminality. Poverty, psychological stress, lack of parental affection in childhood, working mothers, and the decline of the extended family have all been suggested as additional or alternative predisposing factors, and some evidence has been produced to support each of them. But none of this evidence can explain why some people succumb to predisposing factors and become criminals while others, exposed to the same factors, do not.
Deep ethical problems are also involved. To what extent do predisposing factors affect culpability? To what extent should crime be regarded merely as a deviation from social norms? Should punishment fit the crime or the criminal and to what extent should it attempt to be therapeutic? Criminologists have, as yet, no satisfactory answers to most of these questions. Research continues in such institutions as the Institute of Criminology, Cambridge University.

● **crinoid** ▶ A marine invertebrate animal belonging to a class (*Crinoidea*; about 700 species) of ▷echinoderms, including the sea lilies and feather stars. It has a small cup-shaped body covered with calcareous plates and with five radiating pairs of feathery flexible arms surrounding the mouth at the top. Sea lilies, most of which are now extinct, are fixed to the sea bottom, coral reefs, etc., by a stalk. Feather stars, e.g. *Antedon*, are free-swimming and are usually found on rocky bottoms. Crinoids occur mainly in deep waters and feed on microscopic plankton and detritus caught by the arms and conveyed to the mouth. The larvae are sedentary. ⌐fossil.

● **Crippen, Hawley Harvey** ▶ (1862–1910) US murderer. He poisoned his wife in London and attempted to escape to the USA with his mistress. He was arrested on board ship (following one of the first uses of shore to ship radio) and returned to England, where he was convicted and hanged.

● **Cripps, Sir (Richard) Stafford** ▶ (1889–1952) British Labour politician. A barrister, Cripps became solicitor general in 1930, before entering parliament in 1931. In 1939 he was expelled from the Labour Party for campaigning for a Popular Front against Neville ▷Chamberlain's appeasement policy. He was ambassador to Moscow (1940–42), minister of aircraft production (1942–45), and, once more in the Labour fold, chancellor of the exchequer (1947–50), when his austere economic policy set Britain on the road to recovery after World War II.

● **Cristofori, Bartolommeo** ▶ (1655–1731) Italian harpsichord maker and inventor of the ▷piano. He constructed the escapement system in which the hammer falls away from the string immediately after striking it, leaving it free to vibrate. A damper stops the sound when the key is released.

● **critical mass** ▶ The mass of fissile substance that is just capable of sustaining a ▷chain reaction within it. Below the critical mass, too many of the particles that might have induced a reaction escape and the chain reaction dies away.

● **critical-path analysis** ▶ A planning method based on the use of a schematic representation of the network of activities and events involved in a project. Its aim is to aid coordination by identifying the optimum schedule. A critical path is a sequence of activities in which the key parameters, usually time and cost, cannot be increased without endangering the whole project. In large networks, which often need to be analysed by computer, there may be more than one critical path. The method is used in large construction projects.

● **critical state** ▶ The state of a gas at its critical temperature, pressure, and volume. The critical temperature is the temperature above which a gas cannot be liquefied by increased pressure alone. The vapour pressure of the gas at this temperature is the critical pressure and its volume, the critical volume. In the critical state the density of the vapour is equal to the density of the liquid.

● **Crivelli, Carlo** ▶ (c. 1430–95) Venetian painter, who settled in Marche in the late 1460s. He is set apart from the Venetian school by his sharp linear style, influenced by ▷Mantegna, and the decorative detail that appears in such paintings as *The Annunciation* (National Gallery, London).

● **croaker** ▷*See* drumfish.

● **Croatia** ▶ (Serbo-Croat name: Hrvatska) A republic in SE Europe, on the Adriatic Sea. It is chiefly mountainous, descending to plains in the NE, where it is drained by the River Drava.
Economy: chiefly agricultural, producing cereals, potatoes, tobacco, fruit, and livestock. Industries include food processing, metallurgy, and the manufacture of textiles. The economy was severely damaged by the conflicts of 1991–95. Tourism, previously a major source of revenue, all but disappeared but has since revived.
History: settled by the Croats in the 7th century AD, the region was successively controlled by Hungary, Turkey, and Austria until the formation of the kingdom of the Serbs, Croats, and Slovenes (later Yugoslavia) in 1918. Following the occupation of Yugoslavia by the Axis Powers in World War II, Croatia was proclaimed an independent state (1941), ruled over by the fascist dictator Ante Pavelić (1889–1959). In 1945 Croatia once more became part of Yugoslavia as a people's republic. Nationalist feeling grew during the 1980s and in 1990 a noncommunist government was formed under Franjo ▷Tudjman.

Croatia's declaration of independence in 1991 provoked an invasion by the Serb-led Yugoslav army and fierce fighting ensued. Croatia's independence was recognized by EC and other states in 1992. The mainly Serbian Krajina region declared itself independent from Croatia, but was recaptured by government troops in 1995. Croatia was actively involved in the Bosnian civil war between 1991 and 1995, initially on an opportunistic basis but from 1994 in alliance with the Bosnian government. The authoritarian rule of Tudjman faced growing opposition in the later 1990s. He was re-elected as president in 1998 but the polls were widely condemned as unfair. Following Tudjman's death in 1999, his nationalists were heavily defeated by the centre-left in parliamentary elections.

Croatia

Head of state	President Stipe Mesic
Official language	Croatian
Official currency	kuna
Area	56 538 sq km (22 050 sq mi)
Population (2001 est)	4 393 000
Capital	Zagreb

● **Croatian** ▷*See* Serbo-Croat.

● **Croce, Benedetto** ▶ (1866–1952) Italian philosopher. Orphaned at 17, he studied art, philosophy, and history at Rome University. His system is expounded in the four-volume *Philosophy of Mind* (1900–10). The only reality, mental, is divided into theoretical and practical. Theoretical reality comprises intuition (art and aesthetics) and conception (philosophy or history—essentially the same, both being accounts of reality). Practical reality comprises individual will (political and economic activity) and universal will (morality). His aesthetic ideas, aired in numerous other works, are the most influential.

● **Crockett, Davy** ▶ (1786–1836) US frontiersman. As a colonel in the Tennessee militia and member of Congress he cultivated the image of a rough frontiersman. He fought for Texas in its struggle for independence from Mexico and was killed at the ▷Alamo.

● **Crockford, William** ▶ (1775–1844) The founder of Crockford's Club in St James's Street, London. Crockford was a fishmonger until his successes as a gambler enabled him to open his sumptuous club in 1827. The principal attraction was the game of hazard, over which Crockford himself presided and at which he won more than £1,200,000. After his death, the original Crockford's declined, but was revived in the 20th century as a bridge club and is now, again, one of London's leading gambling clubs.

● **crocodile** ▶ A ⌐reptile belonging to either of two genera, *Crocodylus* or *Osteolaemus*, and distinguished from alligators and caymans by having a more pointed snout and fewer teeth, the fourth tooth of the lower jaw remaining visible when the mouth is closed. Crocodiles occur chiefly in tropical fresh waters although the estuarine crocodile (*C. porosus*), which reaches a length of 6 m, occurs in coastal waters of SE Asia and Australia.
Crocodiles belong to the order *Crocodilia* (about 20 species), along with alligators and caymans. Crocodilians are amphibious mainly nocturnal carnivores living in tropical and subtropical swamps and rivers, where they prey chiefly on fish but also on water birds and land animals. They have long powerful jaws and a covering of thick protective bony plates; the ears and nostrils are placed high on the head and can be closed by valves when under water. The female builds a nest of mud or vegetation in which over a hundred shelled eggs may be laid. She guards the nest until the young, measuring 20–25 cm in length, begin to hatch. Crocodilians may live for over a hundred years. Their skins are used to make leather goods and this has caused a decline in their numbers.

● **crocodile bird** ▶ An African riverbank ▷courser, *Pluvianus aegyptius*, that feeds on parasites picked from crocodiles. It is 23 cm long and is black with white markings on the throat and above the eyes.

● **Crocus** ▶ A genus of low-growing plants (75 species), native to Mediterranean regions and widely planted in gardens. They grow from ▷corms to produce long thin leaves and six-lobed flowers in spring or autumn. Spring-flowering species include *C. vernus*, with white, blue, or purple flowers, and *C. aureus*, with deep-yellow flowers. *C. speciosus* is a purple autumn-flowering species. An Asian species (*C. sativus*) is the source of ▷saffron. Family: *Iridaceae*. *Compare* autumn crocus.

● **Croesus** ▶ (died c. 546 BC) The last king of ▷Lydia (c. 560–c. 546 BC), famous for his wealth. He conquered the Greek cities on the coast of Asia Minor but was defeated by the Persian king ▷Cyrus (II) the Great in 546. According to legend, Croesus was saved by Apollo from execution by Cyrus, whose counsellor he then became.

● **crofting** ▶ A system of subsistence farming that involves the cultivation of a small parcel of land together with access to common grazing land. Crofting was widely practised in the Scottish Highlands until the ▷Highland Clearances. It is still practised, under the control of the Crofters' Commission, established in 1955.

● **Crohn's disease** ▶ An inflammatory disorder that can affect any part of the intestinal tract, most usually the terminal part of the small intestine (ileum) and the colon. Crohn's disease, named after the US physician B. B. Crohn (1884–1983), occurs most commonly between the ages of 20 and 40 years; symptoms include partial obstruction of the ileum leading to abdominal pain and diarrhoea. Its cause is not known but it may be a form of ▷autoimmunity. *Mycobacterium paratuberculosis* can survive pasteurization of milk and has been suspected of causing Crohn's disease. Patients are treated with drugs, such as prednisolone (a steroid) and sulphasalazine (a sulphonamide); some cases require surgical removal of the affected part of the intestine.

● **Cro-Magnon** ▶ A prehistoric race of men believed to be ancestral to modern men. Skeletal remains were found (1868) at Cro-Magnon near Les Eyzies-de-Tayac in the Dordogne (SW France) and similar bones of tall broad-faced individuals have been found at other European sites. They first appeared in Europe about 35 000 years ago and were associated with ▷Aurignacian and subsequent cultures. They hunted reindeer, bison, and wild horse. They were often cave dwellers but seem also to have constructed huts. They produced the earliest known examples of cave art (*see* Lascaux). ▷*See also* Homo.

● **Crome, John** ▶ (1768–1821) British landscape painter and etcher, who founded the ▷Norwich school and became president of its Society of Artists. He was apprenticed to a sign painter but was otherwise self-taught through the study of Gainsborough and 17th-century Dutch masters. The style of his Norfolk landscapes, such as *Mousehold Heath* (Tate Gallery), was imitated by his son **John Bernay Crome** (1793–1842).

● **Cromer** ▶ 52 56N 1 18E A resort in England, on the NE coast of Norfolk. It has a fishing fleet, a lifeboat station, and a lighthouse. Population (1991): 7267.

● **Cromer, Evelyn Baring, 1st Earl of** ▶ (1841–1917) British soldier and diplomat. In 1879 Cromer became controller of finance in Egypt. In 1883 he became consul general and was the virtual ruler of Egypt until 1907.

● **cromlech** ▶ (Welsh: bent stone) A former name for a megalithic table grave or ▷dolmen and other prehistoric stone monuments. ▷*See also* megalith.

● **Crompton, Richmal** ▶ (Richmal Crompton Lamburn; 1890–1969) British children's author. *Just William*, her first collection of stories about the young ruffian William, was published while she was teaching in 1922. She wrote numerous sequels and a few adult novels.

● **Crompton, Samuel** ▶ (1753–1827) British inventor of the spinning mule (1779), so called because it was a cross between ▷Arkwright's water frame and ▷Hargreaves' spinning jenny. It was able to produce yarn of a higher quality and at a greater speed than had previously been possible. Unable to afford a patent, Crompton sold his idea for very little money but in 1812 he was awarded a parliamentary grant of £5,000.

● **Cromwell, Oliver** ▶ (1599–1658) English soldier and statesman; Lord Protector of England (1653–58). Cromwell, a country gentleman, was MP for Huntingdon in the parliament of 1628–29. He

Oliver Cromwell ▶ Dismissing the Rump of the Long Parliament (1653).

emerged as a convinced Puritan and critic of Charles I in the ▷Long Parliament, summoned in 1640. After the outbreak of the ▷Civil War he raised a troop of cavalry, the nucleus of his Ironsides (formed 1643), and fought at Edgehill (1642). He held command at ▷Marston Moor (1644) and was instrumental in the formation of the ▷New Model Army under Fairfax, which with Cromwell as second in command decisively defeated Charles at ▷Naseby (1645). Cromwell acted as mediator between the king, parliament, and the New Model Army but his conciliatory attitude hardened after Charles' flight to the Isle of Wight; when the second Civil War ended in Charles' defeat (1648), Cromwell signed the king's death warrant. In the power struggle between parliament and army, he sided with the army and after the establishment of the Commonwealth turned to the final mopping-up campaigns of the Civil War. He ruthlessly subjected Ireland (1649–50) and, after defeating Charles' heir at Dunbar (1650), finally subdued the Scots at Worcester (1651). In 1653 he expelled the Rump of the Long Parliament and following the failure of the ▷Barebones Parliament accepted the Instrument of Government, which established the ▷Protectorate. As Lord Protector, Cromwell established Puritanism but permitted religious toleration, allowing the Jews to return to England (1656). His attempt to decentralize government by dividing England into ten districts administered by ten major generals was short lived. His foreign policy was dictated by religious and commercial considerations: he ended the first ▷Dutch War, allied with France against Spain (gaining Dunkirk), and conquered Jamaica (1655). His relations with parliament were strained. He failed to find a workable constitutional basis for his rule, refusing parliament's offer of the crown in 1657. He was succeeded as Lord Protector by his son **Richard Cromwell** (1626–1712), who was forced by the army to abdicate in 1659 and lived in exile in France until 1680.

● **Cromwell, Thomas, Earl of Essex** ▶ (c. 1485–1540) English statesman, who drafted the legislation that made the English Church independent of Rome (*see* Reformation). Son of a brewer and blacksmith, he entered Wolsey's service in 1514, became an MP in 1529, and by 1532 was Henry VIII's chief adviser; he became chancellor of the exchequer in 1533. He gained Henry's divorce from Catherine of Aragon by a series of Acts that made the king, rather than the pope, head of the English Church. The legalization of the break with Rome by parliamentary statute contributed to parliament's growing influence in government. Between 1536 and 1540 he organized the dissolution of the monasteries, after which his negotiation of Henry's disastrous marriage to the uncomely Anne of Cleves led to his execution for treason.

● **Cronin, A(rchibald) J(oseph)** ▶ (1896–1981) British novelist. He practised medicine until he published his successful first novel, *Hatter's Castle* (1931). His later novels include *The Citadel* (1937) and *The Judas Tree* (1961). The radio and television series *Dr Finlay's Casebook* was based on his medical stories.

● **Cronje, Piet Arnoldus** ▶ (c. 1840–1911) South African general in the ▷Boer Wars. He captured Potchefstroom (1881) and the raiders led by ▷Jameson (1895) and delayed (Magersfontein, 1899) the British advance to relieve Kimberley. He was captured at Paardeburg (1900).

● **Cronus** ▶ A Greek deity, the youngest of the Titans. He ruled the universe after castrating his father Uranus. He swallowed all the children he fathered by his sister Rhea except Zeus, for whom a stone was substituted. Zeus eventually overthrew Cronus.

● **Crookes, Sir William** ▶ (1832–1919) British physicist, whose work on vacuums led him to investigate the newly discovered phenomenon of ▷cathode rays. Crookes showed that cathode rays consisted of charged particles rather than electromagnetic radiation, since they were deflected by a magnetic field. He invented the Crookes radiometer and Crookes glass, containing cerium, to protect the eyes of the industrial workers. He also discovered thalium.

● **crop rotation** ▶ The growing on the same land of different crops in sequence. Crop rotation helps maintain soil fertility, prevents the build-up of crop pests, and enables cultivation of the soil to clear weeds. The Norfolk four-course rotation originated in the UK during the 18th century and involved growing turnips, spring barley, clover, and winter wheat in sequence. Nowadays, mechanized farming and the use of artificial fertilizers and pesticides have encouraged monocropping (the repeated growing of the same crop).

● **croquet** ▶ A ball-and-mallet game that probably developed from *paille-maille*, a French game played certainly by the 13th century. Croquet was particularly popular in Britain and the USA in the mid- to late-19th century. It is played on a grass court or lawn, ideally 35 × 28 yd (32 × 25.6 m), with an arrangement of six hoops and one peg. Two to four players attempt to follow a prescribed course through the hoops, each using a distinctively coloured ball, the winner being the first to hit the peg with his ball. If a player's ball hits (roquets) another ball, the player may croquet this ball by placing his own ball next to it and striking his own ball so that the opponent's ball is also moved; the object is to advance his own ball towards the peg and to drive his opponent's ball off course.

● **Crosby** ▶ 53 30N 3 02W A town in NW England, in Sefton unitary authority, Merseyside. It is a mainly residential suburb of Liverpool. Population (1991): 52 869.

● **Crosby, Bing** ▶ (Harry Lillis C.; 1904–77) US popular singer. He achieved worldwide fame during the 1930s and 1940s as a crooner and is associated with the best-selling recording of all time, Irving Berlin's *White Christmas* (1942). He starred in many films, often with Bob ▷Hope, and also in his own radio and television shows.

● **crossbill** ▶ A finch of the genus *Loxia* (3 species), 14.5-17 cm long, whose unique cross-tipped bill is specialized for extracting seeds from unopened cones. The common crossbill (*L. curvirostra*) of Eurasia and North America feeds on spruce seeds. The male is red and the female grey-green; both have dark-brown wings and tail. The parrot crossbill (*L. pytyopsittacus*) feeds exclusively on pine seeds, and the Eurasian two-barred crossbill (*L. leucoptera*) feeds on fir seeds. ▷*See* Plate III.

● **crossbow** ▶ A short bow mounted on a stock, used in Europe throughout the middle ages. Crossbows were composite, made of wood, horn, tendons, and by the early 15th century of steel. They were drawn by hand, a belt hook, or a winch. The bolt or *quarrel* was short, iron-tipped, fletched with wood, leather, or brass, and capable of penetrating armour. Slower and less accurate than the ▷longbow, it could be fired from behind cover. It is now used for sport.

● **crosses** ▶ Figures formed by a vertical line or bar intersected by a horizontal. As a symbol, the cross is found in the art of several ancient cultures. One of the earliest Egyptian hieroglyphs is the cruciform ankh (*crux ansata*), the symbol of life. The primary association of the cross is with Christianity, in which it represents the instrument used at Christ's ▷crucifixion. It had several forms, conventionally distinguished by their Latin names: a simple upright stake (*crux simplex*); a stake with a transverse beam towards the top (*crux immissa*), which is known as the Latin cross; a stake topped by a transverse beam (*crux commissa*), also known as the tau cross or cross of St Anthony; and an X-shaped structure (*crux decussata*), known as the cross of St Andrew. In European art, the crucifixion is usually depicted with a Latin cross,

ankh   Greek   Latin   tau   Cross of Lorraine

St Andrews   Celtic   papal   Maltese   Russian Cross

crosses ▶ As a Christian symbol the cross was popularized by Constantine the Great and came into wide use in the 4th century.

and the crucifixes (crosses with the image of the crucified Christ) used on altars, rood screens, etc., are given this form. The Greek cross or cross of St George has vertical and horizontal arms of equal length and is the traditional form in use in Orthodox Churches. The cross has influenced innumerable aspects of religious ritual, dress, and art, including the cruciform plan of churches and cathedrals. It is also one of the earliest of monumental designs (*see* Ruthwell cross). As a charge in ▷heraldry, it is given various elaborated forms; a familiar example is the Maltese cross, the insignia of the ▷Hospitallers and, in Britain, of the St John Ambulance Association.

● **Crossman, Richard (Howard Stafford)** ▶ (1907–74) British Labour politician. An MP from 1945, he was minister of housing and local government (1964–66) and then of health and social security (1968–70). The controversial *Crossman Papers* (1975), which revealed details of cabinet discussions, were published in spite of government attempts to suppress them.

● **Crossopterygii** ▶ An order of bony fish—the lobe-finned fishes—most of which are now extinct. Their fins were fleshy and contained elements of the internal skeleton, permitting movement both on land and in water. The suborder *Rhipidistia* were predatory freshwater fishes of the Devonian and Carboniferous periods (about 400–280 million years ago), some of which evolved into the amphibians. The suborder *Coelacanthini* contains the ▷coelacanth, the only surviving member of the order. Subclass: *Sarcopterygii*.

● **crossword puzzles** ▶ A word puzzle with a series of clues, the answers to which are written into a diagram divided into squares, some of which are blacked out. (In most puzzles the pattern of the black squares has to be symmetrical.) The first modern crossword was devised by an Englishman, Arthur Wynne (d. 1945), and published in the New York *World* in 1913. They became very popular in the USA during the 1920s, reaching the UK in 1924. They are now a feature of many newspapers, each one having its own idiosyncrasies. In the UK the more sophisticated puzzles have clues based on literary references, puns, and cryptic sentences as well as anagrams and synonyms.

● **Croton** ▶ A genus of tropical trees and shrubs (750 species) many of which are of economic importance. *C. tiglium* of SE Asia produces croton oil, a powerful laxative now considered unsafe. The bark of *C. cascarilla* and *C. eluteria*, trees of the Bahamas, produces cascarilla, used in tonics. *C. laccifer* from India and Sri Lanka provides a lac used in varnishes. Several Brazilian species produce dragon's-blood resin. Family: *Euphorbiaceae* (spurge family).

The evergreen ornamental plants called crotons are members of the genus *Codiaeum*, grown as pot plants for their variegated foliage.

● **Crotone** ▶ (ancient name: Croton) 39 05N 17 08E A town in S Italy, in Calabria on the Gulf of Taranto. It was founded in about 700 BC by the Achaeans. There are chemical and zinc industries. Population (latest est): 61 326.

● **crottle** ▶ A large leafy ▷lichen belonging to the genus *Parmelia*, which is widely distributed from seashores to mountain tops and resembles crumpled leather. It has a black underside and sometimes reaches 90–120 cm in diameter. It is used as a dye for fabrics.

● **croup** ▶ An acute infection of the respiratory tract, usually caused by viruses, resulting in inflammation and obstruction of the larynx (voice box). Croup occurs most commonly in children under five years of age; symptoms include difficulty in breathing, which is harsh and noisy. Treatment consists of steam inhalations; severe cases may require the insertion of a tube into the trachea (windpipe), either through the mouth (intubation) or through a hole made surgically in the trachea (tracheostomy).

● **crow** ▶ A large songbird of the widely distributed family *Corvidae* (102 species). 30–65 cm long, crows typically have a black or brightly coloured plumage and a stout bill. They take a variety of food, which often includes carrion, and have a distinctive harsh call. The typical crows are the ▷carrion, ▷hooded, and American crows but the family also includes the ▷rooks, ▷ravens, ▷choughs, ▷jays, and ▷jackdaws.

● **Crow** ▶ A ▷Siouan-speaking North American Indian people of the Plains originally living in the Yellowstone River region. They moved W in the early 18th century to become traders of horses, guns, and other goods between the village Indians and the ▷Shoshoni. They hunted buffalo and were a warlike people among whom warriors underwent severe tests of bravery to attain the rank of chief. They used tobacco ritually and their religion emphasized a quest for a spirit guardian experienced through a vision after fasting and other ordeals.

● **crowberry** ▶ A dwarf procumbent shrub, *Empetrum nigrum*, of N temperate and arctic heathlands. 15–45 cm high, it has oblong leaves, tiny pinkish flowers, and black edible berries. The name derives from the reputation of the fruit for attracting crows. Family: *Ericaceae* (heath family).

● **Crowe, Russell** ▶ (1964–) New Zealand film actor, living in Australia. His films include *Romper Stomper* (1992), *The Quick and the Dead* (1995), *LA Confidential* (1997), *Gladiator* (2000), which earned him a Best Actor Oscar, and *Beautiful Mind* (2001).

● **crowfoot** ▶ A widely distributed herbaceous annual or perennial plant of the genus *Ranunculus*, which also contains the buttercups. They have deeply lobed leaves (hence the name) and white or yellow five-petalled flowers. Some species, such as the European water crowfoot (*R. aquatilis*), are aquatic. Family: ▷*Ranunculaceae*.

● **Crown Agents for Overseas Governments and Administrations** ▶ A UK public service, founded in 1833, that acts in a financial, professional, and commercial capacity for overseas governments and public-sector corporations, such as the railways, universities, and central banks. Between 1967 and 1974 they incurred a loss of some £200 million and following a public inquiry were restructured by the Crown Agents Act (1979).

● **Crown Court** ▷*See* courts of law.

● **Crown dependencies** ▷*See* United Kingdom Overseas Territories.

● **Crown Derby** ▷*See* Derby ware.

● **crown jewels** ▶ Royal insignia and regalia and the personal jewellery inherited or acquired by a sovereign. They are now frequently museum pieces. The British Crown Jewels, kept in the Tower of London, were mainly amassed after the Restoration, the earlier set having been destroyed under Cromwell. Those used for coronations include a replica of St Edward's crown, the Sword of State, the Orb, and the Sceptre. Those used for other state occasions include the Imperial State Crown and another Sword of State.

● **Crown land** ▶ Land that belongs to the UK monarch and is managed by the Crown Estate Commissioners. The profits from the land do not go to the monarch, as all revenues were surrendered by George III in 1760 in exchange for the income provided by the ▷civil list.

● **crown of thorns** ▶ **1.** A Madagascan shrub, *Euphorbia splendens*, often cultivated for ornament. Up to 100 cm high, it has spiny stems at the tips of which are a few leaves and clusters of small flowers,

each surrounded by rounded scarlet bracts. ▷*See* Euphorbia. **2.** A spiny vigorous shrub, *Zizyphus spina-christi*, forming thickets or growing singly as a tree. It is widespread in the Mediterranean region and is said to be the source of Christ's crown of thorns. Family: *Rhamnaceae* (buckthorn family).

● **crown-of-thorns starfish** ▶ A reddish starfish, *Acanthaster planci*, that has a spiny body, up to 45 cm across, with 12–19 arms. With the decimation of its chief predator—the Pacific triton (*Charonia tritonis*)—by shell collectors, it has spread throughout the South Pacific since the mid-20th century and threatens destruction to the coral reefs on which it feeds.

● **Crown Prosecution Service** ▶ An independent prosecuting body established in England and Wales in 1986 to decide whether a case should be pursued in the courts. It deals with cases brought by the police (excluding traffic offences) and is headed by the Director of Public Prosecutions.

● **Croydon** ▶ A mainly residential borough of S Greater London, created in 1965. Its name comes from the original Saxon town of Crogedene (Saffron valley). London's first airport was built here in 1915 and remained the capital's main aiport until Heathrow was opened in 1940. Population (1999 est): 313 510.

● **Cruciferae** ▶ (*or* Brassicaceae) A family of plants (about 1900 species), mainly annual or perennial herbs, particularly abundant in N temperate regions. The flowers are four-petalled and cross-shaped. Many crucifers are of economic importance as food plants, cattle food, ornamentals, and weeds. Some, such as cabbage and other brassicas, have been grown since ancient times.

● **crucifixion** ▶ A form of capital punishment carried out by nailing or binding a person to a ▷cross by the wrists and feet and leaving him to die from previously inflicted wounds or from exhaustion. It was commonly used in Carthage and adopted in the Roman Empire, where it was regarded as a scandalous form of death and so restricted to slaves and the worst criminals; it could not be inflicted on anyone holding Roman citizenship. Scourging customarily preceded crucifixion and the victim's legs were sometimes broken to hasten death. As a legal punishment it was abolished by the emperor Constantine. The crucifixion of Christ is reported in the four Gospels of the New Testament; the mockery, the crown of thorns, and the piercing of his side with a spear are not typical elements of this form of punishment. According to tradition, St Peter was also crucified, but head downwards, and St Andrew was executed on the X-shaped cross that bears his name.

● **Cruden, Alexander** ▶ (1701–70) British scholar and bookseller. Author of the famous biblical concordance (first edition 1737), Cruden was dogged by frequent bouts of insanity. He wrote several pamphlets, including one against John ▷Wilkes.

● **Cruft, Charles** ▶ (1852–1938) British dog breeder. In 1886 he organized a dog show in London, the first of the annual British dog shows known as Cruft's.

● **Cruikshank, George** ▶ (1792–1872) British caricaturist, painter, and illustrator. He achieved early success with his satirical political cartoons, superseding ▷Gillray in popularity. He illustrated such books as Dickens' *Oliver Twist* and Ainsworth's *Tower of London*. His etchings of *The Bottle* and painting of *The Worship of Bacchus* (Tate Gallery) are moralizing sermons on alcoholism.

● **Cruise, Tom** ▶ (Thomas Cruise Mapother IV; 1962–) US film actor. His films include *The Outsiders* (1983), *Top Gun* (1985), *Born on the Fourth of July* (1989), *Mission Impossible* (1995), *Eyes Wide Shut* (1999), and *Magnolia* (2000). He was married to Nicole ▷Kidman.

● **cruise missile** ▷*See* guided missiles.

● **cruiser** ▶ A fast heavily armed warship, smaller than a ▷battleship but larger than a ▷destroyer. Cruisers with increased firepower, nuclear power that greatly extends their range, and greater versatility have replaced most of the world's battleships.

● **Crusades** ▶ The military expeditions organized in western Christendom primarily to recover the Holy Places of Palestine from

Crusades ► This 12th-century book illustration shows knights from the time of the Crusades in hand-to-hand combat.

Muslim occupation. The first Crusade (1095–99) was launched under the aegis of the papacy. Jerusalem was captured and the Crusader states of the Kingdom of Jerusalem, the County of Edessa, Antioch, and Tripoli were created. The fall (1144) of Edessa inspired the unsuccessful second Crusade (1147–48) and the capture of Jerusalem by ▷Saladin in 1187 led to the inconclusive third Crusade (1189–92), led by ▷Philip II Augustus of France, Emperor ▷Frederick (I) Barbarossa, and ▷Richard (I) the Lionheart of England. The fourth Crusade (1202–04) was diverted from its initial objective, Egypt, and sacked Constantinople (1204). The four Crusades of the 13th century failed to recover lost ground and Acre, the last foothold of the West in Palestine, was lost in 1291. The Crusades failed in their stated objective, but Europe benefited greatly from the resultant growth of East–West trade and the introduction of eastern concepts into medieval culture. ▷*See also* Children's Crusade; chivalry.

● **crustacean ►** An ▷arthropod of the subphylum or superclass *Crustacea* (over 35 000 species), which includes the ▷barnacles, ▷woodlouse, ▷shrimps, ▷lobsters, ▷crabs, etc. The head bears two pairs of antennae and three pairs of jaws; the head and thorax together are usually covered by a chitinous carapace. There are numerous pairs of forked appendages, which are modified for different functions. Crustaceans are predominantly aquatic, breathing by means of gills. A few, such as the ▷fish louse, are parasitic on fish, whales, and other aquatic animals. During reproduction the male transfers sperm to the female, which often carries the fertilized eggs until they hatch. The larvae are mainly free-swimming and pass through several stages (*see* metamorphosis) to reach the adult form.

● **Crux ►** (Latin: Cross) A small conspicuous constellation, also called the Southern Cross, in the S sky, lying in the Milky Way. The four brightest stars form a cross, the longer arm of which points roughly towards the S celestial pole.

● **Cruyff, Johann ►** (1947–) Dutch Association footballer, who played for Ajax (1965–73), Barcelona, and the Netherlands. An outstanding centre forward, he captained the Dutch side that reached the final of the 1974 World Cup. He retired from football in 1984.

● **Cruz, Sor Juana Inéz de la ►** (1651–95) Mexican poet. An infant prodigy, she lived at the Spanish viceroy's court before entering a convent in 1669. She died while nursing nuns during an epidemic. In addition to her metaphysical religious poems she wrote a defence of intellectual freedom and of women's rights to education.

● **crwth ►** An ancient Welsh musical instrument, consisting of an oblong wooden frame with six strings across a slanting bridge. Four strings could be bowed and stopped against a fingerboard and the other two plucked as a drone bass.

● **cryogenics ►** The production, effects, and uses of very low temperatures, usually meaning from −150°C down to ▷absolute zero. The most common method of producing cryogenic temperatures is

to use ▷adiabatic processes. In adiabatic demagnetization, a magnetized paramagnetic substance is thermally isolated and demagnetized, thus cooling it. In adiabatic expansion, a thermally isolated gas is expanded. Cryogenic effects include changes in electrical properties, such as ▷superconductivity, and changes in mechanical properties, such as superfluidity (*see* superfluid). Cryogenics has been applied to new methods of food preservation, life-support systems in space, and the use of liquid propellants.

● **cryolite ►** A rare mineral of composition Na_3AlF_6. It is colourless or white and occurs in pegmatite veins. It is only mined in significant quantities in Greenland, although it is known to occur elsewhere. It is used in aluminium refining. Synthetic cryolite is manufactured from hydrofluoric acid, sodium carbonate, and aluminium.

● **cryptogam ►** In old classification systems, any plant that reproduces by means of spores. The nonvascular cryptogams included the mosses and liverworts (bryophytes), lichens, fungi, and algae; the vascular cryptogams were the ferns, horsetails, and related plants (pteridophytes). *Compare* phanerogam.

● **Cryptomeria** ▷*See* Japanese cedar.

● **Cryptozoic time ►** Geological time prior to the ▷Phanerozoic, i.e. the Precambrian, ending about 590 million years ago. It is the eon of "hidden life"; fossils are rare and obscure.

● **Crystal Palace ►** A building designed by Joseph ▷Paxton to house the ▷Great Exhibition of 1851. The Crystal Palace, which had an area of 69 892 sq m (772 289 sq ft), was built in Hyde Park, London, with the highly advanced use of prefabricated glass and iron. It was later dismantled and reassembled at Sydenham (a suburb in SE London) but burnt down in 1936.

● **crystals ►** Solids that have a regular geometrical shape because the constituent atoms, ions, or molecules are arranged in an ordered repeating pattern, known as a crystal lattice. Salt grains, for example, are cubic crystals of sodium chloride with sodium and chlorine ions alternating at the corners of a cubic lattice. There are seven crystal systems, in which all crystals are classified. Crystal structures are studied by a variety of techniques, including ▷X-ray diffraction and electron microscopy. Specialized mathematical notation and stereographic projections are used to describe lattice structure and symmetry. Many crystalline solids are polycrystalline, i.e. they consist of many small crystals. The physical properties of crystals have found many uses, ranging from ▷piezoelectric transducers to gemstones. **Crystallography** is concerned with the study of the structure and properties of crystals. Noncrystalline solids, such as glass, are said to be amorphous.

The classification of crystals

system	edges	angles
cubic	$a = b = c$	$\alpha = \beta = \gamma = 90°$
tetragonal	$a = b \neq c$	$\alpha = \beta = \gamma = 90°$
orthorhombic	$a \neq b \neq c$	$\alpha = \beta = \gamma = 90°$
hexagonal	$a = b \neq c$	$\alpha = \beta = 90°; \gamma = 120°$
trigonal	$a = b \neq c$	$\alpha = \beta = \gamma = 90°$
monoclinic	$a \neq b \neq c$	$\alpha = \gamma \neq \beta = 90°$
triclinic	$a \neq b \neq c$	$\alpha \neq \beta \neq \gamma$

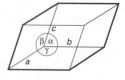

unit cell

crystals ► The classification of crystals.

● **Csokonai Vitéz, Mihaly ►** (1773–1805) Hungarian poet. His autobiographical play *Tempefői* (1793) records the struggles and failures of his life as a poet. His work includes a cycle of love poems addressed to "Lilla," a volume of odes, and the highly popular comic epic *Dorottya* (1804).

● **ctenophore** ▶ A marine invertebrate animal, also called comb jelly, sea gooseberry, and sea walnut, belonging to the phylum *Ctenophora* (about 80 species). Its transparent gelatinous body is usually rounded and bears eight rows of ciliated comblike plates, used for locomotion. Ctenophores are mainly free-swimming and often occur in swarms in coastal waters, feeding on other planktonic animals captured by long branched tentacles. ▷*See also* coelenterate.

● **Ctesiphon** ▶ The capital of ▷Parthian and ▷Sasanian kings near Baghdad (Iraq). Taken temporarily by the Roman emperors ▷Trajan (115 AD) and Carus (283), it fell to the Arabs in 637. The remains of the palace of Khosrow I (reigned 531–79) incorporate the largest known brickwork vault, spanning over 25 m (82 ft).

● **CT scanner** ▷*See* tomography.

● **Cuba, Republic of** ▶ A country in the Caribbean Sea, off the S coast of Florida. It consists of two main islands, Cuba (the largest in the Caribbean) and the Isla de la Juventud, together with over 1500 small islands and keys. On the island of Cuba fertile plains rise to mountains in the centre and SE and there are some lower hills in the NW. The population is mainly of European origin, with large African and mixed minorities.
Economy: mainly state controlled, it is primarily agricultural and very much dependent upon its sugar crop (its main source of export revenue); production levels have been generally low. Tobacco (especially for cigars) is another important export crop and meat production is important in the domestic economy. Fishing has expanded with government help. Important mineral resources include nickel. Although metallurgy, construction, and textiles have all grown, the government's attempts to diversify the economy have largely failed. The end of communism in the Soviet Union and E Europe in 1989–90 deprived Cuba of its only significant trading partners, and both exports and imports fell by abut 75%. As a result the government has been obliged to permit some private enterprise. Since the mid-1990s tourism has been the main source of revenue. In 1995 Cuba negotiated a trade deal with Russia whereby sugar is exchanged for much-needed oil.
History: discovered by Columbus in 1492, it was a Spanish colony (except in 1762–63, when it was occupied by the British) until 1898, when Spain was forced to withdraw following war with the USA. After three years of US occupation Cuba became a republic (1901) but the USA continued to intervene in Cuba's internal affairs and to control its foreign policy until 1934. In 1940 ▷Batista became president, taking Cuba into World War II on the Allied side. His corrupt dictatorship was threatened by ▷Castro's unsuccessful revolt of 26 July, 1953, but in Castro's second attempt (1959) Batista was overthrown. Relations between Castro's socialist government and the USA were increasingly strained, and the USA imposed a trade and economic embargo (still in force, but relaxed somewhat in 2000). As a result Cuba moved closer in its international relations to the Soviet Union. In 1961 an invasion of Cuban exiles with US support was defeated at the ▷Bay of Pigs and in 1962 the Soviet installation of missile bases in Cuba resulted in a US naval blockade (*see* Cuban Missile Crisis). In 1976 a socialist constitution was approved by a referendum. As a result of serious unemployment in the late 1970s many Cubans emigrated to E Europe and South America: there has also been a steady flow of economic migrants from Cuba to Florida. In the 1980s Cuban troops were involved in revolutionary conflicts in both Africa and the Caribbean. Relations with the Soviet Union became strained in 1990 after Castro criticized reforms in communist E Europe: since the collapse of the Soviet Union Cuba has suffered severely from its economic and political isolation.

Republic of Cuba

Head of state	President Fidel Castro Ruz
Official language	Spanish
Official currency	Cuban peso of 100 centavos
Area	148 124 sq km (46 736 sq mi)
Population (2001 est)	11 190 000
Capital and main port	Havana

● **Cuban Missile Crisis** ▶ A crisis that occurred in October 1962, when the USA discovered that Soviet missiles with nuclear warheads were being installed in Cuba. As the USA was well within the range of these missiles, President ▷Kennedy demanded that the Soviet leader, Nikita ▷Khrushchev, should dismantle these missile bases and he imposed a naval blockade against Soviet military shipments to Cuba. With the world hovering on the brink of a nuclear World War III, Khrushchev accepted Kennedy's demands in return for Kennedy's undertaking not to attack Cuba. The positive outcome of the crisis was a direct "hot line" between the two men, maintained by their successors.

● **cubism** ▶ A style of painting and sculpture, originating in the works of ▷Picasso and ▷Braque in about 1907. It started as an intellectual investigation of how a solid form can be represented in two dimensions without resorting to illusionism. Volume was generally suggested by the fusion of multiple viewpoints of an object in one image, which was presented as a complex of geometrical shapes. The subject matter of early cubism was invariably everyday objects of simple form, such as vases, tables, books, pipes, fruit, and musical instruments, many being suggested by the work of a forerunner of cubism, ▷Cézanne. Figures, which are rare, often resemble primitive sculpture, the observation of which helped Picasso to break with Western tradition. After 1911 the development of cubism, in which Juan ▷Gris now also participated, led to the introduction of ▷collage and also to a more decorative approach, monochrome tones being replaced by rich colours. Cubism was the principal catalytic influence on the evolution of ▷abstract art.

● **cubit** ▶ An ancient unit of length equal to between 18 and 22 inches; it is based on the distance from the elbow to the tip of the middle finger.

● **Cubitt, Thomas** ▶ (1788–1855) London carpenter who became a highly successful builder. With his brother **Lewis Cubitt** (1799–1883), he largely created Bloomsbury, Belgravia, and Pimlico. Thomas also built Osborne House (1845–48) on the Isle of Wight to the specification of the Prince Consort and Lewis built King's Cross Station (1837–39). Another brother, **Sir William Cubitt** (1785–1861), became Lord Mayor of London (1860–61) and it is after him that **Cubitt Town** on the Isle of Dogs is named. He developed the area to house workers in the shipyards and docks (1840–50).

● **Cuchulain** ▶ (*or* Cú Chulainn) A legendary Irish hero, resembling ▷Achilles in his strength and courageous exploits. He was the son of the god Lug (*see* Lugus) but was brought up by his mortal uncle, Conchobar, King of Ulster. Cuchulain is the central subject in a series of ancient Gaelic epics and romances known as the Ulster cycle.

● **cuckoo** ▶ A bird belonging to a family (*Cuculidae*; 128 species) occurring worldwide and ranging from 16–70 cm in length. The European cuckoo (*Cuculus canorus*), grey with distinctive white barring and a long tail, belongs to a subfamily of parasitic cuckoos (*Cuculinae*; 47 species); these lay their eggs in the nests of other birds, which rear their young. Parasitic cuckoos' eggs resemble those of the host in order to deceive the host bird. On hatching, the young cuckoo removes the other nestlings from the nest, thus obtaining sufficient food from its adopted parents. Nonparasitic cuckoos include the **coucals** (genus *Centropus*; about 27 species), ranging from Africa through S and SE Asia to Australia, and the **roadrunners** (genus *Geococcyx*; 2 species), extending from the S USA to Central America. Coucals and roadrunners are poor fliers but excellent walkers and runners, actively pursuing their prey, which includes small birds and their eggs. They build their nests on the ground or in low trees. Order: *Cuculiformes* (cuckoos and turacos).

● **cuckoopint** ▶ A perennial herbaceous European plant, *Arum maculatum*, also called lords-and-ladies. 30–50 cm tall, it has large arrow-shaped shiny green leaves and a cylindrical cluster of tiny flowers, which protrudes from a dull-purple funnel-shaped bract (spathe). The flowers give rise to poisonous red berries. Family: *Araceae*.

● **cuckoo-shrike** ▶ A gregarious arboreal songbird of the family *Campephagidae* (70 species), occurring in tropical regions of the Old World. 13–32 cm long, they have a mainly grey plumage, long pointed wings, and a notched bill and feed on insects and fruit.

● **cuckoo-spit insect** ▷*See* froghopper.

● **cucumber** ▶ An annual vine, *Cucumis sativus*, probably originally from Asia but widely cultivated since ancient times. The long green juicy fruits, up to 60 cm long, are eaten raw, cooked, or pickled (*see* gherkin). In northern regions both glasshouse and outdoor (ridge) varieties are grown. Indoor cucumbers produce fruit without fertilization; if pollinated, the fruits taste bitter. Family: *Cucurbitaceae* (gourd family).

● **cucumber tree** ▶ A slender North American tree, *Magnolia acuminata*, 16–30 m high. Hardiest of all magnolias, it is found in moist rich woodlands, often on mountain slopes. It has tulip-shaped greenish-white flowers and cucumber-like fruit—greenish at first, ripening to dull crimson. The light yellow satiny textured wood is used for furniture, flooring, etc. Family: *Magnoliaceae*.

● **Cúcuta** ▶ (or San José de Cúcuta) 7 55N 72 31W A city in N Colombia, on the Pan-American Highway. It is an important commercial centre (especially for coffee). Its university was founded in 1962. Population (1997 est): 589 196.

● **Cudworth, Ralph** ▶ (1617–88) English scholar, a leading member of the ▷Cambridge Platonists. His *True Intellectual System of the Universe* (1678) defends Christianity as the only genuine source of knowledge against the atheism and materialism of ▷Hobbes. His work on ethics is embodied in the posthumously published *Treatise concerning Eternal and Immutable Morality* (1731).

● **Cuenca** ▶ 40 04N 2 07W A city in central Spain, in New Castile. It has a 13th-century cathedral. Industries include tanning, paper milling, and tourism. Population (1991): 45 800.

● **Cuenca** ▶ 2 54S 79 00W A city in S central Ecuador. It is the commercial centre for S Ecuador with a trade in agricultural products, hides, and marble. The university was founded in 1868. Population (1997 est): 255 028.

● **Cuernavaca** ▶ 18 57N 99 15W A city and resort in S central Mexico. It is the site of Cortés' palace (now government offices), a Franciscan cathedral (1529), and a university (1939). Many writers, artists, and film stars have resided here. Its varied industries include flour milling, textiles, and sugar refining. Population (1990): 281 752.

● **Cugnot, Nicolas-Joseph** ▶ (1725–1804) French engineer. In 1769 he developed the first vehicle driven by a steam engine—a gun tractor commissioned by the French government. The following year he produced the first mechanically driven "horseless carriage"; his steam tricycle, driven by a steam engine, carried four passengers and was the forerunner of the modern motor ▷car. It was the difficulty of carrying enough water to generate the steam and the cumbersome nature of a steam engine that gave Otto's ▷internal-combustion engine the edge over steam for this purpose a century later.

● **Cuiabá** ▶ 15 32S 56 05W A city in SW Brazil, the capital of Mato Grosso state on the Rio Cuiabá. It is a collecting centre for cattle, rubber, and palm nuts. The Federal University of Mato Grosso was founded here in 1970. Population (1985 est): 220 500.

● **cuisine minceur** ▶ A health-protecting style of gourmet cookery in which the traditional generous use of butter, cream, and other rich ingredients is minimized. Cuisine minceur was elaborated by the French chef Michel Guérard (1933–) in the 1970s at his restaurant at Eugénie-les-Bains in SW France. This entirely new approach to elegant cooking recommends using concentrated stocks and puréed vegetables to give flavour and texture to sauces and casseroles, eliminating butter, cream, and flour. It emphasizes light delicate food attractively presented, with a liberal use of fresh herbs.

● **Culbertson, Ely** ▶ (1891–1955) US bridge authority, born in Romania, who influenced the development of contract bridge and used his wealth flamboyantly to popularize it. Imprisoned in the Caucasus in his youth for anarchist activity, he emigrated after the Russian Revolution. His life after 1938 was devoted to campaigning for world peace. He founded the magazine *The Bridge World* (1929) and wrote many books on bridge, as well as an autobiography *The Strange Lives of One Man* (1940).

● **Culdees** ▶ (Old Irish *céle dé*: associate of God) Irish and Scottish monks, originally living in solitude but from about the 8th to 12th centuries existing in small groups. They were probably the last surviving remnant of the Celtic Church and were gradually replaced by Roman monastic orders.

● **Culham** ▶ A village in S central England, in Oxfordshire, site of the UK centre for ▷thermonuclear reactor research (part of the Atomic Energy Authority) and of the JET (Joint European Torus) joint undertaking. This nuclear fusion research takes place as part of a coordinated programme by scientists and engineers from the EU countries and Switzerland. It is also the site of the first European school in the UK.

● **Culiacán** ▶ 24 50N 107 23W A city in W Mexico. It is the commercial centre for an irrigated agricultural area. Population (1990): 602 114.

● **Cullinan diamond** ▶ An exceptional diamond weighing 3106 metric carats (c. 621 g) when found in the Premier Mine, South Africa, in 1905. It was cut into 9 major and 96 small stones. The two largest (Star of Africa and Cullinan II) are set in the British royal regalia.

● **Culloden Moor** ▶ A moor in N Scotland, in Highland near Inverness. In 1746 it was the scene of the last land battle to be fought in Britain, in which the Young Pretender, Charles Edward Stuart, was defeated by the Duke of Cumberland, thus ending the ▷Jacobite cause in Britain.

● **Culpeper, Nicholas** ▶ (1616–54) English herbalist, physician, and astrologer. In 1649 he published an unauthorized translation of the official London Pharmacopoeia, which was well received (except by the medical profession). This was followed by his famous and equally popular *Complete Herbal* (1653).

● **Culpeper's Rebellion** ▶ (1677–79) An American colonial uprising, in which tobacco growers in North Carolina opposed British restrictions on their markets. John Culpeper seized the British deputy governor and governed capably himself until his voluntary surrender for trial in England, at which he was acquitted.

● **cultivator** ▶ A farm implement used to till the soil, so destroying weeds and promoting crop growth. Horse-drawn models date from the 19th century but modern tractor-drawn machines consist of a steel frame with curved steel tines to penetrate and disrupt the soil.

● **Cultural Revolution, Great Proletarian** ▶ (1966–68) A political rather than cultural movement launched in China by Mao Tse-tung, with the professed aim of eliminating bureaucracy and reinvigorating revolutionary attitudes. Many leading officials were dismissed, the formal educational system was abolished, and reforms to foster correct political views were introduced. Many universities were closed and young people, mobilized as ▷Red Guards, attacked Party officials and destroyed cultural objects. The result was a reign of anarchy and terror. Although the most turbulent phase of the Revolution was over by 1969, its policies remained in place until Mao's death in 1976.

● **culture** ▶ In microbiology, a colony of micoorganisms grown in a solid or liquid medium for experimental or diagnostic purposes. A widely used medium is agar gel (contained in petri dishes) supplemented with required nutrients, which is inoculated with microorganisms and incubated. Sterile conditions are essential to avoid contamination.

● **Cumae** ▶ The first Greek colony in Italy. Founded near Naples about 750 BC by settlers from Chalcis, Cumae expanded rapidly, spreading Greek civilization in S Italy. It repulsed Etruscan influence but was subsequently subject to Rome (from c. 340 BC).

● **Cumaná** ▶ 10 29N 64 12W A city in N Venezuela. Exports, through its port of Puerto Sucre on the Caribbean Sea, include sugar, cocoa, and tobacco. Its university was founded in 1958. Population (1990 est): 212 000.

● **Cumans** ▶ A nomadic Turkish people, who dominated the W steppes for two centuries until they were driven into Hungary by the Mongol invasions (1237–39). They were absorbed into the Hungarian kingdom in which they had considerable influence.

● **Cumberland** ▶ A former county of NW England. Under local government reorganization in 1974 it became part of the new county of ▷Cumbria.

● **Cumberland, Richard** ▶ (1631–1718) English moral philosopher and Bishop of Peterborough from 1691. One of the ▷Cambridge Platonists, he was renowned for scholarship and virtue. His *De legibus naturae disquisitio philosophica* (1672) opposed ▷Hobbes' egoism in its principle of universal benevolence and anticipated ▷utilitarianism.

● **Cumberland, William Augustus, Duke of** ▶ (1721–65) British general, who was the son of George II. After serving in the War of the Austrian Succession he crushed the ▷Jacobite rebellion at Culloden (1746); his subsequent harsh reprisals earned him the nickname Butcher. His career ended in disgrace after his capitulation to the French in the Seven Years' War.

● **Cumbernauld** ▶ 55 58N 3 59W A town in central Scotland, in North Lanarkshire. Created a new town in 1956 to relieve overcrowding in Glasgow, it has varied light industries. Population (1991): 48 762.

● **Cumbria** ▶ A county in NW England, bordering on the Irish Sea. It was created in 1974 from Westmorland, Cumberland, and parts of NW Lancashire and NW Yorkshire. It consists of the ▷Lake District, enclosed by coastal lowlands and the Pennine uplands. Agricultural activity includes sheep, dairy, and arable farming. New industries, including chemicals, are replacing the traditional ones of coal, iron, and steel, located chiefly in the coastal towns. Granite and limestone are extracted but coal resources are almost exhausted. Atomic energy establishments exist at Sellafield and Calder Hall. Area: 6809 sq km (2628 sq mi). Population (1996 est): 490 600. Administrative centre: Carlisle.

● **cumin** ▶ An annual herb, *Cuminum cyminum*, up to 30 cm high with umbrella-like clusters of small whitish flowers and oblong bristly fruits. Native to the Mediterranean, it has long been cultivated in Europe, India, and China for its bitter fruits, which resemble caraway seeds and are ground for use in curry powders and spicy dishes, to flavour liqueurs, etc. It was once used medicinally as a stimulant and liniment. Family: *Umbelliferae*.

● **cummings, e(dward) e(stlin)** ▶ (1894–1962) US poet. His highly experimental lyric verse is characterized by typographical innovations and eccentric punctuation, which he employed to reinforce the verbal element of his poetry. His works include *Tulips and Chimneys* (1923), *Eimi* (1933), *o Thanks* (1935), and *1 × 1* (1944). He also wrote an experimental novel, *The Enormous Room* (1922), a poetic drama *Him* (1927), and a ballet *Tom* (1935).

● **cumulus cloud** ▶ (Cu) A low type of ▷cloud of convective origin having a heaped appearance and developing vertically from a flat base. Fair-weather cumulus clouds are shallow but others are deep and may become **cumulonimbus cloud**. This cloud is heavy and dense, extending vertically to about 6000 m (20 000 ft), and is associated with thunderstorms. Its upper part often spreads out to form an anvil shape.

● **Cunaxa, Battle of** ▶ (401 BC) The battle fought between ▷Cyrus the Younger and his elder brother Arsaces, who had seized the Persian throne as ▷Artaxerxes II in 404 BC. Cyrus gathered an army of Greek mercenaries (including the historian, Xenophon) and met Artaxerxes at Cunaxa, 70 km N of Babylon. Cyrus was defeated by Artaxerxes' superior cavalry forces and died in the battle.

● **cuneiform** ▶ The oldest ▷writing system of which records survive, used to represent a number of ancient Near Eastern languages. The name derives from the wedge-shaped marks (Latin *cuneus*, a wedge) made by the imprint of a stylus in soft clay. Originally pictographic, by the 3rd millennium BC cuneiform pictures had become stylized in the form of groups of wedge-shaped imprints, many representing the sounds of syllables. Once hardened the clay tablets were almost indestructible and many are extant today. Probably devised by the Sumerians not later than 3100 BC, cuneiform spread to other language groups in the area. By 100 BC, however, it had largely been superseded by the North Semitic script that was used to represent the increasingly dominant Aramaic language.

● **Cunningham, Merce** ▶ (1919–   ) US dancer and choreographer.

He joined the Martha Graham Company in 1945 and founded his own company in 1952. He collaborated frequently with the composer John ▷Cage and his many experimental abstract ballets include *Suite for Five* (1956), *Antic Meet* (1958), *Aeon* (1961), *Scramble* (1967), *Landrover* (1972), *Travelogue* (1977), *Roaratorio* (1983), and *Biped* (2000).

● **Cunobelinus** ▶ (or Cymbeline; died c. 42 AD) British ruler (c. 10–c. 42) of the Catuvellauni tribe. Their lands embraced much of SE England after they overcame the Trinovantes. He founded Colchester (c. 10).

● **cup fungus** ▶ A fungus, belonging to the order *Pezizales*, that produces a cup- or saucer-shaped fruiting body. Cup fungi may or may not have a stalk and the spores are released from the upper surface of the cup. The distinctive scarlet elf cup (*Peziza coccinea*), found on dead branches, is a smooth-rimmed cup, 2–6 cm in diameter, deep red inside and whitish grey or pink outside. Phylum: ▷*Ascomycota*.

● **Cupid** ▶ The Roman god of love, identified with the Greek Eros, and lover of Psyche. He is usually portrayed as a winged boy shooting arrows of love.

● **cuprite** ▶ A red to black mineral of composition Cu_2O, found where deposits of copper have been subject to weathering.

● **cupronickel** ▶ A corrosion-resistant alloy of 75% copper and 25% nickel (by weight). In the UK the Coinage Act (1946) substituted cupronickel coinage for silver alloy; the four cupronickel coins now in circulation are the 5p, 10p, 20p, and 50p pieces.

● **Curaçao** ▶ A West Indian island, the largest in the Netherlands Antilles. Discovered in 1499, it was settled by the Spanish before being colonized by the Dutch in 1634. The refining of oil from Venezuela is of major importance; other industries include the production of Curaçao liqueur and calcium-phosphate mining. Area: 444 sq km (173 sq mi). Population (latest est): 165 011. Chief town: Willemstad.

● **curare** ▶ A resinous substance obtained from South American trees of the genera *Strychnos* and *Chondodendron*, used as an arrow poison by South American Indians. Curare blocks the action of ▷acetylcholine, which is released at the junctions of nerve endings and muscles and causes muscular contraction. Curare therefore causes a relaxed paralysis of muscle. Curare-like compounds (e.g. tubocurarine) are injected during general anaesthesia to relax muscles and provide the surgeon with better access to the part of the body on which he is operating.

● **curassow** ▶ A long-tailed tropical American gamebird belonging to the family *Cracidae*. Curassows have a long neck and long legs and may reach 100 cm in length. The black males have a crest of curly feathers and a yellow bill ornament; females are smaller and brownish in colour. They are mostly arboreal, feeding on buds, insects, and frogs. Chief genera: *Crax*, *Pauxi*, *Mitu*; order: *Galliformes* (pheasants, turkeys, etc.).

● **curia** ▶ An ancient division of the Roman people. There were 30 *curiae*, each with a meeting place that was also known as a *curia*. The Senate house of Rome, attributed to Tullus Hostilius, was called the

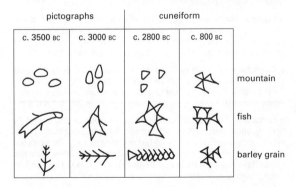

cuneiform ▶ The wedge-shaped strokes of cuneiform writing developed gradually from pictographs.

Curia Hostilia and its replacement, built by Julius Caesar, was known as the Curia Julia.

● **Curia, Roman** ▷*See* Roman Curia.

● **Curia Regis** ▶ The King's Court of early medieval Europe. It fulfilled all the functions of royal government—administrative, legislative, and judicial—and from its specialist departments developed the public government offices, such as, in England, the Chancery and the Exchequer, as well as the courts of law and parliament.

● **curie** ▶ (Ci) A unit of radioactivity equal to the amount of an isotope that decays at the rate of 3.7×10^{10} disintegrations per second. Named after Pierre ▷Curie.

Marie Curie ▶ In her laboratory at the Sorbonne in Paris.

● **Curie, Marie** ▶ (1867–1934) Polish chemist, renowned for her research into ▷radioactivity. Born Marya Skłodowska, she emigrated to France in 1891, studied at the Sorbonne, and married (1895) **Pierre Curie** (1859–1906), a French physicist. Interested in ▷Becquerel's discovery of radioactivity, Marie Curie noticed in 1898 that one particular uranium ore emitted an anomalously large amount of radiation. Realizing that the radiation was caused by a new element, she and her husband spent four years isolating one gram of radium salt from eight tons of the ore. The Curies, together with Becquerel, were awarded the 1903 Nobel Prize for Physics and, for her discovery of radium and polonium, she won the 1911 Nobel Prize for Chemistry. Pierre Curie, before joining his wife's work, had discovered the ▷piezoelectric effect (1880) and shown that ferromagnetism reverts to paramagnetism (*see* magnetism) above a certain temperature, now known as the Curie point (1895). He was killed in a road accident; she died as a result of the radiation to which she had been exposed. Their daughter **Irène Curie** (1896–1956) married the French physicist **Frédéric Joliot** (1900–59) in 1926; after their marriage both took the name **Joliot-Curie**. Working together in the same field as her parents, they were the first to produce radioactivity artificially. For this work they were awarded the Nobel Prize for Chemistry in 1935.

● **Curie's law** ▶ The susceptibility of a paramagnetic substance is inversely proportional to its thermodynamic temperature. The **Curie point** (or Curie temperature) is the temperature above which a ferromagnetic substance becomes paramagnetic. Named after Pierre Curie.

● **Curitiba** ▶ 25 24S 49 16W A city in SE Brazil, the capital of Paraná state. It has two cathedrals and is the site of the Federal University of Paraná (1894). Curitiba is a commercial and industrial centre producing chiefly furniture, tobacco, and maté. Population (2000): 1 586 898.

● **curium** ▶ (Cm) An artificial transuranic element discovered by Seaborg and others in 1944 and named after Marie and Pierre Curie. All 13 isotopes are radioactive and some intensely so; ^{242}Cm gives out about three watts of heat per gram. Curium is a silvery reactive metal. Its compounds include the oxides (CmO_2, Cm_2O_3) and halides (CmF_3, $CmCl_3$). At no 96; at wt (247); mp $1340 \pm 40°C$.

● **curlew** ▶ A streaked brown or grey bird belonging to the genus *Numenius* (8 species). Curlews have a long neck and long curved bill.

They breed in inland subarctic regions and migrate south in winter to marshes and mudflats, feeding on worms and crabs. The common Eurasian curlew (*N. arquata*) is almost 60 cm long and ranges from Britain to central Asia. Family: *Scolopacidae* (snipe, sandpipers, etc.).

● **curling** ▶ A target game played on ice with stones fitted with handles, played since at least the early 16th century in Scotland. Two teams of four players take it in turns to slide two curling stones each up to 36 m (39 yd) along the ice towards the "house," a series of concentric circles at the end of the rink. A team scores one point for each stone finishing nearer the centre of the house than any of its opponents'. Team-mates are allowed to sweep the ice ahead of a moving stone to influence its course. In the UK there was a brief surge of interest in the sport when a Scottish team won a gold medal in the 2002 Winter Olympics.

● **currant** ▶ **1.** One of several species of shrubs belonging to the genus *Ribes*. Some are cultivated for their fruit, for example ▷blackcurrant and ▷redcurrant, and others, such as the ▷flowering currant, are grown as ornamentals. Family: *Grossulariaceae*. **2.** The dried berry of a small seedless ▷grape, grown in the Mediterranean region and used in cooking.

● **currawong** ▶ An Australasian songbird of the genus *Strepera* (6 species). About 50 cm long, currawongs are usually black, sometimes with white markings, and have a long hook-tipped bill. They feed on insects, small mammals, and birds and frequently destroy fruit crops. Family: *Cracticidae* (Australian magpies).

● **currents** ▶ Flows of water masses moving in a particular direction. The major ocean currents form part of the general circulatory system in the oceans and are permanent, although they may vary with the seasons. They result mainly from the action of the prevailing winds on the sea surface; an example is the North Atlantic Drift. Currents are also induced by the tides, by differences in water density (densities vary with temperature, salinity, and turbidity levels), and by rivers discharging into the sea.

● **curricle** ▶ A light two-wheeled carriage usually drawn by two horses harnessed abreast to a pole. Curricles were favoured in the 18th and 19th centuries as rapid and stylish conveyances, equivalents to modern sports cars.

● **curry** ▶ A spicy stew of meat, chicken, vegetables, etc., originating in the Indian subcontinent. Long slow cooking allows the meat to become tender and enables intermingling of the balanced mixture of aromatics: spices (especially turmeric but also cumin, coriander, cardamoms, and ginger), herbs, and seasonings (peppers, chillies, and salt; or sweet seasonings made from sugar or honey; and acid seasonings made from citrus juices). Curries are usually eaten with rice and chutneys. In the West premixed curry powder is often used.

● **Curry, John (Anthony)** ▶ (1949–94) British ice skater and the only British skater to win the world, Olympic, and European figure-skating titles in the same year (1976). After turning professional, he opened a theatrical ice show in London (1977).

● **Curtin, John Joseph** ▶ (1885–1945) Australian statesman; Labor prime minister (1941–45). He implemented many social-welfare policies and developed the military defences of Australia, introducing wide-ranging conscription measures during World War II.

● **Curtiss, Glenn (Hammond)** ▶ (1878–1930) US aviator and aeronautical engineer. Curtiss made the first one-kilometre flight in the US (1908) and designed and constructed the earliest US seaplanes. He manufactured aircraft for the Allies in World War I.

● **Curtiz, Michael** ▶ (Mihaly Kertész; 1888–1962) Hungarian-born film director, who made many films in Europe before moving to Hollywood (1926), where he made many more, including *Mammy* (1930), *Captain Blood* (1935), *Casablanca* (1942), and *White Christmas* (1954).

● **Curwen, John** ▶ (1816–80) British Nonconformist minister and teacher. He perfected the Tonic Sol-fa system invented by Sarah Anna Glover (1785–1867). Curwen resigned from the ministry to propagate Tonic Sol-fa and in 1844 founded the music publishing firm that became J. Curwen and Sons Ltd.

● **Curzon, Sir Clifford** ▶ (1907–82) British pianist. He studied with Schnabel in Berlin and made his debut at the Queen's Hall, London, at the age of 16. He was well known for his interpretations of Beethoven, Mozart, and Schubert; he also championed the works of Rawsthorne. He was knighted in 1977.

● **Curzon, George Nathaniel, 1st Marquess** ▶ (1859–1925) British politician. As viceroy of India (1898–1905) he established the Northwest Frontier Province and overhauled Indian administration but resigned following disagreements with ▷Kitchener. In World War I he was Lord Privy Seal (1915–16) and a member of the War Cabinet (1916–19). As foreign secretary (1919–24) he established a short-lived British protectorate over Persia.

● **Curzon line** ▶ A line between Poland and the former Soviet Union, which they recognized as the border between them in 1945 after World War II. The boundary, which was named after Lord ▷Curzon, had initially been suggested during the Russo-Polish War (1919–20).

● **cuscus** ▶ A cat-sized ▷marsupial mammal belonging to the genus *Phalanger*, found in forests of NE Australia, New Guinea, and nearby islands. Cuscuses have a prehensile tail and climb slowly around trees at night, eating mainly leaves and fruit but sometimes catching lizards or roosting birds. Family: *Phalangeridae* (*see* phalanger).

● **Cush** ▷*See* Nubia.

● **Cushing, Harvey Williams** ▶ (1869–1939) US surgeon, noted for his contributions to brain surgery, particularly of the pituitary gland, and his classification of brain tumours. He was the first to describe ▷Cushing's disease.

● **Cushing's disease** ▶ A disorder resulting from excess ▷corticosteroid hormones in the body, named after H. W. ▷Cushing. The symptoms include obesity, loss of minerals from the bones, and reddening of the face and neck; it may be associated with the symptoms of ▷diabetes mellitus and high blood pressure. It may be caused by a tumour of the pituitary gland or the adrenal gland or by prolonged therapy with high doses of corticosteroids: the treatment is determined by the cause.

● **Cushitic languages** ▶ A subgroup of the ▷Hamito-Semitic languages. Spoken in the Sudan, Somalia, Ethiopia, and Eritrea, they include Beja and ▷Somali. They are closest in sound to the common ancestor Proto-Hamito-Semitic.

● **custard apple** ▶ A small tree of the genus *Annona* of the American tropics, so called because of the custard-like flavour of its fruits. The common custard apple (*A. reticulata*), 5–8 m high and widely grown in the West Indies, produces reddish many-seeded fruits, 8–12 cm in diameter, with a sweetish pulp. ▷*See also* soursop; sweetsop. Family: *Annonaceae*.

● **Custer, George A(rmstrong)** ▶ (1839–76) US cavalry general. After earning distinction in the Civil War, he commanded the Seventh Cavalry during the western campaigns against the Indians. Sent to round up Sioux and Cheyenne forces under Chief ▷Sitting Bull in S Dakota's Black Hills in 1876, an erroneous reconnaissance report led him to divide his force and he and his force of about 260 were massacred by the main Indian strength at the ▷Little Bighorn (Custer's Last Stand).

● **customs and excise duties** ▶ Indirect taxes (*see* taxation) applied to goods and services. In the UK these taxes are collected by the Board of Customs and Excise and comprise customs, excise, assessed taxes, and ▷value-added tax. Customs (*or* tariffs) are duties payable on import of foreign goods. They may be either specific duties assessed according to the weight or quantity, or ad valorem duties assessed according to the foreign or domestic price of the imported goods. They raise revenue and restrict imports. The ▷European Community abolished all internal tariffs between members in 1992 and imposed a common external tariff. Excise tax is a duty chargeable on specific goods produced or consumed within a country, e.g. petrol, intoxicating liquors, and tobaccos. Assessed taxes are duties not properly in the nature of excise but classified under that heading because they are levies on particular activities within a country, e.g. motor-vehicle licences.

● **customs unions** ▶ Associations of countries that agree to abol-

ish customs duties and tariffs for each other's products and to institute ▷free trade between themselves. They usually also agree to common external tariffs for nonmembers. The ▷European Union is an example.

● **Cuthbert, St** ▶ (c. 635–87 AD) English churchman and missionary. As a monk and later a prior at Melrose, he evangelized among the Northumbrians, earning a reputation as a miracle worker. With his abbot, St Eata, he moved to Lindisfarne in 664 and became its bishop in 685. He died on the island of Farne, where he had earlier lived as a hermit. His body was reburied in Durham Cathedral in the 10th century. Feast day: 20 March.

● **Cuttack** ▶ 20 26N 85 56E A city in India, in Orissa. The administrative centre of Orissa, it lies at the centre of a rice-growing region. Population (1991): 402 390.

● **cutter** ▶ **1.** A sailing vessel, similar to a ▷sloop, but with the mast stepped about halfway between the bows and the stern. **2.** A fast armed powerboat used by the US Coast Guard in the enforcement of customs regulations, rescue work, etc.

● **cuttlefish** ▶ A ▷cephalopod mollusc belonging to the family *Sepiidae* (about 100 species), of temperate coastal waters. 2.5–90 cm long, the body is supported by an internal calcareous leaf-shaped shell—the cuttlebone—which gives buoyancy. When alarmed, the animal emits an inky fluid.

● **Cutty Sark** ▶ A clipper ship built at Dumbarton in 1869, preserved as a museum at Greenwich, London.

● **cutworm** ▶ The larva of a ▷noctuid moth of the widely distributed genus *Agrotis*. Cutworms destroy crops, such as cabbage, maize, and pasture grasses, by biting through the stems.

● **Cuvier, Georges, Baron** ▶ (1769–1832) French zoologist and father of the sciences of comparative anatomy and palaeontology. His studies at the Museum of Natural History in Paris showed him how the different parts of an animal skeleton were related to each other. By extending this to fossils he reconstructed entire skeletons from the incomplete ones in existence. His classification, described in *Le Règne animal* (1817), grouped animals (including extinct species) into four phyla. This was an advance on Linnaeus's system although it was later superseded.

● **Cuxhaven** ▶ 53 52N 08 42E A seaport in NW Germany, in Lower Saxony on the Elbe estuary. It is the outport for Hamburg, as well as being a major fishing port and fish-processing centre. Population (1989 est): 55 250.

● **Cuyp, Aelbert Jacobsz** ▶ (1620–91) Dutch landscape painter. He was born in Dordrecht, the son and pupil of **Jacob Gerritsz Cuyp** (1594–1651), a portrait and landscape painter. Aelbert's paintings of cattle, river scenes, etc., are distinguished by their glow of golden light, a fine example being *Herdsmen with Cows by a River* (National Gallery, London).

● **Cuzco** ▶ 13 32S 71 57W A city in S Peru, in the Andes 3416 m (11 207 ft) above sea level. It was the capital of the Inca Empire until 1533; Inca ruins include the Temple of the Sun. It is now a commercial centre serving an agricultural region. It has a university (1962). Population (1993): 257 751.

● **CVS** ▶ (chorionic villus sampling) ▷*See* prenatal diagnosis.

● **Cwmbran** ▶ 51 39N 3 00W A town in South Wales, in Torfaen county borough. Created a new town in 1949, it has engineering, electrical, and food-processing industries. Population (1991): 46 021.

● **cyanide** ▶ **1.** The ion CN⁻ derived from ▷hydrogen cyanide and any salt containing this ion. Most cyanides are very toxic as the ion can combine with haemoglobin, blocking the uptake of oxygen. **2.** (*or* nitrile) Any compound containing the –CN group and having the general formula RCN. An example is methyl cyanide (CH_3CN), which is made by the reaction between potassium cyanide (KCN) and chloromethane (CH_3Cl).

● **cyanide process** ▶ The extraction of gold from its ores by chemical treatment with potassium cyanide. The ore is crushed to a fine powder and mixed with a weak solution of cyanide in water. Once the gold is dissolved by the cyanide the resulting compound is precipitated from the solution and the metallic gold separated out by chemically displacing it from the compound with zinc.

● **Cyanobacteria** ▷*See* blue-green bacteria.

● **cyanocobalamin** ▷*See* vitamin B complex.

● **cyanogen** ► (C_2N_2) A colourless highly poisonous flammable gas with a smell of bitter almonds. It can be prepared by heating mercury cyanide and has been used as a fumigant, war gas, and rocket fuel.

● **Cybele** ► An Asiatic earth goddess identified by the Greeks with ▷Rhea. The centre of her worship was Phrygia, whence her cult spread to Athens and later to Rome. She represented the powers of nature and was a protectress of wild animals. Her priests were eunuchs known as Corybantes.

● **CyberCash** ► An ▷e-commerce technology to enable funds to be moved securely between customers and merchants. When a customer makes a purchase over the Internet, the merchant transfers the transaction to the CyberCash system. This consists of customer software, merchant software, and the CyberCash server. The customer sends details of the transaction and his credit card using his software to encrypt his message to the merchant. The merchant adds his identification details and sends the message, still in code, to the CyberCash server, which decodes the message and instructs the bank or card-processing house to send the money to the merchant. The system, which can also be used between non-commercial e-mail users, is essentially secure and conceals the credit card details of its users.

● **cybernetics** ► The study of communication and control between men, machines, and organizations. The name was derived from the Greek word meaning "steersman" by Norbert ▷Wiener, who was largely responsible for pioneering the subject. It is an aspect of ▷bionics, in which the human ability to adapt to changing circumstances and to make decisions is simulated in the design of computer-controlled systems. Ultimately, the application of cybernetics may extend the process of ▷automation to the point at which almost every operation in a factory is automatic, with very little human supervision.

Cybernetics has also been used as a link between the physical and life sciences, for instance in using ▷information theory to explain how messages are transmitted in nervous systems and in genetic processes.

● **cyberspace** ▷*See* virtual reality.

● **cycad** ► A ▷gymnosperm plant belonging to the phylum *Cycadophyta* (about 100 species), native to warm and tropical regions. They resemble small palms or tree ferns, having short stout stems with a crown of frondlike leaves. Reproductive organs are in the form of separate male and female cones borne on different trees, the female cones often being very large (up to 45 kg). The stems of some species yield a type of ▷sago.

● **Cyclades** ► (Modern Greek name: Kikládhes) A group of some 220 Greek islands in the S Aegean Sea, including Ándros, Delos, Íos, Míkonos, Melos, Náxos (the largest), Páros, and Syros. Total area: 2578 sq km (995 sq mi). Population (1991): 94 005. Capital: Hermopolis (on Syros).

● **cyclamate** ► A salt of cyclamic acid ($C_6H_{11}NHSO_3H$). Sodium and calcium cyclamates were formerly extensively used as artificial sweeteners in soft drinks and for diabetics, but their excessive consumption has been shown to have dangerous side effects and their use has been discontinued.

● **Cyclamen** ► A genus of perennial plants (15 species) native from the European Mediterranean to Iran and widely cultivated as pot and garden plants. The pot varieties are grown from *C. persicum*. The garden cyclamens include attractive dwarf varieties, 5–8 cm high. All cyclamens produce corms but most can be grown from seed. They have marbled heart-shaped leaves and drooping flowers with red, pink, or white reflexed petals. Family: *Primulaceae*.

● **cycloid** ► The curve traced out by a point on the circumference of a circle as it rolls along a flat surface.

● **cyclone** ► An area of relatively low atmospheric pressure with a series of closed isobars around its centre. In the N hemisphere wind circulates in an anticlockwise direction around its centre, in the S hemisphere it is clockwise. Except in the tropics, cyclones are now usually referred to as ▷depressions or lows. Tropical cyclones form over the tropical oceans and are accompanied by strong winds; they include ▷hurricanes and ▷typhoons.

● **Cyclops** ► (Greek mythology) Storm gods who made thunderbolts for Zeus. Homer describes them in the *Odyssey* as one-eyed man-eating giants who lived on an island later identified as Sicily. ▷*See also* Polyphemus.

● **Cyclops** ► (zoology) A genus (44 species) of very small freshwater crustaceans of the class ▷*Copepoda*, so named because of their single median eye. In Africa and Asia they transmit the parasitic Guinea worm larvae to man if accidentally swallowed.

● **cyclostome** ► An eel-like jawless aquatic vertebrate of the class *Cyclostomata*, which includes the ▷lamprey and ▷hagfish. Cyclostomes have a long smooth cylindrical body with fins arranged not in pairs but singly (*compare* fish), a cartilaginous skeleton, and a sucking mouth with numerous horny teeth. They occur mainly in temperate fresh waters and salt waters and many are parasitic on fish. Subphylum: *Agnatha*.

● **cyclotherms** ► Series of beds of sedimentary rocks deposited in a single cycle (in cyclic sedimentation) or repeated group (in rhythmic sedimentation). Carboniferous strata, particularly the Coal Measures, show such sequences, representing the changes in conditions from terrestrial to marine that repeatedly occurred in the period.

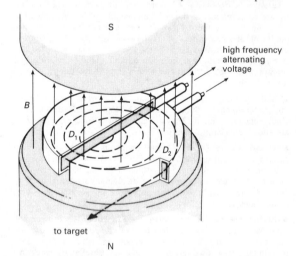

cyclotron ► The charged particles are accelerated in the two D-shaped conductors (D_1 and D_2), which are supported in the magnetic field B.

● **cyclotron** ► A type of particle ▷accelerator in which charged particles are accelerated in an outward spiral path inside two hollow D-shaped conductors (called dees) placed back to back. A magnetic field at right angles to the plane of the dees causes the particles to move in a spiral and, at the same time, they are accelerated by an alternating electric field applied across the gap between the two dees. When the particles reach the edge of the device they are deflected onto the target. The maximum energy of the particles is about 25 MeV. ▷*See also* synchrocyclotron.

● **Cygnus** ► (Latin: Swan) A large conspicuous constellation in the N sky, lying in the Milky Way. The brightest star, ▷Deneb, and four other bright stars form the **Northern Cross**. The constellation contains many interesting ▷variable stars, ▷binary stars, and dark and emission ▷nebulae—including the old supernova remnant, the **Cygnus Loop**. **Cygnus A** is an intense double radio source while **Cygnus X-1**, thought to contain a ▷black hole, is one of several strong X-ray sources.

● **cymbals** ► Circular metal percussion instruments of indefinite pitch. Orchestral cymbals are clashed together, struck with a drumstick, or suspended and rolled with felt-covered timpani sticks. **Choke cymbals** (*or* hi-hat) are a pair of cymbals on a stick, operated by a foot pedal; they are used in dance bands and pop groups. Small tuned cymbals are known as **ancient cymbals**. □musical instruments.

● **Cymbeline** ▷*See* Cunobelinus.

● **Cymbidium** ► A genus of tropical and subtropical ▷orchids (40–70 species), native to Asia and Australia. Most species have pseudobulbs, straplike leathery leaves, and long-lasting sprays of 6–20 flowers on each flower stalk, ranging in colour from white to yellow, maroon, and bronze. Ornamental and very adaptable, cymbidiums are among the most popular orchids in cultivation today.

● **Cynewulf** ► (early 9th century AD) One of the earliest Anglo-Saxon religious poets (*compare* Caedmon). His work shows him to have been a native of Mercia or Northumbria and from a learned background. Four surviving religious poems, preserved in 10th-century manuscripts, carry his runic signature. They are *Elene*, *The Fates of the Apostles*, *The Ascension*, and *Juliana*. All are based on Latin sources and are distinguished by their clear narrative form. Many other Old English poems have been attributed to him.

● **Cynics** ► The followers of the Greek moral philosopher ▷Diogenes of Sinope, who were active from the early 3rd century BC. They are notable less as a coherent school with systematic doctrines than as a succession of flamboyant individuals whose characteristic concern was to discount the pursuit of worldly wealth and success and to demonstrate that basic human needs can be very simply satisfied. They were outspoken critics of accepted social values and often lived notably unconventional lives. Positive freedom could be attained by self-realization, but often it was the negative destructive side of the Cynics' beliefs that was emphasized. Their distinction between natural and artificial values strongly influenced other ancient philosophies, such as ▷Epicureanism.

● **cypress** ► A conifer of the genus *Cupressus* (true cypresses; 20 species), native to S Europe, E Asia, and North America and widely planted for ornament and timber. Cypresses have tiny scalelike leaves, which densely cover the branches and twigs, and rounded cones, 1–4 cm in diameter, usually ripening from green to brown. The Italian or funeral cypress (*C. sempervirens*), of the Mediterranean region, is 25–45 m high. Cultivated forms, usually narrow and columnar, are planted in gardens and cemeteries. Its strong fragrant long-lasting wood is used for chests, furniture, etc. Family: *Cupressaceae*.

Similar and related trees of the genus *Chamaecyparis* (6 species), of North America and SE Asia, are known as false cypresses. The most important species is Lawson's cypress (*C. lawsoniana*), of W North America, where it grows to a height of 60 m. There are many cultivated varieties, up to 38 m high, widely planted for shelter and ornament. ▷*See also* swamp cypress.

● **Cypress pine** ► A coniferous tree of the genus *Callitris* (about 16 species), native to Australia and New Caledonia. Their branches are densely covered with small scale leaves and the cones are small and globular. Several species yield a useful timber. Family: *Cupressaceae*.

● **Cyprian, St** ► (c. 200–58 AD) African churchman; Bishop of Carthage (from c. 248) and Father of the Church, martyred under the Emperor Valerian. In his treatise, *De unitate ecclesiae*, he argues that the bishop's authority provides the basis for the Church's unity. Feast day: 16 Sept.

● **Cyprus, Republic of** ► (Greek name: Kypros; Turkish name: Kibris) An island state in the E Mediterranean Sea, off the S coast of Turkey. A central plain, the Messaoria, rises to the Kyrenia Range in the N, and in the SW the Troödos Massif rises over 1800 m (6000 ft). Most of the population is Greek or Turkish, the former being in a majority of about five to one.

Economy: agriculture is important, with citrus fruits, grapes, and vegetables the main crops. Mineral resources include iron pyrites, asbestos, chromite, and copper ores. Though mining is on the decline, other (mainly light) industries have developed rapidly in the Greek sector. Tourism is now the main source of revenue and employs some 25% of the workforce. The Turkish sector remains relatively poor but

there is now an intensive development programme, largely based on agriculture, with the aim of creating a self-sufficient economy. Exports include wine, citrus fruits, potatoes, and metals.

History: there was already a Greek colony on Cyprus almost 4000 years ago. It was conquered by Egypt in the 6th century BC and later formed part of the Persian, Macedonian, Roman, Byzantine, and Arab empires. In 1193 it became a Frankish kingdom and in 1489 a Venetian dependency. In 1571 it was conquered by the Turks and this occupation lasted until 1878 when it came under British administration. It became a crown colony in 1925. In the 1930s Greek Cypriots began advocating Enosis (Union with Greece), and in 1955 a Greek Cypriot organization (*see* EOKA), led by Archbishop ▷Makarios and Gen Grivas, began guerrilla warfare against the British. Cyprus became a republic in 1960 and a member of the Commonwealth in 1961. The UK, however, retained sovereignty over several military bases. There were fierce clashes between the Greek and Turkish communities in the 1960s and in 1964 a UN peacekeeping force was sent to the island. In 1971 Gen Grivas began a further terrorist campaign in favour of Enosis; he died in 1974. Following a Greek-supported military coup of the same year, in which Makarios was temporarily overthrown, Turkey invaded the island leading to its virtual partition. The Turks set up their own government in the N as the Turkish Federated State of Cyprus, with Rauf Denktash as president, in 1975. This failed to receive international recognition but was, in 1983, declared to be an independent state as the Turkish Republic of Northern Cyprus. In the south Spyros Kyprianou, elected president on the death of Makarios, was succeeded in 1988 by George Vassiliou, who held office until 1993. A UN plan to end the division of Cyprus was proposed in 1992, but has not yet found acceptance; the border area has remained sensitive, with tensions between the communities rising once more in the late 1990s. Cyprus has been formally invited to join the EU early in the 21st century.

Republic of Cyprus

Head of state	President Glafcos Clerides
Official languages	Greek and Turkish; English is also widely spoken
Official currency	Cyprus pound of 100 cents
Area	9251 sq km (3572 sq mi)
Population (1998 est)	861 000
Capital	Nicosia
Main port	Limassol

● **Cyrano de Bergerac, Savinien** ► (1619–55) French writer and dramatist. He became famous in his youth as a soldier and fighter of duels. He wrote a comedy, *Le Pédant joué* (1654), some tragedies on classical subjects, and two fantastic satirical romances describing visits to the moon and sun (published posthumously). He was noted for his comically long nose as well as his chivalrous nature; the conflict between his appearance and his noble character is captured in ▷Rostand's famous play, *Cyrano de Bergerac*.

● **Cyrenaica** ► A region of E Libya, bordering Egypt on the E, largely desert to the S and inhabited mainly by tribesmen of the Senussi, a puritanical Islamic sect. From early pre-Christian times Cyrenaica was colonized or conquered by Greeks, Egyptians, Romans, Vandals, Arabs, Turks, and Italians successively. The scene of many battles in World War II, it was occupied by the British from 1943 until united with Libya in 1951. It was a province of Libya until 1963.

● **Cyrenaics** ► A school of Greek philosophers, founded about 400 BC by ▷Socrates' disciple, Aristippus of Cyrene. The Cyrenaics identified virtue with pleasure and, adopting the ▷Sophists' view that truth and morality are matters for individual judgment, held that the only purpose of life was immediate gratification of the senses. Among them, Anniceris stressed the pleasures of friendship and family affection, whereas Hegesias, believing that pure pleasure was unattainable, advocated rather the avoidance of pain. Their ethical doctrines foreshadowed those of ▷Epicureanism.

● **Cyrene** ► The chief city of ancient Cyrenaica (now in Libya). Founded by colonists from Thera about 630 BC, Cyrene quickly became prosperous, basing its wealth on trade. Its monopoly in silphium, an important Greek medicinal spice, brought the Cyrenaeans fame as doctors. It fell under the control of the Ptolemies of Egypt in the 4th century BC and was bequeathed by Ptolemy Apion to Rome in 96 BC. Excavations of its remains have provided valuable information about ancient art, architecture, and society.

● **Cyril, St** ▶ (c. 827–69 AD) Greek missionary, traditionally the inventor of the ▷Cyrillic alphabet. With his brother **St Methodius** (c. 825–84) he was sent to Moravia to evangelize the Slavs by the Patriarch of Constantinople in 863. Although highly successful, the brothers initially incurred much hostility from the German rulers and ecclesiastics for their use of the vernacular in the liturgy. After Cyril's death, Methodius translated the Bible into Slavonic. Feast day: 19 Feb or 11 May.

● **Cyrillic alphabet** ▶ The alphabet used for Russian, Belarussian, Ukrainian, Bulgarian, Serbian, and various other languages of the former Soviet Union. It was developed from a Greek alphabet of the 9th century AD in the course of Christian missionary work and is traditionally attributed to the Greek brothers, St ▷Cyril and St Methodius. It originally consisted of 43 letters, but modern versions have reduced this number to about 30.

● **Cyril of Alexandria, St** ▶ (c. 375–444 AD) Christian theologian; Patriarch of Alexandria (from 412) and Doctor of the Church. He became a champion of Christian orthodoxy, expelled the Jews from Alexandria, and opposed Nestorius (see Nestorians) on the question of Christ's divinity, eventually succeeding in having him banished as a heretic. He produced numerous works, including biblical commentaries and refutations of paganism. Feast day: 9 June or 27 June.

● **Cyrus (II) the Great** ▶ (d. 529 BC) King of Persia (559–529), who founded the Achaemenian Empire. He staged a successful revolt against his overlord Astyages (reigned c. 584–c. 550), gaining control of the empire of the Medes (see Media). He then conquered Lydia, Ionia, and Babylonia (539), thereby gaining Syria and Palestine, and territories in Central Asia. He was noted for his humane and tolerant policies towards conquered peoples and permitted the Jews to return to Jerusalem in 537. He was killed fighting in Central Asia: his tomb at ▷Pasargadae is still to be seen.

● **Cyrus the Younger** ▶ (d. 401 BC) The son of Darius II (reigned 423–404) of Persia. Appointed commander of Persian forces in Asia Minor in 407, he helped the Spartan admiral ▷Lysander defeat Athens in the ▷Peloponnesian War. When in 404 Cyrus' brother succeeded their father as ▷Artaxerxes II, Cyrus led a Greek mercenary army, which included the historian ▷Xenophon, against him. He died leading a cavalry charge at ▷Cunaxa.

● **cyst** ▶ **1.** A close fluid-filled sac within the body. Cysts may be caused by blockage of the duct of a gland (e.g. a sebaceous cyst in the skin), dilation of an existing body space (e.g. in the ovary), or by parasitic infection. Some cysts are present from birth. **2.** A structure formed during the life cycle of certain lower animals, such as parasitic protozoans and worms. The cysts usually protect the animals when they are most vulnerable.

● **cystic fibrosis** ▶ A hereditary disease affecting the mucus-secreting and sweat glands. The defective gene responsible has now been identified and located; it fails to produce the protein required to transport salts and water across tissues. Symptoms, which appear in early childhood, are due to the production of thick mucus, which obstructs the pancreatic duct, intestinal glands, and bronchi. Patients suffer from malnutrition (because the production of digestive enzymes is blocked) and recurrent chest infections. The sweat contains large quantities of salt, which confirms the diagnosis. Current treatment, which aims to relieve symptoms, includes antibiotics to combat infections, daily physiotherapy, a low-fat high-protein diet, and the administration of pancreatic enzymes. More radical treatment will hopefully be based on ▷gene therapy.

● **cystitis** ▶ Inflammation of the bladder, usually caused by a bacterial infection. Cystitis is most common in women: symptoms include frequent painful urination and occasionally blood in the urine. It is treated with antibiotics.

● **cytochromes** ▶ A group of haem-containing pigments found in the mitochondria of plant and animal cells and involved in cell respiration. Cytochromes b, c_1, c, a, and a_3 form an electron transport chain that captures the energy (in the form of electrons) released by

the ▷Krebs cycle and conserves it for used by the cell through the formation of ▷ATP molecules. The electrons are transferred ultimately to oxygen with the formation of water.

● **cytokinins** ▶ (or kinins) A group of plant growth-stimulating compounds derived from purines. They act in conjunction with ▷auxins to promote cell division and retard senescence. Synthetic cytokinins, such as kinetin, are used commercially in the storage of vegetables.

● **cytology** ▶ The study of the structure and function of cells. It began with the development of techniques for the sectioning, fixation, and selective staining of materials for study under the light microscope, which enabled the ▷nucleus and other organelles to be observed. This led to the identification of chromosomes within the nucleus and of their role in heredity. More recent developments have included the use of phase-contrast and electron microscopy, and the biochemistry and physiology of cells has been studied using such techniques as cell separation and analysis, autoradiography, and tissue culture. Cytology has an important function in medicine. The study of diseased cells can reveal the nature of a disease and how it may be controlled, and cytological tests provide the basis for diagnosis of many diseases, including cancer. ▷See also biological sciences.

● **cytoplasm** ▷See cell (biology).

● **cytotoxic drugs** ▶ Drugs used to kill cancer cells. These drugs, which include cyclophosphamide, cisplatin, and vincristine, have led to major improvements in the treatment of some cancers (e.g. leukaemia). They act by interfering with the multiplication of the malignant cells, but since they may also affect nonmalignant cells they often cause severe side effects, including damage to bone marrow.

● **Czech** ▶ A West Slavonic language related to Slovak and Polish and spoken by over ten million people in the Czech Republic, of which it is the offical language, and in Slovakia. It is written in the Latin alphabet in a standardized form based on the dialect of Prague. Its development as a literary language dates from the 15th and 16th centuries.

● **Czechoslovakia** ▶ (official name: Czech and Slovak Federative Republic) A former country in central Europe. Czechoslovakia was created, under the leadership of Tomáš ▷Masaryk and Edvard ▷Beneš, in 1918 following the collapse of the Austrian Empire. It comprised the former Austrian possessions of ▷Bohemia, ▷Moravia, part of ▷Silesia, ▷Slovakia, and (from 1920) ▷Ruthenia; the population was about two-thirds Czech and almost a third Slovak, with small minorities of Hungarians, Germans, Poles, and others. The new state encountered threats from the diverse national minorities that peopled it and was unable to withstand the expansionist ambitions of Hitler's Germany. In 1938 he secured the ▷Munich Agreement to his annexation of the ▷Sudetenland and in 1939 took control of all Czechoslovakia. During World War II a provisional Czechoslovak government existed in London under Beneš' presidency. Following the war the Allies recognized its former territories, except for Ruthenia, which was ceded to the Soviet Union, and some three million Germans were expelled from Czechoslovakia. By 1948 the Communist Party was in power and Czechoslovakia was closely allied with the Soviet Union. In 1968 a liberalization programme initiated by Dubček provoked a Soviet invasion and Dubček's overthrow. In 1977 Czech dissidents protested against the violation of human rights in Czechoslovakia in a manifesto entitled Charter 77. In 1989 mass unrest, centred on the Civil Forum, led to the resignation of the Communist politburo and of President Gustáv Husák; a new non-Communist government was formed with Václav ▷Havel as president. In 1992 growing pressure for Slovakian independence led to a decision to dissolve the federation. ▷Slovakia and the ▷Czech Republic became separate states on 1 Jan 1993.

● **Czech Republic** ▶ A landlocked country in central Europe. It is mainly wooded; the lowlands in the E surrounding the River Morava rise to the Bohemian plateau in the W and to highlands in the N.
   Economy: industry was entirely nationalized during the communist era (1948–89) and agriculture organized mainly in collectives and state farms. A major privatization programme was embarked upon by the Czechoslovak government in 1992 and has accelerated since the split with Slovakia. The Czech Republic produces a large

number of motor vehicles; glass, beer, ceramics, footwear, and textiles are also major products. Mineral resources are sparse. Principal crops include sugar beet, wheat, potatoes, and barley. Forestry is important, with rich natural forests as well as more recent afforestation.

Czech Republic

Head of state	President Václav Havel
Official language	Czech
Official currency	koruna of 100 haléřů
Area	78 838 sq km (30 431 sq mi)
Population (1998 est)	10 302 000
Capital	Prague

History: the Czech Republic, which comprises the historic provinces of Bohemia and Moravia, was a federal republic of Czechoslovakia until 1 January, 1993, when Slovakia left the federation. Václav ▷Havel, the former president of Czechoslovakia, was elected president of the new state. The government of Václav Kraus implemented vigorous free-market reforms in the mid-1990s but economic progress has been slower than expected. The Czech Republic joined NATO in 1999 and has been formally invited to join the EU early in the 21st century. Elections in 1998 led to the formation of a centrist coalition led by Milos Zeman.

● **Czerny, Karl** ► (1791–1857) Austrian pianist, composer, and teacher. A child prodigy, he had lessons with Beethoven and was influenced by Clementi and Hummel. He was a prolific composer but is best known for his piano studies. He was the teacher of Liszt.

● **Częstochowa** ► 50 49N 19 07E A city in S Poland, on the River Warta. Formed from two separate communities in 1826, it has a monastery that was defended against the Swedes in the Thirty Years' War and to which Roman Catholics make pilgrimages. Its industries include iron and steel production. Population (1996 est): 259 500.

D

● **dab** ▶ One of several ▷flatfish of the family *Pleuronectidae*, especially the genus *Limanda* found in N Atlantic and N Pacific waters. The European *L. limanda*, up to 30 cm long, is light brown, sometimes with dark spots, and is an important food fish.

● **dabbling duck** ▶ A ▷duck that feeds near the surface of water, rarely diving and frequently feeding on land. With relatively small feet and legs set well forward, dabbling ducks walk efficiently on land; they include the ▷mallard, ▷pintail, ▷shoveler, ▷teal, and ▷wigeon. Drakes are usually brightly coloured and generally have a distinctive patch (speculum) on the wing. *Compare* diving duck.

● **dabchick** ▶ A small ▷grebe, *Tachybaptus ruficollis*, common in quiet inland waters of Europe, S Asia, and Africa. It is 23 cm long and has a dark-brown back, pale underparts, and a bright chestnut breast, neck, and cheeks. It feeds on small fish and aquatic invertebrates.

● **Dacca** ▷*See* Dhaka.

● **dace** ▶ A slender lively fish, also called dart or dare, belonging to the family *Cyprinidae*, which includes chub, roach, minnow, etc. The European dace (*Leuciscus leuciscus*) is up to 30 cm long, silvery coloured, and lives in fast-flowing streams and rivers, eating plant and animal material.

● **Dachau** ▶ 48 15N 11 26E A town in S Germany, in Bavaria. It was the site of a Nazi ▷concentration camp (1933–45). Population (latest est): 33 200.

● **dachshund** ▶ A breed of ▯dog originating in Germany, where they were developed to pursue badgers to earth. There are two size varieties—standard and miniature—and three coat types—long-haired, smooth-haired, and wire-haired. Dachshunds are usually brownish or black and tan. Height: 18–25 cm (standard); miniatures are smaller, not exceeding 5 kg in weight.

● **Dacia** ▶ A Roman province in central Europe, created in 105 AD, when the region was invaded by ▷Trajan. The native Daci (called the Getae by the Greeks) had a sophisticated culture and had previously resisted invasion by ▷Domitian (90 AD). The province was defeated by the Goths in the late 3rd century; the area is now occupied by Romania.

● **dacoit** ▶ An armed robber in a gang in India; the term is also applied to members of guerrilla groups in Myanmar (Burma).

● **dactyl** ▷*See* metre (poetry).

● **dada** ▶ A European art and literary movement, beginning in Zürich in 1916: deliberately nihilistic and irrational, it was essentially a protest against prevailing standards of art and morality. Dada was originally the name of a Zürich literary periodical published by the poet Tristan Tzara (1896–1963) and ▷Arp (the name was arbitrarily chosen, being a French children's name for a hobby horse). However, this had no coherent style, and the movement's ideology was more effectively transmitted in poetry periodicals, such as *L'Intransigeant* in France. Manufactured objects were favoured both in graphic art and sculpture, as part of a campaign to deflate the status of the art-object. Their violent effect is seen in the collages of Arp, ▷Ernst, and ▷Schwitters and the ▷ready-mades of ▷Duchamp, who exported dada to the USA. For its most fanatical adherents dada was also a way of life, characterized by calculatedly absurd behaviour. Although dada petered out in the early 1920s, ▷surrealism absorbed many of its characteristics. ▷*See also* conceptual art.

● **Dadd, Richard** ▶ (1817–86) British painter of detailed and complex works, mainly depicting biblical scenes, fairy life, and mythology. His best work was produced in an asylum, to which he was committed after killing his father.

● **Daddi, Bernardo** ▶ (?1290–?1349) Italian Renaissance painter. A pupil of ▷Giotto, he worked in Florence and was influenced by the painters of Sienna. His *Madonna* triptych (1328) and *Madonna Enthroned* (c. 1340) are both in the Uffizi.

● **daddy longlegs** ▷*See* cranefly.

● **Dadra and Nagar Haveli** ▶ A Union Territory of W India, on the Gujarat-Maharashtra border. Formerly a Portuguese colony (1789–1954), it is inhabited largely by tribesmen growing cereals and pulses. Area: 491 sq km (190 sq mi). Population (1994 est): 153 000. Capital: Silvassa.

● **Daedalus** ▶ A legendary Greek craftsman and sculptor, said to have built the labyrinth for King ▷Minos of Crete. Minos imprisoned him but he created wings for himself and his son Icarus and flew away; Icarus was killed when the sun melted his wings but Daedalus reached Sicily safely.

● **daffodil** ▶ A perennial European plant, ▷*Narcissus pseudonarcissus*, widely grown as a garden bulb. It has narrow leaves and yellow flowers, each with a trumpet-shaped central crown surrounded by six segments. The bulbs are poisonous and were once used in medicine as an emetic and cathartic. Family: *Amaryllidaceae*.

● **Dafydd ap Gwilym** ▶ (c. 1320–c. 1380) Welsh poet. Born into an aristocratic family in S Wales, he travelled widely and was acquainted with the work of the continental troubadours. He was trained in the bardic tradition but introduced a personal humour and originality into the intricate and obscure conventional forms of his odes.

● **Dagenham** ▶ A district in the Greater London borough of Barking. Industries include engineering and chemicals; in 2000 it was announced that car assembly at the large Ford motor works here will end in 2002.

● **Dagestan Republic** ▶ A constituent republic of Russia, on the Caspian Sea. The Caucasus Mountains lie in the S and much of central and N Dagestan is also mountainous. Over 30 different nationalities inhabit the republic, many of whom are Muslim.
   Economy: mineral resources remain largely unexploited, although sizable quantities of oil and natural gas have been extracted in coastal areas. There are large engineering, oil, chemical, and food industries and power stations are under construction. Crops include wheat and fruit; cattle breeding is also important.
   History: conquered by Arabs, Turks, Mongols, and Persians, Dagestan was annexed by Russia in 1813. It was an autonomous Soviet republic from 1921 until 1991. The 1990s saw growing agitation by Muslim separatists, leading to armed conflict with Russian troops in 1999. Area: 50 278 sq km (19 416 sq mi). Population (1996 est): 2 098 000. Capital: Makhachkala.

● **Dagly, Gerhard** ▶ (c. 1653–?1714) Belgian artist, a master in baroque lacquer work. At the courts of Electors Frederick William and Frederick III in Berlin (1687–1713) he became known for his cabinet cases, making ▷chinoiserie popular throughout Europe.

● **dagoba** ▷*See* pagoda.

● **Daguerre, Louis-Jacques-Mandé** ▶ (1789–1851) French inventor of the first practicable photographic process (the daguerreotype). Working initially with Joseph Niepce (1765–1833), who had produced the first permanent photographic image (the heliograph), Daguerre succeeded during the 1830s in producing a photograph by focusing light onto a copper plate that had been coated with a silver salt. Daguerreotypes were widely made in the mid-19th century.

● **Dahl, Roald** ▶ (1916–90) British author, whose work is pervaded by ironic black humour. Of Norwegian parentage, he served in the RAF during World War II. He published novels, collections of short stories, including *Kiss Kiss* (1959), and several anarchic children's books, including *Charlie and the Chocolate Factory* (1964).

● **Dahlia** ▶ A genus of herbaceous perennial tropical American plants (12 species), up to 2 m high, originally cultivated as a food crop for their tubers but now grown mainly for ornament. The brightly coloured flowers, 5–15 cm across, may be single or double and are of two main types. The varieties known as flat heads and pompoms are derived from *D. pinnata*; cactus-type flowers with pointed petals are varieties of *D. juarezii*. Family: ▷*Compositae*.

● **Dahomey** ▷*See* Benin, Republic of.

● **Daigo II** ▶ (1287–1339) Emperor of Japan (1318–39), who attempted to restore the power of the throne at the expense of the ▷shoguns (military overlords). Despite superficial success in 1333, Daigo's plans provoked fierce feudal resistance and led to prolonged civil war and his own exile.

● **Dáil Éireann** ▶ The representative assembly of the Republic of Ireland. It is the more important house in the National Parliament, the other house being the Seanad Éireann (the Senate). There are 144 members elected by proportional representation, at least once every 5 years. The president (the nominal head of state) summons and dissolves the Dáil on the advice of the prime minister.

● **Daimler, Gottlieb (Wilhelm)** ▶ (1834–1900) German inventor, who helped to develop the internal-combustion engine. Daimler started to build his own engines in 1883, which were soon sufficiently light and efficient to power machines (⁰motorcycles); in 1890 he founded a company to make motor ▷cars. The name Mercedes was used for Daimler's cars after an Austrian diplomat, Emil Jellinek, used the name of his daughter for a Daimler car in a race. When Daimler merged with Carl ▷Benz's firm in 1925 their products were called Mercedes–Benz cars, later shortened to Mercedes.

● **daimyo** ▶ The feudal lords who rose to control one or more provinces of Japan between the 14th and 16th centuries. Their constant warfare was ended by ▷Tokugawa Ieyasu in 1600 but over 250 *daimyo* ruled their own domains until 1871. They were then given pensions and titles and their lands were incorporated into prefectures.

● **Dairen** ▷*See* Lüda.

● **dairy farming** ▶ The maintenance and management of cattle, goats, and sheep for ▷milk production. Humans have used the milk of domestic animals as a food for thousands of years and the modern dairy cow is an efficient converter of grass into milk. Herds of 50–200 are milked by machine in milking parlours and the milk passes by pipeline under hygienic conditions to await collection in refrigerated bulk tanks.

Advances in breeding and management of dairy cows have resulted in current annual yields of about 4000 litres per cow in the UK, where the Friesian-Holstein breed is the most popular. Registration of producers and control of marketing in the UK was formerly undertaken by Milk Marketing Boards, established by the government, but since 1994 milk producers have been able to choose the buyers for their products. The EU coordinates European dairy farming through the ▷Common Agricultural Policy and the imposition of such measures as milk production quotas. ▷*See also* dairy products.

● **dairy products** ▶ Foods and other products derived from the processing of milk. Separation of milk by centrifugation yields skimmed milk and cream. Churning the cream disrupts the fat globules, removes water, and produces butter, containing over 80% fat, and buttermilk. Cream is retailed in various stages of concentration, for example single cream and double cream; other less concentrated forms include evaporated milk (containing about 65% water) and condensed milk (about 26% water). Yogurt (*or* yoghurt) is produced by inoculating whole milk with bacteria, principally of the genera *Streptococcus* and *Lactobacillus*. The acid they produce during incubation at about 43°C for four to five hours coagulates the milk, to which sweetening and flavouring may be added. Whey is a by-product of ▷cheese manufacture and, as with skimmed milk, may be dried to a powder form for use in the food industry or fed to farm animals in the fresh liquid state. ▷*See also* dairy farming; milk.

● **daisy** ▶ A herbaceous plant of the genus *Bellis* (15 species), native to Eurasia, with flower heads consisting of small central yellow disc florets surrounded by white or purple petal-like ray florets. The entire head is surrounded by bracts (leaflike structures). The flower heads are solitary, arising on long stalks from a basal rosette of simple leaves. Many species are garden ornamentals. The common wild Eurasian daisy is *B. perennis*, a perennial up to 6 cm high, common in grasslands and lawns. Family: ▷*Compositae*.

● **Dakar** ▶ 14 45N 17 08W The capital and main port of Senegal, on Cape Verde peninsula. It was the capital of French West Africa (1904–59). It has a cathedral and a university (1957). The country's main industrial centre and one of Africa's most important cities, its industries include sugar refining and groundnut-oil production. Population (1995 est): 1 500 000.

● **Dakota** ▷*See* North Dakota; South Dakota.

● **Daladier, Édouard** ▶ (1884–1970) French statesman; prime minister (1933, 1934, 1938–40). He signed the ▷Munich Agreement in 1938 and resigned in March, 1940, because of the unpopularity aroused by his failure to assist Finland against Russia (*see* Russo-Finnish War). Arrested by the Vichy government (1940) after the fall of France, he was imprisoned by the Germans from 1942 until 1945.

Dalai Lama ▶ Tenzin Gyatso (1935–　), the 14th Dalai Lama.

● **Dalai Lama** ▶ The title of the spiritual and political ruler of Tibet and head of the Gelukpa Buddhist school. The title, originating in the 14th century, signifies the incarnation of Avalokiteshvara, the ▷Bodhisattva of compassion. Chosen by oracles after the death of the previous incumbent, the Dalai Lama is regarded as infallible. The 14th Dalai Lama went into exile in India in 1959 after a failed uprising against the occupying Chinese; he was awarded the Nobel Peace Prize in 1989. ▷*See also* Panchen Lama.

● **Daldry, Stephen** ▶ (1961–　) British theatre and film director, who made his name with an innovative production of Priestley's *An Inspector Calls* (1992). He was director of London's Royal Court Theatre (1994–98) and directed the highly praised film *Billy Elliot* (2000).

● **Dale, Sir Henry Hallett** ▶ (1875–1968) British physiologist, who, in 1914, isolated the chemical ▷acetylcholine from the fungus ergot. His findings of the effects of acetylcholine on living organs corresponded with the discovery by Otto ▷Loewi, in 1921, that acetylcholine is a chemical transmitter released by the nervous system. Dale shared the 1936 Nobel Prize with Loewi, was president of the Royal Society (1940–45), and was appointed to the OM (1944).

● **d'Alembert, Jean le Rond** ▶ (1717–83) French mathematician. The illegitimate son of an aristocrat, d'Alembert was raised by a glazier and his wife. His works include the study of vibrating strings, during which he derived the general solution to the wave equation, and a theorem in mechanics known as d'Alembert's principle, which is essentially a form of Newton's second law of motion. He also collaborated with ▷Diderot in editing the *Encyclopédie* (*see* Encyclopedists).

● **Dales, the** ▶ The river valleys of the Pennines in the historic county of Yorkshire and other parts of N England. Most of the river valleys drain into the North Sea as tributaries of the Ouse. They include Swaledale, Wensleydale, Wharfedale, and Ribblesdale, which are often called the **Yorkshire Dales**. The Yorkshire Dales National Park (so designated in 1954) occupies an area of some 1761 sq km (680 sq mi) in North Yorkshire and Cumbria. The area is famous for its limestone scenery.

● **Dales pony** ▶ A breed of pony originating in the ▷Dales region of N England. The ponies are strong and compact with a long flowing tail and hairy heels. Brown, bay, black, or grey, Dales ponies were formerly used for draught work; they are now becoming popular for pony trekking. Height: about 1.45 m (14¼ hands).

● **Dalhousie, James Ramsay, 1st Marquess of** ▶ (1812–60) British colonial administrator; governor general of India (1847–56). Elected MP in 1837, he became president of the Board of Trade in 1845 under Peel. The youngest ever governor general, he was criticized for his aggressive annexation of Indian territories. Following the second ▷Sikh War (1848–49) he annexed the Punjab and after the second Burmese War (1852) he annexed Rangoon. His annexation of Oudh (1856) caused unrest that contributed to the outbreak of the ▷Indian Mutiny after his departure.

● **Dali, Salvador** ▶ (1904–89) Spanish surrealist painter. He joined the Paris surrealists (1929) and, inspired by Freudian theories of the unconscious, painted startling dream images with photographic realism during self-induced hallucinatory states. A similar disturbing imagery occurs in *Un Chien Andalou* (1929), a film he made with ▷Buñuel. While living in New York (1940–55), he turned to religious subjects and became a Roman Catholic. His taste for self-advertisement is evident in his autobiographical writings, such as *Diary of a Genius* (1966).

● **Dalian** ▷*See* Lüda.

● **Dallapiccola, Luigi** ▶ (1904–1975) Italian composer and pianist. His interest in composition was stimulated by his acquaintance with Alban Berg and he evolved a personal use of ▷serialism. His compositions include the opera *Ulisse* (1968), as well as many vocal and instrumental works, including the *Songs of Prison* (1938–41).

● **Dallas** ▶ 32 47N 96 48W A city in the USA, in NE Texas on the Trinity River. Founded in 1841, it developed as a cotton market during the late 19th century. The discovery of oil in E Texas during the 1930s accelerated the city's growth, which was further enhanced by the introduction of the aircraft and electronics industries during World War II. Today Dallas is the state's second largest city and the financial and commercial centre of the SW. A notable cultural centre, it is the site of several colleges. President John F. Kennedy was assassinated here on 22 November, 1963. Population (1996 est): 1 053 292.

● **Dalmatia** ▶ A coastal belt in Croatia bordering on the Adriatic Sea. It is penetrated by a narrow corridor giving Bosnia-Hercegovina access to the sea. Predominantly mountainous with an indented coastline and many offshore islands, its picturesque scenery formed the basis of a thriving tourist industry before the civil wars of the early 1990s. Wine production is especially important. The chief towns are Zadar, Split, and Dubrovnik.
  History: Dalmatia formed part of ancient Illyria. Ceded to Yugoslavia in 1920, it was occupied by Italy during World War II before being returned to Yugoslavia in 1947. It became part of independent Croatia in 1991.

● **Dalmatian dog** ▶ A breed named after the Adriatic coastal region of Dalmatia, from where they were exported to the UK. Dalmatians are strongly built and were formerly used as carriage dogs. The short sleek coat has a pure white background with black or liver (brown) spots. Height: 58–61 cm (dogs); 56–58 cm (bitches). □dog.

● **dalton** ▷*See* atomic mass unit.

● **Dalton, John** ▶ (1766–1844) British chemist and originator of the modern ▷atomic theory of matter. Dalton's earliest researches into gases led to his discovery of ▷Dalton's law of partial pressures. He believed that gases consist of particles, extending his theory in 1803 to suggest that all matter is particulate, but he did not distinguish between atoms and molecules. His discovery of the law of multiple proportions in the same year strongly supported his atomic theory.

● **Dalton's law of partial pressures** ▶ The total pressure exerted by a certain volume of a gaseous mixture is equal to the sum of the pressures (called partial pressures) exerted by each gas, if it alone occupied the same volume. Named after John ▷Dalton.

● **dam** ▶ A barrier across a river. Dams are used for diverting the flow of water; raising the water level for navigation purposes; storing water for irrigation, industrial use, or water control; and providing a high-pressure source of water for ▷hydroelectric power. Gravity dams depend on the weight of their bulk to provide strength. Usually made of concrete and having a flat vertical face upstream, they are no longer used for the largest dams. Arch dams consist of curved concrete structures presenting their convex faces upstream, so that pressure is transmitted to the sides of the dams. They can thus be much less massive than gravity dams and are therefore cheaper to build. ▷*See also* Aswan High Dam; Grand Coulee Dam; Grande Dixence Dam; Kariba, Lake; Paraná, Rio.

● **Dam, Carl Peter Henrik** ▶ (1895–1976) Danish biochemist, who discovered vitamin K. He showed that certain symptoms in chicks, such as a tendency to bleed, were due to deficiency of a vitamin, which he named *Koagulations-Vitamin*, or vitamin K. Later, both he and Edward A. Doisy (1893–1986) isolated vitamin K from green leaves. They shared a Nobel Prize (1943).

● **Daman and Diu** ▶ A Union Territory in India, on the Gulf of Cambray. It comprised a district of Portuguese India from 1559 until 1961 and was part of Goa, Daman, and Diu until 1987. Area: 112 sq km (43 sq mi). Population (1994 est): 111 000. Chief town: Daman.

● **Damanhur** ▶ 31 03N 30 28E A city in N Egypt, on the Nile Delta. It has an important cotton trade with cotton-ginning and textile industries. Population (1992 est): 222 000.

● **Damaraland** ▶ An area in N Namibia, named after the Damara people, who, however, now live mainly in the S. It is excellent cattle-grazing country.

● **Damascus** ▶ (Arabic name: Esh Sham) 33 30N 36 19E The capital of Syria, in the SE of the country close to the Lebanese border. It is claimed to be the oldest continually inhabited city in the world. Under Ottoman rule from 1516 until 1918, Damascus was taken by the French (1920) and became capital of independent Syria in 1941. The Great Mosque and the Gate of God are the most notable buildings in the city. The university was founded in 1923. It is now the commercial centre of the fertile plain to the E. Population (1994 est): 1 549 932.

● **damask** ▶ Originally, a woven silk fabric, reversible and elaborately patterned, manufactured in Damascus in the Middle Ages. Crusaders brought it to France, Flanders, and Ireland, where linen damask was later made but cotton is now usually used. A firm glossy fabric with interwoven designs, damask is chiefly used as table linen.

● **damask rose** ▶ An Asian rose, *Rosa damascena*, about 1.5 m high, with spicy-scented pink and white flowers. It is the main source of attar of roses—the rose oil used as the base of many perfumes. Extraction of rose oil is a major industry in Bulgaria and parts of W Asia.

● **Damien, Father** ▶ (Joseph de Veuster; 1840–89) Belgian Roman Catholic missionary. He worked in the leper settlement on the Hawaiian Island of Molokai from 1873 until his death from leprosy.

● **Damietta** ▶ (Arabic name: Dumyat) 31 26N 31 48E A port in Egypt, on the River Nile. Its industries include the manufacture of cotton and silk. Population (1986 est): 121 200.

● **dammar** ▶ A resin used in making varnish, obtained from various trees of SE Asia, especially species of *Shorea* (family *Dipterocarpaceae*) and conifers of the genus *Agathis* (including the New Zealand ▷kauri pine).

● **Damocles** ▶ Legendary courtier of Dionysius I of Syracuse in the 9th century BC. Dionysius seated him at a banquet beneath a sword suspended by a single hair, thus illustrating the insecurity of human life, irrespective of wealth or power.

● **Damodar, River** ▶ A river in NE India. Rising in West Bengal, it flows mainly ESE through Bihar to join the River Hooghly SW of Calcutta. Its valley contains India's most important coalfield, an irrigation works, a hydroelectric project, and important heavy industry. Length: 595 km (370 mi).

● **Dampier, William** ▶ (c. 1652–1715) English explorer. As a buccaneer he carried out several raids on Spanish possessions on the W coast of South America and West Africa in the 1680s, reaching Australia (which had disappointingly little booty to offer) in 1686. In 1699 he was employed by the Admiralty to explore Australia and New Guinea, returning to England in 1701. The Dampier Archipelago, off the NW coast of Australia, was named after him. His last voyage (1708–11), with Capt Woodes Rogers (d. 1732), rescued Alexander ▷Selkirk from the South Seas.

● **damping-off** ▶ A disease, usually affecting seedlings, in which the stem base becomes softened and the plant falls over. Fungus-like organisms of the genus *Pythium* are usually responsible. Soil sterilization may be undertaken as a preventive measure.

● **damselfish** ▶ A lively and aggressive deep-bodied fish, also called demoiselle, belonging to the family *Pomacentridae*. Up to 15 cm long, damselfish are often brightly coloured and live mainly among reefs in the tropical regions of the Atlantic, Indian, and Pacific Oceans. They feed on plant and animal material. Order: *Perciformes*.

● **damselfly** ▶ A slender delicate insect belonging to the suborder Zygoptera, closely related to the ▷dragonflies. It has similar habits but is smaller and has weaker powers of flight. The wings are held over the body at rest. □insect.

● **damson** ▶ The plumlike stone fruit of *Prunus damascena*, a slender twisted tree found across the N hemisphere. It has small white flowers that develop into purple fruits. Damsons may be eaten cooked, used in jam, or pressed into a cake called damson cheese. Family: *Rosaceae*. ▷See also plum.

● **Dan, tribe of** ▶ One of the 12 ▷tribes of Israel. It claimed descent from Dan, the son of Jacob by his concubine Bilhah. Its territory lay N of the Sea of Galilee and its city of Dan was situated at the northernmost point of the Hebrew settlement. Some of its people occupied an area NW of Judah, which was gradually absorbed by Judah.

● **Danae** ▶ In Greek legend, the daughter of Acrisius, King of Argos. He imprisoned her because an oracle said he would be killed by her child; Zeus visited her, however, and she gave birth to ▷Perseus. Acrisius cast mother and son out to sea but Polydectes, King of Seriphos, rescued them.

● **Da Nang** ▶ (former name: Tourane) 16 04N 108 14E A port in S central Vietnam, on the South China Sea. It was the site of a major US airbase during the Vietnam War. Textiles are the chief industry. Population (1992 est): 382 674.

● **Danby, Francis** ▶ (1793–1861) Irish painter, who lived in England and exhibited his romantic historical paintings and sunrise or sunset landscapes at the Royal Academy. His work was influenced by John ▷Martin.

● **Danby, Thomas Osborne, 1st Earl of** ▶ (1631–1712) English statesman. He became an MP in 1665 and as Lord Treasurer (1673–78) implemented successful economic policies. He was twice impeached by parliament: in 1678 for negotiating a secret treaty with France and in 1694, after becoming the 1st Duke of Leeds, for taking a bribe from the East India Company. He is often regarded as the founder of the Tory Party.

● **dance** ▶ A social activity or theatrical art in which the body moves rhythmically, usually to music. In ancient times it was primarily used in religious rituals; such dances still exist today among some primitive tribes. During the middle ages the Church often condemned dancing, particularly when it appeared to be a manifestation of mass hysteria. Dancing as a social activity and as an entertainment largely originated in the European courts. These dances usually developed from peasant dances and among the most popular were the galliard, basse danse, ▷allemande, and volta. The English country dances, so popular at Elizabeth I's court, eventually spread to the continent in the early 18th century and, together with the minuet, dominated ballrooms until the introduction of the ▷waltz. From the late 19th century the USA led the way in social dancing with the ▷cakewalk, foxtrot, and ▷tango; it also introduced the tap dance and contributed to the development of ▷modern dance. Many 20th-century dances were influenced by jazz, notably the ▷Charleston (1920s) and the jitterbug (1940s); others, such as the rumba, samba, and conga, were of Latin-American origin. Popular dancing from the 1960s, commencing with the twist, has become less formal; social dancers often avoid set sequences of steps and bodily contact between partners. Musical trends, such as rock and roll, disco, and rave, have inspired dance styles. ▷See also ballet; choreography; folk dance; modern dance.

● **Dance, George** ▶ (c. 1700–68) British architect. He became surveyor to the City of London in 1735, building several City churches, the façade of Guy's Hospital (1764), and the Mansion House (1753). His son **George Dance** (1741–1825) was also an architect, who acquired a taste for neoclassicism while studying in Italy. He succeeded his father as City surveyor in 1768, building the austere but impressive Newgate Prison (1778), which was demolished in 1902. His gothic south front to the Guildhall (1789), All Hallows, London Wall (1767), and layout for Finsbury Square can still be seen in London. He was one of the original members of the Royal Academy.

● **dance of death** ▶ In late medieval art, literature, and drama, an allegorical dance or procession in which the dead lead the living to the grave; also known as the *danse macabre*. It reflected man's preoccupation with death during an age of plague and warfare and was a popular subject for wall paintings in churches and monasteries in France, Germany, and England during the 14th and 15th centuries. The most famous pictorial version is the series of woodcuts designed by ▷Holbein the Younger between 1523 and 1526.

● **dandelion** ▶ A weedy perennial herbaceous plant of the worldwide genus *Taraxacum*, with a basal rosette of jagged toothed leaves and a solitary flower head of bright-yellow florets, up to 6 cm across, borne on a stalk up to 50 cm high. The seeds have parachutes of fine white hairs and are dispersed by wind. The common dandelion (*T. officinale*) is found throughout the N hemisphere. Its young leaves are edible. Family: ▷Compositae. □fruit.

● **Dandie Dinmont terrier** ▶ A dog breed named after a character in Sir Walter Scott's novel *Guy Mannering* (1812), who owned a pack of them. The Dandie Dinmont has a long body, short legs, and long drooping ears. Its long coat is a mixture of hard and soft hairs and can be either silvery grey to blue-black or fawn to reddish brown. Height: 20–28 cm.

● **Dandolo, Enrico** ▶ (c. 1108–1205) Venetian statesman; ▷doge (1192–1205). He was regarded as the founder of Venice's colonial empire. Dandolo commanded the fleet at the capture of Constantinople during the fourth ▷Crusade (1204) and secured for Venice a substantial portion of the conquered Greek territories. Defeated near Adrianople in 1205, Dandolo, aged and blind, led the army home.

● **dandruff** ▶ Dry scaling of the scalp, which occurs in everybody to some degree. It is presumed to be due to an infection and may extend to the face. Excessive dandruff can be treated with salicylic acid.

● **Danegeld** ▶ A land tax levied by ▷Ethelred the Unready, originally to buy off the Danes from ravaging England. Thereafter it became an intermittent national system of taxation, forming part of the crown's revenue, until its abolition by Stephen in 1136.

● **Danelaw** ▶ The area of Anglo-Saxon England E of Watling Street from the River Tees to the River Thames within which Danish laws and customs prevailed from the late 9th to the late 11th centuries.

● **Dangerfield, Thomas** ▶ (1650–85) English conspirator. He exploited the anti-Catholic hysteria that followed the alleged ▷Popish Plot to murder Charles II in 1678 by falsely accusing his own Catholic employers. He was convicted of libel in 1685 and died after being pilloried and whipped.

● **Daniel** ▶ (6th century BC) An Old Testament prophet and Jewish exile in Babylon. **The Book of Daniel** is credited to him although some believe it to have been written in the 2nd century BC. The first six chapters tell of various mainly supernatural episodes involving Daniel and his companions under Kings Nebuchadnezzar and Belshazzar. The remaining six chapters are mostly apocalyptic visions concerning the future of the Jews.

● **Daniel, Samuel** ▶ (?1562–1619) English poet, dramatist, and critic. From 1604 he enjoyed the patronage of James I. His best-known work is the sonnet sequence *Delia* (1592). Among his other works are a verse history of the Wars of the Roses, *The Civil Wars* (1609), and a prose history of England (1618).

● **Daniell, John Frederic** ▶ (1790–1845) British chemist, whose researches into electrochemistry led him to invent the ▷Daniell cell, the first long-lasting reliable source of electric current. He also invented the hygrometer.

● **Daniell cell** ▶ An ▷electric cell whose positive pole consists of copper immersed in a solution of copper sulphate and whose negative pole consists of zinc in a solution of sulphuric acid or zinc sulphate. It has an almost constant emf of 1.08 volts. Named after J. F. Daniell.

● **danio** ▶ An omnivorous tropical freshwater fish of the genera *Danio* or *Brachydanio*. They have a narrow elongated body, 4–5 cm long, often attractively coloured, and live in shoals. Family: *Cyprinidae*; order: *Cypriniformes*. ▷*See also* zebra fish.

● **Danish** ▶ The official language of Denmark, spoken by about five million people. It belongs to the East Scandinavian branch of the North Germanic languages. Separation from the other Scandinavian languages, to which it is closely related, began in about 1000 AD. It is the most altered form of the common ancestral tongue, having lost the case system and incorporated many words from Low German.

● **Dankworth, John** ▶ (1927–) British jazz composer, clarinetist, and saxophonist. He formed his own band in 1953 and has often worked with his wife, the jazz singer **Dame Cleo Laine** (1927–). His works include *Escapade* (1967), a piano concerto (1972), *Reconciliation* (1987), and scores for various films.

● **D'Annunzio, Gabriele** ▶ (1863–1938) Italian poet, novelist, and dramatist. During the 1890s he wrote several novels strongly influenced by ▷Nietzsche's philosophy, notably *The Triumph of Death* (1894). The erotic novel *The Flame of Life* (1900) described his stormy relationship with the actress Eleanora ▷Duse, who inspired some of his best poetry and for whom he wrote *The Daughter of Jorio* (1904) and other plays. A militant nationalist, he fought heroically in the air force in World War I and headed the Italian occupation of Fiume in 1919. He joined the fascist party but spent his later years in peaceful retirement.

● **Dante Alighieri** ▶ (1265–1321) Italian poet. Born into a noble Guelf family of Florence (*see* Guelfs and Ghibellines), he became actively involved in the political struggle between the Black Guelfs, supported by the Pope, and the White Guelfs, who favoured a democratic commune. After the Black Guelfs gained control of Florence in 1301, he lived in exile in various Italian cities, finally settling in Ravenna about 1318. His major works include *La vita nuova* (c. 1292), an autobiographical work concerning his youthful love for the mysterious Beatrice (probably the Florentine aristocrat Beatrice Portinari, who was married and who died at the age of 24), and two influential treatises on the value of vernacular Italian as a literary language. *The Divine Comedy*, begun about 1307, is Dante's spiritual testament, narrating his journey, guided by ▷Virgil, through Hell and Purgatory and finally, guided by Beatrice, to Paradise.

● **Danton, Georges Jacques** ▶ (1759–94) French revolutionary. A leader of the ▷Cordeliers in 1789 and 1790, he became minister of justice in the new republic in 1792. A member of the first Committee of ▷Public Safety, he began to lose power as the ▷Reign of Terror developed. He and his followers were arrested in March, 1794, charged with a conspiracy to overthrow the government, and Danton was guillotined.

● **Danu** ▶ In Celtic mythology, the mother of the gods. She was particularly associated with the ▷Tuatha Dé Danann, but she was also worshipped in other countries under different names.

● **Danube, River** ▶ The second longest river in Europe after the Volga. Rising in the Black Forest in Germany, it flows ESE across Europe to enter the Black Sea in Romania. Important commercially, it is linked by the River Altmühl with canals to the Rivers Main and Rhine. Cities along its course include Vienna, Budapest, and Belgrade. Length: 2850 km (1770 mi).

● **Danzig** ▷*See* Gdańsk.

● **Daphne** ▶ (botany) A genus of evergreen and deciduous shrubs (70 species) of the Old World, including many important ornamentals. The small, often fragrant, flowers occur in clusters near the ends of branches. They have no petals; the calyx (fused sepals) has four spreading lobes. The fruit is a berry. The genus includes the deciduous mezereon (*D. mezereum*), with reddish-purple flowers and red berries, and the evergreen spurge laurel (*D. laureola*), with greenish flowers and black berries. These shrubs are native to Eurasia and grow to a height of 100 cm; their berries are poisonous. Family: *Thymeleaceae*.

● **Daphne** ▶ (Greek mythology) A mountain nymph who rejected Apollo and, to escape him, was transformed by Gaia into a laurel tree. Apollo made the laurel a symbol of honour and victory.

● **Daphnia** ▷*See* water flea.

● **Daphnis** ▶ In Greek legend, a Sicilian shepherd who was punished with blindness for infidelity in love. He consoled himself with songs and thus invented pastoral poetry and song.

● **Da Ponte, Lorenzo** ▶ (1749–1838) Italian author, originally a priest. Banished from Italy in 1779, he settled in Vienna and there wrote the libretti for Mozart's operas *The Marriage of Figaro* (1786), *Don Giovanni* (1787), and *Così fan tutte* (1790). In 1805 he went to the USA, publishing his memoirs (1823–27).

● **Darby, Abraham** ▶ (1677–1717) British iron manufacturer. He built the first coke-fired ▷blast furnace (1709), at Coalbrookdale, Shropshire, which was used to make parts for the ▷Newcomen steam engine. His grandson, **Abraham Darby III** (1750–91), built the first cast-iron bridge (1779), which still spans the Severn at Ironbridge Gorge, Shropshire.

● **Dardanelles** ▶ (Turkish name: Çannakale Boğazi; ancient name: Hellespont) A strait separating European and Asian Turkey and connecting the Sea of Marmara with the Aegean Sea. It was the scene of an unsuccessful campaign in ▷World War I. Length: 60 km (37 mi); width: 1.5–6.5 km (1–4 mi).

● **Dards** ▶ A number of peoples of N Pakistan and Kashmir of Aryan origin, who speak Indo-European languages. There are three major subgroups: the Western (*or* Kafir), the Central (*or* Khowar), and the Eastern, including Shina and Kashmiri. The Dards were converted to Islam during the 14th century.

● **Dar es Salaam** ▶ 6 48S 39 12E The capital and main port of Tanzania, on the Indian Ocean. Founded in 1862, it was capital of German East Africa (1891–1916) and of Tanganyika (1916–64). The university was established in 1970. It is the terminus of the Tanzam (Tanzania–Zambia) railway and an important commercial centre. Population (latest est): 1 360 850.

● **Darién Scheme** ▶ (1698–99) An attempt by the Company of Scotland to establish a colony in the Darién region, in the E of the Isthmus of Panama. The Scots hoped to control trade between the Atlantic and Pacific Oceans but were forced by the Spanish to abandon their settlement.

● **Darío, Rubén** ▶ (Félix García Sarmiento; 1867–1916) Nicaraguan poet. His interest in contemporary French literature greatly influenced his innovatory experiments in both verse and prose. *Azul* (1888) and *Prosas profanas* (1896) were major works of the Spanish-American modernist movement. After 1898 he lived mostly in Europe, working as correspondent for the Argentine paper *La Nación*. His political convictions are expressed in *Cantos de vida y esperanza* (1905).

● **Darius I** ▶ (c. 558–486 BC) King of Persia (521–486) of the ▷Achaemenian dynasty. He obtained the throne after defeating a usurper and on his accession he was forced to deal with revolts throughout the empire. He crushed a revolt of Ionian Greeks (499–94), which precipitated the ▷Greek-Persian Wars. His invasion of mainland Greece was halted by the Persian defeat at ▷Marathon (490). Darius was a noted administrator, dividing the empire into provinces known as satrapies. He also encouraged trade and improved communications.

● **Darjeeling** ▶ 27 02N 88 20E A town in India, in West Bengal. A popular tourist resort, it has splendid views of the Himalayas. It is a major tea-growing centre. Population (latest est): 57 603.

● **Dark Ages** ▶ In Europe, the period between the collapse of the Western Roman Empire in the early 5th century and the crowning of ▷Charlemagne as Emperor of the West in 800. The period as a whole was one of political instability, accompanied by economic and cultural decline. With the breakdown of Roman authority, Germanic tribes, such as the ▷Ostrogoths and ▷Visigoths, swept through much of W Europe, while the mid-5th century saw Italy sacked by the ▷Vandals and large parts of S central Europe ravaged by the ▷Huns under ▷Attila. By the end of the century the colonization of Britain by pagan ▷Anglo-Saxon tribes was well advanced and the ▷Franks had established control throughout the former Gaul. Although there was a gradual return to stability from the 6th century onwards and Christianity was restored to the NW, the new European kingdoms remained vulnerable to barbarian invasions and learning was confined to a few monastic centres. The military victories of Charlemagne in the late 8th century restored strong government to W Europe and provided the preconditions for a lasting revival of trade and culture. Although "Dark Ages" is still a popular expression, most modern historians avoid it, arguing that the true picture was much more complex than the total collapse of civilization presented by earlier accounts.

● **darkling beetle** ▶ A black or dark brown flightless beetle, also called nocturnal ground beetle, belonging to a widely distributed family (*Tenebrionidae*; 15 000 species), particularly common in warm regions. Darkling beetles vary from 2 to 35 mm in length. Nearly all are scavengers, feeding on decaying vegetation, dung, fungi, or stored grains and cereals. Mealworms (larvae of *Tenebrio molitor*) are common pests of flour mills, etc., and are also reared commercially as food for birds and fish.

● **dark matter** ▶ Matter that is thought to be distributed throughout the universe, although it does not emit or absorb electromagnetic radiation and therefore cannot be observed. Its existence is inferred from its gravitational effects and on this basis it could account for over 90% of the mass of the universe. This dark matter is sometimes referred to as the **missing mass** of the universe. Various theories have been suggested to account for dark matter: some believe that exotic undetected particles exist, e.g. **WIMPs** – weakly interacting massive particles; others believe that massive bodies exist that for various reasons fail to emit or absorb radiation. These are sometimes called **MACHOs** – massive astrophysical compact halo objects. Another possibility, unsupported by experiment, is that ▷neutrinos have a finite, but small, mass.

● **Darlan, Jean (Louis Xavier) François** ▶ (1881–1942) French admiral. He became commander in chief of the navy in 1939 and served in the Vichy government as navy minister and then as vice premier (1941). He lost his post under Laval (1942) and was sent to command French forces in N Africa, where he brought French resistance to the Allies to an end. His assumption of the post of head of state in French Africa aroused hostility. He was assassinated by a French antifascist.

● **Darling, Grace** ▶ (1815–42) British heroine, daughter of a lighthouse keeper on the Northumberland coast. In 1838 she helped her father rescue five people from a ship (*Forfarshire*) that had struck the rocks during a storm.

● **Darling River** ▶ A river in E Australia, rising in the Great Dividing Range and flowing generally SW across New South Wales before joining the Murray River at Wentworth. Length: 2740 km (1702 mi).

● **Darlington** ▶ **1.** 54 31N 1 34W A town in NE England, in Darlington unitary authority, Durham. The Stockton–Darlington ▷railway (1825) was the world's first passenger railway. Darlington has engineering, construction, and communications industries. Population (1991): 86 767. **2.** A unitary authority in NE England, in Durham. Area: 198 sq km (77 sq mi). Population (1997 est): 101 106.

● **Darmstadt** ▶ 49 52N 08 39E A city in central Germany, in Hesse. It has a 16th-century palace and a technical university (1836). Its manufactures include machinery and chemicals. In the decades after World War II the Darmstadt Music Institute became a base for such avant-garde composers as ▷Berio, ▷Boulez, ▷Nono, and ▷Stockhausen: they and their followers are known sometimes as the **Darmstadt School**. Population (1996 est): 138 980.

● **darnel** ▶ A ▷grass, *Lolium temulentum*, also known as poison grass, native to temperate Eurasia. It is often infected by a fungus of the genus *Claviceps* (*see* ergot) and is poisonous; it was formerly a serious contaminant of rye bread but modern techniques can separate darnel seeds from rye seeds.

● **Darnley, Henry Stuart, Lord** ▶ (1545–67) The second husband of Mary, Queen of Scots, and father of James I of England. He married Mary, his cousin, in 1565 and his unpopularity was intensified by his involvement in the murder of her secretary David ▷Riccio (1566). Darnley himself was murdered, probably by ▷Bothwell.

● **Darrow, Clarence** ▶ (1857–1938) US lawyer, famous for his defence of union leaders and of people charged with murder. His defence of Eugene Debs in the case arising from the Pullman strike (1894), although unsuccessful, established his reputation. Through his efforts the labour leader William Haywood (1896–1928) was acquitted (1906) of assassinating the governor of Idaho. He was counsel for the defence in the famous "monkey" trial in Tennessee (1925), in which John Scopes was tried for teaching Darwin's theory of evolution. He was a passionate opponent of capital punishment.

● **darter** ▶ A slender elongated bird belonging to a family (*Anhingidae*; 4 species) occurring in tropical and subtropical inland waters, also called snakebird because of its snakelike neck. Darters are about 88 cm long and black or brown with white markings; males have plumes on the head and neck. They have thin pointed bills for catching fish underwater and are excellent fliers. Order: *Pelecaniformes* (gannets, pelicans, etc.).

● **Dartford** ▶ 51 27N 0 14E A market town in SE England, in Kent, linked with Thurrock (Essex) by the Dartford Tunnel (opened in 1963) under the River Thames; a bridge (the Queen Elizabeth II Bridge) was opened in 1991. The tunnel now carries northbound traffic and the bridge southbound. An industrial, communications, and retail centre, Dartford saw substantial redevelopment in the 1990s as part of the government's Thames Gateway regeneration initiative. The nearby Thames Europort has deepwater and container facilities for freight transportation. Population (1991): 59 411.

● **Dartmoor** ▶ A moorland area of England, in SW Devon. A national park since 1951, it consists of a rolling granite upland rising to tors, the highest of which is High Willhays at 621 m (2039 ft). Its many historic remains include stone circles and Bronze Age and Iron Age settlements. Used extensively as a military training area, its dramatic scenery, picturesque wooded valleys, and outdoor recreational facilities have also made it a major tourist attraction. Dartmoor prison was opened in 1806. Area: 945 sq km (365 sq mi).

● **Dartmoor pony** ▶ A breed of pony originating in the Dartmoor region of SW England. It is placid and hardy with a strong body and small head with tiny ears. The coat is usually bay, brown, or black and the mane and tail are profuse. Dartmoors are used in breeding larger riding ponies (including polo ponies). Height: 1.22–1.32 m (12–13 hands).

● **Dartmouth** ▶ 50 21N 3 35W A port and resort in SW England, in

Devon on the Dart estuary. The Royal Naval College (1905) is situated here. Population (1991): 5676.

● **Dartmouth** ▸ 44 40N 63 35W A city and port in E Canada, in Nova Scotia on Halifax Harbour. It is an industrial and naval centre. Population (1991): 67 798.

● **darts** ▸ A UK indoor target game, probably deriving from archery, in which players throw flighted metal darts at a round board from a set distance. A standard board is divided into 20 irregularly numbered sectors; outer and inner rings score double and treble respectively and there is a central bull's-eye. Various games are played, but the most common in competitions is 301, in which players score downwards from 301 to 0, beginning and ending on a double. In recent years TV coverage has made darts a popular spectator game.

● **Darwin** ▸ 12 23S 130 44E A city in Australia, the capital and chief port of the Northern Territory. The harbour, Port Darwin, adjoins Clarence Strait. It was almost completely destroyed by a cyclone in 1974. It serves a pastoral and mining region; exports include uranium ore. Population (1994): 78 100.

Charles Darwin ▸ In this cartoon from the *London Sketch Book* (1874) Darwin is seen showing an ape how alike they are.

● **Darwin, Charles Robert** ▸ (1809–1882) British naturalist, who originated the concept that living things evolve by means of natural selection. Following attempts to study medicine and theology, Darwin's interest in natural history led him to sail with HMS *Beagle* on an expedition to South America and the Pacific (1831–36). As ship's naturalist, Darwin recorded exhaustive observations of the geology and natural history of the region in a journal, which he later published.

Following the voyage, Darwin set about the task of analysing his observations. In 1858 he presented his findings (jointly with A. R. ▷Wallace) to the Linnaean Society and in 1859 published his famous *Origin of Species by Means of Natural Selection* (*see* Darwinism). His views aroused bitter controversy because they conflicted with the biblical Creation. This culminated in the debate at Oxford in 1860 be-

tween Darwin's supporters, led by T. H. ▷Huxley, and Bishop Samuel Wilberforce. Huxley's arguments won the day. In *The Descent of Man* (1871), Darwin applied his theories to mankind, and—slowly—this fundamental principle of biology gained widespread acceptance. His grandfather **Erasmus Darwin** (1731–1802) was a successful physician noted for his radical views, especially on biology. Among his ideas, which were expounded in verse (*see* poetry), were speculations about the nature of evolution that anticipated later theories, particularly those of ▷Lamarck. By his second marriage, Erasmus Darwin was also the grandfather of the scientist Sir Francis ▷Galton, the founder of eugenics.

● **Darwinism** ▸ The theory of ▷evolution based on the work of Charles ▷Darwin. Darwin drew his conclusions from the following observations: (1) in any population the organisms show individual variations; (2) the size of the population remains constant although more offspring are produced than are necessary to maintain it. He concluded that the forces acting on the population—competition, disease, climate, etc.—resulted in the survival of those best fitted to the environment, a process he called **natural selection**. The survivors would breed, thus passing on their inheritable advantageous variations to their offspring. With time—in a gradually changing environment—this process would result in a change in the whole population and ultimately the evolution of new ▷species. Darwin's theory has now been modified by subsequent discoveries in genetics, which—among other things—have revealed the source of the variation on which it is based (mostly genetic ▷mutations). The modern version of his theory is known as **neo-Darwinism**.

● **Darwin's finches** ▸ A subfamily of ▷finches (*Geospizinae*; 14 species) restricted to the Galápagos Islands and also called Galápagos finches. They appear to have evolved from a single species and differ in such features as bill shape, feeding behaviour, and habitat preference in order to avoid competition for available resources. The study of these finches by Charles ▷Darwin provided evidence for his theory of evolution.

● **dasyure** ▸ A small carnivorous ▷marsupial mammal belonging to a family (*Dasyuridae*; 45 species) occurring in Australia (including Tasmania) and New Guinea, also called marsupial cat or native cat. Dasyures, which vary from 30 cm to 170 cm in length, are nocturnal and good climbers; prey ranges from insects to small wallabies. ▷*See also* Tasmanian devil.

● **database** ▸ A collection of data held on computer so that it can be accessed in different ways. For example, all the entries in this encyclopedia are held on a database and it is possible for the editors to produce lists of types of entry; for example, all people who are still alive, or all US presidents, or all chemical compounds. There are three types of database classified according to the way the records are structured: hierarchical, network, or relational. The software used for accessing, changing, and deleting data is a **database management system** (DBMS).

● **data processing** ▸ The organization, transmission, and storage of information. **Automatic data processing** usually refers to systems using punch-card machines, paper tape, magnetic tape, etc., as opposed to **electronic data processing**, which is based on electronic computers. In batch processing, data is grouped and coded before processing. The alternative is on-line processing in which each user feeds data into the system continuously. Many systems incorporate both of these forms of processing for different types of work. ▷*See also* data protection.

● **data protection** ▸ Legislation to protect individuals who have information about them stored on computers. The Data Protection Convention, signed by members of the EC in 1981, led to the British Data Protection Act (1984). This obliges all computer users who are storing personal information to register with a central body, and to maintain certain standards of security and confidentiality. Individuals have the right to see their entries and, under certain circumstances, to ask for amendments or deletion. A new Data Protection Act (1998; effective from January, 2000) provides further protection by preventing personal details about individuals being used against their will by such organizations as direct-mailing and telephone-sales companies.

● **date** ► A ▷palm tree, *Phoenix dactylifera*, native to N Africa and SW Asia and cultivated from Morocco to India for its fruits, which are rich in sugar and form a staple food in the producing countries. Male and female flowers grow on separate trees (which reach a height of 25 m); the female flowers develop into clusters of up to 1000 single-seeded berries. The trunk yields timber and the leaves are used for basketry, weaving, etc.

● **dating techniques** ▷*See* dendrochronology; fission-track dating; helium dating; potassium-argon dating; radiocarbon dating; radiometric dating; rubidium-strontium dating; thermoluminescence; uranium-lead dating.

● **Datura** ► A worldwide genus of shrubs and herbs (about 10 species), with smooth pointed oval leaves and drooping trumpet-shaped flowers, white, pink, orange, or yellow. The commonest species is the ▷thorn apple. Such species as angel's trumpet (*D. suaveolens*), 5 m high with white flowers, are cultivated in temperate regions. Family: ▷Solanaceae.

● **Daubenton, Louis Jean Marie** ► (1716–1800) French naturalist, who gave anatomical descriptions of many animal species. His other interests included palaeontology, plant physiology, and mineralogy. He was the first director of the Museum of Natural History, Paris (1793).

● **Daubigny, Charles-François** ► (1817–78) French landscape painter. He was associated with the ▷Barbizon school but painted chiefly by the banks of the Seine and Oise, specializing in twilight and moonlight scenes, e.g. *Evening Landscape* (Metropolitan Museum). He strongly influenced the impressionists.

● **Daudet, Alphonse** ► (1840–97) French novelist, born at Nîmes. He wrote a number of naturalistic novels but is best remembered for his sketches on Provençal subjects, which were originally written for *Le Figaro* and later collected as *Lettres de mon moulin* (1868). He also wrote plays, notably *L'Arlésienne* (1872), for which Bizet composed incidental music. His son **Léon Daudet** (1867–1942) was a political journalist and novelist. He was violently right-wing and in 1899 helped to found the royalist periodical *L'Action française*. His essays were published as *Le Stupide XIXᵉ siècle* (1922) and his memoirs, *Souvenirs* (1914–21), cover the years 1890–1905.

● **Daugavpils** ► (name from 1893 until 1920: Dvinsk) 55 52N 26 31E A city in SE Latvia. It is an important rail junction and a commercial and industrial centre. Population (1996 est): 118 500.

● **Daumier, Honoré** ► (1808–79) French caricaturist, painter, and sculptor. In 1832 he was imprisoned for a cartoon depicting the king as Rabelais' gluttonous giant Gargantua. He produced numerous documentary lithographs, such as *Rue Transnonain*. After 1835 he worked for *Charivari*, satirizing the legal and medical professions and other targets. Although his paintings were largely ignored in his lifetime, *The Washerwoman* (Louvre) and *The Third Class Railway Carriage* (Ottawa) were forerunners of ▷impressionism.

● **dauphin** ► From 1350 until 1830 the title of the heirs to the French Crown. It was the personal name, and later became the title, of the rulers of the ▷Dauphiné, which was purchased by the future Charles V in 1350. After becoming king (1364), he granted the Dauphiné and its accompanying title to his son, thus establishing a precedent that was followed until the abdication of Charles X.

● **Dauphiné** ► A former province of SE France, corresponding to the present-day departments of Hautes-Alpes, Isère, and Drôme. It formed part of the Holy Roman Empire until 1343, when it was sold to the King of France. From 1350 to 1457 it was governed by the French king's eldest son, who thus acquired the title ▷dauphin.

● **Davao City** ► 07 05N 125 38E A port in the SE Philippines, in SE Mindanao. The island's commercial centre, it grew rapidly in the 1960s. It has timber and fishing industries and exports hemp and coffee. Population (1994 est): 960 910.

● **Davenant, Sir William** ► (1606–68) English dramatist, poet, and theatrical manager. Rumoured to be the illegitimate son of Shakespeare, several of whose works he "revised," he won popular success and the patronage of Charles I with his early plays, notably *The Wits*

(1634). He was appointed poet laureate in 1638. During the Commonwealth he organized secret theatrical performances and after the Restoration he continued to write and stage spectacular plays.

● **Davenport, Charles Benedict** ► (1866–1944) US zoologist, who introduced the use of statistical techniques into biological research. He applied statistics to his studies of genetics.

● **Davenport, Lindsay** ► (1976–   ) US tennis player, ranked the world's top woman player in 1998–99. She won an Olympic gold medal in 1996, the US Open in 1998, Wimbledon in 1999, and the Australian Open in 2000.

● **Daventry** ► 52 16N 1 09W A town in central England, in Northamptonshire. An overspill area for Birmingham, it has a mixed economy based on light engineering and warehousing and is the site of an important radio transmitter. ▷Althorp House is nearby. Population (1996 est): 19 150.

● **David** ► (d. 962 BC) King of Israel (c. 1000–962). Born in Bethlehem, the son of Jesse, David was anointed by Samuel as the successor of Saul, the first King of Israel. He became a close friend of Saul's son, Jonathan, but his successes against the Philistines, including the slaying of Goliath, aroused Saul's jealousy and he became an outlaw. After the death of Saul and Jonathan, David was proclaimed King of Hebron and then of all Israel. He conquered Jerusalem, making it the nation's political and religious centre, finally defeated the Philistines, and united the tribes of Israel. His reign was troubled by the revolt of his son Absalom, who was eventually defeated and killed. David was succeeded by Solomon, his son by Bathsheba. He was the author of some of the psalms. According to the Jewish prophets, the Messiah must be a descendant of David.

● **David I** ► (1084–1153) King of the Scots (1124–53). The first monarch to recognize Matilda as successor to Henry I of England, he used her cause as an excuse to invade N England (1138) after Stephen had seized the throne. Stephen defeated him in the battle of the Standard (1138), near Northallerton. David founded or refounded over a dozen monasteries.

● **David II** ► (1324–71) King of the Scots (1329–71), succeeding his father Robert the Bruce. He was forced into exile (1334–41) in France by Edward de ▷Balliol. He supported France against Edward III of England and was captured and imprisoned (1346–57) by the English.

● **David, Félicien César** ► (1810–76) French composer, one of the first to combine oriental folk tunes with Western motifs. His works include the symphonic ode *Le Désert* (1844), operas, religious choruses, and piano music.

● **David, Gerard** ► (c. 1460–1523) Netherlandish painter, who was born in Oudewater (Holland) but settled in Bruges. Apart from his use of Renaissance detail in *Judgment of Cambyses* (Bruges), he was little influenced by the current Italianate style.

● **David, Jacques Louis** ► (1748–1825) French neoclassical painter. He trained under Joseph-Marie Vien (1716–1809), before winning the Prix de Rome (1774), which enabled him to study in Italy (1775–80). His mature works depicted heroic scenes from Republican Rome and ancient Greece, e.g. *Oath of the Horatii* (Louvre). During the Revolution he painted some of its martyrs, e.g. *Death of Marat* (Brussels), and supported Robespierre; after Robespierre's fall he was imprisoned (1794–95). As court painter to □Napoleon I from 1804, his paintings illustrate imperial successes, e.g. *Napoleon Crowning Josephine* (Louvre). After Napoleon's fall David was exiled and died in Brussels.

● **David, St** ► (*or* St Dewi; c. 520–600 AD) The patron saint of Wales and first abbot of Menevia (now St David's). He was also a missionary and the founder of many churches in Wales. Feast day: 1 March. Emblem: a dove.

● **David ap Gruffudd** ► (d. 1283) The brother of ▷Llywelyn ap Gruffudd, after whose death (1282) David claimed the title Prince of Wales. He was executed for leading the Welsh in rebellion.

● **Davies, Sir Peter Maxwell** ► (1934–   ) British composer. Some of his works blend medieval musical techniques with modern compositional devices. He lives on the island of Orkney and has been influenced by the Orcadian landscape and culture. His output includes film music, operas, six symphonies, and the ten Strathclyde Concertos (1987–96).

● **Davies, Siobhan** ▶ (1950–) British choreographer and dancer, who made her reputation with the London Contemporary Dance Theatre in the 1970s. She co-founded the Second Stride company in 1982 and has worked extensively with the Ballet Rambert.

● **Davies, W(illiam) H(enry)** ▶ (1871–1940) British poet. He lived for many years as a tramp in England and America before publishing the first of many volumes of simple rural poetry in 1905. His *Autobiography of a Super-Tramp* appeared in 1907.

● **da Vinci, Leonardo** ▷*See* Leonardo da Vinci.

● **Davis, Bette** ▶ (Ruth Elizabeth D.; 1908–89) US film actress. From the 1930s to the 1950s she gave intense and dramatic performances in such films as *Jezebel* (1938), *Dark Victory* (1939), and *All About Eve* (1950). In later years she played elderly eccentric or neurotic women.

● **Davis, Sir Colin** ▶ (1927–) British conductor. During a distinguished career he has conducted the BBC Scottish Symphony Orchestra, the English Chamber Orchestra, the orchestras of the Metropolitan Opera, New York, and the Royal Opera, Covent Garden and became conductor of the London Symphony Orchestra in 1995. He is known for his performances of Mozart, Berlioz, Stravinsky, and Tippett. He was knighted in 1980 and appointed CH in 2001.

● **Davis, Jefferson** ▶ (1808–89) US statesman; president of the Confederate states during the Civil War (1861–65). As senator for Mississippi (1847–51) and then, after serving with distinction in the ▷Mexican War, secretary of war (1853–57), Davis supported slavery and resisted federal interference. However, his loyalty as Confederate president was to the South as a whole: advocates of ▷states' rights were hostile to him and his conscription law was unpopular. He was captured in 1865, imprisoned without trial, and released in 1867.

● **Davis, Joe** ▶ (1901–78) British billiards and snooker player. As well as holding the world snooker championship for nearly 20 years (1927–46), he was world billiards champion (1928–32). His brother **Fred Davis** (1913–98) was also world snooker champion (1948–49; 1951–56) and world billiards champion (1980).

● **Davis, John** ▶ (or J. Davys; c. 1550–1605) English navigator, who went on three voyages in search of the ▷Northwest Passage (1585, 1586, 1587), passing through the strait named after him to Baffin Bay. In 1592, seeking the Magellan Strait, he discovered the Falkland Islands. On his last voyage to the East Indies, he was killed by Japanese pirates.

● **Davis, Miles** ▶ (1926–91) US jazz trumpeter and composer, one of the originators of ▷cool jazz. He studied music at the Juilliard School in New York and formed a series of bands from 1948 (including a famous five-piece with John Coltrane (1926–67) in the 1950s). His albums include *Birth of the Cool* (1948), *Kind of Blue* (1960), and *Bitches Brew* (1969), in which he pioneered the fusion of jazz and rock.

● **Davis, Steve** ▶ (1957–) British snooker player. He won the world professional championship in 1981, 1983, 1984, and 1987–89.

● **Davis Cup** ▶ An international tennis trophy for teams of men, donated in 1900 by Dwight Filley Davis (1879–1945), who played for the US team in the opening contest. Recent winners have been USA (1990, 1992, 1995), France (1991, 1996, 2001), Germany (1993), Sweden (1994, 1997, 1998), Australia (1999), and Spain (2000).

● **Davis Strait** ▶ A section of the Atlantic Ocean, between SW Greenland and Baffin Island (Canada). Length: 640 km (400 mi). Width: 320–640 m (200–400 mi).

● **Davitt, Michael** ▶ (1846–1906) Irish nationalist. He joined the ▷Fenians in 1865 and after seven years' imprisonment founded the ▷Land League (1879). Davitt urged the reconciliation of extreme and constitutional nationalism. In the 1890s he became an MP.

● **Davos** ▶ (Romansh name: Tarau) 46 47N 9 50E A resort in E Switzerland. Comprising two villages at a height of about 1560 m (5118 ft), it is a winter-sports centre, with the renowned Parsenn ski run. Population (1991): 18 099.

● **Davy, Sir Humphry** ▶ (1778–1829) British chemist and inventor

of the miner's safety lamp (1815), known as the Davy lamp. Davy discovered the value of nitrous oxide as an anaesthetic. He was invited to join the Royal Institution in London, where he discovered many new metallic elements. By passing electricity through molten metallic compounds, he discovered potassium in 1807 and sodium, calcium, barium, magnesium and strontium in 1808. He encouraged the young Michael ▷Faraday, his assistant at the Royal Institution.

● **Dawes, Charles G(ates)** ▶ (1865–1951) US financier; who headed a commission to reconstruct the German economy after World War I and enable it to pay reparations to the Allies. This solution, known as the **Dawes Plan** (1924), saved Europe from economic collapse and earned him, jointly with Austen Chamberlain, the Nobel Peace Prize (1925). He was Republican vice president (1925–29) and ambassador to the UK (1929–32).

● **Dawkins, Richard** ▶ (1941–) British zoologist. His works on ▷sociobiology include *The Selfish Gene* (1976) and *River Out of Eden* (1995); *The Blind Watchmaker* (1986) is a study of evolution.

● **dawn redwood** ▶ A deciduous conifer, *Metasequoia glyptostroboides*, thought to be extinct until 1941, when the first specimen of modern times was discovered in SW China. Growing to a height of 35 m, dawn redwood has soft needles grouped in two rows and rounded green long-stalked cones. It is quite widely grown for ornament. Family: *Taxodiaceae*.

● **Dawson** ▶ 64 04N 139 24W A town in NW Canada, in the Yukon on the ▷Klondike River. During the gold rush it had over 25 000 inhabitants. Population (1995 est): 1988.

● **Dawson Creek** ▶ 55 45N 120 15W A town in W Canada, in British Columbia at the beginning of the ▷Alaska Highway. Population (1991): 10 981.

● **day** ▶ The time taken for the earth to make one rotation on its axis relative to the sun (**solar day**) or to the stars (**sidereal day**). The solar day has 24 hours and is the basis of the civil day. The sidereal day, because it takes into account the earth's orbital motion, is 4.09 minutes shorter than the solar day. *Compare* year.

● **Dayak** ▶ (or Dyak) A people of Borneo and Sarawak, speaking Indonesian languages of the Malayo-Polynesian family. Groups include the Bahau of central and E Borneo, the Land Dayak of SW Borneo, and the Iban (or Sea Dayak) of Sarawak. A riverine people, they live in large wooden huts (longhouses) and practise rice cultivation, fishing, and hunting with blowpipes. Head hunting was once common.

● **Dayan, Moshe** ▶ (1915–81) Israeli general. Born in Palestine, during the 1930s he fought with the Haganah (Jewish irregulars) and in World War II in the British Army, losing an eye in battle in 1941. From 1953 until 1958 he was chief of Israel's general staff. As defence minister (1967, 1969–74) he was criticized for not anticipating the October War (1973). In 1977 he became foreign minister and played a major role in the ▷Camp David negotiations, but he resigned in 1979 over disagreement with ▷Begin on policy relating to the ▷West Bank.

● **Day-Lewis, C(ecil)** ▶ (1904–72) British poet and critic. He was a leading left-wing poet of the 1930s but his later verse was more purely lyrical. He published translations of Virgil's *Aeneid* (1952) and other works and was appointed poet laureate in 1968. As "Nicholas Blake" he wrote sophisticated detective stories. His son, **Daniel Day-Lewis** (1958–), is an actor; he won an Oscar for his performance in *My Left Foot* (1988). His other films include *The Last of the Mohicans* (1992), *In the Name of the Father* (1993), and *The Crucible* (1996).

● **day lily** ▶ A herbaceous plant of the genus *Hemerocallis*, native to Europe and Asia and cultivated as garden flowers. They have long narrow leaves and long stalks bearing clusters of orange or yellow lily-like flowers, which wither rapidly. *H. lilio-asphodelinus* is grown for its scent, and garden hybrids of *H. flava* bloom for longer. Family: *Liliaceae*.

● **Dayton** ▶ 39 45N 84 10W A city in the USA, in Ohio on the Great Miami River. It was the home of the Wright brothers; the nearby Wright-Patterson Air Force Base is a centre for military aviation research. Population (1998 est): 167 475.

● **Daytona Beach** ▶ 29 11N 81 01W A resort in the USA, in Florida on on the Atlantic coast. Its hard white beach has been used for motor racing since 1902. Population (1990): 61 921.

● **Dazai Osamu** ▶ (Tsushima Shuji; 1909–48) Japanese novelist. His fiction exploited the conflict between his wealthy background and his radical political beliefs. His postwar novels, notably *No Longer Human* (1948), expressed the nihilism of a generation robbed of traditional values. He committed suicide.

● **DBE** ▷*See* Order of the British Empire.

● **D-Day** ▶ (6 June, 1944) The day on which the Allied invasion of Normandy was launched from Britain during ▷World War II. After months of detailed preparation, US, British, and Commonwealth forces under the supreme command of ▷Eisenhower landed at dawn on five Normandy beaches, thus beginning the greatest amphibious operation in military history. The Normandy landings (code-named "Operation Overlord") led to the liberation of France from German occupation and the final defeat of Germany. ⌐landing craft.

● **DDT** ▶ (dichlorophenyltrichloroethane) An organochlorine compound formerly widely used as a contact ▷insecticide. It is active against many insects, including mosquitoes, flies, fleas, lice, and bedbugs, affecting the central nervous system. However, many insects have become resistant to DDT, which is a very stable compound and accumulates not only in their tissues but also in the tissues of the animals that prey on them, causing toxic effects. Its use is banned in the UK.

● **deacon** ▷*See* holy orders.

● **deadly nightshade** ▶ (*or* belladonna) A branching perennial herb, *Atropa belladonna*, up to 1.5 m tall and native to Eurasia. It has dull green leaves, up to 20 cm long, and solitary purple or greenish bell-shaped flowers. The shiny black berries taste sweet but contain a deadly poison. The plant is a source of a variety of alkaloids, especially hyoscyamine and atropine. Family: ▷*Solanaceae*. ▷*See also* nightshade.

● **dead men's fingers** ▶ A colonial soft ▷coral, *Alcyonium digitatum*, so called because of its fleshy pink finger-like appearance. The individual ▷polyps have an internal skeleton of separate calcareous spicules, which give the tissues a gelatinous consistency. Colonies, which are white, yellow, pink, or orange, are common on rocky coasts of NW Europe.

● **Dead Sea** ▶ A lake in E Israel and W Jordan. It is fed by the River Jordan and, having no outlet, is highly saline and supports no life. Area: 1050 sq km (401 sq mi).

● **Dead Sea Scrolls** ▶ A group of Hebrew and Aramaic manuscript scrolls, originally stored in jars, found in 11 caves in the area of Khirbat ▷Qumeran, NW of the Dead Sea. The first were accidentally discovered in 1947; the rest were recovered as late as the 1950s. Altogether there are about 500 different documents, dating from 250 BC to 70 AD, which seem to have formed the library of a Jewish, perhaps ▷Essene, community that existed from about 125 BC to the Jewish revolt in 66–70 AD, when the scrolls were hidden in the caves for safekeeping. They include texts of many Old Testament books, commentaries, prayers, psalms, and material peculiar to the community, including an apocalyptic prophecy. They are valuable as evidence of the accuracy of previously known Old Testament texts, for the information they provide about a Jewish community contemporaneous with early Christianity, and as examples of the Hebrew and Aramaic scripts of the period.

● **deafness** ▶ A common condition in which hearing is absent or impaired. Deafness is described as either conductive, in which the mechanism for transmitting sound to the inner ear is defective, or sensorineural, when there is damage to the cochlea (in the inner ear), the auditory nerve, or the part of the brain concerned with hearing. Conductive deafness may be caused by wax in the outer ear, infection in the middle ear, or—as with Beethoven—otosclerosis (a disease of the small bones in the middle ear). Sensorineural deafness occurs commonly in old people but can be due to infection, head injury, drugs (such as streptomycin), ▷Ménière's disease, or exposure to continuous loud noise. Some forms of deafness can be treated by removing wax, curing infection, or by microsurgery; untreatable forms can be alleviated with an electronic aid or a cochlear implant (*see* hearing aid).

● **Deák, Ferenc** ▶ (1803–76) Hungarian statesman. After the ▷Hungarian Revolution of 1848, Deák became the country's minister of justice and in 1849, the leader of the opposition to Austrian dominance. Deák believed in the dynastic union of Austria and Hungary but desired separate constitutions and kingdoms and he was largely responsible for the establishment in 1867 of ▷Austria-Hungary.

● **Deakin, Alfred** ▶ (1856–1919) Australian statesman, who was three times prime minister (1903–04, 1905–08, 1909–10). He succeeded Sir Edmund ▷Barton, and like him was a member of the Federal Convention that drafted the constitution for the new Commonwealth of Australia. He introduced policies restricting non-White immigration.

● **Deal** ▶ 51 14N 1 24E A ▷Cinque Port and resort in SE England, in Kent. It is the probable landing place of Julius Caesar (55 BC). Population (1991): 28 504.

● **Dean, Forest of** ▶ An ancient royal forest in W England, in Gloucestershire between the Rivers Severn and Wye. Small independent coalmines have been operating here for centuries.

● **Dean, James** ▶ (James Byron; 1931–55) US film actor. He trained at the Actors' Studio, and became a cult hero for his generation. His films were *East of Eden* (1954), *Rebel without a Cause* (1955), and *Giant* (1955), released following his death in a car crash.

● **Deane, Silas** ▶ (1737–89) US patriot and diplomat. Actively supporting American independence, Deane was sent to Paris by the Continental Congress to buy war supplies and negotiate treaties with France (1776–78). Accused of embezzlement he went into exile, settling in London.

● **Dearborn** ▶ 42 18N 83 14W A city in the USA, in Michigan near Detroit. The birthplace of Henry Ford, it is the headquarters of the Ford Motor Company. Population (1996 est): 91 418.

● **death** ▶ The permanent cessation of all bodily functions in an organism. A person is medically pronounced dead when his heartbeat and breathing movements have ceased, but since the advent of me-

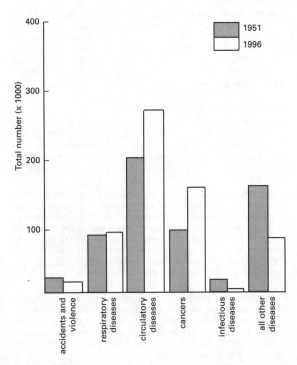

death ▶ Principal causes of death in the UK (1951 and 1996).

chanical ventilators the heartbeat may be maintained long after "natural" breathing has stopped as a result of irreversible brain damage. **Brain death** is defined on the basis of brain function: when the parts of the brain that control breathing, heart rate, and other vital reflexes have ceased to function the patient is said to be brain dead, i.e. truly dead, although his heart may continue to beat for some time with the aid of mechanical life-support systems (*see also* persistent vegetative state). With recent advances in transplant surgery, it is important to establish brain death in those patients who could be suitable donors of kidneys and other organs. The causes of death have changed very markedly in Western countries during the last hundred years. While tuberculosis and other infectious diseases were the main causes of death at the beginning of the 20th century, these are now minor causes in Western countries; circulatory diseases (including heart diseases) and cancer are now the most prevalent causes in the UK (see bar chart).

In general, death rates (mortality) in all age groups in the UK are higher for men than for women. In 1961 the overall crude death rate (i.e. the number of deaths in the year per 1000 of the population) was 12.6 for men and 11.4 for women. By 1996 the rate had fallen more rapidly for men than for women (10.6 for men and 11.1 for women). This apparent anomaly is explained by differing age structures for the male and female populations (*see also* infant mortality).

● **death cap** ▶ A highly poisonous mushroom, ▷*Amanita phalloides*, fairly common in and near deciduous woodlands. Its cap, 7–12 cm in diameter, is usually pale greenish yellow but may be olive green or greyish. The stalk is white or greenish white, with a baglike sheath (volva) at its base. Death cap can be fatal, even in small amounts, and symptoms may not appear for up to 24 hours.

● **death's-head moth** ▶ A ▷hawk moth, *Acherontia atropos*, with a wingspan of 125 mm, found in Europe, Africa, and Asia, whose thoracic markings resemble a skull and crossbones. These moths emit squeaks when handled and may enter beehives to steal honey.

● **Death Valley** ▶ A desert area in the USA, in SE California. The hottest and driest part of North America, its temperatures exceed 39°C (102°F) during summer. The flora and fauna that survive these harsh conditions are of interest to scientists. In 1933 it was declared a national monument.

● **deathwatch beetle** ▶ A widely distributed wood-boring beetle, *Xestobium rufovillosum*, about 7 mm long, that can cause immense damage to old buildings and furniture. It lays its eggs in small crevices in the wood and the larvae tunnel in, eventually reducing it to powder. The pupae often make knocking sounds by repeatedly striking their heads against the walls of their burrows. Family: *Anobiidae*.

● **Deauville** ▶ 49 21N 0 04E A seaside resort in NW France, in the Calvados department. It is linked to Trouville by bridge across the River Touques. Population (latest est): 4769.

● **de Bary, Heinrich Anton** ▶ (1831–88) German botanist and founder of mycology (the study of fungi). He determined the life cycles of many fungi, including important disease-causing species. In 1866 he showed that lichens each comprise a fungus and an alga living in a mutually beneficial partnership. For this he coined the word symbiosis.

● **debenture stock** ▶ A document setting out the terms of a fixed-interest loan to a company. A **secured debenture** is secured against a specified asset belonging to the company (fixed charge) or against all the company's assets (floating charge). An **unsecured debenture** has no such security, but if it cannot be paid back on the repayment date, debenture holders can force the company into liquidation and they then take priority over other shareholders in having their capital repaid. An **irredeemable debenture** is never repaid, being bought only for the interest it earns.

● **de Bernières, Louis** ▶ (L. de Bernière-Smart; 1954–) British novelist. He is best known for *Captain Corelli's Mandolin* (1994), a hugely successful story of love and war filmed in 2001. He has also written three novels set in South America; *The War of Don Emmanuel's Nether Parts* (1990), *Señor Vivo and the Coca Lord* (1991), and *The Troublesome Children of Cardinal Guzman* (1992).

● **debit card** ▶ A card issued by a bank or building society that en-

ables the holder to pay for goods or services at certain retail outlets by using the telephone network to debit his or her cheque account directly. Some debit cards also function as ▷cheque cards and cash cards (enabling cash to be drawn from ▷automated teller machines). ▷*See also* credit card.

● **Debray, (Jules) Régis** ▶ (1940–) French Marxist writer. Formerly active in Latin-American politics, Debray is known for his writings justifying guerrilla warfare as an instrument of social change. The Bolivians sentenced him to 30 years in prison but he served only three years (1967–70), later involving himself in Chilean politics. In the 1980s he was ▷Mitterrand's adviser on third-world affairs.

● **Debré, Michel** ▶ (1912–96) French statesman; prime minister (1959–62). A Gaullist, Debré became prominent as a member of the Saar Economic Mission in 1947. He was the author of numerous works on politics and economics.

● **Debrecen** ▶ 47 30N 21 37E A city in E Hungary. It was a centre of Protestantism in E Europe. Lajos Kossuth proclaimed Hungary independent of the Habsburgs in the Great Church of Debrecen in 1849. There are now various industries and a university (1912). Population (1999 est): 205 032.

● **Debrett, John** ▶ (1752–1822) British publisher. He took over a publishing business 1781; the directory of the peerage, which still bears his name, was first published in 1802.

● **de Broglie, Louis Victor, 7th Duc** ▶ (1892–1987) French physicist, who won the 1929 Nobel Prize for his theory that elementary particles have associated waves, known as ▷de Broglie waves. The theory was confirmed by the subsequent observation of ▷electron diffraction and forms the basis of the branch of quantum mechanics known as ▷wave mechanics.

● **de Broglie wave** ▶ A wave associated with any moving elementary particle with nonzero mass, since such particles exhibit wave properties under appropriate conditions. For example, they may be diffracted by a crystal lattice. The de Broglie wavelength of a particle mass m and velocity v is h/mv, where h is the ▷Planck constant. They were first postulated by Louis ▷de Broglie in 1923.

● **Debs, Eugene V(ictor)** ▶ (1855–1926) US labour organizer. Debs formed the American Railway Union (1893). He was imprisoned several times for labour agitation and in 1918, under the Espionage Law, for pacifist speeches. He ran five times for president as candidate for the Social Democratic Party, which he established. His 1920 campaign conducted from prison won almost a million votes.

● **Deburau, Jean-Gaspard** ▶ (1796–1846) French pantomimist, born in Bohemia. He joined a troupe of acrobats in Paris in 1811 and created the standard pantomime character of Pierrot, the pale and melancholy lover.

● **Debussy, Claude (Achille)** ▶ (1862–1918) French composer. He spent most of his life in Paris and is regarded as the originator of musical impressionism. He married twice and wrote his *Children's Corner Suite* (1906–08) for his daughter Chou-chou. His individual style employed whole-tone, pentatonic, and modal scales as well as unusual harmonies and tone colours. His most famous works include *Prélude à l'après-midi d'un faune* (for orchestra; 1892–94), the opera *Pelléas et Mélisande* (1892–1902), *La Mer* (three symphonic sketches; 1903–05), a string quartet, and a sonata for flute, viola, and harp. He also wrote sonatas for cello and for violin; piano music, including two sets of *Images* (1905, 1907) and 24 preludes (1910–13); and songs.

● **Debye, Peter Joseph Wilhelm** ▶ (1884–1966) Dutch physicist and chemist, who was awarded the 1936 Nobel Prize for Chemistry for his theoretical work on ▷dipole moments and the behaviour of ions in solution. He also extended the technique of X-ray crystallography (*see* X-ray diffraction) so that it could be applied to powders. Most of his work was done in Germany but in 1940 he left Europe for Cornell University (USA), where he remained until his retirement.

● **Decadents** ▶ A group of late-19th-century French symbolist poets and their contemporaries in England. They aimed to create a literature liberated from all moral and social responsibilities. A journal entitled *Le Décadent* was published in France from 1886 to 1889. Poets linked with the movement included ▷Rimbaud, ▷Verlaine, and

▷Mallarmé in France, and Arthur ▷Symons, Oscar ▷Wilde, and Ernest ▷Dowson in England. ▷*See also* Aesthetic movement.

● **Decalogue** ▷*See* Ten Commandments.

● **Decapoda** ▶ A worldwide order of ▷crustaceans (over 8500 species), with five pairs of thoracic appendages—anterior pincers and four pairs of walking legs. They include the ▷shrimps and ▷prawns (suborder: *Natantia*, "swimming forms") and ▷lobsters, ▷crayfish, and ▷crabs (suborder: *Reptantia*, "walking forms"). Class: *Malacostraca*.

● **decathlon** ▶ An athletic competition for men, consisting of ten events over two days. On the first are 100 m sprint, long jump, shot put, high jump, and 400 m sprint; on the second are 110 m hurdles, discus throw, pole vault, javelin throw, and 1500 m run. Competitors score for performances in each event, the winner gaining the highest total. World record: 8891 points (1992) by Dan O'Brien (USA).

● **Decatur, Stephen** ▶ (1779–1820) US naval officer. He established his reputation in the war with the Barbary pirates of Tripoli (1800–05), in which he raided Tripoli harbour and burnt the captured US frigate *Philadelphia* (1804). In the ▷War of 1812 he defeated two British frigates (1812, 1815). He was killed in a duel.

● **Deccan** ▶ A region of India, considered either as the entire peninsula or as the arid plateau between the Rivers Narmada and Krishna. Sloping gently from the Western to the Eastern Ghats, it is cut by many rivers flowing E.

● **Decembrists** ▷*See* Dekabrists.

● **decibel** ▶ (dB) A unit used to compare two power levels on a logarithmic scale. It is one-tenth of a bel, but this unit is rarely used. Two power levels P and P_0 differ by n decibels when $n = 10 \log_{10} P/P_0$. The unit is often used to express a sound intensity in which case P_0 is usually taken as the intensity of the lowest audible note of the same frequency as P. ▷*See also* phon.

● **deciduous plants** ▷*See* evergreen plants.

● **decimal system** ▶ The number system in common use, having a base 10 and thus using ten separate numerals. It also involves the use of a decimal point to express numbers less than one, instead of the method of fractions: for example ¼ is expressed as 0.25. The decimal system was invented by the Hindus and adopted by the Arabs in the 9th century (*see also* mathematics). The use of decimal fractions originated in Italy in the 12th century but was first formalized by the mathematician Simon Stévin (1548–1620) in 1585. The use of the decimal point did not occur until the beginning of the 18th century. Decimalization of currency systems was introduced by France after the Revolution and followed by most other European and American countries, except for Britain, which did not decimalize until 1971. ▷*See also* metric system.

● **Decius, Gaius Messius Quintus Trajanus** ▶ (c. 201–51 AD) Roman emperor (249–51). Decius attempted to restore Roman traditions, persecuting Christians in the name of Roman state cults. He was defeated and killed by the Goths at Abrittus.

● **Declaration of Independence** ▶ (4 July, 1776) The declaration, adopted by the 13 colonies of North America, that announced their independence from Great Britain. Written by Thomas ▷Jefferson between 11 June and 2 July and revised before adoption, the Declaration is both specific (in its enumeration of grievances) and general (in its statement of principles of governance) and is one of the most influential proclamations in the Western political tradition.

● **Declaration of Rights** ▷*See* Bill of Rights.

● **Declaratory Act** ▷*See* Stamp Act.

● **declination** ▷*See* magnetic declination; right ascension.

● **decomposition** ▶ The breakdown of the complex organic molecules of dead plants and animals and animal wastes into their simple components by bacteria and fungi. These microorganisms (**decomposers**) serve as the ultimate link in ▷food chains: the simple nitrogenous compounds released into the soil by decomposition can be used by plants (the producers) to manufacture food. ▷*See also* nitrogen cycle.

● **decompression sickness** ▶ (*or* caisson disease) An occupational hazard of pilots and underwater divers caused by too rapid a return to normal atmospheric pressure. At high pressures large amounts of gas can be carried in the blood. A rapid return to normal pressure causes nitrogen (the main component of inhaled air) to form bubbles out in the blood; this interrupts the blood supply to the tissues, producing joint pain (the bends), general discomfort, and respiratory problems (the chokes). Decompression sickness is prevented by a slow return to atmospheric pressure; it is treated by placing the patient in a hyperbaric chamber.

● **deconstruction** ▷*See* Derrida, Jacques; poststructuralism.

● **Decorated** ▶ The style of ▯gothic architecture predominant in England between 1300 and 1370. In contrast to the geometric restraint of ▷Early English, Decorated is characterized by complex flowing patterns, especially in window tracery (e.g. the Bishop's Eye ▷rose window in Lincoln cathedral, c. 1325). Roof vaults were intricately ribbed and the ogee or double curved ▷arch with ornamentation became common (e.g. the lady chapel of Ely Cathedral, 1321–49). The early 14th-century nave of Exeter Cathedral shows the style's profusion of ribs and arches. *Compare* Flamboyant.

● **decorative arts** ▶ Arts and crafts the function of which is primarily ornamental. The modern concept of the decorative arts was pioneered by such designers as William ▷Morris. Despite attempts to demonstrate that mass production need not compromise design, modern endeavours in the decorative arts tend to centre on small workshops producing individually handmade items in such fields as ▷bookbinding, ▷enamelwork, jewellery, ▷pottery, and wallpaper.

● **Dedekind, (Julius Wilhelm) Richard** ▶ (1831–1916) German mathematician, who gave the irrational ▷numbers the same level of respectability as the rational numbers. He achieved this by means of the Dedekind cut, a method of cutting an infinite line representing the real numbers. He became involved in the controversy between Georg ▷Cantor and Leopold Kronecker (1823–91), taking Cantor's side against Kronecker's attempt to banish all but the integers from mathematics.

● **deduction** ▶ In logic, argument from general principles to particular conclusions. It is thus analytic and certain, in contrast to ▷induction, the conclusions of which are never more than strong probabilities.

● **de Duve, Christian** ▶ (1917–   ) Belgian biochemist, noted for his contributions to cell biology. De Duve discovered lysosomes, components of living cells that are responsible for breaking down substances within the cell. He shared a Nobel Prize (1974) with Albert Claude (1899–1983) and George Emil Palade (1912–   ).

● **Dee, John** ▶ (1527–1608) English mathematician, astronomer, alchemist, and magician. After studying mathematics and astronomy at Cambridge, Dee lectured at Louvain and Rheims. He was distrusted by Mary I, but was consulted by Elizabeth I. He went into partnership with the conjurer and imposter Edward Kelly (1555–95); they travelled to Bohemia and Poland (1583–89). Dee's work and writings reflect Renaissance fascination with magic, but he also wrote an important preface to the first English translation of ▷Euclid.

● **Dee, River** ▶ The name of three rivers in the UK. **1.** A river in NE Scotland, flowing E to the North Sea at Aberdeen. Length: 140 km (87 mi). **2.** A river in North Wales and NW England, rising in Gwynedd and flowing E and N through Chester to the Irish Sea. Length: 112 km (70 mi). **3.** A river in S Scotland, flowing S to the Solway Firth. Length: 80 km (50 mi).

● **deed** ▶ In law, a document in writing, signed and delivered, transferring a right over property (title-deed) or creating an obligation on its maker. To be binding it need not fulfil conditions applicable to a ▷contract. A deed may be between two parties, to establish mutual obligations, or it may involve one party only (deed poll), as, for example, when a person publishes a change of name. A **deed of arrangement** is a written agreement between a debtor and his creditors, when no bankruptcy order has been made, arranging the debtor's affairs for the benefit of the creditors. A **deed of covenant** is an undertaking to pay an agreed amount for a specific period. Such a deed has certain tax advantages when made in favour of a charity. A **deed of gift** is a document in which a donor conveys property to a donee, who makes no consideration in return. The donee can enforce a deed of gift against the donor, but gifts made without a deed are not enforceable.

● **deep freezer** ▷*See* freezing.

● **deer** ▶ A ▷ruminant mammal of the family *Cervidae* (41 species), occurring mainly in the N hemisphere, although a few are found in South America and they have been introduced to SE Asia and Australasia. Nearly all deer have bony antlers that are shed and replaced every year (the ▷Chinese water deer and the ▷musk deer are exceptions). Deer range in size from the ▷elk (up to 2 m high) to the South American pudu, which is only about 40 cm high at the shoulder. Most deer live in herds but some, such as the ▷muntjac, are solitary.

● **deerhound** ▶ A long-established British breed of dog, formerly used for hunting deer. It has a deep-chested long body with long legs and a long tapering head with small ears. The wiry coat is usually blue-grey but may be shades of brown or fawn. Height: 76 cm (dogs); 71 cm (bitches).

● **deer mouse** ▶ A North American rodent belonging to the genus *Peromyscus* (60 species), also called white-footed mouse. 12–37 cm long including the tail (4–20 cm), these climbing and burrowing animals have large eyes and ears; they are omnivorous and are often used as laboratory animals. Family: *Cricetidae*.

● **defamation** ▶ In law, a false and derogatory statement about another person that tends to lower him in the estimation of right-thinking members of the community generally. In English law it is libel if made in a permanent form (e.g. in writing, newspapers, broadcasts, films) and slander if made in a transient form, by spoken words or gestures. The remedy for both types of defamation is by civil proceedings, although libel may also be a crime if its publication is calculated to provoke a breach of the peace. Not only the originator of a libel but everyone who has repeated or published it may be sued by the person libelled. Action for libel cannot be brought against "privileged" proceedings or statements. Judicial and parliamentary proceedings, for example, are "absolutely privileged" and nothing said in them can be the subject of a libel action. A statement judged to be a fair comment on a matter of public interest is not actionable as defamation.

● **Defence, Ministry of** ▶ The UK government department headed by the secretary of state for defence, that administers the country's army, navy, and air force and formulates a coordinated defence policy. It was formed in 1964 from the former Ministry of Defence (established in 1946), the Admiralty, War Office, and Air Ministry. It is the largest user of computers in Europe.

● **Defence Advisory Notice** ▶ An official notice issued by the Ministry of Defence to prevent media coverage of an issue or event for reasons of national security. First used in 1922, they were originally called **D-notices**. As they are voluntarily adhered to they avoid press censorship in the UK.

● **defence mechanisms** ▶ In psychoanalysis, the means by which undesirable and antisocial impulses can be unconsciously avoided or controlled by the subject. ▷Repression, ▷sublimation, and ▷projection are important defences. Others include reaction formation, in which an impulse is turned into its opposite, as when one displays excessive concern for a person whom one secretly hates; and displacement, in which an impulse is transferred onto a more acceptable subject (e.g. kicking the dog instead of the boss). Defence mechanisms are a part of normal life, but if they become excessively strong they can distort the development of personality and even give rise to symptoms of ▷neurosis.

● **Defender of the Faith** ▶ A title given to Henry VIII by Pope ▷Leo X (11 Oct. 1521) for opposing ▷Luther in his treatise *Assertio Septem Sacramentorum*. Parliament confirmed the title after the Reformation and the initials F.D. (Latin: *fidei defensor*) have appeared on British coinage since the reign of George I, being a part of the royal title.

● **deficiency disease** ▶ Any disorder caused by the absence of an essential ▷nutrient, particularly a vitamin, essential amino or fatty acid, or trace element, from the diet. Examples of deficiency diseases are ▷scurvy (due to lack of vitamin C), ▷beriberi (due to lack of vitamin B_1), pernicious ▷anaemia (lack of vitamin B_{12}), ▷pellagra (lack of nicotinic acid), and ▷rickets (lack of vitamin D). ▷Kwashiorkor is a disease caused by lack of protein in the diet. Deficiency diseases are treated by dietary supplements of the missing nutrient.

Plants also develop specific deficiency diseases if grown in soils that lack any of the minerals essential for healthy growth, such as nitrogen, iron, manganese, or boron.

● **deficit financing** ▶ The fiscal policy of stimulating the economy by government spending in excess of revenue by borrowing to finance the resultant deficit. Deficit financing was advocated by the British economist J. M. ▷Keynes as a method of countering the ▷Depression of the 1930s; although Keynes' ideas were not assimilated in time to influence that period, deficit financing became normal practice after World War II (*see* multiplier; national debt).

● **deflation** ▶ A government action to slow down the economy, with the aim of easing ▷inflation or cutting down on imports and thus helping the ▷balance of payments. Both monetary policy (credit "squeeze") and fiscal policy (increasing taxes, cutting government spending) can be used to deflate the economy. ▷*See also* multiplier.

● **Defoe, Daniel** ▶ (1660–1731) British novelist, economist, and journalist. His early career as a merchant ended in bankruptcy in 1692. A Nonconformist, he welcomed the arrival of William of Orange in 1688 and wrote *The True-Born Englishman* (1701) in his defence. He worked as a journalist and informer for both Whigs and Tories and suffered imprisonment for his ironic pamphlet, *The Shortest Way with Dissenters*, in 1702. From 1704 to 1713 he wrote most of the thrice-weekly *Review* himself. His famous novels were written late in his career, *Robinson Crusoe* in 1719 and *Moll Flanders* and *Colonel Jack* in 1722.

● **defoliant** ▶ A chemical applied to foliage in order to cause premature shedding of leaves; examples are ammonium thiocyanate and cacodylic acid. Defoliants are used to aid mechanical harvesting of cotton and for other peaceful uses. They are also employed in ▷chemical warfare.

● **De Forest, Lee** ▶ (1873–1961) US electrical engineer, who invented the triode valve (1906), which became the basic ▷amplifier in all electronic circuits until superseded by the transistor. In the early 1920s he developed a method of converting sound waves into light of varying intensity, which was used as the basis of recording film soundtracks.

● **deforestation** ▶ The removal of large numbers of trees in natural forests by felling or burning in order to obtain timber or fuel wood or to clear the land for farming or mining. About 10 000 years ago, before the advent of agriculture, about half the land surface of the earth was forested. Since then deforestation has removed three-quarters of these forests. The clearing of tropical rain forests in South America and S and SE Asia has accelerated rapidly in the 20th century. Not only has this deprived the world of many rare and potentially useful species of plants and animals but it also has serious ecological consequences. Forest trees bind the soil and help to trap rainwater, which percolates into the soil and thence into rivers. Removal of these trees in upland areas increases the surface run-off of rainwater, which washes away the exposed soil. This results in landslides, soil erosion, and the silting-up of rivers (causing flooding), reservoirs, and oceans (destroying coral reefs and consequently disrupting marine ecosystems). In addition, the burning of felled trees releases large amounts of carbon dioxide, which many scientists believe has contributed to the ▷greenhouse effect and consequent global warming.

● **Degas, (Hilaire Germain) Edgar** ▶ (1834–1917) French painter and sculptor, born in Paris. He trained in the École des Beaux-Arts, where he was influenced by the draughtsmanship of ▷Ingres. His early works were portraits, e.g. *The Bellelli Family* (Louvre), recalling the old masters that he had studied in Italy (1856–60), and history paintings, e.g. *Young Spartans Exercising* (National Gallery, London). From the mid-1860s he turned to painting contemporary scenes, particularly of ballet and racecourses. In these works, characterized by informal poses and unusual angles, Degas was indebted both to Japanese prints and to photography. In 1872 he visited his mother's family in New Orleans and painted the *New Orleans Cotton Office* (Pau, France). His pastels of women at their toilet shocked his contemporaries but are now regarded as being among his finest works. He exhibited frequently with the impressionists but was little influenced by their style.

● **De Gasperi, Alcide** ▶ (1881–1954) Italian statesman; prime minister (1945–53). After imprisonment (1930–31) as an antifascist, De Gasperi withdrew to the Vatican City, where he worked in the library and organized the moderate Christian Democratic party during World War II. From 1945 to 1953 he headed coalition cabinets, which included communists until 1947, when De Gasperi expelled them. A Christian Democratic electoral victory in 1948 gave popular sanction to this measure.

Charles de Gaulle ▶ Attending a wreath-laying ceremony at the tomb of the Unknown Warrior at the Arc de Triomphe after the liberation of Paris in 1944.

● **de Gaulle, Charles André Joseph Marie** ▶ (1890–1970) French general and statesman who was an outstanding international figure in the mid-20th century; president (1958–69). An advocate of mechanized warfare during the 1930s, when he wrote his best-known book, *Vers l'armée de métier* (1934), he was promoted early in World War II to general (1940). He entered the cabinet of Paul ▷Reynaud but opposed the Franco-German armistice, becoming leader of the ▷Free French in London and a symbol of French patriotism. The Free French contributed heroically to the Allied war effort but de Gaulle resented his dependence on Britain and the USA and the antagonism between them was to continue after the war. In 1943 he became head of the newly formed Committee of National Liberation in Algiers and, after the Allied liberation of France (1944), formed a provisional government of which he was president from 1945 until resigning in 1946. In 1947 he formed the unsuccessful Rassemblement du Peuple Français, dissolving it in 1953. In 1958 he was summoned from retirement to deal with the crisis in Algeria, where French settlers, fearing the establishment of Algerian independence, were in revolt. He became president of the new Fifth Republic in 1959 and moved towards the achievement of Algerian independence. Successful by 1962, he subsequently pursued his vision of a Europe of nationally self-conscious states, free of US influence. He thus opposed the postwar multinational organizations, refusing to sign the ▷Nuclear Test-Ban Treaty (1963) and withdrawing France from the military structure of NATO (1966). He was also passionately opposed to UK membership of the EEC. At home his position was greatly weakened by the student and industrial unrest of May, 1968, and in the following year he resigned following defeat in a referendum on constitutional reform. His policies endured in the right-wing Gaullist movement in French politics.

● **degree** ▶ **1.** A unit of plane angle equal to 1/360th of a complete revolution. It is subdivided into 60 minutes, each of which consists of 60 seconds. **2.** An interval on a temperature scale: 1° on the ▷Celsius (centigrade) scale is equal to one-hundredth of the difference in temperature between freezing and boiling water. It is also equal in magnitude to 1 ▷kelvin. 1° on the ▷Fahrenheit scale is 9/5 times the Celsius degree.

● **De Havilland, Sir Geoffrey** ▶ (1882–1965) British □aircraft designer and manufacturer, who produced some of the first jet-propelled aircraft. During both World Wars he designed several military aircraft, including the well-known Mosquito of World War II.

● **Dehra Dun** ▶ 30 19N 78 03E A city in India, in Uttar Pradesh. The Indian Military Academy (1932) is situated here. Population (1981): 294 000.

● **dehydration** ▶ A potentially serious condition resulting from excessive loss of water from the body. The water that is continuously lost from the body in urine, sweat, expired air, and faeces must be replaced by drinking. Dehydration may result from insufficient intake of water in those shipwrecked or too ill to drink or from excessive loss in fever, vomiting, diarrhoea, or from the skin in hot climates. It may lead, if not treated, to shock and death. It can be avoided by ensuring that patients receive fluid in the form of drinks or intravenous infusions. Intravenous fluids can be given slowly to treat those seriously dehydrated.

● **Deighton, Len** ▶ (1929–) British writer of spy thrillers. As well as such spy stories as *The Ipcress File* (1962) and a trilogy based on the character Bernard Samson, he is the author of the war story *Bomber* (1970) and the history *Blood, Tears and Folly* (1993).

● **Deirdre** ▶ The tragic heroine of the Irish legend known as *The Fate of the Sons of Usnech*, of which the earliest surviving account appears in the 12th-century *Book of Leinster*. To escape marrying King Conchobar of Ulster, Deirdre eloped with Noíse, son of Usnech. When they returned, Noíse and his brothers were killed by the king and Deirdre died of grief. The legend has been dramatized by J. M. Synge and W. B. Yeats.

● **deism** ▶ A system of belief in God that, in contrast to ▷theism, discounts revealed religion, especially Christianity, and takes God as the philosophical ▷first cause. More specifically, deism was a rationalistic anti-Christian movement in England in the late 17th and early 18th centuries that criticized and rebutted the Scriptures after the manner of John ▷Locke's ▷empiricism and regarded dogmatic religions as corruptions of man's natural relation with God. Leading deists were Lord ▷Herbert of Cherbury, Matthew Tindal (1655–1733), and the 3rd Earl of ▷Shaftesbury. Deism, often tending towards ▷atheism, had more influence in Germany and France than in England.

● **Dekabrists** ▶ (*or* Decembrists) Members of an anti-Tsarist revolt in December, 1825, following the death of Alexander I. They were members of clandestine organizations formed after the Napoleonic Wars by former military officers, who had become discontented with their country's reactionary government. The revolt failed; five leaders were executed and their followers imprisoned or exiled to Siberia.

● **Dekker, Thomas** ▶ (c. 1572–1632) British dramatist and pamphleteer. His best-known play, *The Shoemaker's Holiday* (1600), expresses his exuberant affection for London life. He often collaborated with ▷Webster, ▷Middleton, and other dramatists. His pamphlets include *The Seven Deadly Sins of London* (1606) and *The Gull's Hornbook* (1609).

● **de Klerk, F(rederik) W(illem)** ▶ (1936–) South African statesman; president (1989–94). Trained as a lawyer, he replaced P. W. ▷Botha as head of the National Party and president. He freed Nelson ▷Mandela in 1990, dismantled ▷apartheid, and in 1993 signed South Africa's new multiracial (transitional) constitution; he was awarded the Nobel Peace Prize (1993) jointly with Mandela. After the ANC won multiracial elections in 1994, de Klerk became second deputy president. In 1996 he withdrew his party from the ruling coalition and in 1997 he resigned as party leader.

● **de Kooning, Willem** ▶ (1904–97) US painter of Dutch birth. Influenced by Arshile ▷Gorky, ▷Picasso, and ▷Miró, he painted both figurative and abstract compositions, some in black and white. By the late 1940s he was regarded as a leader of abstract expressionism. His controversial series of *Women* (1950–53) portrayed females as grotesque and aggressive. In his last years he produced many paintings while suffering from Alzheimer's disease.

● **Delacroix, Eugène** ▶ (1798–1863) French Romantic painter, born near Paris. He studied with Baron Guérin (1774–1883) but was influenced by ▷Géricault, ▷Rubens, and ▷Constable. His richly coloured paintings were often inspired by incidents in Dante, Shakespeare, and Byron, and by contemporary events, e.g. *Massacre at Chios* (1824; Louvre), and *Liberty Leading the People* (1830; Louvre). A visit to Morocco (1832) influenced some of his exotic later works, e.g. *Women of Algiers* (1834; Louvre). From 1833 he worked on decorations in public buildings, such as the Louvre, Palais-Bourbon, and Saint-Sulpice. He was a friend of ▷Chopin and George ▷Sand, both of whom he painted in 1838. His *Journal* contains valuable information on his life and work.

● **Delagoa Bay** ▶ (Portuguese name: Baía de Lourenço Marques) An inlet of the Indian Ocean on the coast of S Mozambique. It is about 30 km (19 mi) across and has Maputo at its edge.

● **de la Mare, Walter** ▶ (1873–1956) British poet, novelist, and anthologist, whose work is imbued with an atmosphere of mystery. The verse collection *Songs of Childhood* (1902) and the romance *Henry Brocken* (1906) were written while he was working for an oil company, from which he retired at 36 to devote himself to writing. Among his works are the poem "The Listeners" (1912), the fantastic novel *Memoirs of a Midget* (1921), and the anthologies *Come Hither* (1923) and *Love* (1943). In 1953 he was appointed to the OM.

● **De la Roche, Mazo** ▶ (1885–1961) Canadian novelist. Her romantic saga of the Whiteoak family ran to over 15 books, beginning with *Jalna* (1927), the name of the family estate.

● **Delaroche, (Hippolyte) Paul** ▶ (1797–1859) French history and portrait painter. Throughout his life he enjoyed great success with such sentimental history paintings as *The Children of Edward IV in the Tower* (1830; Louvre). He was a professor at the École des Beaux-Arts from 1832, for which he produced the mural of the *Apotheosis of Art* (1837–41).

● **De La Rue, Warren** ▶ (1815–89) British astronomer, who pioneered the use of photography in astronomy, discovering solar flares by this process in 1860.

● **Delaunay, Robert** ▶ (1885–1941) The earliest French painter of completely abstract compositions. His first major works represented the Eiffel Tower (1910–11) in cubist style but in his series of *Discs* (1912–13) he pioneered ▷orphism (which he called *simultanisme*), a style in which colour alone was the subject matter. His Russian-born wife Sonia Delaunay (1885–1979) was also an abstract painter, who became well known for her textile designs.

● **Delaware** ▶ The second smallest state in the USA. It occupies part of the low-lying ground of the Atlantic coastal plain with higher ground in the NW, where most of the state's population and industry is concentrated. It is one of the most industrialized states; Wilmington contains the administrative centres of several large chemical companies and is nicknamed "the chemical capital of the world." Motor vehicles, synthetic rubber, textiles, and food products are also produced. There is limited mining of sand and gravel. The state's farmers produce poultry, soya beans, milk, corn, and vegetables. There is some fishing of coastal and inland waters.
History: the Dutch established a settlement (1631) but it was the Swedes who founded the first permanent settlement Fort Christiana (now Wilmington) in 1638. Delaware was captured by the Dutch (1655) and the English (1664). It became part of Pennsylvania in 1682 and shared a governor with that colony until 1776. It was the first of the original 13 states of the USA. Area: 5328 sq km (2057 sq mi). Population (1996 est): 724 842. Capital: Dover.

● **Delcassé, Théophile** ▶ (1852–1923) French politician; foreign minister (1898–1905, 1914–15). His conciliatory policy over the ▷Fashoda incident (1895) and his negotiations leading to the ▷Entente Cordiale with Britain (1904) paved the way to the ▷Triple Entente between Britain, France, and Russia. He urged a strong stand

against Germany during the 1905–06 Moroccan crisis but was forced to resign.

● **Deledda, Grazia** ▶ (1871–1936) Italian novelist. Most of her novels, such as *Ashes* (1904) and *The Mother* (1920), are realistic treatments of peasant life in her native Sardinia. She won the Nobel Prize in 1926.

● **Delescluze, Louis Charles** ▶ (1809–71) French journalist and radical republican. Active in the revolutions of 1830 and 1848, he was deeply opposed to the Second Empire of Napoleon III. A member of the ▷Commune of Paris, he was shot at the barricades.

● **Delft** ▶ 52 01N 4 21E A town in the W Netherlands, in South Holland province. William the Silent was murdered here in 1584. It is famous for its pottery and porcelain known as delftware. Population (1991 est): 89 000.

● **Delhi** ▶ 28 40N 77 14E The capital of India, situated midway between the Ganges and Indus Valleys on the W bank of the River Jumna. It consists of the old city (Old Delhi), which was built in 1639 on the site of former cities of Delhi that date from the 15th century BC, and New Delhi, which replaced Calcutta as the capital of British India in 1912. Both the old and new cities together with the surrounding area comprise the Union Territory of Delhi, an administrative unit of some 1418 sq km (553 sq mi). Within the walls of Old Delhi are the massive Red Fort, which contains the Imperial Palace (1638–48) of Shah Jahan, and the Jami Masjid (Principal Mosque). The narrow streets of the old city contrast with the spacious tree-lined streets and imposing government buildings of New Delhi, which was designed chiefly by Sir Edwin Lutyens. The University of Delhi was established in 1922. Population (1991): 7 206 704.

● **Delian League** ▶ A confederacy of Greek city states formed in 478 BC during the ▷Greek-Persian Wars under the leadership of Athens. Members met on the sacred island of Delos, voted on policy, and contributed funds assessed by ▷Aristides the Just. After the peace between Greece and Persia (c. 450) Athens regarded its allies as subjects. The League treasury was moved to Athens and secession was punished as revolt. The League was disbanded after Athens' defeat (404) in the Peloponnesian War but was revived in defence against Sparta in 378, lasting until the defeat (338) of Athens and Thebes at ▷Chaeronea.

● **Delian problem** ▶ The problem of constructing a cube that has twice the volume of a given cube. Also known as the duplication of the cube, it was first set by the oracle of Delos in the 5th century BC as a condition for ending a plague. The problem cannot be solved by ruler and compass alone, a fact not recognized until the 19th century.

● **Delibes, Leo** ▶ (1836–91) French composer, a pupil of Adolphe Adam. Early in his career he wrote operas and operettas. In 1863 he became accompanist at the Paris Opéra and, later, second chorus master. His best-known works are the ballets *Coppélia* (1870) and *Sylvia* (1876).

● **Delilah** ▷*See* Samson.

● **deliquescence** ▶ The process in which some crystalline substances, such as calcium chloride ($CaCl_2$), absorb water from the atmosphere to such an extent that they dissolve; this is extreme hygroscopic (water-attracting) behaviour. Deliquescent substances are used in several industries to provide dry atmospheres.

● **delirium** ▶ An acute state of mental disturbance in which the patient has hallucinations and delusions and is incoherent, agitated, and restless. It is most commonly associated with a high fever, particularly in children, although it may also be due to a variety of metabolic disorders. It also occurs in association with alcoholic poisoning and with alcohol withdrawal, when it is called **delirium tremens**. It can also be caused by intoxication with other drugs.

● **Delius, Frederick** ▶ (1862–1934) British composer of German descent, born in Bradford. After an abortive career in the family wool business he lived in Florida and subsequently at Grez-sur-Loing, near Paris. Largely self-taught, he was influenced by Debussy and Grieg. His works include *Paris, the Song of a Great City* (1899), *Appalachia* (for orchestra and chorus; 1902), *On Hearing the First Cuckoo in Spring* (1912), and *North Country Sketches* (1913–14). He also wrote four operas, four concertos, chamber music, choral works, and songs. Delius became blind in 1925 but continued to compose with the help of his amanuensis, the musician Eric Fenby (1906–97).

● **Della Robbia, Luca ▶** (1400–82) Florentine Renaissance sculptor. Working first in marble, Luca produced the *Cantoria* (1431–38), his famous relief depicting singers, musicians, and dancers, for the Duomo, Florence. Subsequently he specialized in enamelled terracotta sculptures, the glazing process being his own invention. Their production was carried on by his nephew **Andrea della Robbia** (1435–1525) and Luca's sons **Giovanni della Robbia** (1469–c. 1529) and **Girolamo della Robbia** (1488–1566).

● **Delorme, Philibert ▶** (?1510–70) French Renaissance architect. Influenced by classical architecture, which he studied in Rome, his buildings include the Château d'Anet (c. 1552), designed for Diane de Poitiers, and the palace of the Tuileries (1580). He also wrote two treatises on architecture (1561, 1568).

● **Delors, Jacques (Lucien Jean) ▶** (1925–   ) French politician and economist. As president of the EC (now the EU) Commission (1985–94) he originated the Delors Plan for greater European union. He was previously the French minister of finance (1981–84).

● **Delos ▶** (Modern Greek name: Dhílos) 37 23N 25 15E A Greek island in the S Aegean Sea, one of the Cyclades. It was of great importance in antiquity (*see* Delian League), and many ancient temples and other buildings, an altar built of the horns of sacrificed animals, and nine marble lions have been excavated here. Area: 3 sq km (1 sq mi).

● **Delphi ▶** A village in central Greece. In antiquity, it was the principal sanctuary and oracle of ▷Apollo. The sacred enclosure, still an imposing sight, is set in spectacular mountain scenery. It contained Apollo's temple, "treasuries" where the Greek states stored their offerings, a theatre, and over 3000 statues. A stadium for the ▷Pythian Games, a gymnasium, and other shrines stood nearby. The oracle's advice about religion, morality, commerce, and colonial projects, was interpreted from the trance utterances of a priestess, was widely sought by individuals and states. As traditional beliefs declined after the 4th century BC the oracle lost influence. It was closed by the Christian emperor, Theodosius (390 AD).

● **Delphinium ▶** A genus of annual or perennial herbs (250 species), also called larkspur, up to 2 m high with tall spikes of deep-blue flowers and divided leaves. Delphiniums, native to the N hemisphere, are popular garden plants. Cultivated varieties usually range from 30 to 180 cm high and have single or double flowers in shades of blue, pink, purple, or white. Family: ▷*Ranunculaceae*.

● **delta ▶** A large fan-shaped accumulation of sediment deposited at the mouth of a river, where it discharges into a sea or lake. It forms when the river's flow is slowed down on meeting the comparatively static sea or lake, resulting in a reduction of the river's load-bearing capacity. Clay particles also coagulate on meeting salt water and are deposited. The river is increasingly divided by the deposition into channels. Being fertile, deltas (such as the Nile Delta) are often extensively cultivated but are also prone to flooding.

● **Delvaux, Paul ▶** (1897–1994) Belgian painter, who joined the surrealist group in 1935. Influenced by ▷Magritte and de ▷Chirico, he specialized in scenes of trancelike nudes and half-clothed women in impressive architectural settings.

● **demand ▶** The quantity of goods or services that consumers wish to buy. Demand can be elastic (a small change in price causes a large change in the demand), inelastic (a large change in price results in a small change in demand), or of unitary elasticity (a change in price leads to a proportional demand). The elasticity of demand influences government policy in deciding on which goods to levy a sales tax.

● **Demerara, River ▶** A river in E Guyana, flowing N to enter the Atlantic Ocean at Georgetown. Length: 346 km (215 mi).

● **Demeter ▶** A Greek corn goddess and mother goddess, sister of ▷Zeus. She was worshipped at Eleusis, whose people helped her in her search for her daughter ▷Persephone, abducted to the underworld. In gratitude she instructed them in agriculture and religion (*see* Eleusinian mysteries). She was identified with the Roman goddess Ceres.

● **de Mille, Cecil B(lount) ▶** (1881–1959) US film producer and director. His best-known films were epic productions involving spectacular crowd scenes and special effects. Many were based on biblical themes, notably *The Ten Commandments* (1923; remade 1956), *The King of Kings* (1927), and *Samson and Delilah* (1949). His niece **Agnes de Mille** (1909–93) was a ballet dancer and choreographer. American themes and traditions were a distinctive feature of her work, as in *Rodeo* (1942), choreographed for the Ballets Russes in Monte Carlo. She also choreographed for films and musicals, notably *Oklahoma!* (1943), *Carousel* (1945), and *Paint Your Wagon* (1951).

● **democracy ▶** A form of government in which people either rule themselves (direct democracy), as in ancient Athens, or elect representatives to rule in their interests (indirect democracy), as in most modern democracies. Elections, to be democratic, must be held regularly, be secret, and provide a choice of candidates; the elected assembly must also be free to legislate and to criticize government policy. Modern democratic ideas stem from 18th-century ▷utilitarianism.

Delphi ▶ The sanctuary of Apollo, set in spectacular scenery on the slopes of Mount Parnassus, contains numerous shrines and monuments erected over many centuries. This photograph shows the *tholos*, a round structure of unknown function, designed by Theodoros of Phocaea in about 390 BC.

Much current debate centres on the elitist theory of democracy—that government is by a political elite, which although voted into power invites little participation by the electorate.

● **Democratic Party** ▶ One of the two major political parties in the USA (*compare* Republican Party). Originating in Jefferson's Republican Democrats in 1792, it became the Democratic Party during the presidency (1829–37) of Andrew ▷Jackson. In 1860, just before the Civil War, the Democrats split over ▷slavery and the party, dominated by southern Democrats, was eclipsed until the 1880s. With F. D. Roosevelt's ▷New Deal programme in the 1930s, the Democrats again became a progressive party. Notable Democratic presidents include Woodrow Wilson, F. D. Roosevelt, J. F. Kennedy, Jimmy Carter, and Bill Clinton.

● **Democritus** ▶ (c. 460–370 BC), Greek philosopher and scientist, born at Abdera (Thrace). He developed the first materialist theory of nature. His ▷atomism, developed from ▷Leucippus, considered that all matter consists of minute particles—atoms—the multifarious arrangement of which accounts for different properties of matter apparent to our senses. Democritus wrote also on cosmology, biology, perception, and music. His ethical theory foreshadowed ▷Epicureanism in valuing spiritual tranquillity most highly. Of his works, many fragments, but nothing complete, survives.

● **demography** ▶ A branch of the social sciences concerned with the statistical study of the sizes, distribution, and composition of human populations. The subject also includes collecting and analysing birth, death, and marriage rates for whole populations or groups within them. Demography is a branch of sociology but also overlaps with economics, mathematics, geography, and genetics.

● **demoiselle** ▶ An elegant ▷crane, *Anthropoides virgo*, of dry grassy regions of central Europe and Asia. It is smoky grey in colour with a black head and neck, long black breast feathers, and long white plumes behind each eye.

● **De Morgan, Augustus** ▶ (1806–71) British mathematician and logician. De Morgan was one of the first to recognize that different ▷algebras may exist other than the one corresponding to the real numbers, which was then taken to be the only algebra. He also worked with George ▷Boole.

● **Demosthenes** ▶ (384–322 BC) Athenian orator and statesman. Demosthenes attacked Philip of Macedon's imperial ambitions in Greece in a series of orations called the *Philippics* (351, 344, 341) and promoted an Athenian alliance with Thebes against Philip. This was defeated by Philip at ▷Chaeronea (338), whereby Macedonian supremacy in Greece was assured. After the death of Philip's son, Alexander the Great (323), Demosthenes again encouraged a Greek revolt. Condemned to death by Alexander's successors, Demosthenes fled Athens and committed suicide. His oratory was much admired in antiquity but his politics were anachronistic; the military power of Macedon could not be denied by even Demosthenes' oratory.

● **demotic script** ▶ A form of Egyptian hieroglyphic writing. Pictorial hieroglyphics became less realistic and increasingly cursive from about 2500 BC until in the 7th century BC they developed into the cursive script called demotic. This continued in use until the 5th century AD. ▷*See also* Rosetta Stone.

● **Dempsey, Jack** ▶ (William Harrison D.; 1895–1983) US boxer, who was world heavyweight champion from 1919 to 1926. Renowned for his persistence and ferocious punching, he attracted enormous audiences and gate money. He lost his title to Gene Tunney (1897–1978).

● **Denbighshire** ▶ A county of North Wales, on the Irish Sea. It was absorbed into Clwyd and Gwynedd under local government reorganization (1974) but was reinstated (with different boundaries) in 1996. It is mainly hilly, with the highest mountains in the S: the Vale of Clwyd in the N is low lying and fertile. Agriculture is the chief economic activity. Tourism is important, especially in the coastal resorts of Rhyl and Prestatyn. Area 844 sq km (327 sq mi). Population (1998 est) 90 500. Administrative centre: Ruthin.

● **Dench, Dame Judi (Olivia)** ▶ (1934–) British actress. Her career began at the Old Vic and Royal Shakespeare Companies;

her Juliet and Cleopatra have been highly praised. Her late husband, with whom she appeared in the TV sit-com *A Fine Romance*, was the actor Michael Williams (1935–2001). Her film roles include Queen Victoria in *Mrs Brown* (1997) and Elizabeth I in *Shakespeare in Love* (1999); the latter earned her an Oscar as best supporting actress. She also played Iris Murdoch in *Iris* (2001). She was created DBE in 1988.

● **dendrite** ▷*See* neurone.

● **dendrochronology** ▶ (*or* tree-ring dating) An archaeological dating technique based on the ▷annual rings of trees. Variations in ring widths have been shown to correspond to rainfall and temperature variations and thus very old tree trunks can give a record of past climates. Any construction incorporating timber, for example buildings or ships, can be dated by comparing the timber-ring patterns with a specimen of known age.

● **dendrology** ▷*See* tree.

● **Deneb** ▶ An extremely luminous remote white ▷supergiant star, apparent magnitude 1.25 and about 1600 light years distant, that is the brightest star in the constellation Cygnus.

● **Deneuve, Catherine** ▶ (Catherine Dorléac; 1943–) French film actress. Her films include *Repulsion* (1965), *Belle de Jour* (1967), *Tristana* (1970), *The Scene of the Crime* (1986), *Indochine* (1992), and *Les Voleurs* (1997).

● **dengue** ▶ A tropical disease caused by a virus and characterized by painful joints, fever, and a rash. The virus is transmitted by the bite of a mosquito, and symptoms begin within a week after the bite. Dengue usually lasts for a week and is rarely fatal; there is no specific treatment. Dengue haemorrhagic fever is a severe form of the disease, usually affecting children, marked by internal bleeding.

● **Deng Xiao Ping** ▶ (*or* Teng Hsiao-p'ing; 1904–97) Chinese statesman; vice premier (1973–76; 1977–80) and vice chairman of the Central Committee of the Chinese Communist Party (1977–82). He held prominent Party posts after the establishment of the People's Republic of China in 1949 but was dismissed during the ▷Cultural Revolution. Although rehabilitated in 1973, he was again dismissed three years later. Following his reinstatement in 1977 he emerged as China's de facto leader in the early 1980s. He was Chairman of the State and Party Military Commissions (1982–89). His rule saw liberalization of the economy but continuing political repression. Although he officially retired in 1989 he remained the supreme influence over China's affairs until his death.

● **Denham, Sir John** ▶ (1615–69) English poet. His *Cooper's Hill* (1642), describing the landscape near Windsor, established a minor genre, the topographical poem, and helped to make the ▷heroic couplet a standard English verse form.

● **Den Helder** ▶ 52 58N 4 46E A port in the Netherlands, in North Holland province on the North Sea. It is an important naval and military base. Population (1994): 61 024.

● **denier** ▶ A unit of weight, used to measure the fineness of woven materials, equal to 1 gram per 9000 metres.

● **Denikin, Anton Ivanovich** ▶ (1872–1947) Russian general. After the Russian revolution (1917), he led the ▷White Russian army against the Bolsheviks. He occupied most of Ukraine but internal rifts and Bolshevik counterattacks led to eventual defeat (1920). Denikin fled to France.

● **denim** ▶ A coarse twill-woven cloth, named after the French fabric *serge de Nîmes*. It is made of cotton, often with an admixture of nylon, and is usually dyed blue. Originally popular for work garments, denim became fashionable for jeans and other casual clothes in the 1970s.

● **De Niro, Robert** ▶ (1943–) US film actor, much admired playing tough but sensitive heroes. He won Academy Awards for *The Godfather Part II* (1974) and *Raging Bull* (1979); other films include *Taxi Driver* (1976), *The Deerhunter* (1978), *GoodFellas* (1990), *Casino* (1995), *Analyze This* (1999), and *Showtime* (2002).

● **Denis, Maurice** ▶ (1870–1943) French painter, designer, and art theorist, who was a leading member of the ▷Nabis. He was responsible for decorating many churches and his religious painting influenced succeeding generations of religious artists. In 1919 he helped to found the Studios of Sacred Art, which also encouraged the revival of religious art.

● **Denis, St** ▶ (3rd century) The patron saint of France. Of Italian birth, he was sent to Gaul as a missionary and became the first Bishop of Paris. He was martyred under the Emperor Valerian. His shrine is in the Benedictine abbey at St Denis near Paris. Feast Day: 9 Oct.

● **Denmark, Kingdom of** ▶ (Danish name: Danmark) A country in N Europe, between the Baltic and the North Seas. It consists of the N section of the Jutland peninsula and about a hundred inhabited islands (chiefly Sjælland (Zealand), Fyn, Lolland, Falster, Langeland, and Bornholm). ▷Greenland and the ▷Faeroe Islands are also part of the Danish kingdom, although both now have internal self-government. The country is almost entirely flat.
Economy: agriculture, organized on a partly cooperative basis, is important both for the home and export markets. Since World War II, however, industry has predominated, with manufacturing, engineering, chemicals, brewing, and food processing. Financial and service industries are major employers. Exports include meat and meat products, dairy produce, cereals, fish, porcelain, glassware, and metal goods. The country is self-sufficient in oil and natural gas but nearly all industrial raw materials are imported.
History: Viking kingdoms occupied the area from the 8th century to the 10th century, when Denmark became a united Christian monarchy under Harald Bluetooth. His grandson, Canute, ruled over Denmark, Norway, and England, forming the Danish Empire, which was dissolved soon after his death. In 1363 Norway again came under the Danish Crown by royal marriage. In 1397 Denmark and Norway joined with Sweden to form the Kalmar Union, which lasted until 1523. The Peace of Copenhagen (1660) concluded a long period of conflict between Denmark and Sweden. At this time it became an absolute monarchy, which continued until 1849, when a more liberal government was formed. Having supported Napoleon in the Napoleonic Wars, Denmark was compelled to cede Norway to Sweden by the Treaty of Kiel (1814). In the middle of the 19th century Denmark lost its S provinces of Schleswig, Holstein, and Lauenburg to Prussia, N Schleswig being returned (by plebiscite) in 1920. During World War II Denmark was occupied (1940–45) by Germany but a resistance movement aided the Allied victory. Iceland, which had previously been united with Denmark, became independent in 1944. A new constitution was formed in 1953, with a single-chamber parliament (elected by proportional representation) and executive power in the hands of ministers. In 1973 Denmark joined the EC (now the EU). After decades of government by Social Democrat-led coalitions, Denmark elected a liberal government in 1982. Following elections in 1994 a centrist coalition was formed under Poul Nyrup Rasmussen. In two referenda (1992, 1993) the voters first rejected and then accepted the Maastricht Treaty (*see* European Community). Membership of the single European currency was narrowly rejected in a referendum in 2000. Denmark's first right-wing government for over 75 years was elected in 2001, when Anders Fogh Rasmussen became prime minister. The islands of Sjælland and Fyn were linked by a new suspension bridge (the longest in Europe) in 1998; a bridge and causeway linking Denmark and Sweden was completed in 2000.

Kingdom of Denmark	
Head of state	Queen Margrethe II
Official language	Danish
Official religion	Evangelical Lutheran
Official currency	krone of 100 øre
Area	43 074 sq km (16 631 sq mi)
Population (2000 est)	5 339 000
Capital and main port	Copenhagen

● **Denning, Alfred Thompson, Baron** ▶ (1899–1999) British jurist. He became a High Court judge in 1944, was Master of the Rolls (1962–82), and headed (1963) the enquiry into the resignation of John ▷Profumo. His rulings were frequently controversial for their rejection of legal precedent. His books include *The Family Story* (1981). He was appointed to the OM in 1997.

● **density** ▶ The mass of unit volume of a substance. In ▷SI units it is measured in kilograms per cubic metre; in these units water has a density of 1000 kg m⁻³. **Relative density** (formerly called "specific gravity") is the density of a substance divided by the density of water at 4°C. This value is numerically one thousandth of the density. In the c.g.s. system, density (in grams per cubic centimetre) is numerically equal to relative density. The density of a gas (vapour density) is often expressed as the mass of unit volume of the gas divided by the mass of the same volume of hydrogen at standard temperature and pressure.

● **dentistry** ▶ The branch of medical science concerned with the care of the teeth, gums, and mouth. The first dental school was established in the USA, in Philadelphia, in 1840; the first European school was the Royal Dental Hospital, founded in London in 1858. Restorative dentistry is concerned with the repair of teeth damaged by ▷caries; prosthetic dentistry deals with the replacement of teeth lost through injury or extraction by means of dentures or bridges. Orthodontics deals with the correction of badly positioned teeth, usually by means of braces or other appliances but sometimes by surgery on the jaw. Periodontics (periodontology) includes the care of the gums and other structures supporting the teeth and the treatment of periodontal disease. Oral surgery deals with the extraction of teeth and the surgical repair of fractures or abnormalities of the jaws and facial bones. Preventive dentistry is concerned with preventing tooth decay and gum disease by such measures as education in oral hygiene and ▷fluoridation.

● **Dent du Midi** ▶ 46 11N 6 55E A massif in SW Switzerland, in the Alps. It rises to 3259 m (10 692 ft) at Haute Cime.

● **Denver** ▶ 39 45N 105 00W A city in the USA, the capital of Colorado on the South Platte River. Founded in 1858 during the Colorado gold rush, Denver is the financial, administrative, and industrial centre for an agricultural area. A US Mint is sited here and the city is near 12 national parks. Population (1998 est): 499 055.

● **deodar** ▶ A ▷cedar, *Cedrus deodara*, native to the Himalayas, where it forms vast forests, and planted for ornament in temperate regions and for timber in S Europe. Reaching a height of 75 m in the wild, it has barrel-shaped cones.

● **d'Éon, Charles de Beaumont, Chevalier** ▶ (1728–1810) French secret agent in the service of ▷Louis XV. His fondness for wearing women's clothes, both as a disguise and in normal life, led to wagers in society about his actual sex. Speculation continued until the autopsy after his death in London.

● **deontology** ▶ A system of ▷ethics in which duty, rather than rights, virtue, or happiness, is fundamental to morality. It was the title of a book by ▷Bentham. *Compare* teleology.

● **deoxyribonucleic acid** ▷*See* DNA.

● **Depardieu, Gérard** ▶ (1948–   ) French film actor, noted for his roles in both costume dramas and contemporary stories. His films include *The Last Métro* (1980), *Danton* (1982), *Jean de Florette* (1986), *Trop Belle pour toi* (1989), *Green Card* (1990), *Cyrano de Bergerac* (1991), *A Pure Formality* (1994), and *The Man in the Iron Mask* (1998).

● **depreciation** ▶ The loss in value of capital goods as a result of wear and tear, obsolescence, etc. For example, a machine that costs £10,000 and is expected to last ten years depreciates at the rate of £1,000 a year. To keep its stock of capital goods, therefore, a firm must set aside a certain sum each year to account for depreciation. The calculation of the depreciation provision is sometimes complicated by the difficulty in judging the life of a machine: changes in taste or technological developments may shorten the useful life of a machine. To encourage firms to maintain their capital stock, governments usually allow for depreciation when calculating corporation tax.

● **depression** ▶ (economics) A period during the ▷trade cycle in which demand is low compared to industry's capacity to satisfy it. Profits, and therefore confidence and investment, are also correspondingly low (*see* accelerator principle). A depression is also characterized by high unemployment, as in the 1930s (*see* Depression). The influence of J. M. ▷Keynes led postwar governments to adopt ▷deficit financing policies to counter depressions, but the advent in the 1970s of the previously unknown combination of depression and ▷inflation subsequently led to widespread adoption of the rival doctrine of ▷monetarism. A depression is also called a slump.

● **depression** ▶ (meteorology) A ▷cyclone in the midlatitudes; also called a low or a disturbance. Frequently accompanied by ▷fronts, depressions move towards the NE in the N hemisphere and towards the SE in the S hemisphere. They are characterized by unsettled weather and are the main source of rainfall in the lowland areas of the midlatitudes.

● **depression** ▶ (psychiatry) Severe and persistent misery. It can be a normal reaction to distressing events, such as bereavement. Sometimes, however, it is out of all proportion to the situation or may have no apparent external cause: it can then be a sign of mental illness. In ▷manic-depressive psychosis the depression is severe and can lead the sufferer to delusions of being evil and worthless; sleep, appetite, and concentration can all be disturbed. In dysthymic disorder (depressive neurosis) the symptoms are less extreme but may still lead to ▷suicide. Treatment with ▷antidepressant drugs is often effective and psychotherapy—particularly ▷cognitive therapy—is helpful. Severe cases may need ▷electroconvulsive therapy.

● **Depression** ▶ The period, also called the Slump, during the early 1930s, when worldwide economic collapse precipitated commercial failure and mass unemployment. Starting in the USA in 1929, when share prices fell so disastrously that thousands were made bankrupt (Wall Street Crash), the Depression caused international repercussions. Overseas trade almost ceased, industrial production dropped, millions in industrialized countries were unemployed, and agricultural countries were impoverished. Roosevelt's ▷New Deal (1934) brought Americans hope of recovery, but Britain, despite abandoning free trade to protect its industries, never regained its commercial pre-eminence. In Germany the Depression contributed to the rise of Hitler's Nazi movement.

● **Depretis, Agostino** ▶ (1813–87) Italian statesman; prime minister (1876–78, 1878–79, 1881–87). At first a supporter of ▷Mazzini and opponent of ▷Cavour, Depretis became converted to constitutional monarchism in 1861. He headed several coalitions of moderate Left elements in parliament. His foreign policy contributed to the formation of the 1882 ▷Triple Alliance of Italy, Austria-Hungary, and Germany.

● **Deptford** ▶ A district in the Greater London borough of Lewisham, on the S bank of the River Thames. It was the site of a Royal Naval dockyard (1513–1869).

● **De Quincey, Thomas** ▶ (1785–1859) British essayist. In 1802 he ran away from his family to Wales and then London, where he lived with a young prostitute called Ann. While studying at Oxford he took opium for toothache and became addicted for life. He lived largely by journalism, writing numerous essays. Among his friends were ▷Wordsworth and ▷Coleridge. His *Confessions of an English Opium Eater* first appeared in 1822 (revised 1856).

● **Derain, André** ▶ (1880–1954) French postimpressionist painter. In his bold designs and vibrant colours, particularly in his Thames paintings (1905–06), he was initially a leading exponent of ▷fauvism, but after 1907 he came under the influence of ▷Cézanne and painted in a cubist manner. He later reverted to a traditional style. He produced notable scenery and costume designs for Diaghilev's ▷Ballets Russes.

● **Derby** ▶ A flat race for three-year-old horses, run over 2.4 km (1.5 mi) at Epsom in early June. The most prestigious of the English Classics, it was instituted (1780) by the 12th Earl of Derby.

● **Derby** ▶ **1.** 52 55N 1 30W A city in central England, in Derby unitary authority, Derbyshire, on the River Derwent. Its growth as a manufacturing centre began in the late 17th century; the first silk mill in England was established here in 1719 and by the 18th century Derby had become a centre of porcelain manufacture (*see* Derby ware). All Saints Church became the cathedral of the new diocese of Derby in 1927. Today Derby is an important engineering centre (with Rolls-Royce aero engines) and has large railway workshops. Popula-

tion (1991): 222 500. **2.** A unitary authority in central England, in Derbyshire. Area: 78 sq km (30 sq mi). Population (1996 est): 233 700.

● **Derby, Edward (George Geoffrey Smith) Stanley, 14th Earl of** ▶ (1799–1869) British statesman; Conservative prime minister (1852, 1858–59, 1866–68). He became leader of the Conservative Party after the defection (1846) of the Peelites over the ▷Corn Laws. His government introduced the Jewish Relief Act (1858) and the ▷Reform Act (1867).

● **Derbyshire** ▶ A county in N central England. Under local government reorganization in 1974 it lost part of the NE to South Yorkshire, while gaining part of NE Cheshire; Derby city became an independent ▷unitary authority in 1997. It consists of lowlands in the SE rising to the ▷Peak District in the NW. The main rivers are the Derwent, Trent, Dove, and Rother. Sheep farming is important in the N, while dairy farming predominates in the S. Heavy industry and mining are in decline and service industries are increasingly important. Area (excluding Derby city): 2551 sq km (985 sq mi). Population (1996 est, excluding Derby city): 728 300. Administrative centre: Matlock.

● **Derby ware** ▶ Porcelain first produced by William Duesbury (1725–86) at Derby in the 1750s. Early produce resembles ▷Chelsea porcelain and Duesbury later bought the Chelsea works (1770). Utility products were decorated in blue, red, and gilt "Japan" patterns, but important portrait and fictional figures were also made in quantity. After Duesbury's death the factory was run by his son and the products were known as Crown Derby (1786–1811) from the marks used. In 1811 the factory was bought by Robert Bloor, whose products (1811–48) were known as Bloor-Derby. The products of an entirely new firm, started in 1876 and still running, are also sometimes called Crown Derby (but not by collectors).

● **dermatitis** ▶ Inflammation of the skin, characterized by an itching red rash that may become scaly. Dermatitis usually results from contact with irritant or allergy-provoking substances but it may be a reaction to infections, drugs, or radiation or it may occur without obvious cause, in which case it is more properly referred to as **eczema** (in many contexts, however, the term eczema is used synonymously with dermatitis). Treatment is aimed at removing the cause and easing the condition with creams.

● **dermatology** ▷*See* skin.

● **Dermot MacMurrough** ▶ (?1110–71) King of Leinster. After being defeated by rival kings and banished (1166) from Ireland, he regained his kingdom (1169–70) with English aid.

● **dernier** ▶ A unit of weight, used to measure the fineness of woven materials, equal to 1 gram per 9000 metres.

● **Derrida, Jacques** ▶ (1930–) French philosopher of ▷poststructuralism. He originated the philosophical method known as deconstruction, which assumes that words have no fixed reference point and that all written texts contradict themselves. His works include *Of Grammatology* and *Writing and Difference* (both 1967) and *Of Spirit* (1987).

● **Derris** ▶ A genus of tropical woody vines (80 species), especially *D. elliptica* of the East Indies, the roots of which contain rotenone, a useful insecticide. Family: ▷Leguminosae.

● **Derry** ▶ **1.** A district in NE Northern Ireland, in Co Londonderry. Area: 373 sq km (144 sq mi). Population (1991): 95 371. **2.** ▷*See* Londonderry.

● **dervishes** ▶ Members of Sufi religious brotherhoods (*see* Sufism), which hold various esoteric beliefs and have spread throughout Islam since the 12th century AD. Many of them perform ecstatic rituals, such as hypnotic chanting and whirling dancing, at prayer meetings (called *zikrs*). The dervishes of the Mevlevi order, founded in Anatolia (Turkey) in the 13th century, are famous for their dancing and are commonly called "whirling dervishes."

● **Derwent, River** ▶ The name of several rivers in England, including: **1.** A river in N central England, flowing SE from N Derbyshire to the River Trent. Length: 96 km (60 mi). **2.** A river in N England, flowing S from the North York Moors to join the River Ouse between Selby and Goole. Length: 92 km (57 mi). **3.** A river in NW England, flowing N and W from the Borrowdale Fells in Cumbria to the Irish Sea. Length: 54 km (34 mi).

● **Derwent Water** ▶ A lake in NW England, in Cumbria in the Lake District. A popular tourist area, it is noted for its picturesque scenery. Area: about 8 sq km (3 sq mi).

● **Desai, (Shri) Morarji (Ranchhodji)** ▶ (1896–1995) Indian statesman; prime minister from 1977 until his resignation in 1979. As a young man he was a follower of Mahatma ▷Gandhi. Later, in the Congress Party, he came to oppose Indira Gandhi and during the state of emergency declared during her first administration he was imprisoned. In the 1977 elections he defeated her to become prime minister as leader of the new Janata Party.

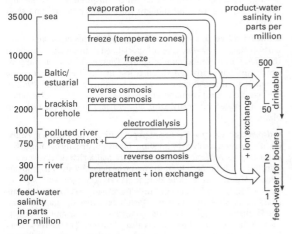

desalination ▶ The initial and final salinities for various desalination techniques and feed-water sources.

● **desalination** ▶ The removal of salt from brine to produce fresh water. Desalination is used to irrigate arid regions in which sea water is available, especially if solar power can be used as an energy source. Several methods are employed, the most common being evaporation of the sea water by heat or by reducing the pressure on it (flash evaporation). The vapour is condensed to form relatively pure water. Freezing is another technique; pure ice forms from brine as it freezes. The method theoretically requires less energy than evaporation but the process is slower and technically more difficult. Reverse ▷osmosis is another method used. Pure water and salt water are contained on either side of a permeable membrane. The pressure of the salt water is raised above the osmotic pressure, causing water to pass from the brine to the pure side. Because the osmotic pressure required is about 25 atmospheres there are difficulties with large-scale application. In electrodialysis, the ions are subjected to an electric field instead of increased pressure, the positive and negative ions being filtered off through separate membranes. Another method used for low salinities is ion exchange; in this method the salt ions are chemically removed from the solution.

● **Descartes, René** ▶ (1596–1650) French philosopher, one of the most original thinkers of all time. After a Jesuit education he spent nine years in travel and military service before turning to study. After 1628 he settled in Holland, where he lived until 1649, when Queen Christina invited him to Sweden. Here the cold climate and predawn tutorials with the queen caused a fatal attack of pneumonia.

Descartes' *Discourse on Method* (1637) introduced his technique of methodical doubt, which he developed in his greatest work the *Meditations* (1641). Asking "How and what do I know?" he arrived by a process of reduction at his famous statement "Cogito ergo sum" ("I think, therefore I am"). From this core of certainty he proceeded to prove to his own satisfaction God's existence (he was a sincere and lifelong Roman Catholic) and hence the existence of everything else. The importance of this approach lies not in what he proves or discards but in making ▷epistemology the gateway to knowledge.

Equally influential was his dualism: he considered that the world was composed of two different kinds of substance—mind (*res cogitans*), which is the essence of human beings, and matter (*res extensa*). Descartes never satisfactorily answered the problem he thus set of how mind and matter can interact—nor has anyone else.

A distinguished mathematician and scientist, Descartes also contributed to the foundations of geometry (*see* coordinate systems) and optics. He held that mathematics was the supreme science in that the whole phenomenal world could be interpreted in terms of mathematical laws. He avoided confrontation with the Church by hiving off the realm of mathematics from that of theology and by cautiously suppressing his acceptance of the correctness of the Copernican system (*see* Copernicus, Nicolaus).

● **descent** ▶ The social recognition of biological relationship to a common ancestor. All societies limit the extent to which such relationships are traced but to differing degrees and in different ways. In many primitive societies the descent system is the basis of group membership, property and other rights, and social status. Unilineal systems count descent in one line only and are termed patrilineal or agnatic when this is through males and matrilineal or uxorial when through females. Double unilineal systems count both lines but for distinct purposes. Cognatic systems, usually found in more advanced societies, count descent in either line. ▷*See also* matriarchy.

● **desensitization** ▶ In immunology, a method of treating some ▷allergies, such as hay fever. Small amounts of the substance (allergen) that provokes the symptoms of the allergy are injected at intervals. This stimulates the production of ▷antibodies in the blood that will combine with the allergen during subsequent exposure and prevent it from reacting with a different set of antibodies, attached to certain cells, to cause the allergic symptoms.

● **desert** ▶ A virtually barren area of land where precipitation is minimal and sporadic, limiting vegetation growth. The mean annual rainfall is usually taken as being below 250 mm (10 in) for desert conditions to exist. Deserts may occur in areas of high atmospheric pressure, such as the ▷Sahara, or near the W coast of continents cooled by cold ocean currents (e.g. the ▷Atacama and ▷Kalahari Deserts). They are also found in continental interiors where mountain barriers restrict precipitation, such as the ▷Gobi Desert. Many deserts are characterized by stony scrublands with occasional resistant rock uplands and some areas of shifting sand dunes. The wind is an important agent of erosion and the rain, falling as violent downpours, is capable of moving large amounts of debris.

● **Desert cultures** ▶ A group of Stone Age North American cultures in Nevada, Utah, Arizona, and New Mexico dating from the period 8000–2000 BC. Adapted to arid or semiarid conditions, they were based upon hunting small game and gathering wild plant foods in small nomadic groups. Baskets, milling stones, bone tools, and chipped stone weapon points were made.

● **desertification** ▶ The process by which arid or semiarid areas

desertification ▶ Fences are built to keep the Sahara sand from encroaching in Mauritania.

become deserts through human action or climatic change. Removal of the topsoil, by artificial means or erosion by wind, water, or desiccation, results in a reduction in the ground's water-storage capacity, which can cause crops to fail. Overintensive farming and the cutting of trees for firewood helped to create the ▷Dust Bowl in the USA and have caused deserts in Africa and SW Asia (including Australia) to advance by several kilometres each year. Solutions are now based on effective management of surface cover and climate as well as restrictions to prevent overpopulation of susceptible areas. ▷See also deforestation.

● **desert rat** ▷See jerboa.

● **De Sica, Vittorio** ▶ (1901–74) Italian film director. His postwar films, in which he treated contemporary social themes with compassion and political awareness, included such examples of ▷Neorealism as *Shoeshine* (1946), *Bicycle Thieves* (1948), and *Umberto D* (1952). His later films included several romantic comedies.

● **Desiderio da Settignano** ▶ (c. 1430–64) Italian Renaissance sculptor. Working chiefly in Florence, he specialized in marble portrait busts. His tomb for the humanist Carlo Marsuppini (Sta Croce, Florence) is renowned.

● **Design Centre** ▶ A British exhibition centre, where selected British products are displayed to promote good design. The first centre opened in the Haymarket, London, in 1956; other centres have since been opened in Glasgow and Cardiff. They are run by the Design Council and are partly funded by the government.

● **desk-top publishing** ▶ (DTP) The use of computers to enable small companies or individuals to produce reports, magazines, etc., to typeset quality. A DTP system usually includes a small computer and a ▷laser printer with suitable DTP software. If the reproduction of photographs is required a scanner is needed. Complete books can also be typeset by DTP, the system either producing camera-ready copy or film, enabling a printer to make printing plates. In the most recent technology PostScript files can be produced to enable the printer to make the printing plates without going through the film stage. ▷See also typesetting.

● **desman** ▶ A small aquatic mammal belonging to the family *Talpidae* (moles). The Russian desman (*Desmana moschata*) is about 20 cm long; the Pyrenean desman (*Galemys pyrenaicus*) is smaller. They have webbed hind feet, live in burrows in river banks, and feed on invertebrates and fish.

● **Des Moines** ▶ 41 35N 93 35W A city in the USA, the capital of Iowa. Founded in 1843, it has developed into an important industrial and commercial centre situated in the heart of the Corn Belt. Population (1996 est): 193 422.

● **Desmond, Gerald Fitzgerald, 15th Earl of** ▶ (c.1538–1583) Anglo-Irish magnate, who opposed the imposition of English authority on Ireland. Periodically imprisoned in the 1560s and 1570s, his 1579 rebellion led to his being outlawed. He was captured and killed. His confiscated estates formed the basis of the Munster ▷Plantation.

● **Desmoulins, Camille** ▶ (1760–94) French revolutionary and journalist. His fiery oratory contributed to the storming of the ▷Bastille (14 July, 1789), and in 1792 he became a stern critic of the Girondins. Subsequently counselling moderation, he was arrested with the followers of ▷Danton and guillotined. His best-known work is his *Histoire des Brissotins* (1793).

● **des Prez, Josquin** ▷See Josquin des Prez.

● **Dessalines, Jean Jacques** ▶ (c. 1758–1806) Emperor of Haiti (1804–06). He rose to military pre-eminence in the slave revolt led by ▷Toussaint-L'Ouverture. When Toussaint was captured by the French in 1802 Dessalines assumed the leadership of the Haitians and with British help defeated the French (1803). His habitual cruelty as emperor provoked a palace revolution, during which he was assassinated.

● **Dessau** ▶ 51 41N 12 14E A city in central Germany, on the River Mulde. Dessau was the former capital of Anhalt state. Many of its historic buildings were destroyed during World War II. Production of armaments, vehicles, and machinery are the main industries. Population (1991): 95 100.

● **destroyer** ▶ A fast heavily armed naval vessel that is smaller than a ▷cruiser, has a displacement of about 3000 tonnes, and is 110–150 m (330–450 ft) long. Destroyers are not armoured. Because of their speed, armament, and versatility, they are employed in antisubmarine warfare, in convoy work, and in "hunter-killer" attack groups consisting of one carrier and five or six destroyers. Smaller **destroyer escorts** were used in World War II mainly to protect convoys.

● **Destutt, Antoine Louis Claude, Comte de Tracy** ▶ (1754–1836) French philosopher and politician. He narrowly escaped the guillotine during the French Revolution. In prison he planned his *Éléments d'idéologie* (1801–15), in which, inspired by ▷Locke and ▷Condillac, he derives all thought from sensory "ideas" and their combinations.

● **detached retina** ▶ A condition in which the inner and outer parts of the ▷retina—the layer of specialized light-sensitive tissue at the back of the eye—become separated from each other. It happens slowly and painlessly and vision is lost in the affected part of the retina. Retinal detachment is caused by injury or inflammation in the eye and is most common in very short-sighted people. Detached retina is treated surgically using a laser beam to weld the retina in place.

● **detective story** ▶ A genre of popular fiction in which a mystery, often a murder, is solved by logic and intuition, usually by an individual detective. Ancient Chinese literature had a rich detective tradition, but in the modern West the first true detective story is probably ▷Poe's "Murders in the Rue Morgue" (1841). The form was popularized in England by Wilkie ▷Collins's *The Moonstone* (1868) and the appearance of Sir Arthur Conan ▷Doyle's detective Sherlock Holmes. The English tradition is typified by Agatha ▷Christie and Dorothy L. ▷Sayers. In the 1930s the tersely realistic "thrillers" of the US writers Dashiell ▷Hammett and Raymond ▷Chandler began a different trend. G. K. ▷Chesterton, "Nicholas Blake" (C. ▷Day-Lewis), Georges ▷Simenon, P. D. ▷James, and Ruth ▷Rendell, among others, have raised it far above a merely popular level.

● **detergents** ▶ Chemicals used for cleansing. Although the term includes ▷soaps it is usually applied in a more restricted sense to synthetic ▷surfactants. Such detergents have large molecules, typically composed of a hydrocarbon oil-soluble part and a water-soluble part. Alkyl sulphonates are common examples. These compounds are thus able to promote the solution of oil, grease, etc., in water. Household detergents also contain builders, water softeners, bleaches, and fabric brighteners.

● **determinant** ▷See matrix.

● **determinism** ▶ The philosophical theory that every event has a cause and that all events are determined by causal physical laws. One view holds that determinism means that every event could be causally explained and could be predicted if the conditions are not too complex for analysis. A stronger view is that a specific event could not have failed to happen, or was predetermined. Applied to human actions, determinism appears to conflict with the concept of ▷free will. If even desires, intentions, and motives are determined or conditioned (as some psychologists believe) and if actions are, in principle, predictable, this contradicts the idea that actions are freely chosen, and hence throws doubt on the concept of moral responsibility. However, some philosophers believe that determinism and free will are compatible and that a person acts freely if his desires are the cause of his actions. ▷See also predestination.

● **Detmold** ▶ 51 56N 08 52E A town in NW Germany, in North Rhine-Westphalia. The capital of the former state of Lippe, it has two palaces. German tribes defeated the Romans here in 9 AD. It has furniture and metallurgical industries. Population (1992 est): 70 970.

● **detonator** ▶ A sensitive primary explosive used to ignite a less sensitive high explosive. Detonators may be initiated by percussion, flash, or electrical current. The less sensitive and safer the high explosive is to handle, the stronger the detonator required. Some high explosives require two-stage detonation. A common detonator is mercury fulminate.

● **Detroit** ▶ 42 23N 83 05W A city in the USA, in Michigan on the Detroit River. Founded in 1701, it was largely rebuilt following a fire in 1805. The fifth largest city in the USA, it is dominated by the motor-vehicle industry. A major port (serving the Great Lakes) and rail centre, its other industries include chemicals, steel, and oil refining. It has two universities. Population (1996 est): 1 000 272.

● **Dettingen, Battle of** ▶ (27 June, 1743) A battle in the War of the ▷Austrian Succession in which British, Austrian, and Hanoverian troops commanded by George II defeated a French and Bavarian army near Dettingen in Bavaria. It was the last time that a British sovereign appeared on a battlefield.

● **Deucalion** ▶ In Greek legend, the son of Prometheus and father of Hellen, the ancestor of the Greek race. Warned of the flood sent by Zeus to destroy mankind, he and his wife Pyrrha survived on a boat and repopulated the earth.

● **Deus, João de** ▶ (1830–96) Portuguese poet. His first book, *Flores do campo* (1868), was praised for its simplicity and directness; after the publication of *Campo de flores* (1893) he was acclaimed as a leading poet. His advanced method of teaching reading was officially adopted in 1888.

● **deus ex machina** ▶ (Latin: god from the machinery) A sudden and improbable intervention that resolves an involved situation. The term refers to the convention in ancient Greek drama in which a god was lowered by a crane to unravel the plot.

● **deuterium** ▶ (D; *or* heavy hydrogen ^{2}H) An ▷isotope of ▷hydrogen having a nucleus consisting of one proton and one neutron. It occurs naturally in hydrogen to an extent of about 0.0156%. It can be separated from the more common isotope by electrolysis of water. It is used as a radioactive tracer. Heavy water (deuterium oxide; D_2O) is used in nuclear reactors (*see also* nuclear energy; thermonuclear reactor). At no 1; at wt 2.014.

● **Deuteronomy** ▶ The fifth book of the Old Testament, traditionally attributed to Moses, although this is no longer accepted by scholars; it may have been compiled in the 7th century BC. It is a series of addresses by Moses to the Israelites immediately before they enter Canaan (Palestine). After repeating the ▷Ten Commandments, he gives a code of religious and civil laws to be observed in Canaan, blesses those who keep the ▷covenant and curses those who disobey the Law, appoints Joshua as his successor, and gives custody of the book of the Law to the ▷Levites. The book closes with the song of Moses and his death.

● **De Valera, Eamon** ▶ (1882–1975) Irish statesman; prime minister (1932–48, 1951–54, 1957–59) and president (1959–73). A commandant in the 1916 ▷Easter Rising, he escaped execution because of his US birth. While in prison he was elected to the British parliament and became the president of ▷Sinn Féin (1918). He escaped from prison in 1919 and became president of the self-declared Irish Republic. However, he rejected the Anglo-Irish treaty of 1921 (*see* Home Rule), which had been negotiated by his own plenipotentiaries (*see* Collins, Michael), because it fell short of complete independence for the whole island. In the ensuing civil war he backed the republican opposition, leading to his imprisonment by the Irish Free State. In 1926 he founded the constitutional ▷Fianna Fáil party, which formed the government from 1932. As prime minister De Valera cut Ireland's remaining links with the UK and kept his country neutral during World War II.

● **de Valois, Dame Ninette** ▶ (Edris Stannus; 1898–2001) British ballet dancer and choreographer, born in Ireland. During the 1920s she worked with Diaghilev's Ballets Russes. In 1931 she founded the Sadler's Wells Ballet, the company that became the ▷Royal Ballet in 1956. She retired in 1963 and was appointed to the OM in 1992.

● **devaluation** ▶ A downward change in the value of one country's currency in terms of other currencies. A country that devalues makes its exports cheaper and its imports more expensive; thus devaluation should help correct a ▷balance-of-payments deficit by increasing the volume of exports and decreasing the volume of imports. The mea-

sure is not always effective, however, because the increased import bill may be larger than the increase in receipts from exports: this is likely if the ▷demand for the country's exports is elastic, while demand for the imports is inelastic. Under the Bretton Woods fixed-rate system (*see* Bretton Woods Conference) devaluations, such as that undertaken by the UK in 1967, only occurred occasionally but were large and destabilizing. In the floating-rate system that replaced it, the value of a currency was determined by supply and demand with a minimum of government interference; as a consequence devaluations were gradual. In the ▷European Community (now the EU), the ▷European Monetary System was intended to stabilize currencies so that devaluation became unnecessary but had clearly failed in this aim by September, 1992. In 1998 11 EU states committed themselves to adopt a single European currency, the euro, which became operational in January, 1999.

● **Devanagari** ▶ An alphabetic ▷writing system used for ▷Sanskrit, ▷Hindi, and certain other languages of India. It has 48 letters and is written from left to right. Vowels are frequently omitted, a short *a* being understood after each consonant unless a different vowel is specified. It was developed from the ancient Brahmi script, which was probably derived from Aramaic in the 7th or 8th century BC. It is therefore related to the Hebrew, Arabic, Greek, and Roman alphabets.

● **developing countries** ▶ Countries that do not have sophisticated industries and consequently have a low per capita income. They include almost all the countries in Africa, Asia, and South America. The economies of these so-called Third World countries are characterized by abundant cheap unskilled labour and a scarcity of capital for investment. Nearly 80% of the world's population lives in developing countries in largely agricultural economies from which poverty, hunger, disease, and illiteracy have not been eliminated. Many of these economies rely shakily on one main crop, which in years of crop failure, poor world demand, or low market prices can cause severe hardship. ▷*See also* Non-Aligned Movement.

● **Deventer** ▶ 52 16N 6 10E A town in the E central Netherlands, in Overijssel province on the River IJssel. During the middle ages it was a major educational centre; Erasmus and Thomas à Kempis studied here. It is the centre of an agricultural area. Population (1994): 69 079.

● **Devil** ▶ In Christian tradition, the personification of evil, who seeks to tempt mankind away from the path of salvation and rules in ▷hell. The name comes from the Greek *diabolos*, meaning accuser or calumniator. Doctrine holds that God created the Devil good and he became evil of his own free will by committing sin (commonly thought to have been the sin of pride).

The Devil is identified with the great red dragon cast out of heaven by Michael (Revelation 12.3–9) and also with such Old Testament figures as the archangel **Lucifer** (who sought to make himself God's equal and was expelled from heaven), the serpent that tempted Eve (Genesis 3.1–6), and **Satan** the tormentor of Job. He is also known as **Beelzebub** (Hebrew: lord of flies). Similar figures exist in other religions originating in the Middle East: ▷Iblis in Islam and Ahriman (*see* Ahura Mazda) in Zoroastrianism.

● **devil ray** ▷*See* manta ray.

● **devil's coach horse** ▶ A large carnivorous beetle, *Staphylinus olens*, also called a cock-tail. About 25 mm long, it occurs commonly in gardens of W Europe. If threatened it curls its flexible abdomen upward and forward and releases an offensive odour. Family: *Staphylinidae* (*see* rove beetle).

● **Devil's Island** ▶ (French name: Île du Diable) 5 16N 52 34W One of the three Îles du Salut, off the coast of French Guiana in the S Caribbean Sea. It contained a leper colony before becoming a French penal settlement (1895–1938). Area: less than 2 sq km (1 sq mi).

● **Devine, George** ▶ (1910–65) British theatre manager, director, and actor. He taught at the London Theatre Studio from 1936 to 1939, and, after World War II, was director of the Young Vic Company. In 1956 he founded the English Stage Company and presented many influential plays by new writers at the Royal Court Theatre in London.

● **Devizes** ▸ 51 22N 1 59W A market town in S England, in Wiltshire. Its 12th-century castle was destroyed by Cromwell. Agricultural products include bacon, ham, and dairy products. Population (1991): 13 205.

● **devolution** ▸ The delegation of political powers from a central government to regional governments. In the UK the establishment of the ▷Stormont parliament in Northern Ireland was the first important act of devolution. Growing nationalist sentiment in Scotland and Wales led to the introduction of two devolution bills in 1976 and the holding of referendums in March, 1979. In Wales there was an absolute majority against devolution; in Scotland the vote in favour fell short of the 40% of the electorate needed to put the plans into effect. In 1997 new plans to establish a Welsh assembly and a Scottish parliament were endorsed in referendums and the first elections to these bodies took place in May, 1999. Following the Good Friday Agreement (1998) an assembly with a power-sharing executive was established in Northern Ireland and power was devolved in late 1999; failure to achieve progress on the decommissioning of terrorist weapons led the British government to suspend the assembly and executive from February to May 2000.

● **Devolution, War of** ▸ (1667–68) The conflict between France and Spain for the Spanish Netherlands, which ▷Louis XIV of France claimed had devolved (descended) to him through his wife Maria Theresa, daughter of Philip IV of Spain (1605–65; reigned 1621–65). Louis' troops, under ▷Turenne and ▷Vauban, invaded the Netherlands but withdrew when an alliance between England, the United Provinces of the Netherlands, and Sweden threatened to intervene. Peace was made at Aix-la-Chapelle.

● **Devon** ▸ A county of SW England, bordering on the Atlantic Ocean in the N and the English Channel in the S. It consists mainly of undulating hills, rising to ▷Dartmoor in the S and ▷Exmoor in the NE. The chief rivers are the Dart, Exe, and Tamar. Agriculture includes dairy farming in the S and E (producing the famous clotted cream), beef cattle in the N and W, and sheep farming in the NE. Cider is also produced. Industry is concentrated on Exeter and Plymouth, a major naval base. Tourism is centred on the coastal resorts, especially Torquay, Paignton, and Ilfracombe. Plymouth and Torbay became ▷unitary authorities in 1998. Area (excluding unitary authorities): 6569 sq km (2536 sq mi). Population (1996 est, excluding unitary authorities): 680 100. Administrative centre: Exeter.

● **Devonian period** ▸ A geological period of the Upper Palaeozoic era, between the Silurian and Carboniferous periods. It lasted from about 415 to 370 million years ago. It is divided into seven stages, based on invertebrate fossil remains, such as corals, brachiopods, ammonoids, and crinoids. The rocks containing these fossils were marine deposits but the Devonian period also shows extensive continental deposits (Old Red Sandstone). Fossils from these rocks include fish, land plants, and freshwater molluscs.

● **Devonshire, Spencer Compton Cavendish, 8th Duke of** ▸ (1833–1908) British Liberal politician, known from 1858 to 1891 as Lord Hartington. Postmaster general in Gladstone's 1868–74 ministry, he led the Liberals during Gladstone's temporary retirement (1874–80). In 1882 he became secretary for war but subsequently failed to persuade the cabinet to hasten the relief of ▷Gordon in Khartoum. He opposed Irish ▷Home Rule, leaving the Liberal Party to form the Liberal Unionist Party, which defeated Gladstone's Home Rule bills (1886, 1893). He subsequently served in Lord Salisbury's coalition ministry (1895–1902) and under Balfour (1902–05).

● **de Vries, Hugo Marie** ▸ (1848–1935) Dutch botanist, who first recognized the importance of ▷mutation. De Vries observed how, occasionally, a new variety would arise from his plant-breeding experiments. He realized that this sudden variation, which he termed mutation, could play an important part in the evolution of living things. De Vries worked out his own laws of inheritance only to discover, in 1900, ▷Mendel's work, which had previously been ignored.

● **dew** ▸ The condensation of moisture, which forms on the ground or on objects near the ground, especially at night. It occurs when the cool air near the ground falls to a temperature, called the **dew point**, at which it becomes saturated and the water vapour present condenses into water droplets.

● **Dewar, Donald (Campbell)** ▸ (1937–2000) Scottish Labour politician and lawyer: first minister of Scotland (1999–2000). He served as secretary of state for Scotland from 1997 until the establishment of the Scottish parliament in 1999.

● **Dewar flask** ▸ (Thermos flask *or* vacuum flask) A flask, used to store a substance at constant temperature. It has double glass walls, the space between the walls being evacuated to prevent heat loss by conduction. The inside wall is silvered to prevent heat loss by radiation and the flask is tightly stoppered to prevent heat loss by convection or evaporation. Also known as the Thermos or vacuum flask, it was invented by the scientist Sir James Dewar (1842–1923).

● **dewberry** ▸ A straggling Eurasian shrub, *Rubus caesius*, very similar to the ▷blackberry but with weaker creeping stems and fewer prickles. The fruit has a purplish bloom. The name is also applied to many trailing North American *Rubus* species. Family: *Rosaceae*.

● **de Wet, Christian Rudolf** ▸ (1854–1922) Afrikaner politician and soldier. De Wet commanded the Orange Free State forces in the second ▷Boer War. He was later minister of agriculture in the Orange Free State (1907–10). In 1914 he led a revolt against Botha's plan to conquer German South West Africa and was imprisoned for treason.

● **Dewey, George** ▸ (1837–1917) US admiral. He first saw action in the Civil War. During the Spanish-American War (1898) he defeated the Spanish fleet in Manila Bay.

● **Dewey, John** ▸ (1859–1952) US philosopher and educationalist. A prominent exponent of ▷pragmatism, Dewey believed thinking arises where practical problems arise. In works such as *Reconstruction in Philosophy* (1920) he urged the reconstitution of philosophy to confront present experience. He held that theorizing was, properly, instrumental in problem-solving—hence the term "instrumentalism," applied to his philosophy; education had concentrated on past experience instead of equipping students to deal with present and future.

● **Dewey Decimal Classification** ▸ An international system for classifying and arranging the books in a library, originated in 1873 by Melvil Dewey (1851–1931) for the Amherst College Library. Books are divided according to subject matter into ten groups, each group having a hundred numbers; principle subdivisions within each group are divided by ten, and with the use of decimal numbers further subdivisions can be generated without limit (e.g. 300: Social Sciences; 370: Education; 372: Elementary Education; 372.3: Elementary Education, Science and Health). Constantly revised, the system is now in its 18th edition. ▷*See also* Universal Decimal Classification.

● **De Wint, Peter** ▸ (1784–1849) British landscape painter of Dutch descent. One of the leading watercolourists of his day, he trained under the London painter and engraver John Raphael Smith (1752–1812) and was influenced by ▷Girtin. Many of his landscapes are of Lincolnshire.

● **Dewsbury** ▸ 53 42N 1 37W A town in N England, in Kirklees unitary authority, West Yorkshire, on the River Calder. It was a centre of the heavy-woollen industry. Population (1991): 50 168.

● **dextrose** ▷*See* glucose.

● **Dhahran** ▸ 26 18N 50 05E A new town in E Saudi Arabia, on the Persian Gulf coast opposite Bahrain. It ships out oil brought by pipeline from the Abqaiq area just inland.

● **Dhaka** ▸ (name until 1982: Dacca) 23 42N 90 22E The capital of Bangladesh, situated in the SE of the country, on the Burhi Ganga River. It is a riverport and commercial and industrial centre producing various textiles and jute. The university was founded in 1921.

History: with a long history of human settlement, it became the capital of the Bengal province of the Mogul Empire in the 17th century. In the 18th century it came under British rule, and upon independence in 1947 was made capital of East Pakistan. Population (1991): 3 839 000.

● **dharma** ▸ A Sanskrit term with various religious and philosophical meanings. In Buddhism it signifies the truth, the teaching of the Buddha in whole or in part. It also denotes the law regarding the ultimate nature of things. In Hinduism, it refers to social law or caste duty.

● **Dhaulagiri, Mount** ▶ 28 39N 83 28E A mountain in NW central Nepal, in the Himalayas. It was first climbed in 1960 by a Swiss team. Height: 8172 m (26 810 ft).

● **dhole** ▶ A wild ▷dog, *Cuon alpinus*, of SE Asia, Sumatra, and Java. Dholes are reddish brown, about 1.4 m long including the tail (40 cm); they hunt in packs of 5–40 individuals, attacking mainly deer and antelope but occasionally even tigers.

● **diabetes** ▶ One of several diseases with a common symptom—the production of large quantities of urine. The term usually refers to **diabetes mellitus** (*or* sugar diabetes), in which the body is unable to utilize sugars to produce energy due to a deficiency of the pancreatic hormone ▷insulin. Symptoms include thirst, weight loss, and a high level of glucose in the urine and in the blood (hyperglycaemia), which—if untreated—leads to coma. Possible long-term complications of diabetes include damage to the arteries, especially in the eyes (which can affect vision). There appears to be a certain tendency to inherit diabetes, which is often triggered by such factors as physical stress. In children the disease appears more suddenly and is usually more severe than in older people. Treatment is based on a carefully controlled diet, often with insulin injections or pills to reduce the amount of sugar in the blood.

    Diabetes insipidus is a rare disease due to a deficiency of the pituitary hormone antidiuretic hormone (ADH, *or* vasopressin), which regulates water balance in the body. The patient produces large quantities of watery urine and is always thirsty. It is treated with doses of the hormone.

● **Diaghilev, Sergei (Pavlovich)** ▶ (1872–1929) Russian ballet impresario. He began his career in the imperial theatres in St Petersburg in 1899 and between 1904 and 1908 organized art exhibitions there and in Paris. His first theatrical production, the opera *Boris Godunov*, staged at the Paris Opéra (1908), was followed by his season of Russian ballet (1909). Its success resulted in the organization of a permanent company (1911), known as the ▷Ballets Russes, which Diaghilev directed until his death.

● **dialect** ▶ A variation of a language, as spoken in a particular district or by a particular group of people. Because it involves the use of nonstandard words and grammatical constructions, dialect should not be confused with ▷accent, which is simply a matter of pronunciation. The distinction between language and dialect is not clear cut. As a general rule any two dialects of a language may be expected to be mutually comprehensible. But, for example, the various "dialects" of Chinese are quite separate, being held together only by a common ideographic writing system, while Dutch, Flemish, and Afrikaans are called separate languages for political reasons, although there is a considerable degree of mutual comprehensibility and they might therefore reasonably be regarded as different dialects of the same language. Dialects develop as a result of geographical separation: slightly differing versions of one original language develop in different places within a generation or so of the time of separation.

● **dialectical materialism** ▶ The official philosophy of ▷Marxism. Materialism, as opposed to ▷idealism, Marx and Engels derived from contemporary (1850) science; dialectic, or argument from thesis and antithesis to synthesis, they borrowed from Hegel's idealism. Engels even proposed a dialectical theory of evolution. As philosophy, not surprisingly, dialectical materialism is obscure and apparently unrelated to Marxist political theory. However, **historical materialism**, expounded in the *Communist Manifesto*, is a coherent account of history on an economic basis: for every system of production there is an appropriate organization of class and property. While economic forces continually develop production systems, the class and property structure remains unchanged, causing tension between economic forces and social relations, which continues until the ultimate rational socialist society evolves.

● **dialysis** ▶ A process, discovered by Thomas Graham (1804–69), for separating mixtures of fluids by diffusion through a semipermeable membrane. Different substances in a solution diffuse at different rates. The passage of large particles, such as ▷colloids, is almost com-

pletely blocked by a semipermeable membrane, whereas salt solutions pass through easily. **Haemodialysis** (the dialysis of blood) is used in artificial kidney machines (**dialysers**), which take over the function of diseased kidneys by filtering waste material from the blood. The technique was introduced in the 1940s and is widely used on patients awaiting a kidney transplant.

● **diamagnetism** ▶ A form of magnetism occurring in materials that when placed in a ▷magnetic field, have an internal field proportional to but less than that outside. Such substances tend to orientate themselves at right angles to the direction of the ▷flux and tend to move from the stronger part of a field to the weaker part. Diamagnetism is caused by the motion of atomic electrons, which, since they are charged, constitute a current. This current tends to oppose the magnetic field in accordance with ▷Lenz's law.

● **diamond** ▶ The hardest known mineral, comprising a cubic variety of crystalline ▷carbon, formed under intense heat and pressure. Diamonds are found in ancient volcanic pipes, mainly in S Africa and Siberia, and in deposits off the coast of Namibia. Over 80% of diamonds mined are used industrially, mainly for cutting and grinding tools; the others are used as gems. One of the largest diamonds discovered is the ▷Cullinan diamond (3106 carats), found in 1905 at Pretoria. Many industrial diamonds are produced synthetically from graphite subjected to very high temperatures and pressures (above 3000°C and 100 000 atmospheres). Birthstone for April.

● **diamondback** ▶ The largest and most dangerous ▷rattlesnake. The eastern diamondback (*Crotalus adamanteus*) and the Western diamondback (*C. atrox*) may reach lengths of 2.5 m.

● **diamondbird** ▶ An Australasian ▷flowerpecker of the genus *Pardalotus* (7–8 species), about 8 cm long with a short tail and a white-spotted plumage. Diamondbirds feed on insects and nest in tree holes and rock crevices.

● **diamorphine** ▷*See* heroin.

● **Diana** ▶ The Roman goddess identified with the Greek Artemis, associated with women and childbirth and with the moon. She is usually represented as a virgin huntress armed with bow and arrows. The position of priest at her shrine of Ariccia (Italy) was customarily held by a runaway slave, who murdered his predecessor.

Diana, Princess of Wales ▶ On a visit to Angola in 1997 to support the Red Cross campaign to outlaw landmines.

● **Diana, Princess of Wales** ▶ (1961–97) Former wife of Prince ▷Charles and mother of Prince William (1982–) and Prince Harry (1984–). As Lady Diana Spencer, daughter of the 8th Earl Spencer (1924–92) and his first wife, Frances Roche (1936–), she married Prince Charles in 1981; they separated in 1993 and divorced in 1996. She was killed in a car crash in Paris, with her companion Dodi Fayed. An icon of fashion and a woman of remarkable beauty, she enhanced the images of many charities, especially those concerned with the victims of AIDS and landmines. She controversially made public her own frailties, including adultery and an eating disorder, her anguish over Prince Charles's relationship with Camilla Parker Bowles, and her disapproval of the Palace establishment. Her premature death caused an unprecedented display of public grief, her funeral procession being witnessed by a sombre crowd estimated at 2 million and a TV audience of some 2.6 billion worldwide. Some public disquiet arising from the apparent indifference shown by members of the House of Windsor to Diana's death, encouraged by critical remarks made by Earl Spencer at his sister's funeral, resulted in a number of changes in royal protocol aimed at modernizing the monarchy. ▷*See also* Althorp House.

● **Diane de Poitiers, Duchesse de Valentinois** ▶ (1499–1566) The mistress of ▷Henry II of France, who was 20 years her junior. She dominated court life until his death in 1559, when she was forced by Henry's wife ▷Catherine de' Medici to retire to Chaumont.

● **Dianthus** ▶ A genus of annual and perennial herbs (300 species), mainly from Europe and Asia, having flower stems (often branched) with swollen joints and showy white, pink, or red flowers. Common species include *D. barbatus* (*see* sweet william), *D. caryophyllus* (*see* carnation), and *D. plumarius* (*see* pink). Family: *Caryophyllaceae*.

● **diaphragm** ▶ 1. In anatomy, a dome-shaped sheet of muscle that separates the thorax (chest cavity) from the abdomen. The diaphragm is attached to the spine, lower ribs, and breastbone and contains a large opening through which the oesophagus (gullet) passes. It plays an important role in producing breathing movements (*see* respiration). 2. ▷*See* contraception.

● **diarrhoea** ▶ The frequent passing of liquid stools, usually more than three times a day. It is a symptom, not a disease; causes include anxiety, infection or inflammation of the intestines, impaired absorption of food, and side effects of drugs. It can be eased by the use of drugs but proper treatment must aim at eliminating the cause.

● **Dias, Bartolomeu** ▶ (c. 1450–c. 1500) Portuguese navigator. In 1486, given command of three ships by John II, he set out to explore the coast of Africa. Blown by a storm round the Cape of Good Hope (which he himself named the Cape of Storms) he reached present-day Algoa Bay on the E coast of Africa but was forced by his unwilling crew to return. He was drowned near the Cape while accompanying ▷Cabral on the expedition that discovered Brazil.

● **diaspora** ▶ (Greek: dispersion) The dispersion of Jewish communities outside Israel. Beginning with the ▷Babylonian exile (6th century BC), Jews spread to most parts of the world, while continuing to regard Israel as their homeland. The most important centres of the diaspora were, in antiquity, Babylonia and Egypt; in the middle ages, Spain and France; and in early modern times, E Europe. In the late 19th century there was a massive exodus of Jews from Russia and Poland, largely to the USA, and the German ▷holocaust destroyed many old European communities. The main centre is now the USA, with some six million Jews.

● **diastole** ▷*See* blood pressure; heart.

● **diastrophism** ▶ The large-scale deformation of the earth's crust resulting in the major structural features of the earth's surface, such as the continents, ocean basins, mountain ranges, fault-lines, etc. It is now widely believed that ▷sea-floor spreading and the consequent movement of the rigid plates that form the earth's crust (*see* plate tectonics) are responsible for diastrophism.

● **diathermy** ▶ The production of heat in the body's tissues by means of a high-frequency electric current passing between two electrodes applied to the patient's skin. It has been used to relieve deep-seated pain in rheumatic conditions. The principle has also been utilized in surgery, one electrode, in the form of a knife, snare, or needle, being used to coagulate blood and therefore seal off blood vessels during incisions or to destroy unwanted tissue.

● **diatoms** ▶ Microscopic ▷algae belonging to a phylum (*Diatoms* or *Bacillariophyta*; about 16 000 species) occurring abundantly as single cells or colonies in fresh water and oceans (forming an important constituent of ▷plankton) and also in soil. They have silicon-rich cell walls, often beautifully sculptured, forming a shell (called a test) composed of two halves (valves) that fit together like a pill box. Fossil-

ized tests form a porous rock called diatomaceous earth (*or* kieselguhr), used in filters, insulators, abrasives, etc.

● **diatonic scales** ▷*See* scale (music).

● **Díaz, Porfirio** ▶ (1830–1915) Mexican soldier, who became president (1876–1911) following a coup. He ruled dictatorially, supported by conservative landowners and foreign capitalists. His promotion of economic development benefited only a small elite and no attention was paid to the needs of the Indians. He fled the country in 1911 in the face of a revolution led by Francisco Madero (1873–1913).

● **diazepam** ▷*See* benzodiazepines.

● **Dibdin, Charles** ▶ (1745–1814) British composer, actor, singer, author, publisher, and theatrical promoter. He was self-taught, apart from several years as chorister at Winchester Cathedral, and left a legacy of fine songs, including "Tom Bowling."

● **Dicentra** ▶ A genus of annual and perennial herbaceous plants (about 300 species) from North America and E Asia, up to 90 cm high. They have divided compound leaves and sprays of hanging flowers that are flattened sideways, with the outer petals pouched and the inner ones joined at the tips. Many species are ornamentals (*see* bleeding heart; Dutchman's breeches). Family: *Fumariaceae*.

● **Dickens, Charles** ▶ (1812–70) British novelist. Son of a naval clerk, he worked in a blacking factory when his father was imprisoned for debt and later as a solicitor's clerk and court reporter. He began his writing career by contributing to popular magazines, many of his early articles being collected in *Sketches by Boz* (Boz being the pseudonym he was then using), which was published in 1836. A year later he achieved sudden fame with *The Pickwick Papers*, which he followed with *Oliver Twist* (1838) and *Nicholas Nickleby* (1839) and the very successful *Old Curiosity Shop* (1840–41); like all his novels, these first appeared in monthly instalments. In the 1840s he travelled abroad, visiting America in 1842, and founded (1846) the liberal *Daily News* and two weekly miscellanies. *David Copperfield* (1849–50) was a strongly autobiographical work, portraying Dickens' father as the feckless Mr Micawber. His later novels, from *Bleak House* (1853) to the incomplete *Edwin Drood* (1870), were increasingly pessimistic in tone; *Great Expectations* (1860–61) and *Our Mutual Friend* (1864–65), in their depiction of the destructive powers of money and ambition, develop most fully Dickens' radical view of society. Dickens' marriage was an

Charles Dickens ▶ The author with his daughters.

unhappy one and in 1856 he and his wife agreed to separate. He formed a relationship with Ellen Ternan, a young actress. In 1858 he began his famous public readings from his work, the strain of which hastened his death.

● **Dickinson, Emily** ▶ (1830–86) US poet. Daughter of a Calvinist lawyer, she lived a largely secluded life after the age of 30, with her family at Amherst, Massachusetts. She wrote numerous letters and over 1700 poems, mostly brief intense lyrics on themes of love, death, and nature; only seven were published during her lifetime. She is now recognized as one of the greatest US poets.

● **dicotyledons** ▶ The larger of the two main groups of flowering plants, which includes hardwood trees, shrubs, and many herbaceous plants (*compare* monocotyledons). Dicots are characterized by having two seed leaves (cotyledons) in the embryo. Typically the flower parts are arranged in fours or fives (or multiples of these) and the leaves have a netlike pattern of veins. ▷*See also* angiosperm.

● **dictionaries** ▷*See* lexicography.

● **Dicynodon** ▶ A large herbivorous ▷therapsid (mammal-like) reptile that lived in the late Permian period, which ended 240 million years ago. It occurred worldwide in large numbers and had a long high-domed skull with a horny beaklike jaw and a single upper pair of teeth.

● **Diderot, Denis** ▶ (1713–84) French philosopher and writer. With ▷Voltaire, Diderot helped create the ▷Enlightenment, mainly through the *Encyclopédie*, which he edited after 1750 (*see* Encyclopedists). Fascinated by science, he developed a form of ▷pantheism. His writings, notably *Lettre sur les aveugles* (1749), were materialistic and anti-Christian.

● **didgeridoo** ▶ An aboriginal musical instrument, consisting of a wooden tube three to four feet long, sounded by blowing across one of the open ends. The other rests against a hole in the ground to increase resonance. It plays two notes: the fundamental, used to set up a basic rhythm, and a harmonic, used in counterrhythm against it.

● **Dido** ▶ In Greek legend, the daughter of a king of Tyre, who fled to Africa when her husband was murdered; there she founded ▷Carthage. According to legend she burnt herself to death on a funeral pyre to avoid marriage to Iarvas of Numidia; in ▷Virgil's *Aeneid* she killed herself after being abandoned by her lover ▷Aeneas.

● **die casting** ▷*See* casting metals.

● **Diefenbaker, John G(eorge)** ▶ (1895–1979) Canadian statesman; Progressive Conservative prime minister (1957–63). His party's victory in 1957 broke 22 years of Liberal government and in 1958 the Conservatives gained an overwhelming majority (208 out of 256 seats). He lost the 1963 election following opposition to proposals to build nuclear weapons and resigned the party leadership in 1967.

● **Diego Garcia** ▷*See* British Indian Ocean Territory.

● **dielectric** ▶ A substance that acts as an electrical ▷insulator and can sustain an electric field. When a voltage is applied across a perfect dielectric there is no energy loss and the electric field strength changes simultaneously with voltage. In the real dielectrics, such as air, ceramics, or wax, which are used in ▷capacitors, there is always a small energy loss.

● **dielectric constant** ▷*See* permittivity.

● **Diels, Otto Paul Hermann** ▶ (1876–1954) German chemist, who shared the 1950 Nobel Prize with Kurt Alder (1902–58) for their discovery of the **Diels-Alder reaction**, by which linear organic molecules are converted into cyclic molecules. The reaction is used in the synthesis of alkaloids, polymers, etc.

● **Diemen, Anthony van** ▶ (1593–1645) Dutch colonial administrator. As governor general of Batavia from 1636, he was responsible for the conquest of Malacca (1641) and parts of Ceylon (1644) important to the spice trade. He also commissioned ▷Tasman to explore the S Pacific in the interest of trade (1642, 1644), expeditions that reached Van Diemen's Land (now Tasmania).

● **Dien Bien Phu, Battle of** ▶ (March–May, 1954) The decisive battle of the Indochina war, in NE Vietnam, in which Vietnamese forces defeated the French. The collapse of the French fortress coincided with the Geneva Conference, which ended French control of Indochina.

● **Dieppe** ▶ 49 55N 1 05E A port and resort in N France, in the Seine-Maritime department on the English Channel. Occupied by the English (1420–35), it became a Huguenot stronghold but declined in importance after the revocation of the Edict of Nantes. It was the scene of heavy fighting during World War II. Population (1990): 36 600.

● **Diesel engine** ▷*See* internal-combustion engine.

● **Diet, Imperial** ▷*See* Reichstag.

● **dietetics** ▶ The study of the principles of ▷nutrition and their application to the selection of appropriate diets both to maintain health and as part of the treatment of certain diseases. A balanced diet should contain foods with adequate amounts of all the ▷nutrients—carbohydrates, fats, proteins, minerals, and vitamins—as well as foods with a high content of dietary ▷fibre. An important aspect of the work of dieticians is to work out the special diets that are required for various diseases. Diabetes mellitus, for instance, requires a diet low in carbohydrate, whereas some liver diseases respond well to a low-protein diet. Obesity can often be managed with a low-calorie diet.

● **Dietrich, Marlene** ▶ (Maria Magdalene von Losch; 1904–92) German film actress and singer. Her image of sultry beauty was developed by Josef von ▷Sternberg in such films as *The Blue Angel* (1930). In 1930 she went to Hollywood, where she made numerous films of varying quality, including *Shanghai Express* (1932), *Blonde Venus* (1932), *Destry Rides Again* (1939), and *Judgment at Nuremberg* (1961). In her later career she gave many cabaret performances.

● **differential calculus** ▷*See* calculus.

● **differential gear** ▶ A gear mechanism that enables the driving wheels on either side of a motor vehicle to rotate at different speeds when cornering. In a rear-wheel-drive vehicle the propeller shaft from the gearbox terminates in a pinion, which drives a crown wheel in the differential. An arrangement of bevels, driven by the crown wheel, enables the half shaft driving the outer wheels during cornering to rotate more rapidly than the half shaft driving the inner wheels.

● **diffraction** ▶ The spreading or bending of light waves as they pass the edge of an object or pass through an aperture. The diffracted waves subsequently interfere with each other producing regions of alternately high and low intensity. This phenomenon, first discovered in 1665 by Francesco Grimaldi (1618–63), can be observed in the irregular boundary of a shadow of an object cast on a screen by a small light source. A **diffraction grating** consists of a plate of glass ruled with close parallel lines, equidistant from each other (usually 1000 lines per millimetre), which splits the light passed through it into a spectrum of its component frequencies. A diffraction grating may also be ruled on a metal sheet, which splits light falling on it into its components after reflection. A similar effect occurs with sound waves. ▷*See also* interference.

● **diffusion** ▶ **1.** The mixing of different fluids, or the distribution of a substance from a region of high concentration to one of lower concentration, by means of the random thermal motion of its constituents. In gases, according to Graham's law (named after Thomas Graham; 1805–69), the rates at which gases diffuse are inversely proportional to their densities. Mixing of fluids is complete after a certain time unless one set of particles is sufficiently heavy for sedimentation to occur. Diffusion also occurs between certain solids; for example gold will slowly diffuse into lead. **2.** The scattering of a beam of radiation on reflection from a rough surface or on transmission through certain media. When diffusion occurs the laws of reflection and refraction are not obeyed.

● **diffusionism** ▶ A theory claiming that all civilization and culture were transmitted from certain circumscribed areas of the ancient world and disregarding the possibility of independent invention and discovery. In its most extreme form it held that this original centre was Egypt. Diffusionism dominated ▷ethnology between 1910 and 1925 but is now largely discredited.

● **Digby, Sir Kenelm** ▶ (1603–65) English courtier and scientist. He entered James I's service in 1623 and led a privateering expedition against French ships off Turkey in 1627–28. A Roman Catholic, he supported Charles I against parliament and was forced to leave England during the Civil War. In Paris he wrote *Of the Nature of Bodies* and *Of the Nature of Man's Soule* (1644). He finally returned to England in 1654. A founder member of the Royal Society (1663), he discovered that plants need oxygen.

● **digestion** ▶ The process by which food is converted into substances that can be absorbed by the ▷intestine. It takes place in the **alimentary canal** and begins in the mouth, where the food is chewed and mixed with saliva, continuing with the action of digestive enzymes secreted by the ▷stomach, duodenum, and ▷pancreas. Rhythmic contractions of the intestinal wall (called peristalsis) ensure a constant mixing of enzymes and food and the propulsion of food along the intestine. The products of digestion include amino acids, various sugars (such as lactose, maltose, and glucose), and fat molecules; these are absorbed by the intestine and conveyed to the bloodstream. ▷*See* Plate II.

● **Diggers** ▶ An English sect that flourished under the ▷Commonwealth, so called because of their attempts to dig common land. Led by Gerrard ▷Winstanley, the Diggers believed in the economic and social equality of men. In April, 1649, they established a community at St George's Hill, Weybridge, based on agrarian communism. Their popularity alarmed the government and they were dispersed in March, 1650. ▷*See also* Levellers.

● **digger wasp** ▶ A solitary ▷wasp of the families *Sphercidae* or *Pompilidae* (*see* spider wasp). Digger wasps are black with yellow or orange markings. They burrow into wood, plant stems, or the ground to build nests, which they stock with insects, such as caterpillars and flies; these have been paralysed to provide food for the developing larvae.

● **digital audio tape** ▶ (DAT) ▷*See* recording of sound.

● **digital compact cassette** ▶ (DCC) ▷*See* recording of sound.

● **digital computer** ▷*See* computer.

● **digitalis** ▶ A crude drug prepared from the leaves of foxglove plants. Digitalis is purified to digoxin and digitoxin. These drugs are used to improve the action of a failing or inefficient heart and to reduce a fast heart rate. Side effects include nausea and pulse irregularities.

● **digital mapping** ▶ The production of a map using a system in which the points and lines that make up a map are converted, or digitized, into computer data; this information is then stored on magnetic tapes. Subsequent reproduction may be of the whole map or of a selected part; it may be at a different scale and/or on a transformed projection. A print of the map can be produced or it may be displayed on a visual display unit. Changes can be made without the whole map having to be redrawn. In the UK the ▷Ordnance Survey began converting its large-scale maps to digital data in 1973.

● **digital photography** ▶ Photography in which the image taken by the camera is converted into digital form and stored on a computer disk as pixels. In this form the digital data can be fed into a computer, viewed on the screen, or printed as a single image using the computer's colour printer. Once the image has been converted to pixels it can be manipulated by computer software. Colour and resolution can be changed and the image can be cropped, retouched, or mixed with other images in a variety of ways. The optical part of a **digital camera** is very similar to an optical camera while the mechanism of recording the image resembles that in a ▷video camera. The results obtained to a large extent depend on the quality of the printer, but digital photography cannot yet produce photographs that compare in quality with those produced by photographic techniques using film.

● **digital recording** ▷*See* recording of sound.

● **Dijon** ▶ 47 20N 5 02E A city in France, the capital of the Côte-d'Or department on the Burgundy Canal. The former capital of Burgundy, it is the site of the palace of the Dukes of Burgundy and has a cathedral (13th–14th centuries). An important railway centre, it has varied industries and is famous for its mustard. Population (1990): 151 636.

● **dik-dik** ▶ A small African antelope belonging to the genus *Madoqua* (7 species), found in the undergrowth of forested areas. 30–40 cm high at the shoulder, dik-diks are generally solitary and only the males have horns. When disturbed, they take flight in a series of erratic leaps.

● **dilatation and curettage** ▶ (D and C) An operation in which the neck (cervix) of the womb is dilatated (widened) and the lining of the womb is scraped out. D and C may be performed for a variety of reasons, including the removal of any residual membranes after a miscarriage or abortion, removal of cysts or tumours, and removal of a specimen of tissue for examination in the diagnosis of various gynaecological disorders.

● **dill** ▶ A widely cultivated annual or biennial European herb, *Anethum graveolens*, 60 cm high. The smooth stem bears feathery leaves and umbrella-like clusters of small yellow flowers, which produce small hard flat fruits. The young leaves and fruits are used to flavour soups, cakes, salads, fish, and pickled cucumbers. Family: ▷*Umbelliferae*.

● **Dilthey, Wilhelm** ▶ (1833–1911) German pioneer of biographical historiography. In contrast to Hegelian reliance on the cosmic spirit and metaphysical enquiry, Dilthey sought to conduct empirical enquiry, using historical facts, biographies, and the surviving records of great personalities.

● **Dimbleby, Richard** ▶ (1913–65) British broadcaster. Having joined the BBC in 1936, he became television's best-known commentator on state events and current affairs (e.g. *Panorama*). The Dimbleby lectures are given in his honour. His sons **David Dimbleby** (1938–) and **Jonathan Dimbleby** (1944–) are also leading broadcasters.

● **dimensional analysis** ▶ A method of testing or deriving a physical equation in which each term is expressed in the dimensions of mass, length, time, and (if electric or magnetic quantities are present) either charge or current. Each term must have the same dimensional formula if the equation is true. Dimensional analysis is also useful in predicting the behaviour of a full-scale system from a model.

● **diminishing returns, law of** ▶ The law that as more of a variable factor of production, such as labour, is applied to a fixed quantity of another factor, such as capital (machinery), the returns to each additional unit of the variable factor will eventually decrease. For example, in a small factory, employing one labourer may increase production by freeing machine operators from some tasks, but employing a second labourer will not increase production by as much again.

● **Dimitrii Donskoi** ▶ (1350–89) Prince of Moscow (1359–89) and Grand Prince of Vladimir (1362–89). His defeat of Khan Mamai at Kulikovo on the Don River in 1380 began the liberation of Russia from the ▷Golden Horde.

● **Dimitrov, Georgi** ▶ (1882–1949) Bulgarian statesman. Dimitrov became a member of the executive committee of the Third ▷International in 1921. Exiled in 1923, he moved in 1929 to Berlin, where in 1933 he was accused with others of setting fire to the Reichstag. Acquitted, he became a citizen of the Soviet Union and secretary general of the Comintern. In 1944 he returned to Bulgaria and became prime minister (1946).

● **Dinan** ▶ 48 27N 2 02W A town and resort in France, in the Côtes-d'Armor department situated high above the River Rance. Its manufactures include hosiery, cider, and beer. Population (1989): 14 157.

● **Dinant** ▶ 50 16N 04 55E A town in S Belgium, on the River Meuse. It was famous for its artistic metalwork (*dinanderie*) in the middle ages. A popular tourist centre, it is overlooked by an 11th-century citadel. Population (1991): 12 200.

● **Dinaric Alps** ▶ (Serbo-Croat name: Dinara Planina) A mountain range in W Croatia, Bosnia-Hercegovina, Montenegro, and N Albania, extending some 700 km (435 mi) NW–SE between the Alps and the Balkan Mountains and rising to 2522 m (8274 ft).

● **D'Indy, Vincent** ▶ (1851–1931) French composer, the pupil and biographer of Franck and the cofounder of the Paris Schola Cantorum (1894). He was influenced by Wagner and wrote large-scale orchestral compositions, as well as operas and chamber music. His most famous work is the *Symphony on a French Mountaineer's Song* (piano and orchestra; 1886).

● **Dinesen, Isak** ▶ (Karen Blixen, Baroness Blixen-Finecke; 1885–1962) Danish author, who took up writing after 20 years spent managing a coffee plantation in Kenya. She is best known for two collections of stories in the gothic style: *Seven Gothic Tales* (1934) and *Winter's Tales* (1942). Her life story was told in the book and film (1986) *Out of Africa*.

● **dingo** ▶ An Australian wild ▷dog, *Canis familiaris* (formerly *C. dingo*), introduced about 3000 years ago from Asia. It is about 120 cm long, including the tail (30 cm), and has a tan-coloured coat. It is nocturnal and generally solitary.

Dinka ▶ An independent cattle-rearing people of the Nile basin.

● **Dinka** ▶ A Nilotic people of the Nile basin region of the Sudan. Warlike and independent, the Dinka move with their cattle from dry-season pastures by the rivers to wet-season settlements, where they grow millet. There are many independent tribes of varying size each with numerous smaller clans and patrilineal kinship units. Age-set organization is important for men, who attain adulthood by undergoing the ordeals of initiation ceremonial. Ritual life emphasizes sacrificing to ancestral spirits and the god Nhial.

● **dinoflagellates** ▶ A group of mostly marine unicellular organisms that form part of the ▷plankton. Usually measuring 0.02–0.1 mm, many have cellulose cell walls. They move by beating two hair-like structures (flagella). Some species contain chlorophyll and can manufacture their own food (by photosynthesis); others engulf food particles. Dinoflagellates are placed in their own phylum (*Dinomastigota* or *Dinoflagellata*) in the kingdom *Protoctista*.

● **dinosaur** ▶ An extinct reptile that was the dominant terrestrial animal during the Jurassic and Cretaceous periods (200–65 million years ago). Dinosaurs first appeared about 225 million years ago, ranging in size from about 60 cm to such mighty creatures as ▷*Diplodocus*, which reached 27 m in length. There were two orders: the ▷*Saurischia*, which were mostly carnivores and included the bipedal ▷*Allosaurus* and ▷*Tyrannosaurus*; and the ▷*Ornithischia*, which were all herbivores and included the bipedal ▷*Iguanodon*, the horned ▷*Triceratops*, and ▷*Stegosaurus*. Why both orders died out at the end of the Cretaceous period along with other reptiles, such as ▷ichthyosaurs, ▷pterosaurs, and ▷plesiosaurs, is still not certain. Dinosaurs had large bodies with heavy bones and protective armour and were probably unable to adapt to climatic changes and the effects of a rise

in the sea level, which flooded their coastal habitats—changes possibly triggered by the impact of a huge meteorite.

● **Dio Cassius** ▶ (c. 150–235 AD) Roman historian, who was twice elected consul and was appointed governor of Africa and Dalmatia. In 80 books, written in Greek, he recorded the history of Rome from Aeneas to his own time.

● **Dio Chrysostom** ▶ (2nd century AD) Greek philosopher and orator. A friend of the Emperor Trajan, he admired the Roman state, from his family estates in Bithynia (Asia Minor), and eulogized its compound of monarchy, aristocracy, and democracy.

● **Diocletian(us), Gaius Aurelius Valerius** ▶ (245–313 AD) Roman emperor (284–305). He was born in Dalmatia and rose to prominence in the army, to which he owed his accession. In 293 he established the tetrarchy to govern the Empire more effectively in a time of civil strife: the Empire was divided into East and West, with each ruled by an emperor and his associate. Diocletian ruled in the East with ▷Galerius, who was probably responsible for the persecution of Christians begun in 303. In 305 Diocletian retired to Salona (now Split, Croatia), where his palace can still be seen.

● **diode** ▷*See* semiconductor diode; thermionic valve.

● **Diodorus Siculus** ▶ (1st century BC) Greek historian, born in Sicily. His *Bibliotheca historica* is a history of the Mediterranean countries from their legendary origins up to his own time; of its 40 volumes, only 15 survive.

● **Diogenes Laertius** ▶ (3rd century AD) Greek compiler of the opinions and biographical details of classical philosophers, including the ▷Presocratics. The historical authenticity of his biographical material, for example about the life of ▷Epicurus, is doubtful.

● **Diogenes of Sinope** ▶ (412–322 BC) The founder of the philosophical sect of the ▷Cynics. Influenced by ▷Antisthenes, Diogenes claimed, in contrast to almost all Greek thinkers, total freedom and self-sufficiency for the individual. Unlike modern anarchists, he saw no need for violent rebellion to assert his independence, which he thought he already had. His ostentatious disregard for social conventions made him the subject of many stories. He is reported to have lived in a large tub in Athens. According to another story, he went about in daylight with a lamp, saying that he was searching for an honest man.

● **Diomedes** ▶ A legendary Greek hero of the Trojan War who commanded 80 ships from Argos. He wounded ▷Ares and ▷Aphrodite, took the place of the absent ▷Achilles in an attack on Troy, and captured the Palladium, the sacred image of ▷Athena.

● **Dionysius of Halicarnassus** ▶ (1st century BC) Greek historian who taught at Rome after 30 BC. He compiled a history of Rome from its origins to the first Punic War in 20 books, of which 10 survive. He also wrote literary criticism and treatises on rhetoric.

● **Dionysius the Areopagite, St** ▶ (1st century AD) Greek churchman. He was converted to Christianity by St Paul and according to tradition was the first Bishop of Athens. In the middle ages he was thought to be the author of several theological treatises in Greek. These are now attributed to the unidentified 6th-century writer known as ▷Pseudo-Dionysius the Areopagite.

● **Dionysius (I) the Elder** ▶ (c. 430–367 BC) Tyrant of Syracuse (405–367), who fought the Carthaginians in a series of wars, which were ultimately unsuccessful, for control of Sicily and the Greek cities of S Italy. His son **Dionysius (II) the Younger**, who succeeded him as tyrant (367–356, 347–344), was a patron of writers and philosophers and was taught briefly by Plato.

● **Dionysus** ▶ (or Bacchus) The Greek god of wine, originally a vegetation god. He was the son of ▷Semele by Zeus, who saved him at her death; he was reared by the nymphs of Nysa. A common theme of many legends concerning him is a people's refusal to accept his divinity and his subsequent retribution: thus Pentheus, King of Thebes, was torn to death by the god's ecstatic female followers, the maenads. Athens held five festivals (**Dionysia**) in Dionysus' honour.

● **Diophantus of Alexandria** ▶ (mid-3rd century AD) Greek mathematician; one of the few Greeks to study algebra rather than geometry. He discovered the method of solving problems by means of algebraic equations. His work was preserved by Arabic mathematicians and, in the 16th century, was translated into Latin, inspiring many advances in algebra. Diophantine equations are named after him.

● **dioptre** ▶ A unit used to measure the power of a lens equal to the reciprocal of its focal length in metres. The power of a converging lens is taken to be positive and that of a diverging lens as negative.

● **Dior, Christian** ▶ (1905–57) French fashion designer, who first became known with his 1947 collection, which introduced the New Look, characterized by fitted bodices and long full skirts. His later designs, which included the H-line and the A-line, aspired to a similar ideal of femininity.

● **diorite** ▶ A coarse-grained plutonic igneous rock of intermediate composition. It consists mainly of plagioclase feldspar and ferromagnesian minerals (often hornblende). It usually occurs in small intrusive masses or in ▷batholiths.

● **Dioscorides Pedanius** ▶ (c. 40–c. 90 AD) Greek physician, who compiled the first pharmacopoeia. He travelled widely as a surgeon in the Roman army and in his work *De materia medica* (c. 77 AD) he described nearly 600 plants and their medicinal properties.

● **Dioscuri** ▷*See* Castor and Pollux.

● **dioxin** ▶ An extremely toxic hydrocarbon, 2,3,7,8-tetrachloro-dibenzo-*p*-dioxin (TCDD), that belongs to a class of similar compounds (called dioxins). An environmental pollutant, it is a by-product of the manufacture of certain herbicides and bactericides and is produced during the incineration of some chemicals and waste products. It causes the skin disease chloracne in humans and developmental abnormalities and cancers in animals. Large amounts were released in an industrial accident at ▷Seveso in 1976.

● **dip circle** ▷*See* magnetic dip.

● **diphtheria** ▶ An acute bacterial infection primarily affecting the throat. It has been virtually eliminated from the UK and most Western nations as a result of immunization, although it formerly caused many child deaths. It still occurs in Africa and India. Diphtheria produces a membrane across the throat that chokes the child. Alternatively death may be caused by poisons damaging the heart. The disease can be cured using penicillin and antitoxin.

● **Diplodocus** ▶ A huge amphibious dinosaur of the Jurassic period (200–136 million years ago) that was the largest terrestrial vertebrate ever to exist, reaching a length of 27 m. It had a narrow body with massive pillar-like legs, a long neck with a tiny head, and a long tail. It fed on soft vegetation and had very few teeth. Order: ▷*Saurischia*.

● **dipole, electric and magnetic** ▶ A pair of equal and opposite electric charges or magnetic poles. The dipole moment is defined as the magnitude of one of the charges or poles multiplied by the distance separating them. Some molecules have an electric dipole moment due to the preferential attraction of the bonding electrons for one of the atoms. In the case of hydrogen chloride, for example, the chlorine atom gains a slight negative charge and the hydrogen atom a slight positive charge. Measurement of dipole moments provides evidence of the shapes of molecules.

● **dipper** ▶ An aquatic songbird of the family *Cinclidae* (4 species), also called water ouzel, of Eurasia and America. Dippers are found near mountain streams, diving into the water to search for insects and fish. The Eurasian white-breasted dipper (*Cinclus cinclus*) is about 17 cm long and has a dense dark-brown plumage with a white breast.

● **Diprotodon** ▶ An extinct Australian giant ▷wombat that was about the size of a rhinoceros. It lived during the Pleistocene epoch, about a million years ago.

● **Diptera** ▶ An order of insects comprising the two-winged, or true, flies. ▷*See* fly.

● **Dirac, Paul Adrien Maurice** ▶ (1902–84) British physicist, who made two fundamental contributions to the development of the quantum theory. In 1928 he introduced a new notation for handling quantum equations that combined ▷Schrödinger's use of differential equations with ▷Heisenberg's approach using ▷matrices. Two years later he incorporated ▷relativity into quantum theory and produced an equation that predicted the existence of antiparticles. For his work he shared the 1933 Nobel Prize with Schrödinger. He was appointed to the OM in 1973.

● **direction finder** ▶ Equipment for locating the source of a radio signal, such as a ship at sea. It consists of one or more directive ▷aerials (usually in the form of a loop), designed to detect signals from a specific direction, and a receiver. Frequencies normally used are between 0.1 and 2 megahertz. The process can be automatic, often using a rotating aerial with a ▷cathode-ray tube to display signal strength and direction. Reflections from mountains or tall buildings can cause errors in a land-based direction-finding system. ▷Radar is a form of direction finding based on picking up reflections of a transmitted signal.

● **Director of Public Prosecutions** ▷*See* Crown Prosecution Service.

● **Directory** ▶ (1795–99) The government of the First Republic of France, comprising five directors elected by a Council of Ancients (men over 40 years old) and a Council of Five Hundred. Less extreme than preceding governments of the ▷French Revolution, the Directory has been criticized for its corruption and administrative incompetence but it achieved successes in the Revolutionary Wars. It was overthrown by a coup on behalf of ▷Napoleon I. The period witnessed the development of the **Directoire style** in furniture, interior decoration, and costume. This style was less ornate than the Louis Seize style (*see* Louis XVI) that preceded it, anticipating the ▷Empire style that followed it.

● **Dire Dawa** ▶ 9 40N 41 47E A town in central Ethiopia. It is in a hot dry region with little cultivation. Local industries include manufacturing cotton goods and cement. Population (1994 est): 194 487.

● **Dirichlet's theorem** ▶ A theorem in ▷number theory stating that there are an infinite number of ▷prime numbers contained in the set of all numbers of the form $(a \times n) + b$, where a and b are themselves prime and n is a natural number, i.e. 1, 2, 3, ... The theorem was first suggested by ▷Gauss and proved by the French mathematician Peter Gustav Lejeune Dirichlet (1805–59).

● **Dis** ▷*See* Hades.

● **disaccharide** ▶ A carbohydrate comprising two linked ▷monosaccharide sugar units. ▷Lactose, maltose, and ▷sucrose are important disaccharides.

● **disarmament** ▶ The reduction of the fighting capability of a nation. Limited disarmament treaties were made under the auspices of the ▷League of Nations in the 1930s, in an attempt to avoid a repetition of the disastrous loss of life in World War I. But German rearmament under the Nazis and Japanese expansionism in Asia thwarted these attempts. After World War II the main concern was to contain the spread of nuclear weapons. An attempt was made by the UN to limit both conventional arms and nuclear weapons, especially of the defeated countries, but during the Cold War both the Soviet Union and the Western powers assisted in the rearmament of their former enemies. In 1963, however, the Soviet Union, the USA, and the UK signed a ▷Nuclear Test-Ban Treaty. In 1967 the same countries signed a treaty banning the use of nuclear weapons in outer space; in the same year 59 countries signed a nuclear nonproliferation treaty. By 1995 178 countries had acceded to the treaty. Talks between the Soviet Union and USA were started in 1969 to limit and reduce strategic nuclear arms; known as SALT (Strategic Arms Limitation Talks) they reached limited agreements in 1974 (SALT I) and again in 1979 (SALT II), which was never ratified and was repudiated by the USA in 1986. New talks—START (STrategic Arms Reduction Talks)—began in 1982. In 1987 the two major powers agreed to reduce medium- and shorter-range nuclear missiles in Europe in an intermediate nuclear forces agreement (INF) and to intensify negotiations on strategic offensive weapons. In 1983 the proposed US ▷Strategic Defence Initiative became an important issue in these talks. Subsequently, following the disintegration of the Soviet Union, Presidents Bush and Yeltsin agreed to cut the nuclear arsenals of the USA and Russia (as well as other countries of the former Soviet Union) by two-thirds by 2003. This was formulated in a START II treaty that was ratified in

1992. In 2002 Presidents Bush and Putin agreed to cut their nuclear stockpiles by 70% over ten years.

● **Disciples of Christ** ▶ (*or* Campbellites) A Christian denomination originating within Presbyterianism in the 19th century but founded as a separate denomination in Philadelphia in 1827 by Alexander Campbell (1788–1866). In Britain they are known as the Churches of Christ. They preach a simple biblical creed, are congregational, and celebrate communion.

● **discount houses** ▶ Financial institutions in the UK that discount ▷bills of exchange and buy and sell ▷treasury bills, activities that they finance by borrowing short-term funds from the ▷commercial banks and other financial institutions. The discount houses take up the whole of the treasury bill issue each week, and in return the ▷Bank of England acts as lender of last resort to the discount houses (*see* open-market operations).

● **discount rate** ▷*See* interest.

● **discus throw** ▶ A field event in athletics. The circular discus is made of wood and metal, the men's weighing 2 kg (4.4 lb) and the women's 1 kg (2.2 lb). It is thrown with one hand from within a circle 2.5 m (8.2 ft) in diameter. World records: men: 74.08 m (1986) by Jürgen Schult (East Germany); women: 76.80 m (1988) by Gabriele Reinsch (East Germany).

● **disinfectant** ▶ A substance or process that kills germs or prevents them multiplying. Carbolic acid (phenol) was introduced for this purpose in medicine in the 1870s by Joseph ▷Lister. It is still used in cleaning materials and, in weaker solutions, in skin disinfectants. Chlorine and such compounds as sodium hypochlorite kill bacteria and also some viruses. Chlorinated phenols, such as hexachlorophane, are also widely used in pharmaceutical products. Other disinfectants include hydrogen peroxide (H_2O_2), iodine (I_2), formaldehyde (HCHO), boiling water, and ultraviolet light. Dry heating to 140°C for about 3 hours will kill all disease-causing germs.

● **dislocation** ▶ Displacement of a bone at a joint, producing severe pain, difficulty in moving the joint, and usually obvious deformity. Shoulders, elbows, hips, vertebrae, and fingers are all commonly dislocated in injuries. Often a bone in the joint will be broken, and it is unwise to attempt to put the joint back before an X-ray film has been taken.

● **Disney, Walt** ▶ (1901–66) US film producer and animator, whose films earned a total of 32 Academy Awards. His most famous cartoon character, Mickey Mouse, was designed in 1928. His films include full-length cartoon features, such as *Snow White and the Seven Dwarfs* (1938), *Pinocchio* (1939), and *Bambi* (1943), nature documentaries, and adventure films, such as *Treasure Island* (1950) and *Mary Poppins* (1964), all made for family audiences. His *Fantasia* (1940) used colourful visual images and cartoons to accompany classical music played by an orchestra under ▷Stokowski. He opened Disneyland, an amusement park, in California in 1955. Walt Disney World was later

Walt Disney ▶ With a model of Donald Duck (1951).

opened (1971) near Orlando, Florida, and a similar park in Tokyo in 1983; Euro Disney opened near Paris in 1992.

● **display** ▶ In zoology, a specialized means by which animals communicate with each other. Displays can be vocal (such as ▷bird song), visual (by posture or colourful plumage), chemical (by means of ▷pheromones), or tactile (for instance bees communicate in a dark hive largely by touch). Displays ensure social integration and cohesion of populations. They are used to establish social rank, maintain territory, synchronize breeding, and give warning of danger.

Benjamin Disraeli ▶ A cartoon from *Punch* (26 August, 1876) showing Queen Victoria rewarding her favourite prime minister with an earldom.

● **Disraeli, Benjamin, 1st Earl of Beaconsfield** ▶ (1804–81) British statesman; Conservative prime minister (1868, 1874–80). Of Italian-Jewish descent, Disraeli was baptized a Christian in 1817. He became an MP in 1837 and led the Young England group of Conservatives. Disraeli was critical of Peel's Conservative Government (1841–46) and opposed the repeal of the ▷Corn Laws. He was three times chancellor of the exchequer in Derby's governments (1852, 1858–59, 1866–68): in 1858 he introduced an unsuccessful parliamentary reform bill but was largely responsible for the 1867 ▷Reform Act. He succeeded Derby in February, 1868, but lost office following the autumn election, which was won by the Liberals under Gladstone. His second ministry carried important social legislation, including the Artisans' and Labourers' Dwellings Improvement Act (1874). In 1875 he bought Britain a major stake in the Suez Canal and in 1876 secured passage of a bill that conferred the title Empress of India on Queen Victoria. He successfully pursued British interests at the Congress of ▷Berlin (1878). Under Disraeli's leadership the Conservative Party came to be clearly identified with policies that upheld the monarchy, Empire, and Church of England, while sponsoring social reform (*see also* Primrose League). A flamboyant and witty parliamentarian, he earned the respect and friendship of the queen. Also a writer, Disraeli's novels include *Vivien Grey* (1826), *Coningsby, or the New Generation* (1844), and *Sybil, or the Two Nations* (1845).

● **Dissenters** ▷*See* Nonconformists.

● **dissociation** ▶ A reversible decomposition of a molecule or ion into smaller molecules or ions. In **electrolytic dissociation** the molecules split into ions, as in the ionization of ▷acids and bases in water (e.g. $HCN \leftrightarrow H^+ + CN^-$). In **thermal dissociation** a definite fraction of a molecule is dissociated at equilibrium at a particular temperature (e.g. $NH_4Cl \leftrightarrow NH_3 + HCl$). The extent of the dissociation is determined by the dissociation constant (*K*) of the reaction at a given temperature. *K* is equal to the ratio of the product of the concentrations of the fragments to the concentration of the dissociating molecule.

● **dissolution of the monasteries** ▶ The suppression (1536–40) of monastic houses and the transfer of their property to the Crown during the English ▷Reformation. Although the policy followed from Henry VIII's break with Rome in 1534, it was driven more by Henry's financial needs than by any zeal for religious reform. In 1535 Thomas ▷Cromwell, the main architect of the policy, prepared a detailed audit of the Church's wealth and sent inspectors to the monastic houses, who soon uncovered the desired evidence of abuses. The process of dissolution began immediately and was formalized in Acts of Parliament in 1536 and 1539. Apart from the ▷Pilgrimage of Grace, a religious uprising in the N that was brutally suppressed, there was little opposition. By 1540 all England's 800 monastic houses had been closed and their 10 000 or so inhabitants cast out, in most cases with minimal compensation.

The dissolution involved the destruction of some of England's greatest religious buildings and the dispersal of their libraries and other treasures. Former monastic lands were granted to the king's supporters or sold on to aspiring members of the gentry, thereby forming the basis of many of England's great estates. The vacuum created by the ending of monastic charity to the poor and sick and the closure of monastery schools led indirectly to the introduction of the ▷Poor Laws and the founding of ▷grammar schools in the later Tudor period.

● **dissonance** ▶ A combination of two or more musical notes that sounds harsh to the ear. This harshness is caused by the ▷beats that are produced when two notes (or their overtones) of similar pitch are sounded together. For example C and F sharp are dissonant because the second overtone of C is G, which beats with F sharp. A common type of dissonance in diatonic music consists of chords that sound incomplete in themselves and need to resolve onto a consonance. All diatonic music relies on the contrast between dissonances and consonances, without which such music would sound predictable and uninteresting. The use of ▷chromaticism in the late 19th century increased the amount of dissonance in music; in the 20th century such composers as Bartok and Stravinsky deliberately cultivated the use of unresolved dissonances.

● **distance learning** ▶ A form of education, mostly for mature students, in which the student and teacher meet face-to-face only occasionally or not at all. Communication is by correspondence, radio and TV broadcasting, audio cassette, and satellite transmission. Some correspondence courses began in the 19th century in Europe, but the leading institution for distance learning in the last 100 years has been the ▷Open University in the UK (founded 1969) and the ▷Open College (founded 1987). Satellite transmission has enabled the University of the South Pacific to become a reality.

● **distemper** ▶ (veterinary science) A highly contagious virus disease affecting dogs, foxes, ferrets, badgers, etc. Canine distemper occurs mainly at 3–12 months; symptoms include fever, loss of appetite, and a discharge from the eyes and nose. Complications may include conjunctivitis, bronchitis, pneumonia, and gastroenteritis. The disease can be prevented by vaccination at about 11 weeks with a booster dose at two years.

● **distemper** ▶ (*or* whitewash) An inexpensive water-based paint for interior decoration. It consists of whiting (calcium carbonate), glue, and water. In dry form it is known as calcine.

● **distillation** ▶ A method of purifying or separating the components of a liquid by boiling or evaporating the liquid and condensing the vapour. It is used for separating either liquids from solids or a mixture of liquids whose components have different boiling points. The latter is known as **fractional distillation**. Distillation is employed in petroleum refineries to separate the various ▷hydrocarbons, in the production of alcoholic spirits, and in extracting pure water from sea water.

In **steam distillation**, steam is bubbled into the liquid to be distilled so that it is heated as the steam gives up its latent heat of vaporization. This causes even heating without the risk of the overheating

and decomposition that can occur in hot spots when external heating is used. Steam distillation is used for such sensitive materials as essential oils. For materials with very high boiling points, which are likely to decompose below their boiling points, **vacuum distillation** is used. In this the vessel in which the distillation takes place is connected to a vacuum pump so that the pressure inside it is reduced, causing the substance being distilled to boil at a lower temperature. This is used in refining petrol.

● **distribution function** ▶ A mathematical function that gives the probability of finding a system in a particular state or within a range of states. For example, the probability of one of the molecules of a gas having a velocity between *v* and *v* + *dv* in a given direction is *Fdv*, where *F* is the distribution function.

● **distributive law** ▶ A law concerning the combination of mathematical operations. In arithmetic, for example, multiplication is said to obey the distributive law, or to be distributive, with respect to addition because $a(b + c) = ab + ac$.

● **District of Columbia** ▶ A federal district of the E USA, coextensive with the federal capital, ▷Washington: it does not form part of any of the 50 states. Area: 178 sq km (69 sq mi).

● **dithyramb** ▶ An ancient Greek hymn to the god ▷Dionysus. Originally sung extempore, it developed into a literary form around the 6th and 7th centuries BC. Its best-known authors include ▷Bacchylides and ▷Pindar. Aristotle believed that Greek drama developed out of this form.

● **dittany** ▶ A perennial European herbaceous plant, *Dictamnus albus*, also known as the gas plant or burning bush. A strong-scented gland-covered plant, it gives off so much aromatic oil that it is said to burst into flames when ignited. Dittany produces a spike of white or pink flowers. Family: *Rutaceae*. The name is also applied to several other plants. Crete dittany (*Origanum dictamnus*) is a herb closely related to marjoram, with thick woolly leaves and pinkish flowers. Family: *Labiatae*.

● **Diu** ▷*See* Daman and Diu.

● **diuretics** ▶ A large class of drugs that increase the excretion of urine by the kidneys. Diuretics are used in the treatment of diseases in which fluid accumulates in the tissues. These illnesses include heart failure, kidney failure, and some liver diseases (such as cirrhosis). Some diuretics cause loss of potassium from the body and are prescribed with a potassium supplement. Diuretics may also be used to treat high blood pressure.

● **diurnal motion** ▶ The apparent daily motion of astronomical bodies from E to W across the sky, in circles parallel to the celestial equator (*see* celestial sphere). It is caused by the earth's W-to-E rotation.

● **diver** ▶ A large aquatic bird belonging to a family (*Gaviidae*; 3 species) occurring in the N hemisphere, also called loon. Divers breed on lakes and ponds and spend the winter in temperate coastal waters. They have small pointed wings and black and white plumage and they dive deeply, feeding on fish, frogs, and aquatic insects. Order: *Gaviiformes*.

● **diverticulum** ▶ A pouch in the wall of any part of the alimentary tract, usually caused by pressure on a weak point. When they occur in the colon they can cause pain as a result of muscular spasm (**diverticular disease**) or of inflammation (**diverticulitis**). Treatment is by increasing dietary fibre and sometimes by antibiotics in diverticulitis.

● **divide** ▷*See* watershed.

● **dividend** ▶ A share in the profits of a company paid to shareholders. The rate of dividend is declared at the company's annual general meeting and will reflect the preceding year's profit. It is usually expressed as a percentage of the par value of the share (e.g. a 5% dividend on a 20p share would pay 1p per share). The dividend **yield** of the share is the income it produces expressed as a percentage of its current value (e.g. a 5% dividend on a 20p share that has a current value of 35p is 20/35 × 5 = 2.86%). Dividends are usually paid twice yearly, an interim dividend and a final dividend.

● **divination** ▷*See* augury; dowsing.

● **divine right of kings** ▶ A political doctrine claiming that ▷monarchy was a divinely ordained institution in which kings and queens were answerable only to God. It therefore followed that it was a sin for the subjects of even the most evil or incompetent monarchs to disobey them. The doctrine evolved in the middle ages, partly as a reaction to interference in the affairs of a nation by the pope and partly to strengthen the hand of monarchs in their dealings with parliaments. In its practical, rather than its mystical, aspects the doctrine can therefore be seen as an early form of the idea of national sovereignty and as an attempt to form a strong centralized executive.

In England, divine right was ardently espoused by ▷James I, not only in his writings and his speeches but also in his dealings with Parliament. The alienation of Parliament became complete when his successor, ▷Charles I, used divine right as a pretext for levying illegal taxes. Although Charles's appointee Archbishop ▷Laud preached that "the king could never depart from God's service," Parliament finally demanded his execution. From the scaffold the doomed king continued to maintain that the people's freedom "consisted in the enjoyment of laws by which their life and liberty would be secure" rather than by sharing in government. In practice the divine right of kings in England died with Charles I, although the theory was revived after the Restoration. Following the deposition of James II in the ▷Glorious Revolution, the theory itself became untenable, and most political thinkers justified the status quo by reference to some form of ▷social-contract philosophy, in which authority derives from the (supposed) consent of the governed, rather than the will of God.

In France, the divine right persisted throughout ▷Louis XIV's reign and in a less pronounced form until the Revolution of 1789. After the Revolutionary and Napoleonic period the theory was revived by conservative thinkers to justify the restoration of hereditary rulers throughout Europe. However, most of the restored monarchies were reduced to constitutional status by the mid-19th century. Only in Russia did an active belief in divine right survive (until the Revolutions of 1918).

In the UK the legacy of divine right survives not only in the religious nature of the coronation service and the mystique that surrounds hereditary constitutional monarchs but also in the doctrine that Parliament is sovereign—i.e. that the Crown, acting in Parliament, cannot be challenged by any other entity (such as the courts or a written constitution).

● **diving** ▶ An aquatic sport in which competitors are judged upon the precision and skill with which they enter the water. Competitors may execute twists, somersaults, and other manoeuvres before entering the water, diving off a springboard 3 m (9 ft 10 in) above the water, or off a platform 10 m (32 ft 10 in) above the water. Such events have been represented at the Olympic Games since 1904.

● **diving beetle** ▶ An aquatic beetle—a true ▷water beetle—belonging to a family (*Dytiscidae*; about 4000 species), occurring worldwide. Diving beetles vary in length from 2 to 38 mm: the largest genera are *Cybister* and *Dytiscus*. The adults and larvae (water tigers) are voracious carnivores.

● **diving duck** ▶ A ▷duck that dives to the bottom of lakes or rivers to feed, aided by a dense high-domed skull. Diving ducks, which include the ▷goldeneye, ▷pochard, and ▷scaup, usually have a drab plumage, thick neck, narrow wings, and large feet; they walk awkwardly on land. *Compare* dabbling duck.

● **Divisional Court** ▷*See* courts of law.

● **division of labour** ▶ The separation of tasks in an industrial process, with the allocation of one worker to each specific task. The term was introduced by Adam ▷Smith in his *Wealth of Nations* (1776). The object is to increase output; however, extreme division of labour, as in a car factory, can condemn a worker to repeating one operation endlessly.

● **divorce** ▶ The legal process by which a marriage is ended. Until the Matrimonial Causes Act (1857), which established a Divorce Court, divorce in England was possible only by special Act of Parliament. Jurisdiction is now vested in the High Court and county courts (*see* courts of law). Since 1971, the only ground for divorce has been

that the marriage has irretrievably broken down. However, the party applying for the divorce (the petitioner) has to substantiate such breakdown by presenting evidence of adultery, desertion, or unreasonable behaviour by the other party (the respondent). If the respondent contests these allegations, the suit has to be heard in open court; if not, a judge can grant an immediate decree nisi (provisional order of divorce). In most cases the decree nisi is followed after six weeks by the decree absolute, which leaves the parties free to remarry. A new Family Law Act was passed in 1996 but never fully implemented. This aimed to replace the emphasis on apportioning blame with a more consensual approach. Under the Act a statement of marital breakdown sworn by one party not earlier than 12 months after the marriage ceremony would have been sufficient to start divorce proceedings. If reconciliation was thought possible, the parties were obliged to seek professional mediation. Otherwise, a compulsory period of reflection was imposed, during which they would be expected to reach an arrangement about money and the care of any children. The divorce would then be granted with immediate effect. However, pilot schemes for the new measures in 1997–99 were considered unsuccessful and implementation was halted. In 2001 the government announced plans to repeal the Act. ▷*See also* separation order.

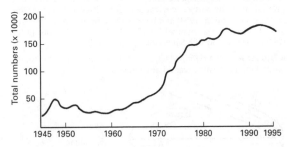

divorce ▶ The total number of divorces in the UK (1945–95). There was an approximately eightfold increase in the period.

● **Diwali** ▶ (Festival of Lights, from Sanskrit *dīpawalī*, row of lights) A Hindu religious festival. Held over the New Year according to the Vikrama calendar (October–November), it is celebrated especially among the merchant classes and honours ▷Lakshmi, the goddess of wealth (or in Bengal, Kali). There is feasting and lighting of lamps in honour of ▷Rama. Jains commemorate the death of their saint ▷Mahavira.

● **Dixieland** ▶ A type of jazz played by Whites in imitation of the ▷New Orleans style, named after the Original Dixieland Jazz Band (founded 1912). It emerged in the early 20th century but declined during the ▷swing and bebop eras.

● **Diyarbakir** ▶ 37 55N 40 14E A town in SE Turkey, on the River Tigris. It was taken by the Turks in 1515 and has 4th-century walls. Gold and silver filigree work is produced here; wool and grain are traded. It has a university (1966). Population (1995 est): 448 145.

● **Djajapura** ▷*See* Jayapura.

● **Djakarta** ▷*See* Jakarta.

● **Djambi** ▷*See* Jambi.

● **Djerba Island** ▶ 33 45N 11 00E A Tunisian island in the Mediterranean Sea, linked to the mainland by a causeway. Area: 510 sq km (197 sq mi). Population (latest est): 92 269.

● **Djibouti, Republic of** ▶ (name until 1977: the French Territory of the Afars and the Issas) A small country in NE Africa, on the Gulf of Aden at its entrance to the Red Sea. It consists chiefly of an arid rocky coastal plain rising to a plateau inland. The main population groups are Somalis and Afars, with Arabic and European minorities.

Economy: the port of Djibouti (a free port since 1949) is the country's economic focus, handling an important transshipment trade. The port is linked by rail to Ethiopia and handles about half of that country's trade. Exports include hides, skins, sugar, and Ethiopian coffee. Inland the predominantly nomadic population tends goats, sheep, and camels.

History: The territory was made a French colony known as French Somaliland in 1896 and proclaimed an overseas territory in 1967. It became independent in 1977 as Djibouti with Hassan Gouled Aptidon (1916–   ) as its first president. In the 1980s and 1990s the country suffered from the disruption of trade caused by civil wars and famine in Ethiopia and Somalia and the arrival of large numbers of refugees from those countries. In 1991 rebels began a guerrilla war against one-party rule. Multiparty democracy was established in 1992 and peace agreements with the rebel groups were signed in 1993 and 2000. Gouled was succeeded by his ally, Ismael Omar Guelleh in 2001.

Republic of Djibouti

Head of state	President Ismael Omar Guelleh
Official languages	Hamitic languages of the Somali people
Official currency	Djibouti franc of 100 centimes
Area	21 783 sq km (8409 sq mi)
Population (1999 est)	669 000
Capital and chief port	Djibouti

● **Djilas, Milovan** ▶ (1911–95) Yugoslav politician and writer. A member of ▷Tito's resistance group in World War II, Djilas became prominent in the postwar government. His criticism of the regime led to his demotion (1954) and he was twice imprisoned (1956–61, 1962–66). His books include *New Class* (1957), *Land Without Justice* (1958), *Conversations with Stalin* (1962), and *Tito* (1980).

● **Djoser** ▶ (*or* Zoser) King of Egypt (c. 2980–c. 2950 BC) of the 3rd dynasty, famous for his pyramid at ▷Saqqarah.

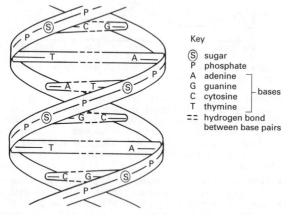

Key

Ⓢ	sugar
Ⓟ	phosphate
A	adenine
G	guanine
C	cytosine
T	thymine

⎦ bases

== hydrogen bond between base pairs

DNA ▶ The structure of a DNA molecule takes the form of a double helix. The sequence of base pairs constitutes the genetic code, which controls the inheritance of characteristics.

● **DNA** ▶ (*or* deoxyribonucleic acid) A nucleic acid that is the chief constituent of the ▷chromosomes, carrying genetic information, in the form of ▷genes, necessary for the organization and functioning of living cells. The molecular structure of DNA was first proposed by J. D. ▷Watson and F. H. ▷Crick in 1953. It consists of a double helix of two strands coiled around each other. Each strand is made up of alternating pentose sugar (deoxyribose) and phosphate groups, with an organic base attached to each pentose group. There are four possible bases: adenine (A), guanine (G), cytosine (C), and thymine (T). The bases on each strand are joined by hydrogen bonds and are always paired in the same way: A always binds with T and G with C. During replication, the strands of the helix separate and each provides a template for the synthesis of a new complementary strand, thus producing two identical copies of the original helix. This special property for accurate self-replication enables DNA to duplicate the genes of an organism during the nuclear divisions for growth (*see* mitosis) and for the production of germ cells for the next generation (*see* meiosis).

● **DNA fingerprinting** ▷*See* genetic fingerprinting.

● **Dnepr, River** ▶ (*or* R. Dnieper) A river in NE Europe. Rising in the Valdai Hills, NE of Smolensk, it flows mainly SE through Russia, Belarus, and E Ukraine to enter the Black Sea. Length: 2286 km (1420 mi).

● **Dneprodzerzhinsk** ▶ (name until 1936: Kamenskoye) 48 30N 34 37E A port in E Ukraine, on the River Dnepr. It produces iron and steel, machine tools, and chemicals. Population (1996 est): 281 000.

● **Dnepropetrovsk** ▶ (name from 1787 until 1796 and from 1802 until 1826: Ekaterinoslav) 48 29N 35 00E A city in the E Ukraine, on the River Dnepr. It is one of the country's largest industrial cities, producing especially iron and steel. Population (1996 est): 1 147 000.

● **Dnestr, River** ▶ (*or* R. Dniester) A river in NE Europe. It flows mainly SE from the Carpathian Mountains through Ukraine and Moldova to the Black Sea near Odessa. Length: 1411 km (877 mi).

● **D-notice** ▷*See* Defence Advisory Notice.

● **Dobell, Sir William** ▶ (1899–1970) Australian artist. Trained as an architect, he subsequently studied art in England and Holland. Returning to Australia in 1934 he became an official war artist and an established portraitist.

● **Dobermann pinscher** ▶ A breed of dog developed by Louis Dobermann in Germany in the late 19th century. It has a powerful streamlined body with a very short tail and a long muzzle. The short smooth coat is black, brown, or blue-grey with tan markings. Dobermanns are widely used as guard dogs. Height: 70 cm (dogs); 64 cm (bitches).

● **Dobruja** ▶ (Bulgarian name: Dobrudzha; Romanian name: Dobrogea) An area in E central Europe, in SE Romania and NE Bulgaria. It consists of a low-lying alluvial plain between the River Danube and the Black Sea.

● **dobsonfly** ▶ A winged insect of the family *Corydalidae*, occurring in all continents except Europe. Male dobsonflies have exaggerated jaws, sometimes over 25 mm long. Eggs are laid near fresh water and the larvae (hellgrammites) are aquatic, using their jaws to feed on insects and invertebrates. They migrate to the soil to pupate. Order: ▷*Neuroptera*.

● **Dobzhansky, Theodosius** ▶ (1900–75) US geneticist, born in Russia. His studies of wild populations of fruit flies revealed the extent of genetic differences between individuals and how, through natural selection, this enabled the populations to adapt rapidly to changing conditions.

● **dock** ▶ A plant (usually perennial) of the genus *Rumex*, of temperate regions. 10–200 cm tall, it has a stout root and lance-shaped leaves, the traditional antidote to nettle stings. The clusters of small greenish flowers produce small nutlets. Family: *Polygonaceae*. ▷*See also* sorrel.

● **Docklands** ▶ An area of over 2000 hectares (5500 acres) in E London that was formerly occupied by the docks, wharfs, and warehouses of the Port of London; since 1981 it has been developed for residential and commercial purposes after the docks became obsolete as a result of an increase in the size of ships, a disinclination on the part of shipowners to waste days negotiating a tidal river, and competition from foreign ports, especially Rotterdam.

The new developments have brought considerable prosperity to the area, with thousands of new residential homes and the tallest building in Europe, the Canary Wharf Tower. The area has its own new Docklands Airport and the Docklands Light Railway connecting it to the City of London.

● **docks** ▶ Structures that enable ships to load and unload cargo or passengers or to undergo repairs. A **wet dock**, on a tidal river or on the coast, has gates to maintain the water level irrespective of the tide. Ships can only enter or leave such a dock when the tide brings the water to the level inside. Where the range of the tide is small (less than 4 m) a **tidal dock** can be used. In this the dock is open to the harbour and ships in dock rise and fall with the tide. In **dry docks** the water enters at one end only and gates enable all the water to be pumped out, so that repairs can be made to a hull. **Floating docks** have the advantage of being movable, but they have a relatively short life. Floating docks also have watertight compartments from which the water can be pumped and they can be used for repairs. ▷*See also* dredger.

● **Doctors' Commons** ► A colloquial name for the College of Advocates and Doctors of Law, situated near St Paul's Cathedral in London between 1572 and 1867 (destroyed in the ▷Fire of London in 1666, it was rebuilt on the same site). It housed the ecclesiastical and Admiralty courts and their advocates, who held doctorates in civil law and were then separate from ▷barristers. With the passing of the High Court of Admiralty Act (1859) and other Acts, the college was closed and the building demolished to make room for Queen Victoria St.

● **documentary film** ► A film that interprets factual reality, often for educational purposes. The term was coined by John Grierson, leader of a school of British documentary film directors in the 1930s, to describe an influential early documentary, Robert ▷Flaherty's *Nanook of the North* (1920). Many political documentaries were produced in the 1930s, including Leni Reifenstahl's pro-Nazi *Triumph of the Will* (1934). During World War II, ▷propaganda documentaries were popular with both sides, notable examples including Frank ▷Capra's *Why We Fight* series (1942–45) and the British-made *London Can Take It* (1940). During the 1950s the advent of light hand-held cameras had a major impact on both the content and the style of documentary films, which became more spontaneous and less staged. In the 1960s such movements as Direct Cinema in the USA and Cinéma Vérité in France pioneered the so-called fly-on-the-wall approach, which attempts to capture reality with a minimum of cinematic artifice. Subsequently television and film drama incorporated many of the techniques associated with the documentary, a notable example of such "documentary dramas" being Ken Loach's essay on homelessness, *Cathy Come Home* (1966). Since the late 1960s the documentary has become primarily associated with television, resulting in such controversial programmes as *Death of a Princess* (1980) and *Death on the Rock* (1988).

● **dodder** ► A twining parasitic plant of the widely distributed genus *Cuscuta* (150 species), which absorbs food by inserting rootlike organs into the stems of other plants. Dodder has no chlorophyll (green pigment): it consists simply of a yellow or pinkish cordlike stem bearing round clusters of tiny yellow or white flowers. The leaves are reduced to scales and there are no roots. Family: *Cuscutaceae*.

● **Dodecanese** ► (Modern Greek name: Dhodhekánisos) A group of Greek islands in the SE Aegean Sea. Although known as the 12 Islands, it in fact consists of some 20 islands and islets, which include Cos, ▷Rhodes (the largest), and Pátmos. They were taken from Turkey by Italy in 1912 and passed to Greece in 1947. Total area: 2719 sq km (1050 sq mi). Population (1991): 162 439. Capital: Rhodes.

● **Dodgson, Charles Lutwidge** ▷*See* Carroll, Lewis.

● **dodo** ► A large flightless bird, *Raphus cucullatus*, that lived on Mauritius but was extinct by 1681, due to hunting by man. Weighing about 23 kg, it had a grey-blue wispy plumage, stout legs, tiny wings, a tuft of white tail feathers, and a large head with a massive hooked bill; it probably fed on fruit or roots. Family: *Raphidae*; order: *Columbiformes*.

● **Dodoma** ► 6 10S 35 40E A town in E central Tanzania. It became the legislative capital in 1983. Population (latest est): 203 833.

● **dog** ► A carnivorous mammal belonging to the family ▷*Canidae*. Ancestors of the modern domestic dog (*Canis familiaris*), probably derived from wolves or jackals, were domesticated over 10 000 years ago (or possibly much earlier than this). Wild dogs generally hunt in packs, relying on speed and cooperation to secure their prey. They are specialized hunters with long legs, sharp teeth, strong jaws, and acute hearing and smell. The intelligence and social nature of dogs have led to their breeding by man for a variety of purposes, principally as sporting dogs, working dogs, and household pets. There are up to 400 modern breeds and in the UK, standards for over 100 recognized breeds are established by the Kennel Club, founded in 1873. The most prestigious dog show, Crufts, is held annually in London. The UK Dangerous Dogs Act (1991) prohibits ownership of dogs bred for fighting, including the pit ▷bull terrier, Japanese Tosa, Dogo Argentino, and Fila Brasiliero; it also strengthens earlier legislation protecting people and property from attacks by dogs. □ p. 380.

● **dogbane** ► A perennial herb of the genus *Apocynum* (about 7 species), found mostly in the tropics and subtropics, especially the American species *A. androsaemifolium*. Up to 1.5 m high, dogbane has simple leaves and small white or pink bell-shaped flowers clustered at the tips of the shoots. The juice contains alkaloids and has been used in arrow poisons. Family: *Apocynaceae*. ▷*See also* Indian hemp.

● **doge** ► The title of the chief magistrate of Venice from about 697 AD to the fall of the Venetian Empire in 1797. The doge was elected for life and wielded considerable power until 1172 when his authority was restricted by the creation of a supreme Great Council of 480 members. Further constitutional checks made the doge little more than a figurehead. The first **Doge's Palace** was built in 814 and destroyed by an uprising in 976. Subsequent structures were destroyed by fire, and the present gothic palace was begun in the early 14th century.

● **Dogen** ► (1200–53) Japanese Buddhist monk, who introduced the ▷Soto school of Zen Buddhism to Japan. An orphan of noble birth, he became a monk at 13 and studied the Buddhist scriptures before visiting several Chinese monasteries (1223–27), where he studied Zen. After returning to Japan, he devoted himself to teaching the form of Zen practice that emphasizes meditation, as in his work *Shobogenzo* (*Knowledge concerning the Dharma*).

● **dogfish** ► A small ▷shark belonging to one of a number of families. *Scyliorhinus stellaris*, up to 1 m long, and *S. canicula*, up to 75 cm long, are brown-spotted dogfish commonly found in Mediterranean and British coastal waters. They are edible and purchased as "rock salmon." Chief families: *Triakidae* (smooth dogfish or smooth hounds); *Squalidae* (spiny dogfish); *Scyliorhinidae* (spotted dogfish).

● **Dogger Bank** ► A vast sandbank in the central North Sea, 17–36 m (55–120 ft) below water. Several naval battles have taken place on the bank, notably the battle of Dogger Bank (24 January, 1915) between British and German forces. It is a major fishing ground.

● **doggerel** ► A crude, naive, form of poetry, often irregular in metre. Early examples are John ▷Skelton's *Colin Clout* (1519) and Samuel ▷Butler's *Hudibras* (1663–78). It is much used in comic verse by Ogden ▷Nash and others.

● **Doggett, Thomas** ► (c. 1670–1721) British actor, who won acclaim as a comedian in plays by William Congreve. At one time a manager of the Theatre Royal, Drury Lane, he offered a prize of a coat and badge in a sculling competition held on the River Thames in honour of the accession of George I; it is still competed for each year on 1 Aug.

● **dog racing** ▷*See* greyhound racing.

● **dog rose** ► A shrubby ▷rose, *Rosa canina*, 1–5 m high. It grows in woods, hedges, and roadsides of Europe, North Africa, and SW Asia. The arching stems have strong curved prickles and bear clusters of scentless white or pink flowers.

● **Dogs, Isle of** ► A district in the Greater London borough of Tower Hamlets, bounded on three sides by the Thames. A former docks area, it now forms the centre of the ▷Docklands redevelopment.

● **dog's tooth violet** ► A spring-blooming plant of the genus *Erythronium* (20 species), also known as adder's tongue, native to Eurasia and North America. They have white, yellow, or purple nodding flowers with two leaves at the base; the fruit is a pod. Several species are grown as rock-garden ornamentals. A European species is *E. dens-canis*, with purple flowers. Family: *Liliaceae*.

● **dogwood** ► A shrub or small tree of the genus *Cornus* (about 45 species), mostly of the N hemisphere. It has oval pointed leaves with prominent curved veins and dense clusters of four-petalled flowers. The fruit is a berry. The common European dogwood (*C. sanguinea*) has white flowers, blood-red shoots and autumn leaves, and black berries; Cornelian cherry (*C. mas*), of central and SE Europe, has small yellow flowers and attractive red berries. The American flowering dogwood (*C. florida*) has showy pinkish blossoms and red berries. Family: *Cornaceae*.

dog

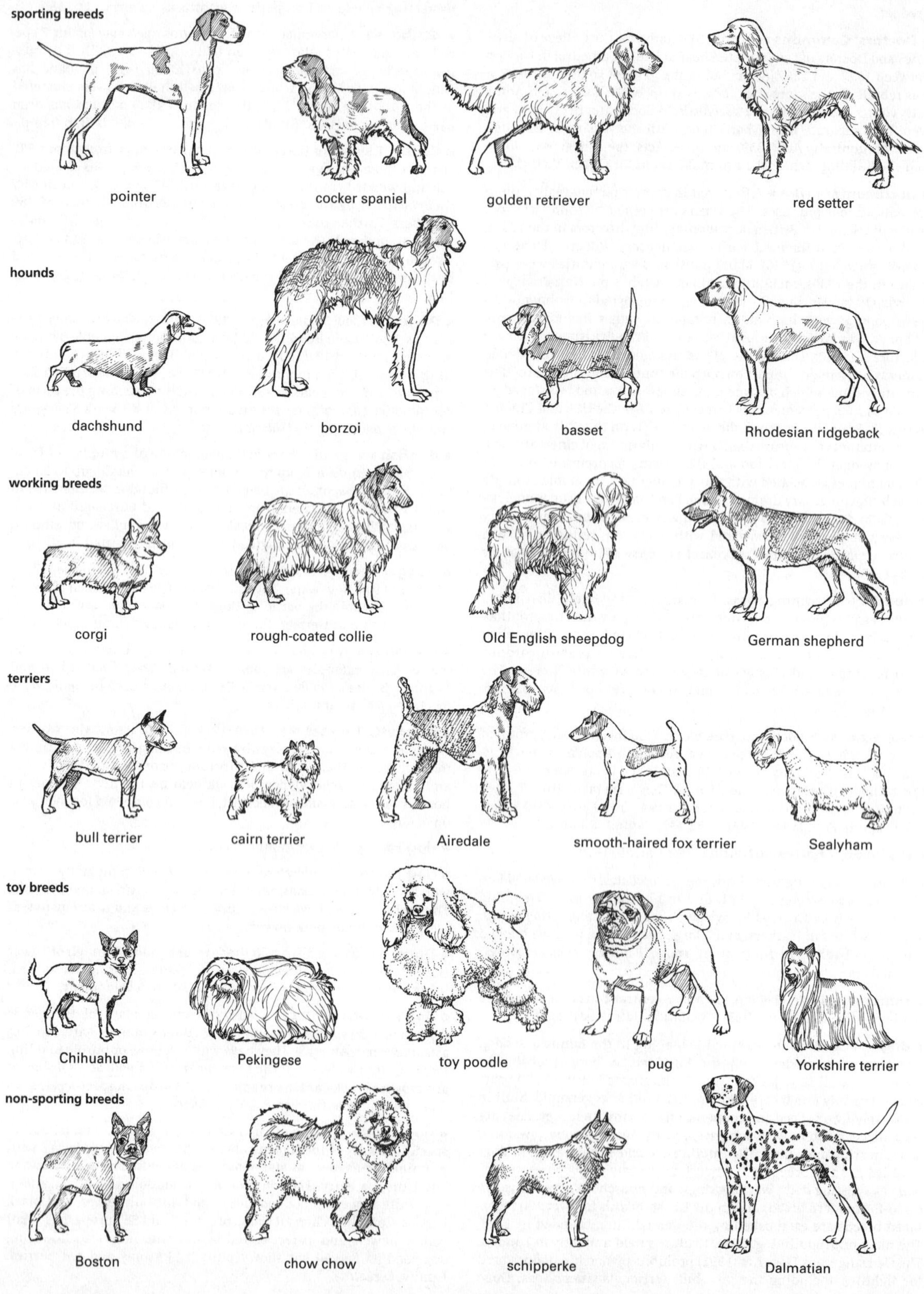

sporting breeds

pointer

cocker spaniel

golden retriever

red setter

hounds

dachshund

borzoi

basset

Rhodesian ridgeback

working breeds

corgi

rough-coated collie

Old English sheepdog

German shepherd

terriers

bull terrier

cairn terrier

Airedale

smooth-haired fox terrier

Sealyham

toy breeds

Chihuahua

Pekingese

toy poodle

pug

Yorkshire terrier

non-sporting breeds

Boston

chow chow

schipperke

Dalmatian

● **Doha** ▶ 25 15N 51 36E The capital of Qatar, on the E coast. Its modern development (including an international seaport and airport) has been funded by oil revenues. Population (1993 est): 339 471.

● **Dohnányi, Ernö** ▶ (Ernst von D.; 1877–1960) Hungarian composer and pianist. He spent his last years in the USA. He was influenced by Brahms, who praised his early works. Unlike Bartók and Kodály, Dohnányi remained uninfluenced by Hungarian folksong. His best-known composition is the *Variations on a Nursery Theme* (for piano and orchestra; 1913), based on the tune "Baa Baa Black Sheep."

● **Dolby system** ▶ Tradename of an electronic device for reducing the hiss in sound reproduction using ▷tape recorders. It was invented by Ray Dolby (1933–   ), who set up a company to make Dolby noise-reduction units. These are now built into most tape recorders, increasingly as an automatic function. Since the late 1970s nearly all commercial audio tapes and film soundtracks have been recorded using the system. The Dolby system selectively boosts the higher frequencies in the signal before recording it, to drown out the hiss produced by the tape, and attenuates them when playing back. Its unique feature is that it operates only when the music is quiet enough for the hiss to be heard. This avoids both distortion that occurs if lower frequencies are boosted to the same level and distortion from boosting already loud higher frequencies.

● **dolce stil nuovo** ▶ (Italian: sweet new style) A style of love poetry founded by the Bolognese poet Guido Guinizelli (c. 1240–76) and perfected by the Florentine poets ▷Cavalcanti and ▷Dante. It is characterized by a spiritualization of ▷courtly love, the use of the vernacular, and the sonnet, ballad, and canzone verse forms. Examples include Dante's lyrics to Beatrice. The style influenced ▷Petrarch, ▷Bembo, Dante Gabriel ▷Rossetti, and Ezra ▷Pound.

● **Dolci, Danilo** ▶ (1924–98) Italian social reformer and writer. The author of many books, including *To Feed the Hungry* (1959), he established centres for the study of economic development, unemployment, and poverty. His international standing brought him a number of awards.

● **doldrums** ▶ The equatorial belt within which the trade-wind zones converge. Winds are light and variable but the strong upward movement of air caused by the meeting of the trade winds produces frequent thunderstorms, heavy rains, and squalls. Navigation by sailing ships was difficult in these areas; ships often became becalmed for several days.

● **dolerite** ▶ A dark-coloured hypabyssal igneous rock, the medium-grained equivalent of gabbros, occurring mainly as dykes, sills, and plugs. It contains calcic plagioclase feldspar and augite, and sometimes olivine, hypersthene, quartz, or feldspathoids. It is called diabase in the USA.

● **Dolgellau** ▶ 52 44N 3 53W A market town and tourist centre in North Wales, in Gwynedd. Population (1991): 2936.

● **Dolin, Sir Anton** ▶ (Sydney Healey-Kay; 1904–83) British ballet dancer and choreographer. Having joined Diaghilev's company in 1921, he founded his own company in 1927, with Alicia ▷Markova; in 1949 they founded the Festival Ballet in London. His original ballets included *Capriccioso* (1940) and *The Romantic Age* (1942).

● **Dollfuss, Engelbert** ▶ (1892–1934) Austrian statesman; chancellor (1932–34). He became prominent as leader of the Lower Austrian Farmers' League. Ruling by decree from 1933, his chancellorship was increasingly strained by his inability to control the Austrian Nazis or to cooperate with the Social Democrats. He suppressed the Social Democratic revolt in February, 1934, and was assassinated in July during an abortive attempt by the Nazis to seize power.

● **dolmen** ▶ (Breton: table stone) A prehistoric tomb made of huge stone slabs set upright and supporting a stone roof. Widely distributed in ▷Neolithic Europe, dolmens were often covered by a ▷barrow.

● **Dolmetsch, Arnold** ▶ (1858–1940) British musician and instrument maker. He pioneered the rediscovery of early music and its performance on contemporary instruments in their original style. His home at Haslemere became a centre for early music festivals and he made viols, lutes, harpsichords, and recorders there, as well as editing early music. His son **Carl Dolmetsch** (1911–97) carried on the tradition and was a virtuoso recorder player.

● **dolomite** ▶ A mineral consisting of calcium magnesium carbonate, $CaMg(CO_3)_2$, colourless, white or grey in colour. Rocks containing over 15% magnesium carbonate are called dolomites, those containing less are magnesian limestones, and those containing both dolomite and calcite are dolomitic limestones. Dolomite occurs as a primary sediment, in metalliferous veins and in limestones altered by the process of dolomitization, by which the calcium carbonate is wholly or partly converted to dolomite by magnesium-rich sea water, or by magnesium-rich solutions permeating joints in the rock.

● **Dolomites** ▶ (Italian name: Alpi Dolomitiche) A section of the Alps in NE Italy. Composed of dolomitic limestone, they are characterized by their steep-sided rocky peaks, the highest of which is the Marmolada at 3342 m (10 965 ft).

● **dolphin** ▶ 1. A toothed ▷whale of the family *Delphinidae* (about 50 species). Agile and streamlined and up to 4.5 m long, dolphins live in large groups, or schools, and feed mainly on fish. They are intelligent creatures with well-developed abilities for social communication and ▷echolocation. The common dolphin (*Delphinus delphus*), which grows to 2.1 m, is blue-black with a white belly and striped body. ▷*See also* bottlenose; porpoise. 2. A fast-moving fish of the family *Coryphaenidae* (2 species). The common dolphin (*Coryphaena hippuras*) has a bluish tapering body, up to 2 m long, with a large blunt head, a forked tail, and a long dorsal fin. It occurs in tropical and temperate seas and feeds on fish and invertebrates. Order: *Perciformes*.

● **Domagk, Gerhard** ▶ (1895–1964) German biochemist, who (in 1932) noticed the powerful effects of a dye, Prontosil, in combating bacterial infection. From this dye was isolated the first of the ▷sulphonamide drugs (sulphanilamide) which paved the way for the treatment of a wide range of bacterial diseases. Domagk received the 1939 Nobel Prize but was prevented from accepting it until 1947, after the fall of Hitler.

● **domain** ▶ (biology) ▷*See* taxonomy.

● **dome** ▶ A roof or ceiling that is hemispherical in section. In classical architecture it was generally supported by a circular drum and topped by a lantern. The Romans developed the technique of building a dome in cast concrete while the Byzantines introduced the use of four pendentives to build a dome over a square section. Another method was invented in the 15th century by ▷Brunelleschi, using a strong brick cone to bear the weight and a lighter outer shell for visual effect. The Pantheon and St Peter's in Rome, Hagia Sophia, Istanbul, and St Paul's, London, all have famous domes. The largest dome in the world is the ▷Millennium Dome in Greenwich, London, followed by the Georgia Dome in Atlanta, USA.

● **Domenichino** ▶ (Domenico Zampieri; 1581–1641) Italian painter, born in Bologna. He trained under Ludovico ▷Carracci. In Rome (1602–31) he painted frescoes of the *Life of St Cecilia* (1615–17; S Luigi dei Francesi) and the altarpiece *Last Communion of St Jerome* (Vatican Museum). His landscapes influenced ▷Poussin and ▷Claude Lorraine.

● **Domenico Veneziano** ▶ (active c. 1438–1461) Italian painter of the early Renaissance, probably born in Venice. He settled in Florence, where he painted his famous *St Lucy Altarpiece* (central panel; Uffizi).

● **Dome of the Rock** ▶ The great mosque in Jerusalem, built in 691 AD by the ▷Umayyad caliph, 'Abd al-Malik, to commemorate the tradition that Mohammed ascended to Paradise from the Temple Mount on which it stands (*see* Temple of Jerusalem). It is the third most holy place of Islam, after ▷Mecca and ▷Medina. The edifice, also erroneously called the mosque of Omar by Europeans, is an impressive example of early Islamic architecture.

● **Domesday Book** ▶ (1086) The survey of England ordered by William I to assess the extent of his own possessions and the value for taxation purposes of the estates of his tenants in chief. Parts of N and NW England and some towns, including London and Winchester, were omitted. Royal commissioners collected, shire by shire, details about each ▷manor, naming its present owner and its owner under Edward the Confessor, changes in its size since Edward's reign, the numbers of its inhabitants and the services or rents they owed, and the numbers of its ploughteams, mills, and fisheries. The survey, in two volumes, is now in the Public Record Office.

● **dominance** ▶ In genetics, the condition in which one of the ▷alleles of a gene predominates in the function of that gene. Gregor ▷Mendel, in his famous experiments, crossed pea plants from a line producing yellow seeds with plants from a line producing green seeds. The resulting offspring all produced yellow seeds, i.e. the dominant allele of the gene determining seed colour was that of the yellow-seeded plants; the allele of the green-seeded plants was recessive.

● **Domingo, Placido** ▶ (1941–) Spanish tenor, educated in Mexico. After making his debut at the Metropolitan Opera, New York, in 1968, he specialized in Puccini and Verdi, starring in film versions of *La Traviata* in 1983 and *Otello* in 1986. In the 1990s he reached a huge international audience through his appearances with the tenors Luciano ▷Pavarotti and José ▷Carreras.

● **Dominic, St** ▶ (Domingo de Guzmán; c. 1170–1221) Spanish churchman, who founded the ▷Dominicans. A canon attached to the cathedral at Osma, Castile, and later its prior, he became a successful missionary to the heretical ▷Albigenses in the south of France. In 1216 with papal encouragement he founded a religious order devoted to preaching. From his headquarters in Rome he sent out preachers to establish houses in many major cities. Feast Day: 4 Aug. Emblems: a star and a dog holding a torch in its mouth.

● **Dominica, Commonwealth of** ▶ An island country in the West Indies, the largest of the Windward Islands. It is of volcanic origin and very mountainous. The population is mainly of African descent.
Economy: chiefly agricultural; exports include bananas, limes, and lime oil. Manufacturing remains limited to food processing and a little light industry. Forestry and fishing are being encouraged.
History: at the time of Columbus's landing in 1493 it was inhabited by Caribs. The island changed hands several times between the French and the British during the 18th century before finally becoming British in 1783. It became internally self-governing in 1967 and an independent republic within the British Commonwealth in November, 1978. Dame Eugenia Charles (1919–) was prime minister from 1980 until 1995.

Commonwealth of Dominica

Head of state	President Vernon Shaw
Official language	English, although Creole French is more commonly spoken
Official currency	East Caribbean dollar of 100 cents
Area	728 sq km (289 sq mi)
Population (1999 est)	77 000
Capital	Roseau

● **Dominican Republic** ▶ A country in the Caribbean Sea, occuping the E two-thirds of the island of Hispaniola (Haiti occupies the W third). It is largely mountainous, rising to over 3000 m (10 000 ft). It is subject to hurricanes. The population is mainly of mixed African and European descent.
Economy: chiefly agricultural. The principal cash crop is sugar, others being coffee, cocoa, and bananas. Mining and light industry have been developed. The principal mineral export is ferro-nickel and gold and silver mining began in 1975. Oil and hydroelectricity are being exploited. Manufacturing and tourism are increasingly important. The country has a large external debt, although large amounts were paid off in the 1990s.
History: the island was visited in 1492 by Columbus, who named it Hispaniola. The E became a Spanish colony, while the French established themselves in the W, in what became Haiti. The Spanish colony was ceded to the French in 1795 and soon fell to the Haitian ▷Toussaint L'Ouverture, who proclaimed himself ruler of all Hispaniola. The Spanish were restored in the E in 1809 and in 1821 the colony gained independence. It was held by Haiti from 1822 until 1844, when the Dominican Republic was founded. Political and economic instability led to US occupation (1916–22) and the establishment (1930) of ▷Trujillo's 30-year dictatorship. Following his assassination Juan Bosch was elected (1962) president only to be deposed (1963) in a military coup. An attempt to reinstate Bosch was

thwarted by the USA in 1965. Joaquín ▷Balaguer was president from 1966 to 1978 and from 1986 to 1996; he was succeeded by Leonel Fernández, who was succeeded in turn (2000) by Hipólito Mejía.

Dominican Republic

Head of state	President Hipólito Mejía
Official language	Spanish
Official currency	Dominican Republic peso of 100 centavos
Area	48 442 sq km (18 700 sq mi)
Population (1999 est)	8 132 000
Capital and main port	Santo Domingo

● **Dominicans** ▶ (Latin *Ordo Praedicatorum*: Order of Preachers) A Roman Catholic order of friars, also known as Black Friars, Friar Preachers, or (in France) Jacobins, founded by St ▷Dominic and formally organized at Bologna in 1220–21. Their purpose was preaching and teaching, the individual friars leading mendicant lives much of the time. Among their great scholars was St Thomas ▷Aquinas. They were prominent defenders of orthodoxy in the ▷Inquisition and leading missionaries to the New World, although the Jesuits superseded them in this role during the Counter-Reformation. There are also two orders of Dominican nuns.

● **Domino, Fats** ▶ (Antoine D.; 1928–) US Black jazz singer, pianist, and songwriter, who became famous in the rock and roll era. His songs, which contained blues elements, include "Blueberry Hill" and "Jambalaya."

● **dominoes** ▶ A game played with rectangular pieces marked at each end with a group of dots or a blank space. In a set of 28 pieces, each group adds up to a number from 1 to 6. Dominoes were used in China in ancient times but not in Europe until the 18th century. There are many games, but in the basic game played in the UK each player first draws seven pieces. The player with the double six places it face up on the table. The next player places next to it a six on the end of another domino; if this domino has, for instance, a two on the other end the third player must match either the two or the remaining six. Doubles are placed crosswise, the others end to end. A player who cannot make a match misses his turn or in some games takes another domino. The first to finish wins.

● **Domitian(us), Titus Flavius** ▶ (51–96 AD) Roman emperor (81–96). His frustrating inactivity under his father ▷Vespasian and his brother ▷Titus made him a harsh ruler. His government became increasingly absolute and from about 84, as censor for life, he controlled the Senate. His suspicion of treachery culminated in a reign of terror, which precipitated his own murder.

● **Domrémy-la-Pucelle** ▶ 48 26N 5 40E A village in NE France, in the Vosges, the birthplace of Joan of Arc.

● **Don, River** ▶ A river in SW Russia, flowing mainly S to the Sea of Azov. A canal links it to the River Volga. Length: 1981 km (1224 mi).

● **Donatello** ▶ (Donato de Nicolo di Betti Bardi; c. 1386–1466) Florentine sculptor. A pioneer of the Renaissance style, Donatello first broke with tradition in his marble sculptures of *St Mark* and *St George* (1415) for the exterior of Orsanmichele. These and his prophets for the campanile of the Duomo are modelled as lifelike rather than idealized figures. Simultaneously he developed a new form of relief sculpture, in which he created perspective by incising the surface of the marble rather than modelling it in depth. Working also in bronze from the early 1420s, he produced *David* (c. 1430–35; Bargello, Florence), the influential equestrian monument in Padua known as the *Gattamelata* (1447–53), and the high altar for S Antonio, Padua (1446–50). His late works include the expressive painted wooden sculpture of *Mary Magdalen* (1454–55; Baptistry, Florence).

● **Donatists** ▶ Members of a schismatic North African Christian group of the 4th and 5th centuries AD, named after Donatus, one of their bishops. They held that the validity of the sacraments depended on the personal holiness of the minister. St ▷Augustine of Hippo's repudiation of their views in the early 5th century crystallized Catholic teaching on these matters. He argued that since the true minister is Christ, the personal worthiness of the priest could not affect the validity of the sacraments.

● **Donatus, Aelius** ▶ (4th century AD) Roman grammarian and rhetorician. Donatus was the tutor of St Jerome, and his Latin grammar, *Ars Grammatica*, became a universally accepted textbook in the middle ages.

● **Donbass** ▷*See* Donets Basin.

● **Doncaster** ▶ **1.** 53 32N 1 07W An industrial town in N England, in Doncaster unitary authority, South Yorkshire, with railway workshops; coalmining is in decline following recent pit closures. Population (1991): 71 595. **2.** A unitary authority in N England, in South Yorkshire. Area: 582 sq km (225 sq mi). Population (1995 est): 292 900.

● **Donegal** ▶ (Irish name: Dún Na Ngall) A county in the NW Republic of Ireland, in Ulster bordering on the Atlantic Ocean. Chiefly mountainous, it has a rugged indented coastline. Agricultural products include barley, oats, and potatoes; cattle and sheep are reared. Linen and tweed are manufactured. Area: 4830 sq km (1865 sq mi). Population (1996 est): 129 000. County town: Lifford.

● **Donets Basin** ▶ (or Donbass) An industrial region in E Ukraine. It is the oldest centre of coal production in the country and still its major coal-producing and steel-manufacturing area. Area: about 25 900 sq km (10 000 sq mi).

● **Donetsk** ▶ (name until 1924: Yuzovka; name from 1924 until 1961: Stalino) 48 22N 40 02E A city in E Ukraine on the River Kalmius. The major city of the ▷Donets Basin, it has important coalmining and metallurgical industries. Population (1996 est): 1 088 000.

● **Dong Hai** ▷*See* China Sea.

● **Dongola** ▶ (or Dunqulah) 19 10N 30 27E A small town in the N Sudan, on the River Nile. It was the capital of the Christian kingdom of Nubia (6th–14th centuries). Population (latest est.): 5937.

● **Dongting, Lake** ▶ (or Lake Tung-t'ing) A lake in SE China. Seasonally fed or drained by the Yangtze River, it regulates the river's flooding. Area: (winter) 3900 sq km (1500 sq mi); (summer) about 10 000 sq km (4000 sq mi).

● **Dönitz, Karl** ▶ (1891–1981) German admiral. He made his name as a U-boat commander in World War I and in the first three years of World War II he developed the "pack" system of submarine attack. In 1943 he became grand admiral and then commander in chief of the German navy. He was appointed chancellor after Hitler's death and was imprisoned from 1946 to 1956 for war crimes.

● **Donizetti, Gaetano** ▶ (1797–1848) Italian composer of operas. He became paralysed and mentally ill towards the end of his life. He wrote with great facility and his 75 stage works rely more on ▷coloratura display than on intrinsic dramatic effect. Revivals of such operas as *Lucia di Lammermoor* (1835) and *Daughter of the Regiment* (1840) have been successful with such singers as Joan Sutherland or Maria Callas in the title roles.

● **Don Juan** ▶ The great aristocratic libertine of European literature. His probable first appearance was in Tirso de Molina's play *El burlador de Sevilla* (1630), in which he kills the father of his latest victim; he mockingly invites the old man's statue to dinner, and it drags him off to hell. This plot is retained in subsequent versions, most notably ▷Molière's *Don Juan* (1665) and ▷Mozart's *Don Giovanni* (1787). In satirical treatments by ▷Byron (*Don Juan*, 1819–24) and G. B. ▷Shaw (*Man and Superman*, 1903) Juan is more hunted than hunter.

● **donkey** ▶ A domesticated ▷ass. Donkeys are more commonly used for pack and draught work than for riding: being stronger in the hindquarters than the forequarters, they must bear the load over the pelvis, which is a less comfortable position for a rider. ▷*See also* hinny; mule.

● **Donleavy, J(ames) P(atrick)** ▶ (1926–　) Irish-American novelist. His successful first novel, *The Ginger Man* (1956), was followed by further comic picaresque novels including *The Onion Eaters* (1971), *The Destinies of Darcy Dancer, Gentleman* (1977), *Are You Listening Rabbi Löw?* (1987), and *The Lady Who Liked Clean Rest Rooms* (1995).

● **Donne, John** ▶ (1572–1631) English poet, greatest of the Metaphysical school. He received a Roman Catholic education, studied at

John Donne ▶ This 19th-century engraving shows the great Metaphysical poet as Dean of St Paul's.

Oxford and Lincoln's Inn, and took part in naval raids on Spain. In 1601 he secretly married the niece of his patron, Sir Thomas Egerton, and was briefly imprisoned. Failing to gain secular advancement, despite having several influential patrons, he became an Anglican priest in 1615 and was appointed Dean of St Paul's in 1621. His poetry combines passionate feeling for God, woman, and humanity with brilliant intellectual wit. Almost all of it, even religious works, such as *La Corona* (1607) and the Holy Sonnets, was written before 1615.

● **Doolittle, Hilda** ▶ (1886–1961) US poet, who wrote under the initials H. D. Born in Pennsylvania, she went to England in 1911 and married Richard ▷Aldington. A leading exponent of Imagism, her books include *Sea Garden* (1916), *Hymen* (1921), and *Helen in Egypt* (1961).

● **dopamine** ▷*See* catecholamines; neurotransmitter.

● **Doppler, Christian Johann** ▶ (1803–53) Austrian physicist, who explained and derived, in 1842, an expression for the change in frequency of a wave when the source is moving relative to an observer (*see* Doppler effect). He attempted to apply this principle to the coloration of stars; although the effect is too small to be observed visually, it is now widely used spectroscopically in astronomy.

● **Doppler effect** ▶ The apparent change in the frequency of a wave caused by relative motion between the source and the observer. When the source and the observer are approaching each other, the apparent frequency of the wave increases; when one is travelling away from the other, the apparent frequency decreases. An example of the Doppler effect is the change in pitch of a train whistle as the train passes through a station. The effect can also be observed as a shifting of the wavelength of light from a receding star towards the red end of the spectrum (*see* redshift). It is named after Christian ▷Doppler.

● **Doráti, Antal** ▶ (1906–88) US conductor and composer, born in Hungary. Conductor Laureate of the Royal Philharmonic, Detroit Symphony, and Stockholm Philharmonic Orchestras, he made over 500 symphonic recordings.

● **dor beetle** ▶ A large shiny black convex beetle, with broad digging legs, belonging to a family (Geotrupidae; about 300 species) of dung feeders. Dor beetles burrow into the soil beneath dung and lay their eggs on plugs of dung.

● **Dorcas gazelle** ▶ A small ▷gazelle, *Gazella dorcas*, of N Africa and S Asia, also called afri. A desert animal, it is light red with a pale flank stripe and distinctive face stripes.

● **Dorchester** ▶ 50 43N 2 26W A market town in S England, the administrative centre for Dorset on the River Frome. It has several Roman remains and features as Casterbridge in Thomas Hardy's novels. Population (1991): 15 037.

● **Dordogne, River** ▶ A river in SW France. Rising in the Auvergne

Mountains, it flows SW to the Gironde estuary NNE of Bordeaux. It is important for hydroelectric power and its vineyards. Length: 472 km (293 mi).

● **Dordrecht** ▶ (*or* Dort) 51 48N 4 40E A port in the SW Netherlands, in South Holland province. It has a thriving timber trade and metallurgical, shipbuilding, and chemical industries. Population (1996 est): 116 196.

● **Doré, (Paul) Gustave (Louis Christophe)** ▶ (1832–83) French illustrator, painter, and sculptor, born in Strasbourg. He established his wide and lasting popularity in the 1850s with his illustrations of Rabelais' books and Balzac's *Contes drôlatiques*. These were followed by illustrations to Dante, Cervantes, Tennyson, etc., showing his taste for the grotesque and dramatic. His realistic scenes of poverty in *London* influenced Van Gogh. □Camelot.

● **Dorgon** ▶ (1612–50) Prince of Manchuria, who controlled China as regent for a child emperor from 1643 to 1650. Continuing the expansionist policy of his father ▷Nurhachi, Dorgon helped to lay the foundations of the ▷Qing dynasty in China, basing its power on centralized government instead of the clan system.

● **Doria** ▶ A family that was prominent in Genoa from the 12th to 18th centuries. The most notable member of the family was **Andrea Doria** (1466–1560). An admiral and condottiere, he served the French against Emperor Charles V, ousted imperial troops from Genoa, and then transferred his allegiance to Charles and expelled the French in return for the emperor's recognition of Genoese liberty (1528). He then became the ruler of Genoa, initiating the period of aristocratic rule (1528–1797) during which the Doria family contributed six doges of Genoa.

● **Dorians** ▶ Iron Age Greek conquerors of the S Aegean region (c. 1100–1000 BC). Moving southward from Epirus and SW Macedonia, they displaced the ▷Achaeans and brought about the final collapse of the Bronze Age ▷Mycenaean civilization. They settled in the S and E Peloponnese, near the isthmus of Corinth, in the S Aegean islands, the Dodecanese, and SW Anatolia. There were three major tribes: the Hylleis, Pamphyloi, and Dymanes. The Doric dialects they spoke belonged to the Western Greek group.

● **Doric order** ▷*See* orders of architecture.

● **dormancy** ▶ A period of reduced metabolic activity during which a plant or animal or a reproductive body (e.g. seeds or spores) can survive unfavourable environmental conditions. The onset of dormancy may be triggered by a number of factors, including changes in temperature, daylength (*see* photoperiodism), and availability of water, oxygen, and carbon dioxide. The dormant phase of a life cycle is represented as spores in bacteria and fungi, cysts in protozoans and some invertebrates, and seeds, buds, and bulbs or similar organs in plants. ▷*See also* aestivation; hibernation.

● **dormouse** ▶ A climbing ▷rodent belonging to the family *Gliridae* (about 10 species) of Eurasia and Africa. The common dormouse (*Muscardinus avellanarius*) is reddish, about 6 cm long with a 5-cm bushy tail. It sleeps in a nest above ground level during the day, feeding at night on nuts, berries, and seeds. During winter it hibernates beneath debris or tree stumps, occasionally waking to feed on stored food.

● **Dorneywood** ▶ A country house in S England, in Buckinghamshire near Burnham Beeches. Administered by the National Trust, it was presented to the nation by Lord Courtauld-Thomson as a residence for ministers of state.

● **Dornier, Claudius** ▶ (1884–1969) German aircraft designer and manufacturer, who constructed the first all-metal aircraft (1911). At his works in Friedrichshafen he manufactured both civil and military planes.

● **Dornoch** ▶ 57 52N 4 02W A resort in N Scotland, in Highland on Dornoch Firth. It was the site of the last execution for witchcraft (1722) in Scotland and it has a well-known golf course. Population (1991): 1196.

● **Dorpat** ▷*See* Tartu.

● **Dorset** ▶ A county of SW England, bordering on the English Chan-

nel. Under local government reorganization in 1974 it gained part of SW Hampshire. Bournemouth and Poole became independent ▷unitary authorities in 1997. It consists of lowlands in the SE with the North Dorset Downs and Cranborne Chase in the N and the South Dorset Downs near the coast. The chief rivers are the Frome and the Stour. Agriculture is predominant, especially livestock farming. Tourism is important, notably in Bournemouth and Weymouth. Many towns and villages are associated with the writings of Thomas ▷Hardy. Area (excluding unitary authorities): 2654 sq km (1024 sq mi). Population (1996 est, excluding unitary authorities): 382 090. Administrative centre: Dorchester.

● **Dort** ▷*See* Dordrecht.

● **Dortmund** ▶ 51 32N 07 27E A city in NW Germany, in North Rhine-Westphalia in the ▷Ruhr. A port on the Dortmund–Ems Canal and a major industrial centre, it produces steel, furniture, textiles, coal, and beer. Its university was established in 1966. Population (1996 est): 598 840.

● **Dortmund–Ems Canal** ▶ A major canal in W Germany. Opened in 1899, it links the Ruhr industrial area with the North Sea near Emden. Length: about 270 km (168 mi).

● **dory** ▷*See* John Dory.

● **dose** ▷*See* gray; radiation sickness; sievert.

● **Dos Passos, John** ▶ (1896–1970) US novelist. He served as an ambulance driver in World War I and worked as a war correspondent in Spain, Mexico, and the Near East. His major work, the trilogy *U.S.A.*—comprising *The Forty-Second Parallel* (1930), *1919* (1932), and *The Big Money* (1936)—is an experimental and radical interpretation of American history.

● **Dostoievski, Fedor Mikhailovich** ▶ (1821–81) Russian novelist. Son of a landowner murdered by his serfs, he graduated as a military engineer in 1843, but resigned his commission and began writing. In 1849 he was sentenced to four years hard labour in Siberia, followed by army service, for printing socialist propaganda. In 1864 his wife and brother died, and he incurred heavy gambling debts. He lived in W Europe from 1867 to 1871 with his new wife, his secretary Anna Snitkina, plagued by his epilepsy and compulsive gambling. He returned to Russia in 1871 and became relatively prosperous, stable, and conservative. His major novels, in which he explored moral and political themes with merciless psychological realism, are *Crime and Punishment* (1866), *The Idiot* (1868–69), *The Possessed* (1869–72), and *The Brothers Karamazov* (1879–80).

● **dotterel** ▶ A small Eurasian ▷plover, *Eudromias morinellus*, that nests in tundra regions and migrates to the Mediterranean and SW Asia for the winter. It is 20 cm long and mottled brown above with a broad white eye stripe and a grey breast separated by a narrow white band from its russet belly.

● **Dou, Gerrit** ▶ (1613–75) Dutch painter of domestic interiors and portraits, born in Leyden. He studied under ▷Rembrandt (1628–31), who influenced his early portrait *Rembrandt's Mother* (c. 1630; Rijksmuseum, Amsterdam). *The Poulterer's Shop* (National Gallery, London) is a more typical work.

● **Douai** ▶ 50 22N 3 05E A town in N France, in the Nord department. It became a centre for English Roman Catholics following the establishment of a college by William Allen in 1568 (*see* Douai Bible). Douai is a coalmining centre and has iron and steel industries. Population (1990): 199 562.

● **Douai Bible** ▶ The Roman Catholic version of the Bible in English, translated from the ▷Vulgate by Catholic scholars from Oxford, who had fled to Europe during the reign of Elizabeth I, becoming members of the English College at Douai. The New Testament was published at Reims in 1582 and the Old Testament at Douai in 1609–10. Its language influenced that of the ▷King James Version.

● **Douala** ▶ 4 04N 9 43E The largest city in Cameroon, on the River Wouri estuary. A deepwater port and the chief export point of the country, it has brewing, food-processing, textiles, and timber industries. Population (1992 est): 1 200 000.

● **double bass** ▶ The lowest-pitched □musical instrument of the violin family. The flat back and sloping shoulders of some double basses are derived from the ▷viol family. Unlike the violin, viola, and cello, its four strings are tuned in fourths (E, A, D, G). It has a range of over three octaves, from the E an octave below the bass stave. The double bass is a member of the symphony orchestra; it is also played in jazz and dance bands, usually by plucking the strings. Music for the double bass is written an octave higher than it sounds.

● **double vision** ► The condition in which a person sees two images of a single object. Known medically as diplopia, it is caused by lack of coordination between the muscles that move the eyes. Temporary double vision may occur after taking drugs or alcohol; alternatively it may be due to damage or disease of one of the nerves that supply the eye muscles.

● **Doubs, River** ► A river in E France. Rising in the Jura Mountains and flowing SW to join the River Saône, it forms part of the Swiss–French border. Length: 430 km (267 mi).

● **Doughty, Charles Montagu** ► (1843–1926) British travel writer and poet. From 1875 to 1877 he travelled in Arabia, which inspired his *Travels in Arabia Deserta* (1888).

● **Douglas** ► 54 09N 4 29W The capital of the Isle of Man, on the E coast. It is a port and resort with legislative buildings, including the House of Keys (parliament house), the Manx Museum, and a casino. Population (1998): 23 487.

● **Douglas, Lord Alfred** ▷*See* Wilde, Oscar.

● **Douglas, Gavin** ► (?1474–1522) Scots poet. His works include a moral allegory, *The Palice of Honour* (1501), and the first translation of Virgil's *Aeneid* into English (or rather Scots) in 1513. After the death of James III at ▷Flodden he became involved in political intrigues and died in London.

● **Douglas, (George) Norman** ► (1868–1952) British novelist. He served in the British diplomatic service in Russia until 1896, when he settled in Italy on the island of Capri, the setting of his novel *South Wind* (1917). *Siren Land* (1911) and *Old Calabria* (1915) are travel books.

● **Douglas fir** ► A conifer, *Pseudotsuga taxifolia*, native to W North America and cultivated for ornament and for its high-quality timber. 60–90 m high, it has flexible blunt needles and cylindrical cones, about 8 cm long, with three-pronged bracts protruding from the scales. Family: *Pinaceae*.

● **Douglas-Home, Sir Alec** ▷*See* Home of the Hirsel, Alec Douglas-Home, Baron.

● **Douglas of Kirtleside, William Sholto, 1st Baron** ► (1893–1969) British air marshal. A much decorated pilot in World War I, he succeeded ▷Dowding as head of Fighter Command (1941–42) after the Battle of Britain, subsequently taking over Middle East Command (1943–44) and Coastal Command (1944–45). He was a highly successful chairman of British European Airways (1949–64).

● **Doukhobors** ► (Russian: fighters against the spirit) Russian nonconformist Christian sect founded in the 18th century. Because of their anarchistic doctrines (denial of the state's right to levy tax, etc.) and heterodox religious views (belief in reincarnation, denial of Christ's divinity), they were for a long time persecuted. With the help of ▷Tolstoy and English Quakers, they emigrated from Georgia to Canada in 1898.

● **Doulton** ► English pottery works, established in 1815 and originally at Lambeth (London), specializing in salt-glazed stoneware. Brown stoneware vessels with relief moulded portrait and landscape ornament were typical of the period to 1850. From 1856 Sir Henry Doulton (1820–97) encouraged artist potters to produce studio pottery in coloured glazes, using wood-fired kilns.

● **Dounreay** ► The site in N Scotland of the world's first fast-breeder reactor (*see* fast reactor); it began generation in 1962 and was closed down in 1977. A second (prototype) fast-breeder reactor began operation in 1974; it was closed in 1994. In 1998 it was announced that the site's nuclear fuel reprocessing plant would close when existing contracts had been fulfilled.

● **Douro, River** ► (Spanish name: Duero) A river in SW Europe. Flowing W from N central Spain, it forms part of the border between Spain and Portugal before entering the Atlantic Ocean at Oporto. Length: 895 km (556 mi).

● **douroucouli** ► A nocturnal ▷monkey, *Aotus trivirgatus*, of Central and South America, also called night monkey or owl monkey. It is 55–75 cm long including the tail (30–40 cm) and moves through trees stalking small animals. It also eats fruit and leaves. Family: *Cebidae*.

● **dove** ▷*See* pigeon.

● **Dover** ► 51 08N 1 19E A port in SE England, in Kent on the Strait of Dover. A ▷Cinque Port, it is the UK's chief ferry and Hovercraft port for the Continent. Population (1993 est): 106 100.

● **Dover** ► 39 10N 75 32W A city in the USA, the capital of Delaware near Delaware Bay. Founded in 1683, it has many 18th- and 19th-century buildings. Population (1990): 27 630.

● **Dover, Strait of** ► (French name: Pas de Calais) A channel comprising the narrowest part of the ▷English Channel. Minimum width: 34 km (21 mi).

● **Dover sole** ▷*See* sole.

● **Dowding, Hugh Caswall Tremenheere, 1st Baron** ► (1882–1970) British air chief marshal, who was head of the RAF Fighter Command in 1940. His strategy played a major role in winning the Battle of Britain (*see* World War II).

● **Dowell, Sir Anthony** ► (1943–) British ballet dancer, director of the Royal Ballet (1986–2001). Noted for his performances in classical ballets, he also danced in such modern works as *The Dream* (1964) and *Four Schumann Pieces* (1975).

● **Dow Jones index** ► A weighted average of the prices on the New York Stock Exchange of 30 industrial shares, computed each working day by Dow Jones and Co. Originally devised in 1884 using only 11 shares, it was reorganized in 1928, when it was given the value 100. It is the principal indicator of movements in share prices in the USA.

● **Dowland, John** ► (1563–1626) English composer and lutenist. He travelled widely and was lutenist at the Danish court (1598–1606). One of the first composers to specialize in writing songs with lute accompaniment, he also composed the famous "Lachrymae" for lutes, viols, or violins.

● **Down** ► **1.** A historic county in SE Northern Ireland, bordering on the Irish Sea. Its administrative powers were devolved to the new district councils in 1973. It consists of lowlands in the E rising to the Mourne Mountains in the SW. Agriculture is the chief occupation. Area: 2466 sq km (952 sq mi). **2.** A district in SE Northern Ireland, in Co Down. Area: 638 sq km (246 sq mi). Population (1998): 60 900.

● **Downing Street** ► A street in the Greater London borough of the City of Westminster, adjoining Whitehall. No 10 is the official residence of the prime minister; the chancellor of the exchequer resides at No 11. It was named after the English statesman Sir George Downing (1623–84).

● **Downing Street Declaration** ► A declaration signed by the British prime minister John Major and Albert Reynolds, prime minister of the Irish Republic, on 15 December, 1993. In it the two governments promised to abide by any decision on the future status of Northern ▷Ireland made by its people and to negotiate with any parties that rejected violence. The Declaration influenced the IRA's announcement of ceasefires (1994–96; 1997–) and led to the settlement agreed in April, 1998 (the Good Friday Agreement).

● **Downpatrick** ► 54 20N 5 43W A market town in Northern Ireland, in Co Down. It is the reputed burial place of St Patrick. Population (1991): 10 257.

● **Downs, North and South** ► Two roughly parallel ranges of chalk hills in SE England, separated by the ▷Weald. The North Downs extend W–E between Guildford, in Surrey, and Dover, in Kent. The South Downs extend generally SE from Winchester, in Hampshire, to Beachy Head. In 1999 plans were announced to designate the South Downs as a National Park. The Downs have traditionally been sheep-farming areas.

● **Down's syndrome** ▶ A condition that results from the presence of one extra copy of chromosome 21 and is present at birth; it is named after J. L. H. Down (1828–96), an English physician who studied the condition. Affected children often have learning difficulties and their faces resemble those of orientals; heart defects may be present. In spite of their handicaps, Down's children are usually cheerful and with special education can live relatively normal lives. The syndrome is more common in babies of mothers over 40; it can be detected during pregnancy (*see* amniocentesis).

● **dowsing** ▶ The use of divining- or dowsing-rods to discover subterranean minerals or water. From the 16th century divining-rods were employed by miners and treasure hunters, a function now largely usurped by metal detectors. Dowsing for water is still of practical value; skilled dowsers can estimate the depth and flow of underground streams. The rod is traditionally a Y-shaped twig which, when its two prongs are grasped, twists in the hands of the dowser as he approaches water. Alternatively metal rods are held parallel a few inches apart and swing across each other. The nature of the stimuli causing these reactions is unexplained.

● **Dowson, Ernest (Christopher)** ▶ (1867–1900) British poet, with Yeats a member of the Rhymers' Club. His poetry explored themes of love and worldly renunciation. From 1894 he lived mostly in France, where he died of tuberculosis, aggravated by poverty and addiction to absinthe.

● **Doyle, Sir Arthur Conan** ▶ (1859–1930) British author, creator of the detective Sherlock Holmes. Conan Doyle graduated in medicine but soon turned to writing. Holmes first appeared in *A Study in Scarlet* (1887), narrated, as are nearly all the stories about him, by his dogged but unimaginative friend Dr John H. Watson. Despite the great success of these works, Conan Doyle valued most highly his historical novels, such as *The White Company* (1890). Knighted in 1902 for his service in the second Boer War, he became a champion of ▷spiritualism after the death of his son in World War I.

● **Doyle, Roddy** ▶ (1958–) Irish novelist and playwright. His novels include *The Commitments* (1988), *The Snapper* (1990), *Paddy Clarke Ha Ha Ha* (1993), awarded the Booker Prize, and *The Woman Who Walked into Doors* (1996).

● **D'Oyly Carte, Richard** ▶ (1844–1901) British theatre impresario and manager. He produced most of the comic operas of Gilbert and Sullivan. The Savoy Theatre, which he opened in 1881, was the first London theatre to have electric lighting. He founded the D'Oyly Carte Opera Company (refounded in 1988), which stages productions of Gilbert and Sullivan.

● **Drabble, Margaret** ▶ (1939–) British novelist. Most of her novels concern the moral and emotional problems of women in contemporary society. They include *The Millstone* (1965), *The Ice Age* (1977), *The Middle Ground* (1980), *The Radiant Way* (1987), and *The Witch of Exmoor* (1996). She also edited the 1985 *Oxford Companion to English Literature*.

● **Draco** ▶ (7th century BC) Athenian lawgiver. His system is reputedly the first comprehensive code of laws drawn up in Athens. It was so harsh that "draconian" has since been used to describe any rigorous or cruel law. Draco's code prescribed the death penalty for most offences, taking retribution out of the hands of private citizens. ▷Solon abolished Draco's code in 590 BC, retaining only his homicide laws.

● **Dracula, Count** ▶ The central character of Bram ▷Stoker's gothic novel *Dracula* (1897) and of many horror films, a Transylvanian ▷vampire. The name, meaning "demon," was applied to Vlad IV the Impaler, a 15th-century Walachian prince who was the prototype of the fictional character.

● **dragonet** ▶ A small spiny-rayed fish, of the family *Callionymidae*, that has a smooth slender body, 10–20 cm long, flattened anteriorly and often brightly coloured. The pelvic fins are located in front of the pectoral fins. Dragonets live on the bottom in temperate and tropical seas and feed on invertebrates. Order: *Perciformes*.

● **dragonfish** ▶ A small ▷bony fish belonging to an order (*Pegasiformes*; about 5 species) found in warm waters of the Indian and Pacific Oceans. They have an elongated body, up to 16 cm long, with bony armour, a long snout, and large horizontal winglike pectoral fins.

● **dragonfly** ▶ A brightly coloured insect belonging to the widely distributed suborder *Anisoptera* (about 4500 species). It has a long body, large eyes, and transparent veined wings (spanning up to 180 mm), which are held horizontally at rest. Both the adults and freshwater nymphs (naiads) are active carnivores and control many insect pests. Order: *Odonata*.

● **dragonroot** ▶ A perennial North American herbaceous plant, *Arisaema dracontium*, also called the green dragon or dragon arum. The flower comprises a central column of sexual organs surmounted by a long tapering cylindrical structure (the spadix) and surrounded by a much shorter pointed green sheath (the spathe). The tuberous roots were formerly used in medicine. Family: *Araceae*.

● **dragon's blood** ▶ A red gum that exudes from the fruit of some palms. It was once used in Europe as a medicine because of its astringent and healing properties. It is used as a varnish for violins and in photoengraving.

● **dragon tree** ▶ A treelike plant, *Dracaena draco*, native to the Canary Islands. Growing 18 m tall and 6 m wide, it has large sword-shaped leaves at the tips of the branches and clusters of greenish-white flowers followed by orange berries. The dragon tree is sometimes grown as a pot plant for its foliage. The trunk was formerly used as a source of a red gum resin, ▷dragon's blood. Family: *Agavaceae*.

● **dragoon** ▶ European mounted soldier of the 16th and 17th centuries who could fight as a light cavalryman (*see also* hussars) or as an infantryman. Named after the muzzle-loading carbine called the dragoon that they carried, they were originally used as an arm of the infantry, being organized in companies, and their officers bore infantry titles. By the 18th century most light cavalrymen were called dragoons (or carabiniers).

● **drag racing** ▶ 1. A form of ▷motor racing that originated in the USA. It is held in heats of two cars on a straight strip a quarter of a mile (402 m) long. Using a standing start, races depend heavily on acceleration with the "elapsed time" (from start to finish) and "terminal velocity" of each vehicle measured electronically. Speeds have reached 403 km per hour (250 mph) in specially constructed light powerful vehicles (slingshots *or* rails), although races are also held for modified production models. 2. A form of motorcycle racing organized in the same way.

● **Drake, Sir Francis** ▶ (1540–96) English navigator and admiral. Drake's first important voyages were trading expeditions to Guinea and the West Indies and in 1567 he accompanied Sir John ▷Hawkins (a relative) to the Gulf of Mexico. In 1572 he embarked on a plundering expedition, destroying towns on the Isthmus of Panama. In 1578 he became the first Englishman to navigate the Straits of Magellan intending, with Elizabeth I's consent, to raid the Pacific coast. Alone out of five ships, his *Golden Hind* sailed N but unable to find a way back to the Atlantic Ocean, returned home via the Cape of Good Hope. He landed at Plymouth in 1580 and was knighted by Elizabeth on board the *Hind* in 1581. Drake crowned his career by helping to defeat the Spanish ▷Armada at Gravelines (1588), his refusal to fight the Spanish until he had finished his game of bowls has passed into legend. He died on an expedition to the West Indies.

● **Drakensberg Mountains** ▶ (*or* Quathlamba) The chief mountain range in S Africa, extending from SE South Africa along the E border of Lesotho to Swaziland, reaching 3482 m (11 425 ft) at Thaba Ntlenyana.

● **drama** ▶ The art form in which actors impersonate fictitious or historical characters to entertain an audience (especially a live audience). Drama is both a genre of literature and a branch of the performing arts. As literature, it includes the great poetry of ▷Sophocles, ▷Shakespeare, and ▷Racine and the highly crafted dialogue of ▷Congreve, ▷Ibsen, ▷Shaw, and ▷Beckett. As a performing art, it encompasses dance, music, mime, and acrobatics, as well as the crafts of the set designer, costumier, and technicians. In most cultures drama has, or had, close links with religious or magical rituals and with popular festivities. This is particularly true of non-Western traditions, such as the ▷No drama of Japan and the many indigenous genres of India, SE Asia, and Africa.

The Western dramatic tradition derives from ancient Greece, where a recognizable form of theatre evolved from rites associated with the god Dionysus in the 6th century BC. The major genres of ▷tragedy and ▷comedy emerged during the 5th century and found their first great exponents in ▷Aeschylus and ▷Aristophanes respectively (see Greek literature). During the later Greek period important innovations were made by ▷Euripides in tragedy and ▷Menander in comedy. Greek traditions were the chief influence on the drama of the Roman world, which included the rhetorical tragedies of ▷Seneca and the intricately plotted comedies of ▷Terence and ▷Plautus (see Latin literature). For some 500 years after the fall of Rome there is no record of any European drama, although it seems probable that various kinds of primitive folk performance continued. When formal theatre resumed in the 10th–11th centuries it was as a natural development of the Church's liturgy, which already included a strong element of the dramatic. The medieval tradition of the religious drama reached its fullest development in the ▷miracle play (14th century) and ▷morality play (15th century), both of which embraced secular and humorous elements.

The foundations of modern European theatre were laid in the Renaissance, with the rediscovery of the Greek and Latin play texts and Greco-Roman ideas of stage design and performance; ▷Aristotle's treatise on drama, The Poetics, also provided an important stimulus. The 16th century saw the construction of Europe's first permanent playhouses and the first professional theatre companies. Europe's greatest flowering of drama occurred in the century 1590–1690, an extraordinarily rich period that produced the great works of ▷Marlowe, Shakespeare, and ▷Jonson in England, Lope de ▷Vega and ▷Calderón de la Barca in Spain, and ▷Molière, ▷Corneille, and Racine in France. While the English and Spanish playwrights drew freely on native and popular traditions (such as the ▷commedia dell'arte) and mixed the genres of comedy and tragedy to great effect, the serious French theatre developed according to strict notions of ▷classicism derived from Aristotle (see unities). Although they never took root in Britain, ideas of classical decorum held sway over the continental stage until the Romantic era, when such playwrights as ▷Schiller and ▷Hugo made a conscious return to the example of Shakespeare. The 18th and 19th centuries saw the triumph of middle-class taste in the theatre, as moral and sentimental dramas banished earlier bawdier works, such as the English Restoration comedies (see Restoration literature), from the stage for many years. Acting conventions and staging techniques grew steadily more naturalistic during this period, with growing attention to such matters as historical accuracy in cos-

tume. At the same time the plots, dialogue, and thematic concerns of both serious and popular drama (see melodrama) were far removed from contemporary realities. This remained the case until the late 19th century, when Ibsen led the movement towards social realism in such plays as A Doll's House (1879). In this he was followed by such dramatists as ▷Chekhov, ▷Strindberg, and ▷Gorki (see Naturalism). Ibsen's use of the theatre as a forum to debate pressing social and moral issues was subsequently extended by such writers as Shaw and ▷Brecht and the numerous left-wing dramatists of the 1950s, 1960s, and 1970s (see Angry Young Men). Despite periodic challenges from such movements as ▷expressionism and symbolism, and a general trend towards more abstract stage settings, realism has remained the dominant mode for serious modern drama. During the last 50 years the ▷Theatre of the Absurd and the "epic theatre" of Brecht (in which the dramatic illusion is deliberately punctured) have offered perhaps the most potent challenge to the realist tradition. ▷See also theatres and staging.

● **Drammen** ▶ 59 45N 10 15E A seaport in S Norway, at the mouth of the River Drammen. It exports timber, wood pulp, and paper. Population (1993): 51 062.

● **draughts** ▶ (US name: checkers) A board game for two players that was developed in 12th-century Europe from an ancient Egyptian game. Each player has 12 disc-shaped pieces (usually black for one and white or red for the other), which are placed on the 12 black squares at the opposite ends of a chessboard. The pieces move only on the black squares and black always starts. One piece per turn is moved diagonally forwards onto a vacant adjacent square. If the next square is occupied by one of the opponent's pieces but the square beyond that is vacant, the playing piece must jump onto the vacant square, removing his opponent's piece from the board. He must make a further jump from there if possible (in the same turn). The 16th-century rule of "huffing" enables a player to remove an opponent's piece that could have jumped but did not. If a piece reaches the opposing back line it becomes a "king" (a second piece is placed on top of it) and it may then move forwards or backwards. The winner is the player who takes or immobilizes all his opponent's pieces.

● **Drava, River** ▶ (or R. Drave) A river in E central Europe, flowing E from N Italy through Austria, then SE forming part of the Croatian-Hungarian border to join the River Danube. Length: 725 km (450 mi).

● **Dravidian languages** ▶ A large language family of up to 20 languages spoken mainly in S India. The major languages of the family are ▷Tamil, which has a literary tradition dating back 2000 years, ▷Kanarese (or Kannada), Telugu, ▷Malayalam, and Tulu. These are all spoken in a continuous area in India, and Tamil is also spoken in Sri Lanka. There is one Dravidian language, Brahui, that is separated

Sir Francis Drake ▶ Queen Elizabeth knights the admiral on board the *Golden Hind* on his return from his voyage round the world (1580).

from the main bloc by almost a thousand miles and is spoken in Pakistan. The Dravidian languages are all agglutinative (*see* languages, classification of) and this is strong evidence for separating them from the other major language bloc of the subcontinent, the ▷Indo-European languages.

● **Drayton, Michael** ▶ (1563–1631) English poet. A prolific writer, he wrote sonnet sequences, pastoral idylls, and many other conventional poems within traditional Elizabethan genres. His most popular work was *England's Heroical Epistles* (1597), a series of imaginary love letters, and his most ambitious was *Polyolbion* (Part 1, 1612; Part 2, 1622), a patriotic attempt to record the history and splendours of England.

● **dreams** ▶ Ideas and images experienced during ▷sleep. Dreams may take place at any stage of sleep, but they are particularly associated with REM (rapid-eye-movement) sleep, in which the eyes move rapidly about. Dreams in this stage of sleep are the most vivid in their imagery and the farthest removed from waking thoughts. Everybody has dreams: most people have REM sleep about four or five times a night, for about 20 minutes at a time; whether or not the dream is remembered depends on how quickly after it the sleeper wakes up.

If a person is repeatedly deprived of the chance to dream (by being woken when a dream starts) he becomes irritable, inefficient, and eventually suffers ▷hallucinations. After such deprivation, he dreams more frequently when he is again allowed to. The new combinations of ideas produced in dreams can be creative and valuable. ▷Psychoanalysis gives much weight to the content of dreams as an approach to understanding the unconscious mind. Experimental studies indicate that the content of dreams is affected by the dreamer's mood and by stimuli that occur while he sleeps. ▷*See also* nightmares.

● **dredger** ▶ A vessel designed to deepen underwater channels in rivers, docks, canals, etc., by removing material from the bottom. The types used include the suction dredger, which sucks up mud through a rubber pipe from the bottom and either deposits it in barges or in its own tanks; the bucket-ladder dredger, which carriers an endless chain of buckets supported on a frame; and the grab dredger, which operates much like a power shovel.

● **Dreiser, Theodore** ▶ (1871–1945) US novelist. The son of a poor German immigrant, he became a journalist and settled in New York in 1894. *Sister Carrie* (1900), his first novel, was attacked for its raw realism but *An American Tragedy* (1925), based on an actual murder case, brought him critical and financial success. He visited the Soviet Union in 1927 and later joined the Communist Party.

● **Drenthe** ▶ (or Drente) A low-lying province in the E Netherlands, bordering on W Germany. Parts of its extensive bogs and heaths have been reclaimed for agriculture; produce includes potatoes, rye, and dairy products. Oil is extracted around Shoonebeek. Area: 2685 sq km (1037 sq mi). Population (1995): 454 864. Capital: Assen.

● **Dresden** ▶ 51 5N 13 41E A city in SE Germany, on the River ▷Elbe, the capital of Saxony. One of the world's most beautiful cities prior to its devastation by Allied bombing in February 1945, it has since been rebuilt. Dresden is a centre of culture, light industry, and market gardening. The china industry moved to Meissen in 1710. It is the site of a music college and a technical university. Population (1996 est): 469 110.

● **Dresden, Battle of** ▶ (26–27 August, 1813) A battle fought near the capital of Saxony between 120 000 French troops led by Napoleon and an Austrian, Prussian, and Russian force of 170 000. Napoleon inflicted a crushing defeat on the allies, who lost 38 000 men.

● **Dresden porcelain** ▷*See* Meissen porcelain.

● **dressage** ▶ The training of a riding (or carriage) horse to make it calm, supple, and responsive to its rider (or driver). It was originally a training for military charges; the present, more humane, methods only developed in the 18th century. The most advanced stage is *haute école* equitation in which a horse is taught to perform intricate leaps and movements. This classical art is practised by the ▷Spanish Riding School in Vienna and the Cadre Noir of the French Cavalry School at

Saumur. Dressage competitions consist of a sequence of complex prescribed movements. ▷*See also* equestrianism.

● **Dreyer, Carl Theodor** ▶ (1889–1968) Danish film director. He began his career in films as a scriptwriter in 1912. His major films concern spiritual and supernatural themes and are distinguished by their atmospheric concentration and intensity. They include *La Passion de Jeanne d'Arc* (1928) and *Ordet* (1955).

● **Dreyer, Johan Ludvig Emil** ▶ (1852–1926) Danish astronomer, who compiled the *New General Catalogue of Nebulae and Clusters of Stars* (1888). This work is still a standard reference catalogue for nonstellar objects, which are referred to by their catalogue number, e.g. the galaxy NGC 175.

● **Dreyfus, Alfred** ▶ (1859–1935) French Jewish army officer. Unjustly accused of revealing state secrets to the German military attaché in Paris, in 1894 Dreyfus, the victim of ▷antisemitism, was deported for life to ▷Devil's Island. His case was reopened in 1898, largely owing to the championship of Zola and Clemenceau, becoming a cause célèbre and the focus of conflict between royalist, nationalist, and militarist elements on the one hand and socialist, republican, and anticlerical factions on the other. Following a retrial in 1899, Dreyfus was pardoned but not completely cleared until 1906, when he was appointed to the Legion of Honour.

● **Driesch, Hans Adolf Eduard** ▶ (1867–1941) German zoologist, whose work gave impetus to modern embryology. His interpretation of studies on developing sea urchin embryos led him to become a lifelong advocate of ▷vitalism.

● **drift** ▶ **1.** The debris, including boulders, sand, clay, and gravel, deposited by glaciers or by glacial meltwater. **2.** The superficial deposits occurring above the solid underlying rock on the earth's surface. Geological maps are published in both drift and solid editions to distinguish between them.

● **drill** ▶ An ▷Old World monkey, *Mandrillus leucophaeus*, of central West Africa, smaller than the closely related ▷mandrill. Drills inhabit inland forests, moving about on the ground in small groups and eating leaves, fruit, and worms.

● **Drinkwater, John** ▶ (1882–1937) British poet, critic, and dramatist. He was a leading contributor to the *Georgian Poetry* anthologies. He helped to found the Birmingham Repertory Theatre in 1913 and wrote several successful historical plays, notably *Abraham Lincoln* (1918) and *Mary Stuart* (1921).

● **driver ant** ▶ An African ▷ant of the genus *Dorylus* or related genera, which has a lifestyle similar to the New World ▷army ant. Subfamily: *Dorylinae*.

● **Drogheda** ▶ (Irish name: Droichead Átha) 53 43N 6 21W A port in the Republic of Ireland, in Co Louth on the River Boyne. Its garrison was massacred by Cromwell in 1649. Drogheda exports cattle and has brewing, linen and cotton, and engineering industries. Population (1991): 23 800.

● **dromedary** ▷*See* camel.

● **drone** ▷*See* bee.

● **drongo** ▶ A songbird belonging to a family (*Dicruridae*; 20 species) occurring in Old World tropical forests. About 22–35 cm long, drongos are usually black, often with long tail plumes, and have a harsh song. They have stout sharp-hooked bills and feed on large insects, which are often caught in flight. These birds are noted for fiercely defending their territories against intruders.

● **dropsy** ▷*See* oedema.

● **dropwort** ▶ A perennial herb, *Filipendula vulgaris*, of grasslands and clearings in Eurasia and N Africa. Up to 70 cm high, it has compound leaves with 8–20 divided toothed leaflets. The flowers, which occur in flat-topped terminal clusters, have 5–6 red-tinged white petals and long prominent stamens. The tuberous roots may be eaten. Family: *Rosaceae*.

● **Drosera** ▷*See* sundew.

● **Drosophila** ▶ A genus of small ▷fruit flies (about 1000 species), also called vinegar flies. Most species feed on fermenting materials, such as rotting or damaged fruit, but a few are predatory or parasitic. Some species, especially *D. melanogaster*, have been used extensively in laboratory studies of heredity and evolution because of the large chromosomes in their salivary glands and their short life cycle. Family: *Drosophilidae*.

● **Droste-Hülshoff, Annette von** ▶ (1797–1848) German poet and novelist. She lived in isolation on her aristocratic family's estate. She wrote poems on religious themes and about her native countryside of Westphalia, and a novella, *The Jew's Beech Tree* (1842).

● **drought** ▶ An extended period of dry weather with a virtual absence of precipitation, causing a lack of moisture in the soil. Droughts in densely populated areas reliant on agriculture, such as India and China, can have disastrous effects. In the UK an **absolute drought** is defined as a period of at least 15 consecutive days on none of which is there more than 0.2 mm of rainfall.

● **drowning** ▶ Suffocation due to water in the air passages. Death occurs much more rapidly in fresh water than sea water. This is because fresh water flows through the lungs into the blood, causing the red blood cells to burst and release potassium, which causes the heart to stop. Salt water mechanically prevents the oxygen reaching the lungs. It can take up to ten minutes to drown, and anybody rescued should immediately be given ▷artificial respiration.

● **drug dependence** ▶ The condition resulting from regular use of a drug such that its withdrawal causes emotional distress (psychological dependence) or physical illness (physical dependence). Drugs causing psychological dependence include cannabis, LSD, some tranquillizers, and the nicotine in tobacco. Physical dependence is associated with such drugs as morphine, heroin, barbiturates, and alcohol. Withdrawal of these drugs causes unpleasant symptoms (withdrawal symptoms) that disappear on taking further doses. Overdosage of such drugs can be fatal. Physical dependence is invariably associated with severe psychological dependence and requires specialist treatment. ▷*See also* alcoholism.

● **drugs** ▶ Compounds that alter the physiological state of living organisms (including humans). Medicinal drugs are widely used for the treatment, prevention, and diagnosis of disease. The wide range of drugs available for this purpose includes the anaesthetics (*see* anaesthesia), ▷analgesics, ▷antibiotics, ▷antidepressants, ▷antipsychotic drugs, ▷cytotoxic drugs, ▷diuretics, and hormonal drugs.

Some drugs are taken solely for the pleasurable effects they produce. Many such drugs are addictive (*see* narcotics) and—despite rigorous controls to restrict their use—illegal trade in them continues. In the UK the Misuse of Drugs Act (1971) restricts the use of these dangerous drugs, which are known as **controlled drugs** and include ▷opium and its derivatives and synthetic substitutes, many stimulants (cocaine, amphetamine, etc.), and some sedatives. ▷*See also* drug dependence.

● **Druids** ▶ Ancient Celtic priests who were also revered as teachers and judges. Information about them is largely derived from Julius Caesar's hostile account in his *Gallic Wars*. They worshipped nature gods, believed in the immortality of the soul and ▷reincarnation, and also taught astronomy. Their central religious rite involved the sacred oak tree, from which they cut mistletoe with a golden knife. They sacrificed humans, usually criminals, on behalf of those near to death. In Gaul and Britain they were wiped out by the Romans, their last stand being in Anglesey (61 AD), but in Ireland they survived until the arrival of Christian missionaries. They had no proven association with ▷Stonehenge, despite the use of the site by the revived 20th-century Druidic Order.

● **drumfish** ▶ A carnivorous fish, also called croaker, belonging to the family *Sciaenidae* (about 160 species), that occurs mainly along warm seashores. They have two dorsal fins and are usually silvery in colour. Most species produce sounds by amplifying muscle movements through the swim bladder. Order: *Perciformes*.

● **drumlin** ▶ A small streamlined hill, formed through glaciation and composed of glacial ▷till or ▷drift, sometimes with a rock core. Drumlins usually occur in groups or swarms (sometimes called basket-of-eggs topography), their long axes parallel to the direction of ice flow. They are common features in Co Down, Northern Ireland.

● **Drummond of Hawthornden, William** ▶ (1585–1649) The first major Scots poet to write in deliberately non-Scottish English. His *Poems* (1614, 1616) were strongly influenced by continental models. He also wrote royalist political pamphlets and was a friend of Ben ▷Jonson and ▷Drayton.

● **drums** ▶ Musical instruments of ancient origin, in which a pitched or unpitched sound is produced by striking a tight skin stretched over a frame or resonating chamber. Drums are played either with sticks of various kinds or with the hands. The family includes the orchestral ▷timpani, the bass drum, ▷snare drum, and ▷tambourine. *Compare* percussion instruments; stringed instruments; wind instruments.

● **drupe** ▶ A stone fruit, such as a cherry, plum, or peach. The fruit wall (pericarp) develops into three layers: an outer skin (epicarp), succulent flesh (mesocarp), and a stone (endocarp) containing the seed.

● **Drury Lane Theatre** ▶ (full name: Theatre Royal Drury Lane) The oldest theatre in London, first opened in 1663. The present building dates from 1813. It has housed every form of dramatic production. Its early managers included Colley ▷Cibber, David ▷Garrick, and R. B. ▷Sheridan, and it has strong associations with the actors Edmund ▷Kean, Charles ▷Macready, and Sir Henry ▷Irving.

● **Druses** ▶ (*or* Druzes) Adherents of the Druse religion, a sect probably named after one of its founders, al-Darazi, who preached the divinity of the Fatimid caliph al-Hakim (996–1021 AD). After his death they won some support in S Syria and developed extreme heterodox ideas. Druses are not generally accepted as Muslims. Their scriptures are based on the Bible, the Koran, and on Sufi writings. Today they live mainly in Syria, the Lebanon, and Israel.

● **dryad** ▶ In Greek mythology, a type of ▷nymph inhabiting trees, especially oak trees. A dryad was believed to die when the tree died.

● **dry cleaning** ▶ Cleaning fabrics using a solvent other than water. Its main advantage over washing is that it rarely affects the shape or colour of the article. Commercial dry cleaning plant is mainly automatic and the most common solvent is perchloroethylene. Like washing, the solvent, which may contain a detergent, loosens and flushes away dirt particles. Drying is by spinning and warm air. The solvent is recycled.

● **Dryden, John** ▶ (1631–1700) British poet and critic. He welcomed the Restoration of the monarchy with two panegyrics to Charles II and was appointed poet laureate in 1668. He wrote several successful plays for the recently reopened theatres, for example *Marriage à la Mode* (1673) and *All for Love* (1677). He also wrote brilliant verse satires, notably *Absalom and Achitophel* (1681) and *MacFlecknoe* (1682). He became a Catholic in 1685 and lost the laureateship on the accession of the Protestant William of Orange in 1688. His last major work was a translation of Virgil (1697).

● **dry farming** ▶ Crop production in regions receiving less than 50 cm (20 in) of rainfall per annum. This involves special farming techniques, especially planting quick-growing drought-resistant crops to make the best use of limited rainfall. Traditionally, winter wheat is grown in alternation with a fallow year, in which moisture and nutrient levels are allowed to recover. Appropriate husbandry, such as leaving a protective layer of crop residue, contour ploughing, and the use of fertilizers, all help to maximize yields under difficult conditions.

● **Dryopithecus** ▶ A genus of extinct apes, also called oak apes, with teeth and jaws similar to those of chimpanzees and gorillas. Most *Dryopithecus* remains come from India dating from the late Tertiary period (between 19 and 1 million years ago).

● **Dryopteris** ▶ A genus of ▷ferns (about 150 species), known as buckler ferns, found mainly in N temperate regions. They have firm feathery branched fronds, often growing in crowns, 15–150 cm high, from short stout scaly rhizomes. Large clusters of spore capsules (sori) occur in two rows on the underside of the leaflets. A common species is the male fern (*D. filix-mas*). Family: *Aspidiaceae*.

● **drypoint** ▶ A technique of engraving. The finished print is characterized by a shadowy effect produced by the ridges thrown up by the incision on the copperplate. Early masters of drypoint include ▷Dürer and ▷Rembrandt.

● **dry rot** ▶ The decay of timber caused by cellulose-digesting fungi, especially *Serpula lacrymans*. Spores are liable to germinate in timber having a moisture content of over 20% and the fungus appears as a whitish mass on the surface. The timber becomes cracked and crumbly and the infection may spread to adjoining dry timbers. Treatment is by removal of infected timbers and application of fungicide to the remaining parts. *Compare* wet rot.

● **Drysdale, Sir (George) Russell** ▶ (1912–81) Australian painter, born in England. After training in Melbourne, London, and Paris, he specialized in scenes of the Australian outback.

● **dualism** ▶ Any philosophical theory asserting either that the universe is made up of two irreducible and independent substances or that it is based on two fundamental principles (for example, good and evil). It is thus distinguished from monism—the belief in just one substance (or principle)—and pluralism, which holds that there are many. One of the most pervasive dualistic theories in philosophy since ▷Descartes is the view that the world is constituted of mental substance (mind or consciousness) and physical substance (body or matter).

● **Dubai** ▷*See* United Arab Emirates.

● **Du Barry, Marie Jeanne Bécu, Comtesse** ▶ (?1743–93) The last mistress of ▷Louis XV of France from 1768 until his death (1774), when she was banished from court. She was guillotined during the French Revolution.

● **Dubček, Alexander** ▶ (1921–92) Czechoslovak statesman. Dubček participated in the resistance to the Nazi occupation and after World War II rose to become secretary of the Czechoslovak Communist Party in 1968. As leader, he granted many liberal reforms, which were opposed by the Soviet Union and precipitated the Soviet-led invasion of Czechoslovakia in August, 1968. Dubček lost his post and was ousted from the Party in 1970. Following the mass uprising of 1989 he re-emerged as a popular leader and was subsequently elected chairman of the new Czech parliament. He died of injuries sustained in a road accident.

● **Dublin** ▶ (Irish name: Baile Átha Cliath) 53 20N 6 15W The capital of the Republic of Ireland, on Dublin Bay. An important commercial and cultural centre, it is also the largest manufacturing centre and the largest port in the Republic. Its industries include whiskey distilling, brewing (it has the largest brewery in the world), clothing, glass, and food processing. It is noted for its wide streets (notably O'Connell Street) and its 18th-century Georgian squares. It has the University of Dublin (founded 1592) and the National University of Ireland (founded 1909); Dublin also contains the famous Abbey Theatre. Literary names associated with the city include W. B. Yeats and James Joyce.

History: during the 18th century Dublin prospered as the second largest city of the British Empire but it declined during the 19th century. The ▷Easter Rising of 1916 took place here. Population (1996 est): 480 996.

● **Dublin** ▶ (Irish name: Baile Átha Cliath) A county in the E Republic of Ireland, in Leinster bordering on the Irish Sea. Chiefly low lying, it rises in the S to the Wicklow Mountains and is drained by the River Liffey. The county is dominated by the city of Dublin. Agricultural produce includes barley, wheat, and potatoes, and cattle are reared. Area: 922 sq km (356 sq mi). Population (1996 est): 1 057 000. Administrative centre: Dublin.

● **Dublin Bay prawn** ▶ (*or* Norway lobster) An edible crustacean, *Nephrops norvegicus*, of the order ▷Decapoda, which is commercially exploited as scampi. Resembling a large prawn, it has a slender pinkish body, up to 20 cm long, with long claws. It is widespread in the Meditarranean and NE Atlantic, living in sandy burrows at a depth of 10–250 m. Dublin Bay prawns are usually fished by trawling and are marketed fresh, frozen, or cooked, shelled or unshelled, whole or as tails.

● **Dubna** ▶ 56 42N 37 09E A town in W Russia. Founded in 1956, it is the site of the United Institute of Nuclear Research. Population (1990 est): 66 000.

● **Dubrovnik** ▶ (Italian name: Ragusa) 42 40N 18 07E A port in W Croatia on the Adriatic coast. It flourished as a city state until the early 19th century, and now, with its picturesque setting and medieval walls, is popular among tourists. The town was damaged by two earthquakes in April, 1979 and again in 1991, when it was shelled by Serbian artillery during the civil war that followed Croatia's secession from Yugoslavia. Population (1991): 49 730.

● **Dubuffet, Jean (Phillipe Arthur)** ▶ (1901–85) French painter and sculptor, who achieved notoriety in 1946 with his "junk" pictures. Using plaster, sand, straw, etc., he produced extremely distorted and flattened images, influenced by graffiti on walls and the art of children and the insane. He showed his own collection of works by children and psychiatric patients in a Paris exhibition entitled *l'Art brut* (raw art) in 1949.

● **Du Cange, Charles du Fresne, Sieur** ▶ (1610–88) French historian. An outstandingly prolific writer, Du Cange wrote glossaries of the middle ages that were a significant and original contribution to historical research. He also wrote widely on the Byzantine Empire and edited the works of the medieval chroniclers Villehardouin and Joinville.

● **Duccio di Buoninsegna** ▶ (c. 1255–c. 1318) Italian painter, founder of the Sienese school. His major works are the *Rucellai Madonna* (Uffizi) for Sta Maria Novella, Florence, and the *Maestà* (1308–11), an altarpiece for Siena Cathedral, which contemporaries hailed

Dublin ▶ A barricade in Talbot Street during the Easter Rising (1916), when 2000 Irishmen fought British troops.

as a masterpiece and carried in procession through the city. A fusion of ▷Byzantine and ▷gothic styles, it illustrates his gift for narrative painting.

● **Duchamp, Marcel** ▶ (1887–1968) French artist. His first success was *Nude Descending a Staircase* (1912; Philadelphia), influenced by ▷cubism and ▷futurism. This was followed by his controversial ▷ready-made objects, for example a urinal, first exhibited in New York. He lived in New York after 1915 and became leader of its ▷dada art movement. His best-known work is the glass and wire picture of *The Bride Stripped Bare by Her Bachelors, Even* (1915–23; Philadelphia).

● **duck** ▶ A small short-necked waterbird belonging to the family *Anatidae* (ducks, geese, and swans), occurring in salt and fresh waters throughout the world except Antarctica. Ducks are adapted for swimming and diving, having a dense waterproofed outer plumage with a thick underlayer of down. The blunt spatulate bill is covered with a sensitive membrane and has internal horny plates for sifting food from water. The 200 species of duck are mostly gregarious; many are migratory and strong fliers. Ducks feed either at the surface of the water (*see* dabbling duck) or dive to forage in deeper water (*see* diving duck). Order: *Anseriformes* (ducks and geese).

● **duck-billed platypus** ▶ An aquatic ▷monotreme mammal, *Ornithorhynchus anatinus*, of Australia and Tasmania. Platypuses grow to 55 cm long and have webbed feet. They use their broad flat toothless beak for sieving invertebrates from stream bottoms. The female lays two eggs in a grass-lined burrow constructed in a river bank, incubates them for two weeks, then suckles the tiny young (about 17 mm long). Family: *Ornithorhynchidae*.

● **duckweed** ▶ A small floating aquatic plant of the genus *Lemna* (about 10 species), forming dense carpets on or just below the surface of ponds, streams, etc. The plants have no distinct stems and leaves, consisting of a group of small round leaflike structures (thalli) that continuously reproduce by budding. Minute petalless flowers are enclosed in a sheath on the margin of the thallus. *L. minor*, *L. gibba*, and *L. polyrhiza* have roots; *L. triscula* is rootless. Duckweeds are the simplest and smallest of flowering plants. Family: *Lemnaceae*.

● **Dudley** ▶ 1. 53 30N 2 06W A town in W central England, in Dudley unitary authority, West Midlands. Dudley has been an important industrial centre since the middle ages: clothing and light engineering have now replaced coalmining and iron smelting as the principal industries. Population (1991): 192 171. 2. A unitary authority in W central England, in West Midlands. Area: 98 sq km (38 sq mi). Population (1997 est): 311 200.

● **Dudley, Robert** ▷*See* Leicester, Robert Dudley, Earl of.

● **Duero, River** ▷*See* Douro, River.

● **Dufay, Guillaume** ▶ (c. 1400–74) Burgundian composer and priest (*see* Burgundian school), associated with Cambrai Cathedral for much of his life. He travelled in France and Italy and was a member of the papal choir for several years. One of the outstanding composers of the middle ages, he wrote masses, motets, magnificats, and French and Italian chansons. He was also a famous teacher.

● **Du Fu** ▶ (or Tu Fu; 712–70 AD) Chinese poet of the Tang dynasty. Du Fu's failure to become a high official forced him to lead a life of poverty and travelling to escape famines and rebellions. The major themes of his poetry are thus the social injustices of his time and the effects of civil strife on Chinese life.

● **Dufy, Raoul** ▶ (1877–1953) French painter, born in Le Havre. His early influences were ▷impressionism and then ▷fauvism. He later developed an individual style in lively and often witty racecourse and regatta scenes, notable for the way forms are drawn sketchily over areas of thinly applied colour. He also designed fabrics, tapestries, and ceramics.

● **dugong** ▶ A marine herbivorous mammal, *Dugong dugon*, of the Indo-Pacific region. Up to 3 m long, dugongs—also known as sea cows—have blue-grey rough skin and a bristly snout; the males have short tusks. Their forelimbs are flippers and they lack hind limbs, having a flukelike tail for swimming. Dugongs feed on sea grass on the sea bed and, together with ▷manatees, are a threatened species. Family: *Dugongidae*; order: *Sirenia*.

● **Duhamel, Georges** ▶ (1884–1966) French novelist. Trained as a doctor, he worked as an army surgeon during World War I. His major works are his two novel cycles, *Salavin* (1920–32), exploring the theme of human aspirations in a materialistic age, and *The Pasquier Chronicles* (1933–44).

● **duiker** ▶ A small nocturnal African antelope belonging to the subfamily *Cephalophinae* (17 species), inhabiting bush or forest. 35–75 cm high at the shoulder, both sexes usually have smooth backward-pointing horns and often a distinct stripe along the back. They plunge into cover when disturbed, hence their name, which in Afrikaans means "diver."

● **Duisburg** ▶ 51 26N 06 45E A city in W Germany, in North Rhine-Westphalia at the confluence of the Rivers Rhine and Ruhr. Heavily bombed in World War II for its armaments industry, it is the largest European inland port and a steel-producing centre. Its university was established in 1972. Population (1996 est): 535 250.

● **Dukas, Paul** ▶ (1865–1935) French composer, teacher, and critic. He is best known for his orchestral scherzo *The Sorcerer's Apprentice* (1897). His works also include the opera *Ariane et Barbe-Bleue* (1907) and the ballet *La Péri* (1912). A perfectionist, he destroyed many of his works shortly before his death.

● **duke** ▷*See* peerage.

● **Dukeries** ▶ A part of NW Nottinghamshire, in the Midlands of England, that includes the parklands associated with the former ducal seats of Clumber, Welbeck, Thoresby, and Rufford. It also includes ▷Sherwood Forest.

● **Dukhobors** ▷*See* Doukhobors.

● **dulcimer** ▶ A musical instrument consisting of a shallow resonating box with strings stretched over two moveable bridges. It is played with two small hammers. Descended from the Persian *santir* and much used in European and Asian folk music, it is particularly popular in Hungarian gipsy music under the name ▷cimbalom.

● **Dulles, John Foster** ▶ (1888–1959) US Republican politician and diplomat. He became a senator and secretary of state (1953–59) under Eisenhower and was delegate to the UN, which he helped to establish (1945). Dulles was influential in forming US Cold War foreign policy. He developed a strategy of brinkmanship to confront the People's Republic of China over Quemoy and Matsu, and the Soviet Union during the Berlin crisis.

● **Dulong and Petit's law** ▶ The product of the mass of 1 mole of a solid element and its specific heat capacity is constant and equal to 25 joules per kelvin. The law is only true for simple substances and at normal temperatures. Named after the French physicists P. Dulong (1785–1838) and A. Petit (1791–1820).

● **dulse** ▶ An edible purplish-red ▷seaweed, *Rhodymenia palmata*, found growing on rocks, shellfish, and other seaweeds on N Atlantic coasts. A red alga, it has flat leathery lobed fronds, about 12–40 cm long, which are often eaten as a salty confection of the same name.

● **Duluth** ▶ 46 45N 92 10W A city in the USA, in Minnesota at the W end of Lake Superior opposite Superior, Wisconsin. It is the commercial and industrial centre of N Minnesota and large quantities of iron ore and grain are shipped from its port. Population (1996 est): 83 699.

● **Dulwich** ▶ 51 27N 0 05W A residential district in the Greater London borough of Southwark. It has a famous public school, Dulwich College (founded in 1619 by the actor Edward Alleyn), and an art gallery.

● **Duma** ▶ The Russian parliament from 1906 to 1917 and from 1993. The Duma, which was established in response to the ▷Revolution of 1905, transformed Russia into a constitutional monarchy. It was composed of an upper chamber, the state council, and a lower chamber. Half the members of the state council were appointed by the monarch and the remainder of the deputies in both chambers were elected. Owing to their radicalism, the first two Dumas (1906, 1907) were quickly dissolved by Emperor Nicholas II but the third (1907–12) and fourth (1912–17) more conservative Dumas lasted their legal five-year terms. At the beginning of the Russian Revolution the Duma established the provisional government that enforced

Nicholas's abdication but it subsequently disintegrated and was abandoned with the triumph of the Bolsheviks. Following the demise of communism, the State Duma was reintroduced in the constitution of 1993: it now comprises the lower chamber of the Federal Assembly, having 450 elected members. In the later 1990s it was dominated by communists, leading to conflict with President Yeltsin and frequent constitutional deadlock.

● **Dumas, Alexandre** ▶ (1802–70) French novelist and dramatist, often called Dumas *père*. His father was a soldier, son of a marquis and a negress, who became a general in the French Revolutionary armies. Brought up in poverty and largely self-educated, he began writing melodramatic historical plays in 1829. After 1839 he began writing his famous historical romances, including *The Count of Monte Cristo* (1844–45), *The Three Musketeers* (1844), and *The Black Tulip* (1850). His works were hugely successful but the uninhibited extravagance of his private life kept him continually in debt.

His illegitimate son **Alexandre Dumas** (1824–95), a dramatist, was often called Dumas *fils*. His best-known work is the novel *La Dame aux camélias* (1848), the basis of a play and Verdi's opera *La Traviata*. His other plays, which include *Le Demi-monde* (1855), were mostly moralistic treatments of such themes as adultery and prostitution.

● **Du Maurier, George (Louis Palmella Busson)** ▶ (1834–96) British caricaturist and novelist. Born in Paris, he moved to London in 1860 and contributed caricatures to *Punch* and other magazines. His novel *Trilby* (1894), remembered for its sinister hypnotist Svengali, is based on his life as an art student in Paris. The best-known works of his granddaughter **Dame Daphne Du Maurier** (1907–89) are romances, usually set in her home county of Cornwall. They include *Rebecca* (1938) and *My Cousin Rachel* (1951).

● **Dumbarton** ▶ 55 57N 4 35W A town in W central Scotland, in West Dunbartonshire ▷unitary authority at the confluence of the Rivers Clyde and Leven. It has engineering and whisky-distilling industries. Population (1991): 21 962.

● **Dumbarton Oaks** ▶ A mansion near Washington DC, at which a conference to lay the foundations of the ▷United Nations organization was held in 1944. The UK, USA, USSR, and China all attended.

● **Dumfries** ▶ 55 04N 3 37W A town in SW Scotland, on the River Nith; the administrative centre of Dumfries and Galloway. Population (1991): 32 136.

● **Dumfries** ▶ (or Dumfrieshire) A former county of SW Scotland. Under local government reorganization in 1975 it became part of Dumfries and Galloway.

● **Dumfries and Galloway** ▶ A council area in SW Scotland, bordering on the Solway Firth. Formed under local government reorganization in 1975 from the counties of Dumfries, Kirkudbright, and Wigtown, it became a ▷unitary authority in 1996. It consists of uplands in the N descending to coastal lowlands in the S and has an indented coastline. The region is mainly agricultural with sheep farming and stock raising. There has been considerable reafforestation since World War II. Area: 6369 sq km (2460 sq mi). Population (1998 est): 147 300. Administrative centre: Dumfries.

● **Du Mont, Allen Balcom** ▶ (1901–65) US engineer, who developed the ▷cathode-ray tube (CRT). He set up a company to manufacture allied electronic devices in 1931 and invented the oscilloscope (see cathode-ray oscilloscope), which incorporated his new durable CRTs. He also utilized them in television receivers from 1937.

● **Dumont d'Urville, Jules Sébastien César** ▶ (1790–1842) French navigator. He twice explored the South Seas (1822–25, 1826–29) and on the second journey circumnavigated the world in the *Astrolabe*, collecting specimens of plants and rocks. In repeating this exploit (1837–40), he discovered the Adélie coast of Antarctica.

● **Dumouriez, Charles François du Périer** ▶ (1739–1823) French general. During the French Revolution he became commander of a division in Nantes (1791). In 1792 he became minister of foreign affairs but resigned to command the northern army against Austria and Prussia. He won victories at Valmy and Jemappes (1792) but after defeat in early 1793 conspired to overthrow France's revolutionary government. Deserted by his troops he went over to the Austrians, eventually settling in England.

● **Dunant, (Jean-)Henri** ▶ (1828–1910) Swiss philanthropist, who inspired the foundation (1864) of the International ▷Red Cross. In 1859 he organized relief for the wounded at the Battle of Solferino, an experience that led him to propose the establishment of an international relief agency. He won the first Nobel Peace Prize in 1901.

● **Dunbar** ▶ 56 00N 2 31W A resort and fishing port in E central Scotland, on the East Lothian coast, scene of Oliver ▷Cromwell's victory over the Scots (1650). Population (1991): 6518.

● **Dunbar, William** ▶ (c. 1460–c. 1530) Scots poet, a courtier of James IV. His talent for vigorous satire is evident in *Dance of the Sevin Deidly Sins* and *Flyting of Dunbar and Kennedie*, an exchange of (probably) goodnatured abuse. *Lament for the Makaris* mourns the death of his fellow poets.

● **Dunbarton** ▶ (or Dunbartonshire) A historic county of W Scotland. Under local government reorganization in 1975 its boundaries were adjusted to form Dunbarton District, in Strathclyde Region. Further reorganization in 1996 involved the creation of two council areas, ▷East Dunbartonshire and ▷West Dunbartonshire.

● **Dunblane** ▶ 56 12N 3 59W A small city in S central Scotland, in Stirling. It is mainly residential and there is a 13th-century cathedral. It was the site of the fatal shooting of 16 primary-school children and their teacher on 13 March, 1996 by a demented gunman, who then killed himself. Population (1996 est): 7000. ▷See also gun laws.

● **Duncan I** ▶ (d. 1040) King of the Scots (1034–40). His claim to the throne was challenged by Macbeth, by whom he was killed.

● **Duncan, Isadora** ▶ (1878–1927) US dancer. She lived mostly in Europe, where she gained a reputation for both her innovative modern interpretive dancing and her flamboyant lifestyle. Her accidental death was caused by her scarf being caught in the wheel of the car in which she was travelling.

● **Duncan Smith, (George) Iain** ▶ (1954–   ) British politician; leader of the Conservative Party (2001–   ). A former army officer, he became an MP in 1992 and held front-bench posts from 1997. He succeeded William ▷Hague as leader following the party's defeat in the 2001 election.

● **Dundalk** ▶ (Irish name: Dún Dealgan) 54 01N 6 25W A port in the Republic of Ireland, the county town of Co Louth. Its chief industries are engineering, brewing, printing, and linen manufacturing, and its main exports are beef and cattle. Population (1991): 25 800.

● **Dundas** ▶ (former name: Thule) 76 30N 68 58W A town in NW Greenland. Founded as an Inuit settlement (1910), it subsequently became a US air and military base, after which the Inuit founded another Thule further N.

● **Dundee** ▶ **1.** 56 28N 3 00W A city in E Scotland, in Dundee City council area, on the Firth of Tay. It is a port and university town. Formerly known for jute goods, it now provides supplies and services for the North Sea oil industry and has engineering industries. It is also a fast-growing centre for biotechnology and genetic research. Population (1993 est): 153 710. **2. Dundee City** A council area in E Scotland. Area: 65 sq km (25 sq mi). Population (1998 est): 146 700.

● **Dundee, John Graham of Claverhouse, 1st Viscount** ▶ (c. 1649–89) Scottish soldier, who led a ▷Jacobite rebellion (1689) in support of the deposed James VII of Scotland (James II of England). He won an outstanding victory against loyalist forces at Killiecrankie but was mortally wounded.

● **Dunedin** ▶ 45 52S 170 30E A port in New Zealand, in SE South Island at the head of Otago Harbour. Founded by Scottish Presbyterians in 1848, it has two cathedrals and the University of Otago (the oldest in the country, founded in 1869). Industries include food processing and the manufacture of woollen goods, agricultural machinery, and footwear. Population (1996 est): 119 612.

● **Dunfermline** ▶ 56 04N 3 29W A town in E Scotland, in Fife on the Firth of Forth. Several Scottish kings, including ▷Robert the Bruce, are buried in the 11th-century abbey. Dunfermline produces electronic equipment and oil-related products and there are rich coal deposits nearby. Population (1991): 55 083.

● **Dungannon** ▶ A district in S Northern Ireland, in Co Tyrone. Area: 763 sq km (294 sq mi). Population (1991): 45 428.

dung beetle ▶ Using its head and paddle-like antennae, this beetle constructs balls of dung, which it buries and feeds on. The females lay eggs in dung balls, which provide food for the larvae.

● **dung beetle** ▶ A ▷scarab beetle, also called a tumblebug, that rolls dung into balls, which serve as a food source for both the adults and larvae. Dung beetles are usually dark and small, varying between 5 and 30 mm in length.

Another group of dung-eating beetles belong to the family *Geotrupidae* (*see* dor beetle).

● **Dungeness** ▶ 50 55N 0 58E A shingle headland in SE England, in Kent extending into the English Channel. Two nuclear power stations and an automatic lighthouse are located here.

● **Dunkirk** ▶ (French name: Dunkerque) 51 02N 2 23E A port in N France, in the Nord department on the Strait of Dover. Sacked by the English (1388), it was ceded to Cromwell in 1658 but was later sold (1662) by Charles II to Louis XIV. During ▷World War II British and other Allied troops were evacuated from its beaches (1940) following the fall of France. Dunkirk is a growing industrial centre and has an oil refinery and naval shipbuilding yards. Population (1990): 71 071.

● **Dun Laoghaire** ▶ 53 17N 6 08W A port in the E Republic of Ireland, in Co Dublin. It is the terminus of a ferry service from Holyhead, Wales, and a resort and yachting centre. Population (1991): 185 400.

● **dunlin** ▶ A common ▷sandpiper, *Calidris alpina*, that breeds in far northern regions, ranging south to N Britain. 20 cm long, it has a bill with a curved tip and a black and russet plumage that changes to grey in winter.

● **Dunlop, John Boyd** ▶ (1840–1921) Scottish inventor, who is credited with inventing the pneumatic tyre (1887). Dunlop began to produce his tyres commercially in 1890. Initially for bicycles, they later contributed greatly to the development of motor cars.

● **Dunmow Flitch** ▶ A flitch (side) of bacon awarded on Whit Monday to a married couple of Great Dunmow in Essex, who have not repented their marriage for a year and a day. Originating in the middle ages, the custom was referred to by ▷Langland and ▷Chaucer and was revived by the Victorian novelist Harrison ▷Ainsworth.

● **dunnock** ▶ A shy inconspicuous songbird, *Prunella modularis*, also called hedge sparrow (although it is an ▷accentor and not a sparrow). About 14 cm long, the dunnock has a dull-brown plumage with a greyish throat and breast. It has a fine sharp bill and feeds on insects. Cuckoos often lay their eggs in dunnocks' nests.

● **Dunois, Jean d'Orléans, Comte de** ▶ (1403–68) French general in the Hundred Years' War. He defeated the English in 1427, then held Orléans until relieved by Joan of Arc (1429). Further victories led to his triumphal entry into Paris (1436). Later he drove the English out of N France.

● **Dunoon** ▶ 55 57N 4 56W A resort in W central Scotland, in Argyll

and Bute on the Firth of Clyde. Holy Loch, formerly the site of a US Navy nuclear submarine base, is nearby. Population (1991): 9038.

● **Dunsany, Edward John Moreton Drax Plunkett, 18th Baron** ▶ (1878–1957) Irish author, famous for his richly fantastic and sinister stories and plays, many of them, such as *The Gods of Pegana* (1905) and *The Gods of the Mountain* (1912), set in worlds recalling Eastern mythology. He was also a sportsman, big-game hunter, and chess master.

● **Dunsinane** ▶ A hill in E Scotland, in Perth and Kinross, in the Sidlaw Hills. The ruined fort on its summit is the main setting for Shakespeare's play *Macbeth*. Height: 303 m (1012 ft).

● **Duns Scotus, John** ▶ (c. 1260–1308) Scottish-born Franciscan philosopher, who, with Roger ▷Bacon and ▷William of Ockham, carried on controversy against ▷Aquinas. Contradicting Aquinas, Duns Scotus held that what makes one thing distinct from another is its form, or essence, that is its essential properties rather than its accidental properties, as the latter may be removed or changed without altering its identity. Although nicknamed the Subtle Doctor by contemporaries, Duns Scotus suffered Renaissance ridicule, his name giving rise to the derisive label "dunce."

● **Dunstable** ▶ 51 53N 0 32W A town in SE England, in Bedfordshire. Its industries include engineering, printing, and the manufacture of commercial vehicles, paper, and cement. The headquarters of the London Gliding Club is situated at the foot of the Dunstable Downs. Population (1991): 49 666.

● **Dunstable, John** ▶ (d. 1453) English composer, mathematician, and astrologer. His music was known outside England and exists chiefly in continental manuscripts, but little is known of his life. Dunstable wrote motets in which the music accurately reflected the rhythm of the words. He also made a famous setting of the chanson "O Rosa bella."

● **Dunstan, St** ▶ (924–88 AD) English churchman and monastic reformer, born near Glastonbury. Of noble birth, he lived as a hermit until appointed Abbot of Glastonbury in 943. He rebuilt its monastery and revived English monasticism. The chief minister under Kings Eadred and Edgar, he became Bishop of Worcester (957), Bishop of London (959), and Archbishop of Canterbury (960). He lost favour under Ethelred II. Feast day: 19 May. Emblem: a pair of tongs.

● **duodecimal system** ▶ A system of numbers that has a base of 12 as opposed to the base 10 of the normal ▷decimal system. For example, the number 31 in the decimal system is 27 in the duodecimal system since $31 = (2 \times 12) + 7$.

● **duodenal ulcer** ▷*See* peptic ulcer.

● **duodenum** ▷*See* intestine.

● **Duparc, Henri** ▶ (Marie Eugène Henri Foucques D.; 1848–1933) French composer, a pupil of Franck. His reputation rests on the 14 songs he wrote between 1868 and 1884, some of which have orchestral accompaniments. In 1885 he suffered a breakdown in health and spent the rest of his life in seclusion in Switzerland.

● **du Pré, Jacqueline** ▶ (1945–87) British cellist. She studied with Paul Tortelier and Mstislav Rostropovich, making her debut in 1961 in Elgar's cello concerto, a work with which she became particularly associated. In 1967 she married the pianist Daniel ▷Barenboim, with whom she gave recitals. Multiple sclerosis put an end to her performing career in 1973, but she subsequently taught gifted cello students.

● **Dupré, Marcel** ▶ (1886–1971) French organist and composer, director of the Paris conservatoire (1954–56). He was well known as a recitalist, improviser, and composer of organ music.

● **Duque de Caxias** ▶ 22 45S 43 19W A city in Brazil, in Rio Grande do Sul. Founded by Italian immigrants in the 19th century, it is a centre of the wine trade. Population (1991): 325 903.

● **Duralumin** ▶ An aluminium ▷alloy containing 3.5% copper and 0.5% magnesium. It becomes harder after heating and quenching and retains this hardness as long as its temperature remains below 150°C. It is used in aircraft manufacture.

● **Durance, River** ▶ A river in S France, flowing mainly SSW to the

River Rhône near Avignon. It provides Marseille with water. Length: 304 km (189 mi).

● **Durango** ▶ 24 01N 104 40W A city in N Mexico. It lies S of Cerro del Mercado, a hill famous for its iron-ore mines. Industries include iron founding, sugar refining, and textiles. Population (1990): 348 036.

● **Duras, Marguerite** ▶ (1914–96) French novelist. Born in Indochina, she went to Paris in 1931. Her novels, often concerned with themes of time and passion, include *The Sea Wall* (1950) and *The Lover* (1984). She also wrote plays and filmscripts, notably *Hiroshima mon amour* (1960).

● **Durazzo** ▷*See* Durrës.

● **Durban** ▶ 29 53S 31 00E The main seaport in South Africa, on the Indian Ocean. Founded in 1835, it has car-assembly and sugar-refining industries, and it is an important tourist centre. It contains part of the University of Natal. Population (1991): 715 669.

● **Dürer, Albrecht** ▶ (1471–1528) German ▷Renaissance painter, engraver, draughtsman, and woodcut designer. The son of a goldsmith, he was born in Nuremberg, where he trained under the woodcut designer and altarpiece painter Michael Wohlgemuth (1434–1519). His first Italian visit (1494–95) resulted in a series of watercolours of the Alps. He was influenced by Italian artists, particularly ▷Mantegna and Antonio ▷Pollaiuolo, but his woodcuts of the *Apocalypse* (1498) are still ▷gothic in style. In about 1500, he became preoccupied with the study of human proportions. Paintings of this period include the *Self-Portrait* as Christ (1500; Alte Pinakothek, Munich) and *Adoration of the Magi* (1504; Uffizi). On his second Italian visit (1505–

Albrecht Dürer ▶ *Dancing Peasant Couple* (1514; copper engraving).

07) he painted *The Feast of the Rose Garlands* (Prague) for the church of the German community in Venice. He worked for Emperor Maximilian I from 1512 to 1519. In this period he executed his most famous engravings, including *Knight, Death, and the Devil* (British Museum, London). His last important work was *The Four Apostles* (Alte Pinakothek, Munich).

● **Durgapur** ▶ 23 30N 87 20E A city in India, in West Bengal. Its heavy industry includes steelmaking. Population (1991): 415 986.

● **Durham** ▶ 54 47N 1 34W A city in NE England, the administrative centre of Co Durham on the River Wear. There is a Norman cathedral (⌐Norman art and architecture) and an 11th-century castle, now part of Durham University (founded 1832). The city has a wide range of manufacturing and service industries. Population (1991): 36 937.

● **Durham** ▶ A county in NE England, on the North Sea. It consists chiefly of undulating lowlands, rising W to the uplands of the Pennines and is drained by the Rivers Wear and Tees. Agriculture includes sheep and dairy farming. Coalmining was formerly of major importance but the last deep pits closed in the 1990s. Iron and steel processing at Consett has declined; food processing, light engineering, services, and clothing manufacture are now the chief industries. Under local government reorganization in 1974 it lost the industrial NE and SE to Tyne and Wear and to Cleveland respectively. In 1996 Cleveland was abolished and the former SE boundary restored for ceremonial and related purposes: these areas are now administered by the ▷unitary authorities of Hartlepool and Stockton-on-Tees. Darlington became an independent unitary authority in 1997. Area (excluding unitary authorities): 2434 sq km (940 sq mi). Population (1996, excluding unitary authorities): 506 900. Administrative centre: Durham.

● **Durham, John George Lambton, 1st Earl of** ▶ (1792–1840) British colonial administrator; governor general of Canada (1838–39). As Lord Privy Seal he helped to draft the 1832 parliamentary ▷Reform Act and was sent to Canada after serving (1835–37) as ambassador to Russia. In Canada he was criticized for giving amnesty to rebellious French-Canadians and resigned. His *Report on the Affairs of British North America* (1839), largely written by the chief secretary for Canada, Charles Buller (1806–48), advocated the union of Upper and Lower Canada and responsible government, influencing subsequent colonial policy (*see* Empire, British).

● **durian** ▶ A tree, *Durio zebethinus*, of SE Asia, up to 30 m tall with oblong tapering leaves and large creamy white flowers. The spherical spiny-coated fruit, 15–20 cm in diameter, is notorious for its noxious smell, but the custard-like pulp is eaten in large amounts by local people and animals. The seeds are roasted. Family: *Bombacaceae*.

● **Durkheim, Emile** ▶ (1858–1917) French sociologist and one of the founding fathers of modern ▷sociology. In opposition to attempts to explain human conduct solely in terms of psychology, he developed an account of stability and change in whole societies in *The Division of Labour in Society* (1893); in *The Rules of Sociological Method* (1895) he set out a methodology for a science of society. His *Suicide* (1897) was a pioneering study in social statistics. Another major work, produced during the latter part of his life, was *The Elementary Forms of Religious Life* (1912), in which he examined the social foundations of religion.

● **durmast** ▶ A Eurasian ▷oak, *Quercus petraea*, up to 40 m tall. It has long-stalked oval leaves with rounded lobes and hairy undersides and unstalked conical acorns (hence its other name—sessile oak). Its durable wood is used for furniture, construction work, and boat building and the bark for tanning.

● **durra** ▶ An economically important variety of ▷sorghum, *S. vulgare* var. *durra*, also called millet, native to the Nile valley. Its grain is used chiefly for livestock feed.

● **Durrell, Lawrence George** ▶ (1912–90) British novelist and poet. Born in India, he lived mostly in the Mediterranean countries. His best-known work is *The Alexandria Quartet*, comprising *Justine* (1957), *Balthazar* (1958), *Mountolive* (1958), and *Clea* (1960), an elaborate exploration of modern love. His later work includes *The Avignon Quintet*, comprising *Monsieur* (1974), *Livia* (1978), *Constance* (1982), *Sebastian*

(1983), and *Quinx* (1985). He also wrote poetry (*Collected Poems*, 1980), humorous sketches, short stories (*Antrobus Complete*, 1985), and travel books. His brother **Gerald Durrell** (1925–95) was a naturalist and popular writer, famous for such books as *The Bafut Beagles* (1954), *My Family and Other Animals* (1956), and *The Stationary Ark* (1976), about his zoo and wildlife conservation trust in Jersey.

● **Dürrenmatt, Friedrich** ▶ (1921–90) Swiss dramatist and novelist. His plays are often experimental and usually satirical, mocking hypocritically conventional values. The best known are *The Visit* (1956) and *The Physicists* (1962). He also wrote short stories and detective novels.

● **Durrës** ▶ (Italian name: Durazzo) 41 18N 19 28E A port in W central Albania, on the Adriatic Sea. It was founded by Greeks in the 7th century BC and is now Albania's major commercial town and principal port. Products include flour, salt, and bricks. Population (1991 est): 86 900.

● **durum** ▷*See* wheat.

● **Duse, Eleonora** ▶ (1858–1924) Italian actress. She acted in plays by contemporary French dramatists and is especially associated with plays by Gabriele D'Annunzio, her lover, and by Ibsen. Her international reputation rivalled that of Sarah Bernhardt. She made one film, *Cenere* (1916).

● **Dushanbe** ▶ (name until 1929: Dyushambe; name 1929–61: Stalinabad) 38 38N 68 51E The capital of Tadzhikistan, on the River Dushanbinka. It has food and textile industries and is a cultural and educational centre. Since 1992 it has been the scene of fighting between rival political factions. Population (1994 est): 524 000.

● **Düsseldorf** ▶ 51 13N 6 47E A city in NW Germany, capital of North Rhine-Westphalia on the River Rhine. The birthplace of Heinrich Heine, it is noted for its art academy (1767). A port and major commercial and industrial centre of the ▷Ruhr, its main industry is iron and steel. Population (1996): 572 638.

● **Dust Bowl, the** ▶ An area in the USA, extending across W Kansas, Oklahoma, and Texas, and into Colorado and New Mexico. During the 1930s droughts and overfarming caused topsoil erosion. The plight of the farmers was illustrated by the photography of Dorothea Lange (1895–1965) and Steinbeck's novel *The Grapes of Wrath* (1939).

● **Dutch** ▶ The national language of the Netherlands, belonging to the West Germanic language group (*see* Netherlandic). In Belgium it is one of the two official languages and is known as Flemish (*or* Vlaams). It is derived from Low Franconian, the speech of the Salic Franks, who settled in this area, and has numerous local variants.

● **Dutch East Indies** ▷*See* Indonesia, Republic of.

● **Dutch elm disease** ▶ A serious disease, first described in the Netherlands in 1919, that reached epidemic proportions in Britain in the 1970s, killing millions of elm trees. The fungus responsible, *Ceratocystus ulmi*, blocks the vessels that carry water to the leaves, which wilt and eventually die. The disease is carried by the ▷elm bark beetle and was probably introduced into the UK on logs imported from Canada. Protective measures can be taken but are too expensive for widespread use.

● **Dutch Guiana** ▷*See* Suriname, Republic of.

● **Dutchman's breeches** ▶ An ornamental perennial herb, *Dicentra cucullaria*, from North American woodlands. Its arching stems bear cream or pale-yellow drooping flowers with saclike spurs. The greygreen fernlike leaves arise from underground tubers. Family: *Fumariaceae* (fumitory family). ▷*See also* Dicentra.

● **Dutchman's pipe** ▶ An ornamental climbing vine, *Aristolochia durior* (or *A. sipho*), from the American Midwest. Up to 9 m long, it has large kidney-shaped or heart-shaped leaves. The brown-and-black patterned tubular flowers are attached to swollen greenish-yellow tubes, bent to resemble a pipe, and are pollinated by carrion flies. Family: *Aristolochiaceae*.

● **Dutch metal** ▶ A highly ductile gold-coloured type of brass that contains between 85% and 88% of copper. It is used for bronzing and imitation gold leaf.

● **Dutch Republic** ▷*See* United Provinces of the Netherlands.

● **Dutch Wars** ▶ **1.** (1652–54) The war between England and the Netherlands precipitated by commercial rivalry, which had been aggravated by Oliver Cromwell's ▷Navigation Act (1651). The English were victorious. **2.** (1665–67) The war between England and the Netherlands (supported by France from 1666). Caused by commercial and colonial rivalry, the English defeated the Dutch off Lowestoft (1665) but in 1667 the Dutch entered the Thames and the Medway, bombarding Chatham. The Treaty of ▷Breda concluded the war. **3.** (1672–78) The war brought about by the invasion of the Netherlands by Louis XIV of France (supported at sea by England). The English were defeated by the Dutch (1672–73) and concluded the Treaty of Westminister (1674). By late 1673 France had been forced to withdraw from the Netherlands but entered the Spanish Netherlands and defeated the alliance of Spain, Austria, and the Dutch. The war was concluded by the Treaties of ▷Nijmegen. **4.** (1780–84) The war between Britain and the Netherlands caused by Dutch support for the American colonies during the ▷American Revolution. The Dutch were defeated.

● **Duval, Claude** ▶ (1643–70) French highwayman celebrated for his courtesy to women. He went to England in 1660. He was hanged.

● **Duvalier, François** ▶ (1907–71) Haitian politician, known as Papa Doc; president (1957–71). He used his secret police, the Tonton Macoutes, to eliminate all opposition and exploited Negro nationalism and voodoo practices to maintain popular sympathy. His son **Jean-Claude Duvalier** (1951–   ), known as Baby Doc, succeeded him but had to flee to France after an uprising in 1986.

● **DVD** ▷*See* compact disc.

● **Dvina, River** ▶ **1.** (Northern *or* Severnaya) A river in NW Russia, formed by the confluence of the Rivers Sukhona and Yug and flowing generally NW to the White Sea. Length: 750 km (466 mi). **2.** (Western *or* Dangava) A river in NE Europe, flowing SW and NW from the Valdai Hills through Russia, Lithuania, and Latvia to the Gulf of Riga. Length: 1021 km (634 mi).

● **Dvinsk** ▷*See* Daugavpils.

● **Dvořák, Antonín** ▶ (1841–1904) Czech composer. He was a friend of Brahms and director of the Prague conservatoire (1901–04). His early life was spent playing the violin and viola in orchestras. After he became famous he made frequent trips to England. From 1892 to 1895 he was director of the National Conservatory in New York, during which time he wrote his famous ninth symphony, entitled "From the New World." Besides the symphonies he wrote concertos for piano, violin, and cello, orchestral tone poems, chamber music, piano music, and songs. His Czech nationalism is particularly evident in his famous *Slavonic Dances* for piano duet (1878–86).

● **dwarfism** ▶ Abnormal smallness. The commonest cause is lack of food, and growth can be accelerated if enough food is given. Dwarfism can also occur in children with disease of the pituitary gland, in which insufficient ▷growth hormone is produced, or an underactive thyroid gland, which fails to produce thyroid hormone. Both conditions can be cured by administration of the deficient hormone. Other chronic diseases, such as heart or kidney disease, can cause dwarfism. Children who are emotionally deprived may also fail to grow. The dwarfs seen in circuses are called achondroplastic dwarfs; their small size is due to faulty bone development.

● **dwarf star** ▷*See* white dwarf.

● **dyarchy** ▶ A system of government, introduced by the UK Government of India Act (1919), for the provinces of India. Devised by Lionel Curtis (1872–1955), dyarchy divided the provincial executives into Crown-appointed councils and ministers responsible to popular assemblies, permitting greater participation in government by Indians. It lasted until the establishment of provincial autonomy in 1935.

● **dybbuk** ▶ (Hebrew: adhesion) In Jewish folklore, an evil spirit, specifically the soul of a sinful person, which, after death, possessed the body of a living person. The dybbuk could be exorcised by invocation of the divine name. Possession by such a spirit is the subject of *The Dybbuk*, a play by the Russian author Solomon Anski (1862–1920).

● **dyeing** ► The process of permanently changing the colour of a material. Natural dyes, such as ▷madder and ▷indigo, have been known since 3000 BC. Mauveine, the first synthetic dye, was discovered in 1856 by W. H. ▷Perkin. Most modern commercial dyes are made from aromatic hydrocarbons extracted from coal tar or oil. To dye fibres or textiles, the material is immersed in a solution containing the dye, so that the dye molecules adhere to the surface of the fibres. The solvent is usually water but occasionally other solvents are used. An inorganic chemical (such as a salt of chromium), known as a **mordant**, may be added to make the dye less soluble once it has adhered to the fibre. Dyes used without a mordant are called **direct dyes**. **Vat dyes** are insoluble in water, but are applied in reduced soluble form and then reoxidized. These are used particularly in cellulosic fibres. ▷*See also* pigments.

● **dyer's broom** ► A stout biennial or perennial plant, *Isatis tinctoria*, also called dyer's greenweed or dyer's furze. 50–120 cm high, it has arrow-shaped leaves and dense clusters of bright-yellow flowers that produce winged fruits. Native to Eurasia but naturalized elsewhere, its leaves ferment to a distinctive blue dye (*see* woad). Family: ▷*Cruciferae*.

● **dyer's rocket** ► A biennial herb, *Reseda luteola*, also called weld. It is widespread on waste ground throughout most of the N hemisphere. Up to 70 cm high, it has lance-shaped leaves with wavy margins and long slender spikes of pale-yellow flowers, 4–5 mm across, formerly used to make a yellow dye. Family: *Resedaceae*.

● **Dyfed** ► A former county of SW Wales. It was created under local government reorganization in 1974 from the counties of Cardiganshire (*see* Ceredigion), ▷Carmarthenshire, and ▷Pembrokeshire. The three historic counties were restored when Dyfed was abolished in 1996.

● **dyke** ► A wall-like body of igneous rock that is intruded (usually vertically) into the surrounding rock in such a way that it cuts across the stratification (layering) of this rock. *Compare* sill.

● **Dylan, Bob** ► (Robert Allen Zimmerman; 1941–   ) US singer and songwriter. An outstanding lyricist, he spoke for the protest movement of the 1960s with such folk albums as *The Times They Are A-changin'* (1964). In *Highway 61 Revisited* (1965) he introduced electronic instruments and rock rhythms. *John Wesley Harding* (1968), following a two-year retirement, and *Blood on the Tracks* (1975) confirmed his inventiveness. His conversion to Christianity in 1979 resulted in religious albums, including *Saved* (1980). More recent records include *Infidels* (1983), *Oh Mercy* (1989), *Unplugged* (1995), and *Time out of Mind* (1997).

● **dynamics** ▷*See* mechanics; Newtonian mechanics.

● **dynamite** ► An explosive plastic solid consisting of 75% nitroglycerine and 25% kieselguhr, a porous form of silicon dioxide (SiO_2). It was invented in 1866 by ▷Nobel. Nitroglycerine alone is very sensitive to shock. The kieselguhr makes it safe to handle. Dynamite is used for blasting, particularly under water.

● **dynamo** ▷*See* electric generator.

● **dyne** ► The unit of force in the ▷c.g.s. system equal to the force that will impart to a mass of one gram an acceleration of one centimetre per second per second.

● **dysentery** ► An infection of the large bowel causing painful diarrhoea that often contains blood and mucus. It may be caused either by bacteria of the genus *Shigella* or by amoebae. It can occur wherever there is poor sanitation, but amoebic dysentery is much more common in tropical countries. Treatment for bacillary dysentery is usually by administration of fluids to prevent dehydration, but for amoebic dysentery drugs to kill the amoebae are also given.

● **dyslexia** ► Difficulty in learning to write, spell, and read. It is commonly discovered at school when a child cannot read as well as would be expected. Dyslexic children are usually of normal intelligence and with special teaching can improve greatly, although some never manage to deal well with the written word. In some cases the cause is genetic.

● **dysmenorrhoea** ► Painful menstrual periods. In most cases the cause is not known. Treatment is usually with pain killers, but starting a course of oral contraceptive pills will also stop the pain. If the pain starts after years of pain-free periods there may be disease of the reproductive organs.

● **dyspepsia** ▷*See* indigestion.

● **dyspraxia** ► Inability to organize movements, also known as clumsy child syndrome. Affected children have difficulties with such tasks as dressing, using cutlery, pedalling a bicycle, and catching a ball. They may have problems in learning to read (due to poor control of eye movements) and write (because of difficulties in manipulating a pen or pencil), but are of average or above-average intelligence. Dyspraxic children benefit from such treatments as physiotherapy and occupational therapy.

● **dysprosium** ► (Dy) A lanthanide element discovered in 1886. It forms the oxide (Dy_2O_3) and halides (for example DyF_3) and can be separated from the other lanthanides by ion-exchange techniques. At no 66; at wt 162.50; mp 1412°C; bp 2567°C.

● **Dzerzhinsk** ► (name until 1919: Chernorech; name from 1919 until 1929: Rastyapino) 56 15N 43 30E A port in central Russia, on the River Oka. It supports chemical, textiles, and cable industries. Population (1995 est): 285 000.

● **Dzhambul** ► (name until 1939: Auliye-Ata) 42 50N 71 25E A city in S Kazakhstan, on the River Talas. Its industries include phosphates, metal, leather, and food processing. Population (1991 est): 312 300.

● **Dzungarian Basin** ▷*See* Junggar Pendi.

E

● **Ea ▶** (*or* Enki) The ancient Mesopotamian god of water and the sea, with Anu and Enlil one of the supreme triad. He created the Tigris and Euphrates rivers. A guardian against demons and patron of the arts and sciences, including magic, his main attribute was wisdom.

● **Eadred ▶** (d. 955) King of England (946–55), who reconquered Northumbria by expelling Eric Bloodaxe (954), its Norwegian king. Eadred bequeathed money to relieve the poor and to aid defence against Viking raids.

● **Eads, John Buchanan ▶** (1820–87) US civil engineer, best known for his design of the steel triple-arched Eads Bridge, which spans the Mississippi River at St Louis, Missouri. Opened in 1874, it is a landmark in civil engineering.

● **Eadwig ▶** (*or* Edwy; d. 959) King of England from 955 to 957, when he lost Mercia and Northumbria, and thereafter of Kent and Wessex only. He forced St ▷Dunstan into exile.

● **eagle ▶** A large broad-winged bird of prey occurring throughout the world, mostly in remote mountainous regions. Eagles have a large hooked bill and strong feet with large curved talons and are typically dull brown but may be a combination of black, grey, white, or chestnut; the head is often crested. With a wingspan of 1.3–2.4 m, they can soar for long periods searching for food—generally live prey, such as mammals or reptiles. Family: *Accipitridae* (hawks and eagles). ▷*See also* bald eagle; golden eagle; harpy eagle; Philippine eagle; sea eagle.

● **eagle owl ▶** A large Eurasian ▷owl of the genus *Bubo*, ranging from cold northern forests to hot southern deserts. It reaches 70 cm in length, is tawny with brown mottling, and has orange eyes and large ear tufts.

● **eaglewood ▶** (*or* aloes wood) The resinous heartwood of a tree of the genus *Aquilaria* (especially *A. agallocha*), of SE Asia. Under certain conditions it becomes resinous and fragrant and is used in perfumery. Family: *Thymelaeaceae*.

● **Eakins, Thomas ▶** (1844–1916) US painter of portraits and everyday life, particularly sports scenes. He lived mainly in Philadelphia, except for visits to Paris (1866–69) and Spain (1870), where he was influenced by the realism of Velázquez. His teaching methods were controversial, as were some of his paintings, such as *Gross Clinic* (1875; Jefferson Medical College, Philadelphia), showing a surgeon operating.

● **ealdorman ▶** The chief royal official of the Anglo-Saxon shire. Almost always of noble rank, he presided over the shire court, sharing one-third of its profits, executed royal orders, and raised the shire military levy. Ealdormen later became the hereditary earls, and the sheriffs succeeded to their duties.

● **Ealing ▶** A borough of W Greater London, created in 1965 from the former municipal boroughs of Acton, Ealing, and Southall. Area: 55 sq km (21 sq mi). Population (1994 est): 289 800.

● **Eanes, António dos Santos Ramalho ▶** (1935–) Portuguese general and statesman; president (1976–86). Eanes became prominent in the military government established in 1974, and helped to suppress the attempted coup of 1975.

● **ear ▶** The organ of hearing and balance in vertebrate animals (including man). The human ear is divided into external, middle, and inner parts. Sound waves are transmitted through the auditory meatus and cause the eardrum (tympanic membrane) to vibrate. These vibrations are transmitted through the three small bones (ossicles) of the middle ear to the fenestra ovalis, which leads to the inner ear. A duct (the Eustachian tube) connects the middle ear to the back of the throat (pharynx), enabling the release of pressure that builds up in the middle ear. The cochlea—a spiral organ of the inner ear—contains special cells that convert the sound vibrations into nerve impulses, which are transmitted to the hearing centres of the brain via the cochlear nerve. The inner ear also contains the vestibular apparatus, comprising the organs of balance: three semicircular canals, each of which registers movement in a different plane. Impulses from the semicircular canals are carried to the brain through the vestibular nerve, which combines with the cochlear nerve to form the auditory (or vestibulocochlear) nerve. The semicircular canals and cochlea are filled with fluid and are known together as the labyrinth of the ear.

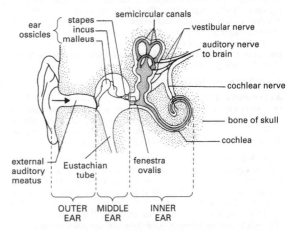

ear ▶ A vertical section through the human ear shows its internal structure; the middle and inner ears are embedded in the bone of the skull. The arrow indicates the direction of sound waves entering the ear.

● **Earhart, Amelia ▶** (1898–1937) US aviator, who was the first woman to fly solo across the Atlantic (1932) and Pacific (1935) Oceans. Her plane was lost over the Pacific on an attempted flight around the world with F. J. Noonan. □ p. 398.

● **earl ▷***See* peerage.

● **Earl Marshal ▶** A hereditary post held by the Dukes of Norfolk since 1672. The Earl Marshal is the senior member of the ▷College of Arms and oversees state ceremonies, when he carries a golden rod with a black ring at each end.

● **Early English ▶** The style of ᵒgothic architecture predominant in England in the 13th century. It is characterized by narrow pointed windows and arches, in contrast to the rounded features of the preceding period (*see* Norman art and architecture). These lancet windows are often grouped in threes or fives (e.g. the Five Sisters window in York Minster). Dog-tooth carving, heavily undercut crockets (stylized foliage) on capitals, and columns with detached shafts in black Purbeck marble are typical decorative elements. Salisbury Cathedral (begun 1220) and the nave of Lincoln Cathedral (begun 1192) show the style at its best.

● **Earp, Wyatt** ► (1848–1929) US frontiersman. After an itinerant youth, Earp, a noted gunslinger, settled in Tombstone, Arizona, where his brother Virgil was marshal. In 1881 a feud between the Earps and their rivals, the Clanton gang, culminated in the famous gunfight at the OK Corral, in which three of the Clantons were killed. Following the murder of another Earp brother, Morgan, in 1882, Wyatt killed the two men he held responsible and fled to escape a murder charge. Thereafter he lived by a mixture of police work, gambling, and confidence trickery. In his old age he successfully created the image of himself as a fearless and incorruptible law officer.

● **earth** ► The third planet from the sun, at an average distance of 149.6 million km (93 million mi) from it. Its diameter at the equator is 12 756 km (7926 mi), slightly less at the Poles; its shape is therefore a flattened sphere (a geoid). It completes an orbit of the sun in 365 days, 6 hours, 8 minutes and makes one rotation on its axis every 23 hours 56 minutes.

The earth is believed to be about 4600 million years old, the oldest rocks so far discovered being 4400 million years old. Geologists divide this time into eras, periods, and epochs (*see* geological time scale). The earth consists of an inner core of solid iron, surrounded by an outer core of molten iron. Surrounding this is the solid mantle, inner and outer, which is separated from the crust by the ▷Mohorovičić discontinuity. The crust consists of basaltic oceanic crust surmounted by less dense granitic continental crust, which forms the continents. The crust varies in thickness from 5 km under the oceans to 60 km under mountain ranges. The composition of the crust is approximately 47% oxygen, 28% silicon, 8% aluminium, 4.5% iron, 3.5% calcium, 2.5% each sodium and potassium, and 2.2% magnesium. All other elements are present to an extent of less than 1% each.

70.8% of the earth's surface is ocean. The greatest ocean depth is over 11 000 m (36 000 ft), in the Marianas Trench; the greatest height of land is 8850 m (29 035 ft), at Mount Everest.

● **earthenware** ▷*See* ceramics.

● **earthnut** ► A slender perennial herb, *Conopodium majus*, of European woods and meadows. Up to 1 m high, it is also called pignut or hognut, as its tubers are eaten by livestock. It has finely divided leaves and clusters of pinkish-white flowers. Family: ▷*Umbelliferae*. The name is also sometimes applied to the ▷groundnut.

● **earthquake** ► A series of shocks felt at the earth's surface, ranging from mild tremblings to violent oscillations, resulting from the fracturing of brittle rocks within the earth's crust and upper mantle. The magnitude of an earthquake depends on the amount of energy liberated when the overstrained rocks fracture. The ▷Richter scale is used for comparing earthquake magnitudes. The point of origin of the ▷seismic waves produced is the focus and the point on the earth's surface directly above this is the epicentre. The majority of earthquakes occur in certain well-defined seismic zones, corresponding with the junction of lithospheric plates (*see* plate tectonics); these include the circum-Pacific belt, the Alpine-Himalayan belt, and the midocean ridges.

● **earth sciences** ► The study of the ▷earth, including such subjects as ▷geology, ▷geochronology, ▷geodesy, ▷geochemistry, ▷geophysics, and physical ▷geography.

● **earthstar** ► A fungus of the genus *Geastrum*, with a starlike inedible fruiting body. Initially globular, the outer layer peels back in segments to form the "rays" of the star, surrounding a thin papery inner globe. Spores are released through a pore in the top. The collared earthstar (*G. triplex*), occurring in woodland, is 6–10 cm across, pale brown, and has five or more rays. Phylum: ▷*Basidiomycota*.

● **earthworm** ► A terrestrial ▷annelid worm belonging to a class (*Oligochaeta*) found all over the world. Earthworms feed on rotting vegetation, pulling the dead leaves down into their burrows and improving the fertility of the soil. The body consists of about 100 segments, each with four pairs of bristles for gripping the surface as the

worm moves. The largest earthworm is *Megascolides australis*, which reaches a length of about 3.3 m.

● **earwig** ► A nocturnal □insect belonging to an order (*Dermaptera*; about 1100 species) found in Europe and warm regions. It has a dark slender body, 5–50 mm long, and a pair of pincers (cerci) at the end of the abdomen. At rest, the membranous semicircular hindwings are covered by short leathery forewings. Most earwigs are herbivorous, sometimes becoming pests. The females lay eggs in the soil and care for them throughout development.

● **East African Rift System** ▷*See* Great Rift Valley.

● **East Anglia** ► A region in E England, consisting of the counties of Norfolk, Suffolk, and parts of Essex and Cambridgeshire. It is predominantly flat and low-lying. Originally an Anglo-Saxon kingdom, it became a famous wool centre in the middle ages. The University of East Anglia was established at Norwich in 1962.

● **East Ayrshire** ► A council area of SE Scotland, consisting of the E part of the historic county of ▷Ayrshire. Absorbed into Strathclyde Region in 1975, it became a ▷unitary authority in 1996. It consists mainly of a rich agricultural plain rising to hills in the S and E. Dairying and cattle breeding are the main agricultural activities, with various industries in Kilmarnock. Area: 1252 sq km (483 sq mi). Population (1999 est): 121 000. Administrative centre: Kilmarnock.

● **Eastbourne** ► 51 00N 0 44W A resort in S England, on the East Sussex coast near Beachy Head, where the South Downs reach the sea. One of the larger English resorts, it developed in the 19th century. Population (1991): 94 793.

● **East Cape** ► 37 42S 178 35E The easternmost point of New Zealand, on North Island.

● **East China Sea** ▷*See* China Sea.

● **East Dunbartonshire** ► A council area of central Scotland, comprising part of the historic county of ▷Dunbarton. Absorbed into Strathclyde Region in 1975, it became a ▷unitary authority in 1996. Mainly low-lying and agricultural, it includes residential suburbs of Glasgow in the S and part of the Campsie Fells in the N. Area: 172 sq km (66 sq mi). Population (1999 est): 110 700. Administrative centre: Kirkintilloch.

● **Easter** ► The feast of the resurrection of Christ, the major feast of the Christian calendar. Associated by the early Church with the Jewish ▷Passover, the date of celebrating Easter was a matter of controversy from earliest times. At the Council of ▷Nicaea in 325 AD, it was agreed that it would be linked to the full moon on or following the vernal equinox and might thus fall on any Sunday between 22 March and 25 April (*see also* Orthodox Church). The keeping of a vigil on the night of Easter Saturday is a traditional part of the observance. ▷*See also* Good Friday; Lent.

● **Easter Island** ► (or Rapanui) 27 05S 109 20W A Chilean island of volcanic origin in the S Pacific Ocean. It is famed for its stone sculptures 3–12 m (10–40 ft) high, of unknown origin. The population is of Polynesian stock. Fruit and vegetables are grown and wool is exported. Area: 166 sq km (64 sq mi). Population (latest est): 2000. Chief settlement: Hanga-Roa.

● **Eastern Cape** ▷*See* Cape Province.

● **Eastern Orthodox Church** ▷*See* Orthodox Church.

● **Eastern Roman Empire** ► (or Byzantine Empire) The Roman territories E of the Balkans as first separated from the western ▷Roman Empire by ▷Diocletian in 293 AD. Thereafter an eastern emperor and magistrates coexisted with their western counterparts at Rome. Under ▷Constantine the Great the Eastern Empire was reunited with the west and became Christian: his capital, Constantinople (previously Byzantium; now ▷Istanbul), was inaugurated as the "New Rome" in 330 AD. The Empire was redivided on the death of the emperor ▷Theodosius (395 AD) and never reunited. After the fall of Rome to the ▷Ostrogoths in 476, the eastern emperors made various attempts to reconquer the west but this was never accomplished. Byzantine civilization reached its first peak during the reign of ▷Justinian I in the 6th century: the Empire later enjoyed an extended period of prosperity and cultural achievement in the 10th, 11th, and

12th centuries. The Eastern Empire survived until the fall of Constantinople to the Ottoman Turks in 1453—almost a millennium after the western Empire. ▷*See also* Byzantine art and architecture.

● **Eastern Townships** ▶ A district of E Canada, consisting of approximately 15 Quebec counties lying S of the St Lawrence River and E of Montreal. A prosperous agricultural area, it also has important asbestos mines. Chief town: Sherbrooke.

● **Easter Rising** ▶ (1916) An armed insurrection in □Dublin against the British Government. Patrick ▷Pearse, a leader of the Irish Republican Brotherhood, and James Connolly with his Citizen Army, a total of 2000 men, occupied strategic positions in the city and proclaimed the establishment of the Irish Republic. Serious street fighting ensued with the government employing artillery. Hopes of German arms and munitions were frustrated and the insurgents surrendered unconditionally. The rising was largely confined to Dublin and minor disturbances in Wexford and Galway. Sixteen of the leaders were subsequently executed by the British, an action that had the effect of rallying Irish opinion, until then largely apathetic, behind the nationalist cause.

● **East Germany** ▷*See* Germany, Federal Republic of.

● **East India Company** ▶ **1.** (British) A commercial company founded in 1600 to trade in East Indian spices; it came to wield great political power in British India. Its dominance in India was established by Robert ▷Clive's victories in the Seven Years' War (1756–63). For the next decade the Company controlled government, its powers then being restricted by the ▷Government of India Acts. Supreme political power was vested in a Board of Control, responsible to the British parliament, while the Company kept administrative and commercial powers. In the 19th century these were gradually limited and the Company ceased to exist in 1873. **2.** (Dutch) A commercial company founded in 1602 to foster Dutch trade in the East Indies. By the late 17th century, it concentrated almost exclusively on the administration of ▷Java. **3.** (French; Compagnie des Indes orientales) A trading company founded by ▷Colbert in 1664 to administer French commerce and colonialism in India. An unsuccessful rival of the British East India Company, it ceased to exist in 1789.

Easter Island ▶ The vast stone statues, of which there are over 600 on the island, occupy stone terraces.

● **East Indies** ▶ A term now usually referring to the ▷Malay Archipelago but sometimes to Indonesia (formerly called the Dutch East Indies). It may also include SE Asia and India.

● **East Kilbride** ▶ 55 46N 4 10W A town in central Scotland, in South Lanarkshire. Designated as a new town in 1947, it has engineering, clothing, printing, and electrical equipment industries. Population (1991): 82 777.

● **East London** ▶ (former name: Port Rex) 33 00S 27 54E A port in S South Africa, on the Indian Ocean. It is an important tourist centre. Population (1996): 212 323 (metropolitan area).

● **East Lothian** ▶ A council area of SE Scotland, on the Firth of Forth and the North Sea. In 1975 the boundaries of the historic county of East Lothian (once called Haddingtonshire) were adjusted to form a district of the same name, in Lothian Region. In 1996 this became an independent ▷unitary authority. Coastal plains in the N rise to the Lammermuir Hills in the SW. Agriculture, fishing, and tourism are the main economic activities. Area: 678 sq km (262 sq mi). Population (1999 est): 90 400. Administrative centre: Haddington.

● **Eastman, George** ▶ (1854–1932) US inventor of the Kodak camera (1888). In 1884 he patented a photographic film consisting of paper base on which the chemicals were fixed rather than being applied to photographic plates when required. The Kodak camera, containing wind-on film, was improved in 1889, when Eastman replaced the paper-based film with celluloid. He founded the Eastman Kodak Company in 1892 and in 1928 developed a process for colour photography.

● **East Pakistan** ▷*See* Bangladesh, People's Republic of.

● **East Renfrewshire** ▶ A council area of W central Scotland, consisting of part of the historic county of Renfrewshire. Absorbed into Strathclyde Region in 1975, it became a ▷unitary authority in 1996. It is mainly an upland farming area apart from the urbanized N, which is now a residential area for Glasgow. Area: 173 sq km (67 sq mi). Population (1999 est): 89 300. Administrative centre: Giffnock.

● **East Riding** ▶ A county of NE England, a historical division of ▷Yorkshire, on the North Sea and the Humber estuary. In 1974 it became part of the new county of Humberside. When this was abolished in 1996, separate ▷unitary authorities were created for the East Riding and its chief city, ▷Hull: the latter is considered part of the East Riding for ceremonial and related purposes. It is mainly flat and low-lying, rising to the Yorkshire Wolds in the N. The main economic activities are arable farming, fishing, and tourism, with various industries in Hull. Area (excluding Hull): 1748 sq km (675 sq mi). Population (1999 est, excluding Hull): 315 700. Administrative centre: Beverley.

● **East River** ▶ A river in the E USA, a navigable waterway flowing through New York City and connecting New York Harbour with Long Island Sound. Length: 26 km (16 mi).

● **East Sussex** ▶ A county of SE England, formerly part of ▷Sussex, on the English Channel. Brighton and Hove became an independent ▷unitary authority in 1997. It is mainly undulating with the South Downs in the S. Cereals, hops, fruit, and vegetables are produced. Industries include electronics and light engineering. Brighton and Eastbourne are tourist centres. Area (excluding Brighton and Hove): 1795 sq km (693 sq mi). Population (1999 est, excluding Brighton and Hove): 496 200. Administrative centre: Lewes.

● **East Timor** ▶ A country in SE Asia, occupying the E part of the island of ▷Timor. It is mountainous, with a monsoon climate. The great majority of the population are Roman Catholics.
　　Economy: lack of natural resources, underdevelopment, and 25 years of repression and conflict have left East Timor the poorest nation in Asia. 90% of the population live off the land; the main crops are coffee (the chief export), coconuts, and sandalwood. Offshore oil and gas are to be exploited from 2004.
　　History: in 1859 Timor was divided between Holland, which took the W part, and Portugal, which took the E. In 1975 East Timor declared its independence but this provoked a military invasion by Indonesia (which had incorporated W Timor in 1949). Wholesale massacres of the Timorese population followed. Although Indonesia formally annexed East Timor in 1976, this was not accepted by the UN. Demonstrations against Indonesian rule in 1991 were severely

repressed, leading to international protests. In September 1999 a referendum on the territory's future was held in East Timor, resulting in a 78.5% vote in favour of independence. There followed a campaign of terror by anti-independence militias, with apparent collusion from government forces. Indonesia finally withdrew its troops in October, leaving a UN administration and peacekeeping force to oversee the transition to full nationhood. East Timor finally achieved independence in May 2002, the former guerrilla leader Xanana Gusmão having been elected president.

East Timor

Head of state	President José Xanana Gusmão
Official languages	Portuguese and Tetum (a lingua franca)
Official currency	US dollar of 100 cents
Area	14 874 sq km (5743 sq mi)
Population (2002 est)	750 000
Capital	Dili

● **East–West Schism** ▶ The breach between the Eastern (Byzantine) and Western (Roman) branches of the Christian Church, which became formal in 1054. The two branches had grown steadily apart since the division of the Roman Empire in 293 AD (*see* Eastern Roman Empire), a process that accelerated after the fall of the west to the barbarians in the 4th century. Initially the differences were more cultural than doctrinal; while the organizational and intellectual structures developed by the Western Church owed much to ▷Roman law, the Eastern Churches were more deeply influenced by the heritage of the Greek world. The very different political situations of the two Churches also led to profound differences of outlook, especially after 800, when the papacy allied itself to the empire of Charlemagne (and subsequently the Holy Roman Empire). By the beginning of the 11th century Rome's growing insistence on its primacy in doctrinal matters was deeply resented in the east. The issue that produced the final breach was a somewhat abstruse point of Trinitarian theology, the so-called ▷Filioque clause added to the ▷Nicene Creed by Rome but rejected in the east. In 1054 Pope Leo IX and the patriarch of Constantinople excommunicated and denounced each other and the schism was complete: any possibility of an early reconciliation was destroyed in 1204, when western forces sacked Constantinople during the Fourth Crusade. Subsequently the Roman Catholic Church and the ▷Orthodox Church developed separately. There was no rapprochement until the 1960s, when the mutual excommunications of 1054 were lifted.

● **Eastwood, Clint** ▶ (1930–) US film actor and director, who became popular playing tough taciturn heroes in such films as *The Good The Bad and The Ugly* (1966) and *Dirty Harry* (1971); as a director his films include *Bird* (1988), the Oscar-winning *Unforgiven* (1992), *The Bridges of Madison County* (1995), *Midnight in the Garden of Good and Evil* (1998), and *Space Cowboys* (2000).

● **eating disorders** ▷*See* anorexia nervosa; bulimia nervosa.

● **Ebbw Vale** ▶ 51 47N 3 12W A town in South Wales, in Blaenau Gwent county borough. Formerly known for coalmining, iron, and steel, it now manufactures tinplate and has varied light industry. Population (1991): 19 484.

● **EBCDIC** ▷*See* character set.

● **Ebert, Friedrich** ▶ (1871–1925) German statesman; first president of the German ▷Weimar Republic (1919–25). A trade union leader, he became a deputy in the Reichstag and from 1913 led the Social Democrats; he accepted the republican presidency when the German Empire collapsed in 1918. As president he suppressed extremists of the Right and Left.

● **Ebla** ▶ An ancient city (modern Tell Mardikh) S of Aleppo (Syria). It was conquered by ▷Sargon of Akkad; over 15 000 Akkadian cuneiform tablets (c. 2300 BC) containing trade and other records were discovered here in 1975.

● **Ebola virus** ▶ A virus causing an acute infection in humans (mortality rate 50–80%), similar to ▷green monkey disease; no cure is known. It is transmitted in blood and other body fluids but its natural host is unknown. Named after the region of the Democratic Republic of Congo (formerly Zaïre) in which it was first identified

(1976), it has caused outbreaks in S Sudan (1976, 1979), Congo (1995), and Gabon and South Africa (1996).

● **ebony** ▶ The valuable heartwood of tropical evergreen trees of the genus *Diospyros*. Very hard, usually deep black, and able to take a high polish, it is used for cabinetwork, inlaying, knife handles, and piano keys. The trees have oval leaves, small white flowers, and round berries. The most important species are *D. ebenum* (up to 15 m high) from India and Sri Lanka and *D. reticulata* from Mauritius. Family: *Ebenaceae*.

● **Eboracum** ▶ (*or* Eburacum) ▷*See* York.

● **Ebro, River** ▶ (Latin name: Iberus) The second longest river in Spain. Rising in the Cantabrian Mountains, it flows SE to the Mediterranean. It is a source of hydroelectricity and irrigation and its delta is canalized. Length: 910 km (565 mi).

● **EC** ▷*See* European Community.

● **Eccles** ▶ 53 29N 2 21W A town in N England, in Salford unitary authority, Greater Manchester, on the Manchester Ship Canal. It manufactures machinery, textiles, and chemicals. Eccles cakes originated here. Population (1991): 36 000.

● **Eccles, Sir John Carew** ▶ (1903–97) Australian physiologist, who (in the 1950s) showed how the different nerve endings (synapses) could either allow the transmission of nervous impulses to other nerves (excitatory) or could prevent their passage (inhibitory). He was awarded the 1963 Nobel Prize together with A. L. ▷Hodgkin and A. F. ▷Huxley.

● **Ecclesiastes** ▶ (Greek: the preacher) An Old Testament book, traditionally ascribed to Solomon (10th century BC) but in fact one of the later books to be accepted as part of the Hebrew Bible. It is pessimistic in tone, consisting of poetic reflections on the futility of human life.

● **ecclesiastical courts** ▶ Tribunals established by the Christian Churches to adjudicate on various matters according to ▷canon law. Although their jurisdiction is now restricted to Church property or personnel, in past centuries it extended into many areas now regarded as secular. In medieval Europe the courts of the Roman Catholic Church rivalled those of the temporal authorities in power. Apart from matters of Church discipline and administration, they had jurisdiction over all cases involving marriage and separation, wills and inheritance, and oaths or vows. They also tried cases of heresy; the ▷Inquisition was a special ecclesiastical court invoked in the most serious cases. The existence of two parallel systems of justice caused considerable controversy and gave rise to various abuses and anomalies, notably in cases in which clergymen were accused of criminal offences (*see* benefit of clergy). By the 16th century the secular authorities had curtailed the scope of the Church courts in most of Europe: nevertheless, they retained vestiges of their former powers in many countries. In England the ecclesiastical courts (now administered by the Anglican Church) continued to preside over cases involving marriage and inheritance until the mid-19th century.

In the present-day Church of England cases involving matters of doctrine or ritual are heard before the Court of Ecclesiastical Causes Reserved, a body established in 1963. Other cases, such as those involving alterations to a church building or "conduct unbecoming" by a clergyman, are heard before a diocesan tribunal known as a consistory court: appeals are heard before the provincial courts of Canterbury or York.

● **Ecclesiasticus** ▶ A book of the ▷Apocrypha, also known as the Wisdom of Jesus the son of Sirach. It was written about 180 BC in Palestine by Joshua (*or* Jesus) ben-Sira. It stresses the need to fear God, gives practical advice for daily living, and underlines the value of having a good name.

● **ecdysis** ▷*See* moulting.

● **ECG** ▷*See* electrocardiography.

● **Echegaray y Eizaguirre, José** ▶ (1832–1916) Spanish dramatist. A mathematician and economist, he was appointed minister of finance in 1874. His plays include *Madman or Saint* (1877) and *The Son of Don Juan* (1895), influenced by ▷Ibsen. He won the Nobel Prize in 1904.

● **echidna** ▶ A ▷monotreme mammal belonging to the family *Tachyglossidae* (5 species), of Australia, Tasmania, and New Guinea.

The Australian echidna (*Tachyglossus aculeatus*), or spiny anteater, is about 45 cm long, with very long spines among its fur, and digs for ants, picking them up with its long sticky tongue; it has no teeth. Echidnas lay a single egg, which is incubated in a pouch on the female's belly. The young echidna is suckled at a teat in the pouch.

● **Echidna** ▶ In Greek legend, a monster, half woman and half serpent. By ▷Typhon she gave birth to many other legendary monsters, including Chimera, Cerberus, Orthus, Scylla, and the Sphinx.

● **echinoderm** ▶ A marine invertebrate animal of the phylum *Echinodermata* (6500 species), including ▷starfish, ▷sea urchins, ▷crinoids, ▷sea cucumbers, ▷brittle stars, etc. Echinoderms usually have a skin-covered skeleton of calcareous plates, often bearing spines. They use hydrostatic pressure created by a water vascular system to extend numerous small saclike organs (tube feet) used in locomotion, respiration, feeding, etc. Echinoderms generally occur on the sea floor, usually feeding on other animals or detritus. The sexes are generally separate and sex cells are fertilized in the sea.

● **Echinoidea** ▶ A class of ▷echinoderms (900 species) in which the body is covered by a rigid calcareous skeleton bearing movable spines. It includes ▷sea urchins, ▷heart urchins, and ▷sand dollars.

● **Echo** ▶ In Greek legend, a nymph deprived of speech by Hera and able to repeat only the final words of others. Her hopeless love for ▷Narcissus caused her to fade away until only her voice remained.

● **echocardiology** ▷*See* ultrasonography.

● **echolocation** ▶ A method by which certain animals can locate surrounding objects by emitting sounds and detecting the echo. Insectivorous bats emit high-frequency sound pulses (12–150 kHz) and locate their prey by detecting the echo by means of large ears or folds of the nostril. Toothed whales and porpoises emit brief intense clicks, enabling them to discriminate objects as small as fine wires. Some shrews and certain cave-dwelling swiftlets also use echolocation.

● **echo sounding** ▶ The use of sound waves to measure the depth of water below a vessel or to detect other vessels or obstacles. It consists of a source of ultrasonic pulses (about 30 kHz, usually at 1 pulse per second) and a circuit to measure the time taken for the pulse to reach the bottom or other vessel and its echo to return. This may be displayed on a ▷cathode-ray tube, paper chart, or neon light. Originally developed by the Allied Submarine Detection Investigation Committee (ASDIC), in 1920 it was formerly known by this acronym. The name was changed to sonar (sound *n*avigation *a*nd *r*anging) in 1963. Echo-sounding devices are now fitted to most ships.

● **Eck, Johann Maier von** ▶ (1486–1543) German Roman Catholic theologian. He was a leading defender of Roman Catholicism during the early years of the Reformation. He publicly disputed with ▷Luther at Leipzig (1519) and with ▷Melanchthon at Worms (1541).

● **Eckermann, Johann Peter** ▶ (1792–1854) German writer. His early work impressed ▷Goethe, whose unpaid assistant he became in 1823. His *Conversations with Goethe* (1836–48) is a brilliant literary account of the poet's last years.

● **Eckert, John Presper, Jr** ▶ (1919–) US electronics engineer, who with **John W. Mauchly** (1907–80) built the first electronic computer (1946). Known as ENIAC (*E*lectronic *N*umerical *I*ntegrator *a*nd *C*omputer), it was commissioned by the US Government and used by the army. Eckert and Mauchly also produced Binac (*Bin*ary *A*utomatic *C*omputer) and Univac I (*Univ*ersal *A*utomatic *C*omputer).

● **Eckhart, Meister** ▶ (Johannes E.; c. 1260–c. 1327) German Dominican theologian and mystic. Joining the Dominicans in 1275, he studied in Cologne and Paris and became provincial of his order in Saxony in 1303. During his professorship at Cologne University (1320–27) he was charged with heresy and in 1329 his writings were condemned by the pope. They have influenced a number of Protestant theologians and Romantic and existentialist writers.

● **eclampsia** ▷*See* pre-eclampsia.

● **eclipse** ▶ The passage of all or part of an astronomical body into the shadow of another. A **lunar eclipse** occurs when the moon enters the earth's shadow at full moon. The gradual obscuration of the moon's surface is seen. A **solar eclipse**, strictly an ▷occultation,

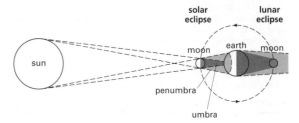

eclipse

occurs at new moon, when the moon passes directly in front of the sun. The moon's shadow moves rapidly across the earth. Observers in the outer shadow region (penumbra) will see a **partial eclipse**, with only part of the sun hidden. Observers in the dark inner (umbral) region will see a **total eclipse**, in which the sun's disc is briefly obscured; the ▷corona can, however, be seen. If the moon is too far away to cover the sun, an **annular eclipse** is observed, in which a rim of light is visible around the eclipsed sun.

● **eclipsing binary** ▷*See* binary star.

● **ecliptic** ▶ The great circle in which the plane of the earth's orbit around the sun meets the ▯celestial sphere. As a result of the earth's orbital motion, the ecliptic marks the apparent path of the sun across the celestial sphere, relative to the background stars, over the course of a year.

● **eclogue** ▶ A short dramatic, originally pastoral, poem. Invented by ▷Theocritus in the 3rd century BC, it was used by Virgil and revived during the Renaissance. Spenser, Marvell, and Swift wrote eclogues; Louis MacNeice and W. H. Auden made ironic use of them.

● **Eco, Umberto** ▶ (1932–) Italian novelist and literary theorist. Best known for the historical thriller *The Name of the Rose* (1981), he has also written such theoretical works as *A Theory of Semiotics* (1975) and the novels *Foucault's Pendulum* (1989) and *The Island of the Day Before* (1995). *Language and Lunacy* (1998) is a volume of essays.

● **E. coli** ▷*See* food poisoning.

● **ecology** ▶ The scientific study of organisms in their natural environment. Modern ecology, dating from the work of such scientists as Charles ▷Elton in the 1930s, is concerned with the relationships of different species with each other and with their surroundings (*see* environment). A ▷community of organisms and their habitat is called an ▷ecosystem. Ecologists can calculate the productivity of various ecosystems in terms of energy, with important applications in agriculture. In addition, the effects of man's intervention on natural ecosystems can be predicted, enabling the effective conservation of wildlife and management of game and fish. Ecologists have also introduced ▷biological control of pests. ▯food chain.

● **e-commerce** ▶ The use of telecommunications, especially the Internet, to buy and sell goods and services. Areas covered include telephone banking, on-line shopping, direct deposits, and EDI (electronic data exchange). The retailer benefits in market reach, time to market, lower administrative costs, etc., and the consumer in quicker access to a much larger range of goods and services. Payment is usually by credit card but other methods, such as ▷smartcards, ▷CyberCash, and digitized e-cash, enable direct anonymous payments to be made. Consumer concerns over privacy and security will hopefully be met by SET (secure electronic transactions), an industry standard for e-commerce designed to create customer confidence in Internet-based transactions.

● **econometrics** ▶ The application of statistical techniques to ▷economics. Econometrics is used in the testing of the validity of economic theories and in forecasting future trends. The usual process is to develop a mathematical model of a specific theory, which is tested against observations of the real world and used to make forecasts.

● **Economic Community of West African States** ▶ (ECOWAS) An organization of African states established by the Treaty of Lagos in 1975 with the aim of removing trade barriers, harmonizing agricultural and industrial policies, and promoting cooperation in social, cultural, and other matters. The original 15 signatories were Benin, Côte d'Ivoire, Gambia, Ghana, Guinea, Guinea-Bissau, Liberia, Mali, Mauritania, Niger, Nigeria, Senegal, Sierra Leone, Togo, and Upper Volta (now Burkina Faso); Cape Verde joined in 1977. In 1993 a new treaty was signed making the creation of a free-trade zone with a single currency a specified objective; there are also plans to establish an ECOWAS parliament and court of justice.

● **economic growth** ▶ An expansion in the output of a nation's economy, measured by an increase in the ▷gross national product (GNP). Economic growth is generally regarded as desirable because it is the best way of raising the standard of living; however, it can have drawbacks, such as increased pollution. The level of ▷investment in the economy is an important factor in the rate of growth, but the reasons for faster growth in some countries than in others are not at all certain. It is also necessary to distinguish between growth and growth per capita. In a developing country the rate of growth may be high but the rate of growth per capita may be low because of a large increase in the population.

● **economics** ▶ A social science concerned with the production of goods and services, their distribution, exchange, and consumption. **Microeconomics** is concerned with the problems facing individuals and firms, while **macroeconomics** is concerned with the economy of a country and regulation of the economy by governments. The division is useful because what is rational for the individual firm or household is not necessarily rational when considering the whole economy. Contemporary problems in economics in the Western democracies centre upon the control of ▷inflation, ▷unemployment, and the ▷balance of payments, as well as the encouragement of ▷economic growth. The conflicting schools of thought of ▷monetarism and Keynesianism disagree about the extent to which governments can influence economies.

● **economies of scale** ▶ An increase in output from a production process that is proportionately larger than the increase in inputs (raw materials, labour, etc.). For instance, a double-decker bus can carry twice as many passengers as a single-decker, using the same crew and only 40% more fuel. Such economies of scale are common in manufacturing.

● **ecosystem** ▶ A ▷community of living organisms and the habitat that they occupy. Examples of habitats are a wood, a seashore, and a pond. Within these habitats there may be one or more much smaller microhabitats (for example, a rotting log in a wood). Some ecosystems are clearly defined (for example, a pond ecosystem); others have no definite boundaries, merging with neighbouring ecosystems. An ecosystem receives inputs of solar energy, nutrients, water, and gases and discharges heat, oxygen, carbon dioxide, and organic compounds. The organisms typically comprise producers (plants, manufacturing organic material from inorganic compounds); consumers (animals, feeding on plants and each other); and decomposers (microorganisms causing decay). Together they form an interdependent ▷food chain or web.

● **ECOWAS** ▷See Economic Community of West African States.

● **ecstasy** ▶ A street name for the illegal ▷hallucinogen 3,4-methylenedioxymethamphetamine (MDMA). Synthesized in Germany in 1914, it became popular in the USA in the 1970s and in the UK in the 1980s. The psychedelic effect results from brain malfunction as a result of depletion of the neurotransmitter ▷serotonin. Users become overheated and drink large quantities of water to assuage their intense thirst. This has led to death through damage to the body's fluid balance.

● **ectopic pregnancy** ▶ Pregnancy occurring elsewhere than in the womb. The commonest site is a Fallopian tube but it may also occur in the cervix of the womb or very rarely inside the abdomen. It may lead to abortion or, more seriously, to rupture of the tube, with pain, bleeding, and shock. The usual treatment is surgical removal of the fetus and tube. Since the patient has a second tube there is usually no reason why she should not subsequently have a normal pregnancy.

● **ECU** ▷See European Currency Unit.

● **Ecuador, Republic of** ▶ A country in NW South America, lying on the Equator, from which it takes its name. It includes the ▷Galápagos Islands 1000 km (600 mi) out in the Pacific. It consists chiefly of a coastal plain in the W, separated from the tropical jungles of the Amazon basin (Oriente) by the Andes (containing several active volcanoes, including ▷Cotopaxi). There are frequent earthquakes. The population is largely of Indian and mixed race, with minorities of European and African descent.

Economy: mainly agricultural, with livestock, cereals, and vegetables in the upland valleys and tropical farming in the lower coastal areas, where the main cash crops (bananas, coffee, and cocoa) are grown. Much of the country is forested and valuable hardwoods are produced. Ecuador is the world's leading producer of balsawood. Fishing is important, especially shrimps, and fishing limits have been extended to 320 km (200 mi). There are some mineral resources; the most important is oil, several oilfields having been discovered in the Oriente since the early 1970s. In 1972 the construction of the Andean pipeline, which brings oil from the E to the coast, was completed and Ecuador is now South America's second largest oil producer (after Venezuela). Ecuador withdrew from OPEC in 1992. Industry is being developed, especially petrochemicals, pharmaceuticals, cement, and steel. Main exports include oil, fish, bananas, cocoa, and coffee. The economy remains hampered by extreme inequalities of land ownership and a massive external debt. In 1999–2000 Ecuador suffered its worst economic crisis in 100 years, with inflation reaching 70%.

History: the Andean kingdom of Quito had already been conquered by the Incas when the Spanish established a colony in 1532. It became part of the viceroyalty of Peru and later of New Granada. It gained independence in 1821 after revolts under Marshal Sucre, and in 1822 joined Gran Colombia under Bolívar. In 1830 it became the independent republic of Ecuador. Apart from a period of stability under liberal governments in the late 19th century, its political history has been one of almost continual turbulence. Between 1934 and 1972 the would-be dictator José Maria Velasco Ibarra (1893–1979) was five times elected president but was each time deposed by the military. A new constitution was introduced in 1979 and free presidential elections were held: since then various governments have faced the same problems of economic crisis, social division and unrest, and threatened military intervention. In the 1990s free-market reforms led to further instability, making possible the election of the maverick Abdale Bucaram (known as "El loco," the madman) to the presidency in 1996. He was dismissed on grounds of mental unfitness in 1997. Following elections in 1998 the centre-left candidate Jamil Mahuad became president. Later that year Ecuador signed a pact with Peru to end a border dispute that had resulted in wars in 1941, 1981, and 1995. Financial and economic crisis in early 2000 led to the resignation of the cabinet, the adoption of the US dollar, and rising disorder. There followed a coup led by the military acting with Indian groups. Gustavo Noboa was installed as president.

Republic of Ecuador

Head of state	President Gustavo Noboa
Official language	Spanish; the main Indian language is Quechua
Official currency	US dollar
Area	270 670 sq km (104 505 sq mi)
Population (1998 est)	12 175 000
Capital	Quito
Main port	Guayaquil

● **ecumenical movement** ▶ A movement among the Christian Churches to re-establish unity. The first major schism within Christianity was caused by the rupture between the Eastern and Western Churches in the 11th century; the second occurred within the Western Church at the ▷Reformation. It was only with the growth of missionary activity in the 19th century that the need for reunion became pressing. Historical divisions meant nothing to the new converts in countries outside the traditional sphere of Christianity. In 1910 the Edinburgh Missionary Conference opened negotiations among the Churches of the Reformation, a process that ultimately led to the foundation of the ▷World Council of Churches in 1948. The Orthodox Churches gradually came to take a more active role in this body, and further encouragement came with Pope ▷John XXIII's invitation to other Churches to send observers to the second ▷Vatican Council. The Church of England's decision (1992) to ordain women priests threatens to impair progress towards greater union with the Roman Catholic and Orthodox churches.

● **eczema** ▷See dermatitis.

● **Edam** ▶ 52 30N 5 02E A town in the NW Netherlands, in North Holland province on the IJsselmeer. It is famous for its round red-skinned cheeses. Population (1991): 24 839.

● **Edberg, Stefan** ▶ (1966–) Swedish tennis player. He won the Wimbledon men's singles title in 1988 and 1990; other victories include the Australian Open Championship (1986, 1987) and the US Open Championship (1991, 1992).

● **Eddas** ▶ Two Old Norse compilations made in Iceland in the early 13th century. Together they comprise the major store of pagan Scandinavian mythology. The **Poetic** (or Elder) **Edda** (c. 1200) contains poems on the gods, heroic legends, and traditional charms and proverbs. The **Prose** (or Younger) **Edda** (1223) was the work of Snorri ▷Sturluson, who planned it as a textbook for writers of ▷skaldic poetry, prefaced by a section on the Norse cosmogony, pantheon, and myths.

● **Eddington, Sir Arthur Stanley** ▶ (1882–1944) British theoretical astronomer, who correctly calculated that the temperature of the sun's interior must be millions of degrees Celsius or it would collapse under gravitational forces. He also showed that the luminosity of a star increases with its mass (the mass-luminosity law). Eddington was a talented popularizer of science: his *Expanding Universe* (1933) contained the novel idea that the galaxies are flying apart. He was appointed to the OM in 1938.

● **Eddy, Mary Baker** ▶ (1821–1910) US religious leader, founder of ▷Christian Science. Brought up as a Congregationalist and frequently ill while young, Mrs Eddy was influenced by the spiritual leader Phineas Parkhurst Quimby (1802–66). She published her beliefs in *Science and Health* (1875) and in 1879 founded the Church of Christ, Scientist, in Boston.

● **eddy current** ▶ An electric current induced in a conductor that experiences a changing magnetic field. In ▷electric generators, motors, and transformers, energy is lost by unwanted eddy currents, either producing heat or opposing motion. In these devices eddy currents are reduced by laminating the iron cores to increase their resistance. Eddy currents are useful in some applications, such as eddy-current heating, mechanical damping and eddy-current brakes, and electricity meters.

● **Eddystone Rocks** ▶ 50 10N 4 16W A dangerous group of rocks off the coast of SW England, in the English Channel. The lighthouse built by John Smeaton (1759) was the first in which dovetail-jointed stones were used; it was replaced in 1882.

● **Ede** ▶ 52 03N 5 40E A town in the central Netherlands, in Gelderland province. Its museum contains a fine collection of Van Gogh paintings. Population (1994): 98 220.

● **edelweiss** ▶ A common perennial alpine plant, *Leontopodium alpinum*, from Europe and South America, often grown in rock gardens. About 15 cm high, it has woolly leaves arranged like a star and tiny yellow flowers. Family: *Compositae* (daisy family).

● **Eden, Anthony** ▷See Avon, (Robert) Anthony Eden, 1st Earl of.

● **Eden, Garden of** ▶ In the Old Testament, the location of Paradise, in which Adam and Eve were created and lived until expelled because of disobedience (Genesis 2–3). Although the narrative may allude to a place in the fertile part of Mesopotamia, the geographical elements are probably mythological.

● **Eden Project** ▷See St Austell.

● **Edessa** ▶ (Modern Greek name: Édhessa) 37 08N 38 45E A town in N Greece, in Macedonia. Originally known as Aegea, it was the earliest capital of ancient Macedonia. Today it is a commercial and agricultural centre; industries include carpet manufacture. Population (latest est): 15 980.

● **Edgar** ▶ (c. 943–75) The first king of a united England (959–75). He allowed his Danish subjects to retain Danish laws. Edgar promoted a monastic revival and encouraged trade by reforming the currency. He improved defence by organizing coastal naval patrols and a system for manning warships.

● **Edgar** ▶ (c. 1075–1107) King of the Scots (1097–1107); a vassal of William Rufus of England. In 1098 he lost the Hebrides to Norway.

● **Edgar the Aetheling** ▶ (c. 1050–c. 1130) The grandson of Edmund II Ironside, his title Aetheling means royal prince. His claim to the English throne was rejected in 1066 owing to his minority and ill health. Although he initially submitted to William I, in 1068 and 1069 he led revolts against the king but came to terms with him in 1074.

● **Edgehill** ▶ A low ridge in the S Midlands of England, in S Warwickshire. It was the scene of the first battle in the Civil War (1642).

● **Edgeworth, Maria** ▶ (1767–1849) Anglo-Irish writer chiefly famous for her novels of Irish regional life, including *Castle Rackrent* (1800), *Patronage* (1814), and *Ormond* (1817), which influenced Sir Walter ▷Scott. She also wrote imaginative but moralizing children's stories.

● **Edinburgh** ▶ 1. 55 57N 3 13W The capital of Scotland, a city in the E centre of the country, in City of Edinburgh council area, on the S shore of the Firth of Forth. It is the financial, legal, and cultural centre of Scotland, and employment depends largely on service occupations. Food, drink, and printing are the primary manufacturing industries; the city's port is at ▷Leith. Edinburgh is distinguished by its spacious layout and attractive buildings. In the old town, atop steep basalt cliffs that rise above the city, stands the castle (which includes an 11th-century chapel). The Royal Mile extends E from the castle rock to the Palace of Holyrood House (begun c. 1500). The other famous thoroughfare in the city is Princes Street, flanked by the picturesque Princes Street Gardens. The new town contains fine Georgian architecture situated around a network of broad streets, squares, and circuses, which were originally designed by James Craig (1744–95) and include the work of such men as Robert Adam, who planned Charlotte Square in 1791. The university (1583) is famous for its medical faculty among other notable faculties; Heriot-Watt University (incorporated 1966) also has premises in the city. The Royal Scottish Academy, the Royal Scottish Museum, and other national institutions are situated in Edinburgh. St Giles Cathedral dates from the 12th century. In 1999 Edinburgh became the seat of the new Scottish parliament.

History: strategically important in medieval times in the wars between England and Scotland, Edinburgh emerged as the national capital in the 15th century. After James VI of Scotland (James I of England) moved his court to London in 1605 Edinburgh suffered a decline. It entered a golden age in the mid-18th century as a centre of learning: the philosopher David Hume and the diarist James Boswell are associated with Edinburgh in this era. The fame of the city as a cultural centre was revived in 1947 with the foundation of the annual Edinburgh International Festival. Population (1991): 401 910. **2. City of Edinburgh** A council area in E central Scotland, created from part of Lothian Region in 1996. Area: 262 sq km (101 sq mi). Population (1996 est): 447 550.

● **Edinburgh, Duke of** ▷See Philip, Prince, Duke of Edinburgh.

● **Edirne** ▶ (former name: Adrianople) 41 40N 26 34E A town in European Turkey, at the confluence of the Rivers Tunca and Maritsa. Round the main square are three mosques, one of which, the Selimiye Mosque, has 19 domes. Population (1995 est): 117 331.

● **Edison, Thomas Alva** ▶ (1847–1931) US inventor, perhaps the most prolific of all time. Most of his discoveries were developed in his own large research laboratory in Menlo Park, New Jersey. His most famous invention, the electric light bulb, took over a year to develop but he finally constructed a long-lasting filament bulb in 1879. By 1881 Edison had built a generating station and was supplying electricity to over 80 customers. Among his other 1300 inventions were the gramophone, a camera and viewing apparatus for moving pictures, and improvements to Alexander Graham ▷Bell's telephone. He also discovered thermionic emission (formerly called the Edison effect), enabling J. A. ▷Fleming to produce the first thermionic valve.

● **Edmonton** ▶ 53 34N 113 25W A city in W Canada, the capital of Alberta on the North Saskatchewan River. A 19th-century trading post, it became an agricultural settlement and grew into a city with the arrival of the railway (1891). The discovery of oil (1947) stimulated an economy already prosperous from agriculture-related industries. Edmonton is the site of the University of Alberta (1906). Population (1991): 616 741.

● **Edmund I** ▶ (921–46) King of England (939–46), who expelled the Norse king Olaf from Northumbria (944). He supported ▷Dunstan's reintroduction of the monasticism of St Benedict. An outlaw stabbed him to death at Pucklechurch.

● **Edmund II Ironside** ▶ (c. 981–1016) The son of Ethelred II of England. His struggle with Canute for the vacant throne ended in Edmund's defeat at Ashingdon (1016). Canute agreed to divide England with Edmund, but after Edmund's sudden death acquired the whole kingdom.

● **Edmund, St** ▶ (Edmund Rich; c. 1175–1240) English churchman; Archbishop of Canterbury. After an academic life at Oxford and Paris he became archbishop (1234). Supported by the barons, he successfully opposed Henry III's policies until his power was diminished by the arrival (1237) of the papal legate, Cardinal Otho. Feast day: 16 Nov.

● **Edmund the Martyr, St** ▶ (c. 841–870) Anglo-Saxon king of East Anglia (855–870), who was killed by Danish invaders and subsequently regarded as a saint. According to the best-known account of his death, which may be legendary, he was shot full of arrows and finally beheaded after refusing to renounce his Christian faith. In the 10th century his body was moved to what is now Bury St Edmunds, which became a major site of pilgrimage. Feast Day: 20 Nov.

● **Edo** ▶ A people of S Nigeria living to the W of the Niger River. Their language belongs to the ▷Kwa subgroup of the Niger-Congo family. Their sacred king (*or oba*) formerly held political, economic, and ritual authority, but most Edo are now Christians or Muslims.

● **Edom** ▶ The mountainous and barren land SW of the Dead Sea, which was traversed in antiquity by important caravan routes. The Edomites, according to the Old Testament, were descendants of ▷Esau and may have been subjected by the Israelites under King David. They were converted to Judaism in the late 2nd century BC after being defeated by the ▷Maccabees. They later migrated to S Judaea.

● **education** ▶ The process of learning. Highly developed systems of learning emerged early in Asia, especially in China. Institutionalized education also occurred in various forms in ancient Greece and Rome, which later influenced the development of formal education in medieval Europe, although the latter owes a great debt to early Arabic and Hebrew scholarship. Medieval European monastic schools originally established for those intending to enter the monasteries gradually admitted other pupils and extended the curriculum to include grammar, logic, rhetoric, geometry, arithmetic, music, and astronomy. A basic education was also provided in some areas for the children of the poor, usually by the local parish priest. Humanist education based upon the classics emerged during the Renaissance; the Gymnasien at Strasbourg provided the model for the academic schools of Protestant Europe, although its influence was slow in reaching England. European schools experienced a decline in standards during the 17th and 18th centuries, especially in England, where the old ▷grammar schools (*see also* public school) degenerated to a very low level.

Widespread education could be said to stem from the introduction of compulsory primary schooling (*see* primary education), first established successfully in Prussia in 1763. The introduction of universal compulsory education and the increasing role of the state in the educational sphere were influenced by the need to supply the skills necessary to the functioning of an industrialized society. The state, however, was slow to intervene in education in England and Wales, since a system of voluntary elementary education provided by the established Church and other religious bodies was already in existence. It was not until the Education Act (1870) that universal ele-

mentary education was introduced and the school boards were set up to establish schools where no voluntary schools existed. In 1902 Local Education Authorities (LEAs) took over from the school boards and in 1918 education was made compulsory until the age of 14. However, until the Education Act (1944), only primary education (in elementary schools) was available to those whose parents were unable to afford school fees or those who were not able to obtain scholarships to public or grammar schools. The 1944 Act inaugurated a system of universal ▷secondary education while maintaining the dual system of independent schools and publicly maintained or aided schools (including voluntary schools, such as those run by religious bodies). During the postwar period many of the ideas of the progressive educationalists, whose origins date back to ▷Rousseau (*see also* Froebel, Friedrich; Montessori system; Neill, A. S.), were adopted in state schools, especially at primary level.

In England and Wales the extent to which children should be selected according to ability remains controversial (*see* secondary education), as does the extent to which parents should be free to choose their children's schools. The Conservative governments of the 1980s and 1990s introduced a number of reforms designed to erode the power of the LEAs. In 1988 legislation was passed permitting primary and secondary schools to opt out of LEA control and become grant-maintained schools, receiving funding from central government directly. All decisions about the overall policy and daily management of such schools are taken by parent-governors, who also control the budget. These principles were later extended to all publicly maintained schools under an initiative known as Local Management of Schools (LMS): LEAs are now required to delegate control of at least 85% of each school's budget to the school itself. Schools have also been encouraged to seek sponsorship and management assistance from businesses. In 1999 the Labour government created a new tripartite structure of community (i.e. LEA-controlled) schools, voluntary schools, and foundation schools (the former grant-maintained schools, which are now funded by the LEAs rather than centrally). In England inspections of schools are carried out by the Office for Standards in Education (OFSTED), led by Her Majesty's Chief Inspector of Schools. Wales, Scotland, and Northern Ireland have their own inspection systems. ▷*See also* adult education; coeducation; distance learning; National Curriculum; preschool education; public examinations; special education; tertiary education.

Scotland's educational tradition has remained quite distinct from that of the rest of the UK in terms of organization, curriculum, and public examinations. The schools system is administered centrally (since 1999 by the Scottish parliament). Responsibility for schools at a local level lies with the local authorities, which are required to establish school boards of parents and teachers to participate in management. In Northern Ireland most secondary pupils are educated in denominational schools maintained or aided from public funds. Since the 1990s the government has encouraged the replacement of segregated schools with integrated ones, whenever this is supported by a ballot of parents. *See also* public examinations.

In Germany education is administered on a regional basis, most *Länder* (states) retaining a selective system of secondary education with approximately 5% of children entering a *Gymnasium* (grammar school). Germany is also noted for its well-developed system of vocational education. The educational state system in France is highly centralized. During the 1960s colleges of general education, which provided a more comprehensive system of education for children aged 11 to 15, were introduced although these usually exist alongside the selective *lycées* (academic secondary schools). In the USA education varies from state to state. Secondary education, however, is nonselective and provides both academic and vocational courses. Approximately 80% of children stay on beyond the compulsory school-attendance age of 16 and about 40% enter higher education. The highly centralized system of education in the Soviet Union provided the model for many of the formerly communist countries. Compulsory education from the age of 7 until 17 is carried out in single nonselective coeducational schools. Vocational courses are provided for students who do not proceed to university.

● **Edward I** ▶ (1239–1307) King of England (1272–1307), succeeding his father Henry III. He married (1254) ▷Eleanor of Castile. In the ▷Barons' War (1264–67) he defeated the barons at Evesham (1265). As king, he encouraged parliamentary institutions at the expense of feudalism and subdued Wales, on which he imposed the English system of administration. He later tried to assert authority over Scotland and died on his way to fight ▷Robert (I) the Bruce.

● **Edward II** ▶ (1284–1327) King of England (1307–27), succeeding his father Edward I. He was born in Caernarvon and became the first English Prince of Wales (1301). He married ▷Isabella of France (1308). His extravagance, his defeats in Scotland, notably at Bannockburn (1314), and the unpopularity of his favourites, Piers ▷Gaveston and Hugh le Despenser (1262–1326), led Isabella and her lover Roger de ▷Mortimer to murder him.

● **Edward III** ▶ (1312–77) King of England (1327–77), succeeding his father Edward II. He married (1328) Philippa of Hainault. Edward assumed effective power in 1330 after imprisoning his mother ▷Isabella of France and executing her lover Roger de ▷Mortimer. Thereafter his reign was dominated by military adventures, his victories in Scotland, especially at ▷Halidon Hill (1333), encouraging him to plan (1363) the union of England and Scotland. Through his mother he claimed the French throne, thus starting (1337) the ▷Hundred Years' War. His son ▷John of Gaunt dominated the government during his last years.

● **Edward IV** ▶ (1442–83) King of England (1461–70, 1471–83) during the Wars of the ▷Roses. He married (1464) Elizabeth Woodville. The Yorkist leader, he was crowned after defeating the Lancastrians at Mortimer's Cross and Towton (1461). He was deposed (1470) by the Earl of ▷Warwick but regained power after victory at ▷Tewkesbury (1471).

● **Edward V** ▶ (1470–?1483) King of England (1483), succeeding his father Edward IV. His uncle, the Duke of Gloucester, imprisoned Edward and his brother Richard in the Tower of London, deposed Edward after a reign of only three months, and had himself crowned as ▷Richard III. The two boys, known as the Princes in the Tower, were probably murdered in 1483.

● **Edward VI** ▶ (1537–53) King of England (1547–53) and the son of Henry VIII, whom he succeeded, and Jane ▷Seymour. Effective power was held by the protector, the Duke of ▷Somerset, until 1550, when the Duke of ▷Northumberland seized power. Edward became a fervent Protestant and during his reign fostered the ▷Reformation in England.

● **Edward VII** ▶ (1841–1910) King of the United Kingdom (1901–10), succeeding his mother Queen Victoria. He married (1863) ▷Alexandra of Denmark. As Prince of Wales he pursued a life of pleasure—possibly as a reaction against his strict upbringing and the early death of his father, Prince Albert—becoming the leader of fashionable London society and a well-known figure in the sporting world. His indiscretions caused Victoria to exclude him from all affairs of state. A popular king, he ably represented Britain abroad.

● **Edward VIII** ▶ (1894–1972) King of the United Kingdom (1936), succeeding his father George V. While both Prince of Wales and king, he expressed sympathy for victims of the Depression. He abdicated on 11 December, 1936, because of constitutional objections to his intention to marry the twice-divorced Mrs Wallis Simpson (1896–1986). The prime minister, Stanley ▷Baldwin, and the Archbishop of Canterbury, Cosmo Lang, joined forces in interpreting public opinion and in resolving the crisis by accepting Edward's abdication and the accession to the throne of the Duke of York (see George VI). The marriage of the ex-King and Mrs Simpson took place in France in 1937. He became Duke of Windsor and was appointed governor of the Bahamas during World War II. He subsequently lived in France, where he remained until his death.

● **Edward, Lake** ▶ (name from 1976 until 1979: Lake Idi Amin Dada) 0 20S 29 35E A lake in the Democratic Republic of Congo and Uganda. Its only outlet, the River Semliki, eventually flows into the River Nile. Area: about 2124 sq km (820 sq mi).

● **Edward (Antony Richard Louis), Prince** ▶ (1964–) Youngest son of Elizabeth II. After Gordonstoun School and Cambridge University, where he obtained a degree in history, he joined the Royal Marines (1986). The following year he began a career in theatre and television production. In 1999 he married Miss Sophie Rhys-Jones (1965–) and the couple were created Earl and Countess of Wessex.

● **Edward, the Black Prince** ▶ (1330–76) Prince of Wales and the eldest son of Edward III. His nickname is probably posthumous and may refer to the black armour he was said to have worn at Crécy (1346). He won victories against France in the ▷Hundred Years' War and ruled Aquitaine from 1360 until ousted (1371) by a revolt, during which he was responsible for the massacre of Limoges (1370).

● **Edwards, Jonathan** ▶ (1703–58) American theologian and philosopher. As minister of the Congregational Church at Northampton, Massachusetts (1727–50), his strongly Calvinistic preaching led to the revival movement known as the ▷Great Awakening. Dismissed because of his overzealous orthodoxy, he continued to preach and became president of the College of Princeton, New Jersey. In *Freedom of the Will* (1754) he discusses determinism.

● **Edward the Confessor, St** ▶ (c. 1003–66) King of England (1042–66), nicknamed for his piety and his foundation of a new Westminster Abbey (consecrated 1065). He lived in Normandy (1016–41) and his early reign was dominated by rivalry between his Norman favourites and his father-in-law Earl ▷Godwin. After 1053 the Godwins were in the ascendant. Edward's childlessness resulted in rival claims to the throne by two named heirs (see Harold II; William (I) the Conqueror) and led ultimately to the Norman conquest. He was canonized in 1161.

● **Edward the Elder** ▶ (d. 924) King of England (899–924), succeeding his father Alfred the Great. He defeated the Danes (918), taking East Anglia, and also conquered Mercia (918) and Northumbria (920).

● **Edward the Martyr, St** ▶ (c. 963–78) King of England (975–78), succeeding his father Edgar. He was murdered at Corfe Castle, reputedly by his stepmother Elfthryth. He was canonized in 1001.

● **Edwin** ▶ (c. 585–633) King of Northumbria (616–33), who became overlord of all English kingdoms S of the Humber, except for Kent. His marriage to Ethelburh, a Christian, led to his conversion and that of his people to Christianity (627). He was killed in battle against Penda of Mercia.

● **Edwy** ▷See Eadwig.

● **EEA** ▶ (European Economic Area) ▷See European Free Trade Association.

● **EEC** ▷See European Economic Community.

● **eel** ▶ A snakelike ▷bony fish of the worldwide order Anguilliformes (or *Apodes*; over 500 species) having, usually, a scaleless body, no pelvic fins, and long dorsal and anal fins continuous with the tail fin. Most species are marine, occurring mainly in shallow waters and feeding on other fish and invertebrates. The freshwater eels (family *Anguillidae*) migrate to the sea to breed—the ▷Sargasso Sea in the case of European and American species. The transparent leaflike larvae (leptocephali) develop into young eels (elvers) and return to rivers and streams. ⌐fish. ▷See also electric eel.

● **eelgrass** ▶ A perennial herbaceous marine plant of the genus *Zostera*, especially *Z. marina*, which grows in muddy intertidal flats and estuaries on the coasts of Europe and North America and is one of the few flowering plants to tolerate sea water. It has creeping underground stems (rhizomes), which help to stabilize mudbanks, and broad dark-green grasslike leaves. Family: *Zosteraceae*.

● **eelpout** ▶ A thick-lipped eel-like fish of the family *Zoarcidae* (about 60 species) that lives on the bottom in cold oceanic waters and feeds on small fish and invertebrates. Up to 45 cm long, eelpouts have small pelvic fins located near the gills. Many produce live young, for example the European *Zoarces viviparus*. Order: *Perciformes*.

● **eelworm** ▶ A very small ▷nematode worm parasitic on plants, causing damage to agricultural crops. Adult eelworms measure up to 1.5 mm long. The larvae, on hatching, penetrate plant roots, which may react by forming root galls around them. Chief genera: *Anguina*, *Ditylenchus*, *Heterodera*.

● **efficiency** ▶ A measure of the performance of an engine, machine, etc., equal to the ratio (often expressed as a percentage) of the energy or power it can deliver to that required to operate it. ▷*See* heat engine; mechanical advantage.

● **Efik** ▶ A people of Calibar province in Nigeria. Their language, Efik-Ibibio, belongs to the ▷Kwa subgroup of the Niger-Congo family. Their territory became a major trading centre, exporting slaves and, later, palm oil. Most Efik live in forest villages where they farm manioc and yams. Political and economic power was vested in the Ekpe or Leopard Society, a graded secret society based upon propitiation of forest spirits.

● **E-FIT** ▷*See* Identikit and Photofit.

● **EFTA** ▷*See* European Free Trade Association.

● **Egas Moniz, Antonio** ▶ (1874–1955) Portuguese neurologist, who in the 1930s developed the original form of prefrontal ▷leucotomy, an operation for relieving severe symptoms of psychiatric illness. For this work he shared (with W. R. Hess) the 1949 Nobel Prize. He also, in the 1920s, pioneered the technique of cerebral angiography, enabling X-ray examination of arteries in the brain. Egas Moniz served as professor of neurology at Lisbon University from 1911 until his retirement in 1944. During this time he also pursued a successful political career: he was ambassador to Spain (1917–18) and—as foreign minister—led Portugal's delegation to the Paris Peace Conference (1919–20).

● **Egbert** ▶ (d. 839) King of Wessex (802–39), who laid the foundations for the supremacy of Wessex over a united England. He faced the first Danish raiders from 835.

● **Eger** ▶ 47 53N 20 22E A town in NE Hungary. It was occupied by the Turks from 1596 to 1687 and has a minaret, 35m (115 ft) high. Wine is produced in the surrounding area. Population (1989): 67 000.

● **Egeria** ▶ A Roman goddess associated with fountains; she also presided over childbirth. According to legend she gave advice to Numa Pompilius (the successor of Romulus as king of Rome), who met her nightly at her sacred fountain near Rome.

● **egg** ▶ (or ovum) The female reproductive cell (*see* gamete), which—when fertilized by a male gamete (sperm)—develops into a new individual of the same species. Animal eggs are surrounded by nutritive material (yolk) and—usually—one or more protective membranes, for example a jelly coat in amphibian eggs, the shell and other layers in birds' eggs. The amount of yolk varies, being greater in the eggs of egg-laying animals since the developing embryo depends on the yolk for nourishment: in mammals the egg is nourished from the maternal circulation and thus has little yolk. ▷*See also* ovary.

● **eggplant** ▷*See* aubergine.

● **eglantine** ▷*See* sweet briar.

● **Egmont, Lamoraal, Graaf van** ▶ (or Egmond; 1522–68) Flemish statesman and soldier, who opposed Philip II of Spain's religious policies in the Netherlands. After distinguished service in the victories against the French he was appointed stadholder (chief magistrate) of Flanders. With William the Silent and other magnates Egmont left the state council in 1565 in protest against the continuing persecution of Protestants by Philip II. He subsequently pledged his loyalty to Philip but was executed as a traitor by the Duke of ▷Alba in 1568. ▷*See also* Revolt of the Netherlands.

● **Egmont, Mount** ▶ 39 18S 174 05E A volcanic mountain in New Zealand, in W North Island. It forms an almost perfect cone and is encircled by a fertile ring plain. Height: 2478 m (8260 ft). ▷*See also* Taranaki.

● **ego** ▶ In ▷psychoanalysis, the part of the mind that is closely in touch with the demands of external reality and operates rationally. It includes some motives (such as hunger and ambition), the individual's learned responses, and his (or her) conscious thought. It has to reconcile the conflicting demands of the ▷id, the ▷superego, and the outside world.

● **egoism** ▶ A philosophical theory of ▷ethics claiming that morality should be based on the self-interest of the individual. Egoism also claims that self-interest both explains and provides a motivating force for a general adherence to a set of moral principles. The argument is that a system of morality ensures a stable society and that an individual is better off in a stable society. Egoism is the opposite of altruism, which claims that morality has to be based on concern for the welfare of others. Altruists claim that while egoism may provide the motivation for others to obey moral rules, it does not provide such a motivation for the self. This can only arise from a concern for the welfare of others.

● **egret** ▶ A white bird belonging to the ▷heron subfamily. The great white egret (*Egretta alba*) has long silky ornamental plumes in the breeding season that were formerly used for decorating hats. The smaller cattle egret (*Aroleola ibis*) is 50 cm long and follows large grazing animals, feeding on insects disturbed by their hoofs.

● **Egypt, Arab Republic of** ▶ (Arabic name: Misr) A country in NE Africa, extending into SW Asia. Most of the country consists of desert—the ▷Sinai Peninsula, the Eastern Desert (a vast upland area), and the Western Desert (an extensive low plateau), while most of the population is concentrated along the fertile Nile Valley.

Economy: despite limited resources of water and cultivable land, the introduction of modern technology and irrigation schemes, such as the ▷Aswan High Dam, have led to an increase in the production of cotton, the chief cash crop, as well as a more diversified agricultural sector (rice, millet, maize, sugar cane, and fruit and vegetables). Nevertheless Egypt is still not self-sufficient in food production. Restriction of land ownership under the Agrarian Reform Law (1952) led to increased private investment in industry but the considerable expansion of the industrial sector from the 1950s to the 1980s, especially heavy industries, such as iron and steel, chemicals, and electricity, was mainly the result of government planning, utilizing aid from communist countries. More recently, however, there has been an increase in private industrial activity. Oil was discovered in 1909 and production has greatly increased; petroleum refining has become an important industry. Natural gas is also being exploited and other minerals include phosphate, iron ore, and salt. Egypt's historical and archaeological remains make tourism an important source of revenue, but this is threatened by recent Islamic terrorist activities. The chief exports are petroleum, cotton, and cotton goods.

History: ancient Egyptian history is traditionally divided into 30 dynasties, beginning in about 3100 BC with the union of Upper and Lower Egypt by Menes and ending in 343 BC with the death of the last Egyptian king, or ▷pharaoh, Nectanebo II. The so-called Old Kingdom (3rd–6th dynasties; c. 2686–c. 2160) reached its peak in the reigns of Khufu and his son Khafre, which saw remarkable building achievements, notably the ▷pyramids at Giza. The 6th dynasty witnessed a decentralization of government and the consequent rise in power of provincial officials, which resulted in the disunity that characterized the First Intermediate Period (7th–11th dynasties; c. 2160–c. 2040). Egypt was reunited by Mentuhotep II (reigned c. 2060–2010), the founder of the Middle Kingdom (12th dynasty; c. 2040–c. 1786), of which the outstanding kings were Sesostris III and Amenemhet III. In the Second Intermediate Period (13th–17th dynasties; c. 1786–c. 1567) Egypt came largely under the control of the invading Asiatic tribes (the Hyksos), which were finally expelled by Ahmose I, founder of the New Kingdom (18th–20th dynasties; c. 1570–1085). During the New Kingdom Thutmose III extended Egypt's frontiers and acquired new territories in Asia and Amenhotep III sponsored buildings at ▷Karnak and ▷Luxor. His own son was the heretic king ▷Akhenaton, but orthodoxy was restored under ▷Tutankhamen. The reign of Ramses II was troubled by the ▷Hittites and that of Ramses III, by the Sea Peoples, and the 20th dynasty also saw the priests' power rise at the kings' expense. The outcome of Egypt's decline under the 21st–25th dynasties (1085–664) was the Assyrian invasion under Esarhaddon (671) and the 26th dynasty (664–525) was brought to an end by the Persian Achaemenians. Achaemenian rule was interrupted by the native 28th, 29th, and 30th dynasties (404–343) and was finally ended by Alexander the Great of Macedon, who obtained Egypt in 332.

On Alexander's death Egypt was acquired by the Macedonian Ptolemy I Soter. The Ptolemies ruled until the suicide of ▷Cleopatra VII in 30 BC, when Egypt passed under Roman rule. In 395 AD, Egypt became part of the Byzantine (Eastern Roman) Empire. The Arabs conquered Egypt in 642 and it was then governed by representatives of the caliphate of Baghdad, under whom Islam was introduced. After 868 it gained virtual autonomy under a series of ruling dynasties. The last of these, the Fatimids, were overthrown by ▷Saladin, who restored Egypt to the caliphate in 1171. It was ruled by the Mamelukes from 1250 until 1517, when it was conquered by the Ottoman Turks. The Turks governed Egypt through a viceroy but by the early 18th century power was largely in the hands of the Mameluke elite.

In 1798 Napoleon established a French protectorate over Egypt, which in 1801 was overthrown by the British and Ottomans. A mutiny among Albanian soldiers in the Ottoman army in Egypt brought Mehemet 'Ali to power as viceroy (1805) and in 1840 he was recognized by the Ottomans as hereditary ruler. British and French interests in Egypt intensified in the mid-19th century and in 1869 the opening of the Suez Canal enhanced Egypt's international significance. An Arab nationalist revolt was suppressed in 1882 by the British, who thereafter dominated Egyptian government in spite of nominal Ottoman suzerainty. In 1914, on the outbreak of World War I, Egypt became a British protectorate until independence under King Fu'ad I was granted in 1922. In 1936 his son Farouk signed a treaty of alliance with Britain, which retained rights in the Suez Canal zone, and in World War II Egypt joined the Allies. The immediate postwar period saw the first Arab-Israeli War (1948–49) and a military coup (1952) that overthrew the monarchy (1953) and brought ▷Nasser to power (1954). Nasser's nationalization of the Suez Canal in 1956 precipitated an invasion by Israeli and Anglo-French forces, which were compelled by the UN to withdraw. In 1958 Egypt, Syria, and subsequently North Yemen formed the ▷United Arab Republic. Conflict with Israel erupted again in 1967, when in the third Arab-Israeli War (the Six Day War) Egypt lost territories that included the Sinai peninsula, partly regained in the fourth war (1973) and finally returned in 1982. In 1970 Nasser was succeeded by ▷Sadat, who in 1972 ended Egypt's close relationship with the Soviet Union. In 1979, under US influence, Egypt and Israel signed a momentous peace treaty and Egypt was expelled from the ▷Arab League. Increasing opposition to Sadat's policies culminated in his assassination by Islamic extremists in 1981. He was succeeded by Hosni ▷Mubarak, who has pursued a pragmatic modernizing policy. Egypt was readmitted to the Arab League in 1989. It suffered a resurgence of terrorist attacks by Islamic extremists in the 1990s; in 1997 over 60 tourists were murdered in Luxor.

Arab Republic of Egypt

Head of state	President Hosni Mubarak
Official language	Arabic
Official religion	Islam
Official currency	Egyptian pound of 100 piastres
Area	1 000 000 sq km (386 198 sq mi)
Population (1999 est)	64 560 000
Capital	Cairo
Main port	Alexandria

● **Ehrenburg, Iliya Grigorievich** ▶ (1891–1967) Soviet author. From 1908 to 1917 he lived in Paris, where he published some poetry; he returned to Russia in 1920 and immediately went back to Paris as a correspondent. He remained in W Europe until 1940. He was a mildly controversial figure under Stalinism but wrote virulent anti-Western propaganda. His novel *The Thaw* (1954) and his memoirs, *Men, Years, Life* (1960–64), were among the earliest open criticisms of Stalin.

● **Ehrlich, Paul** ▶ (1854–1915) German bacteriologist. Ehrlich did much to develop the understanding of acquired immunity to disease in animals and, with ▷Behring, he prepared a serum against diphtheria. In 1910 he announced the discovery of an arsenical compound (Salvarsan) effective in treating syphilis. Ehrlich shared a Nobel Prize (1908) with ▷Metchnikov.

● **Eichendorff, Josef, Freiherr von** ▶ (1788–1857) German Romantic writer. He studied at Heidelberg and Berlin, where he became involved in the Romantic movement, and rose high in the Prussian civil service. His lyrical nature poems were set by many composers. His best-known novel is *Memoirs of a Good-for-Nothing* (1826).

● **Eichler, August Wilhelm** ▶ (1839–87) German botanist, who proposed the system that formed the basis of traditional plant classification. Eichler divided the plant kingdom into four divisions: Thallophyta (algae and fungi), Bryophyta (liverworts and mosses), Pteridophyta (ferns), and Spermatophyta (seed plants).

● **Eichmann, Adolf** ▶ (1906–62) German Nazi politician, appointed at the ▷Wannsee conference during World War II to implement the planned extermination of European Jews (the Final Solution). After the war he went into hiding in Argentina; traced and captured by the Israelis in 1960, he was then tried and hanged for his war crimes.

● **Eid** ▷*See* Id.

● **eider** ▶ A large sea ▷duck, *Somateria mollissima*, of far northern sea coasts. About 55 cm long, males are mostly white with a black crown, belly, and tail; females are mottled dark brown. The soft feathers plucked by the female from her breast to line her nest are the source of eiderdown.

● **Eiffel Tower** ▶ A metal tower in Paris, built for the 1889 Centennial Exposition. The most famous work of the French engineer Alexandre-Gustave Eiffel (1832–1923), the 300 m (984 ft) tower was the highest building in the world until 1930. Although an outstanding engineering achievement, it was originally much disliked, but has become one of the great Parisian landmarks.

● **Eiger** ▶ 46 34N 8 01E A mountain in central S Switzerland, in the Bernese Oberland. Its N face, possibly the most difficult climb in the Alps, was not conquered until 1938. Height: 3970 m (12 697 ft).

● **Eightfold Path** ▶ (or The Noble Eightfold Path) In Buddhism the fourth of the ▷Four Noble Truths, which summarizes the eight ways that lead the Buddhist to enlightenment. They are: right understanding, right resolve, right speech, right action, right livelihood, right effort, right mindfulness, and right meditation. The Path, which is not a series of successive steps but an integrated spiritual attitude, was described in the Buddha's first discourse at Benares.

● **Eijkman, Christiaan** ▶ (1858–1930) Dutch physician, who originated the concept of dietary deficiency disease. As a doctor in the East Indies, Eijkman noticed that chickens fed on polished rice developed symptoms resembling beriberi. By including rice hulls in their diet, the disease was cured—an effect he attributed to a dietary factor (later shown to be thiamine, or vitamin B_1). Eijkmann received the 1929 Nobel Prize with Sir Frederick ▷Hopkins.

● **Eilat** ▶ (Elat or Elath) 29 33N 34 57E A town in S Israel, on the Gulf of Aqaba. Ancient Eilat declined in the 12th century, and the modern city was founded in 1949 as Israel's only port S of the Suez Canal. There is also an oil-refining industry. Population (latest est): 26 000.

● **Eindhoven** ▶ 51 26N 5 30E A town in the S Netherlands, in North Brabant province. It is a manufacturing centre specializing in electronics and producing light bulbs, radios, and televisions. Population (1996 est): 197 374.

● **Einhard** ▶ (or Eginhard; c. 770–840) Frankish historian, a courtier of ▷Charlemagne. His *Vita Caroli magni*, based on intimate knowledge of the emperor's character and government, is one of the major medieval biographies and a probable source of the 12th-century poem, *Chanson de Roland*.

● **Einstein, Albert** ▶ (1879–1955) US physicist born in Germany, in Ulm. Einstein was an undistinguished scholar, being interested only in theoretical physics. In 1901 he obtained a post at the Patent Office in Berne, Switzerland, and became a Swiss citizen. While working there, he continued his researches and in 1905 published four highly original papers. One gave a mathematical explanation of the ▷Brownian movement in molecular terms, the second explained the ▷photoelectric effect in terms of ▷photons, the third announced his special theory of ▷relativity, and the fourth related mass to energy. These papers were so revolutionary that their importance was not immediately recognized and Einstein only secured a university post four years later. In 1916 he extended the theory of relativity to the general case and, when its predictions had been verified in 1919, he became world-famous, receiving the 1921 Nobel Prize for Physics. In 1933, while Einstein was lecturing in California, Hitler came to power; being Jewish, Einstein decided to remain in the USA. He spent

Albert Einstein ► At his home in Princetown, New Jersey (1949).

the rest of his life at the Institute for Advanced Study in Princeton, unsuccessfully seeking a ▷unified field theory. He became a US citizen in 1940. Originally a pacifist, Einstein was persuaded in 1939 to write to President Roosevelt warning him that an atom bomb could now be made and that Germany might make one first. Although he took no part in its manufacture, he was an active postwar advocate of nuclear disarmament, aware that without his theory of relativity the nuclear age could not have dawned.

● **einsteinium ►** (Es) An artificial transuranic element discovered by Ghiorso and others in 1952 in fall-out from the first large hydrogen-bomb explosion. It was named after Albert Einstein. Einsteinium behaves chemically as a trivalent actinide. Its 11 isotopes are all radioactive, the longest-lived having a half-life of 275 days. At no 99; at wt (252).

● **Einthoven, Willem ►** (1860–1927) Dutch physiologist and pioneer of ▷electrocardiography. In 1903 Einthoven devised a sensitive galvanometer to detect the electrical rhythms of the heart. He developed his recording technique until he was able to correlate abnormalities in electrical activity with various heart disorders. He won the 1924 Nobel Prize.

● **Éire** ▷See Ireland, Republic of.

● **Eisenach ►** 50 59N 10 21E A town and resort in S Germany, on the NW slopes of the Thuringian Forest. Among its many notable buildings is Wartburg Castle, where Martin Luther completed his translation of the Bible into German. It is the birthplace of J. S. Bach. It manufactures motor vehicles and chemicals. Population (1989 est): 48 361.

● **Eisenhower, Dwight D(avid) ►** (1890–1969) US general and statesman; Republican president (1953–61). In World War II he was commander of US troops in Europe (1942), of Allied forces in N Africa and Italy (1942–43), and then supreme commander of Allied forces in Europe (1943). He helped to plan and commanded the forces in the D-Day invasion of Normandy. In 1951 he became supreme commander of NATO. A popular president, "Ike" initiated social welfare programmes and used troops to enforce school integration in Arkansas. His administration saw the beginning of space rivalry with the Soviet Union; it spanned the Cold War years and was marred by the anticommunist agitation of Joseph ▷McCarthy. The **Eisenhower Doctrine** (1957) offered economic and military help to Middle Eastern nations against communist advances.

● **Eisenstadt ►** 47 51N 16 31E A city in E Austria, the capital of Burgenland. Joseph Haydn lived here (1766–90); his house is now a museum. Population (1991): 10 506.

● **Eisenstein, Sergei ►** (1898–1948) Russian film director. His films are characterized by their use of montage, an editing technique in which isolated images are juxtaposed to emphasize intellectual points. His experimental theories, developed during his early work in the theatre, brought him into frequent conflict with the Soviet authorities. His films include *Battleship Potemkin* (1925), *Alexander Nevsky* (1938), and *Ivan the Terrible* (1942–46).

● **eisteddfod ►** A Welsh assembly in which bards and minstrels compete for prizes in literature, music, and drama. The main literary prizes are a carved oak chair for the best poem in strict Welsh metre and a silver crown for a poem in free metre. Originating in medieval times, the tradition declined after the 16th century but was revived as the chief national cultural festival during the 19th century.

● **Ekaterinburg ►** (name from 1924 until 1991: Sverdlovsk) 56 52N 60 35E A city in NW Russia. Nicholas II and his family were executed here in 1918. It is a major industrial and cultural centre, with engineering, metallurgical, and chemical industries and many educational institutions. Population (1995 est): 1 280 000.

● **Ekaterinodar** ▷See Krasnodar.

● **Ekaterinoslav** ▷See Dnepropetrovsk.

● **Ekman, Vagn Walfrid ►** (1874–1954) Swedish earth scientist and professor of physics at Lund. He discovered the **Ekman spiral**, a complex interaction between the wind and the surface of the sea, the ▷Coriolis force due to the earth's rotation, and friction forces in the water layers. The **Ekman layer** is the thin top layer of ocean water where flow is at 90° to the wind direction.

● **El Aaiún ►** 27 00N 13 00W The chief city of Western Sahara (a disputed territory occupied by Morocco). Phosphate deposits about 100 km (60 mi) to the SE are exported from here. Population (latest est): 90 000.

● **El Alamein, Battle of** ▷See World War II.

● **Elam ►** An ancient country in SW Iran, roughly corresponding to the present-day province of Khuzistan. The Elamite language, related to no other known tongue, appears in pictographic inscriptions before 3000 BC. Elam's capital was ▷Susa and it was closely linked culturally and politically with ▷Sumer and ▷Babylonia (both of which it temporarily overran in the 2nd millennium BC), before absorption into the Persian ▷Achaemenian empire (6th century BC). The Elamites were believed to be descended from Shem, the son of Noah, and were thus related to the Hebrews.

● **eland ►** An antelope belonging to the genus *Taurotragus* (2 species), of African plains. Up to 180 cm high at the shoulder, both sexes have horns. The common eland (*T. oryx*) is light brown with thin vertical white stripes towards the shoulders. The Derby eland (*T. derbianus*) has a black neck with a white band at the base. Both species have a black-tufted tail and dewlap. Elands live in small herds and have been tamed and used as draught animals.

● **elasticity ►** In physics, the ability of a body to return to its original shape after being deformed. The deforming force is known as a ▷stress, the resulting deformation is the ▷strain (*see* elastic modulus). A body is elastic only below a certain stress. Above this point, known as the *elastic limit*, the body is permanently deformed. A substance permanently deformed by any stress is said to be plastic. ▷See also plasticity.

● **elastic modulus ►** The ratio of the ▷stress on a body obeying ▷Hooke's law to the ▷strain produced. The strain may be a change in length (Young's Modulus) or a change in volume (bulk modulus).

● **elastomer ►** A polymer with elastic properties, i.e. one that can be deformed and will revert to its original shape. ▷Rubber, a natural elastomer, still has many applications, especially for heavy-duty tyres. However, synthetic elastomers of styrene-butadiene, polybutadiene, polyisoprene, ▷silicones, etc., are now far more widely used, not only in car tyres, but also in belting for machines, sponge rubber, footwear, and many other products.

● **Elat ►** (or Elath) ▷See Eilat.

● **Elba ►** An Italian island in the Tyrrhenian Sea. It became famous as the place of exile (1814–15) of Napoleon I. Area: 223 sq km (86 sq mi). Population (1984 est): 28 907.

● **Elbe, River ►** (Czech name: Labe) A river in central Europe, flowing mainly NW from the N Czech Republic, through Germany to the North Sea at Hamburg. It is connected by canals to the Rivers Weser and Rhine as well as to the River Oder. Length: 1165 km (724 mi).

● **El Beqa'a** ▷See Bekaa Valley.

● **Elberfeld** ▷*See* Wuppertal.

● **Elbert, Mount** ▶ A mountain in the USA, in Colorado, highest of the ▷Rocky Mountains. Height: 4399 m (14 431 ft).

● **Elbląg** ▶ (German name: Elbing) 54 10N 19 25E A port in N Poland, on the River Elbląg. Founded in the 13th century, it became a member of the Hanseatic League and an important port for trade with England. Its chief industries include engineering and shipbuilding. Population (1996 est): 128 700.

● **Elbrus, Mount** ▶ (*or* Mt Elbruz) 43 21 N 42 29E A mountain in SW Russia, on the border with Georgia, the highest in the Caucasus Mountains. It is an extinct volcano, with two peaks only 38 m (101 ft) vertically apart, and is a tourist and climbing centre. Height: 5633 m (18 481 ft).

● **Elburz Mountains** ▶ A mountain range in central N Iran, extending 600 km (373 mi) parallel with the S shore of the Caspian Sea. It rises to 5604 m (18 386 ft) at Mount Demavend.

● **Elche** ▶ 38 16N 0 41W A town in SE Spain, in Valencia. Local archaeological finds include a 5th-century Iberian statue, known as *La Dama de Elche*. It produces dates, pomegranates, and figs. Population (1995 est): 192 424.

● **El Cid** ▶ (Rodrigo Díaz de Vivar; c. 1040–99) Spanish warrior, also known as el Campeador (the Champion), who was immortalized in the epic poem *Cantar del mio Cid*. A vassal of Alfonso VI of Castile, he was exiled in 1079 and began a career as a soldier of fortune, fighting for both Spaniard and Moor. Always loyal to his king, he was returned to favour and became protector and then ruler of Valencia.

● **elder** ▶ A shrub or tree (up to 20 m tall) of the genus *Sambucus* (40 species), found in temperate and subtropical areas. The compound leaves have toothed leaflets and the tiny cream-coloured flowers, grouped into flat-topped clusters, can be used in tea or wine. The red or black berries, rich in vitamin C, are used in wine, jams, and jellies. The common European elder is *S. nigra*. Family: *Caprifoliaceae*.

● **Eldorado** ▶ (Spanish: the golden one) An Indian ruler in Colombia who, according to legend, ritually coated himself in gold dust before bathing in a lake. The name was later applied to a rumoured region of fabulous wealth. The conquest of South America in the 16th century was hastened by expeditions seeking Eldorado, notably those of ▷Pizarro (1539) and Jiménez de Quesada (1569–72).

● **Eleanor of Aquitaine** ▶ (c. 1122–1204) The wife (1137–52) of Louis VII of France and, after the annulment of their marriage, the wife (1154–89) of Henry II of England. Henry imprisoned her (1174–89) for complicity in their sons' rebellion. After Henry's death she helped to secure their peaceful accession as Richard I (1189) and John (1199).

● **Eleanor of Castile** ▶ (1246–90) The wife (from 1254) of Edward I of England. A devoted wife, she accompanied Edward on a Crusade (1270–73). He erected the **Eleanor Crosses** wherever her body rested on its way from Nottinghamshire, where she died, to her funeral in London. Of the original 12 crosses, only three survive—at Northampton, Geddington, and Waltham Cross. The last of the stopping places was at ▷Charing Cross in London, where a replica of the original cross stands (erected in 1863; the decayed original was pulled down in 1647).

● **Eleatics** ▶ Greek speculative philosophers, active in the 5th century BC, whose leader was ▷Parmenides of Elea. Their central doctrine was that reality is timeless, motionless, changeless, and indivisible and that any belief to the contrary was illusion occasioned by the frailty of human senses. The early Pythagoreans (*see* Pythagoreanism) were their major opponents. ▷*See also* Zeno of Elea.

● **electoral college** ▶ An electoral device laid down by the US constitution for electing the president and vice president. Each state chooses by popular vote a number of electors to send to an electoral college. This number is equal to its number of representatives in the House of Representatives plus its two senators. All the electors chosen by a state pledge themselves to vote in the electoral college for the presidential candidate with the highest popular vote in the state. Thus the elected president usually obtains a greater majority in

the College than he would have had on the basis of a popular vote throughout the country. This system gives an increased influence to the more populous states.

● **electors** ▶ (1257–1806) The German rulers who elected the Holy Roman Emperor. In 1338 the Archbishops of Mainz, Cologne, and Trier and the dynastic princes of the Palatinate, Saxony, and Brandenburg monopolized the right of election, which was confirmed in 1356. Other electors were the rulers of Bohemia (before 1400 and after 1708), Bavaria (after 1623), and Hanover (after 1708).

● **Electra** ▶ In Greek legend, the daughter of Agamemnon and Clytemnestra. She helped her brother Orestes escape after the murder of Agamemnon and later helped him to kill Clytemnestra and her lover Aegisthus. She is the subject of plays by Aeschylus, Sophocles, and Euripides. Electra is also the name of one of the Pleiades, of a daughter of Oceanus, and of the mother of the Harpies. ▷*See also* Oedipus complex.

● **electrical engineering** ▶ The branch of engineering concerned with the generation, transmission, distribution, and use of electricity. Its two main branches are power engineering and ▷electronics (including telecommunications). Electrical engineering emerged in the late 19th century with the mathematical formulation of the basic laws of electricity by James Clerk ▷Maxwell, followed by the development of such practical applications as the Bell telephone, Edison's incandescent lamp, and the first central generating plants. Electrical power engineers design generators, ▷power stations, and ▷electricity supply systems as well as ▷electric motors and transport and traction systems. Electrical engineering is an applied science involving mathematical skills and a knowledge of physics, in addition to the basic engineering subjects. In the UK the professional body is the Institution of Electrical Engineers (founded 1871, incorporated 1921).

● **electric-arc furnace** ▶ A type of furnace used in making high-grade ▷steels, usually from scrap steel, in which the heat source is an electric arc. Electric furnaces provide clean working conditions and accurate temperature control. They avoid the contamination that occurs when fuel is burnt and are gradually replacing the ▷open-hearth process.

● **electric car** ▶ A car driven by one or more electric motors, which are powered by batteries. Because of diminishing oil reserves and the pollution problems associated with the ▷internal-combustion engine (*see* greenhouse effect), the search for an effective electric car has been intensified in recent years. Electric cars are not new; Queen Alexandra owned an American *Columbia* electric car in 1901 and electric milkfloats and delivery vans have been widely used for short journeys in towns since the 1930s. The basic problem is that even a light car using 280 kg of expensive nickel-cadmium batteries with regenerative braking, only has a 50–60 mile range. Electric motors are several times more efficient than petrol engines but it was not until 1990 that General Motors announced plans to produce an electric car—the *Impact*— to compete with petrol cars. Two lines of research are being pursued: improving batteries and making workable ▷fuel cells. However, unless the batteries are charged by electricity generated centrally by ▷nuclear power or ▷alternative energy sources there will be no net reduction in global pollution. Several commuter cars using special lead accumulators have been produced, with top speeds around 30 mph (44 km per hour), including the unsuccessful Sinclair C5 introduced in 1985 at under £400. The hybrid electric car carries its own petrol-engine-driven generator.

● **electric cell** ▶ (*or* voltaic cell) A device that produces an ▷electromotive force and delivers a current as a result of a chemical reaction. **Primary cells**, such as the ▷Daniell cell and the ▷Leclanché cell, are not reversible (*see also* battery; ▯electricity). **Secondary cells**, however, can be recharged (*see* accumulator). ▷*See also* fuel cell.

● **electric charge** ▶ A property of certain elementary particles (*see* particle physics) that causes them to undergo ▷electromagnetic interactions. The magnitude of the charge is always the same and is equal to 1.6021×10^{-19} coulombs (although quarks, if they exist, would have a fractional charge). Charge is of two kinds, arbitrarily called positive and negative. Like charges repel each other and unlike charges attract each other. The force between them can be regarded as being generated by an exchange of virtual photons between the two particles (*see* virtual particle). On a large scale, charge is always due to an excess or deficiency of ▷electrons compared to the number of protons in the nuclei of a substance.

● **electric constant** ► (ε_0) A constant that appears in ▷Coulomb's law when expressed in SI units. Its value is 8.854×10^{-12} F m^{-1}. It is also known as the absolute ▷permittivity of free space. *Compare* magnetic constant.

● **electric eel** ► An eel-like freshwater fish, *Electrophorus electricus*, that occurs in NE South America. Up to 3 m long, it swims by undulating its long anal fin and has ▷electric organs in the tail, which produce electric shocks capable of killing fish and other prey and of stunning a man. Family: *Electrophoridae*; order: *Cypriniformes*.

● **electric field** ► The pattern of the lines of force that surround an electric charge. The field strength at any point is inversely proportional to the square of the distance of that point from the charge (*see* Coulomb's law). Any other charge placed in this field experiences a force proportional to the field strength and to the magnitude of the

introduced charge. The force is attractive if the charges are opposite and repulsive if they are alike.

● **electric generator** ► A device for converting mechanical energy into electricity, usually by ▷electromagnetic induction. A simple electromagnetic generator, or dynamo, consists of a conducting coil rotated in a magnetic field (⁻electricity). Current induced in this coil is fed to an external circuit by slip rings in an alternating-current generator (alternator) or by a commutator, which rectifies the current, in a direct-current generator. Most of the electricity from ▷power stations is produced by alternators as three-phase ▷alternating current, i.e. there are three windings on each generator, which can have an output of hundreds of megawatts, producing three separate output voltages. For transmission there are three conductor wires with a common neutral wire. This three-phase system optimizes generator design and minimizes transmission losses, if the three loads are balanced. Generally, all three phases are supplied to large factories but the supply is split to single phase for homes, offices, etc. Small generators driven by Diesel engines are used for emergencies in factories, hospitals, etc.

Modern life depends on electricity in so many ways, yet it is not known exactly what it is.

carbon atom

− ve   + ve

electron   proton

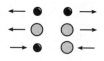

Atoms consist of electrons, protons, and neutrons. The electrons cluster round the central nucleus of protons and neutrons.

Electrons have a negative electric charge — protons are positively charged. The charges are equal but opposite.

Similar charges repel each other, opposite charges attract each other. These are the forces harnessed to make electricity.

helium atom

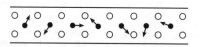

current flow ⟶

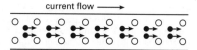

An electrical current consists of a flow of electrons in one direction. But in many atoms, such as helium, they are tightly bound to the nucleus. To flow as a current electrons have to be free.

In a metal wire some of the electrons are free to move about between the metal ions (atoms that have lost an electron). Normally they move about at random and no current flows.

When the majority of electrons flow in one direction this is an electric current. 1 ampere is equivalent to a flow of 6×10^{18} electrons per second.

There are two main methods of making electrons flow to generate a current.

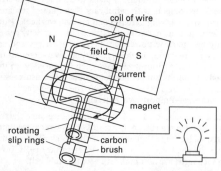

coil of wire

N

field

S

current

magnet

rotating slip rings

carbon brush

One method is to subject them to a changing magnetic field — this is the principle of the dynamo. If a coil of wire is rotated between the poles of a magnet, the electrons are forced round the coil. This is the power-station method; coal or oil is burned to raise steam to drive a turbine, which rotates the coils.

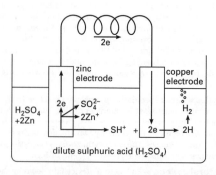

2e

zinc electrode

copper electrode

H_2SO_4 +2Zn

2e

SO_4^{2-}

2Zn$^+$

SH$^+$ +

2e ⟶ 2H

H_2

dilute sulphuric acid (H_2SO_4)

The other way is to make use of a chemical reaction in an electric cell to dissociate the electrons from their atoms and molecules. The separated charges then flow in opposite directions as a result of the forces between them. This is how a battery works. The sulphuric acid dissolves the zinc electrode producing 2 electrons, a sulphate ion (SO_4^{2-}), 2 zinc ions (Zn$^+$), and 2 hydrogen ions (H$^+$).

electricity

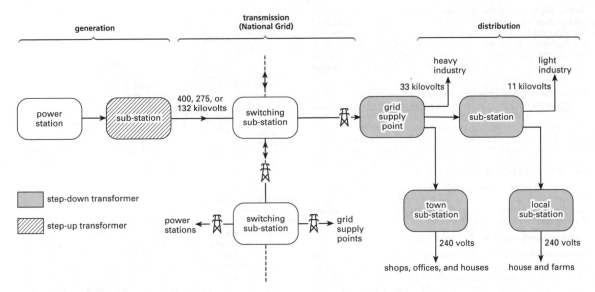

electricity supply ▶ A schematic diagram of the UK system.

● **electricity** ▶ The phenomena that arise as a result of ▷electric charge. Electricity has two forms: ▷static electricity, which depends on stationary charges, and current electricity, which consists of a flow of charges, specifically ▷electrons.

Static electricity, in the form of an attractive force between rubbed amber and pieces of straw, etc., was known to the ancient Greeks but the word electricity was coined in the 16th century by William ▷Gilbert (from the Greek *elektron*, amber). The distinction between positive and negative electricity was made at the beginning of the 18th century, but did not acquire a theoretical basis until the discovery of the electron in 1897 by J. J. Thomson.

Current electricity was first demonstrated by ▷Volta in 1800 and investigated by ▷Ampère during the next 25 years. ▷Oersted's discovery (1820) that a magnetic needle was deflected by an electric current inspired ▷Faraday to investigate the relationship between electricity and magnetism, which led to the discovery of ▷electromagnetic induction, the ▷electric generator, and the ▷electric motor. The theory of electromagnetism was elucidated by Clerk ▷Maxwell in the mid-1850s. The use of electricity as a source of energy developed for heating, lighting, and motive power in the 20th century.

● **electricity supply** ▶ The system that generates (see power station), transmits, and distributes the electric power in an industrialized society. Power stations are interconnected by transmission lines to form a grid. Grid-control centres continuously monitor the load from factories, offices, homes, etc., and match it with the best combination of available generating capacity, maintaining the supply at a constant voltage and frequency. Base-load stations run continuously. These are usually the cheaper-to-run nuclear and gas- or coal-fired stations. Less economic or smaller stations that are easier to start up and shut down are brought in to supply the peak demand. The grid voltage is reduced at substations for area distribution and further reduced at local substations to the UK domestic supply voltage of 240 volts. In the UK, the state-owned Central Electricity Generating Board was split by the Electricity Act (1989) into four: Nuclear Electric plc, National Grid Co. plc, and two non-nuclear generating companies, National Power plc and PowerGen plc, both of which were privatized with the government retaining a 40% holding, which they sold in 1995 by a second flotation. In Scotland and Northern Ireland similar changes were made. ▷*See also* energy. □nuclear power.

● **electric motor** ▶ A device that converts electrical energy into mechanical energy usually for driving machinery. Clean, quiet, and efficient (75–95%), they range from tiny models using less than a watt to those using several megawatts to drive large pumps. They work on the principle that a current-carrying conductor in a magnetic field

experiences a force and that when two electromagnets are placed close together the two magnetic fields force them apart. The simplest motor uses this principle to turn a single coil of wire (the armature or rotor) between the poles of a permanent magnet. Practical motors use a stationary winding (stator) in place of a magnet. Most motors work on alternating-current (ac). In the induction motor, current is fed to the stator, which induces a current in the rotor; interaction between the magnetic field of the stator and the induced rotor current causes the rotor to rotate. In the synchronous ac motor, current is also fed to the rotor (through slip rings) and the rate of rotation is proportional to the supply frequency. In direct-current (dc) motors, current is also fed to both rotor and stator with the two either in series (series wound) or in parallel (shunt wound). In a dc motor current is fed to the rotor through a commutator. ▷*See also* linear motor.

● **electric organ** ▶ In zoology, a group of modified muscle cells in certain fish that generate electric charge to stun prey, as in the ▷electric eel and ▷electric ray. Other species, such as the elephant-snout fishes, generate an electric field for the detection of objects and for navigation.

● **electric ray** ▶ A fish, also called torpedo ray or numbfish, belonging to a family (*Torpedinidae*) found mainly in shallow waters. 30–200 cm long, rays have ▷electric organs on each side of the disclike head to produce electric shocks used in defence and food capture. Order: *Batoidea* (see ray).

● **electrocardiography** ▶ Examination of the electrical activity of the heart. Impulses generated by the contraction of the heart muscle are transmitted through electrodes attached to the skin to a recording apparatus (electrocardiograph). The record, an electrocardiogram (ECG), indicates the rhythm of the heart and aids diagnosis of heart disease. Formerly the patient lay on a couch (resting ECG), however more information is obtained when the heart is under stress and ECGs are now usually taken with the patient walking on a treadmill, the speed of which is controlled by the computer that operates and analyses the electrocardiograph.

● **electroconvulsive therapy** ▶ (ECT) A treatment for mental disorders in which an electric current is passed through the brain causing a convulsion, which is reduced by giving an anaesthetic and drugs to relax the muscles. ECT is used as a treatment for severe cases of endogenous ▷depression but is now being replaced by drug therapy.

● **electrocution** ▶ Injury or death caused by an electric shock. A current over 15 mA passing through the body is normally lethal, upsetting the heart rhythm and causing ventricular fibrillation. The voltage required to cause this current depends on the resistance of the skin, which falls when it is wet. Mains voltage (240 V) can be fatal to a person with wet hands. Electrocution is used for ▷capital punishment in the USA (introduced in 1890 and still used in some states). The prisoner is strapped into the "electric chair" and given repeated shocks of 2000 volts.

● **electroencephalography** ► The measurement of the electrical activity of the brain and the recording of the brain waves in the form of a tracing—an electroencephalogram (EEG). Brain waves were first recorded from electrodes on the scalp by Hans Berger (1873–1941) in 1926. Electroencephalography is now widely used to diagnose diseases of the brain and to study brain function. The frequency of the electrical waves and the way they change with stimuli are related to alertness, responsiveness, and expectation.

● **electroforming** ► A method of manufacturing metallic articles. A metal-coated plastic mould is used as the cathode in ▷electrolysis and the metal is deposited onto the mould. The method is used for making thin intricately shaped articles.

● **electroluminescence** ▷*See* luminescence.

● **electrolysis** ► The chemical decomposition of a substance by passing an electric current through it. If a voltage is applied across two electrodes placed in a liquid (**electrolyte**) containing ions, the positive ions will drift towards the negative electrode (cathode) and the negative ions towards the positive electrode (anode). At the electrodes, the ions may give up their charge and form molecules; for example hydrogen gas is released at the cathode when water is electrolysed. Alternatively, the atoms of the electrode may ionize and pass into solution. Electrolysis is used to electroplate metals and in the manufacture of a number of chemicals, such as sodium and chlorine. It is also a way of separating ▷isotopes. Deuterium (D *or* ^{2}H), for example, is slower than ordinary hydrogen (^{1}H) to pick up electrons at the cathode, and so electrolysed water gradually becomes enriched with heavy water (D_2O).

● **electromagnet** ▷*See* magnet.

● **electromagnetic field** ► A concept describing electric and magnetic forces that, like gravitational forces, act without physical contact (action at a distance). Although both electricity and magnetism have been observed separately for thousands of years, it was not until the 19th century that their interaction was investigated experimentally by Oersted, Faraday, and others. Faraday explained the electromagnetic interaction in terms of magnetic lines of force, forming a field of force, which is distorted by the presence of a current-carrying conductor or by another magnet. James Clerk ▷Maxwell developed the mathematical theory that electricity and magnetism are different manifestations of the same phenomenon (the electromagnetic field), magnetism being the result of relative motion of ▷electric fields.

● **electromagnetic induction** ► The production of voltage in an electrical conductor when it is in a changing magnetic field or if it moves in relation to a steady magnetic field. The direction of the induced ▷electromotive force opposes the change or motion causing it. Since a current-carrying conductor itself induces a magnetic field, if the current changes, **self-inductance** occurs, opposing the current change. **Mutual inductance** occurs between two adjacent conductors that carry changing currents.

● **electromagnetic interaction** ► An interaction that occurs between those elementary particles that possess an electric charge. The interaction can be visualized as the exchange of virtual photons (*see* virtual particle) between the interacting particles. The electromagnetic interaction is 200 times weaker than the ▷strong interaction but 10^{10} times stronger than the ▷weak interaction. ▷*See also* particle physics.

● **electromagnetic radiation** ► Transverse waves consisting of electric and magnetic fields vibrating perpendicularly to each other and to the direction of propagation. In free space the waves are propagated at a speed of 2.9979×10^8 metres per second, known as the speed of light (symbol: *c*). Their ▷wavelength, λ, and ▷frequency, *f*, are

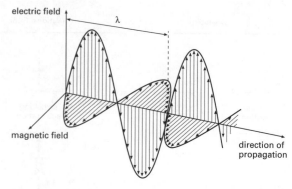

electromagnetic radiation

related by the equation $\lambda f = c$. Those with the highest frequencies are known as ▷gamma radiation; then in descending order of frequency the **electromagnetic spectrum** includes X-rays, ▷ultraviolet radiation, visible ▷light, ▷infrared radiation, ▷microwaves, and ▷radio waves. Electromagnetic radiation exhibits typical wave properties, such as ▷refraction, ▷diffraction, ▷interference, and polarization. However, it can also be regarded as a stream of massless elementary particles called ▷photons. This dual nature of radiation is analogous to the dual nature of massive elementary particles and ▷de Broglie waves. □spectrum.

● **electromotive force** ► (emf) The potential difference or voltage between two points in an electric circuit. It causes the movement of charge that constitutes an electric current, providing a limited analogy to mechanical force and motion.

● **electron** ► A stable negatively charged elementary particle, classified as a ▷lepton, with mass $9.109\,56 \times 10^{-31}$ kilogram and spin ½. Electrons are responsible for almost all commonly observed electrical and magnetic effects and, since they orbit the nucleus in atoms, are also responsible for most chemical processes. A **free electron** is one that has become detached from an atom. An electric current passing through a metal consists of a flow of free electrons; a current of 1 ampere is equivalent to a flow of 6×10^{18} electrons per second. Electrons can also have wave characteristics (*see* de Broglie wave).

● **electron diffraction** ► The ▷diffraction of a beam of electrons as it passes through spaces, the widths of which are comparable to the wavelength of the electrons. Electrons can be diffracted, for example, by the spacing between particles in a crystal lattice, an effect governed by ▷Bragg's law. Electron diffraction demonstrates the wave aspect of electrons (*see* de Broglie wave) since diffraction is specifically a wave effect. The effect is used to investigate the structure of surfaces, films, etc.

● **electronic funds transfer** ► (EFT) A means of charging a sale to a customer's credit-card or bank account by a computer at the retail outlet linked to the telephone network. For example, in garages the customer inserts his credit card into a computer-operated device attached to the petrol pump, taps in his personal identification number (PIN), and his account is instantly debited by the amount shown on the pump.

● **electronic mail** ► (*or* e-mail) A means of transmitting and receiving text using a system of computers connected to the telephone network. Subscribers send messages by keyboarding them into a microprocessor and transmitting them by telephone line to a central computer. To receive a communication a subscriber calls up the central computer, keys in its password, and receives any communications addressed to it on its microprocessor and printer. Telecom Gold is such a system operated by British Telecom in the UK.

● **electronic music** ► **1.** Music consisting of sounds created or recorded electronically. In the late 1940s tape recorders were first used to create ▷musique concrète. This was followed by the development of the ▷synthesizer in the 1960s and the experiments of ▷Cage, ▷Boulez, ▷Berio, ▷Stockhausen, and others. Later composers have experimented with computergenerated electronic music and its use in popular music is now widespread. **2.** Musical sounds generated electronically to represent the sounds of conventional instruments in electronic organs, pianos, and keyboards.

● **electronic publishing** ▶ The publication of books, journals, etc., in computer-readable form, either on disks or on line (*see* Internet). Multimedia reference books on CDs include sound extracts and video clips, in addition to text and pictures. Associated software enables searches for related information to be made. While CDs are cheaper than bound books, the user needs to buy a personal computer to access them. It is expected that the market for electronic books will grow in parallel to the printed book market.

● **electronics** ▶ The study of devices that control and utilize the movement of ▷electrons and other charged particles. Originating with the invention of ▷thermionic valves and their use in radios and record players, it expanded rapidly during World War II to include radar, missile guidance systems, and the first electronic ▷computers. The replacement of bulky thermionic valves by ▷semiconductor components, such as ▷transistors, made possible high-speed digital computers and the miniaturized communications and control systems used in spacecraft. The ▷integrated circuit and the explosive proliferation of **microelectronics** based on microchips were further steps towards more compact and reliable equipment. Tiny wafers of silicon now function as microprocessors.

The social impact of electronics has been immense, with the development of television, communications satellites, and the computerization of office and factory systems.

● **electronic surveillance** ▶ The monitoring of events, conversations, or other activities by electronic means from a distance either overtly or covertly. Wiretapping to listen to telephone conversations can now be achieved simply and secretly using electronic equipment; bugging of rooms by minute microphones may not be used as frequently as films and TV serials imply but it is certainly commonplace. Less sinister uses of electronic surveillance include closed circuit TV cameras in banks, stores, and prisons.

● **electronic tagging** ▶ A method of monitoring the movements of persons convicted of offences for which a court has ordered them to stay at home for a limited period as an alternative to being sent to prison. It has been used in the USA and Canada and to a limited extent in the UK and elsewhere. The offender wears, on his wrist or ankle, a plastic strap containing a microchip device emitting a continuous signal to a transmitter attached to a telephone. If the offender moves out of a 75 m (250 ft) range, the telephone sends a message to the controlling computer.

● **electron microscope** ▶ A type of microscope in which a beam of electrons is focused by means of magnetic and electrostatic lenses onto a specimen and scattered by it to produce an image. The ▷de Broglie wavelength of high-energy electrons is very much less than that of light. Therefore both the ▷resolving power and the magnification of an electron microscope are much greater than can be obtained with an optical microscope. Typically an electron microscope can resolve two points 10^{-9} metre apart and produce magnifications of up to a million. In the **transmission electron microscope** only very thin specimens can be used: the image appears two-dimensional but a high resolution can be obtained. In the **scanning electron microscope** the specimen, which can be of any thickness, is scanned by the beam producing an apparently three-dimensional image but with lower resolution.

● **electron probe microanalysis** ▶ A method of analysing a very small quantity (10^{-16} kg) of a substance by bombarding it with a fine electron beam (about 1 μm in diameter) and examining the X-ray spectrum produced for characteristic lines of the elements. The method can also be used quantitatively.

● **electron spin resonance** ▶ The resonance of an unpaired electron in a paramagnetic substance placed in a magnetic field and exposed to microwaves. Since the electron is unpaired it acts as a magnet and may either align itself with the field or oppose it. If the energy of the microwave ▷photons is equal to the energy difference between the two states the electron resonates. The effect is used to study chemical bonding and structure. ▷*See also* nuclear magnetic resonance.

● **electronvolt** ▶ (eV) A unit of energy, widely used in nuclear physics, equal to the increase in the energy of an electron when it passes through a rise in potential of one volt. 1 eV = 1.6×10^{-19} joule.

● **electroplating** ▶ The process of depositing a layer of one metal on another by making the object to be plated the cathode in an electrolytic bath (*see* electrolysis). Metals used for electroplating include silver (*see* silverplate), gold, chromium, cadmium, copper, zinc, and nickel; they usually form the anode in the bath. The form of the plated layer varies depending on the composition and temperature of the electrolyte, the use of addition agents, and the current density. Some metals do not adhere well to others; for example, chromium does not adhere to steel: steel is usually plated with copper, then nickel, before plating with chromium. ▷*See also* German silver.

● **electroscope** ▶ An electrostatic instrument that detects electric charge or radiation. In a gold-leaf electroscope, the deflection of two suspended gold leaves increases with charge. The quartz-fibre electroscope (QFE), which has a quartz fibre instead of gold leaves, is commonly used to detect radiation. The presence of a radioactive source ionizes the air and causes charge to leak away from the initially charged fibre.

● **electrostatic generators** ▶ Machines that use mechanical or other energy to separate electric charge, creating an electric potential. They are used to create strong electrostatic fields, particularly in high energy nuclear physics for accelerating charged particles to bombard atomic nuclei. ▷*See also* Van de Graaff generator.

● **electrostatics** ▷*See* static electricity.

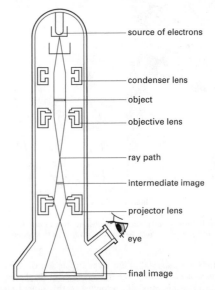

source of electrons

condenser lens

object

objective lens

ray path

intermediate image

projector lens

eye

final image

electron microscope ▶ The beam of electrons in the transmission electron microscope is focused in a similar way to light in an ordinary microscope.

● **electrostatic separation** ▶ The use of a strong electric field to separate substances with different electrical properties. The method is used, for example, in separating out iron ores from a mixture of minerals, and to clean air in chimneys by precipitating charged smoke particles.

● **electroweak theory** ▷*See* weak interaction.

● **electrum** ▶ **1.** An alloy of gold and silver containing 55–80% gold, used in the 7th–6th centuries BC to make the first coins. It occurs naturally, containing some other metals. **2.** A form of ▷German silver containing 52% copper, 26% nickel, and 22% zinc.

● **elementary particles** ▷*See* particle physics.

● **elements** ▶ Substances that cannot be broken down into simpler fragments by chemical means. A sample of an element contains atoms that are chemically virtually identical, since they have the same ▷atomic number and thus the same number of electrons around the nucleus. Samples of a given element may consist of a mixture of ▷isotopes. Over 100 elements are known, of which about 90 occur naturally, the rest having been synthesized in nuclear reactions. Elements are often classified as ▷metals, ▷metalloids, or nonmetals. ▷*See also* periodic table.

African elephant

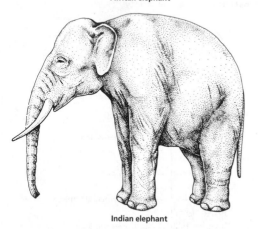

Indian elephant

elephant ▶ The African elephant can be distinguished from the smaller Indian species by its larger ears, flatter forehead, smooth skin, and concave back.

● **elephant** ▶ A mammal of the order *Proboscidea*: the African elephant (*Loxodonta africana*) or the Indian elephant (*Elephas maximus*). (The extinct ▷mammoths also belonged to this order.) Elephants have a tough brownish-grey skin and a muscular prehensile proboscis (trunk)—an extension of the nose and upper lip used to convey food (leaves, branches, and other vegetation) and water to the mouth. The upper incisor teeth are continually growing ▷ivory tusks, for which these animals have long been hunted. Poaching had reduced the number of African elephants from 1.3 million in 1979 to 625 000 in 1989, causing concern for the survival of the species, but by the late 1990s population decline had slowed due to antipoaching measures. It is still considered an endangered species. Elephants live in herds; they have a gestation period of 21–22 months and a lifespan of 60–70 years. The African elephant is the largest land mammal, standing 3–4 m high at the shoulder and weighing 5–7.5 tonnes. The smaller Indian elephant—intelligent and readily trained—is used for transport and heavy work in India, Myanmar (Burma), Thailand, and Malaysia.

● **elephant birds** ▷*See* Aepyornis.

● **elephant grass** ▶ A stout coarse ▷reedmace, *Typha elephanta*, commonly found in marshes and wet habitats from S Europe to the East Indies. It has long tapering leaves, which have been used to make baskets. The name is sometimes also applied to the tropical napier grass (*Pennisetum purpureum*), which resembles sugar cane.

● **elephantiasis** ▶ A condition caused by chronic infection with certain nematode worms, called ▷filariae. It is therefore a form of filariasis. The worms block the lymphatic channels and cause gross swelling of the legs and scrotum (or vulva). Elephantiasis occurs only in the tropics.

● **elephant seal** ▶ A large seal belonging to the genus *Mirounga* (2 species). The male Antarctic elephant seal (*M. leonina*) grows to over 6 m; females are about half that size. The slightly smaller northern elephant seal (*M. angustirostris*) lives off the W coast of North America. Elephant seals feed on fish, crustaceans, octopus, and squid. Family: *Phocidae*.

● **elephant's ear** ▷*See* taro.

● **Eleusinian mysteries** ▶ An esoteric religious cult (*see* mysteries) in ancient Greece, with its centre at Eleusis. It originated before 600 BC in an agrarian fertility cult, and the main deities worshipped were ▷Demeter and ▷Persephone. The myth of Persephone's abduction to the underworld and return was interpreted not only in terms of the dormant seed and the springing corn but also as a symbol of death and resurrection and was probably re-enacted in a darkened room to which only initiates were admitted.

● **eleven-plus** ▶ An examination formerly taken throughout England and Wales by children aged 11 or 12 in order to select pupils for ▷grammar schools. The exam has largely been phased out with the grammar schools, most of which were replaced by ▷comprehensive schools in the 1970s.

● **Elgar, Sir Edward** ▶ (1857–1934) British composer. He was taught largely by his father, the organist at a Roman Catholic church in Worcester. A professional violinist, Elgar became involved as a conductor with the Three Choirs Festival, where many of his important choral works received their first performance. He also wrote two symphonies and concertos for violin and cello; at the end of his life he wrote three important chamber-music works. His most famous works are the *Dream of Gerontius* (for soloists, chorus, and orchestra; 1900), the *Enigma Variations* (for orchestra; 1899), and the *Pomp and Circumstance* marches (1901–30). His incomplete third symphony (completed by Anthony Payne) was given a first performance in 1998.

● **Elgin** ▶ 57 39N 3 20W A town in NE Scotland, in Moray on the River Lossie. Elgin has a ruined 13th-century cathedral and nearby is Gordonstoun school (1934). Its industries include distilling and engineering. Population (1991): 19 027.

● **Elgin Marbles** ▶ Ancient Greek marble sculptures, mostly a frieze from the ▷Parthenon, sold to the British Museum in 1816 by Thomas Bruce, 7th Earl of Elgin, for £35,000. He acquired them from the Turks occupying Athens, who were using the Parthenon for target practice. The British government has not yielded to Greek agitation for their return.

● **Elgon, Mount** ▶ 1 07N 34 35E An extinct volcano in E Africa, on the Uganda–Kenya border. Its crater is about 8 km (5 mi) in diameter and coffee and bananas are grown on the lower slopes. Height: 4321 m (14 178 ft).

● **El Greco** ▶ (Domenikos Theotokopoulos; 1541–1614) Painter of Greek parentage, born in Crete, who worked mainly in Spain. He trained in Venice under Titian in the 1560s and greatly admired the work of Michelangelo, which he saw during a visit to Rome just before he moved to Spain (1577), where he sought the patronage of Philip II. El Greco submitted his *Martyrdom of St Maurice* (1580–82; El Escorial) to Philip but the king rejected it; El Greco then moved to Toledo where he spent most of the remainder of his life, becoming friendly with leading churchmen and scholars. His early Spanish works, such as the *Assumption of the Virgin* (1577; Chicago), were Venetian in inspiration, but his later paintings of saints and his masterpiece, *The Burial of Count Orgaz* (1586–88; Santo Tomé), are characterized by strident colours and dramatically elongated figures. He also painted three stormy landscapes and a number of portraits.

● **Elijah** ▶ An Old Testament prophet, who appears to have lived in the 9th century BC. He attacked the cult of Baal among the Israelites (1 Kings 18) and successfully maintained the monotheistic worship of Jehovah. He was considered the greatest Hebrew prophet. He was taken into heaven without dying (2 Kings 2.1–18), and it was believed that he would return before the final restoration of Israel to the people.

● **Eliot, George** ▶ (Mary Ann Evans; 1819–80) British novelist. Daughter of a Warwickshire estate manager, she was influenced by evangelical Christianity as a girl, but rejected her early religious fervor in 1842. She went to London in 1851, worked on the *Westminster Review*, and lived with the journalist George Henry Lewes, who was married but separated from his wife. After publishing stories based on her childhood she wrote the novels *Adam Bede* (1859), *The Mill on the Floss* (1860), and *Silas Marner* (1861). The pioneering and influential novel *Middlemarch* (1871–72) is a deep and comprehensive depiction of English provincial society. *Daniel Deronda* (1876) contrasts a Jewish family's genuine values with the false ones of society. Lewes died in 1878, and she married a banker, J. W. Cross, six months before her death.

● **Eliot, Sir John** ▶ (1592–1632) English parliamentarian; a leading critic of Charles I. He was imprisoned three times for his views: in 1626 after joining the attack on the 1st Duke of ▷Buckingham; in 1627 after refusing to pay ▷ship money; and in 1628, when he held the speaker of the House of Commons in his chair to prevent his adjournment of parliament before the passing of Eliot's three resolutions against the government. He died, of natural causes, in the Tower of London—a martyr to the parliamentary cause.

● **Eliot, T(homas) S(tearns)** ▶ (1888–1965) Anglo-American poet, critic, and dramatist. Born in Missouri, he was educated at Harvard and in Europe, where he met Ezra ▷Pound. He briefly worked in London as a bank clerk before publication of his first volume of poetry, the innovatory *Prufrock and Other Observations* (1917). *The Waste Land* (1922) is his best-known work, although *Four Quartets* (1935–41) is generally considered to be his major poetic achievement. In 1927 he became an Anglo-Catholic and a British subject. From 1922 to 1939 he edited *The Criterion*, a critical review, and wrote a considerable amount of influential literary criticism. His verse dramas include *Murder in the Cathedral* (1935), *The Family Reunion* (1939), *The Cocktail Party* (1949), and *The Elder Statesman* (1958). He was awarded the Nobel Prize in 1948.

● **Elizabeth** ▶ 40 40N 74 13W A city and port in the USA, in New Jersey on Newark Bay. Part of the New York conurbation, its industries include electronics, aircraft, and chemicals. Population (2000): 120 568.

● **Elizabeth** ▶ 34 45S 138 39E A town in South Australia, near Adelaide. Founded in 1955 as part of a decentralization plan, it was named after Elizabeth II of the UK. Population (latest est): 34 000.

● **Elizabeth** ▶ (1709–62) Empress of Russia (1741–62); the daughter of Peter the Great. Elizabeth came to power in a coup, which ousted the infant Ivan VI (1740–64). She depended on her advisers, such as ▷Bestuzhev-Riumin, and her reign witnessed no reforms and few territorial acquisitions.

● **Elizabeth I** ▶ (1533–1603) Queen of England and Ireland (1558–1603), daughter of Henry VIII and Anne ▷Boleyn. Her mother's execution and Elizabeth's imprisonment by Mary I made her cautious and suspicious but her devotion to England made her one of its greatest monarchs. Her religious compromise (1559–63) established Protestantism in England (*see* Reformation). Several plots to place her Roman Catholic cousin, ▷Mary, Queen of Scots, on the throne led to Mary's execution (1587). England won a great naval victory in 1588 by destroying the Spanish ▷Armada. Elizabeth never married and was called the Virgin Queen, although her relationships with, among others, the Earl of Leicester and the 2nd Earl of Essex caused considerable speculation.

● **Elizabeth II** ▶ (1926–   ) Queen of the United Kingdom (1952–   ),

noted for her scrupulous fulfilment of the roles of constitutional monarch and head of the Commonwealth. She married Prince ▷Philip in 1947; their four children are Prince ▷Charles, Princess ▷Anne (the Princess Royal), Prince Andrew, Duke of ▷York, and Prince ▷Edward. After the death of ▷Diana, Princess of Wales, the Queen agreed to accelerate reforms aimed at modernizing the monarchy. She celebrated her Golden Jubilee in 2002.

Elizabeth the Queen Mother ▶ With the Queen at Sandringham Church in 1994.

● **Elizabeth the Queen Mother** ▶ (1900–2002) The consort of George VI of the United Kingdom. Formerly Lady Elizabeth Bowes-Lyon, she married in 1923 and had two children, ▷Elizabeth II and Princess ▷Margaret. She took the title Queen Mother during her long widowhood (from 1952). Her death at the age of 101 was followed by a ceremonial funeral.

● **Elizabethan literature** ▷*See* English literature.

● **Elizabethan style** ▶ The style of ▷English art and architecture prevalent during the reign of Elizabeth I. A transition between the earlier ▷Tudor style and the ▷Palladianism of Inigo ▷Jones, it produced many country houses, such as ▷Longleat, with characteristically ▷Renaissance features including large windows, decorative gables, and an emphasis on symmetry.

● **Elizabethville** ▷*See* Lubumbashi.

● **elk** ▶ The largest deer, *Alces alces*, found in forests of N Eurasia and also in N North America, where it is called a moose. Up to 2 m high at the shoulder, elks have a broad curved muzzle and a short neck with a heavy dewlap. The coat is grey-brown and males grow large palmate antlers spanning up to 180 cm. They feed on leaves and water plants and form herds in winter. □mammal.

● **elkhound** ▶ An ancient breed of working dog originating in Norway and used for tracking and hunting game animals, especially elk. It has a short compact body with the tail curled over the back and a broad head with pricked ears. The thick coat is grey tipped with black. Height: 51 cm (dogs); 49 cm (bitches).

● **Ellenborough, Edward Law, Earl of** ▶ (1790–1871) British colonial administrator; governor general of India (1842–44). He succeeded ▷Auckland in India and was recalled after unlawfully annexing the Sind.

● **Ellesmere Island** ▶ A Canadian Arctic island W of Greenland, the northernmost part of North America. Mostly rugged plateau with large glaciers, it shelters a few weather stations, police posts, and the remnants of Inuit settlements. Area: 212 688 sq km (82 119 sq mi).

● **Ellesmere Port** ▶ 53 17N 2 54W A port in NW England, in Cheshire on the Mersey estuary and Manchester Ship Canal. Petroleum products, chemicals, paper, and engineering are the main industries. Population (1991): 64 504.

● **Ellice Islands** ▷*See* Tuvalu.

● **Ellington, Duke** ▶ (Edward Kennedy E.; 1899–1974) US Black jazz composer, band leader, and pianist. After leading bands in Washington, DC, Ellington went to New York, where he established a group of musicians that remained the core of his band for 30 years. The success of "Mood Indigo" in 1930 led to European tours and annual concerts in Carnegie Hall. Ellington concentrated on large-scale works, writing the suite *Black, Brown, and Beige* (1943) and the "religious jazz" work *In the Beginning God* (1966).

● **ellipse** ▶ A closed curve having the shape of an elongated ▷circle. The sum of the distances from any point on the circumference to each of two fixed points, known as the foci, is a constant. In the Cartesian ▷coordinate system its equation is $(x - h)^2/a^2 + (y - k)^2/b^2 = 1$, where (h,k) is the centre of the ellipse and a and b are the largest and shortest radii, which are parallel to the coordinate axes. The ellipse is one of a family of curves known as ▷conic sections.

● **Ellis, (Henry) Havelock** ▶ (1859–1939) British psychologist and essayist, noted for his studies of human sexual behaviour. His major work, *Studies in the Psychology of Sex* (7 vols, 1897–1928), was among the first to deal frankly with sexual problems and met with legal opposition. He was also concerned with women's rights and wrote *Impressions and Comments* (3 vols, 1914–24), a series of essays on art.

● **Ellis Island** ▶ 40 42N 74 03W A small island in the USA, in New York Harbor. It served as an entry centre for immigrants to the USA (1892–1943).

● **Ellora Caves** ▶ A cluster of rock-cut Hindu, Buddhist, and Jaina temples in Maharashtra state (W India). They were made mainly between the mid-7th and the early 10th centuries AD. The most sumptuous temple is the Kailashanatha, dedicated to Shiva.

● **Ellsworth Land** ▶ An area in Antarctica, at the base of the Antarctic Peninsula. It contains the highest peak in Antarctica, ▷Vinson Massif. UK claims to the area are contested by Argentina and Chile.

● **elm** ▶ A ▢tree of the genus *Ulmus* (about 30 species), widely distributed in N temperate regions. Up to 40 m high, elms have oval pointed toothed leaves, clusters of small reddish flowers, and rounded or heart-shaped winged nuts. Elms are widely planted for shade and ornament and for their strong durable timber. Unfortunately the number of elm trees in Europe and North America has been greatly reduced by ▷Dutch elm disease. Species include the English elm (*U. procera*), the Eurasian wych elm (*U. glabra*), and the American elm (*U. americana*). Family: *Ulmaceae*. ▷See also slippery elm.

● **elm bark beetle** ▶ A wood-boring beetle, *Scolytus scolytus*, *S. multistriatus*, or *Hylurgopinus rufipes*, that tunnels under the bark of elm trees and carries the fungus *Ceratostomella ulni*, which causes ▷Dutch elm disease. Family: *Scolytidae* (see bark beetle).

● **Elmo, St** ▶ (*or* St Erasmus) ▷*See* St Elmo's fire.

● **El Niño** ▶ (Spanish: the Christ child) A natural phenomenon of widespread weather disruption resulting from reversal of the trade winds and sea currents in the equatorial Pacific region, so called as it tends to begin at around Christmas. Normally, trade winds blow from east to west, pushing warm water westwards and bringing heavy rainfall to Indonesia and cool waters with dry weather to Peru. As a result of El Niño a huge mass of warm water moves eastward, causing torrential rain and floods in Peru—where suppression of the cold ▷Humboldt Current disrupts marine ecosystems and the fishing industry—and the southern USA, while drought and forest fires occur in Indonesia and Australia. El Niño events can extend as far west as Africa, resulting in storms and flooding in E Africa and drought in the S. El Niño usually lasts about 18 months. Since the late 1970s it has recurred on average every 4 years (previously every 10 years).

● **El Obeid** ▶ 13 15N 30 45E A town in the Sudan. It is a trading centre for gum arabic, cereals, and cattle. Population (1993): 228 096.

● **El Paso** ▶ 31 45N 106 30W A city in the USA, in W Texas on the Rio Grande. Situated on the Mexican border, it is the commercial and industrial centre of a mining and cattle-raising area. It is also a major base for the armed forces. Manufactures include refined oil and food products. Population (1996 est): 599 865.

● **Elphanta Island** ▶ 18 58N 72 54E An islet off the W coast of India,

in Bombay Harbour. It is famous for its cave temples and a three-headed bust, 6 m (20 ft) high, of the god Shiva.

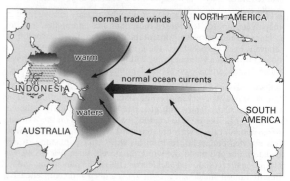

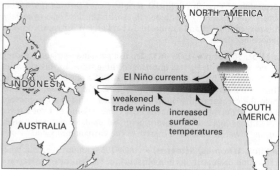

El Niño ▶ Showing the ocean currents that bring flooding to parts of South America, leaving Indonesia and parts of Australia in drought.

● **El Salvador, Republic of** ▶ A country in Central America, on the Pacific Ocean. Narrow coastal lowlands rise to a fertile plateau, which is enclosed by volcanic mountains. The country is frequently subject to earthquakes. Most of the population is of mixed European and Indian descent.
   Economy: mainly agricultural, the economy has been dominated by coffee since the late 19th century. Production of cotton and sugar cane, the other main commercial crops, has declined owing to the political situation in the 1980s and early 1990s. Forests produce hardwoods, such as mahogany and walnut, but also dye woods and balsam of which El Salvador is the world's principal source. Most of the cultivated land is controlled by a few families, which has led to movement and emigration (especially in the 1960s) of farmers, most of whom rent their land. El Salvador has few mineral resources and the main source of power is hydroelectricity. Traditional industries, such as food processing and textiles, remain important, but tourism is also being developed. Coffee production and the banking system are in the process of being privatized. Agriculture and infrastructure were severely affected by Hurricane Mitch in 1998.
   History: the Aztec population was conquered by the Spaniards in 1526 and after the overthrow of Spanish rule the region formed part of the Central American Federation (1823–38). In 1841 it became an independent republic. For most of its modern history El Salvador has been ruled by a series of military leaders, acting on behalf of the landowning oligarchy. Tension arising from the emigration of Salvadoreans to Honduras culminated in war in 1965 and again in 1969, following El Salvador's defeat of Honduras in a World Cup football match. In 1978–79 the repressive regime of Gen Carlos Humberto Romero (1924–) provoked kidnappings of foreigners by left-wing guerrillas of the Farabundo Martí National Liberation Front (FMLN), occupations of foreign embassies, and assassinations. Romero was deposed in 1979 and a junta took control but the violence continued, including the assassination (1980) of the archbishop of San Salvador, Oscar Romero. There was a return to civilian rule in 1982 and in 1984

José Napoléon Duarte was elected president; he was succeeded by Alfredo Cristiani in 1989. After 12 years of virtual civil war peace was finally achieved in 1992, after arbitration through the UN, and in 1994 presidential and parliamentary elections were held in which the FMLN took part. The country has since been governed by a right-wing coalition led by the ARENA party. In 2001 the country adopted the US dollar. El Salvador is a member of the OAS and the Central American Common Market.

Republic of El Salvador

Head of state	President Francisco Flores
Official language	Spanish
Official religion	Roman Catholic
Official currency	US dollar of 100 cents
Area	21 393 sq km (8236 sq mi)
Population (2001 est)	6 238 000
Capital	San Salvador
Main port	Acajutla

● **Elsinore** ▷See Helsingør.

● **Elton, Charles** ▶ (1900–91) British zoologist. In *Animal Ecology* (1927) Elton laid down many of the basic principles of ecology. His work on animal populations has proved of economic value, for example in enabling more effective control of rodent pests. In 1932 he founded the Bureau of Animal Populations at Oxford.

● **Éluard, Paul** ▶ (Eugène Grindel; 1895–1952) French poet, a friend of André ▷Breton and Louis ▷Aragon and with them a leader in the early surrealist movement. Their influence is clear in his early poetry collections, such as *Capitale de la douleur* (1926) and *La Rose publique* (1934). He joined the Communist Party in 1942 and adopted a more realistic style in poems circulated secretly among the Resistance. His postwar poetry was more personal and lyrical.

● **elver** ▷See eel.

● **Ely** ▶ 52 24N 0 16E A city in E England, in Cambridgeshire on the River Ouse. The Isle of Ely, an area of higher ground surrounded by fenland, is famous as the place where Hereward the Wake confronted the Normans. Ely's 11th-century cathedral dominates the fen landscape. Its industries include agricultural engineering, pottery, chemicals, and plastics. Ely is also becoming a waterway cruising centre. Population (1991): 10 329.

● **Elyot, Sir Thomas** ▶ (c. 1490–1546) English diplomat and scholar, author of *The Boke Named the Governour* (1531), a popular treatise on the education of gentlemen to match their responsibilities. He published many translations and an influential Latin-English dictionary (1538).

● **Élysée, Palais de l'** ▶ The official residence of the presidents of France since 1873. The palace, which was built in 1718, was formerly the home of Mme de Pompadour.

● **Elysium** ▶ (or Elysian Fields) In Greek mythology, the fields on the banks of the River ▷Oceanus where those favoured by the gods live in eternal happiness. They are also called (by Hesiod) the Isles of the Blessed. In Roman mythology Elysium is part of the underworld.

● **Elytis, Odysseus** ▶ (O. Alepoudelis; 1912–96) Greek poet. His works, which show the influence of surrealism, include the long poems *Axion Est* (1959) and *Maria Nefeli* (1978). He was awarded the Nobel Prize in 1979.

● **e-mail** ▷See electronic mail.

● **Emancipation Act** ▶ (1861) The edict issued by ▷Alexander II that freed the serfs of Russia (a third of the country's population). The peasants were to receive land from the landlord and pay for it in labour and crops but inequities in land distribution caused considerable discontent.

● **Emancipation Proclamation** ▶ (1863) The edict issued by President Abraham ▷Lincoln that freed slaves in the rebellious southern states of the USA. It was promulgated in part to weaken the Confederate war effort by depriving the South of labourers but Lincoln considered it "the central act" of his administration. The proclamation's

provisions were extended and confirmed by the 13th Amendment, which abolished ▷slavery throughout the nation (1865).

● **Emancipists** ▶ Former convicts in New South Wales (Australia) who campaigned in the late 18th and early 19th centuries for equal civil rights with the free settlers of the colony. Barred from a full political and social life, the Emancipists achieved the abolition of such discrimination with the new constitution of 1842. ▷See also Exclusionists.

● **Emba, River** ▶ A river in W Kazakhstan, flowing mainly SW from the Mugodzhar Hills, through the Emba oilfield, to the Caspian Sea. Length: 611 km (380 mi).

● **embalming** ▶ The techniques for preserving dead bodies from decay. Embalming was frequent in ancient Egypt (*see* mummy). In medieval Europe it was usually carried out by removing the corpse's internal organs, bathing it in spirits of wine, filling cavities made in the flesh with herbs, and finally wrapping it in waxed or tarred sheets. Since the 18th century arterial injections of preservative solutions, now generally a mixture of formaldehyde, alcohols, and salts, have been used.

● **embargo** ▶ A resolution by a country or countries not to supply another country with certain goods, or not to import certain goods from another country, for political reasons. A trade embargo is often imposed on a country as a form of ▷sanctions.

● **embolism** ▶ The sudden blocking of an artery by a clot or other material that has come from another part of the body via the bloodstream (the material is called an embolus). The commonest example is when a clot forms in the leg and pieces break away and lodge in the arteries of the lung—a **pulmonary embolism**. A clot may sometimes come from the heart and lodge in the brain, causing a ▷stroke. Air and fat can also cause embolism. ▷See also thrombosis.

● **embroidery** ▶ The decoration of fabrics with needlework, usually in silk but occasionally in gold and silver thread. It was practised by the ancient Egyptians but the first important Western embroidery was the ▷Bayeux tapestry. From about the 13th century embroidery was chiefly used for state and church vestments, the Syon Cope (Victoria and Albert Museum) being the most famous English 13th-century example. Gros point and petit point are two common kinds of stitch used to form elaborate pictures; from the 17th century such embroidered fabric was much used for curtains, bed hangings, and seat covers.

● **embryo** ▶ An animal or plant in the earliest stages of its development. In vertebrate animals the embryonic stage lasts from the first division of the fertilized egg until the young animal either hatches from the egg or is expelled from the womb at birth. A human embryo is called a ▷fetus from the eighth week of pregnancy. In invertebrate animals the embryo is generally called a ▷larva. In plants, the embryo lies within the ▷seed and consists of a root (radicle), shoot (plumule), and cotyledons for nourishment. **Embryology** is the study of the development of embryos. There is much controversy in the UK over the experimental use of human embryos formed by *in vitro* fertilization, which are produced for implantation as ▷test-tube babies. The unwanted surplus has been used to investigate genetic and congenital diseases. □ p. 418.

● **Emden** ▶ 53 23N 07 13E A town in NW Germany, in Lower Saxony on the Ems estuary. A major seaport for the ▷Ruhr via the Dortmund-Ems Canal, its industries include shipbuilding and car assembly. Population (1991): 51 000.

● **emerald** ▶ A green variety of ▷beryl, the colour being due to the presence of small amounts of chromium. A gemstone, it occurs mainly in metamorphic rocks, particularly mica schists, the finest specimens coming from Muzo, Colombia. It is less resistant to wear than most gemstones. Birthstone for May.

● **Emerson, Ralph Waldo** ▶ (1803–82) US essayist and poet, a leading transcendentalist. He was ordained as a Unitarian minister in 1829, but his wife's death in 1831 provoked a radical re-evaluation of his beliefs. After a tour of Europe, during which he met Wordsworth, Coleridge, and Carlyle, he returned to Concord in 1833. There he wrote the confessional *Nature* (1836), his transcendentalist creed. A prolific lecturer, poet, and essayist he expressed his optimistic humanism in *Representative Men* (1850) and *The Conduct of Life* (1860).

● **emery** ▸ A granular greyish-black rock composed of ▷corundum with magnetite, hematite, or spinel. It occurs mainly in metamorphic rocks or sediments, particularly metamorphosed ferruginous bauxite, and altered limestones. It is used as an abrasive, in grinding wheels, emery cloth, and glass polishes, and in the manufacture of certain concrete floors. The principal producers are Turkey and Greece.

● **emigration** ▷*See* migration, human.

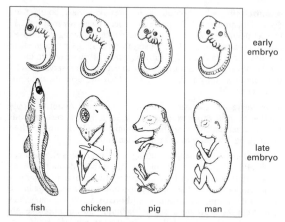

early embryo

late embryo

fish   chicken   pig   man

The different species are hard to distinguish in the early stages of development; later they develop individual characteristics.

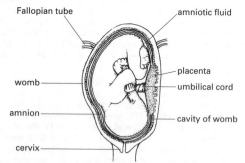

Fallopian tube

amniotic fluid

womb

placenta

umbilical cord

amnion

cavity of womb

cervix

A few weeks before birth this fetus is practically fully formed.

embryo ▸ Various vertebrate embryos (above); a human embryo (below).

● **Emilia-Romagna** ▸ A region in N Italy. It consists of the fertile lowlands of the River Po in the N and E, bounded by the Apennines in the S. It is an important agricultural region producing sugar beet, cereals, vegetables, wine, rice, and fruit. Traditional manufacturing industries associated with agriculture are being replaced by modern chemical and oil-based industries and engineering. Area: 22 122 sq km (8542 sq mi). Population (1994 est): 3 924 348. Capital: Bologna.

● **Éminence Grise** ▷*See* Joseph, Père.

● **Emin Paşa, Mehmed** ▸ (Eduard Schnitzer; 1840–92) German-born physician and naturalist, who became a Muslim and took employment in Egypt. In 1878 ▷Gordon appointed him chief medical officer in the S Sudan, a post he held until "rescued" (1888) by ▷Stanley, who thought he was in danger after Gordon's death in Khartoum. He was murdered by Arabs on his way to explore Lake Victoria, but not before making notable contributions to natural history, anthropology, and geography.

● **Emmen** ▸ 52 47N 6 55E A town in the NE Netherlands, in Drenthe province. It was formerly a peat-digging centre. Industries include metallurgy, timber processing, and chemicals. Population (1994): 93 476.

● **Emmental** ▸ (or Emmenthal) The valley of the upper River Emme, in W central Switzerland. It is famous for its cheese.

● **Emmet, Robert** ▸ (1778–1803) Irish nationalist, who led a rebellion in Dublin for Irish independence in 1803. It amounted to little more than a riot but Emmet's speech before his execution ensured his immortality.

● **emotion** ▸ An aroused state in which bodily changes of pulse rate, respiration, facial expression, glandular secretions, etc., are accompanied by strong feelings of excitement, apprehension, and heightened perception. Rational thought may suffer a disturbance that can impair judgment, and behaviour may be uncharacteristic of that person in the unaroused state. The psychological study of emotion has mostly been concerned with integrating it within a cognitive and physiological understanding of human behaviour.

● **Empedocles** ▸ (c. 490–430 BC) Sicilian Greek philosopher. He modified the teachings of ▷Pythagoras and opposed ▷Parmenides' view of reality as one and unchanging. Empedocles founded the doctrine that earth, air, fire, and water make up the world, and that love and strife (attraction and antipathy) govern their distribution in a cycle of four stages.

● **emperor moth** ▸ A large Eurasian ▷saturniid moth, *Saturnia pavonia*. Males fly by day, attracted by scent to the stationary females. The caterpillars spin a cocoon with an opening that allows easy exit but prevents entrance by predators.

● **emperor penguin** ▸ A large ▷penguin, *Aptenodytes forsteri*. 1.2 m tall and 34 kg in weight, it is the largest seabird and has a blue-grey plumage with a black head and throat, a white belly, and orange patches on the neck. ▷*See* Plate III.

● **emphysema** ▸ A disease of the lungs characterized by destruction of lung tissue and distension of the air spaces. It is most commonly caused by cigarette smoking and is often accompanied by chronic ▷bronchitis. Patients become very breathless on exertion. It is a progressive condition, but the symptoms may be relieved by giving up smoking, breathing exercises, and administration of oxygen.

● **Empire, British** ▸ Britain's overseas possessions from the 16th to early 20th centuries. The Empire's origins lay in the discovery by John ▷Cabot of Cape Breton Island (1497) but permanent settlements in North America were not established until the early 17th century, when colonists, some escaping religious persecution, were granted charters by the Crown to settle Virginia, Maryland, and New England. The loss of the American colonies in 1783 (*see* American Revolution) was a major blow. In Canada the English came into conflict with the French and only established control in the ▷Seven Years' War (1756–63) from which they also emerged victorious in India. The East India Company had received its charter in 1600 but its interests in India had remained commercial until the decline of the Mogul Empire provided the chance for territorial expansion. Robert Clive's victory at Plassey (1757) assured British, rather than French, dominance there and the East India Company continued to govern until 1857, when its authority was replaced by the Crown's (*see* British Raj).

The Napoleonic Wars in the early 19th century brought possessions in the West Indies (Trinidad, Tobago, St Lucia) as well as Mauritius, Ceylon, and, in Africa, the Cape. Britain's first settlement in Africa had been on James Island in the Gambia River (1661) but substantial possessions were not obtained until the late 18th century with the acquisition of what are now Sierra Leone, Ghana, and Nigeria. The 19th-century colonial expansion in Africa was fired by missionary zeal, which motivated such explorers as ▷Livingstone, as well as the commercial activities of such companies as the Royal Niger, the Imperial British East Africa, and the British South Africa. The late 19th century saw the establishment of British dominance in Egypt and the Sudan but in South Africa it was undermined by ▷Afrikaner hostility.

Colonies in Australia were initially penal settlements: New South

Wales was settled in 1778, Tasmania, in 1803, and Queensland, in 1824. New Zealand was controlled by the British from 1840 and the 19th century also achieved the acquisition of Hong Kong (1841) and Burma (1886).

The colonies were supervised from 1801 by the Colonial Office, which became a separate government department in 1854, and were generally self-governing. In the mid-19th century, following the 1839 *Report on the Affairs of British North America* by Lord ▷Durham, the self-governing colonies in Canada, Australia, New Zealand, and South Africa received responsible government, whereby governors were advised by local ministers. In 1907 Canada, Australia, and New Zealand (and in 1910 South Africa), by now federated, were termed dominions and regular ▷Imperial Conferences were instituted. In 1931 the ▷Commonwealth of Nations was established, giving the dominions autonomy, and in the following decades Britain's other colonies gradually achieved full independence with the exception of a few scattered dependencies and other crown possessions (*see* United Kingdom Overseas Territories).

● **Empire style** ▶ The neoclassical style in the decorative arts developing during the Napoleonic empire (1804–14). It was inspired by classical Greek, Roman, and Egyptian models and reflected contemporary interest in archaeology (e.g. ▷Pompeii). Dark woods, such as rosewood, were favoured, sparsely ornamented with ▷ormolu. Shapes tended to be plain but caryatids were used as supports. The effect was of restrained but opulent elegance. The **Second Empire style** was the official architectural style of the French Government under Emperor Napoleon III (1852–70). Grandiose and ideally suited to public buildings, it became popular throughout Europe and America.

● **empiricism** ▶ The philosophical belief that all knowledge is ultimately based on experience, that is, information received through the senses. It is opposed to ▷rationalism and denies that we have any ▷a priori knowledge or innate ideas: we owe all our concepts to experience of the world. Concepts only have meaning if they can be associated with some (actual or possible) experience, and statements asserted to be true can only be justified by appealing to experience. (Mathematical and logical knowlege are often exempted from this requirement by being classified as analytically true—true in virtue of syntax and the meaning of symbols alone.) Since the British empiricists, ▷Locke, ▷Berkeley, and ▷Hume, empiricism has been an influential force in much of Western philosophy.

● **Employment Training** ▷*See* Training, Enterprise and Education Directorate.

● **Empson, Sir William** ▶ (1906–84) British poet and critic. He established his literary reputation with his first book of criticism, *Seven Types of Ambiguity* (1930). Although slight in volume, his poetry, published in *Poems* (1935) and *The Gathering Storm* (1940), had a great influence on the poets of the 1950s and 60s. He taught in Japan and China, and from 1953 at Sheffield University. He was knighted in 1979.

● **EMS** ▷*See* European Monetary System.

● **Ems telegram** ▶ (13 July, 1870) A communication from ▷William I of Prussia to his chancellor ▷Bismarck, the published version of which precipitated the ▷Franco-Prussian War. The telegram described a disagreement between William and the French ambassador concerning the succession to the Spanish throne. Bismarck altered the telegram to make it read as if each party had insulted the other.

● **emu** ▶ A large flightless long-legged Australian bird, *Dromaius novaehollandiae*, found in open plains and forests. Up to 150 cm tall and 45 kg in weight, it has a dark-brown plumage with a naked blue spot on each side of the neck, and can run at speeds of up to 50 km per hour (30 mph). It is the only member of its family (*Dromaiidae*). ▷*See also* ratite.

● **emulsifier** ▶ A ▷food additive consisting of a substance that enables nonmiscible liquids (such as oil and water) to maintain a stable emulsion, as in mayonnaise, margarine, and peanut butter. Natural emulsifying agents, such as egg yolk, agar, and lecithin, have now been largely replaced by synthetic chemical emulsifiers.

● **emulsion** ▷*See* colloid.

● **emu wren** ▶ An Australian ▷wren of the genus *Stipiturus* (3 species). About 7.5 cm long, it has a brownish plumage and a long (9 cm) cocked tail of six wispy grey feathers.

● **enamel** ▶ A glaze that is fused onto the surface of metal. Enamelled gold jewellery dating back to the 13th century BC has been found, and various methods of enamelling have developed since then. Generally, a clear flux made from melted sand, soda potash, and red lead is stained with a metal oxide and left to harden. The resultant enamel cakes are ground and spread on the metal object, which is then placed in a furnace to fuse the enamel with the metal. Painted enamels are applied after the ground enamel has been fired and are not, therefore, true enamels.

● **enamelwork** ▶ The art of decorating metal surfaces with coloured glass that is fused by heat onto the metal. There are three main kinds: ▷cloisonné, ▷champlevé, and painted enamelwork. Painted enamelwork involves painting powdered wet enamel all over the metal before firing. Painted enamel is particularly associated with Limoges (15th and 16th centuries) and England (18th century).

● **encaustic painting** ▶ A method of painting using ground pigments emulsified in hot wax, which are applied thickly with a spatula or brush. Heat is then directed onto the paint to fuse it with the picture surface. Although revived by various artists, it was most successfully employed by ancient Greek and Roman painters.

● **encephalins** ▶ (*or* enkephalins) Short peptide molecules, found in parts of the brain and spinal cord, that are thought to relieve pain. These and similar compounds are called **endorphins**. In the spinal cord encephalins are believed to inhibit painful sensations by reacting with specific receptor sites on the sensory nerve endings. In the brain their function is less certain but may be associated with mood. The pain-relieving effects of acupuncture may be due to the release of the body's encephalins.

● **encephalitis** ▶ Inflammation of the brain. It usually occurs as a result of a virus infection, but can be caused by malaria, fungi, or parasites (rarely by bacteria). The patient is often drowsy and fevered and has a bad headache. There is no specific treatment for viral encephalitis but the patient usually recovers. ▷*See also* sleepy sickness.

● **Encke's comet** ▶ A comet that has a period of only 3.3 years (decreasing by 2.5 hours/revolution) and has been very closely studied during its numerous apparitions. Its period was first established by the German astronomer J. F. Encke (1791–1865).

● **enclosure** ▶ The fencing in of open land to make more efficient use of it. Enclosure has occurred in most parts of Europe but is associated particularly with England, where it reached a peak in the 15th–16th and 18th–19th centuries. The enclosing by landlords, without prior agreement, of land to which tenants had enjoyed traditional grazing rights met much opposition and in the 16th century a series of Acts against enclosure was passed. The movement again intensified in the 18th century, contributing to the ▷agricultural revolution. The General Enclosure Acts (1801, 1836, 1845) established procedures to safeguard tenant rights.

● **encyclical, papal** ▶ A decree of the pope addressed to the whole Roman Catholic Church. The term referred originally to a letter to all the churches in a particular area, such as a diocese. The most famous example of an encyclical in recent times is *Humanae Vitae* (1968), which was issued by Paul VI and expressed the teaching of the Church on contraception.

● **encyclopedia** ▶ A reference book summarizing all human knowledge or comprehensively surveying a particular subject. Greek and Roman encyclopedias, such as ▷Pliny the Elder's *Historia naturalis* (77 AD), were thematically arranged, as were the medieval Latin compilations, such as Vincent of Beauvais' influential *Speculum maius* (c. 1250). After the Renaissance, alphabetical arrangement with articles written in vernacular languages to facilitate use by the layman became accepted. Ephraim Chambers' *Cyclopaedia* (1728) was the earliest to use cross-references. Diderot's 35-volume *Encyclopédie* (1751–65) used specialist contributors and editors (*see* Encyclopedists), but its ideological bias left gaps that the first *Encyclopaedia Britannica* (1768–71) sought to fill. Major encyclopedias that first appeared in the 19th century and are still published in some form include the German *Brockhaus* (1809), the *Encyclopedia Americana* (1833), *Chamber's Encyclopaedia* (1859), and the French *Grand Dictionnaire Universel* (1865–76) of Larousse. In the 20th century the expansion of scientific knowledge has posed particular problems for compilers, in particular the need to keep pace with technology requires frequent updating of reference works. For this reason modern encyclopedias, including this one, are compiled on computer-based systems and typeset by computer. Many encyclopedias are now available on compact discs for use in computers. Multimedia encyclopedias for computers incorporate sounds (e.g. birdsong and famous speeches) as well as illustrations and text. These encyclopedias are often supplied free with multimedia computers.

● **Encyclopedists** ▶ (French name: Encyclopédistes) The French intellectuals who contributed to ▷Diderot's monumental *Encyclopédie*, published in 28 volumes between 1751 and 1772. Five more volumes were published in 1776–77. Over 200 scholarly experts, including such leading figures of the ▷Enlightenment as Voltaire, Rousseau, and d'Alembert, contributed articles that combined scientific facts and radical philosophical thinking. By their appeal to reason rather than faith the Encyclopedists threatened the authority of Church and state.

● **endangered species** ▶ A plant or animal species that is in danger of extinction. It is estimated that nearly 34 000 vascular-plant species and over 5000 animal species are currently endangered, most of them as a result of human activities, notably destruction of natural habitats, pollution, and hunting and trapping. During the 20th century the number of endangered species has grown dramatically, and in 1948 the International Union for the Conservation of Nature and Natural Resources (IUCN) was founded to devise measures to protect endangered species. The IUCN publishes the Red Data Book, which lists all known endangered species. They are divided into three categories—critically endangered, endangered, and vulnerable—based on population decline, scarcity, and distribution. Trade in endangered species is regulated by CITES—the Convention on International Trade in Endangered Species. This has been signed by 96 countries, including the UK. ▷*See also* conservation; World Wide Fund for Nature.

Some examples of endangered species

orang-utan (*Pongo pygmaeus*)
mountain gorilla (*Gorilla gorilla*)
tiger (*Panthera tigris*)
snow leopard (*Panthera uncia*)
black rhinoceros (*Diceros bicornis*)
Indian elephant (*Elephas maximus*)
Tibetan antelope (*Pantholops hodgsoni*)
pygmy hog (*Sus salvanius*)
sloth bear (*Melursus ursinus*)
red wolf (*Canis rufus*)
blue whale (*Balaenoptera musculus*)
Yangtze river dolphin (*Lipotes vexillifer*)
Mediterranean monk seal (*Monachus monachus*)
Californian condor (*Gymnogyps californianus*)
kakapo (*Strigops habroptilus*)
Spix's macaw (*Cyanopsitta spixii*)
crested ibis (*Nipponia nippon*)
loggerhead turtle (*Caretta caretta*)
green turtle (*Chelonia mydas*)
Siamese crocodile (*Crocodylus siamensis*)

● **Enderby Land** ▶ An area in Antarctica, on the Indian Ocean E of Queen Maud Land. The coast is mountainous and the interior consists of an ice-capped plateau. The site of a Russian research station, it is claimed by Australia.

● **Enders, John Franklin** ▶ (1897–1985) US microbiologist, who shared the 1954 Nobel Prize with Frederick ▷Robbins and Thomas Weller (1915–) for their work on ▷viruses. In 1948 they discovered how to grow virus cultures in cultures of human tissue by adding penicillin to prevent the growth of bacteria. Their work paved the

way for the development of vaccines to prevent polio, mumps, and measles—all caused by viruses.

● **endive** ▶ An annual or biennial plant, *Cichorium endivia*, probably native to S Asia and N China and cultivated widely. It has a rosette of shiny leaves, either curled and narrow (var. *crispa*), used for salads, or broad (*latifolia*), used for cooking. The pale-blue daisy-like flowers grow on spikes up to 100 cm high. Family: ▷*Compositae*. ▷*See also* chicory.

● **endocrine glands** ▶ Ductless glands that produce and secrete ▷hormones into the bloodstream. Most are regulated by hormones from the ▷pituitary gland, which is itself controlled by neurohormones secreted by the ▷hypothalamus. Other endocrine glands include the ▷thyroid, ▷adrenal, and ▷parathyroid glands, parts of the ▷pancreas (the islets of Langerhans), and the ovaries and testes. The wall of the intestine also contains many endocrine cells that release hormones, such as secretin and gastrin, controlling the secretion of digestive enzymes. The study of the endocrine glands in health and disease is called **endocrinology**.

● **endorphins** ▷*See* encephalins.

● **endoscopy** ▶ Examination of the interior of the body by means of a viewing instrument (endoscope) as an aid to diagnosis. There are many types of endoscope, specialized for viewing different organs. The modern endoscope for examining the stomach and intestine is a flexible ▷fibre-optic instrument, which is swallowed by the patient. It enables all areas to be observed and photographed and often has attachments for removing tissue specimens for ▷biopsy. Endoscopy of the gastrointestinal tract is particularly useful for identifying sites of intestinal bleeding and for diagnosing peptic ulcers and tumours.

● **endothermic reaction** ▷*See* enthalpy.

● **Endymion** ▶ In Greek legend, a beautiful youth, either a shepherd of Caria or a king of Elis, who was put into an everlasting sleep by Selene, goddess of the moon, so that she could enjoy his beauty forever.

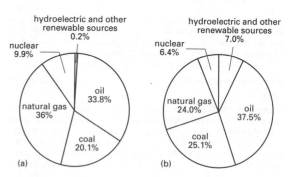

energy ▶ Primary sources: (a) UK in 1996; (b) world in 1993.

● **energy** ▶ A property of a system that enables it to do work, i.e. to move the point of application of a force. ▷Kinetic energy is energy of motion, whereas ▷potential energy is stored energy, for example the energy stored in a body by virtue of its position in a gravitational or electric field. Other forms of energy include thermal energy (the kinetic energy of the atoms and molecules in a body), chemical energy (the potential energy stored in the chemical bonds between atoms in a substance), nuclear energy (the potential energy stored in the atomic nucleus), and radiant energy (the energy associated with electromagnetic waves).

As a consequence of the special theory of relativity, mass (m) has also to be regarded as a special form of energy (E), in accordance with the equation $E = mc^2$, where c is the speed of light. Thus the production of ▷nuclear energy involves a loss of mass in the fuel. However, the sum of the mass and the energy is conserved (*see* conservation laws). Energy is measured in joules (SI units), calories or ergs (c.g.s. units), kilowatt-hours or British thermal units (Imperial units).

Energy sources: man's first use of energy (other than that of his own body or the body of animals) came with the discovery of fire. For combustion is a process in which chemical energy is converted into thermal energy. The first fuel was wood; but fossil fuels (asphalt, coal, oil, natural gas) have been in use for about 8000 years. However, it was the ▷industrial revolution and the later advent of motorized transport that brought explosive increases in the demand for energy and for fossil fuels. These demands have increased during the 20th century, especially with the spread of technology. The total world energy consumption is some 4×10^{20} joules per year, nearly 88% of which is provided by fossil fuels. Concern both about the exhaustion of fossil fuel reserves and the 2.5×10^{10} tonnes of CO_2 they produce each year (*see* greenhouse effect) is directing attention to ▷alternative energy sources as well as nuclear energy. In the UK, the relative merits of coal, gas, and nuclear ▷power stations for the generation of electricity are actively debated. UK-mined ▷coal provides jobs and security of supply but is dearer than some imported coal and environmentally damaging; gas is cheaper and cleaner but the continuity of supply is uncertain; the cost of nuclear-generated electricity is complicated by decommissioning and reprocessing costs—it produces no CO_2 but raises problems of ▷radioactive waste disposal. ▷*See also* energy storage.

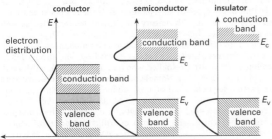

energy band ▶ The distribution of electrons over the various energy levels in a conductor, semiconductor, and insulator. There are no electrons in the "forbidden" band between E_c and E_v in semiconductors and insulators.

● **energy band** ▶ A concept used to explain the electrical properties of solids, particularly ▷semiconductors. Electrons need to have a minimum energy, E_v, to free them from the atoms of the solid. Below this energy they are said to be in the valence band. To be able to move through the solid, so that they constitute a current, they need to be above another energy level, E_c, in the so-called conduction band. In an insulator, E_c is significantly greater than E_v and there are effectively no electrons in the conduction band. In a conductor, there are many electrons with energy greater than E_c, and E_c may be less than E_v, i.e. the conduction and valence bands are very close or overlap. A pure semiconductor at ▷absolute zero behaves like an insulator, but the difference between E_c and E_v is small. With an increase in temperature (a measure of the average energy of the particles in the material), some electrons enter the conduction band. Also, the presence of impurities in a semiconductor crystal brings electrons of an intermediate energy level with it, since E_v and E_c vary from one material to another. Depending on the type of impurity, the number of electrons in either the conduction band or the valence band at a particular temperature, will increase, changing the electrical properties of the solid.

● **energy storage** ▶ The only practical means of storing energy are rechargeable ▷batteries and ▷accumulators (in which electrical energy is stored in the form of chemical energy), pumped storage systems (in which electrical energy is stored as gravitational potential energy; *see* hydroelectric power), and night storage heaters (in which electrical energy is stored as heat). All these methods compare very unfavourably with the natural process involved in the energy storage achieved by ▷fossil fuels. For example, a modern lead accumulator can store some 10^5 joules per kilogram, whereas the combustion of 1 kg of petrol will supply nearly 10^7 joules of stored energy. The storing of energy is important when ▷alternative energy sources are involved. For example, ▷solar power and ▷wind power supply energy intermittently, and not always when it is most needed. Pumped stor-

age is the only practical means of storing electrical energy on a large scale.

● **Enesco, Georges** ▶ (G. Enescu; 1881–1955) Romanian violinist and composer. He settled in Paris and had a long and brilliant performing career; he composed symphonies, sonatas, and nationalistic Romanian rhapsodies. A distinguished teacher, his pupils included Menuhin.

● **Enfield** ▶ A borough of N Greater London, created in 1965 from the former municipal borough. Its various industries included the Royal Small Arms Factory (1815–1989), which manufactured the famous Enfield rifles. Area: 55 sq km (31 sq mi). Population (1999): 257 417.

● **Engadin** ▶ (French name: Engadine) The Swiss part of the upper Inn Valley, divided into Upper Engadin and Lower Engadin. Tourism is important and it contains several winter-sports centres.

● **Engels, Friedrich** ▶ (1820–95) German socialist and chief collaborator of Karl ▷Marx. For a time he managed a factory in Manchester and was able to introduce Marx to English economic conditions and the British working-class movement. Among other works he wrote the *Condition of the Working Class in England in 1844* (1845). His *Anti-Dühring* (1878) systematizes ▷dialectical materialism. After Marx's death, he edited the last volume of *Das Kapital* (1885).

● **engineering** ▶ The systematic application of scientific knowledge to the design, creation, and use of structures and machines. Engineering has its roots in the constructions in classical times by military engineers of harbours, roads, aqueducts, tunnels, canals, and siege machines. ▷Civil engineering arose from the study and design of such static structures as bridges, dams, buildings, etc., whereas ▷mechanical engineering is concerned with dynamical systems, such as machinery and engines. Other important branches of engineering are ▷electrical engineering, aeronautical engineering, and ▷chemical engineering.

● **engineering drawing** ▶ A systematic method of producing a drawing to scale of machines, their components, or other technical structures to convey the shape, dimensions, and other information to the constructor. They usually consist of a series of orthogonal projections, side elevations, plans, and other views or details depending on the complexity of the object.

● **England** ▶ The largest political division in the ▷United Kingdom. With Wales to the W and Scotland to the N, it is separated from the mainland of Europe by the North Sea and the English Channel and from Ireland by the Irish Sea. It consists of two main zones: the lowlands, which extend across the Midlands, the SE, East Anglia, and the Fens, and the highlands of the Pennines and the Lake District in the N and the uplands of Dartmoor and Exmoor in the SW. The chief rivers are the Thames and the Severn. The centre of government and administration of the UK, England is also the wealthiest and most populous of the UK countries.

Economy: the development of industry has been a major contributor to England's wealth. Mineral extraction has historically been of importance and the more recent exploitation of North Sea oil and gas continues to make an important contribution to the economy. The main English coalfields were situated in the Midlands, Yorkshire, and the NE but production has declined greatly since the 1980s; there are now only 13 deep mines in operation (compared to some 800 in the 1950s). The production of iron ore has also declined in recent decades and there is an increased reliance on imports. Tin, mined for about 2000 years in Cornwall, is no longer produced. Other minerals include lead ore, china clay, salt, and potash. Manufacturing industries are centred on Greater London, Birmingham, Lancashire, Yorkshire, Tyneside, and Teeside, although there has been a dramatic decline in manufacturing employment in recent years. Only about 18% of the total workforce are now employed in manufacturing, compared to some 76% in service industries. The production of motor vehicles is centred on Dagenham, Luton, Cowley, and the West Midlands but many formerly British companies are now foreign-owned. Other major industries include heavy engineering, petrochemicals, and pharmaceuticals (Manchester), food processing (Liverpool), and steel processing (Sheffield). Despite the expansion of industries based on advanced technology, together with the reorganization and modernization of older industries, the decline of heavy industry (including shipbuilding), traditionally concentrated in the North and Merseyside, has led to high levels of unemployment in these areas. Agriculture has increased in productivity, although the number of people employed in this sector has decreased. Dairy farming is dominant in the W, while livestock rearing (especially sheep and cattle) is important in the hilly areas of the N and SW. The greatest proportion of crop land is in the E and SE, producing chiefly cereals, potatoes, and sugar beet. Horticulture is important in the E and SE and in the W Midlands. Fishing (centred on Hull and Grimsby) and tourism are also important sources of revenue.

History: there is much archaeological evidence of prehistoric settlement in England but historical records begin with the Roman occupation, from 43 AD until the early 5th century. Christianity was introduced in the 4th century, and conquests between the 3rd and 7th centuries by ▷Angles, ▷Saxons, and ▷Jutes led to the establishment of independent kingdoms (*see* Mercia; Northumbria; Wessex), which were united in the 9th century under the leadership of Wessex. By the late 800s the Danes had established themselves in the area that came to be known as the ▷Danelaw and from 1016 to 1042 the English were ruled successively by the Danish kings ▷Canute and ▷Hardecanute. The ▷Norman conquest (1066) ended the ▷Anglo-Saxon period of English history and established a new dynasty of Norman kings. The Crown was subsequently held by the ▷Angevins, who also ruled an extensive empire in France that was subsequently lost, except for Calais, in the ▷Hundred Years' War (1337–1453). In 1455 the rival claims of the Houses of ▷Lancaster and ▷York precipitated the Wars of the ▷Roses, which lasted until Richard III's defeat at Bosworth (1485) by Henry ▷Tudor. The 16th century saw the establishment of Protestantism in England (*see* Reformation), the formal union of England and Wales (*see* Union, Acts of), and, under Elizabeth I, a significant development in overseas exploration and trade. The consequent rivalry with Spain culminated in the English defeat of the ▷Armada (1588). The Tudors were succeeded by the ▷Stuarts in 1603, when James VI of Scotland ascended the English throne as ▷James I. The unpopularity of James and his son Charles I, especially with parliament, brought about the ▷Civil War, which ended with Charles' execution (1649) and the establishment of republican government. The Stuart ▷Restoration (1660) followed the fall of Oliver Cromwell's ▷Protectorate but the authoritarian and pro-Catholic policies of James II brought about his deposition in 1688 and the succession of William of Orange and his Stuart wife Mary. The crisis of the Glorious Revolution saw the emergence of the rival political groups known as ▷Whigs (later Liberals) and Tories. The Tories' association with the ▷Jacobites, who in 1714 threatened the Hanoverian succession (*see* Settlement, Act of), led to their political isolation until the late 18th century, a century that saw union with Scotland (1707), the development of ▷cabinet government during the administration of Sir Robert Walpole, and the loss of the American colonies (1783; *see* American Revolution). Following union with Ireland in 1801, England, Wales, Scotland, and Ireland became the ▷United Kingdom of ▷Great Britain and Ireland. Area: 130 360 sq km (50 332 sq mi). Population (1995 est): 48 903 000. Capital: London.

● **Engler, Gustav Heinrich Adolf** ▶ (1844–1930) German botanist, who proposed a system of plant classification that is still widely accepted. Engler adapted ▷Eichler's system (1883) to encompass the whole plant kingdom. Engler held several important administrative posts in plant science and was an expert on plant geography.

● **English** ▶ A West Germanic language spoken originally in Britain but now also in the USA, Canada, New Zealand, Australia, and many other parts of the world. It is the world's most widely known and used language. Its history may be divided into three periods. In the Old English period (c. 407–1100 AD), four dialects were spoken: Northumbrian, Mercian, Kentish, and West Saxon. The last became the standard form at this time as many translations of Latin works were made at Winchester during the reign of Alfred the Great. Middle English refers to the period from 1100 to 1500, when five dialects were spoken: Northern (developed from Northumbrian), West and East Midlands (diverging from Mercian), South Western (from West Saxon) and South Eastern (from Kentish). Each developed in

characteristic ways but in general the influence of French after the Norman conquest brought new vocabulary and sound patterns (*see also* Great Vowel Shift). Modern English covers the period from 1500 and was much influenced by the speech of London. English slowly became a relatively uninflected language with great flexibility in the way words may function. Its vocabulary is about half Germanic and half Romance with many other borrowings.

● **English art and architecture** ▶ Before the Norman conquest the art of the British Isles was identified with ▷Celtic art, some Roman, and some Anglo-Saxon art and architecture. Illuminated manuscripts constituted the outstanding contribution of Anglo-Saxon artists, and manuscripts of a high quality continued to be produced in the later middle ages. The Normans introduced ▷romanesque art and architecture, which became the first characteristic English architectural style. The table below shows the development of English architecture from the Norman conquest to the advent of the various international styles in the 20th century.

In painting, art did not become secular until Hans ▷Holbein the Younger came to the court of Henry VIII in the 16th century. Prominent among the followers of Holbein was the portrait miniaturist Nicholas ▷Hilliard, who established a tradition in this type of portraiture that was adopted by such painters as Samuel ▷Cooper and Richard ▷Cosway. In the 17th century the Flemish painters ▷Rubens and his student ▷Van Dyck, who worked in the court of both James I and Charles I, towered above their English contemporaries. Van Dyck greatly influenced the Dutch painter Peter ▷Lely, who also settled in London as did Godfrey ▷Kneller, who founded the first English academy of painting in 1711. Notable painters of the 18th century were ▷Hogarth, ▷Reynolds, and ▷Gainsborough. Romanticism found expression in the work of ▷Turner and ▷Constable and the 19th century also witnessed the formation of the ▷Pre-Raphaelite Brotherhood, which, with the work of William ▷Morris, influenced ▷Art Nouveau in England. The influence of Walter ▷Sickert led to the formation in 1911 of the ▷Camden Town group. The 20th century has produced outstanding sculptors, including ▷Epstein, ▷Hepworth, and Henry ▷Moore, the painters Augustus ▷John, Graham ▷Sutherland, Stanley ▷Spencer, L. S. ▷Lowry, Francis ▷Bacon, and David ▷Hockney, and the architects ▷Lutyens, ▷Spence, ▷Lasdun, and Richard ▷Rogers.

English art and architecture

	style	period
▷Norman		1066–1150
▷Gothic	▷Early English	13th century
	▷Decorated	1300–70
	▷Perpendicular	1370–1550
▷Renaissance	▷Tudor	1485–1560
	▷Elizabethan	1560–1600
	▷Jacobean	1600–25
	▷Palladianism (*see also* baroque)	1600–1750
	▷Queen Anne	1700–14
	▷Georgian	1714–1810
	▷Regency	1790–1830
Victorian	▷neoclassicism	1750–1850
	▷gothic revival	1820–1900

● **English Channel** ▶ (French name: La Manche) An arm of the Atlantic Ocean in NW Europe, between England and France. It is one of the busiest shipping lanes in the world. Many attempts at swimming the Channel (usually across the Strait of ▷Dover) have been made; the first successful one was by Capt Webb (1875). ▷*See also* Channel tunnel.

● **English Heritage** ▶ A public agency, founded in 1983, that protects and preserves historic buildings and monuments throughout England. Properly called the Historic Buildings and Monuments Commission for England, it determines preservation orders by "listing" buildings (*see* listed buildings) and "scheduling" monuments. Archaeological sites in the care of English Heritage include ▷Stonehenge and ▷Maiden Castle. Chairman: Sir Jocelyn Stevens.

● **English literature** ▶ The earliest works of the Old English period (407–1100 AD) are heroic poems, notably the epic *Beowulf*, which belong to a Germanic oral tradition of alliterative unrhymed verse and were not put into written form until the 7th century. There are also a number of remarkable shorter poems, such as the elegies *The Wanderer* and *The Seafarer*, and many poems on Christian subjects. Major Old English religious writers, such as Bede and Alcuin, wrote in Latin; English prose started with the translations from Latin made by King Alfred and developed in the *Anglo-Saxon Chronicle*, the compilation of which he initiated.

Norman-French displaced Old English as the dominant written language after the Conquest, but the native language, enriched by French, was firmly re-established in the 14th century in the Middle English poetry of Chaucer, whose works were indebted to Italian Renaissance authors, especially Dante, Petrarch, and Boccaccio. The native alliterative tradition continued in such poems as *Piers Plowman*, *Pearl*, and *Gawain and the Green Knight*. Printing was introduced in 1476 by Caxton, who published the culminating work of the ▷Arthurian legend, Malory's *Morte d'Arthur* (1485).

Although Chaucer had introduced Renaissance influences, it was not until the 16th century that the full effects of humanism were felt, especially under Elizabeth I and James I, whose reigns mark the golden age of poetry and drama. The sonnet was introduced by Wyatt and Surrey and polished by Sidney and others. Spenser produced the Elizabethan allegorical epic, *The Faerie Queene* (1590–96). The blank-verse plays of Kyd and Marlowe prepared the way for the dramas of Shakespeare (the outstanding figure in the whole of English literature), Jonson, and their 17th-century successors. Donne and the Metaphysical school are the most important poets of the early 17th century, while Milton dominates the latter part. Among the most influential prose works were the Authorized Version of the Bible and Bunyan's *The Pilgrim's Progress* (1678).

During the Restoration (from 1660), Dryden developed the ▷heroic couplet in his satires and made an important contribution to modern English prose in his criticism. Drama, curbed during the Interregnum, was revived in the comedies of Congreve and Wycherley. The classical ideals of the Augustan Age (c. 1690–1740) were embodied in the satirical verse of Pope and the essays of Addison and Steele and were maintained by Johnson, Goldsmith, and Sheridan, etc. Swift was the outstanding prose satirist of the period.

Various economic and social factors during the early 18th century contributed to the emergence of the novel, pioneered by Richardson, Fielding, Defoe, Smollett, Sterne, and various authors of the "gothic" novel of horror. It reached its full development in the works of Jane Austen, Walter Scott, Thackeray, the Brontës, Dickens, George Eliot, Trollope, Hardy, Conrad, and the American Henry James.

In the early 19th century the classicism of the previous period was challenged by the Romantic movement. Its precursor was Blake and its leading figures were Wordsworth, Coleridge, Keats, Shelley, and Byron. Their chief successors in the Victorian era were Tennyson, Browning, Matthew Arnold, and Swinburne. Macaulay, John Stuart Mill, Carlyle, Ruskin, and Pater were among the influential prose writers. At the turn of the century the comedies of Wilde and Shaw enlivened the English theatre; prior to World War I Kipling, Hardy, Yeats, Belloc, Chesterton, Wells, Housman, and de la Mare produced a distinguished body of verse as well as fiction and criticism. The poets associated with the war period include Brooke, Owen, Sassoon, and Graves.

Poetry between the World Wars was dominated by Eliot, Auden, MacNeice, Spender, and the later work of Yeats. Among the leading novelists and prose writers were Forster, Joyce, D. H. Lawrence, Woolf, Aldous Huxley, Orwell, Isherwood, Greene, and Evelyn Waugh. Between World War II and the present appeared the poems of Dylan Thomas, Philip Larkin, John Betjeman, Ted Hughes, and Thom Gunn; the plays of Osborne, Wesker, Pinter, Beckett, Joe Orton, Tom Stoppard, Terrence Rattigan, Peter Schaffer, Alan Ayckbourn, and Alan Bennett; and the novels of Angus Wilson, Kingsley Amis, Muriel Spark, Iris Murdoch, Anthony Powell, Anthony Burgess, Lawrence Durrell, William Golding, Doris Lessing, and Salman Rushdie.

● **English National Opera** ▶ (ENO) The name adopted by the Sadler's Wells Opera Company in 1974, five years after the company moved from the ▷Sadler's Wells Theatre to the London Coliseum. The company continues to present most of its operas in English. Its musical directors have included Sir Charles ▷Mackerras (1970–78), Sir Charles ▷Groves (1978–79), Mark Elder (1947– ; director 1979–93), Sian Edwards (1959– ; director 1993–96), and Paul Daniel (director 1996–). The present managing director is Dennis Marks (1948–).

● **English Nature** ▷*See* nature conservation.

● **English-Speaking Union** ▶ An organization, based in London, that promotes friendship and understanding between English-speaking countries. Founded by Sir Evelyn Wrench (1882–1966) in 1918, it has 160 branches in the UK, North America, Australasia, India, and the Caribbean.

● **engraving** ▶ A method of producing a reproductive plate by chiselling, carving, or biting the design onto a metal or wood plate. Intaglio engraving denotes such methods as ▷etching, ▷mezzotint, and soft- or hard-ground engraving, in which the printed impression pulls ink from inside the carved grooves. By contrast, relief engraving denotes methods, such as ▷woodcut, in which the carved-away areas are not inked. Intaglio engraving allows for extreme delicacy and detail; relief engraving is often exploited for illustrations, where force and clarity are needed.

● **Enigma machine** ▷*See* Bletchley Park.

● **Eniwetok** ▶ 11 30N 162 15E An atoll in the central Pacific Ocean in the ▷Marshall Islands. The population left in the 1940s, after which the USA carried out 47 atomic tests. In spite of the threat of radiation, the population returned in 1980 after contaminated soil was removed. Population (latest est): 715.

● **Enki** ▷*See* Ea.

● **enkephalins** ▷*See* encephalins.

● **Enlightenment** ▶ (*or* Age of Reason) An 18th-century philosophical movement that sought to replace orthodox authoritarian beliefs with rational scientific inquiry. During the 17th century, as scientific knowledge increased, such scholars as Newton, Locke, Pascal, and Descartes questioned accepted beliefs, and criticism of established society and assumptions spread throughout Europe. In France the ▷Philosophes (e.g. Voltaire) attacked established religion (*see* deism) and the Enlightenment beliefs in individual liberty and equality were embodied in the work of Rousseau and other ▷Encyclopedists. The movement provided the intellectual basis for the French Revolution but came to an end in the era of war and political reaction that followed. The so-called **enlightened despots** were those European monarchs (e.g. ▷Joseph II, Frederick the Great of Prussia, and Catherine the Great of Russia) who introduced reforms, based on the ideas of the Enlightenment, by authoritarian means.

● **Enlil** ▶ The Sumerian god of the sky and storms. He was the patron deity of ▷Nippur and with ▷Anu and ▷Ea formed the supreme trinity in the Sumerian pantheon.

● **Ennis** ▶ (Irish name: Inis) 52 50N 8 59W A market town in the W Republic of Ireland, the county town of Co Clare. It has a cathedral and a ruined 13th-century Franciscan friary. Population (1991): 13 750.

● **Enniskillen** ▶ (*or* Inniskilling) 54 21N 7 48W A town in Northern Ireland, in Fermanagh between Upper and Lower Lough Erne. A strongly Protestant town, it resisted James II in 1689 and has two regiments named after it. In 1987, IRA bombing at a Remembrance Day parade resulted in 11 dead and over 60 injured. Population (1991): 11 436.

● **Ennius, Quintus** ▶ (238–169 BC) Roman poet. After service in the second Punic War, he was brought to Rome by the elder Cato in 204 and became a Roman citizen in 184. His works include tragic dramas adapted from the Greek, philosophical poems, epigrams, and the *Annals*, a national epic in 18 books narrating the history of Rome from Aeneas to his own time. Only fragments of his works survive.

● **Enoch** ▶ An Old Testament patriarch. **The Books of Enoch** are two biblical books ascribed to him; they were in fact written in the 2nd century BC and 1st century AD respectively. The first, a composite work of Jewish origin, is a series of apocalyptic visions. The second is of Hellenistic origin and records revelations supposedly given to Enoch, his journey to heaven, and advice to his children.

● **enosis** ▷*See* EOKA.

● **Enragés** ► (French: Madmen) Members of an extremist French Revolutionary group (1793). Led by Jacques Roux (d. 1794), they demanded direct government action to alleviate food shortages and to help the poor. Actively encouraging food riots, their leaders were arrested by the Committee of ▷Public Safety and their extremist role was adopted by the Hébertists (*see* Hébert, Jacques-René).

● **Enschede** ► 52 13N 06 55E A town in the E Netherlands, in Overijssel province. It is an important centre of the Dutch cotton industry. Population (1996 est): 147 832.

● **Ensor, James Sydney, Baron** ► (1860–1949) Belgian painter; his father was English but he was born and spent most of his life in Ostend. He was initially condemned for what was thought his crude technique, but the originality of his grotesque imagery of masks and skeletons, as in *Entry of Christ into Brussels* (1888), was admired in the 1920s.

● **Entebbe** ► 0 05N 39 29E A town in Uganda, in Buganda on the NW shore of Lake Victoria. It was the administrative centre of Uganda until 1958. It contains Uganda's international airport, where, in 1976, Israeli hostages taken from a hijacked French plane by Palestinian guerrillas were rescued by Israeli troops. Population (1991): 41 638.

● **entellus** ▷*See* langur.

● **Entente Cordiale** ► (1904) An agreement between France and Britain. During the 19th century, colonial expansion, especially in Africa, caused tension between France, Britain, and Germany. France feared a German war and Britain and France, partly through Edward VII's efforts, signed the Entente Cordiale. This was not an alliance but a mutual recognition of each other's colonial interests, especially France's in Morocco and Britain's in Egypt. The agreement brought greater diplomatic cooperation against German pressure.

● **enterprise zone** ► An area in the UK in which commercial and industrial properties are exempted from rates and certain taxes. First introduced in 1981, they were designed to attract new business to inner city sites and other depressed regions. The first ten included parts of Belfast, Clydebank, Greater Manchester, the Isle of Dogs, and Tyneside. A further 17 were added in 1983–84 and N Lancashire was added in 1993.

● **enthalpy** ► (*H*) A thermodynamic property of a system equal to its internal energy plus the product of its pressure and volume. The change in enthalpy (Δ*H*) in an **endothermic chemical reaction** equals the heat absorbed; in an **exothermic reaction** the change in enthalpy (−Δ*H*) is the heat evolved.

● **entomology** ► The study of insects. Entomology probably has its origins in the observations of ▷Aristotle. Modern entomology dates from the 17th century, when the introduction of microscopy enabled fine details of insect anatomy to be described; for instance by Jan ▷Swammerdam. Today attention is focused especially on insect pests, to aid their control.

● **entrepreneur** ► An individual who is prepared to commit capital and to initiate a commercial venture. Entrepreneurship is often counted as a fourth (instigating) factor of production (with land, labour, and capital).

● **entropy** ► A measure of the disorder of a system, used in ▷thermodynamics. Thus a solid has less entropy than a liquid since its constituent particles are in a more ordered state. Originally defined by Rudolf ▷Clausius in 1854 in connection with the second law of thermodynamics, the change in entropy of a reversible system is equal to the energy absorbed by the system divided by the thermodynamic temperature at which the change takes place. The entropy of a closed system never decreases during a thermodynamic process: if it increases the process is irreversible; if it is unchanged it is reversible. ▷*See also* heat death of the universe.

● **Enugu** ► 6 20N 7 29E A city in S Nigeria. It developed following the discovery of coal in 1909 and is now a mining, manufacturing, and trade centre. It contains part of the University of Nigeria (1962). Population (1996 est): 316 100.

● **E number** ▷*See* food additives.

● **Enver Pasha** ► (1881–1922) Turkish soldier and politician, who led the ▷Young Turk revolution of 1908. During World War I he was one of the three real rulers of the Ottoman Empire. His aim was to unite the Turks of central Asia with those of Turkey. He was killed in Asia fighting the Bolsheviks.

● **environment** ► The surroundings in which an organism lives, which are affected by physical and chemical factors as well as by the activities of other organisms. The damage to the earth caused by human activities has been a major concern during the last 50 years. In the UK, the Department of the Environment is responsible for a wide range of matters relating to environmental protection, including conservation areas (*see* nature conservation), land use and planning, and ▷energy sources. ▷*See* acid rain; balance of nature; conservation; endangered species; greenhouse effect; ozone layer; pollution.

● **enzymes** ► An important group of proteins that act as biological catalysts, i.e. they speed up (or slow down) the rate of chemical reactions in living organisms. Enzymes are manufactured by cells according to the ▷genetic code carried by the chromosomes; because each enzyme catalyses a specific reaction, it is the enzymes that determine the function of the cell. The structure of enzymes and the nature of their active sites (where they bind to reacting molecules) can be determined by such techniques as X-ray diffraction. Control of ▷metabolism is largely exerted through regulation of enzyme production and activity. Many enzymes require associated nonprotein ▷coenzymes to function properly.

● **Eocene epoch** ▷*See* Tertiary period.

● **eohippus** ► An extinct ancestor of the ▷horse, also called *Hyracotherium* or dawn horse, that lived in the Eocene epoch (55 million to 40 million years ago). About 28 cm tall, it was a browsing forest dweller with a short neck and had four toes on the forefoot and three on the hindfoot. ▷*See* Hipparion.

● **EOKA** ► (Ethniki Organosis Kipriakou Agonos) The National Organization of Cypriot Struggle formed in about 1955 by Georgios ▷Grivas with the support of Archbishop ▷Makarios III. Its aim was to drive the British forces from Cyprus by guerrilla action and to achieve *enosis* (union) with Greece. Disbanded when Cyprus became independent (1959), it was revived by Grivas in 1971 to achieve *enosis*.

● **Eos** ▷*See* Aurora.

● **Eötvös, Roland von, Baron** ► (1848–1919) Hungarian physicist whose studies of gravity established that inertial and gravitational mass are identical, which influenced Einstein. He also developed a torsion balance to measure accurately variations in gravitational force and introduced the concept of molecular surface tension.

● **Epaminondas** ► (c. 418–362 BC) Theban general and military strategist, who defeated Sparta at ▷Leuctra in 371, thereby ending the military supremacy of Sparta in Greece. He was the first to use cavalry to support infantry in a coordinated attack and his military innovations influenced both Philip II and Alexander the Great of Macedon. He died in the battle of Mantinea, in which the Spartans were defeated.

● **Épernay** ► 49 02N 3 58E A town in NE France, in the Marne department on the River Marne. A centre for the wine industry of Champagne, it has famous underground wine cellars. Population (1989): 28 000.

● **ephedrine** ► A drug with effects resembling those of ▷adrenaline. It stimulates the heart, dilates the bronchi (air passages to the lungs), constricts the blood vessels, and has marked effects on the nervous system. Ephedrine is used as a nasal decongestant and also in the treatment of asthma. Side effects include trembling and feelings of anxiety.

● **ephemeral** ► A plant that completes its life cycle—from germination to seed production—in under a year, enabling more than one generation to be produced within a year. Many common weeds, such as groundsel, are ephemerals.

● **ephemeris** ▶ (Greek: diary) A reference manual, usually published annually, that is used in astronomical observation and navigation. It lists the predicted positions of the sun, moon, and planets in the forthcoming year and also gives times of eclipses, stellar positions, etc.

● **ephemeris time** ▷See time.

● **Ephesians, Epistle of Paul to the** ▶ A New Testament book that originated as a circular letter from the Apostle Paul to churches in Asia Minor. Written about 60 AD, it deals with a number of religious and moral points and stresses the equality of Jewish and Gentile Christians.

● **Ephesus** ▶ An ancient Greek city and trading centre on the Ionian coast of ▷Asia Minor. ▷Croesus of ▷Lydia captured it in 550 BC. It thrived under both the Persians and Alexander the Great. In Roman times Ephesus was rivalled only by ▷Alexandria as a commercial centre. It was sacked by the ▷Goths in 262 AD. ▷See also Artemis, Temple of.

● **Ephraim, tribe of** ▶ One of the 12 ▷tribes of Israel. It claimed descent from Ephraim, the son of Joseph and grandson of Jacob and Rachel. It occupied mountainous territory NW of the Dead Sea.

● **epic** ▶ A long narrative poem concerning a heroic theme and written in an appropriately dignified style. The *Iliad* and the *Odyssey* of Homer (8th century BC) are the earliest epics in Western literature and are the models of Virgil's *Aeneid* (c. 29–19 BC), in which the hero Aeneas is seen as representing the national spirit of Rome. The *Aeneid* inspired later national epics, such as Camões' *Os Lusíadas* (1572) and Ronsard's *Franciade* (1572). In English literature, examples include the Old English *Beowulf* (8th century AD), Spenser's *Faerie Queene* (1589–96), and Milton's *Paradise Lost* (1667).

● **epicentre** ▷See earthquake.

● **Epictetus** ▶ (c. 60–110 AD) Stoic philosopher. A freed slave, Epictetus was banished, with other philosophers, from Rome in 89 AD and settled in Epirus. He taught that loving one's enemies, repudiating pleasure, and understanding that all men are brothers are ways to serenity. Epictetus' teachings were preserved by his pupil ▷Arrian. ▷See also Stoicism.

● **Epicureanism** ▶ A school of philosophy founded by ▷Epicurus around 300 BC in Athens. He taught that the highest good was pleasure and the avoidance of pain, based on tranquillity of mind and conscience. Many seeking a licence for the pursuit of pleasure have styled themselves Epicureans, giving the term its common sense of "unashamed sensualist." True Epicureans, however, seek serenity through detachment from worldly affairs.

● **Epicurus** ▶ (341–270 BC) Greek philosopher and founder of the

Epicurus ▶ A Hellenistic portrait bust (Louvre). He taught that it is impossible to live pleasurably , without living wisely, well, and justly and impossible to live wisely, well, and justly without living pleasurably.

school of ▷Epicureanism. In 306 BC he began teaching in a garden in Athens. Virtuous and temperate, he was a good friend and citizen but avoided politics, following his maxim "Live unseen and unknown." His surviving works are few and fragmentary but his philosophy, especially his ▷atomism, was expounded by ▷Lucretius.

● **Epidauros** ▶ A city state of ancient Greece, situated across the Saronic Gulf from ▷Athens. Its sanctuary of ▷Asclepius was famous in antiquity. Patients asleep in the temple were visited by the god in their dreams and treated by his priests next morning; grateful inscriptions record numerous cures. The 4th-century BC theatre (part of the temple complex) is sufficiently preserved to be still used for plays.

● **epidemiology** ▶ The science that investigates the incidence and causative factors of diseases that are associated with a particular environment or way of life. Epidemiologists have enlarged their studies from the classical epidemics of communicable diseases, such as smallpox and cholera, to include noncommunicable diseases. Thus they have demonstrated the connection between cigarette smoking and lung cancer, diet and coronary heart disease, etc.

● **epidermis** ▶ The outermost layer of cells in animals and plants. In lower animals (invertebrates) it often secretes a protective cuticle. In higher animals (including mammals) it forms the outer layer of the ▯skin. In plants the epidermis usually consists of a single layer of cells, but aerial organs gain extra protection from a noncellular waxy cuticle. Both layers prevent dehydration of internal tissues, and lessen damage by bacteria, fungi, and such pests as aphids.

● **epididymis** ▷See testis.

● **epidural** ▷See anaesthesia.

● **epiglottis** ▶ A leaf-shaped flap of cartilage at the root of the tongue that prevents food and fluid from entering the windpipe during swallowing. As it is swallowed, the food presses the epiglottis down against the opening of the larynx (at the top of the windpipe). This, combined with the reflex upward movement of the larynx that occurs during swallowing, effectively seals off the entrance to the windpipe.

● **epilepsy** ▶ A disorder of the brain characterized by recurrent seizures of sudden onset. Epilepsy is common—Dostoievski, Van Gogh, Julius Caesar, and Byron all suffered from it. Generalized seizures affect the whole brain and are of two types. In tonic-clonic seizures (formerly called grand mal) the patient suddenly becomes stiff, loses consciousness, and has convulsions. The seizure lasts a few minutes. Absence seizures (formerly called petit mal) are most common in children, who suddenly lose consciousness but do not fall down; the eyes may stare blankly and twitch. These seizures last only a few seconds. Partial seizures affect one part of the brain, most often the temporal lobe, lasting 0.5–2 minutes. They may feature abnormal movements (e.g. plucking at clothing) and sensory hallucinations. All types of seizure are controlled with antiepileptic (anticonvulsant) drugs.

● **Épinal** ▶ 48 10N 6 28E A town in E France, the capital of the Vosges department on the River Moselle. It is the centre for a region manufacturing cotton goods and artificial fibres. Population (1982): 40 954.

● **epinephrine** ▷See adrenaline.

● **Epiphany** ▶ (or Twelfth Day) A Christian feast celebrated on 6 Jan. In Eastern Orthodox Churches it commemorates the baptism of Jesus. Introduced to the West in the 4th century, it developed as a celebration of the coming of the ▷Magi to Bethlehem, representing the manifestation (Greek: *epiphaneia*) of Christ to the Gentiles. **Twelfth Night** is the night preceding Epiphany and traditionally devoted to festivities and entertainments. In several countries gifts are exchanged on Epiphany rather than at Christmas.

● **epiphyte** ▶ A plant that grows on another plant for support. Epiphytes are not parasites: some obtain nourishment from decaying plant remains and many solve the problem of obtaining water by developing such structures as aerial roots. Some orchids are epiphytic.

● **Epirus** ▶ (or Ípiros) A coastal region of NW Greece and S Albania, bordering on the Ionian Sea. Its tribes were united in the 4th century

BC in a kingdom that reached its peak under ▷Pyrrhus in the early 3rd century BC. Sacked by the Romans in 167, it became part of the province of Macedonia in 148 BC. In the 13th century AD it briefly formed an independent kingdom before falling to the Serbs and Albanians and then (1430) to the Ottoman Turks. It was divided between Greece and Albania in 1913.

● **episcopacy** ▶ In Christian Churches, government by bishops. The biblical basis of episcopacy is equivocal, and many Protestant Churches, for example the Congregational and Presbyterian, have adopted different methods. In the Roman Catholic and Orthodox Churches the episcopal hierarchy is seen as a continuation of the original group of apostles (see apostolic succession). Among the Reformed Churches episcopal government is retained in whole or in part by Anglicans, Methodists, and Lutherans.

● **Episcopal Church** ▷See Anglican Communion.

● **epistemology** ▶ The philosophical discipline that considers the nature, basis, and limits of knowledge. Ancient Greek philosophers examined the relations between knowledge, truth, and belief, and the question of whether knowledge exists independently of a knower. ▷Locke and ▷Kant, however, first treated epistemology as fundamental to all philosophical and scientific enquiry. It is one of the three main branches of modern ▷philosophy.

● **Epistles** ▶ The 21 books of the ▷New Testament that were written as letters. These are arranged in two groups, those by Paul (13) and those by others (7), divided by the Epistle to the Hebrews, of which the author is unknown. Of Paul's letters nine are to specific churches and four to individuals. The remainder are attributed to James, Peter (2), John (3), and Jude. In the liturgy of many Christian Churches, the Epistle is the name of the first of two passages of Scripture recited or sung at the celebration of the Eucharist, the second being the Gospel. It is usually a passage from the New Testament Epistles but may be from the Old Testament, Acts, or Revelation.

● **epithelium** ▶ A tissue that forms the linings of the mouth, nose, pharynx, intestines, respiratory tract, and the skin. There are different types of epithelia specialized for different functions. For example, the cells of the intestinal epithelium are glandular, secreting digestive enzymes, while the skin epithelium produces a tough protective layer of keratin.

● **EPNS** ▷See German silver.

● **epoch** ▷See geological time scale.

● **epoxy resin** ▶ A type of synthetic ▷resin made by polymerizing groups containing a three-membered ring that includes the –O– atom (epoxy group). Epoxy resins are viscous liquids but set to hard clear solids on the addition of such curing agents as amines. They are used as adhesives, the resin and the curing agent being mixed immediately before use.

● **Epping** ▶ 51 40N 0 06E A market and residential town in SE England, in Essex. It stands on the edge of **Epping Forest**, one of the country's largest and most popular recreational grounds, formerly part of the ancient forest of Waltham, which once covered the whole of Essex. Population (1991): 11 413.

● **EPR paradox** ▶ A paradox put forward in 1935 by Albert Einstein, Boris Podolsky, and Nathan Rosen as an attack on the completeness of quantum mechanics (see quantum theory) as a description of reality. Their original idea concerned a thought experiment involving simultaneous measurements of position and momentum. A simplified example is to consider a particle with zero spin decaying into two identical particles with nonzero spin. Since spin is conserved overall, these particles must have equal spins in opposite directions. The particles are assumed to move apart to a considerable separation and the spin direction of one is measured. At that instant the observer also knows the spin direction of the other (because it is opposite). However, according to the ideas of quantum mechanics, the spin of a particular particle is not fixed until the measurement is made—the particle is in an indeterminate state involving superposition of both possible spin directions. It seems, according to quantum mechanics, that making a measurement on one particle forces the other, many metres away, to adopt the opposite spin. Einstein and his collabora-

tors argued that this type of behaviour would imply a form of instantaneous action at a distance, indicating that quantum mechanics is incomplete. They believed that as yet undiscovered hidden variables must be involved in the "true" theory. The alternative quantum-mechanical explanation of the paradox is that the particles are still part of the same system even when widely separated (a condition known as **quantum entanglement**). In 1961 John Bell published work that led to experimental investigation of EPR phenomena (see Bell's theorem). The results supported the quantum entanglement interpretation rather than the hidden-variables theory.

● **Epsom** ▶ 51 20N 0 16W A town in SE England, in Surrey, noted for horse racing on Epsom Downs (the Derby and Oaks are famous races held here). Population (1997 est, with Ewell): 69 700.

● **Epsom salts** ▶ Hydrated magnesium sulphate ($MgSO_4.7H_2O$), which occurs as **epsomite** and in solution in a spring at Epsom (Surrey). It is used as a laxative and for sizing and fireproofing textiles.

● **Epstein, Sir Jacob** ▶ (1880–1959) British sculptor of US birth. Working in London after 1905, he achieved notoriety with his nude figures for the British Medical Association (1907–08; later destroyed) and his memorial tomb to Oscar Wilde (1912) for a Parisian cemetry. After 1912 he experimented with avantgarde sculpture, influenced by primitive art, and provoked criticism with such sculptures as *Rima*, a memorial to the author William Hudson (1925; Hyde Park), and *Genesis* (1931). However, his bronze portrait busts of such celebrities as Conrad (1924), Einstein (1933), T. S. Eliot, and Vaughan Williams (1950) were praised. His last works included *Christ in Majesty* (1957) for Llandaff Cathedral and *St Michael and the Devil* (1958) for Coventry Cathedral.

● **Equal Opportunities Commission** ▷See women's movement.

● **equation** ▶ A mathematical statement in which two expressions, usually containing at least one unknown quantity, are equated. For example, the expression $2x + 4 = 8$ is an equation that can be solved, to give a value of 2 for x: this is known as the root of the equation. Equations are also used to show the general interdependence of several quantities, without necessarily finding their specific values. The degree of an equation is equal to the highest value of the exponent of the variable. A **linear equation** is of the first degree and has the form $y = mx + c$. A ▷graph of such an equation is a straight line, which (in the Cartesian ▷coordinate system) has a ▷gradient equal to m and cuts the y-axis at c. A ▷quadratic equation is of the second degree, i.e. contains terms in x^2. Two or more equations in which all the variables must obey all the equations are called **simultaneous equations**. For a complete solution of simultaneous equations there must be as many equations as variables. ▷See also chemical reaction.

● **equation of time** ▷See sundial.

● **equator** ▶ The great circle around the earth at latitude 0°, lying midway between the poles in a plane at right angles to the earth's axis. It is 40 076 km (24 902 mi) long and divides the N from the S hemisphere.

● **Equatorial Guinea, Republic of** ▶ A small country in W central Africa, on the Gulf of Guinea. It consists of two main parts: mainland Río Muni and the island of Bioko (formerly Fernando Po), as well as the island of Pagalu (formerly Annobón) to the SW and several smaller islands. Río Muni is mainly tropical forest, with a coastal plain rising gradually to over 1000 m (3000 ft) in the interior; Bioko is dominated by three extinct volcanoes, the highest of which reaches 3007 m (9865 ft). The inhabitants are mainly ▷Fang, Fernandinos, and the indigenous Bubi (descendants of slaves from West Africa), who inhabit Bioko.
Economy: chiefly subsistence agriculture, the main cash crops being cocoa on Bioko, and coffee in Río Muni, where timber is also produced. There is little industry, apart from fish processing on Bioko. Although a bonanza from the country's previously unexploited oil resources made Equatorial Guinea the world's fastest growing economy in the early 2000s, it remains one of the world's poorest countries.
History: formerly a Spanish colony, the area became two Spanish provinces in 1959. The country attained some internal self-government in 1964 and was one of the last of the African colonial

territories to become independent (in 1968). In 1975 Nigerian immigrant workers were expelled after 50 years in the country, and this damaged the economy. In 1979 the dictatorial life president Francisco Macías Nguema (1924–79) was overthrown and executed in a coup led by Lt Col Teodoro Obiang Nguema Mbasogo, who became president. In 1992 he appointed a transitional government to establish multiparty democracy and organize elections, which were held in 1993; these resulted in victory for the ruling party but were condemned as unfair by international observers. Further elections in 1996 were boycotted by the opposition parties, which were declared illegal in 1997–98. The United Nations has continued to express concern about violations of human rights in the country.

Republic of Equatorial Guinea

Head of state	President Teodoro Obiang Nguema Mbasogo
Official languages	Spanish and French
Official currency	CFA (Communauté financière africaine) franc of 100 centimes
Area	28 051 sq km (10 831 sq mi)
Population (1997 est)	443 000
Capital and main port	Malabo (formerly Santa Isabel)

● **equestrianism** ▶ The art of horsemanship. As a sport, governed by the Fédération équestre internationale (founded 1921), it involves ▷showjumping, ▷dressage, and ▷horse trials.

● **equilibrium** ▶ The state of a system in which it remains unchanged because opposing forces acting on it balance each other out. A mechanical system is said to be in stable equilibrium if it returned to equilibrium after a small disturbance. In unstable equilibrium the forces only just balance each other and a small disturbance will destroy the equilibrium.

A body is said to be in **thermal equilibrium** if no heat exchange is occurring between it and its surroundings or within it (*see* thermodynamics, zeroth law).

In **chemical equilibrium**, the forward and back reactions of a reversible reaction proceed at such rates that the concentrations of the products and reactants reach stable values. In the reaction aA + bB ↔ cC + dD, the ratio of the products of the concentrations, i.e. $[C]^c[D]^d/[A]^a[B]^b$, is called the **equilibrium constant** of the reaction at a particular temperature.

In economics, equilibrium is achieved when supply and demand in a market balance each other and prices are therefore stable.

● **equinox** ▶ Either of the two points at which the ▷ecliptic intersects the celestial equator (*see* celestial sphere). The ecliptic represents the apparent annual path of the sun around the celestial sphere. The sun crosses the celestial equator from S to N at the **vernal** (*or* spring) **equinox** (21 March). It crosses from N to S at the **autumnal equinox** (23 Sept). At the equinoxes the centre of the sun is above and below the horizon for an equal time, and night and day are then of almost equal duration.

● **Equisetum** ▷*See* horsetail.

● **equity** ▶ (finance) ▷*See* stocks and shares.

● **equity** ▶ (law) The body of rules developed by the Court of ▷Chancery to achieve a fair result in cases in which the application of ▷common law would fail to do so. The historical distinction between the common law and equity is due to the failure of the common law to provide a remedy in certain cases, bringing about the custom of applying for redress to the king, who referred the question to the Lord Chancellor's court. Here the rules of equity developed separately from but by the same method (judicial precedent) as the common law. The two systems were amalgamated in 1875 with the establishment of the High Court of Justice. Now all ▷courts of law administer both law and equity, the rules of equity prevailing if in conflict with the common law. ▷*See also* natural justice.

● **Equity** ▶ (British Actors' Equity Association) A trade union for professional actors in Britain, established in 1929. Professional performance in the theatre, films, TV, or radio is not possible without an Equity membership card, which is very difficult to acquire as Equity strictly controls entry to avoid overcrowding in the profession. Similar organizations exist in Canada, the USA, and elsewhere.

● **equivalence** ▶ The relationship between two mathematical or logical statements linked so that one is true if and only if the other is true. For example "*a* is greater than *b*" is equivalent to "*b* is less than *a*."

● **era** ▷*See* geological time scale.

● **Erasistratus of Ceos** ▶ (3rd century BC) Greek physician, who differentiated between sensory and motor nerves and described the heart as carrying both air and blood around the body.

● **Erasmus, Desiderius** ▶ (1466–1536) Christian humanist and writer, born at Rotterdam. He was perhaps the most influential of Renaissance thinkers and studied and taught all over Europe. He produced many original works and compilations, including *Encomium Moriae* (*Praise of Folly*; 1509), written to amuse his host in England, Thomas ▷More. His translation of the Greek New Testament, the first ever, conclusively exposed the Vulgate as a second-hand document. He opposed dogmatism and priestly power, yet remained impartial throughout the Lutheran conflict with the papacy.

● **Erasmus, St** ▶ (*or* St Elmo) ▷*See* St Elmo's fire.

● **Erastianism** ▶ The subjection of ecclesiastical affairs to secular authority. It is named after Thomas Erastus (1524–83), a Swiss theologian who opposed the strict views of ▷Calvinists. He argued that the civil authority has complete power in affairs both of church and state. Richard Hooker defended the argument in England in *Ecclesiastical Polity* (1594). The ▷Church of England's subjection to the Crown is sometimes called Erastian.

● **Eratosthenes of Cyrene** ▶ (c. 276–c. 194 BC) Greek astronomer; a friend of ▷Archimedes. His calculation of the earth's circumference, obtained by measuring the sun's position at the summer solstice at two different places, was accurate to within a thousand kilometres.

● **Erbil** ▷*See* Irbil.

● **erbium** ▶ (Er) A lanthanide element, named like ▷yttrium, ▷ytterbium, and ▷terbium after Ytterby, a village in Sweden near which lanthanide-rich ores are found. It forms an oxide (Er_2O_3) and halides (e.g. $ErCl_3$). It is added to phosphors, glasses, and alloys. At no 68; at wt 167.26; mp 1529°C; bp 2868°C.

● **Ercilla, Alonso de** ▶ (1533–94) Spanish poet. A courtier of ▷Philip II, he fought the Araucanian Indians in Chile. His epic *La Araucana* (Part I, 1569; Part 2, 1578; Part 3, 1589–90) is noted for its realistic descriptive passages and its sympathetic treatment of the Indians.

● **Erebus, Mount** ▶ 77 40S 167 20E An active volcano on Ross Island, in the Antarctic. Discovered in 1841, it was climbed in 1908. Height: 3794 m (12 520 ft).

● **Eretria** ▶ An ancient Greek city in ▷Euboea. An early leader in commerce and colonization, Eretria was defeated by ▷Chalcis about 700 BC, after which it declined in importance. The Persians sacked Eretria in 490 BC. It was rebuilt and joined the ▷Delian League, but it never regained its former significance.

● **Erevan** ▷*See* Yerevan.

● **Erfurt** ▶ 50 59N 11 00E A city in S Germany, on the River Gera. One of the oldest German cities, it joined the Hanseatic League in the 15th century and was of great commercial importance in the 16th century. Notable buildings include the cathedral (1154–1476) and the 13th-century Church of St Severus. Its university, established in 1392, was closed in 1816. Martin Luther studied there (1501–05). Industries include the manufacture of machinery, electrical equipment, textiles, and footwear. Population (1996 est): 211 108.

● **erg** ▶ The unit of energy in the ▷c.g.s. system equal to the work done when a force of one dyne acts through a distance of one centimetre. 1 erg = 10^{-7} joule.

● **ergonomics** ▶ The study of the psychological and physical factors that can be used to improve the design of both machines and systems for human use. In the USA the term human-factors engineering is widely used and in other parts of the world ergonomics is known as psychological engineering. The study finds application in many fields, including astronautics, the design of aircraft and cars, and a wide variety of industrial processes. Although it is a young science, having largely grown up since World War II, most university engineering courses now include it.

● **ergosterol** ▷*See* vitamin D.

● **ergot** ▶ A disease caused by the fungus *Claviceps purpurea*, which affects cereals and grasses, especially rye. In affected plants a hard black fungal body develops in place of the grain. Consumption of bread made with diseased grain produces the symptoms of **ergotism**—gangrene of the fingers and toes or convulsions. The gangrenous form of ergotism is accompanied by inflammation and pain in the affected part and in the middle ages it was called St Anthony's fire, since a pilgrimage to St Anthony's tomb was believed to result in a cure. Drugs obtained from ergot include ergometrine, used to induce childbirth, and ergotamine, for relieving migraine.

● **Erhard, Ludwig** ▶ (1897–1977) German statesman and economist; Christian Democratic chancellor (1963–66). As minister for economic affairs (1949–63), he was largely responsible for German industrial recovery after World War II. He succeeded Adenauer as chancellor and later became honorary chairman of the Christian Democratic Party.

● **Erica** ▷*See* heath.

● **Ericsson, John** ▶ (1803–89) US naval engineer, born in Sweden, who in 1836 invented the screw propeller, which replaced paddle wheels in ships. Ericsson also designed the ▷ironclad *Monitor*, launched in 1862, which was the first warship to have an armoured revolving turret.

● **Eric the Red** ▶ (late 10th century) Norwegian explorer. Exiled as a child with his father, he was brought up in Iceland. In 982 he set out from Iceland on an exploration westwards and reached Greenland, where he established the first European colony (c. 986). He was the father of ▷Leif Eriksson.

● **Eridanus** ▶ A large constellation in the S sky, named after a river in ancient mythology. The only bright star is ▷Achernar.

● **Eridu** ▶ A city of ancient ▷Sumer, SW of ▷Ur (S Iraq), continuously occupied from around 5000 to 600 BC. Excavations (1946–49) revealed a ▷ziggurat, probably devoted to the worship of Eridu's patron deity ▷Ea.

● **Erie** ▶ 42 07N 80 05W A city in the USA, in Pennsylvania on Lake Erie. Founded in 1753, it is a Great Lakes port and ships coal, timber, iron, and oil. It is also a major industrial business centre. Population (1996 est): 105 270.

● **Erie, Lake** ▶ The fourth largest of the Great Lakes in North America, between Canada and the USA. Linked with Lake Ontario via the Welland Ship Canal, it forms part of the St Lawrence Seaway system. Its shallow depth causes rapid freezing and it is closed to navigation during winter. Area: 25 718 sq km (9930 sq mi).

● **Erigena, John Scotus** ▶ (c. 800–c. 877 AD) Medieval philosopher, probably born in Ireland. He is said to have travelled widely and after about 846 lived under the protection of Charles the Bald in France, where he was made head of the court school at Paris. He defied ecclesiastical orthodoxy in his works on predestination and cosmology, which lean towards ▷Neoplatonism, Pelagianism (*see* Pelagius), and ▷pantheism.

● **Erik XIV** ▶ (1533–77) King of Sweden (1560–68), whose ambitions in the Baltic led to an inconclusive war with Denmark (1563–70). He unsuccessfully sought marriage with Elizabeth I of England. After becoming insane, he was deposed and imprisoned.

● **Erinyes** ▶ (*or* Furies) In Greek legend, spirits of vengeance who lived in the underworld and ruthlessly pursued all evildoers. They were three in number and were named (in later writers) Allecto, Tisiphone, and Megaera. In Roman legend they were known as the Furies (Latin *Furiae* or *Dirae*). ▷*See also* Eumenides.

● **Eris** ▶ A Greek goddess personifying strife. She was the sister of ▷Ares. She threw a golden apple inscribed "To the Fairest" among the gods at the wedding feast of Peleus and Thetis. Aphrodite, Hera, and Athena each claimed the apple. The decision was referred to ▷Paris, who chose Aphrodite because she offered him in return the most

beautiful woman as his wife. This myth, known as the Judgment of Paris, explains the origin of the ▷Trojan War.

Eritrea ▶ Troops of the Eritrean People's Liberation Front, including many women fighters.

● **Eritrea** ▶ A country in NE Africa, bordering on the Red Sea. It consists of a narrow coastal plain rising inland to the Ethiopian plateau.

Economy: agriculture and industry, producing sorghum, livestock, hides, fish, salt, textiles, and footwear, were devastated in the war of independence but are now being restored.

History: made an Italian colony in 1890, it became the base for the Italian invasions of Ethiopia in 1896 and 1936. The area came under British administration in 1941 and was federated as an autonomous unit of Ethiopia in 1952. In 1962 it became an integral part of the Ethiopian empire giving rise to political discontent. During the 1970s this developed into a bloody civil war; many major towns fell to the separatists but the Ethiopian government, anxious to retain its only two ports (Assab and Massawa), refused to grant independence. Despite a major Ethiopian offensive in 1978, backed by Soviet and Cuban aid, the separatists retained control of much of Eritrea throughout the 1980s. In 1991 an alliance of the Eritrean People's Liberation Front and Tigrean forces defeated ▷Mengistu's army; a provisional Eritrean government was formed and full independence was achieved in 1993. In 1998–99 and 2000 border tensions between Eritrea and Ethiopia led to fighting between national forces.

Eritrea

Head of state	President Issaias Afewerki
Official languages	English and Arabic; African languages are also spoken
Official religions	Coptic Christian and Muslim
Official currency	nakfa
Area	93 679 sq km (36 170 sq mi)
Population (1998 est)	3 842 000
Capital	Asmara

● **Erlangen** ▶ 49 36N 11 02E A city in S Germany, in Bavaria on the River Regnitz. The university, shared with Nuremburg, was moved here from Bayreuth in 1743. Its manufactures include electrical equipment and textiles. Population (1996 est): 101 406.

● **Erlanger, Joseph** ▶ (1874–1965) US physiologist, who, with Herbert ▷Gasser, developed techniques for recording the electrical impulses in nerve fibres using a cathode-ray oscilloscope. They demonstrated that the conduction rate of impulses depends on the thickness of the fibre and its function and that different fibres transmit different types of impulses, represented by different waveforms. Erlanger and Gasser shared the 1944 Nobel Prize for this work.

● **ermine** ▶ A ▷stoat in its white winter coat. At the onset of winter in northern latitudes, the brown coat is moulted, leaving a pure white coat except for the tip of the tail: excellent camouflage on snow-covered ground.

● **Ermine Street** ▶ A Roman road built (43–50 AD) between London and York as part of the military communications system of Roman Britain.

● **ERNIE** ▷See premium bond.

● **Ernst, Max** ▶ (1891–1976) German artist, born in Brühl. At first a philosophy and psychiatric student at Bonn University, he achieved prominence in 1919 as a founder of the Cologne ▷dada movement. He excelled in collage, particularly of cut-out illustrations, and became a leading practitioner of ▷surrealism in Paris. He invented the technique of frottage, using pencil rubbings of leaves, wood graining, etc., to suggest images of the unconscious mind. In 1941 he moved to the USA.

● **Eros** ▶ (astronomy) A small (about 20 km diameter) ▷minor planet that moves in a highly elliptical orbit bringing it within 170 million km of the sun, and in 1975 passed within 23 million km of the earth.

● **Eros** ▶ (mythology) The Greek god of love, the son of Aphrodite by Zeus, Hermes, or Ares. A winged youth armed with bow and arrows, he was identified with the Roman Cupid.

● **Erse** ▷See Gaelic.

● **Ershad, Hussain Mohammed** ▶ (1930–   ) Bangladeshi soldier and statesman; president of Bangladesh (1983–90). He seized power in a coup in 1982 and reorganized the country's economy. Martial law was lifted in 1986 but unrest continued, leading to his resignation. He was subsequently imprisoned on corruption and other charges.

● **Erskine, Thomas Erskine, 1st Baron** ▶ (1750–1823) British jurist. An MP (1783–84, 1790–1806) and briefly Lord Chancellor (1806–07), Erskine is best known for his defence of such English radicals as Tom ▷Paine, who were charged with sedition and libel during the French Revolution. He also achieved the acquittal of the leader of the ▷Gordon Riots, Lord George Gordon, in 1781. Another of his famous cases was that of Hadfield (1800), who attempted to kill George III; Erskine defended him successfully on the grounds of insanity.

● **Erté** ▶ (Romain de Tirtoff; 1892–1990) French fashion illustrator and designer, born in Russia. He worked for the US magazine *Harper's Bazaar* (1916–37) and designed extravagant costumes and tableaux for the Folies-Bergère (1919–30) and other theatres. He later produced lithographs and sculpture. Erté comes from the initials of his real name.

● **erysipelas** ▶ A skin infection caused by *Streptococcus* bacteria. It starts suddenly and usually on the face, which is red and hot, and causes a high fever. Penicillin quickly cures it.

● **erythrocyte** ▶ (or red blood cell) A disc-shaped □blood cell, about 0.007 mm in diameter, that lacks a nucleus and contains ▷haemoglobin. Haemoglobin combines reversibly with oxygen and is the means by which blood transports oxygen from the lungs to the tissues. There are normally about 4.5 million erythrocytes per cubic millimetre of blood. A deficiency of red blood cells or haemoglobin is called ▷anaemia.

● **Erzgebirge** ▶ (English name: Ore Mountains; Czech name: Krušné Hory) A range of mountains extending about 130 km (81 mi) along the Czech-German border between the Fichtelgebirge in the W and the River Elbe in the E. They have been heavily worked for silver, copper, lead, uranium, zinc, iron, and tin ores as well as coal and other minerals. They are also a popular tourist area.

● **Erzurum** ▶ 39 57N 41 17E A town in NE Turkey, on the route from Ankara and Trabzon to Iran. Local products include handmade jewellery, and there is a university (1957). Population (1996 est): 247 585.

● **ESA** ▷See European Space Agency.

● **Esaki, Leo** ▶ (1925–   ) Japanese physicist, now working for IBM in the USA. He shared the Nobel Prize (1973) for his discovery of the ▷tunnel effect and Esaki (tunnel) diode.

● **Esarhaddon** ▶ King of Assyria (680–669 BC) in succession to his father ▷Sennacherib after defeating rivals for the throne. In about 674 he attacked Egypt, conquering it in 671.

● **Esau** ▶ In the Old Testament, the son of Isaac (*see* Abraham) and the elder twin brother of ▷Jacob. Because Esau thought little of his birthright as the elder son, he sold it to Jacob for a "mess of red pottage" (i.e. bread and lentils, Genesis 25). Jacob then tricked the blind Isaac into believing that he was Esau, with the connivance of their mother Rebekah, by using a goatskin to give the impression that he was his hirsute brother (Genesis 27). The point of this story is to provide a justification for the domination of ▷Edom (Esau's descendants) by Israel (Jacob's descendants).

● **Esbjerg** ▶ 55 28N 8 28E The largest fishing port in Denmark, in the SW on the North Sea coast. Its exports, mostly to the UK, include fish, fish products, meat, and dairy products. Population (1995 est): 82 579.

● **escalation clause** ▶ A provision in an industrial contract that allows the contractor to increase his price if his costs exceed a stated limit. Escalation clauses are widely used for long-term projects in a time of inflation.

● **escalator** ▶ An automatic moving stairway for transporting passengers from one level to another. Escalators consist of a continuous moving belt of metal stairs, usually driven by an electric motor. The stairs move on tracks between two handrails moving at the same speed. At the top and bottom landings the stairs flatten out and pass through metal combs to dislodge small objects. They are generally about 1.6 m wide and move at 3–3.5 m per second.

● **escape velocity** ▶ The initial velocity required by a projectile to enable it, without any further source of power, to escape from the gravitational field of the earth or a celestial body. The escape velocity varies with the mass and diameter of the body but not with the mass of the projectile. It is also independent of the angle of launch. For the earth the escape velocity is 11 200 metres per second and for the moon, 2370 m s^{-1}.

● **Escaut, River** ▷See Scheldt, River.

● **eschatology** ▶ (Greek *eschatos*: last) The part of Christian theology concerned with the last things, often summarized as death, judgment, heaven, and hell. It refers to the ultimate fate of both the individual and of human society. Eschatological writing is common to both Old and New Testaments, where it is linked with the expectation of a coming Messiah. The teaching of Christ has also been explained as based on the assumption that the end of the world was imminent and that consequently a concern with the last things was urgent. Recent theological work has attempted to restore the relevance of these concepts in a less mythologically inclined world.

● **Escoffier, Auguste** ▶ (1846–1935) French chef. He gained an international reputation while supervising the kitchens at the Savoy and the Carlton hotels in London. He was made a member of the Légion d'Honneur in 1920.

● **Escorial, El** ▶ A royal palace, mausoleum, and monastery near Madrid. Built for Philip II beween 1563 and 1584, El Escorial is an austere, square, granite building, measuring 162 m (530 ft) by 204 m (670 ft). Philip was probably involved in the design, which was begun by Juan Bautista de Toledo (d. 1567) and completed by Juan de ▷Herrera. El Escorial houses a magnificent collection of books and paintings.

● **Esdraelon, Plain of** ▶ (or Valley of Jezreel; Hebrew name: 'Emeq Yizre'el) A lowland area in N Israel, stretching SE from Mount Carmel. In ancient times it was a major commercial route and contains the ancient site of Megiddo. It was swampy until drainage and settlement began in 1921.

● **Esdras, Books of** ▶ Two books of the ▷Apocrypha purporting to be by ▷Ezra. The first is a compilation of various documents, giving a largely parallel account of events recorded in Chronicles, Ezra, and Nehemiah, but adding a legend explaining how King Darius of Persia was persuaded to permit the rebuilding of the Temple at Jerusalem.

The second contains details of several visions consoling the Jews in their suffering and promising them a glorious future.

● **Esfahan** ▷*See* Isfahan.

● **Esher** ► 51 23N 0 22W A town in SE England, in Surrey. It is a dormitory town for London with many historical connections (Thomas Wolsey lived at Esher Place) and a famous racecourse (Sandown Park). Population (1991): 46 599.

● **esker** ► An elongated ridge consisting chiefly of sands and gravels deposited by glaciers. Once the bed of a stream flowing beneath or in a glacier, eskers are left behind once the ice has melted or retreated. They may extend for hundreds of kilometres.

● **Eskilstuna** ► 59 22N 16 31E A town in SE Sweden. A centre of the iron and steel industries, its manufactures include machinery, precision instruments, electrical equipment, and cutlery. Population (1994): 89 761.

● **Eskimo** ▷*See* Inuit.

● **Eskimo dog** ▷*See* husky.

● **Eskişehir** ► 39 46N 30 30E A town in W Turkey, W of Ankara. Its warm springs are well known, and pipes are made from the local meerschaum deposits. There is a university (1973). Population (1994 est): 451 000.

● **ESP** ▷*See* extrasensory perception.

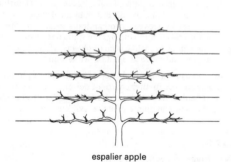

espalier apple

cordon apple   fan-trained peach

espalier ► Espalier and cordon apple trees are trained to bring the fruiting stems within arm's reach. Peach trees are particularly suitable for fan training on wires in greenhouses.

● **espalier** ► A shrub or tree, especially a fruit tree, that is trained to grow flat against a wall or a framework of wood, iron, or wire to support the fruit-laden branches and facilitate picking the crop. The branches are usually arranged in ladder-like tiers. Other methods result in a fanlike arrangement of branches or a single stem (cordon).

● **esparto** ► A perennial ▷grass, *Stipa tenacissima*, also known as alfa or halfa, native to Spain and N Africa, where it is cultivated. It grows in sharp pointed tufts, up to 1 m high, and is used to make paper, cord, and rope.

● **Esperanto** ► An artificial language invented by a Polish philolo-

gist, Lazarus Ludwig Zamenhof (1859–1917), in 1887. It was intended to be a universal medium of communication and is indeed the most successful artificial language, being spoken by over 100 000 people. Grammatically it is entirely regular, its pronunciation is consistent with its spelling, and as well as grammatical rules it has the potential for the formation of new words. The rules of the language are laid down in Zamenhof's *Fundamento de Esperanto* (1905).

● **espionage** ▷*See* intelligence service.

● **Espoo** ► (Swedish name: Esbo) 60 10N 24 42E A town in S Finland, just W of Helsinki. It serves mainly as a dormitory town for the capital. Population (1997 est): 196 260.

● **Esquimalt** ► 48 25N 123 29W A town in W Canada, in British Columbia on the SE coast of Vancouver Island. It is a major naval and military base. Population (latest est): 15 870.

● **ESRO** ▷*See* European Space Agency.

● **essay** ► A short literary prose composition in which a subject is discussed in a personal manner. The word *essai* was coined by ▷Montaigne, whose *Essais* (1580) are informal and intimate discussions of such subjects as vanity and idleness. In contrast, Francis Bacon's *Essays* (1597) were formal treatments of weighty topics. During the 18th and 19th centuries the literary periodicals provided an outlet for the essays of ▷Addison, ▷Steele, ▷Lamb, and ▷De Quincey. Among later essayists are Virginia ▷Woolf and Aldous ▷Huxley.

● **Essen** ► 51 27N 6 57E A city in W Germany, in North Rhine-Westphalia near the River Ruhr. The 9th-century cathedral survived the bombing of World War II. Formerly the site of the Krupp steelworks, it is now the administrative centre of the ▷Ruhr. Population (1996 est): 614 861.

● **Essenes** ► An ancient Jewish sect active between the 2nd century BC and the 2nd century AD in Palestine. Information about them is fragmentary and inconsistent. They seem to have stressed personal purity and asceticism. The ▷Dead Sea Scrolls may be relics of an Essene community.

● **essential oils** ► Substances with a characteristic scent produced by the glands of aromatic plants. Essential oils may be extracted by distillation, mechanical pressing, or organic solvents and are used in perfumes, food flavourings, and medicines. Examples include attar of roses, lavender oil, and clove oil.

● **Essequibo, River** ► A river in Guyana, rising on the Brazilian border and flowing generally N to enter the Atlantic Ocean, draining over half of Guyana. Length: 1014 km (630 mi).

● **Essex** ► A county of E England, bordering on the North Sea and Greater London, which incorporated the SW of the county in 1965. Southend-on-Sea and Thurrock became independent ▷unitary authorities in 1998. It is mainly low lying rising gently towards the NW. Agriculture is varied; the chief crops are wheat, barley, sugar beet, potatoes, and other vegetables. Oyster beds are important, especially in the Colne estuary. Industry is located mainly in the SW. Southend-on-Sea and Clacton are notable coastal resorts and Harwich is a major ferry port. Area (excluding unitary authorities): 3446 sq km (1330 sq mi). Population (1996 est, excluding unitary authorities): 1 281 600. Administrative centre: Chelmsford.

● **Essex, Robert Devereux, 2nd Earl of** ► (?1566–1601) English soldier and courtier to Elizabeth I. He was appointed Master of the Horse (1587) after distinguishing himself against Spain. He commanded an expedition (1591–92) sent to aid Henry IV of France and in 1593 became a privy councillor; he took part in the sack of Cádiz (1596). He was dismissed (1600) after failing to suppress an Irish rebellion and in 1601 raised a riot in London, for which he was executed. His son **Robert Devereux, 3rd Earl of Essex** (1591–1646) was the child of his marriage, unpopular with Elizabeth, to Frances Walsingham, widow of the poet Sir Philip ▷Sidney. The 3rd earl was an unsuccessful parliamentary general in the Civil War, resigning in 1645.

● **Esslingen** ► 48 45N 9 19E A town in SW Germany, in Baden-Württemberg on the River Neckar. It is noted for its gothic church (1321–1516) and its wines. Population (1989 est): 90 540.

● **estate** ▶ An interest in land, which in England may be held in one of two ways: (1) freehold tenure (more properly tenure in fee simple), in which the right over land (all of which belongs to the Crown) is for a period that is neither fixed nor liable to determination by another and for the use of which no payment in kind or money is due to another, except for such taxes as rates; (2) leasehold tenure, in which a tenant holds an estate from a landlord for a fixed period (*see* landlord and tenant). Both freeholders and long leaseholders may raise money on their land by ▷mortgages.

● **Este** ▶ An Italian princely family of Lombard origin, which under **Obizzo II** (1264–93) gained control of Ferrara, Modena, and Reggio. His successors maintained control of these three regions in spite of papal opposition and were a dominant force in Italian Renaissance politics and culture until Ferrara was incorporated into the papal states in 1598. The Estensi continued to hold Reggio until the French invasion of 1796 and Modena until the unification of Italy in the mid-19th century.
The **Villa d'Este**, at Tivoli, near Rome, was designed (1550) for Cardinal Ippolito II d'Este (1509–72).

● **Esterházy** ▶ A family prominent in Hungarian affairs from the 16th to 19th centuries. **Miklós Esterházy** (1582–1645) became imperial governor of Hungary in 1625. His son **Prince Pál Esterházy** (1635–1713) held command against the Turks and became a prince of the Holy Roman Empire (1687). Pál's grandson **Prince Miklós József Esterházy** (1714–90) rebuilt the family castle, Esterháza, and employed Haydn for 30 years. Miklós József's grandson **Prince Miklós Esterházy** (1765–1833) fought against the French in the Napoleonic Wars and accumulated an outstanding art collection. Miklós' son **Prince Pál Antal Esterházy** (1786–1866), a diplomat, was foreign minister in 1848.

● **esters** ▶ Organic compounds produced by the reaction of an alcohol with an acid, with the elimination of water. Common organic esters are formed from carboxylic acids and have the general formula $R.CO.OR'$. The lighter ones often have a pleasant smell and taste and are widely used in perfumes and flavourings. Fats are triesters of long-chain carboxylic acids and glycerol. ▷*See* saponins; soaps.

● **Esther** ▶ A character in the Old Testament who became the queen of the Persian King Ahasuerus. **The Book of Esther** recounts an event in Persia during the reign of ▷Xerxes I (called Ahasuerus in the text), when Esther used her influence to frustrate a plot to massacre the Jews. The deliverance led to the establishment of the Jewish feast of ▷Purim.

● **Estienne** ▶ (*or* Étienne; Latin name: Stephanus) A French family of printers and scholars, who published important classical, lexicographical, and theological works. **Henri Estienne** (c. 1465–1520) established the firm in Paris (c. 1502). His son **Robert Estienne** (1503–59) was printer to Francis I but because of political pressure moved the firm to Geneva (1551). Robert's son **Henri Estienne** (1528–98), a renowned scholar, continued the firm in Geneva.

● **Estonia, Republic of** ▶ A republic in NE Europe. Estonia has many lakes and includes numerous islands in the Baltic Sea. Some 30% of the population are Russians.
Economy: fishing is an important occupation, the main catch being herring. Industries, including machine building, radio engineering, textiles, food processing, and the processing of shale, are being encouraged by free-market reforms. Agriculturally, pig breeding, dairy farming, barley, oats, and potatoes are important. Owing to successful privatization programmes, heavy foreign investment, and flourishing trade with Germany and Scandinavia, Estonia now has perhaps the strongest economy of the former Eastern bloc countries.
History: in the 13th century the N was occupied by the Danes and the S by the Livonian Knights (a German order of knighthood). The Danes withdrew in 1346 and the Knights were replaced by the Swedes in the 16th and 17th centuries. Estonia was ceded to Russia in 1721. Rebellions in the 19th century culminated in a declaration of independence (1918), which was recognized by Soviet Russia in 1920. It was assigned to the Soviet Union by the Nazi-Soviet Pact (1939) and became a Soviet republic in 1940. It was occupied by Germany in

World War II. In 1988 Estonia challenged Soviet control of its internal affairs and in 1991 it unilaterally declared independence, soon afterwards achieving international recognition. Following elections in 1992 Lennart Meri became president and a radical right-wing government was installed. In 1993 a new law denying citizenship to non-Estonian-speaking residents increased tension between Estonians and Russians. Since 1995 the country has been governed by a series of centre-left coalitions. Estonia has been formally invited to join the European Union early in the 21st century.

Republic of Estonia

Head of state	President Arnold Rüütel
Official language	Estonian; Russian is widely spoken
Official currency	kroon of 100 sents
Area	45 100 sq km (17 410 sq mi)
Population (2001 est)	1 363 000
Capital	Tallinn

● **Estonian** ▶ A language of the Baltic-Finnic branch of the Finno-Ugric division of the Uralic language family. It is spoken by the Estonians, who number about one million people in Estonia (in which it is the official language). It is related to Finnish with which it shares the characteristic of distinguishing three degrees of consonant and vowel length. The written language is based on a northern dialect, Tallinn, and has a literature dating from the 16th century.

● **Estoril** ▶ 38 42N 9 23W A resort in W Portugal, on the Atlantic Ocean. It has an outstanding avenue of palm trees between its casino and the sea. Population (1991): 24 850.

● **Estuary English** ▷*See* accent.

● **Esztergom** ▶ 47 46N 18 42E A town in N Hungary, on the Danube opposite the Slovakian town of Stúrovo. Stephen I was crowned here. Population (latest est): 32 100.

● **etching** ▶ A method of making prints from a metal plate covered with an acid-resistant ground, on which a design is drawn with a needle. The plate is then placed in acid, the exposed lines being eaten away. These recessed lines retain ink and the design is transferred to the paper by rolling under pressure. Although the first dated etching was made in 1513, it was ▷Rembrandt who freed the medium from its technical and formal dependence on ▷engraving. The process continues to be widely used, with ▷Picasso among the leading 20th-century exponents.

● **Eteocles** ▷*See* Polyneices.

● **ethanal** ▶ (*or* acetaldehyde; CH_3CHO) A colourless liquid ▷aldehyde with a pungent smell, formed by the oxidation of ▷ethanol. On further oxidation it becomes ▷ethanoic acid.

● **ethane** ▶ (C_2H_6) A colourless gas, the second member of the ▷alkane series. It occurs in ▷natural gas.

● **ethanoic acid** ▶ (*or* acetic acid; CH_3OOH) The acid contained (3–6%) in vinegar. It can be made by the oxidation of ▷ethanol, but is commonly made from ▷ethanal and is used in the manufacture of plastics and as a preservative. **Glacial ethanoic acid** is composed of icelike crystals, which form when the pure acid freezes.

● **ethanol** ▶ (*or* ethyl alcohol; C_2H_5OH) A colourless flammable liquid that is the active constituent of alcoholic drinks. It is prepared by fermentation or by catalytic hydration of ▷ethene. It is used as a solvent, a raw material for producing other chemicals, and a fuel. ▷*See also* alcohol strength.

● **Ethelbert** ▶ (c. 552–616 AD) King of Kent, who became overlord of all England south of the Humber. Encouraging the conversion of his people to Christianity, he received Augustine's mission from Rome. He wrote the first extant English code of laws.

● **Etheldreda, St** ▶ (c. 630–79 AD) The reluctant wife of King Ecgfrith of Northumbria. Greatly influenced by Bishop ▷Wilfrid, who encouraged her to remain a virgin, Etheldreda became abbess of a double monastery at Ely.

● **Ethelred I** ▶ (d. 871 AD) King of England (866–71), in whose reign the Vikings launched a full-scale invasion of England. Ethelred died after his victory at Ashdown, leaving his brother ▷Alfred the Great to fight on.

● **Ethelred the Unready** ► (968–1016) King of England (978–1016). In the face of Danish raids, he was forced to pay huge tributes (*see* Danegeld) to the enemy. He was driven into exile by ▷Sweyn in 1013 but returned after Sweyn's death (1014), dying during ▷Canute's invasion of England (1015–16). His title is a mistranslation of an Anglo-Saxon word meaning "devoid of counsel."

● **Ethelwulf** ► (d. 858 AD) King of Wessex (839–58). Renowned for his military prowess, he reputedly defeated 350 Viking ships (851). Ethelwulf reduced taxation, endowed the Church, made lay lands heritable, and provided a system of poor relief.

● **ethene** ► (*or* ethylene; C_2H_4) A colourless flammable gaseous ▷alkene. It is made by cracking petroleum and is used to make ▷polythene (polyethylene).

● **ether** ► (chemistry) Any member of the group of organic compounds with the general formula R–O–R′, which are formed by the condensation of two alcohols. Diethyl ether, $C_2H_5OC_2H_5$, often known simply as ether, is a volatile liquid made by treating ▷ethanol with concentrated sulphuric acid. It is used as an anaesthetic and solvent.

● **ether** ► (physics) A hypothetical substance (also called the luminiferous ether) once thought necessary, as a medium pervading all space, in order to support ▷electromagnetic radiation. The ▷Michelson-Morley experiment in 1881 showed that no such substance exists and that electromagnetic radiation requires no supporting medium.

● **Etherege, Sir George** ► (c. 1635–c. 1692) English dramatist. A diplomat in Turkey from 1668 to 1671, he fled to Paris after the accession of William III. In his comedies of fashionable London life, *The Comical Revenge* (1664), *She Wou'd If She Cou'd* (1668), and *The Man of Mode* (1674), he introduced the comedy of manners to the British theatre.

● **Ethical Culture movement** ► A movement originating in New York in the late 19th century to promote the importance of morality in all aspects of life (*see* Adler, Felix). The first English Ethical Society was established at the Chapel in South Place, Finsbury (1888).

● **ethics** ► The science of morality, also called moral philosophy. It is one of the three main branches of modern ▷philosophy and seeks to discover a consistent principle by which human actions and character can be judged. Until about a century ago, ethics was prescriptive, aiming to guide men's conduct. Now it is more descriptive, attempting to discover how moral decisions are actually made. In ancient philosophy, ▷hedonism, which held that the greatest goal was happiness, and rationalism, which held that it was reason, were the rival schools. Plato and Aristotle combined hedonism and ▷rationalism. Medieval scholasticism took God's will as the sole ethical standard and grafted this onto Aristotelian ethics. After the Renaissance, pragmatists like ▷Hobbes, ▷Bentham, and John Stuart Mill (*see* Mill, James) developed ▷utilitarianism, in which the good of society rather than of the individual is the criterion. ▷Kant and other idealists were intuitionists, believing that conscience is to ethics as intelligence is to logic. Today utilitarianism is the implicit basis of commercial, legal, and social ethics, but conscience remains the guide of most individuals.

● **Ethiopia, Federal Democratic Republic of** ► (former name: Abyssinia) A country in NE Africa, which consists of deserts in the SE and NE and a central plateau, crossed by river valleys (including that of the Blue Nile) and by mountain ranges rising over 4300 m (11 500 ft). The population consists of many ethnic groups, including the Galla and ▷Amhara. ▷*See also* Falashas.

Economy: Ethiopia remains one of the poorest countries in the world and agriculture is chiefly at subsistence level. All land was nationalized in 1975 and farmed cooperatively until 1992, when economic reforms included converting communal land to private ownership. Mineral resources are sparse, though there are small amounts of gold, platinum, copper, and potash. The disrupted

▷Ogaden region is thought to be a potential source of mineral wealth. Textiles, cement, and food processing are being encouraged. The main export is coffee. The country has a very large foreign debt.

History: Ethiopia has a longer known history than any other country in Africa apart from Egypt and legend claimed the descent of its rulers from Solomon and the Queen of Sheba. From the 2nd to the 9th century AD the Aksumite Empire enjoyed considerable prosperity and expansion, in the 4th century Ethiopia became the first Christian country in Africa. This period was followed by centuries of struggles (especially with the Muslims) and of internal divisions. It was not until the 19th century that the country was once more reunited under Emperor Tewodros II (1818–68). In 1896 Italian attempts to conquer it were defeated by ▷Menelik II. However, in 1935 Italy (under Mussolini) invaded Ethiopia. In spite of Anglo-French attempts (Hoare-Laval Pact) to arrange a settlement and League of Nations sanctions against Italy, in 1936 Addis Ababa fell and the emperor, ▷Haile Selassie, fled to England. For the next five years Ethiopia formed part of Italian East Africa (with Eritrea and Italian Somaliland). In 1941 the Allies liberated Ethiopia and Haile Selassie returned to the throne. ▷Eritrea was fully integrated into Ethiopia in 1962 despite active armed resistance. Haile Selassie was deposed in 1974 and a provisional military government came to power. After the execution of members of the ruling military council in 1977, the government became known as the Derg (Provisional Military Administrative Council) with ▷Mengistu Haile Mariam as president. During this period rebels in Eritrea and the Somali-speaking Ogaden area increased their armed struggle. In 1977 Ethiopia fought off a Somali invasion of the Ogaden. Successive droughts (1982, 1984, 1987, 1989, 1999–2000) led to famine and forced resettlement from the N to the fertile west; one million people died in the famine of 1984. Massive foreign aid was hampered by internal disorganization and civil war. Armed rebellion in the province of Tigré led to further civil war; in

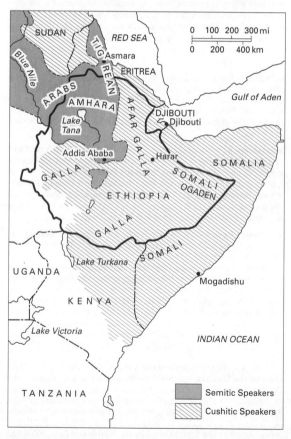

Ethiopia ► Distribution of main ethnic groups.

1991 forces of the Tigrean-led Ethiopian People's Revolutionary Democratic Front (EPRDF) alliance forced the resignation of Mengistu and established a provisional administration. Nine regional councils based on Ethiopia's different ethnic groups were created and a new federal constitution was ratified in 1994. Eritrea became independent in 1993. Elections held in 1995 resulted in victory for the EPRDF and Meles Zenawi became prime minister. A border dispute with Eritrea led to fierce fighting in 1998–99 and 2000.

Federal Democratic Republic of Ethiopia

Head of state	President Negaso Gidada
Official language	Amharic; English is widely spoken
Official religion	Ethiopian Orthodox (Coptic)
Official currency	birr of 100 cents
Area	1 128 221 sq km (435 608 sq mi)
Population (1998 est)	58 390 000
Capital	Addis Ababa

● **ethnic cleansing** ▷*See* genocide.

● **ethnic identity** ▶ The concept that identifies people having a shared set of values and customs deriving from a common history, culture, language, and religion. Ethnic identity is not synonymous with race, nationality, class, or religion although it overlaps with all these concepts. Because its parameters are not well delineated ethnic identity can be hard to define; nevertheless, it has been, and still is, a major cause of social and political unrest in human relations. In Africa the members of one tribe are often willing to kill members of another tribe because they feel their ethnic identity is threatened. In India similar conflicts occur, for similar reasons, often between people of different castes or religions. In Europe the ethnic distinction between Jews and Christians is not solely a result of the different religions, any more than the troubles in Northern Ireland can be dismissed as a conflict between branches of the same religion.

The USA has long claimed to be an ethnically mixed nation, including many Europeans of different ethnic backgrounds in addition to native Amerindians and diverse peoples of African, Hispanic, Chinese, and Japanese origins. While nationhood has unified all these peoples in some respects, ethnicity has continued to segregate them into a nexus of separate communities. In the UK, the native English, Welsh, and Scots have forged a united nation although vestiges of ethnic distinctions endure. Since the end of the British Empire, and the policy of allowing citizens of its former members to settle in the UK, the ethnic mix has diversified. Because intermarriage often results in a loss of ethnic identity for one or both of the partners, as well as their progeny, mixed marriages are often seen as threatening by ethnic communities, ostensibly on religious grounds.

● **ethnology** ▶ The comparative study and theory of contemporary cultures. In most current usages it is synonymous with cultural ▷anthropology. However, it has also been used to refer to the historical study of cultures, especially preliterate cultures, and sometimes as a synonym for social anthropology. It may be distinguished from ethnography, which is the descriptive study of culture and is less concerned with the development of theory.

● **ethnomusicology** ▷*See* musicology.

● **ethology** ▶ The study of animal behaviour. Ethologists are concerned with how animals respond to signals or stimuli (whether from other animals, from their own bodies, or from the environment in which they live), how they sense these signals, and what their response means to other animals and to themselves. They demonstrate the interactions between the inherited (instinctive) aspects of behaviour and those determined by experience (learning).

Ethology was founded in Europe in the 1930s by the work of Konrad ▷Lorenz and Niko ▷Tinbergen. In the USA the approach was one of comparative psychology, using laboratory animals. The work of ethologists has provided insights into some aspects of human behaviour.

● **ethyl alcohol** ▷*See* ethanol.

● **ethylene** ▷*See* ethene.

● **ethyne** ▶ (*or* acetylene; C_2H_2) A colourless toxic inflammable gas. The two carbon atoms in the molecule are joined by a triple bond and it forms a series of compounds called ▷alkynes. Ethyne is made by the action of water on calcium carbide and is widely used as a starting material for many organic compounds. Because of its high flame temperature (about 3300°C) it is used with oxygen in oxy-acetylene ▷welding.

● **Étienne** ▷*See* Estienne.

● **Etna, Mount** ▶ 37 45N 15 00E A volcano in E Sicily. The first recorded eruption was in 476 BC and in the last hundred years significant eruptions have occurred in 1928, 1949, 1971, 1991, and 2000. The coastal town of Catania, 28 km (17 mi) away, has been engulfed twice. Height: 3263 m (10 705 ft).

● **Eton** ▶ 51 31N 0 37W A town in SE England, in Windsor and Maidenhead unitary authority, Berkshire, opposite Windsor on the River Thames. Eton College, the famous public school, was founded by Henry VI in 1440. Population (1991, excluding Eton School): 1974.

● **Etruria** ▶ The region of ancient Italy N of Rome, approximating modern Tuscany. Occupied first by ▷Villanovan peoples, Etruria was inhabited by the ▷Etruscans from the 8th century BC but by the 3rd century BC had come under Roman control.

● **Etruscans** ▶ The ancient inhabitants of Etruria (now Tuscany) in central Italy. From the 8th to the 5th centuries BC their cities, including Clusium (now Chiusi), Tarquinii (Tarquinia), Perusia (Perugia), and Veii (Veio), formed a confederacy that dominated the region; after 396 they were rapidly absorbed by the Romans. The Etruscans' origins are mysterious; oriental traits in their artefacts (exhibiting advanced skills in metalwork and pottery) and the frescoes decorating their tombs suggest that they were invaders from Asia Minor, although these could have arisen through their trading links. Many inscriptions are known and their alphabet is similar to ancient Greek, but their language is still largely untranslated.

● **Etty, William** ▶ (1787–1849) British painter, best known for his studies of the nude. His large-scale *The Combat* (1825; National Gallery of Scotland), exhibited at the Royal Academy in 1828, impressed Delacroix.

● **etymology** ▶ The study of the history of words, in which words are traced back to their earliest recorded forms and, where sufficient evidence exists, beyond these to reconstructed hypothetical forms. Most English words are derived either from Proto-Germanic (*see* Germanic languages) or from Latin and French. Many learned English words were taken from Greek or made up from Greek elements, while in the past 200 years English has borrowed words from most languages in the world.

● **EU** ▷*See* European Union.

● **Euboea** ▶ (Modern Greek name: Évvoia; former English name: Negropont) The second largest Greek island, in the W Aegean Sea. It is separated from the mainland by only a narrow channel and rises to 1743 m (5719 ft) at Mount Delphi. Sheep and cattle are raised and grapes, figs, olives, and cereals, grown. Area: 3908 sq km (1509 sq mi). Population (1990): 209 132. Chief town: Chalcis.

● **Eucalyptus** ▶ A genus of tropical and subtropical evergreen trees (about 600 species) native to Australia but widely cultivated elsewhere. Eucalypts—also known as gum trees and stringybarks—are among the tallest trees in the world, 90–100 m high. The blue-grey bark is smooth and often peeling and the mature leaves are long and narrow (young leaves are rounded or oblong). The flowers are showy, with tiny petals and a fluffy mass of red or white stamens. The fruit is a woody pod. Fast-growing and drought-resistant, eucalypts are important sources of timber. The wood is used as fuel and for buildings and fencing; the bark for paper making and tanning. The best known species are the ▷blue gum and the red gum (*E. ficifolia*). Because they take up much water, eucalypts are used to reclaim marshy land. They are also used for street planting. All parts of the trees contain essential oils (oil of eucalyptus comes from blue gum leaves). Some species are shrubby and are known as ▷mallees. Family: *Myrtaceae* (myrtle family).

● **Eucharis** ▶ A genus of bulb-forming South American plants (10 species), called Amazon lilies. Up to 60 cm tall, they have clusters of large fragrant white flowers, up to 13 cm across, with protruding slender stamens and six backward curling white sepals. The plants are grown for ornament in greenhouses. Family: *Amaryllidaceae*.

● **Eucharist** ▶ (Greek *eucharistia*: thanksgiving) The chief ▷sacrament and central act of worship of the Christian Churches. Also known as Holy Communion, the Lord's Supper, and the Mass, its institution is described in the three Synoptic Gospels. At the last meal of Christ and the apostles, bread and wine were blessed by Christ and shared, representing his death on the cross and the subsequent redemption of mankind. Differing interpretations have been placed on the sense in which Christ is held to be present in the sacrament (*see* consubstantiation; transubstantiation). While in the Orthodox, Anglican, and Reformed Churches communicants receive both bread and wine, in the Roman Catholic Church the wine is usually reserved for the celebrating priest.

● **Eucken, Rudolf Christoph** ▶ (1846–1926) German writer. He upheld idealist metaphysics against 19th-century positivism and materialism and sought to isolate the spiritual content of historical movements. He won the Nobel Prize for Literature in 1908.

● **Euclid** ▶ (c. 300 BC) Greek mathematician, famous for his book entitled *Elements* in which he derived all that was known of geometry from a few simple axioms. The geometry that obeys Euclid's axioms is known as ▷Euclidean geometry, all other kinds being called ▷non-Euclidean geometry.

● **Euclidean geometry** ▶ A system of geometry based on the axioms contained in ▷Euclid's *Elements*. In Euclidean geometry, parallel lines never meet and the angles in a triangle always add up to 180°. The geometry of physical space can be assumed for most purposes to be Euclidean. The surface of a sphere, however, is non-Euclidean. *Compare* non-Euclidean geometry.

● **Eudoxus of Cnidus** ▶ (c. 408–c. 355 BC) Greek astronomer and mathematician, who studied under Plato and later founded a school, first on the NW coast of Asia Minor and then in Athens. He studied the motions of the planets and derived many geometric proofs, some of which were later incorporated by ▷Euclid in his *Elements*.

● **Eugène of Savoy, Prince** ▶ (1663–1736) Austrian general. Born in Paris, he was refused a commission by Louis XIV and entered the service of Emperor Leopold I. He won victories against the Turks at Zenta (1697), which freed Hungary of Turkish domination, Peterwardein (1716), and Belgrade (1717). In the War of ▷Austrian Succession (1701–14), he won, with Marlborough, the victories of ▷Blenheim (1704), Oudenaarde (1708), and Malplaquet (1709).

● **eugenics** ▶ The science that studies the inheritable factors that determine the physical and mental qualities of the human race, with the aim of improving the quality of life for future generations. The term was first coined by Sir Francis ▷Galton in 1883. Eugenics is now concerned primarily with the detection and—where possible—elimination of such genetic diseases as Down's syndrome with the aid of ▷prenatal diagnosis.

● **Eugénie** ▶ (1826–1920) The influential wife (1853–73) of ▷Napoleon III of France. She several times acted as his regent and encouraged French intervention in Mexico. After the fall of the Empire (1870) she retired to England.

● **Euglena** ▶ A genus of single-celled microorganisms found chiefly in fresh water. They are spindle-shaped, with a flexible cell wall (pellicle) and a gullet from which protrudes a long whiplike flagellum, used for locomotion. Some species contain chlorophyll or other pigments and can manufacture food by photosynthesis; others feed on small organisms, such as bacteria. Euglenas were formerly regarded by some authorities as algae of the division *Euglenophyta* and by others as flagellate protozoans. They are now included in the phylum *Discomitochondria*, kingdom ▷*Protoctista*.

● **eukaryote** ▷*See* cell.

● **Eulenspiegel, Till** ▶ A German folk hero, a crafty and often savage joker whose exploits inspired many folktales and literary and musical works, notably the epic poem by Gerhard ▷Hauptmann (1928) and the tone poem by Richard ▷Strauss.

● **Euler, Leonhard** ▶ (1707–83) Swiss mathematician, regarded as the greatest mathematician of the 18th century and the most prolific ever, writing 800 papers during his lifetime. Many more were published posthumously. He did much work on the number e, the base of natural ▷logarithms, which is often known as **Euler's number**. He gave that number its symbol, and introduced the symbol i for the square root of –1 and also the notation $f(x)$ for a function of the variable x.

● **Eumenides** ▶ (Greek: the kindly ones) In Greek legend, spirits identical with the ▷Erinyes. After ▷Orestes was acquitted by the Areopagus of his mother's murder, the pursuing Erinyes became known as the Eumenides.

● **eunuch** ▶ A castrated man or boy. The operation has been practised since antiquity as a punishment or for revenge or humiliation; it was revived by the Germans in their ▷concentration camps in World War II for so-called research. In the East, boys castrated in childhood were sold by their parents as harem attendants until the 20th century. Voluntary emasculation was formerly practised by fanatical Christians as a means of avoiding sexual temptation (Matthew 19:12). ▷Origen, for example, was defrocked for doing so. ▷*See also* castrato.

● **Euonymus** ▶ A genus of widely distributed trees, shrubs, and woody climbers (176 species), often grown as ornamentals for their attractive foliage and fruits, which are surrounded by a bright-pink or orange fleshy coat (aril). The genus includes the ▷spindle tree. Family: *Celastraceae*.

● **Eupen-et-Malmédy** ▶ A region of Belgium, in Liège province. It was ceded by Germany in 1919 by the Treaty of Versailles but was once more occupied by Germany (1940–45). Manufactures include woollen goods, paper, and leather. Population (1995 est): 27 675.

● **euphonium** ▶ Brass instrument with a wide conical bore, a cup-shaped mouthpiece, four valves, and a range of about three and a half octaves above the B flat below middle C. Its range is equivalent to that of a tenor ▷tuba and it is much used in the brass band.

● **Euphorbia** ▶ A worldwide genus of herbs and small trees (1600 species), having small flowers surrounded by petal-like bracts. The genus includes some ornamental shrubs (*see* crown of thorns; poinsettia; snow-on-the-mountain). The herbaceous euphorbias are known as ▷spurges. Family: *Euphorbiaceae*.

● **Euphrates, River** ▶ A river in SW Asia, rising in E Turkey and flowing SE through Syria into Iraq. 190 km (118 mi) from the Persian Gulf, it joins the River Tigris to form the Shatt al-Arab. It flows past the historic sites of Babylon, Ur, Nippur, and Sippara. Length: 2700 km (1678 mi).

● **Euphronios** ▶ (late 6th–early 5th centuries BC) Athenian red-figure potter and vase painter. He signed some 15 surviving vases and is mentioned as a rival by another painter. His drawing shows skill in composition and characterization.

● **Eupolis** ▶ (late 5th century BC) Greek dramatist, a rival of ▷Aristophanes. His comedies satirized contemporary politicians and socialites. Only fragments of his works survive.

● **Eurasia** ▶ Europe and Asia considered as one land mass. Geographically, Europe is a peninsula of the Asian continent, divided from it by the Ural Mountains.

● **EURATOM** ▷*See* European Atomic Energy Community.

● **Eureka project** ▶ A European advanced technology cooperation programme. Originally proposed by the French government as an alternative to the US ▷Strategic Defence Initiative, the project was launched in 1985: its 18 European member-nations aim to find peaceful applications for joint research.

● **Eureka Stockade** ▶ (1854) A miners' rebellion in Victoria (Australia) against oppressive government legislation: prospectors had to pay high licence fees, which were brutally collected, and they were not permitted to vote or to be represented in the Legislative Council. The miners of Ballarat, under Peter ▷Lalor, stockaded themselves into the Eureka goldfield. They were easily routed and about 25 miners were killed.

● **eurhythmics** ▶ A system of teaching music by developing the student's physical response to rhythm. Devised by ▷Jaques-Dalcroze in about 1905, it has since been used in physical education, ▷ballet and ▷modern dance training, and even in mental education. The student is taught a series of body movements to express different musical rhythms; he is then encouraged to improvise his movements.

● **Euripides** ▶ (c. 480–406 BC) Greek dramatist, the third (after ▷Aeschylus and ▷Sophocles) of the three major writers of Attic tragedy. According to tradition he was born in Salamis on the day Xerxes' fleet was defeated in the famous battle. In 408 he went to the court of Archelaus in Macedonia, where he remained for the rest of his life. Of approximately 90 plays, 19 survive, including the tragedies *Medea* (431), *Hippolytus* (428), *Electra* (415), *The Trojan Women* (415), *The Bacchae* (405), and *Iphigenia at Aulis* (405). His technical innovations included naturalistic dialogue and a diminution of the role of the chorus. He also explored feminine psychology. His critical attitude towards traditional religion in some of the plays, which offended his contemporaries, is balanced by incidents portraying real heroism and lyrical passages of great beauty.

● **euro** ▶ The currency unit of 12 member states of the European Union that was launched in January 1999 and replaced the national currencies for all forms of monetary transaction in January–March 2002. It is subdivided into 100 cents. ▷*See also* European Monetary System.

● **Eurodollars** ▶ An international currency based on US dollar balances held by banks outside the USA. The Eurodollar market developed from 1957 onwards as persistent US ▷balance-of-payments deficits (largely due to foreign aid and investment programmes) led to a large outflow of dollars, which were put to use in Europe often to finance international trade. Oil-producing countries often have large holdings of Eurodollars, which they may move between investment centres in order to take advantage of the highest interest rates. Eurodollars and other expatriate currencies together make up the Eurocurrency market, which deals in large amounts of short-term funds the volatility and freedom from government control of which may at times threaten the stability of international money markets.

● **Europa** ▶ (astronomy) ▷*See* Galilean satellites.

● **Europa** ▶ (Greek mythology) The daughter of King Agenor of Tyre. Carried to Crete by Zeus in the form of a bull, she bore him three sons: Minos, Rhadamanthus, and Sarpedon.

● **Europa Nostra** ▶ (Italian: Our Europe) An international federation of about 2000 independent organizations devoted to the preservation of Europe's natural and cultural heritage. Established in 1963, it advises the Council of Europe.

● **Europe** ▶ A continent bordering on the Arctic Ocean (N), the Atlantic Ocean (W), and the Mediterranean Sea (S); the Ural Mountains, the River Ural, and the Caspian Sea form its E boundary. Europe is the second (after Australasia) smallest continent but owing perhaps to its latitude and geography has exerted a disproportionate influence on the rest of the world. It comprises a peninsula of the land mass of Eurasia and all geological eras have contributed to its formation. Its long coastline is much indented with several peninsulas (e.g. Scandinavia, Italy) and offshore islands (e.g. the British Isles, Iceland). A central plain, extending from the Ural Mountains to the Atlantic Ocean and divided by uplands and the English Channel, comprises two-thirds of the continent. It rises in the S to a series of mountain systems (e.g. the Pyrenees, Alps, Apennines, Carpathian Mountains), and in the N to the mountainous region of Scandinavia and Scotland. The chief rivers flow from the Valdai Hills (e.g Volga, Don, Dnieper) or the Alps (e.g. Danube, Rhine, Rhône, Po). Its four climatic zones are characterized by mild winters, cool summers, and rain all the year round (NW); mild winters, hot summers, and chiefly spring and autumn rain (Mediterranean); cold winters, warm summers, and chiefly summer rain (Central Europe); and very cold winters (E Europe). Vegetation zones comprise, from N to S: tundra; a coniferous forest belt, predominantly of Scots pine and Norway spruce; a deciduous forest belt, notably of oak and hornbeam in the E and of oak, birch, and holly in the W, with beech in the central lowlands; and the mainly evergreen and scrub vegetation of the Mediterranean. Steppe and semidesert char-

acterize the SE. Forest once covered some 80% of Europe but intense agriculture since the middle ages and industrialization since the 19th century have reduced it to 30% of the land mass. Europe possesses important mineral resources. Coalfields, especially in Germany, Poland, and what was the Soviet Union, continue to be an important source of power, and oil and natural-gas reserves are found in Russia and neighbouring states, Romania, Albania, and beneath the North Sea. Iron-ore deposits are found on a large scale only in the countries of the former Soviet Union, which also have reserves of nickel, tin, and manganese, but nonmetallic minerals, including kaolinite and rock salt, occur widely. Europe's high-density population is concentrated in its industrial regions, which are found chiefly in a central belt extending from England, through N France, the Netherlands, and Germany, to Moscow; N Italy, however, is also densely populated. Most of the unusually large number of national groups in Europe speak an ▷Indo-European language. The European peoples may be subdivided into racial types (e.g. Nordic, Germanic, Alpine, and Mediterranean) but extensive intermixing has occurred. Christianity, in its various forms, is the dominant religion and has exerted a profound influence on European culture, which also continues to bear the imprint of the civilizations of ancient ▷Greece and Rome (*see* Roman Republic; Roman Empire). Nevertheless Europe's medieval and modern history is that of its diverse nations, conflicts between which culminated in the 20th century in the two World Wars. The postwar period witnessed a split between the communist countries of E Europe, dominated by the Soviet Union until its collapse, and the countries of W Europe, which have sought to resolve their rivalries in the ▷European Union. Area: about 10 400 000 sq km (4 000 000 sq mi). Population (1996 est): 729 370 000.

● **European Atomic Energy Community** ▶ (EURATOM) An international organization founded in 1958 by the Treaty of Rome (1957) to promote and develop the peaceful uses of atomic energy in Europe. In 1967 the executive bodies of EURATOM and the ▷European Coal and Steel Community merged with those of the ▷European Economic Community.

● **European Coal and Steel Community** ▶ (ECSC) A body established in 1952 to coordinate the production of coal and steel in France, Italy, West Germany, and the ▷Benelux countries. In 1967 the executive bodies of the ECSC and the ▷European Atomic Energy Community merged with those of the ▷European Economic Community.

● **European Community** ▶ (EC *or* European Communities) An economic and political organization of European states created in 1967 when the executive and legislative bodies of the ▷European Economic Community merged with those of the ▷European Atomic Energy Community and the ▷European Coal and Steel Community. The original members, Belgium, France, Italy, Luxembourg, the Netherlands, and West Germany, were joined by Denmark, Ireland, and the UK in 1973; Greece joined in 1981, and Spain and Portugal joined in 1986. In 1985 Greenland left the EC, having attained home rule.

Agreements were reached on the removal of customs tariffs between members, the setting of a Common External Tariff for imports from nonmember states, and the abolition of barriers to free movement of labour, services, and capital between member states. The EC established the ▷Common Agricultural Policy (CAP) and initiated a Common Fisheries Policy (1983). British passports in a common European format were introduced in the UK in 1988. Under the terms of the **Maastricht Treaty** (signed Feb 1992) members agreed to steps towards closer political, economic, and monetary union (*see also* European Monetary System), which led to the establishment of the ▷European Union in 1993.

● **European Commission** ▷*See* European Union.

● **European Court of Human Rights** ▶ An international court established (1950) by the ▷Council of Europe to enforce the European Convention on Human Rights (*see* human rights). In 1993 it was merged with the European Commission on Human Rights. Applicants must have exhausted the legal process in their own countries before they can bring a case. The European Court of Human Rights sits in Strasbourg: it should not be confused with the European Court of Justice, which is an institution of the ▷European Union.

● **European Court of Justice** ▷*See* European Union.

● **European Currency Unit** ► (ECU) A monetary unit introduced in 1979 by the European Community as part of the exchange rate mechanism. ▷*See* European Monetary System.

● **European Defence Community** ► (EDC) ▷*See* Western European Union.

● **European Economic Area** ► (EEA) ▷*See* European Free Trade Association.

● **European Economic Community** ► (EEC *or* Common Market) An organization of W European states created by the Treaty of Rome (1957), which was foreshadowed by the Treaty of Brussels (1948), to foster economic cooperation and common development with the eventual aim of economic, and a measure of political, unity. The original six signatories were Belgium, France, Italy, Luxembourg, the Netherlands, and West Germany. The EEC implemented a ▷Common Agricultural Policy (CAP) in 1962 (modified in 1968) and promoted the removal of customs tariffs between members. In 1967 its legislative and executive bodies merged with those of the ▷European Atomic Energy Community and the ▷European Coal and Steel Community to form the ▷European Community.

● **European Free Trade Association** ► (EFTA) An association now consisting of four states (Iceland, Norway, Switzerland, and Liechtenstein), founded in 1960 to foster free trade between members. In 1984 free trade was established between the EC and EFTA. Members may negotiate independent trade agreements with nonmembers. In 1994 EFTA (excluding Switzerland) and the EU together created the **European Economic Area** (EEA), the world's richest open market consisting of over 380 million people.

● **European Monetary System** ► (EMS) A system formed in 1979 for stabilizing exchange rates between members of the European Community (now the EU) and as a possible step towards **European monetary union** (EMU). It originally consisted of an **exchange rate mechanism** (ERM) and a balance of payments support mechanism organized by the **European Monetary Cooperation Fund** (EMCOF)—a fund containing 20% of the participants' gold and gross dollar reserves, to which members had access for credit facilities. The ERM gave each currency a value in European Currency Units (ECUs). If market rates differed by more than an agreed percentage, governments had to intervene. The value of the ECU was calculated as a weighted average of a basket of currencies. The UK joined the ERM in 1990, after much hesitation. In 1992 the British, Italian, and Spanish governments, being unable to support the currencies above their floor values, had to withdraw. Subsequently, the limits of fluctuation permitted among the remaining currencies had to be greatly extended to prevent the collapse of the system. Despite the failure of the ERM, plans to introduce a single European currency (the ▷euro) and a **European Central Bank** (ECB) advanced rapidly in the later 1990s. By 2001, 12 EU countries (all the member states except Denmark, Sweden, and the UK) had committed themselves to EMU. Their currencies were locked together and the ECB was set up (1998) under the presidency of Willem Duisenberg (1935–   ). The euro was launched for all forms of noncash transaction in January 1999; the first notes and coins were issued in January 2002 and the national currencies were withdrawn by March. A referendum (2000) in Denmark rejected the euro and the US and Sweden are committed to referenda before joining. EU countries that remain outside EMU have the option of joining a new exchange rate mechanism (ERM II) based on the euro and supervised by the ECB.

● **European Organization for Nuclear Research** ▷*See* CERN.

● **European Parliament** ▷*See* European Union.

● **European Southern Observatory** ► A major astronomical observatory near La Serena, Chile, operated by a European intergovernmental organization that includes France, Germany, Belgium, the Netherlands, Denmark, Sweden, Italy, and Switzerland. It houses a 3.6 m (142 in) reflecting telescope.

● **European Space Agency** ► (ESA) An organization responsible for Europe's space programme, formed in 1975 from the merger of the European Space Research Organization (ESRO) and the European Launcher Development Organization. There are at present 11 full-member nations, including the UK. Since 1979 all ESA ▷satellites

have been launched by the ESA launcher **Ariane**. In 1996 ESA's most ambitious project, the launcher Ariane-5, was destroyed on its maiden flight.

● **European Union** ► (EU) An organization established in 1993 according to the terms of the Maastricht Treaty. It comprises the ▷European Community, with the addition of a common foreign and security policy and cooperation between members in justice and policing. In 1995 Austria, Sweden, and Finland joined, bringing the numbers of members up to 15. Cyprus, the Czech Republic, Estonia, Hungary, and Poland have all been invited to join early in the 21st century. ▷*See also* European Free Trade Association.

The **European Commission** (until 1993 the Commission of the European Communities) is in Brussels and consists of 20 members (two each from the UK, France, Germany, Spain, and Italy and one each from the other member countries); its president is elected for a four-year term. It acts as an advisory body to, and implements policy decided upon by, the Council of Ministers of the European Union. The current Commission is headed by Romano ▷Prodi. Also in Brussels, the Council comprises ministers from the governments of the member countries. The heads of government meet triannually as the European Council. The **European Parliament** at Strasbourg or Luxembourg comments on the Commission's legislative proposals; it must be consulted on the annual budgets and may dismiss the Commission. Members are (since 1979) elected by direct vote in the member countries and sit as political groups (e.g. Christian Democrats, Socialists) in the Parliament (see diagram). The **European Court of Justice**, at Luxembourg, interprets the treaties that established the European Community, and interprets and applies the laws made by the Council and the Commission. The long-planned single European currency (*see* European Monetary System) was introduced in January, 1999.

● **europium** ► (Eu) A ▷lanthanide element, used in television-tube phosphors. It forms oxides (EuO, Eu$_2$O$_3$), and chlorides (EuCl$_2$, EuCl$_3$). At no 63; at wt 151.96; mp 822°C; bp 1527°C.

● **Europoort** ▷*See* Rotterdam.

● **Eurydice** ► In Greek legend, a ▷dryad, the wife of ▷Orpheus. She died of a snake bite. Orpheus descended to the underworld to recover her but lost her forever when he violated the condition of her release and turned to look at her before emerging.

● **eurypterid** ► An extinct ▷arthropod, also called water scorpion, belonging to a subclass (*Eurypterida*) of the Ordovician and Permian periods, i.e. 500–225 million years ago. Its tapering segmented body, up to 3 m long, bore several pairs of oarlike appendages at the head end. Eurypterids, which lived in salt or brackish waters, were predators of worms and small fish or bottom-dwelling scavengers. ⁰fossil.

● **Eusebius of Caesarea** ► (4th century AD) Christian churchman and historian. As Bishop of Caesarea from 313, he took a moderate position on ▷Arianism and sought a compromise between the views of Arius and Athanasius; he finally accepted the creed proposed by the Council of ▷Nicaea. He is famous for his *Ecclesiastical History*.

● **Eustace, St** ► (2nd century AD) Roman martyr and patron saint of hunters. According to tradition, he was a general who was converted to Christianity after seeing a vision of a stag with a crucifix between its antlers. Feast Day: 20 Sept.

● **Eustachio, Bartolommeo** ► (?1520–74) Italian anatomist and physician, who gave his name to the canal connecting the ear and throat (the Eustachian tube) although this had already been discovered by ▷Alcmaeon (5th century BC). Eustachio's anatomical studies included the ear, kidney, and nervous system but his *Tabulae anatomicae* was not published until 1714.

● **eustasy** ► Worldwide changes in sea level, attributed mainly to the accumulation and release of water in the form of ice. Since the last Ice Age sea level has risen gradually.

● **Euterpe** ► In Greek legend, one of the ▷Muses, the patron of·tragedy, flute playing, or lyric poetry.

● **euthanasia** ► (Greek: easy death) The taking of life to relieve suffering. Whether or not those with painful and incurable diseases

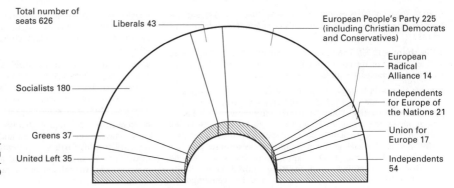

Total number of seats 626
Liberals 43
European People's Party 225 (including Christian Democrats and Conservatives)
European Radical Alliance 14
Socialists 180
Independents for Europe of the Nations 21
Greens 37
Union for Europe 17
United Left 35
Independents 54

European Union ▶ Diagram showing the distribution of seats among the political parties in the European Parliament after the 1999 elections.

should be allowed a painless means of dying if they ask for it remains controversial. Such voluntary euthanasia includes both active steps for taking life (e.g. administration of drugs) and the withholding of life-supporting treatment (passive euthanasia). More unacceptable to some would be compulsory euthanasia, in which the patient—for example, a deformed baby—is unable to express its wishes and the responsibility for deciding to terminate life rests on society or a person acting on authority. Many societies exist to promote voluntary euthanasia (e.g. The Voluntary Euthanasia Society, also known as Exit). Voluntary euthanasia was effectively decriminalized in the Netherlands in 1993 and made fully legal under certain conditions in 2001. Euthanasia has also been legalized in certain strictly defined circumstances in Oregon, USA (1998) and Belgium (2002). ▷*See also* living will.

● **eutrophication** ▶ The overfertilization of lakes, due chiefly to pollution by sewage, runoff from the land, and industrial wastes (inorganic nitrates and phosphates). These compounds act as nutrients, stimulating algal growth to produce huge blooms. Their subsequent decomposition reduces the oxygen content in the water, so killing animals with a high oxygen requirement. Much of the nitrate and phosphate settles to the bottom, to promote further growth at a later stage.

● **Evangelicalism** ▶ A movement within Protestant Churches that advocates traditional concepts of biblical belief. Evangelicals reject the Catholic and Orthodox view of authority residing in the traditions of the Church and the ▷apostolic succession, while remaining faithful to Trinitarian orthodoxy. They resist the liberalizing trend apparent in nonevangelical Protestant circles, emphasizing the importance of personal salvation and the divine inspiration of the Bible.

● **Evans, Sir Arthur John** ▶ (1851–1941) British archaeologist. His interest in Cretan sealstones, while Keeper of the Ashmolean Museum, led him to his life's work, the excavation of ▷Knossos (1899–1935). In *The Palace of Minos* (1921–36) he established the chronology of ▷Minoan civilization.

● **Evans, Dame Edith** ▶ (1888–1976) British actress. Her long career included many celebrated performances in Shakespearean roles and in classic comedies such as *The Rivals* and *The Importance of Being Earnest*. She gave some of her most acclaimed stage and film performances during her eighties.

● **Evans, Sir Geraint** ▶ (1922–92) Welsh opera singer. A baritone, he made his debut at Covent Garden in 1948 in Wagner's *Die Meistersinger*. He was well known for his interpretations of the title roles of Verdi's *Falstaff* and Berg's *Wozzeck*.

● **Evans, Oliver** ▶ (1755–1819) American engineer, who conceived the principle of the continuous production line. In 1784 Evans put his ideas into practice in a flour mill: corn entered one end of an automated production line, was processed, and then discharged as flour at the other end. He also patented a high-pressure steam engine in 1790, which was the first major improvement on James ▷Watt's engine.

● **Evansville** ▶ 38 00N 87 33W A city in the USA, in SW Indiana on the Ohio River. Its industries include plastics, meat packing, refrigeration equipment, flour milling, pharmaceuticals, and aluminium. Population (1998 est): 122 779.

● **evaporation** ▶ The conversion of a liquid into a vapour at temperatures below its boiling point. As it is the most energetic atoms and molecules that escape from the surface in evaporation, the average energy of those that remain is reduced and consequently the liquid is cooled.

● **Evelyn, John** ▶ (1620–1706) English diarist. He travelled in Europe during the Civil War and after the Restoration held several administrative posts and helped to found the Royal Society. He wrote practical works on various subjects but is best known for his *Diary*, covering the years 1641–1706.

● **evening primrose** ▶ A herbaceous plant of the genus *Oenothera* (100 species), 90–100 cm tall, native to the Americas but widespread in Europe. The fragrant yellow flowers, 2–5 cm in diameter, open in the evening. The leaves are spirally arranged and the fruit is a long capsule. Family: *Onagraceae* (willowherb family).

● **event horizon** ▷*See* black hole; singularity.

● **eventing** ▷*See* horse trials.

● **Everest, Mount** ▶ 27 59N 86 56E The highest mountain in the world, on the Nepal–Tibet border in the Himalayas. It was recognized as the highest in 1852, but the height itself was not established until 1955. Climbing attempts started in 1920 and the 12th expedition, led by Col John ▷Hunt, was the first to succeed: (Sir) Edmund ▷Hillary and Sherpa ▷Tenzing Norgay reached the summit on 29 May, 1953. On 5 May, 1978, two Austrians, Peter Habeler (1942–) and Reinhold Messner, became the first to reach the top without the aid of oxygen breathing equipment. Height: 8850 m (29 035 ft). □ p. 438.

● **Everglades** ▶ A subtropical swampy area in the USA, in Florida extending S of Lake Okeechobee. The natural vegetation of sawgrass and rushes is preserved in the Everglades National Park but elsewhere large areas have been drained.

● **evergreen plants** ▶ Plants the foliage of which is retained throughout the year. The leaves of evergreens, which are tough and waxy, are produced and shed at different times all the year round, individual leaves often remaining on the tree for several years. Most conifers and many tropical broad-leaved trees are evergreen. **Deciduous plants** produce softer leaves, which are all shed before winter, leaving only the woody parts and protected buds exposed. Deciduous trees generally occur in temperate regions having seasonal fluctuations in climate.

● **everlasting flowers** ▶ Any flowers that can be dried without losing their shape or colour and are used in floral arrangements and pictures. They include many members of the *Compositae* (daisy family), such as the true everlastings, or immortelles (*Helichrysum* species), the flower heads of which may be dyed various colours. One of the most popular of these is the strawflower of Australia (*H. bracteatum*). Other plants used include *Anaphalis margaritacea* (the pearly everlasting) and *Gnaphalium* and *Helipterum* species, and striking shapes are supplied by ▷teasels (*Dipsacus* species). Grasses with showy panicles are often used, especially wild oats and barley.

● **Evert, Chris(tine)** ▶ (1954–) US tennis player who was Wimbledon singles champion in 1974, 1976 and 1981 and doubles champion in 1976. She won the US singles title 1975–78, 1980 and 1982. She was formerly married to the British tennis player John Lloyd; she retired in 1989.

● **Evesham** ▶ 52 06N 1 56W A market town in W central England, in Worcestershire on the River Avon. The Vale of Evesham is famous for fruit and vegetables. Population (1991): 17 823.

● **evolution** ▶ In biology, the gradual and continuous process by which the first and most primitive of living organisms have developed into the diversity of plant and animal life known today. Speculations about the origin of living things go back to the Greek philosophers, notably Aristotle, but until the 18th century it was generally believed that each group of organisms was separately and divinely created. In the 1760s ▷Linnaeus—in his work on the classification and naming of organisms—recognized the possibility of relationship between similar groups, and his contemporary ▷Buffon suggested that the differences he observed in fossil organisms were brought about by changes in the environment in which they lived.

The first theory of evolution was published by Lamarck, in 1809 (*see* Lamarckism). His explanation of the process—that changes in form acquired during the lifetime of an animal could be inherited—lacked definite proof, although it has had its supporters. A more satisfactory theory was put forward by Charles ▷Darwin and A. R. ▷Wallace in 1858: they proposed that new species arose by a process of natural selection acting on individual inheritable variations in a population (*see* Darwinism). Later work has proved that these heritable changes result from spontaneous genetic mutations, and Darwin's theory—with some modifications—is now generally accepted.

● **Évora** ▶ (ancient name: Ebora) 38 34N 7 54W A town in Portugal. It contains many Roman ruins including a temple known as the Temple of Diana. Population (latest est): 34 072.

● **Évreux** ▶ 49 03N 1 11E A town in NW France, the capital of the Eure department. It has a cathedral (11th–18th centuries) and there are Roman remains nearby. Its manufactures include textiles, rubber, and pharmaceuticals. Population (1990): 51 450.

● **evzones** ▶ Member of a Greek infantry regiment, originally from Epirus, who fought with distinction in the Balkan Wars and World War II. Evzones wear a distinctive white-skirted uniform; their name derives from the Greek word meaning "dressed for exercise."

● **Ewald, Johannes** ▶ (1743–81) Danish Romantic poet and playwright, who ran away at the age of 15 to fight in the Seven Years' War. On returning he began to write; his work was influenced by Klopstock, Shakespeare, and Macpherson's *Ossian*. He was the first Danish writer to use legend and myth as the basis for his works, which include the tragedies *Rolf Krage* (1770) and *Balders Død* (*The Death of Baldur*; 1773).

● **Ewe** ▶ A people of SE Ghana and S Togo, numbering approximately one million, who originated from ▷Oyo in Nigeria. Their language belongs to the ▷Kwa subgroup of the Niger-Congo family. They practise shifting agriculture and, in coastal areas, seafishing. They are divided into independent groups, which form temporary alliances for war.

● **Excalibur** ▶ King Arthur's magic sword. In one legend Arthur succeeds, where others had failed, in drawing it from a stone, thereby proving his claim to the English throne. In another he receives it from the Lady of the Lake, to whom it is thrown back at his death. ▷*See also* Arthurian legend.

● **excavator** ▶ A self-propelled vehicle equipped with a hydraulically powered movable boom and shovel used for excavating trenches, loading earth, etc. Larger models are used for mining and quarrying and usually consist of a crawler vehicle on which is mounted a boom with one or several digging buckets controlled by cables from a winch.

● **exchange control** ▶ Government regulations to control the extent to which a foreign currency can be purchased to prevent a large outflow of foreign exchange, which might precipitate a ▷balance-of-payments crisis. The UK used exchange control extensively in the face of the country's chronic tendency to short-term outflows of foreign exchange, but its impact was limited because of the activities of nonresident holders of sterling, who tend to be the most active in switching funds. In 1979 the UK removed nearly all of its exchange-control restrictions.

● **exchange rates** ▶ The value of one country's currency in terms of another's. Foreign trade and tourism make it essential for currencies to be convertible at a stable rate of exchange. Until World War I and again briefly between 1925 and 1931 international currencies were backed by, and convertible into, gold (*see* gold standard). Between 1931 and 1947 various systems were in use. In the UK, for instance, the Exchange Equalization Account was set up in 1932 to enable the Bank of England to control the official gold and foreign-exchange reserves.

In 1947 the ▷International Monetary Fund (IMF) came into operation, as a result of the ▷Bretton Woods Conference (1944). The IMF fixed par values for members' currencies in terms of gold and these values could not be changed without consulting the IMF. ▷Special Drawing Rights were introduced in 1970 in an attempt to increase world liquidity, but were unable to maintain the stability of the system: the suspension of convertibility from US dollars to gold in 1971 led to an agreement to allow currencies to float (i.e. to find their own value as a result of market forces). Floating rates avoid the problem of large destabilizing devaluation, which took place under the Bretton Woods fixed-rate system.

The aim of the EEC "snake," and its successor, the ▷European Monetary System, was to fix the European currencies in terms of each other. The goal of a monetary union with one European currency was finally realized (for the 11 participating nations) in January 1999.

● **excise tax** ▷*See* customs and excise duties.

Mount Everest ▶ The north face of the world's highest mountain, the summit of which protrudes through two-thirds of the earth's atmosphere. In winter it is relatively free of snow because of the strong northwesterly gales.

● **excitation** ▶ In physics, the raising of a system from its lowest energy level (the ground state) to a higher energy level (the excited state). Usually confined to atoms, molecules, ions, and nuclei, it is most frequently caused by the absorption of a ▷photon. In an atom, ion, or nucleus the photon is absorbed by an electron or ▷nucleon causing it to move to a higher energy level. Molecules can also be excited into higher states of rotational or vibrational energy.

● **Exclusionists** ▶ Free settlers in the colony of New South Wales who wished to debar former convicts from equal civil and political rights. The constitution of 1842 ended this inequality. ▷*See also* Emancipists.

● **exclusion principle** ▷*See* Pauli exclusion principle.

● **excommunication** ▶ The exclusion of a Christian from the community of the Church for misconduct. There are biblical precedents for various forms of excommunication, especially in the Pauline epistles. In the later Church, exclusion from the sacraments was frequently used as a means of censure, and in the middle ages the papacy used it to apply political pressure against sovereigns. It is still used by the Roman Catholic Church as a form of discipline and is theoretically available in some Protestant Churches.

● **excretion** ▶ The elimination of the waste products of metabolism by the body. In higher animals and man this includes the excretion of nitrogenous waste in the form of urine by the ▷kidneys, the egestion of faeces—the waste products of digestion—from the bowel, and the exhalation of carbon dioxide from the lungs in breathing. A small amount of urea is also excreted in sweat. Lower animals have various simple organs for the excretion of waste products.

● **Exe, River** ▶ A river in SW England. Rising on Exmoor in Somerset, it flows SE across Devon to Exeter, where it widens into an estuary, popular for sailing, and flows into the sea at Exmouth. Length: 96 km (60 mi).

● **Exekias** ▶ (6th century BC) Athenian potter and vase painter, known from his signatures on several vases. One of the last black-figure painters, Exekias painted dignified symmetrical compositions in painstaking but fluent detail.

● **Exeter** ▶ 50 43N 3 31W A city in SW England, the administrative centre of Devon on the River Exe. Its 13th-century cathedral, a fine example of gothic architecture, was damaged by bombing in World War II. Exeter's Guildhall is said to be the oldest municipal building in the country. Exeter University (1955) succeeded the University College of the South West. Commercial activities include tourism, distribution, the manufacture of agricultural machinery, and various light industries. Population (1993 est): 105 100.

● **existentialism** ▶ A philosophical movement that rejects metaphysics and concentrates on the individual's existence in the world. The forerunner of existentialism, ▷Kierkegaard, reacted against German ▷idealism and the complacency of established Christianity by developing a pragmatic psychologically realistic philosophy of existence. A similar emphasis was adopted by ▷Heidegger and ▷Husserl in the 1930s. A fully developed philosophy of existentialism was adopted by French intellectuals, especially Sartre, after World War II. Sartre's existentialism allows individuals freedom in a nihilistic universe: "All human activities are equivalent, all are destined by principle to defeat." At the same time a man is responsible for his effect on others, even though only *his* existence is real to him and he is ultimately his own judge. Sartre expounded existentialism chiefly in *Being and Nothingness* (1943), but his plays and novels (and those of ▷Camus) present existentialist ideas more accessibly.

● **Exmoor** ▶ A high moorland and national park of SW England, extending from NE Devon into W Somerset, reaching 520 m (1707 ft) at Dunkery Beacon. It supports heather, bracken, and grass and is grazed by Exmoor ponies, wild red deer, and sheep. Parts are now being ploughed for more intensive agriculture. R. D. Blackmore's novel *Lorna Doone* was set here. Area: 686 sq km (265 sq mi).

● **Exmoor pony** ▶ A breed of pony originating in the Exmoor region of SW England. It is hardy and sure-footed with a broad deep chest, small hard feet, short ears, and large prominent eyes. The coat is bay, brown, or dun and becomes thick and wiry in winter. Exmoors are used as breeding stock. Height: about 1.27 m (12½ hands).

● **Exmouth** ▶ 50 37N 3 25W A town in SW England, in Devon at the mouth of the River Exe. It is a resort and fishing port, with light industry. Population (1991): 28 414.

● **exobiology** ▷*See* astrobiology.

● **Exodus** ▶ (Greek: going out) The second book of the Bible, traditionally ascribed to Moses. It recounts the events culminating in the departure of the Israelites from Egypt, where they had lived as slaves since the time of Joseph, and their arrival at Mount Sinai, where the ▷Ten Commandments are given to Moses. The narrative also includes the story of the birth of Moses, the establishment of the ▷Passover, and the miraculous crossing of the Red Sea. The events themselves perhaps date from the 15th century BC; the book was probably compiled between the 9th and 4th centuries BC.

● **exorcism** ▶ The religious practice of driving out evil spirits by means of prayers and other ritual acts. It is a common rite in a number of religions, including ancient Judaism, and was adopted by Christianity on the basis that it was performed by Christ and the apostles in the New Testament. It refers specifically to the prayers, etc., used to expel evil spirits that supposedly possess a person. Although still available in some Churches, the rite may only be performed by a priest with a bishop's permission.

● **exosphere** ▷*See* atmosphere.

● **exothermic reaction** ▷*See* enthalpy.

● **expanding universe** ▶ The theory that the universe is expanding was first confirmed by Edwin ▷Hubble in 1929 following observations that the light from distant galaxies is subject to a ▷redshift, which arises from the recession of the galaxies from us (and from each other). The expansion can be explained by the ▷big-bang theory. ▷*See also* Hubble constant.

● **expansion** ▶ The general increase in dimensions of a substance with increasing temperature. In solids it is caused by the greater vibrational energy of the atoms leading to increased interatomic distances. In liquids and gases the expansion is caused by the greater velocities of the atoms or molecules. The expansion of an ideal gas is described by ▷Charles's law. The **expansivity** *or* **coefficient of linear expansion** of a substance is its increase in length per unit length caused by a rise in temperature of 1°C.

● **explosives** ▶ Substances that can be made to produce a large volume of gas very suddenly. The energy of the expanding gases may be used for a number of industrial or military purposes. There are three main types. **Mechanical explosives** depend on a physical reaction, such as overloading a container of gas until it bursts. They are little used except in specialized mining applications where the release of gas from chemicals is undesirable. In **nuclear explosives**, a nuclear chain reaction (see nuclear energy) takes place in a sudden uncontrolled manner, releasing energy almost instantaneously. This is used for bombs and occasionally for mining. Most explosives used are **chemical explosives**. These include ▷TNT, ▷nitroglycerin, ▷dynamite, and ▷gelignite. Modern high explosives are often in the form of water gels, which are plastic, water resistant, and easy to handle safely. ▷*See also* Semtex.

● **exponential function** ▶ A mathematical function of the general form Ae^{Bx} where A and B are constants and e is the base of natural ▷logarithms. Bx is called the exponent; if the exponent is a complicated expression, $f(x)$ say, then the function is often written as $\exp[f(x)]$. The function e^x has the important property that its differential is always equal to the function itself. ▷*See also* calculus.

● **exposure meter** ▶ A device for measuring the intensity of light falling on a photographic ▷camera, used to determine the film exposure time and lens ▷f-number needed to suit the lighting conditions. It often consists of a ▷photocell that is directed at the subject from the camera, registering light as a reading on an electric current meter. In some cameras this current is used to control the aperture or shutter speed automatically.

● **expressionism** ▶ A movement in the arts of the early 20th century in which the force of human emotion was allowed to distort the presentation of the external world. It was most important in the visual arts but also significant in cinema, theatre, literature, and music. In painting, the bright colours and distorted forms of ▷Van Gogh and Edvard ▷Munch foreshadow expressionism proper: an even earlier forerunner was the German painter ▷Grünewald. In the 20th century the chief exponents were Die ▷Brücke and Der ▷Blaue Reiter groups in Germany but independent figures, such as ▷Rouault, ▷Soutine, ▷Schiele, and ▷Kokoschka, also worked in an expressionist style. The 1970s and 1980s saw a revival of expressionism by such painters as Georg Baselitz (1938–) and Anselm Kiefer (1945–).

In the cinema, pioneers of expressionism included the German directors Fritz ▷Lang, G. W. ▷Pabst, and F. W. Murnau (1888–1931). Their work is characterized by the use of a non-naturalistic style (including distorted perspective, unusual camera angles, and extreme contrasts of light and shade) to convey disturbed or abnormal states of mind. In drama, expressionism emerged as a definite movement in the German theatre of the 1910s and 1920s, when such writers as George ▷Kaiser, Ernst ▷Toller, and the young ▷Brecht experimented with nonrealistic styles. In literature and music the term is used more loosely: the writings of ▷Kafka and the early music of ▷Berg and ▷Schoenberg are often described as expressionist.

● **extortion** ▶ In law, a misdemeanour committed by someone holding a public office who, under the guise of his office, wrongfully takes from another money or any valuable thing not due to him. It was abolished in England by the Theft Act (1968) and is now mainly covered by ▷blackmail.

● **extrasensory perception** ▶ (ESP) Acquisition of information not accessible through normal perceptual processes. Three phenomena are usually classified as ESP: clairvoyance (knowledge of distant events and concealed objects), telepathy (thought transference between people), and precognition (knowledge of future events). Evidence for all three tends to be anecdotal, but some experiments in which subjects have been asked to guess symbols on cards of which they can see only the backs or to reproduce, without having seen it, a simple sketch done by another person are said to show a statistically significant success rate. ▷*See also* Rhine, Joseph Banks.

● **extreme unction** ▷*See* anointing of the sick.

● **extroversion** ▶ (or extraversion) The tendency to be interested in the outside world more than in oneself. Extroversion is a quality of personality, first described by Carl ▷Jung and still used in modern theories of personality. Extroverts are gregarious and outgoing. They prefer frequent changes of activity; their interests tend to be practical and scientific rather than philosophical; and they tend to be resistant to permanent ▷conditioning. *Compare* introversion.

● **extrusive rock** ▷*See* igneous rock.

● **Eyde, Samuel** ▷*See* nitrogen fixation.

● **eye** ▶ The organ of sight. The human eyes lie within two bony sockets in the skull and are attached by six muscles, which produce eye movements. At the front of the eye the white fibrous outer layer (sclera) is replaced by a transparent curved layer (*see* cornea). A delicate membrane (the conjunctiva) covers the front of the eye and lines the eyelids: it is liable to become inflamed (*see* conjunctivitis). Light entering the eye is refracted by the cornea and passes through the watery aqueous humour and pupil to the lens. The pigmented ▷iris controls the amount of light entering the eye. The shape of the lens can be adjusted by means of the ciliary muscles so that an image is focused through the jelly-like vitreous humour onto the ▷retina. Contraction of the ciliary muscles causes the lens to become flattened for focusing distant objects; relaxation of the muscles increases the curvature of the lens for focusing near objects. Light-sensitive cells in the retina send impulses to the brain via the optic nerve. ▷*See also* blindness; longsightedness; ophthalmology; shortsightedness.

● **eyebright** ▶ A semiparasitic annual herb of the genus *Euphrasia* (over 130 species), of temperate regions. Eyebrights have small toothed leaves and small unstalked two-lipped flowers, usually white with violet and yellow markings. They grow to a height of 15 cm. Family: *Scrophulariaceae*.

● **Eyre, Edward John** ▶ (1815–1901) British explorer and colonial administrator. He led a successful expedition in central Australia (1840–41) and both Lake Eyre and the Eyre Peninsula are named after him. As governor of Jamaica (1864–66) he gained notoriety for his harsh suppression of a revolt (1865), which was followed by over 400 executions. Recalled to England, he was prosecuted by a Jamaican but acquitted.

● **Eyre, Lake** ▶ A shallow salt lake of NE South Australia. It is normally dry except during the rainy season when heavy rains from N Queensland and the Northern Territory are fed into the lake by ▷Cooper Creek and other streams. The last time it was full was in 1950. Lowest point: about 10 m (36 ft) below sea level. Area: about 9100 sq km (3500 sq mi).

● **Eyre Peninsula** ▶ A peninsula of South Australia, situated between the Great Australian Bight and Spencer Gulf. Iron ore is mined in the Middleback Range in the NE.

● **Eysenck, Hans Jürgen** ▶ (1916–97) British psychologist. German-born but educated in France and Britain, Eysenck was appointed professor of psychology at London University in 1955. A critic of conventional psychoanalysis, he developed an alternative treatment—▷behaviour therapy—for neurosis and other mental disorders. Eysenck also developed scientifically based methods of evaluating personality and intelligence, partly based on the distinction between introverts and extroverts. His findings on racial differences in intelligence (*Race, Intelligence and Education*, 1971) caused much controversy. In 1991 he claimed that a link exists between personality types and illness.

● **Ezekiel** ▶ An Old Testament prophet, the successor of ▷Isaiah and ▷Jeremiah. **The Book of Ezekiel** records his prophecies probably written during the ▷Babylonian exile (6th century BC). The prophecies concern the coming destruction of Jerusalem and Israel, denunciations of various foreign states, the renewal of the people, and finally the ideal society and the rebuilding of the Temple at Jerusalem.

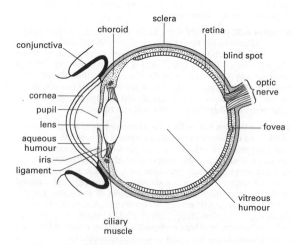

eye ▶ The structure of the human eye is revealed in this section. The blind spot, where the optic nerve leaves the eye, contains no visual cells and is therefore insensitive to light. The fovea is the area of acutest vision.

● **Ezra** ▶ In the Old Testament, a religious reformer, who was sent by the Persian king, possibly ▷Artaxerxes II (c. 436–358 BC), to regulate Jewish affairs in Jerusalem.
The Book of Ezra in the Old Testament is a sequel to ▷Chronicles and was compiled by the author of Chronicles and the Book of ▷Nehemiah. It records the return of the Jews after the ▷Babylonian exile in about 537 BC, the rebuilding of the Temple, and legal and religious reforms introduced by Ezra.

F

● **Fabaceae** ▷*See* Leguminosae.

● **Fabergé, Peter Carl** ▶ (1846–1920) Russian goldsmith and jeweller. He designed elegant *objets d'art* and was patronized by European royalty. He was famous for jewelled Easter eggs containing surprise gifts made for the tsars. He died in exile.

● **Fabian Society** ▶ A society, named after ▷Fabius Maximus, formed in London in 1884 to promote gradual socialist reform through persistent argument and the patient use of constitutional means. Members included George Bernard ▷Shaw, Sidney and Beatrice ▷Webb, and Annie ▷Besant. The Fabians were active in the establishment of the Labour Party and today continue to argue for social reform through public lectures, conferences, and publications.

● **Fabius Maximus, Quintus** ▶ (d. 203 BC) Roman general of the second ▷Punic War. Appointed dictator after ▷Hannibal's defeat of the Romans at Trasimene in 217, Fabius adopted a policy of attrition, harassing Hannibal but avoiding pitched battles. His derogatory title Cunctator (Delayer) became honourable after Hannibal's victory at ▷Cannae proved the wisdom of Fabius' tactics. It was ▷Scipio Africanus' aggressive policies, however, that achieved the final triumph after Fabius' death.

● **fable** ▶ A short narrative in prose or verse, often with animal characters, which illustrates a moral truth. The Western literary form had its origins in the fables attributed to ▷Aesop (6th century BC) and later expanded by ▷Phaedrus (1st century AD). The medieval beast epic developed from this form, which reached its highest degree in the work of ▷La Fontaine. Authors of children's literature, notably ▷Kipling, ▷Carroll, and Beatrix ▷Potter, have used this form extensively. Modern fables have been written by ▷Orwell and ▷Thurber.

● **fabliau** ▶ A medieval French comic and satiric narrative poem, a type that flourished between 1150 and 1400. About 150 examples survive, mostly simple tales the humour of which is usually broad and obscene. Among known authors is Rutebeuf (*see* trouvères). Chaucer's *Miller's Tale* and *Reeve's Tale* (in the *Canterbury Tales*) are the outstanding examples in English.

● **Fabre, Jean Henri** ▶ (1823–1915) French entomologist, noted for his studies of bees, wasps, and other insects. Fabre realized the importance of inherited instinct in insect behaviour. His popular books included *Souvenirs entomologiques* (1879–1907).

● **Fabricius ab Aquapendente, Hieronymus** ▶ (1537–1619) Italian physician. A student of ▷Fallopius, he himself became an eminent teacher, one of his pupils being William ▷Harvey. He studied embryology and fetal development (*De formata foetu*, 1600) and discovered one-way valves in veins.

● **Fabritius, Carel** ▶ (1622–54) Dutch painter of portraits and everyday life. In contrast to his teacher Rembrandt, he specialized in daylight scenes, which had some influence on Vermeer. He was killed in an explosion in Delft, which probably also destroyed many of his works; his masterpiece, *The Goldfinch* (The Hague), survives.

● **Fabry, Charles** ▶ (1867–1945) French physicist, who while working at the Sorbonne discovered ▷ozone in the upper atmosphere (1913). This discovery was made with the Fabry-Pérot interferometer, designed with Alfred Pérot (1863–1925).

● **facsimile transmission** ▷*See* fax.

● **factoring** ▶ The commercial practice of buying trade debts and collecting them on behalf of clients. If a manufacturer sells his products to a number of customers, some of whom may be slow payers, he can sell these debts to a factor, who will usually pay 80% of the debt immediately and the balance (less a service charge) when the debt has been collected. This service is often combined (for an extra charge) with credit insurance, enabling the debt to be guaranteed even if the debtor fails.

● **Factory Acts** ▶ UK parliamentary Acts that regulate conditions of work in factories. A response to the appalling conditions resulting from the ▷industrial revolution, the early Factory Acts (1802, 1819, 1833) were concerned mainly with the employment of children. Ashley (later Lord ▷Shaftesbury), leader of the ten-hour movement, was largely responsible for the Acts of 1844 and 1847. The safety, health, and welfare of factory workers is now regulated by the Factories Act (1961) and the Health and Safety at Work Act (1974).

factory farming ▶ Gathering the eggs in an intensive poultry house.

● **factory farming** ▶ Intensive livestock production in which large numbers of animals are kept in confined artificial environments with feed intake, lighting, temperature, and other factors carefully controlled to maximize production. Battery cages for laying hens and crates for veal calves are the best known methods, but beef cattle, bacon pigs, and even dairy cows can also be reared in "factory" systems. Voluntary or statutory welfare codes set minimum standards for such systems, but critics argue that the animals suffer mental if not physical distress and the edible products of factory farming contain high levels of hormones or antibiotics. In 1999 EU countries agreed to end all battery-egg production by 2013.

● **Fadden, Sir Arthur William** ▶ (1895–1973) Australian statesman; prime minister (1941) following Menzies' resignation. He was leader of the Country Party (1941–58).

● **faeces** ▶ The material that is expelled from the bowels through the anus. It is a solid or semisolid mass consisting of undigested food (chiefly cellulose and other fibres), mucus, bacteria, and material from the liver, including bile pigments (which colour the faeces). Any persistent change in appearance may indicate disease. ▷See also diarrhoea.

● **Faenza** ► 44 19N 11 54E A town in N Italy, in Emilia-Romagna. During the 15th and 16th centuries it was famous for maiolica earthenware, especially ▷faience; a ceramics museum was founded here in 1908. Population (1990): 54 050.

● **Faeroe Islands** ► (or Faroe Islands; Danish name: Faerøerne) A Danish group of self-governing islands in the N Atlantic Ocean, between the Shetland Islands and Iceland. 17 of the 22 islands are inhabited, the chief ones being Strømø, Østerø, and Vaagø. Chiefly hilly, the terrain limits agriculture to sheep raising and the production of hay and potatoes. Fishing and fish processing are important. In 2001 the islands held a referendum on plans to move towards full independence. Official currency: krone of 100 øre. Area: 1400 sq km (540 sq mi). Population (1994): 43 719. Capital: Thorshavn, on Strømø.

● **Fahd Ibn Abdul Aziz** ► (1922–) King of Saudi Arabia and prime minister (1982–). He succeeded his half-brother, Khalid Ibn Abdul Aziz.

● **Fahrenheit scale** ► A temperature scale in which the temperature of melting ice is taken as 32 degrees and the temperature of boiling water, as 212 degrees. Named after the German physicist Gabriel Fahrenheit (1686–1736).

● **Fa-hsien** ▷See Fa Xian.

● **Faidherbe, Louis (Léon César)** ► (1818–89) French soldier and colonial administrator. As governor of Senegal (1854–65), there he established French supremacy and founded Dakar. During the Franco-Prussian War (1870–71), as commander of the Army of the North, he temporarily contained the German advance in the NE. He was also a noted archaeologist.

● **faience** ► Several kinds of tin-glazed earthenware made in France. Strictly, faience is French shorthand for porcellana di Faenza, a species of ▷maiolica made in Italy, and the technique of coating fragile porous earthenware with impervious hard white opaque tin glaze derives from maiolica. Italian potters were using the method in France in the 16th century. Centres of production during the 17th and 18th centuries were Lyons, Marseilles, Moustiers, Nevers, and Rouen. Designs drawn from local history (faience parlante) and revolutionary events (faience patriotique) were popular variations. Richly painted baroque and ▷rococo styles are common.

● **Fairbanks** ► 64 50N 147 50W A town in central Alaska. It is the terminus of the Alaska Railroad and the Alaska Highway. The University of Alaska (1935) is situated here. Population (1990): 30 800.

● **Fairbanks, Douglas** ► (Julius Ullman; 1883–1939) US film actor. With D. W. Griffith, Charlie Chaplin, and his wife Mary Pickford he founded United Artists Corporation in 1919. His films, in which he played the roles of handsome athletic heroes, include The Mark of Zorro (1920) and The Black Pirate (1926). His son **Douglas Fairbanks Jr** (1909–2000) was also a film actor. He played roles similar to those of his father, in films such as The Prisoner of Zenda (1937) and Sinbad the Sailor (1947). He lived for many years in Britain.

● **Fair Deal** ► The programme of social reform pursued by Harry S. Truman, president of the USA (1945–53). It promised more extensive social security and better labour conditions but only some of its recommendations (notably slum clearance and increased old-age benefits) passed Congress.

● **Fairfax, Thomas, 3rd Baron** ► (1612–71) English general, who as commander in chief of the ▷New Model Army defeated Charles I at ▷Naseby. Fairfax subsequently opposed the king's execution and resigned his command in 1650 in protest against the planned invasion of Scotland. After Cromwell's death he participated in the restoration of Charles II.

● **Fair Isle** ► 59 32N 1 38W A sparsely inhabited island in the North Sea, off the N coast of Scotland between the Orkney and Shetland Islands. It is famous for its knitted goods with intricate patterns and

has an important bird-migration observatory; other occupations include fishing. Area: 16.5 sq km (6 sq mi).

● **fairy bluebird** ► A songbird of the genus Irena (2 species), occurring in tropical evergreen forests and feeding chiefly on fruit and nectar. The blue-backed fairy bluebird (I. puella) of Indomalaysia has a glossy black plumage with a bright-blue back and tail and red eyes. Family: Irenidae (leafbirds).

● **fairy penguin** ► The smallest of the ▷penguins, Eudyptula minor, also called little penguin. About 30 cm tall, it is the only penguin commonly occurring on Australian coasts, breeding in dense colonies and nesting in crevices or disused burrows.

● **fairy shrimp** ► A ▷crustacean, belonging to the order Anostraca, that occurs in mainly freshwater pools and ponds of arid regions (compare brine shrimp). It has an elongated body, up to 25 mm long, without a carapace and swims on its back using 11–19 pairs of appendages. Class: ▷Branchiopoda.

● **fairy stories** ► Tales for children of a more or less simple kind, involving fantastic or supernatural elements. Most originate in oral tradition, although some are rewritten in sophisticated form, as with ▷Perrault's Tales of Mother Goose (1697); others, like Oscar ▷Wilde's The Happy Prince (1888), are purely literary in origin. The most famous collection of oral tales is Kinder- und Hausmärchen (1812–13) by the brothers ▷Grimm. Probably the most famous writer of original tales is the Dane Hans Christian ▷Andersen. Fairy tales often transcend national boundaries; similar tales are found throughout all European countries and sometimes even in the Far East.

● **Faisal I** ► (1885–1933) King of Iraq (1921–33). He played an important part in the Arab revolt during World War I. After the war he was briefly King of Syria before the French occupation (1920). In 1921 the British installed him as king in mandatory Iraq.

● **Faisalabad** ► (name until 1979: Lyallpur) 31 25N 73 09E A city in NE Pakistan. It is the centre of an agricultural region specializing in cotton and wheat. Population (1995 est): 1 875 000.

● **Faisal Ibn Abdul Aziz** ► (1905–75) King of Saudi Arabia (1964–75). A son of Ibn Saud, Faisal represented Saudi Arabia at the UN. In 1958 he became the real ruler of Saudi Arabia, although his brother Saud was still nominally king until abdicating in 1964. His reign saw the increased international importance of Saudi Arabia as an oil-producing country. He was assassinated by his nephew.

● **faith healing** ► (or spiritual healing) The curing of illness or disability by supernatural means. The temple of ▷Asclepius at ▷Epidauros was a famous faith-healing centre in antiquity. Christ is credited with several miraculous cures (Matthew 9.2–7, etc.). The need for healing within the framework of the organized churches was recognized by Archbishop William ▷Temple, who founded the Council for Health and Healing in 1944. Some charismatic healers apparently achieve cures unaccountable to science, particularly at mass rallies where powerful emotional effects operate upon the patients: in the Catholic tradition, similar cures are often reported at pilgrimage centres, such as Lourdes. However, the possibilities for deception by callous tricksters are obvious and frauds frequently occur.

● **Faiyum, El** ► (or al-Fayyum) 29 19N 30 50E A city in N Egypt, in the Libyan Desert. Nearby is the ancient site of Crocodilopolis, where the crocodile-god Sobek was worshipped. An agricultural centre, it manufactures cotton textiles. Population (1992 est): 250 000.

● **Fakhr ad-Din II** ► (c. 1572–1635) Ruler of Lebanon (1593–1633). He took advantage of the weakness of the Ottomans to expand into Syria and Palestine, but in 1635 was captured and executed in Istanbul. He is sometimes seen as a forerunner of Lebanese nationalists.

● **fakir** ► (Arabic: poor man) A Muslim mendicant who practises ascetic and religious exercises, often a member of a Muslim sect or of a Sufi religious brotherhood (compare dervishes). In India the term is applied more generally to any (Muslim or Hindu) ascetic or yogi.

● **Falabella** ► The smallest breed of pony, developed by the Falabella family in Argentina using Shetland pony stock. It has a fine soft coat of any colour and is popular as a mount for small children. Height: 38–76 cm (3¾–7½ hands).

● **Falaise** ▶ 48 54N 0 11W A small town in NW France, in the Calvados department. It is the site of the castle of the Dukes of Normandy, in which William the Conqueror was born. The town was virtually destroyed during World War II. Population (latest est): 8820.

● **Falange Española** ▶ The Spanish Fascist party, created in 1933 by José António ▷Primo de Rivera. The Falange wanted to regenerate Spain by means of revolution but rejected socialism as atheistic and alien to Spanish traditions. In 1937 Franco merged the Falange with the various Nationalist parties to create the National Movement, which became Spain's only legal party after the Civil War.

● **Falashas** ▶ An Ethiopian tribe, who practise an early form of Judaism. They adhere closely to the Bible but do not have the postbiblical Jewish literature or observances. In recent years many Falashas have been introduced to modern Judaism and some emigrated to Israel. In early 1985 the Israelis organized a secret airlift of over 7000 Falashas to Israel from famine-stricken Ethiopia.

● **falcon** ▶ A ground-nesting bird of prey belonging to a widely distributed family (*Falconidae*; 58 species). 15–60 cm long, falcons are characterized by long pointed wings and a notched hooked bill. True falcons belong to the genus *Falco;* they kill small birds in flight with their claws or seize small mammals from the ground. The small falconets occur in tropical regions and usually feed on insects. Order: *Falconiformes* (falcons, hawks, etc.). ▷*See also* caracara; gyrfalcon; hobby; kestrel; lanner falcon; merlin; peregrine.

falconry ▶ A falconer holding a seeker falcon at Lisbon airport. After hunters and sirens had failed to scare pigeons and seagulls from the take-off area, the airport authorities resorted to falcons.

● **falconry** ▶ (*or* hawking) The sport of hunting small animals or birds with falcons, other hawks, or sometimes eagles. It was practised in Asia from the 8th century BC and was very popular in Europe from late medieval times to the 17th century. Traditionally the birds are either taken as fledglings (eyasses) or caught as one-year-old birds (passagers) or fully mature birds (haggards), but because many hunting birds are now protected species, they are often bred in captivity. They are then trained to sit hooded on the gloved fist and, by the use of a lure (an imitation bird with meat attached), to hunt and kill (but not retrieve). Large species need open land, while smaller species are used in wooded country.

● **Faldo, Nick** ▶ (1957–   ) British golfer. His successes since turning professional in 1976 have included the US Masters' event (1989, 1990, 1996) and the British Open Championship (1987, 1990, 1992).

● **Falkirk** ▶ 1. 56 00N 3 48W A town in central Scotland, administrative centre of Falkirk council area, on the Forth-Clyde Canal. Here Edward I defeated William Wallace in 1296 and Bonnie Prince Charlie defeated Gen Hawley in 1746. A former centre for iron founding and aluminium rolling, it now has motor vehicle and textile industries. Population (1997 est): 37 228. 2. A council area in central Scotland, on the Firth of Forth. Formerly part of Stirling, it was absorbed into Central Region in 1974 and became an independent ▷unitary authority in 1996. It is mainly agricultural, with petrochemicals in Grangemouth and various industries in Falkirk. Area: 299 sq km (4700 sq mi). Population (1998 est): 144 100. Administrative centre: Falkirk.

● **Falkland Islands** ▶ (Argentine name: Islas Malvinas) An island group and United Kingdom overseas territory in the S Atlantic Ocean. The main islands of the group of about 100 are East and West Falkland; ▷South Georgia and the ▷South Sandwich group to the SE were formerly dependencies of the Falkland Islands but now form a separate overseas territory. The population is almost entirely of British origin. Fishing is a major source of revenue and sheep farming produces wool for export (chiefly to the UK).

History: the first landing was by Capt John Strong in 1690, who named the islands after Viscount Falkland, then treasurer to the Navy. In the early 19th century the islands became a British colony. During World War I the naval battle of the Falkland Islands, in which the Germans were defeated by the British, was fought off Falkland (8 December, 1914). Argentina has long made claims to the group and on 2 April, 1982, invaded the islands, triggering the **Falklands War**. After unsuccessful attempts by the UN and the USA to bring about a peaceful solution, the UK dispatched a task force of some 70 ships with supporting air cover to the islands. Some 10 weeks of fierce fighting ensued in which 254 British servicemen and 750 Argentinians died. 12 000 Argentinian troops surrendered on 14 June. The British victory gave a great boost to British morale and to the popularity of Margaret Thatcher, the prime minister. The defeat of Argentina led to the downfall of its military leader, Gen ▷Galtieri. Argentina refused to declare a cessation of hostilities until 1989. A new airport (1985) improved communications with Britain, and declaration of a fishing zone (1987) led to tripling of the islands' income. The economy has benefited greatly from a new trade in squid, and is expected to be revolutionized by the exploitation of newly discovered oil resources. Official currency: Falkland pound of 100 pence. Area: 12 173 sq km (4700 sq mi). Population (1996): 2221. Capital: Stanley.

● **Falla, Manuel de** ▶ (1876–1946) Spanish nationalist composer. He lived in Paris (1907–14), where he met Ravel and Debussy, and spent his last years in Argentina. His music was heavily influenced by Spanish folksong and he is best known for his ballet scores *Love the Magician* (1915) and *The Three-Cornered Hat* (1919), *Nights in the Gardens of Spain* (1909–15), and a concerto for harpsichord and chamber ensemble.

● **Fallopian tubes** ▷*See* ovary.

● **Fallopius, Gabriel** ▶ (1523–62) Italian anatomist, who discovered the tubes leading from the ovaries to the uterus, which were named after him (Fallopian tubes). A pupil of the great anatomist ▷Vesalius, Fallopius described the semicircular canals of the ear and many features of the reproductive system in his *Observationes anatomicae* (1561).

● **fallout** ▶ Radioactive particles deposited from the atmosphere after a nuclear explosion. If large the particles are deposited within a radius of a few hundred kilometres during the first few hours after the explosion. This is known as local fallout. Tropospheric fallout may occur anywhere along the same line of latitude as the explosion during the first week after the explosion. Particles drawn high into the atmosphere can cause stratospheric fallout for several years.

● **fallow deer** ▶ A ▷deer, *Dama dama*, native to Mediterranean forests but widely kept in parks and woodlands. About 90 cm high at the shoulder, fallow deer are fawn with white spots in summer, becoming greyish in winter; males have flattened antlers with numerous points. They feed mainly on grass but also browse on leaves.

● **Falmouth** ▶ 50 08N 5 4W A resort in SW England, in Cornwall at the mouth of the Fal estuary. It has a magnificent harbour with repair dockyards and fishing, especially oysters. Population (1991): 20 297.

● **False Decretals** ▶ A collection of mostly forged decrees compiled in 9th-century France, but incorporated into ▷Isidore of Seville's compilation of decrees of Church councils. They were used to establish the authority of the papacy at the time of its ascendancy up to the 11th century and were accepted as genuine, being discredited only in 1558.

● **False Dimitrii** ▷*See* Time of Troubles.

● **Falster** ▶ A Danish island in the Baltic Sea, linked by bridge to Sjælland and Lolland. Area: 513 sq km (198 sq mi). Population (1990 est): 42 846. Chief town: Nykøbing.

● **Falun** ▶ 60 37N 15 40E A town in central Sweden. Copper mining, important since early times, declined in the 17th century. Other industries include engineering and chemical industries. Population (1994): 55 014.

● **Famagusta** ▶ 35 07N 33 57E A port in Cyprus, on the E coast. Founded in the 3rd century BC, it did not develop until the 13th century AD, when Christians fled here from Palestine. It has an old walled town and a gothic cathedral (now a mosque). It handles most of the island's freight cargo. Its population was largely evacuated following the Turkish invasion of N Cyprus in 1974. Population (1994): 67 167.

● **family** ▶ (biology) ▷*See* taxonomy.

● **family planning** ▷*See* contraception.

● **family therapy** ▷*See* psychotherapy.

● **fandango** ▶ A Spanish dance with three beats to the bar performed by a man and a woman to the accompaniment of guitar and castanets. The dance begins slowly and becomes gradually faster; the dancers freeze when the music stops.

● **Fang** ▶ A Bantu people of West Africa comprising tribes in N Gabon, Equatorial Guinea, and S Cameroon. They were originally a warlike hunting people but became ivory traders and craftsmen under colonial rule. Cocoa farming is important.

● **Fangio, Juan Manuel** ▶ (1911–95) Argentinian motor-racing driver, who won 24 Grand Prix races and was world champion a record five times (1951, 1954–57).

● **Fa Ngum** ▶ (c. 1316–c. 1373) King of Lan Xang (*or* Lang Chang), which embraced most of present-day Laos, Thai-land, and part of Cambodia (1354–73). He proclaimed himself king after forcing the Lao chiefs of the upper Mekong to accept his sovereignty. He then launched further conquests to the S and W. Wearied by constant warfare, his subjects rebelled in 1373, forcing him to abdicate.

● **Fanning Island** ▶ (*or* Tabuaeran) 03 52N 159 22W A coral atoll in the W central Pacific Ocean, in Kiribati in the Line Islands. Copra is exported. Area: 33 sq km (13 sq mi). Population (1990): 1309.

● **fantail** ▶ A ▷flycatcher of the genus *Rhipidura* (24 species), of S Asia and Australasia, having a long fan-shaped tail. Fantails are 16–22 cm long with a grey, black, or reddish-brown plumage, often with patches of white on the breast, tail, and face.

● **fantasia** ▶ (*or* fantasy) In the 16th and 17th centuries, a piece of music (typically for viols or a keyboard instrument) having a polyphonic character. In the early 19th century the name was applied by such composers as Mozart and Beethoven to extended compositions that did not follow the ▷sonata form. It is also a piece of music constructed from themes from an opera or a number of well-known tunes, such as Liszt's fantasia on Mozart's opera *Don Giovanni*.

● **Fantin-Latour, (Ignace) Henri (Joseph Théodore)** ▶ (1836–1904) French painter, born in Grenoble. He is best known for his flower paintings and portrait groups, particularly of his impressionist friends in *Studio in the Batignolles Quarter* and *Homage to Delacroix* (both Louvre).

● **fanworm** ▶ A marine ▷annelid worm belonging to the family *Sabellidae*, also called peacock or feather-duster worm. Fanworms build a parchment-like tube, up to 45 cm long, from which protrudes a feathery crown of tentacles that trap food particles and absorb oxygen. Class: *Polychaeta*.

● **FAO** ▷*See* Food and Agriculture Organization.

● **farad** ▶ (F) The ▷SI unit of electrical capacitance equal to the capacitance of a capacitor across its plates that, if charged with one coulomb (C) has a potential difference of 1 volt (V), i.e. $1\ F = 1\ CV^{-1}$. Named after Michael ▷Faraday.

● **Faraday, Michael** ▶ (1791–1867) British chemist and physicist. Born into a poor London family, Faraday was apprenticed to a bookbinder where he found the books to excite his first interest in science. After attending lectures at the Royal Institution he persuaded Sir Humphry ▷Davy to take him on as his assistant (1813), eventually succeeding Davy there as professor of chemistry (1833). His earliest scientific work was on the liquefaction of gases (1823) and his first major contribution to science was the discovery of benzene (1825). However, it is with electricity and electrochemistry that his name is permanently linked. After discovering the process of ▷electrolysis (1832) he went on to work out the laws that control it (*see* Faraday's laws of electrolysis), no mean feat for a scientist without mathematical training. In electricity, he discovered the connection between electricity and magnetism and, independently of Joseph ▷Henry, first showed that electromagnetic induction was possible. He used induction to produce the first electrical generator (1831) and also the first transformer. Faraday was a deeply religious man; he had a breakdown in 1839 after which he did little creative work.

● **Faraday constant** ▶ The quantity of electricity equivalent to 1 mole of electrons, i.e. the product of the ▷Avogadro number and the electronic charge. It has the value 96 487 coulombs per mole.

● **Faraday effect** ▶ The rotation of the plane of polarization of plane-polarized light when it travels through certain substances in a direction parallel to the lines of force of an applied magnetic field. The effect occurs in quartz and water and is named after Michael ▷Faraday.

● **Faraday's laws of electrolysis** ▶ Two laws formulated by Michael ▷Faraday in 1813–14. (1) The mass of a substance produced by an electrolytic reaction varies directly with the amount of electricity passed through the cell. (2) The masses of substances produced by a given amount of electricity are proportional to the equivalent masses of the substances. These empirical laws are now understood to hold because electricity is composed of uniform discrete particles (electrons).

● **farce** ▶ (from Latin *farcire*: to stuff) A dramatic genre intended only to amuse its audience, a less sophisticated and less intellectual form than pure comedy. Elements common to most farce include peculiar situations, improbable coincidences, and ridiculous exaggerations of character and physical action. The term originally described comic interludes—"stuffing"—in medieval French religious plays. Some of the best farces were written in the late 19th century by Feydeau, Labiche, Pinero, and W. S. Gilbert.

● **Far East** ▶ The countries and areas of E and SE Asia bordering on the Pacific Ocean. It includes Siberia (Russia), China, North and South Korea, and Japan and sometimes all the countries of E and SE Asia.

● **Fareham** ▶ 50 51N 1 10W A town in S England, in Hampshire on Portsmouth Harbour. A former centre for boatbuilding, it now specializes in information technology and high-quality engineering. It is also a market town and sailing centre. Population (1991): 54 866.

● **Farel, Guillaume** ▶ (1489–1565) French Protestant reformer. Forced to leave France in 1524 because of his beliefs, he settled in Geneva. Although banished from the city, he later returned and succeeded in establishing Protestantism there in 1536. From 1537 he worked with John ▷Calvin, having persuaded him to stay in Geneva.

● **Farewell, Cape** ▶ 59 50N 43 40W The S tip of Greenland, on Egger Island. A headland rising to 600 m (2000 ft), it is edged with rocks and is known for its bad weather.

● **Fargo** ▶ 46 52N 96 49W A city in the USA, in North Dakota on the Red River. Named after the pioneer expressman William Fargo (*see* Wells, Henry), it is the trading centre of an agricultural region. The North Dakota State University was established here in 1890. Population (1996 est): 83 778.

● **Faridabad** ▶ 28 24N 77 18E A city in N India, in Haryana. Founded in 1607, it has grown rapidly in recent years as an industrial centre, with engineering and chemical industries. Population (1991): 613 828.

● **Farnaby, Giles** ▶ (c. 1565–1640) English composer. He wrote some fine canzonets in four parts and more than 50 of his pieces for the virginals were included in the Fitzwilliam Virginal Book.

● **Farnborough** ▶ 51 17N 0 46W A town in S England, in Hampshire. The Royal Aircraft Establishment, the UK's chief aeronautical research centre, is situated here and there are annual air displays. Napoleon III and the Empress Eugénie, who lived here in exile, are buried at Farnborough Hill. Population (1991): 52 535.

● **Farne Islands** ▶ (or The Staples) 55 38N 1 36W A group of about 30 islets and rocks in NE England, off the Northumberland coast. St Cuthbert lived on Inner Farne (the largest) and died here in 687 AD. In 1838 a heroic rescue by Grace ▷Darling took place from Longstone Island lighthouse.

● **Farnese, Alessandro, Duke of Parma** ▶ (1545–92) Italian general in the service of ▷Philip II of Spain (his uncle). In 1571 he fought the Turks at ▷Lepanto and from 1577 served against the ▷Revolt of the Netherlands. As governor general of the Netherlands (1578–92), he regained the southern provinces, making peace at Arras (1579). In 1585 he captured Antwerp following a 13-month siege.

● **Farnham** ▶ 51 13N 0 49W A market town in SE England, in Surrey. It has a 12th-century castle, formerly the palace of the Bishops of Winchester, and Waverley Abbey (1128) is nearby. Population (1991): 36 178.

● **Faro** ▶ 37 01N 7 56W A port in S Portugal, on the Atlantic Coast. Pillaged by the English in 1596, it was almost destroyed in the earthquakes of 1722 and 1755. It is now a popular tourist town with agricultural industries and sardine fishing. Population (1990): 31 970.

● **Faroe Islands** ▷See Faeroe Islands.

● **Farouk I** ▶ (1920–65) The last king of Egypt (1936–52). His inability to prevent British intervention in Egyptian affairs, and defeat in the first Arab-Israeli War (1948–49), led to his overthrow and exile in Monaco.

● **Farquhar, George** ▶ (1678–1707) Irish dramatist. After studying and acting in Dublin he won immediate success in London with his first play, *Love and a Bottle* (1699). His two best-known plays, *The Recruiting Officer* (1706) and *The Beaux' Stratagem* (1707), replaced the mannered and cynical Restoration drama with a more natural sentimental style.

● **Fasciola** ▷See liver fluke.

● **fascism** ▶ A 20th-century political movement. Taking its name from the *fasces*, the bound bundles of rods that symbolized the authority of ancient Roman magistrates, fascism first became an organized movement in Italy in 1919 under ▷Mussolini. Social and economic backwardness, fear of communism, and frustrated national ambitions following World War I encouraged its growth, and in 1922 Mussolini's ▷Blackshirts came to power. Fascism, rejecting ideas of individual liberty and equality, emphasized national or racial superiority and concentrated authority on a dictatorial cult

fascism ▶ Hitler seen here with his ally Mussolini during Hitler's state visit to Italy in May 1938.

figure. In Germany Hitler, who came to power in 1933 as leader of the ▷Nazi Party, added antisemitism to fascist militarism and anticommunism. World War II destroyed Mussolini's and Hitler's dictatorships and fascism won little support in other countries, except in Spain, where Franco's regime survived almost 40 years. The term fascist is now sometimes used pejoratively to describe any advocate of extreme right-wing views.

● **Fashoda incident** ▶ (1898) A confrontation between Britain and France at Fashoda in the Egyptian Sudan over their rival claims to the area. French forces under Jean-Baptiste Marchand (1863–1914) occupied the fort at Fashoda, which quickly brought ▷Kitchener and his Anglo-Egyptian force to the spot. After months of argument, which threatened war, Britain's claims were recognized.

● **Fassbinder, Rainer Werner** ▶ (1946–82) German film director. Working with a small group of actors in Munich, he produced a rapid succession of bleak realistic films on contemporary social themes. These include *The Bitter Tears of Petra von Kant* (1972), *Fear Eats the Soul* (1974), *Despair* (1978), and *The Marriage of Maria Braun* (1979).

● **fast reactor** ▶ A nuclear reactor (*see* nuclear energy) in which natural uranium enriched with uranium-235 or plutonium-239 is used without a moderator, the chain reaction being sustained by fast neutrons. In these reactors the core is surrounded by a blanket of natural uranium into which neutrons escape. These neutrons collide with U-238 nuclei to form U-239 nuclei, which decay to the fissionable isotope Pu-239. By suitable design, more Pu-239 can be produced in the blanket than is required to enrich the fuel in the core. These reactors are therefore called **breeder reactors** and they are 50 times more economical in uranium usage than ▷thermal reactors. Their main disadvantage is that the temperature is so high that a liquid metal (usually sodium) has to be used as coolant: any leakage of sodium could be disastrous. Also, plutonium is both extremely toxic and can be used to make ▷nuclear weapons. The 1200 MW prototype fast reactor Superphénix at Creys Malville in France is a joint European venture, started in 1986. Some 12 fast reactors are in development in the world (four in the EU). The UK ▷Dounreay prototype was closed in 1994.

● **Fatah, al-** ▶ (Arabic: the victory) A militant Palestinian organization established in the early 1960s. Led by Yassir ▷Arafat, al-Fatah began guerrilla warfare against Israel and had become the dominant faction within the ▷Palestine Liberation Organization by 1969. The organization has since split into factions pro and anti Arafat and his role in the Arab–Israeli peace process of the 1990s.

● **Fatehpur Sikri** ▶ 27 06N 77 39E A deserted city in Uttar Pradesh (N India). Founded (1569) by ▷Akbar (I) the Great, it was the Mogul capital until Akbar's move to Lahore (1585). Its palaces, mosques, and gateways are masterpieces of ▷Mogul architecture, notably the Buland Darwaza (Victory Gate).

● **Fateh Singh, Sant** ▶ (1911–72) Sikh religious leader and civil-rights campaigner. He joined with other Indian leaders in opposing British rule. After independence he agitated for an autonomous Punjabi-speaking Sikh state (established in 1966).

● **Fates** ▶ In Greek mythology, three goddesses who determine human destinies. The daughters of Zeus and Themis, they are: Lachesis, who assigns a person's position at birth; Clotho, who spins out the thread of his existence; and Atropos, who cuts the thread at death.

● **Fathers of the Church** ▶ The title given to certain revered writers of the early Christian Church whose works were regarded as carrying special weight in matters of doctrine. The period in which they lived extends from the 1st to the 7th centuries, and they are classified as ante-Nicene or post-Nicene according as to whether they lived before or after the Council of ▷Nicaea (325). They include Tertullian, Athanasius, Ambrose, Augustine, Jerome, and Gregory the Great.

● **fathom** ▶ A unit used to express depths of water. Originally intended to be the distance between a man's fingertips with his arms outstretched, it is equal to six feet. It has now largely been replaced by the metre.

● **Fátima** ▶ 39 37N 8 39W A village in central Portugal. It was here that three children allegedly saw a vision of the Virgin Mary (1917); it is now a place of pilgrimage.

● **Fatimah** ▶ (d. 632) The daughter of ▷Mohammed. She married ▷Ali and was the mother of Hasan and Husayn, from whom most of the Shiite ▷imams were descended. She died shortly after her father. The ▷Fatimids claimed descent from her.

● **Fatimids** ▶ A dynasty of ▷caliphs ruling in N Africa and Egypt (909–1171). The Fatimids claimed descent from ▷Fatimah and formed a subsect of the ▷Ismaili. They seized power in Tunisia in 909 and conquered Egypt in 969. In the 11th century their power declined and in 1171 they were finally overthrown by ▷Saladin. □Cairo.

● **fats and oils** ▶ ▷Lipids formed by the combination of glycerol with ▷fatty acids. Fats occur widely in animals and plants as an energy store and insulating material. Vegetable fats and oils are used in making soaps, margarines, cooking oils, paints, and lubricants. Animal fats are used in foods, soaps, and candles. Oils are distinguished from fats by being liquid at 20°C, whereas fats are solid. Mineral oils are hydrocarbons rather than lipids (*see* oil).

● **fatty acid** ▶ (*or* carboxylic acid) An organic acid that comprises one or more carboxyl groups (–COOH) attached to an alkyl group. Fatty acids combine with glycerol to form glycerides, the main constituents of ▷fats and oils. Animal fats tend to be hard because they contain a high proportion of saturated fatty acids; soft fats, such as vegetable and fish oils, contain more unsaturated and polyunsaturated fatty acids (containing one or more double bonds). The risk of heart disease associated with dietary fat is probably reduced if the fat consumed is rich in polyunsaturated fatty acids. However, the consumption of **trans-fatty acids** has been associated with an increased risk of heart disease. Trans-fatty acids are a form of polyunsaturates produced by hydrogenation, the process used to harden vegetable and fish oils in the manufacture of margarine. Certain essential fatty acids are normally required in small amounts in the diet.

● **fatwa** ▶ An edict issued by a Muslim religious leader. A fatwa issued in 1989 by Ayatollah ▷Khomeini offered a cash reward for the assassination of Salman ▷Rushdie, author of *The Satanic Verses* (1988), which some Muslims regard as disrespectful to Mohammed. The Iranian government withdrew its support for this fatwa in 1998. Most non-Muslims (as well as many Muslims) see the fatwa as an unacceptable attempt to restrict a cherished freedom (of speech) in another country.

● **Faulkner, William** ▶ (1897–1962) US novelist. Born in Mississippi, he abandoned his university education to write. He supported himself with various jobs before publishing his first poetry collection, *The Marble Faun*, in 1924. *Sartoris* (1929), the hero of which is based on Faulkner's great-grandfather, also an author, was the first of his stories set in the fictitious Yoknapatawpha County, based on his native northern Mississippi. His major novels, usually experimental in form and technique, include *The Sound and the Fury* (1929) *Absalom, Absalom!* (1936), and *The Reivers* (1962). He was awarded the Nobel Prize in 1949.

● **fault** ▶ A fracture plane in the rocks of the earth's crust, the rocks on each side being displaced relative to one another, either vertically, horizontally, or obliquely. Faulting occurs as a result of accumulated strain in the rocks, usually at plate margins (*see* plate tectonics). The extent of vertical displacement of the strata is called the throw; the horizontal displacement is the heave. A horst is an upstanding feature between two parallel faults; conversely a graben or rift valley is downthrown between parallel faults.

● **Faunus** ▶ In Roman mythology, a god of fertility and woodland. Associated with agriculture and prophecy, he was usually depicted with the ears, horns, tail, and hindlegs of a goat. He is presumed to have been a Roman equivalent of ▷Pan; recent discoveries indicate that he was also worshipped in Britain.

● **Fauré, Gabriel (Urbain)** ▶ (1845–1924) French composer and organist, a pupil of Saint-Saëns. He became organist at the Madeleine (1877) and director or the Paris conservatoire (1905). He was afflicted with deafness in later life. His works include the well-known *Requiem* (1886–87), incidental music for Maeterlincke's play *Pelléas and*

Mélisande (1898), the opera *Pénélope* (1913), the orchestral *Pavane* (1887), and piano and chamber music. Fauré is best known for his songs, such as those in the cycle *La Bonne Chanson* (1891–92).

● **Faust** ▶ A legendary medieval German scholar and magician who sold his soul to the Devil in exchange for knowledge and power. Stories of magicians in league with the Devil (often personified by Mephistopheles) combined with the historical Johann Faust (c. 1480–c. 1539), a vagrant scholar and mountebank, to produce a figure who has inspired numerous literary works, notably by ▷Marlowe (1592), ▷Lessing (1784), ▷Goethe (1808, 1832), and Thomas ▷Mann (1947), as well as operas by ▷Gounod and ▷Boito. His character has varied from that of Marlowe's power-seeking magician to that of Goethe's rationalist philosopher.

● **fauvism** ▶ A movement in French painting at the turn of the 19th century, characterized by the aggressive use of strong colours. The fauves (French: wild beasts, so called by a critic of their work) included, under the leadership of ▷Matisse, ▷Dufy, ▷Braque, ▷Rouault, and ▷Vlaminck. Most of these painters had become interested in ▷cubism by 1908.

● **Fawcett, Dame Millicent Garrett** ▶ (1847–1929) British suffragette; president of the National Union of Women's Suffrage Societies (1897–1919). A sister of Elizabeth Garrett ▷Anderson, Fawcett opposed the militancy of the Pankhursts. She married **Henry Fawcett** (1833–84), professor of political economy at Cambridge University and an MP (1865–84), who was blind.

● **Fawkes, Guy** ▶ (1570–1606) English conspirator. A convert to Roman Catholicism, he served in the Spanish army in the Netherlands during the 1590s and on his return to England became involved in the Gunpowder Plot, led by Robert Catesby (1573–1605), to blow up James I and parliament. The conspirators were informed upon and Fawkes was discovered (5 November, 1605) with the gunpowder in a cellar of the Palace of Westminister. Catesby was killed while resisting arrest and Fawkes was executed. Nov 5 continues to be celebrated with fireworks and the burning on a bonfire of effigies of Fawkes (so-called "guys").

● **fax** ▶ (facsimile transmission) A method of sending images (text or pictures) by a telecommunications link. Most fax transmissions are via the normal telephone network. The document is scanned optically, line by line, to break it into a pattern of dots, which are transmitted as electrical pulses. The receiving device reconstructs the image from this digital information and outputs it on photosensitive paper or, in some machines, xerographically. The basic technique is not new—for years it has been possible to 'wire' photographs—but recent advances in technology have made it cheap and reliable, and it is now in widespread use.

● **Fa Xian** ▶ (or Fa-hsien; 5th century AD) Chinese Buddhist monk. He travelled to India and Ceylon in about 402 returning to China in about 413 with a large collection of early Sanskrit Buddhist texts. His translation of these and his account of his journey provide important documentation of the beginning of relations between China and India.

● **FBI** ▷*See* Federal Bureau of Investigation.

● **fealty** ▷*See* feudalism.

● **feathers** ▶ The specialized body covering of birds. Thought to have evolved from the scales of reptilian ancestors, feathers arise from definite tracts over the body surface and are of several types: the down feathers of chicks are short and soft, whereas the quill feathers of adult birds typically have a stiff shaft bearing two vanes with interlocking barbs and are specialized for ▷flight as wing and tail feathers. As well as its role in flight, the plumage has several other functions. Like the hair of mammals, it helps to regulate body temperature and provides protection against the environment. It is also responsible for the bird's distinctive coloration, which is particularly important in courtship or aggressive displays. In order to maintain their function the feathers must be periodically renewed, and most birds undergo at least two moults a year. Moulting is controlled partly by hormones and partly by environmental factors.

● **feather star** ▷*See* crinoid.

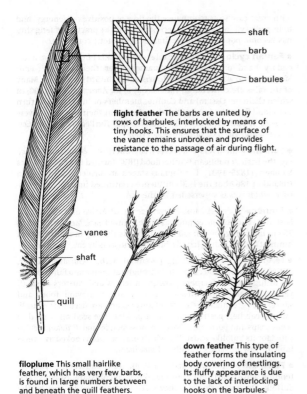

flight feather The barbs are united by rows of barbules, interlocked by means of tiny hooks. This ensures that the surface of the vane remains unbroken and provides resistance to the passage of air during flight.

shaft

barb

barbules

vanes

shaft

quill

filoplume This small hairlike feather, which has very few barbs, is found in large numbers between and beneath the quill feathers.

down feather This type of feather forms the insulating body covering of nestlings. Its fluffy appearance is due to the lack of interlocking hooks on the barbules.

feathers

● **Fécamp** ▶ 49 45N 0 23E A port in N France, in the Seine-Maritime department on the English Channel. It has an important cod-fishing industry and is famous for its Benedictine liqueur. Population (1990): 21 696.

● **Fechner, Gustav Theodor** ▶ (1801–87) German physicist, noted for his work in experimental psychology. Fechner developed techniques for investigating the sensations experienced by human subjects exposed to stimuli of varying strengths. He also proposed a mathematical expression (later shown to be inaccurate) of the theory concerning the difference between two stimuli, advanced by E. H. ▷Weber.

● **Federal Bureau of Investigation** ▶ (FBI) The organization within the US Department of Justice that carries out investigations into possible breaches of federal law, especially those related to security. Founded as the Bureau of Investigation in 1908, it became the FBI in 1935; under J. Edgar ▷Hoover (director 1924–72) it developed considerable autonomy. It was prominent in the campaign against organized crime in the 1930s and also in the anticommunist activities of Joseph ▷McCarthy in the 1950s.

● **federalism** ▶ The political union of separate states, joined together to serve their common interests while retaining a degree of autonomy. A federation usually provides strong central government in such common matters as defence, a national currency system, etc., leaving to state government affairs that depend on local conditions. The attempt by a state or states to withdraw from a federation often leads to warfare, as in the ▷Civil War in the USA and the breakup of the Federal Republic of Yugoslavia in 1990–95. By contrast the breakup of the Soviet Union in 1991 was almost bloodless. In most federations in the 20th century the central government has gained power at the expense of the state government (e.g. in the USA). An exception was the Soviet Union, where republics were given a greater control over their budgets and in the management of industry. Canada is a federation that is under severe strain owing to the sepa-

ratist elements in the province of ▷Quebec. Other federations include those of Malaysia, Australia, Belgium, and Russia. The extent to which the ▷European Union should aspire to a federalist goal remains controversial.

● **Federalist Party** ▶ A US political party, led by Alexander ▷Hamilton and John ▷Adams, that advocated a strong central government for the infant USA. The Federalists emerged in 1787 as those who wanted to replace the ▷Articles of Confederation (the nation's first constitution) by the newly written Constitution; they were opposed in this by the Republicans under Thomas ▷Jefferson, who feared encroachments of individual liberty by a centralized government. The Federalists were in power from 1791 until Jefferson's election as president in 1800 and were responsible for establishing a national administration. After 1800 the Federalist Party declined, their pro-British and aristocratic tendencies being out of touch with America's growing nationalism.

● **Federal Reserve System** ▶ The ▷central bank of the USA, established in 1913, which implements the government's monetary policy. There are 12 Federal Reserve Districts in the USA, each of which has its own Federal Bank, controlled by the Federal Reserve Board in Washington.

● **Fédération internationale de Football association** ▶ (FIFA) The world governing body of association football, formed in Paris in 1904. Based in Zurich, it now has over 140 member organizations. It runs the ▷World Cup competition.

● **feedback** ▶ In electronics and communications theory, the process of returning to the input of a device a fraction of the output signal. **Negative feedback**, in which the feedback opposes and therefore reduces the input, is often used in ▷amplifier circuits. It compensates for noise and distortion in the output signal, although it also reduces the overall amplification. **Positive feedback** reinforces the input signal. If it becomes too high, the circuit oscillates and the output becomes independent of the input. This is the cause of the singing noise heard in a public-address system when the microphone picks up feedback from the loudspeakers. The principle of negative feedback also operates in biological systems, especially in controlling some biochemical reactions: the product of the reaction inhibits further activity of the enzyme catalysing it.

● **Feininger, Lyonel (Charles Adrian)** ▶ (1871–1956) US painter and illustrator, born in New York. He studied painting in Germany and Paris and first worked as an illustrator and cartoonist for various German and French periodicals before concentrating on painting in 1907. His works were exhibited with the ▷Blaue Reiter group and he taught at the ▷Bauhaus (1919–33), eventually returning to the USA in 1937. He developed a personal form of ▷cubism in his oils and watercolours, his favourite subjects being architectural forms and boats.

● **feldspars** ▶ The most important group of rock-forming minerals and the major constituents of igneous rocks. There are four components of feldspars: anorthite (calcium plagioclase, $CaAl_2Si_2O_8$); albite (sodium plagioclase, $NaAlSi_3O_8$); orthoclase (potassium feldspar, $KAlSi_3O_8$); and celsian (barium feldspar, $BaAl_2Si_2O_8$, which is rare). Feldspars ranging between albite and anorthite in composition are plagioclase feldspars; those ranging between albite and orthoclase are alkali feldspars. Calcic plagioclase includes anorthite, bytownite, and labradorite; sodic plagioclase includes andesine, oligoclase, and albite. Alkali feldspars include sanidine, anorthoclase, orthoclase, microcline, and adularia.

● **Felidae** ▶ The ▷cat family: a family of mammals of the order ▷Carnivora. It includes the cats, lion, tiger, leopard, and cheetah.

● **Felix V** ▶ (antipope) ▷See Amadeus (VIII) the Peaceful.

● **Felixstowe** ▶ 51 58N 1 20E A resort in E England, in Suffolk on the North Sea. It has developed rapidly as a container port, with ferry services to Rotterdam and Zeebrugge. Population (1991): 28 606.

● **Fellini, Federico** ▶ (1920–93) Italian film director. He began working in films as an actor and scriptwriter. His films, many of which are characterized by their use of baroque imagery and fantasy, include *La strada* (1954), *8½* (1963), *Roma* (1972), *Amarcord* (1974), *Casa-*

nova (1976), *La città delle donne* (1980), *Intervista* (1987), and *The Voice of the Moon* (1990).

● **felt** ▷*See* textiles.

● **feminism** ▷*See* women's movement.

● **femur** ► The thigh bone: the longest bone in the human body (*see* Plate II). It extends from the pelvis, where it forms part of the ball-and-socket hip joint, to the joint of the knee. The head of the femur is commonly fractured in the elderly after falls.

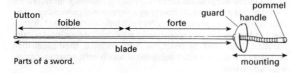

Parts of a sword.

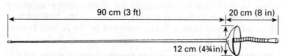

foil The foil weighs a maximum of 500 g. Its blade is quadrangular and very flexible.

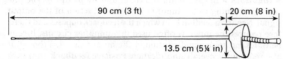

épée The épée weights a maximum of 770 g. Its blade is triangular and stiffer than that of the foil.

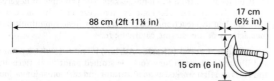

sabre The sabre weighs a maximum of 500 g. Its blade is a flattened V-shape.

fencing

● **fencing** ► The art of combat with a sword, of which there are three main forms in sport: foil, épée, and sabre. Bouts for all three weapons are fought on a *piste*, or marked-out area 2 × 14 m (6.5 × 46 ft) for foil and épée or 2 × 24 m (6.5 × 78.5 ft) for sabre. A hit is scored against a competitor who crosses the rear limit. The winner is the first to score five hits (for men) or four (for women) in a time limit of six minutes (for men) or five (for women), the form of the hit varying between the three weapons. For major competitions the electric foil and épée are used for automatic judging.

● **Fénelon, François de Salignac de la Mothe** ► (1651–1715) French Roman Catholic prelate and theologian. As director (from 1678) of an institution for Roman Catholic converts, he wrote *Traité de l'éducation des filles* (1687), criticizing coercive conversions. In 1689 he became tutor to the Duke of Burgundy and in 1695 Archbishop of Cambrai. His famous *Aventures de Télémaque* (1699) alienated the king and his *Explication des maximes des saints* (1697), containing a defence of ▷Quietism, was condemned by the pope.

● **feng shui** ► An ancient Chinese art that claims to determine the most propitious location for buildings and everything within them. Springing from ideas of harmony important in both ▷Taoism and ▷Confucianism, it combines elements of town planning and interior design with such occult practices as geomancy, divination, and astrology. Buildings, furnishings, and fittings must all be positioned with great care so as to enhance the flow of positive *ch'i* (energy) and to impede evil influences. In recent decades the practice of feng shui has become popular (and profitable) in Western countries.

● **Fenian cycle** ► Irish Gaelic tales and ballads of the Fianna, a legendary band of warrior-poets named after their leader, ▷Finn MacCool, who was said to have flourished in the 3rd century AD. Many of the tales are collected in *The Colloquy of the Ancient Men* (c. 1200) in which Oisin (*see* Ossian) and Caoilte, members of the Fianna, return to Ireland from the Land of Youth and recount their youthful adventures to St Patrick, and in the manuscripts *The Book of the Dun Cow* (c. 1100) and *The Book of Leinster* (c. 1160).

● **Fenians** ► Members of a secret Irish-American revolutionary society, the Irish Republican Brotherhood (IRB), formed in 1858 by James Stephens (1825–1901). The Fenians staged an unsuccessful rising in Ireland in 1867 but the IRB's influence continued into the 20th century, when it was superseded by the IRA.

● **fennec** ► A desert ▷fox, *Fennecus zerda*, of Africa and the Middle East. It is sandy-coloured and has large pointed ears. Measuring up to 70 cm including the tail (30 cm), it spends the day in a burrow and hunts at night, finding lizards, birds, and insects by ear. ⸧mammal.

● **fennel** ► A strong-smelling perennial herb, *Foeniculum vulgare*, native to S Europe and cultivated throughout temperate Eurasia. 0.5–1.5 m high, it has feathery dark-green leaves and clusters of small yellow flowers. The leaves are used mostly to flavour foods and sauces. The greenish seeds taste of aniseed and are used to flavour liqueurs, candies, pastries, and sweet pickles. The seed oil is used to scent soaps and perfumes. Florence, or sweet, fennel (*F. dulce*) is cultivated for its bulblike leafstalks, which may be eaten cooked as a vegetable or raw in salads. Family: ▷Umbelliferae.

● **Fens, the** ► A low-lying area in E England, W and S of the Wash extending across parts of Cambridgeshire, Lincolnshire, Norfolk, and Suffolk. Once waterlogged, they were first drained in part by the Romans. This was resumed during the 17th century by the Duke of Bedford and his engineer, Cornelius Vermuyden, creating the Bedford Level. Now virtually all drained, the Fens form one of the most fertile areas in the UK, producing cereals, vegetables, potatoes, and bulbs.

● **fenugreek** ► An annual herb, *Trigonella foenum-graecum*, native to the Mediterranean but widely cultivated. About 60 cm high, it has toothed compound leaves and small white flowers that develop into slender curved pods. The brownish seeds are used to flavour curry and chutney. Family: ▷Leguminosae.

● **fer-de-lance** ► A venomous tropical American ▷pit viper, *Bothrops atrox*. It is much feared by plantation workers and often visits houses in search of rodents. 1.2–2 m long, it has a triangular head, is grey or brown with black-edged diamond patterning and a yellowish chin, and generally feeds on small mammals, frogs, and lizards.

● **Ferdinand** ► (1865–1927) King of Romania (1914–27), who in 1916 joined the Allies in ▷World War I. In 1918 he annexed Bessarabia from Russia and in 1919 intervened in Hungary to destroy Kun's communist government.

● **Ferdinand (I) the Great** ► (?1016–65) King of Castile (1037–65). He conquered León (1039) and resumed the offensive against the Moorish border kingdoms, reducing the rulers of Toledo, Saragossa, and Seville to tributaries.

● **Ferdinand I** ► (1503–64) Holy Roman Emperor (1558–64). His elder brother, Emperor ▷Charles V, gave him the Habsburg possessions in Germany in 1521 and in 1526 he became King of Bohemia and of Hungary, although his title to the Hungarian crown was challenged by John Zápolya (1487–1540) until 1538. Ferdinand negotiated the religious Peace of ▷Augsburg (1555).

● **Ferdinand I** ► (1751–1825) King of Naples and Sicily (Two Sicilies; 1816–25). As Ferdinand IV he was King of Naples (1759–99, 1799–1806), being twice driven into exile in Sicily by the French. He ruled the Two Sicilies despotically.

● **Ferdinand I** ► (1793–1875) Emperor of Austria (1835–48) and King of Hungary (1830–48). Feeble minded and epileptic, he was dominated by ▷Metternich. He abdicated during the Revolution of 1848.

● **Ferdinand I** ▶ (1861–1948) Prince (1887–1908) and King (1908–18) of Bulgaria. In 1908 Ferdinand declared Bulgaria independent from Turkey but was forced to abdicate in 1918 after supporting the Central Powers.

● **Ferdinand II** ▶ (1578–1637) King of Bohemia (1617–37) and Hungary (1618–37) and Holy Roman Emperor (1619–37), who championed the ▷Counter-Reformation. In 1619 the predominantly Protestant diet (assembly) of Bohemia offered the Bohemian crown to the Protestant, ▷Frederick V of the Palatinate. The ensuing dispute developed into the ▷Thirty Years' War. Initially successful, Ferdinand suffered reverses with the intervention of France and Sweden, forcing him to accept the compromise Peace of Prague (1635).

● **Ferdinand III** ▶ (1608–57) King of Bohemia and of Hungary (1625–57) and Holy Roman Emperor (1637–57). He created a standing army, reformed the imperial council, and helped conclude the ▷Thirty Years' War by signing the Peace of ▷Westphalia (1648).

● **Ferdinand (V and II) the Catholic** ▶ (1452–1516) King of Castile as Ferdinand V (1474–1504) and of Aragon as Ferdinand II (1479–1516). He ruled Castile jointly with his wife ▷Isabella I of Castile and after her death was regent for their daughter Joanna the Mad. Ferdinand's accession to the Aragonese throne effected the union of Castile and Aragon, to which Granada, taken from the Moors in 1492, was added. The introduction of the Inquisition (1480) and the expulsion of the Jews (1492) aimed to strengthen both church and monarchy, to which Ferdinand's reforms in Aragon contributed. His ambitions abroad led to wars with France for hegemony in Italy.

● **Ferdinand VII** ▶ (1784–1833) King of Spain (1808, 1814–33). In 1808 Ferdinand was forced by Napoleon to abdicate but returned to the throne in 1814. His repressive policies caused a liberal uprising (1820) and the establishment of a liberal government until 1823, when it was ousted with French help. Alfonso repudiated the Salic Law of succession to enable his daughter ▷Isabella II to succeed him, an act that led to the emergence of ▷Carlism.

● **Fergana** ▶ (or Ferghana) 40 23N 71 19E A city in eastern Uzbekistan. It is both the industrial and the cultural centre of the fertile Fergana Valley, one of the country's main cotton-, silk-, and fruit-growing districts. Population (1993 est): 191 000.

● **Feriae** ▶ The sacred festival days of ancient Rome, which were usually marked by a public holiday, feasts, prayers, and sacrifices. Feriae were normally held on fixed annual dates.

● **Ferlinghetti, Lawrence** ▶ (1919–   ) US poet. His public readings and his City Lights Bookshop in San Francisco promoted ▷Beat movement poetry. His own poetry, published in *Pictures from the Gone World* (1955), *Tyrannus Nix?* (1969), and other collections, is largely political satire. Prose works include the novel *Love in the Days of Rage* (1988).

● **Fermanagh** ▶ A county and district of SW Northern Ireland, bordering on the Republic of Ireland. In 1973 the new administrative district of Fermanagh was created, having the same boundaries as the historic county. Fermanagh consists of hilly country contained chiefly in the Erne Basin and is divided by the Upper and Lower Lough Erne. It is predominantly agricultural, producing livestock. Manufactures include clothing, cotton thread, and tweeds. Area (including loughs): 1851 sq km (715 sq mi). Population (1995): 54 700.

● **Fermat, Pierre de** ▶ (1601–65) French mathematician. A lawyer by profession, Fermat founded ▷number theory and, with Blaise ▷Pascal, ▷probability theory. He is best known for ▷Fermat's last theorem and ▷Fermat's principle.

● **Fermat's last theorem** ▶ A theorem, first proposed by Pierre ▷Fermat, that there are no natural numbers x, y, z, and n such that $x^n + y^n = z^n$ when n is greater than two. Fermat himself claimed to have proved it but he never recorded his proof. It was finally proved in 1993 by the British mathematician Andrew Wiles.

● **Fermat's principle** ▶ When light travels between two points its path is such that the time taken is a minimum. This holds when the light is reflected or refracted between the two points. Also known as the principle of least time, it is named after P. ▷Fermat.

● **fermentation** ▶ The process by which certain microorganisms respire in the absence of oxygen (i.e. anaerobically). The fermentation of carbohydrates by yeasts to form alcohol is the basis of the baking, brewing, and wine-making industries (*see* beer and brewing; wine). Other types of fermentation produce lactic acid, as in the souring of milk by bacteria, and acetic acid, as in the production of vinegar.

Enrico Fermi

● **Fermi, Enrico** ▶ (1901–54) US physicist, born in Italy. His early work in Italy was concerned with the mathematical statistics of nuclear particles; independently of ▷Dirac he produced the form of statistics known as ▷Fermi-Dirac statistics. For his work on the bombardment of uranium by thermal neutrons he was awarded the 1938 Nobel Prize. Because of his antifascism and because his wife was Jewish, Fermi and his family sailed direct from the Stockholm Nobel ceremony to the USA, where he remained for the rest of his life. He was the first person to achieve a controlled nuclear chain reaction, in a converted squash court at Chicago University (1942). He later played a central role in the development of the atom bomb at Los Alamos. After his return to Chicago (1946) he bitterly opposed ▷Teller in the development of the hydrogen bomb. The **Fermi National Accelerator Laboratory** (Fermilab), the US centre for research in particle physics opened in 1972 at Batavia (Chicago), is named after him.

● **Fermi-Dirac statistics** ▶ A quantum-statistical method of analysing a system of indistinguishable particles to determine the probability of the energy distribution (*see* statistical mechanics). Unlike ▷Bose-Einstein statistics it assumes that these particles, which are known as fermions, obey the ▷Pauli exclusion principle. Named after E. ▷Fermi and P. A. M. ▷Dirac.

● **fermion** ▶ Any elementary particle that obeys ▷Fermi-Dirac statistics. These particles, which have half-integral spin, include ▷leptons and ▷baryons. *Compare* boson.

● **fermium** ▶ (Fm) An artificial transuranic element, named after Fermi. Like ▷einsteinium it was found in debris from the 1952 hydrogen-bomb explosion. The most stable isotope, ^{257}Fm, has a half-life of 100.5 days. At no 100; at wt (257).

● **fern** ▶ A perennial spore-producing vascular plant of the phylum *Filicinophyta* (or *Pterophyta* according to some classification schemes; about 9000–15 000 species), most abundant in shady damp tropical regions but also widely distributed elsewhere. The life cycle of a fern shows marked ▷alternation of generations. The fern plant itself is the asexual (sporophyte) generation, which has a creeping underground stem (rhizome) bearing roots and aerial fronds, which reach a height of 25 m in the ▷tree ferns. The fronds are feather-like and usually divided one or more times into leaflets. Asexual spores are produced in spore capsules, which usually occur in clusters (sori) protected by a covering (indusium) on the underside of the leaflets. The spores develop into the inconspicuous sexual (gametophyte) generation—a tiny heart-shaped plant (called a prothallus) producing egg and sperm cells. The fertilized egg cell develops into a new sporophyte plant, which grows up from the prothallus. Many tropical and subtropical ferns are cultivated as house plants for their attractive foliage.

● **Fernandel** ▶ (Fernand Joseph Desire Contandin; 1903–71) French comedian. Originally a music-hall performer, he later acted in numerous films, notably in the 1950s, as a village priest, Don Camillo, in conflict with the communist mayor.

● **Fernando Po** ▶ Former name of Bioko (*see* Equatorial Guinea, Republic of).

● **Ferrar, Nicholas** ▶ (1592–1637) English mystic, who founded an Anglican religious community at Little Gidding, Huntingdonshire (now in Cambridgeshire), in 1625. Much admired by Charles I, the community was dedicated to prayer and hard work, being particularly skilled in bookbinding. It was disbanded by the Puritans in 1647.

● **Ferrara** ▶ 44 50N 11 38E A town in N Italy, in Emilia-Romagna. Important in Renaissance times as the seat of the Este family, it has a cathedral, castle, citadel, and university (1391). The religious reformer Savonarola was born here. Ferrara has wine, fruit, and grain trades and its manufactures include plastics, sugar, and chemicals. Population (1996 est): 135 135.

● **Ferrara-Florence, Council of** ▶ (1438–45) The Church council at which the last concerted attempt was made to resolve the schism between Eastern and Western Churches. The council endeavoured to reach agreement on doctrinal differences, such as the ▷Filioque clause, and to provide assistance for Constantinople against the Turks. Agreement was reached in 1439 but was short lived.

● **Ferrari, Enzo** ▶ (1898–1988) Italian designer and manufacturer of sports and racing cars. A former racing driver, he designed cars for Alfa Romeo before setting up his own company in 1929. The classic Ferrari marque sports car appeared in 1947. Since the 1950s Ferrari racing cars have proved more successful in competition than those of any rival company.

● **ferret** ▶ A domesticated form of ▷polecat, *Mustela putorius*, that is slightly smaller than the European polecat and lighter in colour (sometimes albino). Ferrets were probably bred from an Asian race (sometimes called *M. eversmanni*) and have been domesticated since at least 400 BC; they are used to drive rats and rabbits from their burrows.

● **Ferrier, Kathleen** ▶ (1912–53) British contralto singer of outstanding ability. She sang Lucretia in the first performance of Britten's *Rape of Lucretia* (1946) and is especially remembered for her performances of Mahler's *Das Lied von der Erde* as well as Britten's settings of English folksongs. She died of cancer at the height of her career.

● **Ferrier, Susan Edmonstone** ▶ (1782–1854) Scottish novelist. Her three satirical novels about Edinburgh society, all published anonymously, were *Marriage* (1818), *The Inheritance* (1824), and *Destiny, or the Chief's Daughter* (1831). She was encouraged by Sir Walter Scott, whom she visited at Abbotsford during his last illness.

● **ferrimagnetism** ▶ A form of magnetism occurring in those ▷antiferromagnetic materials in which the microscopic ▷magnetic moments are aligned antiparallel but are not equal. The behaviour is weakly ▷ferromagnetic below the Néel temperature and ▷paramagnetic above it.

● **ferrite** ▶ **1.** A compound of iron with the general chemical formula MFe_2O_4, where M is a metal. Most ferrites are ▷ferromagnetic or ▷ferrimagnetic ceramic materials and they are used in transformers and computer memories. **2.** Iron in its body-centred cubic crystal structure, either pure or as a constituent of ▷steel.

● **Ferrol del Caudillo, El** ▶ 43 29N 8 14W A city in NW Spain, in Galicia on the Atlantic Ocean. A port and naval base, it has shipbuilding and ship-repairing industries. Gen Franco was born here. Population (1989): 86 271.

● **ferromagnetism** ▶ The property of a material that enables it to become a permanent magnet, i.e. ferromagnetic materials when placed in a ▷magnetic field develop a very strong internal field and

retain some of it when the external field is removed. The most common ferromagnetic substances are iron, cobalt, nickel, and alloys of these metals. Ferromagnetism, like ▷paramagnetism, is caused by the unbalanced spin of atomic electrons, which creates a magnetic dipole moment having the effect of a tiny magnet. In ferromagnetic substances, the application of an external field causes groups of these tiny magnets, called domains, to become aligned; many of them remain aligned when the field is removed. Above a certain temperature, called the Curie point, thermal agitation destroys the domain structure and the substance becomes paramagnetic. The response of a ferromagnetic material to changes in magnetic field is known as the hysteresis effect; the internal field strength remaining after the external field has been reduced to zero is called the remanence.

● **Fertile Crescent** ▶ A strip of land in the Middle East roughly comprising the lower Nile Valley, the E Mediterranean coast, Syria, and ▷Mesopotamia. Formerly enjoying a wetter climate, it was the cradle of civilization, with sites showing evidence of settled communities from at least 9000 BC.

● **fertility drugs** ▶ Drugs given to infertile women to stimulate the release of an egg cell from the ovary. The best known are the ▷gonadotrophins—hormones normally released by the pituitary gland to control activity of the ovary. Another fertility drug is clomiphene. The dosage of these drugs is carefully controlled in order to prevent multiple pregnancies.

● **fertility rate** ▶ A measure required in the calculation of population growth. The most widely used measure is the total period fertility rate (TPFR), which measures the total number of children that would be born, on average, to each woman in a population on completion of her childbearing years. In the UK the TPFR peaked at a value of 2.9 in 1964 and fell to 1.7 in 1977, at which it has since (1994) remained; this is well below the rate of 2.1 required to maintain a steady population. This fall is thought to have resulted from more women postponing motherhood in order to participate in higher education and in senior jobs and from the greater use of family planning, especially the contraceptive pill. However, in other parts of the world the TPFR depends on religious and ethnic beliefs and traditions as well as the value of children on the labour market. In the period 1995–2000 in most European countries the TPFR lay between 1.2 and 1.8. In the USA it was 2.0, in Africa 5.3, and in Asia and Latin America 2.6. ▷*See also* overpopulation.

● **fertilization** ▶ The union of a male and a female ▷gamete, involving the fusion of hereditary material: it is the essential process of sexual ▷reproduction. The resulting cell, called a zygote, undergoes division (*see* cleavage), growth, and development to form a new individual, in which half the chromosomes (and therefore the genes) are of paternal origin and half of maternal origin. In **self-fertilization** both gametes are produced by the same individual; in **cross-fertilization** they derive from different individuals (these terms are applied particularly to the processes in flowering plants). In most aquatic animals the gametes are expelled into the water and fertilization is external; in most terrestrial animals the sperms are introduced into the body of the female, where fertilization takes place.

● **fertilizers** ▶ Substances added to soils to maintain or improve soil fertility. Natural farmyard manures have long been used as a source of plant nutrients and humus, which maintains the physical structure of the soil. Other traditional fertilizers have included bone meal, dried blood, and other animal products. Modern artificial fertilizers, dating from the work of J. B. ▷Lawes and others in the 19th century, provided the means for dramatic increases in crop yields. The major plant nutrients required are nitrogen (chiefly provided as ammonium nitrate derived from fixation of atmospheric nitrogen), phosphate (derived from naturally occurring rock phosphate), and potassium (from mined potash deposits). These fertilizers are used either individually ("straights") or in combined ("compound") form to provide ratios of nutrients matched to the crop requirements.

Artificial fertilizers have been of immense benefit in helping to feed a rapidly expanding human population. The view that they are inferior to natural fertilizers is largely unfounded. Plants take in nitrogen ions, etc., in solution through their roots whether the source is a sack of fertilizer or farmyard manure. However, excessive application of artificial fertilizers can lead to pollution of streams, rivers, and even drinking water. Since the 1970s increased awareness of such environmental effects, coupled with a movement towards a diet free of possibly harmful ▷food additives, has led to the resurgence of organic farming, in which only natural fertilizers are used.

● **Fès ▶** (or Fez; Arabic name: Fas) 34 05N 5 00W A city in N Morocco. In the 14th century the Islamic city reached its peak as a major centre for commerce and learning. It remains important for Arabic and Islamic teaching and has two mosques; the Qarawiyin Mosque is the oldest in Africa and contains a university (859 AD). The city gave its name to the traditional red felt hat worn by Muslims. It is a trade centre for hides and leather, fruit, and traditional crafts. Population (1994 est): 263 828.

● **fescue ▶** A ▷grass of the genus *Festuca* (about 100 species), native to temperate and cold regions of the N hemisphere. It grows in tufts, 46–152 cm high. Meadow fescue (*F. pratensis*) is sown as a pasture grass and used for livestock fodder; sheep's fescue (*F. ovina*) grows on mountains and in dry and exposed soil and the variety *F. ovina glauca* is used in ornamental borders. Red or creeping fescue (*F. rubra*) is common in grass mixtures for lawns.

● **Festival of Britain ▶** A celebration organized in 1951 to commemorate the Great Exhibition of 1851 and to demonstrate Britain's postwar development. Exhibitions in science, architecture, agriculture, and the arts were organized throughout the country. The main exhibition site was in London, on the South Bank of the River Thames, where the Royal Festival Hall (designed by Sir Robert Matthew, J. L. Martin, and Sir Hubert Bennett) was built specially for the occasion. The **Festival Gardens** consisted of a transformed ▷Battersea Park, laid out as a pleasure garden with a tree walk, fountains, and a grotto.

● **Festus, Sextus Pompeius ▶** (2nd century AD) Roman lexicographer. His *De Verborum Significatu*, an important Latin source, is based on the lost work of Marcus Verrius Flaccus.

● **fetishism ▶** 1. In anthropology, the practice of using charms magically. The term derives from the Portuguese *feitico*, something made. Fetishism is found among W African tribes and, hence, in the West Indies. Auguste ▷Comte characterized primitive religion as essentially fetishism, by which he meant the attribution of human qualities to nonhuman bodies. Later ▷Tylor reserved the term for the idea of spirits embodied in or associated with material objects. The term is not very common in modern sociology or anthropology. 2. In psychiatry, the abnormal condition in which sexual satisfaction is obtained by handling or otherwise using nongenital objects (fetishes). The fetish may be an article of clothing (such as shoes or underwear), rubber objects, leather, or fur.

● **fetus ▶** (or foetus) The developing baby in the womb from the beginning of the ninth week of pregnancy until birth. The fetus is protected by a series of membranes enclosing a fluid (amniotic fluid), which can be extracted and used for diagnostic purposes. The fetus is connected through the ▷umbilical cord and ▷placenta to the mother's bloodstream. □embryo. ▷*See also* prenatal diagnosis.

● **Feuchtwanger, Lion ▶** (1884–1958) German novelist and dramatist. Exiled in 1933, he fled to the USA in 1940. His best-known novels are historical romances, notably *Jew Süss* (1925) and *The Pretender* (1936). He collaborated with ▷Brecht on plays and translations.

● **feudalism ▶** The type of land tenure, characteristic of medieval Europe, in which property was held by a **vassal** of a lord in return for military service and a pledge of homage (known as the vassal's **fealty**). Feudalism originated with the collapse of public order in W Europe during the 8th and 9th centuries. Both kings and great lords distributed life grants of lands and offices in return for promises of loyalty and service. This practice developed into the grant of hereditary **fiefs** or fees (Latin word: *feoda*, from which the word feudalism is derived) in return for military service. The resulting fragmentation of authority was reflected in the rapid growth of feudal armies, often engaged in private wars, the development of the castle as an administrative and military centre, and the growth of private justice administered by local lords. From the 12th century these implications of feudal tenure were challenged by the growing power of Western rulers, especially in England, where it was abolished in 1661. Their governments increasingly depended on a royal bureaucracy and an army of mercenaries rather than the feudal bands. The growth of towns, outside the feudal framework, also contributed to the decline of feudalism.

● **Feuerbach, Ludwig Andreas ▶** (1804–72) German philosopher. Critical of Hegelian ▷idealism, Feuerbach saw the power of history not as a nebulous succession of spirits of the ages but as the total material conditions in any given period that caused people to behave as they did. This view and also his writings on religion, in which he argued that people lost their essential selves by applying their own attributes to imaginary beings, impressed ▷Marx and ▷Engels.

● **Feuillants, Club of the ▶** A moderate French Revolutionary political group that met at the former monastery of the Feuillants in Paris. Founded in 1791, the Feuillants opposed extremism, favouring constitutional monarchy. They disbanded in 1792, when the monarchy was abolished.

● **Feuillère, Edwige ▶** (Caroline Cunati; 1910–98) French actress. Her performance in *La Dame aux camélias* in 1937 was one of her earliest successes as a stage actress and her films include *L'Aigle à deux têtes* (1947) and *Le Blé en herbe* (1953).

● **fever ▶** A body temperature greater than 37°C (98.4°F). This is most commonly due to ▷infection, but other causes include tumours, drugs, a heart attack, and a blood clot in the leg. Sometimes no cause can be found (known as p.u.o.—pyrexia of unknown origin). The patient usually has a headache, shivers, and feels ill.

● **feverfew ▶** A perennial aromatic Eurasian herb, *Tanacetum* (or *Chrysanthemum*) *parthenium*, about 50 cm high, with heads of yellow and white daisy-like flowers. Formerly a popular medicinal herb, it was used to reduce fever. Family: ▷*Compositae*.

● **Feydeau, Georges ▶** (1862–1921) French playwright, famous for his many farces, written between 1881 and 1916. They are characterized by fast-moving, intricate, and cheerfully immoral plots, witty dialogue, and complicated stage sets. They include *The Lady from Maxim's* (1889), *Hotel Paradiso* (1894), and *A Flea in Her Ear* (1907).

● **Feynman, Richard Phillips ▶** (1918–88) US physicist, who shared the 1965 Nobel Prize with Julian Schwinger (1918–94) and Shinitiro Tomonaga (1906–79) for their development of quantum electrodynamics. He is best known for his invention of Feynman diagrams, which illustrate the interactions between charged particles by the exchange of virtual photons.

● **Fez** ▷*See* Fès.

● **Fezzan ▶** (or Fazzan; Latin name: Phazania) An area in SW Libya, forming part of the Sahara. It was a province until provinces were abolished in 1963.

● **Ffestiniog ▶** 52 58N 3 55W A village in North Wales, in Gwynedd. It is a tourist centre in picturesque surroundings. At nearby **Blaenau Ffestiniog** there are extensive former slate quarries, a narrow-gauge railway, and a pumped-storage hydroelectric power station. Population (latest est): 800.

● **Fianna Fáil ▶** (Irish: Soldiers of Destiny) Irish political party, founded in 1926 by Eamon ▷De Valera from moderate ▷Sinn Féin members. The ruling party in the years 1932–48, 1951–54, 1957–73, 1977–81, 1982, 1987–94, and from 1997, its leaders have been De Valera (until 1959), Sean Lemass (until 1966), Jack ▷Lynch (until 1979), Charles ▷Haughey (until 1992), Albert ▷Reynolds (until 1994), and Bertie ▷Ahern.

● **Fibonacci, Leonardo ▶** (c. 1170–c. 1230) Italian mathematician. He travelled widely, especially in North Africa, where he learnt the ▷decimal system of numerals and the use of zero, which al-Khwarizmi had, in turn, learnt from the Indians. Fibonacci published the system in Europe, but mathematicians were slow to adopt it. In the **Fibonacci series** (0, 1, 1, 2, 3, 5, 8,...) each number is the sum of the preceding two.

● **fibre ▶** (or dietary fibre) The constituent of the human diet that is not digested. It consists of the cell walls of plants, i.e. cellulose, lignin, hemicellulose, and pectic substances. Significant amounts are present in wholewheat cereals and flour, root vegetables, nuts, and fruit: highly refined foods, such as sugar, have a low fibre content. Dietary fibre is considered helpful in preventing constipation, diverticular disease, obesity, diabetes mellitus, and colonic cancer: societies with high-fibre diets rarely suffer from these conditions.

● **fibreglass** ▶ (glass fibre *or* spun glass) Material made from glass drawn into fine threads. Glass fibre has excellent heat- and fire-resistant properties and is a good electrical insulator. It is spun and woven into curtain material; made into glass wool for heat, electrical, and sound insulation; woven into coarse mats for filters; and used in reinforcing moulded plastics for boats, car bodies, etc.

● **fibre optics** ▶ The use of flexible glass fibres for transmitting light. Each fibre, which may be used singly or in bunches, is usually less than a millimetre thick and has a high refractive index. The light inside the fibre is totally internally reflected and travels through the fibre with little loss of intensity. The fibres are highly polished and coated with a substance of lower refractive index to reduce dispersion further. Glass fibres are used for examining otherwise inaccessible places, for example in medical diagnosis and in specialized industrial processes.

● **fibres** ▶ Threadlike substances of animal, vegetable, or man-made origin. ▷Wool and ▷silk are the most widely used animal fibres. Vegetable fibres include cotton, flax, hemp, jute, and sisal. Man-made fibres fall into two categories: **modified natural fibres**, including ▷rayon made from wood cellulose, and **synthetic fibres**, most of which are made by the polymerization of petrochemicals. They include ▷polyesters, nylon, and ▷acrylics. Some inorganic substances are also used in the form of fibres: examples include glass (*see* fibreglass; fibre optics), ▷asbestos, and ▷carbon fibres.

● **fibrin and fibrinogen** ▷*See* blood clotting.

● **fibrositis** ▶ Inflammation of fibrous tissue, usually of the back muscles and muscle sheaths. This causes sudden pain and stiffness (muscular rheumatism). It is best relieved by rest, but aspirin or similar analgesics may help.

● **fibula** ▷*See* leg.

● **Fichte, Johann Gottlieb** ▶ (1762–1814) German philosopher and follower of ▷Kant. Fichte, however, debunked Kant's world of numinous "things-in-themselves," holding that practical reason and man's autonomously good will originated all that is worthwhile in the world. The outer world, a passive place, is the field of action for this human consciousness; by contrast, the Ego, or self, is the only basic reality. The existence of other Egos was, however, essential for the individual's pursuit of moral perfection. Fichte's philosophical works include *Foundation of the Laws of Nature* (1796) and *System of Moral Philosophy* (1798). His popular works strove to kindle German nationalism against Napoleon.

● **Fichtelgebirge** ▶ A mountain range in central Germany, between Bayreuth and the Czech border. It is mainly wooded (the name means "spruce mountains") and rises to 1051 m (3448 ft) at the Schneeberg. The minerals obtained from it include lead, copper, and marble.

● **Ficino, Marsilio** ▶ (1433–99) Italian Platonist scholar. In 1462, under ▷Medici patronage, he founded the Platonic Academy to disseminate ▷Platonism and reconcile it with Christianity. His system assumed a hierarchical universe, with strata ranging from body to angels and God. Experience consisted of the ascent of man's immortal soul towards God. Ficino's translations of Plato (1484) remained standard for many years.

● **fiddler crab** ▶ A small burrowing ▷crab, 25–30 mm long, belonging to the genus *Uca* (about 65 species). The brightly coloured male has an enlarged claw, which it holds somewhat like a violin. Fiddler crabs are found on salt marshes and sandy beaches of tropical and temperate regions, feeding on algae and other organic material. Tribe: *Brachyura*.

● **fief** ▷*See* feudalism.

● **field** ▶ In physics, a region of space in which a body possessing certain properties can exert a force on similar bodies, when they are not in contact. For example, a body having mass exerts an attractive force on all other massive bodies as a result of its gravitational field. Similarly, an electrically charged body exerts a force (attractive or repulsive, depending on polarity) on other charged bodies and a magnetized body will have a magnetic field around it. A field is often represented by lines of force to indicate the direction in which the force acts at that point. The closeness together of the lines represents the strength of the force, and therefore the field, in that area.

● **Field, Cyrus West** ▶ (1819–92) US businessman, who helped to finance the laying of the first transatlantic telegraph cable, achieved in 1866 after several unsuccessful attempts. He later diversified into railways and newspapers.

● **Field, John** ▶ (1782–1837) Irish pianist and composer, who was taught by Clementi in London. In 1802 they journeyed to Russia and Field settled in St Petersburg as a teacher and composer. After various European tours he returned to Moscow at the end of his life. Field composed much piano music and created the piano ▷nocturne; his music influenced Chopin.

● **field emission** ▶ The emission of electrons from the surface of certain materials when they are subjected to a very high electric field. Typically fields of about 10^{10} volts per metre are required. The effect is also known as cold emission or autoemission. It is utilized in the **field-emission microscope**, in which a magnified image of a surface is obtained by subjecting it to a high electric field and observing the distribution of emitted electrons on a cathode-ray screen.

● **fieldfare** ▶ A ▷thrush, *Turdus pilaris*, of N Europe and Siberia, migrating to S and W Europe. It is about 25 cm long with a speckled brown breast, brown back, white underwings, and blue-grey head.

● **Fielding, Helen** ▶ (1958 –) British humorous writer, best known for her creation of the insecure single woman Bridget Jones. The character first appeared in the *Independent* newspaper (from 1995) and later featured in two bestselling novels, *Bridget Jones's Diary* (1996; filmed 2001) and *Bridget Jones: The Edge of Reason* (1999).

● **Fielding, Henry** ▶ (1707–54) British novelist and dramatist. He wrote about 25 plays, mostly satirical and topical comedies, between 1728 and 1737, when Walpole's Licensing Act effectively banned his vigorous satire; he then turned to journalism and law studies. *Shamela* (1741), a parody of Samuel Richardson's novel *Pamela* (1740), is almost certainly by Fielding. His major novels include *Joseph Andrews* (1742), the ironical *Jonathan Wild* (1743), and *Tom Jones* (1749). In 1749 he was appointed magistrate for Westminster and Middlesex; in this post he helped develop the Bow Street Runners into an efficient ▷police force. He died in Lisbon.

● **fieldmouse** ▶ A small nocturnal long-tailed ▷mouse, *Apodemus sylvaticus*, of Europe, Asia, and N Africa, also called woodmouse. About 9 cm long, with an 8-cm tail, it has a brown coat with white underparts. Fieldmice feed on seeds and grain and can be a pest.

● **Field of the Cloth of Gold** ▶ (1520) The meeting near Calais of Henry VIII of England and Francis I of France. Francis hoped for English support against Emperor Charles V, with whom, however, Henry subsequently formed an alliance.

● **Fields, Gracie** ▶ (Dame Grace Stansfield; 1898–1979) British popular entertainer. She began her career as a music-hall singer and comedian and made several films during the 1930s, notably *Sing as We Go* (1934). During World War II she gave many concerts for the troops; she later lived in Capri.

● **Fields, W. C.** ▶ (William Claude Dukenfield; 1880–1946) US film actor. After working as a vaudeville juggler and comedian he began making films in the 1920s. In *The Bank Dick* (1940), *My Little Chickadee* (1940), and other films, he exploited his eccentricity and intolerance of sentimentality.

● **Fiennes, Sir Ranulph (Twistleton-Wykeham-)** ▶ (1944–) British explorer. After service in the armed forces (including the SAS), he led expeditions in Norway, North Africa, and Canada. In 1979–82 he led the Transglobe expedition, the first surface journey around the earth's polar axis. He failed in two attempts to lead an unsupported expedition to the North Pole (1986 and 1990) but succeeded in his unsupported crossing of the Antarctic continent (1992–93). His publications include *To the Ends of the Earth* (1983) and the autobiography *Living Dangerously* (1987, 1994).

● **Fieschi** ▶ A leading family of Genoa (Italy) during the 13th, 14th, and 15th centuries. The Fieschi, who were ▷Guelfs, wielded much political influence as ambassadors, admirals, generals, cardinals, and even popes—▷Innocent IV and Adrian V (d. 1276; reigned 1276) were Fieschi.

● **Fiesole** ▶ 43 48N 11 17E A town in Italy, in Tuscany on a hill near Florence overlooking the River Arno. It has Etruscan and Roman remains and a romanesque cathedral. It is mainly residential. Population (latest est): 4000.

● **FIFA** ▷*See* Fédération internationale de Football association.

● **fife** ▶ A small transverse ▷flute, pitched in B flat and used in military fife-and-drum bands.

● **Fife** ▶ A council area in E Scotland, bordering on the North Sea, co-extensive with the historic county of Fife. It consists of a lowland peninsula located between the Firths of Forth and Tay. Agriculture is most important in the N, especially on the fertile coastal belt, with the production of cereals, potatoes, and sugar beet. Industry, concentrated in the S, includes light engineering, electronics, and aluminium refining. Coalmining has declined sharply. Area: 1323 sq km (511 sq mi). Population (1998 est): 348 900. Administrative centre: Glenrothes.

● **Fife, Duncan** ▷*See* Phyfe, Duncan.

● **Fifteen Rebellion** ▷*See* Jacobites.

● **Fifteen Years' War** ▶ (1591–1606) A struggle between the Austrian Habsburgs and the Ottoman Turks for the possession of Hungary that followed 50 years of intermittent skirmishing. Neither side gained an ascendency but the stalemate was ended when István Bocksay (1557–1606) of Transylvania rebelled against the Habsburgs, made a treaty with the Turks, conquered Habsburg Hungary, and established Transylvania as an effective buffer state between the two belligerents.

● **fifth column** ▶ A body of enemy sympathizers working within a country. The term originated in the Spanish Civil War when the Nationalist, Gen Emilio Mola (1887–1937), is supposed to have said "I have four columns operating against Madrid and a fifth inside composed of my sympathizers."

● **Fifth Monarchy Men** ▶ An extremist Puritan sect in England in the mid-17th century, which believed in the imminence of the fifth monarchy of Christ that, according to Daniel 2, would succeed the monarchies of Assyria, Persia, Macedonia, and Rome (*see* millenarianism). They supported the ▷Barebones Parliament but turned against Cromwell when he established the ▷Protectorate (1653). Their two rebellions (1657, 1661) were suppressed.

● **fig** ▶ A spreading tree or shrub, *Ficus carica*, 1–12 m high, probably native to W Asia but widely cultivated in warm temperate and subtropical regions. The dark-green leathery leaves, up to 30 × 25 cm, are usually deeply lobed. The tiny flowers are borne inside a fleshy pear-shaped structure, up to 8 cm long, which develops into the edible fig after fertilization of the flowers. Figs—eaten fresh, dried, or preserved—are rich in sugar and iron and have laxative properties. Some other species of *Ficus* are grown as house plants, including the ▷rubber plant. Family: *Moraceae* (mulberry family).

● **fighting fish** ▶ One of several ▷labyrinth fishes, especially of the genus *Betta*, found in SE Asia and the Malay Archipelago. The males are aggressive towards each other and some brood eggs in their mouths. The Siamese fighting fish (*B. splendens*) is about 6.5 cm long and greenish or brown in colour. Long-finned and brightly coloured varieties are bred for use in fighting contests.

● **fig marigold** ▶ A plant of the genus *Mesembryanthemum* (about 200 species), found in warm regions, especially South Africa, and cultivated as ornamentals. They are often succulent, with large brilliant daisy-like flowers and figlike fruits. Family: *Aizoaceae*.

● **figwort** ▶ A herbaceous plant of the genus *Scrophularia* (120 species), of N temperate regions. 30–100 cm tall, they have toothed leaves. The brown, yellow, or green rounded flowers have five small lobes around the opening. A common Eurasian species is *S. nodosa*. Family: *Scrophulariaceae*.

● **Fiji, Republic of** ▶ A country in the S Pacific Ocean. It consists of over 800 islands, only 106 of which are inhabited; the largest are Viti Levu and Vanua Levu. Most of the population are Indians and Fijians with some Europeans, Chinese, and other Pacific islanders.
Economy: chiefly agricultural, sugar cane being the main cash crop; others include copra and ginger. Fishing and livestock rearing are being encouraged. Some gold is mined on Viti Levu and the chief exports are sugar, copra, coconut oil, and gold. Tourism is now the main economic activity after sugar production; manufacture of clothing and textiles is increasing. Fiji is an important staging post on air routes between North America and Australia and New Zealand.
History: reached by the Dutch explorer Tasman in 1643, the islands were visited by Capt Cook in 1774. During the 19th century the search for sandalwood brought many ships and tribal warfare was widespread until Fiji was ceded to Britain in 1874. From 1879 large numbers of Indian workers were brought to Fiji under an indenture system. By the 1950s Indians outnumbered native Fijians and dominated the colony's commercial life, leading to rising ethnic tensions. Fiji became independent within the British Commonwealth in 1970. In 1987 the newly elected Indian-dominated government of Dr Timoci Bavadra was overthrown in a military coup by native Fijians under Maj Gen Sitiveni Rabuka. A second coup led by Rabuka later the same year resulted in the declaration of a republic and withdrawal from the Commonwealth. A new constitution in 1990 guaranteed native Fijians a legislative majority: the result was heavy Indian emigration and the loss of skills and capital. In 1997 the racial elements were removed from the 1990 constitution and Fiji was readmitted to the Commonwealth. Elections in 1999 resulted in a heavy defeat for Rabuka's government and Mahendra Chaudry became Fiji's first ethnic Indian prime minister. In 2000 ethnic Fijian rebels took Chaudry and his cabinet hostage for eight weeks. During this period the military took control, suspended the constitution of 1997, and installed a new government. This government, led by Laisenia Qarase, was returned to power in elections held in August 2001.

Republic of Fiji

Acting head of state	President Ratu Josefa Iloilo.
Official language	English
Official currency	Fiji dollar of 100 cents
Area	18 272 sq km (7055 sq mi)
Population (2000 est)	819 000
Capital and main port	Suva

● **Filarete** ▶ (Antonio Averlino; c. 1400–c. 1469) Italian Renaissance architect. Originally a sculptor, he moved in 1451 to Milan where he designed his masterpiece, the Ospedale Maggiore. He wrote a treatise on architecture (1461–64) and, although he built little, was influential in promoting Italian classicism.

● **filaria** ▶ A parasitic ▷nematode worm, mainly of central Africa, Asia, and the SW Pacific. The species *Wuchereria bancrofti* and *Brugia malayi* cause the disease **filariasis**. The tiny larval worm, measuring about 1.4 mm, enters the body in the saliva of a biting mosquito or mite. It then grows up to 8 cm long in lymph and blood vessels, causing swelling and pain (*see* elephantiasis). Filarial worms of the genus *Onchocerca* cause ▷onchocerciasis.

● **filbert** ▶ A Eurasian shrub, *Corylus maxima*, closely related and similar to the ▷hazel. It is sometimes planted for its nuts, which are larger than hazelnuts and are partly hidden by long bracts.

● **filefish** ▶ A ▷bony fish belonging to a family (*Monacanthidae*) found in warm coastal waters. It has a laterally flattened body, 13–26 cm long, covered with small filelike or velvety scales, two dorsal fin spines, and a very small mouth. Order: *Tetraodontiformes*.

● **filibuster** ▶ To obstruct the passage of legislation through a parliament by making long speeches, raising constant procedural questions, etc. This tactic has been exploited in the British parliament. but is restricted by the use of the **guillotine**, a parliamentary rule that can be invoked to limit the debating time on government business, however contentious. In the US Senate, where filibustering began, if more than one-third of the Senators oppose the closure of a debate, the filibuster can continue until the bill is talked out.

The word comes from the Spanish *filibustero*, a plunderer, and was used to describe the pirates and adventurers who pillaged the Spanish colonies in the 17th century. It was subsequently used to describe any individual who engaged in aggressive tactics against a foreign government. This led to its use for someone who opposed government measures in parliament.

● **Filioque** ▶ (Latin: and the Son) An article of Christian faith in the Western Church, added to the ▷Nicene Creed and referring to the ▷Holy Spirit, "Who proceedeth from the Father *and the Son*" (rather than from the Father alone). It had appeared in Spain as early as 447 but was not adopted at Rome until the 11th century. The Orthodox Church did not accept it and attacked it as an unwarranted addition made to the Creed by Rome. ▷Photius denounced it in the 9th century and it was one of the central issues—together with disagreement over the nature of the primacy of the ▷papacy—that culminated in the ▷East–West Schism in 1054.

● **Fillmore, Millard** ▶ (1800–74) US statesman; president (1850–52). A New York lawyer, as vice president (1849–50) he supported the 1850 Missouri Compromise on the extension of slavery, which helped delay civil war for ten years. Succeeding to the presidency when Zachary Taylor died, he lost abolitionist support by introducing the Fugitive Slave Law and was not nominated as presidential candidate in 1852.

● **film** ▶ A thin flexible strip of cellulose acetate, or similar transparent plastic, coated with a light-sensitive emulsion. A black-and-white photographic emulsion usually consists of gelatin containing tiny suspended crystals of silver halide (usually bromide or chloride). After exposure to light in a ▷camera these crystals are easily reduced to metallic silver when treated with the chemicals in the developer. This produces black deposits of fine particles of metallic silver on the parts of the film upon which the light has fallen, giving a reversed (or negative) image. Fixing of the film consists of bathing it in sodium thiosulphate (hypo) or other fixers to render the unchanged silver halides soluble, enabling them to be washed away with water. The sensitivity (speed) of film is usually quoted as an ▷ASA rating, which determines the amount of light required to form a given amount of metallic silver. ▷*See also* colour photography.

● **films** ▷*See* cinema.

● **filter** ▶ A device that allows one substance to pass through it but not others. For example, a filter is used to remove solid particles from a liquid or gas by passing the mixture through a porous substance, such as paper or ▷fibreglass, the holes in which are fine enough to prevent the passage of the particles. Such filters are used in some airconditioning units, for water purification, etc. In optics, coloured glass filters are used to select light with a certain range of wavelengths. In electronics, filters are circuits used to allow alternating currents of a certain frequency range to pass, while currents with frequencies outside the range are stopped.

● **Final Solution** ▷*See* Wannsee conference.

● **finch** ▶ A songbird belonging to a family (*Fringillidae*; 176 species) occurring in most regions of the world except Australia. Finches have hard conical bills used to crack open seeds, although they also feed on buds and fruit. They range in size from 10 to 27 cm and the plumage varies in colour with the species. There are two subfamilies: the *Fringillinae*, including the finer-billed ▷chaffinch and ▷brambling of the Old World, and the *Carduelinae*, comprising the heavier-billed species found in both the Old World and North America. *Compare* weaverfinch.

● **Finchley** ▶ A district in the Greater London borough of Barnet. Finchley Common, of which little now remains, was once a haunt of highwaymen.

● **Fine Gael** ▶ (Irish: Tribe of Gaels) Irish political party, founded in 1933 by William ▷Cosgrave. It was the senior member of ruling coalitions in Ireland (1948–51, 1954–57, 1973–77, 1981–Jan 1982, Dec 1982–1987, and 1994–97), led by John Costello (1891–1976), Liam ▷Cosgrave, Dr Garret ▷Fitzgerald, and John ▷Bruton. It is more conservative than the rival ▷Fianna Fáil.

● **fineness of gold** ▶ A measure of the purity of gold equal to the number of parts of pure gold in 1000 parts of the alloy. ▷*See also* carat.

● **finfoot** ▶ A secretive semiaquatic bird belonging to a family (*Heliornithidae*; 3 species) found in tropical and subtropical America, Africa, and Asia. Up to 60 cm long, finfoots have olive-brown plumage and large lobed feet, a long neck, and a stiff rounded tail. Order: *Gruiformes* (cranes, rails, etc.).

● **Fingal** ▷*See* Finn MacCool.

● **Fingal's Cave** ▶ A spectacular cave on the Scottish island of Staffa, in the Inner Hebrides, composed of basaltic columns. It is said to have been the home of the legendary Irish hero Fingal (*see* Finn MacCool). Visited by Mendelssohn (1829), it inspired his overture *Fingal's Cave* (1829, revised 1832). Length: 68 m (227 ft). Height: 35 m (117 ft).

● **fingerprint** ▶ The impression made by the pattern of ridges on the palmar side of the end joint of the fingers and thumbs. The taking of a person's fingerprints, which are virtually unique, for the purpose of identifying habitual criminals was introduced into the UK in 1901, largely as a result of the work of Sir William Herschel (1833–1917) and Sir Edward Henry (1859–1931). The print is taken by rolling the fingers and thumbs, one by one or simultaneously, in ink and then rolling them on paper. Fingerprints left at the scene of a crime may be taken by photography. The task of classifying and identifying fingerprints is immensely complicated. Scotland Yard has a library of over two million prints of known criminals and the FBI in the USA has more than 70 million. Classification relies on a numerical value

Fingal's cave ▶ The basalt columns line the entrance to the legendary home of the Irish folk hero, the warrior poet Finn MacCool, otherwise known as Fingal.

given to a print, which identifies the finger and the pattern of ridges (of which there are 1024 primary groups). ▷*See also* genetic fingerprinting.

arch whorl loop

fingerprint ▶ Loops are the commonest form of pattern (c. 65%), followed by whorls (c. 30%), and then arches (c. 5%).

● **Finisterre, Cape** ▶ 42 52N 9 16W The most westerly point in Spain, on the Atlantic coast.

● **Finland, Gulf of** ▶ An arm of the Baltic Sea, extending between Finland on the N, Estonia on the S, and Russia on the E. The ports of Helsinki and St Petersburg lie on the Gulf, which is frozen for 3–5 months of the year. Length: about 400 km (249 mi).

● **Finland, Republic of** ▶ (Finnish name: Suomi) A country in N Europe, with S and W coastlines on the Baltic Sea. It includes the ▷Åland Islands, situated at the mouth of the Gulf of Bothnia, which now have semiautonomous status. The land is generally low lying apart from some small hills in the NW. Over 10% of the area consists of lakes, which, together with rivers and canals, provide an extensive network of inland waterways. The majority of the population are Finns, with minorities of Swedes, Lapps, and Russians.

Economy: agriculture is highly mechanized and, together with cereals, dairy produce is important. Over 70% of the land is forested, providing resources for the timber and pulp and paper industries. Other industries include manufacturing (notably of furniture and metal goods), electronics, chemicals, food processing, and textiles. Hydroelectricity provides the main source of power and the principal mineral resources are copper and iron ore. Tourism is a major source of revenue. The main exports are timber, pulp and paper, and metal products. The economy suffered greatly in the early 1990s from the collapse of its markets in Russia and the former eastern bloc, but there has since been a recovery (largely owing to membership of the EU).

History: prehistorically the Finnic peoples migrated into Finland, gradually driving the Lapps northwards. Conquered by Sweden in the 12th century AD, Finland continued to enjoy considerable independence, becoming a grand duchy in the 16th century. The country suffered considerable hardships, however, in the recurring wars between Sweden and Russia. In the 18th century the SE was occupied by Russia and in 1809 the rest of the country was ceded to Russia, becoming an autonomous grand duchy. During this period nationalism flourished and in 1863 the Finnish language was officially recognized. Finland became independent in 1917, following the Russian Revolution, and a republic two years later. It was invaded by Soviet forces in 1939, 1940, and again in 1944, when it was forced to cede certain territories. A treaty of friendship between the two countries was signed in 1948 and extended in subsequent agreements: as a result the Soviet Union was able to exert considerable influence on Finland's domestic and foreign policies. The friendship treaty was replaced in 1992 by an agreement with Russia. Mauno Henrik Koivisto, president since 1982, was succeeded by Martti Ahtisaari in 1994. General elections in 1995 and 1999 led to the formation of centre-left coalitions under Paavo Lipponen. Finland became a member of the EU in 1995 and adopted the European single currency in 1999–2002.

Republic of Finland

Head of state	President Tarja Halonen
Official languages	Finnish and Swedish
Official currency	euro of 100 cents
Area	305 475 sq km (117 913 sq mi)
Population (2001 est)	5 185 000
Capital and main port	Helsinki

● **Finlay, Carlos Juan** ▶ (1833–1915) Cuban physician, who discovered that yellow fever was transmitted by mosquitoes. By 1900, Finlay had persuaded the authorities to control mosquito populations and so eradicate the disease. ▷*See also* Reed, Walter.

● **Finney, Albert** ▶ (1936–) British actor. Following his early successful performances in plays by modern dramatists he made several films, notably *Saturday Night and Sunday Morning* (1960). He then returned to the theatre to act classic roles, such as Tamburlaine and Hamlet. More recent films include *Under the Volcano* (1984), *The Browning Version* (1994), and *Erin Brockovich* (2000).

● **Finnic** ▶ A group of languages of the ▷Finno-Ugric branch of the Uralic family, which includes Finnish, Estonian, Lapp, Mari, Permic, and a number of other languages, most of which are dwindling. The Finnic peoples, ancestors of the modern Finns and Estonians, migrated in prehistoric times from central Russia to the E Baltic, Finland, and Karelia, bringing grain cultivation with them. Estonia became an important trading area and established a sense of national identity while the Finns inhabited more remote regions and remained fragmented until recent times. The ▷Lapps in the far north retain their separate identity and language but other groups have mainly lost theirs. All these peoples adopted Christianity during the 11th and 12th centuries.

● **Finn MacCool** ▶ (or Fingal) A legendary Irish hero, leader of the Fianna (*see* Fenian cycle). The son of Cumhaill (Cool) and the father of the poet Oisin (*see* Ossian), he killed Goll MacMorna, his father's murderer, and became leader of the company.

● **Finno-Ugric languages** ▶ A large group of languages of the ▷Uralic family, spoken by more than 20 million people in dispersed communities in Scandinavia, E Europe, and W Asia. Thought to have diverged about five millennia ago, the Finnic and Ugric languages can be further divided into the following major groups: Ugric (▷Hungarian and Ob-Ugric) and ▷Finnic (Finnish, Estonian, Mari, Permic, and a number of other languages mostly spoken in the Baltic and in the region of the Volga). Periodically and to varying degrees, neighbouring languages have exercised an influence on the vocabularies of the Finno-Ugric languages. Many Turkic forms, for example, have been absorbed into the Hungarian language. Although phonological processes may be shared by the majority of Finno-Ugric languages no single defining characteristic is common to all members.

● **fins** ▶ Organs of locomotion and balance in fish and some other aquatic animals. The fins of fish are supported by bony or cartilaginous fin rays and are either median or paired. The median fins include the tail (or caudal) fin, typically used for propulsion (in conjunction with the muscular body) and the dorsal and anal fins, used for balancing. The paired pectoral fins, just behind the gills, and pelvic fins, further back, are used for steering (although in rays the large pectorals provide motive force).

● **Finsen, Niels Ryberg** ▶ (1860–1904) Danish physician, who developed the use of light for treating certain bacterial skin diseases. Although now superseded, his work stimulated research into modern radiation therapy. He founded the Medical Light Institute (now the Finsen Institute), Copenhagen, in 1896 and was awarded a Nobel Prize (1903).

● **Finsteraarhorn** ▶ 46 32N 8 08E A mountain in S central Switzerland, the highest in the Bernese Oberland. It was first climbed in either 1812 (disputed) or 1829. Height: 4274 m (14 022 ft).

● **fiord** ▷*See* fjord.

● **Fiordland** ▶ The largest national park of New Zealand, in SW South Island. It is a mountainous region with glacial lakes and fjords, including Lakes Manapouri and Te Anau (famous for its glowworm caves), and Milford Sound. The Homer road tunnel (1953) made more of Fiordland accessible. Area: about 11 400 sq km (4401 sq mi).

● **Fiqh** ▷*See* Islamic law.

● **fir** ▶ A coniferous ▢tree of the genus *Abies* (about 50 species). Mostly native to N temperate regions, these trees are also called silver firs, as many species have leaves with a silvery undersurface. Firs have blunt-tipped needles and erect stout woody cones; they are important softwood trees (*see* timber). The European silver fir (*A. alba*), which forms pure forests in the mountains of central Europe, is widely grown for its timber: it reaches a height of 50 m and its cones are up to 15 cm long. Another widely planted timber tree is the grand, or giant, fir (*A. grandis*), which grows up to 90 m in its native W North America. Family: *Pinaceae*.

● **Firbank, Ronald** ► (1886–1926) British novelist. His wealthy background gave him liberty to write his short witty impressionistic novels, such as *Caprice* (1917), *Valmouth* (1919), and *Prancing Nigger* (1924). His homosexuality and his conversion to Roman Catholicism are major influences on his work.

● **Firdausi** ► (Abul Qasim Mansur; c. 935–c. 1020) The first major Persian poet, author of the epic poem *Shah-nama* (*The Book of Kings*; 1010), which recounts the history of Iran and its rulers up to the conquest of the country by Arabs in 641 AD. It includes the tragic legend of Sohrab and Rustum, familiar to English readers in Matthew Arnold's version. The *Shah-nama* was written in some 60 000 rhyming couplets (*mathnawi*), which are a feature of Persian poetry.

● **fire ant** ► An ▷ant, *Solenopsis saevissima* (or *S. geminata*), that occurs in South America and S North America. Fire ants are serious pests because of their irritant painful sting. Subfamily: *Myrmicinae*.

● **firearms** ► Weapons that use an explosive to discharge a missile. The two main categories are ▷artillery, with barrels having an internal diameter of more than 20 mm, and ▷small arms with calibres below 20 mm (this classification is no longer rigidly adopted).

Although gunpowder was invented in China many centuries before its description by Roger Bacon in the 13th century, a practical ▷cannon was not invented until the 14th century (by a German monk, Berthold Schwarz). ▷Guns, ▷mortars, and ▷howitzers have all evolved from the early cannon. Small-arms development began in the 15th century with the early form of the ▷musket, called a harquebus. They have evolved into the ▷pistol, ▷rifle, and ▷machine gun. ▷Guided missiles constitute a separate class of weapons, but can be considered as firearms in some contexts.

● **firebrat** ► A primitive wingless insect, *Thermobia domestica*: a three-pronged ▷bristletail that is abundant in buildings all over the world. It prefers warm moist places, such as around stoves, furnaces, and bakery ovens, where it feeds on starchy or sugary materials.

● **fireclay** ► A soft unbedded clay often occurring beneath coalseams. It is believed that they are fossil soils or earths in which swamp plants grew. Fireclays consist mainly of aluminium oxide and silica, being deficient in iron and alkalis; kaolin is the principal clay mineral. They are used as refractory materials, and poorer quality fireclay is used in the manufacture of sanitary earthenware.

● **firecrest** ► A tiny European songbird, *Regulus ignicapillus*. It is about 9 cm long and differs from its close relative, the ▷goldcrest, only in its black-and-white eyestripe. It uses its fine sharp bill to seek out small insects and larvae.

● **firefly** ► A nocturnal beetle, also called a lightning beetle, belonging to a family (*Lampyridae*; 2000 species) common in tropical and temperate regions. Fireflies emit a greenish light—often as short rhythmic flashes—from organs on the abdomen (*see* bioluminescence). They are 5–25 mm long and many have conspicuous orange or yellow markings. Most adults never eat (although a few feed on pollen and nectar); the larvae are carnivorous. The wingless females and larvae are called glowworms. *Lampyris noctiluca* is one of the best-known species.

Some ▷click beetles are also called fireflies.

● **Firenze** ▷*See* Florence.

● **Fire of London** ► (2–5 September, 1666) The fire that started in a baker's shop in Pudding Lane and destroyed four-fifths of the City. More than 13 000 buildings, including the medieval St Paul's Cathedral and 87 parish churches, were razed to the ground. Sir Christopher ▷Wren played a major part in the subsequent rebuilding. The **Monument**, which he designed in 1671, stands close to Pudding Lane to commemorate the Fire.

● **fire prevention** ► Fire prevention and control depends on: elimination of the causes (about 25% of fires are caused by electrical faults; smoking, overheating of machinery, furnace and flue defects, and burner flames are also important causes); fire-safe design using fire-retardant coatings and compartmentalized structures to reduce the spread of fire; the provision of such protective equipment as portable **fire extinguishers** and automatic sprinklers; and the existence of an efficient fire-fighting service.

Class A fires (paper, wood, furnishings, and other common solid combustibles) are extinguished by cooling with water, carbon dioxide, foam, etc. A common type of fire extinguisher, the soda-acid device, uses carbon dioxide produced by the reaction of sulphuric acid on sodium hydrogen carbonate to force water out of a container. Class B fires (flammable liquids, such as oil, petrol, etc.) are extinguished by smothering with chemical foam, dry powder, or carbon dioxide, or by extinguishing with halogenated hydrocarbons (e.g. BCF, bromochlorodifluoromethane). Class C fires involve electrical equipment and require nonconducting extinguishers, such as carbon dioxide, dry chemicals, and halogenated hydrocarbons. Class D fires involve burning metals, such as magnesium, sodium, etc., and require special techniques.

Automatic sprinklers are used in factories and warehouses and are usually controlled by thermostats, which turn on the sprinklers at a specified temperature. Smoke detectors are used where materials are expected to produce smoke before flaming and are now also widely used in homes to provide a warning.

● **fire salamander** ► A mainly terrestrial ▷salamander, *Salamandra salamandra*, ranging from S Europe to SW Asia. It is 18 cm long and glossy black with yellow or orange stripes and red patches. If molested it secretes a venom (salamandrin), which can be fatal to small mammals, from pores behind its eyes.

● **firethorn** ▷*See* Pyracantha.

● **fireworks** ► Combustible devices, used for signals, flares, and displays. Gunpowder rockets and fire crackers were first used in ancient China for military purposes and celebrations and in Europe from the middle ages. The basic explosive, usually gunpowder, is coloured by the addition of metallic salts: sodium salts for yellow, barium for green, strontium for red, and copper for blue. Metal filings are added for sparks and aniline dyes provide coloured smokes. Despite safety precautions by firework manufacturers and restrictions on sales to children, fireworks still cause casualties.

● **firn** ► (*or* névé) A stage in the transformation of fresh snow to glacier ice. Compaction and recrystallization of the snow increases its density and it becomes firn at a relative density of 0.5. Under further compaction firn may be transformed to glacier ice, this occurring at a relative density of 0.89–0.90.

● **first aid** ► Procedures that can be carried out by a medically unqualified person on someone immediately after injury in order to save life or facilitate specialist treatment given later. The types of injury requiring first aid include bleeding, burns, choking, drowning, electric shock, fracture, and poisoning. The patient should be removed from the cause of injury unless this would worsen his (or her) condition. The patient's breathing should be checked and constricting clothing loosened. In the absence of breathing ▷artificial respiration should be attempted. Once the patient is breathing he (or she) is put in the recovery position (lying on the stomach with the head to one side and the leg bent at the hip and the knee). In external bleeding the injury is covered and firm pressure applied. Lifting a wounded limb, provided no fractures are suspected, often reduces bleeding. If severe fractures are suspected the patient should not be moved without specialist supervision.

● **first cause** ► In the philosophy of Aristotle, and later more generally, the beginning of all the chains of cause and effect that are supposed to explain events in the world on a deterministic basis. The first cause does not itself require a cause. The necessity of a first cause (*or* prime mover) has been used as an argument for God's existence.

● **First of June, Battle of the Glorious** ► (1 June, 1794) A naval battle during the Revolutionary Wars fought between Britain and France in the Atlantic Ocean 690 km (430 mi) W of Ushant. The British under Richard Howe, in an attempt to prevent a convoy of US grain ships from entering the port of Brest, attacked their French escort ships, capturing six. The grain ships, however, reached their destination.

● **Firth, J(ohn) R(upert)** ▶ (1890–1960) British linguist, noted chiefly for his observation that speech sounds do not have clearcut boundaries (prosodic analysis) and his studies of contextual aspects of meaning and language use.

● **fiscal policy** ▶ Government economic policy in which changes in taxation, social-benefit rates, and government expenditure are used to influence the economy. It has been widely used since World War II, following the widespread acceptance of Keynesianism. According to ▷monetarism, however, such "fine tuning" of the economy may actually destabilize it.

● **Fischer, Bobby** ▶ (Robert James F; 1943–) US chess player. A child prodigy, he became the youngest ever grandmaster at the age of 15. In 1972 he defeated ▷Spassky to become world champion, but thereafter refused to compete, forfeiting his title in 1975. He emerged from 20 years of seclusion to defeat Spassky in a controversial rematch in 1992.

● **Fischer, Emil Hermann** ▶ (1852–1919) German chemist, who discovered a method of separating different ▷sugars from each other. He then determined their structure and showed that their ▷optical activity depended on the three-dimensional arrangement of the atoms in their molecules, thus founding the subject of stereochemistry. For this work he was awarded the Nobel Prize in 1902. In later life, Fischer showed that proteins consist of amino acids; in 1907 he synthesized the first protein molecule from amino acids.

● **Fischer, Hans** ▶ (1881–1945) German chemist. An assistant to Emil ▷Fischer, he became professor at the Technical Institute in Munich, where he analysed the biological molecules haemoglobin and chlorophyll, for which he was awarded a Nobel Prize in 1930. He committed suicide after his laboratory was destroyed in the bombing of Munich.

● **Fischer-Dieskau, Dietrich** ▶ (1925–) German baritone. He is renowned for his performances of *Lieder* and of a wide range of operatic roles. He has recorded all the songs of Schubert.

● **Fischer-Tropsch reaction** ▶ The formation of a variety of organic compounds, chiefly light liquid ▷hydrocarbons, upon passing a mixture of hydrogen and carbon monoxide over catalysts at around 200°C. The reaction is important in the production of synthetic liquid fuels from coal. It was invented by F. Fischer (1852–1932) and H. Tropsch (1839–1935) in 1925 and was used in Germany during World War II.

● **Fischer von Erlach, Johann Bernhard** ▶ (1656–1723) Austrian architect, a genius of German baroque. Fischer trained in Rome under ▷Bernini. Soon after moving to Vienna he became architect to the Habsburg court (1687). The Karlskirche (1716) and Hofbibliotek (1723) in Vienna are probably his finest achievements. He also built numerous palaces and wrote a history of architecture.

● **fish** ▶ A cold-blooded aquatic vertebrate belonging to either of the two classes *Chondrichthyes* (see cartilaginous fish) or *Osteichthyes* (see bony fish), which together comprise over 30 000 species occurring worldwide in seas and fresh waters. Ranging in size from under 10 mm to over 20 m long, they have streamlined bodies with a covering of bony scales, a fin-bearing tail, an anal fin, one or more dorsal fins, and paired lateral, pectoral (anterior), and pelvic (ventral) fins, which are used in swimming. Oxygen is obtained from water by means of ▷gills situated in the wall of the mouth cavity, although a few species can also breathe air (see lungfish). The majority of fish are carnivorous, feeding mainly on other fish and invertebrates, although some eat plants. Large numbers of small eggs are laid (up to several millions in some cases) and are usually fertilized externally. In some species internal fertilization occurs and live young may be born. The branch of zoology concerned with the study of fish is called **ichthyology**. Fish are of major importance as a source of food and other products (see fishing industry) and for sport (see angling). ▷*See also* cyclostome (jawless fish). □ p. 458.

● **Fishbourne Palace** ▷*See* Roman Britain.

● **fisher** ▶ A rare North American mammal, *Martes pennanti* (one of the ▷martens), also called pekan. Fishers are brown and grow to a length of 1 m. They feed on porcupines, small animals, and fruit and are named after their habit of fishing out the contents of baited traps.

● **Fisher, Andrew** ▶ (1862–1928) Australian statesman, born in Scotland; Labor prime minister (1908–09, 1910–13, 1914–15). He pledged Australian support for Britain in World War I.

● **Fisher, John Arbuthnot, 1st Baron** ▶ (1841–1920) British admiral. As an active commander, Fisher effected great improvements in naval training and, as first sea lord (1904–10), introduced far-reaching reforms in response to the German threat. He introduced both the Dreadnought battleships and the Invincible battle cruisers. He resigned in 1915 as a protest against the Dardanelles expedition in World War I.

● **Fisher, St John** ▶ (c. 1469–1535) English prelate and humanist. The chancellor of Cambridge University and Bishop of Rochester from 1504, he opposed Henry VIII's divorce from Catherine of Aragon. He was made a cardinal a month before his execution for refusing to recognize Henry VIII as head of the Church of England. He was canonized in 1935. Feast day: 9 July.

● **Fishguard** ▶ 51 59N 4 59W A port and resort in South Wales, in Pembrokeshire, with ferry crossings to Cork and Rosslare in the Republic of Ireland. It also comprises the original fishing village of Lower Fishguard. Population (1991): 2679.

● **fish hawk** ▷*See* osprey.

● **fishing industry** ▶ The recovery and processing of fish, shellfish, etc., for human consumption and other uses. From ancient times man has fished freshwater rivers and lakes and coastal waters using lines and nets. The modern industry uses vessels with refrigerated holds, echo sounding to locate shoals, and efficient nets and recovery gear; the net is often towed behind the vessel (trawling) or left to drift in the ocean. Fish are also dredged up or sucked up, using powerful pumps. The total world catch in 1994 was about 109.6 million tonnes, of which the anchoveta (a type of anchovy) was the leading species; other commercial species include cod, haddock, whiting, herring, mackerel, pilchards, lobsters, crabs, shrimps, oysters, mussels, octopus, and squid.

Fish are consumed as human food but provide many other byproducts, including fish meal, fish oils, glues, pharmaceuticals, shells, pearls, etc. Overfishing of natural populations has led to a decline in many species and smaller catches, sometimes causing friction between fishing nations (see Cod Wars). International agreement has been sought to regulate fishing and conserve stocks so that yields can be sustained indefinitely, resulting in a Code of Conduct for Responsible Fisheries (1995). One alternative is an increased dependence on **fish farming**, the maintenance and management of fish under controlled conditions to provide food. A long-established practice in China and the Far East, fish farming is now of major importance in many other countries, where trout, salmon, carp, eels, shrimps, and shellfish (including oysters) are commonly reared. Hatching of the eggs and rearing take place under optimum conditions in artificial ponds or enclosures situated in lakes or coastal waters. ▷*See also* whaling.

● **fish louse** ▶ A tiny parasitic ▷crustacean of the subclass *Branchiura* (75 species) that uses sucking mouthparts to attach itself to fresh- and salt-water fish. Its flattened body has a large disclike carapace covering the head and thorax.

● **fish owl** ▶ An ▷owl specialized for feeding on fish and frogs. Fish owls have naked legs and rough scaly feet to grip their slippery prey. Genera: *Ketupa* (Asia; 4 species), *Scotopelia* (Africa; 3 species).

● **fission** ▶ (biology) A form of asexual ▷reproduction in which an individual splits into two (binary fission) or more (multiple fission) equal parts, each part becoming a new individual. It occurs in a variety of plants, bacteria, protozoa, and some multicellular animals (e.g. corals).

● **fission** ▶ (physics) ▷*See* nuclear energy.

● **fission-track dating** ▶ A method of dating based on the sponta-

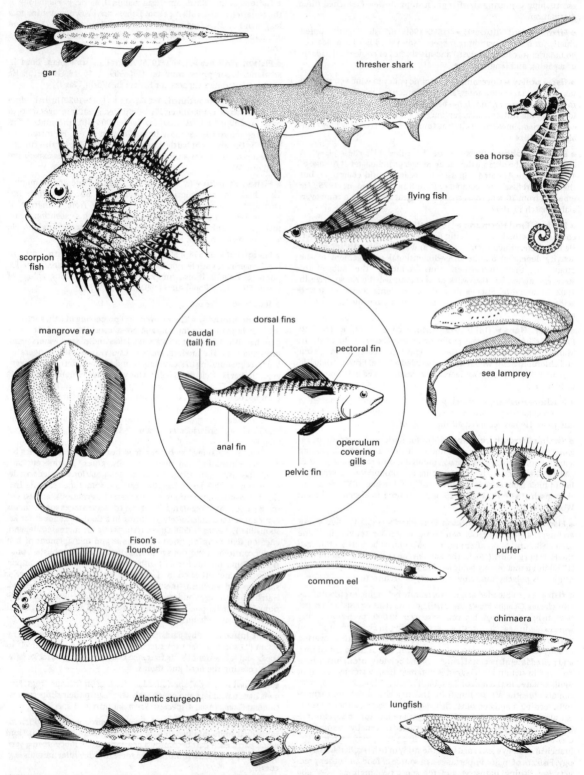

gar

thresher shark

sea horse

flying fish

scorpion fish

mangrove ray

dorsal fins

caudal (tail) fin

pectoral fin

anal fin

operculum covering gills

pelvic fin

sea lamprey

Fison's flounder

common eel

chimaera

puffer

Atlantic sturgeon

lungfish

fish ► There are numerous variations on the structure of a typical bony fish (mackerel: centre). In the flying fish, for instance, the pectoral fins are enlarged as wings; in the lungfish they are fleshy, for moving on land; and in the mangrove ray they are flattened, for swimming. The dorsal and anal fins of the scorpion fish are armed with poisonous spines and the tail of the sea horse is prehensile.

neous nuclear fission of uranium-238 in the sample. The fissions are recorded as tracks, which are then compared to the tracks formed by inducing fission in the uranium-235 present. A comparison of the numbers of tracks is used as a measure of the age of the sample.

● **fistula** ▶ An abnormal channel that has formed between two hollow organs that are not normally connected or between an organ and the exterior. It may result from infection, injury, disease (such as cancer) or occur as a complication of surgery. For example, an anal fistula, connecting the terminal section of the rectum to the exterior, may develop after an abscess in the rectum has burst. A vesicovaginal fistula, between the bladder and the vagina, may result from damage following gynaecological surgery, radiotherapy, or prolonged labour—most commonly in women in developing countries without access to hospitals for childbirth.

● **Fitzgerald, Edward** ▶ (1809–83) British poet. He lived quietly as a country gentleman with literary tastes. His famous *Rubaiyat of Omar Khayyam* (1859) was a free adaptation of the 12th-century Persian original into his own metre and imagery.

Ella Fitzgerald ▶ The "First Lady of Song." Between 1956 and 1967 she produced 19 albums of songs devoted to the works of individual composers, beginning with Cole Porter and including Irving Berlin, Jerome Kern, the Gershwin brothers, and Duke Ellington. These song books, as they were styled, contain almost 250 songs.

● **Fitzgerald, Ella** ▶ (1918–96) US Black jazz singer, known as the "First Lady of Song." Discovered in Harlem by Chick Webb (1902–39), she toured with his band. Later she became famous with the song "A-tisket, A-tasket" (1938), performed with such musicians as Duke Ellington and Oscar Peterson, and made many albums, including *Hello Love*, *Duke Ellington's Song Book*, and the *Gershwin Song Books*.

● **Fitzgerald, F(rancis) Scott (Key)** ▶ (1896–1940) US novelist. The success of his autobiographical first novel, *This Side of Paradise* (1920), enabled him to marry Zelda Sayre (1900–48) and to live out his self-created role as representative of the hedonistic Jazz Age. After 1924 Fitzgerald lived chiefly on the French Riviera, where he wrote his masterpiece *The Great Gatsby* (1925). Zelda suffered increasingly from schizophrenia and after 1930 was confined to an asylum. Fitzgerald, plagued by guilt, declined into alcoholism. His other works include *The Beautiful and the Damned* (1922) and *Tender is the Night* (1934). *The Last Tycoon* was unfinished at his death.

● **Fitzgerald, Garret** ▶ (1926–) Irish statesman; prime minister of Ireland (1981–82, 1982–87). He led ▷Fine Gael (1977–87) and was foreign minister (1973–77). In 1985 he negotiated the controversial Anglo-Irish agreement.

● **Fitzgerald, George Francis** ▶ (1851–1901) Irish physicist, who (independently of ▷Lorentz) suggested that objects become shorter as their velocity increases, as an explanation of the negative results of the ▷Michelson-Morley experiment. Now known as the Lorentz-Fitzgerald contraction, it was incorporated by Einstein into special ▷relativity after Fitzgerald's death.

● **Fitzsimmons, Bob** ▶ (1862–1917) New Zealand boxer, born in England. Of legendary courage and strength, he was world middleweight champion (1891–97), heavyweight champion (1897–99), and light-heavyweight champion (1903–05). He beat many much heavier and bigger men.

● **Fiume** ▷*See* Rijeka.

● **Five, the** ▶ A group of 19th-century Russian composers dedicated to the formation of a nationalist musical tradition based on folk music. Led by ▷Balakirev, the other members were ▷Borodin, César Cui (1835–1918), ▷Mussorgski, and ▷Rimsky-Korsakov. The original name of the group was *mogutchaya kutchka* (Russian: the mighty handful).

● **Five Pecks of Rice Band** ▶ A 2nd-century AD religious cult of the later ▷Han dynasty, so called because its followers paid an annual tribute of five pecks of rice to the sect leader. Together with a sect called the Yellow Turbans, the Five Pecks of Rice Band took part in two mass Taoist rebellions, which lasted over 30 years and played a significant part in overthrowing the Han dynasty (220 AD).

● **Five Power Constitution** ▶ The government constitution drawn up for China by ▷Sun Yat-sen and put into practice by the ▷Guomindang (Nationalists) in 1928. The government exercised five powers—executive, legislative, and judicial and those of examination (of candidates for the bureaucracy) and control (of government efficiency). The Constitution is still used by the Guomindang government of the Republic of China (Taiwan).

● **fives** ▶ A British court game that originated in ▷handball and developed in different forms at three public schools, Eton, Rugby, and Winchester. It is played with gloved hands by two or four players on a three- or four-walled court, each side returning the ball in turn to certain areas of wall. It is played largely in schools, although there are associations for the Eton and Rugby versions.

● **five-year plans** ▶ Economic plans formulated by ▷developing countries as part of the process of industrialization; they usually include targets for construction, investment, and output to be achieved in the following five years. They were first adopted in the Soviet Union. Capitalist countries (*see* capitalism) committed to economies based on market forces tend to avoid the direction implied in five-year plans, but in a ▷mixed economy plans based on exhortation rather than direction are sometimes used (e.g. the plan formulated in the UK by the Department of Economic Affairs in 1965).

● **Fizeau, Armand Hippolyte Louis** ▶ (1819–96) French physicist, who in 1849 was the first to measure the speed of light on the earth's surface. He used the teeth of a rotating gear wheel to switch a light beam on and off. The beam travelled 8 km (5 mi) before being reflected by a mirror back to the gear wheel. The speed of the wheel was adjusted so that it blocked the returning beam, enabling the speed of the beam to be calculated. In 1845, in collaboration with Jean ▷Foucault, he took the first photographs of the sun.

● **fjord** ▶ (*or* fiord) A long narrow sea inlet lying between steep mountain slopes, especially in Norway. Usually U-shaped, fjords are glaciated valleys that have been flooded by the sea. Many are extremely deep, some in excess of 1000 m (3280 ft), but near their mouths they usually have a considerably shallower bar or threshold.

● **flag** ▶ A Eurasian iris, *Iris pseudacorus* (yellow or water flag), growing in marshes and ditches. Up to 1.2 m high, it has yellow flowers and long bladelike leaves. The sweet flag (*Acorus calamus*) is a perennial herbaceous plant native to Asia and North America and naturalized in Britain, growing at the margins of ponds, rivers, etc. About 1 m high, it has wavy-edged leaves, which smell of tangerines when crushed, and the small yellow flowers are tightly packed on a tapering spikelike spadix, 8 cm long. Family: *Araceae*.

● **flagella** ▶ Long threadlike structures that project from the surface of a cell and produce lashing or undulating movements, used for locomotion or food collection. Flagella occur in certain protozoa and algae, motile gametes (usually sperms), and sponges; in all these organisms they have a complex internal structure of protein filaments (microtubules). Bacteria possess flagella of a simpler structure. Because of this difference, many biologists prefer the term "undulipodia" for eukaryotic (nonbacterial) flagella.

● **flagellants** ► In the middle ages, religious fanatics who scourged themselves as part of a public ritual, often to the chanting of processional hymns. Many primitive religions made use of ritual beatings, often as part of fertility or ▷initiation rites. In the Christian Church the use of flagellation as a private penitential practice dates back to the 4th century. Instances of mass public flagellation are first recorded in the 13th century and recurred throughout the medieval period, usually during times of political upheaval or natural disaster, such as the ▷Black Death: the motive seems to have been a belief that God's wrath could be appeased through self-inflicted punishment. In the 14th century organized brotherhoods of flagellants appeared in several European countries. Many of these groups were openly critical of the wealth and corruption of the Church, and some even proclaimed the heresy that flagellation (rather than the sacrament of penance) was the only means of obtaining God's forgiveness. For these reasons the practice was condemned (1349) by the Church authorities and some of the more extreme groups were suppressed. Private use of the "discipline," or scourge, is still practised by some orders of monks and nuns, while public rituals of self-flagellation are occasionally seen in Spain and South America, as well as in some Muslim countries.

● **flageolet** ► A musical instrument similar to the ▷recorder but with two thumb holes on the underside and a more complex head fitted with a slender ivory mouthpiece containing a sponge to absorb condensation. The diarist Pepys was a keen player.

● **flags** ► Emblems of nations, clubs, associations, etc., printed on cloth. The flags of the nations are shown on a coloured plate in the map section.

● **Flagstad, Kirsten Malfrid** ► (1895–1962) Norwegian soprano, famous for her singing of Wagner roles, such as Brünnhilde in *Der Ring des Nibelungen* and Kundry in *Parsifal*. She also sang the role of Dido in Purcell's *Dido and Aeneas* and championed the songs of Sibelius.

● **Flaherty, Robert (Joseph)** ► (1884–1951) US film director. His *Nanook of the North* (1922), filmed during a two-year stay with the Canadian Inuit people, and *Moana* (1926), filmed in the Samoan Islands, were the earliest major documentary films. His later films include *Louisiana Story* (1948).

● **Flamborough Head** ► 54 06N 0 04W A chalk headland in NE England, in the East Riding of Yorkshire extending into the North Sea. Its cliffs, in parts 120 m (400 ft) high, are the breeding ground for many sea birds.

● **Flamboyant** ► In French ▷gothic architecture, the predominant style during the 15th century. Similar to the earlier English ▷Decorated style, Flamboyant takes its name from its characteristic slender and elaborate curves that wind into flamelike patterns, especially in window tracery. St Maclou, Rouen (begun 1432), is a fine Flamboyant church.

● **flamboyant tree** ► An attractive tree, *Delonix regia*, also called royal poinciana, flame tree, and peacock flower. It grows to a height of 6–12 m and has showy flame-coloured flowers with long protruding stamens. Native to Madagascar, it is widely planted in the tropics for shade and ornament. Family: ▷Leguminosae.

● **flamenco** ► A type of Spanish music originating in Andalusia, typically consisting of a song (*cante*) accompanied by dancing, in which the men perform intricate toe and heel tapping steps (*zapateados*) and the women rely on graceful hand and body movements. It was developed by gipsies and shows signs of Moorish influence; the predominant styles are *grande* (anguished) and *chico* (gay and amorous), with a variety of intermediate moods. Flamenco guitar playing has become well known outside Spain; it employs a different technique from that of the "classical" guitar, including a percussive effect obtained by tapping the body of the guitar with the fingers.

● **flame-thrower** ► A weapon that ejects a stream of burning fluid at an enemy either from a hand-held device fed from a backpack or from a similar device mounted on a vehicle. Flame-throwers using burning oil were first employed by the Germans in World War I. In World War II they were used extensively, often mounted on tanks, by most armies. Towards the end of World War II ▷napalm was introduced by the US and British forces.

● **flame tree** ► One of several unrelated trees with flame-coloured showy flowers. The name is most commonly applied to *Brachychiton acerifolium* (or *Sterculia acerifolia*), a deciduous Australian tree that bears masses of small scarlet bell-like flowers on leafless branches. Family: *Sterculiaceae*. It may also refer to the ▷flamboyant tree.

● **flamingo** ► A wading bird belonging to a family (*Phoenicopteridae*; 4 species) occurring in large flocks on saltwater lakes in warm regions of the world. 90–150 cm tall, flamingos have a long neck, a short tail, a broad wingspan, and white plumage, tinged with pink. They separate algae, diatoms, small molluscs, etc., from mud using their bills, which are lined with sievelike filters. Order: *Ciconiiformes* (herons, storks, etc.). ▷*See* Plate III.

● **Flaminian Way** ► A Roman road that extended from Rome to Ariminum (now Rimini) on the Adriatic coast. It was named after Gaius ▷Flaminius, who completed it in 220 BC.

● **Flamininus, Titus Quinctius** ► (c. 230–c. 174 BC) Roman general, who defeated Philip V (237–179; reigned 220–179) of Macedon at Cynoscephalae (198). In 196, at the Isthmian Games, Flamininus proclaimed the independence of the Greek states from Macedonian hegemony.

● **Flaminius, Gaius** ► (d. 217 BC) Roman popular leader. An advocate of the plebeians' rights, he often challenged or disregarded senatorial authority. In 220, as consul, he built the ▷Flaminian Way, Rome's road to N Italy. Popular dissatisfaction with senatorial war policy inspired his election in 217 as leader against ▷Hannibal, who defeated and killed Flaminius at Trasimene.

● **Flamsteed, John** ► (1646–1719) English astronomer, who established, with the permission of Charles II, a national observatory at Greenwich and was appointed the first astronomer royal in 1675. His star catalogue, listing more than 3000 stars, gave their positions with greater precision than ever before. A quarrelsome man, he argued with ▷Newton and ▷Halley over their requests for access to his astronomical observations.

● **Flanders** ► (Flemish name: Vlaanderen; French name: Flandre) A historic region in Europe, in the SW of the Low Countries. It now comprises the Flanders region of Belgium and parts of N France and the Netherlands.

History: in the middle ages Flanders formed an autonomous region ruled by the Counts of Flanders and after the 12th century it became a major industrial and commercial centre, its cloth being especially important. From the 15th century onwards it passed through phases of French, Spanish, Austrian, and Dutch control before becoming part of independent Belgium in 1830. The scene of many battles during its history, Flanders saw heavy fighting in both World Wars. During World War II the Battle of Flanders (10 May–2 June, 1940) comprised the German attack on Holland, Belgium, and France, which resulted in the Allied withdrawal from ▷Dunkirk. A series of amendments to the Belgian constitution from 1977 has given the Flanders region considerable autonomy. ▷*See also* Flemings.

● **flash point** ► The lowest temperature at which an inflammable liquid (generally a hydrocarbon) produces enough vapour to ignite on the application of a small flame under specified conditions. Flash points are useful for setting safety standards, especially for the storage of hydrocarbons and monitoring refinery operations.

● **flatfish** ► Any carnivorous ▷bony fish belonging to the order *Pleuronectiformes* (about 600 species), including many important food fishes, such as ▷halibut, ▷plaice, ▷sole, and ▷turbot. They have a laterally flattened body, 10–200 cm long, fringed with dorsal and anal fins. Both eyes occur on the same side of the head and they lie on their "blind" side, usually on sandy or muddy bottoms of coastal waters; the upper surface is coloured to blend with their surroundings. In the larval stage one eye migrates over the head to lie near the other.

● **flatfoot** ► Obliteration of the longitudinal arch of the foot, so that the entire sole is in contact with the ground on standing. It is common in young children and they usually grow out of it. Rigid flatfoot is more serious and the result of a congenital abnormality.

● **flathead** ▶ A bottom-dwelling carnivorous ▷bony fish of the family *Platycephalidae*, found in tropical Indian, Pacific, and E Atlantic waters. It has a tapering body, up to 1.3 m long, and a large flat head covered with ridges and spines. It is an important food fish. Order: *Scorpaeniformes* (or *Scleroparei*).

● **flat racing** ▶ A form of horse racing in which the horses are not required to jump obstacles. Flat races are usually run over distances between 0.8 km (0.5 mi) and 2.4 km (1.5 mi). ▷Thoroughbred horses are used, mainly as two- and three-year-olds. Weight handicaps are allotted in most races. The most prestigious races are the English ▷Classics, the US ▷Triple Crown, and the French Prix de l'Arc de Triomphe.

● **flatworm** ▶ A flat-bodied wormlike animal of the invertebrate phylum *Platyhelminthes* (9000 species). Some flatworms are free-living (*see* planarian) but the majority are parasitic (*see* fluke; tapeworm). They have a simple body, with sense organs and a primitive brain at the front end, and range in size from 1 mm to 15 m. Many are hermaphrodite.

● **Flaubert, Gustave** ▶ (1821–80) French novelist. The son of a Rouen surgeon he gave up his law studies in 1843 to dedicate himself wholly to literature. He travelled in the Near East (1849–51) and Tunisia (1857) and was a lover of the poet Louise Colet (1808–76). He worked for five years on his first novel, *Madame Bovary* (1856), a controversially explicit study of an overromantic bourgeois wife. His other major works include the exotic romance *Salammbô* (1862), *L'Éducation sentimentale* (1870), *La Tentation de Saint Antoine* (1874), and the brilliant short stories in *Trois contes* (1877).

● **flavour** ▶ (physics) ▷*See* particle physics.

● **flax** ▶ A herbaceous plant of the genus *Linum* (230 species), mostly of the N hemisphere. Cultivated flax (*L. usitatissimum*) is an annual, up to 100 cm high, with narrow leaves and blue five-petalled flowers. Its stem fibres are used to make linen, fine writing paper, and cigarette paper. The seeds contain ▷linseed oil. Flax is cultivated throughout Europe, the main producing countries being the republics of the former Soviet Union, Belgium, Holland, and Northern Ireland. Family: *Linaceae*.

● **Flaxman, John Henry** ▶ (1755–1826) British sculptor and book illustrator. Flaxman chiefly designed and modelled ▷Wedgwood friezes, portrait medallions, etc., until his visit to Rome (1789–94). There, he won an international reputation as a neoclassical artist with his illustrations to the *Odyssey* and *Iliad* (both 1792), Aeschylus' works, and *The Divine Comedy*. His best-known monuments are those of Lord Mansfield (Westminster Abbey) and Nelson (St Paul's). He became the first professor of sculpture at the Royal Academy (1810).

● **flea** ▶ A small wingless □insect belonging to the widely distributed order *Siphonaptera* (about 1600 species). Fleas are bloodsucking parasites of birds and mammals. A flea's body, which is generally brown, is 1–10 mm long and laterally flattened and its legs are modified for jumping. Fleas have irritating bites and change hosts frequently, acting as carriers of some serious diseases. The wormlike larvae use biting mouthparts to feed on dirt, excrement, and dried blood. Two important and widely distributed species are the human flea (*Pulex irritans*) and the oriental rat flea (*Xenopsylla cheopis*), which transmits bubonic plague and typhus to man.

● **fleabane** ▶ A perennial herb of the genus *Erigeron* (about 180 species), from America and Europe. 8–40 cm tall, fleabanes have strap-shaped leaves and small daisy-like flower heads with purple or white ray florets and yellow centres. Herbs of the Old World genus *Pulicaria* are also called fleabane. They have daisy-like yellow flowers, 1–3 cm across. Family: ▷*Compositae*.

● **fleawort** ▶ One of several herbs of the genus *Senecio*, especially *S. integrifolius*, *S. palustris*, and *S. spathulifolius*, from central and N Europe. The plants are 25–100 cm high, with yellow daisy-like flowers, 2–3 cm across. Family: ▷*Compositae*.

● **Flecker, (Herman) James Elroy** ▶ (1884–1915) British poet. A minor diplomat in Turkey and Lebanon, he died of tuberculosis in a

Swiss sanatorium. His best-known works are the poem *The Golden Journey to Samarkand* (1913) and the verse drama *Hassan*, posthumously produced in 1922 with music by ▷Delius; both are lyrical evocations of a richly exotic Orient.

● **Fleet Street** ▶ A street in London between the Strand and Ludgate Circus in which most newspapers had offices until the mid-1980s, when there was a general move out of central London. It is named after the River Fleet (now a covered sewer).

● **Fleetwood** ▶ 53 56N 3 01W A port and resort in NW England, in Lancashire. It is the principal fishing port on the W coast of England. Population (1991): 27 227.

● **Flémalle, Master of** ▶ (c. 1378–1444) One of the founders (with the ▷van Eyck brothers) of the Flemish school of painting (*see* Flemish art). He is usually identified as Robert Campin, an artist active in Tournai from 1406. His name derives from three panels (Frankfurt-am-Main) attributed to him and mistakenly thought to have been commissioned by the abbey of Flémalle near Liège. Other works include the *Mérode Altarpiece* (the Cloisters, New York), the *Annunciation* and *Marriage of the Virgin* (Madrid), and the *Madonna of Humility* (London). His works display the careful realistic rendering of details from everyday life that characterizes the Flemish school as a whole.

Sir Alexander Fleming ▶ The microbiologist is pictured here working in his laboratory at St Mary's Hospital, London.

● **Fleming, Sir Alexander** ▶ (1881–1955) British microbiologist, who discovered the antibiotic ▷penicillin. In 1928 Fleming noticed that a mould contaminating a bacterial culture had destroyed the bacteria in its vicinity. He identified the mould as *Penicillium notatum* and named the antibacterial substance it produced penicillin. Although he found that penicillin was harmless to human cells, Fleming could not isolate or identify the antibiotic. This was later achieved by Lord ▷Florey and Sir Ernest ▷Chain, with whom Fleming shared the 1945 Nobel Prize. Fleming also discovered lysozyme, an antibacterial enzyme found in tears and saliva.

● **Fleming, Ian (Lancaster)** ▶ (1908–64) British author and journalist, famous for his creation of the archetypal secret agent, James Bond, in 12 novels and 7 short stories, most of them filmed. Originally a stockbroker, Fleming served as a foreign correspondent in Moscow, and in World War II he became a senior naval intelligence officer.

● **Fleming, Sir John Ambrose** ▶ (1849–1945) British electrical engineer, who constructed the first rectifying diode in 1904. His invention greatly stimulated the development of radio and led to the invention of the triode two years later by Lee ▷De Forest. He also took part in the development of the electric lamp and studied resistance at low temperatures. He was knighted in 1929. ▷*See also* Fleming's rules.

● **Fleming, Paul** ▶ (1609–40) German poet. A disciple of Martin ▷Opitz, his posthumously published love lyrics and religious hymns were distinguished by their sincerity and directness. Many of his poems were inspired by his thwarted love for Elsàbe Niehus, whom he met on a trading journey to Russia and Persia.

● **Flemings** ▶ Inhabitants of N and W Belgium (▷Flanders) who speak Flemish, a dialect of ▷Dutch known by them as Vlaams. They number approximately 5 500 000. Like the Dutch they are descended from the Salic Franks, a Germanic people, who settled the area during the 3rd and 4th centuries AD. They retain a cultural identity distinct from that of French-speaking Belgians (see Walloons).

● **Fleming's rules** ▶ A mnemonic, invented by Sir John Ambrose Fleming, for the relationship between the directions of motion, magnetic field, and electric current in ▷electric motors and generators. The thumb represents *motion*; the *first* (index) *finger* represents the *field*; and the second finger represents the current. If the right hand is held with the thumb and first two fingers straight and mutually at right angles, the directions in a generator are indicated. The left hand indicates the directions in a motor.

● **Flemish** ▷See Netherlandic.

● **Flemish art** ▶ A tradition of painting that flourished in Flanders, now Belgium, from the 14th to the 18th centuries. The early dominance of manuscript illuminators was replaced in the 15th century by a major school of painters, which included the Master of ▷Flémalle, the ▷van Eycks, van der ▷Weyden, van der ▷Goes, ▷Bouts, ▷Memling, and Gerard ▷David. In the 16th century Flemish art was Italianized by such painters as ▷Gossaert and Frans ▷Floris, although Hieronymus ▷Bosch and ▷Brueghel the Elder remained largely within the Flemish tradition. Major 17th-century figures were ▷Rubens, ▷Van Dyck, ▷Jordaens, and ▷Teniers. Flemish art declined in international importance after the 17th century.

● **Flensburg** ▶ 54 47N 9 27E A town in N Germany, in Schleswig-Holstein on the Baltic Sea. Between 1848 and 1867 it was under Danish rule and in 1945 at the end of World War II the German Government capitulated near here. A port and naval base, its industries include shipbuilding and fishing. Population (1991): 87 240.

● **Fletcher, John** ▶ (1579–1625) English dramatist. He collaborated with Francis ▷Beaumont on *Philaster* (1610), *The Maid's Tragedy* (1611), and many other plays, and probably with ▷Shakespeare on *The Two Noble Kinsmen* and *Henry VIII* (1612).

● **fleur-de-lys** ▶ A heraldic device, which has three everted petals, resembling the bearded iris. It was the coat of arms of the French monarchy from the middle ages.

● **Fleury, André Hercule de, Cardinal** ▶ (1653–1743) French statesman; chief minister (1726–43) of Louis XV. Fleury carried out important reforms, reorganizing finances, building roads, and encouraging commerce. A successful diplomat, he worked to maintain peace in Europe but involved France in the War of the ▷Polish Succession (1733–38).

● **flight, animal** ▶ Aerial locomotion, which is developed to its fullest extent in ▷birds, insects, and bats. A bird's wing has the cross-section of an aerofoil (▯aeronautics) and generates lift in a similar way. Powerful flight muscles are attached at one end to the humerus (the upper wing bone) and at the other to a bony projection—the keel—of the sternum (breastbone). The levator muscle is responsible for the upstroke of the wing, while the depressor muscle propels the wing downwards, providing both thrust (forward propulsion) and extra lift when required. ▯Feathers are also vital for flight, giving the aerofoil shape to the wings, streamlining the body, and providing insulation against heat loss in the cold air. Flight in insects and bats operates on similar principles. A few other animals groups have adopted a passive form of flight—gliding. They include the ▷colugo (flying lemur), ▷flying fish, ▷flying phalangers, and ▷flying squirrels.

● **flight, manned** ▷See aeronautics; aircraft.

● **flight recorder** ▶ A strong box, usually painted orange (in spite of being known as a **black box**), containing a multitrack tape record of an aircraft's flight parameters (instrument readings, control surfaces positions, etc.) and the voice of the pilot and crew; recordings are made every second and the whole tape is recycled after 25 hours.

If found after a crash, it can provide information as to its cause. There are plans to fit similar devices to trains.

● **Flinders, Matthew** ▶ (1774–1814) British navigator and hydrographer. He entered the navy in 1789 and after sailing to the Pacific with Capt ▷Bligh served in the French Revolutionary War. Having explored (1795–1800) the Bass Strait with George Bass (died c. 1812), he was commissioned to survey the coasts of Australia and Tasmania. Flinders Island, River, and Range are named after him.

● **Flinders Island** ▷See Furneaux Islands.

● **Flinders Range** ▶ A mountain range in E South Australia. It extends N from Gulf St Vincent between Lake Torrens and Lake Frome, reaching 1190 m (3904 ft) at St Mary Peak.

● **flint** ▶ A variety of ▷chalcedony. It is grey to black, is dense and tough, and breaks with a conchoidal (curved) fracture, leaving sharp edges (hence its use by Stone Age man for tools and weapons). It occurs in nodules in chalk along the bedding planes and as pebbles in river gravels and beach material.

● **Flint** ▶ 43 03N 83 40W A city in the USA, in Michigan on the Flint River. One of the several cities that surround ▷Detroit, it suffered mass unemployment when its motor-vehicle factories were closed. Population (1996 est): 134 881.

● **flint glass** ▶ A durable, brilliant, and highly refractive glass. It is used in high-quality glassware and also in lenses and prisms since it absorbs very little light. It is also known as lead glass and crystal glass.

● **flintlock** ▷See ▯musket; ▯pistol.

● **Flintshire** ▶ A county of NE Wales, on the Dee estuary and the Irish Sea. Under local government reorganization in 1974 it became part of Clwyd; it was reinstated as a county (with different borders) in 1996. Narrow coastal plains in the E and N rise gradually to the Clwydian Hills in the SW. The Deeside region is heavily industrialized, with chemicals, textiles, and plastics. The S and W is agricultural. Area: 437 sq km (169 sq mi). Population (1996 est): 145 000. Administrative centre: Mold.

● **FLN** ▷See Front de Libération nationale.

● **Flodden, Battle of** ▶ (9 September, 1513) The battle in which the English under Thomas Howard, Earl of Surrey (1443–1524), defeated the Scots under ▷James IV at Flodden Edge, Northumberland. The Scots had invaded England after allying with France against Henry VIII.

● **flood** ▶ The overflowing of a river onto the surrounding land (**flood plain**) or the surging of sea water at high tide onto the coastal land. The flood described in Genesis 6.9 (see Noah) is probably apocryphal, although Sir Leonard ▷Woolley identified at Ur a layer of clay that he believed was deposited during a flood in about 4000 BC. More recent flood disasters include those in Warsaw (1861 and 1964), Paris (1910), the UK's E coast (1953), Florence (1966), Bangladesh (1974, 1985, 1988, 1993, and 1998), Sudan (1988), North Korea (1995), Poland and Germany (1997), and the Yangtze basin in China (1998). However, floods are not always disastrous; the annual floods of the River ▷Nile have provided a fertile flood plain, the site of one of the earliest civilizations.

The prevention of flooding involves accurate prediction of tides and the provision of flood-relief channels and barrages (as in the River ▷Thames).

● **Flood, Henry** ▶ (1732–91) Irish politician. An impressive orator, Flood rapidly became the leader of the patriot party in the Irish parliament. In 1775, however, he accepted a government post and the patriots branded him as an apostate. In 1781 Flood again espoused the patriot cause but quarrelled with its new leader, ▷Grattan, and declined into obscurity.

● **floodgate** ▶ A movable barrier set up on spillways to control the height of water at ▷dams. Closure of some of the floodgates at a spillway in times of water shortage may conserve valuable amounts of water, without reducing the full spillway capacity. Vertical-lift gates are raised to permit flow beneath them, while drum gates (solid circular quadrants) rotate downwards to allow water to flow over them.

● **floppy disk** ▷*See* magnetic disk.

● **Flora** ▶ The Roman goddess of flowers and spring. Her spring festival, the Floralia, instituted in 283 BC, was the occasion for riotous uninhibited behaviour.

● **Florence** ▶ (Italian name: Firenze) 43 47N 11 15E A city in Italy, the capital of Tuscany on the River Arno. Florence is a major market town as well as an administrative and educational centre. The manufacture of luxury goods is important but the principal industry is tourism. Its many famous buildings include the 13th-century cathedral of Sta Maria del Fiore (⌐Brunelleschi, Filippo), the campanile of Giotto, the baptistery, and many churches (including Sta Maria Novella and Sta Croce). The Ponte Vecchio (1345) across the River Arno connects the ▷Uffizi gallery to the Palazzo Pitti (now an art gallery). Art treasures in Florence include works by Michelangelo, Donatello, Masaccio, Giotto, Fra Angelico, Botticelli, Raphael, Titian, and Rubens. The Italian National Library (Biblioteca Nazionale) is situated here and its university was established in 1321.
History: an early Roman colony, it had developed into an important centre of trade and industry by the 12th century. It was torn by the struggles between the ▷Guelfs and Ghibellines (13th and 14th centuries) but flourished financially and culturally (14th–16th centuries). The rule of the ▷Medici family began in 1434 and this continued almost uninterrupted (*see* Savonarola, Girolamo) for three centuries. Following a period of Austrian rule, Florence became part of Italy in 1861 and was the capital (1865–71). Florence has suffered damage in war (including World War II), from floods, especially in November, 1966, and from a terrorist bombing in 1993. Population (1996 est): 383 594.

● **Flores** ▶ An Indonesian island in the Nusa Tenggara group. Mountainous and volcanic, it is largely unexplored. The chief crop is maize; sandalwood and copra are exported. It was devastated by an earthquake and a tidal wave in 1992. Area: 17 150 sq km (6622 sq mi). Chief town: Ende.

● **Florey, Howard Walter, Baron** ▶ (1898–1968) Australian pathologist, who, working with Sir Ernst ▷Chain, isolated and purified the antibiotic ▷penicillin, first discovered by Sir Alexander ▷Fleming in 1928. Florey and Chain developed techniques for producing the pure drug in large quantities. In 1941 they conducted the first clinical trials, in which penicillin proved very effective in combating bacterial infections. Florey shared the 1945 Nobel Prize with Chain and Fleming.

● **Florianópolis** ▶ (former name: Desterro) 27 35S 48 31W A city and port in Brazil, the capital of Santa Catarina state on Santa Catarina island. It is linked to the mainland by a steel suspension bridge. It exports sugar, tobacco, and fruit and has a university (1960). Population (1991): 191 664.

● **floribunda** ▷*See* rose.

● **Florida** ▶ A state in the far SE of the USA, between the Atlantic Ocean and the Gulf of Mexico. It is predominantly a low-lying peninsula with many lakes and rivers, Lake Okeechobee being the largest lake. In the diversified economy manufacturing is important, especially food processing and the chemical industry. The state's mines produce phosphate, titanium, zircon, and other heavy minerals. Tourism, based on its subtropical climate, is the most important industry, with many popular resorts, such as Miami Beach and Palm Beach. Most recently the state has become a centre for space exploration with the John F. Kennedy Space Center at Cape Canaveral. Florida produces some 75% of the USA's citrus fruits, as well as large quantities of vegetables. It is also a major region for breeding thoroughbred horses.
History: following its exploration by the Spanish, it was ceded to the British in 1763 but returned to Spain after the American Revolution. It passed to the USA in 1819, becoming a state in 1845. It was a supporter of the Confederate cause during the US Civil War. The arrival of the railways in the 1880s brought access to the agricultural markets of the N and subsequent economic growth. In 1992 a severe hurricane caused widespread damage. Area: 151 670 sq km (58 560 sq mi). Population (1996 est): 14 399 985. Capital: Tallahassee.

● **Florida Keys** ▶ A chain of small islands in the USA, separated from the S coast of Florida by Florida Bay. It includes the islands of Key West and Key Largo and extends for over 160 km (100 mi). The islands are linked by the Overseas Highway, a complex of roads and 42 bridges.

● **Florio, John** ▶ (c. 1553–1625) English writer, of Italian descent. While teaching at Oxford he published his important Italian-English dictionary (1598). He later held appointments at James I's court. His main work was an English translation of Montaigne's *Essays* (1603).

● **Floris** ▶ Two Flemish artists. **Cornelis Floris** (1514–75) was an architect and sculptor, best known for designing Antwerp town hall (1561–65). His brother **Frans Floris** (c. 1516–70) was a painter. Both studied in Italy and contributed to the spread of the Italian Renaissance style in the Netherlands.

● **Flotow, Friedrich von** ▶ (1812–83) German operatic composer. He had much success in his lifetime but his works, apart from the opera *Martha* (1847), have not survived.

● **flotsam, jetsam, and lagan** ▶ Goods cast into the sea that respectively remain afloat, sink, or would sink but have attached to them a buoy, which keeps them afloat. Unless claimed by the owner, they belong to the Crown.

● **flounder** ▶ A common name for any ▷flatfish or for certain species. An example is *Platichthys flesus*, which is up to 50 cm long and lives in European coastal and fresh waters. It has a greenish or brownish mottled upper surface and is an important food and game ⌐fish.

● **flour** ▶ The powdered grain of wheat or other cereals, used in baking. The chief use of flour is in making bread. When the two proteins in wheat, glutenin and gliadin, are mixed with water they form gluten, which permits the dough to expand and retain the carbon dioxide resulting from fermentation of the yeast in bread dough. Different types of flour are made by varying the percentage of flour separated from the wheat. The principal commercial flours are whole wheat (100%), wholemeal and stoneground (92%), wheatmeal (80–90%), and white flours (70–72%). Many nutritionists consider it important to eat food made from whole wheat and wholemeal flour, rather than white flour. The former retain more of the bran (the outer skin of the wheat grain) and have more iron and calcium than white flour. They are also a good daily source of dietary ▷fibre. Flour with a high gluten content (strong flour) is best when yeast is called for, as in dough for bread. On the other hand a softer flour with a lower gluten content (fine flour) is used for cakes, shortbread, etc. Plain flour is all-purpose, with a moderate gluten content. Self-raising flour is plain flour with the addition of raising agents.

● **flower** ▶ The reproductive organ of flowering ⌐plants (angiosperms), which is essential for the production of seeds and fruits. It is made up of the perianth (petals and sepals) and the sexual organs—the ▷stamens producing pollen (male gametes) and the ▷carpels containing the female gametes. The petals and sepals serve to protect the sexual organs and—in flowers pollinated by animals—are brightly coloured, scented, and secrete ▷nectar to attract insects and birds. Wind-pollinated flowers are typically small and inconspicuous and may lack a perianth.

● **flowering currant** ▶ An ornamental garden shrub, *Ribes sanguineum*, native to North America. Up to 2.5 m tall, it has drooping spikes of pink tubular flowers that appear before the maple-shaped leaves. The fruit is a blue-black berry. The shrub has an odour of blackcurrants. Family: *Grossulariaceae* (*see* currant).

● **flowering quince** ▷*See* japonica.

● **flowering rush** ▶ A perennial freshwater plant, *Butomus umbellatus*, native to Eurasia but common throughout N temperate regions: it is a popular garden plant. It has tapering leaves, up to 1 m long, and an umbrella-shaped cluster of pinkish flowers at the tip of a long stalk. Family: *Butomaceae*.

● **flowerpecker** ▶ A songbird belonging to a family (*Dicaeidae*; 55 species) occurring in S Asia and Australasia. Ranging in size from 8 cm to 20 cm, they have stumpy tails, short bills, and variable plumage. Flowerpeckers feed on berries and nectar, thereby dispersing seeds and pollinating flowers.

● **Fludd, Robert** ▶ (1574–1637) English physician and ▷Rosicrucian. He studied at Oxford and on the Continent, where he was influenced by the works of the Swiss doctor and philosopher ▷Paracelsus. His philosophical books were largely a defence of the allegorical interpretation of the Bible, astrology, palmistry, and alchemy against the new science.

● **fluid dynamics** ▷*See* hydrodynamics.

● **fluidics** ▶ The use of jets of fluid in a circuit to carry out electronic functions. Fluidic circuits can resist much higher temperatures than electronic circuits and are also unaffected by ionizing radiation and magnetic fields. They therefore have uses in nuclear reactors and spacecraft. They are also used as delay lines since they respond much more slowly than electronic circuits.

● **fluidization** ▶ The process of supporting very fine solid particles in a stream of gas so that the combination of solid and fluid behaves like a liquid. The process is used in transporting coal dust and in the cleaning of the catalyst in ▷catalytic cracking in oil refining.

● **fluid mechanics** ▶ The study of the mechanical properties of fluids. ▷Hydrostatics is concerned with the study of fluids at rest and hydrodynamics (or fluid dynamics) with fluids that are flowing. Hydraulics deals with the practical applications of these sciences. Two important aspects of hydrodynamics are the conservation of energy in fluid flow (see Bernoulli's principle) and the distinction between streamline and turbulent flow. ▷*See also* aerodynamics; Reynolds number.

● **fluke** ▶ A parasitic ▷flatworm of the class *Trematoda* (over 6000 species). Typically leaf-shaped, some are elongated to fit the body cavities they inhabit. The monogenetic flukes have a single host and are generally external parasites of fishes; the digenetic flukes have life cycles involving up to four different hosts and are mainly internal parasites of vertebrates, passing early larval stages in various invertebrates.

● **fluorescence** ▷*See* luminescence.

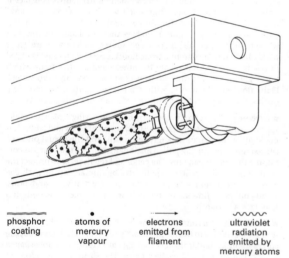

| phosphor coating | atoms of mercury vapour | electrons emitted from filament | ultraviolet radiation emitted by mercury atoms |

fluorescent lamp ▶ Electrons from the filament collide with atoms of mercury vapour in the tube producing ultraviolet radiation. This is converted to visible light by the fluorescent coating on the tube.

● **fluorescent lamp** ▶ A lamp that uses fluorescence (*see* luminescence) as its source of light. It consists of a glass tube containing a low pressure gas, such as mercury vapour. As a current passes through the gas, collisions between the electrons and atoms of the gas excite the atoms, which emit ▷ultraviolet radiation when they return to the ground state. The radiation strikes a phosphor coating on the inner surface of the tube, causing the phosphor to fluoresce emitting visible light.

● **fluoridation** ▶ The addition of fluoride (usually sodium fluoride)

to drinking water to reduce dental ▷caries (tooth decay), especially in children. The fluoride combines with apatite—the chief constituent of tooth enamel—to form fluoroapatite, which has a greater resistance to bacterial decay. The recommended level is one part of fluoride per million and if the natural concentration is below this level it is the policy of some governments to advocate that fluoride is added. In the UK the decision to implement this recommendation rests with local authorities, where controversy sometimes arises on the grounds that "medication" is being forced on people who may not wish to accept it. This measure has been shown to be effective, however, and quite safe in low concentrations (many natural water supplies contain up to four or five parts per million).

● **fluorine** ▶ (F) A highly reactive pale-yellow halogen gas, the most electronegative element known. It was first isolated by H. Moissan in 1886 and occurs naturally in volcanic gases and as ▷fluorite (CaF_2) and cryolite (Na_3AlF_6). It is prepared by electrolysis of potassium hydrogen fluoride (KHF_2) solution in dry hydrofluoric acid (HF). Fluorine became industrially important with the introduction of nuclear power. The gas uranium hexafluoride (UF_6) allows separation of the fissile ^{235}U isotope from ^{238}U by gaseous diffusion. Hydrofluoric acid is used to etch glass and can cause very painful burns to the skin. ▷Fluorocarbons (for example CF_2Cl_2) are chemically unreactive and have many important uses. Trace amounts of fluoride in drinking water are thought to be important in helping to prevent dental decay (see fluoridation). At no 9; at wt 18.9984; mp −219.62°C; bp −188.14°C.

● **fluorite** ▶ (or fluorspar) A mineral consisting of calcium fluoride, white, green, or yellow in colour. It occurs in hydrothermal veins, often as a gangue material in ore deposits, and in some igneous rocks. Most fluorite is used as a flux in iron and steel making; it is also used as a source of fluorine for manufacturing hydrofluoric acid and in the ceramic- and optical-glass industries. Blue John is a deep blue or purple variety used for ornament.

● **fluorocarbons** ▶ Synthetic compounds of carbon and fluorine (sometimes also containing atoms of other halogens). They are extremely resistant to chemical attack, even at very high temperatures, and are nontoxic and nonflammable. They are used as refrigerants, anaesthetics, heat-transfer agents, and high-temperature lubricants. The fluoroanalogue of polythene, polytetrafluoroethylene (Teflon), is a useful plastic in corrosive environments and has a very low coefficient of friction. Its stability at high temperatures enables it to be used for nonstick coatings in cooking utensils. **Chlorofluorocarbons** (CFCs), containing both fluorine and chlorine (many sold under the tradename Freon, e.g. Freon-12 is CCl_2F_2), have been used in enormous quantities as propellants for aerosols, although they have been opposed on environmental grounds as photochemical reactions in the upper atmosphere may lead to depletion of the ▷ozone layer, thereby removing protection against harmful ultraviolet radiation.

● **fluorspar** ▷*See* fluorite.

● **Flushing** ▶ (Dutch name: Vlissingen) 51 27N 3 35E A port in the SW Netherlands, in Zeeland province in Walcheren Island. It was the scene of an Allied invasion in 1944. It has shipbuilding and oil refining. Population (1989): 43 947.

● **flute** ▶ A woodwind instrument of ancient origin, existing in many different cultures. The modern side-blown flute (in which a column of air is made to vibrate by blowing across an elliptical mouth hole) and the ▷recorder are members of the same family. The flute came into prominence in the 16th century, when it was made of wood; today most flutes are metal. The modern orchestral flute (perfected by Theobald ▷Boehm) is about 0.6 m (2 ft) long and has a range of three octaves above middle C. ▯musical instruments.

● **flux** ▶ (brazing and soldering) A substance applied to pieces to be soldered to aid the formation of the joint. Soft solder, used in electrical joints, commonly contains a core of flux, often tallow or a similar substance. For hard soldering, at higher temperatures, zinc chloride is often used. The flux lowers the melting point of the solder and also reacts with or removes surface oxides from the metals, thus keeping their surfaces clean and allowing the liquid solder to adhere to the surfaces.

● **flux** ▶ (physics) The net amount of a directional quantity passing through a surface area at right angles to the surface. The concept of flux is used to describe phenomena that involve forces or the flow of energy, such as electric flux, magnetic flux, and luminous flux.

● **fly** ▶ An insect belonging to the order *Diptera* (over 85 000 species)—the so-called true, or two-winged, flies—of great economic importance in transmitting disease. The adults have only two wings (the front pair), the hind pair being reduced to balancing organs (called halteres). The mouthparts are adapted for piercing or sucking, and most species feed on plant juices or suck the blood of mammals. The larvae—often called maggots—are typically scavengers on plant and animal refuse or parasites of pest status. Bloodsucking species, such as ▷mosquitoes and ▷tsetse flies, may transmit such diseases as malaria, sleeping sickness, and yellow fever. The order also includes the ▷houseflies, ▷blowflies, ▷craneflies, and ▷horse flies. The name fly is used for various flying insects of other orders: the alderfly, caddis fly, firefly, and mayfly are examples of nondipterous flies.

● **fly agaric** ▶ A poisonous mushroom, ▷*Amanita muscaria*, found in woodlands, especially of birch and conifers. Its cap, 6–20 cm in diameter, is scarlet or orange-red with white scales and the white stalk has a membranous collar beneath the cap. Fly agaric is seldom fatal. It was formerly used as a fly killer, hence its name.

● **flycatcher** ▶ A small active songbird belonging to an Old World family (*Muscicapidae*; 378 species) and feeding on insects, typically caught in flight. They have small bills surrounded by stiff bristles and delicate legs used only for perching. The typical flycatchers are dull coloured and include the grey-and-brown European spotted flycatcher (*Muscicapa striata*) and the black-and-white pied flycatcher (*Ficedula hypoleuca*). The tropical blue flycatchers and paradise flycatchers are beautifully coloured and ornamented. *Compare* tyrant flycatcher.

● **flying boat** ▷*See* seaplane.

● **Flying Doctor Service of Australia, Royal** ▶ A scheme begun in 1928 at Cloncurry, Queensland, to transport doctors to patients in remote areas. The development of a Morse radio transmitter-receiver facilitated long-range consultation and emergency treatment. The service, which is free, is financed by state governments, subscriptions from outposts, and charges levied for messages. Similar schemes are run in Canada and East Africa.

● **Flying Dutchman** ▶ In sailors' lore, a ghost ship haunting the sea around the Cape of Good Hope. Its captain, driven back from the Cape by a storm, is supposed to have sworn a blasphemous oath to round it or be forever damned. The story became popular in 19th-century literature and inspired Wagner's opera (1843) of the same name.

● **flying fish** ▶ A □fish of the family *Exocoetidae* (about 40 species). Up to 45 cm long, flying fish swim just below the surface in warm oceanic waters. If disturbed they launch themselves from the water by rapidly beating the tail and glide through the air using large winglike pectoral fins.

● **flying fox** ▶ A fruit ▷bat belonging to the genus *Pteropus* (51 species), ranging from Africa to Australia. Flying foxes have foxlike heads and a wingspan of up to 1.5 m.

● **flying lemur** ▷*See* colugo.

● **flying lizard** ▶ A lizard belonging to the genus *Draco* (15 species) of SE Asia, having large folds of skin between the legs supported by ribs that are spread out when the lizard jumps from a tree. They have greenish bodies and brightly coloured "wings." Family: *Agamidae* (agamas). □reptile.

● **flying phalanger** ▶ A squirrel-like ▷marsupial mammal, also called marsupial glider. Flying phalangers, found in E Australia and Tasmania, range from 14 to 100 cm in length. They all have soft fur and long bushy tails and a flap of skin between the fore and hind legs enables them to glide from tree to tree. Genera: *Acrobates, Petaurus, Schoinobates*; family: *Phalangeridae*.

● **flying saucer** ▷*See* unidentified flying objects.

● **flying snake** ▶ A slender arboreal snake of the genus *Chrysopelea* (3 species), occurring in S Asia and the East Indies. They are diurnal, feed on rodents, bats, birds, and lizards, and glide short distances by launching themselves in the air and flattening their belly scales. Family: *Colubridae*.

● **flying squirrel** ▶ A nocturnal ▷squirrel of the subfamily *Petauristinae* (37 species), occurring in SE Asia, North America, and Eurasia. Flying squirrels have a flap of skin from elbow to knee that is stretched tight by extending the legs, enabling them to glide as they jump. □mammal.

● **Flynn, Errol** ▶ (1909–59) Australian actor, born in Tasmania. After trying a number of odd jobs, he became an actor in Hollywood, playing the handsome adventurous hero in such films as *Captain Blood* (1935), *Gentleman Jim* (1942), and (as John Barrymore) *Too Much Too Soon* (1958). His eventful private life was recounted in two autobiographies, *Beam Ends* (1934) and *My Wicked Wicked Ways* (1959).

● **Fly River** ▶ A river in New Guinea, rising in W Papua New Guinea and flowing generally S, forming part of the border between Papua New Guinea and West Irian, before entering the Gulf of Papua. Length: 1300 km (800 mi).

● **flytrap** ▷*See* Venus flytrap.

● **flywheel** ▶ A large heavy wheel attached to the driving shaft of a motor to act as an energy store and to iron out fluctuations in the speed of the machine. The energy stored depends on the speed of rotation and the weight distribution of the wheel. They are used in ▷internal-combustion engines, power presses, etc.

● **f-number** ▶ The ratio of the focal length of a camera lens to the diameter of the shutter opening (aperture). For example, f-8 means that the focal length is eight times the aperture. The smaller the f-number, the greater the illumination of the film. **Relative aperture** is the reciprocal of f-number.

● **Fo, Dario** ▶ (1926–) Italian playwright and actor-manager, noted for his mimes and for his strongly political plays. His works include *Accidental Death of an Anarchist* (1970), *Can't Pay? Won't Pay!* (1974), and *The Tricks of the Trade* (1991). In 1997 he was awarded the Nobel Prize for Literature.

● **Foch, Ferdinand** ▶ (1851–1929) French marshal. At the outbreak of World War I he commanded the Ninth Army and was largely responsible for halting the German advance at the Marne and the Allied victory at Ypres (1915). After the Somme offensive (1916), he became chief of the general staff (1917). He returned to action in 1918 and as Allied commander in chief forced the Germans back to the Rhine, effecting their defeat.

● **focus** ▷*See* ellipse; □lens.

● **foetus** ▷*See* fetus.

● **fog** ▶ A cloud near the ground surface, within which visibility is reduced to less than 1 km (0.6 mi). Fog is the result of the condensation of water vapour in the lower layers of air, usually through the cooling of air to below its ▷dew point; it often occurs with light wind conditions and a clear sky at night. It can contain dust and smoke particles and in industrial areas ▷smog can develop.

● **Fogel, Robert William** ▶ (1926–) US historian and economist. He was awarded the Nobel Prize for economics in 1993 with Douglass North (1920–) for their four-volume work *Without Consent or Contract: The Rise and Fall of American Slavery* (1989–93).

● **Foggia** ▶ 41 28N 15 33E A city in Italy, in Apulia. It has a castle dating from the time of the Holy Roman Emperor, Frederick II. Olives, grapes, wheat, and tobacco are grown nearby and industries include flour milling, cheese and paper making, and engineering. Population (1996 est): 156 032.

● **föhn** ▶ A warm dry wind that descends down the leeward side of mountains. It is a frequent occurrence in the Alps (where the name originated), the Rocky Mountains (called the **chinook**), and the Andes. In winter it can cause rapid thaws of lying snow, resulting in avalanches.

● **Fokine, Michel** ▶ (Mikhail F.; 1880–1942) Russian ballet dancer and choreographer. From 1909 he worked with Diaghilev's Ballets Russes in Paris, for which he choreographed such revolutionary ballets as *The Firebird* (1910) and *Petrushka* (1911). He went to New York in 1923 and became a naturalized US citizen in 1932.

● **Fokker, Anthony Hermann Gerard** ▶ (1890–1939) Dutch aircraft manufacturer. Fokker opened a factory in Germany in 1912. During World War I he supplied Germany with aircraft and invented a method of firing a machine gun through the propeller of an aircraft. He later became a US citizen.

● **fold** ▶ A buckling of sedimentary rock strata produced by compressional forces acting on it. Large-scale folding produces mountain ranges; this occurs where two continental plates collide (*see* plate tectonics) and the sediment along their margins is compressed and folded. A simple upfold is called an ▷anticline and a downfold, a ▷syncline; however, most folds are much more complex.

● **Foley, John Henry** ▶ (1818–74) British sculptor, born in Dublin. One of the leading Victorian sculptors, his works include the bronze equestrian statues of Hardinge and Canning in Calcutta and the statue of Prince Albert on the Albert Memorial in South Kensington.

● **folic acid** ▷*See* vitamin B complex.

● **Folies-Bergère** ▶ A Parisian variety theatre opened in 1869 and celebrated chiefly for its elaborate revues featuring dancing girls and striptease acts. Maurice ▷Chevalier and many other leading French entertainers have appeared here.

● **folk dance** ▶ A form of dance developed by country people, usually for their own amusement. Folk dances derive from ancient ritual dances used in religious worship and to invoke the fertility of the land (the original purpose of the ▷maypole dance). They have greatly influenced other forms of dances, notably court dancing, 18th- and 19th-century ballroom dances (such as the ▷waltz and ▷polka), and ▷ballet. Many countries have their own traditional dances. In England the most popular types are country dancing and the ▷Morris dance. The revived interest in folk dancing in the 20th century is reflected in the popularity of professional folk-dance companies and folk-dance societies. The English Folk Dance and Song Society was established in 1911 by Cecil ▷Sharp.

● **Folkestone** ▶ 51 5N 1 11E A resort and port in SE England, in Kent, with Channel crossings by ferry and hovercraft to Boulogne. The English terminal of the Channel Tunnel is also here. Just outside Folkestone is the Warren, an extensive wooded area of geologically important chalk landslips. Population (1991): 45 587.

● **folklore** ▶ The social, material, and oral culture of primitive societies. The social culture comprises such forms as festivals, dances, and religious rites; the material culture comprises architecture and arts and crafts; the oral culture includes songs, tales, legends, proverbs, and riddles. The study of folklore, spurred by early collections of folk literature, such as Percy's *Reliques of Ancient English Poetry* (1765) and the *Fairy Tales* (1812–14) of the brothers ▷Grimm, has played an important role in the work of anthropologists, such as Franz ▷Boas and J. G. ▷Frazer.

● **folk music** ▶ Song or dance music developed from a communal aural tradition and not composed by an individual, e.g. Irish ballads and cowboy songs. The melody and words of folksongs are often changed by a succession of performances. Folk music is characterized by modal melody and simple forms, such as dances, lullabies, work songs, and love ballads. Traditional English folksongs include "Black Is the Colour of My True Love's Hair" and "Greensleeves." During the revival of folksong in the USA in the 1950s and 1960s, new music by such composers as Woody Guthrie and Bob Dylan was termed folksong or "folk," owing to its similarity to authentic folk music. More recently the traditional music of Africa, South America, and eastern European countries has won a wide audience in Europe and the USA.

● **follicle-stimulating hormone** ▷*See* gonadotrophin.

● **Folsom point** ▶ A fluted lanceolate (leaf-shaped) stone spearhead made between 9000 and 8000 BC in the western grasslands of the USA. The name derives from Folsom, New Mexico, where one was discovered (1926), with the remains of an extinct form of bison. *Compare* Clovis point.

● **Fomalhaut** ▶ A conspicuous star, apparent magnitude 1.15 and 23 light years distant, that is the only bright star in the S constellation Piscis Austrinus.

● **Fon** ▶ The predominant people of S Benin, who speak a dialect of ▷Ewe. They grow maize, manioc, and yams and palm oil as a cash crop. Their villages are headed by the oldest male. A hereditary headman has general authority to arbitrate in disputes. During the 18th and 19th centuries the Fon formed the kingdom of Dahomey. The king and his chiefs conducted war ceremonies, received tribute, and presided over courts. An ancestor cult involved the sacrifice of prisoners of war in return for supernatural aid.

● **Fonda, Henry** ▶ (1905–82) US film actor and director, associated with the portrayal of men of solid integrity, notably in *The Grapes of Wrath* (1940). Other films include *War and Peace* (1956), *Twelve Angry Men* (1957), which he coproduced, and *On Golden Pond* (1981), which earned him his first Oscar and also starred his daughter **Jane Fonda** (1937–). Her other films include *Barbarella* (1968), an extravaganza of sexual fantasy, *Klute* (1971), *Julia* (1977), *Coming Home* (1978), *Agnes of God* (1985), and *Old Gringo* (1989). His son **Peter Fonda** (1939–) made his name as an actor and director with *Easy Rider* (1969); his other films include *Cannonball Run* (1981) and *Ulee's Gold* (1998). Peter Fonda's daughter **Bridget Fonda** (1964–) has starred in such films as *Scandal* (1989), *Single White Female* (1992), and *Assassin* (1993).

● **Fontainebleau** ▶ 48 24N 2 42E A town in N central France, in the Seine-et-Marne department. The surrounding forest inspired the Barbizon school of painters. The Royal Palace, largely built by Francis I, was the scene of Napoleon I's abdication in 1814. Fontainebleau was the headquarters of NATO from 1954 to 1966. Population (latest est): 18 753.

● **Fontainebleau, school of** ▶ The painters who decorated the Royal Palace of Fontainebleau (France) between about 1530 and 1560. The Italians Giovanni Battista Rosso (1494–1540), Francesco Primaticcio (c. 1504–70), and Niccolò dell' Abbate (c. 1512–71) were chiefly responsible for developing the particularly sensuous and elegant form of ▷mannerism that characterizes the school.

● **Fontana, Domenico** ▶ (1543–1607) Italian architect and engineer. In the employ of the pope in Rome, Fontana designed the Sistine Library (1587–90) and helped complete the dome of St Peter's Basilica. He was also responsible for re-erecting the Egyptian obelisk on its present site in front of St Peter's.

● **Fontane, Theodor** ▶ (1819–98) German novelist. He began writing novels at the age of 56 after varied experience as a journalist and war correspondent. *Vor dem Sturm* (1878) is a realistic historical novel dealing with the Prussian nobility. Of several novels dealing with the place of women in society the best known is *Effi Briest* (1898).

● **Fontanne, Lynn** ▷*See* Lunt, Alfred.

● **Fontenelle, Bernard le Bovier de** ▶ (1657–1757) French philosopher and writer, who joined his uncle, Pierre ▷Corneille, in Paris in 1680, becoming a leading light of the contemporary salons. Renowned for his wit and his learning, he popularized the new scientific theories of Descartes and Newton in such works as *Digressions sur les anciens et les modernes* (1688) and *Éléments de la géométrie de l'infini* (1727). Pouring scorn on ancient myths and beliefs, he was a confirmed "modern," writing his *Théorie des tourbillons cartésiens* when he was 95.

● **Fontenoy, Battle of** ▶ (11 May, 1745) The battle in the War of the ▷Austrian Succession in which France defeated Austria. Fought near Tournai, SE of Brussels, the battle was the French commander de ▷Saxe's most notable victory, leading to the conquest of Flanders. His artillery and cavalry carried the day against the Austrians, and their Dutch and English allies, who retreated toward Brussels.

● **Fonteyn, Dame Margot** ▶ (Margaret Hookham; 1919–91) British ballet dancer. A member of the Sadler's Wells company and the Royal Ballet (1934–59), she also performed with most leading US and European companies, often with Rudolf ▷Nureyev. Her most famous performances, many directed by Sir Frederick ▷Ashton, were in classical ballets such as *Giselle*, *Swan Lake*, and *The Sleeping Beauty*. She married the Panamanian diplomat Roberto Arias (1918–90) in 1955 and lived in Panama after her retirement.

● **Fonthill Abbey** ▶ An architecturally influential country house in SW Wiltshire, designed (1796–1807) in the ▷gothic revival style by James ▷Wyatt for William ▷Beckford. Fonthill was an enormous building, featuring a tower 85 m (278 ft) high. It was quickly and badly built; the tower collapsed in 1827 and the rest was demolished soon after.

● **Foochow** ▷*See* Fuzhou.

● **food additives** ▶ Substances added to food to alter its taste, texture, appearance, keeping qualities, or other properties. Additives have been employed since Roman times; some 3800 are now used, including flavourings (about 3500), colouring agents, emulsifiers, stabilizers, thickening agents, preservatives, antioxidants, flavour enhancers, artificial ▷sweeteners, anticaking agents, and bleaching agents. Although additives can play a vital role in ▷food preservation, consumer resistance to them has grown following recent reports of their toxic, carcinogenic, or allergic effects. In the UK prepacked and processed food must carry a list of ingredients, including any additives (*see* food labelling). About 280 of these currently have an **E number**, meaning that they have been approved for use in the EU. Additives without an E number must be listed by name.

● **Food and Agriculture Organization** ▶ (FAO) A specialized agency of the ▷United Nations constituted in 1945 to coordinate international efforts to raise levels of nutrition and food production and to improve forest management. The agency, with headquarters in Rome, conducts research, makes recommendations, organizes educational programmes, and encourages the export of agricultural products.

● **food chain** ▶ A series of organisms associated in a feeding relationship: each animal feeds on the one below it in the series. Usually, green plants are at the base of a food chain. They are eaten by herbivores, which in turn may be consumed by carnivores. Any parasites are also part of the chain, and different food chains are often interconnected to form a **food web**. Other food chains are based on decomposers—organisms that feed on dead plants and animals.

● **food labelling** ▶ In the EU, packaged and processed food (but not fresh food) must be labelled giving the manufacturer's name, the weight of the ingredients, a list of the ▷food additives, and a "sell by" date (or in some cases a date of manufacture or a "best before" date). It is also common for the label to provide nutritional information.

● **food poisoning** ▶ An acute illness arising from eating contaminated food. Vomiting and diarrhoea are the usual symptoms (*see* gastroenteritis). ▷*Salmonella* is the bacterium that most commonly causes food poisoning (salmonellosis); patients usually recover within a few days. Similar food-borne infections are caused by *Campylobacter* (in poultry, beef, and milk) and ▷*Listeria*. Another kind of food poisoning is due to ▷toxins produced by such bacteria as ▷*Staphylococcus* and ▷*Clostridium* (which is responsible for ▷botulism). Outbreaks of severe food poisoning occurred in Japan, the USA, and Scotland (1996) and NE England (1999) after consumption of food contaminated with toxin-producing *E. coli 0157*, a disease-causing strain of the normally harmless bacterium *Escherichia coli*: several of those affected died from kidney failure.

● **food preservation** ▶ The treatment of food to prevent its deterioration and to maintain its nutritional value. Breakdown of food tissues is caused by enzymes, either contained within the food or produced by microorganisms—bacteria, yeasts, and fungi—growing in the food. These organisms can also produce substances that can cause ▷food poisoning. Oxidation and dehydration also contribute to spoilage. Food preservation therefore aims to alter the condition of food to stop the activities of microorganisms and any chemical change. One of the oldest methods is drying or dehydration—used for meat, vegetables, cereals, milk products, etc. ▷Freezing is now widely used for both industrial and domestic food preservation. ▷Freeze drying involves freezing followed by dehydration, usually in a vacuum. Heating kills mircoorganisms and is the principle of ▷pasteurization, ▷sterilization, etc. Further growth is prevented if food is sealed in airtight containers, such as cans (*see* canning) or bottles. Boiling with sugar (e.g. in jam) and pickling with salt or vinegar (e.g. onions, cucumbers) are traditional methods. Smoking is used to preserve meat and fish. Sodium benzoate, propionates, nitrates, nitrites, sulphur dioxide, and sulphites are also used by the food industry (*see* food additives). In food irradiation gamma radiation is used to kill microorganisms, insects, etc. However, it can also cause chemical changes (e.g. oxidation), which can alter flavour and doubt lingers in the public mind over possible undiscovered side effects. The sale of irradiated food was legalized in the UK in 1991.

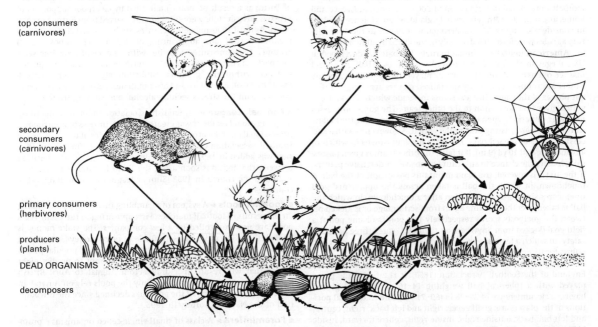

top consumers (carnivores)

secondary consumers (carnivores)

primary consumers (herbivores)

producers (plants)

DEAD ORGANISMS

decomposers

food chain ▶ The feeding relationships between some plants and animals of a meadow habitat are simplified in this food web; in practice many more links and various other organisms are involved.

● **Fools, Feast of** ► A festival held in medieval Europe (especially in France) on, or near, Holy Innocents' Day (28 Dec). It was organized by lower clergy. A mock pope or bishop (sometimes a boy) was elected and presided over burlesque church services. There were also processions and carnival plays as well as festive dancing and drinking.

● **fool's gold** ▷See pyrite.

● **foot** ► The lowermost part of the leg. The human foot contains 14 bones. There are seven tarsal bones, of which one (the talus) forms a hinge joint with the bones of the lower ▷leg and another (the calcaneus) forms the projection of the heel. The five metatarsal bones form the body of the foot and articulate with the phalanges, the bones of the toes. ▷See Plate II.

● **Foot, Michael (Mackintosh)** ► (1913–) British Labour politician and historian, leader of the Labour Party (1980–83). A prominent left-wing intellectual, he has written numerous books, including biographies of Aneurin Bevan (1962, 1973) and H. G. Wells (1995).

● **foot-and-mouth disease** ► A highly infectious viral disease of cattle, sheep, pigs, goats, and other domesticated and wild cloven-hoofed animals. Elephants, rats, and hedgehogs are also susceptible. Typically it causes fever and small blisters on the mouth and feet, with consequent reluctance to feed, listlessness, and lameness. Milk yield may be reduced, and sheep may suffer abortions. The virus can be transmitted to other animals by direct contact, or indirectly by infected saliva, exhaled air, milk, and dung. Airborne transmission can occur over considerable distances and the infection can also be carried by contaminated vehicles, people, and wild animals.

Known since the 16th century, the disease is currently endemic in N South America, central Africa, the Middle East, and S Asia. It also occurs sporadically in China and NW Africa. In Europe it was eradicated by a programme of compulsory mass vaccination of cattle during the 1950s and 1960s, combined with 'stamping out' of any subsequent disease by slaughter of infected animals and contacts, with control of animal movements. Vaccination of animals in areas surrounding an outbreak can also help stem the spread of the disease. Although traditionally free of the disease, the UK suffered major outbreaks in 1967 (2364 cases and over 430 000 animals slaughtered) and in 2001, when by early May there had been over 1500 cases and some 2.6 million animals destroyed.

● **football** ► A field game played throughout the world, the object of which is to score goals with an inflated ball. Team games using a football were played in China around 200 BC, in ancient Greece and Rome, and from the 12th century in England, where violence resulted in considerable injury. The modern games evolved in the 19th century as rules were formalized (largely in the English public schools).

American football is similar to rugby football and developed in US colleges in the 1870s; it is played with an oval ball on a field marked out as a gridiron. There are 22 players on the field at any one time, but groups of differently specialized players are used in different phases of the game. The teams toss to decide which is to kick off, which gives first possession to the other team. The game progresses in downs, or periods when the offensive team is advancing the ball towards the goal by passing or running with it. A down ends with a successful tackle or missed pass. The team has four downs in which to advance the ball 10 yd (9 m). If it fails, the other team is given possession, having the chance to substitute offensive for defensive players. If the 10 yd is covered, the team maintains possession of the ball. A touchdown, in which the ball is taken across the opponents' goal line, scores six points; a conversion after a touchdown, in which the ball is taken over the goal line again from scrimmage or is kicked between the goalposts scores respectively two points or one point; a field goal (kicked from anywhere on the field) scores three points; a safety, in which a team scores a touchdown against itself, scores two points for its opponents.

Association football (or soccer) dates back to the founding in England of the Football Association (1863). It is an 11-a-side game played with a spherical ball weighing 14–16 oz (396–453 g) and having a circumference of 27–28 in (69–71 cm). The traditional positions of the players are: goalkeeper; right and left back; right, centre, and left half-back; outside right, inside right, centre forward, inside left, and outside left. These positions, established early in the 20th century, have become flexible; a modern line-up consists simply of strikers, midfield players, and defenders. The teams toss for the first kick (the kick-off), following which the teams compete, trying to kick or head the ball into the opponents' goal. Only the goalkeeper may use his hands. Played all over the world, the game is governed internationally by the ▷Fédération internationale de Football association.

Australian Rules is an 18-a-side game that originated in the Australian goldfields in the 1850s and is extensively played in some states, especially Victoria. It is a fast open game played with an oval ball measuring 22.75 by 29.5 in (57.2 by 73.6 cm), with which players may run, bouncing it every 9 m (10 yd). The ball must be punched instead of thrown. There are four goalposts without crossbars at each end. A goal, kicked between the two inner posts, scores six points; a behind, kicked between an inner and an outer post, scores one point.

Canadian football is similar to American football but is played with 12-a-side teams on a larger field and has slightly different scoring and rules.

Rugby football uses an oval ball that is kicked or passed by hand. The game was first played at Rugby School, England, according to tradition in 1823. In 1871 the Rugby Football Union was formed, but its ban on professionalism led in 1893 to the secession of the Rugby League (then called the Northern Union); there are therefore two types of rugby. Rugby Union football (or rugger) is a 15-a-side game. The ball is 11–11.25 in (27.9–28.6 cm) long. A try, in which the ball is touched down behind the opponents' goal line, is worth five points; a goal (a try "converted" by kicking the ball over the crossbar of the goalposts), seven points altogether; a penalty goal, resulting from a kick awarded as a penalty against the opposing team, three points; and a drop goal, from the field, three points. A scrum, in which the forwards of both teams battle for the ball in a tight mass, is used to restart the game after minor infringements. For more serious infringements a penalty kick is given to the opposing side. The long-standing ban on professionalism was abandoned in 1995. Rugby League football is a 13-a-side professional game with slightly different rules and scoring; it is played mainly in N England and Australia.

● **football hooliganism** ► Acts of violence and vandalism by certain elements of crowds attending football matches. Unruly crowd behaviour has long been a feature of football matches, particularly in Britain: overcrowding and drunkenness exacerbate feelings of hostility towards rival supporters until these flare into overt violence. The phenomenon reached an unacceptable climax in 1985, when 39 fans (mostly Italians) died at the European Cup Final (Liverpool vs Juventus of Turin) as a result of mob violence led by Liverpool supporters in Brussels. British clubs were subsequently barred from European competitions until 1990 and new measures, such as closed circuit TV, segregation of rival fans, and banning of alcohol, were imposed at all grounds. These measures, together with a policy of providing seats for spectators to replace standing on terraces, have largely eliminated violence within the grounds. Unfortunately, however, football-associated violence before and after matches continues: mobs of supporters roam the streets seeking alcohol and causing trouble.

● **Football League** ► An English association football competition for professional teams. It was created in the N in 1888 to help finance professional clubs by providing a systematic series of matches, as the Football Association Challenge Cup series did not. The Second Division was added in 1892 with a system of promotion and relegation between the divisions soon after; the Third Division was added in 1920 and the Fourth in 1958. Similar leagues exist in many other countries.

● **football pools** ► A system of ▷gambling involving postal betting on the results of football matches. First appearing in the UK in 1923, pools are now controlled by a few companies. The stake money is pooled, some 30% of which is available as prize money (30% goes in running costs and 40% in government duty). The most popular pool is the Treble Chance, in which competitors attempt to predict eight games that will result in a draw. From August to April British matches are used and from May to July the pools rely on Australian matches. The popularity of the pools has declined since the introduction of the National Lottery in 1995.

● **Foraminifera** ► A class of small single-celled organisms (⌐protozoa) found on the sea bed or as part of the ▷plankton. They form cal-

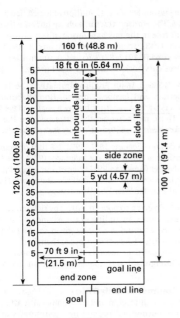

American football

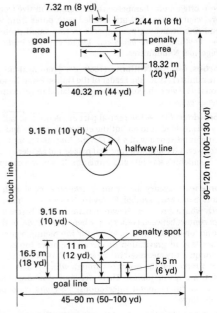

Association football

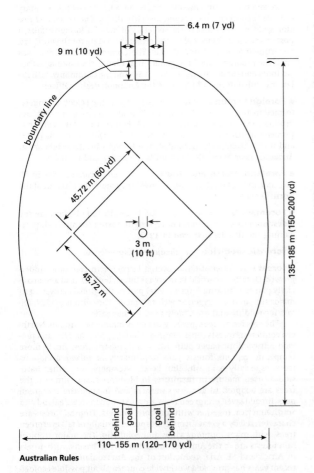

Australian Rules

football ▶ Dimensions of pitches.

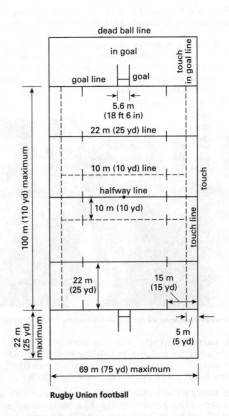

Rugby Union football

careous often multichambered shells, ranging in size from 10 μm to several centimetres, that are studded with pores from which they extend fine branching pseudopodia to trap small protozoans and algae. Phylum: *Granuloreticulosa*; kingdom ▷*Protoctista*. ▷*See also* Globigerina; Nummulites.

● **Forbes, George William** ▶ (1869–1947) New Zealand statesman; prime minister (1930–35). Leader of the United Party, he formed a co-alition (1931) with the Reform Party but failed to solve the problems of the Depression.

● **Forbidden City** ▶ The central part of ▷Beijing, so called because entry was forbidden to all but the emperor's family and servants. It was surrounded by a wall 4 km (2.5 mi) long and from the 15th century onwards it contained the royal palace and residences and offices of the emperor's servants and ministers. It is now a complex of museums.

● **force** ▶ The agency that changes either the speed or the direction of motion of a body (symbol: *F*). Newton's three laws of motion define exactly what a force is (*see* Newtonian mechanics). Forces may involve direct contact between bodies (e.g. when they collide) or they may involve action-at-a-distance, in which the interacting bodies are not in contact (e.g. in gravitation or electromagnetic forces). Force is a ▷vector quantity measured in ▷newtons. Work or energy is the product of a force and the distance through which it acts (measured in newton metres or joules). There are four fundamental forces in nature (*see* fundamental interactions). ▷*See also* centripetal force; Coriolis force.

● **Ford, Ford Madox** ▶ (Ford Hermann Hueffer; 1873–1939) British novelist, grandson of the Pre-Raphaelite artist Ford Madox Brown. Among his 80 or more novels and books of criticism and memoirs are the novels *The Good Soldier* (1915) and *Parade's End* (1924–28), a tetralogy. He founded and edited the *English Review* (1908) and, in Paris, the *Transatlantic Review* (1924), in which he published the early works of ▷Pound, ▷Joyce, ▷Hemingway, and many other writers.

● **Ford, Gerald R(udolph)** ▶ (1913–) US statesman; Republican president (1974–77). Born Leslie King, he later took the surname of his eminent Republican stepfather. A lawyer by profession, Ford was appointed as vice president by ▷Nixon after the resignation of Spiro Agnew in 1973. Following Nixon's resignation, Ford became the first US president to succeed to that office without having been elected. His controversial free pardon granted to Nixon and his visits to the Soviet Union and China did not save him from defeat by Carter in the 1976 election.

Harrison Ford ▶ Promoting *Air Force One* (1997) at the Venice Film Festival.

● **Ford, Harrison** ▶ (1942–) US film actor. His films, most of which are adventure fantasies, include *Star Wars* (1977) and its sequels, *Raiders of the Lost Ark* (1981) and its sequels, *Witness* (1985), *Clear and Present Danger* (1994), and *Six Days, Seven Nights* (1998).

● **Ford, Henry** ▶ (1863–1947) US ▢car manufacturer, who introduced assembly-line production. The Ford Motor Company was founded in 1903 and in 1912 Ford introduced the assembly line to manufacture the famous Model T, 15 million of which had been mass produced by 1928. The Fordson tractor, a cheap but effective vehicle, had an important role in the mechanization of agriculture. His son, **Edsel Ford** (1893–1943), took over the company in 1919 and his grandson, **Henry Ford II** (1917–87), succeeded him in 1945. The company still produces cars both in the USA and Europe.

● **Ford, John** ▶ (1586–c. 1640) English dramatist, the last major figure of Elizabethan and Jacobean drama. He collaborated with ▷Dekker and others at first, writing his own major plays between 1627 and 1638. Those most frequently performed are the revenge tragedies *The Broken Heart* (c. 1630) and *'Tis Pity She's a Whore* (c. 1632).

● **Ford, John** ▶ (Sean O'Feeney; 1895–1973) US film director. He received much critical acclaim for *The Informer* (1935), *The Grapes of Wrath* (1940), and other films on social themes, but is best known as a director of popular westerns. These include *Stagecoach* (1939), *Rio Grande* (1950), and *How the West Was Won* (1962).

● **foreign aid** ▶ Help given to poor countries by richer ones. Foreign aid can take several forms, including gratis payments, cheap loans, gifts in kind, etc. Foreign aid is usually given to the ▷developing countries to relieve natural disasters, to assist them in their efforts to industrialize, or for political reasons. One of the most ambitious programmes of foreign aid was the Marshall Plan (*see* Marshall, George).

● **Foreign and Commonwealth Office** ▶ The UK government department that deals with foreign and commonwealth affairs and is responsible for presenting and promoting the interests of the UK abroad; it was formed in 1968 by an amalgamation of the Foreign Office and the Commonwealth Office and is headed by the secretary of state for foreign and commonwealth affairs. The Foreign Office emerged from the office of the secretary of state for foreign affairs, a post created in 1782 to replace the secretary of state for the northern department (*compare* Home Office). The Commonwealth Office was itself the product of an amalgamation in 1966 of the Colonial Office (an independent department since 1854) and the Commonwealth Relations Office (formed in 1930 as the Commonwealth Office).

● **Foreign Legion** ▶ A French military force, the Légion étrangère, formed in 1831 to serve in France's African colonies. Its recruits are international but its officers are usually French. One of its regiments formed the ▷Organisation de l'Armée secrète (OAS) in Algeria (1961) and was subsequently disbanded. The Legion's headquarters are at Aubagne, near Marseille, with units in Corsica and Djibouti.

● **Foreland, North and South** ▶ Two chalk promontories in SE England, in Kent on the Strait of Dover. They mark the E extent of the North Downs.

● **Foreman, George** ▶ (1948–) US boxer. In 1994 he became the oldest man to win the world heavyweight boxing championship, regaining the title he first won in 1973.

● **forensic medicine** ▷*See* medical jurisprudence.

● **forest** ▶ An area of land covered largely with trees and undergrowth. Over 20% of world land area is forest, both natural and artificially planted, making forests a vital part of the global ecosystem as major suppliers of oxygen as well as timber. They also provide habitats for wildlife and are widely used for recreation.

The species of trees growing depends mainly on climate. Northern coniferous forests consist largely of pine, spruce, and firs and provide softwood for paper pulp, furniture, construction, etc. In more temperate regions forests consist primarily of mixed deciduous trees, especially oak, ash, elm, beech, sycamore, and other hardwoods, used mainly in furniture. In Mediterranean climates, the trees are adapted to hot dry summers and include the evergreen oaks. Broad-leaved evergreen trees are also found in New Zealand and South America, together with southern conifers. Tropical forests are characterized by a great diversity of species, usually of tall evergreen trees, with many climbing vines and epiphytes. The major tropical rain forests are in the Amazon and Orinoco river basins, with others in Africa and SE Asia; reduction of the Amazonian rain forest in recent years has provoked worldwide concern about possible ecological consequences (*see* deforestation; greenhouse effect). In neighbouring regions of lower and more seasonal rainfall, an open savanna forest predominates, consisting of scattered deciduous trees.

● **forestry** ▶ The cultivation and management of forests is of major economic importance. Much research and development has been invested in improving varieties of trees for commercial use and in better methods of planting, pest control, thinning, felling, and extraction and of processing the timber into usable products. In the UK, forestry is controlled by the Forestry Commission (established in 1919), which is now responsible for the production of most home-grown softwoods. It is also involved in ▷nature conservation and the provision of recreational amenities.

● **Forester, C(ecil) S(cott)** ▶ (1899–1966) British historical novelist, famous as the creator of Horatio Hornblower, a heroic but self-doubting British naval officer of Napoleonic times who first appeared in *The Happy Return* (1937).

● **Forest Hills** ▶ A residential district in the USA, in New York City on Long Island. It is noted for its lawn-tennis tournaments at the West Side Tennis Club.

● **forfaiting** ▶ A form of debt discounting in which an exporter can discount, without recourse, a promissory note, bill of exchange, letter of credit, etc., received from an overseas buyer.

● **Forfar** ▶ 56 38N 2 54W A market town in E Scotland, the administrative centre of Angus. Its castle was occupied by early Scottish kings but was destroyed when Robert the Bruce took it from the English in 1308. Forfar manufactures linen and rayon. Population (1991): 12 961.

● **Forfarshire** ▷*See* Angus.

● **forgery** ▶ The crime of making a "false instrument" (document, stamp, cheque, or electronic medium) with the object of making others believe it is genuine. In England and Wales the offence is to create the false instrument, not to pass it off or to be successful in passing it off. In Scotland the offence has not been committed until the forged instrument has been uttered (passed off as genuine to the detriment of the person to whom it is uttered). Forging coins or banknotes is called ▷counterfeiting.

● **forget-me-not** ▶ An annual or perennial herb of the genus *Myosotis* (50 species), of temperate regions. 5–60 cm tall, it has oblong hairy leaves and long spikes of small flowers, usually blue with white centres (young flowers are often pink). The fruits are small nutlets. Family: *Boraginaceae*.

● **Forlì** ▶ 44 13N 12 02E A city in Italy, in Emilia-Romagna. It has some ancient buildings, including a 15th-century citadel. Its various manufactures include furniture, textiles, felt, household appliances, and footwear. Population (1996 est): 108 017.

● **formaldehyde** ▷*See* methanal.

● **Forman, Miloš** ▶ (1932–) Czech film director. His earlier films, such as *The Fireman's Ball* (1967), blend humour and social criticism. In 1968 he went to the USA, where he made *One Flew over the Cuckoo's Nest* (1976). Subsequent films include *Amadeus* (1983), *Valmont* (1989), and *The People vs Larry Flint* (1996).

● **Formby, George** ▶ (George Booth; 1904–61) British comedian, born in Lancashire. The son of a music hall performer, Formby became a leading star of stage and screen, known particularly for his ukelele playing, in such songs as "When I'm Cleaning Windows."

● **formic acid** ▷*See* methanoic acid.

● **Formigny, Battle of** ▶ (15 April, 1450) The battle during the last period of the ▷Hundred Years' War in which the French forces routed the English army near Caen. The victory led directly to the fall of Caen, and then of Normandy, to the French.

● **Formosa** ▷*See* Taiwan.

● **Forres** ▶ 57 37N 3 38W A market town in NE Scotland, in Moray. It contains Sueno's Stone, a sculptured monolith commemorating a Viking victory and believed to date from 900 AD. There are whisky-distilling and engineering industries. Population (1991): 8531.

● **Forster, E(dward) M(organ)** ▶ (1879–1970) British novelist.

Educated at King's College, Cambridge, where he returned as a fellow in 1946, he stressed in his fiction and social criticism the importance of human affection and the need to cultivate both the intellect and the imagination. His novels include *Where Angels Fear to Tread* (1905), *The Longest Journey* (1907), *A Room with a View* (1908), *Howard's End* (1910), and *A Passage to India* (1924). *Maurice*, a novel portraying a homosexual relationship, was published posthumously in 1971.

● **Forsyth, Frederick** ▶ (1938–) British writer. Formerly a radio correspondent, he established his reputation as a thriller writer with *The Day of the Jackal* (1970); subsequent successes have included *The Odessa File* (1972), *The Dogs of War* (1974), *The Fourth Protocol* (1984), and *The Deceiver* (1991).

● **Forsythia** ▶ A genus of shrubs (about 7 species), sometimes called golden bell, native to E Europe and Asia and widely grown as garden ornamentals. The masses of four-petalled yellow flowers appear before the leaves, which are toothed and oval. The slender stems make the plants suitable for wall shrubs and hedges. The most common garden forsythia is the hybrid *F. × intermedia*. Family: *Oleaceae* (olive family).

● **Fortaleza** ▶ (or Ceará) 3 45S 38 35W A city and port in E Brazil, the capital of Ceará state on the Atlantic Ocean. Exports include cotton, rice, coffee, and sugar. Its university was established in 1955. Population (1995 est): 2 660 000.

● **Fort-de-France** ▶ (former name: Fort Royal) 14 36N 61 05W The capital and main port of Martinique since 1680, on the W coast. It was almost destroyed by an earthquake in 1839 and by fire in 1890. It is an important tourist resort and the site of a French naval base. Exports include sugar, cocoa, and rum. Population (1995 est): 104 000.

● **Fortescue, Sir John** ▶ (c. 1394–1476) English jurist; chief justice of the King's Bench (1442–61). A supporter of the Lancastrian party, Fortescue escaped to France with the royal family in 1463, when the Yorkist Edward IV deposed Henry VI. There he wrote his famous works on English law and government, *De laudibus legum Angliae* and *The Governance of England*. Despite his part in the attempted Lancastrian restoration at the battle of Tewkesbury (1471), he was subsequently pardoned by Edward IV.

● **Forth, River** ▶ A river in SE Scotland, rising on the NE slopes of Ben Lomond and flowing 104 km (65 mi) E through Stirling to Alloa. The river then expands into the **Firth of Forth** (an inlet of the North Sea) extending 82 km (51 mi) in length and 31 km (19 mi) wide at its mouth. It is spanned by the cantilever iron Forth Rail Bridge (designed in the 1880s by Benjamin Baker) and a road bridge (1964). The **Forth and Clyde Canal**, 60 km (37 mi) long, links the Rivers Forth and Clyde.

● **Fortin barometer** ▶ A type of mercury ▷barometer, invented in 1810 by the French instrument maker, Nicolas Fortin (1750–1831). The reservoir of mercury is contained in a leather bag attached to an evacuated glass tube marked with a fixed scale. The level of the mercury in the reservoir is set at zero by adjusting the leather bag.

● **Fort Knox** ▶ 37 54N 85 59W A military base in the USA, in N Kentucky. Established in 1917, the US Depository there contains US gold reserves. Population (1989 est): 38 277.

● **Fort Lamy** ▷*See* N'djamena.

● **Fort Lauderdale** ▶ 26 08N 80 08W A city and resort in the USA, in SE Florida on the Atlantic Ocean. It has one of the largest marinas in the world. Population (1996 est): 151 805.

● **Fortran** ▶ (formula *translation*) A computer-programming language. It is a high-level language (*see* program) used for representing mathematical formulae in a form that can be processed by a computer. Widely used among scientists and engineers, it is also used in the business community.

● **Fort Stanwix, Treaties of** ▶ (1768, 1784) Agreements between the British and the Iroquois Indians, in which the British gained present-day W Pennsylvania, West Virginia, New York, and Kentucky for gifts worth $10,000. The fort, located at the site of Rome, New York, was built for defence against the Indians and was renamed Fort Schuyler in 1776.

● **Fort Sumter** ▷*See* Charleston (South Carolina).

● **Fortuna** ▶ The Roman goddess of fortune and good luck. She was usually portrayed standing on a ball or wheel, indicating her mutability, and holding a cornucopia from which she distributes her favours. She is identical with ▷Tyche.

● **Fort Wayne** ▶ 41 05N 85 08W A city in the USA, in NE Indiana on the Maumee River. Founded by the French in 1680, the fort was built in 1794. Its main manufactures are electrical equipment and motor vehicles. Population (1996 est): 184 783.

● **Fort William** ▶ 56 49N 5 07W A town in W Scotland, in Highland at the head of Loch Linnhe. Besides tourism, it has aluminium-smelting, whisky-distilling, and paper-making industries. Population (1991): 10 391.

● **Fort William** ▶ (Canada) ▷*See* Thunder Bay.

● **Fort Worth** ▶ 32 45N 97 20W A city in the USA, in NE Texas near Dallas. It is the centre of an industrial area, manufacturing aircraft, oil, and food products. Population (1996 est): 479 716.

● **Forty-five Rebellion** ▷*See* Jacobites.

● **forty-niners** ▷*See* Gold Rush.

● **Forty-Two Articles** ▷*See* Thirty-Nine Articles.

● **forum** ▶ A Roman marketplace, similar to the Greek ▷agora. The forum was the town's civic centre, containing all the main temples and public buildings. The famous forum in Rome was laid out in the 1st century BC, but later modified.

● **Foscolo, Ugo** ▶ (1778–1827) Italian poet. His early tragedy *Tieste* (1797) and his poem *A Bonaparte liberatore* (1797) reflect the anti-Austrian nationalism that shaped his life. He served in the Napoleonic armies but in 1816 he settled in England. His best-known works are the patriotic poem *Dei sepolcri* (1807) and the unfinished poem *Le grazie* (1822).

● **fossa** ▶ A catlike mammal, *Cryptoprocta ferox*, found only in Madagascar. It is about 150 cm long including the tail (70 cm) and has short legs and short orange-brown fur. It feeds on lemurs. Family: ▷*Viverridae*; order: *Carnivora*.

● **Fosse Way** ▶ A Roman road from Exeter through Cirencester to Lincoln. It marked the frontier in the first phase of the Roman conquest of Britain (c. 47 AD). Its characteristically straight course is now followed partly by the A429.

● **fossil** ▶ The remains or traces of a plant or animal that lived in the past, usually preserved in sedimentary rock. It may be the whole or part of the organism itself that is preserved, usually chemically altered; alternatively it may have dissolved away leaving an impression (mould), which preserves its exact shape, or a cast, when it has been replaced exactly by mineral matter. Examples of fossils are whole mammoths preserved in ice, insects preserved in amber, and coal (the carbonized remains of extinct swamp plants). Trace fossils include excrement, burrows, or fossil tracks. A derived fossil is found in a more recent sediment than the one in which it was originally preserved, because of erosion and redeposition. A zone fossil is used in biostratigraphy to delimit a stratigraphic zone; such fossils must be widely distributed and have a limited vertical range in successive rock strata to be useful for this purpose. The study of fossils is called ▷palaeontology.

● **fossil fuels** ▶ The mineral fuels ▷coal, ▷oil, and ▷natural gas that occur in rock formations. They were formed by the deposition millions of years ago of the remains of vegetation (coal) and living organisms (oil and gas), which were buried under subsequent deposition and later subjected to heat and pressure. Fossil fuels supply much of our energy needs, but the reserves are finite and they cause considerable atmospheric ▷pollution (*see* acid rain; greenhouse effect). Dependence on fossil fuels in the generation of electricity can, to some extent, be reduced by the use of ▷alternative energy sources and by ▷nuclear energy.

● **Foster, Jodie** ▶ (Alicia Christian Foster; 1962–) US actress and film director. A child film star in the 1970s, she later won Academy Awards for *The Accused* (1988) and *The Silence of the Lambs* (1990). She

also starred in *Sommersby* (1993), *Nell* (1995), and *Contact* (1997) and has directed *Little Man Tate* (1991) and *Home for the Holidays* (1996).

● **Foster, Norman, Baron** ▶ (1935–) British architect. With his wife Wendy (d. 1989), and with Richard and Su ▷Rogers, he formed Team 4 (1963–67). A leading advocate of the "High Tech" school, he designed the Willis Faber building in Ipswich (1978), the Sainsbury Centre for Visual Arts (1979) at the University of East Anglia, Stansted Airport, Essex (1991), and an arts centre in Nîmes, France (1993). His Hong Kong airport, the largest covered building in the world, opened in 1998, and his new Reichstag in Berlin in 1999. In 1999 he was commissioned to build a seat for the new Greater London Authority and mayor and was raised to the peerage.

● **Foster, Stephen Collins** ▶ (1826–64) US composer of such songs as "Swanee River" (1851) and "Beautiful Dreamer" (1864). Foster was self-taught and turned to Black plantation songs for melodic inspiration. He died in poverty.

● **Fothergill, John** ▶ (1712–80) British physician, who described the symptoms of diphtheria and migraine. A Quaker and philanthropist, Fothergill supported John ▷Howard in his penal reforms and was an advocate of coffee drinking.

● **Fotheringhay** ▶ 52 32N 0 25W A village in England, in Northamptonshire on the River Nene. Fotheringhay Castle (of which little remains) was the scene of Richard III's birth (1452) and the execution of Mary, Queen of Scots (1587).

● **Foucault, Jean Bernard Léon** ▶ (1819–68) French physicist, after whom the ▷Foucault pendulum (1851) is named. He also measured the speed of light, showing that it decreased in water (1850), and invented the gyroscope (1852).

● **Foucault, Michel** ▶ (1926–84) French ▷poststructuralist historian and philosopher. His *Histoire de la folie* (1961; *Madness and Civilization*), *Les Mots et les choses* (1966; *The Order of Things*), and *L'Histoire de la Sexualité* (1976–84) discuss the history of social attitudes to madness, crime, and sexual deviancy.

● **Foucault pendulum** ▶ A very long pendulum with a heavy bob, capable of oscillating for a long period. It demonstrates the earth's rotation since, as it swings, its plane of oscillation slowly rotates. At the poles it would rotate through 360° in 24 hours; at a latitude λ, the number of hours for a complete rotation is given by $24/\sin \lambda$. It was invented by Jean ▷Foucault and first demonstrated in 1851 in Paris using a 28-kg lead ball suspended from a wire 67 m long.

● **Fouché, Joseph, Duc d'Otrante** ▶ (1759–1820) French politician. A priest and teacher, he became politically active in the French Revolution, being elected a deputy in the National Convention in 1792. He participated in the overthrow of Robespierre (1794) and became minister of police under Napoleon but was forced into exile in 1816.

● **Fountains Abbey** ▶ A ruined ▷Cistercian abbey 5 km (3 mi) SW of Ripon, Yorkshire. Founded in 1132 it became the leading Cistercian community in England. Its well-preserved ruins, mainly 12th-century, testify to its wealth prior to its dissolution (1539) at the ▷Reformation.

● **Fouqué, Friedrich Heinrich Karl, Baron de la Motte** ▶ (1777–1843) German novelist and dramatist. Of French aristocratic descent, he was a prolific writer of chivalric romances and dramas, many based on Scandinavian sagas. His best-known work is the romance *Undine* (1811), the story of a watersprite who marries a human.

● **Fouquet, Jean** ▶ (c. 1420–81) French painter and manuscript illuminator, born in Tours. After visiting Italy, he worked for Charles VII and later for Louis XI, whose tomb he helped design. For the royal treasurer, Étienne Chevalier, he painted *The Virgin and Child* (Antwerp) and *Chevalier with His Patron St Stephen* (Berlin), which were formerly joined as the *Mehun Diptych*. A manuscript of Josephus' *Jewish Antiquities* (Bibliothèque National, Paris) contains his finest illuminations, many depicting French towns and countryside.

● **Fouquet, Nicolas** ▶ (1615–80) French politician; finance minister (1653–61) under Louis XIV. He amassed a large fortune, partly

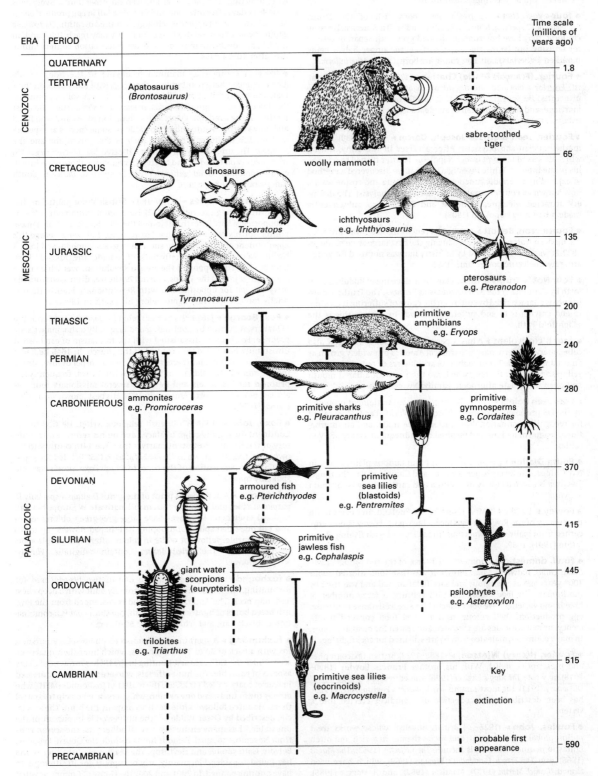

ERA	PERIOD		Time scale (millions of years ago)

CENOZOIC

QUATERNARY — 1.8

TERTIARY

Apatosaurus (*Brontosaurus*)

dinosaurs

woolly mammoth

sabre-toothed tiger

— 65

MESOZOIC

CRETACEOUS

Triceratops

ichthyosaurs e.g. *Ichthyosaurus*

— 135

JURASSIC

Tyrannosaurus

pterosaurs e.g. *Pteranodon*

— 200

TRIASSIC

primitive amphibians e.g. *Eryops*

— 240

PALAEOZOIC

PERMIAN

ammonites e.g. *Promicroceras*

— 280

CARBONIFEROUS

primitive sharks e.g. *Pleuracanthus*

primitive gymnosperms e.g. *Cordaites*

DEVONIAN

armoured fish e.g. *Pterichthyodes*

primitive sea lilies (blastoids) e.g. *Pentremites*

— 370

SILURIAN

primitive jawless fish e.g. *Cephalaspis*

— 415

ORDOVICIAN

giant water scorpions (eurypterids)

psilophytes e.g. *Asteroxylon*

— 445

trilobites e.g. *Triarthus*

CAMBRIAN

primitive sea lilies (eocrinoids) e.g. *Macrocystella*

— 515

Key

extinction

probable first appearance

PRECAMBRIAN

— 590

fossil ▶ Some extinct animals and plants from past geological ages.

through fraudulent dealings, which were revealed to the king by ▷Colbert, and he was imprisoned for life.

● **four-eyed fish** ▶ A freshwater ▷bony fish of the family *Anablepidae* (2 species), found in Central and South America. Up to 30 cm long, they have horizontally divided eyes with separate retinas for cruising just below the water surface, the upper halves being modified for aerial vision. Live young are born. Order: *Atheriniformes*.

● **Fourier, (François Marie) Charles** ▶ (1772–1837) French socialist. Fourier advocated the organization of society on cooperative principles. He sought the abolition of all constrictions, including marriage, and set out his plan of an ideal society in *Le Nouveau Monde industriel* (1829–30).

● **Fourier, Jean Baptiste Joseph, Baron** ▶ (1768–1830) French mathematician and physicist. After a career in the army, during which he served in Egypt under Napoleon, Fourier turned to science, his prime interest. While investigating heat, he discovered a method of expanding a periodic function in terms of sine and cosine waves, now known as **Fourier analysis** (*see* harmonic analysis). The discovery attracted widespread interest and Fourier was subsequently made a baron by Napoleon (1808).

● **Fourneyron, Benoît** ▶ (1802–67) French engineer, who invented the modern water ▷turbine, producing the first large-scale model in 1832. It was quickly adopted by industry but was not used for generating hydroelectric power until 1895.

● **Four Noble Truths** ▶ The fundamental doctrine of Buddhism, set forth by Gautama in the first discourse at Benares. The Truths are: existence is characterized by suffering; the cause of suffering is craving; to end craving is to end suffering; the way to achieve this is the ▷Eightfold Path.

● **four o'clock plant** ▶ A bushy perennial herb, *Mirabilis jalapa*, also called marvel of Peru, native to tropical America but widely grown as an ornamental. 40–75 cm high, it bears clusters of red, pink, white, yellow, or streaked flowers, which are tubular with a flared mouth and open in the late afternoon. Family: *Nyctaginaceae*.

● **Fourteen Points** ▶ (1918) Terms for a peace settlement proposed by the US president, Woodrow Wilson, in World War I. They called for recognition of national aspirations, free trade, and an international league of nations and inspired the subsequent Treaty of ▷Versailles.

● **Fouta Djallon** ▶ (or Futa Jallon) A mountainous plateau area in NW Guinea. The Rivers Niger, Senegal, and Gambia rise in the range. The area is covered chiefly by savanna and cattle raising is the main activity.

● **Fowey** ▶ 50 20N 4 38W A resort in SW England, in Cornwall on the estuary of the River Fowey. Once a busy port, Fowey is now concerned principally with exporting china clay and with fishing. Population (1991): 1939.

● **fowl, domestic** ▶ A domesticated form of the red ▷jungle fowl, *Gallus gallus*, native to Asian forests. It was first domesticated about 4000 years ago as a religious and sacrificial animal and was used by the Romans for food. Since the 19th century, a large number of breeds and varieties have been selected for size, resistance to disease, egg production, shell colour, fertility, and food conversion efficiency. Immature males are castrated and reared for meat as capons. In many countries, males (cockerels) are still used for cockfighting.

● **Fowler, H(enry) W(atson)** ▶ (1858–1933) British lexicographer and prescriptive stylist. With his brother **Francis Fowler** (1870–1918) he wrote *The King's English* (1906) and edited the *Concise Oxford Dictionary* (1911). His most famous work, *Modern English Usage* (1926), has been described as "a collection of prejudices erected into a system."

● **Fowles, John** ▶ (1926–) British novelist, whose works treat philosophical, psychological, and social themes in a rich and often fantastic manner. His novels include *The Collector* (1963), *The Magus* (1966), and *The French Lieutenant's Woman* (1969), which have been filmed, *Daniel Martin* (1977), *Mantissa* (1982), and *A Maggot* (1985). Other books include the short stories in *The Ebony Tower* (1974).

● **fowl pest** ▶ An infectious virus disease, also called Newcastle disease, affecting domestic fowl and certain other birds. Symptoms arise 4–11 days after infection and include a fall in egg production (in laying birds), loss of appetite, lethargy, laboured breathing through a gaping beak, and nasal discharge. Mortality may reach 100% and, in the UK, any outbreak must be reported. Vaccination confers immunity after 10–14 days.

● **fox** ▶ A carnivorous mammal belonging to the ▷dog family (*Canidae*). Foxes have pointed ears, short legs with hairy pads on their feet, and bushy tails. Generally nocturnal, they are solitary hunters, feeding on small mammals, birds, insects, and some fruit. The most familiar is the ▷red fox (*Vulpes vulpes*), found in forest and woodland and now venturing into suburban gardens. Some species are specialized for life in difficult habitats, such as the ▷Arctic fox and the ▷fennec. The unusual South African bat-eared fox (*Otocyon megalotis*) feeds mainly on termites and has teeth resembling those of an insect-eating mammal. Chief genera: *Vulpes* (9 species), *Dusicyon* (South American foxes; 8 species).

● **Fox, Charles James** ▶ (1749–1806) British Whig politician; the first British foreign secretary (1782). He entered parliament (1768) as a supporter of Lord ▷North but joined the ▷Rockingham Whigs in opposing North's American policy. Fox resigned following George III's appointment of ▷Shelburne in succession to Rockingham and joined North in a coalition that briefly took office under the Duke of ▷Portland in 1783. Fox supported the French Revolution, over which issue many Whigs joined the Tories, and in 1798 he was dismissed from the privy council for opposing war with Revolutionary France. He was briefly foreign secretary again before his death in 1806.

● **Fox, George** ▶ (1624–91) English religious leader, founder of the ▷Quakers. A Puritan by upbringing and originally a shoemaker's apprentice, Fox became dissatisfied with the formalism of established Christianity and the state's control of the church. In 1646 he had a personal revelation and thereafter preached a gospel of love, stressing the immediate guidance of the Holy Spirit. He was frequently imprisoned for his beliefs and he made several missionary journeys abroad, notably to North America in 1671. His best-known work is his *Journal* (1674).

● **Foxe, John** ▶ (1516–87) English religious writer. He fled to the Continent during the reign of Mary I and on his return wrote a history of the English Protestant martyrs from the 14th century to his own time. Usually known as *The Book of Martyrs* (1563), it fed the growing Catholic persecution of the time, to which Foxe himself was outspokenly opposed.

● **foxglove** ▶ A herbaceous plant of the genus *Digitalis*, especially *D. purpurea*, a biennial herb, 45–150 cm tall, native to W Europe but naturalized elsewhere. Foxgloves have large grey-green oblong leaves and tall one-sided spikes of drooping bell-shaped flowers, up to 6.5 cm long, purple, yellow, or white in colour, often with purple spots in the centre. The dried leaves contain ▷digitalis. Family: *Scrophulariaceae*.

● **foxhound** ▶ A dog belonging to one of two breeds used for foxhunting. The English foxhound is strongly built with a deep chest and long neck. The American foxhound is descended from the English breed but is of lighter build. In both, the short coat is a combination of black, tan, and white. Height: 56–63 cm.

● **foxhunting** ▶ A sport in which huntsmen on horseback pursue a fox with a pack of 20 to 30 ▷foxhounds, which hunt their quarry by scent. Since the 18th century, hunting in the UK has influenced many aspects of rural life. The hunt officials, who are traditionally dressed in scarlet coats, called pinks, are the master of foxhounds (MFH), who directs the hounds, and one or more whippers-in, who help to control them. Mounted followers (the field) accompany the hunt. The spectacle, described by Oscar Wilde as "the unspeakable in pursuit of the uneatable," has many enthusiastic rural adherents. The season runs from November to April. Famous hunts include the Quorn, Pytchley, Belvoir, Cottesmore, and Heythrop. The League against Cruel Sports has found considerable, mainly urban, support for its attempts to have hunting banned. In 2001 and 2002 the House of Commons voted for an outright ban on hunting with hounds, but the House of Lords blocked the measure on the first occasion and suggested a compromise on the second. Hunting with hounds is now illegal in Soctland following a vote by the Scottish Parliament in 2002. Foxhunting is also popular in the E USA and jackalhunting and draghunting (in which hounds follow a prepared trail) are found as substitutes in other parts of the world.

● **fox terrier** ▶ A breed of ▯dog developed in England for hunting foxes and badgers. It is sturdy with a short tail, a broad tapering muzzle, and small ears that are folded forwards over the face. There are two coat varieties—smooth-haired and wire-haired—and colouring is mainly white with black and tan markings. Height: 37–39 cm.

● **Foyle, Lough** ▶ An inlet of the Atlantic Ocean, in N Ireland. Fed by the River Foyle, it lies between NE Co Donegal in the Republic of Ireland and NW Co Londonderry in Northern Ireland.

fractal ▶ An example of computer-generated art produced using fractal patterns. The representation of the Mandelbrot set occurs on the sphere.

● **fractal** ▶ A type of curve or surface generated by a process involving successive subdivision. A simple example is the **snowflake curve**, which can be produced from an equilateral triangle by dividing each side into three segments. The middle segments are then replaced by two equal segments, which form the sides of a smaller equilateral triangle. This gives a 12-sided star-shaped figure. The next stage is to subdivide each of the sides of this figure in the same way, and so on. The result is a developing figure that resembles a snowflake. In the limit, this figure has "fractional dimension"—i.e. a dimension between that of a line (1) and a surface (2); the dimension of the snowflake curve is 1.26. Fractals are important in ▷chaos theory and in ▷computer graphics. ▷*See also* Mandelbrot set.

● **fracture** ▶ The breaking of a bone. This usually occurs as a result of injury but it may happen very easily in bones diseased with cancer or ▷osteoporosis (pathological fracture). In a simple fracture the ends of the broken bone are not displaced; in a compound fracture the broken bone pierces the skin. A stress fracture is a crack arising in a bone exposed to repeated small injuries, for example in soldiers marching long distances. The bones of children are relatively soft and flexible; such bones are more likely to be bent than completely broken—this is called a greenstick fracture. Fractures are treated by aligning the ends of the broken bone and immobilizing them. Healing will result quickly. Sometimes it is necessary to pin fractures surgically.

● **Fragonard, Jean-Honoré** ▶ (1732–1806) French ▷rococo painter, born in Grasse. He trained with ▷Chardin and ▷Boucher in Paris and studied in Italy (1756–61), concentrating on the work of ▷Tiepolo. He established his reputation with a history painting, *Coresus Sacrificing Himself to Save Callirhoë* (1765; Louvre), but soon turned to more light-hearted and delicately erotic subjects, e.g. *The Swing* (Wallace Collection, London) and *The Progress of Love* (Frick Col-

lection, New York). His interest in Dutch painters was strengthened by a visit to Holland in the 1770s. He suffered financial ruin during the Revolution and died in obscurity.

● **Frame, Janet (Paterson)** ▶ (1924–) New Zealand writer. As a young woman she spent seven years in psychiatric hospitals, where she wrote the stories in her first collection, *The Lagoon* (1951). This was followed by such novels as *Owls Do Cry* (1957), *Scented Gardens for the Blind* (1963), and *The Carpathians* (1988), as well as further volumes of stories. Her three volumes of autobiography—*To the Island* (1983), *An Angel at My Table* (1984), and *The Envoy from Mirror City* (1985)—were made into a film (*An Angel at My Table*, 1990) by Jane ▷Campion.

● **Frampton, Sir George James** ▶ (1860–1928) British sculptor known for his *Peter Pan* (Kensington Gardens) and the Edith Cavell memorial near Trafalgar Square, London.

● **France, Anatole** ▶ (Jacques Anatole François Thibault; 1844–1924) French novelist, son of a Parisian bookseller. His novels are noted for their erudition, scepticism, and elegance. His intervention in the ▷Dreyfus case (1897) marked the beginning of his commitment to socialism and, later, communism. In such novels as *L'Île des pingouins* (1909) and *Les Dieux ont soif* (1913) his view of mankind is deeply pessimistic. He won a Nobel Prize in 1921.

● **France, Republic of** ▶ A country in W Europe, bordering on the English Channel in the N, the Atlantic Ocean in the W, and the Mediterranean Sea in the S. It includes the island of Corsica and several overseas regions (Martinique, Guadeloupe, and French Guiana). Overseas territories include French Polynesia, New Caledonia, and St Pierre and Miquelon. Fertile lowlands cover most of the N and W of France, rising to the Pyrenees in the S, the Massif Central in the SE, and the Vosges, Jura, and Alps in the E. The principal rivers are the Seine, the Loire, and the Rhône.

Economy: compared with other industrial countries in W Europe, agriculture remains important although the number of people employed in this sector has decreased owing to the reorganization of many of the numerous small peasant holdings into larger units. Animal products make up over half the total output and the production of cereals is important; the wine industry is a major source of revenue. There were large-scale developments in the industrial sector in the decades after World War II, especially in iron and steel, motor vehicles, aircraft, mechanical and electrical engineering, textiles, chemicals, and food processing. France's mineral wealth includes iron ore, potash, bauxite, coal, and sulphur. Natural gas is produced in the foothills of the Pyrenees, but a considerable proportion of power still comes from hydroelectric sources. Exports rose dramatically in the postwar period, especially textiles, iron and steel, motor vehicles, and machinery, and France is one of the world's largest exporters of arms. Economic growth has slowed down in recent decades, however, and although inflation has been tamed successive prime ministers have failed to deal with the increasing problems of trade deficits and soaring unemployment. In the mid-1990s most of France's public-sector companies were privatized and severe austerity measures were imposed to prepare the French economy for adoption of the single European currency.

History: present-day France approximates the ancient region of ▷Gaul, which was conquered by Julius Caesar in the 1st century BC. It became part of the Roman Empire and in the 1st century AD Christianity was introduced to the provinces into which Gaul was divided. From the 3rd to the 5th centuries, it was overrun by German tribes, including the Goths, Vandals, and ▷Franks (from whom the name France is derived). The Frankish kingdom reached its peak under Charlemagne (reigned 768–814) and his ▷Carolingian dynasty continued to rule in France until 987, when Hugh Capet became the first ▷Capetian king. During the 10th century Norsemen (Vikings) established themselves in what became Normandy and in 1066 invaded England. The claims of English kings to French territory were realized on a large scale by the ▷Angevins and consequent conflict between France and England culminated in the ▷Hundred Years' War (1337–1453), as a result of which the English were expelled from all of France, except Calais. The Capetians were succeeded by the ▷Valois dynasty (1328–1589), a period that saw the beginning of France's long rivalry with Spain for hegemony in Europe. During the ▷Wars of Religion the last Valois king, Henry III, was succeeded (1589) by the first ▷Bourbon, Henry IV. The first half of the 17th century was dominated by Cardinal de ▷Richelieu and his successor as chief minister, Cardinal ▷Mazarin. They were resonsible for France replacing Spain, after the Thirty Years' War, as the supreme European power (1659). During the reign (1643–1715) of ▷Louis XIV France reached the zenith of its power and brilliance. Decline, however, began before his death and gathered speed in the following decades. The disastrous ▷Seven Years' War forced France to recognize British supremacy in North America and India and the political reaction and economic incompetence of the later Bourbon kings precipitated the ▷French Revolution in 1789. The First Republic was proclaimed (1792) and Louis XVI was guillotined (1793) in spite of the military opposition of the major European powers (*see* Revolutionary and Napoleonic Wars). In 1799 ▷Napoleon Bonaparte overthrew the directory, becoming first consul and, in 1804, emperor. By 1808 he had brought most of continental Europe under his sway but in 1815 he was finally defeated at Waterloo and exiled. The Bourbons were restored until 1830, when the July Revolution raised Louis Philippe to the throne. Overthrown in the ▷Revolutions of 1848, the monarchy was replaced by the Second Republic of which Louis Napoleon became president; in 1852 he proclaimed himself emperor as ▷Napoleon III. During the Second Empire France underwent the beginnings of industrialization but its prosperity was not sufficient to achieve victory in the ▷Franco-Prussian War, in which Napoleon's ignominious leadership led to his overthrow (1870). The subsequent Third Republic lasted until 1940, in spite of scandal (e.g. the ▷Dreyfus and ▷Stavisky affairs), ▷World War I, and political dissension (there were 44 successive governments between 1918 and 1940). After the outbreak of World War II France fell to Germany and a pro-German government was established at Vichy, while ▷de Gaulle led the Free French from London. In 1944 France was liberated by the Allies and de Gaulle established a provisional government that gave way (1946) to the Fourth Republic. The immediate postwar period was overshadowed by war in Indochina and by the crisis in Algeria that precipitated the fall of the Fourth Republic (1958). De Gaulle was recalled from retirement and, as president of the Fifth Republic, instituted a period of firm government. In May 1968, however, the Republic was shaken by student protests and strikes and in 1969 he resigned. Gaullist principles continued to influence government under Pompidou and Giscard d'Estaing. François ▷Mitterrand's election in 1981 made him the first socialist president in 35 years. In the 1993 parliamentary elections there was a swing to the right; this trend continued with the election of Jacques ▷Chirac as president in 1995 but was reversed with the success of the left in the parliamentary elections of 1997. French politics suffered a shock in 2002, when Jean-Marie Le Pen, the candidate of the extreme right, emerged as runner-up to Chirac in the first round of the presidential elections. Chirac was re-elected by a landslide. France adopted the European single currency in 1999–2002.

Republic of France

Head of state	President Jacques Chirac
Official language	French
Official currency	euro
Area	543 814 sq km (209 912 sq mi)
Population (2000 est)	58 835 000
Capital	Paris
Main port	Marseille

● **Franche-Comté** ► A planning region and former province in E France, bordering on Switzerland. Part of Burgundy until 843 AD, it was overrun successively by many powers before being finally annexed to France in 1678. The main occupations are farming, especially dairy farming and cattle rearing, and forestry. Area: 16 202 sq km (6254 sq mi). Population (1999 est): 1 117 059.

● **franchise** ► 1. (politics) The right to vote in a political election. In modern democratic systems all citizens of both sexes over a certain age (18 in the UK) have the franchise. In some countries certain categories are excluded (in the UK prisoners and the mentally ill, and members of the House of Lords may not vote in elections for members of the House of Commons). The franchise has not always been

available so widely. Property, religious, and educational qualifications have been used in the past. In the UK all men (over the age of 21) were given the franchise in 1918, but it was another ten years before the same right was given to women. **2.** (business) The right to sell a particular product granted by a manufacturer to a distributor. For example, a car manufacturer may franchise a chain of garages to sell its vehicles and spares. The franchisor may also sell a right to use a particular trademark, production technique, or know-how in exchange for a fee and usually a percentage of the sale price of the goods or services supplied.

Republic of France

Regions	Area (sq km)	Population (1999)	Chief town
Alsace	8 280	1 734 145	Strasbourg
Aquitaine	41 308	2 908 359	Bordeaux
Auvergne	26 013	1 173 878	Clermont-Ferrand
Basse-Normandie	17 589	1 422 193	Caen
Bourgogne (Burgundy)	31 582	1 276 846	Dijon
Bretagne (Brittany)	27 208	2 906 197	Rennes
Centre	39 151	2 440 329	Orléans
Champagne-Ardenne	25 606	1 342 363	Châlons-sur-Marne
Corse (Corsica)	8 680	260 196	Ajaccio
Franche-Comté	16 202	1 117 059	Besançon
Haute-Normandie	12 317	1 780 192	Rouen
Île-de-France	12 012	9 962 011	Paris
Languedoc-Roussillon	27 376	2 295 648	Montpellier
Limousin	16 942	710 939	Limoges
Lorraine	23 547	2 310 376	Metz
Midi-Pyrénées	45 348	2 558 687	Toulouse
Nord-Pas-de-Calais	12 414	3 996 588	Lille
Pays de la Loire	32 082	3 222 061	Nantes
Picardie	19 399	1 857 834	Amiens
Poitou-Charentes	25 810	1 301 407	Poitiers
Provence-Alpes-Côte d'Azur	31 400	4 476 151	Marseille
Rhône-Alpes	43 698	5 645 407	Lyon

Overseas departments	Chief town
Guadeloupe	Basse-Terre
Guiana	Cayenne
Martinique	Fort-de-France
Réunion	Saint-Denis

Territorial collectivities	Chief town
Mayotte	Dzaoudzi
St Pierre and Miquelon	St Pierre

Overseas territories	Chief town
Southern and Antarctic Territories	–
New Caledonia	Nouméa
French Polynesia	–
Wallis and Futuna	Mata-Utu

● **Francis I** ► (1494–1547) King of France (1515–47). His reign was dominated by rivalry with the Holy Roman Emperor ▷Charles V. In the course of the conflict, which continued intermittently until 1544, Francis was taken prisoner at ▷Pavia (1525). At home, he won control over the French church through the Concordat of Bologna (1516), suppressed French Protestantism, and ordered an attack on the ▷Waldenses in S France (1545).

● **Francis I** ► (1708–65) Duke of Lorraine (1729–37), Grand duke of Tuscany (1737–65), and Holy Roman Emperor (1745–65). He married (1736) ▷Maria Theresa, who succeeded to the Austrian dominions in 1740 in the face of much opposition. He was elected emperor during the consequent War of the ▷Austrian Succession (1740–48).

● **Francis I** ► (Emperor of Austria) ▷*See* Francis II (Holy Roman Emperor).

● **Francis II** ► (1544–60) King of France (1559–60); the son of ▷Henry

II and ▷Catherine de' Medici and husband (1558–60) of ▷Mary, Queen of Scots. He was dominated by the ▷Guise family, which used him in its struggle against the Protestant ▷Condé early in the ▷Wars of Religion.

● **Francis II** ▶ (1768–1835) The last Holy Roman Emperor (1792–1806) and, as Francis I, the first Emperor of Austria (1804–35). Following three defeats by the French in the Napoleonic Wars, he allied with ▷Napoleon I until 1813. After the Congress of ▷Vienna (1815), he was guided by his conservative chief minister ▷Metternich.

● **Francis Ferdinand** ▶ (1863–1914) Archduke of Austria and heir apparent to his uncle, Emperor ▷Francis Joseph. He was known to favour the development of national cultures within the Empire. His assassination (28 June, 1914) by a Serbian nationalist at Sarajevo precipitated ▷World War I.

● **Francis Joseph** ▶ (1830–1916) Emperor of Austria (1848–1916) and King of Hungary (1867–1916). His long reign saw the rise of national tensions in the Empire, which led to the establishment of the Dual Monarchy of ▷Austria-Hungary, under which Austria and Hungary coexisted as equal partners under the Austrian Crown. He was defeated by the Prussians in the Austro-Prussian War of 1866 but in 1879 he allied with the recently formed German Empire and in 1882 with Italy, forming the ▷Triple Alliance. His ultimatum to Serbia, following the assassination by a Serbian nationalist of his nephew, Archduke ▷Francis Ferdinand (1914), was the spark that led to the conflagration of ▷World War I.

● **Francis of Assisi, St** ▶ (Giovanni di Bernardone; c. 1182–1226) Italian friar and founder of the ▷Franciscans, born in Assisi. The son of a merchant, he renounced his worldly life in 1205 to live in poverty and devote himself to prayer and charitable works. By 1209 he had a band of followers with whom he went to Rome (1210), where he obtained papal approval of his new order. He travelled in Spain, the Holy Land, and Egypt, later retiring to Assisi and giving up the leadership of his order. A profoundly humble man, in paintings he is often portrayed among animals and birds, which he called his sisters and brothers. His love of nature is also reflected in his hymn, *Canticle of the Sun*. He received the ▷stigmata in 1224, was canonized in 1228, and was proclaimed patron saint of ecology in 1980. Feast day: 4 Oct.

● **Francis of Sales, St** ▶ (1567–1622) French Roman Catholic prelate and devotional writer, born in Savoy. He played a leading part in the Counter-Reformation by reconverting the people of Chablais from Calvinism to Roman Catholicism. As Bishop of Geneva from 1602 he cofounded the Order of the Visitation, an order of nuns. Feast day: 29 Jan.

● **Francis Xavier, St** ▶ (1506–52) Spanish ▷Jesuit missionary, known as the Apostle of the Indies. While studying in Paris (1523–34) he met St ▷Ignatius Loyola and helped him found the Jesuit order. From 1541 he established missions in the Indies, India, and Japan. Feast day: 3 Dec.

● **Francis, Sir Philip** ▶ (1740–1818) British politician, who was probably the author of the Letters of ▷Junius. He campaigned for the impeachment (1788) of Warren ▷Hastings, governor general of India, whom he fought in a duel in 1780.

● **Franciscans** ▶ An order of friars founded in 1209 by St ▷Francis of Assisi. His rule was devised to impose both personal and corporate poverty on the order's members. The rule was revised in 1221 and again in 1223, when it was confirmed by the pope. Within Francis' lifetime the expanding order found complete poverty practically difficult, and a schism ensued in the early 14th century regarding how strictly the rule should be followed. Despite a resulting decline, the order survived and has remained an important missionary and charitable branch of the Roman Catholic Church.

● **francium** ▶ (Fr) The heaviest alkali metal, a very unstable radioactive element discovered in 1939 by Perey. The longest-lived isotope ^{223}Fr has a half-life of 22 minutes; traces of the element exist in nature, as decay products of ^{227}Ac. At no 87; at wt (223); mp 27°C; bp 677°C.

● **Franck, César Auguste** ▶ (1822–90) Belgian composer, organist, and teacher, who settled in Paris in 1834. He became organist of Ste

Clotilde in 1858, a post he held until his death. His pupils included D'Indy and Chausson. Franck was influenced by Bach and evolved a highly chromatic form of harmony. He also developed "cyclic form," the use of the same theme in more than one movement of a work. His compositions include *Symphonic Variations* (for piano and orchestra; 1885), a symphony (1886–88), a violin sonata (1886), and a string quartet (1889).

● **Franck, James** ▶ (1882–1964) US physicist, born in Germany, whose experiments in collaboration with Gustav Hertz (1887–1975) on the excitation of gases when bombarded with electrons won them the Nobel Prize in 1925. Their experiments provided evidence that the energy levels inside atoms were quantized. He also made valuable contributions to photochemistry. During World War II Franck worked on the atom bomb but opposed its use on populated areas.

● **Franco, Francisco** ▶ (1892–1975) Spanish general and statesman; dictator from 1939 until his death. He entered the Infantry Academy in 1907, aged 14, was posted to Spanish Morocco in 1912, and became the youngest captain in the Spanish army in 1915. By 1935 he was chief of the General Staff and in the following year, on 18 July, staged a military uprising against the Republican Government of ▷Azaña that precipitated the ▷Spanish Civil War. In October, 1936, he became head of state in the Nationalist Zone and commander in chief of the rebel forces. By 1939, with help from Hitler and Mussolini, he had defeated the Republican forces and become the absolute leader of Spain. Franco's government, in which the National Movement (*see* Falange Española) was the only political party, remained sympathetic to Hitler but maintained a neutral position throughout World War II. Spain was excluded from the newly formed UN in 1945 but its isolation was broken during the Cold War, when Franco's anticommunism made him a more attractive ally. In 1953 he signed a military-assistance agreement with the USA. Although his government achieved considerable economic advance for Spain, he operated a ruthless dictatorship. However, during his last years he permitted a perceptible liberalization, which foreshadowed the country's move to democracy under his successor, King ▷Juan Carlos.

● **francolin** ▶ A ▷partridge belonging to a genus (*Francolinus*; 41 species) occurring in Africa and Asia. 27–46 cm long, francolins are usually a dull brownish colour with black, white, or chestnut markings and are popular gamebirds.

● **Francome, John** ▶ (1953–) British jockey who retired in 1985 after having ridden 1036 National Hunt winners. He subsequently trained horses on the flat.

● **Franconia** ▶ A duchy of early medieval Germany, now in Rhineland-Palatinate, Baden-Württemberg, Hessen, and Bavaria. Its duke, Conrad, was the first elected king of Germany (911–18) but by the 13th century the duchy had been fragmented into small principalities.

● **Franco-Prussian War** ▶ (1870–71) A war between France and Prussia. Fearing Bismarck's proposals to make a relative of William I of Prussia the king of Spain (*see* Ems telegram), France declared war. Napoleon III was defeated at ▷Sedan but French resistance continued. Napoleon was deposed and the Third Republic was established but the Prussians besieged Paris, which eventually capitulated. The Treaty of Frankfurt imposed a huge indemnity on France, which ceded Alsace and Lorraine to the new German Empire; France was left economically weakened and politically divided.

● **frangipani** ▶ A tropical American tree, *Plumeria rubra*, cultivated throughout the tropics and known in Asia as pagoda tree or temple flower. Up to 6 m tall, it has tapering long-stalked leaves and round clusters, up to 25 cm across, of fragrant pink, reddish-purple, white, or yellow flowers, used to make perfume. Family: *Apocynaceae*.

● **Frank, Anne** ▶ (1929–45) German Jewish girl, who died in a German concentration camp. Her diary, which has been translated into 30 languages, became a symbol of Jewish resistance and courage following its publication in 1947. She wrote it while hiding from the Nazis in occupied Amsterdam in 1942–43. After she and her family had been betrayed, she was sent to Belsen, where she died of typhus.

● **Frankfort** ▶ 38 11N 84 53W A city in the USA, the capital of Kentucky on the Kentucky River. Its major industry is whiskey distilling. Population (latest est): 25 973.

● **Frankfurt am Main** ► 50 06N 8 41E A city in W Germany, in Hessen on the River Main. A major banking and commercial centre, it is famed for its trade fairs, especially the annual book fair. Its gothic cathedral is 13th-century and the university was established in 1914. It is the birthplace of Goethe and the original home of the Rothschilds. Its industries include the manufacture of chemicals, pharmaceuticals, and machinery.

History: it was the seat of the imperial elections (9th to 18th centuries) and coronations (1562–1792) of the Holy Roman emperors. The first German national assembly met here (1848–49). Population (1996 est): 650 055.

● **Frankfurt an der Oder** ► 52 20N 14 32E A town in E Germany, on the River Oder. Severely damaged in World War II, the part E of the river was incorporated into Poland in 1945. A trading centre since medieval times, its manufactures include machinery and furniture. Population (1991): 85 360.

● **Frankfurter, Felix** ► (1882–1965) US jurist, born in Vienna. He was a professor at Harvard Law School from 1914 until 1939, when he was appointed to the US Supreme Court. During this period he also served as secretary of war (1911–13) and as legal adviser to Woodrow Wilson at the Paris Peace Conference (1919) and to Franklin Roosevelt in the 1930s. Although he helped to found the American Civil Liberties Union (1919), he also supported some measures to limit civil liberties.

● **Frankfurt School** ► A movement founded in 1923 at the Institute of Social Research at the University of Frankfurt. Its leaders, ▷Marcuse, ▷Fromm, ▷Adorno, and Max Horkheimer (1895–1973), attempted to combine the insights of psychology, philosophy, and economics to forge a new critique of Western capitalism based on updated Marxism. Its major work was *Authority and the Family* (1936). With the rise of the Nazis, many members moved to New York but only some returned to Frankfurt after World War II. The movement ceased to function after Adorno's death in 1969.

● **frankincense** ► (or olibanum) An aromatic gum resin obtained chiefly from trees of the genus *Boswellia*, especially *B. carteri*, which grows in the Middle East. It is usually supplied commercially in yellowish blocks covered with white dust, smells of balsam when heated, and burns brightly giving off a fragrant odour. Frankincense was known in ancient Egypt; it is still used as an ▷incense, in fumigants, and in perfumes.

● **Franklin** ► A former district of N Canada, in the ▷Northwest Territories, consisting of Canada's Arctic archipelago and some northerly peninsulas. In April 1999 most of it was absorbed into the new territory of ▷Nunavut, a semiautonomous homeland for the Inuit people.

● **Franklin, Benjamin** ► (1706–90) US diplomat, scientist, and author. He established a printing business in Philadelphia and became well known for his *Poor Richard's Almanac* (1732–57), which contained many maxims on the virtues of thrift and hard work. His experiments with static electricity, especially the famous episode in which he flew a kite during a thunderstorm (and was lucky not to be killed), led him to invent the lightning conductor. His political prominence began in 1737, when he became deputy postmaster of Philadelphia, where he promoted street lighting and the establishment of a city police force. Prior to the American Revolution he represented Pennsylvania's case to Britain (1757–62, 1766–75) and as a member of the ▷Continental Congress helped frame the Declaration of Independence (1775). Famous as a diplomat in Paris (1776–85), he enlisted French help for the colonies and negotiated peace with Britain (1783). Franklin also founded (1743) the American Philosophical Society. His *Autobiography* was published in 1868.

● **Franklin, Sir John** ► (1786–1847) British explorer. After service in the Royal Navy, during which he fought at Trafalgar (1805), he was subsequently governor (1836–43) of Van Dieman's Land (now Tasmania). In 1845 he sailed with two ships, never to return, to look for the ▷Northwest Passage. Successive search expeditions failed to find the men until 1859, when their skeletons and records were found on King William Island. Franklin had virtually discovered the passage

but had become ice-bound and he and his companions died of scurvy or starvation.

● **Franklin, Rosalind Elsie** ► (1920–58) British scientist, whose work in X-ray crystallography contributed to the discovery of the structure of ▷DNA in conjunction with James ▷Watson and Francis ▷Crick. She was working on the structure of tobacco mosaic virus at the time of her premature death from cancer.

● **Franks** ► A Germanic people, who invaded Roman ▷Gaul from the Rhineland between the 3rd and 5th centuries AD. One of the Frankish tribes, the Salian Franks, gained control of most of Gaul under their ruler ▷Clovis (d. 511) and were converted to Christianity. The Frankish state was ruled by the ▷Merovingian dynasty (named after Clovis' grandfather, Merovech) until its replacement by the ▷Carolingians (named after ▷Charlemagne) in 751. The Carolingian empire lasted until its division in 843. The western Frankish kingdom was the nucleus of France.

● **Franz Josef Land** ► (Russian name: Zemlya Frantsa Iosifa) A Russian archipelago of 85 islands in the N Barents Sea, the largest being Aleksandra Land, George Land, Graham Bell Island, Salisbury Island, and Wilczek Land. They were discovered in 1873 by Austrians and annexed by the Soviet Union in 1926. They are 90% icebound and have no permanent population. Total area: about 20 700 sq km (79 905 sq mi).

● **Frasch process** ▷See sulphur.

● **Fraser, (John) Malcolm** ► (1930–) Australian statesman; Liberal prime minister (1975–83). Appointed caretaker prime minister on the dismissal of ▷Whitlam, he remained in office until the Liberals were defeated in the 1983 elections, when he also resigned as leader of the Liberal party.

● **Fraser, Peter** ► (1884–1950) New Zealand statesman; Labour prime minister (1940–49). Born in Britain, he helped form the Democratic Party (1913; the Labour Party from 1916) and entered parliament in 1918. He influenced Allied strategy in the Pacific during World War II and helped to establish the UN (1945).

● **Fraser River** ► A river in W Canada, the chief river of British Columbia. Rising near Mount Robson, it flows rapidly through mountain gorges until it reaches flat farmland in the SW, where it empties into the Strait of Georgia near Vancouver. Length: 1370 km (850 mi).

● **fraud** ► In law, making a false representation, by words or conduct or by withholding facts where there is a duty to disclose them, in order to obtain a material advantage. To prove fraud it is necessary to show that a false representation was made (1) knowingly, (2) without belief in its truth, or (3) recklessly, without concern whether it was true or not. To obtain damages it must be shown that the defendant intended the injured party to act on the fraudulent representation and that he did so to his detriment. A contract based on fraud may be declared void.

● **Fraunhofer, Joseph von** ► (1787–1826) German physicist, who greatly improved the quality of lenses and prisms and made improvements to the design of optical instruments. His superior equipment enabled him to detect numerous dark lines in the sun's spectrum (1814), now known as **Fraunhofer lines**. The eight most prominent lines are still known by the letters he gave them.

● **Fray Bentos** ► 33 10S 58 20W A port in W Uruguay, on the River Uruguay. It is an important meat-packing centre, especially of corned beef. Population (1995): 21 400.

● **Frazer, Sir James George** ► (1854–1941) British anthropologist, mythologist, and writer. Frazer's major work *The Golden Bough* (first edition 1890) was a description of "the long evolution by which the thoughts and efforts of man have passed through the successive stages of magic, religion, and science." Although his interpretation of his observations was sometimes unsound, the results of his work were far reaching, influencing people outside the anthropological field, including T. S. Eliot.

● **Frazier, Joe** ► (1944–) US boxer, who was Olympic heavyweight champion (1964), world heavyweight champion (1971–73), and the first to beat Muhammad ▷Ali professionally. He was defeated by George ▷Foreman.

● **Fredericia** ▶ 55 34N 9 47E A seaport in Denmark, in SE Jutland at the narrow N end of the Little Belt. It has a large oil refinery. Its exports include frozen fish, silverware, and textiles. Population (1990): 28 000.

● **Frederick (I) Barbarossa** ▶ (c. 1123–90) Holy Roman Emperor (1152–90; crowned 1155), who was engaged in a long struggle with the papacy. He made six expeditions to Italy and was ultimately unsuccessful against the Lombard cities, which regained their independence in 1183. Papal opposition to his ambitions was exacerbated when he set up an antipope to ▷Alexander III, who excommunicated Frederick in 1160. He finally made peace with the pope in 1177. He failed to subdue his powerful cousin, ▷Henry the Lion, but he established his authority in Poland, Hungary, Bohemia, and Burgundy. In 1189, he set out on the third ▷Crusade during which he died.

● **Frederick I** ▶ (1657–1713) The first King of Prussia (1701–1713) and, as Frederick III, Elector of Brandenburg (1688–1701). Austria conceded his royal status in return for military aid in the War of the ▷Spanish Succession (1701–14). He encouraged Prussian industry and agriculture and also fostered the arts and learning; he was a patron of ▷Leibniz.

● **Frederick I** ▶ (King of Sicily) ▷See Frederick II (Holy Roman Emperor).

● **Frederick II** ▶ (1194–1250) Holy Roman Emperor (1220–50), the last emperor of the ▷Hohenstaufen dynasty and, as Frederick I, King of Sicily (1198–1250). As leader of the sixth Cru-sade (1228–29) he captured Jerusalem but remained an opponent of papal policy and was excommunicated three times (1227, 1239, 1245). A man of wide learning, he was a noted patron of the arts and sciences but neglected the government of his possessions, which consequently declined.

● **Frederick (II) the Great** ▶ (1712–86) King of Prussia (1740–86), who made Prussia a major European power. He succeeded to the throne after an extraordinarily severe childhood at the hands of his father ▷Frederick William I. An exponent of enlightened despotism (see Enlightenment), he liberalized the Prussian legal code and introduced economic and social reforms that reinvigorated Prussian society and institutions. His conquest of Silesia (1740) gave rise to the War of the ▷Austrian Succession (1740–48), after which his possession of the region was confirmed. His victory in the ▷Seven Years' War (1756–63) confirmed the military supremacy of Prussia, both in Germany and in Europe. At his palace of Sans Souci, near Potsdam, a distinguished circle of artists and writers, including ▷Voltaire, gathered around Frederick, who was himself a writer and composer.

● **Frederick III** ▶ (1415–93) The last Holy Roman Emperor to be crowned by the pope (1452) and, as Frederick IV, German king (1440–93). As Archduke of Austria from 1424, Frederick unified the Habsburg domains, but failed to win the Bohemian and Hungarian crowns and to resist the Turks. In 1485 ▷Matthias I Corvinus of Hungary conquered Austria, which was recovered in 1490 by Frederick's son ▷Maximilian I.

● **Frederick (III) the Wise** ▶ (1463–1525) Elector of Saxony (1486–1525), whose silvermines made him Germany's richest ruler. A devout Catholic, he nevertheless protected ▷Luther at the castle of Wartburg after the papal ban of 1521.

● **Frederick III** ▶ (Elector of Bradenburg) ▷See Frederick I (King of Prussia).

● **Frederick (V) the Winter King** ▶ (1596–1632) Elector of the Palatinate (1610–23). Frederick, who was the son-in-law of James I of England, accepted the Bohemian Crown in 1619 and led the Protestant revolt against Emperor Ferdinand II (see Thirty Years' War). He was defeated at the Battle of White Mountain (1620) and died a throneless exile.

● **Frederick IX** ▶ (1899–1972) King of Denmark (1947–72), who as regent (1942–47) had encouraged Danish resistance to the Germans in ▷World War II.

● **Frederick Henry** ▶ (1584–1647) Prince of Orange and Count of Nassau. The younger son of ▷William the Silent, he became stadholder and captain general of the United Provinces in 1625. He successfully waged war against Spanish rule but his autocratic outlook was unpopular. His attempts to make peace were fulfilled at ▷Westphalia (1648), shortly after his death.

● **Frederick William** ▶ (1620–88) Elector of Brandenburg (1640–88), known as the Great Elector. He inherited Germany's weakest electorate. By furthering dynastic claims in Prussia, Pomerania, and the lower Rhineland, he created for his Hohenzollern family the strongest territorial state in N Germany. His reforms established the base upon which the great power of ▷Prussia was created in the 18th century.

● **Frederick William I** ▶ (1688–1740) The second King of Prussia (1713–40), who made his country strong and prosperous. He strengthened the army, passed financial reforms, resettled the east, freed his serfs (1719), and instituted compulsory primary education (1717); he also centralized administration and in 1720 acquired most of Swedish Pomerania.

● **Frederick William II** ▶ (1744–97) King of Prussia (1786–97), who pursued a policy of territorial aggrandizement. He profited from the second and third partitions of Poland in 1793 and 1795 and from 1792 until 1795 he joined Austria against Revolutionary France. At home his Religious Edict (1788) granted religious toleration, but was limited in effect, and the law code of 1794 included some liberal statutes.

● **Frederick William III** ▶ (1770–1840) King of Prussia (1797–1840). His neutral attitude towards Napoleon damaged the prestige of Prussia, which was subjected to France by the Treaty of ▷Tilsit (1807) following defeat at ▷Jena and Auerstädt. After Prussia's liberation (1813), Frederick William introduced some reforms but became more repressive in the face of liberal attacks.

● **Frederick William IV** ▶ (1795–1861) King of Prussia (1840–61) in a period of social unrest and nationalism. His conservatism triggered off the ▷Revolution of 1848, which forced him to grant a constitution (1850). This failed to prevent a resumption of reactionary government, which, owing to Frederick William's insanity, was in the hands of his brother, later ▷William I, from 1858.

● **Fredericton** ▶ 45 57N 66 40W A city in E Canada, the capital of New Brunswick. Its industries include the manufacture of wood and plastic products. Tourism, military administration, and distribution are important. The University of New Brunswick was established here in 1785. Population (1991): 45 364.

● **Fredrikstad** ▶ 59 15N 10 55E A port in SE Norway, at the mouth of the River Glomma. Founded in 1567, its industries include saw milling and fishing. Population (1990): 26 546.

● **free energy** ▶ A thermodynamic quantity that measures a system's ability to do work. The Gibbs free energy, G, is the energy liberated or absorbed in a reversible process, and is equal to $H - TS$, where H is the ▷enthalpy and S the ▷entropy of the system. Applied to chemical reactions, if ΔG is positive, the reaction will only occur if energy is supplied to the system; if ΔG is negative it will occur spontaneously. The Helmholtz free energy F equals $U - TS$, where U is the internal energy of the system, ΔF representing the work available in a reversible isothermal process.

● **free fall** ▶ Motion resulting only from a gravitational field in which neither air resistance nor any other frictional force impede the fall. In the earth's gravitational field bodies in free fall have a constant acceleration of 9.806 metres/second^{-2}, known as the ▷acceleration of free fall (formerly acceleration due to gravity).

● **free-form jazz** ▶ A style of US ▷jazz developed by Ornette Coleman (1930–), John Coltrane (1926–67), and others in the 1960s. Free-form jazz is based on a single theme that is subject to any form of melodic, harmonic, or rhythmic improvisation; it espouses highly complex musical relationships that often result in ▷atonality.

● **Free French** ▶ French forces organized in London by Gen ▷de Gaulle in defiance of Marshal Pétain's surrender to Germany in World War II. ▷See also resistance movements.

● **freehold** ▷*See* estate.

● **freemasonry** ► A secret society for men, which declares itself to be based on brotherly love, faith, and charity. Its origins are uncertain but it probably developed from the medieval stonemasons' guilds. In its modern form freemasonry dates from the establishment (1717) in England of the Grand Lodge, to which some 9250 private lodges are now affiliated. The movement runs a hospital, a benevolent institution, and a school for the orphans of former masons. During the 18th century masonry spread to America and the colonies as well as to continental Europe. Its ceremonies, which are allegorical and illustrated by symbols (many of which are the tools of a working mason), demand a vow of secrecy as well as a belief in God (the great architect of the universe) and are based on the Old Testament. Opposition to masonry orginated with a papal bull (1738) excommunicating masons, since when Roman Catholics have never accepted it. In France and some other European countries it assumed a political character during the 18th and 19th centuries and was condemned as subversive. More recently, there has been some concern that freemasons in the UK may have an undue influence within certain professions, such as the police and judiciary.

● **free port** ► A port (such as Hong Kong or Singapore) forming a free-trade area, where goods may be landed, handled, processed, and re-exported without incurring ▷customs and excise duties. Such duties become payable when the goods are moved into adjacent territory. The Hanseatic towns were early examples of free ports. British free ports are Southampton, Liverpool, Prestwick, Cardiff, Belfast, and Birmingham.

● **free radicals** ▷*See* radical.

● **Freesia** ► A genus of ornamental South African plants (20 species), cultivated commercially, especially as a source of cut flowers. Growing from corms to a height of 75 cm, they have sword-shaped leaves and funnel-shaped lemon-scented flowers, white, orange, yellow, blue, purple or pink in colour, growing in one-sided clusters. Most cultivated varieties are hybrids derived from *F. refracta* (with yellowish flowers) and *F. armstrongii* (rose-purple flowers). Family: *Iridaceae*.

● **Free State** ▷*See* Orange Free State.

● **Freetown** ► 8 20N 13 05W The capital and main port of Sierra Leone, on the Atlantic coast. It was founded in the late 18th century as a refuge for freed slaves and was capital of British West Africa (1808–74), becoming the capital of Sierra Leone in 1961. The University of Sierra Leone was founded here in 1967. It has trade in ginger, diamonds, and gold; industries include fish processing. Population (1990 est): 669 000.

● **free trade** ► International trade that takes place without tariffs or quotas. World production is maximized by free trade, but the distribution of a particular product may be inequitable and countries may encounter domestic pressures from their own producers to apply ▷tariffs. Conditions in international trade came closest to free trade in the mid-19th century following the demise of ▷mercantilism, but since then tariff barriers have been erected again. A group of countries may agree between themselves to lower tariffs and achieve a measure of free trade (*see* Ottawa Agreements) or they may form a free-trade area (e.g. the ▷European Union) surrounded by a tariff barrier.

● **free verse** ► Poetry without regular metre or form and depending on the rhythms and patterns of natural speech. The original French term, *vers libre*, was coined during the 1880s by poets who wished to emphasize rhythm as the essential principle of poetic form. Major exponents of this form include Ezra Pound, D. H. Lawrence, and William Carlos Williams.

● **free will** ► In philosophy and theology, the ability of man to choose his own destiny, as opposed to the idea that everything that happens to him is inevitable. Philosophers are concerned to discover what the presuppositions and implications of free will are, compared to those of ▷determinism. They are also concerned to discover to what extent free will and determinism can be compatible. The problem has confronted philosophers since man began to think about ab-stract matters and is one to which there is no easy solution. In a theistic context, determinism is replaced by ▷predestination, the view that all events, including human choice, are fixed by the will of God. In the Christian Church, controversy arose in the 5th century between followers of Pelagius, who taught that man is able to choose salvation or damnation, and St ▷Augustine of Hippo, who held that man could only be saved by divine grace. The controversy again became a live issue at the Reformation, the Calvinists rejecting free will and claiming that men were consigned from eternity to salvation or damnation, irrespective of merit.

● **freeze drying** ► A method of drying foods for preservation in which the food is rapidly frozen under very low pressure. Any water present freezes and then sublimes under the low pressure. ▷*See* food preservation.

● **freezing** ► The preservation of food by keeping it frozen. The basic principle in all food preservation is to arrest the development of the microorganisms responsible for the decay of the food. Home **deep freezers** achieve this by keeping food at a temperature of about $-18°C$ ($-0.4°F$). On thawing, the deterioration process restarts. Most foods are well preserved by freezing, with little loss in nutritional value, but some with a high water content within the cells of the food, such as strawberries and cucumbers, become soggy after freezing as a result of damage to the cell structure by ice formation. Most vegetables are blanched (boiled for 2–4 minutes) before freezing to arrest the action of enzymes. It is the residual enzymic action that determines the recommended storage time.

● **Frege, Gottlob** ► (1848–1925) German mathematician and logician, who extended ▷Boole's work on symbolic logic by using logical symbols not already used in mathematics (symbols for *or*, *if-then*, etc.). This is now standard practice in logic. Frege published a massive work in which he applied symbolic logic to arithmetic. This, however, was invalidated by a paradox presented by Bertrand ▷Russell. In Frege's system, some sets, or classes, of things are not members of themselves; for example, the set [all cats] is not itself a cat. Others are; for example, the set [all things that are not animals] is itself not an animal. Russell's paradox is: is the set [all sets that are not members of themselves] a member of itself?

● **Frei (Montalva), Eduardo** ► (1911–82) Chilean statesman, who defeated Salvador ▷Allende in 1964 to become the first Christian Democratic president of Chile. His promises of radical reform were not enough to win him re-election and he was defeated by Allende in the 1970 elections. His son **Eduardo Frei Ruíz-Tagle** (1942–   ), a politician of the centre left, was president from 1994 until 2000.

● **Freiburg** ▷*See* Fribourg.

● **Freiburg im Breisgau** ► 48 00N 7 52E A city in SW Germany, in Baden-Württemberg in the Black Forest. It has a university (1457) and a notable gothic cathedral, built of red sandstone. A major tourist centre, its manufactures include precision instruments and pharmaceutical products. Population (1996 est): 199 273.

● **Fréjus** ► 43 26N 6 44E A town in SE France, in the Var department. There are several Roman remains, including an amphitheatre, and it has a 13th-century cathedral. In 1959 several hundred inhabitants lost their lives when the Malpasset Dam collapsed. Its industries include olive oil and wine. Population (latest est): 32 698.

● **Frelimo** ► (Front for the Liberation of Mozambique) The coalition of Mozambique nationalist groups that fought a successful guerrilla war against the Portuguese in 1964–75 (sometimes called the **Frelimo War**). After training in Algeria and Egypt, Frelimo fighters began operations against Portuguese troops in 1964 and by 1968 controlled about one fifth of Mozambique. Having failed in its increasingly brutal attempts to suppress Frelimo, which was armed and supplied by the Soviet Union, Portugal conceded independence in 1975. The movement's leader, Samora Machel (1933–86), became Mozambique's first president and established a Marxist state with Frelimo as the single permitted party. This led to a 17-year civil war with the rival Renamo (Mozambique National Resistance), which was not resolved until Frelimo largely abandoned its Marxist-Leninist policies (from 1989) and legitimized rival political parties (1991–92).

● **Fremantle** ▶ 32 07S 115 44E A major seaport in Western Australia, SW of Perth at the mouth of the Swan River. Kwinana, an important industrial complex with oil and nickel refineries and bulk-grain facilities, is nearby. Population (latest est): 23 981.

● **Frémont, John C(harles)** ▶ (1813–90) US explorer, cartographer, and politician. In the 1840s he explored and mapped large areas of the USA W of the Mississippi. He fought in the Mexican War (1846–48) before making a fortune in the Gold Rush (1848–49). In 1856 he became the first Republican Party presidential candidate but was defeated by James Buchanan.

● **French** ▶ A Romance language spoken by 45 million people in France, and extensively in Canada, Belgium, Switzerland, and elsewhere. It is the official language of 21 countries. Standard French, based upon the Parisian dialect known as Francien, has been France's official administrative language since 1539. It has replaced most northern dialects, known collectively as *langue d'oïl*, and has superseded the Occitan dialects of S France, known as *langue d'oc* (*see* Provençal). During the 17th century the ▷Académie Française and the publication of a standard dictionary (1680) quickly stabilized the language. French grammar has been simplified from Latin and the phonology has greatly altered. There are no noun case declensions and the verb is conjugated for three persons. Pronunciation does not, however, distinguish as many grammatical differences as the written form.

● **French, John, 1st Earl of Ypres** ▶ (1852–1925) British field marshal. Before World War I he distinguished himself as a cavalry officer in the Sudan and South Africa and in 1914 was made commander in chief of the ▷British Expeditionary Force in France. Criticized for indecisiveness, he resigned in 1915 and ended his career as lord lieutenant of Ireland (1918–21).

● **French and Indian War** ▶ (1754–63) The conflict for empire in North America between France and Britain that constituted the American front of the ▷Seven Years' War. France and its Indian allies had the initial advantage of superior land forces but British sea blockades eventually defeated the French. The war's climax was reached in the battle for Quebec in which the commanders of each side, ▷Montcalm and ▷Wolfe, were mortally wounded. In the concluding Treaty of ▷Paris (1763) Britain gained Canada and all lands E of the Mississippi.

● **French art and architecture** ▶ The styles of art and architecture in France from the early middle ages. Until the ▷Renaissance, architecture dominated French artistic expression. Many French cathedrals and churches date from the Merovingian or Carolingian periods, which evolved features that anticipated the ▷romanesque architecture of the 11th and 12th centuries. The ▷gothic style is celebrated in the cathedrals of Notre-Dame and at Chartres, Rheims, and Amiens. The 13th century also produced some outstanding miniature painting, especially in Paris, a school that reached its height in the 1320s with the work of Jean ▷Pucelle. The Renaissance in France found expression chiefly in domestic architecture and decoration, notable examples including the chateaux at Amboise and Chambord. The school of ▷Fontainebleau, founded by Francis I, was profoundly influenced by Italian ▷mannerism; the 16th century also saw the work of the ▷Clouet family, who were portraitists, and of the sculptor Jean ▷Goujon. The great exponents of classicism—▷Poussin, ▷Claude Lorraine, and Georges de ▷La Tour—dominated French art in the first half of the 17th century, and the influence of ▷Versailles was felt throughout Europe. The ▷rococo style of the 18th century was exemplified by the work of ▷Watteau, ▷Fragonard, and ▷Boucher and contrasted the contemporaneous naturalism of ▷Chardin. The outstanding exponent of late-18th-century ▷neoclassicism was ▷David. The latter's followers, ▷Géricault and ▷Delacroix, were notable among the Romantics of the 19th century, which also saw the work of ▷Ingres, ▷Courbet, and the ▷Barbizon school. French art in the late 19th century is associated with ▷impressionism, but the period also witnessed the work of ▷Gauguin, ▷Van Gogh, and ▷Cézanne, an important influence on the development of ▷modern art. In the first half of the 20th century Paris was the world centre of modern art, providing a focus for such movements as ▷fauvism, ▷cubism, and ▷surrealism. ▷*See also* Louis XIV; Louis XV; Louis XVI.

● **French bean** ▶ An annual herb, *Phaseolus vulgaris*, also called kidney bean, probably native to South America but widely cultivated. It has large heart-shaped leaves and white pealike flowers. Both dwarf and twining varieties are grown for their ▷beans, usually eaten in the pod. Family: ▷*Leguminosae*. ▷*See also* haricot bean.

● **French Canadians** ▶ French-speaking citizens of Canada descended from immigrants who settled, mainly in Quebec, as farmers during the 17th and 18th centuries. They comprise approximately 30% of the Canadian population, are mainly Roman Catholic, and have a distinct culture. The desire to preserve their identity has promoted a strong separatist movement.

● **French Community** ▶ An association of states comprising France and certain of its former colonies, now overseas regions or departments. Established by the new Fifth Republic after a constitutional referendum (1958), it succeeded the French Union, which in turn replaced the empire. In addition to France it includes Guadeloupe, French Guiana, Martinique, Mayotte, La Réunion, St Pierre and Miquelon, Southern and Antarctic Territories, French Polynesia, New Caledonia, and Wallis and Futuna.

● **French Equatorial Africa** ▶ (French name: Afrique Équatoriale Française) A former federation of French territories in W central Africa comprising (1910–59) the present-day independent states of the Central African Republic, Chad, the Republic of Congo-Brazzaville, and Gabon.

● **French Guiana** ▶ A French overseas region on the NE coast of South America. A narrow fertile coastal belt rises to a mountainous interior, which is covered in dense forest rich in valuable timber.
Economy: timber is the principal export and sugar is the main commercial crop, although the large reserves of minerals, land, timber, and fish have as yet been little developed.
History: Europeans in search of ▷Eldorado explored the region from the early 16th century, but it was not settled until the 17th century, when the French, Dutch, Portuguese, and English competed for possession. In 1817 it was finally obtained by the French, who established penal colonies there, including the notorious one on Devil's Island. The French Guianese have had full French citizenship since 1848 and have been represented in the National Assembly since 1870. Area: about 91 000 sq km (34 740 sq mi). Population (1990): 114 900. Capital: Cayenne.

● **French horn** ▶ An orchestral brass instrument, which evolved from the hunting horn. It consists of a long narrow coiled tube with a wide bell and a cup-shaped mouthpiece. In its original form the horn could only play its own natural harmonic series of notes; in the 18th century crooks of tubing of different length were inserted to enable it to play in a variety of keys. In the 19th century valves were fitted giving the horn in F a complete range of about three octaves above B below the bass stave. It is a transposing instrument, its music being written a fifth higher than it sounds.

● **French India** ▶ A former French overseas territory in India, comprising Chandernagor (an enclave in Bengal) and the coastal settlements of Pondicherry, Karikal, Yanam, and Mahé. It was restored to India (1949–54).

● **French literature** ▶ Writings in Old French, the *langue d'oïl*, date from the 10th century AD; major works appeared only in the 12th century. The *chansons de geste* celebrated the military exploits of the French nobility in the Crusades and other wars. From classical and Arthurian romances by Chrétien de Troyes and others developed such allegorical romances as *Le Roman de la rose* (c. 1230) of Guillaume de Lorris. The lyric poetry of courtly love of the southern ▷troubadours and the northern ▷trouvères was followed in the 15th century by the more personal poetry of Charles d'Orléans and François Villon.
During the 16th century Pierre de Ronsard and the other members of the ▷Pléiade rivalled the poets of Renaissance Italy, while the major prose works were the comic masterpieces of Rabelais and the *Essais* of Montaigne. The influence of classicism during the 17th century, the golden age of French literature, is seen in the tragic dramas of Corneille and Racine, the comedies of Molière, and the prose of Descartes and Pascal. During the 18th century the greatest writing

was that of Rousseau, Voltaire, and Montesquieu, in the field of social philosophy.

Among the leading figures of the Romantic movement during the early 19th century were Chateaubriand and Victor Hugo. Reacting against Romanticism, such novelists as Stendhal, Balzac, Flaubert, and Zola favoured realism and naturalism. Baudelaire, reacting against the Romantic poets de Vigny and de Musset and the Parnassian Gautier, was one of the first Symbolist poets; he was succeeded by Verlaine, Mallarmé, Rimbaud, and, in the 20th century, by Valéry, a contemporary of the surrealist poet Apollinaire.

Major French novelists of the 20th century include Proust, Gide, and Montherlant as well as the existentialists Sartre and Camus. French drama flourished with plays by Anouilh, Cocteau, and the Absurdist writers Ionesco and Beckett. Such novelists as Alain Robbe-Grillet and Nathalie Sarraute pioneered the ▷nouveau roman. More recent novelists include Michel Butor, Marguerite Duras, and Michel Tournier.

● **French polishing** ▷See varnish.

● **French Polynesia** ▶ (former name: French Settlements in Oceania) A French overseas territory in the S Pacific Ocean consisting of several island groups. The most important of these are the Gambier Islands, the Society Archipelago, the Tuamotu Archipelago, the Tubuai Islands, and the Marquesas Islands. The islands produce copra and phosphates. Official currency: franc CFP of 100 centimes. Area: about 4000 sq km (1500 sq mi). Population (1990 est): 167 000. Capital: Papeete.

● **French Republican calendar** ▶ The calendar adopted (1793) in France during the French Revolution; the Gregorian ▷calendar was reintroduced in 1806. The revolutionaries' purpose was to design a calendar without ecclesiastical associations. The year began on 22 Sept (the date in 1792 when the Republic came into being) and had 365 days divided into 12 months of 30 days each. The remaining 5 days (17–22 Sept) were festivals, an extra one being added in a leap year. Each month was divided into 3 periods of 10 days (a décade) and was renamed: Vendémaire (French: vintage; 22 Sept–21 Oct), Brumaire (mist), Frimaire (frost), Nivôse (snow), Pluviôse (rain), Ventôse (wind), Germinal (seedtime), Floréal (blossom), Prairial (meadow), Messidor (harvest), Thermidor (heat), Fructidor (fruits).

● **French Revolution** ▶ The overthrow of the French monarchy as a reaction to the corrupt, feudal, and incompetent government of the Bourbon kings. In 1789 Louis XVI was forced to summon the ▷States General but its Third Estate, opposing aristocratic attempts to dominate proceedings, formed its own National Assembly. Riots followed, the ▢Bastille was stormed, the king was mobbed at Versailles, and the Assembly (from July the Constituent Assembly) promulgated the Declaration of the ▷Rights of Man. Feudalism was abolished and in September, 1791, a new constitution was accepted by the king following his thwarted attempt to flee France (the flight to Varennes). However, his continuing uncooperativeness fostered the growing republicanism of what became the Legislative Assembly (October, 1791) and then the National Convention (September, 1792). The Convention proclaimed a republic and in January, 1793, Louis was executed. The moderate ▷Girondins, discredited by France's war reverses (see Revolutionary and Napoleonic Wars), were now ousted by the ▷Jacobins and power passed to the Committee of ▷Public Safety. Under ▷Robespierre the Committee conducted a ▷Reign of Terror in which thousands of suspected antirevolutionaries were executed but his extremism brought (1794) his downfall on 9 Thermidor (27 July; see French Republican calendar). The so-called Thermidorean reaction led to the establishment of the ▷Directory (1795), which struggled for four years with economic crises until Napoleon's coup d'état of 18 Brumaire (1799) brought the Revolution to an end.

● **French Somaliland** ▷See Djibouti, Republic of.

● **French Southern and Antarctic Territories** ▶ A French territory (since 1955) comprising ▷Terre Adélie in Antarctica with the islands of Amsterdam and St Paul and the Kerguelen and Crozet archipelagos in the Indian Ocean.

● **French Sudan** ▷See Mali, Republic of.

● **French West Africa** ▶ (French name: Afrique Occidentale Française) The former French territories in West Africa comprising (1895–1958) the present-day independent countries of Benin, Guinea, Côte d'Ivoire, Niger, and Senegal.

● **Freneau, Philip** ▶ (1752–1832) US poet. He described his experience as a prisoner during the American Revolution in The British Prison Ship (1781). After independence he became a sea captain and later edited the popular National Gazette (1791–93). He then went back to sea before retiring to his farm, where he wrote philosophical nature poetry.

● **Freon** ▷See fluorocarbons.

● **frequency** ▶ The number of cycles completed by a vibrating system in unit time, usually one second (symbol: v or f). The unit of frequency is the ▷hertz. The angular frequency, ω, is related to the frequency by the equation $\omega = 2\pi f$ and is measured in radians per second.

● **frequency modulation** ▷See modulation.

● **fresco** ▶ A classical and Renaissance method of wall decoration in which pure pigments dissolved in water were applied to the wet lime-plastered surface of a wall, producing a chemical reaction that made the colours a permanent part of the wall. Up to about 1500 the design was sketched freehand onto the rough plaster surface (the arricciato). Separate areas of the sketch were then filled in with fine smooth plaster (the intonaco) and detailed colour was applied in layers of different pigments. Subsequently the ▷cartoon, as used by ▷Michelangelo, ▷Raphael, ▷Holbein the Younger, and others, allowed for more complicated premeditated design. The composition was drawn on sheets of paper, later applied to the wall, and the design pricked through with a stylus or with charcoal dust forced through the stylus piercings. Fresco painting was revived in the 20th century by the Mexican muralists ▷Orozco and ▷Rivera.

● **Frescobaldi** ▶ A family of bankers, which dominated Florence until it was divided in the dispute between the ▷Guelfs and Ghibellines at the end of the 13th century. The Frescobaldi opened a bank in London in the 1270s and financed the wars of Edward I and II. Receiving privileges as reward, they were increasingly unpopular, fleeing the country in 1310.

● **Fresnel, Augustin Jean** ▶ (1788–1827) French physicist, who (with Thomas ▷Young) used his work on interference to formulate the wave theory of light. ▷See also Fresnel lens.

● **Fresnel lens** ▶ A convex optical lens used principally in spotlights. It is thinner and therefore absorbs less light and heat than a normal convex lens with an equally short focal length. This is achieved by stepped concentric rings, each with the same curvature as the equivalent normal convex surface at that radius. Named after A. ▷Fresnel.

● **Fresno** ▶ 36 45N 119 45W A city in the USA, in California. A major centre for the sale of agricultural produce, it is the financial centre of the San Joaquin Valley. Population (1996 est): 396 011.

● **Freud, Sigmund** ▶ (1856–1939) Austrian psychiatrist and pioneer of psychoanalysis. Freud studied medicine and, in 1882, joined the staff of a psychiatric clinic in Vienna. An interest in hypnosis developed through his collaboration with Josef ▷Breuer and his meeting, in 1885, with Jean-Martin ▷Charcot. Following the publication with Breuer of Studies in Hysteria (1895), Freud evolved his theory that neuroses were rooted in suppressed sexual desires and sexual experiences of childhood, either real or imagined. In The Interpretation of Dreams (1899), he analysed the content of dreams in terms of unconscious desires and experiences, often dating from childhood. His emphasis on the sexual origin of mental disorders aroused great controversy, particularly his view that the sexual desires of children dated from birth, not puberty. In 1902 Freud established a circle of his colleagues in Vienna, which later (1910) became the International Psycho-Analytical Society. However, many of its members, including Carl ▷Jung and Alfred ▷Adler, resigned over disagreements with its founder. Freud left Vienna in 1938, following the Nazi invasion, joining his son, in London, where he remained until his death. Although subsequently modified, Freud's theories shed light on the workings of the unconscious mind and the motives, desires, and conflicts involved in human behaviour. His other books include *The Psychopathology of Everyday Life* (1904), *Totem and Taboo* (1913), *Beyond the Pleasure Principle* (1920), and *Moses and Monotheism* (1939).

His daughter **Anna Freud** (1895–1982) was a founder of child psychoanalysis. Coming to London with her father in 1938, she directed the Hampstead Child Therapy Clinic from 1952 until her death. Sigmund Freud's grandsons include **Lucian Freud** (1922–), the painter, who became a British citizen in 1939. His portraits and nudes, which tend to be meticulously detailed and bleakly realistic, have acquired a considerable reputation and command extremely high prices. He was appointed to the OM in 1993. Lucian's youngest brother, **Sir Clement Freud** (1924–), is a television personality, caterer, and former Liberal MP.

● **Freyja ▶** (*or* Freya) The Norse goddess of love and fertility, the sister of Frey, the god of sunshine, rain, and fertility. She is the Norse counterpart of Venus and is the leader of the ▷Valkyries. In some sources she is identified with ▷Frigga.

● **friar** ▷*See* monasticism.

● **friarbird ▶** A noisy chattering ▷honeyeater of the genus *Philemon* (16 species), also called leatherhead. Friarbirds resemble jackdaws but have naked patches on the head and horny outgrowths on the bill.

● **Fribourg ▶** (German name: Freiburg) 46 50N 7 10E A town in W Switzerland. Its many medieval buildings include the Cathedral of St Nicholas (13th–15th centuries) and it has a university (1889). Industries include the production of beer, chocolate, and machinery. Population (1989): 35 000.

● **friction ▶** A force exerted at the boundary between two solids or fluids that retards motion between them. In solid friction a distinction is drawn between sliding friction and rolling friction. Sliding friction is further divided into dynamic friction, defined as the minimum force needed to keep a body sliding, and static friction, defined as the minimum force needed to move a stationary body. The latter is slightly greater than the former. In rolling friction the force of resistance is less than in sliding friction as the rolling body moves up the side of a depression made in the stationary body. This accounts for the effectiveness of wheels and ball bearings. The coefficient of friction is defined as the ratio of the frictional force to the perpendicular reaction between the surfaces. Friction is caused primarily by the two surfaces interlocking at the microscopic level. It is reduced by the use of lubricants, such as grease or graphite (*see* tribology). Where it is sometimes desirable to increase friction between surfaces, as in brake linings, clutch plates, and shoe soles, rough hard-wearing materials are used.

● **Friedan, Betty ▶** (1921–) US feminist writer. In her best-known work, *The Feminine Mystique* (1963), Friedan described the frustration felt by many women of her generation at being confined to a domestic role. She subsequently founded (1966) the National Organization for Women, which campaigned for equal rights and employment opportunities for women. Her later writings include *The Fountain of Age* (1993).

● **Friedland, Battle of ▶** (14 June, 1807) A battle in the Napoleonic Wars fought near Friedland, East Prussia (now Pravdinsk, Russia). The French under Napoleon defeated the Russians, under Gen Levin Bennigsen (1745–1826). The victory enabled the French to occupy Königsberg and led to the Treaty of ▷Tilsit.

● **Friedman, Milton ▶** (1912–) US economist. Friedman is known for his theories on monetary supply, which contradict those of ▷Keynes. His published work, which argues for the free market economy, includes *A Theory of the Consumption Function* (1957), *Capitalism and Freedom* (1962), and *Money Mischief* (1992). With his wife **Rose Friedman** he wrote *Free to Choose* (1980) and *Tyranny of the Status Quo* (1984). He won the 1976 Nobel Prize.

● **Friedrich, Caspar David ▶** (1774–1840) German Romantic landscape painter, who studied at the Copenhagen Academy (1794–98). His first major work, an altarpiece painted in 1808, initiated a controversy over the use of landscape in religious subjects; successive works, such as *Wreck of the Hope* (1822; Kunsthalle, Hamburg) are not-

able for their symbolism of despair and man's insignificance in relation to nature.

● **Friel, Brian ▶** (1929–) Irish playwright, born in Northern Ireland. His plays include *Philadelphia, Here I Come!* (1965), *Faith Healer* (1979), *Translations* (1981), the award-winning *Dancing at Lughnasa* (1990), and *Give Me Your Answer Do* (1998).

● **Friendly Islands** ▷*See* Tonga, Kingdom of.

● **friendly societies ▶** Voluntary mutual-aid associations the members of which regularly contribute money to central funds that provide financial assistance in times of need caused by illness, old age, or death. First formed in the 17th century, the societies enjoyed their greatest popularity in the 19th century and inspired many other self-help and insurance schemes, including the UK National Insurance Act (1911). There are over 4000 friendly societies in Britain.

● **Friends of the Earth ▶** A British environmental pressure group. Established in 1971, it campaigns on environmental issues through demonstrations, public meetings, and parliamentary legislation. Targets have included motorway projects, commercial whaling, and industrial pollution (including nuclear power plants). The organization also has branches in 25 countries, directed from the Netherlands.

● **Friese-Greene, William ▶** (1855–1921) British photographer. With Mortimer Evans, he invented the first practical motion-picture camera in the 1880s. He was also the first to use celluloid film.

● **Friesian cattle ▶** A breed of black-and-white cattle originating from Friesland in the Netherlands. They were exported to America by early settlers and there developed as Holstein-Friesians. They are high-yielding milk producers and crosses, especially with a Charolais or Hereford bull, give good beef.

● **Friesland ▶** A province in the N Netherlands, bordering on the IJsselmeer. Much of the land is below sea level and there are dykes and canals. Cattle raising and dairy farming are important (*see* Friesian cattle). Area: 3803 sq km (1468 sq mi). Population (1995): 609 579. Capital: Leeuwarden.

● **frigate ▶** A naval vessel, smaller than a ▷destroyer, used mainly for carrying guided missiles and displacing about 2400 tonnes. Revived as the name of a class by the Royal Navy during World War II, earlier sailing frigates included the *Constitution* ("Old Ironsides"), a vessel that acquired fame in early US history.

● **frigate bird ▶** A seabird belonging to the genus *Fregata* and family *Fregatidae* (5 species), occurring in tropical and subtropical oceanic regions, also called man-of-war bird because it often steals food from other birds in midair. 80–115 cm long, frigate birds have narrow wings spanning up to 2.3 m, a long hooked bill, and a forked tail. Males are glossy black and develop an inflatable red throat sac in the breeding season; females are brownish black with white underparts. Order: *Pelecaniformes* (gannets, pelicans, etc.).

● **Frigga ▶** (*or* Frigg) The Norse goddess of married love and the hearth, the wife of ▷Odin. In some legends she is identified with ▷Freyja; her name is preserved in *Friday*.

● **frilled lizard ▶** A slender pale-brown arboreal lizard, *Chlamydosaurus kingi*, occurring in dry regions of Australia and feeding chiefly on ants. Up to 1 m long, it has a scaly membrane around its neck that forms a large frill, thereby deterring likely enemies. Family: *Agamidae*.

● **Friml, Rudolf ▶** (1879–1972) Czech-born composer and pianist, who settled in the USA in 1906. He is remembered for his operettas, such as *Rose Marie* (1924) and *The Vagabond King* (1925). He also wrote for the piano.

● **Frink, Dame Elisabeth ▶** (1930–93) British sculptor. Having trained at the Guildford School of Art and the Chelsea School of Art, she attracted critical attention with such works as *Horseman* and *Running Man*. She was made a DBE in 1982.

● **Frisch, Karl von ▶** (1886–1982) Austrian zoologist, best known for his work on animal behaviour. He found that by means of a circling "dance" or by wagging movements bees indicate the location of a source of food from the hive. Von Frisch also worked on the sensory abilities of fish. He shared a Nobel Prize (1973) with ▷Lorenz and Niko ▷Tinbergen.

● **Frisch, Max** ▶ (1911–91) Swiss dramatist and novelist. Many of his plays are Brechtian parables attacking complacency. They include the black comedy *The Fire Raisers* (1958) and *Andorra* (1961), a tragedy about antisemitism. His novels include *Stiller* (1954) and *Homo Faber* (1957).

● **Frisch, Otto Robert** ▶ (1904–79) Austrian-born physicist, nephew of Lise ▷Meitner, with whom he worked in Copenhagen on nuclear fission. During World War II he worked at Los Alamos on the atom bomb. In 1947 he became professor of physics at Cambridge University.

● **Frisch, Ragnar** ▶ (1895–1973) Norwegian economist. As professor of economics at Oslo University and editor of *Econometrica*, Frisch was concerned with the application of statistics to economics. He received, with Jan ▷Tinbergen, the first Nobel Prize for Economics (1969).

● **Frisches Haff** ▷*See* Vistula Lagoon.

● **Frisian** ▶ A West Germanic language formerly spoken along the North Sea coastal region of Holland as far as Schleswig in Germany. It is now principally confined to Friesland province in Holland and certain offshore islands including Heligoland. It is the language most closely related to English. The Frisians were a seafaring and commercial people before turning to dairy and beef farming.

● **Frisian Islands** ▶ A chain of islands in the North Sea extending along the coast of, and politically divided between, the Netherlands, Germany, and SW Denmark. The chain comprises three main groups: the West, North, and East Frisian Islands. The chief occupations are fishing, sheep and cattle raising, and tourism.

● **fritillary** ▶ (botany) A bulbous perennial plant of the genus *Fritillaria* (80 species), mostly native to N temperate regions. The leaves are narrow and the bell-shaped flowers droop from slender stalks. The European snake's head (*F. meleagris*), also called leopard lily and toad lily, has reddish-purple chequered flowers. The crown imperial (*F. imperialis*), native to N India, has a cluster of pendant red flowers at the top of a tall (120 cm) stem, topped by a tuft of leaves. Both species are popular garden plants. Family: *Liliaceae*.

● **fritillary** ▶ (zoology) A ▷nymphalid butterfly, usually brown or orange marked with black. The caterpillars feed at night—often on violets—but many species hibernate soon after hatching. Chief genera: *Boloria*, *Melitaea*.

● **Friuli-Venezia Giulia** ▶ A region in the extreme NE of Italy. It was formed in 1947, incorporating Trieste in 1954 and is semiautonomous. It consists of mountains along the N border with Austria and a coastal plain in the S. The region's farmers produce cereals and maize in the lowlands, fruit and vines in the foothills, and livestock in the mountains. Industries include textiles, food processing, chemicals, and shipbuilding. Area: 7850 sq km (3031 sq mi). Population (1994 est): 1 193 217. Capital: Trieste.

● **Frobisher, Sir Martin** ▶ (c. 1535–94) English navigator. He made three attempts (1576, 1577, 1578) to discover the ▷Northwest Passage, giving his name to a bay on Baffin Island and bringing back "black earth," which was mistakenly thought to contain gold. He later served against the Spanish ▷Armada and raided Spanish treasure ships.

● **Frobisher Bay** ▶ A settlement in N Canada, in Nunavut on Baffin Island. It has police, radio, and weather stations. Population (1985): 2954.

● **Fröding, Gustaf** ▶ (1860–1911) One of the most important and popular of Swedish lyric poets. His career was repeatedly interrupted by ill health apparently due to hereditary mental instability. His native Värmland inspired his first highly successful collection, *Guitarr och dragharmonika* (*Guitar and Concertina*; 1891). His later poetry, collected in *Nya Dikter* (*New Poems*; 1894) and *Stänk och flikar* (*Splashes and Rags*; 1896), was influenced by Nietzschean ideas and brought a new level of technical perfection to Swedish verse.

● **Froebel, Friedrich Wilhelm August** ▶ (1782–1852) German pioneer of ▷preschool education. Throughout his life, Froebel was fascinated by the underlying unity of all things. His view of man was one of harmonious growth, and he applied this concept to the development of children in *The Education of Man* (1826). Although influenced by ▷Pestalozzi, Froebel disagreed with his theory that young children should remain only with their mothers. His view that children should spend time together in creative play led him to found the first kindergarten (1837) at Blankenburg.

● **frog** ▶ A tail-less amphibian of the family *Ranidae*, which includes bullfrogs, hairy frogs, and leopard frogs. Many other so-called frogs, such as ▷tree frogs, are actually toads. The European frog (*Rana temporaria*) grows to 10 cm. Greenish-brown with black markings, it spends most of its life on land, feeding on insects, and only returns to water to breed. Other species, such as the edible frog (*R. esculenta*), may spend most of their lives in water. Order: ▷*Anura*.

● **frog-bit** ▶ A Eurasian perennial water plant, *Hydrocharis morsus-ranae*, found in ponds, ditches, etc. It has floating stems arising from submerged roots, rounded leaves, and white flowers, 2 cm in diameter. Family: *Hydrocharitaceae*.

● **frogfish** ▶ A slow-moving carnivorous fish belonging to a family (*Antennariidae*; about 60 species) occurring on the bottom, usually in shallow tropical waters. Frogfish have a robust body, up to 30 cm long, with camouflaging patterned fleshy flaps and warty skin, limblike pectoral fins, and often a wirelike projection from the snout, which lures prey. Order: *Lophiiformes*.

● **froghopper** ▶ A small jumping insect belonging to the family *Cercopidae* (about 2000 species). Froghoppers feed on plant juices, sometimes becoming pests. Eggs are laid on stems or roots and the ▷nymphs remain stationary until adult. They often protect themselves against predators and desiccation with a cover of white froth ("cuckoo spit"), produced by blowing air mixed with fluid from the anus through a valve in the abdomen. For this reason they are often known as cuckoo-spit insects and spittlebugs. Order: ▷*Hemiptera*.

● **frogmouth** ▶ A nocturnal bird belonging to a family (*Podargidae*; 12 species), occurring in forests of SE Asia and Australasia. 25–55 cm long, frogmouths are well camouflaged with a mottled grey and brown plumage. They have a wide-gaping bill and prey chiefly on beetles, frogs, mice, and small birds. Order: *Caprimulgiformes* (nightjars, etc.).

● **Froissart, Jean** ▶ (1337–c. 1400) French chronicler and poet. He travelled widely in Europe and served at the court of Edward III of England. His *Chronicles*, covering the years from 1325 to 1400, are a detailed and colourful record of the Hundred Years' War. He also wrote a verse romance, *Méliador*, and many ballades.

● **Fromm, Erich** ▶ (1900–80) US psychologist and philosopher, born in Germany. Fromm left Germany for the USA in 1934 and became well known for his controversial analyses of social ills in modern industrial society. In *The Sane Society* (1955), he charged the consumer society with being responsible for isolation, loneliness, and doubt among individuals. His other works include *The Art of Loving* (1956) and *The Revolution of Hope* (1968).

● **Fronde** ▶ (French: sling) French uprising between 1648 and 1653 so called because the combatants employed slingshots. The first Fronde, a protest against excessive tax demands and the administration of ▷Mazarin, was led by the Paris parlement. It was quickly suppressed (1649) by the royal army led by ▷Condé. In 1650 Condé himself led a second, aristocratic, revolt against Mazarin's authority. Contention among its leaders and an upsurge of support for the monarchy led to its collapse.

● **front** ▶ In □meteorology, the interface between two air masses of different thermal characteristics and origins. Where the air masses converge the warm air, being lighter, rises and slopes over the cold air. Distinctive weather phenomena are associated with fronts, particularly the development of depressions, and they are very important in short-term weather forecasting.

● **Front de Libération nationale** ▶ (FLN) An Algerian nationalist group that organized the war of independence against France (1954–

62). Formed in 1954, the FLN began a campaign of terrorism and sabotage. In 1956 it organized itself like a government, sending diplomatic missions abroad, and in 1958 set up a provisional government in Tunis under Ferhat Abbas (1899–1985). In 1962 the French agreed to Algerian independence and when ▷Ben Bella became president in 1963 the FLN became Algeria's sole political party.

● **Frontenac, Louis de Buade, Comte de Palluau et de ▶** (1620–98) French soldier; governor of New France (1672–82, 1689–98), who promoted French expansion in North America. His fur-trading activities, challenged by the Iroquois Indian confederacy, and his policy of expansion, caused dissension that led to his recall. When war broke out with England in 1689 he was reinstated. He attacked New England settlements with the help of Indian allies, defended Quebec, and eventually subdued the Iroquois.

● **frost ▶** A weather condition that occurs when the temperature falls below 0°C (32°F). It is recognized by the icy deposit that forms but if the air is very dry this will not occur. In weather forecasting grades of severity of frost are distinguished as slight (–0.1 to –3.5°C), moderate (–3.6 to –6.4°C), severe (–6.5 to –11.5°C), and very severe (below –11.5°C). A distinction is made between ground frost, measured at grass level, and air frost, measured at a height of 1.4 m (4 ft).

● **Frost, Robert Lee ▶** (1874–1963) US poet. In 1885 his family moved from San Francisco to New England, where he worked as a teacher and farmer. The poetry collections *A Boy's Will* (1913) and *North of Boston* (1914), published during a stay in England, brought him fame. His work, often pastoral and lyrical, has a dark undercurrent of fear and suffering relieved only by stoical acceptance.

● **frostbite ▶** Damage to part of the body, usually a hand or foot, resulting from exposure to extreme cold. The blood vessels to the affected limb constrict so that little blood (and therefore essential oxygen) reaches the skin, nerves, and muscles. This may lead to loss of sensation, ulcers, and eventually gangrene, necessitating amputation. Initial treatment is gently to warm the affected part.

● **froth flotation ▶** A method of separating mineral ore from waste or one ore from another. The unpurified pulverized ore is agitated with water and a reagent that binds preferentially with the desired ore and alters its surface properties. Air is then passed through the mixture and the ore is carried to the surface by the bubbles to form a froth, which can then be removed.

● **frottola ▶** (Italian: untruth, silly story) A popular Italian song form of the early 16th century. It was a setting of fashionable verse in four parts, the voice being accompanied by three instrumental parts and the music being repeated for each stanza.

● **Froude, James Anthony ▶** (1818–94) British historian. A defector from the ▷Oxford Movement, Froude was influenced by ▷Carlyle. Froude's *History of England* (1856–70) established his reputation as a historian, which rested on his literary talent rather than his historical understanding. His older brother, **Richard Hurrell Froude** (1803–36), played an important part, with John ▷Keble and John Henry ▷Newman, in initiating the ▷Oxford Movement. His essays and diaries encouraged the development of Anglo-Catholicism. Another brother, **William Froude** (1810–79), was a naval architect, who developed the bilge keel and developed the **Froude number** as a measure of the effect of gravity on fluid motion.

● **fructose ▶** A simple sugar ($C_6H_{12}O_6$) that is sweeter than sucrose and present in green leaves, fruits, and honey. Its phosphate derivatives are important in the carbohydrate metabolism of living organisms.

● **fruit ▶** The fertilized ovary of a flower, which contains the seed (or seeds) and may incorporate other parts of the flower (e.g. the receptacle in strawberries, the bracts in pineapples). The variation in the structure of fruits reflects the different means they have evolved to ensure dispersal of the seeds, which is essential to prevent overcrowding and enable the plant to spread and colonize new habitats. Fleshy fruits, for example, are usually eaten by animals, the seeds passing out with their faeces. Animals can also carry hooked or sticky fruits on their bodies. Seeds dispersed by wind are usually very light: they are either forcibly ejected from their fruits, for example from

the ▷capsule of poppy and the pods of leguminous plants, or they remain attached to the fruit, which can itself remain airborne for considerable distances, for example the winged fruits of sycamores and ash trees. Some fruits are distributed by water: coconut fruits can be transported several hundred miles by sea. The word fruit is popularly restricted to the fleshy edible fruits, many of which are of economic importance to man: **fruit farming** constitutes an important branch of commercial ▷horticulture. In terms of world production the most important fruit crops are: apples, pears, and cherries (in cool temperate regions); grapes, peaches, and figs (warm temperate); citrus fruits and dates (subtropical); bananas and pineapples (tropical). □ p. 486.

● **fruit bat ▶** A vegetarian ▷bat belonging to the family *Pteropidae* and suborder *Megachiroptera* (150 species). Fruit bats occur in tropical and subtropical regions of the Old World. With a body length of up to 40 cm, they are typically larger than insect-eating bats and have better vision; only one genus (*Rousettus*, 13 species) uses ▷echolocation. Most eat fruit although some feed on flowers or nectar. Certain tropical trees are adapted for pollination by fruit bats. ▷*See also* flying fox. □mammal.

● **fruit fly ▶** A fly belonging to the family *Trypetidae* (1200 species)—the true fruit flies. (Insects of the family *Drosophilidae* are known as small fruit flies: *see* Drosophila.) True fruit flies have spotted or banded wings and the larvae of many species feed on fruit, often causing serious damage. For example, the Mediterranean fruit fly (*Ceratitis capitata*) is a pest of almost all succulent fruits, while the North American apple maggot (*Rhagoletis pomonella*) tunnels into apples.

● **Frunze** ▷*See* Bishkek.

● **Fry, Christopher ▶** (C. Harris; 1907–) British dramatist. The verbal excitement of his earliest verse plays, *A Phoenix Too Frequent* (1946) and *The Lady's Not for Burning* (1948), seemed to presage a revival of poetic drama, but the popularity of his work declined after the early 1950s. His other plays include *Venus Observed* (1950), *The Light Is Dark Enough* (1954), and *Curtmantle* (1962).

● **Fry, Elizabeth ▶** (1780–1845) British prison reformer. A Quaker, Elizabeth Fry first visited Newgate Prison in 1813. She aimed to improve the lot of women prisoners by seeing that they were properly fed and clothed, segregated from men, supervised by women, and provided with light work. Later, she travelled throughout Europe, reforming prisons, hospitals, and mental asylums.

● **Fry, Roger (Eliot) ▶** (1866–1934) British painter and art critic. He was educated at Cambridge University, where he later became Slade Professor of Fine Art (1933). He is best known for his influential writings on art, e.g. *Vision and Design* (1920), and artists, e.g. *Bellini* (1899) and *Cézanne* (1927). Through exhibitions (1910, 1912) he promoted the French postimpressionist painters in Britain.

● **Fu'ad I ▶** (1868–1936) King of Egypt (1922–36). He became sultan in 1917 under the British protectorate and king when Britain granted limited independence in 1922. He tried to curb the nationalist Wafd Party and in 1931 suspended the 1923 constitution, but was forced to restore it in 1935.

● **Fu-chien** ▷*See* Fujian.

● **Fu-chou** ▷*See* Fuzhou.

● **Fuchs, (Emil Julius) Klaus ▶** (1911–88) British physicist and spy, born in Germany. During World War II he worked on atomic bomb research in Britain and the USA and in 1950 was tried and found guilty of having passed secret information to the Soviet Union since 1943. His motives were idealistic. Released from prison in 1959, he lived and worked in East Germany until his death.

● **Fuchs, Sir Vivian (Ernest) ▶** (1908–99) British explorer. He was director of the Falkland Islands Dependencies Survey Scientific Bureau (1947–50) and later led the Commonwealth Trans-Antarctic Expedition: with help from Sir Edmund ▷Hillary he covered and surveyed 3500 km (2173 mi) between 24 November, 1957, and 2 March, 1958. He was again director of the Falkland Islands Survey (British Antarctic Survey from 1962) from 1960 until 1973.

● **Fuchsia** ► A genus of shrubs and herbs (100 species) mostly native to tropical America and widely cultivated as ornamentals. The plants range from creeping forms, bushes, and small trees to epiphytes. They have deep-pink, red, or purple drooping flowers all along the branches; each flower has four long flaring coloured sepals surrounding the shorter petals, below which the stamens and stigma protrude. Most cultivated forms are varieties of *F. magellanica*, *F. coccinea*, and *F. arborescens* or hybrids between them. Family: *Onagraceae* (willowherb family).

● **Fucus** ▷*See* wrack.

● **fuel cell** ► A device that converts the energy of a chemical reaction directly into an electric current. In the simplest type oxygen and hydrogen are fed through two separate porous nickel plates into an electrolytic solution. The gases combine to form water and thus set up a potential difference between the two plates. Fuel cells are distinguished from ▷accumulators in that the latter need to be recharged and do not consume their chemicals (which in fuel cells need to be replenished). Fuel cells provide a clean source of power; prototype buses, running on hydrogen fuel cells, are due to be tried in London during 2003. On a much smaller scale, attempts are being made to design methanol fuel cells small enough to power computers and mobile phones by 2004.

● **fuel injection** ► The pumping of fuel in the form of a spray directly into the cylinders of an ▷internal-combustion engine. It is used in diesel engines, and in petrol engines it is increasingly used to replace the ▷carburettor as it gives a more even fuel distribution in the combustion chamber. In many cases the petrol is injected into the inlet part, rather than the combustion chamber. Car models using fuel injection usually have the initial "i" after their model number. Fuel injection is also used in continuous-combustion engines.

● **fuels** ▷*See* fossil fuels.

● **Fugard, Athol** ► (1932–) White South African dramatist and actor. His plays include *Sizwe Banzi is Dead* (1973) and *A Place with the Pigs* (1988), which depict the plight of outcasts under the apartheid system, *Sign of Hope* (1992), and *Sorrows and Rejoicings* (2002).

● **Fugger, Hans** ► (1348–1409) German weaver, who founded a family business that dominated European finance in the 15th and 16th centuries. Through diligence and advantageous marriage the family weaving business expanded under his grandson **Jakob Fugger** (1459–1525) to include mining interests and to handle papal financial business. For a time Fugger financial strength influenced European politics—in 1519 they backed Charles V's election as Holy Roman Emperor—but the family's fortunes subsequently declined and the firm was dissolved after the Thirty Years' War (1618–48).

● **Fugitives** ► An influential group of US poets and critics associated with Vanderbilt University, Nashville, Tennessee, during the 1920s. They included Allen ▷Tate, Robert Penn ▷Warren, and Cleanth Brooks (1906–94). The themes of their writing derived from their concern with the history and traditional culture of the American South. They published the poetry magazine *The Fugitive* (1922–25).

● **fugue** ► A piece of polyphonic music, generally having three or

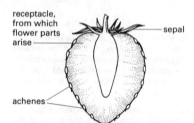

strawberry The true fruits, which are formed from the ovary and contain the seeds, are the achenes on the surface of the fleshy receptacle.

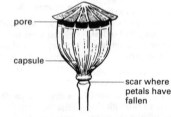

poppy The seeds within the capsule are shaken out through the pores.

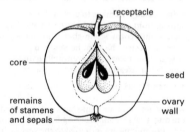

apple The flesh of the apple is the receptacle; the core develops from the ovary and contains the seeds (pips).

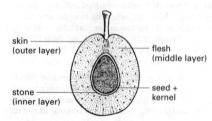

plum This fruit, like all drupes (stone fruits), is made up of three layers.

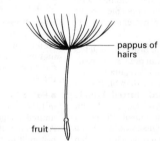

dandelion The pappus acts as a parachute.

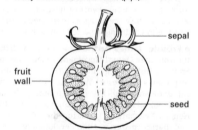

tomato The flesh of the tomato (a berry) is formed from the ovary.

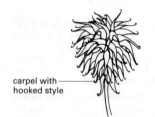

herb bennet The hooks cling to the fur of animals, which thus disperse the seeds.

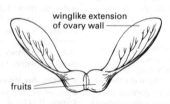

sycamore The two winged fruits separate and are carried away by the wind.

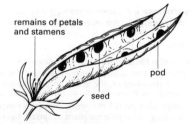

lupin When ripe, the pod splits open and curls back, ejecting the seeds.

fruit

four parts (*or* voices), in which each part enters in turn with a statement of the main theme (*or* subject). After stating the subject each voice continues with the secondary theme (*or* counter-subject). Fugues are not composed to strict patterns; episodes in different tonalities are often interspersed with subsequent groups of entries of the voices. At the climax the voices are overlapped in close succession (*stretto*).

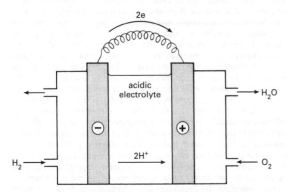

fuel cell ▶ Hydrogen gas (H_2) is passed over a negative electrode containing a catalyst, which ionizes the gas into ions (H^+) and electrons (e). In an acidic electrolyte the ions migrate to the positive electrode over which oxygen is bubbled. The electrons flow through an external circuit as a current. At the positive electrode water is formed according to the equation $2H^+ + \frac{1}{2}O_2 + 2e \rightarrow H_2O$.

● **Fujairah** ▷*See* United Arab Emirates.

● **Fujian** ▶ (Fu-chien *or* Fukien) A province in SE China, on Taiwan Strait, famous for its beauty. Over a hundred dialects have arisen among its mountain population. Since the 17th century food shortages resulting from insufficient agricultural land have prompted much emigration. It is opposite Taiwan and its military strength has been considerably increased since 1950. Chief products are sugar, rice, tea, timber, and fish. There is some light industry. Area: 123 000 sq km (47 970 sq mi). Population (1995 est): 31 830 000. Capital: Fuzhou.

● **Fujiwara** ▶ The most illustrious of Japan's noble families. Fujiwara greatness reached a peak between the 9th and 12th centuries. From 858 the office of regent became a Fujiwara monopoly and government was mainly conducted through the Fujiwara family council. Intermarriage with the imperial family became so common that most emperors were partly of Fujiwara blood. The other base of Fujiwara power was their proprietorship of numerous private estates. From the late 11th century, however, their predominance was challenged by the reinvigorated imperial family and in the 12th century they were forced to yield most of their authority to new provincial warrior leaders.

● **Fujiwara style** ▶ A sophisticated and refined sculptural style, also called the Heian style, prevailing in Japan from the 9th to the 12th centuries, when the Fujiwara clan was politically dominant.

● **Fujiyama** ▶ (English name: Mount Fuji) 35 23N 138 42E The highest mountain in Japan, it is a dormant volcano in S central Honshu. Long regarded as a symbol of Japan, it has a symmetrical snow-capped (Oct-May) cone and a Shinto shrine. Height: 3776 m (12 388 ft).

● **Fukien** ▷*See* Fujian.

● **Fukuoka** ▶ 33 39N 130 21E A port in Japan in N Kyushu on Hakata Bay. An ancient commercial centre, ▷Kublai Khan was twice defeated here (1274, 1281). Kyushu University was established in 1910. Industries include textiles and shipbuilding. Population (1995): 1 284 741.

● **Fukushima** ▶ 37 44N 140 28E A city in Japan, in N Honshu. A major commercial centre, its chief industry is silks. Population (1995): 285 745.

● **Fukuyama** ▶ 34 29N 133 21E A city in Japan, in SW Honshu. It de-

veloped around a 17th-century castle and is now a commercial and industrial centre. Population (1995): 374 510.

● **Fulani** ▶ A Muslim people scattered over a large area of W Africa from Lake Chad to the Atlantic coast. They are a mixed Negroid and, probably, Berber racial type. Their language, known as Fulfulde (*or* Fula), belongs to the Atlantic division of the Niger-Congo family. Their social and cultural patterns are varied, reflecting influences from surrounding peoples. They were originally nomadic herdsmen but many have adopted agriculture and a sedentary way of life. The herdsmen remain egalitarian while the latter are organized more hierarchically. They are generally polygynous and favour cousin marriage, which reflects Islamic influence. In N Nigeria many adopted the ▷Hausa language and culture and, as a result of religious wars (1804–10), established a Muslim empire in which they were the ruling elite.

● **Fulbright educational program** ▶ An international exchange scholarship programme, devised by Senator J. W. Fulbright (1905–95) of Arkansas (USA) after World War II. The programme is ultimately the responsibility of the US Department of State, which, in association with other governments, has made more than 100 000 awards to students and teachers under the scheme.

● **Fulham** ▶ A district in the Greater London borough of Hammersmith, on the N bank of the River Thames. It contains Fulham Palace, residence of the Bishop of London.

● **Fuliang** ▶ (former name: Ching-te-chen *or* Jingdezhen) 29 17N 117 12E A town in E China, in Jiangxi province on the Chang River. It has been known for its porcelain since the 6th century AD. Population (1990): 281 183.

● **Fuller, J(ohn) F(rederick) C(harles)** ▶ (1878–1966) British soldier and military theorist. He served with the infantry in South Africa and in World War I became staff officer of the tank corps and planned the successful armoured attack at Cambrai (1917). His advocacy of tank warfare and of combined operations by air and land had considerable influence, especially in E Europe. His publications include *Tanks in the Great War* (1920), *Field Service Regulations III* (lectures, 1937), and *A Military History of the Great War* (1954–56).

● **Fuller, Richard Buckminster** ▶ (1895–1983) US inventor and architect. One of Fuller's main concerns was making the best use of energy sources. His Dymaxion house (1928) and car (1933; improved version 1943) were designed to reduce waste and environmental pollution. His chief contribution was the **geodesic dome**, a lightweight and cheap structure of mutually supporting interlocking rods that can span large areas. His biggest dome, in Louisiana, has a diameter of 117 m (384 ft). He also experimented with inexpensive mass-produced housing (the "Wichita House," 1948), which can be dismantled and rebuilt as required. His writings include *Operating Manual for Spaceship Earth* (1969).

● **Fuller, Roy (Broadbent)** ▶ (1912–91) British poet and novelist, who was also a practising solicitor. His early poetry, beginning with *Poems* (1939), was concerned with social and political themes; his later volumes, including *Buff* (1965), *New Poems* (1968), and *Available for Dreams* (1989), are more personal and philosophical. He was professor of poetry at Oxford from 1968 to 1973. He wrote several novels, notably *Image of a Society* (1956).

● **Fuller, Thomas** ▶ (1608–61) British historian. Known chiefly in his own lifetime as a preacher, he wrote many historical works, of which the best known is the *History of the Worthies of England* (1662), a biographical dictionary of famous Englishmen.

● **fullerene** ▷*See* carbon.

● **fuller's earth** ▶ A nonplastic ▷clay rich in montmorillonite, with the property of absorbing and decolorizing oil and grease. It was formerly used for whitening and removing the grease from fleeces (fulling). It is still used in the textile industry and in refining fats and oils. It was probably formed by very fine-grained volcanic ash settling in water.

● **fulmar** ▶ A maritime North Atlantic bird, *Fulmarus glacialis*. It is about 46 cm long and dark grey above with white underparts. Its range and numbers have increased, as a result of food in the form of offal from trawlers and whalers. Family: *Procellariidae* (petrels).

● **Fulton, Robert** ► (1765–1815) American inventor, who built one of the earliest steamships, the *Clermont* (1807), and made steam a practical source of power on the sea. He had earlier constructed a submarine for the French government but its use against the British was not a success.

● **fumaric acid** ▷*See* maleic acid.

● **fumitory** ► A branching annual herb of the genus *Fumaria* (about 60 species), native to Eurasia and also found in North America. It has much-divided compound leaves (feathery in some species) and dense spikes of pink, white, or reddish-purple flattened tubular flowers. The fruit is a nutlet. A common species is *F. officinalis*. Family: *Fumariaceae*.

● **Funchal** ► 32 40N 15 55W The capital of the Madeira Islands, on the S coast of Madeira. Its mild climate and picturesque setting make it a popular tourist resort and it has a cathedral (1485–1514). The islands' chief commercial centre, it exports Madeira wines, embroidery, and wickerwork. Population (latest est): 44 111.

● **functionalism** ► (architecture) A doctrine principally associated with the ▷international style. Its main tenet is that the more fitted to its purpose a building is, the more beautiful it will be. The doctrine was developed under Louis ▷Sullivan in the 1890s, but found its most vocal advocate in ▷Le Corbusier, who defined a house as a machine for living in. Functionalism led to a very severe style, lacking in all ornamentation and idiosyncracy. Although still influential, its dominance faded after 1930, and function is no longer accepted as the sole attribute of beauty in architecture.

● **functionalism** ► (sociology) A perspective, based on an analogy with the workings of a biological organism, which emphasizes the contribution constituent parts of a society (groups and institutions) make to the continuity or change of the whole society. Also known as structural-functionalism, the approach was used by ▷Durkheim and was a major influence in sociology in the USA and the UK after World War II as a result of the work of Talcott ▷Parsons.

● **fundamental constants** ► Any of several constants that frequently appear in physical equations. The fundamental constants are often regarded as the five constants: the speed of ▷light (c), the ▷Planck constant (h), the charge (e) and mass (m_e) of the ▷electron, and the fine structure constant (α). The latter is defined as $e^2/2hc\varepsilon_0$, where ε_0 is the electric constant; its value is approximately 1/137 and it is a measure of the strength of the ▷electromagnetic interaction. These constants may be regarded as fundamental in that their values determine the magnitude of many physical effects. Other constants sometimes taken as fundamental include the electric constant, the magnetic constant, Avogadro's number, the Boltzmann constant, and the gravitational constant.

● **fundamental interactions** ► The basic ▷forces that occur in nature. ▷*See* electromagnetic interaction; gravitational interaction; strong interaction; weak interaction.

● **fundamentalism** ► A form of religion in which traditional beliefs are held uncompromisingly and often aggressively. Jewish and Christian fundamentalists reject any scientific theories, such as those of cosmology and evolution, that conflict with a literal interpretation of the Bible. Christian fundamentalism has strong support among some Protestants in parts of the USA. Islamic fundamentalists similarly adhere strictly to the teachings of the Koran and expect the state to adopt Islamic law. A strong upsurge of Islamic fundamentalism began in the late 1970s when Ayatollah ▷Khomeini replaced the Shah as leader of Iran and attempted to rid the country entirely of Western and secular influences. Other fundamentalist regimes include the Sunni Muslim ▷Taleban regime in Afghanistan, which has banned all education and paid employment for women. Islamic fundamentalism has also inspired terrorist groups in Algeria, Egypt, Israel, and Lebanon, among other countries.

● **Fundy, Bay of** ► An inlet of the Atlantic Ocean in SE Canada, between Nova Scotia and New Brunswick. Long and narrow, it has tides up to 20 m (66 ft) high, from which electricity is generated.

● **Fünen** ▷*See* Fyn.

● **Fünfkirchen** ▷*See* Pécs.

● **fungi** ► Unicellular or multicellular organisms belonging to the kingdom *Fungi* (about 50 000 known species) and including mushrooms, mildews, moulds, yeasts, etc. Fungi were formerly classified as plants; however, all fungi lack chlorophyll and therefore (unlike plants) cannot manufacture their own food by photosynthesis. Their cell walls, unlike those of plants, are composed mainly of ▷chitin, and the cells often contain more than one nucleus. Some fungi are saprotrophic, feeding on dead organic matter by means of digestive enzymes; others are parasites of plants or animals. The body of most fungi consists of a network of branching threadlike structures (hyphae), forming a mycelium. Sexual reproduction results in the formation of spores, which may be produced in a specialized structure called a fruiting body: this is the visible part of mushrooms, puffballs, etc. Other fungi consist of single cells, which can reproduce asexually by simple division into two daughter cells. Fungi are distributed worldwide in terrestrial, freshwater, and marine habitats. Some live in the soil and play a vital role in bringing about ▷decomposition of dead organic matter. Other fungi (e.g. *Penicillium* and *Streptomyces*) are of great importance as a source of ▷antibiotics. Many parasitic fungi cause disease in animals and man (*see* infection) or in plants (e.g. the smuts and rusts), while some saprotrophs are destructive to timber (*see* dry rot). Some fungi form associations with other organisms, most notably with algae to form ▷lichens. ▷*See also* Ascomycota; Basidiomycota.

● **funnel weaver** ► A ▷spider, also called funnel web spider, belonging to a worldwide family (*Agelenidae*). It builds funnel-shaped webs in grass, among debris, and under rocks and floorboards. The grass spider (*Agelena naevia*), 18–19 mm long, is a common North American species.

● **fur** ► The skin of certain mammals including its covering of hair. The hair is usually short and soft next to the skin for insulation with longer guard hairs forming an outer protective layer. The untreated skins (pelts) of such animals as sheep, mink, rabbits, chinchilla, etc., are cleaned and stretched before undergoing tanning to make the skin into ▷leather. Many wild fur-bearing species are now protected and "furs" made from synthetic fibres have replaced many natural fashion furs.

● **Furies** ▷*See* Erinyes.

● **furlong** ► A unit of length traditionally based on the length of a furrow. It is equal to 220 yards (⅛ mile) and is still used in horseracing.

● **Furneaux Islands** ► 40 0S 148 0E An Australian group of islands, in Bass Strait off the NE coast of Tasmania. The chief islands are Flinders (the largest), Cape Barren, and Clarke. Sheep farming is the principal activity.

● **Furness** ► A peninsula in NW England, in Cumbria between the Irish Sea and Morecambe Bay. The Cistercian monks of Furness Abbey (founded 1127) exploited the local iron-ore deposits and during the 19th century Furness became a major industrial centre. Tourism and farming are now important. Chief town: Barrow-in-Furness.

● **furniture** ► Movable domestic artefacts, which are indispensable for civilized life. Examples exist from as early as 3000 BC in Egypt. In Europe medieval furniture was gothic in style and consisted principally of ▷chests, beds, seats, and tables, but Renaissance designers and craftsmen, working exclusively for the noble and rich, produced work in which function was subordinated to art, such as cabinets, richly ornamented with jewels and precious metals. During the 17th and 18th centuries architects, such as Robert ▷Adam, were increasingly concerned with the design of furniture for the interiors of their buildings. Such furniture ranked with paintings and other arts, both socially and economically.

In the 19th century, factory production led to debased design against which a few progressive designers, notably William ▷Morris, struggled. The 20th century has seen the introduction of simplified design and new materials, such as steel and plastic, reflecting modern functional needs.

furniture

Ancient Egyptian (c. 1330 BC) Furniture found in the tomb of Tutankhamen is made from imported timber, inlaid with semiprecious stones, ebony, and ivory, and opulently gilded to testify to the wealth and status of its owner.

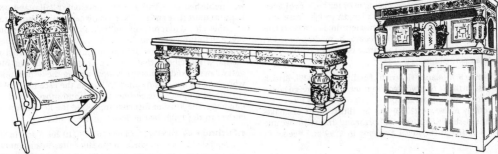

Elizabethan (16th century AD) In England and N Europe gothic detail survived on domestic furniture until the 17th century. Solid oak was the most common wood.

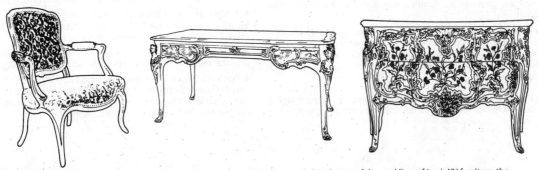

Louis XV (1723–74) The reaction in French taste against Louis XIV's monumental baroque led to the graceful curved lines of Louis XV furniture, the epitome of rococo elegance.

Modern (20th century) Although Mies van der Rohe's Barcelona chair (1929) is the product of a skilled craftsman, new materials (plastic, plate glass, etc.) and mass-production have generally predominated in 20th-century furniture making.

● **Fürstenbund** ► A league of German princes founded in 1785 and led by Frederick the Great of Prussia. Intended as a temporary expedient against Habsburg ambitions in Germany, the league was Prussia's first attempt to unite the other German states under its leadership, finally achieved in 1871.

● **Fürth** ► 49 28N 11 00E A city in S Germany, near Nuremberg in Bavaria on the River Regnitz. The Fürth-Nuremberg railway line (1835) was the first in Germany. Toys and mirrors are manufactured. Population (1996 est): 108 418.

● **further education** ▷*See* tertiary education.

● **Furtwängler, Wilhelm** ► (1886–1954) German conductor. He took over the Leipzig Gewandhaus concerts in 1922 and conducted the Berlin Philharmonic Orchestra from 1922 to 1954. He conducted opera at Bayreuth and Covent Garden and excelled as a conductor of Beethoven and Wagner.

● **furze** ▷*See* gorse.

● **fuse, electrical** ► A length of wire designed to melt when the electric current passing through it exceeds a specified safe level, thus breaking the circuit. It is used to protect electrical equipment and low-voltage wiring, ▷circuit breakers being used for higher voltages. Domestic fuses commonly consisted of a length of bare fuse wire (usually tin or copper alloys) connecting two terminals in a porcelain holder, which fitted into a central fuse board. In modern practice, cartridge fuses (wire enclosed in a ceramic or glass cartridge) are fitted into 13-ampere plugs.

● **Fuseli, Henry** ► (Johann Heinrich Füssli; 1741–1825) British painter of Swiss birth. He first worked as a translator of foreign books in London before studying art in Rome (1770–78). On his return his paintings, notably *Nightmare* (1782) and his illustrations of Shakespeare and Milton, showed his taste for horror and drama. He became professor of painting at the Royal Academy in 1799 and Keeper in 1804.

● **fusel oil** ► A liquid mixture of organic substances including butanol and iso-amyl alcohol. It has an unpleasant smell and taste and is a by-product of the distillation of alcohol produced by fermentation.

● **Fushun** ► 41 51N 123 53E A city in NE China, in Liaoning province. Its oil, steel, and chemical industries are based on its oil-shale and vast coal deposits. Aluminium production is also important. Population (1991 est): 1 202 388.

● **fusion** ► (physics) ▷*See* nuclear energy.

● **Fust, Johann** ► (1400–66) German printer, who financed ▷Gutenberg's development of the printing press. Fust sued Gutenberg for the repayment of his loan and, when Gutenberg was unable to repay it, took possession of his equipment and set up the first successful printing firm.

● **Futa Jallon** ▷*See* Fouta Djallon.

● **Futuna Islands** ▷*See* Wallis and Futuna.

● **futures** ► Commodities, currencies, or securities bought or sold for a fixed price for delivery at a fixed date in the future. Unlike ▷options, a futures contract involves a definite purchase or sale. Futures provide an opportunity for those who make regular purchases of goods to hedge against changes in price and for speculators to play the markets. Futures are traded in a number of London markets, including the London Metal Exchange, the International Petroleum Exchange, the London International Financial Futures and Options Exchange (currencies, interest rates, and share indexes), and the associated LIFFE Commodity Products (cocoa, coffee, etc.).

● **futurism** ► **1.** In Italy, an early 20th-century movement in the arts. It was founded in 1909, when the poet ▷Marinetti published a literary manifesto demanding the obliteration of past Italian culture and the establishment of a new society, literature, and art glorifying the speed and mechanization of modern life. A second manifesto (1910) was published by artists led by ▷Boccioni, ▷Balla, and ▷Severini. Using a cubist style and such subjects as cars, trains, moving animals, etc., they aimed to represent multiple phases of motion in one painting. Italian futurism died during World War I but its influence was sustained in subsequent art movements, notably ▷vorticism. **2.** In Russia, a movement that rejected traditional Russian literature. ▷Mayakovskii and ▷Khlebnikov were among the writers and artists who signed a manifesto called "A Slap in the Face for Public Taste" (1912) and adopted an experimental and innovatory attitude towards language. The Russian futurists supported the Revolution but were curbed in the 1930s by the Soviet government.

● **Fuzhou** ► (Fu-chou *or* Foochow) 26 10N 119 20E A port in SE China, the capital of Fujian province on the Min delta. An ancient capital, it was the centre of foreign trade from the 10th to the 19th centuries. It is the site of Fujian Medical University. It has varied industries and its exports include timber and sugar cane. Population (1990): 1 270 000.

● **Fylde** ► An area in NW England, in Lancashire between the estuaries of the River Wyre and Ribble. It is a rich agricultural area and has several resorts, notably Blackpool, along its coast.

● **Fylingdales** ► The site of an early-warning radar station in NE England, in North Yorkshire, built to give warning of nuclear attack.

● **Fyn** ► (German name: Fünen) The second largest Danish island, situated between the Little Belt and the Great Belt. Fishing is important and its fertile soil supports cereal growing, dairy farming, and cattle rearing. Area: 3481 sq km (1344 sq mi). Population (1995 est): 605 868.

G

● **gabbro** ▶ A dark-coloured coarse-grained basic igneous rock formed by the crystallization at depth of basalt magma. It is the plutonic equivalent of basalt. Calcic plagioclase feldspar (usually labradorite), clinopyroxene (usually augite), and frequently olivine are the main constituents. Gabbro usually occurs in layered complexes or igneous intrusions.

● **Gaberones** ▷*See* Gaborone.

● **Gabin, Jean** ▶ (Jean-Alexis Moncorgé; 1904–76) French film actor. He is best known for his portrayals of brave but vulnerable heroes in films during the 1930s, notably *La Grande Illusion* (1937) and *Le Jour se lève* (1939). His later films include *L'Affaire Dominici* (1973).

● **Gable, Clark** ▶ (1901–60) US film actor. He established his popularity as a leading man during the early 1930s, when he played many tough masculine roles. His films include *A Free Soul* (1931), *It Happened One Night* (1934), *Gone with the Wind* (1939), and *The Misfits* (1961).

● **Gabo, Naum** ▶ (Naum Neemia Pevsner; 1890–1977) Russian sculptor. A pioneer of ▷constructivism, he and his brother Antoine ▷Pevsner formulated its main ideals in their *Realist Manifesto* published in Russia in 1920. Working later in Berlin (1923–33), England (1936–45), and the USA after 1946, he made numerous constructions of glass, plastic, metals, etc., a favourite device being nylon threads stretched over a plastic framework.

● **Gabon** ▶ (official name: Gabonese Republic) An equatorial country in West Africa, on the Gulf of Guinea. Coastal plains rise to plateaus on either side of the Ogooué basin. The population is mainly Fang.
   Economy: almost three-quarters of the land is forested and timber was formerly the most important resource, especially okoumé, a soft wood used for plywood. Now the exploitation of its large offshore oilfields forms the basis of the economy, making Gabon one of Africa's wealthiest countries. Gabon was a member of OPEC from 1975 until 1996. There are also large deposits of natural gas and valuable mineral resources, including diamonds, gold, iron ore, uranium, and manganese. Industry has been hindered by transport difficulties but the position was improved by the opening (1986) of the trans-Gabon railway. Agriculture consists chiefly of subsistence farming. The main exports are oil, timber, manganese, and uranium.
   History: trading posts were set up by the Portuguese in the late 15th century and the area later became a centre of the slave trade. Settled by the French in the mid-19th century, it became one of the four territories of French Equatorial Africa in 1910. It gained internal self-government as a member of the French Community in 1958 and became independent in 1960. A one-party political system was instituted in 1967, under Omar Bongo (1935–   ); in the 1980s the opposition was led by an underground group known as the *morena*. Unrest led to multiparty legislative elections in 1990, which were won by the ruling Parti Démocratique Gabonais (PDG), and in 1993 Bongo was re-elected in the country's first multiparty presidential elections: both elections were marred by accusations of fraud.

Gabon

Head of state	President Omar Bongo
Official language	French; Bantu languages are widely spoken
Official currency	CFA (Communauté financière africaine) franc of 100 centimes
Area	267 000 sq km (103 089 sq mi)
Population (1997 est)	1 190 000
Capital and main port	Libreville

● **gaboon viper** ▶ A highly venomous ▷puff adder, *Bitis gabonica*, occurring in African rain forests. Up to 2 m long, it has a thick body and a broad head with hornlike projections on its snout and is patterned with buff, brown, and purple rectangles and triangles. It feeds on small vertebrates.

● **Gabor, Dennis** ▶ (1900–79) British electrical engineer, born in Hungary. He won the 1971 Nobel Prize for Physics for his invention of ▷holography.

● **Gaborone** ▶ (former name: Gaberones) 24 45S 25 55E The capital of Botswana. The seat of government was transferred here from Mafeking in 1965. It contains part of the University of Botswana and Swaziland. Population (1995 est): 182 000.

● **Gabriel** ▶ In Jewish and Christian tradition, one of the ▷archangels. The name Gabriel is Hebrew for "man of God" and in Jewish theology he is regarded as the messenger of divine comfort. In the Old Testament Gabriel appears to ▷Daniel to interpret his visions, while in the New Testament he foretells the birth of ▷John the Baptist to Zacharias before announcing the conception of Jesus Christ to the Virgin Mary (Luke 1.26–38). His role in the Annunciation story has frequently been depicted in Western art and poetry.

● **Gabriel** ▶ (c. 1776–1800) The leader of the first significant US slave uprising. He planned to attack Richmond, Virginia, with a thousand slaves, seize the arsenal, and establish an independent Black state. An informer warned the governor and Gabriel was captured and hanged.

● **Gabrieli, Andrea** ▶ (c. 1520–86) Italian composer and organist. He became chief organist of St Mark's, Venice, in 1585; he composed madrigals, motets, and instrumental and organ music. His nephew **Giovanni Gabrieli** (c. 1557–1612) became second organist of St Mark's in 1585. He was one of the first composers to incorporate instrumental parts into vocal works and to write antiphonal music for several choirs or orchestras.

● **Gad, tribe of** ▶ One of the 12 ▷tribes of Israel. It claimed descent from Gad, the son of Jacob and his concubine Zilpah. Its territory was in Transjordan, NE of the Dead Sea.

● **Gaddafi, Moammar al-** ▶ (*or* Qaddafi; 1942–   ) Libyan colonel and statesman. In 1969 he led the overthrow of the Libyan monarchy and in 1970 became chairman of the Revolutionary Command Council. In 1977 he took the title "Leader of the Revolution." His Arab nationalist and Islamic socialist policies have led to a reorganization of Libyan society and an active foreign policy, bringing him into conflict with the West, which has accused him of backing international terrorism.

● **Gaddi, Taddeo** ▶ (c. 1300–?1366) Florentine painter, who was the pupil and assistant of ▷Giotto. His independent works include the frescoes of the *Life of the Virgin* (Baroncelli Chapel, Sta Croce, Florence). His son **Agnolo Gaddi** (c. 1350–96), also influenced by Giotto, painted frescoes of the *Story of the True Cross* at Sta Croce and the *Life of the Virgin* (Duomo, Prato).

● **gad fly** ▶ A ▷bot or ▷warble fly whose parasitic larvae irritate animals, arousing them to bursts of frantic running.

● **gadolinium** ▶ (Gd) A ▷lanthanide element named after the Finnish chemist J. Gadolin (1760–1852). It is used in television-tube phosphors. At no 64; at wt 157.25; mp 1313°C; bp 3273°C.

● **Gadsden Purchase** ▶ (1853) About 77 700 sq km (30 000 sq mi) of land in what are now New Mexico and Arizona, bought by the USA from Mexico for $10 million. The purchase was named after its negotiator, James Gadsden (1788–1858), US minister to Mexico (1854–56).

● **gadwall** ▶ A ▷dabbling duck, *Anas strepera*, that breeds in sheltered inland fresh waters of North America and Eurasia and winters in S Europe, Africa, and the southern United States. 48–51 cm long, it has grey barred plumage, a brown head and rump, and white and reddish wing markings.

● **Gaea** ▷*See* Gaia.

● **Gaelic** ▶ A language of the Goidelic group of ▷Celtic languages. Irish Gaelic is spoken in Ireland as a first language by approximately 100 000 people and as a second language by around 700 000. It is an official language of the Republic of Ireland. Scottish Gaelic (*or* Erse), spoken in the NW coastal region of Scotland and in the Hebrides, is an offshoot of Irish Gaelic that became a distinct dialect around the 13th century.

● **Gaeta** ▶ 41 13N 13 36E A fishing port and resort in S central Italy, in Lazio on the Bay of Gaeta. A popular resort in Roman times, it has Roman remains. Industries include an oil refinery and glass making. Population (latest est): 22 605.

● **Gafsa** ▶ (Arabic name: Qafsah) 34 28N 8 43E A town in W central Tunisia, set in an oasis. Its main activities are irrigated fruit growing and the export of phosphates. Population (latest est): 60 870.

● **Gagarin, Yuri Alekseevich** ▶ (1934–68) Soviet cosmonaut, who on 12 April, 1961, became the first person to orbit the earth. He remained in orbit for 89 minutes, reaching a height of about 301 km (187 mi). He died when a plane he was testing crashed.

● **Gage, Thomas** ▶ (1721–87) British soldier; commander in chief of British forces in North America (1763–74). His hostility to the grievances of the colonists contributed to the outbreak of the ▷American Revolution. He helped to draft the ▷Intolerable Acts in response to the ▷Boston Tea Party. He was replaced by William ▷Howe after military failures at the start of the Revolution.

● **Gaia** ▶ (*or* Gaea) A Greek goddess personifying the earth. The wife and mother of Uranus (Heaven), by whom she bore the ▷Titans, the ▷Cyclops, and the ▷Gigantes, she incited the revolt of the Titans against him. From the blood of the wounded Uranus were born the ▷Erinyes.

● **Gaia hypothesis** ▶ The hypothesis put forward by the British scientist James Ephraim Lovelock (1919–) in 1969 that the earth, including its living and nonliving matter, functions as a single self-regulating system. It proposes that the interaction of living organisms with the environment results eventually in changes to the environment that make the earth better adapted to support life. It also suggests that the earth is capable of ridding itself of any species that adversely affects the environment. Named after the Greek earth goddess, the hypothesis is accepted by many conservationists but rejected by most mainstream scientists.

● **Gaillardia** ▶ A genus of herbaceous plants (about 20 species), native to North America. Several species are cultivated in gardens, especially the blanket flowers *G. aristata* and *G. grandiflora* (perennials) and *G. pulchella* (an annual). The single or double daisy-like flowers have purple centres and yellow, orange, or white fringed ray florets. Family: ▷Compositae.

● **Gainsborough, Thomas** ▶ (1727–88) British portrait and landscape painter, born in Sudbury, Suffolk. His London training (1740–46), initially with the French engraver Gravelot, introduced him to ▷rococo portraiture. In 1759 he moved to Bath, seeking a fashionable clientele. There he studied the art of ▷Van Dyck, whose elegant style is reflected in Gainsborough's *Countess Howe* (Kenwood House, London) and the *Blue Boy* (San Marino, California). His landscapes were at first influenced by ▷Ruisdael and ▷Hobbema and later by ▷Rubens, particularly in the *Harvest Wagon* (Barber Institute, Birmingham). On his return to London in 1774 he successfully rivalled ▷Reynolds for commissions and royal favour. In his later years he painted idyllic rustic scenes, the so-called fancy pictures. He was a founder member of the Royal Academy.

● **Gaiseric** ▷*See* Genseric.

● **Gaitskell, Hugh (Todd Naylor)** ▶ (1906–63) British politician; leader of the Labour Party (1955–63). He became an MP in 1945 and was minister of fuel and power (1947–50), minister of economic affairs (1950), and then chancellor of the exchequer (1950–51). He succeeded Attlee as Labour leader, defeating Aneurin Bevan in the leadership bid. After the defeat of the Labour Party in the 1959 general election, Gaitskell unsuccessfully attempted to change the constitution. At the 1960 party conference his opponents voted in favour of unilateral nuclear disarmament, against the policy of the executive. This led to Gaitskell's "Fight, and fight, and fight again" speech, the reversal of the disarmament policy at the 1961 conference, and the reuniting of the party. He opposed British membership of the EEC.

● **galago** ▷*See* bushbaby.

● **Galahad** ▶ In ▷Arthurian legend, the son of ▷Lancelot and Elaine. As the most perfect exemplar of knighthood, he was (in many romances) the only knight to succeed in the quest of the ▷Holy Grail.

● **galangal** ▶ A flavouring obtained from the rhizomes of a Chinese perennial herb, *Alpinia officinarum*, that may be used in place of ginger. The plant grows to a height of 6 m, with long leathery leaves and pink, yellow, or white fragrant flowers in long dense clusters. Family: *Zingiberaceae*.

● **Galápagos finches** ▷*See* Darwin's finches.

● **Galápagos giant tortoise** ▶ A large rare ▷tortoise, *Geochelone* (*or Testudo*) *elephantopus*, found on the Galápagos Islands, where they

Galápagos giant tortoise ▶ A mating pair. The tortoises on each of the Galápagos Islands differ slightly in form, being adapted to the particular conditions of their habitat.

were formerly slaughtered for meat. Up to 1.5 m long and weighing up to 150 kg, there are numerous subspecies, some now extinct, distinguishable by their different shell shapes. The only other surviving species of giant tortoise is *T. gigantica* of the Seychelles.

● **Galápagos Islands** ▶ (Spanish name: Archipiélago de Colón) An archipelago in the Pacific Ocean, W of Ecuador. It consists of 12 main islands and several smaller ones, all of volcanic origin. They became well known following Charles ▷Darwin's visit in 1835, during which he collected evidence that influenced his theories on natural selection. The islands contain a large number of endemic species, including the giant tortoise; many islands now form nature reserves. Area: 7428 sq km (2868 sq mi). Population (1996 est): 13 976.

● **Galatea** ▶ **1.** In Greek legend, a nymph who loved the shepherd Acis and was loved by Polyphemus. When Acis was killed by his rival she turned him into a river. **2.** The name of a statue that came to life in answer to the prayers of ▷Pygmalion.

● **Galați** ▶ 45 27N 28 02E A port in E Romania, on the River Danube. Largely rebuilt after World War II, it has a naval base, the country's largest shipyards, and iron, steel, and textile industries. Population (1994 est): 326 728.

● **Galatians, Epistle of Paul to the** ▶ A New Testament book written by the Apostle Paul to churches in central Asia Minor in the middle of the 1st century AD. In it he defends his claim to be the apostle to the Gentiles, expounds justification by faith, and warns against those who were encouraging the converts to rely on Jewish ceremonial rites for their acceptance by God.

● **galaxies** ▶ Huge assemblies of many millions of stars, gas, and dust, bound together by gravitational interactions. The majority are members of ▷clusters of galaxies. **Spiral galaxies** are large flattened systems with spiral arms winding outwards from a central nucleus. The spiral arms contain much interstellar gas and dust from which stars can form. Spirals have a mass of 10^{10} to 10^{11} solar masses. **Elliptical galaxies** are actually spheroidal with no clear internal structure. There is little interstellar matter so that most of the stars are old. They vary greatly in size and mass, the largest giant ellipticals exceeding 10^{12} solar masses. The third general category, **irregular galaxies**, have no definite shape or structure and are relatively small, with a high content of interstellar matter.

● **Galaxy** ▶ (*or* Milky Way system) The spiral ▷galaxy to which the sun belongs. It contains about a hundred thousand million (10^{11}) stars. Most lie in the flattened galactic disc, comprising two spiral arms that wind out from a bulging central nucleus; the disc is about 120 000 light years across, the sun lying about 33 000 light years from the centre. The roughly spherical galactic halo surrounds the nucleus and disc; it is only sparsely populated with stars and globular ▷star clusters, which are considerably older than the stars of the spiral arms. Light cannot penetrate the dust in the innermost regions of the Galaxy but radio, infrared, and X-ray observations have shown complex phenomena to be occurring, possibly arising from the presence of a ▷black hole at the galactic centre.

● **Galbraith, John Kenneth** ▶ (1908–) US economist and diplomat. An economist in the Keynesian tradition, Galbraith became professor of economics at Harvard University in 1949. His works include *American Capitalism: The Concept of Countervailing Power* (1952), *The Affluent Society* (1958), *Economics and the Public Purpose* (1973), and an autobiography *A Life In Our Times* (1981). He also served as US ambassador to India (1961–63) and adviser to President Kennedy.

● **Galen** ▶ (129–c. 199 AD) Greek physician and scholar, whose ideas dominated medicine until the Renaissance. From his studies of such animals as monkeys and dogs, Galen showed the importance of the spinal cord in muscle activity, the role of the ureter in kidney and bladder function, and that arteries carry blood rather than air. However, he held mistaken views on blood circulation, including the idea that blood seeped through minute pores in the wall of the heart separating the two ventricles. Galen also wrote on philosophy, law, and mathematics.

● **galena** ▶ The principal ore of lead. It is a lead-grey dense but soft metallic mineral, found as cubic crystals of lead sulphide in hydro-thermal veins and as replacement deposits in limestones. Galena ore bodies usually contain silver.

● **Galerius** ▶ (Gaius Galerius Valerius Maximianus; c. 250–311 AD) Eastern Roman emperor (305–11) after the abdication of Diocletian. Galerius was probably responsible for continuing the persecution of the Christians begun by Diocletian in 303 but in 311 he proclaimed a limited toleration of Christianity. His authority was challenged by the emperor in the West and the ensuing conflict lasted until 308.

● **Galicia** ▶ **1.** A medieval kingdom in NW Spain, now an autonomous region. Colonized by the ▷Visigoths from the 6th century, it became a subkingdom of Castile in the late 11th century. It has retained its own flourishing language and culture. **2.** A historical region of E Europe, now in Poland and Ukraine. It became an independent principality in 1087 until conquered by the Mongols in the 13th century. Later part of Poland (14th century) and Austria (18th century), Galicia was divided between Poland and Austria after World War I and Poland and the Soviet Union after World War II.

● **Galilean satellites** ▶ The four largest ▷satellites of ▷Jupiter—Io, Europa, Ganymede, and Callisto—discovered by ▷Galileo (1610) and studied in detail by the US ▷Voyager probes (1979). Io, orbiting closest to Jupiter, is the most active volcanic body known in the solar system. Ganymede is the brightest Galilean and the largest satellite in the solar system. Callisto and Ganymede are heavily cratered.

● **Galilee** ▶ A district of N Israel, bordering on the River Jordan and the Sea of Galilee. It comprised northernmost Palestine and was the scene of Jesus Christ's early ministry. Under the Romans, Galileans were noted for their religious zeal and nationalism; from the fall of Jerusalem (70 AD) to the middle ages Galilee was a centre for rabbinic scholarship. From 1892, Zionist settlements were established in Galilee, which formed part of the state of Israel (1949). ▷*See also* Zealots.

● **Galilee, Sea of** ▶ (Sea of Tiberias; Lake of Gennesaret; Lake Kinneret) A lake in NE Israel. It is fed mainly by and drained by the River Jordan; its surface is 209 m (686 ft) below sea level. It was the scene of many episodes in the life of Christ. Area: 166 sq km (64 sq mi).

Galileo Galilei ▶ Portrait by Ottavio Leoni (c. 1578–1630).

● **Galileo Galilei** ▶ (1564–1642) Italian mathematician, physicist, and astronomer, whose emphasis on mathematical analysis anticipated the experimental method of scientific inquiry. Born in Pisa, legend has it that he demonstrated that the rate of fall of a body is independent of its mass by dropping weights from the Leaning Tower of Pisa. He is also reputed to have worked out that the period of a pendulum is independent of its amplitude by watching a swinging chandelier in Pisa Cathedral. In 1609 Galileo, on learning of the invention of a simple telescope, designed one himself and used it to study the sky. He soon made a number of discoveries, including sunspots and Jupiter's satellites, which convinced him of the superiority of ▷Copernicus' heliocentric system over the ▷Ptolemaic system. He wrote a witty and vigorous book, *Dialogue on Two World Systems* (1632), in which he made Ptolemy's system look foolish. As the Roman Catholic Church had condemned Copernicus' work in 1616, Galileo was forced by the Inquisition to recant his views and placed under house arrest for the rest of his life. Galileo, following his recantation, is said to have murmured "Eppur si muove" ("Still it moves," referring to the earth, which the Church insisted was stationary at the centre of the universe). He was finally cleared of heresy by a Vatican commission in 1992.

● **Galileo probe** ► A US ▷planetary probe. Launched in October 1989 from the space shuttle *Atlantis*, it entered the atmosphere of Jupiter in December 1995.

● **gall** ► A swelling or excrescence on plants caused by abnormal proliferation of cells due to mechanical injury or attack by insects, mites, fungi, bacteria, or viruses. Some galls are self-limiting, including the oak apples caused by the ▷gall wasp, while others are tumorous, such as the crown gall induced by the bacterium *Agrobacterium tumefaciens*.

● **Gall, Franz Joseph** ► (1758–1828) German physician and founder of ▷phrenology. He thought that the shape of the skull reflected the shape of the underlying brain and hence the character of the individual. Although this idea is now discredited, his work provided a stimulus for research on the brain.

● **Galla** ► A people of Ethiopia numbering about 10 million and making up about 40% of the Ethiopian population. They were originally nomads who spread from the SE region during the 16th century to many other areas, where they largely adopted a sedentary existence and local customs. Their language belongs to the ▷Hamito-Semitic family.

● **gall bladder** ► A saclike organ (7–10 cm long), close to the liver, that receives and stores ▷bile (formerly called gall) formed by the liver. The gall bladder is connected to the liver by the hepatic ducts and to the intestine by the common bile duct. Crystallization of bile components forms ▷gallstones, which may block the bile duct or cause gall bladder infections (cholecystitis). ▷*See* Plate II.

● **Galle** ► (former name: Point de Galle) 6 01N 80 13E A seaport in SW Sri Lanka. The country's chief port under the Portuguese and its capital under the Dutch, it declined with the growth of Colombo. It has a cement factory. Population (1990 est): 84 000.

● **Galle, Johann Gottfried** ► (1812–1910) German astronomer, who was the first to observe ▷Neptune. ▷Leverrier predicted (1846) the existence of Neptune and asked Galle to search the area in which he expected it to be. Galle discovered it the same day.

● **galleon** ► A large oceangoing sailing vessel of the 15th–18th centuries, usually having a tall stern and high sides. Galleons were typically square-rigged on the foremast and mainmast and lateen-rigged on one or two after masts. They were widely used by the Spanish as transport between Europe and the New World and were often attacked by pirates. Several sunken galleons, with their treasures still aboard, have been located in the Caribbean Sea.

● **galley** ▷*See* ships.

● **Gallicanism** ► A movement in France asserting the rights of the French Roman Catholic Church, clergy, and monarchy against papal interference. It was an issue as early as the 13th century but reached its zenith in 1682 with the promulgation by the French bishops, at Louis XIV's instigation, of Four Gallican Articles defending the king's authority in temporal affairs and recognizing the authority of a general council of the Church over that of the pope.

● **Gallico, Paul (William)** ► (1897–1976) US writer. He is best known for the short novel *The Snow Goose* (1941); other works include comic novels based on Mrs 'Arris, the novel *The Poseidon Adventure* (1969; filmed 1972), and writings on sport.

● **Galli-Curci, Amelita** ► (1882–1963) Italian coloratura soprano. Largely self-taught, she made her debut in Rome in 1909 as Gilda in Verdi's *Rigoletto*, playing the same role at her New York debut (1916). She retired in 1930.

● **Gallic Wars** ► (58–51 BC) The campaigns in which Julius Caesar an-

nexed Transalpine ▷Gaul (France). Caesar's intervention in Gallic intertribal warfare was prompted by concern for Italian security; his ambition to conquer Gaul developed later. NE Gaul was pacified by 57 BC and the tribes along the Atlantic coast by 56 BC. In 52 Caesar defeated the tribes of central Gaul, led by ▷Vercingetorix. Caesar's own account of the Gallic Wars has survived.

● **gallinule** ► A bird belonging to the family *Rallidae* (rails). Gallinules are widely distributed, occurring on semistagnant water, such as ponds, edged by dense vegetation, and commonly have blue, green, or purple plumage for camouflage. They are 30–45 cm long and have long slender toes enabling them to run over floating vegetation. ▷*See also* moorhen.

● **Gallipoli** ► (Turkish name: Gelibolu) 40 25N 26 41E A seaport in European Turkey, on the NE coast of the Dardanelles. Taken by Turkey in about 1356, it is strategically important to Istanbul. The town had to be rebuilt after the Gallipoli campaign (*see* World War I). Population (latest est): 14 721.

● **gallium** ► (Ga) A metallic element with a low melting point and high boiling point, discovered in 1875 by Lecoq de Boisbaudran. Gallium is found as a trace element in a number of minerals and in chimney soot. **Gallium arsenide** (GaAs) is a ▷semiconductor that is used in electronic devices, particularly the field-effect ▷transistor and the Gunn diode (*see* Gunn effect). At no 31; at wt 69.72; mp 29.77°C; bp 2205°C.

● **Gällivare** ► 67 10N 20 40E A town in N Sweden. The main industry is ironmining, based on the rich deposits discovered in the 18th century. Population (1990): 22 400.

● **gall midge** ► A small delicate fly with hairy antennae, also called a gallfly and gall gnat, belonging to the family *Cecidomyiidae*. Most species eat plants and lay their eggs in galls. Others are general scavengers or predators and parasites upon other insects. ▷*See also* gall wasp.

● **gallon** ► An Imperial unit of volume equal to the volume occupied by ten pounds of distilled water under defined conditions. The US gallon is equal to 0.832 68 British gallons. The gallon is subdivided into 8 pints (still used for beer). However, the gallon has now been replaced for most purposes by the litre. 1 gallon = 4.546 litres.

● **Galloway** ► An area in SW Scotland, now in Dumfries and Galloway council area. The Mull of Galloway forms the most southerly point in Scotland. Dairy farming is important and the area is noted for its breed of hornless black cattle.

● **gallstones** ► Stones in the ▷gall bladder formed from ▷cholesterol, ▷bile pigments, or both. In some people they cause no symptoms; in others they may give rise to pain, indigestion, nausea, and vomiting. The usual treatment is surgical removal of the gall bladder (cholecystectomy).

● **Gallup, George Horace** ► (1901–84) US public-opinion pollster. His techniques for gauging public opinion became a feature of political life following his successful prediction of the result of the US presidential election in 1936. ▷*See* opinion polls.

● **gall wasp** ► A small ▷wasp (6–8 mm long), also called gallfly, of the family *Cynipidae*. Gall wasps lay eggs in plant tissues, particularly oak trees and rose plants, which respond by producing ▷galls. Thus, *Biorhiza pallida* produces the oak apple gall and *Diplolepis rosae*, the robin's pincushion gall.

● **Galois, Évariste** ► (1811–32) French mathematician, who pioneered the branch of modern mathematics known as group theory. His life was dogged by ill luck; three papers that he submitted to the Académie des Sciences were rejected or lost and he was refused admission to the École Polytechnique. He turned to politics, supporting the Republican cause, and was twice arrested. He died following a duel.

● **Galsworthy, John** ► (1867–1933) British novelist and dramatist. He studied law but embarked on a literary career in 1897 with a volume of short stories, published pseudonymously. *The Man of Property* (1906) began the famous novel series *The Forsyte Saga*, chronicling the decline of a rich English family. His plays, usually rather artificial expositions of moral and social issues, include *The Silver Box* (1906) and *Strife* (1909).

● **Galt, John** ▶ (1779–1839) Scottish novelist. As a young business-man he travelled in the Mediterranean countries, where he befriended Byron, and from 1826 to 1829 he worked in Canada. His novels of Scottish rural life include *The Annals of the Parish* (1821) and *The Provost* (1822).

● **Galtieri, Leopold (Fortunato)** ▶ (1926–) Argentinian army officer and politician. As commander-in-chief of the army (1979–82) he was the leading member of the ruling military junta in Argentina before becoming president (1981–82). In April 1982 he ordered the invasion of the ▷Falkland Islands (Malvinas), a British crown colony, thus provoking the Falklands War with Britain. Following Argentina's military defeat and the return of civilian rule, Galtieri was tried and acquitted (1985) of human-rights violations but found guilty (1986) of negligence in starting and losing the Falklands War. He was released from prison in 1989.

● **Galton, Sir Francis** ▶ (1822–1911) British scientist, a grandson of Erasmus ▷Darwin (by his second wife). He studied methods of improving the mental and physical abilities of human populations by selective mating, a science that he called ▷eugenics. Galton argued that mental as well as physical attributes were inherited, an idea that his cousin Charles ▷Darwin later endorsed. Galton also made contributions to meteorology and pioneered the use of fingerprinting for personal identification.

● **Galuppi, Baldassare** ▶ (1706–85) Venetian opera composer, known as Il Buranello. His comic operas written in collaboration with ▷Goldoni earned him the appellation "the father of opera buffa." He was also an excellent harpsichordist.

● **Galvani, Luigi** ▶ (1737–98) Italian physician, who pioneered research into the electrical properties of living things. He observed how frog muscles twitched when they were touched by metal contacts but he wrongly attributed this to innate "animal electricity" (the current was actually produced by the metal contacts). The ▷galvanometer was named after him.

● **galvanized steel** ▶ Steel coated with zinc to prevent corrosion. The zinc may be deposited by electroplating the steel in molten zinc, spraying with molten zinc, or by coating it with zinc powder and heating it.

● **galvanometer** ▶ An instrument for measuring small electric currents. The moving-coil galvanometer consists of a coil of wire suspended in a magnetic field. A current passing through the coil causes it to rotate until balanced by the opposing torsion in the suspending thread. The angle of rotation is used to measure the current. In the moving-magnet instrument the magnet is suspended in the earth's magnetic field and deflection is caused by a current passing through the surrounding coil.

● **Galveston** ▶ 29 17N 94 48W A city in the USA, in Texas on the Gulf of Mexico. Subject to hurricanes (one of which killed 8000 people in 1900), it has had to undertake large protective schemes. Its port handles sulphur, cotton, and wheat and industries include chemicals and hardware. Population (latest est): 61 601.

● **Galway** ▶ (Irish name: Gallimh) 53 16N 9 03W A port in the Republic of Ireland, the county town of Co Galway. It has the University College (founded 1845), part of the National University of Ireland, and a Roman Catholic cathedral (begun 1957). The Galway Theatre produces Irish-language plays. Salmon and eel fishing are important. Population (1991): 50 853.

● **Galway** ▶ (Irish name: Contae Na Gaillimhe) A county in the W Republic of Ireland, in Connacht bordering on Galway Bay and the Atlantic Ocean. Low lying E of Lough Carrib, it rises to mountains in the W with ▷Connemara in the extreme W. Its many offshore islands include the Aran Islands. Cattle and sheep rearing are important. Area: 5939 sq km (2293 sq mi). Population (1996 est): 189 000. County town: Galway.

● **Galway, Sir James** ▶ (1939–) Irish flautist of worldwide reputation. He studied in Paris with Jean-Pierre Rampal (1922–). His silver and gold flutes were made to his own specifications. The com-

poser Rodrigo wrote his *Concierto pastorale* (for flute and orchestra; 1978) for him. He was knighted in 2001.

● **Gama, Vasco da** ▶ (c. 1469–1524) Portuguese navigator. In 1497, under the patronage of ▷Manuel I, he departed with three ships to continue ▷Dias' search for the route to India. He rounded the Cape of Good Hope and reached Mozambique and Malindi (now in Kenya). Aided by an Indian pilot he crossed to Calicut (1498). Received with hostility by the Indians, he withdrew. Following the murder of the Portuguese settlers left by Cabral's expedition to Calicut, da Gama was sent out on a punitive expedition (1502) to establish Portugal's influence in the Indian Ocean. He bombarded Calicut and returned to Portugal with large amounts of booty. Some 20 years later he went back to India as Portuguese viceroy and died there.

● **Gambetta, Léon** ▶ (1838–82) French statesman. A lawyer, Gambetta, who was an opponent of ▷Napoleon III (1868), was elected to the Legislative Assembly in 1869. Strongly republican, he took advantage of the capture of Napoleon in 1870 in the ▷Franco-Prussian War to proclaim a provisional government of national defence. He was instrumental in founding the Third Republic but his term as prime minister (1881–82) was unsuccessful because of opposition to his democratic policies and he was forced to resign.

● **Gambia, Republic of The** ▶ A country in West Africa, on the Atlantic Ocean, occupying a narrow strip along the River Gambia and surrounded by Senegalese territory. Swamps along the river give way to drier savanna. The majority of the inhabitants are Mandingo.
Economy: overwhelmingly agricultural, producing groundnuts for export and rice for the home market. Mineral resources are sparse and manufacturing industries remain very limited. In 1988 a free-trade zone was agreed with Senegal. Tourism has grown rapidly in recent years. There is a large foreign debt.
History: the mouth of the River Gambia was explored in the 15th century by the Portuguese and in the 16th century by the English, who established a trading settlement on James Island in 1661. The area was administered from the British colony of Sierra Leone from 1807 until 1843, when it became a crown colony until again coming under Sierra Leone in 1866. Separated again in 1888, it achieved internal self-government in 1963 and independence in 1965 with Sir Dawda Jawara as president, becoming a republic within the British Commonwealth in 1970. An attempted coup in 1981 was subdued with military aid from Senegal; close ties between the two countries were reinforced with the formation of the Senegambia Confederation (1982–89) and a treaty of friendship and cooperation (1991). In 1994 Lt Yayah Jammeh became president, having ousted Jawara in a military coup. A civilian constitution was adopted in 1996 and Jammeh was given a mandate in presidential and parliamentary elections; he was re-elected in 2001.

Republic of The Gambia

Head of state	President Yayah Jammeh
Official language	English
Official currency	dalasi of 100 butut
Area	10 689 sq km (4125 sq mi)
Population (2000 est)	1 367 000
Capital and main port	Banjul

● **Gambia, River** ▶ A river in West Africa. Rising in the Fouta Djallon plateau in Guinea, it flows mainly NW through Senegal and The Gambia to enter the Atlantic Ocean. It is navigable to oceangoing vessels for 320 km (200 mi). Length: 1126 km (700 mi).

● **Gambier Islands** ▶ 23 10S 135 00W A group of coral islands in the S Pacific Ocean, in French Polynesia forming an extension of the Tuamotu Archipelago. They have been used for French nuclear tests. Area: 30 sq km (11 sq mi). Population (latest est): 582. Chief settlement: Rikitea.

● **Gamblers' Anonymous** ▶ An organization founded in the USA in 1957 and in the UK in 1964 to bring compulsive gamblers together so that they may help each other to give up their addiction. **Gam-Anon** is an affiliated organization that supports the families of compulsive gamblers.

● **gambling** ▶ Playing a game of chance, or betting on the outcome of an uncertain event, in the hope of winning money. Games of chance, betting, financial speculation, lotteries, and similar activities, have been a part of human activity for all of recorded history. Attempts to suppress these activities, or to control them, have an equally long history. Christian Churches, especially the more Protestant denominations, have often opposed gambling on moral and theological grounds. Kings and governments have in the past regarded it as a distraction from "honest" hard work and imposed laws against gambling, often aimed at the working classes. Thus, gaming houses and betting shops have frequently been banned. In England, for example, Henry VIII banned gaming houses, because they distracted young men from their "proper" military pursuits. This ban remained in force until the 1960s, when the Betting, Gaming and Lotteries Act (1963) and the Gaming Act (1968) permitted gaming under licence. However, the wealthy have always been able to engage freely in gambling on stocks, shares, currencies, and commodities: the desire to gain money without having to work for it knows no class barriers. Official attitudes have sometimes been guided by an assumption that the rich will gamble responsibly, while the poor, in desperation, will not.

In the UK, gaming is now a major industry, with ▷football pools, betting on horseraces and greyhound races, casinos, gaming clubs, and amusement arcades licensed by the Gaming Board of Great Britain. Horseraces and greyhound races have an immense following: the annual amount of off-course betting on horseraces in the 1990s exceeded £6 billion. The **National Lottery**, introduced in 1994, regulated (from 1999) by the National Lottery Commission, and run by Camelot plc, is estimated to attract some two-thirds of the adult population, who spend on average about £2.60 each per week on the lottery tickets. Of the billions of pounds staked each year, 50% goes in prize money, 12% goes to the government as tax, and 28% is divided between certain approved good causes (the remainder is divided between Camelot and the retailers). However, the National Lottery was not the first organized attempt by the British government to cash in on the gambling instinct. ▷Premium bonds, introduced in 1956, enable savers to gamble with the interest on their savings (retaining the right to recover the value of the bond at any time).

The urge to gamble exists everywhere in the world and is usually now catered for by governments, who seek ways of taking a share of the stake money (the major exception is in Islamic states, where gambling is forbidden). However, gambling, like drinking and taking illegal drugs, can become addictive with dire consequences to the gambler's life and family (*see* Gamblers' Anonymous).

● **gamboge** ▶ (*or* camboge) A hard brittle gum resin obtained from various SE Asian trees of the genus *Garcinia*. Orange to brown, it turns bright yellow when powdered. Artists use gamboge as a pigment and to colour varnishes. In medicine and veterinary medicine it is used as a purgative.

● **gamebird** ▶ A bird that is hunted for sport and legally defined as such by game laws, which control the hunting season, etc. Gamebirds include pheasants, grouse, partridges, turkeys, guinea fowl, ducks, bustards, snipe, and woodcock.

● **gamelan** ▶ A type of orchestra common in Indonesia and Thailand, consisting mainly of tuned percussion instruments (particularly gongs and bells). A gamelan was heard at the Great Paris Exhibition of 1889; Debussy was influenced by its sonorities.

● **gamete** ▶ A reproductive cell—either male or female—containing half the number of ▷chromosomes present in a body (somatic) cell. On ▷fertilization the new individual therefore has a complete set of chromosomes, half from each parent. The female gamete (*see* egg) is large and immotile and contains abundant cytoplasm, while the male gamete (*see* sperm) is motile, with little cytoplasm. In higher organisms gametes are produced in specialized sex organs. ▷*See* reproduction.

● **gamete intrafallopian transfer** ▷*See* GIFT.

● **game theory** ▶ The branch of mathematics that seeks to analyse and solve problems arising in economic, business, or military situations on the assumption that each participant adopts strategies that will maximize gain (payoff) and minimize loss, as in playing a game.

Worked out originally by John von ▷Neumann and Oskar Morganstern (1907–77), it was successfully used in World War II in an analysis of submarine warfare.

Distinction is made between games for one player (patience, solitaire) in which no conflict arises, games for two players or teams (chess, football) in which conflict is an essential aspect of strategy, and games in which there are more than two participants (poker, roulette) and one person's gain is not directly reflected by another person's loss. When chance is important, information is incomplete, or participants' goals are obscure, the theory is more complex.

● **gametophyte** ▷*See* alternation of generations.

● **Gamliel** ▶ The name of several important rabbis. **Gamliel the Elder** (Greek name: Gamaliel; early 1st century AD), a grandson of ▷Hillel, was president of the Jewish council of Jerusalem and a teacher of St ▷Paul. His grandson **Gamliel II** succeeded Johanan ben Zakkai as head of the school at Jabneh (Yavneh) and is regarded as one of the founders of rabbinic Judaism.

● **gamma globulin** ▷*See* globulin.

● **gamma radiation** ▶ Highly energetic electromagnetic radiation emitted by certain radioactive substances as a result of transitions of nucleons from a higher to a lower energy level and when an elementary particle and its antiparticle annihilate each other. The wavelength of gamma radiation is between 10^{-10} and 10^{-14} metre. ▷*See also* astronomy.

● **Gamow, George** ▶ (1904–68) Russian-born US physicist who worked in Copenhagen and Cambridge before settling in Washington in 1934. He revived the ▷big-bang theory in cosmology and contributed to the Alpher–Bethe–Gamow (αβγ) theory (*see* Alpher, Ralph). In molecular biology he identified the codon as the unit of the ▷genetic code.

● **Ganda** ▶ A Bantu people of the region W and N of Lake Victoria. They are agriculturalists, whose staple crop is bananas. The largest tribe in Uganda, they were formerly ruled by a king (Kabaka) in their own kingdom of ▷Buganda.

● **Gander** ▶ 48 58N 54 34W A town in E Canada, in Newfoundland. A major World War II base, it has one of the world's largest airports, responsible for air-traffic control over the North Atlantic. Population (1991): 10 339.

● **Gandhara** ▶ An ancient region now in NW Pakistan. It was conquered by the Achaemenians (6th century BC) and by ▷Alexander the Great (327–325 BC). In the early centuries AD it became a centre for a Buddhist art that combined Greco-Roman and oriental characteristics. ▷*See also* Taxila.

● **Gandhi, Indira** ▶ (1917–84) Indian stateswoman; prime minister (1966–77; 1980–84). Daughter of Jawaharlal ▷Nehru, in 1942 she married Feroz Gandhi (d. 1960), who was not a relation of Mahatma Gandhi. She was a Congress Party cabinet minister under Lal Bahadur ▷Shastri, whom she succeeded as prime minister. She won substantial victories in the 1971 and 1972 elections. In 1975 she was accused of electoral malpractices; a state of emergency was subsequently declared and strict authoritarian government imposed. She was defeated in the elections of 1977 by Morarji Desai but returned to power in 1980. In the wake of sectarian violence, she was assassinated in 1984 by Sikh members of her bodyguard. Her elder son **Rajiv Gandhi** (1942–91) worked as an airline pilot before succeeding his mother as prime minister. His government also came under pressure as a result of conflict between Sikhs and Hindus; this was a contributory factor in his electoral defeat and subsequent resignation in 1989. He was assassinated while campaigning for re-election. Rajiv's widow, **Sonia Gandhi** (1946–), was elected leader of the Congress (I) Party in 1998. ▷*See also* Indian National Congress.

● **Gandhi, Mohandas Karamchand** ▶ (1869–1948) Indian nationalist leader. Mahatma ("Great Soul") Gandhi was born in W India and went to England in 1888 to study law. In 1893 he moved to South Africa to practise law and became a champion of the rights of the Indian community, introducing a policy of noncooperation with the civil authorities (*see* civil disobedience; satyagraha), which he utilized after his return to India (1914). There he took up the cause of home rule, becoming leader of the ▷Indian National Congress. His noncooperation policy was inaugurated in 1919 and was then extended to civil disobedience (e.g. nonpayment of taxes). Following imprisonment (1922–24), Gandhi withdrew from national politics to travel around India. He campaigned against the degradation of untouchables and encouraged the development of Indian craft industries. It was in this period that he came to be regarded as a saint by many Indians. Returning to politics in 1927, in 1930 he made his famous walk from Ahmedabad to the sea, where he distilled salt from sea water in protest against the government's salt monopoly, and was again imprisoned. In 1932 he undertook his first "fast unto death," against the government's attitude to untouchables, and in 1933 retired to his ashram at Wardha. Returning to political life in the late 1930s, he became committed to the aim of complete independence for India. World War II presented Gandhi with his greatest challenge. Recognizing Hitler as an aggressor, he had to reconcile Indian support for Britain with his own policy of nonviolence; moreover, he had to reconcile his belief in an independent India with cooperation with the imperial power. In 1942, when the Japanese were threatening India, the British Government offered India complete independence after the war in exchange for cooperation in winning it. Describing this offer as "a post-dated cheque on a failing bank," Gandhi demanded that the British should withdraw immediately from India. The British responded by gaoling Gandhi and the other Congress leaders until 1944, when they were released to discuss independence and partition.

Gandhi, with Nehru, played a crucial part in the independence talks and although initially opposed to partition he finally accepted the establishment of Pakistan. When violence broke out in Bengal between Hindus and Muslims, Gandhi undertook a fast in an attempt to halt the conflict. His advocacy of friendship between Hindus and Muslims caused intense resentment among Hindu fanatics, one of whom (Nathuram Godse) assassinated him as he went to a prayer meeting. Gandhi was never a member of the cabinet, but for many years before his death was regarded as the supreme Indian leader. Even the British Government, with which he maintained an ambivalent relationship, respected this remarkable and enigmatic man.

● **Gandzha** ▶ (name from 1813 until 1920: Yelisavetpol; name from 1935 until 1990: Kirovabad) 40 39N 46 20E A city in NW Azerbaidzhan. A medieval commercial centre, it is now an important industrial centre, producing especially textiles, building materials, and wine. Population (1991 est): 282 200.

● **Ganesa** ▶ One of the principal Hindu deities, portrayed as having an elephant's head on a human body. His father ▷Shiva beheaded him, but then decided to save him and replaced his human head with that of the first creature he found. A popular god, he is the teacher of the gods and is invoked at the start of any undertaking since he is believed to remove obstacles.

● **Ganga** ▶ Two related dynasties in medieval India. The **Western Ganga** ruled over much of Mysore in S India (present-day Karnataka) from the 2nd century until the early 11th century, when they were overthrown. The **Eastern Ganga** ruled Kalinga from the 11th to the 15th centuries and were responsible for many glorious monuments, including the Jagannath temple at Puri.

● **Ganges, River** ▶ (or Ganga) The great river of N India. Formed by several headstreams in the Himalayas, one of which emanates from an ice cave, it flows generally E across the broad Ganges plain to join the Brahmaputra River, thereafter continuing as the River Padma, which empties into the Bay of Bengal by way of the largest delta in the world. It is used to irrigate the Ganges plain, which contains several of India's main cities (Delhi, Agra, Varanasi, and Lucknow) and which, after the Yangtze Valley (China), is the world's most populous agricultural area. It is of immense religious importance, being the Hindus' most sacred river. Length: 2507 km (1557 mi).

● **ganglion** ▶ (anatomy) A collection of nerve cell bodies, especially one outside the central ▷nervous system. Sensory ganglia carry out preliminary analysis of the information coming from sense organs. Motor ganglia coordinate the discharges from a number of nerve fibres. ▷See also neurone.

● **ganglion** ▶ (cyst) A small fluid-filled swelling occurring under the skin and close to a joint, usually the wrist. They are most common in children. Treatment is needed only if the cysts are large or painful, in which case they are surgically removed. A former treatment was to hit them with the family Bible.

● **Gang of Four** ▷See Jiang Qing.

● **gangrene** ▶ Death of tissues, most commonly those of a limb. This usually results from narrowing of the blood vessels of the legs by ▷atherosclerosis or because of diabetes. If the tissues become infected the condition is called wet gangrene. Treatment is aimed at improving the blood flow to the limbs by surgery to the vessels or by rest; in advanced cases amputation may be necessary.

● **Gangtok** ▶ 27 20N 88 39E A city in India, the capital of Sikkim. It is an agricultural trading centre. Population (1991): 24 971.

● **gannet** ▶ A seabird belonging to the family *Sulidae*, distributed worldwide. (Tropical members of the family are called ▷boobies.) The North Atlantic gannet (*Sula bassana*), also called solan goose, reaches 90 cm in length. White with black wingtips, it has a long stout bill and a long wedge-shaped tail. Gannets feed on fish and nest in colonies on rocky islands and cliffs. Order: *Pelecaniformes* (cormorants, pelicans, etc.).

● **Gansu** ▶ (or Kansu) A mountainous province in N China, prone in the E to severe earthquakes. Livestock is kept and cereals, cotton, and tobacco are grown in the river valleys. It has oil, coal, hydroelectric power, and a nuclear plant.

History: it became a part of China in the 3rd century BC, but after the introduction of Islam in the 13th century its Muslim population was continually rebellious and it only came under full Chinese influence in the 19th century. On the route to China from the Middle East, along which travelled Marco Polo, it is strategically important. Area: 355 100 sq km (137 100 sq mi). Population (1995 est): 23 780 000. Capital: Lanzhou.

● **Ganymede** ▶ (astronomy) ▷See Galilean satellites.

● **Ganymede** ▶ (mythology) In Greek legend, a Trojan prince of great beauty carried off by Zeus to be his cupbearer in exchange for some immortal horses or a golden vine.

● **Gao** ▶ 16 19N 0 09W A town in S central Mali, on the River Niger. It was the centre of a powerful Islamic empire (15–16th centuries). Population (latest est): 54 784.

● **gaon** ▶ (Hebrew: eminence) A Jewish scholar and communal leader. The geonim were the heads of the Jewish Babylonian academies from the 6th to 11th centuries. Much of their surviving work is in the form of *responsa*, replies to questions on the Bible, ▷Talmud, or ▷Mishnah. The most celebrated gaon was Sa'adya (892–942), Talmudic scholar, philosopher, poet, grammarian, and the translator of the Bible into Arabic.

● **Gaoxiong** ▶ (or Kao-hsiung; Japanese name: Takao) 22 36N 120 17E A city in SW Taiwan, the second largest on the island and its leading port. Under Japanese occupation (1895–1945) it became an important naval base. It is a major industrial centre, its industries including oil refining, fishing, and food processing. Population (1997 est): 1 434 907.

● **gar** ▶ A freshwater ▷bony fish, also called garpike, of a family (*Lepisosteidae*; 7 species) found in North and Central America. Gars have a slender body, up to 3.5 m long, covered with enamelled scales, and a long alligator-like snout with sharp teeth; they feed on fish. Order: *Semionotiformes*. □fish.

● **Garbo, Greta** ▶ (Greta Gustafson; 1905–90) Swedish actress. Her exceptional beauty and aloofness contributed much to her portrayal of tragic heroines in such films as *Grand Hotel* (1932), *Queen Christina* (1934), *Anna Karenina* (1935), and *Camille* (1936). As a comedienne she excelled in *Ninotchka* (1939). She retired into seclusion in 1941. □ p. 498.

● **García Lorca, Federico** ▶ (1898–1936) Spanish poet and dramatist. He began writing poems while a student in Granada and Madrid, winning international fame with *Gipsy Ballads* (1928), noted for their boldly original imagery. His visits to the USA and Cuba (1929–30) inspired the anguished poems of *Poet in New York* (1940). His masterpiece is the trilogy of folk tragedies *Blood Wedding* (1933), *Yerma* (1934), and *The House of Bernarda Alba* (1936). He was shot by Nationalists at the outset of the Spanish Civil War.

Greta Garbo ► In her reclusive later years this legendary beauty of the cinema became identified with the much-quoted line from her film *Grand Hotel*: "I want to be alone." Here she is seen wearing jewellery, given by Napoleon to Empress Marie Louise in 1811, for her role in the film *Madame Walewska*.

● **García Márquez, Gabriel ►** (1928–) Colombian novelist. His novels include *One Hundred Years of Solitude* (1967) and *Chronicle of a Death Foretold* (1981), about the imaginary town of Macondo, and *The General in his Labyrinth* (1989). His other works include *Strange Pilgrims* (1993) and other collections of stories, and the nonfiction *News of a Kidnapping* (1996). He won a Nobel Prize in 1982.

● **Garda, Lake ►** (Latin name: Lacus Benacus) A lake in central N Italy. Sheltered on the N by the Alps, it has a temperate climate that attracts holidaymakers. Area: 370 sq km (143 sq mi).

● **garden city ►** A town surrounded by countryside and designed to have community land ownership, adequate facilities, and recreational space. The garden city was a reaction to the chronic urban overcrowding produced in England by the industrial revolution. Its main advocate was Ebenezer ▷Howard, and the earliest examples, notably Letchworth (1903), were imitated throughout Europe. Many English town-planning schemes after World War II were strongly influenced by its example.

● **garden cress** ▷*See* cress.

● **Gardenia ►** A genus of ornamental shrubs and trees (60–100 species) native to tropical and subtropical Africa and Asia. Many are richly scented and used in perfumes and tea. The shiny evergreen leaves are oval and pointed. Single flowers have four or five strap-shaped petals, often creamy white, but many cultivated varieties have showy double flowers. The fruits are large and berry-like. *G. jasminoides* is a popular pot plant. Family: *Rubiaceae* (madder family).

● **Garden of the Gods ►** An area in the USA, in Colorado. It consists of remarkable formations of eroded red sandstone rocks, some of which resemble animals, gargoyles, and cathedral spires.

● **Gardiner, Sir John Eliot ►** (1943–) British conductor, noted for his carefully researched performances using period instruments. He founded the Monteverdi Choir in 1965 and the Orchestre Révolutionnaire et Romantique in 1990. He was knighted in 1998.

● **Gardiner, Stephen ►** (c. 1490–1555) English churchman. Appointed Bishop of Winchester in 1531, he negotiated with Rome over annulling Henry VIII's marriage to Catherine of Aragon. He later opposed the radical Protestant policies of Thomas ▷Cromwell and was imprisoned (1548) under Edward VI and deprived of his see (1551). He was reinstated by Queen Mary, who made him Lord High Chancellor.

● **Gardner, Ava ►** (1922–90) US film actress, who became a Hollywood sex symbol in the late 1940s. Her films include *The Killers* (1946),

Show Boat (1951), *Mogambo* (1953), *The Sun Also Rises* (1957), and *Night of the Iguana* (1964). She was also famous for her marriages to film star Mickey Rooney, jazz musician Artie Shaw, and Frank Sinatra.

● **Garfield, James Abram ►** (1831–81) US statesman; Republican president (1881). He fought on the Union side in the American Civil War, reaching the rank of major-general before resigning from the army to enter Congress (1863). He led the Republican Party there until 1880, when he fought and won the presidential election. Only months after taking office he was assassinated by a former supporter who had been disappointed in his hopes of gaining a public appointment. Garfield's assassination led to major reforms (1883) in the system for appointing federal employees in the USA.

● **garfish** ▷*See* needlefish.

● **garganey ►** A small ▷dabbling duck, *Anas querquedula*, that breeds in shallow fresh waters of N Eurasia and winters along African and Asian coasts. 36–40 cm long, the male is brown with pale underparts, grey wings, green and white wing bars, and a white eye stripe; females are mottled brown.

● **gargoyle ►** A water spout, in the shape of a grotesque person or animal, that appears chiefly in gothic architecture. Gargoyles project from parapet gutters to carry water draining from the roof clear of the walls.

● **Garibaldi, Giuseppe ►** (1807–82) Italian soldier, a hero of the movement for Italian unification (*see* Risorgimento). Influenced by Mazzini, he joined an attempted republican revolution in Sardinia-Piedmont (1834) and was forced to flee to South America, where he spent ten years fighting in a series of wars of liberation. He returned to Italy to join the ▷Revolution of 1848, fighting the Austrians and, after the flight of Pope Pius IX, playing a leading part in the heroic but unsuccessful defence of Rome against the French. Following another period of exile, he gave his support to the unification movement led by Cavour and Victor Emmanuel II of Sardinia-Piedmont. In 1860 he set out from Genoa on the Expedition of a ▷Thousand, which was to achieve the conquest of Sicily and Naples and their incorporation in the new kingdom of Italy. He continued to serve Victor Emmanuel in the 1860s and also fought for the French in the Franco-Prussian War (1870–71).

● **Garland, Judy ►** (Frances Gumm; 1922–69) US singer and film actress. She began her career at the age of five as a singer in vaudeville. Her films included *The Wizard of Oz* (1939), in which she sang "Over the Rainbow" and established herself as a star, *Meet Me in St Louis* (1944), *A Star is Born* (1954), and *Judgment at Nuremberg* (1961). She married five times; although an unhappy private life interfered with her career, she maintained her reputation as an enormously popular singer. Her daughter **Liza Minnelli** (1946–) is also a singer and actress. She is best known for her starring roles in such films as *Cabaret* (1972), *Arthur* (1981), and *Stepping Out* (1991).

● **garlic ►** A widely cultivated perennial herb, ▷*Allium sativum*, native to Asia and naturalized in S Europe and North America. Its leafless flower stem grows to a height of 60 cm. The garlic bulb has a membraneous skin enclosing up to 20 bublets, called cloves. The bulb has a pungent aroma and taste and is a classic flavouring agent in cooking.

● **garlic mustard ►** A biennial or perennial Eurasian herb, *Alliaria petiolata* (*A. officinalis, Sisymbrium alliaria*), up to 100 cm high, also called Jack-by-the-hedge and hedge garlic. The heart-shaped toothed leaves smell of garlic when crushed. Small white four-petalled flowers are borne in a terminal cluster. Family: ▷*Cruciferae*.

● **garnet ►** A group of minerals with compositions varying within the series pyralspite (pyrope, $Mg_3Al_2Si_3O_{12}$; almandine, $Fe_3^{2+}Al_2Si_3O_{12}$; and spessartite, $Mn_3Al_2Si_3O_{12}$) or ugrandite (grossular, $Ca_3Al_2Si_3O_{12}$; andradite, $Ca_3(Fe^{3+}, Ti)_2Si_3O_{12}$; and uvarovite, $Ca_3Cr_2Si_3O_{12}$). Garnets occur chiefly in metamorphic rocks. They are used as abrasives, almandine being the most important, and flawless crystals are semiprecious stones. Birthstone for January.

● **Garonne, River ►** A river in SW France. Rising in the central Pyrenees, it flows N through Toulouse and joins the River Dordogne near Bordeaux, entering the Atlantic Ocean by the Gironde estuary. It is linked to the Mediterranean Sea by the Canal du Midi. Length: 580 km (360 mi).

● **garpike** ▷See gar.

● **Garrick, David** ▶ (1717–79) English actor. He went to London with Samuel ▷Johnson in 1737 and began his long theatrical career with a highly acclaimed performance as Richard III in 1741. His natural style of acting contrasted with the prevailing formal conventions. As manager of the Drury Lane Theatre from 1747 to 1776, he introduced innovations in production, lighting, and scenery.

● **Garter, Order of the** ▶ A British order of knighthood, traditionally founded by Edward III in 1348 and comprising chiefly the sovereign and 25 knights companions. Its motto is *Honi soit qui mal y pense* (The shame be his who thinks badly of it), supposedly the words of Edward III on tying to his leg a garter dropped by a lady at a party. The motto is inscribed on the dark blue garter worn by the knights of the order on the left leg below the knee. The order's chapel is St George's Chapel, Windsor. Since 1987 the order has been open to women.

● **Gary** ▶ 41 34N 87 20W A city in the USA, in Indiana on Lake Michigan. Founded by the US Steel Corporation (1905), it is one of the world's major steel producers. Population (1996 est): 110 975.

● **Gascoigne, Paul** ▶ (1967–) British footballer, known as "Gazza." A midfielder, he has played for Newcastle United (1985–88), Tottenham Hotspur (1988–92), Lazio, Italy (1992–95), Glasgow Rangers (1995–98), and Middlesbrough (1998–). Known for his controversial behaviour both on and off the pitch, he played for England in the 1990 and 1994 World Cups but was dropped in 1998.

● **gas constant** ▶ (R) The constant that occurs in the ideal ▷gas law: $pV = RT$. Its value is 8.314 joules per kelvin per mole.

● **Gascony** ▶ A former duchy of SW France. After Roman rule Gascony was conquered by the Visigoths and then by the Franks. By the end of the 10th century its dukes had achieved autonomy from the French Crown but in 1052 it fell to Aquitaine and came under English control in the 12th century. It formed the nucleus of English possessions in France until regained by the French at the end of the Hundred Years' War (1453).

● **gas engine** ▷See internal-combustion engine.

● **gases** ▶ Substances that distribute themselves evenly throughout a closed container. The behaviour of a gas under variations of temperature, pressure, and volume is fairly accurately described by the ▷gas laws and the ▷kinetic theory of gases. When gases are cooled or compressed they become ▷liquids. However, above the critical temperature (*see* critical state) a gas cannot be liquefied by pressure alone.

● **Gaskell, Elizabeth Cleghorn** ▶ (1810–65) British novelist. In 1832 she married a Unitarian minister and settled in Manchester, the industrial setting of her first novel, *Mary Barton* (1848). Her other novels include *Cranford* (1853), based on her childhood in a rural village, and *North and South* (1855). She also wrote the first biography of her friend Charlotte Brontë (1857).

● **gas laws** ▶ Relationships between the thermodynamic temperature (*T*), pressure (*p*), and volume (*V*) of a gas. The simplest laws are ▷Boyle's law ($p \propto 1/V$) and ▷Charles's law ($V \propto T$), which are combined in the ideal gas equation: $pV = RT$, where *R* is the ▷gas constant. However, no real gas obeys this equation exactly. Most later gas laws are modifications of this equation, taking into account the volume occupied by the molecules themselves and the attractive forces between the molecules. The best known of these is ▷Van der Waals equation.

● **gas meter** ▶ A meter for measuring the volume of gas passing through a pipe. The common household gas meter is a positive displacement meter in which two bellows are alternately filled and emptied by means of valves, the motion of the bellows being connected to the valves and a counting mechanism. Larger volumes are measured by a rotary meter, in which the gas flow causes an impeller to rotate.

● **gas oil** ▶ A petroleum product used as fuel for Diesel engines. Diesel buses and lorries use high-quality fuel with a ▷cetane number of 50. Slower engines, such as those in ships, use lower grade more viscous oil.

● **Gassendi, Pierre** ▶ (1592–1655) French physicist and philosopher, an ardent believer in the experimental approach to science. He advocated the atomic theory of matter (*see* atomism) and in this influenced the ideas of Robert ▷Boyle. His astronomical works supported Galileo's ideas. In philosophy he wrote extensively on ▷Epicureanism and formulated objections to ▷Descartes' *Meditations*.

● **Gasser, Herbert Spencer** ▶ (1888–1963) US physiologist, who shared a Nobel Prize (1944) with Joseph ▷Erlanger for their work on the function of nerve fibres.

● **gastric juice** ▶ A mixture of hydrochloric acid, protein-digesting enzymes (including the precursor of ▷pepsin), and mucus secreted by glands in the mucous membrane lining the stomach.

● **gastric ulcer** ▷See peptic ulcer.

● **gastrin** ▶ A hormone released by cells of the stomach wall in the presence of food. Gastrin stimulates secretion of gastric juice by the gastric glands.

● **gastritis** ▶ Inflammation of the lining of the stomach. Acute gastritis usually results from such irritants as alcohol or aspirin. If the patient stops taking the irritant, the condition usually resolves quickly. Chronic gastritis is usually caused by the presence of the bacterium ▷*Helicobacter pylori*; it is common in old people and often symptomless, but may be associated with pernicious ▷anaemia.

● **gastroenteritis** ▶ Infection of the stomach and intestines. ▷Food poisoning is one cause of gastroenteritis, but usually it cannot be related to a meal and no particular bacteria can be incriminated. Gastroenteritis is characterized by diarrhoea and vomiting and usually occurs in areas where hygiene is poor. The fluid loss may be severe, and this is particularly dangerous in babies, who may require intravenous fluid replacement.

● **gastroenterology** ▶ The study of the alimentary canal and the functions associated with it. This medical specialty is concerned with treating diseases not only of the stomach, intestines, and other parts of the digestive tract but also of the liver, pancreas, and gall bladder.

● **gastropod** ▶ A single-shelled ▷mollusc belonging to the class *Gastropoda* (about 40 000 species), including ▷snails and ▷slugs, ▷limpets, and ▷sea hares. Measuring 0.1–20 cm in length, gastropods occupy terrestrial, freshwater, and marine habitats. They move by undulating the muscular foot and have two pairs of retractable sensory head tentacles, one pair bearing simple eyes. They feed by scraping plant or animal matter with a rasping tongue (radula). Most gastropods have internal fertilization: the mating individuals may be of separate sexes or hermaphrodite.

● **Gastrotricha** ▶ A phylum of minute wormlike animals (about 400 species) found in salt and fresh waters. 0.1–1.5 mm long, they have a scaly or spiny cuticle and a ciliated underside; they feed on decaying vegetation. Many are ▷hermaphrodites and one group exhibits ▷parthenogenesis.

● **gastrula** ▶ A stage in the embryonic development of an animal in which the cells of the ▷blastula (the preceding stage) undergo complex movements, resulting in the formation of three distinct germ layers. These layers—the ectoderm, mesoderm, and endoderm—will later differentiate into the tissues and organs of the body. A central cavity (archenteron) is the primitive gut.

● **gas turbine** ▶ A form of ▷internal-combustion engine consisting of a ▷turbine in which the power to drive the blades is provided by hot gas. The gas turbine is a flexible engine with many applications, the most useful being in aviation (*see* jet engine). It consists of a ▷compressor, a combustion chamber, and the turbine. Atmospheric air is fed under pressure from the compressor to the combustion chambers, where a fuel, such as natural gas, paraffin, or oil is burnt; the hot gases then drive the turbine, which in turn drives the compressor. Power is supplied either in the form of thrust from a jet or rotation of the turbine shaft. □heat engine.

● **Gates, Bill** ▶ (William Henry G; 1955–) US businessman, whose Microsoft company (founded 1975) has dominated the computer software industry worldwide since the early 1980s. The company's success was founded on its MS-DOS ▷operating system and consolidated by its Windows system, introduced in 1985 and replaced ten years later by Windows 95. In 1991 he was ranked the world's richest man.

● **Gates, Horatio** ▶ (?1728–1806) American general. British-born, he saw action in America in the ▷Seven Years' War and returned to settle there in 1772. During the American Revolution, his army defeated the British under ▷Burgoyne at ▷Saratoga (1777). Defeated by Cornwallis at ▷Camden (1780), he retired, joining Washington's staff (1782).

● **Gateshead** ▶ 1. 54 58N 1 35W A town in NE England, in Gateshead unitary authority, Tyne and Wear, on the River Tyne. Industries include engineering, clothing, paints, plastics, and glass. The Metro Centre (opened in 1986) is one of the world's largest shopping complexes. Major redevelopment of the quayside area in 1998–2002 includes an international art gallery, the Baltic Millennium Bridge, and Norman Foster's Music Centre. In 1997 the UK's largest sculpture, Anthony Gormley's "Angel of the North" (wingspan 53 m), was erected on the outskirts of the town. Population (1991): 83 159. 2. A unitary authority in NE England, in Tyne and Wear. Area: 142 sq km (55 sq mi). Population (1996 est): 201 100.

● **Gatling gun** ▷See machine gun.

● **GATT** ▷See General Agreement on Tariffs and Trade.

● **Gatting, Mike** ▶ (Michael William G.; 1957–) British cricketer, who played for Middlesex and England (1978–95). A pugnacious batsman, he captained England from 1986 to 1988, when he was dismissed.

● **Gatwick** ▶ 51 08N 0 11W A village in SE England, 43 km (27 mi) S of London, in West Sussex. It is the site of one of London's two subsidiary airports (see also Stansted), constructed in 1956–58.

● **gaucho** ▶ A nomadic cattleherder of the Argentine, Uruguayan, and Paraguayan pampas in the 18th and 19th centuries. Often mestizos (of mixed European and Indian ancestry), gauchos were at first independent herders but, like the US ▷cowboys, became employees of ranchers. They disappeared following the ploughing of the pampas and the introduction of pure-breed stock raising.

● **Gaudier-Brzeska, Henri** ▶ (1891–1915) French sculptor. Henri Gaudier adopted the name Gaudier-Brzeska from 1911, the year after he met the Polish novelist Sophie Brzeska in Paris. Working in London, Gaudier-Brzeska became a leading member of the vorticist movement (see vorticism). He produced sculptures influenced by cubism and primitive art, the best known being Red Stone Dancer (1913; Tate Gallery). He was killed in action in World War I.

● **Gaudí y Cornet, Antonio** ▶ (1852–1926) Spanish architect with a highly individual approach. Gaudi's work had strong affiliations to ▷Art Nouveau, but also drew inspiration from gothic and ▷Mudéjar sources. He also made use of the style of the ▷gothic revival in the incomplete Sagrada Familia in Barcelona (1880s). He worked exclusively in Barcelona, beginning with the Casa Vicens (1878) and a house for his patron, Count Güell. In the 1890s his style changed radically, and certain later buildings, for example the Casa Battló (1905), tended to resemble natural growths.

● **gauge theories** ▶ Mathematical descriptions predicting the behaviour of all the fundamental interactions, except gravitation. Gauge theories are based on the concept of symmetry, i.e. that the solution of a set of equations remain unchanged even when a characteristic of the system they describe is varied. The ▷quantum theory applied to the ▷electromagnetic interaction, known as quantum electrodynamics, is a gauge theory in which the electromagnetic force is visualized as a result of the exchange of massless ▷photons between charged particles, the equations describing the motions of the charged particles remaining unchanged during local symmetry operations. The success of this theory enabled it to be extended to the ▷weak interaction and to the formulation of the gauge theory applying to ▷strong interactions, known as quantum chromodynamics. In general, in gauge theories, interactions are seen as the exchange of **gauge bosons** (e.g. photons, gluons) between particles (see particle physics; grand unified theory).

● **Gauguin, Paul** ▶ (1848–1903) French postimpressionist painter, born in Paris. After five years at sea he became a stockbroker (1871),

painting only as a hobby. His early works were influenced by the impressionists with whom he exhibited (1881–86). He became a full-time painter in 1883 and moved to Brittany in 1886, where he developed a style called ▷synthetism in such paintings as Vision after the Sermon (National Gallery, Edinburgh). He visited Martinique in 1887 and stayed with ▷Van Gogh in Arles in 1888. Seeking the inspiration of a primitive civilization, he moved to Tahiti (1891), where the symbolism in such paintings as Nevermore (Courtauld Institute, London) was influenced by native superstitions. He also revived the art of woodcutting.

● **Gauhati** ▶ 26 10N 91 45E A city in India, in Assam. The former centre of British administration in Assam, Gauhati is an important trading centre and has an oil refinery. Its many temple ruins make it a Hindu pilgrimage centre. Its university was established in 1948. Population (1991): 577 591.

● **Gaul** ▶ An ancient region of Europe. It was divided by the Romans into Transalpine Gaul (the area bound by the Rhine, Alps, and Pyrenees) and Cisalpine Gaul (N Italy). Transalpine Gaul was settled from about 1500 BC by Celtic tribes, who inhabited Cisalpine Gaul after around 500 BC. Subsequent Gallic expansion southwards brought conflict with Rome, which the Gauls sacked in 390, and the Roman conquest of Cisalpine Gaul was not completed until the mid-2nd century. In 121 the Romans annexed S Transalpine Gaul, which they called Gallia Narbonensis, and between 58 and 50 Caesar subdued the rest of Gaul, finally crushing the Gallic tribal leader ▷Vercingetorix at Alesia. Augustus organized Transalpine Gaul into four provinces—Narbonensis, Belgica, Lugdunensis, and Aquitania. During the 1st century AD Gaul, especially Narbonensis, was extensively romanized and prospered until the barbarian invasions in the 5th century.

● **Gaullists** ▶ The supporters of the policies of Gen ▷de Gaulle, especially his independent foreign policy and drive towards industrial expansion, which were motivated by a wish to re-establish France as a world power. De Gaulle's Rassemblement du Peuple français (1947–53) was succeeded by the Union de Démocrates pour la République, which was reorganized by Jacques ▷Chirac as the Rassemblement pour la République in 1976.

● **gaur** ▶ The largest of the wild cattle, Bos gaurus, of hilly forests in S Asia. Up to 200 cm high at the shoulder, bulls can weigh up to 1 tonne. Gaurs are dark brown with white socks and both sexes have horns, the tips pointing upwards in bulls and inwards in cows.

● **gauss** ▶ (G) The unit of magnetic flux density in the ▷c.g.s. system equal to a flux density of one maxwell per square centimetre. Named after Karl Friedrich ▷Gauss.

● **Gauss, Karl Friedrich** ▶ (1777–1855) German mathematician, regarded (with ▷Newton and ▷Archimedes) as one of the greatest mathematicians of all time. His greatest contributions were in the fields of probability theory, number theory, complex numbers, algebra, and electricity and magnetism.

● **Gauteng** ▷See Transvaal.

● **Gautier, Théophile** ▶ (1811–72) French Romantic poet and critic. Influenced by Victor ▷Hugo, his early writings include Poésies (1830) and Les Jeunes-France (1833). The brief lyrical poems in Émaux et camées (1852) embody his belief in the value of art for its own sake. He wrote much influential art, ballet, and dramatic criticism and travelled widely.

● **Gavaskar, Sunil Manohar** ▶ (1949–) Indian cricketer, who played for Bombay, Somerset, and India (1971–90) and captained India (1978–83, 1984–85). In 1987 he became the first batsman to score 10 000 runs in Test cricket.

● **Gaveston, Piers** ▶ (c. 1284–1312) Favourite of King ▷Edward II of England, who appointed him Earl of Cornwall and regent of England (1307–08). A Gascon, he was brought up at the English court as a foster brother to Edward, who became infatuated with him. His influence over the young king and his arrogant behaviour provoked the jealousy of the barons, who insisted on his banishment in 1308 and again in 1311. When Gaveston made an unauthorized return to court, the barons took up arms against Edward, who deserted his favourite. Gaveston was captured and beheaded near Warwick.

● **gavial** ▶ (or gharial) A long-snouted ⁰reptile, *Gavialis gangeticus*, occurring in N Indian rivers and sacred to Hindus. 4–5 m long, it has long slender sharp-toothed jaws, which it sweeps from side to side to catch fish. It is the only member of its family (*Gavialidae*). Order: *Crocodilia* (*see* crocodile).

● **Gävle** ▶ 60 41N 17 10E A seaport in E Sweden, on an inlet of the Gulf of Bothnia. Ice free for nine months of the year, it exports timber, wood pulp, and paper. Its industries include shipping and electronics. Population (1994): 90 270.

● **Gawain** ▶ In Arthurian legend, a knight of the Round Table, the nephew of King Arthur and the son of King Lot of Norway and the Orkneys. He was known for his purity.

● **Gay, John** ▶ (1685–1732) British poet and dramatist, a friend of Pope, Swift, and other members of the Scriblerus Club. His *Fables* (1727, 1738) were the most successful of his satirical poems. His best-known work is the ballad opera *The Beggar's Opera* (1728), a parody of Italian opera.

● **Gaya** ▶ 24 48N 85 00E A city in NE India, in Bihar. A centre of Hindu pilgrimage, it lies 10 km (6 mi) S of Buddh Gaya, which is sacred to Buddhists. Population (1991): 291 220.

● **gayal** ▶ A species of domestic cattle, *Bos frontalis*, of Myanmar (Burma). Gayals are similar to the wild ▷gaur, but are smaller, measuring about 150 cm at the shoulder, and have a wider spread of horns.

● **Gay Liberation** ▷*See* homosexuality.

● **Gay-Lussac, Joseph Louis** ▶ (1778–1850) French chemist and physicist. He discovered the element boron (1808) and the law that gases combine in a simple ratio by volume (**Gay-Lussac's law**). He also discovered ▷Charles's law independently of Charles and published his results first.

● **Gaza** ▶ (Arabic name: Ghazzah) 31 30N 34 28E The largest town in the ▷Gaza Strip. Gaza has been inhabited continuously for over 3000 years; in biblical times it was a Philistine centre, where Samson was killed (Judges 16). Its products now include pottery and textiles. Population (1999 est): 388 031.

● **Gazankulu** ▷*See* Bantu Homelands.

● **Gaza Strip** ▶ A strip of coastal territory, 50 km (30 mi) long, on the SE corner of the Mediterranean Sea. Following the Arab-Israeli War of 1948–49, the only part of Palestine held by Egypt was a strip of land on the coast that became known as the Gaza Strip. Held by the Israelis for a short time in 1956–57, it was taken by them again in 1967. Under the Camp David agreement (1979) between Israel and Egypt, eventual self-government for the area was planned. The Gaza Strip suffers from extreme overpopulation, many Palestine refugees being housed in squalid camps. Palestinian self-government officially commenced in 1994 (*see* Palestine Liberation Organization) but living conditions have not improved. Violent protests intensified in 2000–01, provoking Israeli air and rocket attacks and repeated military incursions. ▷*See also* intifada. Population (2000 est): 1 147 000.

● **gazelle** ▶ A slender antelope of the genus *Gazella* (about 12 species), of Africa and Asia. 50–90 cm high at the shoulder, gazelles are distinguished from other antelopes by light and dark horizontal stripes on the face. Brown to grey in colour, gazelles may also have a dark band along the sides above the lighter belly. In most species both sexes have horns, which are generally lyre-shaped, ridged, and backward-curving with a forward-pointing tip.

● **Gaziantep** ▶ 37 04N 37 21E A city in S Turkey, near the Syrian border. Known for its Hittite remains, Gaziantep is near ancient trade routes and has changed hands frequently. It is an important market town. Population (1995 est): 730 435.

● **GBE** ▷*See* Order of the British Empire.

● **GCSE** ▶ (or General Certificate of Secondary Education) An examination for 16-year-old schoolchildren in the UK (except Scotland). Introduced in 1988 to replace GCE O-level and CSE, it is intended to

have a more practical base and to give greater weight to continuous assessment of coursework than its predecessors. Administered by six groups of boards in England, Wales, and Northern Ireland, there is a seven-point scale (A–G corresponding to the former O-level grades). ▷*See also* public examinations.

● **Gdańsk** ▶ (German name: Danzig) 54 22N 18 41E A port in N Poland, on the Baltic Sea. It is an industrial centre with metallurgy, chemicals, and food processing; exports include coal, grain, and timber. The city's famous shipyards closed in 1997. Its university was founded in 1970.
    History: it developed as a trade centre during the Renaissance. It was under Prussian control (1793–1807 and 1814–1919), becoming a free city under the League of Nations in 1919. In 1939 it was annexed by Germany, an act that precipitated World War II; the city was returned to Poland in 1945. It was the birthplace of the trade union ▷Solidarity. Population (1999 est): 458 988.

● **GDP** ▶ (gross domestic product) ▷*See* gross national product.

● **Gdynia** ▶ 54 31N 18 30E A port in N Poland, on the Baltic Sea. Originally a fishing village, it was developed (1924–39) to replace Danzig (*see* Gdańsk) becoming Poland's main shipbuilding centre and naval base. Population (1999 est): 253 521.

● **Ge** ▶ A group of South American Indian peoples of Brazil and N Paraguay who speak languages of the Macro-Ge group. Its numerous tribes are very diverse in cultural patterns. They are largely hunters and gatherers but some have adopted cultivation. Besides clan divisions, social rankings are based on age, sex, occupation, etc., each controlling its own sphere.

● **gean** ▷*See* cherry.

● **gear** ▶ A toothed wheel used to transmit power between rotating shafts. The ratio of the number of teeth on two meshing gears determines the ratio of the speeds of rotation of the two shafts to which they are attached. For example, if the driving shaft is attached to a gear with twice as many teeth as the gear attached to the driven shaft, the driven shaft will rotate at twice the speed of the driving shaft. The driven shaft, however, will exert half the torque of the driving shaft. To enable two shafts to turn in the same direction, three meshing gears are required; to transmit power between two shafts at right angles to each other, bevelled gears are used.

● **Geber** ▶ (14th century) Spanish alchemist, whose suggestion that different metals consist of mercury and sulphur in different proportions laid the foundation for the belief in the ▷philosopher's stone. He was also an experimental chemist, preparing nitric and acetic acids and white lead. He assumed the name Geber, which is the Latin form of Jabir, in honour of the 8th-century Arab alchemist Jabir ibn Hayyan.

● **gecko** ▶ A slender long-tailed nocturnal lizard that belongs to the widely distributed family *Gekkonidae* (650 species) and is found in a wide range of habitats including deserts and rain forests. 3–35 cm long, many geckos have fleshy toe pads covered with microscopic hooks enabling them to cling to smooth surfaces, such as ceilings. They feed on insects. The tokay (*Gekko gecko*) of E Asia is a large arboreal gecko and lays its eggs in crevices (⁰reptile).

● **Gediminas** ▶ (c. 1275–1341) Grand Duke of Lithuania (1316–41). A great ruler, he founded the state by unifying the Lithuanian tribes and made Vilnius the capital. He extended his dominions, which he defended against the ▷Teutonic Knights. He was converted to Christianity in 1323.

● **Geelong** ▶ 38 10S 144 26E A city and major port in Australia, in S Victoria on Corio Bay. Wool, wheat, and oil are the principal exports. Population (1998 est): 186 307.

● **gegenschein** ▶ (German: counterglow) A very faint glow in the night sky that can sometimes be seen on the ▷ecliptic in a direction directly opposite the sun's position. It is part of the ▷zodiacal light.

● **Gehenna** ▶ In the Bible, the Valley of Hinnom, outside Jerusalem. At one time it was apparently the site of human sacrifices and was therefore considered unclean, becoming the place where the city's refuse was dumped and burned. In Jewish thought it came to represent a place where sinners are punished and in the New Testament it is a name for hell.

• **Gehry, Frank O(wen)** ► (1929–) Canadian-born US architect and furniture designer, who set up his own practice in California in 1962 and made his name with such buildings as the Loyola Law School in Los Angeles (1981–84). His adventurous designs include the titanium-clad Guggenheim Museum in Bilbao, Spain (1997), one of the most celebrated buildings of the late 20th century.

• **Geiger, Hans** ► (1882–1945) German physicist, who in 1913 invented the ▷Geiger counter for detecting ionizing radiation in connection with his work on cosmic rays. During World War II he participated in Germany's attempt to build an atomic bomb.

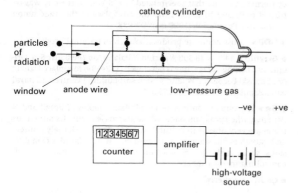

cathode cylinder

particles of radiation

window   anode wire   low-pressure gas

–ve   +ve

1 2 3 4 5 6 7
counter

amplifier

high-voltage
source

Geiger counter ► The radiation entering the tube causes an electrical discharge through the gas between the anode and cathode, sending an electrical pulse to the counter.

• **Geiger counter** ► A device that detects and counts ionizing radiation and particles. Essentially it consists of a metal cylinder containing low-pressure gas and a wire anode running along its central axis. The anode is held at a potential difference just less than that required to produce a discharge in the gas. Ionizing particles passing into the tube through a window at one end induce discharges, which can be counted by a suitable circuit. Named after Hans ▷Geiger.

• **geisha** ► A Japanese woman whose profession is to entertain men in a restaurant. Geishas, who are not prostitutes, sing and dance or engage their clients in conversation. In modern Japan geishas are employed primarily for the benefit of tourists.

• **gel** ▷See colloid.

• **Gela** ► 37 04N 14 15E A town in Italy, in Sicily. Founded by Greek colonists in 689 BC, it flourished under Hippocrates in the 5th century BC. Abandoned in 281 BC, it was refounded in 1233. Its industries include fishing and petrochemicals. Population (latest est): 79 380.

• **gelada** ► A large ▷Old World monkey, *Theropithecus gelada*, of the Ethiopian mountains. 120–150 cm long including the tufted tail (70–80 cm), it has a cape of dark-brown hair with two bare chest patches and lives in large groups, feeding on roots, leaves, and fruit.

• **gelatin** ► A protein derived from bones and skins. In solution it forms a reversible gel that becomes fluid as the temperature rises and solidifies on cooling. Because of this, it is widely used in the food industry as a stabilizer in jellies and confectionery, in drug preparations, and in photographic emulsions.

• **Gelderland** ► A province in the E Netherlands, bordering on Germany. The fertile soils of the Rhine Valley produce vegetables, fruit, and dairy products. The NW is an important tourist area. Manufactured products include cotton and paper. Area: 5131 sq km (1981 sq mi). Population (1996): 1 876 300. Capital: Arnhem.

• **Geldof, Bob** ► (1954–) Irish rock musician. Geldof sang with the Boomtown Rats before becoming involved in fund raising for the starving in Africa in 1984. He organized a massive concert held simultaneously in the UK and the USA in 1985, raising huge sums for charity. He received an honorary knighthood in 1986.

• **gelignite** ► A high explosive consisting of nitroglycerin, cellulose nitrate, potassium nitrate, and woodpulp.

• **Gell-Mann, Murray** ► (1929–) US physicist, who won the 1969 Nobel Prize for his theoretical work on elementary particles. In 1953 he introduced the concept of ▷strangeness to account for the absence of certain expected interactions. He also formulated the theory of ▷unitary symmetry and introduced the concept of quarks (*see also* particle physics). His books include *The Quark and the Jaguar* (1994).

• **Gelsenkirchen** ► 51 30N 7 05E A city in NW Germany, in North Rhine-Westphalia. A ▷Ruhr coalmining centre and port on the Rhine-Herne Canal, it has a moated palace (16th–18th centuries). Its manufactures include steel, chemicals, and glass. Population (1996 est): 291 164.

• **Gemara** ▷See Talmud.

• **Gemini** ► (Latin: Twins) A conspicuous constellation in the N sky near Orion, lying on the ▷zodiac between Cancer and Taurus. The brightest stars are ▷Pollux and ▷Castor.

• **gemsbok** ▷See oryx.

• **gemstones** ► Minerals or mineral fragments used for decorative purposes, particularly jewellery. Desirability is usually based on the gem's beauty (in terms of colour, transparency, and lustre), its durability (gemstones must be hard), and rarity. Diamond, ruby, sapphire, and emerald are precious stones, the others (amethyst, agate, jasper, onyx, aquamarine, topaz, garnet, etc.) are semiprecious. Not all are crystalline; for example, opal and jade are amorphous. Gemstones are usually artificially cut (either faceted or rounded) and polished; some, such as onyx, are suitable for engraving, as cameos for instance. Many can be synthetically produced.

• **gene** ► A unit of the hereditary material of an organism that provides the genetic information necessary to fulfil a single function. The term was coined by W. L. ▷Johannsen (1909). Genes were initially conceived as a string of beads comprising the ▷chromosome; they were later defined as lengths of the chromosome that were physically indivisible during the exchange of chromosomal material that occurs during ▷meiosis. Alternatively, a gene was defined as the shortest length of the chromosome that could undergo ▷mutation. A gene is now regarded as being a functional unit (cistron) of ▷DNA corresponding to a specific sequence of the ▷genetic code. ▷See also genome.

• **General Agreement on Tariffs and Trade** ► (GATT) An organization set up in 1948 by a UN initiative to regulate world trade. Its charter was never ratified but 125 countries have contracted to operate within it and a further 22 did so *de facto*. It aimed to provide an international forum and reduce barriers to trade, especially in developing countries. It completed eight "rounds" of negotiations: the eighth (Uruguay) round was successfully completed in 1993. GATT was succeeded by the ▷World Trade Organization in 1996.

• **General Certificate of Secondary Education** ▷See GCSE.

• **General Strike** ► (1926) A national strike by workers in Britain's major industries, lasting from 3 to 12 May. It began when the Trades Union Council (TUC) called out its members in support of the miners, who had refused to accept a reduction in wages. The Strike affected over two million men in transport, the iron and steel industries, the building and printing trades, and gas and electricity services. However, the government under Stanley ▷Baldwin kept essential services going and the TUC called off the Strike. The miners gained nothing and trade unions were worse off after the Trade Union Act (1927).

• **generative grammar** ▷See grammar.

• **gene sequencing** ► Determining the order of the ▷nucleotides that make up a length of ▷DNA. Since a ▷gene is a sequence of nucleotides concerned with a particular function, this process will reveal the order in which the genes occur. The method usually used is that developed by Frederick ▷Sanger; it forms the basis of the work on the Human Genome Project (*see* genome).

• **Genesis** ► The first book of the Bible, traditionally ascribed to Moses. It recounts the Creation, the fall of Adam and his exclusion from the Garden of Eden, the Flood, the scattering of the nations at

▷Babel, and the lives of Abraham, Isaac, Jacob, and Joseph. It also introduces the theme of the ▷covenant between God and Israel.

● **genet** ▶ A carnivorous mammal of the genus *Genetta* (9 species) of Africa and Europe. Genets range in size from the 50-cm Abyssinian genet (*G. abyssinica*) to the 100-cm African giant genet (*G. victoriae*). They have retractile claws, long tails (up to 50 cm), foxlike heads, and pale fur with dark spots or stripes. Genets are nocturnal hunters. Family: ▷Viverridae.

● **Genet, Jean** ▶ (1910–86) French novelist and dramatist. *A Thief's Journal* (1948) tells of his life in reformatories and prisons and among criminals and prostitutes. In his novels, which include *Our Lady of the Flowers* (1944) and *Miracle of the Rose* (1946), he describes this underworld with poetic intensity. His plays are *Deathwatch* (1947), *The Maids* (1947), *The Balcony* (1956), *The Blacks* (1958), and *The Screens* (1961).

● **gene therapy** ▶ The treatment of diseases by introducing selected genes into the body of the patient using the techniques of ▷genetic engineering. Still undergoing clinical trials, it is targeted at somatic (body) cells rather than germ cells, so that the patient will benefit from the transferred gene but this will not be inherited by subsequent generations. Germ-line therapy is currently considered to be ethically unacceptable. Genetic diseases, such as severe combined immune deficiency (SCID) and cystic fibrosis, are caused by a faulty gene failing to produce a vital protein; treatment is designed to introduce into the patient's body the correct version of the gene, which can restore production of the missing protein. As knowledge of the human ▷genome is increasing, gene-based therapies have the potential for curing not only genetic diseases but also other disorders, including cancer, diabetes, and cardiovascular disease, in which genes are known to play a role.

● **genetic code** ▶ The way in which information encoded in ▷DNA and ▷RNA molecules is used for the organization and function of living cells. The nature of the code was elucidated in the 1960s by ▷Crick, M. W. Nirenberg (1927–), ▷Khorana, and others. The basic symbol of the code is a sequence of three consecutive bases of messenger RNA (which is transcribed from DNA). According to the combination of the four possible bases—adenine, guanine, cytosine, and uracil—different triplet sequences (or codons) specify the 20 or so amino acids commonly used by cells for protein synthesis. There are 64 possible triplet sequences; therefore some amino acids are coded for by more than one triplet, and some triplets have other functions (in stopping and starting the process).

● **genetic counselling** ▶ Advice given to those in whose families there is a history of inherited diseases, such as cystic fibrosis and muscular dystrophy. Families at risk are told of their chances of developing the disease, the likelihood of their children being affected, and what means of prevention and treatment are available.

● **genetic engineering** ▶ (genetic modification *or* recombinant DNA technology) Alteration of the genetic constitution of organisms in order to obtain gene products beneficial to humans. Typically, a sequence of desirable genes is inserted into the DNA of a vector, which is usually a virus or a plasmid (a piece of bacterial DNA that can replicate independently of the bacterial chromosome). The vector containing this altered DNA (or recombinant DNA) is then transferred to a host cell (usually a bacterium) and the recombinant DNA directs the bacterial cell to synthesize the desired gene product. As bacteria can be cultured quickly and easily, large quantities of products, such as insulin and human growth hormone, can be obtained. Genetic modification is also used to improve crop plants, for example by conferring resistance to pests or nonspecific herbicides, prolonging storage time, or increasing nutrient content. Although such plants are not yet grown commercially in the UK, some genetically modified (GM) foods are now available in this country, including tomatoes (in the form of paste and purée) and maize and soya (both of which are present in many food products). Genetic modification of plants to produce oral vaccines is still in the experimental stage but offers the potential for preventing such diseases as hepatitis and AIDS. Genetic engineering may also be used to produce transgenic animals (e.g. mice and sheep) containing foreign genes inserted during early embryonic life. In studying the genetic basis of disease, animals are bred to lack certain genes thought to prevent diseases. When the animal

contracts the disease the function of the gene in question is confirmed. ▷*See also* gene therapy.

● **genetic fingerprinting** ▶ (*or* DNA fingerprinting) An identification technique based on DNA examination. DNA is extracted from sample cells (e.g. from blood or semen) and broken into fragments using enzymes. These fragments, containing the genetic code unique to each individual, are graded for size and compared with fragments obtained from a blood sample of the test subject. Since 1987 it has been used in the UK as forensic evidence.

● **genetic modification** ▷*See* genetic engineering.

● **genetics** ▶ The study of heredity and variation in living organisms. The science of genetics is founded on the work of Gregor ▷Mendel, who, in 1865, established the basic laws of inheritance. In the early 20th century ▷chromosomes and their ▷genes were established as the carriers of information determining inheritable characteristics, and with the discovery of the structure of ▷DNA in 1953, the molecular basis of genetics was revealed. Genetics is important in plant and animal breeding and in understanding inherited diseases and abnormalities. □ p. 504.

● **Geneva** ▶ (French name: Genève; German name: Genf) 46 13N 6 09E A city in SW Switzerland, on the SW corner of Lake Geneva. It is a cultural and commercial centre with over two-thirds of the population employed in the service sector, mainly in banking and international finance. Industries include the production of watches, precision instruments, and chemicals. It is the base of many international organizations including the International Red Cross and the World Health Organization. The European headquarters of the United Nations occupy buildings that formerly housed the League of Nations. It has a cathedral (12th–13th centuries) and a university (founded as the Academy in 1559).
History: originally a prehistoric lake dwelling, it was later a Roman city. It became the centre of the Calvinist Reformation and a refuge for persecuted Protestants. Population (1996 est): 173 549.

● **Geneva, Lake** ▶ (French name: Lac Léman; German name: Genfersee) A lake on the River Rhône lying partly in Switzerland and partly in France. Geneva (at its W end) and Lausanne and Montreux are on the Swiss N shore; the French resort of Evian lies on its S shore. It is dominated by the Alps to the N. Area: 577 sq km (223 sq mi).

● **Geneva Bible** ▶ An English translation of the Bible published in 1560 by Puritan exiles in Geneva. It is also called the Breeches Bible because the word is used in translating Genesis 3.7.

● **Geneva Conferences** ▶ **1.** (1932–34) An international conference on ▷disarmament. 59 states attended the opening meeting, chaired by the British foreign secretary Arthur ▷Henderson, but the major powers failed to agree and in 1933 Hitler withdrew Germany from both the conference and the ▷League of Nations. The conference did not reassemble after 1934. **2.** (1954) A conference held after the conclusion of the ▷Korean War, attended by the USA, Soviet Union, the UK, France, North Korea, South Korea, and the People's Republic of China; it ended without agreement. The war in ▷Indochina was also discussed by the USA, the Soviet Union, the UK, France, China, Vietnam, Cambodia, Laos, and the ▷Viet Minh; a ceasefire line was settled along the ▷seventeenth parallel.

● **Geneva Conventions** ▶ International agreements covering the care of noncombatants and wounded troops in wartime. Inspired by the establishment of the International ▷Red Cross, the first conference, attended by 16 countries, met in Geneva in 1864 to formulate a code of practice for the treatment of wounded soldiers. Later conventions (1906, 1929) ratified further agreements, covering assistance for forces at sea and treatment of ▷prisoners of war. In 1949 a fourth convention concerning the protection of civilians was incorporated and the others revised. Neutral countries and the International Red Cross have a supervisory role in war but enforcement is difficult as violation cannot be punished.

● **Genghis Khan** ▶ (c. 1162–1227) The founder of the Mongol empire. Originally called Tamujin, he adopted the title Genghis Khan (Emperor of All) in 1206 after uniting under his command the nomadic Mongol tribes of the Siberian steppes and destroying Tatar power. Having organized his horsemen into highly mobile and disciplined squadrons called *ordus* (hence "hordes"), he attacked China's frontiers. Although his armies breached the Great Wall and captured Beijing, they failed to conquer China completely. Advancing westwards, Genghis, by ruthless massacres, crushed all resistance in Afghanistan, Persia, and S Russia. After his death his son Ogadai (1185–1241) executed Genghis's plans for the empire's organization.

● **genipap** ▸ The fruit of *Genipa americana*, a small West Indian tree. Resembling a brown orange, it is used in preserves and beverages. Family: *Rubiaceae* (madder family).

● **Genk** ▸ 50 58N 5 30E A town in NE Belgium. Its main manufacture was mining machinery until Belgium's coal industry went into decline. Population (1995 est): 61 996.

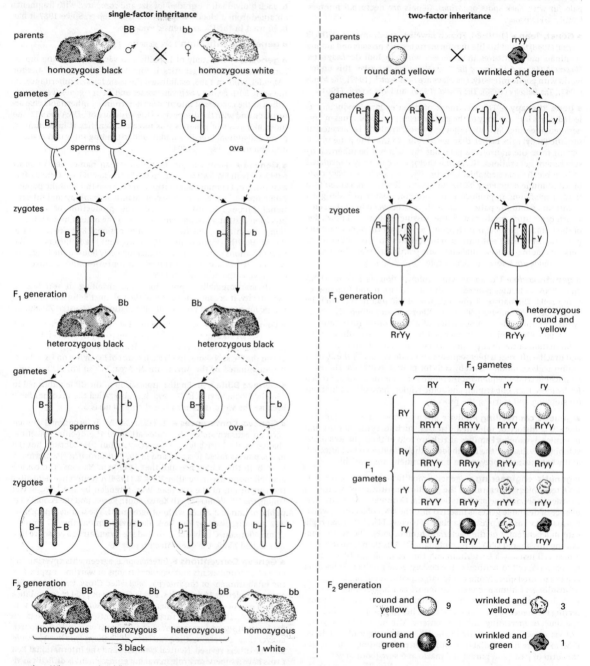

genetics ▸ When a purebred (homozygous) black guinea pig (BB) mates with a purebred white one (bb) all the offspring (F₁ generation) will be black (Bb), since the gene for black is dominant. Mating of this heterozygous F₁ generation will produce both black and white guinea pigs (F₂ generation) in the ratio 3:1, since each of the parents carries a white recessive gene. The same principle applies to the inheritance of two factors — seed colour and texture — in pea plants. When a plant with round yellow seeds (RRYY — dominant) is crossed with one producing wrinkled green seeds (rryy — recessive) the offspring will all have round yellow seeds (RrYy — heterozygous). Crossing of this generation results in the segregation and reassortment of the genes so that their offspring will show all four possibilities of seed colour and texture in the proportions 9:3:3:1. These examples of single- and two-factor inheritance obey Mendel's laws.

● **Gennesaret, Lake of** ▷*See* Galilee, Sea of.

● **Genoa** ▶ (Italian name: Genova) 44 24N 08 56E A port in NW Italy, the capital of Liguria on the Gulf of Genoa. A major maritime city during the middle ages, it possesses many notable buildings dating from then. These include the cathedral of San Lorenzo (1118) and a university (1471). Genoa is Italy's chief port and also a major industrial centre with heavy engineering, steel processing, and oil refining. Population (1996 est): 659 116.

● **genocide** ▶ The systematic killing of the members of a nation, religion, ethnic group, or race. Although history records numerous massacres of vanquished peoples by their conquerors, it was the Germans in the years 1935–45 who defined the modern concept of genocide by murdering some six million Jews and smaller numbers of other ethnic groups, such as Gipsies and Slavs (*see* holocaust; Wannsee conference). In 1948 the UN responded to these crimes by adopting its convention on the Prevention and Punishment of the Crime of Genocide. Unfortunately, human behaviour cannot be controlled by convention. Genocide has subsequently been practised in Cambodia (1970s), Rwanda (1990s), and elsewhere. In the 1990s the genocide of Bosnian Muslims by Serbs became known by the euphemism **ethnic cleansing**. Despite general outrage, the international community failed to stop any of these genocides. In 1999 NATO used air power to halt Serb attacks on ethnic Albanians in ▷Kosovo, thus setting a new precedent for military intervention in such cases.

● **genome** ▶ The full complement of genes within a single (haploid) set of chromosomes; by extension, the genetic constitution of a species or individual. The **Human Genome Project**, begun in 1988, is a 15-year programme to identify and determine the sequence of all the genes comprising the human genome (*see* gene sequencing). By 2001 a complete "first draft" of the human genome had been published, indicating that the total number of human genes is about 30 000. This knowledge will be used to identify the genes responsible for many common diseases, which will enable accurate genetic testing—and, in the long term, the development of gene-based drugs and other treatments—for these diseases. ▷*See also* gene therapy.

● **genotype** ▶ The genetic constitution of an individual organism, which comprises its ▷genes and determines the physical characteristics (*see* phenotype) of that individual.

● **genre painting** ▶ A type of painting representing some aspect of everyday life. Although earlier examples exist, genre painting first became popular in 17th-century Holland, where it was developed by such painters as ▷Vermeer, ▷Steen, de ▷Hooch, and Jacob Duk. Notable 18th-century examples are the works of ▷Hogarth and ▷Chardin. In the 19th century the impressionists and Victorian painters enthusiastically adopted it. In the 20th century it was overshadowed by abstract art, but was still practised by such artists as ▷Bonnard.

● **Genseric** ▶ (*or* Gaiseric; d. 477 AD) King of the ▷Vandals (428–77), who helped destroy the ▷Roman Empire. He led the Vandals from Spain to N Africa, which he conquered after seizing Carthage from the Romans in 439. In 455 he sacked Rome.

● **Gent** ▷*See* Ghent.

● **gentian** ▶ A herbaceous plant of the widely distributed genus *Gentiana* (about 400 species), which includes many alpine perennials. The leaves are opposite and unstalked. The flowers have four or five petals, usually blue, forming a bell or funnel with spreading lobes. The fruit of most species is a capsule. Family: *Gentianaceae*.

● **gentian violet** ▶ A purple dye derived from ▷aniline. It is used as an antiseptic, a chemical indicator, and as a dye.

● **Gentile, Giovanni** ▶ (1875–1944) Italian philosopher. Gentile held to Hegelian theories about the dominance of the will; a thinking person had a spiritual unity that was realized in the *pure act*—hence his doctrine of "actualism." As Mussolini's minister of public education he purged the educational system of teachers suspected of democratic or liberal tendencies.

● **Gentile da Fabriano** ▶ (Niccolo di Giovanni di Massio; c. 1370–1427) Florentine painter of the ▷international gothic style. His fresco cycles (completed by ▷Pisanello) for the Doge's Palace, Venice, and

the Lateran Basilica, Rome, have perished. The *Adoration of the Magi* (Uffizi) shows his decorated style.

● **Gentileschi, Orazio** ▶ (Orazio Lomi; 1562–c. 1647) Italian Baroque painter. Born in Pisa, he worked in Rome from the early 1580s and became a follower of Caravaggio. He subsequently worked in France and (from 1526) England, where he became court painter to Charles I. His masterpiece is usually considered to be *The Annunciation* (1623, Turin). His daughter **Artemisia Gentileschi** (1597–c. 1652) was also a painter in the dramatic style established by Caravaggio. With such works as the violent *Judith and Holofernes* (c. 1622, Florence) she soon outstripped her father's fame. She worked in Florence and England before settling in Naples (1639).

● **Gentlemen at Arms, Honourable Corps of** ▶ The ceremonial bodyguard of the British monarch, first organized in 1509 by Henry VIII. Its members are now chosen from decorated officers of the Army or Royal Marines and are led by a captain, who is the government chief whip in the House of Lords.

● **gentrification** ▶ Upgrading a former working-class street or district for habitation by the middle classes. For example, in London Islington was gentrified in the 1960s and Limehouse in the 1980s by converting artisans' cottages into small but smart (bijou) residences, usually by knocking down walls to enlarge rooms and adding modern bathrooms and kitchens.

● **gentry** ▷*See* yeoman.

● **genus** ▷*See* taxonomy.

● **geocentric system** ▷*See* Ptolemaic system.

● **geochemistry** ▶ The study of the chemical composition of the earth. It involves estimating the abundance of the constituent elements and their isotopes, as well as their distribution in the geochemical environments (lithosphere, atmosphere, biosphere, hydrosphere) and in the rocks and minerals that make up the earth. In the earth's crust, oxygen (47%), silicon (28%), and aluminium (8%) are the most abundant elements.

● **geochronology** ▶ The study of dating geological events, rocks, sediments, and organic remains, either absolutely or relatively. Absolute dating involves radioactive dating techniques giving an actual date BP (before present). Relative dating establishes the order of geological events in relation to each other, using fossil correlation, pollen analysis, archaeological evidence, etc.

● **geodesic dome** ▷*See* Fuller, Richard Buckminster.

● **geodesy** ▶ The science of determining the shape and size of the earth or portions of it, using precise surveying and exact calculations of gravitational force. Related topics, such as the earth's rotational effects and tides, are also studied. Geodetic surveying is the large-scale surveying of the earth's surface, taking into account its curvature. This provides the data for fixing control points for detailed surveying.

● **Geoffrey Martel** ▶ (1006–60) Count of Anjou (1040–60). Through his marriage (1032) to Agnes the widow of the Duke of Aquitaine he unsuccessfully claimed Aquitaine. However, Geoffrey subsequently acquired Touraine and much of Maine.

● **Geoffrey of Monmouth** ▶ (c. 1100–54) English chronicler. His major work, *Historia Regum Britanniae*, was the main source for the whole body of medieval European literature concerned with the Arthurian legend and included the stories of King Lear, Cymbeline, and other legendary figures.

● **Geoffroy Saint-Hilaire, Étienne** ▶ (1772–1844) French naturalist, who suggested that all animals conformed to the same basic structural plan or "unity of composition." Geoffroy saw modern species as unchanging but derived from ancestral species through the appearance of successful "monstrosities."

● **geography** ▶ The study of the features of the earth's surface, together with their spatial distribution and interrelationships, as the environment of man. The Greeks, notably Herodotus, Eratosthenes of Cyrene, and Ptolemy, studied the shape of the earth and the location of land and sea. Modern geography was founded in the early 19th century by the German scholars Humboldt and Ritter. During the 20th century geography has moved away from regional studies to

geology

stages in the evolution of the geological strata of a small area

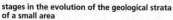

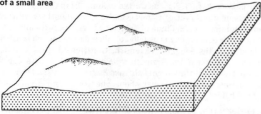

1 Desert conditions resulted in the lowest rock layer being sandstone.

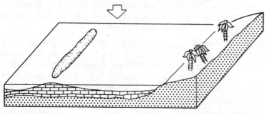

2 The advance of a warm sea over much of the area saw the deposition of chalk.

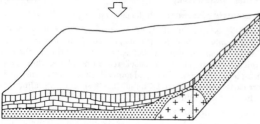

3 Following the retreat of the sea the area was covered with a fine sediment eventually forming clay and an igneous intrusion of granite was forced up by volcanic activity into the overlying strata.

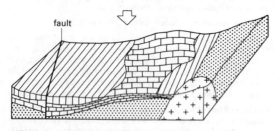

fault

4 The area was then subjected to folding, faulting, and erosion to form the present day landscape.

geological map

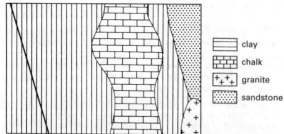

clay

chalk

granite

sandstone

The map of the same area shows the rock types that would be exposed if the overlying soil and vegetation were stripped away.

geological time scale

era	period	epoch	millions of years ago
Cenozoic	Quaternary	Holocene	
		Pleistocene	
		Pliocene	1.8
	Tertiary	Miocene	
		Oligocene	
		Eocene	
		Palaeocene	
			65
Mesozoic	Cretaceous		
			135
	Jurassic		
			200
	Triassic		
			240
Palaeozoic	Permian		
			280
	Carboniferous		
			370
	Devonian		
			415
	Silurian		
			445
	Ordovician		
			515
	Cambrian		
			590
Precambrian	Precambrian		
			4500

a more systematic approach. Physical geography includes geomorphology (the study of landforms), biogeography (the study of soils and the distribution of animals and plants), and climatology (*see* climate). The main branches of human geography are historical geography (studying spatial change in an area over a period of time or reconstructing past landscapes), economic geography, urban geography, and political geography.

● **geological time scale** ▶ A time scale covering the whole of the earth's history from its origin about 4600 million years ago to the present. The largest divisions are eras (Palaeozoic, Mesozoic, and Cenozoic); these are subdivided into periods and the Tertiary and Quaternary periods are further subdivided into epochs; epochs consist of several ages, and ages can be divided into chrons. A number of eras together is an eon. This is known as the chronomeric standard scale of chronostratigraphic classification. The stratomeric standard scale refers to the bodies of rocks formed in these time intervals; the corresponding terms are group (era), system (period), series (epoch), stage (age), and chronozone (chron). The divisions are not uniform time intervals but are based mainly on major evolutionary changes. For example, at the beginning of the Cambrian, about 590 million years ago, marine organisms suddenly became abundant and varied.

● **geology** ▶ The study of the earth: its origin, history, structure, composition, and the natural processes acting on it. The branches of geology are historical (including geochronology, stratigraphy, and palaeontology); physical (including geomorphology, geophysics, petrology, mineralogy, crystallography, and geochemistry); and economic, involving the distribution and occurrence of the economically important rocks and minerals, such as petroleum.

● **geomagnetic field** ▶ The earth's magnetic field, causing a compass needle to align north–south. It is believed to be caused by the liquid-iron core acting as a dynamo resulting from the convection currents moving in it. The magnetic poles do not coincide with the geographic poles, and their positions vary with time. Complete reversals of the earth's magnetic field have occurred in the past; relic magnetism in rocks, which coincides with the magnetic alignment adopted at the time of their formation, provides strong evidence for the theory of sea-floor spreading and continental drift (*see* plate tectonics). The three **magnetic elements** of the earth's field are the ▷magnetic dip, the ▷magnetic declination, and the horizontal field strength, which together completely define the earth's field at any point on its surface.

● **geometrid moth** ▶ A moth of the family *Geometridae*, occurring in Europe, Asia, and North America. The name is derived from the looping method of locomotion of the caterpillars, which are known as inch worms, loopers, or measuring worms. The adults, known as pugs, umbers, carpet moths, etc., have slender bodies, a weak flight, and camouflaging coloration, often resembling dead leaves.

● **geometry** ▶ A branch of mathematics concerned with the properties of space and shapes. In ▷Euclidean geometry the space corresponds to common notions of physical space and the shapes are idealizations of the common shapes that occur in real life. Other branches of geometry include ▷non-Euclidean geometry, such as the geometry of the surface of a sphere; ▷Riemannian geometry, which is used in ▷relativity theory; and ▷analytic geometry, in which algebra is used to solve geometrical problems. ▷*See also* topology.

● **geophysics** ▶ The study of the physical forces acting on, and particularly within, the earth. Sophisticated equipment is used to study the properties, structure, composition, and evolution of the earth. Important branches of geophysics are seismology, geomagnetism, vulcanology, natural radioactivity, and the earth's rotation and gravitational field. Much geophysical data has been collected in recent years as a result of geophysical prospecting, particularly for petroleum.

● **geopolitics** ▶ The study of the influence of geographical factors upon international politics. It suggest that a state's foreign policy is influenced by its desire to obtain, for example, sufficient agricultural land. The term was coined by the Swedish political scientist Rudolf Kjellen (1864–1922) and was used by the Nazis, who justified their expansionist ambitions as the seeking of *Lebensraum* (living space). As a result geopolitics was discredited and has become outdated by technological developments.

● **George I** ▶ (1660–1727) The first Hanoverian King of Great Britain and Ireland (1714–27) and Elector of Hanover (1698–1727). He divorced his wife, Sophia Dorothea, for infidelity (1694) and imprisoned her for 32 years. A successful soldier and a shrewd diplomat, he was none the less unpopular in Britain because he seemed to subordinate British to Hanoverian interests. He never learnt English and left government to his Whig ministers, particularly after they saved George and his mistresses from disgrace in connection with the ▷South Sea Bubble.

● **George II** ▶ (1683–1760) King of Great Britain and Ireland and Elector of Hanover (1727–69), succeeding his father George I. He married ▷Caroline of Ansbach in 1705. His reliance on such ministers as Sir Robert ▷Walpole influenced the development of constitutional monarchy. In the War of Austrian Succession he fought at Dettingen (1743), the last British king to appear in battle. He was a patron of musicians, notably Handel.

George III ▶ His long reign saw the agricultural and industrial revolutions and eventual victory over France in the Napoleonic Wars. Somewhat unfairly, however, he is mainly remembered as the mad king who lost Britain its American colonies. He is seen here in a portrait by Allan Ramsay, whom he appointed court painter in 1767, before the onset of his illness.

● **George III** ▶ (1738–1820) King of Great Britain and Ireland (1760–1820) and Elector (1760–1815) and King (1815–20) of Hanover, succeeding his grandfather George II. He married Charlotte Sophia of Mecklenburg-Strelitz (1744–1818) in 1761. The political instability of the 1760s was blamed by the Whigs unjustly on George's alleged attempts to influence parliament through corrupt "king's friends." He shared with Lord ▷North the blame for the loss of the American colonies but was more astute in backing William ▷Pitt the Younger as prime minister (1783–1801). From the 1780s he suffered periods of madness (attributed to the metabolic disease acute intermittent porphyria) and was permanently insane by 1811, after which the Prince of Wales (later George IV) acted as regent (*see also* Regency style).

● **George IV** ▶ (1762–1830) King of the United Kingdom and of Hanover (1820–30), succeeding his father George III, for whom he was regent (1811–20). He secretly married a Roman Catholic, Maria Fitzherbert, in 1785 but the marriage was invalid and in 1795 he married ▷Caroline of Brunswick. They were separated in 1796. Although intelligent and artistic, George's dissipation and extravagance and his heartless treatment of Caroline undermined the prestige of the monarchy.

● **George V** ▶ (1865–1936) King of the United Kingdom (1910–36), second son of Edward VII, whose heir he became on the death (1892) of his elder brother Albert Victor. In 1893 George married ▷Mary of Teck. He gave valuable political advice during the many crises of his reign.

● **George VI** ▶ (1895–1952) King of the United Kingdom (1936–52).

Second son of George V, he succeeded to the throne when Edward VIII abdicated. He married (1923) Lady Elizabeth Bowes-Lyon (*see* Elizabeth the Queen Mother). His example inspired Britain in World War II.

● **George, St** ▶ The patron saint of England and of soldiers. His cult was brought to England by Crusaders returning from Palestine, where he was believed to have been martyred during Emperor Diocletian's rule. In art he is usually portrayed slaying a dragon to rescue a maiden, a legend that may derive from the ▷Pegasus myth. Feast day: 23 April.

● **George, Stefan** ▶ (1868–1933) German poet. He studied in Paris, where he was associated with the Symbolist poets, and in Germany, where he assembled and dominated a group of disciples. In his manifesto *Über Dichtung* (1894) he advocated rigid formal perfection and metrical regularity, goals that he achieved in *Das Jahr der Seele* (1897) and *Der Teppich des Lebens* (1899). His later work glorified a godlike youth, Maximin. The Nazis favoured him, but he rejected them, voluntarily exiling himself in 1933.

● **George-Brown, Baron** ▶ (1914–85) British statesman, born George Brown; deputy leader of the Labour Party (1960–70) and foreign secretary (1966–68). He entered parliament in 1945, representing Belper until created a life peer in 1970. His disagreement with government policies led to his resignation as foreign secretary and in 1976 he left the Labour Party. Later he helped found the ▷Social Democratic Party.

● **George Cross** ▶ The highest British decoration for civilian bravery, awarded since 1940. A silver cross superscribed *For Gallantry*, it has twice been awarded collectively: to the island of Malta (1942) and the Royal Ulster Constabulary (1999). The **George Medal**, the second highest decoration for civilian bravery, was also instituted in 1940.

● **Georgetown** ▶ (*or* Penang) 5 26N 100 16E A city in NW Peninsular Malaysia, the capital of Penang state. The first British Malayan settlement, it is now Malaysia's chief port, exporting tin, rubber, and copra. Population (1991): 219 376.

● **Georgetown** ▶ 6 46N 58 10W The capital and main port of Guyana, on the Atlantic Ocean at the mouth of the River Demerara. Founded by the British in 1781, it was later occupied by the French and the Dutch. It has twice in recent years (1945, 1951) been badly damaged by fire. Exports include sugar, rice, and bauxite. Its university was founded in 1963. Population (1995 est): 254 000.

● **Georgia** ▶ (USA) A state on the SE coast of the USA. It can be divided into two physical regions: the Appalachian Mountains in the N and a rolling coastal plain with forests and swamps in the S. Manufacturing is important although largely rurally orientated. It is the major textile producer in the USA; other industries include motor-vehicle and aircraft assembly, chemicals, and food processing. The

state is also a major source of building stone. Agriculture is important; poultry has replaced cotton as the major item and Georgia is a leading producer of peanuts. Other products include tobacco, water melons, and other fruits (especially peaches) with some cattle and pig raising. Forest products are produced throughout the state. Its capital Atlanta is the cultural and economic centre of the SE and the state has a rich traditional folk culture.

History: named after George II, it was founded in 1732, the youngest of the 13 original colonies. Settlement of the state expanded after the American Revolution with the development of agriculture. A supporter of the Confederate cause in the US Civil War, it suffered considerable damage during Gen Sherman's March to the Sea (1864). During the 20th century it has experienced many of the problems of the S, such as the decline in the cotton industry and racial unrest. Area: 152 488 sq km (58 876 sq mi). Population (1997 est): 7 486 242. Capital: Atlanta.

● **Georgia** ▶ (Asia) A republic in W Asia. It is a mountainous region with holiday resorts on the Black Sea coast. The population is mostly Georgian, with Russian and Armenian minorities.

Economy: Georgia is rich in minerals, especially manganese and coal, but these remain largely unexploited: gold was discovered in 1941. The region has hydroelectric resources. The main crops are tea, citrus fruits, grapes, and tobacco. The economy was brought to the brink of total collapse in the mid-1990s by the ending of Georgia's special trading relationship with Russia and a series of internal conflicts, which disrupted industry and virtually destroyed the Black Sea tourist trade. The economy has since stabilized, although black marketeering remains a major problem. Georgia signed economic cooperation agreements with Russia in 1994 and the EU in 1996.

History: Christianity was introduced in the 4th century AD. An independent kingdom for most of the middle ages, Georgia enjoyed a golden age of culture and prosperity in the 12th century but was divided between Persia and Turkey in 1555. Control of the whole region passed to Russia in the early 19th century. It became independent in 1918 but subsequently formed part of the Transcaucasian Soviet Federated Republic (*see* Transcaucasia). It became a separate Soviet republic in 1936. The late 1980s saw rising nationalist feeling with demonstrations for independence, which was unilaterally declared in 1990. Opposition to the dictatorial government of President Zviad Gamsakhurdia led to his overthrow by armed rebels in January 1992, control passing to a state council under Eduard ▷Shevardnadze. Georgia's independence was recognized in March 1992 and free elections were held in October. In the early 1990s Georgian troops fought supporters of Gamsakhurdia as well as separatists in ▷Abkhazia and ▷South Ossetia. The economy collapsed and peace was only achieved after Russia, in return for Georgia joining the Commonwealth of Independent States and signing a special cooperation treaty (1994), stopped supporting the separatists. In 1995 a new constitution granted considerable autonomy to both Abkhazia and South Ossetia

Georgian style ▶ The Royal Crescent (1767–75) at Bath, designed by John Wood the Younger. The linking of many residences to form a single architectural block is a major feature of the style.

(which was renamed Tskhinvali) but pressure for complete independence has continued.

Georgia

Head of state	President Eduard Shevardnadze
Official language	Georgian
Official currency	lari of 100 tetri
Area	69 493 sq km (26 831 sq mi)
Population (1997 est)	5 377 000
Capital	Tbilisi

● **Georgian** ▶ The language spoken by the Georgian peoples of Georgia, Azerbaidzhan, NE Turkey, and Isfahan province in Iran. It belongs to the ▷South Caucasian group and is written in a script derived from Aramaic with Greek influences and has a literature dating from the 5th century AD. It is the official language of Georgia.

● **Georgian Bay** ▶ A large bay in central Canada, in NE Lake Huron in Ontario. It is a popular recreational area.

● **Georgian style** ▶ A style of British architecture prevalent during the reigns of George I to George IV (1714–1830). The period was dominated by ▷Palladianism and ▷neoclassicism. Well-proportioned elegance was the keynote of Georgian architecture, characterized by the symmetrical use of twelve-paned sash windows in domestic architecture and the restrained use of classical features in public buildings. ▷*See also* Regency style.

● **geostationary orbit** ▷*See* communications satellite.

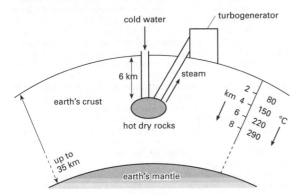

geothermal power ▶ In the UK the absence of volcanoes and geysers means that hot-dry-rock (HDR) technology has to be used. In this, cold water is pumped some 6 km down in the earth's crust, where it percolates through fissures in the hot dry rocks; the resulting superheated steam is brought to the surface, where it drives a turbogenerator. HDR technology is still experimental.

● **geothermal power** ▶ Heat produced in the earth's interior, which can provide a source of ▷alternative energy. Volcanoes, geysers, and hot springs are all sources of geothermal power, although only the latter two provide convenient energy sources. Countries that make use of geothermal power include Iceland, Italy, New Zealand, and the USA. Although geothermal power is being actively explored, it currently supplies only about 0.1% of the world's energy. In the UK, although theoretically it could supply a high proportion of electrical energy, in practice the very deep drilling required involves unsolved technical problems.

● **Gera** ▶ 50 53N 12 6E A city in E Germany, on the Weisse Elster River. Machinery, textiles, and furniture are manufactured; uranium is mined nearby. Population (1996 est): 123 555.

● **Geraldton** ▶ 28 49S 114 36E A port in W Western Australia, on Champion Bay. Wheat, copper, zinc, and mineral sands are the main exports; crayfishing is important. Population (1991): 20 587.

● **geranium** ▶ A herbaceous plant of the genus *Pelargonium* (250 species), most species of which are native to South Africa and widely cultivated as house and garden plants. They have roundish leaves and rounded clusters of showy flowers, usually red or pink. Most horticultural geraniums are hybrids, of which the most important are the zonal pelargoniums, with a dark ring near the centre of each leaf. Family: *Geraniaceae*.

Horticultural geraniums should be distinguished from related plants of the genus *Geranium* (*see* cranesbill).

● **Gérard, François (Pascal Simon), Baron** ▶ (1770–1837) French painter, born in Rome. He was the pupil of ▷David but later rivalled him at the court of Napoleon with his elegant portraits, *Josephine Bonaparte* (Louvre), and history paintings. After Napoleon's fall, he became painter to Louis XVIII, who ennobled him in 1819.

● **gerbil** ▶ A small ▷rodent belonging to the subfamily *Gerbillinae* (over 100 species) of Africa and Asia, also called jird and sand rat. Ranging in size from 5–20 cm, gerbils have long hind legs. They inhabit dry open country and spend the day in underground burrows, feeding at night on seeds and roots. Chief genera: *Gerbillus, Tatera*; family: *Cricetidae*.

● **gerenuk** ▶ A long-necked antelope, *Litocranius walleri*, of E African bush country. About 100 cm tall at the shoulder, gerenuks are bright chestnut with white underparts; only males have the curved backward-pointing horns. They feed by rearing up on their hind legs and cropping leaves from thorny shrubs.

● **geriatrics** ▶ (*or* geratology) The medical specialty that deals with the diseases and problems of old age. With improved standards of living and medical care, the number of people surviving to old age has increased and the suitable care of elderly patients is of great importance. In the past little active treatment was given, the patients being virtually bedridden in hospitals, almshouses, etc. Now, however, the aim is to restore as much function and activity as possible, by encouraging patients to engage in suitable activities with the aid of physiotherapy and occupational therapy.

● **Géricault, (Jean Louis André) Théodore** ▶ (1791–1824) French painter, born in Rouen. His famous *Raft of the Medusa* (1819; Louvre), for which he used corpses in the morgue as models, was based on a contemporary shipwreck, which had become a political issue. While visiting England (1820–22), he produced a number of lithographs depicting poor people. He also painted his favourite subject—horses (e.g. *Derby at Epsom*; Louvre). His last works, inspired by a psychiatrist friend, were five portraits of the insane. Despite his early death after a riding accident, he greatly influenced French Romantic painters, especially ▷Delacroix.

● **German** ▶ A language of the West ▷Germanic language group. It is the official language of Germany and Austria and one of the four official languages of Switzerland. High German, the official and written form, developed from dialects of the highland areas of Germany and Austria. Old High German was spoken before 1100 AD when Middle High German, based on Upper German dialects, became the standard form. Modern High German developed from the 16th-century dialect of Luther, whose biblical translations spread this form. Low German exists only in a spoken form in the lowland areas of N Germany and is derived from Old Saxon and Middle Low German speech. The main difference between Low and High German is the sound system, especially the consonants.

● **germander** ▶ A herbaceous plant of the worldwide genus *Teucrium* (300 species), with square stems and simple toothed leaves. The small tubular two-lipped flowers, borne in groups in the axils of leaflike bracts, are usually pinkish-purple. The perennial water germander (*T. scordium*) is a Eurasian species. Family: ▷*Labiatae*.

● **Germanic languages** ▶ A subgroup of the ▷Indo-European language group. Its member languages are spoken in Britain, Scandinavia, Germany, the Netherlands, and Iceland. There are three recognized subgroups: East Germanic, North Germanic, and West Germanic. The first of these is now extinct but it included Gothic, one of the earliest Germanic languages. North Germanic covers the ▷Scandinavian languages. West Germanic includes modern English and German among its descendants as well as Netherlandic (Dutch and Flemish) and ▷Frisian. These developed from their earlier forms High and Low German, Anglo-Saxon, Middle English, and Old Saxon. Also developed from Germanic origins are ▷Yiddish and Afrikaans (see Afrikaner). All three branches can be traced back to an unrecorded Proto-Germanic language, which has been reconstructed by philologists by comparing and tracing back similar modern languages using such generalizations as those stated in Grimm's Law (see Grimm).

● **Germanicus Julius Caesar** ▶ (15 BC–19 AD) Roman soldier, who was adopted by his uncle, Emperor Tiberius, in 4 AD. In 17 he was appointed to govern Rome's eastern provinces and died mysteriously in Antioch, perhaps as a result of poison. Germanicus married ▷Agrippina the Elder and was the father of Caligula.

● **germanium** ▶ (Ge) A brittle grey-white metalloid, discovered by C. A. Winkler (1838–1904) in 1886. Like ▷gallium it is present in coal and is concentrated in chimney soot as well as in the flue dusts of zinc smelters, from which it is obtained commercially. The element is a ▷semiconductor and its most important uses are in the electronics industry. Germanium compounds include the volatile tetrachloride ($GeCl_4$) and the dioxide (GeO_2), which has a high refractive index and is used in lenses. At no 32; at wt 72.61; mp 938.35°C; bp 2834°C.

● **German literature** ▶ Little vernacular German literature earlier than the 12th century survives. The fragmentary *Hildebrandslied* (c. 800) is the only extant example of early heroic verse. The major works of medieval German literature were the epics the *Nibelungenlied* and *Gudrun*, several court epics based on French models, and the love lyrics of the wandering minnesingers, notably those of Walther von der Vogelweide. The Reformation had a great influence, especially through Luther's translation of the Bible (1522; 1534); Lutheran ideals were often expressed in the poetry of the ▷Meistersingers, the best known of whom was Hans Sachs. The Thirty Years' War, portrayed in Grimmelhausen's novels, resulted in cultural insecurity in the 17th and early 18th centuries and adherence to French models. An upsurge of national feeling in the 18th century resulted in a literary revival; the literature of the Enlightenment, represented most notably by Lessing, was succeeded by the ▷*Sturm und Drang* movement and at the end of the century by Romanticism.

Goethe and Schiller outgrew *Sturm und Drang* emotionalism and espoused classicism instead, although Goethe's *Faust* remains balanced by warmth of feeling. The poets Hölderlin and Heine, the novelist and dramatist Kleist, and the dramatist Büchner were not associated with particular literary movements.

The aestheticism of the late 19th and early 20th centuries, found in the poems of George and the plays of Hofmannsthal, was paralleled by the realism of Fontane's novels. The social malaise of Germany at the time of World War I was reflected in Expressionism, elements of which appear in the works of various writers, influencing the mysticism in Rilke's poetry, the nightmare visions in Kafka's novels, and the search for new social and aesthetic values in the novels of Thomas Mann and Hesse and the dramas of Brecht. During the Nazi period virtually every author of worth was silenced or exiled.

The economic and political character of West Germany after World War II, and its reluctance to confront the Nazi past, were analysed in the novels of Böll and Grass. German-language writers to deal directly with the Holocaust include the poets Paul Celan and Nelly Sachs. In East Germany postwar literature suffered from an official insistence on a restrictive form of socialist realism, although a number of authors, such as the novelist Christa Wolf (1929–   ), were able to transcend these limitations.

● **German measles** ▶ A common contagious disease of children and young adults caused by a virus. Known medically as rubella, it is a mild infection producing a pink rash and a sore throat. If a woman is infected in early pregnancy she may give birth to a malformed child. For this reason immunization is encouraged: in the UK it is recommended that the combined MMR (measles, mumps, rubella) vaccine be given to all children in their second year.

● **German shepherd dog** ▶ (*or* Alsatian) A breed of large strongly built ⃞dog originating in Germany. It has a coarse coat that can range in colour from white to black but is often black and tan. German shepherds are used as working dogs, especially for police work, as guard dogs, and as guide dogs for the blind. Height: 61–66 cm (dogs); 56–61 cm (bitches).

● **German silver** ▶ (*or* nickel silver) An alloy of copper, zinc, and nickel, usually in the ratio 5:2:2, used in cheap jewellery as a silver substitute and as a base for ▷electroplating with silver (an article marked **EPNS** is electroplated nickel silver). ▷*See also* electrum.

● **Germany, Federal Republic of** ▶ A country in central Europe: since 1990 it has comprised both the former West Germany (the Federal Republic of Germany) and the former East Germany (the German Democratic Republic). For administrative purposes, Germany is divided into 16 *Länder* (German *Land*, state). The N part of the country, which borders on Denmark, the North Sea, and the Baltic, and includes the island of ▷Rügen, is generally low-lying and contains many lakes. The central area rises to the Harz Mountains and the Thuringian Forest, with the Erzgebirge to the SE and the peaks of the Alps in the extreme S. The chief rivers are the Danube, Elbe, Ems, Oder, Rhine, and Weser.

Economy: rapid reconstruction, particularly of the industrial sector, followed World War II, especially heavy industry in the centre and N of what was then West Germany, with electrical engineering, iron and steel, motor vehicles, shipbuilding, and chemicals. By the 1970s West Germany was well established as the dominant economic force in Europe. East Germany's industrial sector was also highly industrialized, but state-owned and planned in close cooperation with the Soviet Union: industries included precision engineering, electronics, machinery, and chemicals. By Western standards the economy of the East was backward and undynamic, and the cost of restructuring and modernizing it following unification has proved far higher than anticipated. As a result, Germany spent most of the 1990s in recession, with unemployment reaching its highest levels since the 1930s. Further austerity measures were taken in the later 1990s to meet the criteria for joining the single European currency. Germany's main mineral resources are lignite, iron ore, lead and zinc, and potash. There is also a well-developed nuclear power industry, although the current government has responded to environmentalist pressures by promising to shut this down. The agricultural sector (formerly organized in collectives and state farms in East Germany) has declined in importance although there is a considerable amount of forestry (mainly under state control) and a successful wine industry, especially in the Rhine and Moselle valleys. Tourism is also an important source of revenue. Manufacturing industry remains the mainstay of the economy. The main exports include motor vehicles, machinery, chemicals, electronic goods, lignite, potash, textiles, optical and other scientific instruments, and photographic equipment and paper.

History: The region was occupied by German tribes from about 500 BC and came repeatedly into conflict with the Romans from the 2nd century BC. Overrun by the Huns in the 4th and 5th centuries, the area was dominated by the ▷Franks from the 6th century and was christianized in the late-7th to 8th centuries. After the death of the Carolingian Louis the Pius his empire was divided (843), the E part becoming the eastern Frankish kingdom, the nucleus of Germany. After the failure of the Frankish dynasty the German kings became nominally elective (see electors) but medieval Germany was in practice ruled by a series of hereditary dynasties. The first of these, the Saxons, was founded by Henry the Fowler in 919 and from the election (963) of his son as Holy Roman Emperor (see Otto (I) the Great), the German kings claimed the imperial title by right. The 11th to 13th centuries were dominated by struggle between the emperors and popes over the ▷investiture controversy, which with the conflict between ▷Guelfs and Ghibellines gave rise to a sustained period of civil strife. In the 13th century, following the fall of the ▷Hohenstaufen dynasty, the first ▷Habsburg emperor was elected and from the 15th century the imperial title remained almost continuously in the family. In the later middle ages the power of the princes was challenged by the ▷Hanseatic League of northern ports, which wielded political as well as commercial power. The 16th and 17th centuries were dominated by religious strife, following Luther's inception of the ▷Reformation at Wittenberg in 1520 and the subsequent division of Germany into a predominantly Protestant N and Roman Catholic S. The religious conflict was not resolved until the conclusion (1648) of the ▷Thirty Years' War. In the 17th century the Hohenzollern Electors of Brandenburg acquired Prussia, which, as a kingdom from 1701, became the dominant German state and, under

▷Frederick (II) the Great, a major European power. In 1806 the Holy Roman Empire was brought to an end by Napoleon, who formed the ▷Confederation of the Rhine in its place. The post-Napoleonic German confederation was dominated by Austria and Prussia and in 1834 the latter was the moving influence behind the formation of the ▷Zollverein (customs union). Prussian power increased further with victory in the ▷Austro-Prussian War (1866) and in the ▷Franco-Prussian War (1870–71). In 1871 Bismarck achieved his cherished ambition of creating a German Empire. The late 19th and early 20th centuries saw rapid industrialization, an aggressive armaments programme, and the rise of Germany as a colonial power, especially in Africa; its international aspirations were a major cause of ▷World War I. Defeated in 1918, the Empire came to an end (1919) and was replaced by the ▷Weimar Republic, which was plagued by the economic difficulties that facilitated ▷Hitler's rise to power in the early 1930s. His aggressive foreign policy, aimed at the establishment of a new German empire, led to ▷World War II. Following Germany's defeat the country was divided into British, French, Soviet, and US occupation zones before the subsequent formation of two separate states, East Germany and West Germany.

East Germany, or the German Democratic Republic (GDR; German name: Deutsche Demokratische Republik), lay to the E of the Harz Mountains and was formed from the Soviet-occupied zone of Germany following World War II. It was given a provisional constitution as the German Democratic Republic in 1949, becoming independent in 1954 and being given its own seat in COMECON and the UN, as well as full membership of the Warsaw Pact. The capital was East Berlin. The leading architect of the new state was Walter Ulbricht; in 1960, following the death of President Wilhelm Pieck, he became chairman of the newly established Council of State. The early years of economic austerity and curbs on civil liberties led in 1953 to serious riots, particularly in East Berlin, which were suppressed by Soviet troops, but the flow of refugees to West Germany continued until 1961, when the Berlin Wall was erected. Relations with West Germany improved in the 1970s and 1980s, but living standards lagged behind those in the West, leading to a steady flow of emigrants, which became a flood in 1989 when border restrictions were relaxed. Having resisted the *glasnost* and *perestroika* policies adopted by the Soviet Union, the government of Erich ▷Honecker was faced with mass demonstrations and demands for reform; the Communist politburo resigned and a multi-party democracy was instituted. A conservative alliance won free elections in March 1990, under Lothar de Maizière, and reunification with West Germany was achieved in Oct 1990.

West Germany, or the Federal Republic of Germany (FRG; German name: Bundesrepublik Deutschland), was formed from the British-, French-, and US-occupied zones following World War II; it became fully independent in 1955 and was a founder member of the EEC (now EU) in 1957. The capital was transferred to Bonn although West Berlin remained a part of the Federal Republic. In the postwar years it enjoyed a spectacular economic recovery making it the most prosperous country in W Europe. The import of foreign labour ("guest workers") became essential to continued industrial expansion, leading to social and ethnic tensions. Christian Democratic Union (CDU) governments under Adenauer and Ehrhard were followed in the early 1970s by the Social Democrats under Willi Brandt, and this contributed to better relations with E European countries. In 1982 the Social Democrat coalition led by Helmut Schmidt collapsed and a new coalition was formed under Helmut ▷Kohl. When a reformist government took over in the GDR in 1989, the West German government led moves towards the reunification of Germany.

Monetary union and the dismantling of border controls between the two German states took place in July 1990 and the postwar occupying powers gave up their role in Berlin. East Germany dropped its planned economy and agreed a treaty for social and economic union. Full reunification was achieved on 3 October, 1990. All-Germany elections in December resulted in victory for President Kohl and the Christian Democrats, who continued to dominate politics until 1998, when they were heavily defeated by the Social Democrats. Gerhard ▷Schröder became chancellor and a centre-left coalition (including several Greens) was formed. Germany is a member of NATO; in 1993

Germany's constitution was revised to allow German forces to take part in joint campaigns or peacekeeping missions outside the NATO area (forbidden since World War II). German forces saw military action for the first time since 1945 in the NATO air war against Yugoslavia (1999). Germany adopted the single European currency in 1999–2002.

Federal Republic of Germany

Head of state	President Johannes Rau
Official language	German
Official currency	euro of 100 cents
Area	356 798 sq km (137 746 sq mi)
Population (2000 est)	82 225 000
Capital	Berlin
Main port	Hamburg

● **germination** ▶ The process by which an embryo plant within a seed is transformed into a recognizable plant with roots, stem, and leaves. Water, warmth, and oxygen stimulate germination, which begins with the emergence of the root (radicle) and is followed by the shoot (plumule). Energy for the process is provided by the ▷cotyledons (seed leaves), which either remain below ground (hypogeal germination, as in the broad bean) or form the first leaves of the seedling (epigeal germination, as in the marrow).

● **Germiston** ▶ 26 15S 28 10E A city in N South Africa. It contains the world's largest gold refinery and serves the Witwatersrand mines. An important railway junction, it has railway-engineering industries. Population (1991): 134 005.

● **Gerona** ▶ 41 59N 2 49E A city in NE Spain, in Catalonia. It was besieged several times in the 17th–18th centuries. The fine gothic cathedral (1312–1598) has an exceptionally wide single nave. Industries include textiles, paper, and food processing. Population (latest est): 30 200.

● **Geronimo** ▶ (1829–1909) US Apache Indian chief. He led several raids, resisting resettlement of his people on a barren reservation in Arizona, but surrendered in 1886. Eventually they became farmers in Oklahoma. He dictated his autobiography *Geronimo: His Own Story* shortly before he died.

● **Gershwin, George** ▶ (Jacob Gershvin; 1898–1937) US composer and songwriter. He wrote songs for musical shows and films, perhaps the best-remembered being "The Man I Love," "I Got Rhythm," and "Lady Be Good." His jazz-inspired orchestral works include *Rhapsody in Blue* (1924) and *An American in Paris* (1928); the opera *Porgy and Bess* (1935) is still widely performed. His brother **Ira Gershwin** (1896–1983) wrote the lyrics to many of his songs.

● **Gerson, Jean de** ▶ (1363–1429) French theologian and chancellor of the University of Paris. He was one of the earliest advocates of restricting papal power (*see* Gallicanism). His efforts to end the ▷Great Schism by calling a general council were rewarded at the Council of ▷Constance (1415), of which he was a leading member.

● **Gesner, Conrad** ▶ (1516–65) Swiss physician, who was a founder of modern zoology and botany. He compiled a survey of knowledge of animal life, the *Historiae animalium* (5 vols, 1551–87), and described many plant species, often in the form of woodcut illustrations. His other works include a bibliography of authors and their works, a survey of world languages, and a compendium of recorded knowledge.

● **Gestalt psychology** ▶ A school of ▷psychology that originated in Germany in the early 20th century: Wolfgang ▷Köhler and Kurt ▷Koffka were its founders. It regards mental processes as wholes (gestalts) that cannot be analysed into smaller components. According to this theory, when something is learned the individual's entire perception of the environment has been changed.

● **Gestalt therapy** ▶ A type of psychotherapy that does not derive directly from ▷Gestalt psychology, although it makes use of the totality (gestalt) of a patient's experiences, sensations, emotions, and memories in its group therapy sessions. Conflicts experienced by individual patients are often explored by role play and in weekend workshops in the belief that the holistic approach can release the tensions and remove the impediments to growth that are making the patient ill. This form of therapy was largely developed by the German-born US psychoanalyst Fritz Perls (1893–1970) and has been widely used in the USA since the 1960s.

● **Gestapo** ► (German: *Ge*heime *Sta*atspolizei, secret state police) The Nazi secret police formed in 1933 under Hermann ▷Goering. Administered from 1936 by the ▷SS, the two organizations were the chief instruments of atrocities carried out by the Nazi Party in Germany and German-occupied Europe.

● **gestation** ▷*See* pregnancy.

● **Gesualdo, Carlo, Prince of Venosa** ► (c. 1560–1613) Italian composer. His madrigals employ extraordinary harmonic effects. He was also famous for his lute playing and notorious for the murder of his first (unfaithful) wife.

● **Gethsemane, Garden of** ► In the New Testament, the place in which ▷Judas Iscariot betrayed ▷Jesus Christ. It is situated at the foot of the W slope of the ▷Mount of Olives.

● **Getty, J(ean) Paul** ► (1892–1976) US businessman, who lived in the UK. He made his fortune in oil, becoming a millionaire at the age of 22. He founded the J. Paul Getty Museum at Malibu, California. His son, the philanthropist **Sir Paul Getty Jr.** (1932–   ), is now a British citizen.

geysers ► A geyser at Rotorua in New Zealand.

● **Gettysburg, Battle of** ► (1–3 July, 1863) The most significant battle of the US ▷Civil War, fought in S central Pennsylvania as part of the Confederacy's second invasion of the North. The battle was joined unintentionally at Gettysburg, both armies having been uncertain of the other's position. The first day ended with a slight Southern advantage but a delayed attack by the Confederates on the second day shifted the advantage to the Federal troops. On the third day the Confederates charged the enemy's centre, holding their line briefly despite massive fire, but ultimately withdrawing in defeat. The North lost 23 000 men and the South, 25 000. The **Gettysburg Address**, one of the shortest and most famous of modern speeches, was delivered (19 November, 1863) by President Abraham Lincoln at the dedication of a cemetery at the Gettysburg battlefield.

● **Geulincx, Arnold** ► (1624–69) Belgian-born philosopher. He was converted to Protestantism and settled in Holland. In response to ▷Descartes' mind–body relationship problem Geulincx originated the "two clock" theory, whereby body and mind are conceived of as keeping perfect time, side by side, without interaction. For Geulincx, when a mental or physical process takes place, God occasions it, hence "occasionalism" (*see also* Malebranche, Nicolas).

● **geysers** ► Jets of hot water and steam issuing intermittently from holes in the earth's crust, some reaching heights of up to 70 m. Geysers are found in volcanically active or recently active regions, for example, in Iceland. They occur when water from deep within the crust becomes superheated and suddenly boils, gushing up to the surface like a fountain. Cones of sinter (deposits of silica) frequently build up around the vents of geysers.

● **Gezira, El** ► (*or* al-Jazirah) A triangular plain in the Sudan, between the Blue and White Nile Rivers. The Gezira irrigation scheme using water from the Makwar Dam (completed 1925) makes possible the production of cotton, millet, fodder crops, and groundnuts.

● **Ghana, Republic of** ► A country in West Africa, on the Gulf of Guinea. Coastal plains rise to undulating country around Accra, and, in the centre, the basin of the River Volta rises to plateaus, especially in the N and W. The inhabitants are chiefly of Black Sudanese stock but there are a large number of tribal units.
Economy: chiefly agricultural. Food crops are varied, and increased production has been encouraged through various government schemes. The main cash crop is cocoa, of which Ghana is among the world's chief producers. Such crops as rubber and cotton are produced to provide raw material for industry, in an effort to diversify the economy. The gold-mining industry, which is one of the world's largest producers, was privatized in 1994: diamonds, manganese, bauxite, and limestone are also mined. Hydroelectricity is generated by the Volta Dam and exported to Togo and Benin; oil was found offshore in 1978 but still awaits development. Forestry is also important. Fishing limits were extended from 48 km to 322 km (30 mi to 200 mi) in 1977. Since the early 1980s adherence to an IMF recovery programme, government action to promote manufacturing industry and tourism, and a crackdown on the major problem of smuggling have combined to produce steady economic growth. The main export is cocoa; others include timber and gold.
History: from the middle ages several small kingdoms flourished in what is now Ghana. From 1472 the Portuguese and subsequently other Europeans set up trading posts in the region, which they called the Gold Coast. It became a centre of the slave trade and the scene of rivalry between the British and Dutch. The British abolition of slavery led to prolonged wars with the Ashanti slavetraders in the 19th century. The area became the British colony of the Gold Coast in 1874. In 1957, together with the British part of Togo, it became independent, its new name, Ghana, being that of a medieval N African empire. In 1960 it became a republic within the British Commonwealth, with Dr Kwame Nkrumah as its first president. His government became increasingly dictatorial and in 1966 he was overthrown in a military coup. Military rule continued until 1969, when civilian government was re-established. In 1972, however, a second military coup took place under Col Ignatius K. Acheampong (1931–79). He was forced to resign in 1978 and, with his successor, Lt Gen Fred Akuffo (1937–79), was executed following a military coup (1979) led by Fl Lt Jerry Rawlings (1942–   ). A new civilian government was formed (1979) with Dr Hilla Limann (1934–98) as president but this was overthrown in another military coup led by Fl Lt Rawlings in December, 1981. To stem smuggling activities all borders were closed in 1982. The expul-

sion from Nigeria of one million Ghanaians created a national emergency. Although the 1980s saw famine and the collapse of the cocoa industry, there has since been steady economic improvement and Ghana has repaid much of its foreign debt. Multiparty elections in 1992 led to victory for Rawlings, although opposition parties refused to accept the result. Rawlings was re-elected as president in 1996 but defeated by the opposition leader John Kufuor in 2000.

Republic of Ghana

Head of state	President John Kufuor
Official language	English
Official currency	cedi of 100 pesewas
Area	238 305 sq km (92 010 sq mi)
Population (1999 est)	18 888 000
Capital	Accra
Main port	Takoradi

● **gharial** ▷*See* gavial.

● **Ghats** ▶ Two mountain ranges lying along the W and E coasts of India. The **Western Ghats**, which extend about 1500 km (932 mi) from N of Bombay to Cape Comorin, are the higher, rising to 2693 m (8840 ft). With the plentiful rain brought by the W winds, they have dense natural vegetation and are used for tea planting. The **Eastern Ghats** extend, with several breaks, about 1400 km (880 mi) from near Cuttack to the Nilgiri Hills.

● **Ghaznavids** ▶ A Turkish dynasty that ruled in E Iran, Afghanistan, and N India (977–1186). The Ghaznavids created the first powerful Muslim state in India and prepared the way for the spread of Islam there. Founded by Sebuktigin (d. 997), a Turkish soldier, the dynasty's territories centred on Ghazna (Afghanistan) and reached its peak with ▷Mahmud of Ghazna. Following the battle of Dandanqan in 1040, the Ghaznavids lost their lands in Persia to the Seljuqs.

● **Ghazzah** ▷*See* Gaza.

● **Ghegs** ▶ One of the two major ethnic divisions of the Albanian people (*see also* Tosks). The Ghegs live N of the Shkumbi River and differ from the Tosks in dress and other customs.

● **Ghent** ▶ (Flemish name: Gent; French name: Gand) 51 02N 3 42E A city in Belgium, at the confluence of the canalized Rivers Scheldt and Lys. One of Belgium's oldest cities, it has a university (1816) and a gothic cathedral. It is a major port and the textile centre of the country; other economic activities include metallurgy, chemicals, and banking. Population (1996 est): 226 424.

● **gherkin** ▶ A trailing West Indian vine, *Cucumis anguria*, with lobed leaves and small yellow flowers. It is cultivated for its prickly edible fruit, 2.5–7.5 cm long, which is borne on a crooked stalk and used when immature for pickling. The "gherkins" sold in pickle mixtures are immature ▷cucumbers. Family: *Cucurbitaceae* (gourd family).

● **ghetto** ▶ Any slum area occupied by an ethnic minority. Originally a ghetto was that quarter of a city to which Jews were restricted by law. The term originated in Venice in the middle ages when the Jews were forced to live on an island on which there were a number of iron foundries (*getto* is Italian for the act of casting metal). Ghettos were subsequently established during the ▷Counter-Reformation in many European cities. During the 19th century legal restrictions fell into disuse in W Europe and the communities became bound solely by customs and religion. However, in the 20th century ghettos were revived by the Germans, for example in ▷Warsaw.

● **Ghibellines** ▷*See* Guelfs and Ghibellines.

● **Ghiberti, Lorenzo** ▶ (c. 1378–1455) Florentine Renaissance sculptor. Ghiberti trained as a goldsmith and painter but made his name as a sculptor in 1402, when he won the competition for the bronze relief sculptures for the north doors of the Baptistry of the Florentine Duomo. Finished in 1424, these New Testament scenes, mainly in the ▷international gothic style, were followed by Old Testament scenes in the Gates of Paradise (1425–52), strongly influenced by antique sculpture. Simultaneously he wrote *I commentarii*, which included histories of ancient and early Renaissance art and an auto-

biography. His other works include three statues of saints (1416–25) for Orsanmichele.

● **Ghirlandaio, Domenico** ▶ (Domenico di Tommaso Bigordi; 1449–94) Florentine painter of the early ▷Renaissance. From 1481 to 1482 he worked on a fresco in the Sistine Chapel but his major undertaking was the fresco cycle (1486–90) in Sta Maria Novella, Florence. These scenes from the life of the Virgin and St John the Baptist are notable for their portrayal of Florentine personalities in contemporary dress. The tenderly painted *Old Man and Boy* (Louvre) is a fine example of his portraiture.

● **ghost** ▶ The disembodied spirit of a dead person, believed in many cultures to be capable of manifesting itself to the living. Ghosts are still venerated in tribal societies in Africa, Asia, and Polynesia (*see* ancestor worship). Certain feasts in the Roman calendar were devoted to their propitiation. Post-Reformation ghosts exhibited more secular interests, demanding revenge or restitution of such wrongs as misappropriated inheritances. Scepticism grew in the 18th century but the ▷gothic revival initiated a revival in ghost stories. Hauntings continue to be reported (*see also* spiritualism).

● **ghost shark** ▷*See* chimaera.

Alberto Giacometti ▶ Modelling one of his characteristic elongated forms (1960).

● **Giacometti, Alberto** ▶ (1901–66) Swiss sculptor and painter. Working chiefly in Paris after 1922, he was influenced initially by ▷cubism and primitive art and later by ▷surrealism, particularly in his abstract construction of sticks, glass, wire, etc., entitled *The Palace at 4 am* (New York). After breaking with surrealism in 1935, he developed a unique figure style, featuring spindly elongated forms.

● **Giambologna** ▶ (Giovanni da Bologna *or* Jean de Boulogne; 1529–1608) Italian mannerist sculptor of Flemish birth. Working from 1557 in Florence, where he was patronized by the Medici, he produced fountains, religious sculptures, and small bronze statues. His works include *Samson and a Philistine* (1567; Victoria and Albert Museum).

● **giant planet** ▷*See* planet.

● **Giant's Causeway** ▶ 55 14N 6 32W A promontory in N Northern Ireland, in Antrim on the North Channel. It consists of several thousand closely packed basaltic columns, mainly hexagonal in shape, formed by an outpouring of lava into the sea. According to legend it was built as a bridge for the giants to cross between Ireland and Scotland.

● **giant star** ▶ A large very luminous star that has a very tenuous atmosphere but a dense core. It is in a late stage of evolution, having exhausted the normal source of energy in its core (hydrogen), and must obtain energy from other nuclear fusion reactions. This causes its size and temperature to alter as it evolves. ▷*See also* red giant.

● **giant tortoise** ▷*See* Galápagos giant tortoise.

● **giant water bug** ► A large brown ▷water bug of the family *Belostomatidae* (up to 200 species), found in tropical and temperate regions. Sometimes over 10 mm long, they are strong fliers and are often attracted to light. In some species, such as *Belostoma plumineum*, the female forcibly lays her eggs onto the back of the male, attaching them with a glue.

● **Gibberd, Sir Frederick** ► (1908–84) British architect and town planner. His designs for new towns included Harlow in the UK and Santa Teresa in Venezuela; other works included the Liverpool Roman Catholic Cathedral (1960–67) and the mosque in Regent's Park, London (1977).

● **gibberellins** ► A group of organic compounds that stimulate plant growth. First isolated from the fungus *Gibberella fujikuroi*, over 30 gibberellins are now known. When applied to plants they stimulate growth and break the dormancy of seeds and tubers; hence their importance in horticulture and agriculture.

● **gibbon** ► A small ▷ape belonging to the genus *Hylobates* (7 species), of S Asia. 45–65 cm long, they have long arms with slender hands and hooked fingers used to swing through trees. On the ground they walk upright or run on all fours. They live in family groups, feeding chiefly on fruit and leaves, and have a loud whooping call. Family: *Hylobatidae*. ▷*See also* siamang.

● **Gibbon, Edward** ► (1737–94) British historian. Sent to Lausanne in 1753 by his father because of his conversion to Roman Catholicism, which he soon renounced, he travelled in Switzerland and later (1764–65) in Italy. His ironic treatment of Christianity in his monumental *The History of the Decline and Fall of the Roman Empire* (1776–88) aroused controversy, but the work gradually gained acceptance.

● **Gibbon, Lewis Grassic** ► (James Leslie Mitchell; 1901–35) Scottish writer. He published *Stained Radiance* (1930) and *Spartacus* (1933) under his own name. The trilogy *Scots Quair* (1932–34), for which he is best known, was published under his pseudonym. *Scottish Scene*, with Hugh ▷MacDiarmid, is a celebration of Scottish prose and verse.

● **Gibbons, Grinling** ► (1648–1721) English wood carver and sculptor, born in Rotterdam. Patronized by Charles II and subsequent British monarchs, he produced decorative carvings of flowers, swags of fruit, etc., in wood and occasionally stone, for Windsor Castle, Kensington Palace, Blenheim Palace, and Petworth House. His best-known works, however, are the choir stalls and organ screen in St Paul's Cathedral.

● **Gibbons, Orlando** ► (1583–1625) English composer, organist, and virginalist. He became organist of the Chapel Royal at the age of 21. His church music includes services and anthems. Of his madrigals, "The Silver Swan" is the best known. He also wrote string fantasias and contributed pieces to *Parthenia* (1611), the first English anthology of keyboard music.

● **Gibbs, James** ► (1682–1754) British architect. Gibbs trained under Carlo Fontana (1634–1714) at Rome, where he was influenced by the Italian ▷baroque style. His notable works include St Mary-le-Strand (1714–17) and St Martin's in the Fields (1722–26) in London and the circular Radcliffe Camera (1737–49) in Oxford.

● **Gibbs, Josiah Willard** ► (1839–1903) US physicist, who was a professor at Yale University (1871–1903). Gibbs founded chemical thermodynamics, which is largely based on the function known as the Gibbs ▷free energy. He is also known for his ▷phase rule, relating the number of parameters that can be varied in a system of more than one phase.

● **Gibraltar** ► A United Kingdom overseas territory (formerly a crown colony) occupying a tiny peninsula at the southern tip of Spain. The sandy isthmus that links it to the Spanish mainland rises sharply to the 427 m (1400 ft) limestone Rock of Gibraltar, which contains numerous caverns and galleries. The population is mainly of Spanish, Genoese, and Portugese descent.
Economy: Britain's defence presence on Gibraltar was the mainstay of the economy until the mid-1980s, when the naval dockyards closed. Offshore financial services and tourism are now the main economic activities; tourist attractions include the colony's barbary

apes, the only monkeys native to Europe. Fees for services to shipping are also an important source of revenue.
History: settled by the Moors in 711 AD, the Rock of Gibraltar was taken by Castile in 1462, becoming part of united Spain. It was captured in 1704 by the British to whom it was formally ceded by the Treaty of Utrecht (1713). The colony became an important British naval base. Claims to Gibraltar have long been made by Spain but a UN proposal to end British occupation was defeated in a referendum in 1967. In 1969 Spain closed its frontier with Gibraltar leading to a manpower shortage (as much of its workforce was Spanish). The border was reopened in 1985. In 1998–99 a new dispute led to Spain imposing a semi-blockade. Anglo-Spanish talks aimed at agreeing a new international status for Gibraltar began in 2001. Governor: Sir Richard Luce. Chief minister: Peter Caruana. Official languages: English and Spanish. Official currency: Gibraltar pound of 100 pence. Area: 6.5 sq km (2.5 sq mi). Population (1997 est): 27 100.

● **Gibraltar, Strait of** ► A strait between Europe (Spain and Gibraltar) and Africa (Morocco), joining the Atlantic Ocean and the Mediterranean Sea, of which it is the only outlet. It narrows to 13 km (8 mi) and is of great strategic importance.

● **Gibran, Khalil** ► (1883–1931) Lebanese mystic and poet. He studied in Beirut and Paris and settled in New York in 1912. His major work in English is *The Prophet* (1923), a romantic blending of religion, mysticism, and philosophy.

● **Gibson, Mel** ► (1956–) Australian film actor and director, who works mainly in Hollywood. He starred in *Mad Max* (1979), *Lethal Weapon* (1987) and its three sequels, and *Hamlet* (1990), *Maverick* (1994), and *What Women Want* (2000). *Braveheart* (1995) earned him Oscars for best director and best film.

● **Gibson Desert** ► A desert in central Western Australia. It consists of a vast arid area of active sand dunes and desert grass. Area: 220 000 sq km (85 000 sq mi).

● **Gide, André** ► (1869–1951) French novelist and critic. Much of his work is semiautobiographical and deals with the conflict between desire and discipline, reflecting the conflict between his homosexuality and conventional morality. His visits to North Africa from 1893 to 1896 gave him a sense of freedom, celebrated in *Fruits of the Earth* (1897). In 1895 he married his cousin Madeleine Rondeaux, the inspiration of two short works, *The Immoralist* (1902) and *Strait Is the Gate* (1909). In 1908 he was a founder of the literary journal, *La Nouvelle Revue française*. His longer novels are *The Vatican Cellars* (1914) and *The Counterfeiters* (1926). His *Journal*, which he kept from 1885 until his death, is a major literary autobiography. He won the Nobel Prize in 1947.

● **Gielgud, Sir (Arthur) John** ► (1904–2000) British actor. He was noted for his fine speaking voice and his many performances in Shakespeare. His *Hamlet*, first performed in 1929, received special acclaim. He also acted in plays by modern dramatists, such as Harold Pinter, Edward Bond, and John Mortimer, in films, and on television. In 1989 he became the first honorary fellow of the ▷Royal Academy of Dramatic Art, having been its president (1977–89). He was knighted in 1953 and appointed OM in 1997.

● **Gierek, Edward** ► (1913–2001) Polish statesman, who succeeded ▷Gomułka as first secretary of the Polish United Workers' Party (1970–80). Born in Poland, he lived in France and Belgium from 1923 to 1948. A communist from 1931, he became a member of the politburo in 1956 and came to power following demonstrations against food prices.

● **Giessen** ► 50 35N 08 42E A town in central Germany, in Hessen on the River Lahn. The university (1607) contains the chemist Liebig's laboratory. Manufactures include rubber, machine tools, and leather. Population (latest est): 71 750.

● **GIFT** ► (gamete intrafallopian transfer) A technique used to improve the chances of a woman becoming pregnant, which has been successful in some cases of infertility. Several egg cells, stimulated to mature simultaneously by ▷fertility drugs, are removed from the woman's ovary, mixed with her partner's sperm, and inserted into one of her Fallopian tubes, where fertilization can occur. ▷*See also* test-tube baby.

● **Gifu** ▶ 35 27N 136 46E A city in Japan, in central Honshu. It was ▷Nobunaga's headquarters in the 16th century. Manufactures include paper lanterns and textiles. Population (1995): 407 145.

● **Gigantes** ▶ In Greek mythology, the giant sons of ▷Uranus (Heaven) and ▷Gaia (Earth), whose rebellion against the Olympian gods was defeated with the help of Heracles. They were later associated with earthquakes and volcanoes.

● **Gigli, Beniamino** ▶ (1890–1957) Italian tenor. He became a world-famous opera singer and was regarded as the successor to Caruso. Toscanini brought him to La Scala, Milan, in 1920, where he made his debut as Faust in Boito's *Mefistofele*. He gave his final concert in 1955.

● **Gijón** ▶ 43 32N 5 40W A port in NW Spain, on the Bay of Biscay. Its ancient buildings include Roman baths and medieval palaces. It has manufacturing, metallurgical, and chemical industries. Population (1995 est): 270 867.

● **Gila monster** ▶ A rare venomous lizard, *Heloderma suspectum*, occurring in the SW USA and N Mexico. 50 cm long, it has a stout black body with pink blotches and bands and feeds at night on eggs. It has a strong bite and grooved teeth that inject a nerve poison. Family: *Helodermatidae*.

● **gilbert** ▶ (Gb) The unit of magnetomotive force in the ▷c.g.s. system equal to the magnetomotive force produced by a current of 40π amperes passing through a single coil. Named after William ▷Gilbert.

● **Gilbert, Sir Humphrey** ▶ (c. 1539–83) English navigator. Half-brother of Sir Walter ▷Raleigh, Gilbert was a soldier in Ireland (1567–70, 1579) and the Netherlands (1572). In 1583 he landed at St John's, Newfoundland, which he claimed for Elizabeth I. He was lost at sea on his return voyage.

● **Gilbert, William** ▶ (1544–1603) English physicist and physician to Elizabeth I. One of the early adherents of the experimental method, his *De magnete* (1600) listed many experimental observations concerning magnets, including the discovery of magnetic dip. He suggested that the earth is a spherical magnet, that other magnets point towards its poles, and that the planets are held in their orbits by magnetic attraction. He was the first English scientist to accept the ideas of ▷Copernicus; he was also responsible for many new terms, including *electricity* and *magnetic pole*.

● **Gilbert, Sir William Schwenk** ▶ (1836–1911) British comic dramatist. He wrote comic verses, published as *Bab Ballads* (1869), while studying law. In 1870 he met Arthur ▷Sullivan, the composer for whom he wrote the libretti for 14 popular operas. His plays written after Sullivan's death in 1900 were less successful.

● **Gilbert and George** ▶ The British artists Gilbert Proesch (1943–) and George Passmore (1942–). Originally known as performance artists, they now produce large garish photo-pieces, such as their *Cosmological Pictures* (1993).

● **Gilbert Islands** ▷*See* Kiribati, Republic of.

● **Gilbert of Sempringham, St** ▶ (c. 1083–1189) English priest, who founded the Gilbertines, the only indigenous religious order of medieval England, at Sempringham, Lincolnshire. Composed of nuns, lay sisters and brothers, and canons, it was dissolved by Henry VIII. Feast day: 4 Feb.

● **Gilded Age** ▶ In the USA, an era (1865–1900) marked by ostentatious materialism and governmental corruption. *The Gilded Age* (1873) by Mark ▷Twain (with Charles Dudley Warner; 1829–1900) described and named the period.

● **Giles, Carl Ronald** ▶ (1916–95) British cartoonist. Working for the *Daily Express* and *Sunday Express* from 1943, he satirized the activities of a typical British family, his best-known character being the fearsome Grandma.

● **Gilgamesh** ▶ An ancient Mesopotamian hero whose adventures are related in the collection of fragmentary texts known as the *Epic of Gilgamesh*. These are inscribed on 12 tablets discovered in the library of the Assyrian king, Ashurbanipal (reigned 669–626 BC), at Nineveh.

They relate how Gilgamesh defeats and then befriends the savage man Enkidu, rejects the love goddess ▷Ishtar, journeys to consult an immortal wise man, Utnapishtim, about the secret of eternal life, and gains and then loses the plant of immortality.

● **Gill, (Arthur) Eric (Rowton)** ▶ (1882–1940) British sculptor, engraver, and typographer. Gill's best-known sculptures are the *Stations of the Cross* (1914–18) for Westminster Cathedral and *Prospero and Ariel* (1931) on Broadcasting House, London. He illustrated many books and designed two new printing typefaces, Perpetua (1928) and Gill Sans (1929).

● **Gillespie, Dizzy** ▶ (John Birks G.; 1917–93) US Black jazz trumpeter, band leader, and composer, who was one of the originators of ▷bop. Gillespie played with many different bands in the 1930s and 1940s before forming his own band in 1945. In later years Gillespie incorporated singing and comedy into his performances. His recordings include *Groovin' High* and *Hot vs Cool*; in 1980 he published his autobiographical *To Be or Not to Bop*.

● **Gillingham** ▶ 51 24N 0 33E A town in SE England, in Medway unitary authority, Kent. It is the largest of the towns situated on the Medway estuary. There were formerly extensive dockyards at Chatham. Locally fruit growing is important. Population (1991): 94 923.

● **Gillray, James** ▶ (1756–1815) British caricaturist. After training as a letter engraver and at the Royal Academy, he specialized in political and social cartoons. Targets included George III, whom Gillray called "Farmer George," George IV, Burke, Napoleon, and Pitt.

● **gills** ▶ The respiratory organs of aquatic animals: specialized thin-walled regions of the body surface through which dissolved oxygen is taken into the blood and carbon dioxide released into the water. The gills of fish lie in gill slits on each side of the gullet. Each gill consists of many leaflike gill filaments, which provide a large surface area over which water is pumped. The gills of molluscs (such as the mussel) and fanworms are ciliated and trap food particles in the respiratory currents. The external gills of amphibian larvae (tadpoles) are feathery structures projecting from the body wall.

● **gillyflower** ▶ (or gilliflower) A name given to various clove-scented flowers, originally applied to plants of the pink family (Caryophyllaceae), such as the carnation.

● **gilt-edged security** ▶ A UK government fixed-interest stock. Some, such as **Consols**, are irredeemable (no date is stipulated for the return of the capital); others are redeemable at par on a specified date. Short-term gilts ("shorts") are redeemable within 5 years, "mediums" in 5–15 years, and "longs" in over 15 years. The price of gilts depends upon prevailing interest rates, the price rising as interest rates fall and vice versa. Most gilts are issued in units of £100 (the par value) although the issue price may be above or below this figure, depending on the interest rate offered and the redemption date. The *flat yield* of a stock is the interest rate calculated on the market price rather than the par value. The *yield to redemption* takes into account any capital loss or gain between the market price and the par value, averaged over the years remaining to redemption. Gilts purchased through a bank or a stockbroker are entered on the Bank of England register, but they can also be bought by post through the National Savings Register.

● **gin** ▶ A ▷spirit distilled usually from grain flavoured with juniper berries (the name is derived from the Dutch *jenever*, juniper). Gin is almost pure alcohol, with little flavour. It is generally drunk with tonic water, ▷vermouth, fruit juice, etc. Martini cocktails are a mixture of gin and dry vermouth served very cold with ice. Dry or London Dry gin is the gin most frequently used for mixed drinks.

● **ginger** ▶ A perennial herbaceous plant, *Zingiber officinale*, native to SE Asia and widely grown in the tropics for its pungent underground stems (rhizomes), used as a spice, food, and flavouring and in medicine. Its leafy stems grow about 1 m high; the leaves are 15–30 cm long and the flowers grow in dense conelike spikes. The plants are sterile, and propagation is by cuttings from the rootstocks. Family: *Zingiberaceae*.

● **gingivitis** ▶ Inflammation of the gums. It may be caused by ill-fitting dentures or by infection in debilitated people or those taking antibiotics.

● **Ginkel, Godert de, 1st Earl of Athlone ▶** (1644–1703) Dutch general. As William III's commander in chief in Ireland after the king's victory at the Boyne, he crushed the remaining Roman Catholic resistance and was created Earl of Athlone (1692). He later fought under Marlborough.

● **ginkgo ▶** A deciduous ▷gymnosperm tree, *Ginkgo biloba*, also called maidenhair tree, that is the sole living representative of a group of trees that flourished in the Carboniferous period (370–280 million years ago). Growing to a height of 30 m, it has lobed fan-shaped leaves, 12 × 10 cm, which are pale green and turn yellow in autumn, and fleshy plumlike yellow fruits containing edible kernels. The ginkgo is native to China and widely planted for ornament. Family: *Ginkgoaceae*; phylum: *Ginkgophyta*.

● **Ginsberg, Allen ▶** (1926–97) US poet. His first book, *Howl* (1956), an attack on contemporary America, was a popular work of the ▷Beat movement. *Kaddish* (1961) deals with the madness and death of his mother. In the 1960s he travelled in Asia, India, and South America. His later work, in *The Fall of America* (1973) and other books, is fragmentary and rhapsodic.

● **ginseng ▶** An extract of the forked roots of either of two herbs, *Panax quinquefolium* or *P. schinseng*, used as a stimulant drug in the Far East and to make aromatic bitters. It is said to have aphrodisiac and life-prolonging properties. *P. quinquefolium* is grown commercially in North America; *P. schinseng* in Korea and Japan. Family: *Araliaceae* (ivy family).

● **Giordano, Luca ▶** (1632–1705) Neapolitan painter, nicknamed Luca fa presto (Luca works quickly). His enormous output of religious and mythological paintings, at first influenced by ▷Ribera but later by Venetian art, includes ceiling frescoes in the ballroom of the Palazzo Medici-Riccardi, Florence, and in El Escorial, Spain, where he was court painter (1692–1702).

● **Giorgione ▶** (c. 1477–1510) Italian painter of the Venetian school, born in Castelfranco. He trained under Giovanni ▷Bellini and worked with ▷Titian, whom he influenced, on frescoes for the façade of the German Exchange in Venice (1508). Most of his paintings are small-scale secular pictures of a type previously unknown. Their subject matter is often inexplicable, particularly in the *Tempest* (Accademia, Venice), notable for its atmospheric landscape. *The Sleeping Venus* (Gemäldegalerie, Dresden), completed by Titian, and *The Three Philosophers* (Kunsthistorisches Museum, Vienna) show the romantic and dreamlike mood of his paintings. His portraits, e.g. *Laura* (Vienna), influenced many Venetian painters. He probably died of the plague.

● **Giotto ▶** (Giotto di Bondone; c. 1266–1337) Italian painter and architect, who laid the foundation for ▷Renaissance painting. He was probably the pupil of ▷Cimabue. The fresco cycle of St Francis, in the upper church of S Francesco, Assisi, is thought to be an early work. He painted the frescoes of scenes from the lives of Joachim and Anne and the Virgin and Christ in the Arena Chapel, Padua, and frescoes in Sta Croce, Florence. In 1334 he became city architect and surveyor of Florence Cathedral, for which he designed the campanile.

● **Gipsies ▶** A wandering people found on most continents. The name "Gipsy" is derived from "Egyptian," but they probably originated in India. One group is thought to have migrated through Egypt and North Africa and another through Europe reaching NW Europe during the 15th and 16th centuries. They travel by motorized caravan and live by seasonal work, itinerant trade, and fortune telling. They have been persecuted frequently, half a million being killed by the Nazis during World War II. Their native language is ▷Romany.

● **Gir ▶** A breed of ▷zebu cattle originating from the Gir forest of W India. They have characteristic domed foreheads with backward-curving horns and long ears and are yellowish red to black in colour. Traditionally a dairy breed, they are also used for draught purposes.

● **giraffe ▶** A hoofed ▷mammal, *Giraffa camelopardalis*, of tropical African grasslands. Measuring 3 m at the shoulder, with a neck 2.5 m long, giraffes are marked with a patchwork of reddish-brown blotches on a buff-coloured background. They feed on leaves, using their long necks and prehensile lips and tongues. Both sexes have permanent skin-covered horns. Giraffes live in small groups led by a mature male and can go for long periods without drinking. They usually sleep standing up. Family: *Giraffidae*.

● **Giraldus Cambrensis ▶** (c. 1146–c. 1223) Welsh chronicler. His chronicles of Ireland and Wales, *Expugnatio Hiberniae* (c. 1189) and *Itinerarium Cambriae* (1191), written while in the service of Henry II, contain a number of interesting folk tales. His unfulfilled ambition to become bishop of St David's, Pembrokeshire, is recorded in his autobiography, *De rebus a se gestis* (c. 1204).

● **Girardon, François ▶** (1628–1715) French classical sculptor, best known for his work for Louis XIV at Versailles. His most famous pieces are *Apollo Tended by the Nymphs* (1666) and *The Rape of Persephone* (1677–79).

● **Giraudoux, Jean ▶** (1882–1944) French dramatist, novelist, and diplomat (from 1910 to 1940). His early literary reputation was established by a series of poetic novels, including *Elpénor* (1919) and *Suzanne et le Pacifique* (1921). His stylized plays, often blending elements of tragedy, comedy, and fantasy, include *Amphitryon 38* (1929), *Tiger at the Gates* (1935), *Ondine* (1939), and *The Madwoman of Chaillot* (1949).

● **Girl Guides Association** ▷*See* Guides Association.

● **giro ▶** A low-cost system for transferring money. It originated in Austria in 1883 and the British National Giro was set up by the Post Office in 1968, becoming independent as Girobank plc in 1988. All accounts are held at the Giro Centre (in Bootle, Merseyside), which transfers money from one account to another on receipt of a completed form. Bank giro operates similarly, but accounts are held at bank branches.

● **Gironde, River ▶** A wide estuary in SW France, on the Bay of Biscay. Formed by the confluence of the Rivers Garonne and Dordogne near Bordeaux, it is used by oceangoing vessels. Length: 72 km (45 mi).

● **Girondins ▶** A French Revolutionary political group. Named from the Gironde, where their support was strong, the Girondins were moderate republicans. They became prominent in the newly formed Legislative Assembly (1791), where, suspicious of counter-revolution and seeking to unite the Revolution's supporters, they involved France in war against Austria and Prussia. Military failure undermined their influence and, after the overthrow of the monarchy, they were themselves ousted by the more radical ▷Jacobins (1793). Many Girondins were subsequently executed.

● **Girtin, Thomas ▶** (1775–1802) British landscape painter, famous for being among the first to perfect watercolour technique. His use of broad transparent washes without the old monochrome underpainting produced heightened atmospheric effects, as in *White House at Chelsea* (Tate Gallery). Other works include his etchings of Paris during a visit (1801–02) and drawings for a lost painting of a panoramic view of London.

● **Gisborne ▶** 38 41S 178 02E A port in New Zealand, in E North Island on Poverty Bay. It serves an agricultural region; the chief exports are wool, meat, and dairy produce. Population (1994): 31 700.

● **Giscard d'Estaing, Valéry ▶** (1926–) French statesman; president (1974–81). He was minister of finance and economic affairs from 1962 until 1966, when he established the Independent Republican Party. He returned to this post (1969) under Pompidou, whom he succeeded as president. In the 1981 presidential elections he was defeated by Mitterrand. His attempts at liberal reform were thwarted by his party's dependence on Gaullist support.

● **Gish, Lillian ▶** (1893–1993) US actress, who began her career as a child actress on stage with her sister **Dorothy Gish** (1898–1968). Both acted for the director D. W. ▷Griffith in several early silent films, including *The Birth of a Nation* (1915) and *Intolerance* (1916), and subsequently worked in both films and the theatre. The later films of Lillian Gish include *Duel in the Sun* (1946), *The Night of the Hunter* (1955), and *The Whales of August* (1987).

● **Gislebertus ▶** (early 12th century) French ▷romanesque sculptor. Probably trained in the workshop associated with the Abbey of

Cluny, Gislebertus developed an original and powerfully expressive style. His best-known sculptures are those around the west doorway and on the capitals of columns at the Cathedral of St Lazarus, Autun (c. 1125–35).

● **Gisors** ▶ 49 17N 1 47E A market town in NW France, in the Eure department; it is noted for its 11th- to 12th-century castle. Population (latest est): 8720.

● **Gissing, George Robert** ▶ (1857–1903) British novelist. Of 20 novels written between 1880 and his death, the best known are the autobiographical *New Grub Street* (1891) and *The Private Papers of Henry Ryecroft* (1903). He specialized in realistic portrayals of poverty and never attained popular success. His two marriages to uneducated working-class girls were both unhappy. He separated from his second wife and from 1899 lived with his French mistress in France, where he completed *By the Ionian Sea* (1901), a travel book that contains some of his best writing.

● **gittern** ▶ An early type of guitar with four gut strings, played with a plectrum. It is known to have been a popular instrument for accompanying the voice at various periods between the 13th and 17th centuries but it lost favour after the Restoration.

● **Giulini, Carlo Maria** ▶ (1914–) Italian conductor, musical director of the Los Angeles Philharmonic (1978–84). He was well known in the UK for his work at Covent Garden and with the Philharmonia Orchestra, being particularly noted as a conductor of Verdi.

● **Giulio Romano** ▶ (Giulio Pippi; c. 1499–1546) Italian mannerist painter and architect, born in Rome (*see* mannerism). He was the pupil of ▷Raphael, whom he assisted in the decoration of the Vatican apartments and the Villa Farnesina. After Raphael's death, Giulio completed some of his works. In 1524 he settled in Mantua, where he designed and decorated the Palazzo del Tè, notable for its Room of the Giants, completely covered with illusionistic frescoes.

● **Giza, El** ▶ (*or* al-Jizah) 30 01N 31 12E A city in N Egypt, forming a suburb of Cairo on the River Nile. Nearby are the great pyramids of ▷Khafre, ▷Khufu, and Menkaure, one of the Seven Wonders of the World, and the Sphinx. Tourism is important; there are also film and textile industries. Population (1990 est): 2 516 000.

● **Glace Bay** ▶ 46 11N 59 58W A town in E Canada, on ▷Cape Breton Island. Coal has been mined since 1858; it is now a fishing centre. From here Marconi sent his first wireless message (1902). Population (1992 est): 19 501.

● **glacier** ▶ A mass of ice and ▷firn of limited width lying chiefly, or completely, on land and moving downslope from its source. Different glacier forms exist; **cirque glaciers** are contained in depressions on mountain slopes or valley heads. **Valley glaciers** are contained within pre-existing valleys and are frequently tongue-shaped in plan, originating either from cirque glaciers as an alpine type or from an icesheet as an outlet type. The longest of these is the Lambert Glacier, 400 km (250 mi) long. Where a glacier emerges from a valley onto a lowland area, a lobe-shaped **piedmont glacier** results; an example is

the Malaspina Glacier in Alaska (USA). **Glaciation** is the action of glacier ice on the land surface. The most recent period of extensive glaciation took place during the Pleistocene epoch, when about 30% of the world's surface area was ice covered (*see* Ice Age). The main landforms resulting from glaciation are either erosional or depositional. Erosional features include U-shaped valleys and ▷cirques. Those of depositional origin include glacial ▷drift and ▷till. When water is also involved the term fluvioglacial is used; fluvioglacial deposits include ▷eskers and ▷kames.

● **gladiators** ▶ The slaves, prisoners of war, condemned criminals, or volunteers who fought in amphitheatres for the entertainment of the ancient Roman people. Gladiatorial combats began as a feature of funeral games but their popularity was soon so great that statesmen sponsored shows to enhance their political prestige. Pairs of gladiators would fight to the death unless the audience spared the loser.

● **Gladiolus** ▶ A genus of ornamental perennial herbaceous plants (300 species), native to Europe, Africa, and the Mediterranean regions and widely cultivated. Growing from a corm, the flowering stem reaches a height of 1.2 m, with funnel-shaped flowers, usually red, yellow, orange, or white, grouped on one side. The leaves are sword-shaped. Gladioli cultivated for cut flowers have been developed mainly from South and East African species. Principal garden forms are *G. cardinalis*, *G. primulinus*, *G. psittacinus*, *G. purpurea-auratus*, and *G. saundersii*. Family: *Iridaceae*.

● **Gladstone, W(illiam) E(wart)** ▶ (1809–98) British statesman; Liberal prime minister (1868–74, 1880–85, 1886, 1892–94). Elected to parliament in 1832, he was initially a Tory, becoming president of the Board of Trade (1843) under ▷Peel. He supported the Peelites in the repeal of the ▷Corn Laws, which split the Tories with the Peelites joining the Whigs (shortly to be termed Liberals). As chancellor of the exchequer (1852–55, 1859–66) Gladstone introduced a series of budgets that reduced tariffs and government expenditure. In 1867 he succeeded Lord ▷Russell as leader of the Liberal Party. His first ministry disestablished the Irish Church (1869) and introduced the Education Act (1870), the first Irish ▷Land Act (1870), and the Ballot Act (introducing secret ballots). Defeated in the 1874 election, he resigned the Liberal leadership. In 1875 he re-emerged to criticize the apathetic attitude of his rival ▷Disraeli to the Turkish atrocities in Bulgaria. He again became an MP and prime minister in 1880. His second ministry achieved a second Irish Land Act (1881) and further parliamentary reform (1884) but its failure to save ▷Gordon from Khartoum led to Gladstone's resignation. His last ministries followed his conversion to Irish ▷Home Rule but both his Home Rule bills were rejected (1886, 1893).

An impressive speaker, Gladstone with Disraeli dominated British politics in the second half of the 19th century.

● **Glamis** ▶ 56 37N 3 01W A village in E Scotland, in Angus. Macbeth was thane of Glamis. Nearby Glamis Castle was the childhood home of Queen Elizabeth the Queen Mother and birthplace of Princess Margaret.

El Giza ▶ The Sphinx with the pyramids of Khafre and Khufu visible in the background. Dating from about 2550 BC, the Sphinx is thought to be a portrait statue of King Khafre.

● **Glamorgan ►** A historic county of South Wales. Under local government reorganization in 1974 it was divided to form the counties of Mid Glamorgan, South Glamorgan, and West Glamorgan (with part of the E going to Gwent). In 1996 administrative powers passed to the new county of ▷Swansea and the county boroughs of Bridgend, Caerphilly, Cardiff, Merthyr Tydfil, Neath and Port Talbot, Rhondda Cynon Taff, and Vale of Glamorgan.

● **gland ►** An organ or group of cells that is specialized for synthesizing a specific chemical substance (secretion) from constituents of the blood and releasing its secretion for use by the body. Man and higher animals have two kinds of glands. The ▷endocrine glands lack ducts and release their secretions (which are hormones) directly into the bloodstream. The exocrine glands have ducts through which their products are secreted. Exocrine glands include the salivary glands, the sweat and sebaceous glands in the skin, and the pancreatic cells that secrete digestive enzymes.

Plants also have glands, which secrete a variety of products including latex, resin, nectar, and tannin.

● **glanders ►** A highly contagious disease of horses, donkeys, and related animals caused by the bacterium *Pfeifferella mallei*, which can also infect other animals and man. Onset of symptoms can occur several months after infection and include the formation of nodules in the lungs, liver, spleen, etc., ulceration of the mucous membranes, enlarged lymph nodes, nasal discharge, and pus-filled blisters. The disease is usually chronic. Slaughter of infected animals is compulsory in most countries; human patients usually recover without treatment or after antibiotic or sulphonamide therapy.

● **glandular fever ►** (*or* infectious mononucleosis) An infection characterized by fatigue, sore throat, headache, muscular pain, and enlarged lymph nodes. Most common in children and young adults, it is caused by the Epstein–Barr virus, which can be transmitted in saliva (for example during kissing). Symptoms develop after an incubation period of up to one week and a blood test reveals increased level of monocytes (*see* leucocyte). Treatment is with bed rest and painkillers, but it may be months before full recovery.

● **Glanville, Ranulf de ►** (d. 1190) English jurist; chief minister (1180–89) under Henry II. He assisted with extensive legal reforms and reputedly wrote the *Tractatus de legibus et consuetudinibus regni Angliae*, the earliest treatise on English common law. He died at Acre during the third Crusade.

● **Glaser, Donald Arthur ►** (1926–) US physicist, who was awarded the 1960 Nobel Prize for his invention of the ▷bubble chamber (1952). His first bubble chamber measured only 15 cm across and contained ether.

● **Glasgow ►** 1. 55 53N 4 15W A city in central Scotland, mainly in City of Glasgow council area, on the River Clyde. The largest city in Scotland and the third largest in the UK, it is Scotland's chief commercial and industrial centre. Formerly an important port with a tradition of shipbuilding, Glasgow also has major engineering, textile, chemical, brewing, and whisky-blending industries. Tourism, culture, and service industries are of rising importance.

History: Glasgow was of early religious and educational importance: St Mungo's cathedral dates from the 12th century and the university was founded in 1451. The city's wealth grew rapidly through trade after the union with England (1707), especially in tobacco and sugar from the New World, and through the industrial revolution. Population (1991): 662 954.

2. Glasgow City A council area in W central Scotland. Area: 175 sq km (68 sq mi). Population (1996): 623 850.

● **Glashow, Sheldon Lee ►** (1932–) US physicist. Working at Harvard on particle physics, he independently developed a theory that unified ▷weak interactions and ▷electromagnetic interactions. Known as the GWS model (Glashow–Weinberg–Salam model), the theory won a share of the 1979 Nobel Prize for its three authors (*see also* Weinberg, Steven; Salam, Abdus). Glashow also extended Murray ▷Gell-Mann's theory of quarks.

● **glasnost ►** A policy of increased freedom in social and cultural matters introduced in the Soviet Union by Mikhail ▷Gorbachov in 1986. A Russian word meaning openness, glasnost was adopted by the Soviet government in conjunction with *perestroika* (meaning progress), which heralded a new (though still limited) flexibility in the economy of the USSR, and facilitated the improvement of relations with the West.

● **glass ►** A translucent and usually transparent noncrystalline substance that behaves as a solid although it has many of the properties of a liquid. Glass itself was known in the 3rd millennium BC and glass objects survive from Egypt's 18th dynasty (1570–1320 BC), but glass-blowing was not invented until about 100 BC (in Syria) and windows, which were originally made of blown glass, were not in use until about 100 AD. Ordinary soda glass, used for windows, etc., consists of silica (sand), sodium carbonate, and calcium carbonate (limestone). Flint glass, used for crystal glassware, contains silica, potassium carbonate, potassium nitrate, and lead oxide. Heat-resistant glass also contains borates and alumina; optical glass contains additional elements to control the refractive index and other optical properties, homogeneity being obtained by repeated heating and slow cooling. Blown glass is melted and blown inside a mould until it fills the mould; bottles and lightbulbs are made in this way by a fully automatic process. Flint glass is also blown to make glassware, but this is usually done by hand. Pressed glass, to make domestic bowls and headlamp lenses, is made by pressing the molten glass into a mould. Plate glass, for windows, etc., was formerly made by pouring molten glass onto a flat table and rolling it through heated rollers into sheets, which were then polished. Since 1959 the last stage has been replaced by floating the rolled sheet of glass on molten tin. ▷*See also* fibreglass; stained glass.

● **Glass, Philip ►** (1937–) US composer. A pupil of Nadia ▷Boulanger and Ravi ▷Shankar, he is known for such minimalist works as *Music in Fifths* (1970) and the operas *Einstein on the Beach* (1976), written with Robert Wilson, *Akhnaten* (1984), *The Fall of the House of Usher* (1988), *The Voyage* (1992), and *Monsters of Grace* (1998).

● **glassfish ►** A fish of the family *Centropomidae* (about 24 species), especially the genus *Chanda*, having a transparent body and a cleft dorsal fin. Glassfish occur along coastlines, in estuaries, and in fresh waters from Africa to the Indian and Pacific regions. Order: *Perciformes*.

● **glass harmonica** ▷*See* harmonica.

● **glass snake ►** A legless lizard belonging to the genus *Ophisaurus*, occurring in Europe, S and E Asia, N Africa, and North America. Glass snakes feed on insects, lizards, mice, and birds' eggs. Unlike true snakes, they have ears and eyelids. When attacked, they shed their tail. Family: *Anguidae*.

● **glasswort ►** (*or* marsh samphire) An annual or perennial plant of the genus *Salicornia* (at least 7 species), native to European salt marshes, with jointed succulent stems that turn red in autumn. The fleshy leaves sheath the stem and the flowers are inconspicuous. The plant was once used in glassmaking as a source of soda. Family: *Chenopodiaceae*.

● **Glastonbury ►** 51 09N 2 43W A market town in SW England, in Somerset. Here by tradition Joseph of Arimathea founded England's first Christian church; Glastonbury is also the reputed burial place of King Arthur. There are the ruins of an early Benedictine abbey and the site of an excavated iron age lake village. Population (1991): 7747.

● **glaucoma ►** An eye disease caused by raised pressure inside the eye. Acute glaucoma is often caused by a sudden block to the drainage of the watery fluid (aqueous humour) inside the eye. It leads to pain and disturbed vision, which will result in blindness without treatment. Chronic glaucoma, a common cause of blindness, comes on slowly and painlessly.

● **Glazunov, Aleksandr Konstantinovich ►** (1865–1936) Russian composer and pupil of Rimsky-Korsakov. He became director of the St Petersburg conservatoire in 1906 but left Russia in 1928 and died in Paris. Glazunov's works, which were influenced by Wagner and Liszt, included eight symphonies, concertos, ballets, and string quartets.

● **Gleiwitz** ▷*See* Gliwice.

● **Glencoe ►** A glen in W Scotland, in Highland council area extending to Loch Leven. It was the scene of the massacre of the Macdonalds by the Campbells and English (1692).

● **Glendower, Owen** ▶ (Welsh name: Owain Glyndwr; c. 1359– c. 1416) Welsh rebel. He led a Welsh rising that became a national war of independence. Allying with Henry IV's opponents, Glendower controlled most of Wales by 1404 but was subsequently defeated and turned to guerrilla warfare. He disappeared in 1416.

● **Glen More** ▷*See* Great Glen.

● **Glenn, John** ▶ (1921–   ) US astronaut and politician, who on 20 February, 1962, became the first American to orbit the earth. Previously a test pilot, he became an astronaut in 1959. He remained in orbit in Friendship 7 for 4 hours 56 minutes, reaching a height of about 261 km (162 mi). He subsequently entered politics, becoming a US senator in 1975. In 1998 he returned to space at the age of 77, as part of a research project investigating the effects of space travel on the ageing human body.

● **Glenrothes** ▶ 56 12N 3 10W A town in E central Scotland, the administrative centre of Fife. Developed since 1948 as a new town, it has light and electronic engineering, food-processing, and plastics industries. Population (1991): 38 650.

● **gliders** ▶ Light fixed-wing engineless aircraft, sometimes called sailplanes. They are launched into the air by a winch or catapult or by being towed by a car or powered aircraft. Once airborne a glider slowly loses height unless it is lifted by a rising air current created by warm air rising from the ground (a **thermal**), a ground contour, or a thunderstorm. The height record is 14.1 km (P. F. Bikle; 1961) and the distance record 1460.8 km (H. W. Grosse; 1972).

Pioneered by Otto ▷Lilienthal in the USA, gliders were used by Orville and Wilbur ▷Wright in designing their powered aircraft. Gliders towed by aircraft were used in World War II to carry men and equipment, notably by the British in the ill-fated Arnhem expedition. Gliding is a popular sport, controlled in the UK by the British Gliding Association (1924). ▷*See also* hang-gliding.

● **Glinka, Mikhail Ivanovich** ▶ (1804–57) Russian composer. He studied with John Field, made many journeys abroad, and is regarded as the founder of Russian musical nationalism. He composed the first truly Russian opera *Ivan Susanin* (*A Life for the Tsar*; 1836), various works in a Spanish style, piano music, songs, and a second opera, *Russlan and Ludmilla* (1842).

● **Gliwice** ▶ (German name: Gleiwitz) 50 20N 18 40E A town in S Poland. Within Upper Silesia, it has coal, steel and chemical industries. Population (1996 est): 214 000.

● **Global Positioning System** ▶ (*or* GPS) A US satellite-based system enabling people, ships, aircraft, etc., equipped with a GPS receiver to determine their position on the earth (including the oceans and airspace) to a horizontal accuracy of 100 metres (standard positioning service). For military and certain other uses the accuracy can be 22 metres (precise positioning service).

The system consists of 24 ▷navigation satellites, each in orbit 11 000 nautical miles above the earth and taking 12 hours to complete an orbit. The first GPS satellite was launched in 1978, the last in 1994.

The satellites are positioned to enable users to receive signals from six satellites at any one time, as this number provides the best positional information. Each satellite has a precise clock and sends out a continuous time signal together with its identification signal. These signals enable a receiver to determine exactly how long the signal from a particular satellite takes to reach it. Taking this information from between three and six satellites enables the receiver to calculate its exact position. The satellites are monitored by a number of unmanned ground stations and the whole system is controlled by a US Air Force base in Colorado.

The system, which has extensive military uses and was first used in operation in the Gulf War (1991), was developed for the US Department of Defense. It also has a wide range of civilian uses, including the police, fire, and ambulance services.

● **global warming** ▷*See* greenhouse effect; pollution.

● **globe artichoke** ▷*See* artichoke.

● **globefish** ▷*See* puffer.

● **globeflower** ▶ A herbaceous plant of the genus *Trollius* (about 15 species), found throughout Europe. It has lobed toothed leaves and globe-shaped flowers, yellow or orange, borne on stems 10–70 cm high. Family: ▷*Ranunculaceae*.

● **Globe Theatre** ▶ An Elizabethan theatre, in Southwark, in which most of Shakespeare's plays were first produced. A cylindrical wooden building open to the sky, it was built in 1599, burnt down in 1613, rebuilt in 1614, and finally demolished in 1644. A reconstruction of the Globe, instigated by the US actor Sam Wanamaker (1919–93), was erected near the original site and opened in 1996, enabling Shakespeare's plays to be performed in a theatre that closely resembles the Elizabethan building in which many of them were first staged. The foundations of the first Globe were located in 1989. ▢theatres and stages.

● **globe thistle** ▶ A stout perennial ▷thistle of the genus *Echinops* (about 15 species), of central and S Europe. 50–200 cm high, it has lobed leaves and large usually blue spherical flower heads. They are planted in gardens.

● **Globigerina** ▶ A genus of protozoans (*see* Foraminifera) that are common components of marine plankton. 0.3 to 2 mm, their chalky skeletons are a major constituent of the grey mud on some sea beds, forming globigerina ooze.

● **globular cluster** ▷*See* star cluster.

● **globulin** ▶ A type of protein that is generally insoluble in water. Serum (gamma) globulins of the blood include the immunoglobulins (antibodies), which are manufactured by the animal to combat infections (*see* immunity). Other globulins occur in eggs, nuts, and seeds.

● **glockenspiel** ▶ (German: bell play) A tuned percussion instrument having a keyboard-like arrangement of steel bars played with two small hammers. The notes of its two-and-a-half-octave compass above bottom G of the bass stave sound two octaves higher.

● **Glomma, River** ▶ (Norwegian name: Glåma) A river in SE Norway and the longest river in Scandinavia. Flowing S from a small lake SE of Trondheim, it enters the Skagerrak at Fredrikstad. It is important for hydroelectric power and for transporting timber. Length: 588 km (365 mi).

● **Glorious Revolution** ▶ (1688) The overthrow of James II of England and the establishment of his daughter Mary and her husband William of Orange on the throne. The opposition to James' pro-Catholic and absolutist policies requested William's armed intervention; James, offering no resistance, fled to France. William and Mary accepted the ▷Bill of Rights, establishing constitutional monarchy in England.

● **glory pea** ▷*See* Clianthus.

● **glottis** ▷*See* larynx.

● **Gloucester** ▶ 51 53N 2 14W A city in W England, the administrative centre of Gloucestershire on the River Severn. Gloucester first developed as a regional centre under the Romans (Glevum) in the 1st century AD. Its principal building is its cathedral, noted for its inventions in the Perpendicular style and its medieval cloisters. Formerly known for engineering, Gloucester is now a centre for service industries, including distribution, retail, leisure and tourism, and finance. Population (1997 est): 107 400.

● **Gloucester, Humphrey, Duke of** ▶ (1391–1447) The youngest son of Henry IV and brother of John, Duke of ▷Bedford, with whom he was protector during the minority of Henry VI. Despite his political incompetence and quarrelsome nature his patriotism and patronage of literature earned him the nickname, the Good Duke Humphrey. He died, apparently naturally, shortly after being arrested for treason.

● **Gloucestershire** ▶ A county of W England, bordering Wales. Under local government reorganization in 1974 it lost the SW part to the new county of Avon. In 1996 this area became the unitary authority of ▷South Gloucestershire, which is considered part of Gloucestershire for ceremonial and related purposes but is administered separately. Physically Gloucestershire consists of three regions: the Cotswold Hills, the Severn Valley, and the Forest of Dean. It is mainly agricultural; wheat and barley are the chief crops and dairy farming is important. Industry includes engineering and timber production. Coal is mined in the Forest of Dean. Area (excluding South Gloucestershire): 2643 sq km (1020 sq mi). Population (1995 est, excluding South Gloucestershire): 552 700. Administrative centre: Gloucester.

• **glowworm** ▷*See* firefly.

• **gloxinia** ▶ An ornamental herb, *Sinningia speciosa*, native to Brazil. Gloxinias have rosettes of large simple velvety leaves and bell-shaped flowers, usually violet, purple, or pink. New plants can regenerate from the base of the leafstalks. The numerous hybrids are popular house plants. Family: *Gesneriaceae*. The genus *Gloxinia* (6 species) of the same family is not cultivated.

• **Glozel** ▶ An archaeological site SE of Vichy (central France). During the 1920s finds here included engraved pebbles and clay tablets with an alphabetic script. An international commission investigated the site (1927) and cast grave doubts on its authenticity. Scientific dating of Glozel artefacts in the 1970s revived the puzzle, as some objects are undoubtedly ancient.

• **Glubb, Sir John Bagot** ▶ (1897–1986) British soldier and writer, known as Glubb Pasha. After service in World War I he organized the police force in Iraq and (from 1930) the Arab Legion in Transjordan, becoming its commander in 1939. Dismissed in 1956 after Arab moves to eliminate British influence, he became a writer, mostly on Arab affairs.

• **glucagon** ▶ A polypeptide hormone, produced by the islets of Langerhans in the ▷pancreas, that increases the level of glucose in the blood by stimulating the breakdown of ▷glycogen in body tissues and promoting the utilization of protein and fat as energy sources. At high levels in the blood glucagon stimulates the secretion of ▷insulin.

• **Gluck, Christoph Willibald** ▶ (1714–87) German composer. He reformed ▷opera seria, making it less artificial. Inspired by Calzabigi's librettos, he composed the operas *Orfeo ed Euridice* (1762) and *Alceste* (1767) in which the music reflected the dramatic situation and merely musical repetition and vocal ornamentation were excluded. He composed over 40 dramatic works as well as other music.

• **glucose** ▶ (or dextrose) A simple sugar ($C_6H_{12}O_6$) and an essential substance in the carbohydrate metabolism of living organisms. Carbohydrates (such as starch and glycogen) in food or tissue reserves are broken down to glucose, which is easily transported to cells where it undergoes ▷glycolysis to provide energy for the cell. Organisms can also manufacture glucose from fats and proteins. Glucose levels in blood are regulated by the hormones ▷insulin and ▷glucagon. Fruits and honey are good sources of glucose.

• **glue** ▷*See* adhesives.

• **glue-sniffing** ▷*See* solvent abuse.

• **gluon** ▷*See* particle physics.

• **gluten** ▶ A protein mixture derived from wheat. In bread making, dough rises because the gluten in wheat flour expands, trapping the carbon dioxide bubbles in an elastic network. The properties of gluten vary according to the mixture of the proteins, chiefly gliadin and glutenin. ▷*See also* coeliac disease.

• **glutton** ▷*See* wolverine.

• **glycerol** ▶ (or glycerine; $CH_2OHCHOHCH_2OH$) A colourless syrupy liquid with a sweet taste. It is made from fats and oils or by fermentation and is used in explosives, cosmetics, and antifreeze solutions.

• **glycogen** ▶ A starchlike carbohydrate found in animal tissues as a reserve energy source. Chemically, it consists of branched chains of ▷glucose molecules: when required to provide energy, glycogen is broken down to glucose under the influence of hormones, chiefly ▷adrenaline and ▷glucagon.

• **glycolysis** ▶ The sequence of chemical reactions occurring in most living cells by which glucose is partially broken down to pro-

vide usable energy for the cell in the form of ▷ATP. Glycolysis can take place in the presence or absence of oxygen but only a small amount of the available energy is released, the major proportion being released via the ▷Krebs cycle.

• **Glyndebourne** ▶ An estate near Lewes, in East Sussex, home of an annual international festival of opera. The opera house was built on the estate by its owner John Christie (1882–1962), a British patron of music, who founded the Glyndebourne Festival in 1934 for his wife, the opera singer Audrey Mildmay (1900–53). The opera house was completely rebuilt (1992–94).

• **Glyptodon** ▶ An extinct giant ▷armadillo, whose remains have been found in South America. Glyptodons had a rigid bony shell (unlike the jointed modern armadillo shell) and some had a spiky macelike knob at the end of the tail. They became extinct about 100 000 years ago.

• **GMT** ▷*See* Greenwich Mean Time.

• **gnat** ▶ Any of the smaller delicate species of two-winged flies, the males of which fly in dancing swarms. The term is applied to the less virulent mosquitoes and phantom gnats (family *Culicidae*), winter gnats (family *Trichoceridae*), fungus gnats (family *Mycetophilidae*), craneflies (family *Tipulidae*), and several others.

• **gnatcatcher** ▶ A small active songbird belonging to a family (*Polioptilidae*; 11 species) ranging from S Canada to Argentina. 10 to 14 cm long, gnatcatchers have long wagging tails and fine pointed bills used to pick insects from leaves and crevices. The plumage is typically greyish blue above with lighter underparts and white outer tail feathers.

• **Gneisenau, August (Wilhelm Anton), Graf Neithardt von** ▶ (1760–1831) Prussian field marshal, who was instrumental in effecting major reforms in the Prussian army following its defeat by Napoleon (1807). He subsequently played an important part in the wars of liberation (1813–14) and in the defeat of Napoleon at Waterloo (1815).

• **gneiss** ▶ A coarse-grained metamorphic rock consisting predominantly of bands of quartz and feldspar alternating with bands of micas and amphiboles. These bands are often irregular or poorly defined. Gneisses are formed during regional metamorphism; those derived from igneous rocks are termed **orthogneiss**, while those from sedimentary rocks are called **paragneiss**.

• **Gniezno** ▶ 52 32N 17 32E A city in W central Poland. One of the oldest cities in Poland, it contains many notable historical buildings, including its 10th-century cathedral. It is a commercial centre specializing in food processing. Population (latest est): 63 500.

• **Gnosticism** ▶ A religious movement that flourished in the early Christian era. It manifested itself in many ways and contained many elements of pagan thought and magic, but is most fully recorded as a group of heretical Christian sects, attacked by Church Fathers, such as ▷Tertullian. The Gnostics' defining characteristic was their belief in *gnosis* (Greek: knowledge)—a special and secret revelation from God to initiates, which would ensure their salvation (*compare* mysteries). Their world view was dualistic: God and the spirit were good and created matter evil. Accordingly they made a distinction between God and the creator and ruler of the world, or Demiurge, whom they saw as an evil being. They interpreted Christ (whose humanity they denied) as being sent to rescue particles of spirit (souls) entrapped in matter. Gnosticism influenced ▷Manichaeism and several medieval heresies, notably the ▷Albigenses and the ▷Cathari. ▷*See also* Mandaeanism.

• **GNP** ▷*See* gross national product.

• **gnu** ▶ A large ungainly antelope belonging to the genus *Connochaetes* (2 species), also called wildebeest, of African plains. The brindled gnu (*C. taurinus*) grows to 140 cm high at the shoulder and is blue-grey with a long black mane, black facial tufts, and a black-tufted tail. The smaller white-tailed gnu (*C. gnou*) has a long white tail and is very rare, surviving only in game reserves.

• **go** ▶ (or i-go) A board game that originated in China (as *Wei-ch'i*), possibly in the 3rd millennium BC, and is especially popular in Japan.

The board is marked with a grid of 19 vertical and 19 horizontal lines, making 361 intersections. There are 361 counters: 181 black "stones" for one player and 180 white for the other. Black begins by placing a stone on any intersection of the empty board. Play alternates, one stone being placed at a time; once played a stone may not be moved except to remove it from the board. The object is to conquer territory by enclosing empty points with one's own stones. Opposing stones that are encircled are captured and removed. The score is calculated by deducting the number of stones a player has lost from the number of intersections he has captured.

● **Goa** ► The 25th state of India, formerly part of Goa, Daman, and Diu Union Territory. A Portuguese overseas territory from 1510 until annexed by India in 1961, it has many fine examples of Portuguese colonial architecture, including the church in which the remains of St Francis Xavier are preserved. Goa depends economically on agriculture, fishing, and tourism. Area: 3702 sq km (1429 sq mi). Population (1994 est): 1 235 000.

● **Goa, Daman, and Diu** ► A former Union Territory of W India. ▷Goa is on the central W coast; Daman lies inland N of Bombay; Diu is an island off the coast of Gujarat. In 1987 Goa became the 25th state of India, while the remainder became the Union of ▷Daman and Diu.

● **goat** ► A hoofed ▷ruminant mammal belonging to the genus *Capra* (the so-called "true goats"; 5 species). Related to sheep, goats are 60–85 cm tall at the shoulder and have hollow horns, less curled than those of sheep; males have a scent gland beneath the tail and a beard. Wild goats, found in mountainous regions of Eurasia, are greyish in winter, reddish in summer, and live in herds of 5–20 individuals. Goats were first domesticated over 10 000 years ago; descended from the wild Asian species *C. aegagrus*, they are still used to provide milk, meat, and hides in many semiarid regions of the world. Other wild species include the ▷ibex and ▷markhor. Related to the true goats are the so-called "goat antelopes," which have features of both goats and antelopes. They include the Rocky Mountain goat (*Oreamnus americanus*), the ▷goral, and the ▷serow. Family: *Bovidae*.

● **goat moth** ► A large moth, *Cossus cossus*, of Europe, Asia, and N Africa. Mottled grey and brown, it has a wingspan of 70 mm. The reddish caterpillar bores under the bark of trees and emits a characteristic strong odour. It may hibernate for up to four years.

● **goatsbeard** ► A perennial herb, *Aruncus dioicus* (or *A. sylvestris*), native to N temperate wooded regions, especially Siberia. Often grown as a border plant, goatsbeard is 120–180 cm tall and has fine compound leaves and branched plumes of small stalkless hay-scented creamy-white flowers. Family: *Rosaceae*.

● **Gobbi, Tito** ► (1915–84) Italian baritone. He sang in all the world's major opera houses and was a well-known teacher. His most famous parts included the title roles in Mozart's *Don Giovanni* and Verdi's *Falstaff* and Scarpia in Puccini's *Tosca*. He also produced opera.

● **Gobelins, Manufacture nationale des** ► A French state-controlled tapestry factory, founded in Paris as a dyeworks in the 15th century by Jean and Philibert Gobelin. Manufacturing tapestries from 1529, it was incorporated by Henry IV in 1607. In 1662 Louis XIV purchased it and it was directed from 1663 to 1690 by his First Painter Charles ▷Le Brun. Since 1826 carpets have also been made here.

● **Gobi Desert** ► A vast desert of SE Mongolia and N China, one of the largest in the world. On a plateau 900–1500 m (2950–4920 ft) high, it is largely rocky with salt marshes and streams that disappear into the sand. It is rich in prehistoric remains including fossils and stone implements. Area: about 1 295 000 sq km (500 000 sq mi).

● **Gobind Singh** ► (or Govind S.; 1666–1708) The tenth and last Guru of the Sikhs (1675–1708). As a religious reformer he remodelled the Sikh religious belief and practice and renounced social inequality and caste distinctions. He was assassinated by a Muslim.

● **Gobineau, Joseph Arthur, Comte de** ► (1816–82) French writer and diplomat. He wrote novels, notably *Les Pléiades* (1874), short stories, and scholarly studies, including *La Renaissance* (1877). His influential *Essai sur l'inégalité des races humaines* (1853–55) argued that the continuing strength of the Aryan race depended on its racial purity.

● **goblin shark** ► A carnivorous ▷shark, *Scapanorhynchus owstoni*. Up to 4.2 m long, it has long upper teeth that overlap the lower set, a long paddle-shaped nose, and a very long tail fin. It has been found in deep water off Japan, India, and Portugal and is probably the only member of its family, *Scapanorhynchidae*.

● **goby** ► A fish of the suborder *Gobioidei* (over 800 species), especially the family *Gobiidae* (true gobies). True gobies have smooth elongated bodies, two dorsal fins, and a suction disc formed from fused pelvic fins. Most are 5–10 cm long, although *Pandaka pygmaea* of the Philippines is the smallest known vertebrate at under 13 mm long. They are chiefly marine and inhabit sand or mud burrows in tropical coastal regions, sometimes in association with other animals. Order: *Perciformes*.

● **God** ► The supreme being postulated as the creator and ruler of the universe. The concept of God perhaps originated in man's fear and isolation in the face of natural phenomena and may have developed first as ▷polytheism, as in India and ancient Greece and Rome. In some religions, principally Judaism, Christianity, and Islam, God is seen as not only the architect of the universe (god the creator) but also as being actively involved (god the intervener) with its inhabitants and its destiny (*see* theism). In ▷deism, God is the creator of the universe who leaves its destiny to natural forces and the will of its in-

Gobi Desert ► The Mongolian nomads of the Gobi Desert still follow a traditional pastoral lifestyle based on animal breeding. They live in yurts, tents made of felt erected on wooden poles.

habitants. In ▷Hinduism, Brahman, the supreme spirit and ultimate reality, is conceived as operating through the triad Brahma, Vishnu, and Shiva (*see* Trimurti). ▷Buddhism is, strictly speaking, nontheistic, being concerned more with the attainment of ▷nirvana than with the nature of a supreme being. The concept of a single deity (*see* monotheism) originated with the Jews (*see* Yahweh). Jews, Christians, and Muslims believe that a wholly good and all-knowing God reveals himself in their scriptures (*see* Bible; Koran). This God of revelation requires an act of faith. However, theologians have also tried to prove the existence of God by rational means or by means of observed facts (natural theology). Most of the traditional arguments are associated with St Thomas ▷Aquinas; these include: the argument from design or the teleological argument (there is an observable design, order, and regularity in the universe and therefore it must have been designed, which argues a designer); the cosmological argument (the mere fact that there is a universe demands further explanation); the degrees of perfection argument (if every thing or quality in the universe can be traced back to a more perfect thing or quality, there must be some ultimate perfect being, i.e. God); the First Cause argument (if everything is caused by something else, at the beginning there must have been an uncaused First Cause). Another important argument is the ontological argument (*see* Anselm of Canterbury, St).

Believers in God in the UK in 1995

religion	millions
Christians	
Anglicans	26.1
Roman Catholics	5.7
Nonconformists	4.5
Others	3.1
Non-Christians	
Muslims	1.2
Sikhs	0.6
Hindus	0.4
Jews	0.3
Others	0.3
total	42.2 million (i.e. 72% of the population)

● **Godalming** ▶ 51 11N 0 37W A residential town in SE England, in Surrey on the River Wey. Charterhouse (a famous public school established in 1611) was moved here from London in 1872. Population (1991): 20 630.

● **Godard, Jean-Luc** ▶ (1930–) French film director. During the 1950s he wrote for the magazine *Cahiers du Cinéma* and emerged as a leading director of the ▷New Wave. His films, which are characterized by experimental narrative and editing techniques and by his Marxist political convictions, include *À bout de souffle* (1960), *Alphaville* (1965), *Week-End* (1967), *Tout va bien* (1972), *Je Vous Salue, Marie* (1985), and *JLG/JLG* (1995).

● **Godavari, River** ▶ A river in central India. Rising in the Western Ghats, it flows ESE across the Deccan, through the Eastern Ghats, and into the Bay of Bengal. Its delta has an extensive canal irrigation system, which is linked to the Krishna delta. It is sacred to the Hindus. Length: 1500 km (900 mi).

● **Goddard, Robert Hutchings** ▶ (1882–1945) US physicist, who pioneered the technology of rockets. His first liquid-fuelled rocket (petrol and liquid oxygen) was launched in 1926. Throughout the 1920s and 1930s he continued to make improvements to his rockets but was largely ignored by the US Government. During World War II he invented the ▷bazooka but died before the space-rocket age, although the German ▷V-2 was largely based on his work.

● **Gödel, Kurt** ▶ (1906–78) US mathematician, born in Austria, who derived probably the most important proof in modern mathematics. Known as **Gödel's proof**, it states that, in a mathematical system based on a finite number of axioms, there will always exist statements that can be neither proved nor disproved. Gödel's proof, pub-

lished in 1931, thus ended the search by mathematicians for a complete and self-consistent system.

● **Goderich, George Frederick Samuel Robinson, Viscount** ▶ (1827–1909) British politician and colonial administrator; governor general of India (1880–84). Elected a Liberal MP in 1852, he served under Gladstone before succeeding ▷Lytton in India. There, he ended the second Afghan War (1878–80) and pursued an enlightened policy of reform, increasing the powers of local government and relaxing restrictions on the vernacular press. He was subsequently colonial secretary (1892–95). He became the 2nd Earl of Ripon at the death of his father **Frederick John Robinson, Viscount Goderich and 1st Earl of Ripon** (1782–1859), who had been Tory prime minister from 1827 to 1828.

● **Godesberg** ▶ (or Bad Godesberg) 50 41N 7 10E A spa in W Germany, in North Rhine-Westphalia on the River Rhine; since 1968 a district of Bonn. Chamberlain and Hitler met here in 1938. The site of ministries and embassies, it has a pharmaceutical industry.

● **Godfrey of Bouillon** ▶ (c. 1060–1100) Crusader and Duke of Lower Lorraine. In 1096 Godfrey joined the first Crusade and played a major role in the siege and capture of Jerusalem. He then became defender of the Holy Sepulchre and effective King of Jerusalem. His exploits were celebrated in the medieval song cycle, the *Chansons de Geste*.

● **Godiva, Lady** ▶ (d. ?1080) The English woman who, according to the chronicler Roger of Wendover (d. 1236), rode naked through the market place of Coventry in order to persuade her husband Leofric, Earl of Mercia, to reduce the taxes he had imposed on the town. The story was later embellished with a Peeping Tom who, ignoring Godiva's request that the townspeople remain indoors, was struck blind.

● **Godolphin, Sidney, Earl of** ▶ (1645–1712) British Whig politician; Lord Treasurer (1685–88, 1700–01, 1702–10). Under Anne (reigned 1702–14) he and ▷Harley were the most powerful men in politics until the unpopularity of their pursuit of the War of the ▷Spanish Succession caused their downfall. Godolphin was also a noted importer of racehorses, including the famous Godolphin Arabian.

● **Godoy, Manuel de** ▶ (1767–1851) Spanish statesman; chief minister (1792–97, 1801–08) of Charles IV of Spain. He rose to power through the influence of Charles' wife María Luisa (1751–1819), whose lover Godoy became. He allied Spain with France during the Napoleonic War and, extremely unpopular, was overthrown together with Charles.

● **Godthåb** ▷*See* Nuuk.

● **Godunov, Boris (Fedorovich)** ▶ (c. 1551–1605) Russian statesman and tsar (1598–1605). Godunov rose to power in the reign of ▷Ivan the Terrible and became regent for Fyodor I, whose younger brother and heir, Dimitrii, Godunov may have murdered in 1591. After Fyodor's death (1598), Godunov was elected tsar. His authority was challenged by the first False Dimitrii, a pretender who succeeded Godunov (*see* Time of Troubles). Godunov was the subject of a play by Pushkin, on which Mussorgsky based his famous opera.

● **Godwin** ▶ (or Godwine; d. 1053) Earl of Wessex. An Anglo-Danish noble, he rose to power under Canute, after whose death Godwin supported the accession of Edward the Confessor and became a dominant figure in royal government. In 1045 his daughter Edith married Edward. He was overthrown in 1051 but regained his position by force in 1052. He was succeeded by his son Harold (later Harold II).

● **Godwin, William** ▶ (1756–1836) British political philosopher and novelist. A utilitarian of the extreme radical kind, Godwin in *Political Justice* (1793) advocated anarchy and communism. As a determinist, he held that the notion of moral desert was irrelevant; Christianity was also a harmful influence, distracting men with bogus promises of immortality. His major novel, *Caleb Williams* (1794), propagates his views on justice. He married Mary ▷Wollstonecraft (1797) and was the father of the future Mary ▷Shelley.

● **Godwin Austen, Mount** ▷*See* K2.

● **godwit** ▶ A long-legged long-billed migratory bird belonging to a genus (*Limosa*; 4 species) that breeds in N Eurasia and North America. The black-tailed godwit (*L. limosa*) is 40 cm long and has a distinctive black-banded white tail, white wing stripe, and, in summer, a chestnut neck and breast. Family: *Scolopacidae* (plovers, sandpipers, etc.).

● **Goebbels, (Paul) Joseph** ▶ (1897–1945) German politician. From 1926, when he became Nazi Party leader in Berlin, he was well known for his skilful ▷propaganda techniques. In 1928 he entered the Reichstag and in 1933 was appointed minister of propaganda by Hitler. He established a vast machine for the control of public information, the arts, cinema, and theatre, all of which he manipulated with a cynical disregard for truth to achieve Nazi aims. He committed suicide with his wife after taking the lives of his six children during the collapse of the Third Reich.

● **Goehr, Alexander** ▶ (1932–) British composer. Professor of music at Cambridge University since 1976, he has employed serialism and classical elements in his works, which include the operas *Arden Must Die* (1976), *Behold the Sun* (1985), and *Arianna* (1995) and the choral work *The Death of Moses* (1992).

● **Goering, Hermann Wilhelm** ▶ (1893–1946) German politician. He served in the air force in World War I and became a Nazi in 1922, taking command of Hitler's Brownshirts. He was elected to the Reichstag in 1928 and became its president in 1932. When Hitler came to power in 1933, Goering was appointed air minister of Germany and prime minister of Prussia. He established the ▷Gestapo and ▷concentration camps and probably engineered the Reichstag fire (1933). He directed the development of the Luftwaffe and in 1936 was given charge of mobilizing the economy for war. Hitler declared Goering his successor in 1939 but expelled him from the party shortly before the Nazi collapse. "When I hear the word culture I reach for my gun" was an appropriate epigram for a Nazi who looted occupied Europe for some £20 million worth of art treasures. Condemned to hang at Nuremberg, he committed suicide before the execution could take place.

● **Goes, Hugo van der** ▶ (c. 1440–82) Flemish painter, who worked in Ghent until about 1478. He spent the rest of his life in a monastery near Brussels. His *Portinari Altarpiece* (Uffizi), painted for a Florentine patron, is uncharacteristically large for Flemish paintings. The unharmonious colours and emotional intensity of his last work, *The Death of the Virgin* (Bruges), are perhaps related to mental illness, from which he suffered in the last years of his life.

Goethe ▶ A portrait by Johann Tischbein (1751–1829), painted during the poet's visit to Italy in 1787.

● **Goethe, Johann Wolfgang von** ▶ (1749–1832) German poet, scholar, and statesman. He studied law at Leipzig and Strasbourg, where his discovery of Shakespeare inspired him to write an epic drama, *Götz von Berlichingen* (1773). The autobiographical novel *The Sorrows of Young Werther* (1774) won him international fame. In 1775 he settled at the court of the Duke of Saxe-Weimar, whom he served

as prime minister until 1785 as well as directing the state theatre and scientific institutions. At Weimar he fell in love with Charlotte von Stein, who inspired some of his greatest lyric poetry. A visit to Italy (1786–88) made him an enthusiastic advocate of classicism, influencing such plays as *Iphigenia on Tauris* (1787) and *Torquato Tasso* (1790). After the novel *Wilhelm Meister's Apprentice Years* (1795–96) he published the first part of his greatest work *Faust* (1808), a poetic drama of the aspirations of man. Other novels and scientific publications followed, until in 1829 he published *Wilhelm Meister's Journeyman Years*. The second, more philosophical, part of *Faust* he completed shortly before his death. Goethe's interests included stagecraft, biology, physics, astrology, and philosophy, both orthodox and occult; he knew six languages and translated many works into German.

● **Gog and Magog** ▶ In Revelation and other books of the Bible, attendant powers of Satan. In British folklore they appear as the survivors of a race of giants destroyed by Brutus, the legendary founder of Britain. A famous pair of statues depicting them are located in the Guildhall, London.

● **Gogol, Nikolai Vasilievich** ▶ (1809–52) Russian novelist and dramatist. Early ambitions to become a poet and an actor and to emigrate to the USA all failed, but two volumes of stories based on his Ukrainian childhood won him acclaim from ▷Pushkin and other leading writers. To escape the controversy aroused by his satirical play *The Government Inspector* (1836) he went to Rome, where he wrote his best-known work, *Dead Souls* (1842), a grotesque lampoon of Russian feudalism. In his last years he became a depressive and a religious maniac.

● **Goiânia** ▶ 16 43S 49 18W A city in central Brazil, the capital of Goiás state on the Pan-American Highway. Founded in 1933 to replace the old capital, it serves a cattle-raising and coffee-growing area and has two universities. Population (1995): 1 033 000.

● **Goidelic languages** ▷*See* Celtic languages.

● **goitre** ▶ Swelling in the neck caused by enlargement of the thyroid gland. A goitre is called simple if the thyroid is functioning normally; this occurs in areas where iodine is deficient in the water supply and it may occur sporadically in adolescent girls. A goitre may also be seen when the thyroid is overactive (*see* hyperthyroidism) or underactive (*see* cretinism; myxoedema).

● **Golan Heights** ▶ A range of hills in SW Syria, under Israeli administration. They are of great strategic importance; Syrian artillery positioned here was able to fire into the upper Jordan and Hula Valleys in Israel. Israeli forces stormed the heights in June, 1967, when most of the local populace fled; Jewish settlements have since been established.

● **Golconda** ▶ 17 24N 78 23E A ruined city in S India, in Andhra Pradesh near Hyderabad city. The impressive tombs of the Qutb Shahi dynasty and the fortress, built on a granite ridge, recall the city's former status as capital of one of the five Islamic kingdoms of the Deccan (1518–1687).

● **gold** ▶ (Au) A soft dense yellow metal known and valued since ancient times. It occurs in nature as the element and in compounds with tellurium, in rock veins and alluvial deposits. The metal is the most malleable and ductile known. It alloys with other metals, is a good conductor of heat and electricity, and is chemically unreactive. The major uses for the element are for jewellery, electrical contacts, and as a currency standard (*see* gold standard). Gold dissolves in aqua regia (a mixture of one-third nitric acid and two-thirds hydrochloric acid) and the most common compound is the chloride ($AuCl_3$). Purity is measured in ▷carats. At no 79; at wt 196.967; mp 1064.43°C; bp 2857°C.

● **Gold, Thomas** ▶ (1920–) Austrian-born astronomer, who spent 20 years in England (at Cambridge University) before emigrating to the USA in 1956 and becoming a professor at Cornell University. With ▷Bondi and ▷Hoyle he proposed the ▷steady-state theory of the universe. He is also known for describing (1948) pulsars as spinning neutron stars.

● **Goldberg, Whoopi** ▶ (1949–) US stage and film actress and comedian. Her films include *The Color Purple* (1986), *Ghost* (1990), *Sister Act* (1992), *The Associate* (1997), and *How Stella Got Her Groove Back* (1999).

● **Gold Coast** ▶ The name applied by Europeans to the coastal zone in West Africa between Axim and the River Volta on the Gulf of Guinea. An important source of gold, it came under British control in the 19th century as part of the British colony of Gold Coast (present-day Ghana).

● **Gold Coast, City of** ▶ 27 58S 153 20E A resort city of Australia, on the coast of Queensland. It stretches 32 km (20 mi) S of Brisbane, from Southport, the administrative centre, to the New South Wales border. Population (1995 est, with Tweed): 326 900.

● **goldcrest** ▶ A tiny agile songbird, *Regulus regulus*, occurring chiefly in coniferous woodland of N Europe and Asia and feeding on insects and spiders. It is about 9 cm long and has a yellow-green plumage with white wing stripes and an orange crest, brighter in the male than the female. Family: *Muscicapidae* (Old World ▷flycatchers).

● **Golden Age, Latin** ▶ The period (70 BC–18 AD) during which some of the highest achievements of Latin literature were produced. The first part of the period (70–43 BC) was dominated by ▷Cicero. The major writers of the subsequent Augustan age (43 BC–18 AD) include ▷Virgil, ▷Horace, ▷Livy, and ▷Ovid.

● **Golden Bull of 1222** ▶ A charter of liberties granted by Andrew II of Hungary (1175–1235) that curbed monarchical powers and confirmed the rights of the nobility. The nobles gained important concessions on military service, taxation, and the administration of justice. They had the right to resist if the king violated the Charter's articles.

● **golden calf** ▶ An idol made by Aaron for the Israelites to worship when they believed that Moses would not return from Mt Sinai, where he was receiving the tables of the Law (Exodus 32). Moses destroyed the idol upon his return. A similar idol was made by King Jeroboam I (937–915 BC) and set up at Bethel and Dan (I Kings 12.28).

● **golden cat** ▶ A small ▷cat of SE Asia and Sumatra, *Felis temmincki*, also called Temminck's cat. It is about 125 cm long, with a plain golden coat and strikingly marked head; it lives among rocks preying on rodents and ground-dwelling birds. The closely related African golden cat (*aurata*) is found on the fringes of forests in West Africa.

● **golden chain** ▶ (or golden rain) ▷See laburnum.

● **golden eagle** ▶ A large dark-brown ▷eagle, *Aquila chrysaetos*, occurring in mountainous regions of North America and Eurasia. It is 70–85 cm long and has golden neck feathers, a grey beak, fully feathered legs, large yellow feet, and powerful talons. Golden eagles have a wingspan of up to 230 cm and catch small mammals, rabbits, and gamebirds.

● **goldeneye** ▶ A ▷diving duck, *Bucephala clangula*, that breeds in forested areas of N Eurasia and winters in more southerly regions. It is 41–45 cm long and males are black and white with a greenish head and a circular white patch on the cheek; females are grey with white markings and a brown head.

● **Golden Fleece** ▶ The fleece of a sacred winged ram, the recovery of which was the goal of ▷Jason and the ▷Argonauts. Athamas, King of Thebes, had two children, Phrixus and Helle, by his first wife Nephele. His second wife, Ino, hated her stepchildren and plotted their death. They fled across the sea on the golden ram but Helle fell in and drowned. Phrixus reached Colchis, sacrificed the ram to Zeus, and hung the fleece in a grove sacred to Ares, where it was guarded by a dragon.

● **Golden Fleece, Order of the** ▶ A chivalric order founded by ▷Philip the Good, Duke of Burgundy, in 1430, taking as its badge the fleece captured by Jason in Greek mythology. When Burgundy was united to the Habsburg empire (1477) the Order became increasingly aristocratic and was eventually confined to Austria and Spain.

● **Golden Gate bridge** ▶ A suspension bridge for road traffic over the Golden Gate strait near San Francisco (USA). Completed in 1937, its total length of 1280 m (4200 ft) made it the longest bridge in the world until the completion of the Verrazano–Narrows bridge (1964) across New York Harbor. ▷See also Humber.

● **Golden Horde** ▶ The Mongol army that invaded Russia and E Europe (1237–41) led by Batu Khan, grandson of ▷Genghis Khan. It established the khanate of the Golden Horde, which controlled most of W Russia and parts of NW Asia, traded with Europe, and adopted Islam. The Horde was attacked by ▷Timur and its remnants destroyed in 1502 by the Crimean Tatars.

● **Golden Horn** ▶ (Turkish name: Haliç) An inlet of the Bosporus in NW Turkey, on the N side of the peninsula upon which the old quarter of Istanbul stands. It is 7 km (4.5 mi) long and serves as the city's harbour.

● **golden mole** ▶ A burrowing insect-eating mammal belonging to the African family *Chryochloridae* (15 species). 7–23 cm long, they are stout-bodied, blind, and almost tailless, with two of the four digits on each forefoot greatly enlarged. Their fur is an iridescent golden-brown. Order ▷Insectivora.

● **golden pheasant** ▶ A small ▷pheasant, *Chrysolophus pictus*, native to mountainous regions of E Asia but widespread as an ornamental bird. Its plumage is gold, scarlet, black, and green and the male has a large ruff of broad feathers.

● **goldenrain tree** ▷See lacquer tree.

● **golden ratio** ▶ A way of dividing a line (or figure) into two parts so that the ratio of the smaller part to the larger part is equal to the ratio of the larger part to the whole, i.e. $a{:}b = b{:}(a + b)$, where a is the smaller part. This ratio is 1:1.618. The ratio, also called the **golden mean**, has been regarded since classical times as having an inherent aesthetic value. It frequently features in classical architecture and was used in the planning of many Renaissance works of art.

● **golden retriever** ▶ A large strongly built breed of ▢dog whose ancestors possibly included labradors, setters, and spaniels. The dense water-resistant wavy coat is gold or cream and these dogs are strong swimmers. They are used as gun dogs, guide dogs, and police dogs. Height: 56–61 cm (dogs); 51–56 cm (bitches).

● **goldenrod** ▶ A perennial herb of the genus *Solidago* (about 120 species), up to 2.5 m tall and mostly native to North America. The stem bears one-sided cylindrical heads of small yellow flowers, forming a branching plumelike inflorescence. Canadian goldenrod (*S. canadensis*) is often grown as a garden ornamental. Family: ▷Compositae.

● **goldfinch** ▶ A Eurasian ▷finch, *Carduelis carduelis*, once popular as a cagebird. About 12 cm long, it has a brown back, black wings with a broad yellow stripe, black-and-white tail and head, and a red face. It uses its pointed bill to extract seeds from thistles and dandelions and flocks of goldfinches (called charms) are commonly seen on farmland.

● **goldfish** ▶ A freshwater fish, *Carassius auratus*, also called golden carp, of E Asian origin but introduced elsewhere as an ornamental fish. In its natural state it is greenish brown or grey and up to 30 cm long. However, the breeding of abnormal specimens, originally in China and Japan, has produced over 125 varieties, such as the "pop eye," "veiltail," and "lionhead," often with a characteristic red-gold coloration. The goldfish requires cold well-oxygenated water and is omnivorous.

● **Golding, Sir William** ▶ (1911–93) British novelist. He served in the Royal Navy and became a schoolteacher. His best-known novel, *Lord of the Flies* (1954), concerns a group of schoolboys who are isolated on a desert island and revert to savagery. His other novels include *Pincher Martin* (1956), *The Spire* (1964), *Darkness Visible* (1979), *Rites of Passage* (1980), which won the Booker prize, *A Moving Target* (1982), *The Paper Men* (1984), *Close Quarters* (1987), and *Fire Down Below* (1989). He won the Nobel Prize in 1983.

● **Goldoni, Carlo** ▶ (1707–93) Italian comic playwright. A prolific writer of over 250 plays, he revolutionized the rigid conventions of the ▷commedia dell'arte with his realistic characters and witty dialogue. His plays include *The Liar* (1759), *Mine Hostess* (1753), and *The Fan* (1764). In 1762 he went to Paris, where he wrote his *Mémoires* (1787) and was from 1769 tutor to the daughters of Louis XV.

● **Gold Rush** ▶ The transcontinental journey of eastern profiteers after the discovery of gold in California (1848). Those (some 80 000) who arrived in the first year were called forty-niners. Harsh living conditions and the violent life of the gold fields took many lives and only a few made fortunes. There were gold rushes in Australia, South Africa, and the Klondike, Canada, in the next half century.

● **Goldschmidt, Richard Benedict** ▶ (1878–1958) US geneticist. His view of the chromosome as a large-chain molecule led to advances in genetic research. He demonstrated that differences between races were genetically determined and showed how drastic changes in environmental factors could cause changes in the external appearance of fruit flies.

● **Goldschmidt process** ▶ The reduction of a metal oxide to the metal by reacting it with aluminium to form aluminium oxide and metal. The process, which produces a great deal of heat, is used to extract chromium from chromium ore. Named after Hans Goldschmidt (1861–1923).

● **Goldsmith, Oliver** ▶ (1730–74) Anglo-Irish writer. Born in Ireland, he was sent to study medicine in Edinburgh and arrived penniless in London in 1756. A friend of Johnson and Boswell, he was inarticulate in conversation and a compulsive gambler. His best-known works are the poem *The Deserted Village* (1770), the novel *The Vicar of Wakefield* (1776), and the play *She Stoops to Conquer* (1773).

● **gold standard** ▶ A monetary system in which paper money was convertible on demand into gold. Banknotes were issued fractionally backed by gold (i.e. gold reserves were a fixed proportion of the value of the notes in circulation). Rates of exchange between countries were fixed by their currency values in gold. In classical economics imbalances in international trade were rectified automatically by the gold standard. A country in deficit would have depleted gold reserves and would therefore have to reduce its money supply. The resulting fall in demand would reduce imports and the lowering of prices would boost exports; thus the deficit would be rectified. Most financially important countries were on the gold standard from 1900 until its suspension during World War I because of the problems of transporting gold. It was reintroduced in 1925 but finally abandoned in 1931. ▷*See also* International Monetary Fund.

● **Goldwyn, Samuel** ▶ (S. Goldfish, originally Schmuel Gelbfisz; 1882–1974) US film producer, born in Poland. In 1916 he cofounded Goldwyn Pictures, a production company that merged with other concerns to become Metro-Goldwyn-Mayer (MGM) in 1924. His many successful films as an independent producer include *Wuthering Heights* (1939) and *Guys and Dolls* (1955).

● **golem** ▶ In medieval Jewish folklore, an automaton or artificial human being that can be brought to life by a charm. The best-known legend is that of the golem created by a Rabbi Loew of Prague, which he used as a servant until it ran amok and had to be destroyed: the story probably influenced the later development of the Frankenstein legend. The word originally referred to anything incomplete or embryonic.

● **golf** ▶ A club-and-ball game for two or four players played on a golf course. It was well established in Britain by the 15th century and almost certainly originated in Scotland. A standard course is usually between 4572 m (5000 yd) and 6400 m (7000 yd) and is divided into 18 holes (9 on a small course), each of which is between 90 m (100 yd) and 540 m (600 yd) long. A "hole" comprises the flat starting point, called the "tee," a strip of mown grass about 27–90 m (30–100 yd) wide, called the "fairway," and a smooth putting green. On the green is the actual hole, which has a diameter of 10.8 cm (4.25 in). There are also obstacles around the course, such as trees, ditches, and sand bunkers. The object of the game is to hit the ball from each tee into each hole with as few strokes as possible ("par" for a hole is the standard number of strokes needed by a first-class player; one stroke less than par is called a "birdie," and an "eagle" is two strokes less). To achieve this a player has a set of clubs of which there are three basic types: woods, irons, and putters. The rubber-cored ball must not be less than 41.15 mm (1.62 in) in diameter or weigh more than 45.93 g (1.62 oz).

● **Golgi, Camillo** ▶ (1843–1926) Italian cell biologist, whose staining technique using silver nitrate revealed fine details of cells. Golgi distinguished different types of nerve cells in the brain (Golgi cells) and demonstrated a network of tubules and granules within cells (the ▷Golgi apparatus). He shared the 1906 Nobel Prize with ▷Ramón y Cajal.

● **Golgi apparatus** ▶ (*or* Golgi complex) A structure present in the cytoplasm of nearly all □cells, composed of stacks of flattened sacs bounded by membranes and associated with vesicles. Discovered by Camillo ▷Golgi, it is thought to function in the synthesis and concentration of certain materials, especially secretory products, which are then packaged into the vesicles and transported within the cell.

● **Golgotha** ▷*See* Calvary.

● **goliards** ▶ Wandering scholars (often students or lesser clerics) of medieval Europe who were notorious for their scurrilous verses. They were frequently condemned by the Church for their poetry and riot-

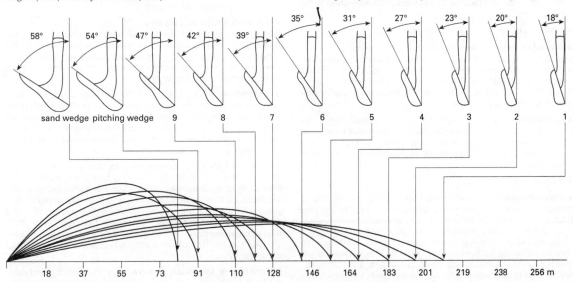

golf ▶ Irons are numbered according to the angle of the face; the greater the angle of inclination, the higher the ball is hit into the air. Thus a good player, under normal conditions, knows the range of each iron. The Number One wood (driver) is used from the tee for the maximum distance and the putter is used on the green.

ous behaviour. By the 14th century the term had lost its earlier connotations, being applied to all minstrels. The largest collection of goliard poetry was published as the ▷*Carmina Burana* in the 19th century.

● **Goliath** ▷*See* David.

● **goliath beetle** ▶ A large beetle belonging to the group of flower ▷chafers. The African goliath beetle (*Goliathus giganteus*) has the largest body of all the insects, measuring about 96 mm in length. It is white with black stripes and brown wing cases. The larvae are found in rotten logs.

● **goliath frog** ▶ The largest known living frog, *Rana goliath*, which grows up to 35 cm long. This rare shy frog inhabits deep river pools in Africa. Its bones are supposed to have magical properties.

● **Gollancz, Sir Victor** ▶ (1893–1967) British publisher and writer. In 1928 Gollancz founded his publishing company in Henrietta Street, London. During the 1930s he campaigned vigorously against fascism, setting up the Left Book Club, and in 1951 he founded the charity War on Want.

● **Golovkin, Gavril Ivanovich, Count** ▶ (1660–1734) Russian statesman. A relative of ▷Peter (I) the Great, he accompanied the tsar on his early visits to western Europe. In 1706 he became foreign minister and in 1709, state chancellor. In the reign (1725–27) of Catherine I (?1684–1727), he became a member of the supreme privy council. In the 1730 accession crisis, he supported ▷Anna Ivanovna.

● **Gombrich, Sir Ernst (Hans Josef)** ▶ (1909–2001) Austrian-born British art historian. From 1936 he taught at the Warburg Institute in London, becoming its director in 1959. He was best known for *The Story of Art* (1950), a hugely popular and influential general history of the subject. His other publications include *Art and Illusion* (1960) and other studies of the psychology of visual perception.

● **Gomel** ▶ 52 25N 31 00E A port in SE Belarus, on the River Sozh. It is an important industrial centre, producing fertilizers, machinery, timber products, foodstuffs, and textiles. Population (1996 est): 512 000.

● **Gómez, Juan Vicente** ▶ (1857–1935) Venezuelan soldier and statesman, who was brought to power in 1908 by a military coup. Elected president in 1910, he governed, either directly or through puppets, until his death. He did much to modernize Venezuela, simultaneously accumulating a vast personal fortune. His power base was in the army and he brutally suppressed all opposition to his regime.

● **Gomorrah** ▷*See* Sodom and Gomorrah.

● **Gomułka, Władysław** ▶ (1905–82) Polish statesman. Gomułka was secretary general of the Polish Workers' Party from 1945 until 1948, when his criticism of the Soviet Union led to his demotion and imprisonment (1951–54). Following the ▷Poznań Riots, Gomułka became first secretary of the Party. In 1970 he resigned after demonstrations over price increases.

● **gomuti** ▶ A ▷palm tree, *Arenga pinnata* (or *A. saccharifera*), also called sugar palm, occurring in SE Asia. The sap yields palm sugar and the fermented juice (palm wine) is distilled to produce arrack. A form of sago is obtained from the pith and the leaf fibres are used to make cord, ropes, etc.

● **gonad** ▷*See* ovary; testis.

● **gonadotrophin** ▶ One of several hormones that control the activity of the testes and ovaries (the gonads) in mammals. The pituitary gland, under the influence of the hypothalamus, produces three gonadotrophins: luteinizing hormone (LH), which stimulates ovulation and ▷oestrogen production by the ovaries and the production of ▷androgens by the testes; follicle-stimulating hormone (FSH), which promotes ovulation and sperm production; and ▷prolactin, which triggers lactation. LH and FSH are glycoproteins and are usually released together. Human chorionic gonadotrophin (HCG) is produced by the placenta, reaching a peak level in the urine in early pregnancy. Measurement of urinary HCG is the basis of pregnancy tests. Gonadotrophins are also used in ▷fertility drugs.

● **Gonaïves** ▶ 12 29N 72 42W A port in W Haiti, on the Gulf of Gonaïves. Exports include coffee, bananas, and mangoes. Population (1992): 63 291.

● **Goncharov, Ivan Aleksandrovich** ▶ (1812–91) Russian novelist. Apart from a voyage to Japan (1852–55), he led an uneventful life as a civil servant. The conflict between traditionalism and pragmatism is a recurrent theme of his work, most notably of *Oblomov* (1859), in which the inactive aristocratic hero loses his beloved to his more prosaic, practical friend, and sinks deeper into absurd idleness.

● **Goncourt, Edmond de** ▶ (1822–96) French writer, who collaborated with his brother **Jules de Goncourt** (1830–70) on art criticism, social histories of France, and a series of carefully researched naturalistic novels, most notably *Germinie Lacerteux* (1864) and *Madame Gervaisais* (1869). They are best known for their *Journal*, a lively record of French literary life from 1851 to 1895, and for Edmond's legacy, the Académie Goncourt, which awards France's most prestigious annual literary prize.

● **Gondar** ▶ 12 40N 37 45E A town in central Ethiopia. A former capital of Ethiopia, Gondar was built after the Portuguese Jesuits had been expelled in the 16th century and is now a tourist attraction. Population (1994 est): 166 593.

● **Gondomar, Diego Sarmiento de Acuña, Conde de** ▶ (1567–1626) Spanish diplomat. He twice served as ambassador to England (1613–18, 1619–22), becoming a close friend of James I. He encouraged the proposed marriage between the Prince of Wales and the Spanish princess, thereby contributing to James' poor relations with parliament.

● **Gondwanaland** ▶ The supercontinent in the S hemisphere believed to have existed prior to 200 million years ago, when the drift of the continents to their present positions began. It probably consisted of South America, Africa, Australia, Antarctica, Arabia, and India. ▷*See also* Laurasia.

● **gong** ▶ A percussion instrument of indefinite pitch. The orchestral gong (*or* tam-tam) is a disc of metal about 1 m (3 ft) in diameter with a turned-over edge, hanging in a wooden frame.

● **gong chimes** ▶ A set of gongs tuned to different pitches, used in many countries of the Far East. The instrument exists in a number of forms, the most elaborate of which, found in Myanmar (Burma) and Thailand, consists of 15–20 small gongs set in a circular wooden frame. The player kneels inside the frame and plays the gongs with hammers. ⌐musical instruments.

● **Góngora y Argote, Luis de** ▶ (1561–1627) Spanish poet. Son of a judge, he was court chaplain in Madrid from 1617. He wrote many conventional sonnets and satirical verses but is best known for his longer works, *Polifemo* (1612) and *Soledades* (1613), in which he used esoteric allusions and elaborate diction and syntax to create a deliberately obscure and artificial style.

● **gonorrhoea** ▶ A sexually transmitted disease caused by a bacterium (the gonococcus; *see* coccus). It is now one of the commonest infections in developed societies. Symptoms in men are discharge from the penis and a burning pain on passing urine. Women may have vaginal discharge and pain on urinating. Gonorrhoea can be treated with penicillin and other antibiotics.

● **Gonzaga** ▶ An Italian dynasty that ruled Mantua (1328–1707) and Montferrato and Casale (1536–1707). The family was established in Mantua by **Luigi Gonzaga** (c. 1268–1360). His distinguished successors included **Gianfrancesco Gonzaga** (?1394–1444), a soldier and patron of learning under whom ▷Vittorino da Feltre established a famous school at Mantua, and **Francesco Gonzaga** (1466–1519), who commanded Italian forces against the French invasion in 1494 and was the husband of the distinguished patron of arts Isabella d'Este (*see* Este).

● **González de Mendoza, Pedro** ▶ (1428–95) Spanish churchman; cardinal, Archbishop of Toledo, and Primate of Spain (from 1482). He was the most powerful supporter of Isabella in her successful claim to the Spanish throne.

● **González Márquez, Felipe** ▶ (1942–) Spanish statesman;

prime minister of Spain (1982–96). Leader of the Spanish Socialist Workers' Party, he formed Spain's first left-wing government in modern times and led Spain into the ▷European Community (1986). He won further elections in 1986, 1989, and 1993 but lost to José Maria Aznar in 1996.

● **Gooch, Graham (Alan)** ▶ (1953–) British cricketer. A batsman, he played for Essex (1973–97) and England (1975–82, 1986–95), captaining England (1988; 1989–93).

● **Good Friday** ▶ The Friday before ▷Easter, when Christ's crucifixion is commemorated. It is a fast day, and in the Roman Catholic Church the Mass is not celebrated. In the Anglican Church Holy Communion is rarely held.

● **Good Friday Agreement** ▷*See* Ireland, Northern.

● **Good Hope, Cape of** ▷*See* Cape of Good Hope.

● **Goodman, Benny** ▶ (Benjamin David G.; 1909–86) US clarinetist, prominent in the development of ▷swing. He led big bands and played in small jazz groups from the 1930s to the 1950s. Bartok and Copland wrote for him.

● **Good Neighbor Policy** ▶ A US policy between World Wars I and II intended to allay Latin American fears of US domination. Initiated by President F. D. Roosevelt in 1933, its measures included the withdrawal of troops, the lifting of trade barriers, and the preparation of common defences.

● **Goodwin Sands** ▶ A range of dangerous sandbanks off the SE coast of England, in the Strait of Dover. At low tide large areas of sand are exposed, which shelter the Downs roadstead.

● **Goodyear, Charles** ▶ (1800–60) US inventor of a method of treating rubber with sulphur at a high temperature to make it strong and elastic (the ▷vulcanization process). Patented in 1844, his process facilitated rubber-manufacturing.

● **Goole** ▶ 53 42N 0 52W A major port in E England, in the East Riding of Yorkshire at the confluence of the Rivers Ouse and Don. Its industries include flour milling, boatbuilding, chemicals, and machinery. Population (1991): 19 410.

● **goosander** ▶ A large migratory ▷duck, *Mergus merganser*, that breeds in North America and N Eurasia, also called sawbill. The male is 75 cm long and has a green head, black back, and white body; females are 57 cm long and have a chestnut head and grey body. Goosanders feed on fish.

● **goose** ▶ A large long-necked waterbird belonging to the family *Anatidae* (ducks, geese, and swans), occurring in the N hemisphere. Geese have short bills, humped at the base, and short webbed feet. They chiefly feed inland on grass, grain, roots, etc., and are highly migratory, flying in characteristic V-formations and honking loudly in flight. Domesticated geese are probably descended from the ▷greylag goose. Genera: *Anser* (grey geese), *Branta* (black geese); order: *Anseriformes*. ▷*See also* barnacle goose; brent goose; Canada goose; Hawaiian goose.

● **gooseberry** ▶ A fruit bush of the genus *Ribes*, especially *R. uva-crispa* (or *R. grossularia*), which is widely cultivated in the Old World for its hairy prickly-coated berries used for preserves, wine, and in desserts. The bush, 1–1.5 m high, may be upright, spreading, or drooping, with three-lobed toothed leaves and spiny stems. The small greenish flowers arise in the axils of the leaves. Family: *Grossulariaceae*.

● **goosefish** ▷*See* anglerfish.

● **goosefoot** ▶ A herb or small shrub of the genus *Chenopodium* (110 species), of temperate regions, also called pigweed. The stem, 15–1500 cm high, is grooved or angular and the leaves are often fleshy. The whole plant may have a whitish mealy appearance. The small greenish flowers are borne on a branched inflorescence. Family: *Chenopodiaceae*.

● **goosegrass** ▷*See* cleavers.

● **Goossens, Sir Eugene** ▶ (1893–1962) British conductor and composer of Belgian descent. He was well known for his performances of modern music and wrote an oboe concerto for his brother **Leon Goossens** (1896–1988), a leading oboist.

● **gopher** ▷*See* pocket gopher; souslik.

● **Gorakhpur** ▶ 26 45N 83 23E A city in N India, in Uttah Pradesh. There is sugar refining and fertilizer production and a university (1956). Population (1991): 489 850.

● **goral** ▶ A small hoofed mammal, *Naemorhedus goral*, of mountainous regions in S Asia. About 65 cm high at the shoulder, gorals have short horns and a woolly coat, which varies from grey to red. Family: ▷*Bovidae*. ▷*See also* goat.

● **Gorbachov, Mikhail Sergeevich** ▶ (1931–) Soviet statesman; general secretary of the Soviet Communist Party (1985–91) and president (1988–91). Born in the Stavropol region into a peasant family, he studied law at Moscow university before entering politics. He became a member of the Politburo in 1980. Succeeding ▷Chernenko as leader, he embarked upon an ambitious programme of political and economic reform (*see* glasnost), including the agreement of major arms limitation treaties (1987, 1990), the creation of a new Congress of People's Deputies, strengthening the role of president, and ending the Communist monopoly of power. These reforms stimulated nationalist movements in many Soviet republics and led indirectly to the end of Soviet domination of Eastern Europe and the ▷Cold War. In August 1991 he survived a coup attempted by Communist hardliners but found his authority greatly weakened. He resigned later that year following his failure to prevent the break-up of the Soviet Union. He was awarded the Nobel Peace Prize in 1990.

● **Gordian knot** ▶ A knot binding the yoke and beam of the chariot of Gordius, a legendary king of Phrygia. The knot was extremely complex. According to legend, whoever could unloose the knot would become the ruler of Asia. In 333 BC Alexander the Great is said to have cut the knot with his sword.

● **Gordimer, Nadine** ▶ (1923–) White South African novelist and short-story writer. Her earlier novels, which include *The Lying Days* (1953), the Booker-Prize-winning *The Conservationist* (1974), and *My Son's Story* (1990), describe the destructive effects of ▷apartheid; later works, such as *The House Gun* (1997), explore the subsequent changes in South Africa. She was awarded the Nobel Prize in 1991.

● **Gordon, Charles George** ▶ (1833–85) British general. Gordon served in the Crimean War and then in China, where he earned the nickname Chinese Gordon after suppressing the ▷Taiping Rebellion (1864). In 1874 he was employed by the Khedive of Egypt to open up the country and from 1877 to 1880 was British governor of the Sudan. In 1884 he was sent back to the Sudan, following al ▷Mahdi's revolt. Gordon was besieged for ten months in Khartoum, which was taken two days before a relief force arrived. Gordon himself was murdered.

● **Gordon Riots** ▶ (1780) Anti-Roman Catholic riots in London fomented by Lord George Gordon (1751–93), who opposed the Roman Catholic Relief Act (1778). The riots were crushed; Gordon was arrested but acquitted of treason.

● **Gordonstoun** ▶ A British public school founded by Kurt ▷Hahn in 1935 near Elgin in Scotland. It emphasizes outdoor activities; Prince ▷Philip and his sons were pupils there.

● **Gore, Al(bert)** ▶ (1948–) US politician; vice-president of the United States (1993–2001). A Democrat, he was elected to the Senate in 1985 and served as vice-president to Bill ▷Clinton during both his terms of office. In 2000 he stood against George W. ▷Bush in a presidential election that proved the closest and most disputed of modern times. After a protracted legal battle Bush was eventually declared the winner.

● **Górecki, Henryk** ▶ (1933–) Polish composer, whose sombre third symphony (1979) achieved great popularity in the early 1990s. He has written two other symphonies (1959, 1973) as well as choral and chamber music.

● **Gorgon** ▶ In Greek legend, an underworld monster. Hesiod refers to three Gorgons, the sisters Stheno, Euryale, and ▷Medusa. They were usually portrayed as winged females with snakes for hair and boars' tusks for teeth.

● **Gorgonzola** ► 45 32N 9 23E A town in N Italy, in Lombardy, famous for Gorgonzola cheese. Population (latest est): 14 571.

● **gorilla** ► The largest living ▷ape, *Gorilla gorilla*, of tropical African forests. Male gorillas can grow to 1.8 m with a weight of 300 kg. They walk on their feet and knuckles, feeding on plant stems and also climbing to reach fruit. Troops are led by a dominant adult male and are generally not aggressive, preferring retreat to attack, although they will fight when cornered. Three races are recognized: the rare shaggy mountain gorilla and two lowland forms—light-coloured in the west and black in the east.

● **Gorizia** ► (German name: Görz; Serbo-Croat name: Gorica) 45 57N 13 37E A town in Italy, in Friuli-Venezia Giulia on the Slovenian border. It was a noted cultural centre under Habsburg rule. Industries include tourism, textiles, and machinery. Population (1990): 39 230.

● **Gorki** ► (Gorkii *or* Gorky) ▷*See* Nizhnii Novgorod.

● **Gorki, Maksim** ► (Aleksei Maksimovich Peshkov; 1868–1936) Russian novelist. His hard nomadic early life is recounted in his autobiographical trilogy *Childhood* (1913–14), *In the World* (1915–16), and *My Universities* (1923). He established his literary reputation with romantic short stories and followed these with several novels and plays, including *Mother* (1906) and *The Lower Depths* (1906). He lived in exile in Italy from 1906 to 1913 and again from 1921 to 1928. He then returned to Russia, becoming first president of the Soviet Writers Union and an exponent of Stalinism.

● **Gorky, Arshile** ► (Vosdanig Adoian; 1905–48) US painter, born in Armenia, who emigrated to the USA in 1920. He worked in most 20th-century styles before adopting, in about 1940, an individual and abstract form of ▷surrealism. Such works as *The Liver Is the Cock's Comb* (1944; New York) anticipate ▷action painting in their free application of paint. His promising career was cut short by his suicide.

● **Görlitz** ► 51 11N 15 0E A town in E Germany, on the River ▷Neisse where it marks the boundary with Poland. Famous since the middle ages for clothmaking, its many industries also include vehicle and machinery manufacture and lignite mining. Population (1991): 70 450.

● **Gorlovka** ► 48 17N 38 05E A city in SE Ukraine, in the ▷Donets Basin. It is one of the largest coalmining and industrial centres of the area. Population (1996 est): 322 000.

● **Gorno-Altai** ▷*See* Altai Republic.

● **Gorno-Badakhshan** ► (*or* Badakhshan) An autonomous region in E Tadzhikistan, formed in 1925 as the Special Pamir Province. Its population consists mainly of ▷Tadzhiks. Chiefly agricultural, it produces wheat, fruit, and fodder crops; cattle and sheep are bred. Gold, coal, and mica are mined. Area: 63 700 sq km (24 590 sq mi). Population (1991 est): 167 100. Capital: Khorog.

● **gorse** ► (*or* furze) A very spiny densely branched shrub, *Ulex europaeus*, up to 4 m high, with bright-yellow sweet-scented flowers. The leaves, which consist of three leaflets, are reduced to spines or scales on mature plants. The fruit is a black hairy pod that splits open explosively to release the seeds. Gorse is native to grassy areas and heaths throughout Europe and has been introduced elsewhere. Family: ▷Leguminosae.

● **Gorton, Sir John Grey** ► (1911–   ) Australian statesman; Liberal prime minister (1968–71). His administration was responsible for greater federal government intervention in the field of education, and he fostered Australia's involvement in the Vietnam War. In 1971 he lost a vote of no confidence and resigned.

● **goshawk** ► A large powerful ▷hawk, *Accipiter gentilis*, ranging throughout forests of the N hemisphere and formerly used in falconry. It is 60 cm long with a wingspan of 130 cm and has a finely barred grey plumage. It feeds chiefly on other birds.

● **Goslar** ► 51 57N 10 28E A city in N Germany, in Lower Saxony. An imperial residence in the middle ages, the palace remains. Silver has been mined here since the 10th century. Population (1989): 46 000.

● **gospel music** ► A form of US popular music deriving from the worship in Black ▷Pentecostal Churches. In its expressive vocal stylings, gospel music shows the influence of Pentecostal preaching (with its accompaniment of "Amens" and "Alleluias" from the congregation) and the phenomenon of "speaking in tongues" (glossolalia). More strictly musical influences include spirituals, blues, and popular hymnody. From the 1930s gospel music spread through recordings and radio, and such leading performers as Mahalia Jackson (1911–72) began to enjoy fame and commercial success. Gospel has had a major influence on ▷soul and other forms of Black popular music since the 1960s: famous pop performers who began their singing careers in the churches include Aretha Franklin, Sam Cooke, and Whitney Houston.

● **Gospels** ► (Old English: good news) The four New Testament accounts of Christ's life, ascribed to ▷Matthew, ▷Mark, ▷Luke, and ▷John. The word originally referred to the message of Christ's redemptive work rather than to the writings. The first three are known as the **Synoptic Gospels**, since they report approximately the same synopsis of the events. According to most biblical scholars Mark is the oldest of these and was used as a source by the authors of Matthew and Luke. Material that is not found in Mark but is common to Matthew and Luke is believed to derive from a single lost source, known as Q. The fourth Gospel, John, emphasizes the divinity of Christ and may presuppose a knowledge of the Synoptic Gospels.

● **Gosport** ► 50 48N 1 08W A port in S England, in Hampshire on Portsmouth Harbour. It is a naval base, linked with Portsmouth by ferry, and has yacht-building and marine-engineering industries. Population (1997 est): 75 061.

● **Gossaert, Jan** ► (c. 1478–c. 1532) Flemish painter, whose popular surname, Mabuse, derives from his birthplace Maubeuge. As one of the first Flemish artists to work in the Italian Renaissance style, after visiting Italy (1508) he painted sculptural nudes against Italian architectural backgrounds, e.g. *Neptune and Amphitrite* (Berlin). As a portraitist he was noted for his expressive treatment of hands.

● **Gosse, Sir Edmund** ► (1849–1928) British critic. His *Father and Son* (1907) recounts his painful self-emancipation from his dominating Victorian father. He translated plays by Ibsen, and his critical books include studies of French literature and biographies of Donne (1899) and Ibsen (1908).

● **Göta Canal** ► A canal in S Sweden, linking Göteborg on the Kattegat in the W with Stockholm in the E. Opened in 1832, it enters the Baltic Sea near Söderköping. Length: 93 km (58 mi).

● **Göteborg** ► (English name: Gothenburg) 57 45N 12 00E An important ice-free port in SW Sweden, at the mouth of the River Göta. Sweden's second largest city, it expanded through Napoleon's Continental System and with the opening of the Göta Canal (1832). Notable buildings include the town hall (1750), the cathedral (1633), and the university (1891). Industries include shipbuilding, oil refining, and the manufacture of cars. Population (1997 est): 454 016.

● **Gotha** ► 50 56N 10 42E A town in Germany, on the N edge of the Thuringian Forest, former capital of the duchy of Saxe-Coburg-Gotha. It is noted for the *Almanac de Gotha* (an annual record of the royal and noble houses of Europe, published here from 1764 to 1944). Gotha manufactures machinery, vehicles, textiles, and chemicals. Population (1989 est): 57 360.

● **Gothenburg** ▷*See* Göteborg.

● **gothic art and architecture** ► The styles flourishing in Europe from the mid-12th to the end of the 15th centuries. "Gothic" originated as a derisory term used by Renaissance artists, who blamed the destruction of classical art on the Goths who invaded the Roman Empire. The gothic is most closely associated with church architecture, the hallmarks of gothic design being the rib and shaft ceiling, the pointed ⌐arch, the flying buttress, and later great height and the impression of weightlessness. Gothic architecture was initiated in France in the chevet of the Abbey of Saint-Denis, near Paris. It was followed by the cathedrals of ▷Notre-Dame de Paris (begun 1163), Chartres (begun c. 1194), Reims (begun 1211), etc. (*see also* Flamboyant). In England it has been subdivided into three phases named by the architect and antiquarian Thomas Rickman (1776–1841) as

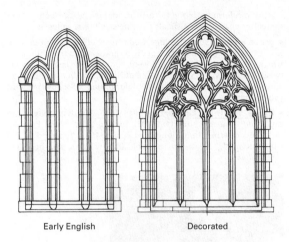

Early English   Decorated

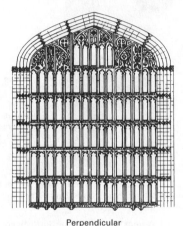

Perpendicular

gothic art and architecture ▶ In England the three phases of gothic architecture are characterized by distinctive window designs.

▷Early English (c. 1200–c. 1300; e.g. Lincoln Cathedral), ▷Decorated (c. 1300–70; e.g. Exeter Cathedral), and ▷Perpendicular (c. 1370–1540; e.g. Winchester Cathedral). Although used during the ▷romanesque period, ▷stained glass was only fully developed in the gothic period, being characterized by elaborate tracery, brilliant colours, and the reduction of stonework between the windows to very thin stone bars. Gothic sculpture mirrored the development of the architecture it adorned, renouncing its early naturalism for a stylized elegance and an emphasis on line and silhouette. In painting, the early gothic manifested itself chiefly in manuscript illumination. In the 14th century elements of it appear in the art of Simone ▷Martini, Rogier van der ▷Weyden, and others, but its full flowering in panel and manuscript painting came with the ▷international gothic style of the early 15th century. The gothic was revived in the 19th century by the Victorians, who considered it a perfect embodiment of religious intensity (see gothic revival).

● **gothic novel** ▶ An English genre, popular in the late 18th and early 19th centuries, characterized by a prevailing atmosphere of mystery and terror and pseudomedieval—"gothic"—settings. Examples include Horace Walpole's *Castle of Otranto* (1765), Ann Radcliffe's *The Mysteries of Udolpho* (1794), and Matthew Gregory Lewis' *The Monk* (1796). The genre wilted under parodies, such as Jane Austen's *Northanger Abbey* (1818), but influenced later writers, among them the Brontë sisters, Poe, and Bram Stoker in *Dracula* (1897).

● **gothic revival** ▶ An architectural style initially associated with ▷Romanticism. The revived popularity for ▷gothic architecture began in England in the late 18th century, with such buildings as ▷Fonthill Abbey. Common throughout W Europe and the USA, it was particularly dominant in Britain after 1818, when parliament voted £1 million to be spent on building 214 new Anglican churches. Of these over 170 were built in the gothic style. The culmination of the gothic revival was perhaps the new Houses of Parliament (1834–45) built by Charles ▷Barry and ▷Pugin. Other leaders of the revival were George Gilbert ▷Scott, ▷Ruskin, ▷Butterfield, and ▷Waterhouse. One of the last important gothic-revival buildings in London was the Law Courts (1882) by G. E. Street (1824–81).

● **Goths** ▶ Germanic peoples who originated in Scandinavia (Gotland) and had moved into the Ukraine by the end of the 2nd century AD. Shortly afterwards they invaded the Roman Empire N of the Danube and expanded into the Balkans. Converted to Arian Christianity (*see* Arianism) in the mid-4th century, their empire was soon destroyed by the ▷Huns and their two groups, the ▷Ostrogoths and ▷Visigoths, separated. ▷*See also* Dark Ages.

● **Gotland** ▶ (Gothland *or* Gottland) The largest of the Swedish islands, in the Baltic Sea. Long disputed between Denmark and Sweden, it was finally ceded to Sweden in 1645. Its economy is based chiefly on agriculture (cattle and sheep raising) and tourism. Area: 3140 sq km (1225 sq mi). Population (1994 est): 58 237, including associated islands. Capital: Visby.

● **Gottfried von Strassburg** ▶ (13th century) German poet. Nothing is known of his life apart from what can be inferred from the erudition and poetic skill of his epic *Tristan und Isolde*, a retelling of the original Celtic legend according to the conventions of courtly love. It inspired Wagner's famous opera.

● **Göttingen** ▶ 51 32N 9 57E A city in central Germany, in Lower Saxony. With its famous university, founded in 1734 by George II of Great Britain, and the Max Planck Association for the furtherance of science, it is a noted educational centre. Its manufactures include precision instruments and aluminium goods. Population (1996 est): 126 253.

● **Gottsched, Johann Christoph** ▶ (1700–66) German critic, who introduced French classical and rationalist critical principles into German literature. His dramatic academy in Leipzig and his own plays, such as *Der sterbende Cato* (1732), and translations helped to raise the literary standards of German theatre.

● **gouache** ▷*See* watercolour.

● **Gouda** ▶ 52 01N 4 43E A town in the W Netherlands, in South Holland province. Its most notable church, the Grote Kerk (1552), has exceptional stained-glass windows (1556–1603). It is famous for its gouda cheese. Population (1994): 69 917.

● **Goujon, Jean** ▶ (c. 1510–68) French Renaissance sculptor. His best-known works are the marble relief of the *Deposition* (Louvre) for St Germain l'Auxerrois, Paris, *The Tribune of the Caryatids* supporting a gallery in the Louvre, and reliefs of nymphs for the Fontaine des Innocents. The first two were produced in collaboration with the architect Pierre ▷Lescot.

● **Goulburn** ▶ 34 47S 149 43E A city in Australia, in SE New South Wales. It is the commercial centre of an agricultural region. Population (latest est): 22 800.

● **Gounod, Charles François** ▶ (1818–93) French composer. A pupil of Halévy, he began serious composition after studying theology and deciding not to become a priest. His most successful works were the operas *Faust* (1852–59) and *Romeo and Juliet* (1864). Towards the end of his life he composed a large quantity of sacred music, including oratorios and masses.

● **gourami** ▶ One of several freshwater tropical ▷labyrinth fishes, especially *Osphronemus goramy*. It has a brown or grey oval body, up to 60 cm long, and a filamentous ray extending from each pelvic fin. Native to the E Indies, it has been introduced elsewhere and cultivated for food; young fishes can be kept in aquaria.

● **gourd** ▶ The fruit of certain plants of the family *Cucurbitaceae*, especially the white-flowered bottle gourd (*Lagenaria siceraria*), a trailing annual herb widely grown in the tropics. Its fruits have woody shells used locally as bottles, pipes, and utensils. Other gourds are grown as ornamentals, having attractive shapes, colours, and surface patterns. The dishcloth gourd (*see* loofah) is used as a bath sponge and the ▷snake gourd is grown for food.

● **gout** ▶ Sudden attacks of arthritis caused by the presence of uric acid crystals in the joints. The big toe is most commonly affected, becoming hot, red, and very painful. Gout is commonest in older men and tends to recur; if not treated (by drugs to reduce the uric acid in the blood) it may lead to destruction of the joint. Acute attacks are treated with anti-inflammatory drugs. Gout is associated with an increased incidence of heart disease.

● **Government of India Acts** ▶ The laws passed by the British parliament from 1773 to 1935 concerning the government of India prior to the establishment of independence (1947). The Acts of 1773, 1780, 1784, 1786, 1793, and 1830, known as the East India Company Acts, regulated the administration of India by the Company and vested supreme power in a government-appointed board of control. In 1833 the Company lost its monopoly of trade and gradually also lost its administrative functions (1833, 1853, 1858). The 1919 Act set up a central parliament in Delhi and provincial parliaments, which were strengthened by the 1935 Act to favour a federal form of government.

● **Govind Singh** ▷*See* Gobind Singh.

● **Gower, David Ivon** ▶ (1957–) British cricketer, who played for Leicestershire (1978–89), Hampshire (1990–93), and England (1978–93). An excellent left-hand batsman, he captained England from 1984 to 1986 and again in 1989. In 1992 he became the highest-scoring batsman in English test cricket.

● **Gower, John** ▶ (c. 1330–1408) English poet. He was a friend of Chaucer and enjoyed the patronage of Henry IV. His works are moral allegories. They are *Mirour de l'homme* (1376–79), written in French; the Latin *Vox clamantis* (c. 1382), in which he attacks the government of Richard II; and his major work, the English *Confessio amantis* (1390), illustrating the virtues of Christian and courtly love.

● **Gower Peninsula** ▶ A peninsula in South Wales, in the county of Swansea. Agriculture (especially dairy farming) and tourism are the principal economic activities. The National Trust owns some of the picturesque S coast as well as stretches of sand dunes in the W.

● **Goya (y Lucientes), Francesco (Jose) de** ▶ (1746–1828) Spanish painter, born near Saragossa. After studying in Italy, he settled in Madrid (1775), where he painted scenes of Spanish life for the royal tapestry factory. As court painter from 1789 he produced realistic portraits of the royal family. He became deaf in 1792, and his works grew pessimistic and sometimes nightmarish, as in his etchings *Lôs Caprichos* and *The Disasters of War*, condemning the French invasion of Spain. He settled in France in 1824. Among his best-known paintings are *Maja Clothed*, *The Shootings of 3 May 1808*, and the so-called black paintings, such as *Saturn Devouring His Children* (all Prado).

● **Goyen, Jan Josephszoon van** ▶ (1596–1656) Dutch landscape painter and etcher, who was born in Leiden but after 1630 lived in The Hague. His river and winter scenes were characterized by large expanses of sky and near-monochrome colours.

● **Gozzi, Carlo** ▶ (1720–1806) Italian dramatist. He opposed the theatrical reforms of ▷Goldoni and attempted to revive the techniques of the ▷commedia dell'arte. His plays, often including elements of fantasy and the grotesque, include *Turandot* (1762), on which Puccini's opera is based, and *L'Augellin Belverde* (1764).

● **Gozzoli, Benozzo** ▶ (Benozzo di Lese; 1420–97) Florentine painter. His major works are the frescoes of the *Journey of the Magi* (Palazzo Medici-Riccardi, Florence), which are noted for their detailed landscapes, and portraits of his contemporaries.

● **GPS** ▷*See* Global Positioning System.

● **Graafian follicle** ▷*See* ovary.

● **Gracchus, Tiberius Sempronius** ▶ (163–133 BC) Roman reformer, who as tribune (133) proposed land reforms intended to create a class of small landowners. He was killed in a riot. His brother **Gaius Sempronius Gracchus** (153–121 BC) was tribune in 123 and renewed Tiberius' attempts at land reform. He was killed in riots over his proposal to grant Roman citizenship to Latins. The Gracchi's at-

tempts at reform polarized the aristocracy into hostile factions and thereafter change was difficult to achieve without violence.

● **grace** ▶ In Christian theology, God's freely offered forgiveness to his sinful creatures. The nature of divine grace and the conditions on which it is offered and accepted were central to the controversy between ▷Pelagius and St ▷Augustine of Hippo, and between the Calvinists and their opponents at the Reformation. ▷*See also* free will; predestination; sin.

● **Grace, W(illiam) G(ilbert)** ▶ (1848–1915) British cricketer, who captained Gloucestershire (1871–98), London County, and England in 13 Test matches. In his long career (1865–1908) he scored 54 896 runs, including 126 centuries, took 2876 wickets, and held 877 catches.

W. G. Grace ▶ Known as "the Doctor" in cricketing circles, because he was a medical practitioner, he is still regarded as the greatest all-rounder the game has ever known. This photograph was taken in 1877.

● **Graces** ▶ In Greek mythology, the three daughters of Zeus and Hera, representing beauty, grace, and charm. They were named ,Aglaia, Euphrosyne, and Thalia.

● **grackle** ▶ An omnivorous black bird of the North American genus *Quiscalus*. Grackles are about 30 cm long and have strong pointed bills used to dig for insect larvae, to kill small vertebrates, and to crack open nuts. They can cause damage to crops. Family: *Icteridae* (American orioles).

● **gradient** ▶ A measure of the inclination of a slope, often expressed as the rise in height divided by the length of the slope, i.e. the sine of the angle of the slope. Mathematically, however, the gradient is the ratio of the vertical rise to the horizontal distance covered, i.e. the tangent of the angle. For gentle gradients the difference between the sine and the tangent is small. In ▷calculus the gradient is the slope of the ▷tangent at any point on a curve in a Cartesian ▷coordinate system. If the curve is represented by the function f(x), then the gradient is the first derivative of this function.

● **Graf, Steffi** ▶ (1969–) German tennis player. Her victories include the Wimbledon singles championship in 1988, 1989, 1991, 1992, 1993, 1995, and 1996. In 1988 she became the fourth woman to complete a grand slam of the four major singles championships and won an Olympic gold medal. She retired from professional tennis in 1999 and married André ▷Agassi in 2001.

● **grafting** ▶ **1.** (horticulture) The transfer of part of one plant, usually a shoot or a bud, onto another plant. It is often used as a means of vegetative propagation, particularly for fruit trees and roses. The ▷cambium (a region of actively dividing cells) of the transplanted piece (called the scion) is aligned with that of the recipient plant (called the stock): the wound tissue formed by the two cambia binds the graft together. Grafts will "take" only if the scion and stock are closely related. Genetically identical scions on different stocks may differ considerably, but this is due solely to environmental effects and there is no transfer of genetic material between stock and scion.

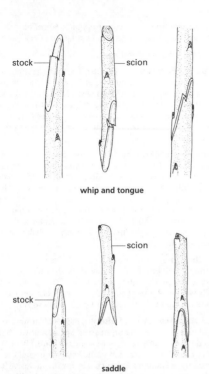

stock — scion

whip and tongue

scion

stock

saddle

grafting ► Two commonly used grafting methods. After stock and scion are fitted together they are held securely by tape, string, etc., and protected from desiccation by covering the point of union with wax or moist material.

Occasionally graft hybrids (*see* chimaera) arise from the graft junction, but these are mixtures of the two cell types rather than true hybrids. **2.** (surgery) ▷*See* transplantation.

● **Grafton** ► 29 40S 152 56E A city in Australia, in NE New South Wales. It is an agricultural trading centre. Population (latest est): 17 500.

● **Graham, Billy** ► (1918–) US evangelist. He began as an evangelist with the Youth for Christ movement before forming the Billy Graham Evangelistic Association (1950) and conducting worldwide crusades. His association with prominent personalities and carefully staged meetings, in which the audience are invited to "take a decision for Christ," have attracted very large crowds.

● **Graham, Martha** ► (1893–1991) US ballet dancer and choreographer. After establishing her own academy in 1927 she became one of the most influential teachers of modern dance. Her ballets, often psychological explorations of mythological themes, include *Primitive Mysteries* (1931), *Night Journey* (1947), *Circe* (1963), and *Acts of Light* (1981).

● **Graham, Thomas** ► (1805–69) British physicist, who investigated gaseous diffusion, discovering **Graham's law** (1831), which states that the rates at which gases diffuse are inversely proportional to the square roots of their densities. After being appointed Master of the Royal Mint (1854), he continued to study diffusion, investigating the flow of solutions through semipermeable membranes. He coined the terms osmosis, crystalloids, and colloids.

● **Grahame, Kenneth** ► (1859–1932) British children's writer. His best-known book is the children's classic, *The Wind in the Willows* (1908), concerned with Toad, Mole, Rat, and other animal characters that inhabit an ideal riverside world. It was adapted as a play, *Toad of Toad Hall* (1929), by A. A. ▷Milne.

● **Graham Land** ► A mountainous peninsula in Antarctica, bordering on the Weddell Sea and comprising part of ▷British Antarctic Territory. It was formerly a dependency of the Falkland Islands.

● **Grahamstown** ► (Afrikaans name: Grahamstad) 33 19S 26 32E A town in SE South Africa. It was the focus of British settlement in 1820. It is an important religious and educational centre with a Roman Catholic procathedral and an Anglican cathedral; Rhodes University was founded here in 1904. Population (latest est): 75 000.

● **Graiae** ► In Greek legend, three goddesses personifying old age, the sisters and protectors of the ▷Gorgons. They shared one eye and one tooth. ▷Perseus stole the eye in order to take the Gorgons by surprise.

● **Grail** ▷*See* Holy Grail.

● **Grainger, Percy Aldridge** ► (1882–1961) Australian composer and pianist, trained in Germany. He lived in London (1900–15) and thereafter in the USA, becoming a US citizen in 1918. Grainger was a friend of Grieg and Delius and studied and recorded English folksong. Many of his compositions incorporate folk-music intervals and rhythms; they include the orchestral *Shepherds' Hey* (1913), *English Dance* (1925), and *Harvest Hymn* (1933), as well as the "clog dance" *Handel in the Strand* (1913).

● **gram** ► (g) A unit of mass equal to 1/1000 of a ▷kilogram. The gram is itself one of the basic units in the ▷c.g.s. system, but in ▷SI units the basic unit is the kilogram.

● **Gram, Hans Christian Joachim** ► (1853–1938) Danish bacteriologist and physician, who in 1884 devised a method for staining bacteria (**Gram's stain**). Bacterial cells are stained with a violet dye (e.g. crystal violet), then treated with iodine solution (to fix the dye) and alcohol, and finally counterstained with a red dye (such as carbolfuchsin). Bacteria that retain the violet dye are described as **Gram-positive**; those that do not (i.e. they appear pink) are **Gram-negative**. This distinction reflects differences in cell-wall structure and is important in identifying and classifying bacteria and in treating bacterial infections: Gram-positive bacteria are susceptible to penicillin, whereas Gram-negative are not.

● **grammar** ► The study of the forms of the words of a language (morphology) and their relationships with one another (syntax). Until 1957 there were two basic types of grammar: **prescriptive grammar**, which expressed value judgments about the correctness of particular expressions, and **descriptive grammar**, which aimed to give an accurate account of the structures observable in recorded texts of a language. The earliest known descriptive grammar is by ▷Panini (c. 5th century BC) of ▷Sanskrit. Many grammars of the ancient Greek and Latin languages are still influential today; for example, the traditional parts of speech—noun, verb, adjective, etc.—were invented by Greek grammarians. Descriptive grammarians have been able to show that the judgments of prescriptivists are founded on no more objective basis than the willingness of the community to accept their judgments. Each language has its own patterns; attempts to resolve disputes or difficulties by appealing to authority, history, logic, or the structure of some other language are at best irrelevant, at worst confusing.

Publication in 1957 of *Syntactic Structures* by Noam ▷Chomsky introduced a new view of the study of grammar—namely that it should be predictive. Chomsky argued that, since the potential number of grammatical sentences in a language is literally infinite, a grammar must predict whether any given utterance is or is not a grammatical sentence of a particular language. Chomsky invented the concept of **generative grammar**, the finite set of linguistic rules that generate an infinite number of grammatical sentences in the language. Every speaker of a language acquires these rules at a very early age in a form to some degree idiosyncratic and different from those of other speakers. The raw material from which sentences are generated (words, phrases, etc.) form in a speaker's memory a store the exact nature of which is disputed. The concept of **transformational** (or transformational-generative) **grammar** seeks to explain the relationships among words in a sentence and among sentences themselves by logical structural analysis. Ambiguities and certain other problems are explained by postulating that behind the "surface structure" of a sentence lies a "deep structure," an abstract underlying form that determines the sentence's meaning. The surface structure is generated from the deep structure by generative rules, some of which are similar to the transformations of theoretical ▷logic.

● **grammar schools** ► Secondary schools in the UK providing an academic education for children between the ages of 11 or 12 and 18, in preparation for further education or the professions. Most of the grammar schools that existed in England and Wales in the 1960s were established following the Education Act (1944) and a large number of the longer-established schools date only from the beginning of the 20th century, created after the Education Act (1902). The original grammar schools, established in the middle ages, were preparatory institutions for university or for jobs in which a knowledge of Latin was essential. Their role expanded during the Renaissance to provide a broader education, and academic standards were generally high. The standard of instruction subsequently fell, however, and by the early 19th century comparisons with the USA, France, Germany, and especially Scotland led many legal and political reformers to conclude that the English secondary schools were among the most backward in Europe. The main emphasis of the reform movement of the 19th century was one of high moral tone and self-discipline (*see* public school). In the years immediately following World War II, with the growing demand for academic excellence in an increasingly meritocratic and technological society, grammar schools were compelled to become selective, restricting entry to those passing the ▷eleven-plus examination. Those not selected for grammar schools had to attend secondary modern schools or independent schools. The principle of selection at the early age of 11 was regarded as unfair, and in an attempt to provide equality of opportunity most grammar schools were replaced by ▷comprehensive schools in the 1970s; those that remain (in 1998, 161 schools concentrated in a few local authorities in S and E England) select mainly by a twelve-plus exam. Opponents of the move to comprehensive education claim that the abolition of grammar schools, many of which were centres of excellence, resulted in a levelling down of educational standards, making English and Welsh schools inferior to many of those in continental Europe and elsewhere in the industrial world.

● **gramophone** ▷*See* recording of sound.

● **Grampian Region** ► A former administrative region in NE Scotland, bordering on the North Sea. It was created under local government reorganization in 1975 from the counties of ▷Aberdeenshire, Banff, Kincardine, and ▷Moray. Under further local government reorganization in 1996 it was abolished and Aberdeenshire and Moray were restored with adjusted borders; the city of Aberdeen became an independent ▷unitary authority.

● **Grampians** ► A range of mountains in central Scotland, mainly in Perth and Kinross and Aberdeenshire. It extends generally SW–NE, bordered in the S by the Central Lowlands; the Cairngorm Mountains form a northerly extension. Its chief summits include Ben Nevis at 1343 m (4406 ft) and Ben Macdhui at 1309 m (4296 ft).

● **Grampians** ► A mountain range in Australia. It extends SW from the Great Dividing Range, in SW central Victoria, reaching 1166 m (3827 ft) at Mount William.

● **grampus** ► A small toothed ▷whale, *Grampus griseus*, of warm and temperate waters, also called Risso's dolphin. About 3.7 m long, dark-grey with a pale belly, grampuses live in small herds and migrate towards the Poles in summer and the equator in winter.

● **Gramsci, Antonio** ► (1891–1937) Italian politician and Marxist theorist. In 1914 he joined the Italian Socialist Party but, dissatisfied with its moderation, broke away in 1921 to form the Italian Communist Party. In 1924 he became its leader in the chamber of deputies. The party was banned by the fascists in 1926 and Gramsci was imprisoned from 1928 until shortly before his death. His voluminous Marxist writings, mostly the work of his prison years, were publishd posthumously as *Prison Notebooks* (1947).

● **Granada** ► 37 10N 3 35W A city in S Spain, in Andalusia. Formerly the capital of the kingdom of Granada, the last Moorish stronghold in Spain, it was conquered in 1492. Much frequented by tourists, its splendid architecture includes many Moorish buildings (notably the ⁕Alhambra), a cathedral (1523–1703), and the 16th-century Capilla Real, containing the tombs of Ferdinand and Isabella. Population (1995 est): 272 738.

● **Granada** ► 11 58N 85 59W A town in SW Nicaragua. It is the centre of an area producing cotton, sugar, and coffee; manufactures include furniture, soap, and rum. Population (1995 est): 74 396.

● **granadilla** ▷*See* passionflower.

● **Granados, Enrique** ► (1867–1916) Spanish composer and pianist. His music was influenced by Spanish folk music. He and his wife were drowned during World War I when HMS *Sussex*, on which they were returning from the USA, was torpedoed. Granados is best remembered for the two sets of piano pieces entitled *Goyescas* (1911), inspired by ▷Goya. These became the basis for an opera of the same name (1916).

● **Granby, John Manners, Marquess of** ► (1721–70) British soldier. As a cavalry officer in the ▷Seven Years' War, he made amends for his commander's disgrace at Minden (1759) by his part in the victory of Warburg (1760). Promotion to commander in chief of the army (1766) and popular acclaim followed, but he subsequently resigned as a result of political criticism. He spent much of his fortune on the welfare of wounded veterans of his campaigns, many of whom he set up in public houses (hence the many English pubs that carry his name) and died in debt.

● **Gran Chaco** ► A vast plain in S central South America, mainly in N Argentina, E Bolivia, and Paraguay. It consists of a vast alluvial lowland region, drained by the W tributaries of the Rivers Paraguay and Paraná. It was the cause of the ▷Chaco War between Paraguay and Bolivia (1932–35). Area: 780 000 sq km (300 000 sq mi).

● **Grand Alliance, War of the** ► (1689–97) The war in which a grand alliance led by England, Austria, Spain, and the Netherlands attempted to curb the expansionist policy of Louis XIV of France. Precipitated by the French invasion of the Palatinate (1688), the war was fought mainly in Flanders. Exhausted by the inconclusive battles and sieges, the participants accepted the Treaty of ▷Rijswijk in 1697. The conflict was renewed, however, in 1701, with the War of the ▷Spanish Succession.

● **Grand Banks** ► A section of the North American continental shelf in the N Atlantic Ocean, extending SE of Newfoundland with a depth of about 40–100 m (130–330 ft). It is an internationally important fishing ground in which cod is especially plentiful. Area: about 1 280 000 sq km (494 000 sq mi).

● **Grand Canal** ► (Chinese name: Da Yunhe) A canal in E China, the longest in the world, extending about 1600 km (1000 mi) N–S from Beijing to ▷Wuhan. Begun possibly in the 4th century BC, it was built in sections over two millenniums. 30–61 m (100–200 ft) wide and 0.6–4.6 m (2–15 ft) deep, it is still used, chiefly in the S.

● **Grand Canyon** ► A vast gorge in the USA, in Arizona on the Colorado River. It has been eroded through a varied series of virtually horizontal beds of multicoloured rock, creating spectacular steps and rock formations. A popular tourist area, it was designated the **Grand Canyon National Park** in 1919. Length: 451 km (280 mi). Width: 6–29 km (4–18 mi). Greatest depth: over 1.5 km (1 mi).

● **Grand Coulee Dam** ► A large gravity ▷dam on the Columbia River in Washington (USA). Completed in 1942, it is 1272 m long at its crest, 108 m high, and has a reservoir capacity of 11 600 million cubic metres for irrigation, flood control, and hydroelectric power.

● **Grande Dixence Dam** ► A gravity ▷dam on the River Dixence (Switzerland). Until 1970 it was the tallest dam in the world (284 m high). It is 670 m wide at the crest and has a reservoir of 400 million cubic metres.

● **Grand Guignol** ► A type of popular sensational drama, exploiting situations of violence and terror, that flourished in Paris in the late 19th century. The term derives from the name of a theatre in Montmartre at which these plays were performed, which was itself named after Guignol, a stock character in French puppet shows.

● **grand mal** ▷*See* epilepsy.

● **Grand National Steeplechase** ► The world's most famous and exacting ▷steeplechase, run in March at Aintree near Liverpool (England), over a course of 7.2 km (4 mi 856 yd) with 30 assorted obstacles. It was first run in 1839.

● **Grand Pré** ▶ A village in E Canada, in Nova Scotia. It was the centre of French-speaking ▷Acadia until Britain deported its inhabitants for refusing to swear allegiance to the Crown (1755).

● **Grand Rapids** ▶ 42 57N 86 40W A city in the USA, in W central Michigan on the Grand River. Founded in the 1820s, its industries include the manufacture of furniture, motor bodies, paper, and paint. Population (2000): 197 800.

● **Grand River** ▶ **1.** A river in the N central USA, the longest river in Michigan. It rises in the S of the state and flows N then NW into Lake Michigan. Length: 418 km (260 mi). **2.** A river in the N central USA. It rises in North Dakota and flows through South Dakota to join the Missouri. Length: 336 km (209 mi).

● **Grand Remonstrance** ▶ (1641) A list of grievances drawn up by the ▷Long Parliament on the eve of the English ▷Civil War. It itemized the past faults of Charles I, the reforms achieved by the Long Parliament, and grievances outstanding.

● **grand unified theory** ▶ (GUT) A theory that attempts to include ▷electromagnetic, ▷weak, and ▷strong interactions into a single ▷gauge theory. Most GUTs assume that these interactions merge at around 10^{15} GeV into a single interaction, some assume that protons decay, and others that neutrinos have mass in certain circumstances. No GUTs are so far supported by conclusive evidence.

● **Grangemouth** ▶ 56 01N 3 44W A port in Scotland, in Falkirk lying on the Firth of Forth at the E end of the Forth–Clyde Canal. Its industries include oil refining, engineering, saw milling, and chemicals. Population (1991): 18 739.

● **granite** ▶ A coarse-grained plutonic rock of acid composition resulting from the high silica content. Granites contain quartz, feldspar (usually alkali), and mafic (dark-coloured) minerals, usually muscovite and biotite (micas). Most granites crystallize from magma in large igneous intrusions known as batholiths, but some are produced by granitization, which is the transformation of pre-existing rocks into granite by the action of granitic fluids rising from great depths. There are many different types of granite with different modes of formation and mineral content.

● **Gran Paradiso** ▶ 45 33N 7 17E The highest mountain entirely in Italy, in the Alps. Height: 4061 m (13 323 ft).

● **Grant, Cary** ▶ (Archibald Leach; 1904–86) US film actor, born in England. He went to Hollywood in 1932 and established his reputation as an actor of debonair sophistication in such films as *Holiday* (1938) and *The Philadelphia Story* (1940). He acted in more than 70 films, including several directed by Alfred Hitchcock, notably *To Catch a Thief* (1955) and *North By Northwest* (1959).

● **Grant, Duncan James Corrowr** ▶ (1885–1978) British painter and designer. He was influenced by the postimpressionists and was associated with Roger ▷Fry and the ▷Bloomsbury group. His work includes designs for rugs and fabrics, murals, stage costumes and scenery, and a portrait of his partner, Vanessa Bell (Tate Gallery).

● **Grant, Hugh (John Mungo)** ▶ (1960–) British film actor. He made his commercial debut in *Maurice* (1987) and went on to star in the hugely successful romantic comedies *Four Weddings and a Funeral* (1994), *Notting Hill* (1999), and *Bridget Jones's Diary* (2001). Other films include *Sirens* (1994) and *About a Boy* (2002).

● **Grant, Ulysses S(impson)** ▶ (1822–85) US general and statesman; Republican president (1869–77). As supreme commander of the Federal armies (1864–65) he defeated the Confederates by means of strategy and battering them into submission. The consequently great losses to his own side earned him the nickname Grant the Butcher. As president, he acquiesced in Reconstruction attempts to enfranchise Blacks, fought inflation, and unsuccessfully planned to annex the Dominican Republic. Subsequently he became so poor that he had to sell his swords and war souvenirs.

● **Grantham** ▶ 52 55N 0 39W A town in E central England, in Lincolnshire. Margaret Thatcher was born here and Sir Isaac Newton was born nearby and attended the grammar school (1528). An important agricultural centre, Grantham has agricultural and general engineering industries. Population (1991): 33 243.

● **grant-maintained school** ▷*See* education.

● **Granville, Granville George Leveson-Gower, 2nd Earl** ▶ (1815–91) British Liberal politician; foreign secretary (1870–74, 1880–85) under Gladstone. He was one of the few Liberals to support Gladstone on Irish ▷Home Rule.

● **Granville, John Carteret, 1st Earl** ▶ (1690–1763) British statesman; secretary of state (1742–44). A bitter opponent of Robert ▷Walpole, Granville became secretary of state after Walpole's fall. During the War of the ▷Austrian Succession he was criticized for putting George II's Hanoverian interests above Britain's and George was forced to dismiss him.

● **Granville-Barker, Harley** ▶ (1877–1946) British theatre director, critic, and dramatist. As comanager of the Royal Court Theatre from 1904 to 1907 he produced many plays by G. B. Shaw and by modern European dramatists. His most influential practical criticism is contained in *Prefaces to Shakespeare* (1927–47). His own plays include *The Voysey Inheritance* (1905) and *The Madras House* (1910).

● **grape** ▶ The fruit of vines of the genus *Vitis* (about 60 species), especially *V. vinifera*, native to N Asia but cultivated throughout Mediterranean regions. The grapevine is up to 30 m long, twining by means of tendrils, with lobed toothed leaves and dense clusters of small greenish flowers. The fruit—a berry—is green, red, or blue-black and used to make ▷wine, brandy, and liqueurs or eaten fresh or dried (in the form of raisins, sultanas, and currants).

● **grapefruit** ▶ A tree, *Citrus paradisi*, 6–12 m high, cultivated in the tropics and subtropics. It has shiny oval leaves and clusters of white flowers that mature into fleshy yellow-skinned fruits, 10–15 cm in diameter. Grapefruits are eaten fresh, tinned, or crushed to make beverages. ▷*See* Citrus.

● **grape hyacinth** ▶ A perennial herbaceous plant of the genus *Muscari* (50 species), mostly native to the Mediterranean region and widely grown as garden bulbs. The leaves are long and narrow and the blue, pink, or white urn-shaped flowers are borne in a dense cluster at the tip of a leafless flower stalk, up to 15 cm high. *M. botryoides*, with blue flowers, is a popular species. Family: *Liliaceae*.

● **graph** ▶ A method of providing a visual representation of relationships between quantities, usually in the Cartesian ▷coordinate system. In mathematics graphs are used to solve equations, represent functions, etc. Histograms, in which the height of columns represents the frequency of a result in each of a series of ranges, and pie charts, which show percentages as segments of a circle, are also sometimes referred to as graphs.

● **graphics** ▷*See* computer graphics.

● **graphite** ▶ An iron-grey to black form of pure carbon, found in many metamorphic rocks, especially metamorphosed coals or other carbonaceous sediments. It occurs in a laminar or massive form. It is very soft, flaky, and greasy to the touch. Graphite is used for making metallurgical crucibles, as a lubricant, in paint, rubber, and pencil leads, in batteries and for other electrical purposes, and as a moderator in nuclear reactors. It has often been called plumbago or black lead, since it was formerly mistaken for lead.

● **Grappelli, Stephane** ▶ (1908–97) French jazz violinist, who played in the quintet of the Hot Club de France (1934–39). He made many recordings, with Yehudi ▷Menuhin among others.

● **graptolite** ▶ A small colonial marine animal belonging to the extinct class *Graptolithina*, possibly related to ▷cnidarians. Their fossils, in the form of carbonaceous impressions, occur in rocks of the Upper Cambrian to Carboniferous periods, about 420–250 million years ago. Graptolites were floating animals, individual polyps living in the cuplike tips of simple or branched hollow tubes.

● **Grasmere** ▶ 54 28N 3 02W A village in NW England, in Cumbria on Lake Grasmere. It is famous for its associations with William Wordsworth (whose cottage is now a museum) and other Lakeland poets. Population (latest est): 1100.

● **grass** ▶ A monocotyledonous annual or perennial herbaceous plant belonging to the family *Poaceae* (or *Gramineae*; 6000–10 000 species), distributed worldwide. The leaves consist of a basal sheath,

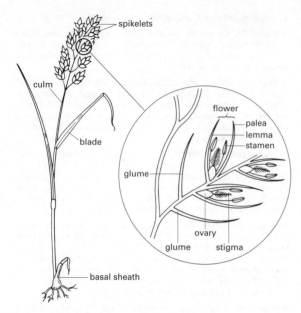

spikelets

culm

blade

flower
palea
lemma
stamen

glume

glume

ovary

glume   stigma

basal sheath

grass ► The typical structure of a grass is seen in the meadow fescue (*Festuca pratensis*). The flowers are grouped into spikelets and each consists only of male and female parts surrounded by bracts; petals and sepals are absent.

which encircles the stem, and a long narrow blade. The flowering stems (culms) bear spikelets of inconspicuous flowers; each spikelet has two basal bracts (glumes) and each flower is enclosed by two other bracts—a lower lemma and an upper palea. The hard single-seeded fruit (the grain) is known botanically as a caryopsis, with the ovary wall (pericarp) and seed coat fused. Many species are important in agriculture as a source of food (*see* cereals; sugar cane) and as pasture grasses.

● **Grass, Günter ►** (1927–   ) German novelist, poet, and political activist. His first novel, *The Tin Drum* (1959), an epic picaresque treatment of modern German history, established him as a moral spokesman for his generation. His other works include the play *The Plebeians Rehearse the Uprising* (1966), the travel journal *Headbirths or The Germans are Dying out* (1982), and the novels *Dog Years* (1963), *The Flounder* (1978), *The Meeting at Telgte* (1981), *The Rat* (1986), and *Toad Croaks* (1992). He received the Nobel Prize for Literature in 1999.

● **Grasse ►** 43 40N 6 56E A town and resort in SE France, in the Alpes-Maritimes department. It is the centre of the French perfume industry. Population (latest est): 50 000.

● **grassfinch ►** A songbird belonging to a subfamily of ▷weaver-finches, occurring chiefly in arid regions of Australasia. About 10 cm long, grassfinches have long tails and stout bills. The group includes a number of colourful popular cagebirds, such as the Gouldian finch (*Poephila gouldiae*) and the ▷zebra finch.

● **grasshopper ►** A jumping insect belonging to the family *Acrididae* (about 5000 species). Grasshoppers, 24–110 mm long, are usually green or brown and have short stout antennae and tail appendages. Both sexes produce sound by rubbing the hind legs against the front wings. Some species can fly, sometimes forming dense migratory swarms (*see* locust). Grasshoppers live and feed on grass and low vegetation and the females lay eggs in the soil. Order: ▷Orthoptera.

● **grass monkey ►** A small African ▷guenon monkey, *Cercopithecus aethiops*, inhabiting thinly wooded regions. The West African green monkey, the East African grivet monkey, and the South African vervet or blue monkey are all local races of grass monkey.

● **grass of Parnassus ►** A tufted perennial herb of the genus *Parnassia* (about 50 species), especially *P. palustris*, found in wet places throughout Europe and temperate Asia. The basal leaves are stalked

and heart-shaped. The solitary white five-petalled flower is borne on an erect stalk with a single unstalked leaf near the base. Family: *Parnassiaceae*.

● **grass snake ►** A nonvenomous snake, *Natrix natrix*, also called water snake, occurring throughout Europe, usually near ponds, streams, and marshes. 75–95 cm long, it has a green back with two rows of black spots, vertical black bars along its sides, and a yellow neck patch. It can be distinguished from the ▷adder, which has a black zigzag line along its back. Its prey includes frogs, tadpoles, fish, lizards, and small mammals. Family: *Colubridae*.

● **grass tree ►** A woody plant of the genus *Xanthorrhoea* (about 5 species), native to E Australia. They often have palmlike stems, 5 m tall, that end in a tuft of rigid grasslike leaves, from which extend flower spikes resembling those of the ▷reedmace, about 3 m tall. A red or yellow gumlike resin, used for varnishes, exudes from the bases of old leaves. Family: *Xanthorrhoeaceae*.

● **Gratian(us), Flavius ►** (359–83 AD) Western Roman emperor (367–83). He was a Christian and abandoned (382) the pagan title *pontifex maximus* (supreme priest). He was deposed by Magnus Maximus (d. 388) and murdered.

● **Grattan, Henry ►** (1746–1820) Irish politician, who with ▷Flood was one of the greatest orators in the Irish parliament. From 1775 he led the patriot party and in 1782 obtained Irish free trade and legislative independence from Britain. He opposed, unavailingly, the union of England and Ireland and in 1805 sat in the British parliament, where he pressed for ▷Catholic emancipation.

● **gravel ►** Unconsolidated rock fragments ranging between 2 and 60 mm in particle size, or between coarse sand and cobbles. The term is loosely used for any unconsolidated material coarser than sand, for instance river gravels and glacial gravels.

● **Gravenhage, 's** ▷*See* Hague, The.

● **Graves, Robert (Ranke) ►** (1895–1985) British poet, critic, and novelist. His early autobiography, *Goodbye to All That* (1929), recounts his experiences in World War I. In 1929 he emigrated to Majorca. He published several editions of *Collected Poems*, historical novels including *I Claudius* (1934) and *Claudius the God* (1934), and studies of mythology, notably *The White Goddess* (1948). His later works include *They Hanged My Saintly Billy* (1980).

● **Gravesend ►** 51 27N 0 24E A port in SE England, in Kent on the River Thames. It is a customs and pilot station for the Port of London and has printing, engineering, and paper-making industries. Population (1991): 51 435.

● **Gravettian ►** A culture of the Upper ▷Palaeolithic, succeeding the ▷Aurignacian in W Europe. Named after the cave at La Gravette in the Dordogne (SW France), the Gravettian is characterized by small pointed stone blades with one blunted edge (Gravette points) and dates from between 26 000 and 20 000 BC. The well-known small female figurines called Venuses are of Gravettian origin. The term Eastern Gravettian is applied to similar material from mammoth hunters' camp sites in Russia and E Europe. *Compare* Perigordian.

● **gravitation ►** An attractive force that occurs between all bodies that possess mass. It was first described by Sir Isaac ▷Newton in a law stating that the force between two bodies is directly proportional to the product of their masses and inversely proportional to the square of the distance between them. The constant of proportionality is called the **universal gravitational constant**, G, which has the value 6.673×10^{-11} newton metre squared per kilogram squared. Gravitation is now more accurately described by the general theory of ▷relativity. In this theory a mass distorts the ▷space-time continuum around it so that the geometry of the space is locally no longer Euclidean. The **force of gravity** and the ▷acceleration of free fall are the result of the attractive force between a body and the earth.

● **gravitational collapse ►** The sudden collapse of the core of a ▷star when thermonuclear fusion eventually ceases. The star's internal gas pressure can no longer support the weight of the star and the initial result may be a ▷supernova explosion. The gravitational pull of all the constituents of the star, or its remains, causes it to contract.

The extent of the contraction depends on the mass of the object, producing a ▷white dwarf, ▷neutron star, or ▷black hole.

● **gravitational interaction** ▶ One of the four kinds of interaction that occur between elementary particles (*see* particle physics) and by far the weakest (about 10^{40} times weaker than the ▷electromagnetic interaction). The interaction occurs between all particles with mass and can be explained as the exchange of ▷virtual particles called **gravitons**. Such particles have not yet been detected.

● **gray** ▶ (Gy) The ▷SI unit of absorbed dose of ionizing radiation equal to the energy in joules absorbed by one kilogram of irradiated material.

● **Gray, Asa** ▶ (1810–88) US botanist, who compiled *Flora of North America* (2 vols, 1838–43), a comprehensive taxonomic guide to the region's plants. He also wrote many popular books on botany, including a *Manual of the Botany of the Northern United States* (1848). Gray was a firm supporter of Darwin's theories of evolution, although he believed that the process of natural selection was controlled by God.

● **Gray, Thomas** ▶ (1716–71) British poet. The only survivor of 12 children, he was educated at Eton and Cambridge, where he spent most of his life in scholarly retirement. He published only a few odes apart from his most famous poem, *Elegy Written in a Country Churchyard* (1751), a classical meditation on the graves of the humble villagers of Stoke Poges, Buckinghamshire.

● **grayling** ▶ A troutlike fish of the genus *Thymallus*, sometimes placed in a distinct family (*Thymallidae*). Graylings have a silvery-purple scaly body, up to 50 cm long, with a sail-like dorsal fin, and live in cold clear fresh waters of Eurasia and N North America, feeding on aquatic insects. They are important food and game fish. Family: *Salmonidae*.

● **Gray's Inn** ▷*See* Inns of Court.

● **graywacke** ▷*See* greywacke.

● **Graz** ▶ 47 05N 15 22E The second largest city in Austria, the capital of Styria. Its numerous historical buildings include a cathedral (1438–62) and a notable clock tower (1561). It has a university (1586). An industrial centre, it produces iron and steel and chemicals. Population (1991): 237 810.

● **Great Artesian Basin** ▶ An artesian basin of E Australia. The largest area of artesian water in the world, it extends S from the Gulf of Carpentaria in Queensland into South Australia and New South Wales, underlying the catchments of both the Darling River and Lake Eyre. Area: 1 750 000 sq km (676 250 sq mi).

● **Great Australian Bight** ▶ A wide bay of the Indian Ocean, in S Australia situated between Capes Pasley and Carnot. Width: 1159 km (720 mi).

● **Great Awakening** ▶ A religious revival in the American colonies in the 18th century. It began in the 1720s among members of the Dutch Reformed Church of New Jersey but flourished in New England in 1740–43, after which it spread to other colonies. It was largely inspired by the preaching of George ▷Whitefield and Jonathan ▷Edwards, who, however, disapproved of the excessive enthusiasm or hysteria that was often manifested by those claiming to be converted.

● **Great Barrier Reef** ▶ The largest coral reef in the world, situated in the Coral Sea off the coast of NE Australia. Approximately 15 000 years old, it consists of a complex of coral reefs, shoals, and islets extending 2012 km (1250 mi) from Breaksea Spit to the Gulf of Papua. Its many fish, crustaceans, birds, exotic plant life, and some 350 species of colourful corals make it popular with tourists. In recent years 30% of the reef has been destroyed by the ▷crown-of-thorns starfish and further damage has been caused by global warming.

● **Great Basin** ▶ A large semiarid area in the USA. Situated between the Sierra Nevada and the Wasatch Mountains, it extends over most of Nevada, Utah, and parts of California and Oregon. It consists of a series of basins, mountain ranges, deserts (including the ▷Mojave Desert), and salt lakes (including the ▷Great Salt Lake).

● **Great Bear** ▷*See* Ursa Major.

● **Great Bear Lake** ▶ A lake in N Canada, in Mackenzie district on the Arctic Circle. Frozen eight months of the year, it is the fourth largest lake in North America. It drains into the Mackenzie River via the Great Bear River, 112 km (70 mi) long. Area: 31 792 sq km (12 275 sq mi).

● **Great Belt** ▶ (Danish name: Store Bælt) A channel between the Danish islands of Fyn and Sjælland, linking the Kattegat and the Baltic Sea. Since 1998 it has been spanned by the Store Bælt (*or* East) Bridge, a road and rail link whose central span (1624 m; 5328 ft) forms the longest suspension bridge in Europe.

● **Great Britain** ▶ ▷England, ▷Wales, and ▷Scotland including those adjacent islands governed from the mainland (i.e. excluding the Isle of Man and the Channel Islands). The United Kingdom of Great Britain was formed by the Act of Union (1707), although the term Great Britain had been in use since 1603, when James VI of Scotland became James I of England (including Wales). Later unions created the United Kingdom of Great Britain and Ireland (1801) and the United Kingdom of Great Britain and Northern Ireland (1922). Area: 229 523 sq km (88 619 sq mi). Population (1992 est): 56 388 200.

● **great circle** ▶ A circle that is the intersection on the surface of a sphere of a plane passing through the centre of that sphere. On the earth, each meridian of longitude is half of a great circle; the equator is the only parallel of latitude that is a great circle.

● **great crested grebe** ▶ A large ▷grebe, *Podiceps cristatus*, occurring in Eurasia. It is dark brown above with a white face, neck, and underparts, a black two-horned crest and neck frill, and chestnut patches at the sides of the face. They perform an elaborate courtship display. ▷*See* Plate III.

● **Great Dane** ▶ A breed of large dog originating in Germany, where they were developed for hunting boar. The Great Dane has a large powerful frame with long legs and a large head with a square muzzle. The short sleek coat can be golden, black, streaked brown, blue-grey, or white with black patches. Height: 76 cm minimum (dogs); 71 cm minimum (bitches).

● **Great Dividing Range** ▶ (Great Divide *or* Eastern Highlands) The E highlands of Australia, which extend 3700 km (2300 mi) from Cape York Peninsula to the Grampians of Victoria and include the ▷Blue Mountains and Australian Alps, reaching 2230 m (7316 ft) at Mount ▷Kosciusko.

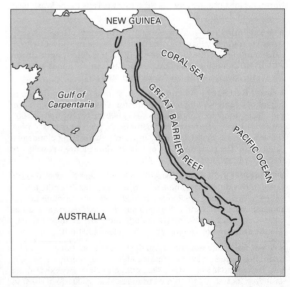

Great Barrier Reef

● **Greater Antilles** ▶ The four largest West Indian islands, comprising Cuba, Hispaniola, Jamaica, and Puerto Rico.

● **Greater London** ▷*See* London.

● **Greater Manchester** ▶ A metropolitan county of NW England, created in 1974 from SE Lancashire and parts of NE Cheshire and SW Yorkshire. In 1986 administrative powers were devolved to the ▷unitary authorities of Wigan, Bolton, Bury, Rochdale, Salford, Oldham, Manchester, Trafford, Stockport, and Tameside. Area: 1285 sq km (496 sq mi).

● **Great Exhibition** ▶ (1851) A display of the products of industrial Britain and Europe, planned by Prince Albert and held in the ▷Crystal Palace. It contained about 13 000 exhibits and showed the technical supremacy of Britain. The exhibition lasted for 23 weeks and was seen by over 6 million people.

● **Great Glen** ▶ (or Glen More) A rift valley extending across N Scotland from Fort William to Inverness. A number of lochs lie along the valley, including Loch Ness and Loch Linhe; the ▷Caledonian Canal was constructed along its length.

● **Great Indian Desert** ▷See Thar Desert.

● **Great Lake** ▶ A shallow freshwater lake in Australia. It lies on the central plateau of Tasmania, at an altitude of 1030 m (3380 ft), and is used as a storage reservoir for hydroelectric power. Area: 114 sq km (44 sq mi).

● **Great Lakes** ▶ Five large lakes in E central North America, mostly along the US-Canadian border: Lakes ▷Superior, ▷Michigan, ▷Huron, ▷Erie, and ▷Ontario. The world's largest freshwater surface, they drain into the ▷St Lawrence River and form part of the ▷St Lawrence Seaway. Canals also link them to the Mississippi River, making them a major transportation route. Their basin is an important economic region, with agriculture, fishing, forestry, mining, hydroelectricity, manufacturing, commerce, and tourism. Recently water pollution has become a major problem, compounded by the many governments with jurisdiction over the lakes.

● **Great Leap Forward** ▶ A nationwide campaign in China to promote economic and industrial growth. The movement started in 1958 and aimed to increase industrial production dramatically by using manpower rather than capital in large-scale rural communes and backyard steel furnaces and factories. Ambitious production targets were reached but it proved impossible to coordinate production and control quality, and the movement was revoked in 1960.

● **Great Ouse River** ▶ (or R. Ouse) A river in E England, rising in Northamptonshire and flowing NE across the Fens to the Wash near King's Lynn. Length: 257 km (160 mi).

● **Great Plains** ▶ An extensive area in North America. It consists of a system of rolling plains extending from the Mackenzie River Delta in Canada in the N to the Rio Grande in the S. It is chiefly agricultural with livestock raising and grain production. Length: about 4828 km (3000 mi). Average width: about 644 km (400 mi).

● **Great Red Spot** ▶ An immense reddish oval feature in the atmosphere of ▷Jupiter, lying S of the equator. Observed for over a century, its prominence, colour, and size (14 000 km N-S by up to 40 000 km E-W) have been found to fluctuate. Pioneer planetary probes showed it to be a vortex of cold anticlockwise-rotating clouds elevated above the surrounding cloud layer and coloured possibly by traces of phosphorus.

● **Great Rift Valley** ▶ (or East African Rift System) An extensive rift valley in the Middle East and East Africa. It extends from the Jordan Valley in Syria along the Red Sea into Ethiopia and through Kenya, Tanzania, and Malawi into Mozambique. It is marked by a chain of lakes (Lakes Turkana (formerly Rudolf) and Natron) and volcanoes (Mount Kilimanjaro). Length: about 6400 km (4000 mi).

● **Great Salt Lake** ▶ A salt lake in the USA, in NW Utah in the Great Basin. It is bordered by the Wasatch Mountains and the Great Salt Lake Desert and has no outlet. A salt extraction industry exists along its shores. Its area has fluctuated from less than 2500 sq km (1000 sq mi) to over 5000 sq km (2000 sq mi).

● **Great Sandy Desert** ▶ A desert of N Western Australia. It consists of a vast arid region of sand dunes and salt marshes stretching SE from Eighty Mile Beach on the Indian Ocean to the Gibson Desert. Area: 415 000 sq km (160 000 sq mi).

● **Great Schism** ▶ (1378–1417) The split in the Roman Catholic Church following the election of two rival popes to succeed Gregory XI. Criticisms of the residency of the papacy in Avignon (see Avignon papacy) forced its return to Rome and the election of an Italian, Urban VI. He determined to reform the College of Cardinals, which responded by electing an ▷antipope at Avignon, Clement VII. The Schism was ended by the Council of ▷Constance (1414–18) and the election of Martin V in 1417. (For the schism in 1054 between the E and W Christian churches, see East–West Schism.)

● **Great Slave Lake** ▶ A very deep lake in N Canada, in Mackenzie district. The fifth largest lake in North America, it drains into the Mackenzie River. Area: 28 438 sq km (10 980 sq mi).

● **great tit** ▶ The largest of the ▷tits, *Parus major*: a common European bird of woodland, farmland, and gardens feeding on caterpillars, aphids, scale insects, and other pests. It is about 14 cm long and has a black head with white cheeks, a green back, and a black stripe down its yellow breast.

● **Great Trek** ▶ The movement from the mid-1830s to mid-1840s of Dutch settlers (Afrikaners) in South Africa northwards across the Orange and Vaal Rivers from the Cape. The so-called Voortrekkers, under such leaders as Andries ▷Pretorius, moved away from British rule at the Cape in search of more farmland that they could administer themselves. They are considered by Afrikaners to be the founding fathers of South Africa. They established the republics of the Transvaal and the Orange Free State.

● **Great Victoria Desert** ▶ A desert of Western and South Australia, between the Gibson Desert and Nullarbor Plain. It consists of a vast arid region of sand hills and salt marshes. Area: 323 750 sq km (125 000 sq mi).

● **Great Vowel Shift** ▶ The phrase coined by ▷Jespersen to describe the change in English pronunciation that took place mainly during the 15th century; it accounts for many of the existing anomalies in English spelling and pronunciation. The highest Middle English long vowels became diphthongized (e.g. ī originally pronounced as in *machine* came to be pronounced like the *i* in *mice*) and other vowels, affected by this, shifted to higher positions.

● **Great Wall of China** ▶ A medieval defensive fortification in N China. Stretching from the Yellow Sea N of Beijing nearly 2400 km (1500 mi) inland, the Great Wall is the world's largest building achievement. Originally begun in 214 BC as a defence against nomadic tribes, it was improved and largely rebuilt of stone in the 15th and 16th centuries. It is about 9 m (30 ft) high, with numerous higher watch towers along its length.

● **Great War** ▷See World War I.

● **Great Yarmouth** ▶ (or Yarmouth) 52 37N 1 44E A resort and port in E England, in Norfolk at the mouth of the River Yare. Once a major herring-fishing port, it is now the service centre for the S sector of the North Sea gas fields. Its main industries are electronics and engineering, tourism, and food processing and packaging. Population (1997 est): 89 000.

● **Great Zimbabwe** ▶ The largest of the ruined Bantu royal centres on the Zambezian plateau in Zimbabwe. The word *zimbabwe* is derived from the Bantu for "revered houses." Great Zimbabwe reached its zenith in the late 14th century but suffered abrupt decline after about 1440. Traces of widespread trade, based on local gold, have been discovered, including Chinese pottery. Parts of the so-called Elliptical Building (a compound enclosing now vanished huts) stand 10.5 m (35 ft) high and consist of regular dry stone courses of dressed granite.

● **grebe** ▶ A bird belonging to a primitive family (Podicipedidae; 21 species) occurring in rivers and lakes worldwide. Grebes are adapted for swimming and diving by having short wings, a very small tail, and partially webbed feet with lobed toes. They have a long neck and a long pointed bill and feed chiefly on fish and aquatic invertebrates. Grebes are grey, black, or brown, usually with white underparts, and in the breeding season many have brightly coloured erectile crests and ear tufts. Order: *Podicipediformes*. ▷See also dabchick; great crested grebe.

● **Greece** ▶ (official name: Hellenic Republic; Greek name: Ellás) A country in SE Europe, occupying the S of the Balkan Peninsula between the Mediterranean and Aegean Seas. Numerous islands, comprising about one-fifth of the total area, lie to the S, E, and W; the largest is ▷Crete. The mainland is largely mountainous, with plains in Thrace and Macedonia in the N and Thessaly in the centre.

Economy: since the early 1970s industry has replaced agriculture as the mainstay of the economy. The rapid expansion of the industrial sector (especially metallurgy, chemicals, textiles, rubber, plastics, and electrical machinery) began in the 1960s. Mineral resources, including lignite, bauxite, and iron ore, have been intensively exploited and processed and there has been a dramatic increase in electricity output. Incentives for the decentralization of industry have led to a rapidly changing pattern of growth in N Greece aided by the discovery of natural gas and oil near the island of Thásos. There has been considerable diversification of agriculture and the principal crops include wheat, barley, maize, tobacco, sugar beet, tomatoes, and dried and fresh fruits. Tourism is also an important source of revenue. In the 1990s economic policy was dominated by privatization schemes and the imposition of austerity measures with the eventual aim of joining the single European currency.

History: the centuries following the collapse of the ▷Mycenaean civilization (c. 1200 BC) saw the rise of the Greek city states. From the 8th century, trading activities led to the establishment of colonies around the Mediterranean, in Asia Minor, N Africa, S Italy and Sicily, and in S France. The first half of the 5th century was dominated by the ultimately abortive attempt of the Persians to annex Greece (*see* Greek-Persian Wars) and the late 5th century, by the Peloponnesian War between rival Athens and Sparta. Sparta's subsequent supremacy in Greece lasted until its defeat by Thebes in 371. Greece fell to Philip of Macedon in 338 and was incorporated in the empire of his son Alexander the Great. Following the division of Alexander's possessions at his death (323), the Greek city states remained within the Macedonian orbit but repeatedly attempted to assert their independence until the last Macedonian War (171–168) allowed Rome to dominate Greece. Roman rule lasted until 395 AD, when the Roman Empire was divided between W and E and Greece became part of the Byzantine (Eastern Roman) Empire, centred on Constantinople. In the middle ages Greece was subject to invasions by the Franks, Normans, and the Latin Crusaders. In the early 14th century Byzantium reasserted its control over the area but in 1453 Constantinople fell to the Ottoman Turks; by 1460 they controlled all Greece. Apart from a brief period (1686–1715) of partial Venetian occupation, Greece remained under Ottoman rule until achieving independence in 1829 (*see* Greek Independence, War of). In 1832 the Greek Crown was offered to a Bavarian prince, who became Otto I (1815–67), but his despotic rule precipitated his deposition in 1862. In 1863 a Danish prince became king as George I (1845–1913). In the same year Greece acquired the Ionian Islands from Britain and in 1881, in the after-math of the Congress of Berlin, Thessaly and part of Epirus from Turkey. Greek demands for Crete led to a disastrous war with Turkey in 1897, but in the Balkan Wars (1912–13) Greece gained the island together with territory in Thrace and Macedonia. In 1917 Venizelos took Greece into World War I on the Allied side and the immediate postwar period saw renewed territorial conflict with Turkey, in which Greece lost Smyrna. Greece was a republic from 1924 until George II was restored in 1935. In World War II an unsuccessful Italian invasion (1940) was followed by German occupation (1941–44), after which Greece was plunged into a civil war between monarchists and communists that lasted until 1949. The 1950s were dominated by the question of union with Cyprus, which Greece supported (see EOKA), and the 1960s saw a military coup (1967), which exiled Constantine II and established the rule of the colonels under Papadopoulos. He was overthrown in 1973 and succeeded by Gen Phaidon Ghizikis (1917–   ). The government's involvement in the coup against Makarios in Cyprus led to its collapse (1974). A constitution (1975) saw the reintroduction of democratic government. Greece became a member of the EC (now the EU) in 1981. The Socialist government (1981–89) under Andreas ▷Papandreou was followed by a brief interim government under Xenophon Zolotas and three years (1990–93) of Conservative government under Constantine Mitsotakis. The Socialists were returned to power in 1993, with Costas Simitis succeeding Papandreou in 1996. Greece adopted the single European currency in January 2001.

Greece

Head of state	President Constantine Stefanopoulos
Official language	Greek
Official religion	Greek Orthodox
Official currency	euro; the drachma of 100 leptae will remain in use until 2002
Area	131 986 sq km (50 960 sq mi)
Population (1999 est)	10 561 000
Capital	Athens
Main port	Piraeus

● **Greek art and architecture** ▶ The arts of ancient Greece from the 8th century BC until Greece's absorption in the Roman Empire after 27 BC, conventionally divided into three main periods: archaic (before c. 550), classical (550–323), and Hellenistic (323–27). Most extant paintings are on pottery. Nonfigurative all-over designs of the earliest period gradually gave way to the more naturalistic black-figure technique in the 7th and 6th centuries BC. The greatest achievements are the Athenian red-figure vases (530–400 BC). As is also the case with sculptors, the work of many Greek painters (e.g. ▷Zeuxis) is known only through Roman copies, but magnificent Hellenistic wall paintings have recently been uncovered at Vergina. In sculpture, the monumental Egyptian-influenced solidity of the early

Great Wall of China ▶ One of the best conserved and most frequently visited parts of the Wall is this section at Badeling Pass, N of Beijing. This stone-faced and turreted section was completed considerably later than the rest of the Wall, having been rebuilt by the Ming in the 16th century.

▷kore and ▷kouros statues yielded to the idealized naturalism of the classical period (480–323 BC). This is exemplified in the ▷Elgin marbles and in the work of ▷Phidias and ▷Praxiteles. In the subsequent Hellenistic period sculpture is characteristically represented by dramatic subject matter and highly complex figure poses and groupings. The small-scale arts of coin engraving, gem carving, jewellery making, and the sculpting of bronze and terracotta figures (see Tanagra figurines) also reached a peak of perfection in the Hellenistic era. Greek architecture is perhaps the greatest legacy that the ancient Greeks have left us, for almost all subsequent European architecture is indebted to it. Although the Egyptians invented the colonnade (c. 2500 BC) and the Romans were the first to make use of arches, domes, and vaults as structural features, it was the Greeks who invented the entablature to surmount the colonnade in order to support a hipped roof. They also perfected the design of columns and created the concept of an architect as an artist, engineer, and town planner. Archaic Greek architecture had its roots in Crete (the first palace at Knossos was built about 2000 BC) and in Mycenae (the famous Lion Gate was erected about 1450 BC). However, classical (or Hellenic) Greek architecture did not emerge until about 700 BC, when the Greeks began to build in stone (limestone or marble) instead of wood, rubble, and mud bricks. This development followed slightly different courses on opposite sides of the Aegean Sea. During the 6th century BC the Doric order (see orders of architecture; □architecture) emerged as a consistent style in mainland Greece; at about the same time the Ionic order developed on the eastern shores of the Aegean. Both styles reached their zenith in the time of Pericles (490–429 BC); on the Athenian Acropolis the ▷Parthenon is the prime example of a Doric temple, while the Erechtheum (built by Mnesicles in 405 BC) contains three different Ionic orders. During the Hellenistic period the Doric gave way to the Ionic, and this in turn yielded to the third order of Greek architecture, the Corinthian. This style is exemplified by the Olympieium at Athens, built by Cossutius in 174 BC.

● **Greek Independence, War of ►** (1821–32) The war that established a Greek state independent of the Ottoman Empire. The rebels had some initial success until in 1825 the Ottomans were strengthened by Egyptian help. The UK, France, and Russia offered to mediate and when rebuffed by the Ottomans defeated the Ottoman and Egyptian fleet at the battle of ▷Navarino (1827). The Ottomans fought on briefly but peace negotiations were begun in London in 1829 and independence was proclaimed, being recognized by the Ottoman Empire in 1832, when a Greek monarchy was established. European sympathizers for the Greek cause included Lord Byron, whose death (1824) at Missolonghi did much to create popular and official support for the Greeks.

● **Greek language ►** An Indo-European language spoken chiefly in Greece and the E Mediterranean islands. Well documented since the 14th century BC (see Linear B), ancient Greek was a highly complex inflected language. It had many dialect forms, the main groupings being Ionic (E Greece and Asia Minor), Aeolic (Boeotia and Thessaly), and Doric (the Peloponnese). From Ionic developed the Attic dialect, centred on Athens, which became the chief literary language of classical Greece. When the Greek city states lost their independence (4th century BC), their dialects gave way to a new common dialect (koine), which became the language of Hellenistic Greece and the New Testament. During the Byzantine Empire, Greek diverged from classical forms, with simplified pronunciations and foreign borrowings. Modern Greek has two widely differing versions: the classically based Katharevusa (purified tongue) used in official publications, and Demotic, the living language of speech, poetry, and fiction.

● **Greek literature ►** The epics of ▷Homer date from the 8th century BC, though their echoes of ▷Mycenaean civilization suggest that they may have existed in oral form for considerably longer. A little later (c. 700) ▷Hesiod's poems portray the lives and concerns of farmers. ▷Archilochus of Paros and Alcman (both 7th century) were early masters of lyric verse; they were followed by ▷Alcaeus, ▷Sappho, ▷Solon, and ▷Anacreon in the 6th century and ▷Pindar in the early 5th century. Incipient philosophical speculation in 6th-century Ionia stimulated the development of prose, but the earliest prose work to survive entire is the mid-5th-century history of ▷Herodotus. After the defeat of the Persians (480 BC) Attic writers brought about the flower-

ing of classical Greek literature; major figures were the tragedians ▷Aeschylus, ▷Sophocles, and ▷Euripides, the comedian ▷Aristophanes (see Old Comedy), and the historian ▷Thucydides. Prose achieved its acme in the 4th century with the works of ▷Plato, ▷Xenophon, and the orators ▷Isocrates and ▷Demosthenes. During the Hellenistic age Alexandria became the cultural centre of the Greek world; it was the home of the poets ▷Apollonius of Rhodes and ▷Callimachus, as well as of mathematicians, astronomers, and others who enhanced the status of Greek as a scientific and scholarly medium. Notable among Hellenistic writers elsewhere were the Sicilians ▷Theocritus and Moschus (c. 150 BC). Under the Roman Empire Greek remained an international literary language, as the works of ▷Marcus Aurelius, ▷Plutarch, and the Greek Church Fathers testify. After the 6th century AD, when Byzantium became the centre of Greek culture, histories (see Procopius), theological works, and scholarly commentaries became the main output. The 10th-century compilation known as the Greek Anthology comprises over 6000 poems ranging in date from the 7th century BC to the 10th century AD. A popular (demotic) tradition also survived, which expressed itself in folksong and epic (e.g. the late 10th-century epic, Digenis Akritas) and led eventually to modern Greek literature. ▷See also Greek language.

● **Greek Orthodox Church ►** Strictly, the Orthodox Church in Greece, although the term is often applied to the ▷Orthodox Churches as a whole, to distinguish them from the Latin Church of the West. The Church in Greece dates from the 1st century and St Paul's activities, especially at Corinth. Under the patriarchate of Constantinople Greece was, from the acceptance of Christianity by ▷Constantine, one of the main Christian centres. With the eventual fall of Constantinople to the Turks, it ceased to be identified with the Byzantine Empire and is now a self-governing Church, the see of Athens holding a primacy of honour after the separation from the patriarchate of Constantinople in 1833.

● **Greek-Persian Wars ►** An intermittent conflict between the Greeks and Persians. Persian encroachment on Greek territory began in 499 BC, when the Greek cities of ▷Ionia revolted against their Persian overlords and were crushed by ▷Darius I. In 490 the Persians were defeated by a small force of Athenians at ▷Marathon. In 480 ▷Xerxes I crossed the Hellespont with a large force. The Greeks and Persians fought at ▷Thermopylae, where the Spartans (under ▷Leonidas I) heroically held the pass. Xerxes now attacked Attica and Athens was evacuated. At the battle of ▷Salamis the Persians were defeated by the Greek fleet under ▷Themistocles and were again defeated at ▷Plataea (479). Intermittent warfare continued until 449, when the Persians abandoned hope of annexing Greece.

● **Greek religion ►** The polytheistic religion of ancient Greece. From at least the time of Homer (9th century BC) the myths and deities of the various Greek states were integrated into a more or less coherent system, with a pantheon of 12 anthropomorphic gods who lived on Mount Olympus: ▷Zeus, ▷Hera, ▷Poseidon, ▷Athena, ▷Apollo, ▷Artemis, ▷Hephaestus, ▷Aphrodite, ▷Ares, ▷Demeter, ▷Hermes, and ▷Hestia. All these had appropriate festivals and observances throughout Greece. The orgiastic rites of ▷Cybele and ▷Dionysus were slightly later imports from Asia Minor. Deified heroes, such as ▷Heracles, were also worshipped and there were innumerable local cults for lesser supernatural beings, such as the ▷nymphs. For those who found the traditional eschatology of ▷Hades unsatisfactory, the ▷mysteries held a powerful attraction. During the Hellenistic age king-worship, another oriental import, became important. Religious centres honoured throughout Greece included ▷Delphi, ▷Delos, Dodona, ▷Epidauros, and ▷Olympia. The forms of the ancient religion were not finally abolished until the Christian emperors closed these shrines (4th century AD), and even today local saints sometimes retain some of the attributes of the pagan gods.

● **Greeley, Horace ►** (1811–72) US political journalist, who in 1841 founded the New York Tribune, championing temperance, liberal reforms, and protectionism; Karl Marx was a contributor. In the 1860s Greeley vigorously opposed slavery. He made several attempts to enter politics, unsuccessfully standing as presidential candidate for the Liberal Republican Party in 1872.

● **Green, Henry ►** (Henry Vincent Yorke; 1905–73) British novelist.

He worked for his family engineering business for many years, eventually becoming managing director. His novels, satires of English social life written in a distinctive impersonal style, include *Living* (1929), *Loving* (1945), *Back* (1946), and *Concluding* (1948).

● **green algae** ► ▷Algae of the phylum *Chlorophyta* (about 6000 species), which are bright green, owing to the predominance of the green pigment chlorophyll. Green algae range from simple unicellular organisms, for example *Chlamydomonas*, to complex seaweeds, for example ▷sea lettuce. They are aquatic (mainly freshwater) or terrestrial in moist areas. Reproduction can be sexual or asexual.

● **Greenaway, Kate** ► (1846–1901) British artist and book illustrator. The daughter of an engraver and draughtsman, she is famous for her charming representation of children in such books as *Kate Greenaway's Birthday Album* and *The Language of Flowers*.

● **Greenaway, Peter** ► (1942–) British film director, noted for his complex cerebral style. Films include *The Draughtsman's Contract* (1982), *Drowning by Numbers* (1988), *Prospero's Books* (1991), *The Pillow Book* (1996), and *8½ Women* (1999).

● **Green Bay** ► 44 32N 88 00W A city and port in the USA, in E Wisconsin at the head of an inlet of Lake Michigan. Its main industries are paper manufacture and food and dairy processing. Green Bay is the home of the National Railroad Museum. Population (1996 est): 102 076.

● **green belt** ► A zone of open, mostly agricultural, land surrounding a town to prevent it from spreading uncontrollably. The concept, which has biblical origins, has been cherished, usually unsuccessfully, by utopians throughout the centuries. Sir Ebenezer ▷Howard's ▷garden cities of the early 1900s provided the first practical examples; in 1935 the London County Council initiated the steps towards a London green belt that were realized in the Green Belt Act (1938) and the Town and Country Planning Act (1947). Since the 1950s successive governments have been made aware of the shortcomings of the concept—unacceptable overcrowding for the poor inside the belt combined with spacious acres for the privileged within the green zone. Restrictions were considerably relaxed in 1987 and the 1990s saw growing pressure for major residential developments in the countryside (necessary not because of a growing population but because of the trend for people to live in single-occupant households). Since 1997 government policy has strongly favoured the reclamation of vacant "brown-field" sites within urban areas rather than further incursions into the countryside, not least because of a wish to reduce car dependence.

● **greenbrier** ► A green-stemmed often evergreen vinelike plant, *Smilax rotundifolia*, that grows in North American woods and thickets, also called catbrier. The leaves are heart-shaped and leathery, and the plant climbs by means of tendrils. The six-part flowers are borne in stalked clusters in the leaf axils and produce blue-black berries. Family: *Liliaceae*.

● **Greene, (Henry) Graham** ► (1904–91) British novelist. His first novel, *The Man Within*, was published in 1929. He was converted to Roman Catholicism in 1927, and an intense concern with questions of morality is central in many of his novels, including *Brighton Rock* (1938), *The Power and the Glory* (1940), *The End of the Affair* (1951), *The Honorary Consul* (1973), *The Human Factor* (1978), *Monsignor Quixote* (1982), and *The Captain and the Enemy* (1988). He also wrote literary thrillers, which he labelled "entertainments," including *The Ministry of Fear* (1943), *The Third Man* (1950), and *Our Man in Havana* (1958). His other works include plays, film scripts, short stories, essays, and a biography, *Getting to Know the General* (1984). He was appointed to the OM in 1986.

● **Greene, Nathaneal** ► (1742–86) American general, who commanded (1780–83) the southern army in the American Revolution in succession to Horatio ▷Gates. Greene conducted a strategic retreat into Virginia and by long marches and skilful deployments so exhausted the pursuing British that he was able to retake the Carolinas.

● **Greene, Robert** ► (c. 1558–92) English pamphleteer and dramatist. His works include *Pandosto* (1588), a prose pastoral, the source of Shakespeare's *A Winter's Tale*, and the romantic comedy *Friar Bacon and Friar Bungay* (c. 1591). His pamphlet, *A Notable Discovery of Cosenage* (1592), describes Elizabethan low life. *Greene's Groatsworth of Wit* (1592), in which he repented of his dissolute life, contains references to his contemporaries, including Shakespeare.

● **greenfinch** ► A Eurasian ▷finch, *Carduelis chloris*, about 14 cm long with an olive-green body and a pale bill. The male has a bright yellow-green breast and both sexes show bright-yellow wing flashes in flight.

● **greenfly** ▷*See* aphid.

● **greengage** ► A bush or small tree, *Prunus italica*, related to the ▷plum, probably native to Asia Minor and widely cultivated. It bears round green fruits, often tinged with red, which are scented and used in preserves and for canning.

● **Greenham Common** ► A US airbase near Newbury in S England, designated as the first UK site for cruise missiles. A protest peace camp set up in 1981 by women, who organized demonstrations of up to 30 000 people, failed to prevent the deployment of the missiles in 1983. The base closed and the missiles were removed by 1991.

● **greenheart** ► An evergreen South American timber tree, *Nectandria rodiaei*, native to Guiana, also called sweetwood or bebeeru. Up to 30 m tall, it has small flowers and the fruit is surrounded by an acorn-like cup. The wood, which is very hard, is used for underwater construction and ships. Family: *Lauraceae* (laurel family).

● **greenhouse effect** ► An atmospheric effect in which some of the energy of ultraviolet radiation and light from the sun is retained by the earth as heat. The radiation is transmitted through the atmosphere to the earth's surface, where it is reradiated as longer wavelength infrared radiation. This is only partially transmitted back into space as some of it is absorbed by atmospheric gases ("greenhouse gases"), especially carbon dioxide and methane, causing a heating effect. The phenomenon takes its name from a greenhouse, in which a similar effect occurs. In recent years the amount of carbon dioxide in the atmosphere has greatly increased, due to increased use of fossil fuels, which now produce some 2.5×10^{10} tonnes CO_2 per year. The burning of forests (*see* deforestation) has produced a further 1×10^{10} tonnes CO_2 per year and reduced the amount of CO_2 absorbed by plants (for ▷photosynthesis) from the atmosphere; at the same time damage to the ▷ozone layer has increased the amount of ultraviolet radiation reaching the earth. The result is **global warming** (in the past century the world's average temperature has risen by 0.6%, 1998 and 2001 being the warmest years since records began in 1860). In 1997 a world conference on climatic change was held in Kyoto, Japan; this eventually resulted in the ▷Kyoto agreement, under which 38 nations agreed to reduce greenhouse gases by 5.2% by 2012. The USA opted out of the agreement before it was finalized in July 2001. □ p. 540.

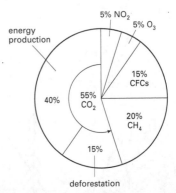

greenhouse effect ► The extent to which the various greenhouse gases cause global warming, taking into account their abundance in the atmosphere and their effectiveness as infrared absorbers.

● **Greenland** ► (Danish name: Grønland; Greenlandic name: Kalaallit Nunaat) A large island off NE North America bounded by the N Atlantic Ocean and the Greenland and Norwegian Seas. Lying chiefly within the Arctic Circle, it is largely covered by a vast ice cap through which nunataks protrude around its rim. Many glaciers emerge from this, including the Humboldt Glacier, breaking off to form icebergs along the coast. Inuit form about 80% of the population, the remainder being chiefly Danish.

Economy: fishing is the chief occupation, principally for cod and halibut but other catches include shrimps and sea trout. Whaling and seal hunting have declined in recent years. The harsh environment makes agriculture difficult but sheep are reared in the SW. Greenland possesses potentially important mineral resources, notably lead, zinc, and uranium. *History*: in about 986 AD the Norwegian Eric the Red discovered the island, which he named Greenland to attract settlers. Norse colonies on the island disappeared during the 15th century and until 1721, when a new Danish settlement was established, the Inuit were the sole inhabitants. A Danish colony from 1721, Greenland became an integral part of Denmark in 1953. In 1979 it gained self-government under Danish sovereignty with its own parliament. In 1985 Greenland left the EC. Prime minister: Jonathan Motzfeldt. Official language: Inupik (Greenland Inuit). Official currency: Danish krone of 100 øre. Area: 2 175 600 sq km (840 000 sq mi). Population (1995): 55 700. Capital: Nuuk.

● **Greenland Sea** ► An extension of the Arctic Ocean, between Greenland, Svalbard, and Iceland. Covered by drifting ice, it links with the Atlantic Ocean.

● **Greenland shark** ► An omnivorous ▷shark, *Somniosus microcephalus*, up to 7 m long, found in deep waters of the N Atlantic and Arctic Oceans. Family: *Squalidae*.

● **green monkey disease** ► An acute, often fatal, viral infection first described in Marburg, Germany (it is sometimes called Marburg disease). It occurs in vervet monkeys and may be transmitted to laboratory workers by contact.

● **Green Mountain Boys** ► Irregular forces formed (1770) and originally commanded by Ethan ▷Allen to oppose colonial New York's claim to control the Green Mountain region (now Vermont). They fought in the American Revolution, notably at Fort Ticonderoga (1775) and Bennington (1777). Their purpose was attained when Vermont was granted statehood (1791).

● **Greenock** ► 55 57N 4 45W A town in W central Scotland, in Inverclyde council area on the Clyde estuary. Its industries include engineering and chemicals. James Watt was born here. Population (1991): 50 013.

● **Green Party** ► A British political party, founded in 1973 as the Ecology Party. Dedicated to protecting the environment, the party attracted growing support in the 1980s before being eclipsed by the increasingly "green" attitudes of the major political parties. Similar parties have achieved greater power in Europe, notably in Germany, where several leading Greens were included in the centre-left coalition formed by Gerhard Schröder in 1998.

● **Greenpeace movement** ► An international environmental pressure group founded in 1971 to protest at nuclear tests in the Aleutian Islands. It campaigns primarily against nuclear power, dumping nuclear waste, and commercial whaling. Its use of direct action has sometimes led to confrontation. In 1985 French saboteurs sank a Greenpeace vessel in New Zealand, killing one crew member.

● **Green Revolution** ▷*See* agriculture; arable farming.

● **Greensboro** ► 36 03N 79 50W A city in the USA, in North Carolina. It is a major centre of the cotton, textile, and rayon industries. Population (1994 est): 196 167.

● **greenshank** ► A bird, *Tringa nebularia*, that breeds in N Eurasian moorland and tundra and winters in South Africa and S Eurasia. It is 30 cm long and greyish in colour with greenish legs, a white rump, and a long slightly upturned blue-grey bill. Family: *Scolopacidae* (sandpipers).

● **green turtle** ► A large brown-green marine turtle, *Chelonia mydas*, which has green fat and has been used to make turtle soup. Up to 1 m long and weighing up to 140 kg, they occur in warm Atlantic coastal waters feeding on marine algae and migrate to lay their eggs on Central American beaches. The green turtle is an ▷endangered species. □reptile.

● **Greenwich** ► A borough of E Greater London, on the S bank of the River Thames. Created in 1965 from the former metropolitan boroughs of Greenwich and ▷Woolwich, it has important royal and maritime connections. The first Renaissance building in England, the Queen's House designed by Inigo ▷Jones (1616), was completed in 1637. The Greenwich Royal Hospital, designed by ▷Wren, became the Royal Naval College in 1873. Wren also designed the original ▷Royal Greenwich Observatory. The tea clipper *Cutty Sark* and Sir Francis Chichester's *Gipsy Moth IV* are at Greenwich Pier. In 1997–99 a massive dome was built here to commemorate the millennium (*see* Millennium Dome). Area: 46 sq km (18 sq mi). Population (1995): 211 400.

● **Greenwich Mean Time** ► (GMT) The local time at Greenwich, London, located on the 0° meridian (*see* latitude and longitude), from which the standard times of different areas of the globe are calculated, 15° longitude representing one hour in time. In 1986 it was succeeded by coordinated ▷universal time (UTC).

● **Greenwich Village** ► A residential section of New York City (USA), in Manhattan. It became a haunt of authors and artists early in

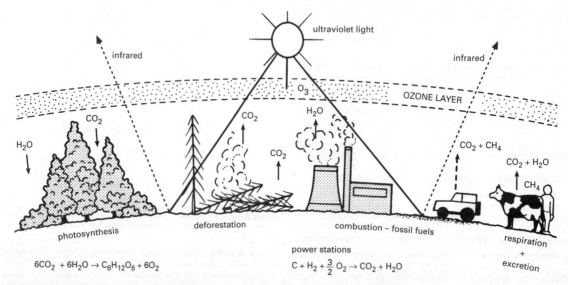

greenhouse effect ► The sun's ultraviolet light is reradiated as infrared radiation, some of which is absorbed by the greenhouse gases (CO_2, CH_4, etc.).

the 20th century, acquiring a reputation for bohemianism. It is the site of the campus of New York University.

● **Greenwood, Walter** ▶ (1903–74) British novelist. *Love on the Dole* (1933) was based on his own experience of unemployment. Later novels include *How the Other Man Lives* (1959).

● **Greer, Germaine** ▶ (1939–) Australian feminist writer. A leader in the women's movement since 1970, her books include *The Female Eunuch* (1970), *Sex and Destiny* (1984), and *The Whole Woman* (1998). In *The Change* (1991) she discussed attitudes to the menopause and the ageing of women.

● **Gregorian calendar** ▷*See* calendar.

● **Gregorian chant** ▶ The official liturgical ▷plainchant of the Roman Catholic Church as codified during the papacy of ▷Gregory I. It consists of single unaccompanied melodic lines based on a system of ▷modes and flexible rhythms.

● **Gregory I, St** ▶ (c. 540–604 AD) Pope (590–604), known as Gregory the Great. Of senatorial rank, he gave himself to charitable works and was a monk before becoming a papal official. As pope he reorganized and increased papal power in Italy, making peace with the Lombards and limiting imperial authority over the Church. He reformed the papal states and sponsored ▷Augustine (of Canterbury) in his mission to convert England. Gregory's many pastoral and doctrinal works were of considerable influence, and he introduced the use of ▷Gregorian chant into the liturgy. He was canonized on his death. Feast day: 3 Sept.

● **Gregory VII, St** ▶ (Hildebrand; c. 1021–85) Pope (1073–85). Before his election he worked closely with ▷Leo IX and Alexander II to reform the Church. As pope, he condemned simony, lay investiture, and clerical marriage. He was ultimately largely successful in asserting the independence of the Church from lay control but during his lifetime he created considerable opposition, especially in France and Germany, where Emperor ▷Henry IV declared his deposition (1076). He in turn excommunicated Henry and released his subjects from allegiance. Henry was soon forced to accept the pope's reforms and submitted to him at Canossa (1077). The conflict continued, however, when the emperor appointed Wibert, Archbishop of Ravenna, antipope (1080), invaded Italy, and captured Rome (1084). Gregory was rescued by Norman troops whom he had summoned but was nevertheless forced to flee from Rome. He died at Salerno. Feast day: 25 May.

● **Gregory IX** ▶ (Ugolino of Segni; c. 1148–1241) Pope (1227–41). He was employed as a papal legate by his uncle, ▷Innocent III, and preached the fifth Crusade (1217). On his election as pope, he immediately excommunicated Emperor ▷Frederick II for his delay in fulfilling crusading vows. His papacy was marked by conflict with the emperor, and he died while Frederick was besieging Rome. He was a noted canon lawyer and was a friend of St ▷Francis of Assisi, whom he canonized.

● **Gregory XIII** ▶ (Ugo Buoncompagni; 1502–85) Pope (1572–85). His pontificate was marked by support of the ▷Counter-Reformation and the sponsorship of colleges and reformed orders, especially the ▷Jesuits and the Oratorians. He founded the English College at Rome (1579) and was responsible for instituting the Gregorian ▷calendar (1582).

● **Gregory, Lady Augusta** ▶ (1852–1932) Irish theatre patron and dramatist. With W. B. Yeats, in 1899 she founded the Irish Dramatic Movement, a national theatre company that moved into the Abbey Theatre in 1904. She collaborated with Yeats on *The Pot of Broth* (1902) and *Cathleen ni Houlihan* (1902) and wrote many comedies and translations, notably of Molière. Her own plays include *Spreading the News* (1904) and *The Rising of the Moon* (1907).

● **Gregory, James** ▶ (1638–75) Scottish mathematician and astronomer. He was the first to investigate converging number series, which have an infinite number of terms but a finite sum. He also designed a reflecting ▷telescope, but failed to build it because the glass could not be ground accurately enough. Similar telescopes are still in use.

● **Gregory of Nazianzus, St** ▶ (c. 330–c. 389 AD) Cappadocian

Father of the Church, son of the Bishop of Nazianzus. He was educated in Athens, where he became a friend of St ▷Basil the Great. With Basil and St ▷Gregory of Nyssa he defended orthodox Christianity against ▷Arianism. He was Bishop of Caesarea from 370 to 379 and briefly served as Patriarch of Constantinople in 380. Feast Day: 9 May.

● **Gregory of Nyssa, St** ▶ (c. 335–c. 394 AD) Cappadocian Father of the Church. A leader of the orthodox party, which opposed ▷Arianism, he was made Bishop of Nyssa in 372 by his brother, St ▷Basil the Great. He was deposed in 376 but reinstated in 378 on the death of the Arian emperor, Valens. He wrote many theological works. Feast day: 9 March.

● **Gregory of Tours, St** ▶ (c. 538–594 AD) French churchman and historian; Bishop of Tours (573–94). He is best known for his *Historia Francorum*, which is a history of the world from its creation to the 6th century AD. It is a valuable source of information on early European history. Feast Day: 17 Nov.

● **Grenada** ▶ An island country in the West Indies, in the Windward Islands in the E Caribbean Sea off the NE coast of Venezuela. It also includes some of the Grenadine Islands, the largest of which is Carriacou. The majority of the population is of mixed European and Indian descent.

Economy: largely agricultural; the chief products are cocoa, bananas, citrus fruits, sugar, and nutmeg (the main export). Tourism is of growing importance and fishing is also being developed.

History: reached by Columbus in 1493, it was colonized by the French and ceded to the British in 1763. In 1967 it became an Associated State under the West Indies Act and in 1974, an independent state within the British Commonwealth. In March, 1979, the government of Sir Eric Gairy (1922–) was overthrown in a nearly bloodless coup led by Maurice Bishop (1944–83), who became prime minister. After an uprising of armed forces in 1983, during which Bishop was killed, the USA invaded to protect US interests. The current prime minister, Dr Keith Mitchell, took office following elections in 1995.

Grenada

Head of state	Queen Elizabeth II, represented by the governor-general, Sir Daniel Williams
Official language	English
Official currency	East Caribbean dollar of 100 cents
Area	344 sq km (133 sq mi)
Population (1997 est)	98 400
Capital	St George's

● **grenade** ▶ A small explosive weapon thrown by hand (hand grenade) or fired from a rifle (rifle grenade). It may contain metal fragments to maim or kill or a chemical agent, such as tear gas, or it may be a smoke or fire bomb. Hand grenades have a time fuse, which will make them explode some four seconds after the safety pin has been removed by the thrower. This time is long enough for the missile to reach its target but too short for the enemy to pick it up and throw it back. Grenades were introduced in the late 16th century, when they were used by special units called **grenadiers**. Early grenadiers, chosen for their height, strength, and courage, had special uniforms, higher pay, and a reputation as elite troops. In the British army this reputation remained with the grenadiers until the middle of the 19th century. Grenadiers have since ceased to be special infantrymen, and all ground combat troops are now trained to use grenades.

● **grenadier** ▶ 1. ▷*See* grenade. 2. A carnivorous bottom-dwelling fish, also called rat-tail or torpedo, belonging to a family (*Macrouridae*; about 300 species) found in deep warm and temperate marine waters. It has a stout body, usually 30–60 cm long, with a long ratlike tail and a large head.

● **Grenadine Islands** ▶ A chain of West Indian islets, extending for about 100 km (60 mi) between St Vincent and Grenada and administratively divided between the two.

● **Grenoble** ▶ 45 11N 5 43E A city in SE France, the capital of the Isère department. The capital of the Dauphiné until 1341, it has a cathedral (12th–13th centuries) and a university (1339). It is the principal tourist centre of the French Alps and has metallurgical, textile, cement, and paper industries. It is also the site of a nuclear research centre. Population (1990): 153 973.

● **Grenville, Sir Richard** ▶ (?1541–91) British sailor. In 1585 Grenville commanded the seven ships taking Sir Walter Raleigh's colonists to Virginia. In 1591, as commander of the *Revenge*, he refused to withdraw before a Spanish fleet off the Azores and put four Spanish ships out of action. Eventually prevailed upon to surrender, he died aboard a Spanish ship. The exploit is the subject of Tennyson's ballad *The Revenge*.

● **Grenville, William (Wyndham), Baron** ▶ (1759–1834) British statesman; prime minister (1806–07). He was foreign secretary (1791–1801) under his cousin William ▷Pitt the Younger, with whom he resigned when George III rejected Catholic emancipation. As prime minister he led the coalition Ministry of All the Talents, which took office after Pitt's death and was notable for its abolition of the slave trade (1807). His government fell owing to royal opposition to the Catholic Relief bill. His father **George Grenville** (1712–70) was prime minister from 1763 to 1765. His government, which was hindered by George III's continued reliance on Grenville's predecessor ▷Bute, was noted for its ▷Stamp Act (1765) and prosecution of John ▷Wilkes.

● **Gresham, Sir Thomas** ▶ (c. 1519–79) English financier and philanthropist. He founded Gresham College and the Royal Exchange, both in London, but is best known for the so-called **Gresham's Law**, attributed to him in the 19th century, that "bad money drives out good": if there are two different types of coin in circulation, and one sort of coin is suspected of being debased, the more valuable coin will be hoarded and will eventually disappear from circulation.

● **Gretna Green** ▶ 55 00N 3 04W A village in S Scotland, in Dumfries and Galloway council area on the English border. It is famous as the scene of marriages of eloping English couples following the prohibition of clandestine marriages in England (1753). From 1856 three weeks residence in Scotland was required and in 1939 these marriage ceremonies were declared illegal. Population (1991): 3149.

● **Grétry, André Ernest Modeste** ▶ (1741–1813) Belgian composer, who lived and died in France. One of the leading opera composers of his time, he was an exponent of ▷opéra comique. Of his large output little is known today, although Beecham made well-known arrangements of his music.

● **Greuze, Jean-Baptiste** ▶ (1725–1805) French painter, born in Tournus. Settling in Paris, he achieved early acclaim with his *Father Reading the Bible to His Children* (1755; Louvre). After an unsuccessful attempt at history painting (1769), he concentrated on sentimental and vaguely erotic portraits of girls, e.g. *The Broken Pitcher* (Louvre).

● **Greville, Fulke, 1st Baron Brooke** ▶ (1554–1628) English poet and biographer. A diplomat and administrator, he was chancellor of the exchequer from 1614 to 1622. He wrote a collection of sonnets, *Caelica* (1633), but is now mainly remembered as the author of *The Life of the Renowned Sir Philip Sidney* (published 1652), a memoir of his friend.

● **Grey, Dame Beryl** ▶ (1927–   ) British ballet dancer. She was prima ballerina with the Sadler's Wells Company (1942–57) and directed the London Festival Ballet (1968–79).

● **Grey, Charles, 2nd Earl** ▶ (1764–1845) British statesman, who as Whig prime minister (1830–34) secured the passage of the parliamentary ▷Reform Act of 1832 by persuading William IV to create sufficient new peers to carry the bill through the House of Lords. His son **Henry George, 3rd Earl Grey** (1802–94) was Whig colonial secretary (1846–52) and, in advance of his time, advocated colonial self-government. The 2nd earl's nephew **Edward, 1st Viscount Grey of Fallodon** (1862–1933) was Liberal (formerly termed Whig) foreign secretary from 1905 to 1916. He negotiated the ▷Triple Entente of Britain, France, and Russia (1904–07) and supported France against Germany in the Morocco crises of 1905–06 and 1911. At the outbreak of World War I he remarked: "The lamps are going out all over Europe; we shall not see them lit again in our lifetime."

● **Grey, Sir George** ▶ (1812–98) British colonial administrator. After serving as governor of South Australia (1841–45) he was governor of New Zealand (1845–53), where he suppressed the initial hostilities of the ▷Maori Wars. He subsequently fostered good relations with the Maoris before being posted to Cape Colony, where as governor (1854–61) he dealt effectively with hostilities between Africans and Europeans. He was again governor of New Zealand (1861–68) following the resumption of the Maori Wars and was later prime minister of New Zealand (1877–79). He retired to Britain in 1894.

● **Grey, Lady Jane** ▶ (1537–54) Queen of England for nine days (1553). On the death of Edward VI, Lady Jane, the Protestant great-granddaughter of ▷Henry VII, was proclaimed queen by the Duke of ▷Northumberland in preference to Mary, who was the rightful heiress but a Catholic. However, Mary had popular support and Jane abdicated. She was executed for treason with her husband Lord Guildford Dudley, Northumberland's son.

● **greyhound** ▶ An ancient breed of dog used for hare coursing and racing. It has a slender deep-chested streamlined body with long legs and a long muscular neck. The short smooth coat can be of various colours. Greyhounds can reach speeds of up to 70 km per hour. Height: 71–76 cm (dogs); 68–71 cm (bitches).

● **greyhound racing** ▶ (or dog racing) A form of racing popular for betting, in which greyhounds pursue an electrically propelled mechanical hare round a circular or oval track. The sport evolved from ▷coursing in the USA in the early 20th century and is especially popular in the UK and Australia. Races may be on the flat or over hurdles, with distances ranging from 210 m (230 yd) to 1100 m (1200 yd). ▷*See also* gambling.

● **greylag goose** ▶ A grazing ▷goose, *Anser anser*, occurring in N and E Europe and central Asia. 75–87 cm long, it has a heavy orange bill and is dark grey above with pale wings, a finely barred neck, and pink legs.

● **greywacke** ▶ (or graywacke) A dark-coloured sedimentary rock with sand-sized angular rock particles in a finer matrix. Greywackes display a wide range of sedimentary structures and are commonly found in geosynclines.

● **gribble** ▶ A wood-boring marine crustacean of the genus *Limnoria* (about 20 species). It feeds on algae, driftwood, and the submerged sections of docks and piers. *L. lignorum*, common in the N hemisphere, has a grey body up to 5 mm long. Order: ▷*Isopoda*.

● **Grieg, Edvard Hagerup** ▶ (1843–1907) Norwegian composer, who studied in Leipzig and Copenhagen. He spent the latter part of his life in a house called Troldhaugen near Bergen and is buried there. The influence of Norwegian folk music is apparent in many of his works, which include the *Lyric Pieces* (for piano; 1867–1901), a very popular piano concerto (1868), incidental music to Ibsen's play *Peer Gynt* (1876), chamber music, and many songs.

● **Grierson, John** ▶ (1898–1972) British film director. He developed the concept of ▷documentary film and helped to establish film production units in Britain, Canada, and the USA. His own documentary films include *Drifters* (1929), *Industrial Britain* (1933), and *Granton Trawler* (1934).

● **griffin** ▶ A mythological creature with the head and wings of an eagle, the body of a lion, and often a serpent's tail. It is common in many ancient eastern mythologies.

● **Griffith, Arthur** ▶ (1872–1922) Irish journalist and nationalist, who organized ▷Sinn Féin in 1905. He was imprisoned three times (1916, 1918–19, 1920–21) by the British authorities. In 1918 Sinn Féin won the majority of parliamentary seats in Ireland and declared a republic, of which Griffith was acting head during ▷De Valera's absence abroad (1919–20). In 1921 he led the Irish delegation to the conference that determined the treaty establishing the Irish Free State. On De Valera's rejection of the terms, Griffith was elected (1922) president of the Free State assembly (the Dáil Éireann) but died later that year.

● **Griffith, D(avid) W(ark)** ▶ (1875–1948) US film director. His intuitive understanding of the artistic potential of the cinema and his innovations in editing and narrative techniques made him the most influential pioneer of the cinema in the USA. His major films include *The Birth of a Nation* (1915), an ambitious epic concerning the Civil War, *Intolerance* (1916), *Broken Blossoms* (1919), and *Isn't Life Wonderful* (1924).

● **griffon** ▶ (dog) A breed of toy dog originating in Belgium and of terrier ancestry. It has a square compact body, a docked tail, and a large head covered with long coarse hair. The coat is either rough and wiry or short and tight and may be red, black, or black and tan. Weight: 2–5 kg.

● **griffon vulture** ▶ One of the largest Old World ▷vultures, *Gyps fulvus*. It is 100 cm long and occurs in mountainous regions of S Europe, South Africa, and Asia. It is grey-brown with darker wingtips, a white head and ruff, and whitish downy patches on the neck.

● **Grignard reagents** ▶ Organomagnesium compounds, discovered by F. A. V. Grignard (1871–1935) and usually prepared by adding an organic halide to magnesium under ether. They are invaluable in a host of organic syntheses, giving addition products with almost all groups.

● **Grillparzer, Franz** ▶ (1791–1872) Austrian dramatist. He worked in government service until his retirement in 1856 and was appointed court dramatist at the Hofburgtheater after the success of his first tragedy, *Die Ahnfrau* (1817). His tragedies ranged from adaptations of Greek myth, such as *The Golden Fleece* (1821), to fantasy plays, such as *A Dream Is Life* (1834).

● **Grimaldi, Joseph** ▶ (1779–1837) British clown. His popular success at Covent Garden between 1806 and 1823 was based on his skills as a dancer, acrobat, and singer, as well as his instinct for pathos and comedy.

● **Grimm** ▶ Two brothers, German philologists and folklorists. After early work on medieval German texts, **Jakob Grimm** (1785–1863) and **Wilhelm Grimm** (1786–1859) set about collecting German folktales, published in 1812–14 as *Kinder- und Hausmärchen*. The *Deutsche Grammatik* (1819, 1822) is a historical and descriptive German grammar containing observations on the regularity of sound changes in Indo-European languages, known as **Grimm's law**. Their *Deutsches Wörterbuch* is a historical and descriptive German dictionary.

● **Grimmelshausen, Hans Jacob Christoph von** ▶ (c. 1625– 76) German novelist. Orphaned when a child, he served in the Imperial and Swedish armies during the Thirty Years' War and later worked as a steward, bailiff, and innkeeper. His picaresque *Simplicissimus* novels (1669–72) are a realistic and satirical record of his unsettled times.

● **Grimond, Jo(seph), Baron** ▶ (1913–93) British politician; leader of the Liberal Party (1956–67). He campaigned for British membership of the EEC and developed the idea of a "copartnership in industry" of management and labour, contributing greatly to Liberal successes in the general elections of 1959 and 1964. He resigned the leadership following electoral reverses in 1966.

● **Grimsby** ▶ 53 35N 0 05W A seaport in NE England, in North East Lincolnshire unitary authority, Lincolnshire, near the mouth of the Humber estuary. Although it is the largest fishing port in England, the extension of Iceland's fishing limits (1975–76) combined with overfishing in many of the traditional grounds has led to a considerable reduction in the size of the fishing fleet. Population (1991): 90 703.

● **Grindelwald** ▶ 46 38N 8 03E An alpine village in central Switzerland, in the Grindelwald Valley. It is a major mountaineering centre and a summer and winter resort at the foot of the Wetterhorn and Eiger mountains at a height of 1037 m (3402 ft). Population (1989): 3600.

● **Gris, Juan** ▶ (José Victoriano González; 1887–1927) Spanish-born cubist painter, who worked in Paris from 1906. In contrast to ▷Picasso and ▷Braque, his approach to ▷cubism was mathematical; his starting points were simple fragmented shapes from which he developed real objects in geometrically constructed still lifes, landscapes, and portraits. He also promoted the art of collage, created book illustrations, and wrote an influential study of painting entitled *Les Possibilités de la peinture* (1924).

● **grison** ▶ A mammal belonging to the genus *Grison* (2 species) of Central and South America. Grisons are about 60 cm long and greyish black, hunting through forest and grassland for invertebrates and small mammals. Family: ▷*Mustelidae* (weasels, stoats, etc.).

● **Grivas, Georgios** ▶ (1898–1974) Greek general, born in Cyprus. Known as Dighenis, he was the leader of ▷EOKA, which fought for the union of Cyprus with Greece.

● **grizzly bear** ▷*See* brown bear.

● **Grodno** ▶ 53 40N 23 50E A port in W Belarus, on the River Neman. Possessed by Lithuania and then by Poland, it includes a medieval castle and ▷Stephen Báthory's 16th-century palace. It is an important railway centre and major industrial city, producing fertilizers, textiles, food products, and tobacco. Population (1996 est): 301 000.

● **Gromyko, Andrei** ▶ (1909–89) Soviet diplomat; foreign minister (1957–85) and president of the Soviet Union (1985–88). Gromyko began his diplomatic career in 1939 and served as ambassador to the USA (1943–46) and the UK (1952–53). He was Soviet representative at the UN between 1946 and 1949.

● **Groningen** ▶ 53 13N 6 35E A city in the N Netherlands, the capital of Groningen province. It has a notable church (the 15th-century Martinikerk) and a university (1614). An important commercial and market centre, its industries include textiles, clothing, and sugar refining. Population (1996 est): 169 627.

● **Groningen** ▶ A province in the Netherlands, bordering on the North Sea and West Germany. Low lying and fertile, it is intensively cultivated and agriculture forms the chief occupation. Natural gas is extracted at Slochteren. Area: 2350 sq km (900 sq mi). Population (1991): 554 604. Capital: Groningen.

● **Groote Eylandt** ▶ 12 20S 135 15E An Australian island, in the Gulf of Carpentaria off the coast of the Northern Territory. It forms part of the Arnhem Land Aboriginal Reserve. Manganese deposits have recently been discovered and exploited. Area: 2460 sq km (950 sq mi). Population (latest est): 1961.

● **Gropius, Walter** ▶ (1883–1969) German architect, one of the pioneers of the international modern style of architecture. Gropius was influenced by William ▷Morris and Frank Lloyd ▷Wright and trained under ▷Behrens until 1910. His first major building, a factory at Alfeld (1911) is a very early example of the new style. As director of the ▷Bauhaus (1919–28) he was able greatly to influence all aspects of contemporary design. The rise of Nazi power forced him to leave Germany (1934) for England. In 1937 he moved to America, where he spent 14 influential years teaching at Harvard. He continued to design a few buildings, for example the US Embassy in Athens (1960), and to influence European architecture.

● **Gros, Antoine Jean, Baron** ▶ (1771–1835) French painter. A pupil of ▷David, he later travelled with Napoleon's armies, painting such scenes as *Napoleon Visiting the Plague-Stricken at Jaffa* (1804; Louvre). Although initially successful under the restored Bourbons, he fell into obscurity in the 1820s and finally drowned himself. His style, influenced by that of ▷Rubens, anticipates the work of ▷Delacroix and ▷Géricault.

● **grosbeak** ▶ A finch with a particularly heavy bill used to crack open hard seeds and nuts. The name is given to birds of several genera found in N Eurasia, America, and the tropics. The reddish-brown Eurasian pine grosbeak (*Pinicola enucleator*) uses its bill as a hammer to obtain seeds from pine cones.

● **gross domestic product** ▷*See* gross national product.

● **Grosseteste, Robert** ▶ (c. 1175–1253) English ecclesiastical reformer and scholar; Bishop of Lincoln (1235–53). Grosseteste brought about many reforms in his diocese and was a regular and stringent visitor of monasteries. His opposition to clerical laxity and nepotism led him to quarrel with both his chapter and the papacy. His writings included translations of the church fathers and philosophical commentaries. His scientific experiments inspired Roger ▷Bacon.

● **Grossglockner** ▶ 47 05N 12 44E The highest mountain in Austria, in the Alps. The Grossglockner Road (built 1930–35) crosses it, rising to 2576 m (7852 ft). Height: 3797 m (12 457 ft).

● **Grossmith, George** ▶ (1847–1912) British singer and entertainer. From 1877, he played in many of the main roles in the operas of Gilbert and Sullivan. His brother **Weedon Grossmith** (1854–1915) wrote and acted in social comedies. They collaborated on an extremely successful novel, *Diary of a Nobody* (1892), which satirized lower-middle-class pretensions.

● **gross national product** ► (GNP) A measure of the total annual output of a country, including net income from abroad; it provides a measure of the economic strength of that country. GNP can be calculated in three ways: based on income, output, or expenditure. If income is used as the basis, all incomes accruing to residents of the country as a result of economic activity (excluding, for instance, pensions) are summed (national income is thus synonymous with GNP calculated in this way). On the basis of output, the value added to a product at each stage of production is summed. If expenditure is used, the value of all consumption products is calculated. All three methods should give the same result. **Gross domestic product** (GDP) is GNP excluding net income from abroad and gives some indication of the strength of industry within a country. **Net national product** differs from GNP in that it makes a provision for ▷depreciation, i.e. the using up of the country's capital stock.

● **Grosz, George** ► (1893–1959) German painter and draughtsman, born in Berlin. A member of the ▷dada art movement, he is famous for his bitter satirical depictions of war, the bourgeoisie, the church, and German social evils. He was fined and charges of blasphemy were brought against him because of his work. He emigrated to the USA in 1932.

● **Grotefend, Georg Friedrich** ► (1775–1853) German philologist. He did important work on ancient ▷Italic languages, but after 1800 was increasingly occupied with attempts to decipher Persian ▷cuneiform inscriptions. He established several facts, including the alphabetic (as opposed to syllabic) nature of the characters, which facilitated their successful decipherment by ▷Rawlinson.

● **Grotius, Hugo** ► (or Huig de Groot; 1583–1645) Dutch jurist and diplomat, the founder of international law. Sentenced to life imprisonment in 1619 by Prince Maurice of Nassau for his support of the Arminian faith in the religious controversies of the time, he escaped to France in 1621. There he wrote his famous *De jure belli et pacis* (1625), arguing that natural law should be applied to nations as well as individuals and that war should only be waged for justified causes. He was Swedish ambassador to France from 1635 until his death.

● **ground beetle** ► A heavily armoured long-legged beetle belonging to a family (*Carabidae*; 25 000 species) that is particularly common in temperate regions. Ground beetles are dark in colour or have a metallic sheen and are from 2 to 85 mm long. Most are nocturnal and can be found under stones, logs, and debris during the day. The adults and most larvae are active carnivores, preying on insects, slugs, and snails. ▷*See also* bombardier beetle.

● **ground bug** ► A ▷plant bug belonging to the worldwide famiy *Lygaeidae* (about 3000 species). Ground bugs have elongated brown or black bodies, 3–15 mm long, often with red markings. They live in moss or rubbish or under stones or low bushes and feed on a variety of plants, in many cases becoming serious pests (*see* chinch bug).

● **ground elder** ► A perennial herbaceous plant, *Aegopodium podagraria*, also called goutweed, bishop's weed, or herb Gerard, common in Europe on waste ground and as a garden weed. 49–100 cm tall, it has compound leaves with three leaflets (like those of elder) and umbrella-like clusters of small white flowers. The leaves may be eaten as a salad or vegetable. Family: ▷*Umbelliferae*.

● **groundhog** ▷*See* marmot.

● **ground ivy** ► A creeping perennial herb, *Glechoma hederacea* (or *Nepeta glechoma*), found in woods and grasslands across Eurasia. It has long-stalked heart-shaped toothed leaves and its stems, 10–30 cm high, bear groups of tubular violet two-lipped flowers. Family: ▷*Labiatae*.

● **groundnut** ► The fruit of *Arachis hypogea*, also called peanut or earthnut, native to tropical South America but widely cultivated in the tropics. The plant is an erect or creeping annual, 30–45 cm high, with compound leaves and yellow flowers. After fertilization the flower stalk elongates, pushing the developing pod below the soil to ripen under ground. The pod has a thin spongy wall and contains one to three seeds (the nuts), which are highly nutritious. They are used in cookery, canned, and made into peanut butter and groundnut oil (used for cooking and in margarine). Family: ▷*Leguminosae*.

● **groundsel** ► A weedy herbaceous plant of the genus *Senecio*, especially *S. vulgaris*, 8–45 cm high and common in Eurasia and N Africa. It has lobed toothed leaves and small yellow flower heads, which lack ray florets and are almost enclosed by the sepals. Family: ▷*Compositae*.

● **ground squirrel** ► A ▷squirrel that lives in an underground burrow rather than in a tree. Ground squirrels have short strong legs, small ears, and shorter tails than tree squirrels, inhabiting open country in North America, Eurasia, and Africa. Chief genera: *Citellus* (34 species), *Lariscus* (2 species), *Xerus* (4 species). ▷*See also* prairie dog; chipmunk; souslik; marmot.

● **groundwater** ► The water that has percolated into the ground and become trapped within pores, cracks, and fissures. It is important in ▷weathering processes through its chemical effects. With depth the ▷water table is reached, below which all pore spaces are filled.

● **grouper** ► One of several sedentary food and game fish of the family *Serranidae* (*see* sea bass), especially the genera *Epinephelus* and *Mycteroperca*, widely distributed in warm seas. Groupers have a dull-green or brown heavy body, up to or exceeding 2 m long, and a large mouth. Some are poisonous when consumed.

● **Group Theatre** ► **1.** A US theatre company founded in 1929 and dedicated to the production of socially relevant plays and the development of ▷Stanislavsky's theories of "method" acting. It produced many of the plays of the US playwright Clifford Odets (1906–63), notably *Waiting for Lefty* (1935), before disbanding in 1940. **2.** A British theatre society founded in 1933. Among its experimental productions of the 1930s were plays by ▷Auden and ▷Isherwood, T. S. ▷Eliot, and Stephen ▷Spender.

● **group therapy** ► A form of ▷psychotherapy in which several patients meet together to understand and overcome their problems, usually with the help of a therapist. There are many forms of group therapy: sometimes the aim is to increase patients' insight in psychoanalytic terms, sometimes to teach social skills, sometimes to act out distressing events from the past, and sometimes to support one another in overcoming a common problem (such as alcoholism).

● **grouse** ► A fowl-like game bird, 30–88 cm long, belonging to a family (*Tetraonidae*; about 18 species) of the N hemisphere. Grouse are mostly ground-living, with short round wings, a short strong bill, and feathered legs. They are noted for their spectacular courtship displays (called *leks*). The family includes the ▷black grouse, ▷red grouse, and ▷capercaillie of N Europe (including Britain); the ▷ptarmigans; and the North American ruffed grouse (*Bonasa umbellus*) and ▷sage grouse. In Britain the grouse-shooting season is from 12 Aug to 10 Dec. Order: *Galliformes*. ▷*See also* gamebird.

● **Grove, Sir George** ► (1820–1900) British musicologist, founder and first editor of *Grove's Dictionary of Music and Musicians* (1879–89). A Londoner, he trained and practised as a civil engineer. His interest in the arts led to extensive musical and biblical research during which he travelled widely. He was founder and first director (1883–94) of the Royal College of Music and was knighted in 1883. *The New Grove Dictionary of Music and Musicians* was published in 1980.

● **Groves, Sir Charles** ► (1915–92) British conductor. Trained at the Royal College of Music, he became successively conductor of the BBC Northern Symphony Orchestra, the Bournemouth Symphony Orchestra, and the Royal Liverpool Philharmonic Orchestra. Knighted in 1973, he was musical director of English National Opera (1978–79).

● **growth hormone** ► (or somatotrophin) A protein hormone that promotes the metabolic processes involved in growth of bone and muscle. It is secreted by the pituitary gland and stimulates protein synthesis, mobilizes fat reserves, increases glucose levels in the blood, and affects mineral metabolism. Lack of growth hormone in children causes dwarfism. Somatotropin is a genetically engineered form of growth hormone used to treat such children.

● **growth rings** ▷*See* annual rings.

● **Grozny** ▶ 43 21N 45 42E A city in S Russia, the capital of Chechenia, in one of the country's oldest and richest oil-producing areas. In 1994–95 conflict between Russia and Chechen separatists left Grozny devastated. It was the de facto capital of independent Chechenia from 1995 until 1999–2000, when Russian troops reoccupied the city amidst further devastation. Population (1993 est): 364 000.

● **Grub Street** ▶ A street in E London, now renamed Milton St, associated in the 18th century with writers of little talent, who earned their livings by whatever literary work they could obtain. ▷Pope satirized such hacks in *An Epistle to Dr Arbuthnot* (1755) and the name is referred to in the title of George ▷Gissing's novel *New Grub Street* (1891).

● **Grünewald, Matthias** ▶ (Mathis Gothardt; d. 1528) German painter, born in Würzburg. His earliest known work is *The Mocking of Christ* (c. 1503; Alte Pinakothek, Munich). For much of his career, he was court painter at Mainz. His favourite subject was the crucifixion, of which perhaps his most tragic treatment is the *Isenheim Altarpiece* (Colmar, France), noted also for its dazzling colour. His style, characterized by a distortion of form, influenced 20th-century German expressionists (*see* expressionism).

● **grunt** ▶ A small food fish, belonging to the family *Pomadasyidae* (about 75 species), that can produce piglike grunts. It has a colourful elongated body and a large mouth; it occurs in tropical coastal waters. Order: *Perciformes*.

● **Gruyère** ▶ A district in Switzerland, in the middle Saane Valley, famed for its cheese and cattle.

● **Guadalajara** ▶ 20 30N 103 20W The second largest city in Mexico, at an altitude of 1650 m (5413 ft). Founded by the Spanish (1530), it has several notable buildings including the cathedral (16th–17th centuries) and the Governor's Palace (begun 1763); there are two universities (1792, 1935). Its key position as a communications centre across the Sierra Madre Occidental has led to its rapid expansion in recent years and it now has a large industrial complex. Its handicraft industries (especially glassware and pottery) also remain important. Population (1990): 2 846 000.

● **Guadalajara** ▶ 40 37N 3 10W A town in NE Spain, in New Castile. Its notable palace was virtually destroyed during the Spanish Civil War but has since been restored. Industries include textiles and tanning. Population (1991): 67 200.

● **Guadalcanal** ▶ 9 30S 160 00E The largest of the Solomon Islands, in the S Pacific Ocean. During World War II the first major US offensive in the Pacific against the Japanese took place here; it was captured after six months of jungle fighting (1942–43). Copra, rubber, and some gold are produced. Area: 6475 sq km (2500 sq mi). Population (1997 est): 61 243. Chief settlement: Honiara.

● **Guadalquivir, River** ▶ The main river of S Spain. It flows mainly WSW from the Sierra de Segura to the Gulf of Cádiz and is navigable to Seville by oceangoing vessels. Length: 560 km (348 mi).

● **Guadalupe Hidalgo** ▶ (name from 1931 until 1971: Gustavo A. Madero) 19 29N 99 07W A city in central Mexico, a NE suburb of Mexico City. The Basilica of the Virgin of Guadalupe, which was built after an Indian convert reported seeing a vision of the Virgin Mary here in 1531, is a famous place of pilgrimage. The Treaty of ▷Guadalupe Hidalgo was signed here. Population (1990): 535 332.

● **Guadalupe Hidalgo, Treaty of** ▶ (1848) The treaty that ended the ▷Mexican War. In exchange for $15 million and the payment of the claims of US citizens, the USA received what are now the states of California, Nevada, Utah, parts of Colorado, Wyoming, and Arizona and most of New Mexico.

● **Guadeloupe** ▶ A French overseas region in the West Indies, in the E Caribbean Sea. It comprises two main islands, Grande Terre and Basse Terre, together with the island dependencies of Marie Galante, La Désirade, Îles des Saintes, St Barthélemy, and the N part of ▷St Martin. The economy is based on agriculture; sugar cane is the chief crop. Area: 1702 sq km (657 sq mi). Population (1998 est): 434 000. Capital: Basse-Terre.

● **guaiacum** ▶ A small evergreen tree of the genus *Guaiacum*, especially *G. officinale* of tropical America, also called lignum vitae. It has blue flowers, yellow heart-shaped fruits, and very dense hard wood, used to make pulleys, axles, and bowling balls. The greenish resin is distilled for medicinal use. Family: *Zygophyllaceae*.

● **Guam** ▶ 13 30N 144 40E An island and US unincorporated territory in the West Pacific Ocean, the largest of the Mariana Islands. Mountainous in the S, it is mantled by jungle. Spanish from 1565 to 1898, it was occupied by the Japanese (1941–44). It is a major naval and air base, especially important during the Vietnam War. Industries include ship repairing. Area: 450 sq km (210 sq mi). Population (1992 est): 139 000. Capital: Agaña.

● **guanaco** ▶ A hoofed mammal, *Lama guanacoe*, closely related to the ▷llama and found at altitudes of up to 5000 m in W South America. Red-brown with a pale face and pale underparts, guanacos grow up to 110 cm high at the shoulder and live in small herds on open grassland. Family: *Camelidae*.

● **Guan Di** ▶ (or Kuan Ti) In Chinese mythology, the god of war. A historical figure and hero of numerous romantic exploits, he was captured and executed in 219 AD. His popularity grew until he was pronounced a god in 1594. Various professions and trades, including writers, adopted him as patron and hundreds of temples were built in his honour.

● **Guangdong** ▶ (Kuang-tung *or* Kwangtung) A mountainous province in S China, including Hainan and other islands. Heavily populated, it produces rice, sugar cane, tobacco, silk, fish, timber, and minerals.
History: Chinese from 222 BC, it only came under Chinese cultural influence in the 12th and 13th centuries AD. As China's main trading area, it later had considerable contact with the West and from the mid-19th century overpopulation led to overseas emigration. During the 19th and early 20th centuries it was a centre of revolutionary movements. Area: 231 400 sq km (90 246 sq mi). Population (1996 est): 66 680 000. Capital: Canton.

● **Guangxi Zhuang Autonomous Region** ▶ (or Kwangsi Chuang AR) A mountainous administrative division in S China, on the North Vietnamese border. It has seen great economic growth since 1949, producing sugar cane, rice, timber, manganese, and tin.
History: its non-Chinese minorities have rebelled periodically and the ▷Taiping Rebellion started here (1851). It became a centre of communist opposition to ▷Chiang Kai-shek and heavy fighting against the Japanese invasion took place here during World War II. Area: 220 400 sq km (85 956 sq mi). Population (1996 est): 45 430 000. Capital: Nanning.

● **Guang Xu** ▶ (or Kuang-hsü; 1871–1908) The title of Cai Tian (or Tsai-t'ien) of the Qing dynasty, who became emperor (1875) at the age of four with his aunt ▷Zi Xi as regent. When after coming of age he sponsored the ▷Hundred Days of Reform she imprisoned him for the rest of his life.

● **Guangzhou** ▷*See* Canton.

● **guano** ▶ The accumulated excrement of certain animals, especially seabirds, seals, and bats. It contains 10–18% nitrogen, 8–12% phosphoric acid, and 2–3% potash, according to the age and origin of the deposit. Large amounts were formerly found on islands off the Peruvian and other coasts and it has been widely used as a fertilizer.

● **Guantánamo** ▶ 20 09N 75 14W A city in SE Cuba, N of Guantánamo Bay. It is the centre of an agricultural area producing sugar cane and coffee. Population (1994 est): 207 796.

● **Guan Yin** ▶ (or Kuan Yin) In Chinese Buddhism, the goddess of compassion. She is the same ▷Bodhisattva who was worshipped in India in male form as Avalokiteshvara and in Japan as the multiheaded or multiarmed Kannon. In Chinese art Guan Yin became female in the 12th–13th centuries.

● **guarana** ▶ A climbing plant, *Paullinia cuparia*, of the Amazon Basin, with large compound leaves and clusters of short-stalked flowers. The fruit is about 2 cm long and contains one seed. The seeds are roasted to produce a stimulant drink containing more caffeine than coffee or ground to make bread. Guarana is also a source of starch, gum, saponin, oils, and drugs. Family: *Sapindaceae*.

• Guarani ► A group of South American Indian peoples of Paraguay and neighbouring areas of Brazil and Argentina who speak languages of the Tupian group. About a million Paraguayans speak Guarani. Few now retain their original culture, typical of the tropical forest, based on hunting and maize cultivation, warfare, and cannibalism.

• Guardi, Francesco ► (1712–93) Venetian painter, who studied under and sometimes collaborated with his elder brother, **Giovanni Antonio Guardi** (1699–1760). His views of Venice were sometimes copied from ▷Canaletto but they are distinguished by their romantic style and impressionistic technique.

• guardian angels ► Divine beings that figure in several religions. They derive from the belief that every individual has an angel assigned by God as his guardian. In the Roman Catholic Church they may be invoked as intercessors; feast day: 2 Oct.

• Guarini, Giovanni Battista ► (1538–1612) Italian poet. He served at the court of the Duke of Ferrara and in Rome and Florence. His best-known work, *The Faithful Shepherd* (1590), emulating Torquato ▷Tasso's *Aminta* (1573), helped to establish the genre of pastoral drama.

• Guarini, Guarino ► (1624–83) Italian baroque architect, philosopher, and mathematician. Most of Guarini's work was done in his native Piedmont. Although influenced by ▷Borromini, his work shows great originality and technical skill. Most notable is the church of S Lorenzo, Turin (1668–87).

• Guarneri ► An Italian family of violin makers, famous in the 17th and 18th centuries. The first of the line was **Andrea Guarneri** (d. 1698), who was a pupil (with Stradivari) of Amati in Cremona. Andrea's grandson **Giuseppe Guarneri** (1698–1744), known as "del Gesù," was the most famous member of the family; influenced by the makers of the Brescian school, he produced violins with a characteristically powerful tone, signing them "Guarnerius."

• Guatemala, Republic of ► A country in Central America, on the Pacific Ocean, with a small outlet on the Caribbean Sea. The tropical forests of the Petén in the N and a narrower plain on the Pacific rise to a central mountainous region, containing a fertile plateau. The country is subject to hurricanes and earthquakes, which have caused havoc throughout its history. About half the population are ▷Maya Quiché Indians and most of the rest are of mixed Spanish and Indian descent.

Economy: mainly agricultural, the land being fertile but subject to erosion. The main crops are coffee, sugar, and bananas, which are the principal exports. Essential oils, rubber, chicle, and timber are also produced. Minerals include zinc and lead concentrates. Oil was discovered in 1974 and is now exported. Efforts have been made to promote growth in plastics, as well as more traditional industries. Economic development has been retarded by extreme inequalities of land ownership (which is concentrated in the hands of a small Hispanic elite) and the consequent political unrest and guerrilla insurgency. It has been further set back by the severe effects of Hurricane Mitch in 1998. There is a large foreign debt.

History: there is extensive archaeological evidence of pre-Spanish civilizations, especially that of the Maya, and, from the 12th century, the Aztecs. From 1524 to 1821 the area was part of the Spanish captaincy general of Guatemala, which included most of Central America. It formed the nucleus of the Central American Federation until 1839, when it became independent. During the last 40 years periods of democracy have alternated with military dictatorships; there has been almost continuous fighting between government forces and left-wing URNG guerrillas, most of whom are Maya Quiché Indian. Following a military coup in 1983 Gen Oscar Humberto Mejia Victores became president; in 1986 civilian rule returned with the election of Vinicio Cerezo as president. In 1991 he was replaced by Jorge Serrano (1945–   ), who tried to acquire dictatorial powers in 1993 but was ousted and forced to flee the country. Guatemala has been frequently criticized for its human rights record: Ramiro de Léon Carpio, the human rights ombudsman, was elected president in 1991. In 1996 Alvaro Arzú became president and signed a peace agreement with the URNG guaranteeing the rights of the indigenous peoples. The conservative Alfonso Portillo was elected president in 1999.

Republic of Guatemala

Head of state	President Alfonso Portillo
Official language	Spanish
Official religion	Roman Catholic
Official currencies	quetzal of 100 centavos; US dollar of 100 cents
Area	108 889 sq km (42 042 sq mi)
Population (2001 est)	11 687 000
Capital	Guatemala City
Main port	Puerto Barrios

• Guatemala City ► 14 38N 90 22W The capital of Guatemala, situated in the S of the country in a high valley. Founded in 1776, it was the capital of the captaincy general of Guatemala and later of the Central American Federation. It has four universities; the oldest was founded in 1776. Population (1995): 1 167 495.

• guava ► A tropical American tree, *Psidium guajava*, about 10 m tall. Its white four-petalled flowers develop into yellow pear-shaped fruits with white or pink pulp containing many small seeds. Guava fruits, rich in vitamin C, are used to make jam and jelly, stewed for desserts, or canned. Family: *Myrtaceae* (myrtle family).

• Guayaquil ► (*or* Santiago de Guayaquil) 2 13S 79 54W The largest city and chief port of Ecuador, on the River Guayas. It is a major commercial centre; industries include food processing, tanning, and textile manufacture. Its university was founded in 1867. Population (1997 est): 1 973 880.

Francesco Guardi ► His romantic Venetian cityscapes include this view of the island and church of San Giorgio Maggiore from across St Mark's Basin.

● **Gudbrandsdal** ▶ The fertile valley of the River Lågen, in S central Norway. Farming is important and it has been a trade route for many centuries. Ibsen's *Peer Gynt* is set here.

● **gudgeon** ▶ A freshwater shoaling fish, *Gobio gobio*, related to ▷carp, found in Europe and N Asia. It has a slender greenish or greyish body, up to about 20 cm long, with a row of blackish spots along each side and a pair of barbels at the corners of the mouth. It is used as food and bait.

● **guelder rose** ▶ A small tree or shrub, *Viburnum opulus*, 4–5 m high, found throughout Eurasia. It has three-lobed leaves and flat-topped clusters of flowers, 5–10 cm across, in which the outer flowers are large and sterile and the inner ones are small and fertile. The fruits are clusters of red translucent berries. The cultivated form, grown as a garden shrub, is sterile: it has rounded heads of flowers and is called snowball tree. Family: *Caprifoliaceae* (honeysuckle family).

● **Guelfs and Ghibellines** ▶ The propapal and proimperial factions respectively in medieval Germany and Italy. Commencing in a German struggle between rival claimants to the Holy Roman Empire, the Guelfs (named after Welf, the family name) and Ghibellines (after Waiblingen, a ▷Hohenstaufen castle), their conflict acquired an Italian context because of papal opposition to the Hohenstaufen. The Italian city states were led by Florence (Guelf) and Pisa (Ghibelline). Both sides, however, had factions within each city. Defeat of the Hohenstaufen (1268) contributed to Ghibelline decline, while the Guelfs espoused the ▷Angevin cause in Italy. By the end of the 14th century the factions had only local significance, reflecting urban rivalries.

● **Guelph** ▶ 43 34N 80 16W A city in central Canada, in SW Ontario. Founded in 1827, it is an agricultural research and farming centre, especially at the University of Guelph (1964). Manufactures include electric motors, wire, and rubber products. Population (1991): 87 976.

● **guenon** ▶ An ▷Old World monkey belonging to the genus *Cercopithecus* (10 species), of African forests. They are 83–160 cm long including the tail (50–88 cm) and move through the trees in troops, feeding on leaves, fruits, insects, and snails. The mona monkey (*C. mona*), dark with creamy-white underparts and rump patches, is a strikingly marked guenon. ▷*See also* grass monkey.

● **Guercino** ▶ (Giovanni Francesco Barbieri; 1591–1666) Italian painter, born at Cento, near Bologna. His masterpiece, the ceiling frescos in the Casino Ludovisi, Rome, commissioned by Pope Gregory XV in 1621, were influenced by the ▷Carracci, under whom he had studied. While in Rome (1621–23) he also painted the *Burial of St Petronilla* (Capitoline Museum, Rome), which his later work never equalled.

● **Guericke, Otto von** ▶ (1602–86) German physicist, renowned for his investigation of vacuums. In 1650 he invented the air pump, which he used to perform a series of experiments culminating in a demonstration in which two teams of horses failed to separate a pair of large hemispheres (called the Magdeburg hemispheres after his home town) placed together and evacuated. When air was admitted to the hemispheres they fell apart on their own.

● **Guernica** ▶ 43 19N 2 40W A historic Basque town in N Spain, on the Bay of Biscay. During the Spanish Civil War it was bombed and virtually destroyed by German planes supporting the Nationalists on 27 April, 1937. This is depicted in a famous painting by Picasso. Population (1989): 16 378.

● **Guernsey** ▶ 49 27N 2 35W The second largest of the Channel Islands, in the English Channel. Roughly triangular in shape, it is low lying in the N and hilly in the S with rugged coastal cliffs. The finance industry is a major source of income; agriculture and horticulture are important, especially dairy farming (the Guernsey breed of cattle originated here) and the production of tomatoes and flowers for export. Guernsey is a popular tourist resort. Area: 63 sq km (24.5 sq mi). Population (1992 est): 64 200. Capital: St Peter Port.

● **Guernsey cattle** ▶ A breed of dairy cattle originating from Guernsey. They have a yellowish coat with a white tail switch and produce high-quality creamy milk.

● **guerrilla warfare** ▶ (Spanish: small war) Military action by small irregular armed forces, often supported by a hostile foreign power, intended to erode the war potential and political stability of a country. Relying on hit-and-run techniques and avoiding combat with better equipped regulars, guerrillas usually attempt to gain local support rather than territory. The word was first adopted in reference to the Spanish–Portuguese action against the French conquest in the ▷Peninsular War. In the 20th century, the activities of T. E. ▷Lawrence's Arab irregulars in World War I and of the various national ▷resistance movements in World War II showed how effective guerrilla action could be when used in support of a larger conventional strategy: by threatening vital enemy communications, tiny groups of guerrillas were able to tie down large conventional forces that would otherwise have been available for action on the main battlefronts. Although guerrillas have rarely been able to defeat conventional armies, they can cause such expense, havoc, and damage to morale over a potentially indefinite period that governments are obliged to meet their demands. Successful campaigns of this kind include the IRA activity in Ireland in 1919–21 and the anticolonialist struggles in various part of Africa and Asia in the decades after World War II. When guerrilla action is aimed at "soft" civilian targets in an attempt to blackmail governments or generate publicity it is usually known as ▷terrorism.

● **Guesclin, Bertrand du** ▶ (c. 1320–80) French commander in the ▷Hundred Years' War. As constable of France from 1370 he was instrumental in recovering the territory previously lost to the English in S and W France.

Che Guevara ▶ A photograph taken in 1965.

● **Guevara, Che** ▶ (Ernesto G.; 1928–67) Argentine revolutionary and theorist of guerrilla warfare, who became the hero of left-wing youth in the 1960s. A doctor by training, he joined ▷Castro's invasion of Cuba (1956) and became one of his chief lieutenants in the subsequent guerrilla war. After Castro's victory, Che Guevara influenced Cuba's procommunist foreign relations and directed the land-reform policies. In 1967 he was captured and killed by government troops while attempting to instigate a revolt in Bolivia. In 1997 his remains were discovered and returned to Cuba, where he was given a state funeral.

● **Guggenheim, Meyer** ▶ (1828–1905) Swiss-born US industrialist, who with his sons established the world's largest mineral extraction and metal-processing empire: the family's wealth subsequently funded a number of educational, philanthropic, and artistic ventures. Meyer Guggenheim emigrated to the USA in 1847 and made his fortune as an importer of Swiss embroideries. From the 1880s he acquired major interests in US copper mines, while his seven sons, especially **Daniel Guggenheim** (1856–1930), bought smelting and refining companies. After consolidating their operations and gaining control of their main rival in 1901, they enjoyed a virtual monopoly of the US industry for some 30 years. Daniel, who ran the empire during this period, also expanded into South America and Africa.

Three of the brothers made notable contributions to culture and philanthropy. Daniel established various charitable and scientific foundations; **Simon Guggenheim** (1867–1949) endowed (1925) the Guggenheim Fellowships for US scholars and artists studying abroad; and **Solomon R. Guggenheim** (1861–1949) created a superb collection of modern art and financed the building of New York's Guggenheim Museum (1959, designed by Frank Lloyd ▷Wright) to house it. **Peggy Guggenheim** (1898–1979), the daughter of another brother (who died on the *Titanic*), was also a major collector and patron of modern art. She lived a colourful Bohemian life in Europe and married the painter Max ▷Ernst. Her collection is split between the Guggenheim Museum and the Peggy Guggenheim Collection, Venice, which occupies her former palazzo on the Grand Canal.

● **Guicciardini, Francesco** ▶ (1483–1540) Florentine statesman and historian. He was Florentine ambassador to Aragon (1512–14) and then active in Florentine politics before entering the service of the papacy and becoming governor of Modena (1516) and Reggio (1517). After the sack of Rome (1527) by the imperial army, Guicciardini concentrated on his writings, including his famous *Storia d'Italia*, which deals with contemporary events in Italy between 1494 and 1534.

● **guided missiles** ▶ Rocket-powered missiles without wings or other lift surfaces that are guided throughout their flight. They comprise a power unit, a guidance system, and a warhead. In most, propulsion is by solid-fuel rocket. The most common guidance systems depend on a trailing wire or a radio, radar, or laser beam. Some have preset on-board computers, others depend on ▷inertial guidance, and some home on sources of infrared radiation. Warheads range from small antitank high explosives to nuclear devices in the kiloton range. All missiles are vulnerable to electronic countermeasures (ECM). Cruise missiles have wings and are driven continuously by an airbreathing turbofan. Guided by an inertial system updated during flight by matching the contours of the land they overfly with contour maps stored in their computer memories, they fly so low that they are difficult to detect by radar. Missiles may be launched from aircraft (air-to-air or air-to-surface) or from the land or sea (surface-to-air or surface-to-surface). ▷*See also* MIRV; MX missile; Polaris missile; Scud missile; Trident missile.

● **guide dogs** ▶ Dogs trained to guide the blind. The first training schools were established in Germany (1911–18); the British Guide Dog Association was founded in 1931. Suitable breeds for the four-month training course are German Shepherds (Alsatians), Labradors, and golden retrievers.

● **Guides Association** ▶ An organization founded (as the Girl Guides Association) by Robert and (his sister) Agnes ▷Baden-Powell in 1910 to encourage the physical, mental, and spiritual development of girls. The three classes of members are Brownie Guides (aged 7–10), Guides (10–15), and Ranger Guides (14–20). There are some 7 million Guides throughout the world, of which 750 000 are in the UK. The Association dropped the word "Girl" from its title in 1992. Its counterpart for boys is the ▷Scout Association.

● **Guido d'Arezzo** ▶ (c. 990–c. 1050) Italian monk and musical theorist. He developed the hexachord, a six-note scale used to aid sight-singing. The notes were named after the first syllables of the first six lines of a Latin hymn: ut, re, mi, fa, sol, and la. This became the basis of later systems of ▷solmization. He also developed the Guidonian hand, a mnemonic device that gave note names to the tips and joints of the fingers, and popularized the use of coloured lines in written music to indicate pitch.

● **Guildford** ▶ 51 14N 0 35W A market town in SE England, in Surrey on the River Wey. The historic county town of Surrey, it is the site of the University of Surrey (1966) and Guildford Cathedral (1936). It is an important regional centre, with administration and services as the main employers. Population (1991): 65 998.

● **guilds** ▶ (or gilds) Associations formed in medieval Europe to further their members' common purposes. Originally religious or social in character, the first guilds are recorded in the 9th century. Merchant guilds were created in the 11th century to organize local trade and became a powerful force in local government. Craft guilds, confined to specific crafts or trades, were formed from the 12th century and became very powerful, exercising a monopoly over both production and trade and controlling recruitment by the apprenticeship system. From the later middle ages their activities were largely superseded by the development of capitalism. The ▷livery companies of London are descended from the craft guilds.

● **Guild Socialism** ▶ A movement, influential from about 1906 to 1925 in Britain, which sought the abolition of capitalism and the establishment of guilds of workers to control industry within government guidelines. The National Guilds League was formed in 1915 but had its greatest support immediately after World War I, when the National Building Guild was formed. However, this only lasted until 1922 and in 1925 the National Guilds League was dissolved.

● **Guillaume de Lorris** ▶ (13th century) French poet, author of the first 4000 lines of the *Roman de la rose* (c. 1230–40), a highly influential medieval poem, translated into English by ▷Chaucer. Nothing certain is known about him.

● **guillemot** ▶ A bird, *Uria aalge*, occurring in coastal regions of the N hemisphere. It is 40 cm long and has a dark-brown plumage with a white belly and wing stripe and a slender bill, feeding on fish, shellfish, and worms. The eggs are shaped so that they do not roll off the cliff ledges where they are laid (*see* Plate III). Family *Alcidae* (auks).

● **guillotine** ▶ 1. A device for beheading people. It consists of two vertical posts and a horizontal blade that is dropped onto the victim's neck. Invented by Joseph Ignace Guillotin (1738–1814), it was introduced as a method of capital punishment in France in 1792, during the French Revolution. 2. ▷*See* filibuster.

● **Guimarães** ▶ 41 26N 8 19W A town in NW Portugal. It was Portugal's first capital (12th century) and the birthplace of Alfonso I (1112–85), Portugal's first king. Its manufactures include cutlery. Population (latest est): 22 092.

● **Guinea, Gulf of** ▶ A large inlet of the E Atlantic Ocean, bordering on the ▷Guinea Coast of West Africa, between Cape Palmas, Liberia, and Cape Lopez, Gabon.

● **Guinea, Republic of** ▶ A country on the coast of West Africa. A coastal plain, partly swamp, rises steeply to plateaus and mountains. The population is mainly Fulani and Mandingo.

Economy: chiefly agricultural. Rice, palm oil, nuts, coffee, peanuts, fruits, and livestock are important. The chief mineral resources are diamonds, iron ore, and bauxite (alumina is the main export). Most trade and industry is nationalized but privatization has begun.

History: the N formed part of Ghana from the 5th to the 8th centuries AD and of the Mali empire in the 16th century. From the mid-15th century European traders were active along the coast. In 1849 the French established a protectorate over part of Guinea, which became a colony in 1891. In 1895 it became part of French West Africa. In 1958 French Guinea became an independent republic, with Ahmed Sékou ▷Touré as its first president, rather than joining the French Community. Under Touré's repressive regime Guinea became almost entirely isolated from the rest of the world. Economic relations with France were re-established in 1963. The army took over after Touré's death in 1984. Accusations of violations of human rights continued, and after civil disturbances in 1991 the government introduced a multiparty system. Gen Lansana Conté, president since 1984, was re-elected in 1993 in the country's first multiparty elections. In 1996 the post of prime minister was created and Sidia Touré became its first holder; he was replaced by Lamine Sidime in 1999.

Republic of Guinea

Head of state	Major-General Lansana Conté
Official language	French and the languages of eight ethnic groups
Official currency	Guinea franc of 100 centimes
Area	245 857 sq km (95 000 sq mi)
Population (1997 est)	7 405 000
Capital and main port	Conakry

● **Guinea-Bissau, Republic of** ▶ (name until 1974: Portuguese Guinea) A small country on the coast of West Africa, including the archipelago of Bijagós. It consists chiefly of a coastal plain, cut by wide river estuaries and rising to savanna-covered plateau inland. The majority of the population are Fulani, Mandyako, and Mandingo.

Economy: chiefly agricultural, the principal crops being groundnuts (the main export), rice, palm oil, and nuts. Cattle breeding is important in the interior. Land was nationalized and cooperative farming introduced in the 1980s, but free-market reforms have subsequently been introduced. Important bauxite deposits have been discovered. Industry is also being developed. Guinea-Bissau joined the French Franc Zone in 1997.

History: explored by the Portuguese in the mid-15th century, the area became a centre of the slave trade. It became a Portuguese colony in 1879 and an overseas province of Portugal in 1951. In 1974 it became an independent republic. Luis de Almeida Cabral became the first president; he was replaced by Maj João Bernardo Vieira and a Marxist government following a coup in 1980. Constitutional rule returned in 1984, with Vieira as head of state. The first multiparty elections, held in 1994, were won by the ruling party and Vieira was re-elected president. In 1998 an attempted coup was suppressed with the help of troops from neighbouring Guinea. However, fighting broke out again and Vieira was overthrown by the military in 1999. Following free elections in 2000 Kumba Ialá became president.

Republic of Guinea-Bissau

Head of State	President Kumba Ialá
Official language	Portuguese; Crioulo is widely spoken
Official currency	CFA (Communauté financière africaine) franc of 100 centimes
Area	36 125 sq km (13 948 sq mi)
Population (1999 est)	1 235 000
Capital	Bissau

● **Guinea Coast** ▶ The coastlands of West Africa extending from Gambia to Cape Lopez in Gabon.

● **guinea fowl** ▶ A bird belonging to an African family (*Numididae*; 7-10 species). About 50 cm long, domesticated guinea fowl are descended from the helmet guinea fowl (*Numida meleagris*), which has a large bony crest, a bare face with red and blue wattles, and a grey white-spotted plumage. Guinea fowl scratch for seeds and insects, especially termites. Order: *Galliformes* (pheasants, turkeys, etc.).

● **guinea pepper** ▶ The spicy aromatic fruit of a West African tree, *Xylopia aethiopica*, source of the condiment "Negro pepper." The tree has fragrant flowers producing aggregates of berries. Family: *Annonaceae*.

● **guinea pig** ▶ A domesticated rodent, *Cavia porcellus*, descended from the ▷cavy. Guinea pigs were originally bred for food but are now popular as pets. They feed on grain, roots, green food, and hay.

● **guinea worm** ▶ A parasitic ▷nematode worm, *Dracunculus medinensis*, that is a serious parasite of man in Africa, India, and the Middle East. The larvae are carried by water fleas (genus *Cyclops*) often present in drinking water. When swallowed by the human host, they burrow into the tissues and grow to maturity: the females reach a length of up to 120 cm, causing ulcers on the feet and legs.

● **Guinevere** ▶ In ▷Arthurian legend, the wife of King Arthur and lover of ▷Lancelot. Malory's *Morte d'Arthur* (1485) describes her abduction by Modred, Arthur's nephew, and her adulterous love for Lancelot.

● **Guinness, Sir Alec** ▶ (1914-2000) British actor. He established his reputation as a stage actor in the late 1930s and played Hamlet in modern dress in 1938. After World War II he achieved success as a character actor in films, including *Oliver Twist* (1948), *Kind Hearts and Coronets* (1949), *The Bridge on the River Kwai* (1957), *Star Wars* (1977), and *A Passage to India* (1984). He was knighted in 1959 and made a Companion of Honour in 1994.

● **Guinness Peat Aviation Literary Prize** ▶ A prize of £47,000 for a literary work by an author born in or living in the Republic of Ireland. Awarded every three years, it was first bestowed in 1989.

● **Guiscard, Robert** ▶ (c. 1015-85) Norman knight, who took part in the Norman invasions of S Italy and Sicily. He established himself in Calabria and gained papal recognition as Duke of Apulia (1059). He died while campaigning in the Balkans. His brother and nephew later ruled Sicily as Roger I (1031-1101; reigned c. 1071-1101) and ▷Roger II.

● **Guise** ▶ A French noble family prominent during the 16th century. The duchy of Guise was the reward (1528) of **Claude I, Duke of Aumale** (1496-1550) for services to France. His daughter **Mary of Guise** (1515-60) married James V of Scotland and was the mother of Mary, Queen of Scots. Claude's sons **François, 2nd Duke of Guise** (1519-63) and **Charles, Cardinal of Lorraine** (1524-74) led the Roman Catholic party in the French ▷Wars of Religion. François was assassinated by a Huguenot and the Catholic leadership passed to his son **Henri I, 3rd Duke of Guise** (1550-88), who directed the ▷St Bartholomew Day's Massacre of Huguenots in 1572. Following Henri's assassination the Guise's influence on French politics diminished.

● **guitar** ▶ A plucked stringed instrument of Moorish origin, which came to Europe via Spain. The modern Spanish guitar has a flat back, a round sound hole, a fretted fingerboard, and six strings tuned chiefly in fourths. It has a range of over three octaves from the E below the bass stave. Music for it is written an octave higher than it sounds. Guitar technique was developed by Fernando Sor (1778-1839) and in the 20th century by Andrés ▷Segovia. The electric guitar, which has an electronic pick-up linked to an amplifier instead of a soundbox, was developed in the USA in the 1950s and became the main instrument in pop and rock music.

● **guitar fish** ▶ A ▷ray fish, belonging to the family *Rhinobatidae*, that has a pointed flattened head with fused pectoral fins and a long muscular sharklike tail. Guitar fish live in shallow waters of tropical and temperate seas and feed on bottom-dwelling animals, especially crustaceans.

● **Guitry, Sacha** ▶ (1885-1957) French actor and dramatist. He wrote many light comedies, often concerning the lives of famous men, such as Napoleon and Mozart. He acted in these and occasionally in films, including *Le Comédien* (1949) and *Napoléon* (1955).

● **Guiyang** ▶ (or Kuei-yang) 26 35N 106 40E A city in S China, the capital of Guizhou province. Industries, developed since 1949, include steel, machinery, and aluminium. Population (1991 est): 1 530 000.

● **Guizhou** ▶ (Kuei-chou *or* Kweichow) A province in S China, a rather infertile high plateau. There were frequent rebellions among the minority non-Chinese groups, which have rich folk cultures. Rice, maize, tobacco, tea, and timber are grown and silk and minerals produced. Area: 174 000 sq km (69 278 sq mi). Population (1997 est): 36 060 000. Capital: Guiyang.

● **Guizot, François (Pierre Guillaume)** ▶ (1787-1874) French statesman and historian. A professor of history at Paris University (1812-30), he was prominent in the revolution that brought Louis Philippe to the throne in 1830 and served as foreign minister (1840-48). He was forced by the Revolution of 1848 to resign and devoted the rest of his life to historical writing.

● **Gujarat** ▶ A state in W India, on the Arabian Sea SE of Pakistan. Lowlands merge into hills in the S and E and into marshes in the NW. Cotton, tobacco, peanuts, and other crops are raised. An industrial area, Gujarat produces textiles, machinery, and chemicals.

History: a flourishing area under Muslim princes (13th-17th centuries), Gujarat was conquered by the Maratha in the 18th century before passing to Britain. In January 2001 a severe earthquake left at least 30 000 dead and 600 000 homeless. Area: 116 024 sq km (44 788 sq mi). Population (1994 est): 44 235 000. Capital: Gandhinagar.

● **Gujarati** ▶ An Indo-Aryan language spoken by 20 million people in Gujarat and Maharashtra in India. It is related to Rajasthani, uses a modified Devanagari script, and has a long literary tradition.

● **Gujranwala** ▶ 32 06N 74 11E A city in NE Pakistan. The Sikh ruler Ranjit Singh was born here. Manufactures include textiles and leather goods and it has a famous ceramics industry. Population (1995 est): 1 663 000.

● **Gulf States** ► The nations situated on the Persian Gulf. They are Oman, the United Arab Emirates, Qatar, Bahrain, Saudi Arabia, Kuwait, Iraq, and Iran. They comprise the world's major oil-producing area.

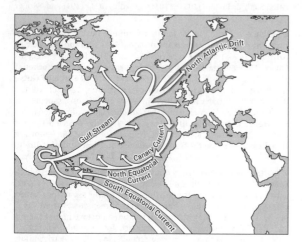

Gulf Stream

● **Gulf Stream** ► One of the major ocean currents of the world, flowing from the Florida Strait parallel to the North American coast as far as the Newfoundland banks. It bears NE across the Atlantic as the North Atlantic Drift, branching into two main directions, one flowing N towards Spitsbergen and the other flowing S to form the Canary Current. Water from the North and South Equatorial Currents builds up in the Gulf of Mexico and escapes with force through the Florida Strait as the Florida Current, one of the strongest major ocean currents. The water is warm and has an ameliorating effect on the climate of NW Europe.

● **Gulf War** ► **1.** (1991) A conflict between Iraq under Saddam ▷Hussein and a US-led multinational force including troops from the UK, France, Saudi Arabia, Egypt, Syria, Kuwait, and other Arab states. It was precipitated by Iraq's invasion of Kuwait (2 August, 1990) and refusal to comply with UN resolutions demanding its withdrawal. The coalition built up a large military force in Saudi Arabia and launched massive air attacks on Baghdad and other targets on 17 January, 1991. Iraq responded with ▷Scud missile attacks on Israel and Saudi Arabia. On 24 Feb the coalition forces began a ground attack, swiftly overwhelming the Iraqi troops in Kuwait and advancing into southern Iraq. The coalition attack ceased on 28 Feb when Iraq agreed to comply with UN resolutions. Tensions between Iraq and the West have continued; in 1993, 1996, and 1998 the USA bombed Iraqi bases in response to Iraq's violation of ceasefire agreements. **2.** ▷See Iran-Iraq War.

● **gulfweed** ▷See Sargasso Sea.

● **gull** ► A seabird belonging to the subfamily *Larinae* (about 40 species), ranging throughout the world's coastal regions and also found inland. Up to 75 cm long, gulls have long pointed wings and a strong slightly hooked bill. Gulls are typically grey and white, often with dark markings. Some gulls feed on fish but most are scavengers. Family: *Laridae* (gulls and terns); order: *Charadriiformes* (gulls, plovers, etc.).

● **gullet** ▷See oesophagus.

● **gums** ► Adhesive substances exuded by plants. They are odourless tasteless amorphous ▷carbohydrates that form either clear liquid solutions or gelatinous mixtures with water. **Gum arabic** (or gum acacia), the most widely used of the water-soluble gums, is obtained from trees of the genus *Acacia*, although the name is also applied to substitute gums from other plants. It is used for making sweets, cosmetics, gummed labels, and textile finishes. **Gum tragacanth** is extracted from shrubs of the genus *Astragalus*: it is not completely

water-soluble, but forms a thick mucilage. It is used as an adhesive in pills and as a sauce thickener.

● **gum tree** ► A tree of the genus ▷*Eucalyptus* (about 600 species), so called because it is rich in resin and aromatic oils.

● **gun cotton** ▷See cellulose nitrate.

● **gun laws** ► Legislation to restrict the possession and supply of firearms. Such laws vary considerably from one country to another. In the USA the right of citizens to bear arms is enshrined in the Second Amendment to the Constitution and supported by powerful interest groups. In the UK the Firearms Act of 1968 restricted certain classes of weapon (such as automatics) to the armed services and police and made it illegal for a civilian to possess any firearm without a valid licence. It also became illegal to supply firearms to a minor, anyone with a criminal record, or anyone who is mentally ill. These controls were strengthened by acts in 1982 and 1988. However, public concern over the ▷Dunblane massacre of 1996 led the government to introduce legislation to remove all large-calibre (over .22 in) handguns from civilian life; an amendment was subsequently passed converting this into a total ban (the recent legislation does not apply in Northern Ireland).

● **gun metal** ► A type of ▷bronze containing about 90% copper and sometimes a little zinc. Being easy to cast, it was originally used for making cannons. Admiralty gun metal (88% copper, 10% tin, 2% zinc) is used in shipbuilding.

● **Gunn, Thom(son William)** ► (1929–) British poet, living in California. His books include *Fighting Terms* (1954), *My Sad Captains* (1961), and *Jack Straw's Castle* (1976). *The Man With Night Sweats* (1992) deals with the AIDS epidemic.

● **Gunn effect** ► The effect used in solid-state ▷semiconductor microwave generators (Gunn diodes). When a sufficiently high steady electric field (typically several thousand volts per centimetre) is applied across a sample of n-type gallium arsenide, microwave frequency current oscillations are set up. Named after J. B. Gunn (1928–).

● **gunnel** ► An eel-like fish of the family *Pholididae* (about 8 species), found among seaweed or rocks in N Atlantic and N Pacific coastal waters. The rock gunnel (or butterfish; *Pholis gunnellus*) is 30 cm long and brownish with 9–13 black spots along the dorsal fin. Order: *Perciformes*.

● **Gunnell, Sally** ► (1966–) British athlete. At the Barcelona Olympics (1992) she won the 400 m hurdles and became world record holder (52.74 secs) in 1993. She retired in 1997.

● **gunpowder** ► An explosive mixture of saltpetre (potassium nitrate), sulphur, and powdered charcoal. Invented by the Chinese many centuries before its description by Roger ▷Bacon in the 13th century it has had a profound effect on human conflict (*see* firearms). It is still used in fireworks.

● **Gunpowder Plot** ▷See Fawkes, Guy.

● **guns** ► ▷Artillery firearms that discharge high-velocity shells with a relatively flat trajectory. A modern breech-loading gun has a rifled barrel. Its sliding or interrupted screw-thread breech blocks contain linked levers activating the firing pin, which strikes the primer, located either in the round or the block. Buffers absorb the firing shock and recuperators return the barrel to its firing position. Controls elevate and traverse the gun, sometimes electronically. Most ammunition is fused to burst before, on, or after impact. Specialized shells are used in ▷antitank guns and ▷anti-aircraft guns. Some shells have nuclear warheads. Guns may be towed or mounted on vehicles or in aircraft or ships. ▷*See also* small arms.

● **Gunter's chain** ▷See chain.

● **Guomindang** ► (or Kuomintang) The National People's Party of ▷Taiwan (Republic of China). Organized in 1912, following the overthrow of the imperial government, from ▷Sun Yat-sen's Alliance Society, it formed, under Soviet influence, an alliance with the new Chinese Communist Party (CCP) in 1924 (*see* United Fronts). Following Sun's death (1925), the Guomindang was led by ▷Chiang Kai-shek and with the CCP had gained control of most of China from the ▷warlords by 1926. A break between the two parties (1927) led to civil war until

Japanese conquests in China (*see* Sino-Japanese Wars) necessitated renewed cooperation in 1937. After Japan's defeat (1945), civil war was resumed until a communist victory in 1949 drove Chiang Kai-shek and his Guomindang followers into exile in Taiwan.

● **guppy** ► A freshwater fish, *Lebistes reticulatus*, native to N South America and the West Indies. Male guppies are up to 4 cm long and brightly coloured, marked with black eyespots and having variably shaped and coloured fins. Females, slightly larger and less colourful, are prolific breeders, producing live young (rather than eggs) at monthly intervals. Guppies are popular aquarium fish and—in their native regions—control mosquitoes. Family: *Cyprinodontidae*.

● **Gupta** ► A powerful Indian dynasty founded in the late 4th century AD. Its founder ▷Chandra Gupta I was succeeded by ▷Samudra Gupta and the throne then passed to ▷Chandra Gupta II. His son Kumara (d. 455; reigned c. 415–55) was followed by Skanda Gupta (reigned 455–67), during whose reign foreign invaders began to conquer parts of the empire. The early Gupta kings fostered Buddhism and presided over a golden age of artistic and cultural achievement. The dynasty was overthrown by the Huns in the 6th century.

● **Gurdjieff, George Ivanovitch** ► (1873–1949) Russian occultist of Greek parentage, who established a teaching centre near Paris in the 1920s. Teaching that man is not usually fully conscious, he claimed to be able to lead his students to a higher level of perception. Part mystic, part bon viveur, and reputedly part charlatan, this enigmatic man had a considerable following, including P. D. Ouspensky, whose books have outlived Gurdjieff's own *All and Everything, Beelzebub's Tales to his Grandson* (1950).

● **gurdwara** ► A Sikh place of worship, housing a copy of the ▷Ádi Granth. Although every Sikh home contains one, public gurdwaras are used for meetings, weddings, and services. The most sacred is the Golden Temple or Harimandir at Amritsar.

● **Gurkhas** ► Soldiers from Nepal who served in the British Indian Army from 1815 until 1947. The Brigade of Gurkhas now serves in the British Army, Hong Kong. The name derives from that of the ruling dynasty of Nepal. The force was halved when Hong Kong was returned to China (1997).

● **gurnard** ► A carnivorous bottom-dwelling fish, also called sea robin, belonging to a family (*Triglidae*; about 40 species) found in temperate and tropical seas. It has a tapering body, up to 70 cm long, a large armoured head, and finger-like pectoral fin rays and produces sound by vibrating its swim bladder. The flying gurnards belong to the family *Dactylopteridae*. Order: *Scorpaeniformes*.

● **guru** ► In ▷Hinduism, a venerated spiritual teacher who personally instructs and guides the disciple. In Tibetan Buddhism the guru embodies the Buddha himself and is correspondingly revered. In Sikhism, guru is the title of the first ten patriarchs (*see* Nanak).

● **Gustaf V** ► (1858–1950) King of Sweden (1907–50), succeeding his father Oscar II. His marriage to Victoria, daughter of the Grand Duke of Baden, unified the Bernadotte and Vasa dynasties. He was succeeded by his son Gustaf VI.

● **Gustaf VI Adolf** ► (1882–1973) King of Sweden (1950–73), succeeding his father Gustaf V. An expert on archaeology and ceramics, he was succeeded by his grandson ▷Carl XVI Gustaf.

● **Gustavus II Adolphus** ► (1594–1632) King of Sweden (1611–32), who displayed military genius in the ▷Thirty Years' War. He inherited wars with Denmark, Russia, and Poland, which he successfully terminated in 1613, 1617, and 1629 respectively. With the help of his chancellor ▷Oxenstierna, he consolidated his internal position and in the 1620s instituted important reforms. In 1630 he entered the Thirty Years War on the Protestant side, inspired by religious aims as well as a desire for Sweden to dominate the Baltic. He defeated Tilly at ▷Breitenfeld (1631) and at the Lech (1632) and Wallenstein at ▷Lutzen, where he was mortally wounded.

● **Gustavus I Vasa** ► (1496–1560) King of Sweden (1523–60), who achieved Swedish independence of Denmark and founded the Vasa dynasty. He was captured in the 1517–18 war against Denmark but escaped to Sweden and led a successful rebellion against the Danes (1521–23). As king, he made Lutheranism the state religion (1527–29).

● **GUT** ▷*See* grand unified theory.

● **Gutenberg, Johann** ► (c. 1400–c. 1468) German printer, who invented the method of printing with movable metal type (*see* typesetting). Gutenberg worked on his printing process from the 1430s. In 1448 he received the financial backing of ▷Fust and by 1455 had produced his great 42-line Bible (the Gutenberg Bible). Fust successfully sued Gutenberg in 1455 for repayment and set up a printing business with Gutenberg's machinery. He produced a famous psalter (1457), which was largely Gutenberg's work.

● **Guthrie, (William) Tyrone** ► (1900–71) British theatre director. He directed the Old Vic and other British companies and frequently worked abroad, notably at Stratford, Ontario, where he founded the Shakespeare Festival in 1953. He was known for his modern-dress productions of Shakespeare.

● **Guthrie, Woody** ► (Woodrow Wilson G.; 1912–67) US folksinger and songwriter, many of whose songs reflected the social injustice of the Depression. His songs, which include "This Land Is Your Land" and "Grand Coulee Dam," were the main influence on the US folk revival of the 1960s. His son, **Arlo Guthrie** (1947–), is also a singer and songwriter.

● **gutta percha** ► A brownish leathery material obtained from the ▷latex of various trees of the family *Sapotaceae*, especially those of the SE Asian genus *Palaquium*. It was once extensively used, for example as an electrical insulator and in golf balls but it has largely been replaced by synthetics.

● **Guyana, Cooperative Republic of** ► (name until 1966: British Guiana) A country in the NE of South America, on the Atlantic Ocean. Narrow fertile coastal plains give way to higher undulating areas, rich in minerals and forests. The main rivers, the Demerara, Essequibo, and Berbice give their names to its three counties. Most of the population is of African and East Indian descent.
Economy: agriculture is important, the main crops being rice and Demerara sugar. Fishing, livestock, and cotton growing are being developed. The most important minerals were formerly gold and diamonds, but these have now been overtaken by bauxite. Alumina is another major export. Most power comes from hydroelectric sources. Guyana's rain forests have become increasingly popular as an international tourist attraction. There is a massive external debt.
History: the coast was first explored by the Spanish in 1499 and settlements were founded by the Dutch in the 17th century. The area was occupied by the British (1796–1802, 1803–14) and then formally ceded to Britain, becoming a colony as British Guiana in 1831. In 1961 it gained internal self-government under Cheddi ▷Jagan. In 1966, as Guyana, it became independent within the British Commonwealth. It is also a member of CARICOM. Guyana became a Cooperative Republic in 1970. In 1978 an agricultural commune (Jonestown) was the scene of the mass suicide of some 900 members of the People's Temple Sect. The 1980s saw deepening economic crisis and social unrest. In 1992 the first free elections for 28 years resulted in victory for the veteran Jagan, who became president. After his death in 1997 Jagan's widow, Janet, was elected to the presidency. She was succeeded by Bharrat Jagdeo in 1999.

Cooperative Republic of Guyana

Head of state	President Bharrat Jagdeo
Official language	English
Official currency	Guyana dollar of 100 cents
Area	210 000 sq km (83 000 sq mi)
Population (1999 est)	787 000
Capital and main port	Georgetown

● **Guyenne** ► A former region of SW France. Ruled by the English kings in the late middle ages, it was regained by France after the Hundred Years War. The scene of fierce fighting in the 16th-century Wars of Religion and the 17th-century Fronde, Guyenne was later merged with Gascony.

● **Guzmán Blanco, Antonio** ► (1829–99) Venezuelan statesman. He was president three times (1870–77, 1879–84, 1886–88) but retained despotic power throughout the period 1870–88. He prompted foreign investment and public works, including the country's first railway.

● **Gwalior** ► 26 12N 78 09E A city in India, in Madhya Pradesh. Strategically important, it developed around its impressive fortress, believed to date from the 6th century AD. Gwalior is also a commercial and industrial centre. Jiwaji University was established here in 1964. Population (1991): 692 982.

● **Gwelo** ▷See Gweru.

● **Gwent** ► A former county of SE Wales, on the English border. It was created under local government reorganization in 1974 from most of ▷Monmouthshire and part of Breconshire. In 1996 it was abolished; administrative powers passed to the county of Monmouthshire (restored with reduced boundaries) and the county boroughs, of Blaenau Gwent, Newport, Torfaen, and Caerphilly.

● **Gweru** ► (name before 1982: Gwelo) 19 25S 29 50E A town in central Zimbabwe. It is the centre of a mining area (with chrome-ore and asbestos deposits) and a cattle-rearing area. Industries include ferrochrome processing. Population (1992): 124 735.

Nell Gwyn ► Described by Samuel Pepys as "Pretty, witty Nell," she was the only one of Charles II's mistresses to become popular with the public. Mistaken once for her rival, the Roman Catholic Louise de Kéroualle, she called out to an angry crowd "Pray, good people, be civil; I am the Protestant whore." This engraving is after a painting by the court painter, Sir Peter Lely.

● **Gwyn, Nell** ► (1650–87) English actress. Originally an orange seller in Drury Lane, she achieved fame as an actress and became Charles II's mistress, bearing him two sons. "Let not poor Nellie starve," are said to have been his last words. She helped to establish the Royal Hospital at Chelsea.

● **Gwynedd** ► A county of NW Wales, bordering on the Irish Sea. It was created under local government reorganization in 1974 from the counties of ▷Anglesey, Caernarfonshire, Merionethshire, and part of W Denbighshire. In 1996 it became a ▷unitary authority: at the same time Anglesey was restored as an independent county and part of the NE went to the new county borough of ▷Conwy. It is predominantly mountainous, rising to 1086 m (3563 ft) in ▷Snowdon. Most of the county lies within the Snowdonia National Park. Slate quarrying, formerly a major occupation, has declined. Area: 1027 sq km (397 sq mi). Population (1996 est): 80 000. Administrative centre: Caernarfon.

● **gymkhana** ► **1.** An event with a number of different games and contests on horseback. Gymkhanas originated among British soldiers in India during the 19th century. In England the Prince Philip Cup (instituted in 1957) is the ▷Pony Club gymkhana championship. **2.** A timed event, especially in the USA, testing the skill of a car driver over an obstacle course.

● **gymnastics** ► Exercises designed to perfect balance, strength, and coordination, popular as a sport for individual performers and teams. The modern sport developed in Germany and Sweden in the 19th century from **calisthenics**, rhythmical exercises performed without apparatus or weights. The ancient Persians, Chinese, Indi-

ans, Greeks, and Romans also exercised in this way. Competitions consist of prescribed programmes of exercises and optional routines, the apparatus being for men the horizontal bar, parallel bars, pommel horse, vaulting horse, and rings and for women the balance beam, asymmetrical bars, and vaulting horse; both men and women do floor exercises. The sport's popularity increased, especially among girls, after the victories of Olga Korbut (1972) and Nadia ▷Comaneci (1976) in the Olympics. The world governing body is the Fédération internationale de Gymnastique (founded in 1881).

● **gymnosperms** ► A group of plants, most of which are trees, whose sole consistent characteristic is that their seeds are not enclosed within a fruit but are borne naked, in many species on ▷cone scales. Gymnosperms originated in the late Devonian period (about 380 million years ago). They were formerly classified as a class, *Gymnospermae*, but are now generally split into separate phyla (or divisions): *Coniferophyta* (*see* conifer); *Ginkgophyta* (*see* ginkgo); *Cycadophyta* (*see* cycad); *Gnetophyta* (e.g. ▷welwitschia); and several extinct orders, including the *Cycadofilicales* (*see* seed fern) and the ▷*Cordaitales*.

● **gymnure** ► An insectivorous mammal belonging to the family *Erinaceidae* of SE Asia, also called hairy hedgehog. There are four species, including the ▷moon rat. Short-legged and flat-footed, 15–60 cm long, they resemble ▷hedgehogs without spines. They are shy, usually living in thick undergrowth and hunting mainly at night.

● **gynaecology** ► The branch of medicine and surgery concerned with diseases of women and girls, particularly those affecting the reproductive system. The closely related specialty of **obstetrics** deals with the care of women during pregnancy, childbirth, and the period immediately after delivery. Doctors specializing in these fields work in close association: a gynaecologist is often also an obstetrician.

● **Györ** ► 47 41N 17 40E A city in NW Hungary, near the confluence of the Rivers Rába and Danube. Györ's include many old buildings a 12th-century cathedral (rebuilt in the 18th century). It has heavy engineering and lies in an area famous for horse breeding. Population (1997 est): 127 000.

● **Gypsies** ▷See Gipsies.

● **Gypsophila** ► A genus of slender annual or perennial herbs (about 120 species), native to the Mediterranean area. Up to 1.5 m high, they have grey-green strap-shaped leaves and large clusters of white or pink flowers. Some species are grown in rock gardens; others are popular for flower arrangements. Family: *Caryophyllaceae* (pink family).

● **gypsum** ► A colourless or white mineral consisting of hydrated calcium sulphate found in clays, shales, and limestones. It occurs mainly as a result of the evaporation of saline water. Rock gypsum is often red-stained, granular, and found in layers. Gypsite is impure and earthy, occurring as surface deposits. ▷Alabaster is a pure compact fine-grained translucent form. Satin-spar is fibrous and silky. Selenite occurs as transparent crystals in clays and mudstones. Gypsum is used in the manufacture of cement, rubber, paper, plaster of Paris, and blackboard chalk.

● **gypsy moth** ► A moth, *Lymantria dispar*, distributed throughout the N hemisphere. Males are brownish grey and females white. The greyish larvae, which feed on a variety of trees, were introduced to North America in 1869 and have become a serious pest. ▷*See also* tussock moth.

● **gyrfalcon** ► The largest ▷falcon, *Falco rusticolus*, which breeds in N Eurasia, North America, and mountainous regions of Asia. It is 60 cm long and its plumage varies from pure white speckled with black to dark grey with dense black barring. It hunts for hares, rodents, and ground-dwelling birds.

● **gyroscope** ► A device consisting of a heavy wheel mounted in a double gimbal so that it is free to rotate about three mutually perpendicular axes. Once spinning, the wheel maintains the same orientation in space, even when the gimbals are turned. This is made use of in the **gyrocompass** (▯compass) and the gyrostabilizer.

H

● **Haakon IV Haakonsson ▶** (1204–63) King of Norway (1217–63), who added Iceland and Greenland to Norwegian territories (1262). He subdued rebellions and strengthened the monarchy by improving royal administration and by extensive legislation. In 1247 he was crowned by the pope's legate. He died in an invasion of the Isle of Man and the Hebrides.

● **Haakon VII ▶** (1872–1957) The first King of Norway (1905–57) following the restoration of Norwegian independence. In 1896 he married Maud (d. 1938), the daughter of Edward VII of the UK. His refusal to abdicate during the German occupation (1940–45), during which he was in England, encouraged Norwegian resistance.

● **Haarlem ▶** 52 23N 4 38E A city in the W Netherlands, the capital of North Holland province. Surrounded by flower fields, it is a major trade centre for bulbs. Industries include textiles and printing. It is noted for its Frans Hals museum and its fine cathedral (14th–15th centuries). Population (1996 est): 147 617.

● **Habakkuk ▶** An Old Testament prophet of Judah, who lived at the time when a Babylonian invasion was imminent (c. 605 BC). **The Book of Habakkuk** records his perplexity that a just God should make use of an evil nation to inflict punishment on his own people, but the prophet is told to trust in God, who will see to it that all evil will eventually be punished.

● **habeas corpus ▶** (Latin: have the body) A remedy against unlawful confinement, which takes the form of a writ ordering the person alleged to have unlawful custody of a prisoner to produce him before the court issuing the writ and to submit to whatever the court directs. The writ may be used to test the legality of imprisonment but not to appeal against a lawful conviction or sentence. Applications for habeas corpus, made to the Lord Chief Justice's court, take precedence over all others, the counsel interrupting the court by the cry: "My Lord, I have a matter concerning the liberty of the subject."

● **Haber, Fritz ▶** (1868–1934) German chemist and inventor of the Haber process (*see* Haber-Bosch process). Haber won the 1918 Nobel Prize. ▷*See also* Bosch, Carl.

● **Haber-Bosch process ▶** A method for the bulk production of ammonia from atmospheric nitrogen and hydrogen. The pure gases are passed over an iron catalyst at about 500°C and a pressure of 500 atmospheres. Ammonia is chiefly used to make nitrate for fertilizers and ▷explosives. The process was devised by Fritz ▷Haber in 1908 and adapted by Carl ▷Bosch, who added a process for making the hydrogen from ▷water gas and steam. The process was essential to Germany's supply of explosives in World War I.

● **habitat ▶** *See* ecosystem.

● **Habsburgs ▶** (*or* Hapsburgs) The most prominent European royal dynasty from the 15th to 20th centuries. The family originated in Switzerland in the 10th century. In 1273 ▷Rudolph I was elected Holy Roman Emperor and consolidated through marriage and conquest his family's possession of Austria, Carniola, and Styria. After Rudolf's death (1291) the Habsburgs lost the imperial title until 1438 but thereafter kept it until 1740, holding it again from 1745 to 1806. In 1516 ▷Charles V inherited the Spanish Crown, adding Spain with its European and American possessions to the Habsburg domains. When he abdicated in 1556 he left the Spanish Crown to his son, ▷Philip II, and his Austrian possessions to his brother, ▷Ferdinand I. The Spanish branch ruled until 1700, when it died out and was replaced by the

Bourbons. The Austrian Habsburgs continued to rule, becoming emperors of Austria in 1804 and of ▷Austria-Hungary in 1867, which they ruled until World War I ended.

● **hacking ▶** Gaining unauthorized access to a computer system using the telephone network and, usually, a microcomputer. The objective is often to obtain confidential information. In the UK computer users are protected by the Computer Misuse Act (1990). ▷*See also* data protection.

● **Hackney ▶** A borough of N central Greater London, created in 1965 from the former metropolitan boroughs of Hackney, Shoreditch, and Stoke Newington. Hackney Marsh, a former haunt of highwaymen, is now one of London's largest playing fields. Area: 19 sq km (8 sq mi). Population (1996 est): 193 800.

● **hackney coach ▶** A four-wheeled vehicle drawn by two horses, containing seats for six people. Hackney coaches, which appeared in England in the early 17th century, were hired out for town journeys. The phrase "hackney carriage" still appears on the municipal licence plate of English taxis. ▷*See also* cab.

● **Hackney horse ▶** An English breed of trotting horse developed from Norfolk trotters. It has a compact body with strong short legs and powerful shoulders, a full tail, and a fine chestnut bay, brown, or black coat. Hackneys were once fashionable carriage horses and are now used mainly for shows. Height: 1.50–1.60 m (14¾–15¾ hands). A smaller version of the Hackney horse is the **Hackney pony**. Standing at 1.22–1.42 m (12–14 hands), it is bred mainly for the show ring.

● **hadal zone ▶** *See* abyssal zone.

● **Haddington ▶** 55 58N 2 47W A town in E Scotland, in East Lothian. It has an important agricultural market and manufactures woollens and hosiery. John Knox was born here. Population (1991): 8844.

● **haddock ▶** A carnivorous food fish, *Melanogrammus aeglefinus*, related to ▷cod, that usually occurs in shoals near the bottom of N Atlantic coastal waters. It has an elongated body, up to 1 m long, grey or brown above and silvery below with a black spot behind each pectoral fin, two anal and three dorsal fins, a small chin barbel, and a dark lateral line. It is eaten both fresh and smoked.

● **Hades ▶** (Pluto *or* Dis) The Greek god of the dead; also the name of the underworld he ruled. He was the brother of Zeus and Poseidon and husband of ▷Persephone. The dead were ferried to Hades across the River Styx by ▷Charon.

● **Hadhramaut ▶** A region in S Yemen. It consists of a mountain range parallel to the coast rising to over 2000 m (6562 ft) and an inland valley. With irrigation, the production of dates, grain, and tobacco is the main industry, and the chief town is Mukalla, on the coast.

● **Hadith ▶** (Arabic: tradition) Traditional records of sayings and deeds attributed to Mohammed not contained in the Koran but accepted as authoritative. Compilations of such traditions made after the Prophet's death include that by al-▷Bukhari.

● **Hadlee, Sir Richard (John) ▶** (1951–) New Zealand-born cricketer. A brilliant all-rounder, he played for Nottinghamshire (1978–87) and New Zealand (1972–90). A fast bowler, in 1988 he passed Ian

▷Botham's record of test wickets; he lost this record to Kapil Dev in 1994. He was knighted in 1990.

● **Hadrian** ▶ (76–138 AD) Roman emperor (117–38). He was admitted to the imperial household as ▷Trajan's ward in 85 and a successful military career included special responsibility in Trajan's Parthian campaign. On Trajan's death he became emperor, crushed a conspiracy against him (118), and from 120 to 131 toured the provinces. His foreign policy was generally defensive (he sponsored the building of ▷Hadrian's Wall in Britain) but he subdued a Jewish revolt (132–35) with considerable severity. From 131 until his death he lived in Rome, instigating building projects, including the ▷Pantheon and the mausoleum (Castel Sant' Angelo) in which he was buried.

● **Hadrian IV** ▷*See* Adrian IV.

● **Hadrian's Wall** ▶ A Roman frontier defence work. Begun in 122 AD, it was the N frontier of Roman Britain for 250 years. Designed to control the Scottish tribes, it stretched 120 km (75 mi) from Tyne to Solway. It comprised ditch, stone and turf wall (incorporating 16 forts, smaller forts every mile, and signalling turrets), road system, and "vallum" (earthworks delimiting the military area), with supporting troop installations. Temporarily superseded by the ▷Antonine Wall and several times rebuilt, it was finally abandoned in 383 AD. Substantial portions still stand.

● **hadron** ▶ Any elementary particle that takes part in ▷strong interactions. The group thus includes all baryons and mesons but not leptons or the photon. ▷*See* particle physics.

● **Haeckel, Ernst Heinrich** ▶ (1834–1919) German zoologist, noted for his speculative theories concerning the origin of life and evolution. A firm advocate of ▷Darwin's theories, Haeckel went even further. He suggested that life originated through spontaneous combination of the elements and he drew genealogical trees to represent the course of evolution. His recapitulation theory (i.e. that stages in the embryological development of an individual reflect stages in the evolution of the species) is now regarded as unsound.

● **haematite** ▶ (*or* hematite) The principal ore of iron, ferric oxide, varying in colour from red to grey to black. It contains over 70% iron. It occurs either in crystalline form (specular iron ore) or in massive form. Most ore deposits are derived from altered iron carbonates and silicates in sedimentary rocks.

● **haematology** ▶ The study of blood and its diseases. This medical specialty is concerned particularly with treating ▷leukaemias, ▷haemophilia, and rare kinds of anaemia.

● **haemodialysis** ▷*See* dialysis.

● **haemoglobin** ▶ The substance, contained within the red blood cells (*see* erythrocyte), that is responsible for the colour of blood. In humans haemoglobin consists of a protein (globin) combined with an iron-containing pigment (haem). Haem combines with oxygen, which is absorbed into the blood at the lungs, to form oxyhaemoglo-

bin, which gives arterial blood its bright-red colour and is the means by which oxygen is transported around the body. Oxygen is released at the tissues and the pigment acquires a bluish tinge, responsible for the bluish-red colour of venous blood.

● **haemophilia** ▶ A hereditary disease in which the blood does not clot properly due to absence of one of the clotting factors, usually Factor VIII, caused by an abnormal gene on the X chromosome (*see* sex chromosomes). Some of the children of both Queen Victoria and Tsar Nicholas II had this disease, which is almost entirely restricted to boys but is transmitted through the mother. If an affected person (a haemophiliac) cuts himself seriously he needs immediate treatment; haemophiliacs also bleed easily into their joints. The disease can be controlled by administration of Factor VIII, obtained from human blood. A genetically engineered form of this factor is now available, which does not have the danger of being infected with the AIDS virus.

● **haemorrhage** ▶ Bleeding. Large amounts of blood may be lost in severe injuries, from bleeding peptic ulcers, during operations, in childbirth, or if the patient has a clotting disorder (such as ▷haemophilia). In these circumstances it may be necessary to give a blood transfusion to avoid ▷shock and death. If haemorrhage occurs in a confined space, such as the brain or the eye, damage results from destruction of normal tissue.

● **haemorrhoids** ▶ (*or* piles) Swollen (varicose) veins in the anal canal, which may enlarge sufficiently to hang down outside the anus. They are very common, usually resulting from chronic constipation, and tend to run in families. Piles may cause bleeding from the anus and itchiness, but rarely severe pain. In severe cases they may be surgically removed or injected with a sclerosing agent, which makes them shrivel up. External haemorrhoids are painful swellings at the side of the anus, caused by rupture of an anal vein.

● **Ha-er-bin** ▶ (English name: Harbin) 45 45N 126 41E A port in NE China, the capital of Heilongjiang province on the Songhua River. A trading and industrial centre, the site of Heilongjiang University, it was developed by Russia and was a haven for refugees from the Russian Revolution (1917). Population (1991 est): 2 830 000.

● **Hafiz, Shams al-Din Muhammad** ▶ (?1326–90) Persian lyric poet, born at Shiraz, where he worked as a religious teacher and copyist of manuscripts. He subsequently became court poet. He is the acknowledged master of the *ghazal*, a short lyric poem on the subjects of love and wine, which are often treated symbolically (the beloved representing God and wine symbolizing ecstasy). About 500 *ghazals* are attributed to him; Goethe's German translations are perhaps the best known.

● **hafnium** ▶ (Hf) A dense ductile metal, first detected in zircon (ZrSiO$_4$) in 1923 and named after the Latin (Hafnia) for Copenhagen, where it was discovered. It is chemically similar to zirconium and the two elements are difficult to separate. The capacity of hafnium to absorb neutrons is used to control nuclear reactors, especially in sub-

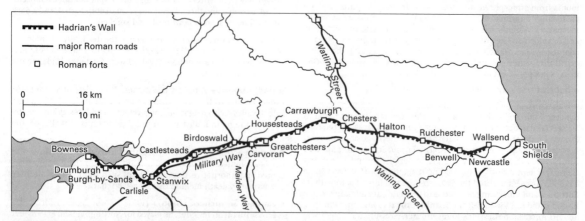

Hadrian's Wall ▶ The most extensive of the Roman remains in the UK.

marines. Its compounds include the chloride ($HfCl_4$) and other halides, the oxide (HfO_2), the carbide (HfC), and the nitride (Hf_3N_4). At no 72; at wt 178.49; mp 2331±20°C; bp 4603°C.

● **Haganah** ▶ (Hebrew: defence) The irregular organization of the early Jewish settlers in Palestine established in 1920 counteract the attacks of the Palestinian Arabs. After the partition of Palestine in 1947, the Haganah became the defence force of the Jewish state, coordinating opposition to the Palestinian and British forces, and in 1948 the national army of the state of Israel.

● **Hagen** ▶ 51 22N 7 27E A city in NW Germany, in North Rhine-Westphalia in the ▷Ruhr. It has iron and steel, textile, and paper industries. Population (1998 est): 209 027.

● **Hagen, Walter Charles** ▶ (1892–1969) US golfer, who did much to popularize the game with his exhibition matches and his extrovert personality. Between 1914 and 1929 he won four British and two US Open championships and five US Professional Golfers Association championships.

● **hagfish** ▶ A fishlike vertebrate, 40–80 cm long, sometimes called slime eel, belonging to a family (*Myxinidae*; about 20 species) of ▷cyclostomes. The eel-like body has 5–16 pairs of gill slits and a sucking mouth surrounded by several thick barbels. Hagfishes occur on or near the sea bottom in cold regions and feed on dead or dying fish. They are initially hermaphrodites but develop either male or female sex organs; fertilization is internal and the eggs hatch to produce young that resemble adults.

● **haggadah** ▶ (*or* aggadah) **1.** Nonlegal portions of the Jewish ▷Midrash, as opposed to ▷halakhah. **2.** The liturgy recited in the Jewish home over the ▷Passover meal (*seder*). It contains a narrative of the Exodus from Egypt and various commentaries and hymns.

● **Haggai** ▶ An Old Testament prophet. **The Book of Haggai** contains four addresses delivered after the ▷Babylonian exile (c. 520 BC). Their purpose is to encourage the completion of the Temple; the prophet rebukes the people's failure to complete the rebuilding of it, but prophesies a return of divine favour when it is rebuilt.

● **Haggard, Sir H(enry) Rider** ▶ (1856–1925) British adventure novelist. His five years in government service in South Africa provided the background of his first and most popular novel, *King Solomon's Mines* (1885), which is notable for a sympathetic treatment of Black Africans. Of his many later romances, *She* (1887) is the best known.

● **haggis** ▶ A traditional Scottish meat dish, called by Burns "great chieftain o' the puddin' race" and eaten especially on Burns' Night (25 Jan). Haggis is made from minced sheep's heart, liver, and lungs with onion, oatmeal, suet, seasonings, lemon juice, and stock. The ingredients are stuffed into a bag, made from the sheep's stomach or a substitute, and boiled for several hours.

● **Hagia Sophia** ▷See St Sophia.

● **Hague, The** ▶ (Dutch name: 's Gravenhage *or* Den Haag) 52 05N 4 16E The seat of government of the Netherlands and capital of South Holland province. It developed as a settlement surrounding a 13th-century hunting lodge and became the seat of the States General of the United Provinces of the Netherlands in the 16th century. It is the residence of the court and the International Court of Justice is located here. Buildings include the 13th-century Binnenhof, in which the government is housed. It is a commercial and residential centre with some light industry. Its port, Scheveningen, is a major herring-fishing centre and the most popular Dutch seaside resort. Population (1999 est): 440 743.

● **Hague, William (Jefferson)** ▶ (1961–) British politician; leader of the Conservative Party (1997–2001). A former Welsh minister (1995–97), he succeeded John ▷Major as leader following the party's heavy defeat in the 1997 election. As leader he reformed the party's structures and attempted to unite it around a policy of opposition to further European integration. After a second crushing defeat for the Conservatives in 2001 he resigned and was succeeded by Iain ▷Duncan Smith.

● **Hague Agreement** ▶ (1949) A treaty ending the hostilities between the Netherlands and the Republic of Indonesia that had erupted after the establishment of the Republic in 1945. A federal government composed of the Republic and 15 autonomous states was created to administer the former Dutch East Indies, excluding West New Guinea. The treaty proved unacceptable to Indonesian nationalists and was revoked by the Indonesian parliament in 1956.

● **Hague Peace Conferences** ▶ (1899, 1907) Two international congresses on ▷disarmament, held at The Hague (Netherlands). The first conference, attended by representatives of 26 countries, codified some of the rules of war as recommended by the ▷Geneva Convention and instituted the permanent Court of Arbitration at The Hague. However, no agreement was reached on disarmament. The second conference, attended by 44 delegates, adopted further conventions on war (*see* neutrality) but again failed to limit armaments.

● **Hahn, Kurt** ▶ (1886–1974) German progressive educationalist. The headmaster of Salem school in Germany (1920–33), Hahn was arrested by the Nazis. He fled to Britain, where he founded ▷Gordonstoun school and was instrumental in establishing the Duke of Edinburgh's Award and the Outward Bound schemes for young people.

● **Hahn, Otto** ▶ (1879–1968) German chemist and physicist. With Lise ▷Meitner he discovered protactinium in 1918. He continued to work with Meitner until she was forced to leave Germany in 1938. Together they discovered the process of nuclear fission. Hahn was unwilling to publish the results of this work, but Meitner did so from Sweden in 1939 and ▷Bohr took the information to the USA. Although Hahn remained in Germany, he did not work on Germany's unsuccessful attempt to make an atom bomb. In 1944 he was awarded the Nobel Prize for Chemistry.

● **Hahnemann, Samuel Christian Friedrich** ▶ (1755–1843) German physician and founder of ▷homeopathy. Hahnemann's methods aroused controversy among his contemporaries and he was forced to leave his practice in Leipzig, eventually settling in Paris.

● **hahnium** ▶ (Ha; element 105) An artificial transuranic element, synthesized in the USA in 1970 by bombarding californium-249 with nitrogen-15 in a particle accelerator and possibly also in the Soviet Union in 1967 by a different method. Named after Otto Hahn. At no 105; at wt (260).

● **Haifa** ▶ 32 49N 34 59E A town in NW Israel, on the Mediterranean coast by Mount Carmel. It was the scene of fighting in the 1948–49 Arab-Israeli conflict and has since developed into a manufacturing town based on the deepwater port (opened 1933). Haifa University was founded in 1963. Population (1999 est): 265 700.

● **Haig, Douglas, 1st Earl** ▶ (1861–1928) British field marshal. After service in N Africa and India, Haig in World War I became commander of the first army corps in France and later commander in chief of the British Expeditionary Force (1915). Haig has been criticized for the appalling losses of the Somme and Passchendaele campaigns but his task was made difficult by the lack of support from ▷Lloyd George's War Cabinet. Under the supreme command of ▷Foch, Haig directed the final victorious assault on the Hindenburg line. He organized the ▷Royal British Legion after the war.

● **hail** ▶ The approximately spherical ice pellets that fall from cumulonimbus clouds. These have been known to weigh almost 1 kg (2.2 lb). They originate within clouds as small ice particles around which layers of ice freeze. Hailstorms occur most often in the continental interiors of temperate latitudes.

● **Haile Selassie I** ▶ (Ras Tafari Makonnen; 1892–1975) Emperor of Ethiopia (1930–36, 1941–74). In 1916 he became regent and heir to Empress Zauditu, succeeding her in 1930 and adopting the name Haile Selassie (Might of the Trinity). He led the resistance to the Italian invasion (1935) and gained world sympathy by taking his case to the League of Nations. In 1936 he had to flee to England but was restored to the throne by the Allies in 1941. An autocratic ruler, who did much to modernize Ethiopia, he was deposed by a military coup and assassinated. ▷See also Rastafarians.

● **Hailsham of St Marylebone, Quintin McGarel Hogg, Baron** ▶ (1907–2001) British lawyer and Conservative politician;

Lord Chancellor (1970–74, 1979–87). A fellow of All Souls College, Oxford (1931–38), he entered parliament in 1938. From 1959 to 1963 he was minister for science and technology. In 1950 he succeeded his father **Douglas McGarel Hogg, 1st Viscount Hailsham** (1872–1950), Lord Chancellor (1928–29, 1935–38), but disclaimed his viscounty in 1963, when he made an unsuccessful bid for the Conservative Party leadership. In 1970 he became a life peer. His grandfather **Quintin Hogg** (1845–1903), a philanthropist, founded the Regent Street Polytechnic in 1882. Lord Hailsham's son, **Douglas Hogg** (1945–   ), was minister of agriculture, fisheries, and food from 1995 to 1997, during the ▷BSE crisis.

● **Hailwood, Mike** ▶ (Stanley Michael Bailey H.; 1940–81) British racing motorcyclist, who between 1961 and 1967 won nine world championships and 12 TT races. He later switched to motor racing (1969) and in 1973 was awarded the George Medal for saving another driver.

● **Hainan Island** ▶ A Chinese island (the largest in the South China Sea apart from Taiwan) separated from the mainland by **Hainan Strait**. It is sparsely populated and mainly undeveloped; in 1988 it became a province as part of a development plan. The aboriginal population has moved into the mountainous centre and S as Chinese farmers have settled the N. Rubber and timber are produced and iron ore and other minerals are mined. Area: 33 991 sq km (13 124 sq mi). Population (1997 est): 7 430 000. Capital: Haikou.

● **Hainaut** ▶ (Flemish name: Henegouwen; French name: Hainault) A province in SW Belgium, bordering on France. It has important coalfields and iron and steel industries. Area: 3997 sq km (1466 sq mi). Population (1996 est): 1 284 761. Capital: Mons.

● **Haiphong** ▶ 20 50N 106 41E A city in N Vietnam, on the Red River delta. As Hanoi's outport and an industrial centre, it was severely bombed during the Vietnam War. Textiles, phosphates, and plastics are manufactured and minerals and rice exported. Population (1992 est): 783 133.

● **hair** ▶ The threadlike structures forming the body covering of mammals. Each hair grows from the base of a sheath (**hair follicle**) embedded in the inner layer (dermis) of the □skin but only a few cells at its root are living. The rest consists of scaly dead cells made largely of ▷keratin and other proteins. Colour is determined by the amount of ▷melanin pigment in hair. In most mammals hair forms an insulating and protective coat (the pelage), which reduces heat loss from the body and often provides camouflage. In humans hair is important only for personal adornment and display. Similar structures in lower animals (e.g. insects) often have a sensory function, and plants possess hairs on roots, stems, and leaves.

● **hairstreak** ▶ A butterfly belonging to the family Lycaenidae and characterized by fine white streaks on the underwings and a small "tail" on each hindwing. Both Old and New World species show a great variety of coloration. ▷See also blue.

● **hairy frog** ▶ A ▷frog, Astylosternus robustus, of the Cameroons. In the breeding season the skin on the sides and thighs of male frogs develops hairlike filaments, containing many blood vessels, that assist in breathing and compensate for its much reduced lungs. The females grow no hairs.

● **Haiti, Republic of** ▶ A country in the Caribbean Sea, occupying the W third of the island of Hispaniola (the Dominican Republic occupies the E two-thirds). Much of Haiti is mountainous and forested, with fertile plains between three main mountain ranges. It is subject to hurricanes. Most of the population is of African descent, with a minority of mulattoes.
Economy: mainly agricultural, mostly organized in small farms. The main crops are coffee (the chief export), sugar, rice, bananas, and sisal. Mineral resources are largely unexploited although some bauxite and copper are mined. Hydroelectricity is an important source of power. Privatization of state industries began in the later 1990s, as did a policy of redistributing land from the large agricultural estates to small producers. Haiti joined the Caribbean Community in 1997. There is a large foreign debt.
History: Columbus landed on the island in 1492 and it became a Spanish colony. The Spanish virtually wiped out the native Indian

population and large numbers of African slaves were brought in. The W part was ceded to France in 1697, becoming the most prosperous of the French colonies; the remainder was temporarily ceded between 1795 and 1809. The slave leader ▷Toussaint L'Ouverture briefly ruled the whole island and in 1804, under Gen ▷Dessalines, Haiti gained its independence. A period of unrest was followed by union with the rest of the island (1822–44). For most of the time since it has been a republic; it was briefly occupied by the USA (1915–34). After a series of coups Dr François ▷Duvalier ("Papa Doc") came to power in 1957 and was succeeded in 1971 by his son, Jean-Claude Duvalier ("Baby Doc"). In 1986 Duvalier's brutal regime fell in a military coup; a government was then set up under Lt-Gen Henri Namphy. There was a further coup in 1988. After a landslide electoral victory in December 1990, Jean Bertrand ▷Aristide became president on a human-rights platform. In October he was deposed by the military, who violently suppressed all dissent, and the UN imposed sanctions. In 1994, with the aid of US troops, Aristide returned to Haiti and assumed the presidency. His associate René Préval took over following elections in 1996. In 1999 President Préval's disputes with parliament led to a state of constitutional crisis. Aristide was re-elected president in 2000 but the result was widely disputed, leading to further crisis.

Republic of Haiti

Head of state	President Jean Bertrand Aristide
Official languages	French and Creole
Official religion	Roman Catholic
Official currency	gourde of 100 centimes
Area	27 750 sq km (10 700 sq mi)
Population (2000 est)	6 868 000
Capital and main port	Port-au-Prince

● **Haitink, Bernard** ▶ (1929–   ) Dutch conductor. He was permanent conductor of the Amsterdam Concertgebouw Orchestra (1964–88), conductor of the London Philharmonic Orchestra (1967–79), and musical director at Glyndebourne (1978–88). He was music director at Covent Garden from 1987 until 2002.

● **hajj** ▶ The pilgrimage to Mecca that every able Muslim is required to make, if means permit, at least once in his lifetime during the first half of the last month of the Islamic year. The pilgrimage includes circumambulations of the ▷Kaaba and visits to other holy places.

● **hake** ▶ A food fish, of the genus Merluccius, that is related to ▷cod and occurs off European, African, and American coasts. Its body, up to about 1 m long, is dark grey above and lighter below, with two dorsal fins, the second running to the tail and matching the anal fin.

● **Hakka** ▶ A Chinese ethnic minority group found in the provinces of Canton and Fujian and in Taiwan and Chinese settlements in East Asia. The Hakkas (guest people) migrated S from N China in the unrest of the 12th and 13th centuries and for several centuries were social outcasts, having brought with them the different dialect and customs that they still retain.

● **Hakkinen, Mika** ▶ (c. 1968–   ) Finnish motor-racing driver. He was Formula One world champion in 1998 and 1999.

● **Hakluyt, Richard** ▶ (c. 1553–1616) English geographer. As a clergyman he served in various posts, but his chief interest was in exploration, navigation, and the establishment of a colony in Virginia. His major work, *The Principal Navigations, Voyages, Traffics, and Discoveries of the English Nation...* (1 vol, 1589; 3 vols, 1598–1600), stimulated English overseas trade and colonization.

● **Hakodate** ▶ 41 46N 140 44E A port in Japan, in SW Hokkaido on the Tsugaru Strait. It contains Japan's only Western-style fort (1855). Industries include fishing and shipbuilding. Population (1995): 298 868.

● **Halab** ▷See Aleppo.

● **halakhah** ▶ Jewish law. The Hebrew word is used in different ways, either for the law as a whole or an individual regulation. The main halakhic sources are the ▷Torah, ▷Mishnah, and ▷Talmuds, the gaonic responsa (*see* gaon), and the medieval codes (e.g. those of ▷Maimonides and Joseph ▷Caro). The halakhah embraces more than law: it governs every aspect of life and also embodies theological ideas. The authority of halakhah is one of the main points of disagreement between traditional and ▷Reform Judaism.

● **Halberstadt** ▶ 51 53N 11 2E A town in central Germany. Many of its historic buildings, including the gothic cathedral, survived the bombing during World War II. Its varied industries include sugar refining, engineering, and chemicals. Population (1989 est): 47 500.

● **Halcyone** ▶ In Greek legend, daughter of ▷Aeolus. She threw herself into the sea after her husband, Ceyx of Thrachis, drowned, and they were both transformed into kingfishers.

● **Haldane, Richard Burdon, 1st Viscount** ▶ (1856–1928) British army reformer. A Liberal MP (1885–1911) until becoming a peer, he was secretary for war from 1905 to 1912. He created a general staff on the German model (1906), formed the Territorial Force (*see* Territorial Army), and facilitated the mobilization of the British Expeditionary Force at the outbreak of World War I. Becoming Lord Chancellor in 1912 he was dismissed in 1915 because his knowledge of Germany brought accusations that he was pro-German. Also a philosopher, he wrote a study of the philosophical implications of ▷relativity, *The Reign of Relativity* (1921). He helped to found the London School of Economics (1895). His brother **John Scott Haldane** (1860–1936) was a physiologist, noted for his investigations of human respiration. Haldane established that the rate of breathing was regulated according to the concentration of carbon dioxide in the blood. He also investigated the effects of high altitude and deepsea pressures on respiration and improved mine safety by demonstrating the toxic effects of carbon monoxide. J. S. Haldane's son **John Burdon Sanderson Haldane** (1892–1964) was a geneticist and philosopher, who contributed to many aspects of biology, including evolution and population genetics. Haldane was a Marxist and during the 1930s edited the communist *Daily Worker* (London). He left the Communist Party because of his disillusionment with the prominence given to the theories of ▷Lysenko in the Soviet Union. In 1957 Haldane emigrated to India in protest against British policy.

● **Hale, Sir Matthew** ▶ (1609–76) English lawyer and judge. Hale defended such royalists as Archbishop ▷Laud during the Civil War but nevertheless became a judge and MP under Cromwell. After the Restoration he was appointed chief baron of the Exchequer (1660) and later chief justice of the King's Bench (1671). He was the author of an important legal work, *The History of the Common Law of England* (1713).

● **Hale Observatories** ▶ The group of observatories comprising the Palomar Observatory, Mount Wilson Observatory, Big Bear Solar Observatory, all in California, and Las Campanas Observatory, near La Serena, Chile. They are sponsored by the Californian Institute of Technology and the Carnegie Institution, Washington. The principal telescopes are the famous 5 m (200 in) reflector and a 1.2 m (48 in) ▷Schmidt telescope (Palomar), the oldest 2.5 m (100 in) reflector (Mount Wilson), and a new 2.5 m reflector (Las Campanas). They are named after the US astronomer G. E. Hale (1868–1938), who helped to develop the Mount Wilson and Palomar Observatories.

● **Halévy, Jacques François** ▶ (Fromental Elias Levy; 1799–1862) French composer of Jewish origin. A pupil of Cherubini at the Paris conservatoire, he won the Prix de Rome in 1819. He composed ballets, incidental music, cantatas, and over 30 operas, including *La Juive* (1835).

● **Haley, Bill** ▷*See* rock and roll.

● **half-life** ▶ The time taken for half the atoms in a sample of a radioactive isotope to decay. It is therefore a measure of the activity of an isotope. A very active isotope may have a half-life of only a millionth of a second, whereas some more stable isotopes have half-lives of millions of years.

● **half-timber work** ▶ A building technique used since ancient times. It involves constructing a wooden skeleton for a building, which is then filled out with either plasterwork or brick. Frequently the frame is left exposed. A quickly built and strong structure, it is best suited to temperate climates. The technique was frequently used in 15th- and 16th-century England.

● **halibut** ▶ A ▷flatfish of the genus *Hippoglossus*, especially *H. hippoglossus*—a large food fish, up to about 2 m long, found in N Atlantic coastal waters. The eyed (right) side is brown or dark green with mottling. Family: *Pleuronectidae*.

Other halibuts include the Greenland halibut and the California halibut, which belong to the family *Bothidae*.

● **Haliç** ▷*See* Golden Horn.

● **Halicarnassus** ▶ (modern name: Bodrum) An ancient city of ▷Caria on the SW coast of Asia Minor. Its rulers included ▷Artemisia and Mausolus, who made Halicarnassus his capital (c. 370 BC) and is remembered chiefly for his tomb, the ▷Mausoleum. Herodotus, the Greek historian, was born here.

● **halides** ▷*See* halogens.

● **Halidon Hill, Battle of** ▶ (19 July, 1333) The battle between English forces under ▷Edward III and Scots attempting to relieve Berwick-upon-Tweed. Using archers to great effect, the English victory ensured the temporary success of Edward's vassal, Edward de ▷Balliol, in his claims to the Scottish throne.

● **Halifax** ▶ 53 44N 1 52W A town in N England, in Calderdale unitary authority, West Yorkshire, on the River Calder. Halifax has a strong wool textile tradition going back to the 13th century. Carpets, woollens, and worsteds are manufactured as well as machine tools and textile machinery. Population (1991): 91 069.

● **Halifax** ▶ 44 38N 63 35W A city and major port in E Canada, the capital of Nova Scotia on the Atlantic Ocean. Founded as a British naval base (1749), it dominates the cultural life, commerce, and industry of the ▷Maritime Provinces. Its industries include shipbuilding, oil refining, steel, and food processing. Population (1991): 114 455.

● **Halifax, Charles Montagu, 1st Earl of** ▶ (1661–1715) English statesman. A Whig MP (1689–95), as a lord of the treasury (1692–94) he initiated the national debt and set up the ▷Bank of England (1694) and as chancellor of the exchequer (1694–95) he introduced a new coinage. In 1697 he became first lord of the treasury but in 1699 was forced by the Tories to resign; he again held the post in 1714–15. He was a patron of writers, including the playwright ▷Congreve.

● **Halifax, Edward Frederick Lindley Wood, 1st Earl of** ▶ (1881–1959) British politician and colonial administrator. As viceroy of India (1925–31) he was sympathetic to the nationalists, collaborating with Gandhi. As foreign secretary (1938–40), he supported Neville Chamberlain's policy of ▷appeasement. He was passed over as Chamberlain's successor and served as ambassador to the USA (1941–46).

● **Halifax, George Savile, 1st Marquess of** ▶ (1633–95) English politician, nicknamed the Trimmer because of the inconsistency of his views. He became a privy councillor in 1672 but was dismissed in 1676 for opposing Charles II's pro-French and pro-Roman Catholic policies. Again a privy councillor in 1679, he opposed the exclusion of the Catholic Duke of York (later James II) from the succession. He lost office at James' accession (1685) and supported the ▷Glorious Revolution. He wrote *The Character of a Trimmer* (1688).

● **halite** ▷*See* salt.

● **halitosis** ▶ Bad breath. Very foul-smelling breath may be caused by infection in the mouth, teeth, tonsils, or lungs and sometimes by stomach disease. Regular cleaning of the teeth can abolish the mild odour that many people have.

● **Hall, Sir Peter** ▶ (1930–   ) British theatre director. He was director of the Royal Shakespeare Company from 1960 to 1968 and director of the National Theatre Company from 1973 to 1988. He is best known for his Shakespearean productions, but he has also directed plays by Harold Pinter and other contemporary playwrights, as well as operas and films. He formed his own company on leaving the National Theatre.

● **Hall, (Marguerite) Radclyffe** ▶ (1883–1943) British writer. After publishing volumes of poetry and short stories and several novels, she achieved critical acclaim for her novel *Adam's Breed* (1926). However, she is now remembered mainly as the author of *The Well of Loneliness* (1928), a novel whose frank discussion of lesbianism led to a trial for obscenity and its banning despite support from literary figures.

● **Halle** ► 51 30N 11 59E A city in central Germany, on the River Saale. The birthplace of Handel, Halle has many old buildings. Industries include sugar refining and coalmining. The university was founded in 1694. Population (1996 est): 282 784.

● **Hallé, Sir Charles** ► (Karl Hallé; 1819–1895) German conductor and pianist. He settled in Britain in 1848 and in 1857 established a series of concerts in Manchester, for which he founded and conducted the **Hallé Orchestra.**

● **Hall effect** ► If a conductor carrying an electric current is placed in a magnetic field, so that the field and the current are at right angles to each other, an electric field appears across the material. The electric field is perpendicular to both the current and the magnetic field. The effect is due to the force experienced by all moving charges in a magnetic field: the charges flowing in the material are displaced to one side thus creating a potential difference. Named after Edwin H. Hall (1855–1938).

● **Haller, Albrecht von** ► (1708–77) Swiss biologist, poet, and one of the founders of modern physiology. Haller showed how the stimulation of a nerve caused contraction of the muscle to which it was attached. He also studied the brain, heart, breathing mechanisms, and embryology; his works include *Elementa physiologiae corporis humani* (8 vols, 1757–66) and four large bibliographies of botany, anatomy, surgery, and medicine. His best-known poem is *Die Alpen.*

● **Halley, Edmund** ► (1656–1742) British astronomer, who was appointed professor of geometry at Oxford University in 1703. He was the first to realize that ▷comets do not appear randomly but have periodic orbits. In 1705 he identified a particular comet, now known as **Halley's comet**, as having a period of 76 years (appearing 1986, 2062, etc.). In 1986 it was intercepted and photographed at close range by the European probe Giotto. He also discovered that stars have a proper motion of their own (1718) and was appointed astronomer royal to succeed ▷Flamsteed (1720). A friend of Sir Isaac Newton, he financed the publication of Newton's *Principia* from an inheritance.

● **hallmarks** ► A set of marks stamped onto gold, silver, and (since 1975) platinum objects manufactured in the UK, as a guarantee of purity. Each article has up to five marks: the mark of the assay office (or hall), an assay mark to indicate quality, a date mark, a duty mark (1784–1890) consisting of the sovereign's head showing that the excise duty had been paid, and the maker's mark. Gold articles also have a mark to indicate their purity, in ▷carats prior to 1975 but as the number of parts per 1000 thereafter (e.g. 14 carat = 583, 9 ct = 375). From January 1999 all articles made of a precious metal in the EU must carry an indication of purity in this numerical form. The future of hallmarks is under discussion as part of the same move to make the marking of precious metals consistent throughout Europe.

● **Hallowe'en** ► 31 Oct, the eve of All Saints' Day. The name is a contraction of All Hallows (hallowed or holy) Eve. In pre-Christian Britain, 31 Oct was the eve of New Year, when the souls of the dead were thought to revisit their homes. After it became a Christian festival supernatural associations continued; customs include the shaping of a demon's face from a hollow turnip or pumpkin, in which a candle is then placed. Children go from door to door on Hallowe'en demanding "treats" on penalty of "tricks."

● **Hallstatt** ► The phase of the central European Iron Age (700–500 BC) preceding ▷La Tène. It is named after the site in the Salzkammergut in Austria, which is famous for its salt mines. Earlier Bronze Age (*see* Urnfield) people in the same area (1200–700 BC) are often included under the term. The wealth of Iron Age Hallstatt depended on extensive trade. Characteristic artefacts were iron swords and elaborate bronze vessels decorated with geometric patterns, solar symbols, or ducks. Wagon burial was practised, e.g. at Vix (France).

● **hallucination** ► A vivid but false perception of something that is not really there. Any sense can be affected. It may be a result of mental illness, especially ▷psychosis, when the commonest forms

are hearing voices and seeing frightening visions. It can also be caused by drugs, epilepsy, disease of the brain, and sensory deprivation. Transient hallucinations can be experienced by normal people, especially when they are falling asleep (hypnagogic hallucinations) or waking up (hypnopompic hallucinations) or if they have been bereaved (grief hallucinations, of the person who has been lost).

● **hallucinogens** ► Drugs that produce hallucinations due to their effect on the brain. Such drugs are also described as psychedelic. Hallucinogens, which include ▷cannabis, ▷ecstasy, and ▷LSD, tend to lead to some form of ▷drug dependence. The ability of any given hallucinogen to produce a hallucination depends very much on the personality of the individual. Some unlikely drugs (e.g. digitalis) may provoke hallucinations in susceptible individuals.

● **halogens** ► The elements forming group 17 of the ▷periodic table: fluorine, chlorine, bromine, iodine, and astatine. In chemical reactions they tend to form negative ions or covalent bonds and have a valence of 1. All are reactive, particularly fluorine and chlorine. They produce salts (**halides**) on contact with metals ("halogen" means salt-yielding) and react with other nonmetals and many organic compounds.

● **Hals, Frans** ► (c. 1581–1666) Dutch painter of portraits and scenes of everyday life. He was born in Antwerp but worked mainly in Haarlem. Apart from his *Laughing Cavalier* (1624; Wallace Collection, London), he is best known for his group portraits, such as those of the companies of archers and musketeers, which are characterized by lively expressions and gestures. Later works, such as *Lady-Governors of the Almshouse at Haarlem* (1664; Frans Hals Museum, Haarlem), influenced by ▷Rembrandt, are more sombre and show a greater sympathy for character.

A typical hallmark, from a sterling silver article assayed in London in 1796.

marks of present assay offices
Some variations in the surrounding shields occur.

London
A leopard's head introduced in 1300 (crowned between 1478 and 1821).

Birmingham
An anchor introduced in 1773.

Sheffield
The crown, introduced in 1773, was replaced by the rose in 1975.

Edinburgh
The castle introduced in the mid-16th century. The thistle was introduced in 1759. The castle is now used.

marks of some former assay offices

Chester

Newcastle-on-Tyne

York

Norwich

Exeter

Glasgow

standard marks

Sterling silver

Britannia silver

9 carat gold

Platinum

All assay offices employ the same marks for both Britannia silver (95.84% pure) and Sterling silver (92.5%), except London, which, before 1975, used a separate Britannia mark.

hallmarks

● **Halsey, William F(rederick)** ▶ (1882–1959) US admiral. A naval aviator, he commanded the South Pacific area (1942–44) and the Third Fleet (1944–45). He contributed to the battles of Guadalcanal, the Coral Sea (1942), ▷Leyte Gulf (1944), and Okinawa (1945), which marked the transition in naval warfare from guns to aircraft as the decisive weapons.

● **Hälsingborg** ▷*See* Helsingborg.

● **Halton** ▶ A unitary authority in NW England, in Cheshire, consisting of the towns of Runcorn and Widnes on either side of the River Mersey. Administrative centre: Runcorn. Area: 75 sq km (29 sq mi). Population (1996 est): 123 300.

● **Hama** ▶ 35 09N 36 44E A town in W Syria. It dates from Hittite times and medieval water-wheels up to 27 m (89 ft) in diameter for irrigation still stand. It is mainly an agricultural and commercial centre. Population (1992 est): 229 000.

● **Hamadan** ▶ 34 46N 48 35E A town in W central Iran. Hamadan lies at a high altitude, and visitors are attracted by the cool summers; the winters, however, are severe. A university was founded here in 1973. Population (1994 est): 406 070.

● **hamadryas** ▶ A small ▷baboon, *Papio hamadryas*, of NE Africa and Saudi Arabia. 100–140 cm long including the tail (40–60 cm), hamadryas baboons have a long silvery-brown mane, pinkish face, and red buttocks and live in groups with a complex social structure. They were sacred to the ancient Egyptians.

● **Hamamatsu** ▶ 34 42N 137 42E A city in Japan, in S central Honshu. A commercial and industrial centre, its manufactures include musical instruments, textiles, and motor cycles. Population (1995): 561 568.

● **Hamas** ▶ (*or* Islamic Resistance Movement) An organization formed in 1976 by Sheikh Yassin Ahmed as a nonmilitant Islamic group with the aim of creating an Islamic Palestinian state. However, Hamas became increasingly militant in the early 1990s, launching terrorist attacks on Israel. Israel deported hundreds of its members to S Lebanon in 1992, although many were allowed to return later. Considering the peace agreement between Israel and the ▷Palestine Liberation Organization to be surrender, militant Hamas members have carried out a series of suicide bombings in Israeli cities since 1996, killing many people and incurring the wrath of both Israeli and Palestinian authorities.

● **Hamburg** ▶ 53 33N 10 00E A city in N Germany, on the Rivers Elbe and Alster. A major port, it is also a cultural centre, with a university (1919), art gallery, and opera house (1678). It is the birthplace of Mendelssohn and Brahms. Its industries include shipbuilding, engineering, and food processing.
History: in 834 AD it was made the seat of a missionary archbishop. Its alliance with Lübeck (1241) became the basis of the Hanseatic League. It was a trading centre from the middle ages and the first German stock exchange was established here (1558). It was severely bombed during World War II. Population (1996 est): 1 707 901.

● **Hamburg** ▶ A small *Land* in N Germany, comprising the city of ▷Hamburg, the surrounding area, and two islands in the Elbe estuary. Area: 748 sq km (289 sq mi). Population (1995 est): 1 705 900.

● **Hamelin** ▶ (German name: Hameln) 52 06N 9 21E A town in N Germany, in Lower Saxony on the River Weser. Its many Renaissance houses include the Ratcatcher's House (1602–03), associated with the legendary Pied Piper, and the Wedding House. Manufactures include carpets and chemicals. Population (latest est): 58 000.

● **Hamersley Range** ▶ A mountain range of N Western Australia. It extends W–E between the Fortesque and Ashburton Rivers, reaching 1227 m (4024 ft) at Mount Bruce, and contains large deposits of iron ore.

● **Hamhŭng** ▶ (*or* Hamheung) 39 54N 127 35E A city in E central North Korea. Its industry was bombed by US forces during the Korean War (1950–53) but has been restored and developed. The principal manufactures are synthetic textiles, chemicals, and machinery. Its seaport, Hungnam, lies to the SE of the city. Population (latest est): 701 000.

● **Hamilcar Barca** ▶ (died c. 229 BC) Carthaginian general and Hannibal's father. Commander in Sicily during the first ▷Punic War, he negotiated peace in 241. After suppressing rebellious mercenaries in Carthage, he invaded Spain, accompanied by the young Hannibal. He was drowned after the siege of Helice.

● **Hamilton** ▶ 43 15N 79 50W A city and port in central Canada, in S Ontario on Lake Ontario. Canada's main centre of heavy industry, it is important for iron and steel, motor vehicles, machinery, chemicals, and electrical goods. It is also a financial, agricultural, transportation, and educational centre. McMaster University (1887) was moved here from Toronto in 1930. Population (1991): 318 499.

● **Hamilton** ▶ 37 46S 175 18E A city in New Zealand, in N North Island on the Waikato River. It is the most important inland centre and serves a pastoral and lumbering region. The University of Waikato was established here in 1964. Population (1996 est): 106 700.

● **Hamilton** ▶ 55 47N 4 03W A town in W central Scotland, the administrative centre of South Lanarkshire in the Clyde valley. Metal goods, carpets, and electrical equipment are manufactured, local coalmining having declined. Population (1992 est): 63 827.

● **Hamilton, Alexander** ▶ (?1755–1804) US statesman; the first US secretary of the treasury (1789–95); leader of the ▷Federalist Party. He established the first national bank (1791) and set up the national debt. He believed in representative central government and collaborated in the *Federalist* (1788), which was influential in securing ratification of the Constitution. He was killed in a duel by Aaron ▷Burr, a long-standing political opponent, after denouncing him as candidate for the governorship of New York.

● **Hamilton, Lady Emma** ▶ (c. 1761–1815) The mistress of Horatio ▷Nelson. She was previously the mistress of Charles Greville (1749–1809) and of his uncle Sir William Hamilton (1730–1803), envoy to the court of Naples (1764–1800). She married Hamilton (1791) and met Nelson in Naples in 1793. They became lovers and had a daughter, Horatia (1801–81). After Nelson's death (1805), Lady Emma squandered her inheritance and fled, a bankrupt, to Calais (1814), where she died. ▷Romney painted many portraits of her.

● **Hamilton, Iain Ellis** ▶ (1922–2000) Scottish composer. Trained at the Royal Academy of Music, he wrote symphonies, concertos, and chamber music as well as the operas *Royal Hunt of the Sun, Anna Karenina,* and *Raleigh's Dream.*

● **Hamilton, James, 1st Duke of** ▶ (1606–49) Scottish royalist in the English Civil War. As Charles I's commissioner in Scotland (1638–41) he tried to moderate the king's unpopular religious policy and opposed his minister Strafford. After the outbreak of the Civil War, however, he joined Charles. Defeated by Cromwell at Preston, he was executed.

● **Hamilton, Sir William Rowan** ▶ (1805–65) Irish mathematician. A child prodigy, he had mastered 13 languages by the age of 13 and at 22 was appointed professor of astronomy at Trinity College, Dublin. His most important work was the discovery of quaternions, three-dimensional equivalents of ▷complex numbers. He also made important contributions to the mathematics of light rays and helped to establish the wave theory of light. A **hamiltonian**, introduced by William Hamilton, is a function that expresses the energy of a system in terms of its momentum and positional coordinates. It is used in quantum mechanics and wave mechanics.

● **Hamito-Semitic languages** ▶ A language family spoken in N Africa and S Asia. It is more appropriately known as Afro-Asiatic, especially since the Hamitic section of the name describes no particular characteristics. It has five branches that descend from an ancestor language, Proto-Hamito-Semitic, which was spoken between the 6th and 8th millenniums BC. The five branches are Egyptian, Berber, Cushitic, Semitic, and Chadic. There is some doubt about the membership of the Chadic languages in this group.

● **Hamm** ▶ 51 40N 7 49E A city in NW Germany, in North Rhine-Westphalia. The rail centre of the ▷Ruhr, it has the largest marshalling yards in the country. Its chief manufactures are wire, cable, and machinery. Population (1996 est): 183 408.

● **Hammarskjöld, Dag (Hjalmar Agne Carl)** ► (1905–61) Swedish international civil servant; the son of Hjalmar Hammarskjöld (1862–1953), who was a prime minister of Sweden (1914–17). As deputy foreign minister (1951–53) he headed the Swedish delegation to the UN and in 1953 succeeded Trygve ▷Lie as secretary general of the UN. He dealt with the Suez crisis (1956) and the civil war arising from the grant of independence to the Congo (1960). He was killed in a plane crash and awarded the Nobel Peace Prize posthumously in 1961. His diary *Markings* was published in 1964.

● **Hammerfest** ► 70 40N 23 44E A port in N Norway, on the W coast of the island of Kvaløya (*or* Kvaløy). It is the most northerly town in the world. Its ice-free harbour permits fishing all year. Population (1991): 6900.

● **hammerhead** ► A dark-brown bird, *Scopus umbretta*, that is the only member of its family (*Scopidae*) and occurs in marshes and mangrove swamps of tropical Africa, Madagascar, and the Arabian Peninsula. It has a large bill and a long backward-pointing crest. Hammerheads feed on frogs, fish, and aquatic invertebrates and build a large domed nest of sticks cemented together with mud. Order: *Ciconiiformes* (herons, storks, etc.).

● **hammerhead shark** ► A ▷shark of the family *Sphyrnidae*, found in warm and temperate salt waters. Up to 4.5 m long, the head is flattened and extended laterally into two hammer- or spade-shaped lobes, which bear the eyes and nostrils. They feed primarily on fish but may attack other animals, including man.

● **Hammersmith and Fulham** ► A borough of W Greater London, on the River Thames. It was created in 1965 from the former metropolitan boroughs of Hammersmith and ▷Fulham. It contains Olympia (an exhibition centre) and the BBC television centre. Area: 16 sq km (6 sq mi). Population (1994 est): 156 600.

● **Hammerstein II, Oscar** ► (1895–1960) US lyricist and librettist, who collaborated with several well-known musical comedy composers. With Richard Rodgers he wrote *Oklahoma!* (1943), *Carousel* (1945), *South Pacific* (1949), *The King and I* (1951), and *The Sound of Music* (1959).

● **hammer throw** ► A field event for men in athletics. The hammer is an iron or brass sphere weighing 16 lb (7.26 kg) attached to a spring-steel wire handle and grip. It is thrown with both hands from within a circle 7 ft (2.13 m) in diameter. A competitor has six tries in which to throw the hammer the furthest. World record: 86.74 m (1986) by Yuri Sedykh (Soviet Union).

● **Hammett, Dashiell** ► (1894–1961) US novelist. He worked as a private detective for eight years before writing his first detective stories. His novels, the realistic and economical style of which influenced Raymond ▷Chandler and other detective-story writers, include *The Maltese Falcon* (1930) and *The Thin Man* (1932), both of which were made into successful films.

● **Hammond, Dame Joan** ► (1912–96) British soprano, born in New Zealand. She studied in Sydney, London, and Vienna, making her operatic debut in Vienna in 1929 and thereafter appearing in the principal opera houses of the world. She was created a DBE in 1974.

● **Hammond, Wally** ► (Walter Reginald H.; 1903–65) British cricketer, who played for England and Gloucestershire. A great all-rounder, he played in 85 Test matches and in his career hit 167 centuries (22 in Tests).

● **Hammurabi** ► (d. 1750 BC) King of Babylon (1792–1750). After defeating the kingdoms of Eshunna, Elam, and Ashur, Hammurabi turned against his former allies, the kingdoms of Larsa and Mari. The Code of Hammurabi, a collection of Babylonian laws, has survived in the Akkadian language.

● **Hampden, John** ► (1594–1643) English parliamentarian, who opposed the policies of Charles I. Elected an MP in 1621, he was imprisoned (1627–28) for refusing to pay a forced loan. In 1636 he was tried for failing to pay ▷ship money but the king only narrowly won the case and the widespread opposition to the tax was intensified. A vocal critic in the ▷Long Parliament (summoned in 1640), he was one of the five MPs whom Charles tried to arrest in 1642. Hampden was killed near Thame in a minor battle of the Civil War.

● **Hampshire** ► A county of S central England, on the English Channel. Under local government reorganization in 1974 it lost part of the SW, including Bournemouth, to Dorset. Portsmouth and Southampton became independent ▷unitary authorities in 1997. It consists mainly of undulating lowlands, rising to chalk downs in the N and E. The chief rivers, the Test and Itchen, drain into the Solent, which separates the Isle of ▷Wight from the mainland. It is mainly agricultural with dairy and arable farming. Industries, centred on Southampton, include shipbuilding and oil refining and there are important naval bases at Portsmouth and Gosport. Tourism is important in the ▷New Forest. Area (excluding unitary authorities): 3780 sq km (1459 sq mi). Population (1996 est, excluding unitary authorities): 1 222 100. Administrative centre: Winchester.

● **Hampstead** ► A district in the Greater London borough of Camden. It contains Hampstead Heath, an extensive open space, and the exclusive residential area of Hampstead "village."

● **Hampton** ► 37 02N 76 23W A port in the USA, in SE Virginia on Hampton Roads Harbour. Founded in 1610, it has large fish-packing and shipping industries. Several military installations are situated nearby. Population (1996 est): 138 757.

● **Hampton, Lionel** ► (1913–96) US Black jazz band leader and vibraphone player, who played with Benny Goodman before forming his own orchestra in 1940. Hampton was the first jazz musician to popularize the vibraphone; one of his biggest successes was the record *Flyin' Home* (1942).

● **Hampton Court** ► A Tudor and Stuart palace on the River Thames near London. Built by Cardinal Wolsey, it was given in the 1520s to Henry VIII, who made substantial alterations, including the addition of the Great Hall. In the 1690s ▷Wren began a further rebuilding project for William III, which included the Fountain Court and the east and south fronts. The palace, now open to the public, has an important collection of paintings, formal gardens (including a maze), as well as the prolific and long-lived Valentine grape vine. In 1986 it was damaged by fire, causing considerable loss to the King's Audience Chamber.

At the **Hampton Court Conference** (1604) the millenary petition was presented to James I by Puritans who wished to see a number of changes to Anglican liturgical practices (*see* millenarianism). James I rejected all these calls for change, except the demand for a new translation of the Bible. This became the Authorized ▷King James Version, which was published in 1611.

● **hamster** ► A small ▷rodent of the family *Cricetidae*. The common hamster (*Cricetus cricetus*), native to Europe and W Asia, is solitary and aggressive and has a red-brown coat with white patches on the flanks, neck, and cheek. It feeds on seeds and grains, storing them in underground burrows. The golden hamster (*Mesocricetus auratus*) is a domestic pet and all are thought to have descended from a single family found at Aleppo, Syria, in 1930.

● **Hamsun, Knut** ► (1859–1952) Norwegian novelist. His early novels, *Hunger* (1890), *Mysteries* (1892), and *Pan* (1894), reflected his interest in nature and the irrational. Much of his subsequent work was influenced by Nietzsche and Strindberg and revealed a distrust of society and civilization; it includes the novels *Vagabonds* (1927) and *Markens grøde* (*The Growth of the Soil*; 1917). He won the Nobel Prize in 1920. He was accused of pro-Nazi tendencies after World War II but was not tried; his own attitude towards the war is commented on in the autobiographical *På gjengrodde stier* (1949).

● **Han** ► (206 BC–220 AD) A Chinese dynasty founded by the general Liu Bang (*or* Liu Pang; 256–195 BC), who overthrew the preceding Qin dynasty. The power of the Han was consolidated by the emperor, Wu Di (*or* Wu Ti; 157–87 BC; reigned 140–87), who completed the conquest of a vast empire. Confucianism was recognized as the state philosophy, Chinese export of silk increased, and a vast canal-building programme was started. Paper was invented by the Han Chinese, who also produced early forms of porcelain and kept detailed historical records. The programme of expansion led to financial difficulties that enabled Wang Mang to usurp the throne in 8 AD. However, he was toppled in turn and the Han dynasty was restored for a second period, known as the Later Han (23–220 AD).

● **Hancock, Tony** ▶ (Anthony John H.; 1924–68) British comedian. He is best known for his radio series of the 1950s, *Hancock's Half Hour*, which was characterized by his unique style of lugubrious humour. He also appeared on television and in several films. Unable to control his alcoholism and depressed by his failing fortunes, he committed suicide in Australia.

● **hand** ▶ The terminal part of the arm. The human hand contains 27 bones. There are 8 carpal bones, which form the wrist and articulate with the forearm at a hinge joint; 5 metacarpals, in the palm of the hand; and 14 phalanges (the bones of the fingers and thumb). The thumb of man and other primates is unique in being opposable, i.e. it can be rotated to touch each of the other fingers, making possible a wide range of manual skills (including using tools and writing). This—combined with its sensitive skin—has produced a manipulative and exploratory organ that has contributed to the success of man as a species. ▷*See* Plate II.

● **handball** ▶ **1.** A court game related to ▷pelota and ▷fives that probably originated in the Roman baths. It is played in a court against one, three, or four walls with a small rubber ball that is hit with the gloved hand. **2.** An 11-a-side field game (or seven-a-side indoor game) introduced in about 1890 and adapted to Association football rules, played by catching and throwing the ball.

● **Handel, George Frederick** ▶ (1685–1759) German composer. He studied in Halle and travelled to Italy, where he became famous as a harpsichordist and as a master of the Italianate style of composition. In 1710 he became kapellmeister to the Elector of Hanover but did not return there after visiting England in 1712. He received a court pension from Queen Anne, which was doubled by the forgiving elector when be became George I of Great Britain on Anne's death in 1714. Handel became musical director to James Brydges, first duke of Chandos (1673–1744), in 1718. He subsequently became music master to the family of the Prince of Wales and director of the Royal Academy of Music on its foundation in 1720. His Italian operas were successfully produced in London and Handel triumphed over his greatest rival, Giovanni Bononcini (1670–1747). The effort needed to sustain his position affected his health and from 1739 he turned from opera to oratorio, producing such masterpieces as *Saul* (1739), *Israel in Egypt* (1739), and *Messiah* (1742), which maintained his public popularity. In 1751, however, he began to be afflicted with loss of sight and despite operations for cataract became completely blind, although he continued to compose with the aid of an amanuensis until his death. His mastery of composition is reflected in the range of his works, which include the *Water Music* (1717), a favourite of the king's, *Music for the Royal Fireworks* (1749), concerti grossi, sonatas, organ concertos, harpsichord suites, and anthems. He was buried in Westminster Abbey.

● **Handley Page, Sir Frederick** ▷*See* Page, Sir Frederick Handley.

● **Handy, William Christopher** ▶ (1873–1958) US Black jazz musician, remembered chiefly for the song "St Louis Blues" (1914). In later life he became a music publisher, continuing to work until his death, even after becoming blind.

● **Han fei zi** ▶ (d. 233 BC) Chinese diplomat and philosopher of law. Although an author of antiquity, he has been studied, along with the Taoists, in the modern period in China. He is best known for his conception of government by law and his advocacy of statecraft.

● **Hangchow** ▶ (*or* Hang-chou) ▷*See* Hangzhou.

● **hang-gliding** ▶ Unpowered flight in a hang-glider, consisting of a large bat-shaped cloth wing on a light metal framework from which the pilot hangs in a harness, holding a horizontal control bar. In flight, the wing fills to form an aerofoil (*see* aeronautics). The first hang-glider was built by Otto ▷Lilienthal, but the prototype for modern design was the sail-wing invented by Frances Rogallo (1912–　) as a means of recovering space vehicles. Hang-gliding became popular in the late 1960s, acquiring a reputation as a dangerous sport largely because hang-gliders are relatively easy to attempt to fly without instruction. A powered hang-glider was first used to cross the English Channel in 1979. In **para-gliding**, a mattress-like canopy is used, allowing greater manoeuvrability.

● **hanging** ▷*See* capital punishment.

● **Hanging Gardens of Babylon** ▶ Ancient gardens in the palace of Nebuchadnezzar II (604–562 BC) on the E side of Babylon. One of the Seven Wonders of the World, they were built on stone arches 23 m (75 ft) above ground and watered from the Euphrates by a complex mechanical system.

● **Hangzhou** ▶ (Hang-chou *or* Hangchow) 30 18N 120 07E A city in E China, the capital of Zhejiang province on Hangzhou Bay, an inlet of the East China Sea. It was the capital (1132–1276) of the Southern ▷Song dynasty. A tourist centre, it has three universities. Its varied industries include silk production. Population (1991 est): 1 340 000.

● **haniwa** ▶ Japanese terracotta sculptures, originally cylindrical in shape, placed on the outside of tomb mounds between about 330 and 552 AD. By the 5th century modelled houses and later horses and human figures were placed on top of the cylinders.

● **Hankou** ▶ (*or* Hankow) ▷*See* Wuhan.

● **Hanks, Tom** ▶ (1956–　) US film actor, who made his name with such comedies as *Splash* (1984) and *Big* (1988). Later films include *Philadelphia* (1993) and *Forrest Gump* (1994), both of which earned him Academy Awards as best actor, *Apollo 13* (1995), *Saving Private Ryan* (1998), and *You've Got Mail* (1999).

● **Hannibal** ▶ (247–c. 183 BC) Carthaginian general. Appointed commander in Spain in 221, he deliberately provoked the second ▷Punic War with Rome. Advancing swiftly, in 218 he crossed the Alps in winter, reaching N Italy with the loss of about 10 000 of his 35 000 men. For two years he devastated Italy but, after disastrous Roman defeats at Trasimene and ▷Cannae, Hannibal lost ground in the face of ▷Fabius Maximus' guerrilla tactics. Recalled to defend Carthage after ▷Scipio Africanus' invasion of Africa, Hannibal was defeated at Zama (202). Domestic politics occupied him until, suspected of rebellion, he was forced to flee Roman retribution. He committed suicide to avoid capture.

● **Hanoi** ▶ 20 57N 105 55E The capital of Vietnam, in the NE of the country on the Red River. The capital of the Vietnamese empire from the 11th until the 17th centuries, it was occupied by the French in 1873 and became the capital of French Indochina. Following World War II it became the capital of the Democratic Republic of Vietnam. Despite the frequent bombing by the USA during the Vietnam War, many ancient buildings in the Vietnamese quarter remain, together with several imposing buildings in the European quarter built by the French. Its university was established in 1956. Population (1993 est): 2 154 900.

● **Hanover** ▶ (German name: Hannover) 52 23N 9 44E A city in N Germany, the capital of Lower Saxony on the River Leine. It is a transshipment port and a commercial and industrial centre, where an important industrial fair is held annually. After the destruction of World War II it was largely rebuilt and some buildings, such as the old town hall (1435–80), were reconstructed. The Leine Palace (founded 1636) is now the *Land* parliament building. Hanover's manufactures include machinery, rubber, textiles, and motor vehicles.
　History: in 1638 Hanover became the capital of an area of Brunswick that was later the electorate and then the kingdom of Hanover. In 1714 Elector George Louis became George I of Great Britain, inheriting the British throne through his mother Sophia (*see* Settlement, Act of). He is buried in Hanover. The Kings of Great Britain were Electors (later Kings) of Hanover until 1837 when Victoria, as a woman, was debarred from succeeding to the Hanoverian throne. Population (1996 est): 523 147.

● **Hanoverian** ▶ A breed of horse developed in Hanover and originally used for draught purposes. During the 19th and 20th centuries crosses with English Thoroughbreds produced the modern Hanoverian, which is popular for showjumping and hunting. Height: 1.63–1.73 m (16–17 hands).

● **Han River** ▶ A river in E central China, rising in S Shenxi province and flowing SE to join the Yangtze River at Wuhan. Length: about 1450 km (900 mi).

● **Hansard** ▶ The official reports of debates in the UK ▷parliament. The name, which was officially adopted in 1943, is that of the family that first printed the reports. From 1774 the House of Commons' journals were printed by **Luke Hansard** (1752–1828). From 1807 his son **Thomas Curson Hansard** (1776–1833) printed the unofficial reports of parliamentary debates that Cobbet had begun to compile in 1804. The Stationery Office published Hansard from 1890.

● **Hanseatic League** ▶ An association of N German trading towns (the Hanse) formed in the 13th century to protect their economic interests overseas. By the mid-14th century, the League, comprising some hundred towns, had become powerful and established trading monopolies in NE Europe. It faced opposition from Denmark and England, with which it conducted several trade wars. The rise of the non-German Baltic states during the 15th and 16th centuries, as well as changing trade routes, contributed to the League's declining influence. It was dissolved in 1669.

● **Hansen's disease** ▷*See* leprosy.

● **hansom cab** ▷*See* □cab.

Hanukka ▶ The candles in this menorah are lit each day of the festival.

● **Hanukka** ▶ A Jewish festival, commemorating the revolt of the ▷Maccabees and the rededication of the Temple in Jerusalem in 164 BC. An eight-day festival, it falls in midwinter and is celebrated by lighting a lamp or candle each day in an eight-branched candelabrum called a **menorah**. In addition to the eight branches, a Hanukka menorah has an extra candle (called a **shammes**) from which the other candles are lit. The menorah used in the Temple had only seven branches; it is now used as an emblem of the State of Israel.

● **Hanuman** ▶ In Hindu mythology, a monkey god and one of the principal characters in the ▷*Ramayana*, in which he helps Rama to recover his wife Sita from the demon Ravana. There are numerous temples dedicated to him in both India and Japan.

● **Hanyang** ▷*See* Wuhan.

● **Hapsburgs** ▷*See* Habsburgs.

● **hara-kiri** ▶ The honourable way of death for Japanese ▷samurai. In its strict form it involved ceremoniously cutting one's stomach open with a dagger before one's head was struck off by the single blow of another samurai's sword. In later times, there was often only a token gesture of disembowelment before decapitation. Now illegal, it is still sometimes practised by Japanese suicides.

● **Harald V** ▶ (1937–) King of Norway (1991–). Educated at Oxford, he subsequently served in the Norwegian forces, succeeding his father Olaf V after 30 years as Crown Prince.

● **Harappa** ▶ The site in the Punjab in Pakistan of a great city of the ▷Indus Valley civilization. Its cemeteries and brick buildings (excavated 1920s, 1946) equal ▷Mohenjo-Daro in importance.

● **Harar** ▶ (*or* Harer) 9 20N 42 10E A city in E Ethiopia, the capital of Harar province. Situated at 1800 m (6000 ft), it is Ethiopia's only walled city. Its capture by British forces (1941) led to the eventual collapse of Mussolini's African colonial empire. Trade is based on coffee and grain. Population (1994 est): 122 932.

● **Harare** ▶ (name until 1982: Salisbury) 17 50S 31 02E The capital of Zimbabwe, on a plateau in the NE. Founded in 1890 it was the capital of the Federation of Rhodesia and Nyasaland (1953–63). The University of Zimbabwe (formerly Rhodesia) was founded here in 1970 and Harare has Anglican and Roman Catholic cathedrals. The centre of a tobacco-growing area, it has an important trade and industry in tobacco. Other industries include textiles and engineering. Population (1992): 1 184 169.

● **Harat** ▷*See* Herat.

● **Harbin** ▷*See* Ha-er-bin.

● **harbour seal** ▶ The common ▷seal, *Phoca vitulina*, of coastal Pacific and Atlantic waters. Up to 1.8 m long, with a blotchy grey coat, harbour seals inhabit sandbanks and river estuaries, feeding on fish. Family: *Phocidae*. □mammal.

● **Hardanger Fjord** ▶ A fjord in SW Norway, S of Bergen, penetrating inland from the North Sea for 110 km (68 mi). It is edged by spectacular mountains and many waterfalls.

● **Hardecanute** ▶ (*or* Harthacnute; c. 1019–42) The last Danish King of England (1040–42), succeeding his illegitimate half-brother Harold I Harefoot, and King of Denmark (1035–42). As the legitimate son of Canute, he ordered Harold's corpse to be disinterred and thrown into the Thames as a revenge for Harold's seizure of the throne after Canute's death. He razed Worcester after a riot against his tax collectors. He died of a seizure at a marriage feast.

● **Hardenberg, Karl (August), Fürst von** ▶ (1750–1822) Prussian statesman. He was foreign minister under Frederick William III from 1804 to 1806 and prime minister in 1807, when Prussia was subjected to Napoleonic rule. Again prime minister from 1810 until his death, he introduced reforms that enabled Prussia to break away from French control in 1813. However, monarchist opposition resulted in his declining influence after 1815.

● **Hardie, J(ames) Keir** ▶ (1856–1915) British politician, who was an important figure in the early parliamentary Labour Party. Born in Scotland, he became a coalminer at the age of ten and was active in the trades-union movement before founding (1888) the Scottish Parliamentary Labour Party. As an Independent Socialist MP (1892–95) he helped to found (1893) the Independent Labour Party. Again an MP (1900–15), he became chairman of the parliamentary Labour Representation Committee in 1906, shortly before it was renamed the ▷Labour Party. He was an ardent pacifist.

● **Hardinge of Lahore, Henry, 1st Viscount** ▶ (1785–1856) British soldier and colonial administrator; governor general of India (1844–48) after 24 years as an MP (1820–44), during which time he was twice secretary for war (1828–30, 1841–44). He became commander in chief of the British army in 1852 but was demoted in 1855 during the Crimean War. His grandson **Charles, 1st Baron Hardinge of Penshurst** (1858–1944) was viceroy of India (1910–16).

● **hardness of water** ▷*See* water softening.

● **Hardouin-Mansart, Jules** ▶ (1646–1708) French ▷baroque architect, who succeeded Le Vau as court architect to Louis XIV. He built Les Invalides, Paris (1680–91), but is most famous for his huge extensions to ▷Versailles, begun in 1678. These include the Galérie des

Glaces (Gallery of Mirrors) and the orangery. He was also a town planner and designed the Place Vendôme (1699) in Paris.

● **Hardwar** ▶ 29 58N 78 09E A town in N India, in Uttar Pradesh. One of the most sacred Hindu pilgrimage centres, its bathing ghat (or steps) along the River Ganges is believed to contain the footprint of the god Vishnu. Population (1991): 148 882.

● **hardware** ▷*See* computer.

● **Hardy, G(odfrey) H(arold)** ▶ (1877–1947) British mathematician, who championed pure mathematics and despised its applied aspects. He discovered one of the fundamental results in population ▷genetics, which gives the proportion of dominant and recessive genes in a large mixed population, but he regarded the work as unimportant.

● **Hardy, Oliver** ▷*See* Laurel and Hardy.

Thomas Hardy ▶ Photographed at Max Gate, his home near Dorchester, in the early 1920s. Hardy used his training as an architect to build this house, a large and somewhat ostentatious villa, in 1883–84; he lived here for the rest of his life and wrote all his late masterpieces in its study. It stands only two miles from the much humbler cottage in which he was born.

● **Hardy, Thomas** ▶ (1840–1928) British novelist and poet. The son of a mason, he went to London in 1862 to study architecture. His major novels, which include *The Return of the Native* (1878), *The Mayor of Casterbridge* (1886), and *Tess of the D'Urbervilles* (1891), are tragic tales set in his native Dorset (called "Wessex" in the novels). After the public outrage caused by the alleged immorality of *Jude the Obscure* (1895) he published only verse, beginning with *Wessex Poems* (1898), and an epic drama, *The Dynasts* (1903–08). After the death of his first wife, Emma, he married his secretary, Florence Dugdale, in 1914. He was appointed to the OM in 1910.

● **hare** ▶ A mammal belonging to the widely distributed family *Leporidae* (which also includes the ▷rabbits). Hares are typically larger than rabbits (the European hare (*Lepus europaeus*) weighs up to 4 kg) and have long black-tipped ears. They live and breed in the open (rather than in burrows) and are mainly nocturnal, feeding on grass and bark. The young are born fully furred with open eyes. Chief genus: *Lepus* (about 26 species); order: ▷Lagomorpha.

● **Hare, Sir David** ▶ (1947–) British playwright and director. As well as screenplays for television and the cinema, he has written such plays as *Plenty* (1978), *Pravda* (1985), the trilogy *Racing Demon* (1990), *Murmuring Judges* (1991), and *The Absence of War* (1993), *Amy's View* (1997), and *The Blue Room* (1998), an adaptation of Arthur Schnitzler's *Reigen* (*La Ronde*). He was knighted in 1998.

● **Hare, William** ▷*See* Burke, William.

● **harebell** ▶ A herbaceous perennial plant, *Campanula rotundifolia*, of N temperate regions, growing to a height of 60 cm. It has rounded leaves and blue nodding bell-shaped flowers on slender stems. Harebell grows in a variety of open habitats. Family: *Campanulaceae*.

● **Hare Krishna movement** ▶ (Sanskrit: hail Krishna) An international quasi-religious cult, the International Society for Krishna Consciousness (ISKCON), founded in New York in 1966 on Hindu principles by an Indian, Swami Prabhupada (1895–1977). Members follow a vegetarian regime that also prohibits gambling, extramarital sex, and drugs. They dress in saffron robes and the men have shaved heads. Daily worship includes the chanting of the Hare Krishna mantra. The movement is financed by begging, the sale of literature and incense, and donations. Its detractors claim that the sect recruits by brainwashing vulnerable young people, whom it separates from their families and exploits for financial gain.

● **harelip** ▷*See* cleft palate.

● **Harfleur** ▶ 49 31N 0 12E A port in N France, in the Seine-Maritime department on the Seine estuary. A major port in the middle ages, it declined with the rise of Le Havre. Population (latest est): 9700.

● **Hargeisa** ▶ 9 20N 43 57E A town in N Somalia, near the Ethiopian border. It was the summer capital of former British Somaliland (1941–60). It is a watering and trading place for nomadic herdsmen. Population (latest est): 400 000.

● **Hargreaves, James** ▶ (d. 1778) English inventor, who around 1764 invented the spinning jenny, a machine (named after his daughter) with which several threads could be spun simultaneously. After local spinners, believing that their jobs were threatened by the jenny, broke into his home near Blackburn, Lancashire, and broke up his machines, Hargreaves set up (1768) a small mill in Nottingham.

● **haricot bean** ▶ A variety of ▷French bean (*Phaseolus vulgaris*) grown in warm climates. The seeds, which are dried for storage and soaked before use, are either brown or light-coloured and are used for making baked beans.

● **Haringey** ▶ A residential borough of N Greater London, created in 1965 from the former municipal boroughs of Hornsey, Tottenham, and Wood Green. Area: 30 sq km (12 sq mi). Population (1991): 201 704.

● **Harishchandra** ▶ (1850–85) Hindi poet, dramatist, and essayist, also known as Bharatendu. He founded two literary Hindi magazines and through his writings and patronage of other writers he contributed to the literary development of Hindi, which eventually became the official language of India. In *Bharat durdasa* (1880) and other plays he attributed the decline of Indian civilization to Muslim and Western influences.

● **Harlan, John Marshall** ▶ (1833–1911) US jurist. As associate justice of the US Supreme Court from 1877 until his death, he opposed many of the court's rulings. He was an ardent supporter of civil rights, particularly those of Blacks. In the case of *Plessy versus Ferguson* (1896) he opposed the Supreme Court's decision that racial segregation in US schools was justified on the principle of "separate but equal."

● **Harlech** ▶ 52 52N 4 07W A historic town in NW Wales, in Gwynedd on Cardigan Bay. It is a resort with a ruined castle begun in 1285 by Edward I. Population (1991): 1233.

● **Harlem** ▶ 40 49N 73 57W A residential district of New York City, USA, in Manhattan. It is a political, social, and cultural focus for Blacks. The poets Langston Hughes (1902–67) and Countee Cullen (1903–46) were leading figures in the literary and cultural revival of the 1920s known as the Harlem renaissance.

● **Harlem Globetrotters** ▶ A Black American professional basketball team formed by Abraham Saperstein (1903–66) in 1927. They play exhibition matches all over the world.

● **Harlequin** ▶ A stock character of the ▷commedia dell'arte. Known as Arlecchino in Renaissance Italy, Harlequin began as a comic and covetous servant but developed by the 18th century into the capricious lover of Columbine and the central comic figure of the **harlequinade**, a type of theatrical entertainment that became popular in Britain. Dressed in a diamond-patterned costume, masked, and carrying a wooden club (called a slapstick), he was played in England by such leading actors as David Garrick. In the 19th century Harlequin was gradually eclipsed by the greater popularity of ▷Pierrot, a minor character in the harlequinade, and the development of that genre into ▷pantomime.

● **harlequin duck** ▶ A short-billed ▷diving duck, *Histrionicus histrionicus*, occurring in coastal waters of Iceland and Greenland. The female is brown with white patches around the eyes; the male is grey-blue with white markings and chestnut flanks.

● **Harley, Robert, 1st Earl of Oxford** ▶ (1661–1724) English statesman under Queen Anne. An MP from 1688, he was a Tory but allied with the Whigs, becoming speaker of the House of Commons (1701) and then secretary of state (1704). Intriguing against his Whig colleagues ▷Godolphin and ▷Marlborough, he was dismissed in 1708 and rejoined the Tories. After the fall of the Whigs, he became Anne's chief minister as chancellor of the exchequer (1710–11) and Lord Treasurer (1711–14). The machinations of his rival ▷Bolingbroke brought his dismissal and after the accession of George I he was imprisoned (1714–17) for his Tory (and, by implication, ▷Jacobite) views. **Edward Harley, 2nd Earl of Oxford**, was the ground landlord after whom **Harley Street**, in the London district of Marylebone, is named. Since about 1845 Harley St has been renowned for the eminent doctors who have their consulting rooms there.

● **Harlow** ▶ 51 47N 0 08E A town in SE England, in Essex. It is a new town, developed since 1947 as a satellite town of London with light industries (surgical and scientific instruments, electronics, engineering, furniture, glass). Population (1991): 74 629.

● **Harlow, Jean** ▶ (Harlean Carpentier; 1911–37) US film actress. Her well-publicized sex appeal and her talent for comedy won great popularity during the 1930s in such films as *Platinum Blonde* (1931) and *Bombshell* (1933). She died from kidney failure while making *Saratoga* (1937).

● **harmonica** ▶ **1.** The mouth organ: the smallest member of the reed-organ family; its invention is attributed to Sir Charles ▷Wheatstone in 1829. Notes and chords are obtained by blowing or sucking rows of parallel reeds. It is used mainly in light music, although ▷Vaughan Williams and ▷Milhaud have written works for the instrument's most celebrated exponent, Larry ▷Adler. **2.** The glass harmonica: an obsolete instrument consisting of tuned glasses rubbed with a damp finger.

● **harmonic analysis** ▶ A procedure, developed in 1822 by Joseph ▷Fourier, by which complicated periodic functions, such as sound waves, can be written as the sum of a number of simple wave functions known as a Fourier series. One wave function, called the fundamental, has the same frequency as the original function. Those that have frequencies that are integral multiples of the fundamental are called harmonics.

● **harmonics** ▶ (overtones *or* partials) The components of a musical note with frequencies that are simple multiples of the fundamental. If a string or column of air is made to vibrate, the fundamental frequency is the frequency at which the whole string or column vibrates. Associated with this vibration are separate, but weaker, vibrations of a half, a third, a quarter, etc., of the string or column. The frequency at which the two halves vibrate is double that of the fundamental; the frequency at which the three thirds vibrate is treble that of the fundamental; and so on. The relative prevalence of the harmonics gives the notes from different instruments or voices their particular ▷timbre (tone or quality). The richness of tone of an oboe, for example, is a consequence of the large number of harmonics that occur. All instruments produce their characteristic harmonics when played normally, but certain harmonics can be emphasized in brass instruments when the player changes the embouchure (configuration of the lips) or by light stopping in some string instruments.
    The series of notes produced by a fundamental and its harmonics is called a **harmonic series**.

● **harmonium** ▶ A keyboard instrument of the reed organ family, patented in 1848 by Alexandre Debain (1809–77) in Paris. It is a free ▷reed instrument, the air being blown by a bellows activated by foot pedals. It may have several stops (*see* organ).

● **harmony** ▶ In music, the combining of notes into chords, so that they are heard simultaneously. Harmony can be defined as the "vertical" aspect of music in contrast to **melody**, its "horizontal" aspect; it has greater importance in Western music than in any other musical

tradition. Before about 1650 composers made use of ▷polyphony, in which the combination of a number of melodic lines based on ▷modes was of prime importance. Between about 1650 and about 1900 (the **harmonic period**) a system of harmony evolved based on diatonic chords (*see* scale). Such chords consist of three notes sounded simultaneously; a note of the scale of the ▷tonality of the composition and the notes a third and a fifth above it. The constituent notes of any chord can be rearranged to provide variety. A **harmonic progression** consists of a particular sequence of chords, especially one leading (*or* modulating) into another tonality. When chords are subject to increasing ▷chromaticism the harmony becomes more complex and the tonality of the music becomes ambiguous. During the last half of the 19th century the music of Wagner, Liszt, and Richard Strauss became increasingly chromatic. In the early years of the 20th century Schoenberg first adopted ▷atonality and later invented ▷serialism as a substitute for traditional harmony. Debussy developed novel harmonic practices, such as harmonizing melodies with chords from unrelated tonalities and chords derived from whole-tone and pentatonic scales. Composers of the 20th century have made use of a wide range of harmonic styles, some following Schoenberg, some deliberately cultivating dissonance, and others modifying traditional harmonic practice in various ways.

● **Harmsworth, Alfred** ▷*See* Northcliffe, Alfred Charles William Harmsworth, 1st Viscount.

● **Harmsworth, Harold** ▷*See* Rothermere, Harold Sidney Harmsworth, 1st Viscount.

● **Harnack, Adolf von** ▶ (1851–1930) German Protestant theologian. A professor at the Universities of Leipzig, Marburg, and Berlin, Harnack was considered the greatest scholar of his day on the early Church Fathers. His influential *History of Dogma* (1886–90), which traced the history of Christian doctrine down to the Reformation, was strongly criticized by conservative theologians.

● **harness racing** ▶ A form of horse racing in which each horse pulls a light two-wheeled ▷sulky with a single driver. The races are of two sorts, according to the pace that the horses are trained to use: trotting (a two-beat gait with legs moving in diagonal pairs) or pacing (a two-beat gait with legs moving in lateral pairs). Races are usually run over 1.6 km (1 mi) on oval dirt tracks. The sport is particularly popular in the USA and Australia.

● **Harold I Harefoot** ▶ (d. 1040) Danish King of England (1037–40). The illegitimate son of Canute, he became king while Hardecanute, Canute's legitimate son, was preoccupied in Denmark. Before Hardecanute could oust him, Harold died.

● **Harold II** ▶ (c. 1022–66) The last Anglo-Saxon King of England (1066), reputedly designated heir by the dying Edward the Confessor. He was the son of Earl ▷Godwin. After becoming king, he crushed the forces of his brother ▷Tostig and ▷Harold III Hardraade of Norway, who claimed the throne, at Stamford Bridge (1066). Harold was killed in the battle of ▷Hastings by the army of another, successful, claimant to the throne, ▷William the Conqueror.

● **Harold III Hardraade** ▶ (1015–66) King of Norway (1047–66). His nickname means Hard Ruler. Until 1045 he served in the Byzantine army, his exploits in which became the subject of Norse sagas. After his return to Norway he briefly shared the throne with Magnus I (d. 1047); when he became sole ruler, he tried unsuccessfully to conquer Denmark. In 1066 he invaded England in support of ▷Tostig against Harold II and died at Stamford Bridge.

● **harp** ▶ A plucked stringed instrument of ancient origin, consisting of an open frame with strings of varying length and tension. The modern orchestral harp is triangular in shape with about 45 strings stretched between the long soundbox, which rests against the player's body, and the curved neck, which takes the tuning pegs. The pillar, which completes the triangle, contains a mechanism invented in 1810 by Sébastien Érard (1752–1831). This enables the player to raise each string by one or two semitones by means of pedals at the base. It gives the harp a full chromatic range of six and a half octaves from the B below the bass stave. ⬚musical instruments.

● **Harpers Ferry Raid** ▶ (1859) The capture of the Federal arsenal at

Harpers Ferry, West Virigina, by John ▷Brown. An abolitionist (*see* Abolition Movement), Brown seized the arsenal as a base for a slave insurrection. Robert E. ▷Lee assaulted and captured Brown's position. Brown was hanged, a martyr to the abolitionist cause.

● **Harpies** ▶ In Greek mythology, malicious spirits, originally conceived as winds, who carried off their victims to their deaths. They were later portrayed as rapacious birds with ugly women's faces.

● **harpsichord** ▶ A keyboard instrument with strings plucked by quills, rather than hit by hammers (*see* spinet; virginals; *compare* clavichord; piano). In the 16th, 17th, and 18th centuries it was an instrument of great importance and it was successfully revived in the 20th century. It lacks the sustaining power and dynamic variation of the piano; the tone can be changed by the addition of stops, which sound strings an octave below or above the note depressed. A muted effect can be obtained by use of the lute stop.

● **harpy eagle** ▶ A tropical South American ▷eagle, *Harpia harpyja*, that lives in rain forests. It is the largest of the eagles, 100 cm long, and has a huge hooked bill and extremely powerful feet for gripping prey, which includes monkeys, sloths, opossums, and parrots. Mottled grey with a dark-banded tail, it has a large erectile crest.

● **harquebus** ▶ (*or* arquebus) ▷*See* musket.

● **harrier** ▶ (bird) A slender long-legged ▷hawk belonging to a widely distributed genus (*Circus*). Harriers are about 50 cm long and are usually brown (in some species the males are grey), with a small bill and a long tail. They fly low over fields and marshes, searching for small animals. ▷*See also* marsh harrier.

● **harrier** ▶ (dog) A breed of hound used for hunting hares. It is similar to the ▷foxhound but smaller. The short smooth coat is usually black, tan, and white but may be mottled blue-grey. Height: 46–56 cm.

● **Harriman, W(illiam) Averell** ▶ (1891–1986) US diplomat; ambassador to the Soviet Union (1943–46) and to the UK (1946). He was governor of New York (1955–58) and helped to negotiate the ▷Nuclear Test-Ban Treaty (1963). He was ambassador to the Vietnam peace talks (1968–69).

● **Harrington, James** ▶ (1611–77) English republican, an admirer of ▷Hobbes and ▷Machiavelli. He believed a nation's distribution of land was the factor determining the form of its government, but ignored mercantile and financial influences. His ideal form of government was a "commonwealth," described in his *Oceana* (1656).

● **Harris** ▷*See* Lewis with Harris.

● **Harris, Sir Arthur Travers** ▶ (1892–1984) British air marshal. Known as "Bomber" Harris, he served in the Royal Flying Corps in World War I; during World War II he was commander-in-chief of RAF Bomber Command (1942–45). The controversy surrounding his strategy of mass bombing of German industrial cities was reopened with the erection of a statue to him in London (1992).

● **Harris, Joel Chandler** ▶ (1848–1908) US novelist and short-story writer. His Uncle Remus stories, drawing on his knowledge of Negro folklore, were published in several volumes, starting with *Uncle Remus, His Songs and His Sayings* (1880).

● **Harris, Roy** ▶ (1898–1979) US composer. He studied with Nadia Boulanger in Paris. His compositions, which include 11 symphonies, show the influence of folk music.

● **Harris, Thomas** ▶ (1940–) US novelist and screenwriter, best known for his creation of the brilliant cannibalistic psychopath Dr Hannibal Lecter. The character features in the novels *Red Dragon* (1981; filmed as *Manhunter*, 1986), *The Silence of the Lambs* (1988; filmed 1991), and *Hannibal* (1999; filmed 2001).

● **Harrisburg** ▶ 40 17N 76 54W A city in the USA, the capital of Pennsylvania on the Susquehanna River. A rail centre, it manufactures bricks, steel, and clothing. In March, 1979, a failure in the cooling system at the nuclear power plant at nearby Three Mile Island caused widespread concern. Population (1992 est): 53 430.

● **Harrison, George** ▶ (1943–2001) British rock musician, a member of the ▷Beatles. When the group disbanded, Harrison embarked on a solo career, his albums including *All Things Must Pass* (1970), *Extra*

Texture (1975), and *Cloud Nine* (1987). He also established the film company Handmade Films.

● **Harrison, John** ▶ (1693–1776) British clockmaker, who invented the first practical chronometer that enabled navigators at sea to calculate their longitude. His spring-driven device, regulated by a compensating balance wheel, won the British government's prize of £20,000 for the first chronometer with which longitude could be calculated to within 0.5 ° at the end of a journey to the West Indies.

● **Harrison, Sir Rex** ▶ (Reginald Carey H.; 1908–90) British actor. His stage successes included *French Without Tears* (1936), *Heartbreak House* (1983), and *The Admirable Crichton* (1988); his films include *Major Barbara* (1940), *Blithe Spirit* (1946), and *My Fair Lady* (1964; he also starred in the 1956 stage production). He was knighted in 1989.

● **Harrison, Tony** ▶ (1937–) British poet and playwright. His works include the long poem *V* (1985) and the collections *Loiners* (1970) and *The Gaze of the Gorgon* (1992), as well as poems for television and many translations for the stage.

● **Harrison, William Henry** ▶ (1773–1841) US soldier and statesman; president (1841). As governor of the Indiana Territory (1800–11) he secured it for White settlement by subduing ▷Tecumseh (1811). He served in the ▷War of 1812 and died a month after being elected as a "frontiersman president." His grandson **Benjamin Harrison** (1833–1901) was Republican president (1889–93). His administration passed the Sherman Anti-Trust Act (1890).

● **Harrogate** ▶ 54 00N 1 33W A residential town and former spa resort in N England, in North Yorkshire. It now hosts conferences and trade fairs and is a centre for tourism and the antiques trade; there are various light industries. Population (1998 est): 70 000.

● **Harrow** ▶ A residential borough of NW Greater London, created in 1965 from the former municipal borough. Harrow School, founded by John Lyon in 1571, with St Mary's Church (1087) dominates Harrow-on-the-Hill. Area: 51 sq km (20 sq mi). Population (1999 est): 200 100.

● **Harsa** ▶ (*or* Harsha; c. 590–c. 647 AD) King of N India (c. 606–47). He ruled an extensive empire from his capital of Kanauj. In later life he became a devout Buddhist and combined his successful rule with the pursuit of poetry and the arts. His life was documented by ▷Bana.

● **Hart, Moss** ▶ (1904–61) US dramatist. He collaborated with George S. ▷Kaufman on a number of Broadway comedies, including *You Can't Take It with You* (1936) and *The Man Who Came to Dinner* (1939). He also wrote librettos for Irving ▷Berlin and Kurt ▷Weill, notably *Lady in the Dark* (1941).

● **Harte, (Francis) Bret(t)** ▶ (1836–1902) US short-story writer. He gained international fame with stories about the miners, gamblers, and prostitutes of California, collected in *The Luck of the Roaring Camp* (1870). He collaborated with Mark Twain on the play *Ah Sin* (1877).

● **hartebeest** ▶ A long-faced antelope, *Alcephalus busephalus*, of African plains. About 120 cm high at the shoulder, hartebeests are slender fast-running animals. There are several races, ranging in colour from dark chestnut to fawn; their horns are united at the base and are generally lyre-shaped. They live in small herds, grazing by day.

● **Hartford** ▶ 41 45N 72 42W A city in the USA, the capital of Connecticut. Founded in 1633, it has many notable buildings. Trinity College (1823) and the law and insurance schools of the University of Connecticut are situated here. Hartford is a leading commercial, industrial, and financial centre. Population (2000 est): 135 523.

● **Harthacnute** ▷*See* Hardecanute.

● **Hartington, Lord** ▷*See* Devonshire, Spencer Compton Cavendish, 8th Duke of.

● **Hartlepool** ▶ 1. 54 41N 1 13W A port in NE England, in Hartlepool unitary authority, Durham: it has included West Hartlepool and the resort of Seaton Carew since 1967. Originally an old fishing port and medieval walled town, Hartlepool's main industries are engineering, clothing manufacture, and timber working as well as services for North Sea oilfields. Population (1991): 87 310. 2. A unitary authority in NE England, in Durham: from 1974 to 1996 part of the county of Cleveland. Area: 93 sq km (36 sq mi). Population (1999 est): 92 000.

● **Hartley, L(eslie) P(oles)** ▶ (1895–1972) British novelist. His most ambitious achievement is a trilogy (*The Shrimp and the Anemone*, 1944; *The Sixth Heaven*, 1946; *Eustace and Hilda*, 1947) concerning the growth to adulthood of a brother and sister. His other novels include *The Go-Between* (1953).

● **Hartmann, (Karl Robert) Eduard von** ▶ (1842–1906) German philosopher. In *Philosophy of the Unconscious* (1869) he sought to reconcile all previous systems and all sciences by means of the hypothesis of the unconscious mind.

● **Hartmann, Nicolai** ▶ (1882–1950) Russian-born German philosopher. He was troubled by the problem of cultural relativism pervading all branches of philosophy. Ideas, and even the concepts of logic, were historically conditioned, so that no thinker could begin without preconceptions. Systematic metaphysics, as presented by 19th-century idealists, was impossible, and the task of the philosopher was to draw the boundary between the rational and the irrational.

● **Hartnell, Sir Norman** ▶ (1901–79) British fashion designer. He designed uniforms for the WRAC and Red Cross and was official dressmaker to Queen Elizabeth II and Elizabeth the Queen Mother. He was knighted in 1977.

● **Harun ar-Rashid** ▶ (?766–809 AD) The fifth caliph (786–809) of the 'Abbasid dynasty of Islam. He relied greatly on the support of the powerful Barmecide family until it fell from power in 803. His reign was troubled by revolts in subject territories and saw the beginning of Tunisian independence. Harun sent expeditions against the Byzantines and forced them to accept a humiliating treaty in 806. He has become an almost legendary figure because of the references to him in *The Arabian Nights*. Muslim sources, however, say nothing of his alleged close relations with Charlemagne.

● **Harvard classification system** ▶ A system by which stars are classified according to features in their spectra; it was introduced in the 1890s by astronomers at the Harvard College Observatory (USA), notably Annie Jump Cannon (1863–1941) and Edward Pickering (1846–1919). Stellar spectral differences arise mainly from differing surface and atmospheric temperatures, and the stars are grouped accordingly into seven major spectral types: O, B, A, F, G, K, and M, in order of decreasing temperature. These types range in colour from blue (O and B) through white, yellow, and orange, to red (M). There are 10 subdivisions for each spectral type, indicated by a digit (0–9) placed after the letter. Stars of one spectral type can be further classified into supergiants, giants, etc., according to their ▷luminosity. ▷See also Hertzsprung-Russell diagram.

● **Harvard University** ▶ The oldest university in the USA (founded 1636), at Cambridge, Massachusetts. It is named after John Harvard (1607–38), who bequeathed half his estate and his books to the college. The associated women's college, Radcliffe College, dates from 1879.

● **harvestman** ▶ An ▷arachnid, also called harvest spider, belonging to the order *Opiliones* (or *Phalangida*; 2200 species), found in tropical and temperate regions. It has an undivided body, 1–22 mm long, and very long delicate legs. It is found in fields, woods, and buildings, feeding on insects and plant materials, and is particularly common in late summer in temperate regions.

● **harvest mite** ▶ A ▷mite, also called chigger and scrub mite, belonging to the genus *Trombicula*. Its larvae are parasitic on vertebrates, including man, feeding on skin to cause intense itching and inflammation. Certain species transmit diseases, including scrub typhus.

● **harvest mouse** ▶ A tiny ▷mouse, *Micromys minutus*, of Europe and Asia. Light red-brown with white underparts, harvest mice are about 4 cm long with a prehensile tail of the same length. They weave a nest of grass among the stems of plants in cornfields and reedbeds, but are becoming rarer as a result of mechanical farming methods.

● **Harvey, William** ▶ (1578–1657) English physician and anatomist, who discovered the circulation of the blood. Harvey studied under the great anatomist ▷Fabricius ab Aquapendente and later became physician to James I and Charles I. From his numerous dissections and experiments on animals, Harvey concluded that blood flowed from the heart to the lungs, returned to the heart, and was pumped out via the arteries to the limbs and viscera, returning to the heart through the veins. His findings, published in *On the Motion of the Heart and Blood in Animals* (1628), aroused controversy, but by his death the circulation of blood was generally accepted. Harvey also made valuable studies of the development of chick embryos.

● **Harwell** ▶ 51 37N 1 18W A village in S central England, in Oxfordshire, site of an atomic research station built in 1947.

● **Harwich** ▶ 51 57N 1 17E A seaport in E England, in Essex on the estuary of the Rivers Stour and Orwell. It has passenger services to Scandinavia and the Continent. Population (1991): 18 436.

● **Haryana** ▶ A state in N India, mostly in the fertile Upper Ganges plain. Predominantly rural, it produces wheat, other grains, cotton, sugar cane, and oilseeds. There is some light industry, including textiles, agricultural implements, and sugar refining.
    History: an important centre of Hinduism, Haryana lies on the migration route into India. Britain merged it with the Punjab, but it was separated in 1966. Area: 44 222 sq km (17 070 sq mi). Population (1994 est): 17 925 000. Capital: Chandigarh.

● **Harz Mountains** ▶ A mountain range extending about 90 km (56 mi) across Germany W of Halle. They are the northernmost range of the European mountain system. The highest peak is the ▷Brocken.

● **Hasan al-Basri, al-** ▶ (d. 728) Muslim ascetic and religious thinker. He was active in Basra in Iraq and is important in the development of Muslim theology, although little is known about him. He is said to have supported the idea of human free will against that of divine predetermination.

● **Hasdrubal (Barca)** ▶ (d. 207 BC) Carthaginian general; the son of ▷Hamilcar Barca and the brother of ▷Hannibal. Hasdrubal commanded the Carthaginian army in Spain following Hannibal's departure to campaign in Italy but was recalled to Africa after being defeated by the Romans in 217. He returned to Spain in 212, campaigning successfully before following Hannibal across the Alps in 207. He was defeated at Metaurus and died in battle.

● **Hašek, Jaroslav** ▶ (1883–1923) Czech novelist, who established an early reputation as a satirist and anarchist. During World War I he was captured by the Russians, joined the Czech liberation army, and became a communist. His unfinished novel sequence *The Good Soldier Schweik* (1920–23) is a bawdy and irreverent satire upon bureaucracy and bourgeois values.

harvest mouse ▶ Seen here on an ear of corn.

● **Haselrig, Sir Arthur** ▷*See* Hesilrige, Sir Arthur.

● **Hashemites** ▶ The Arab descendants of the prophet Mohammed, including the fourth caliph ▷Ali and the line of hereditary emirs of Mecca. The late King Hussein of Jordan is the best-known modern representative of the line.

● **hashish** ▷*See* cannabis.

● **Hasidism** ▶ A Jewish religious movement, founded by the ▷Ba'al Shem Tov. Essentially a blend of ▷kabbalah and popular pietism, Hasidism spread, against strong opposition, throughout the Jewish communities of E Europe in the 18th and 19th centuries. Led by charismatic teachers (*zaddikim*), the Hasidim stressed simple piety and ecstatic prayer and denounced what they saw as the arid scholasticism of the talmudic academies. A more intellectual approach was adopted by the Habad Hasidim, whose leader is the Lubavitch Rabbi, now based in New York. Most European Hasidic communities did not survive the ▷holocaust, but Hasidism still thrives in North America and Israel. Hasidic men are bearded and wear black suits with broad-rimmed 18th-century black hats.

● **Haskalah** ▶ (Hebrew: enlightenment) The intellectual movement for spreading modern European culture among the Jews. It began in Germany in the 18th century, largely under the influence of Moses ▷Mendelssohn, and spread to Russia in the 19th century. Linked to the movement for the political emancipation of the Jews, it attempted to provide them with a modern Hebrew culture and rejected the previous alternatives of the medieval ghetto culture or total assimilation. In its day it exercised an enormous influence, giving birth to modern ▷Judaism, ▷Zionism, and the modern Hebrew language and literature. In the West it succumbed to linguistic and cultural assimilation; in Russia it yielded, in the face of the growing ▷antisemitism of the 1880s, to attempts to find a political solution to the Jewish problem.

● **Hassall, John** ▶ (1868–1948) British artist. After studying in Antwerp and Paris, he exhibited paintings at the Royal Academy and worked as a newspaper cartoonist. He is best known for his humorous theatre and trade posters, of which the most famous is *Skegness Is So Bracing.*

● **Hassan II** ▶ (1929–99) King of Morocco (1961–99). Educated in France, Hassan maintained autocratic rule in Morocco. He introduced some reforms in 1971 following an attempted coup; he was succeeded by his son, Mohamed VI (1963–).

● **Hasselt** ▶ 50 56N 5 20E A town in NE Belgium. It was the site of a Dutch victory over the Belgians (1831). Industries include brewing and distilling. Population (1995 est): 67 486.

● **Hastings** ▶ 39 39S 176 42E A city in New Zealand, in E North Island. Rebuilt after an earthquake (1931), it is the centre of a fruit-growing district and is known as "The Fruit Bowl of New Zealand." Population (1995 est): 58 700.

● **Hastings** ▶ 50 51N 0 36E A town on the S coast of England, in East Sussex, including the resort of St Leonards. Formerly a port (chief of the Cinque Ports), it is now a resort and residential town with a ruined castle built by William the Conqueror, who landed at nearby Pevensey in 1066 (*see* Hastings, Battle of). Population (1997 est): 82 100.

● **Hastings, Battle of** ▶ (14 October, 1066) The battle between the Normans and the English at Senlac Hill (*see* Battle), near Hastings, in which William, Duke of Normandy, claiming the English throne, defeated Harold II of England. The battle was dominated by the Norman use of archery supported by cavalry to break through the defensive ranks of infantry, which alone made up the English army. Both sides suffered heavy losses but the death of Harold allowed William to conquer England (*see* Norman conquest).

● **Hastings, Francis Rawdon-Hastings, 1st Marquess of** ▶ (1754–1826) British soldier and colonial administrator; governor general of Bengal (1813–23). He joined the army in 1771 and fought (1775–82) in the American Revolution. In India he asserted British control over the Maratha states of W and central India and in 1819 negotiated the purchase of Singapore. He was governor of Malta (1824–26).

● **Hastings, Warren** ▶ (1732–1818) British colonial administrator. He first went to India in 1750 in the employ of the East India Company and by 1761 had become a member of its Calcutta council. In 1769 he became second in council in Madras; in 1771 governor of Bengal; and then (1774–85) governor general of Bengal with responsibility for the British territories in India—in effect, the first governor general of India. His outstanding administration consolidated British control of India and introduced administrative, legal, and financial reforms that provided the basis of subsequent British government there. In 1782 he negotiated peace with the Maratha states and in 1784 with Mysore. Hastings was unpopular with his colleagues, especially Sir Philip ▷Francis, with whom he fought a duel in 1779. He was also criticized for the hanging for forgery of one Maharaja Nandakumar and was impeached for corruption. The trial before the House of Lords, which lasted until 1795, cost Hastings £70,000 but ended in his acquittal.

● **hatchetfish** ▶ A carnivorous hatchet-shaped fish, up to 10 cm long, belonging to one of two unrelated groups. Deepsea hatchetfish (family *Sternoptychidae*; 15 species) are related to ▷salmon and occur in warm and temperate waters down to about 1000 m. The freshwater or flying hatchetfish (family *Gasteropelecidae*; about 9 species) of South America are related to ▷carp. They swim near the surface and are able to leap out of the water and "fly" short distances by flapping their large pectoral fins. ▯oceans.

● **Hatfield** ▶ 51 46N 0 13W A market town in SE England, in Hertfordshire, extended as a new town since 1948. The old town contains the 17th-century Hatfield House and remains of the 15th-century Hatfield Palace where Elizabeth I learnt of her accession. Industries include light engineering. Population (1991): 31 104.

● **Hathaway, Anne** ▶ (c. 1556–1623) The wife of William ▷Shakespeare. She was born at Shottery, near Stratford. She married Shakespeare in 1582 and bore him three children. The house known as "Anne Hathaway's cottage" (actually the property of her brother) may still be seen near Stratford.

● **Hathor** ▶ An Egyptian sky goddess, worshipped as goddess of fertility and of love, happiness, and beauty. She was usually portrayed as a cow or with a cow's horns and is sometimes identified with ▷Isis.

● **Hatshepsut** ▶ Queen of Egypt (c. 1490–1468 BC) of the 18th dynasty. The half-sister and widow of ▷Thutmose II, she overshadowed the young ▷Thutmose III, and assumed the status of pharaoh. During her reign direct communications with Punt (now S Eritrea) were reopened. Illustrated accounts of her expedition there and of the transport of her obelisks from Aswan are carved on her funerary temple at

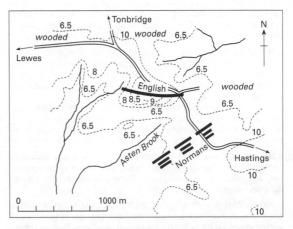

Battle of Hastings ▶ The three lines of Norman troops were led by archers, including crossbowmen (making their first recorded appearance in battle), who were able to undermine the advantage of the English position on a ridge above.

Dayr al-Bahri. After her death Thutmose III attempted to obliterate her memory by defacing her monuments.

● **Hatteras, Cape** ► 35 14N 75 31W A low sandy promontory in the USA, in North Carolina on Hatteras Island. Its shallows are a danger to navigation.

● **Hattersley, Roy (Sydney George), Baron** ► (1932–) British Labour politician and journalist. Having been a junior minister at the Foreign Office (1974–76) and secretary of state for prices and consumer protection (1976–79), he became deputy leader of the Labour Party (1983–92) under Neil ▷Kinnock. He became a life peer, Baron Hattersley of Sparkbrook, in 1997.

● **Hattusas** ► The ancient capital of the ▷Hittite empire (c. 1700–1230 BC) situated at Boğazköy (*or* Boğazkale) in central Turkey. The massive fortifications still visible date from the reign of ▷Suppiluliumas (c. 1375–c. 1335 BC). Thousands of tablets, forming part of the royal archives, have been found here and provide invaluable evidence for diplomatic and commercial activity in the period.

● **Haughey, Charles** ► (1925–) Irish statesman; prime minister of Ireland (1979–81, 1982, and 1987–92). He served in several ministerial posts and was president of Fianna Fáil (1979–92). A controversial figure, he resigned following a series of financial and other scandals.

● **Hauptmann, Gerhart** ► (1862–1946) German dramatist. After studying sculpture he turned to writing plays, making his reputation with *Before Dawn* (1889). Early work was influenced by ▷Naturalism, as in *The Weavers* (1892). This later alternated with a mystical and ▷Symbolist strain, as in *The Assumption of Hannele* (1893). He also wrote novels (*The Fool in Christ*, 1910), novellas (*Flagman Thiel*, 1888), and poetry (*Der Grosse Traum*, 1942). He won a Nobel Prize in 1912.

● **Hauraki Gulf** ► A large inlet of the South Pacific Ocean, in New Zealand on the E coast of North Island. Waitemata Harbour, on which stands Auckland, is situated in the SW. Area: about 2290 sq km (884 sq mi).

● **Hausa** ► A people of NW Nigeria and S Niger, numbering about nine million. Their language belongs to the Chadic subgroup of the ▷Hamito-Semitic family, but has absorbed many Arabic words and influences. It is an official language of Nigeria and a second language in much of West Africa. The Hausa are mainly Muslim. There were once several Hausa states ruled on feudal lines by emirs and titled office holders who held villages as fiefs. Slavery was practised but slaves could attain high office. The economy is based on maize, millet, sorghum, and other crops. Crafts are highly developed and trade is extensive. Cities, such as ▷Kano, date from precolonial times but most Hausa live in small rural settlements.

● **Haussmann, Georges-Eugène, Baron** ► (1809–91) French town planner, responsible for extensive rebuilding in Paris under ▷Napoleon III. Haussmann's long avenues and dramatic vistas, for example the avenues radiating from the ▷Arc de Triomphe, form much of the city's character. His schemes, while improving sanitation and public utilities, destroyed many remnants of the medieval town.

● **Havana** ► (Spanish name: La Habana) 23 00N 82 30W The capital of Cuba, a port in the NW. It exports sugar, cotton, and tobacco. The city has been modernized under Castro but much of the Spanish-colonial element remains, including the cathedral. The university was founded in 1728.
History: the first settlement was on the S coast; the city's present site dates from 1519. It became the capital in the late 16th century. Because of its natural harbour, Havana has long been of great strategic and commercial importance. Population (1995 est): 2 241 000.

● **Havana cat** ► A breed of short-haired cat, formerly known as Chestnut Brown Foreign. The Havana has a lithe slender body with a long tail, a long head, and large ears. The coat is chestnut-brown and the eyes are green and slanting.

● **Havel, Václav** ► (1936–) Czech statesman and writer; president of Czechoslovakia (1989–92) and of the Czech Republic (1993–). The author of such plays as *The Garden Party* (1963), *Largo Desolato* (1984), *Temptation* (1985), and *Redevelopment* (1989), he was imprisoned (1979–83) for involvement in the dissident Charter 77 movement and again in 1989. A founder of the Civil Forum political group, he became pres-

ident after the fall of the Communist regime. He resigned as president of Czechoslovakia following his failure to prevent the break-up of the country, subsequently becoming the first president of the new Czech Republic.

● **Havering** ► A borough of NE Greater London, created in 1965 from the former municipal borough of Romford and the urban district of Hornchurch. Area: 120 sq km (46 sq mi). Population (1996 est): 230 900.

● **Hawaii** ► (former name: Sandwich Islands) A state in the USA, occupying a chain of over 20 volcanic islands in the central Pacific Ocean. These include the islands of Hawaii (the largest), Maui, Oahu, Kauai, and Molokai. Its population, concentrated mainly on Oahu, is more ethnically diverse than that of any other US state, the largest groups being White Americans and Japanese. Its industry relies heavily on imported raw materials; manufactures include oil and chemical products, steel, textiles, and food. Agriculture is important, the main crops being sugar and pineapples. The principal industry, however, is tourism. There is some lumbering and fishing. There are many US military bases.
History: under the rule of several kings when discovered by James ▷Cook in 1778, Hawaii remained a kingdom until becoming a republic in 1894. It was annexed by the USA in 1898 and became a territory in 1900. The Japanese attack on Pearl Harbor (1941) brought the USA into World War II. Hawaii became a state in 1959. Area: 16 641 sq km (6425 sq mi). Population (1996 est): 1 183 723. Capital: Honolulu.

● **Hawaiian goose** ► A rare ▷goose, *Branta sandvicensis*, native to Hawaii and Maui, where it is called néné. It has a grey-brown plumage barred with white and an orange neck. Its numbers are now increasing by breeding programmes.

● **Hawaiian guitar** ► (*or* steel guitar) A type of guitar held flat on the player's lap. The strings are stopped by a sliding steel bar, which produces a characteristic glissando.

● **Hawarden** ► 53 11N 3 02W A market town in NE Wales, in Flintshire. Gladstone lived at Hawarden Castle, built in 1752. Population (latest est): 44 373.

● **hawfinch** ► A large ▷finch, *Coccothraustes coccothraustes*, of Eurasia and N Africa. 18 cm long, it has a reddish-brown plumage with paler underparts, a black bib, and black-and-white wings. Its massive bill is used to crack open the stones of cherries, sloes, and damsons to extract the seeds.

● **Haw-Haw, Lord** ▷*See* Joyce, William.

● **Hawick** ► 55 25N 2 47W A town in SE Scotland, in Scottish Borders on the River Teviot. The site of a 12th-century castle, it produces knitwear and tweeds and is an important market town for livestock. Population (1991): 15 812.

● **hawk** ► A bird of prey belonging to a widely distributed family (*Accipitridae*; 205 species) that includes buzzards, eagles, harriers, kites, and vultures. Hawks range in size from small ▷sparrowhawks to the ▷harpy eagle and have down-curved pointed bills, powerful gripping feet, and highly developed eyesight. Hawks typically fly fast in pursuit of live prey, using their strong claws for killing, and have broad rounded wings; they usually nest in trees or crags. Order: *Falconiformes*. *Compare* falcon. ▷*See also* falconry.

● **Hawke, Edward, 1st Baron** ► (1705–81) British admiral, who destroyed the French fleet in Quiberon Bay in 1759. He thus prevented the French invasion of England.

● **Hawke, Robert (James Lee)** ► (1929–) Australian statesman; Labor prime minister (1983–91). He was president of the Australian Council of Trade Unions (1970–80) before becoming president (1973–78) and leader (1983–91) of the Labor Party. In 1990 he risked unpopularity by pushing forward a radical privatization programme but won a fourth election, resigning a year later after losing his party's support.

● **Hawkesbury River** ► A river in SE Australia, rising in the Great Dividing Range in New South Wales and flowing NE to the Tasman Sea at Broken Bay. Length: 472 km (293 mi).

● **hawking** ▷*See* falconry.

● **Hawking, Stephen (William)** ▶ (1942–) British physicist, a leading figure in the field of general relativity and the theory of black holes. Although a victim of a progressive nervous disease and forced to rely upon mental calculation, he has described the particle emission of black holes (1974) and shown that general relativity supports the big-bang theory. His publications include the best-selling book *A Brief History of Time* (1987) and *The Universe in a Nutshell* (2001). He was made a Companion of Honour in 1989.

● **Hawkins, Sir John** ▶ (1532–95) English navigator. In 1562 he became the first English slave trader, transporting slaves from West Africa to the Spanish West Indies. His third expedition (1567–69), in which Drake participated, met with the Spaniards on its way home and only the ships of Drake and Hawkins escaped. In 1577 he became treasurer of the navy, instituting reforms that greatly contributed to Eng-land's victory against the Spanish ▷Armada (1588), and died at Puerto Rico on a new expedition with Drake. His son **Sir Richard Hawkins** (c. 1562–1622) served against the Armada and in a subsequent round-the-world plundering expedition was seized by the Spanish and imprisoned (1594–1602). His *Observations in His Voyage into the South Sea* (1622) influenced Charles Kingsley's *Westward Ho!* (1855).

● **hawk moth** ▶ A moth belonging to the widespread family *Sphingidae* (about 1000 species), also called sphinx moth or hummingbird moth. They have large bodies with relatively small wings (spanning 5–20 cm), which they beat rapidly, hovering over flowers and sipping nectar through their long proboscis. The leaf-eating larvae pupate in soil or litter.

● **hawk owl** ▶ An ▷owl, *Surnia ulula*, that occurs in coniferous forests of Eurasia and North America. It is 40 cm long and has a long tail, a small head, and short pointed wings, which give a hawklike silhouette in flight. It hunts by day.

● **Hawks, Howard** ▶ (1896–1977) US film director. He started as a writer but from 1938 produced and directed numerous comedies and fast-paced action dramas such as *Scarface* (1932), *His Girl Friday* (1940), *Sergeant York* (1941), and *The Big Sleep* (1946).

● **hawksbill turtle** ▶ A small sea turtle, *Eretmochelys imbricata*, found in warm waters worldwide. It has hooked jaws, feeds on algae, fish, and invertebrates, and is usually 40–55 cm long. The polished translucent mottled brown shell is the tortoiseshell used to make combs, etc.

● **Hawksmoor, Nicholas** ▶ (1661–1736) English baroque architect. Hawksmoor was trained by ▷Wren and collaborated with ▷Vanbrugh at ▷Blenheim Palace and Castle Howard. He was easily Vanbrugh's superior in technical skill. His finest individual work was at Easton Neston (1702), All Souls', Oxford (1729), and St Anne's, Limehouse (1714).

● **hawkweed** ▶ A perennial herb of the genus *Hieraceum* (about 1000 species), of temperate regions and tropical mountains. It grows to a height of about 60 cm and usually has yellow flower heads. The name derives from the old belief that hawks ate these plants to improve their eyesight. Family: ▷Compositae.

● **Haworth** ▶ 53 50N 1 57W A village in N England, in Bradford unitary authority, West Yorkshire, on the edge of the Pennine moorland. Haworth parsonage (now a museum) was the home of the Brontë family from 1820; Emily and Charlotte are buried in the church. Population (1991): 4956.

● **Haworth, Sir Walter Norman** ▶ (1883–1950) British biochemist, who first synthesized artificial vitamin C (ascorbic acid), thus enabling its cheap production for medical use. He shared a Nobel Prize (1937) with the Swiss chemist Paul Karrer (1889–1971).

● **hawthorn** ▶ A thorny shrub or tree of the N temperate genus *Crataegus* (about 200 species). Hawthorns have lobed leaves, usually about 4 cm long, white spring-blooming flowers, and yellow, black, or red fruits. The common hawthorn, or may (*C. monogyna*), is found in hedgerows and thickets in Europe and the Mediterranean. Up to 10 m high, it has red fruits (haws). Horticultural forms include double-flowered varieties. Family: *Rosaceae*.

● **Hawthorn, Mike** ▶ (John Michael H.; 1929–58) British motor-racing driver, who had many successes in the 1950s and was world champion in 1958. He was killed in a road accident after retiring.

● **Hawthorne, Nathaniel** ▶ (1804–64) US novelist and short-story writer. His two best-known novels, *The Scarlet Letter* (1850) and *The House of the Seven Gables* (1851), concern the psychological effects of Puritanism in New England. He was a friend of Herman ▷Melville, who visited him in England after his appointment as consul at Liverpool in 1853. In 1857 he travelled in Italy, the setting of *The Marble Faun* (1860).

● **Hay, Will** ▶ (1888–1949) British comedian. After many years as a music-hall comedian he began acting in films in 1934. His films include *Oh, Mr Porter!* (1937) and *Ask a Policeman* (1939).

● **Haya de la Torre, Victor Raúl** ▶ (1895–1979) Peruvian politician. In exile following an attempt at revolution in 1923, he founded the radical Alianza Popular Revolucionaria Americana (APRA). He ran for the presidency in 1931 and, successfully, in 1962, only to have the result cancelled by a military coup.

● **Haydn, Franz Joseph** ▶ (1732–1809) Austrian composer, born in Rohrau. He became a cathedral chorister in Vienna at the age of eight and subsequently worked as a freelance musician and music teacher, studying the works of C. P. E. Bach. He later studied with the Italian composer Nicola Porpora (1686–1768) and in 1760 made an unfortunate marriage. In 1761 he became kapellmeister to the Esterházy family, a post he held for the rest of his life. In 1791 and 1794 he visited London and wrote his last 12 symphonies, which include the *Oxford* and *London* symphonies. Haydn's compositions include piano sonatas, piano trios, string quartets, masses, concertos, 104 symphonies, operas, and the oratorios *The Creation* (1798) and *The Seasons* (1801).

● **Hayek, Friedrich August von** ▶ (1899–1992) British economist, born in Austria. A historian of economic doctrine, Hayek argued for the free-market economy and the reduction of trade-union and government power. His works include *The Road to Serfdom* (1944). He shared the 1974 Nobel Prize.

● **Hayes, Rutherford B(irchard)** ▶ (1822–93) US statesman; Republican president (1877–81) who ended southern ▷Reconstruction after the Civil War. As governor of Ohio (1868–72, 1876–77) Hayes had pressed for social reforms and ratified the 15th Amendment protecting Black suffrage. As president he continued to support the welfare of minority groups and initiated civil-service reform.

● **hay fever** ▶ An ▷allergy to pollen, which leads to sneezing, a streaming nose, and inflamed eyes. If the sufferer is allergic to only one kind of pollen it may be possible to desensitize him or her (*see* desensitization); otherwise treatment is with ▷antihistamines or, in severe cases, steroids.

● **hazard** ▶ A dice game of great antiquity, played in Europe since the middle ages and popular among gamblers since the 17th century. William ▷Crockford's famous gambling club (opened 1827) was a favourite venue for the game. Two dice are used. The person throwing the dice calls a number between 5 and 9; to win he must throw either this number or a 12 if he has called 6 or 8, or an 11 if he has called 7. An ace loses him the throw, as does an 11 if he has called 5, 6, 8, or 9, or a 12 if he has called 5, 7, or 9. He continues to throw until he either wins or loses. ▷*See also* craps.

● **hazel** ▶ A hardy shrub or tree of the N temperate genus *Corylus* (15 species), cultivated since ancient times for its edible nuts, also called cob nuts. Flowers appear in spring, before the rounded toothed leaves. The male flowers are yellow catkins; each female flower, which consists only of two bright-red stigmas, develops into a nut partly enclosed in a green fringed husk. The best-known species is the European hazel (*C. avellana*), up to 12 m high. Family: *Betulaceae* (birch family) or, according to some authorities, *Corylaceae*.

● **Hazlitt, William** ▶ (1778–1830) British critic and essayist. The son of a Unitarian minister, he studied art and philosophy before becoming a journalist on various dailies and periodicals, including the *Edinburgh Review*. A friend of Wordsworth and Coleridge who later vehemently attacked both men, Hazlitt held independent opinions in politics and literary matters and expressed them in a style notable for its brilliant invective. He also wrote vivid sketches on diverse subjects, such as prize fighting. His collections of essays and lectures include *Lectures on the English Poets* (1818) and *The Spirit of the Age* (1825).

● **Healey, Denis (Winston), Baron** ▶ (1917–) British Labour politician; chancellor of the exchequer (1974–79). He entered parliament in 1952 and from 1964 to 1970 was defence minister. He was deputy leader of the Labour Party (1981–83).

● **health physics** ▶ The study of the problems that arise from the use of radiation of various kinds, especially those emitted by radioactive substances. Particular areas of study include ▷radioactive waste disposal, the maximum levels of radiation to which workers may reasonably be exposed, and the causes and effects of ▷radiation sickness. Health physics is a multidisciplinary subject involving physics, medicine, mathematics, chemistry, biology, and hygiene.

● **Heaney, Seamus (Justin)** ▶ (1939–) Irish poet. His early poems reflect his childhood in rural Northern Ireland, before he moved to Belfast in the 1960s (and subsequently to the Republic of Ireland). He later wrote on wider themes in *North* (1975), *The Haw Lantern* (1987), *Seeing Things* (1991), and *The Spirit Level* (1997); *Opened Ground* (1998) is a major collection of his work. He was Professor of Poetry at Oxford University (1989–94) and published an acclaimed translation of the Old English *Beowulf* in 1999. In 1995 he was awarded the Nobel Prize.

● **Heard and MacDonald Islands** ▶ A group of uninhabited subantarctic islands in the S Indian Ocean, under Australian control since 1947. Heard Island is mountainous and ice covered; its elephant seals and penguins were hunted in the 19th century. The MacDonald Islands are rocky islets.

● **hearing aid** ▶ A device used by the partially deaf to increase the loudness of sounds. Modern hearing aids are electronic and, since the advent of microcircuitry, unobtrusive; they consist of a microphone to convert the sound into electrical signals, which are passed into an amplifier. The amplified signal is then fed into an earphone to convert the signal back into a sound wave of increased intensity. In bone-anchored hearing aids the amplified signal passes to a metal (titanium) screw that is fixed into the skull bone behind the ear and from there to the cochlea. Profoundly deaf people may now benefit from a cochlear implant, consisting of electrodes implanted in the cochlea (inner ear) that convey signals from an external microphone directly to the auditory nerve.

● **Hearst, William Randolph** ▶ (1863–1951) US newspaper proprietor. Beginning with the *San Francisco Examiner*, which he took over from his father, and the New York *Morning Journal*, which he bought, he built up a vast newspaper empire based on popular sensationalism. His career inspired Orson ▷Welles' film *Citizen Kane* (1941). His granddaughter **Patty Hearst** (1955–) was imprisoned after she sided with her Symbionese Liberation Army kidnappers in 1974.

● **heart** ▶ A four-chambered muscular organ that pumps blood around the body (*see* Plate II). Two chambers—the left and right atria—dilate to receive oxygen-rich blood from the lungs and oxygen-depleted blood from the rest of the body, respectively (this is called diastole). Contraction of the heart (called systole) starts in the atria, forcing blood into the two ventricles. The left ventricle then contracts to force blood into a large artery—the aorta, which leads from the heart and feeds all the other arteries. The right ventricle pumps blood into the pulmonary artery and to the lungs, where it receives oxygen. Valves between the atria and ventricles and at the arterial exits of the heart prevent the backflow of blood. The rhythm of the heartbeat is maintained by the electrical activity of specialized cells within the heart (*see* pacemaker). ▷*See also* circulation of the blood; heart disease; transplantation.

● **heart attack** ▷*See* myocardial infarction.

● **heartburn** ▶ A burning pain felt behind the breastbone. It is usually due to regurgitation of the contents of the stomach into the gullet and may be associated with inflammation of the gullet. It is relieved by antacids (drugs that neutralize stomach acids).

● **heart disease** ▶ Any disorder affecting the muscle or valves of the heart or the blood vessels supplying the heart. The most common form of heart disease in industrial societies is ▷atherosclerosis of the

coronary arteries: it may lead to a heart attack (*see* coronary heart disease; myocardial infarction). Diseases of the heart valves include mitral stenosis, i.e. narrowing of the mitral valve, which controls the passage of blood from the left atrium to the left ventricle; it may result from rheumatic fever and, in severe cases, may require surgical treatment. Congenital heart disease, which is present at birth, usually takes the form of an atrial or ventricular septal defect ("hole in the heart"), a hole in the partition between the right and left sides of the heart. In babies with large defects the hole can be closed surgically; small defects do not require surgery. Heart failure occurs when the left ventricle ceases to function effectively, resulting in breathlessness and ▷oedema. It can result from high blood pressure (*see* hypertension) or disease of the valves or coronary arteries and is treated by rest and drugs (including ▷diuretics, ▷ACE inhibitors, and ▷digitalis drugs). ▷*See also* transplantation.

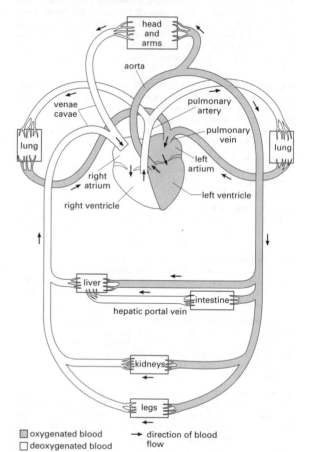

heart ▶ In humans and other mammals the right and left chambers of the heart are completely separate from each other. This ensures that oxygenated and deoxygenated blood do not mix and enables oxygen-depleted blood to receive a fresh supply of oxygen from the lungs before circulating to the rest of the body.

● **heart-lung machine** ▶ An apparatus that temporarily replaces the functions of the heart and the lungs during heart surgery. Using this apparatus the heart can be stopped for several hours to enable delicate surgery to be performed on the heart or its valves. Blood from two main veins is drained from the body through tubes to an apparatus that bubbles oxygen through it and removes the carbon dioxide. The oxygenated blood is then returned to a large artery in the body by a mechanical pump. It was first used in 1953 in the USA.

● **heartsease** ▷*See* pansy.

● **heart urchin** ▶ A marine invertebrate animal belonging to an order (*Spatangoida*) of ▷echinoderms. It typically has a rigid heart-shaped body, covered with short fine spines used for locomotion and defence. It lives in burrows lined with mucus and uses long tentacles (modified tube feet) to pick up particles of food. Class: ▷*Echinoidea*.

● **heat** ▶ The form of energy that is transferred from one body or region to another at a lower temperature. The amount of heat gained or lost by a body is equal to the product of its ▷heat capacity and the temperature through which it rises or falls. Heat is transferred by conduction, convection, or radiation (*see* heat transfer). The **internal energy** of a body (U), the *total* kinetic energy of its component atoms and molecules, was formerly also called its heat, although this can lead to confusion in ▷thermodynamics. According to the first law of thermodynamics $\Delta U = q - w$, where ΔU is the change in the internal energy of a body as a result of a change of temperature; q is the heat lost to or absorbed by the body from its surroundings and w is the work done on or by the surroundings at the same time. To call both U and q heat obviously leads to confusion and this sense is no longer used. Heat is measured in joules, but older units, such as calories and British thermal units, are still sometimes used.

● **heat capacity** ▶ The amount of heat needed to raise the temperature of a body through one degree Celsius (symbol: C). It is measured in joules per kelvin. For a gas, the heat capacity may be measured under conditions of either constant pressure or constant volume. ▷*See also* specific heat capacity.

● **heat death of the universe** ▶ A hypothetical final state of the universe in which its ▷entropy is at a maximum and no heat is available to do work. In any closed system the total entropy can never decrease during any process. Thus the entropy of the universe will eventually reach a maximum value and when that happens all matter will be totally disordered and at a uniform temperature. This assumes that the universe can be treated as a closed system.

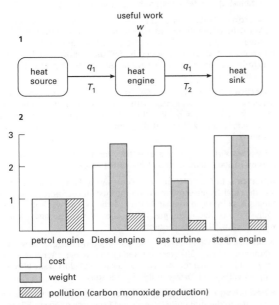

heat engine ▶ The efficiency of a heat engine depends on the temperature T_1 at which heat is fed to it and the temperature T_2 at which waste heat is discharged (1). A comparison of cost, weight, and pollution for various types of heat engine is shown at (2).

● **heat engine** ▶ A device that converts heat energy into work. Examples are petrol and Diesel engines, gas turbines, and steam engines. In terms of ▷thermodynamics, the heat engine converts a quantity of heat q_1 at temperature T_1 into work w; but the conversion can never be complete, some of the heat q_2 will be wasted and can be regarded as being discharged into a heat sink at a temperature T_2. The efficiency of the engine is defined as the work output divided by the heat input (w/q_1). As the work, w, is equal to q_1-q_2 (according to the first law of thermodynamics), the efficiency is $1-q_2/q_1$, or $1-T_2/T_1$. It is therefore important to make T_1 as high as possible and T_2 as low as possible. ▷*See also* Carnot cycle; internal-combustion engine; Stirling engine.

● **heath** ▶ An evergreen shrub or tree of the genus *Erica* (about 500 species) of Europe and Africa (about 470 species are native to South Africa). Heaths have small whorled often needle-like leaves and spikes of bell-shaped or tubular flowers, white, pink, purple, or yellow in colour. Dwarf heaths, such as the European species *E. tetralix* (bog heather) and *E. cinerea* (bell heather), are abundant on acid peaty soils, such as moorlands. There are many cultivated varieties, which are popular in rock gardens. Some tree heaths grow to a height of 6 m. Family: *Ericaceae*.

● **Heath, Sir Edward (Richard George)** ▶ (1916–) British statesman; Conservative prime minister (1970–74), who took the UK into the EC (1973). He entered parliament in 1950 becoming minister of labour in 1959. He was Lord Privy Seal (1960–63) and secretary of state for industry (1963–64) and in 1965 succeeded Douglas-Home as leader of the Conservative Party. His Industrial Relations Act (1971) was badly received by the trade unions and his government was twice challenged by miners' strikes: in 1972 he was forced to submit to their demands but in 1974 went to the country. Defeated in both the elections of that year (February, October), he relinquished the party leadership to Margaret Thatcher and became an outspoken critic of Mrs Thatcher's policies from the back benches. An enthusiastic musician, he was also known as a yachtsman.

● **heather** ▶ (*or* ling) An evergreen shrub, *Calluna vulgaris*, up to 60 cm high, with scaly leaves and clusters of pale-purple bell-shaped flowers. It grows—often with ▷heath—on acid soils of heaths, moors, and bogs throughout Europe and in parts of N Africa and North America (where it was probably introduced). Family: *Ericaceae*.

● **Heathrow** ▶ (*or* London Airport) 51 28N 0 27W The chief international airport in the UK, in the Greater London borough of Hounslow. Begun in 1944, it was opened to passengers in 1946. An underground railway connection covering the 24 km (15 mi) from central London was opened in 1977. A major interchange for transatlantic and other long-distance flights, it is the busiest airport in the world, handling some 58.2 million passengers in 1997.

● **heat pump** ▶ A device that extracts heat from one substance at a low temperature and supplies it to another substance at a higher temperature. Such a process would violate the second law of ▷thermodynamics if it occurred spontaneously; therefore the heat pump necessarily consumes energy in the process. Heat pumps are used to extract the low temperature heat from rivers that flow through towns and to convert it to a higher temperature so that use can be made of it, for example in space- and water-heating units. ▷*See also* refrigeration.

● **heatstroke** ▶ A rise in body temperature associated with ▷dehydration and exhaustion, caused by overexposure to high temperatures. The emergency treatment is to cool the patient down with water or fans, but medical treatment may be needed in addition.

● **heat transfer** ▶ The transference of energy between two bodies or regions by virtue of the difference in temperatures between them. The three methods of transference are: ▷convection, ▷conduction, and ▷radiation. In convection the heat is transferred by a hotter region flowing into a colder region, either as a result of density differences (natural convection) or by using a fan (forced convection). In conduction, on the other hand, the heat is transferred by direct contact without any apparent relative motion. In radiation the heat is transferred by means of either ▷infrared radiation or ▷microwaves. Radiation is the only method of transferring heat through a vacuum. The ▷Dewar (Thermos) flask is designed to minimize heat transfer, whereas the heat exchanger or radiator is designed to maximize it.

● **heat treatment** ▶ The process of heating a metal to a temperature below its melting point and then cooling it in order to change its physical properties. Metals are made up of tiny crystals (grains). Their hardness, strength, and ductility is determined by the concentration and distribution of irregularities (dislocations) in the crystal lattice.

In response to stress the dislocations move and change the shape and orientation of the grains. Heating creates and redistributes dislocations, relieving any internal stresses that have built up. This makes the metal softer and more ductile; a process known as annealing. Dislocation movement is restricted by the boundaries between grains and by the presence of impurities, which "pin" the dislocations making the metal harder and less ductile. Because both the impurity distribution and the grain structure are affected by heating and the rate of cooling, so also is the metal's strength. In steel manufacture, rapid cooling (quenching) by immersion in water or oil hardens the steel, leaving it brittle. Slow cooling makes it soft and ductile. Heating steel to around 900°C and quenching it, followed by warming to about 300°, is known as hardening and tempering. This results in a tough springy steel. ▷*See also* case hardening; work hardening.

● **heaven** ▶ In Christian belief, the abode of God and the angels, in which the souls of the virtuous will be rewarded with everlasting life (*see also* afterlife). The iconography of heaven is based upon the account in the Book of Revelation. The peace, light, and harmony of heaven are generally interpreted as metaphors for the bliss enjoyed by beings in the uninterrupted praise and contemplation of God (*compare* hell). Analogous concepts exist in other major religions.

● **Heaviside, Oliver** ▶ (1850–1925) British physicist, who pioneered the mathematical study of electric circuits and helped to develop vector analysis. Independently of ▷Kennelly, he predicted and then discovered a charged layer of the upper atmosphere that was capable of reflecting radio waves. This region, now known as the E-region of the ▷ionosphere, was formerly called the Heaviside layer or Heaviside-Kennelly layer.

● **heavy water** ▶ Deuterium oxide (D_2O), the form of water containing the isotope of hydrogen with mass number 2. It is chemically less reactive than normal water and has a relative density of 1.1; its boiling point is 101.42°C. It is present to an extent of 1 part in 5000 in natural water and it is used as a moderator and coolant in some nuclear reactors.

● **Hebbel, (Christian) Friedrich** ▶ (1813–63) German dramatist. Coming from a poor family in Holstein, he was largely self-taught. His pessimistic plays, all tragedies, often have historical or legendary settings, *Maria Magdalena* (1844) being the only exception. Among his other plays are *Herodes und Marianne* (1850), *Gyges und sein Ring* (1856), and *Die Nibelungen* (1862).

● **Hebe** ▶ In Greek mythology, the personification of youth. She was the daughter of Zeus and Hera and is described by Homer as cupbearer to the gods and the wife of Heracles.

● **Hebei** ▶ (Ho-pei *or* Hopeh) A province in NE China, on the Yellow Sea. Its fertile S plain is one of the earliest areas of civilization. Chief products are cereals, cotton, coal, and iron. Area: 202 700 sq km (79 053 sq mi). Population (1995 est): 63 880 000. Capital: Shijiazhuang.

● **Hébert, Jacques-René** ▶ (1757–94) French journalist and revolutionary. With his newspaper *Le Père Duchesne* he attained a wide following among the Parisian working class (*see* sans-culottes), becoming their leading demagogue. In 1792 he helped engineer the overthrow of the monarchy and became the procurator general of the Paris Commune. His unsuccessful attempt to incite a popular uprising against the Committee of ▷Public Safety resulted in his execution.

● **Hebrew** ▶ A Semitic language. It is written from right to left in an alphabet of 22 letters, all consonants, with vowels indicated by subscript and superscript diacritical marks. The oldest and best-known works of Hebrew literature are those preserved in the ▷Bible (Old Testament). Mishnaic Hebrew is a somewhat different language, spoken in Palestine until the 2nd century AD. It is the language of the ▷Mishnah and the oldest extant Jewish prayers. Hebrew continued to be a literary language throughout the middle ages, with a particularly rich poetic tradition, besides prose writing. The study of Hebrew grammar was developed by the ▷masoretes, and by the ▷gaon Sa'adya and later grammarians. In more modern times the ▷Haskalah movement led to a renaissance in Hebrew writing, and from the late 19th century Hebrew was revived as a spoken language,

particularly in Russia and Palestine. The ▷Ashkenazim and ▷Sephardim differ in their pronunciation of Hebrew. In 1948 it became an official language of Israel.

● **Hebrew literature** ▶ A body of literature originating as early as 1200 BC in Old Testament writings and still flourishing in the modern secular idiom of Israel. Not synonymous with Jewish literature (which was frequently composed in other languages, e.g. Arabic or Yiddish), Hebrew literature reflects the vicissitudes of the Hebrew language, being confined after about 200 AD to religious and legal texts and commentaries (*see* Mishnah; Talmud). Medieval Spain produced some original talents, including the poets ▷Judah ha-Levi and ▷Ibn Gabirol and the philosopher ▷Maimonides. The 18th-century Haskala (enlightenment) in E Europe initiated the renaissance of secular literature, and the rise of Zionism encouraged the novelist ▷Agnon and the poet ▷Bialik, among others, to mould Hebrew into a modern literary language.

● **Hebrews, Epistle to the** ▶ A New Testament book by an unknown author (formerly believed to be Paul), probably written between 62 and 69 AD. The book asserts that Christ is the high priest and greater than any of the ▷Levites and that his work fulfils and renders obsolete the old ▷covenant between God and Israel. The book is obviously addressed to readers who had a thorough knowledge of Judaism and is intended to confirm such converts in their new faith.

● **Hebrides, the** ▶ A group of about 500 islands off the W coast of Scotland. The islands are subdivided into the Inner and Outer Hebrides, separated by the Minch. The chief islands of the Outer Hebrides include Lewis with Harris and the Uists; those of the Inner Hebrides include Skye, Mull, Islay, and Jura. The Outer Hebrides now comprise an island authority (*see* Western Isles Islands Area) while the Inner Hebrides are divided between the authorities of Highland, Argyll and Bute, and North Ayrshire. The main occupations are stock rearing, fishing, and crofting (producing fodder crops, potatoes, and vegetables). Harris tweed is produced, especially in the Uists.

● **Hebron** ▶ (Arabic name: Al Khalil) 31 32N 35 06E A town on the ▷West Bank of the River Jordan. One of the oldest continuously inhabited cities in the world, it is revered by Jews and Muslims as the burial place of Abraham. Since early 1997 most of the town has been controlled by the Palestinian National Authority. Population (1990 est): 80 000.

● **Hecate** ▶ A primitive Greek fertility goddess and a ruler of the underworld. She was associated with witchcraft and magic and was worshipped at crossroads. She witnessed the abduction of ▷Persephone and accompanied ▷Demeter in her search for her daughter.

● **hectare** ▶ (ha) A unit of area in the ▷metric system equal to 100 ares or 10 000 square metres. 1 ha = 2.471 acres.

● **Hector** ▶ In Greek legend, the eldest son of Priam, King of Troy, and the chief Trojan warrior. He was the husband of Andromache. He fought Ajax in single combat, killed ▷Patroclus, and was killed in revenge by ▷Achilles. Priam pleaded for the return of his body, which was buried with great ceremony.

● **Hecuba** ▶ In Greek legend, the wife of Priam, King of Troy, and mother of ▷Hector. She was captured by the Greeks after the fall of Troy, but in revenge for the death of her son Polydorus, she blinded King Polymestor of Thrace and killed his sons.

● **hedgehog** ▶ A nocturnal prickly-coated insectivorous mammal belonging to the subfamily *Erinaceinae* (15 species), of Africa, Europe, and Asia. The European hedgehog (*Erinaceus europaeus*) grows up to 30 cm long and has brown and cream spines and soft grey-brown underfur. It feeds on worms, beetles, slugs, and snails, hunting mainly by scent and hearing along ditches and hedgerows. Hedgehogs hibernate in colder climates. Family: *Erinaceidae*. ▯mammal.

● **hedgehog cactus** ▶ A cactus of the North American genus *Echinocactus* (10 species), some species of which are cultivated as pot plants. They have round or cylindrical strongly ribbed woolly stems bearing many spines and—at the top—mainly yellow flowers.

● **hedge sparrow** ▷*See* dunnock.

● **hedging** ► A commercial operation enabling a trader or speculator to protect himself against unpredictable changes in price. In ▷commodity trading markets, trading in futures (goods for delivery in the future) provides a hedging facility. For example, a manufacturer may wish to purchase a year's supply of a commodity for regular deliveries throughout the year but may expect the price to fall over the period. In this case he could hedge his purchase by selling short (i.e. selling without buying) on a futures market so that he could cover (buy back) the sales at a lower price if there was a fall.

● **hedonism** ► The ethical theory holding that pleasure is the greatest good. Varying definitions of pleasure distinguished the classical hedonistic schools but all considered individual rather than communal happiness. ▷Utilitarianism, the most important modern form of hedonism, uses a social criterion: "The greatest good of the greatest number." *Compare* Epicureanism.

● **Heenan, John Carmel, Cardinal** ► (1905–75) British Roman Catholic prelate; Archbishop of Westminster (1963–75). Ordained in 1930, he worked as a priest in the East End of London until 1947. He was appointed Bishop of Leeds (1951–57) and Archbishop of Liverpool (1957–63) before being created cardinal in 1963.

● **Hefei** ► (or Hofei) 31 55N 117 18E A city in E China, capital of Anhui province. The capital of a 10th-century kingdom, it is now an industrial centre with an industrial university and a scientific university. Population (1991 est): 733 278.

● **Hegel, Georg Wilhelm Friedrich** ► (1770–1831) German philosopher, one of the greatest and most influential thinkers of the 19th century. He followed ▷Kant, ▷Fichte, and ▷Schelling but exceeded them all in the scale and erudition of his work. He developed his ideas slowly and steadily; his first major work, *The Phenomenology of Mind*, was published in 1807, the *Encyclopedia of the Philosophical Sciences* in 1817, and *The Philosophy of Right* in 1821. Besides these major works, he left voluminous lecture notes on history, religion, and aesthetics. He became an eminent and respected figure, collecting disciples, appointments, and decorations before dying, in Berlin, of cholera. ▷*See also* Hegelianism.

● **Hegelianism** ► The idealist school of thought based on the philosophy of ▷Hegel. His followers built on his idea that philosophy is the highest available form of knowledge and that all other forms (scientific, religious, etc.) must be referred to it. Ambiguity in Hegel's own thought has encouraged considerable diversity in interpreters of Hegelianism. The so-called Old Hegelians thought religion could be brought into harmony with philosophy, while the Young Hegelians saw philosophy as essentially critical of religion. Karl ▷Marx was influenced by the Young Hegelians, especially ▷Feuerbach.

● **Hegira** ► (Arabic *hijrah*: migration) The usual English name for the Muslim era. Based on lunar months, it is reckoned from 622 AD (or 1 AH, from Latin *anno hegirae*), the date of Mohammed's migration from Mecca to Medina. Most Muslim countries now use both the Hegira calendar and the Christian or Common Era calendar.

● **Heidegger, Martin** ► (1889–1976) German philosopher. His main philosophical work was *Sein und Zeit* (*Being and Time*; 1927). As rector of Freiburg University (1933–34) he supported Hitler and this association, together with logical flaws in his work, has damaged his reputation. Although his preoccupation with *Angst* (dread) as a fundamental part of human consciousness is typical of ▷existentialism, Heidegger himself denied that he was an existentialist.

● **Heidelberg** ► 49 25N 08 42E A city in SW Germany, in Baden-Württemberg on the River Neckar. A tourist centre, it has a ruined castle (mainly 16th-17th centuries) and the oldest university in Germany (1386), famed for its student prison. Its varied manufactures include printing presses, cigars, and electrical appliances.
History: the capital of the Palatinate until 1685, it was devastated during the Thirty Years' War and later by the French. In 1952 it became the European headquarters of the US army. Population (1996 est): 138 781.

● **Heifetz, Jascha** ► (1901–87) Russian-born violinist. A child prodigy, he entered the St Petersburg conservatoire in 1910, and at the age of 12 toured Russia, Germany, and Scandinavia, the beginning of a worldwide career. He commissioned important works for the violin, including Walton's violin concerto. He became a US citizen in 1925.

● **Heilbronn** ► 49 08N 9 14E A city in SW Germany, in Baden-Württemberg on the River Neckar. Many historic buildings, including the town hall (1540), were reconstructed after World War II. It is a transshipment point and a centre for electrical engineering. Population (1996 est): 121 509.

● **Heilongjiang** ► (Hei-lung-chiang or Heilungkiang) A province in NE China, bordering on Russia, comprising N Manchuria. The Da Hinggan Ling (mountains) provide valuable timber, while wheat is grown on the S plain. Oil, coal, and gold are produced. Area: 464 000 sq km (179 000 sq mi). Population (1995 est): 36 720 000. Capital: Haer-bin.

● **Heilungkiang** ▷*See* Heilongjiang.

● **Heimdall** ► The Norse god of light and dawn, who guarded the Bifrost bridge between ▷Asgard (the home of the gods) and ▷Midgard (the earth). He possessed miraculously sharp sight and hearing.

● **Heimlich manoeuvre** ► An emergency procedure to treat a person who is choking; it was devised by a US physician, H. J. Heimlich (1920–). The victim is clasped from behind with both arms, the clenched fist of one hand, grasped by the other hand, being placed just beneath the breastbone. A sudden upward thrust under the breastbone should dislodge the piece of food or other object that is obstructing the victim's airway.

● **Heine, Heinrich** ► (1797–1856) German Jewish poet and writer. Before establishing himself as a writer, he worked in banking and studied law. His early works include *Buch der Lieder* (1827), a collection of poetry, and his prose *Reisebilder* (1826–31), in which accounts of his travels are mixed with satirical comment. Sympathetic to revolutionary politics, he moved to Paris in 1831 and remained there until his death. In this period he wrote essays on French and German culture and some satirical poetry, notably *Atta Troll: Ein Sommernachtstraum* (1847).

● **Heinkel, Ernst Heinrich** ► (1888–1958) German aircraft designer. He designed military aircraft in World War I and—having founded his own company in 1922—again in World War II; he also designed and built the world's first jet-powered aeroplane (1939).

● **Heisenberg, Werner Karl** ► (1901–76) German physicist, who, with ▷Schrödinger, was the main architect of quantum mechanics. In 1927 Heisenberg created a mathematical system, known as matrix mechanics, to explain the structure of the hydrogen atom. ▷Dirac soon showed that matrix mechanics and Schrödinger's wave mechanics were equivalent. In the same year he put forward the theory known as the ▷Heisenberg uncertainty principle, which has had a profound effect on both physics and philosophy. For this discovery he was awarded the Nobel Prize in 1932. Heisenberg was one of the few major physicists to remain in Germany during the Nazi period; during World War II he was in charge of Germany's unsuccessful attempts to make an atom bomb at the Max Planck Institute in Berlin. After the war he became director of the Max Planck Institute for Physics in Göttingen.

● **Heisenberg uncertainty principle** ► If a simultaneous measurement is made of the position and momentum of a particle then, no matter how accurate the measurements, there is always an uncertainty in the values obtained. The product of the uncertainties is of the same order as the ▷Planck constant. A similar uncertainty exists with the simultaneous measurement of energy and time. The uncertainty arises because the act of observing the system interferes with it in an unpredictable way. Uncertainty is only important at the atomic and subatomic levels and at this level throws the principle of causality into doubt. Named after Werner ▷Heisenberg.

● **Hejaz** ► (or Western Province) A province in Saudi Arabia, on the Red Sea. Hilly inland, its coastal plain supports some agriculture; income is also derived from light industry and from pilgrims to the holy Muslim cities of Mecca and Medina. The largest town is Jidda. Hejaz, formerly independent, joined ▷Najd in a dual kingdom in 1926; both became part of Saudi Arabia in 1932. Area: about 350 000 sq km (135 107 sq mi). Population (latest est): 3 043 189.

● **Hel** ► In Norse mythology, the underworld; also called Nifleheim. It was covered with ice and guarded by the dog Garm. It is also the name of the goddess of death and ruler of the underworld, who was the daughter of the giant ▷Loki.

● **HeLa cell** ► A type of human cancer cell that has been maintained in continuous culture since February 1951, when the parent cells were removed from a tumour in a Black American patient, *Henrietta Lacks* (hence the name). Used in cancer research, HeLa cells are extremely virulent and propagate readily in cell culture; they are frequently found as contaminants in cultures of normal cells.

● **Helder, Den** ▷*See* Den Helder.

● **Helen** ► In Greek legend, the daughter of Zeus and ▷Leda, famed for her supreme beauty. She married Menelaus, King of Sparta, but later fled to Troy with ▷Paris, thus precipitating the ▷Trojan War.

● **Helena** ► 46 35N 112 00W A city and resort in the USA, the capital of Montana. It is the commercial centre for an agricultural and mining region. Population (1990): 24 569.

● **Helena, St** ► (c. 248–c. 328 AD) Roman empress, mother of Constantine the Great. A Christian from 313, she made a pilgrimage to the Holy Land (c. 326), where, according to tradition, she rediscovered the cross used at the crucifixion. Feast day: 18 Aug. Emblem: the cross.

● **Helgoland** ► (*or* Heligoland) 54 09N 7 52E A German island in the North Sea, in the North Frisian group. Ceded to Britain in 1814, it was transferred to Germany in exchange for Zanzibar (1890) and was a major German naval base during both World Wars. With the end of World War II its fortifications were destroyed. Area: about 150 ha (380 acres).

● **Helicobacter** ► A genus of spiral Gram-negative bacteria. The species *H. pylori* occurs in the inner layer of the stomach wall in humans; it causes ▷gastritis and ▷peptic ulcers, and is suspected of being associated with some forms of stomach cancer. The bacterium can be eradicated by a combination of antibiotics, bismuth, and drugs that reduce acid secretion in the stomach.

● **Heliconia** ► A genus of perennial herbaceous plants (about 120 species), native to tropical America and cultivated for ornament in the tropics. They have stout or reedlike stems and the leaves are often coppery with an ivory and pink midrib. The small flowers are contained within brightly coloured pointed bracts: *H. psittacorum* has green-yellow black-spotted flowers and red bracts. Family: *Heliconiaceae.*

● **helicopter** ► An aircraft that obtains both its lift and its thrust from aerofoils (rotors) rotating about a vertical axis (*compare* autogiro). The principle was known to Leonardo da Vinci, but the first successful helicopter was made in 1939 by Igor ▷Sikorsky in the USA (his 1909 model, made in Russia, failed to lift a man). A helicopter using a single rotor requires an anti-torque tail propeller and some models also use a vertical propeller for forward thrust. Helicopters can rise and drop vertically, hover, and move backwards, forwards, and sideways by control of the pitch of the rotors. First used in World War II, helicopters were widely employed for military purposes in the Korean War. They have since been developed for rescue services, police observation, and urban passenger services.

● **Heligoland** ▷*See* Helgoland.

● **heliocentric system** ► Any model of the solar system in which the planets move around the sun. The geocentric ▷Ptolemaic system was accepted for centuries until the heliocentric system of ▷Copernicus was published in 1543 and, after much religious and scientific controversy, shown to be true in essence (although not in detail).

● **Heliopolis** ► An ancient Egyptian city near present-day Cairo dedicated to the cult of the sun god Re. ▷Cleopatra's Needles came from here.

● **Helios** ► The Greek sun god, usually represented as a charioteer driving the sun across the sky each day. In later legends he was identified with Hyperion or Apollo. Because he was all-seeing he was called to witness oaths and promises.

● **heliotrope** ► A herb or shrub of the genus *Heliotropium* (220 species), found in tropical and temperate regions and having heads of blue or white flowers. Many will withstand cold, but none will survive frost. Many horticultural varieties of the cherry-pie plant (*H. peruvianum*) and *H. corymbosa* are used as bedding plants in cooler climates. Family: *Boraginaceae.*

● **helium** ► (He) The lightest noble gas, first detected in 1868 by Janssen (1838–1904) as an unexpected line in the spectrum of the sun. The term is derived from Greek *helios*, sun. Helium was discovered on earth in 1895 in the uranium mineral, clevite, as a radioactive decay product. Because of its low density and chemical inertness, it is used for filling balloons. It is also used as a gas shield in arc welding, and to replace nitrogen in the breathing mixture used by divers. Helium has the lowest melting point of any element. At no 2; at wt 4.0026; mp −272.2°C; bp −268.9°C.

● **helium dating** ► A method of dating materials that utilizes the production of helium in the form of ▷alpha particles during the radioactive decay of uranium-235, uranium-238, or thorium-232. The amount of helium trapped in the sample may be used to measure its age, after correction to allow for diffusion. The method is used mainly for rocks, minerals, and fossils.

● **hell** ► In Christian belief, the place in which the fallen ▷angels under Lucifer (*see* Devil) and the souls of the wicked are imprisoned in everlasting torment. The concept of hell as a dark and fiery pit derives from the Book of Revelation. Some Christians insist upon the physical reality of hellfire but most consider it a metaphor for the misery of a soul deprived forever of the vision of God (*compare* heaven). According to the doctrine often condemned as a heresy and known as apocatastasis, hell is not everlasting but will eventually be destroyed and all creatures, even the fallen angels, will be restored to God's grace. Other religions have similar concepts in which a tormented existence is visited upon the wicked in an ▷afterlife. *Compare* purgatory.

● **hellbender** ► The largest North American ▷salamander, *Cryptobranchus alleganiensis*. Growing to over 60 cm, it is dark olive-green with a wrinkled shiny skin. Hellbenders inhabit fast-moving oxygen-rich water, emerging from under rocks to feed at night on small animals and carrion. Family: *Cryptobranchidae.*

● **hellebore** ► A poisonous perennial herb of the genus *Helleborus* (20 species), of Europe and W Asia. The stinking hellebore (*H. foetidus*) grows to a height of 30–50 cm and bears clusters of cup-shaped purple-edged green flowers. Family: *Ranunculaceae*. ▷*See also* Christmas rose.

● **helleborine** ► A terrestrial ▷orchid of either of the genera *Cephalanthera* (about 14 species) or *Epipactis* (about 24 species), native to N temperate regions. They have tall thin stems, crinkled leaves, and clusters of flowers, which are either small, stalked, and drooping (*Epipactis*) or larger, stalkless, and held erect (*Cephalanthera*).

● **Hellen** ► In Greek mythology, the grandson of Prometheus and eponymous ancestor of the Greeks, who called themselves the Hellenes and their country Hellas. The four subgroups of the Hellenes, the Aeolians, Dorians, Ionians, and Achaeans, were named after his sons and grandsons.

● **Hellenistic age** ► The period, between the death of Alexander the Great of Macedon (323 BC) and the accession of the Roman emperor Augustus (27 BC), when Greek culture spread throughout the Mediterranean. Alexander's conquests took Greek ideas to the East and in the political confusion that followed his death city states became cosmopolitan and Greek colonists, following in Alexander's footsteps, implanted Greek ideas in their new environments. In the Hellenistic period Alexandria in Egypt was the major commercial city and centre of intellectual life, including scholarly literature and grandiose art, ▷Epicureanism, ▷Neoplatonism, Stoic philosophy, ▷Gnosticism, and Christianity. The Koine, common Greek, was the universal language.

● **Heller, Joseph** ► (1923–99) US novelist. He served in the Air Force during World War II and subsequently worked in advertising. His best-known novel, *Catch-22* (1961), is a satirical portrayal of modern warfare and bureaucracy. He also wrote the novels *Something*

Happened (1974), *Picture This* (1988), and *Closing Time* (1994), a sequel to *Catch-22*, as well as a play, *We Bombed in New Haven* (1968), and the memoir *Now and Then* (1998).

● **Hellespont** ▷*See* Dardanelles.

● **Hell Fire Club** ▷*See* High Wycombe.

● **Hellman, Lillian** ▶ (1905–84) US dramatist. Her plays, often concerning political themes, include *The Little Foxes* (1939) and *The Searching Wind* (1944). She was a close friend of Dashiell ▷Hammett and published volumes of memoirs, including *An Unfinished Woman* (1969), *Pentimento* (1973), and *Scoundrel Time* (1976).

● **Helmand, River** ▶ (R. Helmund *or* R. Hilmand) The longest river in Afghanistan. Rising in the E of the country, it flows generally SW then N to the marshy lake of Halmun Helmand on the Afghan-Iranian border. Length: 1400 km (870 mi).

● **helmet shell** ▶ A ▷gastropod mollusc belonging to the family *Cassidae* (about 60 species), also called bonnet shell. Found in shallow tropical seas and measuring 2–25 cm long, they feed mainly on sea urchins. ⨀shells.

● **Helmholtz, Hermann Ludwig Ferdinand von** ▶ (1821–94) German physicist and physiologist, who made contributions to many fields of science. In physiology his main interest was the sense organs, discovering the function of the cochlea in the inner ear and developing T. ▷Young's theory of colour vision (now known as the Young-Helmholtz theory). This work was published in his *Physiological Optics* (1856). His study of muscle action led him to formulate a much more accurate theory concerning the conservation of energy than that earlier proposed by Julius ▷Mayer and James ▷Joule. He played a considerable part in the development of thermodynamics, especially in formulating the concept of ▷free energy.

● **Helmont, Jan Baptist van** ▶ (1580–1644) Belgian alchemist and physician, who discovered the gas now called ▷carbon dioxide. A skilled and careful experimenter, Helmont helped to transform alchemy into chemistry.

● **Helmund, River** ▷*See* Helmand, River.

● **Heloise** ▷*See* Abelard, Peter.

● **helots** ▶ Indigenous Peloponnesian Greeks who lost their lands and freedom under Sparta. They formed the farming communities of Messenia and Laconia.

● **Helpmann, Sir Robert** ▶ (1909–86) Australian ballet dancer, choreographer, and actor. He went to England in 1933 and worked mainly with Sadler's Wells Ballet until 1950. He became artistic director of the Australian Ballet in 1955. His ballets include *Comus* (1942) and *Hamlet* (1942), and he also acted in films and plays, including productions of Shakespeare.

● **Helsingborg** ▶ (name until 1971: Hälsingborg) 56 05N 12 45E A seaport in S Sweden, on the Sound opposite Helsingør, Denmark. It changed hands several times between Denmark and Sweden before finally becoming Swedish in 1710. An industrial centre, it has an important shipbuilding industry. Population (1997 est): 114 866.

● **Helsingfors** ▷*See* Helsinki.

● **Helsingør** ▶ (*or* Elsinore) 56 03N 12 38E A seaport in Denmark, in NE Sjælland situated on the ▷Sound opposite Helsingborg. The fortress of Kronborg (1580) is famous as the scene of Shakespeare's *Hamlet*. Its industries include shipbuilding, brewing, and food processing. Population (1995): 56 855.

● **Helsinki** ▶ (Swedish name: Helsingfors) 60 13N 24 55E The capital of Finland, a port in the S on the Gulf of Finland. It is the country's commercial and administrative centre; industries include metals, textiles, food processing, and paper. Among its fine pale granite buildings are the 18th-century cathedral and the old senate house. The city is well laid out and spacious in appearance and is renowned for its 20th-century architecture. The university was moved here from Turku in 1828. *History*: founded by Gustavus I Vasa of Sweden in 1550 it was largely rebuilt following a fire in 1808. It replaced Turku as capital of

Finland (then under Russian rule) in 1812. It was badly bombed in World War II. Population (1997 est): 532 053.

● **Helvellyn** ▶ 54 32N 3 02W A mountain in NW England, in Cumbria, in the Lake District. It lies between the lakes of Thirlmere and Ullswater; a sharp ridge, Striding Edge, descends E of the summit. Height: 950 m (3118 ft).

● **Helvetia** ▷*See* Switzerland, Confederation of.

● **Helvetii** ▶ A Celtic tribe that settled about 200 BC in what is now Switzerland. Defeated by Caesar as they migrated southwards, they nevertheless retained their former territory, which was a buffer state between Rome and the Germans for over 400 years.

● **Helvétius, Claude Adrien** ▶ (1715–71) French philosopher. He followed Hume in holding that self-interest was the only motive of human action. His principle of the artificial identity of interests (i.e. interests manipulated by government) influenced ▷Bentham. *De l'esprit* (1758), expounding these views, was furiously denounced and burned by the public hangman.

● **hematite** ▷*See* haematite.

● **Hemel Hempstead** ▶ 51 46N 0 28W A market town in SE England, in Hertfordshire. Designated a new town in 1946, the principal industries include light engineering (scientific, electronic, and photographic equipment), paper, and pyrotechnics. Population (1991): 79 235.

● **Hemichordata** ▶ A phylum of marine invertebrate animals (about 100 species), found in coastal sand or mud and on the sea bed. The gill slits and nervous system show similarities with those of chordates—hence their name. The group comprises the ▷acorn-worms (class *Enteropneusta*) and the pterobranchs (class *Pterobranchia*). The latter are up to 7 mm long and have tentacle-bearing arms. They often form colonies and reproduce both sexually and by budding.

Ernest Hemingway ▶ Photographed at his desk in his Cuban home in 1945.

● **Hemingway, Ernest** ▶ (1899–1961) US novelist. After serving in the Red Cross during World War I he joined the American expatriate community in Paris. His first successful novel was *The Sun Also Rises* (1926). He was a keen sportsman, and in his short stories and his later novels, including *For Whom the Bell Tolls* (1940), about the Spanish Civil War, and *The Old Man and the Sea* (1952), he celebrated courage and stoicism in a forceful economical style. Other works include *A Farewell to Arms* (1929), *To Have and Have Not* (1937), and *Islands in the Stream* (1970). He won the Nobel Prize in 1954. Subject to severe depressions after leaving his home in Cuba in 1960, he committed suicide. In 1985 the $150,000 Ritz Paris Hemingway prize for fiction was instituted. The winning author receives $50,000 and the rest is shared by educational institutions.

● **hemiplegia** ▷*See* paralysis.

● **Hemiptera** ▶ An order of insects (about 50 000 species)—the true bugs—having piercing mouthparts for sucking the juices from plants or animals. The suborder *Heteroptera* includes plant and animal feeders (*see* plant bug; water bug). The forewings of these insects have both a leathery and a membranous region and are held flat over the body at rest. The suborder *Homoptera*, including the ▷froghoppers, ▷aphids, ▷cicadas, and ▷scale insects, are all plant feeders and have uniform front wings, held over the body at rest.

● **hemlock** ► **1.** A poisonous biennial plant, *Conium maculatum*, native to Europe, W Asia, and N Africa. It grows in damp places to a height of 2 m and has branching purple-spotted stems that bear much divided leaves and clusters of tiny white flowers. The plant is notorious as the means by which Socrates died. Family: ▷*Umbelliferae*. **2.** A coniferous tree of the genus *Tsuga* (15 species), native to S and E Asia and North America. The narrow bladelike leaves, up to 2 cm long, are grouped in two rows along the stems and the brown egg-shaped cones are 2–3 cm long. The western hemlock (*T. heterophylla*) of W North America, up to 60 m tall, is grown for timber and ornament. Family: *Pinaceae*.

● **hemp** ► An annual herb, *Cannabis sativa*, native to central Asia. It grows to a height of 5 m and bears small yellow flowers. Hemp is cultivated in many temperate regions (e.g. Italy and the Soviet Union) for its fibre, obtained from the inner stem bark and used for ropes, sacking, and sailcloth. The flowers, bark, twigs, and leaves contain a narcotic resin (*see* cannabis), source of marihuana and related drugs. Family: *Moraceae*. ▷*See also* Indian hemp.

● **Henan** ► (or Honan) A province in E central China. The Yellow and the Huai Rivers irrigate the E fertile plain. Densely populated, it has been a centre of Chinese culture since about 2000 BC. Chief products are cereals, cotton, silk, and coal. Area: 167 000 sq km (65 000 sq mi). Population (1995 est): 90 270 000. Capital: Zhengzhou.

● **henbane** ► A strong-smelling poisonous annual or biennial herb, *Hyoscyamus niger*, native to Europe and N Africa. Up to 80 cm high, it has funnel-shaped yellow flowers, veined with purple, and grows in sandy places. It contains the medicinal alkaloid hyoscyamine. Family: ▷*Solanaceae*.

● **Henbury Craters** ► A group of 13 meteoric craters in the central Australian desert near Henbury. The three largest are believed to have been formed by explosions and the others by impact. Meteoritic fragments in the area are composed of nickel-iron, some of great age.

● **Henderson, Arthur** ► (1863–1935) British Labour politician; foreign secretary (1929–31). An iron moulder, he became an MP in 1903 and later led the parliamentary Labour Party (1908–1910, 1914–1917). He served in Asquith's coalition government (1915–16) and then in Lloyd George's war cabinet (1916–17). As foreign secretary under MacDonald, he ardently supported the League of Nations and the Disarmament Conference, of which he became chairman in 1932. In 1934 he won the Nobel Peace Prize.

● **Hendon** ► A district in the Greater London borough of Barnet. Hendon airfield, from which the first UK aerial postal delivery was made, was an important flying centre (1909–57) and is now the site of an RAF museum (1972).

● **Hendrix, Jimi** ► (James Marshall H.; 1942–70) US rock singer and virtuoso electric guitarist. His group, the Jimi Hendrix Experience, recorded such hits as "Purple Haze" and "Foxy Lady" and the double album *Electric Ladyland* (1968). He died as a result of a drug overdose.

● **Hendry, Stephen** ► (1969–) British snooker player. In 1990, at the age of 21, he became the youngest winner of the world championship, which he won again each year from 1992 to 1996. In 1999 he won again, becoming the only player to win the title seven times.

● **henequen** ► A perennial herbaceous plant, ▷*Agave fourcroydes*, native to Mexico and cultivated for its leaf fibres called Yucatan, or Cuban, sisal. The plant stems grow to an average height of 90 cm in cultivation and the lance-shaped leaves form a dense rosette. Each plant yields 25 leaves annually from 5 to 16 years after planting. The fibres, which have an average length of 1.3 m, are made into twines used in agriculture, shipping, and rope. Family: *Agavaceae*.

● **Hengist and Horsa** ► Legendary leaders of the first Anglo-Saxon settlers in Britain. According to the Anglo-Saxon Chronicle (late 9th century AD) Horsa was killed in 455 AD and his brother Hengist ruled over Kent from 455 to 488.

● **Hengyang** ► 26 58N 112 31E A city in S China, in Hunan province on the Xiang (*or* Siang) River. It is a long-established communications, commercial, and cultural centre and many historic buildings survive. Chemicals and machinery are manufactured. Population (1990): 487 148.

● **Henley-on-Thames** ► 51 32N 0 56W A town in S central England, in Oxfordshire on the River Thames. It is chiefly a residential and recreational town with an annual Royal Regatta (first held in 1839). Population (1991): 10 558.

● **Henman, Tim** ► (1974–) British tennis player, ranked Britain's top male player in 1996 and 1998.

● **henna** ► A shrub, *Lawsonia inermis*, occurring in Egypt, India, and the Middle East. Up to 2 m high, it has fragrant white-and-yellow flowers. The leaves are powdered and used for tinting the hair and nails a reddish colour. It also has medicinal uses. Family: *Lythraceae*.

● **Henrietta Maria** ► (1609–69) The wife of ⌐Charles I of England. As a French Roman Catholic she was unpopular in England. During the Civil War she negotiated abroad for men, money, and munitions for the Royalist cause. Impeached by parliament, she escaped to France in 1644 and settled there.

● **henry** ► (H) The ▷SI unit of inductance equal to the inductance of a closed circuit such that a rate of change of current of one ampere per second produces an induced e.m.f. of one volt. Named after Joseph ▷Henry.

● **Henry (I) the Fowler** ► (c. 876–936) Duke of Saxony (912–36) and German king (919–36), founder of the Saxon dynasty (918–1024). In 925 he recovered Lotharingia for Germany, in 933 he defeated the Hungarians, and in 934, after invading Denmark, he won Schleswig for Germany.

● **Henry I** ► (1069–1135) King of England (1100–35); the youngest son of ▷William (I) the Conqueror. Henry became king on the death of his brother William Rufus, successfully defending his throne against the claims of his eldest brother Robert II Curthose, Duke of Normandy, from whom he won the duchy in 1106. In England his reign is notable for legal and administrative reforms, especially in the Exchequer, and for the resolution of the ▷investiture controversy involving Archbishop ▷Anselm. Abroad Henry waged several campaigns against Louis VI of France (1081–1137; reigned 1108–37), Fulk V, Count of Anjou (1092–1143), and Norman rebels to expand his continental possessions.

● **Henry (II) the Saint** ► (973–1024) German king and Holy Roman Emperor (1002–24; crowned 1014). After a protracted conflict with Poland he was forced to cede Lusatia but in Italy he successfully defended the papacy against the Greeks and Lombards. He sponsored Church reform, founding monasteries and schools. He was canonized in 1145.

● **Henry II** ► (1133–89) King of England (1154–89); the son of Matilda and Geoffrey of Anjou and the grandson of Henry I. Henry succeeded Stephen. Married (1152) to ▷Eleanor of Aquitaine, he ruled an empire that stretched from the River Tweed to the Pyrenees (*see* Angevins). In spite of frequent hostilities with the French king, his own family, and rebellious barons (culminating in the great revolt of 1173–74) and his quarrel with Thomas ▷Becket, Henry maintained control over his possessions until shortly before his death. His judicial and administrative reforms, which greatly increased royal control and influence at the expense of the barons, were of great constitutional importance.

● **Henry II** ► (1519–59) King of France (1547–59); the husband from 1533 of ▷Catherine de' Medici. He concluded war against the Emperor ▷Charles V at Cateau-Cambrésis (1559), after winning the bishoprics of Metz, Toul, and Verdun. An ardent Roman Catholic, he began the systematic persecution of Huguenots, which ultimately led to the ▷Wars of Religion. He died of blood poisoning following injury in a tournament.

● **Henry III** ► (1017–56) German king and Holy Roman Emperor

(1039–56; crowned 1046), who greatly enhanced the power of the Empire. He became interested in Church reform under the influence of his second wife, Agnes, and at the synod of Constance (1043) announced his desire to reform the Church. His suppression of heresy, however, was unpopular and towards the end of his reign he faced rebellions in Germany, Hungary, and S Italy.

● **Henry III** ▸ (1207–72) King of England (1216–72), succeeding his father John. Hubert de ▷Burgh controlled the government from 1219 until dismissed in 1232 and Henry's personal government began in 1234. Baronial discontent simmered, boiling over in 1258, when Henry, facing financial disaster, attempted to raise large sums from his magnates. Reforms—the Provisions of ▷Oxford—were agreed upon but then renounced by Henry. Simon de ▷Montfort led a rebellion against the king (*see* Barons' Wars), which was defeated after initial success. Thereafter, the aged Henry ceded much power to his son, the future Edward I.

● **Henry III** ▸ (1551–89) King of France (1574–89) during the ▷Wars of Religion. Elected King of Poland in 1573, he abandoned that country on succeeding to the French throne. In France he was caught between the Huguenot and Roman Catholic parties and after fleeing Paris following an uprising (1588) allied with the Huguenot Henry of Navarre (the future ▷Henry IV). He was assassinated while besieging Paris.

● **Henry IV** ▸ (1056–1106) German king (1056–84) and Holy Roman Emperor (1056–1106; crowned 1084), famous as the opponent of Pope Gregory VII in the ▷investiture controversy. The conflict over Henry's right to appoint bishops led him in 1076 to depose Gregory, who proceeded to excommunicate Henry. In 1077, however, Henry did penance at Canossa but was then dethroned by the German princes (1078–80). Again excommunicated, in 1084 he entered Rome, deposed Gregory, and nominated the antipope Clement III (d. 1100) by whom he was crowned emperor. He subsequently faced a further rebellion of the German princes and his sons Conrad and the future Emperor Henry V.

● **Henry IV** ▸ (1366–1413) King of England (1399–1413); the eldest son of ▷John of Gaunt. As Henry Bolingbroke, he seized the throne from Richard II. In the early years of his reign Henry faced considerable opposition from Richard's supporters, led by the Earl of Northumberland and his son Hotspur (*see* Percy, Sir Henry), and from the Welsh under ▷Glendower. Successful in defeating his enemies, the costs of these wars and resultant taxation led to protracted struggles between king and parliament for control of royal expenditure. Increasingly incapacitated by illness, Henry's last years were marked by bitter factional struggles within his council.

● **Henry IV** ▸ (1553–1610) The first Bourbon King of France (1589–1610), who restored peace and prosperity following the ▷Wars of Religion. A Protestant, he succeeded his mother to the throne of Navarre in 1572. Shortly afterwards he married Charles IX's sister ▷Margaret of Valois and was forced to renounce his religion and confine himself to court. In 1576 he escaped and became a ▷Huguenot (Protestant) leader in the Wars of Religion. His succession to the throne was only secured in 1594, when he became a Roman Catholic, and civil war continued until he granted the Huguenots freedom of worship by the Edict of ▷Nantes (1598). Thereafter he sponsored the efforts of his minister ▷Sully to restore France's shattered economy. Henry died at the hands of an assassin.

● **Henry V** ▸ (1081–1125) German king (1089–1125) and Holy Roman Emperor (1106–25; crowned 1111); son of Emperor ▷Henry IV and first husband of Matilda of England. His reign saw the settlement of the ▷investiture controversy with the papacy by the Concordat of Worms (1122), which brought him control of the German Church but antagonized his bishops.

● **Henry V** ▸ (1387–1422) King of England (1413–22); the eldest son of Henry IV. He vigorously resumed the ▷Hundred Years' War, partly as a distraction from domestic tensions. His first campaign culminated in the battle of ▷Agincourt (1415) and by 1420, in alliance with Burgundy, he controlled much of N France. He married Catherine of Valois and gained recognition (1420) as the heir of her father

▷Charles VI (1420). He was noted by contemporaries as much for his personal piety and love of justice as for military prowess.

● **Henry VI** ▸ (1165–97) German king (1169–97) and Holy Roman Emperor (1190–97). Son of ▷Frederick Barbarossa, he acquired Sicily through his marriage (1189) to Constance of Sicily (1152–98). His reign was dominated by his attempts to secure Sicily and to subdue ▷Henry the Lion. In 1193 he imprisoned the English king, Richard the Lionheart, and received a large ransom in return for his release.

● **Henry VI** ▸ (1421–71) King of England (1422–61, 1470–71), succeeding his father Henry V. He married (1445), and was dominated by, ▷Margaret of Anjou. His inability to govern led to bitter struggles that culminated in the Wars of the ▷Roses. Deposed and imprisoned by the Yorkists (1461), he was briefly restored to power (1470–71), only to be again defeated and probably murdered. He was a notable patron of learning and religion: he founded Eton College (1440) and King's College, Cambridge (1447).

● **Henry VII** ▸ (c. 1275–1313) Holy Roman Emperor (1309–1313; crowned 1312) and, as Henry VI, Count of Luxembourg (1288–1313). He became King of the Lombards in 1313 but had to contend with ▷Guelf (anti-imperial) opposition in Italy. He arranged a brilliant match between his son John, the future Count of Luxembourg, and Elizabeth of Bohemia.

● **Henry VII** ▸ (1457–1509) King of England (1485–1509). As Henry Tudor, Earl of Richmond, he defeated Richard III at ▷Bosworth Field (1485) and his marriage (1486) to Richard's niece Elizabeth of York (1465–1503) united the Houses of ▷Lancaster and ▷York, effectively ending the Wars of the ▷Roses. Until 1499, however, he faced Yorkist plots, such as those of ▷Simnel and ▷Warbeck. His domestic rule was noted for its harsh financial exactions, efficient royal administration, and growing prosperity. His foreign policy temporarily put an end to war with France (on favourable terms, 1492), while treaties with Burgundy and the Holy Roman Empire resulted in a new pattern of European alliances.

● **Henry VIII** ▸ (1491–1547) King of England (1509–47), who initiated the English ▷Reformation. In 1512 he joined a European alliance against France, which he defeated at the battle of the ▷Spurs (1513),

Henry VIII ▸ Detail from a portrait (1540) by his court painter, Hans Holbein the Younger (Galleria Nazionale, Rome).

gaining Tournai, and in the same year his army thwarted a Scottish invasion at ▷Flodden. His desire to make England a notable European power was pursued from 1515 by his Lord Chancellor, Cardinal ▷Wolsey, who arranged the meeting between Henry and ▷Francis I of France at the ▷Field of the Cloth of Gold, near Calais (1520). From 1527 Henry was preoccupied by his wish to divorce ▷Catherine of Aragon, who had been the widow of his elder brother Arthur (d. 1502). He blamed her failure to produce a son (she had given birth to the future Mary I in 1516) on the canonical prohibition against marrying one's brother's widow, a conviction that was enforced by his love affair with Anne ▷Boleyn. Wolsey's failure to gain a papal annulment of Henry's marriage brought about the cardinal's fall in 1529 but only in 1533, after Thomas ▷Cromwell had initiated the legislation that made the English Church, under Henry's supreme headship, independent of Rome, could the king marry Anne. In the same year she gave birth to the future Elizabeth I. In 1535 Thomas ▷More was executed for refusing to acknowledge royal supremacy over the Church and in the following year Anne met the same fate for adultery. Henry then married Jane ▷Seymour, who died shortly after giving birth to the future Edward VI (1537). His next marriage, arranged by Cromwell, to ▷Anne of Cleves was short lived, ending in divorce and the execution of Cromwell (1540). Shortly afterwards Henry married Catherine ▷Howard, who was executed in 1542, and finally, in 1543, Catherine ▷Parr, who outlived him. Henry's last years were dominated by war with France and Scotland, consequent economic problems, and his attempts to hold back the forces of Protestantism, which "the King's great matter" had unleashed.

● **Henry, Joseph** ▶ (1797–1878) US physicist, who made important contributions to the investigation of electromagnetism. He built the largest electromagnet then known, which could lift over 300 kilograms; he also discovered electromagnetic induction independently of ▷Faraday. Henry invented an early form of the telegraph and the electrical relay. In 1846 he was appointed secretary of the Smithsonian Institution and he was one of the founders of the National Academy of Sciences. The unit of inductance (*see* henry) is named after him.

● **Henry, O.** ▶ (William Sidney Porter; 1862–1910) US short-story writer. He adopted his pseudonym while serving a prison sentence for embezzlement. He subsequently worked in New York, where he published *Cabbages and Kings* (1904), the first of many volumes of short stories characterized by the use of coincidence and unexpected endings.

● **Henry, Patrick** ▶ (1736–99) American Revolutionary orator; first governor of Virginia (1776–79). As a lawyer and member of the Virginia assembly (the House of Burgesses), Henry defended colonial rights against British rule. The mobilization of a Virginia militia on the eve of the American Revolution was ensured by Henry's famous speech ending "give me liberty or give me death." He was again governor of Virginia from 1784 to 1786.

● **Henryson, Robert** ▶ (15th century) Scottish poet. A schoolmaster at Dunfermline Abbey, he was, with ▷Dunbar and Gavin ▷Douglas, one of the Scottish disciples of Chaucer (the Scottish Chaucerians). His works include *The Testament of Cresseid* (a sequel to Chaucer's *Troilus and Criseyde*) and 13 *Moral Fables of Esope the Phrygian*, noted for their colloquial style.

● **Henry the Lion** ▶ (?1129–95) Duke of Saxony (1142–81), whose wealth and power brought him into conflict with the Holy Roman Emperors. He gave support to ▷Frederick Barbarossa in return for regaining Bavaria (1154) but when he broke with Frederick in 1176 most of his lands were confiscated and he was exiled. In 1194, after further conflict, he was reconciled with Frederick's son and successor Emperor ▷Henry VI.

● **Henry the Navigator** ▶ (1394–1460) Portuguese patron of explorers; the fourth son of John I. He won a military reputation at the capture of Ceuta (1415) in N Africa, which kindled his interest in the exploration of the continent. Becoming governor of the Algarve (1419) he set up a school of navigation at Sagres and inspired and sponsored explorers. Under his auspices Madeira, the Azores, and the Cape Verde Islands were colonized, the W coast of Africa was ex-

plored, probably as far as Sierra Leone, and many trading stations were established.

● **Henze, Hans Werner** ▶ (1926–) German composer, a pupil of Wolfgang Fortner (1907–87). His piano concerto won the Schumann Prize in 1951 and he settled in Italy in 1953. He has organized an annual festival at Montepulciano since 1977. Henze has composed in a number of different styles, including serialism and neoromanticism. His Marxist sympathies are evident in such works as the oratorio *The Raft of the Medusa* (1968). He has composed nine symphonies; concertos for piano, violin, viola, and double bass; ballet music; and the operas *Elegy for Young Lovers* (1961), *The Bassarids* (1966), *We Come to the River* (1976), *The English Cat* (1983), and *Das verratene Meer* (1990).

● **heparin** ▶ An ▷anticoagulant that occurs naturally in the tissues and is also used in medicine. Heparin is a complex carbohydrate produced and secreted by special cells (mast cells) in connective tissues, especially in the lungs. It inhibits the enzymes responsible for blood clotting.

● **hepatitis** ▶ Inflammation of the liver, most commonly caused by viruses. The three main types of infectious hepatitis are hepatitis A, usually contracted by ingesting the virus from food or drink; hepatitis B (formerly called serum hepatitis), which is contracted from contaminated hypodermic needles or blood products or is sexually transmitted; and hepatitis C (formerly called non-A, non-B hepatitis), contracted in similar ways to hepatitis B. Some chemicals (e.g. alcohol) can also cause hepatitis. Symptoms include fever, loss of appetite, and jaundice. Hepatitis often resolves without specific treatment, but sometimes chronic disease develops. Vaccines are available for hepatitis A and B.

● **Hepburn, Audrey** ▶ (Edda Hepburn-Ruston; 1929–93) US actress, born in Belgium of Anglo-Dutch parents. After acting in the theatre and playing minor roles in British films, she moved to Hollywood in the early 1950s. Her first major Hollywood film, *Roman Holiday* (1953), won her an Oscar. Subsequent films included *The Nun's Story* (1959), *Breakfast at Tiffany's* (1961), and the musical *My Fair Lady* (1964).

● **Hepburn, Katharine** ▶ (1909–) US actress. Her performances in both films and the theatre are distinguished by her intelligence and versatility. She made several films with Spencer ▷Tracy, and her other films include *The Philadelphia Story* (1940), *The African Queen* (1952), *The Lion in Winter* (1968), and *On Golden Pond* (1981).

● **Hephaestus** ▶ The Greek god of fire and crafts, the son of Zeus and Hera. According to Hesiod he created ▷Pandora, the first woman. He is identified with the Roman ▷Vulcan.

● **Hepplewhite, George** ▶ (1727–86) British furniture designer and cabinetmaker, who established a business in London. His neoclassical furniture is a simplified and more functional version of the designs of Robert ▷Adam, with whom he sometimes collaborated. Usually in inlaid mahogany or satinwood, it is characterized by straight tapering legs and heart- or oval-shaped chairbacks filled with openwork designs.

● **heptane** ▶ (C_7H_{16}) A colourless flammable liquid ▷alkane. It is obtained from ▷oil and is used as a solvent and to make other chemicals. Heptane is also a standard in determining the ▷octane number of petrol.

● **Hepworth, Dame Barbara** ▶ (1903–75) British sculptor. She studied in Leeds and at the Royal College of Art. A friend of Henry ▷Moore, she was also influenced by ▷Brancusi and ▷Arp. Her abstract carving in wood and stone developed after *Pierced Form* (1931), creating massive shapes broken by holes with wires stretched across their openings. Twice-married, to sculptor John Skeaping (1901–80) and painter Ben ▷Nicholson, she received the DBE in 1965.

● **Hera** ▶ In Greek mythology, the daughter of Cronus and Rhea and the sister and wife of Zeus. She was jealous of Zeus' many mistresses and cruel to their children but gave loyal support to ▷Jason and ▷Achilles. She was worshipped as a goddess of women and marriage. She is identified with the Roman ▷Juno.

● **Heracles** ▶ (or Hercules) A Greek legendary hero, famed for his strength and courage. He was the son of Zeus and Alcmene (*see*

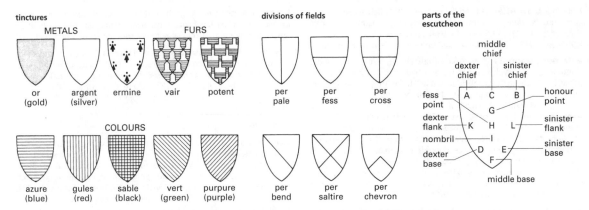

tinctures					divisions of fields			parts of the escutcheon

METALS · FURS

or (gold) · argent (silver) · ermine · vair · potent · per pale · per fess · per cross

COLOURS

azure (blue) · gules (red) · sable (black) · vert (green) · purpure (purple) · per bend · per saltire · per chevron

middle chief · dexter chief · sinister chief · fess point · honour point · dexter flank · sinister flank · nombril · sinister base · dexter base · middle base

heraldry ▶ The terminology of heraldry, of which a few terms are illustrated, reveals the science's French origins.

Amphitryon). After killing his wife and children in a fit of madness inflicted by Hera, he went to the court of King Eurystheus of Tiryns, where he performed the Twelve Labours in expiation: he killed the Nemean lion and the ▷Hydra of Lerna, captured the Hind of Ceryneia and the Boar of Erymanthus, cleaned the Augean stables, chased away the Stymphalian birds, captured the Cretan bull and the horses of Diomedes, stole the girdle of Hippolyte, captured the oxen of Geryon, stole the apples of the ▷Hesperides, and finally captured and bound ▷Cerberus in Hades.

● **Heraclitus ▶** (c. 535–c. 475 BC) Greek philosopher of ▷Ephesus. His treatise *On Nature* postulates that fire is the universe's basic constituent. Rejecting ▷Parmenides' doctrine of a unitary static reality, Heraclitus maintained that reality is transitory and every object "a harmony of opposite tensions." Everything was always changing ("you cannot step into the same river twice") and wisdom consisted in seeking to understand this eternal principle (*see* logos).

● **Heraclius ▶** (c. 575–641 AD) Byzantine emperor. Between 613 and 628 he faced the Persians, who took Syria, Palestine, and Egypt and besieged Constantinople (626). Following a campaign in 626–28, Heraclius restored the Holy Cross to Jerusalem (629), a deed that was immortalized in medieval legend. His success was short-lived for in 634 the Arabs attacked the empire, defeating the Byzantines at Yarmuk (636) and taking Palestine, Syria, and Egypt. He divided Anatolia into military units, from which peasants were enlisted for military service in return for land.

● **Herakleion** ▷*See* Iráklion.

Barbara Hepworth ▶ Photographed with one of her characteristic concave forms in her garden at St Ives, Cornwall, in 1954.

● **heraldry ▶** A system of pictorial devices on shields originally used to identify individuals when wearing armour. Personal devices on shields are of great antiquity but in the early 12th century armorial devices became hereditary in Europe. They were also used as ▷seals. Coats of arms are also granted to institutions. In England heraldry is controlled by the ▷College of Arms. The Court of the Lord Lyon has a similar function in Scotland. Coats of arms comprise the shield, a helmet surmounted by a crest, a mantling (stylized drapery behind the shield), a wreath, and a motto. The shield bears the heraldic signs (charges), which have ancient fixed meanings. From these heralds can determine the genealogy of the bearer.

● **Herat ▶** (*or* Harat) 34 20N 62 10E A city in W Afghanistan. Near the site of several ancient cities, including one built by Alexander the Great, Herat developed as a scientific and cultural centre under the rule of the Turkish conqueror Timur, who seized the city in 1393. An agricultural and commercial centre, Herat's industries include flour milling and textiles. Population (1990 est): 186 800.

● **herbaceous plant ▶** A plant that lacks woody stems and the aerial parts of which die each winter. Many herbaceous plants are ▷annuals but some are ▷perennials, surviving the winter as underground bulbs, corms, rhizomes, etc.

● **herbalism ▶** (*or* herbal medicine) A system of ▷alternative medicine that uses plants or parts of plants to treat or prevent disease. Many drugs used in orthodox medicine are derived from plants (for example, digoxin and digitoxin are derived from ▷digitalis, an extract from the leaves of the foxglove plant). Herbalism, however, differs in using the whole plant or a part of it, such as the flowers, roots, bark, or leaves, as the basis for its remedies, rather than the individual chemical constituents of the plant. It is regarded by its proponents as a ▷holistic form of therapy, the multiple ingredients of herbal remedies being required for treating all aspects of a disease. It has a long history, and in many parts of the world, notably in India and China, herbal medicines remain the only form of therapy widely used. In Western countries herbal medicines have acquired a niche market among those who believe that, as natural products, herbal remedies are a safer alternative to orthodox medicines, some of which have unacceptable side-effects. Many orthodox medical practitioners acknowledge that—at best—some patients may benefit from herbal medicines and—at worst—they will probably not be harmed by them. They argue, however, that it is impossible to prove their clinical effectiveness in a controlled trial because of the difficulty in standardizing preparations.

● **Herbart, Johann Friedrich ▶** (1776–1841) German educational theorist, who pioneered the application of psychology to teaching. Rejecting ▷Fichte's philosophy with its emphasis on freedom, he preferred ▷Kant's pluralism, believing that beyond the phenomenal world there existed many real "things-in-themselves," which are inaccessible to the mind. Herbart, like Kant, sought to make psychology a mathematical science and wasted time developing fruitless systems that had no experimental foundation.

● **Herbert, Sir A(lan) P(atrick)** ▶ (1890–1971) British writer and politician. Notable as a humourist, he wrote *Misleading Cases in the Common Law* (1927), *Holy Deadlock* (1934), and a novel, *The Writer Gypsies* (1930). As an MP (1935–50) he worked for reform of the marriage laws.

● **Herbert, George** ▶ (1593–1633) English poet. A member of a distinguished Anglo-Welsh family, Herbert had a brief career in secular life as Public Orator at Cambridge and as MP for Montgomery before pursuing a religious vocation. In 1630 he was appointed rector of Bemerton, Wiltshire. A friend of Francis ▷Bacon and ▷Donne, he wrote religious lyrics, collected in *The Temple* (1633), which rank among the finest in the language. He died of consumption. His brother **Edward, 1st Baron Herbert of Cherbury** (1583–1648) was a philosopher and poet. He was appointed ambassador to France (1619–24), during which time he completed a philosophical treatise, *De veritate* (1624), a controversial work that had wide contemporary influence. His *Autobiography* (1764) covers his life to 1624. His poems are collected in *Occasional Verses* (1665).

● **herbicide** ▶ (or weedkiller) A chemical used to kill unwanted plants (*see* pesticide). Selective weedkillers kill the target without harming the plants among which it is growing. Some of these act by interfering with the growth of the weed and are often based on plant hormones. An example is 2,4-D, a synthetic ▷auxin, which is used to control broadleaved weeds in cereal crops. Herbicides used to clear waste ground are nonselective and kill every plant with which they come into contact. An example is ▷Paraquat.

● **herbivore** ▶ Any animal whose diet consists solely of plants. Herbivores occupy the position of primary consumers in ▷food chains. Herbivorous mammals include the browsing and grazing ungulates (*see* Artiodactyla; Perissodactyla) as well as rodents, rabbits, and other groups. Their teeth and alimentary canals are specialized for eating and digesting vegetation: powerful grinding molars and premolars break up the cellulose cell walls of plants, which are digested by bacteria within the caecum, the section of the alimentary canal between the small and large intestines. ▷Ruminants have a four-chambered stomach, enabling them to "chew the cud."

● **herb Paris** ▶ A perennial herbaceous plant, *Paris quadrifolia*, native to woodlands of Europe and Asia. Up to 30 cm high, it has a whorl of usually four leaves and a solitary flower with prominent sepals and narrow yellow petals. The fruit is a fleshy capsule. Family: *Trilliaceae*.

● **herb Robert** ▶ An annual or biennial herb, *Geranium robertianum*, growing up to 50 cm high and found in woods and hedgerows throughout temperate Eurasia and introduced to North and South America. The small flowers are pink or red. Family: *Geraniaceae*.

● **herbs and spices** ▶ The fresh or dried parts of aromatic or pungent plants used in food, drink, medicine, and perfumery. Herbs are generally the leaves of plants and are best used fresh. They grow in temperate zones. Common culinary herbs are ▷basil, ▷bay leaves, ▷marjoram, ▷mint, ▷parsley, and ▷thyme. Spices generally grow in hot countries. They were formerly a valuable trade commodity; the Roman Empire's spice trade extended to Indochina and Zanzibar and the quest for spice routes motivated 15th-century European exploration of the East and the Americas. Spices are usually dried and may be obtained from the root (e.g. ▷ginger), bark (e.g. ▷cinnamon), flower (e.g. ▷clove), seed pod (e.g. ▷chilli), or, most commonly, from the seed itself (e.g. ▷coriander, ▷cumin, ▷pepper).

● **Hercegovina** ▷*See* Bosnia-Hercegovina.

● **Herculaneum** ▶ An ancient city near ▷Naples in Italy. It was destroyed by the same eruption as ▷Pompeii (79 AD). It was smaller, better planned, and wealthier than Pompeii. Entombment beneath solidified volcanic mud makes excavation there very difficult; much remains buried.

● **Hercules** ▷*See* Heracles.

● **hercules beetle** ▶ A giant green and black beetle, *Dynastes herculeus*, occurring in Central and South America. The male may reach a length of 15 cm, nearly two-thirds of which is taken up by an enormous pair of horns, extending from the thorax and head. Family: *Scarabeidae* (*see* scarab beetle).

● **hercules moth** ▶ A large Australian ▷saturniid moth, *Coscinoscera hercules*. The adult has broad dark-brown wings, spanning about 28 cm, with a wing area that is possibly the largest of any insect.

● **Herder, Johann Gottfried** ▶ (1744–1803) German philosopher and poet. At first a disciple and later a critic of ▷Kant, he developed a form of religious humanism based on his readings of Shakespeare, Homer, and the Bible. His works include *A Treatise upon the Origin of Language* (1772) and *Outline of a Philosophy of the History of Man* (1784–91).

● **heredity** ▷*See* genetics.

● **Hereford** ▶ 52 04N 2 43W A city in W England, the administrative centre of Herefordshire on the River Wye. Situated in an important agricultural area, Hereford deals mainly in agricultural produce, manufacturing cider, beer, leather goods, and chemicals. It has given its name to a famous breed of cattle. The cathedral, begun in 1079, contains a Mappa Mundi, one of the oldest maps in the world (about 1314). Population (1991): 54 326.

● **Hereford and Worcester** ▶ A former county of W England. It was created in 1974 from the historic counties of Herefordshire and Worcestershire but abolished in 1998 when Herefordshire became an independent ▷unitary authority.

● **Hereford cattle** ▶ A breed of beef cattle originating from Herefordshire and surrounding areas in W England. They are large and stocky with red coats and white faces. Hardy and maturing quickly, Herefords are often mated with dairy breeds to produce a white-faced beef cross.

● **Herefordshire** ▶ A county of W England, on the Welsh border. Under local government reorganization in 1974 it became part of ▷Hereford and Worcester but in 1998 it was reinstated as an independent ▷unitary authority. Herefordshire consists of a rolling plain separating the Malvern Hills in the E from the Black Mountains and other hills of the Welsh border in the W. The chief river is the Wye. It is predominantly agricultural; hop production is surpassed only by Kent, pear and apple orchards produce perry and cider, and the Hereford breed of cattle is renowned throughout the world. Industry is concentrated in Hereford. Area: 2180 sq km (842 sq mi). Population (1998 est): 166 750. Administrative centre: Hereford.

● **Herero** ▶ A group of Bantu-speaking peoples of SW Africa, Botswana, and Angola. They are traditionally cattle, sheep, and goat herders but some adopted agriculture after European contact. Their social organization is based on the common principle of counting descent in the male line for some purposes and in the female line for others.

● **heresy** ▶ Any opinion, belief, or doctrine, especially in religion, that disagrees with the orthodox view. Although Judaism and Islam have been assailed by heretics, their heresies have been less pertinent to the development of these religions than has been the case in Christianity. Indeed, the early history of Christianity is inextricably interconnected with such movements as ▷Gnosticism and the heresies associated with the ▷Nestorians, ▷Pelagius, and many others, because the orthodox creeds were formulated specifically to correct what the Church regarded as erroneous doctrines. Roman Catholic teaching distinguishes between a "formal" heresy, which is deliberate, and a "material" heresy, which reflects ignorance of the orthodox view. Heresy must also be distinguished from **apostasy**, which entails abandoning one's religion in its entirety.

The Catholic Church, always alert to the dangers of heresy, established the ▷Inquisition (or Holy Office) in the 13th century to track down heretics. Those found guilty of the offence were handed over to the secular authorities: if they refused to renounce their heresies, in many European countries they were burnt at the stake. These activities continued after the Reformation (*see also* Counter-Reformation), but since the 18th century the Church has adopted less drastic measures to deal with heresy. Owing to such factors as the rise of theological liberalism and the ecumenical movement, the term "heresy" is rarely used in modern Church circles: however, most Churches maintain some form of internal discipline to prevent the teaching of eccentric or unacceptable doctrines. In the Roman Catholic Church, unorthodox theologians may be prevented from teaching or publishing.

● **Hereward the Wake** ▶ (11th century) Anglo-Saxon thegn, who led a raid on Peterborough Abbey (1070) as a protest against William I's appointment of a Norman abbot. He and other disaffected Anglo-Saxon nobles took refuge on the Isle of Ely, until its capture by William (1071) forced Hereward to flee.

● **Hermann von Reichenau** ▶ (1013–54) German poet and chronicler, known as Hermann the Lame. He was a monk at the monastery at Reichenau. One of the most gifted thinkers of his age, he wrote on theology, mathematics, and astronomy. He may have written *Salve Regina* and *Alma Redemptoris Mater*, among many other hymns and antiphons.

● **hermaphrodite** ▶ (*or* bisexual) A plant or animal possessing both male and female reproductive organs. Such organisms may show cross- or self-▷fertilization: the latter method is particularly common when the opportunity of finding a mate is remote, for example in parasitic invertebrates and deepsea fish. True hermaphroditism rarely occurs in humans. More common is **pseudohermaphroditism**, in which an individual develops secondary characteristics appropriate to the opposite sex (e.g enlarged external genitals in a woman or breasts in a man), due to hormone imbalance.

● **Hermes** ▶ In Greek mythology, the messenger and herald of the gods and the guide of travellers. He was regarded as the god of riches and good luck, the protector of merchants and thieves, and the god of dreams. He was usually portrayed as an athletic youth wearing a cap and winged sandals and carrying a golden staff. He was the son of Zeus and Maia. He conducted the souls of the dead to Hades and is credited with the invention of the lyre, which he gave to Apollo. He is identified with the Roman ▷Mercury.

● **Hermes Trismegistos** ▶ (Greek: Hermes the thrice great) The name applied by Greek Neoplatonists to the Egyptian god ▷Thoth. It is also the name given, after the third century AD, to the author of certain Neoplatonic writings.

● **Hermeticism** ▶ An Italian literary movement of the early 20th century. Its leading writers were the poets Ungaretti, Quasimodo, and Montale, whose early poetry was influenced by the theories of the French ▷Symbolists and characterized by verbal experiment and esoteric symbolism. After World War II all three poets developed more accessible styles.

● **hermit crab** ▶ A ▷crab with a soft unprotected abdomen, belonging to the worldwide families *Paguridae* and *Coenobitidae*. It lives in portable hollow objects, such as snail shells, for protection and changes these for successively larger ones as it grows. Hermit crabs are found in sandy or muddy-bottomed waters and occasionally on land and in trees. Tribe: *Anomura*.

● **Hermite, Charles** ▶ (1822–1901) French mathematician, who (in 1873), discovered the first transcendental number: e, the base of natural ▷logarithms. Such numbers cannot be expressed as a root of a polynomial equation, i.e. an equation of the form $a_0 + a_1x + ... + a_nx^n = 0$, where n and the a's are integers. ▷Liouville had already shown that such numbers exist but could not identify any.

● **Hermon, Mount** ▶ 33 24N 35 50E A mountain on the Syrian-Lebanese border, at the S end of the Anti-Lebanon Mountains. It is the highest point near the E coast of the Mediterranean Sea. Height: 2814 m (9232 ft).

● **Hermosillo** ▶ 29 15N 110 59W A city in NW Mexico. It is an important commercial centre for the surrounding agricultural areas and has a university (1938). Population (1990): 406 417.

● **Herne** ▶ 51 32N 7 12E A city in NW Germany, in North Rhine-Westphalia on the Rhine-Herne Canal. It developed in the 19th century as a coalmining and industrial centre. Population (1996 est): 179 897.

● **hernia** ▶ The protrusion of an organ or tissue through a weak spot in the wall that normally contains it. The most common types are the inguinal hernia (popularly called a rupture), which is a swelling in the groin caused by the protrusion of the abdominal contents, and the hiatus hernia, in which part of the stomach protrudes into the chest cavity. Other common hernias are femoral (also in the groin) and umbilical (at the navel). Hernias should usually be surgically repaired, otherwise they may become painful and cut off from their blood supply (strangulated).

● **Hero and Leander** ▶ Legendary lovers whose story was recounted by the Greek poet Musaeus (4th or 5th century AD). Hero was a priestess of Aphrodite at Sestos and Leander swam to her each night across the Hellespont from Abydos. After a stormy night Hero found her lover's drowned body and in despair drowned herself.

● **Herod (I) the Great** ▶ (c. 73–4 BC) King of Judaea (37–4); the son of ▷Antipater the Idumaean. Supported by Mark Antony, he became the Romans' king in Judaea. A Jew of Arab origins, he was regarded as a usurper by nationalists, who resented his encouragement of Greek culture; he retained power by control of the religious establishment and rigorous suppression of opposition. His jealousy and cruelty were exacerbated by feuds among his ten wives and their sons. Shortly before his death he ordered the massacre of the infants of Bethlehem.

● **Herod Agrippa I** ▶ (c. 10 BC–44 AD) King of Judaea (41–44); the grandson of ▷Herod the Great. An impecunious adventurer, he was educated at the Roman imperial court after the execution of his father by Herod the Great. He intrigued in imperial family politics and helped Emperor ▷Claudius to power, for which he was made King of Judaea. He was a popular ruler but persecuted Christians, executing St James, the son of Zebedee, and imprisoning St Peter.

● **Herod Agrippa II** ▶ (died c. 100 AD) King of Chalcis (50–c. 100) in S Lebanon; the son of ▷Herod Agrippa I. In 60 he heard the case of the arrested St Paul and found him innocent. He attempted to prevent the Jewish rebellion of 66, during which his troops fought on the Roman side, and helped to take Jerusalem in 70.

● **Herod Antipas** ▶ (21 BC–39 AD) Tetrarch (governor) of Galilee (4–39 AD) after the partition of the realm of his father ▷Herod the Great. He divorced his wife to marry Herodias, the divorced wife of his half-brother, for which he was censured by John the Baptist. Herodias persuaded her daughter Salome to ask for John's head in return for dancing at Antipas' birthday celebration and John was executed. Jesus Christ, as a Galilean, was brought before Antipas after his arrest, but Antipas returned him to Pontius Pilate of Judaea without passing judgment. After the death of Antipas' friend Emperor ▷Tiberius, religious riots gave ▷Caligula an excuse to exile Antipas.

● **Herodotus** ▶ (c. 484–c. 425 BC) Greek historian. Born at Halicarnassus, he was exiled for political reasons and moved to Samos. He subsequently moved to Athens and then to the Athenian colony of Thurii in S Italy, where he died. Called "the father of history" by Cicero, he was the first historian to subject his material to critical evaluation and research. His narrative account of the wars between Greece and Persia in nine books contained much incidental anthropological and geographical information gathered on his travels in the Mediterranean countries, Egypt, and Asia, and was written in a lively dramatic style.

● **heroic couplet** ▶ In English poetry, a rhymed pair of iambic pentameters (*see* metre), as for example ▷Pope's:
> Know then thyself, presume not God to scan,
> The proper study of Mankind is Man.

Although it was used by Chaucer and the Elizabethans, the heroic couplet is mainly associated with the poets of the Restoration and the 18th century, when it became the standard form for both serious poetry on elevated subjects and for satire. It is so named because of its use in the "heroic dramas" of ▷Dryden and other Restoration playwrights, which were modelled on the rhyming tragedies of Racine and other French authors. The heroic couplet was perfected by Pope but rejected by the Romantics as rigid and artificial. The so-called **heroic stanza** is a quatrain of pentameters rhyming *abab*: this form is particularly associated with elegiac or meditative works, such as ▷Gray's *Elegy Written in a Country Churchyard* (1751).

● **heroin** ▶ (*or* diamorphine) A pain-killing drug with a stronger action and fewer side effects than ▷morphine, from which it is made. Heroin is used to alleviate the suffering of terminal illness. Because the regular use of heroin readily leads to physical dependence its use in medicine has been restricted. It is widely abused. ▷*See* drug dependence.

● **heron** ▶ A wading bird belonging to a subfamily (*Ardeinae*; 60 species) occurring on lakes and rivers worldwide, especially in the tropics. 75–150 cm long, herons have a slim body, longish legs, long toes, broad wings, a short tail, and a loose plumage coloured grey, blue, greenish, white, purple, or reddish. Herons hunt by standing at the water's edge and seizing fish and insects with the long pointed bill. In the breeding season herons may develop ornamental plumes and perform elaborate courtship displays. Family: *Ardeidae* (herons and bitterns). ▷*See also* egret; night heron.

● **Hero of Alexandria** ▶ (mid-1st century AD) Greek engineer and mathematician, best known for his invention of the aeolipile, the earliest known steam engine. It consisted of a sphere containing water with two bent tubes extending from it. When heated, steam issued from the tubes, causing the sphere to rotate. It was only used for trivial purposes, such as controlling doors and causing statues to move. He also discovered the well-known formula for calculating the area of a triangle from the lengths of its sides.

● **Herophilus** ▶ (c. 335–c. 280 BC) Greek physician, who founded one of the earliest medical schools in Alexandria. Herophilus performed public dissections of human cadavers, distinguished between sensory and motor nerve trunks, and described parts of the brain, duodenum, and other organs.

● **herpes** ▶ A virus of which there are several forms. Herpes zoster virus (*or* varicella-zoster) causes chickenpox and ▷shingles. Herpes simplex virus I causes cold sores, occurring usually on or around the lips. Herpes simplex virus II causes the sexually transmitted genital herpes, which produces painful blisters in the genital area.

● **Herrera, Juan de** ▶ (1530–97) Spanish architect. After having studied in Italy, Herrera designed a palace in Aranjuez (1569) and the Exchange in Seville (1582) in an Italianate style that had great influence in Spain. He is best known for his completion of the ▷Escorial.

● **Herrera the Younger, Francisco de** ▶ (1622–85) Spanish baroque painter and architect, born in Seville, the son of the painter and engraver **Francisco de Herrera the Elder** (1576–1656). After leaving his father's tutelage, he studied in Italy. On his return, he introduced the dramatic style of Italian baroque in such religious works as *Triumph of St Hermengild* (Prado). He later worked in Madrid, where he designed the high altar of the church of Montserrat.

● **Herrick, Robert** ▶ (1591–1674) English poet. A friend of Jonson and other members of London literary society, he was ordained (1623) after graduating from Cambridge and served as rector of Dean Prior, Devonshire, from 1630 to 1646 and again after the Restoration. The majority of his secular and religious poems, collected in *Hesperides* (1648), are short lyrics influenced by classical models.

● **herring** ▶ An important food fish, *Clupea harengus*, found mainly in cold waters of the N Atlantic and the North Sea. It has a slender silvery blue-green body, up to about 40 cm long, with a single short dorsal fin and swims in large shoals, feeding on plankton. A related species (*C. pallasi*) occurs in the N Pacific. Many other small silvery fish of the family *Clupeidae* are called herring. Herrings have long been fished in N Europe, where they are eaten fresh, pickled, and smoked. In the UK, smoked herring are known as kippers, and are produced mainly in Scotland. Overfishing and pollution have greatly reduced European catches in recent years. Order: *Clupeiformes*. ▷*See also* whitebait.

● **herring gull** ▶ A large grey and white ▷gull, *Larus argentatus*, occurring around coasts in the N hemisphere. It is omnivorous and is commonly seen scavenging at refuse tips. Adults are 57 cm long and have pink legs and a yellow bill marked with a red spot on the lower mandible.

● **Herriot, Édouard** ▶ (1872–1957) French statesman and writer; prime minister of a Radical-Socialist coalition (1924–25, 1926 (for two days), 1932). During World War II, he opposed the Vichy Government and spent the years 1942–45 in prison. From 1947 to 1953 he served as president of the national assembly.

● **Herriot, James** ▶ (James Alfred Wight; 1916–95) British veterinary surgeon and writer. His stories, based on his experiences in the Yorkshire Dales, became popular books, film, and TV series. They include *If Only They Could Talk* (1970) and *All Creatures Great and Small* (1972).

● **Herschel, Sir William** ▶ (1738–1822) British astronomer, born in Germany. Working with his sister **Caroline Herschel** (1750–1848), he became expert in grinding lenses and built the largest telescopes then known. In 1781 Herschel discovered the planet ▷Uranus, the first such discovery since prehistoric times. His other discoveries include binary stars, two new satellites of Saturn, and ▷infrared radiation from the sun (1800). His son **Sir John Herschel** (1792–1871) was also an astronomer. Using his father's telescope, he continued with the work of mapping binary stars and nebulae. In order to observe stars in the S hemisphere, he set up an observatory in Capetown in 1834. He was also greatly interested in photography, using it for astronomical purposes. He was the first to use sodium thiosulphate (hypo) as a fixer and he developed a sensitized photographic paper.

● **Herstmonceux** ▶ (*or* Hurstmonceux) 50 53N 0 20E A village in SE England, in East Sussex. Its castle (built in 1440) housed the ▷Royal Greenwich Observatory from 1950 until 1988, when it moved to Cambridge. The Isaac Newton telescope was moved to the Canary Islands in 1979 because of unacceptable levels of atmospheric and light pollution.

● **Hertford** ▶ 51 48N 0 05W A market town in SE England, the administrative centre of Hertfordshire on the River Lea. Industries include printing, brewing, and brush manufacturing. The castle remains include a Norman tower. Population (1991): 21 665.

● **Hertfordshire** ▶ A county of S England, bordering on Greater London. It lies mainly in the Lower Thames Basin rising to the Chiltern Hills in the NW and is drained by the Rivers Lea, Stort, and Colne. The chief agricultural activity is arable farming, producing barley for the brewing industry. Dairy farming, market gardening, and horticulture are also important. There is a mixture of modern and traditional industries. It has four new towns including Hemel Hempstead and Stevenage. Area: 1634 sq km (632 sq mi). Population (1996 est): 1 015 800. Administrative centre: Hertford.

● **Hertogenbosch, 's** ▷*See* 's Hertogenbosch.

● **hertz** ▶ (Hz) The ▷SI unit of frequency equal to one cycle per second. Named after Heinrich ▷Hertz.

● **Hertz, Heinrich Rudolf** ▶ (1857–94) German physicist, who first produced and detected ▷radio waves (1888). ▷Maxwell's equations had predicted the existence of ▷electromagnetic radiation over a wide spectrum of frequencies but, until Hertz's discovery, radio-frequency radiation was unknown. The unit of frequency is named after him.

● **Hertzog, James Barry Munnik** ▶ (1866–1942) South African statesman; prime minister of the Union of South Africa (1924–39). In the second ▷Boer War he led the Orange Free State forces. He was a member of Botha's government from 1910 to 1912 but formed the Afrikaner Nationalist Party in 1914 in opposition to Botha, becoming prime minister in 1924. In 1933 he formed a coalition government with ▷Smuts but resigned in 1939, when his motion against entering World War II was defeated. With ▷Malan he then revived the Nationalist Party but retired in 1940.

● **Hertzsprung-Russell diagram** ▶ A graphic representation of the classification of stars according to spectral type (*see* Harvard classification system) and brightness—usually absolute ▷magnitude. The stars are not uniformly distributed. Most, including the sun, lie on a diagonal band, the main sequence, the brightest stars of which are spectral types O and B and the faintest are M stars. Main-sequence stars are normal stars, obtaining their energy from the nuclear fusion of hydrogen in their cores. The somewhat brighter ▷giant stars, the even brighter ▷supergiants, and the faint ▷white dwarfs fall into their own distinct groupings and are at later stages of evolution. The diagram was originally produced, independently, in 1911 by E. Hertzsprung (1873–1967) and in 1913 by H. N. Russell (1877–1957).

● **Herzen, Aleksandr (Ivanovich)** ► (1812–70) Russian political philosopher. The illegitimate son of a nobleman, he was exiled to the provinces from 1834 to 1842 for his political activities. After 1848 he lived mostly in Paris and London, where he founded several emigré political journals. His early enthusiasm for W European progressive ideals dwindled as he came to believe in Russian peasant communes as a basis for a socialist society. His major literary work was his memoirs, *My Past and Thoughts* (1861–67).

● **Herzl, Theodor** ► (1860–1904) Hungarian-born journalist and playwright, who founded the movement to establish a Jewish nation (*see* Zionism). Living mostly in Vienna, he published the pamphlet *The Jewish State* (1896), calling for a world council to discuss finding a Jewish homeland. At a world congress of Zionists in Basle (1897) the World Zionist Organization was established, Herzl becoming the first president. This congress advocated Palestine as the homeland and set up the Jewish National Fund to buy land there.

● **Herzog, Werner** ► (1942–) German film director. In *Fata Morgana* (1971), *Aguirre, Wrath of God* (1973), *The Enigma of Kaspar Hauser* (1975), and *Nosferatu* (1979) he uses an allegorical or historical framework to express his bleak vision of human society. His other films include *Wozzeck* (1979), *Fitzcarraldo* (1982), *Little Dieter Needs to Fly* (1999), and *Invincible* (2002).

● **Heseltine, Michael (Ray Dibdin), Baron** ► (1933–) British Conservative politician; deputy prime minister (1995–97). He was previously secretary of state for the environment (1979–83; 1990–92), for defence (1983–86), and for trade and industry and president of the board of trade (1992–95). A leading pro-European, he resigned from the government in 1986 over the Westland Affair and in 1990 unsuccessfully contested the leadership of the Conservative Party, precipitating the fall of Margaret Thatcher. He was raised to the peerage in 2001.

● **Hesilrige, Sir Arthur** ► (*or* Haselrig; d. 1661) English parliamentarian. He played a prominent part in the ▷Long Parliament (summoned in 1640) and was one of the five MPs whom Charles I attempted to arrest (1642). He fought through the Civil War but opposed the ▷Protectorate. At the ▷Restoration, he was imprisoned in the Tower of London, where he died.

● **Hesiod** ► (8th century BC) Greek poet, the earliest known after Homer. He was a farmer near Mount Helicon in Boeotia in central Greece and was involved in a long dispute with his brother Perses concerning their inheritance. His two major works are the *Theogony*, concerning the gods and their myths, and *Works and Days*, on farming life.

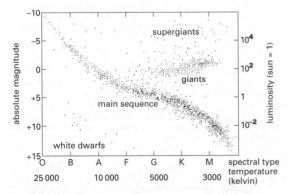

Hertzsprung-Russell diagram ► This graph for bright stars is important in studies of stellar evolution and in determining distance.

● **Hesperides** ► (Greek: daughters of evening) In Greek mythology, three nymphs who guarded the sacred golden apples of Hera in a garden in the far west. The apples were stolen by ▷Heracles, with the help of Atlas, as one of his Twelve Labours.

● **Hesperornis** ► A genus of extinct flightless seabirds whose fossils

date from the Cretaceous period (125–60 million years ago). It was 2 m long and adapted for swimming and catching fish in shallow seas, having large powerful feet and legs, a long slender neck, a small head, and a long bill (possibly with teeth), but only tiny wing bones and reduced flight muscles.

● **Hess, Dame Myra** ► (1890–1965) British pianist. She made her London debut in 1907. During World War II she initiated daily lunchtime concerts at the National Gallery and was created a DBE in 1941.

● **Hess, Rudolf** ► (1894–1987) German Nazi politician. Hess joined the Nazi Party in 1920, becoming Hitler's close friend and deputy party leader (1933). However, his declining influence led to his unsuccessful secret mission to Scotland to negotiate a separate peace with Britain in 1941. He was convicted at the Nuremberg war trials and sent to Spandau prison. The only prisoner there from 1966, he committed suicide.

● **Hess, Victor Francis** ► (1883–1964) US physicist, born in Austria. Using a balloon to investigate atmospheric background radiation, he discovered that, contrary to expectation, the radiation increased with altitude. This work led to the discovery of ▷cosmic rays, for which he shared a Nobel Prize in 1936 with Carl ▷Anderson.

● **Hesse** ► (German name: Hessen) A *Land* in central Germany. Formed in 1945, it consists of the former duchies of Hesse-Darmstadt and Nassau. Hilly and forested, it is chiefly agricultural, producing potatoes, sugar beet, and wheat. Industry, concentrated in the S, includes publishing and the manufacture of machinery and chemicals. Iron ore, salt, and coal are mined. Area: 21 112 sq km (8150 sq mi). Population (2000 est): 6 052 000. Capital: Wiesbaden.

● **Hesse, Hermann** ► (1877–1962) German novelist and poet. He worked as a bookseller until publication of his first novel, *Peter Camenzind* (1904). His early themes of art and self-knowledge were later extended by his interest in Indian mysticism and Jungian psychology, reflected in *Siddharta* (1922). His other major novels are *Steppenwolf* (1927), *Narziss und Goldmund* (1930), and *The Glass Bead Game* (1943); he won a Nobel Prize (1946). From 1911 he lived in Switzerland.

● **Hestia** ► The Greek goddess of the hearth, daughter of Cronus and Rhea and the oldest of the Olympian deities. She vowed to remain a virgin, rejecting both Apollo and Poseidon. She is identified with the Roman ▷Vesta.

● **heterotroph** ▷*See* autotroph; nutrition.

● **Hevesy, George Charles von** ► (1885–1966) Hungarian-born chemist, who worked in Denmark and Sweden. He discovered the use of ▷radioactive tracers to follow the course of compounds in a system, for which he received the 1943 Nobel Prize. He also discovered the element ▷hafnium in 1923.

● **hexadecimal number system** ► A number system using the base 16. It uses the 10 digits 0–9 plus the letters A–F. The number 12E in hexadecimal would, in decimal, be $(1 \times 16^2) + (2 \times 16) + 14 = 302$. Hexadecimal (*or* hex) notation is used in computers because it corresponds to the ▷binary system used in machine operations.

● **Heydrich, Reinhard** ► (1904–42) German Nazi who joined the SS in 1931 and became head, under ▷Himmler, of the Gestapo in 1934. A notorious Jew-baiter, he was selected by Hitler to chair the ▷Wannsee conference, early in 1942, at which the Final Solution (of exterminating European Jewry) was planned. He administered Bohemia and Moravia as "Protector" from 1941. His excessive brutality in this capacity led to his assassination by three Czech nationalists parachuted into Czechoslovakia from Britain. The Germans retaliated with hundreds of indiscriminate executions and by murdering the entire male population of the villages of ▷Lidice and Ležáky.

● **Heyerdahl, Thor** ► (1914–2002) Norwegian ethnologist, who led the ▷Kon-Tiki expedition (1947). The *Kon-Tiki* was a balsawood raft that Heyerdahl built and sailed with five companions from the Pacific coast of South America to Polynesia to show that the pre-Incan inhabitants of Peru might thus have migrated to Polynesia. In 1969–70 he attempted to cross the Atlantic Ocean from Morocco to South America in a papyrus boat—the *Ra*; he reached Barbados, showing the possibility of Egyptian influence on the Precolumbian civilization of America. Later he led a series of archaeological expeditions to Easter Island (1986–88).

● **Heysham** ▷*See* Morecambe.

● **Heywood, Thomas** ► (c. 1574–1641) English dramatist. An actor as well as a prolific writer, he wrote numerous comedies, chronicle plays, and scripts for pageants and masques. His best-known work is the domestic tragedy *A Woman Killed with Kindness* (1607).

● **Hezbollah** ▷*See* Hizbollah.

● **Hezekiah** ► King of Judah (c. 715–c. 686 BC), noted as a religious reformer. Allied with Egypt, he rebelled against ▷Sennacherib of Assyria, against Isaiah's advice, and was defeated.

● **Hiawatha** ► The legendary chief of the Onondaga tribe of American Indians, who formed the ▷Iroquois League. He is the subject of Longfellow's *Song of Hiawatha* (1855).

● **hibernation** ► A state of ▷dormancy in winter experienced by many fish, amphibians, reptiles, and mammals of temperate and Arctic regions: it is an adaption to avoid death by heat loss, freezing, or food scarcity. True hibernation is seasonal and not simply a reaction to a drop in temperature. It occurs in a few mammals, including bats and hedgehogs, and some birds. Hibernation involves a period of sleep during which the body temperature drops almost to that of the surroundings, the body processes are slowed, and the hibernator lives on a reserve of body fat until it awakens in the spring.

● **Hibiscus** ► A genus of tropical and subtropical herbs, shrubs, and trees (about 150 species). Several species are cultivated for their showy five-petalled flowers; two popular shrubs, up to 3 m high, are the Chinese *H. rosa-sinensis* (rose of China), which has red, pink, or yellow flowers with prominent stigmas, and the Syrian *H. syriacus* (rose of Sharon), which has pink, blue, or white hollyhock-like flowers. Both can be grown as pot plants. The genus also includes plants cultivated for their food value (*see* okra; roselle) and for their fibre. Family: *Malvaceae*.

● **hiccup** ► (*or* hiccough) A sudden involuntary intake of breath interrupted by closure of the glottis (in the larynx), producing a characteristic sound. Hiccups are often due to indigestion but may be associated with kidney disease or alcoholism.

● **Hickok, James Butler** ► (1837–76) US lawman known as Wild Bill Hickok, a celebrated gunman. After army service in the Civil War and against the Indians he was appointed marshal in Kansas (1869–71). He was shot dead from behind while playing poker.

● **hickory** ► A tree of the genus *Carya* (20 species), native to E North America and Asia and cultivated for timber, nuts, and ornament. They grow to a height of about 30 m and have compound leaves consisting of paired leaflets. Commercially important species are the shagbark (*C. ovata*), which yields hard durable timber, and the pecan (*C. illinoensis*), which produces thin-shelled nuts resembling walnuts. Both species are North American. Family: *Juglandaceae*.

● **hide** ► A unit of land measurement in Anglo-Saxon England based on the approximate area of land needed to support a peasant household. Tax assessments were often calculated on numbers of hides. The size varied from 40 to 120 acres.

● **Hideyoshi** ► (1536–98) Japanese military ruler. Of humble birth, Hideyoshi became by sheer ability a leading commander of ▷Oda Nobunaga, aiding him to become master of central Japan. Succeeding to Oda's power in 1582, he achieved national hegemony by 1590 but failed to conquer Korea.

● **hieroglyphics** ► Originally, an Egyptian system of picture writing in use from about 3000 BC to 300 AD; the term now denotes any ▷pictographic or ▷ideographic writing system. The Egyptians used hieroglyphics largely for monumental inscriptions. The characters are careful reproductions of people, animals, and objects and may be interpreted as representing either the objects they portray or the sounds that are featured in the pronunciation of the referent. Hieroglyphic records are coextensive with hieratic, a more cursive stylized form appropriate to brush and ink and the smooth surfaces of papyrus and wood.

● **Higgs boson** ► A massive ▷boson the existence of which was proposed by the Scottish physicist Peter Higgs (1924–   ) to explain the ▷weak interaction in terms compatible with the standard model (*see* particle physics). In his theory Higgs suggested that the nonzero masses of the ▷intermediate vector bosons (the W and Z bosons) are acquired by the particles in interacting with an all-pervading field, known as the **Higgs field**. CERN's large hadron collider (LHC), which is due to be completed in 2006, is being constructed to test this theory.

● **high-fidelity sound systems** ► (*or* hi-fi) Systems of recording and reproducing sound in which the quality of the reproduced sound is as close as possible to that of the original source. A typical reproducing system now consists of a ▷compact disc player, a stereophonic amplifier, and two or more loudspeakers. To achieve high fidelity, total distortion in such a system must be less than 2% and the frequency response must be constant between 20 and 20 000 hertz. While two frontal stereophonic speakers can reproduce the spatial pattern of the sound source, reproduction of the reverberation characteristics of the place at which the recording was made can be reproduced more fully by a quadraphonic system with two additional rear speakers.

● **Highgate** ► A residential district mainly in the Greater London borough of Haringey. It derived its name from the tollgate erected by the Bishop of London in the 14th century. Highgate Cemetery contains the graves of Karl Marx, George Eliot, and Herbert Spencer. The Whittington Stone marks the point at which Dick ▷Whittington turned back to London.

● **high jump** ► A field event in athletics in which jumpers compete to clear a horizontal bar. A competitor is allowed three attempts at a height and is eliminated if he fails to clear it. World records: men: 2.45 m (1993) by Javier Sotomayor (Cuba); women: 2.09 m (1987) by Stefka Kostadinova (Bulgaria).

● **Highland** ► A council area in N Scotland, created in 1975 (as Highland Region) under local government reorganization from the N part of Argyll, Caithness, Inverness, Nairn, Ross and Cromarty, and Sutherland. It became a ▷unitary authority in 1996. Highland consists of glaciated highlands divided from NE to SW by the fault valley, the Great Glen, and includes part of the Inner Hebrides. Sheep farming is the main agricultural activity. Industries associated with North Sea oil have developed, especially on the coast, as have aluminium smelting, pulp and paper production, distilling, and tourism. Salmon farming is a growing industry in the sea lochs of the W coast. Area: 25 425 sq km (9814 sq mi). Population (1998 est): 208 300. Administrative centre: Inverness.

● **Highland Clearances** ► The mass evictions of tenant farmers from the Scottish Highlands in the 19th century. An important cause was the ▷agricultural revolution, which had two effects: it provided the aristocratic landowners with such economically attractive alternatives to ▷crofting as sheep farming (introduced to the Highlands in 1762) and, by increasing food production, contributed to a population explosion that, by the early 19th century, could no longer be supported. Another factor was the suppression of the ▷clans after the Forty-five Rebellion (*see* Jacobites). By the late 18th century people were moving to towns or overseas (principally to Canada); but the Highlands' population grew, and in the 19th century the landowners resorted to compulsory relocation or to eviction. Such instances as the clearances of the Countess of Sutherland's estates (1811–20) and

eye   to fly   old age

hieroglyphics ► A picture was used to represent objects, related ideas, and sounds.

of Glengarry (1853)—notorious for its brutality—mean that the Highland Clearances are remembered with bitterness.

● **Highland dress** ► The traditional male costume (since the 17th century) of the Scottish Highlands. It consists of the kilt (a wrapover skirt pleated at the back) and the plaid (a cloak worn over one shoulder). Accessories include the sporran (a goatskin pouch), cap, kilt pin, and dagger (worn in the right sock). This form of dress was probably preceded by "trews" (close-fitting trousers), often checkered, and then by the plaid, a long length of woollen cloth, half being pleated round the waist, the other half forming a cloak. Highland dress was banned (1746–82) following the Jacobite rebellions.

Tartan, the material used for the kilt and plaid, is a woollen cloth woven of differently coloured threads at regular intervals both in the weft and the warp; this gives a design of large-meshed cross stripes. Clan tartans date from the 17th century.

● **Highland Games** ► Scottish athletics meetings, usually professional, held in the Highlands. Events include standard track and field events as well as such Scottish sports as ▷caber tossing, and there are also competitions in highland dancing and playing the bagpipes. The modern games date from the early 19th century but they originated far earlier in clan assemblies. The most famous meeting, the Braemar Games, can be traced back to the 8th century AD.

● **Highland pony** ► A breed of pony originating in the Highlands of Scotland. There are two varieties, both with a deep muscular frame, strong legs, and a profuse mane. The Western Isles variety is smaller than the mainland variety (or Garron). The Highland is usually black, brown, or grey and is now used for pony trekking as well as for pack work. Height: 1.27–1.47 m (12½–14½ hands).

● **high priest** ► The chief official of the ancient ▷Temple of Jerusalem. The office was hereditary in the family of Aaron. The Hasmonean rulers (*see* Maccabees) claimed the title themselves, and in the last century of the temple the high priests were appointed by political rulers. With the destruction of the temple (70 AD) the office ceased to exist.

● **Highsmith, Patricia** ► (1921–95) US author of crime fiction. Her novels, characterized by great suspense and psychological exploration of character, include *Strangers on a Train* (1950), *Ripley's Game* (1974), and *Ripley Under Water* (1991).

● **High Wycombe** ► 51 38N 0 46W A town in SE England, in Buckinghamshire. It has a long tradition of furniture making and also produces paper, precision instruments, and clothing. Hughenden Manor, between High Wycombe and Great Missenden, was the home of Disraeli. At nearby **West Wycombe** are the Hell Fire caves, excavated in the 18th century and made notorious by the **Hell Fire Club** (1745–63), founded by Sir Francis Dashwood (1708–81), whose members (including John ▷Wilkes and the Earl of ▷Bute) indulged in debauchery, black masses, etc. Population (1991): 71 718.

● **hijacking** ► The unauthorized seizure of a vehicle, often together with its cargo and passengers. A form of piracy, hijacking developed in the 1920s with the seizure of freight lorries. The hijacking of aircraft ("skyjacking") became relatively frequent in the 1950s and 1960s, often involving the diversion of US aircraft to Cuba. Since then hijackings have become a feature of terrorist strategy, being perpetrated by Shia Muslim activists, among others (*see also* September 11). Counter-measures include X-ray inspection of baggage and pressure on governments to refuse a safe haven to such criminals.

● **Hilary of Poitiers, St** ► (c. 315–c. 367 AD) French churchman; bishop and Doctor of the Church. He was converted to Christianity from Neoplatonism and became Bishop of Poitiers (c. 353). His works include *De trinitate* and *De synodis*. Feast day: 14 Jan.

● **Hilbert, David** ► (1862–1943) German mathematician, who gave geometry a mathematically rigorous foundation. In a book entitled *Foundations of Geometry* (1899), he defined such concepts as the point, the line, and the parallel relationship, which ▷Euclid in his *Elements* had assumed to be intuitively obvious. Hilbert then developed geometry from a much more rigorous set of axioms than those of Euclid. He also studied the properties of infinite-dimensional space, known as Hilbert space, which is used in quantum theory.

● **Hildebrand** ▷*See* Gregory VII, St.

● **Hildegard of Bingen, St** ► (1098–1179) German mystic and composer. Born into a noble family, she was sent to a convent at Diessenberg at the age of eight. She became prioress in 1136 and in 1147 moved the community to Bingen, where she became abbess. A woman of wide learning, she wrote a manual on herbal medicine (*De simplicines medicae*; 1163) and composed probably the earliest surviving mass music by a woman. Some 70 lyric poems set to music made her one of the most important medieval composers of chants. She has been unofficially regarded as a saint since the 15th century.

● **Hildesheim** ► 52 09N 9 58E A city in N Germany, in Lower Saxony. The romanesque 11th-century cathedral survived World War II. Notable Roman silver plate was found nearby in 1868. Manufactures include machinery, textiles, and carpets. Population (1996 est): 106 101.

● **Hill, Archibald Vivian** ► (1886–1977) British physiologist, noted for his work on muscle contraction. Hill found that oxygen was needed not for the contraction of a muscle but for its recovery, which provided a clue to the underlying biochemistry involved. Hill shared the 1922 Nobel Prize with Otto ▷Meyerhof.

● **Hill, David Octavius** ► (1802–70) Scottish painter and photographer. He first collaborated with **Robert Adamson** (1821–48) in 1843, on a portrait of the founders of the Free Church of Scotland. For greater accuracy Hill and Adamson, a chemist, photographed each clergyman, using the calotype method developed by ▷Talbot. Numerous portrait photographs and views of Edinburgh followed until Adamson's death, when Hill returned to landscape painting.

● **Hill, Geoffrey** ► (1932–   ) British poet and critic. His volumes include *For the Unfallen* (1959), *King Log* (1968), *Tenebrae* (1978), and *Canaan* (1996), and the long poems *The Mystery of the Charity of Charles Péguy* (1983), *The Triumph of Love* (1999), and *Speech! Speech!* (2001).

● **Hill, Graham** ► (1929–75) British motor-racing driver, who was world champion in 1962 and 1968 and runner-up from 1963 to 1965. Despite breaking both legs in an accident (1969) he continued to race. He died in an aircrash. His son, **Damon Hill** (1962–   ), was world champion in 1996.

● **Hill, Octavia** ► (1838–1912) British philanthropist and leader of the open-space movement, which resulted in the establishment of the ▷National Trust. With an inheritance left to her by John ▷Ruskin she financed housing projects in London.

● **Hill, Sir Rowland** ► (1795–1879) British postal expert. In *Post Office Reform* (1837) he advocated a single postage rate within the British Isles that would be prepaid by buying an adhesive stamp (which he invented). Having achieved the introduction in 1840 of the penny postage stamp, he was secretary to the Post Office (1854–64).

● **Hillary, Sir Edmund (Percival)** ► (1919–   ) New Zealand mountaineer and explorer. In 1953 he and ▷Tenzing Norgay were the first to reach the summit of Mount Everest, for which he was knighted. In 1958–59 he participated in the Commonwealth Trans-Antarctic Expedition, preparing the way for Sir Vivian ▷Fuchs' crossing of Antarctica. From 1984 to 1989 he was New Zealand High Commissioner in Delhi.

● **Hillel** ► (1st century BC) Jewish teacher, lawyer, and biblical scholar. Many of his teachings subsequently became authoritative in rabbinic Judaism. His tolerant views are often contrasted with those of his contemporary Shammai.

● **Hiller, Dame Wendy** ► (1912–   ) British actress. Stage successes have included Walter Greenwood's *Love on the Dole* (1935), Bolt's *Flowering Cherry* (1959), and Wilde's *The Importance of Being Earnest* (1987); among her films are *Pygmalion* (1938), *Major Barbara* (1940), *Sons and Lovers* (1960), and *The Elephant Man* (1980).

● **Hillery, Patrick (John)** ► (Gaelic name: Pádraig Óhlrighile; 1923–   ) Irish statesman; president (1976–90). In 1951 he entered the Dáil and in 1959 he assumed office as minister for education, becoming minister for industry in 1965, for labour in 1966, and for foreign affairs in 1969.

● **Hilliard, Nicholas** ► (1547–1619) English portrait miniaturist. Like his father, he trained as a jeweller, later becoming court painter

Nicholas Hilliard ▶ Miniature painting of a man (thought to be Shakespeare) painted in 1588 (Victoria and Albert Museum, London).

to Elizabeth I and James I. His high reputation led many prominent Elizabethans to have their portraits done by him; many of these are in the royal collection at Windsor Castle. In his *Treatise on the Art of Limning* (c. 1600), he describes his style and technique. The elegance and symbolism of his *Unknown Man Against a Background of Flames* (Victoria and Albert Museum, London) is typical of his best work.

● **Hillingdon ▶** A borough of W Greater London, created in 1965 from Uxbridge and several urban districts, all in Middlesex. Area: 110 sq km (43 sq mi). Population (1996 est): 247 700.

● **Hillsborough ▶** A soccer stadium in Sheffield, which was the scene (15 April, 1989) of the worst disaster in British football. At the FA Cup semifinal between Liverpool and Nottingham Forest the police opened a main gate to the terraces causing the death of 95 fans already on the terraces as the surge of incomers crushed them against the perimeter fence. In addition some 400 people were injured. The disaster had an important influence on the subsequent design of all-seater stadiums (with no standing on terraces) and the removal of perimeter fences.

● **hill mynah ▶** A glossy black songbird, *Graculus religiosa*, native to India and the East Indies. 25–37 cm long, it has a yellow bill and yellow wattles on the neck and beneath the eyes. It is a popular cagebird able to mimic human speech. Family: *Sturnidae* (starlings). ▷*See also* mynah.

● **Hilmand, River** ▷*See* Helmand, River.

● **Hilton, James ▶** (1900–54) British novelist. His two most popular novels are *Lost Horizon* (1933), set in the Tibetan monastery of Shangri-La, and *Goodbye, Mr Chips* (1934). From 1935 he worked as a scriptwriter in Hollywood, where he died.

● **Hilversum ▶** 52 14N 5 10E A town in the central Netherlands, in North Holland province. It is a summer resort and commuter town for Amsterdam and is the country's main radio and television broadcasting centre. Population (1994): 84 213.

● **Himachal Pradesh ▶** A state in NW India, in the W Himalayas beside Tibet's border. Long part of the ▷Punjab, it was formed by the combination of various hill states (1948). Most of the inhabitants are

Pahari-speaking Hindus who farm grains, potatoes, maize, and livestock. The forests yield timber and bamboo, and enormous hydroelectric potential is being exploited. Area: 55 673 sq km (21 490 sq mi). Population (1994 est): 5 530 000. Capital: Simla.

● **Himalayas ▶** A vast mountain system, the highest in the world, structurally the southern edge of the great plateau of central Asia. They extend about 2400 km (1550 mi) along the N Indian border in a W–E arc, 200–400 km (125–250 mi) wide, reaching 8848 m (29 028 ft) at Mount ▷Everest. The region is the subject of disputes between China and India and India and Pakistan.

● **Himeji ▶** 34 50N 134 40E A city in Japan, in SW Honshu. It developed around its famous 16th-century castle, one of the few remaining castles in Japan. Its industries include textiles and steel. Population (1995): 470 986. ⌐Japanese art and architecture.

● **Himmler, Heinrich ▶** (1900–45) German Nazi politician, infamous for his direction of the ▷SS. He joined the Nazi Party in 1925 and became head of the SS in 1929. From 1936 he also directed the Gestapo and supervised the extermination of Jews in E Europe. After the Nazi collapse he was captured by the Allies and committed suicide.

● **Hims** ▷*See* Homs.

● **Hinckley ▶** 52 33N 1 21W A town in central England, in Leicestershire. It has an engineering industry and manufactures cardboard boxes and hosiery; the traditional footwear industry is depleted but continues. Population (1999 est): 27 100.

● **Hincmar of Reims ▶** (c. 806–82) French theologian, archbishop of Reims (845–82). He came into conflict with the emperor Lothair I and successive popes over the extent of his jurisdiction. He also engaged in controversy with the Benedictine monk Gottschalk (d. 868) over the doctrine of predestination.

● **Hindemith, Paul ▶** (1895–1963) German composer and viola player. From the age of 11 he supported himself by playing in dance halls and later studied in Frankfurt am Main, where he led the opera orchestra (1915–23). He also played the viola in the Amar Quartet. In 1927 he began teaching in Berlin. His music was banned by the Nazis in 1933; he moved to Turkey and in 1939 went to the USA. His early works were highly dissonant; he later evolved his own system of tonal harmony. Many of his compositions are neoclassical in character (*see* neoclassicism); they include the operas *Cardillac* (1926) and *Mathis der Maler* (1938), the ballet *Nobilissima Visione* (1938), many concertos, instrumental sonatas, and much *Gebrauchsmusik* (German: utility music).

● **Hindenburg, Paul von Beneckendorff und von ▶** (1847–1934) German general, who was recalled from retirement at the outbreak of World War I and with ▷Ludendorff won a great victory at ▷Tannenberg (1914). In 1916 Hindenburg became commander in chief and, again with Ludendorff, effectively controlled Germany. He directed the German retreat to the **Hindenburg line** (fortified defence on the Western Front). After Germany's defeat he again retired but became president in 1925. Re-elected in 1932, he was forced to appoint Hitler as chancellor early in 1933.

● **Hindi ▶** The national language of India and the most widely spoken, having approximately 134 million speakers. It is an ▷Indo-Aryan language, showing strong ▷Sanskrit influence in its written form but with a much simpler grammar. The standard form, written in Devanagari script, is based on the Khari Boli dialect of Delhi. This belongs to the western dialect division from which ▷Urdu also developed.

● **Hinduism ▶** The religious beliefs and institutions of about 400 million inhabitants of India and parts of neighbouring countries. Hinduism is not a religion with a formal creed, but the complex result of about 5000 years of continuous cultural development. It includes a number of extremely diverse traditional beliefs and practices and over the centuries it has influenced and been influenced by younger religions, including Buddhism, Jainism, Christianity, Islam, and Sikhism. One of its central concepts is that the necessary result of one's actions in life leads to ▷reincarnation at a higher or lower level of life (*see* karma), a belief that has given rise both to the system of ▷castes and to a deep respect for all forms of life (*see* ahimsa). The goal of the religion is to find a release (*moksha*; the Sanskrit word for liberation) from the cycle of rebirth and to return to the ultimate unchanging reality, ▷Brahman. Release may be sought through good works, devotion to a particular god, such as the popular deity ▷Krishna, or through various types of meditation and asceticism (*see* samadhi; yoga). The principal gods are Brahma, Vishnu, and Shiva, together known as the ▷Trimurti; the last two are especially venerated by the two major sects, the Vaishnavas and the Shaivas. These and all the innumerable lesser gods and spirits are seen by many Hindus as manifestations of one reality (Brahman). Popular devotion consists mainly of temple worship and the celebration of numerous festivals. Hinduism originated in early ▷animism and ▷totemism (before 2750 BC) and developed a sacrificial worship of a pantheon of nature gods, such as ▷Indra, during the period of the ▷Vedas (c. 1500–500 BC). ▷Brahmanism was the dominant form of Hinduism in the 6th century BC, when Buddhism and Jainism were established in reaction to it. The great Hindu texts, the ▷*Mahabharata* and the ▷*Ramayana*, were composed at this time. Vishnu and Shiva became the prominent deities in the medieval period (after 800 AD). New schools have continued to emerge in recent times, most of them concerned with universalizing Hindu thought. ▷*See also* Arya Samaj; Brahmo Samaj; Ramakrishna; Vedanta; Vivekananda.

● **Hindu Kush** ▶ A mountain range in central Asia, extending about 800 km (500 mi) W from the Pamirs to the Koh-i-Baba Mountains of Afghanistan. Its highest peak is Tirich Mir, at 7692 m (25 236 ft).

● **Hindustani** ▶ An ▷Indo-Aryan language that originated in the dialect of the Delhi district. The Moguls and the British promoted its use as a lingua franca throughout India. ▷Urdu and ▷Hindi are the literary forms developed from it.

● **Hines, Earl (Fatha)** ▶ (1905–83) US Black jazz pianist and songwriter, who trained as a concert pianist but formed his own jazz band in 1928. He worked with Louis Armstrong from 1948–51 and was well known for his virtuosic piano playing. He wrote the songs "The Earl" and "I Got It Bad."

● **Hingis, Martina** ▶ (1980–) Czech-born Swiss tennis player. In 1997 she won the US Open, Australian Open, French Open, and Wimbledon Singles championships to take the Grand Slam title at the age of 16. She won the Australian Open again in 1998 and 1999 and the French Open in 1999.

● **Hinkler, Herbert John Lewis** ▶ (1892–1933) Australian aviator. He went to England in 1912, served in the Royal Naval Air Service in World War I, and in 1928 flew solo to Australia in a record 15½ days. He died in a crash in Italy.

● **hinny** ▶ The sterile offspring of a female ass and a male horse. Smaller than the more common ▷mule, hinnies are used as pack animals, especially in hot climates.

● **Hinshelwood, Sir Cyril Norman** ▶ (1897–1967) British chemist, who became professor at Oxford University in 1937. He pioneered the investigation of reaction kinetics and discovered several chain reaction mechanisms. He shared the Nobel Prize with N. N. Semyonov (1896–1986) in 1956.

● **hip** ▶ The part of the body where the legs are joined to the trunk (*see* Plate II). The skeleton of the hip consists of the ▷pelvis and the part of the spine (the sacrum) to which it is attached. The hip joint—the articulation between the pelvis and femur (thigh bone)—is a common site for arthritis: in severe cases the whole joint may be replaced by an artificial one or pins or other devices may be inserted.

● **Hipparchus** ▶ (c. 190–c. 120 BC) Greek astronomer, born in Nicaea. He produced the first accurate map of over 1000 stars, using latitude and longitude. He also discovered the precession of the equinoxes and accurately measured the distance to the moon by parallax. In mathematics he invented trigonometry by constructing a table of the ratios of the sides of right-angle triangles.

● **Hipparion** ▶ An extinct ▷horse that lived in the Pliocene epoch (about seven million years ago). It was slender and fast-running, about the size of a modern pony, and lived on open plains. Its foot had a distinct hoof, the remaining toes being small and not touching the ground. ▷*See also* eohippus.

● **Hippeastrum** ▶ A genus of herbaceous plants (60 species), native to tropical and subtropical America and cultivated for ornament. They have large bulbs (about 10 cm in diameter), broad straight-sided leaves, and a stout flower stem terminating in a cluster of white, pink, or red flowers, each 10 cm across. The genus includes the Barbados lily (*H. equestre*), with scarlet flowers. Family: *Amaryllidaceae*.

● **hippie movement** ▶ An international movement of the 1960s, closely associated with the use of hallucinatory drugs. The hippie movement, or "flower power," was particularly strong in the USA where it focused on such issues as opposition to the Vietnam War. Followers grew their hair long, listened to "psychedelic" or folk-based music, and favoured liberal attitudes towards sex. Relaxed, anarchic, and opposed to both the work ethic and material possessions, the movement faded with the economic recession of the 1970s.

● **Hippocrates** ▶ (c. 460–c. 377 BC) Greek physician and founder of the Hippocratic school of medicine, which greatly influenced medical science until the 18th century. Hippocrates seems to have been a prominent physician, who travelled widely in Greece and Asia Minor. His followers believed that health was governed by the balance of four body fluids, or humours: phlegm, blood, black bile, and yellow bile. The Hippocratic Collection of 60 or so medical works is ascribed to various authors. The **Hippocratic Oath** was probably not written by Hippocrates, but most of the ethical principles it enjoins, including doctor–patient confidentiality, are still followed by medical practitioners, although they are not now required formally to take the oath.

● **Hippolytus** ▶ In Greek legend, the bastard son of ▷Theseus and Hippolyta, Queen of the Amazons. A devotee of ▷Artemis, his dedication to chastity led him to reject the advances of Theseus's wife ▷Phaedra, and he was destroyed by a bull from the sea sent by Poseidon.

● **hippopotamus** ▶ A large hoofed mammal, *Hippopotamus amphibius*, of tropical Africa. About 150 cm high at the shoulder and weighing around 3.5 tonnes, hippos have virtually naked dark-brown skin and tusks up to 60 cm long. They spend the day in rivers or waterholes, emerging at night to graze on surrounding pasture. Herds usually number 10–15 individuals. Hippos are highly territorial, marking the boundaries of their grazing ground with piles of dung. Family: *Hippopotamidae*. ▷*See also* pygmy hippopotamus.

● **hire purchase** ▶ The buying of goods on credit terms. The buyer pays a deposit, contracts to make periodic payments, and obtains possession of the goods on hire. The seller retains ownership until the full price plus interest has been paid, and can repossess the goods if the buyer defaults; however, in England and Wales a court order has to be obtained if the buyer has paid more than one-third of the value of the goods. Government control of the minimum deposit and the maximum repayment period has frequently been used to regulate consumer demand.

● **Hirohito** ▶ (1901–89) Emperor of Japan (1926–89), having previously been regent for five years after his father Yoshihito (1879–1926) had been declared insane. He married (1924) Princess Nagako Kuai. Ruling as divine emperor until Japan's defeat in World War II, he became no more than a constitutional monarch under the 1946 constitution (introduced under US pressure). He was an expert on marine biology; his role in World War II remains unclear.

● **Hiroshige** ▶ (Ando Tokitaro; 1797–1858) Japanese colour-print artist of the ▷ukiyo-e movement. Under Toyohiro (1774–1829), Hiroshige first specialized in prints of women. From about 1830 he turned to landscapes, which he often depicted in snow, rain, or moonlight.

● **Hiroshima** ▶ 34 23N 132 27E A city in Japan, in SW Honshu on the River Ota. A former military base and seaport, it was largely destroyed (6 August, 1945) by the first atomic bomb to be used in warfare; over 130 000 people were killed or injured. Leading architects helped rebuild the city and it is now a major industrial centre. A conference is held here annually to oppose nuclear weapons. Its university was established in 1949. Population (1995): 1 108 868.

● **Hirst, Damien** ▶ (1965–) British artist and sculptor, best known for his installations involving dead animals preserved in formaldehyde. He was awarded the Turner Prize for 1995.

● **Hispaniola** ► The second largest West Indian island, in the Greater Antilles. It is divided between the ▷Dominican Republic and ▷Haiti. Area: 18 703 sq km (29 418 sq mi).

● **Hiss, Alger** ► (1904–96) US public servant, who was imprisoned in 1950 for perjury after denying that he had communicated with Soviet spies while an adviser to President Roosevelt. His case contributed to ▷McCarthy's anti-Communist measures in the 1950s and remains controversial.

● **histamine** ► An amine, derived from the amino acid histidine, that is released from body tissues after injury or in an allergic reaction, such as asthma or hay fever. It dilates blood vessels, producing inflammation; contracts smooth muscle, which in the lungs leads to breathing difficulties; and stimulates the secretion of gastric juice. Its effects can be counteracted with ▷antihistamines.

● **histology** ► The study of ▷tissues. Originally histology was limited to the study of tissues by light microscopy, but the development of such techniques as electron microscopy, immunofluorescence, and autoradiography has enabled the details of subcellular structure to be revealed. ▷*See also* cytology.

● **history** ► The story of the past. The student of history discovers, examines, and interprets the records of past human societies. Records of events are found in the inscriptions of the ancient Egyptians but history as a literary activity is generally regarded as beginning with the ancient Greeks, among whom ▷Herodotus, ▷Thucydides, and ▷Xenophon were outstanding. The desire of ancient historians for accuracy was sometimes subordinated to their purely literary ambitions and the Romans (notably ▷Sallust, ▷Cicero, ▷Livy, and ▷Tacitus) were also concerned to glorify Rome. Early Christian history writing (historiography) was influenced by Jewish historians, such as ▷Josephus, and Christian preconceptions and subject matter continued to influence the writing of history throughout the middle ages. Medieval historiography consisted largely of chronicles, such as those of ▷Bede, Matthew ▷Paris, and Jean ▷Froissart. The later middle ages were influenced by Byzantine historians, including ▷Anna Comnena, and by such Arabs as ▷Ibn Khaldun and al-▷Tabari. The classical interests of early Renaissance scholars (*see* humanism) led to a new concern for textual criticism, which resulted in the outstanding work of ▷Machiavelli and ▷Guicciardini in the early 16th century. Their critical approach to sources was continued by 17th-century historians but the 18th-century Enlightenment enlarged the interests of historians to include a more fundamental study of the pattern of change in human societies. This concern is reflected in the work of the 18th-century British historian Edward Gibbon, who tried to show that the history of mankind is one of continuous progress. In the 19th century, under the influence of the German school of historians, which included von ▷Ranke and ▷Mommsen, history was established as an academic discipline in the universities. Outstanding British historians of the 19th century included William Stubbs and F. W. Maitland (1850–1906) and the more literary—and more widely read—Macaulay and Carlyle. The 19th century also saw various attempts to establish history on a "scientific" basis by deducing general laws to explain and predict events: these include the positivist philosophy of ▷Comte and the dialectical materialism of ▷Marx. The scope of historiography widened greatly in the 20th century under the influence of sociology, anthropology, and psychology, and new techniques, such as the use of computers to analyse statistical data. The late 20th century also saw a growth in studies that examined the roles of groups previously excluded from most historical accounts, such as women and ethnic minorities.

● **Hitachi** ► 36 35N 140 40E A city in Japan, in E Honshu on the Pacific Ocean. Copper has been mined here since 1591 and the city is Japan's leading producer of electrical equipment. Population (1995 est): 199 241.

● **Hitchcock, Sir Alfred** ► (1899–1980) British film director. He worked almost exclusively in Hollywood from 1940. He specialized in sophisticated thrillers, using calculated cinematic effects to create tension and suspense. His technique influenced the ▷New Wave. His

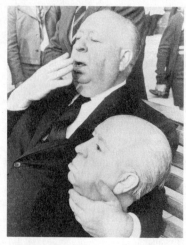

Alfred Hitchcock ► Photographed in 1972 during the filming of *Frenzy*. One of Hitchcock's whims was that he liked to appear fleetingly in his own films—usually in a non-speaking role in a crowd scene.

films include *Blackmail* (1929), *The Thirty-Nine Steps* (1935), *Rebecca* (1940), *Notorious* (1946), *Rear Window* (1954), *Vertigo* (1958), *Psycho* (1960), and *The Birds* (1963).

● **Hitler, Adolf** ► (1889–1945) German dictator. Born in Austria, the son of a customs officer, his youth was spent in poverty in Vienna and Munich (he worked as a housepainter although he aspired to be an artist). He fought in World War I, rising to the rank of lance corporal and winning the Iron Cross. In 1919 he joined the German Workers' Party, renamed the National Socialist (abbreviated to ▷Nazi) Party in 1920. He became its president in 1921 and two years later staged an abortive coup—the Munich Putsch—against the Bavarian Government. During a brief imprisonment he wrote most of *Mein Kampf* (*My Struggle*), setting out his political philosophy, based on a notion of the innate superiority of the Aryan race, the culpability of the Jews for Germany's defeat in World War I, and a violent anticommunism. In the economic crisis of the late 1920s and early 1930s Hitler's powers of oratory and his propaganda machine (headed by ▷Goebbels) brought the Nazis increasing support, especially from German industrialists, and in 1930 they won 107 Reichstag seats. In 1933, aided by von ▷Papen, Hitler was offered the chancellorship by ▷Hindenburg, the German president. The ▷Reichstag fire enabled him to discredit the opposition, gain a majority in the subsequent elections (in coalition with the Nationalists), and acquire the dictatorial powers he sought; following Hindenburg's death in 1934 he assumed the title of Führer (leader). He proceeded to crush his opponents, institute his fanatical persecution of the Jews by the establishment of ▷concentration camps, and rearm in preparation for the wars of conquest that he planned for the Third Reich. He lent his support to Mussolini in Italy and Franco in Spain, precipitating ▷World War II by invading Austria (1938) and then Czechoslovakia and Poland (1939). Having conquered and occupied most of continental Europe, in early 1942 he set up the ▷Wannsee conference under Reinhard ▷Heydrich to exterminate the European Jews in the so-called Final Solution. Military reverses in 1943 led to Stauffenberg's unsuccessful attempt (1944) to assassinate Hitler, but as the Third Reich collapsed in the face of Allied victory the Führer committed suicide with Eva ▷Braun (whom he had married shortly before) in the bunker of the chancellory in Berlin. How Hitler was able, unchecked for over a decade, to implement policies of an unparalleled barbarity with the support of a nation supposed to be civilized, is a question that continues to plague historians.

● **Hittites** ► An Indo-European people who appeared in Anatolia around the beginnning of the second millennium BC. By 1340 BC they had emerged as a major power, with their capital at ▷Hattusas (or Boğazköy) from which they conquered much of Anatolia and also Syria (*see* Carchemish). In their polytheistic religion, their king was believed to be the representative of god on earth and became a god himself on death. The society was feudal in organization and also upheld the institution of slavery. Their language is extinct, but is known from cuneiform tablets and inscriptions (*see* Indo-Hittite languages).

● **HIV** ▷*See* AIDS.

● **hives** ▷*See* urticaria.

● **Hizbollah** ▶ (or Hezbollah; Arabic: Party of God) A Shiite Muslim organization, based in Lebanon, that emerged as a powerful influence on events in the Middle East in the late 1980s. With Iranian backing, it became notorious for its terrorist methods, including hijackings and hostage-taking. In April 1996 Hizbollah rocket attacks provoked Israel to mount a fierce air and missile offensive against S Lebanon, causing hundreds of civilian deaths. Hizbollah activities provoked further Israeli attacks on Lebanon in March 1999 and February 2000. However, in May 2000 a successful Hizbollah offensive obliged Israel to withdraw completely from Lebanon.

● **HMSO** ▷*See* Stationery Office, The.

● **Hoad, Lewis Alan** ▶ (1934–94) Australian tennis player, who was Wimbledon singles champion in 1956 and 1957 and doubles champion in 1953, 1955, and 1956 but then became a professional (1957).

● **Hoare-Laval Pact** ▷*See* Laval, Pierre.

● **hoarhound** ▷*See* horehound.

● **hoatzin** ▶ A primitive bird, *Opisthocomus hoazin*, that occurs in tropical South American swamps. It is 65 cm long and has a small head with a wispy crest and a long tail. Its plumage is streaked brown with yellowish underparts and it feeds chiefly on flowers and fruit. It is the only member of its family (*Opisthocomidae*). Order: *Galliformes* (pheasants, turkeys, etc.).

● **Hobart** ▶ 42 54S 147 18E A city in Australia, the capital and chief port of Tasmania on the Derwent River estuary. It has an excellent natural harbour with small tidal changes. Industries include zinc refining and food processing; the chief exports are apples, wool, timber, and dairy produce. The University of Tasmania was established here in 1890. Population (1995 est): 194 700.

● **Hobbema, Meindert** ▶ (1638–1709) Dutch landscape painter, born in Amsterdam. He often sketched with ▷Ruisdael but, unlike him, Hobbema specialized in peaceful woodland and rural scenes with watermills. Through his marriage (1668) he gained a minor post in the local excise department but continued with his painting, producing in this period perhaps his best work, *The Avenue, Middelharnis* (1689; National Gallery, London).

● **Hobbes, Thomas** ▶ (1588–1679) English political philosopher. Hobbes was a vigorous proponent of scientific ▷materialism, particularly with regard to human nature. His interests lay in mathematics, geography, and the classics until the breakdown of English political and social order in the 1640s inspired him to devise his own political theory. *Leviathan* (1651) argues that because people are inherently selfish they need to be ruled by an absolute sovereign, whose function is to enforce public order. Contemporary theories of natural rights, and the civil rights thought to derive from them, were anathema to him. His theories made him a loyalist both to the English monarchy and, during the Interregnum, to its opponents.

● **Hobbs, Jack** ▶ (Sir John Berry H.; 1882–1963) British cricketer. The world's greatest batsman between ▷Grace and ▷Bradman, he played for Surrey and for England in 61 Test matches. During his career (1905–34) he scored 61 237 runs and 197 centuries (98 made after the age of 40). He was the first cricketer to be knighted (1953).

● **hobby** ▶ A ▷falcon, *Falco subbuteo*, occurring in open regions of Eurasia and NW Africa. It is 33 cm long and has a dark-grey back, whitish underparts streaked with black, and red "trousers." It feeds on large insects and small birds caught in flight.

● **Hochhuth, Rolf** ▶ (1933–) Left-wing Swiss dramatist, who writes in German. His controversial plays include *The Representative* (1962), criticizing the attitude of Pius XII to the Nazi persecution of the Jews, *The Soldiers* (1966), accusing Winston ▷Churchill of complicity in the death of the Polish general Sikorski, and *Wessis in Weimar* (1992). His novel *German Love Story* (1980) analyses the extent of the involvement of the German people in Nazi atrocities.

● **Ho Chi Minh** ▶ (Nguyen That Thanh; 1890–1969) Vietnamese statesman, who led Vietnam in its struggle for independence from the French. As a young man he lived in England (1915–17) and then in France (1917–23), where in 1920 he joined the French Communist Party. In 1924 he went to communist-controlled Canton, where he formed the Association of Young Vietnamese Revolutionaries (Thanh Nien), the forerunner of the Indochinese Communist Party (1930). Returning to Vietnam in 1941, following the French defeat by the Germans in World War II, he formed the ▷Viet Minh, which waged the long and ultimately victorious colonial war against the French (1945–54; *see* Indochina). According to the Geneva Accords, which Ho Chi Minh attended, Vietnam was divided on either side of the 17th parallel into North Vietnam, of which Ho became president, and South Vietnam. In 1959 he extended support to the ▷Viet Cong guerrilla movement in the South (*see also* Vietnam War) with the aim of Vietnamese unification, which was achieved after his death.

● **Ho Chi Minh City** ▶ (name until 1976: Saigon) 10 46N 106 43E A city in S Vietnam, on the River Saigon. The University of Saigon (now Ho Chi Minh City) was established in 1917. It is the major commercial and industrial centre of the S, with shipbuilding, metalworking, textile, and chemical industries.

History: an ancient Khmer town, it was the capital of ▷Cochinchina and then of French Indochina (1887–1902). During the ▷Vietnam War, as the capital of South Vietnam, US presence brought an economic boom but left problems of prostitution, crime, and drug addiction. Population (1993 est): 4 322 300.

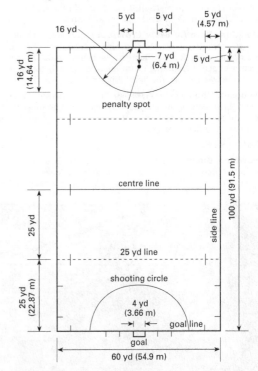

hockey ▶ The dimensions of the pitch.

● **hockey** ▶ An 11-a-side field game for men and women, the object of which is to score goals. It has been played in various forms for at least 4000 years. A team comprises a goalkeeper, two full-backs, three half-backs, and five forwards (left wing, inside left, centre, inside right, and right wing), each of which carries a curved stick for hitting the ball. Play is started at the beginning of the two 35-minute periods (and after each goal) with a bully-off in the centre of the field. In this brief ritual two opposing players cross their sticks and tap the ground three times. Play proceeds by dribbling the ball with the stick and passing it by hitting it along the ground or through the air. ▷*See also* ice hockey.

● **Hockney, David** ► (1937–) British painter, draughtsman, printmaker, and photographer, born in Bradford. After studying at the Royal College of Art (1959–62), he travelled widely in the USA, where he developed his realistic but witty style, his favourite subjects being figure studies and aquatic themes. The latter play a prominent part in a quasi-documentary film about him entitled *A Bigger Splash* (1974). Later work includes still lifes and landscapes, notably the spectacular *A Bigger Grand Canyon* (1998). He has also designed stage sets and illustrated books. Hockney was appointed a Companion of Honour in 1997.

● **Hoddinott, Alun** ► (1929–) Welsh composer. He was professor of music at University College of South Wales from 1967 to 1987. His works include six operas, seven symphonies, concertos, chamber music, and orchestral pieces.

● **Hoddle, Glenn** ► (1957–) British soccer player and manager. He played for Tottenham Hotspur (1976–86), England (1980–88), Monaco (1986–91), and (as player-manager) Swindon Town (1991–93). He managed Chelsea from 1993 to 1996 and was coach of the England team from 1996 to 1999.

● **Hodeida** ► (or Al Hudaydah) 14 50N 42 58E A town and port in W Yemen, on the Red Sea coast. It is the country's principal port, exporting cotton and mocha coffee. Population (1993 est): 246 068.

● **Hodgkin, Sir Alan Lloyd** ► (1914–98) British physiologist, who discovered the chemical changes associated with the propagation of a nerve impulse (*see* action potential) along a nerve fibre. He wrote *Conduction of the Nervous Impulse* (1964) and shared a Nobel Prize (1963) with A. F. Huxley (his colleague) and Sir John Eccles.

● **Hodgkin, Dorothy Mary Crowfoot** ► (1910–94) British biochemist, who determined the structure of several complex molecules by means of ▷X-ray diffraction. She helped to determine the structure of penicillin (in the 1940s) and of vitamin B$_{12}$ (in the early 1950s). She was awarded the Nobel Prize in 1964.

● **Hodgkin, Thomas** ► (1798–1866) British physician, who described the disease of the lymphatic system now known as **Hodgkin's disease** (*see* lymphoma). Hodgkin made a considerable contribution to the pathology of diseases.

● **Hofei** ▷*See* Hefei.

● **Hoffman, Dustin** ► (1937–) US film actor. He made his reputation in the films *The Graduate* (1967) and *Midnight Cowboy* (1969). He was awarded Oscars for his performances in *Kramer vs Kramer* (1980) and *Rain Man* (1989). Other films include *Lenny* (1974), *Tootsie* (1982), *Billy Bathgate* (1991), and *Wag the Dog* (1997).

● **Hofmann, Joseph Casimir** ► (1876–1957) Polish-born pianist. A performer from the age of six, he composed under the name "Michael Dvorsky." He toured extensively and became a US citizen in 1926.

● **Hofmannsthal, Hugo von** ► (1874–1929) Austrian poet and dramatist. In 1901, after studying law and philology, he devoted himself to writing. His influential essay "The Letter of Lord Chandos" (1902) divides the aestheticism of his short early plays from the social concern of his later ones, such as *Der Turm* (1925). He was librettist for several Richard ▷Strauss operas, including *Der Rosenkavalier* (1911) and *Ariadne auf Naxos* (1912). He was a cofounder of the Salzburg Festival in 1920.

● **Hofmeister, Wilhelm Friedrich Benedict** ► (1824–77) German botanist, who pioneered the science of comparative plant morphology. His major work established the relationship between the cryptogams (algae, mosses, ferns, etc.), the gymnosperms (e.g. conifers), and the angiosperms (flowering plants). Hofmeister also discovered that regular alternation between sexual and asexual generations occurs in mosses, ferns, and seed plants.

● **Hogan, Ben** ► (William Benjamin H.; 1912–97) US professional golfer, most of whose major successes, including winning the Masters Tournament in 1951 and 1953, came after a car accident that was expected to cripple him (1949).

● **Hogarth, William** ► (1697–1764) British painter and engraver. He studied under a silverplate engraver and later under Sir James Thornhill (whose daughter he married), before establishing his reputation with the paintings and engravings of *A Harlot's Progress* (1731–32). He excelled in moralizing social satires in such narrative series as *A Rake's Progress, Industry and Idleness, Gin Lane*, and the paintings of *Marriage à la Mode* (Tate Gallery), works that led him to campaign for an Engraving Copyright Act (the so-called Hogarth's Act, 1734). As a portraitist the naturalism and vivacity of *Captain Coram* (Foundling Hospital, London) and *Hogarth's Servants* (National Gallery, London) were influential, although unpopular with his contemporaries. His artistic theories are expressed in his *The Analysis of Beauty* (1753).

● **hogfish** ► A beautifully coloured tropical marine fish belonging to a genus (*Bodianus*) of ▷wrasses. They change colour while growing and are very popular in aquaria.

William Hogarth ► The vivid detail and satirical spirit of Hogarth's works are seen here in "Canvassing for Votes," a copperplate engraving from the series *Parliamentary Elections* (1757). In the centre foreground a voter slyly pockets bribes from agents of both parties; on the right the Tory candidate woos two women (on the balcony) with trinkets. In the background a violent mob attacks the office of the rival party.

● **Hogg, James** ▶ (1770–1835) Scottish poet and writer. Originally a shepherd (hence his nickname "The Ettrick Shepherd"), he was self-educated and became famous as a writer of ballads and narrative poems under the patronage of Sir Walter Scott. His modern reputation rests chiefly on the novel *The Confessions of a Justified Sinner* (1824).

● **Hogg, Quintin** ▷*See* Hailsham of St Marylebone, Quintin McGarel Hogg, Baron.

● **Hoggar Mountains** ▷*See* Ahaggar Mountains.

● **hogweed** ▶ A biennial herb, *Heracleum sphondylium*, also called cow parsnip, native to Eurasia and N Africa and introduced to North America. Up to 2 m high, it has hollow ridged stems, divided leaves, and umbrella-like clusters of white or pinkish flowers. The giant hogweed (*H. mantegazzianum*) may reach a height of 3.5 m and is grown as an ornamental. Family: ▷*Umbelliferae*.

● **Hohenlinden, Battle of** ▶ (3 December, 1800) The battle in the Napoleonic Wars in which the French under Jean Victor ▷Moreau defeated the Austrians. It was fought 31 km (16 mi) E of Munich. The French victory brought the collapse of the second coalition against Napoleon. ▷*See* Revolutionary and Napoleonic Wars.

● **Hohenlohe-Schillingsfürst, Chlodwig Karl Viktor, Fürst zu** ▶ (1819–1901) German statesman; chancellor (1894–1900). He came to prominence during the 1860s as a vigorous supporter of Bismarck's policy of German unification. He served as ambassador to Paris (1874–78) and as governor of Alsace-Lorraine (1885–94) before becoming chancellor, when he attempted to exercise a moderating influence on William II. He was succeeded by his protégé Bernhard von Bülow.

● **Hohenstaufen** ▶ A German dynasty, founded by Frederick, Duke of Swabia (d. 1105), that ruled the Holy Roman Empire from 1138 to 1254. ▷Conrad III was the first Hohenstaufen emperor and of his successors the most important were ▷Frederick (I) Barbarossa and ▷Frederick II. Frequently in conflict with Italian city states and the papacy, the dynasty was destroyed by its defeat at Tagliacozzo by a papal alliance (1268).

● **Hohenzollern** ▶ A dynasty, originating in Swabia, that ruled ▷Brandenburg, then ▷Prussia, and later Germany. First prominent in the late 12th century, the Hohenzollerns became Electors of Brandenburg in the 15th century. During the next 300 years they acquired other territories, including Prussia, of which ▷Frederick I became king in 1701. From 1871 they ruled the German Empire until 1918.

● **Hohhot** ▶ (*or* Huhehot) 40 49N 111 37E A city in NE China, the capital of Inner Mongolia AR. An old frontier trading town, its industry

was developed after 1949. The university was established in 1957. Population (1990): 652 534.

● **Hojo** ▶ Hereditary holders of the regency for the military overlordship (*see* shogun) of Japan between 1204 and 1333. Hojo Tokimasa (1138–1215) became the first regent in 1204 although he had held actual power from the death (1199) of his son-in-law, the first shogun ▷Minamoto Yoritomo. The Hojo regents were notable for their codification of feudal law, their encouragement of Zen Buddhism, and their repulse of the Mongols (1274, 1281). Their power was destroyed in 1333 by other feudal lords and ▷Daigo II.

● **Hokan languages** ▶ An American Indian language group spoken mainly in the NW of the USA and in California. Some Hokan languages are found in Mexico, including the most widely spoken, Tlapanecan and Tquistlatecan. The Yuman subdivision found in Colorado and California also has a comparatively large number of speakers. The Mohave language is a member of this subgroup.

● **Hokkaido** ▶ (former name: Yezo) The second largest and northernmost of the four main islands of Japan, separated from Honshu by the Tsugaru Strait and from the Russian island of Sakhalin by La Perouse Strait. Since 1985 it has been linked to Honshu by the 54 km (33.5 mi) long Seikan tunnel, the longest rail tunnel in the world. Mountainous, volcanic, and forested, with a relatively cool climate, it is popular for winter sports. It has a sizable aboriginal population and the N is largely uninhabited. Main industries are coalmining, agriculture, and fishing.
History: the Japanese began to settle on the island in the 16th century but did not develop it seriously until after 1868. It became administratively autonomous in 1885. Area: 78 508 sq km (30 312 sq mi). Population (1995 est): 5 692 000. Capital: Sapporo.

● **Hokusai** ▶ (Katsushika H.; 1760–1849) Japanese painter and book illustrator, the most famous ▷ukiyo-e designer of colour prints. He began as a wood engraver, becoming in 1778 a pupil of the painter and printmaker Shunsho (1726–92). From the 1790s he illustrated historical novels, verse anthologies, etc., and designed greeting and announcement cards. His early prints were chiefly of women and actors but he is best known for his later landscapes, which deeply influenced the impressionists and postimpressionists. His most famous works include his *Views of Mount Fuji* (1835) and his collection of sketchbooks, the *Hokusai Manga*, published from 1814 onwards.

● **Holbein the Younger, Hans** ▶ (c. 1497–1543) German painter, born in Augsburg. In 1515 he settled in Basle, where he designed woodcuts of the *Dance of Death*. Through his friend Erasmus he obtained the patronage of Sir Thomas More in England (1526–28). Settling in England in 1532, he painted portraits of merchants before

Hokusai ▶ A colour woodcut, *The Wave*, based on a view of Mount Fuji (centre background) from the sea near Kanagawa. Hokusai's 46 *Views of Mount Fuji* are usually seen as the finest products of the Japanese landscape tradition. The daring use of perspective in this picture influenced the French postimpressionist painters in the late 19th century.

becoming court painter and designer to Henry VIII (1536). His portrait of Henry VIII in a wall painting (destroyed) for Whitehall Palace became the prototype for other paintings of the king. He was also commissioned to paint Henry's prospective wives, *Christina, Duchess of Milan* (National Gallery, London) and *Anne of Cleves* (Louvre) and established a thriving portrait-painting business, e.g. *The Ambassadors* (National Gallery, London). Many of the preparatory drawings for his English portraits are in the Royal Collection, Windsor. Holbein died of the plague. His father **Hans Holbein the Elder** (c. 1465–1524) was also a painter, whose major work is the *S Sebastian Altar* (Alte Pinakothek, Munich).

● **Holberg, Ludvig, Baron** ▶ (1684–1754) Danish playwright, poet, and historian, the founder of modern Danish literature. Born in Norway, he was educated in Copenhagen and settled in Denmark after travelling throughout Europe. After publishing historical and legal works, he wrote a satirical poem, *Peder Paars* (1719), one of the earliest classics in modern Danish, and subsequently (1722–27) wrote over 30 comedies for the first Danish-language theatre, including *Jeppe paa Bjerget*, *Erasmus Montanus*, and *Henrik og Pernille*. Much of his later work is historical and philosophical with the exception of the comic satire *Nicolai Klimii iter subterraneum* (*Journey of Niels Klim to the World Underground*; 1741).

● **Hölderlin, (Johann Christian) Friedrich** ▶ (1770–1843) German poet. Trained as a Lutheran minister, he found Christianity incompatible with his enthusiasm for Greek mythology. While working as a private tutor, he fell in love with his employer's wife, who is portrayed in his novel *Hyperion* (1797–99). After her death in 1802 his life was dominated by his schizophrenia, from which he never recovered. His great lyrical talent was unrecognized until the 20th century, when a comprehensive edition of his poetry was published.

● **hole** ▷*See* semiconductors.

● **Holguín** ▶ 20 54N 76 15W A city in E Cuba. It is an important commercial centre; the chief exports through its port Gilbara (to the NE) are sugar and tobacco. Population (1994 est): 242 085.

● **Holiday, Billie** ▶ (Eleanor Gough McKay; 1915–59) US Black jazz singer, known as "Lady Day." She was discovered in Harlem by Benny Goodman and made her first recording in 1933. She subsequently sang with the bands of Count Basie and Artie Shaw. Addiction to heroin caused her death.

● **Holinshed, Raphael** ▶ (d. 1580) English chronicler. A translator in the printing office of Reginald Wolfe, Holinshed continued the compilation of their universal history after Wolfe's death (1573). Pared down to cover only the British Isles, the *Chronicle* was published in 1578. Lucid, patriotic, and uncritical, it inspired many Elizabethan dramatists, including Shakespeare.

● **holistic medicine** ▶ An approach to therapy in which all the physical, mental, and social aspects of the patient's life are taken into account in understanding and curing his disease, as opposed to merely treating his symptoms. A basic tenet of—and often used as a synonym for— ▷alternative medicine, the principle is gaining acceptance among orthodox practitioners. ▷*See also* Ayurvedic medicine.

● **Holland** ▶ The low-lying NW region of the Netherlands, now comprising the provinces of ▷North Holland and ▷South Holland. A county of the Holy Roman Empire from the 12th century, Holland came under Burgundy in the 15th century and then (1500) under the Habsburgs. Prominent in the 16th-century ▷Revolt of the Netherlands, Holland became the chief province of the independent United Provinces of the Netherlands. When the Kingdom of the ▷Netherlands was established in 1814, its importance diminished. Nevertheless the whole country is still commonly called Holland.

● **Holland, Henry** ▶ (1745–1806) British architect. Trained under Capability ▷Brown, Holland began his career by designing Brooks's Club in London (1776). Carlton House, London (1783), exemplified his dignified neoclassicism.

● **Holland, Parts of** ▷*See* Lincolnshire.

● **Holland, Sir Sidney (George)** ▶ (1893–1961) New Zealand statesman; National Party prime minister (1949–57). His government was repressive in industrial disputes and unable to control inflation. His party was defeated shortly after his retirement in 1957.

● **Hollar, Wenceslaus** ▶ (1607–77) Bohemian etcher, born in Prague. He worked in Germany and Antwerp before settling permanently in England (1652), where he produced book illustrations and views of London before the Great Fire.

● **Holles, Denzil, 1st Baron** ▶ (c. 1599–c. 1680) English politician. Prominent in the parliamentary opposition to Charles I, he was imprisoned (1628–30) for helping to hold the speaker in his chair to prevent the adjournment of parliament until the three resolutions of Sir John ▷Eliot had been passed. Holles fought in the Civil War but, a moderate, fled to France (1648) when the army gained the upper hand. He returned in 1653 and participated in the Restoration.

● **Holliger, Heinz** ▶ (1939–) Swiss oboist, conductor, and composer. He is a leading performer of modern music; Berio and Henze have written works for him.

● **holly** ▶ A tree or shrub of the widely distributed genus *Ilex* (300 species). The evergreen English holly (*I. aquifolium*) grows to a height of 15 m and has spiny lustrous dark-green leaves and small white male and female flowers growing on separate trees: the female flowers develop into red berries. It is widely cultivated for hedging and used for Christmas decorations. Family: *Aquifoliaceae*. ▷*See also* maté.

● **Holly, Buddy** ▶ (Charles Hardin Holley; 1936–59) US rock and roll singer and guitarist. With his band The Crickets, he recorded many of the early classic songs of rock and roll, including "That'll Be The Day" (1957) and "Peggy Sue" (1957); he was killed in an air crash.

● **hollyhock** ▶ A perennial herb, *Althaea rosea*, native to China but widely cultivated (usually as biennials). Up to 3 m high, it bears large white, yellow, or red flowers. Family: *Malvaceae*.

● **holly oak** ▷*See* holm oak.

● **Hollywood** ▶ 34 00N 118 15W A NW suburb of Los Angeles, in California in the USA. Founded in the 1880s, it has been the centre of the US film industry since 1911. Population (1996 est): 127 894.

● **Holmes, Oliver Wendell** ▶ (1809–94) US essayist and poet. He became dean of the Medical School at Harvard and wrote several important medical works. He is best remembered for his occasional verse, especially "Old Ironsides" (1830) and "The Chambered Nautilus" (1858), and for his collections of conversational essays beginning with *The Autocrat of the Breakfast Table* (1857). His son **Oliver Wendell Holmes** (1841–1935) was a jurist, known as the Great Dissenter. He became a professor at Harvard University in 1882 and served as a judge in the Supreme Court of Massachusetts from 1882 until 1902, when he was appointed to the US Supreme Court. He opposed legislative restriction of individual rights but dissented from the famous 14th Amendment to the constitution, which specifically restricted state interference with private citizens. His best-known work is *The Common Law* (1881).

● **holmium** ▶ (Ho) A metallic lanthanide element, discovered in 1879 by P. T. Cleve (1840–1905) and named after his native city, Stockholm. Holmium occurs in rare-earth minerals, such as monazite ($CePO_4$). It forms an oxide (Ho_2O_3) and halides (HoX_3), but has few uses. At no 67; at wt 164.93032; mp 1474°C; bp 2700°C.

● **holm oak** ▶ An evergreen ▷oak tree, *Quercus ilex*, also called holly oak, native to S Europe and cultivated for ornament and for its wood. Growing to a height of 30 m, it has a dense crown and the leaves of young trees resemble holly leaves.

● **holocaust** ▶ The attempted extermination of European ▷Jews by the Nazis (1935–45). Altogether some six million Jews from many countries, approximately two-thirds of European Jewry, were killed. The holocaust is usually divided into two phases. During the first (1935–41), Jews in Germany and Austria were deprived of their civil rights under the antisemitic Nuremberg Laws (1935) and subjected to officially sanctioned acts of terror. The result was mass emigration. During the second phase (1941–45), Jews throughout occupied Europe were brutally massacred, initially through mass shootings and forced labour but then (following the adoption of the so-called "final solution" at the ▷Wannsee conference of 1942) through a policy of systematic extermination in Auschwitz and other ▷concentration camps. The Jewish populations of eastern Europe were the most grievously affected. Nearly half the victims of the holocaust (about 2.6 million people) were from Poland, where some 85% of the Jewish population perished: other countries to lose vast numbers of Jews included Romania, the Soviet Union, Hungary, and Lithuania. The holocaust has raised serious questions about the nature of European civilization in general and German culture in particular. Pope ▷Pius XII, who knew what was happening to the Jews in Germany and occupied Europe, brought the Roman Catholic Church into disrepute by failing to criticize the ▷genocide. The UK's first Holocaust Memorial Day was held on 27 January, 2001.

● **Holocene epoch** ▶ The present, or Recent, epoch in ▷geological time, including the last 10 000 years from the end of the Pleistocene. It is sometimes called the Postglacial, although some authorities consider it to be only an interglacial phase of the Pleistocene. At the beginning of the Holocene the general rise in sea level resulting from the melting of the ice isolated Britain from the rest of Europe.

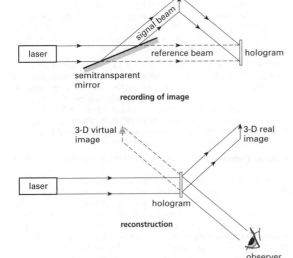

object

signal beam

laser

semitransparent
mirror

reference beam

hologram

recording of image

3-D virtual
image

3-D real
image

laser

hologram

reconstruction

observer

holography ▶ A three-dimensional image formed by two beams of light is recorded as an interference pattern on a single plate. The two images, giving a 3-D effect, are reconstructed by shining a similar beam through the hologram.

● **holography** ▶ A method of producing a stereoscopic image without using a camera. A monochromatic beam of ▷coherent radiation from a laser is split into two using a semitransparent mirror; one beam falls directly onto a photographic film or plate and the other is reflected by the subject onto the film. The two beams form ▷interference patterns on the film, which is called a hologram. To reconstruct the image, light of the same wavelength from a laser is shone onto the hologram. The interference pattern on the hologram diffracts the beam and splits it into two parts. One part gives a real two-dimensional image and the other a virtual three-dimensional image. The theory of holography was suggested by Dennis ▷Gabor in 1947 but could not be put into practice until the laser was invented 16 years later.

● **Holst, Gustav (Theodore)** ▶ (1874–1934) British composer and teacher. He studied composition with Charles Villiers Stanford (1852–1924) at the Royal College of Music, where he met his lifelong friend Vaughan Williams. He taught at the Royal College of Music, Morley College, and St Paul's Girls' School, for whose string orchestra he wrote the *St Paul's Suite* (1913). His interest in oriental philosophy inspired the chamber opera *Savitri* (1908) and other works. Among his most famous compositions are the choral work *The Hymn of Jesus*

(1917), the tone poem *Egdon Heath* (1927), and the orchestral suite *The Planets* (1914–16).

● **Holt, Harold (Edward)** ▶ (1908–67) Australian statesman; Liberal prime minister from 1966 until his death. His government relaxed immigration and citizenship laws and supported involvement in the Vietnam War. He apparently drowned while swimming in the sea but his body was never recovered.

● **Holy Ghost** ▷*See* Holy Spirit.

● **Holy Grail** ▶ In medieval legend and romance, a vessel or dish having supernatural power. Originally the grail may have had some significance in pre-Christian Celtic mythology; but by the 12th century, in romances by ▷Chrétien de Troyes and Robert de Boron's *Joseph d'Arimathie*, it was associated with the chalice used by Christ at the Last Supper and later given to ▷Joseph of Arimathea, who received the blood of Christ in it at the crucifixion. Chrétien had combined the grail legend with the ▷Arthurian legend, and the knightly quest for the Holy Grail, undertaken by Percival, Galahad, and other Knights of the Round Table, is a dominant theme in many Arthurian romances. According to a passage in ▷William of Malmesbury, Joseph brought the Holy Grail to Glastonbury, where he also allegedly built the first church in England.

● **Holyhead** ▶ 53 20N 4 38W A port and resort in North Wales, in Anglesey on Holy Island. It has steamer services to Dun Laoghaire in the Republic of Ireland. Extensions to its fine harbour were completed in 1977. The major London–Holyhead road (A5) was built by Telford. Population (1991): 11 796.

● **Holy Island** ▶ **1.** (or Lindisfarne) 55 41N 1 48W An island, in NE England off the NE coast of Northumberland. Its monastery was founded by St Aidan (635 AD); St Cuthbert was a bishop here (685–87). **2.** 53 20N 4 35W An island off the NW coast of Anglesey.

● **Holy Lance** ▶ The lance said to have pierced Christ's side at the crucifixion. This relic was discovered (1098) after a visionary revelation to a peasant, Peter Bartholomew, at the siege of Antioch during the first ▷Crusade. Accepted as genuine by most, but not all, of the Crusaders, its discovery raised morale and inspired the capture of Antioch from the Muslims.

● **Holy League** ▶ Any of several alliances formed in the 15th, 16th, and 17th centuries usually for the furtherance of papal or Roman Catholic interests. The best known are those formed against the French invasion of Italy (1494) and against the Huguenots in the French ▷Wars of Religion (1576).

● **Holyoake, Sir Keith Jacka** ▶ (1904–83) New Zealand statesman; prime minister (1957, 1960–72). He entered parliament in 1932, became deputy leader of the National Party in 1947, and was deputy prime minister and minister for agriculture from 1949 until ▷Holland's resignation in 1957. He was governor general of New Zealand (1977–80).

● **Holy of Holies** ▶ The central shrine of the Jewish ▷tabernacle (Exodus 25–31, 35–40) and later of the ▷Temple of Jerusalem. Originally it contained the ▷Ark of the Covenant (the receptacle of the two tablets of the law) and other cultic objects. In the second Temple it was apparently empty. The ▷high priest entered it once a year, on ▷Yom Kippur, to make atonement for the people.

● **holy orders** ▶ In Christian Churches, specifically those accepting ▷episcopacy, the ranks of bishop, priest, etc., conferred by a bishop. They are traditionally divided into major and minor orders, the former being the ranks of bishop, priest, deacon, and (in the Roman Catholic Church) subdeacon. The Roman Catholic Church also has four minor orders: porters (or doorkeepers), lectors (or readers), exorcists, and acolytes. Holy orders are considered a ▷sacrament by the Orthodox and Roman Catholic Churches; they are also held to impose an "indelible character" on the recipient, so that they remain valid after the most serious sin and can be conferred only once. The first Anglican deaconesses were charged in the 1960s and the first women deacons ordained after reforms in 1985. After a vote of the General Synod (1992) women priests were first ordained in the Church of England in 1994. The first woman bishop in the worldwide Anglican Communion was ordained in the USA in 1989.

● **Holy Roman Empire** ▶ The successor to the western ▷Roman Empire of antiquity. The name itself was not employed until the mid-13th century but the institution dates from 800, when ▷Charlemagne was crowned emperor of the West by Pope Leo III. Its territory came to comprise much of W and central Europe, being centred on Germany and Austria and including areas of E France and N Italy. After the failure of Charlemagne's ▷Carolingian dynasty the imperial title, which was nominally elective (*see* electors), passed (962) to the German kings, who retained it until the Empire's abolition in 1806; from the 13th century the emperors were almost always ▷Habsburgs. Between the 11th and 13th centuries the emperors (especially those of the ▷Hohenstaufen dynasty) vied with the popes for dominance in Europe (*see* investiture controversy; Guelfs and Ghibellines), a conflict from which the Empire emerged much weakened. It was further undermined by the Protestant ▷Reformation in the 16th century, the ▷Thirty Years' War in the 17th century, and the rise of Prussia and was finally broken by Napoleon's conquest of imperial territories in the early 19th century.

● **Holyrood House** ▶ A palace in Edinburgh, which is the Scottish residence of the British monarch. A medieval building, it was substantially modified in the classical style from 1671 onwards by Sir William Bruce (d. 1710).

● **Holy Spirit** ▶ (*or* Holy Ghost) In Christian theology, the third person of the Trinity, coequal and of one substance with the Father and the Son. Old Testament references to the spirit of God are given a more specific application in the New Testament Gospels; in St John's Gospel the Holy Spirit is seen as the "Paraclete" or Comforter, sent to inspire Christ's followers after the ▷Ascension. In Acts, the descent of the Holy Spirit upon the Apostles is described, an event commemorated at the Feast of Pentecost (the 50th day after Easter). The Holy Spirit is usually symbolized by a dove.

● **Home, Daniel Douglas** ▶ (1833–86) British spiritualist and medium. In 1868 he astonished distinguished witnesses by appearing to float out of one third-storey window and into another, but their testimony is now doubted.

● **Home Counties** ▶ The counties in England nearest to London, traditionally consisting of Buckinghamshire, Essex, Hertfordshire, Kent, Berkshire, Surrey, and Middlesex (now part of Greater London).

● **Home Guard** ▶ A World War II British defence force of unpaid volunteers aged between 17 and 65, first recruited in 1940 as the Local Defence Volunteers (LDV). Originally formed to provide a local defence force in case of invasion, its responsibilities included guard duties, patrolling key areas, and manning anti-aircraft guns and searchlights. Disbanded at the end of World War II, it was raised again between 1951 and 1957. At its highest, its strength reached 1.75 million.

● **Home Office** ▶ The government department, headed by the home secretary, that is responsible for domestic affairs in England and Wales. It was formed in 1782, when the secretary of state for the southern department became the secretary of state for home affairs (*compare* Foreign and Commonwealth Office). The Home Office's responsibilities include immigration and race relations, broadcasting regulation, prisons, and some aspects of police administration.

● **Home of the Hirsel, Alec Douglas-Home, Baron** ▶ (Alexander Frederick D.-H.; 1903–95) British statesman; Conservative prime minister (1963–64). He was an MP (1931–45, 1950–51) before becoming the 14th Earl of Home. He was foreign secretary (1960–63) and then, to widespread surprise, succeeded Macmillan as prime minister, renouncing his peerages. Following the Conservative electoral defeat (1964) he resigned the party leadership (1965). He received a life peerage in 1974.

● **homeomorphism** ▶ In mathematics, a one-to-one correspondence. In ▷set theory it is a property of two sets in which every member of one set is capable of being paired with one member of the other set and vice versa. In ▷topology, two shapes are homeomorphic if one can be transformed into the other by a continuous deformation, without being cut; for example, the surfaces of a sphere and a cube are homeomorphic.

● **homeopathy** ▶ The system of treating illness developed by Samuel ▷Hahnemann at the end of the 18th century and based on the principle of "like cures like." To treat a particular disease homeopathists prescribe small doses of a drug that in larger quantities would cause the symptoms of the disease in a healthy person. *▷See also* alternative medicine.

● **homeostasis** ▶ The self-regulating process by which living organisms tend to maintain their bodies in a constant physiological state regardless of environmental extremes. The extent to which this is achieved by a particular group is a measure of its success: protozoans, for instance, are affected by many external factors, whereas man is relatively independent. In man, reflex activity of the nervous system and hormonal action are important in achieving homeostatic control. Claude ▷Bernard was one of the first to recognize the importance of this kind of regulation.

● **Homer** ▶ (8th century BC) Greek epic poet, presumed author of the *Iliad* and *Odyssey*. He is believed to have lived in Ionia in Asia Minor and according to legend was blind. Working within a primitive oral tradition, he ordered a wealth of traditional material into a monumental and unified poetic structure. The *Iliad* concerns the Trojan War, and its basic tragic theme is enlivened by the variety and human sympathy of its individual episodes. The *Odyssey* relates the various adventures of ▷Odysseus during his voyage home from the Trojan War to his kingdom of Ithaca. Both poems were revered by the ancient Greeks for their moral as well as their literary value and have had a profound influence on Western culture.

● **Homer, Winslow** ▶ (1836–1910) US painter of landscapes and seascapes. In his native Boston he trained under a lithographer. In New York he worked as an illustrator and as an artist-correspondent of the Civil War, achieving prominence with his painting *Prisoners from the Front* (1866; Metropolitan Museum). After a visit to England (1881–83), he settled in Prouts Neck (Maine), where he painted a number of watercolours of fishermen and the sea, often in conflict, as in *The Gulf Stream* (1899; Metropolitan Museum).

● **Home Rule** ▶ An Irish political movement to repeal the Act of ▷Union (1800) with Britain and give Ireland a legislature responsible for domestic affairs. Founded by Isaac Butt (1813–79) in 1870, the Home Rule movement achieved parliamentary prominence under the leadership of ▷Parnell from 1880. ▷Gladstone's conversion to Home Rule produced the Home Rule bills of 1886 and 1893 but both were defeated. In 1914 the third Home Rule bill was passed but suspended for the duration of the war. A modified act was passed in 1920 providing separate parliaments for northern and southern Ireland. This was accepted by the north but rejected by the south, which in 1922 gained dominion status as the Irish Free State.

● **homicide** ▶ The killing of one person by another. In English law it is divided into unlawful and lawful homicide. Unlawful homicide includes ▷murder, ▷manslaughter, and ▷infanticide. Lawful homicide is the killing of a person in self-defence or defence of others or by misadventure or when attempting to prevent a crime or arrest an offender (also called excusable or justifiable homicide).

● **homing instinct** ▷*See* migration, animal.

● **hominid** ▶ A member of the *Hominidae* family of primates, to which modern humans (*Homo sapiens*) belong. Besides *H. sapiens*, there are no surviving hominids: the others are known only from fossil remains. One of the earliest hominids was *Ardipithecus ramidus*; fossils found in Ethiopia are dated at about 4.4 million years old. The *Hominidae* also includes the genera ▷*Australopithecus* and ▷*Homo*. The hominids appeared between 4.4 and one million years ago in Africa and Asia. The first to appear in Europe date from about 600 000 years ago.

● **Homo** ▶ A genus of ▷hominids with a large cranial capacity, erect posture, bipedal gait, a thumb capable of a precision grip, and the ability to make and use tools. The earliest species, *Homo habilis and H. rudolfensis*, first appeared about 2.5 million years ago in Africa and made simple stone tools. *H. erectus* (formerly called ▷*Pithecanthropus*) first appeared about 1.8 million years ago and made hand axes; specimens have been found in Java (Java man) and Beijing (Peking man) as well as Africa. A contemporaneous species was *H. ergaster*, which is

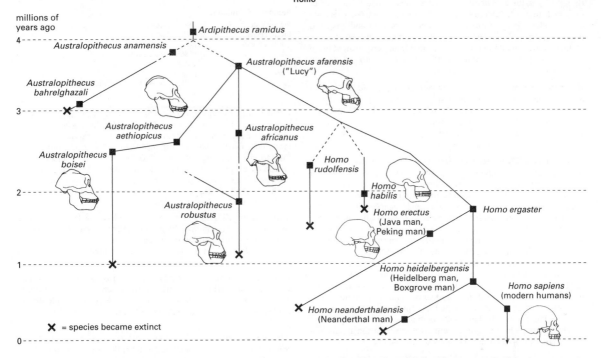

Homo

millions of years ago

Ardipithecus ramidus

Australopithecus anamensis

Australopithecus afarensis ("Lucy")

Australopithecus bahrelghazali

Australopithecus aethiopicus

Australopithecus africanus

Australopithecus boisei

Homo rudolfensis

Homo habilis

Australopithecus robustus

Homo erectus (Java man, Peking man)

Homo ergaster

Homo heidelbergensis (Heidelberg man, Boxgrove man)

Homo sapiens (modern humans)

Homo neanderthalensis (Neanderthal man)

X = species became extinct

The human evolutionary tree is still far from complete: the picture is constantly changing as new fossil evidence comes to light. Palaeoanthropologists are still debating many of the relationships shown on this chart (indicated by the broken lines).

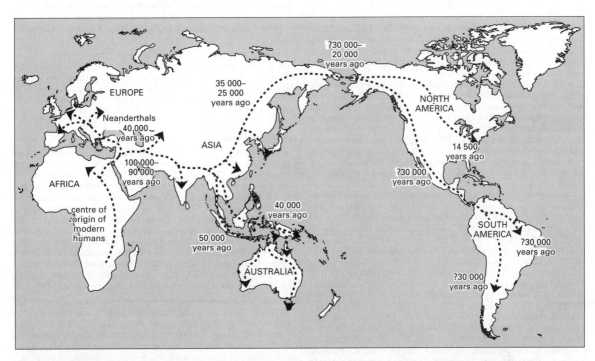

Evidence from DNA studies of different populations indicates that modern humans (*Homo sapiens*) probably evolved in Africa 150 000–100 000 years ago and subsequently spread from there to other parts of the world. The map shows possible routes of dispersal of these early humans. The dates are based on the ages of existing populations, which have been calculated from the number of mutations in each population and a knowledge of the rate at which mutations occur.

thought by many authorities to be the earliest direct ancestor of modern humans. *H. heidelbergensis* evolved around 600 000 years ago and includes remains from Europe (Heidelberg man and Boxgrove man) and Africa. ▷Neanderthal man also belongs to the genus *Homo*, as does ▷Cro-Magnon man, who was probably an early form of *Homo sapiens*; they probably evolved from *H. heidelbergensis* around 100 000 years ago. ▷*See also* Australopithecus.

● **homoiothermy** ▶ The condition of being warm-blooded, i.e. of maintaining a fairly constant body temperature by physiological mechanisms. Birds and mammals are warm-blooded: in cold climates body heat is conserved and also produced by muscle activity, such as shivering, while in hot weather body heat is lost by sweating and panting. *Compare* poikilothermy.

● **homosexuality** ▶ Sexual attraction or relations between persons of the same sex. It is known as lesbianism when the persons involved are females. Homosexuality is an ancient and widespread phenomenon that can involve moral stigma and even punishment, as in the Judaeo-Christian tradition, but just as often is regarded as neither abnormal nor immoral, as in ancient Greece. Related phenomena are bisexuality (when an individual is attracted by people of both sexes) and ▷transvestism. Liberalization of attitudes in the UK had largely occurred by the time of the ▷Wolfenden Report (1957), which recommended that homosexual acts between two consenting adults in private should not be illegal; this is now the case in all EU countries. In 1994 the age of consent for homosexual men in the UK was lowered from 21 to 18, and in 2000 the age of consent for both homosexuals and heterosexuals was equalized at 16, despite opposition from the House of Lords. Since the late 1960s, such movements as Gay Liberation and Outrage have sought to counter discrimination against homosexuals in a predominantly heterosexual society.

● **Homs** ▶ (Arabic name: Hims) 34 44N 36 43E A town in Syria, on the River Orontes close to the border with N Lebanon. There is a large Crusader fortress here, and Homs is an important trading and industrial town. Population (1994 est): 644 204.

● **Honan** ▷*See* Henan.

● **Honduras, Republic of** ▶ A country in Central America, with a N coastline on the Caribbean Sea and a short S one on the Pacific Ocean. Narrow coastal plains rise to mountainous country, dissected by river valleys. The majority of the population is of mixed Indian and Spanish descent.
Economy: mainly agricultural, the chief crops being bananas and coffee (the principal exports). Almost half the land is forested, with valuable hardwoods in the NE and pine in the interior. Fishing is important, especially shrimps for export. The considerable mineral resources, some as yet unexploited, include gold, silver, lead, tin and zinc, and mercury. Hydroelectricity is being developed. Economic development has been set back many years by the hurricane, flooding, and mudslides of 1998, which destroyed about 75% of agricultural produce and 65% of national infrastructure. There is a very large external debt.
History: the area was a centre of Mayan culture from the 4th to the 9th centuries AD and was later occupied by the Lenca Indians. Discovered by Columbus in 1502, it became part of the Spanish captaincy general of Guatemala. It gained independence from Spain in 1821 and then formed part of the Central American Federation (1823–38). For the next 145 years Honduras was ruled by a series of military dictators with only brief periods of civilian rule. The country has suffered much internal unrest as well as a long conflict with Guatemala and, more recently, with El Salvador: in 1969 war broke out following El Salvador's defeat of Honduras in a World Cup football match. In 1972 a former (1966–71) president, Gen Oswaldo López, seized power in a coup but was overthrown in 1975. There was a further coup in 1978. Military rule ended in 1982, when Dr Roberto Suazo Córdova became president. In 1988 3000 US troops arrived to stem Nicaraguan incursions. Honduras suffered its worst natural disaster of modern times in November 1998, when torrential rains in the wake of Hurricane Mitch caused floods and mudslides across the whole country, devastating Tegucigalpa and leaving some 8000 dead and 250 000 homeless. Honduras is a member of the OAS and the Organization of Central American States.

Republic of Honduras

Head of state	President Ricardo Maduro
Official language	Spanish
Official currency	lempira of 100 centavos
Area	112 088 sq km (43 227 sq mi)
Population (2001 est)	6 626 000
Capital	Tegucigalpa
Main ports	Amapala on the Pacific and La Ceiba on the Atlantic

● **Honecker, Erich** ▶ (1912–94) East German statesman; first secretary of the Socialist Unity Party (1971–89). After his release from Nazi imprisonment, Honecker led a German youth group (1946–1955). From 1958 to 1971 he was responsible for security matters. His refusal to agree to liberal reforms led to his resignation as head of state and party leader (1989) and he went into exile in the Soviet Union. In 1992 he was extradited to Germany to face charges over shootings at the Berlin Wall. He was released by the courts on grounds of ill health (1993) and went to live in Chile.

● **Honegger, Arthur** ▶ (1892–1955) French composer, born in Switzerland. He was a pupil of Widor and d'Indy and one of Les ▷Six. His compositions include five symphonies, the stage works *King David* (1921) and *Joan of Arc at the Stake* (1934–35), chamber music, and piano music.

● **honesty** ▶ A herbaceous plant of the European genus *Lunaria* (3 species). Up to 1 m high, it is often grown in gardens for its decorative disc-shaped papery seed heads. *L. annua* has white to purple flowers while *L. variegata* has crimson flowers and variegated foliage. Family: *Cruciferae*.

● **honey** ▶ A sweet thick yellow syrup collected from the honeycomb of bee hives. Bees suck nectar from flowers and empty it into the cells of their hives, where they convert the sugar it contains from sucrose into dextrose and laevulose. Honey from heather is golden and that from white clover is greenish-white. It is extracted by heating the honeycomb. It consists of about 70% sugars, 18% water, and small amounts of minerals, pollen, and wax. Honey was used for embalming in ancient Egypt and was a favourite food of the ancient Greeks. Mildly antiseptic due to its acidity, it has been used medicinally.

● **honey ant** ▶ An ▷ant belonging to subfamilies (*Camponotinae* or *Dolichoderinae*) occurring in North America, Africa, Australia, and New Guinea. Certain members of the colony, called repletes, gorge themselves with honeydew (mainly from aphids and scale insects) gathered by other workers. They then hang from the ceiling of their underground chamber and regurgitate this food store when stimulated by the other ants.

● **honey badger** ▷*See* ratel.

● **honeybee** ▶ A social ▷bee, *Apis mellifera*, also called hive bee. Native to Europe, it is reared worldwide for its ▷honey and ▷beeswax. Honeybees have large colonies with 50 000–80 000 workers during the summer and a well-defined caste system. Workers attend to nest building, food gathering, and brood care; they use dances to communicate the location of food sources to other colony members. The queen lays her eggs in wax chambers (cells). Developing drones and workers are fed on protein-rich "royal jelly" for a few days and then changed to a diet of pollen and honey. Larvae hatching from fertilized eggs and fed on royal jelly throughout their development become queens, rather than workers. New colonies are formed by a swarm of workers led by the old queen (*compare* bumblebee); a young queen continues the established colony. Family: *Apidae*.

● **honeycreeper** ▶ A songbird belonging to a family (*Drepanididae*; 22 species) restricted to the Hawaiian Islands, where they appear to have evolved from a single species. Honeycreepers are of two types: nectar feeders with colourful plumage and long slender curved bills and drab-green seed eaters with short bills. Some honeycreepers face extinction due to man's destruction of their specialized habitats.

● **honeyeater** ▶ An arboreal songbird belonging to a family (*Meliphagidae*; 160 species) occurring chiefly in SE Asia and Australasia. They are 10 to 35 cm long and have a drab plumage with wattles or naked patches on the face. The slender bill is down-curved and the long extensible tongue has a central trough, through which nectar is drunk, and a brushlike tip for collecting pollen and small insects.

● **honey guide** ▶ An arboreal bird belonging to a tropical Old World family (*Indicatoridae*; 12 species). Honey guides are 11.5–20 cm long and dull-brown, grey, or greenish in colour. They feed mainly on bees and wasps and certain species guide ratels or men to bees' nests by chattering and flying in the direction of the nest; the mammal robs the nest and the bird feeds on the remains. Order: *Piciformes* (woodpeckers, etc.).

● **honey locust** ▶ A tree of the genus *Gleditschia* (11 species), occurring in America, Africa, and Asia. The American species *G. triacanthos* is planted for ornament in Europe. It has stout thorns, compound leaves with paired leaflets, and small green flowers producing long pods. Family: ▷*Leguminosae*.

● **honey mouse** ▶ A small marsupial, *Tarsipes spenserae*, of SW Australia, also called honey possum or phalanger. It has a grey-brown body (70–85 mm long) with three dark stripes along the back; a long snout; and a very long prehensile tail (88–100 mm). It climbs shrubs to extract nectar from the flowers, using its long bristly tongue. Family: *Phalangeridae*.

● **honeysuckle** ▶ A shrub or twining plant of the genus *Lonicera* (100 species). The common European honeysuckle (*L. periclymenum*), also called woodbine, is a trailing shrub with clusters of tubular yellowish flowers. Some species are cultivated as ornamentals, including the fragrant climbing honeysuckle (*L. japonica*). Family: *Caprifoliaceae*.

● **Hong Kong** ▶ A special administrative region of S China, formerly (until 1 July, 1997) a British crown colony. It consists of the island of Hong Kong, the mainland peninsula of Jiulong, the New Territories, and Stonecutters Island. Much of the land is steep and barren. The majority of the population is Chinese.
Economy: owing to its strategic position and natural harbour, it is an important entrepôt and banking centre. Much of China's foreign trade passes through Hong Kong. The export of manufactured goods has become increasingly important following industrial expansion since World War II and the textile and clothing industry (developed by immigrants from Shanghai) accounts for over half the exports. Electronics and plastics are also important and there is some heavy industry, such as shipbuilding and repair and iron and steel manufacture. Agricultural land is scarce and the reclamation of land from the sea has long been important in the colony's history. Tourism is a major source of revenue. A new airport, the world's largest, opened in 1998.
History: the island was ceded to Britain by China after the first Opium War (1842) and Kowloon (Jiulong) was added in 1860. In 1898 the New Territories were granted on a 99-year lease. Hong Kong was occupied by the Japanese during World War II. In 1984, a joint declaration of the British and Chinese governments agreed that Hong Kong should become a special administrative region of China in 1997, with its social and economic systems remaining unchanged for at least 50 years. The number of Hong Kong residents permitted to emigrate to the UK was set at 50 000 in 1990. During the 1980s nearly 50 000 Vietnamese refugees claimed political asylum in Hong Kong, causing enormous administrative problems; the first forced repatriations took place in 1989. Direct elections to the legislative council were held for the first time in 1991. In 1992 Chris Patten was appointed governor to oversee the transition to Chinese rule. Despite British assurances, in 1996 the legislative council was replaced by an appointed body dominated by pro-China elements. Tung Chee-hwa was appointed chief executive. Both English and Cantonese are widely spoken. Official currency: Hong Kong dollar of 100 cents. Area: 1031 sq km (398 sq mi). Population (1997 est): 6 491 000. Administrative centre and main port: Victoria.

● **Hong-wu** ▶ (*or* Hung-wu; 1328–98) The title of Chu Yuan-zhang (*or* Chu Yüan-chang), who became the first emperor (1368–98) of the Ming dynasty. A monk, he became a rebel leader and outstanding military tactician, ousting the Yuan dynasty and declaring himself emperor. He made Nanjing his capital and by 1382 he had united China.

● **Hong Xiu Quan** ▶ (*or* Hung Hsiu-ch'uan; 1814–64) Chinese religious leader and revolutionary. After failing to get a place in the civil service, he espoused a strongly political Protestant Christianity, declaring himself God's second son and saviour of China. He led the ▷Taiping Rebellion, but committed suicide in Nanjing shortly before it fell.

● **Honolulu** ▶ 21 19N 157 50W A city in the USA, the capital of Hawaii on SE Oahu in the central Pacific Ocean. Famed for its beauty, it is the economic centre of the islands and a transpacific route stop. It is the site of three universities and of Iolani Palace, the former royal residence. ▷Pearl Harbor is still an important naval base. Population (1996 est): 423 475.

● **Honorius II** ▶ (Lamberto Scannabecchi; d. 1130) Pope (1124–30). An architect of the Concordat of Worms, which ended the ▷investiture controversy (1122), he re-established relations between the papacy and Empire, supporting the claims of Lothair II against Conrad III. Fearing the growing strength of the Normans under Roger II in Sicily, he led an army against him and was defeated and forced to accept Roger as Duke of Apulia.

● **honours list** ▶ A list of awards given to men and women who have distinguished themselves in the service of the UK. The lists are compiled by the prime minister, approved by the sovereign, and published twice each year (on New Year's Day and the sovereign's official birthday). Senior civil servants, prominent politicians, high-ranking serving officers, and distinguished people in the arts, universities, and charities are traditionally given honours, which range from membership of the ▷Order of the British Empire to the ranks of the ▷peerage (usually now life peerages).

● **Honshu** ▶ The largest of the four main islands of Japan, situated between the Pacific Ocean and the Sea of Japan. It is now linked to Hokkaido by the 54 km (33.5 mi) long Seikan tunnel (1985), the longest rail tunnel in the world, and to Shikoku by the 3.91 km (2.43 mi) long Akashi Kaikyo Bridge (1998), the world's longest suspension bridge. It is mountainous, volcanic, and prone to earthquakes, with a great difference in climate between the subtropical S and the cooler N. The historic centre of Japan, it has been the site of its capital since earliest times. Most of Japan's major ports and cities are here, although agriculture is also very important; rice, fruit, cotton, and tea are grown. Mineral wealth includes oil, zinc, and copper. The traditional industry is silk but the many modern industries include shipbuilding, iron and steel, chemicals, and textiles. Area: 230 448 sq km (88 976 sq mi). Population (1995): 100 995 000. Chief town: Tokyo.

● **Honthorst, Gerrit von** ▶ (1590–1656) Dutch painter. Working in Rome (c. 1610–1620), Utrecht, London (1628), and The Hague, he painted biblical, mythological, and everyday scenes influenced by ▷Caravaggio. His portraits include one of Charles I and Henrietta Maria (Hampton Court).

● **Hooch, Pieter de** ▶ (1629–c. 1684) Dutch painter, born in Rotterdam. Working in Delft, Leiden, and Amsterdam, he excelled in small paintings, such as *The Pantry* (Rijksmuseum, Amsterdam), depicting household tasks in courtyards or dark interiors that open into sunlit rooms.

● **Hood, Samuel, 1st Viscount** ▶ (1724–1816) British admiral, who achieved eminence in the American Revolution, when he defeated the French off Dominica (1782). In the French Revolutionary Wars he captured Toulon (1793) and destroyed the defences of Corsica (1794).

● **Hood, Thomas** ▶ (1799–1845) British poet. He became a friend of ▷Hazlitt and Charles ▷Lamb through his work for various periodicals. He followed his successful *Odes and Addresses* (1825) with further volumes of humorous verse, and also wrote serious poems of social and political protest, such as *The Song of the Shirt* (1843).

● **hooded crow** ▶ A crow, *Corvus corone cornix*, identical to the ▷carrion crow except for its grey back and underparts. It is found in N and E Europe, where the carrion crow does not occur, but in the narrow zone where the two races overlap they hybridize, producing birds of mixed coloration.

● **hooded seal** ▶ A ▷seal, *Cystophora cristata*, of deep Arctic waters, also called bladdernose, or crested seal. About 3 m long, pale grey with dark blotches, hooded seals have a red inflatable bladder on top of the nose. In males the inflated bladder may be used to frighten enemies. Hooded seals are solitary except when breeding. Family: *Phocidae*.

● **Hooft, Pieter Corneliszoon** ▶ (1581–1647) Dutch poet and historian, who travelled in France and Italy, where he was influenced by Renaissance art and literature. He gathered a circle of writers, artists, and musicians at the castle at Muiden, of which he was made steward in 1609. Hooft expressed his humanistic and pacifist philosophy in the pastoral play *Granida* (1605), while his love poetry echoed that of Petrarch. His history of the Dutch revolt against Spain, *Nederlandsche Historien* (1628–47), remained a model of Dutch prose for over 200 years.

● **Hooghly, River** ▶ (R. Hoogli *or* R. Hugli) A river in India, rising in West Bengal. The W stream of the Ganges delta, it flows S through Calcutta to the Bay of Bengal. Length: 233 km (145 mi).

Robert Hooke ▶ An unsigned etching of the scientist demonstrating his "dark room" (for copying landscapes) to the Royal Society, London, in 1694.

● **Hooke, Robert** ▶ (1635–1703) British physicist and instrument maker, who became professor of geometry at Gresham College, London, in 1665. In 1660 he discovered ▷Hooke's law. His work on springs led him into horology and he claimed to have invented the hair spring (also claimed by ▷Huygens). He was one of the first scientists to examine vegetable matter with a microscope, in 1667 discovering the existence of cells in cork. Many of his microscope studies were published in *Micrographia* (1665). Appointed a city surveyor after the Fire of London, he designed several buildings, including the College of Physicians.

● **Hooker, Richard** ▶ (c. 1554–1600) English churchman and theologian. Educated at Oxford, becoming a Fellow of Corpus Christi College, and later a parish priest, Hooker emerged as the chief apologist of his day of Anglican doctrine. His most famous work, *On the Laws of Ecclesiastical Polity* (from 1594), strongly influenced Anglican theology and the theory of both church and state government.

● **Hooker, Sir William Jackson** ▶ (1785–1865) British botanist and first director of Kew Gardens. Under his directorship (1841–65) Kew became a world centre for the study of plants. His son **Sir Joseph Dalton Hooker** (1817–1911) achieved equal distinction as a botanist. He travelled widely, making important contributions to plant geography and providing supporting evidence for Darwin's theories of evolution. His many works include a world flora, *Genera plantara* (3 vols, 1862–83), written with George Bentham (1800–84). Hooker succeeded his father as director of Kew Gardens (1865–85) and was president of the Royal Society (1872–77).

● **Hooke's law** ▶ For an elastic body, the ▷stress is directly proportional to the ▷strain. For example, if a heavy mass is hung from a wire, the fractional extension is directly proportional to the mass. The law applies only up to the elastic limit (*see* elasticity). Named after its discoverer Sir Robert ▷Hooke, who stated it in the form *ut tensio, sic vis*.

● **Hook of Holland** ▶ (Dutch name: Hoek van Holland) 51 59N 4 07E A port in the SW Netherlands, in South Holland province at the North Sea end of the Nieuwe Waterweg (New Waterway). A ferry service operates from here to Harwich, England.

● **hookworm** ▶ A parasitic ▷nematode worm inhabiting the intestine of animals and man. About 1 cm long, hookworms attach themselves to the gut lining and feed by sucking blood and body fluids. The two main species infecting humans are *Necator americanus*, of the southern USA and Africa, and the Eurasian *Ancylostoma duodenale*. Both cause lowered resistance to disease, anaemia, and malnutrition. The larvae enter the body through the skin, usually the feet, and migrate to the intestine. Infection can be prevented by wearing shoes and improving sanitation.

● **hoopoe** ▶ A bird, *Upupa epops*, of S Eurasia and Africa. 28 cm long, it has a pink-brown plumage with black and white barred wings, a long tail, and a long black-tipped crest. It feeds on insects and larvae with its long downcurved bill. It is the only member of its family (*Upupidae*). Order: *Coraciiformes* (hornbills, kingfishers, etc.).

● **Hoorne, Filips van Montmorency, Graaf van** ▷*See* Horn, Filips van Montmorency, Graaf van.

● **Hoover, Herbert (Clark)** ▶ (1874–1964) US statesman; Republican president (1929–33). As secretary of commerce (1921–29) he was chairman of commissions that initiated construction of the Hoover Dam (named after him) and the St Lawrence Seaway. Although chief of Allied World War I programmes for relief of famine, Hoover's belief in individual freedom led him to reject federal relief for urban unemployment during the Depression and he was defeated in the 1932 election by F. D. Roosevelt.

● **Hoover, J(ohn) Edgar** ▶ (1895–1972) US lawyer, director of the Federal Bureau of Investigation (FBI) from 1924 to 1972. He fought the gangsters of the 1930s with his reformed FBI and established the first fingerprint file and crime-detection laboratory. Since his death it has been alleged that he abused his powers to indulge in political intrigue.

● **hop** ▶ A perennial climbing herb, *Humulus lupus*. Native to Eurasia, where it grows to a length of 3–6 m in hedges and thickets, it is widely cultivated for its pale yellow-green female flowers ("cones"), which are used in brewing to flavour beer. The male flowers are smaller. The young shoots have been eaten as a vegetable. Family: *Cannabiaceae*.

● **Hope, Anthony** ▶ (Sir Anthony Hope Hawkins; 1863–1933) British novelist. He gave up careers in law and politics after the immediate success of *The Prisoner of Zenda* (1894), a tale of adventure set in the imaginary country of Ruritania. He wrote many other successful romances of this kind.

● **Hope, Bob** ▶ (Leslie Townes Hope; 1903–) US comedian, born in Britain. He starred in many popular films during the 1940s, including *Road to Zanzibar* (1941) and other "Road" films in which he partnered Bing ▷Crosby. He performed for US troops both in and after World War II; he has also acted as compère of the Academy Award presentations. Hope was awarded an honorary British knighthood in 1998.

● **Hopeh** ▶ (*or* Ho-pei) ▷*See* Hebei.

● **hop-hornbeam** ▶ A tree of the N temperate genus *Ostrya* (7 species). Related to hornbeams, they have hard wood, furrowed bark, flowers in catkins, and conelike fruits resembling those of the hop. The European hop-hornbeam (*O. carpinifolia*) may grow to a height of over 20 m. Family: *Corylaceae*. ▷*See also* ironwood.

● **Hopi** ▶ North American Indians of NE Arizona whose language belongs to the Uto-Aztecan family (*see* Aztec-Tanoan languages). They live in stone and adobe houses forming small towns built on rocky plateaus (mesas). They are peaceful cultivators and sheep farmers, much given to religious ceremonial. There are about 6000 now living. ▷*See also* Pueblo Indians.

● **Hopkins, Sir Anthony** ▶ (1937–) Welsh actor. After his London debut in *Julius Caesar* (1964) he appeared in many Shakespearean roles. His films include *The Elephant Man* (1980), *The Silence of the Lambs*

(1991), *Howards End* (1992), *The Remains of the Day* (1993), *Shadowlands* (1994), *Nixon* (1995), and *Hannibal* (2001).

● **Hopkins, Sir Frederick Gowland** ► (1861–1947) British biochemist, who discovered that certain substances—now known as ▷vitamins—are essential in the diet in trace amounts. He also showed that some amino acids (called essential amino acids) cannot be manufactured by certain animals. He shared a Nobel Prize (1929) with ▷Eijkman and was president of the Royal Society (1930–35).

● **Hopkins, Gerard Manley** ► (1844–89) British poet. He was converted to Roman Catholicism in 1866 and ordained as a Jesuit priest in 1877. In verse of daring originality he rejected conventional metres in favour of a flexible "sprung rhythm." "The Wreck of the Deutschland" and "The Windhover" are among his best-known poems. His poetry, which deeply influenced 20th-century verse, was published by his friend Robert ▷Bridges.

● **Hopkins, Harry (Lloyd)** ► (1890–1946) US administrator. His interest in social welfare projects culminated in his administration of ▷New Deal relief programmes during the Depression. As aide to President Roosevelt during World War II he headed the US lend-lease programme (*see* Lend-Lease Act).

● **Hopkinson, John** ► (1849–98) British electrical engineer, who devised the three-phase system for the transmission of electricity. He was killed mountaineering in the Alps.

● **Hoppner, John** ► (1758–1810) British portrait painter, of German descent. He was rumoured to be the illegitimate son of George III, one of his chief patrons. His portraits of famous contemporaries, e.g. Nelson and Wellington, were strongly influenced by Reynolds.

● **Horace** ► (Quintus Horatius Flaccus; 65–8 BC) Roman poet. He was the son of a freed slave. Although he was reduced to poverty after fighting for Brutus in the Civil War, he became a leading poet under the emperor Augustus and acquired a farm near Rome, celebrated in his poetry. His *Odes*, *Satires*, and verse *Epistles* portray contemporary Roman society and express his own humane personality.

● **Horae** ► Greek goddesses of the seasons. They were originally three in number, the daughters of Zeus and Themis, and associated with the concepts of order, justice, and peace. They later became the four seasons, daughters of Helios and Selene (the sun and moon).

● **Horatii and Curiatii** ► In Roman legend, two sets of three brothers who fought on opposing sides in the war between Rome and Alba in the reign of Tullus Hostilius, legendary king of Rome. The single survivor, Horatius, killed his grief-stricken sister on finding she had been engaged to one of the Curiatii, but was acquitted after appealing to the people of Rome.

● **Hordern, Sir Michael (Murray)** ► (1911–95) British actor. He acted in a wide range of plays—including Ibsen's *Ghosts*, Pinter's *The Collection*, Stoppard's *Jumpers*, and Shakespeare—and films, often portraying eccentrics.

● **Hore-Belisha, (Isaac) Leslie, 1st Baron** ► (1893–1957) British politician. A National Liberal, he was minister of transport (1934–37), introducing belisha beacons to mark pedestrian crossings. As secretary for war (1937–40) he introduced conscription in 1939. His unpopularity with the army establishment brought about his dismissal.

● **horehound** ► (or hoarhound) Either of two Eurasian perennial herbs growing in waste places and waysides. White horehound (*Marrubium vulgare*) reaches a height of 3 m and has white flowers while black horehound (*Balleta nigra*) has purple flowers and a disagreeable odour. Both have been used medicinally. Family: ▷Labiatae.

● **hormone** ► A substance that is secreted into the blood in small quantities to cause a response in a specific target organ or tissue of the body. Hormones are produced and secreted by ▷endocrine glands and by specialized nerve cells (*see* neurohormone) under the control of the nervous system or in response to changes in the chemical composition of the blood. Hormones regulate short-term physiological processes, such as digestion, and long-term changes, such as those associated with growth and reproduction; they also help to maintain a constant internal environment in the body (*see* homeostasis). The first demonstration of hormone activity was made in 1905, by ▷Bayliss and Starling, working with the digestive hormone secretin. Important hormones include ▷ACTH, ▷gonadotrophin, ▷growth hormone, and ▷prolactin (secreted by the pituitary); ▷corticosteroids, ▷aldosterone, and ▷adrenaline (from the adrenal glands); ▷androgens and ▷oestrogens (from the sex glands); thyroid hormone (from the ▷thyroid gland); ▷insulin and ▷glucagon (from the pancreas). Most hormones are proteins or steroids. The study of hormones—and the diseases caused by their under- or over-production—is endocrinology. Substances that regulate plant growth (▷auxins, ▷gibberellins, ▷cytokinins, etc.) are sometimes called plant hormones.

● **hormone replacement therapy** ► (HRT) Oestrogenic hormones administered to women in small doses, in tablets, implants, or skin patches or gels, to relieve symptoms of the menopause, such as vaginal dryness and hot flushes, and to prevent ▷osteoporosis. It is also given when the menopause is induced, as by surgical removal of the ovaries. Oestrogens cause thickening of the lining of the uterus, which may lead to cancer. To prevent this, HRT is taken in cycles with a progestogen, which causes periodic shedding of the lining.

● **Horn, Filips van Montmorency, Graaf van** ► (or Hoorne; ?1524–68) Flemish statesman and admiral, who played a leading part in the resistance to Philip II's religious policies in the Netherlands. He served his Spanish rulers in military, naval, and administrative capacities, becoming stadholder (chief magistrate) of Gelder and Zutphen in 1555. However, he joined ▷Egmont and William the Silent in resigning from the state council (1565) and demanding the abolition of the Inquisition. He was executed for treason and heresy by the Duke of ▷Alba. ▷*See also* Revolt of the Netherlands.

● **hornbeam** ► A tree of the genus *Carpinus* (26 species), of N temperate regions. The common Eurasian hornbeam (*C. betulus*) grows to a height of 30 m in the wild (cultivated trees are up to 19 m tall); it has smooth grey bark, oval pointed leaves with prominent veins, and small nuts with conspicuous winged bracts. It is planted for ornament and for its hard fine-grained timber. Family: *Corylaceae*.

● **hornbill** ► A bird belonging to a family (*Bucerotidae*; 45 species) occurring in Old World tropical regions. 38–150 cm long, hornbills are characterized by a huge bill, often bearing a large bony "helmet," and feed on fruit and berries. Most hornbills nest in treeholes in which the female imprisons herself by plastering the entrance with mud, leaving only a small hole through which the male feeds her, until the young hatch. Order: *Coraciiformes* (kingfishers, etc.).

● **hornblende** ► A mineral of the ▷amphibole group, which occurs widely in igneous and metamorphic rocks. It consists mainly of silicates of sodium, calcium, magnesium, and iron. It is black or greenish black and occurs in crystalline or massive form. Hornblende schist is a rock consisting mainly of orientated hornblende crystals.

● **Hornby, Nick** ► (1958–) British writer. His first book, the memoir *Fever Pitch* (1992; filmed 1997), was followed by the best-selling novels *High Fidelity* (1995; filmed 1999), *About a Boy* (1998; filmed 2002), and *How To Be Good* (2001). His books are mainly concerned with the emotional lives of modern men.

● **horned lizard** ▷*See* horned toad.

● **horned poppy** ► One of two herbs belonging to the ▷poppy family and having hornlike seed pods. The perennial or biennial yellow horned poppy (*Glaucium flavum*) of Eurasia grows to 90 cm on seashores. The red horned poppy (*G. corniculatus*) is an annual of the Mediterranean region.

● **horned toad** ► A desert-dwelling lizard, also called horned lizard, belonging to the genus *Phrynosoma*, occurring in North and Central America and characterized by hornlike spines on its head. 8–13 cm long, they have a flattened oval body with a fringe of scales along the sides and hide by wriggling sideways until buried in sand. In defence, they may squirt blood from their eyes. Family: *Iguanidae*.

● **horned viper** ► A mildly venomous desert ▷viper, *Cerastes cornutus*, that occurs in Africa and the Middle East and has a hornlike scale over each eye. Up to 60 cm long, it has a broad head and is pale with dark spots and bars.

● **hornet** ► A social ▷wasp, *Vespa crabro*, that is common throughout Europe and has spread to North America and elsewhere. 35 mm long, it is tawny-yellow with brown markings and nests in hollow trees. It feeds chiefly on insects, nectar, and fruit juices and its painful sting can be dangerous to man. Members of the genera *Dolichorespula*, *Paravespula*, and *Vespula* may also be known as hornets.

● **hornpipe** ▶ A traditional British dance, originally accompanied by a wooden pipe. It was popular with sailors as it requires no partners and little space. Like the jigs and reels to which it is related, it was often danced in clogs.

● **horntail** ▶ A ▷wasp, also called wood wasp, belonging to the family *Siricidae* (about 60 species), having a hornlike projection on its abdomen. Horntails are usually brown, blue, or black with yellow bands and can be up to 37.5 mm long. The females have strong ovipositors to insert their eggs into hardwood trees, particularly elm, beech, and maple, in which the larvae develop.

● **hornwort** ▶ **1.** A plant of the widely distributed genus *Ceratophyllum* (3 species), which grows submerged in ponds and streams. *C. demersum* is rootless, with a stem 20–100 cm long and simple forked leaves, 1–2 cm long. The small flowers produce a three-spined nutlike fruit. Family: *Ceratophyllaceae*. **2.** (*or* horned liverwort) A nonvascular plant of the phylum *Anthocerophyta* (or class *Anthocerotae*; about 100 species), formerly classified as a ▷liverwort. Distributed worldwide, hornworts consist of a flat leaflike gamete-producing plant from which arises a long-lived spikelike spore-producing structure, 2–5 cm long. ▷*See also* bryophytes.

● **horoscope** ▷*See* astrology.

● **Horowitz, Vladimir** ▶ (1904–89) Russian pianist. He settled in the USA in 1940. Horowitz excelled in Russian music and in his own transcriptions.

● **horse** ▶ A hoofed mammal, *Equus caballus*, domesticated worldwide for pack and draught work, riding, and sport (*see* equestrianism). The earliest horse is believed to have been ▷eohippus, which is thought to have originated in North America and spread to Asia. Successive larger forms evolved, in which the central toe became enlarged as the hoof and the remaining toes became smaller and fewer (*see* Hipparion). These horses developed from forest browsers to become grazing animals of the plains with well-developed senses to detect predators.

The many breeds of modern horse—thought to have evolved from several different Asian and European forms, including ▷Przewalski's horse and the ▷tarpan—are commonly grouped into ponies, light horses, and draught horses. They range in size from the tiny ▷Falabella to the massive ▷Shire horse and are measured in hands (1 hand = 4 in = 10.16 cm) to the top of the shoulders (the withers). According to the breed, horses mature at 3½–5 years of age and the lifespan is usually 20–35 years. Mares have a gestation period of 11 months, producing usually a single foal. Except for breeding stallions, males are usually castrated, being called geldings. Horses belong to the family *Equidae*, which also includes ▷asses and ▷zebras.

● **horse chestnut** ▶ A broad spreading □tree, *Aesculus hippocastanum*, native to SE Europe and widely planted as an ornamental. It grows to a height of 25 m, producing large compound leaves and erect clusters of white flowers; the green spiny fruits ripen to release large brown shiny seeds (conkers). The red horse chestnut (*A × carnea*) is similar but has red flowers. It is a hybrid between the horse chestnut and *A. pavia*. Family: *Hippocastanaceae*.

● **horse fly** ▶ A stout-bodied fly of the genus *Tabanus* (the term is also used loosely for the other genera—*Chrysops* (deerflies) and *Haematopota* (cleg flies)—of the family *Tabanidae*; 2500 species). Male horse flies feed on nectar but the females are bloodsuckers and inflict painful bites on man, horses, cattle, etc. A few species transmit diseases, such as tularemia and anthrax. The carnivorous larvae live in damp soil.

● **horsehair worm** ▶ A long thin hairlike aquatic invertebrate of the phylum *Nematomorpha* (about 80 species), found mostly in fresh water. They range in length from 1–100 cm, with a diameter of only 0.3–2 mm. Their larvae are parasitic in beetles, crickets, and grasshoppers.

● **horse latitudes** ▶ Two belts of high pressure and calm in the oceans on either side of the equator (30°N and 30°S). The name is said to refer to the jettisoning of horses when ships travelling from Europe to the Americas were becalmed.

● **horsepower** ▶ (hp) A unit of power equal to 550 foot-pounds per second. It was devised by James ▷Watt, who found that a strong horse could raise a weight of 150 pounds 4 feet in 1 second. ▷*See also* watt.

● **horse racing** ▶ A form of contest in which horses are ridden or driven. Its three main forms are ▷flat racing, ▷steeplechase and hur-

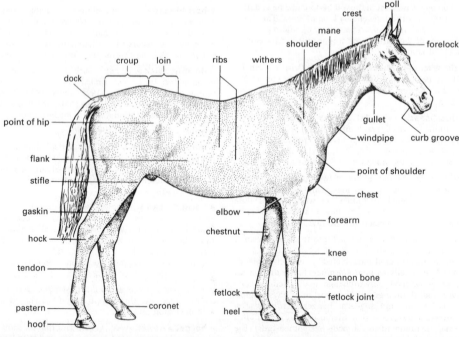

horse ▶ The points of a horse.

dling (known collectively in England as National Hunt racing), and ▷harness racing.

● **horseradish** ▶ A perennial herb, *Armoracia rusticana*, probably native to SE Europe and W Asia and widely cultivated. Growing to a height of 125 cm, it has thick fleshy pungent roots from which horseradish sauce is made and it bears small white flowers. Family: *Cruciferae*.

● **horseshoe bat** ▶ An insect-eating ▷bat belonging to the genus *Rhinolophus* (74 species), found in temperate and tropical regions of the Old World. Horseshoe bats are named after the fleshy structure surrounding the nostrils, which focuses the ultrasonic signals that the bat emits when navigating. They also have large ears for receiving the echoes. Family: *Rhinolophidae*.

● **horseshoe crab** ▶ A large nocturnal marine ▷arthropod (up to 50 cm long), also called king crab, belonging to the class *Merostomata* (4 species), most members of which are now extinct. There are three living genera, found in shallow seas: *Limulus* off the E coast of North America and *Trachypheus* and *Carcinoscorpinus* in the Indo-Pacific region. They have a hinged body covered by a brown horseshoe-shaped carapace and a long tail spine. They can swim but usually burrow in sand, feeding on worms and thin-shelled molluscs.

● **horsetail** ▶ A rushlike perennial flowerless plant, also called scouring rush, belonging to the only living genus (*Equisetum*; about 30 species) of the phylum or division *Sphenophyta* (which includes such giant extinct forms as ▷*Calamites*). Horsetails grow in moist soils everywhere except Australasia. Their creeping rhizomes give rise to aerial jointed stems of two kinds—green sterile stems, often branched in whorls, and fertile stems, bearing cone-shaped clusters of spore capsules. The leaves are sheaths encircling each stem joint. Tropical horsetails grow to a height of 6 m, but temperate species are smaller. They are used in folk medicine.

● **horse trials** ▶ (*or* eventing) Contests to test a horse's abilities and the rider's skill. The three-day event is an Olympic sport involving on successive days: ▷dressage; speed, endurance, and jumping tests on ▷steeplechase and cross-country courses; and ▷showjumping.

● **Horsham** ▶ 51 04N 0 21W A market town in SE England, in West Sussex. Shelley's birthplace and Christ's Hospital School are both nearby. Economic activities now include financial services (especially insurance) and high-tech electronics and engineering. Population (1998 est): 45 000.

● **horst** ▷*See* fault.

● **Horta, Victor** ▶ (1861–1947) Belgian architect. His early work, particularly the Hôtel Tassel (1892) and the Maison du Peuple (1896) in Brussels, are fine examples of ▷Art Nouveau. He later abandoned Art Nouveau for classicism.

● **Horthy de Nagybánya, Miklós** ▶ (1868–1957) Hungarian admiral and statesman. After the collapse of ▷Austria-Hungary (1919), he organized an army against Béla ▷Kun's communist government. Elected regent of Hungary in 1920, he preserved an independent constitutional system, despite alliance with Nazi Germany. When he attempted to surrender to Russia (1944) the Germans deposed him.

● **horticulture** ▶ The cultivation of vegetables (also known as market gardening) and fruit for food and of trees, shrubs, and other plants for ornament. Traditionally practised in small gardens and orchards, horticulture is now both a popular domestic pastime and an important commercial activity using large field and glasshouse acreages. Higher-yielding and more disease-resistant plant varieties, increased mechanization, the use of new cultivation techniques, such as ▷hydroponics, and the application of fertilizers and pesticides have all contributed to improved productivity and quality. Also, modern refrigeration, storage, and transport mean that many crops are now available throughout the year.

● **Horus** ▶ The Egyptian sun-god, usually portrayed as a falcon or with a falcon's head. He was the son of ▷Osiris and ▷Isis and avenged his father's death by killing ▷Set. The pharaohs were conceived as the incarnations of Horus as earthly ruler and added the god's name to their titles.

● **Hosea** ▶ (8th century BC) An Old Testament prophet of Israel. In the **Book of Hosea** the unfaithfulness of Israel to God is presented in terms of a spiritual adultery. This familial analogy was later developed in the Christian concepts of the Fatherhood of God and of the Church as the bride of Christ.

● **hospice movement** ▶ A movement that provides care for the terminally ill. Originally conceived by religious orders in medieval Europe, hospices specialize in easing the physical and mental distress of the patients and supporting their families. Most modern hospices are modelled on St Christopher's hospice, founded in London in 1967 by Dame Cicely ▷Saunders.

● **hospital** ▶ An institution providing diagnostic and therapeutic services for the sick on a residential (in-patient) or nonresidential (out-patient) basis. In the ancient world such medical services as existed were provided by religious organizations (e.g. the Temple of Aesculapius at Epidaurus in Greece). In Europe in the middle ages many institutions for the care of the sick were founded by monastic orders and later, during the Crusades, by orders of knighthood. St Bartholomew's (1123) and St Thomas's (1207) in London date back to this period. In the UK, during the 18th and 19th centuries, many new voluntary hospitals were founded by philanthropists and staffed by doctors who gave their services free. Municipal hospitals arose alongside the voluntary hospitals and were based on Elizabeth I's Poor Law relief system; they had paid medical staff. The two systems existed side by side until they were both nationalized by the National Health Service Act (1946). Since then all National Health hospitals have provided free services for all who want them, although some have a number of paybeds for those willing to pay a small charge for private rooms. Some NHS hospitals also make accommodation available to private patients, who pay the full cost of their stay to the hospital (in addition to medical fees paid to their doctor). Many hospitals now have units for day-case surgery, in which patients can undergo certain surgical procedures in a single day, without the need for an overnight stay. Teaching hospitals, of which there are at least one per health region, provide training for medical students. The National Health Service and Community Care Act (1990) enabled hospitals to become self-governing NHS trusts, which obtain their income by providing services to Health Authorities and fund-holding GPs. In 1999 the Labour government replaced this "internal market" in NHS services with a system under which the NHS trusts contract long-term service agreements with teams of doctors and nurses (primary care groups). Under the Private Finance Initiative, a scheme introduced in 1992, hospitals can now be built, financed, and operated by private interests who lease them to the NHS.

● **Hospitallers** ▶ (Order of the Hospital of St John of Jerusalem) A religious order of knighthood that began as a hospital for pilgrims to Jerusalem (c. 1070) and during the ▷Crusades took on a military function. Immensely wealthy, the Hospitallers were the great rivals of the ▷Templars. After the fall of Acre (1291) they established themselves in Cyprus, Rhodes, and finally Malta.

● **Hosta** ▶ A genus of perennial herbaceous plants (10 species), native to China and Japan and widely planted in gardens. They are grown chiefly for their foliage—the leaves are large (12–25 cm long), oval, and pointed and come in a variety of colours, often variegated—but they also produce attractive spikes of purplish or white funnel-shaped flowers. Family: ▷*Liliaceae*.

● **hot spring** ▶ A spring from which hot water flows continuously from within the earth's crust. Like ▷geysers, hot springs normally occur in areas that are (or have recently been) volcanically active. A distinction is sometimes made between hot springs (at a temperature above that of the human body) and *thermal springs* (above the mean annual temperature of the place where they emerge). The water is charged with minerals and deposits of travertine or sinter usually build up.

● **Hotspur** ▷*See* Percy, Sir Henry.

● **Hottentot** ▷*See* Khoisan.

● **Hottentot fig** ▶ A perennial herb, *Carpobrotus edulis*, native to South Africa but naturalized in many warm temperate regions. It has creeping woody stems, fleshy leaves, showy magenta or yellow flowers, and edible fruits. Family: *Aizoaceae*.

Harry Houdini ► Observers watching the magician carrying out a stunt in a hotel in New York in 1926. He is about to be submerged in a pool in which he apparently remained under water for 1½ hours.

● **Houdini, Harry** ► (Erich Weiss; 1874–1926) US magician. His ability to escape from handcuffs, straitjackets, and locked containers, even under water, gained him an international reputation. He wrote articles and books on magic and was interested in spiritualism.

● **Houdon, Jean Antoine** ► (1741–1828) French sculptor. Houdon's highly successful career began in Rome (1764–68) with his *St Bruno* (1767; Sta Maria degli Angeli, Rome). Although he made many religious and mythological sculptures, he was most popular as a portrait sculptor; famous sitters included Voltaire, Benjamin Franklin, Catherine the Great, Napoleon, and Washington.

● **Hounslow** ► A borough of W Greater London, bordering on the River Thames in the S. Created in 1965 from parts of Middlesex, it contains Hounslow Heath, a former haunt of highwaymen, and ▷Heathrow airport. Area 59 sq km (23 sq mi). Population (1999 est): 204 397.

● **Houphouët-Boigny, Félix** ► (1905–93) Côte d'Ivoire statesman; president (1960–93). In 1946 he founded the Côte d'Ivoire (then Ivory Coast) branch of the Rassemblement démocratique africain and was a member of the French Constituent Assembly (1945–46) and National Assembly (1946–59). In 1959 he became prime minister and, on independence in 1960, president. The massive basilica at Yamoussoukro was built on his orders.

● **housecarl** ► A member of the household bodyguard of the Danish kings of England (1016–51). Originally warriors from the Scandinavian army, the housecarls performed strictly organized military and administrative services for which they were rewarded with gifts of money and land.

● **housefly** ► A dull-grey fly, *Musca domestica*, that is a worldwide household pest. The adult is 5–7 mm long, with mouthparts used for sucking up organic liquids of all kinds. Through the contamination of food it spreads many serious diseases, such as typhoid, tuberculosis, and dysentery. The scavenging larvae grow quickly on practically any decaying organic matter, especially dung. Family: *Muscidae*.

● **houseleek** ► A European perennial herb, *Sempervivum tectorum*, that has a basal rosette of fleshy leaves and bears heads of dull-red flowers on stems up to 60 cm long. Growing on walls and roofs, it was formerly believed to guard against fire, sorcery, and death and had many medicinal uses. Family: *Crassulaceae*.

● **house martin** ▷*See* martin.

● **house sparrow** ► A Eurasian ▷sparrow, *Passer domesticus*, that originated in Africa and spread north with Neolithic man: it is now

also found in the New World. The male has a black-streaked brown plumage with grey underparts and a black bib and eye stripe; the female has a paler drabber plumage. ▷*See* Plate III.

● **Housman, A(lfred) E(dward)** ► (1859–1936) British poet and scholar. Although he failed his degree at Oxford, his classical erudition was eventually rewarded with professorships at London and Cambridge. His two volumes of lyrics, *A Shropshire Lad* (1896) and *Last Poems* (1922), are concerned with themes of human vanity and transience and are imbued with an atmosphere of romantic pessimism. He also published editions of the Roman poets Juvenal and Manilius.

● **Houston** ► 29 45N 95 25W A city in the USA, the main port in Texas. Founded in 1836, it is named after the Texan leader Sam(uel) Houston (1793–1863). It expanded rapidly following the building of a canal (1912–14), linking it to the Gulf of Mexico, and the development of coastal oilfields. Today it is one of the world's major oil and petrochemical centres; other industries include shipbuilding and the manufacture of steel. Among its many educational institutions is Texas medical centre, and the Lyndon B. Johnson Space Center is nearby. Population (2000): 1 953 631.

● **Hove** ► 50 49N 0 10W A town in S England, in Brighton and Hove unitary authority, on the East Sussex coast. It is a resort and residential town adjoining Brighton. Sussex county cricket ground is situated here. Population (1991): 67 602.

● **Hovell, William Hilton** ▷*See* Hume, Hamilton.

● **hovercraft** ► (or air-cushion vehicle) A shiplike vehicle equipped with powerful horizontal blowers capable of lifting it off a surface so that it rides on a cushion of air, which is contained within a rubber skirt. It can navigate on almost any kind of surface (water, swamp, or land) and is moved forward at high speed by vertical propellers. The first hovercraft was built by Christopher ▷Cockerell in 1959. Hovercraft were used as ferries between England and France, and elsewhere, but have largely been superseded by high-speed ▷hydrofoils, which use less fuel.

● **hoverfly** ► A fly, also called a flowerfly or syrphid fly, belonging to the family *Syrphidae* (about 4000 species). Many species are black and yellow, resembling bees and wasps, but they do not sting. The larvae of many hoverflies are scavengers in decaying organic matter or the nests of ants, termites, or bees. Others eat aphids and plant lice, while a few are plant pests. ▷*See also* maggot. insect.

● **Howard, Catherine** ► (c. 1520–42) The fifth wife (1540–42) of Henry VIII of England. She was beheaded for treason when Henry learnt of her premarital love affairs.

● **Howard, Sir Ebenezer** ► (1850–1928) British theorist of town planning. His book *Garden Cities of Tomorrow*, first published under this title in 1902, propounds his concept of ideal spacious suburbs. This was first realized in the planning of Letchworth (1903), ▷Lutyens' design for Hampstead (1908), and Welwyn Garden City (1920). His ideas continue to be influential. ▷*See also* garden city.

● **Howard, Henry** ▷*See* Surrey, Henry Howard, Earl of.

● **Howard, John** ► (c. 1726–90) English prison reformer. Horrified by conditions in Bedford gaol, which he inspected while high sheriff of Bedfordshire, Howard campaigned for sanitary improvements and wages, rather than prisoners' fees, for gaolers. An act of 1774 achieved his aims. The **Howard League for Penal Reform**, founded in 1866 as the Howard Association, was named after him.

● **Howard, John (Winston)** ► (1939–) Australian politician; prime minister (1996–). The leader of the Liberal Party from 1985 to 1989 and again from 1995, he led his party to victory in elections in 1996 and 1998.

● **Howard, Leslie** ► (Leslie Howard Stainer; 1890–1943) British actor of Hungarian descent. He became famous for his performances as the romantic leading man in both British and US films, including *The Scarlet Pimpernel* (1935), *Pygmalion* (1938), and *Gone with the Wind* (1939). He was killed when the aeroplane in which he was travelling was shot down by German aircraft in 1943.

● **Howard, Trevor** ► (1916–88) British actor. After working in the theatre in the 1930s he concentrated on films from the 1940s, often appearing in leading romantic roles. His films include *Brief Encounter* (1946), *The Third Man* (1949), *Mutiny on the Bounty* (1962), *Ryan's Daughter* (1970), *Conduct Unbecoming* (1975), and *White Mischief* (1987).

● **Howard of Effingham, Charles, 2nd Baron** ▶ (1536–1624) English Lord High Admiral (1585–1618), who commanded the English victory against the Spanish ▷Armada (1588). He was a commander of the expedition that sacked Cádiz (1596), for which he was created 1st Earl of Nottingham.

● **Howe, Elias** ▶ (1819–67) US inventor, who invented a lockstitch sewing machine, patented in 1846. It was not at first successful but by the 1850s large numbers were being manufactured in infringement of Howe's patent rights. After winning a series of legal suits, he earned a fortune from royalties.

● **Howe, (Richard Edward) Geoffrey, Baron** ▶ (1926–) British Conservative politician; deputy prime minister (1989–90). He was minister for trade and consumer affairs (1972–74), chancellor of the exchequer (1979–83), and foreign secretary (1983–89). His resignation in 1990 was a key factor in the fall of Margaret Thatcher as prime minister.

● **Howe, Richard, Earl** ▶ (1726–99) British admiral. In the Seven Years' War (1756–63) he fought with distinction off the N French coast. In 1776 he became commander of the British fleet in the American Revolution. He is best known for the victory in the French Revolutionary Wars of the Glorious ▷First of June (1794). His brother **William, 5th Viscount Howe** (1729–1814) gained fame in the army. He fought under ▷Wolfe in North America during the Seven Years' War and in the American Revolution commanded at ▷Bunker Hill (1775), after which he became commander in chief in America. Although he scored successes, notably at ▷Brandywine (1777), he resigned after the failure at ▷Valley Forge (1778).

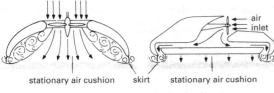

stationary air cushion   skirt   stationary air cushion

plenum-chamber type   **annular-chamber type**

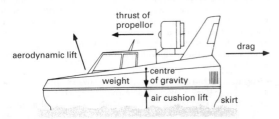

hovercraft ▶ In the plenum chamber the air cushion is produced by a horizontal fan; the cushion in the centre is almost at rest and is surrounded by a fast-moving ring of turbulent air. In the annular chamber the cushion is formed within an annular ring of jets, the nozzles of which are sloped inwards. The lower figure shows the forces acting on a hovercraft.

● **Howel Dda** ▷*See* Hywel the Good.

● **howitzer** ▶ A low-velocity ▷artillery firearm with a shorter barrel and a larger bore than a ▷gun but a smaller bore and longer barrel than a ▷mortar. They are often mounted on carriages that enable them to fire either flat gun-type trajectories or arched mortar-type trajectories. They were widely used in World War I but the distinction between a gun and a howitzer in modern practice is now much reduced. The word comes from the Dutch *houwitzer*, catapult.

● **howler monkey** ▶ A large monkey belonging to the genus *Alouatta* (6 species), of Central and South American forests. Howlers are 115–180 cm long including the tail (58–91 cm) and are named

after their loud voices. They have beards over their enlarged throats, prehensile tails, and live in groups of up to 40 individuals. Family: *Cebidae*.

● **Howrah** ▶ 22 35N 88 20E A city and port in India, in West Bengal situated on the River Hooghly opposite Calcutta. Its industries include shipbuilding, jute milling, engineering, and chemicals. Population (1991): 946 732.

● **Hoxha, Enver** ▶ (1908–85) Albanian leader (1946–85). In World War II Hoxha led Albania's struggle against Italy and founded the country's Communist Party (1941), becoming (1943) its general secretary. He was prime minister (1946–54) and then first secretary (1954–85) of the newly named Party of Labour. After the Sino-Soviet disagreement in 1961, Hoxha supported China until 1978.

● **Hoya** ▷*See* waxplant.

● **Hoyle, Edmond** ▶ (1672–1769) British authority on card games. His book *A Short Treatise on the Game of Whist* (1742) was highly successful and his revised rules of 1760 governed whist until 1864. The idiom "according to Hoyle" (meaning according to the rules) is an allusion to this book.

● **Hoyle, Sir Fred** ▶ (1915–2001) British astronomer, who with H. ▷Bondi and T. ▷Gold proposed the ▷steady-state theory of the universe. His other theoretical studies were mainly concerned with stellar evolution. He was also a leading science writer, his *Galaxies, Nuclei and Quasars* (1965) being a standard work, and a notable science-fiction writer.

● **Hradec Králové** ▶ (German name: Königgratz) 50 13N 15 50E A town in the N Czech Republic, in E Bohemia on the confluence of the Rivers Elbe (Labe) and Orlice. Industries include the manufacture of musical instruments and photographic equipment. Population (1996 est): 100 528.

● **HRT** ▷*See* hormone replacement therapy.

● **Hsia Kuei** ▷*See* Xia Gui.

● **Hsiang-t'an** ▷*See* Xiangtan.

● **Hsi Chiang** ▷*See* Xi Jiang.

● **Hsi-ning** ▷*See* Xining.

● **Hsiung-nu** ▷*See* Xiong Nu.

● **Hsuan-tsang** ▷*See* Xuan Zang.

● **Hua Guo Feng** ▶ (or Hua Kuo-feng; 1920–) Chinese communist statesman; chairman of the Chinese Communist Party (1976–81). Party secretary in Hunan, he survived a ▷Red Guard attack during the Cultural Revolution to succeed Chou En-lai as prime minister (1976–80) and Mao Tse-tung as chairman. Hua's pragmatic policies were regarded as being in part the result of the influence of ▷Deng Xiao Ping.

● **Huainan** ▶ 32 41N 117 06E A city in E China, in Anhui province. Situated on a rich coalfield, it produces iron and steel and chemicals. Population (1999 est): 823 395.

● **Huambo** ▶ (name until 1973: Nova Lisboa) 12 47S 15 44E A town in W Angola. It is a commercial centre with important railway industries. Population (1999 est): 400 000.

● **Huancayo** ▶ 12 05S 75 12W A city in W Peru, the chief commercial centre of the central Andes. It has a cathedral and a university (1962). Population (1998 est): 305 039.

● **Huang Hai** ▷*See* Yellow Sea.

● **Huang Ho** ▷*See* Yellow River.

● **Huari** ▶ An ancient city in the central Peruvian Andes that was briefly the centre of an empire (c. 600–800 AD). Huari itself remained prosperous until abandoned about 1000 and the influence of its pottery styles prevailed over most of its central Peruvian neighbours until the rise of the ▷Chimú.

● **Huascar** ▶ (c. 1495–1532) Ruler of the Incas, who was defeated in civil war by his half-brother ▷Atahuallpa in 1532. Their conflict helped ▷Pizarro to conquer the Incas.

● **Huascarán** ▶ (or Nevado Huascarán) 9 08S 77 36W The highest mountain in Peru, in the Andes. In 1962 an avalanche buried the village of Raurahirca killing about 3500 people. Height: 6768 m (22 205 ft).

● **Hubble, Edwin Powell** ▶ (1889–1953) US astronomer, who used the 100-inch telescope at Mount Wilson Observatory to show that there were celestial bodies (▷galaxies) beyond our own Galaxy and that these were receding from us, thus confirming the idea of an expanding universe. He stated that the velocity of recession of the galaxies is proportional to their distance from the earth (*see* Hubble constant).

● **Hubble constant** ▶ (H_o) The rate at which the velocity of expansion of the universe changes with distance. It relates the recessional velocity, V, of a distant galaxy to its distance, D. **Hubble's law**, proposed in 1929 by Edwin ▷Hubble, states that recessional velocity and distance are directly proportional: $V = H_oD$. One value for H_o is 55 km s^{-1} megaparsec^{-1}, although higher values have been used.

● **Hubble space telescope** ▶ A powerful telescope launched into space by the USA in 1990, in the hope that, unhampered by the earth's atmosphere, it would be possible to probe deeper into the universe than can be done by terrestrial observatories. At first, a faulty mirror limited observation but in 1993 astronauts from the space shuttle *Endeavour* were able to correct it. In 1996 astronomers published the Hubble Deep Field Image, a remarkable composite photograph showing some 2000 galaxies. The telescope is named after Edwin Powell ▷Hubble.

● **Hubei** ▶ (*or* Hupei) A province in E central China. Its fertile E plain has many lakes and rivers, including the Yangtze River. It was devastated during the Taiping Rebellion (1851–64) and the 1911 revolution began here. Products include wheat, rice, cotton, fish, and steel. Area: 187 500 sq km (72 394 sq mi). Population (1996 est): 57 720 000. Capital: Wuhan.

● **Hubli** ▶ 15 20N 75 14E A city in India, in Karnataka. With Dharwar, it forms one of the state's most populous areas. Industries include cotton and newspapers. Population (1991): 647 640.

● **hubris** ▶ (*or* hybris) The ancient Greek concept of human pride that leads to a transgression of the natural order and subsequent retribution by the gods. The concept is important in Greek tragedies, the protagonists of which, being talented and powerful, were especially prone to this fault.

● **Huddersfield** ▶ 58 39N 1 47W A town in N England, in Kirklees unitary authority, West Yorkshire, at the confluence of the Rivers Colne and Holme. Formerly a major wool textile town, Huddersfield now has important manufacturing and chemical industries; it is also a centre for culture and sport. Population (1991): 143 726.

● **Huddleston, Trevor** ▶ (1913–98) British missionary and bishop. While a missionary in South Africa (1943–56) he wrote *Naught for Your Comfort* (1952), about apartheid. He was Bishop of Massai, in Tanzania (1960–68), Suffragan Bishop of Stepney, London (1968–77), Bishop of Mauritius (1978–83), Archbishop of the Indian Ocean (1978–83), and from 1981 president of the Anti-Apartheid Movement (which became a solidarity movement in 1994).

● **Hudson, Henry** ▶ (d. 1611) English navigator. In 1607, in a small ship with ten sailors, he sailed in search of the ▷Northeast Passage to China, reaching Spitzbergen. He tried again, unsuccessfully, in 1608. On a third voyage, under the auspices of the Dutch East India Company, he sailed some 240 km (150 mi) down what came to be called the Hudson River, establishing Dutch claims to the area. His fourth voyage (1610–11), in the *Discovery*, took him to what is now Hudson Bay (NE Canada), where his men mutinied and cast him adrift. Nothing more was heard of him.

● **Hudson, W(illiam) H(enry)** ▶ (1841–1922) British naturalist and writer. Born in Argentina, he came to England in 1869. His books, which achieved little popular success, include ornithological studies, works on the English countryside, and several prose romances, of which the best known is *Green Mansions* (1904).

● **Hudson Bay** ▶ A huge shallow oceanic bay in N central Canada, linked to the Atlantic Ocean by Hudson Strait and to the Arctic Ocean

by Foxe Channel. Frozen during winter, in summer it carries grain ships from W Canada to Europe.

● **Hudson River** ▶ A river in the NE USA, flowing from the Adirondack Mountains to New York Bay, where it forms part of New York Harbor. An important commercial waterway, it is linked by canals with the ▷Great Lakes and the ▷St Lawrence Seaway. Length: 492 km (306 mi).

● **Hudson's Bay Company** ▶ A fur-trading company, formed in 1670, that was given settlement and trading rights in Canada; its first governor was Prince ▷Rupert (*see also* Rupert's Land). The company engaged in bitter rivalry with the ▷Northwest Company from the 1780s until 1821, when they were united under the name of the Hudson's Bay Company. It maintained a monopoly of the fur trade in Rupert's Land until 1859. In 1870 it sold its territories to Canada but remained a major fur-trading agency with headquarters in London.

● **Hue** ▶ 16 28N 107 35E An ancient city in central Vietnam, on the Huong estuary. The University of Hue was established in 1957. A commercial centre, Hue has textile, timber, and cement industries.

History: a Chinese military stronghold from about 200 BC, Hue later fell to Champa and after 1635 was the capital of ▷Annam and after 1802 of the short-lived Vietnamese empire. It suffered heavily during the Vietnam War, during which it was a part of South Vietnam, and it lost many of the historic buildings and treasures of the imperial citadel. Its population was also increased sixfold by refugees. Population (1992 est): 219 149.

● **Huelva** ▶ 37 15N 6 56W A port in SW Spain, in Andalusia on the Odiel estuary. It ships copper from the Riotinto mines and also iron, manganese, and wine. Population (1995 est): 145 712.

● **Huesca** ▶ 42 08N 0 25W A town in NE Spain, in Aragon. Quintus Sertorius (c. 123–72 BC) founded his school here in 77 BC. It has a cathedral (13th–16th centuries). Population (1991): 50 020.

● **Huggins, Sir William** ▶ (1824–1910) British astronomer, who pioneered the application of spectroscopy to astronomy, using the technique to discover that stars consist of the same elements as those found on the earth. He also discovered the ▷redshift in the lines of a star's spectrum. He was knighted in 1897.

● **Hugh Capet** ▶ (c. 940–96 AD) The first ▷Capetian King of France (987–96). Son of the Count of Paris, Hugh seized the throne after the failure of the ▷Carolingian line.

● **Hughes, Howard (Robard)** ▶ (1905–76) US aviator, film producer, and entrepreneur, who established a huge fortune in the oil business. After founding the Hughes Aircraft Company he broke the landplane speed record in 1935, reaching 352 mph in a craft of his own design. His films include *Hell's Angels* (1930), *Scarface* (1932), and *The Outlaw* (1944), the last of which he directed. From 1950 he lived in seclusion.

● **Hughes, Richard** ▶ (1900–76) British novelist. His best-known novel is *A High Wind in Jamaica* (1929), concerning a family of children captured by pirates. *The Fox in the Attic* (1961) and *The Wooden Shepherdess* (1973) are the first two parts of an unfinished work concerning British and German society during the interwar years.

● **Hughes, Ted** ▶ (1930–98) British poet. His first volume, *The Hawk in the Rain* (1957), contained many poems concerned with the natural world written in a forceful style. The poems in *Crow* (1970) and other volumes of the 1970s were characterized by increased violence of language and subject matter. He was married to Sylvia ▷Plath from 1956 until her suicide in 1963 and became poet laureate in 1984. Later works include *Flowers and Insects* (1987), the adaptation *Tales from Ovid* (1997), and *Birthday Letters* (1998), a sequence of poems about his doomed marriage to Plath that won numerous literary prizes and became a bestseller; he also wrote stories for children. He was appointed to the OM in 1998.

● **Hughes, Thomas** ▶ (1822–96) British writer. *Tom Brown's Schooldays* (1857), his best-known novel, is a celebration of the public-school ethos formulated by Thomas ▷Arnold. He was a Christian Socialist and a Liberal MP (1865–74).

● **Hughes, William M(orris)** ▶ (1864–1952) Australian statesman, born in London; prime minister (1915–23) as leader of the Labor Party (1915–16) and then of the newly founded Nationalist Party. An advocate of Australian federation in the 1890s, he was attorney general (1908–09, 1910–13, 1914–21, 1939–41). As prime minister he attended the Paris Peace Conference (1919) after World War I.

● **Hugh of Saint-Victor** ▶ (1096–1141) French theologian. He joined the abbey of St Victor in Paris as a canon regular and, under his direction, its school became a major centre of learning. His best-known book is *The Sacraments of the Christian Faith*.

● **Hugli, River** ▷*See* Hooghly, River.

● **Hugo, Victor (Marie)** ▶ (1802–85) French poet, dramatist, and novelist. After several early novels and volumes of poetry, his leadership of the Romantic movement was confirmed by the success of his drama *Hernani* (1831). During the 1840s he became increasingly involved in politics as a champion of republican ideals and, after the coup d'état by the future Napoleon III in 1851, he went into exile in the Channel Islands until 1870. His later major works included *Les Contemplations* (1856), a volume of poems, and the novel *Les Misérables* (1862). The greatest French poet of the 19th century, he was honoured as a national literary figure. He died in Paris and was buried in the Panthéon.

● **Huguenots** ▶ French Protestants. Their name is derived from the Swiss-German *Eidgenoss*, confederate. The Huguenots, chiefly followers of John Calvin, were soon an influential national minority. The rivalry of their leaders, especially the ▷Condé, with the prominent Roman Catholic ▷Guise family gave rise to the ▷Wars of Religion (1562–94). The Edict of Nantes (1598) guaranteed the Huguenots freedom of worship but in Louis XIV's reign they were increasingly persecuted and after the revocation of the Edict (1685) over 250 000 Huguenots emigrated. Persecution continued until the French Revolution.

● **Huhehot** ▷*See* Hohhot.

● **Hui** ▶ Chinese Muslims of NW China, mainly in the provinces of Hebei, Xinjiang, Gansu, and Qinghai. Numbering about 3.5 million, they are descended from Chinese who were converted as a result of contact and intermarriage with ▷Turkic peoples during the 14th and 15th centuries. They are also known as Dungan (*or* T'ung-kan).

● **huia** ▶ An extinct New Zealand songbird, *Heteralocha acutirostris*, 45 cm long, that had a glossy black plumage with a white-tipped tail and orange wattles at the base of the bill. The bill of the male was strong and straight; that of the female was long, slender, and curved. Huias were hunted for the feathers by Maoris but their extinction was caused by the destruction of their habitat and excessive collection of specimens as curios by European settlers. Family: *Callaeidae* (wattlebirds).

● **Huitzilopochtli** ▶ The Aztec sun- and war-god. He was portrayed as a hummingbird, or with armour of hummingbird feathers, and dead warriors were believed to be reincarnated as this bird. His temple at Tenochtitlan, founded in 1325 in the Valley of Mexico, was the principal Aztec religious structure. He was identified with the sun as a warrior who defeated the night stars, was reborn each day, and depended for nourishment on the blood of human sacrificial victims.

● **Huizinga, Johan** ▶ (1872–1945) Dutch historian. Huizinga was professor of history, first at Groningen and then at Leyden University. His best-known book, *The Waning of the Middle Ages* (1919), was a study of life, thought, and art in late medieval France and the Netherlands. He also wrote *Erasmus* (1924), *In the Shadow of Tomorrow* (1935), an analysis of the malaise of contemporary Western society, and *Homo Ludens* (1938).

● **Hull** ▷*See* Kingston-upon-Hull.

● **Hull** ▶ 45 26N 75 45W A city in E Canada, in SW Quebec on the Ottawa River opposite Ottawa. One of North America's main pulp-and-paper and timber centres, it has acquired many federal government offices in recent years. Population (1991): 60 707.

● **Hull, Cordell** ▶ (1871–1955) US Democratic politician; secretary of state (1933–44) under F. D. Roosevelt. He did much to foster good relations with Latin America (*see* Good Neighbor Policy), attending the important Montevideo Conference in 1933, and supported China against Japanese ambitions in East Asia. He was instrumental in the foundation of the UN, for which he won the Nobel Peace Prize in 1945.

● **Hulse, Russell** ▷*See* Taylor, Joseph Hooton.

● **Human Genome Project** ▷*See* genome.

● **humanism** ▶ 1. The intellectual movement that formed the inspiration and the basis of Renaissance culture. Humanist scholars based their programme upon the rediscovery and study of classical Greek and Roman authors, which had been initiated in Italy by such men as ▷Petrarch and ▷Boccaccio. They turned away from the exclusively theological bias of their medieval forerunners and concentrated instead upon human achievements in the arts and sciences. ▷Erasmus was the greatest N European humanist. For him and the other Renaissance thinkers humanism by no means implied rejection of Christianity. 2. A 20th-century philosophical viewpoint that is based on ▷atheism, holding religion to be an outmoded superstition unworthy of serious consideration.

● **human rights** ▶ Privileges claimed or enjoyed by a human being simply by virtue of being human. The concept developed from Roman ideas of "natural law" entailing "natural rights," via ▷Locke, ▷Paine, and the American Declaration of Independence (1776), to 20th-century liberal acceptance of the idea that human beings should have certain equal civil, political, and economic rights. Since the horrors of World War II, moves have been made to ensure international enforcement of human-rights agreements as embodied in the UN Charter. The UN Universal Declaration of Human Rights (1948), itself not a legally binding code, has spawned various subsequent agreements, such as the Covenants on Civil and Political Rights and on Economic, Social, and Cultural Rights (1966); in 1989 the UN adopted the Convention on the Rights of the Child. A UN High Commissioner for Human Rights was first appointed in 1994. Europe has its own European Convention on Human Rights, set up in 1950 by the ▷Council of Europe, under which the ▷European Court of Human Rights (1959) was established. In 1998 the UK parliament passed the Human Rights Act, under which the European Convention on Human Rights was incorporated into British law.

● **Humber** ▶ An estuary in N England, flowing from the confluence of the Rivers Ouse and Trent to the North Sea past the ports of Hull, Immingham, and Grimsby. The **Humber Bridge** (opened 1981), formerly the world's longest single-span suspension bridge with a main span of 1410 m (4626 ft), spans the estuary. Length: 64 km (40 mi).

● **Humberside** ▶ A former county in NE England. It was created in 1974 from N ▷Lincolnshire, most of the ▷East Riding of ▷Yorkshire, including the city of Kingston-upon-Hull, and part of the West Riding of Yorkshire. In 1996 Humberside county council was abolished and administrative powers were devolved to the ▷unitary authorities of North Lincolnshire, North East Lincolnshire, East Riding of Yorkshire, and Kingston-upon-Hull. The historic county boundaries of Yorkshire and Lincolnshire were restored for ceremonial and related purposes.

● **Humboldt, (Karl) Wilhelm von** ▶ (1767–1835) German scholar and statesman; friend of Schiller and Goethe. As minister of education he founded Berlin University (1809) and was subsequently employed as a diplomat. His writings on language are especially profound: he saw language as a generative process rather than a lifeless structure. He perceived that language and thought are inseparable and identified various kinds of structures by which languages may be differentiated. His brother **(Friedrich Wilhelm Karl Heinrich) Alexander von Humboldt** (1769–1859) was a scientist and explorer. In 1799 he set off with Aimé Bonpland (1773–1858) to explore Central and South America and in the following five years the two men collected a large number of samples and much data relating to earth sciences. He subsequently explored central Asia, again collecting scientific material of great importance. In his great work *Kosmos* (5 vols, 1845–62) he set out his views on the universe. The ▷Humboldt Current and Glacier were named after him.

● **Humboldt Current** ▶ (*or* Peru Current) An ocean current constituting part of the South Pacific oceanic circulation system. It flows N off the Peruvian coast of South America. Because of its Antarctic origins and the upwelling of cold water along the W coast of South America, it is a cold current rich in plankton and the fish that feed on them, giving rise to Peru's prosperous fishing industry.

● **Humboldt Glacier** ▶ The largest known glacier in the N hemisphere, in NW Greenland. At its end in Kane Basin it is 100 km (60 mi) wide and 91 m (300 ft) high.

● **Hume, Basil George, Cardinal** ▶ (1923–99) British Roman Catholic churchman. He joined the Benedictine order and taught languages at Ampleforth College in Yorkshire from 1952 until 1963, when he became Abbot of Ampleforth. He succeeded Cardinal Heenan as Archbishop of Westminster in 1976, the first monk to hold this office, and was created a cardinal in the same year. He was appointed to the OM shortly before his death.

● **Hume, David** ▶ (1711–76) Scottish philosopher and historian. He spent three years in France (1734–37) but for the rest of his life lived in either London or Edinburgh. In *A Treatise of Human Nature* (1739–40) he developed his influential distinction between impression and ideas, claiming that impressions have more force than ideas. We receive impressions from an unknown source and ideas derive from them through the operations of memory and imagination. For Hume almost nothing about existence was demonstrable; regarding the existence of God, his position throughout his numerous works is an incisive ▷agnosticism. Although an empiricist like ▷Locke and ▷Berkeley, Hume modified problematic aspects of their philosophies in favour of psychological explanations. Another aspect of Hume's thought that is influential among 20th-century philosophers is his analysis of cause and effect as no more than "constant conjunction": we can *observe* that one thing follows another but we can never *know* that it must follow, because of the limitations of human understanding. Hume's *History of England* (1754–62), written while he was librarian of the Advocates' Library in Edinburgh, was a bestseller.

● **Hume, Hamilton** ▶ (1797–1873) Australian explorer. His most important journey (1824–25) was with an English immigrant **William Hilton Hovell** (1786–1875) with whom he travelled from Sydney to Port Phillip, Victoria, discovering the Murray River. The Hume Highway (Melbourne to Sydney) is named after him.

● **Hume, John** ▶ (1937–2001) Northern Irish politician: leader of the Social Democratic and Labour Party (1979–2001). A leader of the Catholic civil rights movement of the late 1960s, he cofounded the moderate nationalist SDLP in 1970. He has been a member of the Westminster parliament since 1983 and of the European parliament since 1979. In 1998 he was awarded the Nobel Peace Prize (jointly with David ▷Trimble) for his role in the peace process that led to the Good Friday Agreement.

● **Hume, Joseph** ▶ (1777–1855) British radical politician. After early employment by the East India Company he briefly became an MP (1812). Re-elected in 1818, he advocated free trade, opposed flogging in the army, and consistently questioned public expenditure.

● **humerus** ▷*See* arm.

● **humidity** ▶ A measure of the amount of water vapour in the atmosphere. Absolute humidity is the mass of water vapour in unit volume of air, measured in kilograms per cubic metre. Relative humidity is the ratio of the absolute humidity at a given temperature to the maximum humidity without precipitation at the same temperature, usually expressed as a percentage.

● **Hummel, Johann Nepomuk** ▶ (1778–1837) Hungarian pianist and composer. He numbered Mozart and Haydn among his teachers. He toured Europe as a concert pianist and was famous as an improviser. His compositions include concertos and many piano solos.

● **hummingbird** ▶ A brightly coloured bird belonging to a New World family (*Trochilidae*; 320 species). Hummingbirds are 5.5–20 cm long and have a slender often downcurved bill and a brush-tipped tongue for feeding on nectar and small insects. Hummingbirds can hover, fly backwards, and produce a humming noise during the rapid vibration of their wings during flight. Order: *Apodiformes* (swifts, etc.).

● **humpback whale** ▶ A ▷rorqual whale, *Megaptera novaeangliae*,

found in coastal waters throughout the world. It is 15 m long with long flippers and a large dorsal fin with lobes down to the tail. It is an acrobatic swimmer and lives in communities, feeding on crustaceans and small fish. ▢oceans.

● **Humperdinck, Engelbert** ▶ (1854–1921) German composer. He assisted Wagner with the score of *Parsifal* in 1880–81. Of his operas only *Hänsel und Gretel* (1893) is still popular: it blends German folklore with Wagnerian techniques.

● **Humphrey, Hubert Horatio** ▶ (1911–78) US Democratic politician; vice president (1965–69) under President Johnson. A liberal democrat, he championed civil rights but his defence of Johnson's Vietnam policies cost him liberal support. He was the Democratic presidential candidate in the election of 1968 but lost to Richard Nixon.

● **humus** ▶ The black organic matter in soil resulting from the ▷decomposition of dead plants and animals (humification). It is rich in such elements as carbon, nitrogen, phosphorus, and sulphur, which are useful in maintaining soil fertility and hence in promoting plant growth. Humus also improves water absorption and workability of the soil.

● **Hunan** ▶ A province in S central China, mountainous and forested in the S and W. The population includes an aboriginal minority. The chief products are rice, cereals, tea, cotton, timber, and such minerals as lead, zinc, tungsten, and gold.

History: it was devastated during the Taiping Rebellion (1851–64). Mao Tse-tung was born here. Area: 210 500 sq km (82 095 sq mi). Population (1999 est): 65 320 000. Capital: Changsha.

● **hundred** ▶ A subdivision of the shire in England, first mentioned in the 10th century. Of varying size, it may originally have consisted of a hundred ▷hides. It corresponded to the ▷wapentake in the areas under Danish law. An administrative and judicial unit, it had its own court sitting every four weeks until the 13th century, when its importance began to decline. Hundreds survived, however, until the 19th century. ▷*See also* Chiltern Hundreds.

● **Hundred Days** ▶ (20 March–28 June, 1815) The period from ▷Napoleon I's return to France, after his escape from Elba, until his final defeat by the allies at ▷Waterloo.

● **Hundred Days of Reform** ▶ (1898) A programme of reforms announced by the Chinese emperor ▷Guang Xu, with the help of the reformer ▷Kang You Wei, to modernize the educational system, administration, and the armed forces and to develop trade, commerce, and industrialization on a Western model. Most of the reforms were repealed by Guang Xu's mother ▷Zi Xi, who with the support of the army imprisoned her son and became regent, thus frustrating a reform movement that might have prevented the overthrow of the ▷Qing dynasty.

hummingbird ▶ A broad-tailed hummingbird (*Selasphorus platycercus*) about to extract nectar from a flower.

● **Hundred Flowers** ► A Chinese government campaign to allow greater freedom of speech, particularly among intellectuals. It began in 1956 under the slogan "Let a hundred flowers bloom together, let a hundred schools of thought contend." It led to much open criticism of the government and was harshly suppressed a year later.

● **Hundred Years' War** ► (1337–1453) A war between England and France. It was precipitated by Edward III's claim to the French throne, although there had long been hostility occasioned by disputes over English territory in France and French support for the Scots. The Treaty of ▷Brétigny (1360) recognized initial English successes at ▷Sluys (1340), ▷Crécy (1346), and Poitiers (1356) but thereafter the war was waged intermittently with frequent truces. Conditions were exacerbated by growing French and Burgundian rivalry, the Burgundians supporting Henry V of England, who achieved recognition as heir to the French throne after his victory at ▷Agincourt (1415). His early death, the accession of the weak ▷Henry VI, and more vigorous French prosecution of the war (inspired by ▷Joan of Arc) reversed his triumph and by 1453 England had been expelled from all French territory except Calais.

● **Hungarian** ► A language of the ▷Finno-Ugric branch of the ▷Uralic family. It is spoken by 14 million people mainly in Hungary, where it is the official language, and in Slovakia, Romania, and the Union of Serbia and Montenegro. Hungarian uses a modified Latin alphabet and has borrowed many words from surrounding languages. Vowel harmony is characteristic of its sound system and its grammar is based on the use of suffixes. ▷See also Magyars.

● **Hungarian National Council** ► (1918–19) A political coalition formed in October, 1918, by Mihály Károlyi (1875–1955) and dedicated to establishing constitutional government in Hungary. In November, after Károlyi had become prime minister, it proclaimed Hungary a republic but the decline of the economy and the opposition of Hungary's minority nationalities forced its resignation (March, 1919) in favour of the communists under ▷Kun.

● **Hungarian Revolution** ► (1956) An uprising against Soviet dominance of Hungary. Following the Soviet acceptance of ▷Gomułka as leader in Poland, a demonstration of students and workers in Budapest demanded the end of the Soviet presence in Hungary and of one-party government. The protestors were joined by army units. Imre ▷Nagy formed a coalition government, withdrew Hungary from the ▷Warsaw Pact, and sought UN help. An opposition government was formed by János ▷Kádár, and Soviet troops attacked Budapest and crushed the rebellion; Nagy and his associates were captured and executed. About 190 000 people left Hungary as a result of the Revolution.

● **Hungary, Republic of** ► (Hungarian name: Magyar Köztársasag) A country in central Europe. It lies mainly in the basin of the middle Danube, which forms the NW boundary with Slovakia before running N–S across the centre of the country. To the E of the Danube lies the Great Hungarian Plain, crossed by the River Tisza; to the W an undulating plain rises to some low hills in the SW and in the NW to the hilly Bakony Forest, S of which lies Lake ▷Balaton. The people are mainly Magyars, with minorities of Germans, Slovaks, and others.

Economy: under Communism agriculture was organized collectively, though individuals could own small plots; many farms are still cooperatives. The main crops are wheat and maize as well as fruit and vegetables. The wine industry is being encouraged, including the redevelopment of the Takaj region in the NE. Mineral resources include bauxite, oil, coal, and natural gas, but most fuel supplies and many raw materials come from Russia. After 1949 all industry was nationalized and there was considerable expansion, particularly in engineering and chemicals. From 1968 there was a certain amount of decentralization and encouragement of individual initiative, although overall state control was maintained. In 1992 it was agreed that some 75% of industry should eventually be privatized. Exports include transport equipment, machinery, computer software, fruit and vegetables, and meat.

History: the Magyars reached the Danube area in the 9th century AD and settled there under the Árpád dynasty. In the 11th century St ▷Stephen I converted the country to Christianity and became the first Hungarian king. After a long period of dynastic struggles and threats from foreign powers, Hungary was conquered by the Turks in

1526 and in the 17th century it became part of the Habsburg Empire. The 19th century saw the rise of Hungarian nationalism. A revolt under ▷Kossuth (1848) was suppressed by the Austrians but in 1867 Hungary gained internal self-government as part of the Dual Monarchy of ▷Austria-Hungary. Following military defeat in World War I and the collapse of the Dual Monarchy in 1918, Hungary became a republic. However, after a short period of communist rule, a constitutional monarchy was formed (1920) with ▷Horthy de Nagybánya as regent. Although allied to the Germans in World War II, it was occupied by them in 1944 and liberated by Soviet troops in 1945. After the war it became a republic and in 1949 the communists gained control. In 1956 an anti-Stalinist uprising was crushed by Soviet forces and János ▷Kádár came to power. Pressure for liberal reform led Kádár's successor Karoly Grosz to step down in 1989, following which the Communist Party reconstituted itself as the Hungarian Socialist Party. A new constitution was adopted and multiparty democracy was established. The Socialist Party was elected in 1994 but defeated at the polls in 1998 by the right-wing Fidesz movement. In 2002 the Socialists returned to power in alliance with the Liberals. Hungary joined NATO in 1999 and has been formally invited to join the EU early in the 21st century.

Republic of Hungary

Head of state	President Árpád Göncz
Official language	Hungarian (Magyar)
Official currency	forint of 100 fillér
Area	93 035 sq km (35 911 sq mi)
Population (2001 est)	10 190 000
Capital	Budapest

● **Hung Hsiu-ch'uan** ▷See Hong Xiu Quan.

● **Hungnam** ▷See Hamhŭng.

● **Hung-wu** ▷See Hong-wu.

● **Huns** ► Nomadic peoples, originating in Mongolia, who overran much of SE Europe in the late-4th and 5th centuries, overthrowing the ▷Ostrogoths and then invading the Roman Empire. Renowned and feared for their military prowess, especially their use of cavalry, the failure of the Empire to continue payment of tribute to them inspired ▷Attila, under whom the Huns were now united and controlled, to invade Greece, Gaul, and finally Italy (452). The death of Attila (453) fragmented their empire and after defeat by a coalition of tribes at Nedao (455) they ceased to be of importance.

● **Hunt, Henry** ► (1773–1835) British radical, known as Orator Hunt, who presided over the demonstration that ended in the ▷Peterloo Massacre (1819). He was imprisoned (1820–23) but was subsequently elected to parliament (1830), where he campaigned for parliamentary reform.

● **Hunt, James** ► (1947–93) British motor-racing driver, who became world champion in 1976 and won ten Grand Prix races. He retired in 1979.

● **Hunt, (Henry Cecil) John, Baron** ► (1910–98) British army officer and mountaineer, who led the successful 1953 expedition to climb Mount Everest. Teamwork and planning enabled ▷Hillary and ▷Tenzing to reach the summit.

● **Hunt, (James Henry) Leigh** ► (1784–1859) British poet and journalist. In essays for periodicals he supported Keats and other Romantic poets and promoted political reform. In 1813 he was imprisoned for his attacks on the Prince Regent. His books include *Autobiography* (1850).

● **Hunt, William Holman** ► (1827–1910) British painter. After studying in the Royal Academy, he helped found the ▷Pre-Raphaelite Brotherhood, to the principles of which he alone remained faithful. His symbolic but technically realistic paintings include *The Light of the World* (Keble College, Oxford) and *The Scapegoat* (Port Sunlight), inspired by a visit to Syria and Palestine (1854).

● **Hunter, John** ► (1728–93) British physician and one of the founders of modern surgery. Hunter learnt anatomy under his elder brother William and qualified as a physician, becoming surgeon extraordinary to George III. Hunter also investigated various diseases, most notably venereal diseases, inoculating himself in the process. His brother **William Hunter** (1718–83) was a leading anatomist and obstetrician, attending Queen Charlotte during three pregnancies. He bequeathed his collection of coins, pictures, medals, etc., to Glasgow University.

● **Hunter River** ▶ A river in SE Australia, in New South Wales. It rises in the Eastern Highlands and flows generally S through Glenbawn Reservoir to enter the Pacific Ocean at Newcastle. Length: 467 km (290 mi).

● **Huntingdon** ▶ 52 20N 0 12W A town in E England, in Cambridgeshire on the Great Ouse River. A market town with printing, brewing, and knitwear industries, Huntingdon is the birthplace of Oliver Cromwell, who attended the grammar school (now a Cromwell museum), as did Samuel Pepys. Population (1994): 15 575, with Godmanchester.

● **Huntingdon, Selina Hastings, Countess of** ▶ (1707–91) British Methodist leader. She joined the Wesleys' Methodist society but supported the Calvinistic beliefs of George ▷Whitefield rather than the Arminianism of the Wesleys. After being widowed in 1746, she founded many chapels, known as the Countess of Huntingdon's Connexion.

● **Huntingdon and Peterborough** ▶ A former county of E England, formed in 1965 from the county of **Huntingdonshire** and the Soke of Peterborough (an administrative county; 1888–1965). In 1974 it became part of Cambridgeshire.

● **Huntington's disease** ▶ (*or* Huntington's chorea) ▷*See* chorea.

● **Huntsville** ▶ 34 44N 86 35W A city in the USA, in NE Alabama. Founded in 1805, it is a centre for rocket and guided-missile research. Industries include textiles and agricultural implements. It was badly damaged by a hurricane in 1989. Population (1996 est): 170 424.

● **Hunyadi, János** ▶ (c. 1387–1456) Hungarian military leader and statesman. Following his successful Long Campaign against the Turks (1443–44), he was elected (1446) governor and regent for King Ladislas (1440–57). In 1456, shortly before dying of the plague, he routed the Turkish forces before Belgrade, thus securing a 70-year peace.

● **Hupa** ▶ An Athabascan-speaking North American Indian people of the lower Trinity River region of N California. They lived along the river banks in villages consisting of women's houses and men's lodges. They hunted elk and deer, fished for salmon, and gathered acorns. Wealth consisted of dentalium shells and woodpecker scalps. Their religion was characterized by ▷shamanism and the performance of seasonal ceremonies.

● **Hupei** ▷*See* Hubei.

● **Hurd, Douglas (Richard), Baron** ▶ (1930–) British Conservative politician; home secretary (1985–89); foreign secretary (1989–95). After service overseas with the Foreign Office, he became an MP in 1974 and secretary of state for Northern Ireland in 1984. He became a life peer, Baron Hurd of Westwell, in 1997. He is also a writer of political thrillers.

● **hurdling** ▶ A track event in athletics in which sprinters jump ten hurdles in the course of each race. The standard distances are 110 m and 400 m for men and 100 m and 400 m for women. For the 110 m the height of the hurdles is 106.7 cm (3.5 ft), for the 100 m, 84 cm (2.75 ft), and for the 400 m, 91.1 cm (3 ft) for men and 75.9 cm (2.5 ft) for women. Racers are not normally disqualified for knocking hurdles over. World records: men's 110 m: 12.91 seconds (1993) by Colin Jackson (Great Britain); men's 400 m: 46.78 seconds (1992) by Kevin Young (USA); women's 100 m: 12.21 seconds (1988) by Jordanka Donkova (Bulgaria); women's 400 m: 52.61 seconds (1995) by Kim Batten (USA). ▷*See also* steeplechase.

● **hurdy-gurdy** ▶ A stringed instrument sounded by a rosined wheel, turned by the right hand, and stopped by a set of keys played by the left hand; there are also two drone strings. It was very popular in medieval times and survives as a folk instrument in parts of Europe.

● **hurling** ▶ (*or* hurley) An Irish 15-a-side stick-and-ball field game

similar to ▷hockey, over 3000 years old. The ball is hit or carried through the air with a broad-bladed curved stick, the hurley (Gaelic word: *caman*), and may be caught in the hand. A standard field measures 137 × 82 m (150 × 90 yd). A goal, hit under the crossbar, scores three points; a hit between the posts but above the bar scores one.

● **Huron** ▶ An Iroquoian-speaking North American people of the St Lawrence River region. They cultivated maize, beans, squashes, and tobacco. Families of matrilineal descent occupied villages of bark-covered dwellings. Groups of villages formed bands governed by a council of village chiefs and band chief. Band chiefs formed a tribal council. Women were prominent in public affairs and the appointment of chiefs. The Huron were attacked and displaced by the ▷Iroquois during the 17th century.

● **Huron, Lake** ▶ The second largest of the Great Lakes in North America, situated between the USA and Canada. It is an important shipping route carrying iron ore, coal, grain, and oil. Area: 59 570 sq km (23 000 sq mi).

● **Hurrians** ▶ A people living in E Anatolia and N Mesopotamia during the 2nd millennium BC. The Hurrians probably originated in the Armenian mountains before their expansion. Their language, which is extinct, was neither Indo-European nor Semitic, but may be related to ▷Georgian and the Caucasian languages. It is largely known from cuneiform tablets from Hattusas, the capital of the ▷Hittites, whose civilization the Hurrians greatly influenced. There was never a Hurrian empire, but the powerful kingdom of Mitanni (1550–1400 BC) was largely Hurrian in population. ▷*See also* Nuzi.

● **hurricane** ▶ **1.** A tropical ▷cyclone with surface-wind speeds in excess of 64 knots (32.7 m per second) that occurs around the Caribbean Sea and Gulf of Mexico. Tropical cyclones also occur in the W Pacific Ocean, Bay of Bengal, and Queensland but are identified by their own local names (*see* typhoon). The centre (eye) of a hurricane is an area of light winds around which strong winds, cloud, and rain bands spiral. **2.** Any wind reaching force 12 on the ▷Beaufort scale (in excess of 64 knots or 32.7 metres per second).

● **Hurstmonceux** ▷*See* Herstmonceux.

● **Hus, Jan** ▶ (c. 1369–1415) Bohemian religious reformer and martyr. Ordained as a priest in 1401, he became a university teacher in Prague and a popular preacher. Under the influence of the writings of ▷Wycliffe, he criticized the ecclesiastical establishment, chiefly on moral grounds, emphasizing the role of the Scriptures. In 1415, while defending his beliefs at the Council of ▷Constance, where he had been lured by a promise of safe conduct, he was tried, condemned, and burnt at the stake. His followers in Bohemia became known as ▷Hussites.

● **Husák, Gustáv** ▶ (1913–91) Czechoslovak statesman. Husák, a lawyer, became first secretary of the Czechoslovak Communist Party in April, 1969, after the fall of ▷Dubček, and later became president of Czechoslovakia (1975–89). An opponent of liberal reform, he was replaced as head of the Communist Party in 1987 and as president in 1989.

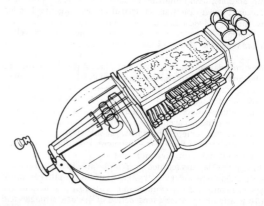

hurdy-gurdy

● **Husaynids** ▶ The ruling dynasty of Tunisia from 1705 to 1957. Their founder, al-Husayn ibn Ali, was recognized as governor of Tunisia by the Ottomans, but he and his successors, who had the title of *bey*, were practically independent. In 1883 their land became a French protectorate. The *beys* lost popularity because it was thought they were too servile to the French and in 1957, when Tunisia became a republic, the dynasty came to an end.

● **husky** ▶ One of several breeds of compact sturdy deep-chested dogs used for pulling sledges in Arctic regions. The Siberian husky has small erect ears, a long muzzle, and a brushlike tail curved over the back. The dense double-layered coat may be of various colours and provides insulation against the severe climate. The Inuit (Eskimo) dog, bred in Greenland, closely resembles the Siberian husky, from which it is probably descended. Height: 51–63 cm. ▷*See also* Samoyed.

● **Hussain, Nasser** ▶ (1968–) British cricketer, born in India. He has played for Essex since 1987 and for England intermittently since 1989, becoming captain in 1999. He led England to four successive test series wins in 2000 and is widely credited with the recent successes of English cricket.

● **hussars** ▶ Light-cavalry regiments originating in Hungary in the 15th century. Most European armies have used hussars for reconnaissance and raids. Their uniform included the characteristic dolman, a cloak worn hanging from the left shoulder.

● **Hussein (ibn Talal)** ▶ (1935–99) King of Jordan (1953–99). He became king following the deposition because of mental illness of his father Talal. Of his four wives, his second (1961–72) was an Englishwoman, Antoinette Gardiner, who took the name Muna, and his fourth was an American, Lisa Halaby (1951–), who took the name Noor. Hussein led Jordan into the 1967 Arab-Israeli War, in which its possessions on the West Bank of the River Jordan were occupied by Israel. The large Palestinian population of the area moved to the East Bank, where al-▷Fatah guerrillas established themselves, posing a threat to Hussein's government. In 1970 he ruthlessly crushed the guerrillas in the fighting of "Black September" but in 1974, under pressure from other Arab countries, accepted the claims of the Palestine Liberation Organization to the West Bank. Following the peace agreement between Israel and the PLO in 1993, he signed a treaty between Jordan and Israel (1994) and played a role in the Israeli-Palestinian peace process. He was succeeded by his son ▷Abdullah II.

● **Hussein, Saddam** ▶ (1937–) Iraqi Ba'athist statesman; president of Iraq (1979–). Acting as his own prime minister, he led Iraq into the ▷Iran-Iraq War and established his own cult following, violently repressing such minority groups as the Kurds using war gases. His invasion of Kuwait (1990) precipitated the ▷Gulf War in which his army was routed. Subsequently antigovernment uprisings by Shiites, Kurds, and others were savagely repressed. In 1993 and 1998 his defiance of UN ceasefire terms led to further US air raids on Iraq.

● **Husserl, Edmund** ▶ (1859–1938) German philosopher, influential in the phenomenological tradition (*see* phenomenology). He taught at Halle, Göttingen, and Freiburg Universities. His philosophy rejected presuppositions about what actually exists (and why it does) and studied instead purely "subjective" data.

● **Hussites** ▶ The followers of the Bohemian heretic, Jan ▷Hus. They demanded a reformed national Church with a vernacular liturgy. In spite of papal and imperial crusades led by the Holy Roman Emperor ▷Sigismund, the Hussites, who were supported by many of the Bohemian aristocracy, remained undefeated until a compromise was reached at the Council of ▷Basle in 1433. Their more radical wing, the Taborites, rejected this but were defeated. The moderate Utraquists gained many of their demands and, in spite of schisms, survived until the 17th century. ▷*See also* Moravian Brethren.

● **Huston, John** ▶ (1906–87) US film director. He began his career as a scriptwriter. His first film as director was *The Maltese Falcon* (1941); subsequent films included *The Treasure of the Sierra Madre* (1948), for which he wrote the script and in which he also acted, *The African Queen* (1951), *The Misfits* (1960), *The Man Who Would Be King* (1975), *Annie* (1982), *Prizzi's Honour* (1985), and *The Dead* (1987). His father **Walter Huston** (1884–1950) was a character actor who starred in such films as *Abraham Lincoln* (1930) and *Dodsworth* (1936), as well as appearing in

several films by his son. John Huston's daughter **Anjelica Huston** (1952–) began her career in her father's films and later emerged as a major star in such movies as *Enemies* (1989), *The Grifters* (1990), *The Addams Family* (1991), *The Crossing Guard* (1995), and *The Golden Bowl* (2000).

● **Hutcheson, Francis** ▶ (1694–1746) Scottish philosopher. He was a professor at Glasgow University (1729–46) and author of works on ethics and aesthetics. The posthumously published *System of Moral Philosophy* (1755) holds that man has an innate moral sense, so that he is born knowing what is good and right. Hutcheson's phrase, "the greatest happiness of the greatest number," as the criterion of virtuous action, was taken up by the exponents of ▷utilitarianism.

● **hutia** ▶ A large ▷rodent of the family *Capromyidae* (which also includes the ▷coypus), found in Cuba and the West Indies. Hutias are 20–60 cm long excluding the naked tail (3–30 cm). They are mainly vegetarian and are either diurnal and arboreal (genus *Capromys*; 4 species) or nocturnal and terrestrial (genus *Geocapromys*; 3 species).

● **Hutten, Ulrich von** ▶ (1488–1523) German humanist, who became poet laureate of the Holy Roman Empire in 1517. His reputation was established as a wit and satirist before he devoted himself to the cause of the Reformation and German nationalism. Joining the war against the German princes, he was driven into exile shortly before his death.

● **Hutton, James** ▶ (1726–97) Scottish physician, generally regarded as the founder of geology. His investigations led him to believe that the earth was very much older than generally believed at that time. These views were expressed in his book *Theory of the Earth* (1795) which met with strong objections from those who accepted the view of creation contained in Genesis.

● **Hutton, Len** ▶ (Sir Leonard H.; 1916–90) British cricketer, who played for Yorkshire and England and became the first professional English captain (1953). He made a record Test score against Australia of 364 (1938) and in his career (1934–60) hit 129 centuries.

● **Hutu** ▶ A Bantu-speaking largely peasant farming people, some 9–10 million of whom inhabit the republics of Burundi and Rwanda. Although the Hutu form the majority (some 80%) in both countries, they have traditionally been dominated by the warrior-farmer **Tutsi** minority. Ethnic violence between the two has had a long history. In the later 20th century it led to escalating revenge killings on both sides, culminating in the attempted ▷genocide of the Rwandan Tutsis by a Hutu militia known as the *interahamwe*, in which between 500 000 and one million were slaughtered. In the subsequent civil war a flood of refugees (mostly Hutu) fled to neighbouring countries. This has caused further instability, especially in the Democratic Republic of Congo (the former Zaïre), where the presence of large numbers of Hutu refugees controlled by the *interahamwe* helped to provoke the Tutsi-led rebellion of 1996–97, which deposed ▷Mobutu. A further Tutsi uprising in 1998 led to military intervention by Rwanda, Angola, Zimbabwe, and Uganda, leading to fears of a full-scale regional conflict. In 1999 *interahamwe* members killed eight Western tourists in Uganda. ▷*See* Burundi, Republic of; Rwanda, Republic of.

● **Huxley, Thomas Henry** ▶ (1825–95) British biologist, whose impact spanned both biology and philosophy. A qualified surgeon, Huxley developed his interest in natural history while serving as a ship's surgeon in the Far East. He was a staunch supporter and friend of Charles ▷Darwin and led the debate against opponents of Darwinism at Oxford in 1860. After valuable work in palaeontology Huxley held numerous public posts and was instrumental in bringing enlightened change to educational methods. From 1880 onwards he challenged orthodox theology and coined the term agnosticism to describe his own position. He served as president of the Royal Society (1883–85). Three of his grandsons achieved fame in the fields of science and literature. **Sir Julian Huxley** (1887–1975) was a zoologist and scientific administrator, who also made valuable contributions to the philosophy of science. He was involved in the improvement of the London Zoo at Regent's Park and in developing its offshoot at ▷Whipsnade and was appointed first director general of UNESCO (1946–48). His brother **Aldous Huxley** (1894–1963) was a novelist and writer. During the 1920s he lived mostly in Italy and in 1937 settled in California. The witty satirical novels *Antic Hay* (1923) and *Point*

Counter Point (1928) were followed by *Brave New World* (1932), *Eyeless in Gaza* (1936), and *After Many A Summer Dies the Swan* (1939). His later essays, including *The Doors of Perception* (1954) and *Heaven and Hell* (1956), explore such subjects as mysticism and the use of drugs. **Sir Andrew Fielding Huxley** (1917–), half-brother to Sir Julian and Aldous, is a biologist noted for his researches into the mechanisms of nerve-impulse conduction and muscle contraction. For their work on nerve impulses Huxley and his collaborator A. L. ▷Hodgkin shared a Nobel Prize (1963) with Sir John ▷Eccles. He was awarded the OM in 1983.

● **Huygens, Christiaan** ▶ (1629–95) Dutch astronomer and physicist, who discovered Saturn's rings in 1656. He also built the first pendulum clock and designed an arrangement of lenses called a Huygens eyepiece, which is still in use on some telescopes and microscopes. He devised a wave theory of light to explain double refraction. He claimed to have invented the hairspring (a claim also made by ▷Hooke).

● **Huysmans, Joris Karl** ▶ (1848–1907) French novelist. In his best-known novel, *À rebours* (1884), he epitomized the contemporary taste for decadent aestheticism in the character of Des Esseintes, who devoted his life to the sensual indulgence of his esoteric tastes. He also wrote art criticism and a series of partly autobiographical novels, including *Là-bas* (1891), that charted his spiritual progress and ultimate acceptance of Roman Catholicism.

● **Hwange** ▶ (name until 1982: Wankie) 18 20S 26 25E A town in W Zimbabwe. It is a tourist centre near Hwange National Park and has coalmining. Population (1989): 40 000.

● **hyacinth** ▶ A perennial herbaceous plant of the genus *Hyacinthus* (about 30 species), native to the Mediterranean region and tropical Africa and widely planted as ornamental garden and pot plants. Growing from bulbs, the flower stems, up to 35 cm high, bear a dense head of bell-shaped flowers, varying from white and yellow to deep purple. The plants have slender leaves, up to 30 cm long. The common garden hyacinths are derived from *H. orientalis*. Family: *Liliaceae*.

● **Hyades** ▶ A young open ▷star cluster in the constellation Taurus, the brightest stars forming a V-shaped group visible with the naked eye. The star ▷Aldebaran lies in the direction of the cluster but is much nearer the sun.

● **hyaena** ▷*See* hyena.

● **hybrid** ▶ The offspring resulting from the mating of two unrelated individuals. The hybrid offspring often shows greater general fitness than either of the two parents, a phenomenon called hybrid vigour (*or* heterosis). This is commonly used by plant breeders to produce a generation of crop plants giving higher yields and showing improved resistance to disease. Hybrid vigour cannot be maintained in subsequent generations and new hybrids have to be produced for each season.

● **Hyde, Douglas** ▶ (1860–1949) Irish scholar, whose translations of Irish literature influenced such writers as Yeats and Synge. He was also a senator in the Irish parliament (1925, 1938) and was president of Eire (1938–45). He founded, and was first president (1893–1915) of, the Gaelic League. His books include *The Love Songs of Connacht* (1893), *A Literary History of Ireland* (1899), and *Legends of Saints and Sinners* (1915).

● **Hyde Park** ▶ An extensive park in the Greater London borough of the City of Westminister. Adjoining Kensington Gardens, it is divided by the Serpentine, a popular boating lake, and crossed by Rotten Row, a horse-riding track. The Great Exhibition (1851) was held here and the park remains a venue for open-air meetings with Speakers' Corner in the NE, opposite Marble Arch. Area: about 1.4 sq km (0.55 sq mi).

● **Hyderabad** ▶ 17 22N 78 26E One of the largest cities in India, the capital of Andhra Pradesh situated on the River Musi. Formerly the capital of the princely state of Hyderabad, it was founded in 1590 by the Muslim Qutb Shahi sultans. The old city was planned around the Charminar (1594), a rectangular building surmounted by four minarets; other notable buildings include the Mecca Masjid, a mosque modelled on the one at Mecca. An educational centre, Hyderabad is the site of Osmania University (1918), an agricultural university, and several research institutes. There has been considerable industrial growth in recent years, giving Hyderabad a higher standard of living than many other Indian cities. The chief manufactures include bus and railway equipment, textiles, and pharmaceutical goods. Population (1991): 3 145 939.

● **Hyderabad** ▶ 25 23N 68 24E A city in SE Pakistan, on the River Indus. A focal point of rail and road routes, it has light industries and several institutions of higher education, including the University of Sind (1947). Population (latest est): 1 107 000.

● **Hyder Ali** ▶ (1728–82) Muslim Indian ruler of Mysore. A volunteer in the Mysore raja's army from 1749, he became a commander (1759) and in about 1761 deposed the raja. When the British refused to support him against his Indian enemies, he invaded British territory and was narrowly defeated near Madras, coming closer than any other Indian ruler to ousting the British from S India.

● **Hydra** ▶ (Greek mythology) A monster with many heads who grew two more whenever one was cut off. It was killed by ▷Heracles, whose own death was later caused by the monster's poisonous blood or gall.

● **Hydra** ▶ (zoology) A widely distributed genus of solitary freshwater invertebrate animals belonging to an order (*Hydroida*) of ▷cnidarians. They are flexible ▷polyps, 10–30 mm long, with the mouth at the top surrounded by 6–10 tentacles. Hydras are usually attached to stones, sticks, or aquatic vegetation and feed on small animals. Reproduction is asexual in summer and sexual in winter. Class: ▷*Hydrozoa*.

● **Hydrangea** ▶ A genus of shrubs (about 80 species) native to Asia and North and South America, which includes several popular ornamentals. The showy heads of white, pink, or blue flowers may be sterile and sometimes change colour according to the acidity or alkalinity of the soil. *H. macrophylla* is a popular pot plant. Family: *Hydrangeaceae*.

● **hydraulics** ▶ The study of the applications of ▷hydrostatics and ▷hydrodynamics to design problems. In civil engineering it is used to study the flow of water in pipes, rivers, canals, etc., especially with reference to the construction of dams, reservoirs, and hydroelectric power stations. In mechanical engineering, applications include the design of machinery involving fluids, such as hydraulic presses, ▷turbines, propellers, etc. Hydraulics is concerned with the bulk properties of fluids, such as density, viscosity, elasticity, and surface tension, rather than their molecular properties.

● **hydraulis** ▶ (Greek: water pipe) An early type of ▷organ in which the air pressure was maintained by water. A clay model found in the ruins of Carthage has three ranks of pipes and suggests an actual height of about 3 m (10 ft). The loud sound it produced made it useful for signalling in battle; it was also played in Roman amphitheatres, Emperor Nero being a keen performer.

● **hydrocarbons** ▶ Compounds containing carbon and hydrogen. The saturated hydrocarbons are classified as ▷alkanes. Unsaturated hydrocarbons include the ▷alkenes and ▷alkynes. ▷Aromatic hydrocarbons include ▷benzene and its many derivatives.

● **hydrocephalus** ▶ An excess of fluid in the brain. The brain is normally bathed in cerebrospinal fluid, which is constantly being produced and reabsorbed. A block in the flow or reabsorption of the fluid will result in hydrocephalus. In a baby, the bones of whose skull are not yet joined, the head becomes enlarged. Congenital defects, meningitis, tumours, and injury can all be causes. Hydrocephalus may resolve spontaneously or may require surgical treatment.

● **hydrochloric acid** ▶ A solution in water of the colourless pungent gas hydrogen chloride (HCl). It is made by the action of sulphuric acid on salt or by the direct recombination of hydrogen and chlorine from the electrolysis of sea water. It is very soluble in water and forms a strong acid. Concentrated hydrochloric acid contains about 40% HCl by weight and is a clear fuming corrosive liquid. The acid in the human stomach is dilute hydrochloric acid (0.4%).

● **hydrocyanic acid** ▷*See* hydrogen cyanide.

● **hydrodynamics** ▶ (*or* fluid dynamics) The branch of mechanics concerned with the study of ideal fluids in motion. An ideal fluid is assumed to be incompressible and to be free from frictional forces. Although never achieved, this simplification is often necessary to analyse a complex situation. The velocity, acceleration, and pressure at each point in the flow of an ideal liquid gives an indication of what will happen in a real liquid. ▷*See also* aerodynamics; hydraulics.

● **hydroelectric power** ▶ Electricity generation using the energy of falling water. The water turns a ▷turbine connected to an alternator, generating electricity with an efficiency of over 90% at full load and generally over 60% at quarter-load. Water is led through pipes from high-level natural or artificial reservoirs to the power station. Lower-level reservoirs and dammed rivers are also used in some situations. The higher the reservoir, the less water is needed for the same power output. Hydroelectric power is, therefore, a cheap power source in mountainous areas with high rainfall. Unfortunately these are not usually near the industrial communities that consume the most power. Also, because it depends on rainfall, hydroelectricity has to be backed by other power sources (*see* power station). In **pumped storage** stations, electricity is stored by using it to drive pumps that raise the water to a high-level reservoir. In times of high demand this water is run back through the turbines. Hydroelectricity is a renewable energy source causing no pollution; it currently provides 2.4% of world ▷energy needs but only 0.2% of UK energy.

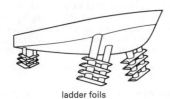

ladder foils

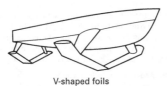

V-shaped foils

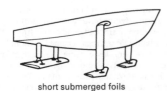

short submerged foils

hydrofoil

● **hydrofoil** ▶ A ship the hull of which is raised out of the water by foils as its speed increases. The foils provide lift in much the same way as an aerofoil; once the hull is clear of the water the drag is greatly reduced and the speed can be increased far above that of a normal ship of the same size and weight. The first hydrofoil was built in 1906 by Enrico Fortanini (1848–1930); this had a stack of foils arranged like a ladder. Modern craft use a large V-shaped foil, to provide stability in turns or in rough seas, or small totally submerged foils, which support the hull on streamlined struts. Propulsion is by propeller or by pumped-water jet. Hydrofoils of 150 tonnes are in use in many parts of the world, including a cross-Channel service; some are capable of reaching speeds of up to 112 km per hour (70 mph).

● **hydrogen** ▶ (H) The lightest of all gases, recognized as an element

by Cavendish in 1766 and named by Lavoisier after water (Greek *hudro*, water). Hydrogen makes up about three-quarters of the mass of the universe. It is the simplest element, its nuclei consisting of one proton. Heavier elements are formed by nuclear fusion (*see* nuclear energy) from hydrogen in stars. The heavier isotope of hydrogen, ▷deuterium (D *or* ^{2}H), occurs as about one part in 6000 of ordinary hydrogen. ▷Tritium (^{3}H) also occurs but is unstable. As well as the gaseous element (H_2) and water (H_2O), hydrogen occurs in organic compounds and in all inorganic ▷acids and alkalis. The gas itself is used as a fuel for rockets, in welding, for filling balloons, and in chemical manufacture. It combines (explosively if in the right proportions) with oxygen to form water and can be obtained from water by electrolysis. Liquid hydrogen is used for experiments in low-temperature physics. At no 1; at wt 1.00794; mp −259.34°C; bp −252.87°C.

● **hydrogen arsenide** ▷*See* arsine.

● **hydrogen bomb** ▷*See* nuclear weapons.

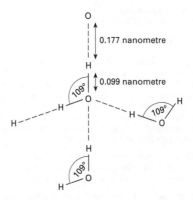

● **hydrogen bond** ▶ The hydrogen bonding between water molecules (H_2O) in ice crystals.

● **hydrogen bond** ▶ A weak attraction (much weaker than a covalent or ionic ▷chemical bond but much stronger than ▷Van der Waals forces) between an oxygen, nitrogen, or fluorine atom in one molecule and a hydrogen atom in a neighbouring molecule. The hydrogen atom must itself be linked to a similar electronegative atom by a covalent bond. The attraction arises because the atom bonded to the hydrogen atoms exerts a strong pull on the shared electrons and thus confers a partial positive charge on the hydrogen. Consequently electrostatic attraction occurs between this hydrogen atom and the oxygen, fluorine, or nitrogen in the other molecule. Hydrogen bonding is responsible for the anomalous physical properties of many compounds, including water. It is particularly important in biological systems, being responsible for maintaining the structure of proteins and nucleic acids.

hydrogen cyanide ▶ (HCN) A highly toxic colourless gas. It is made from ammonia and methane reacted with air in the presence of a catalyst. HCN forms weakly acidic solutions in water (called **hydrocyanic** or **prussic acid**) and is used in making synthetic fibres and as a fumigant. The gas was used by the Germans in the gas chambers of the ▷holocaust.

● **hydrogen ion concentration** ▷*See* pH.

● **hydrogen peroxide** ▶ (H_2O_2) A colourless liquid made by various processes, including the catalytic oxidation of hydrogen and water in the presence of oxygen. It readily decomposes to give water and oxygen. It is sold by volume strength, for example, 20-volume H_2O_2 yields 20 volumes of oxygen for each volume of the solution. It is widely used as an oxidizing agent, antiseptic, and bleach for hair and cloth. It is also used as an oxidant in rockets.

● **hydrography** ▶ The description, measurement, and charting of the waters of the earth's surface (oceans, seas, lakes, rivers, and streams), particularly for navigational purposes. Tides, currents, and waves are also involved. The term is sometimes used for the shape of the sea floor and the deposits covering it.

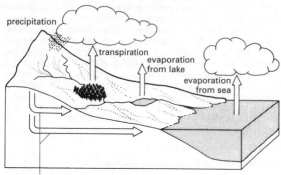

water returning to sea through streams, rivers, and underground flow.

hydrology ▶ The hydrological cycle.

● **hydrology** ▶ The science that studies the occurrence and movement of water on and over the surface of the earth. The **hydrological cycle** is the cyclic movement of water from the sea to the atmosphere and back, via precipitation, streams, and rivers. The main processes with which hydrology is concerned are precipitation, evaporation and transpiration, stream flow, and groundwater flow. Applications include flood control and the supply of water for domestic and industrial purposes, irrigation, and hydroelectric power.

● **hydrolysis** ▶ The reaction of a chemical compound with water; usually water is the solvent in which the reaction occurs. An example is the hydrolysis of ▷esters to form alcohols and carboxylic acids.

● **hydrometer** ▶ An instrument for measuring the relative ▷density of a liquid. It consists of a weighted and sealed glass bulb with a long neck on which a scale is calibrated. The relative density is measured by placing the hydrometer in the liquid and noting the level to which it sinks.

● **hydrophobia** ▷*See* rabies.

● **hydrophone** ▶ A type of ▷microphone that converts underwater sound waves into electrical signals. It consists essentially of a diaphragm, a ▷transducer, and an ▷amplifier. It is used in ▷echosounding equipment, depth sounding, and underwater communications.

● **hydroponics** ▶ The cultivation of plants in a liquid nutrient solution instead of soil. A carefully prepared aqueous solution of all the nutrients required for healthy growth is used, usually in conjunction with an inert medium, such as sand or gravel, which provides support for the plant-root system. On a small scale, the solution is simply poured over the substrate and the excess allowed to drain into containers for re-use. On a commercial scale, this is done by an automatic pumping system in which the solution is monitored to maintain nutrient levels and acidity.
  Hydroponics enables crops to be produced in arid regions or where the soil is infertile or toxic, but its high cost restricts its use to high-value crops, such as flowers and vegetables.

● **hydrostatics** ▶ The branch of mechanics concerned with fluids at rest (*compare* hydrodynamics). It is generally considered to have been instigated by Archimedes. Applications include the design of storage tanks, gates, and valves for hydraulic structures, dams, etc.

● **Hydrozoa** ▶ A class of aquatic invertebrate animals (3700 species) — ▷cnidarians—whose life cycle usually alternates between generations of mainly marine sessile colonial ▷polyps and free-swimming solitary ▷medusae. ▷*See also* Hydra; Obelia; Portuguese man-of-war.

● **hyena** ▶ (*or* hyaena) A carnivorous ▢mammal of the family *Hyaenidae*. There are three species: the African spotted hyena (*Crocuta crocuta*); the Asian striped hyena (*Hyaena hyaena*); and the brown

hyena (*H. brunnea*) of South Africa, also called strandwolf. Hyenas are doglike in appearance, up to 1.5 m long including the tail, and stand about 90 cm high at the shoulder. They hunt in packs, feeding on carrion and killing young or sick animals.

● **Hyères** ▶ 43 07N 6 08E A resort and spa in S France, in the Var department on the French Riviera. It has a notable beach and offshore are the Îles d'Hyères, a small group of islands (Porquerolles, Port-Cros, I'Île du Levant, and two islets). Population (latest est): 41 739.

● **Hygiea** ▶ The Greek goddess of health, worshipped together with ▷Asclepius, god of medicine, and sometimes identified as his daughter or wife. She was usually portrayed in the act of feeding a serpent from a dish.

● **hygrometer** ▶ An instrument that measures the relative ▷humidity of the atmosphere. In mechanical hygrometers, a material (usually human hair) is used, the length of which varies with the humidity; the variations being transformed into the movement of a pointer along a scale. In the wet-and-dry bulb hygrometer, two thermometers are placed side by side, one having its bulb covered by a moist cloth. The cooling caused by the evaporation from this wet bulb depends on the atmospheric moisture and thus the difference between the two thermometer readings can be related by standard tables to the relative humidity.

● **Hyksos** ▶ A nomadic Asiatic tribe, known to the ancient Egyptians as Shepherd Kings or Princes of Foreign Lands. Moving southwards about 1750 BC through Palestine and Syria, the Hyksos invaded Egypt and, until driven northwards again by the Egyptians about 1570 BC, ruled the Delta area, introducing metallurgy, bronze weapons, the wheel, and, traditionally, the use of horse and chariot.

● **Hymen** ▶ The Greek god of marriage. He was the son of Apollo or of Dionysus and Aphrodite.

● **Hymenoptera** ▶ A large worldwide order of insects (over 100 000 species) including the ants, sawflies, ichneumons, wasps, and bees. Many species show a high degree of social organization. Typically they have two pairs of membranous wings and the first segment of the abdomen is constricted to form a "waist." A tubular egg-laying structure (ovipositor) is generally present and in higher groups is modified for sawing, piercing, or stinging. The larvae (except the sawflies) are legless and have well-developed heads. Males develop from unfertilized eggs. Many species benefit man as they pollinate flowering plants and prey on or parasitize insect pests.

● **Hymettus, Mount** ▶ (Modern Greek name: Imittós Óros) 37 57N 23 49E A mountain ridge in SE Greece, running N–S for about 15 km (9 mi) immediately E of Athens. The Kara marble used in ancient times was quarried here. Height: 1026 m (3366 ft).

● **hymn** ▶ A song of praise in honour of a deity or saint, often in a metrical verse form. Hymns have been an important part of Christian congregational worship since the end of the 4th century. During the middle ages polyphonic settings became common but after the Reformation Lutheran chorales became the basis of the German and English hymn traditions. Famous hymn writers include Martin Luther, Charles Wesley, and Isaac Watts (1674–1748); many of the hymns sung in the Anglican church today were written in the 19th century. In many modern churches traditional forms of hymn have been largely replaced by simple and repetitive "worship songs" based on contemporary folk and pop styles.

● **hyoscine** ▶ (*or* scopolamine) A drug similar to ▷atropine. It is used to relieve painful spasms of the intestine and, because of its depressant effect on the brain, to prevent travel sickness.

● **Hypatia** ▶ (d. 415 AD) Neoplatonist philosopher and mathematician. She lectured on philosophy at ▷Alexandria, where her wisdom and learning endeared her to both pagans and Christians. The patriarch Cyril resented her influence, and she was brutally murdered by a Christian mob.

● **hyperactivity** ▷*See* attention deficit disorder.

● **hyperbola** ▶ The curve, or pair of curves, formed by a ▷conic section and defined in Cartesian coordinates (*see* coordinate systems) by the equation $x^2/a^2 - y^2/b^2 = 1$, where a and b are constants. Its two parts have a common axis and are separated by a minimum distance

2*a* along this axis. As it goes out to ▷infinity, the curve becomes increasingly close to two straight lines, called ▷asymptotes.

● **hyperbolic functions** ▶ A set of mathematical functions written sinh *x*, cosh *x*, tanh *x*, and their inverses csch *x*, sech *x*, and coth *x* respectively. Sinh *x* is defined as ½(e^x − e$^{−x}$), where e is the base of natural logarithms; cosh *x* is ½(e^x + e$^{−x}$), and tanh *x* is sinh *x*/cosh *x*. Hyperbolic functions are defined by analogy with the trigonometric functions sin *x*, etc., and are so named because they are related to the ▷hyperbola in much the same way as the trigonometric functions are related to the circle.

● **Hyperboreans** ▶ In Greek mythology, a people who lived in the far north, beyond the north wind (Boreas), in a land of sunshine and luxury. According to ▷Herodotus, they were devotees of Apollo and sent offerings to him at Delos but did not come themselves.

● **hyperglycaemia** ▶ A high concentration of sugar in the blood. This occurs in ▷diabetes mellitus and may, if severe and uncontrolled, lead to coma.

● **Hyperion** ▶ In Greek mythology, one of the ▷Titans, the son of Uranus and Gaia and father of Eos (*see* Aurora), ▷Helios, and ▷Selene. He was himself a sun god and was often identified with his son Helios.

● **hypermetropia** ▷*See* longsightedness.

● **hypersensitivity** ▷*See* allergy.

● **hypertension** ▶ High ▷blood pressure. This is a common condition, which can be caused by kidney disease, hormonal disorders, and some congenital diseases; for most cases, however, no cause can be found (this is known as essential hypertension). Usually there are no symptoms, with the consequent danger that untreated hypertension may lead to heart failure, kidney failure, cerebral haemorrhage, and blindness. In some cases surgery can be curative, but usually only drug treatment (*see* ACE inhibitors; beta blocker; diuretics) is necessary and must continue indefinitely.

● **hyperthyroidism** ▶ Overactivity of the thyroid gland, which occurs most commonly in women. It may lead to the syndrome of thyrotoxicosis: restlessness, irritability, heat intolerance, weight loss, and palpitations, sometimes with protruding eyes and swelling of the neck (*see* goitre)—this is called exophthalmic goitre (*or* Graves's disease). It can be treated by surgery, radioactive iodine to destroy part of the gland, or drugs that suppress the production of thyroid hormones.

● **hypocaust** ▶ A domestic bot-air heating system used by the Romans from about 100 BC. Hot air from a furnace was allowed to circulate within a hollow floor supported on tile piers. It was used both for baths and for space heating. In a later development, in the first century AD, the hot air was also allowed to circulate in hollow walls and in the roof space to ensure even heating throughout a building.

● **hypnosis** ▶ The production of a trance state by means of firm suggestion, with the cooperation of the subject. People who have been deeply hypnotized can carry out instructions that would not be possible in a normal waking state; for instance, they can become insensible to pain or regress to childish behaviour. First used for therapeutic purposes by ▷Mesmer in the 18th century, it was developed (and given the name hypnosis) by James Braid in the 19th century. In France it was used by ▷Charcot (under whom ▷Freud studied), and by the turn of the century it was established as a means of treating certain 19
psychiatric disorders (especially those of psychosomatic origin). It has, however, always been regarded as somewhat disreputable, first because of its misuse on the stage as a form of entertainment and second because the mechanism is still not understood. Although it is alleged that a hypnotist cannot force a patient under hypnotism to do anything he would not be willing to do when awake (e.g. commit a crime), the dangers inherent in one person controlling another's actions are obvious. It is, however, now used with moderate success in treating overeating and some phobias and addictions.

● **hypnotics** ▶ Drugs that cause sleep. Ideally hypnotics should produce natural sleep without "hangover" effects on awakening. Some
▷benzodiazepines and newer drugs, such as zopiclone (Zimovane), produce little or no hangover effect but they can cause unpleasant symptoms when withdrawn (*see* drug dependence). They should therefore only be used for short-term treatment of insomnia. Certain ▷antihistamines with a sedative action are also used as hypnotics.

● **hypoglycaemia** ▶ A low concentration of sugar in the blood. This is most often seen in diabetics who have taken too much insulin. The patient feels weak, sweaty, and shaky. ▷*See* diabetes.

● **hypothalamus** ▶ A part of the ▷brain, surrounding the lower part of the third ventricle, that is an important coordinating centre for the functions of the autonomic ▷nervous system. It is particularly involved with the control of body temperature, with regulating how much is eaten and drunk, and with the emotions. It also releases ▷neurohormones affecting other organs, especially the ▷pituitary gland.

● **hypothermia** ▶ Lowering of the body temperature. This is most commonly seen in old people and young babies—whose body temperature is less well controlled—if they are living in poorly heated rooms. If the body temperature falls to a very low level, severe internal changes may occur, but otherwise gentle warming will help the patient to recover. Hypothermia may be deliberately induced for heart surgery.

● **hyrax** ▶ An African ▷mammal belonging to the order *Hyracoidea* (7 species), also called coney. 30–60 cm long, hyraxes are related to ungulates (hooved mammals), having hooflike toes and a two-chambered stomach for digesting their vegetable diet. They are nimble and live in small colonies in trees or among rocks, being most active at twilight.

● **hyssop** ▶ A perennial herbaceous plant, *Hyssopus officinalis*, native to S Europe, Asia, and Morocco. It is grown elsewhere as a garden ornamental and was formerly cultivated as a medicinal herb. Growing to a height of 60 cm, it has whorls of violet-blue flowers along the stem. Family: ▷*Labiatae*.

● **hysterectomy** ▶ The surgical removal of the womb. A subtotal hysterectomy (now rarely performed) involves removing the body of the womb but leaving the neck (cervix); in total hysterectomy (or panhysterectomy) the entire womb is removed. It is most commonly performed when the womb contains large fibroids—benign tumours that cause heavy menstrual periods—or for treating cancer of the womb. The operation is usually performed through an incision made in the abdominal wall: it invariably precludes subsequent pregnancy but does not affect sexual activity.

● **hysteresis** ▶ Any of several physical phenomena in which an induced effect lags behind the inducing cause. The term is most often applied to magnetic hysteresis in which the magnetic induction produced in a ferromagnetic material lags behind the magnetic field. Thus a graph of magnetic induction plotted against a magnetizing field is a closed S-shaped loop (hysteresis loop). The area within the loop is equal to the energy dissipation per unit volume during one cycle of magnetization. Other forms of hysteresis include thermal, dielectric, and elastic hysteresis.

● **hysteria** ▶ A neurotic condition of emotional instability and immaturity in which patients are vulnerable to suggestion and may develop physical symptoms. Hysterical symptoms are unconsciously adopted by the individual because they bring some gain. The symptoms may be those of conversion disorder, characterized by physical symptoms, such as paralysis; or of dissociative disorder, with changes in thinking, such as multiple personality. Treatment is usually by ▷psychotherapy.

● **Hythe** ▶ 51 05N 1 05E A resort in SE England, in Kent on the English Channel. It is an ancient Cinque Port, long silted up. A light railway, claimed to be the world's smallest, runs to Dymchurch and Romney. Population (1991): 14 569.

● **Hywel the Good** ▶ (Howel Dda; d. 950 AD) Welsh prince (c. 909–50 AD). A friend of the English king Athelstan, Hywel eventually united S and N Wales in his remarkably peaceful reign. His famous codification of Welsh law remained effective for over three hundred years.

● **iamb** ▷*See* metre (poetry).

● **Iapetus** ► In Greek mythology, one of the ▷Titans, the son of Uranus and Gaia and father of Atlas and Prometheus. When the rebellion of the Titans was defeated by Zeus, he was imprisoned in Tartarus.

● **Iaşi** ► (German name: Jassy) 47 09N 27 38E A city in NE Romania, near the Moldovan border. The former capital of Moldavia, it possesses many historic buildings and academic institutions, including a university (1860). It has metal, chemical, and pharmaceutical industries. Population (1994 est): 339 889.

● **Ibadan** ► 7 23N 3 56E The second largest city in Nigeria. The arrival of the railway (1901) aided its commercial development and it is now an important industrial, commercial, and administrative centre although there are few modern industries. Cocoa, palm products, and cotton are traded. It contains the University of Ibadan (1962). Population (1996 est): 1 432 000.

● **Ibagué** ► 4 35N 75 30W A city in central Colombia, on the E slopes of the Central Cordillera. The surrounding area produces cocoa, tobacco, rice, and sugar cane. Tolima University was founded here in 1945. Population (1997 est): 419 883.

● **Ibáñez, Vicente Blasco** ▷*See* Blasco Ibáñez, Vicente.

● **Ibarruri, Dolores** ► (1895–1989) Spanish politician. She was a leading Spanish communist in the 1930s: her oratory during the Spanish Civil War (1936–39) earned her the name La Pasionaria. Ibarruri went into exile in 1939 and lived in the Soviet Union until the legalization of the Communist Party allowed her to return to Spain (1977). She became a member of the Cortes (Spanish national assembly) at the age of 82.

● **Iberian Peninsula** ► A peninsula in SW Europe, occupied by Portugal and Spain. It is separated from the rest of Europe by the Pyrenees and its flora and fauna are similar to those of N Africa. Area: 593 250 sq km (229 054 sq mi).

● **Iberians** ► A Bronze Age people of S and E Spain in the 1st millennium BC. Their non-Indo-European language, which was displaced by Latin, is known from a variety of inscriptions on stone and other materials. The culture of the tribes of the coastal region of Valencia and in the NE showed considerable Greek influence while that of the SE tribes owed much to the Carthaginians. This is shown, for example, in differences in the alphabets used in each area. The economic basis was agriculture, mining, and metalworking. They lost their identity by cultural assimilation to the ▷Celts in Roman times.

● **Ibert, Jacques** ► (1890–1962) French composer. A pupil of Fauré, he won the Prix de Rome in 1919. He directed the Academy of Rome from 1937 to 1955. His compositions include operas, chamber and orchestral music, and songs. His best-known work is the humorous orchestral *Divertissement* (1930).

● **Iberville, Pierre le Moyne, Sieur d'** ► (1661–1706) French-Canadian explorer. After serving in the French navy he returned to Canada and led raids on the English fur-trading posts on Hudson Bay (1686–97). In 1699 he founded a colony at present-day Biloxi (Mississippi) and in 1700, the first French colony in Louisiana (near present-day New Orleans).

● **ibex** ► A rare wild ▷goat, *Capra ibex*, of Eurasian and N African mountains. About 85 cm high at the shoulder, ibexes have backward-curving horns up to 65 cm long and their coat is brownish-grey with variable markings.

Other species known as ibex include the tur (*C. caucasica*) of Russia and the Spanish ibex (*C. pyrenaica*).

ibis ► A white ibis (*Eudocimus albus*) standing on a partly submerged rock.

● **ibis** ► A long-necked wading bird belonging to the subfamily *Threskiornithinae* (20 species), distributed worldwide in warm regions. 55–75 cm long, ibises have a characteristic slender downcurved bill, and unfeathered face or head and neck, which may be black or brightly coloured. Wading in shallow lakes, bays, and marshes, they feed on small fish and aquatic invertebrates. Family: *Threskiornithidae* (ibises and spoonbills); order: *Ciconiiformes* (herons, storks, etc.).

● **Ibiza** ► (Iviza *or* Ivica) A Spanish island in the Mediterranean Sea, in the Balearic Islands. Its climate and fine beaches have made it a popular tourist centre. Exports include almonds, dried figs, apricots, and salt. Area: 541 sq km (209 sq mi). Population (latest est): 45 000. Chief town: Ibiza.

● **Iblis** ► The Muslim name for the devil, perhaps derived from Greek *diabolos*. He is also called *al-Shaytan* (Satan). Because of his disobedience and pride, the devil was expelled from Paradise by God, but given power to lead astray those who do not serve God. Muslim tradition gives him a number of names before his fall, such as Azazil. It is disputed whether he was an angel, as in the Koran, or a jinni.

● **Ibn al-'Arabi, Muhyi-l-din** ► (1165–1240) Muslim mystic and poet born in Murcia (Spain). The leading mystic of his age, he was one of the great geniuses of ▷Sufism. In philosophy, he was a Neoplatonist. Some scholars believe that Islamic sufism, as represented by Ibn al-'Arabi, was an imitation of Christian monastic mysticism.

● **Ibn Battutah** ▶ (1304–?1368) Arab traveller. From 1325 to 1354 he travelled extensively in Asia Minor, the Near and Far East, Europe, and Africa. He then settled at Fez and wrote an invaluable and amusing account of his work—the *Rihlah*.

● **Ibn Ezra, Abraham Ben Meir** ▶ (1093–1167) Hebrew poet and scholar, born in Toledo, who travelled to England, Italy, France, North Africa, and perhaps to Palestine. His works include a set of famous commentaries on the Hebrew Bible, poems, riddles, and epigrams.

● **Ibn Gabirol, Solomon** ▶ (c. 1021–c. 1058) Jewish philosopher and poet, born in Málaga (Spain). He was one of the earliest philosophers of Moorish Spain and a leading Neoplatonist. His outstanding philosophical work, *The Fountain of Life*, influenced generations of Western medieval thinkers. *The Kingly Crown* is the summit of his poetic achievement.

● **Ibn Khaldun** ▶ (1332–1406) Arab historian and philosopher, who held court posts in Spain and was chief judge in Cairo, where he died. In the *Kitab al-'ibar* (*Book of Examples*) he outlined the history of Islam and a historical theory of cyclical progress and regression in which nation states develop out of, and are subsequently destroyed by, nomadic communities.

● **Ibn Saud** ▶ (c. 1880–1953) The first King of Saudi Arabia (1932–53). With the military help of al-▷Ikhwan, he extended his territory from the Sultanate of Najd, which he reconquered in 1902, to encompass much of Arabia by 1924, when he took Hejaz. The name Saudi Arabia was adopted in 1932. In 1933 Ibn Saud came to an agreement with a US oil company, which discovered oil in his country in 1936, using the resultant revenues to introduce modernization programmes.

● **Ibo** ▶ (or Igbo) A people of SE Nigeria who speak Igbo, a language of the Kwa subgroup of the ▷Niger-Congo family. Subsistence cultivators of yams, cassava, and taro, they traditionally lived in scattered small holdings or village clusters of patrilineal kin headed by the eldest male descendant of the founder. Small federations of villages were the largest political units before colonial times. Many have now adopted Christianity. A growing sense of ethnic identity led to the proclamation of the short-lived Ibo secessionist republic of ▷Biafra (1967–70).

● **Ibrahim Pasha** ▶ (1789–1848) Ottoman general; the son (or adopted son) and right-hand man of the viceroy of Egypt, ▷Mehemet Ali. In Egypt from 1805, he was given various offices by his father, culminating in the command of the Egyptian army after Mehemet Ali had quarrelled with the Ottomans (1831). Ibrahim occupied Syria, becoming governor general (1833), until forced to withdraw by the European powers (1840). His modernizing policies were severely imposed and provoked much opposition. In 1848 he succeeded his infirm father as viceroy of Egypt but died after only 40 days in office.

● **Ibsen, Henrik** ▶ (1828–1906) Norwegian playwright and poet, the founder of modern prose drama. The son of a rich merchant who became bankrupt when his son was eight, Ibsen was preparing to study medicine when he wrote his first, unsuccessful, play. After working in theatres in Bergen and Kristiania and continuing to write plays, none of which was outstanding, he wrote *Kongsemnerne* (*The Pretenders*; 1864), for which he was granted a scholarship. He travelled to Rome and from 1864 to 1891 lived in Italy and Germany, with occasional visits to Norway. His fame as a dramatist grew with *Brand* (1865) and *Peer Gynt* (1867). In his next several plays he turned to the presentation of social issues: women's emancipation in *A Doll's House* (1879), inherited disease and guilt in *Ghosts* (1881), and public corruption in *An Enemy of the People* (1882), plays which earned him a wide and controversial reputation. Subsequent works, such as *The Wild Duck* (1884) and *Hedda Gabler* (1890), dealt with the problems of individuals. In his last plays, *The Master Builder* (1892), *John Gabriel Borkman* (1896), and *When We Dead Awaken* (1899), he turned to the treatment of autobiographical themes in a symbolic manner.

● **Icarus** ▶ (astronomy) A very small (about 1 km diameter) ▷minor planet with the smallest known ▷perihelion (0.19 astronomical units). It passed only 600 000 km from earth in 1968.

● **Icarus** ▶ (mythology) ▷*See* Daedalus.

● **Ice Age** ▶ A period in the earth's history when ice spread towards the equator with a general lowering of temperatures. The most recent of these was the ▷Pleistocene epoch ending about 10 000 years ago, during which four major ice advances occurred. Other ice ages occurred in Permo-Carboniferous times about 250 million years ago and in Precambrian times over 500 million years ago. Between 1550 and 1850 the **Little Ice Age** occurred, with a significant lowering of temperatures in the N hemisphere.

● **iceberg** ▶ A large mass of ice in the sea that has originated on land. Many result from the breaking off, or calving, of ice from glaciers. In the N hemisphere icebergs originate chiefly from Greenland, in the S hemisphere most break off from the Antarctic ice. A large part of an iceberg is submerged, causing a hazard to shipping (e.g. the loss of the *Titanic* in 1912).

● **icefish** ▶ A name given to several unrelated fish including the family *Chaenichthyidae* (175 species) of the order *Perciformes*, also called white-blooded fish, which occur in Antarctic waters. Others include the semitransparent icicle or glass fish of E Asia (family *Salangidae*) and certain species of ▷smelt. Order: *Salmoniformes*.

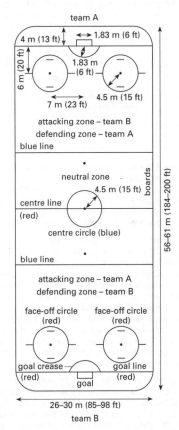

ice hockey ▶ The dimensions of the rink.

● **ice hockey** ▶ A six-a-side team game played with stick and puck on a rink. It derives from field hockey and was first played by Englishmen on the frozen Kingston Harbour, Ontario (c. 1860). Canada is the true home of the game, but it is widely played in the USA, the countries of the former Soviet Union, Sweden, the Czech Republic, Germany, and Finland. Each team consists of a goalkeeper, right and left defence, centre, and right and left wing and is allowed eight reserves. The premier competition is the National Hockey League (NHL) of

North America (instituted 1917). The premier trophy is the Stanley Cup, won by the Montreal Canadians more than any other team. The Canada Cup is an international tournament, and ice hockey is also played at the Winter Olympics.

● **Iceland, Republic of** ▶ (Icelandic name: Ísland) An island country in the N Atlantic, just S of the Arctic Circle, off the SE coast of Greenland. It consists mainly of an uninhabited plateau of volcanoes, lava fields, and glaciers; most of the population live around the deeply indented coast.

Economy: some crops and livestock are produced for local needs, but the basis of the economy is fishing. Tourism is of growing importance. Hydroelectricity and geothermal power (from the numerous geysers and thermal springs) are important sources of energy. There is also an aluminium-smelting industry. The main exports are fish, fish products, ferrosilicon, and aluminium. Iceland is a member of the European Free Trade Association.

History: the Vikings reached Iceland about 874 AD and by the 10th century it had become an independent state with its own parliament, the Althing, considered to be the oldest in the world. In 1264 it came under Norwegian rule and, with Norway, passed to the Danish Crown in 1381. In the late 19th century it gained a degree of self-government and in 1918 became an independent state under the Danish Crown, attaining full independence as a republic in 1944. In the 1960s and 1970s, following extensions of its fishing limits, it was involved in several ▷Cod Wars with the UK; falling fish prices have since created economic strain. In 1995 parliamentary elections were won by the Independence Party under David Oddson.

Republic of Iceland

Head of state	President Olafur Ragnar Grimsson
Official language	Icelandic
Official religion	Evangelical Lutheranism
Official currency	króna of 100 aurar
Area	103 000 sq km (39 758 sq mi)
Population (1997 est)	271 000
Capital and main port	Reykjavik

● **Icelandic** ▶ A North Germanic language of the Western Scandinavian subgroup. It is the official language of Iceland. Developed from the ▷Old Norse spoken by the original settlers of Iceland during the 9th and 10th centuries, Icelandic remains the most conservative of the Scandinavian languages in vocabulary, grammar, and orthography, but there has been much change in pronunciation.

● **Icelandic literature** ▶ The greatest period of Icelandic literature was between 1100 and 1350, when the language was a dialect of ▷Old Norse and the Roman alphabet had only recently replaced the indigenous ▷runic script. Much of the material then written down drew upon considerably older oral sources. ▷Skaldic poetry, originating in the pre-Christian (pre-1000) era, remained an important form throughout the middle ages (*see also* Eddas). In prose, stories previously recited were written down for reading aloud (*see* sagas) and the influence of this classical prose has remained strong. Despite the small number of Icelandic speakers there was a considerable revival in prose and poetry during the 19th century. In 1955 the Icelandic novelist Halldór ▷Laxness won the Nobel Prize for Literature.

● **Iceland moss** ▶ An edible ▷lichen, *Cetraria islandica*, that grows on moors and alpine areas of the N hemisphere and on lava slopes and plains of Iceland. Up to about 10 cm high, it has a dark-brown to grey-white upright body with numerous flattened branches. It contains about 70% digestible starch and a brown dye.

● **Iceland spar** ▶ A variety of ▷calcite consisting of pure colourless transparent crystals having the property of double refraction. It is therefore used for optical purposes and formerly for the nicol prisms in polarizing microscopes. It occurs in large steam cavities in basalt lava in Iceland.

● **Iceni** ▶ A British tribe that inhabited the area that is now Norfolk and Suffolk. They accepted Roman rule after the Roman invasion in 43 AD. However, when their king, Prasutagus, died (60 AD) the Romans attempted to steal his wealth and mistreated his widow ▷Boadicea

and his daughters. Their revolt against Roman rule was brutally suppressed.

● **ice plant** ▶ A succulent annual or biennial plant, *Cryophytum crystallinum*, that is covered in glistening papillae and has long prostrate stems reaching 75 cm. Native to South Africa, it is naturalized in California and the Mediterranean region and widely grown as a garden or pot plant. It is easily propagated from seed. Family: *Aizoaceae*.

● **ice skating** ▶ The recreation and sport of sliding over ice on steel-bladed skates. It originated over 2000 years ago and was widely practised in the middle ages in Scandinavia and on Dutch canals. The main forms of the sport, which is governed by the International Skating Union and is predominantly amateur, are speed skating (long-distance outdoor racing) and two events judged on style—figure skating (a freestyle performance to music, either singly or in pairs) and ice dancing (a combination of dancing and pairs figure skating). ▷*See also* ice hockey.

● **I-ch'ang** ▷*See* Yichang.

I Ching ▶ The eight trigrams known as the *pa kua* (shown here) are the basis of the 64 hexagrams of the I Ching, each of which has a particular significance.

● **I Ching** ▶ A Chinese classic work on divination, also called the Book of Changes, attributed to Wen Wang (12th century BC). It is based on eight named trigrams (*bagua* or *pa kua*) made up of broken and unbroken lines (representing ▷yin and yang respectively) and arranged in different sequences. Study of the I Ching and its cosmology has exercised many Chinese philosophers.

● **ichneumon** ▶ An insect, also called ichneumon fly and ichneumon wasp, belonging to a family (*Ichneumonidae*; about 40 000 species) occurring in Europe, North America, and elsewhere. About 12 mm long, ichneumons resemble wasps but have longer antennae. They are parasitic upon other insects thereby controlling many insect pests. The female uses a long tubular ovipositor to lay eggs on or in the host. The larvae feed on the host's body fluids and eventually cause its death. Order: ▷*Hymenoptera*.

● **ichthyology** ▷*See* fish.

● **Ichthyornis** ▶ A genus of extinct seabirds whose fossils date from the Cretaceous period (125–60 million years ago). It was 20 cm long and was probably an active flier, having a large-keeled breastbone and strong wing bones.

● **ichthyosaur** ▶ An extinct dolphin-like marine reptile that lived through much of the Mesozoic era but was most abundant in the Jurassic period (200–135 million years ago). 1–12 m long, it had broad flexible paddles, a large tail fin, and a triangular dorsal fin. Most ichthyosaurs had a long snout and jaws armed with sharp teeth and hunted fish near the surface of the sea but some had few or no teeth and fed on molluscs. □fossil.

● **Icknield Way** ▶ A prehistoric trackway in SE England. Like its westward extension, the ▷Ridgeway, it follows high ground and runs NE from the Thames Valley along the Chilterns towards the East Anglian coast.

● **icon** ▶ A painted or mosaic image of Christ or a saint, peculiar to the Byzantine and Orthodox churches. Reverence of icons was castigated as idolatry by the Byzantine iconoclasts (*see* iconoclasm) and they were temporarily banned (730–843 AD). The decree reinstating them proclaimed that an icon must be a recognizable portrait of its subject with his accepted attributes, a formula resulting in a high degree of standardization. Unlike other paintings, therefore, icons have undergone little stylistic development and are characterized by a symbolic rather than realistic approach to colour, perspective, etc.

● **Iconium** ▷*See* Konya.

● **iconoclasm** ► The rejection of the veneration of ▷icons in the Byzantine Church. The movement gained much support, especially in Asia Minor, during the 8th and 9th centuries. Imperial prohibition of icons lasted from 730 to 787 and from 815 to 843, during which times icon worshippers were severely persecuted. Iconoclasm was an expression both of long-standing Christological disputes and of the antagonism towards the portrayal of divinity that was also common to Islam and Judaism in the Near East.

● **iconography** ► The branch of art history dealing with the interpretation of images and symbols associated with a particular subject in art. Although the term was first used in the 18th century in the study of engravings, it was largely promoted by Aby Warburg (1866–1929) and Erwin Panofsky (1892–1968). ▷*See also* iconology.

● **iconology** ► The interpretation of the content of a picture in relation to its historical context. The term was adopted by Erwin Panofsky (1892–1968) from the title, *Iconologia*, of a 16th-century book on symbols. Iconology attempts to place ▷iconography in a broader context and to study visual imagery as a bridge to wider aspects of history and civilization.

● **Ictinus** ► (5th century BC) Greek architect. With ▷Callicrates, he designed the ▷Parthenon, the most perfect of classical Greek buildings. He also helped rebuild the Telesterion for the temple at Eleusis and possibly designed the temple of Apollo Epicurius at Bassae.

● **id** ► In ▷psychoanalysis, the part of the unconscious mind that is governed by irrational instinctive forces, such as ▷libido and ▷aggression. These forces seek immediate (actual or symbolic) relief and the id is therefore said to be ruled by the pleasure principle and not by reality or logic. ▷*See also* ego; superego; unconscious.

● **Id** ► (*or* Eid; Arabic: festival) Either of two annual Muslim festivals. **Id-ul-Adha** (Festival of Sacrifice) is held in late February or early March to mark the end of the pilgrimage to Mecca (*see* Hajj) and to commemorate the sacrifice of ▷Abraham. Traditionally the festival is celebrated by cooking meat and distributing it to the poor. **Id-ul-Fitr** (Festival of Fast Breaking) is held in early December, marking the end of ▷Ramadam, when families gather for a festive meal and the exchange of presents.

● **Ida, Mount** ► (Turkish name: Kaz Daği) A mountain range in NW Asian Turkey, rising to 1767 m (5797 ft). It was important in classical times as it overlooks the plain on which Troy was built.

● **Idaho** ► A state in the NW USA, dominated by the N Rocky Mountains. The valley of the Snake River, famous for its canyons and cataracts, lies in the S. It is chiefly agricultural. On the better soils potatoes, wheat, and sugar beet are grown while the poorer lands support herds of beef cattle and sheep. Rich in minerals, Idaho is a leading US producer of silver and antimony. Natural gas and oil are increasingly exploited. The forested uplands make lumbering important.
History: first settled in the early 19th century, it became a state in 1890. Area: 216 412 sq km (83 557 sq mi). Population (1998 est): 1 228 684. Capital: Boise.

● **ide** ▷*See* orfe.

● **ideal gas** ► A hypothetical gas that exactly obeys the ideal gas equation (*see* gas laws). Such a gas has no intermolecular forces and the volume of its molecules is negligible. Also known as a perfect gas, it is closely approximated by real gases at low pressure.

● **idealism** ► Any doctrine that equates reality with mind, spirit, person, soul, thought, or, as in ▷Plato, archetypal ideas. George ▷Berkeley was an idealist in holding that all we perceive is sensible ideas. He escaped from ▷solipsism on the ground that other people were, like himself, spirits—ideas in the mind of God, perceivers of the collections of ideas that were "material objects." In the early 18th

century the term came to be used for the belief that the world of common sense was only a projection of our minds. Later it was publicized by ▷Kant, who called his theory of knowledge "transcendental idealism," the view that the synthetic knowable is confined to the world of phenomena as contrasted with the real world of ideas, or things-in-themselves. ▷Hegel's absolute idealism conceived the real as being perfect, whole, and complete. ▷Bradley and ▷Bosanquet developed this in England, and it is Hegelian idealism that has led to the organic theory of the state (*see also* Hegelianism).

● **Identikit and Photofit** ► Systems for reconstructing the facial appearance of a suspect from details recollected by witnesses. Identikit, which was developed by Hugh McDonald (1913–   ) and first used in Los Angeles, is based on artists' drawings of portions of the face (hair line, nose, eyes, etc.), put together to make up a composite picture. It was first successfully used in Britain in 1961. Photofit, based on photographs of various features, produces a more realistic picture and has replaced Identikit. More sophisticated computerized systems (notably the **E-FIT system**) are also now used. ▷*See also* fingerprint.

● **ideographic writing systems** ► (*or* ideography) Writing systems in which each concept is represented by a symbol. All ideographic systems were probably derived from ▷pictographic writing systems, stylized representations of abstract concepts being added to the list of symbols. Languages such as Chinese still use ideographic writing systems. However, the huge number of symbols required to represent even a practical selection of the words in a language places a great strain on a person's memory, and hinders the acquisition of literacy skills. Moreover, ideographic systems are inflexible and cannot easily represent new coinages, words borrowed from foreign languages, etc. They have, therefore, been largely replaced by the more efficient phonetic writing systems (*see* alphabets).

● **Idi Amin Dada, Lake** ▷*See* Edward, Lake.

● **Idomeneus** ► In Greek legend, a king of Crete, grandson of ▷Minos. He was a suitor of ▷Helen and fought in the ▷Trojan War. On returning to Crete he killed his son, having sworn to Poseidon to sacrifice the first being he met. Thereafter he lived in exile in Italy.

● **If** ► A French islet in the Gulf of Lions. Its 16th-century fortress, Château d'If, was used as a state prison and made famous by Alexandre Dumas in *The Count of Monte Cristo*.

● **Ife** ► 7 33N 4 34E A town in SW Nigeria. It is the holy city of the Yoruba tribe and is famed for its terracotta and bronze pieces. Today it is primarily an agricultural trade centre, the chief products being cocoa and cotton. It contains the University of Ife (1961). Population (1996 est): 296 800.

● **Ifni** ► An area in Morocco, on the Atlantic coast. First settled by the Spanish (1476), it formed part of Spanish West Africa (1946) and was returned to Morocco in 1969. Chief town: Sidi Ifni.

● **Igarka** ► 67 31N 86 33E A port in N Russia, on the River Yenisei. It is one of the country's largest sawmilling centres and a major timber port. Population (latest est): 39 000.

● **Igbo** ▷*See* Ibo.

● **igloo** ► A temporary dome-shaped dwelling made from blocks of snow by Inuits of the region between the MacKenzie River delta and Labrador in N Canada. The blocks are cut with a long knife and the joints filled with snow. The igloo is entered by a low and narrow semi-cylindrical passageway about three metres long.

● **Ignatiev, Nikolai Pavlovich, Count** ► (1832–1908) Russian diplomat, who was instrumental in expanding Russian interests into the Far East and the Balkans. After successful diplomatic missions to Bukhara and China (1858–60), Ignatiev served as ambassador to Turkey (1864–77). In 1878 he negotiated the Treaty of ▷San Stefano, which ended the Russo-Turkish War. He was subsequently minister of the interior (1881–82).

● **Ignatius Loyola, St** ► (1491–1556) Spanish founder of the ▷Jesuits. Of noble birth, his deep interest in religion dated from 1521, after reading the life of Christ while convalescing from a war wound. After visiting the Holy Land (1523), he studied in Spain and in Paris. There, in 1534 he made vows of poverty, chastity, and obedience, with St

▷Francis Xavier and other followers. He was ordained in 1537 and then moved to Rome, where he founded the Society of Jesus with the approval of Pope Paul III in 1540. As its first superior general, he sent out missionaries to Japan, India, and Brazil and founded Jesuit schools. His *Spiritual Exercises* (1548) has had lasting influence on the Roman Catholic Church. Feast day: 31 July.

● **Ignatius of Antioch, St** ▸ (1st century AD) Christian martyr; Bishop of Antioch. Little is known of his life apart from a series of letters to Churches in Rome and Asia Minor, written as a prisoner on his way to Rome to be executed. They provide valuable information on the beliefs and organization of the early Church. Feast day: 1 Feb.

● **igneous rock** ▸ One of the three major categories of rock (*compare* metamorphic rock; sedimentary rock) consisting mostly of crystalline rocks cooled directly from magma. That cooled at the surface forms extrusive rocks—volcanic lavas with small crystals because they have cooled rapidly (*see also* pyroclastic rock). Some extrusive rocks, such as obsidian, are like glass. Igneous rocks cooled at depth are called intrusive or plutonic. They have larger crystals, for example granite. A third category contains the hypabyssal rocks, cooled in dykes or sills at intermediate depth and usually having intermediate crystal sizes, for example dolerite. Silica is the dominant chemical constituent of igneous rocks and the silica content, resulting from the chemical composition of the magma from which the rock cooled, determines whether the rock is acidic (over 66% silica), intermediate (55–66%), basic (45–55%), or ultrabasic (under 45%).

● **ignis fatuus** ▸ (*or* will-o'-the-wisp) A phenomenon sometimes observed on marshy ground or graveyards, appearing as a small bluish light. It is believed to be the flame of burning marsh gas (mostly methane), ignited by traces of hydrogen phosphide sometimes found near decaying organic matter.

● **Iguaçú Falls** ▸ (*or* Iguassú Falls) 25 35S 54 22W A waterfall in South America, on the border between Brazil and Argentina on the Rio Iguaçú. The spectacular falls are a major tourist attraction. Height: 82 m (269 ft). Width: about 4 km (2.5 mi).

● **iguana** ▸ A lizard belonging to the predominantly New World family Iguanidae (700 species), comprising desert-dwelling, arboreal, and amphibious species. The green common iguana (*Iguana iguana*) reaches a length of 1.8 m including the long tail (about 1.3 m) and has a short spiny crest along the back; males have a dewlap beneath the throat. They feed on vegetation and are excellent swimmers. The marine iguana (*Amblyrhynchus cristatus*) of the Galápagos is the only lizard that feeds in the sea. ▷*See also* anole; basilisk; chuckwalla.

● **Iguanodon** ▸ A large dinosaur that lived in the Jurassic and Cretaceous periods (200–65 million years ago). It stood on powerful hind legs about 5 m tall and measured 11 m from its head to the tip of its heavy balancing tail. Iguanodons were herbivorous, tearing off leaves with their tongues and cutting them with bladelike teeth. Order: ▷Ornithischia.

● **Iguvine tablets** ▸ Nine inscribed bronze plaques, discovered (1444) at Gubbio (ancient Iguvium) in central Italy. Seven survive, containing ritual records of a priestly brotherhood between 400 and 90 BC. They are important evidence for ancient Italian religion as well as the extinct Umbrian language.

● **IJmuiden** ▸ 52 28N 4 38E A port in the central Netherlands, in North Holland province on the North Sea. It is connected to Amsterdam by canal and has major iron and steel and fishing industries. Population (latest est): 66 474.

● **IJsselmeer** ▸ (*or* Ysselmeer) A freshwater lake in the NW Netherlands, formed from the S part of the ▷Zuider Zee by the dam completed in 1932. Out of the original area of 3440 sq km (1328 sq mi) approximately 1400 sq km (540 sq mi) will remain under water. In 1986 the reclaimed area became the province of Flevoland.

● **Ik** ▸ A small tribe of N Uganda, also known as the Teuso, one of the remnants of the original East African hunter-gatheres of Palaeolithic times. Their language is unrelated to any other. Resettled and forbidden to hunt, they adopted farming but unsuitable conditions and lack of knowledge resulted in rapid social disintegration.

● **ikebana** ▸ The art of Japanese flower arrangement, first practised

in Japan in the 6th century for Buddhist rituals. It became a formal art, practised only by men until the 19th century. Famous styles include the *shoka*, developed in the 18th century and using three asymmetrically arranged branches.

● **Ikhnaton** ▷*See* Akhenaton.

● **Ikhwan, al-** ▸ (Arabic: the Brethren) Arabian tribesmen united to extend the power of ▷Ibn Saud in Arabia between 1912 and 1930. Ibn Saud organized the Ikhwan in encampments and with their military help conquered most of Arabia. They then attempted revolt but were defeated by Ibn Saud at the battle of Sabala (1929). He later incorporated the Ikhwan into the National Guard of Saudi Arabia.

● **Île-de-France** ▸ A planning region and former province in N France, surrounding Paris and enclosed by the Rivers Seine, Marne, Beuvronne, Thève, and Oise. Originally known as Francia, the region gave its name to the country as a whole. It is the most densely populated region of France, with highly developed industries. Area: 12 012 sq km (4637 sq mi). Population (1995 est): 10 977 700.

● **Ilesha** ▸ 7 38N 4 45E A city in SW Nigeria. Cocoa is exported and it is the centre of a gold-mining area. Population (1995 est): 369 000.

● **Ilhéus** ▸ 14 50S 39 06W A port in E Brazil, in Bahía state on the Atlantic Ocean. Fomerly an important export centre for cocoa, chief exports now include timber and piassava. Population (1991): 135 117.

● **Iliescu, Ion** ▸ (1930–   ) Romanian statesman; president of Romania (1990–96). A leading member of the Romanian Communist Party in the early 1970s, he was subsequently deposed by ▷Ceauşescu. In the 1989 revolution he emerged as leader of the National Salvation Front, which won the 1990 elections. Accused by his liberal opponents of blocking further reform, he retained the presidency in the 1992 elections but lost it in 1996.

● **Ilipa, Battle of** ▸ (206 BC) A battle in S Spain between ▷Scipio Africanus and the Carthaginians. Scipio's victory established Roman control of Spain, enabling him to invade Africa.

● **Ilkeston** ▸ 52 59N 1 18W A town in central England, in Derbyshire. Situated in a former coalmining region, some opencast mining remaining, Ilkeston has engineering, iron founding, textile, clothing, plastics, furnishings, and pipe-making industries. Population (1991): 35 134.

● **Ilkley** ▸ 53 55N 1 50W A town in N England, in West Yorkshire on the River Wharfe. The parish church (13th century) is built on the site of a Roman fort. **Ilkley Moor**, reaching 403 m (1321 ft), lies to the S. Population (1991): 13 530.

● **illegitimacy** ▸ The status of children who are neither conceived nor born within marriage. In England and Wales, some 4% of live births were to unmarried mothers in 1900; with peaks during both World Wars, this figure crept up to 6% in 1961. However, it rose sharply in the 1980s, i.e. from 11% in 1980 to 29% in 1990. By 1997 it was 37%. Of this percentage about four-fifths of the babies were jointly registered by both parents, but less than 60% of the babies born to unmarried mothers had both parents living at the same address. The social stigma formerly suffered by illegitimate children has, in recognition of this large increase in their numbers, virtually disappeared. The Family Law Reform Act (1987) removed all property and inheritance disadvantages, and children formerly referred to pejoratively as illegitimate are now known as children born outside marriage. In Europe there are wide differences, with nearly half the babies being born outside marriage in Sweden and Denmark but only 2% in Greece. ▷*See also* single-parent families.

● **Illich, Ivan** ▸ (1926–   ) Austrian educationalist and radical social critic. A former Roman Catholic priest, who worked in Latin America, Illich seeks a "convivial" society brought about by a cultural revolution. In books such as *Deschooling Society* (1971) he attacks technology, capitalism, and consumerism.

● **Illinois** ▸ A group of Algonquian-speaking North American Indian tribes of Wisconsin, Illinois, Missouri, and Iowa. Their villages were of rush-mat-covered dwellings, each housing several families. Separate chiefs were responsible for matters of war and for civil affairs. Men hunted forest game and prairie bison. Women cultivated maize and corn. The Illinois were much reduced in population through wars with other tribes and eventually dispersed from their territory.

● **Illinois** ▶ A state in the USA, in the Midwest. It consists largely of flat prairies crossed by the Illinois and Kaskaskia Rivers. Approximately half its population is concentrated in the Chicago metropolitan area, the principal grain market of the US interior. Primarily an agricultural state, its farmers are major producers of soya beans, as well as maize, corn, pork, beef, and dairy products. Manufacturing includes machine tools, electrical machinery, printing and publishing, chemicals, iron and steel, motor vehicles, and food processing. It is also an important coalmining state. A deep division exists between upstate Illinois, which contains the Chicago metropolitan area, and the predominantly rural S.

History: the first Europeans to visit Illinois were the French in the 17th century. It formed part of the French province of Louisiana but was ceded to Britain (1763). It came under US control (1783), becoming a territory in 1809 and a state in 1818. The Illinois and Michigan Canal (1848) ensured its importance by linking Lake Michigan with the Mississippi River. Area: 146 075 sq km (56 400 sq mi). Population (1996 est): 11 846 544. Capital: Springfield.

● **illiteracy** ▶ The inability to read or write. The ever-increasing demands of a technological society and the concomitant need for a numerate and literate population has led to a growing awareness of the scale of the problem: although exact numbers are difficult to determine there are an estimated six million adults with reading and writing problems in the UK (*see* literacy levels). Anti-illiteracy campaigns are run by voluntary helpers and coordinated by a small agency of central government, the Adult Literacy Unit, and Local Education Authorities.

illuminated manuscripts ▶ The 13th-century mass book of King Louis IX of France. The initial letter is illustrated with the Ascension of Christ; the plainchant for the mass text is given in the musical notation above.

● **illuminated manuscripts** ▶ Manuscripts of gospels, books of hours, prayers, etc., decorated with designs in opaque or transparent watercolour and frequently gold leaf. The art was first practised by monastic scribes in the early middle ages, as in the 8th-century Book of Kells. Although it began as the elaboration of capital letters and decoration of margins, by the time printing was invented (mid-15th century) it had become a form of miniature painting, perfected by professional illuminators. The Duke of Berry's book of hours by the de ⌐Limburg brothers is an outstanding example of late medieval illumination. Such illumination laid the basis for medieval panel painting.

● **Illyria** ▶ The Adriatic coastal region W of the Balkans. Inhabited from the 10th century BC by warlike independent tribes, Illyria constantly harassed Macedonia and Epirus. Piratical raids in the Adriatic provoked Roman intervention from 228 BC; Illyria became the Roman province of Illyricum in 167 BC.

● **ilmenite** ▶ A black metallic mineral of composition $FeTiO_3$, found in basic igneous rocks, in veins, and as a detrital mineral in sands. It is an ore of titanium.

● **Iloilo** ▶ 10 41N 122 33E A port in the central Philippines, in SE Panay. The island's commercial centre, famed for its fabrics, it exports sugar and rice. Population (1994 est): 302 200.

● **Ilorin** ▶ 8 32N 4 34E A city in W Nigeria. It is an important trading centre for local products, with modern industries producing sugar, matches, and cigarettes. Its university was founded in 1976. Population (1996 est): 475 800.

● **Ilyushin, Sergei Vladimirovich** ▶ (1894–1977) Soviet aircraft designer. He became known for the Il-2 Stormovik, a dive bomber used by the Soviet Union in World War II. He later worked on commercial aircraft, designing the jet airliner Il-62.

● **imaginary number** ▷*See* numbers; complex numbers.

● **Imagism** ▶ A literary movement begun in Britain in 1912, dedicated to composing poetry characterized by the concise expression of pure visual images. It profoundly influenced British and American poetry for a decade. It derived from the criticism of T. E. Hulme, (1883–1917) who rejected the prevailing sentimental romanticism in favour of clarity and hardness. *Des Imagistes* (1914), an anthology edited by Ezra Pound, included poems by Richard Aldington, Hilda Doolittle (H. D.), John Gould Fletcher, and Amy Lowell, who succeeded Pound as leader of the movement.

● **imago** ▶ (zoology) The sexually mature adult form of any insect.

● **imam** ▶ (Arabic: leader) A Muslim title. **1.** Among Shiite Muslims, the title of the successors of Mohammed, who must be descendants of the fourth caliph ▷Ali. The imams were regarded as infallible and exercised complete authority. Various Shiite sects recognize different lines of imams and believe that the last of the line (usually considered either the 7th or the 12th after Ali) will return at the end of time. **2.** A title often used by the caliphs and also given to certain religious leaders, such as ▷Abu Hanifah. **3.** The title of the leader of prayers in a mosque.

● **Imbros** ▷*See* Imroz.

● **Imhotep** ▶ (c. 2600 BC) Egyptian physician, architect, and adviser to pharaoh ▷Djoser of the 3rd dynasty. Revered in later times as a healer and magician, Imhotep was eventually deified. He was identified with Asclepius by the Greeks.

● **Immaculate Conception** ▶ A dogma of the Roman Catholic Church stating that the Virgin Mary, although conceived in the natural way, was free from ▷original sin from the moment of her conception. Although there is little or no biblical support for such a belief, it can be traced back to the early centuries of the Church; the feast of the Conception of the Blessed Virgin Mary (8 Dec) had been celebrated since the 7th century. However, the belief remained a subject of controversy and in the middle ages it was opposed by prominent theologians, such as St Bonaventure and St Thomas Aquinas. It was generally accepted by the Church from the 16th century and promulgated as dogma in 1854 by Pope Pius IX.

● **immigration** ▷*See* migration, human.

● **Immingham** ▶ 53 37N 0 12W A port in NE England, in North East Lincolnshire unitary authority, Lincolnshire, on the Humber estuary. The docks, built in 1912, have been expanded to incorporate a petrochemical complex with bulk handling facilities for the import of iron ore. Exports include chemicals, iron and steel, and petroleum products. Population (1991): 12 278.

● **immortelle** ▷*See* everlasting flowers.

● **immunity** ▶ In medicine, resistance to infection. Nonspecific immunity is achieved by such agents as phagocytic white blood cells and ▷macrophages (which engulf invading bacteria) and ▷interferon, but the term immunity usually refers to that specifically ac-quired due to the presence of ▷antibodies. This may be passive, when antibodies derived from another individual are introduced into the body. For example, newborn babies have a temporary passive immu-nity from antibodies transferred from the mother's blood through the placenta. Active immunity is produced when an individual forms his (or her) own antibodies after exposure to an antigen, such as occurs following an infection. There are two different kinds of immune response produced by antibodies derived from two popula-tions of lymphocytes (white blood cells). Cell-mediated immunity is due to activity of the **T-lymphocytes** (*or* T-cells), which are produced in the bone marrow but complete their development in the ▷thymus. In the presence of antigens these lymphocytes produce cells with an-tibody bound to their surface. They can attack whole cells and are re-sponsible for such reactions as graft rejection, allergic responses, and delayed hypersensitivity reactions. Humoral immunity is produced by the **B-lymphocytes** (*or* B-cells), so called because in chickens they are formed in an organ called the bursa of Fabricius. In humans they are probably formed by lymphatic tissue in the gut. B-lymphocytes produce cells that release free antibody into the blood, neutralizing bacterial toxins and coating bacteria to facilitate their ingestion by the phagocytic cells. Patients with an immune system that has failed to develop completely are said to be **immunodeficient**; those whose immune system has become deficient, as a result of infection (as in ▷AIDS) or for any other reason, are **immunocompromised**. ▷*See also* immunosuppression.

   Immunization is the production of immunity by artificial means. This may be achieved by injecting antibodies against specific diseases (e.g. tetanus and diphtheria), providing temporary passive immunity, or by ▷vaccination to produce active immunity.

● **immunology** ▶ The study of the processes by which the body reacts to foreign substances. This includes the action of ▷antibodies both in protecting the body against infection (*see* immunity) and in rejecting foreign tissues (*see* transplantation). Immunologists are also concerned with disorders of the immune system. ▷*See* allergy; autoimmunity.

● **immunosuppression** ▶ The condition in which the ▷immunity of the body is reduced. This can occur in various diseases (e.g. leukae-mia and severe infections) or may be deliberately induced by drugs (such as azathioprine and cyclophosphamide). Immunosuppressive drugs are administered after transplant surgery to enable the body to accept the foreign tissues; they are also used to treat rheumatoid ar-thritis and other conditions associated with ▷autoimmunity.

● **impala** ▶ A common antelope, *Aepyceros melampus*, of central and S African savanna. About 100 cm high at the shoulder, impalas have a red-brown coat and white underparts; males have lyre-shaped ridged horns. In the rutting season the herds, numbering several hundreds, break up into smaller groups, each led by a mature male. Impalas are known for their springing leaps, especially when they are alarmed.

● **Impatiens** ▶ A genus of annual and perennial herbaceous plants (about 700 species), widely distributed in temperate and tropical re-gions. They have irregular often spurred flowers and (usually) fleshy stems. The genus includes ▷touch-me-not and various cultivated species, such as the garden ▷balsam and busy Lizzies—red-, pink-, purple-, and orange-flowered hybrids that are popular pot plants. Family: *Balsaminaceae*.

● **impeachment** ▶ In the UK, a prosecution brought by the House of Commons as prosecutor and tried by the House of Lords as judge, es-pecially against a minister of the Crown for a serious public offence. Although still legal, the last impeachment was that of the 1st Vis-count Melville (1742–1811) in 1804, tried in 1806 for alleged financial mismanagement of the Admiralty. In the USA impeachments (e.g. of the president) for treason or "high crimes and misdemeanours" are brought by the House of Representatives and tried by the Senate.

● **impedance** ▶ (Z) A measure of the ability of a circuit to resist the flow of an alternating current. It is given by $Z = R + iX$, where R is the ▷resistance, and X is the reactance. The reactance of an inductance L is ωL and that of a capacitance C is $1/\omega C$, where ω is the angular fre-quency. Impedance and reactance are measured in ▷ohms.

● **imperial cities** ▶ The German cities of the Holy Roman Empire subject directly to the Emperor (by whose officials they were gov-erned). They grew in number during the middle ages, when cities took advantage of political disturbance to assert their freedom. Those that survived flourished, forming themselves into leagues (of which the ▷Hanseatic League was the most important) and from 1489 were represented in the imperial diet (assembly). In subsequent centuries most cities were incorporated into the provinces; only Hamburg and Bremen maintain their free status today.

● **Imperial College of Science, Technology and Medicine** ▶ A school of the University of London originally formed in 1907 by the amalgamation of three institutions: the Royal College of Science (1845), the Royal School of Mines (1851), and the City and Guilds Col-lege (1884); St Mary's Hospital Medical School joined in 1988 and the Royal Postgraduate Medical School and the Charing Cross and West-minster Medical School joined in 1997. Since the 1950s the college has more than doubled in size. It is the premier academic institution in the UK for science and engineering.

● **Imperial Conferences** ▶ Meetings between the British Govern-ment and representatives of the self-governing dominions held be-tween 1907 and 1937 to discuss questions of common interest. Imperial Conferences, which replaced the Colonial Conferences of 1887, 1897, and 1902, discussed such matters as migration, natu-ralization (1911), defence (1917–18, 1921, 1923), trade (1923), intraimperial relations (1926), and dominion status (1930). The last Conference (1937) discussed the foreign policy of the newly estab-lished ▷Commonwealth of Nations. The Conferences gave way during World War II to the meetings of Commonwealth prime minis-ters. ▷*See also* Ottawa Agreements.

● **imperialism** ▶ The territorial expansion of a nation and its domi-nation over other countries. Powerful nations generally formed their empires by conquest until the 19th century, when imperialism became an economic policy. European powers, especially Britain (*see* Empire, British), ambitious for prestige and anxious for new indus-trial trading outlets, established their rule over countries in other continents (⁻Africa). Until World War I ended such imperialism these countries depended on their rulers for government, commerce, and protection. Since World War II the term imperialism has often been used to describe the efforts of world powers to impose, by persuasion or force, their political ideologies on less prosperous nations.

● **Imperial War Museum** ▶ A British museum founded in 1917 to house collections of military equipment, uniforms, insignia, and art, relating mainly to the two World Wars. It has a photograph collec-tion and a reference library. It occupies what was formerly ▷Bedlam (the Bethlem Royal Hospital) in S London. The museum opened a Manchester branch in 2000, in a building by Daniel Libeskind.

● **impetigo** ▶ A highly infectious skin disease, usually caused by staphylococci. Children are most commonly affected and epidemics may occur in crowded schools. Usually occurring on the face, hands, and knees, it starts with a red mark that develops into a blister, which later forms yellow crusts. Antibiotics will cure the condition.

● **Imphal** ▶ 24 47N 93 55E A city in India, the capital of Manipur. During World War II, Imphal was the scene of an Anglo-Indian vic-tory over the Japanese. Population (1991): 196 268.

● **impotence** ▶ Sexual inadequacy in men, with failure to achieve or maintain an erection (erectile dysfunction) or to ejaculate at orgasm. It may have a physical cause, such as tiredness, illness (such as diabetes), drunkenness, depression, or taking certain drugs (such as diuretics), or it may have psychological causes. If the causes are psychological, the condition can usually be treated by counselling or psychotherapy. If they are physical, drugs may be appropriate for treatment, depending on the particular cause of the impotence. Of these drugs, sildenafil (Viagra) is available in the form of tablets.

● **impressionism** ▶ A French art movement that flourished from the late 1860s to the late 1880s. Its name was derived from Monet's painting *Impression: Sunrise* (1872; Musée Marmottan, Paris), shown at the first of the eight impressionist exhibitions (1874, 1876, 1877, 1879, 1880, 1881, 1882, 1886). The leading impressionists were ▷Monet, ▷Pissarro, ▷Sisley, and ▷Renoir. Among their many forerunners were ▷Constable, ▷Turner, ▷Boudin, ▷Daubigny, and ▷Corot. ▷Manet shared some of their aims and ▷Degas, although stylistically independent of them, participated in their exhibitions. Painting mainly in the open air, the impressionists aimed to capture fleeting effects of light and weather in paint with dabs of bright colour and a minimum of drawing.

● **imprinting** ▶ In ▷ethology, a rapid and irreversible form of learning that takes place in some animals in the first hours of life. Animals attach themselves to whatever creatures they are exposed to at that time—usually, but not necessarily, their mothers. This behaviour was first described by Konrad ▷Lorenz working with newly hatched ducks and geese.

● **Imran Khan** ▷*See* Khan, Imran.

● **Imroz** ▶ (*or* Imbros) A Turkish island close to the Gallipoli Peninsula. It was occupied by Britain (1914–23) and used as a base in the Dardanelles campaign (*see* World War I). Area: 280 sq km (108 sq mi). Population (latest est): 4802.

● **inbreeding** ▶ Mating between closely related individuals. (The term is also used for self-fertilization in plants.) Inbreeding often occurs in small isolated populations of organisms. The effect is to increase the tendency for harmful ▷recessive genes to express themselves, thus affecting fitness and survival. For example, inbreeding in rats reduces fertility and increases mortality. In human societies close inbreeding is prevented by custom and law (*see* incest).

● **incandescent lamp** ▶ An electric lamp in which light is produced by passing an electric current through a filament, usually inside a glass bulb containing an inert gas. The filament, of tungsten in the common light bulb, is heated to over 2600°C so that it glows with a white light.

● **Incarnation** ▶ The central tenet of Christian belief, that the second person of the Trinity took human form as the man Jesus Christ. Although in other religions gods temporarily appear in human form, in Christianity the Incarnation is a unique event occurring at a particular time; the union of the divine and human in Christ is permanent and the integrity of both the divine and human natures is maintained. The doctrine is stated in the Gospel of St John and in St Paul's Epistle to the Colossians and was further defined by the Councils of ▷Nicaea (325) and ▷Chalcedon (451).

● **Incas** ▶ A Quechua-speaking South American Indian people of the Peruvian Andes. From their capital of ▷Cuzco, they established, during the 15th century, an empire extending from Ecuador to central Chile. It was destroyed in the 16th century by the Spaniards. The Incas assimilated much of the culture of such people as the ▷Chimú, whom they conquered. Their hierarchical society, ruled by the King of Inca and a class of aristocratic officials, was highly centralized. Although the wheel and writing were unknown, imperial messengers and an extensive road system enabled the ruler to maintain contact with all parts of his empire. The complex religion was concerned with the propitiation of the sun god Inti, the creator god Viracocha (*see also* Kon-Tiki), the rain god Apu Ilapu, and others. ▷*See also* Machú Picchu.

● **incense** ▶ A mixture of gums and spices (especially gum benzoin) that is burnt for its aroma (*see also* frankincense). It was employed in pagan rituals in ancient Egypt, Greece, and Rome as well as in Judaic ritual and was a valued trade commodity. In the Book of Revelation it is a symbol of the prayers of saints and has been used in Christian worship since the 6th century AD. It is used predominantly by the Orthodox and Roman Catholic Churches, but in England its use was revived by the ▷Oxford Movement. The vessel for burning incense is called a censer or thurible.

● **incense cedar** ▶ A conifer, *Calocedrus* (or *Libocedrus*) *decurrens*, native to W North America and planted for ornament in Europe, where it is usually narrow and columnar and may reach a height of 45 m. It has small scalelike leaves covering the twigs and branches and bright-yellow pointed cones, 2 cm long, which split open to release the seeds. Family: *Cupressaceae* (cypress family).

● **incest** ▶ Proscribed sexual relations between close kin. Such proscriptions are universal, but vary considerably. For instance, the An-

glican prayerbook sets out the partners prohibited by the Church of England. The most common prohibitions, however, apply to members of the same nuclear family, such as relations between parents and children and between brothers and sisters. These taboos, founded in folklore, have a sound basis in genetics (unfavourable recessive genes can become dominant when consanguineous relatives breed). However, folklore is not always a reliable guide to what constitutes ▷consanguinity, as in the case of taboos forbidding marriage between a man and his mother-in-law. ▷*See also* child abuse.

● **Inchcape Rock** ▷*See* Bell Rock.

● **Inchŏn** ▶ 37 30N 126 38E A city in NW South Korea, Seoul's main seaport on the Yellow Sea. It has a private university (1954). A UN attack here (1950) during the Korean War halted the North Korean invasion. Population (1995): 2 307 618.

● **incomes policy** ▷*See* prices and incomes policy.

● **income support** ▷*See* social security.

Incas ▶ A gold female figurine (1430–1530) of one of the *mamaconas* ("chosen women" or "Virgins of the Sun"), who were the concubines of the Inca emperor. These figurines are often found in Inca burials.

● **income tax** ▶ A direct tax on income and a major source of government revenue in many countries. In most countries, including the UK and the USA, it is a progressive tax (the rate charged increasing with the taxable income) in which a certain amount can be earned without attracting tax. For example, in the UK in 2001–2002, the first £4,385 (for those under 65) is free of tax, the next £1,880 pays tax at 10% (the starting rate), and the next £27,520 pays tax at 22% (the basic rate). Above this figure the rate of tax is 40% (the higher rate). Thus, those with higher incomes pay more tax in proportion to their incomes than the lower paid; therefore the tax, to a certain extent, balances unequal distribution of incomes in the community. However, it acts as a disincentive to increasing income and makes it difficult for the low paid to escape from the ▷poverty trap (compare tax-credit system). Income tax makes no distinction between income that is spent and income that is invested (furthering the productive potential of the economy); higher indirect taxation and lower direct taxation is advocated as a remedy for this. In the UK, most income tax is collected by ▷PAYE.

● **incubus** ► In medieval folklore, a demon that has sexual intercourse with women while they sleep. The female equivalent is a **succubus**. The resulting offspring were said to be witches and demons.

● **incunabula** ► Books printed during the infancy of modern printing (before 1500) after the invention of movable type by ▷Gutenberg. N European incunabula have a heavy type design known as black letter; Italian books have a more elegant roman typeface; both were based on current manuscript writing. Paper leaves and a binding of calf leather over wooden boards were usual. Editions were small (200–500), the preferred subjects being religious or scientific.

● **Independence** ► 39 04N 94 27W A city in the USA, in Missouri. Situated in an agricultural area, its industries include oil refining and cement. It was the home of President Harry S. Truman. Population (1998 est): 116 832.

● **Independence Day** ► The national holiday in the USA that marks the anniversary of the adoption of the ▷Declaration of Independence by the Continental Congress on 4 July, 1776.

● **Independents** ► In English ecclesiastical history, the members of groups in the 17th century and later who believed in self-government for each congregation and advocated toleration of Nonconformity. The term was at first synonymous with ▷Congregationalism; after the Restoration and the Act of Uniformity (1662), it was more widely applied to dissenting bodies the ministers of which were expelled from the Church of England for refusing to subscribe to the Act.

● **independent school** ► A UK school that receives no funds from central government or a local authority. Such schools are funded chiefly by fees charged to parents; many are also charitable trusts. The main groups are the ▷public schools (for 13–17 year olds), the preparatory schools ("prep" schools; 8–13 year olds) that feed them, and the independent primary schools ("pre-prep" schools; 4–7) that feed the prep schools. Other independent schools include a small number of religious schools and schools specializing in progressive methods or providing for children with special needs. Independent schools are not obliged to follow the ▷National Curriculum but must satisfy standards set by the national education departments. Between 1981 and 1991 the percentage of UK schoolchildren attending independent schools increased from 5% to 7%, a percentage that has since declined slightly.

● **indeterminacy principle** ▷See Heisenberg uncertainty principle.

● **indexation** ▷See price index.

● **Index Librorum Prohibitorum** ► (Latin: *Index of Prohibited Books*) In the Roman Catholic Church, a former list of publications considered dangerous to spiritual wellbeing and not to be read without a bishop's permission. The first list was produced under Pope Paul IV (1555–59); a comprehensive guide was issued in 1564. The Second ▷Vatican Council (1962–65) abolished it.

● **India, Republic of** ► (Hindi name: Bharat) A country in S Asia, the seventh largest in the world and the second most populous. Bordering on Pakistan, China, Nepal, Bhutan, and Myanmar (Burma), it comprises 25 states and 7 Union Territories, reorganized since 1946 according to linguistic groupings. The Himalayas, in which the River Ganges rises, form a natural barrier to the N. Central India consists of a plateau (the Deccan), flanked by the mountains of the Western and Eastern Ghats. N of this lies the Indo-Gangetic plain, with the Thar Desert in the W. There are many ethnic and cultural groups and about 1600 languages and dialects are spoken. The chief religions are Hinduism (83% of the population) and Islam (11%). The ▷caste system still survives, although untouchability has been abolished. *Economy:* 70% of the workforce is engaged in agriculture, with rice, pulses, and cereals as the main food crops; sugar cane, tea, jute,

cotton, and tobacco are also important. Despite land irrigation and reclamation, production is hampered by floods, droughts, insufficient mechanization, and the small size of agricultural units. Fishing and forestry are also important. India's mineral resources include iron ore, manganese, bauxite, mica, and ilmenite. Coal is mined, oil is produced from the Arabian Sea, and India also has nuclear power. Many major industries were state owned until the 1990s, when privatization was implemented. India is the world's tenth greatest industrial power. Industries include steel, chemicals, electronics, cotton and silk textiles, and handicrafts. The economic policy of 1977 channelled resources into agriculture and aimed to stimulate rural employment by allowing capital intensive industries to be established for goods that could not be produced by small-scale industries; this was replaced by a policy of deregulation in 1991 and central planning, protectionism, and restrictions on foreign investors were abandoned in 1993. Chief exports are cotton goods, tea, leather, iron ore, and jute, while chief imports are petroleum, wheat, and machinery. There is a large external debt. In 2001 the NW was devastated by an earthquake that left some 30 000 dead and 600 000 homeless.

History: the ▷Indus Valley was the site of a civilization for a millennium before the invading Aryans established theirs (c. 1500 BC) between the Indus and the Ganges. From this civilization Hinduism evolved and it has remained India's dominant religion. The Mauryan Empire followed (c. 320 BC–c. 185 BC), which unified most of India. The 4th–6th centuries AD saw a flowering of Hindu culture in the N under the ▷Gupta dynasty. Muslim raids on the N from the 10th century culminated in the establishment of a Muslim sultanate based on Delhi (1129), under which much of India was again unified. A later Muslim invasion resulted in the magnificent ▷Mogul empire (established 1526). At this time Europeans were also arriving. The British ▷East India Company, grown powerful in the 17th century, fought with French traders in the 18th century for a monopoly as the Mogul Empire declined. With Robert Clive's victory at ▷Plassey (1757), the British established their supremacy and from 1784 a series of ▷Government of India Acts shifted power from the East India Company to the British Government. Some of the territory was directly administered by Britain and came to be called British India. The rest of India was administered by Indian princes, with Britain only exercising general supervision; such areas were called princely states. The Indian economy suffered under British trading arrangements, which allowed British goods into India duty free but barred Indian goods from Great Britain by high tariffs, thus provoking social and political unrest. After the ▷Indian Mutiny (1857–59) reforms were introduced, including the transfer of the East India Company's administrative powers to the India Office, represented by a viceroy and provincial governors. Subsequent reforms allowed greater Indian involvement in government, and in 1919 a parliament was created, most of whose members were elected. However, the nationalist movement (*see* Indian National Congress) became increasingly forceful in its demand for home rule and, under the leadership of Mahatma ▷Gandhi, pursued a policy of civil disobedience. During World War II Gandhi and other Nationalist leaders were imprisoned for refusing to support Britain unless independence was immediately granted. This was finally achieved in 1947 on condition that a Muslim state should be established to satisfy the Muslim faction, active since the late 19th century (*see* Muslim League). The creation of ▷Pakistan (1947) led to upheavals in which 500 000 people were killed and war between the two countries over Kashmir. Trouble between Hindus and Muslims has continued, leading to serious violence in the 1990s. Hostilities with Pakistan erupted again in 1965 and 1971 (*see also* Bangladesh, People's Republic of). Having become a sovereign state in 1950, India incorporated former French and Portuguese territories (1956 and 1961) and Sikkim (1975); the Kashmir border dispute continues, having led India and Pakistan to the brink of war in 1990, 1999, and 2001–02. Indira ▷Gandhi dealt forcibly with separatists, suppressing a Sikh movement advocating autonomy for the Punjab in 1984. Later that year she was assassinated; she was succeeded by her son, Rajiv Gandhi. In foreign affairs India has followed a policy of nonalignment, although it became the world's sixth nuclear power (1974) and in 1987 sent troops to subdue rebels in Sri Lanka. Gandhi was replaced as prime minister by V. P. Singh in 1989 and killed by a terrorist bomb in 1991. Chandra Shekhar became prime minister in

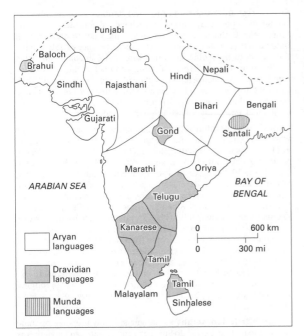

India ▶ The distribution of major language groups in the Indian subcontinent.

1990 but was replaced by Narasimha Rao in 1991. Following the heavy defeat of Rao's Congress Party in the elections of 1996, there was a series of shortlived coalitions. Elections in 1998 produced no clear result and the militant Hindu BJP formed a minority government under A. B. Vajpayee. In May, 1998, India incurred international disapproval by carrying out five underground nuclear tests. In 1999 India's third general election in three years resulted in a clear victory for the BJP.

Republic of India

Head of state	President K. R. Narayanan
Official languages	Hindi and English
Official currency	Indian rupee of 100 paisa
Area	3 287 590 sq km (1 269 072 sq mi), including Jammu and Kashmir
Population (2000 est)	1 014 004 000
Capital	New Delhi

● **Indiana** ▶ A state in the USA, in the Midwest, forming part of the Mississippi Basin. It is largely undulating prairie with glacial lakes in the N. Agriculture is important in the central plain, the major crops being soya beans, maize, wheat, and vegetables (especially tomatoes); pigs are the primary livestock. Its industry produces steel, diamond tools, agricultural machinery, motor vehicles, and domestic appliances. Coal and building stone are also exploited. It is a transport centre with the Ohio River linking Indiana with the Mississippi River.

History: explored by the French in the 17th century, the area was ceded to Britain in 1763, passing to the USA in 1783. Increased settlement followed the defeat of the Indians (1794); it became a state in 1816. Area: 93 993 sq km (36 291 sq mi). Population (2000 est): 6 080 485. Capital: Indianapolis.

● **Indianapolis** ▶ 39 45N 86 10W A city in the USA, the capital of Indiana. A rail, road, and air centre, its varied manufactures include car and aircraft parts and chemicals. It is the scene of the **Indianapolis 500**, a 500-mile race for 33 cars first held in 1911. Population (1998 est): 741 304.

● **Indian art and architecture** ▶ Evidence for many art forms in the Indian subcontinent is incomplete, as the hostile climate damages perishable materials, such as wood. The art of the ▷Indus Valley

civilization is represented by carved steatite sealstones and miniature sculptures and its architecture by the massive brick ruins at ▷Harappa and ▷Mohenjo-Daro. Between about 324 and 185 BC the Buddhist ▷stupa appeared, decorated with stone or stucco reliefs of scenes from the Buddha's life. Greek and Roman influence is apparent in the art of the N Indian Buddhist kingdom of Gandhara (1st–7th centuries AD). The 10th-century Muslim invasions drove indigenous art to the S. The central spire of Hindu temples grew more massive, symbolizing the mythological cosmic mountain; luxuriant carvings, often of erotic scenes, covered every surface, as in the 13th-century Sun Temple at Konarak (Orissa). The Tamil kingdom of Cola (c. 850–1279) is famous for its small bronzes. With the spread of Mogul dominance, ▷Mogul art and architecture became the main tradition until its decline under British rule.

● **Indian corn** ▷*See* maize.

● **Indian hemp** ▶ A North American perennial herb, *Apocynum cannabinum*, that grows to 1.5 m and bears small greenish flowers. The stem fibres were used by Indians to make matting and ropes and the dried roots have medicinal properties. Family: *Apocynaceae*. True ▷hemp is sometimes called Indian hemp.

● **Indian languages** ▶ Languages of widely differing origins spoken in the Indian subcontinent. The two major language families to be found are the ▷Indo-European and the ▷Dravidian. On the NW borders of India, Baluchi and ▷Pashto, members of the ▷Iranian subgroup of the Indo-European family, are spoken. Most of the other Indo-European languages of India are of the ▷Indo-Aryan subgroup. This includes the lingua franca Hindustani; ▷Hindi, the official national language; Rajasthani, ▷Punjabi, ▷Gujarati, and Sindhi in the west; ▷Bengali and ▷Bihari in the east; and Kashmiri. Most of S India is covered by the Dravidian language family. There are also scattered languages of the ▷Munda group in the NE, and languages of ▷Sino-Tibetan origins are spoken in the Himalayas.

● **Indian liquorice** ▶ An Indian plant, *Abrus precatorius*. The roots have been used as a liquorice substitute although they contain poisonous resins. The poisonous red and black seeds are used to make necklaces. Family: ▷*Leguminosae*.

● **Indian literature** ▶ Sanskrit literature, the most important division of ancient Indian literature, is divided into three periods: the Vedic period (c. 1500–c. 200 BC), during which the vast and complex sacred literature of Hinduism was accumulated (*see* Vedas; Upanishads); the Epic period (c. 400 BC–c. 400 AD), in which the great Indian epic, the ▷*Mahabharata*, which includes the ▷*Bhagavadgita*, and the shorter epic, the *Ramayana*, were composed; and the Classical period (from c. 200 AD), characterized by various literary forms including romances, drama, and lyric poetry. ▷Kalidasa is considered the greatest writer of this period. During the 19th century various regional vernacular literatures developed, adopting new Western forms and reviving traditional ones: leading writers were the Bengali poet Rabindranath ▷Tagore and the Urdu poet Mohammed ▷Iqbal.

● **Indian Mutiny** ▶ (1857–59) A revolt of about 35 000 sepoys (Indian soldiers in the service of the British East India Company), which developed into a bloody Anglo-Indian War. It began with a massacre of Europeans at Meerut in May, 1857, following which the mutineers captured Delhi. The sepoys then rose in many other N Indian towns and were joined by local princes. Extensive British reinforcements were able under Colin ▷Campbell to regain Delhi in Sept and relieve besieged Lucknow in Nov; by July, 1858, the revolt had largely been contained. The consequent Government of India Act (1858) transferred the administrative powers of the East India Company to the British Crown.

● **Indian National Congress** ▶ The political party, founded in 1885, that governed India after the declaration of independence in 1947. Though earlier a moderate party, a section of it took up the cause of home rule in 1907. From 1920, chiefly under the guidance of Mahatma ▷Gandhi, it advocated noncooperation with the British and in World War II refused to support Britain without being promised Indian independence. The party was led by Jawarhalal ▷Nehru from 1951 to 1964, by Lal Bahadur Shastri (1904–66) until 1966, and then by Mrs Indira ▷Gandhi. In 1969 the party split into Congress (I), led by Mrs Gandhi, and Congress (II), led by Morarji ▷Desai. The leadership of Congress (I) passed to Rajiv Gandhi in 1984 and to Narasimha Rao in 1991. In 1996 exposure of corruption in Rao's government led to shattering electoral defeat. Sitaram Kesh then became leader but was succeeded by Sonia Gandhi (Rajiv's widow) in 1998.

● **Indian Ocean** ▶ The world's third largest ocean, extending between Asia, Africa, Australia, and Antarctica. Lying mainly in the S hemisphere, most is within the tropical and temperate zones. It contains coral and volcanic islands while others, such as the Seychelles, are the peaks of underwater ridges or, like Madagascar, are continental. The ocean floor is extremely rich in minerals.

● **Indian pipe** ▶ A fleshy waxy-white to pinkish herb, *Monotropa uniflora*, of North America and Asia, also called corpse plant. Up to 30 cm high, it has tiny scalelike leaves, lacks chlorophyll, and obtains nutrients from woodland humus. The stem and single cup-shaped flower resemble a small pipe. Family: *Monotropaceae*.

● **Indian Territory** ▶ The land W of the Mississippi, corresponding to present-day Oklahoma, set aside (1834) for settlement of Indians ejected, sometimes forcibly, from the E. These included the Cherokee, whose journey was known as the Trail of Tears because so many died on the way.

● **indicator** ▶ A substance used to indicate through changes in colour, fluorescence, etc., the presence of another substance or the completion of a chemical reaction. Indicators are usually weak organic acids or bases that yield ions of a different colour to the unionized molecule. For example, litmus is red in the presence of acids but blue in the presence of alkalis.

● **indicator species** ▶ A plant or animal species that is sensitive to a particular environmental factor, such as soil acidity or atmospheric pollution, and whose presence or absence is thus indicative of that factor. For example, the absence of certain lichens indicates atmospheric pollution.

● **indigestion** ▶ (*or* dyspepsia) Abdominal discomfort or pain due to disordered digestion. Most people experience indigestion at some time and there is usually no serious cause, but peptic ulcers, a hiatus hernia, and gall bladder disease may all give symptoms that are described as indigestion. The burning pain felt behind the breastbone, which may appear to rise towards the throat, is often due to the acid contents of the stomach flowing back up the oesophagus (gullet). Drugs, including antacids, are usually effective in treating indigestion.

● **indigo** ▶ A blue dye formerly obtained from plants, particularly of the genus *Indigofera*, and present in the woad plant (*Isatis tinctoria*). It is now synthesized from ▷aniline. ▷*See also* dyeing.

● **indium** ▶ (In) A soft silvery metal, named after the bright indigo line in its spectrum. It is used in making transistors, rectifiers, thermistors, and alloys of low melting point. At no 49; at wt 114.82; mp 156.63°C; bp 2073°C.

● **individual savings account** ▷*See* ISA.

● **Indo-Aryan languages** ▶ A subgroup of the ▷Indo-Iranian language group, spoken in India, Sri Lanka, and Pakistan. Sometimes called the Indic group, it descends from ▷Sanskrit, and the earliest Indo-Aryan language dates from about 1100 AD. The most important languages of the group are ▷Hindi and ▷Urdu, which are the national languages of India and Pakistan respectively; these are both literary languages with many borrowings of Persian and Arabic words dating from the Mogul period. More colloquial ▷Hindustani is also a member of this group, as are the widely spoken Sindhi, ▷Bengali, ▷Gujarati, ▷Punjabi, and Sinhalese. The Dardic (*see* Dards) languages of Pakistan, Afghanistan, and Kashmir are often included in the Indo-Aryan group.

● **Indochina** ▶ The area of SE Asia comprising ▷Vietnam, ▷Cambodia, ▷Myanmar (Burma), ▷Thailand, ▷Malaysia, and ▷Laos. It was so called by Europeans because it has been influenced by both Indian and Chinese culture. During the 19th century the French established control over the E part of the region, forming (1887) the Union of Indochina from ▷Cochinchina, Cambodia, ▷Tonkin, and ▷Annam; Laos was added in 1893. Its capital was Saigon (now Ho Chi Minh City). Except in Cochinchina the royal families were retained, although most power lay with the French federal government. During World War II the Japanese occupied Tonkin (1940) and then all Indochina (1941–42). Following Japan's defeat France established the Federation of Indochina, to which Laos and Cambodia submitted while nationalists in Annam, Tonkin, and Cochinchina demanded complete independence for a new state of Vietnam (*see* Ho Chi Minh). In 1946 fighting broke out between nationalists (*see* Viet Minh) and the French, bitter conflict continuing until 1954, when the ▷Geneva Conference ended the French presence in Indochina.

● **Indo-European languages** ▶ The largest language family of the world, sometimes called Indo-Germanic. They are spoken throughout Europe as well as in India, Iran, and in parts of what was formerly the central and E Soviet Union, and the family is generally thought to include the following subgroups: ▷Germanic; ▷Italic; ▷Indo-Iranian; ▷Celtic; ▷Baltic; Slavic (*see* Slavonic); ▷Albanian; ▷Greek; ▷Armenian; ▷Tocharian; and ▷Anatolian. Of these, the oldest recorded is Anatolian and the most recent Albanian. Armenian and Greek are single languages rather than subdivided groups like Indo-Iranian or Germanic. Anatolian and Tocharian are now extinct. The only living languages of Europe that do not come from Indo-European origins are ▷Turkish, Finnish, ▷Hungarian, and ▷Basque. The Indo-European group relates languages as apparently separate as English, a subgroup of Germanic, and ▷Sanskrit, an ancestor of modern Indian languages. Most of the research needed to support this wide grouping was done by German philologists in the 19th century. ▷*See also* Indo-Hittite languages.

● **Indo-Hittite languages** ▶ A language family proposed by some scholars to include the ▷Indo-European and ▷Anatolian languages as subgroups. There has been some confusion about the relation of Hittite, an Anatolian language (*see* Hittites), to the Indo-European group. Indo-Hittite has been suggested as an ancestor of both Indo-European and Anatolian. It is more generally accepted that Indo-European is the parent language and Anatolian a subgroup on the same level as the ▷Celtic or the ▷Germanic languages.

● **Indo-Iranian languages** ▶ A subgroup of the ▷Indo-European language group, spoken in India, Pakistan, Bangladesh, Nepal, and Sri Lanka. It is subdivided into two branches: ▷Indo-Aryan and ▷Iranian. These are among the oldest of the Indo-European group, spoken originally in Turkistan, and there is debate about the relation of these languages to the Hittite languages of Anatolia. ▷Sanskrit was a language of Indo-Iranian origin and the ▷Romany language spoken by ▷Gipsies is a member of this group.

● **Indonesia, Republic of** ▶ (name from 1798 until 1945: Dutch East Indies) A country in SE Asia, consisting of a series of islands extending E–W for some 5150 km (3200 mi) in the Pacific and Indian Oceans. The main islands are Sumatra, Java and Madura, Bali, Sulawesi, Lombok, and the Moluccas together with the W part of Timor, part of Borneo (Kalimantan), and Irian Jaya (the W half of New Guinea). Plans to link Sumatra, Java, and Bali by tunnels and bridges were approved in 1986. Most of the islands are mountainous and volcanic. Its ethnically diverse population, which belongs mainly to the Malaysian race, may be broadly divided into three groups: the Hindu rice growers of Java and Bali (who make up over half the population), the Islamic coastal peoples, and a group of tribal peoples. The Chinese are the largest nonindigenous group.

Economy: although rich in natural resources, with large deposits of oil, natural gas, coal, and other minerals, as well as some of the richest timber stands in the world, Indonesia has a mainly agrarian economy of which the staple crop is rice; cash crops include rubber, palm oil, copra, sugar cane, and coffee. Heavy industry and manufacturing, which includes shipbuilding, textiles, chemicals, and glass, are being encouraged by the government. The main exports include crude oil, timber, sand, and rubber. In early 1998 Indonesia's economy suffered a virtual collapse owing to the effects of the general economic crisis in SE Asia. An IMF programme to rebuild the economy is being implemented.

History: in the middle ages kingdoms and empires flourished, including the Hindu Srivijaya empire (7th–13th centuries), based on Palembang, and the Majapahit, which, centred on Java, ruled most of the area in the 15th century. In the 16th century it was occupied successively by the Portuguese, the British, and the Dutch, and from 1602 to 1798 it was ruled by the Dutch East India Company. It became a colony of the Netherlands and, after Japanese occupation during World War II, declared itself a republic in 1945 under the leadership of Dr Sukarno. Dutch colonial interests continued in conflict with the Indonesian nationalists until the country was formally granted independence (1949–50) as a single state. In 1956 ties with the Netherlands were broken off. From 1957 Sukarno pursued an essentially nationalist policy; Irian Jaya was incorporated in 1963 and there was confrontation with Malaysia (1963–66). A military coup in 1966 replaced Sukarno's government with a harsh military dictatorship under Gen Suharto; left-wing elements were virtually eliminated. Changes in foreign policy led to an influx of capital from the West and Japan and improved relations with Malaysia. In 1975 Indonesia occupied ▷East Timor leading to thousands of civilian deaths: Indonesia's formal annexation of East Timor in 1976 was not recognized by the UN. Separatist movements there and in Irian Jaya were violently suppressed in the 1980s and 1990s. Indonesia suffered a major ecological disaster in 1997, when forest fires produced a cloud of poisonous smog over most of the country. In early 1998 the economy collapsed, provoking riots and disorder. Following mass protests Suharto resigned in favour of his deputy, B. J. Habibie, who promised reform. The period 1998–99 saw mounting disorder, including conflict between Christians and Muslims, ethnic fighting in Kalimantan, and separatist violence in the northern province of Aceh. In September 1999 East Timor voted for independence in a referendum; savage fighting followed before Indonesia recognized the result and withdrew its troops. Indonesia's first free elections for 45 years took place in June 1999 and resulted in victory for the opposition Democratic Party of Struggle; Abdurrahman Wahid, a veteran Muslim leader, became president. In 2001 Wahid was impeached for alleged corruption and replaced by Megawati Sukarnoputri, Sukarno's daughter.

Republic of Indonesia

Head of state	President Megawati Sukarnoputri
Official language	Bahasa Indonesia
Official currency	rupiah of 100 sen
Area	1 903 650 sq km (735 000 sq mi)
Population (2000 est)	209 342 000
Capital and main port	Jakarta

● **Indore** ▶ 22 42N 75 54E A city in India, in Madhya Pradesh. Formerly the capital of the princely state of Indore, it is an important trading centre with cotton mills and engineering works. Its university was established in 1964. Population (1991): 1 086 673.

● **Indra** ▶ The principal Hindu deity of the Vedic period, god of war and storm, who slew the dragon Vritra, releasing the fertile water and light necessary to create the universe. He is portrayed as wielding a thunderbolt. In later Hinduism, he is supplanted by ▷Vishnu, ▷Shiva, and ▷Krishna and appears as the relatively powerless ruler of the firmament and the east.

● **Indre, River** ▶ A river in W central France. Rising in the Auvergne mountains, it flows NW to join the Loire near Tours. Length: 170 km (115 mi).

● **indri** ▶ The largest Madagascan woolly lemur, *Indri indri*. Up to 70 cm long, it is grey and black, with long hind legs, a short tail, and a doglike head. It lives in treetops, eating leaves, and has a loud howling cry. Indris are threatened by the destruction of their forest habitats. Family: *Indriidae*.

● **induction** ▶ (electromagnetism) ▷*See* electromagnetic induction.

● **induction** ▶ (embryology) The process by which an embryonic tissue influences adjacent cells to develop in a certain way, i.e. to differentiate into a particular adult tissue. Absence of the inducer tissue may result in abnormal development or nondevelopment of the induced cells.

● **induction** ▶ (logic) The process of making an empirical generalization by observing particular instances of its operation. The conclusion goes beyond the facts, since not all possible instances can be examined. From induction predictions can be made but they are always liable to falsification. *Compare* deduction.

● **indulgences** ▶ In the Roman Catholic Church, remissions of the temporal penalties incurred for sins already forgiven by God in the sacrament of penance. Indulgences are based on the belief that a sin, although forgiven, must still have a penalty on earth or in purgatory. The Church may remit these penalties by virtue of the merits of Christ and the saints. The practice of indulgences arose in the early Church when confessors and those about to be martyred were permitted to intercede for penitents and so mitigate the discipline imposed on them. During the later middle ages, indulgences came to command a financial value, which led to widespread abuse and was one of the chief causes of Luther's attack on the Church at the Reformation. Their sale was prohibited in 1567. Today the grant of indulgences, to encourage piety and good works, is largely the prerogative of the pope.

● **Indus, River** ▶ A river in S central Asia, one of the longest in the world. Rising in SW Tibet in the Himalayas, it flows NW through Kashmir, then SSW across Pakistan to its large delta near Karachi on the Arabian Sea. Its main tributary is the Panjnad, which is formed from the Rivers Jhelum, Chenab, Ravi, Beas, and Sutlej. The Indus carries large amounts of sediment and it is also subject to severe flooding but it is an important source of irrigation and hydroelectric power. Waterlogging and salinization have threatened cultivation on the Indus plain and projects have been undertaken to provide an effective drainage system. The Indus contained one of the earliest organized cultures, which lasted from about 2500 until 1700 BC (*see* Indus Valley civilization). Length: 2900 km (1800 mi).

● **industrial democracy** ▶ The participation of workers in decisions regarding their work, factory, or company. Various forms of industrial democracy are used in different countries. In the USA, the method widely advocated is an extension of ▷collective bargaining. In Germany, workers' representatives sit on supervisory boards, which vet the decisions of the board of directors. However, German experience has been that the supervisory boards have had relatively little effect on decision making. Other forms of workers' participation include ▷profit-sharing schemes and works' councils.

● **industrial relations** ▶ Relations between the two sides of industry, employers and employees, usually represented respectively by management and trade unions. In industries with good industrial relations, **industrial action**, such as strikes and lockouts, is rare or nonexistent and both sides cooperate to achieve, and to share in, their objectives, whether they be profits, the provision of an efficient service, or simply job satisfaction. Poor industrial relations are easily recognized by frequent and damaging strikes. The key to good industrial relations is probably some measure of ▷industrial democracy, ▷profit sharing, and unacrimonious ▷collective bargaining.

● **industrial revolution** ▶ The name given to the process of change that transformed Britain and then other countries from agricultural to industrial economies. The industrial revolution began about 1750 when the ▷agricultural revolution was well under way. Inventions were made in the textile industry by such men as James ▷Hargreaves, Richard ▷Arkwright, and Samuel ▷Crompton, which made the production of cloth much faster and the yarn produced of better quality. These new machines could not be used in the home and necessitated the building of factories to house them, at first near rivers for water power and then, when the steam engine was invented, near coalfields. In the factories working conditions were usually intolerable: long hours were worked for low wages and the employment of children was common. Industrial towns sprang up, where living conditions were pitiable, but the current belief in ▷laissez-faire meant little was done to interfere with the progress of industrial growth. Advances were also made in the production of iron, especially by Henry ▷Cort, and in communications. The ▷canals were extended and from about 1830 ▷railways were built. By the mid-19th century British industrial methods had spread to continental Europe and the USA, laying the foundations for further progress in the 20th century.

● **Indus Valley civilization** ▶ A homogeneous culture flourishing between about 2500 and 1700 BC in the area of modern Pakistan. Excavations from the 1920s onwards in the great centres of ▷Mohenjo-

Daro and ▷Harappa have revealed grid-planned streets, municipal drainage, workmen's barracks, granaries and other large public buildings of baked brick, and a standardized system of weights and measures, all testifying to effective centralized administration. Sealstones bearing undeciphered hieroglyphics have also been found. The economy was primarily agricultural but there was some trade with ▷Sumer and ▷Akkad. The final downfall of the civilization (c. 1500 BC) was probably because of the ▷Aryans' incursion.

● **Ine** ► (died c. 726) King of Wessex (688–726), whose code of law provides valuable information on economic and social life in his time. A patron of the Church, he abdicated (726) to retire to Rome.

● **inequality** ► A mathematical statement that one quantity is greater or less than another.

    $a<(>)b$ means a is less (greater) than b.

    $a≤(≥)b$ means a is less (greater) than or equal to b.

● **inert gases** ▷See noble gases.

● **inertia** ► A property of a body that causes it to resist changes in its velocity or, if stationary, to resist motion. When the body resists changes in its linear motion its mass is a measurement of its inertia (see mass and weight). When it resists changes in rotation about an axis its inertia is given by its ▷moment of inertia.

● **inertial guidance** ► A means of guiding a missile or submarine without communicating with its destination or point of departure. It consists of a set of three gyroscopes, with their axes mounted mutually perpendicular to each other, connected to a computer. The gyroscopes provide a frame of reference, which enables the computer to adjust the controls of the vehicle to steer a preset course.

● **INF** ► (Intermediate Nuclear Forces) ▷See disarmament.

● **infallibility** ► A dogma of the Roman Catholic Church promulgated at the first ▷Vatican Council (1870). It stated that the pope cannot err in defining the Church's teaching in matters of faith and morals when speaking *ex cathedra* (Latin: from the throne), i.e. when intending to make such a pronouncement. The pope is not held thereby to be inspired by God but only to be preserved from error.

● **infanticide** ► The killing of newborn children. In advanced societies it is generally considered a crime but in many communities, especially in India and China, it has been used to limit population numbers in circumstances of poverty, overpopulation, or famine. Frequently female children and the weak or deformed were at greater risk because they were considered unproductive. In some societies, for instance among the ancient Phoenicians, a firstborn child would be offered as a sacrifice to the gods.

● **infant mortality** ► The number of deaths that occur in infants under one year of age. This includes neonatal mortality, occurring in the first four weeks of life, from such causes as asphyxia and other birth injuries, prematurity, and developmental abnormalities. Neonatal deaths account for about two-thirds of infant mortalities in

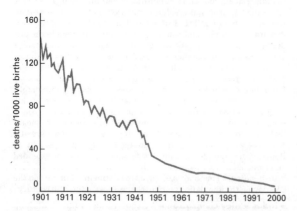

infant mortality ► The decline in infant mortality in the UK during the 20th century.

prosperous countries. The quality of a country's obstetric and antenatal care is reflected in its perinatal mortality rate: the number of stillbirths and deaths occurring in the first week of life per 1000 births. In Europe, the Scandinavians have the lowest perinatal mortality rates, e.g. 5.0 in Sweden (1996). In 1996 the UK rate was 6. In developing countries the figures are considerably higher; for example, in Africa the average is 86. ▷See also cot death.

● **infantry** ► A force of soldiers who fight on foot. Infantry was predominant in ancient warfare, declined when the emphasis shifted to cavalry (c. 400 AD), and became important again with the development of firearms in the late middle ages. World War I, with its trench warfare, was still essentially an infantry war. The development of armoured vehicles, air power, and the landing craft made World War II a war of combined operations in which infantry played a decisive role. In modern warfare the extensive use of armour and guided missiles has turned the emphasis away from confrontation between massed infantry towards infiltration and ▷guerrilla warfare.

● **infection** ► Illness caused by microorganisms, including bacteria, viruses, fungi, and protozoa. Examples of bacterial infections are diphtheria, some kinds of pneumonia, scarlet fever, tuberculosis, and whooping cough. Viruses cause chickenpox, the common cold, influenza, AIDS, measles, polio, rabies, and herpes (among others); malaria and sleeping sickness result from protozoan infection, and fungi cause ringworm and candidiasis. Infectious diseases (also called contagious or communicable diseases) are the commonest cause of sickness and—except in modern industrial societies—have always been the main cause of death. Methods of transmission include contact with an infected person, a human or animal carrier, contaminated objects, and infected droplets. The spread of infectious diseases can be prevented by such measures as improving public health and ▷vaccination. ▷Antibiotics are active against many disease-causing organisms, but there are few effective drugs for viral diseases. Antiviral drugs have, however, been developed for treating herpes infections and AIDS; although the drugs cannot cure these diseases they can delay their progress.

● **inferiority complex** ► An unconscious belief, first described by Alfred ▷Adler, that one is severely inadequate in some particular way. This leads to defensive behaviour and often to an overcompensation, such as open aggressiveness. ▷See also complex.

● **infertility** ▷See sterility.

● **infinity** ► In mathematics, a quantity larger than any that can be specified. The symbols $+∞$ and $-∞$ are read as "plus infinity" and "minus infinity" respectively. They indicate infinitely large positive and negative values. $x → +∞$ means that the value of a variable quantity, x, continues to increase and has no maximum.

● **inflammation** ► The reaction of the body's tissues in response to injury, infection, chemicals, and poisons, which is characterized by redness, heat, swelling, and pain. Blood flow to the inflamed area increases and white blood cells infiltrate the tissues and begin to engulf the invading bacteria (or other foreign particles). This may result in the accumulation of dead cells and bacteria, which form pus. Inflammation is an essential part of the healing process.

● **inflation** ► A general sustained increase in prices resulting from excessive demand for goods (demand-pull inflation), increased pricing by sellers in the absence of increased demand (cost-push inflation), or an expansion of the money supply (monetary inflation). **Deflation** is the opposite process and causes a reduction in both output and employment. In the 19th century periods of deflation and inflation alternated regularly in Europe. However, the abnormal length and severity of deflation in the 1930s has been followed in the postwar years by a protracted period of inflation, rising in the 1970s to over 20% per annum in many countries, including the UK. Remedies vary according to the importance ascribed to each contributory factor: control of wages and prices (see prices and incomes policy), increased taxation, reduced government spending, alterations in interest rates, and a controlled money supply have been among recent policies. However, none of them is likely to succeed when the basic cause is an increase in the cost of imported raw materials, such as oil. The measurement of inflation is also controversial; a ▷price index

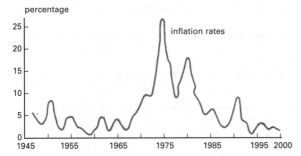

inflation ▶ UK percentages (1948–2000; annual averages).

will be a main component but other factors, such as the mortgage rate, are taken into account by some countries (including the UK) but not others. *Compare* depression.

● **inflorescence** ▶ The arrangement of a group of flowers borne on the same main stalk. In a racemose (or indefinite) inflorescence the tip of the main stem continues to grow and flowers arise below it. Examples are the raceme (e.g. foxglove), the spike (e.g. wheat), and the catkin (e.g. the male flowers of birch and hazel), which is a kind of spike that often hangs down from the stem. Flat-topped racemose inflorescences include the umbel (*see* Umbelliferae), the capitulum (e.g. daisy), and the corymb (e.g. candytuft). A cymose (or definite) inflorescence, or cyme, is one in which a flower is produced at the tip of the main stem, which then ceases to grow. Growth is continued either by one lateral bud, to produce a monochasium (e.g. buttercup), or by a pair of buds, giving a dichasium (e.g. stitchwort).

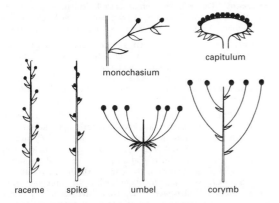

inflorescence ▶ All plants except those with solitary flowers show characteristic arrangements of their flowers on the main flowering stalk. All the types shown here, with the exception of the monochasium, are racemose inflorescences.

● **influenza** ▶ An acute viral infection characterized by fever, headache, weakness, aching joints, and loss of appetite. Cases vary from mild to very severe (particularly if a secondary bacterial infection occurs). Epidemics occur because of the development of new strains of influenza viruses, which are resistant to the body's immune system and to vaccines against existing strains. The worst epidemic in the 20th century occurred in 1918–19, when as many as 20 million people died.

● **information technology** ▶ (IT) The technology involved in producing, storing, processing, and communicating information by computers, microelectronics, and ▷telecommunications. The explosive growth of IT during the 1970s and 1980s arose mainly as a result of a fall in the cost of electronic equipment, as ▷integrated circuits became more reliable and cheaper, combined with a merging of computer technology and telecommunications (*see* Internet). In retail trades the perfection of ▷bar codes combined with ▷electronic funds transfer has enabled chain stores to bank their takings and control their stocks in one operation. In manufacturing industries, many machine tools are operated by computer and their products monitored electronically to a high degree of accuracy. In addition to the making and selling of products, design has now also been profoundly influenced by IT. Software packages for computer-aided design (*see* CAD) enable subjects of engineering drawing to be displayed on computer screens in three dimensions from a number of different angles.

● **information theory** ▶ The mathematical theory of communication, involving analysis of the information content of messages and the processes used in their transmission, reception, storage, and retrieval. Statistical concepts, such as probability, are used to assess the extra information (redundancy) necessary to compensate for spurious signals (noise) occurring during communication. The ▷bit is the basic unit of information and the channel capacity is a measure of the ability of the transmission medium, e.g. a telegraph line, to carry information. Information theory was developed in the 1940s by Claude E. Shannon (1916–2001). It has been applied widely in such fields as computer science and ▷cybernetics and has aided the understanding of many processes, ranging from the laws of thermodynamics to the use of language.

● **infrared radiation** ▶ Electromagnetic radiation with wavelengths between about 750 nanometres and 1 millimetre. In the electromagnetic spectrum it lies between the red end of visible light and microwaves. It was discovered in 1800 by William ▷Herschel, who noticed that the solar spectrum contained invisible rays with a heating effect. Infrared radiation is emitted by all bodies at temperatures above absolute zero and is the predominant radiation emitted up to temperatures of about 3000°C.

● **infrared telescope** ▶ A reflecting ▷telescope for detecting and studying infrared radiation from astronomical sources, such as stars enveloped in dust clouds or cool ▷molecular clouds of gas and dust. Semiconductor detectors are used, and these (and in some cases the telescope optics) must be cooled to very low temperatures. Infrared telescopes are normally sited at high altitudes to reduce infrared absorption by the atmosphere or are carried on satellites. Several major telescopes are located at the summit of Mauna Kea (4200 m) in Hawaii.

● **infrasonics** ▶ The study of sound waves with a frequency below the threshold of human hearing, i.e. below about 20 hertz. They are produced naturally by earthquakes and tidal waves; in cars travelling at high speeds they have been suspected of having adverse effects on the drivers.

● **Inge, William Ralph** ▶ (1860–1954) British Anglican churchman, nicknamed the "Gloomy Dean." He was professor of divinity at Cambridge (1907–11), Dean of St Paul's (1911–34), and wrote theological works on mysticism and Neoplatonism as well as two widely read volumes of *Outspoken Essays* (1919; 1922).

● **Ingenhousz, Jan** ▶ (1730–99) Dutch physician and plant physiologist, who discovered the process of ▷photosynthesis in green plants. Ingenhousz found that plants took in carbon dioxide and gave off oxygen, but only when exposed to light.

● **Ingleborough** ▶ 54 10N 2 23W A hill in N England, in North Yorkshire, one of the highest points in the Pennine Hills. Ingleborough Cave in the S contains stalagmites and stalactites. Height: 723 m (2373 ft).

● **Ingres, Jean-Auguste-Dominique** ▶ (1780–1867) French painter, born in Montauban, the son of an artist. He became a pupil of ▷David in Paris in 1797. His three paintings of the Rivière family (Louvre) established him as a portraitist. From 1806 to 1820 he lived in Rome, where he produced numerous pencil portraits as well as paintings. Many of his historical and mythological paintings aroused criticism but, on returning to Paris in 1824, his *Vow of Louis XIII* (Cathedral, Montauban) established him as an opponent of ▷Romanticism. After teaching at the École des Beaux-Arts, he returned to Rome as the director of the French Academy (1835–41). He is noted for his nudes, e.g. *Valpinçon Bather* (Louvre); his draughtsmanship influenced ▷Degas and ▷Picasso.

● **Ingushetia** ▶ A constituent republic of Russia, in the SW. It was part of the former Checheno-Ingush Autonomous Republic until 1992, when Chechenia and Ingushetia separated following border disputes; Ingushetia gained republic status in 1993. Capital: Nazran; a new capital is currently being built at Magas. For area and population, *see* Chechenia.

● **inheritance tax** ▶ A UK tax introduced in the 1986 Budget to replace capital-transfer tax. The first £250,000 (2002–2003) of an inheritance is tax-free; thereafter a flat rate of 40% is applied. The tax on lifetime gifts was replaced with a tapered charge on gifts made within seven years of death. Exemptions include gifts between spouses.

● **inhibitor** ▶ A substance that retards a chemical reaction; often called a negative catalyst. Examples include antioxidants, enzyme inhibitors, and antipolymerization agents.

● **initiation rites** ▶ Rituals performed on the transition from childhood to adult status or on joining certain professions or associations. During this period adolescents among primitive peoples are often educated in the duties of adulthood. ▷Circumcision may be practised at this time. Initiation rites are frequently performed on admission to religious orders, secret societies, and guilds. ▷*See also* rites of passage.

● **initiative** ▷*See* referendum and initiative.

● **injection** ▶ The introduction of medicinal fluids into the body using a syringe and hollow (hypodermic) needle. The three basic injection routes are under the skin (subcutaneous), for example for insulin; into a muscle (intramuscular), for slow absorption; and into a vein (intravenous), for rapid absorption. Drugs are injected when high concentrations are needed or when they are poorly absorbed by the intestines.

● **injection moulding** ▶ A process, similar to die-casting, for moulding thermoplastic materials (plastics that soften on heating and harden on cooling). Injection-moulding machines are often fully automatic; the plastic is heated in a cylinder until it has melted and is then forced under pressure into a cooled moulding chamber.

● **injunction** ▶ A court order addressed to a particular person to prohibit them from doing something (a **prohibitary injunction**) or to compel them to do something (a **mandatory injunction**). A prohibitory injunction may be used to stop a nuisance or to protect a copyright, while a mandatory injunction may be used to force a person to demolish something he has built in breach of a covenant. Failure to comply with an injunction constitutes ▷contempt of court and may incur a fine or a prison sentence.

● **ink** ▶ A coloured fluid for writing or printing. Blue-black writing ink contains ferrous sulphate, mineral organic acid, and other dyes. Coloured inks contain only synthetic dyes; washable inks use water-soluble synthetic dyes. Marking ink is a mixture of inorganic and organic salts that precipitates aniline black on the surface. Indian ink, used for drawing, is a black waterproof ink containing carbon black and ▷shellac. Printing ink consists of pigments suspended in linseed oil, resins, and solvents. Ballpoint pen ink resembles printing ink, consisting of synthetic dye dissolved in organic liquids with a resinous binder.

● **Inkatha** ▶ A South African political organization founded in 1975 by Chief ▷Buthelezi, leader of the country's Zulu population, to promote Zulu autonomy. Although Inkatha supported the campaign against ▷apartheid, many non-Zulu Blacks accused it of covert collaboration with the White authorities; in the earlier 1990s there were violent clashes with supporters of the ▷African National Congress. Three of its members became government ministers following multiracial elections in 1994. Inkatha formed an electoral pact with the ANC in 1999.

● **ink cap** ▶ A ▷mushroom belonging to the genus *Coprinus*, the gills of which are digested after release of the spores to form an inky fluid that drips from the cap. The common ink cap (*C. atramentarius*) grows in clusters, usually at the base of trees, and has a brownish-grey cap, 3–7 cm high.

● **Inkerman, Battle of** ▶ (5 November, 1854) A decisive battle of the Crimean War, in which the French and British defeated the Russians at Inkerman, near Sevastopol. In spite poor direction the Anglo-French force withstood the Russian attack: the Russians lost about 12 000 men, the British, about 2500, and the French, about 1000.

● **INLA** ▶ (Irish National Liberation Army) ▷*See* Irish Republican Army.

● **Inland Sea** ▶ (Japanese name: Seto Naikai) A shallow section of the NW Pacific Ocean between the Japanese islands of Honshu, Shikoku, and Kyushu.

● **Inner Mongolia Autonomous Region** ▶ (Chinese name: Nei Menggu AR) An administrative division in NE China, bordering on Mongolia and the Gobi Desert in the W. Its steppes are now partly irrigated and cultivated, producing mainly wheat; nomadic Mongol herdsmen, now only 7% of the population, are beginning to settle. Some coal is mined. Area: 1 177 500 sq km (459 225 sq mi). Population (1999 est): 23 620 000. Capital: Hohhot.

● **Inner Temple** ▷*See* Inns of Court.

● **Innocent III** ▶ (Lotario de' Conti di Segni; 1160–1216) Pope (1198–1216). He was an outstanding canon lawyer, and as pope his policy was directed to the extension of papal power in all areas of temporal and spiritual government. He successfully intervened in the disputed imperial succession in Germany. In France he condemned the marital behaviour of ▷Philip II Augustus and in England forced the submission of King ▷John, who recognized the pope as feudal overlord. He also proclaimed the fourth ▷Crusade (1198). The fourth ▷Lateran Council (1215) represents the climax of his spiritual rule and the apogee of the medieval papacy.

● **Innocent IV** ▶ (d. 1254) Pope (1243–54). Before election to the papacy he was a teacher of canon law at Bologna. Much of his pontificate was taken up with the conflict between the papacy and Emperor ▷Frederick II. Innocent was forced to flee Rome (1244) and at the Council of Lyon (1245) condemned and deposed the emperor. Only after Frederick's death did Innocent return to Rome (1253).

● **Innocents' Day** ▶ In the Roman Catholic calendar, the day on which the children massacred by Herod following the birth of Christ are remembered. Also called Childermass, it is celebrated on 28 Dec.

● **Innsbruck** ▶ 47 17N 11 25E A city in W Austria, the capital of the Tirol on the River Inn. Chartered in 1239, it developed as the junction of several important trade routes, including the ▷Brenner Pass. It has many fine medieval buildings, and a university (1677). It is a popular tourist and winter-sports centre. Industries include glass and textiles. Population (1999): 110 454.

● **Inns of Court** ▶ Assocations with the exclusive right to confer the rank or degree of barrister-at-law, known as "calling to the Bar." For the English bar, the Inns are the Honourable Societies of Lincoln's Inn (established 1310), Middle Temple (1340), Inner Temple (1340), and Gray's Inn (1357). They are administered by a body of senior barristers and judges known as "benchers," who have absolute discretion as to admission of students to the Bar. Their previous disciplinary functions and power to deprive a barrister of his status, "disbarring," were transferred in 1974 to the Senate of the Inns of Court and the Bar, which in 1987 was replaced by the General Council of the Bar. Most barristers' offices (known as chambers) in London are in one of the Inns. An Inn of Court of Northern Ireland was established in Belfast in 1926; its governing body is the Honourable Society of the Inn of Court of Northern Ireland.

● **inoculation** ▷*See* vaccination.

● **Inönü, Ismet** ▶ (1884–1973) Turkish statesman; prime minister (1923–37, 1960–65) and president (1938–50). After a successful military career he joined ▷Atatürk and commanded the fighting against the Greeks in Anatolia (1921). He was prime minister under Atatürk and succeeded him as president. Following defeat in the elections of 1950 he led the Republican People's Party opposition to the Democratic Party government and after the 1960 coup formed three successive coalition governments (1961–65).

● **inorganic chemistry** ▷*See* chemistry.

● **inquest** ▷*See* coroner.

● **inquilinism** ▶ An animal relationship in which one species lives in the nest of another species or makes use of its food. For example, some termites live only in the mounds of certain other termite species, although in completely separate compartments.

● **Inquisition** ▶ (*or* Holy Office) An institution of the medieval and early modern Church designed to combat ▷heresy and moral offences. Formally instituted (1231) by Pope ▷Gregory IX in response to the growing threat of heresy, especially of the ▷Cathari and ▷Waldenses, it attempted to place all control of heresy in papal hands. Inquisitors, appointed by the pope, especially from the Dominican and Franciscan orders, and possessing considerable powers, often merited their reputation for cruelty. The use of torture was authorized in 1252 and trials were held in secrecy; fines and various penances were imposed on those who confessed, while those who refused were imprisoned or executed by burning. Almost entirely confined to S Europe, the Inquisition lapsed during the 14th and 15th centuries but was revived in Spain in 1478 against apostate Jews and Muslims. Operating with great severity, especially under the first grand inquisitor, de ▷Torquemada, the **Spanish Inquisition** later operated against Protestants in Spain and (with little success) the Netherlands, and achieved some notoriety for its arrest of St ▷Ignatius Loyola. The growth of Protestantism led to the establishment (1542) of a Roman Inquisition by Pope Paul III. It was given complete independence in matters of doctrine and control of heresy and among its victims was ▷Galileo. In 1965 the Holy Office became a branch of papal bureaucracy and was renamed the Sacred Congregation for the Doctrine of the Faith; it is now concerned with maintaining Roman Catholic discipline.

● **INRI** ▶ Abbreviation for *Iesus Nazarenus Rex Iudeorum* (Jesus of Nazareth King of the Jews). According to St John (19.19–20) this inscription, written in Hebrew, Greek, and Latin, was placed by order of Pilate on the cross upon which Jesus was crucified. The initials often appear on the representation of the cross in Christian painting and sculpture.

● **insanity** ▶ In law (although not a legal term), defect of reason caused by disease of the mind, making a person not responsible for his acts. A person is presumed sane until the contrary is proved. If a jury finds an accused person committed an act as charged but was insane, it must return a verdict of not guilty by reason of insanity. According to **M'Naghten's Rules** (established following the acquittal in 1843 on the ground of insanity of Daniel M'Naghten, charged with murder) an accused person is insane if he was unaware of the nature or quality of his act or did not know it was morally wrong. Insanity may affect a person's capacity to make binding contracts or a will or his fitness to plead, i.e. answer to a criminal charge and therefore to stand trial. An insane person contracting with someone aware of his insanity is only bound by contracts for necessaries, such as food, but is liable to pay only a reasonable price irrespective of the contract price. In cases of a person with partial insanity, i.e. with intermittent periods of lucidity, a defence must show that at the relevant time the person was insane.

● **insect** ▶ An invertebrate animal (an ▷arthropod), 0.2–350 mm long, belonging to the largest class in the animal kingdom (*Insecta* or *Hexapoda*; about a million known species). Insects occur throughout the world and account for 83% of all animal life. An insect's body, covered by a waterproof cuticle, is divided into three sections: the head, which bears a pair of antennae; the thorax, with three pairs of legs and typically two pairs of wings; and the abdomen. With biting or sucking mouthparts they feed on almost all plant or animal materials. The majority of insects lay eggs, which go through a series of changes (*see* metamorphosis) to reach the adult stage. In the more primitive orders, for example ▷*Orthoptera* and ▷*Hemiptera*, the young (called nymphs) resemble the adults, but in the higher orders, for example ▷*Hymenoptera*, *Diptera* (flies), and *Coleoptera* (beetles), the young (called larvae) are unlike the adults, often have a different diet, and go through a resting pupal stage. Insects are important in nature as predators, parasites, scavengers, and as prey. Many are plant or animal pests and disease carriers. Others pollinate crops or kill insect pests and some produce useful substances, such as honey, beeswax, and silk. □ p. 630.

● **insecticides** ▶ ▷Pesticides used specifically to kill insects. Originally, strong inorganic poisons, such as arsenic compounds and cyanides, were used but these were also toxic to humans and livestock. Synthetic organic substances, beginning with DDT in 1945 and including aldrin, endosulphan, and parathion, were then widely used, mainly because of their selectivity, but also because of their cheapness and ease of application. Insecticides are classified according to mode of action or application; for example, **contact insecticides** are applied directly to the insects, while **residual insecticides** are sprayed on surfaces that the insects touch. Many insecticides cause environmental pollution, becoming concentrated in food chains; DDT and aldrin are now banned in the UK for this reason. Because of this, and problems of insect immunity, alternative methods involving ▷biological control are being researched.

● **Insectivora** ▶ The order of ▷mammals, comprising about 375 species, that includes ▷shrews, ▷tenrecs, ▷hedgehogs, ▷moles and ▷desmans, ▷golden moles, and ▷solenodons. Feeding mainly on invertebrates, insectivores are fairly primitive mammals with narrow snouts and sharp simple teeth; their eyes and brains are generally small. Inconspicuous and frequently nocturnal, insectivores are found in nearly all regions; they are absent from the Poles and Australasia.

● **insectivorous plant** ▷*See* carnivorous plant.

● **insolation** ▶ The amount of solar radiation falling on a planet, natural or artificial satellite, or comet per square metre of surface per second. The insolation falling on the earth's atmosphere is called the ▷solar constant. Slightly less than half this energy reaches the earth's surface; the rest is absorbed in the atmosphere or reflected back into space.

● **insolvency** ▶ The inability of a person or company to pay their debts. A creditor may petition a court to declare an insolvent debtor bankrupt (*see* bankruptcy), in which case all his property is sold and the proceeds distributed to his creditors. An insolvent company or partnership is put into liquidation, the court appointing a liquidator, who realizes its assets for distribution to creditors.

● **insomnia** ▷*See* sleep.

● **instinct** ▶ **1.** A complex pattern of behaviour, the form of which is determined by heredity and is therefore characteristic of all individuals of the same species. Although the behaviour may be released and modified by environmental stimuli, its basic pattern does not depend on the experience of the individual. Birdsong and the complex behaviour of social insects (such as bees) are examples. **2.** An innate drive, such as hunger or sex, that urges the individual towards a particular goal.

● **insulator** ▶ A material that is a poor conductor of electric current and therefore has a high resistivity. Solids, such as glass, rubber, ceramics, and PVC, are used in electric circuits to separate conducting wires and prevent current loss. In overhead power transmission, air acts as the insulator between high-voltage lines. ▷*See also* energy band.

● **insulin** ▶ A protein hormone that is secreted by the islets of Langerhans in the ▷pancreas in response to a high concentration of glucose in the blood. It stimulates the uptake of glucose and amino acids from the blood by the tissues and the formation of ▷glycogen. Its effects are counteracted by the hormone ▷glucagon. Insulin was first isolated in 1921 by ▷Banting and ▷Best and its amino acid composition and three-dimensional structure were revealed by Frederick ▷Sanger and Dorothy ▷Hodgkin. A deficiency of insulin causes the symptoms of ▷diabetes mellitus.

● **insurance** ▶ A method of providing monetary compensation for a misfortune or loss that may not occur. Events that must occur at some time, such as death, are provided for by ▷assurance. In the UK and some other countries insurance against unemployment, sickness, and retirement is provided by the government (*see* National Insurance). Other types of insurance are undertaken by the private sector, either by insurance companies or by ▷Lloyd's. Almost any risk can be insured against, the most common being ▷marine insurance; aviation insurance; ▷motor insurance; fire, burglary, and household insurance; ▷private medical insurance; and weather insurance. The public does not deal directly with the underwriters (insurers) but arranges to cover a risk through an insurance broker, who works for a commission paid by the insurer and advises the client as to the best

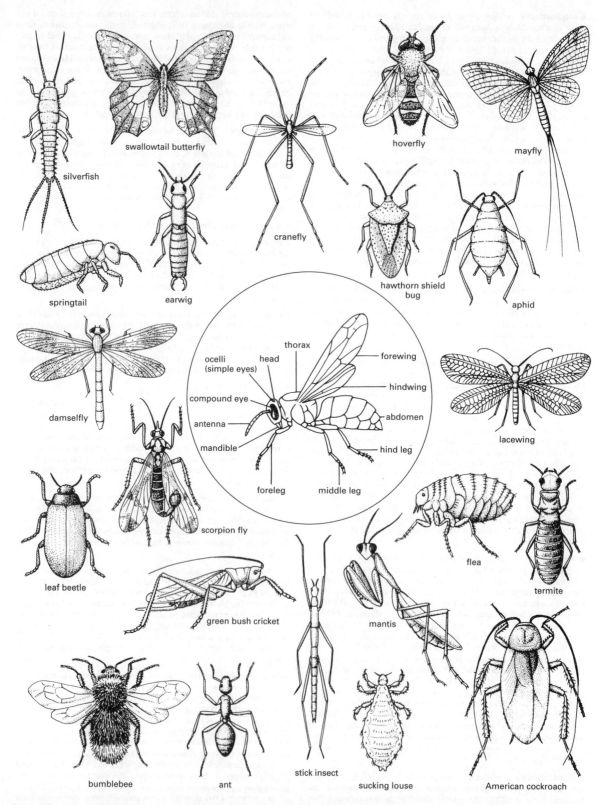

silverfish

swallowtail butterfly

cranefly

hoverfly

mayfly

springtail

earwig

hawthorn shield bug

aphid

damselfly

scorpion fly

ocelli (simple eyes)

head

thorax

forewing

compound eye

hindwing

antenna

abdomen

mandible

hind leg

foreleg

middle leg

lacewing

leaf beetle

flea

termite

green bush cricket

mantis

bumblebee

ant

stick insect

sucking louse

American cockroach

insect ► The structure of a typical insect (centre), with representatives from all the principal insect orders.

cover available, taking into account the cost and reliability of the insurer. Claims are also settled through brokers. The cost to the insured of covering the risk (premium) is calculated by the insurer's ▷actuary on the basis of the probability of the risk occurring. If the event occurs the insured's claim is paid by the insurer, as calculated by an insurance assessor or as stipulated in the insurance policy. *See also* credit insurance.

● **intaglio** ► The production of a sunken image, especially in metal or stone, by etching or engraving. It is used in sculpture, gems, and seals, and in the plates for gravure printing, in which ink is transferred to the paper from only the sunken areas of the plate, the rest having been wiped clean.

● **integers** ▷*See* numbers.

● **integrated circuit** ► (IC) A solid-state ▷semiconductor circuit contained in a single wafer of semiconductor. ICs are made by a process of etching and diffusing a pattern of impurities into the semiconductor surface, forming tiny p-n junctions, which make up individual diodes, ▷transistors, etc.

Since the 1970s computers have been used to make ICs smaller and more complex, in spite of the fact that further reducing the size makes the doping pattern imprecise. A silicon chip (*or* microchip) is covered with circuits, and computer-controlled microscopic probes search out the best points for connections for each specific device. The application of this technique has revolutionized many areas of industry and commerce, making cheap ▷microprocessors available for the automation of production processes.

● **integration** ▷*See* calculus.

● **intellectual property** ► A form of property that includes ▷copyrights, ▷patents, and ▷trademarks. In the UK and most other countries, intellectual properties are protected by laws. In addition, international agreements drawn up by the The World Intellectual Property Organization (a UN agency) ensure the intellectual property laws of individual countries are consistent with each other and that any attempts at piracy are exposed and stamped out.

● **intelligence** ► The ability to reason and to profit by experience. An individual's level of intelligence is determined by a complex interaction between his heredity and environment; the Swiss psychologist Jean ▷Piaget greatly contributed to present-day understanding of intellectual development. The first **intelligence tests** were devised by Alfred ▷Binet in 1905 and there are now many tests for assessing intellectual ability. An individual's performance in a test is represented by his **intelligence quotient** (IQ), the product of 100 and the ratio of mental age (obtained from the test results) to actual age. Tests are constructed so that the average IQ is 100 and over 95% of the population come between 70 and 130. However, since it is now widely thought that true intelligence can be expressed only through speech and writing (and is therefore inaccessible to testing) and since each test reflects the constructor's view of the nature of intelligence, the predictive value of the tests as a basis for selection for secondary education is questionable. Tests that measure a wide range of abilities, such as the Weschler Intelligence Scale for Children (WISC), are now regarded as the most useful and relevant for diagnosing educational difficulties.

● **intelligence service** ► The government department responsible for obtaining information about the military and economic capabilities and political intentions of another country (intelligence) or for thwarting the attempts of a foreign country to obtain such information for itself (counterintelligence). Sources of intelligence information may be open, such as diplomatic reports, newspapers, and radio broadcasts, or secret, such as aerial reconnaissance, "bugging," and the fieldwork of spies. Intelligence services existed in antiquity and the first known treatise on the subject is Sun Tzu's *The Art of War* (c. 400 BC). Elizabeth I of England had a notable intelligence service, organized by Sir Francis ▷Walsingham, as did Cardinal de Richelieu in 17th-century France and Frederick the Great in 18th-century Prussia. The first specifically military service was established in France under ▷Fouché (1802) during the Napoleonic Wars, which the British countered (1808) with the Peninsular Corps of Guides in Spain. This was disbanded after Napoleon's fall but a similar corps was set up

(1855) during the Crimean War. The subsequent Intelligence Department was active in the second ▷Boer War (1899–1902), using balloons for reconnaissance and pigeons for the speedy relaying of messages. In 1909 and 1912 respectively the army general staff's Directorate of Military Operations organized MO-5 (counterintelligence) and MO-6 (intelligence), which soon became the Military Intelligence services: MI-5 (the Security Service) and MI-6 (the Secret Intelligence Service). Elsewhere, intelligence services have included the ▷Central Intelligence Agency, the ▷Federal Bureau of Investigation (counterintelligence), and the National Security Agency (dealing with cryptology) in the USA and the ▷KGB in the former Soviet Union. The development of intelligence services since World War II is linked with technological advances. Modern methods of obtaining secret information about a foreign state, including photoreconnaissance by such aircraft as the U-2 and by satellites, as well as the work of spies, depend on the use of microfilm, recording machines, and computers. The activities of spies have become less significant but remain a popular theme for books and films and those real-life agents who have been uncovered, such as Julius and Ethel ▷Rosenberg, Burgess and ▷Maclean, and ▷Philby, have attracted enormous interest. Since the end of the ▷Cold War in the early 1990s there has been some reappraisal of the role played by Western Intelligence services, with suggestions that they should concentrate on fighting organized crime and international terrorism. There have also been calls for such services to be made more publicly accountable.

● **Intelsat** ▷*See* communications satellite.

● **interactive compact disc** ► (CD-i) A ▷compact disc that stores digitized information, such as text, sound, and pictures, in a form in which the user can interact with and control the information. CD-is are mostly used in education, as the learner may, for example, search for topics or request related information about a particular subject. It is also used for sophisticated computer games with high-quality graphics. ▷*See also* multimedia system.

● **Inter-American Development Bank** ► An international bank founded in 1959 to provide assistance for developing countries in Latin America and the Caribbean by making loans at very low ▷interest rates. The UK joined in 1974.

● **interest** ► The amount of money charged by a lender to a borrower for the use of a loan. The principal (P) is the amount on which interest is calculated; the term (t), the length of time in years for which the money is lent; and the interest rate (r), the annual rate of return per 100 units of principal. In **simple interest**, the principal each year is the sum originally lent. The lender is paid $Prt/100$ in interest and repaid P after t years. In **compound interest**, the interest each year is not paid to the lender but is added to the principal, so that the principal for the next year becomes $P(1 + r/100)$. After t years the lender is paid $P(1 + r/100)^t$. In the UK, if the interest rate on a loan is quoted for a period of less than one year, the equivalent **annual percentage rate** (APR) must be stated.

The basic rate of interest in the UK (i.e. the rate at which the Bank of England lends to the discount houses) is set by the Bank of England; this is known as the **base rate** (or sometimes the **bank rate**). Between 1972 and 1981 it was called the **minimum lending rate**. In the USA, the interest rate charged by the US Federal Reserve Banks when lending to other banks is called the **discount rate**. In practice, customers of UK banks pay a premium over the base rate when they borrow, to enable the banks to make a profit and cover the risks involved.

● **interference** ► A wave phenomenon in which two waves combine either to reinforce each other or to cancel each other out, depending on their relative phases. The pattern of light and dark strips so produced is called an **interference pattern** (*or* interference fringe). The effect occurs when the two beams have the same frequency and have approximately the same amplitude. Thomas ▷Young discovered interference (1801); it provided strong evidence for the wave theory of light.

An **interferometer** is used to produce interference patterns, mainly for the accurate measurement of wavelengths. Several different types are in use, the older instruments being devices for splitting a beam into two parts and then recombining them to form interference patterns after each part has travelled a different distance. In the Michelson interferometer (⌐Michelson-Morley experiment) the beam is split by a half-silvered mirror in which part of the beam is reflected and the rest transmitted. In the Fabry-Perot interferometer two parallel half-silvered mirrors are placed close to each other. Modern instruments use two lasers as separate coherent sources.

• **interferon** ► A protein that appears in the plasma during viral infections: released from infected cells, it inhibits the growth of viruses. Interferon contributes to ▷immunity as it can enter uninfected cells and render them immune to viral infections. It was discovered in 1957 by a British virologist, Alick Isaacs (1921–67). Genetically engineered human interferon can be used to treat certain viral infections (e.g. hepatitis B) and cancers (as it acts against viruses causing tumours) and also multiple sclerosis.

• **interior design** ► The part of architectural design that deals with the placing and layout of rooms within a building. It chiefly involves the decoration of walls and ceilings and design of normally immovable types of furniture, such as mirrors and fireplaces. Since Robert ▷Adam it has increasingly concerned movable furniture as well, a field previously left to the skill of the individual craftsman. In the 20th century greater attention has been given to creating a harmonious and functional style for buildings, down to the smallest object of furniture. A notable practitioner of this was Arne ▷Jacobsen, who sometimes specified exact positions for his furniture.

• **Interlaken** ► 46 42N 7 52E A resort in central Switzerland in the Bernese Oberland. One of Switzerland's oldest tourist resorts, it is surrounded by spectacular scenery with a fine view of the Jungfrau mountain. Population (latest est): 4900.

• **intermediate vector boson** ► (W) A hypothetical elementary particle thought to be exchanged by particles undergoing a ▷weak interaction. It would be an unstable ▷boson, either charged or neutral, and have a mass greater than about 800 MeV. ▷See also particle physics.

• **internal-combustion engine** ► A ▷heat engine in which fuel is burnt inside the engine, rather than in a separate furnace (see steam engine). This category includes all piston engines, ▷jet engines, and ▷rockets. The first practical internal-combustion engine was patented by N. ▷Otto in 1876. This was a four-stroke **gas engine**, i.e. an engine using gas as a fuel. It was the invention of the ⌐carburettor and the development of the ▷oil industry that made the liquid-fuelled Otto engine a source of power for the horseless carriages emerging in the late 19th century (see car).

The modern petrol engine has a compression ratio of 8 or 9 to 1, which requires special fuels (see tetraethyl lead) to avoid ▷knocking although lead pollution is causing manufacturers to design engines suitable for lead-free petrol. A simpler but less efficient variety of the petrol engine is the two-stroke. This does not have the complicated inlet and exhaust valves of the Otto engine, the explosive mixture entering and leaving the cylinder through ports in its walls that are covered and uncovered by the movements of the piston. Two-stroke engines are used where low power is required and in some motorcycles.

The main alternative to the petrol engine is the oil engine, based on a cycle invented by the German engineer Rudolf Diesel (1858–1913). In the Diesel engine, air is compressed alone inside the engine, causing its temperature to rise to over 550°C; oil is then pumped into the combustion chamber as a fine spray and ignites on contact with the hot air. In this case the compression ratio has to be 15 or 16 to 1, making the engine considerably heavier and more expensive than the petrol engine. The efficiency of both Otto and Diesel engines is limited by their compression ratios and thus their working temperatures (⌐heat engines). Also, combustion is intermittent and therefore incomplete, causing pollution. Moreover, being reciprocating engines, they have inherent vibrations. This last problem is partly overcome in the ▷Wankel engine. The ▷gas turbine, however, uses continuous combustion and with a compression ratio of up to 30:1 can reach a working temperature of 1200°C. It is therefore more efficient and creates less pollution than piston engines. Jet engines based on the gas turbine are used in aircraft and as an easily started prime mover in some power stations. As internal-combustion en-

gines rely on fossil fuels they produce much carbon dioxide (see greenhouse effect; electric car).

• **internal energy** ▷See heat.

• **International** ► An association of national socialist or labour parties formed to promote socialism or communism. The **First International** was an organization of labour and socialist groups founded in London in 1864 as the International Working Men's Association. Karl Marx soon assumed its leadership and its first congress was held in Geneva in 1866. Although the First International was successful in disseminating socialist ideas among workers, it failed to make any political changes, largely because of the conflicting socialist views of its members, especially those of Marx and ▷Bakunin. Its last meeting was held in 1876 in Philadelphia.

The **Second International** was founded in Paris in 1889; its headquarters were in Brussels. The organization was composed primarily of European, North American, and Japanese social democratic parties, which believed in parliamentary democracy, and of trade unions. Its leaders included Ramsay ▷Macdonald. At the outbreak of World War I, the organization collapsed because of division between pro- and anti-war groups. A postwar attempt to revive it failed.

The **Labour and Socialist International** was founded in Vienna in 1921; its goal was to create a socialist commonwealth. It has been called the "second and a half International" because it was composed of those out of sympathy with the Second and Third Internationals. It opposed fascism and also communist dictatorship while supporting the Soviet Union. The organization came to an end following Hitler's invasions in W Europe in 1939.

The **Third International** (or Comintern), an organization of world Communist Parties, was founded by Lenin in March, 1919, to encourage worldwide proletariat revolution. Throughout its existence it adjusted its programme to political exigencies and to the power struggles within the Soviet party leadership. As a gesture of reconciliation with his Western allies, Stalin dissolved the International in 1943 (see also Cominform).

The **Fourth International** was founded by ▷Trotsky in Mexico City in 1937 in opposition to Stalin and the Third International. It held its first conference in France in 1938 and was composed primarily of those who supported Trotsky's transitional programme, which aimed to undermine capitalism in preparation for its revolutionary overthrow.

The **Socialist International** was founded in 1951 as an association of socialist parties that believe in parliamentary democracy and oppose communism. Its headquarters are in London.

• **International Atomic Energy Agency** ► A specialized agency of the ▷United Nations established in 1957 to promote peaceful applications of atomic energy. Based in Vienna, it stages an influential annual conference.

• **International Atomic Time** ► The scientific standard of time derived from the ▷SI unit, the second, which is based on the ▷caesium clock. By means of atomic clocks and satellites, the major nations of the world are able to synchronize their time standards. ▷See universal time.

• **International Bank for Reconstruction and Development** ► (IBRD) A specialized agency of the ▷United Nations, known as the World Bank, with headquarters in Washington, DC. It finances development in member countries by making loans to governments or under government guarantee. It was set up at the 1944 ▷Bretton Woods Conference to facilitate reconstruction after World War II. All members must belong to the ▷International Monetary Fund.

• **International Brigades** ► A volunteer army recruited during the Spanish Civil War (1936–39) by the Comintern to aid the Republicans against Franco. Comprising at its largest some 20 000 volunteers, of which about 60% were communists, it was organized by nationality into 7 brigades. Ill-armed and badly led, it was disbanded in 1938.

• **International Civil Aviation Organization** ► (ICAO) A specialized agency of the ▷United Nations established in 1947 to promote high operating standards and fair competition among international airlines. With headquarters in Montreal, it formulates agreed standards in telecommunications, personnel training, and air-traffic protocols. Its council of representatives of 33 of the member countries implements the decisions of the assembly, its legislative body, and when necessary settles disputes between members.

● **International Confederation of Free Trade Unions** ▶ (ICFTU) An international body of national trades-union federations formed in 1949 by federations that had withdrawn from the ▷World Federation of Trade Unions (WFTU) following disagreements with the communist members of the WFTU.

● **International Court of Justice** ▶ The judicial body set up by the UN to pass judgment on disputes between states. The court, which normally sits at The Hague, comprises 15 judges, each from a different state, elected by the UN General Assembly. The court may only hear disputes between states that have agreed to be brought before it by any other state, either generally or in a specific case. Judgments of the court are enforced by application to the UN Security Council. The court also advises the UN and other bodies on public ▷international law.

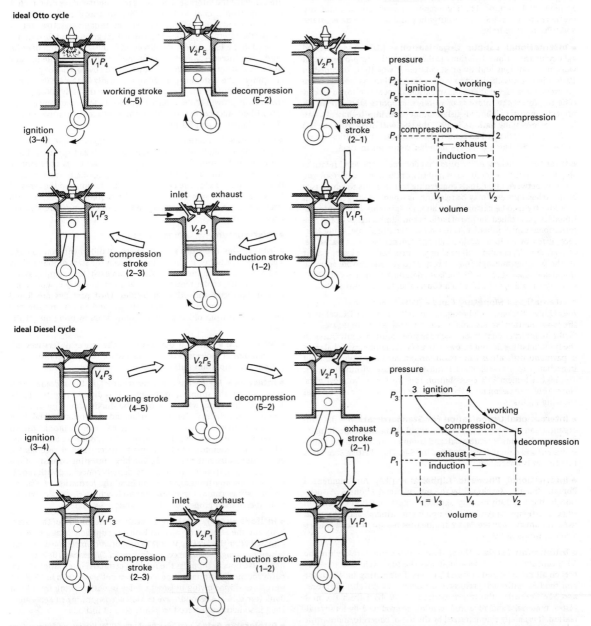

internal-combustion engine ▶ In the ideal Otto-cycle (four-stroke) engine, there are four piston strokes (movements up and down) for explosion. The petrol-air mixture is drawn into the cylinder by the induction stroke (1–2) and compressed by the compression stroke (2–3). A spark then ignites (3–4) the mixture causing the pressure to rise from P_3 to P_4 before the piston descends (combustion at constant volume). The piston then descends in the working stroke (4–5) and rises again in the exhaust stroke (2–1), when the burnt gases are pushed out of the cylinder through the exhaust valve. The graph illustrates the pressure and volume changes during the cycle. In the Diesel cycle, ignition is caused by the high compression achieved by the compression stroke (2–3) and the piston descends, increasing the volume of the burning gas from V_3 to V_4, before the pressure has time to rise (combustion at constant pressure).

● **International Criminal Police Organization** ▷*See* Interpol.

● **International Date Line** ▶ A line following the 180° meridian, deviating to avoid some land areas. The date immediately E of the line is one day earlier than to the W.

● **international gothic** ▶ A style of painting and sculpture dominant in W Europe between about 1375 and 1425. Originating in France and Burgundy, it later spread to Italy, Bohemia, and other German states. International gothic retained the figure stylizations of ▷gothic but introduced naturalism in the depiction of landscape, animals, and costume. Leading exponents were the de ▷Limburg brothers and Claus ▷Sluter in Burgundy and ▷Gentile da Fabriano and ▷Pisanello in Italy.

● **International Labour Organisation** ▶ (ILO) A specialized agency of the ▷United Nations dedicated to the improvement of working conditions and living standards. It was first convened in 1919, when it was affiliated to the ▷League of Nations, and its headquarters are in Geneva. The organization advocates a world labour code to protect the interests of workers, supports labour research projects, monitors labour legislation, and provides technical assistance to developing nations. In 1977 the USA withdrew from the ILO on the grounds that it had come to be dominated by politics but rejoined in 1980. There were 174 member countries in 1998.

● **international law** ▶ The rules that determine the legal relationship between independent states (public), or the method of resolving disputes between individuals concerning transactions to which two or more legal systems may be relevant, as when a contract made in one country is to be performed in another (private). Public international law, also called the law of nations and administered by the ▷International Court of Justice, is based on: (1) natural law, being laws recognized by civilized nations; (2) agreements between states, i.e. conventions; (3) customs followed in practice; and, to a lesser extent (4) the writings and opinions of respected jurists. Private international law, also called conflict of laws, determines the laws of which country should apply and which courts should have jurisdiction.

● **International Monetary Fund** ▶ (IMF) A specialized agency of the ▷United Nations, with headquarters in Washington, DC, set up at the 1944 ▷Bretton Woods Conference to stabilize exchange rates and facilitate international trade. Each member country contributes to the fund in both gold and its own currency. A member with balance-of-payments difficulties can obtain foreign currency from the fund in exchange for its own, which it must repurchase within five years. The higher a member's contribution the greater its voting rights. Horst Köhler of Germany is the managing director. ▷*See also* Special Drawing Rights.

● **International Organization for Standardization** ▶ (ISO) An organization, situated in Geneva, for establishing and controlling international scientific, industrial, and commercial standards of measurement and design. It was founded in 1946. The ▷British Standards Institution is a member.

● **International Phonetic Alphabet** ▶ (IPA) An augmented Roman alphabet, developed by the International Phonetic Association in the late 19th century and kept under continuous revision since. It attempts to symbolize, on phonetic principles, every sound used in human language. Many dictionaries represent the pronunciation of words in IPA.

● **international style** ▶ The predominant architectural style of the 20th century, so called because it was the first style effectively to breach all national and cultural barriers. Originating in W Europe and the USA with such architects as ▷Gropius, ▷Wright, ▷Behrens, and ▷Le Corbusier, the international style evolved from the new tastes, materials, and advanced technology produced by industrialization. It is chiefly characterized by the use of concrete, monolithic uniformity in the use of undecorated cubic forms, and a functional asymmetry. ▷*See also* brutalism.

● **International Telecommunication Union** ▶ (ITU) An international organization founded in 1934 to promote agreement on standards of telecommunications systems, since 1984 a specialized agency of the ▷United Nations. It makes recommendations on radio frequencies, operating procedures, and the establishment of telecommunications systems in developing countries. Its headquarters are in Geneva.

● **International Union for the Conservation of Nature** ▷*See* endangered species.

● **International Working Men's Association** ▷*See* International.

● **Internet** ▶ A worldwide network linking computers through modems, telephone lines, optical cables, and communications satellites. Users of the Internet have access to a number of services, including ▷electronic mail and the ability to transfer files between computers and access information on remote databases. **Usernet** is a part of the Internet organized for discussion groups and forums. Developed in the 1970s under the direction of the US Department of Defense, the Internet was originally used mainly by academic and research institutions. With the growth in the ownership of personal computers, the system expanded dramatically in the 1990s—in particular, in the use of the ▷World Wide Web. By the early 2000s the extraordinary growth of the Internet had begun to revolutionize many established practices in the fields of entertainment, information provision, shopping, and business.

● **Interpol** ▶ (*International Criminal Police Organization*) An association of 169 national ▷police forces, formed in 1923 to promote international cooperation in the prevention of crime. Its constitution precludes activities of a political, military, religious, or racial nature. Its major concerns are the exchange of information and the arrest of those who are the subject of an extradition order. Interpol has been effective in the control of smuggling and of currency offences and counterfeiting.

● **Interregnum** ▷*See* Commonwealth.

● **interstellar medium** ▶ The matter, mainly hydrogen gas and some dust, contained in the region between the stars of the ▷Galaxy and concentrated in the spiral arms. It can exist, for example, as hot ionized clouds, cooler tenuous neutral areas, or dense clouds of molecular hydrogen and other molecules. Dust particles are found throughout the interstellar region. The gas and dust is probably material cast off from old stars, with young stars forming out of the dense clouds.

● **interstitial** ▶ An atom that exists in the spaces (interstices) between atoms or molecules in a crystal lattice. Some interstitial compounds are important ▷alloys or ▷semiconductors.

● **intestine** ▶ The part of the digestive tract, in the abdomen, that extends from the stomach to the anus. It is divided into two parts. The small intestine, which includes the duodenum, jejunum, and ileum, is the principal site of digestion and absorption of food. It secretes digestive enzymes and mucus and its inner surface is thrown into finger-like processes, which increase the absorptive area. The duodenum is a common site for a ▷peptic ulcer, since it receives the acid contents from the stomach. The large intestine consists of the colon, caecum, rectum, and anus. It is largely concerned with the absorption of water from digested food and the formation of ▷faeces. The intestines contain specialized muscle whose rhythmic contractions (peristalsis) propel food to the anus. ▷*See* Plate II.

● **intifada** ▶ (Arabic: uprising) A revolt by Palestinians of the ▷West Bank and the ▷Gaza Strip against Israeli occupation. Israeli rule was imposed after the Six-Day War (1967); sporadic protests led to a sustained campaign of violence, beginning in December 1987. Israel's harsh attempts to suppress the intifada attracted international sympathy for the Palestinians. A peace agreement was signed in 1993 but unrest continued owing to Israel's delay in withdrawing from West Bank territories. A second wave of violence beginning in September 2000 is sometimes referred to as the second intifada.

● **Intolerable Acts** ▶ (*or* Coercive Acts; 1774) British parliamentary Acts to control the American colonies following the ▷Boston Tea Party. The Boston Port Bill (1774) closed the port until reparation for the lost tea had been made. The Massachusetts Government Act repealed the colony's charter and imposed military rule on Massachusetts; the Administration of Justice Act allowed British officials to return home for trial in a criminal case; and the Quebec Act gave the fur trade between Ohio and Mississippi to Quebec. The Acts contributed to the outbreak of the ▷American Revolution.

● **intoxication** ▶ Any form of acute poisoning: in popular language it usually refers to alcoholic poisoning (*see* alcoholism). The law in the UK states that it is illegal to drive with an alcohol concentration in the blood greater than 80 mg/100 ml. Most other countries have a similar law.

● **intra-uterine device** ▶ (IUD) ▷*See* contraception.

● **introversion** ▶ (*or* intraversion) A quality of personality characterized by interest in oneself rather than in the outside world: it is the opposite of ▷extroversion. Introverts are reflective and introspective, with a tendency to have a small circle of friends. They are good at persisting for a long time at one task; their interests tend to be philosophical; and they are highly susceptible to permanent ▷conditioning.

● **intrusive rock** ▷*See* igneous rock.

● **intuitionism** ▶ Any doctrine in which what appears to be self-evident is regarded as the basis of knowledge ("I just *know* that such-and-such is the case"). From the model of mathematics, the Pythagoreans believed that intuition is superior to observation and in modern times the mathematical school of L. E. J. ▷Brouwer was called intuitionist regarding its views about the nature of mathematics. In contemporary philosophy, intuitionism has been most emphasized in ▷ethics; the so-called Oxford Intuitionists regarded the faculty of moral judgment (the individual's conscience) as nonrational and autonomous and opposed ▷utilitarianism and teleology in ethics.

● **Inuit** ▶ A Mongoloid people of the Arctic regions of Canada and Greenland who speak Inupik. The related peoples of Siberia and South Alaska speak Yupik (*see* Inuit-Aleut languages). The men are traditionally hunters of seals, whales, walrus, and caribou, using harpoons, canoes (*or* kayaks), dogs, and sleds. Fishing is also important. Their clothes, made by the women, are of animal skins. Only some of the many different groups build snow dwellings (igloos). Others construct semisubterranean sod shelters or snow-covered skin tents. There is no overall sense of identity among them and the main units are family bands. Their small ivory or stone carvings are prized. The term "Eskimo", which was formerly used to refer to these people, is now considered offensive by most Inuit. In 1999 the semi-autonomous region of ▷Nunavut was established in NE Canada as a homeland for the Inuit people.

● **Inuit-Aleut languages** ▶ A language group, sometimes included in the classification of American Indian languages. It consists of three distinct languages: Inupik (Inupiaq *or* Inuk), spoken by the Inuit in Greenland and in many dialects along the N coast of Canada, Yupik, spoken by the Arctic peoples of Siberia and S Alaska, and ▷Aleut, spoken by a few hundred people in the Aleutian Islands.

● **Inuvik** ▶ 68 16N 133 40W A settlement in N Canada, in the Northwest Territories on the Mackenzie River delta. Built (1954–62) as the regional administration headquarters, it has a largely Inuit population. Population (1990): 2790.

● **Invar** ▶ An ▷alloy of iron with 36% nickel, which expands by only 0.9 mm per km for each Celsius degree rise. This is about one-tenth the expansion of platinum and titanium and less than one-twentieth that of most other metals. Discovered in 1896, it has been used for accurate chronometer parts.

● **Inveraray** ▶ 56 13N 5 05W A town in W Scotland, in Argyll and Bute on Loch Fyne. Inveraray Castle, seat of the dukes of Argyll, was built around 1780 on the site of an earier castle. Population (1991): 512.

● **Invercargill** ▶ 46 26S 168 21E A city in New Zealand, in S South Island on the Waihopai River. It lies in a sheep- and dairy-farming region. Population (1995): 51 600.

● **Inverclyde** ▶ A council area of W central Scotland, on the Firth of Clyde. It was created from part of Strathclyde Region in 1996. The S bank of the Clyde is highly industrialized, with engineering and chemicals in Greenock and in Port Glasgow; inland, the main activity is agriculture. Area 162 sq km (63 sq mi). Population (1999 est): 85 400. Administrative centre: Greenock.

● **Inverness** ▶ 57 27N 4 15W A city in N Scotland, the administrative centre of Highland council area, at the head of the Moray Firth. It has tourist, boatbuilding, distilling, iron-founding, and woollen industries. It has a 19th-century cathedral and castle, which occupies the site of an earlier castle destroyed in 1746. It was granted city status in 2000. Population (1991): 41 234.

● **Inverness** ▶ (*or* Inverness-shire) A former county of N Scotland. In 1975 its boundaries were adjusted to form Inverness District, in Highland. The district was abolished in 1996.

● **invertebrate** ▶ Any animal without a backbone. All animals except vertebrates belong to this category, including the tunicates and lancelets—animals that possess a rodlike skeletal notochord. The term is not employed in taxonomic systems.

● **invert sugar** ▶ A mixture of the sugars glucose and fructose resulting from the action of heat or the enzyme invertase on cane or beet sugar (sucrose). It is sweeter than sucrose and widely used in foods and confectionery.

● **investiture controversy** ▶ A dispute between the papacy and the Holy Roman Empire during the late 11th and early 12th centuries concerning the right of secular rulers to appoint bishops in return for pledges of loyalty. The conflict arose between Pope ▷Gregory VII and the Holy Roman Emperor ▷Henry IV and later also involved the Norman kings of England. Compromise was reached with England in 1106 and with the Emperor in 1122. This issue focused the struggle for supremacy between lay and ecclesiastical powers.

● **investment** ▶ **1.** The purchase of capital goods (plant and machinery) used in the production of consumer goods and services. Investment and consumption together comprise the national income. A high level of investment is a necessary part of a nation's economic wellbeing and helps to promote ▷economic growth. In most countries incentives, in the form of tax relief, are available on investment expenditure. What actually motivates investment is a matter of debate: some economists believe the rate of interest is the most important factor, while others assign more importance to the level of demand in the economy. Certainly investment varies a great deal over the ▷trade cycle. **2.** The use of money to obtain an income or a capital gain in the future. This can be achieved by depositing it with a bank or building society to provide income without capital growth; government stocks and bonds will provide certain limited gains and income; while shares, unit trusts, etc., provide an opportunity for larger capital gains (or losses) and some income, with an element of speculation. Investment also includes the purchase of any asset that can be expected to increase in value and can also be linked with insurance policies.

● **investment bank** ▷*See* issuing house.

● **investment company** ▶ (*or* investment trust) A company that buys and sells ▷securities to make profits for its shareholders. The company has a fixed capital and its shares are bought and sold on the ▷stock exchange. Investors (shareholders) thus become part owners of a professionally managed portfolio of securities. In the USA it is called a closed-end investment company. *Compare* unit trust.

● **in vitro fertilization** ▷*See* test-tube baby.

● **Io** ▶ (astronomy) ▷*See* Galilean satellites.

● **Io** ▶ (Greek legend) A priestess of Hera, loved by Zeus, who transformed her into a heifer to protect her from discovery. Hera ordered Argus, a herdsman with eyes covering his entire body, to guard her, but she escaped with the help of Hermes and was finally restored to Zeus in Egypt.

● **Ioánnina** ▶ (*or* Yannina) 39 40N 20 51E A town in NW Greece, in Epirus on Lake Ioánnina. Conquered by the Turks in 1430, it became the seat (1788–1822) of Ali Pasha. It was captured by the Greeks in 1913. The university was founded in 1970. Population (1991 est): 56 496.

● **iodine** ▶ (I) A purple-black lustrous solid ▷halogen that evaporates slowly at room temperature to give a purple gas. It was discovered in 1811 by B. Courtois (1777–1838). It is insoluble in water but dissolves readily in organic solvents, such as chloroform ($CHCl_3$) or carbon tet-

● io moth ●

rachloride (CCl_4), to give pink-purple solutions. Iodine is present in sea water and concentrated by seaweeds; it also occurs in saltpetre deposits, such as those in Chile. Potassium iodide (KI) is widely used in photography. The radioactive isotope ^{131}I, with a half-life of 8.1 days, is produced in nuclear reactors; its accidental release into the atmosphere would cause serious problems. It is also used in the diagnosis and treatment of thyroid disorders as it is concentrated in the thyroid gland. Tincture of iodine is used as an antiseptic. At no 53; at wt 126.904; mp 113.5°C; bp 184.35°C.

● **io moth** ▶ A large common American ▷saturniid moth, *Automeris io*. Males are yellow and the larger females reddish brown, with a wingspan of 70 mm. The greenish spiny larvae feed on trees and are poisonous to touch.

● **ion** ▶ An atom or group of atoms that has lost or gained one or more electrons and consequently has an electric charge. Positively and negatively charged ions are called **cations** and **anions** respectively. The sign and magnitude of the charge is indicated by a superscript, as in the potassium ion, K^+, or the doubly charged sulphate ion, SO_4^{2-}. Many compounds (electrovalent compounds) are combinations of positive and negative ions; sodium chloride, for example is formed from sodium ions (Na^+) and chloride ions (Cl^-). ▷*See also* chemical bond; ionization.

● **Iona** ▶ 56 19N 6 25W A small sparsely populated island in NW Scotland, in the Inner Hebrides. It has many religious associations; St Columba landed here in 563 AD, establishing a monastery that became the centre of the ▷Celtic Church. It later became a burial ground for Scottish, Irish, and Norwegian kings. In the early 1900s work began on restoring the 13th-century abbey church and associated buildings, a task brought to completion by the Iona Community (founded 1938) in the 1960s. The Community comprises both ministers (mainly of the Church of Scotland) and laymen who spend three months of each year on the island as preparation for missionary and social work elsewhere. Area: 854 ha (2112 acres).

● **ion engine** ▷*See* rocket.

● **Ionesco, Eugène** ▶ (1912–94) French dramatist, born in Romania of French and Romanian parents; he settled permanently in France in 1938. He inaugurated the ▷Theatre of the Absurd with his first play, *The Bald Prima Donna* (1950), which exposed the poverty of language as a means of communication. His later plays, which include *The Lesson* (1951), *The Chairs* (1951), *Rhinoceros* (1960), *Exit the King* (1962), and *Man With Bags* (1977), use a variety of surrealistic techniques to express a nihilistic vision of society.

● **Ionia** ▶ In antiquity, the central W coast of Asia Minor and the adjacent islands, settled by Greeks about 1000 BC. Between the 8th and 6th centuries BC ▷Miletus, ▷Sámos, ▷Ephesus, and other Ionian cities led Greece in trade, colonization, and culture. The first Greek philosophers, including ▷Thales, ▷Pythagoras, and ▷Anaximander, were Ionian. After 550 BC Ionia was dominated by ▷Lydia and later Persia. The Ionian revolt against Persian rule (499–494 BC) resulted in defeat, economic ruin, subjugation by outsiders, and comparative eclipse.

● **Ionian Islands** ▶ A group of Greek islands in the Ionian Sea, extending from Corfu in the N to Zacynthus in the S and including Páxos, Lévkas, Ithaca, and Cephalonia. They belonged to Britain from the Treaty of Paris (1815) until 1864, when they were ceded to Greece. Several were devastated by earthquakes in 1514, 1893, and 1953. Total area: 2307 sq km (891 sq mi). Population (1990): 191 003.

● **Ionian Sea** ▶ The section of the central Mediterranean Sea, bounded by Italy, Sicily, and Greece, that contains the Ionian Islands.

● **Ionic order** ▷*See* orders of architecture.

● **ionization** ▶ The process of producing ▷ions from neutral atoms or molecules. Solvation (surrounding of an ion by polar solvent molecules), heating (thermal ionization), or bombardment with particles or radiation provides the necessary energy for the process. The minimum energy required to ionize an atom A (i.e. $A \rightarrow A^+ + e^-$) is called its **ionization potential**, which is usually measured in electronvolts.

● **ionization chamber** ▶ An instrument used for measuring the intensity of ▷ionizing radiation. It consists of a gas-filled chamber containing two electrodes with a large potential difference between them. When radiation enters the chamber it ionizes some of the gas atoms or molecules. The ions flow towards the electrodes creating a current, whose magnitude is a measure of the intensity of the radiation. ▷*See also* Geiger counter.

● **ionizing radiation** ▶ Any radiation that ionizes the atoms or molecules of matter. It may consist of particles (such as ▷electrons) or it may be electromagnetic (*see* ultraviolet radiation; X-rays; gamma radiation). Ionizing radiation occurs naturally and is emitted by radioactive substances. It is produced artificially in X-ray machines, particle accelerators, nuclear reactors, etc. Ionizing radiations are used in medical diagnosis and therapy and in sterilization of food. In biological tissue these radiations create reactive free radicals, especially by ionizing water molecules, which attack proteins, nucleic acids, etc., and can cause damage by changing their structure and function. This is how they kill cancerous cells, which are more susceptible than normal cells (*see* radiotherapy). Higher doses can change normal cells into cancerous cells and cause other illnesses (*see* radiation sickness). However, man has evolved in an environment in which there is a background of radiation and is therefore adapted to a certain level of it. On average we each receive about 2150 microsieverts from the air (37%), the earth (19%), within the body (17%), ▷cosmic rays (14%), medical X-rays (11.5%), fall-out from nuclear tests and air travel (0.5% each), industry (0.4%), and ▷radioactive wastes (0.1%).

● **ionosphere** ▶ A region of the upper □atmosphere that reflects short radio waves, enabling transmissions to be made round the curved surface of the earth by sky waves. The gases in the ionosphere are ionized by absorption of radiation from the sun. Its existence was suggested in 1902 by A. E. Kennelly and independently by O. Heaviside. Sir Edward Appleton (1892–1925) provided proof by bouncing radio waves off the different layers of the ionosphere, which vary in behaviour with the position of the sun and with the

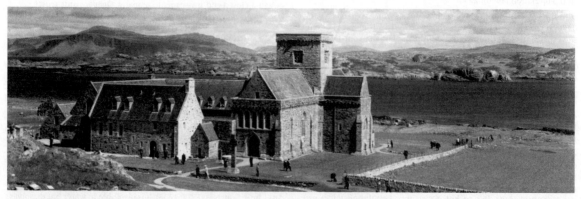

Iona ▶ The restored 13th-century abbey seen from the west, with the island of Mull in the background.

sunspot cycle. The ionization of the D region, at between 50 and 90 kilometres altitude, disappears during the day. The E region is between 90 and 160 kilometres high and the F region (sometimes called the Appleton layer) is from 160 kilometres up to about 400 kilometres. The lower part of the ionosphere (E region) is sometimes called the Heaviside-Kennelly layer. The gas particles in the F region do not lose their charge as quickly as those below because the gas is less dense and therefore ions and electrons are subject to fewer collisions. This enables radio transmissions to continue at night.

● **Iowa** ▶ A state in the USA, in the Midwest bounded on the E by the Mississippi River and by the Missouri River in the W. The land rises slowly from the Mississippi Valley to form a gentle rolling landscape, with the higher land in the NW. Iowa is predominantly an agricultural state and has associated industries, particularly the manufacture of agricultural machinery and food processing. It is famed for its livestock, particularly pigs. Major crops are corn, oats, soya beans, and other fodder crops. There is also some mining for portland cement and gypsum. The scattered population and lack of urban areas limit the cultural institutions the state can support. *History*: explored by the Frenchmen Jolliet and ▷Marquette in 1673, it formed part of the Louisiana Purchase (1803) by the USA. It became a territory (1838) and then a state (1846). The end of the US Civil War and the arrival of the railway opened up the state to immigrants. Area: 145 790 sq km (56 290 sq mi). Population (1996 est): 2 851 792. Capital: Des Moines.

● **ipecacuanha** ▶ A South American herbaceous plant, *Uragoga ipecacuanha*, cultivated in the tropics for its root, which yields medicinal alkaloids used as an expectorant and emetic. Large doses cause vomiting and diarrhoea. Family: *Rubiaceae*.

● **Iphigenia** ▶ In Greek legend, the eldest daughter of ▷Agamemnon and ▷Clytemnestra. When the Greek fleet was delayed at Aulis at the beginning of the ▷Trojan War, Agamemnon was told that Artemis demanded the sacrifice of his daughter before the fleet could sail to Troy. According to some versions Artemis took pity on Iphigenia and transported her to Tauris, where she became a priestess of Artemis. The story is the subject of two plays by ▷Euripides.

● **I-pin** ▷*See* Yibin.

● **Ipoh** ▶ 4 36N 101 02E A city in NW Peninsular Malaysia, the capital of Perak state. The tinmining centre of Malaysia, it has noted Chinese rock temples. Population (1991): 382 633.

● **Ipswich** ▶ 52 04N 1 10E A town in SE England, the administrative centre of Suffolk at the head of the Orwell estuary. It is a port and regional centre; the main economic activities are shipping, financial services, telecommunications, and high-tech industries. Cardinal Wolsey was born here. Population (1997): 112 959.

● **Ipswich** ▶ 27 38S 152 40E A city in Australia, in SE Queensland. It is the state's second largest coal producer. Population (latest est): 73 680.

● **Iqbal, Sir Mohammed** ▶ (?1875–1938) Indian Muslim poet and philosopher, born in Sialkot (Punjab). He came to England in 1905 (already a noted romantic poet and promoter of Indian nationalism) to read philosophy and law at Cambridge University. From 1908 Iqbal lived in Lahore where he became a leading member of the ▷Muslim League. He is generally credited with the formulation of the political theory of Pakistan as a separate Muslim state in the Indian subcontinent.

● **Iquique** ▶ 20 15S 70 08W A port in N Chile, on the Pacific Ocean. Industries include fishmeal plants and canneries; the chief exports are nitrates, iodine, and fishmeal. Population (1995 est): 152 592 (metropolitan area).

● **Iquitos** ▶ 3 51S 73 13W A port in NE Peru, on the River Amazon 3700 km (2300 mi) from its mouth. The furthest point upstream accessible to oceangoing vessels, it exports rubber, timber, and nuts. Its university was founded in 1962. Population (1993): 274 759.

● **IRA** ▷*See* Irish Republican Army.

● **Iráklion** ▶ (*or* Herakleion; Italian name: Candia) 35 00N 25 08E The chief port of the Greek island of Crete, on the N coast. It is pictur-

esque, possessing many Venetian fortifications, and has become a tourist centre. Exports include raisins, grapes, and olive oil. Population (1991): 117 167.

● **Iran, Islamic Republic of** ▶ (name until 1935: Persia) A country in the Middle East lying between the Caspian Sea and the Persian Gulf. Its central plateau, containing deserts and marshes, is surrounded by mountains, the ▷Zagros Mountains in the W, the ▷Elburz Mountains and the Kopet Mountains in the N, and a barren region of peaks and sand in the E. It suffers great extremes of temperature and severe earthquakes. The most populous areas are the NW and the Caspian coast, which have the greatest rainfall. The population is mainly Persian with groups of Turks, Kurds, Armenians, Arabs, and such tribes as the Bakhtyari.

Economy: agriculture supports 75% of the population, although lack of rain hampers productivity and much food has to be imported. Agricultural improvements (most notably the development of irrigation) were held back by the political situation in the 1970s and the subsequent war with Iraq (1980–88). Wheat, rice, tobacco, fruit, sugar beet, and tea are grown; sheep and goats are kept. Iran's chief source of revenue is its oil; it possesses 10% of the world's reserves and profited greatly from the oil price increases of the 1970s. More recently production has been hampered by the long war with Iraq and a failure to modernize. The main oilfields are in the Zagros Mountains, where oil was first discovered (1901). The industry was nationalized in 1979. Other minerals include coal, copper, iron ore, lead, natural gas, and precious stones. The textile industry uses local cotton and silk, and carpet manufacture is an important handicraft. Iran's steel industry is the largest in the Middle East. Although the regime of the Shah saw ambitious attempts to improve Iran's industry and infrastructure, these were mainly abandoned after the Islamic Revolution. Since 1994 there has been a series of economic and financial crises, greatly exacerbated by the imposition of US trade sanctions from 1995 to 1999.

History: the Caspian coast and the plateau are among the earliest centres of civilization. Early Persian dynasties include the ▷Achaemenians and the ▷Sasanians (*see also* Greek-Persian Wars). Arab domination, which established Islam in the mid-7th century, was followed by that of the Turks and Mongols before the Persian Safavid dynasty (1502–1736) came into power. Following a period of great prosperity (1587–1629) Persia again declined, encroached on by Uzbeks, Arabs, Afghans, Turks, and Russians. The next great dynasty, the Kajar dynasty (1794–1925), was marked largely by rivalry for domination between Britain and Russia. Western influence was felt increasingly during the latter half of the 19th century. Repressive rule provoked opposition that became open in about 1900 and was intensified by resentment against the oil and other concessions granted to Britain and Russia, made necessary by the Shah's financial difficulties. The Shah was forced to grant a constitution and National Assembly (the Majlis; 1906); his successor disbanded this and was then deposed and replaced (1909). Further disorders resulted in the army coup that established Reza Khan in power (1921), from 1925 as ▷Reza Shah Pahlavi. Under his virtual dictatorship order returned and the country was industrialized and extensively westernized; he was forced to abdicate in favour of his son ▷Mohammed Reza Pahlavi (1941). Iran's oil has been a major source of political unrest. In 1945 the Soviet Union supported an Azerbaidzhan and Kurdish revolt to gain oil concessions (later withdrawn). Oil was also a major issue for the militant National Front movement, which nationalized the oil industry (1951); the British responded with a blockade resulting in serious economic difficulties and the Shah was forced to flee the country temporarily. Martial law was ended after 16 years in 1957 but economic and political instability continued; the Shah's reform programme, which included in 1963 the enfranchisement of women, the redistribution of land, and compulsory education, was opposed by major religious and political groups. There were riots in the early 1960s and unrest was further provoked by harsh repression, with many dissidents executed or imprisoned. By 1978 different opposition groups, including intellectuals, students, Muslims, and communists, had united under the exiled Muslim leader Ayatollah Ruholla ▷Khomeini. Demonstrations and riots in 1977–78 were reinforced by strikes, despite the imposition of martial law; by February, 1979, an estimated 10 000 people had died in political violence, while anti-Western feeling had forced foreigners to leave the country. The Shah then left the country, later dying in exile (1980), and Khomeini took over the government in the so-called Islamic Revolution. Unrest continued, with Khomeini's strict Muslim administration opposed by progressive groups and Kurdish rebels. In 1979 students occupied the US embassy in Tehran and took 52 of the personnel hostage, only releasing them in January, 1981. Abolhassan Bani-Sadr, elected Iran's first president in 1980, was dismissed and forced to flee the country in 1981; his successor, Muhammad Ali Radjai, was killed in a bomb explosion (1981). War with Iraq broke out in September, 1980 (*see* Iran-Iraq War). Iran's international relations improved after the war ended (1988) but deteriorated in 1989 over Khomeini's threats against the novelist Salman ▷Rushdie (not effectively lifted until 1998). After Khomeini's death in 1989, Seyed Ali Khamenei succeeded him as the country's religious leader and Ali Akbar Hashemi ▷Rafsanjani was elected president. Although Rafsanjani succeeded in improving relations with the West in the early 1990s, Iran's alleged involvement in international terrorism led the USA to impose sanctions from 1995 to 1999. In 1996 Ayatollah Mohammed Khatami was elected president and began a cautious programme of liberal reform, while also aiming to normalize Iran's international relations. The general election of 2000 produced a clear victory for pro-reform groups and Khatami was re-elected by a landslide in 2001.

Islamic Republic of Iran

Head of state	Leader of the Islamic Revolution Ayatollah Seyed Ali Khamenei
Official language	Persian (Farsi)
Official religion	Shiite Muslim
Official currency	Iranian rial of 100 dinars
Area	1 648 000 sq km (636 160 sq mi)
Population (2000 est)	62 704 000
Capital	Tehran

● **Iranian languages** ► A subgroup of the ▷Indo-Iranian language family. Iranian languages are spoken in Iran, Afghanistan, Turkey, and parts of the Caucasus. Like its counterpart the ▷Indo-Aryan group, the Iranian languages are closely related to ▷Sanskrit. Modern Iranian languages include Persian, Kurdish, ▷Pashto, and ▷Ossetic.

● **Iran-Iraq War** ► (*or* Gulf War; 1980–88) An indecisive conflict in the Persian Gulf, between Iran and Iraq. Iraqi forces invaded Iran shortly after the Iranian revolution in pursuit of claims over border territory. A war of attrition developed, costing both sides heavy casualties. The conflict also saw the use of toxic gas (by Iraq). Peace was achieved in 1988 through UN mediation with no significant territorial gains on either side.

● **Iraq, Republic of** ► A country in the Middle East, bordering on the Persian Gulf. The SE consists of an alluvial plain around the delta of the Rivers Tigris and Euphrates; this floods in spring. The W is a vast desert while the N is mountainous. The population is about 90% Muslim divided evenly between Shiite and Sunnite sects. The Kurds, who live in the mountainous NE, form 15–20% of the population. *Economy*: most of the population lives by agriculture, the chief crops being wheat, barley, rice, maize, sorghum, sesame, dates, and cotton. Since 1958 collective farms have been set up and mechanization and irrigation schemes have increased production but the problems of salinity and soil erosion remain. The main industry is oil (first discovered at Kirkuk in 1927) and Iraq is a member of OPEC. Before the ▷Gulf War and the UN's imposition of a worldwide ban on Iraqi oil exports in 1990, oil production accounted for about 45% of GNP and almost 100% of government revenue. Natural gas, textiles, processed foods, cement, and electrical and leather goods are also produced. Cereals, meat, machinery, chemicals, and consumer goods were imported until UN sanctions were imposed. The damage to industry in the Gulf War and continuing restrictions on oil exports have led to a severe economic crisis. *History*: as ▷Mesopotamia, Iraq was the site of the world's first civilization; it is rich in archaeological remains. It was conquered by the Arabs and became Muslim in the 7th century AD and was part of the Ottoman Empire from 1534 until World War I, when UK troops expelled the Turks. As a British mandate (1920–32), Iraq became a king-

dom (1921). From this period on it has been politically unstable, with ethnic and religious unrest and frequent coups; the monarchy was overthrown in 1958. Since the 1960s the Kurds in the NE have been in intermittent rebellion and have opposed the Ba'athist government (in power since 1968). Although a member of the ▷Arab League and formerly of the ▷Baghdad Pact, Iraq has been in dispute with Iran and Syria since the 1970s. In 1980 Iraq invaded Iranian border territory, thus beginning the long ▷Iran-Iraq War. In 1990 Saddam ▷Hussein, president since 1979, ordered the military seizure of Kuwait and defied UN demands for withdrawal despite the imposition of sanctions. A huge multinational force, led by the USA, then waged the ▷Gulf War (1991) against Iraq. Following Iraq's defeat, antigovernment uprisings were crushed: oppression of the Kurds in N Iraq and of the Marsh Arabs in S Iraq led to the flight of thousands of refugees. Iraq's defiance of UN ceasefire terms provoked US air raids in 1993. In 1996 the Iraqi military intervened in Kurdish factional fighting in the N, leading to further US missile strikes. In the same year the UN agreed to a partial lifting of the oil-sales ban on condition that the revenue was used for medical and humanitarian purposes. Iraq's failure to cooperate with UN monitoring of its strategic weapons led to US and British air raids in late 1998 and 2001. In 2002 President Bush gave strong indications that Iraq would be the next target in the USA's ▷war on terrorism. UN sanctions have remained in place, causing growing suffering among the Iraqi population.

Republic of Iraq

Head of state	President Saddam Hussein
Official language	Arabic
Official currency	Iraqi dinar of 1000 fils
Area	438 446 sq km (169 248 sq mi)
Population (2000 est)	22 676 000
Capital	Baghdad

● **Irbil** ► (Arbil *or* Erbil) 36 12N 44 01E A town in N Iraq close to the Turkish and Iranian borders. It was important in Assyrian times and is now a trading centre for a productive agricultural region. Population (latest est): 485 968.

● **Ireland** ► The second largest island in the British Isles, separated from Great Britain by the North Channel, the Irish Sea, and St George's Channel. It consists of a central lowland area of fertile plains, bogs, and moorland, rising to hills and mountains in the N and S. The River Shannon is the chief river, draining N–S, and Ireland contains many lakes, particularly in the N and W, including Lough Neagh. Since 1920 Ireland has been politically divided, the NE part forming Northern Ireland in the UK and the remainder comprising the Republic of Ireland. *History*: rich in archaeological remains, Ireland was invaded in the 4th century BC by the Celts. The country came to be divided into the five tribal kingdoms (the Five Fifths) of Ulster, Meath, Leinster, Munster, and Connaught, which nominally acknowledged the overlordship of the High Kings of Ireland (the rulers of Tara). In the 5th century the country was converted to Christianity—a process in which St Patrick was the outstanding figure—and in the following centuries the Irish Church fostered scholarship, art, and missionary work. The 9th and 10th centuries saw Viking invasions, which were brought to an end by Brian Boru's great victory at Clontarf (1014). In the mid-12th century Ireland was invaded by the Norman conquerors of England and in 1172 Henry II gained the allegiance of the Irish kings. English law and administration were introduced in the 13th century, but effective English rule was restricted to the area around Dublin (called the Pale) until the 16th century, when the subjection of the Irish became the aim of the Tudor monarchs of England. Revolts, inspired in part by Roman Catholic opposition to the Reformation, were suppressed and the ▷Plantation of Ireland by English and later by Scottish settlers was begun, being most successful, in terms of permanence, in Ulster. Irish resistance continued, culminating in the rebellion of 1641, which, centred on the NE, was not suppressed until Oliver Cromwell's notorious expedition in 1649–50. The subsequent confiscation of the rebels' land and its redistribution among English colonists established the economic and political ascendancy of the Protestant minority in Ireland. It was strengthened by the Restoration settlement, which extended Protestant landholdings, and by events after William of Orange's defeat (1690) of the Irish supporters of the deposed Catholic king, James II: the usual land confiscations were accompanied on this occasion by new anti-Catholic penal laws. In the 18th century Ireland's subservience to England came to be opposed by many Irish Protestants and in 1782, under the leadership of Henry Grattan, the Irish parliament obtained legislative independence. However, the abortive Irish rebellion of 1798 (*see* United Irishmen, Society of) persuaded Pitt the Younger of the need for the complete union of Britain and Ireland (1800; *see* Union, Acts of). It also convinced him of the need for ▷Catholic emancipation, which was not fully obtained until 1829 (*see also* O'Connell, Daniel). The appalling social conditions suffered by the majority of Irish renewed Catholic militancy in the 19th century. Attempts by the Young Ireland group to repeal the Act of Union failed, and nationalist agitation was taken up after the Irish (potato) famine first, abortively, by the ▷Fenians and then by the ▷Home Rule movement. While the ▷Land League pursued agrarian reform with some success, Home Rule, in spite of Gladstone's conversion to the cause, was delayed. It was nominally obtained in 1914 but was opposed both by the Republicans, who wanted a greater degree of independence, and the Protestant Ulster Unionists, who feared for their future in a self-governing country with a Catholic majority. Following the ▷Easter Rising of 1916, the proclamation of an Irish republic (1919) by ▷Sinn Féin leaders in Dublin, and virtual civil war between the ▷Irish Republican Army and British forces, Britain proposed partition (1920), with separate parliaments in the predominantly Protestant NE and Catholic S and W, both of which would become self-governing provinces of the UK. This formula was accepted in the north but rejected in the south, where nationalist feeling now demanded full independence. Negotiations between Republican leaders and the British government resulted in the Anglo-Irish Treaty (1921; effective 1922), which created the Irish Free State, independent of the UK but with dominion status within the Commonwealth, in the S.

Northern Ireland The province is divided into 26 administrative districts. There are also six nonadministrative traditional counties: Antrim, Armagh, Down, Fermanagh, Londonderry, and Tyrone.

Economy: since the 1950s, the traditional industries of shipbuilding and linen manufacture have declined in importance, as has agriculture. Diversification of industry has taken place (chemicals, rubber products, man-made fibres, and engineering) and there has been a large rise in the number of people employed in the service sector. The economy has suffered, however, from the political upheavals of the last 30 years.

History: following the Government of Ireland Act (1920) and the Anglo-Irish Treaty (1921), which provided for the division of Ireland, six of the nine counties of ▷Ulster became an autonomous province of the UK. From 1922 until 1972 Northern Ireland was governed by a parliament, which met at Stormont in Belfast and had legislative responsibility for most matters. Executive power lay with a prime minister and cabinet. Foreign policy was decided by the British government. The Northern Ireland MPs were retained at Westminster to represent the province. The Protestant majority dominated politics and economic life, while the Catholic minority (most of whom wanted Northern Ireland united with the Republic) grew increasingly dissatisfied, and in 1968 violence broke out. By 1969 this had escalated and a British army peacekeeping force was sent in. A terrorist campaign by the ▷Irish Republican Army led to the British government suspending Stormont in 1972 and imposing direct rule from Westminster. In 1973 a Northern Ireland Executive, comprising Protestant and Catholic representatives and responsible to an Assembly, was established but, following a general strike in 1974, direct rule was resumed. In 1980 a group of imprisoned members of the IRA went on hunger strike in an attempt to gain political rather than criminal status. Ten strikers died as a result. An Anglo-Irish agreement signed by Margaret ▷Thatcher and Garret ▷Fitzgerald (1985), which gave the Republic of Ireland a greater influence in the province, provoked Unionist protests. In the ▷Downing Street Declaration of 1993 the UK and Dublin governments announced their willingness to negotiate with all political parties that renounced violence. Subsequently (1994) ▷Sinn Féin announced a complete IRA ceasefire and Protestant paramilitaries followed suit. However, prog-

ress foundered on disagreements over the decommissioning of IRA weapons and the IRA ceasefire broke down in early 1996. Following its resumption in July 1997, talks involving the British and Irish governments and most of the Northern Irish parties (including Sinn Féin) began in September. These resulted in the **Good Friday Agreement** of April 1998, which proposed a comprehensive settlement for the province involving the creation of three new bodies: a Northern Ireland assembly with a powersharing executive, a North-South ministerial council, and a "Council of the Isles" with members drawn from the British and Irish governments and the devolved bodies in Northern Ireland, Wales, and Scotland. The agreement allowed for the phased release of paramilitary prisoners and required the complete decommissioning of terrorist arms within two years. In a subsequent referendum (May 1998) the agreement was backed by 71% of the Northern Irish voters. Following elections to the new assembly in June 1998, David ▷Trimble became Northern Ireland's first minister. After further negotiations an executive including Sinn Féin members was established in December 1999 and power was belatedly devolved to the new bodies; however, lack of progress on IRA decommissioning led Britain to suspend the political institutions in February 2000. The assembly and executive were re-established in May, following a new IRA offer to put its weapons "beyond use." In 2001 a further crisis in the process was resolved when the IRA announced that it had finally decommissioned some weapons (October). Area: 14 121 sq km (5452 sq mi). Population (1999 est): 1 691 800. Capital: Belfast.

Republic of Ireland (Irish name: Éire) The country is divided into 26 counties.

Economy: predominantly agricultural, cattle rearing being of major importance, especially in the E lowlands, where cattle are fattened for beef. Dairy farming is also practised, particularly in the S. Arable crops include barley, wheat, oats, potatoes, and sugar beet. Tourism is another major source of revenue. Industries have expanded considerably since the 1950s. They include food processing, brewing, distilling, textiles, and clothing. Peat is extensively cut as a fuel. In 1977 Europe's largest lead-zinc mines were opened at Navan. In the later 1990s the Republic had the fastest growing economy in the developed world.

History: after the establishment of the Irish Free State in 1922 a significant number of Republicans, led by ▷De Valera, continued to oppose partition and fought a civil war against the new governments; they were quelled by 1923. In 1932 De Valera, now leader of the constitutional ▷Fianna Fáil party, became prime minister and, in 1937, introduced a new constitution by which the Irish Free State was renamed Éire. In 1949 a coalition led by ▷Fine Gael took the country, as the Republic of Ireland, out of the Commonwealth. Since 1969 successive Irish governments have declared their desire to see the establishment in Northern Ireland of a form of government acceptable to both Roman Catholics and Protestants. In 1973 Ireland became a member of the EC (now the EU). Charles J. ▷Haughey led a Fianna Fáil government (1979–81; 1982) until replaced by Dr Garret ▷Fitzgerald, heading a Fine Gael–Labour coalition. Haughey returned to power in 1987 but resigned in 1992, to be replaced by Albert ▷Reynolds. Reynolds resigned in 1994 when his coalition collapsed. John ▷Bruton, leader of the Fine Gael, replaced him, heading a new coalition. Following elections in 1997, Fianna Fáil formed a government under Bertie ▷Ahern. In a referendum in May 1998 the Irish electorate endorsed the Good Friday Agreement on the future of Northern Ireland, in which the Republic agreed to abandon its constitutional claim to the province. Ireland adopted the European single currency in 1999–2002. Ahern's Fianna Fáil were re-elected by a large margin in 2002.

Republic of Ireland

Head of state	President Mary McAleese
Official languages	Irish and English
Official religion	Roman Catholic
Official currency	euro of 100 cents
Area	68 893 sq km (26 599 sq mi)
Population (2000 est)	3 783 000
Capital and main port	Dublin

● **Ireland, John Nicholson** ▶ (1879–1962) British composer, a pupil of Stanford and teacher of Britten and E. J. Moeran (1894–1950). His works include orchestral and chamber music, songs, and piano pieces. *The Forgotten Rite* (for orchestra; 1913) and *Sarnia* (for piano; 1941), were inspired by the history of the Channel Islands.

● **Irene** ► (c. 752–803 AD) Byzantine empress and saint of the Greek Orthodox Church. After the death of her husband Leo IV (reigned 775–80), Irene ruled jointly with their son Constantine VI (771–?797) until 790, when she was banished from court. In 797 she returned, blinded and imprisoned Constantine, and ruled alone. She opposed iconoclasm. In 802 she was overthrown and exiled to Lesbos.

● **Ireton, Henry** ► (1611–51) English soldier, who fought for the parliamentarians in the ▷Civil War. Ireton fought at the battles of Edgehill (1642), ▷Marston Moor, and ▷Naseby (1645). In 1646 he became Cromwell's son-in-law. Initially favouring negotiations with Charles I, he proposed a constitutional solution to the conflict of power (Heads of the Proposals, 1647) but in 1649 he was a signatory to the king's death warrant. During the Commonwealth, Ireton served in Ireland, where he died of fever at the siege of Limerick.

● **Irgun Zvai Leumi** ► (Hebrew: National Military Organization) A Jewish guerrilla movement, founded in Palestine (1931), that agitated for a Jewish state during the 1930s and 1940s. Its bombings and assassinations targeted both British people and Arabs. It disbanded (1948) on the creation of Israel.

● **Irian Jaya** ► (former name: West Irian) A province in E Indonesia comprising W ▷New Guinea. Mountainous and densely forested with coastal swamps, it possesses important mineral resources including oil, nickel, and copper. Formerly under Dutch rule, it was transferred to Indonesia in 1963. Indonesia's exploitation of the province's minerals has caused serious environmental damage and provoked unrest among the aboriginal tribespeople. In early 1998 a severe drought led to thousands of deaths from malnutrition and disease. Area: 416 900 sq km (161 000 sq mi). Population (1995 est): 1 956 300. Capital: Jayapura.

● **iridium** ► (Ir) A hard brittle metal, discovered in 1803 by C. Tennant (1768–1838), in the residue left after dissolving platinum in aqua regia. Its salts are highly coloured, whence its name (Latin *iris*, rainbow). Its principal use is as a hardening agent for platinum and in electrical contacts. At no 77; at wt 192.22; mp 2477°C; bp 4428°C.

● **iris** ► (anatomy) The muscular tissue in the ▢eye that surrounds the pupil and is situated immediately in front of the lens: it is responsible for eye colour. Reflex contraction of the muscles in the iris cause it to become smaller in dim light (which enlarges the pupil and allows more light to enter the eye) and larger in bright light (making the pupil smaller).

● **Iris** ► (botany) A genus of perennial herbaceous plants (about 300 species), native to N temperate regions and widely planted in gardens. Irises grow from bulbs or rhizomes (underground stems) and their flowers, which have three erect inner petals and three drooping outer sepals, can be three or more colours, often with a contrasting "beard" on the lower petals. Many garden varieties are derived from *I. germanica*: up to 1 m high, they have purple, white, or yellow flowers. Family: *Iridaceae*. ▷*See also* flag.

● **Iris** ► (mythology) The Greek goddess of the rainbow and messenger of the gods, especially of ▷Hera. She is portrayed as carrying a herald's staff and often bearing water that could put perjurers to sleep.

● **Irish elk** ► A large extinct European ▷deer belonging to the genus *Megaloceros*, which was abundant during the Pleistocene epoch (2.5 million–10 000 years ago). It stood 1.8 m at the shoulder and its massive palmate antlers spanned up to 4 m. Several species are known and remains of the largest have been found in Irish bog deposits.

● **Irish famine** ► (1846–51) The starvation and death of almost a million Irish people following a blight that ruined the potato crop (the staple diet) in 1846. Another million emigrated.

● **Irish Literary Renaissance** ► A period of literary activity in Ireland in the late 19th and early 20th centuries inspired by the resurgence of political nationalism and of interest in traditional Gaelic culture. The strongest individual influence was that of W. B. ▷Yeats, in his early poems and plays. Other writers included the poet George

Russell (pseudonym AE; 1867–1935), the novelist George Moore (1852–1933), and the dramatist J. M. ▷Synge.

● **Irish literature** ► The Gaelic literature of Ireland. The earliest literature, as in other parts of the Celtic world, was the responsibility of an official learned class, the *filid* (or ▷Druids), who transmitted orally the ancient traditions of the people. The earliest written literature, however, dates from the 7th to 10th centuries. Of most interest in this period are the heroic sagas, written in prose and preserved mainly in three 12th-century manuscript collections, the Book of the Dun Cow, the Book of Leinster, and the Yellow Book of Lecan. These epics, which are shorter than Icelandic sagas, deal with both heroic (warfare, voyages, etc.) and romantic elements. They were grouped in the middle ages into two cycles, the early pagan Ulster cycle and the much later ▷Fenian cycle. ▷Deirdre and ▷Cuchulain are the prominent figures in the Ulster cycle and appear in the two most famous stories, the *Longes Mac Nusnig* (*Exile of the Sons of Usnech*) and the *Táin Bó Cúalnge* (*Cattle-Raid of Cooley*). From the 13th century bardic poets preserved Gaelic culture from the impact of Norman English; their main productions were panegyrics written for aristocratic patrons, but they also responded to influences introduced by the Normans and English, such as the theme of courtly love. Despite a revival of Gaelic poetry in the 16th century, it declined with the submergence of the Irish aristocracy, particularly after the coming of Cromwell (1649). The work of the poet and historian Geoffrey Keating (c. 1580–c. 1645) is the most important prior to this date; two outstanding poets of the period were David O'Bruadair (1625–98) and Egan O'Rahilly (1670–1728). Gaelic literature was at its lowest ebb during the 18th century, but was revived in the 19th century, after having splintered into several dialects. Such 20th-century writers as Liam ▷O'Flaherty and Brendan ▷Behan produced distinguished work in Gaelic, but generally there has been nothing to equal the work of the major modern Irish poets and writers in English. ▷*See also* Irish Literary Renaissance.

● **Irish moss** ▷*See* carrageen.

● **Irish Republican Army** ► (IRA) A militant organization established in 1919 to fight British rule in Ireland. Under Michael ▷Collins it fought a successful guerrilla war against British forces (1919–21) but the subsequent Anglo-Irish treaty, which involved the partition of Ireland, was rejected by some IRA members. The antitreaty faction (keeping the name IRA) was defeated by Irish government forces in 1922–23 but continued its fight for an all-Ireland republic with sporadic terrorist incidents. The movement was reactivated when the Northern Irish troubles began in 1968. In 1970 both the IRA and ▷Sinn Féin, to which many IRA members belong, split into the Officials, who abandoned the policy of abstaining from constitutional Irish politics and later renounced violence, and the Provisionals, who began a concerted terrorist campaign to expel the British from the North. Subsequent IRA outrages included the murder of Lord Mountbatten (1979), the attempted assassination of the British prime minister in Brighton (1984), the Remembrance Day bombing in Enniskillen (1987), and a mortar attack on the cabinet in Downing Street (1991). The Irish National Liberation Army (INLA), a breakaway group, murdered the British MP Airey Neave (1979). In 1986 there was a further split between Provisional IRA/Sinn Féin, who adopted a policy of constitutional activity backed by terror, and the so-called Continuity IRA/Republican Sinn Féin, who remained outside politics. Following the ▷Downing Street Declaration, the Provisional IRA announced a complete ceasefire in 1994: this was abandoned in 1996 but resumed in 1997. Although Sinn Féin accepted the Good Friday Agreement of 1998 (*see* (Northern) Ireland), the IRA repeatedly refused to begin decommissioning its weapons, a key element of that agreement. In May 2000 the organization announced that it would allow third-party inspection of its arms dumps as part of a process of putting weapons "beyond use." The inspection process began in June. The IRA finally announced that some weaons had been put beyond use in October, 2001. The so-called "Real IRA," a splinter group hostile to the agreement, has continued with terrorist violence, most infamously the Omagh bombing of August 1998, in which 28 people were killed. The Continuity IRA also remains committed to violence.

● **Irish Republican Brotherhood** ▷*See* Fenians.

● **Irish Sea** ► A section of the Atlantic, separating England, Scotland, and Wales from Ireland. Area: about 100 000 sq km (40 000 sq mi). Maximum width: 240 km (149 mi).

● **Irish terrier** ▶ A breed of dog originating in Ireland and used for hunting. It has a sturdy streamlined body, a long head, and an alert appearance. The hard wiry coat is red to yellowish-red. Height: 41–46 cm.

● **Irish wolfhound** ▶ An ancient breed of large hunting dog originating in Ireland. It has a powerful body and a long narrow head with small ears. The rough wiry coat can be grey, brindle, red, black, white, or fawn. Height: 78 cm minimum (dogs); 71 cm minimum (bitches).

● **Irkutsk** ▶ 52 18N 104 15E A city in S Russia. It is a major railway junction and is the industrial, cultural, and educational centre of E Siberia. Its industries include ship, aircraft, and vehicle production; machinery, chemicals, textiles, and food are produced. Population (1999 est): 596 400.

● **iron** ▶ (Fe) A metallic transition element that has been known and used since prehistoric times. It is the fourth most abundant element in the earth's crust, occurring in the ores haematite (Fe_2O_3), magnetite (Fe_3O_4), and siderite ($FeCO_3$). It is widely used in toolmaking, construction, shipbuilding, car manufacture, and a host of other applications, almost always alloyed with other elements, such as carbon, manganese, chromium, titanium, and vanadium (*see* steel). It is obtained from its ores by smelting in a ▷blast furnace to give pig iron, which is then converted into cast iron, wrought iron, or steel. Iron has two important valence states forming iron II (ferrous) and iron III (ferric) compounds. Common compounds include the sulphates ($FeSO_4$, $Fe_2(SO_4)_3$), chlorides ($FeCl_2$, $FeCl_3$), and oxides (FeO, Fe_3O_4, Fe_2O_3). Iron is vital to animal life owing to its presence in ▷haemoglobin. Studies of meteorites and of the magnetic and seismic properties of the earth suggest that the earth has an iron-nickel core, molten on the outside but solid in the interior. At no 26; at wt 55.847; mp 1538°C; bp 2862°C. ▷*See also* ferromagnetism.

● **Iron Age** ▶ The cultural phase during which iron replaced bronze metal technology (*see* Bronze Age). Despite spasmodic earlier use of meteoric iron, it was not until about 1500 BC that iron-working techniques were perfected by the ▷Hittites. Initially a prestige metal, the superior hardness of which was prized for weapons, iron gradually spread throughout the Middle East after about 1100 BC. It was used in ▷Hallstatt Europe in the 7th century BC. The Chinese were both forging and casting iron about 500 BC, preceding Europe by about 1700 years in casting. Australia and pre-Columbian America never developed iron metallurgy but African societies moved directly from stone to iron.

● **Ironbridge** ▷*See* Darby, Abraham.

● **ironclad** ▶ A wooden warship protected by iron armour, the forerunner of the modern battleship. Both the French and the British used ironclad barges against the Russians in the Crimean War (1854–56) but the first ironclad warship, the *Gloire*, was built by France in 1859. The first battle between ironclads occurred in 1862 in the US Civil War.

● **Iron Cross** ▶ The highest German decoration for bravery in battle, instituted by Frederick William III of Prussia in 1813. An iron Maltese cross edged in silver, it was reinstituted by Hitler in 1939.

● **Iron Curtain** ▶ The ideological barrier between the democratic and communist countries in Europe after World War II. The term was made famous by Winston Churchill in 1946. The concept had become obsolete by 1990 with the reunification of Germany and the overthrow of communist regimes in E Europe.

● **Iron Gate** ▶ (Romanian name: Porţile de Fier; Serbo-Croat name: Gvozdena Vrata) 44 40N 22 30E The deepest gorge in Europe, on the Romanian-Serbian border, through which the River Danube flows. A canal, which is used by larger shipping, bypasses the gorge on the Romanian side. A Romanian-Yugoslav hydroelectric plant was opened here (1972). Length: about 3 km (2 mi).

● **iron lung** ▷*See* respirator.

● **iron pyrites** ▷*See* pyrite.

● **Ironside, William Edmund, 1st Baron** ▶ (1880–1959) British field marshal. A secret agent in the second Boer War, in World War I he commanded the Allied forces against Soviet Russia at Archangel (1918). In World War II he was chief of the imperial general staff (1939–40) and commander in chief of the home forces (1940).

● **ironwood** ▶ One of several unrelated trees with very hard wood, including *Mesurea ferrea* of India and Malaysia (family *Guttiferae*), used in cabinetwork, and a ▷hop-hornbeam, *Ostrya virginiana*, of E North America.

● **Iroquois** ▶ North American Indian tribes of the NE region, between the Hudson River and Lake Erie, who spoke the Iroquois language belonging to the Iroquois Caddoan family. They were cultivators and hunters who lived in villages of longhouses that housed many families, organized into matrilineal clans. These were grouped into tribes and nations ruled by councils of delegates chosen by the senior clanswomen. The ▷Mohawk, Oneida, Onondaga, Cayuga, and Seneca tribes formed the famous **Iroquois League** during the 16th century, which was allied with the British against the French and, except for the Oneida and Tuscarora (members of the League from 1715), against the colonists in the American Revolution (1775–83). The League collapsed following the second Treaty of ▷Fort Stanwix (1784).

● **irrational numbers** ▷*See* numbers.

● **Irrawaddy River** ▶ The chief river in Myanmar (Burma), flowing SSW across the country. Joined by the River Chindwin at Mandalay, it enters the Andaman Sea through a swampy delta (one of the great rice bowls of Asia). Length: 2010 km (1250 mi).

● **Irredentists** ▶ Italians who sought to bring all Italian-speaking areas into newly unified Italy in the late 19th century, in particular the Austrian-controlled Trentino in the NE. The Irredentists, so called from *Italia irredenta* ("unrecovered Italy"), urged Italy to join the UK and France in World War I. The postwar distribution of territories, giving Italy the Trentino and the Istrian peninsula on the N Adriatic, realized their chief ambitions.

● **irrigation** ▶ The artificial watering of land for crop production. Irrigation was practised in ancient Egypt; traditional systems linked to seasonal changes in river level, using earth banks and channels with water-lifting devices, are still used in many areas. Modern methods involve artificial reservoirs, canals, and pumping systems; the entire field may be flooded, as in rice growing, or the water may run in channels between the rows of the crop. High-pressure sprinklers are also used, especially where the land is undulating.

● **Irtysh, River** ▶ (*or* R. Irtish) A river in central Asia. Rising in the Altai Mountains of China, it flows W and NW through Kazakhstan to join the River Ob in Russia. Length: 4444 km (2760 mi).

● **Irvine** ▶ 55 37N 4 40W A port in W Scotland, in North Ayrshire at the mouth of the River Irvine on the Firth of Clyde. It was scheduled for development as a new town in 1966. Population (1991): 32 988.

● **Irving, Sir Henry** ▶ (John Henry Brodribb; 1838–1905) British actor and manager. He established his reputation in London during the early 1870s and remained the leading actor of the London stage for the next 30 years. From 1878 to 1902 he was manager of the Lyceum Theatre, where, with Ellen ▷Terry as his leading lady, he acted in a notable series of Shakespearean productions. He made several tours in the USA, and in 1895 became the first actor to receive a knighthood.

● **Irving, Washington** ▶ (1783–1859) US short-story writer and historian. From 1815 to 1832 he lived mostly in Europe, where he wrote *The Sketch Book* (1819–20), which contains his best tales, including "Rip Van Winkle" and "The Legend of Sleepy Hollow." After returning to the USA he reinforced his reputation as the first American professional man of letters with several biographies, notably one of *George Washington* (5 vols, 1855–59).

● **ISA** ▶ (*or* individual savings account) A form of savings account available in the UK from 6 April, 1999, to replace ▷personal equity plans and ▷TESSAs. Individuals are currently (until 2006) entitled to save up to £7,000 per annum free of tax.

● **Isaac** ▷*See* Abraham.

● **Isaacs, Jorge** ▶ (1837–95) Colombian novelist of British Jewish origin, who worked as a journalist and later became a diplomat. He is chiefly remembered for *María* (1867), a romantic novel set in the Colombian countryside.

● **Isabella** ▶ (*born* Elizabeth Farnese; 1692–1766) The second wife (1714–46) of Philip V of Spain, whom she dominated. Her ambitions centered on the acquisition of Italian possessions for her sons, the eldest of whom ruled Naples and Sicily before becoming ▷Charles III of Spain.

Isabella (I) the Catholic ▶ Also known as Isabella of Castile, she revived the Inquisition in Spain, which—under Torquemada—resorted to appalling brutality against Jews and Muslims.

● **Isabella (I) the Catholic** ▶ (1451–1504) Queen of Castile (1474–1504). Her marriage (1469) to Ferdinand of Aragon brought about the union of the two major Spanish kingdoms, to which Granada was added following its reconquest from the Moors in 1492. The introduction of the Inquisition (1480) and the expulsion of the Jews (1492) were largely due to Isabella's influence. She also supported Columbus' voyages of discovery. ▷*See also* Ferdinand (V and II) the Catholic.

● **Isabella II** ▶ (1830–1904) Queen of Spain (1833–68). Her succession was contested by her uncle Don Carlos and only secured in 1839, after the first Carlist War (*see* Carlism). During a politically turbulent reign she became increasingly unpopular and was finally deposed.

● **Isabella of France** ▶ (1292–1358) The wife (1308–27) of Edward II of England; the daughter of ▷Philip (IV) the Fair. Increasingly isolated by Edward's favourites, she left England in 1325. She became the mistress of Roger de ▷Mortimer and together they returned to overthrow and murder Edward (1327). In 1330 her son Edward III executed Mortimer and confined Isabella to a nunnery.

● **Isabey, Jean Baptiste** ▶ (1767–1855) French portrait painter and miniaturist, born in Nancy. He trained under ▷David and was patronized successively by Marie Antoinette, Napoleon, and the restored Bourbon kings. His son **Eugène Isabey** (1804–86) was also a painter.

● **Isaiah** ▶ (8th century BC) Old Testament prophet. Influential at the court of the rulers of Judah until the Assyrian invasion (701 BC), he was later martyred. **The Book of Isaiah** contains his prophecies, although most scholars attribute chapters 40–66 to others. The prophecies condemn the corruption of both Judah and the surrounding nations, counsel against entering foreign alliances, and predict the captivity of the nation in Babylon and its return. Several sections announce the coming of a Messiah. These passages formed the basis of the messianic expectations of the Jews and were interpreted by the writers of the New Testament as referring to Jesus.

● **ISBN** ▶ (International Standard Book Number) ▷*See* library.

● **Ischia, Island of** ▶ 40 44N 13 57E A volcanic island in Italy, in the Bay of Naples. A resort, it is noted for its picturesque scenery and mineral springs. Area: 47 sq km (18 sq mi). Population (latest est): 16 100. Chief town: Ischia.

● **Ise** ▶ 34 29N 136 41E A city in Japan, in S Honshu on the Pacific Ocean. It is the site of Japan's most sacred Shinto shrines, some of which possibly date back to the 1st century BC. Population (1995): 102 631.

● **Isfahan** ▶ (*or* Esfahan) 32 41N 51 41E A town in central Iran. It has some fine examples of Persian architecture, including the 17th-century royal mosque. An industrial quarter was established in the 1930s, and a university was founded in 1950. Population (1994 est): 1 220 595.

● **Isherwood, Christopher** ▶ (1904–86) British novelist. His experiences while teaching in Berlin in the 1930s are described in the novel *Mr Norris Changes Trains* (1935) and in the stories *Goodbye to Berlin* (1939), which were filmed as *Cabaret* (1968). He collaborated with W. H. ▷Auden on several plays. In 1939 he moved to California, where he cultivated an interest in Vedanta. His other works include the novels *The World in the Evening* (1954), *Down There on a Visit* (1962), and *A Single Man* (1964). In these and several autobiographical works, including *Christopher and His Kind* (1977), homosexuality is a recurrent theme.

● **Ishiguro, Kazuo** ▶ (1954–) British novelist, born in Japan. He has lived in the UK since 1960; his novels include *A Pale View of the Hills* (1982), *An Artist of the Floating World* (1986), which won the ▷Whitbread Book of the Year Award, *The Remains of the Day* (1989), which won the ▷Booker Prize and became a successful film, and *The Unconsoled* (1995).

● **Ishmael** ▶ In the Old Testament, the son of Abraham and Hagar, the maid of his wife Sarah, who expelled him with his mother into the desert. Muslims believe the Arabs to be descendants of Ishmael.

● **Ishtar** ▶ The supreme Babylonian and Assyrian goddess, the daughter of the sky god Anu or of the moon god Sin. She combined aspects of a beneficent mother goddess and fierce goddess of war and fertility. She descended to the underworld in search of her lover ▷Tammuz.

● **Isidore of Seville, St** ▶ (c. 560–636 AD) Spanish churchman; Doctor of the Church and the last of the Western Fathers of the Church. Archbishop of Seville from about 600, he is famous for his encyclopedia of knowledge, the *Etymologiae*. In dealing with such subjects as grammar, mathematics, history, and theology Isidore included etymological explanations of words (hence the title), but these were allegorical rather than scientific. Feast day: 4 April.

● **isinglass** ▶ A form of gelatin, about 90% pure, made from the swim bladders of fish. It is used in glues and to clarify jellies and alcoholic drinks.

● **Isis** ▶ (mythology) An Egyptian goddess, the sister and wife of ▷Osiris, whose dismembered body she magically restored to life, and mother of ▷Horus. She was usually portrayed as holding the child Horus and wearing on her head the solar disc and a cow's horns, the same attributes as ▷Hathor. She was essentially a goddess of protection, being the perfect mother with powers of healing. Her cult spread throughout the Roman Empire.

● **Isis** ▶ (river) ▷*See* Thames, River.

● **Iskenderun** ▶ (former name: Alexandretta) 36 37N 36 08E A port in central S Turkey. Its main activities are fishing and trading in tobacco, silk, bananas, and cereals. Until 1939 it was in Syria. Population (1995 est): 153 871.

● **ISKON** ▷*See* Hare Krishna movement.

● **Islam** ▶ (Arabic: submission to God) A major world religion, which originated in Arabia in the 7th century AD. The essential creed of Islam, whose adherents are called Muslims, is that there is one God, Allah, and that ▷Mohammed is his prophet. The revelations received by Mohammed are recorded in the ▷Koran, which is the basis of Islamic belief and the source of a complex legal and social system (*see also* Islamic law). Islam shares a number of beliefs with Judaism and Christianity and accepts the Books of Moses and the Gospels of Jesus as parts of the same scripture that is definitively expressed in the Koran. There is no organized church or priesthood. Instead, five fundamental duties are incumbent upon the individual Muslim: belief in the one God, Allah, and in the prophethood of Mohammed; observance at set times of five daily prayers, which are recited facing Mecca; fasting during ▷Ramadan; payment of a special tax for charitable purposes; and a pilgrimage to Mecca (*see* hajj) at least once, if means permit. Given the impetus of the *jihad* or holy war against unbelievers originally prescribed as a duty, the Muslim armies of Arabia extended Islam through the Middle East and N Africa in the 7th and 8th centuries AD. It later spread to sub-Saharan Africa, India, China, SE Asia, parts of Russia, the Balkans, and Spain. It early divided into sects, which originally differed as to who should be the leader of Islam and what should be his powers. The main sects are the ▷Sunnites (*or* Sunni) and the ▷Shiites (*or* Shiah; *see also* Ahmadiya; Wahhabiya). In the late 1970s and 1980s Islamic fundamentalism became an important political force in many countries; in the early 1990s the Sunni faith especially spread quickly through central Asia following the break-up of the Soviet Union. There are an estimated 800 million Muslims, about one million of whom are UK citizens.

● **Islamabad** ▶ 33 40N 73 08E The capital of Pakistan, situated in the N of the country on the Potwar Plateau. The site was chosen in 1959 and construction began in 1961. The Quaid-i-Azam University was founded in 1965 and the People's Open University in 1974. Population (1995 est): 204 364.

● **Islamic art and architecture** ▶ A distinctive style of art and architecture created and developed by the Muslims in the countries they conquered. Islamic art is generally classified by scholars into five regional groupings: Syrian-Egyptian; Persian; Ottoman-Turkish; Moorish (i.e. North African and Spanish); and Indian. Its most distinctive feature is its elaborate patterning in architecture, painting, ceramics, metalwork, woodwork, glassware, textiles, and carpets. Of all these arts architecture is the most individual, its main characteristics being the dome and the horseshoe ⬚arch. Religious objections to the depiction of human and animal forms inhibited sculpture. Islamic painting is usually associated with Persian, Mogul, and Turkish miniatures, although there were many schools of painting during the middle ages and later. Calligraphy is regarded as an art form in a class of its own. ▷*See also* Mogul art and architecture; Persian art and architecture.

● **Islamic law** ▶ The sacred law of ▷Islam, *shari'ah* (Arabic: path), prescribes every aspect of the life of a Muslim in this world and provides a route to divine approval in the next. *Fiqh* (Arabic: understanding), an interpretation of *shari'ah*, was largely completed in the 9th century AD, when the ▷Koran and the practice of Mohammed (the *sunna*) came to be accepted as the main sources of the law. The law covers marriage, divorce, and inheritance; it forbids usury, depicting living beings, drinking alcohol, eating pork, etc., and prescribes punishments for crimes. When a problem could not be solved by reference to the Koran or *sunna*, other sources were allowed and different legal interpretations developed. Thus among the ▷Sunnite majority, four equally orthodox schools have arisen, which agree on fundamentals but differ in their interpretation of specific points. In modern times most Muslim states have adopted partially secular legal systems, although the 1980s and 1990s saw a reversion to strict Islamic law in some countries.

● **island** ▶ A piece of land surrounded by water (excluding the continents). The world's largest island is Greenland (2.2 million sq km, 840 000 sq mi). Continental islands, such as Britain, lie on the continental shelves, separated usually by a narrow shallow stretch of water from the mainland. Oceanic orogenic islands, such as the Japanese islands, frequently occur in island arcs at the junction of two lithospheric plates (*see* plate tectonics); they are volcanic in origin. Oceanic volcanic islands, such as the Hawaiian islands, occur in the central parts of the deep oceans. They are believed to be formed over "hot spots" in the earth's crust, where molten magma rises to the surface. Many coral islands have a volcanic base. ▷*See also* reef.

● **Islay** ▶ An island of the Inner Hebrides in the Atlantic Ocean, off the W coast of Scotland. Its economy is based on whisky distilling, tourism, agriculture, and fishing. Area: 606 sq km (234 sq mi). Population (1981): 3792.

● **Islington** ▶ A borough of N Greater London, created in 1965 from the former metropolitan boroughs of Islington and Finsbury. Many of the 19th-century squares and terraces have been gentrified. Area: 16 sq km (6 sq mi). Population (1994 est): 175 200.

● **Ismaili** ▶ A ▷Shiite Muslim sect. In the 8th century AD a group of Shiites recognized Ismail the son of Jafar al-Sadiq as ▷imam, while the rest of the Shiites supported his brother Musa. In 909 the Fatimid caliphate was established, the rulers of which were Ismaili imams. The Ismaili Fatimids ruled in Egypt and N Africa until 1171, contesting control of the Muslim world with the ▷'Abbasid dynasty of Baghdad. They developed several doctrines that diverge from non-Ismaili Islam and eventually split into many subsects (including that headed by the ▷Aga Khan).

● **Ismailia** ▶ (Arabic name: al Isma'iliyah) 31 36N 32 15E A city in NE Egypt, midway along the Suez Canal on Lake Timsah. Dependent on the canal trade, much of the population moved elsewhere during the canal's closure (1967–75). It is the centre of an irrigated area producing market-garden crops. Population (1992 est): 255 000.

● **Isma'il Pasha** ▶ (1830–95) Viceroy of Egypt for the Ottoman Empire (1863–79). He introduced important reforms but the huge foreign debts that his policies incurred eventually led to his deposition (1879) by the Ottomans, and ultimately to the British occupation of Egypt (1882). Under Isma'il the ▷Suez Canal was opened in 1869.

● **ISO** ▷*See* International Organization for Standardization.

● **isobar** ▶ **1.** A line on a map or chart connecting points of equal atmospheric pressure. In meteorology, the distance between isobars is a measure of weather conditions: the closer they are together the more unsettled (cyclonic) the weather to be expected. **2.** One of two isotopes of different elements with the same mass numbers but different atomic numbers, e.g. $^{115}_{50}$Sn and $^{115}_{49}$In.

● **Isocrates** ▶ (436–338 BC) Athenian teacher of rhetoric and political pamphleteer. Isocrates opened a school, where his method of teaching rhetoric as a preparation for life began the literary tradition of education. His appeals for unity of the feuding Greek states against Persia culminated in the *Philippus* (346 BC), addressed to ▷Philip (II) of Macedon.

● **isolationism** ▶ The policy that opposes participation in world affairs, except in self-defence. The term is most usually used to describe policies pursued after World War I in the USA, where isolationism reached its peak in the Neutrality Acts (1935–37). The Japanese attack on Pearl Harbor in World War II ended isolationism.

● **isomers** ▶ Chemical compounds that have the same molecular formulae but different arrangements of atoms in their molecules. In **structural isomerism** the molecules have different molecular structures. Thus, ethanol (C_2H_5OH) and dimethyl ether (CH_3OCH_3) both have the molecular formula C_2H_6O, although they are quite different compounds. A form of structural isomerism is that in which functional groups occur at different positions in the molecule. For example, there are two alcohols derived from propane: propan-1-ol ($CH_3CH_2CH_2OH$) and propan-2-ol ($CH_3CH_2OHCH_3$), which differ in the position of the OH group on the chain. In **stereoisomerism** the molecules have the same structure and groups but the isomers differ in their spatial arrangements. **Cis-trans isomerism** occurs as a result of the positioning of groups in a planar molecule. A common type occurs in organic molecules with double bonds. Since rotation cannot occur about the bond it is possible to have two isomers: one with groups on both sides of the bond (the cis isomer) and the other with groups on opposite sides of the bond (trans isomer). Similar types of isomer are found in square inorganic complexes depending on opposite (trans) or adjacent (cis) positioning of ligands. Another form of stereoisomerism is **optical isomerism**, in which the two isomeric forms of the molecule are asymmetric and differ in that one molecule is a mirror image of the other. Asymmetric molecules of this type exhibit optical activity, i.e. they rotate ▷polarized light passed through their solutions. One isomer rotates the light in one sense, the other rotates the light the same amount in the opposite sense. Many naturally occurring organic compounds are optically active. Isomers of all types have different physical properties and, to a greater or lesser extent, different chemical properties. In some cases isomers can exist in equilibrium, a phenomenon known as **tautomerism**. ⬚ p. 644.

structural isomers Ethanol and dimethyl ether have the same atoms in the molecule but different functional groups.

cis-trans isomers A form of stereoisomerism occurring as a result of a double bond.

optical isomers Another form of stereoisomerism in which two forms of tartaric acid have different optical properties.

isomers

● **isomorphism** ► The existence of different chemical compounds with the same crystal structure. Usually it is a reflection of analogous chemical bonding patterns. The ▷alums, for instance, are all isomorphic compounds.

● **Isopoda** ► A widely distributed order of ▷crustaceans (4000 species). The group includes the most successful terrestrial crustacean—the ▷woodlouse—as well as aquatic forms, such as the ▷gribble; some marine species are parasites. Isopods have oval flattened bodies, covered by armour-like plates, and—usually—seven pairs of walking legs. The young develop within a brood pouch on the female.

● **isoprene** ► ($CH_2:C(CH_3)CH:CH_2$) A colourless volatile liquid made from chemicals extracted from oil, coal, or tar and used to make synthetic rubber. Natural rubber is mainly a polymer of isoprene. ▷See also polymerization.

● **isostasy** ► The principle that segments of the earth's outer crust of equal area have the same mass; the higher the feature rises, the deeper the sial of which it is composed extends into the denser sima below. If a change in this equilibrium condition occurs, movements of the crust occur to restore the equilibrium (this is called isostatic compensation). For example, areas of deposition sink, while areas of erosion rise.

● **isotherm** ► A line on a map joining points of equal temperature. Corrections are usually made to compensate for the effect of altitude on temperature.

● **isothermal process** ► Any process that occurs without a change in the temperature of a system (*compare* adiabatic process).

● **isotopes** ► Atoms of the same element that contain equal numbers of ▷protons but different numbers of ▷neutrons in their nuclei. They have identical chemical properties but different physical properties. An isotope is indicated by combining its nucleon number and its name or symbol in various ways, for example uranium-235, U-235, ^{235}U. All naturally occurring elements are mixtures of isotopes; hydrogen, for example, consists mainly of ^1H (98.44%) with small amounts of ^2H (deuterium). A third isotope, ^3H (tritium), also exists in

nature in minute quantities (1 part in 10^{17}) but can be made artificially. Radioactive isotopes (radioisotopes) are important in nuclear reactors and nuclear weapons. For these purposes sophisticated methods of separation have had to be devised, based on differences in their physical properties. Methods used depend on different rates of gaseous and thermal diffusion, centrifuging, electrolysis, and electric or magnetic effects.

● **isotopic spin** ► (*or* isospin) A ▷quantum number used to distinguish between elementary particles (*see* particle physics) having the same properties, except that of electric charge. The concept is not based directly on the idea of rotation but it is analogous in mathematical terms to angular momentum, different charge states of the same particle (e.g. the nucleon) being regarded as having different orientations in a fictitious "isotopic space."

● **isotropy** ► Any property of a body or medium that is independent of the direction in which it is measured. A body or medium that is not isotropic is said to be anisotropic.

● **Israel, State of** ► A country in the Middle East, bordering on the Mediterranean Sea. There are mountains in the N, a narrow coastal plain in the W, and the Negev Desert in the S. The River Jordan flowing through the ▷Great Rift Valley forms part of the E border. The population varies greatly in language and culture, as it consists largely of Jews who have immigrated since 1948. Many Palestinian Arabs left the area when Israel was created but some have since returned. The remaining Arab population lives mainly in the N, with some nomadic Bedouins in the Negev Desert. In 1948 the population consisted of 650 000 Jews and 155 000 Arabs; the population since then has more than quadrupled, with Jews now forming 82% and Arabs 16%; immigration is now decreasing. Some 3% of the population live in *kibbutzim* (see kibbutz) and about 5% live in *moshavim*; rural settlements established since 1948 are usually on these lines.

Economy: both industrial and agricultural output has increased rapidly since 1948, boosted by investments and gifts of capital from abroad. There are resources of copper ore and phosphates; potash and bromine from the Dead Sea are also exploited. One of the chief centres of diamond cutting and polishing, Israel also has food-processing, textile, chemical, plastics, electronics, aircraft, and military industries and exports finished diamonds and light manufactures. Fishing and tourism are also important. 6% of the work force is employed in agriculture, which depends heavily on artificial irrigation. Between 1949 and 1970 the area of irrigated land increased by six times, with a corresponding increase in production. There has also been extensive reafforestation, with a land reclamation scheme in the Negev Desert. Thus, although in 1948 Israel produced only 30% of its food requirements, it now imports only grain in large quantities and exports citrus and other fruit, vegetables, and flowers.

History: Israel's history prior to 1948 is that of ▷Palestine, in which Zionists had demanded the creation of a Jewish state since the late 19th century. According to a UN recommendation and against Arab opposition, Palestine was to be divided into a Jewish state, an Arab state, and a small internationally administered zone around Jerusalem. As soon as the state of Israel was proclaimed following British withdrawal (1948), however, Arab forces (Egypt, Transjordan, Iraq, Syria, and Lebanon) invaded; by early 1949 Israeli forces had not only repulsed them but had gained control of 75% of Palestine. The rest was annexed by Jordan (the ▷West Bank) and Egypt (the ▷Gaza Strip). Jerusalem was divided between Jews and Arabs. In 1956, following Nasser's nationalization of the Suez Canal, Israeli forces occupied the Gaza Strip and the ▷Sinai Peninsula and gained access to the Red Sea, which boosted its international trade. In the Six Day War (1967) Israel defeated attacks by Egypt, Syria, and Jordan and again occupied the Gaza Strip and Sinai as well as the ▷Golan Heights, the West Bank, and the Arab sector of Jerusalem. Israel's annexation of these territories is not recognized by the UN or international law. After the Yom Kippur War (1973), in which the Israelis were taken unawares by Egyptian forces, a peace agreement with Egypt was finally achieved at the Camp David talks (1979), following which Israel withdrew from Sinai (1980–82). In 1982 Israel invaded Lebanon and forced the ▷Palestine Liberation Organization (PLO) to leave West Beirut. Israel withdrew from Lebanon in 1985 but retained de facto control of the S border region. A policy of economic austerity brought astronomical inflation under control. In 1988 Palestinians in Israeli-occupied territories began a violent protest campaign (*see* intifada). A coalition government formed in 1988 was replaced by a right-wing government under Yitzhak ▷Shamir in 1990. In 1991 Israel came under missile attack from Iraq during the ▷Gulf War. Tentative peace talks with the Palestinians led to the collapse of Shamir's government in 1992 but continued under the Labour government of Yitzhak ▷Rabin. In 1993 Israel and the PLO signed a breakthrough peace agreement in Oslo, Norway; in 1994–95 Israel gave autonomous status to the Gaza Strip and Jericho, handing over power to a new Palestinian National Authority (1995) under Yassir ▷Arafat. A peace treaty with Jordan (1994) followed. In 1995 Rabin was murdered by a Jewish extremist opposed to the peace process. He was succeeded by Shimon ▷Peres. In 1996 ▷Hamas launched a series of suicide bombings in Israeli cities. Attacks by ▷Hizbollah fighters based in S Lebanon provoked Israel to launch (April 1996) an air and missile offensive, causing heavy casualties. In May 1996 a right-wing government was elected under Binyamin ▷Netanyahu. The peace process then stalled, owing mainly to disagreement over the extent and timing of Israel's withdrawal from the West Bank. In 1998 Israel and the PLO signed a further peace agreement, under which Israel agreed to transfer various West Bank territories to Palestinian control in return for greater cooperation on security. In the general election of 1999 Netanyahu's government was defeated by Labour under Ehud ▷Barak. In 2000 an offensive by Hizbollah guerrillas forced Israel to abandon S Lebanon, its worst military defeat since 1973. That same year talks with the PLO collapsed over the issue of Arab E Jerusalem, leading to violent protests by Palestinians and heavy retaliation by Israel. Barak resigned as prime minister and lost the ensuing elections (2001) to Likud's Ariel ▷Sharon, widely seen as a hardliner. Violence then escalated sharply. Rising casualties from Arab suicide bombings prompted Israel to reoccupy large areas of the Palestinian West Bank in 2001–02. In particular, Arafat was imprisoned in his headquarters in Ramallah (until May 2002) by Israeli troops, who also caused considerable devastation in Janin and elsewhere. Accusations of an Israeli massacre in Janin led to worldwide condemnation and calls for an enquiry. Despite US demands that Israel should withdraw from the West Bank, Sharon refused to do so, citing the continuing threat from Arab suicide bombing.

State of Israel

Head of state	President Moshe Katzav
Official languages	Hebrew and Arabic
Official currency	Israeli shekel of 100 new agora
Area (excluding occupied territories)	20 770 sq km (8018 sq mi)
Population (2000 est)	6 107 000
Capital (de facto)	Jerusalem (the UN recognizes only Tel Aviv)
Main port	Haifa

● **Issachar, tribe of** ▶ One of the 12 ▷tribes of Israel. It claimed descent from Issachar, son of Jacob and Leah. It occupied territory to the S and SE of the Sea of Galilee.

● **Issas** ▷*See* Somali.

● **Issigonis, Sir Alec (Arnold Constantine)** ▶ (1906–88) British car designer, born in Smyrna. He joined Morris Motors in 1936. His post-war Morris Minor (1948) established his reputation and led to his record-breaking Mini (1959; □car).

● **issuing house** ▶ A financial institution in the UK (often a ▷merchant bank) that acts as an intermediary between a company seeking to raise capital on a stock exchange and investors. It advises a client on when and how to issue ▷securities, advertises to the public, and often underwrites the issue (i.e. guarantees to buy all the securities left over). In the USA this function is performed by an investment bank.

● **Issus, Battle of** ▶ (333 BC) The battle in which Alexander the Great of Macedon defeated an enormous Persian army under Darius III, which was caught in a narrow pass. Victory here opened Alexander's way into Persia proper.

● **Issyk Kul, Lake** ▶ A lake in Kirgizstan in the N Tien Shan. It is 702 m (2303 ft) deep, 1609 m (5279 ft) above sea level, and never freezes. Area: about 6220 sq km (2401 sq mi).

● **Istanbul** ▶ (*or* Stamboul) 41 02N 28 57E A city in W Turkey, on both sides of the Bosporus. Ancient buildings include the mainly 6th-century Hagia Sophia (originally a church and now a museum; □St Sophia), the Blue Mosque, and the Topkapi Palace (the former sultans' harem). It is a major port and industrial centre and has three universities (15th century, 1773, and 1971); tourism is a major source of revenue.

History: ancient Byzantium was renamed Constantinople in 330, when the emperor Constantine I declared it the capital of the Eastern Roman Empire. It was the capital of the Byzantine Empire until captured by the Ottoman Turks (1453), although it had been held by Crusaders from 1204 to 1261. The Ottomans renamed it Istanbul and made it the capital of their empire in 1457. After World War I, Istanbul (the city's official name from 1926) became the largest city of the Turkish Republic. Population (1995 est): 7 774 169.

● **Isthmian Games** ▶ In ancient Greece, the biennial festival held near Corinth in Poseidon's honour. Established in 581 BC these light-hearted games included music and poetry competitions as well as athletic events and horse racing.

● **Istria** ▶ A peninsula in NW Croatia. Passing to Italy at the end of World War I, it was ceded to Yugoslavia (1947) except for Trieste, which was divided between Italy and Yugoslavia in 1954. It became part of independent Croatia in 1991.

● **IT** ▷*See* information technology.

● **Itaipu Dam** ▷*See* Paraná, Rio.

● **Italian** ▶ A language of the ▷Romance family spoken in Italy. The standard literary and official form is based upon the Tuscan dialect of Florence, the dialect used by ▷Dante.

● **Italian art** ▶ The style of art found in Italy after the collapse of the Roman Empire. Antique motifs continued but were gradually replaced by Christian imagery and the influence, especially in Ravenna and Venice, of ▷Byzantine art and architecture. The ▷romanesque style of the 11th and 12th centuries gave way to the ▷gothic in the 13th century. A truly Italian art developed in the late-13th and 14th centuries, when the foundations of ▷Renaissance art were laid by ▷Giotto, ▷Duccio, and the sculptor Nicola ▷Pisano. Independent styles arose in regional centres, especially in Florence (which dominated the 15th century), Venice (where the Venetian school was founded by the ▷Bellini family), and Rome. The giants of the Renaissance, ▷Leonardo, ▷Michelangelo, ▷Raphael, and the Venetians ▷Giorgione and ▷Titian dominated the late 15th and early 16th centuries. Their work merged into □mannerism, exemplified by the architect ▷Giulio Romano, the painter ▷Parmigianino, and in Venice the painters ▷Tintoretto and ▷Veronese. Mannerism gave way around 1600 to the ▷baroque, the outstanding Italian exponents of which worked in Rome: the architects ▷Bernini (also a sculptor) and ▷Borromini and the painter ▷Caravaggio. After the 17th century Italian art lost its impetus, except in Venice, where it briefly flowered in the 18th century with the work of ▷Canaletto, ▷Guardi, and ▷Tiepolo. Outstanding Italian painters of the modern period are ▷Modigliani and de ▷Chirico.

● **Italian East Africa** ▷*See* Somaliland.

● **Italian literature** ▶ Latin remained the literary language of Italy until the 13th century, when poets at the Sicilian court of Frederick I (later Emperor Frederick II) began to imitate the poetry of Provence in native Italian. The delicate love poetry of the ▷*dolce stil nuovo* school of Florentine poets was followed in the 14th century by the allegorical works of ▷Dante, the love sonnets of ▷Petrarch, and the prose tales of ▷Boccaccio. The gradual development of the Italian language culminated in the Renaissance works of ▷Ariosto, ▷Machiavelli, and ▷Tasso. There followed a long period of decadence until, in the late 18th century, a literary revival was brought about by the dramatists ▷Alfieri and ▷Goldoni and the poet ▷Foscolo. In the 19th century the influence of Romanticism, epitomized in the poetry of ▷Leopardi, was followed by a reaction represented by the classicism of the poet ▷Carducci and the realism of the novelist and dramatist Giovanni Verga (1840–1922). Major writers of the early 20th century include the poet ▷D'Annunzio, the dramatist ▷Pirandello, and the critic Benedetto ▷Croce. Italy's best-known 20th-century poets include the so-called "hermetic" poets, ▷Ungaretti, ▷Quasimodo, and ▷Montale. Literary exploration of social and moral themes was curbed during the fascist regime from 1922 to 1943, but recommenced after World War II, with such writers as Alberto ▷Moravia, Cesare ▷Pavese, Italo ▷Calvino, and Primo ▷Levi.

● **Italic languages** ▶ A subgroup of the ▷Indo-European language family spoken in central and NE Italy in the thousand years before the rise of Rome. A parent of modern ▷Romance languages, this group comprised four related dialects: ▷Latin, Faliscan, Osco-Umbrian, and Venetic. At the beginning of the 1st millennium BC Osco-Umbrian was the most widely spoken, but with the growth of Roman civilization, Latin quickly came to dominate other dialects, which are now known only through Latin sources.

● **italic script** ▶ A style of handwriting adopted in 15th-century Italy by papal scribes and later (c. 1500) adapted for printing. Italic cursive letters eliminate unnecessary lifts of the pen, permitting rapid legible handwriting. *In print its characteristic sloped letters, such as those used in this sentence, are used mainly for display, emphasis, or to indicate that a word is in a foreign language.*

● **Italy, Republic of** ▶ A country in S Europe, occupying a peninsula bordered by the Tyrrhenian Sea (W), the Ionian Sea (S), and the Adriatic Sea (E). The principal offshore islands are Sicily and Sardinia. Except for small coastal areas and the Po Valley in the N, the country is generally rugged and mountainous. The main rivers are the Po, Tiber, Arno, and Adige.

Economy: agriculture is still important, especially in the S, the main crops being wheat, maize, grapes, and olives. Industry has expanded considerably since World War II and is now the most important sector. The principal manufactures are textiles (including silk) and clothing, and machinery, motor vehicles, and chemicals, which together with fruit and vegetables are the principal exports. The wine industry is also important. Mineral resources are small and Italy is dependent on imported fossil fuels, although oil and gas are now being extracted, especially in Sicily, and hydroelectricity has been developed. There are plans to develop nuclear energy. Tourism is an important source of revenue. During the 1970s, however, Italy was faced with severe inflation and economic stagnation and the long-standing problem of integrating the poorer agricultural S with the affluent industrial N remains unresolved. In 1993 economic reforms, including mass privatization and cuts in state spending, were introduced; however, the state-owned sector remains large.

History: pre-Roman Italy was inhabited from the 7th century BC by the ▷Etruscans in the N, Italics (including the Samnites) and Latins in central Italy, and Greek colonists in the southern mainland and Sicily. By 275 BC most of the peninsula had come under the rule of Rome (*see* Roman Republic). As the western ▷Roman Empire declined from the 4th century AD, Italy was invaded by a succession of barbarian tribes, including the Visigoths and the Vandals. The last Roman emperor was deposed in 476 by the German king, Odoacer, who in 493 was in turn overthrown by the Ostrogoths. They were expelled in the early 6th century by the Eastern (Byzantine) Roman Empire, the position of which was threatened from the mid-6th century by successive invasions: the Lombards were followed by the Franks in the 8th and 9th centuries, a period that also saw the origins of the pope's temporal power (*see* papal states); the Muslims invaded the S in the 9th and 10th centuries, Magyars, the N in the 10th century, and Normans, the S in the 11th century. The claim of the German kings to rule Italy was established in 962, when Otto the Great was crowned Holy Roman Emperor in Rome. The conflict from the 11th century between successive popes and emperors over the ▷investiture controversy embroiled the Italian city states (notably Milan, Pisa, Genoa, Venice, and Florence), which in the 12th century were further divided by the struggle between ▷Guelfs and Ghibellines. The economic and political development of the city states in the first half of the 14th century was facilitated by the removal of the papacy to Avignon and the preoccupation with German affairs of the Holy Roman Emperors. Many of the Italian cities came to be dominated by single families, such as the ▷Visconti and then the Sforza in Milan and the ▷Medici in Florence, who during the Renaissance were often outstanding patrons of culture and learning. Following the French invasion of Italy in 1494 Italy became the scene of conflict between

France and Spain and from the 16th to early 18th centuries was largely dominated by the latter. Spain ruled Milan, Naples, Sicily, and Sardinia directly and influenced Savoy, Genoa, and Tuscany; of the major Italian states only the papal states and Venice remained independent. During the 18th century Spanish hegemony was destroyed, passing to Austria until 1796, when Italy was conquered by the French Revolutionary armies under Napoleon. The French occupation gave Italy the experience of unity (*see* Cisalpine Republic). After Napoleon's fall and the restoration of Austrian rule this developed into the movement for independence and unification (the ▷Risorgimento). By 1861, under the leadership of Victor Emmanuel II of Sardinia-Piedmont and his chief minister Cavour, aided by Garibaldi in the S, the Austrians had been expelled and the kingdom of Italy proclaimed with Victor Emmanuel as its first king; unification was virtually complete by 1870. In the late 19th century Italy acquired a colonial empire, notably Somaliland and Eritrea in East Africa, but its attempt to seize Ethiopia was defeated at Adowa in 1896. In 1915 Italy entered World War I on the side of the Allies, obtaining the Trentino and the Istrian peninsula (*see* Irredentists). The postwar rise of fascism brought Mussolini to power in 1922. In 1936 he conquered Ethiopia and in 1939, Albania. In 1940, loyal to his alliances (1936, 1939) with Hitler, Mussolini took Italy into World War II on Germany's side (1940). The Allied conquest of Sicily (1943) brought Mussolini's fall and in 1946 Umberto II abdicated following a referendum rejecting the monarchy. The repeated failure of the Christian Democrats to deal with a stagnating economy, widespread corruption, and lawlessness exacerbated by such groups as the ▷Red Brigades and fascists led to gains for the Communist Party in the late 1970s. Following the general elections of 1983 Bettino ▷Craxi became Italy's first socialist prime minister, heading a coalition government. He resigned in early 1987. In 1992 Giulio ▷Andreotti was replaced by the socialist Giuliano Amato; however, the exposure of widespread corruption in government and industry, in which both Craxi and Andreotti were implicated, caused Amato to resign in 1993. Following the adoption (1993) of a new electoral system, elections in 1994 resulted in victory for a right-wing coalition led by the controversial tycoon Silvio Berlusconi, but he was forced to resign seven months later. In 1996 elections were won by a left-wing coalition led by Romano ▷Prodi. Further centre-left coalitions were formed in 1998 and 2000. The general election of 2001 resulted in victory for a right-wing coalition led by Berlusconi, who formed Italy's 59th government since 1945. Italy was a founder member of the EC (now the EU). It adopted the European single currency in 1999–2002.

Republic of Italy

Head of state	President Carlo Ciampi
Official language	Italian
Official religion	Roman Catholic
Official currency	euro of 100 cents
Area	301 425 sq km (116 350 sq mi)
Population (2000 est)	57 723 000
Capital	Rome
Main port	Genoa

● **itch mite** ▶ A parasitic ▷mite, *Sarcoptes scabei*, that produces ▷scabies in man and mange in domestic animals. The female burrows into the skin, where it lays eggs and causes intense itching and irritation. Family: *Sarcoptidae*.

● **Ithaca** ▶ (Modern Greek name: Itháki) A Greek island in the Ionian Sea, one of the Ionian Islands. It is widely believed to have been the home of Homer's Odysseus. Area: 85 sq km (33 sq mi). Population (latest est): 3646.

● **Ito Hirobumi** ▶ (1841–1909) Japanese statesman, who played a leading part in the abolition of feudalism and the adoption of modern methods and institutions. During the 1880s he assumed responsibility for drafting the Meiji constitution (1889) and between 1885 and 1901 he was prime minister four times. During his second ministry Japan defeated China in the ▷Sino-Japanese War (1894–95). Ito was assassinated by a Korean nationalist.

● **Itúrbide, Agustín** ▶ (1783–1824) Mexican soldier prominent in the independence movement; emperor (1822–23). He used the general unrest in Mexico to further his own advancement in the army. Appointed commander of the combined rebel forces when Mexico declared itself independent of Spain (1820), he subsequently proclaimed himself emperor. Within months ▷Santa Anna forced his abdication; Iturbide returned from exile in 1824 but was executed.

● **IUCN** ▶ (International Union for the Conservation of Nature) ▷*See* endangered species.

● **Ivanovo** ▶ 57 00N 41 00E A city in W central Russia on the River Uvod. It played an important part in both the 1905 and 1917 Russian Revolutions. It is one of the country's major textile centres. Population (1997 est): 469 000.

● **Ivan (III) the Great** ▶ (1440–1505) Grand Prince of Muscovy (1462–1505). Ivan greatly expanded Muscovite territory and ended Russian subordination to the Tatars. In 1497 he introduced a new legal code. Ivan married (1472) Zoë Palaeologus (d. 1503), the niece of the last Byzantine emperor, and adopted the Byzantine two-headed eagle as his arms.

● **Ivan (IV) the Terrible** ▶ (1530–84) Grand Prince of Muscovy (1533–84), who was crowned tsar in 1547. Ivan reformed the legal code and local administration (1555), conquered Kazan and Astrakhan, and established commercial relations with England. After 1560 his reign was marred by his brutality: thousands were executed and in a fit of rage Ivan murdered his son (1581). The effects of his tyranny were aggravated by financial strains resulting from the ▷Livonian War (1558–82).

● **Ivanišević, Goran** ▶ (1971–) Croatian tennis player, known for his powerful serve and fiery temperament. He won the Wimbledon singles title in 2001, having been runner-up in 1992, 1994, and 1998.

● **Ives, Charles (Edward)** ▶ (1874–1954) US composer. An early experimenter with polyrhythms, polytonality, quarter tones, and the superimposition of disparate musical styles, he composed four symphonies, five violin sonatas, songs, and other works. His second piano sonata, subtitled *Concord, Mass* (1909–15), was inspired by US writers associated with the town of Concord, having movements entitled "Emerson," "Hawthorne," etc. One of his best-known works is *Central Park in the Dark* (1898–1907). Of his many works, most remained unpublished. For his Symphony No. 3 (1904) he was awarded a Pulitzer Prize. He was also senior partner of the insurance firm of Ives and Myrick.

● **ivory** ▶ The close-grained white tissue forming the tusks of elephants, walruses, and narwhals and the teeth of hippos. So-called fossil ivory is obtained from mammoths. Plastics have now generally replaced ivory for such mundane domestic artefacts as knife handles, but, being easy to carve and polish, ivory is still such a valuable commodity that its main source, the African elephant, is threatened with extinction. In 1989 many countries agreed to a worldwide ban on ivory trading. Ivory carving is a very ancient art; objects from France date to Palaeolithic times and fine examples survive from Egyptian, Minoan, Mycenaean, Assyrian, Greek, and Roman civilizations. In Europe ivory plaques with relief carving became important during the early middle ages for small religious icons, book covers, caskets, etc. India, SE Asia, China, and Japan (*see* netsuke) have ancient traditions of skilled ivory carving. Inuit carvings in walrus ivory are greatly prized by connoisseurs.

● **Ivory, James** ▷*See* Merchant, Ismael.

● **ivory-billed woodpecker** ▶ A very rare (possibly extinct) black-and-white ▷woodpecker, *Campephilus principalis*, occurring in North American forests. 45 cm long, it has a white bill and the male has a red crest. It feeds on woodboring insects and requires a large feeding territory, hence its decline due to the expanding timber industry.

● **Ivory Coast, Republic of** ▷*See* Côte d'Ivoire, Republic of.

● **ivy** ▶ An evergreen woody climbing plant, *Hedera helix*, that has glossy three- to five-lobed leaves, aerial roots (with which it clings to supports), clusters of small greenish-yellow flowers, and small round fruits ripening from green to black. Native to Europe and W Asia, it is widely cultivated (ornamental ivies often have variegated foliage). Family: *Araliaceae*.

● **Ivy League** ▶ A number of universities in the NE USA of high prestige. They include ▷Harvard, ▷Yale, and ▷Princeton and are all members of a conference for intercollegiate sports known as the Ivy League, which dates back to the 1870s.

● **Iwo** ▶ 7 38N 4 11E A town in SW Nigeria. Its main activity is the export of agricultural products, especially cocoa. Population (1996 est): 362 000.

● **Iwo Jima** ▶ 24 47N 141 19E A Japanese island in the W Pacific Ocean, the largest of the Volcano Islands. Captured by US forces after a severe struggle (1945), it was returned in 1968. Sulphur and sugar are produced. Area: 20 sq km (8 sq mi).

● **Izanagi and Izanami** ▶ In Japanese mythology, the male and female creator deities of Japan. They stirred the sea with a spear and drops from its tip formed the Japanese islands, for which they then created other *kami* (spirits) as inhabitants and guardians (*see* Amaterasu).

● **Izetbegović, Alija** ▶ (1925–) Bosnian politician; president (1992–2000). A Muslim, he was imprisoned for nationalist activities (1945–48) and for Islamic activities (1983–88). Having become president of the Yugoslav republic of Bosnia-Hercegovina in 1990, he led the country to independence in 1992 and throughout the ensuing civil war (1992–95). Following elections in 1996, he became chairman of a new tripartite presidency.

● **Izhevsk** ▶ 56 49N 53 11E A city in W central Russia, the capital of Udmurt Republic. It is a major metallurgical centre. Population (1995 est): 654 000.

● **Izmir** ▶ (former name: Smyrna) 38 25N 27 10E A port in W Turkey, on the Aegean Sea. Much was destroyed by fire in 1922, the rebuilt town being a modern commercial centre with a university (1953). There is trade in silk, cotton, carpets, figs, raisins, and sponges. Population (1997 est): 2 081 556.

● **Izmit** ▶ (*or* Kocaeli) 40 47N 29 55E A town and naval port in NW Turkey, on the Sea of Marmara. As ancient Nicomedia it was the seat of the kings of Bithynia. Izmit was devastated by an earthquake in 1999. Population (1997 est): 198 200.

J

● **Jabalpur** ► (*or* Jubbulpore) 23 10N 79 59E A city in India, in Madhya Pradesh. An important railway junction, its manufactures include cement, textiles, and military equipment. Its university was established in 1957. Population (1991): 739 961.

● **Jabir** ▷*See* Geber.

● **jabiru** ► A large ▷stork, *Jabiru mycteria*, ranging from Mexico to Argentina. 140 cm long, it is white with a dark-blue head and neck with a red patch at the base and has a heavy bill.

● **jaborandi** ► A tropical American plant of the genus *Pilocarpus* (22 species), the dried leaves of which yield an alkaloid, pilocarpine, used to treat glaucoma. Family: *Rutaceae*.

● **jacamar** ► A bird of a family (*Galbulidae*; 15 species) of tropical American forests. 12–27 cm long, jacamars have a large head, long tail, and iridescent blue, green, or bronze plumage. They feed on insects. Order: *Piciformes* (woodpeckers, etc.).

● **jacana** ► A waterbird of the tropical family *Jacanidae* (7 species), also called lily trotter. Jacanas have long legs with elongated toes and claws, enabling them to run over floating vegetation. 25–32 cm long, they are reddish to dark-brown and swim well. Order: *Charadriiformes* (gulls, plovers, etc.).

● **Jacaranda** ► A genus of ▢trees and shrubs (50 species) of South and Central America and the West Indies, often grown as ornamentals. *J. mimosifolia*, up to 15 m tall, has compound leaves and blue or violet tubular flowers. Some species yield valuable timber. Family: *Bignoniaceae*.

● **jackal** ► A carnivorous mammal of the genus *Canis*, found in Asia and Africa. Jackals are closely related to dogs and have pricked ears and bushy tails. The African black-backed jackal (*C. mesomeles*) is up to 110 cm long including the tail (25–33 cm) and often hunts in packs for carrion. The African side-striped jackal (*C. adustus*) is smaller.

● **jackdaw** ► An intelligent Eurasian crow, *Corvus monedula*, about 32 cm long, having a black plumage with a grey nape, an erectile crest, and pale-blue eyes. Often found in colonies, jackdaws may be seen flying around cliffs, ruins, and buildings. They feed on insects, grain, and carrion and rob nests.

● **Jacklin, Tony** ► (1944–) British professional golfer, whose successes include the British open championship (1969), the US open championship (1970), and the British Professional Golfers Association championship (1972, 1982). He captained two victorious European Ryder Cup teams (1985 and 1987).

● **Jack Russell terrier** ► A breed of dog developed in England from the fox terrier by the Rev John Russell (1795–1883) for flushing foxes from earth. It has a stocky body and a strong muscular head with small drooping ears. The short coat is white, black, and tan. Height: up to 38 cm.

● **Jackson** ► 32 20N 90 11W A city in the USA, the capital of Mississippi on the Pearl River. Founded in 1821, it was virtually destroyed by Gen Sherman in 1863. Industries include oil and gas, textiles, and glass. Population (1998 est): 198 419.

● **Jackson, Andrew** ► (1767–1845) US statesman and military hero; Democratic president (1829–37). A Tennessee frontiersman, he became the "Hero of New Orleans" when his defence of the city boosted US morale at the end of the ▷War of 1812. Jacksonian democ-

racy, the movement that made him president, advocated universal White male suffrage. He supported ▷states' rights; his distribution of federal deposits from the Bank of the United States to local banks caused land speculation and inflation.

● **Jackson, Colin Ray** ► (1967–) British athlete. He broke the world record for the 110 m hurdles (12.91 secs) in 1993 and for the 60 m hurdles (7.3 secs) in 1994.

● **Jackson, Glenda** ► (1936–) British actress and politician. She first achieved popular success playing Elizabeth I in a television series (1971). Her films include *Women in Love* (1969), *Hedda* (1976), *Stevie* (1978), and *The Rainbow* (1989). She became a Labour MP in 1992 and was subsequently a junior transport minister (1997–99).

● **Jackson, Jesse** ► (1941–) US Black civil-rights leader. A Baptist preacher, he supported Martin Luther ▷King and subsequently championed Black activists in the Democratic Party; he failed to win the presidential nomination in 1984 and 1988.

● **Jackson, Michael** ► (1958–) US pop singer, who became a solo star after success in the 1970s with his brothers, as The Jackson Five. His solo recordings include *Thriller* (1982), *Bad* (1987), and *Invincible* (2001). In 1993–94 his career was threatened by allegations of sexual abuse of a minor (the case was withdrawn after a private settlement).

● **Jackson, Peter** ► (1961–) New Zealand film director, screenwriter, and producer. His earlier work included the cult horror movie *Bad Taste* (1987) and *Heavenly Creatures* (1994), a psychological thriller. However, Jackson is now best known for his spectacular three-part film adaptation of ▷Tolkien's *The Lord of the Rings* (2001–2003).

● **Jackson, Stonewall** ► (Thomas Jonathan J.; 1824–63) US Confederate general in the Civil War. In the first battle of ▷Bull Run, he was described as standing "like a stone wall" in the face of the Federal advance. Jackson was a master of rapid tactical movement, as in the Shenandoah valley campaign (1862). His accidental death at Chancellorsville left a gap in the Confederate command.

● **Jacksonville** ► 30 20N 81 40W A city and port in the USA, in NE Florida on the St Johns River near its mouth on the Atlantic Ocean. Named after President Jackson (formerly the first territorial governor of Florida), it is the state's largest commercial centre. A major naval base, its industries include ship repairing, paper, and chemicals. Population (1998 est): 693 630.

● **Jack the Ripper** ► An unidentified murderer who killed and mutilated at least six prostitutes in the East End of London in late 1888. One theory suggests that he was Vassily Konovalov, a Russian who committed similar murders in Paris and St Petersburg and who died in a Russian asylum.

● **Jacob** ► In the Old Testament, the son of Isaac and Rebekah and the ancestor of the entire Jewish nation. His story is told in Genesis 25–50. Having deprived his brother ▷Esau of his birthright by trickery, he received a vision of God in which he was promised special blessing and numerous descendants (Genesis 28.10–22). He then lived in Mesopotamia, where he married Leah and Rachel, the daughters of Laban, and became prosperous. On his return journey to Canaan, Jacob wrestled with a mysterious supernatural being and was given the name Israel. His 12 sons gave their names to the 12 ▷tribes of Israel, all of whose members could claim descent from Jacob.

● **Jacobean style** ► A style of English architecture that evolved in the reign (1603–26) of James I. Incorporating Renaissance elements, drawn largely from Flemish carvers, into the ▷Elizabethan style, it led to ▷Palladianism. Hatfield House is an example of lavish Jacobean ornamentation. Furniture incorporated more complex carving.

● **Jacobins** ▶ An extremist group in the ▷French Revolution. The Jacobin Club was founded in 1789 and (meeting in a Dominican (*or* Jacobin) monastery) became more radical. Helped by ▷Danton's rabble-rousing speeches, they proclaimed the republic, had the king executed, and overthrew the ▷Girondins (1792–93). Through the Committee of ▷Public Safety, the Jacobins, influenced by ▷Robespierre, instituted the ▷Reign of Terror, which collapsed after Robespierre's execution.

● **Jacobites** ▶ Supporters of the exiled ▷Stuart king, James II (Latin name: Jacobus), and his descendants. Between 1688, when the ▷Glorious Revolution overthrew James II, and 1745, the Jacobites (mainly Roman Catholics and/or Tories), were the rallying point for opposition to the Hanoverian monarchs. Two Jacobite rebellions, in 1715 (the "15 Rebellion" led by ▷James Edward Stuart, the Old Pretender) and 1745 (the "45 Rebellion" led by ▷Charles Edward Stuart, the Young Pretender), were suppressed and thereafter the movement lost its political force.

● **Jacobsen, Arne** ▶ (1902–71) Danish architect and designer of furniture, wallpaper, etc., the foremost modern Danish architect. Jacobsen's work featured neat clear lines and elegant masses. His most important buildings were Rødovre Town Hall (1955) and the SAS Hotel, Copenhagen (1960). In England he designed St Catherine's College, Oxford (1960–64).

● **Jacob's ladder** ▶ A perennial herb, *Polemonium caeruleum*, native of Eurasia and widely cultivated as a garden flower. Growing to a height of 90 cm, it has bright-blue flowers and leaves consisting of paired ladder-like leaflets. Family: *Polemoniaceae*.

● **Jacopo della Quercia** ▶ (c. 1374–1438) Italian Renaissance sculptor, who was the Sienese counterpart to ▷Donatello. His Sienese works include the Fonte Gaia (1416–19), the now dismantled fountain for the Piazza del Campo, and the Baptistry font, on which he collaborated with ▷Ghiberti. However, Jacopo's most powerful works are the marble reliefs (1425–35) of scenes from Genesis, which surround the portal of S Petronio, Bologna.

● **Jacopone da Todi** ▶ (c. 1236–1306) Italian religious poet. On the death of his wife, he joined the "Spirituals," the strictest group of the Franciscan order. In 1298 he was imprisoned by Pope Boniface VIII, whom he had attacked in verse, but was released on the pope's death in 1303. The Latin poem *Stabat mater dolorosa* is attributed to him, but most of his poetry was written in the Umbrian dialect of Italian. His *laudi spirituali* (spiritual praises) are devotional poems.

● **Jacquard, Joseph-Marie** ▶ (1752–1834) French inventor of the Jacquard loom, completed in 1801. Its design allowed for the weaving of figured patterns by means of punched cards, which were later employed in the calculator developed by Charles ▷Babbage and in subsequent computers.

● **Jacquerie** ▶ (1358) A peasant revolt in NE France during the ▷Hundred Years' War. Jacquerie was the aristocrats' nickname for a peasant, Jacques Bonhomme. Caused by famine, plague, and war, the rebellion was rapidly suppressed.

● **jade** ▶ A hard semiprecious stone, usually green, consisting of either the rare jadeite, $NaAlSi_2O_6$, mostly from river beds in Myanmar (Burma) or the more common nephrite, $Ca_2(Mg,Fe)_5Si_8O_22(OH,F)_2$, from New Zealand, Alaska, China, and the USA. It has been used for carved ornaments and jewellery since prehistoric times, especially by the Chinese. Aztecs and Maoris also used nephrite for weapons and tools.

● **Jadotville** ▷*See* Likasi.

● **Jael** ▶ An Old Testament Israelite heroine, who was the wife of Heber the Kenite. After Deborah had led the Israelites to victory over the Canaanites, Sisera, the Canaanite leader, fled seeking rest in the tent of Jael and Heber, as the Kenites were not involved in the battle. Here Jael gave him "milk and butter...in a lordly dish," lulling him into such a sense of security that he fell asleep. Jael then drove a tent peg through his temple, ensuring peace for the Israelites from the Canaanites for 40 years. The story is told in Judges 4.15–22.

● **Jaén** ▶ 37 46N 3 48W A town in S Spain, in Andalusia. It has a fine Renaissance cathedral. Once famous for silk, it now produces chemicals and lead. Population (1995 est): 113 141.

● **Jaffa** ▷*See* Tel Aviv-Jaffa.

● **Jagan, Cheddi Berrat** ▶ (1918–97) Guyanese statesman, who as leader (from 1950) of the People's Progressive Party (PPP) was the first prime minister (1961–64) of British Guiana. He was president of Guyana from 1992 until his death. His wife **Janet Jagan** (1920–) was general secretary of the PPP (1950–70) and became prime minister of Guyana in 1997.

● **Jagannatha** ▶ A Hindu deity in some contexts synonymous with Krishna. Devotees of Jagannatha have been known to throw themselves under the massive chariot on which its idol is annually wheeled during a festival at Puri, in Orissa, and from which the term "juggernaut" is derived.

● **Jagger, Mick** ▶ (1944–) British rock singer, who studied at the London School of Economics before joining the ▷Rolling Stones. He became notorious for his aggressive performances on stage and was arrested in 1967 for possessing drugs. He acted in the films *Ned Kelly* (1969) and *Performance* (1970). His solo albums include *Wandering Spirit* (1993).

● **Jagiellons** ▶ The ruling dynasty of Poland and Lithuania (1386–1572), Hungary (1440–1441, 1490–1526), and Bohemia (1471–1526). The dynasty was founded by Jagiełło (1350–1434), Grand Duke of Lithuania, who became King of Poland as Władysław II in 1386, when he married Queen Jadwiga of Poland (1370–99; reigned 1384–99). His son, Władysław III (1424–44), also became King of Hungary (1440). Władysław III's nephew Władysław (1456–1516) became Vladislav II of Bohemia in 1471 and of Hungary in 1490. After defeat by the Turks at the Battle of ▷Mohács (1526), the Jagiellons lost Hungary and Bohemia to the Habsburg ▷Ferdinand I. The last Jagiellon ruler was Sigismund II Augustus (1520–72; ruled Poland 1548–72), under whom a Polish-Lithuanian commonwealth was created by the Union of ▷Lublin.

● **jaguar** ▶ The largest New World ▷cat, *Panthera onca*, found in the southern USA and Central and South America. Up to 2.5 m long including the tail (70–90 cm), it has dark rosette-shaped spots on its yellow coat. Jaguars inhabit forest and scrub and can swim well and may catch fish. They also hunt peccaries, turtles, and capybaras and attack livestock.

● **jaguarundi** ▶ A weasel-like ▷cat, *Felis yagouaroundi*, of Central and South America. Up to 110 cm long, it stands only 28 cm high at the shoulder. It has a red or grey coat, long tail, and small ears. Jaguarundis eat birds and fruits.

● **Jahangir** ▶ (1569–1627) Emperor of India (1605–27); the son of ▷Akbar the Great, from whom he inherited a powerful empire. After expanding it further he ruled wisely and justly, fostering sport and the arts. He enjoyed good relations with the British ▷East India Company.

● **Jainism** ▶ The religion of between two and three million Indians, followers of ▷Mahavira. Founded in the 6th century BC in opposition to Vedic religion, Jainism stresses ▷ahimsa (not harming living things), asceticism, and meditation. Right belief, knowledge, and conduct are the means of release from the perpetual round of rebirth caused by ▷karma. This release is possible only for monks; the laity aim only for a better rebirth. Jainism is atheistic, although lesser spirits and demons proliferate. The universe, containing heavens and hells revolving eternally in ascending and descending cycles, is seen as the mechanistic interaction of six principles: souls, space, time, matter, right, and wrong. □ p. 650.

● **Jaipur** ▶ 26 53N 75 50E A city in India, the capital of Rajasthan. Formerly the capital of the princely state of Rajasthan, it has many fine buildings built in pink sandstone, an 18th-century observatory, and a university (1947). Jaipur is famous for its enamel work and jewellery, textile printing, and stone, marble, and ivory carving. Population (1991): 1 454 678.

Jainism ► This huge monolithic statue of the Jain saint Lord Bahubali stands on the summit of Indragiri Hill at Sravana Belgola in Mysore, India. The nude meditative pose of the effigy epitomizes the Jain spirit of renunciation and peace.

● **Jakarta** ► (or Djakarta; name until 1949: Batavia) 6 09S 106 49E The capital of Indonesia, in NW Java linked by canal to its port, Tanjung Priok. The Dutch set up a fort here in the early 17th century and it became the headquarters of the Dutch East India Company. The University of Indonesia was founded in 1950. Population (1995 est): 9 160 500.

● **Jalandhar** ► (former name: Jullundur) 31 18N 75 40E A city in India, in Punjab. An important communications and agricultural centre, it manufactures sporting goods. Population (1991): 519 530.

● **jalap** ► A climbing plant *Ipomoea purga*, of Mexico and South America, that has crimson flowers. The dried tubers yield a resin that is used as a laxative. Family: *Convolvulaceae*.

● **Jamaica** ► An island country in the Caribbean Sea, off the S coast of Cuba, W of Haiti. A high plateau is crossed by the Blue Mountains, which reach 2255 m (7400 ft). The population is mainly of African and mixed African and European descent.
Economy: sugar, bauxite, bananas, and tourism form the basis. Jamaica is the world's second largest producer of bauxite and alumina although a decline in the demand for bauxite contributed to the devaluation of the Jamaican dollar in the 1980s. An oil refinery has been constructed with Mexican aid. The Peoples' National Party (PNP) governments of the last decade have adopted policies of deregulation and austerity.
History: after Columbus reached the island in 1494, it was occupied by the Spanish, who exterminated the original Arawak inhabitants. Captured by the British in 1655, it became a colony and a centre of the slave trade until the abolition of slavery in 1833. Self-government was introduced in 1944 and extended in 1959, and in 1962 Jamaica became an independent state within the British Commonwealth. The 1970s saw considerable political unrest and clashes between supporters of the Labour Party (JLP) led by Edward Seaga and

the PNP led by Michael ▷Manley, an advocate of democratic socialism and republican status for Jamaica, who was prime minister from 1972 to 1980. A state of emergency existed in 1976-77 following riots. Parts of the island were devastated by a hurricane in 1988. Following the 1989 election Manley replaced Seaga as prime minister for his second term in office, retiring in 1992. He was replaced by the PNP's Percival J. Patterson, who was re-elected in 1993 and 1997. Jamaica is a member of the OAS and CARICOM.

Jamaica

Head of state	Queen Elizabeth II, represented by the governor-general, Sir Howard Cooke
Official language	English
Official currency	Jamaican dollar of 100 cents
Area	10 991 sq km (4244 sq mi)
Population (1997 est)	2 536 000
Capital and main port	Kingston

● **Jambi** ► (Djambi or Telanaipura) 1 36S 103 39E A port in Indonesia, in SE Sumatra. It is a commercial centre producing chiefly rubber and oil. Its university was established in 1963. Population (1995 est): 410 400.

● **James (I) the Conqueror** ► (1208-76) King of Aragon (1213-76). James, who became effective ruler in 1227, was the greatest medieval Aragonese monarch. He reconquered the Balearic Islands and Valencia from the Moors and thus laid the basis for Aragonese expansion in the Mediterranean in the next century. James also prompted the compilation of the *Chronicle* of his exploits.

● **James I** ► (1394-1437) King of the Scots (1406-37), whose actual rule began on his release (1424) from English imprisonment. He strengthened royal authority at the expense of the nobles, whom he treated with some harshness, and extended royal control over the administration of justice and commerce. He was assassinated by a group of disaffected nobles. He is believed to be the author of the poem "The Kingis Quair" ("The King's Book").

● **James I** ► (1566-1625) The first Stuart King of England and Ireland (1603-25) and, as James VI, King of the Scots (1567-1625). He succeeded to the Scottish throne after the abdication of his mother Mary, Queen of Scots, and was brought up, a Presbyterian, by a series of regents. As king he reasserted royal authority against the encroachments of the nobility and, less successfully, of the Presbyterians. In 1589 he married ▷Anne of Denmark. In England, James encountered opposition from his parliaments (1604-10, the 1614 "Addled" Parliament, 1621-22), which resented his assertion of the ▷divine right of kings and attempted to make financial grants dependent on the king's redress of its constitutional grievances. James was also unpopular for his choice of favourites—after the death (1612) of Robert Cecil, 1st Earl of Salisbury (see Burghley, William Cecil, Lord), he was influenced by Robert Carr, Earl of ▷Somerset, and then by George Villiers, Duke of ▷Buckingham—and for his attempts to obtain a Spanish marriage for his son. One of the great achievements of his reign was the publication (1611) of the ▷King James Version of the Bible.

● **James II** ► (1430-60) King of the Scots (1437-60). He established his authority over rival factions and continued the extension of royal control and justice begun by his father James I. He was killed while besieging the English at Roxburgh Castle.

● **James II** ► (1633-1701) King of England, Scotland, and Ireland (1685-88). The second son of Charles I, James (as Duke of York) escaped to Holland (1648) after his father's defeat in the Civil War and during the 1650s fought for the French and then the Spanish. In 1659 he married the daughter of the Earl of Clarendon, Anne Hyde (1637-71), by whom he had two daughters (later Queens Mary II and Anne). At the Restoration (1660) of his brother Charles II, James became Lord High Admiral. In about 1669 he became a Roman Catholic and when this became public was forced to resign (1673). Successive attempts to exclude him from the succession failed and in 1684 he was reappointed Lord High Admiral and in 1685 became king. The Protestant rebellion of the Duke of ▷Monmouth was suppressed, Roman Catholics were admitted to public office, and religious freedom for all denominations was announced (1687). In 1688 James prosecuted the Archbishop of Canterbury and six bishops who refused to proclaim religious toleration from the pulpit but lost the case. This defeat and the threat of a Roman Catholic succession with the birth of a son (*see* James Edward Stuart, the Old Pretender) to his second wife, Mary of Modena (1658–1718), precipitated his overthrow in the ▷Glorious Revolution. James was forced to flee and his subsequent attempt to regain the Crown from Ireland failed with his defeat by William III's forces at the ▷Boyne (1690) and ▷Aughrim (1691). He died an exile in France.

James I ▶ The first Stuart King of England with his queen, Anne of Denmark.

● **James III** ▶ (1452–88) King of the Scots (1460–88). Until 1469 Scotland was ruled by a regency and his personal rule was marked by baronial revolts. He was killed after defeat by rebel barons near Stirling.

● **James IV** ▶ (1473–1513) King of the Scots (1488–1513). In 1503 he married ▷Margaret Tudor. He defeated the rebels who had killed his father James III, procuring internal stability and respect for the monarchy. Recurrent hostility with England culminated in the invasion of Northumberland (1513) and his defeat and death, with most of his nobles, at ▷Flodden. He encouraged literature and was a patron of the Scottish Chaucerians, William ▷Dunbar and Gavin ▷Douglas.

● **James V** ▶ (1512–42) King of the Scots (1513–42). During his minority (1513–28) Scotland was controlled by rival pro-French and pro-English factions. James favoured the French, to whom he was allied by his marriage to Mary of Guise (1515–60). He died shortly after the failure of an invasion of England and was succeeded by his daughter Mary, Queen of Scots.

● **James VI** ▶ (King of the Scots) ▷*See* James I (King of England).

● **James, Henry** ▶ (1843–1916) US novelist and critic. Much of his childhood was spent in Europe, and in 1875 he moved to Paris, where he met Turgenev, Flaubert, and others who influenced his concern with the technique of fiction. From 1876 he lived mainly in England, becoming a British citizen in 1915. His novel *Roderick Hudson* (1875) introduced the international theme of Americans confronting European culture that he was to develop in many other novels, such as *The*

Portrait of a Lady (1881), although he occasionally returned to strictly American settings, as in *Washington Square* (1881) and *The Bostonians* (1886). He wrote more than a hundred shorter works of fiction, of which *The Turn of the Screw* (1898) is perhaps the best known. In his later novels, *The Wings of the Dove* (1902), *The Ambassadors* (1903), and *The Golden Bowl* (1904), action is subordinated to a searching psychological analysis rendered in a highly elaborate style. He was an influential critic; the Prefaces to his novels are important theoretical statements on the novel. He also wrote plays, but they were not successful, although many of his works have been adapted for dramatic performance. His brother **William James** (1842–1910) was a psychologist and philosopher, who developed the theory of ▷pragmatism in ethics. He held that the truth or falsity of classical philosophical systems made little difference to everyday life and that the function of a theory should be to solve practical difficulties. Religious and moral beliefs were treated in the same nondogmatic way, especially in his *Varieties of Religious Experience* (1902) and *The Meaning of Truth* (1909).

● **James, Jesse (Woodson)** ▶ (1847–92) US outlaw. After fighting with southern guerrilla groups during the Civil War he formed the James gang and by 1867 was robbing banks, stagecoaches, and trains in his native Missouri and surrounding states. He was shot and killed by Robert Ford, a James gang member who claimed the $10 000 reward offered by the state of Missouri.

● **James, P(hyllis) D(orothy), Baroness** ▶ (1920–   ) British novelist, best known for her detective fiction. Her novels include *Cover Her Face* (1962), *Death of an Expert Witness* (1977), *A Taste for Death* (1986), *Devices and Desires* (1990), *Original Sin* (1994), and *A Certain Justice* (1997). She received a life peerage, becoming Baroness James of Holland Park, in 1991.

● **James, St** ▶ In the New Testament, the name of three followers of Christ. **1.** A leader, with St Peter, of the early Christians of Jerusalem. He is described as "the Lord's brother" (Mark 6.3), but the exact relationship is uncertain. He was a devout follower of Jewish practice, being converted to Christianity at the time of the resurrection. He was condemned to death by the Sanhedrin in 62 AD. The **Epistle of James** in the New Testament was traditionally attributed to him and was possibly written early in the 1st century AD. **2.** The Apostle, known as St James the Great, son of Zebedee and brother of ▷John. He was beheaded by Herod Agrippa I in 44 AD. In the middle ages it was believed that he had preached in Spain and was buried at Santiago de Compostela. Feast day: 25 July. **3.** The Apostle, known as St James the Less, son of Alphaeus. Feast day: 1 May.

● **James Edward Stuart, the Old Pretender** ▶ (1688–1766) The son of James II, the deposed Roman Catholic King of England. In exile, he was urged by his supporters, known as ▷Jacobites, to claim the English throne. After their invasion of Scotland failed in 1715, James abandoned his claim and lived in permanent exile in Rome.

● **Jameson, Sir Leander Starr** ▶ (1853–1917) South African statesman, born in Scotland, who worked closely with Cecil ▷Rhodes; prime minister of Cape Colony (1904–08). In 1895 he led the **Jameson Raid** into the Transvaal to support British immigrants against the Afrikaners. Imprisoned for three months in England he returned to Cape Colony to become a member of parliament and, on Rhodes' death, leader of the Progressive Party.

● **James River** ▶ A river in the central USA, flowing ESE through Virginia to ▷Chesapeake Bay. ▷Jamestown was established along its lower course. Length: 547 km (340 mi).

● **Jamestown** ▶ The first permanent English colony in America, established in 1607 on a peninsula in the James River (Virginia) by Captain John Smith. It is preserved as a historical park.

● **Jammu and Kashmir** ▶ A state in N India, forming part of the disputed area of ▷Kashmir. Area: 100 569 sq km (38 820 sq mi). Population (1991): 7 718 700. Capital: Jammu (winter); Srinagar (summer).

● **Jamnagar** ▶ 22 28N 70 06E A city in India, in Gujarat on the Gulf of Kutch. Formerly the capital of the princely state of Nawanagar, it has a fine palace. Industries include textiles and cement. Population (1991): 325 475.

● **Jamshedpur** ▶ 22 47N 86 12E A city in India, in Bihar. Founded in

1907 by the industrialist Dorabji Jamsetji Tata, it is the site of India's principal iron and steel works. Population (1991): 461 212.

● **Janáček, Leoš** ► (1854–1928) Czech composer. He studied at the Leipzig and Vienna conservatoires and became professor of composition at Brno conservatoire in 1919. He was over 60 before he gained wide recognition as a composer. In his vocal works he attempted to reproduce natural speech rhythms; he was also influenced by folk music. His works include the operas *Jenufa* (1894–1903), *The Excursions of Mr Brouček* (1908–17), and *The Makropulos Case* (1923–25), two string quartets, and the *Glagolithic Mass* (1926).

● **Janissaries** ► The elite troops of the Ottoman sultans. First raised by Sultan Orkhan (1279–1359; reigned 1326–59) about 1330, and organized by his successor Murad I (1319–89; reigned 1359–89) as a professional army, the Janissaries were carefully selected from the Ottoman subject peoples, especially from Christian families. Highly trained, powerful, and close to palace politics, during the 17th and 18th centuries they engineered palace coups, murdering two sultans, and forcing others to abdicate. After their insurrection in 1826 ▷Mahmud II killed the entire corps.

● **Jan Mayen** ► 70 10N 9 00W A volcanic island in the Arctic Ocean. It was annexed to Norway in 1929 and has a meteorological station and a NATO radio and navigation station. Area: 373 sq km (144 sq mi).

● **Jansen, Cornelius Otto** ► (1585–1638) Dutch Roman Catholic theologian and founder of ▷Jansenism. The director of episcopal colleges in Bayonne (1612–14) and Louvain (1617–30), he became dean of the University of Louvain in 1635 and Bishop of Ypres in 1636. His major work, *The Augustinus* (1640), is the basis of Jansenist doctrine and was condemned as heretical by Pope Innocent X in 1653.

● **Jansenism** ► A movement in the Roman Catholic Church in the 17th and 18th centuries based on the teaching of Cornelius ▷Jansen. Stressing the more rigorously predestinarian aspects of St ▷Augustine of Hippo's teaching, it brought the Jansenists into conflict with the Jesuits and was condemned by the Church as constituting a threat to traditional sacramentalism. Among other points, Jansenists argued that the efficacy of the sacraments depended on the moral character of the recipient. One of the most famous Jansenists was ▷Pascal. ▷*See also* Port Royal.

● **Jansky, Karl Guthe** ► (1905–50) US radio engineer, who discovered a source of radio waves outside the solar system (1932), while investigating static interference. Jansky's discovery led to the new science of ▷radio astronomy.

● **Januarius, St** ► (Italian name: San Gennaro; d. ?305) Italian churchman; Bishop and patron saint of Naples. He was probably martyred during the persecution of ▷Diocletian. The phial of solidified blood in the cathedral in Naples, believed to liquefy miraculously several times each year, is revered as one of his relics. Feast day: 19 Sept.

● **January Insurrection** ▷*See* Congress Kingdom of Poland.

● **Janus** ► The Roman god of doors, thresholds, and beginnings, after whom the month January is named. He is usually portrayed as having two heads facing forwards and backwards. His blessing was invoked for the sowing of crops and the beginning of any other major activity.

● **Japan** ► (Japanese name: Nippon *or* Nihon) A country in E Asia, consisting of a series of islands lying between the Pacific Ocean and the Sea of Japan. The four main islands are ▷Honshu, ▷Kyushu, ▷Hokkaido, and ▷Shikoku. They have long indented coastlines and much of the land is mountainous, with the highest mountain, ▷Fujiyama, rising to 3778 m (12 399 ft). The country has long been subject to earthquakes. The population is of mixed Malay, Manchu, and Korean descent; the original inhabitants, the ▷Ainu, survive in small numbers on Hokkaido.
  Economy: Japan is a highly industrialized country, manufacturing electronic and electrical goods, computers, motor vehicles, and petrochemicals; it now produces about a third of the world's ships. Paper and textile industries are also important. Mineral resources, which include limestone, copper, chromite, and coal, are on the whole sparse and Japan relies heavily on imports. There is some oil and natural gas; hydroelectricity is an important source of power. Although only 20% of the land area is cultivable, agriculture is inten-

sive: rice is still the main crop, but wheat, barley, and soya beans are also grown. Vast forests cover over half the land and there is considerable timber production. Japan is one of the world's leading fishing nations and in 1977 fishing limits were extended to 200 miles. Exports include machinery, motor vehicles, metals, textiles, and chemicals. Japan is now one of the foremost financial centres of the world, although its institutions suffered severely from the Asian financial crisis of 1997–98.
  History: about 200 BC the country was united under the ▷Yamato dynasty, already rulers of one of its component kingdoms for about 500 years. Their religion formed the basis of ▷Shinto, the native religion of Japan, and until 1946 Japanese emperors were regarded as divine descendants of the sun goddess. From 1186 AD real power was in the hands of the military ▷shoguns until Emperor ▷Mutsuhito regained power for the House of Yamato in 1867. 1871 saw the end of Hoken Seido (the feudal system) and from the mid-19th century the country was opened up to Western communications and ideas, from which it had been virtually isolated for 200 years. It expanded colonially, especially in successful wars against China and Russia, and it occupied several Asian countries. It fought against the Allies in World War II and surrendered after the dropping of atomic bombs on Hiroshima and Nagasaki in 1945. Until 1951 it was under US occupation. In 1956 Japan joined the UN and in 1972 regained the Ryukyu Islands. By a new constitution of 1947 Emperor ▷Hirohito renounced his former claim to divinity and became a constitutional monarch. Recent years have seen criticisms from abroad of Japan's large international trade surplus and a series of political scandals leading to a rapid succession of premiers. In 1993 the Liberal Democratic Party (LDP), which had held power since 1955, lost a vote of confidence; after elections, a coalition government was formed. In 1995 an earthquake in Kobe killed over 5000 people. In 1997–98 Japan's financial system was hit severely by the general crisis in SE Asia and the economy entered its worst recession since World War II. Following elections in 1998, a new coalition was formed under the LDP's Keizo Obuchi. The current prime minister is Junichiro Koizumi (from April 2001).

Japan	
Head of state	Emperor Akihito
Official language	Japanese
Official currency	yen of 100 sen
Area	372 480 sq km (143 777 sq mi)
Population (1999 est)	126 680 000
Capital	Tokyo
Main port	Yokohama

● **Japan, Sea of** ► A section of the NW Pacific Ocean between Japan and the Asian mainland.

● **Japanese** ► The language of the people of Japan. Its relationship to other languages is uncertain, but it is probably a member of the Ural-Altaic family of languages and related to Korean. Of the many regional dialects, the most widely recognized is that of Tokyo. It is polysyllabic and usually stresses all syllables equally, although different pitches often distinguish adjacent syllables. The writing system is complex. In about the 5th century the Japanese adopted Chinese ideographic characters (*kanji*), which have both Chinese-like (*on*) and native Japanese (*kun*) pronunciations. About 2000 *kanji* are now used. In about the 9th century the Japanese supplemented the *kanji* by deriving from them two phonetic syllabaries, of 48 symbols each, called *hiragana* and *katakana*. *Hiragana* is mainly used for suffixes and grammatical functions and for words for which there are no *kanji*, and *katakana* for foreign names, loanwords, and scientific words.

● **Japanese art and architecture** ► Neolithic Japanese art consisted of crudely executed terracotta figurines and some ceramic ware. The introduction of Buddhism via Korea in the 6th century and the influence of Chinese culture initiated a great period of temple building, sculpture (chiefly of the Buddha), and the development of the art of flower arrangement (*see* ikebana). In the Kamakura period (12th–14th centuries) the refined ▷Fujiwara style was replaced in sculpture by a vigorous naturalism. In painting, a uniquely Japanese style developed in continuous narrative paintings on horizontal

Japanese art and architecture ▶ The 14th-century Himeji Castle, built by the Akamatsu family of warriors.

scrolls and realistic landscapes. Another entirely Japanese art form was the coloured woodblock print of the Tokugawa period (1630–1867). These prints, portraying the transient world of theatre, teahouse, etc., and produced by such artists as ▷Hokusai and ▷Kitagawa Utamaro, enjoyed a popularity in Europe in the late 19th century, being particularly influential among impressionist painters (*see* ukiyo-e). Examples of applied arts are the small wood and ivory carvings (netsuke) and the gold inlaid sword guards (tsuba). Ceramic art is illustrated by the ▷cha-no-yu wares.

Japanese architecture, like Chinese, dates from the introduction of Buddhism, with many Chinese styles being preserved. One of the earliest Japanese buildings to survive is the 7th-century Buddhist monastery at Horyuji, the pillared hall of which is the basis for all Japanese temples (*see also* pagoda). Japanese houses are usually simple single-storey buildings with distinguishing decorative fixtures. In the 19th century native architecture was heavily influenced by Western styles, which culminated in Frank Lloyd ▷Wright's Imperial Hotel, Tokyo (1916, now demolished). Modern Japanese architects, influenced by ▷Le Corbusier, include Kenzo ▷Tange.

● **Japanese cedar ▶** A conifer, *Cryptomeria japonica*, native to China and Japan, where it is an important timber tree reaching 55 m; elsewhere it is grown for ornament and rarely exceeds 35 m. Japanese cedar has narrow curved leaves that point towards the tips of the branches and spiny cones, 2 cm across. Family: *Taxodiaceae*.

● **Japanese literature ▶** Before the mid-8th century AD Chinese was the more prestigious language in Japan and in the 8th century Chinese characters were adapted to render spoken Japanese (*see* Japanese). Vernacular Japanese folksongs, however, gave rise to a type of lyric poem, the *waka*, which remained a standard poetic form for over a millennium. This native form appears in the earliest Japanese anthology, the *Manyoshu* (compiled after 759), which contains about 4500 poems. The emperors of the Heian period (794–1185) encouraged literature, and further anthologies were published, as well as prose tales (*monogatari*) and fictionalized diaries (*nikki*). Fiction was particularly the province of women; its most famous practitioner was ▷Murasaki Shikibu, author of the *Genji Monogatari* (*Tale of Genji*; c. 1015). Unsettled conditions in the following 500 years led to a decline in this essentially aristocratic literary output. The last official anthology appeared in 1439. The ▷No drama, mainly Buddhist in inspiration, flowered during the late 14th and early 15th centuries, and the *haiku* (an epigram comprising 17 syllables) was a product of the early 16th century.

In the Tokugawa period (1603–1867) literature of all kinds en-

joyed a renaissance under the patronage of the leisured warrior class and the new mercantile middle class. The *haiku* reached its peak in the hands of ▷Matsuo Basho. Fiction encompassed many forms and moods, and nationalistic pride led to official encouragement for writers of philosophy, history, and other learned works. The *joruri* (puppet theatre) at first prospered with playwrights of the calibre of Monzaemon writing for it but during the late 18th century it declined in competition with the popular *kabuki* theatre. After 1868 European influence manifested itself in every branch of literature, mainly with adverse effects. In the years after World War II, however, several writers established international reputations, including ▷Kawabata Yasunari, Yukio ▷Mishima, and Kenzaburo ▷Oë.

● **Japanese maple ▶** A ▷maple tree, *Acer palmatum*, up to 13 m tall, the 5–11 lobed leaves of which turn scarlet in autumn. Native to Japan, it is a popular ornamental in many cultivated varieties, including purple-leaved and dwarf types.

● **japonica ▶** A shrub or tree of the genus *Chaenomeles* (or *Cydonia*), native to Japan but widely cultivated as an ornamental. Flowering quince (*C. japonica*) and Japanese quince (*C. speciosa*) are the most popular species. These have toothed oval glossy leaves and clusters of scarlet five-petalled flowers, 5 cm across. The apple-like fruit is used in marmalade and jelly. Family: *Rosaceae*.

● **Japurá, River ▶** A river in NW South America, rising as the Río Caquetá in SW Colombia and flowing SE to join the River Amazon near Tefé in Brazil. Length: 2800 km (1750 mi).

● **Jaques-Dalcroze, Émile ▶** (1865–1950) Swiss composer and educationalist. While professor of harmony at the Geneva conservatoire he developed ▷eurhythmics, a system of coordinating musical rhythms and bodily movement. The London School of Dalcroze Eurythmics was founded in 1913.

● **Jarman, Derek ▶** (1942–94) British film director and writer. His challenging and controversial films include *Sebastiane* (1975), *Jubilee* (1977), *Caravaggio* (1986), *Edward II* (1991), *Wittgenstein* (1993), and *Blue* (1993). He was a leading advocate of gay rights.

● **jarrah ▶** A shrub or tree, ▷*Eucalyptus marginata*, of W Australia, that has extremely durable weather-resistant timber, known as West Australian mahogany. It can grow to a height of 16 m and is found in dry areas. Family: *Myrtaceae*.

● **Jarrow ▶** 54 59N 1 29W A town in NE England, in South Tyneside unitary authority, Tyne and Wear. The Venerable Bede lived in the monastery here. The Jarrow hunger march (1936), from Tyneside to London, was provoked by high local unemployment and poverty following the decline of the shipbuilding industry. Jarrow has foundries, oil installations, and chemical works. Population (1991): 29 325. □ p. 654.

● **Jarry, Alfred ▶** (1873–1907) French dramatist. His play, *Ubu Roi* (1896), is an outrageous satire on bourgeois conventions of respectability. He wrote several sequels and also novels and poems and is regarded as a precursor of ▷surrealism and the ▷Theatre of the Absurd.

● **Jaruzelski, Wojciech ▶** (1923–) Polish general and statesman; defence minister (1968–81); prime minister and first secretary of the Polish Communist Party (1981–89); president (1989–90). Coming to power to halt the liberal reforms obtained by the independent trade union Solidarity, he instituted martial law (1981–83), detained Lech ▷Wałęsa and other union leaders (1981–82), and dissolved Solidarity (1982–89). In 2001 he was put on trial for the shooting of protesters when he was defence minister.

● **jasmine ▶** A shrub of the genus *Jasminum* (about 300 species), native to tropical and subtropical regions and widely cultivated. Many species yield an essential oil used in perfumery. Two species suitable for temperate gardens are the common jasmine (*J. officinalis*) from S Asia, up to 6 m tall with fragrant white flowers, and the Chinese winter jasmine (*J. nudiflorum*), 3–6 m tall, the yellow flowers of which open in winter before the leaves. (Winter jasmine can be distinguished from ▷Forsythia by its green stems.) Family: *Oleaceae*.

● **Jason ▶** A legendary Greek hero, heir to the throne of Iolcos in Thessaly. Sent by his uncle, the usurper Pelias, to fetch the ▷Golden

Fleece, he and the ▷Argonauts underwent many adventures before recovering the Fleece from Colchis with the help of ▷Medea. After years of wandering he died at Corinth.

● **jasper** ► An impure variety of ▷chalcedony, usually red or reddish brown. It is slightly translucent and is regarded as a semiprecious stone. It is an abundant mineral, occurring mainly in veins and in cavities in volcanic rocks.

● **Jaspers, Karl (Theodor)** ► (1883–1969) German philosopher, a forerunner of ▷existentialism. He studied medicine and psychology and believed philosophers should be acquainted with the scientific method. His philosophy, expounded in *Philosophie* (1932), is about the nature of human choice. He thought ▷Kierkegaard and ▷Nietzsche were exceptional in showing the variety of possibilities open to man.

● **Jassy** ▷*See* Iaşi.

● **Jatakas** ► In the Pali Buddhist canon, a collection of 550 moral tales describing previous existences of the Buddha before his enlightenment. Each story is related to an event in the Buddha's present life.

● **jaundice** ► Yellowing of the skin and whites of the eyes due to the presence of ▷bile pigments. Bile pigments are normally produced by the liver from the breakdown of red blood cells and then excreted in bile into the gut. Jaundice may result if there is excessive breakdown of red blood cells, as in haemolytic anaemia, or in disease of the liver, such as ▷hepatitis, or blockage of the bile duct by ▷gallstones.

● **Jaurès, Jean** ► (1859–1914) French socialist leader and journalist; a proponent of the international unity of the working class. He was a supporter of Dreyfus and advocated the separation of church and state. In 1905 he helped to found the French socialist party (the Section française de l'internationale Ouvrière). He helped found *L'Humanité* in 1904 and was its editor until he was assassinated.

● **Java** ► An Indonesian island, the smallest of the Greater ▷Sunda Islands. Its chain of volcanic mountains has formed exceptionally fertile soil, and its many rivers feed its intensive wet-rice agriculture. Other food crops, sugar cane, and kapok are grown and forest products include teak. Indonesia's administrative and industrial centre, Java has its three largest cities and is heavily overpopulated. The textile industry is of particular importance, especially synthetic textiles, although the village batik industry has declined. Java is subsidized by other islands, which has provoked much unrest.
    History: Indian colonies in the early centuries AD developed into Hindu and Buddhist kingdoms, with Hindu-Javanese culture reaching its height in the 14th century. Later Islamic control barely influenced the culture. The Dutch East India Company was centred here from 1619. During the anticommunist purges (1965–67) between 500 000 and 1 000 000 people were killed. Area: 132 174 sq km (51 032

sq mi). Population (1995 est): 102 910 500, with Madura. Capital: Jakarta.

● **Java man** ▷*See* Homo.

● **javelin throw** ► A field event in athletics in which a spearlike javelin is thrown as far as possible. The men's javelin is 2.6–2.7 m (8.5–8.9 ft) long and weighs 800 g (1.8 lb). The women's measures 2.2–2.3 m (7.2–7.5 ft) and weighs at least 600 g (1.3 lb). It is thrown with one hand, over the shoulder, after a run-up of about 36 m (120 ft), and the head must hit the ground first. Each competitor has six tries. World records: men: 95.66 m (1993) by Jan Zelezny (Czech Republic); women: 80.00 m (1988) by Petra Felke (East Germany).

● **jaw** ► One of the two bones of the face that form a framework for the mouth and provide attachment for the teeth. The lower jaw (*or* mandible) is a horseshoe-shaped bone with a vertical process at each end that forms a joint with the temporal bone of the skull, just in front of each ear. The upper jaw consists of two closely connected bones (maxillae) each containing an air ▷sinus.

● **Jawara, Sir Dawda** ► (1924–) Gambian statesman; president (1970–94). A Muslim, he became minister of education in 1960 and prime minister in 1962, in which post he led his country to independence in 1965. When The Gambia became a republic in 1970 Jawara became president. He was ousted in a military coup.

● **jay** ► A crow, *Garrulus glandarius*, of Eurasia and N Africa. It is about 34 cm long and brownish pink, with a black tail, white rump, black-barred blue wing patches, and a black-and-white erectile crest. Jays are found mainly in woodland, feeding on insects and larvae in summer and storing acorns, beechmast, and other seeds for winter food.

● **Jay, John** ► (1745–1829) US Revolutionary patriot; the first chief justice of the USA (1789–95). He led peace negotiations with Britain after the American Revolution and negotiated the so-called **Jay Treaty** averting war with Britain and securing favourable commercial terms. As chief justice he affirmed the subordination of states to the federal government.

● **Jaya, Mount** ► (*or* Mount Sukarno) 4 05S 137 09E The highest mountain in Indonesia, in Irian Jaya in the Sudirman range. Height: 5029 m (16 503 ft).

● **Jayapura** ► (*or* Djajapura; former name: Sukarnapura) 2 37S 140 39E A port in E Indonesia, the capital of Irian Jaya province on the Pacific Ocean. Liberated from Japanese occupation by US forces in 1944, it became Gen MacArthur's headquarters. Population (1995 est): 180 400.

● **Jayewardene, J(unius) R(ichard)** ► (1906–96) Sri Lankan statesman; prime minister (1977–78) and then president (1978–89).

Jarrow ► The famous hunger march of 1936, when some 200 unemployed men marched the 385 km (240 mi) to London to draw attention to the great distress brought to this Tyneside town by the decline of the shipbuilding industry.

He became a significant politician in the years before Ceylon (Sri Lanka from 1972) obtained independence in 1948 and as a member of the United National Party, which he led from 1970, held various posts before becoming prime minister.

● **jazz** ▶ A form of popular music that originated in New Orleans around 1900, characterized by improvisation and syncopated rhythms. The musical influences responsible for its creation included French and Spanish popular music, ragtime, blues, brass-band music, and African slave songs. It first became popular in the Storyville district of New Orleans and as an accompaniment to funerals, weddings, and country outings. Early jazz bands featured improvised solos on such instruments as the cornet, clarinet, and trombone. Louis Armstrong and Jelly Roll Morton are associated with New Orleans jazz (*see* New Orleans style). In the 1920s jazz spread to larger US cities, such as New York and Chicago; the original band was enlarged with saxophones and additional cornets and trumpets. Large dance bands emerged in the era of ▷swing (the 1930s), in which the bandleaders Paul Whiteman (1891–1967), Benny Goodman, Glenn Miller, and Count Basie were especially important. In the 1940s Dizzy Gillespie and Charlie "Bird" Parker revolted against swing with ▷bop, using a smaller band and introducing harmonic and rhythmic innovations. ▷Cool jazz of the late 1940s and 1950s adopted a relaxed behind-the-beat approach as in the playing of Miles Davis and Stan Getz (1927–91). In the 1960s and 1970s such musicians as Gunther Schuller (1925–　) and John Lewis (1920–　) integrated jazz idioms with classical forms and techniques to form ▷third stream. Ornette Coleman (1930–　) and John Coltrane (1926–67) expanded the boundaries of jazz to include atonality in a style called ▷free-form jazz. Trends since the 1970s have included the fusion of jazz with rock, funk, and African styles.

● **Jean de Meun** ▶ (c. 1240–c. 1305) French poet. His conclusion (18 000 lines) of the verse allegory *Roman de la rose*, contrasting in both style and content with the earlier part written by ▷Guillaume de Lorris, is valued chiefly for its lengthy and informative digressions on topics of contemporary interest.

● **Jean Paul** ▶ (Johann Paul Friedrich Richter; 1763–1825) German Romantic novelist. His novels, such as *Hesperus* (1795) and *Das Leben des Quintus Fixlein* (1796), combine fantasy with humour and psychological realism and later influenced ▷Keller and ▷Mörike.

● **Jeans, Sir James Hopwood** ▶ (1877–1946) British mathematician and astronomer. His early work was on the kinetic theory of gases and on the quantum theory. Later he concentrated on cosmogony, putting forward a now discredited theory of planetary formation. After 1928 he devoted himself to writing books popularizing science: *The Universe around Us* (1930), *Science and Music* (1937), and *The Growth of Physical Science* (1947) are examples. He was knighted in 1928 and appointed to the OM in 1939.

● **Jedburgh** ▶ 55 29N 2 34W A town in SE Scotland, in Scottish Borders. The royal castle was destroyed in 1409 but the abbey (founded 1118) remains. Jedburgh's chief industries are textiles (tweeds, woollens, and rayon) and precision tools. Population (latest est): 4168.

● **Jedda** ▷*See* Jiddah.

● **Jeeps, Dickie** ▶ (Richard Eric Gautrey J.; 1931–　) British Rugby Union footballer, who played for Northampton, England, and the British Lions. An outstanding scrum half, he played 24 times for England (1956–62) and 13 times for the British Lions. He became chairman of the Sports Council (1978).

● **Jefferies, Richard** ▶ (1848–87) British novelist and naturalist. He published several collections of essays and sketches about rural life, notably *Hodge and His Masters* (1880). In his autobiography *The Story of My Heart* (1883) and other later works he developed a personal philosophy of mysticism.

● **Jeffers, Robinson** ▶ (1887–1962) US poet. From 1916 he lived in isolation near Carmel on the coast of California. *Tamar and Other Poems* (1924) and other volumes of long narrative poems and short lyrics express a bleak view of mankind. He also wrote plays, notably an adaptation of Euripides' *Medea* (1946).

● **Jefferson, Thomas** ▶ (1743–1826) US statesman; the third president (1801–09) of the USA. A lawyer, Jefferson began his political career (1769) in Virginia's House of Burgesses. He was elected a delegate to the second ▷Continental Congress in 1775 and was the chief author of the ▷Declaration of Independence. Jefferson served as governor of Virginia (1779–81), minister to France (1785–89), secretary of state (1789–93), and vice president (1797–1801) under John Adams. During Jefferson's two terms as president, he approved the ▷Louisiana Purchase (1803) and encouraged US neutrality in the Napoleonic Wars. In private life after 1809, Jefferson founded the University of Virginia. Both he and John Adams died on 4 July, 1826, the 50th anniversary of American independence.

● **Jefferson City** ▶ 38 33N 92 10W A city in the USA, the capital of Missouri on the Missouri River. Primarily an administrative centre, it is the site of Lincoln University (1866). Population (1990): 35 481.

● **Jeffrey, Francis, Lord** ▶ (1773–1850) Scottish literary critic and judge. He is best known as cofounder (1802) and editor (1802–29) of the *Edinburgh Review*. For this brilliant and controversial periodical Jeffrey wrote essays denouncing the work of the Romantics, particularly Wordsworth.

● **Jeffreys of Wem, George, 1st Baron** ▶ (c. 1645–89) English judge. A supporter of the Crown, he became a leading prosecutor of suspected traitors following the ▷Popish Plot and, in 1685, James II's Lord Chancellor. He is notorious for the harsh punishments and death sentences he imposed during the Bloody Assizes, after Monmouth's rebellion (1685). He was captured after the fall of James II and died in the Tower of London.

● **Jeffries, John** ▷*See* Blanchard, Jean Pierre François.

● **Jehol** ▷*See* Chengde.

● **Jehovah** ▷*See* Yahweh.

● **Jehovah's Witnesses** ▶ A religious movement, first known as Bible Students, organized in the early 1870s by Charles Taze Russell (1852–1916) in Pittsburgh. From 1884 the Watch Tower Bible and Tract Society became their legal publishing agency. Jehovah's Witnesses accept the Bible as their sole authority, worshipping the Creator, Jehovah, and acknowledging Jesus Christ to be God's son and spokesman. They look for the end of wickedness and of the present world order in the near future. They believe that 144 000, the Christian congregation, will rule with Christ Jesus in his heavenly kingdom over the rest of obedient mankind, who will live on a paradise earth. Following the example of the first Christians, they do not engage in politics and are conscientious objectors.

● **Jekyll, Gertrude** ▶ (1843–1932) British landscape gardener. Failing eyesight persuaded her to give up her interest in painting and take up gardening; she subsequently designed gardens, many in collaboration with Edwin ▷Lutyens. Her gardens were characterized by simplicity and the use of native plants.

● **Jellicoe, John Rushworth, 1st Earl** ▶ (1859–1935) British admiral; commander of the grand fleet (1914–16) in World War I. He was criticized after the battle of ▷Jutland, in which the German fleet escaped relatively unscathed.

● **jellyfish** ▶ A free-swimming aquatic invertebrate animal belonging to a class (*Scyphozoa*; about 200 species) of ▷cnidarians. The translucent gelatinous body, 1.5–2000 mm in diameter, is bell- or umbrella-shaped, with a central tubular projection that hangs down and bears the mouth. Jellyfish occur in all oceans, especially in tropical regions, and usually propel themselves through the water by contracting muscles around the edge of the bell. Stinging tentacles are used to capture and paralyse prey, ranging from plankton to small fish, and can seriously affect man. The term jellyfish is also used for the free-swimming sexual form of any other cnidarian (*see* medusa).

● **Jena** ▶ 51 00N 11 30E A town in central Germany, on the River Saale. Its university (1558) became famous in the 18th century when Fichte, Hegel, Schelling, Schiller, and August Schlegel taught there. As well as the Zeiss optical works, founded in 1846, Jena has chemical and engineering industries. Population (1996 est): 101 061.

● **Jena and Auerstädt, Battles of** ▶ (14 October, 1806) Simultaneous battles in which Napoleon defeated the Prussians. Following ▷Austerlitz, Auerstädt and Jena broke Prussia as a military power and left Russia to face Napoleon alone. Prussia remained in the orbit of the French Empire until 1813, when it rejoined the alliance against Napoleon.

● **Jenkins, Roy (Harris), Baron Jenkins of Hillhead** ► (1920–) British politician and historian. He entered parliament in 1948 as a Labour member and joined the cabinet of Harold ▷Wilson in 1964. As home secretary (1965–67; 1974–76) he oversaw the abolition of hanging and introduced liberal social reforms; he was also chancellor of the exchequer (1967–70) and deputy leader of the Labour Party (1970–72). After serving as president of the EC Commission (1977–81) he helped to found the ▷Social Democratic Party in 1981 and served as leader (1982–83). His books include biographies of Asquith (1964) and Gladstone (1995).·In 1987 he was elected Chancellor of Oxford University and made a life peer. He was appointed to the OM in 1993. In 1997–98 he headed a commission on the question of voting reform (*see* proportional representation). His wife, **Dame Jennifer Jenkins** (1921–), was chairman of the ▷National Trust (1986–90).

● **Jenkins' Ear, War of** ► (1738–48) A war that arose out of Britain's illicit trade in Spanish America and merged into the War of the ▷Austrian Succession (1740–48). It followed the accusation of Capt Robert Jenkins that his ear had been cut off by Spanish coastguards in the West Indies.

● **Jenner, Edward** ► (1749–1823) British physician, who developed the first effective vaccine—against smallpox. Jenner noticed that people who caught the mild disease cowpox never contracted smallpox. In 1796 he inoculated a small boy with cowpox and, two months later, with smallpox. The boy did not get smallpox. Jenner published his findings in 1798 and vaccination—a word that Jenner coined—became a widespread protective measure against smallpox.

● **Jensen, Johannes (Vilhelm)** ► (1873–1950) Danish novelist and poet, many of whose works were inspired by his travels. His novel sequence *Den lange Rejse* (*The Long Journey*; 1908–22) is a Darwinian account of the origin of mankind.

● **Jenson, Nicolas** ► (c. 1420–80) French printer, who produced the first distinctive roman typeface, which replaced Gothic (*or* black letter) type. After studying printing under Gutenberg, Jenson opened a printing shop in Venice in 1470.

● **jerboa** ► A small hopping ▷rodent belonging to the family *Dipodidae* (25 species) of Asian and N African deserts, also called desert rat. Jerboas are 4–15 cm long and have kangaroo-like hind feet, a long tail, large eyes and ears, and soft sandy-coloured fur. They feed at night on seeds and tubers.

● **Jeremiah** ► (7th century BC) An Old Testament prophet. He is believed to have been born about 650 BC in a village near Jerusalem. The **Book of Jeremiah** contains his prophecies relating to the fall of Judah, its conquest by Nebuchadnezzar, and the ▷Babylonian exile of the Jews. A Messiah is prophesied, who will rule over Jews and Gentiles.

● **Jerez de la Frontera** ► 36 41N 6 08W A city in SW Spain, in Andalusia. It is renowned for its wine industry and gave its name to sherry. Population (1995 est): 191 394.

● **Jericho** ► 31 52N 35 27E A town in the Jordan Valley, N of the Dead Sea, in the Israeli-occupied ▷West Bank. The nearby site of the old city was excavated by Kathleen ▷Kenyon, revealing one of the earliest known towns (before 8000 BC), with massive stone fortifications. Later Neolithic burials yielded skulls with features modelled in plaster and shells inset for eyes. Of the biblical Bronze Age city attacked by ▷Joshua (Joshua 6) nothing remains. The ruins of the magnificent palace, Khirbat al-Mafjar, built (739–44 AD) by the Umayyad caliph Hisham (d. 743) can still be seen. In accordance with to the 1993 peace agreement between Israel and the PLO, Palestinian self-rule was granted in Jericho in 1994.

● **Jerome, Jerome K(lapka)** ► (1859–1927) British humorist, novelist, and playwright. His plays include *The Passing of the Third Floor Back* (1908) but he is best known for his novel *Three Men in a Boat* (1899).

● **Jerome, St** ► (c. 342–420 AD) Italian biblical scholar; Doctor of the Church and author of the ▷Vulgate Bible, the first Latin translation of the Bible from the Hebrew. After a period as a hermit, he was ordained by St ▷Paulinus of Nola in Antioch. A secretary to Pope Damasus I (reigned 366–94) from 382 until 385, he later settled in Bethlehem, where he established a monastery. He also wrote biblical commentaries and theological works. Feast day: 30 Sept.

● **Jersey** ► 49 13N 2 07W The largest of the Channel Islands, in the English Channel. Colonized from Normandy in the 11th century, French influence remains strong and French is the official language. It consists chiefly of a plateau incised by deep valleys. Agriculture, particularly dairy farming, is important and the famous Jersey cattle are bred for export. Finance and tourism are major sources of income. In 1959 the Jersey Zoological Park was founded by Gerald Durrell to protect rare species of wildlife. In 1992 it decided to review its constitutional links with the UK. Area: 116 sq km (45 sq mi). Population (1991): 84 082. Capital: St Helier.

● **Jersey cattle** ► A breed of dairy cattle originating from Jersey. Relatively small and fine-boned, Jerseys are golden-brown to black in colour, adaptable, and mature rapidly. They produce high-quality creamy milk.

● **Jersey City** ► 40 44N 74 04W A city in the USA, in New Jersey. Founded in 1629, it is connected to nearby New York City by the Hudson River tunnels. Its 20 km (12 mi) of waterfront forms part of the port of New York. It is a major industrial and commercial centre with oil refineries; its products include paper and cigarettes. Population (1996 est): 229 039.

● **Jerusalem** ► (Arabic name: El Quds) 31 47N 35 13E The de facto capital of Israel, in the Judaea Heights between the Mediterranean and the Dead Sea. Jerusalem is a religious centre for three major world religions: Christianity, Judaism, and Islam. Most employment is found in government and the city's main industry, tourism. The Hebrew University of Jerusalem was founded in 1918. The modern city spreads out extensively on the W side of the Old City, which is walled (1537–40) and contains most of the religious shrines, including the Western (Wailing) Wall (Jewish), the Dome of the Rock (begun 661 AD; Islamic), and the Church of the Holy Sepulchre, which was founded in about 335 on the traditional site of Christ's burial and resurrection, although most of the present structure is 19th-century. To the W of the city is the Yad WaShem Holocaust Remembrance complex, including the Ohel Yizkor museum and the memorial column to the six million Jews who perished in the German camps.
History: Jerusalem was conquered by King David in 1005 BC and the first ▷Temple was built by his son, Solomon, in 969 BC; it became the capital of Judah in 930 BC. Nebuchadnezzar, King of Babylon, destroyed the city in 586 BC, when the Jewish inhabitants were exiled to Babylon. In 538 BC, 40 000 Jews returned to the city, whose walls were rebuilt under Nehemiah in 445 BC. It was occupied by Alexander the Great (4th century BC) and the Romans (63 BC), under whose fifth procurator, Pontius Pilate, Jesus Christ was put to death. Occupation by the Arabs and Turks was succeeded by the establishment of the Kingdom of Jerusalem, a feudal state created in 1099 following conquest by the Crusaders. It was enlarged in the early 12th century by ▷Baldwin I and his successors, but fell to Saladin in 1187. The Ottoman Turks took the city in 1516 and in 1538 ▷Suleiman the Magnificent rebuilt the city walls, which are those still standing. The Ottoman period lasted until 1917, when it was taken by the British, who held it under mandate until 1948. Jerusalem was then divided between the new state of Israel, which declared the city its capital (1950), and Jordan. Israel occupied the whole city, including the E Arab section, in June, 1967, but this annexation is not recognized by the UN, which does not accept Jerusalem as Israel's capital. The city has since been troubled by ethnic unrest (*see* intifada), including Arab riots in October, 1990, in which 18 protesters died. Population (1997 est): 591 400.

● **Jerusalem artichoke** ► A North American perennial herb, *Helianthus tuberosus*, that grows to a height of 2 m, and has edible sweet-tasting tubers up to 10 cm long. Their yellow flowers appear only in hot summers. Family: *Compositae*.

● **Jerusalem cherry** ► A small shrub, *Solanum pseudocapsicum*, probably of Old World origin, growing to a height of 1.3 m and bearing cherry-sized red or yellow highly poisonous fruits. The false Jerusalem cherry (*S. capsicastrum*) of Brazil is similar. Both are grown as ornamentals. Family: *Solanaceae*.

● **Jervis Bay** ▶ An inlet of the Tasman Sea, in SE Australia. It forms a fine natural harbour and was transferred to the Australian Capital Territory (1915) for development as an outlet port. It contains the Royal Australian Naval College (1915). Area: about 73 sq km (28 sq mi).

● **Jespersen, Otto** ▶ (1860–1943) Danish linguist. His principal works are *Growth and Structure of the English Language* (1905), *A Modern English Grammar on Historical Principles* (1909–31), *The Philosophy of Grammar* (1924), and *Analytic Syntax* (1937). His approach to language is traditional and historical.

● **Jesselton** ▷*See* Kota Kinabalu.

● **Jesuits** ▶ Members of the Society of Jesus, an order founded by St ▷Ignatius Loyola in 1533 to propagate the Roman Catholic faith. The order was organized along military lines; in addition to the traditional vows of chastity, poverty, and obedience, Jesuits were sworn to go wherever the pope might send them. They quickly established themselves as educators and missionaries, becoming one of the dominant forces of the ▷Counter-Reformation; their argumentative subtlety was proverbial. They also played a prominent role in missions to the New World and the East. Their power and rigorous organization eventually brought them into conflict with civil authorities throughout Europe, and they were expelled from several states. In 1773 Pope Clement XIV suppressed the order, and it was not reinstated until 1814. Today Jesuits are active in most countries and are noted for their schools and universities, including the Gregorian University in Rome. In 1986 the Pope appointed Fr Paolo Dezza to lead and to impose discipline upon the order.

● **Jesus** ▶ (c. 6 BC–c. 30 AD) The founder of ▷Christianity; called by his followers the ▷Messiah or Christ (Greek *khristos*, anointed one). Most of the information concerning Jesus comes from the New Testament ▷Gospels of Matthew, Mark, and Luke. This material was arranged in order to proclaim and interpret his life and teachings to early Christians and therefore does not provide neutral biographical detail, although it is based on historical facts. According to these sources, Jesus was born at Bethlehem in the last years of the reign of ▷Herod the Great; he was the son of the Virgin ▷Mary of Nazareth in Galilee. Mary's husband, Joseph, was a carpenter who belonged to the tribe of Judah and the family of David, and it is usually assumed that Jesus was trained as a carpenter in Nazareth. About 27 AD, ▷John the Baptist, who was related to Jesus, began to preach that the Kingdom of God (a divine last judgment) was approaching and to urge repentance and baptism as a preparation for it. Jesus was baptized by John and shortly (after John had been imprisoned by Herod Antipas) began his public ministry, travelling in Galilee and in the area NW of Lake Gennesaret. He taught in synagogues and in the open, not using sacred texts but adopting a popular style by preaching in parables and proverbial expressions. His teaching, which is summarized in the Sermon on the Mount (Matthew 5–7; *see also* Beatitudes), emphasized the approaching Kingdom of God, the need for repentance, and the importance of such virtues as charity, faith, and humility instead of the ceremonial observance of the Law. Miracles were attributed to him, including healing, driving out demons, and miraculously feeding a multitude of 5000. The beginnings of a movement are evident in Galilee when Jesus summoned the disciples, traditionally 12 in number, instructing them to leave their families and their work in order to preach the imminence of the Kingdom of God. The Gospels devote most attention to the last week of Jesus' life. He went with the disciples to Jerusalem for Passover, apparently aware of the serious opposition that awaited him. There he was acknowledged as the Messiah by many people, but, after betrayal by Judas, was arrested and condemned to death by the chief Jewish tribunal, the Sanhedrin, for the blasphemous claim to Messiahship. The Gospels tend to exonerate Pontius ▷Pilate in the proceedings against Jesus, but he was executed according to Roman law as a criminal (*see* crucifixion). In the New Testament his death is presented as the fulfilment of a divine purpose that was made clear to the disciples only at the resurrection (on the next day but one after the crucifixion) and by a number of appearances to individuals and groups of disciples. His ascension into heaven is mentioned in the Gospels and in Acts (1.3), where it is said to have occurred 40 days after the resurrection.

(a)

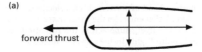

(b)

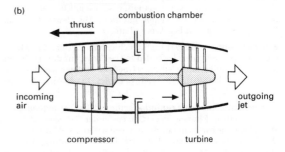

(c)

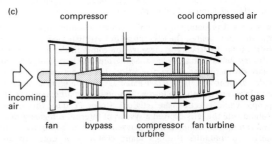

jet engine ▶ (a) The principle: equal pressure from the expanding gas inside the engine meets equal resistance except rearwards. The result is a forward thrust. The lower the outside pressure, the greater the thrust. (b) The turbojet, used for subsonic and supersonic flight (especially with reheat). (c) The turbofan, used for subsonic flight: cool air, compressed by the fan, bypasses the engine and mixes with the hot jet.

● **jet engine** ▶ A form of ▷gas turbine (*see also* internal-combustion engine) in which part of the energy released by burning the fuel drives a turbine, which in turn drives a compressor to increase the pressure of the air required for combustion, and part is used as a high-velocity jet to provide thrust to drive an aircraft. The jet engine was patented in 1930 in the UK by Sir Frank ▷Whittle, the first practical Whittle engine powering a Gloster aircraft in 1941. Except for light aircraft, most military and commercial aircraft are now powered by jet engines. Thrust in these engines is equal to the mass of the gas produced multiplied by its acceleration and is due to the pressure of the expanding gas on the engine itself rather than on the air through which it is flying. It is therefore more efficient at higher altitudes, where the atmosphere is thinner.

Early postwar commercial aircraft (e.g. the Vickers Viscount) used a **turboprop** engine, in which a propeller is driven by the turbine shaft. For greater speed and fuel economy the turboprop has been replaced by the **turbojet**, in which the turbine drives one or more compressors but most of the energy of combustion is used to provide **jet propulsion**. For bursts of extra energy, especially in military aircraft, extra fuel can be burnt in the exhaust gases (called **reheat** or **afterburning**). In the **turbofan** a large fan, driven by an inner shaft from the turbine, precedes the usual compressor and compresses the cool air, which bypasses the combustion chambers and mixes directly with the exhaust jet, giving greater fuel economy and quietness. These are used on modern subsonic jumbo jets.

At over twice the speed of sound (Mach 2), the forward pressure of the air is sufficient for the compressor, and therefore the turbine, to be dispensed with. The resulting engine is called a **ramjet** or, colloquially, a flying drainpipe. The main drawback of the ramjet is that it needs a rocket-assisted take-off. Turboshaft engines, similar to the turboprop, are also in use for driving helicopters, hovercraft, ships, trains, turbogenerators in power stations, and (experimentally) cars. In these the turbine shaft is used to provide all the working power. ▷See also rockets.

● **jet stream** ► A narrow band of westerly high velocity wind, in excess of 95 mph (150 kph), that encircles the earth in the upper troposphere. It can reduce the flying time across the Atlantic Ocean from west to east and retard flights in the opposite direction.

● **Jevons, William Stanley** ► (1835–1882) British economist, logician, and statistician. Jevons' reputation was established by his writings on contemporary economic questions. His *Theory of Political Economy* (1871) sets out his theory of utility.

● **Jewel, John** ► (1522–71) Anglican churchman. From 1547 a leading Protestant reformer, Jewel fled to the Continent during Queen Mary's reign. As Bishop of Salisbury (1560–71) he defended Anglicanism against both Puritans and Catholics in *Apologia Ecclesiae Anglicanae* (1562).

● **Jewish autonomous region** ► (*or* Birobidzhan) An autonomous region (*oblast*) in SE Russia, on the Chinese border. Formed in 1934 for Soviet Jews, the harsh climate discouraged settlers, and Russians and Ukrainians outnumber Jews. Industries include metallurgy, timber, and engineering. Area: 36 000 sq km (13 895 sq mi). Population (1995 est): 216 000. Capital: Birobidzhan.

● **Jews** ► A predominantly Semitic people, claiming descent from the ancient Israelites. The Jews spread or were dispersed in antiquity from the land of Israel, and there are now communities in most countries (*see* Ashkenazim; diaspora; Sephardim). Although they do not share distinctive racial characteristics, they have a strong sense of cultural identity (*see* Bene Israel; Falashas). Their religion is ▷Judaism (but in recent times some Jews have professed an attachment to the people while rejecting the religion). Under Persian, Greek, and Roman rule the Jews evolved a system of internal self-government and communal administration that enabled them to survive as minority communities through many centuries of Christian and Muslim domination, despite adverse discrimination and frequent persecution (*see* antisemitism). Since the late 18th century they have gradually achieved equal rights as citizens in most countries, although the slaughter of six million Jews (*see* holocaust) by the Germans is one of the ugliest episodes in history. It did, however, provide the claim for a national home for the Jews with unanswerable force (*see* Israel, State of; Zionism). In the 1990s, there were estimated to be 17.6 million Jews, 6.9 million of whom are US citizens, 3.5 million Israeli, and 1.4 million European (of whom 110 000 are British). It is said that Jews wield an influence in the arts, politics, and commerce disproportionate to their numbers.

● **Jew's harp** ► A musical instrument consisting of a metal tongue set in a small frame, held between the teeth. The tongue vibrates when plucked; different notes are produced by varying the size of the mouth cavity.

● **Jezreel, Valley of** ▷See Esdraelon, Plain of.

● **Jhansi** ► 25 27N 78 34E A city in India, in Uttar Pradesh. The heroism of the Rani (female ruler) of Jhansi during the Indian Mutiny has become legendary. It is primarily an agricultural trading centre. Population (1991): 301 304.

● **Jhelum** ► 32 58N 73 45E A town in Pakistan, on the River Jhelum. It has a thriving timber industry and there are several oilfields nearby. Population (latest est): 106 000.

● **Jhelum, River** ► A river in India and Pakistan, the most westerly of the five rivers of the Punjab. Rising in Kashmir it flows SSW to join the River Chenab. It is a source of irrigation and hydroelectric power. Length: about 720 km (450 mi).

● **Jiang Jing Guo** ▷See Chiang Kai-shek.

● **Jiang Qing** ► (*or* Chiang Ch'ing; c. 1913–91) Chinese communist politician; the third wife (from 1939) of Mao Tse-tung. A former actress, she attempted with three associates (Zhang Chunjao, Wang Hungwen, and Yao Wenyuan) to seize power on Mao's death. Known as the **Gang of Four**, they were arrested within a month. Following a

public trial she remained in prison until 1984, when she was released for medical treatment. She committed suicide.

● **Jiangsu** ► (Chiang-su *or* Kiangsu) A low-lying province in E China on the Yangtze delta. It is the most densely populated area and one of the richest agricultural regions. It was the centre of European trade after 1842 and was badly damaged by Japanese occupation (1937–45). It produces wheat, rice, tea, cotton, salt, fish, and silk. A severe earthquake in 1920 killed 180 000 people. Area: 102 200 sq km (39 860 sq mi). Population (1995 est): 70 210 000. Capital: Nanjing.

● **Jiangxi** ► (Chiang-hsi *or* Kiangsi) A mountainous province in SE China. It was a centre of Confucianism (960–1279), and in the 20th century the Communist-Nationalist conflict originated here (*see* Jiangxi Soviet). One of China's main rice-producing areas, it has mineral resources, including coal and uranium, and is known for its porcelain. Area: 164 800 sq km (64 300 sq mi). Population (1995 est): 40 150 000. Capital: Nanchang.

● **Jiangxi Soviet** ► (*or* Kiangsi Soviet; 1931–34) A communist republic proclaimed in the Chinese province of Jiangxi. It was a revolutionary base from which Mao Tse-tung and ▷Zhu De were able to build up their forces in the civil war with the ▷Guomindang under Chiang Kai-shek. They withstood four encirclement campaigns but in 1933 Chiang Kai-shek launched a massive fifth campaign in response to which Mao set off on the ▷Long March.

● **Jiang Zemin** ► (1926–) Chinese communist statesman. A member of the Communist Party of China (CPC) from 1946, he was elected its general secretary in 1989 and became president of China in 1993. Following the death of ▷Deng Xiao Ping in 1997, he emerged as China's paramount leader.

● **Jiddah** ► (*or* Jedda) 21 30N 39 10E A town in Saudi Arabia, on the Red Sea coast. It is a modern industrial city and the chief port for Muslim pilgrims to Mecca. The King Abdulaziz University was opened here in 1967. Population (1992 est): 1 500 000.

● **jihad** ▷See Islam.

● **Jilin** ► (Chi-lin *or* Kirin) A province in NE China, in Manchuria. The E is mountainous, while the W lies on the fertile Manchurian plain. Soya beans, cereals, timber, and minerals are produced. Area: 187 000 sq km (72 930 sq mi). Population (1995 est): 25 740 000. Capital: Changchun.

● **Jilong** ► (Chi-lung *or* Keelung) 25 10N 121 43E A port and naval base in N Taiwan. It was developed under Japanese occupation (1895–1945). Industries include fishing, chemicals, coal- and gold-mining, and shipbuilding. Population (1996 est): 370 049.

● **Jim Crow Laws** ► Legislation passed by southern US states in the late 19th century to enforce racial segregation; the name derives from that of a Black character in a popular song. Legislation in Oklahoma, for example, provided separate telephone booths for Blacks and Whites. Most of the laws were invalidated by the civil-rights legislation of the 1950s and 1960s.

● **Jiménez, Juan Ramón** ► (1881–1958) Spanish poet. His early works, such as *Sonetos espirituales* (1915), were influenced by French symbolism but he later developed an abstract style in such works as *La estación total* (1946). He also wrote *Platero y yo* (1914), about a boy and his donkey.

● **Jimmu** ► The legendary first ruler of Japan. According to the oldest Japanese writings, Jimmu was descended from the sun-goddess Amaterasu and embarked upon the unification of Japan in 660 BC. This legend was intended to glorify the imperial dynasty and anticipated the dynasty's actual establishment by about seven centuries.

● **jimsonweed** ▷See thorn apple.

● **Jinan** ► (Chi-nan *or* Tsinan) 36 41N 117 00E A historic city in E China, the capital of Shandong province. An ancient cultural centre, it now has textile, chemical, and machine-building industries. Population (1991 est): 2 320 000.

● **jinja** ► A Shinto shrine dedicated to a deity or nature spirit, situated in a place of exceptional natural beauty. It consists of three parts: the *haiden*, a hall where the laity pray and worship; the *heiden*, where religious ceremonies are performed; and the *honden*, the main inner sanctuary usually accessible only to priests. Before the jinja is a sacred gateway. The architecture is simple and traditional. Larger jinja may incorporate other elements, such as a dance platform, an ablution basin, and animal statues.

● **Jinja** ► 0 27N 33 14E The second largest city in Uganda, on the N shore of Lake Victoria. Founded by the British (1901), it has developed as an industrial centre since the opening of the Owen Falls Dam (1954) with steel rolling, copper smelting, and other industries. Population (1991): 61 000.

● **Jinjiang** ► (Chen-chiang *or* Chinkiang) 32 15N 119 20E A port in E China, in Jiangsu province on the Yangtze River and the ▷Grand Canal. It is a trading centre with food-processing and other industries. Population (1990): 368 316.

● **Jinmen** ► (Chin-men *or* Quemoy) 24 26N 118 20E A Taiwanese island in Taiwan Strait. It is near the Chinese mainland and was bombed from there in 1958, an event that caused an international incident. Area: 130 sq km (50 sq mi). Population (latest est): 57 847.

● **Jinnah, Mohammed Ali** ► (1876–1948) Indian statesman, who was largely responsible for the creation of Pakistan. Born in Karachi, he studied law in England and embarked on an extremely successful legal practice in India before becoming involved in politics. As a member of both the ▷Muslim League and the ▷Indian National Congress he championed Hindu-Muslim unity until 1930, when he resigned from the Congress in opposition to Gandhi's policies. He was president of the League in 1916 and 1920 and from 1934, and came to advocate the establishment of a separate state for Indian Muslims. This was achieved with the creation in 1947 of Pakistan, of which he was the first governor general.

● **Jiulong** ► (*or* Kowloon) 22 20N 114 15E A port in SE China, on the Jiulong peninsula, opposite Hong Kong island and from 1860 to 1997 part of the British colony. Population (1991): 2 030 683.

● **Joachim, Joseph** ► (1831–1907) Hungarian violinist and composer. A child prodigy, he studied at the Leipzig conservatoire. His interpretations of Bach and Beethoven and his musical perfectionism influenced many composers: Brahms dedicated his violin concerto to him.

● **Joachim of Fiore** ► (c. 1132–1202 AD) Italian mystic and abbot. He is best known for his philosophy of history, which divided history into three periods: The Age of the Father (Old Testament), The Age of the Son (New Testament and 42 subsequent generations), and The Age of the Spirit, in which all humanity would be converted. Joachim's monastic order, which he founded at San Giovanni in Fiore, was dissolved in 1505.

● **Joan, Pope** ► A legendary female pope first referred to in the 13th century. She is said to have been elected pope in male disguise about 1100 or earlier, to have ruled for more than two years, and then to have given birth to a child while in a procession, dying immediately thereafter. The legend may be based on a Roman folktale.

● **Joanna the Mad** ► (1479–1555) Queen of Castile (1504–16). The death of her husband, Philip the Handsome of Castile in 1506, drove her mad. Her father Ferdinand (V and II) of Aragon ruled for her until his death, when she was succeeded by her son, later Emperor ▷Charles V. He kept Joanna imprisoned in the castle of Tordesillas, where she died.

● **Joan of Arc, St** ► (French name: Jeanne d'Arc; c. 1412–31) French patriot, known as the Maid of Orléans, whose courageous military and moral leadership against the English invaders led to a reversal of French fortunes in the ▷Hundred Years' War. Of peasant origin, she claimed to have been told by Saints Michael, Catherine, and Margaret that it was her divine mission to expel the English from France and enable Charles VII to be crowned. She persuaded Charles to allow her to lead an army to relieve the besieged city of Orléans. Her success resulted in Charles' coronation at Rheims (July, 1429). Other victories followed but she failed to recapture Paris and was subsequently seized by the Burgundians, who sold her to their English allies. They

Joan of Arc ► A contemporary portrait on parchment (c. 1420).

tried her and burned her as a heretic. She was canonized in 1920. Feast day: 30 May.

● **João Pessoa** ► (name until 1930: Paraíba) 7 06S 34 53W A port in E Brazil, the capital of Paraíba state near the mouth of the Rio Paraíba do Norte. The chief exports are cotton, sugar, and coffee. Population (1991): 666 279.

● **Job** ► An Old Testament figure. **The Book of Job**, probably written between the 5th and 2nd centuries BC, develops the theme of the suffering of the innocent. Job experiences the loss of his family, property, and health, but adamantly denies his friends' suggestions that sin is the cause of his misfortunes, for he knows himself to be innocent. No final explanation of the dilemma is reached, but Job is brought to see that man cannot understand the ways of God. Humbled by this knowledge, he prays for his friends and is ultimately granted greater prosperity, etc., than he formerly had.

● **Jocasta** ▷*See* Oedipus.

● **Jochho** ► (d. 1057) Leading Japanese sculptor of the Fujiwara period (*see* Fujiwara style). His serene and refined statues of the Buddha for the Fujiwara family temple and his joined-wood technique were influential.

● **Jochum, Eugen** ► (1902–87) German conductor. He studied piano and organ at the Augsburg conservatoire and held appointments in Berlin, Hamburg, Munich, and Amsterdam (with the Concertgebouw Orchestra). He was made conductor laureate of the London Symphony Orchestra in 1975.

● **Jodhpur** ► 26 18N 73 08E A city in India, in Rajasthan. Formerly the capital of the princely state of Jodhpur, the city is noted for its handicraft industries, such as ivory carvings and lacquerware. It also gave its name to a style of riding breeches that were introduced into Britain during the 19th century. Jodhpur University was established in 1962. Population (1991): 648 621.

● **Jodl, Alfred** ► (1890–1946) German general, who was responsible for much of German strategy in World War II. His diaries revealed the part he had played in many of the crimes committed by Hitler. He was tried at Nuremberg and executed as a war criminal.

• **Jodrell Bank ►** The site, at Macclesfield, Cheshire (UK), of the Nuffield Radio Astronomy Laboratories of Manchester University. The principal instrument is the 76.2 m (250 ft) fully steerable radio-telescope dish.

• **Joel ►** An Old Testament prophet of Judah. **The Book of Judah** records his prediction of a plague of locusts and other disasters as punishment for Judah's sins, followed eventually by a restoration of God's favour and the nation's final triumph over its enemies.

• **Joffre, Joseph Jacques Césaire ►** (1852–1931) French marshal; commander in chief of the French armies (1915–16) in World War I. As chief of staff he won the victory of the Marne (1914) but the French failure at Verdun (1916) led to his resignation.

• **Jogjakarta ►** (or Yogyakarta) 7 48S 110 24E A city in Indonesia, in S Java. It was the capital of the 1945–49 Indonesian Republic. A cultural centre, its university was established in 1949. It is rich in Buddhist monuments, notably the temple of Borobudur. Population (1990): 412 392.

• **Johannesburg ►** 26 10S 28 02E The largest city in South Africa, on the Witwatersrand. It was founded in 1886 following the discovery of gold in the area and developed rapidly as the centre of the gold-mining industry. During the second Boer War it was taken by the British (1900). Today it is a major industrial, commercial, and banking centre containing the South African Stock Exchange (1887). Its industries include engineering, chemicals, diamond cutting, and textiles. Linked to the city is the complex of towns known as ▷Soweto, inhabited by Black Africans. Johannesburg has a number of cultural and educational institutions, notably the University of Witwatersrand (1922) and the Rand Afrikaans University (1966). The fine Johannesburg Art Gallery (1911) was designed by Sir Edwin Lutyens. Population (1991): 1 712 507.

• **Johannsen, Wilhelm Ludvig ►** (1857–1927) Danish geneticist, whose work with plants demonstrated that the physical appearance (phenotype) of individuals was the result of the interaction of their hereditary constitution (genotype) and their environment. He also provided supporting evidence for the mutation theory of ▷de Vries. Johannsen coined the word *gene* for a unit of heredity as well as the terms phenotype and genotype.

• **John ►** (1167–1216) King of England (1199–1216), nicknamed John Lackland; the youngest son of Henry II, he succeeded his brother Richard I. His reign saw the renewal of war with ▷Philip II Augustus of France, to whom he had lost several continental possessions, including Normandy, by 1205. Struggles with Pope Innocent III over John's objection to the election of ▷Langton as Archbishop of Canterbury led to the imposition of an interdict over England (1208) and the king's excommunication (1212). He came into conflict with his barons and was forced to grant the ▷Magna Carta at Runnymede. His subsequent repudiation of the Charter led to the first ▷Barons' War (1215–17), during which John became ill and died.

• **John I ►** (1357–1433) King of Portugal (1385–1433). The head of the military order of Aviz, John led the nationalist opposition to the succession to the Portuguese throne of John I of Castile (1358–90; reigned 1379–90). After securing the throne, John soundly defeated the Castilians at Aljubarrota. In 1415 he captured Ceuta, the first possession of any European nation in Africa.

• **John I Tzimisces ►** (925–76 AD) Byzantine emperor (969–76). He increased the power of the Byzantine empire by subjecting the Bulgarians and defeating the Russians (971) and by conquering cities in Syria (974–75).

• **John (II) the Good ►** (1319–64) King of France (1350–64), who was taken prisoner by the English at the battle of Poitiers (1356) during the ▷Hundred Years' War. He remained in captivity in London, where he was forced to sign the unfavourable Treaty of ▷Brétigny, until 1360. Released in 1360, he was unable to raise the ransom demanded by the English and was forced to return to London, where he died.

• **John (II) the Perfect ►** (1455–95) King of Portugal (1481–95). John encouraged Portugal's overseas expansion, supporting Bartolomeu Dias, and concluded the Treaty of Tordesillas with Spain (1494), which demarcated their respective fields of action in the New World. His home policies reduced the power of the aristocracy.

• **John II Casimir ►** (1609–72) King of Poland (1648–68), whose reign is known as the Deluge. John faced a revolt of the Ukrainian Cossacks, on whose behalf Russia invaded Poland in 1654, and in 1667 he was forced to cede the eastern Ukraine. Sweden's invasion of Poland in 1655 resulted in the loss of N Livonia (1660). John Casimir abdicated and died in France.

• **John III ►** (1502–57) King of Portugal (1521–57). John's reign saw the flourishing of culture in the works of Camoens and others. Spending his country's wealth on his lavish court (rather than economic development), he was responsible for the start of Portugal's decline.

• **John III Sobieski ►** (1624–96) King of Poland (1674–96), famous as an adversary of the Turks. A brilliant military commander, John Sobieski was elected king after defeating the Turks at Khotin (1663). In 1683 he saved Vienna from the Turks in the great victory at Kahlenberg. His subsequent failure to conquer Moldavia and Wallachia led to a loss of personal prestige, which aggravated the domestic unrest that was a feature of his reign.

• **John (IV) the Fortunate ►** (1604–56) King of Portugal (1640–56). As Duke of ▷Bragança, John led a revolt in 1640 against Spanish rule that brought him to the throne. He revived the Cortes and formed foreign alliances against Spain but lost most of Portugal's Asian possessions to the Dutch.

• **John VI ►** (?1769–1826) King of Portugal (1816–26), having been prince regent from 1799. John lived in Brazil during Napoleon's occupation of Portugal. Returning to Portugal in 1821, he faced a revolt of the reactionaries against constitutional monarchy, which was only defeated with French and British help. In 1825 John recognized the independence of Brazil, which was ruled by his son ▷Pedro I.

• **John XXII ►** (Jacques d'Euse; c. 1249-1334) Pope (1316-34) during the ▷Avignon papacy, a man of great administrative and financial ability. In 1317 he dissolved the austere group of the ▷Franciscans known as Spirituals, whose cause was taken up by Emperor Louis IV. Aided by the philosophers Marsilius of Padua and William of Ockham, Louis denounced papal supremacy and in 1328 set up an antipope in Rome. John's last years were dominated by theological disputes.

• **John XXIII ►** (Baldassare Cossa; d. 1419) Antipope (1410-15), one of three claimants to the papacy during the ▷Great Schism. In 1414 John summoned the Council of ▷Constance to end the Schism but fled when it demanded his resignation. He was arrested, imprisoned, and deposed.

• **John XXIII ►** (Angelo Roncalli; 1881-1963) Pope (1958-1963). A papal diplomat and then patriarch of Venice (1953-58) before his election at the age of 77, John was the most popular and innovative pope of modern times. In 1962 he summoned the second ▷Vatican Council, which marked the climax of John's pursuit of Church reforms and Christian unity. His best-known encyclical, *Pacem in Terris* (*Peace on Earth*; 1963), advocated reconciliation between the Western democracies and eastern communist countries. His diary was published as *The Journal of a Soul* (1965). He was beatified in 2000.

• **John, Augustus (Edwin) ►** (1878-1961) British painter. He studied at the Slade School, London (1894-98), displaying a precocious drawing talent, and exhibited at the ▷New English Art Club from 1903. A flamboyantly unconventional character, he travelled widely, often in Gipsy style. His strongly characterized portraits of contemporaries, such as James Joyce and T. E. Lawrence, are indebted to tradition. His sister **Gwen John** (1876-1939) was also a painter. Noted for her restrained portraits of women, she lived in France from 1904 and became a Roman Catholic convert in 1913.

• **John, Barry ►** (1945-) Welsh Rugby Union footballer, who played for Llanelli, Cardiff, Wales, and the British Lions. A brilliant fly half, he won 25 international caps.

● **John, Sir Elton** ▶ (Reginald Kenneth Dwight; 1947–) British rock pianist and singer, who became popular in Britain and the USA with such songs as "Rocket Man" and "Daniel" in the 1970s. In 1997 a reworked version of his hit song "Candle in the Wind" was released as a charity tribute to ▷Diana, Princess of Wales, and became the world's biggest-ever selling single. He was knighted in 1998.

● **John, St** ▶ In the New Testament, one of the 12 Apostles, son of Zebedee and brother of James. He was present at a number of events in the life of Jesus as recounted in the Gospels and is also thought to be the anonymous disciple "whom Jesus loved" present at the crucifixion. Tradition states that he escaped martyrdom and died at Ephesus. Feast day: 27 Dec.

The Gospel according to St John is the fourth book of the New Testament traditionally ascribed to St John and probably written in the late 1st century AD. It is markedly different in a number of details from the other three synoptic Gospels and was specifically written with the intention of inspiring faith in Jesus as the Son of God. It begins with a prologue portraying Jesus as the *Logos* or Word, a theme familiar to current Greek philosophy. Having spoken of his incarnation, it concentrates on his public ministry and especially on claims made in a number of discourses and conversations not recorded in the other Gospels. Over half the book is devoted to the events and teaching occurring during the last week before the crucifixion.

The Epistles of John are three New Testament books traditionally ascribed to St John and written towards the end of the 1st century. The first is addressed to the Churches at large and defines the distinctive marks of a true Christian. The others are brief personal letters. The second warns an unnamed lady against false teachers, while the third commends and encourages a certain Gaius. Tradition also ascribes the Book of ▷Revelation to John.

● **John Birch Society** ▶ A right-wing group in the USA, founded in 1958. John Birch was a US Army intelligence officer who was killed by the Communist Chinese in August, 1945, and is represented by the Society as the first hero of the ▷Cold War.

● **John Bull** ▶ The personification of England or the English national character. The character first appeared in *The History of John Bull* (1712) by John Arbuthnot, and was popularized in 18th- and 19th-century political cartoons. He is usually portrayed as a stocky countryman noted for his honesty and stubbornness.

● **John Dory** ▶ (*or* dory) A fish of the family *Zeidae*, found worldwide in moderately deep marine waters. It has a round narrow body with deep sides, each having a black spot surrounded by a yellow ring, and spiny-rayed fins extended into filaments. *Zeus faber*, up to 90 cm long, is a food fish of the Atlantic and Mediterranean. Order: *Zeiformes*.

● **John Frederick (I) the Magnanimous** ▶ (1503–54) Elector of Saxony (1532–47), who led the Protestant Schmalkaldic League against Emperor ▷Charles V. He was imprisoned (1547–52) after the League's defeat at the battle of Mühlberg and was deprived of his territory and electoral rank.

● **John of Austria, Don** ▶ (1545–78) Spanish soldier. The illegitimate son of Emperor ▷Charles V, his half-brother ▷Philip II entrusted him with major military commands. He suppressed the revolt of the Moriscos (Moors converted to Christianity) in S Spain in 1569 and in 1571 he commanded the combined fleets of Spain, Venice, and the papacy against the Turks, winning a great victory at ▷Lepanto. In 1573 he conquered Tunis and in 1576 became governor general of the Netherlands, where he died.

● **John of Damascus, St** ▶ (c. 675–c. 749 AD) Greek Orthodox theologian and Doctor of the Church, born in Damascus. While a tax official at the caliph's court at Damascus he wrote several treatises defending the use of images in church worship against ▷iconoclasm. In about 716 he retired to a monastery near Jerusalem, where he was ordained. There he wrote his most influential work, *The Fount of Wisdom*, which deals with philosophy, heresies, and the Orthodox faith. Feast day: 4 Dec.

● **John of Gaunt** ▶ (1340–99) The fourth son of Edward III of England, born at Ghent; Duke of Lancaster from 1362. After a distinguished career in the ▷Hundred Years' War he assumed an increasingly important role in domestic government during the se-

nility of Edward and the minority of Richard II. Never popular, John, who supported ▷Wycliffe and the ▷Lollards, was opposed by a clerical group led by ▷William of Wykeham. From 1386 to 1389 he attempted without success to realize his claim, through his second wife Constance, the daughter of ▷Pedro the Cruel, to Castile. In 1396 he married his mistress Catherine Swynford, and in 1397 their descendants were legitimized but excluded from the royal succession. They included Margaret ▷Beaufort, the mother of Henry VII.

● **John of Leiden** ▶ (Jan Beuckelszoon; 1509–36) Dutch ▷Anabaptist leader. In 1534 he pronounced himself King of Münster, an Anabaptist stronghold that had expelled its civil and religious authorities. During his brief rule he legalized polygamy and made property communal. The town was recaptured in 1535 and he was executed.

● **John of Luxembourg** ▶ (1296–1346) Count of Luxembourg (1310–46) and, by marriage, King of Bohemia (1311–46); son of Emperor Henry VII. His almost constant warfare and consequent levy of high taxes made him unpopular in Bohemia. He died at Crécy fighting for the French.

● **John of Nepomuk, St** ▶ (c. 1340–93) The patron saint of Bohemia. As vicar general of Prague, he opposed Wenceslas IV's plans to create a second bishopric in the city. At the king's instigation he was tortured and drowned. Feast day: 16 May.

● **John of Salisbury** ▶ (c. 1115–80) English churchman, philosopher, and a leading classical scholar of his age. After studying in Paris under ▷Abelard he became secretary to Thomas Becket and later Bishop of Chartres (1176). His principal works are the *Polycraticus*, a treatise criticizing contemporary political and courtly life, and the *Metalogicon*, a defence of the study of grammar, logic, and rhetoric.

● **John of the Cross, St** ▶ (Juan de Yepes y Alvarez; 1542–91) Spanish mystic, poet, and since 1926 Doctor of the Church. With St ▷Teresa he founded the Discalced ▷Carmelites, a reformed branch of the Carmelite order. His poems, which include *Cántico espiritual* and *Noche oscura del alma*, are regarded as the finest examples of Spanish mystical literature. Feast day: 14 Dec.

● **John O'Groats** ▶ 58 39N 3 02W A village at the NE tip of Scotland, site of the house of John de Groot, a 16th-century Dutch immigrant. John O'Groats is 970 km (603 mi) in a straight line from Land's End, Cornwall.

● **John Paul II** ▶ (Karol Wojtyła; 1920–) Pope (1978–). A Pole, he is the first non-Italian pope since 1522 and the longest-serving pontiff of the 20th century. He taught at Lublin and Kraków universities before becoming Archbishop of Kraków (1964). His visits to Poland (1979 and 1987) made him the first pope to visit a communist state and have been credited with hastening the demise of communism in that country and hence throughout the Eastern bloc. In 1981 he sur-

John Paul II ▶ The pope during a mass in St Peter's Basilica on 1 January, 1999, celebrating the 32nd annual day of world peace.

vived an assassination attempt. His condemnation of homosexuality and his uncompromising position on contraception, abortion, *in vitro* fertilization, and a male celibate clergy have aroused considerable criticism both within the Church and outside it. He succeeded **John Paul I** (Albino Luciani; 1912–78; reigned August–September, 1978), who took the names of his two predecessors, John XXIII and Paul VI.

● **Johns, Jasper** ▶ (1930–) US artist, a major influence on ▷pop art. He worked as a commercial artist before establishing his reputation at a one-man show in New York (1958) with paintings of targets and flags. The collages and constructions that followed made a similar use of everyday objects, for example the bronze *Beer Cans* (1960).

● **Johnson, Amy** ▶ (1903–41) British aviator. She established several long-distance records with her solo flights to Australia (in the *Jason*, 1930), to Tokyo (1932), and to the Cape of Good Hope and back (1936). In 1932 she married Jim Mollison (1905–59), another pilot, with whom she flew the Atlantic in 1936. During World War II she was killed when her plane crashed into the sea off the Kent coast, possibly as a result of friendly fire from anti-aircraft guns.

● **Johnson, Andrew** ▶ (1808–75) US statesman; Democratic president (1865–69), who saw himself as a spokesman for ordinary people. He became president after Lincoln's assassination. Despite his veto, the largely Republican Congress passed ▷Reconstruction measures after the Civil War ensuring Republican domination of the South. Impeachment proceedings were begun when Johnson defied the Tenure of Office Act limiting presidential power but he was acquitted.

● **Johnson, Cornelius** ▶ (Janssen van Ceulen; 1593–1661) English portrait painter, born in London of Dutch parents. Until Van Dyck's arrival (1632), Johnson was the leading portraitist at the courts of James I and Charles I, where he specialized in oval-shaped bust portraits. He settled in Holland in 1643.

● **Johnson, Lyndon Baines** ▶ (1908–73) US statesman; Democratic president (1963–69). A Texan, he succeeded to the presidency after Kennedy's assassination. His Great Society programme initiated broad social reform including a tax-reduction Act to stimulate economic growth and various civil-rights Acts. He became unpopular for increasing US military involvement in the ▷Vietnam War.

● **Johnson, Michael (Duane)** ▶ (1967–) US sprinter. Having won gold medals in both the 200 m and the 400 m at the 1995 World Championships, he repeated this double at the 1996 Olympics, while also setting a new world record (19.32 secs) for the shorter distance.

● **Johnson, Samuel** ▶ (1709–84) British poet, critic, and lexicographer. He left Oxford without a degree, married a wealthy widow in 1735, and went to London in 1737. Early publications include a biography of his friend Richard ▷Savage (1744) and a long poem, *The Vanity of Human Wishes* (1749). From 1750 to 1752 he produced the weekly *Rambler* almost single handed. His *Dictionary* appeared in 1755 after nine years' work and was well received, but he still relied on hackwork for money, writing *Rasselas* (1759), a moral fable, in a week to pay for his mother's funeral. His last major works were an edition of Shakespeare (1765) and his *Lives of the Poets* (1779–81). From the early 1760s he enjoyed the security of a pension and the friendship of Reynolds, Goldsmith, Burke, and other men of letters, including his biographer ▷Boswell, who became a close friend in the 1770s. His last years were clouded by the deaths of friends and his estrangement from his companion, Mrs Thrale (*see* Piozzi, Hester Lynch).

● **Johnson, Virginia Eshelman** ▷*See* Masters, William Howell.

● **John the Baptist, St** ▶ In the New Testament, the son of a priest, Zacharias, and Elizabeth, a relative of the Virgin ▷Mary; known as the "Forerunner of Christ." Born in his mother's old age, he was six months older than Jesus. After living in the desert, he began about 27 AD preaching on the banks of the River Jordan, urging repentance and baptism because of the imminent approach of the Kingdom of God. He baptized Christ, recognizing him as the Messiah. He was beheaded by ▷Herod Antipas, at the request of ▷Salome, for denouncing his second marriage to Herodias as illicit. Feast days: 24 June (birth); 29 Aug (beheading).

● **John the Fearless** ▶ (1371–1419) Duke of Burgundy (1404–19), a great military leader who earned his nickname on a Crusade in 1396. He competed with the Armagnacs for control over the mad Charles the Well-Beloved of France and arranged the assassination (1407) of their leader (and his cousin) Louis, Duc d'Orléans. His own death, however, was at the hands of an Armagnac assassin.

● **Johor** ▶ A swampy forested state in S Peninsular Malaysia. It is economically linked to Singapore, depending on it for trading facilities and supplying it with water. Chief products are rubber, copra, pineapples, palm oil, tin, and bauxite. Area: 18 958 sq km (7330 sq mi). Population (1993 est): 2 106 700. Capital: Johor Baharu.

● **Johor Baharu** ▶ 1 29N 103 44E A city in S Peninsular Malaysia, the capital of Johor state. A trading centre with a notable sultan's residence, it is linked to Singapore by a causeway across the Johor Strait. Population (1991): 328 646.

● **joint** ▶ The point at which two or more bones are connected to each other. There are three broad categories. Immovable joints allow no movement of the bones; examples are the sutures between the bones of the skull. Slightly movable joints allow a certain degree of movement, as in the joints connecting the individual bones of the spine. Freely movable joints (diarthrodial, or synovial, joints) permit a variety of movements. They include the hinge joints at the knee and elbow, the ball-and-socket joints at the hip and shoulder, and the gliding joints at the wrist and ankle. The bone ends at movable joints are covered by ▷cartilage and enveloped in a tough capsule thickened in parts to form ▷ligaments. The inside of the capsule is lined by synovial membrane, which secretes a lubricating fluid. ▷*See* Plate II.

● **Joinville, Jean de** ▶ (c. 1224–1317) French chronicler. His record of the seventh Crusade (1248–54), on which he accompanied Louis IX and shared his captivity, constitutes the main part of his *Histoire de Saint Louis*. His work is noted for its vivid descriptions and its human sympathy.

● **Joliot-Curie, Frédéric and Irène** ▷*See* Curie, Marie.

● **Jolliet, Louis** ▷*See* Marquette, Jacques.

● **Jolson, Al** ▶ (Asa Yoelson; 1886–1950) US popular singer and songwriter, born in Russia. He sang in circuses, vaudevilles, and minstrel shows, becoming famous for his blacked-up face and the song "Mammy." In 1927 he appeared in the first full-length sound film *The Jazz Singer* and subsequently made the films *The Singing Fool* (1928) and *Swanee River* (1940).

● **Jonah** ▶ (8th century BC) An Old Testament figure. **The Book of Jonah** was probably written after the ▷Babylonian exile of the Jews. It relates how Jonah was commanded by God to preach to the Gentiles in Nineveh, the Assyrian capital. Attempting to escape this task, he fled by ship, but was thrown overboard, swallowed by a great fish (probably a whale), and after three days was safely cast ashore. He repented of his disobedience and fulfilled God's commandment. The purpose of the story was to emphasize that God was the God of the Gentiles as well as the Jews.

● **Jones, (Alfred) Ernest** ▶ (1879–1958) British psychoanalyst. A follower and friend of Sigmund ▷Freud, Jones helped to establish psychoanalysis in Britain and North America. He wrote many papers, especially on the psychology of literary works, including a famous analysis of *Hamlet* in *Hamlet and Oedipus* (1949). In 1920 he founded the *International Journal of Psychoanalysis* and he also wrote *Sigmund Freud: Life and Work* (3 vols, 1953–56).

● **Jones, Bobby** ▶ (Robert Tyre J.; 1902–71) US amateur golfer. Between 1923 and 1930 he won four US and three British Open championships, five US amateur championships, and one British amateur championship. In 1930 he won all four championships, after which he retired.

● **Jones, Daniel** ▶ (1881–1967) British phonetician. His most influential work was the description (or prescription) of ▷Received Pronunciation—the socially prestigious dialect of English spoken especially in public schools and the BBC (*see also* accent). It is set out in his *English Pronouncing Dictionary* (1917) frequently revised since its first publication. He also established a system of cardinal vowels, by reference to which individual variations may be described.

● **Jones, Daniel** ► (1912–93) Welsh composer. His large output includes *Dance Fantasy* (1976), 13 symphonies, chamber music, and a sonata for three kettledrums (1947).

● **Jones, David** ► (1895–1974) Anglo-Welsh writer and artist. His writings, which combine prose and free verse, are dense with allusions to Anglo-Welsh history and folklore, Arthurian legend, and Christian symbolism. They include *In Parenthesis* (1937), based on his experience of World War I, and *The Anathemata* (1952).

● **Jones, Henry** ▷*See* Cavendish.

● **Jones, Inigo** ► (1573–1652) English classical architect. He was closely associated with the courts of James I and Charles I, for whom he designed masques and many major buildings. One of the first Englishmen to study architecture in Italy and to understand the rules of classicism, Jones was particularly influenced by ▷Palladio in his two best-known buildings, the Queen's House, Greenwich (1616–35), and the Banqueting Hall, Whitehall (1619–22). His career effectively ended with the outbreak of the Civil War in 1642. His style became strongly influential in England in the 18th century, when it was adopted by Lord ▷Burlington and others.

● **Jones, John Paul** ► (1747–92) American naval commander, born in Scotland. He went to America after working in mercantile shipping and on the outbreak of the American Revolution was commissioned into the American navy (1775). Jones captured and sank a number of ships in American and British waters (1776, 1778). In 1779 in the *Bon Homme Richard* Jones defeated the British frigate *Serapis* in a desperate battle lasting almost four hours. He subsequently became a rear admiral in the Russian navy, fighting in the Black Sea against the Turks (1788–89).

● **Jones, LeRoi** ► (1934–) US dramatist and poet. In *Dutchman* (1964) and other works he deals with social relationships between Black and White people in the USA. As a leading editor and publisher he has encouraged Black writers. He changed his name to Imamu Baraka to emphasize his Black heritage and culture.

● **Jones, Marion** ► (1975–) US athlete. In 1998 she was ranked world no. 1 in the 100 m, the 200 m, and the long jump. At the 2000 Sydney Olympics she won gold medals in the 100 m, the 200 m, and the 1600-m relay, and bronzes in the long jump and the 400-m relay—a total unmatched by any other female athlete at a single Olympics.

● **Jones, Sir William** ► (1746–94) British jurist, linguist, and orientalist. He was a supreme-court judge in Calcutta (1783–94) and published a Persian grammar (1771). He is noted for his observation in 1786 that the resemblances between Sanskrit, Latin, Greek, Gothic, Persian, and Celtic languages might be accounted for by their common descent from an earlier language, now lost. This insight inaugurated the study of ▷Indo-European languages.

● **Jongkind, Johan Barthold** ► (1819–91) Dutch landscape painter and etcher, who settled in Paris in 1846. He was influenced by the Dutch landscape tradition but the atmospheric effects he achieved in his seascapes and watercolours anticipate ▷impressionism.

● **Jönköping** ► 57 45N 14 10E A town in S Sweden, at the S end of Lake Vättern. Its manufactures include matches, paper, textiles, and footwear. Population (1997 est): 115 636.

● **jonquil** ▷*See* Narcissus.

● **Jonson, Ben** ► (1572–1637) English dramatist and poet. In *Every Man in His Humour* (1598) he introduced the "comedy of humours," each character being driven by a particular obsession. Other major satirical plays include *Volpone* (1606), *The Alchemist* (1610), and *Bartholomew Fair* (1614). In collaboration with Inigo ▷Jones he produced many court masques. He also published two collections of poems and translations. Ranked above Shakespeare in the 17th century, Jonson based his finest work on classical principles and influenced a number of younger poets known as "the Tribe of Ben." He is buried in Westminster Abbey.

● **Joplin, Janis** ► (1943–70) US rock singer. During the 1960s her powerful blues-style vocals attracted a large following. Her records included "Ball and Chain" and "Me and Bobby McGee"; she died of a drugs overdose.

● **Joplin, Scott** ► (1868–1917) US Black pianist and composer of ▷ragtime music. One of the first to write down such music, Joplin is remembered for his syncopation in such rags as "Maple Leaf Rag" and "The Entertainer." The revival of the latter, in the film *The Sting* (1973), renewed interest in Joplin's music. His ragtime operas *A Guest of Honour* (1903), now lost, and *Treemonisha* (1907) were failures and Joplin, having known success, died in an asylum in poverty.

● **Jordaens, Jakob** ► (1593–1678) Flemish painter, born in Antwerp. Although he painted many altarpieces, influenced by ▷Rubens, he is best known for his allegorical and everyday scenes of merrymaking peasants, such as *The King Drinks* (Brussels). His commissions from the House of Orange included murals for their country house near The Hague.

● **Jordan, Dorothy** ► (1761–1816) British actress. She was a brilliant comic actress and her first London appearance in *The Country Girl* at Drury Lane in 1785 was a great success. She was mistress of the Duke of Clarence, the future William IV, and bore him ten children.

● **Jordan, Hashemite Kingdom of** ► A country in the Middle East, its only sea outlet being on the tip of the Gulf of Aqaba. It is mainly desert but more fertile in the W and N, where the population is concentrated. The people are Arab, and most are Sunnite Muslims, with Christian and other minorities.

Economy: Jordan's major industries include the extraction and processing of phosphates, which are exported from Aqaba and also used locally in fertilizers, oil refining, and tourism. Agriculture is concentrated in the irrigated Jordan Valley. Produce includes cereals, vegetables, wool, and such fruit as melons and olives. Potash from the shore of the Dead Sea is also exploited and some copper is mined. There are sufficient reserves of natural gas to supply the country's electricity requirements (since 1989). Tourism is a growing source of revenue. In the earlier 1990s Jordan's economy suffered badly from the international isolation of Iraq, its main trading partner. The situ-

Jordan ► One of the two Roman amphitheatres at Jerash, an ancient city N of Amman that flourished in the 2nd and 3rd centuries. The best-preserved Palestinian city of Roman times, it also contains a colonnaded street, a triumphal arch, and many temples.

ation has improved since the conclusion of a trade agreement with Israel (1995).

History: the area that is now Jordan appears to have flourished in the Bronze Age and was part of the Roman Empire by 64 BC. It was controlled by Arabs from the 7th century, Crusaders in the 11th and 12th centuries, and Turks from the 16th century until 1918. In 1920 the part E of the River Jordan was named Transjordan and a League of Nations mandate for its control was given to the UK. It became an independent kingdom in 1946 and was named the Hashemite Kingdom of Jordan in 1949. In the Arab-Israeli War of 1948–49, Jordan overran the ▷West Bank, but it was occupied by Israel in the Six-Day War of 1967. Palestinians, many of whom were refugees from the West Bank, then began raids on Israel from the East Bank; they were, however, subdued by Jordanian forces in the civil war of 1970–71 to avoid Israeli retaliation against Jordan. This brought Jordan into disfavour with other Arab states, which was only temporarily alleviated by Jordanian participation in the Arab-Israeli War of 1973. Jordan has since recognized the ▷Palestine Liberation Organization as the body entitled to govern the West Bank and in 1988 it recognized the West Bank as a state. After riots over price rises, liberal reform was promised in 1989; the first multiparty elections for 37 years were held in 1993. In 1990–91 Jordan gave political and diplomatic support to Iraq in the ▷Gulf War; the international crisis caused massive disruption to the Jordanian economy and the return of thousands of expatriate workers from the Gulf states. It also had to cope with a massive influx of refugees. In 1994 Jordan and Israel signed a peace treaty and border agreement ending the state of war existing since 1948. ▷Hussein, king since 1952, died in 1999 and was succeeded by his son, ▷Abdullah II.

Hashemite Kingdom of Jordan

Head of state	King Abdullah II
Official language	Arabic
Official currency	Jordanian dinar of 1000 fils
Area	about 97 740 sq km (37 738 sq mi), including the West Bank
Population (1997 est)	4 333 000, including the West Bank
Capital	Amman

● **Jordan, Michael** ▶ (1963–) US basketball player. He played for the Chicago Bulls (1984–93, 1995–), was a member of the victorious US basketball team in the 1992 Barcelona Olympics, and was named as the highest paid athlete in the world in 1993. He announced his retirement in 1999.

● **Jordan, River** ▶ A river in the Middle East. It rises in Syria and Lebanon and flows due S through the Sea of Galilee to the Dead Sea. It forms for some of its course part of the border between Israel and Jordan. Length: 320 km (199 mi).

● **Jos** ▶ 9 54N 8 53E A city in central Nigeria. It developed following the discovery of tin (1903); tinmining remains important and it is a major source of columbite. It has a university (founded 1975). Population (1996 est): 206 300.

● **Joselito** ▶ (José Gómez; 1895–1920) Spanish matador, regarded as one of the greatest. At 17, he was the youngest ever to qualify; together with ▷Belmonte, he introduced the current style of fighting, working very close to the bull. He died in the ring.

● **Joseph** ▶ In the Old Testament, the 11th son of ▷Jacob (*see also* Abraham) and his first by Rachel. Joseph was sold into slavery in Egypt by his jealous half-brothers because Jacob had marked him out as his favourite by giving him a multicoloured coat (Genesis 37–50). As a slave in Egypt, Joseph correctly interpreted Pharaoh's dreams; he was rewarded by being appointed to high office, his foresight having saved Egypt from famine. When Joseph's brothers came to Egypt seeking food, he forgave them and encouraged Jacob and all his family to settle there. Joseph's sons, Ephraim and Manasseh, became founders of two of the ▷tribes of Israel.

● **Joseph, Père** ▶ (François le Clerc du Tremblay; 1577–1638) French Franciscan friar and diplomat, known as the Éminence Grise (Grey Eminence), who as Richelieu's secretary (from 1611) encour-

aged French participation against Protestant forces in the Thirty Years' War.

● **Joseph, St** ▶ In the New Testament, the husband of the Virgin ▷Mary. He was a devout Jew belonging to the line of David but worked humbly as a carpenter. He eventually settled in Nazareth. ▷Jesus grew up there and remained in his house for at least 12 years. He was certainly dead by the time of the crucifixion. Feast day: 19 March.

● **Joseph II** ▶ (1741–90) Holy Roman Emperor (1765–90), ruling with his mother ▷Maria Theresa until 1780. As sole ruler, Joseph, an enlightened despot (*see* Enlightenment), introduced religious freedom and reforms in education, law (issuing a legal code in 1786), and administration, and emancipated the serfs. His reforms encountered some opposition, especially in Hungary and the Austrian Netherlands, and his attempt to subject church to state involved the dissolution of over 700 monasteries and much hardship for monks.

● **Joséphine** ▶ (1763–1814) The wife (1796–1809) of Napoleon Bonaparte and Empress from 1804. Her first husband was Alexandre, Vicomte de ▷Beauharnais, who was guillotined in the French Revolution. She presided over a brilliant court until divorced by Napoleon because of their childlessness.

● **Joseph of Arimathea, St** ▶ In the New Testament, a man described as a councillor. He asked Pontius Pilate for the body of Christ after the crucifixion and arranged for its burial on the same day. According to medieval legend, he came to England after the crucifixion, bringing with him the ▷Holy Grail, and built the first English church, at Glastonbury. Feast day: 17 March.

● **Josephson, Brian David** ▶ (1940–) British physicist, who shared the 1973 Nobel Prize for his work on tunnelling effects in superconductors and semiconductors. He discovered that when two superconductors are separated by a thin dielectric an oscillating current is set up if a steady potential difference is applied between them (Josephson effect).

● **Josephus, Flavius** ▶ (Joseph ben Mattityahu; c. 38–c. 100 AD) Jewish historian and apologist. During the Jewish revolt of 66 AD against the Romans he helped organize the defence of Galilee, but was captured and subsequently accompanied ▷Vespasian to Rome. Here he wrote his surviving works: a history of the Jewish war, a history of the Jews from the creation up to the war, a defence of Judaism (*Against Apion*), and an autobiography.

● **Joshua** ▶ In the Old Testament, the successor of Moses as leader of the Israelites in the period shortly after the ▷Exodus. **The Book of Joshua**, which follows Deuteronomy in the Old Testament, relates the history of the Israelites between the death of Moses and the death of Joshua. It describes the invasion and conquest of Canaan (Palestine) and its division among the 12 tribes. Among the well-known episodes are the Israelites' miraculous crossing of the River Jordan and the capture of Jericho, the walls of which collapsed at the blast of the Israelites' trumpets.

● **Joshua tree** ▶ A treelike plant, ▷*Yucca brevifolia*, native to desert regions of the SW USA. Growing to a height of more than 10 m, its branching stem can assume unusual shapes: the name is said to derive from its supposed resemblance to the prophet Joshua extending his arms in blessing. It has stiff sword-shaped leaves and bears waxy white flowers in dense clusters at the tips of the branches.

● **Josiah** ▶ (d. 609 BC) King of Judah (c. 640 BC–609 BC). According to biblical sources, he was inspired by his discovery of the book of Deuteronomy during repairs to the Temple to outlaw the worship of Baal and other foreign gods and to make Jerusalem the centre of religious practice. He was killed by the Egyptians at the Battle of Megiddo.

● **Josquin des Prez** ▶ (c. 1450–1521) Flemish composer. A pupil of Ockeghem, he served at the courts of Milan, Ferrara, and Rome and sang in the papal choir between 1486 and 1494. He was choirmaster at Cambrai Cathedral from 1495 to 1499. His compositions were either elaborately contrapuntal or expressively homophonic; they include masses, motets, and chansons.

● **Jotunheimen** ▶ A mountain range in S central Norway. It rises to

2472 m (8110 ft) at Glittertinden, the highest mountain in the country.

● **Joubert, Piet** ▶ (Petrus Jacobus J.; 1831–1900) Afrikaner general and politician. He commanded the Transvaal's forces in the first ▷Boer War and negotiated the consequent ▷Pretoria Convention, which restored independence to the Transvaal. He became vice president (1883) and supported the English-speaking people against the dominance of the Afrikaners. He also held command at the start of the second Boer War.

● **joule** ▶ (J) The ▷SI unit of work or energy equal to the work done when the point of application of a force of one newton moves through a distance of one metre. Named after James ▷Joule.

● **Joule, James Prescott** ▶ (1818–89) British physicist, who performed a series of experiments during the 1840s to determine the mechanical equivalent of heat. His result, announced in 1847, attracted little attention at first but, supported by Lord ▷Kelvin, his work greatly contributed towards ▷Helmholtz's formulation of the law of conservation of energy. He also investigated the heating effect of an electric current (*see* Joule's law) and, with Lord Kelvin, discovered the fall in temperature that occurs when a gas expands adiabatically (*see* Joule-Kelvin effect). The unit of energy is named after him.

● **Joule-Kelvin effect** ▶ (*or* Joule-Thomson effect) The change in temperature of a gas when it is expanded adiabatically. In most gases it produces a cooling as energy is needed to overcome the attractive forces between molecules when the gas is expanded. The effect is utilized in ▷refrigeration and in the ▷liquefaction of gases. It was discovered by James ▷Joule and William Thomson (later Lord ▷Kelvin).

● **Joule's law** ▶ A law formulated by James ▷Joule describing the rate at which a resistance in an electrical circuit converts energy into heat. The heat energy produced per second (in watts) equals the product of the resistance (in ohms) and the square of the current (in amperes).

● **journalism** ▶ The gathering, writing, and publication or broadcasting of news. Journalism developed together with ▷newspapers and periodicals and its modern origins lie in the 17th century. Most early English journalists were essentially propagandists for political parties, although a campaign for freedom from government control was hotly fought throughout the 18th century. The role of journalists became that of objective reporters and investigators only after newspapers became independent of direct political control in the mid-19th century, a period that saw the work of some of the most celebrated journalists, including Sir Henry Morton ▷Stanley and William Howard ▷Russell. The late 19th century saw the introduction of sensational journalism (the "yellow" press) in the USA, which greatly increased circulation. The first academic courses providing training in journalism were established around the beginning of the 20th century. Awareness of the social responsibilities of journalists and the new specialized demands of radio and television broadcasting increased this trend towards professionalism. ▷*See also* Press Complaints Commission.

● **Jouvet, Louis** ▶ (1887–1951) French actor and theatre director. As a director of the Comédie Française from 1936, he directed the first productions of most of the plays of Jean ▷Giraudoux and gave notable performances in productions of Molière. He published *Réflexions du comédien* in 1939.

● **Jovian, Flavius** ▶ (c. 331–64 AD) Roman emperor (363–64). He served with the emperor ▷Julian the Apostate in Persia. After Julian's death (363), Jovian was named emperor by the army. He made an unpopular peace with the Persians and died before his return to Constantinople.

● **Jowett, Benjamin** ▶ (1817–93) British theologian and classical scholar. Jowett's *Epistles of St Paul* (1855) provoked a storm of theological prejudice from the Anglican establishment, which regarded biblical criticism as tantamount to heresy. His classical works include the translation of Plato's *Dialogues* (1871). Master of Balliol College at Oxford from 1870, he was called "the great tutor" and was renowned for his kindness to undergraduates.

● **Joyce, James** ▶ (1882–1941) Irish novelist and poet. After a distin-guished student career at a Jesuit college, Joyce graduated from University College, Dublin, in 1902, having decided to devote himself to writing. Accompanied by Nora Barnacle (whom he did not marry until 1931), he left Ireland in 1904, living first in Trieste (until 1915) and later in Zurich during World War I and Paris (1920–40). *Dubliners* (1914), a volume of short stories, was followed by the semiautobiographical novel *A Portrait of the Artist as a Young Man* (1916). In 1922 he published *Ulysses*, an epic novel that uses various experimental techniques (including the "stream of consciousness" or "interior monologue") to portray a single day in the lives of several Dubliners. He carried linguistic experiment to further extremes in *Finnegans Wake* (1939), a dream recounted in multilingual puns and word play. Joyce died in Zurich.

● **Joyce, William** ▶ (1906–46) Nazi broadcaster, known as Lord Haw-Haw. Born in the USA of Irish parents, he became a supporter of the British fascist Sir Oswald ▷Mosley and in 1939, having obtained a British passport, went to Germany. He broadcast Nazi propaganda to Britain throughout World War II and was subsequently tried as a British subject for treason and executed.

● **JP** ▷*See* justice of the peace.

● **Juan Carlos** ▶ (1938–) King of Spain (1975–). The grandson of Alfonso XIII, he was designated heir to the throne by Francisco ▷Franco and became king when he died, presiding over Spain's peaceful transition to democracy. In 1962 Juan Carlos married Sophia (1938–), daughter of King Paul of Greece.

● **Juan de Fuca Strait** ▶ A strait between ▷Vancouver Island (SW Canada) and the Olympic Peninsula (USA), linking the Pacific Ocean to Puget Sound and Georgia Strait.

● **Juan Fernández Islands** ▶ A Chilean group of three volcanic islands, in the S Pacific Ocean. Alexander Selkirk, who inspired Daniel Defoe's *Robinson Crusoe* (1719), lived on the largest island Más-a-Tierra (1704–09). Area: about 180 sq km (70 sq mi).

● **Juárez** ▷*See* Ciudad Juárez.

● **Juárez, Benito (Pablo)** ▶ (1806–72) Mexican statesman, who was the first Indian president of Mexico (1861–65, 1867–72). He became acting president in 1857 but was forced by conservative opposition to flee from Mexico City. In 1861 he returned and was elected president, winning popularity by nationalizing ecclesiastical property. He led the successful opposition (1864–67) to the French invasion (*see* Maximilian) and was re-elected president in 1867 and 1871, dying in office.

● **Juba, River** ▶ A river in East Africa. Rising in S central Ethiopia, it flows S across Somalia to enter the Indian Ocean near Kismayu. Length: 1660 km (1030 mi).

● **Jubbulpore** ▷*See* Jabalpur.

● **Juchen** ▶ Nomadic tribes that originated in the area N of Korea and around the Liaodong peninsula. The Juchen became especially powerful in ▷Song times, when they founded their own dynasty (1122–1234) modelled on the Chinese system of government.

● **Judaea** ▶ The southern division of ancient Palestine. The Old Testament kingdom of Judah survived Syrian, Assyrian, and Philistine attacks following Solomon's death but came to an end after conquest by ▷Nebuchadnezzar II of Babylon, when its capital, Jerusalem, was destroyed (586 BC) and the Jews were exiled. Judaea came next under Persian domination, when the Jews were allowed to return and rebuild Jerusalem, but under the Seleucids Antiochus IV Epiphanes' desecration of the temple in 167 BC instigated the ▷Maccabees' revolt. Judaea achieved a shortlived independence until the Roman conquest in 63 BC. After years of unrest the Roman province of Syria absorbed it in 135 AD.

● **Judah ha-Levi** ▶ (*or* Halevy; c. 1075–1141) Jewish poet and philosopher. He was born and spent most of his life in Spain, living in both Christian (Toledo) and Muslim (Cordoba) centres, where he practised as a physician. Some 1100 of his poems, on religious and secular subjects, are extant and he is considered one of the greatest of Jewish poets and the most important one to emerge from medieval Arabic culture. His major prose work, *Sefer ha-Kuzari*, is a philosophical dialogue on Judaism and the nature of religious truth. According to tradition, he left Spain in the last year of his life on a pilgrimage to Jerusalem; he was enthusiastically received by the Jews of Alexandria and Cairo but died before reaching the Holy Land.

● **Judah, tribe of** ▶ One of the 12 ▷tribes of Israel. It claimed descent from Judah, the son of Jacob and Leah, and occupied territory W of the Dead Sea, which included Jerusalem and Bethlehem. It became the royal house of David in fulfilment of Jacob's dying prophecy. After the division of Israel (*see* Ten Lost Tribes of Israel), it formed with the tribe of ▷Benjamin the southern kingdom of Judah.

● **Judaism** ▶ The religion of the ▷Jews. Its fundamental tenet is trust in a single, eternal, invisible God, who created the world and desires its welfare. Man's duty is to serve God with all his being. Judaism's most sacred text is the ▷Torah, which, according to tradition, contains not only a record of history and revealed law but a complete guide to human life and the mysteries of the universe (*see also* kosher dietary laws). Judaism has no official creed and no central authority; it lays stress on right behaviour (*see* halakhah) rather than on doctrine.

There is no agreement as to when Judaism began. Tradition attaches importance to the early figures of ▷Abraham and ▷Moses, but many of the characteristic ideas and institutions emerged during the ▷Babylonian exile and the period of the second ▷Temple of Jerusalem. After the destruction of the temple the ▷rabbis codified and elaborated the traditional teachings (*see* Midrash; Mishnah; Talmud), and in the middle ages philosophy and the ▷kabbalah exerted a great influence. The modern enlightenment (*see* Haskalah) undermined traditional values and gave rise to several conflicting movements. Orthodox Judaism asserts the supernatural authority of Torah and halakhah, which is challenged by ▷Reform Judaism. Conservative Judaism and Reconstructionism, which are strongest in the USA, attempt to reach a compromise between these extreme views.

● **Judas Iscariot** ▶ In the New Testament, one of the 12 Apostles. Described as the group's treasurer, he betrayed the whereabouts of ▷Jesus to the Romans for 30 pieces of silver, identifying him with a kiss. Subsequently he killed himself.

● **Judas Maccabee** ▷*See* Maccabees.

● **Judas tree** ▶ A shrub or small tree of the genus *Cercis* (7 species), also called redbud, native to S Europe, Asia, and North America, and cultivated for ornament. The pinkish-red clusters of flowers appear before the heart-shaped leaves have opened. The name is used particularly for *C. siliquastrum*, from which Judas Iscariot is said to have hanged himself. Family: ▷Leguminosae.

● **Jude, St** ▶ In the New Testament, one of the 12 Apostles. He is generally identified with Thaddeus and also known as Judas Thaddeus. Referred to as "Judas of James," he was probably the brother of ▷James ("the Lord's brother") and therefore a half-brother of Jesus. According to tradition he was martyred in Persia with St ▷Simon, whose feast is held on the same day. Feast day: 28 Oct.

The Epistle of Jude in the New Testament is ascribed to him. Of uncertain date, it is a brief warning against certain immoral teachers who were currently infiltrating the Church.

● **judge** ▶ An officer who decides legal disputes and passes sentence on offenders. In England and Wales judges try cases in the House of Lords (the Lords of Appeal in Ordinary, or law lords), the Court of Appeal (the Lords Justices), the High Court of Justice (high-court judges), the Crown Court (high-court judges and circuit judges), and County Courts (circuit judges). A judge is appointed by the Crown on the recommendation of the Lord Chancellor (*see* chancellor; Lord Chief Justice; Master of the Rolls) and must be a barrister (or in some cases a solicitor) of at least ten years' standing. (A part-time recorder, who must also be a solicitor or barrister of ten years' standing, may be appointed to serve in the Crown Court; a ▷justice of the peace or stipendiary ▷magistrate serves in Magistrates' Courts.)

A judge is not answerable for anything he says or does in his judicial capacity unless he exceeds his jurisdiction. He can only be removed from office for bad behaviour on the recommendation of both Houses of Parliament. ▷*See also* courts of law.

● **Judges** ▶ An Old Testament book of unknown authorship, as-

cribed by Jewish tradition to Samuel. It covers the history of Israel from the death of Joshua to the monarchy under Saul (11th century BC). It introduces a philosophy of history in which God causes nations to oppress Israel, as punishment for its apostasy, and then delivers it through the "judges" or virtuous leaders, such as Gideon and Samson.

● **judicial separation** ▷*See* separation order.

● **Judith** ▶ A Jewish widow who deceived and assassinated a general of Nebuchadnezzar's invading army and thus caused the Assyrian army to flee from her home city. The incident is recorded in the **Book of Judith**, a book of the ▷Apocrypha. Its purpose was probably to inspire Jewish resistance to the policy of ▷Antiochus IV Epiphanes.

judo ▶ The 1986 Asian Games in Seoul, South Korea.

● **judo** ▶ An international form of wrestling developed from ▷jujitsu in Japan by Jigoro Kano (1860–1938). It was included in the Olympic Games for the first time in 1964. Contestants wear belts to indicate their proficiency. The six *kyu* (pupil) grades wear white, yellow, orange, green, blue, or brown belts in order of increasing skill, the 12 *dan* (master) grades all wear black belts. Contests take place on a mat 9 m (30 ft) square. Points are scored by executing prescribed throws, ground holds, and locks. Balance, speed, and the ability to use an opponent's strength characterize the skilful judoka. ▷*See also* martial arts.

● **Jugendstil** ▶ The German equivalent of the ▷Art Nouveau style. Named after the magazine *Jugend* (*Youth*), which was first published in 1896, Jugendstil originated in about 1894 in the embroideries of curving plant forms by Hermann Obrist (1863–1927). Other leading exponents were the architects Peter ▷Behrens and Henry ▷van der Velde.

● **juggernaut** ▷*See* Jagannatha.

● **jugular vein** ▶ A vein that drains blood from the head and neck to the larger veins passing to the heart. There are two jugular veins on each side of the neck: a large internal and a smaller external jugular. ▷*See* Plate II.

● **Jugurtha** ▶ (c. 160–104 BC) King of Numidia (118–105). He was the illegitimate grandson of Masinissa (d. 148) and initially ruled with Masinissa's legitimate grandsons Hiempsal and Adherbal. He assassinated Hiempsal and the Romans divided Numidia, a Roman dependency, between Jugurtha and Adherbal. Jugurtha's attack (112) on Adherbal caused Rome to declare war (the Jurgurthine War), which continued until 105, when Jugurtha was captured, taken to Rome, and executed.

● **Juiz de Fora** ▶ 21 47S 43 23W An industrial city in SE Brazil, in

Minas Gerais state on the Rio Paraibuna. It specializes in the manufacture of textiles, especially of knitted goods, and has a university (1960). Population (1991): 377 538.

● **jujitsu** ► (Japanese name: *yawara*) The form of self-defence, usually unarmed, used by the Japanese ▷samurai. The object was to disable, cripple, or kill an opponent by using his own momentum and strength against him. It evolved in about the 16th century and was taught in many forms in different schools. It was misused and fell into disrepute in the late 19th century, when the activities of the samurai were curtailed, but ▷judo, ▷aikido, and ▷karate developed from it.

● **jujube** ► A small thorny tree of the genus *Zizyphus* that produces sweet edible fruit. *Z. jujuba*, native to China, has been widely introduced to other hot dry regions. It grows up to a height of 9 m and has small yellow flowers; blood-red berries are collected and eaten fresh or made into glacé fruits. Family: *Rhamnaceae*. ▷*See also* crown of thorns.

● **Juliana** ► (1909–) Queen of the Netherlands (1948–80) following the abdication of her mother Wilhelmina. In 1937 she married Prince Bernhard von Lippe-Biesterfeld (1911–). In 1980 Queen Juliana abdicated in favour of her eldest daughter ▷Beatrix. Her other daughters are Princess Irene (1939–), whose marriage (1964–81) to a Spanish prince involved her conversion to Roman Catholicism and renunciation of her right of succession to the Dutch throne; Princess Margriet (1943–); and Princess Maria (1947–).

● **Julian calendar** ▷*See* calendar.

● **Julian of Norwich** ► (c. 1342–c. 1413) English mystic. As a recluse in Norwich, she wrote her famous *Revelations of Divine Love*, describing her many visions.

● **Julian the Apostate** ► (Flavius Claudius Julianus; 332–63 AD) Roman emperor (360–63). Julian was the only non-Christian emperor after Constantine. The army proclaimed Julian emperor and he attained power after the death in 361 of Constantius II. In spite of a Christian upbringing, Julian embraced paganism and restored pagan temples and deprived Christian churches of subsidy. He was killed fighting the Persians.

● **Julius II** ► (Giuliano della Rovere; 1443–1513) Pope (1503–13). The protégé of his uncle, ▷Sixtus IV, Julius became a cardinal in 1471 but lived in exile during the pontificate of his rival Alexander VI. Following his election he restored and extended the papal states in Italy. In 1511 he formed a Holy League against the invading Louis XII of France, who, after trying to depose Julius, was forced to withdraw. Julius is best known as a patron of artists, especially Michelangelo and Raphael; he began the building of St Peter's, Rome.

● **Jullundur** ▷*See* Jalandhar.

● **July Revolution** ► Three days of rioting in Paris in July, 1830, which brought ▷Louis Philippe to the French throne. Rebelling against ▷Charles X's reactionary ordinances, bourgeoisie and workers alike barricaded the streets. Charles abdicated, and the Chamber of Deputies elected Louis Philippe as king.

● **Jumna, River** ► (R. Jamuna *or* Yamuna) A river in N India. Rising in Uttar Pradesh, it flows S and SE past Delhi to join the River Ganges near Allahabad. This confluence is sacred to the Hindus. Length: 1385 km (860 mi).

● **jumping bean** ► A Mexican shrub, *Sebastiana pringlei*, the seeds of which may contain the caterpillars of a moth, *Carpocapsa saltitans*. When warmed (for example, when held in the hand) the caterpillars wriggle, causing the seed to jump. The seeds of *Colliguaja* of South America may also contain these caterpillars. Family: *Euphorbiaceae*.

● **jumping mouse** ► A small long-legged rodent belonging to the subfamily *Zapodinae* (5 species), of North America and Asia. 8–10 cm long, jumping mice have long tails (10–15 cm) and are grey, golden, or yellow-brown in colour. Living either in nests on the ground or in very shallow burrows, they feed at night on fruit, seeds, and insects. They hibernate in winter. Family: *Zapodidae*.

● **Junagadh** ► 21 32N 70 32E A town in India, in Gujarat. An agricul-

tural trading centre, it is famous for its Buddhist caves (3rd century BC) and temples. Population (1991): 130 132.

● **junction transistor** ▷*See* transistor.

● **Juneau** ► 58 20N 134 20W A city in the USA, the capital of Alaska on the Gastineau Channel. A supply centre for a fur-trading and mining region, it is also an ice-free port. Industries include salmon fishing and sawmilling. Willow South is to replace Juneau as the state capital. Population (1990): 26 751.

● **June beetle** ► A brown beetle, also called May beetle or June bug, belonging to a genus (*Phyllophaga*) of ▷chafers. 12–25 mm long, June beetles are commonly seen during early summer evenings, being attracted to lights. They can sometimes be serious pests, destroying crops of corn, potato, and strawberry. The adults feed on the foliage and flowers, while the larvae (white grubs) attack the roots.

● **Jung, Carl Gustav** ► (1875–1961) Swiss psychiatrist and pioneer psychoanalyst. Jung worked in Zurich and collaborated with Sigmund ▷Freud until, in 1912, their differences became irreconcilable. Jung originated the concept of introvert and extrovert personalities and made valuable studies of mental disorders, including schizophrenia. In his major work, *Psychology of the Unconscious* (1912), Jung regarded the unconscious part of the mind as containing both the personal experiences of the individual and the common inherited cultural experiences (*see* collective unconscious) of the particular social group to which he belongs. Jung later applied his theories to historical studies of religion and to the way in which the layers of the unconscious become manifest in dreams. He also developed psychiatric methods to treat the elderly.

● **Jungfrau** ► 46 33N 7 58E A mountain peak in S central Switzerland, in the Bernese Oberland. It forms a massif with the Eiger and the Mönch. A railway climbs to 3454 m (11 333 ft) at the **Jungfraujoch**, the pass between the Jungfrau and the Mönch. Height: 4158 m (13 632 ft).

● **Junggar Pendi** ► (English name: Dzungarian Basin) A region in NW China, in Xinjiang Uygur Autonomous Region. A semidesert plateau among mountains, it is inhabited chiefly by nomadic herdsmen. There are some state farms and oil and coal are produced.

● **jungle fowl** ► An Asian forest bird belonging to the genus *Gallus* (4 species). The males have a large fleshy comb and wattles at the sides of the bill and, in the breeding season, fight fiercely using their sharp leg spurs. The red jungle fowl (*Gallus gallus*) is the ancestor of the domestic ▷fowl. Family: *Phasianidae* (fowl and pheasants).

● **juniper** ► A coniferous tree or shrub of the genus *Juniperus* (60 species), widely distributed in the N hemisphere. Junipers have two kinds of leaves: needle-like and scalelike. All species have needles when young and some have both needles and scales when mature. Male and female flowers grow on separate trees and the cone is a fleshy "berry." The common juniper (*J. communis*) is native to N Europe, North America, and SW Asia; it rarely exceeds 4 m in height and is often planted for ornament. It has needle-like leaves and blue-black cones, 6–9 mm in diameter, used for flavouring gin and foods, as a source of oil, and as a diuretic. Family: *Cupressaceae*. ▷*See also* cade; pencil cedar; savin.

● **Junius, Letters of** ► A series of letters, written by a still unidentified author, criticizing the government of George III. They appeared in the *Public Advertiser* between 21 January, 1769, and 21 January, 1772. Sir Philip ▷Francis is the most likely author, although Edmund Burke and Tom Paine, among others, have been suggested.

● **junk bond** ► A ▷bond that gives a high rate of interest because it is associated with a high risk of default. Junk bonds have been used, especially in the USA, to finance the takeover of large companies with readily saleable assets that will provide funds once the company is acquired.

● **Junkers** ► A class of Prussian aristocrats. From small landowners the Junkers rose from the 15th century to control land, industry, and trade. Encouraged by Frederick the Great and Bismarck, they became notorious for arrogance and privilege, enjoying a monopoly of power in the army and civil service that remained unbroken until the 1930s.

• **Junkers, Hugo** ► (1859–1935) German aircraft designer. He founded an aircraft factory in Dessau in 1910 and went on to produce many successful aircraft, including an early monoplane (1915) and transport aircraft much used in both civilian and military roles, especially in World War II.

• **Juno** ► (astronomy) A ▷minor planet (247 km diameter), the orbit of which lies between those of Mars and Jupiter.

• **Juno** ► (mythology) A principal Roman goddess, the wife of Jupiter. She was concerned with all aspects of women's life, especially marriage and childbirth, and is usually portrayed as a matronly figure. In 390 BC the warning given by her sacred geese on the Capitoline hill saved Rome from the Gauls. The word *money* is derived from *moneta*, which was one of Juno's names; her temple served as a mint in ancient Rome. She was identified with the Greek ▷Hera. The ▷month June is probably named after her.

• **Jupiter** ► (astronomy) The largest and most massive planet, orbiting the sun every 11.86 years at a mean distance of 778.3 million km. Its rapid axial rotation (in less than 10 hours) has produced a nonspherical shape: equatorial diameter 142 800 km, polar diameter 135 500 km. In a telescope light and dark bands of clouds are visible, running parallel to the equator, together with spots and streaks. Jupiter is composed mainly (99%) of hydrogen and helium (in the ratio 82:17). Ammonia, methane, and other compounds are present in the cloud layers. The gaseous atmosphere is 1000 km thick. The planetary interior is liquid hydrogen with possibly a small rocky core. Jupiter radiates, as heat, about twice as much energy as it receives from the sun, suggesting an internal energy reservoir. It is also a source of radio waves. It has a magnetic field, radiation belts of great intensity, 16 known satellites (including the four large ▷Galilean satellites), and a satellite ring of rocks, discovered in 1979. ▷*See also* Galileo probe; planetary probe.

• **Jupiter** ► (mythology) The principal Roman god, identified with the Greek ▷Zeus. Originally a sky god, he controlled the weather and used the thunderbolt as his weapon. His temple on the Capitoline hill was the principal Roman temple. He was a protective god and the guardian of honour, being concerned with oaths, treaties, and marriages.

• **Jura** ► An island in W Scotland, in the Inner Hebrides, separated from the mainland by the Sound of Jura. It is mountainous and sparsely populated. Area: 381 sq km (147 sq mi). Population (latest est): 239, with Colonsay.

• **Jura Mountains** ► A mountain range in E France and NW Switzerland. It extends along the border in a NE–SW arc between the Rivers Rhine and Rhône, rising to 1723 m (5653 ft) at Crêt de la Neige. The area is chiefly agricultural.

• **Jurassic period** ► A geological period of the Mesozoic era, between about 200 and 135 million years ago, following the Triassic and preceding the Cretaceous periods. The dinosaurs and other reptiles flourished and diversified in this period. Fossils of the earliest birds and mammals have also been found in Jurassic rocks.

• **jurisprudence** ▷*See* law; medical jurisprudence.

• **Juruá, Rio** ► A river in South America, rising in E central Peru and flowing NE through NW Brazil to join the River Amazon. Length: 1900 km (1200 mi).

• **jury** ► A body of people, usually 12, who have taken an oath to decide questions of fact arising in a court case (now usually a criminal case but occasionally a civil case) according to the evidence before them. The English jury developed under the Normans as a body of people familiar with the case. The modern civil jury developed as the jurors became differentiated from witnesses and constituted an impartial body ignorant of the facts and sworn to decide solely on the evidence produced in court. To qualify for jury service a person must be a registered elector between 18 and 70 years old and resident in the UK for at least 5 years since the age of 13. Persons ineligible for jury service are members of the judiciary and anyone involved in administering justice, the clergy, and the mentally ill. Others (MPs, medical personnel, etc.) have a right to be excused from jury service, while those who have received certain types of convictions are dis-

qualified. Before being empanelled, jurors may be "challenged" (rejected) for various reasons by either side in a court case. They may claim compensation for loss of income while serving and are also paid travel expenses and subsistence. By the Criminal Justice Act (1967) a majority verdict (normally ten to two) was permitted in criminal trials and the Courts Act (1971) permitted similar verdicts in civil proceedings in the High Court. In 2000 the government introduced legislation to remove a defendant's automatic right to choose jury trial for lesser offences.

• **Jussieu** ► A French family of botanists. **Antoine de Jussieu** (1686–1758) was a physician, who wrote many papers on natural history and made a collection of European plants. He became director of the Jardin des Plantes, Paris. His brother **Bernard de Jussieu** (1699–1777) originated a method of classifying plants that was developed by his nephew **Antoine-Laurent de Jussieu** (1748–1836). The youngest brother of Antoine, **Joseph de Jussieu** (1704–79), spent many years in South America and introduced the garden heliotrope to Europe.

• **justice of the peace** ► (JP) An unpaid ▷magistrate appointed by the Lord Chancellor to keep the peace within a county, with statutory power to try summarily certain cases in a Magistrates' Court and to commit other more serious cases for trial by a higher court. Justices have the power to grant licences to sell intoxicating liquor, to deal in gaming, and to rule on certain matrimonial matters, such as maintenance.

• **justiciar** ► The royal deputy in the late 12th and 13th centuries, having full powers to govern England during the king's absence. The office became pre-eminent under Henry II, especially with the appointment (1180) of Ranulf Glanville (d. 1190). The justiciar's duties were chiefly administrative but might also include presiding over courts in the king's name, issuing writs, and controlling finance.

• **Justinian I** ► (482–565 AD) Byzantine emperor (527–65). His reign saw chiefly defensive wars on the eastern frontier but in the west his general ▷Belisarius crushed the Vandals in Africa (533) and the Ostrogoths in Italy (535–53). Justinian, who was greatly influenced by his wife ▷Theodora, reformed provincial administration and codified ▷Roman law, which he issued in the *Corpus Juris Civilis* (Body of Civil Law), informally known as the Justinian Code. An orthodox Christian, he attempted to wipe out paganism and built the great church of ⌐St Sophia at Constantinople.

• **Justinian II** ► (c. 669–711 AD) Byzantine emperor (685–95, 705–11), the last of the Heraclian dynasty. He was a notoriously harsh ruler and after a revolt in 695 his nose was cut off (hence his nickname Rhinotmetus) and he was banished to the Crimea. With Bulgar support he returned to Constantinople as emperor, instigating savage reprisals. He was killed in a second revolt.

• **Justinian Code** ▷*See* Roman law.

• **Justin Martyr, St** ► (c. 100–c. 165 AD) Christian apologist and martyr, born in Samaria. After his conversion (c. 130) he taught in Ephesus and founded a school of Christian philosophy at Rome, where he was later beheaded. His only certain works are two *Apologies* addressed to the emperor Marcus Aurelius and the Roman Senate and the *Dialogue*, defending Christianity against Judaism. Feast day: 1 June.

• **just in time** ► (JIT) A management technique used in the manufacturing industry that aims to reduce waste, queues, and bottlenecks. It relies on the ability of a skilled workforce to exercise personal responsibility to ensure that materials only flow when they are needed (*see* kanban). ▷Total quality management is also a feature of the technique. JIT relies heavily on computerization and computer-aided manufacturing systems.

• **jute** ► Either of two Indian annual plants, *Corchorus capsularis* or *C. olitorius*, cultivated in India, Pakistan, and Thailand for their fibres. Growing to a height of 3 m, they have straight spearlike stems and small yellow flowers. The stems are cut, soaked in water, and beaten to remove the fibres, which are processed into cloth, etc. There are many grades, used for ropes, sacks, carpet backings, hessian, and tarpaulin. Blending jute with man-made fibres has increased its uses. Family: *Tiliaceae*.

● **Jutes** ► A Germanic people, probably from Jutland, who invaded Britain together with the ▷Angles and ▷Saxons in the 5th century AD. Archaeological evidence supports ▷Bede's statement that the Jutes settled in what are now Kent, the Isle of Wight, and Hampshire.

● **Jutland** ► (Danish name: Jylland) A peninsula in N Europe, between the North Sea, the Skagerrak, the Kattegat, and the Little Belt. It is occupied by the continental part of Denmark and part of the German *Land* of Schleswig-Holstein. The **Battle of Jutland**, fought off the peninsula in 1916, was a major naval engagement in ▷World War I. Both sides claimed victory, but the British retained control of the North Sea while the German surface fleet remained in its home ports for the rest of the war.

● **Juvenal** ► (Decimus Junius Juvenalis; c. 60–c. 130 AD) Roman satirist. The biographical records are unreliable, but it is probable that he was born in Aquinum, SE of Rome, and that he was exiled to Egypt under the emperor Domitian but later became relatively prosperous under Hadrian. His 16 *Satires*, probably written in the period 98–128 AD, are savage indictments of the corruption of contemporary Roman society and of the absurd follies of mankind.

● **juvenile delinquency** ► Offences against the law by persons under 17 years old, for which in the UK special punishments exist (*see* criminal law). Most juvenile offenders are tried in special Magistrates' Courts called youth courts, in which one of the magistrates must be a woman: the press and public are not admitted, the identity of the offender cannot be published (unless this is ordered by the court or the home secretary), and the term "conviction" may not be used (the offender is instead "found guilty"). In these courts the juvenile offender may be bound over to a parent or guardian, put under the supervision of a local authority or (if 16 or over) a probation officer, or fined (the fine of an offender aged under 16 is normally paid by a parent or guardian). Juvenile delinquency, which appears to be a problem only of the developed countries, is often thought to be related to the breakdown of stable family life.

● **Jylland** ▷*See* Jutland.

● **K2** ► (*or* Mt Godwin Austen) 35 53N 76 32E The second highest mountain in the world (after Mount Everest), in N Pakistan in the Karakoram Range. As it was the second peak to be measured in the range it was given the symbol, K2. The summit was first reached on 31 July, 1954, by an Italian team. Height: 8611 m (28 250 ft).

● **Kaaba** ► The cube-shaped building at the centre of the great mosque at Mecca. Muslims believe that it was built by Abraham and Ishmael for the worship of God, was corrupted by Arab paganism, but was then purified and adopted for Islam by Mohammed. In the annual pilgrimage the Muslims circumambulate it and kiss the Black Stone, supposedly brought to Abraham by the angel Gabriel, which is fixed in the interior in the southeast corner.

● **kabaddi** ► A seven-a-side team game played in India, in which each player in turn tries to catch and touch members of the other team while holding his breath.

● **Kabardino-Balkar Republic** ► A constituent republic of Russia, in the S on the N side of the Caucasus Mountains. A large part of this mountainous region is unsettled and without roads. The population is 45% Kabardinian, 10% Balkar, and 40% Russian. The Kabardinians, most of whom are Muslims, speak a Northwest Caucasian language, while the Balkars are Turkic-speaking. The principal industries of the region are mining, timber, engineering, and food processing. The main crops are cereals, and livestock, poultry, and dairy farming are also important.

History: the Kabardinians were associated with the Russians from 1557 and, although the Balkars resisted Russian rule, the region was annexed by Russia in 1827. It was an autonomous Soviet republic from 1936 until 1991. In 1943 the Balkars, accused of collaborating with the Germans, were deported; they were returned in 1956. In 1992 the Balkars voted to establish a separate Balkar republic. Area: 12 500 sq km (4825 sq mi). Population (1995 est): 787 000. Capital: Nalchik.

● **kabbalah** ► (Hebrew: tradition) An esoteric Jewish theosophical system. The classical kabbalistic text is the ▷*Zohar* (*Book of Splendour*), written in Aramaic in 13th-century Spain, but kabbalah has much older roots. It has strong connections with ▷Gnosticism and also with magical practices. An important 16th-century kabbalistic school flourished at Safed, in Galilee, around Isaac ▷Luria, and Christian interpretations of the kabbalah blended with ▷Neoplatonism in the 16th and 17th centuries. In modern times a thirst for occult teachings has revived interest in the kabbalah.

● **Kabinda** ▷*See* Cabinda.

● **Kabuki** ► A form of Japanese popular theatre that developed from the aristocratic ▷No theatre during the 17th century. The earliest notable dramatist was Chikamatsu Monzaemon (1653–1724). The plays are performed with musical accompaniment on a wide revolving stage and emphasize visual effects and acting skills. The conventional scenery, costumes, and make-up are elaborate. Female roles are played by male actors. A traditional programme consists of both historical and domestic dramas separated by dance plays.

● **Kabul** ► 34 30N 69 10E The capital of Afghanistan, situated in the NE of the country at an altitude of 1830 m (6000 ft) on the River Kabul. It is over 3000 years old, with a strategic position commanding high mountain passes. It has been destroyed and rebuilt many times, being in the path of the great invasions of India by Alexander the Great, Genghis Khan, and others. It was capital of the Mogul Empire (1504–1738), becoming capital of Afghanistan in 1773. The university was founded in 1932. The scene of fighting between rival Mujahidin factions in the earlier 1990s, it was occupied by the fundamentalist ▷Taleban militia in 1996. Population (1993 est): 700 000.

● **Kabwe** ► (former name: Broken Hill) 14 29S 28 25E A town in central Zambia. The first Rhodesian (Zambia was formerly Northern Rhodesia) railway was built here to serve the mines that now produce some of the world's highest grades of lead, zinc, and vanadium. In 1921 prehistoric hominid fossils were discovered here (*see* Homo). Population (1990): 166 519.

● **Kabyle** ► A ▷Berber people of NE Algeria. They are Muslims and speak the Sanhajah dialect of the Berber language. The Kabyle are mainly settled cultivators living in autonomous villages (firquahs) occupied by patrilineal clans and governed by assemblies of adult males. There are also several castelike groups of inferior status, such as smiths and butchers.

● **Kádár, János** ► (1912–89) Hungarian leader. Head of the Hungarian secret police (1948–50), Kádár joined Imre ▷Nagy's government during the ▷Hungarian Revolution (1956) but after the Soviet invasion that suppressed it became first secretary of the Hungarian Socialist Workers' Party. He was also prime minister (1956–58, 1961–65). Effectively the head of state for over 30 years, he was finally dismissed in 1988.

Kabuki ► A scene from *The Revenge of Lord Masakado*, showing the stylized costumes and make-up of the Kabuki theatre. Female roles, such as the queen (left), are played by men.

● **Kaduna** ▶ 10 28N 7 25E A city in Nigeria. Formerly a colonial administrative centre, it developed as a railway junction and is a major textile and local trade centre. Population (1996 est): 342 200.

● **Kaesŏng** ▶ 37 59N 126 30E A city in SW North Korea, a former Korean capital (938–1392). Many historic buildings here were destroyed during the Korean War (1950–53). Population (latest est): 120 000.

● **kaffir corn** ▶ A variety of sorghum, ▷*Sorghum vulgare* var. *cafforum*, originating in S Africa and cultivated here and in the USA for its grain. It has stout short-jointed stems, up to 5 m high, and a whitish bloom to stems and leaves.

● **Kaffirs** ▶ The former collective name for the Pondo and Xhosa peoples of central South Africa, with whom the advancing White settlers fought the ▷Cape Frontier Wars in the late 18th and 19th centuries.

● **Kafirs** ▶ A people of the Hindu Kush mountains of Afghanistan and Pakistan, who speak a Dardic language (*see* Dards). Their name (Arabic *kafir*: infidel) was acquired from their Muslim neighbours on account of their traditional religion, which is polytheistic and involves sacrifice and divination by shamans.

● **Kafka, Franz** ▶ (1883–1924) Czech writer. Born in Prague (then in Bohemia), the son of German Jewish parents, he studied law and worked in an insurance company until tuberculosis forced him to leave. His own inner conflicts are reflected in fantasies and parables that portray the individual isolated in an incomprehensible and uneasy environment. Most of his work was published posthumously, against his instructions, by his friend Max Brod. Among his best-known writings are the stories *Metamorphosis* (1912) and *In the Penal Settlement* (1919) and the novels *The Trial* (1925) and *The Castle* (1926).

● **Kafuan stone tools** ▶ Quartz pebbles apparently flaked by human agency, found along the Kafue River (Zambia). They are now considered to be of natural origin.

● **Kafue River** ▶ A river in Zambia, rising on the frontier with the Democratic Republic of Congo and flowing generally S and E to join the Zambezi River. Length: 966 km (600 mi). The **Kafue Dam** (1972) provides about two-thirds of Zambia's hydroelectric power.

● **Kagoshima** ▶ 31 37N 130 32E A port in Japan, in S Kyushu on Kagoshima Bay. It was the site of ▷Francis Xavier's landing in Japan (1549). Its university was established in 1949. It has porcelain and textile industries, a naval yard, and a rocket base. Population (1995): 546 294.

● **kagu** ▶ A rare virtually flightless bird, *Rhynochetus jubatus*, occurring on remote forested mountains of New Caledonia. 55 cm long, it has a dark-barred grey plumage, an erectile crest, and reddish eyes, legs, and downcurved bill. It feeds at night on insects and snails. It is the only member of its family (*Rhynochetidae*). Order: *Gruiformes* (cranes, rails, etc.).

● **Kahlo, Frieda** ▷*See* Rivera, Diego.

● **Kahn, Herman** ▶ (1922–83) US scientist and futurologist. Originally a physicist and military analyst (1948–61), Kahn won recognition for his dispassionate analysis of nuclear war in his books *On Thermonuclear War* (1960) and *Thinking About the Unthinkable* (1962). Later books included the optimistic *The Year 2000* (1967) and *Why ABM?* (1969). In 1961 he founded the influential Hudson Institute in New York to make reasoned predictions on world affairs.

● **Kahn, Louis I(sadore)** ▶ (1901–74) US architect. Kahn's first major building was the Yale University Art Gallery (1951–53). He then developed a striking and individual form of ▷functionalism, for example at the Medical Research Building, University of Pennsylvania (1957–60). Other designs include the Kimbell Art Museum in Fort Worth, Texas (1966–72), and the Yale Center for British Art, New Haven, Connecticut (1969–74).

● **Kaieteur Falls** ▶ 5 09N 59 29W A waterfall in central Guyana, on the River Potaro. It is an important feature of the Kaieteur National Park. Height: 226 m (741 ft). Width: about 107 m (350 ft).

● **Kaifeng** ▶ 34 47N 114 20E A city in E China, in Henan province. It was a ▷Song dynastic capital, and a Jewish colony was established here (12th–19th centuries). It is a commercial and industrial centre. Population (1990): 507 763.

● **Kaikoura Ranges** ▶ Twin mountain ranges in New Zealand, comprising the Inland and the Seaward Kaikouras. They extend SW–NE in NE South Island, reaching 2885 m (9465 ft) at Tapuaenuku in the Inland Kaikouras, and are separated by the Clarence River.

● **Kairouan** ▶ (or Qairouan; Arabic name: al Qayrawan) 35 42N 10 01E A city in N central Tunisia. An ancient holy city of Islam, it is now a local trade centre producing carpets and other craft goods. Population (1994): 102 600.

● **kaiser** ▶ The title (derived from the Latin: Caesar) adopted by the German kings as Holy Roman Emperors (800–1806). It was assumed by William I of Prussia in 1871 and borne by the German emperors until 1917.

● **Kaiser, Georg** ▶ (1878–1945) German dramatist. His carefully structured expressionist plays reveal a conflict between his desire for spiritual regeneration and his inherent pessimism. They include *Von Morgens bis Mitternachts* (1916), *Gas I* (1919), and *Gas II* (1920).

● **Kaiserslautern** ▶ 49 27N 7 47E A city in SW Germany, in Rhineland-Palatinate. The site of Barbarossa's ruined castle (1153–58), it shares a university with Trier (1970). Its manufactures include car parts, machinery, and textiles. Population (1996 est): 102 002.

● **kakapo** ▶ A rare nocturnal New Zealand ▷parrot, *Strigops habroptilus*, also called owl parrot. It is the largest and only flightless parrot, having discs of stiff feathers around the eyes resembling an owl. Its green plumage is barred with yellow and brown and it has a heavy bill for grinding plant material.

● **Kakinomoto Hitomaro** ▶ (c. 680–710) Japanese poet. He is considered the greatest of the poets whose works appear in the Man'yoshu, an 8th-century anthology of lyric poetry. He was poet to the court of Empress Jito and Emperor Mommu and many of his poems describe court life.

● **kala-azar** ▷*See* leishmaniasis.

● **Kalahari Desert** ▶ A semiarid area in S Africa, chiefly in Botswana. It is sparsely inhabited by nomadic Bushmen, and although its few rivers are generally dry there is some vegetation. Wildlife is concentrated in the game reserves in the S. Area: about 250 000 sq km (96 505 sq mi).

● **Kalamazoo** ▶ 42 17N 85 36W A city in the USA, in Michigan on the Kalamazoo River. It produces aircraft components, paper, fishing tackle, and stoves. Population (1996 est): 77 460.

● **Kalanchoe** ▶ A genus of small tropical shrubs (over 100 species) having fleshy leaves and clusters of colourful flowers on tallish stems. They are popular house plants, requiring warm temperatures. Most flower in winter, having white, red, yellow, or pink flowers. Family: *Crassulaceae*.

● **Kalat** ▶ (or Khelat) A region of SW Pakistan, in S Baluchistan. A former princely state, it was incorporated into Pakistan in 1948.

● **kale** ▶ A variety of ▷cabbage, also called borecole, grown for its large edible leaves, which are used as a winter vegetable and as livestock food. Curly kales, which have curled and crimped leaves, are the most popular as vegetables. Some produce tender spring shoots. They are more hardy than most other brassicas.

● **Kalemie** ▶ (name until 1966: Albertsville) 5 57S 29 09E A city in the Democratic Republic of Congo, on Lake Tanganyika. A port, it handles the Indian Ocean and Congo–Tanzania trade. Industries include fishing and textiles. Population (1994 est): 101 309.

● **Kalevala** ▶ The Finnish national epic, recounting the legendary exploits of the seer Väinämöinen and other heroes. It was compiled from folk ballads and other traditional material by Elias Lönnrot and published in two volumes (1835, 1849).

● **Kalgan** ▷*See* Zhangjiakou.

● **Kalgoorlie** ▶ 30 49S 121 29E A city in S central Western Australia. It is the centre of Australia's largest gold- and nickel-mining region.

Because of the arid climate water is piped 563 km (250 mi) from Mundaring Weir in the Darling Range. Population, with Boulder (1991 est): 26 079.

● **Kali** ▶ In Hindu mythology, the goddess of death. The wife of ▷Shiva in her destructive aspect, she is represented as a hideous four-armed black woman, adorned with skulls, and is propitiated by nocturnal sacrifices of animals.

● **Kalidasa** ▶ (5th century AD) Indian poet, considered to be the greatest writer in classical Sanskrit. Almost nothing is known of his life, but he is traditionally associated with the court of Chandra Gupta II. The seven works attributed to him include two epics, two shorter poems, and three dramas, of which the most famous is the *Sakuntala*, concerning the love of King Dusyanta for a semidivine nymph.

● **Kalimantan** ▶ The Indonesian part of ▷Borneo, comprising the SE two-thirds of the island. It is little developed, but its dense forests provide valuable timber. Small-scale agriculture includes the growing of rice, tobacco, sugar cane, coffee, and rubber. It is a long-standing source of gold and also produces oil and coal. Since Indonesian independence in 1949 the province has seen recurrent ethnic and political violence, including the mass slaughter of Muslim Madurese by indigenous Dyaks (from 1997). Area: 550 203 sq km (212 388 sq mi). Population (1995 est): 10 520 500. Chief towns: Banjarmasin and Pontianak.

● **Kalinin** ▷*See* Tver.

● **Kalinin, Mikhail Ivanovich** ▶ (1875–1946) Soviet statesman. A loyal supporter of Stalin, he was formally head of state (1919–46) as chairman of what came to be called the presidium of the Supreme Soviet.

● **Kaliningrad** ▶ (name until 1946: Königsberg) 54 40N 20 30E A port in W Russia, on the River Pregolya near its mouth at the Baltic Sea, an exclave within Lithuania. Founded in 1255 as a fortress for the Teutonic Knights, it passed to Prussia in the 16th century and became a German naval base. It was ceded to the Soviet Union in 1945. In 1991 plans were announced to make it a free economic zone. Its industries include shipbuilding, timber, paper, textiles, and food processing. Population (1995 est): 419 000.

● **Kalisz** ▶ 51 46N 18 02E A town in W central Poland. Originally called Calissia, it is one of the oldest towns in Poland, being mentioned by Ptolemy in the 2nd century AD. Population (1996 est): 106 800.

● **Kalmar** ▶ 56 39N 16 20E A port in E Sweden, on Kalmar Sound. The Union of Kalmar (1397) united Sweden, Denmark, and Norway under one ruler. It has a notable 13th-century castle, Kalmar Slott. Shipbuilding is important and nearby are the famous Orrefors glassworks. Population (1994): 58 070.

● **Kalmyk Republic** ▶ (Kalmykia *or* Republic of Khalm Tangch) A constituent republic of Russia, on the Caspian Sea. The Kalmyk people, who speak a Mongolian language, are traditionally Buddhists. Industries include fish processing, canning, and the manufacture of building materials, but the economy is predominantly agricultural and cattle breeding and fodder crops are particularly important. The Kalmyks were deported to Siberia for collaborating with the Germans in World War II but some were returned in 1957. Since the later 1990s there has been growing support for secession from Russia. In 1998 the Republic printed its own money and refused to pay federal taxes, leading Moscow to cut off subsidies. Area: 75 900 sq km (29 300 sq mi). Population (1996 est): 319 000. Capital: Elista.

● **Kaluga** ▶ 54 31N 36 16E A port in central Russia, on the River Oka. It produces railway equipment, electrical equipment, textiles, and consumer goods. Population (1995 est): 347 000.

● **Kama** ▶ In Hindu mythology, the god of love. He is the son of ▷Shiva and his popular epithet of Ananga (bodiless) derives from his having been reduced to ashes by a glance from his father's eye when Kama playfully shot his arrows at him.

● **Kama, River** ▶ A river in central Russia, rising in the Ural Mountains and flowing mainly SW to the River Volga. It is a main waterway. Length: 2030 km (1260 mi).

● **Kamakura** ▶ 35 19N 139 33E A city in Japan, in SE Honshu on an inlet of the Pacific Ocean. A former Japanese capital (1192–1333), it is now a religious centre, noted for its shrines and temples and for its bronze Buddha, 13 m (43 ft) high. Population (1995 est): 170 319.

● **Kamchatka** ▶ A peninsula in the extreme E of Russia. It is about 1200 km (746 mi) long and separates the Sea of Okhotsk from the Bering Sea. There are many lakes, rivers, and forests, two mountain chains, and about 20 active volcanoes. Area: about 270 000 sq km (104 225 sq mi).

● **kame** ▶ A mound consisting chiefly of stratified sands and gravels, deposited by meltwater from a glacier or icesheet. ▷*See also* esker.

● **Kamehameha I** ▶ (c. 1758–1819) King of Hawaii (1810–19), who founded the Kamehameha dynasty. Ruler of part of Hawaii from 1782, by 1810 he had united all the Hawaiian islands. He maintained Hawaiian independence despite the arrival of European explorers, the first of whom was James Cook in 1778. His encouragement of foreign trade established Hawaiian prosperity.

● **Kamehameha IV** ▶ (1834–63) King of Hawaii (1854–63). He instituted social reforms, including free medical care, and encouraged greater commercial activity. He successfully opposed annexation by the USA in 1853–54 and curbed the political influence of US missionaries by inviting representatives of the Church of England to share their educational work.

● **Kamenev, Lev Borisovich** ▶ (1883–1936) Soviet politician. Kamenev failed to win a favourable position in the power struggle after Lenin's death and he was arrested for participating in ▷Kirov's assassination (1934). He was tried in the first public purge trial and executed.

● **Kamet, Mount** ▶ 30 55N 79 36E A mountain in N India, in the Himalayas. It was first climbed in 1931. Height: 7756 m (25 446 ft).

● **Kamikaze** ▶ A Japanese aircraft crashed deliberately by its pilot into its target. Such suicide missions were first flown at the Battle of Leyte Gulf (1944) in World War II; at Okinawa (1945) some 3000 sorties sunk 21 US ships. Kamikaze means divine wind and refers to the typhoon that scattered Kublai Khan's invasion fleet in 1281.

● **Kampala** ▶ 0 20N 32 30E The capital of Uganda, N of Lake Victoria. Founded by the British in the late 19th century, it became the capital in 1962. In 1979 its fall to the combined forces of Tanzanians and exiled Ugandans effected the end of President Idi Amin's regime. It has two cathedrals and Makerere University (1970). It is chiefly an administrative centre with some small industries. Population (1995 est): 954 000.

● **Kampuchea, Democratic** ▶ The name given to ▷Cambodia by the ▷Khmer Rouge, after they took over the government in 1975 and reformed the constitution (1976). The country's former name of Cambodia was reinstated in 1989.

● **Kananga** ▶ (name until 1966: Luluabourg) 5 53S 22 26E A city in the central Democratic Republic of Congo, on the River Lulua. A major commercial centre, it serves an agricultural and diamond-producing area. Population (1994 est): 393 030.

● **Kanarese** ▶ A ▷Dravidian language of SW India, also called Kannada. It is the official language of Mysore. Texts written in the Kanarese alphabet date from the 6th century.

● **Kanazawa** ▶ 36 35N 136 38E A city in Japan, in central Honshu. It is renowned for its landscape garden. Its university was established in 1949. Industries include textiles, porcelain, and lacquerware. Population (1995): 453 977.

● **kanban** ▶ A Japanese-devised method of controlling the movement of materials through a ▷just-in-time system. *Kanban* is the Japanese word for "visual record"; the system relies on kanban cards showing when boxes of parts need refilling to ensure that the parts arrive at the appropriate point in the production line just in time, thus avoiding unnecessary stocks building up throughout a factory. It also ensures that no bottlenecks or delays occur. Pioneered by the

Toyota Motor Company after World War II, the method is now used worldwide.

● **Kanchenjunga, Mount** ▷*See* Kangchenjunga, Mount.

● **Kanchipuram** ▶ (*or* Conjeeveram) 12 50N 79 44E A city in India, in Tamil Nadu. It is one of the oldest cities in S India and is sacred to the Hindus. It is noted for its silk and cotton fabrics. Population (1991): 145 028.

● **Kandahar** ▶ (*or* Qandahar) 31 36N 65 47E A city in S Afghanistan. Situated on main routes to central Asia and India, it is built on the site of several ancient cities. It was the first capital (1747) of a unified Afghanistan. Kandahar is a major commercial centre. Population (1990 est): 237 500.

● **Kandinsky, Wassily** ▶ (1866–1944) Russian expressionist painter and art theorist, born in Moscow, where he graduated in law. In 1896 he moved to Munich to study. Here he painted the first purely abstract pictures in European art (c. 1911). These are characterized by freely applied paint and dazzling colours, from which he drew analogies to music in his book *Concerning the Spiritual in Art* (1911). He was a founder of the ▷Neue Künstlervereinigung (1909) and Der ▷Blaue Reiter (1911); following a stay in Russia (1914–21), he taught at the ▷Bauhaus school, where his style became more geometrical. He settled in France in 1933.

● **Kandy** ▶ 7 17N 80 40E A city in central Sri Lanka. Capital of the kingdom of Kandy from 1480 until 1815, when it was occupied by the British, it has a famous Buddhist temple, Dalada Malagawa. Kandy is the commercial centre for Sri Lanka's major tea-producing region. Population (1990 est): 104 000.

● **Kanem Bornu** ▶ An African empire that controlled the area around Lake Chad. Kanem, situated on the eastern trade routes, became a centre of Muslim civilization in the 11th century. The king was expelled in 1389 and founded a new dynasty in Bornu, which in the 16th century conquered Kanem and expanded the empire. Torn by internal strife, the empire collapsed in about 1800.

● **kangaroo** ▶ The largest ▷marsupial mammal. There are two species, the red kangaroo (*Macropus rufus*) of Australia and the grey kangaroo (*M. giganteus*) of Australia and Tasmania. Red kangaroos can reach a height of 2 m and a weight of 90 kg. Kangaroos have short front legs and long hind legs and feet: they travel by a succession of leaps. When moving slowly, they use their long heavy tail as a prop. The red kangaroos graze across the plains while grey kangaroos live in open woodland. Family: *Macropodidae*. ▷*See also* wallaby; wallaroo; tree kangaroo. □mammal.

● **kangaroo paw** ▶ A stiff hairy plant of the Australian genus *Anigozanthos* (10 species), also known as Australian sword lilies and sometimes planted in gardens in warm regions. The flowers, borne in short branched terminal clusters, are long, tubular, and hairy, with six pointed flaring lobes, usually yellow, green, or red. Unopened flowers resemble kangaroos' paws. Family: *Haemodoraceae*.

● **kangaroo rat** ▶ A North American desert rodent of the genus *Dipodomys* (22 species). Up to 20 cm long, kangaroo rats have long back legs and very long hairy tails. They do not need to drink as they obtain water from their food (seeds, tubers, and other vegetation).

They spend the day in relatively cool humid burrows, in which they store food during droughts. □mammal.

● **Kangchenjunga, Mount** ▶ (*or* Mt Kanchenjunga) 27 44N 88 11E The third highest mountain in the world (after Mount Everest and K2), on the Sikkim (India)–Nepal border in the Himalayas. It was first climbed in 1955 by a British expedition; however, George Band and Joe Brown (1930–) stopped just short of the actual summit in deference to the religious wishes of the Sikkimese. On 16 May, 1979, a British team climbed it without oxygen-breathing equipment. Height: 8598 m (28 208 ft).

● **KaNgwane** ▷*See* Bantu Homelands.

● **Kang Xi** ▶ (*or* K'ang-hsi; 1654–1722) Chinese emperor (1661–1722) of the Qing dynasty, who completed the Qing conquest of China started by ▷Nurhachi. He was a powerful ruler, who led his armies in person against the Mongols and carried out tours of inspection of his vast empire. He built the imperial summer palace at Jehol (now Chengde) and sponsored engineering works to prevent the Yellow River from flooding and to improve communications. His greatest achievement was probably in his sponsorship of the arts.

● **Kang You Wei** ▶ (1858–1927) Chinese reformer. A major influence on the ▷Hundred Days of Reform (1898), he was subsequently forced to flee China and in 1907, in British Columbia, founded the China Reform Association. Back in China (1914), he opposed Sun Yatsen.

● **Kano** ▶ 12 00N 8 31E A city in N Nigeria. It was an important trade centre for caravans crossing the Sahara. It was captured by the British (1903) and trade developed with the S. It is now an important trade centre, particularly for groundnuts and cattle, with some local industries. Population (1996 est): 674 100.

● **Kanpur** ▶ (former name: Cawnpore) 26 27N 80 14E A city in India, in Uttar Pradesh on the River Ganges. Ceded to the British East India Company (1801), it became an important British frontier station and during the Indian Mutiny was the scene (1857) of a massacre of British soldiers. Today Kanpur is one of India's largest cities and a major communications and industrial centre; the chief manufactures are wool, cotton, jute, leather goods, plastics, and chemicals. Several educational institutions are located here, including a university (1966) and an Institute of Technology (1960). Population (1991): 2 111 284.

● **Kansas** ▶ A state in the centre of the USA. It consists mainly of undulating prairie, forming part of the Great Plains, and is crossed by the Kansas and Arkansas Rivers. Manufacturing is significant with aircraft production, food and meat processing, and a range of different processing industries. Its large mineral resources yield oil, natural gas, coal, sand and gravel, cement, stone, chalk, zinc, and lead. Kansas is the USA's main wheat-growing area; other crops include sorghum grains and hay. Beef production is especially important.

History: first explored by the Spanish in the 16th century, it was claimed by the French (1682) and formed part of the Louisiana Purchase (1803) by the USA. It became a state (1861) and the arrival of the railway in the late 1860s and 1870s brought many cattlemen. The ▷Mennonites introduced wheat into the area (1874). Area: 213 063 sq km (82 264 sq mi). Population (1996 est): 2 572 150. Capital: Topeka.

● **Kansas City** ▶ 39 05N 94 37W A city in the USA, in Missouri at the

kangaroo ▶ A grey kangaroo. Their enormously powerful hind legs enable these marsupials to achieve speeds of up to 60 kph (38 mph) over short distances. When leaping, the tail is held out stiffly behind and acts as a counterbalance; at rest it functions as an extra leg.

confluence of the Missouri and Kansas Rivers. Settled in 1821, it expanded rapidly with the arrival of the railways in the mid-18th century. A major trading and distribution centre for a vast agricultural region, it is the site of the annual Royal Livestock and Horse Show. Industries include food processing, metals, chemicals, and machinery and there are several military installations nearby. Population (1996 est): 441 259.

● **Kansu** ▷*See* Gansu.

● **Kant, Immanuel** ▶ (1724–1804) German philosopher, who made many original and influential contributions to thought. He spent much of his life (1755–97) teaching at the university in his native Königsberg (now Kaliningrad in Russia). His early works, notably *Theory of the Heavens* (1755), sought to examine metaphysics in the light of the work of ▷Newton and ▷Leibniz. Acquaintance with Hume's ▷empiricism, however, initiated his so-called "critical period" in which he evolved his doctrine of transcendental idealism. In the famous *Critique of Pure Reason* (1781) he explored the limitations of reason by which mankind interprets experience. The *Critique of Practical Reason* (1788) and the *Critique of Judgment* (1790) deal respectively with ▷ethics and aesthetic and teleological judgments. Reason makes experience possible by imposing upon the raw data supplied by the senses the forms of understanding. Kant identified 12 of these basic forms (which he called "categories"), such as causality; they were transcendental in as much as they were found in pure reason independently of experience. But reason is also practical and as such he identified it with morality. He maintained that there was an absolute moral law, which can never be modified by expediency (it can never be right to tell a lie), and called the obligation to obey this moral law the "categorical imperative."

● **Kao-hsiung** ▷*See* Gaoxiong.

● **kaolin** ▶ A group of clay minerals consisting of hydrous aluminium silicates. It includes kaolinite (the most important), nacrite, and dickite. Kaolin is the main constituent of ▷china clay. It has many other industrial uses, particularly as a mineral filler in the manufacture of paper, paint, textiles, rubber, plastics, and cosmetics. It is also used in medicine, to treat diarrhoea and as a constituent of poultices.

● **Kapil Dev** ▶ (Kapil Dev Ramlal Nikhanj; 1959–) Indian cricketer, who played for Haryana, Northamptonshire, Worcestershire, and India (1978–94; captain 1983–84). In 1994 he became Test cricket's highest wicket-taker, having taken 432 wickets, before announcing his retirement.

● **Kapitza, Peter Leonidovich** ▶ (1894–1984) Soviet physicist, who went to Cambridge in 1921 and worked with ▷Rutherford on high transient magnetic fields. Returning to the Soviet Union in 1934 he transferred his attention to low-temperature physics, which led him to the discovery of superfluid helium (1941). For this work he was awarded the 1978 Nobel Prize.

● **kapok** ▶ The fine silky hairs covering the seeds of the silk-cotton tree (*Ceiba pentandra*), which are used for stuffing mattresses, etc. Impervious to water, kapok can also be used to fill life jackets and oil from the seeds is used in soap making and is edible. The tree is native to tropical America and widely cultivated in the tropics. Growing to 35 m, it has large buttresses at the base of the trunk and clusters of white or red flowers. Family: *Bombacaceae*.

● **Kara-Bogaz-Gol** ▶ A shallow gulf in W Turkmenistan, on the E Caspian Sea. Its water evaporates fast, drawing more in from the Caspian and creating the richest natural deposits of marine salts in the world. Area: about 13 000 sq km (5018 sq mi).

● **Karachai-Cherkess Republic** ▶ A constituent republic of Russia, in the W. It was formed in 1922 for the Muslim Karachai and Cherkess peoples. Mining, engineering, and chemical industries are important, and the chief agricultural activities are livestock raising and cereal production. Area: 14 100 sq km (5440 sq mi). Population (1995 est): 435 000. Capital: Cherkessk.

● **Karachi** ▶ 24 51N 67 02E The largest city and chief seaport in Pakistan, situated on the Arabian Sea just NW of the Indus delta. A modern city, it developed rapidly from the mid-19th century as a

port. It became the capital of Pakistan (1947) following partition, which brought a further influx of refugees to an already overcrowded city. The removal of the capital to Islamabad (1959) and the building of new satellite towns has eased the housing situation. The University of Karachi was established here in 1957. The city is Pakistan's principal naval base and its port is a major outlet for the agricultural produce of the Sind and Punjab provinces. Its industries include textiles, chemicals and plastics, and engineering. Population (1995 est): 9 863 000.

● **Karadžić, Radovan** ▶ (1945–) Bosnian Serb leader. Born in Montenegro, he worked as a psychiatrist and became known as a poet before entering politics. In 1990 he was a cofounder of the nationalist Serbian Democratic Party and following the break-up of Yugoslavia he became leader (1992) of the self-declared Serbian Republic in Bosnia-Hercegovina. His policy of "ethnic cleansing" of non-Serbs during the Bosnian civil war led to his indictment for genocide and crimes against humanity by an international ▷war crimes tribunal in 1995.

● **Karafuto** ▷*See* Sakhalin.

● **Karaganda** ▶ 49 53N 73 07E A city in E Kazakhstan. Founded in 1857, Karaganda grew rapidly in the 1920s and 1930s as the Karaganda coal basin was exploited. It was one of the largest producers of bituminous coal in the former Soviet Union. Although coalmining and the production of coalmining equipment dominate the city's industries, it also produces building materials and has light industries. Population (1995 est): 573 700.

● **Karageorge** ▶ (George Petrović Karadordević; c. 1762–1817) Serbian revolutionary leader. In 1804 he led a successful revolt against Turkey and in 1808 became the "Supreme Serbian hereditary leader." Turkey regained control of Serbia in 1813 and after a five-year exile in Austria Karageorge was murdered, probably by his rivals, the ▷Obrenović family.

● **Karajan, Herbert von** ▶ (1908–89) Austrian conductor. Educated at Vienna and the Salzburg Mozarteum, he was musical director of the Vienna State Opera (1957–64). He founded the Salzburg Easter Festival in 1967 and conducted the Berlin Philharmonic Orchestra (1955–89).

● **Kara-Kalpak Autonomous Republic** ▶ (*or* Kara-Kalpakia) An administrative division in NW Uzbekistan, on the Aral Sea. The population consists mainly of Kara-Kalpaks, a Turkic-speaking people closely related to the Kazakhs. Kara-Kalpakia's main industries are the manufacture of bricks, leather goods, and furniture and canning and wine making. It was the former Soviet Union's chief producer of alfalfa, and other crops grown include cotton, rice, corn, and jute. Cattle and karakul sheep are raised.

History: the Kara-Kalpaks were under the rule of the ▷Kazakhs before passing under Russian rule in the late 19th and early 20th centuries. Kara-Kalpakia was within the Kazakh SSR (1925–30), then within the RSFSR (1930–36), becoming an autonomous republic in 1932, before passing to the Uzbek SSR (1936–91). Area: 165 600 sq km (63 900 sq mi). Population (1993 est): 1 343 800. Capital: Nukus.

● **Karakoram Range** ▶ A mountain range mainly in SW China, NE Pakistan, and NW India. It extends about 450 km (280 mi) between the Pamirs and the Himalayas and includes ▷K2, the second highest mountain in the world. In 1978 the **Karakoram Highway** was opened connecting China with Pakistan over the Khunjerab Pass, 4933 m (16 188 ft) high.

● **Karakorum** ▶ The former Mongol capital founded (c. 1220) by ▷Genghis Khan in the upper valley of the River Orhon Gol (Outer Mongolia). It replaced the nearby Uighur capital of the same name. After ▷Kublai Khan moved the capital from Karakorum (1267) the city declined and was eventually destroyed (1388).

● **karakul** ▶ A breed of sheep originating in central Asia. The young lambs bear a coat of fine tightly curled black wool, known as Persian lamb.

● **Kara Kum** ▶ A desert in Turkmenistan, between the Caspian Sea to the W and the River Amu Darya to the E, comprising most of the republic. Area: about 300 000 sq km (115 806 sq mi).

● **Karamanlis, Constantine** ▶ (1907–98) Greek statesman; prime minister (1955–63, 1974–80), president (1980–85, 1990–95). Karamanlis resigned in 1963 and went into exile, returning in 1974, after the fall of the military dictatorship, to form a civilian government.

● **Kara Sea** ▶ A section of the Arctic Ocean off the N coast of Russia, between Novaya Zemlya and Severnaya Zemlya. It is frozen for much of the year but is used to reach the port of Novy Port some 600 km (373 mi) inland on the Gulf of Ob.

● **karate** ▶ An oriental form of unarmed combat that was systematized in Okinawa, one of the Ryukyu Islands, in the 17th century and spread to Japan in the 1920s, where it absorbed elements of ▷ju-jitsu. Breath-control techniques as well as philosophical attitudes, such as the necessity of mental calm, were taken from Zen Buddhism. The aim is to focus the body's total muscular power in one instant. Hands, feet, elbows, etc., are toughened in stylized training sequences against padded or wooden blocks, and karate fighters also perform feats of strength, such as wood breaking. In actual fights, however, which last two or three minutes, blows are stopped short before impact. As in ▷judo, grades are distinguished by coloured belts and points are awarded in combat. ▷*See also* martial arts.

● **Karatepe** ▶ A fortified hilltop site near Adana (S Turkey), founded (c. 740 BC) by Asitawandas, King of the Danuna (possibly the same people as the Danaoi, mentioned by Homer). King Sanduarri of Karatepe was beheaded by ▷Esarhaddon (676 BC). A palace with sculptured reliefs and an important bilingual Phoenician and Hittite hieroglyphic inscription have been found.

● **Karbala** ▶ (*or* Kerbela) 32 37N 44 03E A town in central Iraq, S of Baghdad. Muslim pilgrims are attracted to the tomb of Husan (the son of ▷Ali), who was martyred here. It is a trading centre for dates and other agricultural produce. Population (latest est): 296 705.

● **Karelian Republic** ▶ (*or* Karelia) A constituent republic of Russia. In NW Russia, it is forested and also possesses thousands of lakes and rivers. The Karelians speak a Finno-Ugric language, and W Karelia has formed part of Finland for much of its history, but was ceded to the Soviet Union in 1940. Industries include mining, timber, and chemicals. Some cereals, potatoes, and fodder crops are grown and fishing is very important. Area: 172 400 sq km (66 560 sq mi). Population (1996 est): 785 000. Capital: Petrozavodsk.

● **Karelian Isthmus** ▶ A land bridge in NW Russia, situated between the Gulf of Finland in the W and Lake Ladoga in the E. It connects Finland with Russia and was ceded to the Soviet Union in 1944. It is 40–113 km (25–70 mi) wide and 145 km (90 mi) long and its principal cities are St Petersburg and Vyborg.

● **Karen** ▶ A group of peoples of S Myanmar (Burma) who speak tonal languages distantly related to those of the Tibeto-Burman branch of the ▷Sino-Tibetan family. There are many distinct groups and languages broadly divided into the White Karens (including Sgaw and Pwo) and the Red Karens (including Bre, Padaung, Yinbaw, and Zayein). Only Sgaw and Pwo have written forms and all are influenced by surrounding languages. Their religion is animistic. Karen guerrillas have been in conflict with the government since the 1950s.

● **Kariba, Lake** ▶ A reservoir in Zambia and Zimbabwe. It is formed by the Zambezi River above the **Kariba Dam** (completed 1959) and is used for generating hydroelectric power. Length: 282 km (175 mi).

● **Karl-Marx-Stadt** ▷*See* Chemnitz.

● **Karloff, Boris** ▶ (William Pratt; 1887–1969) British character actor, who worked mostly in US films. Following his great success as the monster in *Frankenstein* (1931), he was typecast in a number of sinister roles in horror films.

● **Karlovy Vary** ▶ (German name: Karlsbad) 50 14N 12 53E A spa town in the W Czech Republic, in W Bohemia. It has many hot sodium sulphate springs, including the Vřídlo (Sprudel) at a temperature of 72°C (162°F). Population (1991): 56 290.

● **Karlsbad** ▷*See* Karlovy Vary.

● **Karlsburg** ▷*See* Alba-Iulia.

● **Karlskrona** ▶ 56 10N 15 35E A seaport in S Sweden, on the Baltic

coast. It has been the main naval station of Sweden since 1680. Its industries include the manufacture of naval equipment, quarrying, and sawmilling. Population (1994): 60 642.

● **Karlsruhe** ▶ 49 00N 8 24E A city in SW Germany, in Baden-Württemberg, the capital of the former *Land* of Baden. Built in the 18th century as a planned city, it is the site of the federal court of justice and a university (1825). It has a harbour on the Rhine; industries include oil refining and machinery manufacturing. It is a centre for nuclear research and development. Population (1996 est): 275 690.

● **Karlstad** ▶ 59 24N 13 32E A port in SW Sweden, on the N shore of Lake Vänern, at the outlet of the River Klar. Its industries are based on timber and heavy machinery and it has a university (1967). Population (1990): 76 467.

● **karma** ▶ (Sanskrit: action) The sum of all human actions, which according to Hinduism and Jainism is passed from one individual existence to the next and determines the nature of the individual's rebirth. In ▷Buddhism, karma is associated with mental and physical elements passed on in the cycle of rebirth until the personal self is annihilated in attaining ▷nirvana.

● **Karnak** ▶ 25 44N 32 39E A village near ▷Thebes (Upper Egypt), the site of the huge temple of ▷Amon, built (c. 1320–1237 BC) mainly by the pharaohs Seti I (reigned 1313–1292) and ▷Ramses the Great. ▷*See also* Luxor.

Karen ▶ A 12-year-old Karen girl wearing brass neck rings. A long neck is regarded as a sign of great beauty in Karen society, the optimum effect being achieved with a maximum of 32 rings.

● **Karnataka** ▶ (name until 1973: Mysore) A state in SW India, on the Arabian Sea stretching E over the Western Ghats onto the Deccan plateau. Rice and sugar cane are grown along the coast, coffee and tea on the Ghats, and rice, cotton, and fruit on the Deccan. Hill forests provide teak and most of the world's sandalwood. Iron ore, gold, manganese, and bauxite are mined. Industries include iron and steel, food products, and silk. Most of the population are Kanarese-speaking Hindus.

History: long ruled by Hindu dynasties, Karnataka was conquered (1761) by a Muslim, Hyder Ali, whose son Britain dispossessed (1799). Area: 191 773 sq km (74 024 sq mi). Population (1991): 44 817 398. Capital: Bangalore.

● **Karpov, Anatoly** ▶ (1951–) Russian chess player, who became an International Grandmaster at 19 and subsequently world champion (1975). He successfully defended his title against ▷Korchnoi in 1978 and 1981 but was defeated by ▷Kasparov in 1985, 1986, 1987, and 1990. He regained the title in 1993 (Kasparov having been excluded from the championships) and defended it successfully in 1996. He was a member of the Soviet parliament (1989–91).

● **karri** ▶ A tree, ▷*Eucalyptus diversicolor*, native to SW Australia and cultivated elsewhere. It grows to a height of over 35 m in moist areas and produces excellent timber. The attractive leaves are dark green above and lighter below.

● **Karroo** ▶ A plateau in S South Africa, divided by the Groot-Swartberge range into the **Great Karroo** and, to the S, the **Little Karroo**. Seasonal rains turn them into rich pasture for sheep.

● **Kars** ▶ 40 35N 43 05E A town in NE Turkey. It was fortified in the 16th century and captured by Russians three times during the 19th century before being restored to Turkey after World War I. Population (latest est): 58 799.

● **karst region** ▶ An area of the earth's surface typified by sink holes, uvalas (depressions), and underground drainage, produced by the solution of limestone or dolomite. Such features are notable in the Karst region, along the Dalmatian coast of Croatia.

● **karting** ▶ (*or* go-karting) A form of ▷motor racing that originated in the USA in the 1950s. A kart usually has a tubular chassis, no body or suspension system, and a single driving seat. It has a maximum wheelbase of 50 in (1.27 m) and is usually powered by a single-cylinder two-stroke engine. 100 cc, 200 cc, and 270 cc are among the more common engine capacities. Most karts are capable of about 160 km per hour (100 mph).

● **karyotype** ▶ The number and appearance of the ▷chromosomes of an organism. When a cell's chromosomes are stained and fixed, they can be sorted in pairs on the basis of their length and other features to form a **karyogram**. This is characteristic for that particular species, and can be used, for example, to identify chromosomal abnormalities.

● **Kasai, River** ▶ A river in central Africa. Rising in Angola, it flows N into the Democratic Republic of Congo to join the Congo River as its main tributary. It forms part of the Angola–Congo border and is rich in alluvial diamonds. Length: 2100 km (1300 mi).

● **Kasavubu, Joseph** ▶ (c. 1917–69) Congolese statesman; president (1960–65). A teacher, Kasavubu joined with ▷Lumumba to lead the Belgian Congo to independence as the Democratic Republic of Congo. In 1961, helped by ▷Mobutu, he deposed Lumumba, until then prime minister, but was himself deposed in Mobutu's coup in 1965. He retired to his farm, where he died.

● **Kashi** ▶ (K'a-shih *or* Kashgar) 39 29N 76 02E A city in NW China, in Xinjiang Uygur AR on a fertile oasis. It is a centre of trade with the republics of the former Soviet Union and the Middle East. Chinese rule has been intermittent here since the 2nd century BC and rebellion among the Muslim population was common in the period 1862–1943. Cloth is manufactured and handicrafts include rug-making. Population (1990): 174 570.

● **Kashmir** ▶ The northernmost region of the Indian subcontinent, bordered by China to the NE and Afghanistan to the NW. The S Jammu lowlands rise into the Himalaya and Karakoram Mountains. Except for the Indus Valley and the Vale of Kashmir, the valleys are small. Rice, other grains, silk, cotton, fruits, and sheep are farmed.
History: most Kashmiris became Muslims in the 14th century but in the 19th century Hindu princes won power under British control. Britain's withdrawal (1947) was followed by a Muslim revolt; the Hindu maharajah acceded to India but Pakistan intervened and fighting between the two sides resulted in the partition of the region. Pakistan rules 78 932 sq km (30 468 sq mi) of the W and barren N. China occupies 42 735 sq km (16 496 sq mi) in the E. The remainder forms the Indian state of ▷Jammu and Kashmir. Sporadic fighting continues between Indian and Pakistani forces around the border. In recent years civil unrest has reduced the area to anarchy. Severe

floods caused thousands of deaths in 1992. Area: 222 236 sq km (85 783 sq mi).

● **Kasparov, Gary** ▶ (Gary Weinstein; 1963–) Chess player of Armenian-Jewish origin, born in Azerbaidzhan. At 22 he became the youngest ever world champion, beating ▷Karpov in 1985, 1986, 1987, and 1990. In 1993 Kasparov and Nigel Short (1965–) left the official chess organization, the Fédération internationale des Échecs (FIDE), and set up the Professional Chess Association (PCA). As a result he was stripped of his world title by the FIDE (but is regarded as world champion by the PCA). He was deputy leader of the Soviet Union's Democratic Party in 1990–91.

● **Kassala** ▶ 15 24N 36 30E A city in the NE Sudan. It has declined as a centre for cotton but has an important fruit trade. Population (1993): 234 270.

● **Kassel** ▶ 51 18N 9 30E A city in central Germany, in Hessen. Notable buildings include the Orangery Palace (1701–11). Its manufactures include railway engines and textiles. Population (1996 est): 201 573.

● **Kassem, Abdul Karim** ▶ (1914–63) Iraqi soldier and statesman; prime minister (1958–63) after leading an army coup that overthrew the monarchy. An opponent of Arab unity, he survived a rebellion (1959) of those who wanted federation with the United Arab Republic but was killed in a revolt led by army officers.

● **Kassites** ▶ A people of mysterious racial origins who moved SW from the Zagros Mountains to overrun ▷Babylonia in the 16th century BC. Although Indo-European gods were apparently worshipped, the Kassite language is neither Indo-European nor Semitic. The Kassites ruled Babylon for about 400 years until overthrown by Assyria.

● **Kästner, Erich** ▶ (1899–1974) German novelist and poet, best known for his children's books, such as *Emil and the Detectives* (1929). His satirical poetry, novels, and later plays combine humour with social concern.

● **Katanga** ▷See Shaba.

● **Kathiawar Peninsula** ▶ A peninsula in W India, in Gujarat, roughly 190 km (118 mi) square, projecting into the Arabian Sea between the Gulfs of Kutch and Cambay.

● **Kathmandu** ▶ (*or* Katmandu) 27 42N 85 19E The capital of Nepal, near the confluence of the Rivers Baghmati and Vishnumati. Founded in the 8th century AD, it possesses numerous historical buildings and a university (1959) and is the site of several religious festivals. Its development as the country's main commercial centre has been assisted by a programme of road building. Population (1993 est): 535 000.

● **Katmai, Mount** ▶ An active volcano in the USA, in S Alaska in the Aleutian Range. Following its violent eruption in 1912, the ▷Valley of Ten Thousand Smokes was formed. Height: 2100 m (7000 ft). Depth of crater: 1130 m (3700 ft). Width of crater: about 4 km (2.5 mi).

● **Katowice** ▶ (former name (1953–56): Stalinogrod) 50 15N 18 59E A city in S central Poland. It is an important industrial centre within the Upper Silesia coalfield; manufactures include iron and steel. The Silesian University was established here in 1968. Population (1996 est): 354 200.

● **Katrine, Loch** ▶ A lake in central Scotland, in Stirling. Noted for its beautiful scenery, it also supplies Glasgow with water. Length: 15 km (8 mi). Maximum width: 1.6 km (1 mi).

● **Katsina** ▶ 13 00N 7 32E A city in N Nigeria. From its early foundation (c. 1100), it was an important centre for trans-Saharan trade. Active until the 18th century, it has now declined in importance. Population (1996 est): 206 500.

● **Katsura Taro** ▶ (1847–1913) Japanese soldier and statesman, who was instrumental in introducing into the Japanese army a general-staff system on German lines. He was prime minister three times (1901–06, 1908–11, 1912–13) and presided over the victorious ▷Russo-Japanese War (1904–05) and the annexation of Korea (1910).

● **Kattegat** ▶ A strait between Denmark and Sweden linking the Skagerrak with the Baltic Sea. Length: about 240 km (149 mi).

● **katydid** ► A ▷bush cricket of the subfamily *Pseudophyllinae*, common in the tropics and E North America. It takes its name from the repetitive song—"katy-did, katy-didn't"—of male katydids of the genus *Pterophylla*. Katydids are generally green and have long wings but never fly. They are mainly herbivorous, although some species eat insects.

● **Katyn Massacre** ► The execution during World War II of 4250 Polish officers in the Katyn forest, near Smolensk in Russia. The bodies of the Poles, who had been interned by the Russians following the Soviet occupation of Polish territory in 1939, were discovered by the Germans in 1943. The Russians denied responsibility, counter-charging the Germans with the massacre. The Soviet Union forbade the Red Cross investigation requested by the Polish Government in exile, with which it broke diplomatic relations. The Soviet Union finally admitted responsibility for the massacre in 1990.

● **Katz, Sir Bernard** ► (1911–   ) German-born British biophysicist, who shared a Nobel Prize (1970) with Julius Axelrod (1912–   ) of the USA and Ulf von Euler (1905–83) of Sweden for his work on the transmission of signals in the nervous system.

● **Kauffmann, Angelica** ► (1741–1807) Swiss painter, who divided her career between London and Rome. In England (1765–81) she painted portraits influenced by ▷Reynolds and was employed on decorative work in country houses designed by Robert and James ▷Adam.

● **Kaufman, George S(imon)** ► (1889–1961) US dramatist. He worked as a newspaper columnist while collaborating, especially with Moss ▷Hart, on an enormous number of Broadway comedy hits, including *Bandwagon* (1931) and *The Man Who Came to Dinner* (1939). With George ▷Gershwin he wrote *Of Thee I Sing* (1932), and he also wrote the scripts of two ▷Marx brothers films. He was a leading wit at the ▷Algonquin Round Table.

Kathmandu ► A temple dedicated to Hanuman, the Hindu monkey god.

● **Kaunas** ► (Russian name: Kovno) 54 52N 23 55E A port in central Lithuania at the confluence of the Rivers Neman and Viliya. It was held successively by Lithuania, Poland, and Russia. The capital of Lithuania from 1918 until 1940, it was occupied by German forces during World War II. It is a major educational and industrial centre; industries include chemicals, textiles, and iron production. Population (1996 est): 410 800.

● **Kaunda, Kenneth (David)** ► (1924–   ) Zambian statesman; president (1964–91). He joined the African National Congress in 1949 but in 1958 founded the more militant Zambia African National Congress and was imprisoned for subversion. On his release in 1960 he became president of the United National Independence Party, which took Northern Rhodesia to independence as Zambia in 1964. Under his leadership Zambia became a one-party state in 1972. In 1991 he was defeated in the country's first free elections since 1968. Although he then announced his retirement, he went on to serve as leader of Zambia's main opposition party from 1995 to 2000. In 1997–98 he was imprisoned for alleged complicity in an attempted coup but released without charge. He was subsequently stripped of Zambian citizenship, on the grounds that his parents were born in Malawi.

● **Kaunitz, Wenzel Anton, Count von** ► (1711–94) Austrian statesman. As chancellor (1753–92) he controlled Habsburg foreign policy under Empress Maria Theresa and her son Emperor Joseph and was also influential in the reform of internal administration. His most striking achievement was to reverse (1756–57) the European alliances of the War of the ▷Austrian Succession, making France and Russia Austria's allies in the ▷Seven Years' War against Prussia.

● **kauri pine** ► A coniferous tree, *Agathis australis*, from New Zealand. Growing to a height of 46 m, it has oblong leaves, 5 cm long and 2 cm wide, and spherical cones, 5–8 cm in diameter. It yields a resin (kauri copal or gum) used in making varnishes; the best resin is fossilized, derived from extinct trees and dug out of the ground. Its timber is used for building. Family: *Araucariaceae*. ▷See also dammar.

● **kava** ► A shrub, *Piper methysticum*, of the Pacific Islands and Australia, the ground and fermented roots of which are made into a narcotic drink. The roots are also chewed, and continued use produces inflammation and ulcers of the mouth. It has been used medicinally and as a local anaesthetic. Family: *Piperaceae*.

● **Kaválla** ► (or Kavála; ancient name: Neopolis) 40 56N 24 24E A port in NE Greece, in Macedonia on the Aegean Sea. A Roman naval base, it was visited by St Paul (50–51 AD). It was ceded by Turkey to Greece in 1912. Tobacco is the chief export. Population (1991): 58 576.

● **Kawabata Yasunari** ► (1899–1972) Japanese novelist. He was one of a group known as the Neo-Impressionists, which opposed the preceding realist movement in Japanese literature. His novels, which include *Snow Country* (1935–47) and *The Sound of the Mountain* (1949–54), are characterized by melancholy and loneliness, probably related to his being orphaned at an early age. In 1968 he was awarded the Nobel Prize. He committed suicide.

● **Kawasaki** ► 35 32N 139 41E A city in Japan, in SE Honshu. Part of the Tokyo-Yokohama industrial complex, it has shipbuilding, iron and steel, and chemical industries. Population (1995): 1 202 811.

● **Kawasaki disease** ► (or mucocutaneous lymph node syndrome) A disease of infants and young children involving enlargement of the lymph nodes, fever, and reddening of the palms and soles. Later the heart and coronary arteries may be affected. The disease was first described in 1967 by Tomisaku Kawasaki, a Japanese physician.

● **Kay, John** ► (1704–c. 1764) British inventor of the flying shuttle (patented in 1733), which contributed to the mechanization of weaving. Kay was defrauded of most of the royalties due to him and died in poverty in France.

● **kayak** ► A native Inuit canoe consisting of waterproofed animal skins stretched over a light framework and having one or two openings in the top with flexible watertight closures for one or two occupants.

● **Kaye, Danny** ► (David Daniel Kaminski; 1913–87) US actor, singer, and comedian. *Wonder Man* (1944) established his reputation as a cinema comedian. Other films included *The Secret Life of Walter*

Mitty (1946), in which he played a nondescript character who saw himself as a world hero, and the musical *Hans Christian Andersen* (1952). Danny Kaye also performed as a stand-up comic and worked for a number of charities, including UNICEF.

● **Kayseri** ▶ 38 42N 35 28E A town in central Turkey on the site of ancient Caesarea Mazaca. Kayseri has remains of the Seljuq civilization, notably the Great Mosque built in 1136. Population (1994 est): 454 000.

● **Kazakh** ▶ A Turkic people of Kazakhstan and Xinjiang Uygur AR in China. With the Kirgiz, ▷Bashkir, and ▷Tatars they form the Kipchak division of the Turkic peoples. They were traditionally nomadic herders of horses, sheep, and goats who lived on milk products and mutton. Their movable dome-shaped dwellings (yurts) consisted of wooden frames across which skins were stretched. Except in Xinjiang Uygur AR they are now settled stock breeders. Clan units, comprising extended-family groups and headed by chiefs, were the main social organization. ▷See Turkic languages.

● **Kazakhstan, Republic of** ▶ A republic in central Asia, extending over a vast area from the Caspian Sea in the W to the Chinese border in the E. Fertile steppes in the N give way to arid plateaux in the S, including sand desert E of the Aral Sea: the SE is mountainous. The ▷Kazakhs comprise some 30% of the population, which includes Russians (43%) and Ukrainians (7%).
Economy: the area is rich in mineral resources, especially tungsten, coal, copper, and iron ore. In 1993 Kazakhstan agreed to the development and exploitation of its oilfields by international companies. The atomic power station on the Mangyshlak peninsula has the world's first industrial fast-breeder reactor. An important agricultural area, it produces cereals, cotton, rice, and fruit. Kazakhstan is also noted for its sheep, bred for their wool. A privatization programme was announced in 1993.
History: conquered by Mongols in the 13th century, the region came under Russia in the 18th and 19th centuries. A national uprising was suppressed by the Red Army in 1917. Kazakhstan, which became a constituent Soviet republic in 1936, suffered enormously during the Stalinist era, when the enforced collectivization of agriculture resulted in the deaths of thousands of Kazakh nomads. Nationalist riots in 1989 caused several deaths. It became an independent republic on the break-up of the Soviet Union in 1991. The Communist Party remained in power (as the Socialist Party) under President Nursultan Nazarbayev. Although multiparty elections were held in 1994, a subsequent constitution, approved by referendum in 1995, gave Nazarbayev power to dismiss parliament and rule by decree. The country's first contested presidential elections (1999) saw a landslide victory for Nazarbayev but were condemned by observers as unfair. In 1997 the official capital was moved from Alma Ata to Akmola, which was renamed Astana. Kazakhstan is a member of the Commonwealth of Independent States.

Republic of Kazakhstan

Head of state	President Nursultan Nazarbayev
Official language	Kazakh
Official currency	tenge of 100 tein
Area	2 717 300 sq km (1 049 155 sq mi)
Population (1997 est)	16 544 000
Capital	Astana (Akmola)

● **Kazan** ▶ (*or* Kasan) 53 45N 49 10E A city in W Russia, on the River Volga, the capital of the Tatar Republic. It is a major cultural and commercial centre and has oil refining, electrical engineering, chemical production and food processing industries.
History: founded in the 14th century by the ▷Tatars, it became the capital of an independent khanate and was captured (1552) by Ivan the Terrible. Its industry developed during the 19th century. Lenin and Tolstoy studied at Kazan's university (1804). Population (1995 est): 1 085 000.

● **Kazan, Elia** ▶ (E. Kazanjoglous; 1909–) US stage and film director and novelist, born in Turkey of Greek parentage. He helped to found the ▷Actors' Studio in 1947. For the stage he directed *The Skin of Our Teeth* (1942), *A Streetcar Named Desire* (1947), *Death of a Salesman*

(1949), and other outstanding plays. His films include *Viva Zapata* (1952), *On the Waterfront* (1954), *East of Eden* (1955), and *The Arrangement* (1969), which is based on his own novel. Other novels include *America, America* (1963) and *The Anatolian* (1982). In 1999 he was awarded an honorary Oscar for his lifetime's achievement, a decision that caused some controversy owing to his cooperation with the ▷McCarthy investigations into Hollywood in the 1950s.

● **Kazantzakis, Nikos** ▶ (1885–1957) Greek writer of novels, plays, travel books, and poetry. His epic poem *I Odysseia* (1938), a continuation of Homer's *Odyssey*, embodies many of his ideas. He is best known for the novels *Zorba the Greek* (1946) and *Christ Recrucified* (1954).

● **Kazvin** ▶ (*or* Qazvin) 36 16N 50 00E A town in NW Iran. It is the trading centre for a fertile plain and was the national capital in the 16th century. Population (1991): 278 826.

● **KBE** ▷*See* Order of the British Empire.

● **Kean, Edmund** ▶ (c. 1787–1833) British actor. He was particularly successful as Shylock in *The Merchant of Venice*, his first London success in 1814, Richard III, Macbeth, Iago in *Othello*, and Barabas in Marlowe's *The Jew of Malta*, all roles suited to his passionate style of acting.

● **Keating, Paul** ▶ (1954–) Australian statesman; Labor prime minister (1991–96). As finance minister (1983–91) he introduced sweeping economic reforms. As prime minister he opposed Australia's constitutional links with the UK and supported Aboriginal rights. He was re-elected in 1993 but led Labor to a massive defeat in the general election of 1996.

● **Keaton, Buster** ▶ (Joseph Francis K.; 1895–1966) US comedian of silent films. He worked with his parents in vaudeville before starting his film career in 1917. He developed his character of the unsmiling and resilient clown in a series of classic silent comedies, including *The Navigator* (1924), *The General* (1926), and *The Cameraman* (1928). He was awarded a special Academy Award in 1959. His autobiography is *My Wonderful World of Slapstick* (1962).

● **Keats, John** ▶ (1795–1821) British poet. The son of a London ostler, he trained as a surgeon before being encouraged by Leigh ▷Hunt to devote himself to poetry. Despite the failure of his first volume, *Poems* (1817), which contained the sonnet "On First Looking into Chapman's Homer," and the savage criticism directed at his second, *Endymion* (1818), Keats persisted and between 1819 and 1820 wrote most of his best-known poems. His short life was dogged by tragedies, especially the death of his brother from tuberculosis in 1818 and his unfulfilled love for Fanny Brawne. Such poems as *La Belle Dame Sans Merci*, *The Eve of Saint Agnes*, and the great odes ("To a Nightingale," "On a Grecian Urn," etc.), all published in 1820, eventually established his reputation as one of the principal Romantic poets. He died in Rome in search of a cure for his tuberculosis and was buried there.

● **Keble, John** ▶ (1792–1866) British churchman. While professor of poetry at Oxford (1831–41) he preached a famous sermon, entitled "National Apostasy," which effectively began the ▷Oxford Movement. His book of poetry, *The Christian Year* (1827), was widely read. Keble College, Oxford, was founded in his memory (1870).

● **Kebnekaise** ▶ A mountain range in N Sweden. It rises to 2123 m (6965 ft) at Kebnekaise Sydtopp, the highest mountain in Sweden.

● **Kecskemét** ▶ 46 56N 19 43E A town in central Hungary. It lies on a wide fertile plain that is Hungary's most important agricultural area, notably its soft fruit as apricots. Population (1997 est): 105 000.

● **Kedah** ▶ A state in NW Peninsular Malaysia, bordering on Thailand. Rice is grown on the W coastal plain; other products include rubber, tin, tungsten, and iron. Area: 9425 sq km (3639 sq mi). Population (1993 est): 1 412 000. Capital: Alor Star.

● **Keegan, Kevin** ▶ (1951–) British footballer and manager. A forward, he played for Liverpool (1971–77), England (1972–84), Hamburg (1977–80), Southampton (1980–82), and Newcastle United (1982–84). He managed Newcastle United from 1992 until 1997 and is now manager of Fulham. In 1999 he was appointed coach for the English national side.

● **Keeler, Christine** ▷*See* Profumo, John.

● **Keeling Islands** ▷*See* Cocos Islands.

● **Keelung** ▷*See* Jilong.

● **Keene, Charles Samuel** ▶ (1823–91) British artist and illustrator, famous for his gentle satirization of lower- and middle-class characters in *Punch* (1851–90). He also illustrated Charles Reade's *The Cloister and the Hearth* and George Meredith's *Evan Harrington* in the periodical *Once a Week*.

● **Keeshond** ▶ A breed of dog traditionally used by the Dutch as barge dogs. It has a compact body with a foxlike face and a long thick grey coat with black-tipped hairs. The tail is carried over the back and a dense ruff surrounds the neck. Height: 43–45 cm.

● **Keewatin** ▶ A former district of the ▷Northwest Territories of Canada, consisting of the mainland E of 102°W and N of 60°N plus most islands in Hudson Bay. In April 1999 it was absorbed into the new territory of ▷Nunavut, a semiautonomous homeland for the Inuit people.

● **Kefallinía** ▷*See* Cephalonia.

● **Keflavík** ▶ 64 01N 22 35W A town and fishing port in SW Iceland. It has a NATO air base. Population (1994): 7627.

● **Keighley** ▶ 53 52N 1 54W A town in N England, in Bradford unitary authority, West Yorkshire, on the River Aire. The main products are woollens and worsteds, textile machinery, and machine tools. It is the N terminus of the Worth Valley Railway (steam trains). Population (1991): 49 567.

● **Keitel, Wilhelm** ▶ (1882–1946) German field marshal who, as Hitler's chief military adviser throughout World War II, bore a considerable responsibility for the behaviour of the German army in occupied Europe. In 1945 in Berlin he confirmed the German surrender. He was tried at Nuremburg and hanged as a war criminal.

● **Kekulé von Stradonitz, (Friedrich) August** ▶ (1829–96) German chemist, whose main interest was in valence. He was the first chemist to establish the valence of the elements and to introduce the notion of single, double, and triple bonds. He went on to deduce the structural formulae of many organic molecules, including that of benzene (**Kekulé formula**), which he claimed to have thought of in 1865 while dozing on a bus. ▷*See also* aromatic compound.

● **Kelantan** ▶ A state in central Peninsular Malaysia, bordering on Thailand. It was ruled by Siam (now Thailand) from the early 19th century until 1909. Rice is grown on the NE coastal plain, and rubber, copra, and minerals are produced. Area: 14 931 sq km (5765 sq mi). Population (1993 est):1 221 700. Capital: Kota Baharu.

● **Keller, Gottfried** ▶ (1819–90) German-Swiss poet and novelist. His early poetry (1846) won him a scholarship to study in Germany. His works include the novel *Der grüne Heinrich* (1854–55) and short stories, including *Die Leute von Seldwyla* (1856–74), describing life in a small town.

● **Keller, Helen Adams** ▶ (1880–1968) US social worker and writer. At the age of 19 months she lost her sight and hearing through an illness. Despite these handicaps, with the aid of her teacher, Annie Sullivan (1866–1936), she learnt to speak, read, and write and finally graduated from Radcliffe College, Cambridge (Massachusetts), in 1904. She lectured in many countries and raised money for the education of handicapped people. Her books include *The Story of My Life* (1902).

● **Kellogg-Briand Pact** ▶ (1928) An international agreement that condemned war as a means of settling disputes. The pact of perpetual friendship, negotiated by the US secretary of state, Frank B. Kellogg (1856–1937) and French foreign minister, ▷Briand, was signed in Paris in 1928 by representatives of 15 nations, and later by 48 others. Some success in South American disputes was achieved by invoking the treaty, but it proved ineffective against the Japanese invasion of Manchuria (1931), the Italian invasion of Ethiopia (1938), and against Hitler's aggression.

● **Kells** ▶ (Irish name: Ceanannus Mór) 54 48N 6 14W A market town in the Republic of Ireland, in Co Meath. A monastery was founded here in the 6th century AD by St Columba in which *The Book of Kells*, an 8th-century illuminated manuscript of the Gospels, is reputed to have been written. Population (latest est): 2623.

● **Kelly, Grace** ▶ (1929–82) US film actress. Her films include *High Noon* (1952), *The Country Girl* (1955), *To Catch a Thief* (1955), and *High Society* (1956). She retired from acting when she married Prince Rainier III of Monaco in 1956. She died following a road accident.

● **Kelly, Ned** ▶ (1855–80) Australian outlaw. He and his brother Dan formed a gang in 1878 that became notorious for its daring robberies in Victoria and New South Wales. He was captured and hanged in 1880 after a gunfight with the police in which the other gang members were killed.

● **Kelmscott Press** ▶ A private printing press established in Hammersmith, London, by William ▷Morris in 1890. Of the 52 books issued by the press, the best known was an edition of Chaucer (1896) celebrated for its design, its typography, and its illustrations by ▷Burne-Jones. **Kelmscott Manor**, a 16th-century manor house near Lechlade, Oxfordshire, was Morris's home from 1871 and now houses a museum of his life and work.

● **kelp** ▶ A large brown ▷seaweed belonging to the order *Laminariales* (about 30 genera), found in cold seas, usually below the level of low tide, and often covering large areas. The giant kelp *Macrocystis*, of the E Pacific coast, reaches a length of 65 m. Its branching fronds are kept afloat by air bladders. The name kelp is also used for the ashes of seaweed, from which potassium and sodium salts and iodine were once obtained. ▷*See also* Laminaria.

● **kelpie** ▶ A breed of short-haired dog developed in Australia from the Border Collie and used for herding sheep and cattle. Named after a champion sheepdog of the 1870s, the kelpie has a long muzzle and pricked ears. The coat may be black or red (with or without tan), fawn, chocolate, or smoke-blue. Height: 43–50 cm.

● **kelvin** ▶ (K) The ▷SI unit of thermodynamic ▷temperature equal to 1/273.16 of the thermodynamic temperature of the triple point of water. Named after Lord ▷Kelvin.

● **Kelvin, William Thomson, 1st Baron** ▶ (1824–1907) Scottish physicist, who was professor at Glasgow University (1846–99). Kelvin was the first physicist to take notice of ▷Joule's work on heat and to press for its recognition. The two physicists then worked together, discovering the ▷Joule-Kelvin effect; both also made great contributions to the new science of thermodynamics. In 1848 Kelvin postulated that there is a temperature at which the motions of particles cease and their energies become zero. He called this temperature ▷absolute zero and suggested a scale of temperature, now known as the Kelvin scale, in which the zero point is absolute zero. In 1852 he suggested the feasibility of a ▷heat pump. He also studied electricity; during the 1860s he worked on the electrical properties of cables in conjunction with the laying of the first transatlantic cable in 1866. He was knighted for his contribution to this work in the same year and was created baron in 1896. The unit of temperature (*see* kelvin) is named after him.

● **Kemal, (Mehmed) Namik** ▶ (1840–88) Turkish poet, novelist, and dramatist. He was strongly influenced by European Romanticism and became one of the founders of modern Turkish literature. He was a member of a literary group known as the "Young Ottomans" and was imprisoned for the liberal and patriotic ideas he expressed in his most famous play, *Vatan yahnut Silistre* (*Fatherland or Silistria*; 1871).

● **Kemble, Roger** ▶ (1722–1802) British travelling actor and founder of a famous family of actors. His eldest daughter was the tragic actress Sarah ▷Siddons. His sons included **John Philip Kemble** (1757–1823), who played many classical tragic roles and managed both the Drury Lane and the Covent Garden theatres, and **Charles Kemble** (1775–1854), who played supporting roles and managed the Covent Garden Theatre from 1822. Charles' daughter **Frances Ann Kemble** (1809–93), known as Fanny Kemble, made a successful debut at Covent Garden in 1829, where she appeared in order to save her father from bankruptcy. She toured the USA several times. Three daughters of Roger were also well-known actresses in London and New York.

● **Kemerovo** ► 55 25N 86 05E A city in S Russia on the River Tom. It is the centre of the ▷Kuznetsk Basin coalfield and is one of the country's major chemical-producing cities. Population (1995 est): 503 000.

● **Kempe, Margery** ► (c. 1373–c. 1440) English mystic. After experiencing a conversion following a period of insanity, she undertook a series of pilgrimages in Europe and Palestine. These and her mystical experiences are recounted in her autobiography, *The Book of Margery Kempe*, which she dictated between about 1432 and 1436.

● **Kempe, Rudolf** ► (1910–76) German conductor, formerly an oboist. He was conductor of the Royal Philharmonic Orchestra from 1961 to 1963 and from 1964 until his death. He excelled in performances of Wagner and Richard Strauss.

● **Kempis, Thomas à** ▷*See* Thomas à Kempis.

● **Kendal** ► 54 20N 2 45W A town in NW England, in Cumbria, called the Gateway to the Lakes. It manufactures footwear, textiles, and Kendal mint cake. Catherine ▷Parr was born in the Norman castle. Population (1991): 25 461.

● **Kendall, Edward Calvin** ► (1886–1972) US biochemist, who shared the 1950 Nobel Prize in medicine and physiology with Phillip Hench (1896–1965) and Tadeus Reichstein (1897–1996) for their work on hormones. In 1916 he isolated the hormone thyroxine produced by the thyroid gland and later isolated several hormones from the adrenal cortex. This work laid the basis for modern endocrinology.

● **Kendall, Henry** ► (1841–82) Australian poet. He held a succession of menial jobs in Melbourne and Sydney. In three volumes of poetry, including *Leaves from Australian Forests* (1869) and *Songs from the Mountain* (1880), he described the landscape and atmosphere of Australia.

● **kendo** ► A Japanese ▷martial art deriving from ▷samurai sword fighting. Combatants using bamboo staffs or wooden swords try to deliver blows on specified target areas of each other's bodies. Two hits constitute a win.

● **Kendrew, Sir John Cowdery** ► (1917–97) British biochemist, who shared the 1962 Nobel Prize for Chemistry with Max ▷Perutz for his discovery of the structure of the myoglobin molecule. Kendrew, working at Cambridge University, used the technique of ▷X-ray diffraction, analysing his results with a computer. He was knighted in 1974.

● **Keneally, Thomas Michael** ► (1935–) Australian writer. A former schoolteacher, he published 16 novels before writing *Schindler's Ark* (1982), which won the 1982 ▷Booker Prize and was made into a prize-winning film (*Schindler's List*; 1994) by Steven ▷Spielberg. His other works include *The Chant of Jimmie Blacksmith* (1972), *The Playmaker* (1987), *Jacko: the Great Intruder* (1994), the memoir *Homebush Boy* (1995), and *The Great Shame* (1998).

● **Kenilworth** ► 52 21N 1 34W A town in central England, in Warwickshire. Kenilworth Castle, built in the 12th century, was presented to Robert Dudley, Earl of Leicester, by Elizabeth I in 1563 and described in Sir Walter Scott's novel *Kenilworth*. In the **Siege of Kenilworth** Henry III attacked the castle in 1266, besieging de ▷Montfort and his supporters during the second ▷Barons' War. In the **Dictum of Kenilworth** (31 October, 1266), between Henry III and de Montfort, the king's powers were restored and the means by which the barons could recover their lands were stated. The town has engineering and tanning industries. Population (1991): 21 623.

● **Kenitra** ► (former name: Port Lyautey; Arabic name: Mina Hassan Tani) 34 20N 6 34W A port in NW Morocco, on the Atlantic Ocean. It handles agricultural products, minerals, and timber. Population (1994 est): 150 113.

● **Kennedy, Cape** ▷*See* Canaveral, Cape.

● **Kennedy, Charles (Peter)** ► (1959–) British politician, leader of the Liberal Democrats (1999–). An MP from 1983, he is also well-known as a journalist and broadcaster.

● **Kennedy, Joseph Patrick** ► (1888–1969) US businessman and diplomat. A millionaire by the age of 30, he was ambassador to Brit-

ain (1937–40). He had five daughters and four sons, three of whom entered public life. **Joseph Patrick Kennedy, Jr** (1915–44), a naval pilot, was killed in World War II. **John Fitzgerald Kennedy** (1917–63), a Democrat, was the first Roman Catholic president of the USA (1961–63). His liberal domestic policies—the so-called New Frontier—involved tax and social reforms and an extension of racial integration. He also established the ▷Peace Corps. Abroad, he presided over the ▷Bay of Pigs invasion (1961), planned under his predecessor Eisenhower, and confronted the Soviet Union over its installation of missile bases in Cuba (1962; *see* Cuban Missile Crisis). In 1963, however, he negotiated the ▷Nuclear Test-Ban Treaty with Khrushchev and Macmillan, which eased relations between the superpowers. Kennedy's presidency also saw the beginning of US military involvement in Vietnam. He was assassinated in Dallas, apparently by Lee Harvey ▷Oswald. In 1953 he married Jacqueline Bouvier (1929–94), who became the wife of Aristotle ▷Onassis in 1968. **Robert Francis Kennedy** (1925–68), attorney general (1961–64) and then a senator (1965–68), campaigned for the Democratic presidential nomination in 1968, during which he too was assassinated. **Edward Moore Kennedy** (1932–) is a lawyer and Democratic Senator. In 1980 he competed for the presidential nomination.

● **Kennedy, Nigel** ► (1956–) British violinist, noted for his flamboyant style. Recordings include Elgar's violin concerto and Vivaldi's *The Four Seasons*.

● **Kennelly, Arthur Edwin** ► (1861–1939) US electrical engineer. On learning that ▷Marconi had succeeded in transmitting radio waves across the Atlantic, despite the earth's curvature, Kennelly guessed that the waves were being reflected by an electrically charged layer in the upper atmosphere. The existence of this layer was confirmed independently by ▷Heaviside and it was known as the Kennelly-Heaviside layer (now known as the E-layer of the ▷ionosphere).

● **Kenneth I MacAlpine** ► (died c. 858) King of the Scots of Dalriada (c. 844–c. 858). He formed the kingdom of Alba, the foundation of modern Scotland.

● **Kensington and Chelsea** ► A royal borough of W central Greater London, created in 1965 from the metropolitan boroughs of ▷Chelsea and Kensington. **Kensington Palace**, a Jacobean mansion restructured by Wren for William III and Mary II, was the main royal residence from 1690 to 1760; it was later the birthplace of Queen Victoria and the home of Diana, Princess of Wales. The grounds now form Kensington Gardens, a public park, which contains the famous Peter Pan statue by ▷Frampton. The borough is a centre for museums and colleges, including the Victoria and Albert Museum, the Science Museum, the Natural History Museum, and the Imperial College of Science, Technology and Medicine. Area: 12 sq km (5 sq mi). Population (1999 est): 138 394.

● **Kent** ► A county of SE England, bordering on the English Channel and Greater London. It consists chiefly of undulating lowlands, crossed by the North Downs from W to E, and rising to the The Weald in the SW. The chief rivers are the Thames, Medway, and Stour. There are impressive chalk cliffs, notably at Dover. Often called the Garden of England, it is the country's leading fruit and hop-growing area. Other important agricultural activities include market gardening and arable, cattle, and sheep farming. The main industries are paper manufacture and oil refining. Rochester and Gillingham became an independent ▷unitary authority, known as Medway, in 1998. Area (excluding Medway): 3526 sq km (1361 sq mi). Population (1996 est, excluding Medway): 1 317 800. Administrative centre: Maidstone.

● **Kent, William** ► (1685–1748) English architect, landscape gardener, and interior designer, possibly the most famous exponent of English ▷Palladianism. Starting as a painter in Rome, he returned to England in 1719 as the protégé of Lord Burlington, with whom he frequently worked. His most notable buildings include Holkham Hall, Norfolk (1734) and the Horse Guards, London (built after his death). His furniture and interior designs were noticeably influenced by the ▷baroque. Kent's greatest contribution to English art was his development of ▷landscape gardening, later continued by such designers as Capability ▷Brown.

William Kent ▶ The Palladian portico on the south front of Holkham Hall in Norfolk.

● **Kentucky** ▶ A state in the central USA, lying to the E of the Mississippi River. It consists of the Appalachian Mountains in the E, the Bluegrass region in the centre, an undulating plain in the W, and the basins of the Tennessee and Ohio Rivers in the SW. Manufacturing in the state includes machinery, iron and steel products, paints, varnishes, textiles, whiskey, and food products. It is an important coal-mining state and also produces petroleum and natural gas. Local timber is used in the furniture and wood industries. The principal agricultural products are tobacco, corn, hay, soya beans, cattle, sheep, and pigs. It is also an important region for the breeding of thorough-bred horses.

History: Daniel Boone explored the area (1769) and after rapid settlement it became a state (1792). Area: 104 623 sq km (40 395 sq mi). Population (1997 est): 3 908 124. Capital: Frankfort.

● **Kenya, Mount** ▶ 0 10S 37 30E An extinct volcano in Kenya, the second highest mountain in Africa. It includes 12 small glaciers. Height: 5200 m (17 058 ft).

● **Kenya, Republic of** ▶ A country in East Africa, on the Indian Ocean. The land rises gradually from the coast to the highlands of the interior reaching heights of over 5000 m (17 000 ft). In the W the Great Rift Valley runs N–S. Most of the inhabitants are Africans, including ▷Kikuyu, ▷Luo, ▷Masai, and Kamba.

Economy: agricultural production and processing forms the basis of the economy. A variety of subtropical and temperate crops are grown. The chief cash crops are coffee, tea (of which Kenya is Africa's leading producer), sisal, and pineapples; livestock rearing and dairy farming are also important. Forestry is being developed and mineral resources include soda ash, gold, limestone, and salt. Hydroelectricity is a valuable source of power and the country is now self-sufficient in electricity. Industry has expanded greatly since the early 1980s, especially food processing, steel, textiles, and small-scale manufacturing; oil is refined at Mombasa and piped to Nairobi. Tourism, exploiting Kenya's wealth of big game, is important; wildlife reserves include the Tsavo National Park.

History: some of the earliest known fossil ▷hominid remains have been found in the region by the ▷Leakey family. The coastal area was settled by the Arabs from the 7th century AD and was controlled by the Portuguese during the 16th and 17th centuries. It became a British protectorate (East Africa Protectorate) in 1895 and a colony (Kenya) in 1920. In the 1950s independence movements, especially among the Kikuyu, led to the ▷Mau Mau revolt. Kenya gained independence in 1963 and in 1964 became a republic within the Commonwealth, with Jomo ▷Kenyatta as its first president. The late 1980s saw border clashes with Uganda and criticisms of Kenya's human rights record. In 1992 President Daniel arap ▷Moi agreed to hold the first multiparty elections since the 1960s. Although he was re-elected president and his party won a parliamentary majority, the opposition alleged fraud, causing a political crisis. In 1997 protestors demanded sweeping constitutional change, leading to violent clashes. Although elections in 1997 produced another victory for Moi, the opposition refused to accept the result. In an important constitutional change, parliament voted to restrict Moi's powers in 1999.

Republic of Kenya

Head of state	President Daniel T. arap Moi
Official languages	Swahili and English
Official currency	Kenya shilling of 100 cents
Area	582 600 sq km (224 960 mi)
Population (1998 est)	28 337 000
Capital	Nairobi
Main port	Mombasa

● **Kenyatta, Jomo** ▶ (c. 1891–1978) Kenyan statesman; president (1964–78). Son of a poor farmer of the Kikuyu tribe, Kenyatta studied anthropology in London, where his doctoral thesis on the Kikuyu was published in 1938. On his return to Kenya he became (1947) president of the Kenya African Union and in 1953 was imprisoned for seven years for his part in the ▷Mau Mau rebellion (complicity in which he always denied). While in gaol he was elected leader of the Kenya African National Union (1960), which achieved Kenya's independence in 1963. Kenyatta was prime minister before becoming president of a one-party state.

● **Kenyon, Dame Kathleen** ▶ (1906–78) British archaeologist. Under the influence of Sir Mortimer ▷Wheeler she promoted sophisticated excavation techniques. Her excavations at ▷Jericho (1952–58), through which the site's great age was revealed, and at ▷Jerusalem (1961–67) are renowned.

● **Kepler, Johannes** ▶ (1571–1630) German astronomer, who was one of the first supporters of ▷Copernicus' heliocentric theory of the solar system. In 1597 he went to Prague to study under Tycho ▷Brahe; on Tycho's death, Kepler inherited his astronomical observations. Kepler used this data to deduce that the shape of planetary orbits is elliptical. He published this discovery, the first of ▷Kepler's laws, together with his second law in *Astronomia Nova* (1609). In 1619 he published his third law relating a planet's year to its distance from the sun. In 1610 he received a telescope built by ▷Galileo, which he used to observe Jupiter. In 1611 he constructed an improved version, now known as a Keplerian ▷telescope.

● **Kepler's laws** ▶ Three laws of planetary motion proposed by Johannes Kepler in 1609 and (third law) 1619. They state that: (1) each planet moves round the sun in an elliptical orbit with the sun at one focus of the ellipse; (2) the line joining a planet to the sun sweeps out equal areas in equal times, i.e. orbital velocity decreases as distance from the sun increases; (3) the square of the ▷sidereal period (P) of a planet is directly proportional to the cube of its mean distance (a) from the sun. For P in years and a in ▷astronomical units, $P^2 = a^3$.

● **Kerala** ▶ A state in SW India, extending along the W coastal plain and Western Ghats to India's S tip. Tropical, beautiful, and poor, it is India's most densely populated state, with little industry or mining. Rice, tea, coffee, pepper, rubber, nuts, and fruit are farmed. Fishing is also important.

History: a civilization separate from Aryan N India, Malayalam-speaking Kerala has traded with the East since ancient times, flourishing in the 9th and 10th centuries. Area: 38 855 sq km (14 998 sq mi). Population (1994 est): 30 555 000. Capital: Trivandrum.

● **keratin** ▶ An insoluble fibrous protein that is the major constituent of hair, nails, feathers, beaks, horns, and scales. Keratin is also found in the outer protective layers of the skin.

● **Kerbela** ▷*See* Karbala.

● **Kerch** ▶ 45 22N 36 27E A port in S Ukraine, on the Black Sea on the Strait of Kerch. Founded in the 6th century BC by Greek colonists, it was captured from the Tatars by Russia in 1771. Fishing is important, and related activities, together with iron and steel production, form the basis of its industry. Population (1991 est): 178 000.

● **Kerenski, Aleksandr Feodorovich** ▶ (1881–1970) Russian revolutionary. A member of the Socialist Revolutionary Party, after the outbreak of the Russian Revolution in February, 1917, Kerenski became minister of justice and then minister of war in ▷Lvov's provisional government. In July, after Lvov's fall, he became prime minister. His insistence that Russia remain in World War I, and his mismanagement of internal economic affairs, led to the Bolshevik coup d'état in October. Kerenski fled to Paris and in 1940 to the USA.

● **Kerguelen Islands** ▶ 49 30S 69 30E An archipelago in the S Indian Ocean, in the French Southern and Antarctic Territories. Kerguelen Island, the largest, is mountainous and glacial and the site of several scientific bases. Area: 7215 sq km (2786 sq mi).

● **Kérkira** ▶ (or Kérkyra) ▷*See* Corfu.

● **Kerman** ▶ 30 18N 57 05E A town in E Iran. It is an agricultural trading centre and carpet-making town. Kerman University was founded in 1974. Population (1994 est): 349 626.

● **Kermanshah** ▷*See* Bakhtaran.

● **kermes** ▶ A scale insect of the genus *Kermes*, especially *K. ilices* of Europe and W Asia, the dried bodies of which were formerly used to produce a red dye. They feed on the small evergreen kermes oak (*Quercus coccifera*), which is native to S Europe, N Africa, and W Asia and grows to a height of 7 m.

● **Kern, Jerome (David)** ▶ (1885–1945) US composer of musical comedies, the most famous of which was *Show Boat* (1927), written in collaboration with Oscar ▷Hammerstein II. After 1939 he devoted himself to film music. Two of his best-known songs are "Ol' Man River" and "Smoke Gets in Your Eyes."

● **kerosene** ▷*See* paraffin.

● **Kerouac, Jack** ▶ (1922–69) US novelist. He was a leading figure of the ▷Beat movement, of which his novel *On the Road* (1957) was a seminal work. His other loosely structured autobiographical works include *The Dharma Bums* (1958), *The Subterraneans* (1958), *Big Sur* (1962), and *Desolation Angels* (1965).

● **Kerr effects** ▶ Two effects concerned with optical changes produced by magnetic or electric fields. In the magneto-optical effect, plane-polarized light is slightly elliptically polarized when reflected by the pole of an electromagnet. In the electro-optical effect, the plane of polarization of a beam of light is rotated when passed through certain liquids or solids across which a potential difference is applied. This effect is utilized in the **Kerr cell**, which consists of a transparent cell containing a liquid, such as nitrobenzene; two parallel plates immersed in the liquid enable a field to be applied so that the passage of a beam of polarized light can be interrupted. The cell is used as a high-speed shutter and to modulate ▷laser beams. Named after the discoverer John Kerr (1824–1907).

● **Kerry** ▶ (Irish name: Chiarraighe) A county in the SW Republic of Ireland, in Munster bordering on the Atlantic Ocean. Chiefly mountainous with a deeply indented coastline, it rises in the S to ▷Macgillicuddy's Reeks and contains the famous Lakes of Killarney, noted for their beauty. The chief occupations are fishing, farming, and tourism. Area: 4701 sq km (1815 sq mi). Population (1996 est): 126 000. County town: Tralee.

● **Kertanagara** ▶ (d. 1292) King of Java (1268–92). Honoured as Java's greatest leader, he took advantage of the disunited Malay world in the 13th century to unite Java and became the most powerful ruler in SE Asia. He protected Indonesia from Kublai Khan's efforts to exact tribute and upheld Buddhism and Javanese culture.

● **Kertész, André** ▶ (1894–1985) US photographer, born in Hungary, whose work had a profound influence on contemporary photography. His books include *Day of Paris* (1945) and *Distortions* (1976).

● **Kesey, Ken** ▶ (1935–) US novelist. His best-known novel, *One Flew Over the Cuckoo's Nest* (1962), a satire based on his own experience in a mental hospital, was made into a successful film by Miloš ▷Forman. Later works include *Sometimes a Great Notion* (1964) and *Kesey's Garage Sale* (1973).

● **Kesselring, Albert** ▶ (1885–1960) German general, who commanded the Luftwaffe in World War II. He held the air command in the invasions of Poland (1939) and France (1940) and in the battle of Britain (1940). In 1943 he became commander of land and air forces in Italy and in 1945 on the Western Front. His death sentence as a war criminal was commuted to life imprisonment and he was released in 1952.

● **Kesteven, Parts of** ▷*See* Lincolnshire.

● **kestrel** ▶ A small ▷falcon characterized by a long tail and the ability to hover, with the tail fanned out, before diving on its prey. The common kestrel (*Falco tinnunculus*), 32 cm long, is widespread in Eurasia and Africa and hunts small rodents, birds, and insects. The female has a brown streaked plumage; the male is blue-grey with black-streaked pale-brown underparts, a black-tipped tail, and a black eye stripe.

● **Keswick** ▶ 54 37N 3 08W A town in NW England, in Cumbria. One of the main tourist centres of the Lake District, it is situated on the River Greta close to Derwentwater and Skiddaw. It has many associations with the Lakeland poets; Robert Southey is buried here. Population (1991): 4836.

● **ketch** ▶ A fore-and-aft-rigged □sailing vessel with two masts, a taller one set approximately one-third of the boat's length from the bows, a shorter one just forward of the rudder post. Ketches are a favoured rig for yachts, for the split rig reduces the area of each sail, making handling easier. Ketches do not sail as well towards the wind as ▷sloops do. ▷*See also* yawl.

● **Ketch, Jack** ▶ (d. 1686) English hangman, notorious for his cruelty. He was appointed public hangman in 1663, and was responsible for the executions of Lord William ▷Russell (1683) and the Duke of ▷Monmouth (1685), both of which he badly bungled. Subsequently all English executioners were popularly known by his name.

● **ketone** ▶ A class of organic chemicals having the general formula RCOR′, where R and R′ are hydrocarbon groups. Ketones are prepared by the oxidation of secondary alcohols. ▷Propanone (dimethyl ketone) is a common example.

● **Kettering, Charles Franklin** ▶ (1876–1958) US engineer, whose inventions, notably the electric starter (1912), greatly improved motor cars. He also developed leaded petrol, antiknock compounds, and a high-compression car engine (1951).

● **kettledrums** ▷*See* timpani.

● **Kew Gardens** ▶ The Royal Gardens at Kew, near Richmond, Greater London, which occupy land once owned by the royal family. The first botanic garden was created there in 1759, by Augusta (d. 1772), Princess of Wales, and in the late 18th and early 19th centuries Kew became internationally famous as an advisory centre, with many exotic plants, largely due to the efforts of Sir Joseph ▷Banks. Between 1848 and 1876 William and Joseph ▷Hooker founded the Museum of Economic Botany, the Library, Herbarium, and Jodrell Laboratory. Kew has played a major role in the distribution of many economic plants, notably the rubber plant, and is now renowned as a scientific institute. In Oct 1987 hurricane-force winds caused extensive damage.

● **key** ▷*See* tonality.

● **Keynes, John Maynard, 1st Baron** ▶ (1883–1946) British economist and member of the ▷Bloomsbury group. After attending the Versailles peace conference as a Treasury representative, Keynes published *The Economic Consequences of the Peace* (1919), which attacked the war reparations imposed on Germany. In his greatest work, *General Theory of Employment, Interest and Money* (1936), written during the Depression years, he argued that unemployment can only be alleviated by increased public spending. During World War II he worked for the government on war finance and in 1944 was the chief British representative at the Bretton Woods conference, at which the ▷International Monetary Fund was established. **Keynesianism** has been a powerful influence in economics; its central departure from established theory is the premise that what is rational for the individual and the firm is not necessarily rational for the government, and that rather than reinforcing the ▷trade cycle the government should counter it by public spending with money raised by ▷deficit financing. This was developed by later thinkers into a doctrine of expansive ▷fiscal policy and government interventionism.

● **Keystone Kops** ▶ A zealous but incompetent police force that featured in the silent film comedies produced by Mack ▷Sennett for the Keystone Film Company between 1912 and 1917. They were the butt of much irreverent slapstick comedy, preserving their imperturbable masks of dignity even during the absurd accelerated chase sequences.

● **Key West** ▶ 24 34N 81 48W A city in the USA, in Florida situated at the tip of the Florida Keys. A naval, air, and coastguard base, Key West is a tourist centre and was the home of Ernest Hemingway. Population (1990 est): 30 000.

● **KGB** ▶ (Committee of State Security) The former Soviet secret police concerned with internal security and intelligence. It was founded in 1954, after the fall of ▷Beria, and replaced the more brutal MGB (Ministry of State Security; 1946–53), which itself replaced the notorious NKVD (People's Commissariat of Internal Affairs; 1934–46). It was abolished in 1991 but formed the basis of separate units responsible for Russian intelligence, counter-intelligence, and border control.

● **Khabarovsk** ▶ 48 32N 135 08E A port in E Russia, on the River Amur. On the Trans-Siberian Railway, it is an important transport centre. Industries include engineering and oil refining. Population (1995 est): 618 000.

● **Khachaturian, Aram Ilich** ▶ (1903–78) Soviet composer of Armenian birth. He studied composition at the Moscow conservatoire. His music was deeply influenced by the scales and rhythms of Caucasian folk music. His compositions include concertos for piano (1936) and violin (1940) and the famous ballets *Gayaneh* (1942) and *Spartacus* (1954).

● **Khafre** ▶ (Greek name: Chephren) King of Egypt (c. 2550 BC) of the 4th dynasty. He emerged victorious from the dynastic strife that followed the death of his father ▷Khufu. Khafre built the second pyramid and (probably) the Sphinx at ▷Giza.

● **Khajuraho** ▶ 24 50N 79 55E A village in Madhya Pradesh, India, which was the capital of the Candella kingdom. Of the original 85 sandstone temples built there (950–1050), 20 survive.

● **Khakass Republic** ▶ A constituent republic of Russia, in the S. It was formed in 1930 for the Turkic-speaking Khakass people, who are Orthodox Christians. Khakass is rich in minerals, including gold, coal, iron ore, and copper, and timber and woodworking industries are also important. Livestock is raised. Area: 61 900 sq km (23 855 sq mi). Population (1995 est): 583 000. Capital: Abakan.

● **khaki** ▶ (Hindi-Urdu: dust-coloured) A yellowish-brown fabric of cotton, wool, or synthetic fibre used chiefly for military uniforms. Khaki was first worn by British troops in India as a form of ▷camouflage. Since 1900 it has been adopted by most other nations.

● **Khalid Ibn Abdul Aziz** ▷*See* Saudi Arabia, Kingdom of.

● **Khalifa** ▷*See* Abd Allah.

● **Khama, Sir Seretse** ▶ (1921–80) Botswanan statesman; president (1966–80). Trained as a barrister in London, Seretse Khama married Ruth Williams, an Englishwoman, as a result of which he had to renounce the chieftaincy of the Bamangwato tribe before returning to what was then Bechuanaland in 1956. In 1961 he founded the Bechuanaland Democratic Party, which gained independence for Botswana in 1966.

● **khamsin** ▶ A hot dry southerly wind that blows across Egypt from the Sahara Desert. Most common in April and June, it precedes ▷depressions moving E along the N African coast. According to Arab tradition it blows for 50 days.

● **Khan, Hashim** ▶ (1916–) Pakistani squash player, who is the senior member of a family that has dominated world squash for over 40 years. A native of Nawakilla in Peshawar, he won the British open championship seven times. His brother **Azam Khan** (1925–) won the British open championship four times under Hashim's coaching. Hashim's brother **Roshan Khan** and another brother, **Mohibullah Khan**, also won British titles in 1956 and 1963 respectively. Roshan's son, **Jahangir Khan** (1963–) won the first of a record nine successive British open championships in 1982 and secured five consecutive world open championships (1981–85), winning again in 1988. He retired in 1993.

● **Khan, Imran** ▶ (1952–) Pakistani cricketer. An all-rounder, he played for Worcestershire (1971–76), captaining the side (1976), and Sussex (1977–88). He also captained Pakistan (1982–84; 1985–87; 1988–92). In 1995 he married Jemima Goldsmith, daughter of the entrepreneur Sir James Goldsmith, and launched his own political party in Pakistan in 1996.

● **Kharga, El** ▶ (or al-Wahat al-Kharijah) A large oasis in Egypt, in the Libyan Desert. It produces dates, figs, olives, and vegetables; efforts have been made to increase irrigation by sinking deep wells. Chief town: El Kharga.

● **Kharkov** ▶ (or Karkiv) 50 00N 36 15E A city in E Ukraine. It was almost totally destroyed in World War II, when its importance as a road and railway junction led to bitter fighting. The nearby Donets Basin coalfield supports a major engineering industry. Population (1996 est): 1 555 000.

● **Khartoum** ▶ (or al-Khurtum) 15 40N 32 52E The capital of the Sudan, at the confluence of the Blue and the White Nile Rivers. An Egyptian army camp in the early 19th century, it later became a garrison town. In 1885 ▷Gordon was besieged and killed here and the town destroyed by the forces of the ▷Mahdi but was recaptured by Anglo-Egyptian forces in 1898 and rebuilt. It has several cathedrals and two mosques; its university was founded in 1956 and it also houses part of Cairo University (1955). It produces textiles and glass. Population (1993): 924 505.

● **Khazars** ▶ A Turkic people who inhabited the lower Volga basin from the 7th to 13th centuries. Noted for their laws, tolerance, and cosmopolitanism, the Khazars were the main commercial link between the Baltic and the Muslim empire. In the 8th century the Khazars embraced Judaism. Slavonic and nomadic Turkic invaders brought the downfall of the Khazars in the 11th century. Itil, near modern Astrakhan, was their capital.

● **khedive** ▶ The title bestowed in 1867 by the sultan of the Ottoman Empire on the hereditary viceroy of Egypt. It was used until 1914, when Egypt became a British protectorate.

● **Khelat** ▷*See* Kalat.

● **Kherson** ▶ 46 39N 32 38E A port in S Ukraine, on the River Dnepr. It is 25 km (15 mi) from the Black Sea and, founded in 1778, was Russia's first naval base on the Sea. Shipbuilding remains the chief industry. Population (1996 est): 363 000.

● **Khiva** ▶ 41 25N 60 49E A town in Uzbekistan, on the River Amu Darya. It may have existed in the 6th century AD and was the centre of the khanate of Khiva from the 16th century until 1873, when it was captured by Russia. Its architectural remains attract many tourists. Cotton spinning is also important.

● **Khlebnikov, Velimir** ▶ (Victor K.; 1885–1922) Russian poet, who founded the Russian futurist movement (*see* futurism) with ▷Mayakovskii. His poetry was characterized by verbal experimentation and technical virtuosity; much of it was written on scraps of paper during his many travels. He died of typhus and starvation while returning from Persia.

● **Khmer** ▶ A people of Cambodia, Thailand, and Vietnam who speak the Khmer language, belonging to the Mon-Khmer Division of the ▷Austro-Asiatic languages, which includes Vietnamese, ▷Mon, and Palaung. They are rice cultivators and fishers, living in village communities headed by an elected chief. Their religion is Theravada Buddhism, but magical beliefs and practices survive from pre-

Buddhist times. The Khmer empire was founded in 616 AD and between the 9th and 13th centuries Khmer kings presided over the advanced civilization that was responsible for the great stone buildings of ▷Angkor. The name Khmer was adopted by the anti-French nationalist movement of Cambodia (which was called the Khmer Republic from 1971 to 1975) and by the ▷Khmer Rouge movement.

● **Khmer Rouge** ▶ A Cambodian communist and nationalist movement formed in the early 1970s to resist the US-backed regime of Lon Nol. Under the leadership of ▷Pol Pot it took over the government in 1975 and renamed the country Democratic Kampuchea. In its fanatical attempt to create an ethnically and ideologically "pure" agrarian society, the regime caused some two million deaths from forced labour, starvation, and mass executions. The Vietnamese invasion of 1978 toppled the regime and forced the Khmer Rouge to retreat to Thailand, from where they continued to fight a guerrilla war. With other exiled factions, the Khmer Rouge subsequently (1982) formed the Coalition Government of Democratic Kampuchea (CGDK), which took over Cambodia's seat at the UN. Following the UN peace agreement of 1991, the Khmer Rouge participated in Cambodia's coalition government but withdrew before the elections of 1993 in order to resume its guerrilla activities. From 1996 the movement was increasingly split by internal conflicts. In 1997 elements of the Khmer Rouge captured and imprisoned Pol Pot, who died the following year. Most of its remaining members surrendered or defected to government forces in 1998–99. In 2001 Cambodia passed a law to allow the trial of Khmer Rouge leaders for genocide.

● **Khodzhent** ▶ (name from 1936 until 1991: Leninabad) 59 55N 30 25E A city in Tadzhikistan, on the River Syr Darya. Located on the ancient ▷Silk Road, it supports a major silk industry. Consumer goods are also produced. Population (1994 est): 164 500.

● **Khoisan** ▶ The racial grouping comprising the Hottentot and Bushmen people of S Africa. The Khoisan languages, of which the Hottentot Nama and the Bushman Kung have been most studied, are noted for their click sounds. Formerly widespread S of the Zambezi River, the Khoisan tribes have been decimated by Bantu and European encroachments since 1700 and their traditional culture almost exterminated. The Hottentots were nomads, herding sheep and cattle. They were divided into clans, each with its own territory and chief. The Bushmen were traditionally hunters and gatherers, but are now farm workers. Until the early 2000s, some groups in the deserts of W Botswana still roamed in bands, with the men hunting with bows and arrows, but all have now been forcibly resettled in villages. Bushman rock paintings survive in many areas of South Africa.

● **Khomeini, Ayatollah Ruholla** ▶ (1902–89) Iranian Shiite Muslim leader (ayatollah). Following the overthrow of the shah (1979) he returned from 16 years of exile to lead the Islamic Revolution. Advocating strict Islamic principles, he attracted international criticism for his reactionary views and hostility towards the West, as in the ▷Rushdie affair (1989).

● **Khorana, Har Gobind** ▶ (1922–   ) US biochemist, born in India, who was responsible for deciphering the ▷genetic code. Khorana shared a Nobel Prize (1968) with R. W. Holley (1922–93) and M. Nirenberg (1927–   ). In 1976 Khorana and his team constructed the first entirely synthetic yet biologically active gene.

● **Khosrow I** ▶ King of Persia (531–79 AD), who came to the throne after prolonged social disturbance and took measures to restore prosperity and to reform the state. He reorganized the army, strengthened his frontiers, and expanded his territory. His only serious rival, the Byzantine empire, was forced to concede tribute and territory but remained hostile. Khosrow's firm yet benevolent rule over an empire stretching from the River Oxus (now Amu Darya) to the Yemen marked the summit of ▷Sasanian power.

● **Khosrow II** ▶ (d. 628 AD) King of Persia (590–628) of the Sasanian dynasty, who accepted Byzantine aid to secure his throne, conceding territory in return. Its subsequent recovery and the conquest of Anatolia, Syria, and Egypt overtaxed Persian resources. The Byzantine counterattack reached his capital, Ctesiphon, and Khosrow was assassinated; the Sasanian empire disintegrated and was soon overrun by the Arabs.

● **Khrushchev, Nikita S(ergeevich)** ▶ (1894–1971) Soviet statesman; first secretary of the Soviet Communist Party (1953–64) and prime minister (1958–64). Khrushchev was a close associate of Stalin and emerged victorious from the power struggle that followed his death. In 1956 Khrushchev began a programme of destalinization and the degree of liberalization that ensued within the Soviet Union gave rise to revolts in other communist countries, such as the ▷Poznań Riots in Poland and the ▷Hungarian Revolution. Owing to the failure of his economic policies, his humiliation in the ▷Cuban Missile Crisis, and his antagonism towards China, he was ousted by ▷Brezhnev and ▷Kosygin.

● **Khufu** ▶ (or Cheops) King of Egypt (c. 2600 BC) of the 4th dynasty; the father of ▷Khafre. He built the Great Pyramid at ▷Giza, which was said to have taken 20 years to construct. Khufu's funeral barge has been discovered in good condition.

● **Khulna** ▶ 22 49N 89 34E A city in S Bangladesh, on the Ganges delta. An agricultural trading centre, its industries include shipbuilding and the manufacture of cotton cloth. Population (1991): 545 849.

● **Khyber Pass** ▶ (Khaybar Pass or Khaibar Pass) 34 06N 71 05E A mountain pass in the Safid Kuh range of the Hindu Kush, connecting Kabul in Afghanistan with Peshawar in Pakistan. Rising to 1072 m (3518 ft) in barren country, it is of strategic importance, having been used many times over the centuries by invading armies, the progress of which has often been impeded by hostile Afridi tribesmen.

● **kiang** ▶ A wild ▷ass, *Equus hemionus kiang*, of the Himalayas. It is the tallest wild ass, 1.4 m at the shoulder, and has a chestnut-coloured coat. ▷*See also* onager.

● **Kiangsi** ▷*See* Jiangxi.

● **Kiangsi Soviet** ▷*See* Jiangxi Soviet.

● **Kiangsu** ▷*See* Jiangsu.

● **kibbutz** ▶ An Israeli collective settlement in which land and property are owned or leased by all its members and work and meals are organized collectively. Adults generally have private quarters but children are housed together. About 3% of the population live in *kibbutzim*. A **moshav** is a smallholders' cooperative in which machinery is shared but land and property is generally privately owned. About 5% of the Israeli population live in *moshavim*.

● **Kicking Horse Pass** ▶ A pass through the Canadian Rocky Mountains, NW of Banff. It is the highest point on the Canadian Pacific Railway. Height: 1627 m (5339 ft).

● **Kidd, William** ▶ (c. 1645–1701) Scottish sailor. He spent his youth privateering for the English against the French off the North American coast and in 1695 he was given a royal commission to suppress pirates in the Indian Ocean. He reached Madagascar, a pirates' centre, where he seems to have joined them. He was arrested on his return to Boston, sent to England, and executed (possibly unjustly).

● **Kidderminster** ▶ 52 23N 2 14W A market town in W central England, in Worcestershire on the River Stour. It is famous for carpet manufacture, begun in 1735. Woollen yarn, textile machinery, and beet sugar are also produced here. Population (1991): 54 644.

● **Kidinnu** ▶ (4th century BC) Babylonian mathematician and astronomer, who discovered the precession of the equinoxes, an effect that causes the position of the sun at equinox to move slowly backwards through the zodiac. He also calculated the interval of time between successive new moons to within a second.

● **Kidman, Nicole** ▶ (1967–   ) Australian film actress, born in Hawaii. She made her name in the thriller *Dead Calm* (1989) and starred with her then-husband Tom ▷Cruise in *Far and Away* (1992) and Kubrick's *Eyes Wide Shut* (1999). Other films include *To Die For* (1995), *The Portrait of a Lady* (1996), and the musical *Moulin Rouge* (2001). Her stage work has included Hare's *The Blue Room* (1998, London).

● **kidneys** ▶ The two organs of excretion in vertebrate animals and humans, which also regulate the amount of salt and water in the blood. The human kidneys are bean-shaped, each about 12 cm long and weighing about 150 g, and situated on either side of the spine below the diaphragm. They contain millions of tubules organized into units called **nephrons**. Each nephron has a cup-shaped outer part (Bowman's capsule), which filters water and dissolved substances from blood supplied by the renal artery. Most of the water and some substances are reabsorbed back into the blood further down the tubule: the remaining fluid (*see* urine) contains waste products of protein metabolism and passes on to the pelvis of the kidneys and out through the ureters to the ▷bladder. The reabsorption of water is controlled by a hormone (vasopressin) from the pituitary gland. The kidneys also secrete a hormone (*see* renin) that assists in controlling blood pressure.

If one kidney ceases to function or is removed the other will enlarge and take over its function. Removal of both kidneys requires the use of a kidney machine to perform haemodialysis (*see* dialysis) until a suitable donor kidney is available for ▷transplantation.

● **Kiel** ▶ 54 20N 10 08E A city in N Germany, the capital of Schleswig-Holstein. A Baltic port, it was the chief naval port of Germany by the late 19th century. A naval mutiny here in 1918 sparked revolutions throughout Germany. It has a university (1665) and a 13th-century palace, restored after World War II. Industries include shipbuilding and engineering. Population (1998 est): 240 516.

● **Kiel Canal** ▶ (German name: Nord-Ostsee Kanal; former name: Kaiser Wilhelm Canal) A canal in Germany, in Schleswig-Holstein, linking Kiel on the Baltic Sea with the Elbe estuary on the North Sea.

● **Kielce** ▶ 50 51N 20 39E A town in S central Poland. During World War II it contained four German concentration camps. Notable buildings include its cathedral (12th century). It is a major industrial centre. Population (1999 est): 212 383.

● **Kielder Water** ▶ A reservoir in Northumberland, constructed in 1974–82 by damming the North Tyne. One of the largest man-made lakes in Europe, it supplies water to towns in NE England. The nearby **Kielder Forest** (*or* Border Forest), planting of which began in 1922, is the largest woodland area in the UK and one of the largest forest plantations in Europe.

● **Kierkegaard, Søren** ▶ (1813–55) Danish philosopher. Although critical of ▷Hegel, particularly in *The Concept of Irony* (1841), he remained under his influence. Kierkegaard was a prolific writer; much of his work is poetic and paradoxical even in its titles, for example *Either-Or* (1843) and *Concluding Unscientific Postscript* (1846). Suspicious of both science and the established Church, he saw man as existing in isolation and relating only to God. Among his specifically religious books is *Works of Love* (1847). His journal reveals him as a deeply religious, if unorthodox, thinker. He greatly influenced 20th-century ▷existentialism.

● **Kieślowski, Krzysztof** ▶ (1941–96) Polish film director. His works include *Decalogue* (1988–89), a series of ten short films for television, *The Double Life of Véronique* (1992), and the trilogy *Three Colours*, comprising *Blue* (1993), *White* (1993), and *Red* (1994).

● **Kiev** ▶ 50 28N 30 29E The capital city of Ukraine, on the River Dnepr. Industries include metallurgy, the manufacture of machinery and instruments, chemicals, food-processing, and textiles.

Among its many educational institutions is the Kiev State University (1833), and its opera and ballet companies have a worldwide reputation. Outstanding buildings include the 11th-century St Sophia cathedral, now a museum, and the Golden Gate of Kiev.

History: Kiev, "the mother of cities," was probably founded in the 6th or 7th century AD and from the 9th to the 13th centuries was the centre of a feudal state ruled by the Rurik dynasty—Kiev-Rus, the historical nucleus of Russia. In 1240 Tatar attacks virtually destroyed the city, which subsequently passed to Lithuania and then to Poland. Russian rule was established in the 17th century. After the Russian Revolution Kiev became the capital of the short-lived Ukrainian republic and in 1934, the capital of the Ukrainian SSR. In World War II the city was occupied after a long siege by the Germans and thousands of its inhabitants were massacred. Its postwar reconstruction has been spectacular; in 1986 it absorbed many inhabitants of Chernobyl after the nuclear disaster. Population (1998 est): 2 620 900.

● **Kigali** ▶ 1 58S 30 00E The capital of Rwanda (since 1962).A centre of the mining industry and the coffee trade, it was damaged during the civil war in 1994. Population (1991): 232 733.

● **Kikuyu** ▶ A Bantu-speaking tribe of Kenya. They cultivate cereals and sweet potatoes and keep livestock, particularly cattle. Small groups of patrilineal kin occupy scattered homesteads of conical-shaped huts. These groups are organized into clans but there is little hierarchical organization or centralization of authority. Age grades are an important basis of social organization, boys being initiated by circumcision. Political authority is held by a council of members of the senior grade. The largest tribe in Kenya, the Kikuyu were involved in the ▷Mau Mau movement during the 1950s and have a dominant voice in government.

● **Kilauea** ▶ A volcanic crater in the USA, in Hawaii on the E side of Mauna Loa. It is one of the largest active craters in the world. Height: 1247 m (4090 ft). Width: 3 km (2 mi).

● **Kildare** ▶ (Irish name: Contae Chill Dara) A county in the E Republic of Ireland, in Leinster. It consists chiefly of a low-lying fertile plain containing part of the Bog of Allen in the N and the Curragh, an area noted for its racehorse breeding and race track. Cattle rearing and arable farming are also important. Area: 1694 sq km (654 sq mi). Population (1996 est): 135 000. County town: Naas.

● **Kilimanjaro, Mount** ▶ 3 02S 37 20E A volcanic mountain in Tanzania on the Kenyan border, the highest mountain in Africa. It has two volcanic peaks: Kibo at 5895 m (19 340 ft), and Mawenzi at 5273 m (17 300 ft).

● **Kilkenny** ▶ (Irish name: Contae Chill Choinnigh) A county in the SE Republic of Ireland, in Leinster. Chiefly hilly, it is drained by the Rivers Suir, Barrow, and Nore. Agriculture is the chief occupation with cattle rearing and dairy farming. Area: 2062 sq km (796 sq mi). Population (1996 est): 75 000. County town: Kilkenny.

● **Kilkenny** ▶ (Irish name: Cill Choinnigh) 52 09N 7 15W A city in the Republic of Ireland, the county town of Co Kilkenny. One of Ireland's oldest towns, it has two cathedrals and a 12th-century castle. Population (latest est): 9500.

killer whale ▶ This specimen is hunting sealion pups on an Argentinian beach; the white patches behind its eye and dorsal fin are characteristic markings of the species. Killer whales prefer to hunt aquatic mammals but they will also prey on penguins, fish, and squid.

● **Killarney** ► (Irish name: Cill Airne) 52 03N 9 30W A town in the Republic of Ireland in Co Kerry. A tourist centre, it is famous for its lake, mountain, and forest scenery. Population (1991): 7250.

● **killer whale** ► A large toothed whale, *Orcinus orca*, common in Pacific and Antarctic waters but found in all other oceans. Up to 9 m long, killer whales are black above and pure white beneath, with an erect dorsal fin as tall as a man. They are notorious for their voracious appetites, hunting in packs and tackling even sharks and other whales. Like other dolphins, they are intelligent and trainable in captivity. Family: *Delphinidae* (dolphins). □ p. 685.

● **Killiecrankie, Pass of** ► 56 43N 3 40W A pass in the Grampian Mountains, Scotland, in Perth and Kinross. It was the scene of a massacre of William III's troops by Jacobite Highlanders (1689).

● **killifish** ► One of several small elongated fish, also called egglaying top minnows, belonging to the family *Cyprinodontidae*, especially the genus *Fundulus*. Killifish occur chiefly in tropical America, Africa, and Asia and feed at the surface on plant or animal material. Up to 15 cm long, many are brightly coloured and kept as aquarium fish. Similar related fish are the live-bearing top minnows of the family *Poeciliidae*. Order: *Atheriniformes*.

● **Kilmarnock** ► 55 37N 4 30W An industrial town in SW Scotland, the administrative centre of East Ayrshire. Industries include engineering, carpets, woollens, and whisky. The Burns museum contains many of his manuscripts. Population (1991): 44 307.

● **kilogram** ► (kg) The ▷SI unit of mass equal to the mass of the platinum-iridium prototype kept at the International Bureau of Weights and Measures near Paris.

● **kiloton** ► A measure of the explosive power of a nuclear weapon. It is equivalent to an explosion of 1000 tons of trinitrotoluene (TNT).

● **kilowatt-hour** ► (kW-hr) A unit of energy. It is equal to the work done by a power of 1000 watts in 1 hour.

● **kilt** ▷*See* Highland dress.

● **Kilvert, Francis** ► (1840–79) British clergyman and diarist. His diary, vividly recording scenes of rural life in the Welsh marches in the 1870s, was discovered in 1937 and published in 1938–40.

● **Kimberley** ► 28 45S 24 46E A city in N South Africa. It was founded (1871) following the discovery of diamonds and is today the world's largest diamond centre. The Kimberley Open Mine, 1.6 km (1 mi) in circumference, was closed in 1915. Industries include engineering, clothing, and diamond cutting. Population (1995 est): 183 000.

● **Kimberleys** ▷*See* Western Australia.

● **Kim Dae Jung** ► (1925–   ) Korean politician; president of South Korea (1997–   ). A leading human-rights campaigner, he was elected to the national assembly in 1961 and first ran for president in 1971. During the 1970s and 1980s he was subjected to repeated arrest, imprisonment, and assassination attempts by the South Korean authorities. Following his election to the presidency, he negotiated (2000) an agreement ending 50 years of hostility with North Korea and was awarded the 2000 Nobel Peace Prize.

● **Kim Il Sung** ► (Kim Song Ju; 1912–94) North Korean statesman; prime minister (1948–72) and then president (1972–94). He became leader of the Soviet-dominated N in 1945 and with the establishment there of the Democratic People's Republic of Korea in 1948, its first prime minister and chairman of the Korean Workers' Party. In 1950 he ordered the invasion of South Korea in an unsuccessful attempt to reunite Korea (*see* Korean War). He was succeeded by his son, **Kim Jong Il** (1942–   ), who was effectively ruler of the country from 1994 but was not declared head of state until 1998.

● **kimono** ► The traditional costume of Japan for men and women from the 7th century AD, now worn mainly by women for formal occasions. It is an ankle-length wide-sleeved robe, often silk, wrapped over at the front and tied with an *obi* (sash) in a large bow at the back.

● **Kincardine** ► (*or* Kincardineshire) A former county of NE Scotland. In 1975 it became part of Grampian Region; when this was abolished in 1996 it became part of Aberdeenshire.

● **kindergarten** ► A school for young children aged three to five years. A German word meaning "children's garden," it was coined by the German educationalist Friedrich ▷Froebel. The education of young children in the UK is now generally referred to as ▷preschool education.

● **Kindertransport** ► (German: child transport) Any of the trains in which some 10 000 Jewish children escaped from Germany and German-occupied Europe to the UK. Before the war and the "final solution" (*see* Wannsee conference), Germany's main aim was to expel all Jews. Unfortunately, no countries were willing to accept them; in 1938, therefore, a desperate appeal was made to all nations at least to save the Jewish children. Only the UK offered to help by taking 10 000 children and accepting the German conditions: £50 per child had to be paid, the children had to be between 3 and 17, and no parents or adults could travel with them. The first *Kindertransport* left in December 1938 and the last on 1 September, 1939. In England, the children were welcomed into Jewish and non-Jewish homes and orphanages. Some 80% never saw their parents again. All, however, were spared the fate of one and a half million children who were unable to find places on the *Kindertransport*.

● **kinematics** ▷*See* mechanics.

● **kinetic art** ► A type of art, usually sculpture, in which movement occurs. This may result from air currents, as in the mobiles of Alexander ▷Calder, or from electric motors built into the piece.

● **kinetic energy** ► The energy of a moving body. If the body, mass m, is moving in a straight line with velocity v, its kinetic energy is $\frac{1}{2}mv^2$. If it is rotating its rotational kinetic energy is $\frac{1}{2}I\omega^2$, where I is its moment of inertia and ω its angular velocity.

● **kinetics** ▷*See* mechanics.

● **kinetic theory** ► A theory developed in the 19th century, largely by ▷Joule and ▷Maxwell, in which gases are regarded as consisting of tiny dimensionless particles in constant random motion. Collisions, either between the particles or between the particles and the walls of the container, are assumed to be perfectly elastic. The theory explains the pressure of a gas as being due to collisions between the particles and the walls, its temperature as a measure of the *average* ▷kinetic energy of the particles, and the internal energy of the gas (sometimes called its ▷heat) as the *total* kinetic energy of the particles. The kinetic theory is based on the concept of an ▷ideal gas; real gases consist of molecules having a finite volume (*see* Van der Waals' equation). The kinetic theory is extended to all matter and regards the internal energy of a body as the total of the translational, rotational, or vibrational energy of its constituent particles.

● **King, Billie Jean** ► (*born* Moffitt; 1943–   ) US tennis player, who was Wimbledon singles champion in 1966, 1967, 1968, 1972, 1973, and 1975. She won many other titles and took her 20th Wimbledon title in 1979 for the women's doubles, thus beating the previous record of 19 held by Elizabeth Ryan (1892–1979).

● **King, Jr, Martin Luther** ► (1929–68) US Black civil-rights leader. An outstanding orator, he followed principles of nonviolent resistance in organizing demonstrations against racial inequality and was one of the leaders of the great March on Washington (1963), joined by over 250 000 people. His campaigns contributed to the passing of the Civil Rights Act (1964) and the Voting Rights Act (1965) and earned him the Nobel Peace Prize in 1964. He was assassinated in Memphis, Tennessee, by James Earl Ray.

● **King, William Lyon Mackenzie** ► (1874–1950) Canadian statesman; Liberal prime minister (1921–26, 1926–30, 1935–48). His administration enacted welfare legislation and increased trade with the USA and UK. His chief aim was national unity, achieved by enlisting the support of Progressives and French Canadians.

● **King Charles spaniel** ► A breed of ▷spaniel having a compact body, short legs, a short neck, and a large head with a short upturned nose. There are four colour varieties: Blenheim, ruby, tricolour, and black and tan, the last being associated with King Charles II. Weight: 3.5–6 kg; height: about 25 cm. The Cavalier King Charles spaniel has a similar coloration but is lighter bodied, with relatively longer legs and a longer muzzle. Weight: 5–8 kg; height: about 30 cm.

● **king crab** ▷*See* horseshoe crab.

● **kingcup** ▷*See* marsh marigold.

● **kingdom** ▶ (biology) ▷*See* taxonomy.

● **kingfisher** ▶ A bird belonging to a family (*Alcedinidae*; 85 species) divided into two subfamilies: the *Alcedininae* are narrow-billed and live near water, feeding on small fish; the *Dacetoninae* are broad-billed insectivorous birds not closely associated with water. Kingfishers are 12–45 cm long, mostly compact with a bright plumage of blues, greens, purples, and reds, and are often crested; they have large heads with often brightly coloured bills and usually nest in burrows in banks. Order: *Coraciiformes* (hornbills, kingfishers, etc.).

● **King George's War** ▶ (1744–48) An indecisive conflict between Britain and France for control of North America. It was an aspect of the War of the ▷Austrian Succession.

● **King James Version** ▶ The Authorized Version of the ▷Bible that appeared in 1611 under the patronage of James I (*see* Hampton Court). A scholarly translation from the original, it preserved the best from previous versions. It was based on the Bishops' Bible (1568), but the translators also consulted the ▷Geneva Bible and the ▷Douai Bible. It was much indebted to the translations of William ▷Tyndale. Its vigorous language deeply influenced English prose style.

● **King Philip's War** ▶ (1675–76) A war of resistance on the part of the Indians, led by King Philip of the Wampanoags, to the westward expansion of English settlers in Massachusetts, Connecticut, and Rhode Island. War broke out when three Wampanoags were executed by the settlers for the murder of an informer. Indian resistance collapsed after the death of King Philip.

● **Kings, Books of** ▶ Two Old Testament books of unknown authorship. They are the major source for the history of the Hebrew kings after David, continuing the narrative from the end of the Books of Samuel. The first book traces the reign of Solomon (c. 970–933 BC) and his building of the Temple at Jerusalem. After his death, the kingdom was divided into Judah and Israel, the histories of which are continued alternately in the second book. The work of the prophets Elisha and Elijah is treated in detail. After the fall of Israel to Assyria in 722 BC the narrative records the history of Judah up to the ▷Babylonian exile.

● **king's evil** ▷*See* scrofula.

● **Kingsley, Charles** ▶ (1819–79) British clergyman and writer. A supporter of "Christian socialism," he championed social reforms in such works as *Alton Locke* (1850). He became chaplain to Queen Victoria (1859) and canon of Westminster (1873). His works include the popular children's book *The Water Babies* (1863), historical romances, and a volume of lectures on history, *The Roman and the Teuton* (1864). His niece **Mary Henriette Kingsley** (1862–1900) was a noted traveller, chiefly in W Africa, and wrote perceptive accounts of her experiences, including *Travels in West Africa* (1897). She died in Africa, nursing sick Boer prisoners.

● **King's Lynn** ▶ (Lynn *or* Lynn Regis) 52 45N 0 24E A historic market town in E England, in Norfolk near the mouth of the Great Ouse River. Its importance as a port has declined since the middle ages. Industries include food canning and refrigeration, sugar-beet refining, brewing, engineering, and inshore fishing. Population (1991): 41 281.

● **King's Medals** ▶ Two awards instituted in 1945 to recognize the work of foreign civilians in the British interest during World War II. They are awarded for service and courage, respectively, in the cause of freedom.

● **Kingston** ▶ 17 58N 76 48W The capital and main port of Jamaica, in the SE. Founded in 1692, it became the capital in 1872. In the early 20th century it suffered damage from hurricanes and an earthquake. The University of the West Indies was founded in 1962. Most industry is associated with agriculture. Population (1991): 103 771.

● **Kingston** ▶ 44 14N 76 30W A city and port in central Canada, in SE Ontario at the point where Lake Ontario becomes the St Lawrence River. Founded as a fort (1673), it has Canada's Royal Military College, as well as numerous prisons and Queen's University (1841). Kingston's industry includes ship repairing, aluminium, chemicals, and food processing. Population (1991): 56 597.

● **Kingston-upon-Hull** ▶ 1. (or Hull) 53 45N 0 20W A city and port in NE England, in the East Riding of Yorkshire, on the Humber estuary. An important fishing port, Hull also has vast modern docks for ocean-going vessels and serves as a container port for much of the North and Midlands; there are also busy passenger services to the Continent. Industries include food processing, chemicals, and engineering, as well as fish-related industries, and there are also varied services, including a growing conference business. Educational institutions include Hull University (established 1927) and the University of Lincolnshire and Humberside. William Wilberforce was born here and his house is now a museum. Population (1995 est): 268 600. **2.** A unitary authority in NE England, in the East Riding of Yorkshire. Area: 71 sq km (27 sq mi). Population (1999 est): 266 900.

● **Kingston-upon-Thames** ▶ A royal borough of SW Greater London, on the S bank of the River Thames. Created in 1965 from several former Surrey boroughs, it is mainly residential. Although no longer within Surrey, it functions as the administrative centre for that county. Area: 38 sq km (15 sq mi). Population (1999 est): 132 996.

● **Kingstown** ▶ 13 12N 61 14W A port in SW St Vincent, in the West Indies in the E Caribbean Sea. Exports include bananas, copra, arrowroot, and cotton. Population (1995 est): 15 908.

● **kinins** ▷*See* cytokinins.

● **kinkajou** ▶ A nocturnal arboreal mammal, *Potos flavus*, of Central and South American forests. Up to 110 cm long including the prehensile tail (40–55 cm), it has a soft woolly golden-brown coat and feeds mainly on fruit and honey. Family: *Procyonidae* (*see* raccoon).

● **Kinneret, Lake** ▷*See* Galilee, Sea of.

● **Kinnock, Neil (Gordon)** ▶ (1942–) British politician. As leader of the Labour Party (1983–92) he reunited the Party but failed to win general elections in 1987 and 1992. He became a European commissioner in 1995. As vice-president of the Commission (from 1999) he attempted to rid it of corruption and waste.

● **kinnor** ▶ A musical instrument, the ancient Jewish form of the ▷kithara. It is a type of ▷lyre and is the biblical instrument traditionally reputed to have been played by David.

● **Kinross** ▶ A former county of SE Scotland. Under local government reorganization in 1975 it became part of Perth and Kinross District, in Tayside Region. With adjusted borders, this became an independent ▷unitary authority in 1996.

● **Kinsey, Alfred** ▶ (1894–1956) US zoologist and sociologist, who initiated surveys of human sexual behaviour. His reports *Sexual Behaviour in the Human Male* (1948) and *Sexual Behaviour in the Human Female* (1953) helped create more open attitudes to sex.

● **Kinshasa** ▶ (name until 1966: Léopoldville) 4 18S 15 18E The capital of the Democratic Republic of Congo, on the Congo River on the S shore of Malebo Pool. It has a long history of human settlement and was occupied by the Humbu when ▷Stanley visited it in the late 19th century. A campus of the National University was founded in 1954. One of Africa's largest cities, it is an important industrial and commercial centre and has food-processing, woodworking, and textile industries. Population (1994 est): 4 655 313.

● **kinship** ▶ The social recognition of real or ascribed blood relationship. It is usually distinguished from affinity (relationship by marriage). Kinship implies genetic relationship but this is defined very differently in different societies. Many people deny the genetic contribution of either the father or the mother to the child and count the kin of only one parent as their own. These are known respectively as matrilineal and patrilineal systems. Different societies recognize relationships of very different degrees of distance, some counting as kin those descended from common ancestors many generations back. In primitive societies kinship is the basis of social organization.

● **Kintyre** ▶ A peninsula in W Scotland, in Argyll and Bute, between the Atlantic Ocean and the Firth of Clyde. The **Mull of Kintyre** headland, its most southerly point, is the nearest point on the British coast to Ireland, 21.5 km (13.5 mi) from Runabay Head in Co Antrim.

● **Kioga, Lake** ▷*See* Kyoga, Lake.

● **Kiowa** ▶ A North American Indian people of Oklahoma. With the

▷Comanche, they were among the most warlike tribes, raiding settlers in Texas during the 19th century. They also fought against the US Government and were one of the last tribes to be subdued. Their culture was typical of the Plains region. Their language forms part of the ▷Aztec-Tanoan family.

Rudyard Kipling ► The frontispiece of William Strang's book (1901) of 30 etchings illustrating the works of Kipling.

● **Kipling, (Joseph) Rudyard ►** (1865–1936) British writer and poet. Born in Bombay, he was educated in England, returning to India in 1882 to work as a journalist. When Kipling returned to London in 1889, he was already famous for his satirical verses and for stories, such as those in *Plain Tales from the Hills* (1888). His popularity was confirmed with *Barrack Room Ballads and Other Verses* (1892), a volume that includes such well-known poems as "The Road to Mandalay," "If," and "Gunga Din." From 1892 to 1896 he lived with his American wife in New England, where he wrote *The Jungle Books* (1894, 1895). *Kim* (1901) is his best novel and the last he wrote with an Indian setting. Among his many other works are *Just So Stories* (1902) and *Puck of Pook's Hill* (1906), both for children, and the story collections *Debits and Credits* (1926) and *Limits and Renewals* (1932). He won the Nobel Prize in 1907.

● **kipper** ▷*See* herring.

● **Kipp's apparatus ►** A laboratory apparatus for producing a gas as a result of a reaction between a liquid and a solid. It is often used to produce hydrogen sulphide by reacting hydrochloric acid with sticks of ferrous sulphide ($2HCl + FeS = FeCl_2 + H_2S$). The device is named after its Dutch inventor, Petrus Jacobus Kipp (1808–64).

● **Kirchhoff, Gustav Robert ►** (1824–87) German physicist, who was appointed professor at Heidelberg University in 1854. There, working with Robert ▷Bunsen, he invented the technique of spectroscopy. Using this technique, Kirchhoff and Bunsen discovered the elements caesium and rubidium in 1861. Kirchhoff, working alone, also discovered several elements in the sun, by investigating the solar spectrum. He is also known for his work on thermal radiation and on networks of electrical wires (*see* Kirchhoff's laws).

● **Kirchhoff's laws ►** Two laws applying to electrical networks, discovered by G. R. ▷Kirchhoff. The first states that the net current flowing into and out of any point in the network is zero. The second states that the algebraic sum of the voltages in any closed loop of the network is equal to the algebraic sum of the products of the currents and the resistances through which they flow.

● **Kirchner, Ernst Ludwig ►** (1880–1938) German expressionist painter and printmaker, who helped found the art movement called Die ▷Brücke (The Bridge) in 1905 (*see also* expressionism). His diverse influences ranged from ▷Grünewald to ▷Munch and African art in paintings notable for their eroticism, vibrant colours, and angular outlines. He painted many satirical street scenes in Berlin (1911–17) before moving to Switzerland, where he concentrated on landscapes. After Nazi criticism he committed suicide.

● **Kirgizstan, Republic of ►** (Kyrgyzstan *or* Kirghizia) A republic in central Asia. It is chiefly mountainous with spacious valleys and deep lakes, rising to the Tian Shan range in the S and E. The lower plains to the W are subject to hot desert winds. The Kirgiz, a traditionally nomadic Turkic-speaking people, comprise over half of the population; there are large minorities of Russians and Uzbeks.

Economy: Kirgizstan has important deposits of coal, lead, mercury, and antimony, as well as oil and natural gas, but apart from coal these remain largely unexplored. Gold is mined and constitutes the country's main export. Apart from mineral extraction, industries include the manufacture of machinery and building materials and food processing. The industrial sector grew by nearly 50% in 1997. Agriculture is the chief economic activity. Wheat, cotton, and tobacco are grown and livestock, especially cattle, sheep, horses, and yaks, are important. The illegal cultivation of opium poppies is also widespread. A privatization programme began in 1992.

History: the Kirgiz came under Russian rule in the 19th century and fought the new Soviet Government after the Russian Revolution. This resulted in a famine in 1921–22, in which over 500 000 Kirgiz died. The Kirgiz SSR was established in 1936. Nationalist unrest grew in the 1980s, and on the break-up of the Soviet Union in 1991 Kirgizstan became an independent state. A new constitution was approved in 1994 and the country's first multiparty elections were held the following year. Recent years have seen some tension between the rural Kirgiz and the urban Russians and Uzbeks.

Republic of Kirgizstan

Head of state	President Askar Akayev
Official languages	Kirgiz and Russian
Official currency	som of 100 tyin
Area	198 500 sq km (76 642 sq mi)
Population (1997 est)	4 595 000
Capital	Bishkek

● **Kiribati, Republic of ►** (name until 1979: Gilbert Islands) A country in the S Pacific Ocean comprising the Gilbert Islands, the Phoenix Islands, some of the Line Islands, and ▷Ocean Island. Most of the inhabitants are Micronesians.

Economy: chiefly fishing and subsistence agriculture, including such crops as coconuts, pandanus palm, and breadfruit. The phosphates on Ocean Island, formerly a major source of revenue, are now exhausted and the chief exports are copra, coconuts, and fish.

History: first sighted by the Spanish in the 16th century, the islands became a centre for sperm whale hunting in the 19th century. Part of the British protectorate of the Gilbert and Ellice Islands from 1892, they became a colony in 1915. Links with Ellice Islands (*see* Tuvalu) were severed in 1975 and the remaining islands became independent in 1979 as the Republic of Kiribati.

Republic of Kiribati

Head of state	President Teburoro Tito
Official languages	I-Kiribati and English
Official currency	Australian dollar of 100 cents
Area	861 sq km (332 sq mi)
Population (1997 est)	82 400
Capital and main port	Bairiki, on Tarawa

● **Kirin** ▷*See* Jilin.

● **Kiritimati** ▷*See* Christmas Island.

● **Kirk, Norman (Eric) ►** (1923–74) New Zealand statesman; Labour prime minister (1972–74). He implemented social-welfare and housing measures and recognized the People's Republic of China.

● **Kirkcaldy ►** 56 07N 3 10W A town in E central Scotland, in Fife on the Firth of Forth. It is a port, mainly for coastal trade, and manufactures linoleum and coarse textiles. It is the birthplace of Adam Smith. Population (1991): 47 155.

● **Kirkcudbright** ▶ A former county of SW Scotland. In 1975 it became part of Dumfries and Galloway Region.

● **Kirklees** ▶ A unitary authority in N England, in West Yorkshire. Area: 410 sq km (158 sq mi). Population (1996 est): 388 800.

● **Kirkuk** ▶ 35 28N 44 26E A town in NE Iraq, in a rich oilfield. It is the origin of pipelines to Syria, Lebanon, and, until it was cut in the war of 1948, Haifa (Israel). Population (latest est): 418 624.

● **Kirkwall** ▶ 58 59N 2 58W A town in NE Scotland, the administrative centre and main port of Orkney, on the island of Mainland. It has fishing and distilling industries. Population (1991): 6469.

● **Kirov** ▶ (name from 1780 until 1934: Vyatka) 58 38N 49 38E A port in NW Russia, on the River Vyatka. Founded in 1181, it fell to the Russians in the 15th century and became important as a stopping place on the Moscow–Siberia route. It was renamed in honour of S. M. Kirov. Population (1995 est): 464 000.

● **Kirov, Sergei Mironovich** ▶ (1888–1934) Soviet politician. As one of Stalin's closest associates Kirov quickly rose to power and became first secretary of the Leningrad branch of the Communist Party. His assassination, which Stalin claimed to be part of a plot against the entire Soviet leadership and led to the Great Purge trials (1934–38), was probably instigated by Stalin himself.

● **Kirovabad** ▷*See* Gandzha.

● **Kirov Ballet** ▶ A Russian ballet company based at the Kirov State Theatre of Opera and Ballet (formerly the Maryinsky Theatre) in St Petersburg. The theatre was renamed in honour of S. M. ▷Kirov in 1935. The company's style of dancing owes much to the Imperial Russian Ballet, founded in 1935, of which ▷Nijinsky was a product. During the Soviet era some of the Kirov's leading dancers, including Rudolf ▷Nureyev, Natalia ▷Makarova, and Mikhail ▷Baryshnikov, defected to the West and earned international reputations.

● **Kirovohad** ▶ (name until 1924: Yelisavetgrad; name from 1924 until 1936: Zinoviyevsk; name from 1936 until 1939: Kirovo; name from 1939 until 1992: Kirovograd) 48 31N 32 15E A city in S central Ukraine. It is a major agricultural trading centre. Population (1996 est): 276 000.

● **kirsch** ▶ (*or* kirschwasser) A ▷spirit distilled from fermented liquor of wild cherries (German *Kirsch*, cherry). It is drunk neat, or used in cooking, especially in fondue or poured over pineapple.

● **Kiruna** ▶ 67 53N 20 15E A town in N Sweden, within the Arctic Circle. In area, it is the largest town in the world. It has vast iron-ore deposits. Population (1990): 26 150.

● **Kisangani** ▶ (name until 1966: Stanleyville) 0 33S 25 14E A riverport in the NE Democratic Republic of Congo, on the Congo River. It is an agricultural centre and industries include furniture, brewing, and clothing. The National University was founded here in 1963. Population (1994 est): 417 517.

● **Kish** ▶ A city of ancient ▷Sumer, near Babylon. Built on Mesopotamia's fertile alluvial plains, Kish was one of the oldest centres of civilization, retaining its pre-eminence until eclipsed by ▷Ur (c. 2600 BC). Under the Babylonian empire Kish became obscure but remained inhabited until the 2nd century AD. Excavated between 1923 and 1933, its site has produced valuable evidence of Sumerian civilization, including the earliest known example of writing—pictograms on a limestone tablet dating to soon after 3500 BC.

● **Kishinev** ▶ (Romanian name: Chişinău) 47 00N 28 50E The capital city of Moldova. Founded in the 15th century, it passed from the Turks to the Russians (1812), becoming the capital of Bessarabia; it was under Romanian rule (1918–40). It is an important food-processing centre. Population (1994 est): 662 000.

● **Kissin, Evgeny** ▶ (1971–) Russian pianist. A child prodigy, he became internationally famous with a performance of both Chopin concertos at the Moscow Conservatory when he was 12. He made his first European tour in 1988 and his US debut in 1990. He is known for performances of Chopin, Beethoven, and Tchaikovsky.

● **Kissinger, Henry (Alfred)** ▶ (1923–) US diplomat and political scientist, born in Germany; secretary of state (1973–76). As President Nixon's adviser on national security (1969), Kissinger was awarded the Nobel Peace Prize (1973, jointly with ▷Le Duc Tho) for helping to negotiate an end to the Vietnam War. Under President Ford he became well known for his flying-shuttle style of diplomacy while negotiating a truce between Syria and Israel (1974). His publications include *The White House Years* (1979) and *Years of Upheaval* (1982).

● **Kisumu** ▶ 0 03S 34 47E A town in W Kenya, on the NE shore of Lake Victoria. It is an important commercial and industrial centre with trade links with Mombasa. Population (1991 est): 201 100.

● **Kiswahili** ▷*See* Swahili.

● **kit** ▶ A tiny high-pitched violin used by dancing masters in the 18th century. Its neck, to accommodate the fingers, is disproportionately large.

● **Kitagawa Utamaro** ▶ (1753–1806) Japanese artist of the ▷ukiyo-e, whose colour woodblock prints were the first to be popularized in Europe. His book of *Insects* (1788) introduced naturalistic observation into the art of colour print. However, he specialized in scenes of women engaged in everyday tasks or pastimes and half-length portraits of women, such as the series *Ten Physiognomies of Women*. In 1804 his prints of the military ruler's wife and mistresses so offended the government that he was handcuffed for 50 days.

● **Kitaj, R(onald) B(rooks)** ▶ (1932–) US artist, living in the UK from 1960. A mainly figurative painter, Kitaj was associated with the emergence of ▷pop art in the UK in the 1960s. His later work shows an interest in literary, historical, and Jewish themes.

● **Kitakyushu** ▶ 33 52N 130 49E A city in Japan, in N Kyushu on the Shimonoseki Strait. Formed in 1963 from the cities of Wakamatsu, Yawata, Tobata, Kokura, and Moji, it is one of Japan's leading trade and deepsea fishing ports as well as an important centre of heavy industry. Population (1995 est): 1 019 562.

● **Kitasato, Shibasaburo** ▶ (1852–1931) Japanese bacteriologist, who, during an epidemic of bubonic plague in Hong Kong, identified the bacillus responsible. In Berlin Kitasato worked with ▷Behring on tetanus and diphtheria, demonstrating the value of antitoxin in conferring passive immunity. Kitasato founded a laboratory near Tokyo that was incorporated with the university in 1899. In 1914 he founded the Kitasato Institute.

● **Kitchener** ▶ 43 27N 80 30W A city in central Canada, in SW Ontario. Established by German-speaking settlers after 1800, it was called Berlin until 1916. Kitchener is a financial, distribution, and manufacturing centre, producing furniture, foods, and leather and rubber goods. Population (1991 est): 168 282.

● **Kitchener of Khartoum, Horatio Herbert, 1st Earl** ▶ (1850–1916) British field marshal. After service with the Royal Engineers, he was appointed to the Egyptian army (1883), becoming commander in chief in 1892. By 1898, with the battle of Omdurman, he had reconquered the Sudan, becoming its governor general (1899). In the second ▷Boer War he suppressed the guerrillas by a scorched-earth policy and the internment of civilians in concentration camps. In 1914, as war secretary, his recruitment campaign was successful but he lost power in the direction of strategy to ▷Haig and (Sir) William Robertson (1860–1933). He was drowned when his ship was sunk on the way to Archangel.

● **kite** ▶ A ▷hawk belonging to the subfamily *Milvinae*, which occurs throughout the world, most commonly in warm regions. Typically reddish brown and 52–57 cm long, kites have long narrow wings, a long often forked tail, and a narrow bill and feed on insects, small mammals, and reptiles; some are scavengers.

● **kithara** ▶ An ancient Greek wooden-framed lyre, traditionally believed to have been invented by Apollo. Greek vases show it held against the player's body. It was used to accompany epic song and declamation.

● **Kitimat** ▶ 54 05N 128 38W A port in W Canada, in British Columbia on the Pacific Ocean. It was built (1951–54) to house a vast aluminium smelter using cheap local hydroelectricity. Fishing, timber, and pulp and paper are also important. Population (latest est): 12 814.

● **kitsch** ► (German: rubbish) Any artefact that aspires to have artistic integrity but is judged to be pretentious, sentimental, or out of step with current notions of good taste. While this clearly includes cheap mass-produced souvenirs created to satisfy a market that is unable to distinguish between what is kitsch and what is not, it is also true that many objects now regarded as kitsch have been coveted as original creations in other periods. Some 20th-century artists and sculptors, particularly those associated with ▷postmodernism, have purposely produced items that they themselves regard as kitsch.

● **kittiwake** ► A North Atlantic ▷gull, *Rissa tridactyla*, that is adapted for nesting on narrow cliff ledges. It is 40 cm long and has a white plumage with black-tipped grey wings, short black legs, dark eyes, and a yellow bill. It feeds at sea on fish and offal, going ashore only to breed. Kittiwakes nest in dense colonies, anchoring their seaweed nests with mud.

● **Kitt Peak National Observatory** ► An observatory sited near Tucson, Arizona, with an assembly of optical telescopes, notably a 4 m (158 in) reflector, and some radio telescopes.

● **Kitwe** ► 12 48S 28 14E A town in N central Zambia. It is the chief commercial, industrial, and communications centre of the ▷Copperbelt. Population (1990): 338 207.

● **Kitzbühel** ► 47 27N 12 23E A town in W Austria, in the Tirol in the Kitzbühel Alps. A famous winter-sports centre, it is also a health and tourist resort. Population (1991): 8223.

● **Kivi, Alexis** ► (A. Stenvall; 1834–72) Finnish poet, dramatist, and novelist, who was chiefly responsible for establishing the western dialect as the modern literary language of Finland. His greatest work was the novel *Seitsemän veljestä* (*Seven Brothers*; 1870), a naturalistic portrayal of rural life.

● **Kivu, Lake** ► 1 50S 29 10E A lake between the Democratic Republic of Congo and Rwanda. It is 96 km (60 mi) long and drained by the River Ruzizi S into Lake Tanganyika.

● **kiwi** ► (bird) A secretive flightless bird belonging to a family (Apterygidae; 3 species) occurring in forested regions of New Zealand. 25–40 cm long, kiwis have tiny wings hidden in coarse grey-brown plumage and strong legs with large claws. Kiwis are nocturnal and have weak eyes but well-developed hearing; the long bill is used to probe the soil for worms, insect larvae, etc. The kiwi is the national emblem of New Zealand. Order: *Apterygiformes*.

● **kiwi** ► (plant) A Chinese climbing shrub, *Actinidia chinensis*, also called Chinese gooseberry, cultivated in New Zealand and elsewhere. It has white or yellow flowers and its fruit, up to 5 cm long, has a rough brown skin and edible greenish flesh with a gooseberry-like flavour. Family: *Actinidiaceae*.

● **Klagenfurt** ► 46 38N 14 20E A city in S Austria, the capital of Carinthia. It has a cathedral (1578–91) and is a tourist centre. Industries include metals, clothing, and shoe production. Population (1991): 89 415.

● **Klaipeda** ► (German name: Memel) 55 43N 21 07E A port in Lithuania, on the Baltic Sea. It has shipyards and other industries include fish canning, textiles, and fertilizers.
  History: dating from the 7th century AD, it was conquered by the Teutonic Knights in 1252, subsequently passing under Prussian rule. In 1919, after World War I, the Allies imposed a French administration over the region, which was seized by Lithuania in 1923. The Memel Statute (1924) recognized Lithuanian possession. It was occupied by the Germans in World War II. Population (1996 est): 201 500.

● **Klaproth, Martin Heinrich** ► (1743–1817) German chemist, who pioneered the techniques of analytical chemistry. He isolated the oxides of uranium, zirconium, and titanium from minerals and investigated the rare-earth metals.

● **Klausenburg** ▷See Cluj.

● **Kléber, Jean Baptiste** ► (1753–1800) French general in the Revolutionary Wars distinguished for his suppression of the uprising in

the Vendée (1793). He was recalled from retirement in 1798 and given command in Napoleon's Egyptian campaign. He became governor of Alexandria (1799) but was assassinated after recapturing Cairo.

● **Klebs, Edwin** ► (1834–1913) Prussian bacteriologist, who, with Friedrich ▷Loeffler in 1884, isolated the bacillus responsible for diphtheria (the **Klebs-Loeffler bacillus**, *Corynebacterium diphtheriae*). He also demonstrated the presence of bacteria in infected wounds and showed that tuberculosis could be transmitted via infected milk.

● **Klee, Paul** ► (1879–1940) Swiss painter and etcher, born in Berne. After training in the Munich Academy, he worked initially as an etcher, influenced by ▷Beardsley and ▷Goya in the grotesque and symbolic character of his works. Returning to Germany (1906), he became associated with Der ▷Blaue Reiter and taught at the ▷Bauhaus school of design (1920–33), but remained an original and independent talent. Inspired by a visit to Tunisia (1914), he turned to painting. Initially he produced small watercolours in brilliant colours; after 1919 he used oils, incorporating signs and hieroglyphs to create a fantasy world influenced by children's art.

● **Klein, Melanie** ► (1882–1960) Austrian psychiatrist, who moved to England in 1926. She is noted for her psychoanalytical studies of children, which were influenced by Sigmund ▷Freud and his associates. Using children's play in place of free association, she analysed the behaviour of children in terms of their desires and anxieties, their relationship with their parents, and the significance of their experiences in their emotional and sexual development.

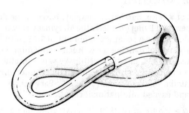

Klein bottle ► A solid with no edges and only one side.

● **Klein bottle** ► In ▷topology, a surface that has no edges and only one side. It is made by putting the small end of a tapering tube through the side of the tube, stretching it, and joining it to the large end. It was discovered by the German mathematician Christian Felix Klein (1849–1925).

● **Kleist, Heinrich von** ► (1777–1811) German dramatist. Coming from an old Prussian family, he gave up his early career in the army. His plays vary in mood between the comedy of *Der zerbrochene Krug* (1808), the demonic violence of *Penthesilea* (1808), the romanticism of *Das Käthchen von Heilbronn* (1810), and the spirit of self-discipline of *Prinz Friedrich von Homburg* (1821). A unifying theme, also present in his short stories, is the confusion between illusion and reality. He committed suicide.

● **Klemperer, Otto** ► (1885–1973) German conductor. He studied in Berlin and became conductor of the German Opera in Prague on the recommendation of Mahler in 1907. He was expelled by the Nazis in 1933 and became first a US and subsequently an Israeli citizen. He was principal conductor of the Philharmonia Orchestra from 1959 until his death and is particularly remembered for his performances of Beethoven's symphonies.

● **Klimt, Gustav** ► (1862–1918) Viennese Art Nouveau artist, who founded the Vienna Sezession (1897), an avantgarde exhibiting society. He achieved notoriety with the pessimistic and erotic symbolism of his murals for Vienna University (1900–03). Subsequent paintings and mosaics, allegories or female portraits, are characterized by large patterned areas often predominantly in gold, as in *The Kiss* (Vienna).

● **Klinger, Friedrich Maximilian von** ► (1752–1831) German dramatist. After touring with a troupe of actors, he made a career in the Russian army. From his tempestuous play *Der Wirrwarr, oder Sturm und Drang* (1776), the ▷*Sturm und Drang* movement took its name.

● **Klint, Kaare** ▶ (1888–1954) Danish furniture designer, the originator of the contemporary Scandinavian style of design. Trained as an architect, he founded the Danish Academy of Arts in 1924 and became its first professor of furniture. His pioneering designs in natural unvarnished wood combined craftsmanship with modern functional needs and were influenced by ▷Chippendale as well as 20th-century styles.

● **klipspringer** ▶ A small antelope, *Oreotragus oreotragus*, of rocky regions of S and E Africa. 60 cm high at the shoulder, klipspringers have a matted bristly yellowish-brown speckled coat with white underparts; males have short horns, ringed at the base. They are agile and agile named "cliff-springers."

● **Klondike** ▶ The valley of the Klondike River in NW Canada, in the central ▷Yukon, where gold was discovered in 1896. The subsequent gold rush opened up the Yukon, although the population later dwindled after 1900.

● **Klopstock, Friedrich Gottlieb** ▶ (1724–1803) German poet. Inspired by what he felt to be his divine mission as a poet, he achieved success with his epic *Der Messias* (1745–73) and later with his odes (*Oden*, 1771). In rejecting rationalism and emphasizing emotion, nature, religion, and history, he anticipated Romanticism. He also wrote plays.

● **klystron** ▶ An electronic device used to generate or amplify ▷microwaves. It consists of a sealed evacuated tube in which a steady beam of electrons from an electron gun is alternately accelerated and retarded by high-frequency radio waves (velocity ▷modulation) as it passes through a cavity. The resultant radio-frequency pulses are picked up at a second cavity, either as a voltage oscillation or, if connected to a ▷waveguide, as electromagnetic waves. The second cavity can be tuned to the input frequency or a harmonic of it. ▷*See also* magnetron.

● **knapweed** ▶ One of several plants of the genus *Centaurea*, of Eurasia and N Africa, having knoblike purplish flower heads. The lesser knapweed (*C. nigra*), also called hardheads, is a plant of grasslands and open places and has been introduced to New Zealand and North America. Family: ▷*Compositae*.

● **Knaresborough** ▶ 54 00N 1 27W A town in N England, in North Yorkshire on the River Nidd. It has a ruined 14th-century castle and the Dropping Well, in which objects are petrified with lime. Population (1991): 13 380.

● **Kneller, Sir Godfrey** ▶ (1646–1723) Portrait painter of German birth. He trained in Holland and Italy, before beginning a successful career in England (1674), working successively for Charles II, William III, Queen Anne, and George I, and founding the first English academy of painting (1711). His best portraits, those of the Whig Kit Cat Club (c. 1702–17; National Portrait Gallery), established a standard British portrait type, known as the kit cat (less than half-length but including a hand). □Newton, Sir Isaac.

● **Knesset** ▶ The representative assembly of Israel; the present building was inaugurated in 1966. There are 120 members elected every four years to a single chamber. The assembly is loosely based on the Kneset ha-Gedola of Jewish leaders following the return (538 BC) from the Babylonian Exile.

● **Knight, Dame Laura** ▶ (*born* Johnson; 1877–1970) British painter, famous for her scenes of circus, gipsy, and ballet life. She exhibited at the Royal Academy, becoming a member in 1936. With her husband, the portraitist **Harold Knight** (1874–1961), she was a prominent member of the Newlyn School of painters based in Newlyn, Cornwall. She was made a DBE in 1929.

● **knighthood, orders of** ▶ Societies, found in many countries, to which persons are admitted as a mark of honour. In medieval Europe, companies of knights (e.g. the ▷Hospitallers) bound by monastic vows to defend Christendom (*see* Crusades). Subsequently, secular orders were instituted, usually by rulers who sought the sworn loyalty of their nobles. The oldest British orders are those of the ▷Garter, ▷Thistle, and ▷Bath. Others include the ▷Order of St Michael and St George, the ▷Royal Victorian Order, and the ▷Order of the British Empire.

● **Knightsbridge** ▶ A street and a district in the London royal borough of Kensington and Chelsea. Its name, dating back to the 11th century, commemorates a legendary duel between two knights on a bridge crossing the Westbourne river (now piped). There are many famous department stores in the district, including Harrods and Harvey Nichols. The tower-block barracks, designed by Sir Basil Spence in 1966, houses the men and horses of the Household Cavalry.

● **knitting** ▶ The chain looping of yarn to form a network fabric that is more elastic than woven fabric; it is very suitable for clinging garments, such as sweaters and stockings. Hand knitting, using two or three needles, is an old craft. In addition to shaped flatwork in various relief patterns, tubular shapes can be knitted. Since the 19th century knitting machines have been developed. The Cotton machine can make shaped work like hand knitting, but the Tompkins system is more versatile.

● **Knock** ▶ A village in the Republic of Ireland, in Co Mayo. Visions of the Virgin Mary were allegedly seen here, the first in 1879, and it has become a place of pilgrimage. A new church was opened in 1976 and in 1979 the village was visited by Pope John Paul II; since 1986 it has had its own international airport, sited at nearby Charlestown.

● **knocking** ▶ A metallic knock heard in petrol engines as a result of combustion of the explosive charge ahead of the flame front. This is caused by local areas of high pressure in the combustion chamber. It greatly reduces the efficiency of the engine and has been controlled by additives, such as ▷tetraethyl lead. However, owing to the problem of pollution of the atmosphere by lead, methyl tertiary butyl ether (MTBE) is now widely used in unleaded petrol.

● **Knossos** ▶ The principal city of Minoan Crete, near present-day Heraklion. It was occupied between about 2500 and 1200 BC. Excavated and reconstructed (1899–1935) by Sir Arthur ▷Evans, the Palace of Minos was luxurious and sophisticated. It is the probable original of the legendary labyrinth in which ▷Theseus fought the ▷Minotaur. Frescoes showing processions, bull sports, and seascapes decorated its walls, there was an elaborate water system, and goods were imported from Egypt. About 1450 BC the palace was burnt down. □Minoan civilization.

● **knot** ▶ (bird) A short-legged bird, *Calidris canutus*, that breeds in Arctic tundra and winters on southern coasts. 25 cm long, it has a short black bill and its plumage is mottled grey in winter and reddish in summer. In winter, knots feed in flocks, probing mud and sand for snails, worms, and crabs. Family: *Scolopacidae* (sandpipers, snipe, etc.).

● **knot** ▶ (unit) A unit of speed, used for ships and aircraft, equal to 1 nautical mile per hour (i.e. 1.15 miles per hour).

● **knotgrass** ▶ A spreading annual plant, *Polygonum aviculare*, widely distributed except in polar regions: it is common on cultivated land, waste ground, and the seashore. Knotgrass has long creeping stems with prominent nodes where silvery sheaths enclose the bases of the lance-shaped leaves; spikes of small pinkish flowers arise in the leaf axils. Family: *Polygonaceae*.

● **knots** ▶ Fastenings formed by looping and tying pieces of rope, cord, etc. The mathematical theory of knots, a branch of ▷topology, draws on ▷matrix theory, algebra, and geometry. A simple closed curve in space may be knotted in various ways, each with specific topological properties. These are classified by knot theory and can be expressed in matrix form. □ p. 692.

● **Knowsley** ▶ A unitary authority of NW England, in Merseyside. Area: 97 sq km (38 sq mi). Population (1994 est) 154 000.

● **Knox, John** ▶ (c. 1514–72) Scottish Protestant reformer. He adopted the reformed faith under the influence of ▷Wishart in the 1540s. In 1547 he joined the Protestants who had murdered Cardinal Beaton in revenge for Wishart's execution in St Andrew's Castle. The castle was stormed by the French, who imprisoned Knox as a galley slave. After his release (1549) he became a chaplain to Edward VI in England and contributed to the revision of the Second Book of Common Prayer. On Queen Mary's accession he escaped to the Continent, where he met ▷Calvin in Geneva. Returning to Scotland in 1559, he became its leading reformer. In 1560 the Scottish parliament adopted Knox's *Confession of Faith*. His *First Book of Discipline*

knots

overhand knot This is used either to make a knob in a rope or as the basis for another knot.

reef knot A non-slip knot for joining ropes of similar thickness.

quick release knot A tug on "a" will quickly unfasten this knot.

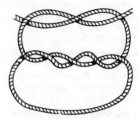

surgeon's knot The extra twist in the first part of the knot prevents it from slipping loose while the second part is tied.

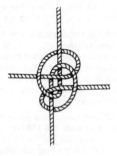

Hunter's bend A strong easily tied knot invented in 1978 by Dr Edward Hunter.

bowline A knot to form a non-slip loop.

running bowline A knot for making a running noose.

sheepshank A means of temporarily shortening a rope.

sheet bend A knot for securely joining two ropes of different thickness.

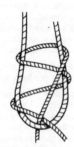

double sheep bend This follows the same principles as the sheet bend.

fisherman's knot Used especially for joining lengths of fishing gut.

carrick bend A knot well suited to tying heavy ropes together.

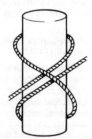

clove hitch A simple knot for attaching a rope to a ring, rail, etc.

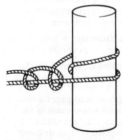

round turn and two half hitches Used for similar purposes as the clove hitch, this knot does not easily work loose.

anchor bend A secure means of attaching a cable to an anchor.

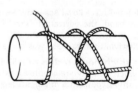

rolling hitch A quickly made and quickly unfastened knot for attaching a rope to a rail or another, standing rope.

(1561) outlined a reformed Church of Scotland that included education and poor relief.

● **Knox, Ronald (Arbuthnott)** ▶ (1888–1957) British Roman Catholic priest and author, son of an Anglican bishop. He wrote about his faith and his conversion to Roman Catholicism (1917) in such works as *A Spiritual Aeneid* (1918). The Catholic chaplain at Oxford University from 1926 to 1939, he is best known for his modern translation of the ▷Vulgate (1945–49). He also published several detective novels.

● **Knox-Johnston, Sir Robin** ▶ (Sir William Robert Patrick K.-J.; 1939–) British yachtsman; the first person to sail alone around the world nonstop (1968–69). In 1981 he set the British transatlantic sailing record (11 days 7 hours 45 mins). He was knighted in 1995.

● **Knoxville** ▶ 36 00N 83 57W A city in the USA, in Tennessee on the Tennessee River. It is the site of the University of Tennessee (1794) and the headquarters of the Tennessee Valley Authority. An inland port and agricultural trading centre, its industries include meat packing and marble processing. Population (1994 est): 169 311.

● **Knutsford** ▶ 53 18N 2 23W A town in N England, in Cheshire, serving as a dormitory town for Manchester. Mrs Gaskell lived here and it is the setting for her novel *Cranford*. Population (1991): 13 352.

koala ▶ A female with her eight-month-old cub.

● **koala** ▶ An arboreal ▷marsupial, *Phascolarctus cinereus*, of E Australia. About 60 cm high, koalas have thick greyish fur, tufted ears, a small tail, and long claws. Groups of koalas move slowly through eucalyptus forests, each adult eating more than 1 kg of the leaves every day. The pouch opens towards the female's tail—unusual in herbivorous marsupials—and the young are weaned on half-digested eucalyptus soup from their mother's anus. The population is threatened by infection with *Chlamydia psittaci*, which causes infertility and death. Family: *Phalangeridae*.

● **kob** ▶ An antelope, *Kobus kob*, of African savanna regions, also called Buffon's kob. Males stand about 90 cm high at the shoulder; females are smaller. The coat ranges from orange-red to nearly black, with white markings on the face, legs, and belly and a black stripe down the foreleg. They are generally found in small groups near water.

● **Kobarid** ▶ (Italian name: Caporetto) 46 16N 13 35E A village in Slovenia, near the Italian border. Part of Italy until 1947, it was the site of the defeat of the Italians by the Austro-German army in 1917.

● **Kobayashi Masaki** ▶ (1916–96) Japanese film director. He established his reputation with *The Human Condition* (1959–61), a trilogy concerned with the dignity of the individual. His other films include *Kwaidan* (1964), an anthology of ghost stories, *Rebellion* (1967), *Kaseki* (1974), and *Glowing Autumn* (1979).

● **Kobe** ▶ 34 40N 135 12E A port in Japan, in S Honshu on Osaka Bay. It forms the W end of the Osaka-Kobe industrial area and has two shipbuilding yards. Other industries include engineering, sugar, chemicals, and rubber. Its university was established in 1949; Oxford University opened a branch of St Catherine's College here. In 1995 a major earthquake caused considerable damage and loss of life. Population (1995): 1 423 830.

● **København** ▷*See* Copenhagen.

● **Koblenz** ▶ (English name: Coblenz) 50 21N 7 36E A city in W Germany, in Rhineland-Palatinate at the confluence of the Rivers Rhine and Moselle. The seat of Frankish kings during the 6th century AD, it was annexed by France in 1798, passing to Prussia in 1815. Notable buildings, many rebuilt after World War II, include the Ehrenbreitstein fortress (c. 1000) and the birthplace of Metternich. It is a wine-trading centre and manufactures furniture, pianos, and clothing. Population (1996 est): 109 219.

● **Koch, Robert** ▶ (1843–1910) German bacteriologist, who was responsible for major discoveries in the study of disease-causing bacteria. As a young doctor, Koch successfully cultured the bacillus causing anthrax in cattle and determined its life cycle. Devising new and better culture methods, Koch succeeded in 1882 in identifying and isolating the bacillus responsible for tuberculosis. He was, however, frustrated in his efforts to find an effective cure for the disease. Koch investigated other diseases, including cholera, bubonic plague, and malaria. He was awarded a Nobel Prize (1905).

● **Köchel, Ludwig von** ▶ (1800–77) Austrian naturalist and musical bibliographer. He compiled a thematic catalogue of Mozart's works, which was published in 1862; a particular work is referred to by a **Köchel number**, consisting of the letter K followed by the appropriate catalogue number.

● **Kodály, Zoltan** ▶ (1882–1967) Hungarian composer. He was educated at Budapest University and conservatoire, where he developed an interest in Magyar folk music. With ▷Bartók he collected Hungarian peasant songs, which influenced his composition. He achieved recognition with his *Psalmus Hungaricus* (1923); other works include the opera *Háry János* (1926), *Dances of Galanta* (1933), masses, chamber music, and orchestral music.

● **Kodiak** ▶ 57 20N 153 40W An island in the USA, off the S coast of Alaska in the Gulf of Alaska. First settled by Russians in 1784, it became a base for seal hunting and whaling. In 1964 it suffered an earthquake that lowered it by about 1.8 m (6 ft). Area: 8974 sq km (3465 sq mi). Population (1990 est): 13 309.

● **Kodiak bear** ▷*See* brown bear.

● **Kodok** ▶ (former name: Fashoda) 9 51N 32 07E A small town in the S central Sudan, on the White Nile River. The ▷Fashoda incident took place here (1898), causing a crisis between Britain and France. Population: about 3000.

● **Koestler, Arthur** ▶ (1905–83) British writer, born in Hungary and educated as an engineer in Vienna. As a journalist in Berlin, he was a member of the Communist Party (1931–38). He settled in Britain in 1940, writing in English thereafter. His novel *Darkness at Noon* (1940), depicting the Moscow purge trials, calls on his experience as a prisoner in the Spanish Civil War. Other novels include *Thieves in the Night* (1946) about Palestine and *The Call Girls* (1972). His nonfiction was concerned with politics (*The Yogi and the Commissar*, 1945), scientific creativity (*The Sleepwalkers*, 1959; *The Act of Creation*, 1964; *The Ghost in the Machine*, 1967), and parapsychology (*The Roots of Coincidence*, 1972). His autobiographies include *Arrow in the Blue* (1952) and *The Invisible Writing* (1954). He and his wife committed suicide when he became terminally ill.

● **Koffka, Kurt** ▶ (1886–1941) US psychologist, born in Germany, who was one of the founders of ▷Gestalt psychology. Among his works was *Growth of the Mind* (1921). He made an influential distinction between the behavioural and the geographical environments—the perceived world of common sense and the world studied by scientists.

● **Koh-i-noor** ▶ A famous diamond of 108 carats owned by the Mogul dynasty until the Shah of Iran looted it from Delhi (1739). Although reclaimed for India by the Sikhs, it became Crown property in 1849, when Britain annexed the Punjab. It was set in the coronation crown of George VI's consort, Queen Elizabeth.

• **Kohl, Helmut** ▸ (1930–) German statesman: chancellor (1982–98). A Christian Democrat, he led the opposition in the Bundestag (1976–82). As chancellor, he was prominent in the formation of EU policy and in German reunification, becoming leader (1990) of the united country. He was elected for a fourth term in 1994, becoming Germany's longest-serving leader since Bismarck. However, owing mainly to high unemployment and economic stagnation, he failed to be re-elected in 1998, when Gerhard ▷Schröder replaced him as chancellor. In 2000 he faced a criminal investigation on charges of improperly channelling party donations.

• **Köhler, Wolfgang** ▸ (1887–1967) US psychologist and a founder of ▷Gestalt psychology. Kohler's experiments on problem solving in apes (*The Mentality of Apes*, 1917) led to his exploration of the physiological basis of perception and the process of learning.

• **kohlrabi** ▸ A variety of ▷cabbage, sometimes called turnip-rooted cabbage. The green or purple stem base, which swells like a turnip, is used as a vegetable and as livestock food.

• **Kokand** ▸ 40 33N 70 55E A city in NE Uzbekistan in the Fergana Valley. Fertilizers and chemicals are produced. Population (1996 est): 184 000.

• **Koko Nor** ▷*See* Qinghai, Lake.

• **Kokoschka, Oskar** ▸ (1886–1980) Austrian expressionist painter and writer. In Vienna and Berlin, he specialized in probing portraits and allegorical poems, plays, and paintings, expressing the struggle of life. After World War I he taught at the Dresden Academy and travelled widely, painting landscapes and city views, particularly of London, where he lived (1938–53). From 1953 he lived in Switzerland.

• **Kokura** ▷*See* Kitakyushu.

• **kola** ▸ (*or* cola) Either of two trees, *Cola nitida* or *C. acuminata*, native to West Africa and widely grown in the tropics, that produce **kola nuts**. These are rich in caffeine and chewed in Africa and the West Indies for their stimulating effects. The nuts, which resemble conkers, are skinned and packed between leaves to keep them fresh. Family: *Sterculiaceae*.

• **Kola Peninsula** ▸ A promontory in NW Russia, between the Barents Sea to the N and the White Sea to the S. The area is largely granite but is mined for apatite (for its phosphorus) and nephelinite (for its aluminium). Tundra is extensive with some swampy pine and other forests in the S. The chief town is Murmansk. Area: about 130 000 sq km (50 182 sq mi).

• **Kolar** ▸ 13 10N 78 10E A town in India, in Karnataka. To the NW lie the Kolar Gold Fields, which produce almost all India's gold output. Population (1991 est): 83 219.

• **Kolarovgrad** ▸ (*or* Shumen) 43 17 N 26 55E A town in NE Bulgaria. It was an important fort under Turkish rule (15th–19th centuries) and has a notable brewing industry. Population (1992 est): 112 091.

• **Kolbe, (Adolf Wilhelm) Hermann** ▸ (1818–84) German chemist, who became professor at Marburg University in 1851. He was one of the first chemists to synthesize organic compounds, his most important discovery being the Kolbe reaction, for synthesizing salicylic acid. This led to the large-scale manufacture of aspirin.

• **Kolchak, Alexander Vasilievich** ▸ (1874–1920) Russian admiral. After the Russian Revolution (1917) he became leader of anti-Bolshevik elements at Omsk, clearing Siberia and linking with ▷Denikin in the south. However, Bolshevik counterattacks, discontent in his territories, and divisions among his followers destroyed Kolchak's forces. He was betrayed by the Allied powers to the Bolsheviks and shot.

• **Koldewey, Robert** ▸ (1855–1925) German archaeologist. After digging at several classical sites (e.g. ▷Baalbek), Koldewey excavated ▷Babylon (1899–1917). Here his training as an architect greatly facilitated recovery of the ancient street plan and reconstruction of the mud-brick buildings.

• **Kolhapur** ▸ 16 40N 74 15E A city in India, in Maharashtra. An early centre of Buddhism, its industries include sugar processing and textiles and it has a university (1962). Population (1991): 405 118.

• **Kolmogorov, Andrei Nikolaevich** ▸ (1903–87) Soviet mathematician, who made notable contributions to many fields, particularly topology, probability theory, functional analysis, and geometry. His work in the branch of probability theory known as stochastic processes has found applications in the science of ▷cybernetics. He was the foremost Russian mathematician of the 20th century and his influence on younger mathematicians has been considerable.

• **Köln** ▷*See* Cologne.

• **Koloszvár** ▷*See* Cluj.

• **Kolyma, River** ▸ A river in NE Russia. Rising in the Kolyma Range of NE Siberia, it flows mainly NE to the East Siberian Sea. Length: 2600 km (1615 mi).

• **Komeito** ▸ A Japanese political party, known in English as the Clean Government Party, formed in 1964 by the Soka-gakkai, a branch of the extreme Nichiren Buddhists. It advocates the establishment of a nonaligned Japan free from extremes of wealth and poverty. Komeito rapidly increased its parliamentary representation to become Japan's third strongest political party. Accused of wishing to impose Nichiru Shoshu as the state religion and of reviving fascism, Komeito severed its links with the Soka-gakkai in 1970.

• **Komi Republic** ▸ A constituent republic of Russia. In NW Russia, it comprises chiefly tundra (in the NE) and coniferous forests. It was established in 1921 as an administrative region for the Komi people, who speak a Finno-Ugric language, and was an autonomous Soviet republic from 1936 to 1991. Timbering and mining (notably of coal and oil) are the most important economic activities; livestock raising is the main branch of agriculture. Area: 415 900 sq km (160 540 sq mi). Population (1996 est): 1 185 000. Capital: Syktyvkar.

• **Kommunizma Pik** ▷*See* Communism Peak.

• **Komodo dragon** ▸ A rare ▷monitor lizard, *Varanus komodoensis*, which, at 3 m long and weighing 135 kg, is the largest living lizard. It has a stout neck and body, a long powerful tail, and short strong legs and is powerful enough to attack and kill a man. Komodo dragons feed mainly on carrion but also eat smaller monitors. They occur only on Komodo Island and some of the Lesser Sunda Islands of Indonesia. □reptile.

• **KOMSOMOL** ▸ (All-Union Leninist Communist League of Youth) A Soviet youth organization. Organized in 1918, its members fought in the civil war (1918–21). In 1922 it became a social organization to promote communist ideology through social activities. Membership, which was for those aged between 14 and 28, provided good employment opportunities. It was disbanded in 1991.

• **Komsomolsk-na-Amur** ▸ 50 32N 136 59E A city in W Russia, on the River Amur. It is named after the ▷KOMSOMOL, members of which built much of the city (founded 1932). Its industries, including engineering and machine building, are based on the Amurstal steelworks, located here; oil from Sakhalin is refined. Population (1995 est): 309 000.

• **Konakry** ▷*See* Conakry.

• **Koniecpolski, Stanisław** ▸ (1591–1646) Polish soldier and statesman. Koniecpolski fought many victorious battles against the Turks, Tatars, and Swedes. In 1632 he became commander in chief and subsequently influenced the government of Władysław IV (1595–1648; reigned 1632–48). Koniecpolski was extremely wealthy and acquired huge estates in Ukraine.

• **Koniev, Ivan Stepanovich** ▸ (1897–1973) Soviet marshal. A commander in World War II in Ukraine and the southern front, he ended the war encircling Berlin from the south. He commanded all Warsaw Pact forces in Europe (1955–60).

• **Königsberg** ▷*See* Kaliningrad.

• **Konoe Fumimaro, Prince** ▸ (1891–1945) Japanese noble, who was prime minister three times. His first cabinet (1937–39) escalated the conflict between Japan and China; his second (1940–41) took

Japan into alliance in World War II with Germany and Italy; and his third (1941) made the decision to attack the USA. After Japan's surrender he avoided trial as a war criminal by committing suicide.

● **Konstanz** ▷*See* Constance.

● **Kon-Tiki** ► The name given by Thor ▷Heyerdahl to the raft built of nine balsawood logs on which, between 28 April and 7 August, 1947, he and five companions travelled the 5000 miles between Peru and the Tuamotu islands near Tahiti. The purpose of the voyage was to demonstrate the possibility that ancient peoples of South America could have reached Polynesia. Kon-Tiki was an older name for the Inca creator god, Viracocha, allegedly known in Polynesia as Tiki.

● **Konya** ► (ancient name: Iconium) 37 51N 32 30E A town in SW central Turkey. It is the centre of the Whirling Dervish sect, and the monastery around the tomb of its founder is a religious museum. The town was visited by St Paul and was the capital of the Seljuq kingdom of Rum. Population (1997 est): 623 333.

● **kookaburra** ► A large grey-brown Australian ▷kingfisher, *Dacelo novaeguineae*, also called laughing jackass because of its chuckling call. 43 cm long, it is arboreal and pounces on snakes, lizards, insects, and small rodents from a perch.

● **Köprülü** ► A family, of Albanian origin, of viziers (public servants) of the Ottoman Empire. **Köprülü Mohammed** (c. 1583–1661), grand vizier (1656–61), reformed the Ottoman navy and economy. His son **Köprülü Ahmed** (1635–76), grand vizier (1661–76), conquered Crete. Ahmed's brother **Köprülü Mustafa** (1637–91), grand vizier (1689–91), instituted many financial and military reforms. Their cousin **Köprülü Hussein** (d. 1702), grand vizier (1697–1702), negotiated the Treaty of Karlowitz (1699), in which the Ottoman Empire lost much territory to Austria.

● **Koran** ► (or Quran) The sacred scripture of Islam. According to tradition, the divine revelations given to ▷Mohammed (d. 632 AD) were preserved by his followers and collected as the Koran under the third caliph, Uthman (d. 656). Written in classical Arabic, they were arranged in 114 suras or chapters according to length, the longer ones first. Admonitions to worship God alone and legal prescriptions predominate. The Koran is one of the main sources of ▷Islamic law. Although the revelations were given to Mohammed piecemeal, Muslims believe that they exist complete in a heavenly book.

● **Korçë** ► 40 38N 20 44E A town in SE Albania. It is the centre of a wheat-growing area. Population (1991 est): 67 100.

● **Korchnoi, Victor** ► (1931–   ) Soviet-born chess player. An International Grandmaster, he became Soviet champion in 1960, 1962, and 1964. He defected from the Soviet Union (1976) and later took part in two much publicized matches with ▷Karpov (1978 and 1981).

● **Korda, Sir Alexander** ► (Sandor Kellner; 1893–1956) British film producer and director, born in Hungary. After settling in London in 1930, he boosted the British film industry during the 1930s and 1940s with a series of extravagant productions, including *The Private Life of Henry VIII* (1932), *The Scarlet Pimpernel* (1934), and *Anna Karenina* (1948).

● **kore** ► (Greek: maiden) In archaic Greek sculpture, a draped standing female figure, derived (c. 650 BC) from Egyptian models. During the next two centuries the drapery, pose, and expression became increasingly naturalistic. *Compare* kouros.

● **Korea** ► A former country in NE Asia, occupying a peninsula between the Sea of Japan and the Yellow Sea, now divided (see below) into the Democratic People's Republic of Korea (North Korea) and the Republic of Korea (South Korea). Plains in the W rise to mountains in the N and E. Both North and South Koreans are ethnically related to the Mongoloid race. From the 1st century AD three kingdoms flourished in the peninsula: the Koguryo in the N, the Paechke in the SW, and the Silla in the SE. In 668 they were united under Silla and Buddhism subsequently became the state religion. The country long had ties with China but in 1905 became a Japanese protectorate, coming formally under Japanese rule in 1910. In 1945, following Japan's defeat in World War II, the Allies divided Korea at the ▷thirty-eighth parallel. The communist Democratic People's Republic of Korea under ▷Kim Il Sung was established in the Soviet-occupied N and the

Republic of Korea under Syngman ▷Rhee, in the US-occupied S (1948). Soviet and US troops had withdrawn by 1949 and in 1950 the ▷Korean War broke out, ending in 1953 with the country still divided. Although the early 1990s saw greater cooperation between the two Koreas, tensions returned owing to North Korean incursions into South Korean territory. In June 2000 the leaders of the two countries met for the first time since the Korean War. A friendship agreement was signed committing the Koreas to social, cultural, and economic cooperation, with peaceful reunification as the acknowledged long-term goal.

Korea, Democratic People's Republic of (Korean name: Chosŏn) The division of Korea left the North with almost all the country's mineral wealth (coal, iron ore, lead, zinc, molybdenum, gold, graphite, and tungsten) and most of the industries developed by the Japanese. Although industry was devastated during the Korean War, reconstruction proceeded rapidly. Textiles, chemicals, machinery, and metals are among the chief manufactures: all industry is nationalized. In the 1990s the economy suffered from the ending of preferential trade terms with the Soviet Union and China. Agricultural land was collectivized in the 1950s and is farmed in large cooperatives. Exports include metals and metal products. In 1994 Kim Il Sung handed effective control of the country to his son, Kim Jong Il. North Korea has remained one of the most secretive and authoritarian countries in the world. In 1995 floods left at least 500 000 people homeless, leading to famine, disorder, and economic collapse. Industrial and agricultural output fell by about two thirds and it is estimated that starvation, epidemics, and a mass refugee exodus have caused the population to fall by nearly 20%.

Democratic People's Republic of Korea

Head of state	General Secretary Kim Jong Il
Official language	Korean
Official currency	won of 100 jun
Area	120 538 sq km (46 540 sq mi)
Population (2000 est)	21 688 000
Capital	P'yŏngyang

Korea, Republic of (Korean name: Han Kook) The repressive government led by Syngman Rhee was ended by a military coup in 1961, followed by the rise to power of Gen ▷Park Chung Hee, who was assassinated in 1979. The South was primarily agricultural when separated from the North but the injection of US aid led to the predominance of the industrial sector. Mineral resources are not large, although it has one of the world's largest deposits of tungsten. The main exports include electrical goods, clothes, textiles, and cars. The corrupt and repressive regime of President Rhee was overthrown in 1960. After a confused period, the military, headed by General Park Chung Hee, seized power the following year. The 1960s and 1970s saw successful reconstruction of the economy but continued suppression of dissent. Park Chung Hee was assassinated in 1979 and General Chun Doo Hwan took over in a coup. The 1980s saw remarkable economic growth but increasing political unrest: in 1987 a more democratic constitution was adopted and Roh Tae Woo, leader of the Democratic Justice Party, was elected president. In 1993 Kim Young Sam became the first civilian president for 32 years. In 1995–96 Roh Tae Woo was imprisoned for corruption and Chun Doo Hwan was sentenced to death for his role in the coup of 1979: both were later freed. In 1997 the currency and the stock market collapsed and the country suffered financial and economic breakdown. The former dissident leader ▷Kim Dae Jung was elected president in 1997.

Republic of Korea

Head of state	President Kim Dae Jung
Official language	Korean
Official currency	won of 100 chon
Area	98 447 sq km (38 002 sq mi)
Population (2000 est)	47 275 000
Capital	Seoul
Main port	Pusan

● **Korean** ► The language of the people of Korea. It is probably distantly related to ▷Japanese and has a somewhat similar grammatical structure. The standard and official form is based on the dialect of Seoul. It is written in a phonetic script called onmun, devised in the mid-15th century to replace the Chinese characters in use before then. Korean literature also dates from about this time, with a royal college of literature being founded in 1420.

Korean War ▶ A Korean girl offers to share her slice of bread with the US Army corporal who saved her life.

• **Korean War ▶** (1950–53) An indecisive conflict between communist and noncommunist forces in Korea. In 1948 two Korean states were established on either side of the ▷thirty-eighth parallel: the communist Democratic People's Republic in the N and the Republic of Korea in the S. Growing friction led to the invasion of South Korea by Northern forces in 1950. The UN condemned the invasion, and 16 nations sent troops, under the command of the US general, Douglas ▷Macarthur, to support the South. The North Koreans were joined by Chinese Communist troops. An armistice was eventually signed on 27 July, 1953, by which time some five million people had died.

• **Kórinthos** ▷See Corinth.

• **Kornberg, Arthur ▶** (1918–) US biochemist, who discovered how DNA is replicated in bacterial cells. Kornberg and associates were able to reproduce the conditions necessary for DNA replication in a test tube. They found that the "building blocks" (nucleotides) of the new DNA strand were joined together by an enzyme—DNA polymerase I—using existing DNA as a template.

• **Kornilov, Lavrentia Georgievich ▶** (1870–1918) Russian general. After the Russian Revolution (1917) he led the anti-Bolshevik White armies in S Russia. After his death in action, the command was assumed by ▷Denikin.

• **Koroliov, Sergei Pavlovich ▶** (1906–66) Soviet aeronautical engineer, who designed missiles, rockets, and spacecraft. During the 1930s he headed development of the Soviet Union's first liquid-fuel rocket. After World War II he worked on ballistic missiles and later supervised the Vostok and Soyuz manned spaceflight programmes.

• **Kortrijk** ▷See Courtrai.

• **Koryŏ ▶** An ancient Korean kingdom founded and ruled by the Wang dynasty (935–1392). Both Buddhism and Confucianism were influential and Koryŏ was divided by rivalry between pacifist Confucianists and militarist nationalists. The weakened state succumbed to Mongol invasions in the 13th century and virtually became a Mongol dependency in 1231. The last Wang ruler was deposed by the Yi in 1392.

• **Kos** ▷See Cos.

• **Kosciusko, Mount ▶** 36 28S 148 17E The highest mountain in Australia, in SE New South Wales in the Snowy Mountains. It was discovered in 1840 by the Polish-born explorer P. E. Strzelecki, who named it after his heroic countryman T. A. B. ▷Kosciuszko. It lies within the Kosciusko National Park, a popular area for winter sports. Height: 2230 m (7316 ft).

• **Kosciuszko, Tadeusz Andrezei Bonawentura ▶** (1746–1817) Polish general and statesman, who served in the American Revolution with George Washington (1776–83). Returning to Poland (1784), he distinguished himself in the war against the Russian invasion, which ended in the partition of Poland. Kosciuszko withdrew to Saxony but returned in 1794 to lead a revolt. He was defeated at Maciejourice and imprisoned until 1796.

• **kosher dietary laws ▶** (Yiddish: proper, clean) The dietary laws of ▷Judaism laid down in the ▷Torah, as observed by Orthodox Jews but not by Reform or Liberal Jews. The laws are complex and, in general, are appropriate for hot climates with no refrigeration. Meat must come from animals that chew the cud (see ruminant) and have cloven hooves. Thus cattle and sheep are permitted but pig meat is forbidden. Slaughter must be carried out according to certain rules and milk products must not be cooked or eaten with meat or fowl. Fish must have scales and fins, which excludes all shellfish.

• **Košice ▶** (German name: Kaschau; Hungarian name: Kassa) 48 44N 21 15E A city in E Slovakia. It has a 13th-century cathedral and a university (1959). It has a large iron and steel complex. Population (2000 est): 241 874.

• **Kosovo ▶** An autonomous province of S Serbia, in the Union of Serbia and Montenegro. The region formed the heartland of Serbia in the middle ages and most Serbs still consider it central to their cultural and religious heritage. However, in 1389 the Ottoman Turks defeated the Serbs here in a decisive battle. The region subsequently became Muslim and was settled by large numbers of ethnic Albanians, who still form about 90% of the population. An autonomous province of the Yugoslav republic of Serbia from 1945, Kosovo declared independence in 1990, prompting the government of ▷Milošević to rescind its autonomous status. In 1992 unauthorized elections were decisively won by pro-separatists. In 1998 demonstrations by ethnic Albanians led to severe repression by Serb forces, which in turn provoked armed resistance from the Kosovo Liberation Army (KLA). Mounting evidence of "ethnic cleansing" by Serb forces led NATO to threaten airstrikes against the Serbs in October 1998; subsequent talks broke down when Serbia refused to accept a negotiated peace and resumed its aggression. As a result, NATO began a campaign of airstrikes against targets in Yugoslavia in March 1999. The Serb forces intensified their campaign of terror against ethnic Albanians, leading to a mass exodus of some 800 000 refugees seeking shelter in Macedonia, Albania, and Montenegro; a similar number were displaced within Kosovo and at least 10 000 are thought to have been massacred. In June 1999 the Serbs surrendered, agreeing to the complete withdrawal of their military forces, the presence of international peacekeepers, and the return of all refugees. About 170 000 Serbs have since fled the province. Kosovo's political status remains unresolved. Population (1997 est): 2 227 742. Capital: Priština.

• **Kossuth, Lajos ▶** (1802–94) Hungarian statesman, who was one of the leaders of the Hungarian ▷Revolution of 1848. In March, 1848, when Hungary was granted a separate government by Austria, Kossuth was appointed finance minister. He became governor of an independent Hungarian republic in April, 1849. After Russia destroyed the republic in August, he lived in exile in Turkey, England, and Italy.

• **Kosygin, Aleksei Nikolaevich ▶** (1904–80) Soviet statesman;

Plate I

Butterflies and Moths

The normal pale-coloured form of the peppered moth (below) is conspicuous against trees blackened by pollution in industrial areas and is readily taken by predators. In such areas it has largely been replaced by a dark (melanic) form (bottom), which is better camouflaged.

Camouflage

Camouflaging coloration in two Trinidad moths. Manduca florestan *(top) – a hawk moth – can barely be distinguished from the tree bark on which it rests. The geometrid moth below (genus* Aeschropteryx) *closely resembles the foliage among which it is found, even down to the veinlike marking on its wings.*

The underside of the wings of this West Indian butterfly (top) resembles a frog's head; the upper surface is plain. A bird predator will be startled by the sudden change when the butterfly folds its wings. If it attacks, the eyespot on the wing will draw its attention from the insect's more vulnerable body.

Life Cycle

American monarch butterflies mate during their northerly migrations in spring.

The eggs are laid on milkweed.

A caterpillar hatches from an egg and begins to feed on the milkweed.

eggs laid within 7 to 10 days

hatching 10 to 15 days

mating within 3 days

larval development 1 month

emergence 90 secs to 30 mins

pupal stage 9 to 15 days

A butterfly, just emerged from the chrysalis, rests until its wings are expanded.

The developing butterfly.

A fully grown caterpillar about to be transformed into a chrysalis.

Plate II **Birds**

Scarlet Macaw

House Sparrow ♂

Osprey

Lady Amherst's Pheasant ♂

Lesser Bird of Paradise ♂

Little Owl

Emperor Penguin

Mallard ♂

*The size, shape and plumage of birds is of astonishing variety, and
is largely governed by their environment*

Birds

Plate II

When identifying birds it is important to note the exact position of patches of colour and other distinguishing marks. For this it is helpful to know the names of the precise areas involved, as shown in this picture of a female reed bunting, Emberiza schoeniclus. The only feature not exhibited by the reed bunting is a dark line through the eye, called the eyestripe (not to be confused with the line over the eye, the supercilium).

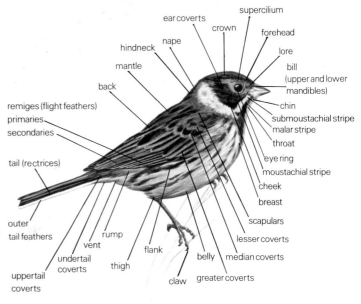

Labels: ear coverts, supercilium, crown, forehead, hindneck, nape, lore, mantle, bill (upper and lower mandibles), back, chin, remiges (flight feathers), submoustachial stripe, primaries, malar stripe, secondaries, throat, tail (rectrices), eye ring, moustachial stripe, cheek, breast, outer tail feathers, scapulars, rump, lesser coverts, vent, flank, belly, median coverts, undertail coverts, thigh, greater coverts, uppertail coverts, claw

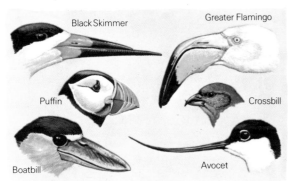

The shape of a bird's bill often indicates its feeding habits: the boatbill, for instance, scoops up its prey from shallow water. The colourful sheath of the puffin's bill is part of its breeding display, being shed in winter.

Labels: Black Skimmer, Greater Flamingo, Puffin, Crossbill, Boatbill, Avocet

Many birds, including the great crested grebe, adopt a special breeding plumage. In a few species (e.g. the ruff) plumage varies between individual males during the breeding season, while others, such as the great spotted woodpecker, show different plumage according to sex and age.

Labels: Ruff, summer, Great Crested Grebe, Great Spotted Woodpecker, winter, ♂ ♀ juv.

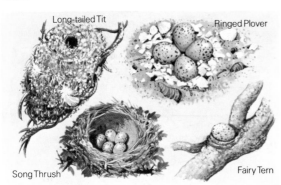

Labels: Long-tailed Tit, Ringed Plover, Song Thrush, Fairy Tern

Nests vary enormously, from the elaborate feather-lined structure of the long-tailed tit to the shallow scrape of the ringed plover. Eggs too vary greatly in size and colour, and those that are vulnerable to predators are

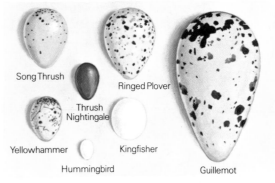

Labels: Song Thrush, Ringed Plover, Thrush Nightingale, Yellowhammer, Kingfisher, Hummingbird, Guillemot

often patterned and coloured so as to match their background. Their shape is also significant: guillemots' eggs are shaped so that they do not roll off the narrow cliff ledges.

Plate III   **Human Body**

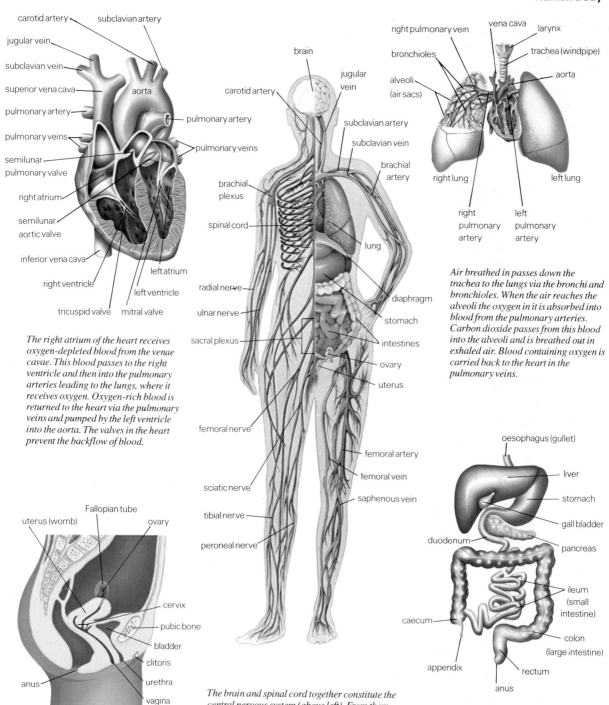

carotid artery
subclavian artery
jugular vein
subclavian vein
superior vena cava
aorta
pulmonary artery
pulmonary artery
pulmonary veins
pulmonary veins
semilunar pulmonary valve
right atrium
semilunar aortic valve
inferior vena cava
left atrium
right ventricle
left ventricle
tricuspid valve
mitral valve

The right atrium of the heart receives oxygen-depleted blood from the venae cavae. This blood passes to the right ventricle and then into the pulmonary arteries leading to the lungs, where it receives oxygen. Oxygen-rich blood is returned to the heart via the pulmonary veins and pumped by the left ventricle into the aorta. The valves in the heart prevent the backflow of blood.

brain
jugular vein
carotid artery
subclavian artery
subclavian vein
brachial artery
brachial plexus
spinal cord
lung
radial nerve
diaphragm
ulnar nerve
stomach
sacral plexus
intestines
ovary
uterus
femoral nerve
femoral artery
sciatic nerve
femoral vein
tibial nerve
saphenous vein
peroneal nerve

right pulmonary vein
vena cava
larynx
bronchioles
trachea (windpipe)
alveoli (air sacs)
aorta
right lung
left lung
right pulmonary artery
left pulmonary artery

Air breathed in passes down the trachea to the lungs via the bronchi and bronchioles. When the air reaches the alveoli the oxygen in it is absorbed into blood from the pulmonary arteries. Carbon dioxide passes from this blood into the alveoli and is breathed out in exhaled air. Blood containing oxygen is carried back to the heart in the pulmonary veins.

Fallopian tube
uterus (womb)
ovary
cervix
pubic bone
bladder
clitoris
anus
urethra
vagina

The female reproductive system is quite separate from the urinary system. The womb (uterus) is connected to the exterior via the vagina, through which the baby passes during labour, while urine is conveyed from the bladder via the urethra.

The brain and spinal cord together constitute the central nervous system (above left). From them arise pairs of nerves that carry messages between the central nervous system and the different parts of the body they supply. A part of the nervous system called the autonomic nervous system (ANS) controls the heart, intestines, lungs, reproductive system, and other internal organs (right). The ANS is not under conscious control (one cannot, for example, consciously control heart rate and intestinal movements), but thoughts and emotions often influence the ANS: fear, for instance, makes the heart beat faster.

oesophagus (gullet)
liver
stomach
gall bladder
pancreas
duodenum
ileum (small intestine)
caecum
colon (large intestine)
appendix
rectum
anus

Food passes down the oesophagus to the stomach, where digestion begins. This process is continued in the duodenum and ileum, where digested food is absorbed into the bloodstream. Undigested remains pass through the colon, where water is absorbed from them, and the resulting semisolid faeces are channelled into the rectum and out through the anus.

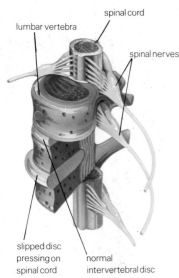

spinal cord

lumbar vertebra

spinal nerves

slipped disc pressing on spinal cord

normal intervertebral disc

The bones (vertebrae) of the backbone are separated by intervertebral discs made of cartilage. If a crack develops in a disc, the softer core may bulge out and press on the spinal cord or a spinal nerve, causing pain. This is called a slipped disc and it most commonly occurs in the lower back (lumbar) region. When the slipped disc presses on the spinal cord the pain may be felt in the neck, chest, or back.

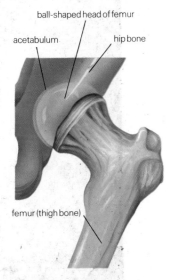

ball-shaped head of femur

acetabulum

hip bone

femur (thigh bone)

The type of joint between the femur (thigh bone) and the hip bone is called a ball-and-socket joint. The head of the femur fits into a cup-shaped socket (called the acetabulum) in the hip bone. The joint itself is lined with cartilage and synovial membrane, which secretes a fluid that lubricates the joint.

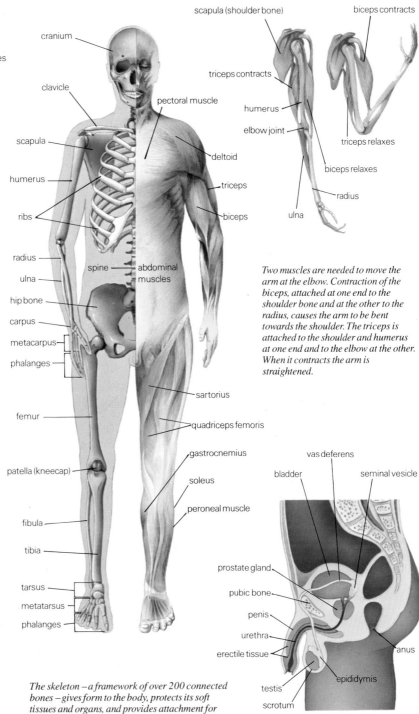

scapula (shoulder bone)

biceps contracts

cranium

triceps contracts

clavicle

pectoral muscle

humerus

elbow joint

triceps relaxes

scapula

deltoid

humerus

triceps

biceps relaxes

ribs

biceps

radius

radius

spine

abdominal muscles

ulna

ulna

hip bone

carpus

metacarpus

phalanges

sartorius

femur

quadriceps femoris

gastrocnemius

patella (kneecap)

soleus

peroneal muscle

fibula

tibia

tarsus

metatarsus

phalanges

Two muscles are needed to move the arm at the elbow. Contraction of the biceps, attached at one end to the shoulder bone and at the other to the radius, causes the arm to be bent towards the shoulder. The triceps is attached to the shoulder and humerus at one end and to the elbow at the other. When it contracts the arm is straightened.

The skeleton – a framework of over 200 connected bones – gives form to the body, protects its soft tissues and organs, and provides attachment for muscles. It also forms a system of levers, which are worked by contractions of the muscles attached to them. The muscles themselves are responsible for all movements of the body. In men the muscles are relatively larger, accounting for about 42% of body weight (compared with 36% in women). There are also differences in the skeleton; for example a woman's pelvic cavity is wider to accommodate the baby during labour.

vas deferens

bladder

seminal vesicle

prostate gland

pubic bone

penis

urethra

erectile tissue

anus

testis

epididymis

scrotum

In males the reproductive system is very closely associated with the urinary system. The urethra provides a route both for urine from the bladder and for semen. Sperms are carried in the vas deferens from the testis to the prostate gland, which contributes to the fluid part of the semen.

Flags

Argentina

Australia

Austria

Azerbaidzhan

Bahamas

Bangladesh

Belarus

Belgium

Bolivia

Brazil

Bulgaria

Burma (Myanmar)

Canada

Chile

China

Colombia

Croatia

Cuba

Cyprus

Dem. Rep. of the Congo

Denmark

Ecuador

Egypt

Ethiopia

Finland

France

Georgia

Germany

The Gambia

Ghana

Greece

Guyana

Hungary

Iceland

India

Indonesia

Iran

Iraq

Ireland (Republic)

Israel

Italy

Jamaica

Japan

Jordan

Kenya

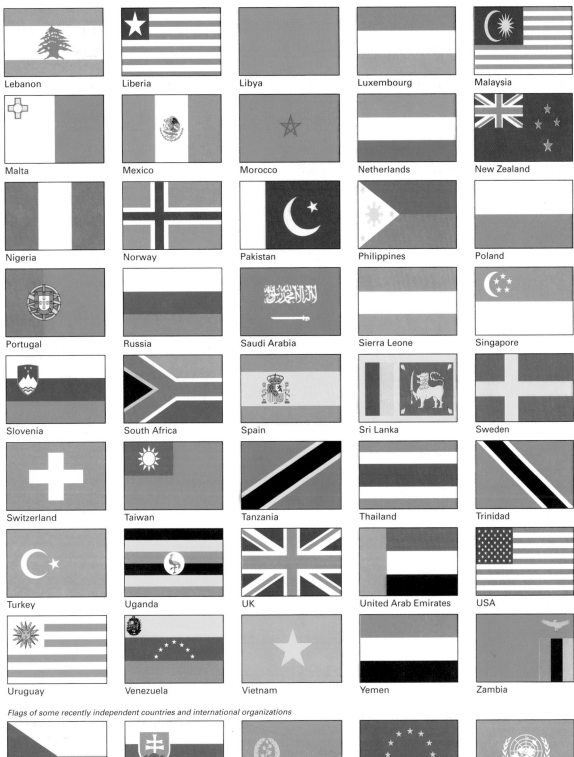

Lebanon	Liberia	Libya	Luxembourg	Malaysia
Malta	Mexico	Morocco	Netherlands	New Zealand
Nigeria	Norway	Pakistan	Philippines	Poland
Portugal	Russia	Saudi Arabia	Sierra Leone	Singapore
Slovenia	South Africa	Spain	Sri Lanka	Sweden
Switzerland	Taiwan	Tanzania	Thailand	Trinidad
Turkey	Uganda	UK	United Arab Emirates	USA
Uruguay	Venezuela	Vietnam	Yemen	Zambia

Flags of some recently independent countries and international organizations

Czech Republic	Slovakia	Eritrea	EC	UN

ARCTIC OCEAN

Ellesmere Island

Queen Elizabeth Islands

Greenland

BEAUFORT SEA

Banks I.

Victoria Island

Baffin Bay

Baffin Island

Davis Strait

Denmark Strait

Iceland

NORWEGIAN SEA

Scan

Bering Strait

Brooks Range

Arctic Circle

Gt. Bear Lake

C. Farewell

British Isles

NORTH SEA

North

Yukon

Alaska Range

Mt. McKinley 6194 m

Mackenzie Mts.

Gt. Slave Lake

Alaska Pen.

Gulf of Alaska

Peace

Hudson Bay

Mt. Robson 3954 m

NORTH

Churchill

Nelson

Saskatchewan

L. Winnipeg

Laurentian Plateau

Newfoundland

Bay of Biscay

Mt. Blanc 4807 m

Alps

E

Rocky Mountains

AMERICA

L. Superior

Huron

St. Lawrence

Pyrenees

Greenpines

Queen Charlotte Is.

Spokane

Columbia

Missouri

L. Michigan

Appalachian Mts.

C. Sable

NORTHE

Azores

MEDITERR

Atlas Mts.

Great Basin

Mt. Elbert 4399 m

Ohio

Mississippi

ATLANTIC

Mid-Atlantic Ridge

Mt. Toubkal 4167 m

Mt. Whitney 4418 m

Colorado

OCEAN

North East Atlantic Basin

Sierra Madre

Rio Grande

Bermuda

North American Basin

Canary Is.

Hoggar

Tropic of Cancer

Hawaiian Is.

C. San Lucas

Gulf of Mexico

1023m

Bahama Is.

6493m

Canary Basin

Sahara

AFRI

150

Citlaltepetl 5700 m

Greater Antilles

Milwaukee Depth 9200m

L. Chad

Jos Plateau

Guatemala

8869m

CARIBBEAN SEA

Lesser Antilles

Cape Verde Is.

Cape Verde

Fouta Djalon

Mt. Cameroon 4095 m

PACIFIC

G. of Panama

Llanos

Orinoco

Guiana Highlands

6390m

Cape Verde Basin

L. Volta

Equator

Galapagos Is.

Chimborazo 6267 m

Amazon

Gulf of Guinea

5110m

OCEAN

Negro

Selvas

SOUTH

C. São Roque

São Francisco

Ascension

Angola Basin

East Pacific Ridge

Andes

L. Titicaca

Mato Grosso

AMERICA

Brazilian Highlands

Brazil Basin

St. Helena

Peru Basin

Peru Current

Atacama Desert

Paraná

Paraguay

Namib

metres

Tropic of Capricorn

8055m

Pampas

Parana

SOUTH

6000

Easter I.

Andes

ATLANTIC

5000

4000

Aconcagua 6960m

OCEAN

Mid-Atlantic Ridge

3000

2000

Tristan da Cunha

Cape Basin

1000

500

Patagonia

200

Argentine Basin

0

land below sea level

Falkland Is.

6245m

South Georgia

2000

Tierra del Fuego

4000

C. Horn

South Sandwich Is.

6000

Projection : Modified Winkel's

Pacific-Antarctic Basin

SCOTIA SEA

8000

0   1000   2000   3000 km

Magellan Strait

South Shetland Is.

5265m

Antarctic Pen.

180   150   120   90   60   30

World - Geographical Statistics	
Continents	
Asia	43 608 000 km^2
Africa	30 335 000 km^2
North America	25 349 000 km^2
South America	17 611 000 km^2
Europe	10 498 000 km^2
Australasia	8 923 000 km^2

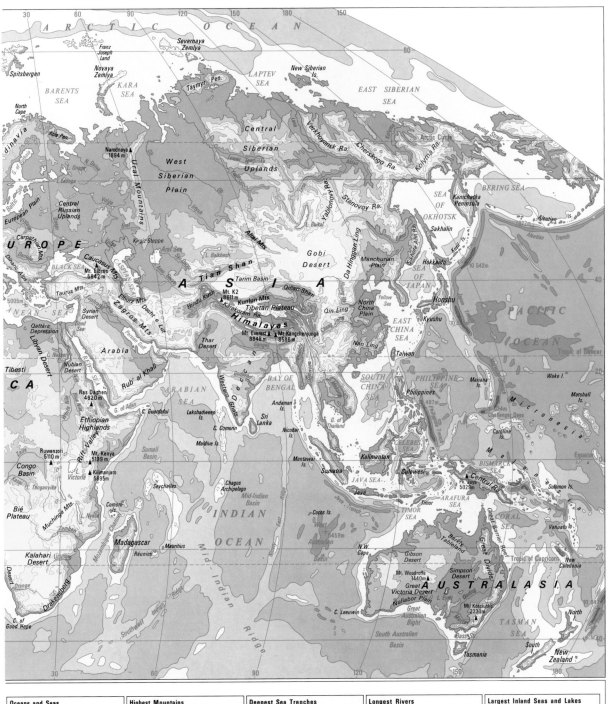

Oceans and Seas	
Pacific Ocean	165 384 000 km²
Atlantic Ocean	82 217 000 km²
Indian Ocean	73 481 000 km²
Arctic Ocean	14 056 000 km²
Mediterranean Sea	2 505 000 km²
South China Sea	2 318 000 km²

Highest Mountains	
Mt. Everest, Nepal/China	8 848 m
Mt. K2, Pakistan/China	8 611 m
Mt. Kangchenjunga, Nepal/China	8 586 m
Mt. Makalu, Nepal/China	8 482 m
Mt. Dhaulagiri, Nepal	8 222 m
Mt. Nanga Parbat, Pakistan	8 126 m

Deepest Sea Trenches	
Marianas Trench, Pac. Oc.	11 034 m
Tonga Trench, Pac. Oc.	10 882 m
Japan Trench, Pac. Oc.	10 595 m
Kuril Trench, Pac. Oc.	10 542 m
Philippine Trench, Pac. Oc.	10 497 m
Kermadec Trench, Pac. Oc.	10 047 m

Longest Rivers	
Nile, Africa	6 695 km
Amazon, South America	6 516 km
Mississippi-Missouri, N. America	6 019 km
Chang Jiang, Asia	5 470 km
Ob-Irtysh, Asia	5 410 km
Huang He, Asia	4 840 km

Largest Inland Seas and Lakes	
Caspian Sea, Asia	372 000 km²
Lake Superior, U.S.A./Canada	82 400 km²
Lake Victoria, East Africa	67 900 km²
Aral Sea, Asia	66 500 km²
Lake Huron, U.S.A./Canada	59 600 km²
Lake Michigan, U.S.A.	58 020 km²

WORLD – POLITICAL

Projection: Modified Winkel's

0 1000 2000 3000 km

International boundary ——
Capital city ■
Important town ○

Abbreviations

ALB.	Albania	LEB.	Lebanon
ARM.	Armenia	MACE.	Former Yugoslav
Aust.	Australia		Republic of Macedonia
AUST.	Austria	MOLD.	Moldova
AZER.	Azerbaidzhan	NETH.	Netherlands
BEL.	Belgium	N.Z.	New Zealand
BOS.-HERC.	Bosnia-Hercegovina	Nor.	Norway
CRO.	Croatia	REP.	Republic
Den.	Denmark	SLOV.	Slovenia
DOM. REP.	Dominican Republic	SW.	Switzerland
EST.	Estonia	U.A.E.	United Arab Emirates
Fr.	France	U.K.	United Kingdom
FR. GUIANA	French Guiana	U.S.A.	United States of America
HOND.	Honduras	YUG.	Yugoslavia
HUNG.	Hungary	ZIMB.	Zimbabwe
ISR.	Israel		

ARCTIC OCEAN

GREENLAND (Denmark)

Spitsbergen (Nor.)

Jan Mayen I. (Nor.)

Melville I.
Banks I.
Victoria I.
Baffin Bay
Baffin I.
Davis Str.
Arctic Circle
Denmark Str.

ICELAND
Reykjavik

ALASKA (U.S.A.)
Fort Yukon
Anchorage
Mackenzie
Gt. Bear L.
Gt. Slave L.
Nuuk
Faeroe Is. (Den.)

NORWAY
SWEDEN
Oslo
Stockholm

Bering Sea
Yukon
Hudson Bay
Churchill

C A N A D A

UNITED KINGDOM
Edinburgh
DENMARK
Dublin
REP. OF IRELAND
London
Berlin
GERMANY
POL.
BEL.
Bonn
CZECH REP.
Paris
AUST.
SLOV.
CRO.
FRANCE
SW.
BOS.-HERC.
ITALY
Rome

Vancouver I.
Vancouver
Winnipeg
Quebec
Montreal
Ottawa
Toronto
Newfoundland
St. John's
Halifax
St. Lawrence
Seattle

UNITED STATES OF AMERICA
Salt Lake City
Chicago
New York
Philadelphia
Washington

San Francisco
Los Angeles
Houston
New Orleans
Miami
Missouri
Mississippi

Gulf of Mexico

PORTUGAL
Lisbon
Madrid
SPAIN
Gibraltar
Mediterranean
Tunis
Algiers
TUNISIA
Tripoli

Azores (Port.)

Bermuda I. (U.K.)

NORTH ATLANTIC
Tropic of Cancer

Madeira (Port.)
Rabat
MOROCCO
Canary Is. (Sp.)
El Aaiún
WESTERN SAHARA
ALGERIA
LIB

Hawaiian Is. (U.S.A.)
150

MEXICO
Mexico City
Havana
CUBA
BAHAMAS
HAITI
DOM. REP.
Puerto Rico (U.S.A.)
JAMAICA

OCEAN

Nouakchott
MAURITANIA
MALI
NIGER

CAPE VERDE
SENEGAL
Dakar
THE GAMBIA
Bamako
Niamey
GUINEA BISSAU
BURKINA FASO
N'djaména
Conakry
GUINEA
BENIN
NIGERIA
SIERRA LEONE
Freetown
CÔTE D'IVOIRE
TOGO
GHANA
Abuja
Lagos
CAMEROON
Monrovia
LIBERIA
Accra
Yaoundé
EQ. GUINEA
Libreville
REP. OF CONGO
GABON

BELIZE
GUATEMALA
HOND.
EL SALVADOR
NICARAGUA
COSTA RICA
PANAMA
Panama City
BARBADOS
TRINIDAD & TOBAGO
Caracas
VENEZUELA
Georgetown
GUYANA
SURINAME
FR. GUIANA
Bogotá
COLOMBIA

PACIFIC

Equator

Galapagos Is. (Ecuador)
Quito
ECUADOR
Guayaquil
Amazon
Belém
Manaus

OCEAN

Brazzaville
Kinshasa
Luanda
AN

Marquesas Is. (Fr.)

Recife
Ascension (U.K.)
SOUTH ATLANTIC
St. Helena (U.K.)

PERU
Lima
B R A Z I L

BOLIVIA
La Paz
Brasília
Salvador

NAMIBIA
Windhoek

Tuamotu Arch. (Fr.)
Tropic of Capricorn

CHILE
PARAGUAY
Asunción
São Paulo
Rio de Janeiro
Paraná
OCEAN

Pitcairn I. (U.K.)

Easter I. (Chile)

URUGUAY
Valparaíso
Santiago
Buenos Aires
Montevideo
ARGENTINA
Bahía Blanca

Tristan da Cunha (U.K.)

Gough I. (U.K.)

Punta Arenas
Magellan Str.

Falkland Is. (U.K.)

S. Georgia (U.K.)

West of Greenwich

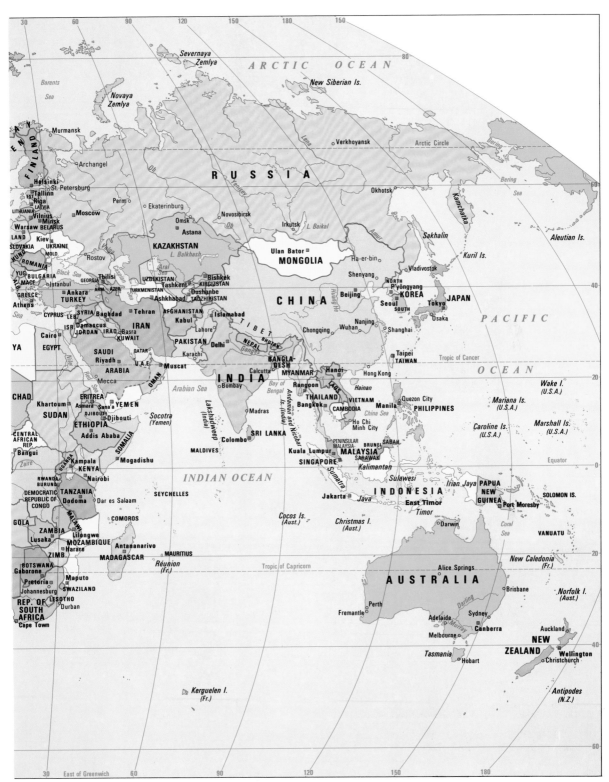

World – Time Zones

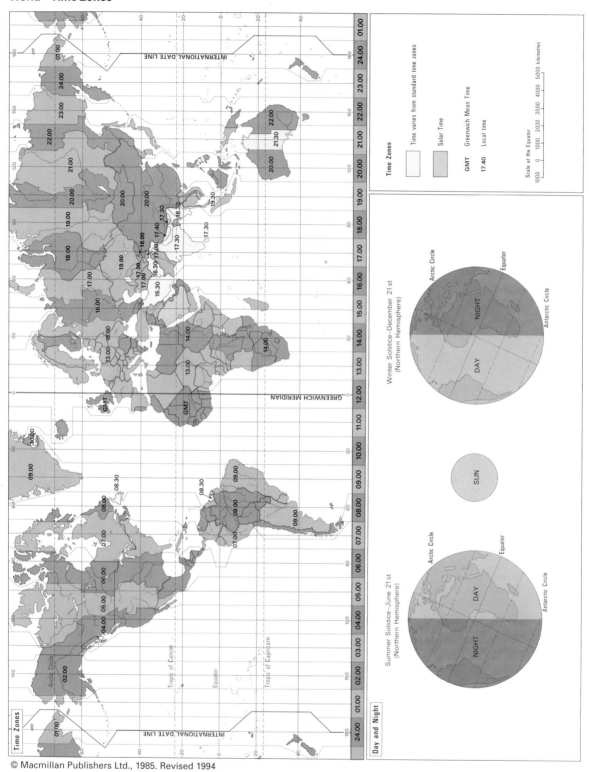

Time Zones

- Time varies from standard time zones
- Solar Time
- GMT — Greenwich Mean Time
- 17.40 — Local time

Scale at the Equator
1000 0 1000 2000 3000 4000 5000 kilometres

Day and Night

Winter Solstice – December 21st
(Northern Hemisphere)

Arctic Circle
Equator
NIGHT
DAY
Antarctic Circle

SUN

Summer Solstice – June 21st
(Northern Hemisphere)

Arctic Circle
Equator
DAY
NIGHT
Antarctic Circle

World – Tectonic Plates

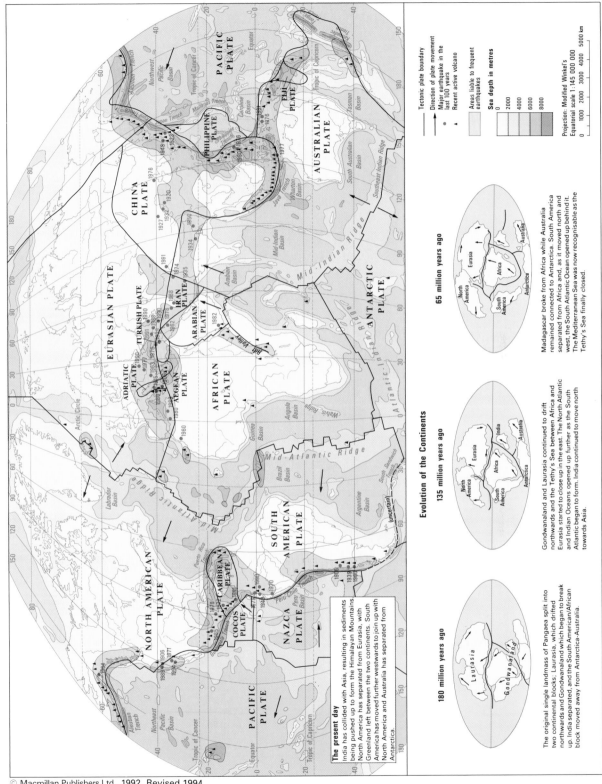

Evolution of the Continents

180 million years ago

The original single landmass of Pangaea split into two continental blocks; Laurasia, which drifted northwards and Gondwanaland which began to break up. India separated, and the South American/African block moved away from Antarctica-Australia.

135 million years ago

Gondwanaland and Laurasia continued to drift northwards and the Tethy's Sea between Africa and Eurasia started to close up in the east. The North Atlantic and Indian Oceans opened up behind it. The South Atlantic began to form. India continued to move north towards Asia.

65 million years ago

Madagascar broke from Africa while Australia remained connected to Antarctica. South America separated from Africa and, as it moved north and west, the South Atlantic Ocean opened up behind it. The Mediterranean Sea was now recognisable as the Tethy's Sea finally closed.

The present day

India has collided with Asia, resulting in sediments being pushed up to form the Himalayan Mountains. North America has separated from Eurasia, with Greenland left between the two continents. South America has moved further westwards to join up with North America and Australia has separated from Antarctica.

Legend

Tectonic plate boundary

Direction of plate movement

Major earthquake in the last 100 years

Recent active volcano

Areas liable to frequent earthquakes

Sea depth in metres

0 · 2000 · 4000 · 6000 · 8000

Projection: Modified Winkel's
Equatorial scale 1: 145 000 000

0 1000 2000 3000 4000 5000 km

British Isles – Counties and Unitary Authorities

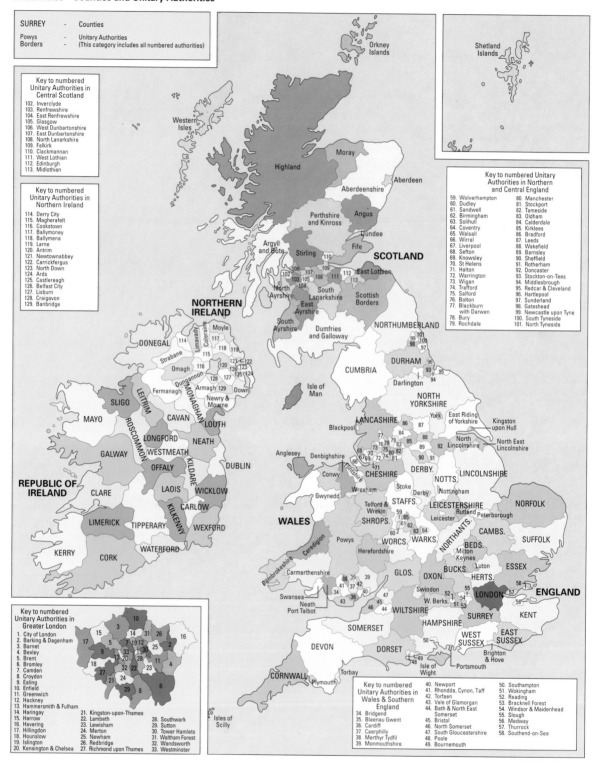

SURREY   –   Counties
Powys   –   Unitary Authorities
Borders   –   (This category includes all numbered authorities)

Key to numbered Unitary Authorities in Central Scotland
102. Inverclyde
103. Renfrewshire
104. East Renfrewshire
105. Glasgow
106. West Dunbartonshire
107. East Dunbartonshire
108. North Lanarkshire
109. Falkirk
110. Clackmannan
111. West Lothian
112. Edinburgh
113. Midlothian

Key to numbered Unitary Authorities in Northern Ireland
114. Derry City
115. Magherafelt
116. Cookstown
117. Ballymoney
118. Ballymena
119. Larne
120. Antrim
121. Newtownabbey
122. Carrickfergus
123. North Down
124. Ards
125. Castlereagh
126. Belfast City
127. Lisburn
128. Craigavon
129. Banbridge

Key to numbered Unitary Authorities in Northern and Central England
59. Wolverhampton
60. Dudley
61. Sandwell
62. Birmingham
63. Solihull
64. Coventry
65. Walsall
66. Wirral
67. Liverpool
68. Sefton
69. Knowsley
70. St Helens
71. Halton
72. Warrington
73. Wigan
74. Trafford
75. Salford
76. Bolton
77. Blackburn with Darwen
78. Bury
79. Rochdale
80. Manchester
81. Stockport
82. Tameside
83. Oldham
84. Calderdale
85. Kirklees
86. Bradford
87. Leeds
88. Wakefield
89. Barnsley
90. Sheffield
91. Rotherham
92. Doncaster
93. Stockton-on-Tees
94. Middlesbrough
95. Redcar & Cleveland
96. Hartlepool
97. Sunderland
98. Gateshead
99. Newcastle upon Tyne
100. South Tyneside
101. North Tyneside

Key to numbered Unitary Authorities in Greater London
1. City of London
2. Barking & Dagenham
3. Barnet
4. Bexley
5. Brent
6. Bromley
7. Camden
8. Croydon
9. Ealing
10. Enfield
11. Greenwich
12. Hackney
13. Hammersmith & Fulham
14. Haringay
15. Harrow
16. Havering
17. Hillingdon
18. Hounslow
19. Islington
20. Kensington & Chelsea
21. Kingston-upon-Thames
22. Lambeth
23. Lewisham
24. Merton
25. Newham
26. Redbridge
27. Richmond upon Thames
28. Southwark
29. Sutton
30. Tower Hamlets
31. Waltham Forest
32. Wandsworth
33. Westminster

Key to numbered Unitary Authorities in Wales & Southern England
34. Bridgend
35. Blaenau Gwent
36. Cardiff
37. Caerphilly
38. Merthyr Tydfil
39. Monmouthshire
40. Newport
41. Rhondda, Cynon, Taff
42. Torfaen
43. Vale of Glamorgan
44. Bath & North East Somerset
45. Bristol
46. North Somerset
47. South Gloucestershire
48. Poole
49. Bournemouth
50. Southampton
51. Wokingham
52. Reading
53. Bracknell Forest
54. Windsor & Maidenhead
55. Slough
56. Medway
57. Thurrock
58. Southend-on-Sea

BRITISH ISLES – PHYSICAL AND POLITICAL

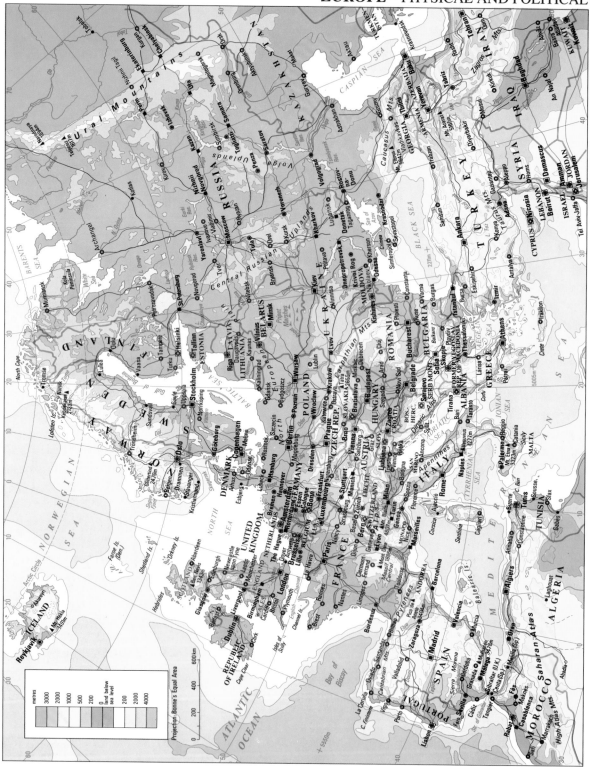

ASIA – PHYSICAL AND POLITICAL

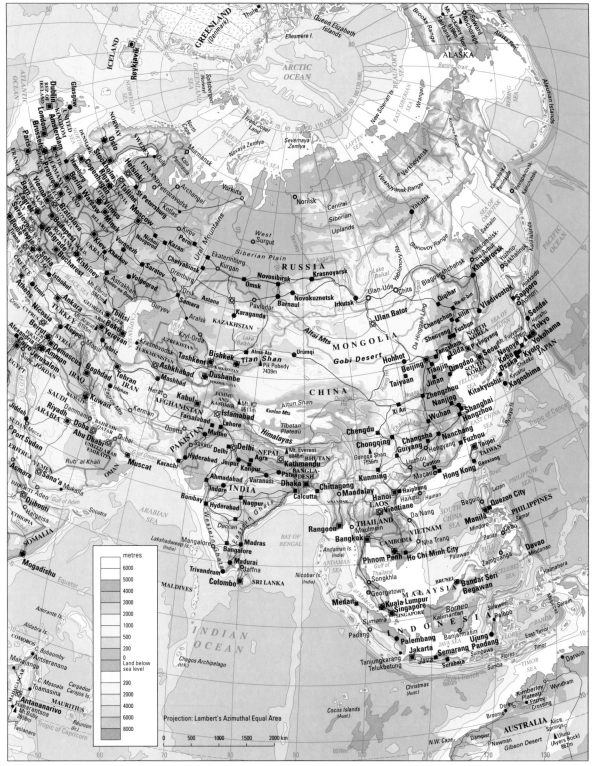

Projection: Lambert's Azimuthal Equal Area

metres
6000
5000
4000
3000
2000
1000
500
200
0
Land below
sea level
200
2000
4000
6000
8000

0   500   1000   1500   2000 km

MIDDLE EAST – PHYSICAL AND POLITICAL

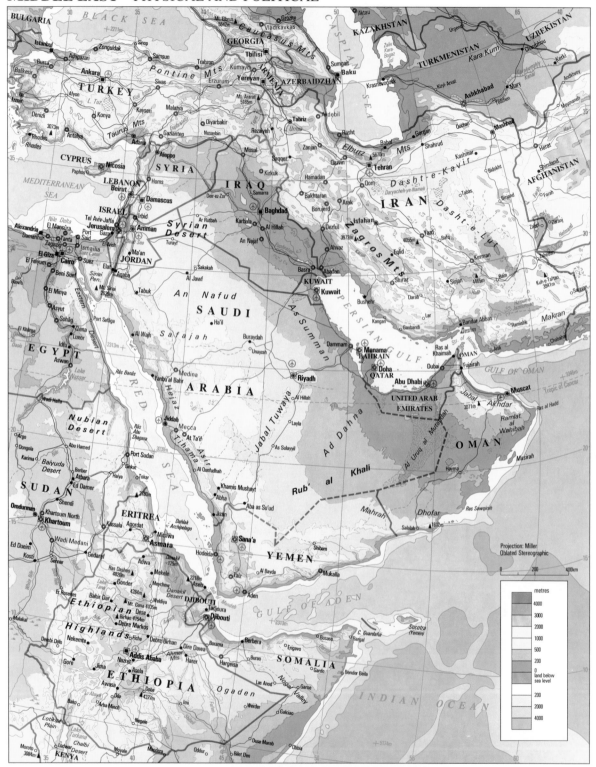

metres

4000	
3000	
2000	
1000	
500	
200	
0	land below sea level
200	
2000	
4000	

Projection: Miller
Oblated Stereographic

0   200   400km

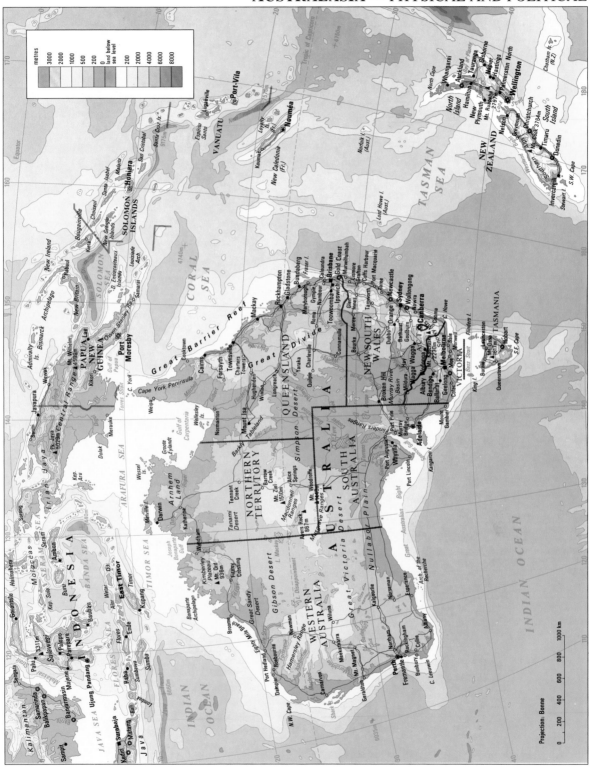

NEW ZEALAND - PHYSICAL AND POLITICAL

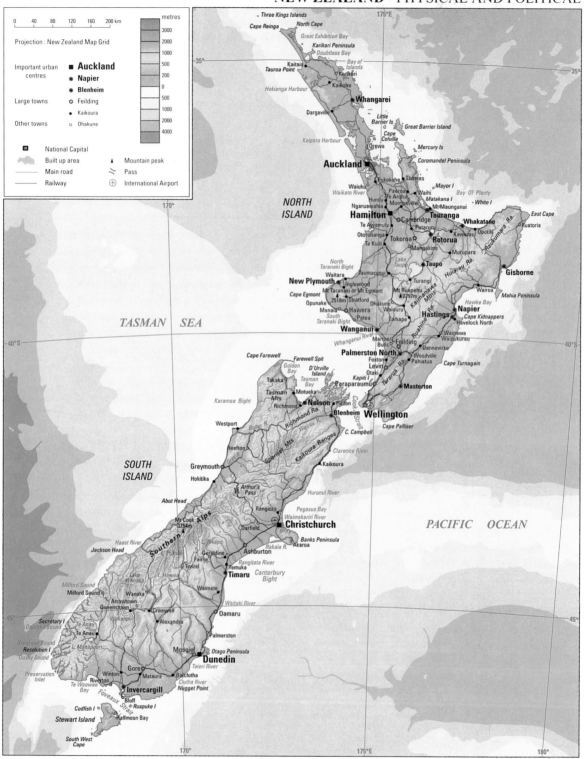

0   40   80   120   160   200 km

Projection : New Zealand Map Grid

metres
3000
2000
1000
500
200
0
500
1000
2000
4000

Important urban
centres

■ Auckland
● Napier
● Blenheim

Large towns
○ Feilding
▲ Kaikoura

Other towns
○ Ohakune

National Capital
Built up area
Main road
Railway

▲ Mountain peak
∕ Pass
⊕ International Airport

Three Kings Islands
Cape Reinga   North Cape
Great Exhibition Bay
Karikari Peninsula
Kaitaia   Doubtless Bay
Tauroa Point   Bay of Islands
Kerikeri
Hokianga Harbour   Kaikohe
Whangarei
Dargaville
Little Barrier Is   Great Barrier Island
Kaipara Harbour   Cape Colville
Orewa   Mercury Is
Coromandel Peninsula
Auckland
Pukekohe   Thames
Waiuku   Paeroa   Mayor I
Waikato River   Te Aroha   Waihi   Bay Of Plenty
Huntly   Matakana I   White I
Ngaruawahia   Morrinsville   Mt Maunganui
Hamilton   Cambridge   **Tauranga**   **Whakatane**
Te Awamutu   Putaruru   Opotiki   Ruatoria
Otorohanga   Tokoroa   **Rotorua**   East Cape
Te Kuiti   Mangakino   Murupara   Raukumara Ra.

NORTH ISLAND

North Taranaki Bight
Waitara   Lake Taupo   **Taupo**   **Gisborne**
Taumarunui
New Plymouth   Inglewood   Turangi   Kaimanawa Mts   Wairoa
Cape Egmont   Mt Taranaki or Mt Egmont   Mahia Peninsula
2518m   Stratford   Mt Ruapehu   Hawke Bay
Opunake   Ohakune   2797m
Manaia   Hawera   Waiouru   Ruahine Ra.   **Hastings**   **Napier**
Patea   Taihape   Cape Kidnappers
South Taranaki Bight   **Wanganui**   Havelock North
Whanganui River   Marton   **Feilding**   Waipawa
Bulls   Woodville   Waipukurau
Cape Farewell   **Palmerston North**   Foxton   Dannevirke
Farewell Spit   Levin   Pahiatua
Golden Bay   D'Urville Island   Otaki   **Masterton**   Cape Turnagain
Takaka   Tasman Bay   Kapiti I
Nelson   Tararua Ra.
Tasman Mts   Motueka   **Paraparaumu**
Richmond   Picton
Karamea Bight   Richmond Ra.   **Wellington**
Westport   Wairau R.   **Blenheim**   Cape Palliser
Buller R.   Cook Strait
C. Campbell

SOUTH ISLAND

Reefton   Spenser Mts   Kaikoura Ranges
Greymouth   Grey R.   **Kaikoura**
Hokitika   Clarence River
Arthur's Pass
Abut Head   Hurunui River
Rangiora   Pegasus Bay
Mt Cook   Southern Alps   Waimakariri River
3754m   Darfield   **Christchurch**
Haast River   Tekapo   Banks Peninsula
Jackson Head   L. Pukaki   Rakaia R.   Akaroa
Ashburton
Geraldine   Rangitata River
Fairlie   Temuka   Canterbury Bight
L. Tekapo   Twizel
Milford Sound   L. Wanaka   **Timaru**
Milford Sound   Waimate
Wanaka
Arrowtown   Waitaki River
Queenstown   Cromwell   Oamaru
L. Wakatipu
Secretary I   Alexandra
Deepwater Sound   Te Anau   Palmerston
Breaksea I   L. Te Anau
Resolution I   L. Manapouri   Mosgiel   Otago Peninsula
Dusky Sound   **Dunedin**
Preservation Inlet   Gore   Taieri River
Winton   Mataura   Balclutha
Te Waewae Bay   Riverton   Clutha River
Nugget Point
Invercargill
Bluff   Ruapuke I
Codfish I
Stewart Island   Halfmoon Bay
South West Cape

TASMAN SEA

PACIFIC OCEAN

175°E
35°
170°
40°S
45°
180°

AFRICA – PHYSICAL AND POLITICAL

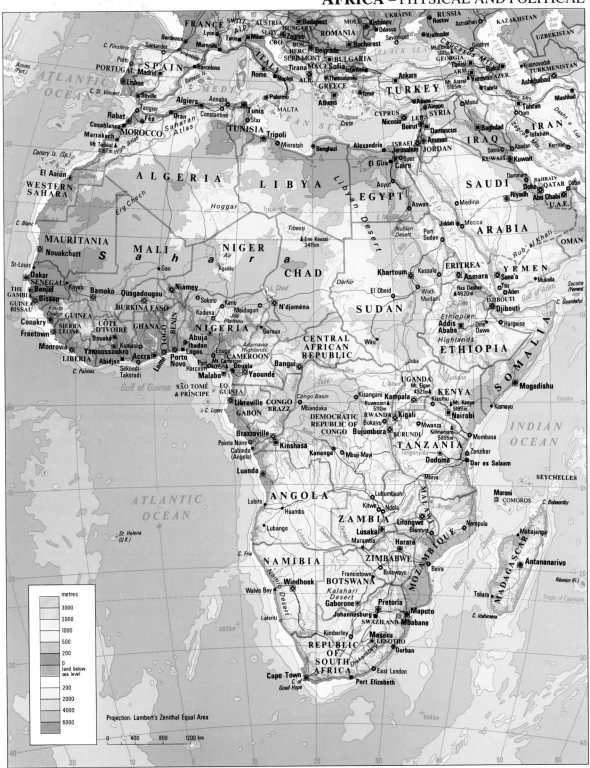

metres
3000
2000
1000
500
200
0
land below
sea level
200
2000
4000
6000

Projection: Lambert's Zenithal Equal Area

0   400   800   1200 km

NORTH AMERICA – PHYSICAL AND POLITICAL

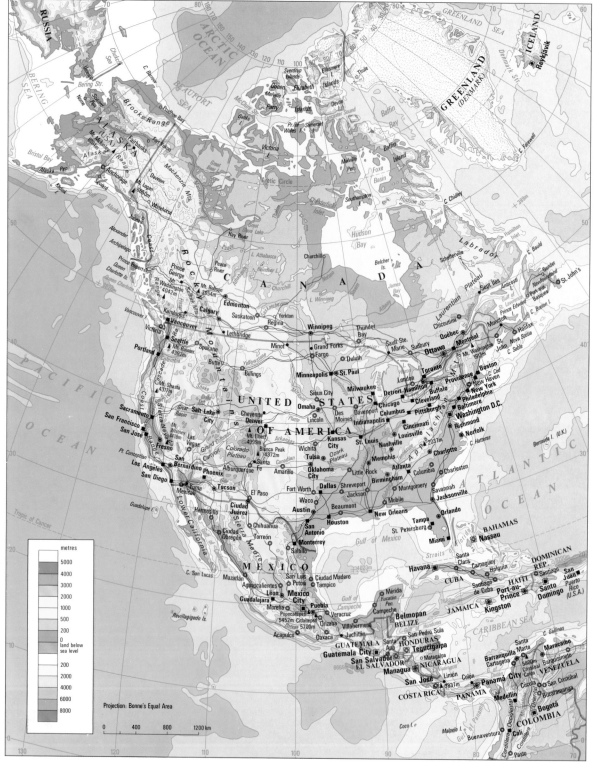

metres

5000	
4000	
3000	
2000	
1000	
500	
200	
0	land below sea level
200	
2000	
4000	
6000	
8000	

Projection: Bonne's Equal Area

0   400   800   1200 km

USA – Political

Capital City
State Capitals
Other Important Towns

International Boundaries
State Boundaries
Major Roads
Major Railways

400 Kilometres
200
0
200

Hawaii

100 Kilometres
50
0
100

Alaska

600 Kilometres
300
0
300

© Macmillan Publishers Ltd.,1980. Revised 1994

SOUTH AMERICA – PHYSICAL AND POLITICAL

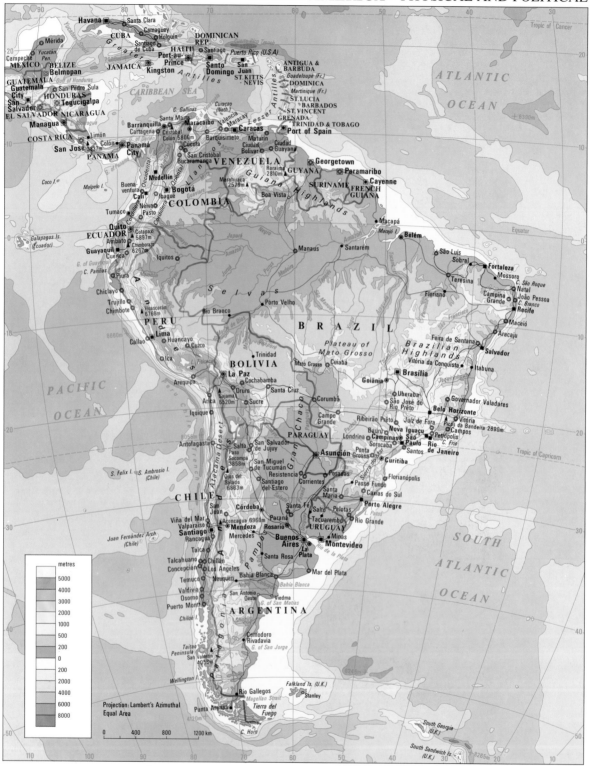

Projection: Lambert's Azimuthal Equal Area

metres
5000
4000
3000
2000
1000
500
200
0
200
2000
4000
6000
8000

0   400   800   1200 km

prime minister (1964–80). Kosygin rose in the Communist Party in the 1940s as an economics expert. He served in the politburo from 1948 to 1952. In 1960 he was elected to what was now the presidium; after Khrushchev's fall he became prime minister. He initially shared power with ▷Brezhnev but in the late 1960s his influence declined.

● **Kota Baharu** ▶ 6 07N 102 15E A town in NE Peninsular Malaysia, the capital of Kelantan state. It has a major power station. Population (1991): 219 713.

● **Kota Kinabalu** ▶ (former name: Jesselton) 5 59N 116 04E A port in Malaysia, the capital of Sabah state on the South China Sea. Industries include fishing and rice milling; rubber is exported. Population (1991): 208 484.

● **koto** ▶ A Japanese stringed instrument of the ▷zither family. The narrow 2-metre sound board has 13 strings, which the player, sitting on his heels, plucks with plectra attached to two fingers and the thumb of the right hand. ⌐musical instruments.

● **Kotor** ▶ 42 27N 18 46E A port in S Serbia and Montenegro, on the Gulf of Kotor. The oldest town in Montenegro with a remarkable 12th-century cathedral, it is now protected as a monument. The town was damaged during an earthquake in April, 1979. Population (latest est): 20 455.

● **Kottbus** ▷See Cottbus.

● **Kotzebue, August von** ▶ (1761–1819) German dramatist and novelist. He was a prolific writer of popular sentimental plays, most notably the comedy *Die deutschen Kleinstädter* (1803). He was assassinated as a suspected spy while working for the Russian tsar.

kouros ▶ A marble horseman found on the Acropolis. Its "archaic smile" is typical of the Greek sculpture of the second quarter of the 6th century BC.

● **kouros** ▶ (Greek: youth) In archaic Greek sculpture, a nude standing male figure, often more than life-size, derived (c. 650 BC) from Egyptian models. The modelling of the face and body became increasingly naturalistic. *Compare* kore.

● **Koussevitsky, Sergei** ▶ (1874–1951) Russian composer. Originally a virtuoso double-bass player, he conducted the State Symphony Orchestra in Petrograd (now St Petersburg) but left Russia in 1920. He worked in Paris and subsequently in the USA, where he directed the Boston Symphony Orchestra from 1924 to 1949. An advocate of contemporary music, he founded the Koussevitsky Music Foundation, which continues to commission new musical works.

● **Kovno** ▷See Kaunas.

● **Kowloon** ▷See Jiulong.

● **Koxinga** ▷See Zheng Cheng Gong.

● **Kozhikode** ▶ (former name: Calicut) 11 15N 75 45E A seaport on the W coast of India, in Kerala. Formerly famous as a cotton-manufacturing centre (Calicut gave its name to calico), it was visited by the Portuguese explorer Vasco da Gama (1498) and in 1664 the British East India Company established a trading post here. Tea, coffee, coconut products, and spices are exported. Population (1991 est): 420 000.

● **Kozirev, Nikolai Aleksandrovich** ▶ (1908–) Russian astronomer, who first observed volcanic activity on the moon. In 1958 he observed a cloud in one of the moon's craters. Kozirev discovered that the cloud contained carbon and deduced that it was formed by volcanic activity.

● **Kra, Isthmus of** ▶ The neck of the Malay Peninsula connecting it to the Asian mainland. It is occupied by Myanmar (Burma) and Thailand and is 64 km (40 mi) across at its narrowest point.

● **Krafft-Ebing, Richard von** ▶ (1840–1902) German psychiatrist, who studied many aspects of mental and nervous disorders. He established the link between syphilis and general paralysis of the insane and made pioneering studies of sexual aberrations in *Psychopathia sexualis* (1886).

● **kraft process** ▶ An industrial process for producing cellulose for paper manufacture from pine-wood chips by digestion with alkali. Rosin and fatty-acid soaps are by-products. The pulp produced is especially strong, hence the name (German *kraft*, strong).

● **Kragujevac** ▶ 44 01N 20 55E A town in E Serbia and Montenegro, in Serbia. A former centre of the Serbian struggle against the Turks, it was the capital of Serbia (1818–39). Its industries include a large car factory. Population (2000 est): 154 489.

● **krait** ▶ A highly venomous snake belonging to the genus *Bungarus* (12 species) occurring in S Asia. Kraits have shiny scales and are usually patterned with blue-and-white or black-and-yellow bands; they prey chiefly on other snakes. The common blue krait (*B. caeruleus*) of India and China is 1.5 m long and its venom can be fatal to humans. Family: *Elapidae* (cobras, mambas, coral snakes).

● **Krakatoa** ▶ (Indonesian name: Krakatau) 6 11S 105 26E A small volcanic Indonesian island in the Sunda Strait. During its eruption in 1883, one of the greatest ever recorded, 36 000 people were killed, many by the tidal waves that swept the coasts of Java and Sumatra. Today the island remains uninhabited.

● **Kraków** ▶ (or Cracow) 50 03N 19 55E The third largest city in Poland, on the River Vistula. It was the capital of Poland from 1305 to 1609 and remains famous as a cultural centre. The Jagiellonian University, one of the oldest in Europe, was founded here in 1364. Other notable buildings include the cathedral (14th century) and many architecturally distinguished churches. Its industry is based at Nowa Huta 10 km (6 mi) to the E. Population (1996 est): 745 400.

● **Kramatorsk** ▶ 48 43N 37 33E A city in E Ukraine, in the Donets Basin. An iron-and-steel centre, it manufactures machinery and machine tools. Population (1998 est): 190 800.

● **Krasnodar** ▶ (name until 1920: Ekaterinodar) 45 02N 39 00E A city in SW Russia, on the River Kuban. It is the centre of an agricultural region and food processing is the most important industry. Population (1999 est): 643 400.

● **Krasnoyarsk** ▶ 56 05N 92 46E A city in E central Russia, on the River Yenisei. It was founded in 1628, developing greatly after the discovery of gold in the region in the 19th century. It produces aluminium, having one of the largest outputs in the country, and has a notable hydroelectric station. Population (1999 est): 877 800.

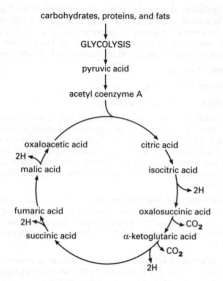

carbohydrates, proteins, and fats

GLYCOLYSIS

pyruvic acid

acetyl coenzyme A

oxaloacetic acid — citric acid
2H
malic acid — isocitric acid
2H
fumaric acid — oxalosuccinic acid
2H — CO_2
succinic acid — α-ketoglutaric acid
— CO_2
2H

Krebs cycle ▶ For every two atoms of hydrogen transferred, three ATP molecules are generated.

● **Krebs, Sir Hans Adolf ▶** (1900–81) British biochemist, born in Germany. Working in Germany until 1933, Krebs discovered the cycle of reactions by which waste nitrogenous products are converted to ▷urea by the body. After his move to Britain came his major achievement—the ▷Krebs cycle. Krebs was awarded a Nobel Prize (1953) with Fritz Lipmann (1899–1986).

● **Krebs cycle ▶** (citric acid cycle *or* tricarboxylic acid cycle) The sequence of chemical reactions, taking place in the mitochondria of cells, that is central to the metabolism of virtually all living organisms. Named after its principal discoverer, Sir Hans ▷Krebs, the cycle involves the conversion of acetyl coenzyme A, derived from the carbohydrates, proteins, and fats of food, into hydrogen atoms or electrons, from which usable energy in the form of ▷ATP is produced by the ▷cytochrome electron transport chain. Intermediate products of the Krebs cycle are used for the manufacture of carbohydrates, lipids, and proteins by cells.

● **Krefeld ▶** 51 20N 6 32E A city in NW Germany, in North Rhine-Westphalia on the River Rhine. It is known especially for its silk and velvet industries. It was the site of a Prussian victory (1758) during the Seven Years' War. Population (1996 est): 249 606.

● **Kreisky, Bruno ▶** (1911–90) Austrian statesman; Socialist chancellor (1970–83). After Austria fell to Nazi Germany, he escaped to Sweden (1938), where he lived until 1945. He was foreign minister (1959–66) before becoming chancellor.

● **Kreisler, Fritz ▶** (1875–1962) Austrian violinist. A child prodigy, he studied at the Vienna and Paris conservatoires and toured the USA in 1889. He frequently played his own compositions, written in the style of older composers and (until 1935) ascribed to them.

● **Kremenchug ▶** 49 03N 33 25E A city in E central Ukraine, on the River Dnepr. It has a large hydroelectric station and metallurgical and engineering industries. Population (1996 est): 246 000.

● **Kremlin ▶** The citadel of any Russian city, now referring usually to that of Moscow. Built in 1156 but continually extended, it contains the Cathedral of the Assumption (1475–79), the Cathedral of the Annunciation (1484–89), the Great Kremlin Palace (1838–49), etc. Except for the period between 1712 and 1918 it has been the seat of the Russian government and is now also a public museum of architecture.

● **Křenek, Ernst ▶** (1900–91) Austrian composer, a pupil of Franz Schreker (1878–1934) in Berlin. His jazz-influenced opera, *Jonny spielt auf* (1925–26), is atonal; he later made use of ▷serialism. He became a US citizen in 1954.

● **Kreutzer, Rodolphe ▶** (1766–1831) French violinist and composer, renowned for his violin studies. Beethoven's *Kreutzer Sonata* for violin and piano (1803) was dedicated to him.

● **Krewo, Union of ▶** (1385) The union of Poland and Lithuania under Jagiełło, Grand Duke of Lithuania (*see* Jagiellons), whose rule there was threatened by rivals in the ducal family and by the ▷Teutonic Knights. He agreed to marry the young Polish queen and to accept Christianity while Lithuania was to be annexed to Poland. The union was only made permanent by the Union of ▷Lublin (1569).

● **krill ▶** Shrimplike marine ▷crustaceans, 8–60 mm long, of the order *Euphausiacea* (82 species). Periodically krill swarms occur in certain regions, for example the Arctic and Antarctic Oceans, to become an important source of food for fishes, birds, and baleen whales.

● **Kripke, Saul ▶** (1940–) US philosopher and logician, who has made significant contributions to truth theory, metaphysics, theory of mind, and linguistics. In the paper "Naming and Necessity" (1972) he investigated the relationship between proper names and the things or persons they denote. He has also argued against the materialist theory of consciousness, according to which states of mind are identical with neurophysiological events in the brain.

● **Krishna ▶** A popular Hindu deity, the eighth incarnation of ▷Vishnu and the subject of much devotional worship, art, and literature. In the ▷*Bhagavadgita* he is revealed as the creator, sustainer, and destroyer of the universe (*see* Trimurti). Elsewhere he is worshipped as a fertility god, whose flute playing entrances all and whose erotic love for young maidens expresses God's love for man. He is commonly represented as a beautiful youth with bluish skin wearing a crown of peacock feathers.

● **Krishna Menon** ▷*See* Menon, Krishna.

● **Kriss Kringle ▶** A name for Santa Claus (*see* Nicholas, St) used principally in the USA. It is a changed form of the German *Christkindl*, little Christ child.

● **Kristallnacht ▶** (German: night of glass) 9–10 November, 1938, when mobs led by the ▷Nazi brownshirts (*Sturm Abteilung*) roamed German and Austrian towns setting fire to synagogues and smashing the windows of shops and homes owned by Jews. This first intimation of the coming ▷holocaust led many Jews, including the academics who later developed the A-bomb in the USA, to leave Germany.

● **Kristiansand ▶** 58 8N 08 01E A major seaport in S Norway, on the ▷Skagerrak. Industries include shipbuilding, textiles, smelting, and food processing. Population (1994): 73 543.

● **Kristianstad ▶** 56 02N 14 10E A town in Sweden, on the River Helge. Originally a Danish fortress (1614), it finally became part of Sweden in 1678. Its industries include textiles and engineering. Population (1994): 73 543.

● **Krivoi Rog ▶** 47 55N 33 24E A city in SE Ukraine. Founded by the Cossacks in the 17th century, it is now an important ironmining centre. Population (1996 est): 720 000.

● **Krochmal, Nachman ▶** (1785–1840) Jewish philosopher and historian, born in Poland. His influential *Guide to the Perplexed of Our Time* (1851) offers an original philosophy of Jewish history.

● **Kroger affair ▶** The case of Morris and Lona Cohen, a US couple living an outwardly normal life in the W London suburbs under the names of Peter and Helen Kroger; in 1961 they were exposed as Soviet spies. A Special Branch surveillance operation established that the "Krogers" were part of a spy ring centring on the KGB agent Gordon ▷Lonsdale and that their Ruislip bungalow was being used to radio stolen secrets to Moscow. They were sentenced to 20 years' imprisonment.

● **Kronstadt ▶** 60 00N 29 40E A port in NW Russia, on Kotlin Island in the Gulf of Finland. Scene of the ▷Kronstadt Rebellion (1921), it is still an important naval base. Population (1994 est): 44 400.

● **Kronstadt Rebellion ▶** (1921) An uprising among Soviet sailors in Kronstadt. The sailors, who had supported the Bolsheviks in the Russian Revolution, demanded economic reforms and an end to Bolshevik political domination. The Red Army crushed the rebels and

Lenin's ▷New Economic Policy (1921) was introduced to relieve the privations that had given rise to the revolt.

● **Kropotkin, Peter, Prince** ▶ (1842–1921) Russian anarchist. A geographer and geologist, Kropotkin joined the anarchist movement in the 1870s, was arrested, and escaped abroad. He settled in England in 1886 and later wrote his famous autobiography, *Memoirs of a Revolutionist* (1899). In 1917, Kropotkin returned to Russia to retire.

● **Kroto, Sir Harold (Walter)** ▶ (1939–) British chemist. In 1985 he discovered ▷buckminsterfullerene, a form of carbon molecule in which the atoms are arranged in a ball-like structure. In 1996 he was knighted and awarded the Nobel Prize for Chemistry.

● **Kruger, (Stephanus Johannes) Paul(us)** ▶ (1825–1904) Afrikaner statesman; president (1883–1902) of the South African Republic (Transvaal). A farmer of Dutch descent, Kruger settled with his parents in the Transvaal after taking part in the ▷Great Trek. He led the struggle to regain independence for the Transvaal from the British, achieved in 1881, after the first ▷Boer War. As president he resisted British immigrant demands for equality with the Afrikaners, a policy that led to the second Boer War (1899–1902). During the war he went to Europe to seek aid for the Afrikaners. Unsuccessful, he settled in Holland and then Switzerland, where he died.

● **Kruger National Park** ▶ A game and plant reserve in NE South Africa, adjacent to the border with Mozambique. About 325 km (202 mi) long and 20–50 km (12–31 mi) wide, it serves to protect such species as lions, leopards, zebras, and elephants. Area: about 21 000 sq km (8106 sq mi).

● **krugerrand** ▶ A South African coin containing one troy ounce of gold, minted since 1967 for overseas issue and bought for investment purposes. It has never been a true currency coin and was minted to enable investors to escape restrictions on the private ownership of gold. Since 1975 an import licence has been required to bring them into the UK. In the late 1980s they lost popularity for political reasons and because other countries produced similar coins.

● **Krugersdorp** ▶ 26 06S 27 46E A town in N South Africa. Founded in 1887, it is an important mining and industrial centre producing gold, uranium, and manganese. Population (latest est): 73 767.

● **Krum** ▶ (d. 814 AD) Khan of the Bulgars (802–14). After defeating a Byzantine army in 811, Krum besieged Constantinople in 813 and 814, dying during the campaign. Krum introduced a state administrative system to Bulgaria.

● **Krupp** ▶ A German family of arms manufacturers. Under **Arndt Krupp** (d. 1624), the family settled in Essen, where in 1811 **Friedrich Krupp** (1787–1826) established a steel factory. His son **Alfred Krupp** (1812–87) diversified the family business into arms manufacture, contributing to Prussian victory in the ▷Franco-Prussian War (1870–71). Under Alfred's son-in-law **Gustav Krupp von Bohlen und Halbach** (1870–1950), the company developed Big Bertha, the World War I artillery piece named after Gustav's wife **Bertha Krupp** (1886–1957). Their son **Alfried Krupp** (1907–67) developed Gustav's ties with the Nazis, using concentration-camp internees in his factories. After World War II he was imprisoned for war crimes until 1951.

● **krypton** ▶ (Kr) A noble gas discovered in 1898 by Sir William Ramsay and M. W. Travers (1872–1961), in the residue left after boiling liquid air. Compounds include KrF_2 and some ▷clathrates. It is used for filling some fluorescent light bulbs and the ▷metre was defined (1960–83) by the wavelength of a specified isotropic transition. At no 36; at wt 83.80; mp −157.37°C; bp −153.23°C.

● **Kuala Lumpur** ▶ 3 10N 101 40E The financial and commercial capital of Malaysia, in central Peninsular Malaysia; the administrative capital moved to ▷Putrajaya in 1999. Kuala Lumpur became capital of the Federated Malay States in 1895. The University of Malaya was founded in 1962 and the Technological University of Malaysia in 1972. It is a major commercial centre serving an important tin-mining and rubber-growing area. Population (1991): 1 145 075.

● **Kuang-chou** ▷*See* Canton.

● **Kuang-hsü** ▷*See* Guang Xu.

● **Kuan Ti** ▷*See* Guan Di.

● **Kuang-tung** ▷*See* Guangdong.

● **Kuan Yin** ▷*See* Guan Yin.

● **Kuban, River** ▶ A river in SW Russia. Rising in the Caucasus Mountains, it flows mainly NW into a swampy delta that enters the Sea of Azov. Its main port is Krasnodar. Length: 906 km (563 mi).

● **Kubelik, Rafael** ▶ (1914–96) Czech conductor. He left Prague for the UK in 1948 and subsequently worked in Germany and the USA. He was music director of the Royal Opera, Covent Garden (1955–58), and of the New York Metropolitan Opera (1972–74). In 1973 he took Swiss citizenship. His father, **Jan Kubelik** (1880–1940), was a violinist.

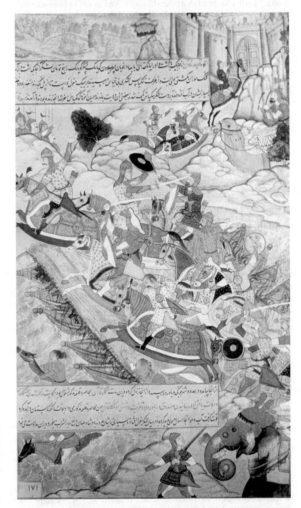

Kublai Khan ▶ A 16th-century illustration of Kublai Khan's armies crossing a pontoon over the Yangtze River to besiege the Chinese fortress of O-Chou.

● **Kublai Khan** ▶ (1215–94) Emperor of China (1279–94), who founded the Yuan dynasty. Genghis Khan's grandson, Kublai established himself (1259) as chief of the Mongols after years of conflict with his brother Mangu (d. 1259). The conqueror and ruler of all China from 1279, he administered from Beijing an empire extending from the River Danube to the East China Sea. More humane than his predecessors and much influenced by Chinese culture, he opened up trade and communications with Europe, largely through Marco ▷Polo. However, his preoccupation with China and attempts to conquer SE Asia weakened his hold on the rest of the empire.

● **Kubrick, Stanley** ▶ (1928–99) US film writer, director, and producer working mainly in the UK. His first major film, *Paths of Glory*

(1957), concerned an unjust courtmartial. Subsequent films, often satirical and highly imaginative, include *Lolita* (1962), *Dr Strangelove* (1963), *2001: A Space Odyssey* (1968), *A Clockwork Orange* (1971), *Barry Lyndon* (1975), *The Shining* (1980), *Full Metal Jacket* (1987), and *Eyes Wide Shut* (1999).

● **Kuching** ▶ 1 32N 110 20E A port in Malaysia, the capital of Sarawak state on the River Sarawak. It exports rubber, sago, and pepper. It has Anglican and Roman Catholic cathedrals. Population (1991): 147 729.

● **kudu** ▶ A large antelope, *Tragelaphus strepsiceros*, of African bush regions. About 130 cm high at the shoulder, kudus are red-brown with thin white vertical stripes on the flanks. Males have long corkscrew-shaped horns, a fringe on the lower side of the neck, and a mane along the back. The lesser kudu (*T. imberbis*) is smaller and found only in NE Africa.

● **kudzu** ▶ A climbing vine, *Pueraria lobata*, with entire or lobed leaves and fragrant purple flowers. Native to E Asia, it has been introduced to North America for its edible tubers, fibre, and as a quick-growing ornamental along highways, etc. Family: ▷*Leguminosae*.

● **Kuei-chou** ▷*See* Guizhou.

● **Kuei-yang** ▷*See* Guiyang.

● **Kufah** ▶ A town 145 km (90 mi) S of Baghdad, in Iraq. Founded as an Arab garrison town in 638 AD, Kufah became one of the most important centres of Islam. From the 10th century it began to decline and it is now an archaeological site. Its suburb of Najaf is the burial place of ▷Ali and a flourishing centre of ▷Shiite Islam.

● **Kuibyshev** ▷*See* Samara.

● **Kukai** ▶ (774–835) Japanese Buddhist monk, famous as a scholar and artist. The founder of the Kongobuji monastery on Mount Koya, Kukai reputedly invented hiragana, the syllabary system of ▷Japanese writing.

● **Ku Klux Klan** ▶ (KKK) A US secret society active against the Blacks. It originated in Tennessee after the Civil War to deter newly enfranchised Blacks from voting. Klansmen in white cloaks and hoods, burning fiery crosses, killed Blacks and destroyed their property. It was revived in 1915, supporting White protestants in business and politics against immigrants, Catholics, Jews, and Blacks. Membership dropped during the Depression and the KKK became quiescent. Bitterness in the South against the ▷civil-rights movement led to another revival in the 1950s. The Un-American Activities Committee investigated its leaders in 1965, after a civil-rights demonstrator was murdered. Klansmen opposed desegregation orders; they are still active, especially in the South.

● **kulaks** ▶ Wealthy peasants in late imperial and early Soviet Russia. Before the Russian Revolution (1917) they were prominent in village affairs. After the Revolution, they were favoured by the ▷New Economic Policy (1921) until 1927, when Stalin raised their taxes and then transformed their lands into ▷collective farms. The de-kulakization programme led to the exile of many kulaks to remote regions.

● **Kulturkampf** ▶ (German: conflict of beliefs) The struggle between ▷Bismarck and the German Roman Catholic Church during the 1870s and 1880s. Bismarck opposed the church's involvement in politics and subordinated it to the state. However, opposition to the persecution of priests had forced Bismarck to restore the church's rights by 1887.

● **Kumamoto** ▶ 32 50N 130 42E A city in Japan, in W Kyushu on the River Shira. One of the strongest centres in feudal Japan, it has a 17th-century castle. Its university was established in 1949. It is an agricultural centre, with bamboo, pottery, textile, and advanced technological industries. Population (1995): 650 322.

● **Kumasi** ▶ 6 45N 1 35W The second largest city in Ghana. Formerly the capital of Ashanti, it was taken by the British in 1874. It is the commercial and transportation centre of Ghana's chief cocoa-growing area. The University of Science and Technology was founded here in 1961. Population (1988 est): 385 192.

● **Kumayri** ▶ (name from 1840 until 1924: Aleksandropol; name from 1924 until 1991: Leninakan) 40 47N 43 49E A city in NW Armenia. Its textile industries are of major importance. In 1988 it was devastated by an earthquake. Population (1994 est): 120 000.

● **Kumbh Mela** ▷*See* Allahabad.

● **kumquat** ▶ A shrubby plant of the genus *Fortunella* (6 species), of E and SE Asia, with fruits resembling small oranges. They are acid-tasting and mainly used for pickling and preserves and kumquats can be grown farther N than citrus trees. Family: *Rutaceae*.

● **Kun, Béla** ▶ (1886–?1939) Hungarian revolutionary. Kun founded the Hungarian Communist Party in 1918 and led the Soviet Republic that succeeded Károlyi's government in March, 1919. Opposition to his nationalization programme led to a reign of terror, which with his unsuccessful campaigns against Romania forced him to flee in August to Vienna and then to Russia. He reportedly died in Stalin's purges.

● **Kundera, Milan** ▶ (1929–   ) Czech novelist and writer, living in France since 1975. His ironic sexual comedies include *Life is Elsewhere* (1973), *The Unbearable Lightness of Being* (1984), *Immortality* (1990), and *Slowness* (1996).

● **kung fu** ▶ An ancient Chinese form of combat, mainly for self-defence. Among the other ▷martial arts it is most closely related to ▷karate, which possibly developed from it. In the later 20th century the *wing chun* style (according to tradition devised as a means of self-defence for women) became particularly well known, partly because of the publicity given it by Bruce ▷Lee. Like other martial arts, it embodies a philosophy as well as a method of combat.

● **Kunlun Mountains** ▶ A mountain system in W China, separating Tibet from the Tarim Basin. It extends 1600 km (1000 mi) E–W, reaching 7723 m (25 378 ft) at Ulugh Muztagh.

● **Kunming** ▶ 25 04N 102 41E A city in S China, the capital of Yunnan province. A major commercial and cultural centre, it is noted for its Ming bronze temple and is the site of Yunnan University. Industries include iron and steel, engineering, and chemicals. Population (1991 est): 1 520 000.

● **Kuomintang** ▷*See* Guomindang.

● **Kuo Mo-jo** ▶ (1892–1978) Chinese man of letters, translator of many Western classics. Born in Szechwan, he went to Japan in 1913, where in 1921 he founded the Creation Society, dedicated to the reform of Chinese language and literature. He was a prolific poet, novelist, playwright, and critic. He returned to China in 1937 a committed communist and held many major cultural posts under Mao.

● **Kura, River** ▶ A river in W Asia. Rising in NE Turkey, it flows E through Georgia and Azerbaidzhan to enter the Caspian Sea near Baku. It is used for hydroelectric power and irrigation. Length: 1515 km (941 mi).

● **Kurchatov, Igor Vasilievich** ▶ (1903–60) Soviet physicist, who headed his country's research into nuclear fission during World War II. His team constructed a nuclear reactor in 1946 and built the Soviet Union's first atomic bomb in 1949 and its first hydrogen bomb in 1952. The element kurchatovium is named after him.

● **kurchatovium** ▶ (Ku) An artificial transuranic element and the first transactinide. It was first detected by Soviet scientists in 1964 and named after I. V. ▷Kurchatov. The claim is disputed by scientists at Berkeley, USA, who proposed the name **rutherfordium** (Rf) after Lord ▷Rutherford, following their independent synthesis. At no 104.

● **Kurdistan** ▶ An area in the Middle East inhabited by ▷Kurds, comprising parts of SE Turkey, N Syria, N Iraq, and NW Iran, including the Iranian province of Kordestan. The Turkish part includes a plateau that supports some agriculture, the remainder being mainly mountainous; the chief towns are Diyarbakir (Turkey), Kirkuk (Iraq), and Kermanshah (Iran). The area was split between different countries on the dissolution of the Ottoman Empire at the end of World War I, and subsequent attempts to form a Kurdish state have been only partially or temporarily successful. In 1992 Kurdish groups set up an unofficial government in N Iraq. Area: 192 000 sq km (74 600 sq mi).

● **Kurds** ▶ The major population group in ▷Kurdistan. Their language, Kurdish, is one of the ▷Iranian languages and is written in either a modified Arabic or a modified Cyrillic script. The Kurds grow cereals and cotton and are now mostly detribalized but a few nomadic groups still exist. They are Muslims but do not restrict their women to the same extent as other Islamic peoples. Known from Assyrian records (6th century BC), the Kurds have never enjoyed political unity, and nationalistic aspirations issuing in rebellions in the 19th and 20th centuries have led to reprisals in Turkey (1925), Iraq, and Iran. Iraq devastated Kurdish mountain villages in 1988 and again in 1991 following a Kurdish rebellion during the ▷Gulf War. Recent years have seen continuing conflict with Iraqi and Turkish forces and fighting between rival Kurdish factions.

● **Kure** ▶ 34 14N 132 32E A port in Japan, in SW Honshu on Hiroshima Bay. An important naval base since 1886, an enormous battleship, the *Yamato*, was built here during World War II. Other industries include engineering and steel. Population (1995 est): 209 477.

● **Kurgan** ▶ 55 30N 65 20E A city in W Russia, on the River Tobol. Machinery is produced and food processed. Population (1995 est): 363 000.

● **Kuria Muria Islands** ▶ A group of five islands off the coast of Oman, in the Arabian Sea. Area: 72 sq km (28 sq mi).

● **Kuril Islands** ▶ A Russian chain of 56 islands extending 1200 km (746 mi) NE–SW between Kamchatka (Russia) and Hokkaido (Japan) and separating the Sea of Okhotsk and the main body of the Pacific Ocean. Discovered in 1634 by the Dutch, the islands were Japanese until seized by the Soviet Union in 1945; in 1986 and 1992 Japan demanded their return. The largest are Paramushir, Urup, Iturup, and Kunashir. There are 38 active volcanoes. About 200 km (124 mi) to the E is the **Kuril Trench**, which has a maximum depth of 10 542 m (34 587 ft). Total area: about 15 600 sq km (6022 sq mi).

● **Kurosawa Akira** ▶ (1910–98) Japanese film director. His best-known films are costume dramas such as *Rashomon* (1950) and *Seven Samurai* (1954). Often working with the actor Toshiro Mifune (1920–97), he made films on contemporary themes of social injustice and literary adaptations, notably *Throne of Blood* (1957) and *Ran* (1985) (from Shakespeare's *Macbeth* and *King Lear*, respectively); other films include *Kagemusha* (1980) and *Rhapsody in August* (1991).

● **kuroshio** ▶ A warm ocean current forming part of the N Pacific circulation. Analogous to the Gulf Stream of the Atlantic, it flows NE along the Pacific coast of Japan, then veers across the N Pacific as the North Pacific Drift.

● **Kursk** ▶ 51 45N 36 14E A city in W Russia. Food processing and metallurgy are important. Population (1995 est): 442 000.

● **Kusunoki Masashige** ▶ (1294–1336) Japanese samurai. His steadfast loyalty to Emperor ▷Daigo II and heroic defence of Chihaya castle became one of the most famous examples of *bushido* (the way of the warriors).

● **Kut** ▷*See* Al Kut.

● **Kutaisi** ▶ 42 15N 42 44E A city in W Georgia, on the River Rioni. It is a historic Transcaucasian city and the 11th-century Bagrati Cathedral survives. It is a major industrial centre. Population (1991 est): 238 200.

● **Kutch, Rann of** ▶ An area of salt waste in central W India, near the border with S Pakistan. It consists of the Great Rann in the N and the Little Rann in the SE. It was a navigable lake in the 4th century BC, but is now salt marsh in the wet season and salt desert in the dry. Total area: about 23 000 sq km (8878 sq mi).

● **Kutenai** ▶ A North American Indian people of the plateau region between the Rocky and Cascade Mountains of British Columbia. They were a hunting and fishing people, occasionally moving on to the Plains to hunt buffalo. Their language is distantly related to the ▷Algonquian family.

● **Kutná Hora** ▶ (German name: Kuttenberg) 49 58N 15 15E A mining town in the Czech Republic, in E Bohemia, famous during the 13th century as a silvermining centre. It contains the fine gothic Ca-

thedral of St Barbara (13th century), in the form of an imperial crown. Population (latest est): 21 628.

● **Kutuzov, Mikhail Ilarionovich, Prince of Smolensk** ▶ (1745–1813) Russian field marshal. After service in Poland, Austria, and against the Turks, he commanded the forces opposing Napoleon's invasion of Russia. When Napoleon withdrew from Moscow, Kutuzov's army harassed his retreat until barely 100 000 French soldiers remained.

● **Kuwait, State of** ▶ A country in the Middle East, in Arabia situated at the head of the Persian Gulf. The country is flat, sandy, and barren and has a harsh climate with extremes of temperature. The inhabitants are predominantly Arab, although about half are foreigners, and the Kuwaitis are mainly Sunnite or Shiite Muslim.

Economy: Kuwait is one of the largest oil producers in the world and has one of the highest per capita incomes; oil revenues account for over half the gross national product and oil-related services for most of the remainder, as the country has almost no other natural resources. Kuwait is a member of OPEC. Production capacity was gravely damaged by the ▷Gulf War but has returned to about 80% of prewar levels. There are some manufacturing industries, such as plastics and fertilizers, and fruit and vegetables are cultivated in the small arable areas. Traditional fishing (especially for shrimp) has declined owing to oil pollution but the building of dhows (Arab sailing craft) continues.

History: Kuwait was originally settled in the early 18th century by nomads from the Arabian interior, who established a sheikdom in 1756. In 1899, to counter German and Ottoman expansionism, Kuwait made an agreement giving Britain control over its foreign affairs and on the outbreak of World War I it became a British protectorate. Its borders were fixed in 1922–23, including those of a neutral zone, the oil revenues from which are shared by Saudi Arabia and Kuwait. Oil was discovered in 1938 and transformed the Kuwaiti economy after World War II. On gaining independence in 1961, Kuwait had to request troops from Britain to avert the threatened annexation by Iraq. In August 1990 Iraq invaded, claiming Kuwait to be its 19th province; the country was then systematically looted. The UN passed resolutions demanding Iraq's withdrawal which Iraq ignored, precipitating the Gulf War. Iraq's routed retreating army devastated the country, setting fire to hundreds of oil wells. In early 1993 Iraqi troops made minor raids across the border, which the UN then moved a few metres northwards. Demands for the restoration of parliamentary democracy under the 1962 constitution, suspended by the ruling al-Sabah family since 1976, led to elections being held in 1992. Despite only a small proportion of the population being eligible to vote, several opposition candidates won seats in the National Assembly. Crown Prince Sheikh Saad al-Abdullah al-Salim al-Sabah became prime minister.

State of Kuwait	
Head of state	the Amir of Kuwait, Sheikh Jaber al-Ahmad al-Jaber al-Sabah
Official language	Arabic
Official currency	Kuwait dinar of 1000 fils
Area	17 819 sq km (6880 sq mi)
Population (1997 est)	1 809 000
Capital	Kuwait City

● **Kuwait City** ▶ 29 20N 48 00E The capital of the sheikdom of Kuwait, on the Persian Gulf. It has a good natural harbour, and its livelihood was based on sea trade, fishing, and boatbuilding until oil became the major industry in the early 1950s and it developed into a metropolis with modern facilities including a university (1962). It was badly damaged during the ▷Gulf War. Population (1995 est): 28 859.

● **Kuznets, Simon** ▶ (1901–85) US economist, born in Russia. His theory of the ▷gross national product as a measure of economic output is contained in his major work *National Income and Its Composition (1919–1938)* (1941). Other works include *Economic Growth of Nations* (1971). Kuznets was awarded the Nobel Prize in 1971.

● **Kuznetsk Basin** ▶ An area in S Russia comprising the river basin of the Tom from Novokuznetsk to Tomsk. It has vast coal deposits, which have brought heavy industry to the area, notably iron- and steel-works.

● **Kuznetsov, Alexander** ▶ (1929–79) Russian writer who published his first novel, *The Continuation of a Legend*, in 1957. *Babi Yar* (1966), a novel about the massacre of Ukrainian Jews by the Germans in 1941, was heavily censored in the Soviet Union. He moved to Britain in 1969.

● **Kwa** ▶ A major division of the ▷Niger-Congo language family that includes many languages of West Africa, such as Yoruba, Igbo (*see* Ibo) ▷Ewe, Twi, and Anyi.

● **Kwajalein** ▶ 9 15N 167 30E The largest atoll of the Marshall Islands, in the W Pacific Ocean. It was the first Pacific territory captured by US forces in World War II and is now a US military base.

● **Kwakiutl** ▶ A North American Indian people of the coastal region of British Columbia. They speak a ▷Wakashan language. Their vigorous traditional culture was typical of the NW coast and characterized by extreme competition for status and rank through ostentatious disposal and even destruction of wealth (*see* potlatch). There was an elaborate religious and ceremonial life and a distinctive artistic tradition based upon carving of wooden totem poles, masks, and other objects. Their economy was based on an abundance of salmon and other fish, game, and wild fruits and agriculture was not practised.

● **Kwangju** ▶ 35 07N 126 52E A city in SW South Korea. An ancient commercial and administrative centre, it has industries that include motor-vehicle manufacture. Its university was established in 1952. Population (1990): 1 257 636.

● **Kwangsi Chuang Autonomous Region** ▷*See* Guangxi Zhuang Autonomous Region.

● **Kwangtung** ▷*See* Guangdong.

● **kwashiorkor** ▶ Severe protein deficiency in children under five years. **Marasmus** is deficiency of not only protein but also of carbohydrate and fat. Kwashiorkor and marasmus often occur together in some combination. Kwashiorkor, which develops in babies soon after they are weaned, occurs in poor countries, especially parts of West Africa, where the diet does not contain sufficient protein (the name derives from a Ghanaian word). The children fail to grow, are apathetic, have swollen stomachs and ankles, sparse hair, diarrhoea, and enlarged livers. The slightest infection is usually fatal but the children recover rapidly with a good diet.

● **KwaZulu** ▷*See* Bantu Homelands.

● **KwaZulu/Natal** ▷*See* Natal.

● **Kweichow** ▷*See* Guizhou.

● **Kwinana** ▷*See* Fremantle.

● **Kyd, Thomas** ▶ (1558–94) English dramatist. A friend of Christopher ▷Marlowe, Kyd inaugurated the genre of revenge tragedy with *The Spanish Tragedy* (1592). Among his probable works is a play about Hamlet, now lost, which influenced Shakespeare.

● **Kyoga, Lake** ▶ (or Lake Kioga) A lake in central Uganda. Formed by the Victoria Nile River, it is shallow and reedy and has many arms. Length: about 130 km (81 mi).

● **Kyoto** ▶ 35 2N 135 45E A city in Japan, in S Honshu. It has been a leading cultural centre since early times, when it was the Japanese capital (794–1192 AD) and the old imperial palace and ancient Buddhist temples still remain. Kyoto university was established in 1897. It is also the centre of Japanese Buddhism. Situated within the Osaka-Kobe industrial complex, it is famed for its silk, porcelain, and handicrafts. It suffered a major earthquake in 1995. Population (1995): 1 463 601.

● **Kyoto agreement** ▶ An international agreement to limit the emission of greenhouse gases (*see* greenhouse effect) negotiated between 1997 and July 2001. The agreement commits 38 industrialized countries to reducing their emissions of greenhouse gases by an average of 5.2% from 1990 levels by 2012. The USA opted out of the agreement in March 2001 but the EU countries are participants.

● **Kyprianou, Spyros** ▶ (1932–2002) Cypriot statesman; president (1977–88). When Cyprus became independent in 1960 he became minister of justice and then foreign minister (1960–72). In 1976 he founded the Cyprus Democratic Party.

● **Kyrgyzstan** ▷*See* Kirgizstan, Republic of.

● **Kyushu** ▶ The southernmost of the four main islands of Japan, separated from Korea by the Korea Strait and from Honshu by Shimonoseki Strait. Mountainous and volcanic, it has hot springs and a subtropical climate and is the most densely populated of the Japanese islands. There is a rice-growing area in the NW, drained by the River Chikugo, while heavy industry is centred on the N coalfield. Other important products are silk, fish, timber, fruit, and vegetables. It is noted for its Satsuma and Hizen porcelain. Area: 35 659 sq km (13 768 sq mi). Population (1999 est): 13 462 534. Chief cities: Kitakyushu, Fukuoka, and Nagasaki.

● **Kyzyl Kum** ▶ A desert in central Asia, in Kazakhstan and Uzbekistan, lying between the Rivers Amu Darya and Syr Darya. Area: about 300 000 sq km (115 806 sq mi).

● **Laaland** ▷*See* Lolland.

● **Laban, Rudolf von** ▶ (1879–1958) Hungarian dancer and chore-ographer, who invented the system for recording dance movements known as **Labanotation**. ⸠ballet.

● **labelled compounds** ▷*See* radioactive tracer.

● **Labiatae** ▶ (*or* Lamiaceae) A family of herbaceous plants and shrubs (about 3500 species), widely distributed but particularly abun-dant in the Mediterranean region. They typically have square stems, hairy simple leaves, and clusters of tubular two-lipped flowers. Many of the plants are aromatic and yield useful oils (lavender, rosemary, etc.) and many are used as culinary herbs (marjoram, mint, sage, thyme, etc.).

● **Labiche, Eugène** ▶ (1815–88) French dramatist. His numerous popular farcical comedies include *The Italian Straw Hat* (1851) and *The Journey of Mr Perrichon* (1860). They are characterized by intricate plots and the satirical portrayal of contemporary bourgeois manners and conventions.

● **Labor Party** ▶ The Australian democratic socialist party. It was formed in New South Wales in 1891 and first held federal office in 1904. World War I provoked a split in the party with the Labor prime minister W. M. ▷Hughes leading the proconscription majority out of the party to form the National Party (1916). The Labor Party did not regain power until 1929 and in 1931 policies in dealing with the De-pression caused another split. In power from 1939 to 1949, the party introduced important social legislation but in opposition in the 1950s another split occurred over attitudes to communism. Labor were again in power from 1972 until 1975, under Gough ▷Whitlam. Subsequent Labor premiers were Bob ▷Hawke (1983–91) and Paul ▷Keating (1991–96). The current leader is Kim Beazley (1946–).

● **Labour Day** ▶ The day on which the labour movement is cele-brated. In 1889, the Second International declared an international labour holiday on ▷May Day, which has since been thus celebrated in many countries. In Britain, Labour Day was the first Sunday in May until 1977, when the first Monday of the month was declared a public holiday. It is celebrated in Australia at different times in different states, in New Zealand on the fourth Monday in October, and in the USA on the first Monday in September.

● **Labour Party** ▶ The democratic socialist party in the UK. The party was formed in 1900 as the Labour Representation Committee, being renamed the Labour Party in 1906. Its origins lie in the trades-union movement of the 19th century, and the trade unions continue to provide most of its funds. The ▷Fabian Society was also a powerful influence on its formation and beliefs. In 1922 the Labour Party re-placed the divided Liberal Party as one of the two major UK parties (*compare* Conservative Party) and in 1924 and 1929–31 Labour formed minority governments under Ramsay ▷MacDonald. After World War II, under Clement ▷Attlee, the party won a huge majority in the gen-eral election of 1945 and was able to introduce radical policies. In office until 1951, the Labour administration undertook widespread ▷nationalization and set up a comprehensive system of ▷social secu-rity. The party was in office again from 1964 to 1970 and from 1974 to 1979, under Harold ▷Wilson (1964–76) and then James ▷Callaghan. The increasing prominence of the left caused splits within the party and in 1981 four members defected to form the ▷Social Democratic Party. Subsequent leaders of the party (but not the country) were Mi-chael ▷Foot (1980–83), Neil ▷Kinnock (1983–92), and John ▷Smith (1992–94), who died in office. His successor, Tony ▷Blair, modernized the party's constitution and image, leading it to landslide victories in the general elections of 1997 and 2001.

● **labour relations** ▷*See* industrial relations.

● **labour theory of value** ▶ The economic theory that the value of a product can be determined by the amount of labour needed to pro-duce it, e.g. a product needing twice as many man hours (of equal skill) to produce it as another is worth twice as much.

● **labour union** ▷*See* trade union.

● **Labrador** ▶ (*or* Coast of Labrador) A district of NE Canada, on the Atlantic Ocean. Although the coast has belonged to Newfoundland for several centuries, the interior was finally awarded to Newfound-land in 1927 by a judicial decision, which is still not recognized by Quebec. Labrador is mostly a rolling swampy plateau within the Ca-nadian Shield. Generally barren except for forested river valleys, it has vast reserves of high-grade iron ore, which are being mined. Its hydroelectric potential is enormous. Churches and missions are very influential in Labrador, especially in the sphere of education. Area: 258 185 sq km (99 685 sq mi). Population (latest est): 33 052. ▷*See also* Churchill Falls.

● **Labrador Current** ▶ A major ocean current of the N Atlantic, flowing S from the polar seas down the W coast of Greenland and past Newfoundland, until it meets the Gulf Stream and, being cold and dense, sinks beneath it. The Labrador Current carries icebergs S and is a cause of frequent fogs in the region of Newfoundland.

● **Labrador retriever** ▶ A breed of dog originating in Newfound-land and brought to Britain by fishermen in the early 19th century. It is solidly built with a tapering otter-like tail and a short dense water-resistant coat, usually black or yellow-brown. Height: 56–57 cm (dogs); 54–56 cm (bitches).

● **La Bruyère, Jean de** ▶ (1645–96) French satirist. He studied law and then served in the household of Louis II, Prince of Condé. His single work, *Caractères de Théophraste, avec les caractères ou les moeurs de ce siècle* (1688), consists chiefly of satirical portrait sketches (often of real persons under disguised names) and contemporary illustrations of vices; it achieved immediate and lasting popularity.

● **Labuan** ▶ A Malaysian island in the South China Sea. It became part of the state of Sabah in 1946. Copra, rubber, and rice are pro-duced. Area: 98 sq km (38 sq mi). Population (1990): 54 307. Chief town: Victoria.

● **laburnum** ▶ A tree of the genus *Laburnum*, especially *L. ana-gyroides*, which is native to mountainous regions of central Europe and widely grown for ornament. Up to 7 m high, it has smooth olive-green or brown bark and its leaves each consist of three dark-green leaflets. The bright-yellow flowers grow in hanging clusters, 10–30 cm long, and produce slender brown pods. All parts of the plant are poisonous, especially the seeds. Family: ▷*Leguminosae*.

● **labyrinth fish** ▶ A small elongated laterally compressed fish of the family *Anabantidae* (about 70 species), found in fresh waters of tropical Asia and Africa. They have an accessory respiratory organ (labyrinth) with which they obtain oxygen from air gulped at the sur-face—of benefit in poorly oxygenated water. The males often build a floating nest of bubbles to protect the eggs. Some species are popular aquarium fish. Order: *Perciformes.* ▷*See also* climbing perch; fighting fish; gourami.

● **Lacan, Jacques (Marie Emile)** ▶ (1901–81) French psychoanalyst and philosopher, whose unorthodox views led to his expulsion from the International Psychoanalytic Society in 1963; he founded his own École Freudienne de Paris a year later. His reinterpretation of Freud in terms of the ▷structuralist theory of language made him a cult figure in the ▷poststructuralist movement that emerged in the late 1960s. His major publication was his *Écrits* (1966).

● **Laccadive, Minicoy, and Amindivi Islands** ▷*See* Lakshadweep.

● **lace** ▶ An ornamental network of threads of silk, linen, etc., used mainly for dress collars, cuffs, altar cloths, etc. Needlepoint lace, originating in Italy in the early 16th century, is made with a needle on parchment or fabric. Pillow or bobbin lace, reputedly invented by Barbara Uttmann (b. 1514) in Saxony, is formed by twisting threads around pins stuck in a pillow. The best work was done in Italy, Flanders, France, and England in the 17th and 18th centuries, famous types of lace being Brussels, Valenciennes, Mechlin, and Honiton. Lace making as an art declined in the 19th century after machine manufacture was introduced.

● **La Ceiba** ▶ 15 45N 86 45W A port in N Honduras, on the Gulf of Honduras. It is a major port exporting chiefly coconuts, abaca fibre, and oranges. Population (latest est): 61 900.

● **lacewing** ▶ An □insect belonging to one of several families of the suborder *Plannipennia.* Lacewings have delicate net-veined wings and are carnivorous, with biting mouthparts. Green lacewings (*Chrysopidae*), also called golden-eyed lacewings, are about 10 mm long and occur worldwide near vegetation. Eggs are laid individually on hairlike stalks and the larvae feed on aphids, scale insects, etc. The brown lacewings (*Hemerobiidae*) are smaller and often have spotted wings. Order: ▷*Neuroptera.*

● **Lachish** ▶ An ancient city in ▷Canaan, W of Hebron (Israel), occupied from before 1580 BC. The Israelites held it from about 1220 until its destruction by the Babylonians (588). Inscriptions discovered here are important evidence for the early evolution of the alphabet.

● **Lachlan River** ▶ A river in SE Australia, in New South Wales. Rising in the Great Dividing Range it flows generally NW to join the Murrumbidgee River. Length: 1483 km (922 mi).

● **lac insect** ▶ An insect of the family *Lacciferidae,* found mainly in tropical and subtropical regions. The legless females have globular bodies covered with a layer of hardened resin. In the Indian species, *Laccifer lacca,* the females become encrusted on twigs to form sticklac, from which ▷shellac is produced. Suborder: *Homoptera*; order ▷*Hemiptera.*

● **Laclos, Pierre Choderlos de** ▶ (1741–1803) French novelist. He was a professional soldier and died while serving as a general under Napoleon in Italy. His novel, *Les Liaisons dangereuses* (1782), written in the form of letters between the main characters, concerned sexual corruption and intrigue in aristocratic society. The seducer Valmont, his accomplice Mme de Merteuil, and their victims are depicted with keen psychological insight.

● **La Condamine, Charles Marie de** ▶ (1701–74) French geographer. After service in the army he travelled widely and joined a geographical expedition to Peru (1735–43). He later went down the River Amazon on a raft, studying the region, and brought the drug curare to Europe.

● **Laconia** ▶ (modern Greek name: Lakonía) The SE region of the Peloponnese. Once a prosperous Mycenaean kingdom, Laconia was conquered by invading ▷Dorians about 1000 BC. Settling in ▷Sparta, the newcomers became rulers of Laconia, using the indigenous inhabitants as serf labourers, called ▷helots.

● **La Coruña** ▶ (or Corunna) 43 22N 8 24W A port in NW Spain, in Galicia on the Atlantic Ocean. The Spanish Armada sailed from here on 26 July, 1588, and in 1589 the city was sacked by Sir Francis Drake. During the Peninsular War Sir John ▷Moore was mortally wounded here after ensuring a British victory against the French. An impor-

tant fishing centre, it also manufactures tobacco and linen. Population (1995 est): 254 822.

● **lacquer** ▶ Coloured and often opaque varnish applied to metal or wood for protection and decoration. In Chinese and Japanese artwork, the sap of the ▷lacquer tree is used as wood lacquer. Other types of lacquer consist of ▷shellac dissolved in alcohol, which dries to form a protective film.

● **lacquer tree** ▶ A tree, *Rhus vernicifera,* of SE Asia, also called varnish tree. Up to 30 m tall, it has compound leaves each with up to nine pairs of leaflets, which turn red in autumn. Japanese ▷lacquer is obtained from the milky resin that oozes from cuts in the bark. Family: *Anacardiaceae.*

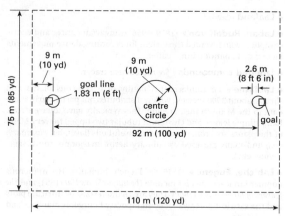

The optimum dimensions of the women's ground, although the game is played with no boundaries.

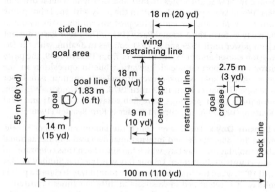

The dimensions of the men's ground.

lacrosse

● **lacrosse** ▶ A 10-a-side field game (12 for women) played with a ball and a long-handled stick (the crosse), which has a triangular head with a raw-hide strung pocket for catching, throwing, and picking up the ball. Of North American Indian origin, it is played mainly in the USA, Canada, Britain, and Australia. The object is to score goals by running with the ball and passing it. Each team consists of a goalkeeper, three defensive players (point, cover point, and first defence), three attackmen (first attack, in home, and out home) and three midfielders (second defence, centre, and second attack). Tackling and striking an opponent's stick to dislodge the ball are allowed, and protective clothing is worn.

● **lactation** ▶ The secretion of milk from the breasts or mammary glands. In women lactation is controlled by hormones released from the ovary, placenta, and pituitary gland (*see* prolactin; oxytocin) and starts shortly after childbirth, in response to the sucking action of the baby at the nipple: it will continue for as long as the baby is breastfed. A protein-rich fluid called colostrum is secreted in the first few days of lactation, before the milk has been produced. It contains antibodies that give the baby temporary immunity to disease.

● **lactic acid** ▶ (or 2-hydroxypropanoic acid) A carboxylic acid ($CH_3CH(OH)COOH$) that is the end product of ▷glycolysis in animal muscles and of ▷fermentations (such as the souring of milk) by certain bacteria. A commercial preparation is used as a flavouring and preservative in pickles and salad dressings and in tanning leather.

● **lactose** ▶ (or milk sugar) A disaccharide carbohydrate ($C_{12}H_{22}O_{11}$) consisting of one molecule of glucose linked to one of galactose. Lactose is found in the milk of all animals and is less sweet than sucrose.

● **Ladakh Range** ▶ A mountain range mainly in NW India, extending about 370 km (230 mi) between the Karakoram Range and the Himalayas and rising to over 6000 m (19 685 ft).

● **Ladin** ▶ A language spoken in the Dolomite region of Italy that belongs to the Rhaetian branch of the ▷Romance family. It is related to French and the Occitan dialects, to Romansh, and to Friulian, which is spoken around Udine in N Italy.

● **Ladino** ▶ A ▷Romance language originally spoken by Sephardic Jews in Spain but taken by them after their exile in 1492 to the Balkans, the Near East, N Africa, Greece, and Turkey. It is an old form of Castilian Spanish mixed with Hebrew elements and written in Hebrew characters.

● **Ladoga, Lake** ▶ A lake in NW Russia, the largest lake in Europe. It discharges via the River Neva into the Gulf of Finland. A canal forming part of the water route from the Gulf of Finland to the River Volga and the White Sea has been built parallel to its S shore to avoid the storms on the lake. ▷See also St Petersburg. Area: about 17 700 sq km (6836 sq mi).

● **ladybird beetle** ▶ A small round beetle, 8–10 mm long, that belongs to the widely distributed family Coccinellidae (5000 species). Most species are red or yellow with black spots and are of great benefit to humans. Both the larvae and adults feed on a variety of plant pests, including aphids, scale insects, mealybugs, and whiteflies. When attacked, ladybirds exude a toxic fluid.

● **Lady Day** ▶ The Christian feast of the ▷Annunciation of the Virgin Mary. Celebrated on 25 March, it began the calendar year in England from 1155 to 1752 and is still a ▷quarter day.

● **lady fern** ▶ A delicate ▷fern, Athyrium filix-femina, found in moist shady temperate regions. It has a short stout scaly rhizome that produces a circular cluster of large light-green feathery branched fronds, usually 50–70 cm long. The clusters of spore capsules (sori) are curved or horseshoe-shaped. Family: Aspidiaceae.

● **Ladysmith** ▶ 28 34S 29 47E A town in E South Africa. Founded in 1850, it was besieged for four months (1899–1900) by the Boers during the second Boer War, with the death of 3200 British soldiers. Population (1989): 56 599.

● **lady's slipper** ▶ A terrestrial orchid, Cypripedium calceolus, native to N Europe and Asia. Up to 45 cm high, it has broad leaves and the flowers are grouped singly or in twos and threes. Each flower has small twisted red-brown petals and an inflated yellow slipper-like lip. The lady's slipper is nearly extinct in Britain. ▷See also slipper orchid.

● **lady's smock** ▶ A perennial herb, Cardamine pratensis, also called cuckoo flower, found in damp meadows of N temperate regions. 15–60 cm high, it has compound leaves and a tall spike of pink or violet four-petalled flowers on slender stalks. Family: ▷Cruciferae.

● **Laënnec, René Théophile Hyacinth** ▶ (1781–1826) French physician and inventor of the stethoscope. Laënnec listened to the chest sounds of his patients using a foot-long wooden cylinder, from which he was able to diagnose diseases of the heart and respiratory system.

● **Lafayette, Marie Joseph Gilbert Motier, Marquis de** ▶ (1757–1834) French general and politician, prominent at the beginning of the French Revolution. His early career was distinguished by his military successes (1777–79, 1780–82) against the British in the ▷American Revolution. In France as a representative in the ▷States General, he presented the Declaration of the ▷Rights of Man (1789)

and after the storming of the Bastille he became commander of the new National Guard. In 1792 the rising power of the radicals threatened his life and he gave himself up to France's enemy, Austria. Lafayette was also prominent in the July Revolution (1830), which overthrew Charles X.

● **La Fayette, Mme de** ▶ (Marie Madeleine, Comtesse de L. F.; 1634–93) French novelist. She was a friend of ▷La Rochefoucauld and many other prominent writers. Her best-known novel is La Princesse de Clèves (1678), a study of the conflict between passion and duty in marriage.

● **Lafontaine, Henri-Marie** ▶ (1854–1943) Belgian jurist and statesman. A senator (1894–1936) and president of the International Peace Bureau (1907–43), he is best known for his contribution to international law. In 1913 he received the Nobel Peace Prize.

● **La Fontaine, Jean de** ▶ (1621–95) French poet. He was a friend of many prominent writers and patrons. His major work was the Fables (1668–94), sophisticated verse treatments of traditional fables from the collections of ▷Aesop, ▷Phaedrus, and later writers. His many other works included the bawdy verse tales, Contes (1664), which he is said to have repudiated after his religious conversion in 1692.

● **Laforgue, Jules** ▶ (1860–87) French poet, one of the ▷Symbolists. He was born in Montevideo (Uruguay) and wrote most of his poetry in Berlin while serving as reader to the Empress Augusta (1858–1921). His ironic and slangy poetry in vers libre greatly influenced several later French and foreign poets, notably T. S. Eliot.

● **Lagash** ▶ A city of ancient ▷Sumer, N of ▷Ur, flourishing about 2500 to 2100 BC. ▷Cuneiform tablets found here bear witness to social, legal, and commercial conditions in Sumerian society.

● **Lagerkvist, Pär (Fabian)** ▶ (1891–1974) Swedish novelist, poet, and dramatist. His early works were pessimistic in tone and influenced by expressionism. In the novels Bödeln (The Hangman; 1934) and Dvärgen (The Dwarf; 1944) he explored the problems of evil and human brutality. His best-known work is the novel Barabbas (1950), after which he achieved a worldwide reputation, winning the Nobel Prize in 1951.

● **Lagerlöf, Selma Ottiliana Lovisa** ▶ (1858–1940) Swedish novelist, who drew her inspiration from myth, legend, and her early life in Värmland. Her works include Gösta Berlings Saga (1891) and the children's storybook The Wonderful Adventures of Nils (1907). She was the first woman to be awarded the Nobel Prize (1909).

● **Lagomorpha** ▶ An order of mammals (66 species) comprising ▷pikas, ▷rabbits, and ▷hares. Lagomorphs have teeth similar to rodents, with four continuously growing incisors. They are vegetarians and eat their own faecal pellets, thus obtaining the maximum value from their food. Lagomorphs are found all over the world except Antarctica.

● **Lagos** ▶ 6 27N 3 28E The former capital and main port of Nigeria, on Lagos Island on the Bight of Benin. First settled by Yoruba fishermen in the 17th century, it became the centre of the Portuguese slave trade in W Africa and was ceded to Britain in 1861. Its university was founded in 1962. One of Africa's largest cities, it is an important commercial and industrial centre. Exports include palm oil and kernels and groundnuts. Population (1996 est): 1 518 000.

● **Lagrange, Joseph Louis, Comte de** ▶ (1736–1813) Mathematician and astronomer, born in Italy of French parents. In 1788, he published a book entitled Mechanique analytique, in which mechanics is developed algebraically and a wide variety of problems are solved by the application of general equations. In astronomy he solved the problem of predicting how two or more bodies move under each other's gravitational force and worked with ▷Laplace on planetary perturbations. **Lagrangian points** are the five points in the vicinity of two orbiting masses at which the gravitational forces balance each other out. The **lagrangian** (L) is the difference between the kinetic energy (K) and the potential energy (P) of a system; i.e. $L = K - P$. Lagrange also headed the commission that produced the metric system of units in 1795.

● **La Guardia, Fiorello Henry** ▶ (1882–1947) US politician; mayor of New York City (1933–45). As a lawyer and Congressman (1917–21,

1923–33) La Guardia helped initiate the Norris-La Guardia Act (1932), which allowed organized labour to strike, boycott, and picket. As mayor of New York he fought municipal corruption and supported action for civic improvement.

● **Lahore** ► 31 34N 74 22E The second largest city in Pakistan, near the River Ravi. Traditionally the chief city of the Punjab, Lahore is situated close to the Indian border and has been the scene of much bloodshed and violence. It is a major railway, commercial, and political centre and the headquarters of the Muslim League. The famous Shalimar gardens lie to the E of the city. An important educational centre, it is the site of the University of the Punjab (1882) and Pakistan University of Engineering and Technology (1961).

History: founded about the 7th century AD, it fell to the Moguls in 1524 and in 1798 it became the seat of Ranjit Singh's Sikh empire. It came under British rule in 1849. Population (1995 est): 5 085 000.

● **Lahti** ► 61 00N 25 40E A town in S Finland. A winter-sports resort and growing industrial centre, it has sawmilling, furniture, and textile industries and is the site of Finland's main radio and television stations. Population (1994): 94 706.

● **LAIA** ▷*See* Latin America.

● **Laibach** ▷*See* Ljubljana.

● **Laing, R(onald) D(avid)** ► (1927–89) British psychiatrist. He is best known for regarding schizophrenia as a defensive façade and madness as a journey of self-realization (*The Divided Self*, 1960). *The Politics of Experience* (1967) became influential among radical movements and his views on family life (*Sanity, Madness and the Family*, 1965 and *The Politics of the Family*, 1971) aroused controversy.

● **Laird, Macgregor** ► (1808–61) Scottish explorer. In 1830 he formed a merchant company to trade with Africa and took the first oceangoing vessel (*Alburkah*) up the lower Niger, with a loss, however, of 39 lives. He also sailed up the Niger's tributary, the Benue. In 1854 he promoted an expedition that advanced 240 km (150 mi) up the Niger; the use of quinine prevented any loss of life.

● **laissez-faire** ► The economic theory that governments should not interfere with market forces based on self-interest and the profit motive. The concept, originally proposed by the 18th-century French economists led by François ▷Quesnay (*see also* Physiocrats), was advocated by Adam ▷Smith and widely accepted until the beginning of the 19th century. By then the growth of capitalism had exposed its principal weaknesses: the rise of monopolies, the grossly inequitable distribution of wealth, and the exploitation of labour. In the 20th century laissez-faire policies were largely abandoned for ▷mixed economies in Western countries. However, since the 1970s there has been a revival of free-market ideas in both the developed and the developing world.

● **lake** ► (landform) An extensive body of water occupying a hollow in the earth's surface. Rivers generally flow both into and out of lakes although some are landlocked with no outlet. An **oxbow lake** is crescent shaped and is formed when a river ▷meander is cut off by the river flow breaching its neck. The larger saline lakes form inland seas, such as the ▷Caspian Sea. Many lakes are man made, for water supply, hydroelectric-power generation, and irrigation; Lake ▷Kariba in S Africa is an example.

● **lake** ► (pigment) An insoluble pigment formed by the combination of an organic dyestuff with a metallic compound (salt, oxide, or hydroxide). Lakes are used in paints and printing ▷inks.

● **Lake District** ► (*or* Lakeland) An area in NW England, in Cumbria, a national park since 1951. It consists of a high dome incised by a radial system of glaciated valleys, many of which contain ribbon lakes including Derwentwater, Ullswater, and Windermere. High mountains rise between the valleys, the highest being ▷Scafell Pike and ▷Helvellyn. Its spectacular scenery, popularized by the **Lakeland poets** (notably Wordsworth and Coleridge), is now a major tourist attraction, together with facilities for hill walking, rock climbing, and water sports. Other traditional occupations include hill farming, forestry, and quarrying. Area: about 1813 sq km (700 sq mi).

● **Lakeland terrier** ► A breed of dog originating in the English Lake District and used to flush foxes from cover. It has a robust body and a long flat head with small folded triangular ears. The rough dense coat may be black or blue (with or without tan), red, or dark brown. Height: up to 36 cm.

● **Lakshadweep** ► (name until 1973: Laccadive, Minicoy, and Amindivi Islands) A Union Territory of India comprising 27 islands in the Indian Ocean, 300 km (186 mi) W of Kerala. Ruled by Britain from 1792, it was handed over to India in 1956 and depends economically on fish, coconuts, grains, bananas, and vegetables. Area: 32 sq km (12 sq mi). Population (1991): 51 681. Administrative headquarters: Kavaratti Island.

● **Lakshmi** ► In Hinduism, the goddess of wealth and happiness, the benign aspect of Shakti, the supreme goddess. As the wife of Vishnu she appears in various forms according to his several incarnations. Many festivals are held in her honour (*see* Diwali). Lakshmi is also revered by the Jains.

● **Lalande, Joseph-Jérôme Le Français de** ► (1732–1807) French astronomer, who published (1801) the most complete catalogue of the stars then known. It listed some 47 000 stars, one of which was found by ▷Leverrier a hundred years later to be the planet Neptune.

● **La Línea** ► 36 10N 5 21W A town in SW Spain, in Andalusia on the Strait of Gibraltar. Many of its inhabitants work in Gibraltar. Industries include textiles and cork. Population (latest est): 56 282.

● **Lalique, René** ► (1860–1945) French ▷Art Nouveau jeweller and glassmaker. His jewellery is usually asymmetric with motifs of plants, snakes, etc. He later designed glassware with frosted patterns in relief, establishing a factory at Wingen-sur-Moder (1920).

● **Lallans** ► The dialect of the lowlands of Scotland, in which Robert ▷Burns wrote. A movement to re-establish it as a literary medium occurred after World War I (*see also* MacDiarmid, Hugh).

● **Lally, Thomas, Comte de** ► (1702–66) French general of Irish ancestry. He took part in the ▷Jacobite rebellion of 1745 and subsequently became commander in chief in the French East Indies (1756), coming into conflict with the British. Forced to surrender in 1761, his action was construed as treason and he was beheaded.

● **Lalo, (Victor Antoine) Édouard** ► (1823–92) French composer of Spanish descent. He is best remembered for his *Symphonie espagnole* (for violin and orchestra; 1873), a cello concerto (1876), and the ballet *Namouna* (1882).

● **Lalor, Peter** ► (1827–89) Australian engineer and politician, born in Ireland, who led the ▷Eureka Stockade uprising (1854). He was subsequently postmaster general (1875), commissioner of trade and customs (1875, 1877–80), and speaker of the Legislative Assembly of Victoria (1880–87).

● **lamaism** ▷*See* Tibetan Buddhism.

● **Lamarck, Jean-Baptiste de Monet, Chevalier de** ► (1744–1829) French naturalist, noted for his speculations about the evolution of living things, particularly his theory of the inheritance of acquired characteristics (*see* Lamarckism). Lamarck studied botany under Bernard de ▷Jussieu and published a flora of France in 1778. In 1793 he became professor of invertebrate zoology at the Museum of Natural History, Paris. Here Lamarck worked on a system of classification for invertebrate animals, published in his *Histoire naturelle des animaux sans vertebres* (7 vols, 1815–22). In 1809 Lamarck published his theory of evolution (in *Philosophie zoologique*). Lamarck's speculations about the physical and natural world found little favour among his contemporaries and he died blind and poverty stricken.

● **Lamarckism** ► The first theory of ▷evolution as proposed by Jean-Baptiste ▷Lamarck in 1809, based on his concept of the inheritance of acquired characteristics. He suggested that an organism develops structural changes during its lifetime as an adaptation to its particular environment and that these features are then inherited by successive generations through sexual reproduction. A classic example of these acquired characteristics are the forelegs and neck of a giraffe, which he believed became longer through its habit of browsing on tall trees. There is now little support for Lamarck's theory, although it was revived in a slightly modified form (neo-Lamarckism) by the Soviet geneticist T. D. ▷Lysenko.

● **Lamartine, Alphonse de** ► (1790–1869) French poet, one of the major figures of the Romantic movement. He established his reputation with *Méditations poétiques* (1820), a volume of lyrical poetry inspired by an unsuccessful love affair. During the 1820s he served as a diplomat in Naples and Florence and in the 1830s he became an active political champion of republican ideals. He was briefly head of the provisional government after the Revolution of 1848. He also wrote the poems *Jocelyn* (1836) and *La Chute d'un ange* (1836).

● **Lamb, Lady Caroline** ▷*See* Byron, 6th Baron; Melbourne, 2nd Viscount.

● **Lamb, Charles** ► (1775–1834) British essayist and critic. He worked as a clerk for the East India Company, devoting his private life to caring for his sister Mary (1764–1847), who had killed their mother in 1796 during one of her recurrent fits of insanity. He collaborated with Mary on *Tales from Shakespeare* (1807), a children's book. He is best remembered for his *Essays of Elia* (1822).

● **Lamb, Henry** ► (1885–1960) Australian-born British painter, the son of the mathematician and engineer **Sir Horace Lamb** (1849–1934). After studying medicine, he became a painter of portraits, notably *Lytton Strachey* (1914; Tate Gallery), and was an official war artist during World War II.

● **Lamb, William** ▷*See* Melbourne, 2nd Viscount.

● **Lambaréné** ► 0 41S 10 13E A town in W Gabon, on an island in the River Ogooué. Its hospital (1913) was founded by the missionary Albert ▷Schweitzer. Industries include palm products. Population (latest est): 50 800.

● **lambert** ► A unit of luminance equal to the luminance of a surface that emits one lumen per square centimetre. Named after J. H. ▷Lambert.

● **Lambert, Constant** ► (1905–51) British composer and conductor, a pupil of Vaughan Williams. Diaghilev commissioned his ballet *Romeo and Juliet* (1925–26) and he was musical director of the Sadler's Wells from 1928 to 1947. He also wrote the choral work *Rio Grande* (1929) and a famous book about music entitled *Music Ho!* (1934).

● **Lambert, Johann Heinrich** ► (1728–77) German mathematician and astronomer, who first derived the ▷hyperbolic functions and proved that π is an irrational ▷number. As an astronomer he measured the luminosities of stars and planets and introduced the term ▷albedo; a unit of luminance (*see* lambert) is named after him.

● **Lambert, John** ► (1619–83) English parliamentary general in the ▷Civil War. He commanded the cavalry at ▷Marston Moor (1644) and against the Scots at Preston (1648), Inverkeithing (1650), and Worcester (1651). He was largely responsible for the overthrow of Richard Cromwell (1659) and helped to rule the country until the Restoration of Charles II (1661). Convicted of treason, he died in prison.

● **Lambeth** ► A borough of S central Greater London, on the River Thames. Created in 1965 from the former metropolitan borough and E Wandsworth, it contains the Royal Festival Hall (*see* Festival of Britain), the ▷Royal National Theatre building (1976), the Oval cricket ground, and Lambeth Palace (since 1197 the London residence of the Archbishop of Canterbury). Area: 27 sq km (11 sq mi). Population (1994 est): 244 834.

● **Lambeth Conferences** ► Assemblies normally convened every ten years under the chairmanship of the Archbishop of Canterbury at Lambeth Palace, London, to which all bishops of the Anglican Church are invited. The first Lambeth Conference was held in 1867. Although their decisions have no binding power, the conferences are important indications of the Anglican episcopate's views and policies.

● **Lambeth walk** ► A British ballroom dance popularized in the 1930s by the musical *Me and My Girl* (1937). It purported to imitate the strutting walk of the Lambeth cockney.

● **lamb's lettuce** ▷*See* corn salad.

● **Lamentations of Jeremiah** ► An Old Testament book, a sequel to the Book of ▷Jeremiah and traditionally attributed to him, al-though it is more likely a work of the 5th century BC. It consists of a series of five dirgelike chapters concerned with the capture and destruction of Jerusalem and its Temple by the Babylonians in 586 BC. The event is graphically described, as are the accompanying slavery and famine. Jeremiah sees it as a divine judgment and closes with a prayer for mercy.

● **Lamerie, Paul de** ► (1688–1751) English silversmith of French Huguenot parents. Establishing his shop in 1712, he progressed from an unornamented Queen Anne style to ▷rococo designs, for which he is most famous.

● **Lamian War** ► (323–322 BC) The conflict that confirmed Macedon's supremacy in Greece after Alexander the Great's death. ▷Antipater, the Macedonian regent, was besieged in Lamia by rebellious Greek forces but eventually crushed the city states and reimposed his authority more firmly.

● **Lamiaceae** ▷*See* Labiatae.

● **laminar flow** ► Fluid flow in which the particles move in parallel layers, as in a fluid moving slowly along a horizontal straight pipe. Above a velocity given by the ▷Reynolds number, the layers no longer remain parallel and the flow becomes turbulent.

● **Laminaria** ► A genus of large brown seaweeds (*see* kelp), also called oarweed, that occurs in abundance along British and Pacific coasts. *L. digitata* (tangle) is a fan-shaped seaweed that may grow to a length of 50 m. *Laminaria* is a good source of alginic acid and alginates, used in ice cream, tyres, etc.

● **Lammas** ► The medieval festival of harvest (1 Aug). No longer observed in England, it remains a ▷quarter day in Scotland. An annual Lammas Fair is still held at Ballycastle, Co. Antrim, in Northern Ireland. The word comes from the Old English *hlāfmaesse*, loaf mass, because the festival originally involved consecrating the bread loaves made from the new season's wheat.

● **lammergeier** ► A large ▷vulture, *Gypaetus barbatus*, also called bearded vulture because of the long bristles on its chin. It is over 1 m long with a wingspan of 3 m and occurs in mountainous regions of S Europe, central Asia, and E Africa. It is brown with tawny underparts and a black-and-white face. Lammergeiers feed on bones and other carrion.

● **Lammermuir Hills** ► A range of hills in SE Scotland, in East Lothian and Scottish Borders. It extends NE between the Vale of Gala Water and the North Sea, reaching 535 m (1755 ft) at Meickle Says Law.

● **Lampedusa, Giuseppe Tomasi di** ► (1896–1957) Italian novelist. He lived an adventurous early life as a wealthy Sicilian aristocrat. During his last years he wrote *The Leopard* (1958), a historical novel concerning Sicily in the late 19th century. His works all appeared posthumously.

● **Lampeter** ► (Welsh name: Llanbedr Pont Steffan) 52 07N 4 05W A market town in SW Wales, in Ceredigion on the River Teifi. St David's College (founded in 1822) is part of the University of Wales. Population (1991): 1989.

● **lamprey** ► A fishlike vertebrate belonging to a family (*Petromyzonidae*; about 22 species) of ▷cyclostomes. 15–100 cm long, lampreys have an eel-like body with one or two dorsal fins and seven pairs of gill slits. They occur in fresh or salt water and many are parasitic on fish, attaching themselves with a circular sucking mouth and feeding on the blood and flesh. Sexually mature adults move into fresh water to breed and then die after the eggs are laid. The burrowing larvae (ammocoetes) feed on microorganisms and take three to seven years to grow before their metamorphosis into adults and return to the sea. □fish.

● **lamp shell** ▷*See* Brachiopoda.

● **Lanark** ► 55 41N 3 48W A town in S central Scotland, in South Lanarkshire overlooking the middle Clyde Valley. Nearby New Lanark, founded as a cotton-spinning centre in 1784 by David Dale and Richard Arkwright, is well known for the social experiments carried out there by Robert Owen. Population (1991): 8877.

● **Lanarkshire** ► A historic county of S central Scotland, mainly occupied by the valley of the River Clyde. Although sometimes considered part of the geographical county, ▷Glasgow has long been administered separately. Under local government reorganization in 1975 Lanarkshire became part of Strathclyde Region. When this was abolished in 1996, administration passed to three ▷unitary authorities: Glasgow, industrial ▷North Lanarkshire, and rural ▷South Lanarkshire.

● **Lancashire** ► A county of NW England, bordering on the Irish Sea. It consists of lowlands in the W rising to the high plateaus of the Pennines in the E, with the chief river, the Ribble, flowing SW to the Irish Sea. The lowlands are important agriculturally, mainly for dairy farming and market gardening. Industry is based chiefly on textiles and engineering. Tourism is important in the coastal towns of Blackpool and Morecambe.
  History: it became a county palatine in 1351. With industrialization, exploitation of the coalfields accelerated and by the 19th century Lancashire had become the greatest cotton-manufacturing centre in the world. Under local government reorganization in 1974 it lost the S (including Liverpool and Manchester) to Merseyside and Greater Manchester, and the Furness Peninsula to Cumbria. Central Lancs New Town (1970) comprising Preston, Fulwood, Bamber Bridge, Leyland, and Chorley became the new county focus. Blackburn with Darwen and Blackpool became independent ▷unitary authorities in 1998. Area (excluding unitary authorities): 2889 sq km (1115 sq mi). Population (1996 est, excluding unitary authorities): 1 134 000. Administrative centre: Preston.

● **Lancaster** ► 54 03N 2 48W A town in NW England on the River Lune, formerly the administrative centre of Lancashire. The castle, partly 13th-century and enlarged by Elizabeth I, stands on the site of a Roman garrison. Port trade, once of considerable importance, has declined. Lancaster manufactures textiles, floor coverings, and plastic goods. A university was founded here in 1964. Population (1991): 44 497.

● **Lancaster** ► 40 08N 76 18W A city in the USA, in SE Pennsylvania. Settled by German Mennonites in the early 18th century, it developed as an armaments centre during the American Revolution. Today it is an agricultural and industrial centre, producing tobacco, grain, livestock, and electrical products. Population (1996 est): 115 675.

● **Lancaster** ► A ruling dynasty of England descended from Edmund, the second son of Henry III, who was created Earl of Lancaster in 1267. In 1361 the title passed by marriage to the third son of Edward III, ▷John of Gaunt. His son seized the throne from Richard II and ruled (1399–1413) as Henry IV. He was succeeded by Henry V, whose son Henry VI led the Lancastrians against the Yorkists (*see* York) in the Wars of the □Roses (1455–85), in which their emblem was a red rose. Following Henry VI's death (1471) the royal dynasty came to an end.

● **Lancaster, Burt** ► (Stephen Burton L.; 1913–94) US actor and film producer. A former circus acrobat, Lancaster made his screen debut in 1946 and became well known for athletic swashbuckling roles in such films as *The Flame and the Arrow* (1950) and *The Crimson Pirate* (1952). He later gave strong performances in such varied films as *From Here to Eternity* (1953), *The Sweet Smell of Success* (1957), *Elmer Gantry* (1960), *The Birdman of Alcatraz* (1962), *The Leopard* (1963), *The Swimmer* (1967), and *Atlantic City* (1981).

● **Lancaster, Duchy of** ► A territory with its own courts and administration created in 1267 by Henry III for his son Edmund (1245–96). After the last Duke of Lancaster became Henry IV in 1399 the Duchy was attached to the Crown, retaining its own jurisdiction. The Crown continues to hold the Duchy's revenues and the chancellor of the Duchy of Lancaster is usually a member of the cabinet.

● **Lancaster, Sir Osbert** ► (1908–86) British cartoonist. He graduated from Oxford before studying painting and stage design at the Slade School. Although also a writer on architecture, he is best known for his *Daily Express* cartoons (from 1939), satirizing the upper classes.

● **lancelet** ► A small slender fishlike animal, formerly called amphioxus, belonging to the phylum *Cephalochordata* (23 species). Up to 5 cm long, they occur in shallow coastal waters, living mostly in burrows with the front end protruding; food particles are filtered from the water, which enters the mouth and leaves through the gill slits. There is a supportive rodlike ▷notochord and a nerve cord running the length of the body. Genera: *Branchiostoma*; *Epigonichthys*.

● **Lancelot** ► In ▷Arthurian legend, a knight of the Round Table, the son of King Ban and Queen Helaine of Benoic. While a child he was kidnapped by the Lady of the Lake, who educated him and later sent him to serve King Arthur. He was a celebrated warrior but failed in the quest of the ▷Holy Grail because of his adulterous love for ▷Guinevere.

● **lancers** ► Originally foot soldiers armed with a lance, they subsequently became cavalrymen belonging to one of the regiments called lancers, both on the continent and in the UK. The name is retained in some armoured regiments.

● **lancewood** ► Dense strong wood obtained from various trees of the family *Annonaceae*, especially *Oxandra lanceolata*, native to the West Indies and South America. It is used in whip handles, fishing rods, etc., which require an elastic wood. Australian lancewood comes from several trees, including *Acacia doratoxylon* (family *Leguminosae*).

● **Lanchester, Frederick William** ► (1868–1946) British engineer, who built the first British car in 1896. He formed the Lanchester Engine Company producing high-quality vehicles. He later became interested in aeronautics.

● **Lanchow** ► (*or* Lan-chou) ▷*See* Lanzhou.

● **Land** ▷*See* Germany, Federal Republic of.

● **Land, Edwin Herbert** ► (1909–91) US inventor of ▷Polaroid, who set up the Polaroid Corporation in 1937 for its manufacture. He also invented the Polaroid Land Camera in 1947, in which pictures are printed inside the camera.

● **Land Acts, Irish** ► A series of laws passed between 1870 and 1903 to deal with Irish agrarian problems. The three Fs (freedom to sell, fixity of tenure, and fair rents) were obtained in Gladstone's acts of 1870 and 1881. Later acts (especially of 1885 and 1903) provided for the tenant to buy his holding; Ireland thus became a land of owner occupiers.

● **landau** ► A four-wheeled coach drawn by two or four horses. Landaus, first made in Landau (Germany) in the late 18th century, have fully collapsible tops and are still used in European royal processions.

● **Landau, Lev Davidovich** ► (1908–68) Soviet physicist, who pioneered the mathematical theory of magnetic domains (*see* ferromagnetism). Working with Peter ▷Kapitza on ▷superfluid helium he was able to explain its properties in terms of quantum theory. For this work on superfluidity he was awarded the Nobel Prize in 1962.

● **land crab** ► A large square-bodied ▷crab of the tropical family *Gecarcinidae*, specialized for a terrestrial existence. It feeds on plant and animal materials. *Cardisoma guanhumi*, 11 cm across the back, is found in the West Indies and S North America. It lives in fields, swamps, and mangroves, sometimes several miles inland. Tribe: *Brachyura*.

● **Landes** ► An area of heath and marshland in SW France, bordering on the Bay of Biscay and consisting chiefly of the Landes department. It is bordered by a strip of sand dunes, many over 45 m (148 ft) high, that have been fixed by the planting of pine forests. Area: 14 000 sq km (5400 sq mi).

● **landfill gas** ▷*See* biomass energy; waste disposal.

● **landing craft** ► Amphibious craft used for military assaults on beaches. Developed mainly by the US Marine Corps in World War II, they were first used on a large scale in the Anglo-American invasion of Sicily (June, 1943), and later were important in the ▷D-Day invasion of Normandy (1944) and in the Pacific campaign from Guadalcanal onwards.

● **Land League** ► An Irish agrarian organization established by Michael ▷Davitt in 1879 to press for land reforms. Its most famous tactic was one of organized ostracism (boycotting; *see* Boycott, Charles

Cunningham). After Gladstone's 1881 ▷Land Act, the League's aims were achieved and it disbanded.

● **landlord and tenant** ▶ The relationship arising from a grant (lease) of exclusive possession of land by a landlord to a tenant for a fixed period and, usually, for a regular payment of rent. The relationship is defined by a ▷contract, which is contained in the lease or, for short terms, in a tenancy agreement. Some measures of security of tenure and the fixing of a rent fair to both tenant and landlord have been the subject of a number of Acts of Parliament. The present legislation is embodied in the Rent Act (1977) and the Housing Acts (1988 and 1996). **Regulated tenancies** give full protection under the Rent Act at a rent agreed between landlord and tenant or at a fair rent as assessed by the local rent officer, with a right of appeal to a rent assessment committee. Since the Housing Act (1988; in force since Jan 1989) no new regulated tenancies can be created but existing ones remain protected. Instead, **assured tenancies** came into force, which are similar to regulated tenancies except that if landlord and tenant do not agree a rent, an open-market rent is fixed by the rent assessment committee. The Rent Act (1974) gave tenants of furnished and unfurnished accommodation equal security of tenure (unless the landlord occupied part of the premises). The Housing Act (1988) also created **assured shorthold tenancies** for a fixed term (not less than six months). Unlike assured tenancies, the landlord is entitled to recover possession without having to show grounds for repossession. Under the Housing Act (1996; in force since 28 February, 1997) all new residential tenancies are assured shorthold tenancies unless the landlord gives the tenant a notice specifically stating that the tenancy is an assured tenancy (with security of tenure).

Under the Leasehold Reform Act (1993) the law was changed to allow holders of long leases on flats in certain circumstances to buy their freeholds or extend their leases.

● **landmine** ▷*See* mine.

● **Landor, Walter Savage** ▶ (1775–1864) British poet and prose writer. He lived for many years on the Continent, chiefly in Florence. He wrote poems and dramas based on classical models, and is best known for his *Imaginary Conversations of Literary Men and Statesmen* (1824–28).

● **Landowska, Wanda** ▶ (1877–1959) Polish-born harpsichordist and authority on its repertoire. She established a school for advanced performers in Paris and later lived in the USA.

● **Landrace** ▶ A breed of pig originating in Denmark, where it has been developed to produce high-quality lean bacon. It has a relatively small head and neck with light shoulders and long flanks. It can also produce good-quality pork.

landing craft ▶ US landing craft prepare to set out from a British port on D-Day (6 June, 1944), carrying troops to the Normandy beaches as part of the largest amphibious invasion in history.

● **Land Registry, HM** ▶ An official registry of titles to land, established in 1862 and subject to the Land Registration Acts (1925 to 1988). The purpose of establishing a registry of land is to simplify conveyancing when the property is sold: by searching in the Registry, outstanding leases, mortgages, etc., may be discovered. In England and Wales land registration on sale is now compulsory, although existing owners are not obliged to register their title.

● **landscape gardening** ▶ The designing and planting of a pleasing garden or park. Landscape gardening was carried out in the ancient Middle East, Greece, and Rome. In Europe, rigidly organized geometric spaces predominated as in the work of André ▷Le Nôtre) until the mid-18th century, when William ▷Kent and Capability ▷Brown demonstrated the possibilities of large-scale remoulding of the landscape to achieve a naturalistic impression. Apparently random planting of trees, strategic siting of focal points, and sinuous expanses of water, as at ▷Blenheim Palace, are key components. With the 20th-century decline of the ▷country house, landscape gardening principles have come to be applied on a smaller scale, e.g. by Gertrude ▷Jekyll.

● **Landseer, Sir Edwin Henry** ▶ (1802–73) British artist, the son of an engraver. He first exhibited at the Royal Academy at the age of 12, becoming a member in 1831. His success, particularly with Queen Victoria, relied on his sentimental animal and Highland subjects, notably *Dignity and Impudence*. He also sculpted the four bronze lions in Trafalgar Square.

● **Land's End** ▶ (Cornish name: Pednanlaaz) 50 03N 5 44W The extreme western point of England. A granite headland in Cornwall, it lies at a distance of 970 km (603 mi) from John o'Groats at the N tip of Scotland. The rugged beauty of Land's End has been compromised by the theme park that now attracts tourists to the promontory. ▷*See also* Lizard Point.

● **Landshut** ▶ 48 31N 12 10E A town in SE Germany, in Bavaria on the River Isar. It is an industrial centre and the site of a 13th-century castle. The Bavarian university was sited here (1800–26). Population (1991): 56 670.

● **Landskrona** ▶ 55 53N 12 50E A seaport in SW Sweden, on the Sound. A centre for shipping and trade, it has flour milling, sugar refining, and chemical industries. Population (1989 est): 35 847.

● **landslide** ▶ (*or* landslip) The sudden downward movement of a mass of rock or earth. This may be triggered by an earthquake, an increase in the weight borne by a steep slope owing to heavy rain, etc., or the undercutting of a slope by water, as in a riverbank or sea cliff.

● **Landsteiner, Karl** ▶ (1868–1943) Austrian immunologist, who (in 1900) discovered human ▷blood groups and devised the ABO system of classification. Landsteiner's discovery enabled safe blood transfusions: by matching the blood groups of donor and recipient the immunological rejection of "foreign" blood by the recipient was avoided. He also discovered, in 1940, the ▷rhesus (Rh) factor in blood and made valuable contributions to poliomyelitis research. He was awarded the Nobel Prize (1930).

● **Lane, Sir Allen** ▶ (1902–70) British publisher, who founded Penguin Books Ltd in 1935 to produce the first paperbacks in Britain. After his death, the company was bought by Longman (publishers), which in turn was bought by the entertainment and media group Pearson plc.

● **Lanfranc** ▶ (c. 1010–89) Italian churchman and theologian; Archbishop of Canterbury (1070–89). In about 1043 he founded and became prior of a Benedictine abbey at Bec in Normandy; under the direction of his pupil St Anselm, the abbey became one of the most famous medieval schools. As archbishop under William the Conqueror from 1070, he launched a programme of Church reform, which included appointing Normans as abbots of English monasteries and enforcing celibacy among the clergy. His famous tract, *De Corpore et sanguine Domini* (1079), is a defence of the doctrine of transubstantiation against the teachings of Berengar of Tours (c. 998–1088).

● **Lang, Andrew** ▶ (1844–1912) Scottish writer and literary critic. One of the most versatile writers of his day, Lang published historical and anthropological works, in addition to journalistic articles. He also wrote poetry and compiled several books of fairytales. As a classical scholar he is known for his translations of Homer.

● **Lang, Fritz** ▶ (1890–1976) German film director, a leading exponent of ▷expressionism in the cinema. The best known of his early films are *Dr Mabuse the Gambler* (1922), *Metropolis* (1926), a nightmare vision of the future, and *M* (1931), a study of a psychopathic murderer. He left Germany in 1933 for Hollywood, where he made commercially successful thrillers and westerns.

● **Lange, David Russell** ▶ (1942–) New Zealand politician; Labour prime minister (1984–89). Trained as a lawyer, he became an MP in 1977 and two years later was appointed deputy leader of the opposition. Becoming leader in 1983, he led his party to victory in the 1984 elections. Controversy surrounded his refusal to allow nuclear armed ships to dock in New Zealand.

● **Langland, William** ▶ (c. 1330–c. 1400) English poet and probably a minor cleric. He is generally credited with the authorship of the allegorical Middle English alliterative poem, *The Vision of Piers Plowman*. Its theme of spiritual pilgrimage is combined with a depiction of 14th-century English society and criticisms of ecclesiastical abuse.

● **Langley, Samuel Pierpont** ▶ (1834–1906) US astronomer, whose work on aerodynamics contributed to the design of early aircraft. Langley himself failed to build a working aircraft, in spite of a $50,000 grant from the US Government.

● **Langmuir, Irving** ▶ (1881–1957) US chemist, whose early work on gases led to the invention of the Langmuir condensation pump. He also developed gas-filled filament lamps. He was awarded the 1932 Nobel Prize for his work on monomolecular layers and surface chemistry.

● **Langton, Stephen** ▶ (c. 1150–1228) English theologian; Archbishop of Canterbury (1207–28). A student and later the chancellor at the University of Paris, he was appointed Archbishop of Canterbury by Pope Innocent III. However, he was unable to occupy the see until 1213 because King John opposed his election. He sided with the barons against John and supported the Magna Carta.

● **Langtry, Lillie** ▶ (Emilie Charlotte le Breton; 1853–1929) British actress, known as the Jersey Lily. After marrying a wealthy shipping owner, she became well known in London society and was an intimate friend of the Prince of Wales, later Edward VII. Separating from her husband when he became bankrupt, Lillie Langtry went on the stage in order to support herself and her daughter, making her debut in 1881. She was the first woman in Britain to prove that high social position was not incompatible with a successful acting career, although her fame was based more on her beauty and high spirits than her acting talents.

● **language** ▶ The chief means by which human beings communicate with one another. Among the features that distinguish human language from other animals' communication systems are that it is learned, not inborn; the connection between a word or expression and that to which it refers is in principle arbitrary; it can be used to talk about itself, about events, objects, etc., not immediately present, or about any novel or unforeseen situation; and it is organized in recognizable patterns on two levels: ▷grammar and phonology. The origins of language are unknown, but since it is unique to man and all speech organs have some other more basic physiological function it is probably of quite recent origin in evolutionary terms. It is estimated that there are some 4000 languages spoken in the world today; countless thousands of others have perished, generally without trace. ▷*See also* accent; dialect; linguistics.

● **languages, classification of** ▶ The division of languages into groups. There are three methods of classification. The first method is that of geographical or political division, in which languages are grouped together according to the continent or country in which they occur. Examples of the former include ▷Indian languages and European languages. The latter is represented by the similar but politically distinct languages ▷Swedish, ▷Danish, and ▷Norwegian. Such divisions do not always follow the genetic relationships that exist between languages. This relationship forms the basis for the second method of classification, which maps the historical development from one form of the language to another, as in the relation between Old English and modern ▷English. Further back both these and other languages can be traced to their common ▷Indo-European ancestor. However, some languages, such as ▷Basque, have no discoverable ancestry or relations. The third possible method of classification is on typological evidence, which depends on the grammatical structure of the language. The original three classes were devised by W. von ▷Humboldt: analytic (or isolating), agglutinative, and inflecting languages. **Analytic languages** (e.g. English, Chinese) show little variation in the forms of words but rely on strict word order to express grammatical relations (compare "The speaker thanked the chairman" with "The chairman thanked the speaker"; the words are the same in both sentences and the subject-object relations are understood purely by the order). In **agglutinative languages** (e.g. Turkish) words have the capacity to be split up into individual components with separate grammatical roles (in Turkish *sev/mek* means "to love"; *sev/dir/il/mek* means "to be made to love"; *sev/ish/mek/* means "to love one another"; and *sev/ish/dir/il/mek* means "to be made to love one another"). In **inflecting languages** (e.g. Latin, Sanskrit) words are characteristically built up of a root plus a component (morpheme) that represents several different grammatical categories (the Latin word *lavo* (I wash) consists of the root *lav-* and a suffix *-o*, the suffix here indicating the distinct grammatical elements of first person, singular number, present tense, indicative mood, and active voice. No language is entirely in one or other of these categories and the system itself has been modified and expanded by 20th-century linguists; nevertheless, it is possible, on the grounds of predominant characteristics, to make general classifications.

● **Languedoc** ▶ A former province in S France, on the Gulf of Lions. Its name derived from *langue d'oc*, the language of its inhabitants (*see* Provençal). In the 10th–12th centuries it flourished as an important cultural centre. It is now incorporated chiefly into the planning region of **Languedoc-Roussillon** and is a very important wine-producing area. Area: 27 447 sq km (10 595 sq mi). Population (1995 est): 2 221 300.

● **langur** ▶ A leaf-eating ▷Old World monkey of tropical Asia. Langurs have specially adapted stomachs to digest their food. The largest is the hanuman, or entellus langur (*Presbytis entellus*), 75 cm long with a 95-cm tail. The douc langur (*Pygathrix nemaeus*) of Vietnam is mainly grey with white forearms and is now an endangered species. Chief genera: *Presbytis* (14 species), *Rhinopithecus* (4 species).

● **Lanier, Sidney** ▶ (1842–81) US poet. As a Confederate soldier in the Civil War he was imprisoned and contracted tuberculosis, from which he eventually died. His poetry, notably "Corn" (1875), "The Symphony" (1875), and "The Marches of Glyn," was greatly influenced by his musical skills.

● **Lankester, Sir Edwin Ray** ▶ (1847–1929) British zoologist, whose wide-ranging contributions to biology included work on protozoan parasites of vertebrate animals and the embryology of invertebrates. He was director of the British Museum of Natural History (1898–1907) and helped found the Marine Biological Association.

● **lanner falcon** ▶ A large ▷falcon, *Falco biarmicus*, occurring in SE Europe and Africa. Up to 45 cm long, it has a grey-brown back, white underparts flecked with black on the breast, a tawny head, and a black moustache. Lanner falcons feed chiefly on birds and are used in falconry.

● **lanolin** ▶ A purified ▷wax extracted from wool. It is a mixture of cholesterol and other sterols, aliphatic alcohols, and esters. Because it is easily absorbed by the skin, lanolin is used as a base for creams, soaps, and other skin preparations.

● **Lansbury, George** ▶ (1859–1940) British Labour politician. He became an MP in 1910 but resigned in 1912 to fight a by-election on a women's suffrage ticket. Mayor of Poplar (1919–20), he was imprisoned (1921) together with most of the borough council for refusing to raise the rates. Again an MP from 1922 to 1940 he led the Labour Party in opposition (1931–35), resigning because, as a pacifist, he opposed the party's militant response to Mussolini's seizure of Ethiopia.

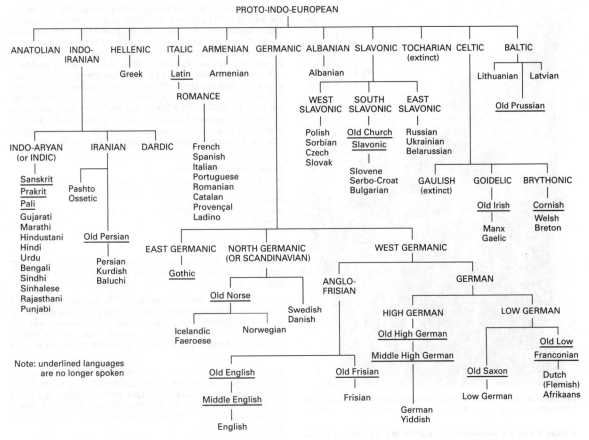

classification of languages ▶ A simplified family tree shows the relationships of the Indo-European languages, spoken by about half the world's population.

● **Lansdowne, Henry Charles Keith Petty-Fitzmaurice, 5th Marquess of** ▶ (1845–1927) British politician and colonial administrator. After holding office under Gladstone he was governor general of Canada (1883–88) and then viceroy of India (1888–94). As secretary for war (1895–1900) he was criticized for early British failures in the second Boer War but was nevertheless appointed foreign secretary in 1900. In 1917, during World War I, he wrote the notorious **Lansdowne Letter** to the *Daily Telegraph*, in which he advocated a negotiated peace with Germany.

● **Lansing** ▶ 42 44N 85 34W A city in the USA, the capital of Michigan on the Grand River. The site of the Michigan State University (1855), it contains part of the Detroit motor-vehicle industry, manufacturing car components. Population (1996 est): 125 736.

● **lantern fish** ▶ A deepsea ▷bony fish belonging to the family *Myctophidae* (about 150 species). 2.5–15 cm long, lantern fish have large mouths and eyes and numerous light-producing organs on the head, underside, and base of the tail. At night, many species migrate towards the surface. Order: *Myctophiformes*.

● **lanthanides** ▶ (or rare-earth metals) A group of 15 ▷transition elements, atomic numbers 57–71, which all have remarkably similar physical and chemical properties as a result of their electronic structures. They occur together in monazite and other minerals. They are used as catalysts in the petroleum industry, in iron alloys and permanent magnets, and in glass polishes. The **rare earths** are the oxides of these metals.

● **lanthanum** ▶ (La) The first of the series of rare-earth metals (*see* lanthanides), all of which have similar chemical properties. It is used in ▷misch metal to make lighter flints. Its compounds include an oxide (La_2O_3) and a chloride ($LaCl_3$). At no 57; at wt 138.9055; mp 918°C; bp 3464°C.

● **Lanzarote** ▷*See* Canary Islands.

● **Lanzhou** ▶ (Lan-chou *or* Lanchow) 36 01N 103 45E A city in N China, the capital of Gansu province at the confluence of the Yellow and Wei Rivers. It is an ancient trade and communications centre and the site of a university. Industries include oil refining, plutonium processing, and the manufacture of chemicals and machinery. Population (1991 est): 1 510 000.

● **Laocoon** ▶ In Greek legend, a Trojan priest of Apollo who warned against accepting the Greek gift of the ▷Trojan Horse. He and his two sons were killed by sea serpents, sent in some versions by Athena but in others by Apollo, and the Trojans then opened their gates to the wooden horse. □ p. 712.

● **Laodicea** ▶ 37 46N 29 02E An ancient city of Asia Minor, near present-day Denizli (SW Turkey), founded by ▷Antiochus II about 250 BC. On an important trade route Laodicea soon prospered; early Christians condemned its worldliness. Under Diocletian it became Phrygia's metropolis (mother city). Its Roman remains include theatres and an aqueduct.

● **Laois** ▶ (Laoighis *or* Leix; former name: Queen's County) A county in the E central Republic of Ireland, in Leinster. Predominantly low lying with bogs and drained chiefly by the Rivers Barrow and Nore, it rises to mountains in the NW. Agriculture is the main occupation with dairy farming and cattle rearing. Area: 1719 sq km (664 sq mi). Population (1996): 52 000. County town: Portlaoise.

● **Laon** ▶ 49 34N 3 37E A town in N France, the capital of the Aisne department. A former leading town of the kingdom of the Franks, notable buildings include the cathedral (begun in the 12th century) and the bishop's palace. It has metallurgical and sugar-refining industries. Population (latest est): 29 074.

Laocoon ► A plaster cast of the original marble statue by Hagesandros, Athenodoros, and Polydoros of Rhodes (c. 25 BC; Vatican Museum, Rome).

● **Laos, People's Democratic Republic of** ► A landlocked country in SE Asia, in the Indochina peninsula between Vietnam and Thailand. Except for the valley of the River Mekong along its western border, the country is mountainous and forested. Over half the population are Lao (descendants of the Thai) and there are minorities of Vietnamese, Chinese, and others.

Economy: predominantly agricultural. The difficult terrain, combined with recurrent political upheavals from the 1940s until the mid-1970s, has hindered development and Laos remains one of the poorest nations in the world. There has been some economic growth since 1986, when the government began a programme of liberalizing the economy and encouraging private enterprise. The main crops are rice, corn, coffee, cotton, tea, and tobacco; opium cultivation is illegal but widespread. The valuable mineral resources (tin, iron ore, gold, and copper) have yet to be fully exploited. There is still little industry. Hydroelectricity is an important source of power, especially since the opening of the Nan Ngum Dam in 1971. The supply of hydroelectricity to Thailand now constitutes the country's main export; other exports include tin and teak wood. Communications are difficult; there are no railways and river traffic is hindered by rapids and waterfalls. The situation has been improved by the opening (1994) of a major road bridge across the Mekong on the border with Thailand, thus creating a continuous road link from Singapore to China.

History: the origins of the area as a nation date from the rule of Fa Ngum, who founded a Buddhist kingdom in the mid-14th century. European contacts were initiated in the 17th century and in 1893 Laos became a French protectorate. It was occupied by the Japanese from 1941 to 1945, when the Lao Issara (Free Lao) proclaimed an independent government. This movement collapsed when the French returned in 1946 and a constitutional monarchy was formed in 1947. In 1949 Laos became independent within the French Union. In 1953 civil war, which was to last for 20 years, broke out between the government (supported by the USA and by Thai mercenaries) and the

communist-led Pathet Lao movement (supported by the North Vietnamese). In 1974 a provisional coalition government was formed but following the collapse of the South Vietnamese the Pathet Lao gained power (December, 1975) and the People's Democratic Republic of Laos was formed with Prince Souphanouvong (1902–95) as president; he resigned because of illness in 1986. After the acting presidency (1986–91) of Phoumi Vongvichit, the long-serving prime minister Kaysone Phomvihan (1920–92) was elected president. In 1991 a new constitution was published, reaffirming the Lao People's Democratic Party (the former Pathet Lao) as the sole legal party. The prime minister, General Khamtay Siphandon, was re-elected in 1997. That same year Laos was admitted to the Association of South-East Asian States (ASEAN). Recent years have seen border clashes with Thailand.

People's Democratic Republic of Laos

Head of state	President Nouhak Phounsavanh
Official language	Laotian; French is widely spoken
Official currency	kip of 100 at
Area	236 800 sq km (91 429 sq mi)
Population (1997 est)	5 117 000
Capital	Vientiane

● **Laotian** ► A language of SE Asia belonging to the Thai language family. It is a tonal and monosyllabic language and written in an alphabet derived from ▷Khmer.

● **Lao Zi** ► (or Lao Tzu; ?6th century BC) The founder of ▷Taoism. A shadowy, possibly legendary, figure, he was eventually deified. His purpose, propounded in books compiled about 300 years after his likely date of death, was to reach harmony with the *Tao* (way) by dwelling on the beauty of nature, being self-sufficient, and desiring nothing.

● **La Paz** ► 16 30S 68 00W The administrative capital of Bolivia, situated in the W of the country. At an altitude of 3577 m (11 735 ft), it is the world's highest capital. Founded by the Spanish in 1548, it became the seat of government in 1898. The University of San Andrés was founded here in 1830. Population (1993 est): 784 976. ▷*See also* Sucre.

● **lapis lazuli** ► A blue semiprecious stone composed mainly of a sulphur-rich variety of the mineral haüyne (a feldspathoid) called lazurite. It is formed by the metamorphosis of limestone. It often contains specks or threads of yellow iron pyrites. Lapis lazuli has been mined in Afghanistan for over 6000 years. The pigment ultramarine was formerly made by grinding up lapis lazuli.

● **Laplace, Pierre Simon, Marquis de** ► (1749–1827) French mathematician and astronomer. Laplace worked with ▷Lagrange on the effects, known as perturbations, of the small gravitational forces that planets exert on each other. (Newton's work considered only the gravitational force of the sun on the planets.) They deduced that the perturbations only cause small oscillations in the planets' motions and not any permanent movement, thus proving the stability of the solar system. Laplace published their results in a five-volume work, *Mécanique céleste* (1799–1825). At the end of the work, Laplace speculated that the solar system was formed from a condensing rotating cloud of gas.

● **Lapland** ► (or Lappland) A vast region in N Europe, inhabited by the ▷Lapps and extending across northern parts of Norway, Sweden, Finland, and into the extreme NW of Russia. Lying mainly within the Arctic Circle, it consists of tundra in the N, mountains in the W, and forests in the S; there are many lakes and rivers. For centuries the Lapps were reduced to virtual slavery by their more powerful neighbours. Subsistence farming, fishing, trapping, and hunting are the main occupations and reindeer are a particularly important source of income. There are rich deposits of iron ore in Swedish Lapland. High unemployment, however, has led to considerable emigration S although there are plans to develop Lapland's fishing potential and to establish fur farms (especially the silver fox). Recent industrial successes include the new steel works at Tornio on the border between Finland and Sweden. A Lapp parliament was established in 1993.

● **La Plata** ► (name from 1952 until 1955: Eva Perón) 34 52S 57 55W

A city in E Argentina, near the Río de la Plata. Its industries include meat packing and oil refining and it has a university (1884). Population (1991): 542 567.

● **Lapps** ▶ (*or* Sami) A people of N Scandinavia and the Kola peninsula of Russia. They speak a ▷Finno-Ugric language, which differs from the related Finnish and ▷Estonian mainly in its sound system. There are three major Lapp dialects, which are very different from one another. The mountain Lapps are nomadic reindeer herders who follow their herds on their seasonal migrations using them as pack animals or to pull sledges. Other Lapps are seminomadic hunters and fishers.

● **Laptev Sea** ▶ A section of the Arctic Ocean off the coast of Russia, between the Taimyr Peninsula and the New Siberian Islands. Half of its supply of fresh water comes from the River Lena and it is frozen for most of the year.

● **laptop computer** ▶ A single-unit computer that includes a keyboard, screen, and both hard- and floppy-disk drives, but is still small enough to rest on the operator's lap. The screen usually occupies the inside of the lid and makes use of a liquid-crystal display, rather than a bulky cathode-ray tube.

● **lapwing** ▶ A Eurasian ▷plover, *Vanellus vanellus*, also called peewit and green plover. It occurs commonly on farmland, where it feeds on harmful insects, such as wireworms and leatherjackets. 28 cm long, it has a greenish-black and white plumage, a long crest, short rounded wings, a short tail, and pink legs. Lapwings perform acrobatic courtship displays.

● **Lara, Brian** ▶ (1969–   ) Trinidadian cricketer, who plays for the West Indies (1991–   ). In 1994 he broke the record for the highest Test innings with 375 runs and also the highest score in first class cricket (playing for Warwickshire against Durham) with 501 runs. In 1998 he returned to Warwickshire as team captain and also became captain of the West Indies.

● **Laramie** ▶ 41 20N 105 38W A city in the USA, in SE Wyoming on the Laramie River. Founded (1868) with the arrival of the Union Pacific Railroad, it is a commercial centre for a timber, mining, and livestock region. The University of Wyoming was established here (1886). Population (1990): 26 687.

● **larceny** ▷*See* theft.

● **larch** ▶ A deciduous conifer of the genus *Larix* (10 species), native to the cooler regions of the N hemisphere. Larches are graceful trees, with needles growing in bunches on short spurs and producing small woody cones. The common European larch (*L. decidua*), from the mountains of central Europe, is widely cultivated both for timber and ornament. It reaches a height of 40 m and its cones, 2–4 cm long, ripen from pinkish-red to brown. The Japanese larch (*L. kaempferi*) is commonly grown on plantations. Family: *Pinaceae*. □tree.

● **Lardner, Ring** ▶ (1885–1933) US short-story writer. He worked as a sports reporter and his early stories concern the life of a baseball player. His best-known stories are collected in *How to Write Short Stories* (1924) and *The Love Nest and Other Stories* (1926).

● **Laredo** ▶ 27 32N 99 22W A city in the USA, in Texas on the Rio Grande. Situated opposite Nuevo Laredo (Mexico), it was founded by the Spanish in 1755 and is a centre for US and Mexican trade. It has a thriving tourist industry and is the commercial centre for an oil-producing and agricultural region. Population (1996 est): 164 899.

● **Lares and Penates** ▶ Roman household gods. The Lares were originally gods of cultivated land who were worshipped at crossroads and boundaries. The Penates were gods of the storeroom. Together with the ▷Manes, they were later worshipped as guardians of the family, household, and state.

● **Large White** ▶ A breed of pig originating in Yorkshire, England, also called the Yorkshire. Relatively large-framed, Large Whites are white-skinned with a sparse coat of fine hair. They are extensively used for bacon production. A derivative breed, the Middle White, was once popular as a porker.

● **Lárisa** ▶ (*or* Larissa) 39 38N 22 25E A town in E Greece, in Thessaly.

It is a commercial centre; products include silk cloth and tobacco. Population (1991): 269 300.

● **lark** ▶ A slender long-winged songbird belonging to a family (*Alaudidae*; 75 species) found mainly in mudflats, marshes, grasslands, and deserts of the Old World and characterized by a beautiful song. Larks commonly have a brown or buff streaked plumage that often matches the local soil colour. They have long slender bills and feed on seeds and insects. The only New World lark is the horned lark, or shorelark (*Eremophila alpestris*) of North America. ▷*See also* skylark.

● **Larkin, Philip** ▶ (1922–85) British poet. His poetry expresses a resigned acceptance of the limitations of daily existence. His volumes include *The Whitsun Weddings* (1964) and *High Windows* (1974). He became librarian at Hull University in 1955, edited *The Oxford Book of Twentieth Century English Verse* (1973), and published two novels and jazz criticism. His *Collected Poems* were published in 1988 and his *Selected Letters* in 1992.

● **larkspur** ▶ An annual herb of the genus *Consolida*, especially *C. ajacis*, *C. ambigua*, or *C. orientalis*, native to Eurasia but commonly grown for ornament. Larkspurs have feathery leaves and tall stems with branching spikes of white or blue spurred flowers. The name "larkspur" is also applied to species of the genus ▷*Delphinium*. Family: *Ranunculaceae*.

● **Larnaca** ▶ (Greek name: Larnax) 34 55N 33 36E A port, industrial town, and tourist resort in S Cyprus, on Larnaca Bay. Larnaca Airport is the island's main international airport: the British military base at Dhekelia is nearby. Historic buildings include a 17th-century Turkish fort (now a museum). Population (1990 est): 62 600.

● **Larne** ▶ **1.** A district in Northern Ireland, in Co Antrim. Area: 337 sq km (130 sq mi). Population (1991): 29 500. **2.** 54 51N 5 49W A port in Northern Ireland, in Co Antrim at the entrance to Lough Larne. Larne is a tourist centre and has the shortest searoute between Ireland and Britain (Stranraer). Population (1991): 17 575.

● **La Rochefoucauld, François, Duc de** ▶ (1613–80) French moralist. He was born into an ancient aristocratic family and played an active part in intrigues against Richelieu and in the ▷Fronde revolts against Mazarin (1648–53). Thereafter he lived in retirement, writing his *Mémoires* (1664) and compiling his celebrated *Maximes* (1665), a collection of cynical epigrammatic observations on human conduct.

● **La Rochelle** ▶ 46 10N 1 10W A port in W France, the capital of the Charente-Maritime department on the Bay of Biscay. A major seaport (14th–16th centuries), it was a Huguenot stronghold until its capture by Richelieu in 1628. Industries include fishing, shipbuilding, fertilizers, and plastics. Population (1990): 73 749.

● **Larousse, Pierre** ▶ (1817–75) French lexicographer, encyclopedist, and reference publisher. In 1852 he founded the publishing firm of Larousse, which specialized in dictionaries, encyclopedias, and other works of reference. His major work was the *Grand Dictionnaire universel du XIXe siècle* (15 vols, 1866–76). His firm continues as a major French publisher, with such reference works as the *Grand Larousse Encyclopédique* (1960–64).

● **Lars Porsena** ▶ (*or* Porsenna; 6th century BC) Etruscan king of Clusium (now Chiusi, near Siena). According to legend, when ▷Tarquin the Proud, the last Etruscan king of Rome, was deposed, Porsena successfully attacked Rome on his behalf. In another version of the story, Porsena made peace with the Romans from admiration of their bravery.

● **Lartet, Édouard Armand Isidore Hippolyte** ▶ (1801–71) French archaeologist, who was one of the founders of palaeontology. Following his first discoveries of fossil remains in SW France, Lartet excavated many cave sites, finding important evidence for dating the various phases of human culture in the region.

● **larva** ▶ The immature form of many animals, which hatches from the egg and often differs in appearance from the adult form. Larvae usually avoid competing for food, etc., with the adults by occupying a different habitat or adopting a different lifestyle. For example, adult barnacles, which are sessile, produce motile larvae, whose role is distribution of the species. Other larvae are responsible for gathering food reserves for the production of a fully formed adult, whose primary function is to breed. Caterpillars and maggots are types of insect larvae with this function. ▷*See also* metamorphosis; tadpole.

● **Larwood, Harold** ▶ (1904–95) British cricketer, known as "Lol", who played for Nottinghamshire and England. A miner at the age of 14, Larwood was a fast bowler who was at the centre of the bodyline controversy during the 1932–33 tour of Australia. His 33 wickets from fast short-pitched balls made him disliked in Australia, although he emigrated there after World War II.

● **larynx** ▶ An organ, situated at the front of the neck above the windpipe (*see* trachea), that contains the **vocal cords**, responsible for the production of vocal sounds. The larynx contains several cartilages (one of which—the thyroid cartilage—forms the Adam's apple) bound together by muscles and ligaments. Within are the two vocal cords: folds of tissue separated by a narrow slit (glottis). The vocal cords modify the flow of exhaled air through the glottis to produce the sounds of speech, song, etc.

● **La Salle, Robert Cavelier, Sieur de** ▶ (1643–87) French explorer in North America. La Salle settled in Montreal in 1666 and in 1669 set out on his first expedition, exploring the Ohio region. From 1679 he concentrated on achieving his ambition to descend the Mississippi River to the Gulf of Mexico. In 1682, after two arduous years, he reached the Gulf and named the area watered by the Mississippi and its tributaries Louisiana, after Louis XIV of France. While attempting to found a permanent colony, he was murdered by mutineers.

● **La Scala** ▶ (*or* Teatro alla Scala) The principal Italian opera house, opened in Milan in 1776. It is noted for its varied repertoire of new and classical works, and attained its highest reputation under Arturo ▷Toscanini, director from 1898 to 1907 and from 1921 to 1931.

● **Las Campanas Observatory** ▷*See* Hale Observatories.

● **Las Casas, Bartolomé de** ▶ (1474–1566) Spanish priest, known as the Apostle of the Indies. As a planter on Hispaniola, Las Casas was horrified by the treatment to which the Indians were subjected. He became a priest (1510) and entered the Dominican order, becoming the defender of the Indians at the Spanish court. His agitation included the publication of *The Brief Relation of the Destruction of the Indies* (1552) and bore fruit with the abolition of Indian slavery in 1542.

● **Las Cases, Emmanuel, Comte de** ▶ (1776–1842) French writer. He held political office under Napoleon and shared his exile on St Helena. His *Mémorial de St Hélène* (1823) recorded Napoleon's final conversations and opinions on politics and religion and greatly influenced his posthumous reputation.

● **Lascaux** ▶ Upper ▯Palaeolithic cave site in the Dordogne (France), discovered in 1940. Lascaux contains rock paintings and engravings of horses, oxen, red deer, and other animals, dating from about 18 000 BC; traps and arrows depicted nearby suggest that the pictures had magical significance in a hunting ritual. Atmospheric changes resulting in deterioration of the paintings caused the cave to be closed again (1963).

● **Lasdun, Sir Denys** ▶ (1914–   ) British architect. One of the foremost contemporary British architects, Lasdun has designed such important buildings as East Anglia University (1962–68) and, in London, the National Theatre (1968–76), the School of African and Oriental Studies (1970–73), and the Royal College of Physicians (RIBA medal, 1992).

● **laser** ▶ (light amplification by stimulated emission of radiation) A device that produces a beam of high-intensity coherent monochromatic radiation (light, infrared, or ultraviolet). Stimulated emission is the emission of a photon when an atomic electron falls from a higher energy level to a lower level as a result of being stimulated by another photon of the same frequency. In the laser large numbers of electrons are "pumped" into a higher energy level, an effect called population inversion, and then stimulated to produce a high-intensity beam. Laser beams have been produced from solids, liquids, and gases. The simplest type is the ruby laser, consisting of a cylinder of ruby, silvered at one end and partially silvered at the other. A flash

lamp is used to excite chromium ions in the ruby to a high energy level. When the ions fall back to their ground state photons (wavelength 694.3 nanometres) are emitted. These photons collide with other excited ions producing radiation of the same wavelength (monochromatic) and the same phase (coherent), which is reflected up and down the ruby crystal and emerges as a narrow beam from the partially silvered end. Lasers are used in civil engineering, in surgery, in laser interferometers to measure very small displacements, in ▷holography, and in ▷compact disc players. ▷*See also* laser printer.

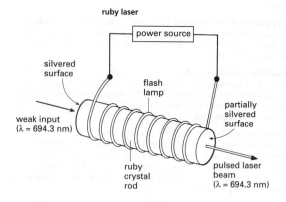

ruby laser

● power source
● silvered surface
● flash lamp
● weak input (λ = 694.3 nm)
● partially silvered surface
● ruby crystal rod
● pulsed laser beam (λ = 694.3 nm)

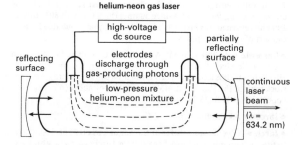

helium-neon gas laser

● high-voltage dc source
● electrodes
● discharge through gas-producing photons
● low-pressure helium-neon mixture
● reflecting surface
● partially reflecting surface
● continuous laser beam (λ = 634.2 nm)

laser ▶ In the solid-state ruby laser, chromium ions are excited by an intense flash of light and then stimulated by weak light of one wavelength to emit a pulse of photons. In the helium-neon gas laser, a continuous laser beam is produced from an electrical discharge through low-pressure gas.

● **laser printer** ▶ A type of printer used with computers, in which the image is formed by scanning a photoconductive drum with a narrow-beam laser. Parts of the surface are charged and, as in a ▷photocopying machine, the image is developed by applying powdered pigment, which adheres to the charged regions. The pigment is transferred to paper and fixed by heat. Laser printers are fast, quiet, and have high resolution, allowing near-typographical print quality in many cases.

● **Lashio** ▶ 22 58N 97 48E A town in NE central Myanmar (Burma). It is a railway terminus and the starting point of the Burma Road to Chongqing, China.

● **Lasker, Emanuel** ▶ (1868–1941) German chess player, who became world champion in 1894 and remained champion until he conceded the title to ▷Capablanca in 1921. A Jew, he left Germany in 1933, finally settling in the USA.

● **Laski, Harold Joseph** ▶ (1893–1950) British political theorist. Laski became professor of political science at the London School of Economics in 1926. A socialist, he was influenced by ▷Burke and John Stuart ▷Mill but became progressively Marxist. His writings include *Authority in the Modern State* (1919) and *Faith, Reason, Civilization* (1944). His niece **Marghanita Laski** (1915–88) was a novelist and critic. Her novels include *Love on the Supertax* (1944), *Little Boy Lost* (1949), and *The Victorian Chaise-longue* (1953).

● **Las Palmas** ▶ 28 08N 15 27W The largest city in the Canary Islands, the capital of Las Palmas province in Gran Canaria. It is a popular resort noted for its palms and is a major fuelling port. Population (latest est): 872 270.

● **La Spezia** ▶ 44 07N 9 48E A port and resort in Italy, in Liguria on the Gulf of Spezia. It is a major naval base, with the largest harbour in Italy. Its industries include shipbuilding and the manufacture of electrical goods. Population (1992): 100 458.

● **Lassa fever** ▶ A severe virus disease occurring in West Africa and first described in 1969 in Lassa, a village in Nigeria. It is a rare and often fatal disease that is transmitted to man by certain species of rat.

● **Lassalle, Ferdinand** ▶ (1825–64) German socialist politician and theorist. Although deeply influenced by Karl Marx, Lassalle developed a distinctive theory of socialism, stressing the formation of workers' cooperatives as a peaceful way to socialism. He headed working-class opposition to Bismarck and helped to found the General German Workers' Association (1863), the precursor to the Social Democratic party. He was killed in a duel.

● **Lassus, Roland de** ▶ (Italian name: Orlando di Lasso; c. 1532–94) Flemish composer. He was born in Mons, where he became a chorister. He obtained appointments in Rome (choirmaster at St John Lateran), Antwerp, and with the Bavarian court in Munich. His madrigals, chansons, and motets exhibit great contrapuntal skill. He was afflicted with depression in later life.

● **Las Vegas** ▶ 36 10N 115 12W A city in the USA, in SE Nevada. Founded in 1855, it grew rapidly after construction of the nearby Hoover Dam. It is famous for its nightclubs and the Strip (a row of luxury hotels and gambling casinos). Population (1996 est): 376 906.

● **László I, Saint** ▶ (1040–95) King of Hungary (1077–95). In 1091, László conquered Croatia, to which he introduced Roman Catholicism, founding the bishopric of Zagreb. He also reformed the criminal code, bringing peace and security to Hungary.

● **Latakia** ▶ (Arabic name: Al Ladhiqiyah) 35 31N 35 47E A town in NW Syria, on the Mediterranean. It dates from Phoenician times and is now Syria's principal port. It is famous for tobacco. Population (1994 est): 306 535.

● **La Tène** ▶ The second phase of the European Iron Age, succeeding ▷Hallstatt from the 5th century BC. Named after the site at La Tène (Switzerland), this recognizably Celtic culture spread throughout Europe, coming into contact with the civilizations of Greece and Rome. Aristocratic chariot burials replaced wagon burials and the geometric patterns of Hallstatt metalwork were superseded by the intricate curvilinear designs of ▷Celtic art. By the 1st century BC Roman expansionism ended La Tène culture. ▷*See also* Celts.

● **latent heat** ▶ The amount of heat absorbed or released by a substance when it undergoes a change of state. For example, a liquid absorbs heat (**latent heat of vaporization**) from its surroundings on evaporation, since energy is needed to overcome the attraction between the molecules as the liquid expands into a gas. Similarly a solid absorbs heat (**latent heat of fusion**) when it melts. The heat absorbed or released per unit mass of substance is called the **specific latent heat**; per amount of substance it is the **molar latent heat**.

● **Lateran Councils** ▶ Five ecumenical councils of the Roman Catholic Church convened in the Lateran Palace, Rome. **1.** (1123) The council that confirmed the settlement of the ▷investiture controversy. **2.** and **3.** (1139, 1179) The councils that were principally concerned with the papal-election procedure. **4.** (1215) The council, attended by most major European ecclesiastical and secular powers, that proclaimed the fifth Crusade (1217–21) and was enormously influential in its formulations of doctrine and Church organization and law. **5.** (1512–17) The council that endeavoured to defend papal power on the eve of the Reformation.

● **Lateran Treaty** ▶ (1929) An agreement between Mussolini and the Vatican. The Vatican City state was created and the papacy abandoned its claims to the former ▷papal states.

● **laterite** ▶ A deposit formed from the weathering of rocks in humid tropical conditions. It consists mostly of iron and aluminium oxides. It occurs either under ground, where it is soft, or as a hardened reddish surface capping where the overlying material has been eroded. Most laterites developed in the Tertiary period.

● **latex** ▶ A liquid, often milky, emulsion found in certain flowering plants. It has a complex composition and its function in the plant is not fully understood. The latex of the ▷rubber tree is used in rubber manufacture, while opium and morphine are obtained from the latex of the ▷opium poppy.

● **lathe** ▶ A machine for turning wood, plastic, or metal into cylindrical or conical parts or for cutting holes or screw-threads in them. The piece to be worked is held in a rotating plate or chuck so that a cutting tool can be held against it. The **turret lathe** has a turret containing a set of cutting tools. Automatic turret lathes perform a sequence of operations on the workpiece without manual interference and are extensively used in mass-production processes.

● **Latimer, Hugh** ▶ (c. 1485–1555) Anglican reformer and martyr. While a university preacher, he was converted to Protestantism (1524) and declared against the legality of Henry VIII's marriage to Catherine of Aragon. He became Bishop of Worcester in 1535, but his opposition to Henry's Six Articles upholding Roman Catholic doctrine resulted in his resignation and imprisonment (1539). A popular preacher under Edward VI, he was arrested at Mary's accession, tried for heresy at Oxford, and burnt at the stake.

● **Latimeria** ▷*See* coelacanth.

● **Latin America** ▶ The countries of Central and South America lying S of the US-Mexican border, including those islands of the West Indies where a Romance language is spoken. Spanish is the most widely used language but Portuguese is spoken in Brazil, the largest country, and French is spoken in Haiti and French Guiana. The population is mainly mestizo (people of mixed Indian and European—usually Spanish—parentage), with minorities of pure Indians, Europeans, and Afro-Caribbeans. The **Latin American Free Trade Association** (LAFTA) was formed in 1961 with the aim of removing restrictions on trade among member countries (Argentina, Brazil, Bolivia, Chile, Colombia, Ecuador, Mexico, Paraguay, Peru, Uruguay, and Venezuela); it was renamed the **Latin American Integration Association** (LAIA) in 1981.

● **Latini, Brunetto** ▶ (c. 1220–c. 1294) Florentine scholar. A friend of ▷Dante, Latini promoted French learning in Italy and wrote an encyclopedia entitled *Li Livres dou trésor*.

● **Latin language** ▶ An Italic Indo-European language, the ancestor of modern Romance languages. First spoken on the plain of Latium near Rome, Latin spread throughout the Mediterranean world as Roman power expanded. An inflected and syntactically complex language, written Latin was gradually moulded to express with equal power Cicero's rhetoric and philosophy, Martial's epigrams, and Virgil's subtle poetry. Educated conversational Latin developed contemporaneously with literary Latin, although, with its freer syntax and vocabulary, it remained less static than the formalized written language. Colloquial Vulgar Latin used prepositions and conjunctions freely to replace inflected forms and had a simpler word order; it became the Latin of the provinces, contributing to the early development of the Romance languages. As the western Roman Empire's official language, Latin was used in W Europe for religious, literary, and scholarly works until the middle ages and beyond, and remained the Roman Catholic Church's official language until the mid-20th century.

● **Latin literature** ▶ The earliest Latin literature dates from after the conclusion of the first ▷Punic War (241 BC). Writers such as ▷Ennius, Naevius, and ▷Plautus (*see* Roman comedy) translated Greek epic, tragedy, and comedy and adapted them to Roman themes. Prose, particularly legal and historical writing, developed along more independent lines until the 1st century BC, when ▷Cicero conclusively established Latin as a mature literary medium. His contemporary ▷Lucretius perfected the Latin hexameter and, together with the lyric poet ▷Catullus, they inaugurated the ▷Golden Age of Latin literature. Their achievements were consolidated in the subsequent Augustan age (43 BC–18 AD), during which the emperor Augustus' adviser ▷Maecenas was patron to ▷Virgil, ▷Horace, and ▷Propertius. Among their important contemporaries were the poets ▷Ovid and ▷Tibullus and the historian ▷Livy. The spirit of the succeeding ▷Silver Age is encapsulated in ▷Seneca's highly rhetorical tragedies. ▷Juvenal and ▷Martial were the major poets and ▷Tacitus, ▷Suetonius, ▷Quintilian, and ▷Petronius Arbiter contributed notable prose works. Imitations, anthologies, and commentaries later predominated over original work. In the 4th and 5th centuries the Latin Church Fathers set Latin on course for becoming the lingua franca of Christian intellectuals. As the literature of learning, Latin literature's characteristic products were encyclopedias and theological texts. Exceptions to this were the medieval Latin lyrics, which have the spontaneity of their vernacular counterparts. ▷*See also* Latin language.

● **Latinus** ▶ A legendary ancestor of the Romans, who gave his name to their language. ▷Aeneas arrived from Troy in his kingdom of Latium, an area S of Rome, and married his daughter Lavinia.

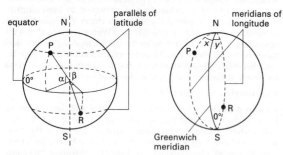

The latitude of P is given by the angle α. In this case it would be α° N. The latitude of R is β° S.

The longitude of P is given by the angle x. In this case it would be x° W. R has a longitude y° E.

latitude and longitude

● **latitude and longitude** ▶ Imaginary lines on the earth's surface, enabling any point to be defined in terms of two angles. **Parallels of latitude** are circles drawn round the earth parallel to the equator; their diameters diminish as they approach the Poles. These parallels are specified by the angle subtended at the centre of the earth by the arc formed between a point on the parallel and the equator. All points on the equator therefore have a latitude of 0°, while the North Pole has a latitude of 90°N and the South Pole of 90°S. Parallels of latitude 1° apart are separated on the earth's surface by about 100 km (63 mi).

Meridians of longitude are half great circles passing through both Poles; they cross parallels of latitude at right angles. In 1884 the meridian through Greenwich, near London, was selected as the **prime meridian** and given the designation 0°. Other meridians are defined by the angle between the plane of the meridian and the plane of the **prime meridian**, specifying whether it is E or W of the prime meridian. At the equator meridians 1° apart are separated by about 112 km (70 mi).

● **latitudinarianism** ▶ An attitude originating with certain 17th-century Anglican clergymen, who deprecated sectarian squabbles over Church government and forms of ritual and considered such matters unimportant in comparison with personal piety and practical morality. Latitudinarian principles characterized the ▷Cambridge Platonists. Between the 1690s and the rise of the ▷Oxford Movement in the 1830s latitudinarianism was predominant in the Church of England.

● **Latium** ▷*See* Lazio.

● **La Tour, Georges de** ▶ (1593–1652) French painter, a native of Lorraine. He excelled in candlelit religious scenes, influenced by such Dutch followers of Caravaggio as ▷Honthorst. His works include *St Joseph the Carpenter* (Louvre) and *The Lamentation over St Sebastian* (Berlin). La Tour's reputation has only been re-established in the 20th century.

● **La Tour, Maurice-Quentin de** ▶ (1704–88) French portrait pastellist, born in Saint-Quentin. He settled in Paris, where he enjoyed an immense and lasting popularity. His sitters included Voltaire, Madame de Pompadour, and Louis XV.

● **Latter-Day Saints, Church of Jesus Christ of** ▷*See* Mormons.

● **Latvia, Republic of** ▶ A republic in NE Europe, on the Baltic Sea. It is a fertile lowland with extensive forests. Latvians, who comprise approximately 52% of the population, are mainly Lutheran Christians.

Economy: Latvia has few natural resources and remains dependent on Russia for its energy needs. Industries include shipbuilding, engineering, chemicals, and textiles. Dairy farming, pig breeding, and fishing are important; Riga, the capital, is a major seaport. The transition from a command to a market economy in the 1990s caused high unemployment: privatization was completed in 1998. Owing to its "crossroads" position and its excellent communications (including seaports), Latvia is fast developing as a major trading and transportation route between Russia and the EU states and between Scandinavia and the rest of Europe. Tourism is also being developed.

History: the Latvians were overrun by Russians and Swedes from the 10th century and conquered by the Livonian Knights (a German order of knighthood) in the 13th century. Thereafter Latvia passed to Poland in the 16th century, to Sweden in the 17th century, and to Russia in the 18th century. Latvia declared its independence in 1918, and this was recognized by Soviet Russia in 1920. However, following the Nazi–Soviet Pact of 1939, Latvia was invaded by the Red Army and incorporated into the Soviet Union as an SSR (1940). It was occupied by Germany in World War II. Mass demonstrations in the late 1980s marked a resurgence of nationalism. In 1990 Latvia voted to leave the Soviet Union, leading to confrontation between Latvian nationalists and Soviet military units. Independence was declared in 1991 and the last Russian troops left in 1994. Since independence the main issue has been the status of the very large (48%) Russian minority. In 1991 a draconian citizenship law was passed, stripping the ethnic Russians of voting and other rights; this was subsequently relaxed in 1994 and 1998 (largely because such a law would hinder any future application to join the EU).

Republic of Latvia

Head of state	President Vaira Vike-Freiburg
Official language	Latvian
Official currency	lats of 100 santimes
Area	63 700 sq km (25 590 sq mi)
Population (1997 est)	2 472 000
Capital	Riga

● **Latvian** ▶ A language belonging to the E division of the ▷Baltic languages group of the Indo-European family, spoken by about two million Latvians. Most live in Latvia, where it is the official language. Also known as Lettish, it is closely related to ▷Lithuanian. It is written in a Latin alphabet and written texts date from the 16th century.

● **Laud, William** ▶ (1573–1645) Anglican churchman, with ▷Strafford the chief adviser to Charles I immediately before the ▷Civil War. Successively Bishop of St David's, Bath and Wells, and London, and then Archbishop of Canterbury (1633–45), he supported Charles I's personal rule and his attempt to enforce liturgical uniformity among both Roman Catholics and Puritans. His pressure on the Scots to accept the Book of Common Prayer led to the ▷Bishops' Wars and paved the way for the Civil War and his own downfall. He was impeached for high treason by the Long Parliament in 1640. Although found not guilty by the Lords, he was executed by a bill of attainder passed by the Commons.

● **Lauda, Niki** ▶ (1949–) Austrian motor-racing driver, who was world champion in 1975, 1977, and 1984. Badly burnt in a crash in 1976, he finally retired in 1985.

● **laudanum** ▷*See* opium.

● **Lauder, Sir Harry** ▶ (Hugh MacLennan; 1870–1950) Scots singer and famous music-hall comedian. He always appeared on stage wearing a glengarry and kilt and carried a crooked stick. His most famous songs included "I Love a Lassie" and "Roamin' in the Gloamin'." He toured in Australia and the USA and gave concerts for the troops during World War I.

● **Lauderdale, John Maitland, Duke of** ▶ (1616–82) Scottish statesman; a member of the political faction called the ▷Cabal under Charles II. He supported parliament in the English Civil War until changing sides in 1647; in 1651 he was captured by the English army and imprisoned until the Restoration (1660). Under Charles II he was an unpopular high commissioner for Scotland from 1667 until 1680.

● **Laue, Max Theodor Felix von** ▶ (1879–1960) German physicist, who became professor at the University of Berlin in 1919. His early investigations of X-rays led him to discover the technique of X-ray crystallography (see X-ray diffraction), now widely used for determining crystal structures. For this work he won the 1914 Nobel Prize. In 1943 he resigned his chair in protest against the Nazis. After the war he was appointed director of the Max Planck Institute for Physical Chemistry.

● **Laugharne** ▶ 51 47N 4 28W A small town in SW Wales, in Carmarthenshire on the estuary of the River Taff near Carmarthen Bay. The poet Dylan Thomas lived and was buried here.

● **laughing jackass** ▷See kookaburra.

● **laughing owl** ▶ A ground-nesting New Zealand ▷owl, *Sceloglaux albifacies*, probably now extinct due to the introduction of predatory mammals. It was 37 cm long and had a speckled brown plumage with whitish facial feathers.

● **Laughton, Charles** ▶ (1899–1962) British actor. His international reputation was based on his numerous films, which included *The Private Life of Henry VIII* (1933), *Mutiny on the Bounty* (1935), and *Rembrandt* (1936). He was married to the actress Elsa Lanchester (1902–86) and lived for many years in Hollywood, but made several late appearances in the English theatre, notably as King Lear in 1959. His one film as director was the classic *The Night of the Hunter* (1955).

● **Launceston** ▶ 41 25S 147 07E A city and port in Australia, in N Tasmania situated at the confluence of the North and South Esk Rivers. It is an important commercial centre; industries include aluminium smelting, heavy engineering, textiles, and sawmilling. Population (1991): 93 347.

● **launch vehicle** ▷See rockets.

● **Laura** ▶ The subject of Petrarch's love sonnets. She has been variously identified, traditionally as Laura de Noves (?1308–48), a married woman living in Avignon. The poems suggest that Petrarch's love for her was not returned.

● **Laurasia** ▶ The supercontinent of the N hemisphere that is believed to have existed prior to 200 million years ago, when the drift of the continents to their present positions began. It probably consisted of Greenland, Europe, Asia (excluding India), and North America. ▷See also Gondwanaland.

● **laurel** ▶ One of several unrelated aromatic shrubs or small trees with attractive evergreen leaves. The so-called true laurels (genus *Laurus*) include the ▷bay tree. Other laurels include the ornamental ▷cherry laurels, the spotted laurels (genus *Aucuba*; family *Cornaceae*), and the mountain laurel (*Kalmia latifolia*; family *Ericaceae*). The spurge laurel is a species of ▷*Daphne*.

● **Laurel and Hardy** ▶ US film comedians. **Stan Laurel** (Arthur Stanley Jefferson; 1890–1965), the thin member of the team and originator of the gags, was born in Britain. He joined with **Oliver Hardy** (1892–1957), who played the pompous fat partner, in 1926. They made numerous outstanding two-reel and feature-length comedy films in the 1920s and 1930s, including *The Music Box* (1932), *Our Relations* (1936), and *Way Out West* (1937).

● **Laurentian Shield** ▷See shield.

● **Laurier, Sir Wilfrid** ▶ (1841–1919) Canadian statesman; the first French-Canadian prime minister of Canada (1896–1911). His Liberal government was notable for the settlement of the West and the defence of Canadian autonomy within the British Empire.

● **laurustinus** ▶ An ornamental evergreen shrub, *Viburnum tinus*, native to the Mediterranean region and up to 3 m tall. It has pointed oval leaves, reddish twigs, and round heads of tiny five-petalled pink-and-white flowers, borne on red stalks and producing blue-black berries. It is often grown as a pot plant. Family: *Caprifoliaceae*.

● **Lausanne** ▶ 46 32N 6 39E A city and resort in W Switzerland, on the N shore of Lake Geneva. A cultural and intellectual centre, it has a notable cathedral (13th century) and a university (1891) founded as a college in the 16th century. Lausanne is the seat of the Swiss Supreme Court and the headquarters of the International Olympic Committee. Industries include chocolate, precision instruments, and clothing. Population (1996 est): 115 878.

● **Lausanne, Conferences of** ▶ **1.** (1922–23) A conference between the Allied Powers and Turkey that modified the post-World War I Treaty of Sèvres (1920), which had been unacceptable to Turkey. By the Treaty of Lausanne, Turkey regained territory from Greece and the Allies recognized Turkey's right to control its own affairs. **2.** (1932) A conference between the UK, France, Belgium, and Italy, which ended the payment by Germany of World War I reparations.

● **Lautréamont, Comte de** ▶ (Isidore Ducasse; 1846–70) French writer, born in Montevideo. Sent to Paris to study, he died after three years and little is known of his life. His prose poems, *Les Chants de Maldoror* (1868), concern a blasphemous misanthropic hero, and fantastic episodes are described with hallucinatory intensity. Lautréamont was later acknowledged as an important precursor by the surrealists.

● **lava** ▶ Magma that has reached the earth's surface through volcanic vents and from which the volatile material has escaped, either molten or cooled and solidified. Basic lavas tend to be liquid and flow over large areas, while acid lavas are viscous.

● **Laval** ▶ 45 33N 73 43W A city in E Canada, in Quebec on the island next to ▷Montreal. Primarily a suburb, it has some industry, including electronics, paper, and metal goods. Population (1991): 314 398.

● **Laval, Pierre** ▶ (1883–1945) French statesman, whose collaboration with Germany during the German occupation of France in World War II resulted in his execution as a traitor. A socialist, Laval was prime minister in 1930, 1931, 1932, 1935, and 1936 and foreign minister in 1934, 1935, and 1936. In 1935, with Sir Samuel Hoare (1880–1959), the British foreign minister, he proposed an unsuccessful plan (the Hoare-Laval Pact) for the settlement of Mussolini's claims in Ethiopia. After the collapse of France (1940) he joined Marshal ▷Pétain's Vichy government. Increasingly powerful, he was dismissed and briefly imprisoned by Pétain (December, 1940) but the support of Germany secured Laval the virtual leadership of the Vichy government in 1942. After the liberation of France (1944) he fled to Germany and then to Spain but later gave himself up for trial in France (July, 1945).

● **La Vallière, Louise de Françoise de la Baume le Blanc, Duchesse de** ▶ (1644–1710) The mistress of Louis XIV of France from 1661 until 1667, when she was replaced by Mme de Montespan. In 1674 she retired to a convent.

● **Lavalloisian** ▶ A Middle ▷Palaeolithic technique of making stone tools by flaking pieces away from a specially shaped lump (prepared core). It is often associated with ▷Mousterian sites.

● **lavender** ▶ A small shrub of the genus *Lavandula* (about 8 species), especially *L. vera* and *L. angustifolia* (or *L. officinalis*). 30–80 cm high, it has aromatic narrow grey-green leaves and long-stemmed spikes of small mauve or violet flowers. Native to the Mediterranean area, it is widely cultivated for its flowers, which retain their fragrance when dried, and for its oil, which is used in perfumes. Family: ▷*Labiatae*.

● **laver** ▶ An edible red ▷seaweed of the genus *Porphyra*, found growing at the high tide mark in both hemispheres. It has wide irregular membranous fronds, which are dried to provide an important food source in the Orient. In the British Isles it is fried and known as laverbread (or sloke).

● **Laver, Rod(ney George)** ▶ (1938–   ) Australian tennis player, who was Wimbledon singles champion in 1961, 1962, 1968, and 1969. In 1962 he took all four major singles titles (Australian, French,

US, and Wimbledon) as an amateur and repeated the feat as a professional in 1969.

● **Laveran, Charles Louis Alphonse** ► (1845–1922) French physician, who (in 1880) first recognized the protozoan parasite responsible for malaria while stationed with the army in Algeria. Laveran also investigated other diseases caused by protozoa, including trypanosomiasis and leishmaniasis. He was awarded the 1907 Nobel Prize.

● **Lavoisier, Antoine Laurent** ► (1743–94) French chemist, regarded as the founder of modern chemistry. Born into an aristocratic family, he became wealthy by investing his money in a private company hired by the government to collect taxes. With his wealth he built a large laboratory where he discovered in 1778 that air consists of a mixture of two gases, which he called oxygen and nitrogen. He then went on to study the role of oxygen in combustion, finally disposing of the ▷phlogiston theory. Lavoisier also discovered the law of conservation of mass and devised the modern method of naming compounds, which replaced the older nonsystematic method. Lavoisier was arrested during the French Revolution and tried for his involvement with the tax-collecting company. He was found guilty and guillotined.

● **law** ► The body of rules that govern and regulate the relationship between one state and another (*see* international law), a state and its citizens (public law), and one person and another when the state is not directly involved (*see* civil law). The study of the principles on which legal systems are based is known as **jurisprudence**. Two great legal systems are dominant in the Western world: ▷Roman law, as used in most countries of continental Europe and South America, and English law. The laws of England, which are enforceable by judicial process, can be divided into: (1) the ▷common law, based on judicial decisions, as opposed to law enacted by parliament; (2) ▷equity, the principles originally applied by the Court of ▷Chancery; and (3) statute law, embodied in specific Acts of Parliament. ▷*See also* courts of law; criminal law.

● **Law, (Andrew) Bonar** ► (1858–1923) British statesman; Conservative prime minister (1922–23). Colonial secretary (1915–16), he fostered the revolt against ▷Asquith's coalition and in the subsequent coalition led by ▷Lloyd George became chancellor of the exchequer and leader of the House of Commons. He became prime minister after Lloyd George's resignation.

● **Law, William** ► (1686–1761) Anglican divine. Deprived of his Cambridge fellowship for refusing to take the oath of allegiance to George I, Law later became a private tutor. His most famous work, *A Serious Call to a Holy and Devout Life* (1728), became a classic of Protestant spirituality, influencing, among others, the ▷Wesleys.

● **Lawes, Sir John Bennet** ► (1814–1900) British agriculturalist, who pioneered the production of artificial fertilizers. Lawes patented a method for chemically improving phosphate rock and in 1842 opened the first fertilizer factory. In 1843 Lawes began a long association with Sir Henry Gilbert (1817–1901), with whom he investigated aspects of crop fertilization and animal nutrition. This marked the foundation of Rothamsted Experimental Station.

● **Lawler, Ray** ► (1921–) Australian dramatist. He worked as actor and producer for the National Theatre Company in Melbourne. He won international fame with his plays *The Summer of the Seventeenth Doll* (1955) and *The Piccadilly Bushman* (1959).

● **Lawrence, D(avid) H(erbert)** ► (1885–1930) British novelist, poet, and painter. The son of a Nottinghamshire miner, he was encouraged by his mother to become a teacher; he published his first novel *The White Peacock*, in 1911. The semiautobiographical *Sons and Lovers* (1913) established his reputation. In 1912 he eloped with Frieda Weekley, the German wife of a professor at Nottingham University College and a cousin of Freiherr von ▷Richthofen. Their extensive travels provided material for the novels *Kangaroo* (1923), reflecting a stay in Australia, and *The Plumed Serpent* (1926), set in Mexico and published after they had lived several years in Taos, New Mexico. Lawrence explored marital and sexual relations in *The Rainbow* (1915) and *Women in Love* (1921). He treated this subject in more explicit detail in *Lady Chatterley's Lover* (privately printed, Florence, 1928); the novel

was not published in Britain in its unexpurgated form until 1961, after a long trial. An exhibition of his paintings was banned in 1929. Lawrence's collected poems were published in 1928 and his *Last Poems* in 1932. *Fantasia of the Unconscious* (1922) develops metaphysical ideas that become increasingly prominent in the novels. He also published criticism and travel writings, and his short stories and letters are considered among the finest in the language. Lawrence died of tuberculosis in Vence (France). An autobiographical novel *Mr Noon* (1920) was published posthumously in 1984.

● **Lawrence, Ernest Orlando** ► (1901–58) US physicist, who in 1930, at the University of California, designed and built the first ▷cyclotron, a type of particle ▷accelerator upon which almost all subsequent models have been based. For his invention he received the Nobel Prize in 1939.

● **Lawrence, Gertrude** ► (1898–1952) British actress. She performed in many revues and was especially successful in Noel ▷Coward's *Private Lives* (1930) and *Tonight at 8.30* (1935–36). She went to the USA and made her final appearance in the musical *The King and I* in 1951.

● **Lawrence, John Laird Mair, 1st Baron** ► (1811–79) British colonial administrator. As chief commissioner in the Punjab (1853–57) he helped to suppress the ▷Indian Mutiny, for which he received a life pension of £2,000 a year and the nickname Saviour of the Punjab. He was subsequently governor general of India (1864–69).

● **Lawrence, St** ► (d. 258) Roman deacon martyred during the reign of Emperor Valerian. According to tradition he distributed ecclesiastical treasure to the poor and was condemned to death by being roasted on a gridiron, which has become his emblem. Feast day: 10 Aug.

● **Lawrence, Stephen** ► (1975–93) British student, whose murder by White racists who were never convicted became a *cause célèbre* in the UK. Of Jamaican parents, he was stabbed to death by a gang of White youths on 22 April, 1993, while waiting for a bus in Eltham, S London. Of the five prime suspects, two were arrested but released without trial, owing to lack of evidence. The case became a cause of national controversy largely as a result of the persistence of the victim's parents, who brought an unsuccessful private prosecution against all five suspects in 1994–96. A subsequent inquiry, headed by Sir William Macpherson of Cluny, published its report in February 1999. The report roundly condemned the Metropolitan Police for appalling incompetence and an "institutional racism" that led officers to treat the killing as an episode in a gang war, rather than the racially motivated murder of an innocent man. In particular, the police failed to give first aid to the stricken youth, showed an unsympathetic attitude to the victim's family and the main witness (a Black youth), neglected to follow many basic evidence-gathering procedures, and—crucially—delayed arresting the alleged perpetrators, despite many reports from members of the public. The report, which recommended various measures to eradicate racism from the police and a number of modifications to the law, was immediately seen as a landmark in Britain's race relations.

● **Lawrence, T(homas) E(dward)** ► (1888–1935) British soldier and writer, known as Lawrence of Arabia. He learned Arabic while excavating Carchemish (1911–14) and after the outbreak of World War I worked for army intelligence in Cairo. In 1916 he joined the Arab revolt against the Turks, leading the Arab guerrillas triumphantly into Damascus in October, 1918. His exploits, which brought him almost legendary fame, were recounted in his book *The Seven Pillars of Wisdom* (subscription edition, 1926). Disillusioned by the failure of the Paris Peace Conference to establish Arab independence, in 1922 he joined the ranks of the RAF, assuming the name John Hume Ross, and then the Royal Tank Corps (1923), as T. E. Shaw. In 1925 he rejoined the RAF, about which he wrote in *The Mint* (1955). He died in a motorcycle accident in Dorset. His house at Bovington is now owned by the National Trust.

● **Lawrence, Sir Thomas** ► (1769–1830) British painter, born in Bristol. He achieved success in London with his portrait of *Queen Charlotte* (c. 1789; National Gallery, London). He became painter to George III (1792) and president of the Royal Academy (1820), establishing a

European reputation with his portraits of the participants in the Congress of ▷Vienna, all now in the Waterloo Chamber, Windsor Castle.

● **lawrencium** ▶ (Lr) A synthetic transuranic element discovered in 1961 and named after E. O. ▷Lawrence. Chemical tests on a few atoms suggest a dominantly trivalent chemistry. At no 103; at wt (262).

● **Law Society** ▶ The body that governs solicitors in England and Wales (separate Law Societies exist for Scotland and Northern Ireland). It controls the training and examination of solicitors, investigates complaints against solicitors (through its Office for the Supervision of Solicitors), and until 1989 managed ▷legal aid (now administered by the Legal Aid Board). Membership of the Society is voluntary but all solicitors contribute to its fund to compensate persons who have been defrauded by solicitors.

● **Lawson, Nigel, Baron** ▶ (1932–) British Conservative politician; chancellor of the exchequer (1983–89). He became an MP in 1974 and was secretary of state for energy (1981–83). His budgets included major reforms of the tax system. His resignation arose over conflict with Mrs Thatcher's private economic adviser Sir Alan Walters and her reluctance to permit the UK to participate in the ▷European Monetary System.

● **laxatives** ▶ (or purgatives) Drugs used to treat constipation. Osmotic laxatives, such as magnesium sulphate (Epsom salts), mix with the faeces and cause them to retain water, which makes them easier to pass. Stimulant laxatives, such as senna, stimulate the bowel directly. Bulk-forming laxatives, such as ispaghula husk and methylcellulose, absorb water and therefore increase the bulk of the stools. Dietary ▷fibre acts in a similar way.

● **Laxness, Halldór (Kiljan)** ▶ (1902–98) Icelandic novelist and essayist. He spent much of his early life travelling in Europe, where he became a Roman Catholic. The novel *Vefarinn mikli frá Kasmir* (*The Great Weaver from Kashmir*; 1927) marked his abandonment of Catholicism and adoption of socialism, a theme of works written after his return to Iceland in 1930. These include *Salka Valka* (1934) and *Sjalfstaet folk* (*Independent People*; 1934–35). He won a Nobel Prize in 1955.

T. E. Lawrence ▶ A rare photograph of "Lawrence of Arabia" in the uniform of a British officer, taken during a visit to Cairo headquarters in 1918. During his desert campaigns Lawrence invariably wore the robes of a high-born Arab, in order to win the trust of his Bedouin followers.

● **Layamon** ▶ (early 13th century) English poet and priest. His alliterative verse chronicle *Brut*, based on the *Roman de Brut* by ▷Wace, relates the history of England from the arrival of Brutus (a legendary Trojan) to the defeat of the Britons by the Saxons in 689 AD and includes ▷Arthurian legends.

● **Layard, Sir Austen Henry** ▶ (1817–94) British archaeologist and diplomat. As excavator of ▷Nimrud and ▷Nineveh (1845–51), Layard stimulated popular interest in Mesopotamian archaeology by his book *Nineveh and Its Remains* (1848)—actually about Nimrud, as he had

at first misidentified the site—and by his feat of transporting colossal statues of winged bulls to Britain.

● **Lazarists** ▶ A Roman Catholic order of lay priests known more formally as the Congregation of the Mission. Established by St ▷Vincent de Paul at St Lazare Priory, Paris, in 1625, the Lazarists now have teaching and missionary communities all over the world.

● **Lazio** ▶ (Latin name: Latium) A region in W central Italy. It consists of an extensive coastal plain in the W and mountains in the E, separated by volcanic hills. The majority of the population live in urban centres, such as Rome. Agriculture is important producing cereals, olives, wine, fruits, sheep, and cattle. Rome is an important centre for manufacturing industries, such as food processing, chemicals, textiles, and paper; there is also a sizable service industry. Area: 17 204 sq km (6642 sq mi). Population (1994 est): 5 185 316. Capital: Rome.

● **LDL** ▶ (low-density lipoprotein) ▷*See* cholesterol.

● **L-dopa** ▷*See* levodopa.

● **Lea, River** ▶ (or R. Lee) A river in S England, rising in S Bedfordshire and flowing SE and S past Luton to join the River Thames at Blackwall. Its valley has been developed as a recreational park. Length: 74 km (46 mi).

● **Leach, Bernard (Howell)** ▶ (1887–1979) British potter, born in Hong Kong. After training in Japan (1909–20), he established a pottery at St Ives in Cornwall (1920) and began producing simple designs indebted to Japanese *raku* ware (moulded rough earthenware with a thick lead glaze). His pottery and writings, notably *A Potter's Book* (1940), have been very influential.

● **Leacock, Stephen (Butler)** ▶ (1869–1944) English-born Canadian humorist. He was educated and taught economics and political science at Canadian universities. *Literary Lapses* (1910) and *Nonsense Novels* (1911) were the first of over 30 popular humorous books.

● **lead** ▶ (Pb) A dense soft bluish-grey metal, known from prehistoric times. It occurs in nature chiefly as the sulphide ▷galena (PbS) but also as cerussite ($PbCO_3$), anglesite ($PbSO_4$), and occasionally as the native metal. The metal is very resistant to corrosion and some lead pipes installed by the Romans are still intact. Lead has been widely used in plumbing although it is now largely replaced by plastics. It is also used to shield X-rays, as ammunition, as cable sheathing, in crystal glass (as lead oxide), and as an antiknock (as ▷tetraethyl lead; $(C_2H_5)_4Pb$), although because of the toxicity of lead compounds lead-free petrol is now preferred. Other common compounds include the sulphate ($PbSO_4$), chromate ($PbCrO_4$), and the oxides red lead (Pb_3O_4) and litharge (PbO). These are coloured white, yellow, red, and orange respectively and were formerly extensively used as paint pigments. Most lead salts are insoluble, with the exception of the nitrate, ($Pb(NO_3)_2$), and acetate ($Pb(CH_3COO)_2$). Acute lead poisoning causes diarrhoea and vomiting, but poisoning is more often chronic and characterized by abdominal pain, muscle pains, anaemia, and nerve and brain damage. Children are particularly vulnerable to excess lead levels from car exhaust fumes. At no 82; at wt 207.2; mp 327.502°C; bp 1750°C.

● **Leadbelly** ▶ (Huddie Ledbetter; 1888–1949) US Black folksinger and songwriter, whose blues and work songs foreshadowed the folk revival of the 1960s.

● **leaf** ▶ An outgrowth from the stem of a □plant in which most of the green pigment chlorophyll, used for ▷photosynthesis, is concentrated. Foliage leaves are typically thin and flat, providing a large surface area for absorbing the maximum amount of light, and they contain pores (stomata) through which exchange of gases and water occurs. They may be simple or compound (composed of a number of leaflets) and with a branching vein system (in ▷dicotyledons) or parallel veins (in ▷monocotyledons). Other kinds of leaves include seed leaves (*see* cotyledon) and ▷bracts. The spines of cacti and the thorns of gorse are modified leaves. □ p. 720.

● **leaf beetle** ▶ A beetle belonging to a large family (*Chrysomelidae*; 26 000 species) occurring in tropical and temperate regions. Leaf beetles are generally small (less than 12 mm) and brightly coloured. Both the adults and larvae feed on leaves and flowers, although the larvae may also eat roots and stems. Leaf beetles have a wide range of habits: one group is aquatic; in others the larvae carry excrement on their backs (*see* tortoise beetle); and many are serious pests, including the notorious ▷Colorado potato beetle. □insect.

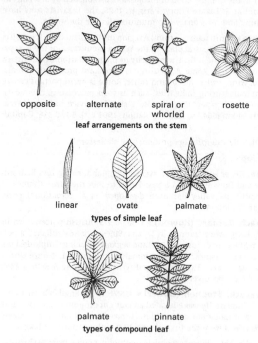

opposite   alternate   spiral or whorled   rosette

leaf arrangements on the stem

linear   ovate   palmate

types of simple leaf

palmate   pinnate

types of compound leaf

leaf ▶ The type and arrangement of the leaves are characteristic for a particular species of plant. For example, the pear has alternate ovate leaves; the horse chestnut has opposite palmate leaves.

● **leafcutter ant** ▶ An ▷ant, also called a parasol ant, belonging to the genus *Atta* and related genera and occurring in tropical and subtropical America. Armies of leafcutter ants damage crops by cutting pieces of leaf and carrying them to their large underground nests. The leaves are used as a medium on which the ants cultivate their diet of fungi. Subfamily: *Myrmicinae*.

● **leafcutter bee** ▶ A solitary ▷bee, about 10 mm long, belonging to a genus (*Megachile*) of the family *Megachilidae*. It nests in rotten wood and soil, lining the chamber and egg cells with pieces of leaf cut with its strong jaws. Leafcutters are similar to ▷honeybees in appearance and have pollen-carrying brushes on the underside of their abdomens.

● **leaf hopper** ▶ A small slender insect (up to 15 mm long) belonging to the family *Cicadellidae*. Leaf hoppers are often brightly coloured and are powerful jumpers. They feed by sucking plant juices and exude honeydew. Some species are serious pests of plants causing discoloration and weakening or spreading disease. Suborder: *Homoptera*; order: ▷Hemiptera.

● **leaf insect** ▶ A plant-eating insect, also called a walking leaf, belonging to the family *Phyllidae*. It is excellently camouflaged against foliage, having a broad leaflike body and wings and leaflike flaps on the legs. The female is much larger than the male and lacks hindwings. Order: ▷Phasmida.

● **League of Nations** ▶ An international organization created (1920) after World War I with the purpose of achieving world peace. The League's Covenant was incorporated into the postwar peace treaties and the USA's failure to ratify the Treaty of ▷Versailles meant its exclusion from the League. Before 1930 the League, from its Geneva headquarters, organized international conferences, settled minor disputes, and did much useful humanitarian work. However, it failed to deal effectively with the aggression during the 1930s of Japan in China, Italy in Ethiopia (in which the League's use of ▷sanctions was

ineffectual), and Germany, which withdrew from the League in 1933. The UN superseded the League after World War II.

● **Leakey, Louis Seymour Bazett** ▶ (1903–72) Kenyan palaeontologist. His work at ▷Olduvai Gorge uncovered evidence for man's early evolution. In 1974 his wife **Mary Leakey** (1913–96) unearthed hominid remains at Laetolil (N Tanzania) dating back 3.75 million years. Their son **Richard Leakey** (1944–) found significant fossils around Lake Turkana (N Kenya) and directed Kenya's Wildlife Service (1990–94; 1998–). In 1995 he formed a new political party to oppose the rule of President Moi.

● **Leamington** ▶ 52 18N 1 31W A spa town in central England, in Warwickshire, noted for its mineral springs. It was named Royal Leamington Spa in 1838 as a result of an earlier visit by Queen (then Princess) Victoria. Motor-car components and gas cookers are manufactured here. Population (1991): 55 396.

● **Lean, Sir David** ▶ (1908–91) British film director. His films in collaboration with Noel Coward include *In Which we Serve* (1942) and *Brief Encounter* (1946). Adaptations of Dickens' *Great Expectations* (1946) and *Oliver Twist* (1947) were followed by *The Bridge on the River Kwai* (1957). Later films included *Lawrence of Arabia* (1962), *Dr Zhivago* (1965), and *A Passage to India* (1984). He was knighted in 1984.

● **Leander** ▷See Hero and Leander.

● **leap year** ▷See calendar.

● **Lear** ▶ A legendary British king, probably invented by Geoffrey of Monmouth, who recounts the story of the old king's division of his kingdom among his three daughters. This story is the basis of Shakespeare's *King Lear* (c. 1605).

● **Lear, Edward** ▶ (1812–88) British artist and poet. After 1837 he lived mainly abroad. He showed inventiveness in his four books of nonsense verse for children, beginning with *The Book of Nonsense* (1846), and he popularized the limerick.

● **learning** ▶ A relatively permanent change in the response of an animal or human that occurs as a result of a reinforced practice. There are many theories that attempt to codify the mechanisms that underlie this process but none has yet achieved universal recognition. ▷Behaviourism achieved some success in accounting for simple animal learning but has not attempted to account for the complex way in which humans learn speech, for example. The view that behaviourism is incomplete has led to the development of ▷cognitive psychology, but no one would claim that cognitive sciences have provided a definite theory of learning. The development of computers and programs that simulate intelligence (see artificial intelligence) has given added urgency to the need to formulate a comprehensive theory of learning. ▷See also conditioning; imprinting.

● **learning disability** ▶ (*or* learning difficulty) **1.** An inability on the part of certain children of normal intelligence to learn certain skills. For example, ▷dyslexia is the inability to learn to read; dysgraphia is the inability to write; and ▷dyspraxia is an inability to coordinate movements. As the sufferers of these disabilities are normal in all other respects it is assumed that the problem arises as a result of a minor dysfunction in part of the brain, which may or may not be genetic. Special training and the use of mechanical aids can often alleviate these problems, although a residual disability is often carried forward into adult life. **2.** The **mental handicap** produced by impaired intellectual development resulting from such genetically determined conditions as Down's syndrome.

● **leasehold** ▷See estate; landlord and tenant.

● **leasing back** ▶ An operation to raise liquid cash from a capital asset. The owner of a property, such as a house, sells it on the condition that the buyer leases it back to the seller.

● **leather** ▶ Specially treated animal skin, chiefly that of domesticated animals, such as cows, sheep, goats, and pigs. Animals killed exclusively for their skins, such as crocodiles and lizards, produce beautiful but very expensive leather. The skin is first stripped of the fleshy inner and hairy outer layers and then tanned by steeping in tannin, a preservative, or using chromium salts. Finishing processes include rubbing to bring out the grain, as in Morocco leather (goatskin); dyeing; oiling; lacquering for patent leather; and sueding to raise a nap. The uses of leather, which is strong, flexible, and waterproof, range from shoes to saddles. Synthetic leather, made since 1850, is usually made from vinyl polymers. See also fur; parchment.

● **leatherback turtle** ▶ The largest living turtle, *Dermochelys coriacea*, found worldwide. Up to 2.1 m long with a weight of 540 kg, it has no horny external shell and its bones are buried in a ridged leathery brown-black skin. It is a strong swimmer and feeds on marine invertebrates, especially large jellyfish. It is the sole member of its family, *Dermochelyidae*.

● **Leatherhead** ▶ 51 18N 0 20W A residential town in SE England, in Surrey. It is the home of the Royal School for the Blind (1799). Population (1991): 42 903.

● **leatherjacket** ▷*See* cranefly.

● **Leavis, F(rank) R(aymond)** ▶ (1895–1978) British literary critic. The moral value of the study of literature was the theme of his teaching at Cambridge University and of his critical journal *Scrutiny* (1932–53). His books include *The Great Tradition* (1948), *The Common Pursuit* (1952), and studies of D. H. ▷Lawrence (1955) and ▷Dickens (1970; with his wife, Q. D. Leavis).

● **Lebanon, Republic of** ▶ A country in the Middle East, on the E coast of the Mediterranean Sea. It contains two mountain ranges (the Lebanon and Anti-Lebanon Mountains) extending N–S separated by the Beqaa Valley. There is a narrow coastal plain. The population is mixed, having Arab, Phoenician, Crusader, and Greek origins. Roughly half are Christian and half Muslim.

Economy: Lebanon was once forested and famous for its cedars, but much land has been converted to arable use. The fertile Beqaa Valley is the main area of production, citrus fruits being the chief crop. Agriculture, industry, and infrastructure suffered badly during the civil war and subsequent violence of 1975–92 and are now being rebuilt as part of a ten-year reconstruction plan (1993–2003), financed largely by foreign loans. International trade, banking, and insurance were formerly important, and there are plans to re-establish Beirut as a financial and commercial centre. Lebanon's two oil refineries have not functioned since the 1970s.

History: From about 1000 BC the coastal plain was the centre of Phoenician civilization, based on the trading cities of Tyre, Sidon, and Byblos. The region subsequently came under Hellenistic and then Roman control. Lebanon was an early convert to Christianity but in the 7th century broke away from the rest of the Church (*see* Maronite Church) and was invaded by Muslim Arabs. The Maronites maintained their culture and religion and supported the Crusaders in the 12th and 13th centuries. Lebanon was held by the Mamelukes during the 14th and 15th centuries and by the Ottoman Turks from the early 16th century to 1918. France was given the mandate over Greater Lebanon after World War I. Lebanon became officially independent in 1941, but France retained control until 1945. In 1958, at the request of President Camille Chamoun (1900–87), US troops were sent to quell a rebellion against his pro-Western policies. Lebanon did not fight in the 1967 and 1973 Arab-Israeli Wars, but Israel has made raids to eliminate Palestinian guerrillas. In 1975, civil war broke out between the dominant Maronite Christians and the Muslims; after 19 months this was ended by a Syrian-backed Arab Deterrent Force but unrest continued, especially in the S. In 1982 Israel invaded S Lebanon, clashing with Syrian forces in the Beqaa Valley and, after besieging Beirut, forcing the Palestine Liberation Organization to leave. Bashir Gemayel (1947–82), the president-elect, was killed in a bomb explosion and his brother, Amin Gemayel (1942–) succeeded him. Israel withdrew her forces from all but the S border region in 1985. The United Nations Interim Force in Lebanon (UNIFIL) was left to maintain peace between the Israeli-armed Christians, the Muslims, Druses, and Palestinian guerrillas. From 1986 various groups took foreign hostages, releasing most of them in 1991. In early 1987 Syrian troops moved into Beirut hoping to end the intermilitia wars. They drove the dominant Shia Muslim Amal militia out of the Muslim sector, but subsequently clashed with other groups. Presidential elections in 1988 failed to produce a winner and led to rival Christian- and Muslim-dominated governments. In 1989 the Christians, led by Gen Michel Aoun, refused to accept a new government led by René Muawad. Muawad was assassinated and succeeded as president by Elias Hrawi. Aoun led the Christian resistance until exiled in 1990. Syria's protection of Lebanon was formalized in a treaty in 1991. In 1992 the first general elections for 20 years were boycotted by most Christian parties. There followed several years of relative peace. In April 1996, however, hostile activity by ▷Hizbollah fighters in the S provoked Israel to launch an air and missile campaign against Beirut and S Lebanon, in which hundreds of civilians were killed. Although Israel launched a further air attack in February 2000, Hizbollah activity forced it to withdraw its forces from S Lebanon in May. In 1998 prime minister Rafik Hariri was replaced by Salim al-Hoss; Hariri became premier again following elections in 2000.

Republic of Lebanon

Head of state	President Emile Lahoud
Official language	Arabic
Official currency	Lebanese pound of 100 piastres
Area	10 452 sq km (4036 sq mi)
Population (1999 est)	3 563 000
Capital	Beirut

● **Lebowa** ▷*See* Bantu Homelands.

● **Le Brun, Charles** ▶ (1619–90) French painter and designer. He was First Painter to Louis XIV, for whom he decorated rooms in Versailles, and became director of the Gobelins tapestry works (1664) and of the French Academy (1683).

● **Le Carré, John** ▶ (David Cornwell; 1931–) British novelist. He worked for the secret service in Germany (1961–64). His spy novels include *The Spy Who Came in from the Cold* (1963), *Tinker, Tailor, Soldier, Spy* (1974), *Smiley's People* (1980), and *The Tailor of Panama* (1996). Novels on other themes include *Single and Single* (1999) and *The Constant Gardener* (2000).

● **Lecce** ▶ 40 21N 18 11E A town in SE Italy, in Apulia. It has Roman remains, a 12th-century cathedral, and a university (1956). It has a wine industry. Population (1996 est): 100 046.

● **Lech, River** ▶ A river in central Europe. Rising in SW Austria, it flows mainly N through S Germany and joins the River Danube. Length: 285 km (177 mi).

● **Le Châtelier, Henri-Louis** ▶ (1850–1936) French chemist, who discovered (1888) **Le Châtelier's principle**, that a chemical system will react to a disturbance of its equilibrium by tending to compensate for the disturbance. He used this principle to assist in the foundation of chemical thermodynamics. He was also the first to use a thermocouple to measure high temperatures and invented an optical pyrometer.

● **lecithin** ▷*See* phospholipid.

● **Leclanché cell** ▶ An ▷electric cell invented in 1867 by the French engineer Georges Leclanché (1839–82). It consists of a carbon anode surrounded by manganese dioxide and crushed carbon held in a porous bag or pot dipping into a solution of ammonium chloride, which also contains a zinc cathode. It delivers 1.5 volts. The common **dry cell** consists of a Leclanché cell or a ▷battery of cells in which the electrolyte is a paste of ammonium chloride in a zinc casing.

● **Leconte de Lisle, Charles Marie René** ▶ (1818–94) French poet. He was born on Réunion Island in the Indian Ocean and settled in Paris in 1846. His poetry, especially in *Poèmes antiques* (1852) and *Poèmes barbares* (1862), contains powerful descriptions of natural physical beauty. His disciples were known as the ▷Parnassians.

● **Lecoq de Boisbaudran, Paul-Émile** ▶ (1838–1912) French chemist, who used the technique of spectroscopy, newly developed by ▷Bunsen and ▷Kirchhoff, to discover the element gallium (1874). He also discovered samarium (1879) and dysprosium (1886).

● **Le Corbusier** ▶ (Charles-Édouard Jeanneret; 1887–1965) French architect, born in Switzerland, one of the most inventive artists of the 20th century. The influence of Le Corbusier's buildings and writings has been enormous. He trained under Auguste Perret (1874–1954) and ▷Behrens. His career falls into two parts. Until World War II he pioneered a rational, almost cubist, form of design, especially

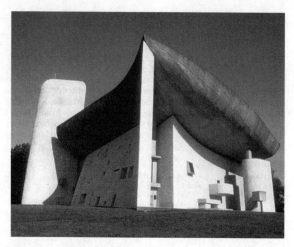

Le Corbusier ▶ Chapel Notre-Dame-du-Haut at Ronchamp (1950–55).

with his villas at Garches (1927) and Poissy (1929). Afterwards he became more individual, for example at his extraordinary chapel at Ronchamp (1950–55). He was also concerned with town planning (e.g. ▷Chandigarh, 1950s) and large-scale housing projects (L'Unité, Marseilles, 1945). He also contributed much to the UN buildings in New York (1946).

● **Le Creusot** ▶ 46 48N 4 27E A town in E central France, in the Saône-et-Loire department. A major metallurgical centre, it produced the first French locomotives and armour plate. Population (latest est): 32 310.

● **LED** ▶ (light-emitting diode) ▷*See* semiconductor diode.

● **Leda** ▶ In Greek myth, the wife of Tyndareus, King of Sparta, and mother, either by her husband or by Zeus, of Clytemnestra, Helen, and Castor and Pollux. Helen was born from an egg after Zeus had visited Leda as a swan.

● **Lederberg, Joshua** ▶ (1925–) US geneticist, who discovered transduction in bacteria. Lederberg found that fragments of bacterial DNA could be transmitted from one bacterium to another by a virus. For this, together with his earlier work on bacterial sex factors, Lederberg shared a Nobel Prize (1958) with George ▷Beadle and Edward ▷Tatum.

● **Le Duc Tho** ▶ (1911–90) Vietnamese politician. He was a founder member of the Indochinese Communist Party (1930) and the Viet Minh (1945). His negotiations with Henry Kissinger towards the close of the ▷Vietnam War were instrumental in securing the ceasefire of 1973; the two men were jointly awarded the Nobel Peace Prize (1974) but Le Duc Tho refrained from accepting it.

● **Lee, Bruce** ▶ (Lee Yuen Kam; 1940–73) US film actor and ▷kung fu expert, whose films include *Enter the Dragon* (1973) and other martial-arts adventures. He became a cult figure with a series of films made in Hong Kong, after only moderate success in Hollywood, and died in somewhat mysterious circumstances. His son **Brandon Lee** (1966–94) also starred in action films before his death in an unexplained shooting accident.

● **Lee, Gypsy Rose** ▶ (Rose Louise Hovick; 1914–70) US entertainer, who brought grace to striptease. She appeared in the Ziegfeld Follies in 1936 and in several films. A film and a musical were based on her autobiography, *Gypsy* (1957).

● **Lee, Jennie** ▷*See* Bevan, Aneurin.

● **Lee, Laurie** ▶ (1914–97) British novelist and poet. He is best known for the autobiographical novel *Cider with Rosie* (1959), about his rural childhood; other works include the autobiographical *As I Walked Out One Midsummer Morning* (1969) and several volumes of poetry.

● **Lee, River** ▷*See* Lea, River.

● **Lee, Robert E(dward)** ▶ (1807–70) US Confederate commander in the Civil War. He initially saw his role as one of defending his native state of Virginia, using superior mobility to defeat Federal attacks in the Seven Days' battles (1862), and subsequently as one of advance to keep the enemy outside Virginia. Losses at ▷Gettysburg (1863), however, again forced a defensive strategy. Lee was the first to use fixed field defences, quick to understand his opponents' intentions and an outstanding leader of men.

● **Lee, Spike** ▶ (Shelton Jackson L.; 1957–) US film director, producer, and screenwriter. His films, which deal with contemporary Black life in the USA, include *She's Gotta Have It* (1985), *Mo' Better Blues* (1990), *Malcolm X* (1992), *Clockers* (1996), and *Summer of Sam* (1999).

● **Lee, Tsung-Dao** ▶ (1926–) US physicist, born in China, who (working with his countryman Chen Ning ▷Yang) showed that parity is not conserved in ▷weak interactions. For this discovery the two shared the 1957 Nobel Prize.

● **leech** ▶ A carnivorous aquatic ▷annelid worm of the class *Hirudinea* (about 300 species). Leeches inhabit fresh and salt water throughout the world and occur in wet soil and cloud forest. They have one sucker around the mouth and a second at the rear. Most feed on the blood of animals and man, using specialized piercing mouthparts; the European medicinal leech (*Hirudo medicinalis*) is used to remove excess blood after reconstructive surgery.

● **Leech, John** ▶ (1817–64) British caricaturist, born in London. He studied medicine before publishing his first caricatures, *Etchings and Sketches by A. Pen*, in 1835. He was principal cartoonist to *Punch* from 1841 until his death and illustrated such books as Dickens' *Christmas Carol*.

● **Leeds** ▶ **1.** 53 50N 1 35W A city in N England, in Leeds unitary authority, West Yorkshire, on the River Aire. Canal links with Liverpool and Goole and the local outcropping of coal promoted Leeds as an industrial and commercial centre. Its traditional industries are clothing, textiles, printing, engineering, and leather goods, but most employment is now in the service sector. The university was founded in 1904. Among Leeds's principal buildings is the imposing town hall, built in 1858 in the classical style. The Leeds international piano competition is held here every three years. The Henry Moore Galleries opened in 1982 and the Royal Armouries Museum in 1999. Population (1991): 424 194. **2.** A unitary authority in N England, in West Yorkshire. Area: 562 sq km (217 sq mi). Population (1999 est): 680 722.

● **leek** ▶ A hardy biennial plant, ▷*Allium porrum*, native to SW Asia and E Mediterranean regions and widely grown in Europe as a vegetable. The bulb is hardly differentiated from the stem, which bears long broad leaves. Cultivated leeks are grown from seed and the stems and leaves are eaten in the first year, before flowering. They are set deep in the soil to ensure blanching. The leek is the national emblem of Wales.

● **Lee Kuan Yew** ▶ (1923–) Singaporean statesman; prime minister (1959–90). As leader of the People's Action Party (PAP) from 1954, he advocated Singaporean self-government within the British Commonwealth and in 1958–59 helped to draft a constitution in preparation for independence. He agreed, in 1963, to lead Singapore into the Federation of Malaysia but constant dissensions led to Singapore's withdrawal in 1965. His government was authoritarian and pro-Western.

● **Leeuwarden** ▶ 53 12N 5 48E A town in the N Netherlands, the capital of Friesland province. An economic centre with trade in cattle and dairy produce, its industries include engineering and glass production. It contains the notable Frisian museum. Population (1994): 87 464.

● **Leeuwenhoek, Antonie van** ▶ (1632–1723) Dutch scientist, noted for his microscopic studies of living organisms. He was the first to describe protozoa, bacteria, and spermatozoa and he also made observations of yeasts, red blood cells, and blood capillaries. Among his many other achievements, Leeuwenhoek traced the life histories of various animals, including the flea, ant, and weevil, refuting many popular misconceptions concerning their origin. Leeuwenhoek ground over 400 lenses during his lifetime, achieving magnifications of up to 300 times with a single lens.

● **Leeward Islands** ▶ **1.** A West Indian group of islands in the Lesser Antilles, in the Caribbean Sea extending SE from Puerto Rico to the Windward Islands. **2.** A former British colony in the West Indies (1871–1956), comprising Antigua, St Kitts-Nevis, Anguilla, Montserrat, and the British Virgin Islands. **3.** A group of islands in French Polynesia, in the Society Islands in the S Pacific Ocean.

● **Le Fanu, (Joseph) Sheridan** ▶ (1814–73) Irish novelist. He studied law before becoming a journalist and writer. His best-known books are stories of mystery and suspense, notably the novel *Uncle Silas* (1864) and the collection of stories *In a Glass Darkly* (1872).

● **leg** ▶ In human anatomy, the lower limb, which extends from the hip to the foot. The bone of the thigh (*see* femur) is connected by a ball-and-socket joint to the pelvis, permitting a wide range of movements. It forms a hinge joint at the knee with the bones of the lower leg—the shin bone (tibia) and the smaller fibula. This joint is overlain at the front by a bone (the patella, or kneecap) embedded in the tendon of the quadriceps muscle of the thigh. ▷*See* Plate II.

● **legal aid** ▶ A UK scheme deriving from the Legal Aid Act (1988), enabling a person to have all or part of the costs connected with legal proceedings (including solicitors' and barristers' fees) paid from public funds. In civil proceedings it is available if the applicant's disposable income and capital are less than amounts fixed by government orders. Eligibility is decided by the Legal Aid Board on the basis of means and the reasonableness of the case. For legal advice and assistance, other than proceedings, a separate arrangement is available, based on similar constraints relating to the disposable income of the applicant. In criminal cases, a defendant is eligible if his means are insufficient to pay for his defence, which is a matter decided by the courts. In practice, legal aid has made civil litigation available to poor individuals; they, and large companies, are now virtually the only litigants to be able to afford it.

In 1998 the Government published plans for replacing the existing legal-aid scheme with a service provided by fewer, but more specialized, lawyers: a Community Legal Service for civil proceedings and a Criminal Defence Service for criminal cases. There will be more stringent qualifying tests for civil legal aid, but legal advice and mediation services will be available from nonlawyer counsellors. In addition, for those who do not qualify for legal aid, there will be an increase in the categories of cases covered by conditional fee ("no win, no fee") agreements.

● **Legaspi** ▶ 13 10N 123 45E A port in the E Philippines, in SE Luzon. It was severely damaged by the eruption of Mount Mayon in 1815. Hemp and copra are exported. Population (1990): 121 000.

● **Legendre, Adrien Marie** ▶ (1752–1833) French mathematician, who made important contributions to number theory and mathematical physics. Due to the jealousy of ▷Laplace, then the foremost mathematician in France, Legendre never in his lifetime received the recognition that he deserved.

● **Léger, Fernand** ▶ (1881–1955) French painter, born in Argentan. He settled in Paris (1900) where, associated with ▷cubism, he produced robotlike figure paintings, followed by an abstract series entitled *Contrasts of Forms* (1913), consisting of brightly coloured tubes. His experiences in World War I inspired the machine imagery of such paintings as *The City* (1919; Philadelphia) but later he often returned to the human figure. Broad areas of bright colours are the most characteristic feature of his work. He also painted murals, designed ballet sets, and made the first non-narrative film, *Le Ballet mécanique* (1924).

● **Leghorn** ▶ (bird) A breed of domestic fowl originating in Italy and widely used in breeding commercial hybrids for egg laying. It has a full rounded breast, a flat sloping back, a short stout beak, long wattles, and a prominent comb in the male. The plumage can be black, blue, reddish brown, white, and black and white. Weight: 3.4 kg (cocks); 2.5 kg (hens).

● **Leghorn** ▶ (port) ▷*See* Livorno.

● **legionnaires' disease** ▶ An acute severe pneumonia, caused by the bacterium *Legionella pneumophila*, first described in 1976 after an outbreak among US legionnaires in Philadelphia. Over 30 people died in Stafford, England, as a result of an outbreak in 1985. Treatment is with the antibiotic erythromycin. The bacterium is transmitted in the droplets produced typically by air-conditioning systems.

● **Legion of Honour** ▶ (French name: Légion d'Honneur) A French order of knighthood, established by Napoleon in 1802. Its five ranks, to which foreigners are admitted, are knight of the grand cross, grand officer, commander, officer, and chevalier. Its grand master is the president of France.

● **Legnica** ▶ (German name: Liegnitz) 51 12N 16 10E An industrial town in SW Poland. Its manufactures include metal products, textiles, and chemicals. Population (1995 est): 107 800.

● **Leguminosae** ▶ (or Fabaceae) A worldwide family of herbs, shrubs, and trees (about 7000 species), which includes many important crop plants, such as peas, beans, clovers, and alfalfa. They all have compound leaves and the fruit is a pod containing a single row of seeds. Both pods and seeds are rich in protein. Most species possess root nodules that contain nitrogen-fixing bacteria and replenish nitrogen in the soil (*see* nitrogen cycle).

● **Lehár, Franz** ▶ (Ferencz L.; 1870–1948) Hungarian composer. He studied at the Prague conservatoire and after a period as a military band conductor (1894–99) turned to the composition of operettas, of which *The Merry Widow* (1905) was his greatest success. Others include *The Count of Luxembourg* (1911) and *Land of Smiles* (1923).

● **Le Havre** ▶ 49 30N 0 06E A port in N France, in the Seine-Maritime department on the English Channel at the mouth of the River Seine. Severely damaged in World War II, its harbour now maintains an important transatlantic cargo service and a car-ferry service to England. Population (1990): 197 219.

● **Lehmann, Lilli** ▶ (1848–1929) German operatic soprano. She was taught by her mother. During a long career she sang many roles, including Brünnhilde in *Die Walküre*, Isolde, Donna Anna in *Don Giovanni*, and Leonora in *Fidelio*.

● **Lehmann, Lotte** ▶ (1885–1976) German soprano, a US citizen from 1938. She studied in Berlin with Mathilde Mallinger (1847–1920); her most famous role was the Marschallin in Richard Strauss' opera *Der Rosenkavalier*.

● **Lehmann, Rosamond Nina** ▶ (1901–90) British novelist. She established her reputation with *Dusty Answer* (1927); subsequent novels, most of which depict family relationships, include *Invitation to the Waltz* (1932), *The Weather in the Streets* (1936), and *The Echoing Grove* (1953).

● **Leibniz, Gottfried Wilhelm** ▶ (1646–1716) German philosopher and mathematician. His philosophy is summarized in his books *New Essays on the Human Understanding* (c. 1705) and *Theodicy* (1710) and numerous essays. Leibniz' best-known doctrine is that the universe consists of an infinite set of independent substances (monads) in each of which a life force is present. In creating the world, God took account of the wishes of monads and this led to a rational harmony in the "best of all possible worlds"—a view satirized in ▷Voltaire's *Candide*. As a rationalist Leibniz founded the distinction between the logically necessary and the merely contingent truth. His claim to have invented the calculus was disputed by ▷Newton.

● **Leibovitz, Annie** ▶ (1950–) US photographer known for her celebrity portraits. As photographer for *Rolling Stone* magazine she produced famous images of rock stars, including John Lennon (1970, 1980) and the Rolling Stones (1975). As chief photographer for *Vanity Fair* (1983–) her subjects have included Hillary Clinton (1998).

● **Leicester** ▶ **1.** 52 38N 1 05W A city in central England, in Leicester unitary authority, the administrative centre of Leicestershire. Ancient Ratae Coritanorum on the Fosse Way, Leicester has many Roman remains including the Jewry Wall and sections of the forum and baths. Parts of the Norman castle also remain. St Martin's Church became a cathedral in 1927 and Leicester university was established in 1957. Other important buildings include the Town Hall and De Montfort Hall, a major venue for classical music. The principal industries are hosiery, knitwear, footwear, engineering, printing, plastics, and electronics. Population (1994 est): 293 400. **2.** A unitary authority in central England, in Leicestershire. Area: 73 sq km (28 sq mi). Population (1996 est): 294 800.

● **Leicester, Robert Dudley, Earl of** ▶ (c. 1532–88) English courtier; the fifth son of the Duke of ▷Northumberland. Dudley's good looks attracted the attention of Elizabeth I, who made him Master of the Horse (1558) and then a privy councillor (1559). It was rumoured that he might marry the queen after the death (for which some believed him responsible) of his wife Amy Robsart (c. 1532–60). His incompetent command (1585–87) of an English force in support of the Revolt of the Netherlands against Spain led to his recall but he retained Elizabeth's favour until his death. A strong supporter of the Protestant cause, he was attacked, probably by a Roman Catholic, in *Leicester's Commonwealth* (1584).

● **Leicestershire** ▶ A county in the East Midlands of England. In 1974 it absorbed the small historic county of ▷Rutland: this became an independent ▷unitary authority in 1997, as did Leicester city. The River Soar, flowing N, separates Charnwood Forest from the uplands of the E. A new forest is being planted on the border with Derbyshire and Staffordshire. It is an important agricultural county with dairy and livestock farming in the E and arable farming in the W. Stilton cheese is produced in the E. Coal extraction came to an end in the 1990s. Hosiery has long been the county's staple industry; others include footwear at Leicester and bell founding at Loughborough. Area (excluding unitary authorities): 2553 sq km (985 sq mi). Population (1996 est, excluding unitary authorities): 597 400. Administrative centre: Leicester.

● **Leichardt, (Friedrich Wilhelm) Ludwig** ▶ (1813–48) German explorer in Australia. In 1844–45 he led an expedition from Moreton Bay, near Brisbane (Queensland), to the Gulf of Carpentaria. He subsequently disappeared while trying to cross Australia from E to W. His unusual character was used by Patrick White in the novel *Voss* (1957).

● **Leiden** ▶ (English name: Leyden) 52 10N 4 30E A city in the W Netherlands, in South Holland province. In 1574 it survived a Spanish siege by cutting the dykes and flooding the countryside. Its famous university was founded in 1575 as a reward for this heroic defence. During the 17th and 18th centuries it was an artistic and educational centre. The painters Rembrandt and Lucas van Leyden were born here. Industries include textiles and metallurgy. Population (1996 est): 116 224.

● **Leif Eriksson** ▶ (11th century) Icelandic explorer; the son of ▷Eric the Red. He was converted to Christianity around 1000 and on his way to promote the faith in Greenland Leif, off course, became the first European to reach America. He landed in a region he called Vinland (perhaps Newfoundland or Nova Scotia). His story is told in Icelandic sagas.

● **Leigh, Vivien** ▶ (Vivien Hartley; 1913–67) British actress. In the theatre, she played many leading Shakespearean roles, frequently appearing with Laurence ▷Olivier, her husband from 1937 to 1960. Her films include *Gone with the Wind* (1939), in which she played the heroine Scarlett O'Hara, and *A Streetcar Named Desire* (1951).

● **Leighton, Frederic, Baron Leighton of Stretton** ▶ (1830–96) British painter and sculptor of classical subjects, born in Scarborough. He studied in Europe and established his reputation with *Cimabue's Madonna Carried in Procession* (1855), which was purchased by Queen Victoria. In 1860 he settled in London. He became president of the Royal Academy in 1878 and was ennobled in 1896.

● **Leinster** ▶ A province in the SE Republic of Ireland. It consists of the counties of Carlow, Dublin, Kildare, Kilkenny, Laois, Longford, Louth, Meath, Offaly, Westmeath, Wexford, and Wicklow. It incorporates the ancient kingdoms of Meath and Leinster. Area: 19 632 sq km (7580 sq mi). Population (1996): 1 992 000.

● **Leipzig** ▶ 51 20N 12 21E A city in E Germany, near the confluence of the Rivers Elster, Pleisse, and Parthe. Important international trade fairs have been held in Leipzig since the middle ages. It was also the centre of the German book and publishing industry until World War II. Notable buildings include the 15th-century Church of St Thomas and Auerbach's Keller, an inn that provided the setting for

Goethe's *Faust*. A famous musical centre, the city has associations with J. S. Bach and Mendelssohn. The university was founded in 1409 and renamed Karl Marx University in 1952. Leipzig is the country's second largest city and one of its chief industrial and commercial centres. Its industries include iron and steel, chemicals, printing, and textiles. Population (1996 est): 470 778.

● **Leipzig, Battle of** ▶ (or Battle of the Nations; 16–19 October, 1813) The battle in which Napoleon was defeated by an alliance including Prussia, Russia, and Austria. The engagement culminated in the allies driving the French into Leipzig and then storming the city. The French army was shattered and its remnants retreated westwards across the Rhine, ending Napoleon's empire in Germany and Poland.

● **leishmaniasis** ▶ A tropical disease caused by infection with parasitic protozoans of the genus *Leishmania*, which are transmitted to humans by the bite of sandflies. The disease may affect the skin, causing open sores or ulcers, or the internal organs, principally the liver and spleen (this form of leishmaniasis is called **kala-azar**). Treatment is by means of drugs that destroy the parasites.

● **Leith** ▶ 55 59N 3 10W A port in E central Scotland, on the Firth of Forth, now part of Edinburgh. There are shipbuilding, engineering, and chemical industries.

● **leitmotif** ▶ (German: leading theme) A short musical phrase characterizing an object, person, state of mind, event, etc. ▷Wagner developed the technique of constructing large-scale compositions from leitmotifs in his mature operas, such as the cycle *Der Ring des Nibelungen*.

● **Leitrim** ▶ (Irish name: Contae Liathdroma) A county in the NW Republic of Ireland, in Connacht bordering on Donegal Bay. Mainly hilly, descending to lowlands in the S, it contains several lakes, notably Lough Allen. Agriculture consists chiefly of cattle and sheep rearing; potatoes and oats are also grown. Area: 1525 sq km (589 sq mi). Population (1996): 25 000. County town: Carrick-on-Shannon.

● **Leix** ▷ *See* Laois.

● **Leland, John** ▶ (c. 1506–52) English antiquary. He served as chaplain and librarian to Henry VIII. The manuscripts and antiquities he collected during an extensive tour of England, recorded in his *Itinerary* (1710), were used by many later antiquaries.

● **Lely, Sir Peter** ▶ (Pieter van der Faes; 1618–80) Portrait painter, born in Germany of Dutch parents. He studied and worked in Haarlem before settling in London (1641), where he was patronized by Charles I and later Cromwell. As court painter to Charles II from 1661, he produced his best-known works, including his *Windsor Beauties* (Hampton Court) and *Admirals* (National Maritime Museum, London).

Vivien Leigh ▶ As Scarlett O'Hara in a scene from *Gone with the Wind* (1939), with Clark Gable as Rhett Butler.

● **Lemaître, Georges Édouard, Abbé** ► (1894–1966) Belgian priest and astronomer, who originated the ▷big-bang theory of the universe (1927). Lemaître based his theory on ▷Hubble's suggestion that the universe is expanding; it went unnoticed until ▷Eddington drew attention to it.

● **Léman, Lac** ▷*See* Geneva, Lake.

● **Le Mans** ► 48 00N 0 12E A city in NW France, the capital of the Sarthe department. Its many historical buildings include the cathedral (11th–15th centuries) in which Queen Berengaria (died c. 1290), the wife of Richard the Lionheart, is buried. The Le Mans 24 Hours, a sports-car race, is held here annually. Le Mans is an agricultural, industrial, and commercial centre. Population (1990): 148 465.

● **Lemberg** ▷*See* Lvov.

● **lemming** ► A ▷rodent belonging to the subfamily *Microtini* (which also includes voles), found in northern regions of Asia, America, and Europe. They range from 7.5 to 15 cm in length and have long thick fur. When their food of grass, berries, and roots is abundant, they breed at a great rate but when food is scarce they migrate southwards, often in large swarms crossing swamps, rivers, and other obstacles. Although able to swim, they sometimes drown through exhaustion. (Contrary to popular belief, they do not deliberately drown themselves.) Chief genera: *Dicrostonyx* (collared lemmings; 4 species), *Lemmus* (true lemmings; 4 species). Family *Cricetidae*. □mammal.

● **Lemnos** ► (Modern Greek name: Límnos) A Greek island in the N Aegean Sea. Remains of the most advanced Neolithic communities in the Aegean have been found here. Area: 477 sq km (184 sq mi). Population (latest est): 15 721.

● **lemon** ► A small tree or shrub, ▷*Citrus limon*, 3–6 m high, probably native to the E Mediterranean but widely cultivated in subtropical climates for its fruit. Its fragrant white flowers produce oval fruits with thick yellow skin and acid-tasting pulp rich in vitamin C. The juice is used as a flavouring in cookery and confectionery and as a drink. Family: *Rutaceae*.

● **lemon sole** ► A ▷flatfish, *Microstomus kitt*, also called lemon dab, found in the NE Atlantic and North Sea. Up to 45 cm long, its upper side is red-brown or yellow-brown with light or dark marbling. It is an important food fish. Family: *Pleuronectidae*.

● **lemur** ► A small ▷prosimian primate belonging to the family *Lemuridae* (16 species), found only in Madagascar and neighbouring islands. Lemurs are mostly arboreal and nocturnal and often live in groups, feeding mainly on fruit, shoots, and leaves and also insects. The ring-tailed lemur (*Lemur catta*) is 70–95 cm long including the tail (40–50 cm) and is mainly terrestrial, sheltering among rocks and in caves. Dwarf lemurs, which belong to a different family (*Cheirogaleidae*), are only 25–50 cm long including the tail (12–25 cm). ▷*See also* indri.

● **Lemures** ► In Roman religion, maleficent spirits of the dead. They haunted their former homes and were ritually appeased at the annual festival of the Lemuria, held in May.

● **Lena, River** ► The longest river in Russia. Rising in S Siberia, W of Lake Baikal, it flows mainly NE to the Laptev Sea. Its large delta, about 30 000 sq km (11 580 sq mi) in area, is frozen for about nine months of the year. Length: 4271 km (2653 mi).

● **Le Nain** ► A family of French painters, natives of Laon, who established a workshop together in Paris (c. 1680). The individual contributions of **Antoine Le Nain** (c. 1588–1648), **Louis Le Nain** (c. 1593–1648), and **Mathieu Le Nain** (1607–77) are uncertain, since their works were not signed and some were probably joint efforts. Louis probably painted the dignified peasant scenes, such as *The Peasant's Meal* (Louvre); small-scale works on copper, often of family life, are credited to Antoine. All three became members of the newly established French Academy in 1648.

● **Lenclos, Ninon de** ► (Anne de L.; 1620–1705) French courtesan, whose salon was the meeting place for many prominent literary and political figures of her day. She herself was much interested in Epicu-

rean philosophy. Her lovers included ▷La Rochefoucauld and the Marquis de Sévigné.

● **Lendl, Ivan** ► (1960–   ) Czech tennis player. He has won all the major Open championships except Wimbledon, being beaten in the final in 1986 and 1987.

● **Lend-Lease Act** ► (1941) Legislation introduced by President Roosevelt enabling Congress to lend or lease information, services, and defence items to any country vital to US defence. Britain and its World War II allies immediately received planes, tanks, raw materials, and food.

● **L'Enfant, Pierre-Charles** ► (1754–1825) US architect and town planner of French birth. His principal achievement was his design for Washington, DC (1791), with its traditional French layout of long parallel avenues and dramatic focal points.

● **Lenglen, Suzanne** ► (1899–1938) French tennis player. She won the Wimbledon singles seven times between 1919 and 1926, when she turned professional. Her grace and daring dress helped to make tennis a spectator sport.

V. I. Lenin ► The revolutionary leader in August 1917, several weeks before he seized power.

● **Lenin, Vladimir Ilich** ► (V. I. Ulyanov; 1870–1924) Russian revolutionary and first leader of communist Russia. Lenin became a Marxist after the execution (1887) of his brother Aleksandr for attempting to assassinate the tsar, Alexander III. In 1893 Lenin joined a revolutionary group in St Petersburg where he practised as a lawyer. In 1895 he was imprisoned and in 1897, exiled to Siberia, where he married (1898) Nadezhda Krupskaya, a fellow Marxist, with whom he worked closely throughout his career. In 1902 he published *What Is to Be Done?*, in which he emphasized the role of the party in effecting revolution. This emphasis led to a split in the Russian Social Democratic Workers' Party between the ▷Bolsheviks under Lenin and the ▷Mensheviks. After the failure of the ▷Revolution of 1905, Lenin again went into exile, settling in Zurich in 1914, where he wrote *Imperialism, the Highest Stage of Capitalism* (1917). In April, 1917, after the outbreak of the ▷Russian Revolution, Lenin returned to Russia. Calling for the transfer of power from the Provisional Government to the soviets (workers' councils), he was forced into hiding and then to flee to Finland. Lenin returned in October to lead the Bolshevik revolution, which overthrew the Provisional Government and established the ruling Soviet of People's Commissars under Lenin's chairmanship. He made peace with Germany and then led the revolutionaries to victory against the Whites in the civil war (1918–20). He founded (1919) the Third ▷International and initiated far-reaching social reforms, including the redistribution of land to the peasants, but in response to the disastrous economic effects of the war he introduced the ▷New Economic Policy (1921), which permitted a modicum of free enterprise.

In 1918 Lenin was injured in an attempt on his life and a series of strokes from 1922 led to his premature death. Subsequently his image became an icon of the Soviet Union; when the Soviet state was finally broken up into independent countries in 1991 statues of Lenin and other creators of the communist system were demolished in many cities and plans were made to remove his embalmed body from the mausoleum in Moscow's Red Square. ▷*See also* Leninism.

● **Leninabad** ▷*See* Khodzhent.

● **Leninakan** ▷*See* Kumayri.

● **Leningrad** ▷*See* St Petersburg.

● **Leninism** ► Developments in the theory of scientific socialism (*see* Marxism) by V. I. ▷Lenin. His theory of imperialism is an account of the final stage of capitalism, in which it dominates the entire world, decisive control resting with finance capital (banks) as opposed to industrial capital. Because of the worldwide nature of capitalism, socialist revolution becomes possible even in economically underdeveloped countries, the "weak link" of imperialism. According to his theory of the revolutionary party, the most conscious element of the proletariat provides the leadership for the rest of the working class and the peasantry in organizing the overthrow of the capitalist class.

● **Lenin Peak** ► (Russian name: Pik Lenina) 39 21N 73 01E The highest mountain in the Trans-Altai range of central Asia, on the border of Tadzhikistan and Kirgizstan. Height: 7134 m (23 406 ft).

● **Leninsk-Kuznetskii** ► (name from 1864 until 1925: Kolchugino) 40 37N 72 15E A city in central S Russia, in the Kuznetsk Basin. Coalmining has been the most important industrial activity since its foundation in 1864. Population (1980 est): 133 000.

● **Lennon, John** ► (1940–80) British rock musician and founding member of the ▷Beatles. After the Beatles disbanded Lennon recorded such solo albums as *Plastic Ono Band* (1970), *Imagine* (1971), *Walls and Bridges* (1974), and *Double Fantasy* (1980), several of which featured his second wife, the Japanese-born artist **Yoko Ono** (1933–). He was assassinated by a deranged fan in 1980.

● **Le Nôtre, André** ► (1613–1700) French landscape gardener. Le Nôtre perfected the French version of the formal garden with his use of imposing vistas and was imitated throughout Europe. His first complete garden was at Vaux-le-Vicomte (1656–61) but his largest and most perfect was for Louis XIV at ▷Versailles, on which he worked for nearly 30 years.

● **lens** ► A piece of transparent material, usually glass, quartz, or plastic, used for directing and focusing beams of light. The surfaces of a lens have a constant curvature; if both sides curve outwards at the middle the lens is called convex, if they curve inwards it is concave. The image formed by a lens may be real, in which case the rays converge to the image point (a converging lens), or virtual, in which the rays diverge from the image point (a diverging lens). The focal length of a lens is the distance from the lens at which a parallel beam of light is brought to a focus. If the focal length of the lens is f, the rays from an object distance u from the lens are focused at a distance v from the lens, where $1/f = 1/u + 1/v$ and u, v, and f all obey certain sign conventions.

● **Lens** ► 50 26N 2 50E A town in N France, in the Pas-de-Calais department. It was badly damaged in both World Wars, especially in World War I. The centre of an important coalmining area, it has metallurgical and chemical industries. Population (latest est): 38 307.

● **Lent** ► The Christian period of fasting and penance preceding Easter. Beginning on ▷Ash Wednesday, the Lenten fast covers 40 days, in emulation of Christ's 40 days in the wilderness (Matthew 4.2). In the middle ages the fast was more or less strictly observed, especially with regard to the prohibition on eating meat, but since the Reformation the rules have been generally relaxed in both Roman Catholic and Protestant Churches.

● **lentil** ► An annual herb, *Lens culinaris*, native to the Near East but widely cultivated. Each pod produces 1–2 flat round green or reddish seeds, which are rich in protein and can be dried and stored for use in soups, stews, etc. Family: ▷*Leguminosae*.

● **Lenya, Lotte** ► (Caroline Blamauer; 1900–81) Austrian-born singer and character actress, famous for her interpretations of songs by her husband, the composer Kurt ▷Weill. She made her name in the Berlin premiere (1928) of his *The Threepenny Opera* and settled in the USA in 1936.

● **Lenz's law** ► The direction of an induced current in a conductor is such as to oppose the cause of the induction. For example, a current induced by a conductor cutting the lines of flux of a magnetic field would produce a magnetic field of its own, which would oppose the original magnetic field. Named after Heinrich Lenz (1804–65).

● **Leo** ► (Latin: Lion) A large conspicuous constellation in the N sky near Ursa Major, lying on the ▷zodiac between Virgo and Cancer. The brightest stars are the 1st-magnitude Regulus, which lies at the base of the **Sickle of Leo**, and the 2nd-magnitude Denebola and Algeiba.

● **Leo (I) the Great, St** ► (d. 461 AD) Pope (440–61). One of the greatest medieval popes, Leo was largely successful in his attempts to extend papal control in the West after the fall of the western Roman Empire, but he failed to find support in the East. His treaties with the invading ▷Huns (452) and ▷Vandals (455) protected Rome from their onslaughts. His Christology, expressed in the *Epistola Dogmatica* (or *Tome of Leo*; 449), defined the doctrine of the Incarnation and was accepted at the Council of Chalcedon (451). Feast day: 10 Nov.

● **Leo (III) the Isaurian** ► (c. 675–741 AD) Byzantine emperor (717–41). He repulsed a Muslim attack on Constantinople in 718 and finally secured Asia Minor in 740 after a great victory over the Muslims at Acroïnon. In 730 he issued a decree that established the policy of ▷iconoclasm (the destruction of Christian images).

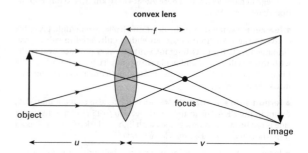

convex lens

object
focus
image

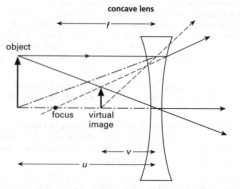

concave lens

object
focus
virtual image

lens ► The lines representing light rays show how a convex lens gives a real inverted image and how a concave lens gives an upright virtual image.

● **Leo III, St** ► (d. 816 AD) Pope (795–816). After his election he was opposed by a Roman faction and was forced to flee to ▷Charlemagne, who supported his return to Rome. There, in 800, Leo crowned Charlemagne Emperor of the West—an act that marks the start of the Holy Roman Empire. His rule was noted for its munificent church building. He was canonized in 1673. Feast day: 12 June.

● **Leo IX, St** ► (Bruno of Egisheim; 1002–54) Pope (1049–54), the first of the great medieval reforming popes. At successive councils clerical marriage and simony were condemned and, assisted by Hildebrand (later ▷Gregory VII) and Humbert of Moyenmoutier (c. 1000–61), he attempted to free the papacy from imperial control. Rival claims with the Normans to gain control of S Italy resulted in Leo's defeat at the battle of Civitella (1053). His conflict with the Eastern Church led to the schism between Rome and Constantinople (1054; *see* Filioque). Feast day: 19 April.

● **Leo X** ▶ (Giovanni de' Medici; 1475–1521) Pope (1513–21), the second son of Lorenzo the Magnificent (*see* Medici), by whose influence Giovanni was made a cardinal at the age of 13. He negotiated the Concordat of Bologna (1516) with Francis I giving the French Crown control over French ecclesiastical appointments. A patron of the arts, he reaffirmed the selling of indulgences in order to raise funds for the rebuilding of ▷St Peter's Basilica. This was one of the factors that provoked ▷Luther to demand reform and attack the papacy, for which Leo excommunicated him (1521).

● **Leo XIII** ▶ (Vincenzo Gioacchino Pecci; 1810–1903) Pope (1878–1903). Elected after a long career as a papal diplomat, Leo fostered relations between the papacy and European powers, the USA, and Japan. He also encouraged learning, foreign missions, and lay piety. His encyclical *Rerum novarum* (*Of New Things*; 1891), while condemning socialism, emphasized the duty of the Church in matters of social justice.

● **Leoben** ▶ 47 23N 15 06E A town in central Austria, in Styria. A lignite-mining centre, it has a university of mining and iron-founding industries (1840). Population (1991): 28 504.

● **León** ▶ (*or* León de los Aldamas) 21 10N 101 42W A city in central Mexico. It is a commercial and distribution centre; industries include the manufacture of footwear and leather goods. Population (1990): 956 070.

● **León** ▶ 42 35N 5 34W A city in NW Spain, in León region. Formerly capital of the kingdom of León, it declined after the 13th century. Medieval in atmosphere, it has a notable gothic cathedral. Population (1995 est): 147 780.

● **León** ▶ 12 24N 86 52W A city in W Nicaragua. Moved to its present site after the original city near Lake Managua was destroyed by an earthquake in 1610, it was the capital of Nicaragua until 1855. It is the country's cultural centre and has a university (1812). Industries include textiles, distilleries, tanneries, and food processing. Population (1995 est): 123 865.

● **Leonardo da Vinci** ▶ (1452–1519) Italian artistic and scientific genius of the ▷Renaissance, born in Vinci, the illegitimate son of a notary. He trained in Florence under ▷Verrocchio and painted the *Adoration of the Magi* (Uffizi) for the monks of S Donato a Scopeto (1481). In 1482 he became painter, engineer, and designer to Duke Ludovico Sforza in Milan, where he painted the fresco of the *Last Supper* (Sta Maria delle Grazie) and the first version of the *Virgin of the Rocks* (Louvre). His promised equestrian sculpture glorifying the Duke was never cast but the studies of horses for the project have survived. After the French invasion of Milan (1499), he returned to Florence, becoming military engineer and architect (1502) to Cesare ▷Borgia. Paintings in this period include the *Battle of Anghiari* for the Palazzo Vecchio, *The Virgin and Child with St John the Baptist and St Anne* (painting, Louvre; cartoon, National Gallery, London) and the *Mona Lisa* (Louvre). Some of his paintings were left unfinished and others, because of his experimental techniques, failed to survive. After working again in Milan (1506–13) and in Rome (1513–15), he was invited by Francis I to France (1516), where he spent his last years in Cloux near Amboise. His notebooks reveal his wide range of interests, including anatomy, botany, geology, hydraulics, and mechanics.

● **Leoncavallo, Ruggiero** ▶ (1858–1919) Italian composer of operas. Only *I Pagliacci* (1892) has met with continuing success, although he composed over 15, including a trilogy on Italian historical subjects and, a year after Puccini, his own *La Bohème* (1897).

● **Leonidas I** ▶ (d. 480 BC) King of Sparta (?490–480), following the suicide of his half-brother Cleomenes. Leonidas was the hero of the battle of ▷Thermopylae, in which with indomitable courage he and a small force held the pass for three days before being killed by the Persians.

● **Leonov, Leonid** ▶ (1899–1994) Soviet novelist and playwright. His moral and psychological themes were most powerfully expressed in his early novels, notably *Barsuki* (*The Badgers*; 1924) and *Vor* (*The Thief*; 1927). His later novels were politically and stylistically more orthodox.

● **leopard** ▶ A large spotted ▷cat, *Panthera pardus*, found throughout Africa and most of Asia. Leopards are slender, up to 2.1 m long including the 90-cm tail, having a yellow coat spotted with black rosettes. Colour variations, such as the ▷panther, sometimes occur. Leopards are solitary and nocturnal, typically lying in wait in a tree for their prey, which includes monkeys, dogs, and antelopes.

● **Leopardi, Giacomo** ▶ (1798–1837) Italian poet. His pessimistic philosophy, which is most fully expressed in the long poem *La ginestra* (1836), was largely conditioned by his unhappy home back-

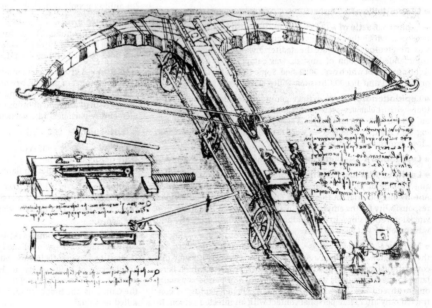

Leonardo da Vinci ▶ The range of Leonardo's scientific and mechanical interests is best seen in the pages of his notebooks. This drawing shows his design for a ballista, or giant crossbow, for use in war; it is mounted on a wheeled chassis.

ground, his poor health, and his failure in love. He is best known for the intense lyric poetry of *I canti* (1831). He died of cholera in Naples.

● **leopard lily** ▶ A perennial herbaceous plant, *Belamcanda chinensis*, also called blackberry lily, native to E Asia and widely planted as a garden ornamental. Growing over 1 m tall from an underground stem (rhizome), it has sword-shaped leaves, orange-spotted red flowers, and blackberry-like clusters of seeds. Family: *Iridaceae*.

The name is also given to several other garden flowers, including the snake's head ▷fritillary and a North American lily (*Lilium pardalinum*).

● **leopard seal** ▶ A solitary Antarctic ▷seal, *Hydrurga leptonyx*, of the pack ice. Leopard seals are fast agile hunters, feeding mainly on penguins. Grey, with dark spots and blotches, females grow to 3.7 m and males to 3.2 m. Family: *Phocidae*.

● **Leopold I** ▶ (1640–1705) Holy Roman Emperor (1658–1705). Leopold was ultimately successful against the Turks, who had besieged Vienna in 1683, freeing most of Hungary from Turkish dominance by 1699. He also came into conflict with Louis XIV of France, whose claims to the Spanish throne he opposed in the War of the ▷Spanish Succession. Under Leopold, Vienna became a great European centre.

● **Leopold I** ▶ (1790–1865) The first King of the Belgians (1831–65). He defended Belgium against William III of the Netherlands (1817–90; reigned 1849–90), who refused to recognize Belgian independence until 1838. A leading diplomat in Europe, at home he encouraged educational and economic reforms. A member of the House of Saxe-Coburg-Saalfield (previously Gotha), he helped to negotiate the marriage of his niece Queen Victoria to Prince Albert. He was briefly (1816–17) married to Charlotte (1796–1817), the daughter of George IV of Great Britain.

● **Leopold II** ▶ (1797–1870) Grandduke of Tuscany (1824–59). Initially a liberal who granted a constitution in 1848, he became increasingly reactionary after a brief period in exile in 1849 and was forced by radical opposition to abdicate.

● **Leopold II** ▶ (1835–1909) King of the Belgians (1865–1909), who sponsored Stanley's exploration of the Congo region of Africa. In 1885 he obtained European recognition of his sovereignty over the Congo Free State, which was annexed as the Belgian Congo in 1908.

● **Leopold III** ▶ (1901–83) King of the Belgians (1934–51). He surrendered to the Germans in ▷World War II, provoking opposition to his return to Belgium in 1945 and forcing his abdication in favour of his son ▷Baudouin I.

● **Léopoldville** ▷*See* Kinshasa.

● **Lepanto, Battle of** ▶ (7 October, 1571) A naval battle off Lepanto, Greece, in which the ▷Holy League routed the Ottoman navy, which was threatening to dominate the Mediterranean. The Christian force, commanded by ▷John of Austria, was composed of about 30 000 fighting men, of which over 7000 died. Some 15 000 Turks were killed or captured and 10 000 Christian galley slaves were freed.

● **Lepidodendron** ▶ An extinct genus of treelike pteridophytes that—with ▷*Calamites*—were dominant forest trees of the Carboniferous period (370–280 million years ago), their fossilized remains forming coal seams. Some species were over 30 m high and 1 m wide. Class: *Lycopsida* (clubmosses, etc.).

● **Lepidoptera** ▷*See* butterflies and moths.

● **Lepidus, Marcus Aemilius** ▶ (died c. 13 BC) Roman politician and protégé of Julius Caesar. After Caesar's death, Lepidus joined Antony and Octavian in the second Triumvirate (43), which divided responsibility for the empire, but in 42 they deprived him of his provincial governorships. In 36 Lepidus attempted to secure Sicily and was forced by Octavian to retire.

● **leprosy** ▶ A chronic disease, also called **Hansen's disease** after the Norwegian bacteriologist Armauer Hansen (1841–1912), who discovered the bacillus that causes it (*Mycobacterium leprae*, which is related to the tuberculosis bacillus). The incubation period is usually one to three years and—contrary to popular belief—leprosy is contracted only after close personal contact with an infected person. In

leprosy ▶ An unfortunate victim begging in the streets of Delhi.

the lepromatous form of the disease lumps appear on the skin, which—together with the nerves—becomes thickened and progressively destroyed, resulting in disfigurement and deformity. Eyes, bones, and muscles may also be affected. Tuberculoid leprosy usually produces only discoloured patches on the skin associated with loss of sensation in the affected areas. There are now potent drugs—including sulphones (which are related to sulphonamides)—available to cure the disease. Tuberculoid leprosy is treated with a combination of dapsone (a sulphone) and rifampicin (an antibiotic); lepromatous leprosy requires multidrug therapy—dapsone combined with several antibiotics. Leprosy is still endemic in many tropical areas with over 20 million people suffering from it.

● **Leptis Magna** ▶ An ancient trading centre near present-day Homs (Libya). Founded by the Phoenicians (6th century BC) Leptis' importance increased during Roman imperial times; ruins of unusually splendid public buildings attest its former grandeur.

● **lepton** ▶ A group of elementary particles, consisting of the ▷electron, ▷muon, ▷tau particle, ▷neutrinos, and their antiparticles. They take part only in the ▷weak and ▷electromagnetic interactions; together with quarks and photons they are thought to be the only truly elementary particles. ▷*See* particle physics.

● **leptospirosis** ▷*See* Weil's disease.

● **Le Puy** ▶ 45 03N 3 53E A town in S France, the capital of the Haute-Loire department. It has a 12th-century cathedral and is famous for its lace making. Population (latest est): 29 024.

● **Lérida** ▶ 41 37N 0 38E A town in NE Spain, in Catalonia. It possesses two cathedrals and a massive Moorish castle. An agricultural centre, its industries include glass and silk. Population (1994 est): 114 234.

● **Lermontov, Mikhail** ▶ (1814–41) Russian poet and novelist. His early Romantic poetry, published while he was a student at Moscow University, was greatly influenced by ▷Byron. As an army officer and an observer of high society he developed the cynical attitudes expressed in his novel *A Hero of Our Time* (1840). He was twice exiled to the Caucasus, the first time for a poem attacking the court, and was killed in a duel.

● **Lerner, Alan Jay** ▶ (1918–86) US lyricist and librettist, who collaborated with the composer Frederick ▷Loewe in the musicals *Brigadoon* (1947), *My Fair Lady* (1956), and *Camelot* (1960). Lerner also wrote the film scripts for *An American in Paris* (1951) and *Gigi* (1958).

● **Lerwick** ▶ 60 09N 1 09W A town in N Scotland, the administrative centre and chief port of the island authority of Shetland, on the E coast of Mainland. The most northerly town in the UK, it has fishing and hand-knitting industries. Population (1991): 7336.

● **Lesage, Alain-René** ▶ (1668–1747) French novelist. His best-known work is the picaresque novel *Gil Blas* (1715–35). He made translations and satirical adaptations of Spanish plays, in addition to writing 60 plays and librettos of his own.

● **lesbianism** ▷*See* homosexuality.

● **Lesbos** ▶ (Modern Greek name: Lésvos) A Greek island in the E Aegean Sea, situated close to Turkey. Settled by Aeolians about 1000 BC, it is associated with the development of Greek lyric poetry (especially through the work of Alcaeus and Sappho). Lesbos was a member of the Delian League and the chief town, Mytilene, was made a free port in the era of Roman power. Olives, grapes, and cereals are grown. Area: 1630 sq km (629 sq mi). Population (1991): 105 082.

● **Leschetizky, Theodor** ▶ (1830–1915) Polish pianist and piano teacher. His method influenced a generation of pianists, including Paderewski. He was a pupil of Czerny in Vienna and moved to St Petersburg in 1852, becoming head of the piano department at the conservatoire.

● **Lescot, Pierre** ▶ (c. 1510–78) French architect. Lescot's most influential work was the square court of the ▷Louvre (1546), the proportions and ornamentation of which set the style of French classicism.

● **Lesotho, Kingdom of** ▶ (name until 1966: Basutoland) A small country in SE Africa, enclosed by South Africa. It is largely mountainous, rising to 3350 m (11 000 ft). Most of the inhabitants are ▷Sotho.
  Economy: chiefly agricultural, the main crops being maize, wheat, and sorghum. Livestock is important but soil erosion due to overgrazing is a serious problem. The main exports, along with diamonds, are cattle, wool, and mohair. Some industry, including tourism, is being developed, but much of the population still works in South Africa.
  History: in 1868, following war with the Orange Free State, Basutoland came under British protection on the request of the Sotho chief, Moshoeshoe. In 1871 it was annexed by the Cape Colony but came under direct British administration in 1884. In 1910 it was placed under the British High Commission in South Africa and in 1966 became an independent kingdom within the Commonwealth under King Moshoeshoe II (1939–96). A state of emergency existed from 1970 to 1973. Chief Leabua Jonathan (1914–87) was deposed as prime minister in a military coup in 1986 and in 1990 the king was deposed and replaced by his son, Letsie III. Military rule lasted until 1993, when elections were held. Moshoeshoe II was reinstated as king in 1995 but died a year later; he was succeeded by Letsie III. Following elections in May 1998 Bethel Pakalitha Mosisili became prime minister. However, allegations of fraud provoked opposition protests and an attempted army mutiny, leading to South African military intervention in October. Following talks, the various parties agreed to set up a transitional body to reform the electoral system in preparation for fresh elections in the early 21st century.

Kingdom of Lesotho

Head of state	King Letsie III
Official languages	Sesotho and English
Official currency	loti of 100 lisente
Area	30 340 sq km (11 716 sq mi)
Population (2001 est)	2 177 000
Capital	Maseru

● **Lesseps, Ferdinand de** ▶ (1805–94) French diplomat, who supervised the construction of the Suez Canal, which was completed in 1869. A subsequent project to construct the Panama Canal ended in disaster when Lesseps was prosecuted for embezzling funds.

● **Lesser Antilles** ▶ (former name: Caribbees) A West Indian group of islands, comprising a chain extending from Puerto Rico to the N coast of Venezuela. They include the Leeward and Windward Islands, Barbados, Trinidad and Tobago, and the Netherlands Antilles.

● **Lessing, Doris** ▶ (1919–) British novelist. Born in Iran and brought up in Rhodesia, she came to England in 1949. Political and social themes predominate in her fiction, notably the novel sequence *Children of Violence* (1952–69) and *The Golden Notebook* (1962). Later works include *Memoirs of a Survivor* (1974), a series of science-fiction works (1979–83), *The Good Terrorist* (1985), and *Love Again* (1996), as well as the autobiographies *Under My Skin* (1994) and *Walking in the Shade* (1997). She was appointed a Companion of Honour in 1999.

● **Lessing, Gotthold Ephraim** ▶ (1729–81) German dramatist and writer. After studying theology and medicine, he became a translator and critic. His *Miss Sara Sampson* (1755) was the first German tragedy to use middle-class protagonists, while his comedy *Minna von Barnhelm* (1767) demonstrates the ▷Enlightenment ideal of reason. In 1765 he was involved in an unsuccessful attempt to create a German national theatre; in his influential essays, the *Hamburgische Dramaturgie* (1767–69), he developed his dramatic theories.

● **Letchworth** ▶ 51 58N 0 14W A town in SE England, in Hertfordshire. Built in 1903 as England's first garden city, preserving the original village, Letchworth has engineering, printing, and rubber industries. Population (1991): 31 418.

● **Le Tellier, Michel** ▷*See* Louvois, Michel Le Tellier, Marquis de.

● **Lethbridge** ▶ 49 43N 112 48W A city in W Canada, in S Alberta. Founded in 1870 as a coalmining centre, it has become an agricultural, distribution, and research centre, housing the University of Lethbridge (1967). Most industry is agriculturally based. Population (1991): 60 974.

● **Lethe** ▶ In Greek and Roman mythology, a river in the underworld, the water of which caused those who drank it to forget their former lives.

● **Leto** ▶ In Greek mythology, a daughter of the ▷Titans loved by Zeus. During her pregnancy she was not welcomed anywhere because of the fear of Hera and was forced to give birth to Apollo and Artemis on the barren island of Delos.

● **letter of credit** ▶ A letter from a bank to a foreign bank authorizing the payment of a specified sum to the person or company named. They are widely used as a means of paying for goods in foreign trade. An **irrevocable letter of credit** cannot be cancelled by the purchaser or the issuing bank. A **confirmed letter of credit** guarantees payment to the beneficiary should the issuing bank fail to honour it. A confirmed irrevocable letter of credit opened at a first-class bank is a safe basis for trading, although it must be negotiated before its expiry date. Unconfirmed or revocable letters of credit do not have great value.

● **Lettish** ▷*See* Latvian.

● **lettres de cachet** ▶ (French: letters of the seal) Administrative and judicial orders issued by the Kings of France. They were much misused during the 17th and 18th centuries to authorize arrest and imprisonment without trial or appeal. As symbols of the monarchy's despotism they were abolished (1790) during the French Revolution.

● **lettuce** ▶ An annual herb, *Lactuca sativa*, probably from the Near East and widely cultivated as a salad plant. It has a tight rosette of juicy leaves, rich in vitamin A, and is usually eaten fresh or cooked in soups. Cos lettuce has long crisp leaves and oval heads while cabbage lettuce has round or flattened heads and often curly leaves. Family: ▷*Compositae*.

● **Leucippus** ▶ (5th century BC) Greek philosopher. He developed from the teachings of ▷Parmenides the theory that there are two ultimate realities: (1) an infinite number of tiny irreducible particles (atoms), randomly circulating in (2) empty space. This theory is remarkably close to modern ▷atomic theory. ▷*See also* Democritus.

● **leucite** ▶ A feldspathoid mineral of composition $KAl(SiO_3)_2$, occurring as whitish or greyish crystals in some volcanic rocks deficient in silica. Where sufficiently concentrated it is a source of potash.

● **Leuckart, Karl Georg Friedrich Rudolph** ▶ (1822–98) German zoologist, who founded the science of parasitology. Leuckart described the life cycles of tapeworms and the liver fluke and revealed the importance of wormlike parasites in causing diseases in man.

● **leucocyte** ▶ (or white blood cell) A colourless □blood cell, up to 0.02 mm in diameter, of which there are normally 4000–11 000 per cubic millimetre of blood. There are several kinds, all involved in the body's defence mechanisms. Granulocytes (or polymorphs), which have granules in their cytoplasm, and monocytes ingest and feed on bacteria and other microorganisms that cause infection (*see also* phagocyte). The lymphocytes are involved with the production of antibodies (*see* immunity). Cancer of the white blood cells is called ▷leukaemia.

● **leucotomy** ▶ The surgical operation of interrupting the course of white nerve fibres within the brain. It is performed to relieve uncontrollable pain or emotional tension in very severe and intractable psychiatric illnesses, such as severe depression, chronic anxiety, and obsessional neurosis. The original form of the operation—prefrontal leucotomy (or lobotomy)—had the serious complications of epilepsy, apathy, and irresponsibility. Modern procedures make small and selective lesions and side effects are less disabling. ▷*See also* psychosurgery.

● **Leuctra, Battle of** ▶ (371 BC) The battle in which the reorganized Theban army under ▷Epaminondas crushed the Spartan invasion of Boeotia in Sparta's first major defeat on land. Sparta's resultant loss of influence allowed Thebes a short-lived ascendency in Greece.

● **leukaemia** ▶ A disease in which the blood contains an abnormally large number of white blood cells (*see* leucocyte). Leukaemia is a type of cancer of the blood-forming tissues, which undergo uncontrolled proliferation to produce many immature and abnormal white blood cells that do not function properly. Leukaemias may be acute or chronic, depending on the rate of progression of the disease. They are also classified according to the type of white cell affected. For example acute lymphocytic leukaemia (affecting the lymphocytes) occurs most commonly in children and young adults; it can now often be controlled by means of radiotherapy or ▷cytotoxic drugs. Chronic leukaemias occur more often in old people and may not need any treatment.

● **Leuven** ▷*See* Louvain.

● **Levant** ▶ A former name for the lands on the E coast of the Mediterranean Sea, now within Turkey, Syria, Lebanon, and Israel. The French mandates (1920–46) of Syria and Lebanon were known as the Levant States.

● **Le Vau, Louis** ▶ (1612–70) French ▷baroque architect. His first building, the Hôtel Lambert, Paris (1642), was remarkable for its ingenious room planning. As first architect to the Crown from 1654, he completed the Louvre, built the Collège des Quatre Nations (begun 1661), and designed the first extension of ▷Versailles (1669), which was later obliterated by the work of ▷Hardouin-Mansart. His most famous building is Vaux-le-Vicomte (begun in 1657), a chateau outside Paris built for Nicolas Fouquet.

● **level** ▶ 1. An instrument (also called a spirit level) for indicating whether or not a surface is level. It consists of a sealed glass tube containing spirit (alcohol) and a bubble of gas. The tube is mounted so that the wooden or metal frame supporting it is level when the bubble is in the centre of the tube. 2. An instrument for obtaining a horizontal line of sight. It consists of a telescope with cross hairs on both sights together with a parallel tubular spirit level, mounted on a tripod. Levelling is achieved by means of screw legs on the tripod table.

● **Levellers** ▶ An extremist English Puritan sect, active 1647–49. Led by the pamphleteer John ▷Lilburne, they were drawn mainly from the lower ranks of the army. They campaigned for a written constitution, radical extension of the franchise, and abolition of the monarchy and other social distinctions (hence their name). Cromwell's refusal to execute this programme led to mutinies (1647, 1649). After suppression of the last of these, the Levellers lost their identity and influence. ▷*See also* Diggers.

● **Leven, Alexander Leslie, 1st Earl of** ▶ (1580–1661) Scottish general. After over 30 years with the Swedish army, he led the Scots against Charles I of England in the ▷Bishops' Wars. In the English Civil War he had charge of Charles between the king's surrender to the Scots (1646) and his delivery to the English (1647).

● **Leven, Loch** ▶ A lake in Scotland, in Perth and Kinross. It has seven islands, one of which contains the ruins of a castle in which Mary, Queen of Scots, was imprisoned (1567–68). Length: 6 km (3.7 mi). Width: 4 km (2.5 mi).

● **lever** ▶ A simple machine consisting of a bar pivoted at a point on its length (the fulcrum) to move the point of application of a force and to obtain a ▷mechanical advantage. The three orders of lever are shown in the illustration.

● **Leverhulme, William Hesketh Lever, 1st Viscount** ▶ (1851–1925) British soap manufacturer and the founder with his brother James Lever of the Lever Brothers company. He introduced profit-sharing, pensions, medical care, and other benefits for his employees and in 1888 established the model industrial town Port Sunlight, now part of ▷Bebington. He was an MP from 1906 to 1910.

● **Leverkusen** ▶ 51 02N 6 59E A city in NW Germany, in North Rhine-Westphalia on the River Rhine. It is the site of the extensive Bayer chemical works. Population (1996 est): 162 252.

● **Leverrier, Urbain Jean Joseph** ▶ (1811–77) French astronomer, who predicted the existence of the planet ▷Neptune (1846) after investigating anomalies in the orbit of Uranus. John ▷Adams had made similar calculations but the planet was actually first observed by Johann Galle (1812–1910), the German astronomer, in 1846 on information supplied by Leverrier.

● **Levi** ▷*See* Levites.

● **Levi, Carlo** ▶ (1902–75) Italian physician, painter, and writer. Exiled to Lucania in S Italy for anti-Fascist activities in 1935, he wrote a widely acclaimed novel about the region, *Christ Stopped at Eboli* (1947). Other works include *The Watch* (1952) and *Words and Stones* (1958), a study of Sicily and the Mafia.

● **Levi, Primo** ▶ (1919–87) Italian novelist, poet, and chemist. A Jew, he survived imprisonment at Auschwitz and related his experiences there in *If This is a Man* (1947). Other works include *The Periodic Table* (1975), *If Not Now, When?* (1982), and *The Drowned and the Saved* (1988), published after his suicide.

● **Leviathan** ▶ An animal mentioned in several passages (Job, Isaiah, Psalms) of the Old Testament and variously interpreted as referring to the whale or crocodile. Leviathan was mythologically associated with evil and the devil.

● **Lévi-Strauss, Claude** ▶ (1908–) French anthropologist, the founder of structural anthropology (*see* structuralism). After teaching in America, Lévi-Strauss became professor of ethnology at the University of Paris (1948) and professor of anthropology at the Collège de France (1959). His works include *The Elementary Structures of Kinship* (1949), *Structural Anthropology* (1958), *Mythologies* (1964–71), and *The Jealous Potter* (1985).

● **levitation** ▷*See* magnetic levitation.

● **Levites** ▶ In ancient Israel, the descendants of Levi, the son of Jacob and Leah, forming the priestly caste and one of the 12 ▷tribes of Israel. They were not allocated territory in Palestine but only settlements with grazing rights and they were partly supported by offerings. After the ▷Babylonian exile, the priesthood was confined to Levites descended from Aaron.

● **Leviticus** ▶ The third book of the Old Testament, attributed to Moses. It gives instruction in the laws governing sacrifice and purification, in which the priestly caste of ▷Levites officiate. It also relates the laws governing diet, hygiene, the five annual national feasts, the use of land, and personal chastity.

● **levodopa** ▶ (or L-dopa) A drug used to treat ▷Parkinson's disease, which is caused by a deficiency of dopamine (a chemical secreted at nerve endings when an impulse passes: *see* neurotransmitter). Levodopa is converted to dopamine in the body; it is given in combination with benserazide (as Madopar) or carbidopa (as Sinemet), which prevents its breakdown in the body before it reaches the brain.

● **Lewes** ▶ 50 52N 0 01E A town in SE England, the administrative centre of East Sussex, on the River Ouse. At the Battle of Lewes (1264) Henry III was defeated by Simon de Montfort. ▷Glyndebourne is nearby. Population (1991): 15 376.

● **Lewes, George Henry** ▶ (1817–78) British author and literary critic. His most successful work was his *Life of Goethe* (1855), but he also publicized Comte's positivism in *Comte's Philosophy of the Sciences* (1853). From 1854 he lived with George ▷Eliot.

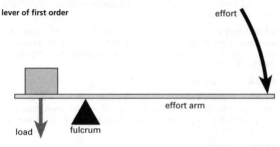

lever of first order

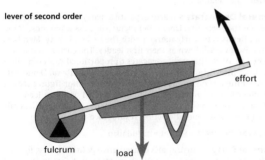

lever of second order

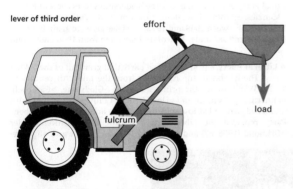

lever of third order

lever In a first-order lever the fulcrum lies between the load and the effort (as in a pair of scissors). In a second-order lever the load falls between the fulcrum and the effort (as in a wheelbarrow). In a third order lever the effort lies between the fulcrum and the load (as in a mechanical digger).

● **Lewis, Carl** ▶ (Frederick Carleton L.; 1961–) Black US athlete, who won four gold medals (long jump, 100 m, 200 m, 4 × 100 m relay) at the 1984 Olympics, equalling Jesse ▷Owens' 1936 performance. In the 1988 Olympics he won a gold medal in the 100 m; in 1991 he won the 100 m world title for the third time, in a record 9.86 seconds.

● **Lewis, C(live) S(taples)** ▶ (1898–1963) British scholar and writer. He taught at Oxford University from 1925 to 1954 and was professor of medieval and Renaissance English at Cambridge from 1954 to 1963. He wrote science fiction including *Out of the Silent Planet* (1938), a series of children's books chronicling the land of Narnia, be-

ginning with *The Lion, the Witch, and the Wardrobe* (1950), and works on religious themes, notably *The Screwtape Letters* (1942) and *A Grief Observed* (1961), which describes his experience of bereavement.

● **Lewis, Denise** ▶ (1977–) British heptathlete. She won Commonwealth titles in 1994 and 1999, the European title in 1998, and came second in the World Championships in 1997 and 1999. She won the bronze medal in the 1996 Olympics and the gold at Sydney in 2000.

● **Lewis, Gilbert Newton** ▶ (1875–1946) US physical chemist. After studying at the University of Nebraska and at Harvard, he spent a period working at Göttingen and Leipzig before returning to teach at Harvard, the Massachusetts Institute of Technology, and the University of California, where he was appointed professor. He introduced the concept of covalent bonds (*see* chemical bond) in 1916 as part of his more general octet theory, published in *Valence and the Structure of Atoms and Molecules* (1923). He is also known for his theory of ▷acids and bases in which he extended the theory of Brønsted and Lowry to include the concepts of the **Lewis acid**, which can accept a pair of electrons, and the **Lewis base**, which can donate such a pair.

● **Lewis, Lennox** ▶ (1965–) British heavyweight boxer. He held the World Boxing Championship title in 1993–94 and regained it in 1997. In 2000 he successfully challenged Evander Holyfield for the World Boxing Association and International Boxing Federation titles, thereby becoming undisputed world champion.

● **Lewis, Matthew Gregory** ▶ (1775–1818) British novelist, known as Monk Lewis. His major work is the gothic novel *The Monk* (1796), written while he was a diplomat in Germany. In 1817 he visited his inherited estates in Jamaica and died on the return voyage.

● **Lewis, (Harry) Sinclair** ▶ (1885–1951) US novelist. He made his reputation with *Main Street* (1920), a satire on provincial materialism. His social satires include *Babbitt* (1922), portraying a well-meaning but dehumanized businessman, *Arrowsmith* (1925), and *Elmer Gantry* (1927). He was the first US writer to win the Nobel Prize (1930).

● **Lewis, (Percy) Wyndham** ▶ (1882–1957) British novelist and painter. After studying art in London and Paris, he helped found ▷vorticism, the manifestos of which were published in *Blast*, a journal he cofounded with Ezra Pound in 1914. In his polemical works and satirical novels, which include *The Apes of God* (1930) and the trilogy *The Human Age* (1928–55), he attacked the liberal establishment.

● **Lewis and Clark expedition** ▶ (1804–06) A journey of exploration across the American continent by Meriwether Lewis (1774–1809) and William Clark (1770–1838). They ascended the Missouri, crossed the Rockies, and went down the Columbia River to the Pacific, exploring the Yellowstone River on the return journey. The expedition established the US claim to the Louisiana Purchase.

● **Lewisham** ▶ A borough of SE Greater London, created in 1965 from the former metropolitan boroughs of Deptford and Lewisham. It includes part of ▷Blackheath. Area: 35 sq km (13 sq mi). Population (1999 est): 230 983.

● **lewisite** ▶ (*or* chlorovinyl dichloroarsine; $ClCH:CHAsCl_2$) A colourless volatile liquid that causes blistering of the skin and is used as a war gas. It can be destroyed by oxidizing agents such as ▷bleaching powder. Named after the US chemist W. L. Lewis (1878–1943).

● **Lewis with Harris** ▶ The largest island of the Outer Hebrides, separated from the coast of NW Scotland by the Minch. Often referred to as separate islands, Lewis in the N is linked with Harris by a narrow isthmus; its most northerly point is the Butt of Lewis. In 1998 a £6.4m-road bridge was opened linking Harris to the small island of Scalpay. The main occupations are crofting, sheep farming, fishing, and weaving of Harris tweed. Area: 2134 sq km (824 sq mi). Population (latest est): 23 510. Chief town: Stornoway.

● **lexicography** ▶ The compilation of dictionaries. Dictionaries can be monolingual (dealing with only one language) or bi- or multilingual (giving equivalents of words in other languages). Both were known in antiquity. Monolingual dictionaries differ in the style and fullness of the definitions, in the audience for which they are intended (e.g. for native speakers or foreign learners), and the principles on which they are compiled. Some are on historical principles (listing definitions of a word in historical order) while others take the language as it is at the time of compilation (listing definitions in order of current usage). Some dictionaries are prescriptive in that they set out to tell the user how the language should be used; most modern dictionaries are only descriptive, recording without comment the way words are currently used. Almost all contain information about spelling and meaning; many also offer guidance on pronunciation, usage, inflected forms, ▷etymology, etc.

The earliest English dictionary was *A Table Alphabeticall of Hard Words* (1604) by Robert Cawdrey; the most famous are Samuel ▷Johnson's *Dictionary* (1755) and the *Oxford English Dictionary on Historical Principles* (1884–1928; chief editor Sir James ▷Murray). Both the latter works contain illustrative quotations. The best-known American dictionary is Noah ▷Webster's *American Dictionary of the English Language* (1828). Both the Oxford and Webster's have several updated and shortened modern versions; a second edition of the *Oxford English Dictionary* was published in 1989.

● **Lexington** ▶ 38 02N 84 37W A city in the USA, in Kentucky. A major horse-breeding centre, Lexington is the market and distribution centre for E Kentucky's farm produce, oil, and coal. The University of Kentucky was established here in 1865. Population (1996 est): 239 942.

● **Lexington and Concord, Battle of** ▶ (19 April, 1775) The first battle in the ▷American Revolution. British troops intending to destroy American stores were attacked at Lexington, Massachusetts, by militiamen alerted by Paul ▷Revere. Going on to Concord they destroyed the stores but were then forced to retreat to Boston.

● **Leyden** ▷*See* Leiden.

● **Leyden jar** ▶ An early form of ▷capacitor, consisting of a glass jar coated with tinfoil on part of its inner and outer surfaces. Named after Leiden (*or* Leyden), the town in the Netherlands in which it was invented.

● **Leyland** ▶ 53 42N 2 42W A town in NW England, in Lancashire. The future of its commercial motor vehicle industry is uncertain. Population (1991): 37 331.

● **Leyte Gulf, Battle of** ▶ (23–26 October, 1944) The battle in World War II in which a US armada of 250 000 men defeated almost the entire Japanese navy. It initiated the reconquest of the Philippines and US command of the Pacific.

● **Lhasa** ▶ 29 41N 91 10E A city in W China, the capital of Tibet. As the traditional centre of ▷Tibetan Buddhism, it has many temples, monasteries, and the Potala, formerly a residence of the ▷Dalai Lama. A trading centre, it has traditional handicrafts and light industry.

History: the Tibetan capital since 1642, it was closed to foreigners in the 19th century. Before the Chinese occupation (1951) monks comprised half the population. There were several riots against the Chinese in the late 1980s. Population (1990): 106 885.

● **liana** ▶ A long-stemmed perennial plant that is supported by trees and bushes, over which it climbs or scrambles. Lianas are prolific in tropical forests, where they climb to the tops of the tallest trees in

order to obtain maximum light at canopy level: their woody stems can reach a length of 70 m. In temperate regions lianas include ▷*Clematis* (e.g. traveller's joy) and ▷honeysuckle.

● **Liaodong Peninsula** ▶ (*or* Liaotung Peninsula) A mountainous peninsula in NE China, in Liaoning province. After rivalry with Russia (1895–1905; *see* Sino-Japanese War; Russo-Japanese War) Japan occupied its S harbours (1905–45).

● **Liaoning** ▶ A province in NE China, on the Yellow Sea in S Manchuria. The Japanese controlled it (1905–45) and developed its industry. Rich in coal and iron, it is one of China's main industrial areas. Area: 150 000 sq km (58 500 sq mi). Population (1997 est): 41 380 000. Capital: Shenyang.

● **Liaoyang** ▶ 41 16N 123 12E A city in NE China, in Liaoning province, one of the oldest Chinese settlements in Manchuria. Industries include food processing, textiles, and engineering. Population (1990): 492 559.

● **Libau** ▷*See* Liepaja.

● **Libby, Willard Frank** ▶ (1908–80) US chemist, who was awarded the Nobel Prize in 1960 for his discovery of ▷radiocarbon dating. He also perfected a similar technique in which water is dated from its tritium content.

● **libel** ▷*See* defamation.

● **Liberal Democrats** ▶ A British political party of the centre, established (as the Social and Liberal Democrats) in 1988 when most of the ▷Social Democratic Party merged with the ▷Liberal Party. Members elected Paddy ▷Ashdown as their first leader. The current name was adopted in 1989. The party advocates ▷proportional representation and closer integration into the EU. From 1997 the Liberal Democrats had an influence on government policy, with senior figures sitting on some cabinet committees. Ashdown retired as party leader in 1999 and was succeeded by Charles ▷Kennedy. In 2001 the Liberals gained their best general election result since the 1920s.

● **Liberal Judaism** ▷*See* Reform Judaism.

● **Liberal Party** ▶ (Australia) A conservative political party, formed in 1944 from the United Australia Party after its defeat in the 1943 election. A coalition of the Liberals and the Country Party (*see* National Party, Australian) under the leadership successively of Robert ▷Menzies, Harold ▷Holt, John ▷Gorton, and William ▷McMahon held office between 1949 and 1972. The Liberals were again in power from 1975 to 1983 under Malcolm ▷Fraser and from 1996 under John ▷Howard.

● **Liberal Party** ▶ (UK) A political party that grew out of the ▷Whig party. The heyday of the party was from the mid-19th century to World War I, under the prime ministers ▷Gladstone, ▷Campbell-Bannerman, ▷Asquith, and ▷Lloyd George. Conflict between Asquith and Lloyd George led to a split in the party and in 1922 the Labour Party replaced the Liberals as the official opposition. Under ▷Grimond (1956–67) and ▷Thorpe (1967–76) there was a slight re-

Lhasa ▶ The imposing Potala palace, former winter residence of the Dalai Lama, stands on a hill crest some 3650 m (12 000 ft) above sea level. The Dalai Lama's summer residence, also in Lhasa, is now a People's Park.

vival. Under David ▷Steel, the party agreed to support the Labour government in return for consultation (the Lib-Lab Pact; 1977–78) and in 1981 formed the Liberal-SDP Alliance with the Social Democratic Party. In 1988 the Liberals merged with the SDP to form the Social and Liberal Democrats, now known as the ▷Liberal Democrats.

● **liberation theology** ► A Christian theological movement introduced by Gustavo Gutierres of Peru in his book *The Theology of Liberation* (1969). Popular among Roman Catholics in developing countries, especially in South America, it insists that the Church must take an active role in the struggle against poverty and oppression, which are seen in essentially Marxist terms. Liberation theologians have often shown sympathy for revolutionary movements, leading to public criticism from Church leaders, including Pope John Paul II.

● **Liberec** ► (German name: Reichenberg) 50 48N 15 05E A town in the N Czech Republic, on the River Neisse. In 1938 it was a centre of the Sudeten-German movement. Population (1996 est): 100 604.

● **Liberia, Republic of** ► A country in West Africa, on the Atlantic Ocean. Coastal plains rise to higher ground inland and to mountains in the N; much of the land is covered with tropical rainforest. Most of the population belongs to indigenous tribes, including the Kpelle, Bassa, and Kru, with a minority descended from American slaves.

Economy: the main food crops are rice and cassava. The 1980s saw efforts to increase rice production and large-scale development in the sugar industry with aid from China. However, since the outbreak of civil war in 1990 agriculture has declined to subsistence levels and almost all forms of economic activity have been suspended. The main cash crop was rubber, some of it grown under concession to US companies. Foreign investment included the exploitation of Liberia's mineral resources, which previously formed the basis of the country's economy, especially high-grade iron ore and diamonds. These, together with rubber and timber, were the main exports. Ships are easily registered in Liberia and, with many foreign vessels, its merchant fleet is the largest in the world.

History: it was founded in 1822 by the American Colonization Society as a settlement for freed American slaves. In 1847 it became the Free and Independent Republic of Liberia with a constitution based on that of the USA. It has had considerable US aid. Liberia has close economic ties with Sierra Leone. William V. S. Tubman (1895–1971) was president from 1944 until 1971. In 1980 his successor, Dr William R. Tolbert, Jr (1913–80), was assassinated in a military coup led by Master Sergeant Samuel Doe, who won a general election in 1985. After months of civil war in 1990, rival rebel forces—under Charles Taylor and Prince Yormie Johnson—seized Monrovia and killed Doe. Although an interim government was set up, several ceasefire agreements failed and fighting continued. In 1995 a peace accord was signed by the six main factions and a transitional government was formed. However, savage fighting broke out again in 1996; in September Ruth Perry became head of state as part of a new peace plan. Charles Taylor was elected president in 1997. Attempts to arrest the cabinet minister and former factional leader Roosevelt Johnson, for allegedly plotting a coup, led to violent clashes in September 1998; Johnson fled abroad but was indicted for treason.

Republic of Liberia

Head of state	President Charles Taylor
Official language	English
Official currency	Liberian dollar of 100 cents
Area	111 400 sq km (43 000 sq mi)
Population (1999 est)	2 924 000
Capital and main port	Monrovia

● **Liberty Bell** ► A large bell (weighing nearly 1 tonne and measuring 3.7 m round the lip) traditionally regarded as a symbol of US liberty. Bearing the inscription "Proclaim liberty throughout all the land unto all the inhabitants thereof" (Leviticus 25.10), it was hung in the State House steeple in Philadelphia in 1753. It was first rung on 8 July, 1776 to celebrate the first public reading of the Declaration of Independence. It was rung for the last time in 1846 to commemorate the anniversary of the birth of George Washington, when it cracked irreparably. In 1976 the Liberty Bell was moved to a new pavilion close to Independence Hall in Philadelphia.

● **Libeskind, Daniel** ► (1946–   ) Polish-born US architect, who established a practice in Berlin in 1989. His buildings include the highly praised Jewish Museum in Berlin (1999) and the Imperial War Museum in Manchester (2000). His proposed extension (1998) to the Victoria and Albert Museum, London, in the form of a glass "spiral," has caused controversy.

● **libido** ► The sexual drive. In ▷psychoanalysis the libido (like the death instinct) is a fundamental source of energy for all mental life, and changes in psychosexual development are responsible for many distortions of the adult personality.

● **Li Bo** ▷*See* Li Po.

● **Libra** ► (Latin: Scales) A constellation in the S sky, lying on the ▷zodiac between Scorpius and Virgo. The brightest star is of 2nd magnitude.

● **library** ► A collection of books, sound recordings, films and videos, photographs, etc., organized for private or public consultation or borrowing. In ancient Mesopotamia libraries were offshoots of royal archives (*see* Nineveh). Aristotle's teaching library at his ▷Lyceum inspired the Ptolemaic rulers of Egypt to found a library at Alexandria that became the cultural centre of Hellenism. Sizable private libraries were assembled by Roman scholars, such as ▷Cicero, and Roman and Byzantine emperors founded large public libraries. With the growth of Christian literature it became customary to attach libraries to churches. Monastic libraries grew from the daily study of religious treatises, especially among the ▷Benedictines. Late medieval and Renaissance nonecclesiastical collections formed the basis of many great libraries, such as the ▷Bodleian, the Vatican (present building opened in 1571), the ▷Bibliothèque Nationale, the ▷British Library, and the US ▷Library of Congress.

The explosion in the numbers of items held by libraries has placed increasing demands on **library science**, a discipline concerned chiefly with the acquisition, classification, and cataloguing of items in a library. The acquisition of materials is dictated by a library's selection policy, which is influenced by its budget, storage space, and readers' requirements. The systems of classification of materials into subject fields that are most widely used today are the ▷Universal Decimal Classification, based on the ▷Dewey Decimal Classification. and the Library of Congress system. Catalogues of holdings generally consist of an alphabetized author catalogue and a subject catalogue. The practice of printing catalogues, with regularly issued supplements, was complemented in the late 19th century by card catalogues, which facilitate the incorporation of new items. More recent developments include the use of ▷microcopy systems for recording holdings and of automatic ▷data processing, which aids the centralization on a regional, national, or international scale of library information. Centralization demands standardization and all publications are now identified by an International Standard Book Number (ISBN) or an International Standard Serial Number (ISSN).

Formal training for librarians was pioneered by the American Library Association (founded 1876). The sister organization in the UK (founded 1877) campaigned for the first school of librarianship, established within London University in 1917. Technical and other specialist libraries have their own association, ASLIB (Association of Special Libraries and Information Bureaux), formed in 1925. The International Library Committee was set up in 1927 to try to achieve internationally accepted conventions in such matters as the transliteration of Cyrillic characters into the Roman alphabet, and UNESCO has a division concerned with libraries.

● **Library of Congress** ► The national library of the USA founded in 1800. First housed in the Capitol, it was moved to its present site in Washington in 1897. It contains over 60 million items, and its system of classification is widely used elsewhere.

● **libretto** ► (Italian: little book) The text of an opera or operetta. The most notable early librettists were the Italians Apostolo Zeno (1668–1750) and Pietro Metastasio (1698–1782), whose elevated style eventually provoked a reaction in favour of greater realism. Dramatists whose plays have been used as libretti include von ▷Hofmannsthal, ▷Maeterlinck, and Oscar ▷Wilde. ▷Wagner, ▷Berlioz, and ▷Tippett wrote their own libretti. Notable partnerships between librettists and composers include Calzabigi (1714–95) and

Gluck, da Ponte (1749–1838) and Mozart, Boito and Verdi, and Gilbert and Sullivan.

● **Libreville** ▶ 0 25N 9 25E The capital of Gabon, a port in the NW on the Gabon Estuary. It was founded by the French in the 19th century, when freed slaves were sent there. The National University was established in 1970. Population (1993): 362 386.

● **Librium** ▷*See* benzodiazepines.

● **Libya** ▶ (official name: Great Socialist People's Libyan Arab Republic) A country in N Africa, on the Mediterranean Sea. It consists chiefly of desert, with a narrow coastal plain, rising to the Tibesti Mountains along its southern border and is divided into the three main areas (provinces until 1963) of Cyrenaica, Tripolitania, and Fezzan. The population is mainly of Berber and Arabic origin.

Economy: between 1955 and 1970 considerable prospecting for oil took place during which time major deposits were discovered, notably at Zelten (1959). Libya subsequently became one of the world's major oil producers, with oil constituting about 95% of exports in value; liquefied natural gas was also exported. There is also some oil refining. From 1992 until 1999 all areas of economic activity were affected by UN sanctions; Libya's foreign assets were frozen in 1993. Subsistence agriculture is important, livestock farming of sheep, goats, and cattle being the main agricultural occupation, nomadic in the S. The aridity of the land restricts crop production to the narrow coastal areas and scattered oases; barley, wheat, and olives are grown here and esparto grass in semidesert areas. In 1983 work was begun on a major irrigation programme, involving the creation of a vast man-made river diverting water to the arid S. Manufacturing industry is based largely on traditional crafts.

History: the area was important within the Roman Empire. During the 16th century it came under Turkish domination and in 1912 was annexed by Italy. It was the scene of heavy fighting in World War II; the French occupied Fezzan and the British occupied Cyrenaica and Tripolitania. In 1951 the United Kingdom of Libya was formed from the federation of these three areas and the Emir of Cyrenaica, Mohammed Idris Al-Senussi (1889–1983), became its first king. He was deposed in a coup led by Col Moammar al-▷Gaddafi in 1969 and Libya was proclaimed a republic. The Revolutionary Command Council was established to rule the country. In 1973 Gaddafi introduced a cultural revolution based on Islamic principles. Since 1969 Libya has been firmly aligned against Israel and has been accused of using terrorist methods abroad; in 1986 such terrorist activity prompted punitive bombing raids on Tripoli and Benghazi by US planes. Libya was involved in armed clashes with neighbouring Chad (1982–88). In 1990 Libya signed a treaty of economic and political cooperation with Sudan. In 1992 sanctions were imposed on Libya by the UN when Gaddafi refused to extradite two men suspected of involvement in the ▷Lockerbie disaster. These were suspended in 1999, when Gaddafi agreed to their trial in the Netherlands.

Libya

Head of state	Leader of the Revolution Col Moammar al-Gaddafi
Official language	Arabic; English and Italian are also spoken
Official currency	Libyan dinar of 1000 dirhams
Area	1 759 540 sq km (679 216 sq mi)
Population (1999 est)	4 993 000
Capital	Tripoli

● **licensed premises** ▶ Premises in the UK that are licensed by licensing justices to sell intoxicating liquor (spirits, wine, beer, porter, cider and any other fermented or distilled liquor), either for consumption off the premises (an off licence) or on the premises (on licence). The hours during which these alcoholic drinks may be sold are currently restricted. Since 1988 in the UK they may be sold between 11 am and 11 pm on Mondays to Saturdays and between noon and 3 pm and 7 pm to 10.30 pm on Sundays. These hours can be extended by the grant of a special licence for special occasions. In 2000 the government announced proposals to remove all the remaining restrictions on opening times and to shift the granting of licenses to local authorities.

● **lichee** ▷*See* litchi.

● **lichens** ▶ A large group of organisms (about 15 000 species) consisting of two components, an alga or a bacterium (usually a green alga or blue-green bacterium) and a fungus (usually an ascomycete), in a mutually beneficial association. Millions of algal or bacterial cells (the phycobiont) are interwoven with fungal filaments (the mycobiont) to form the lichen body (a thallus), which may be crusty, scaly, leafy, or stalked and shrublike in appearance. Lichens were formerly regarded as plants; they are now classified as fungi. They occur in almost all areas of the world, mainly on tree trunks, rocks, and soil, and can survive in extremely harsh ·conditions. They normally reproduce asexually by fragmentation, ▷budding, or by producing special structures (soredia), consisting of a few algal or bacterial cells enmeshed with fungal threads. Lichens are an important source of food for browsing animals of tundra regions (*see* reindeer moss) and they are used by humans for food, dyes, medicine, in perfume, and as pollution indicators. ▷*See also* crottle; oak moss; orchil; rock tripe.

● **Lichfield** ▶ 54 42N 1 48W A city in central England, in Staffordshire. Lichfield cathedral (13th–14th centuries) is noted for its three spires. Dr Johnson was born here. Population (1991): 28 666.

● **Lichtenstein, Roy** ▶ (1923–97) A leading US painter of ▷pop art. His one-man show of comic-strip paintings in 1962 pioneered the use of mass-media techniques in noncommercial art. His works include *Whaam* (1963; Tate Gallery).

● **Liddell Hart, Sir Basil Henry** ▶ (1895–1970) British soldier and military theorist. He served throughout World War I and wrote the official manual on infantry training (1920). His advocacy of mechanized warfare and airpower led to his appointment as adviser (1937–38) to the British secretary for war, ▷Hore-Belisha, and is thought to have influenced the German policy of ▷Blitzkrieg in World War II.

● **Lidice** ▶ 50 03N 14 08E A mining village in the Czech Republic. On 10 June, 1942, it was destroyed by the Nazis in revenge for the assassination of Reinhard Heydrich, their local administrator. The 400 inhabitants were either shot or deported to concentration camps. The site is now a memorial garden.

● **Lie, Trygve (Halvdan)** ▶ (1896–1968) Norwegian Labour politician and international civil servant; the first secretary general of the UN (1946–52). At the UN he dealt with the first Arab-Israeli War and the ▷Korean War. Soviet opposition to his Korean policies resulted in his resignation.

● **Liebig, Justus, Baron von** ▶ (1803–73) German chemist; one of the earliest investigators of organic compounds. His work on fulminates (1920) was followed by the development of a technique for measuring the proportion of carbon and hydrogen in a compound by burning it and determining the amount of carbon dioxide and water released (1831). His later work was concerned with biochemistry and agricultural chemistry. His name is also connected with the Liebig condenser, a much used piece of laboratory equipment.

● **Liebknecht, Wilhelm** ▶ (1826–1900) German socialist. He participated in the ▷Revolution of 1848 and was forced to flee Germany, living in Britain, where he worked with Karl Marx. Returning to Germany in 1862, he was expelled from Prussia in 1865 for his activities but in 1867 became a member of the North German Reichstag. His opposition to the Franco-Prussian War (1870–71) brought imprisonment but he subsequently became a leader of what became (1891) the Social Democratic Party. His son **Karl Liebknecht** (1871–1919) was among the few socialists who refused to support the war effort in 1914. In 1915 he helped to found the revolutionary ▷Spartacus League, which he led with Rosa ▷Luxemburg. They were both murdered following the unsuccessful communist revolt of 1919.

● **Liechtenstein, Principality of** ▶ A small country in central Europe, between Switzerland and Austria. Mountains rise from the Rhine Valley to heights of over 2500 m (8000 ft).

Economy: although there is still a considerable amount of farming, the balance of the economy has shifted since World War II to light industry and technology; the main industries are now high-tech engineering, superconductor technology, and textiles. Tourism and the sale of postage stamps are also important sources of revenue.

History: the principality was formed from the union of the counties of Vaduz and Schellenberg in 1719 and was part of the Holy Roman Empire until 1806. It formed a customs union with Switzerland in 1923 and joined EFTA in 1991 and the European Economic Area in 1995. Until 1984 women were banned from voting in national elections.

Principality of Liechtenstein

Head of state	Prince Hans Adam II
Official language	German
Official religion	Roman Catholic
Official currency	Swiss franc of 100 centimes (or rappen)
Area	160 sq km (62 sq mi)
Population (1999 est)	31 700
Capital	Vaduz

● **lie detector** ▷*See* polygraph.

● **Liège** ▶ (Flemish name: Luik) 50 38N 5 35E A city in E Belgium, on the River Meuse. It has many old churches, including St Martin's (692 AD). Its university was founded in 1817. The centre of a former coal-mining area, its industries include the manufacture of armaments, iron, textiles, and paper. Population (1996 est): 190 525.

● **Liegnitz** ▷*See* Legnica.

● **Liepaja** ▶ (German name: Libau) 56 30N 21 00E A port in W Latvia, on the Baltic Sea. It was founded by the Teutonic Knights (1263), passing to Russia in 1795. The independent Latvian Government met here in 1918. A naval base, it has shipbuilding and metallurgy industries. Population (1995 est): 100 271.

● **Lif and Lifthrasir** ▶ In Norse mythology, a man and woman destined to sleep during the destruction of the world (*see* Ragnarök), awaking afterwards to found a new race.

● **Lifar, Serge** ▶ (1905–86) Russian ballet dancer and choreographer. He joined Diaghilev's Ballets Russes in 1923 and from 1932 to 1958 was ballet master at the Paris Opéra Ballet, which he revitalized with his experimental choreography. His ballets include *Prométhée* (1929), *Icare* (1935), and *Phèdre* (1950).

● **life** ▶ The property that enables a living organism to assimilate nonliving materials from its environment and use them to increase its size and complexity (the process of growth), to repair its existing tissues, and to produce new independent organisms that also possess the properties of life (the process of reproduction). ▷*See also* animal; plant.

Life on earth is thought to have originated between 4500 and 3000 million years ago. The atmosphere then consisted chiefly of methane, hydrogen, ammonia, and water vapour, from which simple organic molecules (such as amino acids, proteins, and fatty acids) were formed as a result of energy supplied by solar radiation, lightning, and volcanic activity. The first "cells" may have arisen spontaneously as complexes of protein molecules surrounded by envelopes of lipid molecules, which functioned as a cell ▷membrane. However, the crucial steps towards life would probably have been the inclusion in a cell of both the enzyme molecules necessary to perform primitive fermentations and the nucleic acid molecules, such as RNA and DNA, capable of directing the metabolic processes of the cell and of self replication, i.e. passing on this information to succeeding generations. These early cells are thought to have arisen in the sea, deriving their energy from the fermentation of simple organic molecules. In time increasingly efficient biochemical pathways evolved, including the process of trapping light energy in cellular pigments, enabling blue-green bacteria—followed by algae and plants—to develop the process of photosynthesis. This led to the gradual build-up of oxygen in the atmosphere, which started about 2000 million years ago; by about 400 million years ago the ▷ozone layer in the upper atmosphere was sufficiently dense to shield the land from harmful ultraviolet radiation, enabling plants and animals to survive. With increasing oxygen levels, aerobic respiration—the most efficient method of energy utilization—was adopted by most living organisms.

The factors involved in the origination of life on earth have prompted a search for similar conditions on other planets and in other solar systems, but so far no evidence of life elsewhere has been discovered. *See* astrobiology.

● **lifeboat** ▶ **1.** In the UK, a powerful motorboat, especially designed to right itself in the event of capsize and equipped with safety devices, used by the ▷Royal National Lifeboat Institution (RNLI) as an emergency vessel in the event of a disaster near the shore. **2.** A boat carried aboard a ship, used by passengers and crew if the ship has to be abandoned.

● **life cycle** ▶ The progressive series of stages through which a species of organism passes from its ▷fertilization or production by asexual means to the same stage in the next generation. The simplest life cycles occur by asexual ▷reproduction, producing offspring similar to the parent. Life cycles involving sexual reproduction are much more complex and the young do not necessarily resemble the adults: marine crustaceans, for example, pass through several different larval stages before becoming adult. In many plants and algae and some animals there is a succession of individuals showing an alternation of sexual and asexual reproduction before completing the cycle (*see* alternation of generations).

● **life expectancy** ▶ The average number of years a person born in a particular year might expect to live, assuming the mortality rate in that year continues unchanged. In the UK, life expectancy at birth has increased from 48 years for men (51.6 for women) in 1906 to 75 for men (80 for women) in 1995 as a result of great improvements in health care and education, housing, nutrition, and sanitation. In the developed countries there is little variation in these figures. In less developed countries, however, the position is quite different; for example in 1995 in Africa life expectancy was 52 (55 for women). In almost all countries women outlive men by 5–7 years; Afghanistan, Nepal, and Bangladesh are exceptions with figures of about 52 for men and two years less for women (possibly due to poor maternity care).

The average life expectancy in different parts of the world for those born in 1995

country	males	females
UK	75	80
EU	74	81
Eastern Europe	62	73
USA	73	80
Canada	76	82
Africa	52	55
China	68	72
Australia	75	81
Latin America	66	73
Asia	65	68

● **Liffey, River** ▶ A river in the E Republic of Ireland, rising in the Wicklow Mountains and flowing mainly W and NE through Dublin to Dublin Bay. Length: 80 km (50 mi).

● **ligament** ▶ A strong fibrous tissue that joins one bone to another at a ▷joint. Ligaments are flexible but inelastic: they increase the stability of the joint and limit its movements to certain directions. Unusual stresses on a joint often damage ("pull") a ligament, as occurs in a "twisted" ankle.

● **ligature** ▶ Any material, such as silk, gut, cotton, or wire, used to tie a blood vessel (to stop bleeding) or the base of a tumour (to constrict it). They are widely used in surgery.

● **liger** ▷*See* tigon.

● **Ligeti, György** ▶ (1923–) Hungarian composer. He worked in Cologne (1957–58) and settled in Vienna. His compositions are largely experimental and include *Volumina* (1961–62) for organ, a Requiem (1963–65), *Continuum* (1968) for harpsichord, and *Melodien* (1971) for orchestra.

● **light** ▶ The form of ▷electromagnetic radiation to which the eye is sensitive. It forms the part of the electromagnetic spectrum from 740 nanometres (red light) to 400 nanometres (blue light), white light consisting of a mixture of all the colours of the visible spectrum. The nature of light has been in dispute from earliest times, ▷Newton supporting a corpuscular theory in which a luminous body was believed to emit particles of light. This theory adequately explained reflection and geometric optics but failed to explain ▷interference and ▷polarized light. The wave theory, supported in the 19th century by ▷Fresnel and ▷Foucault, adequately explains these phenomena and achieved a mathematical basis when James Clerk ▷Maxwell showed that light is a form of electromagnetic radiation. The wave theory, however, does not explain the ▷photoelectric effect and ▷Einstein reverted to a form of the corpuscular theory in using the ▷quantum theory to postulate that in some cases light is best regarded as consisting of energy quanta called photons. The present view, expressing ▷Bohr's concept of complementarity, is that both electromagnetic theory and quantum theory are needed to explain this phenomenon. Light travels at a speed of $2.997\,925 \times 10^8$ m per second in free space. The **speed of light** is, according to the special ▷relativity, the highest attainable speed in the universe.

● **light-emitting diode** ▷See semiconductor diode.

● **lighthouse** ▶ A tall structure, built on a coastal promontory or cape or on an island at sea, equipped with a powerful beacon, visible at some distance, to mark an obstruction or other hazard. Modern lighthouses are also equipped with radio beacons. Both light and radio signals are emitted in a unique pattern to enable vessels to identify the lighthouse.

● **lightning** ▶ An electrical discharge in the atmosphere caused by the build up of electrical charges in a cloud by such methods as friction between the particles in the cloud. The potential difference causing the discharge may be as high as one thousand million volts. The electricity then discharges itself in a lightning flash, which may be between the cloud and the ground or, much more commonly, between two clouds or parts of a cloud. Thunder is the noise made by the discharge. ▷See also ball lightning; thunderstorm.

● **lightning conductor** ▶ An earthed conducting rod placed at the top of buildings, etc., to protect them from damage by lightning. It acts by providing a low-resistance path to earth for the lightning current.

● **lightship** ▶ A vessel, anchored at sea, used as a lighthouse. Once in wide use most lightships have now been replaced by fixed structures or, because of advances in sophisticated navigation devices, have been eliminated entirely.

● **light year** ▶ A unit of distance, used in astronomy, equal to the distance travelled by light in one year. 1 light year = 9.46×10^{15} metres or 5.88×10^{12} miles.

● **lignin** ▶ A complex chemical deposited in plant cell walls to add extra strength and support. It is the main constituent of ▷wood cells, allowing the trunk to support the heavy crown of leaves and branches.

● **lignite** ▷See coal.

● **lignum vitae** ▶ Wood from trees of the genus *Guaiacum*, especially *G. officinale*, a tropical evergreen of the New World. Lignum vitae is hard, dense, greenish-brown, and rich in fat (making it waterproof). It is used for shafts, pulleys, and bowling balls. Lignum vitae was formerly thought to have medicinal properties: its name (from the Latin) means "wood of life." Family: *Zygophyllaceae*.

● **Liguria** ▶ A region in NW Italy. It consists of a narrow strip of land between the Apennines and Maritime Alps in the N and the Gulf of Genoa in the S. It is an important industrial region, concentrating on engineering, shipbuilding, metals, petroleum products, and chemicals. Tourism is a major source of revenue, the region more or less corresponding to the Italian Riviera. Agricultural products include vegetables, olives, and flowers. Area: 5415 sq km (2091 sq mi). Population (1994 est): 1 662 658. Capital: Genoa.

● **Ligurian Sea** ▶ A section of the NW Mediterranean Sea, between Italy (N of Elba) and Corsica.

● **Li Hong Zhang** ▶ (*or* Li Hung-chang; 1823–1901) Chinese soldier and statesman of the ▷Qing dynasty. His armies helped suppress the ▷Taiping Rebellion in 1864 and, as the trusted adviser of the empress ▷Zi Xi, he encouraged commerce and industry, attempting to introduce modernizing projects, and conducted China's foreign affairs. He amassed a huge personal fortune.

● **Likasi** ▶ (name until 1966: Jadotville) 10 58S 26 47E A city in SE Democratic Republic of Congo. Founded in 1917, near the site of old copper workings, it is a major mineral-processing centre refining copper and cobalt. Other industries include chemicals and brewing. Population (1994 est): 299 118.

● **lilac** ▶ A deciduous bush or small tree of the genus *Syringa* (30 species), especially *S. vulgaris*, native to temperate Eurasia and often grown as a garden ornamental. It has heart-shaped leaves and dense terminal clusters of white, purple, or pink tubular fragrant flowers with four flaring lobes. The fruit is a leathery capsule. Family: *Oleaceae*.

● **Lilburne, John** ▶ (c. 1614–57) English pamphleteer; leader of the radical Puritan sect called the ▷Levellers. Imprisoned (1638–40) for his Puritan activities, he joined the parliamentarians in the Civil War but resigned from the army in 1645 to organize the Levellers. Between 1645 and 1647 he was mostly in prison; he was twice tried and acquitted for treason (1649, 1653) but a popular demonstration in his favour led to further imprisonment from 1653 until 1655.

● **Liliaceae** ▶ A family of monocotyledonous plants (about 250 species), mostly herbaceous and native to temperate and subtropical regions. They usually grow from bulbs or rhizomes to produce six-lobed flowers and three-chambered capsular fruits. The family includes many popular garden plants, including the lilies, tulip, hyacinth, and lily-of-the-valley. A few are economically important, for example *Asparagus*. This family can include related plants, such as the onion, leek, etc. (*see* Allium), ▷*Agave*, and ▷*Yucca*.

● **Lilienthal, Otto** ▶ (1848–96) German aeronautical engineer, who pioneered the construction of gliders. A student of bird flight, Lilienthal demonstrated the superiority of a curved wing over a flat wing. He made some 2000 flights before being killed in a crash.

● **Lilith** ▶ In Jewish folklore, a female demon, traditionally the first wife of Adam, who refused to recognize his authority over her. An amulet bearing the names of the three angels who tried to persuade her to return to Adam was worn as protection against her evil powers.

● **Liliuokalani** ▶ (1838–1917) The only queen and last sovereign of Hawaii (1891–95). Hawaiian resistance to US attempts to annex the islands led to an insurrection after which she abdicated. She composed the song "Aloha Oe," as a farewell gift to her people.

● **Lille** ▶ 50 39N 3 05E A city in N France, the capital of the Nord department on the River Deûle. The centre of a large industrial and commercial complex, its industries include textiles, machinery, chemicals, distilling, and brewing. Notable buildings include the citadel (built by Vauban) and the university (1887).
  History: following a prosperous period under the Dukes of Burgundy (14th century), Lille later passed to Austria and then Spain before returning to France in 1668, and was badly damaged in both World Wars. Gen de Gaulle was born here. Population (1990): 178 301.

● **Lillie, Beatrice** ▶ (Constance Sylvia Munston, Lady Peel; 1898–1989) British actress, born in Canada. The sophisticated comedy of her performances in revues and cabaret was successful in both London and New York. Her films included *Exit Smiling* (1926) and *On Approval* (1943).

● **Lilongwe** ▶ 13 58S 33 49E The capital of Malawi. It replaced Zomba as the capital in 1975. Tobacco production is important. Population (1994 est): 395 500.

● **lily** ▶ A perennial herbaceous plant of the genus *Lilium* (80–100 species), native to N temperate regions and widely grown for ornament. Lilies grow from bulbs to produce leafy stems with terminal clusters of showy flowers, usually with backward-curving petals. Some popular species are the tiger lily (*L. tigrinum*), from China and

Japan, 60–120 cm high with purple-spotted golden flowers; the Japanese golden ray lily (*L. auratum*), 90–180 cm high, whose white flowers are marked with yellow and crimson; the Eurasian Madonna lily (*L. candida*), 60–120 cm high with pure-white flowers; and the turk's-cap or martagon lily (*L. martagon*), also from Eurasia, 90–150 cm high, with purplish-pink flowers marked with darker spots. Family: ▷*Liliaceae*.

The name is also applied to numerous other unrelated plants, such as the ▷arum lily, ▷day lily, and ▷leopard lily.

● **lily-of-the-valley** ► A fragrant perennial herbaceous plant, *Convallaria majalis*, native to Eurasia and E North America and a popular garden plant. Growing from creeping underground stems (rhizomes), it has a stem, 13–20 cm long, bearing a cluster of white nodding bell-shaped flowers. Family: ▷*Liliaceae*.

● **Lima** ► 12 06S 77 03W The capital of Peru, situated in the E of the country near its Pacific port of Callao. Founded by Pizarro in 1535, it became the main base of Spanish power in Peru. Notable buildings include the 16th-century cathedral and the National University of San Marcos (1551). Lima has considerable industry; the main manufactures include motor vehicles, textiles, paper, paint, and food products. Approximately one-third of the population live in the shantytown settlements around the city. Population (1995): 421 570.

● **Lima bean** ► A herb, *Phaseolus lunatus*, also called butter bean or Madagascar bean, native to South America but widely cultivated in the tropics and subtropics as a source of protein. It is easily stored when dry. Family: ▷*Leguminosae*.

● **Limassol** ► (Modern Greek name: Lemesós; Turkish name: Limasol) 34 40N 33 03E A town in Cyprus, on the S coast. It is the island's second largest town and a major port, exporting notably wine and fruit. Population (1994 est): 143 400.

● **Limavady** ► A district in Northern Ireland, in Co Londonderry. Area: 585 sq km (226 sq mi). Population (1991): 29 700.

● **limbo** ► In medieval Christian theology, the state of existence of souls that merit neither heavenly bliss nor the torments of hell after death. The two categories of soul destined for limbo were unbaptized babies and the patriarchs and prophets of the Old Testament.

● **Limburg** ► 1. A former duchy in W Europe, divided in 1839 between Belgium and the Netherlands. 2. (French name: Limbourg) A province in NE Belgium, bordering on the Netherlands. In the N, the Kempen heath area has industries including chemicals and glass. The S is chiefly agricultural (especially dairy farming). Area: 2422 sq km (935 sq mi). Population (1995 est): 771 613. Capital: Hasselt. 3. A province in the SE Netherlands. Its traditional coalmining industry has declined in recent years. Agriculture is varied producing cereals, fruit, vegetables, and sugar beet; cattle, pigs, and poultry are raised. Area: 2208 sq km (852 sq mi). Population (1995): 1 130 050. Capital: Maastricht.

● **Limburg, de** ► (*or* de Limbourg) A family (active c. 1400–c. 1416) of manuscript illuminators comprising three brothers Pol, Herman, and Jehanequin, born in Nijmegen (Netherlands), the sons of a sculptor. They worked for the Duke of Burgundy (1402–04) and later for the Duke of Berry, for whom they illuminated *Les Très Riches Heures* (Chantilly, France), a fine example of the ▷international gothic style. They influenced the development of Flemish landscape painting.

● **lime** ► (botany) 1. A large deciduous tree of the genus *Tilia* (about 30 species), also called linden. Growing to a height of 30 m, it has toothed heart-shaped leaves and fragrant pale-yellow flowers that hang in small clusters on a long winged stalk. The small round fruits remain attached to the papery wing when shed. Family: *Tiliaceae*. 2. A tree, ▷*Citrus aurantifolia*, growing to a height of about 4 m and cultivated in the tropics for its fruit. Lime fruits are pear-shaped, 4 cm in diameter, with a thick greenish-yellow skin and acid-tasting pulp; the juice is used to flavour food and drinks.

● **lime** ► (chemistry) Calcium oxide (*or* quicklime; CaO), calcium hydroxide (*or* slaked lime; Ca(OH)$_2$), or, loosely, calcium salts in general. Ca(OH)$_2$ is prepared by reacting CaO with water and is used in

▷cement. CaO is used in making paper, as a ▷flux in ▷steel manufacture, and in softening water.

● **Limehouse** ► A district in the Greater London borough of ▷Tower Hamlets on the Thames. Its name comes from the 14th-century lime kilns built here. A centre of shipbuilding in the 18th century, it became known for its Chinese colony from the late 19th century. Some of it is now being gentrified.

● **limerick** ► A short form of comic and usually bawdy verse having five lines of three or two feet and usually rhyming aabba, as in:

> There was a young lady of Lynn
> Who was so uncommonly thin
> That when she essayed
> To drink lemonade,
> She slipped through the straw and fell in.

The form, the origin of which is uncertain, was popularized by Edward ▷Lear in the 19th century and practised by several notable poets, but the best-known limericks are by anonymous authors. The name is said to have originated in the chorus of an Irish soldiers' song, "Will you come up to Limerick?"

● **Limerick** ► (Irish name: Luimneach) 52 40N 8 38W A port in the Republic of Ireland, the county town of Co Limerick on the Shannon estuary. It was besieged by William III (1691). Notable buildings include two cathedrals. Its industries include flour milling, tanning, and brewing. Population (1995 est): 74 900.

de Limburg ► A page from the 15th-century manuscript book *Les Très Riches Heures*, illustrated by the de Limburg brothers in the style known as international gothic. The stylized human figures contrast with the naturalistic depiction of landscape and architecture.

● **Limerick** ► (Irish name: Luimneach) A county in the SW Republic of Ireland, in Munster bordering on the River Shannon estuary. It consists chiefly of lowlands rising to hills in the S. Lying mainly in the fertile Golden Vale, it is important for dairy farming. Area: 2686 sq km (1037 sq mi). Population (1996 est): 165 000. County town: Limerick.

● **limestone** ► A common sedimentary rock consisting largely of carbonates, especially calcium carbonate (calcite) or dolomite. Most limestones were deposited in the sea in warm clear water, but some limestones were formed in fresh water. Organic limestones, including ▷chalk, consist of fossil skeletal material. Precipitated limestones include evaporites and ▷oolites (spherically grained calcite). Clastic limestones consist of fragments of pre-existing limestones. Marble is metamorphosed limestone. Limestone is used as a building stone, in the manufacture of cement and glass, for agricultural lime, for road metal, and as a flux in smelting.

● **limitation, statutes of** ► The Acts of Parliament that specify a time (period of limitation) within which legal proceedings must be started by any person seeking to enforce a right; failing this, the right of action is barred. If the specified time has passed, some rights, such as those over land, cease to exist, whereas others, for example the right to receive payment of a debt, continue for all purposes, except that there is no right to enforce them by legal action. Proceedings must be started within six years to recover debts on simple ▷contracts and in most civil wrongs (torts).

● **limited liability** ► The restriction of a shareholder's obligation to meet company debts in the event of its ▷insolvency. In the UK those who engaged in business ventures before 1855 (when the concept was introduced) risked losing all their personal property. The ▷Companies Act allows the formation of corporations the liability of whose shareholders is restricted either to the nominal amount of their shares ("company limited by shares") or to the amount that they have respectively undertaken to contribute if the company is wound up ("company limited by guarantee").

● **Limoges** ► 45 50N 1 15E A city in W France, the capital of the Haute-Vienne department on the River Vienne. The centre of the French porcelain industry, Limoges has Roman remains, a cathedral (13th–16th centuries), and a university (1808). It is the birthplace of Pierre Auguste Renoir. Population (1990): 175 646.

● **limonite** ► A naturally occurring mixture of hydrated iron oxides and iron hydroxides, both amorphous and cryptocrystalline, derived from the weathering of minerals containing iron. It ranges in colour from yellow to brown to black and occurs in bog iron ore, in gossan, and in ▷laterite.

● **Limosin, Léonard** ► (or Limousin; c. 1505–c. 1577) French artist, born in Limoges. As court painter to Francis I and later Henry II he was popular chiefly for his enamel portraits, although he also painted plates, vases, etc., and worked in oils.

● **Limousin** ► A planning region and former province in central France, on the W Massif Central. It was in the possession of the English from 1152 until 1369. Area: 16 932 sq km (6536 sq mi). Population (1995 est): 723 000.

● **limpet** ► A marine ▷gastropod mollusc with a flattened shell and powerful muscular foot for clinging to rocks and other surfaces. The true limpets (superfamily *Patellacea*; about 400 species) are oval-shaped and up to 10 cm long whereas the keyhole limpets (superfamily *Fissurellacea*; several hundred species) have an opening in the shell for expelling wastes and tend to be smaller.

● **limpkin** ► A wading bird, *Aramus guarauna*, the sole representative of its family (*Aramidae*), that inhabits tropical American marshes and swamps. Resembling a rail, it is 50–76 cm long, has a dark brown plumage with white markings, and feeds largely on water snails, often at night. Order: *Gruiformes* (cranes, rails, etc.).

● **Limpopo River** ► A river in SE Africa. Rising as the Crocodile River in the Witwatersrand, South Africa, it flows generally NE through Mozambique, to the Indian Ocean, forming part of the border between South Africa and Botswana. Length: 1770 km (1100 mi).

● **linac** ▷See linear accelerator.

● **Linacre, Thomas** ► (c. 1460–1524) English physician and humanist, who (in 1518) founded the Royal College of Physicians in London. This was intended to control the practice of medicine by introducing a system of examining and licensing would-be physicians. Linacre translated the works of ▷Galen from Greek to Latin and taught at Oxford, where his pupils included Erasmus and Sir Thomas More.

● **Lin Biao** ► (or Lin Piao; 1908–71) Chinese communist soldier and statesman. Lin received military training under ▷Chiang Kai-shek at the Whampoa Military Academy. He became a Guomindang (Nationalist People's Party) colonel but led his regiment to join the communist uprising in Nanchang. He became commander of the First Red Army Corps and played a major part in the communist victory against the Guomindang (1949). In 1959 he became defence minister and in 1969, vice chairman of the Chinese Communist Party. Lin seemed destined to become Mao Tse-tung's successor but he was killed in a mysterious aircrash in Outer Mongolia, when he may have been attempting to flee China after making an unsuccessful bid for power.

● **Lincoln** ► 53 14N 0 33W A city in E central England, the administrative centre of Lincolnshire on the River Witham. The British settlement became Lindum Colonia under the Romans, at the intersection of the important routeways Fosse Way and Ermine Street. The castle was begun in 1068 and the cathedral, which is mainly 13th century, in 1075. The principal manufactures are machinery, radios, metal goods, vehicle components, and cattle feed. Population (1991): 80 281.

● **Lincoln** ► 40 49N 96 41W A city in the USA, the capital of Nebraska. It is the centre of a region producing grain and livestock. The University of Nebraska was established here in 1869. Population (1996 est): 209 192.

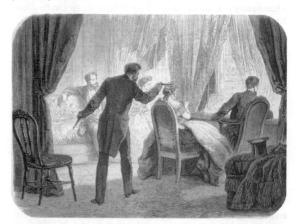

Abraham Lincoln ► The US president being shot by John Wilkes Booth in a box at Ford's Theatre, Washington, DC. Lincoln's wife is sitting next to him. He died the following morning.

● **Lincoln, Abraham** ► (1809–65) US statesman; Republican president (1861–65). A self-educated man, who had been born in a log cabin, Lincoln became a lawyer and, in 1847, member of Congress for Illinois. Holding long-standing convictions against slavery, he opposed its extension to the new western states and in 1856 joined the newly formed antislavery Republican Party. Elected president on the slavery issue just before the outbreak of the ▷Civil War, in 1863 Lincoln proclaimed the freedom of slaves in the South (the Emancipation Proclamation) and gave his famous ▷Gettysburg Address recalling the principles of equality established by America's founding fathers. He oversaw the 13th amendment prohibiting slavery (1865) and advocated magnanimous ▷Reconstruction measures but was assassinated a few days after the South surrendered.

● **Lincolnshire** ► A county in E England, bordering on the North Sea. It is generally low lying, with the Lincolnshire Edge (a limestone escarpment) in the W and the Lincolnshire Wolds in the E. It is mainly agricultural producing arable crops and livestock; horticulture is also important.

History: under Roman occupation drainage of the Fens was attempted. This was achieved in the 17th century, increasing its importance as an agricultural region. Lincolnshire formerly comprised the administrative regions of Lindsey, Holland, and Kesteven. In 1974, under local government reorganization, it lost the N part to Humberside. When Humberside was abolished in 1996, this area was returned to Lincolnshire for ceremonial and related purposes but is now administered by the unitary authorities of ▷North Lincolnshire and ▷North East Lincolnshire. Area (excluding unitary authorites): 5918 sq km (2284 sq mi). Population (1996 est, excluding unitary authorities): 615 900. Administrative centre: Lincoln.

● **Lincoln's Inn** ▷*See* Inns of Court.

● **Lind, Jenny** ▶ (1820–87) Swedish soprano, known as "the Swedish nightingale." Her brilliant career in opera and on the concert platform took her all over Europe and to the USA. She endowed many charities in England and Sweden.

● **Lindbergh, Charles A(ugustus)** ▶ (1902–74) US aviator who made the first solo nonstop flight across the Atlantic, from New York to Paris (1927), in the monoplane *Spirit of St Louis*. After the kidnapping and murder of his two-year-old son in 1932 he and his wife moved to Europe to escape publicity. He advocated US neutrality at the start of World War II but later contributed to the Allied cause. His book *The Spirit of St Louis* (1953) won a Pulitzer Prize.

● **Lindemann, Frederick Alexander, 1st Viscount Cherwell** ▶(1886–1957) German-born British physicist, who became Churchill's scientific adviser in World War II. Criticized for advocating mass bombing of civilians, Lindemann was highly praised by Churchill, who made him paymaster-general (1951–53).

● **linden** ▷*See* lime.

● **Lindisfarne** ▷*See* Holy Island.

● **Lindsay, (Nicholas) Vachel** ▶ (1879–1931) US poet. After failing as a painter he became an itinerant poet, earning his living by reciting his poems. His best-known volumes, *General William Booth Enters into Heaven and Other Poems* (1913) and *The Congo and Other Poems* (1914), show his interest in folklore and his mastery of ballad-like verse.

● **Lindsey, Parts of** ▷*See* Lincolnshire.

● **Linear A** ▶ A syllabic script used (c. 1700–1450 BC) to write the lost language of the ▷Minoan civilization of Crete. It evolved from a pictographic script. Known from fewer than 400 inscriptions, it is still undeciphered, but, like its successor, ▷Linear B, was mainly used on clay tablets to record inventories.

● **linear accelerator** ▶ (*or* linac) An ▷accelerator in which charged elementary particles are repeatedly accelerated along a long straight tube by a radio-frequency electric field. In modern linear accelerators the field is supplied by the electric component of a travelling radio wave in a waveguide. The particles are confined in the tube by a series of magnetic lenses, which focus the beam. The maximum energy attained by a linear accelerator is about 10 GeV for electrons and 2 GeV for protons.

● **Linear B** ▶ A syllabic script apparently adapted (c. 1450–1400 BC) from ▷Linear A by the invading Mycenaeans at ▷Knossos to write their own language (*see* Mycenaean civilization). In 1952 Michael ▷Ventris deciphered this language as an early form of ▷Greek. Several thousand Linear B clay tablets, mainly containing inventories, survive from Knossos, ▷Pylos, and elsewhere, dating between about 1400 and 1100 BC.

● **linear motor** ▶ A form of electric induction motor in which the stator and the rotor are linear instead of cylindrical and parallel instead of coaxial. The development of linear motors as a method of traction for monorail intercity trains has been proposed by E. R. Laithwaite (1921–89). In this arrangement one winding would be in the train and the other on the single rail, thus obviating the need for rotating parts.

● **Line Islands** ▶ A chain of coral atolls in the W central Pacific Ocean. Of the N islands, Palmyra and Jarvis Islands are US territories while Washington, Fanning, and Christmas Islands, the only permanently inhabited ones, form part of Kiribati. Copra is produced.

● **linen** ▶ A fabric manufactured from ▷flax (*Linum usitatissimum*). Probably the first textile of plant origin, specimens 4500 years old have been found in Egyptian tombs. Flax growing was brought to Britain by the Romans and in the 16th century a flourishing trade grew up, especially in Scotland and Northern Ireland. Greatly reduced by the 18th-century expansion of the cotton trade, and even more so by the advent of man-made fibres, these strong absorbent fibres now constitute less than 2% of world fibre production, being reserved for luxury household fabrics and summer garments.

● **line of force** ▷*See* field.

● **ling** ▶ 1. A deep-sea fish, belonging to a genus (*Molva*; 3 species) related to cod, that is cured and dried for food. The common ling (*M. molva*) has a long slim body, up to about 2 m long, mottled brown or green, a long chin barbel, and two dorsal fins. 2. ▷*See* heather.

● **lingua franca** ▶ Any language that is used as a means of communication between speakers with different native languages. It may be a hybrid of other languages, such as ▷pidgin English, or it may refer to an already existing language, such as French, which was formerly the lingua franca of diplomacy. Lingua franca, meaning Frank language, was originally a pidgin used by Mediterranean traders in the middle ages (Frank being the Arabic word for European).

● **linguistic philosophy** ▶ An approach to philosophy that suggests that the way in which language is used, learnt, and developed in everyday exchanges can illuminate and, in some cases, transform many of the problems with which philosophers have grappled. It is therefore a branch of ▷analytic philosophy. Its foundations were laid by ▷Wittgenstein, but it was developed in the 1950s and 1960s by such English philosophers as J. L. ▷Austin and Gilbert ▷Ryle. It differs from linguistics proper in that the features of a language that linguistic philosophers seek to explain are usually determined by the philosophical problems they wish to simplify. Philosophical elucidation is seen as achievable through sensitivity to the language in which a problem is expressed, rather than through the adaptation of a general doctrine or method to the particular problem.

● **linguistics** ▶ The scientific study of ▷language. The earliest recorded studies of particular languages include the Sanskrit grammar of ▷Panini (6th/4th century BC) and the Greek grammar of Dionysius Thrax of Alexandria (2nd century BC). In the 19th century the study of language (then called ▷philology) was mainly concerned with establishing the history and relationships of the ▷Indo-European languages. The chief influences in broadening the scope of linguistics to its present range were Ferdinand de ▷Saussure, the founder of the ▷structuralist approach, Leonard ▷Bloomfield, and Noam ▷Chomsky. Modern linguistics has three main branches, corresponding to the three main components of language: ▷semantics, ▷grammar, and ▷phonetics. Many linguists at present see it as their task to contribute to the building of a formal model of language, in which the theoretical problems are resolved, the components and processes accurately identified, and the relationships among the components and between linguistic systems and other worlds are plausibly described. Other linguists believe that a coherent one-piece model is simply not possible.

Various specialized interests exist within the field of linguistics. **Comparative linguistics** compares languages either to establish the history of and relationships among related languages (e.g. the Indo-European family) or to test theories about linguistic universals by comparing unrelated languages (*see also* etymology). The main contribution of **structural linguistics**, which developed in the early 20th century, was to free linguistics from the historical and comparative approach, viewing language as a unique relational structure. **Sociolinguistics** deals with social aspects of language, including such matters as how language affects and reflects the role and status of individuals within the community, attitudes to dialect and "correctness," linguistic taboos and preferences, bilingualism, etc. **Psycholinguistics** is the comparatively recent branch of linguistics that deals with psychological aspects of language, including how children acquire language, how language is stored in and generated by the brain, the relationship between meaning and memory, etc.

Neurolinguistics, a branch of psycholinguistics, is concerned with the relationship between language and the physiology of the brain, especially with speech disorders that arise from brain damage.

● **Linklater, Eric** ► (1899–1974) Scottish novelist. Born in Orkney, he studied and later taught English literature at Aberdeen and in the USA. His many satirical and picaresque novels include *Juan in America* (1931), *Judas* (1939), and *The House of Gair* (1953).

● **Linköping** ► 58 25N 15 35E A town in SE Sweden. It has a notable romanesque cathedral and its university was established in 1970. Industries include railway engineering and the manufacture of cars and textiles. Population (1997 est): 131 898.

● **Linlithgow** ► 55 59N 3 37W A town in central Scotland, in West Lothian. The palace (now in ruins) was the birthplace of Mary, Queen of Scots. The chief industries are the manufacture of computer components, paper making, footwear, and whisky distilling. Population (1991): 11 866.

● **Linnaeus, Carolus** ► (Carl Linné; 1707–78) Swedish botanist, who established the principles for naming and classifying plants and animals. As a result of his botanical studies, Linnaeus proposed a system for classifying plants based on their flower parts. He published *Systema naturae* in 1735 followed by *Genera plantarum* (1737) and *Species plantarum* (1753). In his system, Linnaeus defined each type of plant by two names: a generic name and a specific name (*see* binomial nomenclature). Furthermore he grouped related genera into classes and combined related classes into orders. Linnaeus also applied his system to the animal kingdom. His was the first major attempt to bring systematic order to the great array of living things and provided a valuable framework that ▷Cuvier and others were able to modify and improve. Linnaeus' manuscripts and collections are kept at the Linnaean Society, London, which was founded in his honour in 1788.

● **linnet** ► A small Eurasian ▷finch, *Acanthis cannabina*, occurring in dry open regions, where it feeds on the seeds of common weed plants. The female has a dull brown-streaked plumage; the male has a crimson crown and breast, a greyish head, and a red-brown back with darker wings and tail. Male linnets have a beautiful flutelike voice and were popular cagebirds in the 19th century.

● **Lin Piao** ▷*See* Lin Biao.

● **linotype** ▷*See* typesetting.

● **linsang** ► A carnivorous mammal belonging to the genus *Prionodon* (2 species) of SE Asia. Linsangs are short-legged, about 75 cm long including the tail (30–35 cm), and have short velvety fur. Nocturnal, with large ears and eyes, they prey on lizards, small mammals, birds, frogs, and insects. Family: ▷Viverridae.

● **linseed** ► The flat oval seed of cultivated ▷flax, which is a source of **linseed oil**, used in paints, inks, varnishes, oilcloth, and sailcloth. The crushed seed residues form linseed meal, an important protein feed for ruminants and pigs.

● **Linz** ► 48 19N 14 18E The third largest city in Austria, the capital of Upper Austria on the River Danube. Its many historical buildings include two 13th-century baroque churches and a cathedral (1862–1924). A cultural centre, it has art galleries, libraries, and theatres. Its industries include iron and steel processing using local hydroelectric power. Population (1991): 203 044.

● **Lin Ze Xu** ► (or Lin Tse-hsü; 1785–1850) Chinese statesman and scholar. Lin Ze Xu served as governor of several provinces. While imperial commissioner of Canton (1839–41) he confiscated opium and tried to put an end to its trafficking through British merchants, thus provoking the ▷Opium War (1839–42). He is also known for his efforts to introduce Western defence techniques to China.

● **lion** ► A large carnivorous ☐mammal *Panthera leo*, one of the big ▷cats. Lions are found mainly in Africa (there are a few in India). They are heavily built with sandy-coloured coats: the shaggy-maned males grow to 2.8 m while females lack a mane and are more lightly built. Both sexes have a thin tail with a tuft at the end.

Lions inhabit grasslands, living in groups (prides) containing be-

tween four and 30 individuals dominated by a supreme male. They hunt mainly at twilight.

● **Lions, Gulf of** ► (French name: Golfe du Lion) An inlet of the NW Mediterranean Sea, on the coast of central S France between Marseille and the Spanish border.

● **Liouville, Joseph** ► (1809–82) French mathematician, who proved that there exists a class of numbers, called transcendental numbers, that cannot be expressed as a solution of a polynomial equation (i.e. one of the form $a_0 + a_1x + \ldots + a_nx^n = 0$, where n and the a's are integers). Liouville could not identify any transcendental numbers, a feat first achieved by ▷Hermite.

● **Lipari Islands** ► (or Aeolian Is; Italian name: Isole Eolie) An Italian group of seven volcanic islands in the Tyrrhenian Sea, off the N coast of Sicily. The largest is Lipari and the islands of Stromboli and Vulcano have active volcanoes. Exports include pumice stone, grapes, wine, and figs. Area: 114 sq km (44 sq mi). Population (latest est): 10 300. Chief town: Lipari, on Lipari.

● **lipase** ► An enzyme that splits the glycerides of fats in food and fatty tissue into their component fatty acids and glycerol. Digestive lipases are secreted by the pancreas and small intestine.

● **Lipchitz, Jacques** ► (1891–1973) Lithuanian cubist sculptor, who lived in Paris from 1909 and New York after 1941. Producing his first cubist sculpture in 1914, Lipchitz developed heavy angular forms in such characteristically cubist subjects as bathers and musicians. In 1925 he began experimenting with the use of voids in bronze sculptures, which he entitled "transparents." His later mythological and religious sculptures explored themes of love, evil, and conflict.

● **Lipetsk** ► 52 37N 39 36E A city in central Russia, on the River Voronezh. Industries include iron and steel and engineering. Its mud spa attracts health devotees. Population (1995 est): 474 000.

● **lipids** ► A group of compounds, generally insoluble in water but soluble in organic solvents, that includes ▷fats and oils, ▷waxes, phospholipids, sphingolipids, and ▷steroids. Fats and oils function as energy reserves in plants and animals and form a major source of dietary energy in animals. Phospholipids are important structural components of cell membranes, and sphingolipids are found predominantly in nerve tissues. Steroids have many important derivatives, including ▷cholesterol, bile salts, and certain hormones. ▷Prostaglandins, ▷carotenoids, and ▷terpenes are also classified as lipids. Lipids often occur in association with proteins as lipoproteins.

● **Lipizzaner** ► A breed of horse long associated with the Spanish Riding School in Vienna, where they are trained for spectacular displays. It is named after the stud founded by Archduke Charles at Lipizza, near Trieste, in 1580. The Lipizzaner has a short back, strong hindquarters, a powerful neck, and a small head. Born black, they mature to a grey colour. Height: 1.47–1.52 m (14½–15 hands).

● **Li Po** ► (Li Bo *or* Li T'ai Po; 705–62) Chinese poet. Li Po and ▷Du Fu together are often considered China's greatest poets. Li Po's poetry is mostly light-hearted and romantic and has its stylistic origins in folk ballads and other old traditions. Legend has it that he drowned trying to embrace the reflection of the moon from a boat.

● **Lippe, River** ► A river in NW Germany, rising in the Teutoburger Wald (forest) and flowing generally W to join the River Rhine at Wesel. **The Lippe Canal** (1929), which runs parallel to the river, is the more important waterway. Length: 240 km (150 mi).

● **Lippershey, Hans** ► (died c. 1619) Dutch lens grinder, who built the first ▷telescope. The Dutch Government tried to keep the invention a secret but news of it eventually reached ▷Galileo, who built his own telescope, which he used for astronomical observations.

● **Lippi, Fra Filippo** ► (c. 1406–69) An early Renaissance Florentine painter, who was a Carmelite monk from 1421 to about 1432. During this time he probably trained under ▷Masaccio. He was frequently patronized by the Medici but his greatest works are his fresco decorations for the choir of Prato Cathedral (1452–64), showing scenes from the lives of St John the Baptist and St Stephen. He is also noted for his idealized Madonnas, e.g. *The Madonna and Child with Two Angels* (Uffizi). He abducted and later married a nun, Lucrezia Buti; their son, **Filippino Lippi** (1457–1504), was also a painter. Filippino trained under ▷Botticelli after his father's death and completed Masaccio's fresco cycle in the Brancacci Chapel. His paintings, such as *The Vision of St Bernard* (Badia, Florence), influenced the Florentine mannerists of the 16th century.

● **Lipscomb, William Nunn** ▶ (1919–   ) US chemist, who won the 1976 Nobel Prize for his elucidation of the structure of ▷boranes. He discovered the arrangement of atoms inside borane molecules by means of X-ray diffraction and showed how groups of three such atoms are bonded by a single pair of electrons.

● **liquefaction of gases** ▶ Gases are liquefied in several ways. If the temperature of the gas is below its critical temperature (*see* critical state), it can be liquefied simply by compressing it. If the critical temperature is too low for this, the cascade process can be used. In this a gas with a high critical temperature is first liquefied by compression and then allowed to cool by evaporation under reduced pressure. This gas cools a second gas below its critical temperature, so that it in turn can be liquefied, evaporated, and cooled still further. Thus the temperature is reduced in stages. Other methods include cooling by the ▷Joule-Kelvin effect, which is used industrially in the Linde process (named after Carl von Linde; 1842–1934), and by adiabatic expansion in which a compressed gas is cooled by performing external work. This is the basis of the Claude process (named after Georges Claude; 1870–1960).

● **liquefied natural gas** ▷*See* natural gas.

● **liquefied petroleum gas** ▶ (LPG) Propane, propene, butane, butene, or a mixture of any of these. LPG is a product of ▷oil refining and is also produced from ▷natural gas. It is transported by pipeline or in specially built tankers by road, rail, or sea. Most of the LPG produced is sold in low-pressure cylinders for heating or used as a raw material for chemical manufacture, although it is also used as engine fuel.

● **liqueurs** ▶ Alcoholic ▷spirits flavoured with herbs or other ingredients, usually heavily sweetened. Liqueurs are generally sipped, neat, from small glasses after dinner. Some liqueurs, such as Benedictine, were originated by monks; the yellow or green Chartreuse is still made by the Carthusians. Other liqueurs include Curaçao, Cointreau, and Grand Marnier, which are made with brandy and oranges; Kümmel made with cumin and caraway seeds; Maraschino made with marasca cherries; and Drambuie made with whisky and honey. Aged high-quality brandy and whisky, drunk neat, are sometimes described as liqueurs.

● **liquid crystal** ▶ A substance exhibiting some liquid properties, especially fluidity, and some crystalline properties, in that large clusters of molecules are aligned in parallel formations. As liquid crystals change their reflectivity when an electric potential is applied to them, they are used in **liquid-crystal displays** to show the digits in a digital watch, calculator or other battery-operated device requiring a simple display.

● **liquidity preference** ▶ The proportion of an individual's total assets held in cash. Liquidity preference is determined chiefly by the general price level (if prices are high people need more cash to finance their purchases) and the rate of interest (if interest rates are high people will wish to invest their assets in interest-bearing bonds rather than in money). The concept was originated by J. M. ▷Keynes to explain the demand for money.

● **liquids** ▶ A state of matter between that of ▷gases and the ▷solid state. Liquids assume the shape of a container in the same way as gases but being incompressible do not expand to fill the container. Intermolecular forces are considerably stronger than in gases but weaker than in solids. Molecules are only maintained in an orderly arrangement by intermolecular forces over relatively small groups of molecules. The theory of liquids is much less well established than that of gases and solids.

● **liquorice** ▶ A perennial herb, *Glycyrrhiza glabra*, native to S Europe but cultivated throughout warm temperate regions. It bears clusters of blue flowers and long flat pods and its sweet roots, up to 1 m long, are a source of flavouring for confectionery, tobacco, and medicines.

The thickened juice of the roots is made into liquorice paste (*or* black sugar). Family: ▷*Leguminosae*.

● **lira** ▶ **1.** Another name for the ▷hurdy-gurdy. **2.** A bowed string instrument of the late middle ages. The **lira da braccio** (Italian: lyre for the arm) resembled the ▷violin but had a flatter body; it was held against the shoulder. The larger **lira da gamba** (Italian: lyre for the leg) was held like a ▷cello or viola da gamba. Both instruments had between 7 and 15 strings, some of which were sympathetic strings.

● **Lisbon** ▶ (Portuguese name: Lisboa) 38 44N 9 08W The capital of Portugal, in the SW on the River Tagus. The country's chief seaport, main exports include wine, olive oil, and cork. Lisbon is also a major industrial and commercial centre. Historic buildings in the suburb of ▷Belém include the Tower of Belém and the Jerónimos Monastery. Lisbon University was founded in 1290.
History: a settlement from very early times, it was an organized community under the Roman Empire but was later overrun by German tribes. Occupied by the Moors in the 8th century AD, it was captured by the Portuguese in the 12th century and became their capital in 1256. It flourished in the 15th and 16th centuries, the great age of Portuguese exploration and colonization, but later suffered a decline. In 1755 it was almost totally destroyed by an earthquake. It has expanded considerably in the 20th century and in 1966 one of the world's longest suspension bridges was opened across the River Tagus, linking Lisbon with Almada. Population (2001): 556 797.

● **Lisburn** ▶ **1.** 54 31N 6 03W A city in Northern Ireland, in Co Antrim. The Irish fine-linen industry was begun here by immigrant Huguenots in the 17th century. Furniture is also manufactured. It is also the headquarters of the British Army in Northern Ireland. Lisburn was granted city status in 2002. Population (1991): 42 110. **2.** A district in Northern Ireland, in Co Antrim and Co Down. Area: 436 sq km (168 sq mi). Population (1999 est): 111 300.

● **Lisieux** ▶ 49 09N 0 14E A town in N France, in the Calvados department. The shrine of Ste Thérèse (1873–1917) attracts many pilgrims to Lisieux. An agricultural trading centre (especially in dairy products), its manufactures include textiles and car components. Population (latest est): 24 506.

● **Lismore** ▶ 52 08N 7 55W A market town in the Republic of Ireland, in Co Waterford. There is a castle (1185) and two cathedrals, one built on the site of a 6th-century monastery that was a centre of learning. Population (latest est): 919.

● **Lissajous figures** ▶ Patterns arising from the addition of two ▷simple harmonic motions at right angles to each other, first studied by Jules Lissajous (1822–80). The shape of the pattern depends on the periods of the two motions and the initial conditions. If one of the two periods is an exact multiple of the other the curve is closed, otherwise the curve is open. Lissajous figures are displayed on a ▷cathode-ray oscilloscope when two sinusoidal signals control the vertical and horizontal motion of the electron beam.

● **Lissitzky, El** ▶ (Eliezer L.; 1890–1941) Russian painter, typographer, designer, and architect, known particularly for his work in advertising and exhibition design. While teaching architecture at Vitebsk (1919–21) he painted his series of abstract geometrical paintings, *Proun*. Between 1922 and 1929 he lived in the West, where he was instrumental in spreading Russian ideas on design (*see* constructivism).

● **List, Friedrich** ▶ (1789–1846) German economist, who was exiled in 1825 and emigrated to the USA. In *Outlines of American Economy* (1827), he argued the need for tariffs to encourage the growth of industry. He also wrote *The National System of Political Economy* (1841).

● **listed buildings** ▶ Buildings in the UK that are of special architectural or historic interest and that according to the Planning (Listed Buildings and Conservation Areas) Act (1990) must be listed to ensure that care is taken in deciding their future. No changes affecting the architectural or historic character of a listed building may be made without special permission. It is a criminal offence to demolish or alter a listed building without consent. In England listed buildings are classified as Grade I, Grade II*, or Grade II; some 500 000 are listed in England, 95% of which are Grade II. ▷English Heritage is always consulted about proposals affecting Grade I and II* buildings, although local planning authorities normally deal with applications to make changes. Almost all buildings built before 1700 are listed, as are most buildings erected between 1700 and 1840. In Scotland the criteria for listing buildings are similar to those in England but they are graded A, B, and C. About 42 000 buildings in Scotland are listed.

● **Lister, Joseph, 1st Baron** ▶ (1827–1912) British surgeon, who pioneered antiseptic techniques in surgery. In 1865, while surgeon at Glasgow Royal Infirmary, Lister realized the significance of ▷Pasteur's germ theory of disease in trying to prevent the infection of wounds following surgical operations. Lister devised a means of eliminating contamination and he introduced carbolic acid as an antiseptic to dress wounds. Mortality arising from infected wounds declined sharply in Lister's ward and his antiseptic procedures eventually became standard practice in hospitals everywhere. Lister was appointed president of the Royal Society (1895–1900) and was awarded the OM (1902).

● **Listeria** ▶ A genus of rod-shaped bacteria. The single species, *L. monocytogenes*, is a parasite of warm-blooded animals. On transmission to humans, especially through eating unpasteurized cheese or yogurt, it may cause **listeriosis**, with symptoms ranging from mild food poisoning to a serious form of meningitis; in pregnant women it can damage the fetus and usually results in termination of the pregnancy.

● **Liszt, Franz** ▶ (Ferencz L.; 1811–86) Hungarian pianist and composer. He made his debut at the age of nine. After studying the piano with Czerny and studying composition he began a career as a virtuoso. From 1835 to 1839 he lived with the Comtesse d'Agoult (1805–76); their daughter Cosima married Wagner, of whose works Liszt was an early champion. From 1848 to 1861 Liszt lived with the Princess Sayn-Wittgenstein. In 1865 he took minor orders in the Roman Catholic Church; he spent most of the rest of his life in Weimar, Budapest, and Rome. As a pianist Liszt was considered the greatest performer of his time. As a composer he invented the symphonic poem and made use of advanced harmonies and original forms. His compositions include much piano music (including a sonata in B minor), the *Faust Symphony* (1854–57) and *Dante Symphony* (1855–56), and the symphonic poem *Les Préludes* (1854).

● **litchi** ▶ (lychee *or* lichee) A Chinese tree, *Litchi chinensis*, cultivated in the tropics and subtropics for its fruits. The fruit is almost globular, 2.5 cm in diameter, with a warty deep-pink rind. The white translucent watery flesh has a sweet acid flavour and encloses a single large brown seed. The fruit is eaten fresh, canned, or dried as litchi nuts. Family: *Sapindaceae*.

● **literacy levels** ▶ Levels that indicate a person's ability to read and write. In 1996 the International Adult Literacy Survey measured the reading skills of people of working age (16 to 65). Performance was graded at five levels; Level 3 is considered by the ▷Organization for Economic Cooperation and Development to be the minimum literacy requirement for coping with life and work in a modern society. The percentages of people in various nations who failed to achieve this level are shown below. ▷*See also* illiteracy.

Percentage of adults at the lowest literacy levels

Poland	75%
Switzerland	54%
UK	51%
Germany	48%
USA	46%
Australia	44%
Sweden	27%

● **litharge** ▷*See* lead.

● **lithium** ▶ (Li) The lightest metal (relative density 0.534), discovered by Arfvedson in 1817. An alkali metal, it gives a crimson colour to flames. It occurs in lepidolite, spodumene (LiAlSi$_2$O$_6$), and other minerals; as well as in brine, from which it is extracted commercially by electrolysis of the molten chloride (LiCl). The metal has the highest specific heat capacity of any solid element. It is corrosive, combusti-

ble, and reacts with water. Because of its efficiency in reflecting neutrons, lithium has important applications as a blanketing material in proposed ▷thermonuclear reactors. It forms salts, like the other alkali metals, and the hydride LiH. Lithium salts are used in the treatment of manic-depressive illness. At no 3; at wt 6.941; mp 180.6°C; bp 1342°C.

● **lithography** ▷*See* printing.

● **Lithops** ▶ A genus of succulent South African desert plants (about 50 species), with no stems and leaves partly buried in the soil. The tips of the leaves are smooth, with a deep cleft across the top, camouflaged to resemble pebbles. The daisy-like flowers are white or yellow. Family: *Aizoaceae*.

● **Lithuania, Republic of** ▶ A republic in NE Europe, on the Baltic Sea. Most of Lithuania comprises a central lowland and is particularly fertile, with forests and peat reserves. The Lithuanians comprise about 80% of the population.

Economy: the economy was subject to rapid industrialization during the Soviet era, when large fertilizer, textile, petrochemical, and metalworking industries were developed. A privatization programme began in 1991 and gathered pace in the later 1990s. The country has few mineral resources and remains dependent on Russia for its energy supply. Agriculture, especially livestock breeding and grains, and forestry are important. Tourism is being developed.

History: one of the largest states in medieval Europe, Lithuania united with Poland under the ▷Jagiellon dynasty in the 14th century. After the partition of Poland in the late 18th century it passed to Russia. Nationalism grew during the 19th century and Lithuania declared its independence in 1918 (recognized by the Soviet Union in 1920). However, following the Nazi–Soviet pact, Lithuania was incorporated into the Soviet Union as an SSR in 1940. It was occupied by Germany in World War II, during which the large Jewish minority was virtually exterminated. Nationalist unrest intensified in the 1980s and in 1990 the independent non-Communist Republic of Lithuania was declared with Dr Vitautas Landsbergis as president. In early 1991 Soviet troops seized buildings in Vilnius and attempted to suppress the nationalists; Lithuania's independence was finally recognized by Russia after the break-up of the Soviet Union later in the year. In 1992 the Lithuanian Democratic Labour (formerly Communist) Party (LDLP) won elections to a new parliament and the following year the former Communist leader Algirdas Brazauskas was elected president. Lithuania applied to join the EU in 1995 and signed a treaty of association the following year. In 1996 Landsbergis' party defeated the LDLP in elections and a centre-right coalition was formed. Valdas Adamkus, an independent, was elected president in 1998. A centre-left government took office in 1999 but was replaced by the former Communists under Brazauskas in 2002.

Republic of Lithuania

Head of state	President Valdas Adamkus
Official language	Lithuanian
Official currency	litas of 100 centas
Area	65 200 sq km (25 170 sq mi)
Population (2001 est)	3 691 000
Capital	Vilnius

● **Lithuanian** ▶ A language belonging to the E division of the Baltic languages division of the Indo-European family; it is the official language of Lithuania. Lithuanian speakers, including those in America, number about 2 750 000. Lithuanian is closely related to ▷Latvian. It is written in a Latin alphabet and texts date from the 16th century.

● **litmus** ▶ A soluble compound obtained from certain lichens. Litmus turns red in an acid solution and blue in an alkaline solution. It is therefore used as an ▷indicator, often in the form of **litmus paper**, strips of paper impregnated with litmus.

● **litre** ▶ A unit of volume in the ▷metric system formerly defined as the volume of one kilogram of pure water under specified conditions. This definition still applies for purposes of the UK Weights and Measures Act (1963), but in ▷SI units the litre is a special name for the cubic decimetre.

● **Little America** ▶ 78 11S 162 10W The main US Antarctic base, near the coast of Ross Dependency. It was established in 1928 as headquarters for the expeditions of Richard ▷Byrd.

● **Little Belt** ▶ (Danish name: Lille Bælt) A strait in SW Denmark, between the mainland and the island of Fyn. It links the Kattegat with the Baltic and narrows to 1 km (0.6 mi) wide.

● **Little Bighorn, Battle of the** ▶ (25 June, 1876) The battle fought on the S bank of the Little Bighorn River in which Gen ▷Custer and his men were massacred by Sioux Indians led by ▷Crazy Horse and ▷Sitting Bull (Custer's Last Stand).

● **little owl** ▶ A small ▷owl, *Athene noctua*, occurring in Eurasia and N Africa. 20 cm long, it has a white-mottled brown plumage with barred underparts, rounded wings, and yellow eyes and hunts over open country at dawn and dusk, feeding on insects, worms, and mice. ▷*See* Plate III.

● **Little Rock** ▶ 34 42N 92 17W A city in the USA, the capital of Arkansas. In 1957, when Black pupils entered the high school for the first time, it was the scene of major race riots. Population (1996 est): 175 752.

● **Littlewood, Joan** ▶ (1914–) British theatre director. In 1945 she founded Theatre Workshop, a company dedicated to the production of plays for working-class audiences. It moved into the Theatre Royal, Stratford, in the East End of London, in 1953. Her best-known productions include *The Hostage* (1958) and *Oh What a Lovely War!* (1963). The company disbanded in 1964.

● **Litvinov, Maksim Maksimovich** ▶ (1876–1951) Soviet diplomat. He was Soviet envoy to London (1917–18), having married an English girl, Ivy Low, in 1916. He headed the Soviet delegation to the League of Nations disarmament conference (1927–29) and became Soviet foreign minister (1930–39). Litvinov, who believed in cooperation between the Soviet Union and the West, obtained US recognition of his country in 1934. In the League of Nations he advocated action against the Axis powers and was dismissed shortly before the German–Soviet nonaggression treaty of 1939. After the German invasion of the Soviet Union, Litvinov was ambassador to the USA (1941–43).

● **Liu Shao Qi** ▶ (*or* Liu Shao-ch'i; 1898–1974) Chinese communist statesman. He joined the Communist Party in Moscow in 1921 and later became a leader of the trades union movement in the ▷Jiangxi Soviet. In 1959 he succeeded ▷Mao Tse-tung as chairman of the People's Republic of China but was condemned as a reactionary during the ▷Cultural Revolution and disappeared from public view.

● **Lively, Penelope (Margaret)** ▶ (1933–) British novelist. Her books include publications for children and the novels *Judgement Day* (1980), *Moon Tiger* (1987), which won the ▷Booker Prize, *Passing On* (1990), *City of the Mind* (1991), *Cleopatra's Sister* (1993), *Heat Wave* (1996), *Beyond the Blue Mountains* (1997), and *Spiderweb* (1998).

● **liver** ▶ A large glandular organ, weighing 1.2–1.6 kg, situated in the upper right region of the abdomen, just below the diaphragm (*see* Plate II). The liver has many important functions concerned with the utilization of absorbed foods. It converts excess glucose into glycogen, which it stores and reconverts into glucose when required; it breaks down excess amino acids into ▷urea; and it stores and metabolizes fats. The liver forms and secretes ▷bile, which contains the breakdown products of worn-out red blood cells, and synthesizes blood-clotting factors, plasma proteins, and—in the fetus—red blood cells. It also breaks down (detoxifies) poisonous substances, including alcohol. ▷Cirrhosis of the liver is commonly caused by a combination of sensitivity to, and excess of, alcohol.

● **liver fluke** ▶ A parasitic ▷flatworm that inhabits the bile duct of sheep, cattle, and man. The common liver fluke (*Fasciola hepatica*) passes its larval stages in a marshland snail before infecting grazing animals (or, rarely, man). The Chinese liver fluke (*Opisthorchus sinensis*), 1–2 cm long, passes two larval stages in a freshwater snail and fish before maturing in a human host.

● **Liverpool** ▶ **1.** 53 25N 2 55W A major city in NW England, in Liverpool unitary authority, Merseyside, on the estuary of the River Mersey. It is the UK's fourth most important port and the foremost for Atlantic trade; Liverpool Free Port opened in 1984. The city is linked with Birkenhead and Wallasey on the Wirral Peninsula by two tunnels under the Mersey. The most famous landmark is the Royal Liver Building (1911) at the Pier Head, alongside the Cunard and Mersey Docks buildings. There is a Roman Catholic cathedral constructed (1962–67) in a modern design of Sir Frederick Gibberd (1908–84); the original design (1929) in modern classical style was by Sir Edwin Lutyens (only the crypt and sacristy were completed before World War II prevented further building). The Anglican cathedral (1904–78), designed by Sir Giles Gilbert Scott, is the country's largest ecclesiastical building. Other notable buildings include St George's Hall (1854). Liverpool has one of the largest provincial universities in the UK (1903). Exports include all kinds of manufactured goods, especially textiles and machinery, from a hinterland covering most of the North and Midlands. The main imports are petroleum, grain, ores, nonferrous metals, sugar, wood, fruit, and cotton. These are reflected in some of Liverpool's industries: flour milling, sugar refining, electrical engineering, food processing, chemicals, soap, margarine, tanning, and motor vehicles; recent years have, however, seen a marked decline in the city's industry.

History: originally trading with Ireland, Liverpool grew rapidly in the 18th and 19th centuries, superseding Bristol as the chief west coast port as a result of trade with the Americas (sugar, tobacco, slaves, cotton) and the industrialization of S Lancashire (raw cotton came through Liverpool). Britain's first wet dock was built here in 1715. Liverpool developed also as a cultural centre, with the Walker Art Gallery (built 1877) the Royal Liverpool Philharmonic Orchestra, the home of which is the Philharmonic Hall (1939), and the Tate Gallery, which was opened in the restored Albert docks in 1988. Population (1994 est): 474 000.
2. A unitary authority in NW England, in Merseyside. Area: 113 sq km (44 sq mi). Population (1996 est): 468 000.

● **Liverpool, Robert Banks Jenkinson, 2nd Earl of** ▶ (1770–1828) British statesman; Tory prime minister (1812–27). He became an MP in 1790 and held office continuously from 1793 until 1827 except for 14 months in 1806–07; he was foreign secretary (1801–04), home secretary (1807–09), and secretary for war and the colonies (1809–12). As prime minister he is remembered for his unenlightened response to the unrest that followed the Napoleonic Wars (1803–15). In 1817 he suspended ▷habeas corpus and following the ▷Peterloo Massacre introduced the repressive Six Acts (1819). He also opposed ▷Catholic emancipation but the last years of his government saw the development of Tory reform under the influence of George ▷Canning and William Huskisson.

● **liverwort** ▶ A ▷bryophyte plant of the phylum *Hepatophyta* (c. 6000 species), found growing on moist soil, rocks, trees, etc. There are two groups: leafy liverworts, in which the plant body is differentiated into stems and leaves; and thallose liverworts, which have a flat lobed liverlike body (thallus). The liverwort plant is the gamete-producing phase (gametophyte) and gives rise to a capsule, the spore-producing phase (sporophyte), which is sometimes borne on a slender erect column. ▷*See also* hornwort.

● **livery companies** ▶ Descendants of the medieval craft ▷guilds, so called because of the distinctive dress (livery) worn by their members on ceremonial occasions. Some occupy notable buildings in the City of London and, in addition to their ceremonial duties, some, such as the Mercers, Haberdashers, and Merchant Taylors, have educational interests. In 1878 the livery companies joined the Corporation of the ▷City of London in setting up the City and Guilds of London Institute to promote technical education.

● **livestock farming** ▶ (*or* animal husbandry) The maintenance and management of domesticated animals for the production of milk, meat, eggs, fibres, skins, etc. Farming methods vary widely throughout the world and modern improvements in livestock breeds and husbandry techniques have enabled dramatic increases to be made in productivity, nutrition and disease control being essential aspects of management.

Cattle produce milk (*see* dairy farming) and beef. Under European conditions, a cow may breed at any time of the year. The gestation period is about 9 months, followed by about 10 months of lactation and a 2-month dry period before calving again. A cow is known as a heifer until her second lactation. Heifers are reared either for beef or as dairy replacements and bull calves are generally castrated and reared for beef, being known as bullocks or steers. Age at slaughter depends on the breed and level of feeding but is generally about 18 months. Calves for veal are reared on a milk-based diet and are slaughtered at about 14 weeks.

Sheep are farmed worldwide for meat and wool (and in some countries for milk), often grazing on poor mountainous or arid pastures. In Europe, the one or two lambs per ewe are born in early spring. Males are castrated and reared for slaughter at weights of 20–45 kg. Selected females are reared as replacement ewes. Each sheep yields 2–5 kg of wool.

Pigs have traditionally been kept outdoors, foraging for roots, seeds, etc. In modern intensive systems, they are housed under controlled conditions. Young females (gilts) are first mated at 7–8 months. Following the gestation period of 115 days, an average of 7–9 piglets are born per litter. Pork pigs are slaughtered at 40–50 kg; those reared for bacon are slaughtered at 80–100 kg.

Poultry are now kept indoors in an artificially controlled environment. Chicks are hatched artificially, the female birds starting to lay after about 20 weeks and producing about 250 eggs per year. Laying flocks are kept in **batteries** of cages with 3–5 birds per cage, feeding, cleaning, and egg collection being automatic. Table birds are fed ad lib and reach a weight of around 2 kg in 8–12 weeks. Turkeys are also reared for meat under intensive conditions.

Apart from food, many livestock, especially horses, mules, and donkeys, provide transport and motive power. Goats provide milk in many traditional agricultural systems.

● **Livia Drusilla** ► (58 BC–29 AD) The wife of Octavian (Emperor ▷Augustus) from 39 BC and the mother by her first husband of Emperor ▷Tiberius. As Augustus' consort Livia's image was one of matronly dignity and reports of her machinations on Tiberius' behalf are probably exaggerated. After Augustus' death (14 AD) she received the honorific name Julia Augusta.

● **living fossil** ► A living organism whose closest relatives are all extinct, being known only as fossils. Such organisms were thought— before their discovery in modern times—to be extinct themselves. Examples of living fossils are the ▷coelacanth and the ▷dawn redwood, discovered in 1938 and 1941, respectively.

● **Livingston** ► 55 51N 3 31W A town in central Scotland, in West Lothian. It was designated for development as a new town in 1962. Population (1991): 41 647.

● **Livingstone** ▷See Maramba.

● **Livingstone, David** ► (1813–73) Scottish missionary and explorer of Africa. Livingstone qualified as a physician at Glasgow University and after his ordination as a missionary in 1840 set out for Bechuanaland (now Botswana). He traced stretches of the Zambezi, Shire, and Rovuma Rivers, and was the first European to see Lake Ngami (1849), the Victoria Falls (1855), and Lake Nyasa (now Malawi). During an attempt to trace the source of the Nile (1866–73) his encounter with Sir Henry Morton ▷Stanley occurred. He died near Lake Bangweulu in Old Chitambo village, where his heart is buried. His body lies in Westminster Abbey.

● **Livingstone, Ken** ► (Kenneth Robert L; 1945–) British politician; mayor of London (2000–). A left-winger, he became famous for his maverick policies as Labour leader of the Greater London Council from 1981 until its abolition in 1986. He subsequently became an MP (1987–). In 2000 he was narrowly defeated in a ballot to decide Labour's candidate for the mayor of London but went on to stand successfully as an independent.

● **Living Theatre** ► An experimental theatre company founded in New York City in 1947 by Julian Beck (1925–85) and Judith Malina (1926–). Their best-known productions include Jack Gelber's *The Connection* (1959), a play about drug addiction, and *Paradise Now* (1968), in which they developed controversial experiments in audience participation.

● **living will** ► A document in which a terminally ill person states that he or she does not want life to be prolonged by artificial means. In 1993 in the UK, a Cambridge hospital, with cautious approval from

the Department of Health, gave terminally ill patients the opportunity to refuse resuscitation in the event of cardiac arrest.

● **Livonian Knights** ► (Livonian Brothers of the Sword) A German military and religious order of knighthood founded in 1202 to conquer and christianize the region, notably Livonia, around the Baltic Sea. They merged with the Teutonic Knights in 1237 and were disbanded in 1561.

● **Livonian War** ► (1558–83) A confrontation over Russian expansion towards the Baltic Sea. In 1558 ▷Ivan the Terrible invaded Livonia and defeated its rulers, the Livonian Knights, who placed Livonia under Lithuanian protection. Russia was defeated by the Polish-Lithuanian commonwealth (*see* Lublin, Union of) and Sweden, losing its Livonian conquests and some towns on the Gulf of Finland.

● **Livorno** ► (English name: Leghorn) 43 33N 10 18E A port in central Italy, in Tuscany on the Ligurian Sea. It has a 16th-century cathedral. Its industries include oil refining, engineering, and the manufacture of straw (Leghorn) hats. Olive oil and marble are exported. Population (1996 est): 164 569.

● **Livy** ► (Titus Livius; 59 BC–17 AD) Roman historian. He was born in Patavium (Padua) in N Italy and settled in Rome about 29 BC. His monumental history of Rome from its legendary foundation to the death of Drusus in 9 BC, written in an elevated style and emphasizing the moral examples of individual lives, was immediately popular. Only 35 of the original 142 books survive, covering the early history up to the 4th century BC, the second Punic War against Hannibal, and the wars against Macedonia up to 166 BC.

● **lizard** ► A ▷reptile belonging to the suborder *Sauria* (3000 species), occurring worldwide but most abundant in tropical regions. They are mainly terrestrial with cylindrical or narrow scaly long-tailed bodies, some with limbs reduced or absent (*see* glass snake; skink), and often with crests, spines, and frills. They range in size from the smallest ▷geckos to the formidable ▷Komodo dragon. Lizards lay leathery-shelled eggs although certain species of colder regions and many skinks bear live young. The female builds a simple nest and may guard her eggs until the young hatch and disperse. Some lizards reproduce by parthenogenesis, i.e. unfertilized eggs develop into races of females. Lizards eat chiefly insects and vegetation and have been known to live for 25 years in captivity.

● **Lizard Point** ► (or Lizard Head) 49 56N 5 13W The most southerly point of mainland Britain, in SW Cornwall on the Atlantic Ocean. It possesses magnificent coastal scenery with distinctive green- and purple-coloured serpentine rock.

● **Ljubljana** ► (German name: Laibach) 46 04N 14 30E The capital of Slovenia, situated in the W of the country. It is the centre of Slovene culture with a university (1595). The old city was largely destroyed by an earthquake in 1895. Population (1996 est): 269 621.

● **llama** ► A hoofed mammal, *Lama glama*, of S and W South America. Up to 120 cm high at the shoulder, llamas are sure-footed, nimble, and hardy, with thick warm coats. They are now only found in the domesticated state, being used for meat, wool, and as pack animals. Family: Camelidae (camels, etc.).

● **Llanberis** ► 53 07N 4 06W A small town in NW Wales, in Gwynedd at the W end of Llanberis Pass. A mountain railway (opened 1896) to the summit of Snowdon starts from here. Population (1991): 1859.

● **Llandaff** ► 51 30N 3 14W A district of Cardiff, in South Wales on the River Taff. It is the oldest bishopric in Wales (6th century). The 12th-century cathedral, severely bombed in World War II, was restored in 1960 with inclusion of a prestressed concrete arch supporting Epstein's *Majestas*.

● **Llandrindod Wells** ► 52 15N 3 23W A town in central Wales, the administrative centre of Powys. It is the largest Welsh spa and a tourist centre. Population (1991): 4362.

● **Llandudno** ► 53 19N 3 49W A resort in North Wales, in Conwy county borough on Conwy Bay. Two limestone promontories, the Great Orme's Head and the Little Orme's Head, lie on either side of the town. Population (1991): 14 576.

● **Llanelli** ► 51 42N 4 10W A port in South Wales, in Carmarthenshire on the Burry Inlet of Carmarthen Bay. It is a tinplate manufacturing centre besides producing steel, copper, chemicals, and bricks. Population (1991): 44 953.

● **Llanfair PG** ▶ (*or* Llanfairpwll) 53 13N 4 12W A village in NW Wales, in Anglesey, famous for its 58-letter full name (lengthened in the 18th century): Llanfairpwllgwyngyllgogerychwyrndrobwll-llantysiliogogogoch (St Mary's Church in the hollow of the white hazel near to the rapid whirlpool of St Tysilio's Church by the red cave). The first Women's Institute in the UK was founded here in 1915.

● **Llangollen** ▶ 52 58N 3 10W A town in North Wales, in Denbighshire. It is a tourist centre on the River Dee, spanned by a 14th-century bridge. An international musical Eisteddfod is held here each summer. Population (1991): 3267.

● **llanos** ▶ The treeless grasslands of South America that cover about 570 000 sq km (220 000 sq mi) of central Venezuela and N Colombia. Drained by the River Orinoco, the llanos are traditionally a cattle-rearing region but the discovery of oil in the 1930s led to considerable population growth and economic development.

● **Llewelyn I** ▷*See* Llywelyn ap Iorwerth.

● **Llewelyn II** ▷*See* Llywelyn ap Gruffudd.

● **Llewellyn, Harry** ▶ (Lt Col Sir Henry Morton L.; 1911–99) British show jumper and equestrian, who won over 150 international competitions. At the 1948 Olympic Games he won a team bronze medal and in the 1952 Olympics won the team gold medal. His horse Foxhunter became world famous.

● **Llewellyn, Richard** ▶ (R. D. V. L. Lloyd; 1907–83) Welsh novelist. After working in films and journalism, he found success with his novel about a Welsh mining village, *How Green Was My Valley* (1939). Other novels include the sequel *Up, Into the Singing Mountains* (1960).

● **Lleyn Peninsula** ▶ A peninsula in NW Wales, in Gwynedd between Caernarfon Bay and Cardigan Bay. It is a stronghold of the Welsh language and a popular tourist area with several coastal resorts, including Pwllheli and Criccieth.

● **Lloyd, Chris(tine)** ▷*See* Evert, Chris(tine).

● **Lloyd, Clive Hubert** ▶ (1944–) West Indian cricketer. A batsman, he captained his country's team (1974–78; 1979–85) in 74 tests. He played for Lancashire (1968–86), captaining the side (1981–84; 1986). He became a UK citizen in 1986.

● **Lloyd, Harold** ▶ (1893–1971) US film comedian. He developed the character of the dogged little man in conventional suit and spectacles in numerous early silent comedies, most of them characterized by his use of dangerous stunts. His films include *Just Nuts* (1915), *Safety Last* (1923), and *The Freshman* (1925).

● **Lloyd, Marie** ▶ (Matilda Wood; 1870–1922) British music-hall entertainer. She began her career on stage in 1885. Her songs, characterized by cockney humour, include "Oh! Mr Porter" and "A Little of What You Fancy."

● **Lloyd George, David, 1st Earl** ▶ (1863–1945) British statesman; Liberal prime minister (1916–22). Born in Manchester of Welsh parents, he entered parliament in 1890 and gained a reputation for radicalism as a Welsh nationalist and a supporter of the Afrikaners in the second Boer War (1899–1902). He was president of the Board of Trade (1905–08) and then chancellor of the exchequer (1908–15), in which post he is best known for the so-called People's Budget (1909). This proposed higher death duties, a land value tax, and a supertax; the rejection of this budget by the House of Lords led ultimately to the 1911 Parliament Act, which removed the Lords' veto power. Lloyd George also introduced old-age pensions (1908) and national insurance (1911). In World War I he served as minister of munitions (1915–16) and secretary for war (1916) before succeeding Asquith as prime minister. His energetic war policy conducted by a small war cabinet included the introduction of the convoy system to thwart the German U-boat aggression. After the war he continued to lead a coalition government increasingly dominated by the Conservatives. He was criticized for negotiating with Irish militants in the establishment of the Irish Free State (1921) and his government fell when Britain came close to war with the Turkish nationalists. Lloyd George never re-

David Lloyd George ▶ The elder statesman with a model of a World War I howitzer.

gained prominence in British politics, although he held his parliamentary seat until he finally resigned on being created an earl in 1945. After the death of his first wife **Dame Margaret Lloyd George** (1864–1941) he married his secretary **Frances Stevenson** (1888–1972), who published (1971) *Lloyd George: A Diary.*

● **Lloyd's** ▶ An association of ▷insurance underwriters named after the 17th-century London coffee house, owned by Edward Lloyd, where underwriters used to meet. Lloyd's was incorporated by Act of Parliament in 1871. The corporation itself does not underwrite insurance business, which is all undertaken by syndicates of private underwriters (names), who are responsible for any losses with unlimited liability and share in any profits; insurance business is conducted by a syndicate manager but names have to deposit substantial sums with the corporation to provide its risk capital. Names are not permitted to deal with the public, all insurance policies with the public being transacted by Lloyd's insurance brokers. Although Lloyd's is situated in London (its new building in Lime St (1986) was designed by Richard ▷Rogers) its business in marine and aircraft insurance is worldwide. Lloyd's will also undertake all other kinds of insurance. During 1988–93 some syndicates made large losses resulting in the financial ruin of some names. In 1993 Lloyd's agreed to admit limited companies as names, breaking its tradition of unlimited liability. **Lloyd's Register of Shipping** is an organization formed by Lloyd's to inspect all oceangoing vessels over 100 tonnes. The *Register*, published annually, gives up-to-date reports on these ships by Lloyd's surveyors. The highest classification, "A1 at Lloyds," indicates that the hull and the trappings are in first class order.

● **Lloyd Webber, Andrew, Baron** ▶ (1948–) British composer. His early musicals, with lyrics by Sir Tim Rice (1944–), include *Jesus Christ Superstar* (1970) and *Evita* (1978); later works include *Cats* (1981), *Phantom of the Opera* (1986), and *Whistle Down the Wind* (1996). He was raised to the peerage in 1997. His brother **Julian Lloyd Webber** (1951–) is a cellist.

● **Llywelyn ap Gruffudd** ▶ (Llewelyn II; d. 1282) The only native Prince of Wales (1258–82) to be recognized as such by England. He aided the English barons against Henry III (1263–67) and refused homage to Edward I (1276), who forced him into submission but let him remain Prince of Wales by title. He was killed in another revolt.

● **Llywelyn ap Iorwerth** ▶ (Llewelyn I; d. 1240) Prince of Gwynedd, N Wales (1194–1238), who achieved supremacy over most other Welsh princes. He supported the barons against his father-in-law, King John of England (1215), obtaining recognition for Welsh rights in Magna Carta.

● **loach** ▶ A small freshwater ▷bony fish of the family *Cobitidae* (over 200 species), found mainly in Asia, but also in Europe and N Africa. Loaches feed at night on bottom-dwelling invertebrates detected by the three to six pairs of barbels around the mouth. Order: *Cypriniformes*.

● **loam** ▸ A type of soil containing approximately equal proportions of sand, silt, and clay. It is an ideal soil for agriculture since it can retain some moisture and plant nutrients but is well aerated and drained and easily worked.

● **Lobachevski, Nikolai Ivanovich** ▸ (1793–1856) Russian mathematician, who (in 1829) produced the first ▷non-Euclidean geometry by examining what is possible if the fifth axiom in Euclid's *Elements* is neglected. In Lobachevski's geometry the angles of a triangle always add up to less than 180°.

● **Lobelia** ▸ A genus of annual and perennial herbs (about 250 species), found in most warm and temperate regions. The leaves are simple and the flowers are tubular, with a two-lobed upper lip and a larger three-lobed lower lip, and are arranged in a terminal spike. Ornamental species, called cardinal flowers, are usually blue or red. Family: *Lobeliaceae*.

● **Lobengula** ▸ (c. 1836–94) King (1870–94) of the Matabele (*or* Ndebele) kingdom in S Rhodesia. Son of ▷Mzilikazi, Lobengula granted land and mineral rights to the British South Africa Company but this was no protection against the conquest of his kingdom in 1893.

● **Lobito** ▸ 12 20S 13 34E A port in W Angola, on the Atlantic coast. Its fine natural harbour has made it the country's busiest port. Population (latest est): 150 000.

● **lobotomy** ▷*See* leucotomy.

● **lobster** ▸ A large marine ▷crustacean of the section *Macrura* that has a long abdomen ending in a tailfan. True lobsters (family *Homaridae*) have segmented bodies, a pair of pincers, four pairs of walking legs, and several pairs of swimming legs (swimmerets). They live on the ocean bottom and are mainly nocturnal, feeding on seaweed and animals. Eggs are carried on the swimmerets and hatch into free-swimming larvae that later descend to the bottom. Species used as food include *Homarus vulgaris* and *H. americanus*. Order: ▷*Decapoda*.

● **local government** ▸ The administration of a locality. In the UK local government developed from the Anglo-Saxon division of the country into ▷shires, ▷hundreds, and ▷boroughs. However, it only became systematized in the 19th century, when the industrial revolution brought social problems demanding local attention. The Municipal Corporation Act (1835) established 178 municipal councils, elected by ratepayers, which in the following decades grew in number and took over a wide range of responsibilities, including the police and public health. County councils were established in 1888. In 1894 the work of local government was distributed by the creation of borough and urban district councils in urban areas and parish councils in rural areas. The Local Government Act (1972; effective 1974) divided England and Wales into 53 ▷counties. These were divided into districts, and they in turn into parishes or, in Wales, communities. District councils were entrusted with providing such services as education, housing, and refuse collection. Parish and community councils have lesser functions, e.g. providing bus shelters. A similar system was established in Scotland in 1973 (effective 1975). Northern Ireland has 26 district councils. In 1996–98 ▷unitary authorities were established to replace the two-tier system of county

and district councils in many parts of the UK, including the whole of Scotland and Wales. 32 unitary councils were set up in Scotland and 22 in Wales. In England a mixed system of one-tier and two-tier local government has been established, involving the abolition of several county councils. Local government is financed by the ▷council tax, business ▷rates, rent, borrowing, and central-government grants.

● **Local Group** ▸ The small irregularly shaped ▷cluster of galaxies to which our ▷Galaxy belongs. Other members include the ▷Andromeda galaxy, the Triangulum Spiral, and both ▷Magellanic Clouds. There are 30 or more members.

● **Locarno** ▸ (German name: Lugarrus) 46 10N 8 48E A resort in S Switzerland, on Lake Locarno. Its church of Madonna del Sasso (1480) is a place of pilgrimage. The ▷Locarno Pact was signed here. Population (1990 est): 14 150.

● **Locarno Pact** ▸ (1925) A series of treaties between Germany, France, Belgium, Poland, Czechoslovakia, the UK, and Italy. The most important was an agreement between France, Germany, and Belgium, guaranteed by the UK and Italy, to maintain the borders between Germany and France and Belgium respectively and the demilitarized zone of the Rhineland. The latter was violated by Hitler in 1936.

● **Loch Lomond** ▷*See* Lomond, Loch.

● **Lochner, Stefan** ▸ (c. 1400–51) German painter of the Cologne School, born in Meersburg on Lake Constance. He probably trained in the Netherlands before settling in Cologne. His *Madonna of the Rose Bower* (Wallraf-Richartz Museum, Cologne) combines the delicacy of the ▷international gothic with the naturalism of Flemish painting.

● **Loch Ness** ▷*See* Ness, Loch.

● **lock** ▸ A section of a canal or river, enclosed by gates, that is used to regulate the water level and raise or lower vessels wishing to navigate the waterway. The more common pound lock consists of two sets of mitred gates set a distance apart pointing into the downward force of the water. A vessel wishing to pass from the lower water level to the higher level enters the lock, the lower gates are closed behind it, and water from the upper level is allowed to flow into the lock through gaps in the upper gates. When the two levels are equal the upper gates are opened and the vessel leaves. The reverse procedure enables vessels to travel from the higher to the lower level.

Locke, John ▸ (1632–1704) English philosopher. His greatest work, the *Essay concerning Human Understanding* (1690), reveals him as a pioneer of ▷empiricism. It maintains, contrary to received tradition, that every one of our ideas comes from sense impressions; at birth the human mind is a *tabula rasa* (blank tablet). The *Essay* also attempts to sustain the distinction between primary qualities (found without exception in all bodies) and secondary qualities (originating in the impressions these bodies make on our senses). Locke's two works *Of Government* (1690) were enormously influential in moulding modern concepts of liberal democracy. He dismissed any divine right to kingship and advocated liberal government, the function of which was, he thought, to preside over the exchange of "natural" for "civil" rights. He held that, in virtue of the occurrence of some form of ▷social contract in antiquity, political rulers were obliged to guarantee as civil rights any liberties that their subjects' ancestors might be supposed to have surrendered. However, there were some inalienable rights that could never be given up to a citizen's ruler.

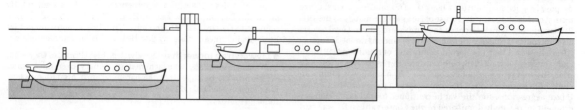

Vessel about to enter lock.   Vessel being raised inside lock.   Vessel emerging from lock at higher level.

lock

● **Locke, Matthew** ▶ (c. 1622–77) English composer. He became Composer in Ordinary to Charles II. His works include the masque *Cupid and Death* (with Christopher Gibbons; 1653). He wrote a pamphlet defending his church music.

● **Lockerbie** ▶ 55 07N 3 22W A town in SW Scotland, in Dumfries and Galloway Region. On 21 Dec 1988 it was the scene of Britain's worst air disaster when a Pan-American jumbo jet flying from Frankfurt to New York was destroyed by a terrorist bomb. 270 people died, 11 of them residents of Lockerbie. In 1991 a US court indicted two Libyan intelligence agents for the bombing but Libya refused to extradite them for trial in the USA or the UK. As a result the UN imposed sanctions on Libya (suspended in 1999). In 1998 Libya accepted a proposal that the men should be tried in a neutral country under Scots law. In 2001 a Scottish court sitting in the Netherlands found Abdul Baset Ali al-Megrahi guilty of murder but acquitted his alleged accomplice. Population (1991): 3982.

● **Lockhart, Sir (Robert Hamilton) Bruce** ▶ (1887–1970) British diplomat and writer, born in Scotland. Acting consul general in Moscow (1915–17), he led a mission to the new Soviet Government in 1918, when he was briefly imprisoned in the Kremlin. He subsequently worked on the *Evening Standard* (London), returning to the Foreign Office in World War II. Among his books is *Memoirs of a British Agent* (1932).

● **Lockhart, John Gibson** ▶ (1794–1854) Scottish biographer and journalist. His best-known work is his biography of Sir Walter Scott (1837–38), whose daughter he married. He also wrote a biography of Robert Burns (1828) and edited the *Quarterly Review* from 1825 to 1853.

● **lockjaw** ▷*See* tetanus.

● **lockout** ▶ The closure of a workplace by an employer to prevent employees from working, in an attempt to persuade them to accept the employer's terms of employment. The measure is now rarely used.

● **Lockyer, Sir Joseph Norman** ▶ (1836–1920) British astronomer, who in 1868 first recognized the existence of an unknown element, which he called helium, in the sun's spectrum. Terrestrial helium was eventually discovered nearly 40 years later by Sir William ▷Ramsay. Lockyer also founded the scientific journal *Nature*.

● **locomotive** ▶ An engine that draws a train on a ▷railway. The first locomotives, designed by ▷Trevithick and ▷Stephenson were driven by steam engines and steam dominated the railways until the end of World War II. Even in the mid-1970s, it was estimated that over 25 000 steam locomotives were still in use throughout the world. However, the steam engine has a low efficiency (about 8% in a locomotive, which does not use a condenser), it takes a long time to become operational while steam is raised, it uses an awkward and dirty solid fuel (which it has to pull with it in a tender immediately behind the engine), and it creates pollution. For these reasons steam locomotives have largely been replaced in the industrial countries by electric, Diesel-electric, or Diesel trains, all of which have efficiencies of about 22%.

Where the traffic justifies the cost of installing overhead wires or a conductor rail, electric trains are usually preferred, as it is more efficient to generate electricity centrally than in the locomotive. Various configurations have been tried, but series-wound direct-current motors are the most widely used, with rectification in the locomotive when the supply is alternating current. In some cases a three-phase supply is used, with ▷thyristor control. For lines in which a permanent installation is not economic, Diesel engines are used as a prime mover. These are either coupled hydraulically to the wheels, using a hydraulic torque converter (or fluid flywheel) and a gearbox, or to an electric generator or alternator, which produces current to power electric motors that drive the wheels. The first Diesel-electric train was used in Sweden in 1912 and the first Diesel-hydraulic in Germany a year later. Because the Diesel provides a very low torque at low speeds, it cannot be used without a hydraulic coupling, but even these units are usually restricted to small trains.

The use of ▷gas turbines on the railways began in 1934, when a turbine powered a Swedish experimental train. A gas turbine-electric train was first tried in Switzerland in 1941. Although the gas turbine is lighter than the Diesel, it is only efficient at high power, and most of the long runs that could utilize its smooth full-power output are already electrified. The outlook for gas turbines is therefore not regarded as very promising. ▷*See also* magnetic levitation; monorail. ☐ p. 748.

● **Locri** ▶ 38 14N 16 15E A city founded by Dorian Greek colonists about 700 BC on the E of the toe of Italy. Well governed by oligarchic rulers, Locri possessed in Zaleucus' legal code (c. 650 BC) Europe's earliest written laws. Its strategic position inevitably brought involvement in Rome's wars with Pyrrhus and Hannibal, and Scipio Africanus conquered it in 205 BC. It later declined and was destroyed by Muslims in 915 AD. Excavations in 1889–1900 and the 1950s revealed a temple and many 5th-century terracotta plaques.

● **locus** ▶ In mathematics, a set of points that satisfy certain conditions. For example, in two dimensions the set of points a fixed distance from a particular point is a circle.

● **locust** ▶ (botany) An evergreen Mediterranean tree, *Ceratonia siliqua*, also called carob tree or St John's bread. 12–15 m in height, it has catkins of petalless flowers and produces leathery pods containing a sweet edible pulp and small flat beans. The black locust (*Robinia pseudoacacia*), also called false acacia, is a North American tree widely cultivated for ornament (it is common in streets and parks). Up to 24 m tall, it has deeply ridged dark-brown bark, paired pale-green leaves, hanging clusters of white flowers, and black pods. Family: ▷Leguminosae.

● **locust** ▶ (zoology) A ▷grasshopper that undergoes sporadic increases in population size to form huge swarms, which migrate long distances and devour all the crops and other vegetation on which they settle. When the population density is high, due to favourable environmental conditions, the nymphs (immature forms), called hoppers, are brightly coloured and crowd together—the gregarious phase, maturing into gregarious swarming adults. Solitary-phase nymphs, whose coloration is that of their surroundings, mature in uncrowded conditions into solitary nonswarming adults. Economically important species include the migratory locust (*Locusta migratoria*), about 55 mm long (all locusts are relatively large), which is found throughout Africa and S Eurasia and eastward to Australia and New Zealand; and the desert locust (*Schistocerca gregaria*), occurring from N Africa to the Punjab. In the late 1980s African food crops were threatened by the simultaneous swarming of five different species: the migratory and desert locusts, the red locust (*Nomadacris septemfasciata*), the brown locust (*Locusta pardalina*), and the Senegalese grasshopper. In 1988 locusts were recorded in the West Indies for the first time.

● **Lod** ▶ (or Lydda) 31 57N 34 54E A town in central Israel, between Jerusalem and Tel Aviv-Yafo. Lod was the scene of many biblical events. Allocated to the Arabs by the UN in 1947, it fell to Israeli forces and is now the site of Israel's international airport. Population (latest est): 42 000.

● **lodestone** ▷*See* magnetite.

● **Lodge, David (John)** ▶ (1935–) British novelist and critic. His popular comic novels lampooning academic life include *Changing Places* (1975), *Small World* (1984), and *Nice Work* (1988), which contrasts university society with the world of industry; later novels include *Paradise News* (1991), *Therapy* (1995), and *Thinks...* (2001).

● **Lodge, Henry Cabot** ▶ (1850–1924) US Republican politician; a senator from 1893 to 1924. An isolationist, he led the group of Republican senators who rejected the Treaty of ▷Versailles (1919) and prevented US membership of the League of Nations (1920).

● **Lodge, Sir Oliver Joseph** ▶ (1851–1940) British physicist; one of the pioneers in the study of radio waves and radio communication, for which he was knighted in 1902. After 1910 he became increasingly involved in attempting to reconcile science and religion, which led him into investigation of psychical phenomena. His books include the spiritualist *The Survival of Man* (1909) and the more scientific *Atoms and Rays* (1924).

● **Lodge, Thomas** ▶ (1558–1625) English poet, dramatist, and writer. His works are very varied. Notable among them is the pastoral

locomotive

Stephenson's "Rocket" The first locomotive to combine a multi-tubular boiler and a blast pipe, the "Rocket" was designed for the Liverpool to Manchester railway, which opened in 1830.

"General" Typical of the commonest type of US locomotive in the 19th century, the "General" was involved in a dramatic sabotage incident in 1862 during the Civil War. One of this class was the first to run at 100 mph (1893).

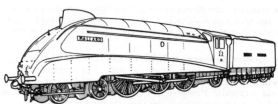

C.R. No. 123 Caledonian Railway's famous locomotive, designed by Dugald Drummond, ran the difficult 100.6 miles between Carlisle and Edinburgh in 102.5 minutes in August 1888.

"Mallard" This locomotive, designed by Sir Nigel Gresley, took the world steam traction speed record in July 1938, achieving 126 mph on a brake-test run.

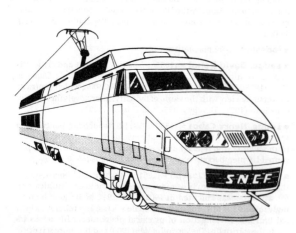

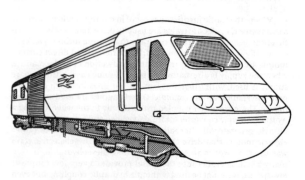

Train à Grande Vitesse (TGV) France's high-speed electric train, which runs on special rails. It established a world record for rail travel of 236 mph in 1981.

High Speed Train (HST) British Rail's Diesel-electric HST set a world record in 1985 for Diesel-powered trains by reaching 144.8 mph. The HST continues to power long-distance services in the UK's privatized system.

romance *Rosalynde* (1590), the source of Shakespeare's *As You Like It*. After studying medicine at Avignon he published medical treatises and translations.

● **Lodi** ▶ 45 19N 9 30E A town in Italy, in Lombardy on the River Adda. It has a 12th-century cathedral. Manufactures include iron, maiolica, silk, and linen; it has a large trade in cheese, especially Parmesan. Population (1993 est): 42 277.

● **Łódź** ▶ 51 49N 19 28E The second largest city in Poland. It developed rapidly during the 19th century and now specializes in textiles, chemicals, and electrical goods. Its university was founded in 1945. Population (1996 est): 825 600.

● **Loeb, Jacques** ▶ (1859–1924) US zoologist, born in Germany, who demonstrated that unfertilized eggs of sea urchins and frogs could develop to maturity by means of controlled changes in their environment, which influenced cell division (*see* parthenogenesis). Loeb also worked on brain physiology, animal ▷tropisms, and tissue regeneration.

● **Loeffler, Friedrich August Johannes** ▶ (1852–1915) German bacteriologist, who (with Edwin ▷Klebs in 1884) first isolated the diphtheria bacillus (the Klebs-Loeffler bacillus: *Corynebacterium diphtheriae*). Loeffler also showed how some animals were immune to diphtheria, which helped ▷Behring to develop an antitoxin.

● **loess** ▶ A deposit consisting of wind-born dust from desert or vegetation-free areas at the margins of ice sheets. Vast thick deposits occur in NW China; in Europe loess occurs in Germany (the Bördeland), Belgium, and NE France. Deep well-drained soils develop from loess.

● **Loewe, Frederick** ▶ (1904–88) Austrian composer of musical comedies, resident in the USA after 1924. He is famous for such musicals as *Brigadoon* (1947), *Paint Your Wagon* (1950), *My Fair Lady* (1956), *Gigi* (1958), and *Camelot* (1960), written with the librettist Alan ▷Lerner.

● **Loewi, Otto** ▶ (1873–1961) US physiologist, who demonstrated that stimulation of nerves releases a chemical transmitter that affects the muscle concerned. He identified it as ▷acetylcholine—a substance first isolated by Sir Henry ▷Dale, with whom Loewi shared the 1936 Nobel Prize.

● **Lofoten Islands** ▶ A large group of islands off the NW coast of Norway, within the Arctic Circle. There are rich cod and herring fisheries in the surrounding waters, to which many Norwegian fishermen come during spring. Area: about 5130 sq km (1980 sq mi). Population (latest est): 66 600.

● **log** ▶ 1. A book containing a detailed record of the events occurring in and navigation of a vessel. 2. A device, towed behind or fastened to a vessel, that records the speed of the vessel through the water. Its name comes from chip log, the device formerly used, which consisted of a chip tossed overboard, at the bow of a vessel; the time required to pass the chip and the distance covered were used to calculate the speed of the vessel.

● **Logan, Mount** ▶ 60 31N 140 22W The highest mountain in Canada, in SW Yukon in the St Elias Mountains. It towers 4200 m (13 780 ft) above glaciers. Height: 6050 m (19 850 ft).

● **loganberry** ▶ A trailing bramble-like shrub that is a cross between a raspberry and a blackberry. It bears heads of juicy wine-red tart-tasting fleshy berries, which are used for preserves, puddings, and wine. It originated in California and is named after James H. Logan (1841–1928), who first grew it in 1881. Family: *Rosaceae*.

● **logarithms** ▶ A mathematical function used to facilitate multiplication and division. Based on the law that $a^x \times a^y = a^{x+y}$, two numbers p and q can be multiplied together by writing them in the form $p = a^x$ and $q = a^y$ and then adding together the values of x and y (the exponents). x is called the logarithm of p to the base a, i.e. $x = \log_a p$. Thus $p \times q$ is found by looking up their logarithms in books of tables, adding them together, and looking up the antilogarithm of the result. Division is carried out in a similar way using subtraction, based on the law $a^x \div a^y = a^{x-y}$.

Logarithms were invented in 1614 by John ▷Napier, who used e,

the exponential function, as the base. These are called Napierian or natural logarithms. Shortly afterwards, the mathematician Henry ▷Briggs made calculations easier by using 10 as the base (i.e. $a = 10$). Such logarithms are known as common logarithms. The conversion from natural to common logarithms is given by: $\log_e a = 2.303 \log_{10} a$. Pocket calculators have obviated the need for logarithms as a method of computation but they remain useful mathematical functions.

● **logic** ▶ In the widest sense, the science of reasoned argument. As a mental discipline, it is concerned not so much with the application of argument in specific instances as with the general rules covering the construction of valid inferences. The dialogues of ▷Plato present ▷Socrates as pursuing wisdom through rational discourse, but ▷Aristotle was the first to make a systematic study of the principles governing such discourse (*see also* syllogism). His six logical treatises, known collectively as the *Organon*, were the sourcebooks for such medieval logicians as ▷Abelard. After the Renaissance philosophers became increasingly aware of limitations in the Aristotelian approach. ▷Leibniz, for instance, was worried by the difference between the logical and grammatical structure of sentences; two grammatically identical sentences may be very different logically. (Suppose, for example, that Jemima is a cat and compare the following two sentences: "Jemima is a cat; Jemima is mine; therefore Jemima is my cat." "Jemima is a mother; Jemima is mine; therefore Jemima is my mother.") Rules must therefore be found to formalize ordinary language in such a way as to make plain its underlying logical structure, before further rules for the construction of valid arguments can be drawn up. Since the 19th century formulation of such rules has become mainly the province of mathematicians. ▷Boole and ▷Frege were important pioneers in what is now called "mathematical logic" to differentiate it from the wider still current sense. ▷Russell, whose work influenced ▷set theory, called "logic...the youth of mathematics, and mathematics...the manhood of logic."

● **logical positivism** ▶ A philosophical movement that arose from the ▷Vienna Circle in the 1920s. Influenced by ▷Mach and ▷Wittgenstein, it insisted that philosophy should be scientific, regarding it as an analytical (rather than a speculative) activity (*see* analytic philosophy), the purpose of which was clarification of thought. Any assertion claiming to be factual (i.e. excluding the axioms of logic or mathematics) has meaning only if its truth (or falsity) can be empirically tested. Metaphysical propositions and those of aesthetics and religion are consequently meaningless, since it is impossible to say how they can be verified. A secondary goal of logical positivism was the analysis and unification of scientific terminology. After the Nazi invasion of Austria, members of the Circle emigrated to Britain and the USA, where the movement continued to be influential.

● **logos** ▶ (Greek: word) A term with several different philosophical interpretations. ▷Heraclitus used it to mean the pervading rational underpinning of the universe. For the ▷Sophists logos could simply mean an argument. For the Stoics it was the kind of god from whom stems all the rationality in the universe. Students of St John's Gospel tend to interpret its occurrence there (John 1.1, 14) in the Stoic sense. In later Christian theology it became a term for the Second Person of the Trinity, the agent of creation and redemption that became incarnate in Jesus Christ. ▷*See also* Stoicism.

● **logwood** ▶ A thorny tropical American tree, *Haematoxylon campechianum*, 9–15 m tall, with a short twisted trunk, leaves comprising many paired leaflets, and clusters of small yellow flowers. The blood-red heartwood yields the black to purple dye haematoxylin, used in the textile industry and as a biological stain. Family: ▷*Leguminosae*.

● **Lohengrin** ▶ In ▷Arthurian legend, the son of Percival (Parzival). He champions a young noblewoman, Elsa of Brabant, whom he agrees to marry on condition that she does not enquire into his origins. When her curiosity overcomes her, he is taken back by his swan guide to the castle of the ▷Holy Grail, whence he came. The story was adapted by ▷Wagner in the opera *Lohengrin* (1850).

● **Loire, River** ▶ The longest river in France. Rising in the Cévennes Mountains, it flows mainly W to the Bay of Biscay at St Nazaire, passing through Orléans, Tours, and Nantes. Its tributaries include the Allier, Vienne, and Maine and it drains an area of 119 140 sq km

(40 000 sq mi), one-fifth of the area of France. The Loire Valley is renowned for its vineyards and chateaux (Amboise, Blois, Chambord, Chaumont, Chenonceaux). It is linked by canal with the River Seine. Length: 1020 km (634 mi).

● **Loki** ▶ In Norse mythology, a mischief-making giant with the ability to change his shape and sex, who lived among the gods until imprisoned in a cave for the murder of Balder. His offspring—Hel, the goddess of death, Jörmungandr, the evil serpent surrounding the earth, and Fenris, the wolf—are among the forces of evil, which he leads against the gods at doomsday (▷Ragnarök).

● **Lolland** ▶ (or Laaland) A Danish island in the Baltic Sea, S of Sjælland. Produce includes cereals, hops, and apples. Area: 1240 sq km (480 sq mi). Population (latest est): 80 500. Chief town: Maribo.

● **Lollards** ▶ The followers of the English reformer ▷Wycliffe. Until his retirement from Oxford in 1378, the preaching of his doctrines attacking the Church hierarchy and transubstantiation and advocating the primacy of Scripture was largely confined to the University. Thereafter his teachings were taken up by nonacademics, including merchants, lesser clergy, and a few members of Richard II's court. Henry IV's reign saw repression of the Lollards culminating in the defeat of ▷Oldcastle's rebellion in 1414. The movement then went underground and became more proletarian. Many of its tenets were adopted by the early Protestants.

● **Lomax, Alan** ▶ (1915–) US compiler of folksongs. With his father **John Avery Lomax** (1867–1948), he compiled *American Ballads and Folk Songs* (1934), *Negro Folk Songs As Sung by Leadbelly* (1936), and *Our Singing Country* (1941).

● **Lombard League** ▶ A confederacy of Lombard towns formed with papal support in 1167 against attempts by the Holy Roman Empire to weaken their liberties. These were confirmed by Frederick (I) Barbarossa at the Peace of Constance (1183). Renewed against the threat of Frederick II the League was disbanded after his death (1250).

● **Lombardo, Pietro** ▶ (c. 1438–1515) Italian sculptor and architect. Lombardo worked mainly in Venice, where he was the leading sculptor of his generation. His works include the Pietro Mocenigo monument (c. 1476–81; SS Giovanni e Paolo) and the design and sculptural decoration of Sta Maria dei Miracoli (1481–89). He was frequently assisted by his two sons **Antonio Lombardo** (c. 1458–c. 1516) and **Tullio Lombardo** (c. 1460–1532).

● **Lombards** ▶ (Latin name: Langobardi) A Germanic people who, under ▷Alboin, invaded Italy and established a kingdom centred on Pavia (572 AD). When ▷Aistulf and then Desiderius (reigned 756–74) threatened Rome, the pope sought Carolingian assistance and in 773–74 the Lombards lost their independence to Charlemagne.

● **Lombardy** ▶ (Italian name: Lombardia) A region in N Italy, consisting mainly of mountains in the N and lowlands in the S. Italy's most industrialized region, its economic prosperity has attracted workers from other parts of the country. The industrial area containing Milan is dominated by textile, chemical, and engineering industries; metal manufacture is also important. Agriculture is the most mechanized in Italy, producing a wide range of foods. There are natural-gas fields and hydroelectric plants. Area: 23 834 sq km (9191 sq mi). Population (1996 est): 8 924 870. Capital: Milan.

● **Lombok** ▶ An Indonesian island in the Nusa Tenggara group. The N and S are mountainous, while the central plain produces rice, coffee, and tobacco. Under Hindu-Buddhist rule until the 15th century, it resisted Islamic influence and came under Dutch control in 1894. The island saw violence between Muslims and Christians in 2000. Area: 4730 sq km (1826 sq mi). Population (1991 est): 2 500 000. Chief town: Mataram.

● **Lombroso, Cesare** ▶ (1835–1909) Italian criminologist. His theories that some criminals can be recognized by physical characteristics are no longer considered valid, but his major work, *L'uomo delinquente* (1876), initiated a new emphasis in criminology on the study of the criminal mind.

● **Lomé** ▶ 6 10N 1 21E The capital and chief port of Togo, on the Gulf of Guinea. The Lomé Convention, providing trade concessions with EC countries for 46 African and Caribbean states, was signed here in 1975, as were its successors in 1979 and 1984. It has a university (1970). Population (1990 est): 513 000.

● **Lomond, Loch** ▶ The largest lake in Scotland, in Argyll and Bute about 40 km (15.5 mi) NW of Glasgow. It is a picturesque tourist area. Length: about 38 km (24 mi). Width: 8 km (5 mi).

● **Lomonosov, Mikhail Vasilievich** ▶ (1711–65) Russian poet and scientist. The son of a fisherman, his work in the natural sciences led to a professorship at the St Petersburg Academy. In 1755 he founded Moscow University. He also wrote classical poetry and works on grammar and rhetoric.

● **Lomu, Jonah** ▶ (1975–) New Zealand Rugby Union player. A forward, he dominated the 1995 World Cup with his gigantic physique and sprinting power.

● **London** ▶ (Latin name: Londinium) 51 30N 0 10W The capital of the UK, in SE England on the River Thames. One of the largest cities in the world, it comprises a succession of village communities that counterbalance its overall size, bustle, and complexity. It is also exceptional in its large number of parks, gardens, and garden squares.

London's financial hub is to be found in its original nucleus, the ▷City of London, on the N bank of the Thames between Blackfriars Bridge and Tower Bridge. The City comprises some 2.6 sq km (1 sq mi) and its large daytime population dwindles to a mere 8000 at night. Attempts to halt its depopulation have included new residential developments, notably the ▷Barbican (1973), designed for about 6500 people. London's East End, centring on the borough of ▷Tower Hamlets, has long provided a home for successive immigrant groups and acquired in the 19th century a reputation for harbouring Britain's leading criminal families. The West End comprises the district around Oxford Street (constructed in the 19th century) and is the city's shopping and entertainment centre. For purposes of local government, a two-tier administrative structure was devised in 1963: 32 (12 Inner London and 20 Outer London) boroughs and the Greater London Council (GLC). However, the Labour-controlled GLC was abolished by the Conservative government in 1986, its functions being transferred to the borough councils and to residuary bodies. In a 1998 referendum Londoners backed plans to create an elected Greater London Assembly and a directly elected mayor, to take over in 2000. Ken ▷Livingstone was duly elected and in 2002 ▷City Hall was opened to house the mayor and assembly. The government of the City is the responsibility of the Corporation of the City of London, which remains administratively separate.

London's cultural life is outstanding. In addition to the private art galleries around Bond Street in Mayfair, there are remarkable collections in the ▷National Gallery, the National Portrait Gallery, the two ▷Tate Galleries, and the ▷Courtauld Institute of Art. Museums include the ▷British Museum (in Bloomsbury), the Natural History Museum—properly the British Museum (Natural History), the ▷Science Museum, the ▷Victoria and Albert Museum (all in South Kensington), and the ▷Imperial War Museum. Most of London's commercial theatres are in the West End but the subsidized National Theatre Company moved in 1975 to Lasdun's building on the South Bank of the Thames, adjacent to the Royal Festival Hall (*see* Festival of Britain), the Queen Elizabeth Hall, the Purcell Room (all concert halls), the Hayward Gallery, the National Film Theatre, and the Museum of the Moving Image. The ▷Barbican Centre (opened 1982) in the City houses the Royal Shakespeare Company and the London Symphony Orchestra. Other concert halls include the Royal Albert Hall and the Wigmore Hall. London has four independent symphony orchestras—the London Philharmonic, the London Symphony, the Royal Philharmonic, and the Philharmonia Orchestras; there is also the BBC Symphony Orchestra. The Royal Opera House at ▷Covent Garden (renovated 1998–99) houses both the ▷Royal Opera and the ▷Royal Ballet, which with the English National Opera (currently at the London Coliseum) was founded at ▷Sadler's Wells. The University of London (1836) comprises colleges scattered throughout the city; the City University (1966) and Brunel University (1966) also lie within Greater London as do another seven universities formed in 1992 from former polytechnics. Other educational institutions include the ▷Royal Academy, the Royal Academy of Music, the Royal College of Music, the Guildhall School of Music and Drama, the ▷Royal Academy of Dramatic Art, and several teaching hospitals. ▷*See also* Inns of Court.

London ► A general view of the city before the Fire of London in 1666. Old St Paul's Cathedral is in the left middle ground, London Bridge and the Tower are on the right, and Southwark Cathedral dominates the foreground.

Economy: the City of London is one of the world's greatest banking, commodity, and insurance centres. Other London markets include ▷Billingsgate (for fish), ▷Smithfield (the largest meat market in the world), and Nine Elms in Vauxhall, which replaced the colourful fruit and vegetable market at Covent Garden, which has been redeveloped as a shopping precinct. London's commercial development depended to a large extent on its port, on which a vast entrepôt trade was based. However, apart from Tilbury Docks, most of the port area has been redeveloped for residential and commercial purposes, including Canary Wharf, a large office development that is London's tallest building (*see* Docklands).

Many industries have now moved from central London to the suburbs but a variety of light industries remain. Activities are often localized: for example, the bespoke tailoring trade is centred on Savile Row, diamonds on Hatton Garden, and Harley Street (in Marylebone) is synonymous with private medicine. London's public-transport system includes an extensive bus service (which was privatized in 1994) as well as the ▷underground railway (the "tube"). Developments in the 1980s included the Docklands Light Railway. London has the chief railway terminuses in the UK (stations include Euston, Paddington, Marylebone, Victoria, King's Cross, St Pancras, and Waterloo); it is served by airports at ▷Heathrow, ▷Gatwick (in Surrey), and ▷Stansted (in Essex). A London City Airport was opened in the former docklands in 1987.

History: the foundations of London Wall are the chief reminder of the City's origins under the Romans, who built London at the highest point at which the Thames could be forded and at the river's tidal limit—on what was later Cornhill and Ludgate Hill. It was sacked by Boadicea in 61 AD and subsequently, on several occasions, by the Vikings. During the reign of William the Conqueror the White Tower (*see* Tower of London) was built, and as London prospered in the middle ages both the Church and the ▷guilds sponsored exceptional building programmes. Parts of St Bartholomew the Great (1123), St John of Jerusalem at Clerkenwell (c. 1150), and the Temple Church (1185), among others, survive from the 12th century; ▷Westminster Abbey dates from the 11th century, being largely rebuilt in the 13th century, when Southwark Cathedral was begun. To the 15th century belong the Guildhall and Lambeth Palace and to the 16th century, when London began to extend westwards, ▷St James' Palace. The early Stuart period saw the great work of Inigo Jones, notably the Queen's House at Greenwich (1617–35) and the Banqueting Hall in Whitehall (1619–22), its ceiling painted by Rubens. London's population was decimated by the Plague (1665) and much of its fabric was destroyed in the Fire of the following year. The greatest loss—Old St Paul's (▷St Paul's Cathedral)—was replaced by Wren, who was responsible for much of the work of reconstruction: of his 49 parish churches, probably the finest is St Stephen Walbrook (1679), the Lord Mayor's church. Many of London's squares were built in the late 17th and early 18th centuries—Grosvenor and Berkeley Squares in Mayfair, Hanover and Cavendish Squares off Oxford Street, and St James's Square, S of Piccadilly all belong to this period. In the second half of the 18th century the Adam brothers designed the Adelphi

estate near the Strand and also Portland Place; to the early 19th century belongs the work of Nash: Regent's Park (in which the zoological gardens are now to be found) and the terraces around it. London's other parks include ▷Hyde Park, Kensington Gardens, St James's Park (in which ▷Buckingham Palace is located), and Battersea Park in S London. New bridges were also being built at this time: Westminster was completed in 1750, Blackfriars in 1769, Waterloo in 1817 (rebuilt 1937–42), and Southwark in 1819. Subsequent river crossings in London include ▷Tower Bridge, the new ▷London Bridge, Lambeth Bridge (1861, rebuilt 1929–31), the ▷Rotherhithe Tunnel, the ▷Blackwall Tunnel, the ▷Dartford tunnel and bridge, and the Millennium Bridge (2000; a footbridge between St Paul's Cathedral and Tate Modern on Bankside). The 19th century produced the ▷Palace of Westminster, the Law Courts, such railway stations as St Pancras, and the Byzantine-style Westminster Cathedral. London, especially the City and the East End, was seriously damaged by bombs during World War II and subsequent rebuilding has consisted largely of high-rise offices and flats, including the National Westminster building (1977). Area: 1580 sq km (610 sq mi). Population (1995 est): 7 007 100.

● **London ►** 42 58N 81 15W A city in central Canada, in Ontario. Founded in 1826, it has become SW Ontario's centre for transportation, manufacturing, finance, and education. Industries include textiles, printing, food processing, chemicals, electrical and metal goods, motor vehicle parts, and engines. It houses the University of Western Ontario (1878). Population (1991): 381 522 (metropolitan area).

● **London, Jack ►** (1876–1916) US novelist. After childhood poverty and imprisonment for vagrancy he embarked on a course of self-education, becoming a socialist and best-selling author. His best-known novel, *The Call of the Wild* (1903), was written after his experience of the Klondike gold rush in 1897. His other novels include *White Fang* (1906) and the autobiographical *Martin Eden* (1909).

● **London Bridge ►** A bridge spanning the River Thames from the SE region of the City of London to the borough of Southwark. Bridges on this site date back to Roman times but the most famous London Bridge was built in stone between 1176 and 1209, had 19 pointed arches and a drawbridge, and was surmounted by shops and houses. It was replaced by a new bridge in the 1820s, designed by John ▷Rennie. The present bridge was completed in 1973.

● **London clubs ►** Establishments, chiefly in and around the London streets of St James and Pall Mall, in which men and/or women (some are single-sex) gather for companionship or to pursue a common interest. Most have restaurants and provide accommodation for short stays. Membership to a London club is by election; subscriptions and entrance fees provide for their maintenance. The origins of the modern club lie in the regular gathering of men over coffee in the 17th and 18th centuries; the first London club was White's, which began as a Chocolate House in 1698. Others include Boodle's (founded 1762), the Athenaeum (1824), ▷Crockford's (1827), the Garrick (1831), the Carlton (1832), the Reform (1836), and the Royal Automobile (1897).

● **Londonderry** ▶ (*or* Derry) 55 00N 7 19W A city and port in North-ern Ireland, in Co Londonderry on the River Foyle. The City of London Corporation was granted Londonderry and the Irish Society estab-lished (1610) to administer it. In a famous siege (1688–89) it held out for 105 days against the forces of James II. Industries include light en-gineering and food processing. Population (1991): 72 334.

● **Londonderry** ▶ (*or* Derry) A historic county of N Northern Ire-land, on the Atlantic Ocean. In 1972 its administrative powers were devolved to the new district councils of Coleraine, Derry, Limavady, and Magherafelt. It consists of central uplands bordered by lowlands with Lough Neagh in the SE. Drained by the Rivers Foyle, Bann, and Roe, it is mainly agricultural, producing flax, cereals, and dairy pro-duce. Fishing is also important. Industries include textiles, chemi-cals, and light engineering. Area: 2108 sq km (814 sq mi).

● **London Eye** ▶ (*or* Millennium Wheel) The world's largest Ferris wheel, built on London's South Bank to commemorate the new mil-lennium and opened in 2000. It has a diameter of 132 m (435 ft) and carries 32 viewing capsules attached to its circumference (each hold-ing 25 people). Taking 30 minutes to complete one revolution, it gives passengers unrivalled views of the capital.

● **London Marathon** ▶ A marathon race held annually in E central London (beginning on Blackheath and finishing on Westminster Bridge). The first such event was organized by Chris Brasher and John Disley in 1981 and proved a huge success, attracting both serious in-ternational athletes and thousands of ordinary runners. It has since grown in size and popularity; by 2000 some 445 000 people had com-pleted the marathon, raising an estimated £100M for charity through sponsorship. A wheelchair race for paraplegics was introduced in 1983.

● **London Museum** ▷*See* Barbican.

● **London pride** ▶ A succulent herb, *Saxifraga umbrosa*, also called St Patrick's cabbage, native to Ireland and Portugal and widely grown as an ornamental. It has a basal rosette of leaves and small white or pinkish five-petalled flowers in clusters on slender stems, 30–50 cm tall. The garden form is a hybrid, *S.* × *urbium*. Family: *Saxifragaceae*.

● **London School of Economics and Political Science** ▶ (LSE) A school of London University founded in 1895 by Sidney ▷Webb using money bequeathed for the purpose by Henry Hutchinson, a member of the ▷Fabian Society. The school has had a profound influence on political and economic thinking throughout the 20th century.

● **Londrina** ▶ 23 18S 51 13W A city in S Brazil, in Paraná state. Founded in 1930, it is the centre of a coffee-growing area and has a university (1971). Population (1991): 355 062.

● **Long Beach** ▶ 33 47N 118 06W A city and port in the USA, in Cali-fornia on San Pedro Bay. It is a major tourist centre, with a beach 13.5 km (8.5 mi) long. The former British liner *Queen Mary*, converted into a hotel and conference centre, is moored here. Industries include aircraft manufacture and oil refining. Population (1996 est): 421 904.

● **longbow** ▶ A bow of straight-grained yew used from about 1400 to about 1600. Originally Welsh, longbows were up to 1.8 m (6 ft) long and could fire a 110 cm (37 in) arrow capable of piercing chainmail and some plate armour at 183 m (200 yd) every 10 seconds.

● **Longfellow, Henry Wadsworth** ▶ (1807–82) US poet. He trav-elled extensively in Europe and was professor of modern languages at Harvard (1834–54). He achieved enormous popularity with such narrative poems as *Evangeline* (1847) and *The Song of Hiawatha* (1855). He also produced a translation of Dante's *Divine Comedy* (1865–67).

● **Longford** ▶ (Irish name: Longphort) A county in the N central Re-public of Ireland, in Leinster. Chiefly low lying with areas of bog, it contains part of Lough Ree in the SW. Agriculture consists of stock rearing and the production of oats and potatoes. Area: 1043 sq km (403 sq mi). Population (1996): 30 000. County town: Longford.

● **Longhi, Pietro** ▶ (Pietro Falca; 1702–85) Venetian painter, who specialized in scenes of upper-class life. Small in scale, they are distin-guished by their doll-like figures and humorous approach, notably in *Exhibition of a Rhinoceros* (National Gallery, London). His son **Alessandro Longhi** (1733–1813) was a portrait painter.

● **Longinus** ▶ (1st century AD) Greek rhetorician, supposed author of *On the Sublime*. This treatise, a critical analysis of the quality of ex-cellence in literature with illustrative quotations, greatly influenced later neoclassical writers, including Dryden, Pope, and Gibbon; it was first translated (1674) into a modern language by Boileau.

● **Long Island** ▶ An island in the USA, in New York state separated from the mainland by Long Island Sound. Chiefly residential with many resorts, it contains the New York City boroughs of ▷Brooklyn and ▷Queens and John F. Kennedy Airport. Its farms provide the city with market-garden produce. Area: 4462 sq km (1723 sq mi).

● **longitude** ▷*See* latitude and longitude.

● **long jump** ▶ A field event in athletics. Competitors sprint up a runway and leap into a sandpit from a take-off board. The competitor who makes the longest jump in three or six tries is the winner. World records: men: 8.95 m (1991) by Michael Powell (USA); women: 7.52 m (1988) by Galina Chistyakova (Soviet Union).

● **Longleat** ▶ A country house near Warminster, in Wiltshire, owned by the Marquess of Bath. Begun in the 1550s, it was burned down in 1567, and rebuilt from 1572 for Sir John Thynne (d. 1580). The house and its grounds, originally laid out by Capability ▷Brown and now containing a lion safari park, are open to the public.

● **Long March** ▶ (1934–35) The flight of the Chinese communists from the ▷Jiangxi Soviet, which they were forced by the ▷Guomindang to abandon, to Yan'an, a distance of 10 000 km (6000 mi). Over 100 000 people, led by Mao Tse-tung, took part in the heroic march but only about 30 000 reached Yan'an. The Long March estab-lished Mao as the leader of the Chinese Communist Party.

● **Long Parliament** ▶ (1640–60) The parliament that was sum-moned by Charles I of England following his defeat in the second ▷Bishops' War. In 1640 it impeached the king's ministers, ▷Strafford and ▷Laud, and in 1641 expressed its grievances against Charles in the ▷Grand Remonstrance. Following his attempt to impeach five MPs by force it assumed control of the militia (1642). Charles' rejec-tion of its demands for reform (Nineteen Propositions) precipitated the Civil War. Its power declined as that of the ▷New Model Army in-creased and in 1648 it was purged of its moderate members (*see* Pride, Thomas). The remaining Rump Parliament was dismissed in 1653 by Oliver □Cromwell, who established the ▷Protectorate. The Rump was reinstated in 1659 and the full Long Parliament was restored by ▷Monck in 1660. Shortly afterwards it dissolved itself, being replaced by the Convention Parliament, which effected the ▷Restoration.

● **longship** ▶ A large sailing vessel equipped with a bank of oars on each side. Longships were used by Scandinavian peoples until the mid-18th century. They had square sails and high prows and were steered by a tiller attached to a large rudder. Longships could carry up to a hundred people and are said to have carried the Vikings from Scandinavia as far as Greenland and to the coast of North America.

● **longsightedness** ▶ (*or* hypermetropia) Inability to see close ob-jects clearly, because the lens of the eye focuses light to a point behind the retina (light-sensitive layer). This is less common than shortsightedness among young people, but, owing to changes in the lens with age, many people need glasses for reading by the time they are 50. This type of longsightedness is known as **presbyopia**.

● **long-tailed tit** ▶ An acrobatic Eurasian tit, *Aegithalus caudatus*, about 14 cm long, with a black, pink, and white plumage and a long (7 cm) black-and-white tail. It feeds on insects and spiders and builds a nest from lichens, hair, cobwebs, and feathers. ▷*See* Plate III.

● **Lonsdale, Gordon Arnold** ▶ (Konon Trofimovich Molody; 1924–?70) Russian secret agent. He worked in Britain from 1954, posing as a Canadian businessman. Arrested in 1961, he was exchanged in 1964 for the British agent Greville Wynne. ▷*See also* Kroger affair.

● **Lonsdale, Dame Kathleen** ▶ (1903–71) Irish physicist. One of the foremost X-ray crystallographers of her time, she used this tech-nique to prove the ring structure of benzene compounds (1929). In 1945 she became the first woman to be elected to the Royal Society.

● **loofah** ▶ The fibrous skeleton of the fruit of the tropical dishcloth gourd, or vegetable sponge (genus *Luffa* (6 species), especially *L. cylindrica*). These vines produce cucumber-like fruits, about 30 cm long. When mature, the pulp and seeds are removed leaving a dense network of fibrous conducting tissue, which is used as a bath sponge, dish washer, and industrial filter. Family: *Cucurbitaceae*.

● **loom** ▷*See* weaving.

● **looper** ▷*See* geometrid moth.

● **Loos, Adolph** ▶ (1870–1933) Austrian architect. One of the pioneers of modern architecture, Loos was influenced by the styles of Otto ▷Wagner and Louis ▷Sullivan. His austere plain style, evident in the Steiner House, Vienna (1910), influenced ▷Gropius and the development of ▷functionalism. Later in his career, however, he became less dogmatic, designing buildings with classical motifs.

● **loosestrife** ▶ Either of two perennial herbs occurring in marshes, ditches, and along river banks. Purple loosestrife, *Lythrum salicaria* (family *Lythraceae*), native to Eurasia, N Africa, and North America, grows to a height of 60–120 cm and bears spikes of purple flowers. The Eurasian yellow loosestrife, *Lysimachia vulgaris* (family *Primulaceae*), grows to a height of 1 m and bears clusters of yellow flowers.

● **Lope de Vega** ▷*See* Vega (Carpio), Lope Félix de.

● **López, Carlos Antonio** ▶ (?1790–1862) Paraguayan statesman. As president (1844–62) he attempted to modernize the country and to end its isolation. He was succeeded by his son **Francisco Solano López** (1826–70), who led Paraguay into the disastrous War of the ▷Triple Alliance.

● **López de Ayala, Pero** ▶ (c. 1332–c. 1407) Spanish poet and chronicler, who became chancellor of Castile in 1399. His works include translations of Livy, Boethius, and Boccaccio, as well as *Rimado de palacio*, a collection of satirical poetry, and *Crónicas de los reyes de Castilla*.

● **Lop Nor** ▶ An area of salt marsh and shallow shifting lakes in NW China, in the ▷Tarim Basin. Nuclear tests have been carried out here. Formerly a large salt lake, its area now varies widely.

● **loquat** ▶ A small evergreen tree *Eriobotrya japonica*, native to China and Japan but cultivated in Mediterranean countries. 6–9 m high, it bears clusters of white flowers. The pear-shaped orange fruit has a woolly skin and is eaten fresh, in preserves, or in stews. Family: *Rosaceae*.

● **Lorca, Federico García** ▷*See* García Lorca, Federico.

● **Lord Chancellor** ▷*See* chancellor.

● **Lord Chief Justice** ▶ The presiding judge of the Queen's Bench Division of the High Court of Justice and the Criminal Division of the Court of Appeal; he is second in the judicial hierarchy to the Lord Chancellor (*see* chancellor). In 2000 Sir Thomas Bingham was succeeded in the post by Harry, Baron Woolf (1933–).

● **Lord Lieutenant** ▶ In the UK, the permanent local representative of the Crown in a county. The office dates from 1557, when the Lord Lieutenant was responsible for maintaining order in the county and for its local defence. The post now involves attending on any members of the royal family who visit the county and making presentations of honours and awards on behalf of the Crown. Most Lord Lieutenants also hold the office of *Custos Rotulorum*, which makes them responsible for appointing magistrates in the county. They also have certain duties in connection with the armed forces (especially reserve forces). The appointment of Lords Lieutenant is now regulated by the Reserve Forces Act (1980) and the appointment is made by the sovereign on the recommendation of the prime minister.

● **Lord Lyon King of Arms** ▶ The highest authority in the deciding of heraldic matters in Scotland. Originally a herald in the 14th century, the Lord Lyon now heads four heralds and two pursuivants at the Lyon Office where, since 1677, all claims to arms must be registered. Also a judge, the Lord Lyon has jurisdiction over issues of clan chieftainship and pedigrees.

● **Lords, House of** ▷*See* parliament.

● **Lord's cricket ground** ▶ The world's most famous cricket ground, owned by the ▷Marylebone Cricket Club and situated in St John's Wood, London. It was founded by Thomas Lord (1757–1832) in

Dorset Square and was moved to its present site in 1814. It has been the home of the Middlesex County Cricket Club since 1877.

● **Lorelei** ▶ A rock in the Rhine River in W Germany noted for its echo and its association with a legend concerning a water nymph whose singing lured sailors to destruction. The legend first appears in the works of Clemens ▷Brentano.

● **Loren, Sophia** ▶ (S. Scicoloni; 1934–) Italian film actress. From working as an extra and then as a supporting actress, she progressed to international stardom in such films as *Two Women* (1961), *The Millionairess* (1961), *Marriage Italian Style* (1964), *The Cassandra Crossing* (1977) and *Saturday, Sunday, and Monday* (1990). She is married to the Italian film producer Carlo Ponti (1913–); she became a French citizen in 1964.

● **Lorentz, Hendrick Antoon** ▶ (1853–1928) Dutch physicist, who was awarded the 1902 Nobel Prize, with his pupil ▷Zeeman, for their work on the relationship between magnetism and radiation. Independently of ▷Fitzgerald, he suggested that bodies become shorter as their velocity increases, in order to explain the negative result of the ▷Michelson-Morley experiment. This phenomenon, now known as the **Lorentz-Fitzgerald** contraction, was later incorporated into Einstein's theory of ▷relativity. The mathematical treatment for transforming a set of coordinates from one frame of reference to another was worked out by Lorentz (**Lorentz transformations**) and also formed part of Einstein's theory of relativity.

● **Lorenz, Konrad** ▶ (1903–89) Austrian zoologist, who was one of the founders of modern ethology (the study of animal behaviour). In the 1930s Lorenz identified the phenomenon of ▷imprinting in young chicks. He aimed to determine the elements of behaviour, how they were stimulated, their development in an individual, and their evolutionary significance. Lorenz wrote several popular books about his work, including *King Solomon's Ring* (1949) and *Man Meets Dog* (1950). He applied his theories to the human species, with controversial implications (*On Aggression*, 1963). He was awarded a Nobel Prize (1973) with Karl von ▷Frisch and Niko ▷Tinbergen.

● **Lorenzetti** ▶ Two brothers, both Italian painters of the Sienese school, who were influenced by Giovanni ▷Pisano and ▷Giotto. They probably both died in the plague of 1348. **Pietro Lorenzetti** (c. 1280–?1348) was probably the pupil of ▷Duccio; he introduced a new humanity into his master's style in such works as *The Birth of the Virgin* (Duomo, Siena). His brother **Ambrogio Lorenzetti** (c. 1290–?1348) is renowned for his frescoes of *Good and Bad Government* (1337–39; Palazzo Pubblico, Siena). They are among the first Italian paintings to show scenes of contemporary life and are remarkable for their early mastery of perspective.

● **Lorenzo Monaco** ▶ (Piero di Giovanni; c. 1370–1425) Italian painter, born in Siena. He settled in Florence, becoming a monk in 1391. Influenced by both the Sienese school and the Florentine tradition of ▷Giotto, his *Coronation of the Virgin* (Uffizi) is his major work.

● **Lorestan** ▷*See* Luristan.

● **Loreto** ▶ 43 26N 13 36E A small town in central Italy, in Marche. Pilgrims travel here to see the Santa Casa (Holy House), which is said to have been the home of the Virgin Mary in Nazareth and to have been brought to Loreto by angels in the 13th century. Population (latest est): 10 500.

● **Lorient** ▶ 47 45N 3 21W A port in NW France, in the Morbihan department on the Bay of Biscay. Formerly the principal naval shipyard in France, it was destroyed in World War II. Today it has important fishing and car component industries. Population (1990): 61 630.

● **loris** ▶ A nocturnal Asian ▷prosimian primate belonging to the subfamily *Lorisinae* (5 species). Lorises are 20–35 cm long with almost no tail and very large dark eyes. They are generally slow-moving and arboreal, feeding on insects and fruit. Family: *Lorisidae*. ▷*See* also angwantibo; potto.

● **Lorraine** ▶ (German name: Lothringen) A planning region and former province in NE France, bordering on Belgium, Luxembourg, and Germany. Its iron-ore deposits are the largest in Europe outside Sweden and the former Soviet Union.

History: it was frequently the scene of conflict between France and Germany. In the 9th century AD it formed part of the kingdom of Lotharingia, later becoming a duchy under the Holy Roman Empire. Disputed between France and the Habsburgs, it finally became a French province in 1766. Following the Franco-Prussian War (1871) part of Lorraine (now Moselle department) was lost to Germany and united with ▷Alsace as the imperial territory of Alsace-Lorraine. Area: 23 540 sq km (9087 sq mi). Population (1995 est): 2 311 500.

● **Lorraine, Charles, Cardinal of** ▷*See* Guise.

● **Lorraine, Claude** ▷*See* Claude Lorraine.

● **lory** ► A small brightly coloured ▷parrot belonging to the subfamily *Loriinae* (62 species), occurring in Australia, New Guinea, and Polynesia. Lories have a slender bill with a brush-tipped tongue and feed on pollen and nectar.

● **Los Alamos** ► 28 54N 103 00W A town in the USA, in New Mexico. The first atom bombs were made here during World War II and the first nuclear explosion took place here on 16 July 1945. The H-bomb was later developed here by the scientific laboratory of the University of California, which now covers an area of 199 sq km (77 sq mi). Government control of Los Alamos ended in 1962. Population (1990): 11 455.

● **Los Angeles** ► 34 00N 118 15W A city and seaport in the USA, in S California on the Pacific coast. Founded in 1781 by Franciscan missionaries, it was made the capital of Mexican California in 1845 but was captured by US forces in the following year. Over the years it has incorporated many neighbouring towns so that today it comprises a large industrial and urban complex, with the second largest population in the USA. The centre of the US film industry, it attracts many tourists and has several television and radio stations. Other major industries include the manufacture of aircraft and oil refining. Industrial pollution, augmented by the high density of cars (Los Angeles is the only major US city without a public system of transport), is a serious problem. An educational centre, it is the site of several universities. The city was badly damaged during riots resulting from social and racial tensions (1992) and by an earthquake (1994). Population (1996 est): 3 553 638.

● **Los Angeles, Victoria de** ► (1923–   ) Spanish soprano. She studied at the Barcelona conservatoire, made her London and New York debuts in 1950, and excelled in the title roles of Massenet's *Manon Lescaut* and Puccini's *Madame Butterfly*.

● **Losey, Joseph** ► (1909–84) US film director. Accused during the McCarthy era of having communist sympathies, he went to Europe in 1952. His fascination with English class structure is evident in *The Servant* (1963), *Accident* (1967), and *The Go-Between* (1971), all scripted by Harold ▷Pinter. His last film was *Steaming* (1984).

● **Lossiemouth** ► 57 43N 3 18W A town in NE Scotland, in Moray on the Moray Firth. It is a small fishing port, resort, and the birthplace of Ramsay MacDonald. Population (1991): 7184.

● **Lost Generation** ► The expatriate US writers of the 1920s whose works expressed their sense of spiritual alienation. The term derives from a remark attributed to Gertrude Stein and used as an epigraph to Ernest Hemingway's novel *The Sun Also Rises* (1926).

● **Lot** ► In the Old Testament, the nephew of ▷Abraham. He and his wife escaped the destruction of Sodom, but his wife disobeyed instructions not to look back and was turned into a pillar of salt (Genesis 19). Lot was subsequently made drunk and seduced by his two daughters, who bore his children.

● **Lot, River** ► A river in S France, flowing mainly W through the departments of Lozère, Aveyron, Lot, and Lot-et-Garonne to the River Garonne. Length: 483 km (300 mi).

● **Lothair** ► (c. 835–69 AD) King (855–69) of an area W of the Rhine, inherited from his father Lothair I, that came to be called Lotharingia. His attempts to divorce his childless wife Theutberga developed into a struggle with Pope Nicholas I.

● **Lothair I** ► (795–855 AD) Coemperor of the West; eldest son of ▷Louis (I) the Pious, whose coemperor he became in 817. On Louis' death in 840 Lothair's position was challenged by his brothers Louis

the German (d. 876) and Charles the Bald and in 843 the Frankish territories were divided between them.

● **Lothair II** ► (1075–1137) Holy Roman Emperor (1133–37) and, as Lothair III, German king (1125–37). He became Duke of Saxony in 1106 in return for supporting Emperor Henry V against his father in 1104 but subsequently turned against Henry, defeating him at the battle of Welfesholz (1115). The Hohenstaufen family contested his election as king until 1135. As emperor, he tried to expel Roger II of Sicily from Italy.

● **Lothian Region** ► A former administrative region in SE Scotland, bounded by the Firth of Forth in the N and the North Sea in the E. It was created under local government reorganization in 1975 from the counties of ▷East Lothian, ▷Midlothian (including ▷Edinburgh), and ▷West Lothian. In 1996 it was abolished and administrative powers were devolved to four ▷unitary authorities: West Lothian, Edinburgh, Midlothian, and East Lothian.

● **Loti, Pierre** ► (Julien Viaud; 1850–1923) French novelist. He served as a naval officer and wrote numerous novels of romance and adventure with exotic settings and several travel books. His best-known novels include three studies of Breton sailors, *Mon frère Yves* (1883), *Pêcheur d'Islande* (1886), and *Matelot* (1893).

● **Lotto, Lorenzo** ► (c. 1480–1556) Venetian painter. He travelled extensively in Italy and his work is consequently marked by a number of influences; he frequently visited Venice but, unable to compete with Titian's success, worked chiefly in Bergamo. He is noted for his altarpieces, e.g. the *Crucifixion* (Monte San Giusto, Bergamo), and the psychological insight of such portraits as *A Young Man* (Kunsthistorisches Museum, Vienna), and *Andrea Odoni* (Hampton Court). He spent his last years in a monastery in Loreto.

● **lotus** ► Any of several different water plants. The sacred lotus of ancient Egypt was probably *Nymphaea lotus*, a sweet-scented white night-flowering ▷water lily with broad petals, or *N. caerulea*, a blue-flowered species. The sacred Indian lotus, *Nelumbo nucifera* (family *Nelumbaceae*), has roselike pink flowers and its seeds, called lotus nuts, are eaten raw or in soups. The genus *Lotus* contains about 70 species of herbs, including the birdsfoot ▷trefoils.

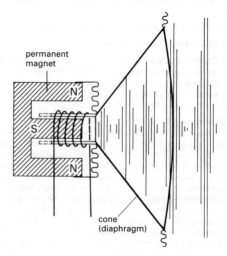

permanent magnet

N

S

N

cone (diaphragm)

loudspeaker ► A moving-coil loudspeaker with a pot-shaped permanent magnet.

● **loudspeaker** ► A device for converting electrical signals into sound. It usually consists of a small coil fixed to the centre of a movable diaphragm or cone. The coil is in an annular gap between the poles of a strong ▷magnet. An audio-frequency electrical signal fed to the coil creates a varying magnetic field, which interacts with the steady field in the gap. This causes the coil, and the attached cone, to vibrate and produce sound waves of the same frequencies as the electrical signal. Generally, larger cones give a better response at low frequencies and the smaller cones are best at high frequencies; for the best results two or more different-sized cones are therefore used, either in the same or in separate cabinets. The loudspeaker cabinet is also an important part of the system since it can act as a sound baffle and improve the frequency response.

● **Loughborough** ▶ 52 47N 1 11W A town in central England, in Leicestershire on the River Soar. Industries include footwear, hosiery, pharmaceuticals, electrical equipment, and bell founding (the great bell of St Paul's, London, was cast here). Loughborough University of Technology was incorporated in 1966. Population (1991): 46 867.

● **Louis (I) the Pious** ▶ (778–840 AD) Emperor of the West (813–40); son of Charlemagne. He fostered Christianity but imperial unity was undermined by his rebellious sons and after his death the Empire was partitioned.

● **Louis (I) the Great** ▶ (1326–82) King of Hungary (1342–82) and Poland (1370–82). Louis encouraged commerce and the arts and in 1367 he founded Hungary's first university at Pécs. His campaigns against Venice had brought Hungary most of Dalmatia by 1381.

● **Louis II** ▶ (1845–86) King of Bavaria (1864–86) renowned for his extravagant castles, especially Neuschwanstein, and patronage of the composer Richard Wagner. His hopes for Bavaria in the newly founded German empire (1871) were disappointed and he subsequently withdrew from politics. In 1886 he was pronounced mad and shortly afterwards drowned himself.

● **Louis (IV) the Bavarian** ▶ (?1283–1347) German king and Holy Roman Emperor (1314–47; crowned 1328). In 1324 Pope John XXII excommunicated Louis in support of Frederick III of Austria (c. 1286–1330), who contested the German throne. Louis deposed John in 1327 and in 1328 was crowned emperor by the antipope Nicholas V. From 1294 Louis was Duke of Bavaria, for which he devised a legal code (c. 1335).

● **Louis (V) le Fainéant** ▶ (967–87 AD) The last Carolingian King of France (986–87), whose frivolity (his nickname means "feckless") helped to discredit the dynasty, bringing the Capetian ▷Hugh Capet to power.

● **Louis (VI) the Fat** ▶ (1081–1137) King of France (1108–37). He succeeded his father, Philip I, and continued his policy of resisting the English in Normandy. For most of his reign he was at war with Henry I of England. A popular monarch, he strengthened royal authority by suppressing the barons and courting the support of the church and the middle classes.

● **Louis (VII) le Jeune** ▶ (c. 1120–80) King of France (1137–80). He was engaged in a bitter struggle with Henry II of England between 1152, when Henry acquired Aquitaine through his marriage to Louis' former wife ▷Eleanor of Aquitaine, until 1174.

● **Louis VIII** ▶ (1187–1226) King of France (1223–26), known as the Lionheart. He was offered the English throne by King John's baronial opponents but his invasion of England was defeated in 1217. He gained Toulouse and Languedoc for the French Crown and in 1226 launched a crusade against the ▷Albigenses.

● **Louis IX, St** ▶ (1214–70) King of France (1226–70), regarded as the model medieval Christian king. After defeating Henry III of England (1242) he set out as leader of the seventh ▷Crusade (1248), during which he was captured by the Egyptians. On his return to France he introduced administrative reforms and fostered learning and the arts. He died on a Crusade in Tunisia and was canonized in 1297.

● **Louis XI** ▶ (1423–83) King of France (1461–83), who united most of France under his rule. In 1447 his father, Charles VII exiled him to Dauphiné for his part in a conspiracy. After becoming king Louis overcame the aristocratic opposition of the League of the Public Weal (1465) and in 1477 finally defeated Charles the Bold of Burgundy. He extended royal authority over the church and encouraged commerce, gaining the support of the middle classes.

● **Louis XII** ▶ (1462–1515) King of France (1498–1515). His reign was dominated by the wars that his father Charles VIII had initiated in Italy, and Louis suffered major defeats (1511–13) on several fronts at the hands of the Holy League.

● **Louis XIII** ▶ (1601–43) King of France (1610–43), whose reign was dominated by his chief minister Cardinal de ▷Richelieu. He was the son of the assassinated Henry IV and of ▷Marie de Médicis, who was regent during his minority. In 1617 he exiled Marie from court and she raised two revolts against him but mother and son were later reconciled by Richelieu, her adviser, who in 1624 became Louis' chief minister. The king defeated two ▷Huguenot uprisings (1622, 1628), taking their fortress of La Rochelle in 1628.

● **Louis XIV** ▶ (1638–1715) King of France (1643–1715), known as the Sun King because of the splendour of his reign. His minority was dominated by Cardinal ▷Mazarin, after whose death in 1661 Louis allowed no single minister to dominate. He was ably served by such men as ▷Colbert, who revived French trade, industry, and agriculture, and ▷Louvois, who with his father made France's army the best in Europe, but insisted that *L'état c'est moi* ("I am the state"). He was a firm advocate of the ▷divine right of kings and subdued the aristocrats, whose rebellion known as the ▷Fronde had threatened the Crown during his minority, by providing diversions at his great palaces—outstandingly ▷Versailles. His patronage of artists, including the writers Molière and Racine, further enhanced the magnificence of his court. In 1660 he married Maria Theresa (1638–83), the daughter of Philip IV of Spain (1605–65; reigned 1621–65). His mistresses included Mme de ▷Montespan and then Mme de ▷Maintenon, whom he secretly married after Maria Theresa's death. Abroad, France became the dominant power in Europe during Louis' reign. His ambitions in the Spanish Netherlands sparked off the War of ▷Devolution (1667–68) and were renewed by a second invasion in 1672. From this, the third ▷Dutch War, France emerged (1678) at the pinnacle of its power, a position Louis was unable to retain through the subsequent Wars of the ▷Grand Alliance (1689–97) and ▷Spanish Succession (1701–14). France was further weakened by Louis' revocation (1685) of the Edict of Nantes, ending toleration of Protestants and driving many of France's most productive citizens into exile. He left a country weakened by the economic demands of his wars and a monarchy that was to prove unequal to the enormous demands placed on it by his personal rule. His reign was nevertheless one of incomparable brilliance.

The **Louis Quartorze style** of late 17th-century interior design was developed in a deliberate attempt by Louis XIV and his designers to establish a French national idiom. The formal baroque furniture made in the new royal workshops derived from Italian antiquity and was sumptuously gilded or veneered for such regal settings as ▷Versailles. The most resplendent items were made of cast silver.

● **Louis XV** ▶ (1710–74) King of France (1715–74), whose weak rule discredited the Crown and contributed to the outbreak of the French Revolution of 1789. His early reign was dominated by ▷Fleury, after whose death in 1743 Louis' indecisiveness and the influence of his mistresses, especially Mme de ▷Pompadour and, later, Mme ▷Du Barry, fostered faction and intrigue. The loss of almost all France's colonies in the ▷Seven Years' War (1756–63) increased his unpopularity, which hasty judicial and financial reforms at the end of his reign did nothing to alleviate.

The **Louis Quinze style** of French interior decoration and furnishing lasted from about 1723 until Louis' death. A sophisticated and informal style, it was a reaction to the formal baroque pomp of Louis XIV's court. The rococo, with its lighthearted use of eccentric scrolls, replaced symmetrical antique and Renaissance motifs. Chairs, formerly ranged around the walls of large rooms, were designed and arranged for ease of conversation in the new, smaller, and more intimate rooms.

● **Louis XVI** ▶ (1754–93) King of France (1774–93), who was guillotined during the ▷French Revolution. The opposition of Louis' wife ▷Marie Antoinette and the aristocracy thwarted the attempted reforms of his ministers ▷Turgot and ▷Necker. The consequent economic crisis forced the king to summon (1789) the States General, the disaffected Third Estate of which precipitated revolution. The royal family was confined to the Tuileries Palace from which they attempted to flee in 1791, reaching Varennes. Brought back to the Tuileries, Louis was deposed after it had been stormed by the Paris mob. In 1793 he was guillotined and was followed to the scaffold by his wife.

The Louis Seize style, a neoclassical French style of furnishing, came into fashion after Louis XVI's accession. It was characterized by rejection of the rococo with straight lines replacing curves and a continuing tendency towards lightness and utility. The predominant idiom was restrained classicism (key patterns, caryatids, garlands, trophies). After the French Revolution (1789–99) this style remained in vogue for some time.

● **Louis XVII** ► (1785–95) King of France in name (1793–95) following the execution of his father Louis XVI during the French Revolution. He died in prison.

● **Louis XVIII** ► (1755–1824) King of France, in name from 1795, following the death in prison of his nephew ▷Louis XVII, and in fact from 1814, following the overthrow of Napoleon. He fled Paris when Napoleon returned from Elba, being restored with diminished prestige after Waterloo "in the baggage train of the allied armies." His attempts to be a moderate constitutional monarch were thwarted by the ultraroyalists.

● **Louis, Joe** ► (Joseph Louis Barrow; 1914–81) US boxer, called the Brown Bomber, who was world heavyweight champion from 1937 to 1948, when he retired. He defended his title 25 times and has been regarded as the world's greatest boxer.

● **Louisiana** ► A state in the S USA, on the Gulf of Mexico. Chiefly low lying, it is crossed by the Mississippi River, the delta of which dominates the coastal lowlands in the S. The main upland area in the state is found in the NW along the Red River Valley. The population lives mainly in the S.
Economy: the state produces chemicals and petrochemicals, paper and food products. Oil is exploited and there are major deposits of natural gas, sulphur, and salt. New Orleans and Baton Rouge are important ports and tourism has become important since the decline of heavy industry. Its favourable climate and fertile soils make it an important agricultural state; the chief products are beef cattle, rice, soya beans, dairy products, sugar cane, and cotton. It is an important cultural region, famous for its jazz music centred on New Orleans.
History: although the Spanish were the first Europeans to discover the territory, it was claimed for France and named after Louis XIV in 1682. It was ceded to Spain (1762) but was restored to France (1800). It was acquired by the USA as part of the Louisiana Purchase (1803), becoming a state in 1812. It was a supporter of the Confederate cause in the US Civil War. Area: 125 675 sq km (48 523 sq mi). Population (1996 est): 4 350 579. Capital: Baton Rouge.

● **Louisiana Purchase** ► (1803) About 2 144 250 sq km (828 000 sq mi) of land between the Mississippi River and the Rocky Mountains, purchased by the USA from France for $27,267,622. The purchase doubled the size of the USA and established US dominance in North America.

● **Louis of Nassau** ► (1538–74) A leader of the ▷Revolt of the Netherlands against Spain. His opposition to the Spanish led to his exile in 1567 but, after gaining support in Germany and France, he invaded the Netherlands with a Protestant army (1568). The campaign was indecisive and in the second invasion, in 1574, Louis and his younger brother were killed.

● **Louis Philippe** ► (1773–1850) King of the French (1830–48), the son of the Duke of ▷Orléans. He supported the ▷French Revolution until 1793, when he deserted to the Austrians, living abroad until 1814. He joined the liberal opposition to the restored Louis XVIII and came to the throne after the July Revolution had ousted Louis' successor Charles X. Styled King of the French rather than of France and described by Thiers as the Citizen King, Louis Philippe relied on the support of the middle class. His initial moderation turned to repression in the face of the many rebellions against his rule and he abdicated in the Revolution of 1848. He retired to England, dying at Claremont, in Surrey.

● **Louisville** ► 38 13N 85 48W A city and port in the USA, in N Kentucky on the Ohio River. The state's largest city, it has many historical buildings and is the site of the University of Louisville (1798). The American Printing House for the Blind is situated here. Since 1875 the famous Kentucky State Derby has been held in Louisville at the Churchill Downs racecourse. Industries include tobacco manufac-

ture, whiskey distilling, milling, and chemicals. Population (1996 est): 260 689.

● **Lourdes** ► 43 06N 0 02W A town in SW France, in the Hautes-Pyrénées department situated at the foot of the Pyrenees. It has been a major pilgrimage centre for Roman Catholics since ▷Bernadette of Lourdes was led by a vision of the Virgin Mary to the Grotte de Massabielle in 1858. This has since been the scene of many reputed cures for a variety of illnesses (*see* faith healing). The Basilica of the Rosary was completed in 1889; however, this became too small to accommodate the annual influx of some 3 million pilgrims (of whom some 50 000 are seeking cures) and in 1958 an enormous underground church was built. Population (1995 est): 17 100.

● **Lourenço Marques** ▷See Maputo.

● **louse** ► A wingless ⬚insect parasitic on warm-blooded animals. The sucking lice (order *Anoplura*; 225 species) suck the blood of mammals. They have hairy flattened bodies, 0.5–6 mm long, and claws for attachment to the host. The eyes are often reduced or absent. One of the most important species is the human louse (*Pediculus humanus*), of which there are two varieties—the head louse (*P. humanus capitis*) and the body louse (*P. humanus corporis*). Both are transmitted by direct contact and lay their eggs ("nits") on hair or clothing. Body lice are carriers of typhus and related diseases. Biting lice (order *Mallophaga*; 2600 species) resemble sucking lice but have biting mouthparts for feeding on the skin, feathers, etc., of birds—their principal hosts.

● **Louth** ► (Irish name: Contae Lughbhaidh) The smallest county in the Republic of Ireland, in Leinster bordering on the Irish Sea. It is chiefly low lying. Agriculture is important with cattle rearing and arable farming producing oats and potatoes. Area: 821 sq km (317 sq mi). Population (1996): 92 000. County town: Dundalk.

● **Louvain** ► (Flemish name: Leuven) 50 53N 04 42E A town in central Belgium. It was a centre of the cloth trade in the middle ages and the capital of the duchy of Brabant. It possesses a gothic town hall and a university (1426). Much of the town was destroyed in World War I. Industries include leather and chemicals. Population (1995 est): 87 165.

● **Louvois, Michel Le Tellier, Marquis de** ► (1641–91) French statesman; minister for war (1666–77). With his father **Michel Le Tellier** (1603–85), war minister (1643–66), he reorganized the French army. Their success was demonstrated by Louis IV's victories. Louvois was the king's chief minister after 1683.

● **Louvre** ► The national museum of France containing the art collection of the French kings and housed in the former royal palace and Tuileries palace in Paris. When the court moved to Versailles in 1678, its conversion to a museum was started but it was not opened to the public until 1793. Napoleon exhibited his war loot here, of which the celebrated Venus de Milo still remains. Other highlights are Leonardo da Vinci's *Mona Lisa* and a collection of impressionist paintings, housed separately in the Jeu de Paumes in the Tuileries gardens. New buildings (opened in 1989) include a controversial glass pyramid designed by I. M. ▷Pei, which sits incongruously in the middle of the magnificent Renaissance courtyard.

● **lovage** ► A perennial herb, *Ligusticum scoticum*, that grows 15–90 cm high and has large compound leaves with pairs of divided toothed leaflets and clusters of greenish-white flowers. It is native to Europe and used as a pot herb and salad plant. Family: ▷Umbelliferae.

● **lovebird** ► A small brightly coloured ▷parrot belonging to a genus (*Agapornis*; 9 species) occurring in Africa and Madagascar. 10–16 cm long, lovebirds typically have a short tail, a red bill, and a prominent eye ring. Lovebirds often feed in large flocks and may damage crops. They are popular cagebirds because they are long-lived, can be taught tricks, and appear to have great affection for each other.

● **Lovecraft, H(oward) P(hilips)** ► (1890–1937) US novelist and short-story writer. He lived virtually as a recluse and wrote science-fiction stories and tales of macabre fantasy, such as *The Case of Charles Dexter Ward* (1928) and *At the Mountains of Madness* (1931).

● **love-in-a-mist** ► An annual herb, *Nigella damascena*, also called fennel flower, native to S Europe and grown as an ornamental in temperate regions. It has fernlike leaves and blue or white flowers, 4 cm across, with many clawed petals surrounded by the leaves. The fruit is a globular head of capsules. Family: *Ranunculaceae*.

● **Lovelace, Richard** ► (1618–57) English Cavalier poet. During the Civil War, although he was not actively involved, he was committed to and spent nearly all his fortune in the royalist cause, and was twice imprisoned. In prison he wrote one of his best-known poems "To Althea, from Prison." *Lucasta* (1649) contains most of his best lyrics.

● **love-lies-bleeding** ▷*See* Amaranthus.

● **Lovell, Sir Bernard** ► (1913–   ) British astronomer. After working on radar during World War II he became interested in ▷radio astronomy and supervised the construction of a 250-foot radio telescope at ▷Jodrell Bank Experimental Station, a part of Manchester University. His books include *The Exploration of Outer Space* (1961) and *Out of the Zenith* (1973).

● **Lovett, William** ► (1800–77) British Chartist leader. He helped to found the London Working Men's Association in 1836 and to draft the People's Charter in 1838. He was imprisoned (1839–40) following riots in Birmingham. His moderate views subsequently alienated him from other Chartist leaders. ▷*See* Chartism.

● **Low, Sir David (Alexander Cecil)** ► (1871–1963) New Zealand-born cartoonist. Self-taught, he was employed by the *Sydney Bulletin* (1911) and in England by the *Star* (1919–27) and the *Evening Standard* (1927–50). He created world-famous characters, notably Colonel Blimp, and cartoons, satirizing Hitler, Mussolini, Churchill, etc., with a uniquely simple drawing technique. He later worked for the *Daily Herald* (1950–53) and the *Guardian* (1953–63).

● **Low Countries** ► The Netherlands, Belgium, and Luxembourg. The Low Countries originally comprised numerous small states, controlled by major powers. In 1568 the N Protestant states revolted against Spanish rule, becoming the independent United Provinces of the Netherlands (*see* Revolt of the Netherlands). Belgium and Luxembourg gained independence in 1830 and 1867 respectively.

● **Lowell** ► 42 38N 71 19W A city in the USA, in NE Massachusetts at the confluence of the Concord and Merrimack Rivers. Its growth began with the establishment of textile mills here in 1822 and it became one of the most famous textile centres in the USA. Population (1996 est): 100 973.

● **Lowell, Amy** ► (1874–1925) US poet and critic. After meeting Ezra ▷Pound in London in 1913, she became the leading propagandist for ▷Imagism. Her *Collected Poetical Works* was published in 1955. She also wrote criticism and a biography of *John Keats* (1925).

● **Lowell, James Russell** ► (1819–91) US poet, critic, and diplomat. He published literary criticism, political works, and poetry ranging from the satirical *Fable for Critics* (1848) to the dialect *Biglow Papers* (1848, 1867). He edited the *Atlantic Monthly* (1857–61). He served as minister to Spain (1877–80) and Britain (1880–85).

● **Lowell, Percival** ► (1855–1916) US astronomer, who first predicted the existence of the planet ▷Pluto, because of certain irregularities in the orbit of Uranus. Lowell never discovered Pluto despite intense searching and it was not found until 14 years after his death. He also made a detailed study of the "canals" on Mars.

● **Lowell, Robert** ► (1917–77) US poet. In 1943 he was imprisoned as a conscientious objector. *Life Studies* (1959) marked a change from his complex and allusive early poetry, such as *Lord Weary's Castle* (1946), to a looser, more personal style. His left-wing political involvement during the 1960s is reflected in *For the Union Dead* (1964). He also published free translations, collected in *Imitations* (1962), and verse dramas. His last book was *Day by Day* (1977).

● **Lower California** ► (Spanish name: Baja California) A peninsula in NW Mexico, between the Gulf of California and the Pacific Ocean. It is chiefly mountainous and arid. Within irrigated areas, especially in the N near the US border, cotton, fruit, vegetables, and vines are grown. Important mineral deposits include copper, silver, and lead. Length: 1223 km (760 mi). Population (1995 est): 2 483 568.

● **Lower Hutt** ► 41 12S 174 54E A city in New Zealand, in S North

Island on Port Nicholson (an inlet of Cook Strait). An important industrial centre, Lower Hutt has meat freezing, engineering, and textile industries. Population (latest est): 62 900.

● **Lower Saxony** ► (German name: Niedersachsen) A *Land* in NW Germany, bordering on the North Sea and the Netherlands. Formed in 1946 from four former states, it lies on the N German plain, with mountains in the S. It is chiefly agricultural but some minerals are extracted, including oil and iron ore. Area: 47 430 sq km (18 301 sq mi). Population (1995 est): 7 715 400. Capital: Hanover.

● **lowest common denominator** ► The smallest common multiple of the denominators of two or more fractions. For example, the group 2/3, 1/6, 5/8 have the lowest common denominator 24.

● **Lowestoft** ► 52 29N 1 45E A fishing port in E England, in Suffolk. It suffered considerable damage in both World Wars and the Royal Naval Patrol Service Memorial stands in Belle Vue Park. Besides fishing and associated industries, Lowestoft is concerned mainly with yachting and tourism. Population (1991): 62 907.

L. S. Lowry ► Putting the finishing touches to *The Cricket Match* in his somewhat cluttered studio.

● **Lowry, L(awrence) S(tephen)** ► (1887–1976) British painter, born in Manchester. He worked as a clerk until his retirement at 65, using his spare time for art lessons and painting. He exhibited regularly in Manchester from the 1920s, when he began his most characteristic works, bleak industrial landscapes and towns dotted with matchstick figures. These first attracted serious attention in the 1940s. A large retrospective exhibition was held at the Royal Academy in 1976.

● **Lowry, (Clarence) Malcolm** ► (1909–57) British novelist. His first novel, *Ultramarine* (1933), was based on his experience as a deckhand on a voyage to China. After studying at Cambridge he lived in Paris before going to Mexico, the setting of his novel *Under the Volcano* (1947), the semiautobiographical account of the self-destruction of an alcoholic ex-consul. He lived in Canada from 1940 to 1954. Further stories and fragments were published posthumously.

● **Lo-yang** ▷*See* Luoyang.

● **Lozi** ► A Bantu-speaking people of Zambia, also known as Barotse. They are cereal cultivators on the fertile flood plain of the upper Zambezi, but hunting and animal husbandry are also important. Political authority is vested in a divine king and subordinate queen who rule from separate northern and southern capitals with a council of ministers and regional chiefs drawn from the aristocracy. There is an elaborate system of taxation, centralization, and redistribution of reserves.

● **LPG** ▷*See* liquefied petroleum gas.

● **LSD** ► (lysergic acid diethylamide) A drug that—in very small doses—produces hallucinations, altered sensory perception, and a sense of happiness and relaxation or, in some people, fear and anxiety. Long-term use of LSD can cause a schizophrenia-like illness and—if taken by pregnant women—may produce deformities in the developing fetus.

● **LSE** ▷*See* London School of Economics and Political Science.

● **Lualaba, River** ▶ A river in SE Democratic Republic of Congo, the headstream of the Congo River. Rising in the Shaba region, it flows N to join the River Luvua and becomes the Congo River at the Boyoma Falls. Length: 1800 km (1100 mi).

● **Luanda** ▶ (former name: São Paulo de Loanda) 8 58S 13 09E The capital of Angola, a port in the NW on the Atlantic Ocean. Founded by the Portuguese in 1575, it became a centre of the slave trade to Brazil. Oil was discovered nearby in 1955 and a refinery was established; main exports include coffee, cotton, diamonds, iron, and salt as well as sugar, timber, and tobacco. The University of Luanda was established in 1963. Population (1995 est): 2 250 000.

● **Luang Prabang** ▶ 19 53N 102 10E A town in N Laos, a port on the River Mekong. The royal capital of Laos (1946-75), it has many Buddhist pagodas and is the trading centre for the surrounding region. Population (1995 est): 59 800.

● **Lubbock** ▶ 33 35N 101 53W A city in the USA, in NW Texas. Settled by Quakers in 1879, it is a market centre for cotton, grain, cattle, and poultry. Population (1996 est): 193 565.

● **Lübeck** ▶ 53 52N 10 40E A city in N Germany, in Schleswig-Holstein on the Trave estuary. A leading city of the Hanseatic League, it has a cathedral (1173) and city hall (13th-15th centuries), both restored after World War II. Buxtehude lived here (1668-1707) and it is the birthplace of Thomas and Heinrich Mann. A major Baltic port, its industries include shipbuilding and metal founding. Population (1996 est): 216 986.

● **Lubitsch, Ernst** ▶ (1892-1947) US film director, born in Germany. Following the success of *Madame Dubarry* (1919), a historical romance, he went to Hollywood, where he made a series of sophisticated comedies for Paramount during the 1920s and 1930s. These include *Forbidden Paradise* (1924), *Bluebeard's Eighth Wife* (1938), *Ninotchka* (1939), and *Heaven Can Wait* (1943).

● **Lublin** ▶ 51 18N 22 31E A city in E Poland. The Union of ▷Lublin, between Poland and Lithuania, was signed here in 1569. Notable buildings include the 16th-century cathedral; its university was founded in 1944. It is an important commercial and industrial centre; manufactures include farm machinery, motor vehicles, and beer. Population (1996 est): 353 300.

● **Lublin, Union of** ▶ (1569) The act that created a Polish-Lithuanian commonwealth. Poland and Lithuania were to share a common monarch and diet (parliament) but each maintained its own laws, administration, treasury, and army.

● **lubricant** ▷*See* friction; tribology.

● **Lubumbashi** ▶ (name until 1966: Elizabethville) 11 30S 27 31E A city in SE Democratic Republic of Congo. Founded in 1910 as a copper-mining settlement, it is the industrial centre of an important mining area. It has a cathedral and a campus (1955) of the National University. Population (1994 est): 851 381.

● **Lucan** ▶ (Marcus Annaeus Lucanus; 39-65 AD) Roman poet, nephew of the Stoic philosopher Seneca. He was born in Spain. The *Pharsalia*, his single surviving work, is an epic poem in ten books concerning the civil war between Caesar and Pompey. He committed suicide after the discovery of his involvement in a conspiracy against the emperor Nero.

● **Lucan, Richard John Bingham, 7th Earl of** ▶ (1934-?1974) British aristocrat. Widely known as "Lucky Lucan" among his gambling associates, he disappeared in November 1974 after the murdered body of his children's nanny, Sandra Rivett, was discovered in the basement of his house. It is assumed that in the unlit basement he mistook the nanny for his wife, whom he had intended to murder. In 1975 a coroner's jury charged him with murder, but a worldwide police search failed to disclose his whereabouts, in spite of many reported sightings. In 1999 Lord Lucan was finally declared dead by the High Court, which enables his son to inherit his title. His great-great grandfather, **George Charles Bingham, 3rd Earl of Lucan** (1800-88), commanded the cavalry division at the Battle of ▷Balaclava. He was responsible for misunderstanding orders from Lord ▷Raglan, as a result of which the disastrous charge of the Light Brigade took place.

● **Lucas, George** ▶ (1945-) US film director, producer, and screenwriter. His films include *American Graffiti* (1973), the hugely successful space adventure *Star Wars* (1977), and (as producer) *Raiders of the Lost Ark* (1981) and several further films in the *Star Wars* series—*The Empire Strikes Back* (1980), *Return of the Jedi* (1983), and *The Phantom Menace* (1999).

● **Lucas van Leyden** ▶ (Lucas Hugensz *or* Jacobsz; c. 1494-1533) Northern Renaissance artist. His early paintings include everyday subjects, notably *The Chess Players* (Berlin), but he mainly painted religious works, his masterpiece being the triptych of *The Last Judgment* (Leiden). Best known as an engraver, he was influenced by Dürer, whom he met in Antwerp (1521). He was probably the first to etch on copper rather than iron and to combine ▷etching with ▷engraving; his portrait of Emperor Maximilian I (1521) uses these techniques.

● **Lucca** ▶ 43 50N 10 30E A town in NW Italy, in Tuscany on the River Serchio. It has Roman remains, an 8th-century church, and a cathedral (11th-15th centuries). Industries include chemicals, engineering, and food processing. It is the birthplace of Puccini. Population (1990 est): 86 676.

● **Luce, Henry R(obinson)** ▶ (1898-1967) US publisher, who was a cofounder of the magazine *Time* (1923), which he edited and published. He also founded *Fortune* (1930), *Life* (1936), and *Sports Illustrated* (1954). His wife **Clare Booth Luce** (1903-87), a playwright, wrote the satire *Kiss the Boys Goodbye* (1938). She sat in the US House of Representatives (1943-47) and was subsequently ambassador to Italy (1953-56) and Brazil (1959).

● **lucerne** ▷*See* alfalfa.

● **Lucerne** ▶ (German name: Luzern) 47 03N 8 17E A town in central Switzerland, on Lake Lucerne. The Lion of Lucerne, a monument to the Swiss guards who fell in Paris (1792), is a notable feature and Lucerne also has a Benedictine monastery and a 17th-century cathedral. It is a major tourist centre. Population (1991): 60 500.

● **Lucerne, Lake** ▶ (German name: Vierwaldstättersee) A lake in N central Switzerland. It has four arms formed from deep winding glaciated valleys. Area: 114 sq km (44 sq mi).

● **Lucian** ▶ (c. 120-c. 180 AD) Greek rhetorician. He was born in Syria and travelled during his early life as a public lecturer in Asia Minor, Greece, Italy, and Gaul (France). He eventually settled in Athens but also held an administrative post in Alexandria. His many lively satirical works attacking contemporary superstitions and religious fanaticism include *Dialogues of the Dead* and *Dialogues of Courtesans*.

● **Lucifer** ▷*See* Devil.

● **Lucknow** ▶ 26 50N 80 54E A city in India, the capital of Uttar Pradesh. Capital of the nawabs of Oudh (1775-1856), it has many notable buildings including the Great Imambara (1784), which is a Muslim meeting place, and the British Residency (1800), which was besieged (but remained uncaptured) in 1857 during the Indian Mutiny. The University of Lucknow was established here in 1921. An agricultural trading centre, its industries include food processing, railway engineering, and the manufacture of chemicals, carpets, and copper and brass products. Population (1991): 1 642 134.

● **Lucretia** ▶ A legendary Roman heroine, wife of Tarquinius Collatinus. After being raped by Sextus, son of Tarquinius Superbus, the Etruscan King of Rome, she committed suicide. Junius Brutus then led a rebellion that expelled the Tarquins and established the Roman Republic.

● **Lucretius** ▶ (Titus Lucretius Carus; c. 95-c. 55 BC) Roman philosopher and poet. The biographical records are unreliable, including St Jerome's statements that he became insane but in moments of sanity wrote books that were edited by Cicero and that he committed suicide. His single work, *De rerum natura*, consists of six books that give the most complete exposition of the philosophy of ▷Epicurus, including his atomic theory of phenomena and the belief that the soul was material (and mortal). His style blends moral intention with poetic sensitivity to the physical world.

● **Lucullus, Lucius Licinius** ► (died c. 57 BC) Roman general. After service with ▷Sulla, he successfully conducted the third war against ▷Mithridates until his troops mutinied and Pompey took command in 67. Lucullus retired to private life and luxury; the splendours of "Lucullan" feasts became proverbial.

● **Lüda** ► (Lüshun or Lü-ta) 38 53N 121 37E A port complex in NE China, at the end of the ▷Liaodong Peninsula. It comprises the two cities **Lüshun** (English name: Port Arthur) and **Dalian** (or Ta-lien; English name: Dairen). Industries include shipbuilding, railway engineering, and fishing.
History: Lüshun, a major naval base from 1878, was the base of the Russian Pacific fleet during the Russian occupation (1898–1905). The Russians began the construction of the commercial port at Dalian, completed under Japanese occupation (1905–45). Population (1991 est): 2 400 000.

● **Luddites** ► A group of Nottingham frameworkers, named after their probably mythical leader, Ned Ludd, who destroyed labour-saving machinery in 1811. Luddism, which spread to other parts of industrial England, showed the hostility of the handicraftsmen to the new machines that were taking their livelihood from them. They were severely repressed.

● **Ludendorff, Erich** ► (1865–1937) German general in World War I. He became chief of staff under ▷Hindenburg in 1914 and was largely responsible for the German victory at ▷Tannenberg. After being appointed quartermaster general (1916) Ludendorff exerted considerable political as well as military influence, forcing the resignation of ▷Bethmann-Hollwegg. He himself resigned after the German defeat and from 1924 to 1928 sat in the Reichstag as a Nazi.

● **Lüderitz** ► (former name: Angra Pequena) 26 38S 15 10E A port in SW Namibia, on the Atlantic coast. It was the first German settlement in SW Africa (1883). The major industry is rock-lobster fishing. Population (1990 est): 6000.

● **Ludhiana** ► 30 56N 75 52E A city in India, in Punjab. An important grain market, its manufactures include textiles, machinery, and agricultural tools. It is the site of Punjab Agricultural University (1962). Population (1991): 1 012 062.

● **Ludlow** ► 52 22N 2 43W A market town in W central England, in Shropshire on the River Teme. Its historical importance resulted from its proximity to the Welsh border and its castle, which has a massive Norman keep. Population (1991): 9040.

● **Ludwigshafen** ► 49 29N 8 27E A city in SW Germany, in Rhineland-Palatinate on the River Rhine. It is a transshipment point and centre of the chemical industry. Population (1996 est): 167 369.

● **Luftwaffe** ► The German air force. The Luftwaffe, which fought in World War I, was developed by Goering in the 1930s. In ▷World War II, countries destined for Nazi invasion were first pounded by aerial bombardment (*see* Blitzkrieg) but the Luftwaffe's failure in the Battle of ▷Britain was disastrous to German plans to invade Britain.

● **Lugano** ► 46 01N 8 57E A town in S Switzerland, on Lake Lugano. Noted for the beauty of its scenery, it is a popular tourist centre. It is also a centre of international finance. Population (1995 est): 26 800.

● **Lugansk** ► (name from 1935 until 1991: Voroshilovgrad) 48 35N 39 20E A city in E Ukraine. In the coal-producing Donets Basin, it manufactures mining machinery and has iron and steel and chemical industries. Population (1996 est): 487 000.

● **Lugard, Frederick Dealtry, 1st Baron** ► (1858–1945) British colonial administrator. After army service he joined the British East Africa Company (1890), gaining control of Buganda. He was high commissioner for Northern Nigeria (1900–06) and then, after uniting N and S, of all Nigeria (1914–19), where he laid the foundations of the modern state.

● **Luger pistol** ► A German automatic ▷pistol developed from a Borchard design by George Luger in 1902. The Parabellum 9-mm

model was the standard sidearm of the German navy (1904) and army (1908) until 1938.

● **Lugus** ► One of the principal Celtic gods. In Ireland he was called Lug and was skilled in many fields, being a warrior, poet, musician, craftsman, magician, etc. His Welsh counterpart was Lleu Llaw Gyffes (skilful hand). Many European placenames, notably Lyon, Laon, and Leiden, derive from his name.

● **lugworm** ► A burrowing ▷annelid worm, *Arenicola marina*, of Atlantic shores, also known as the lobworm. Up to 40 cm long, lugworms have about 20 segments, with tufts of red gills on all but the last few. They feed on organic material in the mud, leaving casts of egested mud on the surface. Class: *Polychaeta*.

● **Lu Hsün** ► (or Chou Shu-jen; 1881–1936) Chinese writer, famous for his short stories criticizing traditional Chinese thought and government. Among the best known are *The True Story of Ah Q* (1921) and those collected in *Call to Arms* (1923) and *Wandering* (1924–25). Although he never joined the Communist Party, the Chinese regard him as a revolutionary hero.

● **Luik** ▷*See* Liège.

● **Lukacs, Giorgi** ► (1885–1971) Hungarian Marxist philosopher. Having shown the resemblance between the philosophies of ▷Hegel and the young ▷Marx in *History and Class Consciousness* (1923), he disowned the book, which was also condemned by Soviet orthodoxy. For Lukacs, a cultural relativist, the dynamic of all art is the historical movement of its time; in the 20th century this is socialist realism.

● **Luke, St** ► A New Testament evangelist, traditionally the author of the third Gospel and of the Acts of the Apostles. Although information about him is scarce, he seems to have been a Gentile doctor and to have accompanied ▷Paul on numerous missions, notably to Greece, Macedonia, and Jerusalem. He is the patron saint of doctors and artists. Feast day: 18 Oct. **The Gospel according to St Luke** was written in the latter part of the 1st century AD. It was written in idiomatic Greek and with Gentile readers in mind. It contains the most complete account of the life of Jesus. Many historic hymns, such as the *Ave Maria*, *Magnificat*, *Benedictus*, *Gloria in Excelsis*, and *Nunc Dimittis*, are taken from it.

● **Luleå** ► 65 35N 22 10E A seaport in N Sweden, on the Gulf of Bothnia. It is icebound in the winter, but exports iron ore from ▷Gällivare and ▷Kiruna during the rest of the year. Its university was established in 1971. Population (1994): 70 694.

● **Lull, Ramón** ► (English name: Raymond Lully; c. 1235–c. 1315) Catalan mystic and poet. After an early secular career, he became a Franciscan and devoted himself to missionary work among the Muslims. His mystical writings foreshadow those of St ▷Teresa and St ▷John of the Cross. His important theological work, *Ars magna*, was condemned by Pope Gregory XI in 1376 for its attempt to show that the mysteries of faith could be proved by reason. According to tradition, he was stoned to death in N Africa.

● **Lully, Jean Baptiste** ► (Giovanni Battista Lulli; 1632–87) French composer of Italian birth. The son of a miller, he worked as a scullion in an aristocratic French household but subsequently became composer, violinist, and dancer to Louis XIV. He composed ballets, incidental music to Molière's plays, and operas, being granted a monopoly of operatic production in 1684. He died from gangrene as a result of striking his foot with a pointed stick while conducting.

● **Luluabourg** ▷*See* Kananga.

● **lumbago** ► Chronic backache. Almost everybody experiences backache at some time and many biologists regard it as the price man pays for walking upright. More serious backache may be caused by arthritis, a slipped disc, muscle strain, or strained ligaments.

● **lumbar puncture** ► A procedure in which ▷cerebrospinal fluid is withdrawn using a hypodermic needle inserted through the spine and into the spinal cord in the region of the lower back. Examination of the fluid assists in the diagnosis of various conditions, for example the presence of blood may indicate a brain haemorrhage.

● **Lumbini** ► A park and Buddhist shrine in the modern village of

Rummindei, in S Nepal. According to legend, the Buddha was born here in about 563 BC.

● **lumen** ▶ (lm) The ▷SI unit of luminous flux equal to the light emitted per second in a cone of one steradian solid angle by a point source of one candela.

● **Lumière, Auguste** ▶ (1862–1954) French photographer, who, with his brother **Louis Lumière** (1864–1948), manufactured photographic equipment and made innovations in the techniques of photography, especially in motion pictures. In 1895 they invented the *cinématographe*, which had a camera and projector combined into one. In the same year they used their invention to film and show the first motion picture, *La Sortie des usines Lumière*, which was an immediate success. They went on to make a great number of short films, nearly all documentaries. They also greatly improved existing methods of colour photography.

● **luminance** ▶ The ▷luminous intensity of a surface in a given direction per unit of orthogonally projected area of that surface. It is measured in candela per square metre.

● **luminescence** ▶ The emission of light by a substance for any reason except high temperature. It occurs as a result of the emission of a ▷photon by an atom of the substance when it decays from an excited state to its ground state. The atom may be excited by absorbing a photon (**photoluminescence**), colliding with an electron (**electroluminescence**), etc. If the luminescence stops as soon as the exciting source is removed, it is known as **fluorescence**; if it persists for longer than 10^{-8} seconds it is called **phosphorescence**. The photons emitted may have a different energy (in visible light, a different colour) from the absorbed energy. Fluorescent dyes in washing powders make clothes look brighter. Luminous paint is phosphorescent. Other examples of luminescence include **triboluminescence**, caused by friction, and ▷chemiluminescence, caused by chemical reaction. ▷Bioluminescence, which is seen in glow worms, seaweeds, and other organisms, is a form of chemiluminescence. **Radioluminescence** is caused by radioactive decay.

● **luminosity** ▶ The intrinsic brightness of an object, such as a star, equal to the total energy radiated per second from the object. A star's luminosity increases both with surface temperature and with surface area: the hotter and larger a star, the greater its luminosity. Stellar luminosity is related (logarithmically) to absolute ▷magnitude.

● **luminous flux** ▶ The rate of flow of light energy, taking into account the sensitivity of the observer or detector to the different wavelengths. For example, the human eye is most sensitive to the colour green. Luminous flux is measured in ▷lumens.

● **luminous intensity** ▶ The amount of light emitted per second by a point source per unit solid angle in a specified direction. It is measured in ▷candela.

● **lumpsucker** ▶ A slow-moving carnivorous ▷bony fish, also called lumpfish, belonging to the family *Cyclopteridae*, found in cold northern seas. They have a thickset body, sometimes studded with bony tubercles, a cleft dorsal fin, and a ventral sucking disc formed from fused pelvic fins. *Cyclopterus lumpus* is the largest species, reaching a length of 60 cm. The roe is used as a substitute for caviar. Order: *Scorpaeniformes*.

● **Lumumba, Patrice (Hemery)** ▶ (1925–61) Congolese statesman; prime minister (1960–61) of the Congo Republic (now the Democratic Republic of Congo). Mission-educated, Lumumba was active in trades unionism before entering national politics. He became prime minister of the newly independent Congo Republic under president ▷Kasavubu in 1960 and opposed the secession of Katanga province under ▷Tshombe. The following year he was deposed and murdered.

● **luna moth** ▶ A large North American saturniid moth, *Actias luna*. It is pale green with a long "tail" on each hindwing, moonlike markings on the forewings, and a wingspan of about 150 mm. The palegreen larvae feed on trees.

● **Lund** ▶ 55 42N 13 10E A town in S Sweden, near Malmö. It has a university (1668) and an 11th-century cathedral. Its varied industries include printing, publishing, and sugar refining. Population (1994): 95 895.

● **Lunda** ▶ A group of Central Bantu tribes speaking languages of the Benue-Congo division of the ▷Niger-Congo family. Historically they were united under a paramount chief but their customs and culture vary considerably. Cultivation, hunting and gathering, and trade are all important to their economy.

● **Lundy** ▶ 51 11N 4 40W An island in SW England in the Bristol Channel, off the N coast of Devon. Once the haunt of smugglers and pirates, it is now a bird sanctuary, owned by the National Trust (since 1969). Area: 4 sq km (1.5 sq mi). Population (1994 est): 20.

● **Lüneburg** ▶ 53 15N 10 24E A spa in N Germany, in Lower Saxony. There are many fine medieval buildings. **Lüneburg Heath** was the site of the surrender of German troops to Montgomery in 1945 at the end of World War II. Population (1990): 61 000.

● **lungfish** ▶ A freshwater ▷bony fish belonging to the formerly abundant order *Dipnoi*, now reduced to six species including *Lepidosiren paradoxa* of South America, *Protopterus annectens* of Africa, and the Australian *Neoceratodus forsteri*. Up to 2 m long, lungfish have slender bodies, narrow paired fins, and tapering tails. Their ▷swim bladders are modified for breathing air, an adaptation for droughts, when some make burrows in the bottom mud, leaving air vents above the mouth. They re-emerge in the rainy season to feed on bottom-dwelling fish, snails, mussels, etc., and to spawn. Subclass: *Sarcopterygii*. ▯fish.

● **lungs** ▶ The respiratory organs of many air-breathing animals and humans. The human lungs are situated within the rib cage on either side of the heart. Each lung is enclosed by a smooth moist membrane (the pleura), which permits it to expand without friction, and contains many tiny thin-walled air sacs (alveoli), through which exchange of oxygen and carbon dioxide takes place during breathing (*see* respiration). Air to the lungs passes through the ▷trachea (windpipe) to the two main airways (bronchi), which subdivide into progressively smaller branches that terminate (as respiratory bronchioles) in the alveoli. ▷*See* Plate II.

Diseases most commonly affecting the lungs and airways are virus infections and bronchitis; cancer and tuberculosis are less common.

● **lungworm** ▶ One of several species of parasitic ▷nematodes that inhabit the lungs and bronchial passages of cattle, pigs, deer, sheep, and other animals. They damage lung tissue, causing coughing, distress, and debilitation, and may act as reservoirs of such diseases as swine influenza.

● **lungwort** ▶ A perennial herb of the genus *Pulmonaria* (about 10 species), especially *P. officinalis*, native to woods of Eurasia. The leaves are heart-shaped or oval, often white-spotted, and the tubular fivelobed flowers, borne in drooping terminal clusters, are pink when young, turning blue later. The plant grows to a height of 30 cm. Family: *Boraginaceae*.

● **Lunt, Alfred** ▶ (1892–1977) US actor, who worked with **Lynn Fontanne** (1887–1983) after their marriage in 1922. They were most successful in sophisticated comedies, such as Noel Coward's *Design for Living* (1933) and Terence Rattigan's *Love in Idleness* (1944), but they also performed in more serious productions, notably Dürrenmatt's *The Visit* (1959).

● **Luo** ▶ A Nilotic people of N Uganda and Kenya, who moved into this area from the SE Sudan after about 1500. They speak a Sudanic language. The Luo cultivate cereal crops and herd cattle. For lakeside groups fishing is important. They lack centralized political institutions or chiefs.

● **Luoyang** ▶ (*or* Lo-yang) 34 47N 112 26E A city in E central China, in Henan province. A commercial and cultural centre, it was the Tang dynastic capital. Manufactures include machinery and ball bearings. Population (1990): 759 752.

● **Lupercalia** ▶ An ancient Roman festival of purification and fertility held annually on 15 Feb. After performing sacrifices, priests carrying whips of goat hide made a circuit of the Palatine. Women struck by their whips were ensured fertility. The ceremony was suppressed in 494 AD by Pope Gelasius.

● **lupin** ▶ An annual or perennial herb of the genus *Lupinus* (about 200 species), native to the N hemisphere and widely cultivated for ornament. They grow 30–120 cm high and have compound leaves with up to 18 radiating leaflets. Lupins produce dense spikes of blue, purple, white, pink, or yellow flowers. Family: ▷*Leguminosae*.

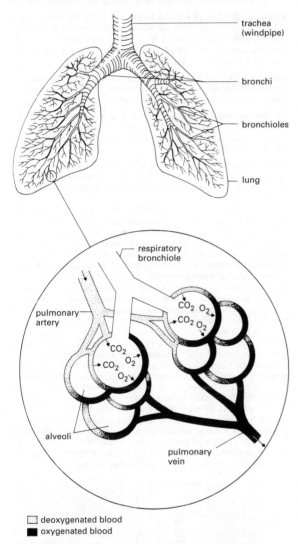

trachea (windpipe)

bronchi

bronchioles

lung

respiratory bronchiole

pulmonary artery

CO_2 O_2
CO_2 O_2
CO_2 O_2
CO_2 O_2

alveoli

pulmonary vein

☐ deoxygenated blood
■ oxygenated blood

lungs ▶ The air passages in the lungs terminate in millions of tiny air sacs (alveoli), into which blood from the pulmonary artery releases its carbon dioxide. Inhaled oxygen in the alveoli is absorbed by the blood, which is carried back to the heart by the pulmonary vein.

● **lupus** ▶ A skin disease of which there are two forms. Used alone, the term usually refers to **lupus vulgaris**, a tuberculous infection of the skin now rare in developed countries. Without treatment the infection will progress to erode the face (hence the name, which is Latin for wolf, implying a gnawing disease), but it is now readily cured by drugs. **Lupus erythematosus** (LE) is a disease in which inflammation of tissues is brought about by the body's own antibodies. Discoid LE is a chronic condition of scaling and scarring of the skin. Systemic LE affects the connective tissues and so can have serious effects, particularly on the joints, skin, kidneys, heart, lungs, and brain. LE can be controlled with steroid drugs.

● **Lurçat, Jean** ▶ (1892–1966) French tapestry designer. A painter in the cubist style until 1936, he established a tapestry factory at Aubusson in 1939, where he played a major part in the 20th-century revival of tapestry weaving and design.

● **Luria, Isaac** ▶ (1534–72) Jewish mystic of Safed (Galilee); the founder of an important school of ▷kabbalah. He attracted a large band of disciples who, after his early death in an epidemic, collected and developed his teachings, which became extremely influential, especially later in ▷Hasidism.

● **Luristan** ▶ (*or* Lorestan) A province in W Iran, comprising part of a larger historical region in which many important archaeological finds have been made since 1929.

● **Lusaka** ▶ 15 03S 28 30E The capital of Zambia, lying on the Tanzam Railway. It became the capital of Northern Rhodesia in 1935 and of Zambia on independence in 1964. The University of Zambia was founded here in 1965. The centre of an important agricultural region, it has expanded rapidly and industries include food processing, paint, clothing, and plastics. Population (1990): 982 362.

● **Lüshun** ▷*See* Lüda.

● **Lusitania** ▶ **1.** A Roman province roughly equivalent to modern Portugal. It was conquered by Rome in 139 BC. **2.** A British liner that, although unarmed, was sunk by a German submarine off the Irish coast on 7 May, 1915, during World War I. Of the 1195 lives lost, some 128 were Americans and the incident contributed to the anti-German feeling in the USA that ultimately brought the country into the war.

● **Lü-ta** ▷*See* Lüda.

● **lute** ▶ A plucked stringed instrument of Moorish origin; the name derives from the Arabic *al'lud*. The European lute, popular during the 15th, 16th, and 17th centuries, had a body in the shape of a half pear, six or more courses of double strings and a fretted fingerboard. The round sound hole was often intricately carved. Music for the lute was written in tablature, a system of notation using letters or numbers to indicate the position of the fingers. The lute was used chiefly as a solo instrument and to accompany singers; it has been revived in the last hundred years.

● **luteinizing hormone** ▷*See* gonadotrophin.

● **lutetium** ▶ (Lu) The heaviest ▷lanthanide element, separated from ytterbium by G. Urbain (1872–1938) in 1907 and named after Paris (Latin name: *Lutetia*), his native city. It was also discovered independently by C. A. von Welsbach, who called it **cassiopeium**, a name used until the 1950s, especially in Germany. It is present in small amounts in monazite ($CePO_4$) and extracted by reduction of $LuCl_3$ or LuF_3 by alkali metals (e.g. sodium). It is separated from the other lanthanides by ion-exchange techniques. At no 71; at wt 174.967; mp 1663°C; bp 3402°C.

● **Luther, Martin** ▶ (1483–1546) German Protestant reformer, founder of ▷Lutheranism. An Augustinian monk and from 1507 a priest, he became professor of theology at Wittenberg University in 1511. After experiencing a personal revelation he came to believe that salvation could be attained by faith alone. Several visits to Rome convinced him of the corruption of the papacy, the Dominican monk ▷Tetzel, who sold ▷indulgences on behalf of papal funds, being a particular target for his hostility. In 1517 he nailed his 95 theses against this practice to the church door at Wittenberg. He disobeyed the papal summons to Rome (1518) and further attacked the papal system in such writings as *On the Babylonian Captivity of the Church of God* (1520). His public burning of a papal bull condemning his theses and writings resulted in his excommunication in 1521. He appeared before Charles V's imperial diet (legislative assembly) at Worms but refused to recant and was declared an outlaw. While in hiding at Wartburg, under the protection of the Elector of Saxony, he completed a German translation of the New Testament. In 1522 he returned to Wittenberg, where he led the reform of its church and in 1525 married the former nun Catherina van Bora (1499–1552). At the same time he lost much popular support because of his opposition to the Peasants' Revolt (1524–25). His contention that human will was incapable of following the good resulted in his rift with ▷Erasmus and in 1529 he also broke with ▷Zwingli, maintaining his belief in ▷consubstantiation. His original intention was reform not schism, but with the ▷Augsburg Confession (1530) a separate Protestant church emerged. The leadership of the German Reformation was then gradually taken over by ▷Melanchthon.

● **Lutheranism** ▶ The belief and practice of the Protestant Churches that derive from the teaching of Martin ▷Luther, especially as formulated in the ▷Augsburg Confession (1530). There is a wide divergence in matters of belief among Lutherans. Essentially Scripture is taken to be the only rule of faith and conservative Lutherans accept Luther's basic doctrine of justification by faith alone, i.e. that redemption is only through faith in Christ. Lutheranism is the national faith in all Scandinavian countries, where there are some 19 million Lutherans. It is the principal Protestant Church in Germany (about 40 million adherents) and is also strong in North America (over 8 million). The Lutheran World Federation, based in Geneva, claims authority over some 80 million Lutherans, which makes it the largest Protestant body.

● **Lutine bell** ▶ The ship's bell taken from the *Lutine*, a ship that sank in the North Sea in 1799 with a cargo of bullion. The bell now hangs in the underwriting room at ▷Lloyd's and was formerly rung when news arrived of a ship previously posted "missing, fate unknown." One ring was for bad news and two for good news; the ringing of the bell ensured that all underwriters received the news simultaneously. It is now rung before important announcements.

● **Luton** ▶ **1.** 51 53N 0 25W A town in SE England, in Luton unitary authority, Bedfordshire. It has important motor-vehicle, mechanical, and electronic engineering industries. Straw-plaiting and millinery industries have survived from the 17th century. London's Luton Airport is located on the outskirts of the town. Population (1995): 181 400. **2.** A unitary authority in SE England, in Bedfordshire. Area: 43 sq km (17 sq mi). Population (1998 est): 183 300.

● **Lutoslawski, Witold** ▶ (1913–94) Polish composer. His early works, such as his first symphony, were influenced by Bartók. From the orchestral *Venetian Games* (1961) onwards most of his works contain ▷aleatoric sections. They include four symphonies, a cello concerto (1970), and *Preludes and Fugue for 13 Solo Strings* (1972).

● **Lutuli, Albert (John Mvumbi)** ▶ (1898–1967) South African Black leader, whose advocacy of nonviolent opposition to racial discrimination won him the Nobel Peace Prize in 1960. A Zulu chief, in 1952 he became president of the African National Congress, formed in 1912 to further the Black cause in South Africa. In 1956 he was arrested for treason and although acquitted in 1957 continued to suffer social and political restrictions.

● **Lutyens, Sir Edwin Landseer** ▶ (1869–1944) British architect. Known as the last English designer of country houses, a notable example of which is Middlefield, Cambridgeshire (1908), he combined classicism with the influence of Norman ▷Shaw and the ▷Arts and Crafts movement. He designed the central square of Hampstead Garden Suburb (1908–10) and the Cenotaph (1919–20) but his most spectacular commission was the layout and viceregal palace of New Delhi (1912–30). His daughter, **Elisabeth Lutyens** (1906–83), a composer, studied in London and Paris and adopted ▷serialism in the 1930s. Her works include *O Saisons, O Chateaux* (1946) for soprano and strings, concertos for horn and viola, operas, and chamber music.

● **Lutzen, Battles of** ▶ **1.** (16 November, 1632) The battle in the ▷Thirty Years' War in which the Swedes under Gustavus II Adolphus clashed with imperial forces in a costly and indecisive battle. Gustavus Adolphus was killed. **2.** (May, 1813) A battle in which Russian and Prussian forces were defeated by Napoleon.

● **lux** ▶ (lx) The ▷SI unit of intensity of illumination equal to the illumination resulting from a flux of one lumen falling on an area of one square metre. Former name: metre candle.

● **Luxembourg** ▶ A province in SE Belgium, bordering on the Grand Duchy of Luxembourg and France. The ▷Ardennes is an important tourist area. Area: 4416 sq km (1705 sq mi). Population (1995 est): 240 281. Capital: Arlon.

● **Luxembourg, Grand Duchy of** ▶ A small country in central Europe, between France and Germany. The generally undulating S with its wide valleys rises to the rugged uplands of the Ardennes Plateau in the N.

Economy: predominantly industrial; iron and steel are especially important although considerable economic diversification has taken place (e.g. chemicals, rubber, and synthetic fibres). Agriculture remains important, especially livestock raising, and wine is produced from the vineyards of the Moselle Valley. The city of Luxembourg is an important international centre, with the headquarters of the European Coal and Steel Community and the secretariat of the European Parliament as well as many international companies. Banking secrecy has made it an important international financial centre.

History: with the Netherlands and Belgium it formed part of the so-called Low Countries. It became a duchy in 1354 and passed to Burgundy in 1443 and to the Habsburgs in 1482. It became a grand duchy in 1815 under the Dutch Crown. In 1830 it joined the Belgian revolt against the Netherlands, W Luxembourg joining independent Belgium and the E forming part of the Netherlands until obtaining independence in 1867. It was occupied by the Germans in both World Wars. In 1921 it formed an economic union with Belgium and in 1948 both joined with the Netherlands to form the ▷Benelux economic union. Luxembourg was a founding member of the EEC (now the EU). In 1998 it chose to enter the single European currency (from January 1999). A centre-left coalition has held power since 1984, with Jean-Claude Juncker as prime minister since 1994. In 2000 Grand Duke Jean abdicated in favour of his son Henri (1955–   ). Luxembourg adopted the single European currency in 1999–2002.

Edwin Lutyens ▶ The Secretariat Buildings in New Delhi from Central Vista Park.

Grand Duchy of Luxembourg

Head of state	Grand Duke Henri
Official languages	Luxembourgish, French, and German
Official currency	euro of 100 cents
Area	2586 sq km (999 sq mi)
Population (2000 est)	439 000
Capital	Luxembourg

● **Luxemburg, Rosa** ▶ (1871–1919) German revolutionary, born in Poland. She was converted to communism in 1890, helped to found the Polish Social Democratic party (later the Communist Party), and from 1898 was a leader of the left wing of the German Social Democratic party. Upon the outbreak of World War I she broke with the majority of German socialists and formed, with Karl ▷Liebknecht, the ▷Spartacus League. She spent most of the war in prison and after her release participated in the abortive uprising of 1919, following which she and Liebknecht were murdered.

● **Luxor** ▶ (or El Aksur) 25 40N 32 38E A town in central Egypt, on the River Nile. It occupies the S part of the ancient city of ▷Thebes. Its numerous ruins and tombs include the temple built by Amenhotep III to the god Amon. The town is a winter resort. Population (1996 est): 360 503.

● **Luzern** ▷See Lucerne.

● **Luzon** ▶ A volcanic island in the N Philippines, the largest and most important. Largely mountainous, its central fertile plain is a major grain growing area with rice terraces to the N. Other products include sugar cane, hemp, timber, and minerals, notably chromite. Most industry is concentrated around Manila.
History: power struggles for the Philippines have been centred here, including the Japanese invasion during World War II (*see* Corregidor). Area: 108 378 sq km (41 845 sq mi). Population (1995 est): 32 558 000. Chief town: Manila.

● **Lvov** ▶ (German name: Lemberg) 49 50N 24 00E A city in W Ukraine. A major industrial and cultural centre, Lvov supports machine building, food processing, and chemical and textile industries, and has a notable university (1661).
History: founded in the 13th century, it subsequently passed to Poland. Under Austrian rule from 1772, it became the capital of Galicia. It was ceded to Poland after World War I and to the Soviet Union in 1939, being occupied by the Germans in World War II; it passed to Ukraine in 1991. Population (1998 est): 793 700.

● **Lvov, Georgi Yevgenievich, Prince** ▶ (1861–1925) Russian statesman. Lvov was the first leader of the provisional government in the ▷Russian Revolution. His unrealistic policies led to the Petrograd uprising in July, 1917, and he resigned. He emigrated to Paris, where he died.

● **Lyallpur** ▷See Faisalabad.

● **Lyautey, Louis Hubert Gonzalve** ▶ (1854–1934) French marshal and colonial administrator. He served in Indochina and then in Madagascar, where he reformed the colonial government. In 1912 he became resident general of the French protectorate of Morocco, where he again reorganized the administration, maintaining the French position there during World War I. He was briefly war minister (1917–18).

● **lycanthropy** ▷See werewolf.

● **Lyceum** ▶ The gardens and gymnasium in ancient Athens in which ▷Aristotle lectured and which gave their name to the school and research foundation that he established there in about 335 BC. The name is now applied particularly to Aristotle's philosophical doctrines.

● **lychee** ▷See litchi.

● **Lycurgus** ▶ A legendary Spartan statesman credited with establishing the constitution and military regime of Sparta after a slave rebellion in the 7th century BC. He is mentioned by ▷Herodotus and his biography was written by ▷Plutarch. The name refers to several other

figures in Greek legend, notably a king of Thrace who opposed the cult of ▷Dionysus and was subsequently blinded or driven mad.

● **Lydda** ▷See Lod.

● **Lydgate, John** ▶ (c. 1370–c. 1450) English poet. He lived at the monastery of Bury St Edmunds. A prolific writer, his major works include the long narrative poems *The Troy Book* (1412–21), written at the request of Henry V, and *The Fall of Princes* (1431–38).

● **Lydia** ▶ In antiquity, a region of W Asia Minor with its capital at ▷Sardis. Its last native king, ▷Croesus (ruled 560–546 BC), enriched by Lydia's alluvial gold, controlled Anatolia eastwards to the River Halys, until his defeat by ▷Cyrus the Great. The Lydians invented coined money (c. 700 BC).

● **Lyell, Sir Charles** ▶ (1797–1875) British geologist, who was mainly responsible for the acceptance of the view that rocks are formed by slow continual processes, such as heat and erosion. Lyell popularized this theory in his *The Principles of Geology* (3 vols, 1830–33). Lyell's work had a great influence on Charles ▷Darwin and, in turn, Lyell became one of the earliest supporters of Darwin's theory of evolution by natural selection.

● **Lyle, Sandy** ▶ (1958–) British golfer, who became the first British player to win the US Masters event (1988). His other successes have included the British Open Championship in 1985.

● **Lyly, John** ▶ (c. 1554–1606) English dramatist and writer. From the elaborate artificial style of his two didactic prose romances *Euphues, the Anatomy of Wit* (1578) and *Euphues and His England* (1580) was derived the term "euphuism." He wrote several comic dramas, courtly precursors of later Elizabethan comedies.

● **Lyme disease** ▶ A disease first described in Lyme, Connecticut, in 1977. It is caused by the spirochaete *Borrelia burghdorferi*, carried by ticks. Symptoms include skin rash, fever, headache, and muscle and joint pains: nearly two-thirds of patients go on to experience recurrent attacks of arthritis; a few suffer carditis (inflammation of the heart) and encephalitis. The disease responds to antibiotics.

● **Lyme Regis** ▶ 50 44N 2 57W A resort in S England, in Dorset on Lyme Bay. Once an important port, the picturesque harbour was the scene of Monmouth's landing (1685). Important prehistoric fossils have been found here. Population (1991): 3851.

● **lymph** ▶ A clear colourless fluid, consisting of water and dissolved substances, that is contained in a network of vessels called the **lymphatic system**. It is derived from blood and bathes the cells, supplying them with nutrients and absorbing their waste products, before passing into the lymphatic vessels. Here the lymph passes through a series of small swellings called **lymph nodes**, which filter out bacteria and other foreign particles, before draining into the main lymphatic vessels—the thoracic duct and the right lymphatic duct—in the neck. These two vessels are connected to veins in the neck and so drain the lymph back into the bloodstream. The lymph nodes, which also produce lymphocytes (a type of white blood cell), sometimes become enlarged during infections. The lymphatic system is one of the routes by which cancer is spread.

● **lymphocyte** ▷See leucocyte.

● **lymphoma** ▶ Cancer of the lymph nodes, which is one of the commonest cancers of young people. There are several different types but the most common is Hodgkin's disease, which can often be cured if chemotherapy is started in the early stages of the disease. The other types of lymphoma are referred to as non-Hodgkin's lymphomas.

● **Lynch, Jack** ▶ (1917–99) Irish statesman; prime minister (1966–73, 1977–79). A former hurling star, he was elected a Fianna Fáil MP in 1948 and served in ministerial posts from 1957. He led Ireland into the EC in 1973.

● **Lynd, Robert Staughton** ▶ (1892–1970) US sociologist. Lynd taught at Columbia University from 1931 to 1961. He collaborated with his wife **Helen Lynd** (1896–1982) on the field study of Muncie, Indiana, their findings being published in *Middletown: A Study in Contemporary American Culture* (1929) and *Middletown in Transition* (1937).

● **Lynn** ▶ 42 29N 70 57W A city in the USA, in Massachusetts. A long-established industrial centre, it was the site of the first ironworks (1643) and the first fire engine (1654) in the USA. A shoe-manufacturing centre since 1636, Lynn also manufactures jet engines and marine turbines. Population (1980): 78 471.

● **Lynn, Dame Vera** ► (Vera Margaret Lewis; 1917–) British singer. Known as the "Forces Sweetheart," she was immensely popular during World War II singing such songs as "We'll Meet Again" and "White Cliffs of Dover."

● **lynx** ► A short-tailed ▷cat, *Felis lynx*, that inhabits forests of Eurasia and North America. Lynxes are about 1 m long with faintly spotted yellow-brown thick fur; their ears are tipped with black tufts. The rare Spanish race has especially bright spots.

Lynxes hunt at night, usually for small mammals (such as lemmings) but sometimes catching moose or reindeer, especially in deep snow. ▯mammal.

● **Lyon** ► (English name: Lyons) 45 46N 4 50E The third largest city in France, the capital of the Rhône department at the confluence of the Rivers Rhône and Saône. Notable buildings include the cathedral (12th–15th centuries) and the *hôtel de ville* and Palais des Arts (both 17th century). The university was founded in 1808. A *métro* (underground railway) was opened here in 1978. The focal point of road and rail routes, Lyon is an important financial centre and has been a leading textile centre since the 15th century. Manufactures include synthetic fibres, cars, chemicals, and hosiery. Population (1990): 422 444.

● **Lyons, Joseph Aloysius** ► (1879–1939) Australian statesman; prime minister (1931–39). At first a Labor politician, he resigned over financial policy in 1931 and with the Nationalist Party formed the United Australia Party (*see* Liberal Party). He died in office.

● **Lyra** ► (Latin: Lyre) A constellation in the N sky near Cygnus. The brightest star is ▷Vega. The constellation contains the **Ring nebula** (a ▷planetary nebula) and the ▷variable stars **RR Lyrae** (a pulsating variable) and **Beta Lyrae** (an eclipsing binary).

● **lyre** ► An ancient plucked string instrument. It consists of a sound box with two symmetrical arms supporting a cross piece from which strings are stretched to a bridge on the belly. Greek vases often show players holding a lyre in the left hand and a large plectrum in the right.

lyre ► A 5th-century BC terracotta vase showing a pupil learning to play the lyre.

● **lyrebird** ► A primitive ground-dwelling passerine bird belonging to a family (*Menuridae*; 2 species) restricted to forests of E Australia. The male superb lyrebird (*Menura superba*), about 130 cm long, is brown with grey underparts. Its magnificent tail is spread out into a lyre shape during the courtship display, which is performed on a mound of mud and debris. The smaller Prince Albert's lyrebird (*M. alberti*) does not build display mounds and has a smaller tail. All lyrebirds sing loudly and are excellent mimics.

● **Lysander** ► (d. 395 BC) Spartan general and politician. He commanded the fleets that defeated the Athenians at Notium (407) and Aegospotami (405) towards the end of the ▷Peloponnesian War. His plot to make the Spartan throne elective rather than hereditary was thwarted by the government but Lysander escaped punishment. He was subsequently killed in action in Boeotia.

● **Lysenko, Trofim Denisovich** ► (1898–1976) Soviet biologist, who achieved notoriety for his maverick ideas and damaging influence on Soviet biology. He claimed that changes induced in wheat by his vernalization experiments could be inherited, thus endorsing ▷Lamarck's discredited theory of evolution through inheritance of acquired characteristics. This led him to attack Mendelian genetics and the chromosome theory of inheritance, which, in the 1930s, were widely accepted elsewhere. With the backing of Stalin, Lysenko's influence grew. In 1939 he attacked the Soviet geneticist ▷Vavilov, who was later exiled to Siberia, and by 1948, Soviet scientific opposition to his views had been stifled. Lysenko's influence was eclipsed after Stalin's death although he retained his post as director of the Institute of Genetics until 1965, after the fall of Khrushchev.

● **lysergic acid diethylamide** ▷*See* LSD.

● **Lysias** ► (c. 459–c. 380 BC) Greek orator. He escaped from Athens during the reign of terror of the Thirty Tyrants (404 BC), but returned to prosecute one of them in his speech "Against Eratosthenes". About 35 of his legal speeches in plain unadorned style survive. He and his family are portrayed in Plato's *Republic*.

● **Lysippus** ► (4th century BC) The court sculptor of Alexander the Great. Long-lived, original, and prolific, Lysippus worked in bronze and was noted for his portraiture and new system of proportions for human figures. Surviving copies of his works (e.g. the Vatican statue of the athlete scraping oil from his arm) indicate his naturalism.

● **lysosome** ► A membrane-bounded structure occurring in large numbers in nearly all ▯cells (except bacterial cells) and containing enzymes responsible for the breakdown of materials both within and outside the cell. Functions of lysosomes include the destruction of bacteria in white blood cells, the digestion of food by unicellular organisms, and the breakdown of cellular material after death.

● **lysozyme** ► An enzyme, present in tears, nasal secretions, and egg white, that destroys bacteria by breaking down their cell walls. It was one of the first enzymes whose molecular structure and mode of action were analysed by X-ray diffraction techniques.

● **Lyttelton, Humphrey** ► (1921–) British jazz trumpeter and band leader, who influenced the revival of New Orleans jazz in England. Lyttelton, an Old Etonian, played with George Webb's Dixielanders, formed his own group in 1948, and has written several books on jazz. He is also a well-known broadcaster.

● **Lytton, Edward George Earle Bulwer-Lytton, 1st Baron** ► (1803–73) British novelist and politician. His long career as a Liberal and then a Tory MP culminated in his peerage in 1866. The best known of his many popular volumes of fiction, verse, and drama are his historical novels, which include *The Last Days of Pompeii* (1834). His son **(Edward) Robert Bulwer-Lytton, 1st Earl of Lytton** (1831–91) was viceroy of India (1876–80), initiating the second Afghan War (1878–80) against Russian influence in Afghanistan. An able administrator, he abolished internal customs duties. He was also a poet and his publications, under the pseudonym Owen Meredith, include *Clytemnestra...and Other Poems* (1855) and *The Wanderer* (1858).

M

● **Ma, Yo Yo** ▶ (1955–) US cellist born in France to Chinese parents. After studying at Harvard and the Juilliard School in New York, he performed with all the world's leading orchestras as well as in many distinguished chamber ensembles. His many recordings have won several Grammy awards.

● **Maas, Nicolas** ▷*See* Maes, Nicolas.

● **Maas, River** ▷*See* Meuse, River.

● **Maastricht** ▶ 50 51N 5 42E A city in the SE Netherlands, the capital of Limburg province on the River Meuse. It has the Netherlands' oldest church (founded in the 6th century) and is a cultural centre. Industries include pottery and cement. On 7 Feb 1992 the Maastricht Treaty (*see* European Community) was signed here. Population (1999 est): 121 479.

● **Maazel, Lorin** ▶ (1930–) US conductor, formerly a violinist. He directed the German Opera in West Berlin (1965–71), was conductor of the Cleveland Orchestra (1972–82), and musical director of the Vienna State Opera (1982–84), the Pittsburgh Symphony Orchestra (1988–96), and the Bavarian Radio Symphony Orchestra (1993–).

● **Mabinogion, the** ▶ A collection of eleven medieval Welsh folktales. Drawing on Celtic, Norman, and French legends, it was compiled in the 14th century and contains the earliest known Arthurian romance, *Culhwch and Olwen* (c. 1100). The four best-known tales are known as "The Four Branches of the Mabinogi".

● **Mabuse** ▷*See* Gossaert, Jan.

● **McAdam, John Loudon** ▶ (1756–1836) British inventor of the macadam road surface. It consisted of rocks interspersed with small chips, bound together with slag or gravel and raised to facilitate drainage. In 1823 McAdam's methods were adopted by the British Government and in 1827 he became general surveyor of roads.

● **Macadamia** ▶ A genus of bushy evergreen trees, 9–15 m tall, native to Australia and often grown as ornamentals. *M. ternifolia* has long stiff leaves and small white or lilac flowers. The round hardshelled fruit contains a single edible seed. Called macadamia or Queensland nuts, they are used as dessert nuts. Family: *Proteaceae*.

● **McAleese, Mary (Patricia)** ▶ (1951–) Irish politician; president of Ireland (1997–). A lawyer, she was pro-vice-chancellor of Queen's University, Belfast (1994–97).

● **Macao** ▶ (Portuguese name: Macáu; Chinese name: Aomen) 22 13N 113 36E A port and special administrative region of S China, situated across the Zhu estuary from Hong Kong. It was an overseas territory of Portugal until 20 December, 1999. The population is mainly Chinese, but has Portuguese cultural traditions. Industries now include gambling and financial services as well as the traditional textiles and fishing. Tourism is also important

History: the Macao peninsula and neighbouring islands became a Portuguese colony in 1557 and the port was a major trading centre until the 19th century. Immigration of refugees from China was stopped after procommunist riots (1966–67). In 1987 it was agreed that Macao would become part of China in 1999. The 1990s saw rapid development of the city as a commercial and financial centre. Official currency: pataca of 100 avos. Area: 16 sq km (6 sq mi). Population (2000 est): 440 000.

● **Macapá** ▶ 9 30S 67 29W A port in N Brazil, the capital of Amapá territory on the N channel of the Amazon delta. Exports include manganese, iron ores, and rubber. Population (1996): 209 663.

● **macaque** ▶ An ▷Old World monkey belonging to the genus *Macaca* (12 species), found mainly in the forests of S Asia. 35–78 cm long (the tail is absent or up to 90 cm long), they have short legs and areas of hard bare skin on the rump. They are mainly terrestrial, feeding on plant and animal matter. ▷*See also* Barbary ape; rhesus monkey.

Douglas MacArthur ▶ Arriving in Inchon Harbour (South Korea) in 1950.

● **MacArthur, Douglas** ▶ (1880–1964) US general. One of the outstanding strategists of World War II, he directed the recapture of the SW Pacific as Allied commander (1942–45). He commanded the occupation of Japan (1945–51) and then commanded the UN forces in the Korean War. After defeating the North Korean army, he advocated active operations against China. This was contrary to US policy and President Harry S. Truman dismissed him (1951).

● **Macarthur, Ellen** ▶ (1976–) British yachtswoman. In 2001 she came second in the Vendée Globe round-the-world race, becoming the youngest person and the fastest woman to circumnavigate the globe single-handed.

● **Macarthur, John** ▶ (1767–1834) Australian sheep farmer. Born in Britain, he went to Australia in 1789 and became a landowner. His experiments in sheep breeding led him to import (1797) the Merino sheep on which the development of Australia's wool industry was to be based. In 1808 he instigated the ▷Rum Rebellion against William ▷Bligh, the governor of New South Wales, and was exiled in Britain (1811–17).

● **Macassar** ▷*See* Ujung Pandang.

● **Macaulay, Dame Rose** ▶ (1881–1958) British novelist. She published her first novel while an undergraduate at Oxford. Subsequent novels, such as *Dangerous Ages* (1921), established her reputation as a social satirist. Her best-known novel is *The Towers of Trebizond* (1956).

● **Macaulay, Thomas Babington, 1st Baron** ▶ (1800–59) British essayist and historian. From 1825 he was a leading contributor to the *Edinburgh Review*. He had a long career in parliament (1830–34,

1839–47, 1852–56) and worked in India from 1834 to 1838. His Whig sympathies are evident in his immensely successful *History of England* (5 vols, 1849–61).

● **macaw** ► A large brightly coloured ▷parrot belonging to one of two genera (*Ara* and *Anodorhynchos*), ranging from Mexico to Paraguay. Up to 100 cm long, macaws have a long tail and a huge hooked bill that is used to crack nuts. ▷*See* Plate III.

● **Macbeth** ► (d. 1057) King of Scots (1040–57), after killing Duncan I in battle at Bothnagowan. He was killed by Duncan's son Malcolm. Although portrayed by Shakespeare as a tyrant, he was regarded as a just and effective ruler by contemporary chroniclers.

● **MacBride, Seán** ► (1904–88) Irish diplomat. The son of the nationalist Maud Gonne (1866–1953), he was a member of the IRA, then of the Irish assembly (1947). He chaired Amnesty International (1961–75) and was UN commissioner for Namibia (1973–77). He shared the Nobel Peace Prize in 1974.

● **McBride, Willie James** ► (1940–) Irish Rugby Union footballer. A lock forward, he won 63 caps for Ireland and made a record 17 appearances for the British Lions (1962–74).

● **Maccabees** ► The Hasmonean dynasty, founded in Jerusalem by the Jewish fighter Judas Maccabee (d. 161 BC). With his father, the priest Mattathias, and his five brothers, he led Jewish resistance to the invasion by the Syrian (Seleucid) king Antiochus IV Epiphanes, who attempted to impose Hellenism on the Jews. Defeating four Seleucid armies, Judas restored the Temple of Jerusalem in 164 BC, an event commemorated in the Jewish festival of ▷Hanukka. Judas achieved political as well as religious freedom from the Seleucids before his death in battle. The struggle was continued by his brothers Jonathan and Simon Maccabee, both of whom were assassinated. The dynasty ended with the capture of Jerusalem by the Romans in 63 BC. In 1895 it was revived in the name of a Jewish athletics organization, Maccabi, the World Union of which was formed in 1921.

The **Books of Maccabees** are four books of the ▷Apocrypha. I and II Maccabees record the revolt (168 BC) of the Maccabees against Antiochus and the establishment of an independent Jewish kingdom. They date from the late second century BC. III and IV Maccabees are unrelated, written probably at the beginning of the Christian era. III Maccabees describes a (probably imaginary) persecution of Jews by Ptolemy IV Philopator of Egypt (late 3rd century BC), while IV Maccabees is a philosophical treatise, on the superiority of intellect over passions.

● **McCarthy, Joseph R(aymond)** ► (1908–57) US Republican senator, who led Senate investigations of supposed communists during the Cold War. His claim to have the names of communist infiltrators into the State Department was not proved and in 1954, after he had been censured by the Senate, his anticommunist witchhunt—commonly known as McCarthyism—came to an end.

● **McCarthy, Mary** ► (1912–89) US novelist and critic. Her novels on American society include *The Groves of Academe* (1952), *The Group* (1963), *Birds of America* (1971), and *Cannibals and Missionaries* (1974). She published criticism, travel books, the autobiographical *Memories of a Catholic Girlhood* (1957), and journalism, notably *Vietnam* (1967).

● **McCartney, Sir Paul** ► (1942–) British rock musician, formerly a member of the ▷Beatles. His solo career was launched with "Maybe I'm Amazed" (1970). With his wife **Linda McCartney** (1942–98) he formed (1971) Wings, the band with which he recorded such albums as *Band on the Run* (1973). His classical composition, the *Liverpool Oratorio*, was premiered in 1991 and his symphonic poem, *Standing Stone* in 1997. He was knighted in 1997.

● **McClellan, George B(rinton)** ► (1826–85) Federal general in the US ▷Civil War. His 1861 campaign preserved Kentucky and separated W Virginia from the Confederacy. He then fortified Washington, rebuilding the Federal forces there. In 1862 he was defeated before Richmond. Despite superior strength he did not counterattack at Antietam and President ▷Lincoln dismissed him (1862).

● **Macclesfield** ► 53 16N 2 07W A town in NW England, in Cheshire on the W edge of the Peak District. Its origins as a centre of the silk industry have left many historic mills and other listed buildings. It is now a base for service-sector businesses, the pharmaceutical industry, plastics, and paper products. Population (1998): 50 810.

● **McClintock, Barbara** ► (1902–92) US geneticist. In 1929–31, working with maize chromosomes, she demonstrated that linkage of genes occurred in plants (it had previously been discovered in animals by T. H. ▷Morgan). In the 1940s she began studying a group of genes in maize that were capable of moving from one part of a chromosome to another, thereby modifying the expression of other genes. For her discovery of these transposable elements (or "jumping genes"), McClintock was awarded the 1983 Nobel Prize.

● **McClure, Sir Robert John Le Mesurier** ► (1807–73) Irish naval officer and explorer. In 1850, in search of Sir John ▷Franklin, McClure entered the Beaufort Sea from the Pacific and was marooned in the strait named after him. He was rescued, returning home via the Atlantic (1854), being the first to traverse the ▷Northwest Passage.

● **McColgan, Liz** ► (Elizabeth M.; 1964–) Scottish long-distance runner, who won the 10 000 m world title (1991) and in 1992 set a world record in the 5000 m (15 mins 3.17 secs).

● **McConnell, Jack (Wilson)** ► (1960–) Scottish Labour politician; first minister of Scotland (2001–). He became a member of the new Scottish parliament in 1999 and first minister on the resignation of Henry McLeish (1948–).

● **McCullers, Carson** ► (1917–67) US novelist and playwright. Her novels, which include *The Heart Is a Lonely Hunter* (1940), *Reflections in a Golden Eye* (1941), and *A Member of the Wedding* (1946), are set in her native South and describe a grotesque and violent world. Other works include *The Ballad of the Sad Café* (1951) and *Clock Without Hands* (1961).

● **MacDiarmid, Hugh** ► (Christopher Murray Grieve; 1892–1978) Scottish poet. A nationalist and a Marxist, he virtually created the "Scottish Renaissance" in literature. His early poetry, notably *A Drunk Man Looks at the Thistle* (1926), was written in a Scots language drawn from regional dialects and Middle Scots writers. Such later poems as *In Memoriam James Joyce* (1955), however, are written in standard English.

● **MacDonald, Flora** ► (1722–90) The Scottish gentlewoman who, after the battle of Culloden in 1746, smuggled the defeated ▷Charles Edward Stuart, the Young Pretender, disguised as her maid, to Skye whence he sailed to exile in Europe.

● **Macdonald, Sir John (Alexander)** ► (1815–91) Canadian statesman; prime minister (1857–58, 1864, 1867–73, 1878–91). He was a member of the British America League, whose proposals formed the basis of the British North America Act giving Canada dominion status within the British Empire (1867). His premiership saw the expansion of Canada to include Manitoba, British Columbia, and Prince Edward Island.

● **MacDonald, (James) Ramsay** ► (1866–1937) British statesman; the first Labour prime minister (1924, 1929–31, 1931–35). He joined the Independent Labour Party in 1894 and became secretary of the Labour Representation Committee in 1900. Elected an MP (1906) he became leader of the parliamentary ▷Labour Party (1911) but resigned in opposition to World War I (1914) and lost his seat in the 1918 election. Re-elected in 1922 he again led the Labour Party, becoming prime minister in 1924. His minority government was defeated in an election held after a vote of no confidence. His 1929–31 government, failing to deal with current economic problems, was broadened into a coalition (1931–35) that was increasingly dominated by the Conservatives and he was replaced by Baldwin in 1935.

● **Macdonnell Ranges** ► A system of mountain ranges in Australia. They extend for about 65 km (40 mi) E and 320 km (200 mi) W of Alice Springs, across S Northern Territory reaching 1510 m (4955 ft) at Mount Ziel.

● **mace** ▷*See* nutmeg.

● **Macedonia** ► The central region of the Balkans. Inhabited from Neolithic times, Macedonia was settled by many migrating northern tribes. About 640 BC Perdiccas I became the first ruler of the kingdom of Macedon. ▷Philip II (359–336 BC) quelled the warlike tribes and founded Macedon's military and economic power, which under his son ▷Alexander the Great was extended to the East. Alexander's successors were harassed by rebellious uprisings and, after defeat (168 BC) in the ▷Macedonian Wars, Macedonia became a Roman province (146), losing its independence but remaining a centre of Hellenistic culture. For most of the 20th century the region was divided between S Yugoslavia (*see* Macedonia, Former Yugoslav Republic of), N Greece, and SW Bulgaria.

● **Macedonia, Former Yugoslav Republic of** ▶ (FYROM) A country in SE Europe, in the Balkans. It is mountainous and landlocked. Most of the population are Macedonians (65%) or Albanians (21%).

Economy: the economy has suffered greatly from the political crisis in the Balkan region; UN sanctions against Serbia (Macedonia's main trading partner), an economic blockade by Greece (1994–95), and a massive influx of Albanian refugees, fleeing Serbian "ethnic cleansing" in Kosovo (1999), have had a particularly damaging effect. Mining, metalworking, chemicals, and textiles are the main industries. Agricultural products include tobacco, wheat, and sugar beet. Since the mid-1990s the government has adopted policies of privatization and deregulation.

History: the country occupies the N part of the region of ▷Macedonia, which was ceded by Turkey to Serbia in 1913. It was a constituent republic of Yugoslavia from 1944 until 1991, when the government declared independence and published a new constitution. Greek fears that the country's use of the name Macedonia implied a claim to the Greek region of Macedonia delayed international recognition of the country until 1993, when it agreed to adopt its current name. Following parliamentary elections in 1994, a centre-left coalition was formed; this was replaced by a right-wing coalition under Ljubčo Georgievski in 1998. In 2001 the NE saw mounting violence between Albanian militants and state forces. A peace agreement involving major constitutional reforms was signed in August.

Former Yugoslav Republic of Macedonia

Head of state	President Boris Trajkovski
Official language	Macedonian
Official currency	denar of 100 deni
Area	25 713 sq km (9925 sq mi)
Population (2000 est)	2 041 000
Capital	Skopje

● **Macedonian Wars** ▶ The three campaigns that secured Roman control of the kingdom of Macedon. The first Macedonian War (214–205 BC) coincided with the intervention of Philip V of Macedon (237–179; reigned 220–179) against Rome in the second ▷Punic War. The second Macedonian War (200–196) ended with the Roman victory at Cynoscephalae, in Thessaly. Rome instigated the third Macedonian War (171–168) against Philip's son Perseus (reigned 179–168) and finally crushed the Macedonians at Pydna.

● **Maceió** ▶ 9 40S 35 44W A city in NE Brazil, the capital of Alagoas state. It has sugar-refining, distilling, sawmilling, and textile industries. Population (1996): 667 827.

● **McEnroe, John (Patrick, Jr)** ▶ (1959–　) US tennis player. He won the US singles title in 1979, 1980, 1981 and 1984, and the doubles title in 1979, 1981, and 1989. An intense competitor noted for his tempestuous court behaviour, he became Wimbledon singles champion in 1981 (defeating Bjorn ▷Borg), 1983, and 1984, and doubles champion in 1979, 1981, 1983, and 1984, partnered by Peter Fleming.

● **McEwan, Ian (Russell)** ▶ (1948–　) British novelist and short-story writer. After the collections *First Love, Last Rites* (1975) and *In Between the Sheets* (1978), which dealt with themes of perverted sexuality and violence, he achieved further success with such novels as *The Child in Time* (1987), *The Innocent* (1990), *The Black Dogs* (1992), *Enduring Love* (1997), *Amsterdam* (1998), which won the Booker Prize, and *Atonement* (2001).

● **Macgillicuddy's Reeks** ▶ A mountain range in the Republic of Ireland, in Co Kerry. It extends W of the Lakes of Killarney, reaching 1041 m (3414 ft) at Carrantuohill, Ireland's highest peak.

● **McGonagall, William** ▶ (1830–1902) Scottish poet. Convinced of his own genius, he wrote memorably bad poetry characterized by naive sincerity and lack of rhythm. He published *Poetic Gems* in 1890.

● **Mach, Ernst** ▶ (1838–1916) Austrian physicist and philosopher, after whom the ▷Mach number is named in recognition of his researches into airflow and his observation that as the velocity of sound is reached the airflow changes. Philosophically he was a positivist and as such argued strongly against the concept of atoms, which he regarded as mystical entities since their existence could not be detected but only inferred. ▷*See also* logical positivism.

● **Machaut, Guillaume de** ▶ (c. 1300–77) French poet and composer, who held a number of court and ecclesiastical appointments in Bohemia and France before becoming canon of Rheims in 1337. He wrote a number of allegorical poems and developed the *ballade* and *rondeau*. He was one of the leading composers of the ▷*ars nova* style and was the first composer to write a complete setting of the mass.

● **Machen, Arthur (Llewellyn)** ▶ (1863–1947) Welsh novelist. His novels of the supernatural include *The Great God Pan* (1894) and *The Hill of Dreams* (1907). His short story "The Bowmen" (1914) gave rise to the World War I legend of the angels of Mons.

● **Machiavelli, Niccolò** ▶ (1469–1527) Italian political theorist. He served the Florentine republic as statesman and diplomat from 1498 to 1512, when the restoration of the Medici family forced him into exile. In *The Prince* (1532), written in 1513, he argued that all means are permissible in the realization of a stable state, and in the *Discorsi* (written 1513–19) he used the example of the ancient Roman Republic to reinforce his arguments. The adjective Machiavellian describes the view, or a supporter of the view, that opportunist or amoral means justify politically desirable ends.

● **machine gun** ▶ A ▷small arm that fires repeatedly without reloading. The first was Puckle's rotating cylinder flintlock (1718). By 1862 the Gatling, named after Richard Jordan Gatling (1818–1903), was firing six rounds in a second by means of its several barrels and a hand-rotated breech. Modern weapons are derived from the recoil-operated belt-fed water-cooled weapons designed by Sir Hiram ▷Maxim towards the end of the 19th century. Ammunition from pan, box, belt, or drum is loaded, fired, extracted, and reloaded automatically by recoil or in later models by gas and piston (*see* Bren gun). Classes are: light machine gun (LMG), developed from the rifle; medium machine gun (MMG), normally having a two-man crew and using belt-fed rifle ammunition; and heavy machine gun (HMG), with calibres up to 20 mm. ▷Submachine guns using pistol ammunition are light derivatives.

● **machine tools** ▶ Power-driven mechanical tools used to turn, form, drill, mill, shape, or plane metal or other materials. In ▷lathes the material to be worked (workpiece) is rotated and the tool is applied to it, whereas in other types of machine tool the workpiece is held stationary and a rotating cutter (milling machine), drill (drilling machine), or reciprocating cutter (shaping machine) is applied to it. In a planing machine the workpiece is reciprocated past the tool. In mass-production techniques a number of operations are carried out on the workpiece without human intervention, often by using a transfer machine to convey it from one machine tool to another. Computer-controlled machine tools are a further step in the automation of production lines.

● **Mach number** ▶ The ratio of the velocity of a body in a fluid to the velocity of sound in that fluid. The velocity is supersonic if the Mach number is greater than one. If it exceeds five the velocity is said to be hypersonic. Named after Ernst ▷Mach.

● **MACHO** ▶ (or massive astrophysical compact halo object) ▷*See* dark matter.

● **Machu Picchu** ▶ A well-preserved ▷Inca town in the Urubamba valley (Peru), discovered in 1911 by the US archaeologist Hiram Bingham (1875–1956). Sited on a precipitous ridge, Machu Picchu is flanked by extensive agricultural terraces and dates from the late 15th century. It contains a central plaza, royal palace, and sun temple, all built of polygonal dressed stone blocks. □ p. 768.

● **McIndoe, Sir Archibald Hector** ▶ (1900–60) New Zealand sur-

Machu Picchu ▶ The remains of the Inca city. The real name of the city is unknown; Machu Picchu is the name of the mountain that rises above it.

geon, who pioneered techniques in plastic surgery. He is particularly noted for his work in Britain with badly burnt RAF airmen during World War II.

● **Macintosh, Charles** ▶ (1766–1843) Scottish chemist, who invented the waterproof garment known as the "mackintosh." He made his discovery in 1823 by noting that rubber dissolved in naphtha could be used to stick together two pieces of cloth, producing a waterproof layer between them. He also patented a steel-making process (1825).

● **Macke, August** ▶ (1887–1914) German painter. During visits to France he was successively influenced by ▷impressionism, ▷fauvism, and ▷cubism. A member of Der ▷Blaue Reiter group, he became known for his light-hearted subjects, particularly parks and zoos, although his best works were watercolours painted in Tunis (1914), shortly before his death in World War I.

● **McKellen, Sir Ian** ▶ (1939–) British stage and film actor. He made his London debut (1964) in *A Scent of Flowers* and became a founder member (1972) of the Actors' Company. His stage roles include Faustus (1974) and Richard III (1990–92; filmed 1996); his films include *Gods and Monsters* (1998). Knighted in 1991, he is a leading spokesman for gay rights.

● **McKenna, Siobhán** ▶ (1923–86) Irish actress. She acted at the Abbey Theatre, Dublin, from 1943 to 1946 and made her London debut in 1947. She was particularly successful in the roles of St Joan in G. B. Shaw's play and of Pegeen in Synge's *The Playboy of the Western World*, a role she also played in the film (1962).

● **Mackenzie** ▶ A former district of N Canada, in the ▷Northwest Territories, comprising the Mackenzie Mountains in the W, the ▷Mackenzie River valley, and barren plains in the E. Parts of the NE were absorbed into ▷Nunavut, a semiautonomous homeland for the ▷Inuit people, in 1999.

● **Mackenzie, Sir (Edward Montague) Compton** ▶ (1883–1972) British novelist. His early novels include the semiautobiographical *Sinister Street* (1913). He served at Gallipoli in World War I and later settled on a Hebridean island. All of his later work is in a lighter vein and includes several volumes of memoirs and many humorous novels, notably *Whisky Galore* (1947).

● **Mackenzie River** ▶ The longest river in Canada, flowing from Great Slave Lake in the North West Territories W and NNW through sparsely settled country to an extensive delta on the Beaufort Sea. Navigable in summer, it carries oil and minerals from the Arctic Ocean to S Canada. Its tributaries generate cheap hydroelectricity. Length: 1705 km (1065 mi).

● **mackerel** ▶ An important food and game fish belonging to the genus *Scomber*, related to tuna. Mackerels live in shoals in tropical and temperate oceans, feeding on fish and invertebrates. They have a streamlined body, two dorsal fins, and a series of finlets running in front of the forked tail. The common Atlantic mackerel (*S. scombrus*), about 30 cm long, is marked with black and green bands above and is silvery-white below.

● **mackerel shark** ▶ A medium to large carnivorous oceanic ▷shark of the family *Isuridae*, which includes the ▷porbeagle and the ▷white shark. They are heavy bodied and have large keels along both sides of the crescent-shaped tail for stability during fast swimming.

● **Mackerras, Sir Charles** ▶ (1925–) US-born British conductor of Australian parentage. He studied conducting in London and Prague. He was director of the Hamburg State Opera (1965–69), of the English National Opera (1970–78), and of the Welsh National Opera (1987–92). He is known for his performances of Janáček's operas.

● **Mackinder, Sir Halford John** ▶ (1861–1947) British geographer. Mackinder developed what he called the "new geography," a discipline that bridged the natural sciences and the humanities. In 1899 he became director of the newly founded Oxford school of geography and subsequently director of the London School of Economics. Mackinder's *Democratic Ideas and Reality* (1919) was an astute and farsighted treatise on the balance of world power. His later theories on the Atlantic Community anticipated NATO. Mackinder was a Conservative MP from 1910 to 1922.

● **McKinley, Mount** ▶ A mountain in the USA, in S central Alaska in the Alaska Range. The highest peak in North America, it was first successfully climbed in 1913 by a party led by the US explorer, Hudson Stuck (1863–1920). It was named after President William ▷McKinley. Height: 6194 m (20 320 ft).

● **McKinley, William** ▶ (1843–1901) US statesman; Republican president (1897–1901). An Ohio congressman, and later governor of Ohio (1891–96), he introduced the McKinley Tariff Act (1890), which established protective duties. Dominated by the war with Spain to protect Cuban investments, his administration, under which business boomed, opened an era of US imperialism, annexing the Philippines and intervening in the Boxer Rising in pursuit of the ▷Open Door trading policy. He died shortly after being shot by an anarchist.

● **Mackintosh, Charles Rennie** ▶ (1868–1928) Scottish architect and designer. One of the most brilliant exponents of ▷Art Nouveau, Mackintosh evolved an austere version of the style, which was highly influential throughout Europe, though less so in Britain. All his best work was in Glasgow, in particular the School of Art (1897–1909) and four tearooms (1897–1912). In 1923 he moved to London, where his practice collapsed, resulting in his retirement.

● **Maclaine, Shirley** ▶ (1934–) US actress, singer, dancer, and writer. Her films include *The Apartment* (1960), *Sweet Charity* (1969), *Desperate Characters* (1971), *Terms of Endearment* (1984), which earned her an Academy Award, *Madame Sousatzka* (1988), *Steel Magnolias* (1989), and *Guarding Tess* (1994). She has published several volumes of autobiography.

● **Maclean, Alistair** ▶ (1923–87) Scottish writer. After five years in the Navy he wrote *HMS Ulysses* (1955). Other novels include *The Guns of Navarone* (1956), *Where Eagles Dare* (1967), and *The Lonely Sea* (1985).

● **Maclean, Donald** ▶ (1913–83) British Foreign Office official and Soviet secret agent. He fled to Russia in company with Guy Burgess (1911–63) in 1951. They had been warned of the British authorities' growing suspicion by Kim ▷Philby. In 1979 it was revealed that Anthony ▷Blunt, the art historian, was implicated in the affair. In 1991 John Cairncross admitted he was the so-called "fifth man" involved in the ring.

● **Macleish, Archibald** ► (1892–1982) US poet. An expatriate writer in France during the 1920s, he later worked in the US government service. Much of his *Collected Poems* (1952) was influenced by his liberal politics. He wrote verse dramas including *Panic* (1935) and *J.B.* (1958), which was awarded a Pulitzer Prize, and a collection, *Six Plays* (1980).

● **Macleod, Iain (Norman)** ► (1913–70) British Conservative politician. After serving as minister of health (1952–55) and minister of labour (1955–59) he was a notable colonial secretary (1959–61). Appointed chancellor of the exchequer in 1970, he died in office. He was also a wellknown bridge theorist who, with his partner, Jack Marx (1904–87), developed the Acol system of bidding.

● **Macleod, John James Rickard** ► (1876–1935) British physiologist, noted for his work on carbohydrate metabolism. He was professor of physiology at Toronto University (1919–28), where F. G. ▷Banting and C. H. ▷Best first isolated insulin. Macleod shared the 1923 Nobel Prize with Banting.

● **McLeod gauge** ► An instrument that uses ▷Boyle's law to measure the pressure of a near vacuum. A sample of the vacuum is compressed into a small volume thus raising its pressure, which may then be measured. It is accurate down to about 10^{-6} millimetre of mercury.

● **Mac Liammóir, Micheál** ► (1899–1978) Irish actor and dramatist. In 1928 he was a founder of the Gate Theatre in Dublin, a platform for international drama and young Irish dramatists. He is best known for his one-man show, *The Importance of Being Oscar* (1960–61), based on Oscar Wilde.

● **Maclise, Daniel** ► (1806–70) Irish portrait and history painter, born in Cork. He moved to London (1827), where he painted his celebrated *Death of Nelson* (Liverpool) and *The Meeting of Wellington and Blücher*.

● **McLuhan, (Herbert) Marshall** ► (1911–80) Canadian sociologist, best known for his controversial views on the effects of technology on society. His books include *The Gutenberg Galaxy* (1962), *The Medium Is the Massage* (1967), and *The City as Classroom* (1977).

● **MacMahon, Marie Edme Patrice Maurice, Comte de** ► (1808–93) French marshal and statesman; president (1873–79). He came to prominence in the Crimean War (1854–56) and in Italy, where his victory at Magenta (1859) brought him the title Duc de Magenta. He helped to suppress the Commune of Paris (1871) succeeding Thiers as president; he attempted to break the influence of the republican party by appointing a royalist cabinet in defiance of the chamber of deputies, but was forced to resign.

● **McMahon, Sir William** ► (1908–88) Australian statesman; prime minister (1971–72) of a coalition of Liberal and Country Parties. He became Liberal deputy leader in 1966 and minister for foreign affairs in 1969. He was knighted in 1977.

● **Macmillan, Daniel** ► (1813–57) Scottish bookseller and publisher, who with his brother **Alexander Macmillan** (1818–96) founded (1843) Macmillan and Company, which became one of the world's largest publishing houses. Apprenticed to a bookseller in Irvine, Scotland, in 1824, Daniel moved (1833) to Cambridge, where he opened a shop in 1843. The first publications appeared in 1844. Daniel's grandson, Harold ▷Macmillan, became a prime minister.

● **McMillan, Edwin Mattison** ► (1907–91) US physicist, who shared the 1951 Nobel Prize with Glenn ▷Seaborg for their discovery of transuranic elements. The first such element, ▷neptunium, was discovered by McMillan in 1940.

● **Macmillan, (Maurice) Harold, 1st Earl of Stockton** ► (1894–1986) British statesman; Conservative prime minister (1957–63). The grandson of Daniel ▷Macmillan, who founded the family publishing business, he was an MP for Stockton (1924–29; 1931–45) and for Bromley (1945–64). During the 1930s he opposed ▷appeasement and in World War II held office under Churchill. In 1951 he became a successful minister of housing and local government and then minister of defence (1954) and foreign secretary (1955). As chancellor of the exchequer (1955–57) he introduced Premium Bonds (1957). He succeeded Sir Anthony Eden as prime minister. His "wind of change" speech in Africa in 1958 marked his government's support of independence for African states; he is also remembered for his speech

Harold Macmillan

during the 1959 election asserting "you've never had it so good." His second ministry failed to deal with inflation and suffered a major blow when de Gaulle frustrated Britain's attempt to join the EEC (1963). However, he improved relations with the USA and helped to achieve the ▷Nuclear Test-Ban Treaty (1963). The last year of his government was marred by the ▷Profumo affair. Macmillan resigned because of ill health; he became chancellor of Oxford University in 1960 and was granted an earldom in 1984.

● **MacMillan, Sir Kenneth** ► (1929–92) British ballet dancer and choreographer. He choreographed many ballets for companies in Europe and the USA, including *Romeo and Juliet* (1965), *Anastasia* (1967), *Sleeping Beauty* (1973), and *The Prince of the Pagodas* (1989). He was director of the Royal Ballet from 1970 to 1977.

● **Macmillan, Kirkpatrick** ► (d. 1878) Scottish blacksmith, who in 1839 built the first ▷bicycle. It was an adaptation of the hobby-horse and was propelled by pedals.

● **MacNeice, Louis** ► (1907–63) British poet, born in Belfast. A friend of ▷Auden, ▷Spender, and ▷Day-Lewis at Oxford in the 1930s, he published his first volume of poetry, *Blind Fireworks*, in 1929. Among his other works are the poetry collections *Autumn Journal* (1939) and *The Burning Perch* (1963) and the radio play *The Dark Tower* (1947). His *Collected Poems* appeared in 1966.

● **Macon** ► 32 49N 83 37W A city in the USA, in Georgia on the Ocmulgee River. It is the industrial centre of a large agricultural area. Population (1998 est): 114 336.

● **Mâcon** ► 46 18N 4 50E A town in E France, the capital of the Saône-et-Loire department on the River Saône. An important trading centre for Burgundy wines, its manufactures include textiles, vats, and machinery. Population (1995 est): 39 700.

● **Macpherson, James** ▷See Ossian.

● **Macquarie, Lachlan** ► (1761–1824) Scottish colonial administrator; governor of New South Wales (1810–21). He encouraged construction and exploration in the colony but his liberal policies towards the ▷Emancipists and the Aborigines made him enemies and he resigned.

● **Macquarie Island** ► A subantarctic volcanic island in the S Pacific Ocean, in the Australian Antarctic Territory. The site of a meteorological research station, it is the only known breeding ground of the royal penguin. Area: about 168 sq km (65 sq mi).

● **McQueen, Steve** ► (1930–80) US film actor. Following his success in *The Magnificent Seven* (1960) he was usually cast as tough laconic heroes. His later films include *The Great Escape* (1963) and *Bullitt* (1968).

● **Macready, William Charles** ► (1793–1873) British actor and theatre manager. One of the most distinguished of 19th-century tragedians, he was particularly successful in the roles of Lear, Hamlet, and Macbeth, and was regarded as the chief rival of Edmund ▷Kean.

● **macrobiotics** ▶ A dietary system that aims to achieve the correct balance of so-called ▷yin and yang foods. It was "discovered" in Japan by George Ohsawa (d. 1965), who introduced it to the West; its supposed Zen Buddhist origin is probably spurious. Yin foods include fruits and vegetables, while meat, eggs, fish, etc., are yang. Some cereals, notably brown rice, contain a harmonious balance of yin and yang.

● **macroeconomics** ▷See economics.

● **macrophage** ▶ An amoeba-like cell (▷phagocyte) found in many tissues and organs of vertebrates. Macrophages engulf cell debris, invading bacteria, and other foreign particles; they also remove dead erythrocytes (red blood cells). They are closely related to monocytes (*see* leucocyte).

● **Madagascar, Republic of** ▶ (name until 1975: Malagasy Republic) An island country in the Indian Ocean, off the SE coast of Africa. A narrow coastal plain in the E and a broader one in the W rise to central highlands, reaching heights of over 2800 m (9000 ft). Most of the inhabitants are Merina, Betsimisaraka, and Betsileo, all speaking ▷Austronesian dialects.

Economy: chiefly agricultural, developed on a cooperative basis. Livestock is important and the main crops include rice and manioc as well as coffee, sugar, and spices, the main exports. Forests produce not only timber, but also gums, resins, and dyes. Clearing of the forests has, however, seriously depleted the unique indigenous fauna, especially the lemurs. Minerals include graphite, chrome, and ilmenite. Industry, previously based mainly on food processing and tobacco, now includes metals, plastics, paper, and oil refining.

History: settled by Indonesians from the 1st century AD and by Muslim traders from Africa from the 8th century, the island was visited by the Portuguese in the 16th century. It remained a native kingdom until the late 19th century, when the French laid claim to Madagascar and, after much bloodshed, established a protectorate (1895). It became a French overseas territory in 1946 and a republic within the French Community in 1958, gaining full independence in 1960. A military government took over in 1972 but was overthrown in 1975. A new socialist constitution was approved by referendum and Admiral Didier Ratsiraka (1936–) became president. The government's socialist policies led to economic disaster and serious unrest. In 1991 a transitional government was appointed, leading to multiparty elections in 1992 and 1993. In 1996 the National Assembly impeached President Albert Zafy for misusing his powers; following elections later that year Ratsiraka became president once more in 1997. Presidential elections in late 2001 produced a narrow victory for Marc Ravalomanana, but Ratsiraka refused to accept the result, leading to chaos and division.

Republic of Madagascar

Head of state	President Admiral Didier Ratsiraka
Official languages	Malagasy and French
Official currency	Malagasy franc of 100 centimes
Area	587 041 sq km (229 233 sq mi)
Population (2000 est)	15 506 000
Capital	Antananarivo
Main port	Taomasina

● **Madariaga y Rojo, Salvador de** ▶ (1886–1978) Spanish historian and diplomat, who was ambassador to the USA (1931) and to France (1932–34). His historical writings include *The Rise and Fall of the Spanish American Empire* (1947) and *Bolivar* (1952).

● **mad cow disease** ▷See BSE.

● **madder** ▶ A perennial herb of the genus *Rubia* (about 38 species), especially *R. tinctorum*, native to Eurasia. It has trailing stems with whorls of narrow leaves, clusters of small yellow flowers, and blackish berry-like fruits. A red dye is extracted from the roots. Family: *Rubiaceae*.

● **Madeira, Rio** ▶ A river in W Brazil, formed by the union of the Rios Beni and Mamoré and flowing generally NE to join the River Amazon. Length: 3241 km (2013 mi).

● **Madeira Islands** ▶ (or Funchal Islands) A Portuguese archipelago in the Atlantic Ocean, about 640 km (398 mi) off the coast of Morocco. It comprises the inhabited islands of Madeira and Porto Santo and two uninhabited island groups. Madeira, the largest and most important island, is densely vegetated and its mild climate attracts many holiday-makers. Its products include basketwork, fruit (such as mangoes), sugar, and the famous Madeira wine. Area: 777 sq km (300 sq mi). Population (1993 est): 253 800. Capital: Funchal.

● **Maderna, Carlo** ▶ (1556–1629) Roman architect. A precursor of the Roman ▷baroque, Maderna's vigorous style is first seen in the façade of Sta Susanna (1597–1603). His major work was the completion of St Peter's Basilica, adding the nave and façade to Michelangelo's design.

● **Madhya Pradesh** ▶ A state in central India, stretching N over highlands to the S edge of the Ganges plain. The largest state, it is predominantly agricultural, producing grains, cotton, and sugar cane. Its hydroelectric potential is harnessed for a few industries, including steel, aluminium, and cement. Coal, iron ore, and other minerals are mined.

History: under Islamic (11th–18th centuries) and Maratha (18th–19th centuries) rule until Britain established control, Madhya Pradesh became a state in 1956. Area: 443 446 sq km (171 179 sq mi). Population (1994 est): 71 950 000. Capital: Bhopal.

● **Madison** ▶ 43 04N 89 22W A city in the USA, the capital of Wisconsin situated on an isthmus between Lakes Mendota and Monona. The commercial and industrial centre of a rich agricultural region, it is the site of the University of Wisconsin (1848). Population (1996 est): 197 630.

● **Madison, James** ▶ (1751–1836) US statesman; president (1809–17). His influence at the ▷Constitutional Convention (1787), which drew up the US constitution, earned him the title "father of the American constitution." Madison urged its ratification and defended federal powers over ▷states' rights in *The Federalist Papers*. As secretary of state under Jefferson he promoted the ▷Louisiana Purchase. While president he declared the expansionist ▷War of 1812 on Britain, described as "Mr Madison's War."

● **Madonna** ▶ (Madonna Louise Veronica Ciccone; 1958–) US pop singer and film actress, who has sold more records than any other female performer. Her album *Like a Virgin* (1985) established her as an international star; subsequent albums included *True Blue* (1986), *Ray of Light* (1998), and *Music* (2000). She has also appeared in such films as *Desperately Seeking Susan* (1985) and the musical *Evita* (1996). She married the British film director Guy Ritchie (1968–) in 2000.

● **Madras** ▶ (official name from 1996: Chennai) 13 05N 80 18N A city and major seaport in India, the capital of Tamil Nadu on the Coromandel Coast. Founded (1639) by the British East India Company, the city developed around the small fort, Fort St George, which now contains state government offices and is the site of the first English church built in India (1678–80). The University of Madras was established here in 1857. An important industrial centre, Madras manufactures cars, bicycles, and cement and its chief exports are leather, iron ore, and cotton textiles. Population (1991): 3 795 028.

● **Madras** ▶ (state) ▷See Tamil Nadu.

● **Madrid** ▶ 40 27N 3 42W The capital of Spain, situated on a high plateau in the centre of the country on the River Manzanares. Madrid is the focal point of rail, road, and air routes and is the financial centre of Spain. Its industries include the manufacture of leather goods, textiles, chemicals, engineering, glassware, and porcelain and the processing of agricultural products. A cultural centre, Madrid possesses a university (transferred from Alcalá de Henares in 1836), notable art galleries (especially the ▷Prado), and the national library (founded in 1712). Buildings include the former royal palace, the parliament, many churches, and the 17th-century cathedral.

History: Madrid was captured from the Moors in 1083 by Alfonso VI. Philip II established it as the capital in 1561. The citizens' uprising against Napoleon's occupation in 1808 provided inspiration for the rest of Spain. In the Spanish Civil War Madrid was a Republican stronghold until it fell to the Nationalists in March, 1939, after being besieged for two years. Population (1995 est): 3 029 734.

● **madrigal** ▶ A secular polyphonic composition (*see* polyphony) for voices, often a setting of a love poem. Its first flowering was in 14th-century Florence, where Landini wrote madrigals in two and three parts for voices and instruments. The Italian madrigal of the 16th and 17th centuries developed as an aristocratic art form in the complex and expressive compositions of Marenzio, Monteverdi, and Gesualdo. The English school (Byrd, Morley, Weelkes, etc.) wrote in a simpler style; many madrigals were composed in praise of Elizabeth I.

● **Madura** ▶ An Indonesian island in the Java Sea, off NE Java. Largely infertile, its chief industries are cattle rearing and fish farming. It is known for its bull races. The population is Muslim and there is a notable mosque at Bangkalan. Area: 5472 sq km (2113 sq mi). Chief town: Pamekasan.

● **Madurai** ▶ 9 55N 78 07E A city in India, in Tamil Nadu. Capital of the Pandya kings (4th–11th centuries AD), it is the site of a large Hindu temple (rebuilt 16th–17th centuries). Its university was established in 1966. Industries include brassware and textiles. Population (1991): 951 696.

● **Maeander, River** ▷*See* Menderes, River.

● **Maecenas, Gaius** ▶ (d. 8 BC) Roman statesman, who was a close adviser of Emperor ▷Augustus. Also noted as a literary patron, Maecenas included in his circle the three most important Augustan poets, Virgil, Horace, and Propertius.

● **Maelstrom** ▶ A violent whirlpool in a channel in the Norwegian Lofoten Islands, a notorious shipping hazard. The word (uncapitalized) is also used for any whirlpool, particularly one of tidal origin occurring in a narrow irregular channel, as between islands.

● **Maes, Nicolas** ▶ (*or* N. Maas; 1634–93) Dutch genre painter, born in Dordrecht. Initially influenced by his teacher ▷Rembrandt in such paintings as *Girl at the Window* (c. 1655; Rijksmuseum, Amsterdam), he later adopted the style of Flemish portraiture, after visiting Antwerp in the 1660s.

● **Maeterlinck, Maurice** ▶ (1862–1949) Belgian poet and dramatist. Having established his reputation as a poet he became the leading dramatist of the ▷Symbolist movement with such plays as *Pelléas et Mélisande* (1892), on which Debussy based his opera, and *L'Oiseau bleu* (1908). He also wrote several philosophical prose works. From 1890 he lived mostly in France. He won the Nobel Prize in 1911.

● **Mafeking** ▶ (*or* Mafikeng) 25 53S 25 39E A town in N South Africa. It was besieged for 217 days by Boers during the second Boer War (1899–1902) but was held by Col ▷Baden-Powell until relieved. Although outside the territory, it was the capital of the protectorate of Bechuanaland (now Botswana) until 1965. The town was officially part of Bophuthatswana from 1980 until 1994. Population (latest est): 6775.

● **Mafia** ▶ A criminal organization that originated as a secret society in 13th-century Sicily. The word (meaning "swank") was coined in the 19th century, when the Mafia was employed by the great landowners of Sicily to manage their estates. By extortion, "protection," ransom, and blackmail, the Mafia formed an organization so powerful that it virtually ruled Sicily. Repeated attempts to end its power, including the almost successful efforts of the fascists, have been hampered by the code of absolute silence enforced by reprisals. Italian emigrants took the Mafia to the USA in the early 20th century, where as Cosa Nostra (Our Affair), it has flourished.

● **Magadha** ▶ An ancient kingdom in NE India, now absorbed by Bihar state. Its early kings included Bimbisara (reigned c. 543–c. 491 BC) and Ajataśatru (reigned c. 491–c. 459). Under ▷Chandragupta Maurya, ▷Asoka, and later the ▷Gupta kings Magadha, and its capital Pataliputra, became a great cultural and political centre.

● **Magdalena, Río** ▶ A river in Colombia, rising in the SW of the country and flowing generally N to enter the Caribbean Sea near Barranquilla. Length: 1540 km (956 mi).

● **Magdalenian** ▶ A culture of the Upper ▷Palaeolithic, succeeding the ▷Solutrean in W Europe. Named after La Madeleine cave in the Dordogne (SW France), the Magdalenian is marked by an abundance of bone and antler tools, notably barbed harpoons and spear throwers. Dating from about 15 000 to 10 000 BC, it was the heyday of prehistoric art with magnificent cave paintings (e.g. at ▷Altamira) and carved and engraved decoration on bone artefacts.

● **Magdeburg** ▶ 52 8N 11 35E A city in E Germany, on the River ▷Elbe. It achieved fame in the middle ages for its judicial system, the "Magdeburg Law," which was used as a model by many other European cities. It was also a leading member of the Hanseatic League. Bombs destroyed much of the city during World War II, including the town hall (1691), but the cathedral (begun in the 13th century) survived. Its industries include iron, oil refining, chemicals, and textiles. Population (1996 est): 257 656.

● **Magellan, Ferdinand** ▶ (c. 1480–1521) Portuguese explorer. He undertook many expeditions to India and Africa for Portugal between 1505 and 1516. In 1519, under Spanish patronage, he set off to seek a passage W to the Moluccas. Magellan's flagship *Trinidad*—with *San Antonio, Concepción, Victoria,* and *Santiago*—crossed the Pacific and late in 1520 sailed through the strait that was named after him. In the spring of 1521, after severe privations, they reached the East Indies, where Magellan was killed. Only the *Victoria* returned to Spain, thus completing under del ▷Cano the first circumnavigation of the world. ▷*See also* Magellanic Clouds.

● **Magellan, Strait of** ▶ A channel separating the mainland of South America from Tierra del Fuego. Discovered in 1520 by the Portuguese explorer Magellan, it is an important passage between the S Atlantic and the S Pacific Oceans. Length: 600 km (370 mi). Maximum width: 32 km (20 mi).

● **Magellanic Clouds** ▶ Two small irregular ▷galaxies, the Small and Large Magellanic Clouds, that are close to our ▷Galaxy. They can be seen, by eye, from the S hemisphere and were first recorded by Ferdinand ▷Magellan (1519).

● **Magendie, François** ▶ (1783–1855) French physiologist, noted for his work on the nervous system. He investigated the finding, first made by the anatomist Sir Charles Bell (1774–1842), that the anterior roots of the spinal cord carry motor nerves and the posterior roots carry sensory nerves. Magendie also experimented on nutritional requirements and studied the effects of drugs on the body.

● **Magenta** ▶ 43 28N 8 52E A town in N Italy, in Lombardy. A decisive battle in the struggle for Italian national independence was fought here in 1859, in which the French and Sardinians defeated the Austrians; Magenta dye was named in honour of the event. Population (latest est): 23 694.

● **Maggiore, Lake** ▶ (Latin name: Lacus Verbanus) A long narrow lake in Italy and Switzerland. Sheltered from the N by the Alps, it enjoys a mild climate: the holiday resorts at its edge include ▷Locarno. Area: 212 sq km (82 sq mi).

● **maggot** ▶ The legless soft-bodied larva of many two-winged flies, such as the ▷blowfly and ▷housefly. Rat-tailed maggots are the aquatic larvae of certain ▷hoverflies, so called because of their long respiratory siphons.

● **Magherafelt** ▶ A district in Northern Ireland, in Co Londonderry. Area: 562 sq km (217 sq mi). Population (1991): 36 100.

● **Maghrib** ▶ (*or* Maghreb; Arabic: west) The area in NW Africa occupied by the states of Morocco, Algeria, Tunisia, and Libya, so called on account of its geographical position in the Arab world. It formerly included Moorish Spain. Its inhabitants are of mixed ▷Arab and ▷Berber stock. Although the peoples of the Maghrib have their own distinctive customs and Arabic and Berber dialects they have always formed an integral part of the Arabic cultural tradition. In 1988 the states concerned formed association, modelled on the European Community, to promote closer political and economic cooperation. *Compare* Mashriq.

● **Magi** ▶ **1.** In antiquity, the priests of Zoroaster, renowned for their astronomical knowledge (*see* Zoroastrianism). **2.** The sages who came from the East, following a star, to worship the infant Christ at Bethlehem (Matthew 2.1–12). Early Christian tradition embroidered the New Testament account, giving them the title of kings and the names of Caspar, Melchior, and Balthazar. Symbolic significance was ascribed to their gifts: gold (kingship), frankincense (divinity), and myrrh (death). Honoured as saints during the middle ages, they became the patron saints of ▷Cologne and a favourite subject in Christian art.

● **magic** ▸ A system of beliefs and practices by which some humans attempt to control the natural and supernatural forces that affect their lives. Generally regarded as "superstition" in industrial societies, magic still lingers in such popular rituals as touching wood to avert ill luck. In many preindustrial societies, magic plays an important social role. Its practitioners may rank next to the chief in prestige and authority, being credited with the ability to communicate with good and evil spirits to ensure success in war and hunting as well as to increase the fertility of land and the wellbeing of livestock.

Some primitive rituals, such as pouring water on the ground to bring rain, are purely magical, as they assume that the performance of certain preordained ritual actions, usually of an imitative nature, can in some way directly affect the natural order (in this case, the mechanics of precipitation). In this they differ from religious rituals (e.g. praying for rain), which involve a submissive appeal to a higher being or beings believed to have power over the natural order (in this case, power to alter the prevailing meteorological circumstances).

● **Maginot line** ▸ Fortifications built (1929–38) to protect the E frontier of France. They were named after André Maginot (1877–1932), French minister of war (1929–32), who authorized its construction. Outflanked in World War II by the invading Germans (1940), the line was never tested.

● **magistrate** ▸ An officer who administers the law. In England magistrates are either ▷justices of the peace or stipendiary magistrates, who are barristers or solicitors appointed to try cases in some metropolitan Magistrates' Courts, have wider powers than justices, and are salaried. Magistrates' Courts are mostly concerned with ▷criminal law and have to decide whether an indictable offence has been committed, in which case the offender is sent for trial in the Crown Court (*see* courts of law). If the offence is less serious (a summary offence), it can be tried by the summary jurisdiction of the magistrates. Some offences can be tried either way, in which case the magistrates must decide whether to send the offender to the Crown Court or to try the case themselves. Magistrates' Courts are also called upon to adjudicate in certain civil-law cases.

● **Maglemosian** ▸ A ▷Mesolithic culture of N Europe, dating from about 8000 to 5000 BC. Named after a site at Mullerup on Sjaelland (Denmark), the Maglemosian extended from E England to NW Russia. Hunters of forest game and fishers in the lakes by which they preferred to live, the Maglemosians used wood, stone, antler, and bone artefacts, including dug-out canoes, but lacked domestic animals (apart from dogs), cultivated crops, and pottery.

● **maglev** ▷*See* magnetic levitation.

● **magma** ▸ Molten rock lying beneath the earth's surface, either in the crust or upper mantle. It may rise to the surface through volcanic fissures and be extruded as lava; if it solidifies under ground it forms intrusive ▷igneous rock. Magma is a hot largely silicate liquid, containing dissolved gases and sometimes suspended crystals.

● **Magna Carta** ▸ (1215) The Great Charter that was sealed at Runnymede by King John of England in response to the baronial unrest that resulted from his disastrous foreign policy and arbitrary government. The Charter defined the barons' feudal obligations to the monarch, opposed his arbitrary application of justice, and confirmed the liberties of the English Church; its enforcement was to be supervised by 25 men elected by the barons. Although it failed to avert the first ▷Barons' War and was annulled by the pope, it was reissued, with changes, in 1216, 1217, and 1225. Originally intended to define the limitations of royal power, the Charter was subsequently upheld as a statement of civil rights. Of the four extant originals, two are in the British Library, and one each in Salisbury and Lincoln Cathedrals.

● **magnesite** ▸ A white or colourless mineral consisting of magne-

sium carbonate. It results from the alteration of magnesium-rich rocks, as in the veins of magnesite in serpentine, and as replacement deposits in limestone and dolomite. It is an important ore of magnesium and is used in making refractory material, fertilizers, abrasives, etc.

● **magnesium** ▸ (Mg) A light silvery-white reactive metal, first isolated by Sir Humphry Davy in 1808. Magnesium is the eighth most common element in the earth's crust and is a major constituent of the earth's mantle as the minerals olivine (Mg_2SiO_4) and enstatite ($MgSiO_3$). It is extracted by electrolysis of magnesium chloride ($MgCl_2$) from sea water. Magnesium forms many other ionic salts, such as the sulphate ($MgSO_4$; Epsom salts), the carbonate ($MgCO_3$; magnesite), the oxide (MgO; magnesia), the nitrate ($Mg(NO_3)_2$), and the hydroxide ($Mg(OH)_2$; milk of magnesia). It also plays a role in plant life, occurring in ▷chlorophyll. When alloyed with aluminium it is used in aircraft construction. It is also used in flares, incendiary bombs, and in refractory furnace linings. At no 12; at wt 24.3050; mp 650°C; bp 1090°C.

● **magnet** ▸ A body that has an appreciable external ▷magnetic field (*see also* magnetism). Every magnet has two distinct areas around which the field is greatest—called the north and south poles. Like poles repel each other and opposite poles attract each other. Ferromagnetic materials (*see* ferromagnetism) are attracted to magnets because the magnet induces a field in the material in line with its own field. **Permanent magnets** are made of ferromagnetic materials and retain their magnetism unless they are heated above a certain temperature or are demagnetized by an opposing field. **Electromagnets** only function when a current flows through their coils. The field strength along the axis of the coil is proportional to the number of turns of the coil and the current flowing through it.

● **magnetic bottle** ▸ An arrangement of magnetic fields designed to contain a ▷plasma. Usually the fields are linear with strong magnetic fields called **magnetic mirrors** at both ends so that the plasma is confined within a cylinder. They are used in experimental ▷thermonuclear reactors.

● **magnetic compass** ▷*See* compass.

● **magnetic constant** ▸ (μ_0) A constant occurring in magnetic equations. Also known as the ▷permeability of free space, its value is $4\pi \times 10^{-7}$ H m^{-1}. It is related to the ▷electric constant (ε_0) by $\mu_0\varepsilon_0 = 1/c^2$, where c is the speed of light.

● **magnetic declination** ▸ The angle between geographical north and the horizontal component of the ▷geomagnetic field. It is also known as the magnetic variation.

● **magnetic dip** ▸ The angle between the horizon and a compass needle swinging in the vertical plane. It thus indicates the direction of the vertical component of the ▷geomagnetic field. It is measured with a **dip circle**, a vertically mounted magnetic needle.

● **magnetic disk** ▸ A disc coated in magnetic material on which computer information is stored, using the same technology as a ▷tape recorder. A **hard disk** (*or* fixed disk) comprises one or more metal discs, usually sealed in an airtight container; it is usually an integral part of its computer. Hard disks have high storage capacities—commonly 100 million characters. A **floppy disk**, made from plastic, is more robust and can be removed but can store only up to 1½ million characters. *Compare* compact disc.

● **magnetic domain** ▷*See* ferromagnetism.

● **magnetic field** ▸ The concept, devised by ▷Faraday, to explain the action-at-a-distance forces produced by a ▷magnet. The magnet is thought of as being surrounded by a field of force, within which its magnetic properties are effective. The strength and direction of the field is indicated by the lines of force that join the magnet's north and south poles. A wire carrying an electric current is surrounded by a magnetic field, with concentric lines of force. An electromagnet usually consists of a coil of wire, in which the lines of force run through the centre of the coil and around its circumference. The strength of the field at the centre of the coil is proportional to the current and the number of turns, and inversely proportional to the coil's radius. ▷*See also* electromagnetic field.

● **magnetic flux** ▶ A measure of the current-inducing properties of a magnetic field (*see* flux). It is measured in ▷webers.

magnetic levitation ▶ The German *Transrapid* maglev train approaching the contact rail that enables it to charge its batteries.

● **magnetic levitation** ▶ (maglev) A magnetic method of raising a vehicle above its tracks to provide almost frictionless propulsion. Experimental maglev trains in Britain (Birmingham's National Exhibition Centre) and Japan (Miyazaki) have shown the system to be fast but expensive. Starting on normal wheels, the train levitates above its elevated track as it gathers speed as a result of the interaction between superconducting magnets buried in the track and those in the base of each coach. Forward propulsion is by ▷linear motor.

● **magnetic moment** ▶ A measure of the strength of a ▷magnet in terms of the torque or twisting force it experiences in a uniform magnetic field. It is equal to the product of the strength of a magnet's poles and the distance between them.

● **magnetic monopole** ▶ A hypothetical particle that would carry a magnetic charge equivalent to either a north pole or a south pole. Such particles would be analogous to charged elementary particles and would provide a complete symmetry between electricity and magnetism. Unlike an electrically charged particle, a stationary magnetic monopole would give rise to a magnetic field and, when moving, an additional electric field.

● **magnetic resonance imaging** ▶ (MRI) A technique used in medicine for producing images of soft tissues, especially in the brain and spinal cord. Based on ▷nuclear magnetic resonance, it produces images in any plane by analysis of variations in the absorption and transmission of high-frequency radio waves by tissues subjected to a strong magnetic field. It enables a variety of diseases to be diagnosed without exposing the patient to X-rays.

● **magnetic storm** ▶ A large transient variation in the ▷geomagnetic field, lasting for minutes or days. It is caused by ▷solar flares producing irregularities in the normal interaction between the ▷solar wind and the ▷magnetosphere. As a result electron densities in the ▷ionosphere are disturbed, causing problems with radio communication and radar transmission, as well as induced currents in electric power lines and in oil and gas pipelines, especially in higher latitudes.

● **magnetism** ▶ A phenomenon in which one body exerts a force on another body with which it is not in contact (action at a distance). The space in which such a force exists is called a ▷magnetic field. Stationary charged particles are surrounded by an ▷electric field; when these particles move or spin, an associated effect, the magnetic field, is created. Thus, an electric current, consisting of a flow of electrons, produces a magnetic field around the conductor. The behaviour of

materials in such a field depends on whether the spinning electrons in its atoms align themselves to reinforce or oppose the external field. ▷*See also* antiferromagnetism; diamagnetism; ferrimagnetism; ferromagnetism; paramagnetism.

● **magnetite** ▶ (*or* lodestone) A black magnetic mineral, a form of iron oxide (Fe_3O_4). It often has distinct magnetic poles and was known around 500 BC for its use as a compass. It is one of the ores from which iron is extracted.

● **magneto** ▶ An ▷electric generator with a permanent ▷magnet, rather than an electromagnet, to create the magnetic field. It consists of one or more conducting coils rotating between magnetic poles. The voltage frequency is equal to the number of magnets times the speed of rotation of the coils. It is used in the ignition of simple petrol engines.

● **magnetohydrodynamics** ▶ (MHD) A method of generating electricity in which current carriers in a fluid are forced by an external magnetic field to flow between electrodes placed in the fluid. Usually the fluid is a hot ionized gas or plasma in which the current carriers are electrons. The electron concentration is increased by adding substances of low ionization potential (e.g. sodium or potassium salts) to the flame. The method has been used to increase the efficiency of generation of a gas turbine, the exhaust flame of which is used for MHD generation.

● **magnetomotive force** ▶ (mmf) A measure of the magnetic effect of an electric current in a coil. It is analogous to ▷electromotive force and is measured in ampere-turns, being dependent on the number of turns in the coil.

● **magnetosphere** ▶ A region surrounding a planet in which charged particles are controlled by the magnetic field of the planet rather than by the interplanetary magnetic field carried by the ▷solar wind; beyond a magnetosphere, solar-wind particles flow undisturbed. Its shape arises from the interaction between solar wind and planetary magnetic field. The earth's magnetosphere, which includes the ▷Van Allen radiation belts, extends 60 000 km from the sunward side of the planet but is drawn out to a much greater extent on the opposite side.

● **magnetostriction** ▶ The mechanical deformation of a ferromagnetic material (*see* ferromagnetism) when it is subjected to a magnetic field. The effect is the result of internal mechanical stress that arises because the energy required to magnetize the crystal domains varies with their orientation in the field. The converse effect, mechanical stress causing a change in magnetization, also occurs. Magnetostriction is used in ▷echo-sounding oscillators to produce the ultrasonic sound wave.

● **magnetron** ▶ An electronic device used to generate and amplify ▷microwaves. It consists of a sealed evacuated tube containing a central cylindrical cathode (source of electrons) inside a cylindrical anode to which electrons are drawn by an electrostatic field. A steady magnetic field applied along the axis of the tube deflects the electrons from their radial path causing them to rotate around the cathode setting up microwave-frequency oscillations. It is widely used in radar generators.

● **magnification** ▶ In optical systems, the ratio of the width of an object to the width of its image, both being measured perpendicular to the axis of the system. For a single lens this reduces to the ratio of the distances of the image and the object from the lens when the image is in focus. For optical instruments the magnification is defined as the ratio of the size of the image on the retina produced by an object with and without the instrument.

● **Magnitogorsk** ▶ 53 28N 59 06E A city in central Russia, on the River Ural. It is an important metallurgy centre but its iron and steel plant—the largest in the country—is based on obsolete technology that causes high levels of airborne pollution. Population (1995 est): 427 000.

● **magnitude** ▶ A measure of the brightness of stars and other astronomical objects. An object's **apparent magnitude** is its brightness as observed from earth and depends primarily on its ▷luminosity and its distance. An object's **absolute magnitude** is its apparent magnitude if it lay at a distance of 10 parsecs (32.616 light years). Both apparent and absolute magnitude are measured at various specific wavebands in the visible, ultraviolet, and infrared regions of the electromagnetic spectrum. Magnitude values range from about +25 for the faintest objects so far detected through zero to negative values for the brightest objects. Magnitude is proportional to the logarithm of the brightness. One star 5 magnitudes less than another is 100 times brighter; a difference of one magnitude thus denotes a brightness ratio of $^5\sqrt{100}$, i.e. 2.512. The difference between the absolute and apparent magnitudes of a body is related to its distance from earth.

● **Magnolia** ▸ A genus of evergreen or deciduous shrubs and ▫trees (35 species), native to North America and Asia and widely grown as ornamentals. Up to 45 m high, they have large simple leaves and big showy flowers, with white, yellow, greenish, or pink petals and many stamens. Papery conelike structures contain the winged fruits. A popular ornamental is the Chinese hybrid *M × soulangeana*, which has pink-tinged flowers. Family: *Magnoliaceae*. ▷*See also* umbrella tree.

● **Magnox** ▸ A magnesium alloy used to encase the fuel in some early nuclear reactors. ▫nuclear energy.

● **magpie** ▸ A noisy black-and-white crow, *Pica pica*, occurring in Eurasia, NW Africa, and W North America. 44 cm long, it has a long wedge-shaped tail and an iridescent blue sheen on the wings. Magpies are omnivorous and notorious predators of eggs and nestlings. The name is also given to Australian songbirds of the family *Cracticidae*, which includes the ▷currawongs.

● **Magritte, René** ▸ (1898–1967) Belgian surrealist painter. Initially a wallpaper designer and commercial artist, he became associated with the Paris surrealists (*see* surrealism) in the late 1920s. Using a realistic but deadpan technique, he made everyday images appear menacing by unusual juxtapositions.

● **Magyars** ▸ The largest ethnic group in Hungary. There are substantial Magyar minorities in neighbouring countries. They originated from mixed Ugric and Turkic stock, who migrated from Siberia during the 5th century and reached their present location during the late 9th century. They subjugated the local ▷Slavs and ▷Huns and for 50 years raided far into Europe. ▷*See also* Hungarian.

● **Mahabharata** ▸ (Sanskrit: great epic of the Bharatas) A Hindu epic poem in 18 books. Probably composed about 300 BC, it may record actual events of a thousand years earlier. The main story relates the feud between the Pandava and Kaurava clans and is interwoven with many myths and other episodes, including the ▷*Bhagavadgita* in the sixth book. The *Mahabharata* and ▷*Ramayana* form the two great classics of Sanskrit literature.

● **Mahalla el-Kubra** ▸ 30 59N 31 10E A city in N Egypt, on the Nile Delta. In a region producing rice, cereal, and cotton, it is an important cotton-manufacturing centre. Population (1992 est): 408 000.

● **Maharashtra** ▸ A state in W central India, on the Arabian Sea. Rising from its coastal plain eastwards over the Western ▷Ghats, it lies mostly on the ▷Deccan plateau. Cotton, millet, wheat, and rice are farmed. Highly industrialized, it produces cotton textiles, chemicals, machinery, and oil products. Bauxite, manganese, and iron ore are mined.
History: conquered by Muslims (1307), the Marathas regained their freedom (16th century) and maintained it until Britain established control (19th century). Maharashtra became a state in 1960. Area: 307 690 sq km (118 774 sq mi). Population (1991): 72 748 215. Capital: Bombay.

● **Mahavira** ▸ Title of **Vardhamana** (?599–527 BC), the 24th and final ▷Tirthankara and founder of ▷Jainism. Born a member of the warrior caste, at the age of 30 he left his family to become an ascetic, following the teaching of the previous Tirthankara. After 12 years of austere self-mortification, he gained the spiritual knowledge he sought. He devoted the rest of his life to teaching Jaina doctrine.

● **Mahayana** ▸ (Sanskrit: Great Vehicle) The school of Buddhism dominant in Tibet, Mongolia, China, Korea, and Japan. Less conservative and academic than the rival school, the ▷Theravada, the Mahayana teaching differs from it primarily in promulgating the ideal of the ▷Bodhisattva—the one who, having gained enlightenment, remains in the world in order to help other beings to their release.

● **Mahdi, al-** ▸ (Arabic: the guided one) In Islamic tradition, a messianic leader who will appear shortly before the end of the world and, for a few years, restore justice and religion. According to some ▷Shiite Muslims, the 12th ▷imam (9th century AD), who is now hidden, will return as the Mahdi. Of a number of claimants to the title, the best known was the Sudanese leader **Muhammad Ahmad** (1844–85). After a religious experience, he proclaimed himself the Mahdi and led an uprising against the Egyptian Government. In 1884 he attacked Khartoum, which was defended by General ▷Gordon, and captured it in January, 1885, after a ten-months siege. He died at Omdurman in June, 1885, probably of typhus. His rule was continued by ▷Abd Allah, the Khalifa.

● **Mahfouz, Naguib** ▸ (1911–) Egyptian writer. A civil servant (1934–71), he acquired a reputation as a writer with *Al-Thulāthyya* (1956–57; known as *The Cairo Trilogy*), *Children of Gebelawi* (1959; banned in Egypt for its treatment of religion), and *Miramar* (1967); his more recent novels include *Adrift on the Nile* (1993). He was awarded the 1988 Nobel Prize.

● **mahjong** ▸ An ancient Chinese game. It is usually played by 4 people using 2 dice and 136 tiles of bone, ivory, or plastic. 108 of the tiles are arranged in 3 suits: circles, bamboos, and characters. Each suit comprises tiles numbered one to nine, with four of each type of tile. There are also four each of red, white, and green dragons and four each of east, south, west, and north winds. Many sets have eight additional tiles, the flowers and seasons. The tiles are built into a square of four walls, symbolizing a walled city. Players score by collecting sequences of tiles according to complex rules.

● **Mahler, Gustav** ▸ (1860–1911) Austrian composer and conductor. He studied at the Vienna conservatoire and directed the Viennese Court Opera (1897–1907). In 1909 he became conductor of the New York Philharmonic Society, but met resistance to his advocacy of modern music. He died of heart disease. His nine symphonies (and uncompleted tenth) were written during vacations. The second (*Resurrection Symphony*), third, fourth, and eighth (*Symphony of a Thousand*) employ vocal soloists. He also wrote the song cycles *Kindertotenlieder* (1901–04) and *Das Lied von der Erde* (1907–10).

● **Mahmud II** ▸ (1785–1839) Sultan of the Ottoman Empire (1808–39). He continued and increased the modernization and westernization of the Empire that had begun under Selim III (1761–1808; reigned 1789–1807). He destroyed the ▷Janissaries in 1826 and in 1829 was forced to recognize Greek independence (*see* Greek Independence, War of).

● **Mahmud of Ghazna** ▸ (971–1030) The third sultan (997–1030) of the Ghaznavid dynasty, which ruled a kingdom comprising modern Afghanistan. During his reign Mahmud led about 17 expeditions into India, conquering Kashmir and the Punjab, and also expanded his state in Iran. He is regarded as the greatest of his dynasty.

● **mahogany** ▸ An evergreen tree of the genus *Swietenia* (7 species), native to tropical America and the West Indies and widely cultivated for timber. Up to about 20 m high, it has large compound leaves with 2–6 pairs of leaflets, greenish-yellow flower clusters, and fruit capsules containing winged seeds. *S. macrophylla* and *S. mahogani* are the most important species: their hard red-brown wood is valued for furniture. Similar wood is obtained from members of other genera, such as *Entandrophragma* (sapele), *Khaya*, and *Trichilia*. Family: *Meliaceae*. ▷*See also* jarrah.

● **Mahón** ▸ (*or* Puerto de Mahón) 39 54N 4 15E A port on the Spanish island of Minorca, on the Mediterranean Sea. It is the site of an important air and naval base. Population (latest est): 22 926.

● **Mahonia** ▸ A genus of evergreen shrubs (70 species), native to N temperate regions and South American mountains and often grown as ornamentals. They have leaves with paired, sometimes spiky, leaflets, and bunches of yellow or orange flowers that produce berries; only those of the Oregon grape (*M. aquifolium*) are edible. Family: *Berberidaceae*.

● **Mahratta** ▷*See* Maratha.

● **Maiden Castle** ▶ The 115-acre site on Fordington Hill, near Dorchester, Dorset (UK), of a prehistoric fortress (*Mai Dun*, "great fort") that may date back to 2000 BC. Excavations (1934–37) by Sir Mortimer ▷Wheeler provided evidence that an Iron Age fortified village occupied the site in the 4th century BC. It was captured by the Romans in 43 AD and abandoned in about 70.

● **maidenhair fern** ▶ An ornamental ▷fern of the genus *Adiantum* (about 200 species), especially *A. capillus-veneris*, found worldwide in moist warm places. From a creeping rhizome arise delicate brown or black stalks, about 2.5–30 cm high, bearing fan-shaped green leaflets. Clusters of spore capsules (sori) are situated on the leaf margins, which are folded onto the underside. Family: *Adiantaceae*.

● **maidenhair tree** ▷*See* ginkgo.

● **Maidenhead** ▶ 51 32N 0 44W A town in SE England, in Windsor and Maidenhead unitary authority, Berkshire. It is mainly residential and its situation on the River Thames makes it a popular tourist centre. Various light industries have been established since World War II. Population (1991): 59 605.

● **Maidstone** ▶ 51 17N 0 32E A town in SE England, the administrative centre of Kent on the River Medway. It is an ancient town and the centre of a fruit- and hop-growing region. Employment is mainly in the service sector, with public administration, health, education, finance, and tourism. Other commercial activities include brewing, distribution, and the manufacture of scientific instruments. Population (1991): 90 878.

● **Maiduguri** ▶ (*or* Yerwa) 11 53N 13 16E A city in NE Nigeria. It comprises the towns of Yerwa and Maiduguri. It exports livestock, crocodile skins, and leather goods. It has a university (1960). Population (1995 est): 312 100.

● **Maikop** ▶ 44 37N 40 48E A city in SW Russia, capital of the Adygei autonomous region. It is the centre of an oil-producing region and is also important for timber and food processing. Population (1996 est): 320 000.

● **Mailer, Norman** ▶ (1923–) US novelist and journalist. He established his reputation with the World War II novel *The Naked and the Dead* (1948). His concern with American society, which provided the themes for novels such as *An American Dream* (1965), is more directly expressed in later works, such as *The Armies of the Night* (1968), concerned with a protest march on the Pentagon, and *The Executioner's Song* (1979), about a convicted murderer, both of which were awarded a Pulitzer Prize. More recent works include the novels *Ancient Evenings* (1983), *Tough Guys Don't Dance* (1984), and *Harlot's Ghost* (1991); *The Time of Our Time* (1998) is a retrospective collection.

● **Maillol, Aristide** ▶ (1861–1944) French sculptor. Originally a painter and tapestry designer influenced by the ▷Nabis and ▷Gauguin, Maillol turned to sculpture in 1896. He made his name in the early 1900s with his monumental female nudes, the best known being *Mediterranean* (c. 1901; New York) and *Night* (1902; Paris). Although influenced by classical Greek models, their extreme simplicity anticipated modern abstract sculpture. Maillol's later works included war memorials and monuments to Cézanne and Debussy.

● **mail-order business** ▶ A method of retail trading in which members of the public purchase goods (clothes, household goods, etc.) through the post, either in response to individual advertisements or from large illustrated catalogues. The customer usually has to pay a postage charge but items are usually cheaper than in shops. This method of trading was pioneered in the USA, being especially appropriate in remote areas, but has become popular in the UK. Newspaper colour magazines carry extensive mail-order advertising. A modern trend is armchair shopping, in which TV shopping channels enable viewers to phone orders while the advertisements are on the screen.

● **Maimonides, Moses** ▶ (Mosheh ben Maymun; 1135–1204) Jewish philosopher and physician. He was born in Córdoba (Spain), then under Moorish rule. After its fall to the ▷Almohads and the religious persecution of Jews, Maimonides and his family left Spain for Cairo (1165), where he later became physician to the Egyptian court. Maimonides' medical theories were advanced for his age. His philosophical work, *The Guide of the Perplexed*, attempted to reconcile faith with reason and led to controversy between Judaism and science.

● **Main, River** ▶ A river in central Germany, flowing W through Frankfurt to join the River Rhine at Mainz. It is linked by canal with the River Danube. Length: 515 km (320 mi).

● **Maine** ▶ A coastal state in the extreme NE USA. The largest of the New England states, it consists of uplands in the W and NW and lowlands along the deeply indented coast in the E. Four-fifths of the state is forested although the famous white pine is now almost extinct. It is the most sparsely populated state E of the Mississippi, most of its inhabitants living in the original settlements along the coast and river valleys. Manufacturing products include paper and pulp, leather goods, food, timber, and textiles. It is an area of considerable mineral wealth; limestone, building stone, and sand and gravel are exploited. The state's major agricultural products are potatoes, poultry, dairying, apples, and beef.
History: although claimed by both Britain and France, it became a British possession (1763). It entered the Union as part of Massachusetts (1788) and later became a separate state (1820). Area: 86 027 sq km (33 215 sq mi). Population (1996 est): 1 243 316. Capital: Augusta.

● **Maine** ▶ A former province in NW France (approximating to Mayenne and Sarthe departments). United with Anjou in 1126, Maine became English territory in 1154. It was reconquered by Philip II Augustus in 1204 and was a province from about 1600 until divided into departments in 1789.

● **Mainland** ▶ **1.** (*or* Pomona) The largest of the Orkney Islands, divided into two main parts by Kirkwall Bay and ▷Scapa Flow. Area: 492 sq km (190 sq mi). Population (1991): 15 128. Chief town: Kirkwall. **2.** The largest of the Shetland Islands. Area: about 583 sq km (225 sq mi). Population (1991): 17 596. Chief town: Lerwick.

● **main sequence** ▷*See* Hertzsprung-Russell diagram.

● **Maintenon, Mme de** ▶ (Françoise d'Aubigné, Marquise de M.; c. 1635–1719) The second wife of Louis XIV of France. In 1652 she married the writer Paul ▷Scarron and after his death became the governess of Louis' illegitimate children (1669) and the king's mistress. She became his wife secretly after the death of Queen Marie Thérèse (1683).

● **Mainz** ▶ (French name: Mayence) 50 00N 8 16E A city and port in SW Germany, the capital of Rhineland-Palatinate at the confluence of the Rivers Rhine and Main. Originally a Celtic settlement, it was the first German archbishopric and in the 15th century Gutenberg set up his printing press here. Its cathedral was founded in 975 AD and its university in 1477 (discontinued 1816–1946). It is a wine-trading centre with varied industries. Population (1996 est): 183 720.

● **maiolica** ▶ Italian pottery originating in the 15th century. Made from calcareous clay, the soft buff body is coated with white tin glaze and brilliantly painted in lustre and rainbow colours. Motifs include narrative pictures, botanical and zoological subjects, grotesques, arabesques, and armorial designs. Items made include tableware, drug jars, and display ornaments. Principal centres of manufacture were Gubbio (famous for lustres by Maestro Giorgio), Deruta (yellow and blue designs on orange backgrounds), Faenza (*see* faience), and ▷Caffaggiolo. The much-imitated manufactures of the early 16th century were often financed by noble patronage.

● **Maistre, Joseph de** ▶ (1753–1821) French monarchist. Settling in Lausanne, he became prominent as an opponent of Revolutionary France with his advocacy of absolutist government, faith in the ▷divine right of kings, and belief, expounded in *Du pape* (1819), that an infallible pope can depose rulers who disregard the laws of God.

● **Maitland** ▶ 32 33S 151 33E A town in Australia, in E New South Wales on the Hunter River. It is an agricultural, industrial, and coalmining centre. Population (latest est): 46 250.

● **maize** ▶ An annual ▷cereal grass, *Zea mays*, also called Indian corn, sweet corn, or corn, native to the New World and widely cultivated in tropical and subtropical regions. 1–4.5 m high, it bears a tassel of male flowers at the top of the stem and spikes of female flowers in the leaf axils; these develop into cobs, each comprising long parallel rows of grains. Maize is used as a vegetable, in breakfast cereals, flour, and livestock feed and for the extraction of corn oil. Cultivated as a grain crop in Central America since at least 2000 BC, maize is a staple food in Latin America and many other countries. In terms of world production it is the third most important cereal crop (after wheat and rice), the USA being the chief producing country.

• **Major, John** ▶ (1943–) British Conservative politician; prime minister (1990–97). Having entered parliament in 1979, he served as chief secretary to the Treasury (1987–89), foreign secretary (July–Oct 1989), and chancellor of the exchequer (1989–90). As prime minister he adopted a more conciliatory approach to Europe than his predecessor, Margaret ▷Thatcher, and initiated new moves towards peace in Northern ▷Ireland (from 1994). However, despite success in the 1992 election and signs of an economic recovery his party was divided over further European integration and troubled by sexual and financial scandals. In May 1997 he led the party to a crushing defeat in the general election. He was appointed a Companion of Honour in 1998.

• **Majorca** ▶ (Spanish name: Mallorca) A Spanish island in the Mediterranean Sea, the largest of the Balearic Islands. Noted for tourism; cereals, legumes, oranges, olives, and figs are produced and marble is quarried. Area: 3639 sq km (1465 sq mi). Population (1990 est): 614 000. Capital: Palma.

• **Majuba Hill** ▶ A mountain in E South Africa, in the Drakensberg range. In 1881 it was the scene of a Boer victory over the British. Height: 1981 m (6500 ft).

• **Makarios III** ▶ (Mikhail Khristodolou Mouskos; 1913–77) Cypriot churchman and statesman; archbishop of the Orthodox Church of Cyprus (1950–77) and president of Cyprus (1960–74, 1974–77). In 1956 he was deported by the British because of his support for Greek-Cypriot union (*see* EOKA). He later abandoned this aim, thus facilitating Cypriot independence. In 1974 he was deposed in a coup backed by Greece but resumed the presidency before the end of the year.

• **Makarova, Natalia** ▶ (1940–) Russian ballerina and actress. She danced with the Kirov Ballet from 1959 until 1970, when she defected from the Soviet Union and settled in the USA. Her most famous roles have included Giselle and Aurora in *The Sleeping Beauty*. She formed her own company in 1980 and has choreographed ballets for the London Festival Ballet.

• **Makassar** ▷*See* Ujung Pandang.

• **Makeevka** ▶ (or Makeyevka) 48 01N 38 00E A city in SE Ukraine, in the Donets Basin. Its industry is based on coalmining and metallurgy. Population (1996 est): 409 000.

• **Makhachkala** ▶ (name until 1921: Petrovsk) 42 59N 47 30E A port in SW Russia, the capital of the Dagestan Republic on the Caspian Sea. It has oil-refining, engineering (especially aircraft), and textile industries. Population (1995 est): 339 000.

• **Malabar Coast** ▶ (or Malabar) The W coast of India from Goa in the N to Cape Comorin in the S. In 1498 Vasco da Gama landed here, making it the first part of India to be brought into contact with Europe. The shore is fringed by sand dunes and coconut palms, while further inland there are long shallow lagoons and paddy fields.

• **Malabo** ▶ (name until 1973: Santa Isabel) 3 45W 8 48E The capital of Equatorial Guinea, a port in the N of the island of Bioko (formerly Macías Nguema), founded by the British in 1827. Population (1991 est): 58 040.

• **Malacca** ▶ (or Melaka) 02 14N 102 14E A historic port in W Peninsular Malaysia, the capital of Malacca state. It was colonized successively by the Portuguese, Dutch, and British after 1511; many Portuguese and Dutch buildings remain. Population (1991): 295 299.

• **Malacca** ▶ (or Melaka) A state in W Peninsular Malaysia, on the Strait of Malacca. Consisting chiefly of a low-lying coastal plain, it produces rice, rubber, copra, tin, and bauxite. Area: 1650 sq km (637 sq mi). Population (1993 est): 583 400. Capital: Malacca.

• **Malacca, Strait of** ▶ (or Strait of Melaka) A channel between Sumatra and Peninsular Malaysia, linking the Indian Ocean with the Pacific Ocean. It is one of the world's most important shipping lanes. Length: about 800 km (500 mi).

• **Malachi** ▶ An Old Testament prophet who rebuked religious hypocrites and the various social evils of the time, predicted a day of judgment, and urged the people to observe the Law of Moses. **The Book of Malachi** is the last book of the Old Testament.

• **malachite** ▶ An ore of copper consisting of hydrated copper carbonate, $Cu_2(OH)_2CO_3$. It is bright green and is found in the oxidized zone of deposits of copper minerals. It occurs in massive form, often with a smooth surface.

• **malachite green** ▶ (aniline green *or* China green; $C_{23}H_{25}ClN_2$) A dye that occurs as lustrous green crystals and is soluble in alcohol. It is used medicinally in dilute solution as an antiseptic and in fish breeding to kill fungus and bacteria. It is also used to dye leather and natural fabrics.

• **Malachy, St** ▶ (1094–1148) Irish prelate, whose Church reforms initiated a religious revival in Ireland. He became Bishop of Connor in 1124 and Archbishop of Armagh in 1132. On his way to Rome (1139) he visited St ▷Bernard of Clairvaux, with whose encouragement he founded the first Cistercian abbey in Ireland, at Mellifont (1142). Feast day: 3 Nov.

• **Málaga** ▶ 36 43N 4 25W A city in S Spain, in Andalusia on the Mediterranean Sea. Founded by the Phoenicians (12th century BC), it passed successively to the Romans, the Visigoths, and the Moors, before falling to Ferdinand and Isabella in 1487. It has a cathedral (begun 16th century) and is the birthplace of the painter Picasso. A major tourist centre and port, it exports olives, almonds, and dried fruits. Population (1995 est): 532 425.

• **Malagasy** ▶ A language of the ▷Austronesian family, related to Malay, spoken in Madagascar. The standard form, written in Roman characters is based on the Merina dialect. It has been influenced by Swahili and Arabic.

• **Malagasy Republic** ▷*See* Madagascar, Republic of.

• **Malamud, Bernard** ▶ (1914–86) US novelist. With such witty and ironic novels as *The Assistant* (1957) and *A New Life* (1961) he built a reputation as a skilful chronicler of Jewish characters and themes. His other works include the story collections *The Magic Barrel* (1958) and *Pictures of Fidelman* (1969) and the novels *The Fixer* (1966), *The Tenants* (1971), *Dubin's Lives* (1979), and *God's Grace* (1982).

• **Malan, Daniel F(rançois)** ▶ (1874–1959) South African politician; prime minister (1948–54). Founder in 1939 with ▷Hertzog of the Nationalist Party, which won the 1948 elections, Malan instituted ▷apartheid in South Africa. A minister of the Dutch Reformed Church, he was a right-wing Afrikaner nationalist.

• **Malang** ▶ 07 59S 112 45E A city in Indonesia, in E Java. It is the site of ancient ruined royal palaces and Indonesian army and air-force bases. Its university was established in 1961. An agricultural centre, it has soap, ceramics, and cigarette industries. Population (1995 est): 763 400.

• **Malaparte, Curzio** ▶ (Kurt Erich Suckert; 1898–1957) Italian political journalist, novelist, and dramatist. He was an active but unorthodox adherent of fascism from the 1920s to the 1940s. His best-known novels are *Kaputt* (1944) and *The Skin* (1949), which drew on his experience as a war correspondent on the Russian front and as a liaison officer with the Allies in Naples during World War II.

• **malaria** ▶ An infectious disease caused by protozoa of the genus ▷*Plasmodium*. Malaria is transmitted by the female *Anopheles* mosquito, which lives only in the tropics. There are four species of *Plasmodium* that infect humans and cause different types of malaria. Malignant tertian malaria (caused by *P. falciparum*) is the most severe; benign tertian malaria (caused by *P. vivax*) is less often fatal but are repeated attacks. The parasites invade the red blood cells and cause them to burst. There is always fever but, depending on the type of parasite and the number of cells affected, there may also be fits, diarrhoea, shock, and jaundice. Chronic infection causes enlargement of the liver and spleen. Drugs used to treat the disease include chloroquine, proguanil, and mefloquine (Lariam) and these can also

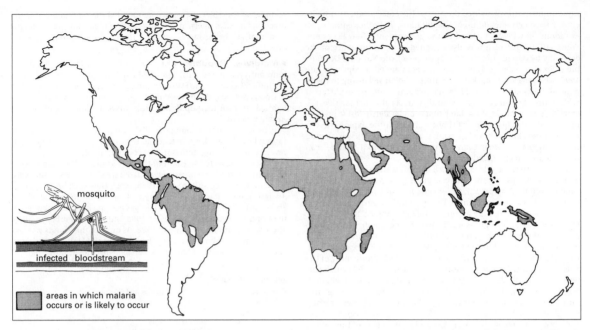

mosquito

infected bloodstream

■ areas in which malaria
   occurs or is likely to occur

malaria ▶ Despite eradication programmes, malaria is still endemic in many parts of the tropics. By sucking the blood of an infected person, the female *Anopheles* mosquito can transmit the malarial parasite to an uninfected person.

be taken to prevent it. Attempts by the World Health Organization to limit malaria, which is a major cause of death and ill health in the tropics, by destroying the mosquito have not yet achieved success.

● **Malatesta** ▶ A family that ruled Rimini (Italy) from 1295 to 1500. **Malatesta da Verrucchio** (d. 1312) led the local Guelf (papal) faction and came to power in 1295 after ousting the Ghibellines (imperial party; *see* Guelfs and Ghibellines). In the 15th century the family lost papal support and its most famous member, **Sigismondo Pandolfo Malatesta** (1417–68), was expelled from Rimini by Pope Pius II (1461). The family's temporary recovery of Rimini (1469–1500) ended when it was taken by Cesare ▷Borgia.

● **Malatya** ▶ 38 22N 38 18E A town in SE central Turkey dating from 1838. It is in a fertile area producing cotton, tobacco, apricots, and grapes and has a university (1975). Population (1995 est): 314 539.

● **Malawi, Lake** ▶ (former name: Lake Nyasa) A lake in Malawi, Tanzania, and Mozambique. Discovered for Europeans by Livingstone in 1859, it is 595 km (370 mi) long and is drained by the Shiré River S into the River Zambezi. Area: about 31 000 sq km (11 966 sq mi).

● **Malawi** ▶ (name until 1963: Nyasaland) A country in SE Africa, between Tanzania, Zambia, and Mozambique. Lake Malawi lies at its E border and the land consists mainly of plateaus reaching heights of over 3000 m (9800 ft). The majority of the population is Bantu.
Economy: chiefly agricultural. The main subsistence crop is maize, and cash crops include tobacco, tea, sugar, and groundnuts, which are the chief exports. Mineral resources are sparse and most power comes from hydroelectric sources, which have been intensively developed. Light manufacturing industries have also been encouraged.
History: the area was visited by the Portuguese in the 17th century and, after Livingstone's exploration, became a British protectorate in 1891. In 1953, in spite of African opposition, it was joined with Northern and Southern Rhodesia to form the Federation of ▷Rhodesia and Nyasaland. This was dissolved in 1963 and Nyasaland gained internal self-government, becoming independent in 1964. In 1966 it became a republic within the British Commonwealth with Dr Hastings ▷Banda as its first president (subsequently life president). Opposition to his authoritarian rule grew in the early 1990s and steps towards implementing multiparty democracy were taken in 1993. Following elections held in 1994 Bakili Muluzi became president and the United Democratic Front formed a government.

Malawi

Head of state	President Bakili Muluzi
Official languages	Chichewa (spoken by over 50% of the population) and English
Official currency	kwacha of 100 tambala
Area	94 079 sq km (36 324 sq mi)
Population (1997 est)	9 609 000
Capital	Lilongwe

● **Malay** ▶ A language of the Indonesian branch of the ▷Austronesian family spoken in SE Asia and Indonesia. The dialect of the S Malay peninsula is the basis of standard Malay. It can be written in Roman or Arabic script. The Malay people probably migrated to this area from China between 2500 and 1500 BC. They became great seafarers, colonizing as far as Madagascar. Predominantly village dwellers, they live in nuclear families in houses raised on piling. Rice and rubber are the main crops. Since the 15th century Islam has been the accepted religion, but vestiges of Hinduism survive.

● **Malayalam** ▶ A ▷Dravidian language of SW India. It is the official language of Kerala. It is related to Tamil from which its script, Koleluttu, is derived.

● **Malay Archipelago** ▶ (former name: East Indies) An island group in SE Asia, the largest in the world. It lies between the Pacific and Indian Oceans and between Asia and Australia. It comprises the Indonesian, Malaysian, and Philippine islands; New Guinea is sometimes included.

● **Malay Peninsula** ▶ (*or* Kra Peninsula) A narrow peninsula in SE Asia, between the Andaman Sea and the South China Sea and separated from Sumatra by the Strait of Malacca. Politically it comprises SW Thailand, Peninsular Malaysia, and Singapore. Length: about 320 km (200 mi). ▷*See also* Malaysia.

● **Malaysia** ▶ A country in SE Asia, consisting of the 11 states of Peninsular Malaysia (formerly the Federation of Malaya) and the states of ▷Sabah and ▷Sarawak in N Borneo. Peninsular Malaysia consists of coastal plains rising to mountains in the interior, reaching heights of 2100 m (7000 ft). Most of the inhabitants are Malays and Chinese with minorities of Indians, Pakistanis, and others.
Economy: formerly an agricultural economy dependent on exports of rubber and other raw materials, Malaysia has undergone

rapid industrialization since the 1970s. The chief products now include cars, electronics, household appliances, and office equipment. Economic growth was fostered by the government's New Economic Policy (1971-90), which was also designed to end dominance of the economy by ethnic Chinese, and its successor the National Development Policy (1990-). The economic boom ended abruptly in late 1997, when the stock market and currency collapsed owing to the financial crisis in SE Asia. Malaysia remains a major exporter of rubber, tin, and palm oil; agricultural products also include rice, the chief food crop. Much of the land area is under dense forest producing considerable quantities of timber, although the exploitation of the rainforest has provoked growing international criticism; fishing is also important. Other than tin, minerals exploited include iron ore, bauxite, ilmenite, and gold.

History: from the 9th to the 14th centuries the Srivijaya empire dominated the area. In the 14th century it was overrun by Hindu Javanese from the Majapahit kingdom and in about 1400 Malacca was established as an Islamic centre. The spice trade flourished, centred on Malacca, attracting the attention of Europeans. In 1511 the port was taken by the Portuguese and in 1641 by the Dutch. British interest in the Malay states began in the 18th century; the East India Company established stations on Penang, Malacca, and Singapore Island, which became the Straits Settlements (1826). With the opening of the Suez Canal, British trade interests increased and in 1909 British protection was extended over the Federated Malay States (Selangor, Negri Sembilan, Perak, and Pahang) and the remaining five unfederated states. Following occupation by the Japanese during World War II, the Federation of Malaya was established (1948). Malaya became independent in 1957 and in 1963 part of the federal state of Malaysia, together with Sabah, Sarawak, and Singapore (which left the federation in 1965). The architect of federation, Tunku >Abdul Rahman, became Malaysia's first prime minister (1963-70). Since the 1960s there has been considerable unrest owing mainly to mutual resentment between the economically dominant Chinese and the politically dominant Malays. Riots in 1969 led to the suspension of parliamentary government and a restructuring of the country's institutions. Since 1971, when parliamentary rule resumed, the country has been governed by the National Front, a Malay-dominated coalition. A resurgence of communist guerrilla activities in the 1970s led to repressive government measures. In foreign policy Malaysia took a generally pro-Western stand during the Cold War period. Dr Mahathir bin >Mohamad became prime minister in 1981. During the 1980s and early 1990s Malaysia experienced continuous economic growth but incurred growing criticism for its human-rights record. In 1997-98 a severe financial and economic crisis led the government to adopt harsh measures, including the expulsion of some two million foreign workers. A political crisis erupted in 1998-99 when the reforming deputy prime minister Anwar Ibrahim was convicted of corruption. His supporters staged mass protests calling for the resignation of Mahathir's government.

Malaysia

Head of state	King Syed Sirajuddin Putra Jamalullail
Official language	Bahasa Malaysia
Official religion	Islam
Official currency	ringgit of 100 sen
Area	329 749 sq km (127 289 sq mi)
Population (2000 est)	23 260 000
Capitals	Putrajaya (administrative), Kuala Lumpur (financial)
Main port	Georgetown

● **Malcolm, George (John)** ► (1917-97) British harpsichordist, pianist, and conductor educated at Oxford and the Royal College of Music. From 1947 to 1959 he was Master of Music at Westminster Cathedral. He was created a CBE in 1965.

● **Malcolm III** ► (c. 1031-93) King of the Scots (1057-93). He became king after killing >Macbeth, the murderer of his father Duncan I (d. 1040; reigned 1034-40). Malcolm married St >Margaret. He became a vassal of William the Conqueror (1072) and was murdered during the last of frequent raids into N England.

● **Malcolm X** ► (1925-65) US militant Black leader. Formerly a

member of the >Black Muslims, he founded the rival militant Organization of Afro-American Unity (1964), which supported violent means of achieving racial equality. He was assassinated while addressing a rally.

● **Maldives, Republic of** ► (Divehi name: Divehi Raajjeyge Jumhooriyyaa; name until 1969: Maldive Islands) A small country in the Indian Ocean, to the SW of Sri Lanka. It consists of a large number of small coral islands, grouped in atolls, of which just over 200 are inhabited. Most of the population is of mixed Indian, Sinhalese, and Arabic descent.

Economy: coconuts, along with fish, are the main export; as crops cannot be cultivated, much food has to be imported. Other sources of revenue are shipping, tourism, and copra production.

History: converted to Islam in the 12th century, the islands were officially under British protection from 1887 to 1965. They were ruled by an elected sultan until 1968, when they became a republic. An agreement allowing the UK staging facilities on the island of Gan ended in 1976. The Republic of Maldives became a special member of the Commonwealth of Nations in 1982 and a full member in 1985. There was an attempted coup in 1988. As most of the islands rise less than 1.8 m (6 ft) above sea level, the future of the Maldives is threatened by the ecological changes associated with global warming.

Republic of Maldives

Head of state	President Maumoon Abdul Gayoom
Official language	Divehi
Official religion	Islam
Official currency	rufiyaa of 100 laari
Area	298 sq km (115 sq mi)
Population (2000 est)	285 000
Capital and main port	Malé

● **Malebo Pool** ► (former name: Stanley Pool) 4 15S 15 25E A broad section of the Congo River in West Africa, on the border between Congo-Brazzaville and the Democratic Republic of Congo. It contains the island of Bamu, which divides the river channel into N and S branches. Area: 450 sq km (174 sq mi).

● **Malebranche, Nicolas** ► (1638-1715) French philosopher and theologian. Like >Descartes, whose work he publicized, Malebranche was concerned with the mind-body relation. In *De la recherche de la vérité* (1674) he held that the two could not interact causally. God brought about all events, including bodily movements, by direct intervention, a doctrine known as occasionalism.

● **maleic acid** ► (or *cis*-butenedioic acid; HOOCCH:CHCOOH) A colourless crystalline toxic >fatty acid. It is an >isomer of **fumaric acid** (*trans*-butenedioic acid) and both are used in making dyes and synthetic resins.

● **Malenkov, Georgi Maksimilianovich** ► (1902-88) Soviet statesman; prime minister (1953-55). A close associate of Stalin, Malenkov became first secretary of the Soviet Communist Party and prime minister after Stalin's death. He was replaced in the former post by Khrushchev but continued as prime minister until forced, owing to agricultural failures, to resign. He was expelled from the Communist Party in 1961.

● **Malesherbes, Chrétien Guillaume de Lamoignon de** ► (1721-94) French statesman, a leading figure of the pre-revolutionary era of reform in France. In 1750 he became director of censorship and gained a reputation for his liberal attitude, permitting, for example, the >Philosophes to publish their work. Criticism of the monarchy led to his banishment from court in 1771 but he was executed as a royalist during the French Revolution.

● **Malevich, Kazimir** ► (1878-1935) Russian painter and art theorist, born in Kiev. He worked in most modern styles before exhibiting (1915) his *Black Square on White Ground*, which launched the art movement called >suprematism and made a significant contribution to >abstract art.

● **Malherbe, François de** ► (1555-1628) French poet and critic. In 1605 he became court poet to Henry IV. His criticism, mostly in letters and commentaries, anticipated classicism by advocating principles of harmony, regularity, and propriety. His poetry consisted chiefly of conventional verses on political and religious themes.

● **Mali, Republic of** ► (name until 1959: French Sudan) A large landlocked country in West Africa. It consists largely of desert, extending into the Sahara in the N, and is crossed by the River Niger, the flood plains of which provide most of the fertile land. The majority of the population are Bambara, Fulani, and Senufo.

Economy: Mali is one of the world's poorest and least developed countries. The main activity is subsistence agriculture, especially the raising of livestock, including cattle, camels, and sheep. The main crops are rice, millet, cassava, cotton, and groundnuts, but all agriculture has been badly affected by recurrent droughts. River fishing is important and dried and smoked fish, together with cattle products and groundnuts, are the main exports. Industry is based mainly on the processing of food and hides and skins. Mineral reserves of bauxite, uranium, and oil are present but only salt and small quantities of gold are exploited. Tourism is being developed, the main attractions being hunting, fishing, and the ancient city of Timbuktu.

History: from the 4th century AD the area was occupied by successive empires, including those of Ghana, Mali (the most famous ruler of which was Mansu Musa), and Gao. In the late 19th century it was conquered by the French and, as French Sudan, it became part of French West Africa. It achieved internal self-government as part of the French Community in 1958. With Senegal it briefly formed the Federation of Mali in 1959, before becoming a fully independent republic in 1960. It broke away from the French Community but, because of economic problems, rejoined the franc zone in 1967. In 1968 the government was overthrown in a military coup led by Lt Moussa Traoré (1936–   ), who became president in 1969. In 1985 Mali fought a war with Burkina Faso over the disputed Agacher area. Rioting, protests, and strikes in early 1991 led to the overthrow of Traoré by Lt Col Amadou Toumani Touré. A transitional government drew up a multiparty constitution and free elections were held in 1992. However, social and tribal unrest has continued. In 1997 legislative elections resulted in victory for the ruling Alliance for Democracy in Mali; the former army leader Touré was elected president in 2002.

Republic of Mali

Head of state	President Amadou Toumani Touré
Official language	French
Official currency	CFA (Communauté financière africaine) franc of 100 centimes
Area	1 204 021 sq km (464 752 sq mi)
Population (2001 est)	11 009 000
Capital	Bamako

● **malic acid** ► (or 2-hydroxybutanedioic acid) A dicarboxylic acid ($C_4H_6O_5$) that occurs widely in fruits (including apples, plums, and grapes) as the free acid or its salts. The anion malate is an intermediate compound in the >Krebs cycle.

● **Malik-Shah** ► (1055–92) The last of the three great Seljuq Sultans of Turkey (1073–92), succeeding his father >Alp Arslan. A noted patron of science and the arts, he built the mosques of Isfahan (his capital) and sponsored the poet >'Omar Khayyam. His government owed its distinction to the work of the vizier >Nizam al-Mulk.

● **Malines** >*See* Mechelen.

● **Malinke** ► A people of West Africa, also known as Mandingo, who speak a language of the Mande division of the >Niger-Congo family. During the 7th century AD one group founded a state with its capital at Kangaba. This spread to become the empire of Mali, which flourished from about 1250 to 1500. The Malinke are agriculturalists, who live in villages of round huts. Descent is patrilineal.

● **Malinowski, Bronisław** ► (1884–1942) Polish anthropologist, regarded as the founder of social anthropology. Between 1914 and 1918 Malinowski lived among the natives of New Guinea and the Trobriand Islands, making a detailed study of their culture. A professor at London University from 1927, he became famous for his functional theory of anthropology, which saw every ritual and belief of a society as fulfilling a particular function. Malinowski's published work includes *The Natives of Mailu* (1915) and *The Father in Primitive Psychology* (1927).

● **Malipiero, Gian Francesco** ► (1882–1973) Italian composer and teacher. His style owes much to the study of 17th- and 18th-century Venetian composers; his works include operas and orchestral, vocal, and chamber music. He published an edition of the works of Monteverdi.

● **mallard** ► A >dabbling duck, *Anas platyrhynchos*, common on ponds and lakes in the N hemisphere. About 55 cm long, females are mottled brown and males greyish with a green head, white collar, reddish breast, black rump, a curly tail, and a broad yellow bill. Both sexes have a purple wing speculum. The mallard is the ancestor of most domestic breeds of duck. >*See* Plate III.

● **Mallarmé, Stéphane** ► (1842–98) French poet. He visited England frequently and until 1871 taught English in schools in the French provinces and in Paris. Influenced by Baudelaire and Poe, he became a major figure of the >Symbolist movement, believing that the function of poetry was to evoke the ideal essences that lay behind the world of actual appearances. His best-known works include *Hérodiade* (1864), *L'Après-Midi d'un faune* (1865), and his obscure final poem, *Un Coup de dés jamais n'abolira le hasard* (1897).

● **Malle, Louis** ► (1932–95) French film director of the >New Wave. Malle's early films included *Ascenseur pour l'échafaud (Frantic;* 1957) and *Les Amants* (1958), both of which starred Jeanne Moreau. In the 1970s *Le Souffle au coeur* (1971), about incest, and *Lacombe, Lucien* (1974), about the German occupation, aroused much controversy, and Malle moved to Hollywood. His later films include *Atlantic City* (1980), *Au revoir les enfants* (1987), and *Damage* (1992).

● **mallee** ► Scrubland vegetation of the coastal regions of S Australia, dominated by small trees and shrubs of the genus >*Eucalyptus*. Most are 2–3 m high, with leathery grey-green leaves and many thick roots that store water.

● **mallee fowl** ► A white-spotted light-brown bird, *Leipoa ocellata*, occurring in semiarid interior regions of Australia. 65 cm long, it feeds on seeds and flowers and builds a large nest mound of fermenting plant material and sand, which may reach 4.5 m across. Throughout the incubation period the male maintains the mound at a constant temperature by adding and taking away sand as necessary. Family: *Megapodidae* (megapodes).

● **Mallorca** >*See* Majorca.

● **mallow** ► A herbaceous plant of the genus *Malva* (30 species), native to N temperate regions. Mallows, which may be creeping or erect, grow up to 90 cm tall. They have hairy lobed leaves and five-petalled flowers, usually purple, pink, or white and 1.5–6 cm across. The name is also given to other plants of the same family. The tree mallow (*Lavatera arborea*) is a shrublike biennial, up to 3 m high, with rose-purple flowers. Family: *Malvaceae*. >*See also* marsh mallow.

● **Malmédy** >*See* Eupen-et-Malmédy.

● **Malmö** ► 55 38N 12 57E A city and port in S Sweden, on the >Sound opposite Copenhagen. It was a prominent trade and shipping centre in the middle ages. Malmö's varied industries include shipbuilding, textiles, and food processing. Population (2000 est): 257 574.

● **malnutrition** ► Ill health resulting from an inadequate diet, usually associated with poverty. The body needs certain amounts of protein, carbohydrate, fat, vitamins, and minerals. Insufficient protein causes >kwashiorkor in children, and a diet deficient in all nutrients causes marasmus. Lack of vitamins causes a wide variety of >deficiency diseases, including >scurvy, >rickets, >beriberi, and >pellagra. >Obesity can be considered as a form of malnutrition resulting from overeating. On the other hand, malnutrition can result from such eating disorders as >anorexia nervosa and >bulimia nervosa.

● **Malory, Sir Thomas** ► (?1400–1471) English writer. He was the author of *Morte d'Arthur* (c. 1469), a narrative in 21 books of the legendary court of King Arthur, drawn mostly from French sources. The work was printed by Caxton in 1485. Malory's identity remains uncertain, but he was probably a Warwickshire knight who had fought in France, became an MP in 1445, and was several times imprisoned.

● **Malpighi, Marcello** ► (1628–94) Italian anatomist, whose microscopical studies of living organisms provided new insights into their function. In 1661 he discovered the fine capillaries that connect arteries with veins, substantiating William ▷Harvey's theory of blood circulation. Malpighi made numerous studies of body organs—the kidney glomeruli (**Malpighian bodies**) and a layer of skin tissue (**Malpighian layer**) are named after him. He also made valuable early studies of embryology, insect physiology (he discovered the excretory **Malpighian tubules** in insects), and comparative plant anatomy (the plant family *Malpighiaceae* is also named after him).

● **Malplaquet, Battle of** ► (11 September, 1709) A battle in the War of the ▷Spanish Succession in which the French faced the armies, under Marlborough and Prince Eugene of Savoy, of Britain, the Netherlands, and Austria, fought 16 km (10 mi) S of Mons. By a strategic retreat the French inflicted severe casualties upon the allies, who, although victorious, were checked in their advance upon Paris.

● **Malraux, André** ► (1901–76) French novelist and essayist. His career included active service with communist revolutionaries in China in the 1920s, with the Republican forces in the Spanish Civil War, and with the French Resistance in World War II. His novels, which are notably objective treatments of the issues involved in these conflicts, include *Man's Estate* (1933) and *Days of Hope* (1938). He was minister for cultural affairs under de Gaulle from 1959 to 1969. He also wrote on art, notably in *Voices of Silence* (1953) and *Museum without Walls* (1967), and a volume of memoirs, *Antimémoires* (1967).

● **malt** ► Barley or other grain prepared for brewing or distilling. The grain is softened by soaking in water, then either heaped on the malting floor and turned by hand or put in revolving drums to encourage germination. Germ growth is stopped by drying the malt by heat, after which it is ready for brewing. Alternatively, after eight to ten days' germ growth the malt may be used for malt ▷whisky.

● **Malta, Republic of** ► A small country in the Mediterranean Sea, to the S of Sicily comprising the two main islands of Malta and Gozo and several islets.

Economy: previously heavily dependent on British military bases, Malta has made efforts to diversify the economy in the decades since independence. The naval dockyards have been converted to commercial use and modern port facilities, including an oil-products terminal, have been developed to encourage the use of Malta as a transit centre for Mediterranean shipping. Shipbuilding and repair are also important. However, the main source of revenue is now tourism, with the island attracting over a million visitors annually. The development of other industries has been aided by foreign investment (especially from Libya, Algeria, and Saudi Arabia). There is some agriculture, both crops and livestock, and fishing. Exports include clothing, textiles, machinery, and food.

History: occupied successively by the Phoenicians, Greeks, Carthaginians, and Romans, the island was conquered by the Arabs in 870 AD. In 1090 it was united with Sicily and in 1530 was granted to the Knights Hospitallers. In 1798 the island was occupied by the French and then by the British, to whom it was formally ceded in 1814. As a crown colony it became an important naval and air base. In World War II Malta's heroic resistance to German attack (1940–42) gained it the George Cross. In 1947 and 1961 it acquired increasing self-government, becoming fully independent in 1964. In 1974 under Dom ▷Mintoff it became a republic within the British Commonwealth. In recent years the main political issue has been the question of EU membership. Malta applied to join the EU in 1990 but in 1993 was instructed to undertake various economic reforms before negotiations could begin. Legislative elections in 1998 resulted in victory for the Nationalist Party under Eddie Fenech-Adami.

Republic of Malta

Head of state	President Ugo Mifsud Bonnici
Official languages	Maltese and English; Italian is widely spoken
Official religion	Roman Catholic
Official currency	Maltese lira of 100 cents
Area	316 sq km (122 sq mi)
Population (1997 est)	375 000
Capital and main port	Valletta

● **Malthus, Thomas Robert** ► (1766–1834) British clergyman and economist, famous for his population theories. In his *Essay on the Principle of Population* (*First Essay*, 1798; *Second Essay*, 1803) Malthus argued that mankind is doomed to remain at near-starvation level as growth in food production, which increases at an arithmetical rate, is negated by the geometrical increase in population. Elaborating ideas from Plato, Aristotle, and Hume, Malthus called for positive efforts to cut the birth rate, preferably by sexual restraint but, failing that, by birth control. ▷*See also* overpopulation.

● **Maluku** ▷*See* Moluccas.

● **Malvern** ► 52 05N 2 20W A town in W central England, in Worcestershire, consisting of Great Malvern and several small villages incorporating the name. It is a spa town lying on the E slopes of the **Malvern Hills**, a narrow range of hills running for some 6.5 km (9 mi) N–S along the Herefordshire–Worcestershire border and reaching 420 m (1378 ft) at Worcestershire Beacon. Malvern has a famous public school (**Malvern College**, founded 1863), the Royal Radar Establishment, and an annual drama and music festival associated with Elgar and G. B. Shaw. Elgar lived and is buried here. Population (1991): 31 537.

● **Malvinas, Islas** ▷*See* Falkland Islands.

● **mamba** ► A large agile highly venomous snake belonging to the African genus *Dendroaspis* (4–5 species). The aggressive black mamba (*D. polylepis*) is 4.3 m long, lives in open rocky regions, and preys on birds and small mammals. The smaller arboreal green mamba (*D. angusticeps*) reaches a length of 2.7 m and is much less aggressive. Mambas are egg-laying snakes. Family: *Elapidae* (cobras, mambas, coral snakes).

● **Mamelukes** ► (Arabic: *mamluk*, slave) The rulers of Egypt and Syria (1250–1517). The Mamelukes were slave soldiers who seized power and then provided a succession of rulers from their own ranks. They drove back the Mongols and finally expelled the Crusaders from Syria. In 1517 the Ottoman Turks conquered Syria and Egypt but the Mamelukes survived and were frequently the effective rulers of Egypt until destroyed by ▷Mehemet Ali in 1811.

● **Mamet, David (Alan)** ► (1947–   ) US playwright, screenwriter, and film director. A cofounder of the St Nicholas Theater Company in Chicago, he made his reputation with such plays as *American Buffalo* (1975), *Glengarry Glen Ross* (1984), and *Speed-the-Plow* (1988), which won praise for their realistic dialogue. *Oleanna* (1992) was a controversial play about sexual harrassment. Mamet's screenplays include *The Untouchables* (1987) and *Wag the Dog* (1998); his films as director include *House of Games* (1987).

● **mammal** ► A warm-blooded animal belonging to the class *Mammalia* (about 4500 species). The evolution of mammals from reptiles involved the development of a temperature-regulation system with an insulating layer of fur and sweat glands in the skin for cooling. This enabled mammals to become highly active, with well-developed sense organs and brains, and to colonize cold climates. The survival of the young was improved by the evolution of milk-secreting ▷mammary glands, and in placental mammals a specialized nourishing membrane (the ▷placenta) in the uterus (womb) enabled the young to be born at an advanced stage of development. The stages involved in this evolution can still be seen in such primitive mammals as the egg-laying ▷monotremes and the ▷marsupials.

The majority of modern mammalian species are terrestrial, ranging in size from tiny shrews to the elephant. However, bats are flying mammals and whales have adapted to a wholly marine existence. □ pp. 782–783.

● **mammary gland** ► The gland in female mammals that secretes milk. Believed to have evolved from sweat glands, there are one or more pairs on the ventral (under) side of the body. The number of glands is related to the number of young produced at one birth; for example, rats and mice have five or six pairs; whales and humans have one pair. Each gland consists of branching ducts leading from milk-secreting cells and opening to the exterior through a nipple. In the most primitive mammals (▷monotremes) there are no nipples and the milk is secreted directly onto the body surface. ▷*See also* breast; lactation.

● **mammography** ▶ ▷Radiography of the breast, used in diagnosing such disorders as breast cancer. Areas of increased density in the breast tissue are revealed as opacities on the X-ray film (**mammogram**), and may indicate the presence of cysts or tumours.

● **mammoth** ▶ An extinct elephant belonging to the genus *Mammuthus*, whose remains have been found in India, Europe, and North America. Of the four types known, the imperial mammoth (*M. imperator*) was the largest, 4.5 m at the shoulder. The woolly mammoth (*M. primigenius*) had thick body hair and tusks up to 2.5 m long. The well-preserved remains of woolly mammoths, which died out about 10 000 years ago, have been found frozen in the permafrost of Siberia. ⁰fossil.

● **Mammoth Cave** ▶ A large cavern in the USA, in W central Kentucky in the Mammoth Cave National Park. It consists of a series of limestone caves with spectacular stalactites and stalagmites. The largest cave reaches 38 m (125 ft) in height and a width of 91 m (300 ft).

● **Mamoré, Río** ▶ A river in South America, rising in the Andes in central Bolivia and flowing generally N. It forms part of the Bolivia–Brazil border before joining the Río Beni to become the Rio Madeira. Length: about 1500 km (930 mi).

● **Ma'mun, al-** ▶ (786–833 AD) The seventh ▷caliph (813–833) of the 'Abbasid dynasty. A son of Harun ar-Rashid, al-Ma'mun seized the caliphate from his half-brother al-Amin (c. 785–813). As caliph he was inclined towards Shiite ideas and encouraged philosophical and scientific work.

● **Man, Isle of** ▶ An island in the Irish Sea, between England and Ireland. It has been a British Crown possession since 1828 but is virtually self-governing with its own parliament, the Court of Tynwald, comprising the lieutenant governor (representing the Crown), the Legislative Council, and the elected House of Keys. It consists of central hills rising to 620 m (2034 ft) at Snaefell, with lowlands in the N and S.
  Economy: tourism is the main source of revenue; attractions include its mild climate, scenery, and the famous annual Tourist Trophy (TT) motorcycle races. The island's low taxation levels encourage a steady influx of retired people. Its agriculture is varied; sheep and cattle are raised and produce includes cereals, turnips, and potatoes. Some manufacturing industry exists including light engineering.
  History: the island was originally inhabited by Celts and the Manx language, a derivative from Gaelic, survived in common usage until the 19th century. The island became a dependency of Norway in the 9th century AD and was ceded to Scotland (1266), coming under English control after 1406. Area: 588 sq km (227 sq mi). Population (1992 est): 70 700. Capital: Douglas.

● **Manado** ▷*See* Menado.

● **Managua** ▶ 12 06N 86 18W The capital of Nicaragua, on the S hore of Lake Managua. Formerly an Indian settlement, it became capital in 1857. It suffered severe damage from earthquakes in 1931 and 1972 and from the civil war (1979). The Nicaragua campus of the Central American University was founded in 1961. It is the country's principal industrial centre. Population (1995 est): 1 195 000.

● **manakin** ▶ A small stocky bird belonging to a family (*Pipridae*; 59 species) occurring in tropical forests of South and Central America. Male manakins are generally dark with bright patches and decorative crests and tail feathers; the females are usually green. Males perform elaborate courtship displays.

● **Manama** ▶ (Arabic name: Al Manamah) 26 12N 50 38E The capital of Bahrain since 1971, situated at the N end of Bahrain Island. An important free port, its economy is based on oil. Population (1992 est): 140 401.

● **Manasseh, tribe of** ▶ One of the 12 ▷tribes of Israel. It claimed descent from Manasseh, King of Judah, son of Joseph and grandson of Jacob. Manasseh's lands lay E and W of Jordan, midway between Galilee and the Dead Sea.

● **Manasseh ben Israel** ▶ (Manoel Dias Soeiro; 1604–57) Rabbi of Amsterdam. His *Hope of Israel* (1650) dealt with the supposed discovery of the ten lost tribes in South America. He presented a petition to Oliver ▷Cromwell (1655), asking for the readmission of the Jews to England (they had been expelled in 1290). He died before he could witness the success of his mission.

● **manatee** ▶ A herbivorous aquatic ⁰mammal belonging to the genus *Trichechus* (3 species), of warm Atlantic waters and coastal rivers of Africa and America. Up to 4.5 m long, manatees have a rounded body with tail fin and flippers and a squarish snout. The American manatee (*T. manatus*) of Florida feeds mainly at night. Slow and placid, it rests on the bottom during the day, rising regularly to breathe. Family: *Trichechidae*; order: *Sirenia*. ▷*See also* dugong.

● **Manaus** ▶ (or Manáos) 3 06S 60 00W A city in NW Brazil, the capital of Amazonas state on the Rio Negro. Founded in 1660, it became the centre of the rubber boom (1890–1920). It remains the chief inland port of the Amazon basin and is accessible to oceangoing steamers. Exports include rubber, brazil nuts, timber, and other forest products. Notable buildings include the Teatro Amazonas (the opera house, 1896) and the University of Amazonas (1965). Population (1995 est): 1 189 000.

● **Manawatu River** ▶ A river in New Zealand, in SW North Island flowing generally W and SW to the Tasman Sea NE of Wellington. The surrounding plain is one of New Zealand's most productive farming areas. Length: 182 km (113 mi).

● **Mancha, La** ▶ An area and former province in Spain. It consists of a sparsely populated arid plateau. Windmills, used to pump water from under ground, are a distinctive feature. It was the setting of Cervantes' *Don Quixote de la Mancha*.

● **Manchester** ▶ 1. 53 30N 2 15W A city in NW England, in Manchester unitary authority, Greater Manchester, situated on the River Irwell and forming part of a large conurbation. Linked with the Mersey estuary by the **Manchester Ship Canal** (opened 1894), it is an important port as well as England's second largest commercial centre (banking, insurance). It was the centre of Lancashire's traditional cotton industry, although most of the cotton mills lay outside the city itself. Industries include chemicals, engineering, clothing, food products, and electrical goods. Education and the leisure industry are also major employers. Manchester is the cultural centre of the North. It has well-known art galleries, concert halls, libraries, the Hallé Orchestra, Manchester Grammar School (1515), the University of Manchester (1851), and the Institute of Science and Technology (1824) and Manchester Business School (now both part of the university). The national newspaper the *Guardian* was founded here as the *Manchester Guardian* in 1821. The 15th-century parish church became Manchester Cathedral in 1847.
  History: the Roman fort of Mancunium, Manchester developed as a regional market place for raw wool and flax and finished pieces. From the mid-18th century onwards a number of factors, such as new technology, the humid climate, and the availability of labour, combined to make it the world's main cotton-manufacturing town. It became the centre of a network of roads, canals, and railways but its rapid growth led to industrial discontent and political agitation (*see* Peterloo Massacre). It also nurtured the basic principles of economic and political liberalism, embodied in the **Manchester School** (a group of political economists, including John ▷Bright and Richard ▷Cobden). Population (1991): 402 889. 2. A unitary authority in NW England, in Greater Manchester. Area: 116 sq km (45 sq mi). Population (1996 est): 430 800.

● **Manchu** ▶ A nomadic people of Manchuria who conquered China during the 16th and 17th centuries and established the ▷Qing dynasty.

● **Manchukuo** ▶ A puppet state set up by the Japanese in Manchuria in 1932 in a bid to occupy all China. It was administered by Chinese with the last Chinese emperor, Henry P'u-i (1906–67), as ruler, and lasted until Japan's defeat in 1945.

● **Manchuria** ▶ A region in NE China bordering on Russia, roughly comprising the provinces of Heilongjiang, Jilin, and Liaoning. It is mountainous in the E and W with a large central fertile plain. The densely populated plain is a major industrial and agricultural area. Products include timber, minerals, such as coal and iron, and fish.

tundra and arctic

reindeer

Norway lemming

musk ox

polar bear

Arctic fox

temperate forest

European flying squirrel

lynx

North American porcupine

elk

wolf

tropical grassland

springbok

chacma baboon

spotted hyena

African mongoose

lion

tropical forest

clouded leopard

common opossum

colobus monkey

bongo

Philippine tarsier

fruit bat

mammal ► This large and diverse group of animals has succeeded in colonizing almost every available habitat on earth, even the most inhospitable. Representative mammals are shown from eight of the world's major habitats (the animals depicted in each habitat are not necessarily from the same geographical region).

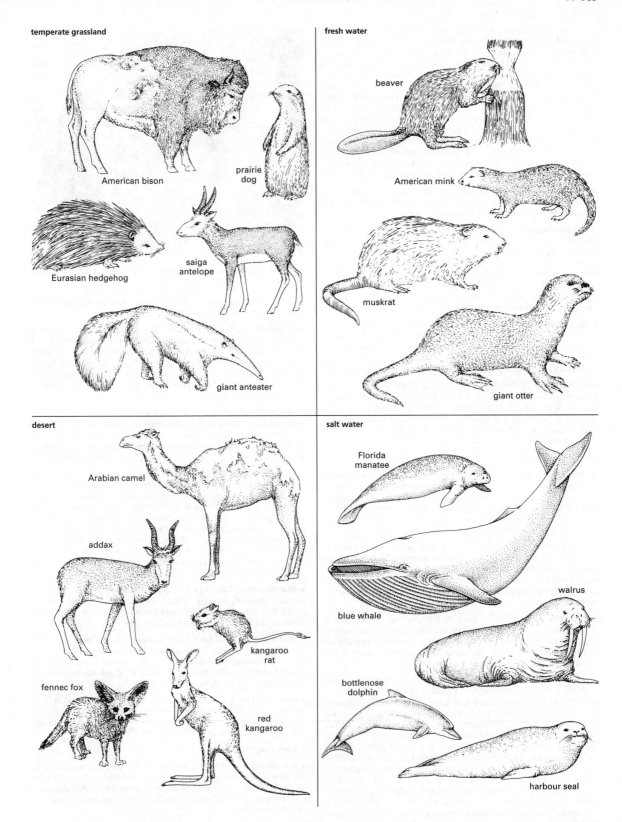

temperate grassland

American bison

prairie dog

Eurasian hedgehog

saiga antelope

giant anteater

fresh water

beaver

American mink

muskrat

giant otter

desert

Arabian camel

addax

kangaroo rat

fennec fox

red kangaroo

salt water

Florida manatee

blue whale

bottlenose dolphin

walrus

harbour seal

History: the area was for centuries inhabited and fought over by the Manchu, Mongols, and Chinese. Their power struggles resulted in empires established over China by the Mongols (1279–1368; *see* Yuan) and Manchus (1644–1912; *see* Qing). Although the S had long been colonized by the Chinese, immigration into the whole area increased greatly under the Qing because of land hunger in China. In the late 19th century this fertile area was dominated by Russia (1898–1904) and then by Japan (1905–45), which developed industrial centres in the region. In 1931, following the Mukden Incident (*see* Shenyang), Japanese forces invaded Manchuria and established a puppet state (*see* Manchukuo). After 1945 the area, staunchly communist, received aid from the Soviet Union until the break between China and the Soviet Union in the 1960s. Since then military forces have been massed along the border. Area: about 1 300 000 sq km (502 000 sq mi).

● **Manchu-Tungus** ▶ A group of languages of the ▷Altaic family, related to ▷Mongolian and ▷Turkic. It comprises only a few languages, of which only Manchu has any literary tradition.

● **Mandaeanism** ▶ A Gnostic sect surviving in S Iraq and SW Iran (*see* Gnosticism). It originated in the 1st or 2nd century AD, but its place of origin and its relationship to Christianity, Judaism, and indigenous Iranian religions, on all of which it draws, are disputed. Mandaeans are hostile to Christ but revere John the Baptist. Their most important rite is frequent baptism. The sacred *Ginza* described their cosmology, which envisages a universe in which hostile spirits (*archons*) endeavour to prevent the soul's ascent to God.

● **mandala** ▶ A Buddhist painted or sometimes metal-wrought symbol used in meditation and other religious practices and particularly associated with Tibetan and Japanese Buddhism. It usually consists of a series of concentric circles, representing universal harmony and containing religious figures, the Buddha being at the centre.

● **Mandalay** ▶ 21 57N 96 04E A city in Myanmar (Burma), on the Irrawaddy River. The last capital of the Burmese kingdom, it fell to the British in 1885. It has numerous monasteries, temples, and pagodas and is the site of a university (1964). Mandalay is the principal commercial centre of the N and E part of the country. Population (1995 est): 677 000.

● **mandarin** ▶ (fruit) ▷*See* tangerine.

● **mandarin** ▶ (official) A Chinese bureaucrat, whose appointment to salaried posts in the civil service was from early Han times until the 1911 revolution by examination. Mandarins occupied a privileged position in society, wore special embroidered robes, and spoke the Mandarin dialect of ▷Chinese, which in its standard, Beijing, form is now spoken by 70% of the population.

● **mandarin duck** ▶ A brilliantly coloured ▷duck, *Aix galericulata*, native to China and widespread as an ornamental bird. It is 43 cm long. The female is grey-brown with a bluish head, a white eye stripe, and a black bill; the male has a red bill, black-and-white head, purple breast, white underparts, and chestnut wing fans and whiskers at the sides of the face.

● **mandate** ▶ The authority given by the League of Nations to the Allied Powers, after World War I, to administer the former German colonies and Turkish territories until the mandatories were ready for self-government. After the UN was established those that had not become self-governing became ▷trust territories.

● **Mandela, Nelson (Rolihlahla)** ▶ (1918–) South African statesman, first Black president of South Africa (1994–99). Mandela practised law in Johannesburg and was active in the ▷African National Congress. He was acquitted of treason in 1961 but retried (1963–64) and sentenced to life imprisonment. He was finally released in 1990. Mandela at once resumed the struggle against ▷apartheid in his capacity as vice-president (from 1991 to 1997 president) of the ANC. In 1993 he signed South Africa's new (transitional) multiracial constitution, marking the complete end of apartheid, and was awarded the Nobel Peace Prize with F. W. ▷de Klerk. In the country's first multiracial election he won an overwhelming victory for the ANC. By the late 1990s, he had become an influential and much respected world statesman. His first wife, **Winnie Mandela** (1934–), campaigned for his release and became a political figure in her own right, but was

Nelson Mandela ▶ With his second wife, Graca, widow of the former president of Mozambique Samora Machel.

found guilty of kidnapping and being an accessory to assault in 1991; they separated in 1992 and divorced in 1996.

● **Mandelbrot, Benoit** ▶ (1924–) French mathematician, born in Warsaw. After studying in Paris and California he became professor of mathematics in Geneva (1955–57); after joining IBM he became professor at Yale (1987–). His work on ▢fractals, geometrical figures in which a shape is repeated on a diminishing scale, was published in *The Fractal Geometry of Nature* (1982). His work has had a marked influence on ▷chaos theory.

● **Mandelbrot set** ▶ A mathematical entity discovered by Benoit ▷Mandelbrot in 1980. It is a set generated by repeated mappings of the type $z \rightarrow z^2 + c$, where z and c are complex numbers. The complex pattern is usually plotted using computer graphics as it contains an infinite number of self-similar copies of itself. ▷*See also* fractal.

● **Mandelson, Peter (Benjamin)** ▶ (1953–) British Labour politician. The grandson of Herbert ▷Morrison, he became the Labour Party's director of communications (its chief "spin doctor") in 1985 and an MP in 1992. He became a cabinet minister on Labour's victory in 1997 but resigned (1998) when it was revealed that he had failed to disclose a loan from a colleague. As secretary of state for Northern Ireland (1999–2001), he oversaw the establishment of new devolved institutions. He was forced to resign again in 2001, over his intervention in a passport application by an Indian businessman, who had made substantial contributions to the Millennium Dome.

● **Mandelstam, Osip** ▶ (1891–?1938) Russian poet, a leading figure in ▷acmeism. His second volume, *Tristia* (1922), contains poems noted for their classical form and spiritual intensity. Arrested in 1934 and 1938, he is presumed to have died in a labour camp.

● **Mandeville, Sir John** ▶ (14th century) The professed author of the immensely popular *Travels* (1356–57), an account that mixes factual and fantastic information about the Middle East, Africa, and Asia. He probably never existed. The book is a translation of a French work itself compiled from other sources.

● **mandolin** ▶ A plucked musical instrument, generally having four double courses of wire strings tuned in the same way as the violin. It is played with a plectrum, using a tremolo effect to sustain longer notes. It is used mainly in informal music making.

● **mandragora** ▷*See* mandrake.

● **mandrake** ▶ A herb of the genus *Mandragora*, especially *M. officinarum*, native to Europe. It has large simple leaves, white flowers, and a thick forked root, which resembles the human form and was formerly believed to have healing and aphrodisiac properties. Family: *Solanaceae*.

● **mandrill** ▶ A large ▷Old World monkey, *Mandrillus sphinx*, of West

African coastal forests. They are 66–84 cm long including the tail (5–7.5 cm), with red and blue muzzle and buttocks and shaggy yellow-brown hair. They live in small family groups and forage for plants and insects, sometimes climbing for berries. ▷*See also* drill.

● **Manes** ▶ In Roman religion, the spirits of the dead. The word, a euphemism meaning "the kindly ones," also referred to the underworld and its gods.

Mandelbrot set ▶ The characteristic shape of the set together with a detail (top left) obtained over a small area of the complex plane.

● **Manet, Edouard** ▶ (1832–83) French painter, born in Paris. After overcoming parental opposition, he trained under the classical painter Thomas Couture (1815–79) between 1850 and 1856. By 1860 he was painting contemporary scenes, but throughout his career he remained indebted to the Old Masters, particularly to Velázquez and Hals. He exhibited mainly at the Paris Salon, where such paintings as *Olympia* and *Déjeuner sur l'herbe* (both Louvre) became targets for considerable scorn and derision. However, his friend Émile ▷Zola spiritedly defended his work in an article published in 1867. In the 1870s he adopted the technique of the impressionists, although he refused to participate in their exhibitions (*see* impressionism). Such paintings as *The Balcony* (Louvre) and *The Luncheon* (Neue Staatsgaleries, Munich) anticipate 20th-century painting by making brushwork, colour, and design more important than the subject matter. His last great work was *A Bar at the Folies-Bergère* (Courtauld Institute, London).

● **mangabey** ▶ A large long-tailed ▷Old World monkey belonging to the genus *Cercocebus* (4 species), of central African forests. Mangabeys are 80–165 cm long including the tail (43–75 cm) and have long limbs and muscular bodies. They live in troops, feeding on fruit high in the trees.

● **Mangalore** ▶ 12 54N 74 51E A port in India, in Karnataka on the Malabar Coast. Its manufactures include textiles and tiles. Population (1991): 273 304.

● **manganese** ▶ (Mn) A hard grey brittle transition element that resembles iron, first isolated in 1774 by J. G. Gahn (1745–1818). It occurs in nature in many minerals, especially pyrolusite (MnO_2) and rhodochrosite ($MnCO_3$), in addition to the extensive deposits of manganese nodules discovered on the deep ocean floors. It is extracted by reduction of the oxide, with magnesium or aluminium, or by electrolysis. The metal is used in many alloys, particularly in steel, in which manganese improves the strength and hardness. Manganese forms compounds in a number of different ▷valence states: for example MnO, Mn_3O_4, MnO_2. The permanganate ion (MnO_4^-) is a well-known oxidizing agent. At no 25; at wt 54.9380; mp 1246±3°C; bp 2062°C.

● **mange** ▶ A contagious skin disease, caused by mites, that can affect domestic livestock, pets, and man (*see* scabies). The parasites bite or burrow into the skin causing hair loss, scaly dry skin, pimples, blisters, and intense itching. Treatment is with such insecticides as gamma benzene hexachloride.

● **mangel-wurzel** ▷*See* beet.

● **mango** ▶ A large evergreen tropical tree, *Mangifera indica*, native to SE Asia but cultivated throughout the tropics for its fruit. Growing 15–18 m high, it has long narrow leaves and large clusters of pinkish flowers. The oblong fruit, up to 2.3 kg in weight, has a green, yellow, or reddish skin and contains a stony seed, surrounded by juicy orange edible flesh that has a spicy flavour. Mangos are eaten fresh and used in preserves or for canning. Family: *Anacardiaceae*.

● **mangosteen** ▶ A tropical fruit tree, *Garcinia mangostana*, native to SE Asia and reaching a height of 9.5 m. The round or oval fruit, up to 8 cm in diameter, has a thick hard purple rind and contains a few seeds surrounded by juicy white edible flesh, which is divided into separate segments and has a slightly sharp taste. Family: *Guttiferae*.

mangroves ▶ Red mangroves in Sarawak, Malaysia. Aerial breathing roots protrude above the waterlogged soil.

● **mangroves** ▶ Shrubs and trees forming dense thickets and low forests on coastal mudflats, salt marshes, and estuaries throughout the tropics. Many are evergreen, with shiny leathery leaves, aerial supporting (prop) roots, and breathing roots with "knees" that protrude above the water or mud. The main species are the common or red mangrove (*Rhizophora mangle*), the black mangrove (*Avicennia nitida*), and *Sonneratia* species.

● **mangrove snake** ▶ A mildly venomous snake belonging to the genus *Boiga* (30 species) occurring in mangrove swamps and lowland forests of Africa, Asia, Australia, and Polynesia. They live on the ground or in trees and prey on frogs, birds, lizards, crabs, fish, etc. The black-and-yellow mangrove snake (*B. dendrophila*) of E Asia can reach a length of 2.5 m. Family: *Colubridae*.

● **Manhattan** ▶ An island in the USA, situated at the N end of New York Bay, between the Hudson, East, and Harlem Rivers, comprising one of the five boroughs of New York City. It is a major commercial and financial centre focused on Wall Street. Other notable features include the famous Broadway theatre district, ▷Greenwich Village, and its many skyscrapers, including the Empire State Building (1931). Area: 47 sq km (22 sq mi). Population (1990): 1 487 536.

● **Manhattan Project** ▶ The code name for a US project set up in 1942 to develop an atomic bomb. Research culminated in the construction of the bombs at Los Alamos, New Mexico. In 1945 a uranium bomb and a plutonium bomb were dropped on Hiroshima and Nagasaki respectively (*see* World War II; nuclear weapons).

● **manic-depressive psychosis** ▶ A severe mental illness, more correctly called bipolar disorder, causing repeated episodes of severe ▷depression, mania (excessive euphoria, overactivity, irritability, and impaired judgment), or both. These episodes can be precipitated by upsetting events but are out of proportion to them. There is a genetically inherited predisposition to this illness; long-term treatment with lithium salts can prevent or reduce the frequency and severity of attacks.

● **Manichaeism** ▶ A religion influenced by both ▷Gnosticism and Christianity. It originated in Persia (c. 230 AD), spread throughout Asia and the Roman Empire, and survived in Chinese Turkistan until the 13th century. It influenced several dualistic medieval heresies (*see* Cathari). Its founder, Mani (c. 216–c. 276), was martyred by the adherents of ▷Zoroastrianism. Fundamental to his creed was the belief that matter is entirely evil, but within each individual is imprisoned a soul, which is a spark of the divine light. By strict abstinence and prayer man can recover consciousness of the light and be liberated at death from material entanglement. Mani's followers were divided into the elect, teachers who lived in poverty and celibacy, and the hearers, who cared for the elect's material needs and could only achieve salvation after a cycle of reincarnation.

● **Manila** ▶ 14 30N 121 12E The capital and main port of the Philippines, on Manila Bay in Luzon. Founded by the Spanish in 1571, it suffered several foreign occupations over the centuries and the old town was destroyed in World War II. The official capital was transferred to Quezon City on the outskirts (1948–76). An educational centre, it has over 20 universities, including the University of Santo Tomas founded in 1611. It has one of the finest harbours in the world and is also an important industrial centre; its industries include textiles, pharmaceuticals, and food processing. Manila suffers from severe traffic congestion; highly decorated jeeps left by US forces provide the main form of transport. Population (1991 est): 1 894 667.

● **Manila Bay** ▶ An inlet of the South China Sea, in the Philippines in SW Luzon. One of the world's finest natural harbours, it was important before the ports of Manila and Cavite were founded. In the battle of Manila Bay in 1898 the US navy defeated the Spanish fleet, and there was again bitter fighting here during World War II. Area: 1994 sq km (770 sq mi).

● **Manila hemp** ▷*See* abaca.

● **Manin, Daniele** ▶ (1804–57) Italian patriot, born in Venice. His opposition to Austrian rule of Venice resulted in his imprisonment in 1847. He was released on the outbreak of the Revolution of 1848, appointed president of the newly restored Venetian Republic, and led a courageous defence of Venice against an Austrian siege. On its surrender (August, 1849) he went into exile in Paris.

● **manioc** ▷*See* cassava.

● **Manipur** ▶ A state in NE India, on the hilly Burmese border. Its largely Mongoloid inhabitants speak many languages. Rice, fruits, sugar cane, and mustard are grown. There is some silk weaving. The jungles yield bamboo and teak.
  History: Burmese threats caused the raja to seek British aid (1824), which became British rule (1891). Manipur became a state in 1972. Area: 22 327 sq km (8617 sq mi). Population (1991): 1 826 714. Capital: Imphal.

● **Manisa** ▶ (ancient name: Magnesia) 38 36N 27 29E A town in W Turkey. Founded in the 12th century BC, Manisa is a commercial town with trade in such crops as tobacco, olives, and raisins. The Romans defeated Antiochus the Great here in 190 BC. Population (1995 est): 191 287.

● **Manitoba** ▶ A province of central Canada, in the centre of North America. Although it is one of the ▷Prairie Provinces, only the SW is true prairie. Further to the NE lies the ▷Red River Valley and three large lakes (Winnipeg, Winnipegosis, and Manitoba) with extensive forests in the N and tundra near Hudson Bay. Manitoba's economy is based on large mechanized farms producing grains and livestock.

Forests, fisheries, and hydroelectricity are also important. Manitoba produces copper, gold, zinc, silver, nickel, and oil. Manufacturing is based on natural resources and agriculture. The province boasts a rich cultural life centred around Greater ▷Winnipeg, which contains over half the population.
  History: originally exploited for furs, Manitoba (then known simply as the Red River Settlement) first attracted dispossessed Scots Highlanders as settlers (1812). Acquisition of the area by Canada (1869) provoked the Riel Rebellion (1869–70), an uprising of French-speaking halfbreeds (Métis). Manitoba became a province in 1870. The transcontinental railway (1882) and steady immigration (especially 1900–14) brought a prosperity that has been interrupted only between the World Wars. Area: 548 495 sq km (211 774 sq mi). Population (1995 est) 1 137 500. Capital: Winnipeg.

● **Manitoulin Islands** ▶ A group of Canadian islands in N Lake ▷Huron. Timber, farming, and tourism are economically important. The main island, Manitoulin Island, is the largest freshwater lake island in the world. Area (Manitoulin Island): 2766 sq km (1068 sq mi).

● **Manizales** ▶ 5 03N 75 32W A city in central Colombia, in the Central Cordillera. It is the commercial centre of the country's chief coffee-growing area. Manufactures include textiles, chemicals, and leather products and it has a university (1943). Population (1997 est): 358 194.

● **Manley, Michael** ▶ (1924–97) Jamaican statesman, who, as leader of the People's National Party, was twice prime minister of Jamaica (1972–80; 1989–92). During his first government he followed socialist policies, including nationalizing 51% of the bauxite industry, developing close ties with Cuba, and speaking out for the developing world. However, his second government adopted austerity measures and a policy of economic liberalization.

● **Mann, Thomas** ▶ (1875–1955) German novelist. Born into a wealthy merchant family, he chose a similar family as the subject of his first novel, *Buddenbrooks* (1901). Art and the artist are his main themes, however, in the novella *Death in Venice* (1912), *The Magic Mountain* (1924), in which a sanatorium is a microcosm of society, and *Doctor Faustus* (1947), a novel about a modern composer of genius. His other works include *Joseph and His Brothers* (1933–44), a series of four novels based on the biblical story of Joseph, and the picaresque *Felix Krull* (1954). Mann opposed Nazism and was forced to emigrate to the USA in the 1930s. He was awarded a Nobel Prize in 1929. His brother **Heinrich Mann** (1871–1950), also a novelist and opponent of fascism, is best known for his novel *Professor Unrat* (1905; filmed as *The Blue Angel*, 1928).

● **manna** ▶ 1. In the Bible, the miraculous food that fell with the dew to sustain the Israelites in the wilderness (Exodus 16.14–15). This phenomenon has been variously identified as an exudation from the tamarisk tree or a form of lichen. 2. A sugary substance obtained from the ash tree and used in medicine.

● **Mannerheim, Carl Gustaf Emil, Baron von** ▶ (1867–1951) Finnish general and statesman. He led the antisocialist forces to victory against the Finnish Bolsheviks in 1918 and then retired until 1931. In 1939, at the outbreak of the ▷Russo-Finnish War, he became commander in chief and, although defeated, was able to obtain good terms for Finland (1941). He re-embarked on war with the Soviet Union (June, 1941) and as president (1944–46) negotiated peace.

● **mannerism** ▶ An art movement dominant in Italy from about 1520 to 1600. Mannerism developed out of the ▷Renaissance style, some of its characteristics being evident in the late work of ▷Raphael and ▷Michelangelo. It aimed to surpass the Renaissance style in virtuosity and emotional impact. In architecture this resulted in a clever and playful misuse of the rules of classical architecture, notably in the buildings of ▷Giulio Romano. In painting it led to a distortion of scale, an elongation of form, and dissonance of colour, which frequently resulted in an effect of tension. Leading mannerist painters were ▷Pontormo, ▷Parmigianino, ▷Vasari, and ▷Bronzino. Features of mannerism also appeared in the work of ▷Tintoretto and ▷El Greco, in the school of ▷Fontainebleau, and in Bohemia in the work of ▷Arcimboldo and Bartholomeus Spranger (1546–1611).

● **Mannheim** ▶ 49 30N 8 28E A city in SW Germany, in Baden-

Württemberg at the confluence of the Rivers Rhine and Neckar. It was the seat of the Electors Palatine (1720–98) and has a notable baroque castle. It is a major port with an oil refinery and its manufactures include motor vehicles and agricultural machinery. Population (1996 est): 311 292.

● **mannikin** ▶ A ▷waxbill of the genus *Lonchura* (30 species) occurring in Africa, S Asia, and Australasia. Mannikins are typically small (about 11 cm long) and brown or black with paler underparts. The chestnut mannikin (*L. ferruginosa*) of the Philippines has become a pest to rice growers.

● **Manning, Henry Edward, Cardinal** ▶ (1808–92) British churchman. A member of the ▷Oxford Movement, he converted to Roman Catholicism in 1851. As Archbishop of Westminster (1865–75) he was a leading defender of papal infallibility at the ▷Vatican Council (1870). A cardinal from 1875, he was active in social reform and temperance.

● **Manolete** ▶ (Manuel Laureano Rodríguez Sánchez; 1917–47) Spanish matador, who became a professional at 17 and achieved a reputation as a bullfighter of great style. He died of injuries received in the ring.

● **manometer** ▶ An instrument for measuring pressure differences. The simplest form consists of a U-shaped tube containing mercury, one arm of which is connected to a source of pressure and the other is open. The difference in height of the liquid in the arms is a measure of the pressure difference.

mannerism ▶ Detail from *The Madonna with the Long Neck* (1532–40; Palazzo Pitti, Florence) by Parmigianino. The elongated proportions of the Madonna's neck and fingers and the baby's body are typical of the reaction against naturalism.

● **manor** ▶ The most common unit of agrarian organization in medieval Europe, introduced into England by the Normans. The manor was essentially the lord's landed estate, usually consisting of the lord's own farm (the demesne), and land let out to peasant tenants, chiefly ▷villeins, who worked for the demesne and were legally dependent upon their lord.

● **Manresa** ▶ 41 43N 1 50E A town in NE Spain, in Catalonia. Below its 17th-century church is the Holy Cave of St Ignatius of Loyola, where he composed his *Spiritual Exercises*. Population (latest est): 65 607.

● **Mansart, François** ▶ (*or* Mansard; 1596–1666) French classical architect. His design for the north wing of the chateau at Blois (1635–38) featured the double-angled (Mansard) roof. He built several houses in Paris, notably the Hôtel de la Vrillière (1635), but is best known for Maisons-Laffitte near Paris (1642). He also designed the church of Val-de-Grâce, Paris (1645). His great-nephew by marriage, who adopted his name, **Jules Hardouin Mansart** (1646–1708), became (1675) architect to Louis XIV, spending much of his life enlarging the Palace of Versailles. He also built the chapel of Les Invalides in Paris and planned the Place Vendôme and Place des Victoires.

● **Mansell, Nigel** ▶ (1954–) British racing driver. He won the European Grand Prix in 1985, becoming Britain's top Formula One driver. His 17th Grand Prix victory in 1991 established a new record for a British driver. In 1992 he was the Formula One world champion. In 1993 he won the US IndyCar championship, but returned to Formula One racing in 1995.

● **Mansfield** ▶ 53 09N 1 11W A town in the Midlands of England, in Nottinghamshire. Coalmining was formerly important; industries now include textiles, engineering, and general manufacturing. Population (1991): 71 858.

● **Mansfield, Katherine** ▶ (Kathleen Mansfield Beauchamp; 1888–1923) New Zealand short-story writer. She came to Europe in 1908, published her first collection of stories in 1911, and in 1918 married John Middleton ▷Murry. *Bliss* (1920) and *The Garden Party* (1922) contain her best-known stories. Two more collections, *The Dove's Nest* (1923) and *Something Childish* (1924), were published posthumously; her *Collected Letters* appeared in 1984. She died of gonorrhoea and tuberculosis in France.

● **Mansfield, William Murray, 1st Earl of** ▶ (1705–93) British judge and politician. He was elected to parliament in 1743 and later became a cabinet minister. As chief justice of the King's Bench from 1756 to 1788 he incurred public hostility because of his views on seditious libel. His London house was a principal target during the ▷Gordon Riots (1780). He transformed the diverse customs of commerce into a code of legal practice.

● **Mansholt, Sicco** ▶ (1908–95) Dutch politician and economist. During World War II he worked secretly to maintain the food supplies of the W Netherlands during the German occupation. After the war he became vice president (1958–72) and president (1972–73) of the EC Commission. In 1953 he prepared the **Mansholt Plan** for a common EC agricultural policy.

● **manslaughter** ▶ The crime of killing a person, which does not amount to ▷murder but is not lawful or accidental. It may arise if the *mens rea* (*see* criminal law) is that required for murder but diminished responsibility, a suicide pact, or provocation can be proved (known as **voluntary manslaughter**) or if there is no *mens rea* for murder and the killing resulted from gross negligence or from a criminally illegal act involving an element of danger to the victim (**involuntary manslaughter**). A person may also commit manslaughter when drunk. The maximum penalty is life imprisonment, although this is rarely imposed.

● **Mansur, Abu Ja'far al-** ▶ (c. 712–75 AD) The second ▷caliph (754–75) of the 'Abbasid dynasty and its effective founder. He built Baghdad (begun 762) and made it the 'Abbasid capital. Influenced by Persia, he developed the bureaucracy.

● **Mansura, El** ▶ (*or* al-Mansurah) 31 03N 31 23E A city in N Egypt, on the Nile Delta. In 1250 it was occupied by Crusaders under Louis IX

(St Louis) of France, who was held for ransom by Muslim forces. It has cotton-ginning and flour-milling industries. Population (1992 est): 371 000.

● **manta ray** ▶ A ▷ray fish, also called devil ray or devil fish, of the family *Mobulidae*. 60–660 cm long, they swim near the surface of warm-temperate and tropical waters, feeding on plankton and small animals swept into the mouth by hornlike feeding fins projecting from the front of the head.

● **Mantegna, Andrea** ▶ (c. 1431–1506) Italian Renaissance painter and engraver, born near Vicenza. He was trained in Padua by his adopted father Francesco Squarcione, an artist and archaeologist. His marriage (1453) to the daughter of Jacopo ▷Bellini connected him with the Venetian school. As court painter to the Duke of Mantua from 1459, he painted nine panels depicting *The Triumph of Caesar* (Hampton Court, London). His fresco decorations for the bridal chamber of the ducal palace include portraits of members of the Mantuan court and an illusionistic ceiling, which anticipates the ▷baroque.

● **mantis** ▶ An insect belonging to the family *Mantidae* (2000 species), found in tropical and warm temperate regions. Up to 125 mm long, mantids blend with the surrounding vegetation and are voracious carnivores, using their forelegs to capture insects and other small animals. The "praying" position held by the forelegs at rest accounts for the name praying mantis, applied in particular to *Mantis religiosa* but also to all other mantids. Eggs are laid in capsules (oothecae) on rocks and plants. Order: *Dictyoptera*. □insect.

● **mantis shrimp** ▶ A marine ▷crustacean of the widely distributed order *Stomatopoda* (over 250 species), especially the genus *Squilla*. 1–300 mm long, it has a short carapace and stalked eyes and the second pair of legs form large pincers for catching prey. Mantis shrimps live in sand burrows or crevices in coastal waters up to depths of 1300 m.

● **mantra** ▶ A sound, word, or verse repeated by Hindus and Buddhists as a chant to aid ▷meditation. Mantras are believed to have spiritual attributes that not only enhance concentration but also protect the persons using them from evil. Hindu mantras include verses from the ▷Vedas or syllabic utterances, such as *om*, which is regarded as representing the ▷Trimurti.

● **Mantua** ▶ (Italian name: Mantova) 45 10N 10 47E A city in N Italy, in Lombardy on the River Mincio. It dates from Etruscan and Roman times and from 1328 to 1708 it was ruled by the Gonzaga family. Notable buildings include a cathedral (10th–18th centuries), the 15th-century church of S Andrea (designed by Alberti), a 14th-century castle, and a ducal palace. The poet Virgil was born nearby. An important tourist centre, Mantua's industries also include tanning, printing, and sugar refining. Population (1990): 54 808.

● **Manu** ▶ In Hindu mythology, the ancestor of mankind. Like the biblical ▷Noah, he survives a flood because supernatural intervention warns him in time to build an ark. He is the reputed author of a Sanskrit code of laws, the *Manusmriti*, probably compiled between 500 and 300 BC.

● **Manuel I** ▶ (1469–1521) King of Portugal (1495–1521) during the great period of Portuguese overseas exploration. The Crown was greatly enriched by the voyages of Vasco da ▷Gama and ▷Cabral, which opened up eastern markets to Portugal. Manuel's reign also saw a revision of the legal code and the expulsion of the Jews (1497–98).

● **Manukau** ▶ 37 03S 174 32E A city in New Zealand, in N North Island on Manukau Harbour (an inlet of the Tasman Sea). It serves as the W coast harbour for ▷Auckland. Population (1996 est): 254 577.

● **Manutius, Aldus** ▶ (Aldo Manucci *or* A. Manuzio; 1449–1515) Italian printer and classical scholar, who founded the famous Aldine Press in Venice in about 1490. He specialized in inexpensive compact editions of the Greek and Latin classics, many of them first printed editions. His edition of *Virgil* (1501) was the first book in italic type. After his death the Press was carried on by his brothers-in-law and later by his son **Paulus Manutius** (1512–74) and grandson **Aldus Manutius the Younger** (1547–97).

● **Manx** ▶ A language of the Goidelic branch of the ▷Celtic family. An offshoot of Irish Gaelic, it was spoken on the Isle of Man until the

19th century. Since 1992 it has been taught in Manx schools in an attempt to revive the language.

● **Manx cat** ▶ A breed of short-haired tailless cat originating from the Isle of Man. The Manx has a short body with deep flanks and a large head. The soft coat has a thick undercoat and may be of any colour.

● **Manzini** ▶ (former name: Bremersdorf) 26 30S 31 22E A town in central Swaziland. It has a cathedral and nearby is the University of Swaziland (1964). It is an important commercial centre serving an agricultural area; industries include meat processing and cotton. Population (latest est): 18 085.

● **Manzoni, Alessandro** ▶ (1785–1873) Italian poet and novelist. After living in France from 1805 to 1810 he returned to Italy and established his reputation with the Catholic poems *Inni sacri* (1815), an ode to Napoleon, and two verse dramas. His patriotism and religious convictions are most fully expressed in his masterpiece, *The Betrothed* (1821–27), a historical novel set in 17th-century Milan during the Spanish occupation.

● **Maoism** ▶ The theories developed by ▷Mao Tse-tung. Mao's strategy for revolution in China gave central importance to peasant armies rather than to the action of the industrial working class in urban centres. Similarly, on a world scale, he believed that the socialist revolutions would develop first in the underdeveloped countries rather than in advanced capitalist countries (*compare* Marxism). Mao laid great stress on moral exhortation, indoctrination, and willpower in overcoming problems in socialist construction. Like Stalin, Mao defended the system of one-party rule and the view that socialism could be constructed in a single country.

● **Maori** ▶ A Polynesian people of New Zealand, who make up about 10% of the population. They trace their origins to migrants, probably from the Cook Islands, who came in canoes from around 1150, possibly earlier. They were an agricultural people who lived mainly in the North Island in large fortified villages of timber dwellings. Descent was counted in both lines and a person could attach himself to either his mother's or father's descent group (hapu) to obtain rights to land and residence. The traditional arts of wood carving and dancing still survive but urbanization and Christianization have largely destroyed the Maoris' way of life.

● **Maori Wars** ▶ The wars between the colonial government of New Zealand and the Maoris, fought intermittently between 1845 and 1848 and between 1860 and 1872. They were caused by the enforced sale of Maori lands in infringement of the Treaty of ▷Waitangi and led to further dispossession. In 1995–98 the New Zealand government granted large tracts of land and sums of money to the Maoris in compensation.

● **Mao Tse-tung** ▶ (*or* Mao Ze Dong; 1893–1976) Chinese communist statesman. Born into a peasant family in Hunan province, he was a Marxist by 1920 and helped to form the Chinese Communist Party (CCP) in 1921. In the late 1920s he became a guerrilla leader against the ▷Guomindang (Nationalist Party) and in 1931 he became chairman of the ▷Jiangxi Soviet. Forced to evacuate Jianxi in 1934, Mao led the communist forces on the ▷Long March with a price of $250,000 on his head. His arrival in Yan'an in 1935 marked his emergence as a leader of the CCP. Following the defeat of Japan in the ▷Sino-Japanese War of 1937–45, in which the communists and Guomindang joined forces, civil war was resumed, ending in communist victory. In 1949 Mao, as chairman of the Communist Party, proclaimed the establishment of the People's Republic of China. Mao's political writings formed the theoretical basis of the new government and led to the founding of communes and the ▷Great Leap Forward. He stepped down as chairman in 1958, purportedly due to ill health, but reappeared with greater standing during the ▷Cultural Revolution. After his death, his third wife (from 1939), Jiang Qing, tried unsuccessfully to seize power and Mao was succeeded by ▷Hua Guo Feng. ▷*See also* Maoism.

● **maple** ▶ A shrub or tree of the genus *Acer* (over 200 species), widespread in N temperate regions and often grown for timber and ornament. Growing 6–35 m high, maples usually bear lobed leaves, which turn yellow, orange, or red in autumn, and small yellow or greenish flowers, which give rise to paired winged fruits (samaras). Popular species are the ▷sycamore, ▷Japanese maple, and ▷box elder. The sap of the sugar maple (*A. saccharum*) of E North America produces maple sugar. Family: *Aceraceae*.

● **mappa mundi** ▷*See* Hereford.

● **map projection** ▶ The representation of the curved surface of the earth on a plane surface. The parallels of latitude and meridians of longitude (*see* latitude and longitude) are represented on the plane surface as a network or graticule of intersecting lines. It is not possible to produce a projection of the earth's surface without some distortion of area, shape, or direction and a compromise between these has to be reached. The basic map projections include conical, cylindrical, and azimuthal (*or* zenithal) projections. In the conical form the globe is projected onto a cone with its point above either the North or the South Pole. In the cylindrical projection the globe is projected onto a cylinder touching the equator; the ▷Mercator projection is of this type. Part of the globe is projected upon a plane from any point of vision in the azimuthal projection; all points have their true compass bearings. Peters' projection is a modified form of cylindrical projection. □ p. 790.

● **Maputo** ▶ (name until 1975: Lourenço Marques) 25 58S 32 35E The capital and chief port of Mozambique, on Delagoe Bay. It became the capital of Portuguese East Africa in 1907. It has a university (1962). A major East African port, its exports include minerals from South Africa, Swaziland, and Zimbabwe. Population (1991 est): 931 591.

● **Maquis** ▶ Groups of provincial guerrillas of the French resistance to the Germans in World War II, as distinct from the urban underground groups. The maquisards took their name from the scrubland (French word: *maquis*) in which they hid.

● **marabou** ▶ A large African ▷stork, *Leptoptilus crumeniferus*. It is 150 cm tall with a wingspan of 2.6 m and has a grey-and-white plumage, a bare black-spotted pink head and neck with a pendulous inflatable throat pouch, and a huge straight pointed bill. It feeds chiefly on carrion.

● **maraca** ▶ A percussion instrument originating in Latin America, consisting of a dried gourd filled with beads, shot, or dried seeds. Maracas are usually played in pairs, chiefly in jazz bands. □musical instruments.

● **Maracaibo** ▶ 10 44N 71 37W The second largest city in Venezuela, a port on the NW shore of Lake Maracaibo. Its economic importance is based on oil production; industries include petrochemicals. The University of Zulia was founded here in 1891. Population (1990): 1 207 513.

● **Maracaibo, Lake** ▶ A lake in NW Venezuela. Oil is drilled both in and around the lake, providing about 70% of Venezuela's total oil production. It is connected with the Gulf of Venezuela by a waterway (completed in 1956). Area: about 13 000 sq km (5000 sq mi).

Mao Tse-tung ▶ Seen casting his vote in a local election of deputies to the People's Congress of Hsitan district on 18 May, 1958. Deputies to the National People's Congress are elected by local People's Congresses.

● **Maracay** ▶ 10 20N 67 28W A city in N Venezuela, NE of Lake Valencia. A military centre with two airfields, its chief industry is textiles. Population (1990): 354 428.

● **Maradona, Diego** ▶ (1960–) Argentinian footballer, who captained the team that won the World Cup in 1986; he has also played for Barcelona and Naples. His use of cocaine resulted in a 15-month ban from world football and a suspended gaol sentence in 1991. He was banned again in 1994 for using stimulants.

● **Marajó Island** ▶ (Portuguese: Ilka de Marajó) The world's largest fluvial island, in NE Brazil in the Amazon delta. Area: 38 610 sq km (15 444 sq mi).

● **Maramba** ▶ (*or* Livingstone) 17 50S 25 53E A city in S Zambia, on the Zambezi River. It was the former capital of Northern Rhodesia (1907–35). It is a tourist centre for the nearby Victoria Falls. Population (latest est): 94 637.

● **Marañón, Río** ▶ The headstream of the River Amazon, in South America. Rising in the Peruvian Andes, it flows generally NE forming the Amazon at its confluence with the Río Ucayali. Length: 1450 km (900 mi).

● **Maraş** ▶ 37 34N 36 54E A town in central S Turkey. Founded by Hittites, it used to manufacture guns and swords but now exports carpets and embroidery. Population (latest est): 228 129.

● **marasmus** ▷*See* kwashiorkor.

● **Marat, Jean Paul** ▶ (1743–93) French politician, journalist, and physician, who devoted himself to radical journalism during the French Revolution. He became editor of *L'Ami du peuple*, supporting the ▷Jacobin cause of radical reform. Elected to the National Convention in 1792, he was murdered by Charlotte ▷Corday, a member of the ▷Girondins, whom Marat had helped to overthrow (1793).

● **Maratha** ▶ (*or* Mahratta) A people of India, who live mainly in Maharashtra and speak Marathi, an ▷Indo-Aryan language. Marathas are strictly the high-ranking castes of this region, who are cultivators, landowners, and warriors. During the 17th century there was a Maratha kingdom, and Maratha leaders resisted the British between 1775 and 1818.

● **marathon** ▶ A long-distance running race over 42 195 m (26 mi 385 yd). The marathon derives its name from the story of a soldier who ran from the Battle of Marathon to Athens with news of the Greek victory. As courses vary, there is no official world record; the fastest time is 2 hours 6 minutes 50 seconds (1988) by Belanyeh Dinsamo (Ethiopia). In the Olympic Games there are marathon races for both men and women.

● **Marathon, Battle of** ▶ (490 BC) The battle during the ▷Greek-Persian Wars in which the Athenians under ▷Miltiades defeated the Persians. ▷Phidippides was sent to summon Spartan help but the Spartans arrived too late.

● **marble** ▶ A rock consisting of metamorphosed limestone or any similar rock that can be cut and polished for ornamental use. Pure marble is white recrystallized calcite, but impurities, such as dolomite, silica, or clay minerals result in variations of colour. Certain quarries in Greece and Italy have been producing large quantities of marble since pre-Christian times. The flawless white marble from Carrara in Tuscany, Italy, is prized by sculptors.

● **Marble Arch** ▷*See* Nash, John.

● **Marburg** ▶ 50 49N 8 36E A town in central Germany, in Hesse on the River Lahn. It has a gothic castle and an important library and is the site of the country's first Protestant university (1527). Population (1995 est): 75 400.

● **Marburg disease** ▷*See* green monkey disease.

● **Marc, Franz** ▶ (1880–1916) German expressionist painter, born in Munich. A member of ▷Neue Künstlervereinigung and a founder of Der ▷Blaue Reiter art group, Marc is known for his symbolic animal paintings, such as *Blue Horses* (1911; Walker Art Center, Minneapolis). He was killed in World War I.

● **marcasite** ▶ A pale bronze mineral form of ▷pyrite. It occurs as

map projection

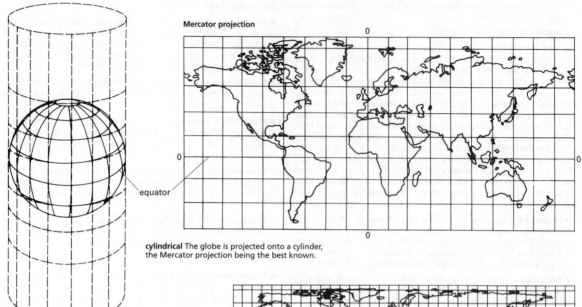

Mercator projection

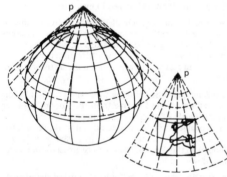

cylindrical The globe is projected onto a cylinder, the Mercator projection being the best known.

conical The globe is projected onto the cone as if it contained a source of light casting a shadow of its features onto the cone, resulting in a flat projection when the cone is unfurled. The cone may touch the globe along one parallel of latitude or intersect along two parallels.

Peters' projection Designed by the German historian, Arno Peters, in 1973, this modified cylindrical equal-area projection draws attention away from Europe, focusing instead on the developing countries, which are placed prominently in the centre of the map. It aims to show countries more accurately in relation to their true size but has an odd appearance in that land surfaces close to the equator are elongated and those in high latitudes are compressed.

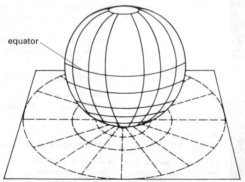

orthographic projection

azimuthal (*or* zenithal) The globe is pictured as a flattened disc. It may be projected as if it were seen from a point in the centre of the earth (gnomonic), from a point on the far side of the earth (stereographic), or from a point in space (orthographic).

Lambert's azimuthal projection

nodules in sedimentary rocks as a replacement mineral, particularly in chalk. Marcasite jewellery is sometimes pyrite but more often polished steel or white metal.

● **Marceau, Marcel** ► (1923–) French □mime. He began to study mime in 1946, gradually developing the original character Bip, a white-faced clown derived from the traditional pantomime figure of Pierrot. As well as giving solo performances, he formed his own mime company.

● **Marcellus, Marcus Claudius** ► (d. 208 BC) Roman general in the second ▷Punic War. After Roman defeats at Trasimene and Cannae, he was chosen to check Hannibal's advance through Italy. After capturing Syracuse, he harassed the Carthaginian armies in S Italy until his death.

● **Marchand, Jean Baptiste** ► (1863–1934) French soldier and explorer. After exploring the Niger, W Sudan, and the Ivory Coast, he narrowly avoided causing a war with the British by occupying Fashoda (see Fashoda incident).

● **Marche** ► (or the Marches) A region in central Italy, consisting of a narrow undulating coastal plain and a large hilly or mountainous interior. It produces wheat, maize, wine, fruit, vegetables, and cattle. Area: 9692 sq km (3742 sq mi). Population (1996 est): 1 443 172. Capital: Ancona.

● **Marches** ► The border areas of England and Wales, conquered between 1067 and 1238 by vassals of the English kings. The so-called **marcher lords** enjoyed enormous powers until the union of Wales and England in the 1530s.

● **March on Rome** ► (1922) The display of armed strength by Mussolini's ▷Blackshirts that established fascist government in Italy. Using threats of violence to support his demands for representation in the government, Mussolini organized the Blackshirts in a march against Rome. They entered unopposed by government or army and Mussolini was asked by Victor Emmanuel III to form a cabinet.

● **Marciano, Rocky** ► (Rocco Francis Marchegiano; 1923–69) US boxer. He took the world heavyweight championship from Joe Walcott in 1952 and retired in 1956, after 6 defences. Unbeaten in his 49 professional fights, a record among world heavyweight champions, he was killed in an aircrash.

● **Marconi, Guglielmo** ► (1874–1937) Italian electrical engineer, who invented, independently of ▷Popov, communication by radio. On reading about the discovery of radio waves, Marconi built a device that would convert them into electrical signals. He then experimented with transmitting and receiving radio waves over increasing distances until, in 1901, he succeeded in transmitting a signal across the Atlantic Ocean. For this work he shared the Nobel Prize for Physics in 1909. During the 1930s he was a fascist supporter.

● **Marcos, Ferdinand E(dralin)** ► (1917–89) Philippine statesman; president (1965–86). He assumed dictatorial powers in 1972. The murder in 1983 of opposition leader Benigno Aquino Jr, with alleged government complicity, caused further unrest and Marcos was overthrown in 1986 by the supporters of Aquino's widow, Corazon Aquino, who succeeded him as president. He fled into exile in Hawaii. In 1988 he and his wife, **Imelda Romualdez Marcos** (c. 1930–), were indicted by US courts on charges of fraud and embezzlement. Marcos died before he could stand trial, while his wife was acquitted in 1990. In 1993 a Filipino court sentenced her to 18 years in jail for corruption but this conviction was quashed on appeal (1998). She ran unsuccessfully for the presidency of the Philippines in 1992 but was elected as a congresswoman in 1995.

● **Marcus Aurelius** ► (121–180 AD) Roman emperor (161–180), in association with Lucius Verus (130–169) from 161 and alone from 169. Although he is known as the philosopher emperor on account of his *Meditations* (12 books of aphorisms in the Stoic tradition), his rule was active: from 170 he fought on the Danube frontier, where he died.

● **Marcuse, Herbert** ► (1898–1979) German-born US thinker. His radical anti-authoritarian philosophy evolved from the Frankfurt School of social research. Marcuse attacked both Western positivism and orthodox Marxism, the former because it led to analysis rather than action, the latter because it lacked relevance to 20th-century

conditions. His books include *The Ethics of Revolution* (1966) and *Counter-Revolution and Revolt* (1973).

● **Mar del Plata** ► 38 00S 57 32W A resort in E Argentina, on the Atlantic Ocean. It possesses extensive beaches, hotels, and a casino. The National University of Mar del Plata was founded in 1961. Population (1999 est): 579 483.

● **Marduk** ► The supreme god in Babylonian mythology. He created order out of the universe after defeating the sea dragon Tiamat and the forces of chaos. This victory, recounted in the Babylonian and Assyrian creation myth, *Enuma Elish*, was celebrated in a festival at the start of each year.

● **Marengo, Battle of** ► (14 June, 1800) A battle, fought 5 km (3 mi) SE of Alessandria, in Napoleon's Italian campaign (see Revolutionary and Napoleonic Wars). Napoleon was surprised by the Austrians with his forces divided and only the timely arrival of reinforcements made French victory possible.

● **Marenzio, Luca** ► (1553–99) Italian composer, noted for his madrigals. Some, published in London, influenced English madrigalists. He spent his life in service to various Italian noble families and lived for a time in Warsaw.

● **mare's tail** ► An aquatic perennial herb, *Hippuris vulgaris*, found in lakes and ponds throughout N temperate regions. It resembles the unrelated ▷horsetails in having stems, rising up to 30 cm above the water surface, bearing whorls of small slender leaves with minute greenish flowers at their bases. Family: *Hippuridaceae*.

● **Margaret** ► (1353–1412) Queen of Denmark, Norway, and Sweden. Daughter of Valdemar IV Atterdag of Denmark, in 1363 she married Haakon VI of Norway (1339–80; reigned 1355–80). Their son Olaf (1370–87) succeeded Valdemar in Denmark (1375) and Haakon in Norway; after Olaf's death Margaret became queen of both countries, which remained united until 1814. In 1388 she was proclaimed Queen of Sweden by discontented Swedish nobles. The union of the three countries was formalized in 1397, when her heir Erik of Pomerania (1382–1459) was crowned at Kalmar. Margaret remained effective ruler until her death.

● **Margaret (Rose)** ► (1930–2002) Princess of the United Kingdom; the younger daughter of George VI and sister of Elizabeth II. In 1955 she abandoned her plan to marry Group Captain Peter Townsend (1914–95), a divorcé, in response to public opposition and in 1960 married Antony Armstrong-Jones (later Lord ▷Snowdon); they were divorced in 1978. Their children are David, Viscount Linley (1961–), and Lady Sarah Chatto (1964–).

● **Margaret, Maid of Norway** ► (?1282–90) Queen of the Scots (1286–90), succeeding her grandfather ▷Alexander III; she was the daughter of Eric II of Norway (reigned 1280–99). Betrothed to the future Edward II of England, she died while travelling to England and Edward I promptly declared himself overlord of Scotland.

● **Margaret, St** ► (1045–93) The wife of ▷Malcolm III of Scotland and the sister of ▷Edgar the Aetheling. She was noted for her piety and reform of the Scottish Church in accordance with Gregorian principles, for which she was canonized in 1250.

● **Margaret of Angoulême** ► (1492–1549) An outstanding patron of Renaissance artists and writers; wife of Henry II of Navarre (1503–55). She wrote a collection of tales (*Heptaméron*, 1558) and of poetry (*Miroir de l'âme pécheresse*, 1531).

● **Margaret of Anjou** ► (1430–82) The wife (1445–71) of Henry VI of England; their marriage constituted an attempt to cement peace between England and France during the Wars of the ▷Roses, in which she was one of the most formidable Lancastrian leaders. She was captured and imprisoned after the Lancastrian defeat in the battle of ▷Tewkesbury (1471), in which her son Edward was killed. Her husband died, probably murdered, shortly afterwards and she returned to France (1476) after Louis XI had paid a ransom for her release.

● **Margaret of Valois** ► (1553–1615) The wife of Henry IV of France, famous for her *Mémoires* (1628). Daughter of Henry II and Catherine de' Medici, her marriage, which took place in 1572, was dissolved in 1599 to enable Henry to marry Marie de Médicis.

● **Margaret Tudor** ▶ (1489–1541) Regent of Scotland (1513–14) for her son James V. The elder daughter of Henry VII of England and the wife of James IV of the Scots (d. 1513), she was ousted from the regency by the English but continued to play an active role in politics until 1534. Her great-grandson, James VI of the Scots, succeeded to the English throne as James I in 1603.

● **margarine** ▶ A butter substitute that is free of dairy-product fat. A type of margarine was first produced in France in 1869 from beef tallow. However, vegetable oils were only able to be used extensively after 1910, when a hydrogenation process was developed to solidify the liquid vegetable oils by adding hydrogen to saturate some of the unsaturated fatty-acid residues in the oils. In modern margarine, pasteurized fat-free milk powder is emulsified with water and such refined vegetable oils as soya-bean oil. Vitamins A and D are also added. The resulting emulsion is cooled, solidified, and kneaded to remove air. Soft margarines contain only lightly hydrogenated oils, retaining some of their unsaturated nature to comply with medical opinion that they are less likely to form damaging ▷cholesterol in the blood than saturated fats. ▷*See also* fatty acid.

● **Margarita Island** ▶ A Venezuelan island in the S Caribbean Sea. Pearl and deepsea fishing are of importance. Area: 1150 sq km (444 sq mi). Population (latest est): 117 700. Capital: La Asunción.

● **Margate** ▶ 51 24N 1 24E A resort in SE England, on the N Kent coast, including the resorts of Westgate-on-Sea and Cliftonville. It developed as a resort in the late 18th century, when Benjamin Beale, a local Quaker, invented the bathing machine. Population (1991): 56 734.

● **margay** ▶ A spotted ▷cat, *Felis wiedi* of Central and South America. It is 90 cm long including the tail (30 cm), and is found in forests and brush, hunting small mammals and reptiles in trees and on the ground.

● **marginal cost** ▶ The cost of producing an additional unit of output. If the marginal cost is less than the market price, it will be profitable to increase output. In **marginal cost pricing**, items are priced on their marginal cost rather than average cost, to keep prices low and boost sales.

● **Margrethe II** ▶ (1940–   ) Queen of Denmark (1972–   ), who succeeded her father Frederick IX after the Danish constitution had been altered to enable a woman to become monarch. In 1967 she married a French diplomat, Henri de Laborde de Monpezat (Prince Henrik; 1934–   ); they have two sons, Prince Frederick (1968–   ) and Prince Joachim (1969–   ).

● **marguerite** ▶ A perennial herb, *Chrysanthemum frutescens*, also called Paris daisy, native to the Canary Isles. Each stem bears a large daisy-like flower. The name is also applied to the ▷oxeye daisy. ▷*See also* Chrysanthemum.

● **Mari** ▶ An ancient city on the middle Euphrates River in Syria. Commanding major trade routes, Mari throve during the early Sumerian period (*see* Sumer) and under the rule of ▷Akkad (c. 2300 BC). Excavated buildings of Mari's final period of prosperity include the palace of the last king, Zimrilim, killed when ▷Hammurabi destroyed the city (c. 1763). Its archive of 25 000 cuneiform tablets throws light on contemporary diplomacy, administration, and trade.

● **maria** ▶ (Latin: seas) Large dark fairly smooth areas on the surface of a planet or satellite. The moon's maria consist of iron-rich basaltic lava that erupted onto the moon's surface (primarily on the nearside) some 3000–3900 million years ago. The lava flooded the immense basins produced by earlier impacts of bodies from space, creating both circular and irregularly shaped maria.

● **Mariana Islands** ▶ (*or* Ladrone Islands) A group of mountainous islands in the W Pacific Ocean, comprising the US unincorporated territory of ▷Guam and the US commonwealth territory of the Northern Marianas. Strategically important, they include the islands of Tinian and ▷Saipan. Discovered by Europeans in 1521, the islands were colonized by Spanish Jesuits after 1668. Guam was ceded to the USA after the Spanish-American War, while the Northern Marianas

were sold to Germany (1899) and occupied by Japan (1914–44) until taken by the USA. They voted in 1975 to leave the UN Trust Territory of the ▷Pacific Islands. Sugar cane, coffee, and coconuts are produced. Area: 958 sq km (370 sq mi). Population (1995 est): 187 400. Administrative centre: Garapan, on Saipan.

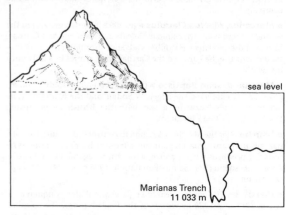

Marianas Trench

● **Marianas Trench** ▶ A deep trench in the earth's crust in the W Pacific; it is the greatest known ocean depth (11 033 m). It marks the site of a plate margin (*see* plate tectonics), where one plate is being submerged beneath another.

● **Mariánské Lázně** ▶ (German name: Marienbad) 49 59N 12 40E A town in the W Czech Republic, in W Bohemia. During the 18th and 19th centuries it was a popular spa, patronized by such famous people as Edward VII of the UK and the composer Richard Wagner. Population (1991 est): 15 380.

● **Maria Theresa** ▶ (1717–80) Archduchess of Austria (1740–80). Her father Emperor Charles VI issued the ▷pragmatic sanction (1713) to enable Maria Theresa, as a woman, to succeed to his Austrian territories. Her accession nevertheless precipitated the War of the ▷Austrian Succession (1740–48), with European powers, especially Prussia, which seized Silesia, hoping to expand their possessions. In 1745 her husband Francis (whom she married in 1736) became Holy Roman Emperor. Under the influence of ▷Kaunitz, and determined to regain Silesia, Maria Theresa substituted her English alliance with a French coalition but in the subsequent ▷Seven Years' War (1756–63) Austria suffered defeat. At home she combined absolutism with a measure of reform, anticipating the Enlightened Despotism (*see* Enlightenment) of her son and successor, Emperor Joseph.

● **Mari El Republic** ▶ A constituent republic of Russia, lying in the W central part and heavily forested. The Mari people, who speak a Finno-Ugric language, are known for their wood and stone carving and embroidery; they came under Russian rule in the 16th century and the region was an autonomous Soviet republic (1936–91). Industries include machinery, metalworking, timber, paper and food processing; agriculture is mainly cereal production. Area: 23 200 sq km (8955 sq mi). Population (1995 est): 766 000. Capital: Yoshkar-Ola.

● **Maribor** ▶ (German name: Marburg) 46 35N 15 40E A town in N Slovenia, on the River Drava. A former Habsburg trading centre, it is now one of Slovenia's largest industrial centres. Its university was established in 1975. Population (1996 est): 134 289.

● **Marie** ▶ (1875–1938) The wife of ▷Ferdinand of Romania. Marie was instrumental in affiliating Romania with the Allies in World War I. A granddaughter of Queen Victoria, Marie wrote several books in English, including an autobiography (1934–35).

● **Marie Antoinette** ▶ (1755–93) The wife of Louis XVI of France, whose uncompromising attitude to the ▷French Revolution contributed to the overthrow of the monarchy. The daughter of Emperor

Marie Antoinette ▶ A portrait (1778) of the young queen by Marie-Louise-Elisabeth Vigée-Lebrun (1755–1842). Vigée-Lebrun, one of the first women to achieve fame as an artist, specialized in portraits of royalty and produced at least 25 pictures of Marie Antoinette.

Francis I and Maria Theresa, she married the dauphin Louis in 1770. Her extravagance and alleged immorality contributed to the unpopularity of the Crown. After the outbreak of the Revolution she is said to have remarked of the Paris mob: "If they have no bread, let them eat cake." After the overthrow of the monarchy and Louis' execution, she was herself guillotined.

● **Marie Byrd Land ▶** (or Byrd Land) An area in Antarctica, between the Ross Ice Shelf and Ellsworth Land. The USA, although laying no claim to it, has long been active in the area and has established a research station.

● **Marie de France ▶** (12th century AD) French poet. Her identity is uncertain, although it has been suggested that she was a daughter of Geoffrey Plantagenet and half-sister of Henry II of England. Her works include several *lais*, verse narratives based on traditional Celtic stories of love, adventure, and the marvellous.

● **Marie de Médicis ▶** (1573–1642) The wife (1600–10) of Henry IV of France and regent (1610–14) for her son Louis XIII. Banished by Louis from court in 1617 she raised two revolts (1619, 1620) and was readmitted to the king's council in 1622. She persuaded Louis to make her protégé Richelieu chief minister in 1624 but she subsequently tried to oust him and in 1631 fled to Brussels. She built the Luxembourg Palace in Paris, the galleries of which were decorated by Rubens (1622–24).

● **Marie Louise ▶** (1791–1847) The second wife of Napoleon Bonaparte, who married her (1810) following the dissolution of his marriage to Empress Josephine. Their son, his longed-for heir, was entitled King of Rome (*see* Napoleon II). After her husband's fall she became Duchess of Parma (1816).

● **Marienbad** ▷See Mariánské Lázně.

● **Mariette, Auguste Ferdinand François ▶** (1821–81) French Egyptologist. Abandoning art teaching, he went to Egypt (1850) to buy Coptic manuscripts for the Louvre, but embarked instead on the excavation of ▷Saqqarah. He established the Egyptian Antiquities Service (1858) and Cairo Museum (1864) and initiated excavations at ▷Abydos, ▷Memphis, ▷Thebes, and elsewhere.

● **marigold ▶** One of several annual herbaceous plants of the family ▷Compositae, popular as garden ornamentals. The pot marigold (*Calendula officinalis*), native to S Europe, bears orange or yellow flowers, which can be eaten in salads. The African and French marigolds (genus *Tagetes*), native to Mexico, have single or double flowers with large outer florets; there are several dwarf varieties. Cape marigolds (genus *Dimorphotheca*) are more daisy-like. ▷See also marsh marigold.

● **marihuana** ▷See cannabis.

● **marine biology ▶** The study of the organisms that live in the sea and on shore and the features of the environment that influence

them. Marine biology is of great economic importance to man in view of his dependence upon the oceans for food, in the form of fish and shellfish, and the effects of pollution upon these organisms. ▷See also fishing industry.

● **marine insurance ▶** ▷Insurance against the perils of the sea, including storm, collision, theft, stranding, fire, and piracy. Marine insurance, which is underwritten by insurance companies or by Lloyd's, falls into three categories: hull, cargo, and freight. Hull insurance provides cover against losses arising from the perils of the sea as well as accidents caused by the crew, faulty machinery, etc., to the ship itself. Cargo insurance is arranged for each cargo and for each voyage; it is the responsibility of the seller in cif (cost, insurance, and freight) contracts and of the buyer in c & f (cost and freight) and fob (free on board) contracts. Cargo is either insured free of particular ▷average (FPA) or with average (WA). FPA insurance covers against total loss and any contribution to general average; WA covers these risks in addition to partial losses or damage. Cargo insurance throughout the world is usually based on the clauses drawn up by the Institute of London Underwriters. Freight insurance is the form of marine insurance enabling a buyer or a seller to cover himself against loss for sums paid out in chartering a ship or hiring cargo space.

● **Mariner probes ▶** A series of highly successful US ▷planetary probes. Mariners 2 and 5 approached Venus in 1962 and 1967, while Mariner 10 flew past Venus in 1974 and then three times past Mercury in 1974–75. Mariners 4 (1965), 6 and 7 (1969), and 9 (1971–72) investigated Mars, with Mariner 9 going into Martian orbit. Mariners 11 and 12 were renamed the ▷Voyager probes. Mariners 1, 3, and 8 did not achieve their missions.

● **Marinetti, Filippo Tommaso ▶** (1876–1944) Italian poet and novelist. His manifesto published in Paris in 1909 calling for the destruction of traditional literary goals and the creation of new means of expression inaugurated the literary and artistic movement of futurism. His glorification of warfare and technology resulted in his commitment to fascism, which he defended in *Futurism and Fascism* (1924).

● **Marini, Marino ▶** (1901–80) Italian sculptor, born in Pistoia. Originally a painter, he turned to sculpture in the late 1920s, becoming professor of sculpture at the Brera Academy, Milan, in 1940. Marini, under the influence of ancient Etruscan and Roman sculpture, continued the figural tradition of European art with his bronze horse-and-rider and dancer series.

● **Maritain, Jacques ▶** (1882–1973) French Roman Catholic thinker. He was interested in applying St Thomas ▷Aquinas' methods to contemporary social problems. *Les Degrés du savoir* (1932) treats mystical, metaphysical, and scientific knowledge as complementary. When the metaphysical pretensions of the sciences are abandoned, Maritain thought they would not conflict with Christian faith. He was for a time associated with the reactionary group Action Française.

● **Maritime Alps ▶** (French name: Alpes Maritimes) A range of mountains in SE France and NW Italy, running about 130 km (81 mi) along the border and constituting the southernmost arm of the Alps. It reaches 3297 m (10 817 ft) at Punta Argentera.

● **maritime law ▶** The branch of law relating to ships and shipping. It evolved from the local customs of certain dominant ports. The Romans, borrowing from the customs of Rhodes, imposed a code in the Mediterranean that was international and uniform in character. This uniformity was preserved until 17th-century nationalism gave rise to various individual codes. The French *Code de Commerce* (1807) treated maritime law as a branch of commercial law and has been widely adopted by other European countries. Outside the Mediterranean the most important early code was the 12th-century Rolls of Oléron (an island off the W coast of France), which codified the customary laws of the Atlantic ports and formed the basis of the maritime law of England, Scotland, France, Flanders, and other countries. The laws of Wisby, the seat until 1361 of the Hanseatic League, were also important and contained the mercantile code of the Baltic. The English **Admiralty Court**, established in the 14th century, developed very broad powers in deciding questions of commercial law, but in the 17th century was restricted to matters "done upon the sea." Today the Admiralty Court is mainly concerned with cases involving ▷salvage and collisions at sea, while other types of cases, such as those involving marine insurance, are referred to the Commercial Court. A certain international uniformity has been achieved by the Comité maritime international (CMI), in which 31 member states have agreed and ratified a number of maritime conventions.

● **Maritime Provinces** ▶ (Maritimes or Atlantic Provinces) The easternmost provinces of Canada, on the Atlantic coast and the Gulf of St Lawrence. They consist of ▷New Brunswick, ▷Nova Scotia, ▷Prince Edward Island, and usually ▷Newfoundland and lie in the Appalachian Highlands.

● **Maritime Trust** ▶ A UK organization established in 1970 "to discover, repair and preserve, for the benefit of the nation, vessels of historic, scientific, or technical interest and to arrange for their berthing at sites ashore or afloat."

● **Maritsa, River** ▶ A river in SE Europe. Rising in the Rila Mountains in W Bulgaria, it flows E then S forming part of the Greek-Turkish border, before flowing into the Aegean Sea. Length: 483 km (300 mi).

● **Mariupol** ▶ (name from 1948 until 1991: Zhdanov) 47 05N 37 34E A port in SE Ukraine, on an estuary leading into the Sea of Azov. A railway (1882) connects it with the Donets Basin and it exports coal. It has a variety of industries and supports a fishing fleet. Population (1996 est): 510 000.

● **Marius, Gaius** ▶ (c. 157–86 BC) Roman general; an opponent of ▷Sulla. Military ability outweighing his undistinguished origins and educational deficiencies, he entered Roman politics after campaigns in Numantia, becoming associated with the popular party. After reorganizing the Roman army, he quelled ▷Jugurtha and crushed Gallic uprisings. In competition with Sulla for the command against ▷Mithridates, he was forced to flee Italy but in 87 returned with ▷Cinna and captured Rome, massacring his political opponents. He died shortly afterwards.

● **Marivaux, Pierre Carlet de Chamblain de** ▶ (1688–1763) French dramatist. His popular comedies, mostly on romantic themes, include La Surprise de l'amour (1722) and Le Jeu de l'amour et du hasard (1730). He also wrote two unfinished novels and much literary journalism.

● **marjoram** ▶ One of several aromatic perennial herbs or small shrubs of the Eurasian genera Origanum (about 13 species) or Majorana (about 4 species). Wild marjoram (O. vulgaris) is a hairy plant, 30–80 cm tall, bearing clusters of small tubular pinkish-purple flowers. Sweet marjoram (M. hortensis) is widely cultivated for its aromatic leaves and flowers, which are used as culinary flavouring. Family: Labiatae.

● **Mark, St** ▶ A New Testament evangelist, traditionally the author of the second Gospel. A cousin of ▷Barnabas, he went with him and Paul on their first mission. Subsequently he seems to have assisted Paul in Rome, where he also acted as interpreter for Peter. He was believed to have founded the Church in Alexandria and is also associated with Venice, of which he is patron saint. Feast day: 25 April.

The Gospel according to St Mark is the earliest of the Gospels and is thought to have been written about 65–70 AD. It is a brief record of the life of Jesus and is believed to have been used by Matthew and Luke in the compiling of their Gospels.

● **Mark Antony** ▶ (Marcus Antonius; c. 83–31 BC) Roman general and statesman. Antony fought under Julius ▷Caesar in Gaul (54–50) and held command in Caesar's civil-war victory at ▷Pharsalus (48). Following Caesar's assassination, Antony came into conflict with Octavian (see Augustus) but they were later reconciled and formed the second ▷Triumvirate with Lepidus (43). In 42 Antony defeated his opponents, Brutus and Cassius, at ▷Philippi. In 41 he met ▷Cleopatra; not until 37 did Antony abandon his wife Octavia (Octavian's sister) to live with Cleopatra in Egypt. His strained relations with Octavian were finally severed in about 33. Subsequently Antony was defeated at ▷Actium. Both he and Cleopatra committed suicide.

● **market forces** ▷See supply and demand.

● **market gardening** ▷See horticulture.

● **marketing** ▶ The process of developing a market for goods or services. It is usually based on **market research** carried out to analyse the extent of a market for a particular product or service. This involves collecting information from a sample of the target market by such methods as interviews, sales in shops, and observation of the sales of competing products or services. From this information the appropriate **marketing mix** is established. This consists of four main parameters (sometimes called the 4 Ps): the quality, packaging, etc., of the product itself; the pricing of the product (e.g. the recommended retail price, discounts, and credit terms); the place in which the product is best sold; and the promotion that should accompany the launch of the product or service.

Marketing also involves anticipating changes in demand and providing advice on the design of a product to meet changing consumer needs and the development of products by competitors. It may also be involved in the provision of appropriate after-sales service.

● **markhor** ▶ A large wild ▷goat, Capra falconeri, of the Himalayas. Over 100 cm tall at the shoulder, markhors are red-brown in summer and grey in winter and have massive corkscrew-like horns. The species is subdivided into four geographical races, which show variations in the horns.

● **Markiewicz, Constance, Countess of** ▶ (?1868–1927) Irish nationalist, who married a Polish count. She fought in the 1916 Easter rising and was imprisoned. She was the first woman to be elected to the British parliament (1918, as a Sinn Féin Member) but did not take her seat.

● **Markov, Andrei Andreevich** ▶ (1856–1922) Russian mathematician, who did important work in probability theory, notably on the type of event series known as the Markov chain. In such series the probability of an event occurring depends upon previous events. His work led to the theory of stochastic processes.

● **Markova, Dame Alicia** ▶ (Lilian Alicia Marks; 1910–   ) British ballet dancer. She joined Diaghilev's Ballets Russes in 1925 and the Vic-Wells Ballet in 1931. Her dancing was noted for its lightness and delicacy, particularly evident in Giselle, Swan Lake, and Les Sylphides. She retired in 1962.

● **Marks, Simon, 1st Baron** ▶ (1888–1964) British businessman, who expanded the company Marks and Spencer, a chain of retail stores selling high-quality clothes, household goods, and food at reasonable prices. The firm was founded by his father **Michael Marks** (d. 1907) and **Thomas Spencer** (d. 1905) in 1887 as a penny bazaar.

● **marl** ▶ A calcareous clay that is soft and plastic when wet; consolidated marl is usually called marlstone. Marls are deposited in water, either fresh or marine. The word is also used for any friable clayey soil. Marls and marlstones are used in the manufacture of cement.

● **Marlborough** ▶ 51 26N 1 43W A market town in S central England, in Wiltshire on the River Kennet. It has engineering and tanning industries and is the site of Marlborough College, a public school founded in 1843. Population (1991): 6429.

● **Marlborough, John Churchill, 1st Duke of** ▶ (1650–1722) British general. He suppressed ▷Monmouth's rebellion against James II (1685) but subsequently supported the ▷Glorious Revolution (1688) against James. In 1691 he lost favour when suspected of Jacobite sympathies but was reinstated (1701) at the beginning of the War of the ▷Spanish Succession. As commander in chief under Queen Anne, he won the great victories of ▷Blenheim (1704), ▷Ramillies (1706), ▷Oudenaarde (1708), and ▷Malplaquet (1709). A Whig, he owed much of his political importance to the influence of his wife **Sarah Churchill** (born Jennings; 1660–1744), a confidante of Anne. Following Sarah's fall from favour, he was charged with embezzlement and dismissed (1711), living in Holland until 1714. ▷See also Blenheim Palace.

● **Marley, Bob** ▶ (Robert Nesta M.; 1945–80) Jamaican reggae singer. A Rastafarian who survived attempted assassination in 1976 for his populist left-wing views, he enjoyed international success with such albums as *Natty Dread* (1975) and *Exodus* (1976).

● **marlin** ▶ A large game fish, also called spearfish, belonging to the genus *Tetrapturus* (or *Makaira*). It has an elongated body, up to 2.5 m long, a spearlike snout, and a long rigid dorsal fin, which extends forwards to form a crest. Marlins are fast swimmers, occurring in all seas and hunting small fish. Family: *Istiophoridae*; order: *Perciformes*.

● **Marlowe, Christopher** ▶ (1564–93) English dramatist and poet. His involvement in secret political activity while a student at Cambridge may have had some bearing on his death in a tavern fight in Deptford. His development of blank verse and dramatic characterization in his plays *Tamburlaine the Great* (written about 1587), *The Jew of Malta* (about 1590), *Faustus* (probably 1592), and *Edward II* (1592), prepared the way for Shakespeare. His poetry included lyrics, translations, and the narrative *Hero and Leander* (unfinished; completed by Chapman, 1598).

● **Marmara, Sea of** ▶ A sea lying between European and Asian Turkey and between the Bosporus and the Dardanelles. In it lies the island of Marmara, where marble (from which the name Marmara comes) and granite have long been quarried. Area: 11 474 sq km (4429 sq mi).

● **marmoset** ▶ A small South American monkey belonging to the genera *Callithrix* (9 species, including a new one discovered in 1992) and *Cebuella* (one species—the pygmy marmoset), with claws instead of fingernails. Marmosets are 20–90 cm long including the long tail (10–38 cm) and have silky fur, often strikingly coloured. They feed on fruit, insects, eggs, and small birds. Family: *Callithricidae*.

● **marmot** ▶ A large ▷ground squirrel belonging to the genus *Marmota* (8 species), also called groundhog, of Europe, Asia, and North America. Marmots are 30–60 cm long and inhabit mountainous or hilly country, feeding on vegetation during the day and living in burrows at night. The woodchuck (*M. monax*) lives in North American woodlands. Marmots live in colonies, which bolt under ground at any sign of danger.

● **Marne, River** ▶ A river in NE France. Rising on the Plateau de Langres, it flows N and W to join the River Seine near Paris. Linked by canal to the Rivers Rhine, Rhône, and Aisne, it was the scene of two German offensives during ▷World War I (1914, 1918). Length: 525 km (326 mi).

● **Maronite Church** ▶ A Lebanese Christian ▷uniat church named after St Maro (died c. 410). The Maronites apparently originated in a Syrian Orthodox Church group that embraced ▷Monothelite doctrines in the 7th century and were consequently excommunicated. In the 12th century Crusader influences caused them to enter into full communion with the Roman Catholic Church and in 1584 a Maronite college was established at Rome. Although Catholic in doctrine, the Maronites retain their own Syriac liturgy and hierarchy.

● **Maros, River** ▷*See* Mureş, River.

● **Marot, Clément** ▶ (1496–1544) French poet. He served in the households of Marguerite of Navarre and of her brother Francis II. Suspected of being a Lutheran, he took refuge several times in Italy and died in Turin. He is best known for his metrical translations of the *Psalms* (1539–43), which received the encouragement of John Calvin. He was one of the first French poets to adopt the sonnet. His work marks the transition from the middle ages to the Renaissance.

● **Marprelate Tracts** ▶ (1587–89) Pamphlets, published under the assumed name Martin Marprelate, in London, attacking the bishops (mar a prelate). John Penry (1559–93) was charged with their authorship and executed. The work of extreme Puritans, they intensified hostility towards Puritanism.

● **Marquand, J(ohn) P(hillips)** ▶ (1893–1960) US novelist. His best-known novels are satirical studies of upper-middle-class New England families adrift in an era of social change. These include *The Late George Apley* (1937), *Wickford Point* (1939), and *H. M. Pulham Esq.* (1941). Another of his characters was Mr Moto, the Japanese detective.

● **Marquesas Islands** ▶ A group of 12 volcanic islands in the S Pacific Ocean, in French Polynesia (annexed 1842). Nuku Hiva is the largest and Hiva Oa, where Gauguin is buried, the second largest. Since the 1850s European diseases have reduced the population to a quarter. Mountainous and fertile, they export copra, pearls, and vanilla. Area: 1287 sq km (497 sq mi). Population (1988): 7538. Capital: Atuona, on Hiva Oa.

● **marquess** ▷*See* peerage.

● **marquetry** ▶ A technique of veneering furniture with different woods, ivory, tortoiseshell, and metals cut into interlocking shapes. It is frequently used on European 17th- and 18th-century fine furniture. ▷*See also* parquetry.

● **Marquette, Jacques** ▶ (1637–75) French explorer. A Jesuit, he worked among the Indians in Canada from 1666 and in 1673, with **Louis Jolliet** (1645–1700), he descended the Mississippi River as far as the mouth of the Arkansas River, establishing that it flows into the Gulf of Mexico.

● **Marrakech** ▶ (or Marrakesh) 31 49N 8 00W The second largest city in Morocco. Founded in 1062, it was for a time the capital of the Moorish kingdom of Morocco. Its notable buildings include the 12th-century Kotubai Mosque. It is a commercial centre, producing carpets and leather goods, and it is also a tourist centre. Population (1994 est): 621 914.

● **marram grass** ▶ A coarse perennial ▷grass of the genus *Ammophila* (2 species), also called beach grass or sand reed, which grows on sandy coasts of temperate Europe, North America, and N Africa. About 1 m high, it has spikelike leaves and scaly underground stems that can stabilize sand dunes.

● **Marranos** ▶ (Spanish: pigs) Spanish and Portuguese Jews, who adopted Spanish names and professed Christianity to avoid death by the ▷Inquisition, but continued to practise Judaism in secret. A small community existed in London in the mid-16th century, which formed the basis of the Sephardim in England. In the 17th century they were joined by more Marrano families who had been living in Holland.

● **marriage** ▶ The socially, and sometimes legally, acknowledged union between men and women, such that the resulting children are recognized as legitimate offspring of the parents. Although societies vary greatly in the rules that govern marriage, such legitimacy is traditionally important in determining rights to property, rank, group membership, etc. Monogamy, in which each spouse may have only one partner, is general in Christianized societies. Most churches treat marriage as an important rite and in the Roman Catholic and Greek Orthodox Churches it is accounted a ▷sacrament. Polygyny, in which a man may be married to more than one woman simultaneously, is widespread and sanctioned by Islam. A few societies allow polyandry, in which a group of men, usually brothers, have a wife between them, as in traditional Nayar communities in India. Polygyny and polyandry are collectively known as polygamy. Many societies proscribe certain unions (*see* incest). Others insist on marriage within a particular group (endogamy) or outside it (exogamy). In most countries, social customs and tax laws presuppose some form of marriage as the basis of family life. However, in industrialized societies there has been a marked decline in the penalization of unmarried cohabiting couples or their children (*see* illegitimacy). Furthermore, changes in the economic status of women, the need for more than one income to support a family, a decline in the sacramental view of marriage, and the widespread use of ▷contraception have combined to change family structure. In the UK some 35% of children were born outside marriage in 1996 (under 5% in 1901). In 1996 21% of all families were headed by single parents (compared with about 8% in 1971). The number of marriages contracted in 1995 was 322 000 (compared with 461 200 in 1971) and the number of ▷divorces more than doubled. In 1995 40% of all UK marriages were remarriages for at least one partner (9% in 1961), suggesting that lifelong monogamy has been replaced by "serial monogamy." ▷*See also* morganatic marriage.

● **marrow** ▶ (botany) A trailing or climbing vine, *Cucurbita pepo*, probably native to the Americas and widely cultivated as vegetable crops. Marrows bear yellow or orange cup-shaped flowers and large elongated fleshy fruits, which have orange, green, or yellow skins and are eaten as cooked vegetables. Family: *Cucurbitaceae*. ▷*See also* courgette.

● **marrow** ▶ (zoology) The soft tissue contained in the central cavities of bones. In early life the marrow of all bones helps to manufacture blood cells: it is called red marrow. In adult life the marrow of the limb bones becomes filled with fat cells and ceases to function: this is yellow marrow.

● **Marryat, Captain Frederick** ▶ (1792–1848) British novelist. His novels based on his naval career include *Mr Midshipman Easy* (1836) and *Masterman Ready* (1841). His children's books include *The Children of the New Forest* (1847).

● **Mars** ▶ (astronomy) The fourth planet from the sun, orbiting the sun every 687 days at a mean distance of 227.9 million km. Its diameter is 6794 km and its period of axial rotation 24 hours 37 minutes 23 seconds. It has two small ▷satellites. The Martian atmosphere is 95% carbon dioxide and is very thin (surface pressure 7 millibars). The dry reddish dust-covered surface is heavily cratered in the S hemisphere while N regions show signs of earlier volcanic activity: there are several immense volcanoes, the largest being **Olympus Mons** (25 km high), and extensive lava plains. Huge canyons and smaller valleys occur in equatorial regions; the valleys are evidence of running water in the past. In 1997 ▷NASA landed a Pathfinder spacecraft on the planet, enabling the remotely controlled Sojourner buggy to send live television pictures of the surface back to earth. In 2001 NASA launched the Mars Odyssey Probe, which will spend two years orbiting the planet 400 km (250 mi) above the surface, carrying out detailed chemical and geological surveys. NASA plans a manned landing by 2020. ▷*See* Viking probes.

● **Mars** ▶ (mythology) The Roman war god, the son of Juno. He was identified with the Greek ▷Ares and is usually portrayed as an armed warrior. Originally a god of agriculture, he was later worshipped at Rome as a major deity and protector of the city. The ▷month March is named after him.

● **Marsala** ▶ (ancient name: Lilybaeum) 37 48N 12 27E A port in Italy, in W Sicily. Founded in 397 BC as a Carthaginian stronghold, it has a baroque cathedral. Marsala wine, grain, and salt are exported. Population (1998 est): 80 177.

● **Marseillaise, La** ▶ The French national anthem, written in 1792 by ▷Rouget de l'Isle. Originally a patriotic song entitled "Le Chant de guerre de l'armée du Rhin", it was taken up by a group of republican soldiers from Marseille and became the revolutionary anthem.

● **Marseille** ▶ (English name: Marseilles) 43 18N 5 22E The principal seaport in France, capital of the Bouches-du-Rhône department. Flanked on three sides by limestone hills, it stands on a bay overlooking the Gulf of Lions. Founded about 600 BC, it was destroyed by the Arabs in the 9th century AD, redeveloped during the Crusades, and came under the French Crown in 1481. Most industry is associated with its large world trade and includes oil refining at Fos, which lies to the W and is an industrial centre. The city is noted for Le Corbusier's L'Unité (multiple dwellings). Population (1999): 797 486.

● **Marsh, Dame Ngaio** ▶ (1899–1981) New Zealand detective-story writer. She came to England in 1928. Her detective novels, which feature Roderick Alleyn of Scotland Yard, include *Final Curtain* (1947) and *Last Ditch* (1977).

● **Marshall, George C(atlett)** ▶ (1880–1959) US general and statesman. As army chief of staff (1939–45), and President Roosevelt's strategic adviser, he organized the build-up of US forces, ensuring that recruitment, training, weapons, and strength allocations conformed. He thus contributed greatly to the Allied victory. As secretary of state (1947–49) he devised the **Marshall Plan**, or European Recovery Programme, in which the USA provided economic aid to Europe after World War II. For this he won a Nobel Peace Prize (1953).

● **Marshall, John** ▶ (1755–1835) US judge. He began his legal career after serving in the American Revolution. He supported strong federal government and was elected to Congress in 1799, becoming secretary of state in 1800. As chief justice of the Supreme Court from 1801 until his death, he was instrumental in shaping US law since he had to interpret the recently drafted constitution and his decisions

created several precedents. In *Marbury versus Madison* (1803), for example, he established the Supreme Court's right to review the constitutionality of federal and state laws.

● **Marshall Islands, Republic of the** ▶ A country in the central Pacific Ocean comprising 29 atolls and five islands including the Ralik (Sunset) and Ratak (Sunrise) chains; the chief islands are Kwajalein, Majuro, and Jaluit.

Economy: coconut oil and copra are the main exports; fishing and service industries are also important.

History: formerly in the UN Trust Territory of the ▷Pacific Islands, it achieved self-government in 1979 but UN recognition of its independence was delayed until 1990. Under a Compact of Free Association the USA retains control of military matters. The islands are threatened by global warming as a 1 m rise in sea levels would submerge 80% of the land.

Republic of the Marshall Islands

Head of state	President Kessai Note
Official language	English
Official currency	US dollar of 100 cents
Area	181 sq km (70 sq mi)
Population (2000 est)	51 600
Capital	Majuro

● **marsh gas** ▷*See* methane.

● **marsh harrier** ▶ A temperate Eurasian ▷hawk, *Circus aeruginosus*, that hunts low over reedbeds and marshes, preying chiefly on water voles, waterbirds, and frogs. It is 53 cm long and its plumage is dark brown; the male has a paler streaked breast, bluish wing patches, and a grey tail and the female has a pale head and throat.

● **marsh mallow** ▶ A stout perennial herb, *Althaea officinalis*, of marshy coastal areas of Eurasia. Its velvety stems, 60–90 cm high, bear lobed leaves and clusters of flesh-coloured flowers, 5 cm in diameter. The roots yield a mucilage formerly used to make marshmallows. Family: *Malvaceae*.

● **marsh marigold** ▶ A stout perennial herb, *Caltha palustris*, also called kingcup, growing in marshes and wet woods throughout arctic and temperate Eurasia and North America. It has erect or prostrate stems, up to 80 cm long, bearing round leaves and bright golden flowers, 2–5 cm across. Family: ▷*Ranunculaceae*.

● **marsh samphire** ▷*See* glasswort.

● **Marsilius of Padua** ▶ (c. 1280–1342) Italian critic of papal imperialism. Marsilius argued in his *Defensor Pacis* (1324) that since the Church is concerned entirely with faith through revelation, and not reason, which belongs to the secular world, it should be regulated by the civil power and should not interfere with government.

● **Mars-la-Tour and Gravelotte, Battles of** ▶ (16–18 August, 1870) Successive battles in the ▷Franco-Prussian War in which the French were defeated. These engagements led to the encirclement of the French in Metz, allowing Prussian forces to march on Paris.

● **Marston, John** ▶ (1576–1634) English dramatist. Initially a verse satirist, he was involved in a literary feud with Ben ▷Jonson until they collaborated (with ▷Chapman) on the satirical comedy *Eastward Ho!* (1605), for which they were both imprisoned. His best-known play is *The Malcontent* (1604). He was ordained priest in 1609.

● **Marston Moor, Battle of** ▶ (2 July, 1644) The battle in the English ▷Civil War in which the parliamentarians and the Scots decisively defeated the royalists at Marston Moor, W of York. The parliamentary victory, which owed much to Oliver Cromwell's cavalry, destroyed the king's hold on N England.

● **marsupial** ▶ A primitive ▷mammal belonging to the order *Marsupialia* (176 species). Most marsupials are found in Australia and New Guinea and include the ▷kangaroos, ▷wallabies, ▷marsupial moles, ▷dasyures, ▷bandicoots, and ▷phalangers. The only American marsupials are the ▷opossums. Marsupials have relatively small brains and they lack a placenta. Young marsupials, which are born in a very immature state, complete their development in a pouch of skin on the mother's belly surrounding the teat, from which they are fed until fully formed. In general, the pouch of herbivorous marsupials opens forwards and that of carnivorous ones opens to the rear.

● **marsupial mole** ► A molelike insectivorous burrowing ▷marsupial, *Notoryctes typhlops*, of Australia. It has short golden fur, powerful forelimbs with digging feet, a sensitive nose, and a cylindrical body. Family: *Notoryctidae*.

● **Marsyas** ► In Greek mythology a Phrygian satyr who discovered the flute that Athena had invented and discarded, and challenged Apollo, who played the lyre, to a musical contest. He lost and was bound and flayed alive by Apollo for his presumption.

● **Martello towers** ► Fortifications containing cannon built in S Britain, Ireland, and Guernsey from 1804 to 1812. The towers were intended to check the potential invasion of Britain by Napoleon—which never materialized. Their construction was proposed after observation of the single tower mounting cannon at Mortella Point, Corsica, whence the term Martello was derived.

● **marten** ► A carnivorous mammal belonging to the genus *Martes* (8 species), of Eurasian and North American forests. Up to 90 cm long including the tail (15–30 cm), martens are arboreal agile hunters with dark lustrous fur: they prey largely on squirrels but also take sitting birds and their eggs. The two European species are the ▷pine marten and the smaller stone marten (*M. foina*). The fur of the American marten (*M. americana*) is called American ▷sable. Family: ▷*Mustelidae*. ▷*See also* fisher.

● **Martenot, Maurice** ► (1898–1980) French musician who invented (1928) the **Ondes Martenot**, an electronic instrument consisting of a keyboard, which determines the frequency of the notes by means of oscillators and a metal ribbon for producing glissandi; lateral movement of the keys causes small changes in pitch. The instrument was used by Messiaen in his symphony *Turangalîla* (1948).

● **martensite** ► The hard brittle form of ▷steel produced after rapid quenching in ▷heat treatment. When steel is heated to red heat (750°C), the carbon in it forms a solid solution in the iron. On quenching the carbon is frozen into this configuration and the crystal structure of the steel has internal strains, which cause its hardness. Named after Adolph Martens (1850–1914).

● **Martha's Vineyard** ► An island in the USA, off the coast of SE Massachusetts. A former whaling and fishing centre, it is now known chiefly as a summer resort. Area: about 260 sq km (100 sq mi). Population (1990): 12 000.

● **Martí, José Julián** ► (1853–95) Cuban poet and patriot. He worked for Cuban independence as a journalist in France, Mexico, Venezuela, and the USA and died during a military expedition to Cuba. He published essays and volumes of poetry, notably *Versos sencillos* (1891) and *Versos libres* (1913).

● **Martial** ► (Marcus Valerius Martialis; c. 40–c. 104 AD) Roman poet. Born in Spain, he went to Rome in about 64 AD and gained the patronage of his fellow Spaniards Seneca and Lucan. His best-known works are his 12 books of epigrams, comprising about 1500 short poems describing the contemporary social scene with satirical wit. Shortly before his death he returned to Spain.

● **martial arts** ► Styles of armed and unarmed combat developed in the East. The Japanese forms, such as ▷karate, ▷judo, ▷aikido, kendo, and sumo, derive largely from the fighting skills of the ▷samurai. Since the late 19th century they have become popular sports, as has the Chinese style, ▷kung fu. They are associated with Eastern philosophies, especially Zen Buddhism. ▷*See also* Bushido.

● **martin** ► A bird belonging to the ▷swallow family (*Hirundidae*; 78 species). The widely distributed brown sand martin (*Riparia riparia*) is about 12 cm long and has white underparts with a brown breast band. It nests in colonies in tunnels excavated in sand or clay banks. The black-and-white Old World house martin (*Delichon urbica*), about 13 cm long, commonly nests beneath the eaves of houses.

● **Martin V** ► (Oddone Colonna; 1368–1431) Pope (1417–31), whose election at the Council of ▷Constance ended the ▷Great Schism. He attempted to increase papal power by condemning the view that

Church councils have supreme authority and by limiting the power of the national Churches. His attempts to suppress the ▷Hussites were largely unsuccessful.

● **Martin, Archer John Porter** ► (1910–) British biochemist, who shared the 1952 Nobel Prize with Richard Synge (1914–94) for their development of the technique of paper ▷chromatography (1944), which they used for separating amino acids. Martin went on to develop gas chromatography in 1953.

● **Martin, John** ► (1789–1854) British painter. His large and grandiose paintings, often on biblical themes, including *The Fall of Babylon* (1819), *Belchazzar's Feast* (1826), and *The Deluge* (1834), brought him fame throughout Europe.

● **Martin, Pierre-Émile** ► (1824–1915) French engineer, who invented the Siemens-Martin process of producing steel. In this process Martin employed the open-hearth furnace developed in 1856 by Sir William ▷Siemens but adopted his own steel-producing process, which utilized pig iron and scrap steel. The Siemens and the Siemens-Martin processes largely replaced the ▷Bessemer process but the Siemens-Martin eventually became the more widespread.

● **Martin, Richard** ► (1754–1834) Irish politician. He was an MP in the Irish (1776–83, 1798–1800) and British (1801–26) parliaments. Nicknamed Humanity Dick by his friend George IV, he was a founder of the RSPCA.

● **Martin, St** ► (c. 316–97 AD) A patron saint of France; Bishop of Tours (372–97). A soldier in the imperial army, he later settled at Poitiers and nearby founded the first monastery in Gaul. After becoming Bishop of Tours, he continued to live as a monk at a monastery that he established outside Tours. His military cloak, part of which he reputedly gave to a naked beggar, has become a symbol of charity. Feast day: 11 Nov.

● **Martin du Gard, Roger** ► (1881–1958) French novelist. After active service in World War I he devoted his life entirely to writing. His major work was *Les Thibault* (1922–40), a cycle of novels analysing contemporary society through family relationships. His other works include the outspoken *Notes sur André Gide* (1951). He won the Nobel Prize in 1937.

● **Martineau, Harriet** ► (1802–76) British writer. Despite deafness and ill health, she was a leading figure in intellectual life. Her work includes novels, books on religion and economics, and the influential *History of England during the Thirty Years' Peace, 1816–46* (1849).

● **Martini, Simone** ► (c. 1284–1344) Italian painter, born in Siena and probably the pupil of ▷Duccio. In 1317 he worked for Robert of Anjou (reigned 1309–43) in Naples, where he was influenced by French gothic art. His *Guidoriccio da Fogliano* (1328), commissioned for the town hall of Siena, is probably the first commemorative equestrian portrait in European art. The *Annunciation* (1333; Uffizi) is the best example of his decorative style and graceful use of line. In about 1340 he moved to Avignon (France), where he worked for the papal court.

● **Martinique** ► A French overseas region in the West Indies, in the Windward Islands of the Lesser Antilles. It consists of a mountainous island of volcanic origin. Agriculture is of importance, the chief exports being sugar, bananas, and rum. Tourism is being developed.
  History: colonized by the French in 1635, it became a French overseas department in 1946. The volcanic eruption of Mont Pelée (1902) destroyed the town of St-Pierre. Area: 1090 sq km (420 sq mi). Population (1996 est): 394 000. Capital: Fort-de-France.

● **Martinmas** ► The feast of St ▷Martin (11 Nov), traditionally the date for slaughtering livestock to be salted as winter food. Fairs, at which servants could be hired, were also held at Martinmas, and in Scotland it is a quarter day recognized in common law.

● **Martinů, Bohuslav** ► (1890–1959) Czech composer. He was largely self-taught apart from a period of study with Roussel in Paris from 1923. During World War II he settled in the USA. He composed many works, including symphonies, concertos, the ballet *La Revue de cuisine* (1927), the opera *Julietta* (1936–37), and a concerto for double string orchestra and timpani (1938).

● **Marvell, Andrew** ► (1621–78) English poet. He was employed as tutor by Cromwell and Fairfax and as secretary by Milton. From 1659 until his death he served as MP for Hull. He published several satires and pamphlets attacking religious intolerance and government corruption. His poetry, most of which was published posthumously, is noted for its combination of intelligent argument and lyricism. "To his Coy Mistress" and "The Garden" are among his best-known poems.

● **marvel of Peru** ▷See four o'clock plant.

Karl Marx ► An 1898 drawing by Shukow.

● **Marx, Karl (Heinrich)** ► (1818–83) German philosopher, economist, and revolutionary. While studying at the University of Berlin, Marx became a member of the Young Hegelians, an antireligious radical group. Unable to obtain a university post because of his radical views, Marx turned to journalism, becoming the editor of a radical paper in 1842. After its suppression Marx left Germany and spent the rest of his life in exile. He stayed first in Paris (until his expulsion in 1845), where he met several leading socialists including Friedrich ▷Engels, who later collaborated in many of Marx's writings and provided him with substantial financial support. While in Brussels, Marx's association with a group of German handicraftsmen led to the writing of The Communist Manifesto (1848). In 1849 Marx moved to London, where he remained for the rest of his life, publishing The Class Struggles in France (1850), The Eighteenth Brumaire of Louis Bonaparte (1852), and A Contribution to the Critique of Political Economy (1859). Following the establishment of the International Working Men's Association in 1864, Marx devoted many years to the affairs of the First ▷International, gaining wide recognition among socialists. The first volume of Das Kapital was published in 1867 but the rest of his work did not appear until after his death. ▷See also Marxism.

● **Marx brothers** ► A US family of comic film actors: **Chico** (Leonard M.; 1886–1961), **Harpo** (Adolph M.; 1888–1964), **Groucho** (Julius M.; 1890–1977), and, until 1933, **Zeppo** (Herbert M.; 1901–79). Their original vaudeville act also included **Gummo** (Milton M.; 1893–1977). Their comedies, characterized by irreverent comic interplay between the fast-talking Groucho, the incompetent Chico, and the dumb harp-playing Harpo, included Horse Feathers (1932), Duck Soup (1933), and A Night at the Opera (1935). The team disbanded in 1949; Groucho subsequently presented a US TV show.

● **Marxism** ► The theory of scientific socialism introduced by Marx and Engels, which purports to explain the origin, historical development, and demise of the capitalist economic system. It relies heavily on the philosophy of Hegel, in particular Hegel's thesis that change has to be explained in terms of contradiction (see dialectical materialism). Class analysis, the central component of Marxism, is not peculiar to Marx but was shared by contemporary political economists, such as Adam Smith and Ricardo. Marxism is distinct in that it developed the theory of proletarian revolution. The transition to a socialist and eventually a classless society would not be a gradual evolution but would involve the violent overthrow of the state power (army, police, bureaucracy, etc.) of the bourgeois class. The working class would have to establish its own state power, which would be more democratic because it would be the rule of the majority of the population, the working class. As classes gradually disappeared, however, state power would also wither away since the state was fundamentally an instrument by which one class ruled over other classes. The classless society of the future would allow the fullest developments of individuals through social cooperation. Many different versions of Marxism have been expounded (see also Leninism; Maoism; communism).

● **Mary** ► 37 42N 61 54E A city in SE Turkmenistan. Located in a cotton-growing oasis of the Kara Kum Desert, it has important textile industries. Population (1991): 94 900.

● **Mary I** ► (1516–58) Queen of England and Ireland (1553–58), succeeding her younger half-brother ▷Edward VI. The daughter of Henry VIII and Catherine of Aragon, Mary faced an uncertain future after her parents' divorce in 1533 until her rehabilitation in the line of succession in 1544. She became queen after the failure of a conspiracy to place Lady Jane ▷Grey on the throne. Her singleminded aim was to restore Roman Catholicism in England: Edward's Protestant legislation was repealed and in 1554 the heresy laws were reintroduced, resulting in almost 300 deaths at the stake and the queen's nickname, Bloody Mary. Her marriage (1554) to Philip II of Spain, the announcement of which had incited the unsuccessful rebellion (1553) of Sir Thomas ▷Wyatt, led to England's entanglement in Philip's foreign policy and the loss in 1558 of its last possession on the Continent, Calais. This disaster, coupled with a series of false pregnancies, hastened Mary's death.

● **Mary II** ► (1662–94) Queen of England, Scotland, and Ireland (1689–94), joint monarch with her husband William III. Daughter of James II, she was brought up as a Protestant and came to the throne after the enforced abdication of her Roman Catholic father during the ▷Glorious Revolution. She was a popular ruler, governing during William's absences abroad, and died prematurely of smallpox.

● **Mary, Queen of Scots** ► (1542–87) The daughter of James V and the French noblewoman Mary of Guise (1515–60) and the great-niece of Henry VIII of England; she succeeded to the throne shortly after her birth. Her mother became regent and from 1547 Mary, a Roman Catholic, lived at the French court, where in 1558 she married the dauphin (later Francis II). After Francis' death (1561) Mary returned to Scotland and in 1565 married, unpopularly, her cousin Lord ▷Darnley. In 1566 he murdered out of (probably unfounded) jealousy her secretary David ▷Riccio. In that year Mary gave birth to the future James VI (James I of England). In 1567 Darnley was murdered by ▷Bothwell, who abducted Mary (so she later alleged) and then married her. The question whether Mary was already the mistress of Bothwell remains unsettled, resting on the evidence of the much debated Casket Letters. A rebellion of Scottish nobles defeated Mary and Bothwell at Carberry Hill (1567) and Mary, imprisoned at Loch Leven, was forced to abdicate in favour of her son. She escaped and raised an army that was defeated at Langside (1568). Fleeing to England, where her claim to the English succession had long been an embarrassment to Elizabeth I, she was imprisoned. The focus of a series of plots against Elizabeth, she was finally tried for complicity in the conspiracy of Anthony ▷Babington (see also Ridolfi, Roberto; Throckmorton, Sir Nicholas) and executed at Fotheringhay Castle, near Peterborough. Her remains were moved to Westminster Abbey by her son.

● **Mary, the Virgin** ► In the New Testament, the mother of ▷Jesus Christ. The fullest accounts of Mary are contained in the birth stories in ▷Luke and ▷Matthew. ▷John (19.25) reports that she was present at the crucifixion, and she appears to have been present at the growth of the early Church in Jerusalem (Acts 1.14). Luke records the Annunciation (the announcement by the Angel Gabriel that she was to conceive the Son of God by the Holy Spirit); her betrothal to ▷Joseph; her meeting with her cousin Elizabeth; and her song of praise (the Magnificat) when Elizabeth had greeted her as the mother of the Lord. The Gospels state that she was a virgin at the time of the conception of Jesus, and Roman Catholic doctrine teaches that she remained one (despite references in the Gospels to Jesus's brothers). Mary's ▷Immaculate Conception has been a dogma of the Roman Catholic Church since 1854 and the belief that she was taken up bodily into heaven (the Bodily Assumption) was defined as doctrine in 1950: neither of these beliefs is mentioned in the Gospels but both can be traced back to the early Church. In the Orthodox and Roman Catholic Churches Mary is venerated as having a secondary mediating role between God and man.

● **Mary Magdalene, St** ▶ In the New Testament, the first person to see Jesus after the resurrection. Jesus cured her of possession by evil spirits. She aided his work in Galilee and was present at the crucifixion and burial. Medieval scholars associated her with the repentant prostitute who annointed Jesus' feet, mentioned in Luke's Gospel. Feast day: 22 July. Emblem: an ointment jar.

● **Mary of Guise** ▷See Mary, Queen of Scots.

● **Mary of Modena** ▶ (1658–1718) The second wife of James II of England. A devout Roman Catholic, the daughter of the Duke of Modena, she fled to France with her husband in 1688 when their son, ▷James Edward Stuart (the Old Pretender), was born, threatening a Catholic dynasty. ▷See also Glorious Revolution.

● **Mary of Teck** ▶ (1867–1953) The wife of George V of England. Previously engaged to Albert, Duke of Clarence (1864–92), George's elder brother, she married George in 1893, following Albert's death. She was noted as a needlewoman and for her interest in art and antique furniture.

● **Maryborough** ▶ 25 32S 152 36E A port in Australia, in SE Queensland. The main industries are timber milling, and the manufacture of heavy machinery; exports include sugar, tropical fruits, coal, and timber. Population (latest est): 22 220.

● **Maryborough** ▶ (Ireland) ▷See Portlaoise.

● **Maryland** ▶ A state on the E seaboard of the USA. It consists of two regions: the Atlantic Coastal Plain, which is split by Chesapeake Bay into a low flat plain in the E and uplands in the W, and an area of higher ground, part of the Alleghenies in the N and W. Manufacturing is important, with primary metals, metal products, food processing, transportation and electrical equipment, printing and publishing, and textiles. The state's farmers produce livestock, poultry, and dairy products as well as some corn, tobacco, soya beans, and vegetables.

History: one of the 13 original colonies, it was first settled by the English. It was granted (1632) to George Calvert, 1st Baron Baltimore by Charles I and named after his wife, Henrietta Maria. Under the 2nd Baron Baltimore, it became a refuge for Roman Catholics. Area: 27 394 sq km (10 577 sq mi). Population (1996 est): 5 071 604. Capital: Annapolis. Chief port: Baltimore.

● **Marylebone Cricket Club** ▶ (MCC) A cricket club founded in London in 1787. Its headquarters are at ▷Lord's cricket ground. The MCC became the leading authority on the laws of cricket and was responsible for the control of English cricket until 1969, when this became the responsibility of the Cricket Council. It voted to admit women in 1998.

● **Mary Rose** ▶ A Tudor warship (Henry VIII's flagship), which sank in 1545 in Portsmouth Harbour while sailing into battle. The wreck was positively identified by underwater archaeologists in 1971. The ship's contents, most of which were remarkably preserved, were raised during the following ten years and the hull itself was lifted in 1982 and placed in a dry-dock in Portsmouth. The Mary Rose Trust, of which the Prince of Wales is president, was formed in 1979.

● **Masaccio** ▶ (Tommaso di Giovanni di Simone Guidi; 1401–28) Florentine painter of the early Renaissance. He collaborated with ▷Masolino on the *Madonna and Child with St Anne* (Uffizi) and on the fresco cycle in the Brancacci Chapel in Sta Maria del Carmine. His in-

dependent paintings include the *Trinity* (Sta Maria Novella, Florence). Influenced by ▷Giotto and the innovations of ▷Brunelleschi and ▷Donatello, Masaccio initiated the use of linear perspective and a single light source in painting.

● **Masada** ▶ 31 19N 35 21E A precipitous rocky hilltop near the W shore of the Dead Sea, in S Israel. The site of one of ▷Herod the Great's fortified palaces, it was later a centre of the ▷Essene sect and a stronghold of the Jews in their revolt against Rome (66 AD). In the last action of the war (73 AD), after a siege lasting almost two years, the defenders, on the eve of the final assault by the Roman besiegers, committed mass suicide. The site is an Israeli national monument.

Masai ▶ The elaborate beadwork decorating these Masai women indicates their ethnic identity, social status, family, and the number of their children.

● **Masai** ▶ A Nilotic people of Kenya and Tanzania who speak a Sudanic language. Age sets are the basis of social organization, with three principal stages for every male: boy, warrior, and elder. This system allowed the nomadic Masai to form large raiding parties to increase their stocks of cattle, which are the basis of their economy. Milk and blood from cattle form an important part of their diet, the blood being drawn from a vein in the animal's neck without killing it. Tall and active, the Masai highly value courage.

● **Masaryk, Tomáš (Garrigue)** ▶ (1850–1937) Czech statesman, who was one of the founders of Czechoslovakia. In Paris, during World War I, he and Edvard Beneš founded the Czechoslovak National Council, which the Allies recognized in 1918. When Austria-Hungary fell in November, 1918, Masaryk was elected Czechoslovakia's first president; he was re-elected in 1920, 1927, and 1934. His administration was marked by a major land reform. He resigned, owing to his age, in 1935. His son **Jan (Garrigue) Masaryk** (1886–1948), a diplomat, was Czechoslovak minister to Britain (1925–38) and foreign minister in Czechoslovakia's provisional government in London (1940–45). Following World War II he returned to Prague but after the communists came to power in 1948 he died in a fall from a window, allegedly a suicide.

● **Mascagni, Pietro** ▶ (1863–1945) Italian opera composer. His fame rests chiefly on his one-act opera *Cavalleria Rusticana* (1889), written as an entry for a competition in which it won first prize. He wrote many other operas, including *L'amico Fritz* (1891).

● **Mascara** ▶ 35 28N 0 02E A town in NW Algeria. In 1832 Abdelkader chose the town as his headquarters but it was razed by the French in 1835. It is noted for the production of red and white wines. Population (latest est): 62 301.

● **Mascarene Islands** ▶ (French name: Îles Mascareignes) The heavily populated islands of Mauritius, Réunion, and Rodrigues in the W Indian Ocean. Discovered by the Portuguese in the early 16th century, they were known earlier to the Arabs.

● **mascons** ▶ Disc-shaped masses that are located beneath the lunar surface in the younger ▷maria and are denser than their surroundings. They were discovered when lunar-satellite orbits were found to be slightly perturbed as a result of the higher gravitational attraction over these regions.

● **Masefield, John** ▶ (1878–1967) British poet and writer. Having served briefly in the merchant navy, he captured the fascination of the sea in his first volume, *Salt-Water Ballads* (1902). He also wrote narrative poems, such as *Reynard the Fox* (1919), and several adventure novels, and children's stories, notably *The Midnight Folk* (1927). He was poet laureate from 1930 until his death.

● **maser** ▶ (microwave amplification by stimulated emission of radiation) A device that works on the same principle as the ▷laser, the radiation produced being in the ▷microwave region instead of in the visible spectrum. Masers are used as oscillators (e.g. the ammonia clock; *see* atomic clock) and amplifiers.

● **Maseru** ▶ 29 19S 27 29E The capital of Lesotho, near the South African border. It was founded in 1869. The University of Botswana, Lesotho, and Swaziland was established nearby in 1966. Population (1995 est): 297 000.

● **Mashhad** ▶ (or Meshed) 36 16N 59 34E A town in NE Iran, close to the Afghanistan and Turkmenistan borders. It is a pilgrimage centre for Shiite Muslims; the shrine of the *imam* 'Ali ar-Rida is a magnificent structure. Mashhad is famous for carpets and turquoise; its university was founded in 1956. Population (1994 est): 1 964 489.

● **Mashonaland** ▶ An area in central and NE Zimbabwe, inhabited by the Shona, a Bantu people. Mashonaland was administered by the British South Africa Company from 1889 to 1923, when it became a part of the new colony of Southern Rhodesia.

● **Mashriq** ▶ (Arabic: east) The Arab countries of SW Asia (the Middle East) as compared with the ▷Maghrib countries of N Africa. Egypt and the Sudan are included in the Mashriq.

● **Masinissa** ▶ (c. 240–148 BC) Ruler of Numidia in North Africa. With the support of Rome, whom he had helped against Carthage in the second Punic War (208–201), he established a strong state among the diverse Numidian tribes.

● **masochism** ▶ Sexual pleasure obtained from the experience of pain. The condition is named after an Austrian writer, Leopold von Sacher-Masoch (1835–95), whose novels depict it. It is often associated with a pathologically strong need to be humiliated by and submissive to one's sexual partner. Frequently, masochistic and sadistic desires are combined in the same individual.

● **Masolino** ▶ (Tommaso di Cristoforo Fini; 1383–?1447) Italian painter, born in Panicale but active mainly in Florence. He was strongly influenced by ▷Masaccio, particularly while working with him on the fresco cycle in the Brancacci Chapel, Florence. Later he painted in the ▷international gothic style. Independent works include *The Miracle of the Snow* (Sta Maria Maggiore, Rome).

● **Mason, A(lfred) E(dward) W(oodley)** ▶ (1865–1948) British novelist. After several popular adventure stories, notably *The Four Feathers* (1902), he wrote detective novels featuring Inspector Hanaud of the Sûreté, starting with *At the Villa Rose* (1910). He was MP for Coventry and served in naval intelligence during World War I.

● **Mason, James** ▶ (1909–84) British film actor, noted for his distinctive speaking voice. His early British films include *The Man in Grey* (1943) and Carol Reed's *Odd Man Out* (1947). After moving to Hollywood he starred in *The Desert Fox* (1952), *A Star is Born* (1954), Hitchcock's *North by Northwest* (1959), and Kubrick's *Lolita* (1962). Later films include *The Verdict* (1982) and *The Shooting Party* (1984).

● **mason bee** ▶ A solitary ▷bee belonging to the genus *Osmia* and related genera, occurring in Europe, Africa, and elsewhere. It builds nests of soil cemented together with saliva in hollows in wood or stones. Family: *Megachilidae*.

● **Mason-Dixon line** ▶ A line drawn in 1767 by two surveyors, Charles Mason and Jeremiah Dixon, to settle the conflict over borders between Pennsylvania and Maryland. Until the Civil War it also represented the division between southern proslavery and northern free states. It has remained a symbolic boundary between the North and South.

● **masoretes** ▶ Transmitters of the textual tradition (*masorah*) of the Hebrew Bible. The textual study of the Bible goes back to antiquity (*see* scribes); in the gaonic period (*see* gaon) various schools of masoretes laboured to establish a correct text and to mark the pronunciation with the help of accents. The text of Aaron ben Asher (930 AD) was recognized as authoritative by ▷Maimonides. The masoretic text is the basis of all Hebrew Bibles printed today.

● **masque** ▶ A form of dramatic court entertainment popular in England during the late 16th and early 17th centuries. It consisted of a combination of verse, dance, and music, usually with a slight dramatic plot based on a mythological theme. The form was perfected in the collaborations of Ben ▷Jonson and Inigo ▷Jones, whose elaborate costumes and scenery were vastly expensive. Other writers of masques include Sir Philip ▷Sidney and Samuel ▷Daniel.

● **mass** ▶ (physics) ▷*See* mass and weight.

● **mass** ▶ (religion) ▷*See* Eucharist.

● **Massachusetts** ▶ A state on the NE coast of the USA, in New England. The uplands in the W, which are cut N–S by the Connecticut River, are separated from the lowlands of the Atlantic Coastal Plain and Cape Cod Peninsula by the rolling country of central Massachusetts. The mainly urban population is concentrated along the coast and river valleys. A major manufacturing state, its industries produce electrical and communications equipment, high-quality instruments, chemicals, textiles, and metal and food products. Boston is an important financial and service centre. Its farmers produce dairy products, eggs, poultry, cranberries, and horticultural goods. Massachusetts is an important centre in the educational and cultural life of the USA.
History: one of the 13 original colonies, the arrival of the ▷Pilgrim Fathers on the *Mayflower* (1620) heralded major settlement. It was a centre for opposition to British colonial policy leading to the American Revolution and became prominent following statehood (1788), although it lost much of its industrial influence in the 20th century. Area: 21 386 sq km (8257 sq mi). Population (1996 est): 6 092 352. Capital: Boston.

● **Massachusetts Bay Company** ▶ A colony of English Puritans established at Salem in 1628. The main body of colonists arrived in 1630 under the leadership of John ▷Winthrop. The Company's charter was withdrawn in 1684.

● **Massachusetts Institute of Technology** ▶ (MIT) A university in the USA, situated at Cambridge, Massachusetts. Founded in 1861 at Boston, it moved to its present site in 1916. It is world famous for scientific education and research.

● **mass action, law of** ▶ The rate of a chemical reaction for a uniform system at constant temperature varies as the concentration of each reacting substance, raised to the power equal to the number of molecules of the substance appearing in the balanced equation. Thus, for the reaction $2H_2 + O_2 = 2H_2O$ the speed of the forward reaction is proportional to the concentration of O_2 (written $[O_2]$) and to $[H_2]^2$; the reverse reaction depends on $[H_2O]^2$. The law is thus useful for calculation of equilibrium concentrations when reaction speeds are known, and vice versa. It was first proposed by C. M. Guldberg (1836–1902) and P. Waage (1833–1900).

● **massage** ▶ Manipulation of the soft tissues of the body for therapeutic purposes. This includes rhythmic stroking (effleurage), kneading (petrissage), and tapping (tapotement); it is used to relieve muscular spasm and pain, improve blood circulation, and reduce swelling. ▷*See also* physiotherapy.

● **mass and weight** ▶ Two physical quantities used to express the extent to which a substance is present; they are sometimes confused. The mass of a body was defined by ▷Newton as the ratio of a force applied to the body to the acceleration it produces. This is now called the **inertial mass**, as it is a measure of the extent to which a body resists a change in its motion. **Gravitational mass** is defined in terms of the gravitational force between two bodies in accordance with Newton's law of gravitation. ▷Eötvös showed experimentally that inertial mass and gravitational mass are equal, a result used by Einstein in his general theory of relativity. Mass was also shown by Einstein, in his special theory of relativity, to be a form of energy, according to the relationship $E = mc^2$ (where c is the speed of light). The total of the mass and the energy of a closed system remains unchanged under all circumstances (the law of the conservation of mass and energy).

Weight is proportional to gravitational mass, being the force by which an object is attracted to the earth. It is therefore equal to the product of the mass and the ▷acceleration of free fall (i.e. $W = mg$). Thus, the weight of a body may vary according to its position; the mass is a constant. In scientific terms mass and weight are different, mass being expressed in units of mass (e.g. kilograms) and weight in units of force (e.g. newtons) although, of course, in everyday usage they are both measured in kilograms, pounds, etc. ▷*See also* amount of substance.

● **Massawa** ▶ (*or* Mitsiwa) 15 37N 39 28E A port in Eritrea, on the Red Sea. It was occupied (1885) by the Italians, who used it as a base for their offensive against Ethiopia in 1935. Massawa has food-processing and chemical industries and a naval base. Population (1992): 40 000.

● **mass defect** ▶ The difference between the total mass of the nucleons in an atom and the mass of the nucleus. This is equal to the ▷binding energy of the nucleus.

● **Masséna, André** ▶ (?1756–1817) French marshal. He fought in Napoleon's Italian campaign, winning an important victory at Rivoli (1797). He subsequently defeated the Russians in Switzerland (1799), fought again in Italy, and against the Austrians (1809–10). He was defeated by Wellington in the ▷Peninsular War and lost his command.

● **mass-energy equation** ▷*See* relativity.

● **Massenet, Jules** ▶ (1842–1912) French composer. He studied at the Paris conservatoire and won the Prix de Rome in 1863. Massenet wrote 27 operas, of which *Manon* (1884) and *Werther* (1892) are still performed today.

● **Massey, Raymond** ▶ (1896–1983) Canadian actor. He first acted on the stage in 1922 and thereafter appeared in a number of films, including *The Scarlet Pimpernel* (1934), *Abe Lincoln in Illinois* (1939), *Arsenic and Old Lace* (1944), and *East of Eden* (1955). He also appeared in the television series *Dr Kildare* (1961–65). His son **Daniel Massey** (1933–98) was an actor, as is his daughter **Anna Massey** (1937–   ).

● **Massey, William Ferguson** ▶ (1856–1925) New Zealand statesman; prime minister (1912–25). He entered parliament in 1894 and became (1903) leader of the Conservative opposition, which in 1909 he named the Reform Party. His administration, in coalition (1915–19) with the Liberals during World War I, supported agrarian interests.

● **Massif Central** ▶ A plateau area in S central France. Generally considered to be that area over 300 m (984 ft) high, it rises to 1885 m (6188 ft) at Puy de Sancy. The central N area is also known as the Auvergne and the SE rim as the Cévennes. There is dairy and arable farming as well as heavy industry. Area: about 90 000 sq km (34 742 sq mi).

● **Massine, Léonide** ▶ (Leonid Miassin; 1896–1979) Russian ballet dancer and choreographer. He joined Diaghilev's company in Paris in 1914 and choreographed his first ballet, *Soleil de nuit*, in 1915. He choreographed for many companies, notably the Ballet Russe de Monte Carlo. Most controversial were *Les Présages* (1933) and *Symphonie Fantastique* (1936).

● **Massinger, Philip** ▶ (1583–1640) English dramatist. He collaborated with several other writers before succeeding John ▷Fletcher in 1625 as chief dramatist for the leading theatrical company, the King's Men. His best-known play is the satirical comedy *A New Way to Pay Old Debts* (1621).

● **mass number** ▶ (*or* nucleon number) The total number of protons and neutrons in the ▷nucleus of an atom.

● **mass spectrometer** ▶ An instrument for identifying ions. In the simplest type, a gaseous sample at low pressure is ionized by a beam

of electrons and the ions produced are accelerated by an electric field and deflected into circular paths by a magnetic field. Both magnetic and electric fields can be continuously varied and successive ions are focused onto a detector, the deflection of an ion depending on its charge-to-mass ratio. A **mass spectrum** is produced consisting of a series of peaks, each corresponding to a different ion. The mass spectrum of a compound can be used to find its formula and chemical structure.

● **Massys, Quentin** ▶ (*or* Matsys, Messys, Metsys; c. 1466–1530) Flemish painter, born in Louvain but active in Antwerp. He was influenced by Italian Renaissance artists, particularly ▷Leonardo. In portraits, such as *Erasmus* (Galleria Nazionale, Rome), he anticipated ▷Holbein by depicting his sitter at work. He also painted scenes of daily life, notably *The Banker and His Wife* (Louvre).

● **mastectomy** ▶ Surgical removal of a breast, usually for the treatment of breast cancer. In a partial mastectomy (or lumpectomy) only the tumour is removed, while in a total mastectomy the entire breast is removed. A radical mastectomy involves removal of the breast together with the lymph nodes in the armpit and the chest muscles associated with it.

● **Master of the Queen's** (*or* King's) **Music** ▶ An English court post established in the reign of Charles I. Originally the holder presided over the monarch's private band. It is now an honorary position held by a composer who may be called upon to write music for ceremonial occasions. The present holder is Malcolm Williamson (since 1975).

● **Master of the Rolls** ▶ The presiding judge of the Civil Division of the Court of Appeal. The office originated as the guardian of all charters, patents, etc., entered upon parchment rolls. They were stored from 1290 in a chapel founded by Henry III in 1233. The Master of the Rolls also advised the Lord Chancellor in the old Court of ▷Chancery, becoming a full judge in 1729 and a member of the Court of Appeal in 1881. As his legal responsibilities increased he became less involved in record-keeping. Since the 19th century the rolls have been kept in the Public Record Office. He also admits solicitors to practice, and appoints the members of the Solicitors' Disciplinary Tribunal.

● **Masters, Edgar Lee** ▶ (1868–1950) US poet. His best-known work is *Spoon River Anthology* (1915), a collection of free-verse monologues by the inhabitants of a small provincial town.

● **Masters, William Howell** ▶ (1915–2001) US physician, noted for his studies of human sexual behaviour using volunteer subjects under laboratory conditions. Masters and his colleague, the US psychologist **Virginia Eshelman Johnson** (1925–   ), measured the physiological changes associated with sex and published their findings in *Human Sexual Responses* (1966). Although criticized, their work established a body of knowledge that is useful in such areas as marriage guidance.

● **mastic** ▶ An evergreen shrub, *Pistacia lentiscus*, up to 1.8 m high, native to the Mediterranean region. An aromatic yellowish-green resin is obtained from the bark and used to make varnishes for coating metals and paintings and as an adhesive. Family: *Anacardiaceae*. The name is also applied to other resin-yielding trees, including the related American mastic (*Schinus molle*) and *Sideroxylon masticho-dendron* (family: *Sapotaceae*).

● **mastiff** ▶ An ancient Eurasian breed of large dog long used as a guard dog and for bull- and bear-baiting. It is powerfully built with a large head and a short deep muzzle. The short smooth coat may be apricot, silver, or fawn; the muzzle, ears, and nose are black. Height: 76 cm (dogs); 69 cm (bitches). ▷*See also* bull mastiff.

● **mastodon** ▶ An extinct elephant that originated in Africa 34 million years ago and spread throughout Europe, Asia, and America. Early mastodons were small and had two pairs of tusks; later forms were larger and more elephant-like. The American mastodons survived until about 8000 years ago and were painted in hunting scenes by early man.

● **mastoid bone** ▶ A nipple-shaped process of the temporal bone of the skull, situated behind the ear and containing many air spaces. Infection of the middle ear may spread through these spaces to affect the mastoid bone. Formerly treated surgically, this infection is now readily cured with antibiotics.

● **Mastroianni, Marcello** ► (1924–96) Italian actor. He became one of the best-known international film stars of the 1960s. He appeared in Visconti's *White Nights* (1957), Fellini's *La dolce vita* (1960), Antonioni's *La notte* (1961), and, more recently, in *Intervista* (1987) and *Splendor* (1989).

● **Matabeleland** ► An area in W Zimbabwe, between the Limpopo and Zambezi Rivers. It was named after the Ndebele, a tribe that was driven across the Limpopo by the Voortrekkers in 1837. Consisting chiefly of extensive plains, the area has important gold deposits. Area: 181 605 sq km (70 118 sq mi).

● **Matadi** ► 5 50S 13 32E The chief port in the Democratic Republic of Congo, on the Congo River. It was founded in 1879 by ▷Stanley. It has one of central Africa's largest harbours and is accessible to ocean-going vessels. Population (1994 est): 172 730.

● **Mata Hari** ► (Margaretha Geertruida Zelle; 1876–1917) Dutch courtesan and secret agent. She lived in Indonesia with her husband, a Dutch colonial officer, from 1897 to 1902. She became a professional dancer in Paris in 1905 and probably worked for both French and German intelligence services. She was executed by the French in 1917.

● **matamata** ▷*See* snake-necked turtle.

● **Matamoros** ► 25 50N 97 31W A city in N Mexico, on the Rio Grande on the US border. It is the manufacturing centre for a region producing cotton and sugar cane and is an important point of entry for US tourists. Population (1990): 303 392.

● **Matanzas** ► 23 04N 81 35W A port in Cuba, on Mantanzas Bay on the N coast. Its chief export is sugar. It is also a popular tourist centre. Population (1994 est): 123 843.

● **Matapan, Cape** ► (Modern Greek name: Ákra Taínaron) 36 23N 22 29E The southernmost point of mainland Greece, off which (March, 1941) the British Mediterranean fleet scored a decisive victory over the Italians during World War II.

● **matches** ► Small lengths of wood, cardboard, etc., tipped with an ignitable substance. The friction match was invented in 1816 (by Dérosne). Modern strike-anywhere matches are usually tipped with phosphorus sesquisulphide, potassium chlorate, and zinc oxide. Safety matches, invented in 1844, have their ignitable substances divided between the tip and a special striking surface. Usually the surface contains red phosphorus and the tip a mixture of antimony sulphide and such oxidizing agents as potassium chlorate and manganese dioxide.

● **matchlock** ▷*See* musket.

● **maté** ► The dried leaves of a ▷holly shrub or tree, *Ilex paraguariensis*, native to Paraguay and Brazil. They are roasted, powdered, and infused with water to make the stimulating greenish tealike beverage, popular in many South American countries.

● **materialism** ► In classical metaphysics, materialism is the doctrine of ▷Democritus and ▷Leucippus that everything in the universe is matter or stuff. All events were explicable in terms of the movements and alterations initiated by this matter. By contrast ▷Plato sought to establish the existence of some incorporeal objects, called by him Forms. ▷Aristotle also did not confine himself to a completely materialist explanation of the world, believing that the soul was immaterial. His doctrines nevertheless led to more refined materialistic views than those of the Presocratics, but ▷Hobbes' uncompromising materialism owed nothing to Aristotle. ▷Marx's economic materialism, whereby human actions and beliefs are explained solely in terms of economic forces was developed by ▷Lenin in ▷dialectical materialism. Some recent materialist philosophers studying the body-mind relationship have reduced thought to (physical) neural processes. In all these senses materialism is a metaphysical doctrine. More popularly, the term has also been used to signify worldly outlooks and behaviour.

● **mathematics** ► The logical study of numerical and spatial relationships. It is usually divided into pure and applied mathematics. In pure mathematics the general theoretical principles are studied, often in abstract. Its branches are ▷arithmetic, ▷algebra, ▷calculus, ▷geometry, and ▷trigonometry. Some form of mathematical calculation is an indispensable part of all financial transactions and all measurements. The ancient Egyptians, Sumerians, and Chinese were all using a form of ▷abacus to carry out these calculations for thousands of years before the Christian era. But it was not until the 9th century AD that ▷al-Khwarizmi introduced the idea of writing down calculations instead of carrying them out on an abacus. The Venetian mathematicians of the 11th and 12th centuries were largely responsible for the introduction of these methods to the West; indeed it was they who showed that commercial calculations based on algorisms (a word derived from al-Khwarizmi's name) were superior to those performed on an abacus. However, the application of mathematics to the physical sciences (including astronomy) was largely a 16th-century development inspired by ▷Galileo. It was from this development that applied mathematics grew. It is now largely concerned with ▷mechanics and ▷statistics. In the 20th century ▷set theory and ▷chaos theory were developed, while the introduction of electronic calculators and computers made calculations extremely easy.

● **Mathura** ► 27 30N 77 42E A city in India, in Uttar Pradesh on the River Jumna. A pilgrimage centre, it is the traditional birthplace of the Hindu god, Krishna. Population (1991): 226 840.

● **Matilda** ► (*or* Maud; 1102–67) The daughter of Henry I of England, who designated her his heir. On his death (1135), his nephew Stephen, seized the throne and Matilda invaded England (1139), inaugurating a period of inconclusive civil war. She and her second husband Geoffrey, Duke of Anjou (1113–51), captured Normandy and in 1152 the Treaty of Wallingford recognized her son Henry as Stephen's heir. Her first husband was Emperor ▷Henry V (d. 1125).

● **Matisse, Henri** ► (1869–1954) French painter and sculptor. Having abandoned his legal studies he became a pupil of the painter Gustave ▷Moreau in the 1890s. Matisse initiated ▷fauvism in the early 1900s with his boldly patterned and vibrantly coloured still lifes, portraits, and nudes, notably the controversial *Woman with the Hat* (1905). He was the only artist to continue fauvist principles after the development of ▷cubism. He was also inspired by Islamic art. By 1909 he had achieved worldwide recognition and he remained inventive until his death, a stained glass design for the Dominican chapel at Vence (S France) being among his last works.

● **Matlock** ► 53 08N 1 32W A town in England, the administrative centre of Derbyshire on the River Derwent. Nearby Matlock Bath was a noted spa during Victorian times. Population (1991): 14 680.

● **Mato Grosso** ► A plateau area in SW central Brazil. It extends across the states of Mato Grosso and Goias, separating the Amazon and Plata river systems. Its height varies between about 100 m (328 ft) and 900 m (2953 ft). It is an important cattle-raising area.

● **Matopo Hills** ► A range of hills in SW Zimbabwe, S of Bulawayo. Cecil Rhodes is buried here at a point named World's View.

● **matriarchy** ► A hypothetical social system in which women dominate the family and the state. Some post-Darwinian 19th-century anthropologists believed that such a system preceded male-dominated societies, but this view is no longer held. In practice, matriarchies do not seem to have existed, although some matrilineal societies are known, in which ▷descent is traced through women and in some cases position and property are inherited through the female line. Such matrilineal societies have been found in India, Africa, and America.

● **matrix** ► A set of numbers, called elements, arranged in rows and columns to form a rectangular array. It is used to assist in the solution of certain mathematical problems. The ▷commutative, ▷associative, and ▷distributive laws of matrix arithmetic and algebra are different from those of ordinary arithmetic. The **determinant** of a square matrix is a number, or algebraic expression, that is obtained by multiplication and addition of the elements in a specified way. It has properties that are useful for simplifying and solving sets of simultaneous equations. Single column matrices may represent ▷vectors, enabling them to be handled algebraically and processed by computer.

● **Ma-tsu** ▷*See* Mazu.

● **Matsuo Basho** ► (Matsuo Munefusa; 1644–94) Japanese poet. Born near Kyoto, he moved to Edo (Tokyo) in 1667 and in 1680 became a recluse. He transformed the traditional 17-syllable lyric verse form, the haiku, introducing the characteristic concentrated elliptical imagery and the philosophical spirit of ▷Zen Buddhism. He also wrote travel diaries, of which *The Narrow Road to the Deep North* (1694) is outstanding.

● **Matsuyama** ► 33 50N 132 47E A port in Japan, in NW Shikoku on the Inland Sea. It is an agricultural and industrial centre, with a university (1949). Population (1995): 460 870.

● **Matsys, Quentin** ▷*See* Massys, Quentin.

● **Matteoti, Giacomo** ► (1885–1924) Italian Socialist politician, who was assassinated by fascists after denouncing their party in the Chamber of Deputies. His murder almost brought the fall of Mussolini's government. Three of his assassins were imprisoned following the reopening of the case after World War II.

● **matter** ► Anything in the universe that has the attributes of mass and extension in space and time. According to ▷Einstein's mass-energy equation, matter is a specialized form of ▷energy. All the matter in the universe is composed of atoms, which are themselves made up from elementary particles (*see* particle physics). In the bulk, matter can exist in three physical states — solid, liquid, or gas (*see* states of matter). ▷Plasma can be regarded as a fourth state of matter.

● **Matterhorn** ► (French name: Mont Cervin; Italian name: Monte Cervino) 45 59N 7 39E A mountain in Europe, on the Swiss-Italian border in the Alps near Zermatt. First climbed in 1865 by the British mountaineer, Edward Whymper, it is conspicuous because of its striking pyramidal shape. Height: 4478 m (14 692 ft).

● **Matthew, St** ► In the New Testament, one of the 12 ▷Apostles. He was a tax collector until he became a follower of Jesus. According to tradition, he preached in Judaea, Ethiopia, and Persia and suffered martyrdom. Feast day: 21 Sept. Emblem: a man with wings. **The Gospel according to St Matthew,** is generally believed to have been written sometime after St Mark's Gospel, from which it drew material. It is a narrative of the life and ministry of Jesus that seeks to convince the Jews that he is the Messiah predicted by the Old Testament. It contains the Sermon on the Mount (chapters 5–7).

● **Matthews, Sir Stanley** ► (1915–   ) British Association footballer, who played for Stoke City (1931–47; 1961–65), Blackpool (1947–61), and England, for which he played 54 times. A skilful winger, he played in 886 first-class matches, his last at the age of 50.

$$\begin{vmatrix} a & b \\ c & d \\ e & f \end{vmatrix} + \begin{vmatrix} p & q \\ r & s \\ t & u \end{vmatrix} = \begin{vmatrix} a+p & b+q \\ c+r & d+s \\ e+t & f+u \end{vmatrix} \quad \text{addition}$$

$$k \times \begin{vmatrix} a & b \\ c & d \\ e & f \end{vmatrix} = \begin{vmatrix} ka & kb \\ kc & kd \\ ke & kf \end{vmatrix} \quad \text{multiplication by a constant}$$

$$\begin{vmatrix} a & b \\ c & d \\ e & f \end{vmatrix} \times \begin{vmatrix} p & q & r \\ s & t & u \end{vmatrix} =$$

matrix multiplication

$$\begin{vmatrix} (ap+bs) & (aq+bt) & (ar+bu) \\ (cp+ds) & (cq+dt) & (cr+du) \\ (ep+fs) & (eq+ft) & (er+fu) \end{vmatrix}$$

the **determinant** of $\begin{vmatrix} a & b \\ c & d \end{vmatrix} = \begin{vmatrix} a & b \\ c & d \end{vmatrix} = ad - bc$

matrix ► Examples of matrix algebra.

● **Matthias** ► (1557–1619) Holy Roman Emperor (1612–19). He became King of Hungary (1608) and of Bohemia (1611) following revolts against his brother Rudolph II and was in turn forced to cede these crowns to Ferdinand of Styria (later Ferdinand II) in 1618 and 1617 respectively. Matthias then tried unsuccessfully to moderate Ferdinand's harsh policies against the Bohemian Protestants.

● **Matthias I Corvinus** ► (?1443–90) King of Hungary (1458–90). The son of János Hunyadi, Matthias brought Hungary to a peak of greatness before its fall in 1526 to the Turks. His reforms embraced administration, law, and the army. He also imposed high taxes, which greatly benefited the treasury but precipitated revolts. His foreign policy was dominated by conflict with Emperor ▷Frederick III and in 1485 Matthias occupied Vienna. He also added Bosnia, Moravia, and Silesia to his domains but failed in his efforts to take Bohemia. A great patron of Renaissance art and scholarship, Matthias founded the great Corvina library.

● **Mauchly, John W.** ▷*See* Eckert, John Presper, Jr.

● **Maud** ▷*See* Matilda.

● **Maudslay, Henry** ► (1771–1831) British engineer, who invented the metal lathe. After working under Joseph ▷Bramah, Maudslay established his own machine-tools business. His other inventions include the slide rule and a method of desalinating seawater. He also designed marine engines.

● **Maugham, W(illiam) Somerset** ► (1874–1965) British novelist and dramatist. Born in Paris, he studied and qualified in medicine but abandoned it after the success of his first novel, *Liza of Lambeth* (1896). His later fiction includes *Of Human Bondage* (1915), *The Moon and Sixpence* (1919), *Cakes and Ale* (1930), and *The Razor's Edge* (1944). He wrote popular comedies of manners, such as *The Circle* (1921), and many short stories with Far Eastern or other exotic settings. From 1928 he lived in the South of France.

● **Mau Mau** ► A secret organization among the Kikuyu people of Kenya, which led a revolt (1952–57) against the British colonial government. Secret oaths were administered to participants, who committed appalling atrocities against Whites and uncooperating Blacks. Jomo ▷Kenyatta was thought to be a Mau Mau leader and was imprisoned from 1953 to 1961.

● **Maundy Thursday** ► The Thursday before ▷Good Friday. Its name derives from Latin *mandatum*, commandment, and its traditional foot-washing and almsgiving ceremonies originated at the Last Supper, when Christ washed the disciples' feet and commanded them to follow his example (John 13). The British sovereign's distribution of special Maundy money in Westminster Abbey and other sites is a survival of these rites.

● **Maupassant, Guy de** ► (1850–93) French short-story writer and novelist. He was introduced into literary circles by Flaubert, his literary mentor, met Zola, and joined his group of naturalist writers (*see* Naturalism). Following the phenomenal success of the first story he published under his own name, "Boule de Suif" (1880), he wrote about 300 short stories and 6 novels, including *Une Vie* (1883) and *Bel-Ami* (1885). He suffered from syphilis and died in an asylum.

● **Maupertuis, Pierre Louis Moreau de** ► (1698–1759) French mathematician, best known for his principle of least action, by which the paths of moving bodies, rays of light, etc., are such that the action (momentum multiplied by distance) is a minimum. A quarrelsome and dislikeable man, Maupertuis argued with ▷Voltaire over his principle and became involved with the controversy between ▷Newton and ▷Leibniz over who first discovered the calculus.

● **Mauretania** ► The coastal area N of the Atlas Mountains in ancient N Africa. Inhabited by Moorish tribes, who retained their independence while permitting settlements of Phoenician traders and later Italian colonists, Mauretania was incorporated in the Roman Empire in 40 AD. It was conquered by the Muslims in the 7th century. ▷*See also* Moors.

● **Mauriac, François** ► (1885–1970) French novelist. He was born into a middle-class Roman Catholic family near Bordeaux. His novels, which include *Le Désert de l'amour* (1925), *Thérèse Desqueyroux* (1927), and *Le Noeud de vipères* (1933), characteristically portray the conflict between worldly passions and religion in provincial marital and family relationships. He also wrote plays and polemical criticism and journalism. He won the Nobel Prize in 1952.

● **Maurice of Nassau** ▸ (1567–1625) Stadholder (chief magistrate) of the United Provinces of the Netherlands (1584–1625), succeeding his father William the Silent. A great military leader and a master of siege warfare, Maurice instituted army reforms that enabled the United Provinces to withstand Spanish attempts to destroy the newly established Protestant republic (*see* Revolt of the Netherlands). He failed to draw the Roman Catholic provinces of the S into the union and was forced to negotiate a 12-year truce with Spain in 1609. His career was marred by the arrest and execution of his colleague ▷Oldenbarneveldt in 1619.

● **Mauritania, Islamic Republic of** ▸ (French name: Mauritanie; Arabic name: Muritaniyah) A country in West Africa, with a coastline on the Atlantic Ocean. The N part is desert while the S is mainly fertile. Most of the inhabitants are Arabs and Berbers with a Negro population, mainly Fulani, in the S.
Economy: chiefly agricultural. Livestock, especially cattle, are important and the main crops are millet, sorghum, beans, and rice. Agriculture has been affected by recurrent droughts since the late 1960s. Fishing is important and fish processing is one of the main industries. Iron ore and copper are exploited and, with dried and salt fish, are now the main exports.
History: Mauritania was dominated by Berber tribes from about 100 AD and converted to Islam during the 11th century. The coast was visited by the Portuguese in the 15th century and by the Dutch, English, and French in the 17th century. The area became a French protectorate in 1903 and a colony in 1920. It achieved self-government within the French Community in 1958 and became fully independent in 1960 with Moktar Ould Daddah (1924–) as its first president. It moved from French to Arab ties in international relations, joining the Arab League and the Arab Common Market. In 1976 Mauritania and Morocco took over the former Spanish colony of ▷Western Sahara and divided the territory between them. This prompted guerrilla attacks from the Polisario, the Western Saharan independence movement. In 1979 Mauritania withdrew from all but the southern tip of Western Sahara, relinquishing its territorial claims. In 1978 Daddah was overthrown and Lt Col Mustapha Ould Mohamed Salek (1935–) became president until his resignation in 1979. He was succeeded by Lt Col Khouna Ould Kaydalla (1940–), who was ousted in a coup in 1984. There has been ethnic unrest in recent years between Arabs and Black Africans. Military rule ended in 1991 and a democratic multiparty constitution was adopted. Col Maaouya Ould Sidi Ahmed Taya, president since 1984, won the country's first open presidential election in 1992. Taya's party was victorious in elections in 1992 and 1996 and he himself was re-elected in 1997; however, all these elections were undermined by accusations of fraud and an opposition boycott.

Islamic Republic of Mauritania

Head of state	Maaouya Ould Sidi Ahmed Taya
Official languages	French and Arabic, known as Hassaniya
Official religion	Islam
Official currency	ouguiya of 5 khoums
Area	1 030 700 sq km (397 850 sq mi)
Population (1997 est)	2 411 000
Capital	Nouakchott

● **Mauritius, Republic of** ▸ An island country in the Indian Ocean, about 800 km (500 mi) to the E of Madagascar. It is mainly hilly and subject to tropical cyclones, which cause severe damage. The smaller Agalega and St Brandon Islands are dependencies of Mauritius. The majority of the population are of Indian descent, with European, African, and mixed minorities.
Economy: sugar production plays a major role although manufacturing, especially of clothing, is of increasing importance. Other cash crops include tea and tobacco. Fishing is being developed, as well as agriculture and tourism, in an effort to reduce unemployment.
History: visited by the Arabs in the 10th century and by the Portuguese in the 16th century, the island was settled by the Dutch in

1598. In 1715 it came under French rule as Île de France and in 1814 it was ceded to Britain following its capture in the Napoleonic Wars. During the 19th century large-scale immigration from British India was encouraged. After riots in 1968 it became independent within the British Commonwealth, with Dr Sir Seewoosagur Ramgoolam (1900–85) as its first prime minister. In the 1970s there was considerable political unrest. Ramgoolam was defeated in the 1982 elections and succeeded by Sir Aneerood Jugnauth of the Mauritius Socialists Party. Following elections in 1995 Navin Ramgoolam became prime minister. Mauritius became a republic in 1992 but remained within the Commonwealth.

Republic of Mauritius

Head of state	President Cassam Uteem
Official languages	English and French; Creole is widely spoken
Official currency	Mauritius rupee of 100 cents
Area	1843 sq km (720 sq mi)
Population (1997 est)	1 143 000
Capital and main port	Port Louis

● **Maurois, André** ▸ (Émile Herzog; 1885–1967) French biographer, novelist, and critic. He served in the British army in World War I and had a lifelong affection for English culture. He wrote several novels and short stories but is best known for his biographical studies of Shelley (*Ariel*, 1923), Disraeli (1927), Byron (1930), Voltaire (1935), Chateaubriand (1937), Proust (1949), and Hugo (1954).

● **Maurras, Charles** ▸ (1868–1952) French political theorist and essayist. In 1899 he helped found ▷Action Française, a political group dedicated to extreme monarchist, antisemitic, and Roman Catholic principles (although condemned and excommunicated by the Church). *Au signe de Flore* (1931) contains his memoirs of his political activities. After World War II, during which he supported the government of Pétain, he was condemned to life imprisonment, but was released because of ill health shortly before his death.

● **Mauryan empire** ▸ (c. 321–185 BC) A dynastic empire that spread across most of the Indian subcontinent. It was founded by ▷Chandragupta Maurya, who made Pataliputra (modern Patna) his capital. The dynasty ended with the assassination of Birhadratha in 185 BC. This Buddhist dynasty has left the earliest surviving architecture and sculpture of India. Its most lasting edifices are the burnished stone pillars set up around Patna and Delhi, with an inverted lotus bell supporting animal sculptures.

● **Mauser rifle** ▸ The first successful metallic-cartridge breech-loading rifle, designed by Paul von Mauser (1838–1914) in 1868. The Model-98 rifle and Model-98a/b carbine were standard in the German infantry in World War I; the Model-98k (1938) was standard in World War II.

● **Mausoleum of Halicarnassus** ▸ An ancient Greek tomb built (363–361 BC) as a monument to Mausolus of Caria by his widow, Artemisia (died c. 350 BC). The building, designed by Pythius, was probably a standard temple form with adorning sculptures, fragments of which are in the British Museum, but raised on a high base and with a stepped pyramid-like roof. It was one of the ▷Seven Wonders of the World.

● **Mawson, Sir Douglas** ▸ (1882–1958) Australian explorer who discovered the magnetic South Pole, on ▷Shackleton's expedition (1907); he later led his own Antarctic expeditions. Australia's Antarctic base is named after him.

● **Maxim, Sir Hiram Stevens** ▸ (1840–1916) British inventor, born in the USA, who in 1884 invented the first fully automatic ▷machine gun. The Maxim gun led him to discover cordite, which being smokeless increased the gun's efficiency.

● **Maximilian** ▸ (1832–67) Emperor of Mexico (1864–67). Maximilian, the brother of Emperor Francis Joseph I, was the Archduke of Austria. He was offered the Mexican Crown by France following its invasion of Mexico in 1863. He had no popular support and when in 1867 the French army withdrew he was captured by Benito ▷Juárez and executed.

● **Maximilian I** ► (1459–1519) Holy Roman Emperor (1493–1519). His ambition to rule all W Europe led him into unsuccessful wars, especially with France. However, his marriage (1477) to Mary of Burgundy (1457–82), and that of his son Philip the Handsome to Joanna the Mad of Castile, provided his grandson ▷Charles V with a vast empire.

● **Maximilian I** ► (1756–1825) King of Bavaria (1806–25); formerly Elector of Bavaria (1799–1806) as Maximilian IV Joseph. In 1799 he joined the second coalition against France (*see* Revolutionary and Napoleonic Wars) but in 1801 made peace. Until abandoning the French alliance in 1813 Maximilian gave military aid to Napoleon, acquiring in return extensive territories. His government was noted for liberalism.

● **maxwell** ► The unit of magnetic flux in the ▷c.g.s. system equal to the flux through one square centimetre perpendicular to a field of one gauss. Named after James Clerk ▷Maxwell.

● **Maxwell, James Clerk** ► (1831–79) Scottish physicist, who achieved the unification of electricity, magnetism, and light into one set of equations (known as **Maxwell's equations**). These equations, first published in their final form in 1873, enabled Faraday's lines of force to be treated mathematically by introducing the concept of the electromagnetic field. Maxwell observed that the field radiated outwards from an oscillating electric charge at the speed of light, which led him to identify light as a form of electromagnetic radiation. Maxwell also made important advances in the kinetic theory of gases, by introducing Maxwell-Boltzmann statistics (developed independently by ▷Boltzmann). ▷*See also* Maxwell's demon.

● **Maxwell, Robert** ► (Robert Hoch; 1923–91) British publisher, born in Slovakia. After serving in the British army as a captain and being awarded the Military Cross, he founded Pergamon Press in 1948. A Labour MP from 1964 to 1970, he became chairman of Mirror Group Newspapers in 1984, controlling several national newspapers; he also had an interest in football clubs. His unexplained death (believed by some to be suicide) aboard his yacht off the Canary Islands led to the disclosure of serious business irregularities, including misappropriation of pension funds, and to the collapse of his publishing empire. In 1996 his sons Kevin and Ian were acquitted of conspiracy to defraud.

● **Maxwell's demon** ► A hypothetical creature, postulated by James Clerk ▷Maxwell in 1871 as a construct to disprove the second law of ▷thermodynamics. The demon was visualized as being able to separate a gas into a hot region and a cold region by opening and closing a shutter to allow only fast-moving molecules to enter the hot region. No violation of the second law on these or any other grounds has ever been observed.

● **may** ▷*See* hawthorn.

● **May, Sir Thomas Erskine, 1st Baron Farnborough** ► (1815–86) British constitutional authority. Clerk to the House of Commons (1871–86), he wrote the standard reference work, *Rules, Orders, and Forms of Procedure of the House of Commons* (1854), and several constitutional histories. He is not to be confused with an earlier **Thomas May** (1595–1650), an English poet and parliamentary historian, who wrote *The History of the Parliament of England* (1647).

● **maya** ► (Sanskrit: illusion) In the Vedas maya is the magic power of a god or spirit. In the ▷Upanishads, maya is illusion or the mundane world, which is ultimately unreal because of its impermanence. Elsewhere maya is seen as the play of ▷Brahma, who splits himself into innumerable parts.

● **Maya** ► An American Indian people of Yucatán (Mexico) Guatemala, and Belize. There are a number of languages in the Totonac-Mayan language family (*see* Mesoamerican languages). Today the Maya live mainly in farming villages and are nominally Roman Catholic, but between 300 and 900 AD they had established an advanced civilization. They developed hieroglyphic writing and had considerable knowledge of astronomy and mathematics. They devised a precise calendar, which regulated elaborate rituals at such sites as ▷Chichén Itzá, ▷Tikal, Copan, and Palenque, where large pyramid temples were constructed for the worship of the sun, moon, and rain

Maya ► A lintel decoration carved in c. 725 AD, showing a warrior receiving his battle garb from his wife.

gods. After 900 the influence of the ▷Toltecs led to a mixed Toltec-Maya culture.

● **Mayagüez** ► 18 13N 67 09W A port in W Puerto Rico, in the West Indies. It has an important needlework industry; other manufactures include beer, rum, and soap. Population (1996 est): 100 937.

● **Mayakovskii, Vladimir** ► (1893–1930) Russian poet. He was a leading member of the futurist movement (*see* futurism) and a prolific propagandist for Bolshevism. Revolutionary politics and his frustrated private life are the main themes of his poetry, which is characterized by aggressive vitality and experimentation. He also wrote two satirical dramas, *The Bedbug* (1929) and *The Bath-House* (1930). He committed suicide.

● **May Day** ► May 1, traditionally a festival associated with spring fertility rites, celebrated in Britain by such customs as dancing round the Maypole. ▷*See also* Labour Day.

● **Mayence** ▷*See* Mainz.

● **Mayer, Julius Robert von** ► (1814–78) German physicist, who (in 1842) was the first to calculate the mechanical equivalent of heat and formulated a form of the law of conservation of energy. However, his work went virtually unrecognized; ▷Joule received credit for the first achievement and ▷Helmholtz for the second.

● **Mayer, Louis B.** ► (1885–1957) US film producer, born in Russia. In 1924 he founded the Metro-Goldwyn-Mayer (MGM) production company, which became Hollywood's largest and most successful studio during the "Golden Age" of the 1930s and 1940s. The studio's style was largely determined by his personal taste for lavish but uncontroversial entertainment. He retired in 1951.

● **Mayer, Sir Robert** ► (1879–1985) German-born British businessman and patron of music. He founded the Robert Mayer Concerts for Children.

● **Mayfair** ▶ A fashionable residential district in the Greater London borough of the City of Westminster. It was named after the annual fair held from the 16th century until 1809.

● **Mayflower** ▶ The ship that carried the ▷Pilgrim Fathers to America. They had intended to settle in Virginia but the ship was blown off course and reached Plymouth (Massachusetts) in December, 1620. There, the Pilgrims drew up the **Mayflower Compact**, which based their government on the colonists' will, not the English Crown.

● **mayfly** ▶ A slender □insect of the order *Ephemeroptera* (1500 species), found near fresh water. Up to 40 mm long, mayflies are usually brown or yellow with two unequal pairs of membranous wings. The adults do not feed and only live long enough to mate and lay eggs. The aquatic nymphs feed on plant debris and algae.

● **May Fourth Movement** ▶ (1917–21) A Chinese movement for social and intellectual reform that culminated in a student demonstration in Beijing on 4 May, 1919, against the allocation of Chinese territory to Japan by the Paris Peace Conference. It aimed to throw off foreign dominance and to build a new modern China.

● **Mayhew, Henry** ▶ (1812–87) British journalist. His best-known work is *London Labour and the London Poor* (4 vols, 1851–62), a combination of vivid reportage and amateur social and economic analysis. He was a founder of *Punch* in 1841 and the author of plays and novels.

● **Maynard Smith, John** ▶ (1920–) British biologist, known for his evolutionary theories influenced by ▷game theory. Professor of biology at Sussex University (1965–85), he postulated an evolutionary stable strategy (ESS), a collection of characteristics in a population that is resistant to replacement by different characteristics. His books include *Theory of Evolution* (1958), *Mathematical Ideas in Biology* (1968), and *Evolution and the Theory of Games* (1982).

● **Mayo** ▶ (Irish name: Contae Mhuigheo) A county in the W Republic of Ireland, in Connacht bordering on the Atlantic Ocean. Mountainous in the W it contains several large lakes. Cattle, sheep, and pigs are raised and potatoes and oats are grown. Area: 5397 sq km (2084 sq mi). Population (1996): 111 524. County town: Castlebar.

● **Mayo** ▶ A family of US physicians, who pioneered the concept of group practice and established the Mayo Clinic in Rochester, Minnesota, along these lines. The family included **William Worrall Mayo** (1819–1911), his sons **William James Mayo** (1861–1939) and **Charles Horace Mayo** (1865–1939), and Charles' son **Charles William Mayo** (1898–1968). The Mayos also made a number of contributions to medical research.

● **mayor** ▶ The chief officer of a municipal council. In the UK a mayor or mayoress is the chairman or chairwoman of a district council having ▷borough status. The mayor's counterpart in Scotland is called a ▷provost. The mayor of the ▷City of London and certain other cities is called a **Lord Mayor** (Lord Provost in Scotland). In the City of London he presides over the three courts that comprise the Corporation and attends all civic functions. In 2000 London voted in its first mayoral elections; Ken ▷Livingstone was duly elected and took office. As leader of the Greater London Assembly, the mayor will integrate services, especially transport, for Londoners. The mayor and assembly are housed in the purpose-built ▷City Hall. Directly elected mayors were instituted in several other major UK cities in 2002.

● **mayor of the palace** ▶ An officer of the royal household and later a viceroy appointed by the Merovingian kings of the early middle ages. The most famous were ▷Pepin of Herstal and his grandson ▷Pepin the Short, who overthrew the Merovingians and founded the Carolingian dynasty.

● **Mayotte** ▶ An island in the W Indian Ocean, in the Comoro Islands group. After the other islands declared independence from France (1975), Mayotte (and the island of Pamanzi) decided by a referendum to remain a French territory. It exports vanilla, ylang-ylang oil, and coconuts. Area: 374 sq km (144 sq mi). Population (1994 est): 109 600. Chief town: Dzaoudzi (on Pamanzi).

● **maypole dance** ▶ A folk dance of ancient origin, traditionally

performed on 1 May as part of the May Day festival. Participants circle round a tall pole, often adorned with ribbons, which they weave into patterns.

● **Mazarin, Jules, Cardinal** ▶ (1602–61) French statesman. A papal diplomat, he rose to prominence as a protégé of Cardinal de Richelieu and shortly after Richelieu's death (1642) became chief adviser to the regent Anne of Austria, Louis XIV's mother. The era of Mazarin witnessed a great expansion in the power of the monarchy, achieved largely through his suppression of rebellious aristocrats during the ▷Fronde. Abroad, he enhanced French supremacy in Europe by the Treaties of ▷Westphalia (1648) and the ▷Pyrenees (1659).

● **Mazatlán** ▶ 23 11N 106 25W A port and resort in W Mexico, on the Gulf of California. The chief industries are textiles manufacture and sugar refining; exports include tobacco and minerals. Population (2000 est): 325 000.

● **Mazu** ▶ (or Ma-tsu) 26 10N 119 59E A Taiwanese island in the East China Sea. It was bombed from the Chinese mainland in 1958, causing an international incident. Area: 44 sq km (17 sq mi). Population (latest est): 8200.

● **Mazurian Lakes** ▶ Several hundred lakes in NE Poland, around which Germany inflicted two heavy defeats on the Russians in 1914 and 1915.

● **mazurka** ▶ A traditional Polish dance that originated in the 17th century in Mazovia, a region of E central Poland. In triple time, with accents on the second and third beats accompanied by heel tapping, the mazurka was danced by groups of 4 to 12 dancers to improvised music. The 55 mazurkas for the piano, written by ▷Chopin, vary in speed and mood to reflect the diversity of the original dances. Glinka and Borodin also composed mazurkas for the piano.

● **Mazzini, Giuseppe** ▶ (1805–72) Italian patriot, who was a leader of the movement for Italian unification (*see* Risorgimento). Forced to live mostly in exile in France, Switzerland, and England, he planned with his ▷Young Italy movement a rising in Piedmont and an invasion of Savoy in the 1830s but both failed. Mazzini was in Italy during the ▷Revolutions of 1848 and became head of a short-lived Roman republic. Although a united kingdom of Italy was formed in 1861, he never realized his ideal of an Italian republic.

● **Mbabane** ▶ 26 30S 31 30E The capital of Swaziland, in the Mdimba Mountains. It was founded in the late 19th century. Tourism is important and nearby is a large iron mine. Population (1998 est): 60 000.

● **MBE** ▷*See* Order of the British Empire.

● **Mbeki, Thabo** ▶ (1942–) South African politician; president (1999–). A leading ANC activist from the 1960s, he took a prominent role in the negotiations that effected South Africa's transition to multiracial democracy (1991–93). As deputy president to the ageing ▷Mandela (1994–99), he became increasingly responsible for the executive functions of government. He succeeded Mandela as president of the ANC in 1997 and succeeded to the national presidency following the elections of May 1999.

● **Mboya, Tom** ▶ (1930–69) Kenyan politician. Mboya was from the Luo tribe and was an active trades unionist and general secretary of the Kenyan Federation of Labour. A founder member and general secretary (1960–64) of the Kenya African National Union, he became, under Kenyatta, minister of justice (1963) and minister of economic planning and development (1964–69). He was assassinated.

● **Mbuji-Mayi** ▶ (name until 1966: Bakwanga) 6 10S 23 39E A city in the central Democratic Republic of Congo. Diamonds were discovered here in 1909 and the region now produces about 75% of the world's industrial diamonds. Population (1994 est): 806 475.

● **Mc–** ▶ Names beginning Mc are listed under Mac.

● **MCC** ▷*See* Marylebone Cricket Club.

● **ME** ▶ (myalgic encephalomyelitis) ▷*See* chronic fatigue syndrome.

● **mead** ▶ An alcoholic drink of fermented honey and water. The honey is dissolved in water and boiled with spices. When cool, after brewer's yeast has been added, the mead ferments in barrel. It should be stored in bottle for at least six months before serving. It was drunk in Anglo-Saxon England and, called hydromel, by the ancient Romans.

● **Mead, Margaret** ▶ (1901–78) US anthropologist. Margaret Mead's anthropological work centred on the study of child rearing and the family. Her field work was done in New Guinea, Polynesia, and other Pacific islands. Her books include *Coming of Age in Samoa* (1929), *Sex and Temperament in Three Primitive Societies* (1935), and *Male and Female* (1949). She also wrote on education, science, culture, and mental health. Her reputation as a field anthropologist has been attacked since her death.

● **Meade, James Edward** ▶ (1907–95) British economist. A professor at the London School of Economics (1947–57) and later at Cambridge (1957–74), he wrote the influential book *The Principles of Political Economy* (1965–76) and was awarded a share in the Nobel Prize (1977).

● **meadowsweet** ▶ A perennial herb, *Filipendula* (or *Spiraea*) *ulmaria*, common in damp places throughout temperate Eurasia. 60–120 cm high, it has large compound leaves, with 8–20 pairs of toothed leaflets and fluffy terminal clusters of small, creamy-white fragrant flowers, with long stamens. An oil distilled from the flower buds is used in perfumes. Family: ▷*Rosaceae*.

● **Meads, Colin Earl** ▶ (1935–) New Zealand Rugby Union footballer, who played for King Country and the All Blacks. A huge lock forward, he won a record 55 New Zealand caps (1957–71).

● **mealworm** ▷*See* darkling beetle.

● **mealybug** ▶ An insect of the worldwide family *Pseudococcidae*, closely related to the ▷scale insects. The female is covered with a white sticky powder, which may be extended into filaments. The species *Pseudococcus citri* is a serious pest of citrus trees in America.

● **mean** ▷*See* average.

● **meander** ▶ A sinuous curve in a river. The velocity of flow in a meandering river is highest on the outside of the meander bends; erosion is concentrated here with deposition occurring on the inside of the bend. The meander will become increasingly looped until the river eventually breaks through its narrow neck creating an oxbow ▷lake.

● **mean free path** ▶ The average distance travelled by a molecule between successive collisions with other molecules. According to the ▷kinetic theory, the mean free path is directly proportional to the viscosity of the substance and inversely proportional to the average velocity of the molecules.

● **mean life** ▶ (*or* lifetime) The average time for which a radioactive isotope, elementary particle, or other unstable state exists before decaying. ▷*See* radioactivity.

● **means test** ▶ An inquiry into a person's resources to establish his entitlement to a welfare benefit. In the UK between 1931 and 1934 a means-tested benefit was paid to the long-term unemployed who had exhausted their ▷National Insurance rights. Introduced as an economy measure and operated by local councils, it was discontinued because of its unpopularity. Means tests are still applied in the UK to certain benefits, e.g. income support, housing benefit, ▷legal aid, and students' maintenance grants. Their defenders claim that they lower the cost of a benefit and direct it where it is most needed, while their opponents assert that they are expensive to apply, represent an invasion of privacy, and create a "poverty trap" in which people are discouraged from saving or increasing their earnings because they will forfeit benefits.

● **measles** ▶ A highly infectious viral disease, which usually affects children. After an incubation period of about two weeks the child becomes irritable and fevered and has a running nose and inflamed eyes. Two or three days later a rash appears on the head and face and spreads over the body. Usually the child recovers after a week, but sometimes pneumonia or encephalitis may develop. There is no specific treatment, but vaccination has reduced the incidence of the disease. *Compare* German measles.

● **Meath** ▶ (Irish name: Contae na Midhe) A county in the E Republic of Ireland, in Leinster bordering on the Irish Sea. Consisting chiefly of fertile glacial drifts it is important for agriculture; cattle are fattened and oats and potatoes grown. Area: 2338 sq km (903 sq mi). Population (1996): 109 000. County town: Trim.

● **Meaux** ▶ 48 58N 2 54E A town in N France, in the Seine-et-Marne department on the River Marne. The commercial and industrial centre of the Brie region, it supplies Paris with agricultural produce. Population (latest est): 45 873.

Mecca ▶ The court of the Al-Haram Mosque in the centre of the city, showing pilgrims crowding around the shrine of the Kabaa.

● **Mecca** ▶ (Arabic name: Makkah) 21 26N 39 49E A city in W Saudi Arabia, in a narrow valley surrounded by barren hills. Mecca and Riyadh are joint capitals of the kingdom, but it is famous as the holiest Muslim city, which every Muslim is expected to visit at least once in his lifetime; nonbelievers are not allowed to enter the city. It has been a holy city since ancient times, but was also the birthplace of Mohammed (c. 570). Inside the court of the al-Haram Mosque in the centre of the city are located the chief shrines: the Kabaa (a small windowless building) and the sacred well of Zamzam. In November, 1979, the al-Haram Mosque was seized by armed militants, who held a number of worshippers hostage before being overpowered by the military forces. Population (1991 est): 630 000.

● **mechanical advantage** ▶ The ratio of the force output of a machine to the force input, i.e. the ratio of load to effort. It is useful only as an analysis of simple machines, such as ▷levers, pulleys, jacks, etc., as no account of friction is taken. The **velocity ratio** of the machine is the distance moved by the effort divided by the distance moved by the load; the **mechanical efficiency** of a machine is the ratio of its mechanical advantage to its velocity ratio.

● **mechanical engineering** ▶ The branch of ▷engineering concerned with the application of scientific knowledge to dynamical structures and systems, rather than the static structures of civil engineering. This branch encompasses the design, manufacture, and maintenance of machines of all kinds, engines, vehicles, and many aspects of industrial manufacturing. The subject has numerous specialized subdivisions, including ▷aeronautics, motor engineering, machine-tool design, etc. In the UK the professional body is the Institute of Mechanical Engineers.

● **mechanics** ▶ The study of the motion of bodies and systems and the forces acting on them. The subject is traditionally divided into statics, the study of bodies in equilibrium, and dynamics, the study of forces that affect the motion of bodies. Dynamics is further divided into kinetics, the effects of forces and their moments on motion, and kinematics, the study of velocity, acceleration, etc., without regard to the forces causing them. Aristotelian (*see* Aristotle) mechanics was based on the erroneous concept that a force is required to maintain motion. ▷Newtonian mechanics recognizes that once a body is moving a force is required to stop it but no force is needed to keep it moving. Newtonian mechanics is the mechanics of classical systems, i.e. large-scale systems moving at relatively low velocities. The more general relativistic mechanics is also applicable to systems moving at speeds comparable to that of light. It reduces to Newtonian mechanics at velocities that are small compared to that of light (*see also* quantum theory; statistical mechanics). ▷Fluid mechanics is the application of mechanical principles to fluids, both stationary (hydrostatics) and flowing (hydrodynamics).

● **Mechelen** ▸ (French name: Malines; English name: Mechlin) 51 02N 4 29E A town in N Belgium, on the River Ryle. Its 12th-century cathedral contains an altarpiece by Van Eyck and there are Rubens masterpieces in two other churches. Famous for Mechlin lace, industries include textiles and tinned vegetables. Population (1995 est): 75 718.

● **Mechnikov, Ilya** ▷*See* Metchnikov, Ilya Ilich.

● **Mecklenburg** ▸ An historic region and former *Land* of Germany on the SW Baltic coast, now part of the *Land* of Mecklenburg-West Pomerania. Mecklenburg was frequently partitioned until its permanent division in 1701 into the Duchies of Mecklenburg-Schwerin and Mecklenburg-Strelitz. After the Congress of Vienna in 1815, both duchies formed part of the German Confederation under Austria, but in 1866 joined Prussia's North German Confederation; thereafter Mecklenburg's history is linked with Prussia's.

● **Mecklenburg-West Pomerania** ▸ A *Land* of NE Germany on the Baltic coast. Reinstated in 1990, it consists of the former *Land* of Mecklenburg and those parts of Pomerania that were not ceded to Poland at the end of World War II. It is thinly populated, with many lakes and forests. Population (1995 est): 1 832 300. Capital: Schwerin.

● **medals** ▸ Pieces of metal fashioned as coins or crosses to commemorate individuals or special occasions, or awarded in recognition of service to a state or institution. During the Renaissance personal medals, usually bearing a portrait of the owner with an emblem and motto on the reverse, achieved high artistic standards. ▷Pisanello, ▷Dürer, and ▷Cellini were notable medallists. Military medals multiplied in Britain during the imperialist expansion of the 18th and 19th centuries. They usually portray the sovereign's head or insignia of the awarding body, bear a commemorative legend, and are worn suspended on a special ribbon. Many reward bravery, such as the ▷Victoria Cross and ▷George Cross, but some commemorate campaigns and state occasions.

● **Medan** ▸ 03 35N 98 39E A city in Indonesia, in N Sumatra. Its two universities were established in 1952. An agricultural and trade centre that grew around tobacco plantations, it has a seaport (Belawan). Population (1995 est): 1 909 700.

● **Medawar, Sir Peter Brian** ▸ (1915–87) British immunologist, noted for his investigation of the development of the immune system, including the phenomenon of acquired immunological tolerance to foreign tissue grafts. He also showed how genetically determined "markers" (antigens) enable the immune system to discriminate between host cells and foreign cells. Medawar shared the 1960 Nobel Prize.

● **Medea** ▸ In Greek legend, a sorceress, the daughter of King Aeetes of Colchis and niece of ▷Circe. She helped ▷Jason steal the ▷Golden Fleece. When Jason deserted her for Glauce, daughter of the Corinthian King Creon, she killed Glauce, Creon, and her own two children and fled to Athens.

● **Medellín** ▸ 6 15N 75 36W The second largest city in Colombia, in the Central Cordillera. It is a leading industrial centre with steel processing and textiles. Its university was founded in 1822. In recent years domination of the city by cocaine barons led to an internationally supported campaign against drug traffickers. Population (1997 est): 1 970 691.

● **Media** ▸ An ancient region SW of the Caspian Sea settled by semi-nomadic tribes of **Medes**. Between the 8th and 6th centuries BC they began to unite against Assyria and in 612 under their sovereign Cyaxares (625–585) destroyed Nineveh with the help of Chaldea and overthrew the Assyrian empire. But in 550 the Medes were amalgamated with the Persians in Cyrus the Great's expanding empire.

● **median** ▸ 1. The line joining the vertex of a triangle to the midpoint of the opposite side. 2. The middle value of a set of numbers arranged in order of magnitude. For example, the median of {2, 3, 3, 4, 5} is 3.

● **medical ethics** ▸ The ethical views that arise in the practice of medicine. The traditional duties of patient–doctor confidentiality and helping the sick to the best of one's ability date back to the Hippocratic oath, of which the Greek physician ▷Hippocrates may or may not have been the author. The limits of confidentiality always involve controversial decisions. If a patient confesses to a doctor that he has committed a murder, should the doctor notify the police? The extent to which a doctor should share the prognosis of a patient's condition with the patient and the extent to which a patient should be involved in planning the appropriate treatment can also involve difficult decisions.

On broader issues, ▷euthanasia, ▷contraception, ▷abortion, ▷prenatal diagnosis, and the turning off of life-support machines in cases of ▷persistent vegetative state are areas in which the doctors' own religious affiliations could influence their treatment or advice. Clinical trials of new drugs or other forms of treatment on human patients and the allocation of medical resources that are in short supply are also issues requiring ethical judgment. Similarly, the practice of transplant surgery (*see* transplantation), in which organs are removed on the death of one patient for the benefit of another, may call for several kinds of ethical decision, which often have to be taken very rapidly if the organs are to be viable.

More recently the advent of in-vitro fertilization (*see* test-tube baby), surrogate motherhood (*see* artificial insemination), and other methods of assisted reproduction have introduced a new set of ethical problems that have not yet been fully resolved; in the UK the Human Fertilization and Embryology Authority, established under the Human Fertilization and Embryology Act (1990), monitors and controls both treatment and research into assisted conception. Rapid advances in ▷genetic engineering are certain to generate ever more complex ethical problems concerned with the genetic manipulation of human tissues, including ▷gene therapy, xenotransplantation (transplantation of animal organs into human beings), and the possibility of human ▷clones. ▷*See also* triage.

● **medical jurisprudence** ▸ (*or* forensic medicine) The legal aspects of medical practice. This includes the application of a country's laws to such practices as the termination of pregnancy, transplantation of organs, sterilization, and artificial insemination. It also covers investigations of the causes of sudden ▷death and the giving of medical evidence in courts of law, for example in cases of murder, assault, infanticide, etc.

● **Medici** ▸ A family that dominated Florence from 1434 to 1494, from 1512 to 1527, and from 1530 to 1737 (as grand dukes from 1532). The Medici, who were merchants and bankers, dominated the government of Florence in the 15th century by manipulating elections to the key magistracies. The family's power was established by **Cosimo de' Medici** (1389–1464), entitled Pater Patriae (Father of His Country), who also initiated the Medici tradition of artistic patronage: Brunelleschi, Ghiberti, and Donatello, among others, were employed by Cosimo. His son **Piero de' Medici** (1416–69) succeeded to his position, which then passed to **Lorenzo the Magnificent** (1449–92). Following the ▷Pazzi conspiracy (1478), in which his brother **Giuliano de' Medici** (1453–78) died, Lorenzo's political prestige was greatly enhanced. An outstanding patron of Renaissance artists (Botticelli, Ghirlandaio, Michelangelo) and scholars (Ficino, Pico della Mirandola, Politian), Lorenzo tended to neglect the family business, which declined in the late 15th century. He was succeeded by his son **Piero de' Medici** (1472–1503), who was forced to flee Florence in a revolt incited by ▷Savonarola. Piero's brother **Giovanni de' Medici** (1475–1521) was restored to Florence in 1512, a year before he became Pope ▷Leo X. The Medici were again ousted, in 1527, but the combined efforts of Emperor Charles V and Pope Clement VII (previously Giulio de' Medici, the illegitimate son of Lorenzo's brother Giuliano) established Clement's illegitimate son **Alessandro de' Medici** (1511–37) as the first Duke of Florence. Subsequent grand dukes included **Cosimo I** (1519–74), **Francesco I** (1541–87), and **Ferdinando I** (1549–1609).

● **medicine** ▶ The science and practice of preventing, diagnosing, and treating disease. The term is also used specifically for the management of disease by nonsurgical methods, for example by drugs, diet, etc. (*compare* surgery). Medicine involves study of the anatomy, physiology, and biochemistry of the body in health as well as the changes that occur in disease (pathology). It is closely connected with pharmacology (the study of drugs).

Medicine has its origins in ancient Greece. The medical school at Cnidos, established in the 7th century BC, was concerned purely with the description of symptoms, whereas that founded later by ▷Hippocrates considered the causes of symptoms in relation to the patient and the environment. In the Alexandrian school the emphasis was on the effects of disease rather than the causes. All existing knowledge of medicine was coordinated and supplemented in the 2nd century AD, by ▷Galen, whose influence prevailed until the Renaissance. Landmarks in the development of modern medicine were the publication of ▷Vesalius' major work on anatomy (1543) and of William Harvey's discovery of the circulation of the blood (1628). The nature, treatment, and prevention of infectious diseases were illuminated by the researches of ▷Pasteur, ▷Koch, and ▷Klebs in the 19th century; their work directed ▷Lister to the discovery of antiseptics, by means of which wound healing and hospital sanitation were greatly improved. Chemotherapy (the treatment of disease by chemical agents) was revolutionized in 1911, when ▷Ehrlich introduced salvarsan for treating syphilis. The late 1930s saw the development of the sulphonamides– the first powerful general antibacterial drugs–and World War II provided the stimulus for the widespread production and use of antibiotics (the first of which was penicillin). Together these drugs enabled many infectious diseases to be cured, but new antibiotics are continually being developed to combat resistant strains of bacteria. Viruses do not succumb to antibiotics and the control of viral diseases has relied largely on vaccination, pioneered by ▷Jenner in 1798, and the continued search for effective antiviral drugs. Since World War II, preventive and public-health medicine have become important, with the establishment of the ▷World Health Organization in 1948, campaigns to eradicate epidemic diseases, and the establishment of antenatal clinics, medical inspections for schoolchildren, dental clinics, welfare centres, etc., in many parts of the world. With advances in molecular biology and genetics (*see* genetic engineering; gene therapy), research has concentrated on the causes, prevention, and treatment of hereditary diseases, cancer, etc. *▷See also* alternative medicine; medical ethics; nuclear medicine.

● **medick** ▶ An annual or perennial herb of the genus *Medicago* (about 120 species), native to Eurasia and N Africa. The stems, 5–90 cm tall, bear compound leaves with three toothed leaflets, dense yellow or purple flower heads and curved or spirally twisted pods. Family: ▷*Leguminosae*.

● **Medina** ▶ (Arabic name: Al Madinah) 24 30N 39 35E A city in W Saudi Arabia, N of Mecca. The tomb of Mohammed is in the mosque at Medina, the second most holy Muslim city after Mecca. Husayn ibn Ali, with the assistance of T. E. ▷Lawrence, contained the Turks during World War I by putting the railway from Damascus out of commission. Date-packing supplements the city's income from pilgrims, and the Islamic University was founded in 1961. Population (1991 est): 400 000.

● **meditation** ▶ Disciplined contemplation, especially as a spiritual or religious practice. Meditation has a place in most religious traditions, as it is considered to increase spiritual awareness and devotion. In Christianity it usually takes the form of reflecting on texts or themes from the Bible with the aim of kindling the will and emotions; a higher form of pure contemplation, in which the mind is fixed solely on God, is also recognized. By contrast, Eastern forms of meditation aim at emptying all conscious thought and feeling from the mind (*see* samadhi). This type of meditation has a central place in Buddhist practice, where it is seen as one of the main paths to enlightenment; many detailed techniques have been evolved, especially in the ▷Zen school. It also plays an important part in the ▷yoga practices of Hinduism and other Indian religions, which aim at self-purification as a precondition of union with the divine. Various techniques are prescribed as aids to meditation; these include the repetition of sacred names, texts, or syllables (such as ▷mantras), special movements, postures, or breathing exercises (as in yoga), or repeated ritual actions (such as the use of rosary beads). In the West, Eastern styles of meditation are now widely practised for nonreligious reasons, as they are thought to reduce stress and bring other mental and physical benefits. ▷*See also* transcendental meditation.

● **Mediterranean Sea** ▶ An almost landlocked sea extending between Africa and Europe to Asia. It connects with the Atlantic Ocean at Gibraltar, the Black Sea via the Sea of Marmara, and the Red Sea via the Suez Canal. It loses twice as much water through evaporation as it receives from rivers and thus is fed continuously by the Atlantic and to a lesser extent by the Black Sea. Although its waters return to the Atlantic in a ten-year cycle, it is saltier and warmer than the oceans; pollution is a serious problem because of the large quantities of waste discharged into its waters. Tidal variation is insignificant.

● **medlar** ▶ A thorny shrub or tree, *Mespilus germanica*, native to SE Europe and central Asia and cultivated for its fruit. Growing to a height of 6 m, it bears oblong toothed leaves, 15 cm long, and white five-petalled flowers. The globular brownish fruit, 5–6 cm across, has an opening at the top, surrounded by the remains of the sepals, through which the five seed chambers can be seen. Medlars are eaten when partly decayed and have a pleasant acid taste; they can also be made into jelly. Family: *Rosaceae*.

● **Médoc** ▶ An area in SW France, bordering on the left bank of the Gironde estuary. Producing some of France's finest red wines, it contains some famous vineyards including Château Latour.

● **medulla oblongata** ▷*See* brain.

● **medusa** ▶ The free-swimming sexual form that occurs during the life cycle of many animals of the phylum *Cnidaria*. Medusae resemble small ▷jellyfish and have separate sexes, releasing eggs and sperm into the water. The ciliated larvae settle and develop into the sedentary asexual forms (*see* polyp). ▷*See also* cnidarian.

● **Medusa** ▶ In Greek mythology, the only mortal ▷Gorgon. Athena, angered by her love affair with Poseidon, made her hair into serpents and her face so ugly that all who saw it were turned to stone. She later sent ▷Perseus to behead her. From her blood sprang ▷Pegasus and Chrysaor, her children by Poseidon.

● **Medway** ▶ A unitary authority in SE England, in Kent. Administrative centre: Gillingham. Area: 204 sq km (79 sq mi). Population (1996 est): 239 500.

● **Medway, River** ▶ A river in SE England. Rising in Sussex, it flows N and E through Kent to join the River Thames by a long estuary. It passes through Tonbridge, Maidstone, Rochester, Chatham, and Gillingham. In 43 AD, near Rochester, the invading Romans defeated the British under Caractacus in the battle of the Medway. Length: 113 km (70 mi).

● **Meegeren, Hans van** ▶ (1889–1947) Dutch painter, notorious for his ▷Vermeer forgeries. He successfully misled the art world, notably with works such as *Christ at Emmaus*, bought by the Boymans Museum, Rotterdam, as an early Vermeer painting. In 1945 he was arrested as a Nazi collaborator, confessed his deceptions, was imprisoned, and died in poverty.

● **meerkat** ▶ A small carnivorous mammal, *Suricata suricata*, also called suricate, of South African grasslands. It is about 60 cm long including the tail (17–25 cm), and lives in large colonies of shallow burrows, emerging to sunbathe in the early morning. Meerkats stay close to home, feeding on insects, grubs, reptiles, birds, and small mammals. Family: ▷*Viverridae* (mongooses, etc.). □ p. 810.

● **meerschaum** ▶ A white mineral consisting of hydrated magnesium silicate, $H_4Mg_2Si_3O_{10}$, found in some magnesium-rich rocks, such as serpentine. Turkey has famous deposits of meerschaum; it also occurs in East and S Africa. It is used for making tobacco pipes.

● **Meerut** ▶ 29 00N 77 42E A city in India, in Uttar Pradesh. The scene of the first uprising (1857) of the Indian Mutiny, Meerut is an important army headquarters and has diverse industries. Population (1991): 753 778.

● **megalith** ▶ (Greek: large stone) A large stone particularly favoured for building monuments in the ▷Neolithic and ▷Bronze Age (in Britain, about 3500 BC to 1500 BC). Megaliths could be placed singly, as in Rudston (N Yorkshire) churchyard; or in lines, as on Dartmoor or at ▷Carnac; or in simple or complex circles as at ▷Stonehenge. Megaliths were also used for tombs and temples in Malta, Egypt, and elsewhere. Stones weighing many tons were set up using simple tackle of timbers and ropes.

● **Megaloceros** ▷See Irish elk.

● **megapode** ▶ A bird belonging to a family (*Megapodiidae*; 12 species) ranging from Australia to Peninsular Malaysia. 48–70 cm long, megapodes are fowl-like and ground-dwelling with brownish or black plumage and build a large nest mound in which the eggs are incubated by the heat of fermenting plant material, the sun, or volcanic heat. They include the ▷mallee fowl and the brush turkeys (e.g. *Alectura lathami*). Order: *Galliformes* (pheasants, turkeys, etc.).

● **Mégara** ▶ 38 00N 23 20E A town in E central Greece. It was an important city state from the 8th century BC fostering many colonies, including ▷Chalcedon and Byzantium, before its decline in the 5th century BC. Population (1991 est): 26 562.

● **Megatherium** ▶ A genus of extinct giant ground sloths that lived in North and South America about a million years ago. *Megatherium* was about the size of a modern elephant and probably ate leaves. Giant mammals like this were common in South America before the Panama isthmus closed at the end of the Ice Age, when most of them—including *Megatherium*—became extinct.

● **megaton** ▶ A measure of the explosive power of a nuclear weapon. It is equivalent to an explosion of one million tons of trinitrotoluene (TNT).

● **Meghalaya** ▶ A state in NE India, NE of Bangladesh on a beautiful plateau falling N to the Brahmaputra Valley. One of the world's wettest areas, it has rich forests but little industry. Rice, potatoes, cotton, and fruits are grown. Meghalaya was separated from Assam in 1972. Area: 22 489 sq km (8681 sq mi). Population (1994 est): 1 960 000. Capital: Shillong.

● **Megiddo** ▶ An ancient site in N Israel. Continuously occupied between about 3000 and 350 BC, Megiddo was strategically positioned on the route between Egypt and Syria and was the scene of many battles. Excavations (1925–39) unearthed hundreds of Phoenician ivories (13th–12th centuries BC) and stabling for about 450 horses, built probably by King Solomon. Megiddo is identified with the biblical Armageddon, where, according to St John the Divine (Revelation 16.16), the last battle will be fought.

● **Mehemet Ali** ▶ (1769–1849) Viceroy of Egypt for the Ottoman Empire (1805–48). An Albanian in the Ottoman army, he was recognized as viceroy after he had seized power in Cairo. His important military, agricultural, and educational reforms have led some to see him as the founder of modern Egypt. In 1840 the Ottomans recognized him as hereditary ruler of Egypt and he was succeeded by his son ▷Ibrahim Pasha. His dynasty survived until 1952.

● **Mehta, Zubin** ▶ (1936–) Indian conductor, director for life of the Israel Philharmonic Orchestra (1981–). Also associated with the Vienna Philharmonic and noted as a pianist, he was music director of the New York Philharmonic (1978–91).

● **Meiji** ▷See Mutsuhito.

● **meiosis** ▶ The process by which the nucleus of a germ cell divides prior to the formation of gametes (such as sperm, pollen, or eggs). Meiosis consists of two successive divisions during which one cell with the normal duplicate (diploid) set of chromosomes gives rise to four cells each with only one chromosome of each type (haploid). Meiosis differs from ▷mitosis in that the chromosomes of each pair become closely associated, enabling the interchange of genetic material between maternal and paternal chromosomes. There is no duplication of chromosomes between the two divisions of meiosis.

● **Meir, Golda** ▶ (1898–1978) Israeli stateswoman, born in Russia; prime minister (1969–74). Brought up in the USA (1906–21), she emigrated to Palestine in 1921. A founder member of the Israeli Workers' Party (Mapai) she was its secretary general (1966–68). She was minister of labour (1949–56) and minister of foreign affairs (1956–66) before becoming prime minister. She was committed to bringing peace in the Middle East and resigned after Israel had been taken unawares in the 1973 Arab-Israeli War.

● **Meissen** ▶ 51 11N 13 23E A town in E Germany, on the River Elbe. Meissen is famous for porcelain manufacture, moved here from Dresden in 1710. The production of the porcelain (known as Dresden china) was begun by J. F. Böttger in 1709. Population (latest est): 38 100.

● **Meissen porcelain** ▶ The first hard-paste porcelain made in Europe following discovery (1710) of the technique by the alchemist Böttger (1682–1719) under the patronage of the Elector of Saxony. Initially, the Elector's oriental collection at Dresden was copied. There followed extensive ranges of domestic ware, figures (shepherdesses, monkey bands, Italian comedy, etc.), chinoiseries, small boxes, seals, and ornaments painted with landscapes, flowers, and insects. The styles were copied by all 18th-century factories.

● **Meissonier, Jean-Louis-Ernest** ▶ (1815–91) French painter, born in Lyons. He achieved great success at the Paris Salon exhibitions from the 1840s onwards with his minutely detailed history paintings, particularly of Napoleonic battles, for example *Campagne de France, 1814* (1864; Louvre).

● **Meistersingers** ▶ (German: master singers) German singing guilds, which flourished from the 14th to the 17th centuries. As the

meerkat ▶ These engaging mongooses adopt the posture shown for basking in the sun outside their burrows. When alarmed they stand on the toes of their hind feet and crane their necks in all directions before seeking refuge in their burrows.

▷Minnesingers declined in Germany, song guilds developed in the artisan class, the first being established in Mainz in 1311. They flourished in most German towns; their contests were closely regulated, as depicted by Wagner in his opera *The Mastersingers of Nuremberg*.

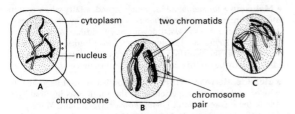

prophase I The four chromosomes appear as thin threads (A), which form pairs (B). Each chromosome divides into two chromatids and exchange of genetic material occurs between the chromatids of each pair (C).

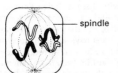

metaphase I The chromosomes of each pair separate from each other and move to opposite poles of the spindle.

metaphase II Two new spindles form and the chromatids of each group separate from each other.

telophase II Four new nuclei form, each containing two chromosomes.

meiosis ▶ The formation of four egg or sperm cells from one parent cell takes place in two divisions, each of which is divided into several phases. Only four phases are shown here.

● **Meitner, Lise ▶** (1878–1968) Austrian physicist. After studying in Vienna under ▷Boltzmann, she worked with Otto ▷Hahn in Berlin (1907–38) until expelled by the Nazis. Together they discovered protactinium (1918) and caused the first fission of a uranium atom by neutron bombardment (1934). Hahn did not publish the results of this work and it was first published by Meitner from Stockholm in 1939. In Stockholm she worked with Karl Manne Georg Siegbahn (1886–1978), becoming a Swedish citizen in 1949. In 1958 she moved to Cambridge.

● **Meknès ▶** 33 53N 5 37W A city in N Morocco. It became known as the "Moroccan Versailles" under Mawlay Isma'il (?1645–1727; reigned 1672–1727), when several palaces were built. It is a trade centre for agricultural produce and carpets. Population (1994 est): 188 224.

● **Mekong, River ▶** A major SE Asian river, rising in Tibet and flowing generally SE through China, Laos, Cambodia, and Vietnam to the South China Sea. It is navigable for about 550 km (340 mi). The extensive delta is one of the greatest Asian rice-growing areas. Length: about 4025 km (2500 mi).

● **Melaka** ▷*See* Malacca.

● **Melanchthon, Philip ▶** (P. Schwarzerd; 1497–1560) German Protestant reformer, who succeeded ▷Luther as leader of the German Reformation movement. Professor of Greek at the University of Wittenberg, Melanchthon was a convinced humanist, influenced by

▷Erasmus, and a supporter of Luther in public confrontations, including the debate with ▷Zwingli over the Eucharist. He was largely responsible for the ▷Augsburg Confession (1530), the main Lutheran statement of belief.

● **Melanesia ▶** A division of Oceania in the SW Pacific Ocean, consisting of an arc of volcanic and coral islands NE of Australia. It includes the Bismarck Archipelago, the Solomon, Admiralty, and D'Entrecasteaux Islands, Vanuatu Republic, New Caledonia, and Fiji. ▷*See also* Micronesia; Polynesia.

● **Melanesians ▶** The people of the Melanesian islands. The term also covers similar peoples of New Guinea, though these are also often known as Papuan. They are of Oceanic Negroid race and speak languages of the ▷Austronesian family. There are a great many very different languages mostly spoken by only small numbers. The Melanesians cultivate yams, taro, and sweet potatoes and live in small, usually dispersed, homesteads. In coastal areas fishing is important. Pigs play a major role in the economy, being used in the ceremonial exchanges of valuables to establish status that are a common cultural trait.

● **melanin ▶** A pigment, varying from brown-black to yellow, that occurs in hair, skin, feathers, and scales. Derived from the amino acid tyrosine, its presence in the skin helps protect underlying tissues from damage by sunlight. Melanin is also responsible for colouring the iris of the eye.

● **melanoma ▶** (*or* malignant melanoma) A form of cancer, mainly affecting the skin, that arises in the cells producing the pigment ▷melanin. Most melanomas develop from an existing ▷mole, and excessive exposure to sunlight is known to be a contributory factor.

● **Melba, Dame Nellie ▶** (Helen Porter Armstrong; 1861–1931) Australian soprano, whose professional name was derived from her native city, Melbourne. She studied in Paris, making her debut in 1887 in Verdi's *Rigoletto*. Her career culminated in a number of farewell performances in 1926.

● **Melbourne ▶** 37 45S 144 58E The second largest city of Australia, the capital of Victoria on Port Phillip Bay. It is a major commercial centre and contains about two-thirds of the state's population. Port Melbourne is sited 4 km (2.5 mi) away, on the mouth of the Yarra River; exports include wool, scrap metal, and dairy products. The chief industries are heavy engineering, food processing, and the manufacture of textiles and clothes. A cultural centre, Melbourne possesses three universities (including the University of Melbourne founded in 1853), and the new Arts Centre of Victoria. Other notable buildings include the State Parliament House and the Anglican and Roman Catholic cathedrals. The Melbourne Cricket Ground, founded in 1853, is world famous.

History: founded in 1835 and named after the British prime minister, Viscount Melbourne, it developed rapidly following the 1851 gold rush. It was the capital of the Commonwealth of Australia from 1901 until 1927. Population (1995 est): 3 218 100.

● **Melbourne, William Lamb, 2nd Viscount ▶** (1779–1848) British statesman; Whig prime minister (1834, 1835–41), who exerted an early influence on Queen Victoria. He was chief secretary for Ireland (1827–28) and then home secretary (1830–34), when he dealt harshly with the ▷Tolpuddle Martyrs. During his second ministry his attempted resignation (1839) precipitated Victoria's ▷Bedchamber Crisis. In 1805 he married Lady Caroline Ponsonby (1785–1828). As **Lady Caroline Lamb** she had a love affair with Lord Byron (1812–13); she separated from her husband in 1825.

● **Melchett, Alfred Mond, 1st Baron** ▷*See* Mond, Ludwig.

● **Melchior** ▷*See* Magi.

● **Melchior, Lauritz ▶** (1890–1973) Danish tenor. He studied at the Royal Opera School in Copenhagen and made his debut in 1913. His performances as Tristan and Siegfried marked him as the leading Wagnerian tenor of the 20th century.

● **Melchites ▶** Christians of the Orthodox Churches in Syria and Egypt who, during the 5th-century ▷Monophysite controversy, adhered to the anti-Monophysite doctrine supported by the Byzantine emperor. Their name was therefore derived from a Syriac word meaning "imperial."

● **Meleager** ▶ In Greek legend, the son of Oeneus, King of Calydon. He killed the Calydonian boar, sent by Artemis because Oeneus had neglected to sacrifice to her.

● **Melilla** ▶ 35 17N 2 57W A Spanish port forming an enclave on the Mediterranean coast of N Morocco. Iron ore is the principal export. Population (1994 est): 58 052.

● **melilot** ▶ A herb belonging to the genus *Melilotus* (25 species), also called sweet clover, occurring in temperate and subtropical Eurasia. The leaves consist of three leaflets and the small yellow or white flowers grow in clusters along the stems. The biennial common melilot (*M. officinalis*) grows to a height of 130 cm. Family: ▷*Leguminosae*.

● **Melitopol** ▶ 46 51N 35 22E A city in SE Ukraine. The centre of a fruit-growing region, it has food-processing industries. Nearby is the site of ancient Merv, an Islamic centre at its height under the Seljuq Turks in the 12th century. Population (1996 est): 174 000.

● **Melk** ▶ 48 14N 15 21E A town in N Austria, in Lower Austria on the River Danube. Its Benedictine abbey is one of the finest baroque buildings. Population (1991): 5163.

● **Mellon, Andrew William** ▶ (1855–1937) US financier and philanthropist. As secretary of the treasury (1921–32) he played a major role in postwar tax reforms. He was also ambassador to Great Britain (1932–33). He donated his art collection to the National Gallery of Art in Washington, DC.

● **melodrama** ▶ A type of theatrical entertainment characterized by fast-moving and sensational plots, overemotional acting, and stock characters representing extremes of virtue or villainy. The genre, which emerged in France and Germany during the 18th century, was so named because of its use of music to accompany spoken dialogue. It reached its zenith in the popular theatres of Victorian London (the "penny gaffs" or "blood tubs"), where melodrama attracted large rowdy audiences, but was also hugely popular in New York, Paris, and Berlin. In the 20th century melodrama transferred to the new mass medium of the cinema, notably in the "cliff-hanging" serials of the silent era.

● **melody** ▷*See* harmony.

● **melon** ▶ An annual trailing vine, *Cucumis melo*, native to tropical Africa but widely cultivated for its edible fruits. Melon plants have coarse hairy five- to seven-lobed leaves, yellow or orange cup-shaped flowers, and round or oval fruits, up to 4 kg in weight, with tough skins and sweet juicy flesh surrounding a core of seeds. Varieties include the muskmelon, with a net-veined skin and pinkish orange flesh; the honeydew melon, with smooth whitish or greenish skin and light-green flesh; the canteloupe, with rough warty skin and orange flesh; and a variety produced in Israel with a green skin and sweet green flesh. Family: *Cucurbitaceae*. ▷*See also* watermelon.

● **Melos** ▶ (*or* Mílos) A Greek island in the Aegean Sea, one of the Cyclades. Minoan cities have been excavated here and the famous statue, the *Venus de Milo*, was discovered here in 1820. Area: 150 sq km (58 sq mi). Population (latest est): 4555.

● **Melpomene** ▶ In Greek religion, one of the nine Muses, the patron of tragedy. She was mother of the ▷Sirens.

● **Melrose** ▶ 55 36N 2 44W A market town in SE Scotland, in Scottish Borders on the River Tweed. It is famous for its associations with Sir Walter Scott and for its 12th-century ruined abbey, where the heart of Robert the Bruce is interred. Population (1991): 2270.

● **meltdown** ▶ A disaster in which a malfunction in a nuclear reactor (*see* nuclear energy; nuclear power) causes the temperature to rise above the melting point of the reactor vessel (over 3000°C), resulting in the reactor melting and burning its way through its concrete foundations. This can release radioisotopes into the earth or the atmosphere, as it did in ▷Chernobyl in 1986.

● **melting point** ▶ The temperature at which the solid form of a substance becomes a liquid, usually at atmospheric pressure.

● **Melton Mowbray** ▶ 52 46N 0 53W A market town in central Eng-

land, in Leicestershire on the Rivers Eye and Wreak. It lies in a stock-raising area and is renowned for its cattle market (one of England's largest), Stilton cheese and pork pies, and as a fox-hunting centre. Population (1996): 25 276.

● **Mélusine** ▶ (*or* Melusina) In French legend, a fairy who was punished for imprisoning her father in a mountain by being changed into a serpent from the waist down every Saturday. When her husband, Count Raymond of Lusignan, broke his promise not to see her on Saturdays, she vanished but her cries were heard at Lusignan castle shortly before the death of each of her descendants.

● **Melville, Herman** ▶ (1819–91) US novelist. In 1841 he joined the crew of a whaler; his experiences in the South Seas inspired *Typee* (1846), *Omoo* (1847), *Mardi* (1849), *Redburn* (1849), and *White Jacket* (1850). His masterpiece, *Moby Dick* (1851), is a narrative about whaling with an underlying philosophical theme on evil. After the failure of *Pierre* (1852), Melville abandoned professional writing. *Billy Budd*, published in 1924, formed the basis of an opera by Benjamin Britten.

● **membrane** ▶ In biology, a thin layer of tissue that covers an organ or lines a canal or cavity. They include serous membranes—such as the peritoneum, lining the abdomen and covering the abdominal organs (*see* peritonitis), and the pleura, covering the lungs and lining the chest wall (*see* pleurisy)—and ▷mucous membranes. **Cell membranes** (*or* plasma membranes) surround the protoplasm of cells and of the organelles within. Only 5–10 nanometres thick, they are made up of ▷phospholipids and proteins. The lipid molecules are arranged in a double layer (bilayer), with the hydrophilic "heads" of the molecules forming the outer and inner surfaces of the membrane, and the protein molecules are randomly distributed within the bilayer. Cell membranes are important in controlling the passage of substances into and out of the cell. Water and certain small molecules can pass freely through the lipid part of the membrane, but the passage of other molecules and of ions is mediated by the membrane proteins, which act as "channels" or "carriers." In addition to lipids and proteins, animal cell membranes contain glycolipids and glycoproteins (sugar-containing lipids and proteins), which function in antigen-antibody reactions and other responses involving cell recognition.

● **Memel** ▷*See* Klaipeda.

● **Memling, Hans** ▶ (*or* Memlinc; c. 1430–1494) Painter of portraits and religious subjects, born in Seligenstadt (Germany). He settled in the Netherlands, where he probably studied under Rogier van der ▷Weyden. About 1465 he moved to Bruges, where *The Shrine of St Ursula* and *The Mystic Marriage of St Catherine* were painted for the Hospital of St John.

● **memory** ▶ The recollection of experiences from the past. Three processes are required: registration, in which an experience is received into the mind; retention, in which a permanent memory trace, or engram, is preserved in the brain, probably in the form of a chemical molecule; and recall, in which a particular memory is brought back into consciousness. Short-term memories are vivid but are forgotten with the passage of time unless they are registered in the long-term memory. Once in the long-term memory, they remain available unless they are interfered with by a similar memory. Failure of memory (*see* amnesia) is a common consequence of diseases of the brain, especially those caused by ▷alcoholism and those affecting the hippocampus (*see also* Alzheimer's disease). An abnormally good memory (hypermnesia) can sometimes be produced by hypnosis and is sometimes found in ▷autism.

● **memory, computer** ▶ The part of a computer that stores information. It usually refers to the computer's internal store, in which the programs and data needed to run the computer are held; this is under the direct control of the central processing unit. In some computers, a cache memory is used between the main memory and the central processing unit to improve performance. Solid-state electronic memory devices, which operate at very high speeds but lose their contents when the machine is turned off, are used for the internal memory. Slower devices, such as ▷magnetic disks, provide permanent data storage, but their contents cannot be accessed directly by the central processing unit; these are sometimes called the external memory.

● **Memphis** ▶ 35 10N 90 00W A city and port in the USA, in Tennessee situated above the Mississippi River. Founded in 1819, it was so called because of the similarity of its riverside position to that of the ancient Egyptian city of Memphis. A major cotton, timber, and livestock market, it produces textiles and chemicals. Memphis State University was established in 1912. Population (1996 est): 596 725.

● **Memphis** ▶ An ancient city of Lower Egypt, S of modern Cairo. A centre for ▷Ptah worship, Memphis was founded as the capital of all Egypt after its unification by ▷Menes (c. 3100 BC), remaining the capital until it was supplanted by ▷Thebes (c. 1570 BC). The necropolis of ▷Saqqarah and the ▷pyramids and sphinx at Giza formed part of its extensive complex of monuments.

● **Menado** ▶ (or Manado) 01 32N 124 55E A port in Indonesia, in N Sulawesi on the Celebes Sea. A trading centre, it exports copra, coffee, and spices. Its university was established in 1961. Population (1995 est): 398 900.

● **Menai Strait** ▶ A channel separating the island of Anglesey from the mainland of NW Wales. It is crossed by a suspension bridge designed by Thomas Telford (1819–26). The Britannia railway bridge, built by Robert Stevenson (1850), was damaged by fire in 1970. It has been rebuilt to carry a road track above the railway (1980).

● **Menander** ▶ (c. 341–c. 290 BC) Greek dramatist. The leading exponent of the ▷New Comedy, he wrote sophisticated comedies on romantic and domestic themes. His single surviving complete play is the *Dyscolus*, recovered from a papyrus in 1958, but many of his plays are known from their adaptations by Plautus and Terence.

● **Menander** ▶ (c. 160–c. 20 BC) Greek King of the Punjab and one of the heirs to ▷Alexander the Great's conquests. His capital was at Sakala (probably present-day Sialkot, Pakistan) and he commanded an extensive empire over NW India. He became a devout Buddhist.

● **menarche** ▷See puberty.

● **MENCAP** ▶ A British charity founded in 1946, as the Association of Parents of Backward Children, to improve understanding of mental handicap. It became the National Society for Mentally Handicapped Children in 1955, being authorized to add Royal to its title in 1981. It provides homes and training for the mentally handicapped and support for their families.

● **Mencius** ▶ (Mengzi or Meng-tzu; 371–289 BC) Chinese moral philosopher. He was taught by pupils of ▷Confucius and produced the *Mencius*, an exposition of Confucian thought read by Chinese schoolchildren until the 20th century. Mencius made benevolence (*ren* or *jen*) the keynote of his political philosophy. He travelled extensively, advocating that rulers should treat their subjects humanely.

● **Mencken, H(enry) L(ouis)** ▶ (1880–1956) US journalist and critic. As editor of *The Smart Set* (1914–23) and *American Mercury* (1924–33) he attacked both the political and the literary establishments. His essays were collected in *Prejudices* (6 vols, 1919–27). In *The American Language* (1919) he surveyed the development of English in America. *Newspaper Days 1899–1908* (1914) and *Heather Days 1890–1936* (1943) are autobiographical. His diaries were published in 1989.

● **Mendel, Gregor Johann** ▶ (1822–84) Austrian botanist, who discovered the fundamental principles governing the inheritance of characters in living things (*see* genetics). Mendel was a monk with a scientific education and an interest in botany. In 1856 in the monastery garden at Brünn, Moravia, he began to inbreed lines of pea plants by means of repeated self-pollination. All the dwarf plants produced dwarf offspring only, but of tall plants, only about one third were true-breeding. The majority each produced both tall plants and dwarf plants in the ratio 3:1. Mendel then crossed pure-bred tall and dwarf plants and found that all the resulting hybrids were tall. Crossing these hybrids resulted in a mixture of pure-bred dwarf, hybrid tall, and pure-bred tall plants in the ratio 1:2:1. Mendel concluded that such characteristics were determined by factors of inheritance that were contributed equally by both parents and that sorted themselves among the offspring according to simple statistical rules. He summarized these findings in two principles (▷Mendel's laws).

Mendel reported his findings in 1865 but his achievement was not appreciated until the rediscovery of his work by C. E. ▷Correns, Hugo ▷de Vries and E. von Tschermak (1871–1962) in 1900.

● **mendelevium** ▶ (Md) A synthetic element, first produced in 1955 by Ghiorso and others, by bombarding einsteinium with helium ions; it is named after the chemist Mendeleyev. At no 101; at wt (258).

● **Mendeleyev, Dimitrii Ivanovich** ▶ (1834–1907) Russian chemist, who was professor at St Petersburg from 1866 to 1890. He became interested in the subject of atomic weights after hearing ▷Cannizzaro lecture on the subject and, in 1869, succeeded in arranging the elements in order of increasing atomic weights so that those with similar properties were grouped together (*see* periodic table). Mendeleyev recognized that the rows of the table were not all of equal length and that there were gaps in the table, representing undiscovered elements. ▷*See also* Newlands, John Alexander Reina.

● **Mendel's laws** ▶ The basic principles governing the inheritance of characters, first proposed by Gregor ▷Mendel in 1865. His first law, the Law of Independent Segregation, states that the factors of inheritance (now called ▷alleles of the gene) that determine a particular characteristic segregate into separate sex cells. His second law, the Law of Independent Assortment, states that the segregation of factors for one character occurs independently of that for any other character. (This is true except for alleles of genes located on the same chromosome, which are segregated together.)

● **Mendelssohn, Felix** ▶ (Jacob Ludwig Felix Mendelssohn-Bartholdy; 1809–47) German composer; the grandson of Moses Mendelssohn. A child prodigy, his education was strictly supervised by his father. His string octet (1825) and the overture to *A Midsummer Night's Dream* (1826) demonstrated his precocious brilliance. In 1836 he became conductor of the Leipzig Gewandhaus orchestra and subsequently founded the Leipzig conservatoire. His music was popular in Britain and he was entertained by Queen Victoria. His compositions include five symphonies, overtures, the oratorios *St Paul* (1836) and *Elijah* (1846), two violin concertos, two piano concertos, chamber music, and piano music. He revived Bach's *St Matthew Passion* in 1829.

● **Mendelssohn, Moses** ▶ (1729–86) German Jewish philosopher and literary critic. He was admired by ▷Kant and ▷Lessing and sought civil rights for the Jews. He also advocated the separation of church and state, the immortality of the soul, in *Phaedon* (1767), and the existence of a personal God, in *Morgenstunden* (1785).

● **Menderes, Adnan** ▶ (1899–1961) Turkish statesman; prime minister (1950–60). His repressive policies led to an army coup in 1960 and his execution.

● **Menderes, River** ▶ (ancient name: R. Maeander; Turkish name: Büyük Menderes) A winding river in W Turkey, flowing WSW into the Aegean Sea. Its ancient name gave rise to the term ▷meander. Length: 400 km (249 mi).

● **Mendes, Sam** ▶ (Samuel Alexander M; 1965–) British theatre and film director. He achieved celebrity as the young director of London's Donmar Warehouse Theatre (from 1992). His first film, *American Beauty* (1999), earned five Academy Awards.

● **Mendès-France, Pierre** ▶ (1907–82) French statesman; prime minister (1954–55). A Radical Socialist, Mendès-France strengthened the executive, ended the war with Indochina, and granted independence to Tunisia.

● **Mendip Hills** ▶ (or Mendips) A range of limestone hills in SW England, in N Somerset, extending NW–SE and reaching 325 m (1068 ft) at Blackdown. Its many limestone features include Cheddar Gorge and the caves of Cheddar and Wookey Hole.

● **Mendoza** ▶ 32 48S 68 52W A city in W Argentina. It is the commercial centre of a wine-producing area and has a university (1939). Population (1991): 773 113.

● **Mendoza, Antonio de** ▶ (?1490–1552) Spanish colonial administrator. Mendoza was the first viceroy (1535–50) of New Spain (Mexico), where he fostered economic development and education, bringing the first printing press to the New World. He was viceroy of Peru (1551–52), where he died.

● **Menelaus** ▶ A legendary Spartan king and husband of ▷Helen. He served under his brother Agamemnon in the ▷Trojan War and after the fall of Troy won Helen back.

● **Menelik II** ▶ (1844–1913) Emperor of Ethiopia (1889–1913). He greatly expanded Ethiopia, limited the power of the nobility, and modernized the administration. In 1896 he was able to repel an Italian invasion.

● **Menem, Carlos (Saúl)** ▶ (1931–) Argentinian politician; president of Argentina (1989–99). A Peronist, he succeeded Raul Alfonsín as president and was re-elected in 1994. His free-market policies led to economic growth but provoked social unrest.

● **Menes** ▶ The first ruler of a united Egypt (c. 3100 BC); the founder of the 1st dynasty. Perhaps a legendary figure, he was said to have founded ▷Memphis.

● **Mengele, Josef** ▶ (1894–?1979) German medical scientist, notorious for atrocities committed in the German concentration camp at Auschwitz (see Oświęcim). Known as "the Angel of Death," he was camp doctor at Auschwitz from 1943 to 1945 and was subsequently held responsible for the deaths of 400 000 people, mostly Jews, many of whom died in bizarre medical experiments. After World War II he was reported to be in hiding in South America and probably died from drowning in Brazil in 1979. In 1985 a body was exhumed and identified as his; to the end of his life he denied that he had done wrong.

● **Mengistu Haile Mariam** ▶ (1937–) Ethiopian soldier and politician; head of state of Ethiopia (1977–91, as president from 1987). He helped to depose ▷Haile Selassie in 1974 and sought aid from Cuba and the Soviet Union against Somalia (1978) and against Eritrean and Tigréan separatists. He resigned in May 1991, shortly before the separatists seized power; he subsequently fled into exile in Zimbabwe.

● **Mengs, Anton Raphael** ▶ (1728–79) German painter, born in Aussig, Bohemia. An early exponent of ▷neoclassicism, he achieved a high reputation particularly in Rome, where he settled (1755), and in Spain, where he worked for Charles III. Apart from numerous portraits, his best-known work is the *Parnassus* fresco (1761; Villa Albani, Rome).

● **Mengzi** ▶ (*or* Meng-tzu) ▷See Mencius.

● **menhir** ▶ (Breton: long stone) A prehistoric ▷megalith set upright either by itself or with others in circles (e.g. ▷Stonehenge) or alignments (e.g. ▷Carnac).

● **Ménière's disease** ▶ A disease of the inner ear causing progressive deafness, tinnitus (ringing in the ear), and vertigo. The disease normally occurs in the middle-aged and elderly and treatment (medical or surgical) is not altogether successful. It is named after a French physician, P. Ménière (1799–1862).

● **Menindee Lakes** ▶ A series of lakes and reservoirs in Australia. They lie in SW New South Wales, forming part of the Darling River Conservation Scheme, and provide water for irrigation and industrial and domestic purposes.

● **meningitis** ▶ Inflammation of the meninges—the membranes that surround the brain. This is usually caused by bacteria or viruses and occurs most commonly in children. Symptoms include headache, vomiting, stiff neck, intolerance to light, tiredness, irritability, and fits. Treatment for bacterial meningitis is with antibiotics and the patient usually recovers rapidly, but meningococcal meningitis, a severe form caused by the meningococcus (*Neisseria meningitidis*), develops rapidly, may spread to the bloodstream (causing meningococcal septicaemia), and can be fatal within a week unless promptly diagnosed and treated. The Hib vaccine protects children against bacterial meningitis caused by *Haemophilus influenzae* type B. Viral meningitis is often mild, requiring no specific treatment.

● **Mennonites** ▶ A Christian sect that originated in Holland and adjacent areas in the 16th century. Their name derives from Menno Simons, who reorganized persecuted ▷Anabaptist groups after 1536. There are sizable Mennonite communities in Holland and in North America, where the first colony settled in 1683. Common ground between the doctrinally diverse Mennonite groups is their rejection of hierarchical Church organization and of infant baptism. In secular life Mennonites are pacifists and avoid public office.

● **Menno Simons** ▶ (c. 1496–1561) Dutch Anabaptist leader. A former Roman Catholic priest, Menno became the travelling shepherd of scattered ▷Anabaptist groups in N Europe, persecuted by both Roman Catholics and Reformers. His preaching of total pacifism became the mark of the ▷Mennonites, one section of the Anabaptist movement.

● **Menon, Krishna** ▶ (Vengalil Krishnan Krishna Menon; 1896–1974) Indian diplomat. In England from 1924 to 1927, he was secretary of the India League from 1929 and a major figure in the campaign for Indian independence. After this was achieved in 1947 he was high commissioner for India to the UK (1947–52) before becoming a member of the Indian legislature; he was a delegate at the UN (1952–62) and defence minister (1957–62).

● **menopause** ▶ The change of life: the time in a woman's life when the menstrual periods become irregular and finally cease because egg cells are no longer produced by the ovaries. The menopause can occur at any age between the late 30s and late 50s. Some women may experience symptoms, including flushing ("hot flushes"), palpitations, and irritability, due to reduced secretion of oestrogens. This deficiency can be helped by ▷hormone replacement therapy.

● **menorah** ▷See Hanukka.

● **Menorca** ▷See Minorca.

● **Menotti, Gian Carlo** ▶ (1911–) Italian-born US composer, living in the USA since 1928. He studied and later taught at the Curtis Institute, Philadelphia. Among his compositions are the operas *The Medium* (1946) and *The Saint of Blecker Street* (1954), which both won a Pulitzer Prize, *Goya* (1986), *Giorno di Nozze* (1988), and the television opera *Amahl and the Night Visitors* (1951). In 1958 he founded the Spoleto Festival.

● **Mensa International** ▶ An international organization, founded in the UK in 1945, the members of which are admitted on the basis of a high score in a standard intelligence test.

● **Mensheviks** ▶ One of the two factions into which the Russian Social Democratic Workers' Party split in 1903 in London. Unlike the rival ▷Bolsheviks, the Mensheviks (meaning those in the minority) believed in a large and loosely organized party. They supported Russia's participation in World War I and were prominent in the Russian Revolution until the Bolsheviks seized power in October, 1917. They were suppressed in 1922.

● **mens rea** ▷See criminal law.

● **menstruation** ▶ The monthly discharge of blood and fragments of womb lining from the vagina. This is part of the **menstrual cycle**—the sequence of events, occurring in women from the menarche (see puberty) to the ▷menopause, by which an egg cell is released from the ▷ovary. The menstrual cycle is controlled by follicle-stimulating hormone (FSH) and luteinizing hormone (LH), produced by the pituitary gland (see gonadotrophin), and ▷oestrogens and ▷progesterone secreted by the ovary. Growth of an egg cell in a follicle of the ovary is stimulated by FSH. As the egg cell matures, large quantities of oestrogen are secreted; ovulation (release of a mature egg cell) is triggered by LH. After ovulation, a corpus luteum forms within the empty follicle and secretes progesterone, which causes the lining of the womb to thicken in preparation for conception. Menstruation is the stage at which this lining breaks down and the egg cell (with blood, etc.) is expelled from the womb if conception has not occurred. Ovulation occurs at around the middle of the cycle: it may be associated with abdominal pain. Depression and irritability are common shortly before menstruation (premenstrual tension).

● **mental handicap** ▷See learning disability.

● **mental retardation** ▶ A state of arrested or incomplete development of the intellect. Mildly retarded people (with an IQ of approximately 50–70) usually make a good adjustment to life after special help with education; their condition is usually caused by inherited disorders or psychological disturbances. Severely retarded people (with an IQ of less than 50) usually require permanent help and may need care in a special home or a hospital. Severe retardation is nearly always caused by physical diseases affecting the brain, but good education improves the outcome. Mental retardation is also known as mental handicap (*see* learning disability). ▷*See also* intelligence.

● **menthol** ▶ ($C_{10}H_{20}O$) A white crystalline solid. It is a constituent of peppermint oil and is responsible for the characteristic smell of the mint plant, but can also be prepared synthetically. Menthol is used in many remedies for coughs and colds as well as in flavouring for sweets and cigarettes.

● **Menton** ▶ 43 47N 7 30E A town in SE France, in the Alpes-Maritimes department on the French Riviera near the Italian border. A popular holiday resort, it produces fruit and flowers. Population (latest est.): 25 449.

Lord Menuhin ▶ Not only outstanding as a solo violinist, Yehudi Menuhin in later years became a respected guru, speaking up for many humanitarian and environmentalist causes.

● **Menuhin, Yehudi, Baron** ▶ (1916–99) British violinist, born in the USA of Russo-Jewish parentage. A pupil of Georges Enesco, he became famous in boyhood; Elgar coached him for performances of the composer's violin concerto. From 1959 to 1968 Menuhin was director of the Bath Festival, where he also participated as a conductor. He founded the Yehudi Menuhin School for musically gifted children in 1963. He was frequently partnered in recitals by his sister, the pianist **Hephzibah Menuhin** (1920–81); another sister, **Yaltah Menuhin** (1921–2001), was also a pianist, as is his son **Jeremy Menuhin** (1951–).

● **Menzies, Sir Robert Gordon** ▶ (1894–1978) Australian statesman; prime minister as leader of the United Australia Party (1939–41) and then of the Liberal Party (1949–66). Elected to the federal parliament in 1934, he was attorney general (1934–39) before becoming prime minister as leader of the United Australia party. He resigned in 1941 and formed the Liberal Party in 1944. As Liberal prime minister he increased US influence in Australian affairs and was strongly anticommunist, attempting to disband the Australian Communist Party in 1951 and later supporting the USA in the Vietnam War. He encouraged immigration from Europe and developed the Australian universities. Loyal to the British Commonwealth, he became Lord Warden of the Cinque Ports in 1965.

● **Merca** ▶ 1 45N 44 47E A town in Somalia, on the Indian Ocean. Merca has a deepwater harbour and exports agricultural produce. Population (latest est): 100 000.

● **mercantilism** ▶ An economic doctrine that flourished in the 17th and 18th centuries. Primarily concerned with international trade, mercantilism attempted to maximize national wealth, which it identified with a nation's bullion reserves. To this end, tariffs were applied to imports in the hope of creating a ▷balance-of-trade surplus and adding to bullion reserves. Mercantilism was replaced by ▷free trade, after ▷Hume and Adam ▷Smith had shown that mercantilism merely served the self-interest of the merchant classes.

● **Mercator, Gerardus** ▶ (Gerhard Kremer; 1512–94) Flemish geographer, best known for his method of mapping the earth's surface, known as the ▷Mercator projection. He worked at Louvain, but was prosecuted for heresy in 1544 and emigrated to Protestant Germany in 1552, where he was appointed cartographer to the Duke of Cleves. In later life he prepared a book of maps, which, since it depicted Atlas supporting the earth on its cover, became known as an atlas.

● **Mercator projection** ▶ A cylindrical □map projection, originally used (1569) by Gerardus Mercator. The parallels of latitude are represented as being straight lines of equal length to the equator. The meridians are equally spaced and intersect at right angles. The correct ratio between latitude and longitude is maintained by increasing the distance between the parallels away from the equator causing increased distortion towards the Poles. Compass bearings are accurately shown and the projection is commonly used for navigation charts. The **Transverse Mercator projection** is a development of the Mercator projection but in this case the cylinder is tangential to a meridian rather than to the equator. It is used chiefly for small areas with a N–S orientation and is used in all British ▷Ordnance Survey maps.

● **Mercer, David** ▶ (1928–80) British dramatist. His plays for both television and the theatre generally concern political disillusion, insanity, and sexual relationships. He also wrote scripts for the films *Morgan, a Suitable Case for Treatment* (1965), *Family Life* (1970), and *Providence* (1977).

● **mercerization** ▶ A finishing process for cotton fabrics and yarns. Named after John Mercer (1791–1866), who investigated the process (1844), mercerization involves treating the cotton by immersion, while under tension, in a caustic soda solution, later neutralized by acid. This process causes the fibres to swell permanently; cotton thus treated dyes better and is stronger and more lustrous.

● **Merchant, Ismael** ▶ (1936–) Indian-born film producer, who is best known for his collaborations with the US director **James Ivory** (1928–). Their films together include *Shakespeare Wallah* (1964) and the literary adaptations *A Room With a View* (1986), *Howards End* (1992), *The Remains of the Day* (1993), and *The Golden Bowl* (2000). His own films as a director include *The Proprietor* (1997).

● **merchant banks** ▶ Financial institutions that became ▷acceptance houses as a result of their foreign trading as merchants. They are now involved in a variety of other businesses, including: the issue, placing, and underwriting of shares and debentures for firms (*see* issuing house); the issue of long-term loans for governments and institutions abroad; advising on the investment of funds and the management of portfolios; advising on and managing takeover bids; and dealings in foreign exchange.

● **Merchants Adventurers** ▶ An English trading company, incorporated in 1407, which controlled the export of cloth to the Continent. Its continental centre was at Bruges until 1446, when it moved to Antwerp; in 1567 it transferred to Hamburg but returned to a series of Dutch marts after 1580. The Adventurers, who rivalled the ▷Hanseatic League, were criticized for furthering their own interests at the expense of England and lost their charter in 1689.

● **Merchant Staplers** ▶ (or Company of the Merchants of the Staple) The company of between 26 and 38 English merchants that controlled the export and sale of wool from the late 13th to late 16th centuries. Exports were sold at one market (the staple), which from 1363 was Calais. At its height in the 15th century, the company declined with the growth of English manufacturing.

● **Mercia** ▶ A kingdom of Anglo-Saxon England. The Mercians were ▷Angles and their territory embraced most of central England S of the Humber between Wales and East Anglia. Mercia became a formidable power under ▷Penda (c. 634–55) and ▷Offa (757–96), who controlled England S of the Humber. Thereafter it declined and was merged in the 9th century into a united England under Wessex.

● **Mercosur** ▶ (Spanish: Southern Market; Portuguese name: Mercosul) A trading group in South America, comprising Argentina, Brazil, Paraguay, and Uruguay; Chile is an associate member. First conceived in 1991, the customs union was formally inaugurated in January, 1994. A cooperation agreement with the EU was signed in 1995.

● **Mercouri, Melina** ▶ (1925–94) Greek actress and politician; minister of culture and science (1981–85); minister of culture, youth, and sports (1985–89); minister of culture (1993–94). Her best-known films were made with the US director Jules Dassin (1911–   ), whom she married, and include *Never on Sunday* (1960) and *Topkapi* (1964). She returned to Greece from the USA in 1974 when civilian government was restored.

● **mercury** ▶ (botany) An annual or perennial herb of the genus *Mercurialis* (8 species), native to Eurasia and N Africa. The perennial dog's mercury (*M. perennis*) of woodland areas has an evil smell and is poisonous to grazing animals. Growing 15–40 cm high, it has large toothed leaves and clusters of small green male and female flowers borne on separate plants. The annual mercury (*M. annua*) occurs on wasteland and as a garden weed. Family: *Euphorbiaceae*.

● **mercury** ▶ (Hg) The only common metal that is liquid at room temperature (it has a high relative density of 13.546). It occurs chiefly as the sulphide cinnabar (HgS), from which mercury is obtained simply by heating in a current of air. The element was known in ancient Egypt, India, and China and occurs rarely in nature in the metallic state. It is used in thermometers, barometers, and batteries and as an ▷amalgam in dentistry. Compounds include the oxide (HgO), mercurous and mercuric chlorides (Hg_2Cl_2, $HgCl_2$), and the explosive mercury fulminate ($Hg(ONC)_2$), which is widely used as a detonator. Mercury and its compounds are highly poisonous and are only slowly excreted by the human body. Organo-mercury compounds, such as dimethyl mercury, $(CH_3)_2Hg$, are particularly toxic (*see* Minamata disease). At no 80; at wt 200.59; mp –38.87°C; bp 356.58°C.

● **Mercury** ▶ (astronomy) The innermost and second smallest (4880 km diameter) planet, orbiting the sun every 88 days at a mean distance of 57.9 million km. Its long period of axial rotation, 58.6 days, is two-thirds of its orbital period. Mercury can only be seen low in the twilight and early morning sky and, like the moon, exhibits ▷phases. Its surface is heavily cratered, with intervening lava-flooded plains. It has a very thin atmosphere, mainly helium and argon. ▷*See also* planetary probe.

● **Mercury** ▶ (mythology) The Roman god of commerce and astronomy, who was also the messenger of the gods. He is usually portrayed as holding a purse, and also with a cap, winged sandals, and staff, the attributes of the Greek ▷Hermes, with whom he was identified.

● **Meredith, George** ▶ (1828–1909) British poet and novelist. Educated in Germany, he returned to England to study law but embarked on a literary career instead. For many years he was dependent on literary hackwork. His long poem *Modern Love* (1862) was partly based on his unhappy marriage to Mary Ellen Nicholls, daughter of Thomas Love ▷Peacock. With his novels, including *The Egoist* (1879) and *The Tragic Comedians* (1880), he achieved critical acclaim.

● **Meredith, Owen** ▷*See* Lytton, Edward George Earle Bulwer-Lytton, 1st Baron.

● **merganser** ▶ A ▷duck belonging to a genus (*Mergus*) of the N hemisphere, also called sawbill. It occurs on inland lakes in summer and coastal regions in winter. 40–57 cm long, mergansers have a long serrated bill for feeding on worms, fish, and eels. Males have a dark-green double-crested head, a chestnut breast, and a grey-and-white back; females are brown with a white wing bar. ▷*See also* goosander.

● **merger** ▶ The amalgamation of two or more companies to form one new company; usually the shareholders of the old companies exchange their old shares for shares in the new company. **Vertical mergers** involve the amalgamation of companies specializing in different parts of the production process (e.g. a car manufacturer and a steelmaker); **horizontal mergers** involve the amalgamation of related product manufacturers (e.g. car and truck manufacturers); and **conglomerate mergers** are between firms unrelated in production. Mergers usually require government approval, as they can lead to ▷monopolies.

● **Mérida** ▶ (Latin name: Augusta Emerita) 38 55N 06 20W A town in W Spain, in Estremadura on the River Guadiana. Founded by the Romans in 25 BC, it has numerous Roman remains, including an aq-

ueduct, temples, two bridges, and a triumphal arch. Population (1911): 49 830.

● **Mérida** ▶ 20 59N 89 39W A city in E Mexico. It is the commercial and industrial centre for an agricultural area specializing in henequen (a fibre) production. It has a 16th-century cathedral and is the site of the University of Yucatán (refounded 1922). Population (1990): 557 340.

● **meridian** ▷*See* latitude and longitude.

● **meridian circle** ▶ (*or* transit circle) An instrument for determining very accurately the position of a celestial body by measuring the body's altitude and the time as it crosses the observer's meridian (which passes through the observer's zenith and N and S celestial poles). It consists of a telescope pivoted on a horizontal E–W axis so that the telescope's line of sight follows the meridian plane.

● **Mérimée, Prosper** ▶ (1803–70) French novelist. His first published works were fake translations of plays and ballads that deceived many leading scholars. His best-known works are his short novels, especially *Columba* (1841) and *Carmen* (1843), the source of Bizet's opera. He was also a distinguished historian and archaeologist, and a friend of the empress Eugénie.

● **Merino** ▶ A breed of sheep originating from Spain and noted for its long thick high-quality white fleece. Merinos are well adapted to hot arid climates and have been exported to many parts of the world, especially Australia.

● **Merionethshire** ▶ A former county of NW Wales. Under local government reorganization in 1974 it was mainly absorbed into ▷Gwynedd.

● **meristem** ▶ An area of actively dividing plant cells responsible for growth in the plant. The main meristematic regions in dicotyledon plants are the shoot tip and root tip (apical meristems) and the ▷cambium (lateral meristem). A damaged meristem produces distorted growth.

● **Merleau-Ponty, Maurice** ▶ (1908–61) French philosopher. He discussed the nature of human consciousness and its interaction with matter in *Le Structure du comportement* (1942) and *Phénoménologie de perception* (1945). In his eyes, causal and behaviouristic theories misinterpreted consciousness, as did dualism, and he accepted the Marxist view of the dependence of consciousness upon material conditions.

● **merlin** ▶ A small ▷falcon, *Falco columbarius*, occurring in moorland and heathland regions of the N hemisphere. The female is 32 cm long and is dark brown with heavily streaked underparts; the male is 26 cm long and has a grey-blue back and tail. Merlins feed chiefly on small birds caught in flight.

● **Merlin** ▶ In ▷Arthurian legend, the wizard who counsels and assists Arthur and his father, Uther Pendragon. There are various accounts of Merlin's life in ▷Geoffrey of Monmouth and later writers. He helped Uther to win Igraine, Arthur's mother, made the Round Table, cared for Arthur as a child, and gave him, or arranged for him to be given, the sword Excalibur. In old age Merlin fell in love with Nimue (*or* Vivien), who tricked him into a cave or hollow tree and left him there forever imprisoned by a spell.

● **mermaid** ▶ A legendary creature with the form of a beautiful woman above the waist and a fish below; the male counterpart is a **merman**. They are generally represented as malicious to man. Such aquatic mammals as dugongs may account for mermaid stories in mythology and folklore.

● **Merneptah** ▶ King of Egypt (c. 1236–1223 BC) of the 19th dynasty. His father ▷Ramses (II) the Great had neglected frontier defence in his old age and Merneptah faced the aggression of Libya and the Sea Peoples, whom he defeated in 1232.

● **Meroë** ▶ The capital of an ancient Nubian kingdom in the area that is now the Sudan. After ruling Egypt (c. 730–670 BC), Nubian kings established Meroë in about 600 BC. Its temples and pyramids show Egyptian influence. Before its abandonment (7th century AD), Meroë may have been the route by which iron technology reached sub-Saharan Africa.

● **Merovingians** ▶ The first Frankish ruling dynasty (*see* Franks). It was founded by Merovech, King of the Salian Franks, in the mid-5th century AD. His grandson ▷Clovis (reigned 481–511) greatly extended Merovingian possessions and the kingdom reached its zenith in the mid-6th century. The last Merovingian king, Childeric III, was deposed in 751 by the Carolingian ▷Pepin the Short.

● **Merseburg** ▶ 51 22N 12 0E A town in E Germany, on the River Saale just S of Halle. Founded in 800 AD, it has a 15th-century castle and a 13th-century cathedral. Industries include tanning, brewing, engineering, lignite mining, chemicals, machinery, and paper. Population (1989 est): 46 250.

● **Mersey, River** ▶ A river in NW England. Formed by the confluence of the Rivers Goyt and Tame at Stockport, it flows W to the Irish Sea by way of a 26 km (16 mi) long estuary, with ▷Liverpool and Birkenhead on its banks. Length: 113 km (70 mi).

● **Merseyside** ▶ A metropolitan county of NW England, created in 1974 from SW Lancashire and NW Cheshire. In 1986 its administrative powers were devolved to the unitary authorities of Sefton, Liverpool, St Helens, Knowsley, and Wirral. Area: 648 sq km (250 sq mi).

● **Mersin** ▶ 36 47N 34 37E A port in central S Turkey, the major port on the S coast. It has an oil refinery and exports wool, cotton, and agricultural produce. Population (1994 est): 523 000.

● **Merthyr Tydfil** ▶ (Welsh name: Merthyr Tudful) **1.** 51 46N 3 23W A town in SE Wales, in Merthyr Tydfil county borough on the River Taff. Formerly a world iron and steel centre based on the surrounding coalfields, it now has light and electrical engineering as its main industries and various services. Population (1991): 39 482. **2.** A county borough in SE Wales, created from part of Mid Glamorgan in 1996. Area: 111 sq km (43 sq mi). Population (1996 est): 58 100.

● **Merton** ▶ A mainly residential borough of SW Greater London, created in 1965 from the former urban district and adjacent boroughs, including ▷Wimbledon. Area: 38 sq km (15 sq mi). Population (1996 est): 182 300.

● **Meru, Mount** ▶ In Hindu mythology, the cosmic mountain at the centre of the universe. It is symbolized in the massive pyramidal towers of Hindu shrines.

● **Merv** ▷*See* Melitopol.

● **mesa** ▶ An isolated flat-topped hill occurring in areas of long-eroded horizontally bedded strata, usually in semiarid climates. The upper slopes are steep, and gentle lower slopes merge into the surrounding plain. The cap rock is of resistant material. Further erosion may reduce the mesa to a ▷butte.

● **Mesa Verde** ▶ A high plateau in the USA, in SW Colorado. It contains the remains of numerous cliff dwellings, spanning four archaeological periods.

● **mescaline** ▶ A hallucinogenic drug obtained from the ▷peyote cactus of Mexico, where it was once widely used in religious ceremonies. The effect of mescaline varies from individual to individual; it does not cause serious dependence and the hallucinations are mostly visual.

● **Mesembryanthemum** ▷*See* fig marigold.

● **Meshed** ▷*See* Mashhad.

● **Mesmer, Franz Anton** ▶ (1734–1815) German physician, who claimed to cure diseases by correcting the flow of "animal magnetism" in his patients' bodies during séance-like group sessions. Investigation of "mesmerism" by a commission concluded that any cures were due to the powers of suggestion. Mesmer's claims stimulated serious study of hypnosis by such men as James Braid (1795–1860).

● **Mesoamerican languages** ▶ A geographical classification of the languages spoken by the American Indian peoples of Mexico, Guatemala, Honduras, Belize, El Salvador, and Nicaragua. It includes around 70 languages. The main families are: the Totonac-Mayan (e.g. Mayan); Uto-Aztecan (e.g. ▷Nahuatl) the Otomangean (e.g. Mixtec); the Hokan-Coahuiltecan; and Tarascan.

● **Mesolithic** ▶ The middle division of the ▷Stone Age, especially in

Mesolithic ▶ A terracotta statuette from the late Mesolithic period (5th millennium BC) found in Serbia.

N Europe, where a distinct cultural stage, the ▷Maglemosian, intervened between the last ice age and the evolution of farming communities. Generally, the Mesolithic is characterized by production of microliths (very minute stone tools), which were hafted into wooden, bone, or other handles. The dog was the only domesticated animal. Outside Europe the Mesolithic distinction is less useful: the Middle Eastern transition between ▷Palaeolithic and ▷Neolithic was less definable and in Japan pottery, a Neolithic characteristic, coexisted with microlith manufacture.

● **mesons** ▶ A group of unstable elementary particles (lifetimes between 10^{-8} and 10^{-15} second) that are classified as hadrons; each meson is believed to consist of a quark-antiquark pair (*see* particle physics). ▷*See* muon.

● **mesophyll** ▶ The inner tissue of the leaf blade of a ⊓plant, between the two layers of epidermis. In dicotyledons the mesophyll consists of two layers: an upper palisade layer containing many chloroplasts and constituting the plant's principal photosynthetic tissue; and a lower spongy mesophyll with intercellular air spaces, linked to the stomata, through which gases pass between the leaf and the atmosphere. In monocotyledons these two layers are often not apparent.

● **Mesopotamia** ▶ The region between the Rivers Tigris and Euphrates, "the land between two rivers." The Sumerians (*see* Sumer) settled in S Mesopotamia about 4000 BC to cultivate the alluvial land left by flooding. They established the world's first civilization and founded city states, such as ▷Ur, ▷Kish, and ▷Uruk. ▷Babylon became Mesopotamia's capital under ▷Hammurabi. After his death Mesopotamia was overrun by Kassites, Assyrians, and Persians.

● **Mesosaurus** ▶ A freshwater reptile of the late Carboniferous and early Permian periods (around 280 million years ago). It was 1 m long and had a long narrow skull with numerous teeth for straining crustaceans from water.

● **Mesozoic era** ► The geological era following the Palaeozoic and preceding the Cenozoic. It contains the Triassic, Jurassic, and Cretaceous periods, and lasted from about 240 to 65 million years ago. The reptiles were at their greatest development during this era but became extinct before the end of it. The Alpine orogeny began at the end of the Mesozoic.

● **mesquite** ► A spiny shrub or small tree, of the genus *Prosopis*, with deep penetrating roots, native to the SW USA and Mexico. Up to 15 m tall, it has compound leaves, with many narrow leaflets, and creamy flower catkins producing long narrow pods, which are used as cattlefeed. The hard wood is sometimes used in furniture. Family: ▷*Leguminosae*.

● **Messager, André (Charles Prosper)** ► (1853–1929) French composer and conductor. His works include the operetta *Véronique* (1898) and the ballet *Les Deux Pigeons* (1886).

● **Messalina, Valeria** ► (c. 26–48 AD) The third wife of Emperor Claudius and mother of Britannicus (41–55) and Octavia (the wife of Nero). Messalina was notorious for her promiscuity and, according to Roman scandal, contracted a bigamous and treacherous marriage to the senator Gaius Silius, for which they were both executed.

● **Messerschmitt, Willy** ► (1898–1978) German ▯aircraft designer. He is best known for his World War II military planes, particularly the Me-109 fighter (1935) and the Me-262, the first jet fighter.

● **Messiaen, Olivier** ► (1908–92) French composer, organist, and teacher. Messiaen was a pupil of Paul Dukas and Marcel Dupré. In 1931 he was appointed organist of La Trinité in Paris. His music was influenced by Catholic mysticism, eastern music, and birdsong. His works include *La Nativité du Seigneur* (1935), the symphony *Turangalîla* (1948), the *Quatuor pour la fin du temps* (1941), and *La Transfiguration* (1965–69). His opera *St Francis d'Assise* had its British premiere in 1986.

● **Messiah** ► The Jewish concept of an anointed (Hebrew: *mashiah*) person sent by God to improve the lot of the Jews, of man, or of the universe. Messianic ideas occur in many religions. The concept occurs in various forms in the ▷Old Testament, but usually looking forward to a kingly redeemer (on the model of David) rather than a godly saviour (as in the New Testament). For the Jews during and after the ▷Babylonian exile, the concept had particular prominence and there are many who believe that the survival of Judaism owes much to the persistent hope of a messianic event.

In ▷Christianity, this event occurred with the birth of ▷Jesus Christ (Greek *christos*: anointed one), though whether or not Jesus claimed to be the Messiah is not clear; the Gospel of St Mark (14:62) claims that he did. The issue of whether or not Jesus is the Messiah remains one of the main differences between Christianity and Judaism.

● **Messier, Charles** ► (1730–1817) French astronomer. In 1760 he began the **Messier catalogue**, which listed 109 bright nonstellar celestial objects and was published in 1784–86. The objects were given a number preceded by the letter M, as in M31—the Andromeda galaxy. They are mainly galaxies and star clusters together with some nebulae.

● **Messina** ► 38 13N 15 33E A port in Italy, in NE Sicily on the Strait of Messina. Originally known as Zancle, it was successively occupied by Greeks, Carthaginians, Mamertines, Romans, Saracens, Normans, and Spaniards. In 1860 it became part of a united Italy. Most of its old buildings were destroyed by severe earthquakes in 1783 and 1903. It has a university (1549) and its manufactures include macaroni, chemicals, and soap. Population (1996 est): 263 092.

● **Messina, Strait of** ► A channel in the central Mediterranean Sea, between Italy and Sicily and narrowing to 3 km (2 mi). The rocks on the Italian side and the whirlpool on the Sicilian are possibly the origin of the myth of ▷Scylla and Charybdis.

● **Messys, Quentin** ▷*See* Massys, Quentin.

● **Meštrović, Ivan** ► (1883–1962) US sculptor, born in Yugoslavia. Trained at the Vienna Academy, Meštrović enjoyed an international reputation with his religious and portrait sculptures. His sitters included Herbert Hoover, Pope Pius XI, and Sir Thomas Beecham. He became a US citizen in 1954.

● **metabolism** ► The processes and chemical reactions that occur in living organisms in order to maintain life. **Anabolism** involves building up tissues and organs using simple substances, such as amino acids, simple sugars, etc., to construct the proteins, carbohydrates, and fats of which they are made. These processes require energy, which is provided by the oxidation of nutrients or the body's own food reserves. Oxidation and all other processes involving the chemical breakdown of substances with the production of waste products are known collectively as **catabolism**. Basal metabolism is the energy required to maintain vital functions (e.g. respiration, circulation) with the body at rest. It is controlled by thyroid hormones (*see* thyroid gland) and expressed in terms of **basal metabolic rate** (BMR)—the amount of heat released per unit of body surface area per unit of time. This is usually calculated by measuring the amount of oxygen consumed by the subject or (less commonly) by estimating the amount of heat produced by the body. The BMR varies between species and between individuals of the same species: among humans it is influenced by the age and sex of the individual, being highest in children.

● **metal** ► An element that is usually a hard crystalline solid, opaque, malleable, a good conductor of heat and electricity, and forms a salt and hydrogen when reacted with an acid and a salt and water when reacted with an alkali. Not all metals have all these properties, however: mercury is a liquid at normal temperatures, sodium is soft, and antimony is brittle. Of the 70 odd metals known, the most important are the heavy metals (iron, copper, lead, and zinc) used in engineering and the rarer heavy metals (nickel, chromium, tungsten, etc.) used in ▷alloys. Other commercially important metals are the ▷noble metals (gold, silver, platinum, and mercury) and the light metals (aluminium and magnesium). Chemically important metals include the ▷alkali metals (sodium, potassium, and lithium), the ▷alkaline-earth metals (calcium, barium, etc.), and the rare-earth metals (*see* lanthanides). Uranium is important in ▷nuclear energy.

Most metals occur in the earth's crust in the combined state and have to be mined (*see* mining and quarrying) before being extracted from their ores (*see* metallurgy). The extracted metal is then usually formed into an alloy (*see also* steel) before being ready for use.

● **metal detector** ► A device for detecting the presence of metal, usually below ground. It is used to trace pipework and by archaeologists and others seeking buried metal. Developed from wartime mine detectors, they usually consist of an electronic circuit that oscillates at a frequency controlled by an induction coil. The inductance of the coil, which is contained in the search head of the device, is altered in the presence of metal. The resulting change in frequency creates an audible tone in headphones or causes a light to flash. Their indiscriminate use on registered archaeological sites is restricted in many countries.

● **metal fatigue** ► The deterioration of metal caused by repeated stresses. Fatigue, which eventually leads to failure, occurs in vibrating parts of machinery, but only when the stresses are above a critical value, known as the endurance limit. It is important in the design of aircraft, where high engine speeds and high stresses are unavoidable.

● **metallography** ► The study of the crystalline structure of metals. It includes various techniques and is used to test steel after ▷heat treatment. Usually a small sample is taken from a batch and polished before being examined under a microscope for cracks, impurities, or holes. The polished surface may also be treated chemically to show up the different constituents of an alloy or to highlight cracks. In 1911 Max von ▷Laue used X-rays to show that the atoms in metals are arranged in a regular geometrical fashion, i.e. they are crystalline. His technique of ▷X-ray diffraction is still used.

● **metalloids** ► Elements displaying the physical and chemical properties both of ▷metals and nonmetals. Examples of metalloids are arsenic and germanium, which both have metallic and nonmetallic allotropes. Chemically, their behaviour is intermediate between metals and nonmetals in that they may form positive ions as well as covalently bonded compounds. They are often ▷semiconductors.

● **metallurgy** ► The science and technology of producing metals. It includes the extraction of metals from their ores, alloying to form materials with specific properties, and ▷heat treatment to improve their properties. The art of working metals was known as early as 3500 BC, when copper, lead, tin, gold, and silver were in use. Modern metallurgy is concerned primarily with metals that are abundant and useful (*see* steel). Metallurgy originally developed by finding new ▷alloys and treatments by trial and error. Techniques, such as ▷metallography, have reduced the element of chance by identifying the factors in the microscopic structure of metals that contribute to hardness, strength, and ductility.

● **metamorphic rock** ► One of the three major rock categories (*compare* igneous rock; sedimentary rock) consisting of rocks produced by the alteration (in the solid state) of existing rocks by heat, pressure, and chemically active fluids. Contact (*or* thermal) metamorphism occurs around igneous intrusions and results from heat alone. Regional metamorphism, extending over large areas, results from the heat and pressure created by crustal deformation. Dislocation metamorphism results from localized mechanical deformation, as along fault planes. Metamorphic rocks tend to be resistant to denudation and often form upland masses. Marble is a metamorphic rock formed from recrystallized limestone.

● **metamorphosis** ► The process in animals by which a ▷larva changes into an adult. This radical change of internal and external body structures may be gradual or abrupt. Certain insects, such as dragonflies, undergo incomplete metamorphosis, during which successive stages (known as nymphs) become increasingly like the adult through a series of moults. In complete metamorphosis, seen in such insects as butterflies and houseflies, the larva passes into a quiescent pupal stage, during which the adult tissues are developed. Metamorphosis also occurs in amphibians (*see* frog). The process in insects and amphibians is controlled by hormones.

● **metaphor** ► A figure of speech in which one thing is described in terms of another. The comparison is implicit, lacking such words as *like* or *as* (*see* simile). The metaphor is a common feature of ordinary language, as in such phrases as "time flies" and "to lose one's head," and is a fundamental poetic device. This example is from Shakespeare's *Macbeth*:

Life's but a walking shadow, a poor player
That struts and frets his hour upon the stage.

● **metaphysical painting** ► A style of painting practised by Carlo Carrà (1881–1966) and Giorgio de ▷Chirico in the second decade of the 20th century. Together they established a school in Ferrara in 1917. They illustrated the mystery behind everyday reality by depicting dreamlike illusions, characterized by hallucinatory lighting, incongruous juxtapositions of objects, and the use of mannequins rather than people. ▷Surrealism adopted many of their ideas.

● **metaphysical poets** ► A group of 17th-century English poets whose work was characterized by intellectual wit and ingenuity, especially in their use of elaborate figures of speech. The leading poet was John ▷Donne, and his successors included George ▷Herbert, Henry ▷Vaughan, Andrew ▷Marvell, and Abraham ▷Cowley. They frequently employed colloquial speech rhythms in both their secular and their religious verse. The influential criticism of T. S. Eliot, who praised their union of intellect and emotion, helped to establish their high reputation in the 20th century.

● **metaphysics** ► The study of existence or being in general. The term derives from the title given to a group of Aristotle's writings by the philosopher Andronicus of Rhodes (1st century BC). The status of metaphysics has been much debated; ▷Kant thought this kind of investigation impossible because our minds can only cope with the phenomenal world or the world of appearances and ▷Ayer used the word in *Language, Truth and Logic* (1936) as a pejorative term to indicate the meaninglessness of much traditional philosophy. However, with ▷ethics and ▷epistemology, metaphysics is still held to be one of the main divisions of philosophy.

● **Metastasio, Pietro** ► (Pietro Antonio Domenico Trapassi; 1698–1782) Italian poet and librettist. In 1730 he was appointed court poet in Vienna, where he wrote classical libretti. These include *L'Adriano* (1731) and *La clemenza di Tito* (1732), which has been set to music by many composers.

● **Metaxas, Ioannis** ► (1871–1941) Greek general; dictator (1936–

41). After the monarchy was re-established in 1935, he became premier and, with George II's support, dictator. He led Greek resistance to the Italian invasion in World War II.

● **metayage** ► A type of land tenure in which rent is paid in kind. Metayage, a French word (from Latin *medietas*, half), was at one time the dominant form of tenure in S France, involving payment of approximately half the tenant's output.

● **Metazoa** ► In traditional classification systems, a subkingdom of animals whose bodies consist of many cells differentiated and coordinated to perform specialized functions. It excludes the single-celled ▷protozoa and the *Parazoa* (*see* sponge). In modern classifications, the protozoa are placed in the kingdom *Protoctista* and the animal kingdom is divided into the subkingdoms *Parazoa* and *Eumetazoa*.

● **Metchnikov, Ilya Ilich** ► (*or* I. I. Mechnikov; 1845–1916) Russian zoologist, who discovered that certain cells in animals could surround and engulf foreign particles, such as disease-causing bacteria. He called these cells ▷phagocytes and was awarded, with Paul ▷Ehrlich, the 1908 Nobel Prize.

● **metempsychosis** ▷*See* reincarnation.

● **meteor** ► A streak of light seen in the night sky when a **meteoroid**—an interplanetary rock or dust particle, usually with a mass from 10^{-7} to 10^{-3} gram but sometimes weighing over 10 kg—enters and burns up in the earth's atmosphere. A decaying ▷comet gradually produces a **meteor stream** of meteoroids around its orbit. When the earth passes through a meteor stream, an often spectacular **meteor shower** is observed, usually at the same time each year. The August Perseids and December Geminids are examples. A **meteorite** is a large piece of interplanetary debris (mass usually over 100 kg) that falls to the earth's surface, usually breaking up in the process. It produces a brilliant meteor. Meteorite composition is either principally iron or stone, or an intermediate mixture. Meteorites were formed early in the history of the solar system and most are believed to be fragments of minor planets. The rare fragile stony carbonaceous chondrites are possibly cometary fragments.

● **meteorology** ► The study of the physics, chemistry, and movements of the ▷atmosphere and its interactions with the ground surface. The troposphere and stratosphere, the lower layers of the atmosphere in which most weather phenomena occur, are the chief focuses of meteorology and much attention has been paid to the explanation of surface weather and to weather forecasting. **Weather** is the state of atmospheric conditions (including temperature, sunshine, wind, clouds, and precipitation) at a particular place and time. A **weather forecast** is a prediction of what weather conditions will be over a stated future period; it is made by studying weather maps, especially those obtained from satellites (often feeding the observations into a computer). Short-term forecasts are made usually for a period of 24 hours (less for specialized uses) and long-range forecasts may be made for a month ahead although they are considerably less accurate. Weather forecasts are essential to shipping and aviation and are of use to many other bodies, including power authorities (predicting cold spells) and transport authorities (predicting snow, ice, and fog), as well as to farmers. Attempts have been made to modify weather, including cloud seeding, hurricane steering, and fog clearance. ▷*See also* climate. □ p. 820.

● **methadone** ► A powerful ▷narcotic drug with pain-relieving effects, which is similar to morphine but produces less sedation. It is used to relieve severe pain in terminal illness and also to treat heroin addiction, as it reduces the withdrawal symptoms of heroin and is said to be less addictive.

● **methanal** ► (*or* formaldehyde; HCHO) A colourless toxic gaseous aldehyde. It dissolves in water to produce a solution known as **formalin**, which is used as a preservative. Methanal is made by the catalytic oxidation of ▷methanol or petroleum gas and is used to make synthetic resins.

● **methane** ► (CH_4) A colourless odourless flammable gas that is the main constituent of ▷natural gas. It is the simplest member of the ▷alkane series and is used as a fuel and a source of other chemicals. Methane is produced in nature by the decay of vegetable matter

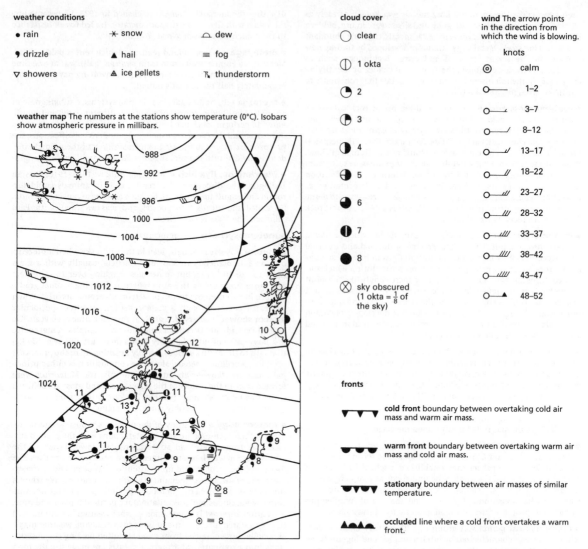

weather conditions

- rain   ✳ snow   ⌂ dew
🮥 drizzle   ▲ hail   ≡ fog
▽ showers   △ ice pellets   ⏚ thunderstorm

weather map The numbers at the stations show temperature (0°C). Isobars show atmospheric pressure in millibars.

cloud cover

○ clear

◖ 1 okta

◕ 2

◕ 3

◑ 4

◕ 5

◕ 6

◐ 7

● 8

⊗ sky obscured
(1 okta = $\frac{1}{8}$ of
the sky)

wind The arrow points in the direction from which the wind is blowing.

knots

◉   calm

○—   1–2

○—⟍   3–7

○—⟍   8–12

○—⟋   13–17

○—⟍   18–22

○—⟍⟍   23–27

○—⟍⟍   28–32

○—⟍⟍⟍   33–37

○—⟍⟍⟍   38–42

○—⟍⟍⟍⟍   43–47

○—▲   48–52

fronts

▼▼▼ **cold front** boundary between overtaking cold air mass and warm air mass.

●●● **warm front** boundary between overtaking warm air mass and cold air mass.

▼●▼ **stationary** boundary between air masses of similar temperature.

▲▲▲ **occluded** line where a cold front overtakes a warm front.

meteorology ► Internationally agreed symbols are used throughout the world by meteorological stations to represent current weather conditions. These are plotted on weather maps from which forecasts can be made.

under water, rising in bubbles from marshes as **marsh gas**. Coal gas also contains methane and is found in coalmines. Recently the generation of methane from sewage has been investigated as an ▷alternative energy source. It burns with a clear blue flame. ▷*See also* greenhouse effect.

● **methanoic acid** ► (*or* formic acid; HCOOH) A colourless corrosive liquid ▷fatty acid with a pungent smell. It is made industrially by treating sodium methanoate (sodium formate; HCOONa) with sulphuric acid and is used in textile finishing and chemical manufacture. Methanoic acid occurs naturally in nettles and insects. The older name, formic acid, comes from the Latin *formica*, ant, whose sting is due to the secretion of formic acid.

● **methanol** ► (methyl alcohol *or* wood alcohol; CH₃OH) A colourless poisonous flammable liquid. Originally produced by distillation of wood, it is now usually made from hydrogen and carbon monoxide by high-pressure ▷catalysis. It is used as a solvent, antifreeze, and a raw material for making other chemicals. ▷*See also* methylated spirits.

● **method acting** ▷*See* Actors' Studio.

● **Methodism** ► The Christian denomination that developed out of

the religious practices advocated by the ▷Wesley brothers. Although not conceived initially as an institution separate from the Church of England, to which it is very close in doctrinal matters, Methodism evolved its own church organization during the 1790s. The supreme decision-making body is the Conference; local societies (congregations) are highly organized and pastoral and missionary work are major concerns. Methodism in the USA, where it dates from the 1780s and is the second largest Protestant denomination (after the Baptists), accounts for 80% of all Methodists. In the UK Methodism has declined more rapidly than any other mainstream denomination, leading to some talk of a possible reunion with the Anglican Churches.

● **Methodius, St** ▷*See* Cyril, St.

● **Methuselah** ► In the Old Testament, a patriarch and the grandfather of ▷Noah. According to Genesis, he lived 969 years.

● **methyl alcohol** ▷*See* methanol.

● **methylated spirits** ► A form of ▷ethanol (ethyl alcohol) that has been made unsuitable for drinking (and is therefore duty free) by the addition of about 9.5% of methanol (methyl alcohol), about 0.5% of pyridine, and a methyl violet dye (as a warning that it is dangerous to drink). In this form it has many household uses, especially as a fuel for spirit burners. It is sometimes drunk by desperate alcoholics, in whom it can cause blindness and other serious medical conditions. Industrial methylated spirits (IMS) consists of ethanol with about 5% of methanol and no pyridine. It is used as a solvent.

● **metre** ▶ (m) The unit of length in the ▷metric system. Originally defined in 1791 as one ten-millionth of the length of the quadrant of the earth's meridian through Paris, it was redefined in 1927 as the distance between two marks on a platinum-iridium bar. It is now defined (General Conference on Weights and Measures, 1983) as the length of the path travelled by light in a vacuum in 1/299 792 458 second, which replaces the 1960 definition based on the emission of a krypton lamp.

● **metre** ▶ (poetry) The rhythmic pattern of a line of verse measured in terms of basic metrical units or feet. In accentual verse, as in English, a foot consists of various arrangements of stressed (′) and unstressed (˘) syllables. In classical Greek and Latin verse, the quantity or length rather than the stress of syllables determines the foot. In English the most common feet are the iamb (˘ ′), the trochee (′ ˘), the anapaest (˘ ˘ ′), the dactyl (′ ˘ ˘), and the spondee (′ ′). A typical line of ▷blank verse with five iambs is known as an iambic pentameter. Most traditional poetic forms, such as the ▷sonnet and ▷heroic couplet, are written according to strict metrical patterns. Many poets of the late 19th and 20th centuries have written in free verse, which has no regular metre or line length, or syllabic verse, in which each line has a fixed number of syllables but no regular pattern of stress.

● **metric system** ▶ A system of measurement based on the decimal system. First suggested in 1585 by Simon Stevin (1548–1620), an inspector of dykes in the Low Countries, it was not given formal acceptance until 1795, when a French law provided definitions for the ▷metre, ▷are, ▷stere, ▷litre, and gram. In 1799 a subsequent law established legal standards, made of platinum, for the metre and the kilogram. However, this form of the metric system was not widely used, even in France, until the 1830s; during this period it was also adopted by most European countries.

Although the metric system was authorized in the UK in 1864, bills for its compulsory adoption were defeated in parliament in 1897 and again in 1907. British reluctance to abandon its own "Imperial units" did not weaken until 1963, when the Imperial yard and pound were given legal definitions in terms of metric units (e.g. the yard is now defined as 0.9144 metre exactly). By 1969 the **Metrication Board** had been set up with the target of completing the metrication of British industry and commerce by 1975. This target was not met and the Board was disbanded in April 1980. From 1 January 2000 an EU regulation was adopted into British law, making it illegal to sell goods in any measure other than grams, kilograms, millimetres, and metres (with exceptions for beer and milk).

In science, former metric systems (such as the ▷c.g.s. system and the ▷m.k.s. system) have been replaced by ▷SI units.

● **metrology** ▶ The science of measurement. The scientific method is based on making accurate measurements, i.e. of expressing the magnitude of a physical quantity (say, length) in terms of a number and a unit (say, metres). Metrologists study methods of making these accurate measurements and of deciding what units should be used and how they should be defined. Modern metrology is based on ▷SI units and the methods of defining the system's seven basic units. The decision to adopt this system was taken in 1960 by metrologists from 30 nations meeting at the Conférence Générale des Poids et Mesures.

● **metronome** ▶ A small device consisting of a pendulum with a small sliding weight on it, which can be regulated to make the pendulum beat at a desired number of beats per minute. The most common type is the clockwork metronome invented by J. N. Maelzel (1770–1838); electric metronomes also exist. Metronome markings are often given in musical scores to indicate the exact speed of the music.

● **Metropolitan Museum of Art** ▶ The principal museum in New York City and one of the most important in the world. Founded in 1870, it was opened in its present premises in Central Park in 1880. Its enormous collection comprises paintings, drawings, sculptures,

ceramics, furniture, etc., from many periods and countries, including China, ancient Egypt, Greece, and Rome. Since 1938 its collection of medieval art has been housed in the Cloisters, built in Fort Tyron Park, Manhattan, from fragments of medieval monasteries and churches.

● **Metropolitan Opera Association** ▶ The principal US opera company, founded in New York in 1883. ▷Caruso sang regularly with the company from 1904 to 1921. The general manager from 1950 to 1972 was Sir Rudolf Bing (1902–97). The company occupied the Metropolitan Opera House until 1966, when it moved into the Lincoln Centre for the Performing Arts, the original building being demolished.

● **Metsu, Gabriel** ▶ (1629–67) Dutch painter, who was born in Leyden but lived in Amsterdam from about 1650. His early subjects were often religious but he is better known for his interiors showing middle-class life in such paintings as *The Duet* (National Gallery, London).

● **Metsys, Quentin** ▷*See* Massys, Quentin.

● **Metternich, Klemens Wenzel Nepomuk Lothar, Fürst von** ▶ (1773–1859) Austrian statesman, the leading figure in European diplomacy from the fall of Napoleon (1815) until the the Revolutions of 1848. As foreign minister (1809–48) he sought to maintain the balance of power in Europe, supporting dynastic monarchies and suppressing liberalism. His policies dominated the great Congresses of ▷Vienna (1814–15), ▷Aix-la-Chapelle (1818), Troppau (1820), Laibach (1821), and Verona (1822). The Revolution of 1848 forced him to seek refuge in Britain, the constitutional monarchy of which he had always condemned.

● **Metz** ▶ (Latin name: Divodorum) 49 07N 6 11E A city in NE France, the capital of the Moselle department on the River Moselle. The centre of the Lorraine coal and metal industries, it trades in wine and agricultural products and has varied manufacturing industries. It has a fine cathedral (13th–16th centuries) and a university (1971).

History: part of the Holy Roman Empire until seized by France (1552), it fell to Germany (1871) but returned to France after World War I. Population (1990): 123 920.

● **Meuse, River** ▶ (Dutch and Flemish name: Maas) A river in W Europe. Rising in NE France and flowing mainly N past Liège in Belgium and Maastricht in the S Netherlands, it enters the North Sea at the Rhine Delta. It was the scene of heavy fighting in World War I (1914) and World War II (1940). Its lower course is a commercial waterway. Length: 926 km (575 mi).

● **Mewar** ▷*See* Udaipur.

● **Mexicali** ▶ 32 36N 115 30W A city in the extreme NW of Mexico, on the US border. It is the commercial centre for a rich irrigated agricultural area. Population (1990): 602 391.

● **Mexican War** ▶ (1846–48) The war between Mexico and the USA over disputed border territory. Military operations began when Gen Zachary ▷Taylor invaded New Mexico and ended with the fall of Mexico City (1847). Peace was concluded with the Treaty of ▷Guadalupe Hidalgo.

● **Mexico, United States of** ▶ A country in North America between the Gulf of Mexico and the Pacific Ocean. Narrow coastal plains rise to high mountain ranges in the interior, which include the volcano Popocatépetl. Much of the N is arid with tropical forest in the S, especially in the Yucatán Peninsula in the SE (the only extensive low-lying area). Most of the population is of mixed Indian and Spanish descent.

Economy: Mexico now ranks among the world's main oil-producing countries following substantial finds in several areas, the most recent being along the E coastline of the states of Tamaulipas and Veracruz. The great majority of exported oil goes to the USA. Mexico also has large reserves of natural gas and there are substantial deposits of uranium; in 1988 its first nuclear power station went into operation. Other minerals extracted include iron ore, zinc, sulphur, silver, and copper, and Mexico is the world's largest producer of fluorite and graphite. Manufacturing industry has grown considerably since the 1970s; the chief manufactured exports include motor vehicles and engines as well as iron and steel goods. Agriculture employs about one fifth of the population but remains relatively underdeveloped. Maize is the main food crop; cash crops include cotton, sugar, coffee, and fruit and vegetables (including chilli peppers); Mexican species of *Agave* yield tequila and sisal hemp. Fishing has been developed considerably in recent decades and important catches include sardines, shrimps, and oysters. Tourism is an important source of foreign currency. Economic pressures in the 1980s led to high inflation, devaluation of the peso, and rescheduling of Mexico's debts by the International Monetary Fund. Despite government austerity measures, the same problems of inflation, unmanageable debt levels, and a soaring trade deficit recurred in the mid- and late 1990s.

History: NW Mexico was the site of the Mayan civilization from the 2nd to the 13th centuries AD, and between the 8th and the 12th centuries the ▷Toltecs flourished in the N central area. The 14th century saw the rise of the ▷Aztecs, whose capital was at Tenochtitlán, the site of present-day Mexico City. The Aztecs were conquered by the Spanish under Cortés in 1521 and Mexico became part of the viceroyalty of New Spain. The struggle for independence from Spain began in 1810 and was achieved under ▷Itúrbide in 1821. A turbulent period dominated by ▷Santa Anna was followed by the ▷Mexican War (1846–48), in which much territory was lost to the USA. In 1864 ▷Maximilian, Archduke of Austria, was installed as emperor by the French, but in 1867 he was shot in the successful anti-French revolution led by Benito Juárez. In 1911 the long dictatorship of Porfirio Díaz (1830–1915) ended in an uprising under Francisco Madera. The Mexican Revolution (1910–40) produced the constitution of 1917, the democratic goals of which have been the declared aims of subsequent governments. Mexican politics has long been dominated by the Party of Institutionalized Revolution (PRI), which remained the governing party from 1929 until 2000 despite repeated allegations of electoral fraud. The PRI lost its parliamentary majority in 1997 and was finally ousted in the elections of 2000, when it was defeated by an Alliance for Change led by Vicente Fox. In 1994 and 1995 there were armed uprisings of indigenous peoples from the poverty-stricken southern states, led by the Zapatista National Liberation Army (ZNLA). Several new guerrilla groups emerged in the late 1990s. Mexico is a member of the OAS and signed the ▷North American Free Trade Agreement in 1993 (effective from 1 January, 1994).

United States of Mexico

Head of state	President Ernesto Zedillo
Official language	Spanish; Indian languages, especially Nahuatl, are widely spoken
Official currency	Mexican peso of 100 centavos
Area	1 967 183 sq km (761 530 sq mi)
Population (1999 est)	97 367 000
Capital	Mexico City
Main port	Veracruz

● **Mexico City** ▶ (Spanish name: Ciudad de México) 19 25N 99 10W The capital of Mexico, in the S of the high central plateau at a height of 2380 m (7800 ft), surrounded by mountains. The 14th-century Aztec city of **Tenochtitlán** (built on a lake, since filled in) had a population of almost half a million when it was destroyed by Cortés in 1521. A new Spanish city was built on the site and it rapidly became the most important in the New World. It was captured by the USA and then by France in the 19th century and in the 20th century was the centre of several revolutions. It now has considerable industry and suffers atmospheric pollution. It is the site of the National Autonomous University of Mexico (founded in 1551), the national library, a famous school of mining engineering, the museum (containing the Aztec Calendar Stone), and the Palace of Fine Arts Theatre. Other famous landmarks include the cathedral (16th–19th centuries) and the 17th-century Palacio National. In 1985 the city was devastated by an earthquake in which at least 10 000 people died. Population (1990): 14 987 051.

● **Meyerbeer, Giacomo** ▶ (Jacob Liebmann Beer; 1791–1864) German composer and pianist. A child prodigy, he studied the piano with Clementi and composition with Abbé Vogler (1749–1814). His early German operas failed while those in the more superficial Italian style were more successful. In Paris he composed the spectacular works *Robert le Diable* (1831), *Les Huguenots* (1836), and *L'Africaine* (performed posthumously; 1865).

● **Meyerhof, Otto Fritz** ▶ (1884–1951) US biochemist, born in Germany, who showed that glycogen in muscles is broken down anaerobically into lactic acid when the muscle is working. He shared the 1922 Nobel Prize with Archibald ▷Hill.

● **Meyerhold, Vsevolod Emilievich** ▶ (1874–?1940) Russian theatre director. He joined the Moscow Art Theatre in 1898, but rejected the naturalism of ▷Stanislavsky and experimented with a symbolic drama in which the actor's individual role was reduced. He supported the Revolution and joined the Bolshevik Party in 1918. In the 1920s he was the first director to specialize in producing Soviet plays, but fell out of favour with the government in the 1930s. In 1938 he was arrested and imprisoned; he was probably executed in 1940.

● **mezuza** ▶ In Judaism a small box or case containing a parchment on which is inscribed the *Shema* (a Hebrew prayer; Deuteronomy 6.4–9). The mezuza is attached to the right front doorpost of Jewish households and to the right doorposts of all inhabited rooms. Its purpose is to serve as a visible reminder to Jews of their obligations to God, especially for having delivered them from slavery in Egypt. When the Egyptian first-born were slain by God, He passed over the houses of the Jews, which were identified by sheep's blood on the doorposts (Exodus 12.5–7). ▷*See* Passover.

● **Mezzogiorno** ▶ (Italian: midday) Southern Italy; the name refers to the heat of the region, which is economically, socially, and politically backward. After the unification of Italy in the 19th century the development of the N received greater attention from the central government than the S, where local government was ineffectual, the ▷Mafia flourished, and the gulf between landowners and peasants was considerable. Despite special government aid during the 20th century, the problems are still largely unsolved.

● **mezzo-soprano** ▷*See* soprano.

● **mezzotint** ▶ A technique of printing tonal areas (as opposed to lines), invented by a German officer, Ludwig von Sieger (1609–?1680). It was thus particularly suitable for reproducing paintings, being popular in 18th- and 19th-century England for printing Reynolds' portraits, Constable's landscapes, etc. The technique involves roughening and indenting a copper or steel plate with a serrated edged tool (rocker). Some of the roughened parts are then scraped away before the plate's surface is coated with ink. The indentations create the dark tones of the print, while the polished parts produce the lighter accents. Mezzotint is often combined with ▷etching and line engraving.

● **Mfecane** ▶ (1818–28) A period of wars and upheaval among Bantu peoples of southern Africa. The Zulu, under their warrior king ▷Shaka, turned on neighbouring tribes, causing them to abandon their cattle and grain stores and to flee into the territory of other tribes. This movement radically altered tribal groupings and led to the formation of new groupings, such as the Swazi, Basuto, Kololo, and Ndebele.

● **MHD** ▷*See* magnetohydrodynamics.

● **Miami** ▶ 25 45N 80 15W A city and port in the USA, in Florida on Biscayne Bay. A major tourist resort and retirement centre, it grew during the Florida land boom of the 1920s and includes Coral Gables (site of the University of Miami, established in 1925) and Miami Beach. It is famous for its citrus fruit and winter vegetables. Industries include aircraft repairing, sponge fisheries, clothing, and concrete. Population (1996 est): 365 127.

● **Micah** ▶ (8th century BC) An Old Testament prophet of Judah and contemporary of Isaíah. **The Book of Micah** records his condemnation of a number of specific sins in the corrupt nation and predicts the fall of Jerusalem, the renewal of the people, and the coming of a Messiah.

● **micas** ▶ A group of common rock-forming silicate minerals that have a layered structure and a complex composition. Muscovite, $K_2Al_4(Si_6Al_2)O_{20}(OH)_4$, is a white mica and economically the most important; it occurs in granitic rocks (often pegmatites), gneisses, and schists. The other principal micas are ▷phlogopite (amber), biotite (dark), paragonite, margarite, zinnwaldite, and lepidolite (a source of lithium). Their perfect cleavage is reflected in the layered structure. In its commercial form it is sold in blocks (sheets), books (flakes resembling the pages of a book), and splittings (loose flakes). Since it is a good insulator and can withstand high temperatures, mica has many electrical uses and is used for furnace windows. Splittings bonded together with shellac or synthetic resins are used to make Micanite.

● **Michael** ► (1596–1645) Tsar of Russia (1613–45) and founder of the ▷Romanov dynasty. Michael's election as tsar ended the ▷Time of Troubles. Michael was a weak ruler, relying upon his father Patriarch Philaret (c. 1553–1633). Serfdom was intensified during his reign.

● **Michael** ► (1921–   ) King of Romania (1927–30, 1940–47). Michael succeeded his grandfather in 1927 but lost the crown in 1930, when his father ▷Carol II returned from exile. After Carol's abdication in 1940, Michael again became king. In 1944 he overthrew the dictatorship of Ion Antonescu and declared war on Germany. He abdicated in 1947. After a long exile he returned to Romania in 2001.

● **Michael** ▷*See* archangels.

● **Michael VIII Palaeologus** ► (1224–82 AD) Byzantine emperor (1259–82), who founded the Palaeologan (the last Byzantine) dynasty (1259–1453). In 1261 Michael captured Constantinople from the Latins and re-established the Byzantine empire there after its 57-year exile. His subsequent policies were determined by the fear of another attack from the West. An alliance with the papacy against Charles I of Naples and Sicily led to the union (1274) of the Greek and Roman Churches, for which he was vilified after his death.

● **Michaelmas daisy** ▷*See* Aster.

● **Michaelmas Day** ► The feast of St Michael the archangel (29 September). It is one of the four quarter days in traditional English business practice.

● **Michelangelo Buonarroti** ► (1475–1564) Italian sculptor, painter, architect, and poet, born at Caprese, in Tuscany. Michelangelo was trained in Florence under the painter ▷Ghirlandaio and in the school in the Medici gardens, under the patronage of Lorenzo de' Medici. Working in Rome from 1496 until 1501, he produced his first major sculptures, notably the *Pietà* (St Peter's, Rome). This was followed (1501–05) by his work in Florence, including *David* (Accademia, Florence), the painting of the *Holy Family* (Uffizi), and the influential cartoon of the *Battle of Cascina*. The last was commissioned as a fresco for the Palazzo Vecchio but was never finished and was painted over by Vasari. Michelangelo's productive but stormy association with Pope Julius II began in 1505, when the pope commissioned Michelangelo to produce his tomb. Although this proved to be his most chequered and lengthy project, it resulted in such masterpieces as the *Slaves* (Accademia, Florence). The celebrated Sistine Chapel ceiling (1508–12), in the Vatican, established his reputation as the greatest painter of his day. Returning to Florence (1516), Michelangelo became the architect and sculptor of the Medici funerary chapel (1520–34) in the church of San Lorenzo and he also designed the Laurentian Library. These architectural projects and the fresco of the *Last Judgment* (1534–41) for the Sistine Chapel were his first major works in the new mannerist style (*see* mannerism). In his last years he worked mainly as an architect, becoming in 1547 chief architect of St Peter's, Rome, in which capacity he designed its great dome. His last sculptures included the *Rondanini Pietà* (Milan, Castello).

● **Michelet, Jules** ► (1798–1874) French historian. He established his academic reputation while still young and was appointed Keeper of the National Archives in 1831. His *Histoire de France* (6 vols, 1833–43; 11 vols, 1855–67) and *La Révolution française* (7 vols, 1847–53) were unashamedly nationalist works, written with romantic imagination. During the Second Empire (1852–70) he retired from public life and wrote works on natural science.

● **Michelin, André** ► (1853–1931) French tyre manufacturer, who founded, with his brother **Édouard Michelin** (1859–1940), the Michelin Tyre Company (1888). In 1895 they became the first to demonstrate the feasibility of using pneumatic tyres on motor cars. The company is now also famous for its maps and guidebooks.

● **Michelozzo di Bartolommeo** ► (1396–1472) Florentine ▷Renaissance sculptor and architect. As a sculptor he collaborated first with ▷Ghiberti and then with ▷Donatello, but after 1433 he turned to architecture. He designed several buildings for the Medici, including the Palazzo Medici (1444–59), which was the first Renaissance palace.

● **Michelson, Albert Abraham** ► (1852–1931) US physicist, born in Germany. He designed a highly accurate interferometer known as the Michelson interferometer and used it to measure precisely the speed of light. He also used it in an attempt to measure the velocity of the earth through the ether. This work, carried out in conjunction with Edward ▷Morley and known as the ▷Michelson-Morley experiment, eventually led ▷Einstein to his theory of relativity. Michelson received the Nobel Prize in 1907.

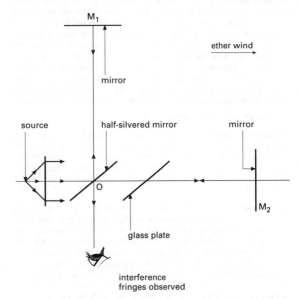

Michelson-Morley experiment ► The Michelson interferometer was used in an attempt to detect changes in the speed of light of the earth's motion through the ether. Distances OM₁ and OM₂ are equal. The glass plate compensates for the thickness of the half-silvered mirror.

● **Michelson-Morley experiment** ► An experiment performed by A. A. ▷Michelson and E. W. ▷Morley in 1881 in an attempt to demonstrate the existence of the luminiferous ether by measuring the earth's velocity relative to it. They used a Michelson interferometer to obtain interference fringes and then rotated the apparatus through 90° expecting to find a shift in the fringes, since the speed of light would be different in the two directions. This difference would result from the earth's motion through the ether. However, no shift was detected. This negative result led to the downfall of the ether theory and was explained by Einstein's theory of ▷relativity in 1905 (*see also* Lorentz, Hendrick Antoon).

● **Michigan** ► A state in the N central USA, bordered largely by water (Lakes Superior, Huron, Michigan, Erie, and St Clair). It is divided by the Straits of Mackinac into the Lower Peninsula in the S (an area of lowlands) and the Upper Peninsula in the N (lowlands in the E and uplands in the W). Michigan is also divided demographically and economically, with most of its population and industry concentrated in the Lower Peninsula. Manufacturing is very important, especially the production of motor vehicles at Detroit; other industries include machinery, iron and steel, and chemicals. The state exploits its large mineral reserves of gypsum, calcium, and magnesium compounds, natural gas and oil. Tourism is the state's second largest industry. It is also an important agricultural state producing vegetables, maize, beans, fruit, and livestock.

History: first explored by the French in the 17th century, it remained under French control until it was acquired by the British (1763) as part of Canada. It came under American control (1783), becoming a state in 1837. Area: 150 779 sq km (58 216 sq mi). Population (2000 est): 9 938 444. Capital: Lansing.

● **Michigan, Lake** ▶ The third largest of the Great Lakes in North America, the only one wholly in the USA. It is linked with Lake Huron via the Straits of Mackinac; the city of Chicago is on its S bank. Area: 58 000 sq km (22 400 sq mi).

● **Mickiewicz, Adam** ▶ (1798–1855) Polish poet. His early poetry was influenced by the Romantics, especially Byron. In 1823 he was arrested with other students of Vilna University and deported to Russia, where he befriended Pushkin. He left Russia in 1829 and settled in Paris in 1832. His works include the drama *Dziadzy* (1823–32) and the epic poem *Pan Tadeusz* (1832–34).

● **microbiology** ▶ The study of microorganisms, or microbes—organisms that are invisible to the naked eye, including bacteria, small fungi (e.g. yeasts and moulds) and algae (e.g. diatoms), protozoa, and viruses. Microorganisms, which are abundant everywhere, are of immense importance to all living things. They bring about ▷decomposition and the recycling of nutrients. They are vital to numerous industries, including brewing, baking, dairying, and food processing, they have revolutionized medical treatment with the discovery of antibiotics, and they are important tools in ▷genetic engineering. Many microorganisms are parasites that cause disease (*see* infection).

● **microchip** ▷*See* integrated circuit.

● **microcomputers** ▶ Small ▷computers designed for a single user. The tiny central processing unit is a ▷microprocessor. Multiple users often have a series of microcomputers linked in a network. Microcomputers were introduced in the 1970s for industrial, commercial, and domestic uses. Laptop and handheld computers are very small and portable.

● **microcopy** ▶ A greatly reduced photographic copy of a printed page, drawing, or other image. **Microfilm** is a strip of standard-width film containing microcopies. It was introduced in the 1920s for use in banks and is now widely used for compact storage and ready reference to documents. Special enlarging viewers can rapidly wind the film to the correct page. **Microfiche** is a similar system on cards holding a single film negative, with even greater reduction of the pictures. The viewers often have a printer attached. Microfiche is widely used in data-processing systems and in libraries.

● **microeconomics** ▷*See* economics.

● **microelectronics** ▷*See* electronics.

● **microlight aircraft** ▶ A small powered aircraft of minimal weight. These aircraft were developed in the 1980s, when such models as the British Optica were considered for traffic monitoring and other roles. Some models can be folded up for ease of transport.

● **micrometer** ▶ An instrument for measuring small lengths with great accuracy. The object to be measured is held between the jaws of a C-shaped metal piece, one jaw of which can be adjusted by a screw. The screw is turned by rotating a drum with a ▷Vernier scale marked on it, from which the required dimension can be read.

● **micron** ▶ (μm) An obsolete name for one-millionth of a metre. The correct name is now the **micrometre** (*see* SI units).

● **Micronesia** ▶ A division of Oceania in the W Pacific Ocean, consisting of an arc of islands E of the Philippines. It includes the Mariana, Caroline, and Marshall archipelagos, and the W Kiribati islands. ▷*See also* Melanesia; Polynesia.

● **Micronesia, Federated States of** ▶ A country in the W Pacific Ocean comprising 600 of the ▷Caroline Islands, including Chuuk, Yap, Pohnpei, and Kosrae.

Economy: most of the population lives by subsistence agriculture, fishing, tourism, or government work. The main exports are copra and fish.

History: the Caroline Islands formed part of the Spanish Empire until 1899, when they were sold to Germany. They were administered by Japan from 1914 until their occupation by US forces in World War II. Forming part of the UN Trust Territory of the ▷Pacific Islands from 1947, Micronesia became fully self-governing in 1986 and was recognized as independent by the UN in 1990. Under a compact of free association, the USA retains responsibility for defence.

Federated States of Micronesia

Head of state	President Jacob Nena
Official languages	English and local languages
Official currency	US dollar of 100 cents
Area	700 sq km (270 sq mi)
Population (2000 est)	118 000
Capital	Palikir, on Pohnpei

● **microphone** ▶ A device that converts sound into electrical signals. It acts like a ▷loudspeaker in reverse and some microphones may also be used as loudspeakers. Most consist of a thin diaphragm, the mechanical vibration of which is converted to an electrical signal proportional to the sound pressure. A telephone mouthpiece usually consists of a carbon microphone in which the sound waves exert a varying pressure on carbon granules, so varying their electrical resistance. In capacitor microphones, commonly used in music recording, the diaphragm forms one plate of a capacitor, across which the sound waves produce a fluctuating potential difference. Crystal microphones rely on the ▷piezoelectric effect. Other types use magnetic induction, magnetostriction, or other electromagnetic effects. Ribbon microphones have a highly directional response. They consist of a strip of aluminium alloy in a strong magnetic field. The ribbon vibrates in the sound waves, inducing in itself an electromotive force proportional to its velocity.

● **microprocessor** ▶ The central processing unit of a ▷microcomputer. Its development was made possible in the 1970s by advances in solid-state electronics, in particular the design of ▷integrated circuits of such complexity that all the main calculating functions can be carried out by a single silicon chip.

● **microscope** ▶ An optical instrument used for producing a magnified image of a small object. There are several distinct types, the most common being the compound microscope, which contains an objective lens system and an eyepiece system. It was invented in 1609 by a Dutch spectacle maker Zacharias Janssen (1580–c. 1638) and his father, but Robert ▷Hooke gave the first extensive description of its use in biology in his *Micrographia* (1665). In a compound microscope the objective produces a real magnified image, which is further magnified by the eyepiece. At low ▷magnifications the system is illuminated by a source the light of which is reflected through the specimen by a mirror. At high magnifications special illuminating systems are needed. The magnification, which may be up to a thousand, is limited by the ▷resolving power of the lenses; the smallest detail capable of resolution by an optical microscope is about 0.2 micrometre. This can be increased by using an ▷oil-immersion lens (*see also* ultramicroscope). Still higher magnifications are obtained by using shorter wavelength radiations as in the ▷electron microscope. ▷*See also* atomic force microscope; scanning tunnelling microscope.

A **photomicrograph** is a photograph of the image obtained using a microscope. This enables a permanent record to be kept and also enables ultraviolet radiation to be used for illumination of the specimen.

● **microsurgery** ▷*See* surgery.

● **microwave background radiation** ▷*See* big-bang theory.

● **microwaves** ▶ Electromagnetic radiation with wavelengths between 1 and 300 millimetres, lying between infrared rays and radio waves in the electromagnetic spectrum. They are used in ▷radar and **microwave heating**. This method is used in the rapid cooking of food as the radiation penetrates to the interior of the food. The microwave photon is the same order of magnitude as the vibrational energy of atoms and molecules and therefore heats the interior directly, rather than by conduction from the surface. It is also used in sterilization and in drying wood, etc. Microwaves are generated by such devices as ▷magnetrons and ▷klystrons.

● **Midas** ▶ In Greek legend, a king of Phrygia whose wish that everything he touched be turned to gold was granted by Dionysus in gratitude for his hospitality to the satyr ▷Silenus. Because he was therefore unable to eat or drink, he was released from this handicap by bathing in the River Pactolus. In another legend, Midas was asked to judge between the music of Pan and Apollo and chose the former.

Apollo punished his tactlessness by changing his ears into those of an ass.

● **Mid-Atlantic Ridge** ► The submarine ridge extending N–S through the Atlantic Ocean. It forms part of the mid-ocean ridge system that crosses all the major oceans. Much of it is over 1000 km (621 mi) wide and rises to between 1 and 3 km (0.6–1.9 mi) above the ocean basin, in places rising above sea level to form islands. Along the crest are rift mountains and a fractured plateau. ▷*See* plate tectonics.

● **Middelburg** ► 51 30N 3 36E A town in the SW Netherlands, the capital of Zeeland province on Walcheren Island. Badly damaged in World War II, a 12th-century abbey survives. Population (1994): 40 118.

● **middle ages** ► The period of European history that is generally regarded as beginning with the fall of the western Roman Empire in the 5th century and ending with the Renaissance a thousand years later. Following a period of chaos and upheaval (the so-called ▷Dark Ages, which are sometimes excluded from the middle ages proper), relative stability returned with the creation of the barbarian kingdoms, which developed into the nation states of W Europe. In Church history, the period covers the rise to supremacy of the Roman Catholic Church, centred on Rome, and the development of the papacy as an international religious and political power (from the 11th century). Socially and economically the period saw the rising power of the great landed magnates and the creation of a feudal society (*see* feudalism), while urban growth and the development of trade reached unprecedented heights. The period can be said to end with the fall of Constantinople to the Turks (1453), the European discovery of America (1492), and the successful challenge to the papacy of the national reform movements.

● **Middleback Range** ► A range of hills in S South Australia. It extends N–S for 64 km (40 mi) in the Eyre Peninsula and possesses rich deposits of iron ore; these are worked at Iron Knob, Iron Monarch, and Iron Baron.

● **Middle Comedy** ► The transitional period of Greek comic drama, lasting from about 400 BC to about 320 BC. Its characteristics are evident in the last two plays of Aristophanes, *Ecclesiazusae* (392) and *Plutus* (388). A more oblique humour replaced the exuberant and scurrilous wit of earlier comedy, perhaps reflecting the Athenians' loss of confidence in themselves after their defeat (404) in the Peloponnesian War. ▷*See also* Old Comedy; New Comedy.

● **Middle East** ► The area comprising Iran and the countries of the Arabian peninsula and the Mediterranean seaboard. The Middle East, sometimes called the cradle of civilization, is the birthplace of three major world religions, Judaism, Christianity, and Islam, and their attendant cultures. A world crossroads, its troubled history has been dominated at different times by the Jews, Assyrians, Babylonians, Tatars, Macedonians, and Arabs. The present instability derives from the competing attempts of the Cold War superpowers to influence an area that produces 40% of the world's oil, conflict between Arab countries and Israel (exacerbated by the displaced Palestinians), the rise of Islamic fundamentalism, and Iraq's hostility to its own minorities and to neighbouring states. Moves towards a settlement of the Palestinian problem and a rapprochement between Israel and its Arab neighbours made considerable progress in 1994–95 but subsequently stalled; Arab–Israeli conflict erupted again in 2000.

● **Middlesbrough** ► **1.** 54 35N 1 14W A town in NE England, in Middlesbrough unitary authority, North Yorkshire, on the Tees estuary. Local iron ore (in the Cleveland Hills) and local coking coal (from the Durham coalfield) gave Middlesbrough early industrial advantages. Until the recessions of the 1980s and 1990s iron and steel, petrochemicals, and constructional engineering were the major industries, with almost all the traffic through the port of Middlesbrough being related to the steel and chemical industries. The economy is now mainly based on the service sector. Population (1998 est): 145 000. **2.** A unitary authority in NE England, in North Yorkshire; formerly (1974–96) part of the county of Cleveland. Area: 54 sq km (21 sq mi). Population (1998 est): 145 100.

● **middle school** ▷*See* primary education.

● **Middlesex** ► A former county of SE England. In 1965 it was for the most part absorbed by Greater London; Staines and Sunbury-on-Thames were transferred to Surrey and Potters Bar to Hertfordshire. It is still used as a postal address.

● **Middle Temple** ▷*See* Inns of Court.

● **Middleton, Thomas** ► (1580–1627) English dramatist. He wrote and collaborated on many comedies and pageants, and achieved popular success with his political satire *A Game at Chess* (1624), which was suppressed after complaints from the Spanish ambassador. His best-known plays are the tragedies *Women Beware Women* (c. 1621) and, in collaboration with William ▷Rowley, *The Changeling* (1622).

● **Middle West, the** ▷*See* Midwest, the.

● **Midgard** ► In Norse mythology, the earth, which lies between Hel or Nifleheim, the land of ice, and Muspelheim, the land of fire, and is reached from ▷Asgard (the home of the gods) by Bifrost, the rainbow bridge. It was formed by the gods from the dead body of the giant Aurgelmir, his flesh being the land, his blood the oceans, etc.

● **midge** ► A small fly, also called a nonbiting midge, belonging to the family *Chironomidae* (over 2000 species). It resembles a mosquito but is harmless. Midges are found near fresh water, often in large swarms. The wormlike aquatic larvae are often red (*see* bloodworm) and live in gelatinous or sand tubes, feeding on algae.
 Unrelated flies, including the biting or bloodsucking midges (family *Ceratopogonidae*) and the ▷gall midges, are also loosely referred to as midges.

● **Mid Glamorgan** ► A former county of SE Wales. It was created in 1974 from industrial central Glamorgan and parts of Breconshire and Monmouthshire. In 1996 it was abolished and administrative powers were handed over to the new county boroughs of Bridgend, Merthyr Tydfil, Rhondda Cynon Taff, and part of Caerphilly.

● **Midlands** ► A collective term for the central counties of England. The area includes the counties of Derbyshire, Leicestershire, Northamptonshire, and Nottinghamshire, which are often known as the **East Midlands**, and the counties of Staffordshire, Warwickshire, Worcestershire, Herefordshire, and the metropolitan county of West Midlands, which comprise the **West Midlands**. The term **South Midlands** is sometimes used to refer to the counties of Buckinghamshire, Bedfordshire, and Oxfordshire.

● **Midlothian** ► A council area of SE Scotland. Under local government reorganization in 1975 the historic county of Midlothian, including the city of Edinburgh (the county was once called Edinburghshire), was absorbed into Lothian Region. A much smaller district council of the same name (excluding Edinburgh and the surrounding industrial area) was created. When Lothian Region was abolished in 1996, this became an independent unitary authority. Midlothian is mainly hilly, rising to the Moorfoot Hills in the S. The chief activity is agriculture. Area: 356 sq km (137 sq mi). Population (1998 est): 80 900. Administrative centre: Dalkeith.

● **midnight sun** ► The sun when it is seen on or above the horizon at midnight at places within the Arctic or Antarctic circles. At the polar circles it is seen only at the summer ▷solstice. At the Poles it is seen for the six months between the summer and winter solstices.

● **Midrash** ► (Hebrew: enquiry, exposition) Exposition of the Hebrew Bible, and more particularly a book consisting of such exposition. There are many Midrashim, mostly dating from the early middle ages, and they are a valuable source for the religious ideas of the Jews of the time. The ▷Talmuds also contain a great deal of Midrash.

● **midshipman** ► A fish, also called singing fish, belonging to a genus (*Porichthys*) of ▷toadfishes. It is able to produce a whistling sound and has rows of light-producing organs on its underside.

● **Midway Islands** ► 28 15N 177 25W A small group of US islands in the central Pacific Ocean. A military base, they are unpopulated apart from US military personnel. The air battle that took place here (3–6 June, 1942) resulted in a major Allied victory. Area: 5 sq km (2 sq mi).

● **Midwest, the** ► (*or* Middle West) An area in the N central USA. Its boundaries are indefinite but it is generally accepted to be N of the Ohio River, W of Lake Erie, and E of the Great Plains. One of the world's most fertile agricultural areas, it produces chiefly maize and wheat.

● **midwifery** ▶ The nursing specialty concerned with the care of women during pregnancy and childbirth and in the postnatal period. Midwives assist in monitoring the health of the mother and baby during labour and deliver the baby in the absence of complications. Midwives undergo extensive training beyond basic nursing training and are registered with the UKCC (*see* nursing).

midwife toad ▶ Mating takes place on land. Soon after fertilization the male twines the eggs around his legs and carries them about, thus protecting them from the predators they would otherwise encounter if laid in water.

● **midwife toad** ▶ A ▷toad, *Alytes obstetricans*, found in W Europe up to 2200 m above sea level. Pale grey and slow-moving, it has an unusual breeding habit. As the eggs are laid, the male winds the two egg strings around his hind legs. He keeps the eggs for about a month, frequently moistening them with dew and finally takes them to hatch in a pool.

● **Mies van der Rohe, Ludwig** ▶ (1886–1969) German architect. A pioneering architect of the 1920s and 1930s, Mies first achieved fame with his glass skyscrapers (1919–21). However, his most influential building was the glass, steel, and marble German pavilion at the Barcelona international exhibition (1929; ⁁furniture). After a short period running the ▷Bauhaus, he moved (1937) to the USA, where he designed such buildings as the Illinois Institute of Technology (1939) and the Seagram building, New York (1958). His last design, a controversial tower block for Mansion House Square in the City of London, was finally rejected in 1985.

● **mignonette** ▶ A bushy annual herb, *Reseda odorata*, native to N Africa and widely grown as an ornamental. Up to 60 cm high, it bears dense terminal clusters of tiny yellow or white flowers, which have a musky fragrance and are used in perfumery. The name is also applied to other species of *Reseda*. Family: *Resedaceae*.

● **migraine** ▶ Recurrent headaches, usually affecting one side of the head and caused by contraction and then dilation of the arteries in the brain. The attacks may be preceded by blurring of vision and flickering lights (called an aura). During the headache itself vomiting commonly occurs and the sufferer cannot tolerate light. Some drugs reduce the incidence of attacks and others relieve the severity of an attack.

● **migration, animal** ▶ The periodic movement of animal populations between one region and another, usually associated with seasonal climatic changes or breeding cycles. Migration is best known among birds. Many European species travel to S Africa to avoid the harsh winter weather and the Arctic tern makes a spectacular migration of 17 600 km (11 000 mi) between its breeding grounds in the Arctic and the Antarctic. The phenomenon is seen in many other animals, including fish (notably salmon), which return each year from

the sea to spawn in the same river that they themselves were spawned, butterflies, bats, lemmings, and whales. The mechanism of navigation and homing is not completely understood. In birds it seems to involve sighting of visible landmarks, such as mountains and vegetation, as well as a compass sense, using the sun or the stars as bearings. Other animals are thought to use similar methods. Land mammals may lay scent trails for local direction finding.

● **migration, human** ▶ The movement of groups of people from one country to another in which they intend to settle. Religious persecution has led many (e.g. the ▷Pilgrim Fathers, the French ▷Huguenots following the revocation of the Edict of ▷Nantes, and the Jews) to flee their homelands and settle elsewhere. The 19th century was a period of migration on a large scale, often prompted by severe population pressures, rural unemployment, and the economic opportunities in the country of destination as well as racial persecution. Many of the major countries able to absorb large numbers of immigrants have had historic policies favouring Europeans (e.g. Australia, South Africa, and the USA). Even European immigration in these countries was severely restricted by legislation in the 1920s. Since World War I governments have been more active in controlling migration and this applies also to controls exercised in the sending countries.

Immigration into the UK increased in the 1950s, when British public services, faced with shortages of labour, began recruiting West Indians to work in the UK. Despite the net fall in population due to emigration, there were demands for controls of immigration from the Commonwealth countries of Asia and the Caribbean, which caused a temporary surge in the number of immigrants before they were enforced. Controls were introduced in 1962, since when approximately 30–50 000 migrants have entered the UK annually. Official statistics show that in the decade 1986–95 there was an average annual net outflow from the UK of 43 200 and a net inflow of 47 800. In the UK about half the number of people seeking ▷political asylum are held in detention centres, often for many months, while awaiting permission to stay.

A specific feature of the postwar period has been the temporary migration of approximately 11 million unskilled "guest workers" (German word: *Gastarbeiter*) from such countries as Turkey and Algeria to the industrial countries of Europe, especially France and Germany.

● **Mihajlović, Draža** ▶ (*or* D. Mihailović; (1893–1946) Yugoslav general. After Germany occupied Yugoslavia in World War II he organized the ▷Chetniks. In 1943 he was appointed minister of war by Peter II (1923–70; reigned 1934–45) but lost the king's confidence and Allied support to ▷Tito. After the liberation he was shot for treason.

● **Míkonos** ▶ (*or* Mykonos) A Greek island in the S Aegean Sea, one of the Cyclades. It is popular with tourists and is noted for having a large number of churches. Area: 90 sq km (35 sq mi). Population (latest est): 5503.

● **Milan** ▶ (Italian name: Milano; Latin name: Mediolanum) 45 28N 9 12E A city in N Italy, the capital of Lombardy on the River Olona. Milan is the focal point of rail and road routes and is the chief commercial and industrial centre of Italy. Its manufactures include motor vehicles, machinery, silk and other textiles, and chemicals and it is a major publishing centre. Milan has a gothic cathedral (duomo), two universities (both founded in the 1920s), the Brera Palace (containing the city's chief art collection), a library, and the opera house of ▷La Scala. The convent of Sta Maria delle Grazie contains Leonardo da Vinci's fresco *The Last Supper*.

History: founded by the Gauls about 600 BC, it was captured by the Romans in 222. Later devastated by the Huns and the Goths, it was involved in much warfare until the 12th century, after which time it enjoyed considerable economic prosperity. It was ruled by the Visconti family from 1310 until 1447, after which it passed to the Sforza family, who ruled until the fall of Milan to Spain (1535). Milan was under Austrian rule (1713–96) and in 1797 Napoleon made it capital of the Cisalpine Republic (1797) and the kingdom of Italy (1805–14). It grew in industrial importance after its unification (1861) with Italy. Population (1996 est): 1 306 494.

● **Mildenhall** ▶ 52 21N 0 30E A market town in E England, in Suffolk on the River Lark. Nearby, Stone Age, Roman, and Saxon remains have been found. Population (1991): 10 468.

● **mildew** ▶ Any fungus that grows as dense filaments forming visible white patches. Many fungal diseases of plants are called mildews: powdery mildews are infestations by fungi of the order *Peronosporales*, while downy mildews are due to infection by fungi of the family *Erysiphaceae*.

● **Mildura** ▶ 34 14S 142 13E A city in Australia, in NW Victoria on the Murray River. It is the centre of the Mallee, an irrigated region producing chiefly fruit, vegetables, and wheat. Population (1990): 19 350.

● **mile** ▶ A unit of length traditionally used in the UK and USA. A statute mile is equal to 1760 yards. A nautical mile (UK) is equal to 6080 feet; a nautical mile (international) is equal to 1852 metres (6076.12 ft). The unit is based on the Roman mile of 1000 paces.

● **Miles, Bernard, Baron** ▶ (1907–91) British theatre director and actor. He founded the Mermaid Theatre, which opened at its present riverside site in Blackfriars, London, in 1959. He contributed as writer, director, and actor to many of its productions.

● **Miles Gloriosus** ▶ (Latin: boastful soldier) A stock character in comic drama who boasts of brave deeds yet is easily shown to be a fool or coward. The term derives from the title of a play by ▷Plautus.

● **Miletus** ▶ An ancient Greek city in ▷Ionia, founded about 1000 BC. Centre of the wool trade, early colonizer of the Black Sea area, and commercially active from Italy to Egypt, Miletus exemplified Ionian energy and enterprise. Milesians were prominent among the 6th-century Ionian thinkers, and even after destruction by Persia (494 BC) Miletus remained commercially important until its harbours silted up.

● **milfoil** ▷*See* yarrow.

● **Milford Haven** ▶ 51 44N 5 02W A port in SW Wales, in Pembrokeshire on the Milford Haven estuary. It was developed as a major oil terminal capable of accommodating large oil tankers. There are oil refineries and a long-established fishing industry. Population (1991): 13 194.

● **Milhaud, Darius** ▶ (1892–1974) French composer, a member of Les ▷Six. He made use of polytonality and jazz in many of his compositions. With Jean Cocteau he wrote the ballets *Le Boeuf sur le toit* (1919) and *Le Train bleu* (1924); with Paul Claudel he wrote the opera *Christophe Colomb* (1928). His other works include 12 symphonies, 15 string quartets (the last 2 of which can be played simultaneously as an octet), concertos, and Jewish liturgical music.

● **Militant Tendency** ▶ A faction formerly within the ▷Labour Party advocating Trotskyist policies, which emerged in the 1970s around the newspaper *Militant*. It attracted notoriety after 1979 in the controversy over reform of the party. In 1982 it was judged to have broken the rules for groups within the party. In 1986 members of the Militant Tendency were expelled from the party.

● **militia** ▶ A military force composed of reservists enlisted in emergencies to reinforce a standing army. The militia is descended from the Anglo-Saxon *fyrd*, to which all free men were compulsorily recruited for short-term local service. This general levy survived the introduction to England of the feudal levy by William I and under the Tudors responsibility for raising so-called "trained bands" fell to the parishes. The militia declined with the establishment (1661) of a standing army and was reorganized in 1757. In the 19th century the militia became voluntary and militiamen served abroad for the first time. It lasted until the Territorial and Reserve Forces Act (1907). ▷*See also* Territorial Army.

● **milk** ▶ A fluid secreted by the ▷mammary glands of mammals to feed their young. Cows' milk consists typically of about 87% water, 3.6% fat, 3.3% protein, 4.7% lactose (milk sugar), small quantities of minerals (mainly calcium and phosphorus), and vitamins (mainly vitamins A and B). (Human milk, in contrast, contains less protein and more lactose.) Although its composition depends on the breed of animal, its diet, and the season, milk forms a well-balanced and highly nutritious food. In the UK most milk is sold, after ▷pasteurization, in bottles or cartons, with daily doorstep deliveries. Sterilized and UHT (ultraheat-treated) milk both have a longer shelf-life (about one month) but sterilized milk has a distinctive flavour. Long-life UHT milk will keep for up to six months in sealed containers. Homogenized milk is processed so that the fat globules are uniformly sized. ▷*See also* dairy farming; dairy products.

● **milk of magnesia** ▶ A suspension of magnesium hydroxide (Mg(OH)$_2$) in water. It is a white milky fluid used as an antacid and a mild laxative.

● **milk sugar** ▷*See* lactose.

● **milkweed** ▶ A herb of the genus *Asclepias* (120 species), native to North America and often grown in the tropics and subtropics for ornament. Up to 1.2 m high, it bears umbrella-shaped clusters of orange, purple, pink, or red flowers and yields a milky latex. The seeds have long silky hairs ("vegetable silk"), often used in upholstery padding or as insulation. Family: *Asclepiadaceae*.

● **milkweed butterfly** ▶ A butterfly belonging to the widely distributed mainly tropical family *Danaidae*. The adults are typically large and colourful and may fly long distances (*see* monarch). The caterpillars feed on milkweed and other plants, which make them taste unpleasant to predators.

● **milkwort** ▶ A perennial herb or small shrub of the genus *Polygala* (500–600 species), native to Europe and North America. The common European milkwort (*P. vulgaris*) has slender branching stems, 7–25 cm long, and spikes of irregular flowers, white, pink, or blue in colour. Family: *Polygalaceae*.

● **Milky Way** ▶ The diffuse band of light that is seen, on a clear moonless night, stretching across the sky. It is composed of innumerable stars that are too faint to be seen individually. They lie around the sun in the flattened and densely populated disc of our ▷Galaxy.

● **Mill, James** ▶ (1773–1836) Scottish writer, historian, and philosophical radical. In the course of a busy journalistic career he met ▷Bentham (1808), whose enthusiastic disciple he became. Mill's *History of India* (1818) secured him an official post at India House for the remainder of his life. His *Elements of Political Economy* (1821) influenced ▷Marx and his philosophical stance is reflected by his son **John Stuart Mill** (1806–73), one of the greatest 19th-century thinkers. In economics, J. S. Mill was influenced by the theories of Adam ▷Smith, ▷Ricardo, and ▷Malthus, and his *Principles of Political Economy* (1848) is little more than a restatement of their ideas. He was also the last of the English philosophers in the empirical tradition of Locke. He was a proponent of ▷utilitarianism, publishing a book under that title (1863). *On Liberty* (1859) shows that he was concerned for the rights of the individual, yet sympathetic to the ideas of contemporary socialists. He believed strongly in the equality of the sexes, publishing his views in *Subjection of Women* (1869). He edited the *London Review* (1835–40).

● **Millais, Sir John Everett** ▶ (1829–96) British painter, born in Southampton. He was one of the founders of the ▷Pre-Raphaelite Brotherhood, the principles of which he applied to his best paintings, notably the controversial *Christ in the House of His Parents* (1850) and *Ophelia* (1852; both Tate Gallery). After abandoning Pre-Raphaelitism in the 1860s, he painted more popular and sentimental works, such as *Bubbles* (1886).

● **Millay, Edna St Vincent** ▶ (1892–1950) US poet. The bohemianism of her early lyrical poetry matured into a more profound disillusion, especially in *The Buck in the Snow* (1928) and *Fatal Interview* (1931), a sonnet sequence. *The Harp Weaver and Other Poems* (1923) won a Pulitzer Prize.

● **millenarianism** ▶ A belief, widespread among early Christians, that Christ will soon return to reign on earth with his elect for a period of a thousand years preceding the Last Judgment. The idea was fostered by literal interpretations of the Book of Revelation (especially chapter 20) but was rejected by ▷Origen, whose views on the matter became generally accepted. At the Reformation millenarianism flourished among persecuted minorities, such as the ▷Anabaptists. Puritan millenarian sects, notably the ▷Fifth Monarchy Men, proliferated in the mid-17th-century turmoils in England. Millenarian beliefs also recurred at the time of the French Revolution. The political frustrations of colonial rule, combined with fundamentalist biblical teaching, fostered millenarianism among the indigenous peoples of Africa and Polynesia, where it sometimes took the form of ▷cargo cults. Contemporary millenarian groups include the ▷adventists and ▷Mormons.

● **millennium** ► A period of 1000 years, especially in the context of the Christian calendar, in which Christ's birth is taken as a (purely notional) year 0. The term originally referred to the 1000 years of Christ's reign on earth that, according to the Book of Revelation, would accompany the Second Coming (*see* millenarianism). By a simple association of ideas, some Christians in both the late 10th century and the late 20th century came to expect the Second Coming at the close of the calendar millennium, although there is no biblical support for such a view.

Apart from this, the end of the first millennium of the Christian era appears to have passed without much notice. By contrast the closing of the second millennium became an occasion for celebration, historical stocktaking, and the dedication of new and notable public buildings. In the UK, the government decided that the event should be celebrated by the erection of the ▷Millennium Dome.

On a less celebratory note, exaggerated fears of the **millennium bug**, a term for any problem affecting computer software caused by a failure to cope with the transition from the year 1999 to the year 2000, cost the users of large computer systems much worry and expense. Governments worldwide are estimated to have spent some £400 billion of public money in attempts to publicize and prevent this problem. In the event, fears that it would have immense and unforseeable knock-on effects (technological, financial, and social) in our computer-dependent world proved totally unfounded. Countries and companies that spent no money at all on prevention seem to have been no more affected than those that spent prodigious sums.

● **Millennium Dome** ► A large ▷dome erected in Greenwich, Greater London, to house the "Millennium Experience," a multimedia exhibition celebrating the year 2000. The site, a previously derelict area beside the River Thames, lies on the Greenwich (0°) meridian (*see* Greenwich Mean Time). With a circumference of just over 1 km (1099 yards) and a height of 50 m (164 feet), it is easily the world's largest dome. Designed by the Richard ▷Rogers Partnership, it consists of a Teflon (PTFE) canopy suspended from 12 100-m (328-ft) steel masts. Construction began in 1997 and was completed a year later at a cost of some £750 M. The Millennium Experience, which ran for 367 days from its opening on 31 December, 1999, received generally poor publicity, attracted only about half the hoped-for 12 million visitors, and had to be bailed out with some £600 M of lottery money. The Dome has since remained empty; in 2002 it was given away to a US company who will stage entertainment and sports events.

● **Miller, Arthur** ► (1915–) US dramatist. As a Jewish liberal intellectual he has played an active role in political life, and one of the main themes of his plays is social responsibility. His plays include *All My Sons* (1947), *Death of a Salesman* (1947), which won a Pulitzer Prize, *The Crucible* (1953), concerning the Salem witch trials of the 1690s, *A View from the Bridge* (1955), *After the Fall* (1964), which is in part a portrait of his late wife, Marilyn Monroe, *The Ride down Mt Morgan* (1991), and *Mr Peters' Connections* (1998).

● **Miller, Glenn** ► (1904–44) US jazz trombonist, band leader, and composer of such popular songs as "Moonlight Serenade". Miller's band, assembled in 1938, recorded many hit swing tunes and entertained the troops during World War II. He died when his plane disappeared on a routine flight between England and France.

● **Miller, Henry** ► (1891–1980) US novelist. During the 1930s he lived in Paris, where he became a close friend of Lawrence ▷Durrell; he lived in California from 1944. He first gained notoriety with the sexually explicit novels *Tropic of Cancer* (1934) and *Tropic of Capricorn* (1939). Later writings include *The Rosy Crucifixion* (1949–60) and *My Life and Times* (1972). His works, which are mostly autobiographical, are anarchic celebrations of life and liberty.

● **Miller, Jonathan (Wolfe)** ► (1934–) British theatre director, who studied medicine at Cambridge and appeared in the successful Footlights revue *Beyond the Fringe* (1960). As a director, his productions include Sheridan's *The School for Scandal* (1972), Chekhov's *Three Sisters* (1976), and Shakespeare. His opera productions include Don

Giovanni (1985), *Tosca* (1986), and *Manon Lescaut* (1992). He has also written, produced, and presented series for television.

● **miller's thumb** ▷*See* bullhead.

● **millet** ► One of various ▷grasses or their seeds, cultivated in Asia and Africa as a cereal crop and in parts of Europe and North America chiefly as a pasture grass and fodder crop. It grows 30–130 cm high and the flowers form spikes or branched clusters. Common or broomcorn millet (*Panicum miliaceum*) is used for poultry feed or for flour milling. Pearl millet (*Pennisetum glaucum*) is grown in arid and infertile soils as a food grain; Italian millet (*Setaria italica*) has been cultivated as a grain crop in Asia since ancient times; and Japanese millet (*Echinochloa crus-galli* var. *frumentacea*) is grown for fodder. A variety of sorghum (*see* durra) is also known as millet.

● **Millet, Jean François** ► (1814–75) French painter of peasant origin. He studied under ▷Delaroche, achieving acclaim in 1844, although later his works were criticized for expressing socialist ideas. After settling in Barbizon (1849), he became associated with the ▷Barbizon school and painted melancholy and sometimes sentimental agricultural scenes, notably *The Gleaners* (1857) and *The Angelus* (1859; both Louvre).

● **millibar** ▷*See* bar.

● **Milligan, Spike** ► (Terence Alan M.; 1918–2002) Irish comedian and writer, born in British India. His surreal humour first found an audience with the cult radio series *The Goon Show* (1951–59), which he scripted and in which he costarred with Harry Secombe, Peter Sellers, and (in early shows) Michael Bentine. He subsequently appeared regularly on television. His numerous publications include children's stories, poetry, and comic memoirs. He was awarded an honorary knighthood in 2000.

● **Millikan, Robert Andrews** ► (1868–1953) US physicist, who first measured the charge on the electron. For this and other work, he was awarded the Nobel Prize in 1932. In **Millikan's oil-drop experiment**, he balanced the effects of an upward electromagnetic attraction and the downward pull of gravity on an electrically charged droplet. As changes in the drop's charge (caused by bombardment with X-rays) occur in whole numbers of units of electronic charge, the size of the unit can be calculated from the movement of the drop. Millikan also studied cosmic rays and hoped to reconcile religion and science.

● **millipede** ► A slow-moving ▷arthropod of the widely distributed class (or subclass) *Diplopoda* (about 8000 species). Its slender cylindrical body, 2–280 mm long, is covered by a calcareous cuticle and consists of 20–100 segments, most of which bear two pairs of legs (*compare* centipede). Millipedes live in dark humid places as scavengers of dead plant and animal materials. In defence they secrete a toxic fluid containing cyanide and iodine. Eggs are usually sheltered in a nest of excrement.

● **Mills, Sir John** ► (1908–) British actor. He appeared in the roles of quiet but gallant heroes in *This Happy Breed* (1944) and other war films and later in character roles, as in *Ryan's Daughter* (1971) and *Gandhi* (1980). His daughters **Hayley Mills** (1946–) and **Juliet Mills** (1941–) are both actresses.

● **Milne, A(lan) A(lexander)** ► (1882–1956) British novelist and dramatist. He contributed to *Punch* and wrote several popular comedies, but is best known for his books for and about his son Christopher Robin. These include *When We Were Very Young* (1924), a collection of verse, and two books about toy animals, *Winnie-the-Pooh* (1926) and *The House at Pooh Corner* (1928).

● **Milner, Alfred, Viscount** ► (1854–1925) British colonial administrator. After serving in Egypt (1889–92) and as chairman of the Board of Inland Revenue (1892–97) he was high commissioner in southern Africa (1897–1906) and governor of Cape Colony (1897–1901). His inflexibility towards Kruger at the Bloemfontein Conference (1899) precipitated the second ▷Boer War. However, he was a distinguished administrator as governor (1902–06), after their annexation, of the Orange River Colony (previously the Orange Free State) and the Transvaal.

● **Milo** ► (late 6th century BC) Greek wrestler of legendary strength, who won six Olympic prizes. He is said to have carried a calf on his shoulders once every day from its birth and eventually to have carried the grown cow round the Olympic stadium.

● **Miloš** ▶ (M. Obrenović; 1780–1860) Prince of Serbia (1815–39, 1858–60), who led a successful revolt against the Ottoman Empire (1815) and founded the ▷Obrenović dynasty. Miloš was the alleged assassin of ▷Karageorge. He was forced to abdicate in 1839 but was recalled in 1858.

● **Mílos** ▷*See* Melos.

● **Milošević, Slobodan** ▶ (1941–) Serbian politician; president of Serbia (1989–97) and of the Federal Republic of Yugoslavia (1997–2000). He authorized military action against the breakaway Yugoslav republics of Croatia and Slovenia in 1991–92 and supported Bosnian Serb aggression and "ethnic cleansing" during the civil war in Bosnia-Hercegovina (1992–95). The result was international isolation and economic disaster for Serbia. Serbia's repression of the majority Albanian population in ▷Kosovo led to NATO airstrikes against Yugoslavia from March, 1999. Milošević was defeated in presidential elections in 2000; when he refused to recognize the result, he was swept from power in a bloodless revolution. In 2001 he was arrested and handed over to the war crimes tribunal at The Hague, becoming the first head of state to stand trial for genocide.

● **Milstein, César** ▶ (1927–2002) British molecular biologist, born in Argentina. He worked in Cambridge, at the Medical Research Council's Laboratory of Molecular Biology, from 1963 until his retirement in 1994. For his role in producing the first ▷monoclonal antibodies, Milstein was awarded in 1984 Nobel Prize, which he shared with Georges Köhler (1946–95) and Niels Jerne (1911–94).

● **Milstein, Nathan** ▶ (1904–92) US violinist, born in Russia, resident in the USA from 1929. A pupil of Leopold Auer and Eugène Ysae, Milstein gave recitals with Vladimir Horowitz in Russia before establishing a European reputation in 1925. He published a number of violin transcriptions.

● **Miltiades** ▶ (c. 550–489 BC) Athenian general and statesman. Sent to govern the Thracian peninsula, he ruled as tyrant and fought with ▷Darius I of Persia in Scythia. After joining the Ionian cities' unsuccessful revolt against the Persians, he had to flee to Athens (493) but escaped punishment. Appointed a general in 490, he devised the strategy by which the Greeks defeated the Persians at the Battle of ▷Marathon.

● **Milton, John** ▶ (1608–74) English poet. After leaving Cambridge University he studied privately and wrote the poems *L'Allegro* and *Il Penseroso* (1632), the masque *Comus* (1633), and the elegy *Lycidas* (1637). In 1638 he travelled in France and Italy. During the 1640s and 1650s he supported the Puritan revolution and wrote many polemical pamphlets, notably *Areopagitica* (1644), a defence of free speech. He also wrote justifying divorce in cases of incompatibility, a position reflecting his own unhappy first marriage. In 1649 he was appointed Latin Secretary to the Council of State, but his sight began to fail and he was totally blind by 1652. After the Restoration he retired from public life to write his great epic *Paradise Lost* (1667), its sequel *Paradise Regained* (1671), and the dramatic poem *Samson Agonistes* (1671).

● **Milton Keynes** ▶ 1. 52 02N 0 42W A city in S central England, in Milton Keynes unitary authority, Buckinghamshire. Since 1967 it has been developed as a new town around the old village of Milton Keynes. It is the headquarters of the Open University (1969) and there are many other educational and training facilities. Diverse industries include electronics, clothing, and machinery, and there is a full range of service sector businesses. The UK's only multidenominational cathedral opened here in 1993. Population (1991): 156 148. **2.** A unitary authority in S central England, in Buckinghamshire. Area: 310 sq km (119 sq mi). Population (1998 est): 203 200.

● **Milwaukee** ▶ 43 03N 87 56W A city and port in the USA, in Wisconsin on Lake Michigan. Originally a fur-trading post, it grew after an influx of German refugees in 1848. The state's largest city and a major shipping centre, Milwaukee is a leading producer of heavy machinery, electrical equipment, and diesel and petrol engines. Population (1998 est): 578 364.

mime ▶ Marcel Marceau seen backstage in his character of Bip (1952).

● **mime** ▶ Acting without words by physical gestures alone. It was practised in ancient Greek and Roman drama and was an important constituent of the ▷commedia dell'arte in the 16th century. Modern mime was developed during the early 19th century in France by ▷Deburau and was revived in the 1920s by Etienne Decroux (1898–1991), whose pupils included Jean-Louis ▷Barrault and Marcel ▷Marceau.

● **mimesis** ▶ (Greek: imitation) A philosophical concept discussed by ▷Aristotle in the *Poetics*. He argues that imitation is the basis of all the arts but they differ as to the means they use and the objects they imitate. Thus, drama is the imitation of an action and the dramatic genres, tragedy and comedy, may be differentiated by their characters, who are either better (in tragedy) or worse (in comedy) than average humanity. Imitation in the arts does not refer to a simple realistic rendering of detail but to the poet's (or artist's) ability to select and present his material so as to express essential truth.

● **mimicry** ▶ The phenomenon of two or more organisms (commonly different species) resembling each other closely, which confers an advantage—usually protection—to one or both of them. In **Batesian mimicry**, named after H. W. ▷Bates, a poisonous or inedible species (the model) has a conspicuous coloration, which acts as a warning to predators. This aposematic (*or* warning) coloration is adopted by a harmless edible species (the mimic), which derives protection against the same predators. In **Müllerian mimicry**, first described by the German naturalist Fritz Müller (1821–97), two or more species—all inedible—have the same warning coloration. After a predator has associated this pattern with an inedible species it will learn not to select similarly coloured species.

● **Mimosa** ▶ A genus of trees, shrubs, and herbs (450–500 species), mostly native to tropical and subtropical America. They have feathery compound leaves and fluffy round catkins of yellow flowers. The genus includes the sensitive plants, *M. pudica* and *M. sensitiva*, in which the leaflets fold upwards and the leafstalks droop at the slightest touch. Florists' mimosas are species of *Acacia* (*see* wattle). Family: ▷Leguminosae.

● **Mina Hassan Tani** ▷*See* Kenitra.

● **Minamata disease** ▶ A form of mercury poisoning that killed 43 people in Minamata, Japan, between 1953 and 1956. The disease was contracted by eating fish contaminated with dimethyl mercury, derived from effluent from a local PVC factory. Symptoms included tremors, paralysis, severe anaemia, and bone deformities.

● **Minamoto Yoritomo** ▶ (1147–99) Japanese military leader descended from a 9th-century emperor, who as the first ▷shogun (military overlord, 1192–99) laid the foundations of feudal government in Japan. After the defeat (1185) of the dominant ▷Taira clan, Yoritomo built up an extensive vassal network based on Kamakura, near modern Yokohama. In 1192 he obtained the title of shogun from the emperor and his administration gradually moved from coexistence with the imperial government to dominance over it. His half-brother **Minamoto Yoshitsune** (1159–89) was a warrior who contributed to the Minamoto triumph against the Taira but who subsequently incurred the jealousy of Minamoto Yoritomo. His adventures before he was hunted down and committed suicide have captivated succeeding generations.

● **minaret** ▶ A tall slender tower attached to a mosque from which the muezzin calls Muslims to prayer five times a day.

● **Minch, the** ▶ A channel in the E Atlantic Ocean. It consists of the **North Minch** between Lewis and mainland Scotland and the **Little Minch** between Harris, North Uist, and Skye.

● **mind** ▶ A philosophical term for whatever it is in a person that thinks, feels, wills, etc. Whether it is immaterial or not is controversial. ▷Materialism denies its existence as an incorporeal entity. For ▷Aristotle mind was *nous* (intellect), the only part of the soul to survive death. For ▷Descartes it is his starting point, an incorporeal mental substance by virtue of whose activity (thought) he knew he existed (*cogito ergo sum*—I think therefore I am). Until recently it has been usual to suppose that nonhuman animals do not have minds, which were taken as a defining characteristic of human beings. ▷Behaviourism identifies mental attitudes with brain states.

● **Mind** ▶ (National Association for Mental Health) A voluntary British organization founded in 1946 to provide for the needs of the mentally ill and handicapped. It campaigns for better services for the mentally ill, runs advice centres, encourages an understanding of mental illness, and promotes mental health. Since 1970, when the name Mind was adopted, it has increased its political role. Director: J. Clements.

● **Mindanao** ▶ An island in the S Philippines, the second largest. Volcanic and rugged, it has suffered soil erosion due to tree felling. Hemp, maize, pineapples, timber, nickel, and gold are produced.
History: the Muslim population has resisted Spanish, US, and now Philippine rule. Separatism, aggravated by rapid economic development in the 1960s, led to recurrent fighting from 1975 onwards. In 1996 a peace agreement was reached giving the island greater autonomy. Area: 101 919 sq km (39 351 sq mi). Population (1995): 14 262 000. Chief towns: Davao and Zamboanga.

● **Minden** ▶ 52 18N 8 54E A town in NW Germany, in North Rhine-Westphalia on the River Weser. In 1759 the English and Hanoverians defeated the French here. Its medieval cathedral was rebuilt after World War II. Products include chemicals and glass. Population (1989 est): 75 175.

● **Mindoro** ▶ A mountainous island in the central Philippines. It produces timber and coal. Area: 10 236 sq km (3952 sq mi). Population (1995 est): 912 000. Chief town: Calapan.

● **Mindszenty, József, Cardinal** ▶ (J. Pehm; 1892–1975) Hungarian Roman Catholic churchman. He opposed the Nazis and later the Communists, who imprisoned him in 1948. Released in the 1956 Hungarian Revolution, he gained asylum at the US legation in Budapest and eventually settled in Rome.

● **mine** ▶ An explosive device used for military purposes on both land and sea. Largely developed in the 20th century, such weapons are buried or submerged and detonated by contact, vibration, nearby magnetic material, a timing mechanism, or noise. The first naval mine was exploded by Samuel Colt in 1843 (*see also* minesweeper). Uncleared antipersonnel landmines are a hazard for soldiers and have killed and injured civilians long after a conflict has ended. In 1997 there were an estimated 110 million uncleared mines in 50 countries, which kill some 10 000 people and maim over 14 000 (many of them children) every year. A campaign to ban antipersonnel mines (supported by ▷Diana, Princess of Wales shortly before her death) resulted in the Ottawa Treaty (1997) forbidding their production, sale, stockpiling, or use; this was signed by 134 countries (excluding the USA, Russia, and China) and came into force in 1999. The 1997 Nobel Peace Prize was awarded to the International Campaign to Ban Landmines and its head, Jody Williams.

● **minerals** ▶ Naturally occurring substances of definite chemical composition (although this may vary within limits). Some consist of a single element but most are compounds of at least two. Strictly defined, minerals are solid (except native mercury) and are inorganically formed, although the constituents of organic limestones, for instance, are considered minerals. Minerals, loosely, are any naturally occurring materials of economic value, especially those obtained by mining. Almost all true minerals are crystalline; a few, such as opal, are amorphous. Minerals are identified by the following properties: crystal system (e.g. cubic) and habit or form (e.g. fibrous), hardness (*see* Mohs' scale), relative density, lustre (e.g. metallic), colour, streak (colour when finely divided), ▷cleavage, and fracture. ▷Rocks are composed of mixtures of minerals (*see* mining and quarrying). **Mineralogy** is the study of minerals: their identification, classification, and formation.

● **Minerva** ▶ A Roman goddess originally of the arts and crafts of wisdom, later identified with the Greek ▷Athena. As goddess of war her importance almost equalled that of Mars. Her annual festival was the Quinquatrus, held in March.

● **minesweeper** ▶ A vessel equipped to cut the cables of floating mines. Partially submerged cables, attached to paravanes that keep them taut, are towed through a minefield so that the cable cuts the mines' anchor chains, allowing the mines to float so that they can be detonated by gunfire. Some mines are now laid on the sea bed; these can be detected by a submersible acoustic or magnetic mine-finder that places an explosive next to the mine to destroy it. To avoid detonating such mines, minesweepers have plastic or wooden hulls. Helicopters have also been used for minesweeping.

● **Ming** ▶ (1368–1644) A native Chinese dynasty, which succeeded the Mongol Yüan dynasty. It was founded by ▷Hong-wu, the first of 17 Ming emperors. The Ming provided stable government personally controlled by the emperor. The examination system to select bureaucrats was restored and overseas expeditions were encouraged. Painting and pottery, especially blue and white porcelain, flourished. The Ming built the Forbidden City in Beijing in the 15th century.

● **Minghella, Anthony** ▶ (1954–) British film director and screenwriter. His films include *Truly, Madly, Deeply* (1991), *The English Patient* (1997), which won eight Academy Awards, and *The Talented Mr Ripley* (2000).

● **Mingus, Charlie** ▶ (1922–79) US Black jazz musician, who experimented with dissonance in jazz. A double-bass player, he played with Louis Armstrong, Lionel Hampton, and others. He also led his own band and appeared in films.

● **Minho, River** ▷*See* Miño, River.

● **miniature painting** ▶ The art of painting on a very small scale, using watercolour on a vellum, card, or (from the 18th century) ivory base. The medieval Persian and Indian miniatures are the first great examples. In Europe it flourished in the form of portraits from the 16th to mid-19th centuries. There it developed from medieval manuscript illumination and ▷Renaissance portrait medals. Although ▷Holbein the Younger produced some miniatures, ▷Hilliard was the first major English specialist. Other British miniaturists were Isaac ▷Oliver, Samuel ▷Cooper, and Richard ▷Cosway.

● **minicomputer** ▶ A small ▷computer, especially one that fits into a single cabinet. Minicomputers were cheaper than large mainframe computers, but were slower and had less memory. They have been superseded by modern ▷microcomputers.

● **Minicoy Islands** ▷*See* Lakshadweep.

● **minimal art** ▶ An abstract style of painting and sculpture developed in New York in the 1960s. In reaction to ▷abstract expressionism, it aims to eliminate self-expression by using geometrical shapes and unmodulated colours. Exponents include the painters Kenneth Noland (1924–) and Frank Stella (1936–) and the sculptor Carl André (1935–).

● **minimal music** ► A style of music that developed in the late 1960s, characterized by the repetition of simple musical elements. Exponents include the Americans Philip ▷Glass and Steve Reich (1936–). Some of the works of ▷Górecki, ▷Pärt, and ▷Tavener have also been described as minimalist.

● **minimally invasive surgery** ▷See surgery.

● **minimum wage** ► A minimum rate of pay for certain forms of employment, or for any form of employment, fixed by a government. The purpose is to prevent exploitation of workers by employers but, in practice, it can mean that some people who would be employed at a low rate are not employed at all because employers cannot afford the minimum rate. Pioneered in Australia at the beginning of the 20th century, it has been widely used in developing countries, although it is sometimes difficult to enforce and some informal or casual forms of employment may escape the regulations. In the EU a minimum wage formed part of the so-called "Social Chapter," a protocol adopted by all signatories to the Maastricht Treaty (1992) except the UK. The UK adopted the social chapter in 1997 and finally introduced (from April, 1999) a minimum wage; this is now set at £4.20 per hour for those aged 22 or over and £3.20 for those aged 18–21.

● **mining and quarrying** ► The extraction of useful minerals from the earth's crust. Quarrying is usually regarded as the extraction of stone, sand, gravel, etc., from surface workings. Mining is the extraction by ▷opencast or underground workings of ores producing metals (gold, silver, zinc, copper, lead, tin, iron, and uranium) and other valuable minerals (coal, limestone, asbestos, salt, precious stones, etc.); mining also includes the extraction of oil from wells and the extraction of alluvial deposits. Some 70% of mineral ores come from surface workings, which using modern equipment can reach down to depths of 500 m (1640 ft). After the overburden of rock or sand has been removed, the underlying mineral is blasted by explosives or broken up by machinery and excavated by power shovels, which load it onto conveyors or trucks. To comply with environmental requirements the overburden is often backfilled (deposited behind the current working face). In underground workings many factors have to be taken into account, such as the size, shape, and hardness of the deposit, the nature of the surrounding rock and the surface terrain, and the risk of subsidence. Ores are loosened and excavated by blasting, drilling, and mechanical shovelling. The waste material after the valuable ore has been extracted is often fed back into the mine (sometimes hydraulically, as a slurry) to reduce the risk of subsidence. ▷See also coalmining; oil.

● **minivet** ► An Asian songbird of the genus *Pericrocotus* (10 species), occurring in forests, where it hunts for insects in small flocks. Male minivets, about 17 cm long, have a black-and-red plumage; the females are yellowish grey. Family: *Campephagidae* (cuckoo-shrikes and minivets).

● **mink** ► A small carnivorous ▢mammal belonging to the genus *Mustela* (weasels, stoats, etc.), prized for its fur. The American mink (*M. vison*) is the largest species (about 70 cm long) and has the most valuable fur. It is bred in captivity in many parts of the world, and escaped animals readily adapt to life in the wild. They are nocturnal, semi-aquatic, and efficient hunters both on land and in water, preying on fish, rodents, and waterfowl. Family: ▷Mustelidae.

● **Minkowski, Hermann** ► (1864–1909) Russian-born German mathematician. His family returned to Germany in 1872 and Minkowski studied at Königsberg University in the same class as David ▷Hilbert. In 1902 Minkowski became professor of mathematics at Göttingen University, where he worked with Hilbert. Minkowski's most important work was in developing the concept of space-time, in which time is treated as a fourth dimension. The resulting four-dimensional ▷space-time continuum (sometimes called **Minkowski space**) was used by Einstein in both special and general ▷relativity.

● **Minneapolis** ► 45 00N 93 15W A city in the USA, in Minnesota on the Mississippi River, adjacent to St Paul. The Twin Cities comprise the commercial, industrial, and financial centre of a large grain and cattle area; flour milling is the main industry. Minneapolis is noted for its wide streets, many lakes, and parks. The University of Minnesota was established here in 1851. Population (2000): 382 618.

● **Minnelli, Liza** ▷See Garland, Judy.

● **Minnesingers** ► (German: singers of love) Aristocratic German singing guilds that flourished in the 12th and 13th centuries; the German equivalent of the French ▷troubadours. Their decline coincided with the rise of the ▷Meistersingers.

● **Minnesota** ► A state in the USA, bordering on Canada in the N and Lake Superior in the NE. It consists of rolling prairies rising to the heavily forested Superior Highlands in the N and contains many lakes, the largest being the Lake of the Woods. Manufacturing industries (especially food processing) now form the most important sector of the economy. The high-grade iron ores, of which it was a major source, are virtually exhausted but mining remains important following new finds of copper and nickel. Agriculture, concentrated chiefly in the S, produces maize and soya beans. Tourism is an important source of revenue.
History: part of the Louisiana Purchase in 1803, it became a state in 1858. During the 1880s many Scandinavians settled in Minnesota and their influence remains strong today. Area: 217 736 sq km (84 068 sq mi). Population (2000): 4 919 479. Capital: St Paul.

● **minnow** ► One of several fish of the family *Cyprinidae*, especially *Phoxinus phoxinus*, found in clear fresh waters of Europe and N Asia. Its slim body is usually about 7.5 cm long, has small scales, and ranges in colour from gold to green. Order: *Cypriniformes*.
The name is also applied to various other small fish, including mudminnows (family *Umbridae*; order *Salmoniformes*) and ▷killifish.

● **Miño, River** ► (Portuguese name: Minho) A river in SW Europe. Rising in NW Spain, it flows mainly SSW, forming part of the border between Spain and Portugal, to the Atlantic Ocean. Length: 338 km (210 mi).

● **Minoan civilization** ► The civilization of Bronze Age Crete, named by Sir Arthur ▷Evans after the legendary King ▷Minos. The most advanced Aegean civilization, the Minoan arose after 2500 BC. It is conventionally divided into three phases: Early (2500–2000), Middle (2000–1700), and Late (1700–1400). During the Middle Minoan period palace building at ▷Knossos, Mallia, and Phaistos attests Crete's growing wealth. Around 1700 these structures were destroyed and replaced by grander ones, the centres of power in a marine empire covering the S Aegean. A catastrophic eruption on ▷Thera (sometime between 1645 and 1450) ended Minoan prosperity as the sterile volcanic fallout temporarily ruined Crete's agriculture. Subsequent occupation levels show increasing Mycenaean influence (*see* Mycenaean civilization).
Excavated frescoes and artefacts show that Minoan material culture was highly sophisticated; craftsmen included architects, potters, painters, stone cutters, goldsmiths, and jewellers. Three scripts were used: hieroglyphics (c. 1900–1700), ▷Linear A (c. 1700–1450), and ▷Linear B (c. 1450–1400). A prominent deity was a snake goddess; the famous bull sports may have had ritual significance. ▢ p. 832.

● **Minorca** ► (Spanish name: Menorca) A Spanish island in the Mediterranean Sea, the second largest of the Balearic Islands. It is generally low lying and dry and agriculture is limited, with livestock raising. Shoe manufacture is important and it has an expanding tourist industry. Area: 702 sq km (271 sq mi). Population (latest est): 55 500. Chief town: Mahón.

● **minor planet** ► (*or* asteroid) A small nonluminous rocky body that orbits a star. Over 100 000 orbit the sun, mostly (probably 95%) in a main belt between the orbits of Mars and Jupiter, 2.17–3.3 astronomical units from the sun. Of the remainder, some, such as Icarus, have highly elliptical orbits that bring them close to the sun while others, including the ▷Trojan group, lie far beyond the main belt. Some are less than 1 km across with only about 200 exceeding 100 km: the largest is ▷Ceres (1003 km). They are probably debris from collisions of bodies that formed between Mars and Jupiter. Most meteorites (*see* meteor) are considered fragments of minor planets.

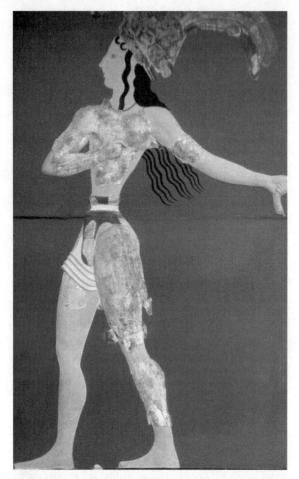

Minoan civilization ▸ Stucco relief of a prince with feather crown found in the procession corridor of the Palace of Minos at Knossos (Crete).

● **Minos** ▸ A legendary king of Crete, son of Zeus and Europa. His wife was Pasiphae, by whom he had two daughters, ▷Ariadne and ▷Phaedra. Although usually regarded as a good ruler, the Athenians portrayed him as a tyrant, who exacted an annual tribute of seven youths and seven maidens who were fed to the ▷Minotaur. According to Herodotus, he was killed in Sicily while pursuing ▷Daedalus after his escape from Crete. He is, with Rhadamanthus and Aeacus, one of the judges of the dead in Hades.

● **Minotaur** ▸ In Greek legend, a Cretan monster with a bull's head and a man's body. It was the offspring of Pasiphae, wife of ▷Minos, and a bull with which Poseidon had caused her to fall in love. It was kept in a labyrinth built by ▷Daedalus and killed by ▷Theseus with Ariadne's help.

● **Minsk** ▸ 53 51N 27 30E The capital of Belarus, in the centre of the country. Dating from at least the 11th century, it came under Lithuanian and then Polish rule; it was restored to Russia in 1793. It was virtually destroyed in World War II, and its large Jewish population exterminated during the German occupation. Industries include machine and vehicle manufacturing, textiles, and food processing. It is a cultural centre. Population (1996 est): 1 700 000.

● **mint** ▸ An aromatic perennial herb of the genus *Mentha* (about 25 species), native to Eurasia and Australia and widely distributed throughout temperate and subtropical regions. It has creeping roots from which arise square stems, bearing simple toothed leaves and terminal clusters of purple, pink, or white flowers. Many species are grown in gardens as herbs, especially ▷peppermint and ▷spearmint:

their leaves are used fresh or dried. An oil extracted from mint stems and leaves is used in perfumes and medicines. Family: ▷*Labiatae*.

● **Mint** ▷*See* Royal Mint.

● **Mintoff, Dom(inic)** ▸ (1916–) Maltese statesman; Labour prime minister (1955–58, 1971–84). He supported Maltese independence from Britain, achieved in 1964, and negotiated the end (1979) of a British military presence on Malta.

● **Minton ware** ▸ Porcelain produced at the pottery founded (1796) by **Thomas Minton** (1765–1836) at Stoke (England). Remarkable products included imitation ▷maiolica, tiles, and Parian (imitation marble) statuary.

● **minuet** ▸ A court dance of the 17th and 18th centuries in triple time. Of rustic origin, it was often included in the instrumental suite and became part of the sonatas and symphonies of Haydn, Mozart, etc. The first statement of the minuet was followed by a second minuet in a related key (called a trio), after which the first minuet was repeated.

● **Minya, El** ▸ 28 06N 30 45E A port in N central Egypt, on the River Nile. It is an important link between the left bank of the Nile and the Bahr Yusuf Canal and trade includes cotton and flour. Population (1992 est): 208 000.

● **Miocene epoch** ▷*See* Tertiary period.

● **Miquelon Island** ▷*See* St Pierre et Miquelon.

● **Mir** ▸ A space station launched into earth orbit by the Soviet Union in 1986. The first permanently manned space station, it included six docking ports for the addition of further units. Used for various experiments and observations, Mir was a refinement of the earlier ▷Salyut stations. In 1997 Mir collided with an unmanned cargo ship causing damage to the solar panels; although the crew were able to make repairs, Russia subsequently decided to abandon the station, effectively ending its manned space programme. Its remains were successfully brought back to earth in 2001.

● **Mirabeau, Honoré Gabriel Riquetti, Comte de** ▸ (1749–91) French statesman. In the years before the ▷French Revolution he gained notoriety as a libertine and profligate. In 1789 he was elected to the States General, championing the cause of the Third Estate at the outbreak of the Revolution. However, he was out of sympathy with the growing republicanism, advocating the establishment of a constitutional monarchy on the British model. By 1790 he was coming under increasing attack from the ▷Jacobins but died of natural causes before a crisis was reached.

● **Mira Ceti** ▸ A ▷red giant in the equatorial constellation Cetus that is a ▷variable star with a mean period of 331 days. Long known to vary considerably in brightness (by 5–6 magnitudes on average), it is the prototype of the **Mira stars**, which are all long-period pulsating variables.

● **miracle plays** ▸ Medieval European dramas based on religious themes. In England, they flourished particularly in the 14th and early 15th centuries. A distinction between **mystery plays** (based on episodes in the Bible) and miracle plays (based on the lives of saints) is often made with regard to French examples, but in England the terms were used interchangeably. They were originally performed in churches on religious holidays, especially Corpus Christi and Whitsuntide. They became increasingly secular and were eventually performed on mobile stages by trade guilds in marketplaces (hence the term "mystery play," from the Middle English *misteri* meaning a skilled trade). Almost complete cycles of plays from York, Coventry, Wakefield, and Chester have survived.

● **mirage** ▸ An optical illusion sometimes observed on hot days. It is caused by the air near the ground being considerably hotter than the air above, causing refraction of light rays from the sky, since the refractive index of air depends on its density and therefore on its temperature. Thus rays near the horizon can be bent upwards sufficiently to appear to be coming from the ground, creating the illusion of a lake.

● **Miranda, Francisco de** ▸ (1750–1816) Venezuelan revolutionary, whose plan to liberate Latin America from Spain failed. He was a leader of the Venezuelan revolutionary army, assuming dictatorial powers when the country formally declared independence in 1811. He surrendered to Spain in 1812 and died in a Spanish prison.

● **Miró, Joan** ▶ (1893–1983) Surrealist painter, born in Barcelona. He moved to Paris (1919), where he participated in the first surrealist exhibition (1925) and began painting in a childlike style. The gaiety of his painting disappeared in the late 1930s with his "savage" paintings, expressing the horrors of the Spanish Civil War; it reappeared, however, in his *Constellations*, painted (during World War II) with his characteristic amoebic shapes. He also created ballet sets, murals, and sculptures.

● **mirrors** ▶ Devices for reflecting light, usually consisting of a sheet of glass with one surface silvered. A plane (flat) mirror forms a laterally inverted virtual image. Spherical mirrors, concave or convex, magnify or reduce the image. If the distances of the object and image from the mirror surface are u and v, then $1/u + 1/v = 1/f$, where f is the focal length of the mirror, taking all distances as positive in front of the mirror and negative behind it. To avoid spherical aberration, parabolic mirrors are used in reflecting ▷telescopes.

● **MIRV** ▶ (multiple independently-targeted re-entry vehicle) A ballistic missile with several separate nuclear warheads, which can be aimed at different targets.

● **misch metal** ▶ An ▷alloy of between 15% and 40% iron with cerium and other rare metals. When rubbed with an abrasive it produces sparks and it is used for flints. The name is from German *Mischmetall*, mixed metal..

● **Mishima, Yukio** ▶ (Kimitake Hiraoka; 1925–70) Japanese novelist and playwright. He also acted in several films. His novels, which include *Confessions of a Mask* (1948) and *Sun and Steel* (1970), dealt with homosexuality, suicide, and traditional Japanese military values. He organized his own military group, the Shield Society, and committed harakiri as a protest against the weakness of postwar Japan.

● **Mishnah** ▶ (Hebrew: instruction) An early code of Jewish law. Written in Hebrew, it is traditionally thought to have been based on earlier compilations and edited in Palestine by the ethnarch Judah I in the early 3rd century AD. It consists of ▷halakhah on a wide range of subjects, derived partly from biblical law as interpreted by the early rabbis (called *Tannaim*) and partly from customs that had grown up over a long period of time. ▷*See also* Talmud.

● **Miskito Coast** ▷*See* Mosquito Coast.

● **Miskolc** ▶ 48 07N 20 47E A city in NE Hungary. Its buildings include a 13th-century gothic church and the National Theatre. The Technical University of Heavy Industry was established here in 1949. Its manufactures include iron, steel, and chemicals. Population (1997 est): 178 000.

● **missiles** ▷*See* antiballistic missiles; ballistic missiles; guided missiles; MIRV; Pershing missile; Polaris missile; Scud missile; Trident missile.

● **missing mass** ▷*See* dark matter.

● **missions, Christian** ▶ Enterprises to spread the Christian faith among those who profess other religions or none. The missionary journeys of St ▷Paul and the Apostles set an example that Christian individuals and organizations have followed ever since. St ▷Patrick, St ▷Columba, and St ▷Augustine of Canterbury were outstanding early missionaries in the British Isles. Isolated medieval missions reached as far as China, but concentrated activity began with the European discovery of the Americas and its diverse gods, and the sea route round Africa in the late 15th century. Roman Catholic orders, such as the ▷Dominicans, ▷Franciscans, and ▷Jesuits, made substantial conversions, especially in the 17th century, but Protestant denominations, with the exception of the ▷Moravian Brethren, did not do so until the 1790s. The 19th century was the peak period of activity with mission stations being established in remote regions. Developing countries frequently recognize the value of this work, which generally includes training in literary, practical, and medical skills, and allow missions to remain in the postcolonial period, sometimes facing hardship and danger. Missionaries now feel their work is countering the indifference and materialism of the Western world.

● **Mississippi** ▶ A state in the S central USA, on the Gulf of Mexico. Mainly low lying, it consists of the cotton-producing alluvial plain of the Mississippi River in the W, an area of extensive swamps in the SW, and a generally infertile region of low hills in the E and NE. The predominantly rural population has a large Black community. Still an important agricultural state, its main products are cotton (although this is no longer the mainstay of the economy), soya beans, poultry, eggs, and livestock. Manufacturing has increased in importance, with ship construction and repair the main industry. Timber and paper products, textiles, chemicals, and food processing are also important. Petroleum is the main mineral but natural gas, clay, and sand and gravel are also exploited. Mississippi is one of the country's poorest states.

History: explored by the Spanish, it was later claimed for France and was ceded to Britain (1763). Colonization followed and the area came under US control (1783). Made a state in 1817, it became a leading cotton producer and slave state until the US Civil War. Due to an oversight, Mississippi did not officially agree to the abolition of slavery until 1995. Area: 123 584 sq km (47 716 sq mi). Population (1996 est): 2 716 115. Capital: Jackson.

● **Mississippian period** ▷*See* Carboniferous period.

● **Mississippi River** ▶ A river in the central USA, the second longest river in North America. Rising in N Minnesota, it flows generally S into the Gulf of Mexico, through several channels (known as the Passes). Together with its chief tributary, the Missouri River, it forms the third longest river system in the world, at 6050 km (3759 mi) long with the world's third largest drainage basin, covering 3 222 000 sq km (1 243 753 sq mi). The lower course has high artificial embankments (levees) to prevent flooding; these failed in 1993 when the river burst its banks. Famous for its steamboats, celebrated by Mark Twain, it is now one of the world's busiest commercial waterways, with major ports at St Louis and New Orleans. Length: 3780 km (2348 mi).

● **Missolonghi** ▶ (Modern Greek name: Mesolóngion) A town in W Greece, on the Gulf of Patras. It is famous for its defence against the Turks during the War of Greek Independence (1821–29). Lord Byron died here in 1824. Population (latest est): 10 164.

● **Missouri** ▶ A state in the central USA, lying immediately W of the Mississippi River. It is divided by the Missouri River into fertile prairies and rolling hills in the N and W and the hills of the Ozark plateau in the S. Highly urbanized, much of its population lives in the two main cities of St Louis and Kansas City. Manufacturing dominates the economy, with transport and aerospace equipment, food processing, chemicals, and printing and publishing. The leading lead producer in the USA, it also exploits barytes, iron ore, and zinc deposits. Agriculture is diversified producing livestock and dairy products, soya beans, corn, wheat, cotton, and sorghum grains.

History: explored by the French from Canada and claimed for France (1682), it was ceded to Spain (1783) before returning to France in 1800. It formed part of the Louisiana Purchase (1803) by the USA, becoming a state in 1821. Area: 180 486 sq km (69 686 sq mi). Population (1996 est): 5 358 692. Capital: Jefferson City.

● **Missouri River** ▶ A river in the central USA, the longest river in North America and chief tributary of the Mississippi River. Rising in the Rocky Mountains, it flows N and E through Montana, then SE across North and South Dakota before joining the Mississippi at St Louis. A series of dams provides irrigation and has considerably reduced the danger of flooding along its lower course. Length: 4367 km (2714 mi).

● **Mistinguett** ▶ (Jeanne-Marie Bourgeois; 1875–1956) French singer and comedienne. She was a leading star of the Moulin Rouge, the Folies-Bergère, and other Paris music halls between the wars. She performed with elaborate costumes and settings, often in company with Maurice ▷Chevalier.

● **mistle thrush** ▶ A heavily built thrush, *Turdus viscivorus*, of Eurasia and NW Africa. It is about 28 cm long and has a greyish-brown upper plumage with a thickly speckled yellowish breast and white underwings. It feeds on berries (especially mistletoe—hence its name), snails, and worms.

● **mistletoe** ► A semiparasitic evergreen shrub of the temperate and tropical family *Loranthaceae* (1300 species), growing on the branches of many trees. The Eurasian mistletoe (*Viscum album*) occurs mainly on apple trees, poplars, willows, and hawthorns. It has rootlike suckers, which penetrate into the host tissues, and woody branching stems, 60–90 cm long, bearing oval leathery leaves and yellow male and female flowers borne on separate plants. The female flowers give rise to white berries, which are eaten by birds (which thereby disperse the seeds). Mistletoe was believed by the Druids to have magical and medicinal properties and is a traditional Christmas decoration.

● **mistral** ► A cold dry northerly wind that is funnelled down the Rhône Valley in S France to the Mediterranean Sea. Thick hedges and tree screens orientated E–W protect crops from its force.

● **Mistral, Frédéric** ► (1830–1914) French poet. In 1854 he helped found the Félibrige, a movement dedicated to the regeneration of Provençal language and culture. His many works in the Provençal vernacular include the epic verse narratives *Mirèio* (1859) and *Lou Pouèmo dóu Rose* (1897). He won the Nobel Prize in 1905.

● **Mistral, Gabriela** ► (Lucila Godoy Alcayaga; 1889–1957) Chilean poet, who worked as a teacher and cultural ambassador. Her volumes of poetry include *Desolación* (1922), published after the suicide of her fiancé, *Tala* (1938), and *Lagar* (1954). She was awarded the Nobel Prize in 1945.

● **Mitchell, Joni** ► (Roberta Joan Anderson; 1943–) Canadian singer and songwriter. Her earlier albums, such as *Clouds* (1967), *Blue* (1971), and *Court and Spark* (1974), are in a folk-based style with introspective lyrics. Later work, such as *The Hissing of Summer Lawns* (1975), *Mingus* (1979), and *Turbulent Indigo* (1994), shows a growing jazz influence.

● **Mitchell, Margaret** ► (1900–49) US novelist. Her single novel, the international bestseller *Gone with the Wind* (1936), is a historical romance set in Georgia during and after the Civil War. It won a Pulitzer Prize (1937) and was made into one of the cinema's most successful films in 1939.

● **Mitchell, R(eginald) J(oseph)** ► (1895–1937) British aeronautical engineer. He joined Vickers in 1916 and was a leading designer of seaplanes entered for the Schneider Trophy in the 1920s. His seaplane designs led to his design for the first Spitfire (1936), although he did not live to see its supremacy as a fighter in World War II. ⁰aircraft.

● **Mitchum, Robert** ► (1917–97) US film actor, noted for his taciturn style. His earlier films, mainly thrillers and westerns, included *The Story of GI Joe* (1945), *Crossfire* (1947), *The Night of the Hunter* (1955), *The Sundowners* (1960), and *Cape Fear* (1962). Later work included the films *Ryan's Daughter* (1970), *The Yazuka* (1975), and *Mr North* (1988), as well as many appearances on television.

● **mite** ► A tiny ▷arachnid (up to 6 mm long) comprising—with the ▷ticks—the worldwide order *Acarina* (or *Acari*; over 20 000 species). It has an unsegmented body and eight bristly legs. Mites occur in a wide range of habitats, including soil, stored foods, water, plants, and decaying organic material; some are parasitic on animals. Some are pests and may transmit diseases (including some forms of ▷typhus). ▷*See also* harvest mite; itch mite; spider mite.

● **Mitford, Nancy** ► (1904–73) British writer; one of four famous daughters of the eccentric Lord Redesdale. Her books include *The Pursuit of Love* (1945) and *Love in a Cold Climate* (1949). Her sister **Lady Diana Mosley** (1910–) was the wife of the notorious British Fascist Sir Oswald ▷Mosley. Another sister, **Unity Mitford** (1914–48), was an admirer and friend of Hitler; she committed suicide. Her sister, **Jessica Mitford** (1917–96) was also a writer, the author of *Hons and Rebels* (1960) and *The American Way of Death* (1963).

● **Mithra** ► A Persian god of light, truth, and justice. He killed a cosmic bull, whose blood was the source of all animals and plants. ▷*See* Mithraism.

● **Mithraism** ► A mystery religion (*see* mysteries) that worshipped ▷Mithra. It spread through Asia Minor, finally reaching Rome in

about 68 BC. Here Mithra was known as Mithras and was worshipped widely among Roman soldiers. He was regarded as the eternal enemy of evil, whose sacrifice of a bull symbolized the regeneration of life. Part of the cult's initiation ceremony was a bath in a sacrificed bull's blood. Mithraism rivalled Christianity until its decline in the 3rd century AD. Remains of a Roman temple to Mithras were discovered (1954) in the City of London; parts of it can still be seen.

● **Mithridates VI Eupator** ► (120–63 BC) King of Pontus and one of Rome's most persistent enemies. Mithridates extended his kingdom by invading Colchis and Lesser Armenia, antagonizing Rome by proceeding to Paphlagonia, Cappadocia, and Greece. Sulla, Lucullus, and Pompey in turn opposed him in three Mithridatic Wars (88–84, 83–81, 74–64) and he finally committed suicide.

● **mitochondria** ► Granular rod-shaped structures that occur in the cytoplasm of all ⁰cells except those of bacteria. They contain their own DNA and various enzymes that function in cellular ▷respiration and the metabolism of fat, glycogen, proteins, etc., to produce energy. It is thought that mitochondria evolved from symbiotic bacteria that lived within the cells of other organisms.

● **mitochondrial Eve** ► (*or* African Eve) The hypothetical ancestral female from whom all modern humans are said to be directly descended. Evidence for such an ancestor comes from a study of DNA from the ▷mitochondria of individuals from widely different racial and geographical backgrounds. This DNA, which is inherited only through the female line (since a sperm contributes no mitochondria when it fertilizes an egg cell), was found to be surprisingly uniform, indicating a common ancestor who lived 100 000–200 000 years ago, probably in Africa. Evidence for an "African Adam"—the male representative of this ancestral population—comes from a similar study of the DNA from Y chromosomes, which are found only in males.

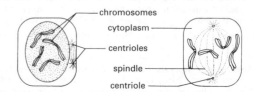

— chromosomes
cytoplasm —
— centrioles
spindle —
centriole —

prophase The genetic material becomes visible in the form of chromosomes and the nuclear membrane disappears.

metaphase The chromosomes become attached to the equator of a fibrous spindle.

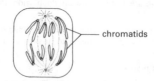

— chromatids

anaphase The two chromatids of each chromosome move to opposite poles of the spindle.

telophase Nuclear membranes form around the two groups of chomatids, which become less distinct.

mitosis ► Division of the nucleus of an animal cell takes place in four phases, which grade into each other.

● **mitosis** ► The process by which the nucleus of a somatic cell (i.e. any cell that is not a germ cell) duplicates itself exactly, producing two daughter nuclei with chromosomes that are identical to those of the parent nucleus. This nuclear division involves the separation of the two chromatids of each chromosome, which move apart to form two groups at opposite ends of the cell. In the final phase each group becomes enclosed in a new nuclear membrane. After this the cytoplasm usually divides to form two new cells. Mitosis occurs in most animals and plants during the normal growth and repair of tissues. *Compare* meiosis.

● **Mitsiwa** ▷*See* Massawa.

● **Mittelland Canal** ► (*or* Ems-Weser-Elbe-Kanal) A canal in central Europe. Opened in 1938, it links the Dortmund-Ems Canal in W Germany with the River Elbe in E Germany. Length: 325 km (202 mi).

● **Mitterrand, François (Maurice)** ► (1916–96) French socialist politician; president (1981–95). He assumed leadership of the newly unified Socialist Party in 1971. After two unsuccessful runs for the French presidency (1965, 1974) he defeated Giscard d'Estaing in 1981 to become the first socialist president in 35 years. Mitterrand assumed a leading role in the formation of EC policy. He retired in 1995, having become France's longest-serving president.

● **mixed economy** ► An economy with neither complete capitalist control of resources, nor complete government control. The aim is to temper the "unacceptable face" of capitalism while retaining its incentives and its efficient allocation of resources. In mixed economies, governments usually seek to control the public services, the basic industries, and those enterprises that cannot raise adequate capital investment from private sources. Ideally, this arrangement enables a measure of economic planning to be combined with a measure of free enterprise. In the 1980s and 1990s many Western societies moved away from mixed economies, with privatization of public services and a renewed emphasis on free-market ideas.

● **Mixtecs** ► An American Indian people originating in W Oaxaca province (S Mexico). After the 10th century they gradually absorbed the neighbouring ▷Zapotecs. The Mixtecs were excellent craftsmen, whose skill in gold working, mosaics, pottery, and painting spread over much of Mesoamerica, influencing both ▷Maya and ▷Aztec art styles.

● **Mizoguchi Kenji** ► (1898–1956) Japanese film director. His films are characterized by a controlled visual style and by a persistent concern with the psychology of women. They include *The Life of Oharu* (1952), *Ugetsu Monogatari* (1953), and *Street of Shame* (1956).

● **Mizoram** ► A state in NE India, in tropical hills between Bangladesh and Myanmar (Burma). Its largely Christian tribes are subsistence farmers of rice, sugar, and potatoes. Mizoram was separated from Assam in 1972 and became a state in 1986. Area: 21 081 sq km (8138 sq mi). Population (1994 est): 775 000. Capital: Aijal.

● **m.k.s. system** ► A ▷metric system of units based on the metre, kilogram, and second. It has now been replaced in science by ▷SI units, which are derived from it. The main difference between the two systems is that in SI units, the m.k.s. electrical units are rationalized (i.e. the factor 4π or 2π is introduced when demanded by the geometry).

● **M'Naghten's Rules** ▷*See* insanity.

● **Mnemosyne** ► In Greek mythology, a daughter of the ▷Titans Uranus and Gaia. She is the personification of memory. After sleeping with Zeus for nine consecutive nights she gave birth to the ▷Muses.

● **moa** ► An extinct flightless bird belonging to an order (*Dinornithiformes*; about 25 species) that occurred in New Zealand. Moas were 60–300 cm tall and had a small head, a long neck, and long legs. They were fast runners but were hunted by early Polynesian settlers for food. Some smaller species may have survived until the 19th century.

● **Moabites** ► A highly civilized Semitic tribe living E of the Dead Sea from the late 14th century BC. Closely associated ethnically with their neighbours and rivals the Israelites, they successfully rebelled against Israelite occupation in the 9th century BC. In 582 BC, according to Josephus, they were conquered by the Babylonians. The Moabite Stone, found at Dibon near Amman (Jordan) in 1868 and dating to the 9th century BC, bears an inscription (in the Moabite alphabet) celebrating a Moabite victory against the Israelites.

● **Mobile** ► 30 12N 88 00W A seaport in the USA, in Alabama on Mobile Bay at the mouth of the Mobile River. Founded in 1710, it was occupied by the French, British, and Spanish before being seized for the USA in 1813. Industries include shipbuilding, oil refining, textiles, and chemicals. Population (1998 est): 202 181.

● **mobile phone** ► A small battery-operated telephone that uses the ▷cellular network to connect to other mobiles or to the main tele-phone system. Some 60% of the UK population now own a mobile. First-generation models used analogue technology and relied on circuit switching. Second-generation phones (*see* WAP), are based on digital technology and include a short-message service (SMS) enabling up to 160 characters of text to be sent. **Texting** in this way is now widespread (1.5 billion messages per month in the UK) and has its own shorthand. Third-generation (3G) phones, in which circuit switching is replaced by the faster packet switching, are expected to enter service in Europe in 2003–04. They provide a permanent connection to the Internet (with instant e-mailing and video messages), many computer functions, and a ▷Global Positioning System.

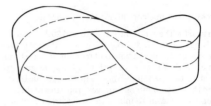

Möbius strip ► A surface with one side and one edge.

● **Möbius strip** ► In ▷topology, a one-sided surface with only one edge, made by taking a strip of paper, twisting it once, and joining the ends. If cut in two lengthwise, it remains in one piece but with a double twist. It was discovered by the astronomer August Ferdinand Möbius (1780–1868).

● **Mobutu, Lake** ▷*See* Albert, Lake.

● **Mobutu Sese Seko** ► (Joseph-Désiré M.; 1930–97) Dictator (1965–97) of Zaïre (the Democratic Republic of Congo). As commander-in-chief of the Congo army he seized power in 1960 and again in 1965. In 1970 he became president and changed the country's name to Zaïre. By the 1990s his authoritarian and massively corrupt rule faced mounting opposition. He was deposed by rebels under Laurent Kabila in 1997.

● **Moçambique** ▷*See* Mozambique, Republic of.

● **Moçâmedes** ▷*See* Namibe.

● **moccasin** ► (snake) ▷*See* water moccasin.

● **Mocenigo** ► A Venetian family from which came many of the ▷doges of the Venetian Republic. They included **Tommaso Mocenigo** (1343–1423), doge (1414–23); his nephew **Pietro Mocenigo** (1406–76), who was a distinguished admiral as well as doge (1474–76); Pietro's brother **Giovanni Mocenigo** (1408–85), doge (1478–85); and Giovanni's grandson **Andrea Mocenigo** (1473–1542), a historian.

● **Mocha** ► (*or* Al Mukha) 13 20N 43 16E A town in SW Yemen, on the Red Sea coast. It was famous for its coffee. Population (latest est): 2000.

● **Moche** ► An ancient Peruvian city near Trujillo, which was the capital (c. 400–600 AD) of the pre-Inca Mochica people. It is noted for its two pyramids (Sun and Moon).

● **mock epic** ► A form of satiric verse that exposes the absurdity or worthlessness of a trivial subject or theme by treating it in the elevated style appropriate to a genuine ▷epic. The form originated in classical literature and was practised by neoclassical writers in the late 17th and early 18th centuries. Examples include *Le Lutrin* (1674–83) by ▷Boileau and *The Rape of the Lock* (1712–14) ▷Pope.

● **mockingbird** ► A songbird that belongs to an American family (*Mimidae*; 30 species) and is noted for its ability to mimic sounds. Mockingbirds live on or near the ground, feeding on insects and fruit. The common mockingbird (*Mimus polyglottus*) is about 25 cm long with a grey plumage and white wing bars.

● **mock orange** ► A shrub, also called syringa, of the genus *Philadelphus* (75 species), native to N temperate regions and cultivated for ornament. They have simple leaves and fragrant white flowers resembling orange blossom. *P. coronarius* is the only native European species. Family: *Philadelphaceae*.

● **Model Parliament** ▷See parliament.

● **modem** ▶ (modulator demodulator) A device that converts digital information into analogue signals, and vice versa. Modems are used mainly to connect computers across analogue transmission systems, such as the telephone network, which gives access to the ▷Internet.

● **Modena** ▶ (ancient name: Mutina) 44 39N 10 55E A city in N Italy, in Emilia-Romagna. Ruled by the Este family (1288–1860), it has an 11th-century romanesque cathedral, several palaces, and a university (1175). The centre of an agricultural area, its industries include agricultural engineering, textiles, and motor vehicles. Population (1998 est): 175 013.

● **moderator** ▷See nuclear energy; thermal reactor.

● **modern art** ▶ The art of the late 19th and 20th centuries, which has largely abandoned traditional subjects, aesthetic standards, and techniques of art. The development of modern art was stimulated by the decline of artistic patronage by church and state, giving the artist more freedom to experiment. These experiments have largely centred round the use of colour and form as properties in their own right and not only as a means to mirror the real world (see photography). They can be traced back to ▷Manet and the impressionists. ▷Cézanne began the dissolution of one of the main foundations of Western painting since the Renaissance—the use of linear ▷perspective. This was completed by ▷cubism in the early 20th century and formed the basis for subsequent work by ▷Picasso. Parallel movements were ▷futurism in Italy and ▷vorticism in England. In Russia a completely nonrepresentational geometric art developed in the form of ▷suprematism and ▷constructivism. Suprematism, constructivism, and neoplasticism (see Stijl, de) were highly influential in the 1920s at the German ▷Bauhaus school of design and geometric abstraction has remained a leading artistic trend in the form of ▷Op art and ▷minimal art. Colour used for its own sake was a major feature of French ▷fauvism in the early 1900s. Die ▷Brücke, the German counterpart of fauvism, was also part of another modern movement—▷expressionism. These two trends were fused in the work of ▷Kandinsky, who produced the first abstract painting in about 1910. His heir in the 1940s, when the centre of modern art shifted to New York, was Jackson ▷Pollock, the leading exponent of ▷abstract expressionism. Other movements have explored such concerns as the world of dreams and the subconscious (see surrealism), the role of the mass media in society (see pop art), and the status of art itself (see conceptual art; dada; performance art). ▷See also abstract art; sculpture.

● **modern dance** ▶ A form of theatrical dance developed in central Europe and the USA in the early 20th century in reaction to the technical virtuosity and fairytale subjects of ▷ballet. The early pioneers were the German dancers Kurt Joos (1901–79) and Mary Wigman (1886–1973) and the US dancers Isadora ▷Duncan and Martha ▷Graham.
  Modern dance has developed new kinds of movement to express feeling, particularly jerking, thrusting, and contracting movements. It is usually performed in simple clothing against austere scenery and often uses music from outside the Western classical tradition. In England it has been promoted by the London School of Contemporary Dance, founded in 1969, and the work of the Rambert Dance Company. Such leading ballet choreographers as ▷Béjart, Jerome ▷Robbins, and Richard Alston (1948–) have been influenced by modern dance. In recent decades such innovative choreographers as Trisha Brown (1936–) and Meredith Monk (1942–) in the USA and Jirí Kylián (1947–) and Pina ▷Bausch in Europe have pioneered a fusion of dance with theatre.

● **modernism** ▶ (arts) A general movement in the earlier 20th century against the traditional subjects, attitudes, and techniques of previous generations of artists. It embraced such developments as the ▷stream of consciousness and ▷free verse in literature, experiments with ▷atonality and ▷serialism in music, and ▷functionalism in architecture. Among its characteristics were formal innovation and complexity, a tone of ironic disenchantment, and the elimination of sentimentalism, decoration, and representationalism (see modern art). In recent decades the concept of ▷postmodernism has been much discussed.

● **Modernism** ▶ (religion) A movement among Roman Catholic theologians that arose independently in several countries in the late 19th century. Its adherents sought to bring Roman Catholic thinking into harmony with modern philosophical and scientific trends. The historical accuracy of the Bible and the problems of dogmatic theology were held to be relatively unimportant. Pope Pius X condemned the movement officially in 1907.

● **modes** ▶ Musical scales derived from ancient Greek music, on which European music was based up to the 16th century. Each mode consists of a different pattern of the five tones and two semitones of the octave. Some of the most common modes were the Ionian (C-C), the Dorian (D-D), the Lydian (F-F), and the Aeolian (A-A). The Ionian and Aeolian modes became the basis of the major and minor scales of the 17th century and after.

● **Modigliani, Amedeo** ▶ (1884–1920) Italian painter and sculptor, born in Livorno of Jewish origin. His mature work, executed in Paris (1906–20), was influenced by ▷Cézanne and ▷Brancusi and, in its angular and elongated character, by Negro masks. From 1909 to 1915 he worked chiefly on sculptures; from 1915 until his death from tuberculosis, aggravated by drink and drug addiction, he painted many nudes and portraits.

● **modulation** ▶ A method of carrying information (the signal) on an electromagnetic wave or an oscillating electric current. In **amplitude modulation** (AM) the amplitude of a carrier wave is changed according to the magnitude of the signal. This is used in mediumwave sound broadcasting in which audio-frequencies (50–20 000 hertz) are carried on radio waves with a frequency of about one megahertz. In **frequency modulation** (FM) the frequency of the carrier wave is changed within a small bandwidth of the reference frequency. FM is used in VHF ▷radio (about 100 megahertz). It offers a better signal-to-noise ratio than AM.
  In **pulse modulation** the carrier is a series of pulses. It is used in digital equipment, such as computers, and in telegraphy and telemetry. A continuous signal alters the height in pulse-amplitude modulation, the width in pulse-duration modulation, or the time between pulses in pulse-position modulation. Pulse-code modulation uses a coded pattern of pulses to carry the signal, e.g. in ▷Morse code.

● **Moers** ▶ 51 27N 6 36E A city in NW Germany, in North Rhine-Westphalia in the ▷Ruhr. It grew rapidly in the 20th century as a coal-mining centre. Population (1998 est): 106 704.

● **Mogadishu** ▶ (or Mogadiscio) 2 01N 45 25E The capital and main port of Somalia, on the Indian Ocean. It was founded as an Arab settlement in the 10th century and sold to Italy in 1905 becoming the capital of Italian Somaliland. It has a university (1969). In 1991 the city was reduced to ruins during Somalia's prolonged civil war. Population (1999 est): 1 162 000.

● **Mogilev** ▶ 53 54N 30 20E A city in E Belarus, on the River Dnepr. Founded in 1267, it passed to Lithuania and then to Poland before being annexed by Russia (1772). It produces metal goods, machinery, and chemicals. Population (1998 est): 369 000.

● **Mogul art and architecture** ▶ A style that developed in N India under the patronage of the Mogul emperors. Originally much indebted to ▷Persian art, Mogul painting developed a more naturalistic style with small-scale scenes of court life and natural history as favoured subjects. Book illustration was highly developed. Architecture reached its peak during the reign (1556–1605) of ▷Akbar the Great, when attempts were made to fuse the opposing traditions of the indigenous Hindu architecture, characterized by solid rocklike masses and use of beams in building, with the Islamic tradition of mathematical clarity in design and use of true arches and internal spaces in construction (see Fatehpur Sikri). ▷See also Indian art and architecture; Taj Mahal.

● **Moguls** ▶ An Indian Muslim dynasty, descended from the Mongol leader ▷Genghis Khan, that ruled from 1526 until 1858. Its founder was ▷Babur (reigned 1526–30); he and the first 5 of his 18 successors, Humayun (1508–56; reigned 1530–56), ▷Akbar the Great (reigned 1556–1605), ▷Jahangir (1605–27), ▷Shah Jahan (1627–58), and

▷Aurangzeb (1658–1707), are known as the Great Moguls, and by the time of Aurangzeb the Empire spread from the far N to the far S of India. During the late 17th and the 18th centuries Mogul power declined in the face of opposition from Hindus to religious intolerance and of European commercial expansion. The last emperor, Bahadur Shah II (1775–1862; reigned 1837–58), was deposed after the ▷Indian Mutiny.

● **Mohács, Battle of** ► (29 August, 1526) The battle in which the Ottoman Turks under ▷Suleiman the Magnificent defeated a vastly outnumbered Hungarian and Bohemian army. It led to the submission of Hungary to Ottoman rule.

● **mohair** ► A wool-like fabric or yarn manufactured from the hair of ▷Angora goats. Warm, light, and durable and frequently blended with wool, silk, or cotton, mohair is used for lightweight suiting, upholstery, and fluffy fashion knitwear.

● **Mohamad, Mahathir bin** ► (1925–) Malaysian statesman; prime minister of Malaysia (1981–). Leader of the United Malays' National Organization (UMNO) since 1981, he successfully encouraged national industrial development in the 1980s and 1990s. However, Malaysia's financial collapse in 1998 led to economic and political crisis. In 1998–99 he faced riots and protests over the sacking and imprisonment of his reforming deputy, Anwar Ibrahim.

● **Mohammed** ► (*or* Muhammad; 571–632 AD) According to Muslims, the last of the prophets and preacher of ▷Islam to the Arabs. Mohammed is said to have been born in Mecca, a member of the Quraysh clan, which dominated the town. In 610, when he was about 40, he received revelations from God and called upon his pagan fellow townsmen to repent. The Meccans rejected him and threatened his life and in 622 he fled to Yathrib (*see* Hegira), where he established the first Muslim community. Yathrib now came to be called Medina, "City of the Prophet." By 629 the Muslims in Medina were strong enough to defeat the Meccans and took control of Mecca. By the time of Mohammed's death, Islam was spreading throughout Arabia. Mohammed's revelations were collected after his death as the ▷Koran. His tomb is venerated at Medina.

● **Mohammed I Askia** ► (d. 1538) Ruler of the West African empire of Songhai (1493–1528), which reached its greatest extent under his able rule. An enthusiastic Muslim, he made the pilgrimage to Mecca in 1495–97.

● **Mohammed II** ► (1430–81) Sultan of the Ottoman Empire (1451–81). Known as the Conqueror, his fame rests mainly on his conquest in 1453 of Constantinople, which as ▷Istanbul became the Ottoman capital. He also extended Ottoman territories in the Balkans and Asia Minor.

● **Mohammed Reza Pahlavi** ► (1918–80) Shah of Iran (1941–79). He became shah when the Allies forced his father ▷Reza Shah Pahlavi, to abdicate in World War II. In 1979 civil war forced him into exile and an Islamic republic was established in Iran under the leadership of Ayatollah Khomeini.

● **Mohave Desert** ▷*See* Mojave Desert.

● **Mohawk** ► An Iroquoian-speaking American Indian tribe of New York state. They were one of the five tribes that formed the league of the ▷Iroquois, said to have been founded by the Mohawk chief ▷Hiawatha.

● **Mohenjo-Daro** ► The site in Sind (Pakistan) of a great city of the ▷Indus Valley civilization. First excavated in the 1920s, it has extensive brick-built remains. ▷*See also* Harappa.

● **Mohican** ► An Algonquian-speaking American Indian tribe of New England. Primarily cultivators, they lived in fortified communities of 20 to 30 houses or in enclosed villages, but were displaced by wars with the Mohawks. Each of their five tribal sections was governed by a chief (sachem) together with an elected council.

● **Mohole** ► An unsuccessful research project embarked upon with US government funds but abandoned in 1966 because of its cost. The aim was to obtain samples of the rocks of the earth's upper mantle by drilling down from the ocean floor through the crust to the ▷Mohorovičić discontinuity. Drilling off W Mexico faced great technological difficulties.

● **Moholy-Nagy, László** ► (1895–1946) Hungarian artist. His most influential work was produced while teaching at the ▷Bauhaus (1923–29), where his experimental abstract paintings and photographs culminated in his *Light-Space Modulators*, plastic mechanical constructions that show continuously changing effects of light. He later taught in Chicago.

● **Mohorovičić discontinuity** ► The boundary between the earth's crust and upper mantle, marked by a sudden increase in velocity in seismic waves as the denser mantle is reached. It lies 33–35 km (20–22 mi) beneath the continents and 5–10 km (3–6 mi) beneath the oceans. It is named after the Andrija Mohorovičić (1857–1936), who discovered it in 1909.

● **Mohs' scale** ► A scale of hardness of minerals named after the mineralogist Friedrich Mohs (1773–1839). The ten standard minerals in the scale, in ascending order of hardness, are: 1. talc, 2. gypsum, 3. calcite, 4. fluorite, 5. apatite, 6. orthoclase feldspar, 7. quartz, 8. topaz, 9. corundum, and 10. diamond. Each can be scratched by any mineral higher up the scale, and other minerals can be assigned numbers in the scale according to which materials will scratch them.

● **Moi, Daniel arap** ► (1924–) Kenyan statesman; president of Kenya (1978–). Trained as a teacher, he was a founder of the Kenya African National Union (KANU). He succeeded Kenyatta as president and presided over Kenya's transition to multiparty politics in the early 1990s, since when he has been re-elected twice.

● **moiré pattern** ► A wavy cloudy fabric design. Originally applied

Mogul art and architecture ► The tomb of Humayun (reigned 1536–56), the second Mogul emperor, at Delhi. Mogul architecture entered its greatest period in the mid-16th century, when a subtle blend of Muslim and Hindu styles was achieved. The tomb's bulbous central dome and bell-shaped turrets are characteristic features.

to mohair (hence its name), this watered effect is obtained by steam pressing the material, usually silk or rayon, between engraved rollers.

● **Mojave Desert** ▶ (or Mohave Desert) A desert area in the USA, in S California. It comprises part of the ▷Great Basin. Area: 38 850 sq km (15 000 sq mi).

● **Moji** ▷See Kitakyushu.

● **moksha** ▷See Hinduism.

● **molarity** ▷See mole (metrology).

● **molasses** ▷See sugar cane.

● **Mold** ▶ 53 10N 3 08W A market town in North Wales, the administrative centre of Flintshire on the River Alyn. Population (1991): 8745.

● **Moldavia** ▶ A former principality in SE Europe. It was occupied by the Mongols in the 13th century, becoming independent in the 14th century and encompassing ▷Bukovina and ▷Bessarabia. It became an Ottoman vassal state in the 16th century, losing Bukovina to Austria in the 18th century and Bessarabia to Russia in the 19th century. In 1859 Moldavia and Walachia formed Romania. Russian Moldavia became the Moldavian Soviet Socialist Republic in 1940 (see Moldova, Republic of).

● **Moldova, Republic of** ▶ A republic in SE Europe. Romanians comprise 64% of the population, which also includes Ukrainians (14%) and Russians (13%).
Economy: the land is very fertile, producing wheat, maize, fruit, and vegetables, as well as supporting many vineyards. The main industries are wine making, tobacco processing, and food canning. The economy suffered gravely from a suspension of Russian trade (including vital fuel supplies) in 1992–94. Privatization and other economic reforms were implemented in the mid-1990s.
History: as the Moldavian Soviet Socialist Republic, it was formed in 1940, mainly from areas of ▷Bessarabia (see also Moldavia). Demands for increased autonomy continued from 1989 until independence from the Soviet Union was declared in 1991. Separatist ambitions in the mainly Russian and Ukrainian Dnestr region led to fierce fighting during 1992; this involved former Soviet troops stationed in the region, who were not withdrawn until 1996. There has been no recurrence of fighting but the situation remains tense. Although Moldova has strong historical and ethnic links with Romania, union with that country was rejected in a referendum in 1994. Later that year a new pluralist constitution was adopted and Moldova joined the Commonwealth of Independent States. The republic's first multiparty elections were held in 1994 and free presidential elections in 1997. The Communists were voted back into power in 2001.

Republic of Moldova

Head of state	President Vladimir Voronin
Official language	Moldovan (a form of Romanian)
Official currency	leu
Area	33 670 sq km (13 000 sq mi)
Population (2000 est)	4 298 000
Capital	Kishinev

● **mole** ▶ (medicine) An area of darkly pigmented skin, known medically as a naevus. Many people have moles and the only reasons for doing anything about them are cosmetic unless they enlarge, bleed, or become painful, any of which may indicate malignant change (see melanoma).

● **mole** ▶ (metrology; symbol mol) The ▷SI unit of amount of substance equal to the amount of substance that contains the same number of entities as there are atoms in 0.012 kg of carbon-12. One mol of any substance contains $6.022\,52 \times 10^{23}$ entities (the ▷Avogadro number). The entities may be atoms, molecules, ions, electrons, etc. The **molarity** of a solution is its concentration expressed in moles of solute per cubic decimetre (litre) of solvent.

● **mole** ▶ (zoology) A burrowing mammal belonging to the family *Talpidae*, of Europe, Asia, and North America. The common Eurasian mole (*Talpa europaea*) is about 14 cm long including its small bristly tail. It is thickset, with velvety-black fur, and has long-clawed digging forefeet. Moles dig extensive underground tunnels, feeding on earthworms. Practically blind above ground, moles rapidly starve when prevented from digging. Order: ▷Insectivora. ▷See also desman.

● **mole cricket** ▶ A large ▷cricket belonging to the family *Gryllotalpidae* (about 50 species). 35–50 mm long, mole crickets are brown and have enlarged and toothed front legs, which are used for digging long shallow tunnels under damp ground. The female lays large numbers of eggs in an underground nest and the young (like the adults) feed on plant roots and insect larvae.

● **molecular biology** ▶ The scientific discipline that deals with the molecular basis of living processes. Molecular biology involves both ▷biochemistry and ▷biophysics: its growth since the 1930s has been made possible by the development of such techniques as ▷chromatography, ▷electron microscopy, and ▷X-ray diffraction, which have revealed the structures of biologically important molecules, such as DNA, RNA, and enzymes. Heredity, and the development, organization, and function of living cells, all depend on the physical and chemical properties of the molecules involved.

● **molecular clock** ▶ The concept that the number of structural differences between corresponding proteins in any two species is proportional to the time elapsed since those species diverged from a common ancestor. The differences are the result of gene mutations occurring at a constant rate over a period of time. For example, if comparison of the haemoglobins of two animal species reveals only a small number of differences, this indicates that the two species have separated relatively recently. The molecular clock can be used to construct taxonomic relationships between species.

● **molecular cloud** ▶ An immense cloud of cool dense matter in the ▷interstellar medium, composed mainly of molecular hydrogen with a very small proportion of other molecules and dust grains. A typical cloud is 130 light years across, has a mass of 500 000 solar masses, and a temperature of 10–20 K. Stars form in these regions and have been detected by radio astronomers in our Galaxy and others. Several thousand molecular clouds are thought to exist in the Galaxy.

● **molecular weight** ▷See relative molecular mass.

● **molecule** ▶ The smallest portion of a compound that can exist independently and retain its properties. The atoms that make up a molecule are either bonded together covalently, as in carbon dioxide, or electrovalently, as in sodium chloride. However, in crystalline substances the bonds extend throughout the whole crystal structure and the molecule has only a notional existence. In covalent gases and liquids, however, the molecule actually exists as a small group of atoms. The **molecular formula** gives the number of atoms of each element present in the molecule; for example, the molecular formula of water is H_2O and of carbon dioxide is CO_2.

● **mole rat** ▶ A burrowing ▷rodent superficially resembling a mole. Mole rats belong to three families found in Africa and Eurasia: *Bathyergidae* (16 species), *Spalacidae* (3 species), and *Rhizomyidae* (14 species). Mole rats of all three families have small eyes and ears, a small tail, and powerful digging feet. They feed on roots and tubers.

● **Molière** ▶ (Jean-Baptiste Poquelin; 1622–73) French dramatist, the father of modern French comedy. He left home in 1643 to establish a theatrical company and toured the provinces from 1645 to 1658. *Les Précieuses ridicules* (1659) was the first of a series of Paris productions that included *Tartuffe* (1664), *Dom Juan* (1665), *Le Misanthrope* (1666), *L'Avare* (1668), *Le Bourgeois Gentilhomme* (1670), and *Le Malade imaginaire* (1673). His ridicule of hypocrisy and his vigorous satire of contemporary manners and types brought him into conflict with the religious authorities. He frequently acted in his own productions and died after collapsing on stage.

● **Molina, Luis de** ▶ (1535–1600) Spanish ▷Jesuit theologian. A professor at Évora in Portugal and later at Madrid, he is best known for his *Concordia liberi arbitrii cum gratiae donis* (1588), which founded Molinism. This was an attempt to reconcile divine grace with man's free will. It precipitated a dispute between Molina's Jesuit supporters and the ▷Dominicans, which lasted for several centuries.

● **Molinos, Miguel de** ► (c. 1640–97) Spanish mystic and priest, who was a leading advocate of ▷Quietism. From 1669 he lived chiefly in Rome, where he wrote his famous *Spiritual Guide* (1675). He was condemned to life imprisonment by the ▷Inquisition in 1687.

● **Molise** ► A mountainous region in S central Italy, part of Abruzzi e Molise until 1963. It is a poor underdeveloped agricultural region producing wheat, potatoes, maize, sheep, and goats. Area: 4438 sq km (1713 sq mi). Population (1991): 320 916. Capital: Campobasso.

● **mollusc** ► An invertebrate animal belonging to the phylum *Mollusca* (about 50 000 species). Molluscs occupy marine, freshwater, and terrestrial habitats. They have a soft unsegmented body with a muscular foot, variously modified for crawling, burrowing, or swimming, and a thin dorsal mantle that secretes a shell of one, two, or eight parts. The shell is usually external, as in snails, but it may be internal, as in cuttlefish, or absent, as in slugs. All except ▷bivalves feed using a ribbon-shaped rasping tongue (radula). Most molluscs are herbivorous with some carnivorous and scavenging species. In the more primitive molluscs there are separate male and female sexes and eggs and sperm are released into the water, where fertilization takes place. Some of the more advanced ▷gastropods and bivalves are hermaphrodite and in some gastropods and all ▷cephalopods fertilization is internal.

● **molly** ► An attractive tropical fish of the genus *Mollienesia*. 5–13 cm long, several colour varieties have been bred for use in aquaria, including the well-known sailfin mollies (*M. latipinna* and *M. velifera*), which have a bluish sheen and, in the male, a large sail-like dorsal fin. Family: *Poeciliidae*; order: *Atheriniformes*.

● **Molly Maguires** ► A secret Irish coalminers' organization set up in Pennsylvania in the 1870s. Their strikes and violence against the coal owners came to an end with prosecutions, hangings, and prison sentences.

● **Molnár, Ferenc** ► (1878–1952) Hungarian dramatist known for his romantic and witty plays, notably *The Devil* (1907) and *The Red Mill* (1923). He also wrote novels and short stories. He emigrated to the USA in 1940.

● **moloch** ► A desert-dwelling Australian lizard, *Moloch horridus*, also called thorny devil. Its yellow-and-brown body is covered in camouflaging thorny spines. Ants are its chief food and microscopic channels on its head collect dew, which drips into its mouth. Family: *Agamidae*.

● **Moloch** ► A Semitic god whose worship involved the sacrificial burning of children. There are several biblical references to his worship by the Israelites during the period of the Kings (c. 961–c. 562 BC).

● **Molokai** ► A mountainous US island in the N Pacific Ocean, in Hawaii. Father Damien worked in its leper colony. Pineapples and cattle are exported. Area: 676 sq km (261 sq mi). Population (latest est): 6700. Chief settlement: Kaunakakai.

● **Molotov** ▷*See* Perm.

● **Molotov, Vyacheslav Mikhailovich** ► (V. M. Scriabin; 1890–1986) Soviet statesman, who assumed his name in 1906 to escape from the Imperial police. As prime minister (1930–41) and foreign minister (1939–49, 1953–56), Molotov signed the Soviet-German nonaggression treaty in 1939; after the German invasion in 1941, he negotiated alliances with the Allies. His subsequent attitude to the West (the frequency with which he said *niet* (no) in the UN was renowned) contributed to the Cold War. Disagreements with Khrushchev led to demotion in 1956 but in 1984/5 he was rehabilitated. The **Molotov cocktail**, named after him, is an incendiary hand-grenade.

● **Moltke, Helmuth, Graf von** ► (1800–91) Prussian field marshal; chief of the general staff (1858–88). His reorganization of the Prussian army led to victories against Denmark (1864) and Austria (1866) and in the Franco-Prussian War (1870–71). His nephew **Helmuth Johannes Ludwig von Moltke** (1848–1916) was chief of the German general staff (1906–14), directing at the outbreak of World War I the strategy devised by ▷Schlieffen. Held responsible for the defeat at the Marne, he was relieved of his command.

● **Moluccas** ► (or Maluku) An Indonesian group of islands between Sulawesi and West Irian. It includes the islands of Ambon, Halmahera, and Ceram. Mountainous and volcanic, most are fertile and humid. The indigenous population fishes, hunts, and collects sago, while along the coasts the tropical rain forest is giving way to shifting cultivation; spices, fish, and copra are exported.

History: before the Portuguese arrival (1512), the islands were ruled by Muslims and already famed for their cloves and nutmeg from which they gained the name of Spice Islands. After great European rivalry, Dutch control was established in the 19th century. With Indonesian independence (1949) the S Moluccas fought to secede but were subjugated by the new government (1950–56). In 1966 S Moluccans in the Netherlands drew attention to their cause with violent protests. Rioting between Muslims and Christians caused hundreds of deaths in 1999–2000. Area: about 74 504 sq km (28 766 sq mi). Population (1995 est): 2 094 700. Chief town: Ambon.

● **molybdenum** ► (Mo) A very hard silvery-grey metal of high melting point, it was first prepared in 1782 by P. J. Hjelm (1746–1813). It occurs in nature as molybdenite (MoS_2) and as wulfenite (lead molybdenate; $PbMoO_4$). It is extracted by the reduction of molybdenum trioxide (MoO_3). Molybdenum is used in high-temperature filaments and as an alloying agent in the production of high-strength steels. Trace quantities of molybdenum are important for plant nutrition. At no 42; at wt 95.94; mp 2623°C; bp 4639°C.

● **Mombasa** ► 4 04S 39 40E A port in Kenya, on an island in an inlet of the Indian Ocean. It was an important port for Arab traders and was taken in the 16th and 17th centuries by the Portuguese; the Arab influence remains strong. The modern deepwater port at Kinlindini handles most of Kenya's trade; industries include oil refining and a pipeline (opened 1977) supplies Nairobi. Population (1991 est): 600 000.

● **moment** ► The product of a force and its perpendicular distance from the axis about which it acts. A moment produces a turning effect and is sometimes called a torque. The inertia of a body to a torque is called its **moment of inertia**. This quantity is equal to mr^2 for a single mass (m) rotating about an axis at a distance r from the axis. The moment of inertia of a system of masses is equal to the sum of these products.

● **momentum** ► The linear momentum of a body is the product of its mass and its linear velocity. The angular momentum of a body is the product of its ▷moment of inertia and its angular velocity. Momentum is an important quantity in physics as during any process, for example a collision between two bodies, the total momentum of the system always remains constant (the law of conservation of momentum).

● **Mommsen, Theodor** ► (1817–1903) German historian and politician. In his major historical work, *The History of Rome* (1854–85), Mommsen adopted a modern critical approach, effectively demythologizing Roman history. He also wrote on law and archaeology.

● **Mon** ► A people of lower Myanmar (Burma) and central Thailand. They speak an ▷Austro-Asiatic language, also known as Talaing. It is written in a script derived from ▷Pali, which the Burmese subsequently adopted. Between about 600 and 1000 AD Mon kingdoms dominated the area. After the fall of rival ▷Pagan, the Mons recovered independence (late 13th to mid-16th centuries) but were subjugated by the Burmese in the 18th century and now survive only as minority groups. They are village-dwelling rice farmers, whose Theravada Buddhism is tinged with earlier pagan beliefs.

● **Mona** ▷*See* Anglesey.

● **Monaco, Principality of** ► A tiny country on the Mediterranean Sea, an enclave within French territory. It consists of three principal localities: the business district around the ports, Monte Carlo with its famous casino, and the capital Monaco.

Economy: the main sources of revenue are real estate, financial services, tourism, and the sale of postage stamps. There is no cultivation.

History: ruled by the house of Grimaldi since 1297, it has been under French protection since 1641 (except for a period, 1815–61, of Sardinian protection). Executive power lies with the hereditary prince and the State Council, and legislative power with the prince and the National Council. Monaco became a member of the UN in 1993.

Principality of Monaco

Head of state	Prince Rainier III
Official language	French; Monégasque, a mixture of French and Italian, is also spoken
Official currency	euro of 100 cents
Area	189 hectares (467 acres)
Population (2000 est)	31 700 (of which only 5000 have citizenship)
Capital	Monaco-Ville

● **monad** ▷*See* Leibniz, Gottfried Wilhelm.

● **Monadhliath Mountains** ▶ (*or* Grey Hills) A mountain range in N Scotland, in Highland. It lies between Loch Ness and the River Spey and reaches 941 m (3087 ft) at Carn Mairg.

● **Monaghan** ▶ (Irish name: Contae Mhuineachain) A county in the NE Republic of Ireland, in Ulster bordering on Northern Ireland. It is generally low lying and undulating. Agricultural produce includes oats and potatoes; cattle rearing and dairy farming are also important. Area: 1551 sq km (499 sq mi). Population (1996): 51 000. County town: Monaghan.

● **mona monkey** ▷*See* guenon.

● **monarch** ▶ A widespread American ▷milkweed butterfly, *Danaus plexippus* (*see* Plate I). Light brown with black borders and white dots, the adults migrate southwards to overwinter in semihibernation. In spring they move north, breeding on the way. Occasionally, individuals may reach Europe. The caterpillars are green with black and yellow bands.

● **monarchy** ▶ A system of government in which sovereignty is concentrated in the hands of one person, who is traditionally considered to have divine, rather than electoral, authority (*see* divine right of kings). The monarch generally acquires this position, and the power that goes with it, on a hereditary basis (usually through the male line). Monarchy was the prevailing form of government in the ancient and medieval worlds, when the condition of society made more democratic methods impractical outside small city states. During the late medieval and Renaissance periods most European monarchies successfully withstood the rival claims of popes, barons, and parliaments to emerge with their powers enhanced. In western Europe, the 16th and 17th centuries constituted the great era of **absolute monarchy**—the age of the Habsburgs in Spain and Austria, the Stuarts in Britain, and the Bourbons in France. However, with the growth of democratic and revolutionary sentiment in the 18th and 19th centuries, most European monarchs were deposed, although a few, such as the British sovereigns, have survived as **constitutional monarchs**. In this adaptation of the system the sovereign deputes government to elected representatives of the Crown, retains a traditional rather than divine authority, and personally performs a largely ceremonial role. However, the British monarchy still includes the **royal prerogative**. These poorly defined powers theoretically give the monarch the right to declare war, make treaties, and dissolve parliament, although in practice they would not be exercised without the advice of the government. Apart from the risk that a rogue sovereign might make use of the royal prerogative, the constitutional monarchy has perhaps two main disadvantages; first, the pomp and ceremony required to maintain its credibility is extremely expensive; secondly, its critics would argue that it perpetuates an elitist and backward-looking society in which birth is more important than merit and tradition more important than innovation. The advantages, however, are that it provides a ceremonial head of state who is not involved in party politics, who acts as a focus of national unity, and who is regarded by a majority of the British public as preferable to the alternative of an elected or appointed head of state.

● **monasticism** ▶ A system under which men or women devote themselves to a religious life either in solitude or in special communities removed from society. St ▷Anthony of Egypt probably inaugurated Christian monasticism by organizing ascetic hermits under a rule (c. 305). They were, however, essentially solitaries; communal

monastic life was introduced by Anthony's disciple, ▷Pachomius. Between 358 and 364 St ▷Basil the Great drew up the rule that still governs the Orthodox Churches' religious communities. In the 6th century St ▷Benedict of Nursia introduced a monastic rule in Italy that remained the basic system in the West (*see* Benedictines). It underwent periodic reform, first at ▷Cluny in the 10th century. The rules of three orders founded in the 11th century—the Camaldolese (1012), ▷Carthusian (1084), and ▷Cistercian (1098)—were also stricter variants of the Benedictine rule. The mendicant friars (*see* Augustinians; Carmelites; Dominicans; Franciscans) also took vows and lived according to a rule, but not in seclusion: they continued to perform duties in the world. They had corresponding rules for women, however, who lived enclosed lives as nuns. Two military orders, the ▷Hospitallers and ▷Templars, followed monastic discipline. Both monks and nuns were required to take vows of poverty, chastity, and obedience and to devote their lives to prayer and work. Until the Renaissance revived secular learning, the monasteries were the main cultural centres. Monasticism was also practised by the ancient Jews (*see* Essenes), and there is a strong monastic tradition in Buddhism (*see* sangha; tri-ratna). ▷*See also* dissolution of the monasteries.

● **Monastir** ▷*See* Bitola.

● **monazite** ▶ A rare-earth mineral that has the composition $(Ce,La,Y,Th)PO_4$ and is yellow to reddish-brown in colour; it is found as an accessory in acid igneous rocks and as placer deposits. Monazite is usually obtained as a by-product of titanium and zircon mining; it is the most common source of the rare earths.

● **Mönchengladbach** ▶ (*or* München Gladbach) 51 12N 6 25E A city in W Germany, in North Rhine-Westphalia. The site of a 13th-century cathedral, it is the centre of the German textile industry and headquarters of the NATO forces in N central Europe. Population (1998 est): 266 505.

● **Monck, George, 1st Duke of Albemarle** ▶ (1608–70) English general. Initially a royalist in the Civil War, he was captured and imprisoned (1644–46). Won over to the parliamentary cause, he defeated the Scots at Dunbar (1650) and pacified Scotland. In the first ▷Dutch War he became a successful general at sea. In command of Scotland from 1654, he supported the overthrow of Richard Cromwell (1659) and was largely responsible for the Restoration of Charles II.

● **Moncton** ▶ 46 04N 64 50W A city and river port in E Canada, in New Brunswick. The transportation hub of the ▷Maritime Provinces, it also has light industry and the French-language University of Moncton (1864). Population (1991): 80 744.

● **Mond, Ludwig** ▶ (1839–1909) German industrial chemist, who lived in Britain from 1862. He discovered nickel carbonyl and its application to the extraction of platinum from its ores, a method now known as the **Mond process**. He also made improvements to the ▷Solvay process. His son **Alfred Mond, 1st Baron Melchett** (1868–1930) was a British industrialist and Liberal politician, who helped to found Imperial Chemical Industries Ltd.

● **Mondrian, Piet** ▶ (Pieter Cornelis Mondriaan; 1872–1944) Dutch painter, born in Amersfoot. His early still lifes and landscapes became increasingly architectural; however, while in Paris (1912–14) he came under the influence of ▷cubism. His first abstract compositions (1917) used only horizontal and vertical lines, primary colours, and black and white. During this period he helped to launch the art movement of de ▷Stijl. After 1919 his style, known as neoplasticism, influenced both the ▷Bauhaus school and the ▷international style in architecture. In New York after 1940 his style became more relaxed with such paintings as *Broadway Boogie Woogie*.

● **Monet, Claude** ▶ (1840–1926) French impressionist painter, born in Paris (*see* impressionism). He spent his childhood in Le Havre, where his teacher ▷Boudin encouraged him to paint in the open air. After military service in Algeria (1860–62) he met ▷Sisley and ▷Renoir in Gleyre's studio. Initially influenced by the ▷Barbizon school, in the late 1860s he developed the impressionist technique in views of Paris and in the 1870s in boating scenes at Argenteuil. He excelled in his series of the same scenes painted at different times of day, e.g. *Gare St Lazare*, *Haystacks*, *Rouen Cathedral*, and the *Poplars*, the last of which anticipates ▷abstract art. His last works were his famous murals of water lilies (Orangerie, Paris).

● **monetarism** ▶ A revision of old-established economic theories that rivals Keynesianism. Monetarism's most celebrated proponent is the US economist Milton ▷Friedman. Monetarists believe that, with the exception of ▷monetary policy, government economic policy does not achieve its aims and is harmful. They believe that responsible regulation of the money supply is essential to the wellbeing of the economy, advocating a gentle expansion of the money supply at roughly the rate of growth of the economy. Monetarists blame ▷inflation on overexpansion of the money supply. The essential difference between neo-Keynesians and monetarists is that the former believe in government regulation of the economy, whereas the latter do not.

● **monetary policy** ▶ An economic policy in which the money supply is managed by the government, in order to influence the economy. During the 1950s and 1960s in the UK, government attention was focused on ▷fiscal policy and, to a lesser extent, on ▷prices and incomes policy. Since the inflation of the 1970s and the impact of monetarist ideas (*see* monetarism), more attention has been paid to monetary policy (*see also* open-market operations).

● **money** ▶ A medium of exchange. To be an efficient medium of exchange, money should be divisible (for small transactions), have a high value-to-weight ratio (to make it easy to carry about), be readily acceptable, and not easily counterfeited. Money also functions as means of credit and a store of wealth, for which purposes its value must remain stable. The depreciation in the value of money (*see* inflation) is an economic problem, at present besetting the West. Money was reputedly invented by the Lydians in the 7th century BC. It originally took the form of something intrinsically valuable (such as a precious metal) but, so long as it is generally acceptable and retains confidence, this is not necessary. Indeed, most money is now in the form of paper, which is itself almost worthless. Individual countries have their own form of money (currency), which cannot be used in other countries; to be used in another country currencies have to be exchanged (*see* exchange rates).
   The total stock of money in the economy is known as the **money supply**. In the UK two definitions of the money supply are used: the narrow M1 (essentially, the total amount of cash and current accounts) and the broad M3 (essentially, the total amount of cash plus both current and deposit accounts). Government regulation of the money supply is known as ▷monetary policy. ▷*See also* Juno.

● **money market** ▶ A market in which money is borrowed and lent for short periods. Participants in the UK money market, in the City of London, include ▷discount houses, the ▷commercial banks, and the ▷Bank of England conducting ▷open-market operations for the government and acting as lender of the last resort.

● **money spider** ▶ A tiny ▷spider of the family *Liniphiidae* (over 250 species). It has a reddish or black body and occurs in enormous numbers in fields, etc. Money spiders build sheetlike webs on vegetation to which they cling upside down, waiting to catch insects that drop onto the web. Immature spiders may be seen drifting considerable distances in the air, attached to silken gossamer threads.

● **moneywort** ▶ A perennial herb, *Lysimachia nummularia*, also called creeping jenny, native to damp places in Europe. It has a creeping stem, up to 60 cm long, shiny heart-shaped leaves, and yellow flowers borne individually on short stalks. Family: *Primulaceae*.
   The Cornish moneywort (*Sibthorpia europaea*) is a small trailing perennial with minute pink flowers. Family: *Scrophulariaceae*.

● **Monge, Gaspard** ▶ (1746–1818) French mathematician. He was one of the founders of descriptive geometry, the mathematics of projecting solid figures onto a plane, upon which modern engineering drawing is based. He became a close friend of Napoleon and was appointed minister for the navy (1792–93), but was stripped of all honours on the restoration of the Bourbons. He died in poverty.

● **Mongolia, State of** ▶ A large sparsely populated country in NE central Asia, between Russia and China. It is mainly high plateau, rising to the Altai and Khangai Mountains in the W and extending into the Gobi Desert in the S.
   Economy: with its nomadic-pastoral tradition, it is still mainly dependent on livestock rearing, organized until 1992 in collectives and state farms. In 1999–2000 nearly 10% of the country's livestock died as a result of the harsh winter, leading to much hardship. In recent decades there have been attempts to increase crop growing. Copper mining has been developed and other minerals include coal, oil, gold, tungsten, lead, and uranium. There is some industry, mainly based on Ulan Bator and Darkhan. Infrastructure and communications remain largely undeveloped. Exports include cattle and horses, wool, and hair. Mongolia remains dependent on Russia for imports of fuel, machine parts, and many basic manufactures. In the early 1990s the end of central economic planning and of special trading arrangements with communist East Europe produced an economic crisis, resulting in considerable hardship. In 1996–2000 the government implemented IMF-backed policies of restructuring and deregulation.
   History: in the 13th century Genghis Khan ruled the vast Mongol empire from Karakoram in the N. As Outer Mongolia, the area comprising the present republic was a province of China from 1691 to 1911, when it became an autonomous monarchy under Russian protection. Again under Chinese influence from 1919 to 1921, it then became independent and the communist Mongolian People's Republic was declared in 1924. Persecution of lama priests (*see* Tibetan Buddhism) precipitated the Lama Rebellion (1932), when several thousand Mongolians with several million head of livestock crossed the border into Inner Mongolia (which had remained a province of China). After World War II its independence was guaranteed by the Soviet Union and China. In 1990 the Communist Party renounced its monopoly of power and multiparty elections were held, resulting in victory for the former Communists. A new constitution was adopted for the newly named State of Mongolia in 1992, enshrining democracy and introducing a free-market economy. In 1996 the ex-Communists were defeated in parliamentary elections and the opposition Democratic Union (DU) formed a government pledged to radical free-market reforms. From 1998 the DU government was beset by corruption scandals and constitutional disputes with President Bagabandi. Elections in 2000 resulted in a landslide for the former Communists under Nambariyn Enkhbayar.

State of Mongolia

Head of state	President Natsagiin Bagabandi
Official language	Khalkha Mongolian
Official currency	tugrik of 100 möngö
Area	1 565 000 sq km (604 095 sq mi)
Population (1999 est)	2 440 000
Capital	Ulan Bator

● **Mongolian languages** ▶ A group of languages that, together with ▷Turkic and ▷Manchu-Tungus, constitute the Altaic language family. Western Mongolian languages are spoken in parts of what was the Soviet Union, the Republic of Mongolia, and Afghanistan; Eastern Mongolian is spoken in China and the Republic of Mongolia. There are more than three million speakers of these languages, the majority of which remain unwritten.

● **Mongoloid** ▶ The racial grouping comprising the populations of E Asia and the Arctic region of North America. They are characterized by medium skin pigmentation, the epicanthic fold of the upper eyelid, straight coarse black hair, a rather flat face with high cheekbones, slight facial and body hair, and a high percentage of B blood type. The American Indian peoples used to be classified as Mongoloid.

● **Mongols** ▶ An Asiatic people united in the early 13th century by ▷Genghis Khan, who built up an empire that encompassed much of central Asia. Under his grandson ▷Kublai Khan the Mongols conquered China and ruled there as the ▷Yuan dynasty until 1368. They were subsequently confined to the area approximating to the present-day Republic of Mongolia.

● **mongoose** ▶ A carnivorous ⬚mammal belonging to the family ▷*Viverridae*, found in warm regions of the Mediterranean, Africa, and Asia. There are about 40 species, ranging in size from 50 to 100 cm including the long tapering furry tail (25–50 cm), with short legs, small ears, and long grey-brown fur. They are renowned for catching snakes and rats and also eat eggs, small mammals, frogs, and birds. Chief genera: *Galidictis, Herpestes, Helogale*. ▷*See also* meerkat.

● **monism** ▷*See* dualism.

● **monitor** ▶ A class of ironclad US warship of the mid-19th century, especially the *Monitor*, a Federal ship that engaged its Confederate counterpart, the *Merrimack*, at Hampton Roads, Virginia (1862). In 1978 the wreck of the victorious *Monitor* was identified in 75 m (230 ft) of water outside the harbour, but was in too fragile a condition to be raised.

monitor lizard ▶ The desert monitor (*Varanus griseus*) thrives in arid country ranging from NW Pakistan to the W Sahara.

● **monitor lizard** ▶ A lizard belonging to the Old World family *Varanidae* (30 species) of tropical and subtropical regions. 0.2–3 m long, monitors have an elongated body and well-developed legs. They feed on mammals, snakes, lizards, eggs, and carrion. The rare Bornean earless monitor (*Lanthanotus borneensis*) lives in tunnels and is a good swimmer, feeding on fish and worms. ▷*See also* Komodo dragon.

● **Moniz, Antonio Egas** ▶ (1874–1955) Portuguese surgeon, who pioneered the use of brain surgery to treat severe mental illness. In 1935 he performed the first prefrontal lobotomy (*see* leucotomy) and shared the 1949 Nobel Prize.

● **Monk, Thelonius (Sphere)** ▶ (1920–82) US Black jazz pianist and composer, a pioneer of ▷bop. He developed a characteristic style and played alone or in small groups; his compositions include "Off Minor" and "Blue Monk."

● **monkey** ▶ A tree-dwelling ▷primate. Monkeys are 20–110 cm long and most have a long balancing tail of up to 100 cm used in climbing, although some are tailless. Agile and intelligent, they have fingernails and an opposable thumb enabling manual dexterity. Most monkeys are omnivorous but they prefer fruit, nuts, and other vegetation. ▷*See also* New World monkey; Old World monkey.

● **monkey flower** ▶ A fragrant annual or perennial herb or shrub of the mostly North American genus *Mimulus* (100 species), growing near streams and rivers. *M. guttatus* is a naturalized European species. Up to 60 cm tall, it has simple toothed leaves and showy yellow tubular flowers with red spots, each with a two-lobed upper lip and a larger three-lobed lower lip. Family: *Scrophulariaceae*. ▷*See also* musk.

● **monkey puzzle** ▶ A coniferous tree, ▷*Araucaria araucana*, also called Chile pine, native to Chile and Argentina and widely grown as an ornamental. Up to 30 m high (ornamental trees are much smaller), it has whorled horizontal branches covered with leathery prickly overlapping leaves, 3–4 cm long. The globular spiny cones, 10–17 cm long, ripen from green to brown and break up to release large seeds, which are ed-ible when roasted. Family: *Araucariaceae*.

● **monkfish** ▶ A ▷shark belonging to the family *Squatinidae*. It has a broad flattened head, an elongated tapering body, winglike pectoral fins, two dorsal fins, and no anal fin. Monkfish occur in tropical and temperate seas and feed on bottom-dwelling fish, molluscs, and crustaceans. A species of ▷anglerfish, *Lophius piscatorius*, is also called monkfish.

● **monkshood** ▷*See* aconite.

● **Monmouth, James Scott, Duke of** ▶ (1649–85) The illegitimate son of Charles II of England and Lucy Walter (d. 1658), who led the Monmouth rebellion against his uncle James II. In 1662 he married, and took the name of, Anne Scott, Countess of Buccleuch. A Protestant, he became a focus of the opposition to the succession of the Roman Catholic James and was banished (1684) after being implicated in the ▷Rye House Plot. After James' accession (1685), Monmouth landed at Lyme Regis to raise a rebellion (known as **Monmouth's Rebellion**) and was defeated at ▷Sedgemoor, captured, and beheaded.

● **Monmouthshire** ▶ A county of SE Wales, bounded by the Bristol Channel in the S and the English border in the E. Under local government reorganization in 1974 the historic county of Monmouthshire was mainly absorbed into Gwent (with small areas going to South Glamorgan and Mid Glamorgan). When Gwent was abolished in 1996, administration passed to a reduced Monmouthshire in the E and N and four county boroughs (Blaenau Gwent, Newport, Torfaen, and part of Caerphilly) in the industrial W. Monmouthshire consists of undulating country, rising to the Black Mountains in the N. It is chiefly agricultural, with tourism and light industry. Area: 851 sq km (329 sq mi). Population: (1996 est): 85 600. Administrative centre: Cwmbran.

● **Monnet, Jean** ▶ (1888–1979) French economist and public official, known for his contribution to European unity. He was deputy secretary general of the League of Nations (1919–23). In 1946 he inaugurated the Monnet Plan for the modernization of French industry and later drafted the ▷Schuman Plan for the establishment of the European Coal and Steel Community, of which he was president (1952–55). His efforts culminated in the establishment of the EEC.

● **monoclonal antibody** ▶ A type of pure antibody that can be produced artificially in large quantities. Mouse lymphocytes producing the required antibody are fused with mouse cancer cells; the resulting hybrid cells multiply rapidly and all produce the same type of antibody as their parent lymphocytes. Monoclonal antibodies are widely used to detect and measure the amounts of particular antigens (e.g. blood-group antigens) or entities (e.g. disease-causing organisms, cancer cells) that can act as antigens. They are also being investigated for the treatment of certain types of cancer.

● **monocotyledons** ▶ The smaller of the two main groups of flowering plants, which includes the palms, bananas, orchids, grasses, lilies, and many garden bulbs and corms—daffodils, irises, tulips, crocuses, etc. (*compare* dicotyledons). Monocots have a single seed leaf (cotyledon) in the embryo. Typically the flower parts are in threes (or multiples of three) and the leaves have parallel veins. Very few monocots produce true wood. ▷*See also* angiosperm.

● **Monod, Jacques-Lucien** ▶ (1910–76) French biochemist, who proposed a mechanism for the regulation of gene activity. Monod and his colleague F. Jacob (1920–) postulated a regulatory gene that controlled the activity of a neighbouring gene for protein synthesis. Their theory was later found to be largely true. Monod and Jacob shared the 1965 Nobel Prize with A. Lwoff (1902–).

● **monody** ▶ A musical style of the 16th century, developed by Giulio ▷Caccini, in which a single recitative-like vocal line has a simple accompaniment of chords. It formed the basis of the first operas.

● **monomer** ▶ A simple molecule or group of atoms forming a repeated unit in a dimer (two molecules), trimer (three molecules), or polymer (*see* polymerization).

● **Monophysites** ▶ (Greek *monos physis*: one nature) Supporters of the doctrine that the incarnate Christ had only a single divine nature. They opposed the orthodox teaching that he possessed two natures, human as well as divine. The doctrine was provoked by the dogmatic formulations of the Council of Chalcedon (451) and, despite attempts at reconciliation, the ▷Coptic and several other Eastern Churches were irrevocably schismatic by the mid-6th century.

● **monopoly** ▶ An industry in which the market is supplied by one supplier. The monopolist can obtain a high profit by restricting supply and demanding a high price. Consumers are thus penalized and it is likely that with a secure market there will also be inefficiency in production. In the public sector of a mixed economy monopolies for the supply of public services (electricity, gas, transport, etc.) are commonplace. In the private sector they are usually restricted by legislation. The **Monopolies Commission** conducts detailed investigations into monopolies and mergers. In the USA the ▷antitrust acts perform a similar function. In a **monopsony**, there is a single buyer in the market, as in the purchase of defence equipment. A monopsonist clearly has great power in determining prices.

● **monorail** ▶ A railway using a single rail, either from which to suspend a carriage or over which a carriage is straddled. The former type was first used in 1884, consisting of an electrically driven truck running on a single rail from which was suspended a load-carrying car (called a **telpher**). The latter type has been demonstrated at Birmingham's National Exhibition Centre, using ▷magnetic levitation. Monorail systems are expensive to instal and are currently only used for special purposes.

● **monosaccharide** ▶ (*or* simple sugar) A ▷carbohydrate consisting of a single sugar unit and possessing either a keto group (C=O) or an aldehyde group (CHO). Monosaccharides are classified according to the number of carbon atoms they possess—the most common being pentoses (with five) and hexoses (with six)—and they can exist as either straight-chain or ring-shaped structures. The most widely occurring monosaccharides are ▷glucose and ▷fructose.

● **monosodium glutamate** ▶ The sodium salt of the amino acid glutamic acid, used widely in the food industry as a flavouring agent, especially in tinned preserved foods.

● **monotheism** ▶ Belief in only one God. The great monotheistic religions are Judaism, Christianity, and Islam. Earlier views that monotheism evolved out of ▷polytheism are now discredited, as Judaism and Islam in particular seem to have grown from conscious opposition to polytheism.

● **Monothelites** ▶ (Greek *monos, thelein*: one, (to) will) Supporters of the doctrine that the incarnate Christ possessed only one divine will. Monothelitism was conceived in 624 as a formula for reconciling the ▷Monophysite churches but failed and was formally branded a heresy in 680.

● **monotreme** ▶ A primitive ▷mammal belonging to the order *Monotremata*, found only in Australia (including Tasmania) and New Guinea. The name means "single hole," and monotremes have the reptilian characteristic of a single vent for passing urine, faeces, and eggs or sperm. Monotremes lay eggs, suckling their young after these hatch. The only living monotremes are the ▷echidnas and ▷duck-billed platypus.

● **Monroe, James** ▶ (1758–1831) US statesman; president (1817–25). He fought in the American Revolution and was later minister to France (1794–96) and Britain (1803–07) before becoming secretary of state (1811). His two peaceful terms as president, known as the "era of good feelings," saw the opening of the West and the acquisition of Spanish Florida. The **Monroe Doctrine** (1823), largely the work of John Quincy ▷Adams, became a basic principle of US foreign policy; it warned European powers not to intervene in the Americas and declared that the USA would likewise refrain from interference in Europe.

● **Monroe, Marilyn** ▶ (Norma Jean Baker *or* Mortenson; 1926–62) US film actress. Her childhood was spent in an orphanage and foster homes. Promoted as a sex symbol, in such films as *Niagara* (1952) and *Gentlemen Prefer Blondes* (1953), she later developed a real acting talent and ability as a comedienne. Her third husband was Arthur ▷Miller, and her last film appearance was in *The Misfits* (1961), which he wrote. She died from an overdose of barbiturates.

Marilyn Monroe ▶ Her girlish voice, sexual appeal, and vulnerability made her a legend. Unfortunately not even marriage to the intellectual Arthur Miller could protect her from the pressures of life in Hollywood, which ultimately drove her to suicide.

● **Monrovia** ▶ 6 20N 10 46W The capital and main port of Liberia, on the Atlantic Ocean. Founded in 1822 as a settlement for freed North American slaves, it was named after President Monroe of the USA. The University of Liberia was founded in 1851. Population (1995 est): 962 000.

● **Mons** ▶ (Flemish name: Bergen) 50 28N 3 58E A town in Belgium, situated between two coalmining regions. Notable buildings include the town hall (1443–67) and the Church of Ste Waudru (1450–1621). The Battle of Mons took place here on 23 August, 1914. Industries include oil, cotton, porcelain, and tobacco. Population (latest est): 89 515.

● **Monsarrat, Nicholas** ▶ (John Turney; 1910–79) British novelist. *The Cruel Sea* (1951) was based on his naval experiences in World War II. Other novels include *The Tribe That Lost its Head* (1956) and *The Pillow Fight* (1965).

● **monsoon** ▶ A seasonal large-scale reversal of winds in the tropics, resulting chiefly from the differential heating of the land and oceans. It is best developed in India, SE Asia, and China; N Australia and East and West Africa have similar wind reversals. The term is derived from the Arabic word *mawsim*, originally applied to the seasonal winds of the Arabian Sea. It is now commonly applied to the rainfall that accompanies the wind reversals, especially the period of heavy rainfall in S Asia extending from April to September.

● **Monstera** ▶ A genus of large tropical American herbaceous plants (50 species) that climb by means of aerial roots. *M. deliciosa* is often grown as a house plant for its foliage and in the tropics for its edible green fruits. The leaves, up to 60 cm long, are perforated with slits or holes and the flowers resemble those of the ▷arum lily. Family: *Araceae*.

● **Montagu, Lady Mary Wortley** ▶ (1689–1762) English writer. Her best-remembered works are her letters, especially those written from Constantinople, where her husband was ambassador and from where she introduced into England the practice of inoculation against smallpox. A friend of many prominent writers, she lived in Italy from 1739 to 1761.

● **Montaigne, Michel de** ▶ (1533–92) French essayist. Soon after the death of his father, a wealthy merchant, in 1568, he resigned his position as magistrate in Bordeaux and began composing his *Essais*. In 1580 he travelled extensively in Europe and was mayor of Bordeaux from 1581 to 1585. His *Essais*, which inaugurated a new literary genre, expressed his mature humanistic philosophy and constitute a moving self-portrait. They were published in two editions in 1580 and 1588, and a posthumous edition incorporated his final revisions. The *Essais* were translated into English by John Florio in 1603 and influenced the development of the English essay.

● **Montale, Eugenio** ▶ (1896–1981) Italian poet. The stoic pessimism and symbolic imagery of his early poetry, especially in *Ossi di seppia* (1925), contrasts with the personal warmth of such later volumes as *Satura* (1971) and *Xenia* (1972). He was an opponent of fascism, and from 1947 literary editor of the newspaper *Corriere della Sera*. He published many translations and literary essays and won the Nobel Prize in 1975.

● **Montana** ▶ The fourth largest state in the USA, bordering on Canada. It is mountainous and forested in the W, rising to the Rocky Mountains, with the rolling grasslands of the Great Plains in the E. Its economy is predominantly agricultural, cattle ranching and wheat production being of greatest importance. Other crops include barley and sugar beet. It possesses important mineral resources, notably copper (at Butte) and coal. The extraction of the latter is possible through strip mining but this has caused environmental problems. There are several Indian reservations within the state, notably the Crow reservation.

History: it formed part of the Louisiana Purchase in 1803. During the mid-19th century a gold rush caused an influx of immigrants to the state; the capital, Helena, originated as a mining camp called Last Chance Gulch. During the Indian wars the battle of ▷Little Bighorn (Custer's Last Stand) took place (1876). Area: 377 070 sq km (145 587 sq mi). Population (2000): 902 195. Capital: Helena.

● **Montanism** ▶ An early Christian sect founded by a shadowy individual called Montanus in Asia Minor in the mid-2nd century. It spread to N Africa, where ▷Tertullian became an adherent. It was characterized by ▷millenarianism, prophesying, and insistence upon strict asceticism.

● **Montauban** ▶ 44 01N 1 20E A town in SW France, the capital of the Tarn-et-Garonne department. It has textile and porcelain industries. Population (latest est): 53 280.

● **Mont Blanc** ▶ (Italian name: Monte Bianco) 45 50N 6 52E The highest mountain in the Alps, on the French–Italian border. It was first climbed in 1786. A road tunnel (1958–62) beneath it, 12 km (7.5 mi) long, connects the two countries. Height: 4807 m (15 771 ft).

● **montbretia** ▶ A perennial herb, *Crocosmia crocosmiflora* (a hybrid between *C. pottsii* and *C. aurea*), native to South Africa but naturalized in Europe and often grown as a garden ornamental. Up to 1 m high, it has long sword-shaped leaves and clusters of orange-red funnel-shaped flowers, up to 7.5 cm across, with spreading petals. The name is also applied to the similar and related flowering herbs of the South African genus *Montbretia* (or *Tritonia*). Family: *Iridaceae*.

● **Montcalm, Louis Joseph de Montcalm-Grozon, Marquis de** ▶ (1712–59) French general distinguished for his command (1756–59) against the British in Canada during the Seven Years' War. In 1756 he regained control of Ontario for the French, in 1757 he took Fort William Henry, and in 1758 repulsed the much larger British force from Ticonderoga. He died defending Quebec from assault by Gen James ▷Wolfe, who, although victorious, was also mortally wounded.

● **Monte Bello Islands** ▶ 20 30S 115 30E A group of uninhabited coral islands in the Indian Ocean, off the W coast of Western Australia. They were used for testing British nuclear weapons in 1952 and 1956.

● **Monte Carlo** ▶ 43 44N 7 25E A resort in the principality of Monaco, on the Riviera. It is famous for its casino, motor rally, and other cultural and sporting events. Population (latest est): 12 000.

● **Monte Cassino** ▷*See* Benedict of Nursia, St; Cassino.

● **Monte Cristo** ▶ An Italian islet in the Tyrrhenian Sea. It is associated with the novel by Dumas, *The Count of Monte Cristo*.

● **Montefeltro** ▶ An Italian noble family that ruled the city of Urbino between the 13th and 16th centuries. Originally rulers of the town of Mons Feretri from which they derived their name, the Montefeltri gave military support to the Holy Roman Emperor in his struggle against the pope (*see* Guelfs and Ghibellines). The best-known member of the family is the illegitimate **Federigo Montefeltro, Duke of Urbino** (1422–82), who distinguished himself as a military leader and as an art patron, especially of ▷Piero della Francesca.

● **Montefiore, Sir Moses** ▶ (1784–1885) British philanthropist, born in Italy, who campaigned for Jewish rights. He travelled widely throughout Europe and the Middle East, furthering with some success the cause of persecuted Jews. He also endowed many hospitals.

● **Montego Bay** ▶ 18 27N 77 56W A port and tourist resort in NW Jamaica. Its chief exports are bananas and sugar. Population (1991): 83 446.

● **Montélimar** ▶ 44 33N 4 45E A town in SE France, in the Drôme department. Famous for its nougat, it is an agricultural centre and has light industry. Population (1990): 32 000.

● **Montenegro** ▶ (Serbo-Croat name: Crna Gora) The smaller of the two republics in the Union of ▷Serbia and Montenegro, bordering on the Adriatic Sea. It is predominantly mountainous and forested. Stock raising is important, especially of sheep, goats, and pigs. Its economy has suffered from the international sanctions imposed on ▷Serbia in the 1990s.

History: declared a kingdom in 1910, it became a province of the kingdom of the Serbs, Croats, and Slovenes (later ▷Yugoslavia) in 1918. Following the disintegration of Yugoslavia in 1991–92, Montenegro and Serbia formed the Federal Republic of Yugoslavia. The later 1990s saw growing opposition to the federation with Serbia, a feeling exacerbated by Belgrade's repressive policy in Kosovo and the resultant war with NATO (1999). Tensions rose in 1999–2000 as the Montenegrin parliament announced plans to withdraw from the federation. However, there has been a rapprochement with Serbia since the fall of the ▷Milošević regime in 2000 and in 2002 the federation was replaced with a new Union of Serbia and Montenegro. Head of state: President Milo Djukanovic. Area: 13 812 sq km (5387 sq mi). Population (1997 est): 631 164. Capital: Podgorica.

● **Monterey** ▶ 36 39N 121 45W A city in the USA, in California on Monterey Bay. One of California's oldest cities, it is a well-known retreat of artists and writers. It forms the background for several of John Steinbeck's novels. Population (latest est): 31 954.

● **Monte Rosa** ▶ 45 57N 7 53E A massif in S Europe, on the Swiss–Italian border in the Alps. The highest peak, the Dufourspitze, is, at 4634 m (15 203 ft), the highest in Switzerland.

● **Monterrey** ▶ 25 40N 100 20W One of the largest cities in Mexico. Founded in 1579, it has many notable buildings including the 18th-century cathedral. Monterrey is a major industrial centre specializing in metallurgy. Population (1995): 1 088 023.

● **Montespan, Françoise Athénaïs de Rochechouart, Marquise de** ▶ (1641–1707) The mistress of Louis XIV of France from 1667 until replaced by the governess of their seven children—Mme de ▷Maintenon. Mme de Montespan remained at court until 1691, when she retired to a convent.

● **Montesquieu, Charles Louis de Secondat, Baron de** ▶ (1689–1755) French historical philosopher and writer. Montesquieu's first work, the *Lettres persanes* (1721), was a satirical portrait of French institutions and society and a forerunner of the ▷Enlightenment. There followed the *Considérations sur les causes de la grandeur et de la décadence des romains* (1734) and the famous *Esprit des lois* (1748). This latter, a comparative study of ideas on law and government, was perhaps the most important book of 18th-century France.

● **Montessori system** ▶ A system of education for young children devised by the Italian doctor **Maria Montessori** (1870–1952). It places emphasis on development of the senses and envisages a limited role for the teacher as the child learns by itself through the use of didactic materials. Her first school opened in Rome in 1907 and her methods continue to be influential in infant schools today.

● **Monteux, Pierre** ▶ (1875–1964) French conductor. He became conductor of Diaghilev's Ballets Russes in 1911 and gave the first performances of Stravinsky's *Petrushka* and *The Rite of Spring*. He subsequently held various posts in Europe and the USA and was principal conductor of the London Symphony Orchestra from 1961 to 1964.

● **Monteverdi, Claudio** ▶ (1567–1643) Italian composer, a pupil of Marco Ingegneri (1545–92). From about 1590 to 1612 Monteverdi was court musician to the Duke of Mantua. From 1613 until his death he was maestro di cappella at St Mark's Cathedral, Venice. Monteverdi was the first great composer of ▷opera; enlarging the orchestra, he employed a new range of instrumental effects and made use of an innovatory harmonic style to achieve dramatic effects. He also influenced the development of the madrigal as an expressive form. His works include the operas *Orfeo* (1607) and *The Coronation of Poppea* (1642), a set of *Vespers* (1610), and many madrigals.

● **Montevideo** ▶ 34 55S 56 10W The capital and main port of Uruguay, in the S on the Río de la Plata. Founded in 1726 by the Spanish as a defence against Portuguese attacks from Brazil, it suffered several occupations in the early 19th century before becoming capital of the newly independent Uruguay in 1828. In the 20th century it has developed rapidly, as both an industrial and a communications centre, and it is now one of South America's largest cities. It is also a popular summer resort. The University of Uruguay was founded here in 1849. Population (1996): 1 378 707.

● **Montez, Lola** ▶ (Marie Gilbert; 1818–61) Irish dancer and mistress of Louis I of Bavaria (1786–1868; reigned 1825–48). The hostility aroused by her influence led to the abdication of Louis in 1848 and her own expulsion. She later lived for several years in the USA.

● **Montezuma II** ▶ (1466–c. 1520) The last Aztec Emperor of Mexico (1502–20). During his reign his empire was weakened by tribal warfare, which enabled the Spaniards, led by Hernán ▷Cortés, to establish themselves in Mexico. The emperor was captured by Cortés and was killed either by the Spaniards or by his own people during the Aztec attack on Cortés' force as it tried to leave Tenochtitlán.

● **Montfort, Simon de, Earl of Leicester** ▶ (c. 1208–65) English statesman, born in Normandy; the son and namesake of the leader of the Crusade against the ▷Albigenses. After serving Henry III of England in Gascony, he joined the antiroyalist faction that demanded greater control of the government, becoming the barons' leader in the subsequent ▷Barons' War. Initially successful, he became virtual ruler of England, summoning a parliament in 1265. In the same year, however, he was defeated and killed at Evesham.

● **Montgolfier, Jacques-Étienne** ▶ (1745–99) French balloonist, who with his brother **Joseph-Michel Montgolfier** (1740–1810) invented the hot-air balloon. The hot-air balloon, so called because it derived its buoyancy from air heated by a fire, was publicly launched in 1782. A much larger balloon, which rose 2000 m, was demonstrated in June 1783 and in October a series of passenger-carrying ascents were made. Jacques-Étienne (who himself never made an ascent) then launched a free-flying balloon and in 1784 Joseph-Michel with five companions ascended in a steerable balloon. Their experiments aroused enormous interest in flying.

● **Montgomery** ▶ 32 22N 86 20W A city in the USA, the capital of Alabama on the Alabama River. Montgomery was the first capital (1861) of the Confederate states during the American Civil War. In the mid-1950s it was the scene of a bus boycott by Blacks, which played an important part in the growth of the civil-rights movement and brought Martin Luther King to the nation's attention. Montgomery is an industrial city and agricultural trading centre. Population (1996 est): 196 363.

● **Montgomery, Bernard Law, 1st Viscount Montgomery of Alamein** ▶ (1887–1976) British field marshal. In World War II he became commander of the Eighth Army (1942) and after the battle of Alamein drove ▷Rommel back to Tunis and surrender (1943), an achievement that brought him enormous popularity. Having played a major role in the invasion of Italy (1943), he became chief of land forces in the 1944 Normandy invasion. He helped plan the Arnhem disaster (September, 1944), but restored his reputation by pushing back the subsequent German offensive, receiving Germany's surrender. After the war he was chief of the imperial general staff (1946–48) and deputy commander of NATO forces (1951–58).

● **Montgomeryshire** ▶ A former county of NE Wales. Under local government reorganization in 1974 it became part of ▷Powys.

● **month** ▶ The time taken by the moon to complete one revolution around the earth. The complicated motion of the moon requires the starting and finishing points of the revolution to be specified. The length of the month depends on the choice of reference point. The **sidereal month**, of 27.32 days, is measured with reference to the background stars. The **synodic month**, of 29.53 days, is measured between two identical phases of the moon. The month is one of the basic time periods used in ▷calendars. The table shows the origins of the names of the months of the Gregorian ▷calendar. ▷*See also* French Republican calendar.

Months

month	named after
January	Roman Republican month *Januaris*—after ▷Janus
February	Roman *Februaris*—from *Februa*, festival of purification
March	Roman *Martius*—after ▷Mars
April	Roman *Aprilis*—from Latin *aprire* to open (of buds)
May	Roman *Maius*—from Maia, goddess of growth
June	Roman *Junius*—probably after ▷Juno
July	Roman *Julius*—after Julius ▷Caesar
August	Roman *Augustus*—after ▷Augustus
September–December	from Latin *septem-, octo-, nove-, decem-*, the 7th to 10th months of the Roman Republican calendar

● **Montherlant, Henry de** ▶ (1896–1972) French novelist and dramatist. He was born in Paris into an aristocratic family. His works celebrate the virtues of austerity and virility and concentrate on physical pursuits and relationships. His novels include *Les Célibataires* (1934), the tetralogy *Les Jeunes Filles* (1936–39), and *Le Chaos et la nuit* (1963), and his plays include *Malatesta* (1946) and *Port-Royal* (1954).

● **Montmartre** ▷*See* Paris.

● **Montparnasse** ▷*See* Paris.

● **Montpellier** ▶ 43 36N 3 53E A city in S France, the capital of the Hérault department. A Huguenot stronghold, it was besieged and captured by Louis XIII in 1622. Notable buildings include the gothic cathedral, the university (founded 1289), and the Musée Fabre. Montpellier trades in wine and brandy and has numerous manufacturing industries. Population (1990): 210 866.

● **Montreal** ▶ 45 30N 73 36W A city and port in E Canada, in Quebec on Montreal Island at the junction of the Ottawa and St Lawrence Rivers. It is a major transportation, trade, and manufacturing centre. Montreal employs cheap hydroelectricity for many industries, including oil refining, meat packing, brewing and distilling, food processing, textiles, and aircraft. It is the headquarters of banks, insurance companies, airlines, and railways. Housing two English-speaking and two French-speaking universities, Montreal is a forum for politics, broadcasting, theatre, film, and publishing. Two-thirds of the population is French speaking, making it the second largest French-speaking city in the world. Among its many beautiful buildings are Notre Dame Church, Christ Church Cathedral, and St James Cathedral.

History: founded as Ville-Marie (1642), Montreal quickly became a commercial centre. Captured by Britain (1760), it acquired an English-speaking merchant community that has dominated Quebec's economy. Montreal was the venue of the 1976 Olympics. Population (1991): 1 017 666.

● **Montreux** ▶ 46 27N 6 55E A winter resort in W Switzerland, on Lake Geneva. Its 13th-century Château de Chillon is immortalized in Byron's poem, the "Prisoner of Chillon". It holds an annual television festival awarding the Golden Rose of Montreux. Population (1990): 19 850.

● **Montrose** ▶ 56 43N 2 29W A resort in E Scotland in Angus. It has fishing, canning, chemical, and distilling industries and services for North Sea oil. Population (1991): 11 440.

● **Montrose, James Graham, 1st Marquess of** ▶ (1612–50) Scottish general. In 1637 he signed the Covenant in support of Presbyterianism but became a rival of the antiroyalist ▷Argyll, who secured his imprisonment in 1641. Montrose fought for Charles I in the English Civil War but after a series of victories (1644) against the Scottish covenanters his army of Highlanders was defeated at

Philipaugh (1645) and he fled to the Continent. He returned in 1650 but was defeated, captured, and executed.

● **Montserrat** ► A British overseas territory comprising one of the Leeward Islands, in the Caribbean Sea to the SE of Puerto Rico. It is largely mountainous with active volcanoes.

Economy: chiefly agricultural; the main exports are cotton, coconuts, fruit and vegetables, and cattle. Forestry is being developed.

History: European discovery of the island (by Columbus) occurred in 1493; it was colonized by the Irish in the 17th century. Formerly administratively joined to the Leeward Islands, it became a separate colony in 1960. It was part of the Federation of the West Indies (1958–62). In 1997 a huge volcanic eruption made two-thirds of the island uninhabitable (including the capital, Plymouth). Half the population have fled, with Britain offering help with voluntary resettlement. The future of the island is uncertain. Official language: English. Official currency: East Caribbean dollar of 100 cents. Area: 106 sq km (40 sq mi). Population (1997 est, since the eruption): 6500.

● **Montserrat** ► 41 36N 1 48E An isolated mountain in NE Spain, NW of Barcelona. On its E slope is a Benedictine monastery housing a well-known carving, supposedly by St Luke, of the Virgin and Child. Height: 1235 m (4054 ft).

● **Mont St Michel** ► 48 38N 1 30W A granite islet in NW France, in the Manche department in the Bay of St Michel. The islet is connected to the mainland by a causeway. It is about 78 m (256 ft) high and is crowned by a Benedictine monastery (founded 966 AD), which was used as a prison from the French Revolution until 1863.

● **Monument** ▷*See* Fire of London.

● **Monza** ► 45 35N 9 16E A city in Italy, in Lombardy. An important commercial city in the 13th century, it has a gothic cathedral. Umberto I was assassinated here in 1900. Its manufactures include machinery and textiles. It is noted for its motor-racing circuit. Population (1996 est): 119 658.

● **Moody, Dwight Lyman** ► (1837–99) US evangelist. A businessman in Chicago, he was a lay worker in a Congregational Church. He first achieved fame as a preacher in England (1873–75), and with his musical colleague Ira David Sankey (1840–1908) compiled the *Sankey and Moody Hymn Book* (1873). He founded the Moody Bible Institute in 1899.

● **Moog synthesizer** ▷*See* synthesizer.

● **moon** ► The natural satellite of the earth. The moon orbits the earth every 27.32 days at a mean distance of 384 400 km, keeping more or less the same face (the nearside) towards the earth. As it revolves, different ▷phases can be seen from earth, together with up to two or three lunar ▷eclipses per year. The moon is only 81 times less massive than the earth and has a diameter of 3476 km. Its origin is uncertain; of the various theories the most common are that it formed from material that separated from the earth, from the debris created when a planet-sized mass collided with the earth, or from a separate body captured by the earth's gravitation.

The major surface features are the light-coloured highlands on the southern nearside and most of the farside, and the much darker lava plains—the ▷maria. The maria and more especially the highlands are heavily cratered. These roughly circular walled depressions, ranging greatly in size, were produced by impacting bodies from space. The extremely tenuous atmosphere exposes the surface to extremes of temperature (−180°C to +110°C). In 1998 a NASA spacecraft detected ice under the lunar poles, prompting speculation that it could supply water for a manned moon base.

Much of our information about the moon has been derived from photographs and other measurements taken from orbiting US and Soviet satellites and later from moonrock samples brought back (1969–72) by the Apollo astronauts (and the unmanned Soviet Luna landers) and from experiments set up on the moon by the astronauts. The first landing on the moon was made by Neil ▷Armstrong and Edwin ▷Aldrin on 20 July, 1969. ▷*See* Apollo moon programme.

● **moonfish** ► A deep-bodied fish, also called opah, belonging to the genus *Lampris* and family *Lamprididae*, widely distributed in warm seas. Up to 2 m long, its body is coloured blue above, rose-pink below,

and is spotted with white; the fins are scarlet. It is uncommon and valued as food. Order: *Lampridiformes*.

● **moonflower** ▷*See* morning glory.

● **Moonies** ▷*See* Unification Church.

● **moon rat** ► The largest living mammal of the order ▷*Insectivora*, *Echinosorex gymnurus*, of Sumatra, Borneo, and S Asia. It is a ▷gymnure about 60 cm long, black with a white head and long whiskery snout. A secretion of the anal glands gives it a characteristic smell.

● **moonstone** ► A gem variety of feldspar, usually transparent or translucent orthoclase, albite, or labradorite. It shows a play of colours resembling that of opal.

● **Moore, Bobby** ► (Robert Frederick M.; 1941–93) British Association footballer, who played for West Ham United (1958–74) and Fulham (1974–76). He also played for England a record 108 times. He captained West Ham United and led the England team that won the 1966 World Cup.

● **Moore, G(eorge) E(dward)** ► (1873–1958) British philosopher. Moore's work centred around language and the analysis of its meaning. He maintained that the common usage of words is often profoundly different from their analytical meaning. Much of his published work is concerned with ethics and 12the analysis of concepts of goodness. His books include *Principia Ethica* (1903) and *Ethics* (1912). He was professor of mental philosophy and logic at Cambridge (1925–39) and editor of the journal *Mind* (1921–47).

● **Moore, Gerald** ► (1899–1987) British pianist. He became one of the leading accompanists of such singers as Dietrich Fischer-Dieskau and Elisabeth Schwarzkopf and such instrumentalists as Pablo Casals.

Henry Moore ► Seen here in his studio at his home in Much Haddam, Yorkshire.

● **Moore, Henry** ► (1898-1986) British sculptor. Moore was born at Castleford, Yorkshire, and studied at Leeds and the Royal College of Art (1921–24). His fascination with primitive African and Mexican art moulded the development of his two characteristic themes: mother and child sculptures and reclining figures. The latter, a lifelong preoccupation, reached its apogee in the sculpture for UNESCO in Paris (1956–57). After devoting himself to abstract work in the 1930s, Moore reverted to the humanist tradition in the early 1940s with his celebrated drawings of sleeping figures in air-raid shelters. These, his *Madonna and Child* (1943–44; St Matthew's, Northampton), and family groups brought him international fame. His later output continued in this vein, together with more experimental abstract works, such as *Atom Piece* (1964–66; University of Chicago).

● **Moore, Sir John** ► (1761–1809) British general, whose fame rests on his command (1808–09) in the ▷Peninsular War. Forced to retreat from Valladolid to Coruña over hazardous terrain and in bad conditions, he then repulsed a French attack but was mortally wounded.

● **Moore, Marianne** ▶ (1887–1972) US poet. Her first volume, *Poems* (1921), contained poems contributed to the Imagist magazine *The Egoist*. She edited the literary magazine *The Dial* from 1925 to 1929. *Collected Poems* (1951) won the Pulitzer Prize. She also translated *The Fables of La Fontaine* (1954).

● **Moore, Sir Patrick (Caldwell)** ▶ (1923–) British astronomer, author, and broadcaster. A self-trained astronomer, he has written numerous books on the subject as well as presenting *The Sky at Night* (1957–), the world's longest-running television programme. He was knighted in 2000.

● **Moore, Thomas** ▶ (1779–1852) Irish poet. He went to London in 1799 and won great popularity with his *Irish Melodies* (1807–34) and his oriental romance *Lalla Rookh* (1817). With the publisher John Murray, he burned the memoirs of his friend Byron in 1824.

● **moorhen** ▶ A grey-brown waterbird, *Gallinula chloropus*, also called common gallinule and waterhen, occurring worldwide except for Australia. It is 32 cm long and has a red bill and forehead and a white patch beneath the tail. It breeds in thick vegetation near ponds and marshes and feeds on seeds, water plants, and aquatic invertebrates. Family: *Rallidae* (rails, etc.).

● **Moorhouse, Adrian** ▶ (1964–) British swimmer. He won an Olympic gold medal (1988) in the 100 m breaststroke event and in 1989 won the European title in the same event for a third time.

● **Moorish idol** ▶ A deep-bodied tropical fish, *Zanclus canescens*, found in shallow Indo-Pacific waters. It has a black and yellow vertically striped body, about 18 cm long and a greatly extended dorsal fin. It is the only member of its family (*Zanclidae*). Order: *Perciformes*.

● **Moors** ▶ A European name for the ▷Arab and ▷Berber inhabitants of NW Africa and, by extension, for the 8th-century Muslim conquerors of the Iberian peninsula, whose armies consisted of both Arab and Berber troops. The word originates in the Roman name for that region of Africa—Mauretania. The Moors ruled Spain until the 11th century, after which they fell under Christian rule (*see* Mudéjars). A highly civilized people, the Moors played a major role in transmitting classical science and philosophy to W Europe.

● **moose** ▷*See* elk.

● **Moose Jaw** ▶ 50 23N 105 35W A city in W Canada, in S Saskatchewan. Founded in 1882, it is a railway and farming centre. Food processing, building materials, and oil refining are economically important. Population (1991 est): 33 953.

● **moped** ▷*See* motorcycles.

● **Moradabad** ▶ 28 50N 78 45E A city in India, in Uttar Pradesh. Founded in 1625, it is an agricultural trading centre and has metalworking, cotton-weaving, and printing industries. Population (1991): 416 836.

● **moraine** ▶ The clay, stone, boulders, etc. (*see* till), carried along or deposited by glaciers. It may have been deposited by former glaciers as particular landforms or be actively transported on the ice surface, within the ice, or beneath the ice.

● **morality plays** ▶ A form of vernacular religious ▷drama popular in England and France from the late 14th to late 16th centuries. Similar in content and purpose to medieval sermons, morality plays were dramatized allegories of good and evil fighting for man's soul. They include *The Pride of Life*, *The Castle of Perseverance*, and *Everyman*, which is best known. They influenced Elizabethan drama and at the Reformation in England provided a vehicle for dramatizing the religious issues at stake. ▷*See also* miracle plays.

● **moral philosophy** ▷*See* ethics.

● **Moral Rearmament** ▶ (MRA) An evangelical movement founded by a US evangelist and former Lutheran pastor, Frank ▷Buchman, in the 1920s. It initially received most support at Oxford University and was called the Oxford Group until 1938. It seeks the regeneration of individuals and nations through conversion, God's personal guidance, and living in purity, unselfishness, honesty, and love.

● **Morandi, Giorgio** ▶ (1890–1964) Italian still-life painter and etcher. Although he also painted landscapes and flowerpieces, he is noted for his austere pictures of bottles and jars. He was associated with the school of ▷metaphysical painting.

● **Moravia** ▶ (Czech name: Morava; German name: Mähren) An area of the Czech Republic, formerly a province (1918–49) of Czechoslovakia. Lying chiefly in the basin of the River Morava, it rises in the N to the Sudeten Mountains and in the E to the Carpathian Mountains. It contains important mineral deposits, including coal and iron ore.

History: settled by Slavic tribes in the late 8th century AD, it formed the centre of an important medieval kingdom (Great Moravia) until incorporated into the kingdom of ▷Bohemia in 1029; in 1849 it was made an Austrian crownland. It was part of Czechoslovakia from 1918 until the end of 1992. Chief town: Brno.

● **Moravia, Alberto** ▶ (Alberto Pincherle; 1907–90) Italian novelist. His early novels, beginning with *The Time of Indifference* (1929), criticized fascism and the corrupt society that allowed it to flourish. His later works, which include *The Woman of Rome* (1947), *Roman Tales* (1954), *Two Women* (1957), *The Lie* (1966), *1934* (1983), and *Erotic Tales* (1985), deal with social alienation and the futility of sexual relationships. His essays are collected in *Man As an End* (1963).

● **Moravian Brethren** ▶ A Protestant denomination that continues the ideals of the Bohemian Brethren, a 15th-century group centred in Prague that practised a simple unworldly form of Christianity. The Moravians date from the establishment of a community in 1722 by Count von ▷Zinzendorf in Saxony. In doctrine they are close to ▷Lutheranism but have a simplified Church hierarchy and liturgy. Hymn singing is important in their services. From the 1730s they were active missionaries; John ▷Wesley was among those whom they influenced. Many now live in North America.

● **Moray** ▶ A council area of NE Scotland on the Moray Firth and the North Sea. Under local government reorganization in 1975 the historic county of Moray was expanded to form a district of the same name in Grampian Region. When Grampian was abolished in 1996, this became an independent ▷unitary authority. Apart from the coastal plain in the N, Moray consists of hills and moors, rising to the Cairngorm Mountains in the S. The main occupations are agriculture, fishing, forestry, and whisky distilling. Area: 2238 sq km (864 sq mi). Population (1999 est): 85 870. Administrative centre: Elgin.

● **Moray, James Stuart, Earl of** ▶ (*or* Murray; c. 1531–70) Regent of Scotland (1567–70) after the abdication of his half-sister Mary, Queen of Scots. The illegitimate son of James V, he was exiled (1565–66) after opposing Mary's marriage to Darnley. As regent he defeated Mary and Bothwell at Langside (1568). He was assassinated.

● **moray eel** ▶ A thick-bodied ▷eel of the family *Muraenidae* (over 80 species). Up to 1.5 m long, it is brightly coloured and lacks pectoral fins. Moray eels live in rocks and reefs of warm and tropical seas and can be dangerous when disturbed. The flesh can be poisonous.

● **Moray Firth** ▶ An inlet of the North Sea in NE Scotland, extending SW from between Tarbat Ness in Highland and Burghead in Moray. Length: 56 km (35 mi).

● **Morazán, Francisco** ▶ (1792–1842) Honduran soldier and statesman; president (1830–39) of the shortlived Central American Federation (*see* Central America). A liberal, he failed to hold the five states together and was driven into exile. He became president of Costa Rica in 1842 but was executed after civil war broke out.

● **Morceli, Nourredine** ▶ (1970–) Algerian middle-distance runner. He set world records for the mile (1993), the 3000 m (1994), the 1500 m (1995), and the 2000 m (1995) and indoor records for the 1000 m and 1500 m.

● **mordant** ▷*See* dyeing.

● **Mordvinian Republic** ▶ (*or* Mordovian Republic) A constituent republic of Russia, in W central Russia; it is heavily forested. The majority of the population is Russian, 35% being Mordvinians, who speak a Finno-Ugric language. The area was annexed by Russia in the 16th century and was an autonomous Soviet republic (1934–91). The region produces timber, building materials, and textiles; the main crops are cereals; sheep and dairy farming are also important. Area: 26 200 sq km (10 110 sq mi). Population (1995 est): 960 000. Capital: Saransk.

● **More, Henry** ▶ (1614–87) English philosopher. One of the ▷Cambridge Platonists, More shared the group's interest in ▷Neoplatonism. ▷Descartes, whose work he helped publicize in England, was an early influence, but More later found his philosophy too materialistic. Although he was an opponent of religious fanaticism, More's own writings, such as *The Immortality of the Soul* (1659) and *Divine Dialogues* (1668), are more poetical and mystical than philosophical.

● **More, Sir Thomas** ▶ (1477–1535) English lawyer, scholar, and saint, whose martyrdom horrified his contemporaries. He joined Henry VIII's Privy Council in 1518 and succeeded Wolsey as chancellor in 1529. He resigned the chancellorship in 1532 in opposition to Henry's assumption of the supreme headship of the English Church. In 1534 More was imprisoned after refusing to swear to the new Act of Succession because it repudiated papal authority in England, and he was brought to trial for treason in 1535. In spite of a brilliant self-defence, he was convicted on false evidence and beheaded. He was canonized by the Roman Catholic Church in 1935. His best-known work is *Utopia* (1516), in which he discussed an ideal social and political system; he also wrote (c. 1513–c. 1518) an unfinished *History of King Richard III*.

● **Moreau, Gustave** ▶ (1826–98) French symbolist painter, best known for his detailed and brilliantly coloured biblical and mythological fantasies and as the enlightened teacher of ▷Matisse and ▷Rouault at the École des Beaux Arts. Most of his works are in the Musée Gustave Moreau, Paris.

● **Moreau, Jean Victor** ▶ (1763–1813) French general. He fought in the Revolutionary Wars and, after Napoleon came to power (1799), became commander of the Rhine army, defeating the Austrians at Hohenlinden (1800). In 1804 he was arrested after becoming involved with anti-Bonapartists and was exiled. In 1813 he joined the coalition army formed to oppose Napoleon and died in the battle of ▷Dresden.

● **Morecambe** ▶ 54 04N 2 53W A resort in NW England, in Lancashire on Morecambe Bay (a wide shallow inlet of the Irish Sea between NW Lancashire and Cumbria). The adjacent port of Heysham forms part of the borough known as Morecambe and Heysham. Population (1991): 46 657.

● **Morecambe and Wise** ▶ The British comedians **Eric Morecambe** (John Eric Bartholomew; 1926–84) and **Ernie Wise** (Ernest Wiseman; 1925–99). Having formed their double act in 1941, they appeared in variety and on radio before making their television debut in 1955. The hugely popular *Morecambe and Wise Show* ran on British television from 1961 until Morecambe's death from a heart attack.

● **morel** ▶ A fungus belonging to the genus *Morchella*. Morels are typically club-shaped with the surface of the cap pitted like a honeycomb. The edible common morel (*M. esculenta*) has a yellowish-brown cap, 4–8 cm high, and a stout whitish stalk. It is found in clearings and hedgerows. Phylum: ▷Ascomycota.

● **Morelia** ▶ (name until 1828: Valladolid) 19 40N 101 11W A city in Mexico, situated on the central plateau. It has a notable cathedral (17th–18th centuries) and is the centre of a cattle-raising area. Population (1990): 489 758.

● **Morgagni, Giovanni Battista** ▶ (1682–1771) Italian anatomist and founder of pathological anatomy. His great work, *On the Seats and Causes of Diseases as Investigated by Anatomy* (1761), was based on over 600 postmortem dissections. Morgagni was professor of anatomy at Padua University.

● **Morgan** ▶ An American all-purpose breed of horse descended from a stallion with some Thoroughbred and Arabian ancestry, born in about 1790 and named after its owner, Justin Morgan. The Morgan has a compact deep-chested body, powerful hindquarters, and a long crested neck and is usually bay. Height: 1.42–1.52 m (14–15 hands).

● **Morgan, Charles** ▶ (1894–1958) British novelist and dramatist. With his novels, which include *The Fountain* (1932), he achieved a reputation in Europe, becoming a member of the French Academy. However, he is now little read.

● **Morgan, Sir Henry** ▶ (c. 1635–88) Welsh buccaneer. Said to have been kidnapped and taken to Barbados, he joined the buccaneers then raiding the Spanish in the Caribbean. In 1671 he led a band over the Isthmus of Panama and sacked the city (1671), thus opening the way to plunder in the S Pacific. He was knighted in 1674 and made lieutenant general of Jamaica.

● **Morgan, John Pierpont** ▶ (1837–1913) US financier, who founded (1895) J. P. Morgan and Co, one of the most powerful banking corporations in the USA. During the 1880s he reorganized many foundering railway companies and later financed such consolidations as the US Steel Corporation and General Electric. His son **John Pierpont Morgan, Jr** (1867–1943) helped to organize credit for the Allies in World War I.

● **Morgan, (Hywel) Rhodri** ▶ (1939–) Welsh Labour politician; first secretary of Wales (2000–). A Labour MP since 1987, he was opposition spokesman on Welsh affairs (1992–97). He became first secretary after the Welsh Assembly forced the resignation of Alun Michael (1943–), the candidate backed by the Blair leadership.

● **Morgan, Thomas Hunt** ▶ (1866–1945) US geneticist, who established that ▷chromosomes carried the units of inheritance proposed by Gregor ▷Mendel. Morgan was sceptical about Mendelian theory until he began his breeding experiments with the fruit fly *Drosophila*. He discovered that a number of genetic variations were inherited together and that this was because their controlling genes occurred on the same chromosome (the phenomenon of linkage). Morgan won a Nobel Prize (1933).

● **Morgan le Fay** ▶ In ▷Arthurian legend, an evil sorceress who plotted the overthrow of her half-brother King Arthur. According to Malory's *Morte d'Arthur* (1485) she betrayed ▷Guinevere's adultery to Arthur. However, in the earlier *Vita Merlini* (c. 1150) by ▷Geoffrey of Monmouth she is a benevolent figure who heals the wounded Arthur in Avalon.

● **morganatic marriage** ▶ A legal form of marriage, of medieval German origin, in which a man from a royal or noble family marries a woman of lower status on the understanding that neither she nor her children will enjoy, or succeed to, his hereditary dignities or property. "Morganatic" may derive from the German *Morgengabe* (morning gift) or the Gothic *maurjan* (restricted or restrained). Such a marriage was suggested for ▷Edward VIII and Mrs Simpson, but was not acceptable. It has been suggested for Prince Charles and Mrs Camilla Parker Bowles.

● **Mörike, Eduard Friedrich** ▶ (1804–75) German poet and novelist. A rural clergyman, he found inspiration in country life, which supplied the subjects of his first distinguished collection of lyrics (*Gedichte*, 1838). The best of his prose works is the novella *Mozart auf der Reise nach Prag* (1856).

● **Moriscos** ▶ Muslims forced to profess Christianity in Spain. Many Muslims continued to live in Spain after the formerly Muslim areas came under Christian rule and by the 15th century they were forced to become Christians or go into exile. Many chose to remain in Spain while privately remaining Muslims and eventually the government ordered their expulsion. Between 1609 and 1614 about 500 000 Moriscos were forced into exile, settling mainly in Africa.

● **Morison, Stanley** ▶ (1889–1967) British typographer, editor, and historian of printing. As typographic adviser to the Monotype Corporation (from 1923), the Cambridge University Press (1923–59), and *The Times* (1929–44), he helped to adapt traditional typefaces to machine composition. He is best known for designing the Times New Roman typeface (first used in 1932).

● **Morisot, Berthe** ▶ (1841–95) French painter, granddaughter of the artist ▷Fragonard. The first female impressionist and an outstanding painter of women and children, she was strongly encouraged by ▷Corot. ▷Manet, whose brother Eugène she married (1874), was influenced by her.

● **Morland, George** ▶ (1763–1804) British painter, born in London. The son and pupil of the painter Henry Morland (c. 1730–97), he exhibited sketches at the Royal Academy when aged only ten. Popularized through engravings, his work, which included such picturesque rustic scenes as *The Inside of a Stable* (Tate Gallery), declined after 1794. His dissolute life finally resulted in imprisonment (1799–1802).

● **Morley, Edward Williams** ► (1838–1923) US chemist, who investigated the relative atomic weights of hydrogen and oxygen. However, he is best known for his collaboration with Albert ▷Michelson in the ▷Michelson-Morley experiment.

● **Morley, Robert** ► (1908–92) British stage and film actor. His long career as a character actor dates from 1929, and his films include *Major Barbara* (1940), *Beat the Devil* (1953), *Oscar Wilde* (1960), and *The Blue Bird* (1976). Many of his later roles were pompous eccentrics. He was the son-in-law of the actress Dame Gladys Cooper (1888–1971).

● **Morley, Thomas** ► (1557–1603) English composer, music printer, organist of St Paul's Cathedral, and member of the Chapel Royal. A pupil of Byrd, he wrote madrigals, songs, church music, and the textbook *A Plaine and Easie Introduction to Practicall Musicke* (1597).

● **Mormons** ► Adherents of the Christian sect that is formally called the Church of Jesus Christ of Latter-Day Saints, founded in 1830 by Joseph Smith in New York state. A series of visions culminated in Smith's claim that he had discovered golden tablets that contained the Book of Mormon, a sacred book named after a primitive American prophet who had compiled it. After Smith's murder by a mob, the persecuted Mormons moved W under Brigham Young, establishing their headquarters at Salt Lake, Utah, in 1847. Attempting to revert to the simple sanctity of the early Christians, Mormons have no professional clergy, reject infant baptism, emphasize self-help, abstain from alcohol and other stimulants, and run educational and missionary programmes. Polygamy (*see* marriage), for which Mormons were once notorious, has been disallowed since 1890.

● **Mornay, Philippe de, Seigneur du Plessis-Marly** ► (1549–1632) French Huguenot (Protestant) leader during the ▷Wars of Religion. Escaping the ▷St Bartholomew's Day Massacre (1572), he rose to a position of considerable influence as one of the chief confidants of Henry of Navarre, later Henry IV of France. When Henry was converted to Roman Catholicism, Mornay retained his Huguenot sympathies and lost the king's favour.

● **morning glory** ► A trailing or twining plant of the genus *Ipomoea*, native to tropical America and Australia and cultivated for its beautiful flowers. The leaves are often heart-shaped and the trumpet-shaped flowers, up to 12 cm across, are deep blue, purple, pink, or white. Popular species are *I. purpurea* and *I. alba* (the moonflower). Some seeds contain hallucinogens. Family: *Convolvulaceae*.

● **Moro, Aldo** ► (1916–1978) Italian statesman; Christian Democratic prime minister (1963–68, 1974–76) and foreign minister (1965–66, 1969–72, 1973–74). He included socialists in his first cabinet and in 1976 was instrumental in gaining communist support for the minority Christian Democratic government. In 1978 he was kidnapped and then murdered by the ▷Red Brigades.

● **Morocco, Kingdom of** ► A country in NW Africa, bordering on the Atlantic Ocean and Mediterranean Sea. The Atlas Mountains crossing the centre of the country rise to 4165 m (13 665 ft) at Mount Toubkal and separate the Atlantic coastal area from the Sahara. The population is mainly of Berber and Arabic origin.
Economy: the chief occupations are agriculture and mining. Wheat, barley, maize, and citrus fruits are grown, mainly in the coastal areas N of the mountains; livestock, especially sheep and goats, is also important. Morocco is a leading exporter of phosphates having over 70% of the world's known phosphate reserves. Other mineral resources are iron ore, coal, lead, zinc, cobalt, and manganese. Industries include chemicals, food processing, textiles, and traditional handicraft industries; a major phosphoric acid plant has been developed and the country now has two oil refineries. There is a thriving fishing industry, sardines and tuna being the chief catch. Morocco's hot sunny climate and Atlantic and Mediterranean beaches make it an increasingly popular tourist centre.
History: part of the Roman province of Mauretania, it fell to the Vandals in the 5th century AD. Conflict between Arabs and Berbers was virtually continuous; in the 15th and 16th centuries Morocco came under attack from Spain and Portugal and until the 19th century was a base for Barbary pirates. Its strategic importance was recognized by the European powers in the 19th century, French and Spanish interests conflicting with those of Germany. The French increased their control in the area and the appearance of a German warship at Agadir (1911) was interpreted by the French as a threat of war. Following the Agadir incident Morocco was partitioned into French and Spanish protectorates (1912) and the international zone of Tangier (1923). In 1956 the protectorates were relinquished and Morocco became a sultanate, later a kingdom (1957) under King Mohammed V; his son, Hassan II, acceded to the throne in 1961. In 1975 agreement was reached providing for the partition of Spanish Sahara (*see* Western Sahara) between Morocco and Mauritania; in 1979 Mauritania withdrew from Western Sahara and the whole area came under Moroccan occupation. The 1980s and 1990s saw armed clashes between Moroccan forces and the pro-independence Polisario movement over the area; a UN peace plan halted warfare in 1988, but broke down in 1991. Following elections to a new national assembly in 1998, the socialist Abderrahmane el Youssoufi became prime minister. Hassan II was succeeded by his son, Mohammed VI, in 1999.

Kingdom of Morocco

Head of state	King Mohammed VI
Official religion	Islam
Official language	Arabic
Official currency	dirham of 100 centimes
Area	458 730 sq km (144 078 sq mi)
Population (1998 est)	28 060 000
Capital	Rabat

● **Moroni** ► 11 40S 43 16E The capital of the Comoro Islands, a port in the SW of Grande Comore island. Population (1991 est): 30 000.

● **Moroni, Giovanni Battista** ► (c. 1525–78) Italian painter, born near Bergamo. Although he painted many altarpieces in Bergamo, he

Morocco ► The Great Kasbah, an imposing Berber citadel, at Skoura, S Morocco.

is best known for his portraits, notably *The Tailor* (National Gallery, London).

● **Morosini** ► A noble Venetian family, prominent from the 10th century, that produced four ▷doges as well as many distinguished generals, admirals, and churchmen. Best known is **Francesco Morosini** (1618–94), who was doge of Venice from 1688 until his death. As commander in chief of the Venetian fleet, he defeated the Turks at sea and in Greece.

● **Morpeth** ► 55 10N 1 41W A town in NE England, the administrative centre of Northumberland, on the River Wansbeck. The site of a ruined medieval castle, it is a service centre for the surrounding area. Population (1991) 14 393.

● **Morpheus** ► In Greek mythology, a god of dreams, a son of Somnus, the god of sleep. He sent human forms into the dreams of sleeping men, while his brothers Phobetor and Phantasus sent animal and inanimate forms.

● **morphine** ► A ▷narcotic analgesic drug obtained from ▷opium and used in medicine for the relief of severe pain. Its depressant effect on the brain accounts for the pain-killing properties; in high doses it also inhibits the breathing and cough centres. Other side effects include constipation, nausea, and vomiting. Morphine is an addictive drug and readily leads to severe physical dependence. Nalorphine is a specific antidote to morphine overdosage. ▷*See also* drug dependence.

● **morphology** ► (biology) The study of the form and structure of plants, animals, and microorganisms. ▷Anatomy is often used synonymously with morphology but in the former the emphasis is on the gross and microscopic structure of organs and parts.

● **morphology** ► (language) ▷*See* grammar.

● **Morphy, Paul Charles** ► (1837–84) US chess player, who between 1858 and 1860 was regarded as the world's best player and whose games still fascinate enthusiasts. He travelled to Europe, defeating all opponents, but gave up chess for his legal career. This was unsuccessful and he became mentally unstable.

● **Morris, Desmond John** ► (1928–) British zoologist, noted for his popularization of biology, especially in his books on human behaviour. *The Naked Ape* (1967), *The Human Zoo* (1969), *Manwatching* (1977), *Bodywatching* (1985), and *Bodytalk* (1994) all set out to prove that human beings are still subject to the basic laws of animal behaviour.

● **Morris, William** ► (1834–96) British designer, artist, and poet. Associated with the ▷Pre-Raphaelite Brotherhood, he later started a firm of decorators and designers (1861), who placed great importance on preindustrial crafts. He designed stained glass, carpets, and furniture, and his wallpaper designs are still used. His ▷Kelmscott Press, founded in 1890, influenced book design and printing generally. The 19th-century ▷Arts and Crafts movement drew much of its inspiration from his work. He was also one of the founders of British socialism.

● **Morris dance** ► A ritual English folk dance performed by groups of white-clad men wearing bells and often carrying sticks or handkerchiefs. A common theme is fertility through death and rebirth, symbolized by the carrying of green branches. Similar dances are found throughout Europe, India, and the Americas, often featuring animal characters or the black-faced Morisco (Moor), whence the name Morris is thought to derive. Morris dancing is a popular pastime, many groups existing in both town and country.

● **Morris Jesup, Cape** ► 83 40N 34 00W The N tip of Greenland, the world's most northerly land point, 708 km (440 mi) from the North Pole.

● **Morrison, Herbert Stanley, Baron** ► (1888–1965) British Labour politician, who was prominent as a member of the London County Council from 1922 to 1945. He was also minister of transport (1929–31) and, in World War II, minister of supply (1940) and home secretary (1940–45), serving in the war cabinet (1942–45). He became deputy leader of the Labour Party in 1951 but resigned when Gaitskell became leader (1955). In 1959 he was made a life peer as Baron Morrison of Lambeth.

● **Morrison, Toni** ► (Chloe Anthony M.; 1931–) Black US novelist and academic. Her works, which include *Sula* (1974), *The Song of Solomon* (1977), *Beloved* (1987), *Jazz* (1992), and *Paradise* (1998), explore the historical experience of African Americans in US society. She was awarded the Nobel Prize in 1993.

● **Morse, Samuel Finley Breese** ► (1791–1872) US inventor, who erected the first telegraph line, between Washington and Baltimore (1844). Messages were sent by a system of dots and dashes that he had invented for the purpose (*see* Morse code).

letters

A	● —	N	— ●
B	— ● ● ●	O	— — —
C	— ● — ●	P	● — — ●
D	— ● ●	Q	— — ● —
E	●	R	● — ●
F	● ● — ●	S	● ● ●
G	— — ●	T	—
H	● ● ● ●	U	● ● —
I	● ●	V	● ● ● —
J	● — — —	W	● — —
K	— ● —	X	— ● ● —
L	● — ● ●	Y	— ● — —
M	— —	Z	— — ● ●

numbers		punctuation marks	
1	● — — — —	.	● — ● — ● —
2	● ● — — —	,	— — ● ● — —
3	● ● ● — —	:	— — — ● ● ●
4	● ● ● ● —	?	● ● — — ● ●
5	● ● ● ● ●	-	— ● ● ● ● —
6	— ● ● ● ●	/	— ● ● — ●
7	— — ● ● ●	(or)	— ● — — ● —
8	— — — ● ●	"	● — ● ● — ●
9	— — — — ●		
0	— — — — —		

Morse code

● **Morse code** ► The code invented by Samuel ▷Morse for transmitting telegraph messages. Each letter of the alphabet and number has a characteristic sequence of dots and dashes (short and long pulses), a dash being three times as long as a dot. The code has been used widely for transmitting messages by sound and by light flashes. The signal SOS (three short pulses, three long pulses, and three short pulses) was for some 150 years the universal distress signal. However, from 1993 satellite technology made the tapping out of distress signals unnecessary and by the late 1990s Morse code was rarely used at sea, except occasionally for flashing lights between ships. From February 1999 it was officially replaced by a worldwide satellite communication system known as the **Global Marine Distress and Safety System** (GMDSS); it is now compulsory for all ships over 300 tonnes to carry the technology for this system (smaller ships have until 2005 to comply). Morse code continues to be used for identifying aeronautical navigation beacons.

● **mortality** ▷*See* death.

● **mortar** ► (building material) A mixture of sand, hydrated lime, and Portland cement, used to bind together building bricks, etc. It is applied wet as a paste, which sets to a durable solid.

● **mortar** ► (weapon) A short-barrelled muzzle-loading artillery piece with a low-velocity high-angled trajectory. Although modern designs date from 1915, it originated before 1600. In World War II the largest Allied mortar had a calibre of 4.2 inches (107 mm), the German version being 8.3 inches (210 mm) with six barrels. Used against an enemy behind cover, mortars are used to fire high-explosive and smoke bombs.

● **mortgage** ► Rights in property (buildings, etc.) given by a borrower (mortgagor) to a lender (mortgagee) as security for a loan. In the UK ▷building societies and banks lend money for house purchase in return for a charge on the property, giving them the right to sell it if the borrower defaults. Successive mortgages may be taken out on the same property for further loans. When all the money borrowed and the interest due under the mortgage have been repaid, it is redeemed. In 1996 there were over 10.6 million building-society mortgages in the UK, 42 560 forced repossessions for default, and about 424 000 accounts in arrears.

● **Mortier, Édouard Adolphe Casimir Joseph, Duc de Trévise** ▶ (1768-1835) French marshal, who fought in the Revolutionary and Napoleonic Wars. In 1803 he occupied Hanover but in 1805 was defeated at Dürnstein by the Russians. He subsequently served in the campaign against Prussia (1806-07) and in the ▷Peninsular War, winning at Ocaña (1809). He was Louis-Philippe's prime minister (1834-35) and died in an attempt on the king's life.

● **Mortimer, Sir John Clifford** ▶ (1923-) British barrister and writer. He was called to the bar in 1948, a year after his first novel, *Charade*, was published. He is best known for the televised tales of Horace Rumpole, a fictional barrister. The first of his many plays was *The Dock Brief* (1958); his novels include *Paradise Postponed* (1985), *Summer's Lease* (1988), *Dunster* (1992), and *The Sound of Trumpets* (1998). Other works have included the autobiographical play *A Voyage Round My Father* (1970) and the memoirs *Murderers and Other Friends* (1994). He was knighted in 1998.

● **Mortimer, Roger de, 1st Earl of March** ▶ (c. 1287-1330) English magnate. He led the baronial opposition to Edward II (1320-22) and was imprisoned before fleeing to France. There he became the lover of Edward's queen ▷Isabella of France with whom he secured Edward's deposition and murder in 1327. He then ruled England in the name of Edward's son, Edward III, until the latter had him executed.

● **Morton, James Douglas, 4th Earl of** ▶ (c. 1516-81) Regent of Scotland (1572-78) for James VI (later James I of England). Under Mary, Queen of Scots, he was involved in the murder of Riccio (1566) and then, for which he was eventually executed, of Darnley (1567).

● **Morton, Jelly Roll** ▶ (Ferdinand Joseph La Menthe; 1885-1941) US Black jazz pianist and composer, who began his career playing the piano in New Orleans' Storyville brothels and made recordings in the 1920s with the group Morton's Red Hot Peppers. Claiming that he "invented jazz in 1902," his reputation has been the subject of controversy.

● **Morton, John** ▶ (c. 1420-1500) English churchman. A supporter of the Lancastrian cause, under Henry VII he became Archbishop of Canterbury (1486), chancellor (1487), and cardinal (1493). He is remembered for his argument—**Morton's Fork**—that both rich and poor could afford to contribute to royal funds: the rich obviously had the money to spare, while those who lived less extravagantly must have saved money by their modest way of life.

● **mosaic** ▶ A picture or ornamental design made from small coloured cubes of glass, stone, tile, etc. Mosaics were common in ancient Greece, where they were principally used for floors and made from coloured pebbles. During the Roman Empire mosaics of opaque glass and glass covered with gold leaf became popular for wall and vault decoration, a development that reached its peak in the early Christian churches in Byzantium and Italy. The 6th-century decorations in S Vitale, in Ravenna, are among the most famous mosaics of the middle ages. During this period mosaics were no longer stylistically dependent on painting but, instead, led artistic trends with their use of two-dimensional forms, rich colour, and lavish use of gold. During the Renaissance frescoes were preferred for church decoration but mosaics have been revived during the 20th century.

● **Mosaic law** ▶ The collective name for the laws contained in the ▷Torah. They purport to have been revealed by God to Moses on Mount Sinai and in ▷Judaism they form the basis of ▷halakhah. In Christianity some of them are accepted, but most are rejected or interpreted allegorically.

● **mosasaur** ▶ A member of an extinct family of huge marine liz-

ards that lived during the Cretaceous period (135-65 million years ago). Up to 10 m long, mosasaurs had broad paddle-like limbs and a long flexible tail and were efficient swimmers, feeding on fish, cuttlefish, and squid.

● **moschatel** ▶ A perennial herbaceous plant, *Adoxa moschatellina*, also called townhall clock, native to Eurasia and North America. Up to 10 cm high, it has compound leaves and greenish flowers. It has a musky smell and is the sole member of its family (*Adoxaceae*).

● **Moscow** ▶ (Russian name: Moskva) 55 45N 37 42E The capital of Russia and of the Moscow region (*oblast*), on the River Moskva. It is the economic and political centre of Russia and an important transportation centre. Industries include heavy engineering, cars, textiles, electronics, chemicals, publishing, and food processing. Moscow is at the centre of the Russian railway system and is an important riverport. Its underground railway (begun 1935) is of note. The city is based on a radial plan; the ▷Kremlin (citadel) and Red Square are at its heart. The Kremlin, triangular in shape, encloses a number of notable ecclesiastical buildings including the Cathedral of the Assumption (1475-79) and the Cathedral of the Annunciation (1484-89). Red Square is the traditional setting for military parades and demonstrations. Beyond its historical centre Moscow is a modern city. It is a major cultural centre; its many educational institutions include the University of Moscow (1755), the People's Friendship University (1960) for foreign students, and the Academy of Sciences. The Tretyakov Gallery of Russian Art (1856) is the most notable of its many museums. Other famous institutions include the Bolshoi Theatre of Opera and Ballet (1780), the ▷Moscow Art Theatre, and the Moscow State Circus.
  History: first documented in 1147, settlement actually dates back to prehistoric times. By the beginning of the 13th century it was the centre of the Muscovy principality and it became the seat of the metropolitan of the Russian Orthodox Church in 1326. In 1712-13 the capital was transferred to St Petersburg but Moscow remained significant. The city was invaded by Napoleon (1812) and the ensuing fire, started either by looting French soldiers or the Moscow people themselves, destroyed much of the city. The workers' movements in Moscow played an important role in the Revolution of 1905. In March, 1918, it became the capital of the RSFSR and following the arrival of Lenin and other communist leaders (1922) the capital of the Soviet Union. Development resumed after World War II, during which the German invasion of the city was only halted by severe weather and strong resistance. Since the war, Moscow has developed an important tourist industry. It was the site of the 1980 Olympic Games. Population (1996 est): 8 400 000.

● **Moscow Art Theatre** ▶ A Russian theatre company that was founded in 1898 by Konstantin ▷Stanislavsky and Vladimir Nemirovich-Danchenko (1859-1948). Its first success was a production of *The Seagull* by Chekhov, whose plays suited the naturalistic acting style developed by Stanislavsky. Other dramatists whose plays were produced include Gorky, Tolstoy, and Maeterlinck. The company gained international acclaim on its tour of Europe and the USA in 1922 and has continued to maintain high standards of ensemble acting.

● **Moseley, Henry Gwyn Jeffries** ▶ (1887-1915) British physicist, who, working under ▷Rutherford, discovered the connection between the frequency of the X-rays emitted by an atom and its atomic number. This discovery provided a theoretical basis for the periodic classification of the elements. He was killed at Gallipoli in World War I.

● **Moselle, River** ▶ (German name: R. Mosel) A river in W Europe, flowing N from NE France to join the River Rhine at Koblenz. It forms part of the border between Germany and Luxembourg. Its valley is a major wine-growing area. Length: 547 km (340 mi).

● **Moses** ▶ In the Old Testament, the lawgiver of Israel, who led the people from slavery in Egypt (Exodus) and, after wandering in the desert for 40 years, brought them to an area E of the River Jordan, the border of the Promised Land. He is the central figure in most of the Pentateuch (the first five Old Testament books). As a child in Egypt (according to the Old Testament), Moses was saved from the slaughter of all Hebrew male children ordered by Pharaoh by being hidden in bulrushes on the Nile; he was found and brought up by one of Pharaoh's daughters. On Mt Sinai he was given the Ten Commandments by Jehovah. He died at the age of 120, before the Israelites entered the Promised Land, which he was allowed to see from Mt Pisgah.

● **Moses, Grandma** ▶ (Anna Mary Robertson M.; 1860–1961) US primitive painter, born in Greenwich, New York (*see* primitivism). Entirely self-taught, she only turned seriously to painting at the age of 67 after a life as a farmer's wife. Her naive and nostalgic scenes of farm life were popularized through prints and Christmas cards.

● **Mosley, Sir Oswald Ernald** ▶ (1896–1980) British fascist. He was a Conservative MP (1918–22), an Independent MP (1922–24), and then a Labour MP (1924, 1926–31), serving as chancellor of the Duchy of Lancaster (1929–30). In 1932 he established the British Union of Fascists, which incited antisemitic violence, especially in the East End of London. In World War II he was interned (1940–43) and in 1948 he founded the Union Movement, which put forward parliamentary candidates between 1959 and 1966 but secured a negligible vote. Mosley retired in 1966, after which the movement collapsed. He married (1936) Diana ▷Mitford.

● **mosque** ▶ A Muslim place of worship. It evolved in various styles from a simple rectangular building, such as the first mosque built by Mohammed at Medina in 622 AD. Larger mosques are usually built around a courtyard, which is surrounded by arcades on all four sides. Prayers are said in a large covered area on the side facing Mecca, the direction being indicated by a niche (*mihrab*) in the wall. Mosques are often domed and have ▷minarets. Painting and sculpture of living beings are forbidden, but elaborate geometrical designs and Arabic calligraphy frequently adorn both exterior and interior walls. The mosque has traditionally been the centre of Muslim life, intellectual and social as well as religious. The three most sacred mosques are those of Mecca, Medina, and Jerusalem.

● **Mosque of Islam** ▷*See* Black Muslims.

● **mosquito** ▶ A small fly belonging to a family (*Culicidae*; about 2500 species) of almost worldwide distribution, being especially abundant in the tropics. It has long legs, elongated mouthparts, and a long slender abdomen. In most species the males feed on plant juices, while the females bite and suck the blood of mammals, often transmitting serious human and animal diseases. The three important genera are ▷*Anopheles*, ▷*Aedes*, and *Culex* (including the common gnat, *C. pipiens*). The active larvae live in fresh water, feeding on algae, bacteria, and organic debris. Most breathe through a siphon at the rear end.

● **Mosquito Coast** ▶ (*or* Miskito Coast) A coastal belt in Central America, bordering on the Caribbean Sea and extending from E Honduras into E Nicaragua. Its name derives from the former inhabitants of the area, the Mosquito (Miskito) Indians. The cultivation of bananas is the chief occupation. Average width: 60 km (40 mi).

● **moss** ▶ A flowerless plant of the phylum *Bryophyta* (about 15 000 species; *see* bryophytes), growing worldwide (except in salt water) on moist soil, trees, rocks, etc. The moss plant is differentiated into stems and leaves and produces sex cells (gametes), which give rise to a spore capsule that grows on a long stalk. Mosses help control erosion by providing surface cover and retaining water. ▷*Sphagnum*, responsible for peat formation, is economically important.

The name is also applied to several unrelated plants, for example ▷Spanish moss.

● **Moss, Sir Stirling** ▶ (1929–) British motor-racing driver, who had innumerable successes on the track in the 1950s, including 16 Grand Prix wins, but never won the world championship— being runner-up from 1955 to 1958. He was knighted in 2000.

● **moss animal** ▷*See* Bryozoa.

● **Mössbauer effect** ▶ The emission of a gamma ray (*see* gamma radiation) by an excited nucleus in a solid. Generally such an emission causes the nucleus to recoil, thus reducing the energy of the gamma ray. In the Mössbauer effect the recoil is distributed throughout the solid. The gamma ray therefore loses no energy and may then raise other nuclei into the same excited state. It was discovered by the German physicist Rudolph Mössbauer (1929–) and enables nuclei and molecules to be examined.

● **moss pink** ▷*See* Phlox.

● **Mostaganem** ▶ 36 04N 0 11E A port in NW Algeria, on the Mediterranean Sea. Founded in the 11th century, it has an 11th-century citadel. It trades in wine, fruit, and vegetables, and is at the head of a natural gas pipeline from Hasse R'Mel in the Sahara. Population (latest est): 504 124.

● **Mostar** ▶ 43 20N 17 50E A town in SW Bosnia-Hercegovina, on the River Neretva. A cultural centre with a university (1977), it lies in hilly wine-producing country. From 1992 to 1994 it was the scene of fighting, mainly between Muslims and Croats. Population (1991): 126 067.

● **most-favoured-nation clause** ▶ A clause in a trade agreement between two countries in which each country agrees that any more favourable agreement either may make with a third country shall also apply to the other country. The mechanism was at the heart of the ▷General Agreement on Tariffs and Trade (GATT), although GATT allowed the clause to be waived in treaties with ▷developing countries, in certain cases involving the formation of a ▷customs union, and formerly for Commonwealth preference arrangements.

● **Mosul** ▶ 36 21N 43 08E A town in N Iraq, close to the Turkish border. From 1534 to 1918 it was an important trading centre in the Ottoman Empire, and Turkey continued to claim the town until 1926. Mosul's modern prosperity is derived from nearby oilfields. Its former Faculties of the University of Baghdad became Mosul University in 1967. Population (latest est): 664 221.

● **motet** ▶ A polyphonic composition (*see* polyphony) for voices, generally unaccompanied. In the medieval motet the fundamental tenor (holding) part was based on a slow-moving plainchant or popular song while the upper triplex (treble) and motetus (worded) parts had a different text and a quicker rhythm. The 16th-century motet with Latin text, used during church services but not a part of the liturgy, is found in its purest form in the works of Palestrina. In England a Latin motet was distinguished from an English ▷anthem. Since the 17th century the word has described a serious though not necessarily religious choral work.

● **mother-of-pearl** ▷*See* pearl.

● **Motherwell, Robert** ▶ (1915–91) US abstract painter. Largely self-taught, he turned to painting during World War II, under the influence of the European surrealists. He became a leading exponent of ▷action painting with his use of dripped and splattered paint, notably in his black and white series *Elegy to the Spanish Republic*. Later paintings were more structured, showing the influence of ▷Rothko.

● **Motherwell and Wishaw** ▶ 55 48N 4 00W A town in central Scotland, in North Lanarkshire on the River Clyde. Formed by the union of the two towns in 1920, its industries include iron and engineering; closure of the Ravenscraig steelworks here was announced in 1992. Population (1991): 60 508.

● **moth orchid** ▶ An epiphytic ▷orchid of the genus *Phalaenopsis* (about 40 species), native to SE Asia and E Australia. It has a short stem bearing broad leaves and larger clusters of flowers. Moth orchids are popular ornamentals; hybrids usually have white or pink long-lasting flowers.

● **moths** ▷*See* butterflies and moths.

● **Motion, Andrew** ▶ (1952–) British poet and writer. His publications include the poetry collection *Pleasure Steamers* (1978), *Natural Causes* (1987), and *Of Salt Water* (1997), biographies of Larkin (1982) and Keats (1998), and the historical novel *Wainewright the Poisoner* (2000). He was appointed poet laureate in 1999.

● **motion sickness** ▷*See* travel sickness.

● **motmot** ▶ A bird of the tropical American family *Motmotidae* (8 species). 16–50 cm long, motmots have short rounded wings, short legs, and long tails. The bill is broad and serrated and the plumage is green, blue, brown, and black. Motmots live in forests and prey on insects, spiders, worms, etc. Order: *Coraciiformes* (kingfishers, etc.).

● **moto-cross** ▶ (*or* scrambling) A form of ▷motorcycle racing invented in the UK in 1927. It takes place on a circuit marked out across rough country. International events are for 250 cc and 500 cc machines.

● **motorcycle racing** ▶ Racing single-seater motorcycles or sidecar combinations, in classes according to engine capacity. In **road racing**, run usually on special circuits, the main classes are 125, 250, 350, and 500 cc. World championships are awarded according to points won in Grand Prix and other races, such as the Tourist Trophy (TT) races on the Isle of Man (first held in 1907). **Motorcycle trials** are usually events in which a cross-country course has to be completed within a certain time, with points lost in observed sections of the course for stopping, touching the ground, etc. ▷See also drag racing; moto-cross; rally; speedway.

● **motorcycles** ▶ Two-wheeled engine-powered vehicles. The evolution of the motorcycle has been closely associated with that of the ▷bicycle, ▷steam engine, and ▷car. The concept of a steam-powered bicycle was first realized by S. H. Roper in the USA in the 1860s. Similar machines were being built in Paris at about the same time by Pierre and Ernest Michaux. However, the true forerunner of the modern motorcycle was Gottlieb ▷Daimler's 1885 bicycle powered by an ▷Otto four-stroke engine. The first production model was Hildebrand and Wolfmüller's 1894 *Pétrolette*. By 1900 there were some 11 000 motorcycles in France and by the start of World War I over 100 000 were registered in the UK. By then the invidious belt drive (which slipped in wet weather) had been replaced by the chain, hot-tube ignition (which often set the whole machine alight) had given way to the sparking plug, and the battery had been augmented by the magneto. During the war, motorcycles (often with sidecars) were extensively used by both sides. The interwar period saw the development of many classic designs: the Harley-Davidson in the USA; the Brough Superior, Triumph Speed Twin, and Ariel Square Four in the UK; and the German DKW two-stroke and BMW four-stroke. All these were in military use in World War II. During and after the war innovations included telescopic forks, sprung near wheels, disc brakes, and starter motors. In the 1950s and 1960s interest in motorcycles in Europe and the USA declined; their inherent danger and the status symbol of car ownership forced most European manufacturers out of business. The motor scooter, a low-powered Italian version of the motorcycle, and the moped, an engine-assisted bicycle, acquired some popularity. In the 1970s, the Japanese, exploiting the closure of European factories, developed a new range of motorcycles, based on European designs. These machines now dominate world markets. □ p. 854.

● **motor insurance** ▶ ▷Insurance against the risks to people and property arising from the use of motor vehicles. It is of two kinds: insurance against damage caused to third parties or their property and insurance against damage to the insured or the insured's own property. Third-party insurance has been compulsory in the UK since the Road Traffic Act (1930) and in most other countries from about the same time. Comprehensive insurance covers both kinds and is considerably more expensive; some insurers offer an intermediate policy covering third-party, fire, and theft insurance. In the UK most policies include a no-claims bonus, which reduces the cost of the premium and discourages the insured from making small claims. In most parts of the world, motor claims are settled on a "knock-for-knock" basis, each insurer settling his own client's claims without attempting to establish blame for an accident.

● **motor nerves** ▷See neurone.

● **motor neurone disease** ▶ A progressive disease that causes degeneration of parts of the brain and spinal cord that control voluntary movements, resulting in muscle wasting. Intelligence and sensitivity to touch, etc., are unaffected. There are several forms: in some speech and swallowing are affected first; in others the paralysis starts in the limbs and progresses upwards. There is, as yet, no cure, although drugs (e.g. riluzole) are being used to ameliorate the symptoms.

● **motor racing** ▶ Racing in cars, from family saloons at club level to highly specialized Grand Prix vehicles. Early races, such as the 1895 race from Paris to Bordeaux and back, were held on roads, but since 1903 they have usually been held on closed-circuit courses, the

first of which in England was Brooklands (1907) in Surrey. (Racing round-the-houses (on roads) was revived in the UK in Birmingham (1986).) The most prestigious form of racing is Grand Prix (Formula One) racing, for which specially built single-seater vehicles are raced by professional drivers for manufacturers or private owners. The Drivers' World Championship (instituted in 1950) is awarded according to points won in certain Formula One races. Championships for less powerful cars include Formula Two, Formula Three, and Formula 5000. **Sports-car racing** is for production-type or modified sports cars; the most famous sports-car race is the Le Mans 24 Hours. **IndyCar** racing originated with the Indianapolis 500 in 1911. **Autocross** races are amateur races over grass, while **rallycross** is a more professional form held on circuits that are half grass and half tarmac. ▷See also drag racing; karting; rally; stock-car racing.

● **Mo-tzu** ▷See Mo-Zi.

● **mouflon** ▶ A wild sheep, *Ovis musimon*, native to Corsica and Sardinia and introduced to other parts of Europe and to North America. Mouflons are about 65 cm high at the shoulder and males have large curved horns, a distinctive rump patch, and a white saddle on the back.

● **mould** ▶ Any fungus that forms a fine woolly mass growing on food, clothing, etc. Examples are the ▷bread mould and species of ▷*Aspergillus* and ▷*Penicillium*. ▷See also slime moulds.

● **Moulins** ▶ 46 34N 3 20E A town in central France, the capital of the Allier department on the River Allier. It manufactures leather, metal goods, and textiles. Population (1990): 23 350.

● **Moulmein** ▶ 16 30N 97 39E A port in Myanmar, on the River Salween. The chief town of British Burma from 1826 until 1852, Moulmein has an important teak trade and exports rice. Population (latest est): 202 967.

● **moulting** ▶ The periodic shedding of skin, fur, or feathers. In mammals and birds moulting occurs once a year or more often. It is usually seasonal and is triggered by hormonal changes; in many species it is coordinated with the breeding cycle, especially when the breeding coat is a different colour from the nonbreeding coat. In amphibians and reptiles the entire skin is shed, the new skin forming underneath the old one. Juvenile arthropods undergo a series of moults; this process, called **ecdysis**, is triggered, in insects, by the hormone ecdysone. A new soft cuticle is secreted beneath the old one, which is cast off; the insect increases its size (e.g. by absorbing water) before the new cuticle hardens.

● **mountain** ▷See orogeny.

● **mountain ash** ▶ A tree, *Sorbus aucuparia*, also called rowan, native to temperate Eurasia and cultivated as an ornamental. Up to 15 m high, it has long leaves with many paired leaflets and large clusters of small cream flowers, which give rise to bright-scarlet berries, used to make wine and jelly. The related American species is *S. americana*. Family: ▷Rosaceae. The Australian mountain ash (▷*Eucalyptus regnans*), up to 105 m high, is the tallest broad-leaved tree.

● **mountain beaver** ▷See sewellel.

● **mountaineering** ▶ A sport that developed in the mid-19th century. Interest in exploring mountains first grew in the 18th century; after Mont Blanc was climbed in 1786 by Michel Paccard and Jacques Balmat interest gradually extended to other areas of the Alps. The English Alpine Club, founded in 1857, was quickly followed by continental clubs. The Matterhorn was climbed in 1865 by Edward ▷Whymper's expedition, Mount Kilimanjaro in 1889 by Hans Meyer and Ludwig Purtscheller, and Mount Kenya in 1899 by Sir Halford Mackinder (1861–1947) and two guides. No peak over 7817 m (25 646 ft) was climbed until after World War II, when modern equipment and generous funding made high-altitude climbing possible. Annapurna I was climbed in 1950 by Maurice Herzog and Louis Lachenal and Mount Everest in 1953 by Sir Edmund ▷Hillary and ▷Tenzing Norgay. Now that the world's highest peaks have been conquered, mountaineering is largely a matter of finding new routes and new methods. Rock climbing and ice climbing, skills always intrinsic to mountaineering, have become independent sports; like mountaineering in general, they make use of such equipment as

motorcycles

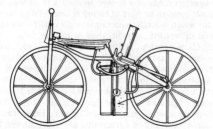

1860s S.H. Roper Velocipede One of the earliest steam-powered cycles, this machine survives in the Smithsonian Institute, Washington, USA.

1885 Daimler The forerunner of the modern motorcycle, it had a wooden frame, iron tyres, and a 264 cc four-stroke engine.

1894 Hildebrand and Wolfmüller "Pétrolette" The first production motor cycle, it had direct rearwheel drive, pneumatic tyres, and a 1488 cc engine. Prodution was ten machines a day.

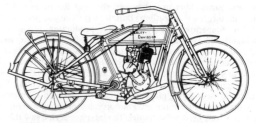

1917 Harley-Davidson This 989 cc Vee-twin chaindrive machine had the first twist-grip throttle control.

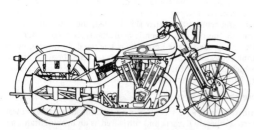

1930 Brough Superior Built from 1919 to 1940 this Rolls Royce of motorcycles had a 980 cc Vee-twin JAP engine. Only 3000 were ever made.

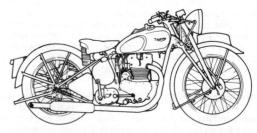

1938 Triumph 500 cc Speed Twin Capable of over 100 mph, it was widely used by the police.

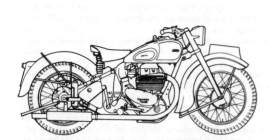

1949 Ariel Square Four The compact arrangement of the four cylinders gave the machine its name. It had telescopic front forks and a sprung rear wheel.

1988 Honda Goldwing Aspencade A Japanese tourer with a flat four 1182 cc engine, 5-speed gearbox, drive shaft, and transistorized ignition.

nylon ropes, eiderdown suits, and crampons and are organized through clubs.

● **mountain lion** ▷*See* cougar.

● **Mountbatten, Louis, 1st Earl Mountbatten of Burma** ▶ (1900–79) British admiral and colonial administrator; son of Prince Louis of Battenberg (1854–1921), who took the name Mountbatten and was created Marquess of Milford Haven in 1917, and of Princess Victoria of Hesse-Darmstadt, the granddaughter of Queen Victoria. He entered the Royal Navy in 1913 and in World War II was supreme Allied commander in SE Asia (1943–45), retaking Burma (now Myanmar). As viceroy of India (1947) he presided over the transfer of power to India and Pakistan and was then governor general of India (1947–48). He was subsequently commander in chief of the Mediterranean fleet (1952–54) and first sea lord (1955–59), becoming an admiral in 1956. He died in Ireland, the victim of an IRA bomb.

● **Mounties** ▷*See* Royal Canadian Mounted Police.

● **Mount Isa** ▶ 20 50S 139 29E A town in Australia, in NW Queensland. Zinc, lead, silver, and copper are mined. Population (latest est): 24 104.

● **Mount Lofty Ranges** ▶ A range of hills in SE South Australia. It consists of an extension of the ▷Flinders Range and reaches 934 m (3063 ft) at Mount Byron.

● **Mount of Olives** ▶ The highest point in a small range of four summits situated just E of Jerusalem. It features in the Old and New Testaments. Its W slope was the site of the Garden of ▷Gethsemane. According to the Acts of the Apostles (1.2–12), Christ ascended to heaven from the Mount of Olives. Many churches and convents have been built here since the 4th century AD or earlier.

● **Mount Palomar Observatory** ▷*See* Palomar, Mount.

● **Mount Rushmore National Memorial** ▶ The gigantic sculpture of the heads of four US presidents—Washington, Jefferson, Lincoln, and Theodore Roosevelt—carved (1927–41) to the design of the sculptor Gutzon Borglum (1871–1941) on the NE cliffs of Mount Rushmore, in the Black Hills of South Dakota. Each head is about 18 m (60 ft) high.

● **Mount St Helens** ▷*See* St Helens, Mount.

● **Mount Vernon** ▶ A national shrine in the USA, in Virginia S of Washington, DC, on the Potomac River. It was the home (1759–99) of George Washington, whose tomb lies in the grounds of the 18th-century mansion.

● **Mount Wilson Observatory** ▷*See* Hale Observatories.

● **Mourne Mountains** ▶ A mountain range in Northern Ireland, in Co Down. It extends SW–NE between Carlingford Lough and Dundrum Bay, reaching 853 m (2798 ft) at Slieve Donard.

● **mourning dove** ▶ A common North American ▷pigeon, *Zenaidura macroura*, that is adapted for survival in hot deserts; it can endure high body temperatures and dehydration and can fly long distances, enabling it to live far from water. 30 cm long, it has a long pointed tail and grey-brown plumage with pink and violet patches on the neck.

● **mouse** ▶ A ▷rodent belonging to the suborder *Myomorpha*. The house mouse (*Mus musculus*) is common in buildings worldwide and has long been associated with man. Greyish brown, it is 14–16 cm long including its tail (7–8 cm) and feeds on a variety of foods, from grain to oil-based paints.

Most mice—together with their larger relatives, the ▷rats—are grouped into the subfamilies *Murinae* of the Old World and *Cricetinae* of the New World (which also includes hamsters). There are separate subfamilies for African tree mice (*Dendromurinae*; 7 species), jumping mice (*Zapodinae*; 3 species), dormice, and other small groups.

● **mousebird** ▷*See* coly.

● **mouse deer** ▷*See* chevrotain.

● **Mousterian** ▶ A stone-tool industry of the Middle ▷Palaeolithic, associated with ▷Neanderthal man. Named after caves at Le Moustier in the Dordogne (SW France), the Mousterian occurs, with variants,

throughout Eurasia from France to China and in N Africa. Spanning roughly the period of 70 000 to 35 000 BC, it is characterized by a wide variety of hand axes, scrapers, points, and blades, often made by the ▷Lavalloisian technique. Mousterian sites have provided the earliest evidence for formal burial of the dead.

● **mouthbrooder** ▶ A fish belonging to one of several genera of ▷cichlid fishes. The eggs are carried in the mouth of the parent, usually the female, until they hatch. Chief genera: *Tilapia*; *Haplochromis*; *Pelmatochromis*. Other mouthbrooders include certain ▷fighting fish, ▷catfish, and cardinal fish.

● **mouth organ** ▷*See* harmonica.

● **Moyle** ▶ A district in Northern Ireland, in Co Antrim. Area: 494 sq km (191 sq mi). Population (1991): 14 700.

● **Mozambique, Republic of** ▶ (Portuguese name: Moçambique) A country in S East Africa, bordering on the Indian Ocean. Extensive coastal plains, at their widest in the S, rise to plateaus inland with mountains reaching over 2000 m (6500 ft). The chief rivers, notably the Zambezi and Limpopo, flow E and provide both irrigation and hydroelectric power. Most of the population is African, mainly Bantu, with diminishing minorities of Europeans and others.

Economy: chiefly agricultural, the staple food crops being rice and maize. The main cash crops of cashew nuts (of which Mozambique is the world's largest producer), cotton, and sugar are also the principal exports. Industry is, at present, based largely on food processing and textiles but there are plans to develop heavy industry. Mineral resources, including natural gas and high-grade iron ore, are largely unexploited except for coal and bauxite. In 1985 two US petroleum companies contracted with Mozambique to explore for oil. The ▷Beira Corridor trade route, running across Mozambican territory from Zimbabwe to the coast, is an important source of income. By the late 1990s government moves to deregulate the economy and attract foreign investment had resulted in a spectacular burst of growth. However, these gains were largely reversed by the floods of 2000.

History: the N coast was settled by Arabs from the 10th century and was explored by Vasco da ▷Gama in 1498, becoming a Portuguese colony in the early 16th century. In 1951 it became an overseas province of Portugal. From 1963 ▷Frelimo waged a guerrilla campaign that achieved the establishment (1975) of Mozambique as an independent socialist one-party state under Samora Moïses Machel (1933–86). Mozambique provided a base for ▷Mugabe's arm of the Zimbabwe guerrilla organization, the Patriotic Front, and its borders with Rhodesia (now Zimbabwe) were closed from 1976 until 1980. From 1977 the South African-backed Mozambique National Resistance (Renamo or MNR) waged war on the state with a campaign of guerrilla raids and sabotage. One-party (Frelimo) rule was abandoned in favour of multiparty democracy in 1990 and Renamo was recognized as a legitimate political party in 1991. A peace treaty ending the civil war was concluded in 1992; the first multiparty elections, held in 1994, were won by Frelimo. Mozambique joined the Commonwealth in 1996, becoming the first member state to have no historical links with the UK. In 2000 and 2001 Mozambique was devastated by cyclones and flooding that left about one million people homeless.

Republic of Mozambique

Head of state	President Joaquim Chissano
Official language	Portuguese; the main African language is Makua Lomwe
Official currency	metical of 100 centavos
Area	784 961 sq km (303 070 sq mi)
Population (1999 est)	19 124 000
Capital and main port	Maputo

● **Mozarabs** ▶ Christians living in Spain under Muslim rule. The Mozarabs (meaning "almost Arabs") were so called because they adopted the Arabic culture of their Muslim rulers. They formed autonomous communities within the Muslim state.

● **Mozart, Wolfgang Amadeus** ▶ (1756–91) Austrian composer, born in Salzburg, the son of the violinist and composer Leopold Mozart (1719–87). Mozart exhibited extraordinary musical talent at the age of four; in 1762 his father took him on a tour of Germany and

Wolfgang Amadeus Mozart ▶ A painting (1819) by Barbara Krafft (1764–1825). Mozart was enormously prolific as a composer. Overwork and poverty undoubtedly contributed to his death at the age of 35. One can only imagine the extent to which he would have enlarged the musical repertoire if he had been granted a more usual lifespan.

to Paris and London, where he received adulation for his abilities. In 1770 in Rome Mozart was able to write out the entire score of a *Miserere* by Gregorio Allegri (1582-1652) after hearing the work twice. He continued to tour, composing piano sonatas, symphonies, and his early operas but failing to find a permanent position worthy of his exceptional talents.

After a period of unhappy service with the Archbishop of Salzburg (1779–81) he settled in Vienna as a freelance musician and teacher, composing such masterpieces as the operas *The Marriage of Figaro* (1786) and *Don Giovanni* (1787). The success of the latter obtained him belated recognition from the emperor but constant travelling, poverty, and frequent overwork contributed to his early death, possibly from typhus. Mozart achieved a fusion of the Germanic and Italianate styles of composition and his immense productivity enriched almost every musical genre. He composed 49 symphonies, over 40 concertos (of which those for piano (25), horn, violin, and clarinet are best known), 7 string quintets, 26 string quartets, numerous divertimenti, piano sonatas, violin sonatas, and much other music. Some of his finest works, such as the operas *Così fan tutte* (1790) and *The Magic Flute* (1791) and the *Jupiter* symphony (1788), were written in the last years of his life. His unfinished *Requiem* was completed after his death by Franz Süssmayr (1766-1803). The "Odense Symphony" (1768), was found in 1982 and first performed in 1984. ▷*See also* Köchel, Ludwig von.

● **Mo-Zi** ▶ (or Mo-tzu; ?470–?391 BC) Chinese philosopher. Originally a follower of Confucius, Mo-Zi criticized him for stressing ritual rather than virtue. In his chief work, the *Mo-Zi*, he taught universal love, pacifism, and simplicity, principles that formed the basis of a religious movement, Moism. Although Moism had ceased to be practised by the 2nd century BC, its philosophy it is still highly regarded.

● **Mpumalanga** ▷*See* Transvaal.

● **MRI** ▷*See* magnetic resonance imaging.

● **MS-DOS** ▶ (Microsoft disk operating system) ▷*See* operating system.

● **Mtwara** ▶ 10 17S 40 11E A deepwater port in S Tanzania, on the Indian Ocean. It exports chiefly local produce, mainly cashew nuts. Population (latest est): 252 000.

● **Mu'awiyah I** ▶ (c. 602–80 AD) The first ▷caliph (661–80) of the Umayyad dynasty. He participated in the conquest of Syria, where he was made governor in 640. After the assassination of his enemy ▷Ali, he became caliph. Renowned for his tactful control of the Arabs, Mu'awiyah is blamed by Islam for turning the caliphate into a worldly kingship.

● **Mubarak, (Mohammed) Hosni (Said)** ▶ (1928–) Egyptian statesman; president (1981–). A general, he commanded (1972–75) the Egyptian air force in the ▷Yom Kippur War (1973). He became vice

president to Anwar ▷Sadat in 1975 and succeeded him on his assassination. A modernizing pragmatist, he has contained inflation, improved relations with the USA and Arab countries, and worked for peace in the Middle East. His hard line against Islamic fundamentalism has provoked terrorist activity, including an assassination attempt in 1995.

● **mucous membrane** ▶ A moist ▷membrane that lines many tracts and cavities, including the digestive and respiratory tracts and the nasal sinuses. It is a type of ▷epithelium containing cells that secrete **mucus**, a slimy substance that protects its surface and—in the digestive tract—also lubricates the passage of food and faeces. In the bronchi the mucus traps particles that are inhaled with air.

● **Mudéjars** ▶ (Arabic: vassal) The Muslims (*see* Moors) of Spain who had, by the 13th century, become subject to Christian rule during the reconquest of Iberia. Frequently of mixed ▷Berber and Spanish descent, they continued to preserve their religion. They created an architectural style notable for its ornamental brickwork and ceramic tiling. Many examples survive in Castile and Aragon.

● **mudfish** ▷*See* bowfin.

● **mudpuppy** ▶ A salamander, *Necturus maculosis*, of North America. Grey-brown, with four well-developed limbs, mudpuppies retain their dark-red gills throughout their lives, even when mature at about five years old and 20 cm long. They are slow moving and generally hunt fish, snails, and other invertebrates at night. The female guards her eggs until they hatch. Family: *Proteidae*. ▷*See also* olm.

● **mudskipper** ▶ A fish of the subfamily *Periophthalminae*, especially the genus *Periophthalmus*, found in swamps, estuaries, and mud flats of Africa, Polynesia, and Australia. Mudskippers have an elongated body, up to 30 cm long, a blunt head, and dorsally protruding eyes. They are able to climb and walk over land using their limblike pectoral fins. Family: *Gobiidae* (*see* goby).

● **mufti** ▶ A Muslim legal expert. They assist judges or private citizens by writing their opinions (*futwas*) on legal matters. These only become precedents in cases of marriage, divorce, and inheritance. In the Ottoman Empire muftis were state officials, the grand mufti being the chief spiritual authority.

● **Mugabe, Robert (Gabriel)** ▶ (1925–) Zimbabwean statesman; prime minister (1980–87); president (1988–). He helped found the Zimbabwe African National Union (ZANU) in 1963 and, after ten years' (1964–74) detention in Rhodesia, formed the ▷Patriotic Front (PF) with Joshua Nkomo, leader of the Zimbabwe African People's Union (ZAPU). Based in Mozambique, he waged guerrilla warfare against the governments of Ian Smith and then Bishop Muzorewa until 1979–80, when he played a major part in the talks that brought Black majority rule to Rhodesia (renamed Zimbabwe). His party's election victory (1980) brought Mugabe the leadership of Zimbabwe. He consolidated his power and restricted opposition by creating a one-party state in 1987. In the late 1990s his authoritarian rule and failure to prevent deepening recession provoked growing protests. His support for the illegal and violent seizure of White-owned farms by Black militants led to controversy in 2000; elections the same year brought an end to his effective monopoly of power.

● **mugger** ▶ A broad-snouted ▷crocodile, *Crocodylus palustris*, found in India, Sri Lanka, and Myanmar (Burma). It was formerly a sacred animal, kept in temples and tended by priests.

● **mugwort** ▷*See* wormwood.

● **Muhammad** ▷*See* Mohammed.

● **Muhammad Ahmad** ▷*See* Mahdi, al-.

● **Mühlhausen** ▶ 51 14N 10 26E A town in central Germany, on the River Unstrut. The headquarters of Thomas ▷Müntzer in the Peasants' War, it has several fine medieval churches. Industries include the manufacture of textiles, machinery, and furniture. Population (1989 est): 44 000.

● **Muir, Edwin** ▶ (1887-1959) Scottish poet. Born in Orkney, he moved to Glasgow in 1901 and to London in 1919. During the 1930s he and his wife Willa moved to Prague, where they translated the novels of Franz ▷Kafka and other major German writers. His reputation as a poet was established rather late in life with *The Voyage* (1946) and *The Labyrinth* (1949). His *Autobiography* (1954) contains much of his best prose.

● **Mujahidin** ▷*See* Afghanistan, Islamic State of.

● **Mujibur Rahman, Sheikh** ▶ (1920–75) Bangladesh statesman; prime minister (1972–75). He was gaoled in 1968 by ▷Ayub Khan's regime in Pakistan for campaigning for the independence of East Pakistan. Following the victory of his party, the Awami League, in the 1970 elections and victory in the subsequent civil war (1971), he became prime minister of the independent state of Bangladesh. Shortly before his assassination he assumed dictatorial powers.

● **Mukden** ▷*See* Shenyang.

● **mulberry** ▶ A tree of the genus *Morus* (12 species), native to N temperate and subtropical regions. The black mulberry (*M. nigra*) is the species most commonly cultivated for its fruit. About 12 m high, it has toothed heart-shaped leaves and round green male and female flower clusters (catkins), borne usually on separate trees. The female flowers give rise to a blackberry-like fruit, which has a pleasant slightly acid taste and is used in jellies, desserts, etc. The leaves of the white mulberry (*M. alba*) are the staple food of silkworms. Family: *Moraceae*. ▷*See also* paper mulberry.

● **mule** ▶ The sterile offspring of a female horse and a male ass. Mules are useful pack and draught animals, being hardy, sure-footed, and strong but smaller than a horse and requiring less food. ▷*See also* hinny.

● **Mülheim an der Ruhr** ▶ 51 25N 6 50E A city in NW Germany, in North Rhine-Westphalia on the River Ruhr. There is a 13th-century castle. Its manufactures include pipes, tubes, and machinery. Population (1996 est): 176 530.

● **Mull** ▶ An island off the W coast of Scotland, in the Inner Hebrides. It is chiefly mountainous; some sheep and cattle are raised. Other occupations include fishing, forestry, and tourism. Area: 909 sq km (351 sq mi). Population (1991): 2708. Chief town: Tobermory.

● **mullein** ▶ A biennial or perennial herb of the genus *Verbascum* (about 300 species), native to N temperate Eurasia. The biennial common mullein (*V. thapsus*), also called Aaron's rod, occurs in dry limy regions. 0.6–2 m tall, it bears large woolly leaves and pale-yellow flowers. Some species, including the European dark mullein (*V. nigrum*), are grown as garden plants. Family: *Scrophulariaceae*.

● **Muller, Hermann Joseph** ▶ (1890–1967) US geneticist, who discovered the ability of X-rays to induce changes (mutations) in genetic material. Although useful as an experimental tool, Muller recognized the danger of X-radiation to man. He was awarded a Nobel Prize (1946).

● **Müller, Paul Hermann** ▶ (1899–1965) Swiss chemist, who discovered the insecticidal properties of ▷DDT (1939). Müller found it was relatively harmless to other forms of life and DDT became widely used to combat insect pests. Müller was awarded the 1948 Nobel Prize for Medicine.

● **mullet** ▶ A food fish, also called grey mullet, belonging to the genus *Mugil* (about 70 species), found in temperate and tropical coastal waters and estuaries. It has a slender silvery-green or grey large-scaled body, 30–90 cm long, with two dorsal fins. It feeds in schools on algae and small invertebrates. Family: *Mugilidae*; order: *Perciformes*. ▷*See also* red mullet.

● **Mulliken, Robert Sanderson** ▶ (1896–1986) US chemist and physicist, who developed ▷Schrödinger's theory of wave mechanics to provide a mathematical explanation of chemical bonding in terms of electron probabilities, orbitals, and energy levels. He received the 1966 Nobel Prize.

● **Mullingar** ▶ (Irish name: Muileann Cearr) 53 32N 7 20W A market town in the Republic of Ireland, the county town of Co Westmeath. Trade includes cattle and it has a cathedral. Population (1995 est): 11 800.

● **Mullis, Kary Banks** ▶ (1944–　) US biochemist. Mullis devised a simple method of producing unlimited copies of DNA fragments, which he named the polymerase chain reaction (PCR). He was awarded the Nobel Prize in 1993.

● **Mulready, William** ▶ (1786–1863) British painter, born in Ireland, best known for his everyday scenes of cottages, schoolrooms, etc., and as the designer of the first penny postage envelope (1840).

● **Mulroney, (Martin) Brian** ▶ (1939–　) Canadian statesman and lawyer; prime minister (1984–93). After practising law in Montreal he became leader of the Progressive Conservative Party in 1983 and prime minister a year later.

● **Multan** ▶ 30 10N 71 36E A city in central Pakistan. An ancient settlement on the key route to S India, it has often been besieged and occupied. It has textile and noteworthy cottage industries. Population (1995 est): 1 257 000.

● **multimedia system** ▶ A computer system capable of producing high-quality moving pictures and sound as well as text, usually from information stored on a ▷compact disc. Such systems are used in education and for entertainment.

● **multinational corporations** ▶ Large business enterprises with headquarters (the parent company) in one country and operating divisions (subsidiaries) in one or more other countries. Strategic decision making usually takes place at the head office. Their command of large resources and ability to manoeuvre around local legislation and taxation have led to demands for international legislation to restrain their activities when these conflict with national interests.

● **multiple sclerosis** ▶ A chronic and usually progressive disease of the nervous system in which the fatty sheaths that surround the nerves in the brain or spinal cord are destroyed, which affects the function of the nerves. The disease is also called disseminated sclerosis, as its effects are disseminated in different parts of the body. It usually begins in young adults, and the commonest initial symptoms are sudden severe blurring of the vision or weakness in one limb. The initial symptoms often resolve completely but later the disease returns, causing permanent handicap. Steroids and interferons are used in treatment.

● **multiple star** ▶ A system of two or more stars that move in complex orbits under mutual gravitational attraction. ▷*See also* binary star.

● **multiplexer** ▶ In ▷telecommunications, a device that combines several signals so that they can be sent along a single transmission path, or channel, and reconstructed at the receiver. One method is to superimpose carrier waves of different frequencies (*see* modulation) on the signals. Multiplexers are used with radio transmissions, telephone lines, etc.

● **multiplier** ▶ A number used in economic theory to indicate how many times a specific increase in income, demand, etc., will be multiplied to produce an increase in the overall income, demand, etc., in a nation's economy. For example, if an individual's income is increased by £10 as a result of a cut in direct taxation, half of this increase may be spent in such a way that it becomes income for others, who may in turn also spend half of their increased income. Thus the original £10 could be multiplied to produce a total of £20 of additional income, in which case the multiplier has a value of 2. Opinions differ as to the practical impact of the multiplier, depending on the view of what motivates consumption.

● **Mumbai** ▷*See* Bombay.

● **Mumford, Lewis** ▶ (1895–1990) US social philosopher. Mumford's academic posts included research professorships at the Universities of Stanford (1942–44) and Berkeley (1961–62). He wrote widely on architecture and cities, arguing that technological society was repressive. His books include *Sticks and Stones* (1924), *Technics and Civilization* (1934), *Values for Survival* (1946), *In the Name of Sanity* (1954), and *The City in History* (1961).

● **mummers' play** ▶ An English folk drama based on the legend of St George and the Seven Champions of Christendom; it was a dumb show (*mummer*, from Middle English *mum*, silent), traditionally enacted on Christmas Day by masked performers. Its plot largely consists of a duel between St George and an infidel knight, in which one of them is killed but is later revived by a doctor. The play is still performed in a few villages in England and N Ireland.

● **mummy** ► A human or animal body prepared and embalmed for burial according to ancient Egyptian religious practice. The internal organs were extracted and sealed in ▷Canopic jars and the body was desiccated by packing in dry natron, anointed, and encased in linen bandages.

● **mumps** ► An acute virus infection that usually occurs in children. After an incubation period of 12 to 20 days the child develops headache and fever; later, the parotid salivary glands (situated under the ear) become tender and swollen. The disease is usually mild and resolves rapidly, but sometimes mild ▷meningitis develops. In adult male patients the infection may spread to the testicles, which may occasionally lead to sterility. In the UK immunization, in the form of the combined MMR (measles, mumps, rubella), is recommended for all children.

● **Munch, Charles** ► (1892–1968) French conductor. He made his debut in Paris in 1932 and directed the Boston Symphony Orchestra from 1949 to 1962. In 1967 he founded the Orchestre de Paris but died on its first US tour.

● **Munch, Edvard** ► (1863–1944) Norwegian painter and printmaker, who was a major influence on 20th-century German ▷expressionism. Largely self-taught, he developed his mature style in Berlin, following visits to Paris where he was influenced by ▷Gauguin and ▷Van Gogh. His symbolic paintings of love, death, and despair, including the famous *Cry* (1893; Nasjonalgalleriet, Oslo), reflect the pessimism caused by family tragedy. After 1910 he lived in Norway, where he painted murals for the festival hall of Oslo University (1913).

● **München** ▷*See* Munich.

● **München Gladbach** ▷*See* Mönchengladbach.

● **Munchausen's syndrome** ► A psychiatric condition in which a person repeatedly seeks hospital treatment, especially surgery, for nonexistent ailments, which are described in vivid and convincing detail. Symptoms are mimicked, often to the extent of self-injury, in order to gain a doctor's attention. **Munchausen's syndrome by proxy** is a related condition in which medical attention is sought by a carer or parent for the child (or other person) in their charge: physical injury is inflicted to provide evidence of disease. Both syndromes are named after Freiherr von ▷Münchhausen.

● **Münchhausen, Karl Friedrich, Freiherr von** ► (1720–97) German soldier famous as a raconteur. His hyperbolic accounts of his feats passed into legend and were the subject of a series of fantasy tales, *The Adventures of Baron Münchhausen* (1793), written by R. E. Raspe (1737–94).

● **Muncie** ► 40 11N 85 22W A city in the USA, in E Indiana on the White River. It is the "typical American" town of the classic sociological study *Middletown* (1929) by Robert and Helen Lynd. An agricultural trading centre, Muncie's varied manufactures include machine tools and glass. Population (1990): 71 035.

● **Munda** ► Aboriginal tribes living mainly in the hills and forests of central and NE India. Munda languages form a subgroup of the ▷Austro-Asiatic language family. The northern branch of the Munda languages includes Santali, the most important. The Munda peoples are mainly slash-and-burn cultivators.

● **mung bean** ► A ▷bean plant, *Phaseolus aureus*, also known as green gram, native to India and cultivated in tropical and subtropical regions chiefly as a vegetable crop. The slender pods contain up to 15 small edible seeds, which can be dried and stored or germinated in the dark to produce bean sprouts. Family: ▷*Leguminosae*.

● **Munich** ► (German name: München) 48 08N 11 35E A city in S Germany, the capital of Bavaria on the River Isar. It has a 15th-century cathedral and many baroque and rococo buildings, including Nymphenburg Palace (1664–1728). Its university was moved here from Landshut in 1826. It is also noted for its technical university, opera, art galleries, and for its annual Oktoberfest (beer festival). A centre of

commerce, industry, and tourism, its manufactures include precision instruments, electrical goods, chemicals, and beer.

History: Munich was from 1255 the residence and from 1506 the capital of the Dukes of Bavaria (from 1806 Kings). During the late 19th and early 20th centuries the city flourished culturally, attracting such figures as the composer Wagner. The Nazi movement began here in the 1920s. Munich was severely bombed during World War II. Population (1996 est): 1 236 370.

● **Munich Agreement** ► (1938) The settlement, resulting from the conference between Neville Chamberlain (UK), Daladier (France), Hitler (Germany), and Mussolini (Italy), that recognized Hitler's territorial claims to the ▷Sudetenland. Described by Chamberlain as achieving "peace in our time," it was followed in March, 1939, by Hitler's invasion of Czechoslovakia and in Sept by World War II.

● **Munich Putsch** ► (1923) The attempt by ▷Hitler to seize power in Germany. Hitler planned to form a national government after first seizing power in Bavaria. This attempt at revolution (German word: *Putsch*) failed and Hitler was imprisoned.

● **Munnings, Sir Alfred** ► (1878–1959) British painter. His immaculate paintings of horses were first exhibited at the Royal Academy in 1898. He was president of the Royal Academy from 1944 to 1951.

● **Munro, Hector Hugh** ▷*See* Saki.

● **Munsell colour system** ► A method of classifying ▷colours based on three parameters: hue (dominant colour), luminosity (brightness), and saturation or chroma (strength, i.e. the degree to which it is a pure spectral colour). The various colours are set out in a chart known as the colour tree, in which the different gradations of colour are exhibited according to the three parameters. The Munsell colour system is widely used in the paint industry. Named after Albert H. Munsell (1858–1918).

● **Münster** ► 51 58N 7 37E A city and port in NW Germany, in North Rhine-Westphalia on the Dortmund-Ems Canal. It was an important member of the Hanseatic League and the capital of the former province of Westphalia. It has a 13th-century cathedral, restored after damage caused during World War II, and a university (1773). Service industries employ most of the workforce. Population (1996 est): 265 061.

● **Munster** ► A province and ancient kingdom of the SW Republic of Ireland. It consists of the counties of Clare, Cork, Kerry, Limerick, Tipperary, and Waterford. Area: 24 125 sq km (9315 sq mi). Population (1996): 1 035 000.

● **Munthe, Axel** ► (1857–1949) Swedish physician and author. Munthe practised in Paris and Rome before retiring to Capri, where he built the Villa San Michele. *The Story of San Michele* (1929) described his early life and the building of the villa. It has been translated into 44 languages.

● **muntjac** ► A small deer belonging to the subfamily *Muntiacinae* (6 species), occurring in forests of Asia, Sumatra, Java, and Borneo. The Indian muntjac (*Muntiacus muntjak*), also called barking deer or rib-faced deer, is 55 cm high at the shoulder, chestnut above and paler beneath with short unbranched antlers and short sharp fangs. Muntjacs are solitary and nocturnal, feeding on grass, leaves, and shoots.

● **Müntzer, Thomas** ► (c. 1490–1525) German Protestant reformer and ▷Anabaptist leader. He began preaching reformed doctrines at Zwickau in 1520 but soon diverged from Luther's teachings. Claiming direct inspiration from the Holy Spirit, he called for radical social, political, and religious reform. A leader of the ▷Peasants' Revolt (1524–25), he was captured at the battle of Frankenhausen (1525) and executed.

● **Muntz metal** ► A relatively hard strong type of ▷brass containing 60% copper and 40% zinc. It is not easily worked at room temperature and is usually shaped while hot or by casting. Named after G. F. Muntz (d. 1847).

● **muon** ► A negatively charged unstable elementary particle (lifetime 2×10^{-6} second; mass 207 times that of the electron) that decays into an electron and two ▷neutrinos. It has a corresponding antiparticle. It was originally thought to be a meson (and was called the mu-meson) but is now classified as a lepton. ▷*See* particle physics.

● **mural painting** ▶ The decoration of walls and ceilings by such varied techniques as ▷encaustic, ▷tempera, and ▷fresco painting. The design of murals is largely dependent on their architectural settings. ▷Renaissance painters often used perspective and architecture in their murals to create the illusion that the painted walls or ceilings were space extensions of the real architecture. Mural painting was revived during the 20th century, principally by the Mexican painters ▷Rivera, ▷Orozco, and ▷Siqueiros, who used it to reach a wider public with their social and political subject matter.

● **Murasaki Shikibu** ▶ (?978–?1014) Japanese writer. She is most famous for *The Tale of Genji*, which is probably the world's earliest novel. It deals with the love life of Prince Genji and is remarkable for its observations of nature and understanding of human emotions.

● **Murat, Joachim** ▶ (1767–1815) French marshal and King of Naples (1808–15). He served in Napoleon's campaigns in Italy (1796–97) and Egypt (1798–99) and fought at ▷Marengo (1800) and ▷Austerlitz (1805). In Naples, Murat introduced administrative reforms. He treated with the Austrians after Napoleon's defeat (1813) but attempts to regain his throne ended in defeat at Tolentino and then in his capture and execution.

● **Murcia** ▶ 38 59N 1 08W A city in SE Spain, in the autonomous region of Murcia. Formerly the capital of the Moorish kingdom of Murcia, it has a cathedral and university (1915). Industries include silk and textiles. Population (1995 est): 344 904.

● **murder** ▶ The crime of killing a person in which, in the UK, the *mens rea* (*see* criminal law) is malice aforethought, i.e. an intention to kill, intention to cause grievous bodily harm, doing something realizing that it would almost certainly or very probably cause death, or realizing that grievous bodily harm could result from the act. There are two defences: diminished responsibility (i.e. having powers of control, judgment, or reasoning that an ordinary man would consider abnormal; *see also* insanity) or provocation (being exposed to conduct or words that would make a reasonable man lose his self-control), which, if proved, can reduce a charge from murder to ▷manslaughter. Since 1965 the punishment has been life imprisonment (*see also* capital punishment). In 1991, for the first time, a case against two suspected murderers (one acquitted and one unprosecuted in the criminal courts) was successfully pursued in a civil action.

● **Murdoch, Dame Iris** ▶ (1919–99) British novelist and philosopher. Born in Dublin, she studied and taught philosophy at Oxford; her philosophical works include *Sartre* (1953) and *Metaphysics as a Guide to Morals* (1992). Her novels include *Under the Net* (1954), *The Bell* (1958), *A Severed Head* (1961), *The Black Prince* (1974), *The Sea, the Sea* (1978), which won the Booker Prize, *The Good Apprentice* (1985), *The Book and the Brotherhood* (1987), and *Jackson's Dilemma* (1995). Her last years were clouded by Alzheimer's disease.

● **Murdoch, (Keith) Rupert** ▶ (1931–) US publisher and entrepreneur, born in Australia. His company, News International, runs several British national papers, including *The Times* and *The Sun*, and the only national Australian newspaper: he also owns US papers, 20th Century-Fox, US TV networks, Collins (UK publishers), and the satellite broadcasting company British Sky TV. In 1998 he launched Sky Digital, the first digital TV system in Britain.

● **Murdock, William** ▶ (1754–1839) British inventor, who pioneered the use of coal-gas for lighting. In 1802–03 he used it to light the Soho engineering works where he was an employee.

● **Mureş, River** ▶ (Hungarian name: Maros) A river in E Europe, flowing W from the Carpathian Mountains in Romania across the Transylvanian Basin to join the Tisza River in Hungary. Length: 803 km (499 mi).

● **murex** ▶ A ▷gastropod mollusc belonging to the family *Muricidae* (about 1000 species), mainly of tropical seas. Murex □shells are elaborately ornamented with spines and frills; the snail feeds on other molluscs by drilling holes in their shells and extracting the flesh with its long proboscis. *Murex trunculus* was the source of the dye Tyrian purple.

● **Murillo, Bartolomé Esteban** ▶ (1617–82) Spanish painter. He spent most of his life in Seville, working for the religious orders and helping to found the Spanish Academy (1660), of which he became first president. After abandoning his early realism, he painted urchins and religious scenes in an idealized style influenced by Rubens and the Venetians. The 20th century saw a reaction against the sentimentality of these works.

● **Murmansk** ▶ 68 59N 33 08E A port in NW Russia, on the Kola inlet of the Barents Sea. Its ice-free harbour was used by the Allied expedition against the Bolsheviks in 1918. Murmansk was formerly an important naval and fishing base but has now declined. The surrounding region is very heavily polluted, having served for many years as the world's leading dump for nuclear waste; an internationally funded clean-up is now planned. Population (1995 est): 407 000.

● **Murphy-O'Connor, Cormac, Cardinal** ▶ (1932–) British Roman Catholic churchman. He became Bishop of Arundel and Brighton in 1977 and succeeded Basil ▷Hume as Archbishop of Westminster in 2000. He was created a cardinal in 2001.

● **Murray, Gilbert** ▶ (1866–1957) British classical scholar. He was professor of Greek at Glasgow (1889–1908) and Oxford (1908–36). His translations of Aeschylus, Sophocles, Euripides, and Aristophanes kindled interest in Greek drama.

● **Murray, Sir James (Augustus Henry)** ▶ (1837–1915) British lexicographer. Largely self-educated, he became a teacher at Mill Hill School in 1870. After joining the Philological Society and editing some early English texts, he was in 1878 appointed editor of the *New English Dictionary on Historical Principles* (later called the *Oxford English Dictionary*), to which he devoted the rest of his life.

● **Murray, Les** ▶ (Leslie Allan M.; 1938–) Australian poet. In such poem sequences as *The Buladelah-Taree Holiday Song Cycle* (1977) and *The Idyll Wheel* (1987) he describes the landscape, wildlife, and society of New South Wales, where he farms. He published his *Collected Poems* in 1991 and the verse novel *Fredy Neptune* in 1999.

● **Murray, James Stuart, Earl of** ▷*See* Moray, James Stuart, Earl of.

● **Murray cod** ▶ A carnivorous food and game fish, *Maccullochella macquariensis*, found in fresh waters of Australia. Up to 2 m long, it has a broad olive-green body with brown spots and a long dorsal fin.

● **Murray River** ▶ The chief river in Australia. Rising near Mount Koscuisko, in New South Wales, it flows generally W and S before entering Encounter Bay on the Indian Ocean through Lake Alexandrina. The main tributaries are the Darling and Murrumbidgee Rivers; it also receives water from the Snowy Mountains hydroelectric scheme. Length: 2590 km (1609 mi).

● **Murrow, Edward R(oscoe)** ▶ (1908–65) US radio and television journalist. He joined CBS in 1935 and became head of the European Bureau in 1937. After World War II he became a CBS vice president and in the 1950s was a fearless critic of Senator Joseph ▷McCarthy. In 1961 he became director of the US Information Agency.

● **Murrumbidgee River** ▶ A river in SE Australia, rising in the Eastern Highlands in New South Wales and flowing to the Murray River. The Burrinjuck Dam provides water for irrigation. Length: 1690 km (1050 mi).

● **Murry, John Middleton** ▶ (1889–1957) British literary critic. He married Katherine ▷Mansfield and was a friend of D. H. ▷Lawrence. He edited the literary magazines *Athenaeum* (1919–21) and *Adelphi* (1923–48). His many books include studies of Keats and Blake.

● **Muscat** ▶ (Arabic name: Masqat) 23 37N 58 38E The capital of Oman, on the Gulf of Oman. Most port traffic is now handled at Matrah to the NW. There is an oil terminal to the W. Population (1993): 51 969.

● **Muscat and Oman** ▷*See* Oman, Sultanate of.

● **muscle** ▶ Tissue that is specialized to contract, producing movement or tension in the body. It contains long spindle-shaped cells (muscle fibres) that convert chemical energy (*see* ATP) into mechanical energy. Most of the body's musculature consists of voluntary muscle, which is consciously controlled via the central nervous system. It is also known as skeletal muscle (because it is attached to the bones) and striated (or striped) muscle (because of its banded appearance under the microscope). Individual muscles are made up of bundles of fibres enclosed in a strong fibrous sheath and attached to bones by tendons. Involuntary muscle occurs in the walls of hollow organs, such as blood vessels, intestines, and the bladder. It is responsible for movements not under conscious control and is regulated by the autonomic nervous system. Cardiac muscle is a special type of muscle found only in the ▷heart: its rhythmic contractions produce the heartbeat. ▷See Plate II.

● **muscovite** ▷See micas.

● **Muscovy Company** ► The first important English joint-stock company. Founded in 1553 to discover a northeast passage to the Orient, it was chartered in 1555 and granted a Russian trade monopoly, which it lost in 1698. It was dissolved in 1917.

● **Muscovy duck** ► A large tropical American ▷perching duck, *Cairina moschata*. It has a glossy black plumage with white wing patches. The domesticated form is larger with a grey, white, or speckled plumage and a large scarlet caruncle on the bill.

● **muscular dystrophy** ► A group of chronic and progressive disorders characterized by wasting and weakening of the muscle fibres. The disease is inherited and the commonest type, Duchenne muscular dystrophy, affects predominantly boys. The muscles affected and the rate of progress of the disease are both very variable. There is no specific treatment but physiotherapy and orthopaedic measures can help sufferers.

● **Muses** ► In Greek mythology, the nine patrons of the arts and sciences, who were daughters of Zeus and ▷Mnemosyne. Calliope was the muse of epic poetry; Clio, history; Euterpe, flute playing and music; Erato, love poetry and hymns; Terpsichore, dancing; Melpomene, tragedy; Thalia, comedy; Polyhymnia, song and mime; and Urania, astronomy.

● **Musgrave, Thea** ► (1928–) Scottish composer. She was a pupil of Nadia Boulanger in Paris. Her works include concertos for horn, viola, and clarinet as well as operas and choral, orchestral, and chamber music.

● **Musgrave Ranges** ► A range of rocky granite hills in NW South Australia. It runs parallel to the Northern Territory border, reaching 1516 m (4970 ft) at Mount Woodruffe.

● **mushroom** ► The umbrella-shaped spore-forming body produced by many fungi. (Sometimes the word toadstool is used for those species that are inedible or poisonous, mushroom being restricted to the edible species.) It consists of an erect stem (stipe) and a cap, which may be flat, conical, spherical, or cylindrical and has numerous radiating gills on its undersurface in which the spores are produced. The well-known edible mushrooms belong to the genus *Agaricus*; they have a smooth white or scaly brown cap with gills that are white, grey, or pink when immature and become deep brown at maturity. The field mushroom (*A. campestris*) has a white cap 4–8 cm in diameter and deep-pink to brown gills. ▷See also agaric.

● **music** ► The art of organizing sounds, which usually consist of sequences of tones of definite ▷pitch, to produce melody, harmony, and rhythm. Musical cultures based on ▷scales evolved in such ancient civilizations as those of China, Persia, India, etc., as well as in Europe. Within each culture both ▷folk music and classical (or "art") music traditions exist. In Western music both traditions evolved from the Greek system of ▷modes established by Pythagoras and codified during the middle ages. In classical music modes became the basis for ▷plainchant and subsequently for ▷polyphony, which reached its peak in the 15th and 16th centuries. With the development of the major and minor scales in the early 17th century harmonic composition for instrumental ensembles and in ▷opera began to evolve. During the 17th and 18th centuries increasing attention was given to the development of musical form in classical music. By the beginning of the 19th century the dominant musical forms were the ▷sonata, ▷symphony, ▷concerto, and string quartet. Opera continued to flourish and ▷oratorio, invented during the 18th century, remained popular. The influence of Romanticism in music gave rise

to the tone poem (*see* symphonic poem) and an increasingly free attitude to traditional forms. ▷Chromaticism in the music of the late 19th and early 20th centuries led to ▷atonality and the adoption by some composers of ▷serialism. In the later 20th century many composers used unpitched sounds, electronic generators, tape recordings, synthesizers, and unconventional instrumental techniques to create music, as well as experimenting widely with musical forms. The 20th century also saw the development of ▷jazz and other important forms of popular music. ▷See programme music; rock and roll; pop music.

● **musica ficta** ► (Latin: false music) A modification of the pitch of certain notes, which, during the 11th to 16th centuries, was made in the course of musical performance. For instance, the harsh tritone F-B, known as *diabolus in musica* (Latin: the devil in music), was avoided by sharpening the F or flattening the B.

● **musical instruments** ► Devices used to produce music. The chief characteristics of a musical instrument are its ▷timbre and range (i.e. the highest and lowest notes it can produce). In the ▷orchestra musical instruments are grouped into families. The ▷stringed instruments (*or* strings) include the violin, viola, cello, double bass, and harp (*see also* piano). The ▷wind instruments are divided into the woodwind (flute, clarinet, oboe, and bassoon) and brass (horn, trumpet, trombone, and tuba). The ▷percussion instruments include a whole range of instruments from the triangle and cymbals to the xylophone and timpani. Many instruments are used chiefly in jazz or pop (e.g. guitar, vibraphone, and maracas) while others, such as the Indian sitar, the Japanese koto, and the Spanish castanets, feature predominantly in the music of particular countries.

● **musicals** ► Light dramas combined with songs and dances. The genre evolved in the USA in the late 19th century and was developed during the 1920s and 1930s by George ▷Gershwin, Cole ▷Porter, Irving ▷Berlin, and Jerome ▷Kern. In *Oklahoma!* (1943) and other musicals of the 1940s, Richard ▷Rodgers and Oscar ▷Hammerstein attempted to integrate the dramatic and musical elements, a trend continued by ▷Lerner and ▷Loewe is the 1950s and culminating in Leonard Bernstein's *West Side Story* (1957). Later successes range from the rock musicals *Hair* (1968) and *Jesus Christ Superstar* (1971), to the more cerebral works of Stephen ▷Sondheim and the spectacular productions of Andrew ▷Lloyd Webber, whose *Cats* (1981) is the UK's most successful musical.

● **music drama** ▷See opera.

● **music hall** ► A type of popular entertainment featuring a variety of performers including singers, dancers, comedians, conjurors, jugglers, and acrobats. It developed from entertainments given in taverns, attained its greatest popularity in 19th-century England, and declined in the 1920s and 1930s with the rise of the rival attractions of cinema and the radio. Notable music-hall performers were Marie ▷Lloyd, Vesta ▷Tilley, Harry ▷Lauder, and Gracie ▷Fields. Revivals of music-hall entertainments are occasionally featured on television and have great nostalgic appeal. The US equivalent is known as vaudeville. Celebrated vaudeville performers include W. C. ▷Fields and Will Rodgers (1879–1935), both of whom later became film actors.

● **musicology** ► The study of the theoretical aspects of ▷music, not including its composition or performance. The aspects usually included in this study are acoustics, aesthetics, notation, harmony, history (including the development of instruments), and biography. **Ethnomusicology** is the study of music from different parts of the world in relation to their cultural and anthropological development. Originally known as comparative musicology, this study was renamed ethnomusicology in the 1930s.

● **Musil, Robert** ► (1880–1942) Austrian novelist. He studied engineering and later philosophy and psychology and served as an officer in World War I. His fame was posthumous and due chiefly to his one major work, *The Man Without Qualities* (1930–43), a long novel describing life during the declining years of the Habsburg empire. Of his other works, only the novel *Young Törless* (1906) is noteworthy.

● **musique concrète** ► A type of musical composition invented by

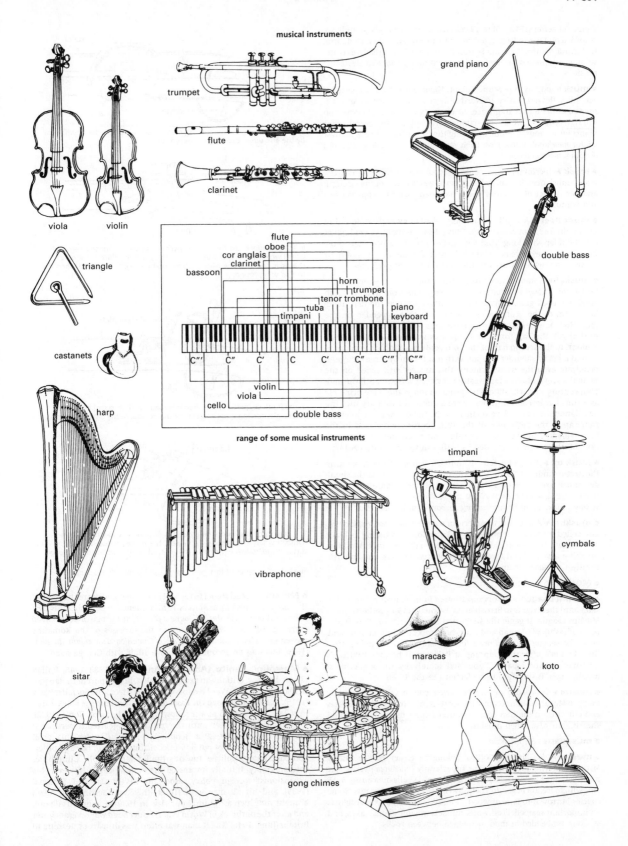

musical instruments

trumpet

flute

clarinet

grand piano

viola

violin

triangle

castanets

harp

bassoon

cor anglais

clarinet

flute

oboe

horn

trumpet

tenor trombone

tuba

timpani

piano
keyboard

C‴′ C″ C′ C C′ C″ C‴ C‴

harp

violin

viola

cello

double bass

range of some musical instruments

double bass

timpani

cymbals

vibraphone

sitar

gong chimes

maracas

koto

Pierre Schaeffer (1910–95) in 1948. Natural or man-made sounds are recorded on tape and arranged, often in an altered or distorted form, to form a composition made up of "concrete" or already existing sounds, as opposed to "abstract" musical tones. ▷*See also* electronic music.

● **musk** ▶ (botany) A perennial plant, *Mimulus moschatus* (a species of ▷monkey flower), native to North America and grown as an ornamental for its musky fragrance. 20–60 cm tall, it has oval leaves and tubular yellow flowers. The name is also applied to several other plants with a musky odour including the ▷moschatel, musk mallow (*Malva moschata*), musk rose (*Rosa moschata*), and musk stork's bill (*Erodium moschatum*).

● **musk** ▶ (perfumery) An odorous substance obtained from the male ▷musk deer. It is included in perfumes because of the strength and persistence of its odour and it has been used as an aphrodisiac and stimulant.

● **musk deer** ▶ A small solitary deer, *Moschus moschiferus*, found in mountain forests of central Asia. Musk deer are about 60 cm high at the shoulder with long hind legs; males have no antlers but grow long fangs. They have been widely hunted for the secretion of their musk gland, which is used in the manufacture of perfumes.

● **musket** ▶ A smoothbore firearm fired from the shoulder. The earliest form, known as a harquebus (*or* arquebus from Middle Dutch *hakebusse*, hook gun), evolved in the 15th century as the first handheld form of the ▷cannon—a development that depended on the matchlock as a means of igniting the charge. With a range of only 110 m (120 yd), the ball from the harquebus was unable to penetrate armour. In the second half of the 16th century a Spanish general invented a heavy shoulder weapon with a sufficiently large charge to penetrate even the finest armour—this musket still relied on the matchlock, essentially a fair-weather device. It was not until the mid-17th century that wheellocks (working on much the same principle as a flint lighter) and flintlocks were adopted for military use. The next landmark in the development of the musket was the ▷percussion cap at the beginning of the 19th century, which led to the breech-loading musket with cartridge and percussion-cap ammunition. Muskets were superseded by ▷rifles in the mid-19th century.

● **musk ox** ▶ A large hoofed ▢mammal, *Ovibos moschatus*, inhabiting the Arctic tundra of North America. About 150 cm high at the shoulder, musk oxen have long dark shaggy hair and prominent curved horns. They live in herds of 20–30 and feed on grass, etc. Bulls have a strong musky scent in the rutting season. Family: ▷*Bovidae*.

● **muskrat** ▶ A large North American water ▷vole, *Ondatra zibethica*, also called musquash. It grows up to 35 cm long, excluding its black hairless tail, and its soft glossy coat is used in the fur trade. Muskrats inhabit marshland and feed on water plants, mussels, and crayfish. Family: *Cricetidae*. ▢mammal.

● **Muslim** ▷*See* Islam.

● **Muslim League** ▶ An organization of Indian Muslims created to safeguard their rights in British India. Formed in 1906 as the All-India Muslim League, it generally supported British rule. In 1940, under the leadership of ▷Jinnah and with the prospect of Indian independence, the League began to press for a separate state for Indian Muslims. In 1947, after the founding of Pakistan, it became Pakistan's dominant political party. Supported mainly by the westernized middle class, it split into three factions in the 1960s.

● **muslin** ▶ A smooth delicately woven cotton fabric. Originally made in Mosul in Mesopotamia (hence its name), it is used for dresses and curtains. In the USA coarser cotton fabrics used for shirts and sheeting are also called muslins.

● **musquash** ▷*See* muskrat.

● **mussel** ▶ A ▷bivalve mollusc belonging either to the family *Mytilidae* (marine mussels) or the superfamily *Unionacea* (freshwater mussels). Marine mussels have wedge-shaped shells measuring 5–15 cm, which are anchored to rocks by strands (byssus threads). Some species burrow into sand or wood. The edible mussel (*Mytilus edulis*) is an important seafood. Freshwater mussels inhabit ponds, lakes, and streams, embedded in mud or wedged between rocks.

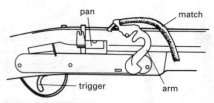

In the matchlock, a slow-burning match was forced into the powder pan by the arm when the trigger was pressed.

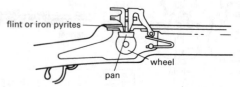

In the wheellock, the flint or iron pyrites was lowered onto a serrated wheel when the trigger was pressed. The sparks produced ignited the charge in the pan. The wheel, wound up by a key, also rotated when the trigger was pressed.

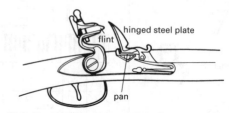

In the flintlock, pressing the trigger caused the flint to strike a hinged steel plate, forcing it back to expose the powder in the pan to the sparks.

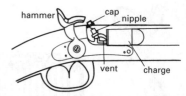

The percussion cap, containing mercury fulminate, was struck by the hammer when the trigger was pressed. The flame produced passed through the hollow nipple into the vent, where it fired the main charge.

musket ▶ The types of lock mechanism used in muzzle-loaders.

● **Musset, Alfred de** ▶ (1810–57) French poet and dramatist, one of the major figures of the Romantic movement. He published his first volume of poetry, *Contes d'Espagne et d'Italie*, at the age of 20. He lived extravagantly, and wrote satires on the excesses of the Romantic movement. His autobiographical *La Confession d'un enfant du siècle* (1836) includes an account of his love affair with George ▷Sand.

● **Mussolini, Benito (Amilcare Andrea)** ▶ (1883–1945) Italian fascist dictator. Initially an ardent socialist, his support of Italian participation in World War I led to his expulsion from the Socialist Party (1915). In 1919 he formed the Fasci di combattimento (*see* Blackshirts) in Milan and came to power following the ▷March on Rome (1922). He was prime minister until the murder of ▷Matteotti persuaded him to establish (1924–29) a dictatorship. As *duce* ("leader") his social policies, programme of public works, maintenance of law and order, and conciliatory policies towards the Roman Catholic Church (*see* Lateran Treaty) initially impressed the Italian people. However, his expansionist foreign policy, especially his invasion of Ethiopia (1935), and his alliance with Hitler (the Rome-Berlin Axis, 1936) brought him increasing unpopularity. In 1939 he annexed Albania and after the outbreak of World War II he declared war on France and Britain (June, 1940). The Italian war effort was disastrous, leading to defeats in E and N Africa and in Greece. Following the Allied invasion of Sicily, Mussolini was forced by the Fascist Grand Council to resign (July, 1943). Rescued by the Germans to head a new fascist republic in N Italy, he was subsequently captured and shot by Italian partisans. His body was hung up in public in Milan before burial.

● **Mussorgski, Modest Petrovich** ▶ (1839–81) Russian composer. An army officer and civil servant, he had little formal training beyond a few lessons with Balakirev. He developed a highly personal style, reproducing Russian speech rhythms in such works as the song cycles *The Nursery* (1868–72) and *Songs and Dances of Death* (1875–77). His masterpieces are the opera *Boris Godunov* (1868–72), the piano work *Pictures at an Exhibition* (1874), and the orchestral tone poem *A Night on the Bare Mountain* (1860–66).

● **mustang** ▶ The wild horse of North America. Mustangs are descended from the domesticated European stock of Spanish settlers and have become tough and small in the harsh conditions. Many were caught and tamed by cowboys and Indians, including the Mustang tribe, which was noted for its horse breeding. Protective legislation was passed in 1971.

● **mustard** ▶ Any of various annual herbs of the genus ▷*Brassica* and closely related genera, native to Europe and W Asia and cultivated chiefly for their seeds—source of the condiment mustard. They have branched stems, up to 1.5 cm high, deeply lobed leaves, and terminal clusters of yellow flowers. The leaves may be used as fodder, fertilizer, vegetables, or herbs. The main species are the white or yellow mustard, *Sinapis alba* (or *B. hirta*), black or brown mustard (*B. nigra*), and Indian mustard (*B. juncea*).

● **mustard gas** ▶ $(S(CH_2CH_2Cl)_2)$ A colourless oily volatile liquid; dichlorodiethyl sulphide. It is a poisonous vesicant first used as a war gas by the Germans during World War I in 1917. It was also used by Iraq against Kurdish rebels in 1988.

● **Mustelidae** ▶ A family of mammals of the order ▷*Carnivora*. It includes the stoats, weasels, martens, badgers, skunks, and others. Mustelids typically have a long body and tail, short legs, and glands that secrete a musky fluid.

● **Mutanabbi, Abu At-Tayyib Ahmad Ibn Husayn al-** ▶ (915–65 AD) Arab poet. From a poor but noble family, he learned his craft from the Bedouins and at Damascus, becoming a court poet in N Syria (948) and later in Egypt. He brought elaborate rhetorical innovations to the traditional odes (*qasidahs*) addressed to his patrons.

● **Mutare** ▶ (name until 1982: Umtali) 19 00S 32 40E A town in E Zimbabwe. Situated on the main railway to Mozambique from Harare, it is an important market centre for an area producing fruit and timber. Industries include papermills, textiles, and food canning. Nearby national parks attract tourists. Population (1992 est): 131 808.

● **mutation** ▶ A change in the hereditary material (*see* DNA) of an organism, which results in an altered physical characteristic. A mutation in a germ cell is inherited by subsequent generations of offspring; a change in any other cell (somatic cell) affects only those cells produced by division of the mutated cell. Gene mutations result from a change in the bases of the DNA molecule; chromosome mutations may be due to the addition or subtraction of bases and can usually be seen under a microscope. Both types of mutation affect the ▷genetic code and hence the corresponding function of the genes.

Very occasionally, mutations occur spontaneously and at random. They can also be induced by certain chemicals, ionizing radiation (such as X-rays), and by ultraviolet light. Most nonlethal mutations are of no benefit to the organism, but they do provide an important source of genetic variation in the population on which natural selection can act, which eventually results in the ▷evolution of new species.

● **Mutesa I** ▶ (c. 1838–84) King of ▷Buganda in East Africa. An absolute ruler, Mutesa tried to play off the Arab intruders into his kingdom against the Europeans so that neither would become too powerful. He traded with both and encouraged Islam and Christianity.

● **mute swan** ▶ An Old World ▷swan, *Cygnus olor*, found in marshy areas and estuaries and, as a semidomesticated ornamental bird, on rivers and lakes. It is 160 cm long and has a long neck, white plumage, black legs, and an orange bill with a black base. Less vocal than other swans, it is also silent in flight.

● **Muti, Riccardo** ▶ (1941–) Italian conductor. He was principal conductor of the Philharmonia Orchestra, London, from 1973 to 1982 and musical director of the Philadelphia Orchestra from 1981 to 1992. He became artistic director at La Scala, Milan, in 1986.

● **Mutsuhito** ▶ (1852–1912) Emperor of Japan (1867–1912), who presided over Japan's transformation into a modern state. The Meiji (Mutsuhito's title as emperor) restoration (1866–68) ended seven centuries of feudal rule and nominally returned full power to the throne, a change that culminated in the constitution promulgated by Mutsuhito in 1889.

● **muttonbird** ▶ A bird whose chicks are collected for meat and oil. The name is used especially for the slender-billed shearwater (*Puffinus tenuirostris*) of Australia and the sooty shearwater (*Procellaria griseus*) of New Zealand. Both belong to the family *Procellariidae* (petrels).

● **mutualism** ▷*See* symbiosis.

● **Muybridge, Eadweard** ▶ (Edward James Muggeridge; 1830–1904) US photographer, born in Britain. He was a pioneer of action photography with his series of animals and humans photographed in consecutive stages of motion. He showed that a trotting horse momentarily raises all four legs simultaneously.

● **Muzorewa, Bishop Abel (Tendekayi)** ▶ (1925–) Zimbabwean statesman and bishop of the Methodist Church. One-time president of the African National Congress and the All Africa Conference of Churches, Muzorewa headed a nominally Black government in ▷Zimbabwe from 1978 to 1980, when Robert ▷Mugabe became prime minister.

● **MX missile** ▶ A US nuclear strategic missile with a range of 9650 km (6000 m). Carrying 10 warheads, the MX missile was developed in response to the vulnerability of the concrete underground silos in which other ICBMs are housed. The MX missile can be launched from ships, aircraft, submarines, mobile land launchers, or from specially reinforced silos. A controversial weapon, the MX programme was begun in 1979 under Jimmy ▷Carter.

● **myalgic encephalomyelitis** ▶ (ME) ▷*See* chronic fatigue syndrome.

● **Myanmar, Union of** ▶ (name until 1989: Socialist Republic of the Union of Burma) A country in SE Asia, on the Bay of Bengal and the Andaman Sea. The principal river system, that of the Irrawaddy and its main tributary, the Chindwin, forms a narrow plain running N–S, rising to the Arakan Mountains and the Chin Hills in the W and the Shan Plateau in the E. The Tenasserim Hills lie along the coast in the SE. The majority of the population, concentrated in the Irrawaddy delta, is Burmese, but there are several minorities, including the Shan, Karen, Chachin, and Chin peoples.

Economy: priority has been given to the development of agriculture, the main crop being rice. Almost half the land (all of which is nationalized) is under forest and teak is a valuable export. Myanmar is also thought to be the world's largest producer of opium. There is some mining, especially of lead and zinc, and petroleum is produced and refined in growing quantities. Other industries are mainly based on food processing; all industry has been nationalized since the 1970s. Inland waterways provide an important means of communication. All foreign trade is carried out through government trading organizations and the main exports include rice and rice products, rubber, jute, and timber. Despite the political situation, tourism increased tenfold during the 1990s. In 1997 the USA imposed economic sanctions.

History: by the 13th century the Burmese had developed a civilization based on Hinayana Buddhism. In the centuries following defeat by the Mongols in 1287, the area was under the rule of the Shans and the Mons. The rule of the Burmese Alaungpaya in the 18th century began a period of increased prosperity. After successive wars Burma came under British rule in 1885 as part of British India. In 1937 it attained a measure of self-government and was separated from India.

In World War II it was occupied by Japanese forces, and fought first with the Japanese and later against them in support of the British. In 1948 it became a republic outside the Commonwealth. In 1962 parliamentary democracy was overthrown in a military coup by Gen U ▷Ne Win. 1974 saw the end of direct military rule and the formation of a one-party socialist republic. In 1981 Gen San Yu was elected president, but Ne Win remained the effective ruler. In 1988 Gen Sein Lwin held power for just 18 days before being replaced amid widespread unrest by President Maung Maung, who was himself replaced by Gen Saw Maung within weeks. Since then strict martial law has been enforced. Elections held in 1990 were won by the National League for Democracy, led by ▷Aung San Suu Kyi, who had been held under house arrest since 1989. However, the military refused to hand over power and suppressed opposition activity. Suu Kyi was released in 1995, rearrested in 2000, and released again in 2002. Since independence there has been recurrent fighting between government forces and armed groups representing the country's various ethnic minorities. In the 1990s a number of these groups surrendered or signed ceasefires. Myanmar was admitted to the Association of South-East Asian States in 1997.

Union of Myanmar

Head of state	General Than Shwe
Official language	Burmese
Official currency	kyat of 100 pyas
Area	678 000 sq km (261 789 sq mi)
Population (2001 est)	41 995 000
Capital and main port	Rangoon

● **myasthenia gravis** ▶ An autoimmune disease (*see* autoimmunity) characterized by muscle weakness and abnormal fatigue. It is caused by antibodies that prevent ▷acetylcholine from stimulating contraction of the muscle. Treatment is by drugs, such as steroids and immunosuppressants (*see* immunosuppression), and surgical removal of the thymus.

● **mycelium** ▷*See* fungi.

● **Mycenae** ▶ An ancient citadel in the Peloponnese (S Greece). Famed in legend as the home of ▷Agamemnon, Mycenae attained its zenith between 1600 and 1200 BC. Massive fortifications, including the famous Lion Gate, attest Mycenae's military readiness and exquisite bronze daggers, gold masks, and silver drinking vessels from its royal graves indicate accompanying affluence.

● **Mycenaean civilization** ▶ The civilization of Bronze Age Greece. It developed after about 1650 BC in mainland centres, such as ▷Mycenae and ▷Pylos, but after the collapse of the Minoan civilization (c. 1450 BC) its influence and political control extended to Crete. The Mycenaeans were a warrior aristocracy, identifiable with Homer's ▷Achaeans. They spoke a form of Greek, used ▷Linear B script, and lived in palaces decorated with frescoes and equipped with luxury stone and metal goods. About 1200 BC the palaces were destroyed, either by invaders or in internecine struggles, but recognizably Mycenaean culture survived in debased form until about 1100 BC.

● **mycology** ▶ The branch of biology dealing with the study of fungi. Mycology was established as a separate discipline in the early 19th century, when the Swedish botanist Elias Fries (1794–1878) published the first scientifically based classification of the fungi (1821–32).

● **mycoplasma** ▶ A minute organism that lacks a cell wall, belonging to a group of bacteria also called pleuropneumonia-like organisms (PPLOs). Mycoplasmas may be rounded, 150–300 nanometres in diameter, or filamentous, up to several micrometres long. They are the cause of several plant and animal (including human) diseases; for example *Mycoplasma pneumoniae* causes a form of pneumonia in humans.

● **mycorrhiza** ▶ An association between a fungus and the roots of a higher plant that is beneficial to both participants. In some mycorrhizas the fungus forms a sheath around the root, with its hyphae penetrating between the root cells; in others the fungus lives between and within the root cells. The plant benefits by more efficient uptake of nutrients, and the fungus obtains carbohydrates and other nutrients from the plant. Certain mycorrhizal associations between grasses and basidiomycete fungi can produce "fairy rings" of toadstools on the soil surface.

● **myelin** ▶ A white fatty material that forms a sheath around the large nerve fibres of vertebrates and some invertebrates. Myelin acts as an insulator, thereby increasing the speed of conduction of impulses along the nerve fibre.

Mycenae ▶ The entrance to the citadel of Mycenae is by the Lion Gate, set between massive walls of Cyclopean stonework.

● **Myers, F(rederic) W(illiam) H(enry)** ▶ (1843–1901) British essayist and poet. As well as poetry and literary criticism, he published several books concerning psychical research, including *Phantasms of the Living* (1886) and *Human Personality and Its Survival of Bodily Death* (1903). He helped to found the Society for Psychical Research in 1882.

● **Mykonos** ▷*See* Míkonos.

● **Mylae, Battle of** ▶ (260 BC) A battle in the first ▷Punic War in which the Romans destroyed the Carthaginian fleet off Sicily. It was Rome's first naval victory.

● **My Lai** ▶ A village in S Vietnam, where a massacre of about 347 civilians by US soldiers took place (16 March, 1968) during the Vietnam War. The incident was only investigated after it had been disclosed by an ex-serviceman (1969) and provoked much criticism of the role of the USA in Vietnam.

● **Mylodon** ▶ A genus of extinct South American ground sloths dating from the Pleistocene epoch (one million years ago). About 300 cm long, they had a specialized toe on the hind limb that was probably used for gripping branches or digging up tubers. ▷*See also* Megatherium.

● **mynah** ▶ A songbird belonging to a genus (*Acridotheres*) native to SE Asia. Mynahs usually have a dark plumage with bright wattles on the face. They feed chiefly on the ground and eat the insects found on cattle. The common mynah (*A. tristis*) lives in close proximity to man and has become a pest in some regions. The Chinese crested mynah (*A. cristatellus*) has been introduced to North America. Family: *Sturnidae* (starlings). ▷*See also* hill mynah.

● **myocardial infarction** ► Death of part of the heart muscle: the cause of what is popularly described as a heart attack. This is the commonest cause of death in advanced societies and usually results from ▷atherosclerosis. The patient usually experiences sudden severe central chest pain, which may spread to the neck and arms and is usually accompanied by sweating and nausea. Most people who recover from heart attacks can eventually lead a full and active life: many have survived for as long as 40 years. ▷*See also* heart disease.

● **myoglobin** ► An oxygen-carrying protein found in the skeletal muscles of vertebrate animals. Like ▷haemoglobin, it contains the pigment haem, which reversibly binds oxygen. Myoglobin serves as an oxygen store, releasing its oxygen only when tissue levels are very depleted, for example during strenuous exercise.

● **myopia** ▷*See* shortsightedness.

● **Myrdal, Gunnar** ► (1898–1987) Swedish sociologist and economist. Joint recipient of the 1974 Nobel Prize, Myrdal is best known for his study of the US racial problem, published as *An American Dilemma* (1944). His wife **Alva Myrdal** (1902–86) won the 1982 Nobel Peace Prize for her work for disarmament.

● **Myriapoda** ► A group (phylum) of terrestrial arthropods comprising the ▷centipedes, ▷millipedes, and centipede-like animals of the classes *Pauropoda* and *Symphyla*. Myriapods have elongated bodies and numerous walking legs.

● **Myrmidons** ► A legendary Greek people from Thessaly. According to one legend, they originated on the island of Aegina when Zeus turned the ants (Greek *myrmex*, ant) into people. They are best known as the loyal warriors commanded by ▷Achilles in the Trojan War.

● **Myron** ► (5th century BC) Athenian sculptor. His *Discus-Thrower* and *Marsyas*, described by ancient critics, are known through Roman copies. These free-standing figures show the new stances (made possible by the novel techniques of bronze working) that superseded the stylized poses derived from ▷kouros and ▷kore figures.

● **myrrh** ► An aromatic yellow to red gum resin obtained from small tropical thorny trees of the genus *Commifera*, especially *C. myrrha*, *C. molmol*, and *C. abyssinica*, native to Africa and SW Asia. Myrrh exudes from the bark through slits and hardens on exposure to air. It is used in incense, perfumes, cosmetics, dentistry, and pharmaceuticals. Family: *Commiphoraceae*.

● **myrtle** ► An evergreen shrub of the genus *Myrtus* (over 100 species). The common myrtle (*M. communis*), native to the Mediterranean area and W Asia, may grow to a height of 5 m. It has aromatic dark-green shiny leaves, fragrant five-petalled white flowers, 2–3 cm across, with numerous stamens, and blue-black berries. An oil obtained from the leaves, flowers, and fruit is used in perfumery. Family: *Myrtaceae*. Other plants known as myrtle include the ▷sweet gale.

● **Mysore** ► 12 18N 76 37E A city in India, in Karnataka. Industries include textiles, chemicals, and food processing and it has a university (1916). Population (1991): 480 692.

● **mysteries** ► Secret religious cults in the ancient Mediterranean world that revealed their mystical rites only to initiates and promised them a life after death. Their initiation ceremonies, of which the details are often vague, involved purification, assimilation of occult knowledge, and acting out a sacred drama. The Egyptian cult of ▷Isis, the Greek ▷Eleusinian and ▷Orphic mysteries, and Roman ▷Mithraism are the most famous.

● **mystery plays** ▷*See* miracle plays.

● **mysticism** ► Belief in a type of religious experience in which the individual claims to achieve immediate knowledge of or temporary union with God. Mysticism is an element in most theistic traditions and the validity of the experience is often claimed to be established by the similarity of the accounts by mystics from totally different cultures of their visions, trances, and ecstasies. The usual preliminary is strict ▷asceticism. Christianity insists that a mystic should demonstrate his spiritual grace by practical works of charity. St ▷Francis of Assisi, St ▷Catherine of Siena, St ▷Teresa of Avila, St ▷John of the Cross, and ▷Julian of Norwich are among the many famous Christian mystics. Official Church attitudes have alternated between regarding mysticism as a special spiritual grace and suspecting it of verging on ▷Gnosticism, ▷pantheism, ▷Neoplatonism, or simply dangerous individualism. ▷*See also* Sufism.

● **mythology** ► Imaginative poetic stories, traditions, etc., concerning religious beliefs, gods, and supernatural and heroic human beings. Mythology often involves a cosmogony—an attempted explanation of the origin of the universe, of mankind, or of a particular race or culture. The term also refers to the formal study of such stories, traditions, etc. Myths have been interpreted in several ways. One ancient theory, first advanced by the Greek Euhemerus (300 BC) and called euhemerism, holds that there is an element of historical truth in myths and that mythical characters are only kings or other heroes given the honour of deification by the populace. ▷Plato also adopted a critical view of Greek mythology because of its immorality and sought to introduce worthier ideals by inventing more rational myths. Anthropology and psychoanalysis have thrown new light on the function of myths. Among primitive peoples they serve to provide an explanation or justification for social institutions. They also appear to embody universal values or patterns with regard to human psychology, as in Freud's interpretation of the child's relationship to its parents in terms of the ▷Oedipus myth. The mythologies of particular cultures have provided the material of most of the world's great literature and art, as in Egypt, Greece and Rome, and in Hinduism.

● **Mytilene** ► (Modern Greek name: Mitilíni) 39 06N 26 34E The chief town of the Greek island of Lesbos, on the Aegean Sea. It is a port trading chiefly in olive oil, citrus fruits, and cereals. Population (1991 est): 25 440.

● **myxoedema** ► Underactivity of the ▷thyroid gland. Patients are slow, tired, dislike the cold, and have a slow pulse and reflexes. The skin may be thick and swollen. Myxoedema can be easily treated with thyroxine, the hormone produced by the thyroid gland.

● **myxomatosis** ► An infectious disease of rabbits and hares that is caused by a virus. Symptoms include swollen eyes, nose, and muzzle, closed eyelids, and fever. The disease is usually fatal although some strains of rabbits show resistance. A vaccine is available to protect domestic rabbits. The disease was introduced to the UK and Australia during the 1950s as a pest-control measure.

● **Mzilikazi** ► (c. 1790–1868) Zulu warrior, who in about 1840 founded the Matabele (*or* Ndebele) kingdom in S Rhodesia. A great military leader and an able administrator, Mzilikazi organized his new kingdom on military lines and withstood attacks from neighbouring tribes and from the Afrikaners. Not long after his death his kingdom, under his son ▷Lobengula, was overwhelmed by the Whites.

N

● **Naas** ▶ (Irish name: Nás na Riogh) 53 13N 6 39W A town in the Republic of Ireland, the county town of Co Kildare. It is a centre for horse racing and hunting. Population (latest est): 8345.

● **Nabis** ▶ (Hebrew: prophets) A group of French artists formed in Paris in 1888. The leading members—Paul Sérusier (1863–1927), ▷Denis, ▷Bonnard, and ▷Vuillard—were united by their admiration for ▷Gauguin and Japanese prints. They applied their famous tenet that "a picture is … essentially a flat surface covered by colours in a certain order" to their activities as painters, poster and stained-glass designers, book illustrators, etc., thus influencing many branches of art. They disbanded in 1899.

● **Nablus** ▶ 32 13N 35 16E A town on the ▷West Bank of the River Jordan. Nablus is the Shechem of the Old Testament: Jacob's Well is nearby. Population (1989 est): 98 000.

● **Nabokov, Vladimir** ▶ (1899–1977) US novelist. Born into an aristocratic Russian family, he was educated at Cambridge University and lived in France and Germany before emigrating to the USA in 1940. He achieved popular success with *Lolita* (1955), whose academic antihero lusts after young girls. His novels, noted for their elegant and witty word play, include *The Defence* (1930), one of several originally written in Russian, *Pale Fire* (1962), and *Ada* (1969). His other works include the autobiographical *Speak, Memory* (1967) and a translation of Pushkin's *Eugene Onegin* (4 vols, 1964).

● **nacre** ▷*See* pearl.

● **Nadar** ▶ (Gaspard Felix Tournachon; 1820–1910) French photographer, caricaturist, and writer, born in Paris. Although better known by his contemporaries as a novelist and essayist, his reputation now rests on his photographs of writers and artists, such as Baudelaire and Delacroix, and his pioneering aerial photographs taken from a balloon (1858).

● **Na-Dené languages** ▶ An American Indian language group covering the northern USA, NW Canada, and Alaska. It includes the Athabascan, Tlingit, Haida, and Eyak subgroups. Athabascan is the largest group, with more than 20 languages, and is also the most widespread, extending from the Yukon almost to the US border. Another Athabascan subgroup, spoken on the N American Plains, includes ▷Navajo and several ▷Apache languages.

● **Nader, Ralph** ▶ (1934–) US lawyer and social campaigner. His book *Unsafe at Any Speed* (1965) criticized the safety standards of the car industry and resulted in legislation in 1966. Among the many consumer issues he has investigated are advertising, nuclear power, and meat processing. He founded the Centre for the Study of Responsive Law in 1969. He was the Green Party candidate for president in 1996 and 2000.

● **Nader Shah** ▶ (1688–1747) Shah of Persia (1736–47). Of Turkoman origin, he overthrew the Safavid dynasty to become shah. He had military successes but his internal policies led to many revolts. His attempt at introducing a new rite of Sunni Islam (*see* Sunnites) into Shiite Persia, and forcing his subjects to join it, failed. He was assassinated.

● **nadir** ▷*See* zenith.

● **Naevius, Gnaeus** ▶ (c. 270–c. 200 BC) Roman poet. He wrote a number of tragedies and comedies and an epic on the first Punic War, in which he related the mythical origins of Rome (making Romulus a grandson of the Trojan Aeneas). Only fragments of his work are extant.

● **naevus** ▷*See* birthmark.

● **NAFTA** ▷*See* North American Free Trade Agreement.

● **naga** ▶ In Hindu mythology, one of a race of minor serpent deities inhabiting an underworld region called Patala, which is filled with gems. They are associated with water and may be regarded as demons and a possible source of evil, but are also worshipped as companions of the gods. ▷Vishnu is often portrayed sleeping on the naga Sesha, and there is a Buddhist legend of a naga raising the Buddha on its coils above a flood sent to prevent his attaining enlightenment. Nagas are variously depicted as half-snake and half-human, as many-headed cobras, or in human form posed beneath a canopy of cobras.

● **Nagaland** ▶ A state in NE India, on the Burmese border. Mostly in the forested Naga Hills, it produces rice, other grains, pulses, sugar cane, and vegetables. Mahogany and other forest products are important. Local industries include weaving.

History: after 1947 the Naga tribes resisted Indian rule as fiercely as they had Britain, winning statehood in 1963. Further talks with the Naga underground movement led to the Shillong Peace Agree-

naga ▶ A 2nd-century sandstone carving showing a young naga—half-human, half-serpent. It was found in Mathura, Uttar Pradesh.

ment in November, 1975. Area: 16 579 sq km (6400 sq mi). Population (1994 est): 1 410 000. Capital: Kohima.

● **Nagarjuna** ▶ (c. 150–c. 250 AD) Indian Buddhist monk and philosopher. Probably originally a brahmin from S India, he founded the Madhyamika (Middle Way) school of Mahayana Buddhism, noted for its highly intellectual approach to defining the nature of reality. Works attributed to him survive only in Tibetan and Chinese.

● **Nagasaki** ▶ 32 45N 129 52E A port in Japan, in W Kyushu on the East China Sea. The first Japanese port to deal with European traders, it became a centre of Christianity following its introduction by the Portuguese in the 16th century. On 9 August, 1945, the second of the two atomic bombs used against Japan was dropped on Nagasaki, killing or wounding about 75 000 people, although the damage was not as extensive as at Hiroshima. Rapid rebuilding followed; it is now a centre of the shipbuilding industry. Its university was established in 1949. Population (1995): 438 724.

● **Nagorno-Karabakh** ▶ An autonomous region in Azerbaidzhan. It was formed in 1923 and its population is about 80% Armenian with the rest chiefly Azerbaidzhani. It has metal and mineral deposits and supports many light industries but is chiefly agricultural: cotton, grapes, and wheat are grown. In 1988 Armenian claims to the area led to riots and the declaration of a state of emergency (1990). In 1991 fighting broke out between Armenian and Azerbaidzhani forces, leading to the displacement of up to one million people. A ceasefire was agreed in 1994 but peace talks have yet to produce any significant result. Area: 4400 sq km (1700 sq mi). Population (1991 est): 193 300. Capital: Stepanakert.

● **Nagoya** ▶ 35 8N 136 53E A port in Japan, in SE Honshu on Ise Bay. The fourth largest city in the country, it was founded in 1610 and by World War II had developed into an important centre for the manufacture of aircraft and ammunition. It was largely rebuilt following heavy bombing in 1945 and its industries now include steel and textiles. Its universities were established in 1939 and 1950. Population (1995): 2 152 258.

● **Nagpur** ▶ 21 10N 79 12E A city in India, in Maharashtra. Founded in the early 18th century, it fell under British control in 1853. It grew with the arrival of the Peninsula Railway (1867) and now has cotton, transport equipment, and metallurgical industries. Its university was established in 1923. Population (1991): 1 622 225.

● **Nagy, Imre** ▶ (1896–1958) Hungarian statesman, who led the revolutionary government of 1956. As prime minister (1953–55) Nagy promised such reforms as an end to the forced development of heavy industry and agricultural collectivization, more consumer goods, occupational mobility, and the closure of labour camps. Opposed by Hungary's Stalinists, he was demoted and in 1956 expelled from the Communist Party. In the subsequent ▷Hungarian Revolution Nagy again became prime minister but was abducted by Soviet troops and executed; he was reburied with honours in 1989.

● **Naha** ▶ 26 10N 127 40E A port in Japan, the main city of the ▷Ryukyu Islands and capital of Okinawa. It is the site of the University of the Ryukyus. Population (1995): 301 928.

● **Nahuatl** ▶ The most widely used American Indian language of the Uto-Aztecan family, spoken in Mexico. It was the language of the ▷Aztecs and ▷Toltecs. A characteristic is the extensive use of the *tl* sound. The Nahua people are slash-and-burn cultivators, growing maize, beans, tomatoes, and chilis. Crafts, especially weaving, are well developed. The Nahua are nominally Roman Catholic, but paganism flourishes.

● **Nahum** ▶ An Old Testament prophet who predicted the imminent destruction of the Assyrian capital of Nineveh by the Medes in 612 BC. **The Book of Nahum** describes this event in detail and interprets it as divine retribution.

● **naiads** ▶ In Greek mythology, a class of ▷nymphs or female spirits of nature associated with rivers, lakes, and springs.

● **Naipaul, Sir V(idiadhur) S(urajprasad)** ▶ (1932–) British writer, born in Trinidad of Indian Brahmin descent. A witty ironic tone characterizes his early comic novels, such as *A House for Mr Biswas* (1961). His later more sombre novels include *A Bend in the River*

(1979), the semiautobiographical *The Enigma of Arrival* (1987), and *Half a Life* (2001). He has also published travel books and a history of Trinidad, *The Loss of El Dorado* (1969). Other nonfiction works include *Among the Believers* (1981), *A Turn in the South* (1989), and *Beyond Belief* (1998). He was awarded the Nobel Prize for Literature in 2001.

● **Nairn** ▶ A former county of N Scotland. Under local government reorganization in 1975 it formed a new district of the same name, in the Highland Region. This district was abolished in 1996.

● **Nairobi** ▶ 1 17S 36 50E The capital of Kenya, situated on a plateau just S of the equator. It was founded as a trading and railway centre in the late 19th century. Its varied manufactures include chemicals, textiles, glass, and furniture. The Nairobi National Park lies on the city's outskirts. The University of Nairobi was established in 1970. Population (1991 est): 2 000 000.

● **naive art** ▷*See* primitivism.

● **Najd** ▶ (or Nejd or Central Province) A province in Saudi Arabia, occupying the centre of the country. It is largely desert and much of the population is nomadic. Formerly an independent kingdom, it became part of Saudi Arabia in 1932. Area: about 1 100 000 sq km (424 621 sq mi). Population (latest est): 3 632 092. Capital: Riyadh.

● **Nakhichevan** ▶ An enclave of Azerbaidzhan in Armenia. It is populated mainly by Azerbaidzhani and was the scene of nationalist unrest in 1990. The economy is predominantly agricultural, producing mainly cereals, cotton, and tobacco. Industries include textiles and food processing. Area: 5500 sq km (2120 sq mi). Population (1994): 315 000. Capital: Nakhichevan.

● **Nakuru** ▶ 0 16S 36 04E A town in Kenya, on the N shore of Lake Nakuru. It has a large European community and is the trading centre of an agricultural area producing wheat, maize, and coffee. Population (1991 est): 124 200.

● **Namaqualand** ▶ (or Namaland; Afrikaans name: Namakwaland) An arid coastal area in SW Africa, extending S from near Windhoek (Namibia) into E South Africa, divided by the Orange River into Little Namaqualand (S) and Great Namaqualand (N). It is occupied chiefly by Namas (Hottentots) and has important diamond reserves.

● **Namib Desert** ▶ A desert chiefly in W Namibia, extending some 1600 km (994 mi) along the Atlantic coast. It is arid and almost devoid of population.

● **Namibe** ▶ (name until 1982: Moçâmedes) 15 09S 40 34E A port in SW Angola, on the Atlantic Ocean, noted for its fishing industry. Population (latest est): 77 000.

● **Namibia, Republic of** ▶ (name until 1968: South West Africa) A country in SW Africa, on the Atlantic Ocean. The narrow coastal plains of the Namib Desert rise to the central plateau, with the Kalahari Desert to the N. The Orange River forms its S boundary, and the Rivers Kunene and Okavango form part of its N boundary. The majority of the population is African, the largest group being the Ovambo.
Economy: chiefly subsistence agriculture with emphasis on stock raising, and some dairy farming. Fishing is important, especially for pilchards. Mineral resources include diamonds (the main export), uranium, copper, lead, zinc, tin, and vanadium. The economy was devastated by 20 years of guerrilla warfare and remains heavily dependent on South Africa. Hydroelectricity is a valuable source of power.
History: the region was originally occupied by Khoisan peoples (Bushmen). European contacts began in the late 15th century but there was no exploration of the interior until the 19th century, when Germany declared a protectorate (1884). During World War I this surrendered (1915) to South Africa, which subsequently administered South West Africa under a League of Nations mandate. In 1966 South Africa refused to acknowledge the declaration by the League's successor, the UN, that the mandate was at an end and was condemned by both the UN and the nationalist South West Africa People's Organization (SWAPO) as illegally occupying the territory. Under the leadership of Sam Nujoma, SWAPO began a guerrilla campaign from neighbouring Angola in the late 1960s. Following negotiations, South Africa accepted Namibian independence in 1989 (effective

from 1990) and returned the major part of ▷Walvis Bay in 1994. SWAPO candidates won multiparty elections held in 1989 and in 1994. Namibia joined the Commonwealth in 1990.

Republic of Namibia

Head of state	President Sam Nujoma
Official languages	Afrikaans and English
Official currency	Namibian dollar of 100 cents
Area	824 269 sq km (318 261 sq mi)
Population (1997 est)	1 727 000
Capital	Windhoek
Main port	Walvis Bay

● **Namier, Sir Lewis Bernstein** ▶ (1888–1960) British historian. Born in Poland, he emigrated to England (1906) and was professor of modern history at Manchester University (1931–53). Among his works on 18th-century politics is *The Structure of Politics at the Accession of George III* (1929). He was well known for his conservative and Zionist views.

● **Namur** ▶ (Flemish name: Namen) 50 28N 04 52E A town in S Belgium, strategically positioned at the confluence of the Rivers Sambre and Meuse. It was besieged and captured many times. Notable buildings include the 18th-century cathedral. Its chief manufactures are glass, paper, and leather and steel goods. Population (1996 est): 105 059.

● **Nanaimo** ▶ 49 08N 123 58W A city and port in W Canada, in British Columbia on the E coast of Vancouver Island. With the main ferry links to the mainland, it is Vancouver Island's distribution centre and the site of primary industries. Population (1990 est): 55 643.

● **Nanak** ▶ (1469–1539) Indian founder of ▷Sikhism. Born near Lahore, a member of the mercantile Hindu class he travelled within and perhaps beyond India, visiting both Hindu and Muslim centres in search of spiritual truth. He settled finally in Kartarpur, where he attracted a large community of disciples. His teachings are contained in a number of hymns, many of which are extant.

● **Nana Sahib** ▶ (Dandhu Panth; c. 1825–c. 1860) A leader of the ▷Indian Mutiny (1857). Adopted into a noble family, he led the revolt at Cawnpore, in which the British were massacred. When defeated in 1859 he was driven into the Himalayan foothills, where he probably died.

● **Nanchang** ▶ 28 38N 115 56E A city in SE China, the capital of Jiangxi province and the site of its university. China's first commune was briefly established here in 1927. An ancient commercial centre, it has varied manufactures. Population (1991 est): 1 350 000.

● **Nan-ching** ▷*See* Nanjing.

● **Nancy** ▶ 48 42N 6 12E A town in NE France, the capital of the Meurthe-et-Moselle department on the River Meurthe. The former capital of the Dukes of Lorraine, it passed to France in 1766. It has a fine collection of 18th-century buildings and is the site of a university (1572). Its varied industries include iron, salt, sodium, machinery, and textiles. Population (1990): 102 410.

● **Nanda Devi, Mount** ▶ 30 21N 79 50E A mountain in NW India, close to the Tibetan border in the Himalayas. Height: 7817 m (25 645 ft).

● **Nanga Parbat, Mount** ▶ 35 15N 74 36E A mountain in NE Pakistan, in the Himalayas. Height: 8126 m (26 660 ft).

● **Nanhai** ▷*See* China Sea (South).

● **Nanjing** ▶ (Nan-ching *or* Nanking) 32 05N 118 55E A port in E China, the capital of Jiangsu province on the Yangtze River. An ancient cultural centre, it was a Chinese capital (1368–1421, 1928–37) and the centre of the Taiping Rebellion (1851–64). The university was established in 1902. It is a centre of heavy industry. Population (1991 est): 2 500 000.

● **Nanning** ▶ 22 50N 108 19E A city in S China, the capital of Guangxi Zhuang AR. The commercial centre of a rich agricultural area, it has many industries, including food processing and the man-

ufacture of paper and agricultural machinery. Population (1991 est): 1 070 000.

● **nanotechnology** ▶ The technology and manufacture of very small objects, especially those that have dimensions of less than 100 nanometres (10^{-7} metre) or involve individual atoms or molecules. The purpose is usually to create minute computers and tiny machines that could be of importance in medicine. Using scanning electron microscopes, which are capable of enabling single atoms or molecules to be seen, and the established techniques of silicon microchip manufacture, minute experimental devices have been made, although technology on this scale has yet to produce a useful artefact.

● **Nansen, Fridtjof** ▶ (1861–1930) Norwegian explorer, zoologist, and statesman. In 1888 he led an expedition across the Greenland icefield and in 1893, in the *Fram*, specially designed to resist icepacks, set sail across the Arctic. He allowed the vessel to drift attached to an icefloe. In 1895, with F. J. Johansen (1867–1923), he left the ship and reached 18 14N, the nearest point to the North Pole then attained. He subsequently contributed greatly to the League of Nations, becoming its high commissioner for refugees in 1920; he pioneered the **Nansen passport**, an identification card for displaced persons (1922). He won the Nobel Peace Prize (1923).

● **Nantes** ▶ 47 14N 1 35W A major port in W France, the capital of the Loire-Atlantique department on the Loire estuary. Its commercial importance dates back to Roman times and it was here that the Edict of Nantes was signed in 1598. It has a 15th-century cathedral and a university (1961). Its port is accessible to oceangoing vessels and its industries include shipbuilding, oil refining, and tanning. Population (1990): 264 857.

● **Nantes, Edict of** ▶ (1598) A decree that guaranteed the French Protestants (*see* Huguenots) religious liberty. The edict, proclaimed by Henry IV, established the principle of religious toleration; by permitting the Huguenots freedom of worship and limited civil equality, Henry hoped to prevent further wars of religion in France. It was revoked in 1685 by Louis XIV.

● **Nantucket** ▶ An island in the USA, off the coast of SE Massachusetts. A former whaling centre, it is now chiefly a resort. Length: 24 km (15 mi). Width: 5 km (3 mi). Population (1990): 6012.

● **napalm** ▶ An inexpensive jelly consisting of a mixture of the aluminium salts of *n*apathenic acid and *palm*itic acid used to thicken petrol so that it can be used in incendiary bombs and ▷flamethrowers. It was used in World War II, the Korean War, and in Vietnam. It ignites easily, burns at temperatures up to 1000°C, and is particularly effective against humans.

● **Naphtali, tribe of** ▶ One of the 12 ▷tribes of Israel. It claimed descent from Naphtali, the son of Jacob by his concubine Bilhah. Its territory was NW of the Sea of Galilee.

● **naphthalene** ▶ ($C_{10}H_8$) A white crystalline aromatic hydrocarbon that occurs in coal tar. It is used in the manufacture of dyes, synthetic resins, and mothballs. **Naphthol** ($C_{10}H_7OH$) is the hydroxy derivative. It consists of two isomers; the most important, beta-naphthol, is used in antioxidants for rubbers and dyes and in drugs.

● **Napier** ▶ 39 29S 176 58E A port in New Zealand, in E North Island on Hawke Bay. It is the most important centre of New Zealand's wool trade. Population (1995 est): 53 500.

● **Napier, Sir Charles James** ▶ (1782–1853) British general and colonial administrator. After service in the Peninsular War (1808–10), against the USA (1813–14), in Greece (1822–30), and at home, he was sent (1841) to Sind (now in Pakistan). By 1843 he had gained control of the country and as governor (until 1847) he established a civil administration.

● **Napier, John** ▶ (1550–1617) Scottish mathematician, who invented ▷logarithms. In 1614 he published a table of logarithms to the base e, now known as Napierian logarithms. Logarithms to the base ten (common logarithms) were later adopted, following a suggestion by Henry ▷Briggs. Napier also produced an elementary calculating machine using a series of rods, known as **Napier's bones**.

● **Napier of Magdala, Robert Cornelis, 1st Baron** ▶ (1810–90)

British field marshal. He fought in the ▷Sikh Wars in India (1845–49) and during the Indian Mutiny helped to relieve Lucknow (1857). In 1868 he led the expedition to release British diplomats imprisoned in Ethiopia, capturing Magdala.

● **Naples** ▶ (Italian name: Napoli; ancient name: Neapolis) 40 50N 14 15E A city in S Italy, the capital of Campania situated on volcanic slopes overlooking the Bay of Naples. It is an important port and a centre of commerce and tourism. As well as traditional industries, such as textiles, food processing, and oil refining, newer industries (including the manufacture of cars and ball bearings) have grown up in recent years as a result of central government assistance. Its many historic buildings include medieval castles, a gothic cathedral (13th–14th centuries), the 17th-century Royal Palace, and the university (1224). The National Museum houses remains from Pompeii and Herculaneum.

History: founded by Greek colonists about 600 BC, it fell to Rome in 326 but retained its Greek culture. It was under Byzantine rule (6th–8th centuries AD) and in 1139 it became part of the Norman kingdom of Sicily. It prospered under Charles I, the first Angevin King of Sicily, who made Naples his capital. Following the revolt known as the ▷Sicilian Vespers (1282), the island of Sicily passed to the House of Aragon and the Italian peninsula S of the Papal States became known as the kingdom of Naples (with Naples as its capital) until it fell to Garibaldi (1860) and was united with the rest of Italy (*see also* Sicily). From this time Naples lagged economically behind the N, resulting in considerable poverty. The city suffered further hardships during World War II, when it was badly damaged. Central government assistance during the postwar period has led to improvements in the infrastructure. Existing industries have been modernized and new industries added. Many thousands of its inhabitants, however, continue to live in slum conditions. An earthquake in 1980 killed 4800 people. Population (1996 est): 1 050 234.

● **Napoleon I** ▶ (1769–1821) Emperor of the French (1804–15). Born Napoleon Bonaparte in Corsica, he became an artillery officer and rose to prominence in 1795, when he turned the guns of the Paris garrison—"a whiff of grapeshot"—on a mob threatening the government of the National Convention. Shortly afterwards he married ▷Joséphine de Beauharnais and in January, 1796, was appointed to command the French army in Italy (*see* Revolutionary and Napoleonic Wars). His Italian campaign (1796–97) took the army from the brink of defeat by the Austrians to the conquest of Milan and Mantua. After Sardinia, Naples, and the papacy had sued for peace Napoleon obtained the Directory's support for his plan to break British imperial power by conquering Egypt and India. In Egypt his great victory of the ▷Pyramids was undermined by Nelson's annihilation of a French fleet at the Battle of the ▷Nile (1798) and in 1799 he returned unobtrusively to France, where he joined a conspiracy against the tottering Directory. In the coup d'état of 18 Brumaire (9–10 November, 1799) he became first consul in a consulate formed on the Roman model; in 1802 he became consul for life and in 1804, emperor.

His outstanding domestic achievement was the legal codification, the ▷*Code Napoléon*, that remains the basis of French law, but Napoleon achieved immortality with his exploits abroad. He negotiated the Treaty of Lunéville (1801), which marked his defeat of the Austrians at ▷Marengo, and the Treaty of Amiens (1802) with the British; however, his designs upon Italy, Germany, and Switzerland led to a renewal of war in 1805. Despite the disaster at ▷Trafalgar (1805), which forced him to abandon his plan for the invasion of Britain, his land victories, especially at ▷Austerlitz (1805), ▷Jena and Auerstädt (1806), and ▷Friedland (1806), drew almost every continental power within the French orbit.

Napoleon's supremacy was short lived. The ▷Continental System failed to break the British by blockade and the protracted ▷Peninsular War (1808–14) drained French resources. In 1812 Napoleon invaded an increasingly recalcitrant Russia with half a million men, of whom nearly 400 000 died in the brutal Russian winter. In 1813 Europe rose against Napoleon, inflicting a massive defeat at Leipzig that forced his abdication and subsequent exile to Elba, of which he was given sovereignty. In 1815, however, he escaped, returned to a rapturous welcome in France, and attempted in the ▷Hundred Days to regain his former greatness. He suffered a decisive defeat at

Napoleon I ▶ David's portrait (1821; Versailles) of the young military commander crossing the Alps evokes the glory of the Napoleonic legend.

▷Waterloo and spent the remainder of his life confined to the island of St Helena. Napoleon's claim to the French Crown was pursued after his death by the son of his second marriage, to Marie Louise of Austria (*see* Napoleon II), and then by his nephew, Emperor ▷Napoleon III. ▷*See also* Bonaparte.

● **Napoleon II** ▶ (1811–32) The title accorded by supporters of the Bonapartist claim to the French throne to the son of Napoleon I and Empress Marie Louise. At birth entitled King of Rome, he was brought up, after his father's fall (1814), in Austria, with the title Duke of Reichstadt.

● **Napoleon III** ▶ (1808–73) Emperor of the French (1852–71); son of Louis Bonaparte and Hortense de Beauharnais and nephew of Napoleon I. Pretender to the French throne during the reign of Louis Philippe (1830–48), Napoleon used the enormous prestige of his name to win the presidential election after the Revolution of 1848. By a coup d'état at the end of 1851, he dissolved the legislative assembly and, a year later, declared himself emperor. His domestic policies fostered industry and, with the planning work of Baron ▷Haussmann, transformed the face of Paris. Abroad, his diplomacy embroiled France in the Crimean War (1854–56), in war against the Austrians in Italy (1859), and in a desultory conflict in Mexico (1861–67). Finally, his aggressive stance towards Bismarck helped to cause the ▷Franco-Prussian War, in which the Second Empire was destroyed and Napoleon was driven into exile.

● **Napoleonic Code** ▷*See* Code Napoléon.

● **Napoleonic Wars** ▷*See* Revolutionary and Napoleonic Wars.

● **Nara** ▶ 34 41N 135 49E A city in Japan, in S Honshu. Japan's first capital (710–84 AD), it contains many historic monuments, including a bronze Buddha 16 m (72 ft) high. Population (1995): 359 234.

● **Narayan, R(asipuram) K(rishnaswamy)** ▶ (1906–2001) Indian novelist and short-story writer. Writing in English and setting his stories in Malgudi, an imaginary version of his hometown Mysore, Narayan drew upon his experiences as a teacher for his first novel, *Swami and Friends* (1935). Later works, such as *The Man-Eater of Malgudi* (1961), *Under the Banyan Tree* (1985), *The Grandmother's Tale* (1993), and numerous short stories, are witty and ironic portrayals of Indian daily life.

● **Narayanganj** ▶ 23 36N 90 28E A city in Bangladesh, the chief riverport of Dhaka. It is a major trading centre and together with Dhaka forms the largest industrial region in the country. Population (1991): 268 952.

● **Narbonne** ▶ 43 11N 3 00E A market town in SE France, in the Aude department. An important Roman settlement, it was formerly a port (silted up in the 14th century). Population (1990): 47 090.

● **Narcissus** ▶ (botany) A genus of perennial herbaceous plants (about 40 species), native to Eurasia and N Africa and widely planted in gardens and parks. Growing from bulbs, they produce strap-shaped or rushlike leaves and erect flower stalks, usually up to 30 cm high. The flowers are usually yellow, orange, or white, with a ring of petal-like segments surrounding a central crown. The ▷daffodils (*N. pseudonarcissus*) have large solitary yellow flowers with trumpet-shaped crowns, which may be orange-tipped; the sweet-scented jonquils (*N. jonquilla*) have clusters of smaller pale-yellow flowers with small cuplike crowns; and the poet's narcissus (*N. poeticus*) has solitary flowers with white petals surrounding a short fringed orange-tipped crown. Family: *Amaryllidaceae*.

● **Narcissus** ▶ (Greek mythology) A beautiful youth who was punished for rejecting the love of the nymph Echo by being made to fall in love with his own reflection in a pool. He died and was transformed into a flower.

● **narcotics** ▶ Drugs that cause stupor or sleep and relieve pain by depressing activity of the brain. The best known natural narcotics are ▷opium and its derivatives (opiates), including morphine and codeine. Synthetic narcotics include heroin, methadone, and pethidine. The main medical use of narcotics is for the relief of severe pain, but their use is strictly controlled by law in most countries because they carry the risk of ▷drug dependence. The term narcotics is also used more loosely for any addictive drug.

● **Narita** ▶ 35 46N 140 20E A town in Japan, NE of Tokyo in central Honshu. It is the site of an international airport, which was for several years the scene of angry protests by the local farming population, student groups, and environmentalists; although completed in 1972 it did not become operational until May, 1978. Population (latest est): 68 418.

● **Narraganset** ▶ An Algonquian-speaking North American Indian people of Rhode Island. They were a woodland people who cultivated maize, hunted, and fished. There were eight divisions of the Narraganset, each headed by a chief. In 1675, after wars with White settlers, they were dispersed.

● **Narragansett Bay** ▶ A bay in the USA, in SE Rhode Island state. It contains many islands including Rhode Island, Prudence Island, and Conanicut Island.

● **Narses** ▶ (c. 480–574 AD) Byzantine general. Originally a slave in Emperor ▷Justinian I's household, Narses rose to become the emperor's confidant. In 551 he replaced ▷Belisarius as commander in Italy. He recaptured Rome and eventually subdued the Ostrogoths, governing Italy until 567.

● **Narva** ▶ 59 22N 28 17E A port in Estonia, on the River Narva near the Gulf of Finland. Peter the Great was defeated by the Swedes in a famous battle here in 1700. It is an important textile centre and has food-processing industries. Population (1995): 77 770.

● **Narvik** ▶ 68 26N 17 25E An ice-free port in N Norway. Two naval battles between the British and Germans were fought here in 1940 and the port was occupied by the Allies from 10 May until 9 June. It exports iron ore from the Kiruna-Gällivare mines in N Sweden. Population (1990): 18 500.

● **narwhal** ▶ A gregarious Arctic toothed ▷whale, *Monodon monoceros*, up to 5 m long and feeding on fish and squid. Male narwhals have a long straight spirally twisted tusk that is derived from a tooth and grows to a length of 3 m; its function is unknown. Family: *Monodontidae*.

● **NASA** ▶ (National Aeronautics and Space Administration) The US civilian agency, formed in 1958, that is responsible for all nonmilitary aspects of the US space programme. Its major projects have included the manned ▷Apollo moon programme, ▷Skylab, reusable ▷space shuttles, and successful ▷planetary probes. In addition it has launched many artificial ▷satellites belonging to the USA and other nations.

● **Naseby, Battle of** ▶ (14 June, 1645) The battle in the English Civil War that decided Charles I's defeat. The ▷New Model Army under Fairfax and Oliver Cromwell routed Prince ▷Rupert's royalist forces at Naseby, near Market Harborough, Leicestershire, and in the following year Charles surrendered.

● **Nash, John** ▶ (1752–1835) British architect of the Regency period. An unsuccessful speculative builder in London, he went bankrupt in 1783 and retired to Wales. There he built up a new practice as an architect specializing in large country houses. Returning to London at the end of the century, he attracted the patronage of the Prince of Wales (later George IV). When the prince became regent (1811) he employed Nash to redevelop parts of London. Central to Nash's plan was the laying out of Marylebone Park (later called Regent's Park) as a formal park surrounded by curved terraces of houses with stucco façades. Regent's Street (1825) was designed to link the park with Westminster. Nash's colonnades were removed later but his All Souls, Langham Place, remains. In London Nash also built Carlton House Terrace (1833), laid out Trafalgar Square and St James's Park (1829), and redesigned ▷Buckingham Palace with the triumphal Marble Arch (1828) as its gateway (it was moved to its present position in 1851). In ▷Brighton he redesigned the Royal Pavilion for the king as an oriental fantasy. His career ended with the death of the king.

● **Nash, Ogden** ▶ (1902–71) US humorous writer. He wrote witty comments on social and domestic life expressed in doggerel verse. He contributed to the *New Yorker* magazine, and his books include *Free Wheeling* (1931), *I'm a Stranger Here Myself* (1938), *You Can't Get There From Here* (1957), *Collected Verse* (1961), and *Marriage Lines* (1964). He collaborated with Kurt Weill and S. J. Perelman on the musical *One Touch of Venus* (1943).

● **Nash, Paul** ▶ (1889–1946) British painter. After studying at the Slade School, he became known for his symbolic war landscapes during World Wars I and II, the finest example being *Totes Meer* (1940–41; Tate Gallery). Nash was also a leading member of Unit One (1933), a group of artists, including Barbara ▷Hepworth and Henry ▷Moore, dedicated to promoting modern art (particularly ▷abstract art) in the UK. His brother **John Nash** (1893–1977) produced fine watercolour landscapes and botanical illustrations.

● **Nash, Richard** ▶ (1674–1762) English gentleman, known as Beau Nash. In 1705 his fondness for gambling led him to Bath, where he became Master of Ceremonies and which he developed into the most fashionable spa town in England. He opposed duelling, smoking, and casual clothes.

● **Nash, Sir Walter** ▶ (1882–1968) New Zealand statesman; Labour prime minister (1957–60). Born in Britain, he introduced successful anti-Depression policies while minister of finance (1934–49) and was also a member of the Pacific War Council (1942–44).

● **Nashe, Thomas** ▶ (1567–c. 1601) British pamphleteer and dramatist. In *Pierce Penilesse* (1592) and other satiric pamphlets he attacked the Puritans and defended the theatres against them. Among other works are the comic masque *Summer's Last Will and Testament* (1592) and the pioneering picaresque novel *The Unfortunate Traveller* (1594). He collaborated with Ben Jonson and others on the satirical play *The Isle of Dogs* (1597).

● **Nashville** ▶ 36 10N 86 50W A city in the USA, the capital of Tennessee on the Cumberland River. Founded in 1779, it is the site of Vanderbilt University (1873) and is a major centre for religious education. It is also a centre of the recording industry for ▷country and western music; the Country and Western Music Hall of Fame and Museum are situated here. Since the 1930s cheap electric power from the Tennessee Valley Authority has made it an important commercial and industrial city. Industries include railway engineering, glass, printing and publishing, and clothing. Population (1996 est, with Davidson): 511 263.

● **Nasik** ▶ 20 00N 73 52E A city in India, in Maharashtra on the River Godavari. It is a Hindu pilgrimage centre. Industries include printing and distilling. Population (1991): 648 896.

● **Nassau** ▶ A former German duchy, now in Hesse and Rhineland-Palatinate *Länder*. In 1544 William the Silent, Count of Nassau, inherited the principality of ▷Orange, thus linking the two states. Nassau joined Napoleon's Confederation of the Rhine in 1806 and in 1866 came under Prussia.

● **Nassau** ▶ 25 2N 77 25W The capital of the Bahamas, a port on New Providence Island. Built in 1729, it is an important tourist centre. Population (1990): 171 000.

● **Nasser, Gamal Abdel** ▶ (1918–70) Egyptian statesman; prime minister (1954–56) and president (1956–70). An army officer, he helped to found the nationalist Free Officers group, which overthrew the monarchy in 1952. He became prime minister and then president of the Republic of Egypt (United Arab Republic from 1958). His nationalization of the Suez Canal led to an unsuccessful Israeli and Anglo-French attack on Egypt (1956), after which he was established as a leader of the Arab world. His socialist and Arab nationalist policies brought him into frequent conflict with the West and the more conservative Arab states.

● **Nasser, Lake** ▷*See* Aswan High Dam.

● **nastic movement** ▶ (*or* nasty) A nondirectional plant movement caused by an external stimulus. For example, physical contact with a twig of the sensitive plants (▷*Mimosa*) will cause folding of the leaves throughout the plant. Here the stimulus is touch and the plant's response is called a haptonasty. Other stimuli include light and heat, causing photonasties and thermonasties, respectively, examples of which are seen in the opening of certain flowers.

● **nasturtium** ▶ An annual garden plant of the genus *Tropaeolum* (90 species), also called Indian cress, native to Central and South America. It has round parasol-like leaves with central stalks, and orange, yellow, pink, or red flowers, which are funnel-shaped with a long spur containing nectar. *T. majus* is the most popular ornamental species and its seeds may be used in salads. The canary creeper (*T. peregrinum*) has twining leafstalks. Family: *Tropaeolaceae*.

● **Natal** ▶ 5 46S 35 15W A port in NE Brazil, the capital of Rio Grande do Norte state near the mouth of the Rio Potengi. The chief exports are sugar, cotton, and carnauba wax; industries include salt refining and textiles. It has a university (1958). Population (1991): 459 827.

● **Natal** ▶ A former province in South Africa. The land rises sharply from the Indian Ocean in the E to the Drakensberg Mountains in the W. Agriculture and forestry are important. Industries include shipping, food processing, chemicals, and sugar and oil refining. Durban is the main industrial centre and port. Coal is the chief mineral.
History: the Boers attempted to establish a republic in Natal (1838) but this was annexed by Britain in 1843. In 1897 Zululand was added to Natal and some parts of Transvaal were annexed to it in 1903. In 1910 it became one of the original provinces of the Union of South Africa. In 1994 it was replaced by the new region **KwaZulu/Natal** as part of an administrative reorganization.

● **Nataraja** ▶ In Hinduism, ▷Shiva in his aspect as lord of the cosmic dance, which symbolizes constant creation and dissolution. During the middle ages, in imitation of this dance, dancing became an important part of temple ritual.

● **Natchez** ▶ A Muskogean-speaking North American Indian tribe of the Lower Mississippi. They were cultivators who, like the ▷Creeks, built mound temples and worshipped the sun. They were ruled by a despotic chief known as the Great Sun and had an elaborate system of social classes. The highest caste, the "suns," were obliged to marry commoners.

● **National Aeronautics and Space Administration** ▷*See* NASA.

● **national anthem** ▶ The official song of a country, sung or played on ceremonial occasions. The British national anthem, "God Save the King," was adopted in the mid-18th century. Its musical origin is earlier and its authorship is unknown.

● **National Book League** ▷*See* Book Trust.

● **National Country Party** ▷*See* National Party, Australian.

● **National Curriculum** ▶ The curriculum of subjects taught in state schools in England and Wales. Established by the Education Reform Act (1988) and introduced progressively from 1989, the National Curriculum comprises ten foundation subjects (eleven in Wales), three of which (maths, science, and English) are core subjects that must be studied by all children from the age of five and taken at GCSE. Of the remaining subjects, some (design and technology, history or geography, a modern language, and physical education) are a compulsory part of secondary education, while others (music, art) are optional. In Wales, Welsh is a core subject in designated Welsh-speaking schools and a compulsory foundation subject in English-speaking schools. Attainment targets detail the knowledge, skills, and understanding a child is expected to acquire by a certain age. Children are assessed formally in the core subjects at the ages of 7, 11, 14, and 16 (the four "key stages"). At the three earlier stages these tests take the form of Standard Assessment Tasks (SATs) while at stage four they mainly take the form of ▷public examinations. In England Local Education Authorities are required to publish school-by-school information showing the percentage of children achieving the expected level of performance at each stage. In 1993 teachers protested that the curriculum created unnecessary bureaucracy and restricted the ability of schools to provide a range of courses; many boycotted the first national tests. The government subsequently agreed to reduce testing at ages 7, 11, and 14 to the core subjects and to reduce the compulsory element of the curriculum.
In addition to the National Curriculum, all schools must provide religious education and (from 2000) lessons in citizenship; they are also expected to teach additional subjects, such as health education, a second foreign language, and home economics, at appropriate stages. Independent schools need not teach the NC but in practice are forced to do so by the public exams syllabuses. Northern Ireland has its own statutory curriculum while in Scotland there are official (but nonstatutory) guidelines about the curriculum and standards.

● **national debt** ▶ The money that a government borrows; together with the revenue from ▷taxation it makes up the government's income. In the UK, the internal debt consists of two parts, the funded debt and the unfunded debt. The funded debt consists of money that the government does not have to repay on a fixed date (e.g. war loan); it makes up about 10% of the national debt. The unfunded debt consists of the floating debt (e.g. treasury bills), ▷gilt-edged securities, and such small savings as Savings Bonds. Money borrowed as unfunded debt has to be repaid on a fixed date. In the USA the national debt is known as the public debt.

● **National Economic Development Council** ▶ (NEDC *or* Neddy) A UK body set up in 1962 to advise the government on economic policy. Its members were drawn from government, industry, and trade unions. The **Economic Development Committees**, set up under its management, studied particular industries. It was abolished in 1992.

● **National Front** ▶ (NF) A British political party of the extreme right; avowedly racist and antisemitic, it is committed to ending non-White immigration and to the forced repatriation of non-Whites (even if born in the UK). It was formed in 1960 from several small neofascist groups. Although its support grew in the later 1970s, when its marches and rallies attracted much publicity, its attempts to enter mainstream electoral politics failed completely. Owing to its violent thuggish image, the revival of respectable right-wing politics under Thatcher in the 1980s, a series of internal splits, and the growing racial tolerance of the British public, it has since dwindled into irrelevance.

● **National Gallery** ▶ An art gallery in Trafalgar Square (London), containing the largest collection of paintings in the UK. Founded for the nation in 1824, it originally contained 38 paintings, housed in a building in Pall Mall until William Wilkins (1778–1839) built the present premises (1832–38). An extension of the building, the Sainsbury Wing, designed by Robert ▷Venturi, opened in 1991.

● **National Health Service** ▶ (NHS) A comprehensive medical service in the UK, financed primarily by national government and local taxation. The National Health Service Act (1946), implemented in

1948, covered all aspects of health care except that of the school child, which was primarily the responsibility of the local education authorities, and that of the worker, which was covered by a series of Factory Acts. Progress was slow during its first ten years with a virtual ban on the building of new hospitals and little relocation of adequate resources to areas of deprivation. It also became apparent that Aneurin Bevan's initial hope that the Service would be a self-eliminating expense was based on a fallacy. The success of the Service in keeping people alive into old age and new treatments resulting from advances in medical science have caused costs to escalate explosively rather than diminish. Complaints during the late 1950s and 1960s that the structure and policies of the NHS did not facilitate medical advance led to substantial reorganization of the Service in 1974; further reforms followed in 1982, 1988, 1990, and 1996 (*see* hospital). In England overall responsibility lies (from 1988) with the secretary of state for health. The service is administered (since 1996) by Health Authorities, which combine the functions of the old District Health Authorities and Family Health Service Authorities. They are accountable to the regional offices of the NHS Executive, which took over the functions of the old Regional Health Authorities. In Wales and Scotland responsibility now lies (since 1999) with the Welsh Assembly or Scottish Parliament, while administration lies with Health Authorities (in Wales) or Health Boards (in Scotland). The strain placed on the NHS by rising costs led the Conservative government to introduce the National Health Service and Community Care Act (1990), empowering hospitals to opt to be run by self-governing NHS trusts, funded by selling their services to Health Authorities and fund-holding GPs. In 1997 the Labour government replaced GP fund-holding with a system of primary care groups (*see* hospital). Long waiting lists for surgical treatment of conditions that are not life-threatening, a shortage of nurses largely resulting from poor pay, and the dilapidated state of some hospitals have led many to conclude that after 50 years the NHS is no longer working as it should. For some economists, the only solution to the problem of rising costs that cannot be met out of taxation is a form of means testing, i.e. to make those who can afford it pay something towards their treatment. Plans to increase annual spending on the NHS by 43% within five years were announced in 2002.

● **National Insurance** ► A UK insurance scheme that operates under various acts, including the Social Security Acts (1968–92). Old-age ▷pensions were first introduced by Lloyd George in 1908 and sickness and unemployment benefits in 1911. A more comprehensive scheme was planned in the ▷Beveridge Report (1942), which became law in the National Insurance Act (1946). National Insurance is financed by compulsory contributions from earners and employers. This fund provides for payments towards the cost of the ▷National Health Service and for contributory and noncontributory benefits. Contributory benefits include the jobseeker's allowance, incapacity benefit, maternity allowance, and widow's benefit. Noncontributory benefits include child benefit, income support, and working families' tax credit. Under the State Earnings-Related Pension Scheme (SERPS) of 1978, the state retirement pension consists of a basic flat-rate pension and an additional pension based on the person's earnings; contributions to the pension are related to earnings and pensions are index linked. State pensions are paid, irrespective of other earnings, at 65 for men and 60 for women. In 2020 the pension age will be equalized at 65. Persons who wish to contract out of SERPS may subscribe instead to an approved occupational or personal pension scheme. By the late 1990s the rising costs of SERPS and the manifest inadequacy of the basic state pension led to pressure for reform. In 2001 the government introduced "stakeholder" pensions as an alternative to SERPS for those without occupational or personal pensions; these will be administered by the private sector but regulated by government. There are also plans to replace SERPS itself with an additional state pension targeted at the most needy.

● **nationalism** ► A doctrine that claims to determine the unit of population entitled to have government of its own. In its revolutionary form it regards existing state boundaries as arbitrary. The doctrine developed in Europe around 1800. The Latin word *Natio* had simply meant a group, regardless of frontiers. After the French Revolution nationalists, such as ▷Fichte and ▷Mazzini, sought to make the boundaries of states coextensive with those of national habitation. Nations were supposed to be recognizable by certain characteristics—for Fichte this was the use of a particular language. ▷Kant's doctrine of the autonomy of the will was used to provide philosophical backing for nationalism. While it was hoped that nationalism would make for peace, in practice it has often resulted in xenophobia, rivalry, oppression of ethnic minorities, and war.

● **nationalization** ► The policy of taking into public ownership industries that were privately owned. In the UK after World War II, ▷Attlee's Labour government (1945–51) nationalized the "commanding heights" of the economy: those industries in which competition appeared wasteful (e.g. the gas and electricity supplies) and those war-damaged enterprises needing huge injections of capital (e.g. coal, railways). In the 1980s and 1990s Conservative governments reversed the trend, returning industries to the private sector to restore competition and efficiency. The same trends have been followed elsewhere in the world, notably in the developing countries of Africa and South America. ▷*See* privatization.

● **National Lottery** ▷*See* gambling.

● **National Parks** ► Designated areas in which scenery, wildlife, and heritage are granted special legal protection and public enjoyment and access are promoted. Most countries now have National Parks or their equivalent. In England and Wales National Parks were first established in 1949. The ten parks (in England, Dartmoor, Exmoor, Lake District, Northumberland, North York Moors, Peak District, and Yorkshire Dales and, in Wales, Brecon Beacons, Pembrokeshire Coast, and Snowdonia) are now the responsibility of the individual National Park Authorities, under the overall guidance of the Countryside Agency (established as the Countryside Commission in 1968) and the Countryside Council for Wales (established in 1991). The Broads (from 1989) and the New Forest (from 1998) have the same legal protection as the National Parks without the administrative machinery. In 1999 the government announced plans to make the New Forest and the South Downs full National Parks. England and Wales also have 41 designated **Areas of Outstanding Natural Beauty** (AONBs)—areas judged to be no less beautiful than the National Parks but to be less suitable for outdoor recreation. Northern Ireland has nine AONBs. Owing to opposition from the big landed estates and fears of disrupting the rural economy, no National Parks were created in Scotland; there are, however, 40 **National Scenic Areas**, which have a similar status to the AONBs; they are the responsibility of Scottish Natural Heritage and the local planning authorities. Plans to designate several Scottish National Parks, beginning with Loch Lomond and the Trossachs, were announced in 1998. In the USA the National Park Service (established in 1916) is responsible for 38 national parks, the largest of which is ▷Yellowstone National Park. Australian National Parks include the ▷Simpson Desert and the Kosciusko National Park. ▷*See also* nature reserve.

● **National Party, Australian** ► An Australian political party, founded in 1919 as the Country Party, to represent the interests of farmers. It has held office only in coalition with the ▷Liberal Party. It was formerly the National Country Party.

● **National Physical Laboratory** ► An establishment financed by the UK government, founded in 1900 at Teddington, Middlesex, which carries out research into subjects connected with physics and monitors standards of measurements.

● **National Portrait Gallery** ► An art gallery in London founded in 1856 to house portraits of famous personalities in British history. Its collection includes works by Holbein, Rubens, Reynolds, and Augustus John and many photographs. The gallery is near the National Gallery; there are annexes in Carlton House Terrace and at Montacute House, Somerset. A major extension opened in 2000.

● **National Service** ▷*See* conscription.

● **National Socialist German Workers' Party** ▷*See* Nazi Party.

● **National Society for the Prevention of Cruelty to Children** ► (NSPCC) A British charity, incorporated in 1884, whose 1000 child- and family-care workers investigate physical, emotional, and sexual abuse of children and child neglect, working with the social services. Its 24-hour helpline handles some 120 000 calls annually.

● **National Theatre Company** ▷*See* Royal National Theatre Company.

● **National Trust** ▶ An independent charity in the UK, founded in 1895, that acquires and preserves country houses, castles, gardens, and places of interest or natural beauty. Properties bequeathed to the Trust are exempt from ▷inheritance tax but to be accepted they must be self-supporting or accompanied by an endowment.

● **National Vocational Qualifications** ▷*See* public examinations.

● **Nation of Islam** ▷*See* Black Muslims.

● **Nations, Battle of the** ▷*See* Leipzig, Battle of.

● **NATO** ▷*See* North Atlantic Treaty Organization.

● **Natron, Lake** ▶ 2 20S 36 05E A lake in N Tanzania, in the ▷Great Rift Valley. It measures about 56 km (30 mi) by 24 km (15 mi) and contains salt and soda.

● **natterjack** ▶ A short-legged European ▷toad, *Bufo calamita*. About 7 cm long when fully grown, the natterjack has a yellow stripe down its back. It runs in a series of short spurts and if alarmed raises its inflated body on its hind legs to appear larger to the enemy.

● **natural gas** ▶ A naturally occurring gas consisting mainly of methane with smaller amounts of heavier hydrocarbons. It is obtained from underground natural reservoirs, often associated with ▷oil deposits. Like oil it originates in the bacterial decomposition of animal matter. It is a relatively cheap fuel, although known reserves are likely to be exhausted in the 21st century. It also contains nonhydrocarbon impurities, including helium, which is extracted commercially. It has largely replaced coal gas in town gas supplies and is now transported by a pipeline grid with underground storage systems in the form of **liquefied natural gas** (LNG). This consists of compressed and cooled natural gas from which the "wet" gases propane and butane have been removed. At a temperature of −160°C, the LNG occupied 1/600th of the volume of the gas and in this form can be transported by special tanker vessels. The gases propane and butane so extracted are used to make ▷liquefied petroleum gas.

● **Natural History Museum** ▷*See* British Museum.

● **Naturalism** ▶ A literary and artistic movement of the late 19th century characterized by the use of realistic techniques to express the philosophical belief that all phenomena can be explained by natural or material causes. It was influenced by the biological theories of ▷Darwin, the philosophy of ▷Comte, and the deterministic theories of the historian ▷Taine. Its literary manifesto was *Le Roman expérimentale* (1880) by ▷Zola, whose sequence of 20 novels known as *Le Rougon-Macquart* (1871–93) was intended to demonstrate, by its concentration on the history of a single family, how human life is determined by heredity and environment. Writers influenced by Naturalism include the dramatists ▷Hauptmann, ▷Ibsen, ▷Strindberg, and, in the 20th century, the US novelist Theodore ▷Dreiser. Its influence is also apparent in the work of such painters as ▷Courbet and the young ▷Van Gogh.

● **naturalization** ▶ In law, the process by which an ▷alien, on taking an oath of allegiance, acquires the rights of a natural-born citizen of a country. In the UK, the requirements for naturalization are governed by the British Nationality Act (1981) and include a period of residence or service abroad with the Crown, good character, a knowledge of English, and the intention to reside in the UK or to be in the service abroad of the Crown or a UK company.

● **natural justice** ▶ The basic rules of fair play that should govern any adjudication between individuals or organizations. These principles were originally developed by the courts of ▷equity and subsequently extended (mostly in the 20th century) to apply to any court or tribunal exercising administrative power. Any decision reached by a court or tribunal that contravenes natural justice is said to be *ultra vires* (Latin: beyond the powers), i.e. going beyond the powers conferred on it. There are two main rules of natural justice. The first is that those fulfilling a judicial role must be totally free of bias and that no decision can be reached by a judicial procedure in which the

judge has a financial or other interest in the outcome or fails in any way to be impartial. The second rule is that no decision can be made by any court or tribunal unless both sides are free to state their cases and both sides know the details of the other side's case. This is known as *audi alteram partem* (Latin: hear the other side).

● **natural selection** ▷*See* Darwinism.

● **nature conservation** ▶ The management of areas deemed worthy of preservation from development on biological, geological, or physiographical grounds. In Britain nature conservation is the responsibility of English Nature (EN), Scottish National Heritage (SNH), and the Countryside Council for Wales (CCW). These agencies were established in 1991, replacing the Nature Conservancy Council (founded 1973). They designate and manage National Nature Reserves and identify and organize protection for Sites of Special Scientific Interest (SSSIs); there are currently over 6000 SSSIs. Other nature conservation areas are Local Nature Reserves, identified and managed by local authorities; Forest Nature Reserves, created by an agency of the Forestry Commission; and Marine Nature Reserves, selected and managed by EN, SNH, and CCW. The Joint Nature Conservation Committee deals with UK and international issues. ▷*See also* nature reserve.

● **nature reserve** ▶ An area set aside for the preservation of fauna, flora, and their natural habitats. Nature reserves differ from ▷National Parks in that their purpose is to maintain plants and animals in their natural environments rather than to provide for public enjoyment. In some reserves the emphasis is on the protection of specific habitats, while others are managed to preserve particular species of plants or animals, including ▷endangered species. Nature reserves for the preservation of game animals for hunting have existed since medieval times, but their creation for the preservation of wild animals for their own sake did not begin until the late 19th century. ▷*See also* nature conservation.

● **naturopathy** ▶ A system of healing that encourages the body's own resources to overcome disease, rather than relying on drugs and surgery. Practitioners place great emphasis on the beneficial effects of a healthy lifestyle, in which exercise, fresh air, sunlight, and a natural diet, using pure water and foods grown without artificial fertilizers or pesticides and prepared without the use of additives, play an important role in ridding the body of the toxins that are believed to be the cause of most diseases. The body's powers of self-healing may be further promoted by the use of herbal remedies or manipulative therapies. ▷*See also* alternative medicine; holistic medicine.

● **Naukratis** ▶ (*or* Naucratis) An ancient town on the W side of the Nile delta in Egypt. An autonomous community of Greek traders flourished here from the 7th century BC.

● **Nauplia** ▶ (Modern Greek name: Návplion) 37 34N 22 48E A port in S Greece, in the E Peloponnese. It was the capital of Greece from 1829 to 1834. Exports include fruit, vegetables, tobacco, and cotton. Population (latest est): 10 609.

● **Nauru, Republic of** ▶ (*or* Naoero; former name: Pleasant Island) A small country in the central Pacific Ocean, NE of Australia comprising a coral island. The small population consists mainly of Nauruans and other Pacific islanders.
Economy: based entirely on the mining of phosphates, the only export. Deposits are expected to run out early in the 21st century, but Nauru has made investments abroad and is developing as a transport centre and tax haven. There is very little fertile land and almost all food is imported.
History: the first Europeans to arrive were the British in 1798. Nauru was administered by Germany from 1888 until World War I. It was under British mandate from 1920 to 1947, when it came under the joint trusteeship of Australia, New Zealand, and the UK. In 1968 it became an independent republic and a special member of the British Commonwealth, with Hammer DeRoburt (1922–92) as its first president. Having been replaced by Bernard Dowiyogo (1946–) in 1976, DeRoburt was re-elected in 1978. In 1983 he was forced to resign after defeats in a libel suit and over the issue of the dumping of nuclear waste in the Pacific, but was re-elected 4 days later. In 1989 he was again replaced by Dowiyogo. After an interval (1995–98) during

which Kinza Clodumar was president, Dowiyogo resumed the office but resigned after losing a confidence vote in 1999. Nauru received some £50 million compensation from Australia in 1993 for environmental damage and loss of mining profits while it was a trusteeship (1947–68).

Republic of Nauru

Head of state	President Rene Harris
Official language	English
Official currency	Australian dollar
Area	21 sq km (8 sq mi)
Population (1997 est)	11 000
Capital and main port	Yaren

● **Nausicaa** ► In Greek legend, the daughter of Alcinous, King of Phaeacia. She helped the shipwrecked ▷Odysseus, and was offered by her father in marriage, but Odysseus, loyal to his wife, refused.

● **nautical mile** ▷*See* mile.

● **nautilus** ► One of several cephalopod molluscs with external shells. The pearly nautiluses (genus *Nautilus*; 3 species) live near the bottom of the Pacific and Indian Oceans. Up to 20 cm across, they have 60–90 tentacles surrounding a horny beak and live in the outermost chamber of their flat coiled shells. The others serve as buoyancy chambers, enabling the animals to float at different depths. The paper nautilus (*Argonauta argo*) is found in the Atlantic and Pacific Oceans. The female, 20 cm long, secretes from one of its tentacles a papery boat-shaped shell in which the eggs are laid and fertilized and develop. The male is smaller (about 2 cm long).

● **Navajo** ► A North American Indian Athabascan-speaking people of New Mexico, Arizona, and Utah. Like their relatives, the ▷Apache, they migrated from the north, probably during the 17th century. Unlike the Apache, they learned farming and adopted many traits from the ▷Pueblo Indians. Their social organization is matrilineal. They are the most numerous North American Indian tribe.

● **Navarino, Battle of** ► (20 October, 1827) A naval battle in the War of ▷Greek Independence. French, Russian, and British ships destroyed an Ottoman-Egyptian fleet in the Bay of Navarinou in the Peloponnese.

● **Navarre** ► A former kingdom in N Spain, corresponding to the present-day Spanish region of Navarra and part of the French department of Basses-Pyrénées. Known as Pampalona until the late 12th century, it was ruled by Muslims until the late 9th century, when a Basque dynasty established control over the kingdom. In 1234 it passed to a French dynasty but in 1512 S Navarre was conquered by Ferdinand the Catholic of Aragon and united with Castile in 1515. French Navarre passed to the French Crown in 1589.

● **navel** ► A depression in the centre of the abdomen that represents the site of attachment of the ▷umbilical cord of the fetus. Its medical name is the umbilicus. Occasionally babies are born with an umbilical hernia, in which the intestines protrude through the navel.

● **navigation** ► (technology) The science required to plot a course for a ship, aircraft, or spacecraft and to direct a vessel or craft so that it follows this course. Until the 20th century navigation was concerned only with sea-going vessels and with the navigational aids required at sea or on remote parts of the land. At sea, early sailors remained in sight of the land until the Phoenicians in about 1000 BC discovered how to make use of celestial bodies to set a course. As successful navigation at sea requires reliable maps and charts, the sciences of navigation and ▷cartography developed together. The earliest instruments used in star-based navigation were the magnetic ▷compass and the ▷astrolabe, which were both invented in the second century BC. These two instruments dominated navigation until the ▷sextant replaced the astrolabe in the 18th century and the gyrocompass replaced the magnetic compass in the 19th century.

In the early 20th century the advent of aircraft made navigation not only a way of finding one's way about the globe, but also a necessity to avoid collisions. Radio, radio beacon, and ▷radar became of increasing value, but it was not until the dawn of the space age and the positioning of **navigation satellites** in orbit that precise navigation

anywhere on earth became possible (*see* Global Positioning System). The science is now dominated by on-board computer-controlled electronic devices that enable the pilots of aircraft and spacecraft to know their exact positions.

● **navigation** ► (zoology) The process enabling animals to follow a particular course, especially when migrating. Birds are believed to use the sun to set a compass bearing, taking additional cues from the direction of the earth's magnetic field, especially when the sun is obscured. Landmarks may also play a part, both in locating a previous nesting site and during migration itself. Homing pigeons may even use smell to locate their own loft.

A magnetic sense is also important for some aquatic animals. Whales and sharks, for instance, migrate by following magnetic contours along the ocean floor. Turtles can return to the beach on which they hatched, to lay their own eggs, sometimes 10 years later. They are thought to use a magnetic sense in conjunction with smell. In the insect world both the sun and moon are used as navigational aids. ▷Honeybees use the sun to fix a compass bearing when foraging and communicate the bearing to other members of the hive by a special dance. North American monarch butterflies migrate some 4000 km in the autumn from the N USA to a small site in Mexico. They are believed to set a bearing by the sun, but temperature, altitude, smell, and magnetism may play a part. In spring the monarchs pass through several generations on the return, indicating a hereditary element in the navigational sense.

● **Navigation Acts** ► A series of Acts originally to foster English shipping (1382, 1485, 1540) but subsequently to protect England's colonial trade, especially against its Dutch rivals. During the Commonwealth (1649–53) two ordinances (1650, 1651) respectively banned foreign trading in the colonies and restricted such trade to English or colonial ships, manned by predominantly English crews. These and similar Acts of 1660, 1672, and 1696 were repealed in 1849.

● **Navratilova, Martina** ► (1956–   ) Czech-born tennis player who defected to the USA in 1975. She was Wimbledon singles champion in 1978, 1979, 1982–87, and 1990 and doubles champion in 1976, 1979, and 1981–86. She also holds a record of 74 consecutive wins. She retired in 1994.

● **navy** ► A nation's warships (*see* ships), together with their crews and supporting administration. Navies were built by the ancient Greek city states at first to protect their Mediterranean trade routes from pirates and later to undermine the sea power of their rivals and enemies. The first recorded sea battle took place between Corinth and Corcyra (*or* Corfu) in 664 BC and navies—typically comprising triremes—played an important part in both the Greek-Persian and Peloponnesian Wars. The first permanent naval administration was organized (311 BC) in ancient Rome, which was the supreme Mediterranean power by the early 2nd century BC (*see* Punic Wars). Rome's naval power passed after the collapse of the western Empire in the 5th century AD to the Byzantine (Eastern Roman) Empire. Meanwhile, the Vikings marauded northern waters, provoking Alfred the Great of England to create (9th century) the origins of the ▷Royal Navy. The later middle ages saw the rise of Italian navies, outstandingly those of Venice and Genoa, and the decline of the Byzantine fleet, under the threat of the Ottoman Turks. By 1571, when, at Lepanto, the Turkish control of the Mediterranean was finally destroyed, Spain had emerged as the supreme naval power. England's defeat of the Spanish ▷Armada (1588) anticipated its subsequent emergence as a great naval power: by the late 17th century it had overtaken the Netherlands (*see* Dutch Wars) and by the early 19th century, France (*see* Revolutionary and Napoleonic Wars). British naval supremacy was threatened in the early 20th century by the German navy, which in spite of defeat in World War I again became a power to be reckoned with in the 1930s. By the end of World War II command of the seas had passed to the US navy. During the Cold War the navies of the USA and the Soviet Union dominated the seas and with their nuclear-powered missile-armed submarines also dominated most of the earth's surface. ▷*See also* Admiralty, Board of; Royal Marines.

● **Naxalites** ► An extremist communist movement centring on the town of Naxalbari in W Bengal (India). Dedicated to Maoist principles, it attempted a violent seizure of land for the landless in 1967.

● **Náxos ▶** A Greek island in the S Aegean Sea, the largest in the Cyclades. Náxos is traditionally the place where Theseus abandoned Ariadne. It was an ancient centre of the worship of Dionysius. Area: 438 sq km (169 sq mi). Population (1981): 14 037. Chief town: Náxos.

● **Nazarenes ▶** A group of young German and Austrian painters who worked in Italy in the early 19th century. Formed in 1809 as the Brotherhood of St Luke (Lukasbröder), they aimed to revive the Christian art of the medieval and early Renaissance periods; they also undertook to work cooperatively in the manner of medieval craftsmen. Leading members of the group included Peter von ▷Cornelius, Friedrich Johann Overbeck (1789–1869), and Franz Pforr (1788–1812). Their chief joint work was a series of frescoes at the Casa Bartholdy in Rome (1816–17; now at the Staatliche Museen, Berlin). Their ideals helped to inspire the ▷Pre-Raphaelite Brotherhood in Britain.

● **Nazareth ▶** 32 41N 35 16E A town in N Israel, between Haifa and the Sea of Galilee. According to the New Testament it was the home of Sts Mary and Joseph and of Jesus Christ before he began his ministry. These associations have made Nazareth a centre of Christian pilgrimage with many churches and shrines, including St Mary's Well and the Church of the Annunciation, built over the supposed home of the Virgin Mary. Population (1989): 51 000.

● **Nazi Party ▶** (*Nationalsozialistische Deutsche Arbeiterpartei*) The National Socialist German Workers' Party, founded in 1919 as the German Workers' Party and led from 1921 until his suicide in 1945 by Adolf ▷Hitler. Having enjoyed the support of virtually the entire German population from the mid-1930s to the humiliating defeat of Germany in World War II, the party was disbanded in 1945. In those ten years it perpetrated some of the most demoniacal crimes in human history (*see* holocaust) and brought Germany into the second half of the 20th century morally shamed and discredited. The revival of the Nazi Party is forbidden by the government of the Federal Republic of Germany. ▷*See also* fascism; Third Reich.

● **Nazirites ▶** (*or* Nazarites) In the Old Testament, a group of Israelites who consecrated themselves to God by taking special vows, originally perhaps for life but later for a certain period only. The vows were to abstain from wine, not to cut the hair, and to avoid contact with dead bodies. Samson and Samuel were Nazirites from birth.

● **N'djamena ▶** (name until 1973: Fort Lamy) The capital of Chad, a port in the SW on the River Chari. It was founded by the French in 1900. The University of Chad was established in 1971. Population (1990 est): 402 000.

● **Ndola ▶** 13 00S 28 39E A city in N Zambia, near the border with the Democratic Republic of Congo. It is an important commercial and distribution centre for the ▷Copperbelt and has copper and cobalt refineries. Population (1987 est): 418 142.

● **Neagh, Lough ▶** A lake in Northern Ireland, divided between Co Antrim, Co Armagh, and Co Tyrone. It is the largest lake in the British Isles. Area: 388 sq km (150 sq mi).

● **Neanderthal man ▶** An extinct ▷hominid race that inhabited Europe and the adjacent areas of Asia between about 150 000 and 30 000 years ago. Characterized by heavy brow ridges, receding forehead, heavy protruding jaw, and robust bone structure, Neanderthal man had a large cranial capacity and upright posture. They were cave-dwelling hunters who made tools and buried their dead in a manner implying some sort of cult and ritual (*see* Mousterian). Neanderthals are generally regarded as a distinct species (*Homo neanderthalensis*), rather than a subspecies of *Homo sapiens*, and may have evolved from *Homo heidelbergensis* (*see* Homo).

● **neap tide ▶** A ▢tide of comparatively small range that occurs near the time of the moon's quarters. The range falls below the average range by 10 to 30% (high low tides and low high tides). *Compare* spring tide.

● **Neath Port Talbot ▶** (Welsh name: Castell-Nedd Port Talbot) A county borough in S Wales, created from part of West Glamorgan in 1996. Area: 442 sq km (170 sq mi). Population (1996 est): 139 500. Administrative centre: Port Talbot.

● **Nebraska ▶** A state in the N central USA, lying W of the Missouri River. Part of the Central Lowlands cover the eastern third of the state, with the higher Great Plains in the W. Traditionally an agricultural state, it is still a leading producer of cattle, corn, and wheat. Most of the population is situated in the industrial E. Food processing (especially meat) is a major industry; machinery, fabricated metal, transport equipment, chemicals, and printing and publishing are also important.
　　History: explored by the French and Spanish, it formed part of the Louisiana Purchase (1803). It became a state in 1867 and, with the arrival of the railways in the same year, it began to develop rapidly as a cattle-ranching region. Area: 200 018 sq km (77 227 sq mi). Population (1996 est): 1 652 093. Capital: Lincoln.

● **Nebuchadnezzar II ▶** (*or* Nebuchadrezzar; c. 630–562 BC) King of ▷Babylon (605–562). Nebuchadnezzar defeated the Egyptians at Carchemish (605 BC) and extended Babylonian power in Elam, N Syria, and S Asia Minor. He captured Jerusalem in 597 and again in 586, when he destroyed the city and forced the Jews into exile (*see* Babylonian exile). He restored Babylon to its former glory. Daniel's story of his madness is probably unhistorical.

● **nebula ▶** A cloud of interstellar gas and dust that becomes visible for one of three reasons. In an **emission nebula** the gas is ionized by ultraviolet radiation, generally from a hot star within the cloud; the ions interact with free electrons in the cloud, and light (predomi-

Nazi Party ▶ The Nazis orchestrated elaborate quasi-military ceremonials in order to consolidate their hold on the public imagination, most notoriously at the annual Nuremberg rallies. The photograph shows a parade of the Nazi National Labour Service (some carrying spades) at the Zeppelinfeld in Nuremberg (September, 1936).

nantly red and green) is emitted. In a **reflection nebula** light from a nearby star is reflected in all directions by dust in the cloud, thus illuminating the cloud. The dust in a **dark nebula** reduces quite considerably the amount of light passing through it (by absorption and scattering) and a dark region is seen against a brighter background.

● **Neckar, River** ▶ A river in SW Germany, flowing mainly N from the Black Forest past Stuttgart and Heidelberg to join the River Rhine at Mannheim. Length: 394 km (245 mi).

● **Necker, Jacques** ▶ (1732–1804) French statesman. A successful banker, in 1768 he became a director of the French East India Company. In 1776 he was appointed director of the treasury and in 1777, director general of finance. In retirement from 1781 to 1788, he was recalled to his former post on the eve of the French Revolution in the hope that he would deal with the economic crisis. He persuaded Louis XVI to summon the States General and suggested reforms that aroused the enmity of the aristocrats, who secured his dismissal. Reappointed after the storming of the Bastille, he resigned in 1790. His wife was the writer and philanthropist **Suzanne Necker** (1739–94) and their daughter became Mme de ▷Staël.

● **necropsy** ▷*See* autopsy.

● **nectar** ▶ A sugary solution produced by glandular structures (nectaries) in animal-pollinated flowers. Nectar attracts insects, birds, or bats and encourages pollination as the animal collects nectar from different sources. ▷*See also* ambrosia.

● **nectarine** ▷*See* peach.

● **needlefish** ▶ A carnivorous fish, also called garfish, belonging to the family *Belonidae* (about 60 species), that occurs in tropical and warm-temperate seas. It has a slender silvery-blue or green body, up to 1.2 m long, with elongated jaws and numerous sharp teeth. Species include the European garfish (*Belone belone*). Order: *Atheriniformes*.

● **Needles, the** ▶ 50 39N 1 34W A group of chalk rocks in S England, off the W coast of the Isle of Wight. A lighthouse stands on the most westerly rock.

● **Neer, Aert van der** ▶ (c. 1603–77) Dutch landscape painter, famous for his moonlight, sunset, and firelight scenes. He also painted ice-bound canals and other winter landscapes.

● **Nefertiti** ▶ (died c. 1346 BC) The cousin and chief wife of ▷Akhenaton of Egypt. She is depicted with her six daughters and the king in scenes of domestic life, a unique exception to the priestly conventions of Egyptian royal portraiture. Her portrait bust is a well-known work of Egyptian art.

● **negative income tax** ▷*See* tax-credit system.

● **Negev** ▶ A desert in S Israel. In recent years large areas have been irrigated by pipeline from the River Jordan and many farming communities established, including over a hundred *kibbutzim*. Area: about 12 000 sq km (4632 sq mi).

● **negligence** ▶ Failure to do something an average responsible person would do or doing something such a person would not do. Negligence may be an element in a number of crimes, the most serious of which is manslaughter. Professional negligence occurs if a professional is proved to have less than the skill of an average member of his profession. If negligence results in damage this could be a ▷tort consisting of breach of a duty.

● **Negrín, Juan** ▶ (1889–1956) Spanish politician. A moderate socialist, Negrín became prime minister of the Republic in 1937 during the ▷Spanish Civil War. He centralized the military forces of the Republic but Negrín's dependence on the Communist Party brought opposition that forced his resignation.

● **Negri Sembilan** ▶ A state in W Peninsular Malaysia, on the Strait of Malacca. It is hilly, producing mainly rubber, rice, coconuts, and tin. Area: 6605 sq km (2550 sq mi). Population (1990): 723 800. Capital: Seremban.

● **Negro, Río** ▶ 1. (Portuguese name: Rio Negro) A river in NE South America. Rising in E Colombia as the Guainía, it flows E into Brazil, joining the River Amazon below Manaus. Length: about 2250 km

(1400 mi). 2. A river in S Argentina, rising in the Andes and flowing SE across Patagonia to the Atlantic Ocean. Length: 1014 km (630 mi).

● **Negroid** ▶ The racial grouping originating in sub-Saharan Africa. They are characterized by heavy skin pigmentation, curly to kinky dark hair, broad nose and lips, slight body hair, and high frequency of blood type Ro in the Rh system. Subtypes are the taller darker Congoloids and the shorter lighter pygmies, Bushmen, and Hottentots, collectively called Capoids.

● **Negros** ▶ A volcanic island in the Philippine Visayan Islands. The chief industry is sugar production. Area: 13 670 sq km (5278 sq mi). Population (1980): 2 749 700. Chief town: Bacolod.

● **Nehemiah** ▶ In the Old Testament, a Jewish leader of the 5th century BC. Cupbearer to the Persian king, he was granted permission to return to Jerusalem in 444 BC, where he planned and supervised the restoration of the city walls. In 432 he visited Jerusalem a second time and initiated a number of religious and social reforms. **The Book of Nehemiah**, recording his activities, is by the author of ▷Chronicles and ▷Ezra.

Jawaharlal Nehru ▶ The Indian prime minister giving *namaste*, the traditional Indian salute.

● **Nehru, Jawaharlal** ▶ (1889–1964) Indian statesman; the first prime minister of independent India (1947–64). Educated in England, he returned to India in 1912 to practise law but soon left his profession to follow Mahatma ▷Gandhi; in 1929 he was elected president of the ▷Indian National Congress in succession to his father Motilal Nehru (1861–1931). Between 1921 and 1945 he served nine prison sentences for noncooperation with the British. After World War II he was a central figure in the negotiations for the creation of an independent India. He carried through many social reforms and maintained a policy of nonalignment with foreign powers, although he was finally forced to enlist US support against Chinese border attacks in 1962. His sister was Vijaya ▷Pandit and his daughter was Indira ▷Gandhi.

● **Neill, A(lexander) S(utherland)** ▶ (1883–1973) Scottish educationalist, child psychologist, and writer. An exponent of child-centred education, Neill founded Summerhill (1921), a coeducational boarding school, famous for its informal atmosphere and liberal educational techniques. His books include *Hearts, Not Heads* (1945) and *Talking of Summerhill* (1967).

● **Neisse, River** ▶ 1. (or Glatzer Neisse; Polish name: Nysa) A river in SW Poland, flowing NE to join the River Oder near Brzeg. Length: 244 km (159 mi). 2. (or Lusatian Neisse) A river rising in the N Czech Republic and flowing mainly N to the River Oder near Gubin in Poland. It forms part of the border between Germany and Poland. Length: 225 km (140 mi).

● **Nejd** ▷*See* Najd.

● **Nekrasov, Nikolai Alekseevich** ▶ (1821–78) Russian poet. After rejecting the military career proposed by his father, he became a successful editor and manager of various literary periodicals. The main theme of his poetry is the oppression and character of the Russian peasants. He frequently drew on traditional folksongs, especially in his poems for children.

● **nekton** ▶ An ecological division of aquatic animals that includes all those swimming actively, i.e. by their own efforts, in the open waters of a sea or lake (*compare* benthos; plankton). The nekton includes fishes, squids, turtles, seals, and whales.

● **Nelson** ▶ 53 51N 2 13W A town in N England, in E Lancashire. It developed in the 19th century around the Lord Nelson Inn. Population (1991): 29 120.

● **Nelson** ▶ 41 18S 173 17E A port and resort in New Zealand, in N South Island on Tasman Bay. It contains the Cawthron Institute, a notable agricultural research centre. Population (1995 est): 51 200.

● **Nelson, Horatio, Viscount** ▶ (1758–1805) British admiral. While serving in the West Indies, he married (1787) Mrs Frances Nisbet (1761–1831). At the outbreak of the French Revolutionary Wars he was given command of the *Agamemnon* in the Mediterranean. In 1794, at Calvi, he lost the sight in his right eye but went on to play an important part in the victory off Cape St Vincent (1797), for which he was knighted. Shortly afterwards he lost his right arm in action but in 1798 he destroyed France's naval power in the Mediterranean by his great victory in the battle of the ▷Nile. Nelson spent the following year in Naples, where he fell in love with Emma, Lady ▷Hamilton. Returning to England in 1800, Nelson, now Baron Nelson of the Nile, received a hero's welcome but his affair with Emma Hamilton, who gave birth to their daughter Horatia late in 1800, caused considerable scandal. Given command in the Baltic, he was responsible for the victory at Copenhagen (1801) and was created a viscount on his return. In 1803 he became commander in the Mediterranean. He blockaded Toulon for 18 months but in 1805 the French escaped, with Nelson hot in pursuit, and the ensuing chase culminated in the battle of ▷Trafalgar (1805). Nelson directed this British triumph from aboard the *Victory* (▢ships) but was himself mortally wounded. He is buried in St Paul's.

● **Neman, River** ▶ (*or* R. Nyeman) A river in E Europe. Rising in Belarus, it flows mainly NW through Lithuania to enter the Baltic Sea. Length: 937 km (582 mi).

● **nematode** ▶ A spindle-shaped colourless worm, also called roundworm, belonging to the phylum *Nematoda* (about 80 000 species). Most nematodes are less than 3 mm long and have a mouth at one end, sometimes containing teeth or stylets, and usually a short muscular pharynx leading to the intestine. The sexes are generally separate. Nematodes live almost everywhere in soil, fresh water, and the sea. Some are parasites of plants or animals; others feed on dead organic matter. Many damage crops or parasitize domestic animals and man. ▷*See also* Ascaris; eelworm; filaria; guinea worm; hookworm; pinworm; vinegar eel.

● **Nemertina** ▷*See* ribbonworm.

● **Nemery, Jaafar Mohammed al** ▶ (1930–) Sudanese statesman; president (1971–85). An army officer, Nemery came to power in a coup in 1969 as chairman of a revolutionary council. In 1972 he negotiated an end to the 17-year revolt of the non-Muslims in the S. After a coup in 1985, he went into exile.

● **Nemesia** ▶ A genus of annual herbs native to South Africa. They are up to 30 cm tall, with narrow leaves and showy white, yellow, red, pink, or purple two-lipped flowers, sometimes spurred, with spotted centres. Many species are popular ornamentals, especially *N. strumosa*, *N. floribunda*, and *N. versicolor*. Family: *Scrophulariaceae*.

● **Nemesis** ▶ In Greek mythology, a goddess personifying the gods' anger at and punishment of human arrogance or ▷hubris. According to Hesiod, she is the daughter of night. She is associated with just vengeance and especially the punishment that befalls the impious.

● **Nemi, Lake** ▶ 41 43N 12 43E A small crater lake in W central Italy, SE of Rome. Two large pleasure ships from the time of the Roman emperor Caligula were raised from the bottom (1930–31) but burned by the retreating German army in 1944.

● **Nennius** ▶ (9th century AD) Welsh antiquary. He is traditionally held to be the author of *Historia Britonum*, a summary of Roman, Saxon, and Celtic legends concerning the early history of Britain. It contains the earliest reference to King ▷Arthur and mentions the poets ▷Aneirin and ▷Taliesin.

● **neoclassicism** ▶ 1. In art and architecture, a style dominant in Europe from the late 18th to mid-19th centuries. Originating in Rome in about 1750, it later spread throughout Europe and to the USA. Although essentially a revival of classical art and architecture (*see* classicism), it was distinguished from similar revivals by its new scientific approach to the recreation of the past. This was largely stimulated by archaeological discoveries at ▷Pompeii, ▷Herculaneum, and elsewhere. Key figures in the early development of neoclassicism were the art historian ▷Winckelmann, who promoted enthusiasm for Greek art, and ▷Piranesi, who did the same for Roman art. Early neoclassical painters included ▷Mengs and Benjamin ▷West but the best known were Jacques Louis ▷David and ▷Ingres, who worked in France. Here neoclassicism developed under the stimulus of the ▷Enlightenment as a reaction to the frivolity of the ▷rococo style. The neoclassical penchant for themes of self-

Horatio, Viscount Nelson ▶ On the quarterdeck of the *Victory* the mortally wounded admiral is supported by his officers and men. Nelson's death in battle became a favourite subject of patriotic paintings and engravings in 19th-century Britain.

sacrifice in painting made it popular during the French Revolution. Other leading neoclassicists were the sculptors ▷Canova and ▷Thorvaldsen and the architects Robert ▷Adam, ▷Soufflot, Claude-Nicholas Ledoux (1736–1806), and Friedrich Gilly (1772–1800). In the UK, the ▷Georgian and ▷Regency styles formed part of the neoclassical movement in architecture. *See also* Empire style.

2. A style of musical composition originating in the 1920s. It was characterized by the use of counterpoint, small instrumental forces, and the use of such 18th-century forms as the concerto grosso. The leading practitioners were ▷Stravinsky and ▷Hindemith.

● **neo-Darwinism** ▷*See* Darwinism.

● **neodymium** ▶ (Nd) A ▷lanthanide element, occurring in the mineral monazite. It is used with lanthanum in ▷misch metal in lighter flints and, as the oxide (Nd_2O_3), together with praseodymium, to produce special dark glasses used in welding goggles. At no 60; at wt 144.24; mp 1021°C; bp 3074°C.

● **neoimpressionism** ▷*See* pointillism.

● **Neolithic** ▶ The final division of the ▷Stone Age. It is characterized by the development of the earliest settled agricultural communities and increasing domestication of animals, apparently occurring first in the Middle East during the 9th millennium BC (*see* Catalhüyük; Jericho). Although man still used only stone tools and weapons, he evolved improved techniques of grinding (as opposed to flaking) stone and the invention of pottery facilitated food storage and preparation.

● **Neo-Melanesian** ▶ The form of ▷pidgin English widely used in Melanesia and New Guinea as a trade and mission language, which has become the native language of some communities. It has a more restricted vocabulary than that of English, on which it is based, a simplified grammar, and a modified sound system.

● **neon** ▶ (Ne) A noble gas present in very small amounts in the earth's atmosphere, discovered in 1898 by Ramsay and M. W. Travers (1872–1961) by fractional distillation of liquid air. In an electrical discharge tube, neon glows orange-red and it is commonly used in advertising signs and voltage indicator lamps. Although some ion-pairs have been reported (for example NeH^+), no stable compounds similar to those of krypton and xenon are yet known. At no 10; at wt 20.179; mp −248.67°C; bp −246.08°C.

● **neoplasticism** ▷*See* Stijl, de.

● **Neoplatonism** ▶ The philosophy, formulated principally by ▷Plotinus that emphasizes an eternal world of order, goodness, and beauty, of which material existence is a weak copy. The chief influences were Plato's concept of the Good, the analysis of love in the *Symposium*, and the speculations about the soul and immortality in the *Phaedo*; Plotinus had little interest in Plato's political and other systems. Neoplatonism helped to shape both medieval Christian theology and Islamic philosophy. ▷*See also* Platonism.

● **neoprene** ▷*See* rubber.

● **Neoptolemus** ▶ In Greek legend, King of Epirus, the son of ▷Achilles. He took part in the ▷Trojan War after his father's death and killed ▷Priam at the altar of Zeus.

● **Neorealism** ▶ An Italian literary movement that originated during the fascist regime in the 1920s and flourished openly after its fall in 1943. Notable writers included the novelists Cesare ▷Pavese, Alberto ▷Moravia, and Ignazio ▷Silone, all of whom suffered persecution for their accurate portrayal of social conditions. The term has also been applied to certain Italian films made during and after World War II. Neorealist films were shot on location, often using nonprofessional actors, and showed a concern for the lives of the poor; classics of the genre include ▷De Sica's *Bicycle Thieves* (1948).

● **neoteny** ▶ A slowing of the rate of growth of the somatic (nonreproductive) parts of the body of an animal, so that larval characteristics may persist when it reaches sexual maturity. The ▷axolotl is a neotenous salamander that rarely assumes the typical adult form under natural conditions, although metamorphosis can be triggered by injection of thyroid hormone. Neoteny is also known in certain tunicates (primitive marine chordates).

● **Nepal, Kingdom of** ▶ A landlocked country in the Himalayas, between China (Tibet) and India. Most of the country consists of a series of mountain ranges and high fertile valleys, with some of the world's highest peaks, including Mount Everest, along its northern border and a region of plain and swamp in the S. Its predominantly Hindu population is of Mongoloid stock, the Gurkhas having been the dominant group since 1769.

Economy: chiefly agricultural, with rice, maize, millet, and wheat as the main crops. Forestry is also important. Mineral resources are sparse, although some mica is being mined. Hydroelectricity is being developed on a large scale and some industry is being encouraged, including jute and sugar. Tourism is the main source of foreign-exchange revenue. Exports, mainly to India, include grains, jute, and timber, as well as medicinal herbs from the mountains.

History: the independent principalities that comprised the region in the middle ages were conquered by the Gurkhas in the 18th century. Nepal was subsequently ruled by the Shah family until 1846, when the throne was seized by Jung Bahadur Rana, whose descendants continue to reign. In 1959 a new constitution provided for an elected parliament, but in 1960 the king dismissed the new government and in 1962 abolished the constitution. A pyramidal structure of local and national councils (*panchayat*) was set up, executive power lying with the king. In 1990 mass unrest led to the restoration of parliamentary democracy under a new constitution. The Nepali Congress Party won multiparty elections in 1991. A Communist-led government was elected in 1994 but was replaced by a series of unstable coalitions from 1996 until 1999, when the Congress Party returned. In 2001 King ▷Birendra, his queen, and six other members of the royal family were shot dead by Crown Prince Dipendra, who then killed himself. Birendra's brother Gyanendra assumed the throne amidst riots and protests. A guerrilla campaign by Maoist insurgents, which began in 1996, escalated dramatically in early 2002.

Kingdom of Nepal

Head of state	King Gyanendra
Official language	Nepali
Official currency	Nepalese rupee of 100 paisa
Area	141 400 sq km (54 600 sq mi)
Population (2000 est)	24 702 000
Capital	Kathmandu

● **nephritis** ▶ (*or* Bright's disease) Inflammation of the kidneys. It may result from infection, as in ▷pyelitis, or from a disorder of the body's system that affects the kidneys (called glomerulonephritis), which causes protein, cells, and blood to appear in the urine and swelling of the body tissues (*see* oedema). This sometimes occurs in children after a streptococcal infection of the throat and often resolves, but other types of glomerulonephritis, occurring more often in adults, may become chronic and result eventually in kidney failure or ▷uraemia.

● **nephron** ▷*See* kidneys.

● **Neptune** ▶ (astronomy) The most distant giant planet, orbiting the sun every 165 years at a mean distance of 4497 million km. It is somewhat smaller (48 600 km in diameter) and more massive (17.2 earth masses) than ▷Uranus, exhibits a similar featureless greenish disc in a telescope, and is thought to be almost identical to Uranus in atmospheric and internal structure. It has eight ▷satellites. Neptune's existence was predicted by John Couch Adams and Urbain Leverrier. It was discovered in 1846 by J. G. Galle, using Leverrier's predicted position. In 1989 it was circumnavigated by ▷Voyager 2.

● **Neptune** ▶ (mythology) An early Italian god associated with water. When seapower became important to Rome, he became the principal Roman sea god and was identified with the Greek ▷Poseidon. He is usually portrayed holding a trident and riding a dolphin.

● **neptunium** ▶ (Np) The first synthetic transuranic element, produced in 1940 at Berkeley, USA, by bombarding uranium with neutrons. Trace quantities are produced in natural uranium ores by the same reaction. It is available in small quantities in nuclear reactors and forms halides (for example NpF_3, $NpCl_4$) and oxides (for example NpO_2). At no 93; at wt (237); mp 639°C; bp 3902°C.

● **nereids** ▶ In Greek mythology, a class of ▷nymphs or female spirits of nature associated with the sea. They were the daughters of the sea god Nereus and Doris, daughter of Oceanus. The best-known Nereids were ▷Amphitrite, wife of Poseidon, and ▷Thetis, mother of Achilles.

● **Nereus** ▶ A primitive Greek sea god, father of the ▷nereids. He had prophetic powers and could change his form.

● **Nergal** ▶ A Mesopotamian god of hunger and devastation and ruler of the underworld. He is also described as a protective god capable of restoring the dead to life and features in the *Epic of Gilgamesh*.

● **Neri, St Philip** ▶ (1515–95) Italian mystic, who founded the Congregation of the Oratory (*see* Oratorians). Settling in Rome (c. 1533), he organized a body of laymen dedicated to charitable works. He was ordained in 1551, becoming a priest at the Church of San Girolamo. Over its nave he built an oratory to hold religious meetings and concerts of sacred music, from which both the name of Neri's order and the word *oratorio* derive. He later ordained his followers, finally installing them in Sta Maria at Vallicella in 1575. Feast day: 26 May.

● **Nernst, Walther Hermann** ▶ (1864–1941) German physical chemist, who first stated the third law of ▷thermodynamics. He also explained the ionization of certain substances when dissolved in water and showed that hydrogen and chlorine combine, when exposed to light, as a result of a chain reaction involving free radicals. He won the 1920 Nobel Prize for Chemistry.

● **Nero (Claudius Caesar)** ▶ (37–68 AD) Roman emperor (54–68), notorious for his cruelty. His early reign was dominated by his mother ▷Agrippina the Younger, ▷Seneca, and Sextus Afranius Burrus but by 62 Nero had thrown off these influences: Agrippina was murdered (59), Burrus died, perhaps by poison (62), and Seneca retired (62). Also in 62, he murdered his wife Octavia in order to marry Poppaea, who herself died in 65 after being kicked by her husband. Nero ruled with a vanity and irresponsibility that antagonized most sectors of society. A conspiracy to assassinate him, after which Seneca was forced to kill himself, failed in 65. In 68, revolts in Gaul, Spain, and Africa and the mutiny of his palace guard forced him to flee Rome and led to his suicide.

● **Neruda, Pablo** ▶ (Neftalí Ricardo Reyes; 1904–73) Chilean poet. He served as a diplomat from 1927 to 1943, was elected a Communist senator in 1943, and was appointed ambassador to France by ▷Allende in 1970. The nihilism of his early poetry, such as *Residencia en la tierra* (1925–31), was replaced by social commitment in *Canto general* (1950) and other works. He won the Nobel Prize in 1971.

● **Nerva, Marcus Cocceius** ▶ (c. 30–98 AD) Roman emperor (96–98), chosen by the Senate to succeed Domitian. Nerva's rule was enlightened: land was allotted to the poor, treason charges were abolished, and administration was improved.

● **Nerval, Gérard de** ▶ (Gérard Labrunie; 1808–55) French poet. His interest in the occult was furthered by travels in the Near East. His works, which anticipate the ▷Symbolists and ▷surrealism, include the story *Sylvie* (1854), the sonnets *Les Chimères* (1854), and the collection of prose and poetry, *Le Rêve et la vie* (1855). He suffered from mental breakdowns from 1841 until his suicide in 1855.

● **nerve** ▷*See* nervous system; neurone.

● **nerve gases** ▶ War gases that inhibit the action of the enzyme acetylcholinesterase, which is essential for the transmission of impulses from nerve to nerve or muscle. Death results from paralysis of the diaphragm leading to asphyxiation. Most nerve gases are derivatives of phosphoric acid and they are toxic in minute quantities (1 mg can be lethal). ▷*See* chemical warfare.

● **Nervi, Pier Luigi** ▶ (1891–1979) Italian engineer and architect, famous for his use of reinforced concrete. His first major building, a stadium in Florence (1930–32), features a concrete cantilevered spiral staircase and curved roof. It was followed between 1935 and 1941 by a series of aircraft hangars (now destroyed). In 1949 he designed the great exhibition hall in Turin and in 1953 was one of the architects of the UNESCO building in Paris. Among his later works were two sports stadiums for the 1960 Rome Olympics and San Francisco Cathedral (1970).

● **nervous system** ▶ The network of nervous tissue in the body. This comprises the central nervous system (CNS), i.e. the ▷brain and ▷spinal cord, and the peripheral nervous system. The latter includes the cranial and spinal nerves with their ▷ganglia and the autonomic nervous system (ANS). The ANS controls unconscious body functions and is coordinated by the ▷hypothalamus. It is divided into the sympathetic and parasympathetic nervous systems, most organs receiving nerves from both systems. The former has such general functions as the regulation of heat loss; the latter controls more localized activities, such as glandular secretion and digestion. The nervous system is chiefly responsible for communication both within the body and between the body and its surroundings. Incoming information passes along sensory ▷neurones to the brain, where it is analysed and compared with ▷memory; nerve impulses then leave the central nervous system along motor nerves, carrying signals to all parts of the body and enabling it to respond continuously. The success of humans as a species is largely due to the complexity of the human nervous system. ▷*See* Plate II.

● **Nesbit, E(dith)** ▶ (1858–1924) British children's writer. Among her best-known books, noted for their realistic characterization of children, are *The Treasure Seekers* (1899), *The Would-be Goods* (1901), and *The Railway Children* (1906).

● **Ness, Loch** ▶ A deep lake in N Scotland, in Highland in the Great Glen. The sighting of a monster (the **Loch Ness monster**) has frequently been reported but never confirmed. Length: 36 km (22 mi). Depth: 229 m (754 ft).

● **Nesselrode, Karl Robert, Count** ▶ (1780–1862) Russian statesman. He represented Russia at the Congress of Vienna (1814–15) and became foreign minister in 1822, dominating the formation of Russian foreign policy until his death. Nesselrode's intransigent policy in the Balkans contributed largely to the outbreak of the ▷Crimean War in 1853.

● **Nessus** ▶ In Greek legend, a centaur who tried to rape Deianira, the wife of ▷Heracles, who killed him with an arrow tipped with the ▷Hydra's poisonous blood. Before he died, Nessus deceitfully told Deianira that she should use his own infected blood as a potion to win back Heracles' love. She smeared the centaur's blood on Heracles' shirt and thus caused his death.

● **nest** ▶ A structure built or taken over by animals to house their eggs, their young, or themselves. Birds' nests are typically bowl-shaped and constructed of twigs, leaves, moss, fur, etc., woven or glued together. The nests of certain swifts are made entirely of saliva and form the major ingredient of bird's nest soup. Some birds nest on the ground, without using any nesting material; others use holes, either naturally occurring or excavated in trees. Nest building in birds is a complex behaviour, triggered by hormones, in which some components are instinctive and others learnt. Nests are also built by ants, termites, bees, and wasps, which construct elaborate tunnel systems, and by fish, amphibians, reptiles, and small mammals.

● **Nestor** ▶ In Greek legend, a king of Pylos. His 11 brothers were killed by ▷Heracles. As a Greek commander in the ▷Trojan War during his old age, he was respected for his wise advice.

● **Nestorians** ▶ The adherents of the Christological doctrines of the Syrian bishop Nestorius (died c. 451). Appointed Patriarch of Constantinople (428), he maintained, probably in overreaction to ▷Monophysite theories, that there were two persons, not merely two natures, in the incarnate Christ. He was accused of heresy and deposed (431). His supporters in his E Syrian homeland formed a church, centred on Edessa. Expelled from Edessa (489), they established themselves in Persia until virtually annihilated by the 14th-century Mongol invasions.

● **Netanyahu, Binyamin** ▶ (1949–   ) Israeli politician and diplomat; prime minister (1996–99). As leader of Likud (1993–99), he was victorious in the election that followed the murder (1995) of Yitzhak ▷Rabin. His premiership was preoccupied with the troubled Palestinian peace process. He was defeated by the Labour leader, Ehud ▷Barak, in the 1999 election.

● **netball** ▶ A seven-a-side court game adapted from ▷basketball and played almost exclusively by girls and women, mainly in English-speaking countries. The court is 100 × 50 ft (30.5 × 15.25 m), divided into three equal zones. The goal is a net mounted 10 ft (3.05 m) above the ground. A team consists of a goal shooter, goal attack, wing attack, centre, wing defence, goal defence, and goalkeeper, who are all restricted to particular areas of the court. The game is played by throwing the ball; players may not run with it.

● **net book agreement** ▷*See* publishing.

● **Netherlandic** ► A subgroup of the Western ▷Germanic languages. It first appears in documents in the 12th century. It is now spoken in Holland and Belgium, where it is called Dutch and Flemish respectively, although the two are in fact the same language. It is the parent language of Afrikaans and is also spoken in parts of Indonesia.

● **Netherlands, Kingdom of the** ► A country in NW Europe, on the North Sea. It is almost entirely flat except for some low hills in the SE, and considerable areas of land have been reclaimed from the sea. Rivers, including the Scheldt, Maas, and Rhine, together with the many canals form an efficient system of inland waterways.

Economy: industry, banking, and commerce are the principal sources of income. Highly developed industries include engineering, petrochemicals and plastics, electronics, metals, and food processing. The production of coal ceased in 1975. Agriculture is highly mechanized and market gardening is important. There is livestock farming, dairy produce being one of the principal exports together with flower bulbs, fuels, chemicals, textiles, and machinery. There is a thriving fishing industry and oysters are a valuable product. Tourism is an important source of revenue as is the port of Rotterdam, which handles a large volume of trade with the European interior.

History: until 1581 the Netherlands formed with present-day Belgium and Luxembourg the region often referred to as the Low Countries. It was under Roman occupation from the 1st century BC to the 4th century AD. It was then overrun by German tribes, of which the Franks had established dominance over the area by the mid-5th century. After the partition of the Frankish empire in 843 the region formed (855) part of Lothair's inheritance and was called Lotharingia. The following centuries saw the rise of powerful principalities, notably the bishopric of Utrecht and the counties of Holland and Guelders, which were fiefs of the German kings before coming under the influence of Burgundy from the 14th century and the Habsburg Emperor Charles V in the early 16th century. Commercial prosperity and the persecution of Protestants fostered a growing movement for independence from the rule of Charles' son Philip II of Spain. In 1581, during the ▷Revolt of the Netherlands, the seven northern provinces—Holland, Zeeland, Utrecht, Overijssel, Gröningen, Drenthe, and Friesland—proclaimed their independence as the United Provinces of the Netherlands under the leadership of William the Silent. War with Spain continued intermittently until, at the conclusion of the Thirty Years' War, Spain recognized the independence of the Dutch Republic in the Peace of Westphalia (1648). In the 17th century, under the rule of the House of Orange-Nassau, from which the stadholder (chief magistrate) was elected until 1795, the Netherlands reached a peak of prosperity (based on trade and fishing) and international prestige, forming a considerable overseas empire. In the 18th century, however, after the death of William III of Orange, who in 1688 had become King of England, the Netherlands declined. In 1795 it fell to Revolutionary France and in 1806 Napoleon made his brother Louis Bonaparte King of Holland. Following Napoleon's defeat the former Dutch Republic was reunited with the southern provinces (the Spanish Netherlands until 1713 and then the Austrian Netherlands), which had remained loyal to the Habsburgs in the 16th century, to form the Kingdom of the Netherlands (1814). In 1830 the S revolted against the union, forming Belgium (1831), and in 1867 Luxembourg became an independent state. The Netherlands, which flourished economically in the second half of the 19th century, remained neutral in World War I but in World War II was occupied by Germany (1940–45) in spite of fierce Dutch resistance. In 1948 the Netherlands joined with Belgium and Luxembourg to form the ▷Benelux economic union; it is now a member of the European Union. The immediate postwar period was dominated by the Dutch colony of Indonesia's fight for independence, achieved in 1950 after bitter and bloody conflict. The 1970s saw terrorist activities by immigrants from the former colony of South Molucca protesting against the In-

donesian occupation of their country. In 1980 Queen Juliana abdicated and was succeeded as head of state by her daughter Princess Beatrix. In the 1980s much argument surrounded the Dutch decision to allow deployment of nuclear weapons on its soil under a 1979 NATO agreement. The Netherlands adopted the European single currency in 1999–2002. A centre-left coalition under Wim Kok (1938–) governed the Netherlands from 1994 until 2002, when the whole cabinet resigned following a report that partly blamed the government for the Dutch army's failure to stop the massacre of Bosnian Muslims at Srebrenica in 1995. During the ensuing election campaign Pim Fortuyn, leader of a populist anti-immigration party, was assassinated, causing deep national shock. The election resulted in the formation of a right-wing coalition under Jan Peter Balkenende, which included some of Fortuyn's followers.

Kingdom of the Netherlands

Head of state	Queen Beatrix
Official language	Dutch
Official currency	euro of 100 cents
Area	41 160 sq km (15 892 sq mi)
Population (2000 est)	15 896 000
Capitals	Amsterdam (legal and administrative); The Hague (seat of government)
Main port	Rotterdam

● **Netherlands Antilles** ► (Dutch name: Nederlandse Antillen) Two groups of West Indian islands in the Lesser Antilles, in the Caribbean Sea some 800 km (497 mi) apart. The S group lies off the N coast of Venezuela and consists of ▷Curaçao and Bonaire; the N group (geographically part of the Leeward Islands) consists of St Eustatius, Saba, and the S part of ▷St Martin. ▷Aruba, geographically part of the S group, became a separate Dutch territory in 1986. Under Dutch control since the 17th century, the islands became self-governing in 1954. The economy is based chiefly on oil refining and ship repairing. Prime minister: S. F. Camelia-Römer. Official currency: Netherlands Antilles guilder of 100 cents. Area: 996 sq km (390 sq mi). Population (2000 est): 221 000. Capital: Willemstad.

● **net national product** ▷*See* gross national product.

● **netsuke** ► A form of sculpture in which small figures or other subjects are carved in ivory, wood, etc. Designed as toggles for purses, pouches, etc., such carvings were perfected in Japan between 1603 and 1867. Early examples were carved from boxwood; later netsukes were inlaid with coral, pearl, and other materials.

● **nettle** ► An annual or perennial herb of the genus *Urtica* (about 30 species), found in temperate regions worldwide. Up to 1.5 m in height, it has simple leaves with toothed margins and bears clusters of small green unisexual flowers. Stems and leaves may have stinging hairs. Family: *Urticaceae*.

Dead-nettles are annual or perennial herbs of the genus *Lamium* (about 40 species), occurring in Europe, temperate Asia, and N Africa. They bear clusters of tubular two-lipped flowers and lack stinging hairs. Family: ▷*Labiatae.*

● **nettle rash** ▷*See* urticaria.

● **Neuchâtel** ► (German name: Neuenburg) 47 00N 6 56E A city in W Switzerland, on Lake Neuchâtel. It has a university (1909) and the Swiss Laboratory of Horological Research. Industries include watch-making and chocolate production. Population (latest est): 32 509.

● **Neue Künstlervereinigung** ► (New Artists' Association) An organization of artists founded in Munich in 1909 by ▷Kandinsky and Alexei von Jawlensky (1864–1941), among others. It organized a major exhibition of international art in 1910 but Kandinsky and Marc defected in 1911, founding Der ▷Blaue Reiter.

● **Neumann, (Johann) Balthasar** ► (1687–1753) German architect, born in Bohemia. One of the greatest rococo architects, Neumann was a military engineer before becoming court architect to the Bishop of Würzburg (1719), for whom he built his most famous palace. His churches include that of Vierzehnheiligen (1743–72).

● **Neumann, John von** ► (1903–57) US mathematician, born in

Hungary. He invented ▷game theory, the branch of mathematics that analyses strategy and is now widely employed for military purposes. He also set quantum theory upon a rigorous mathematical basis.

● **neuralgia** ▶ Sharp or burning pain arising from nerves. Causalgia, one form of neuralgia, is pain in a limb arising from a single nerve and is usually caused by an injury to that nerve. In postherpetic neuralgia, intense pain is experienced at the site of a shingles rash. In trigeminal neuralgia, paroxysms of pain affect one side of the face, particularly the cheek, along the course of the trigeminal nerve.

● **neural network** ▶ A network of interconnected computer elements, called neurons, so designed that an input signal is multiplied by a weighting factor at each neuron before being transmitted to two or more other neurons, and so on. A computer usually simulates the network. For given input data, the overall output signal of the network depends on the weighting factors of the neurons, which can be adjusted to change the output pattern. Such networks, designed to mimic the transmission of impulses in the brain, can be trained to recognize patterns in vast amounts of data and hence to predict the likely trends in future events. They are used in research into artificial intelligence and for making predictions in financial markets.

● **neuritis** ▶ Inflammation of the nerves. This can be caused by leprosy and multiple sclerosis. However, most diseases of peripheral nerves are caused not by inflammation but by degeneration of the nerve, and the word **neuropathy** is used to describe this. Neuropathies can be caused by a variety of conditions, including diabetes, alcoholism, lead poisoning, and vitamin deficiencies, such as beriberi and pellagra.

● **neurohormone** ▶ A chemical (*see* hormone), secreted by nerve cells, that modifies the function of other organs in the body. The ▷hypothalamus, for example, releases hormones that cause the ▷pituitary to secrete its own hormones, the kidney to retain water in the body, and the breast to produce milk.

● **neurology** ▶ The study of the structure (neuroanatomy), function (neurophysiology), and diseases (neuropathology) of the ▷nervous system. A neurologist is a physician who specializes in the diagnosis and treatment of nervous diseases.

● **neurone** ▶ (*or* nerve cell) The functional unit of the ▷nervous system, consisting of a cell body, containing the nucleus; small branching processes called dendrites; and a single long nerve fibre, or axon, which may be ensheathed by fatty material (myelin) and either makes contact with other neurones at ▷synapses or ends at muscle fibres or gland cells. When a neurone is stimulated from outside or by another neurone, a nerve impulse is transmitted electrochemically down the axon (*see* action potential). The frequency of these impulses is the basis for the control of behaviour. Bundles of nerve fibres are bound together to form **nerves**, which transmit impulses from sense organs to the brain or spinal cord (sensory nerves) or outwards from the central nervous system to a muscle or gland (motor nerves).

● **Neuroptera** ▶ An order of slender carnivorous insects (4500 species) with long antennae and two similar pairs of net-veined wings. The order includes the ▷alderflies, ▷snakeflies, and ▷dobsonflies (suborder *Megaloptera*) and the ▷lacewings and ▷antlions (suborder *Plannipennia*).

● **neurosis** ▶ (*or* psychoneurosis) A mental illness in which insight is retained but behaviour is disordered causing suffering to the patient (*compare* psychosis). The symptoms vary considerably: they include a pathologically severe emotional state, as in ▷anxiety or ▷depression; distressing behaviour, as in ▷phobias or ▷obsessions; and physical complaints, as in ▷hysteria. Neuroses are now often referred to as **anxiety disorders**. Interaction between ▷stress and a vulnerable personality usually causes neurotic symptoms. Treatment can include ▷tranquillizers, ▷psychotherapy, and ▷behaviour therapy.

● **neurotransmitter** ▶ A chemical substance released by a nerve ending to transmit an impulse to another nerve cell or to a muscle. In vertebrates the principal neurotransmitters are ▷acetylcholine and ▷noradrenaline; others include gamma amino butyric acid (GABA),

dopamine, and serotonin. When an impulse reaches a nerve ending it triggers the release of neurotransmitter, which diffuses across the gap (synapse) between the adjacent nerve cells and elicits an impulse in the neighbouring cell (or, if it is an inhibitory transmitter, prevents the neighbouring cell from firing). A similar mechanism enables the transmission of nerve impulses to muscle fibres, across neuromuscular junctions.

● **Neusiedl, Lake** ▶ (German name: Neusiedlersee) A lake in Austria and Hungary. Having no natural outlet, its area varies with the rainfall. Many species of bird are to be found on its reedy shore. Area: about 350 sq km (135 sq mi).

● **Neuss** ▶ 51 12N 06 42E A city in NW Germany, in North Rhine-Westphalia near the River Rhine. Known for its annual rifle-shooting contest, it is a canal port and industrial centre. Population (1996 est): 148 796.

● **Neustria** ▶ The western Frankish kingdom created by the partition in 511 of the possessions of ▷Clovis. Approximating in area to N France, it was the rival to ▷Austrasia until 687, when ▷Pepin of Herstal defeated the Neustrians at Tertry.

● **neutrality** ▶ The legal status of a country that remains impartial to other countries at war (belligerents). In ▷international law the rights and obligations of a neutral state are contained in the Hague Conventions V and XIII (1907; *see* Hague Peace Conferences) on neutrality in land war and at sea, respectively. A neutral state must treat belligerents in the same way in matters not relating to war and must not assist either side in its war aims. It must prohibit the use of its territory to equip or recruit men for war, but it may use force to prevent any violation of its neutrality. The most important right conferred by neutrality is inviolability of territory: belligerents may not carry on warfare in a neutral state's territory, which includes its water and air space. The term "nonbelligerence" is used of a state that while neutral is sympathetic to one belligerent, for example the relationship between the USA and the UK from 1939 to 1941.

● **neutrinos** ▶ A group of three elementary particles and their antiparticles. They are classified as leptons, have no charge, and are probably massless. One type of neutrino is associated with the ▷electron, one with the ▷muon, and one with the ▷tau particle. ▷*See* particle physics.

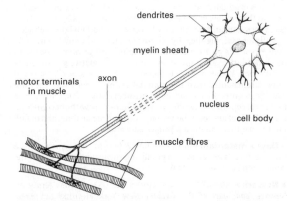

neurone ▶ When a nerve impulse transmitted down the axon of a neurone reaches the motor terminals in muscle fibres, the muscle is stimulated to contract.

● **neutron** ▶ An elementary particle that is a constituent of all atomic nuclei except hydrogen–1. It has no electric charge and its mass is slightly greater than that of the ▷proton. Inside the nucleus the neutron is stable but when free it decays by the ▷weak interaction to a proton, an electron, and an antineutrino (*see* beta decay). Its mean life is about 12 minutes. The neutron was discovered by ▷Chadwick in 1932. The number of neutrons in the nucleus of an atom is called the **neutron number**. ▷*See also* particle physics.

● **neutron activation analysis** ▶ A sensitive method of detecting elements in microgram quantities. The specimen is bombarded with neutrons, some of which are captured by nuclides in the sample to form radioactive nuclides that emit gamma radiation. A gamma-ray spectrometer enables the emitting elements to be identified.

• **neutron bomb** ▷*See* nuclear weapons.

• **neutron star** ▶ A star that has undergone ▷gravitational collapse so that most of the protons and electrons in its atoms have coalesced into neutrons. The density is sufficiently high (about 10^{17} kg m^{-3}) to support the star against further contraction. Neutron stars are thought to form when the mass of the stellar core remaining after a ▷supernova exceeds about 1.4 times the sun's mass. ▷*See also* pulsar.

• **Neva, Battle of the** ▶ (15 July, 1240) The battle in which Sweden was defeated by the forces of Prince Aleksandr Yaroslavich of Novgorod (who thus received the name Nevsky; *see* Alexander Nevsky). His victory ended the expansionist ambitions of Sweden into NW Russia.

• **Nevada** ▶ One of the mountain states in the W USA. Lying mostly within the Great Basin, the state consists of a vast plateau with high mountain ranges rising to well over 1600 m (5249 ft). The only major river is the Colorado in the SE. It is the most arid state in the USA. Most of its population and industry is located in Las Vegas and Reno. Copper smelting is a major industry; others include stone, clay, and glass products, cement, food processing, electronics, and the atomic and space industries. It produces metallic ores and other minerals. Tourism is important. Livestock, especially cattle and sheep, are the principal agricultural products.
History: ceded by Mexico to the USA in 1848, it became a state (1864) during a mining boom (1860–80). Area: 286 297 sq km (110 540 sq mi). Population (1997 est): 1 676 809. Capital: Carson City.

• **Nevers** ▶ 47 00N 3 09N A town in central France, the capital of the Nièvre department on the River Loire. It has a 13th-century cathedral and a palace (15th–16th centuries); industries include engineering and pottery. Population (1990): 43 890.

• **Nevis** ▷*See* St Kitts-Nevis, Federation of.

• **New Age Travellers** ▶ Young men and women who, with their children, lead a nomadic existence, often professing beliefs in Eastern religion (especially Buddhism), meditation and the occult, astrology, homeopathy, organically grown food, and green issues. The attitudes originated on the west coast of the USA and can be traced back to the ▷hippie movement of the 1960s. In the UK New Age Travellers move around the country in convoys of dilapidated vehicles, sometimes camping illegally on private land. For many the lifestyle they espouse is an escape from unemployment or homelessness in the inner cities although others come from relatively prosperous middle-class homes or have dropped out of universities. Most claim to be disenchanted with the materialism of modern life. They are usually resented by conventional members of society, who accuse them of accepting the benefits of the welfare state without contributing to them, of antisocial behaviour, such as drug dealing, and of failing to give their children a proper education.

• **New Amsterdam** ▶ 6 18N 57 30W A port in NE Guyana, on the River Berbice. It serves an area producing sugar cane, rice, and cattle. Population (1990 est): 23 000.

• **Newark** ▶ 40 44N 74 11W A city in the USA, in New Jersey on Newark Bay, part of the Greater New York Metropolitan Area. Founded in 1666, it attracted several inventors, whose developments included patent leather (1818), malleable cast iron (1826), the first photographic film (1888), and electrical measuring instruments (1888). Industries include cutlery, jewellery, and chemicals. Population (1996 est): 268 510.

• **Newark** ▶ (official name: Newark-on-Trent) 53 05N 0 49W A market town in the Midlands of England, in Nottinghamshire on a branch of the River Trent. King John died in the Norman castle, which was later besieged three times in the Civil War. Engineering, building materials, and brewing are important industries. Population (1997): 24 870.

• **New Britain** ▶ A volcanic island in the SW Pacific Ocean, in Papua New Guinea, in the Bismarck Archipelago. Copra and some minerals

are exported. Area: 36 520 sq km (14 100 sq mi). Population (1990): 311 955. Chief town: Rabaul.

• **New Brunswick** ▶ A province of E Canada, on the Gulf of St Lawrence. Heavily forested, it consists of rugged uplands with fertile river valleys; the population is concentrated in the ▷St John River Basin. There is some mixed farming and fishing is important along the Bay of Fundy. Lead, zinc, and some copper are mined at Bathurst. Forestry was a major activity during the 19th century but overcutting and the loss of protected British markets led to a decline in the industry. In an attempt to encourage industrial development the federal government has spent considerable sums of money on improving the infrastructure (factories, roads, etc.).
History: slow settlement by French peasants, beginning in the 17th century, ended shortly after Britain's control of the coastal areas was confirmed in 1713. Colonization from Britain and New England followed, and New Brunswick became a separate colony (1784). It prospered and was a founding member of the Dominion of Canada (1867). Area: 72 092 sq km (27 835 sq mi). Population (1997 est): 762 000; approximately 30% are French speaking. Capital: Fredericton.

• **Newbury** ▶ 51 25N 1 20W A market town in S England, in West Berkshire unitary authority, Berkshire, on the River Kennet. Two indecisive Civil War battles were fought here. Newbury has a famous racecourse and is now a centre of the telecommunications industry. Population (1991): 33 273.

• **New Caledonia** ▶ (French name: Nouvelle Calédonie) An island in the SW Pacific Ocean. With its dependencies (the Isle of Pines, the Loyalty Islands, and others) it forms a French overseas territory. The main industries are nickel mining and meat preserving. Nickel, copra, and coffee are exported. In 1984 violence broke out over plans for independence; in a referendum (1987) the people voted to remain under French sovereignty. Area: 19 103 sq km (7374 sq mi), including dependencies. Population (1994 est): 183 200. Capital: Nouméa.

• **Newcastle** ▶ 32 55S 151 46E A city in Australia, in New South Wales on the mouth of the Hunter River. Iron and steel industries are important. In 1989 12 people died here in Australia's first fatal earthquake. Population (1995 est): 466 000.

• **Newcastle, Thomas Pelham-Holles, 1st Duke of** ▶ (1693–1768) British statesman; Whig prime minister (1754–56, 1757–62). He was secretary of state (1724–54; until 1742 under Sir Robert Walpole). He resigned as prime minister in 1756 because of early reverses in the ▷Seven Years' War but returned in 1757 with foreign affairs in the hands of Pitt the Elder. His brother **Henry Pelham** (1696–1754) was prime minister (1743–54) in the Broad-Bottom administration, which included members of opposing political factions.

• **Newcastle, William Cavendish, Duke of** ▶ (1592–1676) British soldier, author, and patron of the arts. He fought for the royalists in the Civil War and after their defeat at ▷Marston Moor (1644) he went into exile. Returning at the Restoration, he became a patron of writers, including Jonson and Dryden. He wrote books on horsemanship and such plays as *The Triumphant Widow* (1677).

• **Newcastle disease** ▷*See* fowl pest.

• **Newcastle-under-Lyme** ▶ 53 00N 2 14W A town in the Midlands of England, in Staffordshire. There are traces of a 12th-century castle built by John of Gaunt. The principal industries include electrical components and high-tech engineering, as well as the traditional bricks and tiles. Nearby is Keele University (1962) and its science park. Population (1996 est): 122 300.

• **Newcastle upon Tyne** ▶ 1. 54 59N 1 35W A city in NE England, in Newcastle upon Tyne unitary authority, Tyne and Wear; it stands on the N bank of the River Tyne opposite Gateshead, with which it is linked by tunnel and six bridges. It is the principal port and regional centre of NE England, with a 14th-century cathedral and two universities; cultural institutions include the Baltic Centre for Contemporary Art (2000). Industries, which are now very diverse, include marine and electrical engineering, chemicals, flour milling, soap, and paints. Most employment is now in health and education.
History: on the site of a Roman settlement (Pons Aelius), Newcas-

tle derives its name from the castle (1080) built as a defence against the Scots. Newcastle's trade in coal developed in the 13th century, but has now declined. The first locomotives for the Stockton–Darlington Railway were made at George Stephenson's iron works, established here in 1823. Population (1991): 189 150. **2.** A unitary authority in NE England, in Tyne and Wear. Area: 112 sq km (43 sq mi). Population (1995 est): 283 100.

● **Newchang** ▷See Yingkou.

● **Newcombe, John** ► (1944–　) Australian tennis player, who was Wimbledon singles champion in 1967, 1970, and 1971 and US singles champion in 1967 and 1973. Also an outstanding doubles player, he won the Wimbledon doubles championship (1965–66, 1968–70, 1974).

● **New Comedy** ► The final period of Greek comic drama, lasting from c. 320 BC to the mid-3rd century BC and characterized by well-constructed plays on domestic themes. The role of the chorus diminished as the plots became more complicated. The leading writers of this period were ▷Menander and ▷Philemon, whose plays influenced the development of comedy in Rome and later in W Europe. ▷See also Middle Comedy; Old Comedy.

● **Newcomen, Thomas** ► (1663–1729) English blacksmith, who in 1712 constructed an early steam engine. It was based on Thomas ▷Savery's engine and was widely used for pumping water out of mines. It was extremely inefficient, however, and it was not until ▷Watt invented the separate condenser that steam engines became suitable for use in transportation.

● **New Deal** ► (1933–41) Legislation introduced by the US president, F. D. Roosevelt, to ameliorate the effects of the Depression and to initiate social and economic reforms. Emergency legislation enabled sound banks to reopen and regulated credit, currency, and foreign exchange; the gold standard was abandoned and the dollar devalued. Loans on crops, credit, and refinancing of debts and mortgages supported farmers, while the unemployed were helped by direct relief and civil-works programmes. Labour legislation protected the rights of unions to organize and bargain and provided federal agencies to mediate disputes. Ostensibly set up for flood control, the Tennessee Valley Authority (*see* Tennessee River) improved the social and economic status of the backward valley area by developing farming and industry.

● **New Delhi** ▷See Delhi.

● **New Economic Policy** ► (NEP) An economic policy adopted by the Soviet Union between 1921 and 1929. Introduced by Lenin, the NEP replaced War Communism, a period during the civil war of forced labour and brutal requisitioning of food supplies. The NEP, by contrast, gave concessions to private enterprise in agriculture, trade, and industry and aimed at the political neutralization of the peasants. Although the NEP met with considerable success, it was followed under Stalin by more radical policies and the ▷five-year plans.

● **New England** ► An area in the extreme NE USA, bordering on the Atlantic Ocean. It consists of the states of Maine, New Hampshire, Vermont, Massachusetts, Rhode Island, and Connecticut. Explored and named by Capt John Smith (1614), it was first settled by the Puritans (1620). Poor agriculturally, it developed industry early, especially fishing and textiles. Despite the decline of its textile industry the area is now of major economic importance with a flourishing tourist industry. Area: about 164 000 sq km (63 300 sq mi).

● **New England** ► A district of Australia, in New South Wales. Predominantly agricultural, it occupies the N Tableland between the Moonbi Range and the Queensland border. A separatist movement has existed since the early 20th century but so far has been unsuccessful in making the district a separate state.

● **New English Art Club** ► A society of British artists founded in London in 1886 to provide an alternative exhibiting organization to the Royal Academy. Largely catering for avantgarde painters influenced by ▷impressionism, it attracted such artists as ▷Sickert and ▷John. It still exists but is now more conservative.

● **New Forest** ► A woodland area in S England, in Hampshire. Originally an ancient hunting forest it was extended considerably by

William the Conqueror during the 11th century. Today it consists chiefly of oak and beech woodland, coniferous afforestation, and open heathland and is a popular tourist area, noted for its ponies. In 1998 it was given legal protection equivalent to that of a National Park. Area: 336 sq km (130 sq mi).

● **New Forest pony** ► A breed of pony native to the New Forest in S England. Different breeds have been introduced to the wild herds over the years producing marked variations. The smaller ponies tend to be more finely built than the larger ones. They are usually bay or brown and make good childrens' mounts. Height: 1.22–1.47 m (12–14½ hands).

● **Newfoundland** ► A province of E Canada, consisting of the sparsely populated Coast of ▷Labrador on the Atlantic Ocean and the triangular island of Newfoundland, lying between the Ocean and the Gulf of St Lawrence. The island consists of a low forested plateau rolling gently to the NE. Its interior is fairly infertile and most of the population lives along the irregular coast, especially in the SE. Pulp and paper has replaced the declining fisheries as the major industry. Iron, lead, zinc, and copper are mined.

History: discovered by John Cabot (1497), Newfoundland became an English fishing station where settlement was actively discouraged until the 19th century. The island won representative government (1832) and developed steadily until World War I, when it became a dominion. In 1927 it won possession of Labrador's interior and in 1949 became the newest Canadian province. In the last 50 years Newfoundland has not been very prosperous. The island still has a rich tradition of folksong and story-telling. Area: 370 485 sq km (143 044 sq mi). Population (1995 est): 575 400. Capital: St John's.

● **Newfoundland dog** ► A breed of working dog originating in Newfoundland. Massively built and strong swimmers, Newfoundlands have been used for life-saving at sea. The heavy dense black, brown, or black-and-white coat enables them to withstand icy water. Height: 71 cm (dogs); 66 cm (bitches).

● **New France** ► The French colonies in E Canada. From about 1600 French trading posts extended along the St Lawrence River to the Great Lakes. France lost these colonies to Britain in the ▷Seven Years' War (1756–63).

● **Newgate** ► A prison that formerly stood on the present site of the ▷Old Bailey. Originally a gatehouse at the wall of the City of London, it was established as a prison under Henry I. It was twice rebuilt, after the Great Fire (1666) and after the Gordon Riots (1780). Last used as a prison in 1881, it was pulled down in 1902.

● **New Granada** ► A Spanish colony in South America, which in 1717 became a viceroyalty comprising modern Colombia, Ecuador, Panama, and Venezuela (which was later detached). It was liberated by Simón ▷Bolívar in 1819. From 1830 to 1858 Colombia and Panama formed the Republic of New Granada.

● **New Guinea** ► An island in the SW Pacific Ocean, the second largest island in the world, separated from Australia by the Torres Strait. It consists of the Indonesian province of ▷Irian Jaya in the W and ▷Papua New Guinea in the E. Mountainous and forested, it is largely undeveloped and is famed for its unique species of butterflies and birds. Its linguistically diverse tribal population consists of Melanesian, Negrito, and Papuan ethnic groups.

History: known to Europeans from 1511, the island was colonized by the Dutch in the 18th century. In 1828 the Dutch controlled the W part; this became part of Indonesia in 1963. The SE was colonized by Britain and the NE by Germany in the late 19th century. Area: 775 213 sq km (299 310 sq mi). Population (1992 est): 6 475 000.

● **Newham** ► A borough of E Greater London, created in 1965 from the former county boroughs of East Ham and West Ham, and parts of Barking and Woolwich. Area: 36 sq km (14 sq mi). Population (1994 est): 226 800.

● **New Hampshire** ► A state in the NE USA, in New England. It is generally hilly, with many lakes; a low-lying area adjoins the Atlantic Ocean in the SE. Manufacturing is the principal source of employment, centred mainly in the S. Electrical and other machinery together with paper and wood are the principal products. Tourism is the other major industry. The state's farmers produce livestock, dairy and poultry products, and vegetables. Mining is of minor importance and the large deposits of granite are no longer quarried to any great extent.

History: one of the 13 original colonies, it was first settled by English colonists about 1627, becoming a royal province in 1679. One of the first states to declare its independence, it became a state in 1788. Area: 24 097 sq km (9304 sq mi). Population (1996 est): 1 162 481. Capital: Concord.

● **New Haven** ► 41 18N 72 55W A city and seaport in the USA, in Connecticut on Long Island Sound. It is best known as the site of Yale University (1701). It was here that Charles Goodyear invented vulcanized rubber. Industries include hardware, watches, and firearms. Population (1996 est): 124 665.

● **New Hebrides** ▷*See* Vanuatu, Republic of.

● **Ne Win, U** ► (1911–) Burmese statesman; president (1974–81). He fought for Burmese independence and, when this was achieved in 1948, became defence minister. In 1958 he became prime minister after forcing U ▷Nu's resignation and, after leaving office in 1960, again seized power in 1962. In 1972 the 1947 constitution was abolished and replaced (in 1974) by one introducing a single-party assembly and the presidency of Ne Win. He remained effective leader until 1988.

● **New International Economic Order** ► A series of economic measures adopted by the United Nations General Assembly in 1974, aimed at achieving an international distribution of wealth, income, and political power comparable to that of western Europe. Because the existing world economy favours the industrial nations, the most important measures concern the control of basic raw materials supplied by the developing nations, especially by international commodity agreements. Other measures include curbs on multinational companies and taxing nonterritorial airways and waterways.

● **New Ireland** ► A volcanic island in the SW Pacific Ocean, in Papua New Guinea in the Bismarck Archipelago. Copra is exported. Area: 8650 sq km (3340 sq mi). Population (1990): 87 194. Chief town: Kavieng.

● **New Jersey** ► A state in the NE USA, on the mid-Atlantic coast. The Kittatinny Mountains extend across the NW corner of the state, SE of which lies a belt of lowland containing most of New Jersey's major cities. The remaining area to the S consists of coastal plains, which cover more than half the state. One of the most highly urbanized and densely populated states, it is a major industrial centre. The chief manufactures are chemicals, textiles, electrical machinery, and food products. Although mining is relatively unimportant, New Jersey is a centre for copper smelting and refining as well as a major producer of titanium concentrate. Agriculture is also well developed and a variety of crops are grown, including asparagus, tomatoes, peppers, sweet corn, potatoes, and peaches. Its beaches, forests, and mountain regions form the basis of a thriving tourist industry.

History: one of the original 13 colonies, it was first settled by the Dutch in the 1620s, coming under British control in 1664. It became a state in 1787. Area: 20 295 sq km (7836 sq mi). Population (1996 est): 7 987 933. Capital: Trenton.

● **Newlands, John Alexander Reina** ► (1837–98) British chemist whose law of octaves (1864) stated that if the elements were listed in order of their atomic weights, there was a repetition of properties, as in a musical octave, after every seven elements. The idea was ridiculed until Mendeleyev's ▷periodic table was announced in 1869, when the value of Newlands' work was recognized.

● **New London** ► 41 21N 72 06W A city and seaport in the USA, in Connecticut at the mouth of the Thames River on Long Island Sound. The US Coast Guard Academy and a submarine base (1916) are located here. The annual Harvard-Yale boat race is held here. Industries include shipbuilding and textiles. Population (latest est): 28 800.

● **Newlyn School** ► A group of artists based at Newlyn, Cornwall between 1880 and 1890. They included Stanhope Forbes (1857–1947).

● **Newman, John Henry, Cardinal** ► (1801–90) British churchman and a leader of the ▷Oxford Movement, until his conversion to

Roman Catholicism (1845). He was educated at Oxford, later becoming a fellow and tutor there. While vicar of St Mary's, Oxford (1827–43), he published *Parochial and Plain Sermons* (1834–42) and began the series entitled *Tracts for the Times* in 1833. He wrote many of these, including the most controversial one, *Tract 90*, which argued that the Thirty-Nine Articles were not incompatible with Roman Catholicism. In Rome (1846) he joined the ▷Oratorians and later established his own Oratorian congregation at Edgbaston. Of his later works the most famous are *Idea of a University* (1852), his poem, *Dream of Gerontius* (1866), and a theological work, *Grammar of Assent* (1870). His spiritual autobiography, *Apologia pro vita sua* (1864), was a reply to Charles Kingsley's criticisms of Roman Catholicism. He was made a cardinal in 1879. In 1991 he was awarded the title 'Venerable', the first stage of canonization.

Paul Newman ► As the somewhat seedy trickster in the film *The Sting* (1973).

● **Newman, Paul** ► (1925–) US film actor and political activist. He has frequently played the roles of cynical and witty heroes, notably in *Hud* (1963), *Butch Cassidy and the Sundance Kid* (1969), and *The Sting* (1973); among his more recent films are *Absence of Malice* (1981), *The Verdict* (1982), the Oscar-winning *The Color of Money* (1986), and *Twilight* (1998). From 1968 he also directed and produced films. He is married to the US actress Joanne Woodward (1930–).

● **Newmarket** ► 52 15N 0 25E A market town in E England, in Suffolk. It is the centre of British horse racing; many racehorses are bred and trained here and several important racing events take place annually. Caravans and electronic equipment are manufactured. Population (1991): 16 498.

● **New Mexico** ► One of the mountain states in the SW USA. There are three main physical regions: a flat tableland in the E, a central mountainous region cut N–S by the Valley of the Rio Grande, and a region of mountains and plains in the W. The relatively sparse population is mainly concentrated in the urban centres, especially in Albuquerque. Its oil and natural-gas deposits are important, and it is a leading producer of uranium ore, manganese ore, and potash. There are also large commercial forests. Livestock is the main agricultural product, and crops include hay, cotton, wheat, and sorghum grains. Problems of irrigation are mitigated by the Rio Grande and the Pecos rivers. There is limited manufacturing. Tourism is an important source of revenue.

History: a Spanish possession from the 16th century, it was under Mexican rule when it was annexed by the USA in 1848. Following a period of Indian wars and land disputes typical of the Far West at this time, it became a state (1912). Area: 315 113 sq km (121 666 sq mi). Population (1996 est): 1 713 407. Capital: Santa Fe.

● **New Model Army** ► The parliamentary army formed in 1645 during the English ▷Civil War. Organized by Sir Thomas ▷Fairfax, it united the various local armies; its core comprised the forces of the Eastern Association led by Oliver ▷Cromwell. It wielded increasing political power after its success at ▷Naseby (1645), emerging the victor from its power struggle with the ▷Long Parliament. In 1650 Cromwell became its commander in chief.

● **New Netherland** ▶ A Dutch colony in North America. Established in 1613, the colony was centred on New Amsterdam, which after its conquest by the English (1664) was renamed New York.

● **New Orleans** ▶ 30 00N 90 03W A city and major port in the USA, in Louisiana. Known as the Crescent City because of its location on a bend in the Mississippi River, it is one of the leading commercial and industrial centres of the South with food processing, oil, chemical, shipbuilding, and ship repairing industries. The Vieux Carré (French Quarter) has many historic buildings, including St Louis Cathedral (1794) and the Cabildo (1795). An educational centre, New Orleans possesses several universities. The famous Mardi Gras festival is held here annually.
　　History: founded in 1718, New Orleans became the capital of the French colonial region of Louisiana before passing to Spain in 1763. It returned briefly to France in 1803 but passed to the USA in the same year. Jazz had its origins among the Black musicians of New Orleans during the late 19th century. Population (2000): 484 674.

● **New Orleans style** ▶ The original style of jazz, which developed in the Storyville district of New Orleans. The New Orleans style began around 1890 with the band of Buddy Bolden (1868–1941) and continued until the 1920s when ▷swing bands gained popularity. In New Orleans jazz, the melody of a song was treated as a basis for improvisation by the cornet, clarinet, or trombone, supported by double bass, drums, guitar, and piano. Important New Orleans jazz musicians include Louis Armstrong and Jelly Roll Morton. *Compare* Dixieland.

● **New Plymouth** ▶ 39 03S 174 04E A port in New Zealand, in W North Island on North Taranaki Bight. An important dairy centre, it is known for its export of cheese. New Zealand's chief natural gas field is nearby, at Kapuni. Population (1995 est): 49 800.

● **Newport** ▶ 50 42N 1 18W A market town and port in S England, the administrative centre of the Isle of Wight on the River Medina. Nearby are Carisbrooke Castle and Parkhurst Prison. Population (1991): 20 574.

● **Newport** ▶ (Welsh name: Casnewydd ar Wysg) **1.** 51 35N 3 00W A city and port in SE Wales, in Newport county borough, near the mouth of the River Usk. Iron and steel, engineering, chemicals, and electronics are important industries. Its parish church became the cathedral for the Monmouth diocese in 1921. Newport was granted city status in 2002. Population (1991): 115 522. **2.** A county borough in SE Wales, created in 1996 from part of Gwent. Area: 190 sq km (73 sq mi). Population (1999 est): 136 800.

● **Newport News** ▶ 36 59N 76 26W A city and seaport in the USA, in SE Virginia on the James River estuary. A major shipbuilding and ship-repair centre, its manufactures include metal products and building materials. Population (2000): 180 150.

● **New Providence** ▷*See* Bahamas, Commonwealth of the; Nassau.

● **Newry** ▶ 54 11N 6 20W A city and port in Northern Ireland, in Co Down, on Carlingford Lough. Close to the border with the Republic, it has suffered from high unemployment and sectarian violence. It was granted city status in 2002. Population (1991): 82 943.

● **Newry and Mourne** ▶ A district in Northern Ireland, in Co Down. Area: 886 sq km (342 sq mi). Population (1999 est): 87 700.

● **news agency** ▶ An organization that gathers news and sells it to newspapers, broadcasting companies, etc. The four largest international news agencies are Reuters (*see* Reuter, Paul Julius, Baron von), Associated Press, Agence France-Presse, and Itar Tass (Information Telegraph Agency of Russia, Telegraph Agency of Sovereign States).

● **New Siberian Islands** ▶ (Russian name: Novosïbirskiye Ostrova) A Russian archipelago off the N coast, between the Laptev Sea and the East Siberian Sea. Kotelny, Faddeyevskii, and New Siberia are the largest islands and the Lyakhov Islands to the S are sometimes considered

part of the group. There is no permanent population. Total area: 35 100 sq km (13 549 sq mi), including the Lyakhov Islands.

● **New South Wales** ▶ A state of SE Australia, bordering on the Pacific Ocean. It consists of extensive plains in the W, separated from the narrow coastal belt by the ▷Great Dividing Range with the ▷Snowy Mountains and part of the Australian Alps in the SE. The chief rivers are the Murray, Darling, and Murrumbidgee. It is the most populous and economically important state of Australia. Agricultural products include beef cattle, cereals (of which wheat is the most important), fruit and vegetables (especially in the southern ▷Riverina district), wool, and dairy produce, which includes large quantities of butter and milk products processed at cooperative factories along the coast. Fishing, including oyster farming, and forestry are also important. Minerals extracted include coal, silver, lead, zinc, and copper. Over half the population live in Sydney, where most of the industries are located; these include the manufacture of iron and steel, textiles, electrical goods, and chemicals. Separatist movements, resenting the domination of the state, exist in the districts of ▷New England and Riverina. In 1994 bush fires caused considerable damage in the state. Area: 801 428 sq km (309 433 sq mi). Population (1999 est): 6 441 680. Capital: Sydney.

● **New Spain, Viceroyalty of** ▶ (1535–1821) A Spanish colony in the New World comprising modern Mexico, the SW USA, and parts of Central America. It was established under Antonio de ▷Mendoza.

● **newspaper** ▶ A publication issued at regular intervals and containing information and opinion about current affairs. The earliest newspaper may have been the ancient Roman ▷*Acta Diurna* (59 BC) but newspapers in their modern form originated in Europe in the 17th century. Early English newspapers include the *Oxford Gazette* (founded in 1665), which became the *London Gazette* in 1668, and the *Daily Courant* (founded in 1702), the first daily newspaper. In 1785 John ▷Walter I founded the *Daily Universal Register*, which became *The Times* in 1788. The political influence of newspapers was quickly appreciated by governments, which introduced such legislation as the Stamp Act (1712), imposing a duty of a halfpenny on each half-sheet and a penny on each whole sheet. The most notable victory in the campaign for press freedom was made in the 18th century by John ▷Wilkes, who obtained the right to publish parliamentary reports, but not until 1855 was the Stamp Act repealed. The rapid expansion of newspapers during the 19th century was influenced by improvements in printing technology, the establishment of international ▷news agencies, and the increase in literacy. In 1903 the first tabloid, the *Daily Mirror*, was founded by Alfred Harmsworth (*see* Northcliffe, Alfred Harmsworth, 1st Viscount) and introduced to England the popular ▷journalism pioneered in the USA by such newspapers as the *San Francisco Examiner* (1880) and the *Morning Journal* (1895), both founded by William Randolph ▷Hearst.
　　The emergence of the great press families (e.g. Beaverbrook, Thomson) and more recently of multinational communications empires, such as that of ▷Murdoch, has led to the multiownership of newspapers, on which two Royal Commissions have reported critically. Controversy has also focused on the scope of the Official Secrets Acts (1911, 1920, 1939, 1989) and the system for issuing D-notices to restrict publication of sensitive material. There has been concern, too, about distortions and invasions of privacy by the tabloid press. The Calcutt Report (1993; Sir David Calcutt) suggested ways of curbing such invasions, which some editors regarded as unacceptable censorship of the press (*see also* Press Complaints Commission). The advent of computer-aided typesetting in the 1980s broke the power of the print unions and led to an expansion of the British newspaper industry, which relocated from its traditional home in Fleet Street. Great newspapers of the world include the *New York Times* and *Washington Post* in the USA, the *Asahi Shimbun* and *Mainichi Shimbun* in Japan, the *Age* in Melbourne (Australia), the *Corriere della Sera* in Milan (Italy), *Le Figaro* in France, the *Neue Zürcher Zeitung* in Zürich (Switzerland), and the *Frankfurter Allgemeine Zeitung* in Germany.

● **newt** ▶ A salamander of a family (*Salamandridae*) occurring in Europe, Asia, and North America. The European smooth newt (*Triturus vulgaris*) is greenish brown with dark-brown spots and an orange belly. It grows to 10 cm (including a 5-cm tail). Newts live mainly on land, hibernating under stones in winter and returning to water to breed in spring. The European fire salamander (*Salamandra salamandra*) bears live young and produces a poisonous skin secretion when harmed.

● **New Testament** ▶ The 27 books that constitute the second major division of the Christian ▷Bible. The title is intended to convey the belief that the books contain the fulfilment of prophecies made in the ▷Old Testament. Written in Greek, the New Testament has four divisions: the four Gospels (Matthew, Mark, Luke, and John); the ▷Acts of the Apostles; the ▷Epistles, mainly written by St Paul; and the Book of ▷Revelation. It covers a period from the birth of ▷Jesus to the spread of Christianity throughout the Roman Empire and was written between about 50 and 100 AD.

● **newton** ▶ (N) The ▷SI unit of force defined as the force required to give a mass of one kilogram an acceleration of one metre per second per second. Named after Sir Isaac ▷Newton.

Isaac Newton ▶ A stencil drawing after the portrait by Godfrey Kneller, painted in 1702.

● **Newton, Sir Isaac** ▶ (1642–1727) British physicist and mathematician, who was a professor at Cambridge University (1669–1701), MP for the university (1689–90), and Master of the Mint (1699–1727). One of the greatest scientists of all time, Newton did much of his original work in his parents' Lincolnshire home immediately after his graduation, while the university was closed (1665–67) during the Great Plague. His first discovery was the law of gravitation, apocryphally inspired by the realization that an apple falling from a tree is attracted by the same force that holds the moon in orbit. Gravitation required a precise definition of force, this Newton also supplied in his laws of motion (*see* Newtonian mechanics). Newton's second major work in this period was the invention of the calculus; ▷Leibniz and Newton bickered unbecomingly for some years as to who had the idea first. Probably they both invented the method independently. His third contribution was in optics: he recognized that white light is a mixture of coloured lights, which can be separated by refraction. His incorrect belief that the resulting chromatic aberration of a lens could not be corrected, inspired him to invent the reflecting telescope. Newton's principal publications were *Philosophiae naturalis principia mathematica* (1686–87) and *Optics* (1704), which held that light is a corpuscular phenomenon.

Although Newton became a Whig MP he made little impact in politics; he did, however, reform the coinage when he was Master of the Mint. He was president of the Royal Society from 1703 until his death and was knighted in 1705. A considerable amount of Newton's later life was spent delving into alchemy, astrology, and theological speculation. From biblical chronology he calculated the day of the earth's creation to be about 3500 BC. Newton is buried in Westminster Abbey. Einstein said of him: "in one person, he combined the experimenter, the theorist, the mechanic and, not least, the artist in exposition."

● **Newton Abbot** ▶ 50 32N 3 36W A market town in SW England,

in Devon at the head of the Teign estuary. William of Orange was first proclaimed king here in 1688. Population (1991): 23 801.

● **Newtonian mechanics** ▶ The branch of ▷mechanics concerned with systems in which the results of ▷quantum theory and the theory of ▷relativity can be ignored. Based on **Newton's three laws of motion**, it forms an important part of ▷classical physics (also known as **classical mechanics**). Newton's first law of motion states that a body remains at rest or moves with constant velocity in a straight line unless acted upon by a ▷force. This law thus defines the concept of force. The second law, which defines mass, states that the ▷acceleration (*a*) of a body is proportional to the force (*f*) causing it. The constant of proportionality is the mass (*m*) of the body: $f = ma$. The third law states that the action of a force always produces a reaction in the body. The reaction is of equal magnitude but opposite in direction to the action.

● **Newton's rings** ▶ A series of light and dark rings formed in a plano-convex lens if monochromatic light is shone onto the lens when it rests on a plane mirror. First observed by ▷Newton, they are caused by ▷interference between light reflected by the mirror and light reflected at the curved surface of the lens.

● **Newtown** ▶ 52 32N 3 19W A market town in central Wales, in Powys on the River Severn. Designated a new town in 1967, it has a number of light industries. It is the birthplace of Robert Owen. Population (1991): 10 548.

● **Newtownabbey** ▶ A district in Northern Ireland, in Co Antrim. Area: 156 sq km (60 sq mi). Population (1991): 74 035.

● **new towns** ▶ Planned towns built in one phase, as opposed to towns that have evolved gradually in response to economic and social pressures. Under the guidance of Ebenezer Howard ▷garden cities, e.g. Letchworth (1903), were built in the UK to provide an alternative way of life to that in the crowded cities. After World War II new towns were built to cater for the expanding populations of large towns, e.g. ▷Milton Keynes, or to provide economic growth centres in declining areas, e.g. Peterlee, Co Durham.

● **Newtown St Boswells** ▶ 55 34N 2 40W A town in SE Scotland, the administrative centre of Scottish Borders on the River Tweed. Population (1991): 1108.

● **New Wave** ▶ (or Nouvelle Vague) A group of French film directors who emerged in the late 1950s; their films were characterized by a rejection of Hollywood conventions in favour of their own highly original individual styles. The directors, most of whom were associated with the magazine *Cahiers du Cinéma* and the ▷auteur theory of film criticism, included ▷Truffaut, ▷Chabrol, ▷Resnais, and ▷Godard.

● **New Westminster** ▶ 49 10N 122 58W A city and port in W Canada, in British Columbia on the Fraser River. Bordering on E Vancouver, it manufactures wood products, foods, and oil. Population (latest est): 38 550.

● **New World** ▶ A name for the American continent, used especially by early emigrants and in describing the geographical distribution of plants and animals. *Compare* Old World.

● **New World monkey** ▶ A ▷monkey native to the Americas. There are two families: the *Cebidae* (37 species) including ▷sakis, ▷titis, ▷howler monkeys, ▷capuchin monkeys, ▷squirrel monkeys, ▷spider monkeys, ▷woolly monkeys, and the ▷douroucouli; and the *Callithricidae* (33 species) containing ▷marmosets and ▷tamarins. All are restricted to Central and South America and are largely arboreal.

● **New York** ▶ A state in the NE USA. It is basically an upland region, dissected by the valleys of the Mohawk and Hudson Rivers. Traffic flowing from the Great Lakes to the major port of New York City has provided many opportunities for industrial development and today New York is the chief manufacturing state in the USA. Its varied products include clothing, electrical machinery, and processed foods and printing and publishing are among the most notable industries. The presence of New York City also makes it the commercial, financial, and cultural centre of the nation. The most important agricultural activity is dairying; other leading products include apples, grains, and potatoes.

History: one of the 13 original colonies, it was first settled by the

Dutch in the early 17th century. It became an English colony in 1664 and was prominent in the American Revolution. Area: 128 402 sq km (49 576 sq mi). Population (1998 est): 18 175 301. Capital: Albany.

● **New York** ► 40 45N 74 00W The largest city in the USA, situated in New York state on New York Bay at the mouth of the Hudson River. Divided into five boroughs—▷Manhattan, ▷Brooklyn, the ▷Bronx, ▷Queens, and Richmond (coextensive with ▷Staten Island), it is the nation's leading seaport and one of its most important business, manufacturing, communications, and cultural centres. As one of the world's financial centres (*see* Wall Street), it is the site of many large corporations and the New York and American Stock Exchanges. The principal manufactures include furs, jewellery, chemicals, metal products, and processed foods. New York is also the main centre of US television and radio and book publishing. Its most notable features include Central Park, the fashionable shops of Fifth Avenue, the ▷Statue of Liberty, Times Square, ▷Greenwich Village, the Brooklyn Bridge (1883), Rockefeller Center, St Patrick's Cathedral (1858–79), and a large number of extremely tall buildings (⬜skyscrapers), such as the Empire State Building (1931), and the United Nations Headquarters (1951), which give Manhattan its characteristic skyline. As well as the famous Broadway theatre district and the Lincoln Center for the Performing Arts, which houses two opera companies, a symphony orchestra, and a ballet company, there are numerous museums and art galleries, including the Metropolitan Museum of Art (1872), the Museum of Modern Art (1929), and the ▷Guggenheim Museum (founded 1939). Educational institutions include Columbia University (founded as King's College in 1754); the City University of New York (1847), and New York University (1831).
History: on 3 September, 1609, Henry Hudson sailed into New York Bay and his glowing reports attracted its founding Dutch colonists, who arrived in 1620. In 1625 New Amsterdam, situated at the S tip of Manhattan, became the capital of the newly established colony of New Netherland and the following year the whole island of Manhattan was bought from the Indians for the equivalent of $24. In 1664 the city was captured by the English for the Duke of York and promptly renamed. In the 17th century it became a base for prosperous merchants and such pirates as Capt Kidd. From 1789 until 1790 it was the first capital of the USA. The opening of the Erie Canal in 1825 ensured its pre-eminence as a commercial city and seaport. Following the US Civil War, it began to merge with neighbouring towns, such as Brooklyn, and the metropolis began to form. Early in the 20th century the arrival of millions of European immigrants supplied New York with limitless cheap labour. In recent years many of its middle-class inhabitants have moved to the suburbs of the metropolis and the city subsequently lost a considerable amount of tax revenue. During the mid-1970s New York's financial crisis worsened and the city was narrowly saved from bankruptcy by emergency loans. In the 1970s and 1980s it acquired a reputation for street violence, but this was reduced in the later 1990s. On ▷September 11, 2001 New York saw the destruction of one of its great landmarks, the ▷World Trade Center, in a terrorist outrage that cost nearly 3000 lives. Population (1998 est): 7 420 166.

● **New Zealand** ► A country in the Pacific Ocean, to the SE of Australia. It consists of two main islands, ▷North Island and ▷South Island, together with several smaller ones, including ▷Stewart Island to the S. ▷Ross Dependency and the ▷Tokelau Islands are dependencies, and the ▷Cook and Niue Islands are self-governing. Most of the population is of British descent with a large Maori minority.
Economy: the main basis of the economy is livestock rearing, especially sheep farming. Farms are highly mechanized and there is considerable research into agricultural science and technology. Meat, wool, and dairy products are the main exports, which were adversely affected when the UK joined the EC in 1973; since then New Zealand has opened up markets in other parts of the world. Mineral resources include coal, gold, limestone and silica sand; oil and natural gas have been found and are being increasingly exploited. Hydroelectricity now supplies over 95% of New Zealand's power. Timber production has increased and there is a growing pulp and paper industry. Other industries, such as food processing, textiles, engineering, and electronic goods, have also been expanding. Tourism is now the fastest growing economic activity. Until the mid-1980s New Zealand had one of the most highly regulated and subsidized economies in the

capitalist world. Since then both Labour and National Party governments have pioneered radical policies of privatization and deregulation, including the ending of all agricultural subsidy.
History: from about the 12th century the islands were inhabited by the Maoris, a Polynesian people. The first European to discover New Zealand was ▷Tasman in 1642, who called it Staten Land, later changed to Nieuw Zealand; in 1769 the coast was explored by ▷Cook. During the early part of the 19th century it was used as a whaling and trading base. By the Treaty of ▷Waitangi in 1840 the Maori chiefs ceded sovereignty to Britain and a colony was established. British settlement increased and sheep farming developed. After two wars with the Maoris over land rights, peace was reached in 1871. New Zealand was made a dominion in 1907 and became fully independent by the Statute of Westminster in 1931. By the early part of the 20th century its social administration policy was one of the most advanced in the world. Free compulsory primary education was introduced in 1877 and in 1893 New Zealand became the first country in the world to give women the vote. A comprehensive social security system was established in 1898. Since World War II New Zealand has played an increasing role in international affairs, especially in the Far East. In the 1970s its economy suffered from world recession, and efforts to curb inflation included a prices and wages policy. By contrast the 1980s and 1990s saw the implementation of radical free-market policies, including major reconstruction of the welfare state. In 1985 relations with the USA became strained when the new Labour government under David ▷Lange prohibited nuclear vessels from entering New Zealand waters; in 1989 Geoffrey Palmer succeeded Lange as prime minister. In 1990 the National Party was returned to office under James ▷Bolger, who retained the premiership until 1997, when he handed it to Jenny ▷Shipley. The 1999 general election saw a victory for the Labour Party, led by Helen ▷Clark.

New Zealand

Head of state	Queen Elizabeth II, represented by the governor-general, Dame Silvia Cartwright
Official languages	English and Maori
Official currency	New Zealand dollar of 100 cents
Area	268 704 sq km (103 719 sq mi)
Population (2000 est)	3 835 000
Capital	Wellington
Main port	Auckland

● **Nexø, Martin Andersen** ► (1869–1954) Danish novelist. His upbringing in the slums of Copenhagen led him to become a socialist and subsequently a communist. He achieved worldwide fame with his novels *Pelle erobreren* (Pelle the Conqueror; 1906–10) and *Ditte menneskebarn* (Ditte: Daughter of Man; 1917–21), depicting the struggles of the working class. In 1949 he settled in East Germany.

● **Ney, Michel, Prince of Moscow** ► (1769–1815) French marshal, whom Napoleon described as "the bravest of the brave." He served throughout the Revolutionary Wars and, under Napoleon, won the great victory at Elchingen (1805) and fought at ▷Jena and Auerstädt (1806) and ▷Friedland (1807). His extraordinary courage in the French retreat from Moscow (1812–13) prompted Napoleon's accolade. When Napoleon returned from Elba, Ney rallied to the former emperor's cause and after his defeat at Waterloo was shot as a traitor.

● **Nez Percé** ► A North American Indian people of the plateau region of Idaho. Their culture, typical of this area, was based on salmon fishing. After acquiring horses in the 18th century, they frequently left their riverside villages to hunt buffalo on the Plains and thus acquired many Plains Indian traits. They became expert horse breeders. Their language belongs to the Sahaptin division of the ▷Penutian family.

● **Ngo Dinh Diem** ► (1901–63) Vietnamese statesman; president of South Vietnam (1955–63). Unsympathetic to Ho Chi Minh's ▷Viet Minh, he went into exile during the war of independence against France. Returning just before partition, he was appointed prime minister (1954) under US influence and abolished the monarchy and became president (1955). His government was threatened by the guerrilla activities of the ▷Viet Cong against whom he sought US aid (*see* Vietnam War). He was assassinated, together with his brother Ngo Dinh Nhu, in a military coup in 1963.

● **Nguni** ► A division of the ▷Bantu-speaking peoples of S Africa. It includes the ▷Swazi, ▷Xhosa, and ▷Zulu.

● **Nha Trang** ► 12 15N 109 10E An ancient port in S Vietnam, at the mouth of the River Cai. Nearby are four shrines dating from the 7th to 12th centuries. The chief industry is fishing. Population (1992 est): 221 331.

● **NHS** ▷*See* National Health Service.

● **Niagara Falls** ► Two waterfalls on the US-Canadian border, on the Niagara River between Lakes Erie and Ontario. The American Falls, 51 m (167 ft) high and 300 m (1000 ft) wide, are straight while the Horseshoe Falls (Canada), 49 m (162 ft) high and 790 m (2600 ft) wide, are curved. Much of their flow is diverted to generate electricity but they remain spectacular tourist attractions. Shipping between the two lakes avoids the Falls by the Welland Ship Canal.

● **Niamey** ► 13 32N 2 05E The capital (since 1926) of Niger, on the River Niger. It has grown rapidly as the country's administrative and commercial centre. Its university was founded in 1973. Population (1995 est): 495 000.

● **Niarchos, Stavros Spyros** ► (1909–96) Greek businessman and the owner of one of the largest independent shipping lines in the world. In rivalry with his brother-in-law, Aristotle ▷Onassis, he pioneered the construction of supertankers during the 1950s.

● **Nibelungenlied** ► (German: *Song of the Nibelungs*) A Middle High German epic poem composed in the 13th century but drawing on earlier material. Its theme is the disastrous rivalries following ▷Siegfried's killing of the Burgundian princes called Nibelungs and his seizure of their treasure. A variant of the story also occurs in the Old Norse *Volsungasaga* (*see* sagas), in which Siegfried is called Sigurd. ▷Wagner's operatic cycle, *The Ring of the Nibelung*, uses elements from both the Germanic and Old Norse versions.

● **Nicaea, Councils of** ► Two ecumenical councils of the Christian Church held at Nicaea, now Iznik (Turkey). **1.** (325) The council that was summoned by the Byzantine emperor Constantine to establish Church unity and suppress ▷Arianism. The number of participating bishops was, according to later reports, 318. The ▷Nicene Creed was the major doctrinal formulation. **2.** (787) The council that was summoned by the Byzantine empress Irene to condemn ▷iconoclasm. Its initial assembly at Constantinople (786) was disrupted by iconoclasts, but the following year at Nicaea it approved a formula for restoring the veneration of icons.

● **Nicaragua, Republic of** ► A country in Central America between the Caribbean Sea and the Pacific Ocean. Swamp and dense tropical forest on the Caribbean coast, and a broader plain with lakes to the W rise to a central mountain range. Lake Nicaragua in the SW is the largest in Central America. The population is mainly of mixed Indian and Spanish descent, with minorities of African and other descent. *Economy*: chiefly agricultural, with coffee, cotton, peanuts, sugar, rice, and maize as the main crops. Production of bananas in the E has been reduced in recent years. There is considerable livestock rearing, and meat packing is an important industry. Minerals include gold, silver, and copper, and large quantities of natural gas were found in 1974. Oil deposits are being explored. Industries, on a small scale, include food processing, textiles, and oil refining. The main exports are peanuts, sesame seed, cotton, coffee, sugar, beef, and timber. Economic hardship resulting from the civil war of the 1980s has continued to the present. In the mid-1990s the government agreed a free-market reform package with the IMF. Nicaragua has a large external debt. *History*: sighted and visited by Columbus in 1502, it was colonized by Spain from 1522, becoming part of the captaincy general of Guatemala. It broke away from Spain in 1821 and formed part of the Central American Federation until 1838, when Nicaragua became an independent republic. A treaty with the USA in 1916 gave the latter an option on a canal route through Nicaragua as well as naval-base facilities. From 1927 until 1933 the US presence was opposed by a guerrilla movement led by Augusto César Sandino (1893–1934). He was assassinated by the National Guard under Anastasio Garcia Somoza (1896–1956), who seized power in 1936. For over 40 years the government continued to be dominated by the Somoza family, opposition to which culminated in a civil war that forced the resignation (1979) and exile of the president, Gen Anastasio Somoza Debayle (1925–80). The victorious ▷Sandinista National Liberation Front (FSLN) under Daniel ▷Ortega instituted socialist policies. Accusing the Sandinistas of supplying arms to rebels in El Salvador, the USA supported an army of Somoza supporters (Contras) that attacked Nicaragua from Honduras and Costa Rica. Civil strife contributed to record inflation, precipitating Ortega's downfall in 1990, when the US-backed leader of the opposition coalition (UNO), Violeta Chamorro (1929–), won a free election. After several attempts, a ceasefire agreement was signed with the Contras in 1994. In 1996 Chamorro resigned and the conservative Arnoldo Aleman defeated Ortega in presidential elections. In late 1998 the country was devastated by Hurricane Mitch, which left at least 1300 dead, 3000 missing, and 750 000 homeless, as well as causing widespread devastation to the economy and infrastructure. In 2002 Enrique Bolaño, a liberal, was elected president. Nicaragua is a member of the OAS and the Central American Common Market.

Republic of Nicaragua

Head of state	President Enrique Bolaño
Official language	Spanish
Official currency	córdoba of 100 centavos
Area	148 000 sq km (57 143 sq mi)
Population (1997 est)	4 632 000
Capital	Managua
Main ports	Corinto (on the Pacific) and Bluefields (on the Caribbean)

● **Nice** ► 43 42N 7 16E A city in SE France, the capital of the Alpes-Maritimes department on the Baie des Anges. Ceded by Sardinia to France in 1860, it is one of the leading resorts of the French Riviera. Notable landmarks include the Promenade des Anglais and it has a university (1965). It has a large trade in fruit and flowers. Population (1999): 342 738.

● **Nicene Creed** ► A widely used statement of Christian belief based on doctrinal statements accepted by the first Council of ▷Nicaea (325). The Nicene Creed used in the ▷Eucharist service of Orthodox, Roman Catholic, and many Protestant Churches is a version of this creed, with the sections on Christ (*see* Filioque) and the Holy Spirit expanded. ▷*See also* creeds.

● **niche** ► In ecology, the position and role of an organism in its community, determined by all the living and nonliving factors with which it reacts. In different communities, the same niche may be occupied by different species. If two different species occupy the same niche in the same community, competition will occur between them until one has displaced the other.

● **Nichiren Buddhism** ► A popular Japanese Buddhist school named after its founder, a 13th-century monk and prophet. He militantly opposed other Buddhist sects and held that *The Lotus Sutra* contained the true teaching and that the historical Buddha was identical with eternal Buddha-nature, in which all men participate. The sincere invocation of the mantra of homage to *The Lotus Sutra* is sufficient to gain enlightenment. Among the subsects of the school, the Nichiren-sho-shu and the related lay group, the Soka-gakkai, are the largest.

● **Nicholas I, St** ► (d. 867) Pope (858–67 AD). In the West Nicholas successfully defended and expanded papal authority against both secular rulers, such as ▷Lothair, and local bishops, notably ▷Hincmar of Reims. In the East Nicholas strongly opposed the appointment of ▷Photius to the patriarchate of Constantinople and declared him deposed. Photius, in his turn, declared the deposition of Nicholas (867) but Photius' overthrow prevented further hostilities. Feast day: 13 Nov.

● **Nicholas I** ► (1796–1855) Emperor of Russia (1825–55), notorious as an autocrat. His accession was followed by the unsuccessful ▷Dekabrist revolt, which hardened his conservatism. His ambitions in the Balkans precipitated the ▷Crimean War.

● **Nicholas II** ► (1868–1918) The last Emperor of Russia (1894–1917). His ambitions in Asia led to the unpopular ▷Russo-Japanese War, which precipitated the ▷Revolution of 1905. Forced to accept a representative assembly (*see* Duma), Nicholas nevertheless continued to rule autocratically. He took command of Russian forces in World War I, leaving Russia to the mismanagement of the Empress ▷Alexandra and ▷Rasputin. After the outbreak of the Revolution in 1917, Nicholas was forced to abdicate (March). He and his family were imprisoned by the Bolsheviks and executed at Ekaterinburg. In 1995 DNA testing established that bones discovered in 1991 were those of Nicholas. His remains were finally buried with due ceremony in St Petersburg in 1998. The Russian Orthodox Chruch declared Nicholas and his family saints in 2000.

● **Nicholas, St** ▶ (4th century AD) The patron saint of Russia, sailors, and children. He is thought to have been Bishop of Myra in Asia Minor and his alleged relics are in the Basilica of S Nicola, Bari. His legendary gifts of gold to three poor girls for their dowries led to the practice of exchanging gifts on his feast day, 6 Dec. As the patron saint of children, St Nicholas is the original basis for the "Father Christmas" legend. The name **Santa Claus**, by which this benefactor of children is also known, derives from the Dutch dialect name for St Nicholas, Sinte Klaas. In some countries presents are still given on 6 Dec, but in most countries children now expect lavish generosity on Christmas Day in the name of Santa Claus. ▷*See also* Kriss Kringle.

● **Nicholas of Cusa** ▶ (1401–64) German prelate and scholar. He was made a cardinal in 1448, bishop of Brixen (present-day Bressanone) in 1450, and became a papal legate. He wrote works on mysticism, mathematics, biology, and astronomy.

● **Nicholson, Ben** ▶ (1894–1982) British artist. He studied at the Slade before holding his first one-man exhibition (1922), which reflected the influence of ▷cubism and de ▷Stijl. Some of his best abstract works were produced in the 1930s, while a member of the British art group Unit One (*see* Nash, Paul). These include white-painted plaster reliefs of rectangles combined with circles. He was the son of the painter and poster artist **Sir William Nicholson** (1872–1949); his first wife was the painter **Winifred Nicholson** (1893–1981) and his second the sculptor Barbara ▷Hepworth.

● **Nicholson, Jack** ▶ (1937–) US film actor. After success in *Easy Rider* (1969), he became a star in the 1970s. His films include *Chinatown* (1974), *Prizzi's Honor* (1985), *Batman* (1989), *The Two Jakes* (1991), *Wolf* (1994), and *The Crossing Guard* (1996). He won Oscars for *One Flew Over the Cuckoo's Nest* (1976), *Terms of Endearment* (1983), and *As Good as It Gets* (1998).

● **Nicias** ▶ (c. 470–413 BC) Athenian general and politican. An aristocratic opponent of the demagogue ▷Cleon, Nicias negotiated a temporary peace with Sparta in the Peloponnesian War (peace of Nicias, 421). He opposed Alcibiades' imperialist designs and only reluctantly commanded the Athenian campaign to Sicily, during which he and nearly his entire force perished.

● **nickel** ▶ (Ni) A hard silvery metal similar to iron, discovered in 1751 by A. F. Cronstedt (1722–65). It occurs in nature chiefly as pentlandite, NiS, and pyrrhotite, (Fe,Ni)S, which are found in Canada and Australia. Iron meteorites typically contain from 5 to 20% nickel. It is chemically similar to cobalt and copper, and forms a green oxide (NiO), the chloride (NiCl$_2$), the sulphate (NiSO$_4$), and other compounds. It is used in alloys, such as stainless steel, Invar, Monel, armour plating, German silver, and in coinage. Finely divided nickel is used as a catalyst for hydrogenation reactions in organic chemistry. At no 28; at wt 58.6934; mp 1455°C; bp 2914°C.

● **nickel silver** ▷*See* German silver.

● **Nicklaus, Jack William** ▶ (1940–) US golfer, who has won more major championships than any other. Between 1959 and 1986 he won two US amateur championships, four US and three British Opens, five US Professional Golfers Association championships, and six Masters championships.

● **Nicobar Islands** ▷*See* Andaman and Nicobar Islands.

● **Nicolai, Otto Ehrenfried** ▶ (1810–49) German conductor and composer of operas. He held posts in Rome and Vienna and is remembered for *The Merry Wives of Windsor* (1849).

● **Nicolson, Sir Harold (George)** ▶ (1886–1968) British diplomat and literary critic. Born in Iran and educated at Oxford, he worked in the diplomatic service until 1929 and was later an MP (1935–45). In 1913 he married the novelist Victoria ▷Sackville-West. He published political studies, critical appreciations of Verlaine, Byron, Tennyson, and others, and several volumes of his *Diaries*.

● **Nicopolis, Battle of** ▶ (25 September, 1396) The battle in which a coalition of Crusaders under Emperor ▷Sigismund, acting on the request of the Byzantine emperor, Manuel II Palaeologus (1350–1425; reigned 1391–1425), were defeated by the Turks under Sultan Bayezid I (1347–1403; reigned 1389–1403). It led to further Turkish advances and the ultimate fall of the Eastern Roman (Byzantine) Empire.

● **Nicosia** ▶ (Greek name: Leukosia; Turkish name: Lefkosa) The capital of Cyprus, on the River Pedieas. Originally known as Ledra it has been successively under Byzantine, Venetian, Turkish, and British control. It has many old buildings, including the Cathedral of St Sophia (completed 1325), now a mosque. Its industries include textiles, food processing, and cigarettes. Population (1993 est): 177 000.

● **Nicotiana** ▶ A genus of poisonous herbs (over 100 species), native to Central and South America and Australia. 30–300 cm in height, they bear branching clusters of large five-lobed funnel- or bell-shaped flowers, white, yellow, pink, or purple in colour. The fruits are capsules. Many species are cultivated for ornament and certain species are grown commercially for ▷tobacco. Family: ▷Solanaceae.

● **nicotine** ▶ (C$_{10}$H$_{14}$N$_2$) A toxic colourless oily liquid alkaloid that

Nicholas II ▶ The last Russian emperor (centre) photographed with his children and a Cossack escort in 1916. The Grand Duke Alexei is standing next to the emperor; the Grand Duchesses (left to right) are Anastasia, Tatiana, Olga, and Maria.

rapidly turns brown on exposure to air. It is obtained from the dried leaves of the tobacco plant and is present in small quantities in cigarettes. It is also used as an insecticide. Nicotine patches, small plastic patches impregnated with nicotine, can be attached to the skin to provide those giving up smoking with a continuous supply of nicotine to satisfy their craving for the drug. Alternatively, nicotine chewing gum is available to supply the need.

● **nicotinic acid** ▷See vitamin B complex.

● **Niebuhr, Barthold Georg** ► (1776–1831) German historian. Niebuhr served as Prussian ambassador in Rome from 1816 to 1823, when he joined the staff of Bonn University. His *History of Rome* (1811–32) was significantly different from previous works on the ancient world, as he adopted a more critical approach and stressed the importance of external factors in the development of Rome. His ideas and methods influenced many scholars, including Theodor ▷Mommsen.

● **Niedersachsen** ▷See Lower Saxony.

● **Nielsen, Carl (August)** ► (1865–1931) Danish composer and conductor. He began his musical career as a violinist. Nielsen developed the principle of progressive tonality (beginning in one ▷tonality and ending in another) in his six symphonies, of which the fourth, entitled *The Inextinguishable* (1914–16), and the fifth (1922) are the best known. He also composed concertos for the violin, flute, and clarinet, the operas *Saul and David* (1900–02) and *Maskarade* (1904–06), chamber music, and choral music.

● **Niemeyer, Oscar** ► (1907–) Brazilian architect. A disciple of Le Corbusier with whom he worked on the Ministry of Education (1937–43) in Rio de Janeiro, Niemeyer has made a major contribution to modern architecture in Brazil. His first independent buildings included a casino, club, and church at Pampulha in Bel Horizonte. He has achieved international fame for his designs for □Brasília, notably the president's palace (1959) and the cathedral (1964).

● **Niemöller, Martin** ► (1892–1984) German Lutheran pastor and Protestant leader. A U-boat commander in World War I, he was ordained in 1924. In 1933 he became head of the Pastors' Emergency League, which became the ▷Confessing Church, and opposed the nazification of the Church in Germany. Niemöller was dismissed from his pastorate in Berlin in 1934 and in 1937 was sent to a concentration camp, where he remained until the end of the war. After the war he served (1947–64) as the first bishop of the newly established Evangelical Church of Hesse.

● **Nietzsche, Friedrich** ► (1844–1900) German philosopher. A friend of Wagner, Nietzsche was influenced by the writings of ▷Schopenhauer and ▷Goethe. His first book, *The Birth of Tragedy* (1872), argued that Wagnerian opera was the successor to Greek drama. Nietzsche rejected Christianity and its morality and attempted a "transvaluation of all values." He argued that the "will to power" (the title of his posthumously edited notebooks) was the crucial human characteristic. In *Thus Spake Zarathustra* (1883–92), he eulogizes the man who is free, titanic, and powerful, an ideal adopted by the Nazis for the Aryan superman. After 1889 he was permanently insane.

● **Niger, Republic of** ► A large landlocked country in West Africa. Lying mainly in the Sahara, it consists of desert in the N merging to semidesert in the S and rising to the central Aïr mountains. In the extreme SW it is drained by the River Niger, bordered by fertile flood plains. Approximately half the population are Hausa, with large porportions of Zerma, Songhai, Fulani, and Tuareg.

Economy: agriculture, particularly livestock raising, is important but during the last 30 years it has suffered badly from repeated droughts in the Sahel. Crops include groundnuts, millet, beans, and cassava, with cotton and rice being grown in the wetter river districts. Mineral resources include salt, natron, tin, and uranium. The main exports are uranium, livestock, and groundnuts. Trade is mainly with France and Nigeria. The country has a large external debt.

History: the area's early inhabitants, the ▷Tuareg, were displaced by the Hausa during the 18th century. In 1804 the Fulani defeated the Hausa in battle and established the kingdom of Sokoto. The region was subsequently occupied by France (1883–99), becoming a territory of French West Africa in 1904. It was made an autonomous republic

within the French Community in 1958, gaining full independence in 1960 with Hamani Diori as president. Diori was overthrown in a military coup (1974) led by Maj Gen Seyni Kountché (1931–87), who became president. Upon his death Col Ali Seybou took control. In the same year a referendum approved a charter to end military rule. In 1991 an interim government was installed to oversee the transition to democracy. Following free elections held in 1993 Mahamane Ousmane became president and a coalition government was formed. In 1995 a peace agreement was signed by the government and Tuareg rebels, who had been fighting since 1991. Ousmane and the elected government were overthrown by a military coup in 1996. Later that year presidential and legislative elections were won by the coup leader Brig Gen Ibrahim Barre Mainassara and his supporters. However, rival parties have contested these results and unrest continues. In April, 1999, Mainassara was assassinated, apparently by a section of the military. Parliament was suspended and military rule imposed. Following elections in November, Tandja Mamadou became president.

Republic of Niger

Head of state	President Tandja Mamadou
Official language	French
Official currency	CFA (Communauté financière africaine) franc of 100 centimes
Area	1 186 408 sq km (458 075 sq mi)
Population (1999 est)	9 962 000
Capital	Niamey

● **Niger, River** ► The third longest river in Africa. Rising in the S highlands of Guinea, near the Sierra Leone border, it flows NE and then SE through Mali, Niger, and Nigeria to enter the Gulf of Guinea. It has a large hydroelectric-power scheme. Length: 4183 km (2600 mi).

● **Niger-Congo languages** ► An African language family spoken in central and S Africa. It is subdivided into six groups: the ▷West Atlantic languages; the Mande languages spoken in Guinea, Mali, and Sierra Leone; the Voltaic languages spoken in Upper Volta, Ghana, and Côte d'Ivoire; the ▷Kwa languages of West Africa, such as Yoruba and Igbo; the Benue-Congo group, which includes the ▷Bantu languages; and the Adamawa-Eastern group spoken in Nigeria. The family is sometimes included in the larger Niger-Kordofanian classification, which relates it to the Kordofanian languages of the Sudan.

● **Nigeria, Federal Republic of** ► A large country in West Africa, on the Gulf of Guinea. Mangrove swamps along the coast give way to tropical rain forest inland rising to open savanna-covered plateaus, with mountains in the E reaching heights of over 2000 m (5000 ft). The N is semidesert and the River Niger flows through the W. Although the country is ethnically very diverse, the inhabitants are mainly Hausa and Fulani in the N, Yoruba in the W, and Ibo in the E.

Economy: the discovery of oil in the 1960s and 1970s led to a dramatic industrial expansion in the economy. Oil production accounted for about 90% of exports during its peak in the late 1970s but declined dramatically thereafter, causing serious economic problems; Nigeria is still the world's fifth largest producer and is a member of OPEC. There are also important reserves of natural gas, tin, coal, iron ore, and columbite (of which Nigeria is the world's main supplier). Manufacturing industries include brewing, aluminium, motor vehicles, textiles, and cement. Hydroelectricity is a valuable source of power, particularly since the opening of the Kainji Dam on the River Niger (1969). Agriculture is still important and diverse although output has suffered severely through the recurrent droughts in the Sahel. The main cash crops are groundnuts and cotton in the N and palms, coconut, and rubber in the S. Livestock, fishing, and forestry for timber are also important. In the mid-1990s the government lifted exchange controls and took steps to encourage foreign investment. However, Nigeria's poor human-rights record has since led many countries to suspend aid and development programmes.

History: in the middle ages there were highly developed kingdoms in the area, such as those of the Hausa in the N and the Yoruba (e.g. Oyo, Benin) in the SW; the Ibo occupied the SE. The coast was explored in the 15th century by the Portuguese, who developed the slave trade, in which the Dutch and English also participated. In 1861 Lagos was annexed by Britain and in 1886 the Royal Niger Company was incorporated to further British interests. By 1906, the British were in control of Nigeria, which was divided into the protectorate of Northern Nigeria and the colony (of Lagos) and protectorate of Southern Nigeria. These were united in 1914. Nigeria became a federation in 1954, gained independence in 1960, and became a republic within the Commonwealth in 1963. The government was overthrown in a military coup in 1966 and, after a further coup, a new government was formed under Lt Col Gowon. In 1967 the eastern region, which contained the homeland of the Ibo, withdrew to form the Republic of ▷Biafra under Lt Col Odumegwu Ojukwu's leadership. Civil war followed, lasting until Biafra's surrender in 1970. Gowon was overthrown in a coup in 1975 and Brig Olusegun Obasanjo became leader. In 1979, a civilian, Alhaji Shehu Shagari became president. He was reelected in 1983 but his failure to combat corruption and economic decline led to his overthrow (December, 1983) in a military coup led by Maj Gen Mohammed Buhari. A further coup in 1985 brought Maj Gen Ibrahim Babangida to power. Democratic elections held in 1993 were annulled by Babangida, provoking a political and social crisis. Later that year Gen Sani Abacha seized power in a coup and abolished all democratic institutions. Following the execution of Ken Saro-Wiwa and eight other political activists in 1995, Nigeria was suspended from the Commonwealth (until 1999). On the death of Abacha in June, 1998, Gen Abdulsalam Abubakar became president. Over the next months all Nigeria's political prisoners were released and Abubakar announced steps to restore democratic civilian rule. Presidential elections in 1999 resulted in victory for the former military leader Gen Obasanjo amid opposition claims of fraud. The period 1999–2002 saw escalating ethnic and religious strife.

Federal Republic of Nigeria

Head of state	President Obusegun Obasanjo
Official language	English; Hausa, Yoruba, and Ibo are the main African languages
Official currency	naira of 100 kobo
Area	923 773 sq km (356 669 sq mi)
Population (2000 est)	123 338 000
Capital	Abuja
Main port	Lagos

● **nightblindness** ▶ Inability to see in dim light. This is the earliest sign of vitamin A deficiency and is seen most commonly in young children in poor countries. Vitamin A is found in fruit, vegetables, and fish-liver oil. Preparations of vitamin A and cod-liver oil are used in treatment.

● **night heron** ▶ A nocturnal ▷heron belonging to a subfamily (*Nycticoracini*; 9 species) occurring worldwide. They are comparatively short-legged and squat, with a short neck and a broad bill. Birds of the main genus (*Nycticorax*) are mostly black-headed with long white head plumes.

● **nightingale** ▶ A plump woodland bird, *Luscinia megarhynchos*, that winters in tropical Africa and breeds in S Europe and Asia Minor during the summer. It is about 16 cm long with reddish-brown plumage and pale underparts and feeds on ground insects and spiders. Nightingales are noted for their beautiful song and were popular as cagebirds. The thrush nightingale (*L. luscinia*) is a closely related similar species. Family: *Turdidae* (thrushes). ▷*See* Plate III.

● **Nightingale, Florence** ▶ (1820–1910) British hospital reformer and founder of the nursing profession. With strong religious convictions, Florence Nightingale trained as a nurse and was appointed as a nursing superintendent in London in 1853. On the outbreak of the Crimean War, in 1854, she volunteered to lead a party of nurses to work in the military hospitals. She set about transforming the appalling conditions, earning herself the title Lady with the Lamp from her patients. After the war she was instrumental in obtaining improved living conditions in the army and, in 1860, from a Nightingale Fund subscribed by the public, she established the Nightingale School for Nurses at St Thomas's Hospital—the first of its kind. In 1907 Nightingale became the first woman to be appointed to the OM.

● **nightjar** ▶ A nocturnal bird belonging to a subfamily (*Caprimulginae*; 60–70 species) occurring in most temperate and tropical regions, also called goatsucker. About 30 cm long, nightjars have a soft mottled grey, brown, and rufous plumage with spotted and barred underparts and a long tail. Its short bill has a wide gape surrounded by long sensitive bristles enabling it to catch insects in flight. Family: *Caprimulgidae*; order: *Caprimulgiformes* (frogmouths, nightjars, etc.).

● **nightmares** ▶ Frightening ▷dreams, from which the sufferer often wakes with a feeling of suffocation. They are distinguished from **night terrors**, in which a child wakes suddenly in panic but later cannot remember the incident. Nightmares are more common during states of anxiety and depression and in people taking certain sleeping tablets. ▷*See also* sleep.

● **nightshade** ▶ One of several plants of the family ▷Solanaceae. The most notorious is the ▷deadly nightshade (or belladonna). The **woody nightshade**, or bittersweet (*Solanum dulcamara*), is a scrambling shrubby perennial, up to 2 m tall, of Eurasia and N Africa. It has oval leaves, the lower ones much divided, and loose clusters of flowers with five spreading purple lobes and conspicuous yellow stamens. The red berries are poisonous. The **black nightshade** (*S. nigrum*) is an annual, up to 50 cm high, widely distributed as a weed. It has oval pointed leaves, small yellowish flowers, and poisonous black berries.

The unrelated **enchanter's nightshade** (*Circaea lutetiana*), of Eurasia, is a herbaceous perennial of shady places. Up to 60 cm tall, it has

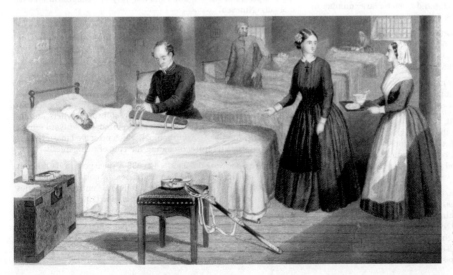

Florence Nightingale ▶ A contemporary steel engraving after a drawing by Robert Hind (1817–79), showing the founder of the nursing profession at work in the military hospital in Scutari.

large heart-shaped leaves and a terminal spike of tiny white flowers. Family: *Onagraceae*.

● **nihilism** ▶ A view that rejects totally all traditional values and institutions. ▷Turgenev invented the label in *Fathers and Sons* (1861) for the philosophy of the character of Basarov, which was based on that of Dmitrii Pisarev (1840–68). The political expression of nihilism is anarchy; in 19th-century Russia, where nihilism became an organized revolutionary movement, proponents held that progress is impossible without the violent destruction of all existing institutions. The nihilists assassinated Tsar Alexander II in 1881 but were themselves later eradicated by the Bolsheviks. Philosophical nihilism also undermines accepted standards in ▷ethics and ▷aesthetics.

● **Niigata** ▶ 37 58N 139 2E A city in Japan, in NW Honshu. The main port for the Sea of Japan, its industries include chemicals and oil refining. Its university was established in 1949. Population (1995): 494 785.

● **Nijinsky, Vaslav** ▶ (1890–1950) Russian ballet dancer. In 1909 he joined Diaghilev's company in Paris, and quickly achieved an international reputation for his daring and sensitive dancing. Michel ▷Fokine created *Petrushka*, *Scheherazade*, and other ballets for him, and from 1913 he also began to choreograph. He retired in 1919 suffering from schizophrenia and was cared for by his wife until his death.

● **Nijmegen** ▶ (German name: Nimwegen) 51 50N 5 52E A city in the E Netherlands, in Gelderland province. The Treaties of ▷Nijmegen (1678–79) were signed here. Its university was founded in 1923. It is an important industrial centre with chemicals and engineering. Population (1996 est): 147 600.

● **Nijmegen, Treaties of** ▶ (1678–79) The peace treaties between France and, respectively, the Netherlands (1678), Spain (1678), and the Holy Roman Empire (1679) that ended the third ▷Dutch War. Terms were least favourable to Spain, Louis XIV securing Franche-Comté and a naturally defensible frontier with the Spanish Netherlands.

● **Nike** ▶ The Greek personification of victory, often portrayed as an aspect of ▷Athena. Among larger representations is the famous statue discovered in Samothrace in 1836 and now in the Louvre, Paris.

● **Nikisch, Arthur** ▶ (1855–1922) Hungarian conductor. A brilliant student at the Vienna Conservatoire, he directed the Leipzig Opera (1879–87), the Boston Symphony Orchestra (1889–93), and then the Leipzig Gewandhaus and Berlin Philharmonic Orchestras concurrently (1895–1922).

● **Nikko** ▶ 36 45N 139 37E A town in Japan, in central Honshu. Situated within Nikko National Park its beautifully ornamented temples and shrines are a place of pilgrimage and attract a large number of tourists. Population (1990): 20 128.

● **Nikolaev** ▶ 46 57N 32 00E A port in S Ukraine, at the confluence of the Rivers Bug and Ingul about 64 km (40 mi) from the Black Sea. Long a naval base, it has important shipbuilding and flour-milling industries. Population (1996 est): 508 000.

● **Nikopol** ▶ 47 34N 34 25E A city in Ukraine, on the River Dnepr. It is important as the centre of a region having the world's largest manganese reserves. Population (1991 est): 159 000.

● **Nile, Battle of the** ▶ (1 August, 1798) A naval battle in which the British, under ▷Nelson, defeated the French in Aboukir Bay during ▷Napoleon's invasion of Egypt (*see* Revolutionary and Napoleonic Wars). This engagement severed communications between France and Napoleon's army in Egypt and gave Britain control of the Mediterranean.

● **Nile, River** ▶ A river in N Africa, the longest river in the world. The longest of its three main tributaries, the White Nile, rises in Burundi as the River Luvironza before joining the River Kagera to enter Lake Victoria, the chief reservoir of the Nile. It emerges as the Victoria Nile at Jinja to flow northwards through Lake Albert becoming the White Nile at its confluence with the Bahr el Ghazal. At Khartoum it is joined by the Blue Nile (which rises in the Ethiopian highlands) and

later by the River Atbara before flowing through a broad delta into the Mediterranean Sea. The Nile's annual floodwaters have supported cultivation on its floodplains since ancient times. To provide the increasing amounts of water required for irrigation vast dams have been constructed, including the Aswan Dam and ▷Aswan High Dam. Length: 6741 km (4187 mi).

● **nilgai** ▶ A large antelope, *Bosephalus tragocamelus*, inhabiting Indian forests and plains. Up to 140 cm high at the shoulder, male nilgais have a slate-grey coat with white underparts and develop short horns and a throat tuft. Females are smaller and tawny brown. They live in small herds, browsing on shrubs and fruit.

● **Nilo-Saharan languages** ▶ A family of African languages that covers the smallest geographical area of all the African language groups. It is also the least clearly defined group, there being very great variety within its constituent languages. It includes the Nilotic languages of the Chari-Nile group, such as Dinka and Nuer.

● **Nilsson, Birgit Marta** ▶ (1918–   ) Swedish soprano, who studied at the Stockholm Royal Academy, making her debut in 1946 in Weber's opera *Der Freischütz*; she was well known in the roles of Brunnhilde, Salome, Elektra, and Turandot. She retired in 1982.

● **nimbostratus** ▶ A form of ▷cloud common in temperate latitudes. Dark grey and solid in appearance it has a low base but may show extensive vertical development. Precipitation of snow or rain is often prolonged although not usually heavy.

● **Nîmes** ▶ 43 50N 4 21E A city in S France, the capital of the Gard department. An important Roman settlement, it was a Protestant stronghold (16th–17th centuries). It has several notable Roman remains, including an amphitheatre and the temple of Diana; the Pont du Gard lies to the NE. A trading centre for wine and brandy, its manufactures include textiles, footwear, and machinery. Population (1990): 133 607.

● **Nimitz, Chester W(illiam)** ▶ (1885–1966) US admiral. In World War II, as commander of the Pacific Fleet after Pearl Harbor (1941), he complemented General Douglas ▷MacArthur's command of the SW Pacific. His victories along the island chains from Japan to New Guinea, which destroyed the Japanese fleet, were made possible by his use of aircraft carriers as support bases.

● **Nimrod** ▶ A legendary biblical figure described in Genesis as a mighty hunter. He founded a Mesopotamian kingdom that included Babel, Erech, and Akkad and is credited with building Nineveh and Kalhu (modern Nimrud).

● **Nimrud** ▶ An Assyrian capital (ancient Kalhu) near Mosul (Iraq). Founded about 1250 BC it was destroyed by the Medes in 612 BC. ▷Layard's excavations (1845–51) of the 9th-century city yielded gigantic sculptures of winged bulls and a library of ▷cuneiform tablets. ▷*See also* Nineveh.

● **Nin, Anaïs** ▶ (1903–77) US novelist, born in Paris, who is best known for her diaries (1966–83). She was also the author of novels, including *House of Incest* (1936), critical writings on D. H. Lawrence and others, and such erotic works as *Delta of Venus* (1977).

● **ninety-five theses** ▷*See* Luther, Martin.

● **Nineveh** ▶ An Assyrian capital (modern Kuyunjik) near Mosul (Iraq). Nineveh was made cocapital with Nimrud by ▷Sennacherib (c. 700 BC). The Medes sacked it in 612 BC. Sculptures, reliefs, and inscriptions illuminate Assyrian life at this period, but ▷Layard's great find was the library of ▷Ashurbanipal, which preserved masterpieces of ▷cuneiform literature, including the epic of ▷Gilgamesh.

● **Ningbo** ▶ (*or* Ning-po) 29 54N 121 33E A river port in E China, in Zhejiang province near the East China Sea. Important for overseas trade (5th–9th centuries), it was also a religious centre. Its industries include textiles and food processing. Population (1995 est): 1 090 000.

● **Ningxia Hui Autonomous Region** ▶ (*or* Ningsia Hui AR) An administrative division in N China. It occupies a plateau and is largely desert, with nomadic herdsmen in the N and some cultivation in the S. Area: 66 400 sq km (25 896 sq mi). Population (1995 est): 5 040 000. Capital: Yinchuan.

● **Niobe** ▶ In Greek mythology, the daughter of Tantalus and wife of the King of Thebes. She took pride in her many children and urged the Thebans to worship her instead of Leto, the mother of only two children, Apollo and Artemis. When the Thebans consented to this, Apollo and Artemis avenged their mother's honour and killed Niobe's children. Overcome by grief, Niobe wandered to Mount Sipylus in Lydia, where Zeus changed her into a stone column or statue, the face of which was said continually to shed tears.

● **niobium** ▶ (Nb) A soft ductile white metal, discovered in 1801. It was formerly known as columbium in the USA. Niobium is used in specialist alloys in spacecraft, and at low temperatures it has superconducting properties. Its compounds include the white oxide (Nb_2O_5), which has interesting structural properties, and the volatile fluoride and chloride (NbF_5, $NbCl_5$). At no 41; at wt 92.9064; mp 2469 ± 10°C; bp 4744°C.

● **nipa** ▶ A small ▷palm tree, *Nipa fruticans*, of brackish waters and estuaries of SE Asia. It has a creeping trunk and large feathery foliage, which is used for thatching and basket making. The fruits are sometimes eaten and the flowers are used commercially as a source of sugar.

● **Nippur** ▶ A city of ancient ▷Sumer (modern Niffer in central Iraq). From about 2600 BC it was Sumer's chief religious centre with a ▷ziggurat dedicated to Enlil (built c. 2000 BC) and temples to ▷Ishtar (Inanna). Tablets bearing religious, literary, and other texts have been discovered.

● **Nirenberg, Marshall Warren** ▶ (1927-   ) US biochemist, who developed a technique for breaking the genetic code. Nirenberg used synthetic RNA of known base sequence and determined for which amino acid it coded. He shared a Nobel Prize (1968) with ▷Khorana and Robert W. Holley (1922–93) for this work.

● **nirvana** ▶ The supreme goal of Buddhism, in which liberation from the limitations of existence and rebirth are attained through the extinction of desire. Whereas the ▷Theravada school sees nirvana as the negation of the mundane, the ▷Mahayana regards it as the ultimate achievement of man's essential Buddha-nature. In Hinduism nirvana also means spiritual release in the sense of freedom from reincarnation or union with God or the Absolute.

● **Niš** ▶ 43 20N 21 54E A city in Serbia and Montenegro, in E Serbia on the River Nišava. For centuries it was a centre for Serbian resistance to Turkish control. Its products include locomotives and textiles, and it has a university (1965). Population (2000 est): 182 583.

● **Nishinomiya** ▶ 34 44N 135 22E A city in Japan, in S Honshu on Osaka Bay. An industrial centre, it is known for its *sake* (a Japanese rice wine). Population (1995): 390 388.

● **Niterói** ▶ 22 54S 43 06W A city in SE Brazil, in Rio de Janeiro state on Guanabara Bay opposite the city of Rio de Janeiro. Although largely residential, it has shipbuilding and textile industries and is a popular resort. Population (1996 est): 450 364.

● **Nithsdale, William Maxwell, 5th Earl of** ▶ (1676–1744) Scottish Jacobite. He was captured during the 1715 ▷Jacobite rising and condemned to death. His wife helped him to escape from the Tower of London dressed as a woman and he fled to France.

● **nitric acid** ▶ (HNO_3) A fuming corrosive liquid made by the oxidation of ammonia by air in the presence of a platinum catalyst or the action of sulphuric acid on sodium or potassium nitrate. It is widely used in the manufacture of fertilizers and explosives and in other chemical processes.

● **nitrocellulose** ▷*See* cellulose nitrate.

● **nitrogen** ▶ (N) A colourless odourless gas, discovered by Daniel Rutherford (1749–1819) in 1772. It makes up 78% of the earth's atmosphere by volume. The element exists as diatomic molecules (N_2) bonded very strongly together. This bond must be broken before nitrogen can react, which accounts for its chemical inertness. It forms a range of chemical compounds including ammonia (NH_3), the oxides (N_2O, NO, N_2O_3, NO_2, N_2O_5), nitric acid (HNO_3), and many **nitrates** (for example $NaNO_3$). Liquid nitrogen has a wide range of cryogenic applications. Ammonia (NH_3) and nitrates are of great

importance as fertilizers. Nitrates are also used in explosives as a source of oxygen, which they liberate when heated. Sodium and potassium nitrates occur naturally in some desert areas. Nitrogen gas is used to provide an inert gas blanket in some welding applications. At no 7; at wt 14.0067; mp -210.0°C; bp -195.8°C.

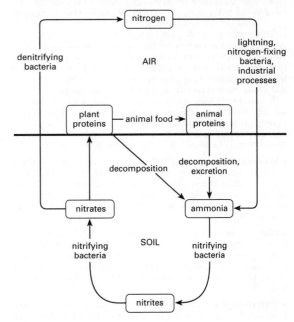

nitrogen cycle

● **nitrogen cycle** ▶ The sequence of processes by which nitrogen and its compounds are utilized in nature. Nitrogen gas in the air is converted (fixed) to ammonia by lightning, cosmic radiation, certain soil bacteria, and fertilizer manufacturers (*see* nitrogen fixation). Nitrifying bacteria in the roots of leguminous plants convert ammonia to nitrites and then to nitrates. Some nitrates are reduced by denitrifying bacteria to nitrogen, but most are used by plants to manufacture amino acids and proteins. When animals eat plants some of this nitrogenous plant material is incorporated into animal tissues. Nitrogenous excretory products and dead organic matter decompose to produce ammonia, so completing the cycle.

● **nitrogen fixation** ▶ The conversion of atmospheric nitrogen gas into nitrogen compounds. The process occurs naturally by the action of certain bacteria in the roots of leguminous plants (*see* nitrogen cycle). Industrial methods of fixing nitrogen are of immense importance in the manufacture of nitrogen fertilizers. One method is the reaction of nitrogen with oxygen to give nitric oxide in an electric arc. This process, devised by the Norwegian physicists Kristian Olaf Birkeland (1867–1917) and Samuel Eyde (1866–1940), is only economical in regions in which cheap hydroelectric power is available. A more efficient method of fixing nitrogen is the ▷Haber-Bosch process for making ammonia.

● **nitroglycerin** ▶ ($C_3H_5(NO_3)_3$) A yellow oily highly ▷explosive liquid. It is used as an explosive either alone or as ▷dynamite or ▷gelignite.

● **Niue** ▶ 19 02S 169 55W A fertile coral island in the S Pacific Ocean, belonging to New Zealand. Copra and bananas are exported. Area: 260 sq km (100 sq mi). Population (1993 est): 1977. Chief town: Alofi.

● **Niven, David** ▶ (1909–83) British film actor. His early films include *The Prisoner of Zenda* (1937) and *Wuthering Heights* (1939), and he later appeared in many stylish comedies and action films, including *Separate Tables* (1958), *The Guns of Navarone* (1961), and *Candleshoe* (1977). He published two volumes of autobiography, *The Moon's a Balloon* (1972) and *Bring on the Empty Horses* (1975).

● **Nixon, Richard Milhous** ▶ (1913–94) US statesman; Republican president (1969–74). A Californian-born lawyer, he contributed to McCarthy's anticommunist investigations and achieved early political power partly by discrediting Democratic opponents as communist sympathizers. He was Eisenhower's vice president from 1953 until 1960, when he became the Republican presidential candidate. He was defeated by Kennedy, and when in 1962 he failed to win the governorship of California his political career seemed over. However, he returned to national politics in the mid-1960s and in 1968 narrowly defeated Hubert Humphrey for the presidency. As president he reduced US troop commitments abroad and in 1973 ended US military involvement in Vietnam. In 1972 he visited China, a move that was to lead to the establishment of diplomatic relations between the USA and China. Participation in illegal efforts to ensure re-election in 1972 and the subsequent cover-up attempt led to the ▷Watergate scandal. Under threat of impeachment he became the first president to resign office. President Gerald ▷Ford granted him a free pardon after succeeding him as president. He wrote *RN: The memoirs of Richard Nixon* (1978), *In the Arena* (1990), and *Seize the Moment* (1991).

● **Nizam al-Mulk** ▶ (c. 1018–92) Persian statesman, who was vizier (minister; 1063–92) to the ▷Seljuq sultans ▷Alp Arslan and Malik-Shah. Wielding almost absolute power, he governed the Seljuq empire at its zenith. He was the author of *The Book of Government*, in which he expressed his political and orthodox religious views. He was assassinated.

● **Nizhnii Novgorod** ▶ (name from 1932 until 1991: Gorki) 56 20N 44 00E A city in central Russia, on the Rivers Oka and Volga. It is an important industrial city, whose manufactures include machinery, chemicals, and textiles. Its trade fair was the most important in Russia until it was discontinued in 1917. Population (1996 est): 1 400 000.

● **Nizhnii Tagil** ▶ 58 00N 59 58E A city in Russia, on the River Tagil and to the E of the Ural Mountains. Its metallurgical industries arise from the surrounding ironmining region. Population (1995 est): 409 000.

● **Nkomo, Joshua** ▶ (1917–99) Zimbabwean politician. Secretary general of the Rhodesian African Railway Union in Rhodesia (1945–50), Nkomo became president of the Zimbabwe African People's Union (ZAPU) in 1961. Based in Zambia, it allied with Robert Mugabe's Zimbabwe African National Union (ZANU) in 1976 to form the ▷Patriotic Front (PF) against the government of Ian Smith in Rhodesia (*see also* Zimbabwe, State of). Nkomo became a minister in Mugabe's government in 1980 but was dismissed (1982) when arms were found on his farms; he returned to the Cabinet in 1988 and became vice-president in 1990.

● **Nkrumah, Kwame** ▶ (1909–72) Ghanaian statesman; prime minister (1957–60) and then president (1960–66). A student in the USA and the UK, after returning home he formed (1949) the Convention People's Party, which with a policy of noncooperation with the British took the Gold Coast to independence as Ghana in 1957. Nkrumah was deposed by a military coup in 1966. He sought exile in Guinea, where Sékou Touré made him cohead of state. An advocate of African unity, he wrote *Towards Colonial Freedom* (1947) and *Handbook of Revolutionary Warfare* (1968).

● **NKVD** ▷*See* KGB.

● **No** ▶ A form of Japanese theatre, the early development of which is associated with the work of the actor and dramatist ▷Zeami Motokiyo (1363–1443). Originating in religious ritual and folk dances and strongly influenced by Zen Buddhism, it is performed with a minimum of scenery and properties and involves the use of dance, mime, and masks. The acting is highly stylized. A traditional No programme lasts several hours and consists of five plays separated by three comic interludes known as *Kyogen*. It has remained an aristocratic form, contrasting with the more realistic ▷Kabuki drama.

● **Noah** ▶ An Old Testament figure. After God had determined to destroy the human race because of its wickedness (Genesis 6–8), he made a covenant with Noah as the only man worthy of being saved from the coming flood. Noah was instructed to build an ark for his family and representatives of each animal species, and they would be preserved after the flood subsided. Noah and his sons Ham, Shem, and Japheth and their wives became the ancestors of the present human race. Several other cultures have similar legends about a catastrophic primeval flood.

● **Nobel, Alfred Bernhard** ▶ (1833–96) Swedish chemist and businessman. From his invention of dynamite (1866) and a smokeless gunpowder (1889) and his exploitation of the Baku oilfields he amassed a considerable fortune, leaving £1.75 million as a foundation for the **Nobel Prizes**. Four of the annual awards (for physics, chemistry, physiology or medicine, and literature) are made by various Swedish academies; the Peace Prize is awarded by a committee elected by the Norwegian parliament. A sixth prize, for economics, instituted in memory of Alfred Nobel, has been financed by the Swedish National Bank since 1969. See Appendix.

● **nobelium** ▶ (No) A synthetic transuranic element discovered in 1957 by bombarding curium with carbon ions in an accelerator. Five isotopes with short half-lives have been discovered. Named after Alfred Nobel. At no 102; at wt (259).

● **Nobile, Umberto** ▶ (1885–1978) Italian aeronautical engineer and aviator. He designed the airships *Norge* and *Italia*, piloting the *Norge* in ▷Amundsen's flight over the North Pole (1926). In 1928 he flew the *Italia* across the Pole but crashed on the return journey, being rescued after 40 days.

● **Noble, Sir Andrew** ▶ (1831–1915) British physicist, who founded the science of ballistics. In conjunction with Sir Frederick ▷Abel he improved the quality of gunpowder and made many innovations in artillery design.

● **noble gases** ▶ (or inert gases) The elements forming group 18 of the ▷periodic table: helium, neon, argon, krypton, xenon, and radon. For many years they were thought to be chemically inert owing to their filled outer electron shells. The first compound of ▷xenon was discovered in 1962, since when fluorides and oxygen fluorides of xenon, krypton, and radon have been prepared.

● **noble metals** ▶ Metals, such as gold, silver, and platinum, that do not rust or tarnish in air or water and are not easily attacked by acids.

● **Nobunaga Oda** ▶ (1534–82) Japanese general, hero of many legends. As the emperor's chief military commander, Nobunaga was virtual ruler of central Japan from 1568. Thereafter he built up his own regular forces, bringing much of Japan under imperial rule. His work of unification was brought to an end by his assassination.

● **Noctiluca** ▶ A genus of flagellate ▯protozoa found in coastal waters. They are pinkish and luminescent.

● **noctuid moth** ▶ A moth belonging to the family *Noctuidae* (about 20 000 species), also called owlet moth, widespread in Eurasia and North America. The adults are usually dull brown or grey and fly at night. The caterpillars, which are also known as ▷army worms and ▷cutworms, are active at night, eating plant roots and stems.

● **noctule** ▶ An insect-eating ▷bat, *Nyctalus noctula*, of Eurasia. About 12 cm long, it has bright-chestnut fur and long narrow wings. Noctules hibernate only from Dec to Jan. Family: *Vespertilionidae*.

● **nocturne** ▶ A musical composition that suggests the serenity associated with the night. Mozart's *Serenata Notturna* is an 18th-century example. The two great exponents of the form in the 19th century were John ▷Field and ▷Chopin, with Field's 18 *Nocturnes for the Piano* serving as a model for the younger composer's 21 piano nocturnes. While Field's piano writing owes much to the lyricism of Italian *bel canto*, Chopin expanded the genre to encompass a wider variety of moods, embellished by his pianistic virtuosity. ▷Debussy at the end of the 19th century composed three nocturnes for orchestra and female choir. In the 20th century Benjamin ▷Britten's song cycle *Serenade* also reflects the quiet of the night.

● **noddy** ▷*See* tern.

● **Noel-Baker, Philip John** ▶ (1889–1982) British campaigner for disarmament and Labour politician. He worked at the League of Nations (1919–22) and helped to draft the UN Charter; he was an MP

(1929–31, 1936–50). The author of *The Arms Race: A Programme for World Disarmament* (1958), in 1959 he was awarded the Nobel Peace Prize.

● **Noguchi, Hideyo** ► (1876–1928) Japanese bacteriologist, who discovered that paralysis in syphilis is caused by spirochaetes in the central nervous system. Noguchi also investigated snake venoms, poliomyelitis, and trachoma. He died of yellow fever while investigating the disease.

● **noise pollution** ► Unwanted sounds that cause inconvenience or nuisance to members of the public. Noise is measured on a decibel scale in which 0 dB is the hearing threshold and 130 dB is the pain threshold. A whisper may register 25 dB, while heavy urban traffic can reach 80–90 dB. Prolonged exposure to noise levels in excess of about 85 dB can lead to permanent hearing impairment.

● **Nolan, Sir Sidney** ► (1917–92) Australian painter. Largely self-taught, he first painted abstract works, influenced by ▷Klee and ▷Moholy-Nagy, but is internationally known for his paintings of Australian historical figures, such as Ned ▷Kelly, and landscapes of the outback. Knighted in 1981, he became a member of the OM in 1983.

● **Nolde, Emil** ► (E. Hansen; 1867–1956) German expressionist painter and printmaker. Although briefly associated (1906–07) with Die ▷Brucke, he developed an independent style characterized by his distorted forms and clashing colours. Deeply religious, he painted many biblical scenes, bleak landscapes of the Baltic coast, and still lifes of flowers.

● **Nollekens, Joseph** ► (1737–1823) British neoclassical sculptor (*see* neoclassicism). After executing several portrait busts in Rome (1760–70), he became highly successful with his portrait sculptures in England. His sitters included George III, Benjamin West, William Pitt the Younger, and Charles James Fox. He was also a sculptor of tombs and mythological subjects.

● **nomads** ► Peoples who live in no fixed place but wander periodically according to the seasonal availability of food, pasture, or trade and employment. Hunters and gatherers (e.g. Australian Aborigines) usually live in small bands that spend anything from a few days to a few weeks in a vicinity, moving within a loosely defined territory. Pastoralists (e.g. many central Asian tribes) often move between summer and winter pastures (*see* transhumance). Traders, tinkers, entertainers, and those who provide certain crafts and services, such as the ▷Gipsies, often travel widely seeking custom.

● **nominalism** ► The medieval philosophical theory that general terms (called universals) have no real existence, that is, there is no abstract entity corresponding to a universal. Thus, there exists no such thing as blueness, but only individual blue things (called particulars). Nominalism, therefore, contrasts with ▷realism. ▷William of Ockham, ▷Hobbes, and certain modern analytic philosophers have all made varying statements of nominalist theory.

● **nomograph** ► (*or* nomogram) A ▷graph showing the relationship between three variable quantities, enabling the value of one variable to be read off if the other two are known. It can take the form of a series of curves on a graph of two quantities, corresponding to constant values of a third. Or it can consist of three straight lines calibrated with the values of the variables. A fourth line is drawn between two known points on two of the straight lines: the point at which this fourth line cuts the third straight line gives the value of the unknown quantity.

● **Non-Aligned Movement** ► An international movement founded in 1961 to represent the interests of third-world countries not aligned with the superpowers of the East and West. Opposing colonialism and holding major conferences every three years, it has over 100 members.

● **Nonconformists** ► In its original early-17th-century sense, the term referred to members of the Church of England who did not conform with its rituals. After the Act of Uniformity (1662), the term's scope widened to include dissenting Protestant sects, such as the Quakers and Methodists.

● **non-Euclidean geometry** ► A form of ▷geometry in which ▷Euclid's postulates are not satisfied. In ▷Euclidean geometry if two lines are both at right angles to a third they never meet (i.e. they remain parallel). In, for example, hyperbolic (or elliptic) geometry they eventually diverge (or converge). Non-Euclidean geometry was developed independently by ▷Lobachevski (published 1831) and ▷Bolyai (published 1836). ▷*See also* Riemann, Georg Friedrich Bernhard.

● **Nonjurors** ► Some 400 Church of England clergy who were deprived of their livings in 1690 for refusing to swear allegiance to William III and Mary II, on the grounds that this would mean breaking their previous oath to James II. In Scotland most ministers of the Episcopal Church, which was disestablished in 1689, were Nonjurors.

● **Nono, Luigi** ► (1924–90) Italian composer. A pupil of Francesco Malipiero (1882–1973), he married Schoenberg's daughter Nuria. Nono's compositions frequently employ serialism; many of them consist of settings of texts by Marxist writers. They include *La fabbrica illuminata* (for mezzo-soprano and tape; 1964) and *Non consumiamo Marx* (for voices and tape; 1969).

● **Nonproliferation of Nuclear Weapons, Treaty on the** ▷*See* disarmament.

● **nonsense verse** ► A genre of comic verse that is structured according to a kind of surreal logic that defies rational interpretation. It is characterized by strict rhyme schemes and the use of meaningless neologisms. The genre, predominantly English, is usually dated from the publication of *The Book of Nonsense* by Edward ▷Lear in 1846. Other outstanding writers of nonsense are Lewis ▷Carroll and Hilaire ▷Belloc. ▷*See also* limerick.

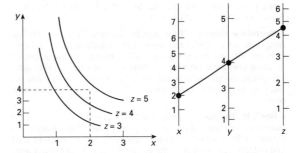

nomograph ► If $x = 2$ and $y = 4$, a value of approximately 4.5 for z is obtained from the two forms of nomograph shown.

● **nonverbal communication** ► Any form of communication between people that does not rely on words (written, spoken, or transmitted by ▷sign language). The principal form is **body language**, which may be deliberate, as in shrugging, winking, making eye contact, facial expression, or gesticulation, or it may be quite involuntary, as in blushing, shivering, or weeping. Deliberate nonverbal communication may be used to reinforce verbal communication (e.g. nodding to reinforce an affirmative response) or to contradict it (e.g. raising the eyebrows when giving an expected response in which the responder does not really believe). Alternatively a deliberate nonverbal gesture may replace verbal communication (e.g. giving the "thumbs-up" sign to indicate pleasure and approval). Involuntary nonverbal responses may also reinforce or contradict a verbal statement. The ▷polygraph (lie detector) makes use of these responses (changes in blood pressure, respiration rate, skin conductivity) to assess the validity of a verbal response.

Some forms of nonverbal communication have universal meanings; others, however, are specific to particular cultures. For example, shaking or nodding the head may have different meanings in different communities. Not all nonverbal communication relies on body language. For example, the presuppositions shared by the communicators or the context within which the communication occurs can affect the meaning of an exchange.

● **Nootka** ► A North American Indian people of the NW Pacific coast region who speak a ▷Wakashan language. They were traditionally hunters, fishers, and expert whale catchers, using large canoes and harpoons. They practised the ▷potlatch as did their neighbours, the ▷Kwakiutl.

● **noradrenaline** ▶ (or norepinephrine) A hormone that is secreted by the central core (medulla) of the adrenal glands. It is a ▷catecholamine, structurally similar to ▷adrenaline but produces different effects in certain target organs, especially the heart, the rate of which it decreases. Noradrenaline is released by nerve endings of the sympathetic nervous system (see neurotransmitter). In the hypothalamus it is thought to inhibit transmission of impulses.

● **Nordenskjöld, Nils Adolf Erik, Baron** ▶ (1832–1901) Swedish navigator. He became the first, in the Vega, to navigate the ▷Northeast Passage (1878–79).

● **Nordic Council** ▶ An international organization founded in 1953 to coordinate action on interests common to its member states. The five members, Denmark, Finland, Iceland, Norway, and Sweden, meet on an annual basis; in 1962 they agreed the Helsinki Convention, which promoted closer cooperation.

● **Nore, the** ▶ A sandbank in SE England, at the mouth of the River Thames. A naval mutiny occurred near here in May, 1797, after the ▷Spithead mutiny, in protest against working conditions (see Royal navy). The mutineers surrendered after about a month and their leader was hanged.

● **norepinephrine** ▷See noradrenaline.

● **Norfolk** ▶ 36 54N 76 18W A seaport in the USA, in Virginia on Hampton Roads. Founded in 1682, it was damaged in the American Revolution and the US Civil War. It is the headquarters of the US Atlantic Fleet. Its industries include textiles, cars, and shipbuilding. Population (1996 est): 233 430.

● **Norfolk** ▶ A county of E England, in ▷East Anglia. It is mainly low lying, with fens in the W and the Norfolk ▷Broads in the E, and agricultural, with arable farming and turkey rearing. Fishing is centred on Great Yarmouth. Tourism is important. Under local government reorganization in 1974 it gained part of NE Suffolk. Area: 5374 sq km (2074 sq mi). Population (1996 est): 777 000. Administrative centre: Norwich.

● **Norfolk, Thomas Howard, 3rd Duke of** ▶ (1473–1554) English statesman; the uncle of two of Henry VIII's wives, Anne Boleyn and Catherine Howard. He became president of the privy council in 1529 and in 1536 suppressed the ▷Pilgrimage of Grace. He lost power after Catherine Howard's execution (1542) and was imprisoned under Edward VI for involvement in the treason (1546) of his son Henry Howard, Earl of ▷Surrey. Surrey's son **Thomas Howard, 4th Duke of Norfolk** (1538–72) was imprisoned (1559–60) by Elizabeth I for planning to marry Mary, Queen of Scots. He participated in ▷Ridolfi's plot and was executed. ▷See also Earl Marshal.

● **Norfolk Island** ▶ 29 05S 167 59E A mountainous Australian island in the SW Pacific Ocean. Formerly a British penal colony, some of the descendants of the Bounty mutineers moved here from ▷Pitcairn Island (1856). Area: 36 sq km (14 sq mi). Population (1986): 1977. Chief town: Kingston.

● **Noriega, Manuel** ▶ (1938–) Panamanian general who, as head of the armed forces, was effective leader of Panama (1983–89). Notorious for corruption, he annulled the result of a presidential election in 1989, provoking the dispatch of a US task force to Panama. Noriega was deposed and brought to the USA, where he was sentenced (1992) to 40 years in prison on drugs charges. In 1996 a Panamanian court sentenced him (in absentia) to 20 years in jail for ordering nine killings while in office.

● **Norman, Greg** ▶ (1955–) Australian golfer. He won the British Open in 1986 and 1993.

● **Norman, Jessye** ▶ (1945–) US soprano. She made her debut in Berlin in 1969 in Wagner's Tannhäuser and is known for both opera roles and solo performances. Her repertoire ranges from Schubert and Schoenberg to Gershwin and Negro spirituals.

● **Norman art and architecture** ▶ The styles that flourished in Normandy and the lands that the Normans had conquered in the 11th and 12th centuries, notably the ▷romanesque architectural style. First appearing in England before the Norman conquest in Westminster Abbey (consecrated 1065), Norman architecture devel-

Norman architecture ▶ The arcade on the north side of the nave of Durham Cathedral, showing the rounded arches and geometrical ornamentation typical of the style.

oped into a distinctive native style. Norman features include rounded arches, two-tower church façades, and geometrical ornamentation. In S Italy it fused with Saracen and Byzantine traditions. ▷See also Bayeux tapestry.

● **Norman conquest** ▶ (1066–72) The conquest of England by William, Duke of Normandy (see William the Conqueror). After defeating Harold II at the battle of Hastings (1066), William captured London and was crowned. English risings in the SW, N, and on the Welsh border were suppressed by 1070 and with the defeat of the Scots in 1072 the conquest was complete. The Norman influence on Anglo-Saxon England was fundamental. Although structures of government continued virtually unaltered, the English lay and ecclesiastical aristocracy was replaced by Normans and other continentals and ▷feudalism was introduced. Latin became the language of government and Norman French, the literary language; the Norman influence was also felt in church organization and architecture.

● **Normandy** ▶ (French name: Normandie) A former province in N France, on the English Channel. It comprises the regions of **Basse-Normandie** and **Haute-Normandie** (see France, Republic of). An agricultural area with sheep and dairy farming, it also produces flax, hemp, and apples.
  History: during the medieval period Normandy flourished. William II, Duke of Normandy, conquered England (1066) to become William I of England. Disputed between England and France during the following centuries, it reverted to France in 1449. The **Normandy invasion**, the Allied counteroffensive in June–August, 1944, consisted of the landing of over 1 million men on a number of Normandy beaches in under four weeks (see D-Day; World War II).

● **Norman French** ▶ The dialect spoken in Normandy during the early middle ages and by the Norman invaders of England. Their speech introduced new words to the English language.

● **Normans** ▶ Viking settlers in N France (later Normandy) whose rule, under their leader Rollo, was formally recognized (911) by Charles the Simple (879–929; reigned 898–923). By the end of the 11th century they had also conquered England (*see* Norman conquest) and much of S Italy and Sicily and had established crusading states in the E, besides gaining a foothold in Wales and Scotland. Noted for their military dynamism and inventiveness (they introduced the castle into England) they successfully adapted existing administrative practices in countries they conquered, normally possessing a stable government working closely with the Church.

● **Norns** ▶ In Norse mythology, the fates, three females who shape the life of man. They are Urth (the past), Verthandi (the present), and Skuld (the future).

● **Norrköping** ▶ 58 35N 16 10E A port in SE Sweden, on an inlet of the Baltic Sea. Its industries include shipbuilding, engineering, and textiles. Population (1997 est): 123 531.

● **Norse** ▷*See* Norwegian; Old Norse.

● **Norsemen** ▷*See* Vikings.

● **North, Douglass** ▷*See* Fogel, Robert William.

● **North, Frederick, Lord** ▶ (1732–92) British statesman; prime minister (1770–82). He was a Lord of the Treasury (1759–65) and chancellor of the exchequer (1767–70) before becoming prime minister, as which his policies were largely dictated by George III. He was criticized for precipitating the ▷American Revolution (1775–83), and resigned.

● **North, Sir Thomas** ▶ (c. 1535–c. 1601) English translator. His translation of Plutarch's *Lives of the Noble Grecians and Romans* (1579) was based on that of the scholar Jacques Amyot (1513–93) but was more vivid. It was widely read in Elizabethan times and used by Shakespeare.

● **Northallerton** ▶ 54 20N 1 26W A market town in N England, the administrative centre of North Yorkshire. The battle of the Standard took place nearby in 1138, in which the English defeated the Scots. Northallerton has light engineering and trailer-manufacturing industries. Population (1991): 13 774.

● **North America** ▶ The third largest continent in the world, in the N of the W hemisphere bordering on the Arctic Ocean, the N Pacific Ocean, the N Atlantic Ocean, the Gulf of Mexico, and the Caribbean Sea. The Isthmus of Panama links it with South America. It is generally accepted as consisting of ▷Canada, the ▷United States of America, ▷Mexico, ▷Central America, ▷Greenland, and the ▷West Indies. The mountains of the Western Cordillera extend down its entire W coast, descending to the Great Plains to the E. The Appalachian Mountains, further E, are separated from the Canadian Shield by the Great Lakes. Area: over 24 000 000 sq km (9 500 000 sq mi). Population (1993 est): 441 000 000.

● **North American Free Trade Agreement** ▶ (NAFTA) A free-trade treaty signed by the USA and Canada in 1988 and by Mexico in 1992. All trade tariffs will be removed, those on certain agricultural products being gradually phased out. In 1994 negotiations about the admittance of Chile commenced.

● **North American Indian languages** ▶ A geographical classification of the languages of the indigenous peoples of North America. These languages originally numbered about 300; at least a third of these are dead or dying out, but the number of speakers of a few, such as Navaho, is increasing. Highly diverse, about 57 families of these languages have been identified. ▷Sapir arranged these into six phyla (1929): ▷Inuit-Aleut; ▷Algonquian-▷Wakashan; ▷Na-Dené; ▷Penutian; ▷Hokan-▷Siouan; and ▷Aztec-Tanoan.

● **North American Indians** ▶ A group of peoples of North America, who ▷Columbus mistakenly believed to be inhabitants of the Indian subcontinent. They are probably descended from migrants who arrived from Asia some 20 000 years ago. Their physical characteristics include dark hair and eyes, scant body hair, and ruddy skin.

Their traditional cultures range from that of warlike primitive hunters and gatherers to peaceful subsistence cultivators. Social organization is usually based on kinship and depends upon a complex tribal system. ▷*See also* American Indians; Algonquian; Apache; Arikara; Blackfoot; Caddo; Cherokee; Cheyenne; Chinook; Choctaw; Comanche; Cree; Creek; Crow; Hopi; Hupa; Huron; Illinois; Iroquois; Kiowa; Mohawk; Natchez; Navajo; Nez Percé; Nootka; Ojibwa; Pawnee; Shoshoni; Sioux; Tlingit.

● **Northampton** ▶ 52 14N 0 54W A town in central England, the administrative centre of Northamptonshire on the River Nene. Notable buildings include St Peter's Church and the Church of the Holy Sepulchre (one of the few round churches in the country), both dating from the 12th century. A centre of the footwear industry, Northampton also manufactures shoe machinery, cosmetics, and motor-car accessories; it was designated as a new town in 1968. Population (1997 est): 193 000.

● **Northamptonshire** ▶ (*or* Northants) A county in the East Midlands of England. An escarpment runs NE–SW, dipping gently to the SE. It is predominantly agricultural producing livestock, cereals, potatoes, and sugar beet. Industrial activities include shoemaking, printing, food processing, and engineering. Area: 2367 sq km (915 sq mi). Population (1998 est): 615 800. Administrative centre: Northampton.

● **North Atlantic Drift** ▶ One of the major ocean currents, flowing NE across the Atlantic from the ▷Gulf Stream.

● **North Atlantic Treaty Organization** ▶ (NATO) An alliance formed in 1949 on the basis of the Treaty of Brussels (1948) by Belgium, Canada, Denmark, France, Iceland, Italy, Luxembourg, the Netherlands, Norway, Portugal, the UK, and the USA; Greece and Turkey joined in 1952, West Germany in 1955, Spain in 1982, and the united Germany in 1990. It was formed during the ▷Cold War to guard against possible Soviet aggression. All member states are bound to protect any member against attack. NATO also seeks to encourage economic and social cooperation. Its secretariat headquarters is in Brussels and its military headquarters near Mons. The **North Atlantic Cooperation Council** (NACC) was formed in 1991 to forge links with the former Eastern-bloc nations, many of which joined a new "Partnership for Peace." In 1997 the NACC was renamed the **Euro-Atlantic Partnership Council**. That same year Russia was given a voice in NATO business in return for accepting NATO's expansion into eastern Europe. The Czech Republic, Poland, and Hungary joined NATO in 1999; a further nine E European nations have applied to join early in the 21st century. In 1995 NATO carried out air strikes against Serb positions around Sarajevo, its first-ever aggressive action. Its first action against a sovereign state took place in 1999, when NATO undertook a major air campaign against the Federal Republic of Yugoslavia (*see* Kosovo).

● **North Ayrshire** ▶ A council area of W central Scotland on the Firth of Clyde, comprising part of the historic county of ▷Ayrshire, including the Isle of Arran. Absorbed into Strathclyde Region in 1975, it became an independent ▷unitary authority in 1996. Apart from Arran, which is mountainous, it is mainly low-lying and fertile; tourism and fishing are important and there are various industries in Irvine. Area: 884 sq km (341 sq mi). Population (1999): 139 660. Administrative centre: Irvine.

● **North Borneo** ▷*See* Sabah.

● **North Brabant** ▶ (Dutch name: Noord-Brabant) A province in the S Netherlands, bordering on Belgium. It produces wheat and sugar beet. Area: 4911 sq km (1896 sq mi). Population (1999 est): 2 337 700. Capital: 's Hertogenbosch.

● **North Cape** ▶ (Norwegian name: Nordkapp) 71 11N 25 40E A promontory in Norway, on the island of Magerøy. It is the most northerly point in Europe.

● **North Carolina** ▶ A state in the USA, on the S Atlantic coast. The extensive coastal plain stretches westwards to the Appalachian Mountains. It is heavily populated and the leading industrial state in the South, producing textiles, furniture, and processed foods. It is the nation's major producer of tobacco and tobacco products.

History: one of the 13 original colonies, it shares its early history with South Carolina. It became a separate colony in 1713 and a state in 1789. It supported the Confederates in the US Civil War. Area: 136 197 sq km (52 586 sq mi). Population (1996 est): 7 322 870. Capital: Raleigh.

● **Northcliffe, Alfred Charles William Harmsworth, 1st Viscount** ▶ (1865–1922) British newspaper proprietor, who pioneered popular journalism in Britain. After founding several periodicals he and his brother (*see* Rothermere, 1st Viscount) bought the *Evening News* (London) in 1894. He founded (1896) the *Daily Mail*, which became the most widely circulated daily in the world. In 1903 he founded the *Daily Mirror* and in 1908 acquired control of *The Times*.

● **North Dakota** ▶ A state in the N central USA. It comprises three main physical regions: the Red River Valley along the E border, the Central Lowlands just W of this, and the Great Plains in the SW. The population is sparse, particularly in the W. Agriculture and mining are the two main economic activities; its coal and oil reserves are among the country's largest and it is a major producer of wheat. The small manufacturing sector is growing, especially food processing. *History*: early attempts to settle were made by Scottish and Irish families at Pembina in 1812, although major settlements did not occur until after 1871 and the arrival of the railway. It formed part of the territory of Dakota from 1861 until 1889 when it was made a separate state. Area: 183 022 sq km (70 665 sq mi). Population (1996 est): 643 539. Capital: Bismarck.

● **North Down** ▶ A district in Northern Ireland, in Co Down. Area: 82 sq km (32 sq mi). Population (1991): 72 900.

● **Northeast Caucasian languages** ▶ A group of about 25 languages of the NE Caucasus, also called the Nakho-Dagestanian family. Chechen, the most important, is part of the Nakh subdivision. The Dagestanian subdivision may be further divided into the Avar-Ando-Dido languages of which Avar is the most important and the only one that is written; the Lakk-Dargwa languages; and the Lezgian languages.

● **North-East Frontier Agency** ▷*See* Arunachal Pradesh.

● **North East Lincolnshire** ▶ A unitary authority of NE England, in Lincolnshire; formerly (1975–96) part of the county of Humberside. Area: 192 sq km (74 sq mi). Population (1996 est): 164 000.

● **Northeast Passage** ▶ (Russian name: Severny Morskoy Put) The sea route along the N Eurasian coast, kept open in summer by Russian icebreakers. It was first traversed (1878–79) by Nils ▷Nordenskjöld. ▷*See also* Northwest Passage.

● **Northern Areas** ▶ The northernmost districts administered by, although technically not part of, Pakistan, principally Baltistan, Hunza, and Gilgit.

● **Northern Cape** ▷*See* Cape Province.

● **Northern Ireland** ▷*See* Ireland.

● **Northern Lights** ▷*See* aurora.

● **Northern Marianas** ▷*See* Mariana Islands.

● **Northern Province** ▷*See* Transvaal.

● **Northern Rhodesia** ▷*See* Zambia.

● **Northern Territory** ▶ An administrative division of N central Australia, bordering on the Timor and Arafura Seas. It consists chiefly of a plateau with Arnhem Land in the N (containing Australia's largest Aborigine reservation) and the Macdonnell Ranges in the S. SW of Alice Springs stands ▷Ayers Rock. The main agricultural activity is the rearing of beef cattle. Minerals are important, especially iron ore, manganese, copper, gold, and bauxite. There are also large deposits of uranium. In 1978 the Northern Territory became an independent state, although the federal government retained control over uranium. Area: 1 346 200 sq km (519 770 sq mi). Population (1996 est): 177 500. Capital: Darwin.

● **Northern Transvaal** ▷*See* Transvaal.

● **Northern War, Great** ▶ (1700–21) The war fought between Russia, Denmark, and Poland, on one side, and Sweden, on the other.

▷Charles XII of Sweden, whose Baltic supremacy was opposed by his neighbours, defeated Denmark, then Russia at Narva (1700), and Poland (1706). He was subsequently overcome by the Russians under Peter the Great (Poltava, 1709) and fled to the Turks, who defeated the Russians at Pruth River (1711). After returning to Sweden Charles was forced to initiate peace negotiations. At the same time he continued hostilities in the course of which he died (1718). The war between Denmark, Poland, and Sweden was ended by the Treaties of Stockholm (1719–20). The Treaty of ▷Nystad (1721) between Russia and Sweden made Russia the major Baltic power.

● **North German Confederation** ▶ (1867–71) An alliance of German states under Prussian leadership formed by Bismarck following the Austro-Prussian War (1866). It formed the basis of the German Empire, proclaimed in 1871.

● **North Holland** ▶ (Dutch name: Noord-Holland) A province in the W Netherlands, between the North Sea and the IJsselmeer. Much of it lies below sea level. The province contains Amsterdam and its industrial activities include shipbuilding, textiles, and motor vehicles. Its farms produce dairy and livestock products. Area: 2912 sq km (1124 sq mi). Population (1995): 2 463 611. Capital: Haarlem.

● **North Island** ▶ The most northerly of the two principal islands of New Zealand, separated from South Island by Cook Strait. It consists chiefly of a central volcanic plateau with fertile coastal and valley lowlands. Area: 114 729 sq km (44 281 sq mi). Population (1996): 2 733 083.

● **North Korea** ▷*See* Korea.

● **North Lanarkshire** ▶ A council area of central Scotland, consisting mainly of the NE part of the historic county of ▷Lanarkshire. Absorbed into Strathclyde Region in 1975, it became an independent ▷unitary authority in 1996. It is heavily urbanized in the S and W, with agricultural land rising to the Campsie Fells in the N. Industries include engineering, metalworking, and electronics. Area: 1771 sq km (684 sq mi). Population (1996 est): 307 100. Administrative centre: Motherwell.

● **North Lincolnshire** ▶ A unitary authority of NE England, in Lincolnshire; formerly (1975–96) part of the county of Humberside. Area: 1497 sq km (578 sq mi). Population (1996 est): 153 000.

● **North Ossetian Republic** ▶ A constituent republic of Russia, in the S. The Ossetians are a Caucasian people, known for their wood and silver carving. The region has metal and oil deposits and industries include textiles and food processing. The main crops are grain, cotton, and grapes. Area: 8000 sq km (3088 sq mi). Population (1995 est): 658 000. Capital: Vladikavkas.

● **North Pole** ▷*See* Arctic Circle.

● **North Rhine-Westphalia** ▶ (German name: Nordrhein-Westfalen) A *Land* in W Germany, bordering on the Netherlands and Belgium. It was formed in 1946. Rich in minerals, including coal, it contains the vast Ruhr industrial region and is one of the world's most densely populated areas. Its many industries include steel, textiles, and chemicals. Area: 34 057 sq km (13 147 sq mi). Population (1992 est): 17 510 000. Capital: Düsseldorf.

● **North Riding** ▷*See* Yorkshire.

● **Northrop, John Howard** ▶ (1891–1987) US biochemist, who isolated and purified various digestive enzymes and showed they were all proteins. He won the 1946 Nobel Prize.

● **North Sea** ▶ A section of the Atlantic Ocean in NW Europe, between the British Isles and the continent N of the Strait of Dover. The entire floor is part of the continental shelf, with an average depth of about 300 m (914 ft). It is fished for over 5% of the world's catch, consisting especially of cod, herring, and mackerel; recent exploitation of ▷North Sea oil and natural-gas finds have further increased its economic importance. Freak high tides have flooded large areas of coastal lowlands in the Netherlands and E England. Concern has been caused in recent years over high levels of pollution.

● **North Sea oil** ▶ The ▷oil deposits that were discovered under the North Sea in the 1960s. Exploration and development has been carried out by multinational companies from the USA and Europe. The area is divided into UK, German, Norwegian, Danish, and Dutch sectors. The UK has the largest of these sectors and became self-sufficient in oil in 1980, since when oil revenues have aided the UK's balance of payments. Total output reached 127.6 million tonnes in 1985, fell to 91.6 million tonnes in 1990, but had recovered to 130 million tonnes by 1995. Exploration is still continuing. The perilous nature of production of oil at sea was underlined in 1988 with the destruction of the Piper Alpha platform, leading to 167 deaths.

● **North Somerset** ▶ A unitary authority of SW England, in Somerset; formerly (1974–96) part of the county of Avon. Area: 375 sq km (145 sq mi). Population (1996 est): 177 000.

● **North Star** ▷See Polaris.

● **North Tyneside** ▶ A unitary authority of NE England, in Tyne and Wear. Area: 84 sq km (32 sq mi). Population (1996 est): 194 100.

● **North Uist** ▷See Uist.

● **Northumberland** ▶ The northernmost county of England, bordering on Scotland and the North Sea. It consists of a coastal plain rising to the Cheviot Hills in the N and the Pennines in the W. The main river, the Tyne, flows SE. The county also includes Kielder Water (opened 1982), the largest man-made lake in N Europe. Roman remains include Hadrian's Wall. The main agricultural activity is sheep farming. In 1974 the industrial SE became part of Tyne and Wear. Area: 5033 sq km (1944 sq mi). Population (1996 est): 307 700. Administrative centre: Morpeth.

● **Northumberland, John Dudley, Duke of** ▶ (1502–53) English statesman, who was virtual ruler of England (1549–53) under Edward VI. On the accession of Edward (a minor) in 1547, Dudley (as Earl of Warwick) became a member of the regency council dominated by the Duke of ▷Somerset. He replaced Somerset in 1549, securing his execution in 1552. In 1553 he married his son Guildford Dudley to Lady Jane ▷Grey, whom he persuaded the king to name as his heir. On Edward's death Jane was proclaimed queen but lack of support forced Northumberland's surrender to Mary (I) and he was executed.

● **Northumbria** ▶ A kingdom of Anglo-Saxon England north of the Humber, formed in the 7th century by the union of the kingdoms of Deira and Bernicia. Northumbria became politically pre-eminent in England in the 7th century under ▷Edwin, Saint ▷Oswald, and ▷Oswiu. Northumbrian scholarship was also unrivalled, boasting such great names as ▷Bede and ▷Alcuin. By 829, however, Northumbria had recognized the overlordship of Wessex and in the late 9th century its unity was destroyed by the Danes.

● **Northwest** ▷See Cape Province; Transvaal.

● **Northwest Caucasian languages** ▶ A group of languages of the NW region of the Caucasus, also called the Abkhazo-Adyghian family. It includes Abkhaz, Abaza, Adyghian, Kabardian (Circassian), and Ubykh. All but Ubykh are written. A distinctive feature is the small number of vowel sounds and great number of consonants.

● **Northwest Company** ▶ A Canadian fur-trading company, founded in 1783, that rivalled the ▷Hudson's Bay Company. Conflict between them ended in their forced merger (1821).

● **North-West Frontier Province** ▶ A province in NW Pakistan, SE of Afghanistan in the Himalayas and lower mountains. Its Pathan inhabitants mostly herd livestock or cultivate grains, fruit, sugar cane, and tobacco. There is little industry, but the province controls the strategic Khyber Pass to Afghanistan. Over the centuries each great power in the region has sought to control the province, but it has usually remained semiautonomous because of its rugged terrain and fierce inhabitants. Since the early 1980s over a million refugees from the civil wars in Afghanistan have fled here. Area: 74 522 sq km (28 773 sq mi). Population (latest est, excluding Afghan refugees): 12 287 000. Capital: Peshawar.

● **Northwest Passage** ▶ The sea route along the coast of North America, between the Atlantic and Pacific Oceans. It was first traversed by Roald Amundsen (1903–06) and since 1969 has been used for transporting Alaskan oil. It is claimed by both Canada and the USA. ▷See also Northeast Passage.

● **Northwest Territories** ▶ A territory of NW Canada. The Northwest Territories formerly occupied a vast area stretching from 60°N to the North Pole and from Baffin Island in the E to the Yukon border in the W. However, in April, 1999, a large area of the NE (the whole of the former district of ▷Keewatin, most of ▷Franklin, and parts of ▷Mackenzie) became the new territory of ▷Nunavut, established as a semiautonomous homeland for the Inuit peoples. The remainder, which is the more populated and developed part of the Canadian north, continues to be known as the Northwest Territories at present, although several new names have been proposed. Rich in mineral resources, the economy is dominated by mining; pitchblende, silver, zinc, lead, tungsten, and gold are extracted. The vast oil reserves are being explored. Area: 2 011 189 sq km (776 319 sq mi). Population (1999 est): 41 800. Capital: Yellowknife.

● **Northwich** ▶ 53 16N 2 32W A town in N England, in Cheshire on the River Weaver. Salt is extracted and there are large chemical works. Population (1991): 34 520.

● **North Yorkshire** ▶ A county in N England, bordering on the North Sea. It was created in 1974 from most of the North Riding and parts of the West and East Ridings of Yorkshire. In 1996 the post-1974 county of ▷Cleveland was abolished and those districts historically belonging to Yorkshire were restored to the county for ceremonial and related purposes: they are now administered by the ▷unitary authorities of Langbaurgh, Middlesbrough, and Stockton-on-Tees. The city of York also became a unitary authority. North Yorkshire consists of two upland areas separated by the Vale of York: the Pennines to the W, and the Cleveland Hills, North York Moors, and Tabular Hills to the E. The River Ouse flows SE to the Humber Estuary. It is chiefly agricultural with cereals in the Vale of York, dairy farming in the Pennine Dales, and sheep farming on the moorlands. There is heavy engineering in Teeside and some industry in the larger towns, such as York. Coal is mined from a field centred on Selby (opened 1983). Tourism is centred on Harrogate, Scarborough, and York. Area (excluding unitary authorities): 8037 sq km (3102 sq mi). Population (1996 est, excluding unitary authorities): 559 600. Administrative centre: Northallerton.

North Sea oil ▶ An oil rig in the North Sea with a tanker taking oil on board.

● **Norway, Kingdom of** ► (Norwegian name: Norge) A country in N Europe occupying the W part of the Scandinavian Peninsula. It borders on the Arctic Ocean (N), the Norwegian Sea (W), and the Skagerrak (S). It is largely mountainous, reaching heights of almost 2500 m (8000 ft), with a heavily indented coastline. There are numerous glaciers and forests cover approximately one-quarter of the country. The archipelago of Svalbard and Jan Meyen Island are also part of Norway together with the dependencies of Bouvet Island, Peter I Island, and Queen Maud Land. Norway is one of the most sparsely populated countries on the Continent.

Economy: abundant hydroelectric power has enabled Norway to develop as an industrial nation. The main manufactured products include industrial chemicals, machinery, and processed foods. Forestry is a major source of wealth: timber products and the pulp and paper industry are important. Norway is one of the world's great fishing nations and fish is one of the principal exports. It also has one of the world's largest merchant fleets. Revenues from tourism are important. Minerals include aluminium, iron ore, limestone, coal, copper, zinc, and lead. Offshore oil was discovered in 1968 and petroleum exports are now a major source of revenue. Norway also has deposits of natural gas. Agriculture is limited as less than 4% of land surface is suitable for cultivation.

History: its early history was dominated by the Vikings. The many local chieftains were not subjected to a single ruler until the reign of Harold I Haar-fager (died c. 930). Christianity was introduced in the 10th century and became established under Olaf II Haraldsson (reigned 1015–28). During the reign (1204–63) of Haakon IV Haakonsson Norway acquired Iceland and Greenland. Following the Union of Kalmar (1397), Norway was united with Sweden and Denmark under the rule of Margaret. Sweden broke free in 1523 but Norway remained under Danish domination until 1814, when it was united with Sweden under the Swedish Crown, while maintaining internal self-government. Only in 1907 was full independence achieved. Norway declared its neutrality in both World Wars but from 1940 to 1945 was occupied by the Germans, who established a government under Quisling. After World War II, Norway joined the UN (of which the Norwegian Trygve Lie was first secretary general) and NATO. Norway has a highly developed social-welfare system. In 1981 Gro Harlem Brundtland became the country's first woman prime minister; she was re-elected in 1993 and resigned in 1996. In a referendum (1994) Norwegians voted against joining the EU. In 2000 the centrist coalition led by Kjell Magne Bondevik collapsed and was replaced by a Labour government. Bondevik formed a new centre-right coalition following elections in 2001.

Kingdom of Norway

Head of state	King Harald V
Official language	Norwegian
Official religion	Evangelical Lutheran
Official currency	krone of 100 øre
Area	323 886 sq km (125 053 sq mi)
Population (2000 est)	4 487 000
Capital and main port	Oslo

● **Norwegian** ► A North Germanic language of the West Scandinavian division, spoken in Norway. There are two distinct forms known as Dano-Norwegian (Bokmål or Riksmål) and New Norwegian (Nynorsk or Landsmål). Bokmål derives from written Danish, the language used during the union with Denmark (1397–1814). Nynorsk was created by the scholar Ivar Aasen (1813–96) to revive the tradition of Old Norwegian, which was closely related to ▷Old Norse speech. Bokmål is more widely used.

● **Norwegian Antarctic Territory** ► The area in Antarctica claimed by Norway, lying S of latitude 60°S and between longitudes 20°W and 45°E. It consists of the end of Coats Land, Queen Maud Land, and islands. There have been many European, South African, and Soviet research stations along the mountainous coast.

● **Norwich** ► 52 38N 1 18E A city in E England, the administrative centre of Norfolk on the River Wensum. Towards the end of the 16th century many weavers from the Netherlands settled in the city and it became a major textile centre. It has a Norman cathedral (1096) and

keep, many medieval churches, and is the site of the University of East Anglia (1963). With the decline of the traditional shoe making, the main economic activities are now financial services, engineering, chemicals, and clothing manufacture. The city is an important regional centre for East Anglia. Population (1993 est): 128 100.

● **Norwich school** ► A school of landscape painters active in Norwich in the first half of the 19th century. Founded as the Norwich Society in 1803, it held regular exhibitions until 1834. Its leading members were ▷Cotman and ▷Crome.

● **nose** ► The organ of smell, which is also an entrance to the respiratory tract. The external nose, which projects from the face, has a framework of bone and cartilage and is divided into two nostrils by the nasal septum. It leads to the nasal cavity, which is lined by ▷mucous membrane, extends back to the pharynx and windpipe, and is connected to the air ▷sinuses of the skull. Hairs in the nostrils filter particles from inhaled air, which is further cleaned, warmed, and moistened in the nasal cavity. The membrane at the top of the nasal cavity contains olfactory cells, which are sensitive to different smells and are connected to the brain via the olfactory nerve.

● **Nostradamus** ► (Michel de Notredame; 1503–66) French physician and astrologer, famous for his *Centuries* (1555–58), in which he made a number of prophecies in the form of rhyming quatrains. Some of his prophecies appeared to come true and Charles IX appointed him his physician on his accession (1560).

● **notary public** ► A legal practitioner, in England and Wales usually a ▷solicitor, who certifies certain documents, protests dishonoured ▷bills of exchange (i.e. re-presents bills dishonoured by nonacceptance or nonpayment and, if still dishonoured, attaches a note to them giving details of the re-presentation), administers oaths, and takes sworn statements for use in court. If the service of a notary is required outside the UK, diplomatic and consular staff may exercise this function. In some countries notaries belong to an independent profession, while in others they are civil servants.

● **nothosaur** ► A primitive marine reptile of the Jurassic period (200–135 million years ago). 0.3–6 m long, nothosaurs had a long neck and tail and long paddle-like limbs. They fed on fish, which were gripped tightly with long sharp teeth.

● **notochord** ► A flexible skeletal rod running the length of the body in the embryos of the ▷chordates (including the vertebrates). In primitive chordates, such as the lancelets and lampreys, the notochord remains the main axial support, but in vertebrates it is incorporated into the backbone as the embryo develops.

● **Notoungulata** ► An extinct order of mammals whose remains have been found mainly in South America. Notoungulates ranged from small rabbit-like forms to the massive *Toxodon*, which stood over 2 m high. They had three-toed feet, with either claws or hooves, and lived from the Palaeocene epoch to the Pleistocene epoch (about 70 million to 2.5 million years ago).

● **Notre-Dame de Paris** ► The gothic cathedral built (1163–1345) on the Île de la Cité, Paris, to replace two earlier churches. The nave, choir, and west front were completed by 1204; the innovatory flying buttresses and the great rose windows, which still retain their 13th-century stained glass, are notable features. Damaged during the French Revolution, Notre-Dame was saved from demolition and redecorated for Napoleon's coronation (1804) and was subsequently fully restored (1845–64) by ▷Viollet-le-Duc.

● **Nottingham** ► 1. 52 58N 1 10W A city in N central England, in Nottingham unitary authority, the administrative centre of Nottinghamshire on the River Trent. Charles I raised his standard here in 1642 at the outbreak of the Civil War. Buildings include the castle (built by William I and restored in 1878) and the "Trip to Jerusalem," reputedly the oldest inn in England. Formerly known for lacemaking and hosiery, it now has textiles, pharmaceuticals, telecommunications, engineering, and brewing as its leading industries. The city has two modern universities. Population (1991): 270 222. 2. A unitary authority in N central England, in Nottinghamshire. Area: 78 sq km (30 sq mi). Population (1999 est): 284 000.

● **Nottinghamshire** ► A county in the East Midlands of England. It consists mainly of lowlands, crossed by the River Trent, with uplands in the W and the remnants of Sherwood Forest (famous for the Robin Hood legend) in the SW. Agriculture is important with arable and dairy farming, orchards, and market gardening. Coalmining was formerly important but many mines have now been closed. Gypsum, limestone, and gravel are also extracted. The main industrial town is Nottingham, which became an independent ▷unitary authority in 1998. Area (excluding Nottingham): 2086 sq km (805 sq mi). Population (1996 est, excluding Nottingham): 747 800. Administrative centre: Nottingham.

● **Notting Hill** ► A residential area of N Kensington in the London borough of Kensington and Chelsea. Recorded in 1356 as Knottynhull (meaning unknown), it was farmland until the 19th century. Its large West Indian community began the **Notting Hill Carnival** in 1966; this is still a spectacular annual street carnival held on August (Late Summer) Bank Holiday.

● **Nouakchott** ► 18 09N 15 58W The capital of Mauritania, in the W near the Atlantic coast. A small village until the 1950s, it was developed as the capital after independence in 1960. Its modern port is situated 6.4 km (4 mi) from the city. Population (1999 est): 881 000.

● **Nouméa** ► 22 16S 166 26E The capital of New Caledonia. A port, it exports nickel, chrome, manganese, and iron. Population (1996): 76 293.

● **nouveau roman** ► An experimental type of the novel pioneered by French writers in the 1950s. The leading exponents include Nathalie ▷Sarraute, Alain ▷Robbe-Grillet, and Michel ▷Butor. Reacting against traditional realistic concepts of character and narrative, their works are characterized by a distrust of psychological motives, detailed descriptions of external reality, and the avoidance of any kind of value judgment.

● **nouvelle cuisine** ► A style of cooking developed in France in the 1970s largely by Michel Guérard (1933–). It avoids fats and rich sauces, concentrating on fresh food in light and elegantly presented dishes.

● **Nouvelle Vague** ▷See New Wave.

● **nova** ► A ▷binary star that suddenly increases in brightness by perhaps 10 000 times or more and then fades over months or years, usually to its original brightness. Nova eruptions occur in close binary systems comprising a ▷white dwarf with a nearby companion star that is expanding and is losing matter to the white dwarf. Gaseous material flowing from the large star forms a disc around the dwarf and gradually spirals down to its surface. When enough has accumulated the resulting thermonuclear explosion is seen as the nova erupting.

● **Novalis** ► (Friedrich Leopold, Freiherr von Hardenberg; 1772–1801) German Romantic poet and writer. After studying law, he became an auditor. The death of his fiancée (1797) inspired his celebration of death and love in the *Hymnen an die Nacht* (1800); he himself died prematurely of tuberculosis. His unfinished novel *Heinrich von Ofterdingen* (1802) typifies the Romantic belief in the power of art.

● **Nova Lisboa** ▷See Huambo.

● **Novara** ► 45 27N 08 37E A town in NW Italy, in Piedmont. It has several notable buildings, including a 13th-century town hall. As well as a rice-milling industry, there are textile and chemical plants. Population (1998 est): 102 404.

● **Nova Scotia** ► A province of E Canada. It consists of a peninsula protruding into the Atlantic Ocean and ▷Cape Breton Island. Mostly rolling hills and valleys, Nova Scotia was originally covered by mixed forest but has been largely replanted with conifers. Economic growth is restricted by limited resources and the distance from important markets. Coal output is down significantly, but Nova Scotia also mines gypsum, salt, and copper. Agriculture includes dairying, mixed farming, livestock, and fruit. Iron and steel, pulp and paper, fishing, and tourism are also economically important.
History: from the first colonization (1605), Britain and France contested the area, Britain eventually gaining possession (confirmed by the Treaty of Paris in 1763). Largely settled by Scots, Nova Scotia prospered in the 19th-century age of sail. But since joining Canada (1867),

its economy has lagged. Area: 52 841 sq km (20 402 sq mi). Population (1999 est): 940 825. Capital: Halifax.

● **Novaya Zemlya** ► A Russian archipelago off the N coast, between the Barents and the Kara Seas. It is a continuation of the Ural Mountains and consists almost entirely of two islands separated by a narrow strait. There is no permanent population, and the N island is always icebound. Total area: about 83 000 sq km (32 040 sq mi).

● **novel** ► An extended work of prose fiction dealing with the interaction of characters in a real or imagined setting. The term derives from Italian *novella*, meaning a short tale or anecdote. Latin forerunners of the novel are the picaresque *Satyricon* of Petronius (1st century AD) and *The Golden Ass* by Apuleius (2nd century AD). Cervantes' *Don Quixote* (1605) is considered the most important early novel. In England, a particular combination of social, economic, and literary conditions led to the development of the novel in the 18th century. The first notable English novelists included ▷Richardson, ▷Fielding, and ▷Defoe. The novels of the great 19th-century writers, notably ▷Dickens in England, ▷Tolstoy and ▷Dostoievski in Russia, and ▷Balzac and ▷Flaubert in France, together constitute one of the great achievements of world literature. In the 20th century the novel has been strongly influenced by developments in psychology and philosophy, and the various proliferating categories of novel—such as ▷science fiction, the ▷detective story, and the ▷*nouveau roman*—appeal to all levels of readership. ▷See also picaresque novel; stream of consciousness.

● **Novello, Ivor** ► (David Ivor Davies; 1893–1951) British composer, dramatist, and actor. He composed the World War I song "Keep the Home Fires Burning," and is best known for such romantic musicals as *Careless Rapture* (1936) and *The Dancing Years* (1939).

● **November Insurrection** ▷See Congress Kingdom of Poland.

● **Novgorod** ► 58 30N 31 20E A city in NW Russia, on the River Volkhov. It has varied industries and is a tourist centre, although many of its magnificent buildings, including the St Sofia Cathedral (1045–50), were badly damaged during World War II.
History: it is one of Russia's oldest towns, dating at least to the 9th century, and was a notable trading centre in the middle ages. Self-governing from 1019, it was forced to acknowledge Tatar overrule in the 13th century and that of Moscow in the 15th century. It was held by the Swedes from 1611 to 1619 and subsequently declined. Population (1997 est): 232 000.

● **Novi Sad** ► 45 15N 19 15E A port in Serbia and Macedonia, in N Serbia on the River Danube. It is a centre of Serbian culture with a university (1960). Population (2000 est): 182 778.

● **Novokuznetsk** ► (name from 1932 until 1961: Stalinsk) 53 45N 87 06E A city in S central Russia, on the Tom River. Founded in 1617, it developed as an industrial centre in the 1930s, producing iron and steel as well as machinery. Population (1997 est): 566 000.

● **Novosibirsk** ► 55 04N 83 05E A city in W central Russia, on the River Ob and the Trans-Siberian Railway. An important economic centre, it has machine-building, textile, chemical, and metallurgical industries. Nearby is the Akademgorodk, a complex of science research institutes. Population (1997 est): 1 367 000.

● **Novotný, Antonin** ► (1904–75) Czechoslovak Communist politician; president (1957–68). A founder member (1921) of the Czechoslovak Communist Party, he played a leading role in the Communist coup of 1948 and became first secretary of the Party in 1953. His unbending Stalinist policies eventually provoked the "Prague Spring" of 1968, in which he was deposed in favour of the more liberal ▷Dubček.

● **NSPCC** ▷See National Society for the Prevention of Cruelty to Children.

● **Nu, U** ► (or Thakin Nu; 1907–95) Burmese statesman; prime minister (1948–56, 1957–58, 1960–62). A leading nationalist from the 1930s, he became prime minister of Burma (now Myanmar) on independence. He sought to establish parliamentary democracy but when his Anti-Fascist People's Freedom League split in 1958 he was forced by ▷Ne Win to resign. He was restored, together with parliamentary government, in 1960 but was again deposed in 1962 and in 1966 went into exile. He returned to Burma in 1980; he declared himself prime minister in 1988, shortly before military rule was imposed, and sought foreign assistance, which was denied.

● **Nubia** ► A region of NE Africa, in the Nile valley, approximately between Aswan (Egypt) and Khartoum (Sudan). Much of Nubia is now drowned by Lake Nasser. From about 2000 BC the Egyptians gradually occupied Nubia, which they called Cush. Trade, especially in gold, flourished. By the 15th century BC Nubia had an Egyptian viceroy. As Egyptian power waned, Nubian kings, based at Napata and ▷Meroë, became influential, even dominating Egypt itself (c. 730–670). Their independent nation and language lasted until the 4th century AD.

● **Nubian Desert** ► A desert in the NE Sudan, between the River Nile and the Red Sea. It consists of a sandstone plateau with peaks of up to 2259 m (7411 ft) near the coast. Area: about 400 000 sq km (154 408 sq mi).

● **nuclear energy** ► The energy evolved by nuclear fission or nuclear fusion. The energy is liberated in fission when a heavy atomic nucleus, such as uranium, splits into two or more parts, the total mass of the parts being less than the mass of the original nucleus. This difference in mass is equivalent to the ▷binding energy of the nucleus and most of it is converted into kinetic energy (i.e. the increased velocity with which the parts move) according to Einstein's law, $E = mc^2$. In a fusion reaction, two light nuclei, such as hydrogen or deuterium, combine to form a stable nucleus, such as helium; as the nucleus formed is lighter than the sum of the component nuclei, again energy is released in accordance with Einstein's law.

In the case of fission, when the nucleus of a uranium-235 atom is struck by a neutron, a U-236 nucleus is formed, which immediately splits into two roughly equal parts, two or three neutrons being liberated at the same time. As these neutrons can then cause further fissions, a chain reaction builds up and a lump of U-235 will disintegrate almost instantaneously with enormous explosive power, provided that it is in excess of the critical mass (*see* nuclear weapons).

In nuclear power stations the fission reaction is harnessed to produce heat at a controlled rate (to raise steam to drive a turbine) in one of two ways. Both use natural uranium, which contains only 0.7% of the fissionable U-235 isotope, nearly all of the rest being the isotope U-238. The U-238 isotope absorbs the fast-moving neutrons emitted by the fission of U-235 and prevents a chain reaction from occurring in natural uranium. There are, however, two ways of producing a chain reaction. One is to use a moderator to slow down the fast neutrons so that they are not absorbed by U-238 nuclei (*see* thermal reactor). The other is to enrich the natural uranium with extra quantities of U-235 (or plutonium-239) so that there are sufficient neutrons to sustain the chain reaction in spite of absorption by U-238 (*see* fast reactor). Most present commercial reactors are thermal, although fast reactors are operating in the UK, France, and the former Soviet Union. They are expected to provide the new generation of reactors by the 2020s.

The fusion process is the basis of the hydrogen bomb (*see* nuclear weapons) and the □thermonuclear reactor, which is unlikely to be a source of energy until the 21st century.

Nuclear energy is an important source of electricity (*see* nuclear power) and is also used to power submarines, a very small quantity of nuclear fuel providing a very large amount of energy–about 7×10^{13} joules per kilogram, compared to about 4×10^7 J/kg for coal.

● **nuclear fission** ▷*See* nuclear energy; nuclear weapons.

● **nuclear fusion** ▷*See* nuclear energy; nuclear weapons; thermonuclear reactor.

● **nuclear magnetic resonance** ► (NMR) An effect observed when an atomic nucleus is exposed to radio waves in the presence of a magnetic field. A strong magnetic field causes the magnetic moment of the nucleus to precess around the direction of the field, only certain orientations being allowed by quantum theory. A transition from one orientation to another involves the absorption or emission of a photon, the frequency of which is equal to the precessional frequency. With magnetic field strengths customarily used the radiation is in the radio-frequency band. If radio-frequency radiation is supplied to the sample from one coil and is detected by another coil, while the magnetic field strength is slowly changed, radiation is ab-

sorbed at certain field values, which correspond to the frequency difference between orientations. An NMR spectrum consists of a graph of field strength against detector response. This provides information about the structure of molecules and the positions of electrons within them, as the orbital electrons shield the nucleus and cause them to resonate at different field strengths. ▷*See also* magnetic resonance imaging; tomography.

● **nuclear medicine** ► The use of ▷radioisotopes in the study and diagnosis of disease. It is widely used in the study of heart disease (**nuclear cardiology**): a gamma-emitting nuclide (e.g. technetium 99 or thallium 201) is injected into the blood, enabling a computerized gamma camera to record images of the heart as the blood passes through it.

● **nuclear power** ► The generation of electricity using ▷nuclear energy. The nuclear power industry expanded rapidly from the 1960s; by the 1990s it provided some 22% of world electricity, 30% of Europe's electricity, and 28% of UK electricity. However, the disaster (1986) at ▷Chernobyl caused universal concern over nuclear safety. The Soviet design of the Chernobyl reactor, using a single shell building, is now considered unsafe, unlike the US water-cooled reactors using double-walled buildings, which prevented disaster at Three Mile Island in 1979. In addition to safety fears, the cost of disposing of radioactive waste and high decommissioning costs have made the price of nuclear-generated electricity uncompetitive with fossil fuels. This has been especially so in the UK since privatization of the industry in 1996, when the £1bn per year subsidy raised by the **nuclear levy** came to an end. Once regarded as the energy source of the future, nuclear power is now becoming, in the UK at least, a thing of the past. Most countries have reconsidered their plans for expansion and in the UK the 15 remaining plants will be closed during the next 20 years (*see* table). This position has been reached in spite of a strong lobby that regards nuclear power as essential in view of diminishing fossil fuel reserves and the global warming they cause (*see* greenhouse effect). ▷*See also* fast reactor; thermal reactor; thermonuclear reactor.

● **nuclear reactor** ▷*See* nuclear energy.

● **Nuclear Test-Ban Treaty** ► (1963) A treaty banning nuclear testing by its signatories on the ground, in the atmosphere, in space, and under water. The signatories were the Soviet Union, the UK, and the USA; many other countries agreed to adhere to the treaty. As it made no attempt to limit nuclear stockpiling it was rejected as ineffectual by France, which performed atmospheric tests until 1974 and carried out underground tests in 1996, and by China, which staged tests in 1996. Subsequent ▷disarmament talks led to a comprehensive testban treaty (1996) but this will only come into force when signed and ratified by all 44 countries deemed to have nuclear potential; so far it has been signed by all but India, Pakistan, and North Korea but ratified only by France and the UK.

● **nuclear waste** ▷*See* radioactive waste.

● **nuclear weapons** ► Missiles, bombs, shells, or land mines that use fission or fusion of nuclear material (*see* nuclear energy) yielding enormous quantities of heat, light, blast, and radiation. The first **atomic bomb** (*or* fission bomb), manufactured by the USA in World War II, was dropped on Hiroshima in 1945. It consisted of two small masses of uranium-235 forced together by a chemical explosion to form a supercritical mass, in which an uncontrolled chain reaction occurred. Below the critical mass (estimated at between 16 and 20 kg) a chain reaction does not occur, as too many neutrons escape from the surface. The bomb had an explosive power equivalent to 20 000 tons of TNT. Later models used plutonium-239 to even greater effect.

The **hydrogen bomb** (fusion bomb *or* thermonuclear bomb) consists of an atom bomb surrounded by a layer of hydrogenous material, such as lithium deuteride. The atom bomb creates the necessary temperature (about 100 000 000°C) needed to ignite the fusion reaction (*see* thermonuclear reactor). Hydrogen bombs have an explosive power measured in tens of megatons (millions of tons) of TNT. The first hydrogen bomb was exploded by US scientists on Eniwetok Atoll in 1952 and although it has never been used in war, hydrogen bombs have been tested by the Soviet Union, Britain, France, and China. ▷*See also* Nuclear Test-Ban Treaty.

UK Nuclear Power Stations

Station	Type	Open/closure	Station	Type	Open/closure
Calder Hall	Magnox	1959–2008	Heysham 1	AGR	1984–2009
Chapelcross	Magnox	1959–2010	Dungeness B	AGR	1985–2008
Bradwell	Magnox	1962–2002	Heysham 2	AGR	1988–2023
Dungeness A	Magnox	1965–2006	Hunterston B	AGR	1989–2023
Sizewell A	Magnox	1966–2006	Torness	AGR	1989–2023
Oldbury	Magnox	1968–2013	Hartlepool	AGR	1989–2023
Wylfa	Magnox	1971–2021	Sizewell B	PWR	1995–2035
Hinkley Point B	AGR	1976–2011			

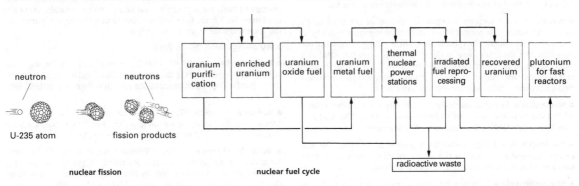

nuclear fission

nuclear fuel cycle

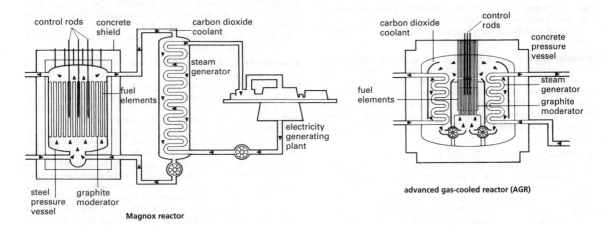

Magnox reactor

advanced gas-cooled reactor (AGR)

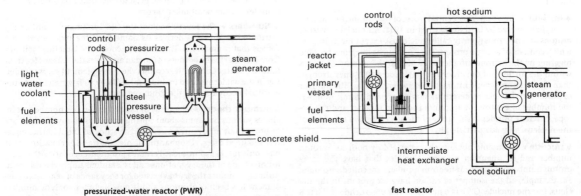

pressurized-water reactor (PWR)

fast reactor

nuclear energy ▸ Natural uranium metal fuel clad in Magnox (magnesium alloy) is used in Magnox thermal reactors. Enriched uranium dioxide pellets clad in steel are used in AGR and PWR fuel elements. Plutonium for fast reactors and recycled enriched uranium is obtained by reprocessing spent fuel from thermal reactors. The electricity generating plant is similar with all reactor types.

The **neutron bomb** (*or* enhanced radiation bomb) is a nuclear weapon designed to maximize neutron radiation. It is lethal to all forms of life but, having reduced blast, leaves buildings, etc., relatively undamaged.

● **nuclear winter** ▶ The period of darkness and low temperatures following a nuclear war, predicted in 1983 by an international group of scientists chaired by Sir Frederick Warner. Using models of global weather systems, they showed how dust from nuclear explosions and smoke from ensuing fires could affect the climate. In the months following a nuclear exchange, sunlight would be drastically cut and temperatures could fall by 20–30°C, with grave ecological consequences and almost total devastation of crops. The concept reinforces the view that nuclear war is unwinnable and suicidal.

● **nucleic acids** ▶ Organic compounds, found in the cells of all living organisms, that consist of a mixture of nitrogenous bases (purines and pyrimidines), phosphoric acid, and a pentose sugar (*see* nucleotide). The sugar is ribose in the ribonucleic acids (*see* RNA) and deoxyribose in the deoxyribonucleic acids (*see* DNA). Nucleic acids store genetic information in organisms and interpret that information in protein synthesis. ▷*See also* nucleoprotein.

● **nucleolus** ▶ A small dense body, one or more of which can be seen within the ▷nucleus of a nondividing cell. It contains RNA and protein and is involved in the synthesis of ▷ribosomes.

● **nucleon** ▶ A collective name for a proton or neutron. The **nucleon number** is the sum of the proton number and the neutron number. ▷*See also* mass number; nucleus; nuclide.

● **nucleoprotein** ▶ A compound consisting of a ▷nucleic acid associated with one or more proteins. The nucleoprotein of cell nuclei—the chromosomes—consists of DNA and proteins, mainly histones; cytoplasmic nucleoproteins—the ▷ribosomes—are ribonucleoproteins comprising some 60% protein and 40% RNA. ▷Viruses also consist of nucleoprotein.

● **nucleotide** ▶ A molecular unit consisting of an organic nitrogenous base (a ▷purine or a ▷pyrimidine) linked to a sugar (ribose or deoxyribose) and a phosphate group. The base–sugar units are called **nucleosides**; thus nucleotides are phosphorylated nucleosides. The nucleic acids (*see* DNA; RNA) consist of long chains of nucleotides, i.e. they are **polynucleotides**. The high-energy compound ▷ATP is an example of a **mononucleotide**, in which the base is adenine and the sugar is ribose.

● **nucleus** ▶ (biology) A large granular component of nearly all cells. It is usually spherical or ovoid in shape and is surrounded by a nuclear membrane, which is perforated with pores to allow exchange of materials between the nucleus and cytoplasm. The nucleus contains the ▷chromosomes, made up of the hereditary material (DNA), and is therefore essential for the control and regulation of cellular activities, such as growth and metabolism. ▷*See also* meiosis; mitosis.

● **nucleus** ▶ (physics) The central core of the atom (*see* atomic theory) discovered by Lord Rutherford in 1911. All nuclei consist of protons and neutrons (jointly called nucleons), except for hydrogen, which consists of a single proton. The constituent nucleons are held together by the ▷strong interaction, which at the minute distances within the nucleus (of the order 10^{-15} m) is some 100 times stronger than the electromagnetic interaction between protons. The number of protons in the nucleus determines its charge and atomic number; the number of neutrons determines the mass number and the isotope. **Nuclear physics** is the study of the structure and reactions of the nucleus. ▷*See also* particle physics.

● **nuclide** ▶ An atomic nucleus characterized by both its ▷proton number and its ▷neutron number. Nuclides that have the same proton number but different neutron numbers are called ▷isotopes. For example, all the isotopes of carbon have six protons in the nucleus, but the nuclide $_6C^{12}$ has 6 neutrons and the nuclide $_6C^{14}$ has 8 neutrons. The subscript 6 preceding the symbol is the proton number; the superscript 12 or 14 following it is the ▷nucleon number.

● **Nuevo Laredo** ▶ 27 30N 99 30W A city in N Mexico, on the Rio Grande. It is an important point of entry into Mexico from the USA. Population (1990): 218 413.

● **Nuffield, William Richard Morris, 1st Viscount** ▶ (1877–1963) British car manufacturer and philanthropist. He established a car factory in Cowley, near Oxford, which in 1913 produced the first Morris Oxford, soon followed by the Morris Cowley. He founded Nuffield College, Oxford, the Nuffield Trust, and the Nuffield Foundation.

● **nuisance** ▶ Any activity that interferes with a person's use or enjoyment of land or rights over land (**private nuisance**) or with public health, safety, comfort, or property (**public nuisance**). A private nuisance is a tort, which can be stopped by removing the nuisance or applying to a court for an injunction and/or damages. A public nuisance is a crime; such nuisances include obstructing the highway and selling food unfit for human consumption.

● **Nu Jiang** ▷*See* Salween River.

● **Nuku'alofa** ▶ 21 09S 175 14W The capital of Tonga in the S Pacific, in N Tongatabu. It is the site of the Royal Palace (1865–67) and Royal Tombs. Copra and bananas are exported. Population (1990 est): 34 000.

● **Nukus** ▶ 42 28N 59 07E A city in Uzbekistan, the capital of the Kara-Kalpak Autonomous Republic on the River Amu Darya. Its industries include food processing. Population (1993 est): 185 000.

● **Nullarbor Plain** ▶ A plain of SW South Australia and SE Western Australia, bordering on the Great Australian Bight. It consists of a treeless arid plateau with extensive limestone areas and is crossed by the Trans-Australian Railway. Area: 260 000 sq km (100 000 sq mi).

● **numbat** ▶ A rat-sized pouchless ▷marsupial, *Myrmecobius fasciatus*, of open eucalyptus woods in SW Australia, also called marsupial (*or* banded) anteater. It is rust-coloured, with white stripes across the back and a long tail; it feeds on ants and termites with its sticky tongue. Family: *Dasyuridae*.

● **numbers** ▶ Mathematical symbols used to denote quantity. The natural numbers, 1, 2, 3, 4, 5..., etc., were developed first by the Hindus and Arabs for simple counting. Subtraction led to negative numbers and to zero, which together with natural numbers make up the set of integers ...–3, –2, –1, 0, 1,.... Division of whole numbers results in fractions or rational numbers. Some numbers, such as √2, cannot be expressed as the ratio of two integers. These are called irrational numbers and they occur as the solutions to simple algebraic equations. They can be calculated to any required accuracy but cannot be written as exact values. Other numbers, called transcendental numbers, do not come from algebraic relationships. Some of these occur as basic properties of space, for example π, the ratio of a circumference of a circle to its diameter. Real numbers include all rational and irrational numbers. The equation $x^2 = -1$ can have no real solution for x, since the square of any number is positive. The imaginary number, i = √–1, was introduced to overcome this problem. ▷*See* complex numbers; number theory.

● **Numbers** ▶ The fourth book of the Old Testament, traditionally attributed to Moses. It derives its name from the two records of a census that it mentions. The narrative covers the Israelites' journey from Mt Sinai to the borders of Canaan and gives the reasons for their failure to enter Canaan. It recounts the subsequent 40 years wandering in the wilderness and includes miscellaneous laws relevant to the eventual occupation of the Promised Land.

● **number theory** ▶ The study of the properties of ▷numbers. It includes various theorems about ▷prime numbers, many of which are unproved but apparently true, and the study of Diophantine equations (named after ▷Diophantus of Alexandria), i.e. equations that have only integer solutions. ▷Fermat's last theorem deals with the solution of one of these equations and is a famous unproved theorem. Although number theory has existed for thousands of years, its development has been continuous and it now includes analytic number theory, originated by ▷Euler in 1742; geometric number theory, which uses such geometrical methods of analysis as Cartesian coordinates (*see* coordinate systems), ▷vectors, and ▷matrices; and probabilistic number theory, based on ▷probability theory.

● **Numidia** ▶ An ancient kingdom of N Africa, W of ▷Carthage. Its ▷Berber population was nomadic until Masinissa (c. 240–149 BC), Rome's ally during the second and third ▷Punic Wars, promoted agriculture and urbanization. After supporting Pompey against Julius Caesar (46 BC), Numidia lost its monarchy and became part of the Roman province of Africa.

● **numismatics** ▶ (or coin collecting) Collecting and studying coins, medals, or banknotes as a hobby or as historical research. Collecting Greek and Roman coins became popular among aristocrats in Renaissance Italy, although collections then often included copies. In the 19th century numismatics became popular among a wider public; catalogues were produced and societies formed. Museums are now the chief collectors, while private collectors usually specialize in one field. Coins in good condition are a form of investment, the best being "proof" coins, struck especially for sale to collectors.

● **Nummulites** ▶ A genus of single-celled organisms (see protozoa), sometimes called money fossils, that was abundant during the Eocene epoch (about 54–38 million years ago) although only one species has survived. Some limestones are almost entirely composed of their disc-shaped biconvex shells. Class: ▷Foraminifera.

● **nunatak** ▶ A rock peak protruding above the surface of an ice sheet. Nunataks occur in Greenland, the word originating from the Inuit language.

● **Nunavut** ▶ (Inupik: Our Land) A territory of NE Canada, created in April, 1999, from part of the Northwest Territories as a semi-autonomous homeland for the Inuit peoples. Occupying about one-fifth of Canada's land mass, it extends from 60°N to the North Pole and incorporates most of Canada's Arctic islands, including Baffin Island in the E and Ellesmere Island in the N. Nunavut is one of the most sparsely populated areas in the world. About 85% of the people are Indians and Inuits, who traditionally live nomadically by hunting, trapping, and fishing. However, the Inuits are increasingly settling in larger communities around cooperatives and government institutions. Although the territory is rich in mineral resources (including copper, silver, zinc, lead, and iron), these remain largely unexploited owing to the severe climate and lack of infrastructure. Nunavut has almost no roads outside settlements and most transport is by snowmobile or by air. The decision to create the new territory was taken following a referendum in 1992 and involved the settlement of some 216 000 sq km (135 000 sq mi) of land on the Inuit people. Elections to the new territorial assembly took place in 1999 and Paul Okalik became premier. The territory has severe economic and social problems, with about two-thirds of the population receiving welfare and high levels of alcoholism and suicide. Area: 1 235 200 sq km (476 787 sq mi). Population (1999 est): 24 000. Capital: Iqaluit.

● **Nuneaton** ▶ 52 32N 1 28W A town in central England, in Warwickshire. Formerly noted for brickmaking, it now has textile and light-engineering industries and is a storage and distribution centre. Its name refers to the 12th-century Benedictine nunnery, now in ruins. Nuneaton was the birthplace of George Eliot. Population (1991): 66 715.

● **Nunn, Trevor (Robert)** ▶ (1940–) British theatre director. He was artistic director of the Royal Shakespeare Company from 1968 to 1986 and of the Royal National Theatre from 1997 to 2002. Renowned for his productions of Shakespeare, he is also known for directing musicals, including Cats (1981) and Les Misérables (1985).

● **Nuremberg** ▶ (German name: Nürnberg) 49 27N 11 05E A city in S Germany, in Bavaria on the River Pegnitz. It was severely bombed during World War II because of its engine industry and is now a major centre of the metalworking and electrical industries. It shares a university with Erlangen.
　History: a medieval trading centre, it became the centre of the German Renaissance, when the mastersingers' contests were held here. It was the site of the ⁿNazi Party congresses (1933–38) and the war-crime trials following World War II. It is the birthplace of Albrecht Dürer and Hans Sachs. Population (1998 est): 489 758.

● **Nuremberg Trials** ▶ (1945–46) The trials of ▷Nazi criminals after World War II. An international military court was set up by the Allied Powers in Nuremberg to try Nazi individuals or groups who had vio-

lated the rules of war or committed crimes against humanity, such as the mass murders of Jews in ▷concentration camps. 12 men were sentenced to hang (including Goering, who committed suicide before the sentence could be carried out, Ribbentrop, Frank, Streicher, and Jodl) and six others were imprisoned for various terms (including Hess, who died in Spandau in 1987). The trials of the war criminals created precedents, chiefly that ▷war crimes are the responsibility not merely of the state but also of the individual.

● **Nureyev, Rudolf** ▶ (1938–93) Russian ballet dancer. He danced with the Leningrad Kirov Ballet from 1958 until 1961, when he defected from Russia. In 1962 he joined the Royal Ballet, where he frequently partnered Margot ▷Fonteyn. In 1977 he starred in the film *Valentino*; other films include *Exposed* (1982). He was artistic director of the Paris Opéra Ballet from 1983 until 1989. He became an Austrian citizen in 1982.

● **Nurhachi** ▶ (1559–1626) Manchu chieftain, who founded the Qing dynasty of China. He unified the Juchen tribes of Manchuria to found the Manchu state. He organized all his subjects under the ▷Banner System, creating a powerful base from which his successors conquered all China.

● **Nurmi, Paavo Johannes** ▶ (1897–1973) Finnish middle-distance and long-distance runner. He broke over 20 world records and won 12 Olympic medals, 9 gold and 3 silver. He was Olympic 10 000 metres champion in 1920 and 1928 and in 1924 won both the 1500 metres and the 5000 metres. He was in the habit of carrying a stopwatch while he ran.

● **nursery education** ▷See preschool education.

● **nursery rhymes** ▶ Traditional verses said or sung to small children. They are usually for amusement only, although some, such as counting rhymes, are also instructional. They vary greatly in age and origin: some probably originate in ancient folklore, while others were composed as popular ballads in the 19th century. The earliest known collection, *Tommy Thumb's Song Book* (1744), includes such perennial favourites as "Sing a Song of Sixpence" and "Who Killed Cock Robin?".

● **nurse shark** ▶ A ▷shark, *Ginglymostoma cirratum*, that occurs in warm shallow waters of the Atlantic Ocean. Yellow-brown or grey-brown and up to 4.2 m long, it is considered dangerous to man only when provoked. Live young are born. Family: *Orectolobidae*.

● **nursing** ▶ The medical specialty concerned with the care of the sick. Nursing originated in the religious orders, becoming increasingly secularized in Protestant countries after the Reformation; the standards of professional nursing were established by Florence ▷Nightingale after her work in the Crimea. Nurses are responsible for the day-to-day welfare of patients and for carrying out routine medical and surgical procedures under the supervision of a doctor. In the UK the profession is regulated by the United Kingdom Central Council for Nursing, Midwifery, and Health Visiting (UKCC); under Project 2000, introduced in 1989, student nurses must undertake a three-year course to gain a diploma in higher education, in addition to hospital training, in order to qualify for registration at the UKCC as a general nurse. The professional organization for British nurses is the Royal College of Nursing. Apart from nursing in hospitals, the profession includes the work of midwives, health visitors, and district, school, and practice nurses. **Nurse practitioners** have the authority to prescribe certain drugs. **Triage nurses** (see triage) are responsible for sorting casualties or patients according to the seriousness of their conditions, so that the seriously ill are seen first by the appropriate doctors.

● **Nusa Tenggara** ▶ (former name: Lesser ▷Sunda Islands) A volcanic island group E of Java, the chief islands being Bali, Lombok, Sumbawa, Sumba, and Flores (all in Indonesia), and ▷Timor. Area: 73 144 sq km (28 241 sq mi). Population (1995 est): 7 237 600.

● **nut** ▶ Loosely, any edible nonsucculent fruit, including the peanut and brazil nut. Botanically, a nut is a large dry fruit containing a single seed that is not released from the fruit at maturity. An example is the chestnut.

● **nutcracker** ▶ A songbird of the genus *Nucifraga* found in coniferous forests of E Europe and Asia. The common nutcracker (*N. caryocatactes*) is dark brown speckled with white, about 32 cm long, and cracks open pine cones with its sharp bill to extract the seeds. Clark's nutcracker (*N. columbianus*) is grey with a black tail and wings patched with white. Family: *Corvidae* (crows, jays, magpies).

● **nuthatch** ▶ A small stocky bird belonging to a family (*Sittidae*: 30 species) occurring everywhere except South America and New Zealand. Nuthatches have long straight bills, for hammering open nuts, and long-clawed toes, for running up and down tree trunks in search of insects. The European nuthatch (*Sitta europaea*), about 14 cm long, has a blue-grey upper plumage with paler underparts and a black eyestripe.

● **nutmeg** ▶ A fragrant tropical evergreen tree, *Myristica fragrans*, native to Indonesia but widely cultivated in SE Asia and the West Indies. Growing to 20 m high, it has oval pointed leaves and tiny male and female flowers borne on separate trees. The yellow fleshy fruit, about 3 cm across, splits when ripe to expose the seed, which has a red fleshy covering (aril). The dried aril (mace) and whole or ground seeds (nutmeg) are used as spices. Family: *Myristicaceae*.

● **nutria** ▷*See* coypu.

● **nutrient** ▶ A substance required for nourishment, providing a source of energy for bodily processes and materials for body components (*see* nutrition). In animals (including humans) nutrients are consumed as part of the diet. A balanced diet must include the so-called major nutrients—▷carbohydrates, ▷fats, and ▷proteins—as well as vitamins and certain minerals (calcium, phosphorus, sulphur, potassium, sodium, chlorine, magnesium, iron, and the ▷trace elements). In plants nutrients are obtained from carbon dioxide (taken in from the atmosphere during photosynthesis) and water and are divided into macronutrients and micronutrients. Macronutrients, which are required in relatively large amounts, include carbon, hydrogen, oxygen, nitrogen, phosphorus, potassium, sulphur, magnesium, calcium, and iron. Micronutrients, required only in minute quantities, include copper, zinc, and manganese.

● **nutrition** ▶ The process by which organisms obtain the ▷nutrients they require to provide a source of energy and materials for maintenance, growth, and repair. There are two types of nutrition: autotrophic, used by most plants and bacteria (*see* autotroph); and heterotrophic, seen in animals (including humans) and fungi. Heterotrophic nutrition relies on the consumption of food, which is broken down to release its nutrients by the process of ▷digestion. The study of nutrition in humans is concerned with the functions of nutrients, the composition of diets, and the effects of dietary deficiency (*see* dietetics; deficiency disease).

● **Nuuk** ▶ (name until 1979: Godthåb) 64 10N 51 40W The capital of Greenland, a port at the mouth of Godthåb Fjord. Founded in 1721, it is the site of a radio station, hospital, and college. Chief occupations are reindeer and sheep raising, hunting, and fishing. Population (1996 est): 12 882.

● **nux vomica** ▶ A poisonous evergreen tree, *Strychnos nux-vomica*, also called the koochla tree, native to lowlands of Myanmar (Burma) and India. It has simple leaves and clusters of tubular flowers, each with five spreading lobes. The seeds of the orange-like fruits contain the highly poisonous substances strychnine and curare. Family: *Strychnaceae*.

● **Nuzi** ▶ An ancient ▷Hurrian city SW of Kirkuk (N Iraq). Nuzi flourished in the 15th century BC before being absorbed into the Assyrian Empire. Excavations here in the 1920s revealed a prosperous trading centre with archives detailing legal, commercial, and military activities.

● **nyala** ▶ An antelope, *Tragelaphus angasi*, of SW Africa. About 100 cm high at the shoulder, nyalas are shy and nocturnal, inhabiting dense undergrowth, and have spiral-shaped horns and a greyish-brown coat with vertical white stripes on the flanks. The mountain nyala (*T. buxtoni*) lives in mountainous regions of S Ethiopia.

● **Nyasa, Lake** ▷*See* Malawi, Lake.

● **Nyasaland** ▷*See* Malawi.

● **Nyeman, River** ▷*See* Neman, River.

● **Nyerere, Julius (Kambarage)** ▶ (1922–99) Tanzanian statesman; president (1962–85). Educated at Makerere College (Uganda) and Edinburgh University, in 1954 Nyerere formed the Tanganyika African National Union, which led the fight for independence (achieved in 1960). He became chief minister (1960), prime minister (1961), and then president of Tanganyika, which was renamed Tanzania in 1964 after union with Zanzibar. Nyerere defended the one-party state as appropriate for developing countries and was a prominent advocate of African unity. Under his leadership Tanzania was instrumental in the overthrow of Amin in Uganda in 1979. He resigned as president in 1985 and as party chairman in 1990.

● **Nyköping** ▶ 58 45N 17 03E A seaport in E Sweden, on the Baltic coast. A centre of commerce and industry, its manufactures include machinery and textiles. Population (1990): 65 908.

● **nylon** ▶ A synthetic material with a translucent creamy white appearance, widely used both in fibre form and in solid blocks because of its lightness, toughness, and elasticity. It is made by ▷polymerization of diamine with ▷fatty acid or by polymerizing a single monomer, in both cases to form a polyamide. Nylon is used to make small engineering components, such as bearings and gears, because it is hard wearing and easy to machine. It is also spun and woven into fabrics for clothing, etc., and can be coloured with pigments. Introduced commercially in 1938, nylon was the first truly synthetic fibre.

● **nymph** ▶ A stage in the life cycle of insects that show incomplete ▷metamorphosis, including dragonflies, grasshoppers, and bugs. The egg hatches into a nymph, which undergoes a series of moults to form a line of nymphs that show increasing similarity to the adult.

● **nymphalid butterfly** ▶ A butterfly belonging to the widely distributed family *Nymphalidae*, also called brush-footed butterfly. Nymphalids are characterized by small hairy forelegs, useless for walking. Many, including the migratory ▷red admiral and ▷painted lady, are strong fast fliers. The adults are generally orange or brown with black markings and the caterpillars are commonly brown or black and covered with branched spines.

● **Nymphenburg porcelain** ▶ Porcelain produced at a factory established (1753) near Munich. It is famed for rococo figures designed by F. A. Bustelli (1723–64). They include Italian comedy, chinoiserie, and mythological models. After Bustelli died table wares, particularly tea services, were made, often based on Meissen. The factory still copies its early models.

● **nymphs** ▶ In Greek mythology, female spirits of nature, often portrayed as youthful and amorous dancers or musicians. They were long lived, though not immortal, and usually benevolent. The several classes of nymphs associated with natural phenomena include the ▷dryads, the ▷naiads, and the ▷nereids.

● **Nyoro** ▶ A Bantu-speaking people of the western lakes region of Uganda. They were traditionally divided into three distinct groups: the Bito clan from whom the hereditary paramount chief (Mukama) always came, the aristocratic Huma pastoralists, and the subordinate Iru cultivators. The Bito and Huma are thought to have originally come from the north as conquering invaders. They are a patrilineal people who live in small scattered settlements.

● **Nysa, River** ▷*See* Neisse, River.

● **Nystad, Treaty of** ▶ (1721) The peace treaty between Russia and Sweden that concluded the Great ▷Northern War. Sweden was obliged to cede large tracts of territory, including Livonia, and Russia gained its long-coveted access to the Baltic Sea, thus becoming a European power.

● **Nyx** ▶ (Latin name: Nox) A Greek goddess, the personification of night. She was the daughter of Chaos and her offspring included Thanatos (Death), Hypnos (Sleep), the ▷Fates, and ▷Nemesis. She lived in Tartarus, from which she emerged as Hemera, the goddess of day.

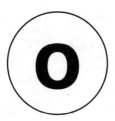

O

● **Oahu** ▶ A US island in Hawaii, the most populous and the administrative centre. The Japanese attack on ▷Pearl Harbor (1941) was decisive in bringing the USA into World War II. Area: 1584 sq km (608 sq mi). Population (latest est): 836 231. Chief town: Honolulu.

● **oak** ▶ A deciduous or evergreen [□]tree or shrub of the genus *Quercus* (over 800 species), found in N temperate and subtropical regions. The leaves usually have lobed or toothed margins and the yellow male catkins and tiny green female flowers are borne on the same tree. The fruit—an acorn—is an oval nut partly enclosed in a round cup. Often 30–40 m high, many species are important timber trees, especially the common or pedunculate oak (*Q. robur*) and the ▷durmast oak (both Eurasian) and the North American white oak (*Q. alba*) and live oaks. Several are planted for ornament, including the Eurasian Turkey oak (*Q. cerris*), the North American red oak (*Q. rubra*), which has a red autumn foliage, and the Mediterranean ▷holm oak. The cork oak (*Q. suber*) is the main commercial source of ▷cork. Family: *Fagaceae*.

● **Oakham** ▶ 52 40N 0 43W A market town in central England, the administrative centre of Rutland. It has a 12th-century castle and a school founded in 1584. The main industries are plastics, engineering, and hosiery. Population (1991): 8691.

● **Oakland** ▶ 37 50N 122 15W A port in the USA, in California on San Francisco Bay and connected with San Francisco by the San Francisco–Oakland Bay Bridge (1936). Oakland's industries include chemicals and shipbuilding. Most of the deaths in the 1989 San Francisco earthquake were caused here when a double freeway collapsed. Population (1998 est): 365 874.

● **Oakley, Annie** ▶ (Phoebe Anne Oakley Mozee; 1860–1926) US gunshooter. From 1885 she and her husband, Frank Butler, performed daring acts of marksmanship in Buffalo Bill's Wild West Show. A musical, *Annie Get Your Gun* (1948) with music by Irving Berlin, was based on her life.

● **oak moss** ▶ An edible ▷lichen, *Evernia prunastri*, found in mountainous regions of the N hemisphere. It has a pale greenish-grey body, 3–8 cm long, with pointed branches. It is used in perfumery and in the preparation of drugs.

● **Oak Ridge** ▶ 36 02N 84 12W A town in the USA, in Tennessee. It contains the Oak Ridge National Laboratory (1943) for nuclear research. Population (latest est): 27 310.

● **Oaks** ▶ A flat race for three-year-old fillies only, run over the ▷Derby course (2.4 km; 1.5 mi) at Epsom, three days after the Derby in early June. One of the English ▷Classics, it was first run in 1779 and was named after the 12th Earl of Derby's hunting lodge.

● **Oakville** ▶ 43 27N 79 41W A town in central Canada, in S Ontario. A dormitory suburb of Toronto, it houses a major motor-vehicle factory and produces plastics, paints, and electrical appliances. Population (1996): 128 405.

● **oarfish** ▶ A ▷ribbonfish of the genus *Regalecus*, especially *R. glesne*, found in all seas. It has a long silvery ribbon-like body, up to 9 m long, a long red dorsal fin that extends forwards to form a crest, long red oarlike pelvic fins situated near the pectoral fins, and no anal or tail fins. [□]oceans.

● **OAS** ▷*See* Organisation de l'Armée secrète; Organization of American States.

● **oasis** ▶ An area within a desert where water is available for vegetation and human use. It may consist of a single small spring around which palms grow or be an extensive area where the water table is at or near the ground surface.

● **Oasis** ▶ British rock band led by the Gallagher brothers Noel (1967–) and Liam (1969–). Their albums are *Definitely Maybe* (1994), *What's the Story (Morning Glory)?* (1995), *Be Here Now* (1997), *Standing on the Shoulder of Giants* (2000), and *Heathen Chemistry* (2002).

● **Oastler, Richard** ▶ (1789–1861) British social reformer. He attacked the employment of children in factories and campaigned for a ten-hour working day, which was achieved in the act of 1847.

● **Oates, Lawrence Edward Grace** ▶ (1880–1912) British explorer. A professional soldier, he was given leave to participate in R. F. ▷Scott's expedition to the Antarctic (1910–12). They reached the Pole but on the return journey Oates, fearing that his lameness (resulting from frostbite) might hinder the already struggling expedition, walked out into the blizzard to die. His gallant act failed to save his companions and was only revealed when Scott's diary was found, together with the bodies of Scott and his companions, by a later expedition.

● **Oates, Titus** ▷*See* Popish Plot.

● **oat grass** ▶ A perennial ▷grass of either of the genera *Arrhenatherum* (about 6 species), native to temperate Eurasia, and *Danthonia* (over 100 species), native to S temperate regions. Tall oat grass (*A. elatius*) has been introduced as a pasture grass to many countries; *Danthonia* species are important forage grasses.

● **oath** ▶ A solemn promise to tell the truth when giving evidence in a court of law or when making a sworn written statement (an **affidavit**), usually to support a particular application or to provide a court with written evidence. The solemnity of the oath is emphasized by a reference to the oath-taker's God (if he or she has one). In British courts witnesses have to take a copy of the New Testament in their right hand and say "I swear by Almighty God that the evidence which I shall give shall be the truth, the whole truth, and nothing but the truth." Jews are expected to hold the Hebrew scriptures in their right hand and take the oath with their heads covered. Muslims swear on the Koran and Hindus use an appropriate sacred text.

For those who do not believe in God, or do not wish to take an oath, the permitted alternative is to **affirm**, i.e. to make the same solemn promise to tell the truth, without calling on God to witness the act. Taking an oath or affirming have the same legal validity; telling an untruth under oath or after affirmation constitutes the offence of ▷perjury.

● **oats** ▶ Annual ▷grasses belonging to the genus *Avena* (10 species), native to temperate regions. The common oat (*A. sativa*) was first cultivated in Europe and is grown in cool temperate regions. Up to 1 m high, it has a branching cluster of flowers; the grain is used as a livestock feed, especially for horses, and for oatmeal, breakfast cereals, etc. The straw is used for livestock fodder and bedding. Wild oats, especially *A. fatua*, can be a serious weed in cereal crops.

● **OAU** ▷*See* Organization of African Unity.

● **Oaxaca** ▶ (*or* Oaxaca de Juárez) 17 05N 96 41W A city in S Mexico, in the Atoyac Valley. Founded in 1486 by the Aztecs, it has flour-milling, cotton, textile, and handicraft industries. Its university was established in 1827. Population (1990): 212 943.

• **Ob, River** ▸ A river in N central Russia, flowing N from the Altai Mountains to the **Gulf of Ob** on the Kara Sea. One of the world's largest rivers, its drainage basin covers an area of about 2 930 000 sq km (1 131 000 sq mi). Length: 3682 km (2287 mi).

• **Obadiah** ▸ An Old Testament prophet who predicted the downfall of Edom, the traditional enemy of Israel. **The Book of Obadiah** is the shortest book of the Old Testament.

• **Oban** ▸ 56 25N 5 29W A port and resort in W Scotland, in Argyll and Bute on the Firth of Lorne. Glassware, pottery, and whisky are manufactured. Population (1991): 8203.

• **OBE** ▷See Order of the British Empire.

• **Obelia** ▸ A genus of marine invertebrate animals belonging to a suborder (*Leptomedusae*) of ▷cnidarians. Their life cycle alternates between a sedentary asexual phase (*see* polyp) and a free-swimming sexual phase (*see* medusa). The polyps occur in small whitish or brownish colonies attached to the sea bottom, rocks, shells, etc., of shallow coastal waters. Order: *Hydroida*; class: ▷Hydrozoa.

• **obelisk** ▸ A stone monument generally shaped as a tall tapering rectangular column of stone, ending in a pyramid-like form. First used by the Egyptians, they have also been employed in the modern age. They were normally made of a single piece of stone and erected for religious or commemorative purposes. Perhaps the most famous are those known as ▷Cleopatra's Needles.

• **Oberammergau** ▸ 47 35N 11 07E A town in S Germany, in the Bavarian Alps. It is noted for its passion play, performed every ten years following a vow made by the villagers (1633) when they were saved from the plague. Population (1989 est): 4740.

• **Oberhausen** ▸ 51 27N 6 50E A port in NW Germany, in North Rhine-Westphalia on the Rhine-Herne Canal in the ▷Ruhr. Population (1996 est): 224 397.

• **Oberon** ▸ In European legend, a king of elves or fairies. In literature he first appeared in the medieval French romance *Huon de Bordeaux*, which formed the basis of ▷Wieland's poem *Oberon* (1780) and ▷Weber's opera of the same name (1826). He also features in English folklore and (with his queen Titania) in Shakespeare's *A Midsummer Night's Dream* (1596). Oberon is probably related to the Alberich of German medieval legends, a Nibelung (dwarf) who steals the magic treasure from the Rhine maidens (*see* Nibelungenlied).

• **obesity** ▸ The condition of being seriously overweight, usually defined as weighing more than 20% above the average for a person's height, build, and gender. The overweight is caused by the consumption of more food than is required to supply a person's energy needs and usually results from subcutaneous deposits of fat in the tissues. Recent evidence suggest that genetic factors may play a part; hunger appears to be controlled by peptide messengers, encoded by specific genes, that act on the ▷hypothalamus in the brain. Obesity, the most common nutritional disorder in the industrialized countries, is particularly prevalent in middle-aged women; it can increase the body's susceptibility to disease and can reduce life expectancy.

The obvious remedies of eating less and exercising more may not always be practicable, especially for those with a disordered appetite-regulating mechanism, and in extreme cases surgical shortening of the intestines may be required.

• **oboe** ▸ A woodwind instrument with a double reed, made in three jointed sections and having a conical bore and small belled end. It derives from the ancient shawm. It has a range of about three octaves above the B flat below middle C and because of its constant pitch usually gives the A to which other orchestral instruments tune.

• **Obote, (Apollo) Milton** ▸ (1925–) Ugandan statesman; prime minister (1962–66) and president (1966–71, 1980–85). He formed (1958) the Uganda People's Congress, which opposed the existence of the kingdom of ▷Buganda within Uganda. On independence he became prime minister and in 1966 deposed Mutesa II of Buganda (1924–69). Overthrown by ▷Amin Dada in 1971, he was re-elected in 1980 but deposed in a military coup in 1985.

• **Obrenović** ▸ A Serbian ruling dynasty that came to power in 1815, when ▷Karageorge was assassinated, probably by ▷Miloš Obrenović. The subsequent feud between the Karadordević and Obrenović families lasted until ▷Alexander, the last Obrenović monarch, was assassinated in 1903.

• **O'Brien, Conor Cruise** ▸ (1917–) Irish writer, politician, and diplomat. He was the UN representative in the Congo (1961). In 1969 he became a Labour MP in Ireland and served in the coalition government of 1973–77. He served as a senator (1977–79) in the Irish parliament and was editor of the *Observer* newspaper (London) from 1979 to 1981. In 1996 he was elected to the Northern Ireland negotiating forum as a member of the new UK Unionist Party. He published *Memoir: My Life and Themes* in 1998.

• **O'Brien, Edna** ▸ (1936–) Irish author. Her novels include *The Country Girls* (1960), *The Lonely Girls* (1962; filmed as *The Girl With Green Eyes*, 1965), *Casualties of Peace* (1966), *Johnnie I Hardly Knew You* (1977), and *Time and Tide* (1992). She has also written plays and short stories.

• **O'Brien, Flann** ▸ (Brian O'Nolan; 1911–66) Irish novelist and journalist. His best-known novel is *At Swim-Two-Birds* (1939), an exuberant comic mixture of folklore, farce, and lyricism that was praised by James Joyce and Dylan Thomas. Other novels include *The Dalkey Archive* (1964) and *The Third Policeman* (1967). He wrote a satirical column for the *Irish Times* under the name Myles na Gopaleen.

• **O'Brien, William** ▸ (1852–1928) Irish nationalist politician and journalist. He made a great impression as a fiery MP (from 1883) in the ▷Home Rule party. He later became more moderate, forming (1910) a short-lived political party that attempted to reconcile different opinions in Ireland.

• **O'Brien, William Smith** ▸ (1803–64) Irish politician. An MP (1828–48), he was at first a moderate constitutionalist but in the 1840s became a prominent member of the ▷Young Ireland group and led the abortive 1848 rebellion. O'Brien was transported to Australia but subsequently pardoned.

• **obscenity** ▷See censorship.

• **observatory** ▸ A collection of optical, ▷infrared, or ▷radio telescopes together with ancillary equipment and housing. Observatories for optical and infrared studies are now sited at high altitudes so that atmospheric disturbance is minimized. Space observatories, orbiting above the earth's atmosphere, permit X-ray, gamma-ray, ultraviolet, and infrared studies to be made and improve optical measurements.

• **obsession** ▸ A recurrent and persistent thought, feeling, or idea that forces itself into the mind and cannot be put aside, although the person is aware of its irrational nature. It is often expressed in the performance of a particular, usually trivial, action (such as patting a door or drawer three times after closing it), which relieves the tension caused by the obsession. Obsessive behaviour of this type is widespread and not regarded as abnormal, provided that it does not interfere with everyday activities. Obsessions that dominate a person's life are a feature of the anxiety disorder (*see* neurosis) known as **obsessive-compulsive disorder**, which may, for example, take the form of repeated hand-washing to dispel an obsessional fear of contamination. Treatment of obsessive-compulsive disorder is by behaviour therapy, psychotherapy, and/or tranquillizing drugs.

• **obsidian** ▸ A black glassy volcanic rock with a conchoidal fracture. It is of rhyolitic composition (*see* rhyolite) and contains less water and less crystalline material than pitchstone, a similar volcanic glass. Obsidian is formed by the rapid cooling of acid lava.

• **obstetrics** ▷See gynaecology.

• **O'Casey, Sean** ▸ (1880–1964) Irish dramatist. Born into a poor Protestant family in Dublin, he was largely self-educated. His early realistic tragicomedies, *The Shadow of a Gunman* (1923), *Juno and the Paycock* (1924), and *The Plough and the Stars* (1926), were produced at the Abbey Theatre and dealt with Ireland in the time of the "Troubles." In 1926 he went to live in England. His later work, which includes the antiwar play *The Silver Tassie* (1929) and *Red Roses for Me*

(1943), is usually considered inferior. He published six volumes of autobiography (1939–54).

● **Occitan** ▷*See* Provençal.

● **occultation** ▶ The temporary disappearance of one astronomical body behind another, as when the moon passes in front of and obscures a star. ▷*See also* eclipse.

● **occultism** ▶ Theories and practices based on a belief in hidden supernatural forces that are presumed to account for phenomena for which no rational or scientific explanation can be provided. Occultists set great store by ancient texts, secret rituals, esoteric traditions, and the powers of the human mind as keys to the understanding of the universe. ▷*See also* theosophy; satanism; alchemy; astrology; kabbalah; Gnosticism; I Ching.

● **occupational disease** ▶ Any disease associated with working in a particular occupation. Occupational diseases include industrial diseases, to which workers in a particular industry are prone and which may result from close contact with a hazardous substance or the use of particular equipment. The most important industrial disease is ▷pneumoconiosis, which is caused by inhaling dust (such as coal, silica, and asbestos dust) and affects coalminers, quarry workers, stone dressers, construction workers, etc. Other occupational diseases include deafness in road workers, white finger in coalminers (from the vibration of the drills used), anthrax in wool handlers, and toxic-metal poisoning in factory workers; in some cases ▷repetitive strain injury can be regarded as an occupational disease. In the UK legislation requires employers to adopt measures to ensure that hazardous substances or equipment in the workplace do not affect their employees' health; sufferers from some occupational diseases may be entitled to the state's industrial injuries disablement benefit.

● **occupational therapy** ▶ The ancillary medical specialty concerned with restoring the physical and mental health of the sick and disabled. It plays an important role in keeping long-stay hospital patients interested and usefully occupied, in helping them gain confidence to return to work, and in training disabled persons for new employment. ▷*See also* geriatrics.

● **oceanarium** ▶ A large display tank in which species of marine animals and plants are maintained in the conditions of their natural environment. The first public oceanarium was founded in 1938 at Marineland, Florida (USA).

● **Oceania** ▶ The islands of the Pacific Ocean, usually taken to exclude Japan, Indonesia, Taiwan, the Philippines, and the Aleutian Islands, but often including Australasia.

● **Ocean Island** ▶ (*or* Banaba) 00 52S 169 35E An island in the SW Pacific Ocean, part of ▷Kiribati. It was annexed by Britain in 1900, when phosphate mining started; mining continued until 1979, when supplies were exhausted. Under Japanese occupation (1942–45), most Banabans were deported to the Gilbert Islands and resettled on Rabi, Fiji; those remaining were massacred in 1945. In 1965 surviving Banabans were paid compensation for overmining and in 1979 were given dual Kiribati and Fijian nationality. Area: 5 sq km (2 sq mi). Population (1990): 284.

● **oceanography** ▶ The study of the oceans, particularly their origin, structure, and form, the relief and sediments of the sea floor, and the flora and fauna they contain. The physical and chemical properties of sea water, waves, currents, and tides are also involved. The structural geology of the oceans is a major element in the theory of ▷plate tectonics. Underwater techniques, such as GLORIA (geological long-range incline ASDIC), based on ▷echo sounding are being developed, especially in the USA, to obtain information about the sea floor and the minerals it contains.

● **oceans** ▶ The large areas of water (excluding lakes and seas) covering about 70% of the earth's surface. The whole water mass is known as the hydrosphere. The oceans are the ▷Pacific (covering about one-third of the world), ▷Atlantic, ▷Indian, and ▷Arctic; the ▷Southern Ocean (waters south of 40°S) is sometimes distinguished. Major structural features are the continental margins (continental shelf and slope), mid-ocean ridges, ocean basins, and trenches. □ p. 910.

● **ocean thermal energy conversion** ▶ (OCET) A source of usable energy deriving from the difference in temperature between the warm surface of an ocean and its cold depths. In one form of this energy the warm water is used to vaporize a volatile liquid, which drives a turbogenerator, before the vapour is condensed back to a liquid in the cold depths. The technique is so far experimental but there are hopes that it could provide useful amounts of energy in some tropical areas.

● **Oceanus** ▶ In Greek mythology, a river issuing from the underworld and encircling the earth. It was personified as a ▷Titan, a son of Uranus and Gaia and father of the gods and nymphs of the seas and rivers.

● **ocelot** ▶ A ▷cat, *Felis* (*Panthera*) *pardalis*, also called painted leopard, of Central and South American forests. 100–150 cm long including the tail (30–50 cm), it has a black-spotted buff coat with stripes on the legs. It frequently hunts by night, searching for small mammals and reptiles.

● **ochre** ▶ A natural pigment, either red or yellow, consisting of hydrated ferric oxide with various impurities. It is therefore a type of ▷limonite deposit. It has been used as a pigment since prehistoric times and was important in medieval frescoes.

● **Ockham's Razor** ▶ The metaphysical principle, associated with the English medieval philosopher ▷William of Ockham, that "Entities should not be multiplied unnecessarily." In analysing a problem one should always choose the hypothesis that makes the least number of assumptions; only indispensable concepts are real.

● **O'Connell, Daniel** ▶ (1775–1847) Irish politician, who aroused popular support in the 1820s for the right of Roman Catholics to sit in the British parliament. Himself a Catholic, his election as MP for Clare in 1828 forced the government to concede ▷Catholic emancipation. Thereafter O'Connell was dubbed the Liberator. He subsequently worked for the repeal of union with Britain but lost the backing of the more revolutionary ▷Young Ireland group.

● **O'Connor, Feargus** ▶ (1794–1855) Irish politician. From 1832 to 1835 he was a radical MP for Cork. He then became a leading Chartist (see Chartism), editing the radical newspaper *Northern Star*. He was elected MP for Nottingham in 1847 and presented the 1848 Chartist petition. In 1852 he was pronounced insane.

● **O'Connor, Frank** ▶ (Michael O'Donovan; 1903–66) Irish short-story writer. During the 1930s he was director of the Abbey Theatre and a friend of W. B. ▷Yeats. He published many collections of stories, from *Guests of the Nation* (1931) to *My Oedipus Complex* (1964), and translations from Gaelic.

● **OCR** ▶ (optical character recognition) ▷*See* computer.

● **octane number** ▶ A measure of the extent to which a fuel causes ▷knocking in a petrol engine. It is the percentage by volume of *iso*-octane (C_8H_{18}) in a mixture of *iso*-octane and *n*-heptane (C_7H_{16}), which has the same knocking characteristics as the fuel under specified conditions.

● **Octavia** ▶ (d. 11 BC) The sister of Emperor Augustus, who married her to Mark Antony (40) to seal their reconciliation. Antony divorced her in 32, when he returned to Egypt and Cleopatra.

● **Octavian** ▷*See* Augustus.

● **octopus** ▶ An eight-armed ▷cephalopod mollusc belonging to the genus *Octopus*, found in most oceans. Octopuses are 5–540 cm long and a large species may have an armspan of 900 cm. The common octopus (*O. vulgaris*), weighing up to 2 kg, has a pair of well-developed eyes, a ring of tentacles around its horny beak, and a saclike body. Octopuses feed mainly on crabs and lobsters and may eject a cloud of ink when alarmed. Family: *Octopodidae*; order: *Octopoda*.

● **Oda Nobunaga** ▶ (1534–82) Japanese feudal lord, who began the reunification of feudal Japan. By careful administration, skilful diplomacy, the selection of able generals, and the adoption of novel military tactics based on formations of infantry armed with the newly introduced arquebus, Nobunaga achieved domination between 1560 and 1582 over Kyoto and central Japan. He was treacherously assassinated.

diving petrel

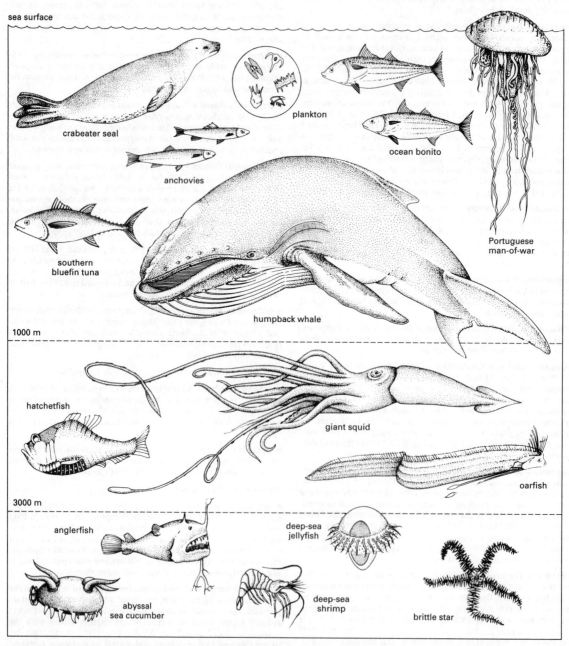

sea surface

crabeater seal

plankton

ocean bonito

anchovies

Portuguese
man-of-war

southern
bluefin tuna

humpback whale

1000 m

hatchetfish

giant squid

oarfish

3000 m

anglerfish

deep-sea
jellyfish

abyssal
sea cucumber

deep-sea
shrimp

brittle star

oceans ► A selection of animals and plants found at different depths of the ocean.

● **Odense** ▶ 55 24N 10 25E A seaport in S Denmark, on the island of Fyn. Its gothic cathedral was founded by ▷Canute II and contains his tomb and shrine. Odense University was established in 1964. It is the birthplace of Hans Christian Andersen. Its varied industries include shipbuilding, sugar refining, textiles, and iron founding. Dairy produce is the main export. Population (1996 est): 183 564.

● **Oder, River** ▶ (Polish and Czech name: Odra) A river in E Europe. Rising in the Oder Mountains in the Czech Republic, it flows N and W through Poland and forms a long stretch of the German–Polish border before entering the Baltic Sea at Szczecin. Linked by canals to E and W Europe, it is of great commercial importance. In 1997 the lower reaches of the Oder overflowed, causing the worst European floods for several centuries. Length: 886 km (551 mi).

● **Oder-Neisse Line** ▶ The boundary between Germany and Poland confirmed by the Allies at the ▷Potsdam Conference (1945) at the end of World War II. The line ran S from Swinoujście on the Baltic Sea to the Czechoslovak border, following the Rivers Oder and Neisse. It was recognized by East Germany and Poland in 1950 but not by West Germany until 1970.

● **Odessa** ▶ 46 30N 30 46E A port in S Ukraine, on the Black Sea. Fishing and whaling as well as ship repairing are important activities and industries include engineering, chemicals, and oil refining.
　History: founded in the 14th century as a Tatar fortress, it passed to Russia in 1791 and became a naval base. It was the scene in the Revolution of 1905 of the mutiny on the *Potemkin*, as filmed by Eisenstein. Population (1991 est): 1 101 000.

● **Odets, Clifford** ▶ (1906–63) US dramatist. He joined the Communist Party in 1934 and was a founding member of the Group Theatre, which produced his first successful play, *Waiting for Lefty* (1935). He later became a Hollywood scriptwriter. His other plays include *Awake and Sing* (1935), *Golden Boy* (1937), and *The Country Girl* (1950).

● **Odin** ▶ The principal god of the Teutonic peoples, the husband of ▷Frigga and, according to some legends, the father of ▷Thor. Also known as Woden and Wotan, he was the god of war, learning, and poetry and possessed great magical powers. He was the protector of slain heroes, who were brought to ▷Valhalla by his servants the ▷Valkyries. His desire for learning was so great that he gave up his right eye to drink from Mimir's well of knowledge. The Old English form of his name, *Woden*, is preserved in *Wednesday*.

● **Odoacer** ▶ (c. 433–93 AD) King of Italy (476–93). A German chieftain, he served with various Roman commanders before rebelling and deposing the last western Roman emperor, ▷Romulus Augustulus. After acknowledging the overlordship of the Eastern Roman emperor, Zeno (reigned 474–91), he ruled Italy competently until overthrown and killed by the Ostrogothic king, ▷Theodoric the Great.

● **Odontoglossum** ▶ A genus of epiphytic ▷orchids (about 250 species) native to mountainous areas of tropical America. Each large swollen stem base bears one or more leaves, and the flowers, which are borne on a spike, vary greatly in colour and size. Many *Odontoglossum* species have been crossed both within the genus and with other orchid genera to produce hundreds of beautiful hybrids, prized by orchid growers.

● **Odo of Bayeux** ▶ (c. 1036–97) Bishop of Bayeux (1049–97). The half-brother of William the Conqueror, he took part in the Norman conquest of England and helped rule the country during William's absences but subsequently rebelled against William II. He died on the first Crusade.

● **Odysseus** ▶ (*or* Ulysses) A legendary Greek king of Ithaca and hero of Homer's *Odyssey*, notable for his cunning. His many adventures during his voyage home from the ▷Trojan War included encounters with the Cyclops ▷Polyphemus, the cannibalistic Laestrygones, the enchantress ▷Circe, and the goddess Calypso, with whom he lived for eight years. Having reached Ithaca, he was reunited with his faithful wife ▷Penelope after killing her suitors with the help of his son Telemachus.

● **Oë, Kenzaburo** ▶ (1935–) Japanese writer, whose works explore the spiritual confusion of postwar Japan. His novels include *Our Age*

(1959), *Screams* (1962), and *The Silent Cry* (1967), while nonfictional writings include *Hiroshima Notes* (1965) and the autobiographical *A Quiet Life* (1990). He won the Nobel Prize in 1994.

● **OECD** ▷*See* Organization for Economic Cooperation and Development.

● **oedema** ▶ The accumulation of fluid in body tissues, leading to swelling, popularly known as dropsy. There are many causes of oedema, including heart failure, kidney failure, liver failure, and malnutrition. Fluid in the lungs (pulmonary oedema) will cause breathlessness. ▷Diuretic drugs can usually resolve oedema by causing the patient to pass more urine. Swelling of the ankles occurs quite commonly: for example, in hot weather and in women before menstruation. It is usually relieved by resting with the legs raised.

● **Oedipus** ▶ In Greek legend, a king of Thebes who unwittingly fulfilled the prophecy of the oracle at Delphi that he would kill his father and marry his mother. He was brought up by Polybus, King of Corinth. He killed his true father, Laius, in a roadside quarrel, and after winning the throne of Thebes by solving the riddle of the ▷sphinx he married his mother, the widowed Jocasta. When they discovered the truth, Jocasta committed suicide and Oedipus blinded himself and went into exile. The story is the subject of Sophocles' best-known tragedy.

● **Oedipus complex** ▶ The unconscious sexual feelings of a boy for his mother, which are accompanied by aggressive feelings for his father. According to psychoanalysis this is a normal desire, made unconscious by ▷repression. The female equivalent (in which a girl desires her father) is called the **Electra complex**.

● **Oehlenschläger, Adam (Gottlob)** ▶ (1779–1850) Danish poet and playwright. Greatly influenced by Goethe, Fichte, Schelling, and the Schlegels, Oehlenschläger was the founder of Danish Romanticism and Denmark's greatest poet. His works include the blank-verse tragedies *Hakon Jarl* and *Baldur hin Gode* (*Balder the Good*), based on Norse legend and published in *Nordiske Digte* (1807). He also wrote lyric poetry and a ballad cycle based on the poetic Edda, *Nordens Guder* (*The Gods of the North*; 1819).

● **Oersted, Hans Christian** ▶ (1777–1851) Danish physicist; professor at Copenhagen University. He discovered the magnetic effect of an electric current and thus established the relationship between electricity and magnetism. He did not, however, take an active part in the elucidation of this discovery. The c.g.s. unit of magnetic field strength is named after him.

● **oesophagus** ▶ The gullet: a muscular tube, about 25 cm long, running from the pharynx at the back of the mouth to the stomach. Contractions of the oesophagus propel swallowed food towards the stomach: the food is lubricated with mucus secreted by the walls of the oesophagus.

● **oestrogens** ▶ A group of steroid hormones that function principally as female sex hormones. The most important oestrogens in mammals are oestradiol and oestrone. Produced by the ovaries under the influence of pituitary ▷gonadotrophins, they promote the development of the reproductive organs and secondary sexual characteristics (such as enlargement of breasts) at puberty and regulate the changes of the menstrual cycle (*see* menstruation). Oestrogens are also produced by the placenta, adrenal glands, and testes. Natural and synthetic oestrogenic preparations are used in medicine to treat menstrual and menopausal disorders (*see* hormone replacement therapy); they are also constituents of ▷oral contraceptives.

● **oestrus** ▶ The period of "heat" in the sexual cycle of female mammals, when the female will attract males and permit copulation. It corresponds to the time of ovulation, so that mating is most likely to result in pregnancy. The oestrous cycle is similar to the menstrual cycle of women, except that the lining of the womb is not shed during oestrus.

● **Offa** ▶ (d. 796) King of Mercia (757–796) and overlord of all England S of the Humber. He engaged in trade with Charlemagne, although Charlemagne had refused to marry his daughter to Offa's son. He accepted greater papal control of the Church, introduced a new currency, and devised a code of laws. **Offa's Dyke**, an earthwork dividing England from Wales, built c. 784–c. 796, marks the frontier established by his wars with the Welsh.

● **Offaly** ▶ (Irish name: Uabh Failghe) A county in the central Republic of Ireland, in Leinster bordered in the W by the River Shannon. It is chiefly low lying containing part of the Bog of Allen in the N. Agricultural produce includes oats, barley, and wheat; cattle are reared. Area: 2000 sq km (770 sq mi). Population (1996 est): 59 000. County town: Tullamore.

● **Off-Broadway theatres** ▶ Small-scale professional theatres in New York City that specialize in noncommercial and experimental productions. They were responsible for the most lively drama in the USA in the 1950s and 1960s. As they became more mainstream and commercial, they were succeeded by the so-called Off-off-Broadway theatres of the late 1960s.

● **Offenbach (am Main)** ▶ 50 06N 8 46E A city in S Germany, in Hesse on the River Main. It is noted for its leather industry. Population (1996 est): 116 533.

● **Offenbach, Jacques** ▶ (J. Eberst; 1819–80) German composer of French adoption and Jewish descent. He adopted the name of his father's home town. A professional cellist, at the age of 30 he began writing a series of popular operettas, including *Orpheus in the Underworld* (1858), *La Belle Hélène* (1864), and *La Vie Parisienne* (1866). He also composed one grand opera, *The Tales of Hoffman* (produced posthumously; 1881).

● **Official Secrets Acts** ▶ Three UK acts of parliament, 1911, 1936, and 1989, that make it an offence to pass on secret government information, including information gleaned while a servant of the crown, whether or not that information could be of use to an enemy. After the publication of *Spycatcher* (1987) by Peter Wright (1917–95), a former member of the secret services, and the government's unsuccessful attempts to suppress it, the restrictive Section 2 of the 1911 Act was replaced under the Official Secrets Act (1989), redefining the classes of information that should not be disclosed.

● **O'Flaherty, Liam** ▶ (1897–1984) Irish novelist. Born in the Aran Islands, he worked his way round the world before starting his literary career in London in 1922. His books, concerned with violence and terrorism, include *The Informer* (1925), *The Assassin* (1928), and *The Pedlar's Revenge and Other Stories* (1976).

● **Ogaden, the** ▶ A semidesert area in E Ethiopia, enclosed by Somalia except to the W. The nomadic inhabitants are chiefly Muslim Somalis and in the 1960s a claim to the area by Somalia provoked border clashes. Somalia invaded in 1977 but withdrew (1978) in the face of counteroffensives launched by Ethiopia with Cuban and Soviet aid. Guerrilla fighting has continued.

● **Ogam** ▶ (or Ogham) A script found in about 400 Celtic inscriptions in Ireland and W Britain, dating from the 5th to the 7th centuries AD. It is alphabetic and consists of 20 letters, each made from a number of oblique or straight strokes on either side of a central dividing line.

● **Ogbomosho** ▶ 8 05N 4 11E The third largest city in Nigeria, on the Yorubaland plateau. Agricultural trade is important and there are local craft industries, including textiles and wood working. There are also shoe and tobacco factories. Population (1996 est): 730 000.

● **Ogden, C(harles) K(ay)** ▶ (1889–1957) British scholar. With I. A. ▷Richards he wrote *The Meaning of Meaning* (1923). He developed ▷Basic English, with a vocabulary of 850 words, intended as a medium of international communication.

● **Ogdon, John** ▶ (1937–89) British pianist. He was joint winner with Vladimir Ashkenazy of the 1962 Tchaikovsky Competition in Moscow. He was particularly well known for his championship of such composers as Scriabin, Busoni, and Messiaen.

● **Ogham** ▷See Ogam.

● **Oglethorpe, James Edward** ▶ (1696–1785) English general and colonizer. While an MP, he obtained a charter for a colony in North America for debtors and persecuted Protestants and in 1733 he led a group of settlers to the colony that became Georgia. He repulsed a Spanish attack against it (1742).

● **Ogooué, River** ▶ (or R. Ogowe) A river in W central Africa. Rising in SW Congo-Brazzaville, it flows mainly NW and W through Gabon to enter the Atlantic Ocean. Length: 970 km (683 mi).

● **O'Higgins, Bernardo** ▶ (?1778–1842) Chilean national hero. The son of an Irish-born soldier who became Spanish colonial governor, he fought with José de ▷San Martin against Spain and liberated Chile. He was made dictator of the country in 1817 but his wide-ranging reforms created much resentment and he was deposed after a revolt in the provinces.

● **Ohio** ▶ A state in the USA, in the Midwest situated to the S of Lake Erie. The flat or rolling land of W Ohio gives way in the E to the hill and valley region of the Appalachian Plateau. A major industrial state, it lies at the centre of the most industrialized area of the USA and is strategically located near many rich markets. The principal manufactures are transportation equipment and raw and fabricated metals. It also exploits its abundant natural resources, including clay and stone, lime, coal, natural gas, and oil. Agriculture is important, especially livestock.
History: disputed by the French and British, it was eventually ceded to Britain in 1763 and to the USA in 1783. It became a state in 1802. Area: 106 764 sq km (41 222 sq mi). Population (1997 est): 11 186 331. Capital: Columbus.

● **Ohio River** ▶ A river in the USA flowing mainly SW from Pittsburgh in W Pennsylvania to join the Mississippi (in Illinois) as its main E tributary. Length: 1577 km (980 mi).

● **ohm** ▶ (Ω) The ▷SI unit of electrical resistance equal to the resistance between two points on a conductor when a potential difference of one volt between the points produces a current of one ampere. This definition replaced the former definition, which was based on the resistance of a specified column of mercury. Named after Georg ▷Ohm.

● **Ohm, Georg Simon** ▶ (1787–1854) German physicist, who discovered in 1827 that the current flowing through a wire is proportional to the potential difference between its ends (see Ohm's law). Ohm also found that the electrical resistance of a wire is proportional to its length and inversely proportional to its cross-sectional area. The unit of electrical resistance is named after him.

● **Ohm's law** ▶ The basic law of electric current, named after its discoverer Georg ▷Ohm. The current, I, flowing through an element in a circuit is directly proportional to the voltage drop, V, across it. It is written as $V = IR$, where R is the resistance of the circuit element.

● **oil** ▶ There are three types of oil: lipids (see fats and oils), ▷essential oils, and mineral oil.
Petroleum (or rock oil) is the thick greenish mineral oil that occurs in permeable underground rock and consists mainly of ▷hydrocarbons, with some other elements (sulphur, oxygen, nitrogen, etc.). It is believed to have derived from the remains of living organisms deposited many millions of years ago with rock-forming sediments. Under the effects of heat and pressure this organic material passed through a number of chemical and physical changes ending up as droplets of petroleum, which migrated through porous rocks and fissures to become trapped in large underground reservoirs, often floating on a layer of water and held under pressure beneath a layer of natural gas (mostly methane).
Mineral oil was used in the 4th millennium BC by the Sumerians to reinforce bricks, and the Burmese were burning it in oil lamps in the 13th century AD. However, the modern oil industry began when oil was discovered in Pennsylvania in 1859 and has grown with the development of the internal-combustion engine, which is entirely dependent on it as a fuel.
The presence of oil in underground reservoirs is detected by geologists, who seek evidence of the type of structures in which oil is known to occur and measure the gravitational force in likely areas to identify variations of rock density; depth is determined by such measures as the behaviour of sound waves produced by small surface explosions. Exploratory narrow-bore drillings are then made to determine the extent of a reservoir. The actual oil well is made by drilling through the rock with a rotating bit supported in a wider shaft; a specially prepared mud is pumped through the hollow bit to

collect the debris, which is forced back up the shaft around the drilling bit. When the oil is reached, the pressure of the mud is used to control the pressure of the oil so that none is wasted by "gushers"; when the mud has been removed from the shaft the flow is controlled by valves. This method of sinking wells enables oil over 5 km (3 mi) below the surface to be mined. Drilling for oil below the sea is achieved in a similar manner, except that the drilling rig has to be supported on a base, which has legs sunk into the sea bed.

Petroleum has no uses in its crude form and has to be refined by fractional distillation (i.e. separating the components according to their boiling points) before it is of commercial value. Natural gas is widely used as a substitute for coal gas and as a source of power in the refinery. Products made by blending the distillation fractions include aviation spirit, petrol, kerosene, Diesel oil, lubricating oil, paraffin wax, and petroleum jelly. In addition to fractional distillation, other processes, such as catalytic cracking, are used to split the larger molecules into smaller ones to increase the yield of petrol and to reduce the viscosity of heavier oils. Catalytic reforming is used to make a number of valuable chemicals (petrochemicals), which are required to manufacture detergents, plastics, fibres, fertilizers, drugs, etc.

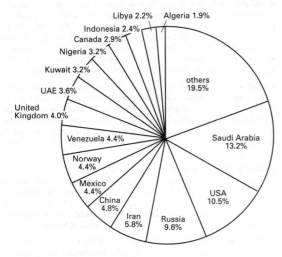

oil ▶ World crude oil production (1995).

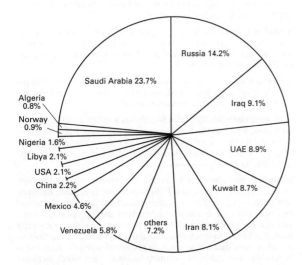

oil ▶ World crude oil reserves (1995).

As one of the world's primary energy sources, the price, conservation, and political significance of oil are extremely controversial issues. In 1961 the ▷Organization of Petroleum Exporting Countries (OPEC) was set up to protect producing countries from exploitation. Its advent ended the era of cheap energy and prices for petroleum products rose sharply during the ensuing decade. In 1974 the International Energy Agency (IEA) was established to protect consumers. Since then various factors, including the flow of North Sea oil, have helped to stabilize prices, although the Iranian revolution of 1979 and the ▷Iran-Iraq War led to world shortages and further price increases. World oil reserves are as difficult to estimate as future world consumption. Reserves depend on undiscovered sources, while consumption depends on usage, the price of oil in relation to its competitors, and the extent to which ▷nuclear energy will be utilized, either because it becomes cheaper or because it does not cause the ▷greenhouse effect. Possible future sources of oil include shale, tar sands, and coal.

● **oil beetle** ▶ A heavy-bodied flightless beetle belonging to the family *Meloidae* (about 2000 species). If disturbed, it discharges evil-smelling oily blood—an example of reflex bleeding—as a defence mechanism. It has a similar lifestyle to the ▷blister beetle.

● **oilbird** ▶ A South American cave-dwelling bird, *Steatornis caripensis*, also called guacharo or quacharo. It is 30 cm long and has a fan-shaped tail, a white-spotted black-barred brown plumage, and a hook-tipped bill surrounded by long bristles. It lives in colonies, uses echolocation in caves, and feeds on fruit. It is the only member of its family (*Steatornithidae*); order: *Caprimulgiformes* (frogmouths, nightjars, etc.).

● **oil-immersion lens** ▶ A lens system used in some ▷microscopes in which the gap between the objective lens and the specimen is filled with oil (usually cedar-wood oil). It increases the amount of light entering the system.

● **oil palm** ▶ A ▷palm tree, *Elaeis guineensis*, native to tropical West Africa and cultivated in Africa, Indonesia, Malaysia, and tropical America as the source of palm oil. Growing to a height of 15 m, the palms produce fleshy fruits, 3 cm long, containing a white kernel within a hard black shell. Palm oil is extracted from the pulp and kernel and used in making soaps, margarine, lubricants, etc. The residual meal from the kernels is a valuable livestock feed.

● **oilseeds** ▶ Oil-bearing seeds of plants from which the edible oil is extracted for making margarine, soaps, etc. Examples include rapeseed, cottonseed, groundnuts, sunflower seed, linseed, sesame seed, castor-oil seed. and soya beans. The oil is obtained from the seeds by expelling it under pressure or by extracting it using a solvent (with a solvent recovery cycle); the **oilcake** remaining after most of the oil has been removed is called expellers or extractions, respectively. Both forms of oilcake are widely used as animal feeds.

● **Oise, River** ▶ A river in N France, flowing mainly SW from the Belgian Ardennes to join the River Seine at Conflans. Length: 302 km (188 mi).

● **Oistrakh, David** ▶ (1908–74) Russian violinist. He made his debut in Moscow in 1933 and won the International Violin Competition in Brussels in 1937. He played frequently in the West, and was well known for his performances of the Brahms, Tchaikovsky, and Prokofiev violin concertos. His son and pupil, the violinist **Igor Oistrakh** (1931–), often gave joint recitals with him and has also conducted.

● **Oita** ▶ 33 15N 131 36E A port in Japan, on the NE coast of Kyushu. An important town in the 16th century, it is now an expanding industrial centre with an oil refinery and iron and steel industries. Population (1995): 426 981.

● **Ojibwa** ▶ A North American Indian people of the Great Lakes region, who speak a language of the Algonquian family. They are also known as Chippewa; those who now live near Lake Winnipeg in Canada are called Saulteaux. They were traditionally hunters, fishers, and gatherers, who wandered in small bands and sheltered in simply made dome-shaped wigwams. Shamans exercised considerable influence.

● **Ojos del Salado** ► 27 05S 68 05W A mountain peak on the border between Argentina and Chile, the second highest peak in the Andes. Height: 6873 m (22 550 ft).

okapi ► A female with her calf. The closest living relative of the giraffe, this nocturnal animal becomes very docile and breeds readily in captivity.

● **okapi** ► A hoofed mammal, *Okapia johnstoni*, of central African rain forests. Okapis are about 150 cm high at the shoulder and have a dark-brown coat with horizontal black and white stripes on the legs and rump, which provide camouflage. The smaller male has short bony backward-pointing horns. They were unknown to science until 1901. Family: *Giraffidae* (giraffes).

● **Okavango Swamp** ► A marshy area in NE Botswana, into which the River Okavango drains. It supports a rich and varied wildlife.

● **Okayama** ► 34 40N 133 54E A town in Japan, in SW Honshu. A commercial and industrial centre, it has a 16th-century castle and a traditional Japanese garden (1786). Its university was established in 1949. Population (1995): 616 056.

● **Okeechobee, Lake** ► A large freshwater lake in the USA, in S Florida. It drains into the Atlantic Ocean through the ▷Everglades. Area: 1813 sq km (700 sq mi).

● **O'Keeffe, Georgia** ► (1887–1986) US painter. Her first one-person show was presented in 1917 by the photographer Alfred ▷Stieglitz, whom she married in 1924. Thereafter she specialized in semiabstract paintings of flowers, bones, architecture, and landscapes inspired by the scenery of New Mexico.

● **Okefenokee Swamp** ► A swamp area in the USA, extending through SE Georgia and NE Florida. In 1937 a large proportion of it was designated the Okefenokee National Wildlife Refuge; the wildlife includes alligators, snakes, and birds.

● **Okeghem, Jean d'** ► (c. 1425–c. 1495) Flemish composer, noted for his innovatory counterpoint. He was composer to Charles VII, Louis XI, and Charles VIII of France and his pupils included Josquin des Prez. He wrote much church music, including 16 masses and 9 motets.

● **Okhotsk, Sea of** ► A section of the N Pacific Ocean off the E coast of the Soviet Union, separated from the main ocean by Kamchatka and the Kuril Islands.

● **Okinawa** ► A mountainous Japanese island, the main one of the ▷Ryukyu group. During World War II it was captured by the USA in a major amphibious operation and was only returned to Japan in 1972, the USA retaining military bases there. Chief products are fish, rice, sugar cane, and sweet potatoes. Area: 1176 sq km (454 sq mi). Population (1995): 1 273 508. Capital: Naha.

● **Oklahoma** ► A state in the S central USA. It has a diverse landscape, with uplands in the W, the lowlands of the Arkansas River Valley and coastal plain in the centre and S, and wooded hills in the E. An oil-rich state, agriculture (especially cattle) remains a major source of revenue. Most industry is located around Oklahoma City and Tulsa (one of the world's leading oil centres). The most important manufacturing industries are food processing, nonelectrical machinery, fabricated metal products, and electrical and transport equipment.
  History: first explored by the Spanish, it formed part of the Louisiana Purchase in 1803. It was reserved as Indian territory (1828) but after the US Civil War White settlement began and it became a state in 1907. Area: 181 089 sq km (69 919 sq mi). Population (2000 est): 3 450 654. Capital: Oklahoma City.

● **Oklahoma City** ► 35 28N 97 33W A city in the USA, the capital of Oklahoma on the North Canadian River. Founded in 1889, it expanded rapidly following the discovery of oil (1920s). Today it is a commercial, industrial, and distribution centre for an oil-producing and agricultural area. Oklahoma City University was established in 1904. In 1995 a right-wing extremist bombed a government office building, killing 168 people. Population (1996 est): 472 221.

● **okra** ► An annual African herb, ▷*Hibiscus esculentus*, also called lady's fingers or gumbo, widely cultivated in the tropics and subtropics. It grows 1–2 m high and has heart-shaped leaves and yellow flowers with a crimson centre. The pods are picked before they are ripe and eaten fresh, canned, dried, or pickled. They may be used to thicken stews and soups. The seeds are a coffee substitute. Family: *Malvaceae*.

● **Olaf I Tryggvason** ► (c. 964–c. 1000) King of Norway (995–c. 1000). He took part in the Viking attacks on England (991–94) but the English king, Ethelred the Unready, became his godfather when Olaf was confirmed as a Christian at Andover (994). Olaf subsequently imposed Christianity on Norway. A hero of Scandinavian literature, he died at the hands of the Danes in the battle of Svolder.

● **Olaf II Haraldsson, Saint** ► (c. 995–1030) King (1015–28) and patron saint of Norway. Baptized in 1013, he attempted to complete the conversion of Norway to Christianity. He was overthrown by Canute II of England and Denmark and died, attempting to regain his kingdom, at the battle of Stikelstad.

● **Olaf V** ► (1903–91) King of Norway (1957–91). A talented sportsman, he took part as a yachtsman in the 1928 Olympic Games. In 1929 he married Princess Märtha of Sweden (1901–54); he was succeeded by his son ▷Harald V.

● **Öland** ► An island in Sweden, in the Baltic Sea separated from the mainland by the Kalmar Sound. Area: 1347 sq km (520 sq mi). Population (latest est): 24 100. Chief town: Borgholm.

● **Olbers, Heinrich Wilhelm Matthäus** ► (1758–1840) German astronomer, who was the first to point out the paradoxical nature of the night sky (*see* Olbers' paradox). He was also one of the first astronomers to detect and study the asteroids, discovering Pallas in 1802 and Vesta in 1804.

● **Olbers' paradox** ► Why is the sky dark at night? Heinrich ▷Olbers argued, in 1826, that if the universe were infinite, uniform, and unchanging, with innumerable stars, then the night sky would be covered in stars and appear as bright as the average star, i.e. the sun. The paradox is resolved by the facts that the universe does not extend infinitely in space and time and is expanding rather than remaining static and unchanging: as the galaxies recede, their radiation suffers a ▷redshift (i.e. is diminished in energy), which increases with distance.

● **Old Bailey** ► A street in the City of London in which the ▷Central Criminal Court is situated. The street takes its name from the Bailey, originally an outwork outside the city wall. The Court is now also called the Old Bailey and occupies the site of the former ▷Newgate prison. The old courthouse, built in 1773, was replaced by E. W. Mountford's building in 1907, which was extended in 1970.

● **Old Believers** ► A schismatic sect of the Russian Orthodox Church that rejected the liturgical reforms of the Patriarch of Moscow (1667). Its members were mainly peasants, who suffered much persecution. The majority, who evolved their own Church hierarchy, was eventually recognized by the state (1881), but the rest split into small and often eccentric sects.

● **Oldcastle, Sir John** ► (c. 1378–1417) English soldier and leader of the ▷Lollards. An ardent supporter of ▷Wycliffe, he was arrested for heresy and imprisoned in the Tower of London (1413). He escaped but was recaptured four years later and hanged. Shakespeare's Falstaff is partly based on him.

● **Old Catholics** ► Churches from several European countries that separated from the Roman Catholic Church at various times and in 1932 entered into communion with the Church of England. They comprise the Church of Utrecht, which supported ▷Jansenism (1724), the Old Catholic Churches of Germany, Switzerland, and Austria, which rejected papal ▷infallibility (1870), the National Polish Church (established 1897), and the Yugoslav Old Catholic Church (1924).

● **Old Comedy** ► The first period of Greek comic drama, lasting up to the end of the 5th century BC. The episodic choral plays of this period contained elements of song, dance, topical satire, and political criticism and ranged in style from bawdy slapstick to lyrical grace. All the surviving examples are by ▷Aristophanes. ▷*See also* Middle Comedy; New Comedy.

● **Oldenbarneveldt, Johan van** ► (1547–1619) Dutch statesman. He supported William the Silent in the ▷Revolt of the Netherlands against Spain and, with ▷Maurice of Nassau, became (from 1586) the leading statesman of the newly formed United Provinces of the Netherlands. He presided over a vast expansion of Dutch trade and the formation of the Dutch East India Company. His moderate Protestantism brought him into conflict with Maurice, whose imprisonment and execution of Oldenbarneveldt was a shameful blot on the early history of the United Provinces.

● **Oldenburg** ► 53 08N 8 13E A city in NW Germany, in Lower Saxony on the River Hunte. The capital of the former duchy of Oldenburg, it has a 17th-century palace. It is an agricultural and industrial centre. Population (1996 est): 151 382.

● **Oldenburg, Claes (Thure)** ► (1929–) US sculptor, born in Sweden. He became a leading exponent of ▷pop art in the 1960s, first with his re-creation of ordinary environments, notably *The Store* (1960–61), and later with his "soft sculptures," in which vinyl and stuffed canvas are shaped into everyday objects, such as bathtubs, typewriters, etc.

● **Old English sheepdog** ► A breed of working □dog originating in England. It has a compact body, a characteristic ambling gait, and a long dense shaggy coat that may be grey or blue-grey with white markings. These dogs are also known as bobtails because their tails are docked at birth. Height: 55–66 cm.

● **Oldfield, Bruce** ► (1950–) British fashion designer. Brought up in a Dr Barnardo's home, he has established a reputation for clothes designed for his many clients, who have included members of the royal family.

● **Oldham** ► **1.** 53 33N 2 07W A town in N England, in Oldham unitary authority, Greater Manchester. Traditionally a cotton-spinning town, Oldham now also has electronics, textile machinery, plastics, and clothing industries. The town hall is a copy of Ceres' Temple in Athens. Population (1991): 103 931. **2.** A unitary authority in N England, in Greater Manchester. Area: 141 sq km (54 sq mi). Population (1996 est): 220 200.

● **old man cactus** ► A succulent desert ▷cactus of the genus *Cephalocereus* (50 species), especially *C. senilis*, native to tropical and subtropical America. Its sturdy stems are coated with long strands of white hair at maturity and may reach a height of 12 m. It is a popular house plant.

● **old man's beard** ▷*See* Clematis.

● **Old Norse** ► A North Germanic language formerly spoken in Iceland and Norway (c. 1150–c. 1350). It is the language of the Norse ▷sagas and was closely related to the contemporary speech of Denmark and Sweden. From this group the modern Scandinavian languages are derived.

● **Old Sarum** ▷*See* Salisbury.

● **Old Testament** ► The collection of 39 books that forms the first of the two major divisions of the Christian ▷Bible (the second being the ▷New Testament). The same writings (traditionally divided into 24 books) form the whole of the Hebrew Bible, the sacred scriptures of Judaism. The Christian title for these writings derives from the Latin word for ▷covenant and refers to the pact between God and Israel, a concept that underlies the authors' view of history and is the major theme throughout. The books claim to cover the period from the creation of the universe and man (Adam) to about 400 BC. They are traditionally divided into three parts: the Law or ▷Torah, the first five books, traditionally ascribed to Moses and often called the Pentateuch by scholars; the Prophets, which are most of the books bearing the names of individual prophets and containing much historical information; and the Writings or Hagiographa (Hebrew: *Kethubim*), the latest books admitted to the Hebrew Bible (c. 100 AD), i.e. Psalms, Proverbs, Job, Ruth, Lamentations, the Song of Solomon, Ecclesiastes, Esther, Daniel, Chronicles, Ezra, and Nehemiah. Christianity has traditionally regarded the Old Testament as a partial revelation that foreshadows (and in places predicts) the full revelation of the New Testament.

● **Olduvai Gorge** ► A site in N Tanzania yielding an important sequence of Lower ▷Palaeolithic fossils and tools. Here L. S. B. ▷Leakey found remains of the ▷*Australopithecus* he called *Zinjanthropus* (c. 1 750 000 years old) and the hominid *Homo habilis* (c. 2 000 000 years old; *see* Homo), which manufactured crude pebble choppers.

● **Old Vic** ► A London theatre built in 1818 and named the Royal Victoria in 1833. It became famous for its music-hall entertainments and, after Lilian ▷Baylis became manager in 1912, its productions of Shakespeare. It was the home (1963–76) of the National Theatre Company and since 1982 has been owned by the Canadian entrepreneur Ed(win) Mirvish (1914–).

● **Old World** ► A name for Europe, Africa, and Asia, used especially by early emigrants from Europe. *Compare* New World.

● **Old World monkey** ► A ▷monkey belonging to the family *Cercopithecidae* (58 species), native to Africa or Asia. There are both terrestrial and arboreal species, active mainly by day and either omnivorous or vegetarian. They inhabit forest, savannah, swamps, and rocks. ▷*See also* baboon; colobus; guenon; langur; macaque.

● **oleander** ► A poisonous evergreen shrub, *Nerium oleander*, also called rosebay, native to the Mediterranean region and widely cultivated in warm regions for its attractive flowers. Up to 7 m high, it has long narrow leaves, clusters of white, pink, or purplish five-petalled flowers (up to 7.5 cm across), and dangling pods. Family: *Apocynaceae*.

● **oleaster** ► A shrub or tree, *Elaeagnus angustifolia*, also called Russian olive, found throughout S Europe and sometimes cultivated for its ornamental silvery foliage. It grows 2–12 m high and bears small fragrant yellowish flowers. The olive-shaped yellowish fruits have a silvery scaly coat and are dried and used in cakes as Trebizond dates. Family: *Elaeagnaceae*.

● **olefines** ▷*See* alkenes.

● **oleum** ▷*See* sulphuric acid.

● **Oligocene epoch** ▷*See* Tertiary period.

● **oligopoly** ► An economic market structure in which there is imperfect competition between a few suppliers. Oligopoly is common in Western economies today. Economic theory is not as successful at predicting the market trends in an oligopoly as it is under the extremes of ▷monopoly and ▷perfect competition, because the action of each firm in an oligopoly affects the policies of the others.

● **olingo** ▶ A mammal belonging to the genus *Bassaricyon* (3 species), found in tropical forests of South America. Olingos are 75–95 cm long including the tail (40–48 cm), with buff-coloured or golden fur. They apparently nest in hollow trees and feed chiefly on fruit. Family: *Procyonidae* (raccoons, kinkajous, etc.); order: *Carnivora*.

● **Oliphant, Sir Mark Laurence Elwin** ▶ (1901–) Australian physicist, who in 1934 discovered ▷tritium while bombarding deuterium with deuterons. His work contributed to the development of the hydrogen bomb. He also designed the first proton synchrotron accelerator.

● **Olivares, Gaspar de Guzmán, Conde-Duque de** ▶ (1587–1645) Spanish statesman. The chief minister of Philip IV (1621–43), he combined reform, especially economic, with a grand imperial vision and attempted to make all the Spanish kingdoms provide him with men and money. Dissatisfaction exploded under the strain of Spain's participation in the ▷Thirty Years' War into revolt in Portugal and Catalonia and led to his downfall. Olivares supported the painters Rubens and Velázquez and the writer Lope de Vega.

● **olive** ▶ An evergreen tree, *Olea europaea*, native to W Asia but cultivated throughout Mediterranean and subtropical regions for its fruits. Up to 12 m high, it has a gnarled grey trunk and lance-shaped leathery grey-green leaves. Small greenish-white flowers produce fleshy oval berries containing a hard stone. Unripe green olives and ripe black olives are usually pickled for use in hors d'oeuvres and other dishes. **Olive oil**, pressed from the fruit, is one of the finest edible oils and can be consumed without refining or processing (when it is known as virgin olive oil). It is also used in making soaps, cosmetics, and textiles. Olive wood resists decay and is used for furniture and ornaments. Family: *Oleaceae*.

● **Oliver, Isaac** ▶ (?1556–1617) Portrait miniaturist, born in Rouen (France). In about 1568 he moved to London with his Huguenot parents to escape religious persecution. Although he studied under ▷Hilliard, his naturalistic style was influenced by Italian and Flemish art. He successfully rivalled his master at James I's court, where he painted many portraits of the queen and Henry Frederick, Prince of Wales (1594–1612).

● **Olives, Mount of** ▶ (*or* Olivet) 31 47N 35 15E A hill to the E of the old city of Jerusalem. Near its foot is the Garden of Gethsemane, the scene of the betrayal of Christ (Mark 14.26–50) and it is the traditional site of Christ's Ascension (Acts 1.2–12). Height: 817 m (2686 ft).

● **olive shell** ▶ A ▷gastropod mollusc of the family *Olividae* (300 species) of warm shallow seas. The shiny ⁰shell, 1–12 cm long, is roughly cylindrical with a short spire and is covered by the mantle. The animals prey on smaller molluscs on sandy seabeds.

● **Olivier, Laurence (Kerr), Baron** ▶ (1907–89) British actor. He played many Shakespearean roles while with the Old Vic Theatre Company from 1937 to 1949 and a number of outstanding modern roles, including Archie Rice in *The Entertainer* (1957). His films include the Shakespeare adaptations *Henry V* (1944), *Hamlet* (1948), and *Richard III* (1956). He was director of the National Theatre Company from 1961 to 1973, during which time he played many leading roles, including Shakespeare's Othello (filmed 1965) and in plays by Chekhov, O'Neill, and Ionesco. His second marriage to Vivien ▷Leigh ended in divorce; in 1961 he married his third wife, Joan ▷Plowright. He was knighted in 1947 and created a life peer in 1970. The Olivier Theatre, part of the National Theatre, was named in his honour.

● **olivine** ▶ A group of rock-forming silicate minerals, varying in composition between the end-members forsterite (Mg_2SiO_4) and fayalite (Fe_2SiO_4). Olivines are green, brownish green, or yellowish green, with a conchoidal fracture. Those rich in magnesium occur in basic and ultrabasic igneous rocks, while fayalite occurs in acid igneous rocks. Peridot is a pale green gem variety. Olivine is believed to be a major constituent of the earth's upper mantle.

● **olm** ▶ A cave-dwelling salamander, *Proteus anguineus*, found in the Carpathian Mountains. Growing to about 30 cm, it is white and has bright-red gills. The eyes are covered with skin but are clearly visible in young larvae. Although sightless, olms prey on small worms and can survive for long periods without feeding. Family: *Proteidae*. ▷*See also* mudpuppy.

● **Olmecs** ▶ An ancient American Indian people of the Gulf Coast of Mexico. Between about 1200 and 400 BC they evolved the first important Mesoamerican culture, with great ceremonial centres at La Venta and San Lorenzo. They invented a hieroglyphic script and a calendar. Outstanding stone carvers, they produced monumental basalt heads and jade figures.

● **Olomouc** ▶ (German name: Olmütz) 49 48N 17 15E An industrial town in the W Czech Republic, in N Moravia. Its notable historic buildings include the gothic cathedral and town hall with a 15th-century astronomical clock. The university was founded in 1576. Population (1996 est): 104 845.

● **Olsztyn** ▶ (German name: Allenstein) 53 48N 20 29E A market town in NE Poland. It was founded in 1334 by the Teutonic Knights. Industries include the manufacture of leather. Population (1995 est): 167 000.

● **Olympia** ▶ A sanctuary of ▷Zeus, established about 1000 BC in the NW ▷Peloponnese, in Greece. From 776 BC until at least 261 AD it was the venue of the ▷Olympic Games. Extensive excavations from 1881 have revealed the 6th century BC temple of Hera and the stadium. In 457 BC the temple of Zeus in the Altis (sacred grove), which later held ▷Phidias' famous statue, was completed. Public buildings and monuments, a gymnasium, wrestling area, baths, and guest houses for officials and competitors were built later. The sanctuary was closed by the Christian Emperor Theodosius (390 AD).

● **Olympia** ▶ 47 03N 122 53W A seaport in the USA, the capital of Washington on Puget Sound. Founded in 1850, it possesses a fine capitol building (1893). Industries include timber, fishing, and mining. Population (1990): 161 238.

Laurence Olivier ▶ Seen here in one of his last major film roles, as Professor Abraham Van Helsing in the 1979 version of *Dracula*. His first Shakespearean role was Katherine, in a special boys' performance of *The Taming of the Shrew* at Stratford in 1922; his last was King Lear in a 1982 television production.

● **Olympic Games** ▶ A quadrennial international amateur sports contest. The modern games derive from the ancient Greek athletic festival held at ▷Olympia, first recorded reliably in 776 BC; however, the games probably date back to the 14th century BC and originated in a religious ceremony. Corrupted in Roman times, they were banned by ▷Theodosius the Great (393 AD). They were revived at Athens in 1896, largely through the efforts of Baron Pierre de Coubertin (1863–1937), a French educator, who wished to improve national and international understanding through sport. The Winter Olympics were first held in 1924. The Games are governed by the International Olympic Committee (IOC). Although officially a contest between individuals, the Games are often seen as a competition between countries and have sometimes been disrupted by international political tensions. In 1999 a corruption scandal led to six expulsions and three resignations from the IOC.

• **Olympus, Mount** ▶ (Modern Greek name: Óros Ólimbos) 40 05N 22 21E A small group of mountains in NE central Greece, held in ancient times to be the home of the gods. Highest point: 2917 m (9570 ft).

Venues of Olympic Games since 1896

1896	Athens	1960	Rome
1900	Paris	1964	Tokyo
1904	St Louis	1968	Mexico City
1908	London	1972	Munich
1912	Stockholm	1976	Montreal
1920	Antwerp	1980	Moscow
1924	Paris	1984	Los Angeles
1928	Amsterdam	1988	Seoul
1932	Los Angeles	1992	Barcelona
1936	Berlin	1996	Atlanta
1948	London	2000	Sydney
1952	Helsinki	2004	Athens
1956	Melbourne	2008	Beijing

Winter Olympics

1924	Chamonix	1972	Sapporo
1928	St Moritz	1976	Innsbruck
1932	Lake Placid	1980	Lake Placid
1936	Garmisch-Partenkirchen	1984	Sarajevo
1948	St Moritz	1988	Calgary
1952	Oslo	1992	Albertville
1956	Cortina d'Ampezzo	1994	Lillehammer
1960	Squaw Valley	1998	Nagano
1964	Innsbruck	2002	Salt Lake City
1968	Grenoble	2006	Turin

• **Om** ▶ In Indian religions, the greatest of the mantras or mystical sounds embodying spiritual power. In Sanskrit *Om* comprises three sounds *A, U, M* (the vowels being equivalent to *O*), which represent the three Vedic scriptures, the three worlds (earth, atmosphere, heaven), the ▷Trimurti or some other triple, and ultimately the essence of the universe.

• **Omagh** ▶ **1.** A district in Northern Ireland, in Co Tyrone. Area: 1123 sq km (434 sq mi). Population (1998 est): 47 000. **2.** 54 36N 7 18W A market town in Northern Ireland, in Co Tyrone. Dairy products and shirts are manufactured. On 15 August, 1998, Omagh was the scene of the worst atrocity of the current Northern Irish Troubles, a terrorist bombing by the so-called Real IRA that killed 28 people (including 9 children). Population (1991): 17 280.

• **Omaha** ▶ 41 15N 96 00W A city in the USA, in Nebraska on the Missouri River. Industries include meat processing and agricultural machinery. Omaha is a centre for medical research. Population (1998 est): 371 291.

• **Oman, Sultanate of** ▶ (name until 1970: Muscat and Oman) A country in E ▷Arabia, on the Gulf of Oman and the Arabian Sea. The main port of Oman is an exclave separated from the rest of the country by the United Arab Emirates. It is mainly flat but rises to 3107 m (10 194 ft) near the N coast. The population is mainly Arab, Ibadhi Muslim, nomadic, and illiterate, although literacy programmes are in operation.
Economy: oil, which has been extracted since 1967, accounts for about 90% of revenue. Although most of the interior is empty sand desert, the coastal plain and some of the mountain valleys are fertile. Beef is produced and cereals, tobacco, dates, limes, and pomegranates are grown. Oman now has two desalination plants, a power station, and several modern factories.
History: Oman became part of the Muslim empire in the 7th century and was settled by the Portuguese, Dutch, and English in the 16th century. Since the 19th century Britain has been influential in Oman. In 1970 the current Sultan deposed his father and adopted the country's present name. A long-running Marxist insurgency was defeated in 1975. Oman is an absolute monarchy; a partially elected State Advisory Council was created in 1991 and an appointed Council of State in 1997.

Sultanate of Oman

Head of state	Sultan Qaboos ibn Sa'id
Official language	Arabic
Official currency	Rial Omani of 1000 baiza
Area	300 000 sq km (120 000 sq mi)
Population (2000 est)	2 416 000
Capital	Muscat

• **Omar** ▶ (*or* Umar) (d. 644 AD) The second ▷caliph (634–44), regarded by Islam as the founder of the Muslim state. Continuing Muslim conquests, he visited Jerusalem after its capture (638). He was murdered in Medina by a discontented slave.

• **'Omar Khayyam** ▶ (?1048–?1122) Persian poet, who was famous as a mathematician and made astronomical observations for the reform of the calendar. His poems, characterized by an agnostic and hedonistic philosophy, were written in the form of *ruba'is* (quatrains). The free translation of 75 of them by Edward ▷Fitzgerald in 1859 became widely popular; more recent translations have been made by the British poets Robert Graves and John Heath Stubbs (1918–   ).

• **Omayyads** ▷*See* Umayyads.

• **ombres chinoises** ▶ (French: Chinese shadows) A form of shadow puppet drama introduced into 18th-century Europe by travellers returning from the Far East. It was popularized in France by the opening of a shadow theatre at Versailles in 1774. The technique involved the representation of brief amusing episodes by black silhouettes cast from solid puppets.

• **ombudsman** ▶ A person appointed to investigate grievances against maladministration. The post originated in Sweden in 1809. New Zealand has had an ombudsman since 1962. In the UK an ombudsman (the parliamentary commissioner for administration) was first appointed in 1967 to investigate complaints against central government departments; complaints against health authorities are investigated by Health Service Commissioners, appointed since 1973; and there have been ombudsmen for local government since 1974. Financial ombudsmen have been set up by UK insurance companies (1981), banks (1986), building societies (1987), unit trusts (1988), investment managers (1989), and pension managers (1993) to investigate complaints from customers.

• **Omdurman** ▶ 15 37N 32 29E A city in the Sudan, on the River Nile. The Mahdi made it his capital in 1885 but his successor, the Khalifa, was defeated by Lord Kitchener in the battle of Omdurman (1898). The Islamic University of Omdurman was founded in 1961. It has trade in hides, textiles, agricultural produce, and handicrafts. Population (1993): 1 267 077 (urban area).

• **Omsk** ▶ 55 00N 73 22E A port in W central Russia, at the confluence of the Rivers Irtysh and Om. Also on the Trans-Siberian Railway, it has important engineering industries and oil refineries. Population (1997 est): 1 158 000.

• **onager** ▶ A small wild ▷ass, *Equus hemionus onager*, of Iran. Onagers have a yellow-brown summer coat, which becomes darker in winter, and they roam over dry grassland in small herds.

• **Onassis, Aristotle Socrates** ▶ (1906–75) Greek businessman, who owned one of the largest independent shipping lines in the world. He started his business in 1932 and during the 1950s became one of the first to construct supertankers. In 1968 he married Jacqueline ▷Kennedy, his second wife, after a long relationship with Maria ▷Callas.

• **Oñate, Juan de** ▶ (d. 1630) Spanish conquistador. In about 1595 he settled the territory NW of Central America, New Mexico, and in 1601 sought the mythical kingdom of Quivira. Later, seeking a strait to the Pacific, he reached the Colorado River and Gulf of California.

• **onchocerciasis** ▶ A tropical disease caused by a parasitic nematode worm, *Onchocerca volvulus* (*see* filaria). The parasite is transmitted to humans by the bite of various species of ▷black fly and settles beneath the skin, causing itching, inflammation, and the formation of small fibrous tumours. Embryo worms released from the adults are carried in the bloodstream to the eyes, where they cause partial or total blindness (**river blindness**). The disease, which occurs in Africa and Central and South America, can be treated with anthelmintics.

● **oncogene** ▶ A gene in viruses and mammalian cells responsible for turning a normal cell into a cancerous cell. Several viruses (called oncogenic viruses) are known to carry oncogenes; when such a virus infects a host cell the oncogene directly transforms it into a cancer cell without altering the host cell's genes.

● **oncology** ▶ The medical specialty concerned with the study and treatment of tumours, especially malignant tumours (*see* cancer).

● **Ondaatje, (Philip) Michael** ▶ (1943–) Canadian novelist and writer, born in Sri Lanka. He is best known for the novels *In the Skin of a Lion* (1987) and *The English Patient* (1992); the latter was joint winner of the Booker Prize and became a highly successful film (1996). Other publications include poetry and the autobiography *Running in the Family* (1993).

● **Ondes Martenot** ▷*See* Martenot, Maurice.

● **Onega, Lake** ▶ A lake in NW Russia, the second largest in Europe. It forms part of the water route from the Gulf of Finland to the White Sea. Area: 9887 sq km (3817 sq mi).

● **Oneida** ▶ 43 04N 75 40W A city in the USA, in New York state. A religious society, the Oneida Community, was established nearby in 1848. Its members held all property in common, but social experiments ceased when it became a joint stock company in 1881. Population (latest est): 10 810.

● **O'Neill, Eugene** ▶ (1888–1953) US dramatist. The son of actors, he began writing one-act plays while recovering from tuberculosis in a sanatorium and won critical recognition with *Beyond the Horizon* (1920), *Emperor Jones* (1920), *Anna Christie* (1921), and *Desire Under the Elms* (1924). *Mourning Becomes Electra* (1931) transplants Aeschylus' trilogy to Civil War New England. His finest plays, including *The Iceman Cometh* (1946) and *Long Day's Journey into Night* (1956; written 1940–41), were written while he was suffering from Parkinson's disease and alcoholism. He won the Nobel Prize in 1936.

● **O'Neill, Terence, Baron** ▶ (1914–90) Northern Irish statesman, who became prime minister in 1963. In 1969 his acceptance of civil rights for the Roman Catholic minority forced his resignation from the Unionist Government. He became a life peer in 1970.

● **One Thousand Guineas** ▶ A flat race for three-year-old fillies only, run each spring at Newmarket over the Rowley Mile course. It was the last of the English ▷Classics to be instituted (1814).

● **onion** ▶ A hardy herbaceous perennial plant, ▷*Allium cepa*, probably native to central or W Asia but now cultivated worldwide, mainly in temperate regions, for its edible bulb. The mature plant has a leafless stalk, about 1 m high, which bears a round head of small white flowers, and six long slender leaves growing directly from the bulb. Onions are grown either from seed or from tiny bulbs called sets, produced in the flower head. Immature bulbs, together with their leaves, are eaten raw in salads, etc.: these are spring, or green, onions (*see* scallion). Family: *Liliaceae*.

● **Onitsha** ▶ 6 10N 6 47E A port in S Nigeria, on the River Niger. It suffered damage during the civil war (1967–71). It is an important trading centre. Agricultural products are the main exports and manufacturing is being developed, including textiles, printing, and tyre retreading. Population (1983 est): 268 700.

● **Ono, Yoko** ▷*See* Lennon, John.

● **Onsager, Lars** ▶ (1903–76) US chemist, born in Norway. His study of the thermodynamics of irreversible processes helped to solve the problems of separating uranium-235 from uranium-238 by gaseous diffusion, which was essential to the production of nuclear fuel. For this work Onsager was awarded the Nobel Prize in 1968.

● **Ontario** ▶ A province of Canada, stretching from the Great Lakes N to Hudson Bay. It lies mainly on the mineral-rich Canadian Shield, a rocky forested plateau with many lakes and rivers. Most of the population live in the gentle fertile lowlands near the S Great Lakes, dominated by the highly industrialized belt stretching from Toronto to Windsor. Manufacturing is very important, especially the produc-

tion of motor vehicles, steel, pulp and paper, textiles, machinery, petrochemicals, and food products. Ontario is Canada's leading mining province, producing half the world's nickel as well as copper, iron, zinc, gold, and uranium. The province's farmers produce tobacco, fruit, vegetables, and dairy products. Ontario is the wealthiest and most populous Canadian province, the country's political and economic heartland, and the cultural and educational centre of English-speaking Canada.

History: penetrated by French explorers and fur traders in the 17th century, Ontario became British (1763) and was settled by United Empire Loyalists after the American Revolution. The province benefited greatly from the formation of Canada (1867), which provided it with a larger domestic market. Area: 891 194 sq km (344 090 sq mi). Population (1995 est): 11 100 300. Capital: Toronto.

● **Ontario, Lake** ▶ A lake in E North America, the smallest and easternmost of the Great Lakes. It is fed by the Niagara River and empties into the St Lawrence River. Area: 18 941 sq km (7313 sq mi).

● **ontogeny** ▷*See* phylogeny.

● **ontological argument** ▷*See* Anselm of Canterbury, St.

● **ontology** ▶ The branch of philosophy that deals with the theory of being and considers questions about what is and what is not. Ontological theories may assert that only minds exist (extreme ▷idealism), or that only physical objects do (*see* materialism). The term was introduced by the rationalist philosopher Christian Wolff (1679–1754) to cover one of the chief concerns of ▷metaphysics.

● **o'nyong-nyong** ▶ An acute viral infection occurring in East Africa. The disease, transmitted by mosquitoes, causes a rash, aching joints, headache, and fever. Patients usually recover with rest and drugs to relieve the pain and fever.

● **onyx** ▶ A semiprecious stone consisting of a variety of ▷chalcedony characterized by straight parallel bands, often distinctly coloured. Onyx occurs in the lower part of steam cavities in igneous rocks. **Sardonyx** (birthstone for August) is a variety with reddish bands.

● **oolite** ▶ A variety of ▷limestone consisting mainly of beds of **ooliths**, approximately spherical concretions of calcite accumulated in concentric layers around a nucleus (for example a grain of sand or fragment of a shell). Ooliths of greater diameter than 2 mm are called pisoliths and the resultant rocks pisolites. Although most oolites are calcareous, oolitic ironstones also occur.

● **Oort cloud** ▶ A cloud of ten million or more comets, thought to move around the sun in orbits whose aphelia (greatest distance from sun) lie in a zone far beyond Pluto's orbit. A comet can be perturbed out of the cloud by, say, a passing star and sent closer to the sun, taking many thousands of years to complete its orbit. The cloud is named after the Dutch astronomer Jan Hendrik Oort (1900–92).

● **opah** ▷*See* moonfish.

● **opal** ▶ A semiprecious stone consisting of a hydrous amorphous variety of silica. Common opal is a dull-white or milky-blue colour, with yellow, brown, or red tinges due to impurities. The precious variety, used as a gem, shows a characteristic internal play of colours (opalescence) resulting from internal reflection and refraction of light passing through adjacent thin layers of different water content. It occurs in cavities in many rocks, deposited by percolating silica-bearing water; geyserite is a variety deposited from hot springs. The variety diatomite, made up of diatom skeletons, is used industrially as an insulator, abrasive, and filtering agent. The main sources of opal gems are Australia and Mexico. Birthstone for October.

● **Op art** ▶ A form of abstract art, developed in the 1950s and 1960s, that exploits optical techniques to produce dramatic effects, such as the illusion of movement. Violent colour contrasts and subtly distorted patterns are commonly used. Exponents include Victor ▷Vasarely and Bridget ▷Riley.

● **OPEC** ▷*See* Organization of Petroleum Exporting Countries.

● **opencast mining** ▶ The ▷mining of an ore that is sufficiently close to the surface to be reached without tunnelling. Iron ore, coal, copper ore, and phosphates are often available for opencast mining.

Any overlying soil is stripped from the ore deposit before explosives are used to break up the deposit. The ore is then transported to a processing plant for extraction of the useful products.

● **Open College** ▶ A nonresidential educational institution in the UK, established in 1987. It provides open-learning courses towards vocational and technical qualifications, supported by programmes on radio and television.

● **Open Door** ▶ A policy promulgated by the USA in 1899 to ensure equal trading rights in China for all countries. Its own trade with China threatened by the growing influence there of the other major powers, the USA sought and received the guarantee by Britain, France, Germany, Italy, and Japan of the maintenance of Chinese integrity.

● **open-hearth process** ▶ A technique for making ▷steel from ▷pig iron, scrap steel, and iron ore. It was developed in the 1850s and is still used, although ▷electric-arc furnaces are being used increasingly, especially for high-grade steel. The process uses gaseous fuel, which is preheated by the exhaust gases from the furnace. The molten metal lies in a shallow pool at the bottom or hearth of the furnace.

● **open-market operations** ▶ The mechanism by which the ▷Bank of England controls domestic credit and interest rates. When conducting a credit squeeze the Bank sells ▷treasury bills to the public (via the ▷discount houses), thus reducing ▷commercial bank assets (as a result of cheques drawn on them by the buyers of the bills) and making the banks call for funds from the discount houses. The discount houses in turn must borrow from the Bank at a high rate. This encourages the discount houses to sell bills, thus repeating the cycle until the commercial banks, faced with a drop in their liquid assets, are forced to cut back their advances to maintain the statutory ratio of liquid assets to total assets.

● **Open University** ▶ (OU) A nonresidential university in the UK, established in 1969 to provide ▷adult education on a part-time basis by means of correspondence courses and radio and television programmes, supported by a tutor-counselling service at regional centres throughout the country. It is open to anyone regardless of previous qualifications, age, or school attended. First mooted by the Advisory Centre for Education, it came to fruition under the administration (1964–70) of Harold Wilson, who made Jennie Lee responsible for the project; the first courses started in 1971. The OU has earned international esteem, giving those who did not have the chance early in life the opportunity to undertake a university education. More recently the OU has launched a variety of nondegree courses, ranging from in-service education for teachers to short courses on such subjects as pregnancy. ▷*See also* distance learning.

● **opera** ▶ A staged dramatic work in which all or most of the text is set to music. Opera originated in Florence in the early 17th century as the result of attempts to revive Greek tragedy and to reproduce its musical elements. These became the aria, recitative, and chorus of operatic convention. Opera began in the court but quickly became a popular public entertainment. The earliest opera still in the modern repertory is Monteverdi's *Orfeo* (1607). In ▷opera seria, developed by such composers as Scarlatti, Lully, and Handel, vocal ability became the dominant feature until Gluck reaffirmed the importance of the dramatic element in the mid-18th century. ▷Opera buffa developed in the early 18th century; it was perfected at the end of the 18th century by Mozart, who gave it greater depth and expression. In the early 19th century the influence of Romanticism gave rise to the works of Weber and Meyerbeer, while the Italian ▷bel canto tradition was maintained by Bellini, Rossini, and Donizetti. In the mid-19th century Wagner evolved the theory of music drama, in which the musical and dramatic elements of opera were integrated. He applied it to his opera cycle *Der Ring des Nibelungen* (1869–1876) and his subsequent operas, which embodied his theory of the *gesamtkunstwerk* (German: complete work of art). Verdi extended the emotional and dramatic range of Italian opera and in his late works assimilated the Wagnerian technique of continuous music in each act in place of the traditional division into separate numbers. The realism of Bizet's *Carmen* (1875) influenced Leoncavallo, Mascagni, and Puccini. In the 20th century a wide variety of operatic styles have flourished, including the dramatic realism of Janáček and the neoclassicism of Stravinsky. Richard Strauss's operas were greatly influenced by Wagner. Schoenberg and Berg applied atonal and serial techniques to opera. Other important operatic composers of the 20th century include Prokofiev, Britten, Henze, and Tippett. ▷*See also* opéra comique; comic opera; operetta.

● **opera buffa** ▶ A form of comic ▷opera containing some spoken dialogue. It evolved in Italy in the 18th century, an early example being ▷Pergolesi's *La serva padrona* (1733). The French genre, *opéra bouffe*, evolved from it in the 19th century and is typified by ▷Offenbach's operettas.

● **opéra comique** ▶ 1. A type of French comic opera of the 18th century with spoken dialogue. 2. In the 19th century, any French opera with spoken dialogue, a category including Bizet's *Carmen* and Gounod's *Faust*.

● **opera seria** ▶ A type of ▷opera common in the 18th century, characterized by a mythological or heroic plot, an Italian libretto, and a formal musical scheme of recitatives and arias.

● **operating system** ▶ The suite of programs that controls the basic operation of a ▷computer, providing an interface between the machine and the users' programs. In small computer systems it handles such tasks as preparing the machine for use, input and output, and loading and executing programs; in larger multitasking systems it also ensures that several programs can run simultaneously. Two of the main operating systems are **MS-DOS** (Microsoft disk operating system), which is used on ▷microcomputers, and **UNIX**, which is used on ▷minicomputers.

● **operetta** ▶ A light or comic ▷opera, usually with spoken dialogue. Lehar's *The Merry Widow* (1905) is a typical example.

● **operon** ▶ A group of closely linked genes in bacteria that together control the synthesis of the enzymes of a particular pathway. It includes an operator gene and one or more structural genes; its operation is controlled by a regulator gene outside the operon.

● **Ophites** ▶ (Greek *ophis*: serpent) A Gnostic sect that worshipped the serpent who brought about man's fall (Genesis 3) as the source of wisdom. ▷*See* Gnosticism.

● **ophthalmia** ▶ The old name for inflammation of the eye (*see* conjunctivitis). **Ophthalmia neonatorum** is conjunctivitis in newborn babies who have caught the infection from their mothers during birth; the most serious condition, due to gonorrhoeal infection, can result in blindness. The babies are treated with antibiotics.

● **ophthalmology** ▶ The medical specialty concerned with the study, diagnosis, and treatment of diseases of the eye. Ophthalmologists are doctors specializing in this. **Ophthalmic surgery** is the branch of surgery concerned with operations to the eye and its surrounding tissues. **Optometry** is the assessment and correction of visual defects, and opticians are not doctors: ophthalmic opticians (*or* optometrists) both test eyesight and prescribe suitable lenses; dispensing opticians make and fit glasses.

● **Ophüls, Max** ▶ (M. Oppenheimer; 1902–57) German film director. He worked mostly in France, Italy, and the USA. His stylish and elaborate romantic films include *La Ronde* (1950), *Madame De* (1953), and *Lola Montes* (1955).

● **Opie, John** ▶ (1761–1807) British portrait and history painter. He was introduced to London (1781) as a prodigy by his teacher John Wolcot (1738–1819) and later became professor of painting at the Royal Academy (1805). His best work was done in the early part of his career.

● **opinion polls** ▶ Surveys that sample public opinion on a matter of current concern, usually in an attempt to gauge the attitudes of the population as a whole (or a particular section of it). They are frequently used to predict election results. Although straw polls and ad hoc surveys have a long history, more scientific attempts to gauge public opinion began with the work of Dr George ▷Gallup of the American Institute of Public Opinion. Under the Gallup system, which was soon widely imitated, trained interviewers were used to question a small but representative sample of the population, carefully selected to reflect the social, economic, and educational balance of society. Sophisticated statistical methods were then used to assess the margin of error in making inferences to the population as a whole. These methods have had some spectacular successes (Gallup predicted the result of the UK's general election of 1945 to within 1%) but also some notable failures (no poll foresaw the Conservative victory in the 1992 general election). The extent to which opinion polls can themselves influence voting intentions is controversial; some countries now ban publication of polls in the days immediately before an election. In the later 1990s advertisers and political parties turned increasingly to so-called "focus groups" as a means of gauging public attitudes. These consist of tiny groups of people chosen to represent very precisely targeted sections of the population, who are subjected to in-depth and often oblique questioning designed to probe their underlying prejudices as well as their more conscious views.

● **Opitz (von Boberfeld), Martin ▶** (1597–1639) German poet and man of letters. Educated at Heidelberg, he served in the courts of various German nobles until he was appointed historiographer to Ladislaus IV of Poland. His own verse, for example *Teutsche Poemata* (1624), was, with his translations and critical works, especially *Buch von der teutschen Poeterey* (1624), influential in providing a model for German verse and in introducing the work of the ▷Pléiade, Sidney's *Arcadia*, and other foreign writers.

● **opium ▶** The dried juice obtained from the seed capsule of the ▷opium poppy. A narcotic drug, opium has been used for centuries in medicine for the relief of pain. Although still sometimes given in the form of laudanum (tincture of opium), its main legitimate uses today include the extraction of its active ingredients—▷morphine (first isolated in 1803), codeine, papaverine, etc.—and preparation of their derivatives (e.g. heroin). Because opium causes ▷drug dependence and overdosage can be fatal, its preparation and use are strictly controlled (in spite of this, illegal trading in opium continues). India, Turkey, and Afghanistan are the main opium-producing countries.

● **opium poppy ▶** An annual ▷poppy, *Papaver somniferum*, cultivated since ancient times in N temperate and subtropical regions as the source of ▷opium. 30–60 cm tall, it has large white to purple flowers with dark centres and the fruit is a round capsule. Opium is extracted from the latex of the plant, which exudes from notches made in the half-ripened capsule and hardens on exposure to air.

● **Opium Wars ▶ 1.** (1839–42) The war between Britain and China precipitated by the confiscation by the Chinese Government of British opium stores in Canton and the murder of a Chinese by British sailors. The British victory was confirmed by the Treaty of Nanking in which five ▷treaty ports were opened to British trade and residence. **2.** (1856–60) The war between Britain and France, on one side, and China. Its immediate cause was the boarding of the British *Arrow* by Chinese officials. The allied victory opened further ports to Western trade (Treaty of Tientsin, 1858, finally ratified by the emperor in the Peking (Beijing) Convention, 1860) and led to the legalization of opium in China.

● **Opole ▶** (German name: Oppeln) 50 40N 17 56E A town in SW Poland, on the River Oder. It was the capital (1919–45) of the German province of Upper Silesia. Industries include the manufacture of machinery, chemicals, cement, and textiles. Population (1996 est): 130 600.

● **Oporto ▶** (Portuguese name: Pôrto) 41 09N 8 37W The second largest city in Portugal, on the River Douro near the Atlantic coast. Built on terraces, it has many tall granite houses and a modernized 13th-century cathedral; its university was founded in 1911. It is famous for the export (chiefly to Britain) of its port wine; other exports include fruit and cork. Population (1991): 309 485.

● **opossum ▶** A New World ▷marsupial belonging to the family *Didelphidae* (65 species). Opossums are the only marsupials outside Australasia. The common, or Virginian, opossum (*Didelphys marsupialis*) is cat-sized, with a large pouch containing up to 16 teats; it produces at least two litters of young every year. After about three months the young ride on their mother's back, leaving the pouch

opossum ▶ Young opossums cling to their mother's fur after emerging from the pouch and remain close to her for about three months before leading an independent existence.

free for another litter. Opossums live in crevices and abandoned burrows, feeding on both animal and vegetable matter. ⬚mammal.

● **Oppeln** ▷*See* Opole.

● **Oppenheimer, J. Robert ▶** (1904–67) US physicist, who contributed to quantum mechanics and particle physics. In 1943 he was put in charge of the development of the atom bomb at Los Alamos, New Mexico. After the war he was appointed chairman of the advisory committee to the Atomic Energy Commission but as a result of his opposition to the development of the hydrogen bomb, he lost his post in 1954 and was labelled a security risk by Senator Joseph ▷McCarthy's committee.

● **opposition ▶** An alignment of two celestial bodies in the solar system, usually the sun and a planet, that occurs when they lie directly opposite each other in the sky. The angle planet-earth-sun is then 180°. Venus and Mercury cannot come to opposition with the sun. For the other planets, opposition is the most favourable time for observation.

● **Ops ▶** A Roman fertility goddess, wife of Saturn, identified with the Greek ▷Rhea. She was usually worshipped together with a primitive rustic god, Consus.

● **optical activity ▶** The rotation of the plane of polarization of plane ▷polarized light as it passes through certain solutions and crystals. The angle through which the plane is rotated is directly proportional to the path length of the light in the substance and, in the case of a solution, to its concentration. If the plane is rotated clockwise (looking at the oncoming light) the substance is said to be dextrorotatory and is indicated by the prefix *d*- (or +). Laevorotatory substances, indicated by *l*- (or –), rotate the plane anticlockwise.

● **optical character recognition ▶** (OCR) ▷*See* computer.

● **optical fibre** ▷*See* fibre optics.

● **optics ▶** The branch of physics concerned with ▷light and vision. Optics is divided into two major branches: geometrical optics and physical optics. Geometrical optics studies the geometry of light rays as they pass through an optical system. Physical optics concerns light's properties (e.g. ▷diffraction, ▷interference, and polarization) and its interaction with matter (e.g. in ▷refraction, ▷scattering, and absorption).

● **option ▶** The right to buy or sell something at an agreed price by a specified date. Usually the option costs a sum of money (the option money), which is not returned if the option is not taken up. Options are sought for such diverse assets as the right to buy a house, the film rights of a book, or a line of shares. Financial options on shares (stock options), foreign currencies, bonds, etc., are dealt with in London on the London International Financial Futures and Options Exchange (LIFFE), while options on commodities are traded on the associated LIFFE Commodity Products. An option to buy shares or commodities (a call option) or to sell them (a put option) are regular features of trading; in most cases the options themselves can be bought and sold (these are called traded options). ▷*See also* futures.

● **optometry** ▷*See* ophthalmology.

● **Opuntia** ▷*See* prickly pear.

● **Opus Dei** ▶ (Latin: God's work) **1.** In Benedictine monasticism, the monk's primary duty of prayer. It specifically refers to the recitation of prescribed prayers (the Divine Office) at set times known as the canonical hours, namely matins, lauds, prime, terce, sext (noon), nones, vespers, and compline. **2.** An international Roman Catholic organization (full name: Prelature of the Holy Cross and Opus Dei) founded by the Spanish priest Josemaría Escrivá de Balaguer (1902–75) in 1928 to spread Christian ideals to all spheres of society. The Prelature now has an estimated 1000 priests and 72 000 lay members. Opus Dei has been attacked for its alleged secrecy and authoritarianism but is supported by the present pope, who canonized its founder in 2002.

● **orache** ▶ An annual herb or small shrub of the genus *Atriplex* (about 100 species), occurring worldwide on sea shores and waste land and growing 1–1.5 m high. The leaves are narrow or triangular and, in some species, may be used as a vegetable. Tiny green flowers develop into fruits surrounded by a winglike membrane. Family: *Chenopodiaceae*.

● **oracle** ▶ A response given by a deity, usually through a priest or priestess, to an inquiry; also, the sacred place at which such responses were sought. Although occurring in Egyptian and other ancient civilizations, the best-known oracles were those of classical Greece. The oldest was that of Zeus at Dodona, where the oracle was interpreted from the rustling of oak leaves. At the oracle of Apollo at Delphi, which attained political influence during the 6th and 7th centuries BC, the pronouncements made by the Pythian priestess in a state of frenzy were interpreted in verse by the priests.

● **Oracle** ▷*See* teletext.

● **Oradea** ▶ 47 03N 21 55E A city in NW Romania, on the River Crişul Repede. It is situated in a wine-producing area where many Neolithic, Roman, and other artefacts have been found. Industries include the manufacture of machine tools, chemicals, and food products. Population (1992): 220 848.

● **oral contraceptive** ▶ A hormonal drug—usually a combination of a synthetic ▷oestrogen and a synthetic progestogen (*see* progesterone)—taken in the form of tablets ("the Pill") by women to prevent conception (*see also* contraception). Oral contraceptives act by preventing the monthly release of an egg cell from the ovary. They are taken every day from the 5th to the 26th day of the menstrual cycle (menstruation occurs during the week in which they are not taken). Combined pills may cause fluid retention (therefore swelling of the ankles), depression, weight gain, and in rare cases thrombosis. Progestogen-only pills contain no oestrogen: they are thought to act on the lining of the womb to make conception less likely. They are associated with fewer side effects than the combined pill, but are slightly less efficient contraceptives.

● **Oran** ▶ (Arabic name: Wahran; French name: Ouahran) 35 45N 0 38W A port in Algeria, on the Mediterranean Sea. Under intermittent Spanish occupation from the 16th to the 18th centuries, it was occupied by France from 1831 until Algerian independence (1962). It has a university (1965). Exports include cereals, wine, wool, and esparto grass. Population (latest est): 610 000.

● **orange** ▶ One of several small evergreen □trees or shrubs of the genus ▷*Citrus*, native to SE Asia but cultivated throughout the tropics and subtropics. The thick oval shiny leaves have winged stalks and the white five-petalled flowers are borne in clusters. The globular fruit has a dimpled orange or yellow rind and a juicy pulp, rich in sugars, acids, and vitamin C. Fruit of the sweet orange (*C. sinensis*) is eaten fresh while that of the Seville orange (*C. aurantium*) is used to make marmalade. Oranges are used in soft drinks and confectionery. Family: *Rutaceae*. ▷*See also* tangerine.

● **Orange** ▶ The ruling dynasty of the Netherlands since 1815. In the 16th century the Princes of Orange, in S France, married into the House of ▷Nassau, a member of which, ▷William the Silent, became Prince of Orange-Nassau (1544) and led the Revolt of the Netherlands against Spain. He and his descendants (one of whom became William III of England) were ▷stadholders (chief magistrates) of the United Provinces of the Netherlands until its collapse in 1795. In 1815 the family were restored as monarchs of the newly established kingdom of the Netherlands. The principality of Orange was seized by Louis XIV in 1660.

● **Orange** ▶ 44 08N 4 48E A town in SE France, in the Vaucluse department. It was the capital of the principality of Orange in the middle ages, the descendants of which formed the House of Orange. There are several notable Roman remains. Population (latest est): 28 136.

● **Orange** ▶ 33 19S 149 10E A city in Australia, in E central New South Wales. It is the centre of a fruit-growing and sheep-rearing region. Its industries include woollen mills and electrical engineering. Population (1991 est): 32 520.

● **Orange Free State** ▶ (Afrikaans name: Oranje Vrystaat) An inland region and former province in South Africa. Consisting mostly of the undulating plain of the Highveld, it is predominantly rural, with agriculture as the leading economic activity. Wheat, maize, and stock rearing are important. Mining has developed recently; diamonds, gold, uranium, and coal are produced. Chemicals, fertilizers, and oil from coal are manufactured. The region has a strong Afrikaner culture.

History: settled by Voortrekkers from the early 19th century, it was under British rule as the Orange River Sovereignty from 1848 until 1854, when it was recognized as the independent Orange Free State. In 1900 it was annexed by the British again, becoming the self-governing Orange River Colony in 1902. It became a province of the Union of South Africa in 1910. In 1994 it became the **Free State** region as part of administrative reorganization. Area: 129 152 sq km (49 886 sq mi). Population (1996): 2 633 504. Capital: Bloemfontein.

● **Orange Order** ▶ An Irish sectarian society, named after William III of England (previously William of Orange) who defeated the Roman Catholic former king James II in 1690. Formed in 1795 following agrarian agitation in County Armagh that culminated in a sectarian confrontation known as the Battle of the Diamond, the Orange Order was originally a secret society modelled on ▷freemasonry. Pledged to maintain Protestantism and the Protestant succession, it provided the backbone of Ulster resistance to the ▷Home Rule movement. The order now has lodges throughout Ireland, Great Britain, and several former British colonies, but is concentrated in Northern Ireland, where it articulates hardline Protestant Unionism and exercises a considerable political influence, particularly through its links with the ▷Ulster Unionist Party. Since 1796 it has held parades with flags, banners, and marching bands, climaxing each year on 12 July, which commemorate the Battles of the ▷Boyne and of ▷Aughrim at which William was victorious. Since 1807 the Orange Order has held a march from Portadown to Dumcree Church; in recent years part of the return route, passing through roads largely inhabited by Catholics, has sparked annual controversy and unrest. Since the Troubles began in 1969 the marches have been seen by some as perpetuating hostility between Protestants and Catholics.

● **Orange Prize** ▶ Britain's richest literary award, worth £30,000. Announced in 1996 and sponsored by the telecommunications company Orange, it is open only to women writers of fiction in English. The 2001 prize was won by Kate Grenville with *The Idea of Perfection*.

● **Orange River** ▶ A river in SW Africa. Rising in NE Lesotho, it flows mainly W across the South African plateau to the Atlantic Ocean. The largest river in South Africa, it forms part of the border with

Namibia. Since 1963 the **Orange River Project** has provided irrigation and hydroelectric power. Length: 2093 km (1300 mi).

• **orang-utan** ▶ A long-armed great ▷ape, *Pongo pygmaeus*, of Borneo and Sumatra. Orang-utans grow up to 120 cm tall, with arms spanning more than 200 cm, and have long reddish-brown hair. Mainly vegetarian, they are fond of durian fruit. The only great apes outside Africa, with fewer than 5000 individuals in the wild, they are an endangered species.

• **Oratorians** ▶ Communities of Roman Catholic priests who live together without taking vows and who devote themselves to teaching, preaching, prayer, and administration of the sacraments. There are two orders: the Italian Oratory of St Philip Neri (founded 1564) and the French Oratoire de Jésus-Christ (1611). The former has oratories in England founded by Cardinal Newman.

• **oratorio** ▶ A musical composition, usually on a religious subject, for soloists, chorus, and orchestra. The name derives from the Oratory of St Philip Neri in 16th-century Rome (*see* Oratorians), where semidramatized versions of biblical stories were performed with musical accompaniment. Among notable oratorios are the *St Matthew* and *St John Passions* of J. S. Bach, Handel's *Messiah*, Haydn's *The Creation*, Mendelssohn's *Elijah*, Berlioz's *Childhood of Christ*, Elgar's *Dream of Gerontius*, and Tippett's *A Child of Our Time*.

• **orbital** ▶ An atomic orbital is the region around the nucleus in which there is an appreciable probability that an electron will be found. In ▷wave mechanics an electron does not have a fixed orbit as it does in the ▷Bohr atom; it has instead an orbital in which there is a probability distribution, given by a wave function, that it will be found in a particular region. Each orbital has a fixed energy and a shape determined by three ▷quantum numbers, one (n) indicating the most probable distance of the electron from the nucleus, one (l) giving its angular momentum, and one (m) giving the orientation of the orbital if it is not spherical. In the formation of a covalent bond between two atoms, a molecular orbital containing two electrons is formed.

• **orb weaver** ▶ A ▷spider belonging to a widely distributed family (*Argiopidae*; over 2500 species), noted for its geometrically designed web. For example, the web of the orange garden spider (*Miranda aurantia*), common in grass and bushes, has a zigzag band and reaches 60 cm across.

• **Orcagna, Andrea** ▶ (Andrea di Cione; c. 1308–c. 1368) Florentine artist. His only certain surviving painting is an altarpiece in Sta Maria Novella, Florence; as a sculptor he is known for his marble tabernacle in Orsanmichele. He became architect to Orsanmichele (1355), to the Duomo in Florence (1357; 1364–67), and in Orvieto (1358).

• **orchestra** ▶ A body of instrumentalists playing music written or arranged for a specific combination of instruments. The modern **symphony orchestra** evolved from the small and variously constituted orchestras of the 18th century; its original instrumentation (first and second violins, violas, cellos, double basses, bassoons, oboes, flutes, horns and timpani) being that of the typical symphony. Such orchestras were directed from a continuo keyboard instrument or by the leader of the first violin section. In the 19th century the orchestra was enlarged and the range of instruments widened by the addition of clarinets, trumpets, trombones, and percussion instruments; later the harp, cor anglais, piccolo, bass clarinet, contra bassoon, and tuba were added. In the late 19th century the number of woodwind and brass was increased, and such instruments as the saxophone, saxhorn, Wagner tuba, glockenspiel, and xylophone were occasionally used. The role of the conductor became increasingly important from the early 19th century onwards. In the 20th century the piano, guitar, mandolin, marimba, vibraphone, as well as various electric and electronic instruments have been incorporated. The modern symphony orchestra comprises at least a hundred players. The **chamber orchestra** corresponds in size to the smaller orchestras of the 18th century.

• **orchid** ▶ A herbaceous perennial plant of the family *Orchidaceae* (about 20 000 species), found worldwide, especially in damp tropical regions. Most temperate orchids grow normally in the soil (i.e. they are terrestrial), while tropical orchids tend to grow nonparasitically on trees (i.e. as epiphytes) and form pseudobulbs (storage organs) at the base of the stem. Orchid flowers vary greatly in shape, colour, and size and occur usually in clusters. Each flower consists of three petal-like sepals and three petals—the lowest (labellum) being very distinctive. The one or two stamens and stigma are fused to form a central column that bears pollen grains grouped into masses (pollinia), which are transferred to other flowers by insects. The flowers of many species are adapted to receive only a particular species of insects in order to restrict natural hybridization; examples are the bee, fly, and spider orchids (genus *Ophrys*). The fruit is a capsule containing enormous numbers of tiny seeds, which are dispersed by wind. Many orchids are cultivated for ornament (*see* Cattleya; Cymbidium; Odontoglossum; slipper orchid); one genus—▷*Vanilla*—is the source of vanilla flavouring.

• **orchil** ▶ (*or* archil) One of several ▷lichens (*Umbilicaria, Roccella, Evernia, Lecanova*, and *Ochrolechia*) from which a violet dye (also called orchil) can be extracted by fermentation.

• **Orczy, Baroness Emmusca** ▶ (1865–1947) British novelist. Born in Hungary, she went to London to study art. *The Scarlet Pimpernel* (1905) concerns an English nobleman who smuggles aristocrats out of Revolutionary France.

• **order** ▶ (biology) ▷*See* taxonomy.

• **Order in Council** ▶ A command or direction issued by the queen with the advice of the ▷Privy Council, although in fact it is issued only with the advice of the cabinet. Apart from the Crown's inherent right (royal prerogative) to issue Orders, for example declarations of war, some Acts of Parliament authorize them to give legal force to administrative regulations made by government departments. Only Orders authorized by act of parliament can make or alter the law.

• **Order of Merit** ▶ (OM) A British order of chivalry, instituted by Edward VII to mark his coronation in 1902. It comprises the sovereign and not more than 24 men and women of great eminence.

• **Order of St Michael and St George** ▶ An order of chivalry founded in 1818 and subsequently enlarged. Mainly awarded to diplomats, its three classes consist of 120 Knights or Dames (GCMG), 390 Knights or Dames Commanders (KCMG or DCMG), and up to 1775 Companions (CMG).

• **Order of the British Empire, The Most Excellent** ▶ A British order of knighthood, instituted in 1917 and having five classes: Knights or Dames Grand Cross (GBE); Knights or Dames Commanders (KBE or DBE); Commanders (CBE); Officers (OBE); and Members (MBE). In 1993 the British Empire Medal was merged with the MBE. Its motto is *For God and Empire*.

• **orders of architecture** ▶ The fundamental elements of classical □architecture, comprising five main types of supportive column—Doric, Tuscan, Ionic, Corinthian, and Composite. The column was first employed by the Egyptians but it was developed by the Greeks and Romans to such an extent that the proportions between the column's constituent parts determined the proportions of the entire building.

Each order usually consists of four main parts, the base, shaft, ▷capital, and entablature, these having individual shapes and types of decoration. The first order to be developed, the Doric, takes two forms: the Greek Doric, which has no base, and the Roman Doric, more slender in proportion and with a base. Roman Doric's unadorned and unfluted counterpart is the Tuscan order. The Ionic first appeared in Asia Minor in about the 6th century BC and was adopted by the Greeks in the 5th century BC. It has slender proportions and a capital adorned with four spiral scrolls (volutes), two at the front and two at the back. The most decorative order, the Corinthian, was developed by the Romans, although it was occasionally used in ancient Greece. The Romans also combined the Corinthian capital of ▷acanthus leaves with the volutes of the Ionic capital to form the Composite order.

A **pilaster** is a rectangular column attached to the wall. It conforms to the system of orders but, unlike the cylindrical column, is usually only decorative in function.

• **ordination** ▷*See* holy orders.

● **Ordnance Survey** ▶ The official map-making body of Great Britain (there is a separate survey for Northern Ireland). Established in 1791, following the mapping of Scotland by Gen William Roy (1726–90), it published its first map in 1801. Maps ranging from the large-scale 1:1250 (used for major urban areas) to the small-scale 1:1 000 000 (covering Great Britain in two parts) have since been produced. The original scale to be used, the 1:63 360 (1 in:1 mi), was converted to the metric scale of 1:50 000 in the 1970s and this remains the most widely used scale. The First Series of the 1:50 000 was completed in 1976 and is gradually being replaced by a Second Series with redrawn maps. Other major scales include the 1:10 000 (formerly 6 in:1 mi) and the 1:250 000 (formerly ¼ in:1 mi). Some maps are produced for specialized uses, such as the archaeological maps. Revisions are produced by the Ordnance Survey Department based in Southampton. ▷*See also* digital mapping.

● **Ordovician period** ▶ A geological period of the Lower Palaeozoic era, between the Cambrian and Silurian periods. It lasted from about 515 to 445 million years ago. It is divided into the Upper and Lower Ordovician, based on the graptolite fossils that are abundant in the deepwater deposits.

● **Ordzhonikidze** ▷*See* Vladikavkas.

● **ore** ▶ A rock body or mineral deposit from which one or more useful materials, usually metals, can be economically extracted. The metal content of the various ores differs; iron ore contains about 20–30% iron, whereas copper ores may contain only 0.5% copper. The gangue is the waste material left when the desired mineral has been extracted. ▷*See* metallurgy.

● **Örebro** ▶ 59 17N 15 13E A city in S Sweden. An ancient city, it was largely rebuilt following a fire in 1854. It has a university (1967) and its manufactures include footwear, machinery, and chemicals. Population (1997 est): 120 774.

● **oregano** ▶ An aromatic perennial herb, *Origanum vulgare*, native to the Mediterranean and W Asia. The dried leaves and flowers are used as a culinary flavouring and the plant is a source of essential oils. Family: ▷*Labiatae*.

● **Oregon** ▶ A state in the USA, on the NW Pacific coast. Its topography is diverse; the Cascade Range extends N–S dividing the state between the valleys of the W and the dry plateau areas of the E. The Willamette Valley contains the major settlements. The economy is based predominantly on agriculture and forestry. Oregon is the nation's leading timber state and approximately half its area is forested; the Douglas fir is especially important. Much of the timber is used to produce plywood, pulp, and paper. Agriculture includes cattle ranching in the drier areas, dairy farming in the valleys, and wheat growing in the NE; specialized crops, such as cherries, are also grown. Hydroelectric-power resources have led to the development of metal-processing industries.
History: originally occupied by several Indian tribes, there was considerable migration of White settlers from the Midwest along the famous ▷Oregon Trail during the 19th century. It became a state in 1859. Area: 251 180 sq km (96 981 sq mi). Population (1996 est): 3 203 735. Capital: Salem.

● **Oregon Trail** ▶ A route from the Missouri to the Columbia Rivers followed first by explorers and fur traders and then by settlers. Some 2000 miles long, it began at Independence, Missouri, crossed the Rockies at the South Pass and went on down the Columbia River. In the Great Emigration of 1843 almost a thousand people followed the trail to settle in ▷Oregon.

● **Orel** ▶ (or Oryol) 52 58N 36 04E A city in W Russia. Founded in 1564, it was severely damaged in World War II. Industries include engineering. The writer Turgenev was born here. Population (1987): 335 000.

● **Orellana, Francisco de** ▶ (1511–46) Spanish soldier and explorer. After serving with ▷Pizarro in the conquest of Peru (1535), he became governor of Guayaquil in 1538. In 1541–43 he became the first European to explore the Amazon river system, navigating from its headstreams in the Andes to the Atlantic Ocean.

● **Orenburg** ▶ (name from 1938 until 1957: Chkalov) 51 50N 55 00E A city in W Russia on the River Ural. It was founded in 1735 by the Cossacks on the site of present-day Orsk, subsequently being moved down stream. Industries include engineering and consumer-goods manufacture. Population (1995 est): 532 000.

● **Orense** ▶ 42 20N 7 52W A town in NW Spain, in Galicia on the River Miño. It possesses a cathedral and a remarkable bridge built in 1230. Industries include iron founding and flour milling. Population (1994 est): 108 547.

● **Oresme, Nicole d'** ▶ (c. 1320–82) French philosopher and churchman. He became master of the College of Navarre at Paris in 1355 and later Bishop of Lisieux (1377). His writings deal with politics, natural science, geometry, and economics. He was also an early advocate of the theory that the earth revolves around other bodies.

● **Orestes** ▶ In Greek legend, the son of ▷Agamemnon, King of Mycenae, and ▷Clytemnestra. Encouraged by his sister ▷Electra, he avenged his father's murder by killing his mother and her lover Aegisthus. In the dramatic trilogy of ▷Aeschylus he is pursued by the ▷Erinyes until acquitted at the Areopagus in Athens by the deciding vote of Athena.

● **Øresund** ▶ (or Öresund) ▷*See* Sound, the.

● **orfe** ▶ A carnivorous food and game fish, *Idus idus*, also called ide, found in rivers and lakes of Europe and NW Asia. Its stout elongated body, 30–50 cm long, is blue-grey or blackish with a silvery belly. The golden orfe is a reddish-gold variety. Family: *Cyprinidae*; order: *Cypriniformes*.

● **Orff, Carl** ▶ (1895–1982) German composer, teacher, conductor, and editor. He developed a monodic style of composition characterized by lively rhythms; his best-known work is the oratorio *Carmina Burana* (1935–36), based on 13th-century Latin and German poems found in a Benedictine monastery in Bavaria. Orff also introduced percussion instruments, such as the stone chimes, into musical education.

● **organ** ▶ A musical wind instrument of early origin, which developed from the reed pipes and the ▷hydraulis. The modern organ consists of a large number of graduated pipes, some of which contain reeds, fitted over a wind chest and blown by manual or electric bellows. The pipes are made to sound by depressing keys or pedals. Each pipe sounds one note, but groups of duplicate pipes, called stops, can be made to sound together or successively. Different stops have different tone colours, many of which resemble orchestral instruments. An organ console may have as many as five or more keyboards, known as the great, swell, choir, solo, and echo, as well as pedals. Each keyboard has a separate range of stops and different characteristics; the swell, for example, has shutters over the pipe holes that allow crescendos and decrescendos. Coupler mechanisms allow one keyboard to become automatically linked to another. These allow, for example the pedals, which normally play the deepest notes, to play notes many octaves higher.
 The action linking keys and pipes consists of a series of rods called a tracker action or wires conveying electrical impulses. The modern **electronic organ** consists of a series of electronic oscillators to produce notes, which are then amplified.

● **organic chemistry** ▷*See* chemistry.

● **organic farming** ▷*See* fertilizers.

● **Organisation de l'Armée secrète** ▶ (OAS) An organization of French settlers in Algeria opposed to Algerian independence from France. The OAS was established in 1961 and led by General Raoul Salan (1899–1984). Its campaign of terrorism in Algeria and France included the attempted assassination in September, 1961, of the French president, de Gaulle, who by March, 1962, had reached agreement with the Algerian nationalists (*see* Front de Libération nationale). Salan was captured in April (and imprisoned 1962–68) and the OAS collapsed.

● **Organisation européenne pour la Recherche nucléaire** ▷*See* CERN.

● **Organization for Economic Cooperation and Development** ▶(OECD) An international organization founded in 1961 to further economic growth among its members, expand world trade, and coordinate aid to developing countries. It succeeded the Organization for European Economic Cooperation, which had been set up in 1948 to coordinate the Marshall Plan (*see* Marshall, George) for European economic recovery after World War II. The headquarters of the OECD are in Paris.

● **Organization of African Unity** ▶ (OAU) An intergovernmental organization of African countries. It was founded in 1963 to provide a forum for discussion of political and economic problems affecting African states and to formulate policies towards such problems. In 2001 the OAU was formally replaced by a new **African Union**, which will involve the creation of an economic community and the establishment of a Pan-African parliament.

● **Organization of American States** ▶ (OAS) A body founded in 1948 to foster mutual understanding and cooperation between American republics and collective security. It is based on the principle of the ▷Monroe Doctrine. In 1962 Cuba was suspended from the OAS because of its acceptance of nuclear missiles from the Soviet Union.

● **Organization of Central American States** ▶ (OCAS) An international organization founded in 1951. Its members include Costa Rica, El Salvador, Guatemala, Honduras, and Nicaragua, and its headquarters are in Guatemala City. Its aim is to promote social, cultural, and economic development through joint action.

● **Organization of Petroleum Exporting Countries** ▶ (OPEC) An organization founded in 1960 to represent the interests of the chief oil-exporting nations in dealings with the major oil companies. OPEC was the only successful primary-product ▷cartel until the mid-1970s, when dissension between member nations and increased supplies from non-OPEC sources reduced its influence. The members of OPEC are Algeria, Indonesia, Iran, Iraq, Kuwait, Libya, Nigeria, Qatar, Saudi Arabia, United Arab Emirates, and Venezuela. Ecuador left in 1992 and Gabon in 1995. The Organization of Arab Petroleum Exporting Countries (OAPEC), established in 1968, has ten members.

● **organ-pipe cactus** ▶ A branching columnar ▷cactus, of the genus *Lemacrocereus* or *Cereus*, especially *L. thurberi*, which resembles a candelabra and is found in deserts of the S USA and Mexico. Up to 10 m high, it is grown in hedgerows and used for fuel and construction. The fruit is edible.

● **organ-pipe coral** ▶ A ▷coral, *Tubipora musica*, occurring in shallow waters of the Indian and Pacific Oceans. It is composed of a colony of long upright stalked ▷polyps supported by bright-red skeletal tubes of fused spicules. Order: *Stolonifera*.

● **organum** ▶ (Latin: organ, instrument) A type of medieval polyphonic vocal composition in which a plainchant melody was accompanied by voices at the fixed intervals of the octave and fourth or fifth. ▷*See also* ars antiqua.

● **oribi** ▶ A rare antelope, *Ourebia ourebi*, of African grasslands. About 90 cm high at the shoulder, oribis have slender legs, large ears, a fawn coat, and a short bristly tail; males have short straight horns. Hiding among long grass during the day, they graze in small herds at dawn and dusk.

● **orienteering** ▶ A navigational sport, held over rugged country, that originated in Sweden in 1918 and is designed to test both intellectual and athletic ability. Using a map and compass, competitors run round a series of control points that must be visited in the prescribed sequence. Distances range from 3 to 13 km (2–8 mi).

● **origami** ▶ The oriental art of paper folding, which developed into a traditional Japanese craft. It is used in the formal ceremonial wrapping of gifts and to make models of birds, animals, sailing boats, etc., which can often be made to move, e.g. birds that flap their wings. It now enjoys a wide popularity outside Japan.

● **Origen** ▶ (c. 185–c. 254 AD) Egyptian theologian and Father of the Church, born at Alexandria, son of a Christian martyr. As head of Alexandria's catechetical school he gained fame as a teacher. He was ordained in Palestine (c. 230), but the Bishop of Alexandria immediately unfrocked him, maintaining that he was unfit for priesthood because he had castrated himself. He then settled in Caesarea, where he founded a school. During the persecution of Emperor Decius (c. 250) he was imprisoned and tortured at Tyre. The most famous of his many influential works are his critical edition of the Bible, the *Hexapla*, and his theological treatise, *De principiis*.

● **original sin** ▶ In Christian doctrine, the teaching that human nature is radically and inescapably flawed, causing alienation from God and the frustration of God's purposes for the world. The fall of man into original sin is described in the biblical story of Adam's misuse of his freedom (Genesis 3): for most of Christian history this story was accepted as historical, but it is now more likely to be interpreted symbolically. After much debate by the Church Fathers, St ▷Augustine of Hippo's diagnosis, that Adam's sin is inescapably transmitted to us by natural propagation and that only the divine initiative of ▷grace can redeem us, was accepted as orthodox (*see also* Pelagius). This had the effect of associating original sin with the sexual act itself, leading to much distorted teaching. The standard Roman Catholic position was defined by St Thomas ▷Aquinas, who accorded greater scope to the human will and reason and placed less emphasis on sex. However, such reformers as ▷Luther and John ▷Calvin emphasized the Augustinian doctrine in its severest form. After the Enlightenment the concept of original sin became unfashionable as belief in human progress and even perfectibility grew. However, the horrors of the 20th century led such theologians as Karl ▷Barth to reemphasize the reality of original sin. Modern teaching on the subject is varied; some thinkers have interpreted the doctrine in existential terms (*see* existentialism), while others have used it to develop an idea of collective or "structural" sin (e.g. as embedded in unjust social or economic systems). ▷*See also* sin.

● **Orinoco, River** ▶ (Spanish name: Río Orinoco) The third largest river system in South America. Rising in S Venezuela, it flows in an arc forming part of the Venezuela–Colombia border before entering the Atlantic Ocean via an extensive delta region. Oceangoing vessels can penetrate upstream for about 364 km (226 mi). Drainage basin area: 940 000 sq km (365 000 sq mi). Length: about 2575 km (1600 mi).

● **oriole** ▶ A songbird belonging to an Old World family (*Oriolidae*; 28 species) occurring mainly in tropical forests. Orioles generally have a black-and-yellow plumage, measure 18–30 cm, and feed on fruit and insects. The golden oriole (*Oriolus oriolus*) is the only species reaching Europe.
American orioles (also called American blackbirds) belong to the family *Icteridae* (87 species). 16–54 cm long, they usually have a black plumage with red, yellow, or brown markings. The family includes the ▷bobolink and the ▷grackle.

● **Orion** ▶ (astronomy) A very conspicuous constellation that lies on the celestial equator and can therefore be seen from most parts of the world. The brightest stars, ▷Rigel and the slightly fainter ▷Betelgeuse, lie at opposite corners of a quadrilateral of stars with Bellatrix and Saiph, both 2nd magnitude, at the other corners. Inside the quadrilateral three 2nd-magnitude stars form **Orion's Belt**, S of which lies the **Orion nebula**, one of the brightest emission nebulae.

● **Orion** ▶ (mythology) A giant of ▷Boeotia who, according to Greek legend, was a son of ▷Poseidon or the offspring of an ox. Famed as a hunter, he either died from a scorpion sting or was killed by ▷Artemis when he tried to rape her.

● **Orissa** ▶ A state in E India, on the Bay of Bengal. Its coastal plain extends through the Eastern ▷Ghats via broad valleys into interior highlands. Orissa is grossly overcrowded and its inhabitants farm rice, turmeric, and sugar cane. Fishing, forestry, and the mining of iron ore, manganese, chromite, and coal are important. There is also some heavy industry.
History: known from ancient times, Orissa ruled a maritime empire during the 1st millennium AD. Partitioned by Muslim conquerors (17th century), it gradually fell under British domination (18th–19th centuries). In 1999 thousands were killed and about 1.5 million made homeless by a cyclone. Area: 155 782 sq km (60 132 sq mi). Population (2001): 36 706 920. Capital: Bhubaneswar.

● **Orizaba** ▶ 18 51N 97 08W A city and resort in E central Mexico. It is the chief centre of the textile industry. Population (2000 est): 118 400.

● **Orkney Islands** ▶ (*or* Orkneys) A group of about 70 islands off the

N coast of Scotland, separated from the mainland by the Pentland Firth. About 20 of the islands are inhabited; the chief ones are Mainland (Pomona), South Ronaldsay, Westray, Sanday, and Hoy. The population is of Scandinavian descent, reflecting the Islands' long connections with Norway and Denmark. Formerly an insular county, it became an island authority under local government reorganization in 1975 and a council area in 1996. Agriculture is of major importance, producing chiefly beef cattle and poultry. It serves as a base for the exploitation of North Sea oil with a pipeline from the Piper field. Other industries include fish curing and woollen weaving. Area: 974 sq km (376 sq mi). Population (1996 est): 19 800. Administrative centre: Kirkwall.

● **Orlando** ► 28 33N 81 21W A city in the USA, in central Florida. A tourist resort, it is the commercial centre for citrus growing. Walt Disney World is situated nearby. Population (1996 est): 173 092.

● **Orlando, Vittorio Emanuele** ► (1860–1952) Italian statesman; prime minister (1917–19). Representing Italy at the Paris Peace Conference (1919) after World War I, his failure to secure sufficiently favourable terms for Italy led to his resignation. He supported Mussolini and ▷Matteotti's murder in 1924, retiring from politics until after World War II. He was elected to the Senate in 1948.

● **Orléans** ► 47 54N 1 54E A city in N France, the capital of the Loiret department on the River Loire. Its cathedral, which was destroyed by the Huguenots in 1568, was rebuilt in the 17th century. Orléans has an extensive trade in wine, brandy, and agricultural produce. Its manufactures include machinery, electrical goods, and textiles. Population (1990): 107 965.

● **Orléans, Charles, Duc d'** ► (1394–1465) French poet. He was captured by the English at the battle of Agincourt (1415) and spent the next 25 years in prison in England, where he wrote a collection of poems in English. His son became Louis XII of France.

● **Orléans, Louis Philippe Joseph, Duc d'** ► (1747–93) French revolutionary. A cousin of Louis XVI of France, he nevertheless supported the dissident Third Estate at the beginning of the ▷French Revolution. He joined the radical Jacobins in 1791 and voted for the execution of the king. He was himself executed after his son (later King Louis Philippe) had joined the Austrian coalition against France.

● **Orléans, Siege of** ► (October, 1428–May, 1429) English siege of the strategically important city of Orléans during the ▷Hundred Years' War. ▷Joan of Arc relieved the city; her success was a notable factor in French military resurgence and signalled the beginning of the end of English occupation.

● **Orlov, Grigori Grigorievich, Count** ► (1734–83) Russian soldier, who was the lover of ▷Catherine (II) the Great. Orlov and his brother **Aleksei Grigorievich Orlov** (1737–1807) led the coup d'état that placed Catherine on the throne in 1762. Grigori Orlov had a favourable position at court but exerted little influence over Catherine.

● **Orly** ► An industrial town in N France, on the S edge of the Paris conurbation. Orly international airport lies 14 km (9 mi) S of the city centre.

● **Ormandy, Eugene** ► (E. Blau; 1899–1985) Hungarian-born conductor, a US citizen after 1927. Originally a violinist, he turned to conducting soon after settling in the USA in 1921. He was conductor (1938–80) of the Philadelphia Orchestra.

● **ormolu** ► (French: *d'or moulu*, powdered gold) Ornamental gilded bronze usually used as embellishment on furniture. The 17th- and early 18th-century technique applied the gold coating by means of a mercuric process, which released poisonous fumes. This was abandoned in favour of applying gold dust in a varnish. Ormolu mounts were frequent on French 18th- and 19th-century furniture.

● **Ormonde, James Butler, 1st Duke of** ► (1610–88) Anglo-Irish general, who in the ▷Civil War commanded the royalist army in Ireland (1641–50). After the Restoration of the monarchy, he was Lord Lieutenant of Ireland (1661–69, 1677–84).

● **Ornithischia** ► An order of herbivorous ▷dinosaurs that lived in the Jurassic and Cretaceous periods (200–65 million years ago). They

had hip bones arranged like those of birds (the name means "bird hips") and a horny beak at the front of the jaw. Some were bipedal while others were quadrupedal and heavily armoured. There were both amphibious and terrestrial forms. ▷*See* Iguanodon; Stegosaurus; Triceratops.

● **Ornitholestes** ► A North American dinosaur of the Jurassic and Cretaceous periods (200–65 million years ago). About 2 m long, it was lightly built with long slender hind limbs and a long stiff tail. Its fore limbs were short with long slender clawed fingers and it probably lived in forests, catching birds, lizards, and mammals.

● **ornithology** ► The scientific study of birds. Professional or amateur ornithologists undertake serious studies into such aspects of bird biology as behaviour, distribution, and ecology. The interest of birdwatchers may be less serious. The term "birder," originating in the USA, is applied to birdwatchers whose main interest is in seeing and identifying a wide variety of species; "twitchers" are birders whose sole interest is in seeing rare birds (often those already discovered by other birdwatchers). Uniquely numbered rings are used to mark birds to trace their migrations, determine mortality rates, and undertake other studies. Birds are caught for this purpose by licensed bird-ringers. Some conservation organizations, including the ▷Royal Society for the Protection of Birds, are devoted wholly to protection and conservation of birds and their habitats. ▷*See also* endangered species.

● **orogeny** ► A period of mountain building. Several major orogenies have occurred in the earth's geological history, including the Caledonian (in the Lower Palaeozoic), Variscan (including the Armorican and Hercynian phases, in the Upper Palaeozoic), and the Alpine (in the Tertiary). **Orogenesis** is the process of mountain building, including folding, faulting, and thrusting, resulting from the collision of two continents, which compresses the sediment between them into mountain chains (*see* plate tectonics).

● **Orontes, River** ► A river in SW Asia. Rising in Lebanon, it flows through Syria and then SW past Antioch (Turkey) to enter the Mediterranean Sea. Length: 370 km (230 mi).

● **Orozco, José** ► (1883–1949) Mexican mural painter. His early watercolours of prostitutes were so bitterly attacked that he sought refuge in the USA (1917–20). In 1922, however, the Mexican Government commissioned him to paint murals in the National Preparatory School, Mexico City. Renewed criticism of his subject matter led to his second visit to the USA (1927–34), where he made his name with murals for several educational institutions.

● **Orpheus** ► A legendary Greek poet and musician, the son of the muse Calliope by either Apollo or Oeagrus, King of Thrace. After sailing with the ▷Argonauts he married ▷Eurydice. After her death, he descended to Hades to recover her. ▷Persephone, charmed by his playing on the lyre, released Eurydice but Orpheus lost her when he disobeyed the gods' command not to look back at her. He met his death at the hands of the Maenads, followers of ▷Dionysus, who dismembered him. He was believed to be the founder of the ▷Orphic mysteries.

● **Orphic mysteries** ► A religious cult (*see* mysteries) in ancient Greece and S Italy based on poems, probably of the 7th century BC, which its adherents believed were written by ▷Orpheus. According to these, the world was made from the ashes of the Titans, whom Zeus destroyed for devouring his son Dionysus. Vegetarianism, mystical rites, and high ethical standards were demanded of initiates.

● **orphism** ► An abstract form of ▷cubism, which developed in France about 1912. Albert Gleizes (1881–1953), Jean Metzinger (1883–1956), and Gino ▷Severini all contributed to this brightly coloured flat patterned style but the chief exponent was ▷Delaunay. His work became purely abstract by 1914, greatly influencing ▷Klee and ▷Kandinsky.

● **orrery** ► A small model of the solar system, often driven by clockwork, and originally called a ▷planetarium (now a picture of the sky on a dome). It was invented by George Graham (d. 1751), who named it after his patron Charles Boyle, 4th Earl of Orrery (1676–1731).

● **orrisroot** ► The fragrant rhizome (underground stem) of several

European plants of the genus ▷*Iris*, chiefly *I. florentina, I. pallida* and *I. germanica*. It is dried and ground for use in perfumes and medicines.

● **Orsini** ▶ A Roman family, originating in the 10th century, that led the propapal (Guelf) faction in Rome during the 13th century. Several members became high-ranking clerics including two popes, Celestine III (reigned 1191–98) and Nicholas III (reigned 1277–80). They remained a dominant force in the politics of Rome and the papacy during the early modern period, attaining princely status in 1629.

● **Orsk** ▶ 51 13N 58 35E A city in W Russia, at the confluence of the Rivers Ural and Or. It has an oil refinery and also manufactures heavy machinery. Population (1995 est): 275 000.

● **Ortega (Saavedra), Daniel** ▶ (1945–) Nicaraguan statesman; president of Nicaragua (1981–90). As leader of the ▷Sandinista National Liberation Front, he deposed Somoza in 1979 and instituted left-wing policies in the face of armed opposition from US-supported Contras.

● **Ortega y Gasset, José** ▶ (1883–1955) Spanish philosopher and writer. He became professor of metaphysics at Madrid University in 1910. His philosophy was chiefly concerned with what he called "the metaphysics of vital reason." In his best-known book, *La rebelión de las masas* (1930), he attacked mass rule, which, he argued, would lead to chaos.

Ortelius ▶ A map of the world by Abraham Ortelius (coloured copperplate engraving, 1571).

● **Ortelius, Abraham** ▶ (1527–98) Flemish cartographer. Ortelius travelled widely, buying and selling antiquities and maps. His *Theatrum orbis terrarum* (1570), a collection of maps charting the whole world, became the definitive contemporary cartographical system. Ortelius became geographer to Philip II of Spain in 1575.

● **orthicon** ▶ A television camera tube in which a low-energy electron beam scans a target screen, consisting of a thin dielectric plate with photosensitive squares on one side and a thin metallic coating on the other. Each square and its metallic electrode form a tiny capacitor; when light falls on a photosensitive element the capacitor becomes charged. The scanning beam discharges these capacitors and thus becomes modulated by the pattern of light falling on the screen.

● **orthoclase** ▶ An alkali potassium ▷feldspar, $KAlSi_3O_8$, that crystallizes in the monoclinic system, often with twinned crystals. Found in acid igneous rocks and many metamorphic rocks, it is white, pink, or green and softer than quartz. Commercially obtained from pegmatites, it is used in the manufacture of glass, glazes, and enamels.

● **orthodontics** ▷*See* dentistry.

● **Orthodox Church** ▶ The federation of self-governing Churches historically associated with the eastern part of the Roman Empire and separated from the Latin Church since 1054 (*see* East–West

Schism; Filioque); also called the Eastern Orthodox Church. The four ancient ▷patriarchs of Orthodoxy are of Constantinople (which has primacy of honour), Alexandria, Antioch, and Jerusalem; in addition there are patriarchs of Moscow, Georgia, Serbia, Bulgaria, and Romania. Independent or autocephalous Orthodox Churches exist in Greece, Cyprus, Albania, the Czech Republic, and Poland. There are numerous congregations in other countries, many established by Russian immigrants after the Revolution. Government is by bishops, who must be unmarried, priests, who may marry but only before ordination, and deacons, who play an important liturgical role. The Orthodox Church claims the authority of ▷apostolic succession and regards itself as the one true Church, accepting as doctrine only the ▷Nicene Creed. Its worship is sacramental and centred on the Eucharist and the ancient liturgies of St John Chrysostom and St Basil, which are always solemnly celebrated and sung without accompaniment. Both bread and wine are given at Communion. The veneration of ▷icons is a distinctive feature of Orthodox worship; three-dimensional images are forbidden. Easter is the main feast of the Church year, which follows the Julian calendar. ▷*See also* Greek Orthodox Church; Russian Orthodox Church.

● **orthopaedics** ▶ The medical specialty concerned with treating deformities caused by disease of and injury to the bones and joints. This includes the use of surgery, manipulation, traction, etc., in correcting deformities and fractures, together with rehabilitation to enable patients to lead an independent life. The availability of artificial joints (especially hip and knee joints) has greatly extended the scope of orthopaedics in the treatment of severe arthritis.

● **Orthoptera** ▶ A mainly tropical order of generally large stout-bodied insects (15 000 species), including the ▷grasshoppers and ▷crickets. The hind legs are enlarged for jumping and the large blunt head has biting jaws for feeding on vegetation. Typically there are two pairs of wings—the front pair thicker—but few species are good fliers. Many species produce sounds by rubbing one part of the body against another (stridulation).

● **ortolan** ▶ A Eurasian ▷bunting, *Emberiza hortulana*, about 16 cm long, having a brown-streaked plumage with a yellow throat and pinkish belly. Prior to its autumn migration to N Africa and the Middle East it stores large amounts of fat and it is therefore trapped in large numbers as a table delicacy.

● **Orton, Joe (Kingsley)** ▶ (1933–67) British dramatist, whose black comedies include *Entertaining Mr Sloane* (1964); subsequent plays on similar themes of sexual perversion and corruption were *Loot* (1966) and *What the Butler Saw* (1969). A homosexual, he was murdered by his lover, Kenneth Halliwell, who committed suicide.

● **Oruro** ▶ 17 59S 67 08W A city in central Bolivia, 3705 m (12 160 ft) above sea level. It lies in a tinmining area; other minerals worked include silver, copper, and wolfram. It has a technical university (1892). Population (1993 est): 201 831.

● **Orvieto** ▶ 42 43N 12 06E A town in central Italy, in Umbria. It is thought to be the site of the Etruscan city Volsinii, which was destroyed by the Romans in 280 BC. Buildings include the gothic cathedral and several palaces. A tourist centre, it is famous for its white wine. Population (1990): 21 575.

● **Orwell, George** ▶ (Eric Blair; 1903–50) British novelist. Born in India, he was educated at Eton and served in the Burmese Imperial Police from 1922 to 1927. In *Down and Out in Paris and London* (1933) and *The Road to Wigan Pier* (1937) he described his experience of poverty. He criticized communism in *Homage to Catalonia* (1936), an autobiographical account of the Spanish Civil War, and expressed anti-Stalinist convictions in the allegory *Animal Farm* (1945). *Nineteen Eighty Four* (1949) is a pessimistic view of a totalitarian future.

● **Oryol** ▷*See* Orel.

● **oryx** ▶ A desert antelope, *Oryx gazella*, which comprises two races, beisa and gemsbok, of S and E Africa. Up to 120 cm high at the shoulder, oryxes have long slender straight horns and are greyish brown with black markings on the face and legs. The herds feed at night on desert plants. The white Arabian oryx (*O. leucoryx*) and the greyish-white N African scimitar-horned oryx (*O. tao*) are both endangered species.

● **Osaka** ▶ 34 40N 135 30E A port in Japan, in SW Honshu on the Yodo delta. The third largest city in Japan, it was a leading commercial centre by the 17th century. Imperial palaces were built here from the 4th century AD and an ancient Buddhist temple (593 AD) still remains. It is overlooked by the 16th-century castle (reconstructed). A cultural centre, it possesses several universities and has a famous puppet theatre. Together with Kobe, Kyoto, and several small cities it now forms the **Osaka-Kobe** industrial area, second in importance only to the Tokyo-Yokohama area, and in common with Tokyo suffers from serious atmospheric pollution as well as traffic congestion. In 1995 an earthquake caused severe damage and loss of life. Major industries are textiles, steel, electrical equipment, and chemicals. Population (1995): 2 602 352.

● **Osborne, Dorothy** ▶ (1627–95) English letter writer. The wife of the diplomat Sir William ▷Temple, she is remembered for her witty and lively letters to him during their courtship (1652–54; published in 1836).

● **Osborne, John** ▶ (1929–94) British dramatist. One of the original ▷Angry Young Men, he gave expression to the rage and frustration of a whole generation in the character of Jimmy Porter, the disillusioned antihero of *Look Back in Anger* (1956). His criticism of contemporary Britain continued in such plays as *The Entertainer* (1957), *A Patriot for Me* (1965), and *West of Suez* (1971). Other plays include *Luther* (1960), *Inadmissible Evidence* (1964), and *The Hotel in Amsterdam* (1967). Jimmy Porter appeared again in *Déjà Vu* (1992), a sequel to *Look Back in Anger*. *A Better Class of Person* (1981) and *Almost a Gentleman* (1991) are autobiographies.

● **Osborne House** ▶ A country house near Cowes, on the Isle of Wight, built for Queen Victoria in 1845 to a design by Prince Albert. It was one of her favourite residences and she died there in 1901. It is now open to the public.

● **Oscar** ▷*See* Academy of Motion Picture Arts and Sciences.

● **Oscar II** ▶ (1829–1907) King of Sweden (1872–1907) and of Norway from 1872 until its final separation from Sweden in 1905. He was also a writer, especially of poetry.

● **oscilloscope** ▷*See* cathode-ray oscilloscope.

● **Oshawa** ▶ 43 53N 78 51W A city and port in central Canada, in S Ontario on Lake Ontario. A prosperous agricultural centre, it houses a major motor-vehicle factory. Other industries include metal goods, furniture, glass, and plastics. Population (1991): 129 344.

● **O'Shea, Katherine Page** ▶ (1846–1921) The wife (1867–90) of William O'Shea (1840–1905), an Irish MP, and then of Charles Stewart ▷Parnell. In 1889 O'Shea filed for divorce, citing Parnell, thus initiating Parnell's political downfall. Parnell married Katherine shortly before his death in 1891.

● **Oshogbo** ▶ 7 50N 4 35E A town in SW Nigeria. It developed as a commercial centre after the arrival of the railway (1906). Its main exports are cocoa and palm oil; there are also local tobacco-processing, cotton-weaving, and dyeing industries. Population (1996 est): 476 800.

● **osier** ▶ A small ▷willow tree, *Salix viminalis*, 3–10 m high, with flexible hairy branches used in basket making. The long narrow leaves are smooth above and white and silky beneath, with inrolled margins. Osiers are found in marshy areas throughout central and S Eurasia and often cultivated.

● **Osijek** ▶ 45 33N 18 42E A town in NE Croatia, on the River Drava. An agricultural centre, it manufactures machinery and footwear. It was the scene of fierce fighting in the Yugoslav conflict of 1991–92. Population (1991): 164 589.

● **Osipenko** ▷*See* Berdyansk.

● **Osiris** ▶ The Egyptian god of the dead, the brother and husband of ▷Isis; as the father of ▷Horus (the sun), he was also the god of renewal and rebirth. He was killed by his evil brother ▷Set. After Isis had magically reconstructed his body, he became ruler of the underworld. The pharaohs, and later all men who passed the judgment of good and evil, became identified with Osiris after death. He is usually portrayed holding the royal flail and crook. He was identified by the Greeks with ▷Dionysus.

● **Osler, Sir William** ▶ (1849–1919) Canadian physician, who pioneered modern clinical teaching methods. In 1872 Osler identified the particles in blood known as ▷platelets. He was appointed professor of medicine at the new Johns Hopkins University, Baltimore, in 1888. Osler encouraged examination of patients in the wards and the use of laboratories by students. In 1905 he became Regius Professor of Medicine at Oxford University.

● **Oslo** ▶ (former name (1877–1925): Kristiania) 59 56N 10 54E The capital and main port of Norway, situated in the SE at the head of Oslo Fjord. It is the financial and industrial centre of Norway. The principal industries include the manufacture of consumer goods and shipbuilding. A cultural centre, Oslo is the site of a university (1811), the National Theatre, and several notable museums. Fine buildings include the 17th-century cathedral and the 19th-century royal palace.

History: founded in the 11th century as a defensive post against the Danes, it became capital in 1299. It developed into an important trading post under the influence of the Hanseatic League and was rebuilt after a fire in the 17th century. It was occupied by the Germans in World War II. Population (1997 est): 493 973.

● **Osman I** ▶ (c. 1258–c. 1326) Emir of the small Turkish state in Asia Minor that later developed into the ▷Ottoman Empire. He was the eponymous ancestor of the Ottoman sultans. Under Osman the state expanded mainly at the expense of the Byzantines.

● **osmiridium** ▶ A naturally occurring alloy of osmium and iridium, with minor quantities of platinum, rhodium, and ruthenium. It is used for fountain pen nibs because it is hard and resistant.

● **osmium** ▶ (Os) An extremely hard bluish-silver metal of the platinum group. It is one of the densest elements known (relative density

Osiris ▶ An illustration from the papyrus *Book of the Dead of Ta-Nafer* of the 21st dynasty. A boat bearing Osiris (right, depicted as a mummy wearing a pharaoh's crown), the dead Ta-Nafer (centre), and his wife is being rowed on the River of the Dead. The bird on the prow of the boat symbolizes the dead man's soul.

22.6). Its major use is in the production of hard alloys with other noble metals, for pen nibs and electrical contacts. The tetroxide (OsO_4) is volatile (bp 130°C) and very toxic; it is used as a fixative in microscopy, as a catalyst, and as an oxidizing agent in organic chemistry. At no 76; at wt 190.2; mp 3033 ± 20°C; bp 5012 ± 100°C.

• **osmoregulation** ▶ The means by which the internal osmotic pressure (*see* osmosis) of animals is controlled, by regulating the amount of water and salts entering and leaving the body. In vertebrates this is effected by the uriniferous tubules of the ▷kidneys.

• **osmosis** ▶ The passage of a solvent from a less concentrated into a more concentrated solution through a semipermeable (partially permeable) membrane (one allowing the passage of solvent, but not solute, molecules). Osmosis stops if the pressure of the more concentrated solution exceeds that of the less concentrated solution by an amount known as the **osmotic pressure** between them. In living organisms the solvent is water and osmosis plays an important role in effecting the distribution of water in plants and animals: the passage of water into and out of cells is determined by the osmotic pressures of the extracellular and intracellular solutions. Osmosis can be used in the ▷desalination of water.

• **Osmunda** ▶ A genus of stout leathery ▷ferns (about 12 species), found in wet tropical and temperate regions. Their branching fronds, 50–180 cm high, are made up of light-green tapering leaflets with expanded bases. The upper leaflets of the larger central fertile fronds are reduced to veins covered with clusters of brown pear-shaped spore capsules, which resemble flower clusters in the royal fern (*O. regalis*). The root and rhizome fibres are used as a culture medium for orchids. Family: *Osmundaceae*.

• **Osnabrück** ▶ 52 17N 8 03E A city in NW Germany, in Lower Saxony on the River Hase. The 13th-century romanesque cathedral and episcopal palace (1667–90) survived the bombing of World War II. It has iron, steel, and car industries. Population (1996 est): 168 618.

• **osprey** ▶ A large ▷hawk, *Pandion haliaetus*, also called fish hawk, occurring worldwide (except in South America) around coasts and inland waters. It is 65 cm long and its plumage is brown above and white below (*see* Plate III). It feeds mostly on fish, caught in its talons, which are covered in rough spikes to help grasp prey. The recent decline in numbers has been due mainly to pesticide poisoning.

• **Ossa, Mount** ▶ 41 52S 146 04E A mountain in Australia, the highest peak of Tasmania in the Duana Range. Height: 1617 m (5305 ft).

• **Ossetia** ▷*See* North Ossetian Republic; South Ossetia.

• **Ossetic** ▶ A language belonging to the ▷Iranian family and spoken in the N Caucasus by the Ossetes. The Ossetes are descended from the ancient Alani, a Scythian tribe. The language is written in the Cyrillic alphabet and has absorbed many influences from Russian and the other Caucasian languages.

• **Ossian** ▶ (3rd century AD) A legendary poet and warrior who, as Oisin, features in the ▷Fenian cycle. The Scots poet James Macpherson (1736–96) claimed to have discovered remains of Ossian's poetry in the Highlands and published his "translations" from the Gaelic between 1760 and 1763. These included the epic poem *Fingal* (1762). Macpherson's work was in fact his own, largely based on a few well-known Gaelic fragments. Although denounced as forgeries by Dr Johnson, the poems were enthusiastically received throughout Europe and had a great influence on European Romanticism.

• **Ossietsky, Carl von** ▶ (1888–1938) German pacifist and journalist. He founded a pacifist organization in 1920 and became editor of a liberal newspaper in 1927. Arrested in 1933, he spent the rest of his life in a concentration camp and in hospitals. He won the Nobel Peace Prize in 1935.

• **Ossining** ▶ 41 10N 73 52W A town in the USA, in New York state. Known as Sing Sing until 1901, it is the site of a once notorious prison. Population (1980): 20 196.

• **Ossory** ▶ A kingdom of ancient Ireland. An independent state within the Kingdom of Leinster, it was absorbed into Leinster in 1110 but survives as a modern diocese.

• **Ostade, Adrian van** ▶ (1610–85) Dutch painter and etcher, born in Haarlem. Influenced by Adriaen ▷Brouwer, he specialized in scenes of peasant life.

• **Ostend** ▶ (Flemish name: Oostende; French name: Ostende) 51 13N 2 55E A seaport in NW Belgium, on the North Sea. Ostend is a pleasure resort, with a casino, a promenade, and a royal chalet. It is the headquarters of the country's fishing fleet and maintains a cross-Channel ferry service to Dover, England. Industries include shipbuilding and fish processing. Population (1995 est): 68 858.

• **osteoarthritis** ▶ A disease of the joints in which their internal surfaces are rubbed away and they become swollen and painful. This becomes increasingly common as people age: almost all very old people have some osteoarthritis, but it may affect younger people as well. The joints that bear most weight are most commonly affected: back, hips, and knees. Drugs can reduce the pain of the joints but cannot reverse the disease. Artificial hips and knees can be surgically installed to relieve the pain and allow greater movement. ▷*See also* arthritis.

• **osteology** ▷*See* bone.

• **osteomalacia** ▶ Softening of the bones due to shortage of vitamin D: adult ▷rickets. It is seen most commonly in pregnant women and in old people whose diet is deficient in vitamin D or who do not have access to much sunshine (which activates vitamin D). Fractures occur very easily in osteomalacia. Treatment is with vitamin D preparations.

• **osteomyelitis** ▶ Infection of bone. This occurs most commonly in poor communities. Children, particularly boys, are more often affected; symptoms are a high fever and acute pain in the bone affected, which is classically around the knee. Before antibiotics were available death or physical handicap often resulted, but these are now rare and the infection is readily cured with antibiotics.

• **osteopathy** ▶ A system of healing by manipulation and massage, based on the theory that nearly all diseases are due to the displacement of bones, especially the bones of the spine. Osteopathy is undoubtedly of use in treating dislocations, fractures, and disorders of the joint, but the theory behind it is controversial and osteopathy is not legally recognized as a branch of orthodox medicine. The British School of Osteopathy was founded in London in 1917.

• **osteoporosis** ▶ Weakening and brittleness of the bones, resulting in an increased tendency for them to fracture. This occurs most commonly in old people, particularly women, but it can also result from long-term steroid therapy, infection, or injury. ▷Hormone replacement therapy is useful in preventing osteoporosis in postmenopausal women, which can also be treated by using drugs called bisphosphonates, such as alendronate (Fosamax) and etidronate (Didronel).

• **Ostia** ▶ A town of ancient Rome, at the mouth of the River Tiber. It was probably founded about 350 BC, although it is dated by tradition to the 7th century BC. A major naval base under the Republic, its prosperity was greatest in the 2nd century AD, when it was an important commercial centre. It was abandoned in the 9th century. Impressive Roman ruins have been excavated.

• **ostracism** ▶ The method in 5th-century BC Athens of banishing unpopular citizens. Each citizen inscribed on a potsherd (*ostrakon*) the name of his candidate for banishment. The man receiving most votes was exiled for ten years. Instituted to curb tyranny, ostracism was in practice uncommon. Prominent ostracized Athenians included Aristides and Themistocles.

• **Ostracoda** ▶ A class or subclass of small ▷crustaceans (2000 species), 1–4 mm long, also called mussel or seed shrimps, found in fresh and salt water. Ostracods have a bean-shaped two-sided carapace, from which protrude two pairs of large hairy antennae and two pairs of legs for swimming or walking. Most ostracods live on or near the bottom and eat anything, but particularly decaying vegetation or small animals. The females lay eggs on stems and leaves of water plants.

• **Ostrava** ▶ 49 50N 18 15E An industrial city in the Czech Republic, in N Moravia on both sides of the River Ostravice. It is a major coalmining centre; other industries include iron and steel processing, engineering, and chemicals. Population (1996 est): 324 813.

● **ostrich** ► A flightless African bird, *Struthio camelus*, occurring in open grassland and semidesert regions. Males may reach 2.5 m tall and are black with white wing and tail plumes; females are smaller and mainly brown. Ostriches have a long almost naked neck, a small head, and a ducklike bill used to feed on plant material. They can reach speeds of up to 65 km per hour (40 mph). Domesticated birds are farmed commercially for meat, leather, and ornamental feathers. It is the largest living bird and the only member of its family (*Struthionidae*). Order: *Struthioniformes*.

● **Ostrogoths** ► A branch of the ▷Goths, originally based in Ukraine, but forced W of the River Dniester by the ▷Huns (375 AD). In the 6th century they frequently invaded N Italy and captured much of the Balkans. Between 493 and 526 ▷Theodoric, their leader, ruled Italy. Following his death the Eastern Roman Empire, after a long struggle, destroyed the Ostrogoths (562).

● **Ostrovskii, Aleksandr Nikolaevich** ► (1823–86) Russian dramatist. He established his reputation with realistic comedies about the merchant class, making use of the knowledge of corruption that he had gained as a civil servant. His best-known plays include *Easy Money* (1856) and the tragedy *The Storm* (1859), which became the basis of ▷Janáček's opera *Katya Kabanova*.

● **Ostwald, (Friedrich) Wilhelm** ► (1853–1932) German chemist, born in Riga, who was a pioneer in the field of physical chemistry. His greatest work was in developing the theory of catalysis for which he was awarded the Nobel Prize in 1909. He also contributed to the philosophy of science and was an ardent positivist.

● **Oswald, Lee Harvey** ► (1939–63) The presumed assassin of US president John F. ▷Kennedy in Dallas, Texas, on 22 November, 1963. Two days later he was killed by Jack Ruby (d. 1967), a nightclub owner, in the Dallas police headquarters.

● **Oswald, Saint** ► (c. 605–41) King of Northumbria (634–41) after defeating and killing the Welsh king, Cadwallader. Converted to Christianity while in exile on Iona, he restored Christianity in Northumbria with the help of St ▷Aidan. Oswald was killed in battle by Penda. Feast day: 5 Aug.

● **Oswald of York, St** ► (d. 992 AD) English churchman. Bishop of Worcester and later Archbishop of York, he founded many new monasteries and was a leading initiator of Anglo-Saxon monastic reform. Feast day: 28 Feb.

● **Oświęcim** ► (German name: Auschwitz) 50 02N 19 11E A town in S Poland, where the Germans established a forced-labour camp in 1940, which was subsequently expanded as Auschwitz II (*or* Birkenau) to accommodate four large gas chambers in which between two and four million victims (mostly Jews) were murdered. The unprecedented scale of the extermination programme organized in Auschwitz by the German government far exceeds any previous or subsequent attempt at what is now called ethnic cleansing in the whole of human history. Parts of the site have been preserved as a memorial to the dead and a perpetual indictment of the perpetrators. Population (latest est): 45 200.

● **Oswiu** ► (*or* Oswy; d. 670) King of Northumbria (655–70) and overlord (655–57) of all England S of the Humber, after his forces had killed Penda of Mercia in battle. He summoned the Synod of ▷Whitby (664) to resolve the differences between the Roman and Celtic Churches.

● **Otis, Elisha Graves** ► (1811–61) US inventor, who in 1852 designed the first safety lift, that is one that would not fall to the ground if the cable broke. In 1854 Otis publicly demonstrated the lift's safety by arranging for the cable of a lift in which he was riding to be cut.

● **O'Toole, Peter** ► (1932–   ) Irish-born British actor. He made his stage debut in 1955 and his first major film appearance was the title role of *Lawrence of Arabia* (1962). Subsequent films included *Becket* (1964), *The Lion in Winter* (1968), *Goodbye, Mr Chips* (1969), *The Ruling Class* (1972), *The Stuntman* (1980), *My Favourite Year* (1982), *High Spirits* (1988), and *Fairytale* (1998).

● **Otranto** ► 40 08N 18 30E A small port in SE Italy, in Apulia on the Strait of Otranto. Dating from Greek times, it became an important Roman port, later destroyed by Turks (1480). Its ruined castle provided the setting for Horace Walpole's gothic novel *The Castle of Otranto*. Population (latest est): 4811.

● **Ottawa** ► 45 25N 75 43W The capital of Canada, in SE Ontario on the Ottawa River. It is two-thirds English speaking and one-third French speaking. Ottawa University was founded in 1848 and the Carleton University in 1942.

History: founded (as Bytown) in the early 19th century as a lumbering centre, it became capital of the United Provinces of Canada in 1858, and national capital in 1867. Population (1991): 920 857 (metropolitan area).

● **Ottawa Agreements** ► (1932) Preferential tariff rates negotiated between the UK and its dominions at the Imperial Economic Conference held at Ottawa (Canada). In 1931 the UK began to tax food imports from outside the Empire, allowing almost all imports from its dominions to enter the country free of duty. The dominions agreed to reciprocate this concession except when it was to the detriment of their own products. The new policy, called imperial preference, was limited by the ▷General Agreement on Tariffs and Trade (1947) and was phased out following the UK's membership of the EC.

● **Ottawa River** ► A river in central Canada, rising in W Quebec and flowing W, then SE down the Ontario-Quebec border to join the St Lawrence River, as its chief tributary, at Montreal. The numerous rapids along its lower and middle courses are used to generate electricity. It is linked with Lake Ontario by the Rideau Canal. Length: 1120 km (696 mi).

otter

● **otter** ► A semiaquatic carnivorous □mammal belonging to the subfamily *Lutrinae* (18 species), distributed worldwide except in Polar regions, Australasia, and Madagascar. Otters have a cylindrical body with waterproof fur, short legs, partially webbed feet, and a thick tapering tail. The Eurasian otter (*Lutra lutra*), grows to a length of about 1.2 m and a weight of about 10 kg. Otters inhabit waterways, lakes, and coasts, feeding on frogs, fish, and invertebrates. Chief genera: *Lutra, Paraonyx*; family: ▷*Mustelidae*. ▷*See also* sea otter.

● **otterhound** ► A breed of dog of uncertain ancestry, used to hunt otters. It is a strongly built powerful swimmer with large webbed feet and a large head with long drooping ears. Otterhounds have a dense water-resistant undercoat and a long shaggy outer coat, which can be any colour. Height: 61–69 cm.

● **otter shrew** ► A semiaquatic carnivorous mammal belonging to the family *Potamogalidae* (3 species), of West and central Africa. Up to 60 cm long, they have long slender brown and white bodies with a shrewlike snout and a flattened tail for swimming. They forage for aquatic invertebrate prey. Order: ▷*Insectivora*.

● **Otto (I) the Great** ► (912–73 AD) Holy Roman Emperor (936–73;

crowned 962). He subdued his rebellious vassals, defeated a Hungarian invasion at the great victory of Lechfeld (955), and extended his influence into Italy. He deposed Pope John XII, replacing him with Leo VIII, and established bishoprics as a means of controlling his domains.

● **Otto IV** ▶ (c. 1175–1218) Holy Roman Emperor (1198–1215; crowned 1209). He was elected emperor in opposition to the candidate of the Hohenstaufen family but was crowned by Pope Innocent III in return for promising to keep out of Italian territorial disputes. In 1210, however, he invaded S Italy and, after being decisively defeated by France, a Hohenstaufen ally, at ▷Bouvines (1214), was formally deposed.

● **Otto, Nikolaus August** ▶ (1832–91) German engineer, who in 1876 devised the four-stroke cycle, known as the Otto cycle, for the ▷internal-combustion engine. His engine made the development of the motor car possible.

● **Ottoman Empire** ▶ A Turkish Muslim empire ruling large parts of the Middle East as well as territories in Europe from the 14th to the 20th centuries. Its capital was ▷Istanbul (formerly Constantinople) and its rulers descendants of its founder ▷Osman I. Originating around 1300 as a small Turkish state in Asia Minor, in 1453 the Ottomans captured Constantinople and destroyed the Eastern Roman (Byzantine) Empire. Ottoman power culminated in the 16th century with the conquest of Egypt and Syria (1517) and, under ▷Suleiman the Magnificent, Hungary (1529) and territories in the Middle East and N Africa. From the 17th century the Empire declined. Attempts at modernization were only partly successful and in the 1908 ▷Young Turks revolution a group of army officers seized power. In World War I the Ottomans supported Germany and defeat brought the loss of territories outside Asia Minor. This humiliation led to the nationalist revolution of Kemal ▷Atatürk, which replaced the Ottoman Empire with the state of Turkey (1922).

● **Otway, Thomas** ▶ (1652–85) British dramatist. His best-known plays are the sentimental tragedies *The Orphan* (1680) and *Venice Preserved* (1682), written for the actress Elizabeth Barry (1658–1713), whom he loved. He also wrote Restoration comedies and adapted plays by Racine and Molière.

● **Ouagadougou** ▶ 12 25N 1 30W The capital of Burkina Faso. Founded in the 11th century as the centre of a Mossi empire, it was captured by the French in 1896. Its university was founded in 1974. It is an important communications centre. Population (1993 est): 690 000.

● **Oudenaarde, Battle of** ▶ (11 July, 1708) A battle in the War of the ▷Spanish Succession in which the British, Dutch, and Austrians defeated the French. The allied commanders, Marlborough and Prince Eugene of Savoy, unexpectedly joined armies and forced the French to fight a surprise battle.

● **Oudry, Jean-Baptiste** ▶ (1686–1755) French ▷rococo painter and tapestry designer. A pupil of Nicholas de Largillière (1656–1746), he was a portrait and still-life painter before specializing (from about 1720) in animal and hunting scenes. He became head of the ▷Beauvais (1734) and ▷Gobelins (1736) tapestry works and favourite painter of Louis XV. His illustrations to La Fontaine's *Fables* are well known.

● **Ouessant** ▷*See* Ushant.

● **Oughtred, William** ▶ (1574–1660) English priest and scholar, noted for his writings on mathematics. In *Clavis Mathematicae* (1631) he introduced new algebraic symbols as well as the symbol × for multiplication. He also invented the earliest form of slide rule.

● **Ouida** ▶ (Marie Louise de la Ramée; 1839–1908) British novelist. Of English and French parentage, she wrote popular adventure novels with fashionable upper-class characters. Her best-known book is *Under Two Flags* (1867).

● **Oujda** ▶ 34 41N 1 45W A city in E Morocco, near the Algerian border. It is a meeting point of the Moroccan and Algerian railways. Population (1991): 646 000.

● **Oulu** ▶ (Swedish name: Uleåborg) 65 00N 25 26E A seaport in NW Finland, on the Gulf of Bothnia. It has a university (1959) and its industries include shipbuilding and saw milling. Population (1997 est): 111 556.

● **ounce** ▷*See* snow leopard.

● **Ouro Prêto** ▶ 20 54S 43 30W A city in SE Brazil, in Minas Gerais state. Founded in 1701, its former prosperity was based on gold. It contains many colonial buildings. It is now a mining centre for manganese and iron and is the site of the National School of Mines (1876). Its university was established in 1969. Population (latest est): 27 821.

● **Ouse, River** ▶ The name of several rivers in England, including: **1.** A river in NE England, flowing mainly NE through Yorkshire to join the River Trent, forming the Humber estuary. Length: 92 km (57 mi). **2.** A river in S England, flowing E and S across the South Downs to the English Channel at Newhaven. Length: 48 km (30 mi). ▷*See also* Great Ouse River.

● **Ouspensky, Peter** ▶ (1878–1947) Russian-born occultist. He trained as a scientist but as ▷Gurdjieff's close associate (1915–24) he became interested in methods of developing man's consciousness. His writings include *Tertium Organum* (1912) and *A New Model of the Universe* (1914).

● **Outer Mongolia** ▷*See* Mongolia, State of.

● **outlawry** ▶ A process by which a person (particularly one convicted of ▷treason or a felony) was deprived of his rights under the law, including the right to own property, to enforce a ▷contract, or to seek redress for injuries. His property was forfeited to the Crown. Outlawry was abolished for civil wrongs in 1879 and for crimes in 1938.

● **Outram, Sir James** ▶ (1803–63) British soldier and colonial administrator. He made his name during the first Afghan War (1839–42). He subsequently took part in the relief of Lucknow (1857) during the Indian Mutiny.

● **ouzel** ▷*See* ring ouzel.

● **ouzo** ▶ A Greek spirit flavoured with aniseed, similar to ▷absinthe. It is drunk with water, in which it becomes cloudy.

● **Oval, the** ▶ A cricket ground at Kennington, London, and the headquarters of the Surrey County Cricket Club. It was first used for cricket in 1845. The final Test match of an English series always takes place here.

● **ovary** ▶ **1.** The organ of female animals in which the ▷egg cells (ova) are produced. In mammals (including women) there are two ovaries close to the openings of the Fallopian tubes, which lead to the uterus (womb). They produce both eggs and steroid hormones in a regular cycle (*see* menstruation). The ovaries contain numerous follicles, some of which—the Graafian follicles—mature to release egg cells at ovulation; maturing follicles secrete ▷oestrogen. After ovulation each follicle forms a yellowish body, the corpus luteum, which secretes ▷progesterone. **2.** The part of a flower that contains the ▷ovules. It becomes the fruit wall after fertilization. ⌐plant.

● **ovenbird** ▶ A small brown passerine bird belonging to a diverse family (*Furnariidae*; 221 species) occurring in tropical America and ranging in size from 12 to 28 cm. Ovenbirds usually build elaborate nests in tunnels and crevices but the family name is derived from the nests of the genus *Furnarius*, which build large oven-like globes from wet clay.

● **Overijssel** ▶ An inland province in the NE Netherlands bordering on Germany. Dairy farming and fodder crops are especially important. Recently developed industries produce textiles, machinery, and salt. Area: 3927 sq km (1516 sq mi). Population (1995): 1 050 389. Capital: Zwolle.

● **Overlanders** ▶ Australian cattle drovers who, in the 19th century, drove cattle across previously unopened territories to markets or new stations.

● **overpopulation** ▶ Too many people living in an area in which the resources—land, food, water, fuel, and an acceptable infrastructure—are inadequate to support them without hardship. The dangers of overpopulation were first realized by the British clergyman

Thomas ▷Malthus at the beginning of the 19th century. He argued that as food production grows arithmetically and population increases geometrically, the living standards of the majority could never rise above subsistence level. In Britain and Europe Malthus was proved wrong, owing to rising national prosperity from industrialization, which was accompanied by a falling birth rate to offset the falling mortality rate. However, his stark analysis of the problem has remained influential.

In 1850 the world ▷population was approximately 1.3 billion. By 1950 it had almost doubled to 2.5 billion. According to UN projections, by 2050 it will be 8.9 billion, i.e. over 3½ times the 1950 figure; it is then expected to level off at around 11 billion by 2200. Most of this growth since 1950 has taken place in developing countries, i.e. in Asia, Africa, and Latin America, where birth rates remained high despite falling mortality rates. In addition to shortages of food, fuel, and minerals, the UN now predicts that overpopulation will lead to serious degradation of the environment. The UN Population Fund calls for a reduction in ▷fertility rates to stem the rising tide of population. This, they believe, can only be achieved by better education and health care, coupled with the widespread use of ▷contraception. However, campaigners for family planning face a number of obstacles, not least the opposition of the Roman Catholic Church to all effective means of contraception (especially important in Latin America). In many poor communities, tradition places a high value on fertility, which is seen as a form of wealth rather than a cause of poverty. In societies dependent on low-level agriculture, children are often seen as a source of extra manpower rather than a drain on resources; parents may also see a large family as a form of insurance for their old age. Such factors have led some analysts to conclude that high birth rates are more often a product of poverty than its cause, and to argue that the real solution to overpopulaton lies in sustained economic development. By the end of the 20th century fertility rates had fallen to 2.1 (the level at which the population stabilizes) in most of Asia and had also fallen substantially in South America. Nonetheless, the age structure of many developing societies, in which a large proportion of the population has yet to reach reproductive age, means that whatever the long-term outcome populations will grow rapidly for the next few decades. Overpopulation remains one of the most serious problems facing human beings and the planet they inhabit.

● **overture** ▶ An orchestral composition introducing an opera, oratorio, or play or a one-movement work with a programmatic title played in the concert hall (**concert overture**). In the 18th century the two principal forms of opera overture were the **Italian overture**, consisting of a slow movement between two quick ones, from which the symphony evolved, and the **French overture**, consisting of a slow introduction, a quick fugal section, and often a slow section or separate dance movement.

● **Ovett, Steve** ▶ (1955–) British middle-distance runner. A gold medallist in the 800 m at the 1980 Olympic Games and the 5000 m at the 1986 Commonwealth Games. He broke world records in the 2 mile (1978) and 1500 m (1980) events.

● **Ovid** ▶ (Publius Ovidius Naso; 43 BC–17 AD) Roman poet. He travelled extensively in Greek territories. His poems include the *Amores* and the *Ars amatoria*, both demonstrating his polished style and his characteristic theme of love; the *Heroides*, love letters addressed by legendary heroines to their lovers; and the *Fasti*, a poetic treatment of festivals and rites in the Roman calendar, which he never completed. His greatest work, the *Metamorphoses*, is a poem in 15 books including mythological and historical tales linked by the theme of transformation. In 8 AD he was exiled by the emperor Augustus to Tomi, a remote township on the Black Sea, possibly because of some association with Augustus' daughter, Julia. Despite appeals for mercy in his poems *Tristia* and *Epistulae ex Ponto*, he remained there until his death.

● **Oviedo** ▶ 43 21N 5 50W A city in N Spain, in Asturias. It possesses a 14th-century cathedral and a university (founded 1608). Industries include mining and food processing. Population (1995 est): 202 421.

● **ovule** ▶ The structure within the ovary of a ▷flower that contains an egg cell and nutritive tissue. After fertilization it develops into the ▷seed containing the embryo. ⬚plant.

● **ovum** ▷*See* egg.

● **Owen, Alun Davies** ▶ (1925–94) British dramatist. Liverpool is the setting of such plays as *Progress to the Park* (1959). Other works include the musical *Maggie May* (1964), written with Lionel Bart, and *Come Home Charlie, and Face Them* (1990).

● **Owen, David (Anthony Llewellyn), Baron** ▶ (1938–) British politician. He entered parliament as a Labour member (1966) and was foreign secretary (1977–79). A cofounder of the Social Democratic Party, he became leader in 1983 but resigned in 1987 in protest against the majority vote to merge with the Liberals. Subsequently (1988) he revived a reduced SDP but wound the party up in 1990 and sat in parliament as an independent social democrat until 1992. In 1992–94 he was involved in attempts to negotiate a peace settlement in Bosnia-Hercegovina.

Michael Owen ▶ The England striker.

● **Owen, Michael (James)** ▶ (1979–) British Association footballer. A striker, he made his League debut for Liverpool at the age of 17 and his England debut the following year. In May, 1998 he became a national hero after scoring a brilliant goal against Argentina in the World Cup.

● **Owen, Robert** ▶ (1771–1858) British philanthropist and manufacturer. Born in Wales, in 1800 he became manager of the mills at New Lanark (Lanarkshire), where he established a model community. He introduced better working conditions and housing and established the first infant school in Britain (1816). His advocacy from 1817 of "villages of unity and cooperation" for the unemployed anticipated ▷cooperative societies and he established such communities at New Harmony, Indiana (1825), Orbiston, near Glasgow (1826), Ralahine, County Cork (1831), and Queenswood, Hampshire (1839). Owen also helped to found the Grand National Consolidated Trades Union in 1834.

● **Owen, Wilfred** ▶ (1893–1918) British poet. His poetry written during World War I was motivated by horror at the brutality of war, pity for its victims, and anger at civilian complacency. His most famous poems include "Strange Meeting" and "Anthem for Doomed Youth." While in hospital near Edinburgh in 1917 he met Siegfried ▷Sassoon, who edited his *Poems* (1920). He was killed in action.

● **Owen Falls** ▶ 0 29N 33 11E A cataract in Uganda, on the Victoria Nile River just below Lake Victoria. The **Owen Falls Dam** (completed 1954) provides hydroelectric power for Uganda and Kenya and controls flood waters.

● **Owens, Jesse** ▶ (John Cleveland O.; 1913–80) US sprinter, long jumper, and hurdler. In 1935 he set six world records in 45 minutes (in the long jump, 100 yards, 220 yards, 220 metres, 220 yards hurdles, and 220 metres hurdles). At the Berlin Olympics (1936) he won four gold medals; Hitler refused to congratulate this Black athlete.

● **owl** ▶ A nocturnal bird of prey of a worldwide order (*Strigiformes*). There are two families: *Strigidae* (typical owls) and *Tytonidae* (barn and bay owls). Owls have a large head with large forward facing eyes surrounded by a facial disc of radiating feathers, soft plumage, usually brown and patterned, and a short sharp hooked bill. With acute vision and hearing and silent flight, owls hunt mammals, birds, and insects, disgorging the remains in hard pellets. They range from the ▷pygmy owls to the large ▷eagle owls; most are arboreal but some live on the ground. ▷*See* barn owl; burrowing owl; fish owl; hawk owl; little owl; snowy owl; tawny owl.

● **owlet frogmouth** ▶ A solitary arboreal bird belonging to a family (*Aegothelidae*; 7 or 8 species) occurring in Australian forests. They have a gaping mouth surrounded by long sensitive bristles and feed at night on insects. The little owlet frogmouth (*Aegotheles cristatus*) is 22 cm long and has a grey-brown plumage with brown underparts. Order: *Caprimulgiformes* (nightjars and nighthawks).

● **owlet moth** ▶ *See* noctuid moth.

● **ox** ▷*See* cattle.

● **oxalic acid** ▶ (*or* ethanedioic acid; $(COOH)_2$) A colourless poisonous soluble crystalline solid. Potassium and sodium salts are found in plants. Industrially it is prepared from sawdust treated with sodium and potassium hydroxides. Oxalic acid is used as a metal cleaner and for bleaching textiles and leather.

● **oxbow lake** ▷*See* lake.

● **Oxenstierna, Axel, Count** ▶ (1583–1654) Swedish statesman; chancellor (1612–54). He gained great power during the reign of Gustavus II Adolphus, being the effective controller of national finance. After Gustavus' death in 1632, he directed Sweden in the Thirty Years' War and gained favourable terms at the Peace of ▷Westphalia. During the minority (1632–44) of Queen ▷Christina he dominated the regency.

● **oxeye daisy** ▶ A perennial herb, *Chrysanthemum leucanthemum*, also called moon daisy or marguerite, found in grassland throughout Europe. 20–70 cm high, it has large solitary flower heads, 2.5–5 cm in diameter, with long white rays surrounding a yellow central disc. Family: ▷*Compositae*.

● **OXFAM** ▶ A British charity founded in 1942, and registered in 1948 as the Oxford Committee for Famine Relief. Its purpose is to relieve suffering caused by natural calamity or lack of resources. Three-quarters of its overseas budget is used to promote long-term projects, including medical, social, and economic research and training schemes. Director: David Bryer.

● **Oxford** ▶ 51 46N 1 15W A city in S central England, the administrative centre of Oxfordshire on the Rivers Thames and Cherwell. Important from Saxon times and heavily fortified, Oxford subsequently became famous as a centre of learning, the first university colleges being founded in the 13th century (*see* Oxford, University of). In the Civil War Oxford was the royalist headquarters. The college buildings dominate the centre of the city with business parks on the outskirts. The motor-car works at Cowley now employs only a fraction of its former workforce. Oxford has one of the world's greatest libraries (the ▷Bodleian Library, 1602). Population (1991): 127 600.

● **Oxford, Provisions of** ▶ (1258) The scheme of constitutional reform imposed upon Henry III by his barons at Oxford following their opposition to excessive taxation. Royal authority was to be contained by an advisory council of 15 barons. The pope absolved Henry from his promise to observe the Provisions (1261), which led to the ▷Barons' War.

● **Oxford, 1st Earl of** ▷*See* Harley, Robert, 1st Earl of Oxford.

● **Oxford, University of** ▶ One of the oldest universities in Europe, dating from the 12th century. It is organized as a federation of colleges, governed by their own teaching staff ("Fellows"), maintain their own property (which includes residential accommodation, libraries, playing fields, etc.), and provide members of the University's legislative bodies, its many faculties, departments, and committees. The University is responsible for organizing a lecture programme, maintaining the large libraries (such as the ▷Bodleian Library), pro-

viding all laboratories, and conducting examinations. The colleges include All Souls, the members of which are all Fellows, Christ Church (founded by Cardinal Wolsey), the college chapel of which is also Oxford Cathedral, and Lady Margaret Hall, which was the first women's college. St Hilda's is now the only single-sex college in the university (Somerville began taking men in 1994). In 1997–98 there were 15 623 students in residence.

Colleges and halls of Oxford University with dates of foundation

College	Date	College	Date
University	1249	Keble	1868
Balliol	1263	Hertford	1874
Merton	1264	Lady Margaret Hall	1878
St Edmund Hall	c.1278	Somerville	1879
Exeter	1314	Mansfield	1886
Oriel	1326	St Hugh's	1886
Queen's	1340	St Hilda's	1893
New College	1379	Campion Hall	1896
Lincoln	1427	St Benet's Hall	1897
All Souls	1438	Greyfriars	1910
Magdalen	1458	St Peter's	1929
Brasenose	1509	Nuffield	1937
Corpus Christi	1517	St Anthony's	1950
Christ Church	1546	St Anne's	1952
Trinity	1554	Linacre	1962
St John's	1555	St Catherine's	1962
Jesus	1571	St Cross	1965
Wadham	1612	Wolfson	1966
Pembroke	1624	Green	1979
Worcester	1714	Kellogg	1990
Regent's Park	1810	Manchester	1990

● **Oxford Group** ▷*See* Moral Rearmament.

● **Oxford Movement** ▶ A movement within the Church of England in the 19th century aimed at emphasizing the Catholic principles on which it rested. Led by ▷Newman, ▷Keble, ▷Pusey, and ▷Froude of Oxford University, it was initiated in 1833 by Keble's sermon "On the National Apostasy." Aided by their *Tracts for the Times*, the Tractarians, as they came to be called, unleashed a spiritual force that did much to invigorate Anglicanism. ▷*See* Anglo-Catholicism.

● **Oxfordshire** ▶ A county in the South Midlands of England. Under local government reorganization in 1974 it gained a large part of NW Berkshire. It consists mainly of a broad vale, crossed by the River Thames, with the ▷Chiltern Hills in the SE and the ▷Cotswold Hills in the NW. It is chiefly agricultural; arable farming is important. Industries include light manufacturing, electronics, and tourism, centred mainly on Oxford. Area: 2611 sq km (1008 sq mi). Population (1996 est): 603 200. Administrative centre: Oxford.

● **oxidation and reduction** ▶ Oxidation is the chemical combination of a substance with oxygen. An example is the combustion of carbon to carbon dioxide: $C + O_2 \rightarrow CO_2$. The converse process, removal of oxygen, is known as reduction; an example is the reduction of iron oxide to iron: $Fe_2O_3 + 3C \rightarrow 2Fe + 3CO$. The terms oxidation and reduction have been extended in chemistry. Thus, reduction also refers to reaction with hydrogen and oxidation to removal of hydrogen. More generally, an oxidation reaction is one involving loss of electrons and a reduction reaction is one in which electrons are gained. Thus, the conversion of ferrous ions to ferric ions is an oxidation: $Fe^{2+} - e \rightarrow Fe^{3+}$. A compound that supplies oxygen or removes electrons is an **oxidizing agent**, whereas one that removes oxygen or supplies electrons is a **reducing agent**. Usually oxidation and reduction reactions occur together. Thus, in the reaction of ferric ions (Fe^{3+}) with stannous ions (Sn^{2+}), the ferric ions are reduced to ferrous ions (Fe^{2+}) and the stannous ions oxidized to stannic ions (Sn^{4+}): $2Fe^{3+} + Sn^{2+} + Sn^{4+}$. Reactions of this type are called **redox reactions**.

● **oxidation number** ▶ (*or* oxidation state) The number of electrons that would have to be added to an atom to neutralize it. Thus Na^+, Cl^-, and He have oxidation numbers of 1, –1, and 0, respectively. Rules have been developed for assigning oxidation numbers to covalently bound atoms depending on the electric charge that the atom would have if the molecule ionized.

● **oxlip** ► A perennial herb, *Primula elatior*, found throughout Europe and W Asia. It is similar to the ▷cowslip but has larger more flattened pale-yellow flowers with a darker yellow throat. The name is also given to hybrids between the primrose and cowslip. Family: *Primulaceae*.

● **oxpecker** ► An African songbird of the genus *Buphagus*, also called tickbird, that feeds on ticks and maggots pecked from the hides of cattle and game animals. The yellow-billed oxpecker (*B. africanus*) is about 20 cm long with sharp claws for clinging to its hosts and a stiff tail used for support in climbing over them. Oxpeckers remove parasites from their hosts but feed on the blood from the sores. Family: *Sturnidae* (starlings).

● **Oxus, River** ▷*See* Amu Darya, River.

● **oxy-acetylene welding** ▷*See* welding.

● **oxygen** ► (O) A colourless odourless gas discovered by J. ▷Priestley. The element exists in two forms—the diatomic molecule (O_2), which constitutes 21% of the earth's atmosphere, and trace amounts of ▷ozone (O_3), which is formed in the ▷ozone layer of the upper atmosphere. Oxygen is very reactive and forms oxides with most elements (for example Na_2O, MgO, Fe_2O_3, Cl_2O_7, XeO_3). In addition to its vital importance for plants and animals, its major use is in the production of steel in blast furnaces. It is obtained by the distillation of liquid air. At no 8; at wt 15.9994; mp −218.79°C; bp −182.97°C.

● **oxygen cycle** ► The process by which oxygen—present in the atmosphere or dissolved in water—is taken in by plants and animals for use in ▷respiration (intercellular combustion of food materials to provide energy) and released into the environment as a waste product, mostly in the form of free oxygen (by plants in ▷photosynthesis). Oxygen is often combined in organic and inorganic compounds, which may also be considered as part of the cycle. ▷*See also* carbon cycle; nitrogen cycle.

● **oxytocin** ► A hormone of female mammals and birds produced in the ▷hypothalamus and transported in the blood to the posterior ▷pituitary gland, where it is stored and from which it is secreted. In mammals oxytocin stimulates contraction of the womb during childbirth and contraction of the milk ducts of the mammary glands during suckling, causing the flow of milk in lactation. A preparation of oxytocin is used to induce labour or abortion.

● **Oyo Empire** ► A kingdom in SW Nigeria and the most powerful state in West Africa from the mid-17th until the mid-18th centuries. Oyo then began to decline relative to Dahomey and during the next century was broken up by ▷Fulani invasions, European intrusions, and civil war. Oyo is now a province in Western State, SW Nigeria.

● **oyster** ► A sedentary ▷bivalve mollusc belonging to the family *Ostreidae* (true oysters), of temperate and warm seas. The lower plate (valve) of the shell is larger and flatter than the upper valve; they are held together by an elastic ligament and powerful muscles. Edible oysters are cultivated for their white flesh; pearl oysters (family *Aviculidae*) are cultivated for their pearls, which they make by coating a grain of sand lodged inside their shell with calcareous material.

● **oystercatcher** ► A black or black-and-white wading bird of a family (*Haematopodidae*; 4 species) occurring in temperate and tropical coastal regions. 40–50 cm long, oystercatchers have long pointed wings, a wedge-shaped tail, pink legs, and a flattened orange-red bill specialized for opening bivalve molluscs and probing in mud. Order: *Charadriiformes*.

● **Ozark Plateau** ► (or Ozark Mountains) An eroded plateau in the USA, in S Missouri and N Arkansas, reaching over 600 m (2000 ft) in the Boston Mountains. Forestry and mining are important; minerals include lead and zinc.

● **ozone** ► (O_3) A pale blue gaseous form of ▷oxygen, formed by passing an electrical discharge through oxygen (O_2). Ozone is a poisonous unstable gas. It is used as an oxidizing agent, for example in water purification. It is present in small amounts in the atmosphere, mostly in the ▷ozone layer.

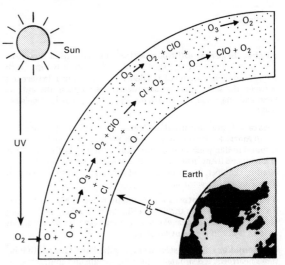

ozone layer ► Solar ultraviolet radiation breaks up oxygen molecules (O_2) into atoms, some of which recombine with oxygen molecules to form ozone (O_3). Chlorine atoms from stable CFCs combine with O_3 to form chlorine monoxide (ClO), which reacts with atomic oxygen to form O_2 and chlorine atoms again. These Cl atoms react again with O_3. Each chlorine atom can react 20 000 times with ozone causing a severe drop in the concentration of ozone in the ozone layer.

● **ozone layer** ► (or ozonosphere) The zone in the upper atmosphere in which the gas ozone (triatomic oxygen; O_3) forms in its greatest concentrations. This is generally between about 11 to 26 km (7–16 mi) above the earth's surface. Ozone forms as a result of the dissociation by solar ultraviolet radiation of molecular oxygen into single atoms, some of which then combine with undissociated oxygen molecules. It absorbs in the 230–320 nm waveband, protecting the earth from dangerous excessive ultraviolet radiation.

Warnings have been given that the use of aerosols could reduce the amount of ozone in the upper atmosphere because the CFCs (*see* fluorocarbons) used as the driver gas, and as refrigerants, are stable and can diffuse up to the ozone layer, where they react with the ozone. In the late 1980s holes in the ozone layer were detected over both poles, prompting the EC to phase out the use of harmful fluorocarbons (by 1997); internationally, several governments signed the Montreal Protocol (1990) limiting such emissions. In 2000 the hole above Antarctica was calculated at some 28.5 million sq km (11 million sq mi)—about three times the size of the USA. *See also* greenhouse effect.

P

● **Pabst, G(eorge) W(ilhelm)** ▶ (1885–1967) Austrian film director. His films are distinguished by their innovatory realistic techniques and their criticism of decadence and nationalism in Germany between the wars. They include *Pandora's Box* (1929), the antiwar *Westfront 1918* (1930), *Die Dreigroschenoper* (1931), and *Kameradschaft* (1931).

● **paca** ▶ A large nocturnal ▷rodent, *Cuniculus paca*, of Central and South America. Up to 60 cm long, with a tiny tail and spotted coat, it is found in damp places near rivers and swamps, feeding on leaves and fruit and living in burrows. Part of the skull is specialized as a resonating chamber. It is hunted by all kinds of predators, including man. Family: *Dasyproctidae*.

● **Pacaraima Mountains** ▶ A mountain range in NE South America. Comprising part of the Guiana Highlands, it extends W–E along part of the Brazil–Venezuela and Brazil–Guyana borders reaching 2810 m (9219 ft) at Mount Roraima.

● **pacemaker** ▶ A small section of specialized heart muscle that initiates heartbeat. It is situated in the right atrium and contracts spontaneously: the impulse to contract is transmitted from the pacemaker to both atria and then to the ventricles. If the pacemaker ceases to function (heart block) it may be replaced by an artificial battery-operated device that stimulates the heart to contract. If required permanently it is surgically implanted under the skin.

● **Pachelbel, Johann** ▶ (1653–1706) German composer and organist. Born in Nuremberg, he was organist at the Sebalduskirche there and also for a time assistant organist at St Stephen's Cathedral in Vienna. His compositions include works for the organ and harpsichord as well as liturgical vocal music. His 78 organ chorales deeply influenced J. S. ▷Bach, and his canon and gigue in D major for three violins and continuo is still extremely popular.

● **pachisi** ▶ A board game popular in India. It is played by two partnerships of players who move pieces round a cross-shaped course according to the throw of dice (or cowrie shells). In the 19th century it was patented in the UK in a modified form as Ludo.

● **Pachomius, St** ▶ (c. 290–346 AD) Egyptian hermit, who founded the first monastery in 318 at Tabenna, on the River Nile, and the first Christian rule involving a uniform communal existence. Until then ▷monasticism had been practised only by solitaries in the desert. Feast day: 14 May.

● **pachyderm** ▶ A thick-skinned ▷mammal, such as the elephant, rhinoceros, or hippopotamus. Early naturalists classified these animals, together with pigs and walruses, in a group called *Pachydermata*. The classification is now abandoned but the term is still used.

● **Pachymeres, Georgius** ▶ (1242–c. 1310) Byzantine historian and writer. Pachymere's most important work was a history of the period 1261 to 1308, under the emperors ▷Michael VIII Palaeologus and Andronicus II Palaeologus (1260–1332; reigned 1282–1328). Other works include an outline of Aristotelian philosophy and a treatise on the Holy Spirit. The latter work is significant in that it accepts the controversial Roman ▷Filioque clause of the formula of St ▷John of Damascus.

● **Pacific, War of the** ▶ (1879–84) The war between Chile and the allies Bolivia and Peru. Also called the Nitrate War, it was provoked by a dispute over Chile's exploitation of nitrate deposits in Bolivia. Within two years Bolivia was defeated, and Peru's capital Lima captured. According to the peace terms, finally agreed in 1884, Peru and Bolivia ceded territories to Chile, Bolivia losing all access to the sea.

● **Pacific Islands, Trust Territory of the** ▶ A former UN trust territory (1947–87) administered by the USA. It comprised the ▷Marshall Islands, the Federated States of ▷Micronesia, the Mariana Islands (until 1978), and ▷Belau. Taken by Japan from Germany (1914), the islands were captured by the USA in World War II (1944).

● **Pacific Ocean** ▶ The world's largest and deepest ocean, covering a third of its surface. It extends between Asia, Australia, Antarctica, and America. It contains a multitude of volcanic and coral islands in the tropical SW and reaches its maximum depth in the ▷Marianas Trench. The S and E are marked by a uniform climate with steady winds, but the W is known for its typhoons, which often cause coastal flooding. The Pacific has some diurnal and mixed tides, while Tahitian tides follow the sun and not the moon. Its vast mineral resources are unexploited.

● **pacifism** ▶ The group of doctrines, religious, moral, or political, that urge nonparticipation either in any war whatsoever or in particular wars that are held to be unjustified. In ancient societies it was assumed that membership of the society involved fighting for it when necessary. This view was not held by early Christians, although not all Christians have been unanimously pacifist; in fact Christian pacifism was relatively unimportant from Constantine's period to the Reformation, when first ▷Anabaptists, and then ▷Quakers, adopted total pacifism. In modern times conscientious objectors have been recognized in both World Wars and have often served with distinction in noncombatant (medical) units. Moreover nonviolent methods of attaining political ends were shown to be effective by ▷Gandhi in the 1920s, despite the slaughter between Hindus and Muslims that followed, and Martin Luther ▷King, Jr in the 1960s (*see* civil disobedience).

● **Pacino, Al** ▶ (1940–   ) US actor. He has appeared on stage but is best known for his films, which include *The Godfather* (1972) and its sequels, *Scent of a Woman* (1992), which earned him an Oscar, and *Looking for Richard* (1996).

● **pack rat** ▶ A North American ▷rodent belonging to the genus *Neotoma* (20 species), also called wood rat. With body length of 15–23 cm, it has a hairy tail and inhabits rocky and wooded country, nesting in a pile of twigs and feeding on seeds and vegetation. Family: *Cricetidae*.

● **Padang** ▶ 1 00S 100 21E A port in Indonesia, in W Sumatra. An early Dutch settlement, it flourished when railways were built in the 19th century. It exports coal, cement, coffee, copra, and rubber. Its university was established in 1956. Population (1995 est): 721 500.

● **Paddington** ▶ A district in the Greater London borough of the City of Westminster. It is noted for Paddington Station, an important railway terminus for trains from the west of England and south Wales.

● **paddlefish** ▶ One of two species of freshwater ▷bony fish, *Polyodon spathula* of North America or *Psephurus gladius* of China, also called duckbill cat. Paddlefishes have a smooth body, with an enormous paddle-shaped snout, and feed by straining planktonic organisms from the water. Family: *Polyodontidae*; order: *Acipenseriformes*.

● **Paderborn** ▶ 51 43N 8 44E A city in NW Germany, in North Rhine-Westphalia. Notable buildings include a cathedral (11th–13th centuries) and a Renaissance town hall (1613–20). Its university was established in 1972. An important agricultural market, it manufactures agricultural machinery, computers, textiles, and furniture. Population (1996 est): 133 717.

● **Paderewski, Ignacy (Jan)** ▶ (1860–1941) Polish pianist, composer, and statesman. Having studied at Warsaw, Berlin, and Vienna, he achieved an international reputation as a performer and composed a piano concerto and many solo pieces. He was the first prime minister (1919) of newly independent Poland but resigned after ten months to return to his musical career.

● **Padua** ▶ (Italian name: Padova) 45 24N 11 53E A city in NE Italy, near Venice. An important city in Roman and Renaissance times, it has several notable buildings, including a 13th-century cathedral and the Basilica of St Anthony, in front of which stands one of Donatello's most famous works, the equestrian statue of Gattamelata. Galileo taught at its university (founded in 1222). Machinery and textiles are produced. Population (1996 est): 212 731.

● **paediatrics** ▶ The medical specialty concerned with the problems and illnesses of infants and children from birth (or premature birth) to adolescence. Paediatricians must have a knowledge of obstetrics, genetics (to deal with inherited diseases), and psychology. Their work includes the management of handicaps at home and in school as well as the treatment and prevention of childhood diseases.

● **Paestum** ▶ The Roman name for Posidonia, a colony of ▷Sybaris founded about 600 BC on the SW coast of Italy. Paestum is famed for the three great Doric temples the remains of which still stand there. Named after the Greek sea god ▷Poseidon, it was conquered by Rome in 273 BC and became celebrated in Latin poetry for its twice-flowering roses.

● **Páez, José Antonio** ▶ (1790–1873) Venezuelan revolutionary. The leader of a band of cowboys (*llaneros*), he allied himself with ▷Bolívar against Spain. After the liberation he took Venezuela out of the confederation of Gran Colombia and became its first president (1831).

● **Pagalu** ▷*See* Equatorial Guinea, Republic of.

● **Pagan** ▶ The former capital of Myanmar (Burma) on the Irrawaddy River SE of Mandalay. Founded in about 849 AD, Pagan was refounded after the decree adopting Buddhism as the state religion (1056). Hundreds of brick-built temples, monasteries, and pagodas survived Pagan's sack by the Mongols (1287) and some, such as the Ananda temple (1090) and Shwezigon pagoda (12th century), are still in use.

● **Paganini, Niccolò** ▶ (1782–1840) Italian virtuoso violinist. After an adventurous youth he toured Europe, astonishing audiences with his techniques, such as left-hand pizzicato, multiple stopping, and artificial harmonics. His skill inspired Liszt and Schumann to compose piano music of transcendent difficulty. He composed six violin concertos, various showpieces for violin, including a set of variations on the G string, and 24 caprices, one of which became the basis for compositions by Rachmaninov, Brahms, and others.

● **Page, Sir Earle (Christmas Grafton)** ▶ (1880–1961) Australian politician, who was leader of the Country Party from 1920 to 1939 and briefly prime minister in 1939. Between 1923 and 1929, he was treasurer in the coalition government under ▷Bruce. He was later minister of commerce (1934–39, 1940–41), establishing the Australian Agricultural Council (1934), and minister of health (1949–56).

● **Page, Sir Frederick Handley** ▶ (1885–1962) British ▢aircraft designer, who in 1909 founded Handley Page Ltd, the first British aircraft company. His Handley Page 0/400 was the first twin-engined bomber and saw action in World War I. He also designed and built the Halifax, a World War II bomber.

● **Pagnol, Marcel** ▶ (1895–1974) French writer and film maker. His works, most of which are set in Provence, include the Marseilles trilogy of plays (1926–36) and the film *Manon des Sources* (1953). Several of his writings were made into successful films in the 1980s and 1990s.

● **pagoda** ▶ A Buddhist shrine in the form of a tower for housing

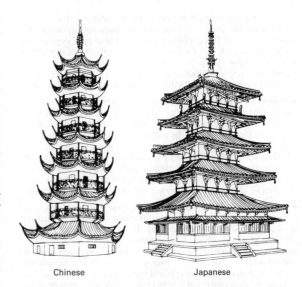

Chinese   Japanese

pagoda ▶ The exuberantly curving roofs of the typical multistoreyed Chinese pagoda contrast with the more restrained Japanese form.

relics of the Buddha. Pagodas originated in India, where their form of a basic unit repeated vertically in diminishing sizes was evolved. The pagoda spread to Sri Lanka (where it is called a dagoba), SE Asia, China, and Japan. Japanese pagodas are usually five-storeyed wooden structures built round a central timber post to provide stability against earthquakes. ▷*See also* stupa.

● **pagoda tree** ▷*See* frangipani.

● **Pago Pago** ▶ 14 16S 170 43W The capital of American Samoa, in SE Tutuila on the S Pacific Ocean. A US naval base (1872–1951), it is a port exporting tinned tuna. Population (1990): 4000.

● **Pahang** ▶ A large state in SE Peninsular Malaysia, on the South China Sea. Lying mainly in the River Pahang basin it rises to the Cameron Mountains in the W. Rubber, rice, coconuts, gold, and tin are produced. Area: 35 931 sq km (13 873 sq mi). Population (1993 est): 1 056 100. Capital: Kuantan.

● **Pahang, River** ▶ The longest river in Peninsular Malaysia, rising in the NW and flowing S then E through the state of Penang to enter the South China Sea. Length: 322 km (200 mi).

● **Pahlavi** ▷*See* Mohammed Reza Pahlavi; Reza Shah Pahlavi.

● **pain** ▶ An unpleasant experience associated with actual or potential tissue damage, or described in terms of such damage. Pain is always subjective. Each individual learns the application of the word through experiences in early life. Because it is always unpleasant, pain is an emotional as well as a sensory experience. Many people report pain in the absence of tissue damage or any likely pathological cause; usually this happens for psychological reasons. There is no way to distinguish this experience from that due to tissue damage; if people regard their experience as pain, and if they report it in the same way as pain, it should be accepted as pain. This definition avoids tying pain to the stimulus. Activity induced in peripheral nerve fibres is not pain, which is always a psychological state. As nerve impulses pass from the peripheral nerves into the spinal cord, they pass through a gate control in which the subsequent passage of the impulse depends on the mixture of the various events in the periphery and on descending controls from the brain, which permit the entry and transmission of the information.

Attention is a crucial component of any sensed experience; if a person switches attention from one event to another the sensation associated with the first event is not experienced. This results in the paradoxical occurrence of painless injuries and introduces the concept of distraction as a basis for pain therapy. Anxiety and depression focus the attention and exaggerate the pain. The pain mechanism is not a hard-wired rigid single system but is modifiable. If messages fail to arrive, the brain reacts and increases the amplification in the disabled pathway. This explains the occurrence of pain in phantom limbs and pain when nerves are destroyed. In some situations it is possible to reduce the gain along the transmission pathways by the use of narcotics; in others it is possible to reduce the signals associated with tissue damage, as in the action of aspirin on inflammation.

● **Paine, Thomas** ▶ (1737–1809) British writer and political theorist. In 1774 he went to America, where his pamphlet *Common Sense* (1776) initiated the American movement towards independence. Returning to England in 1787, he published *Rights of Man* (1791–92) in support of the French Revolution and in opposition to Edmund ▷Burke's *Reflections*. Indicted for treason, Paine fled to France, where he was elected to the French Convention. While imprisoned by Robespierre, he wrote the second part of his *Age of Reason* (1796), a deist manifesto. He returned to America in 1802 and died there in poverty.

● **paint** ▶ A finely powdered insoluble pigment suspended in a binding medium; on application to a surface the volatile components of the binding medium evaporate, the drying oils oxidize, and the resins polymerize, leaving a decorative or protective skin. The pigments impart colour and opacity to the skin and extenders (such as barium sulphate, calcium carbonate, or asbestos) are mixed with the pigments to strengthen the skin and reduce raw-material costs. The binding medium consists of a drying oil (e.g. linseed oil or tung oil), a resin (rosin or a synthetic alkyd), a thinner (turpentine, benzene, etc.), and a drier (e.g. lead linoleate) to accelerate film formation. Water-based emulsion paints consist of emulsions of a synthetic resin (e.g. polyvinyl acetate, polystyrene, acrylic resins) in water.

● **painted lady** ▶ An orange, black, and white ▷nymphalid butterfly, *Vanessa cardui*, of worldwide distribution. It cannot survive cold winters but migrates from warmer regions each year. The caterpillars feed mainly on thistles and nettles. The American painted lady (*V. virginiensis*) is similar but less widespread.

● **painting** ▶ In art, the creation of an aesthetic entity by the skilled covering of a surface with paint. Suitable painting surfaces include paper, canvas, walls, and ivory, and among the many techniques of painting are oil, ▷watercolour, ▷tempera, ▷encaustic, ▷fresco, and, the most modern method, ▷acrylic painting. The main subjects of painting were religious until the Renaissance period, when portraits, landscapes, ▷genre, and ▷still-life began to assume an independent existence. The principal painting styles in art have been classical (ancient Greek and Roman), Byzantine, romanesque, gothic, Renaissance, mannerist, baroque, rococo, neoclassical, realist, impressionist, expressionist, and abstract.

● **Paisley** ▶ 55 50N 4 26W A town in W central Scotland, in Renfrewshire. It has been famous for shawls since the 19th century. The richly coloured abstract design used for the shawls is still known as **paisley pattern**; any fabric printed with such a design is known as paisley. Dyeing, bleaching, engineering, and starch and cornflour manufacturing are also important. Population (1991): 75 526.

● **Paisley, Ian** ▶ (1926–) Northern Irish politician; an uncompromising defender of Protestant unionism. A minister of the Free Presbyterian Church of Ulster from 1946, he was a Protestant Unionist MP in the Northern Irish parliament (1970–72) before becoming an MP in the House of Commons (1970–85; 1986–). He has been leader of the Democratic Unionist Party since 1972 and an MEP since 1979. Since the later 1990s he has been a leading opponent of the Northern Ireland peace process and the Good Friday Agreement of 1998.

● **Pakistan, Islamic Republic of** ▶ A country in S Asia, bordering on Iran, Afghanistan, China, and India. The W is mountainous and the E has areas of desert, while the River Indus rises in the Himalayas in the N and flows S across plateau and the Indus Plain to the Arabian Sea. The country is arid with great extremes of temperature but the plain is very fertile, except in areas that have become saline or waterlogged. The population, which is increasing rapidly, is a mixture of many Asian and Middle Eastern racial groups. Of the languages spoken Punjabi is the most commonly used, although Urdu is the language of the educated. 97% of the population is Muslim. *Economy*: mainly agricultural, producing cotton, rice, wheat, and

sugar cane. Productivity improved during the 1960s and 1970s with increased mechanization, chemical fertilizers, improved strains of crops, and the reclamation of saline land. Irrigation, on which agriculture is dependent, has also been extensively developed since the Indus Waters Treaty was concluded with India (1960). Industry has developed successfully since 1947 but is still largely dependent on imported machinery, petroleum, chemicals, and metals. Pakistan has become a major exporter of cotton and cotton yarn and cloth. Chemical fertilizers, cement, animal products, and engineering goods are also produced, and a steel industry is being developed. Fishing is increasingly important. Resources include coal (mainly low-grade), iron ore, copper, limestone, oil, and large quantities of natural gas. Hydroelectric power is also produced. The economy has been in severe recession since 1996. In 1998 international trade sanctions were imposed in response to Pakistan's nuclear tests.

History: the history of Pakistan is that of ▷India until 1947, when it was created to satisfy the ▷Muslim League's demand for a separate state for the Muslim minority. The partition of the subcontinent led to intense violence between Muslims and Hindus in which over a million people were killed and some 17 million were displaced. Muhammad Ali ▷Jinnah, Pakistan's chief creator, became the country's first president. Pakistan initially consisted of two separate areas: West Pakistan comprised Baluchistan, the Northwest Frontier, West Punjab (now Punjab province), and Sind, while East Pakistan was formed from East Bengal. The question of control over Kashmir is still unsettled and has led to repeated conflicts with India. The most serious problem facing Pakistan has been the unification of its diverse population groups, divided by geography, race, language, and extremes of wealth and poverty. The unifying force of the common religion has not been able to contain demands for regional autonomy and increased democracy. Thus each of Pakistan's three constitutions (1956, 1962, 1973) has been replaced by martial law (an amended version of the 1973 constitution was restored in 1985 and suspended in 1999). Regional unrest was especially serious in East Pakistan, which had a larger population but less political and military power than West Pakistan. The electoral victory in East Pakistan of the Awami League (1970), which demanded regional autonomy, led to its secession as ▷Bangladesh (1971). This was effected after a two-week civil war in which Indian forces intervened and defeated troops from West Pakistan. Regionalism later led to guerrilla fighting in Baluchistan and the Northwest Frontier province (1970s and 1980s) and in Sind (1990s). In 1972 Pakistan withdrew from the Commonwealth. Allegations of ballot rigging in the 1977 elections triggered violent unrest, which led to a military coup led by Gen ▷Zia ul-Haq. The former prime minister, Zulfikar Ali Bhutto, was executed for conspiracy to murder (1979). Gen Zia became president in 1978 but faced increasing opposition from Benazir ▷Bhutto and her supporters during the 1980s. In 1988 Zia died in an air crash caused by a bomb; in the ensuing election Benazir Bhutto became prime minister. Pakistan rejoined the Commonwealth in 1989. In 1990, following increased ethnic violence, Bhutto was dismissed as prime minister. Her successor, Nawaz Sharif, was dismissed in 1993 and Bhutto was re-elected. In 1996 she was dismissed once more on grounds of corruption and mismanagement; Sharif was re-elected the following year. In May 1998 Pakistan carried out underground nuclear explosions in response to similar tests by India. From 1997 to 1999 there was a state of turmoil owing to constitutional disputes between the prime minister and president (1997), ethnic violence in Karachi and elsewhere, and deepening economic crisis. In October 1999 Sharif was deposed in a military coup led by Gen Pervaiz Musharraf, who appointed himself president in 2001. Musharraf's rule was endorsed in a referendum held in April 2002, but this was widely condemned as fraudulent.

Islamic Republic of Pakistan

Head of state	President Pervaiz Musharraf
Official language	Urdu
Official currency	Pakistan rupee of 100 paisa
Area (excluding Jammu and Kashmir)	803 943 sq km (310 322 sq mi)
Population (2000 est)	141 553 775
Capital	Islamabad

● **Palace of Westminster** ▶ The British parliamentary buildings in Westminster, London, containing the House of Commons and the House of Lords (*see* parliament). It is also known as the Houses of Parliament. A royal palace of medieval construction until the 16th century, when it assumed its present function, it was largely burnt down in 1834, only the Great Hall surviving. It was rebuilt in the ▷gothic revival style by ▷Barry and ▷Pugin. ▷*See also* Big Ben.

● **Palaeocene epoch** ▷*See* Tertiary period.

● **palaeography** ▶ The study of ancient handwriting. Palaeography originated as an adjunct to textual criticism of Greek and Latin manuscripts but is now applied to all kinds of scripts. Palaeographers assess the cultural and historical implications of the development of writing styles and the output of individual scriptoria (scribal centres) and scribes. Recent technical aids include computerized surveys of large numbers of manuscripts and ultraviolet photography.

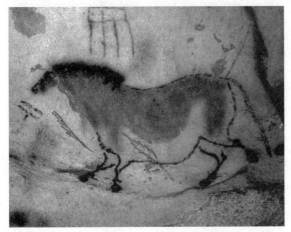

Palaeolithic ▶ Painting of a horse from the Upper Palaeolithic (c. 15 000 BC) found in the caves of Lascaux in the Dordogne, France.

● **Palaeolithic** ▶ The earliest division of the ▷Stone Age. It extends from the emergence of man, or some hominid capable of making simple pebble tools, to the end of the last ice age. The Palaeolithic is usually divided into three phases: Lower, beginning as much as 3 500 000 years ago and characterized by pebble-tool and hand-axe manufacture; Middle, beginning about 70 000 years ago and associated with ▷Neanderthal man and ▷Mousterian industries; and Upper, beginning about 40 000 years ago and associated in Europe with ▷Cro-Magnon man and cave art.

● **Palaeologus** ▶ The ruling dynasty of the Eastern Roman Empire from 1261 to 1453. The first Palaeologus emperor was ▷Michael VIII Palaeologus and they continued to rule until the fall of Constantinople to the Turks in 1453. During this period Byzantine culture underwent a major revival.

● **palaeomagnetism** ▶ The history of the earth's magnetic field (*see* geomagnetic field) as determined from the remanent magnetism of rocks. The study assumes that the principal component of igneous and sedimentary rocks' magnetism was determined at or near to the time at which the rocks were formed. It provides evidence for continental drift (*see* plate tectonics) and the movement of the magnetic poles.

● **palaeontology** ▶ The study of ancient organisms from their ▷fossil remains in the rocks. Their taxonomy, anatomy, ecology, and evolution are studied. Fossils are used to correlate bodies of rock and establish their stratigraphic relationships (biostratigraphy). Modern methods of dating rocks by ▷radiometric means give their absolute dates rather than their order in the stratigraphic column. The study of ancient microscopic organisms (microfossils) is called **micropalaeontology**.

● **Palaeo-Siberian languages** ▶ A group of languages of Siberia comprised of four unrelated groups: Yeniseian; Luorawetlan, which includes Chuckchi, Koryak, and Aliutor; Yukaghir, which includes Yukaghir and also Omok and Chuvan, both now extinct; and Gilyak, the only one of its group. These languages now have fewer than 25 000 speakers altogether.

● **Palaeozoic era** ▶ The era of geological time between the Precambrian and the Mesozoic, lasting from about 590 to 240 million years ago. It is divided into the Lower Palaeozoic, which contains the Cambrian, Ordovician, and Silurian periods, and the Upper Palaeozoic, containing the Devonian, Carboniferous, and Permian. It is the first era of ▷Phanerozoic time. The Caledonian and Variscan orogenies both occurred in this era.

● **palanquin** ▶ An enclosed litter formerly used in the East by high-ranking officials and by women and usually carried by four or six men.

● **palate** ▶ The roof of the mouth, which is divided into two parts. The soft palate at the back of the mouth is composed of mucous membrane and prevents food passing into the nose during swallowing. From its centre hangs down a flap of tissue, the uvula. The hard palate, further forward, is composed of two fused halves made up of the palatine bone and part of the maxillary (upper jaw) bones. ▷*See also* cleft palate.

● **Palatinate** ▶ Two regions of Germany: the Lower (*or* Rhenish) Palatinate is now in Rheinland-Pfalz, Baden-Württemberg, and Hesse and the Upper Palatinate is now in Bavaria. In 1156 the title of count palatine (originally a judicial officer) was bestowed by Emperor Frederick I on his half-brother Conrad, whose territories included what later became the Rhenish Palatinate. When, in 1214, it passed to the ▷Wittelsbach family, their lands in Bavaria became the Upper Palatinate. From 1356 the counts palatine were ▷electors of Holy Roman Emperors. During the Reformation the Palatinate became a centre of Protestantism and the claim by the Protestant, Elector Frederick, the Winter King, to the Bohemian throne precipitated the ▷Thirty Years' War. The two Palatinates were separated from 1648 until 1777 but in the early 19th century the Lower Palatinate was divided between France and various German states and the Upper Palatinate passed to Bavaria. ▷*See also* county palatine.

● **Palau** ▷*See* Belau, Republic of.

● **Palawan** ▶ A mountainous island in the W Philippines, between the South China and Sulu Seas. Sparsely populated, its chief products are timber, mercury, and chromite; fishing is important. Area: 11 785 sq km (4550 sq mi). Population (latest est): 311 548. Chief town: Puerto Princesa.

● **Palembang** ▶ 2 59S 104 45E A port in Indonesia, in S Sumatra on the River Musi. It was the capital of a Hindu Sumatran kingdom (8th century AD) and Dutch trade began here in 1617. Its university was established in 1960. The export centre of local oilfields, it has Indonesia's largest refinery and many oil-based industries. Population (1996 est): 1 352 300.

● **Palencia** ▶ 41 01N 4 32W A town in N central Spain, in León. It possessed Spain's first university, founded in 1208 and moved to Salamanca in 1239. The gothic cathedral contains paintings by El Greco, including *St Sebastian*. Manufactures include iron and porcelain. Population (1991): 77 752.

● **Palermo** ▶ 38 08N 13 23E A port in Italy, the capital of Sicily. Founded by the Phoenicians in the 8th century BC, it established itself as Sicily's chief town under the Arabs (9th–11th centuries). Buildings include the gothic cathedral and the Norman palace (now the regional parliament). It has shipbuilding and textile industries. Population (1996 est): 689 301.

● **Palestine** ▶ (*or* Holy Land) A historic area in the Middle East, consisting of the area between the Mediterranean Sea and the River Jordan. It now comprises ▷Israel and the Israeli-occupied territories. Sacred to Jews, Christians, and Muslims alike, and caught between a succession of surrounding empires, the area has been much fought over. It has been inhabited since prehistoric times. Towards the end of the 2nd millennium BC it was settled by the Hebrew people, who in the Old Testament were led out of Egypt by Moses, and in about 1000

BC a Hebrew kingdom was founded by Saul. Following the reign of Solomon it was split into Israel, later conquered by the Assyrians, and Judah (see Judaea), later conquered by the Babylonians (see Babylonian exile), who destroyed the ▷Temple of Jerusalem (rebuilt in 516 BC under the Persians). The Romans conquered the Jewish state that existed briefly in 142–63 BC and also destroyed the Temple (70 AD) while violently suppressing a Jewish revolt. From the late 4th century AD many Jews left Palestine, which became a centre first for Christian and later for Muslim pilgrimage (following Arab conquest in 636 AD). Christianity was reinstated in the area by the conquest of the Crusaders (1099 until the 13th century). After a period of Egyptian rule it fell to the Ottoman Turks (1516), who ruled it until World War I. During the 1830s Palestine, inhabited chiefly by Arab peasants, was opened up to European influence and from the mid-19th century Jews returned from the ▷diaspora to settle in Palestine. The late 19th century saw the beginning of ▷Zionism and in 1909 Tel Aviv, the first new Jewish city, was founded. By 1914 there were 100 000 Jews in Palestine, although their numbers were reduced by almost half during World War I, in which they were sympathetic to the Allies. In 1918 Palestine was captured by the British; British administration, effective from 1920, was confirmed by a League of Nations mandate (1922). By the ▷Balfour Declaration (1917) the British supported the Jewish demand for a Jewish nation in Palestine. This provoked unrest and terrorism among the Arab population, who felt increasingly threatened by Jewish immigration. The British limits on immigration and land purchase in order to pacify the Arabs (1939) angered the Jews and thus increased tension even further, as did also the large numbers of illegal Jewish immigrants arriving during the war. In 1947 the problem was referred to the UN, which decided to divide Palestine into two separate states, Jewish and Arab. As this was accepted by the Jews but not the Arabs, Britain renounced its mandate in 1948. The state of Israel was then proclaimed and immediately attacked by the surrounding Arab countries. They were repulsed and Israel extended its boundaries at the expense of the proposed Arab state: the remainder was divided between Jordan (the ▷West Bank of the Jordan) and Egypt (the ▷Gaza Strip). Both areas were occupied by Israel in the war of 1967, following which some 750 000 Palestine Arabs fled to Jordan and other neighbouring countries. In 1988 a new Palestinian state was declared by the ▷Palestine Liberation Organization (PLO), but was not recognized by Israel. In 1995 Israel handed over the administration of the Gaza Strip and parts of the West Bank to a new Palestinian National Authority, according to the terms of a peace agreement (1994) with the PLO. Yassir ▷Arafat was elected first president of the Authority in 1996. Further progress was hampered by continuing Arab violence and delays in Israeli troop withdrawals from the West Bank. From 2000 violent protests by Palestinians met with savage reprisals from the Israeli military, who reoccupied large areas of Palestinian territory in 2002. ▷See also intifada.

● **Palestine Liberation Organization** ► (PLO) An organization of various Palestinian groups formed to oppose the Israeli presence in Palestine. Founded in 1964, the PLO has not been able to unite all the Palestinian groups; in particular the Popular Front for the Liberation

of Palestine, led by George Habash, has remained independent. The PLO is under the leadership of Yassir ▷Arafat's al-▷Fatah. Terrorist actions carried out by the PLO include the murder of 11 Israeli athletes at the Munich Olympics (1972). In 1982 PLO forces were expelled from Lebanon, which they had been using as a base, when Israel invaded. In 1988 the PLO set up a parliament in exile (in Tunis) for the newly declared state of Palestine. In the same year Arafat embarked on a more peaceful policy, with US backing. After secret discussions, a peace agreement was signed in 1993 by Arafat and Yitzhak ▷Rabin. The PLO renounced terrorism and recognized Israel's right to exist in return for Israel's offer to withdraw its troops from the ▷Gaza Strip and parts of the ▷West Bank. The Palestinians, under PLO leadership, gained effective autonomy in these areas in 1995. However, the peace process then stalled owing to violence by more extreme Arab factions (see Hamas) and Israeli reluctance to implement troop withdrawals. A further land-for-security deal was signed by Israel and the PLO in 1998 but US-brokered talks in 2000 ended in bitter failure. The result was rising violence on both sides. Claims that the PLO was colluding in Arab suicide bombings were used to justify Israel's reoccupation of Palestinian cities in 2002.

● **Palestrina, Giovanni Pierluigi da** ► (?1525–94) Italian composer. He spent most of his life in Rome, as chorister, choirmaster, or maestro at churches including St Peter's. A master of ▷polyphony, he composed 93 masses, 179 motets, and many other pieces. He was offered posts elsewhere (Venice and Mantua) but he asked too high a salary.

● **Paley, William** ► (1743–1805) British churchman and Anglican theologian. A Fellow of Christ's College, Cambridge, Paley was the author of View of the Evidences of Christianity (1794) and Natural Theology (1802). These were acclaimed apologies for Christian belief against ▷deism.

● **Palgrave, Francis Turner** ► (1824–97) British poet and anthologist. A friend of Tennyson, he published several volumes of verse and became professor of poetry at Oxford. He is best remembered for his influential anthology of English verse, The Golden Treasury (1861).

● **Pali** ► An ▷Indo-Aryan language originating in N India. It is the language of the Theravada Buddhist canon and is used throughout the Theravada countries of SE Asia but disappeared from India itself during the 14th century.

● **Palio** ► A horse race run in July and August in the main piazza of Siena. It is named after the painted silk banner that the winner receives. The Palio first took place in 1482 and is accompanied by considerable pageantry.

● **Palissy, Bernard** ► (1510–89) French potter, famous for his rustic ware, a colourful lead-glazed earthenware. His dishes are ornamental in relief with mythological subjects or reptiles, plants, etc. He enjoyed court patronage in the 1560s but was persecuted as a Huguenot and died in prison. He is also known for his writings on religion, science, and philosophy.

Palladianism ► The Church of Il Redentore (the Redeemer) in Venice, built (1577–92) to a design by Palladio. This is often considered Palladio's most successful attempt to fuse the principles of classical Roman architecture with the requirements of an ecclesiastical building.

● **Palladianism** ▶ An architectural style developed in 16th-century Venetia by ▷Palladio. It was based on classical Roman public architecture and the theories of ▷Vitruvius and it placed great importance on symmetrical room planning and a harmonious system of proportions. Largely disseminated by Palladio's books, *I quattro libri dell' architettura* (1570), it was first introduced into England in the early 17th century by Inigo ▷Jones but had no other followers until it was revived early in the 18th century by Lord ▷Burlington, Colen Campbell (1673–1729), and William ▷Kent. It was widely used in England for public buildings and country houses, eventually being replaced by ▷neoclassicism in the mid-18th century.

● **Palladio, Andrea** ▶ (1508–80) Italian architect, born in Padua. One of the most sophisticated and widely imitated of classical architects, Palladio is famous for developing the architectural style now known as ▷Palladianism. Trained as a stonemason, Palladio designed most of his buildings in and around Vicenza. His first job was the remodelling of the basilica in Vicenza (begun 1549) and from that emerged a successful career. He produced villas, for example the Villa Rotonda (near Vicenza) and Villa Barbaro (Maser); palaces, for example the Palazzo Chericati (1550s); and churches, the most famous being S Giorgio Maggiore in Venice (begun 1566; ▢Guardi, Francesco).

● **palladium** ▶ (Pd) A silvery-white noble metal of the platinum group, discovered by W. H. Wollaston (1766–1828) in 1803, and named after the asteroid Pallas, which was discovered at about the same time. Palladium readily absorbs hydrogen and is used as a catalyst for hydrogenation reactions; it is alloyed with gold to form white gold. At no 46; at wt 106.4; mp 1552°C; bp 3140°C.

● **Palladium** ▶ In Greek and Roman religion, an ancient image of Athena, originally the wooden image kept in the citadel of Troy and believed to have been sent from heaven by Zeus. The safety of the city depended on it. It was stolen by Odysseus and Diomedes, who thus made possible the capture of Troy. It was believed to have been taken to Athens or Sparta, or to Rome (by ▷Aeneas).

● **Pallas** ▶ The second largest (608 km in diameter) ▷minor planet, the orbit of which lies between those of Mars and Jupiter.

● **Pallas Athena** ▷*See* Athena.

● **Pallas's cat** ▶ A small wild ▷cat, *Felis* (or *Otocolobus*) *manul*, of Tibet, Mongolia, and Siberia. About 50 cm long, with a very thick tail and long yellow-grey fur, it has a small face with low-set ears—an adaptation for stalking small mammals from the cover of rocks and boulders.

● **palm** ▶ A monocotyledonous plant of the family *Palmae* (or *Arecaceae*; about 2500 species), occurring in tropical and subtropical regions. Ranging from 1 to 60 m in height, palms typically have an unbranched trunk crowned with a cluster of leaves, which are pleated and fan-shaped or feather-like and often very large (up to 15 m long). The flowers are usually grouped into large clusters and give rise to berries or drupes (stone fruits). Palms are commercially important as a source of food (*see* coconut; date; sago), oil (*see* oil palm), wax (*see* carnauba wax), and various fibres and building materials.

● **Palma** ▶ (*or* Palma de Mallorca) 39 35N 2 39E The capital of the Spanish Balearic Islands, in Majorca on the Mediterranean Sea. Its historic buildings include the gothic cathedral (1230–1601) and the 14th-century Bellver Castle. Noted as a tourist resort, it is also a port and commercial centre; industries include textiles, footwear, and such crafts as pottery. Population (1995 est): 318 030.

● **Palma Vecchio, Jacopo** ▶ (J. Negretti; c. 1480–1528) Italian painter of the Venetian school. He is noted for his *St Barbara Altarpiece* (Sta Maria Formosa, Venice) and his portraits.

● **Palm Beach** ▶ 26 41N 80 02W A town and resort in the USA, in SE Florida on Lake Worth (a lagoon). It is an extension of the much larger West Palm Beach. Population (1990): 9814.

● **palm civet** ▶ A mammal of the family ▷*Viverridae* that is smaller than the true civets and more omnivorous than the ▷genets. Most palm civets are Asian (the two-spotted palm civet (*Nandinia binotata*) is the only African species). The masked palm civet (*Paguma larvata*) of

SE Asia is up to 140 cm long including the tail (50–65 cm) and is mainly arboreal, feeding on fruit, insects, and some vertebrates.

● **Palme, (Sven) Olof** ▶ (1927–86) Swedish Social Democratic politician; prime minister (1969–76, 1982–86). He was a noted advocate of international disarmament and acted as UN special envoy during the ▷Iran-Iraq War. He was assassinated.

● **Palmer, Arnold** ▶ (1929–) US professional golfer, who did much to make golf a spectator sport. US amateur champion in 1954, he won the US Open championship (1960), Masters championship (1958, 1960, 1962, 1964), British Open championship (1961, 1962), and many other events.

● **Palmer, Samuel** ▶ (1805–81) British landscape painter and etcher, born in London. He first exhibited at the Royal Academy at the age of 14 but his best landscapes, often moonlit and either in sepia or watercolour, were painted during his association (1826–35) with a group of painters in Shoreham, who all admired William ▷Blake. His imaginative and mystical approach to art declined into conventionality in the late 1830s.

● **Palmerston, Henry John Temple, 3rd Viscount** ▶ (1784–1865) British statesman; foreign secretary (1830–34, 1835–41, 1846–51) and Liberal prime minister (1855–58, 1859–65). He entered parliament in 1807 as a Tory, serving as secretary for war from 1809 to 1828, but by 1830 he had joined the Whigs (later Liberals). His markedly nationalistic foreign policy sought to defend constitutional states and prevent a Franco-Russian combination. In 1850 he made a famous speech defending the dispatch of a fleet to Greece in support of the claims of Don Pacifico (1784–1854), who had been born in British Gibraltar, against the Greek Government (his house had been burned by a mob), stating that every British subject might "hold himself free from indignity when he could say *Civis Romanus sum*." As prime minister Palmerston supported the Confederacy in the US Civil War but was dissuaded by his colleagues from actively involving Britain.

● **Palmerston North** ▶ 40 21S 175 37E A city in New Zealand, in S North Island. It is a centre for the agricultural area of the Manawatu Plain and is the site of Massey University (founded in 1926; independent since 1963). Population (1995 est): 76 300.

● **palmistry** ▶ The study of the lines and ridges on the palm of the hand in order to interpret character and divine the owner's future. Although without scientific basis, palmistry (or chiromancy as it is also called) provides common-sense evidence of a person's way of life and habits and from these something may be deduced of his character and interests.

● **Palm Springs** ▶ 33 49N 116 34W A city in the USA, in California. Known for its hot springs, it is a resort with golf courses and an aerial tramway. Population (1990): 40 181.

● **Palm Sunday** ▶ In the Christian liturgical calendar the Sunday before Easter, commemorating Christ's last triumphal ride into Jerusalem (Mark 11). In many Churches crosses or palm leaves are distributed on this day.

● **palmyra** ▶ A ▷palm tree, *Borassus flabellier*, cultivated in India and Sri Lanka. The timber is used for construction and the leaves are used for thatch and made into a type of paper. The sugary sap from the flower heads is fermented to give palm wine and the kernels of the fruits are eaten.

● **Palmyra** ▶ (*or* Tadmor) 34 36N 38 15E An ancient Syrian desert city on the route of the E–W caravan trade in the 2nd and 3rd centuries AD. Palmyra came under Roman control in the 1st century AD but under ▷Zenobia regained its independence from 270 until 272, when it was reconquered and then destroyed; subsequently rebuilt, it was taken by the Muslims in 634. The ruins of the ancient city include the remains of the Temple of Bel (Palmyra's chief deity). Inscriptions in the Palmyric alphabet (developed from the ▷Aramaic) provide important information on Palmyra's trade. The modern town has a population (latest est) of 12 722.

● **palolo worm** ▶ (*or* paolo worm) A large marine ▷annelid worm, *Eunice viridis*, of the S Pacific. Palolo worms hunt for small prey among coral reefs and their reproduction is synchronized by the phases of the moon. The rear portion of the worm, containing eggs or sperm, separates and swims to the surface, discharging its gametes in the sea. Swarming worms are a local delicacy. Class: *Polychaeta*.

● **Palomar, Mount** ▶ A mountain in the USA, in California, the site of the Mount Palomar Observatory. Its 508 cm (200 in) reflecting telescope is among the largest in the world. Height: 1870 m (6140 ft). ▷*See also* Hale Observatories.

● **Palomino** ▶ A horse that has a yellow or golden coat and a white or silver mane and tail. Palominos are often Arabs or American Quarter horses but may be of any light saddle-horse breed. They are recognized as a colour breed in the USA but do not breed true.

● **palynology** ▶ (*or* pollen analysis) The study of pollen grains and their distribution in sedimentary rocks in order to provide information about life and environmental conditions of past geological ages. Pollen is extremely resistant to decay and therefore well preserved in rocks. The different genera and species are also very distinctive; therefore the presence of a certain type of pollen indicates the dominant flora—and therefore the climate and other conditions—of the period studied.

● **Pamirs** ▶ (*or* Pamir) A mountainous area of central Asia, situated mainly in Tadzhikistan and extending into China and Afghanistan. It consists of a complex of high ranges rising over 6000 m (20 000 ft), with the Tian Shan in the N, the Kunlun and Karakoram in the E, and the Hindu Kush in the W. Its highest point in Tadzhikistan is Communism Peak, at 7495 m (24 590 ft). In China it reaches 7719 m (25 326 ft) at Kungur.

● **Pampas** ▶ The flat treeless plains of Argentina. These extend W from the Atlantic Ocean to the Andes and are bordered by the Gran Chaco in the N and Patagonia in the S. They are of major agricultural importance in the E, producing wheat, corn, and beef in particular.

● **pampas cat** ▶ A small wild ▷cat, *Felis colocolo*, of South America. About the size of a domestic cat, with a long tail and greyish coat, it once hunted in grassland and swamps but is now very rare.

● **pampas grass** ▶ A perennial ▷grass of the genus *Cortaderia*, native to South America and widely cultivated as an ornamental. *C. argentea* grows in dense clumps, with leaves up to 2 m long and flowering stems over 3 m in length. The flowers usually form silvery or sometimes coloured plumes.

● **Pamplona** ▶ 42 49N 1 39W A city in NE Spain, in the Basque Provinces. It has a cathedral and holds a renowned fiesta (during which bulls are driven through the streets to the bullring) described by Ernest Hemingway, in *The Sun Also Rises* (1926). It is an agricultural centre and its industries include crafts and chemicals. Population (1995 est): 181 776.

● **Pan** ▶ The Greek god of shepherds and their flocks, the son of Hermes. He is usually portrayed with the legs, ears, and horns of a goat. He lived in the mountains and was associated especially with Arcadia, where he sported with the nymphs and played his pipes, known as the syrinx (*see* panpipes). He was believed to be the source of a sudden inexplicable fear, or panic, which sometimes overcame travellers in wild and remote places. The Roman equivalent was Sylvanus.

● **Panama, Isthmus of** ▶ A strip of land linking North and South America, between the Caribbean and the Pacific. Length: 676 km (420 mi). Minimum width: 50 km (31 mi).

● **Panama, Republic of** ▶ A country in Central America, occupying the Isthmus of Panama. Narrow coastal plains rise to volcanic mountains. The population is largely of mixed Indian, European, and African descent.
Economy: considerable revenue comes from receipts from the Panama Canal and from international capital. The main agricultural products are bananas, rice, sugar, and maize and fishing (especially for shrimps) is growing in importance. Industries include cement production and paper and food processing; oil refining was formerly an important source of exports but has now declined. Tourism has grown rapidly in recent decades and is now the main source of foreign revenue. The main exports include bananas, shrimps, and sugar.
History: soon after European discovery of the territory (by Colum-

bus in 1502), it was colonized by the Spanish; in 1513 Balboa made his famous journey across the isthmus. Panama later became part of the viceroyalty of Peru and then of New Granada. In 1821 it became part of the newly independent Gran Colombia, from which it broke free in 1903 after a revolution supported by the USA. In return the USA was given the right to construct and control the Panama Canal. The country's subsequent political history has been turbulent, leading to US military intervention on four occasions between 1908 and 1989. A military coup in 1968 brought Gen Omar Torrijos (1929–81) to power and in 1972 a new constitution gave him full executive powers for six years, while also initiating a presidency. Torrijos retired as head of state in 1978; after his death effective control passed to Gen Manuel ▷Noriega. The USA accused Noriega of involvement in drug trafficking and after a coup in 1989 failed, a US task force arrived. Noriega was deposed and taken to the USA, where he was convicted of drug charges (1992). In 1991 a new constitution abolished the armed forces. The presidential election of 1994 was won by Ernesto Pérez Balladares. In 1999 Mireya Moscoso became Panama's first woman head of state when she defeated Martín Torrijos, son of Gen Torrijos, in presidential elections.

Republic of Panama

Head of state	President Mireya Moscoso
Official language	Spanish
Official currency	balboa of 100 centésimos
Area	78 046 sq km (30 134 sq mi)
Population (1998 est)	2 767 000
Capital and main port	Panama City

● **Panama Canal** ▶ A canal across the Isthmus of Panama connecting the Atlantic and Pacific Oceans. Some 82 km (51 mi) long, it was begun in 1880 by the French Panama Canal Company under Ferdinand de ▷Lesseps but construction was halted in 1889 by bankruptcy. In 1903 the USA acquired the construction rights from newly independent Panama and the canal was opened to commercial traffic in 1914. By the 1903 treaty the USA acquired sovereignty in perpetuity over the **Panama Canal Zone**, a region extending 8 km (5 mi) on either side of the canal. In return Panama received $10 million and an annuity. In 1977–78 two treaties restored Panamanian sovereignty over the canal and the Zone (from 1979) while also ensuring their neutrality and the USA's continued use of its bases. Full control of the canal reverted to Panama on 31 December, 1999. Area: 1676 sq km (647 sq mi).

● **Panama City** ▶ 5 58N 79 31W The capital of Panama, situated in the centre of the country near the Pacific end of the Panama Canal. Founded by the Spanish in 1519 on the site of an Indian fishing village, it was destroyed by Henry Morgan and his pirates in 1671 and rebuilt two years later 8 km (5 mi) to the SW. It became capital of the newly independent Panama in 1904 and has expanded considerably since the opening of the Canal in 1914. The University of Panama was founded in 1935 and that of Santa Maria de la Antigua in 1965. Population (1995 est): 452 041.

● **Pan-American Highway** ▶ A system of highways connecting North and South America. When completed it will consist of about 26 000 km (16 150 mi) of roadway. First proposed as a single route, it is now a whole network of roads. Between Texas and Panama it is called the Inter-American Highway. The sections through the Central American states were built with US aid, while Mexico financed and built its own section. It will eventually connect with roads leading to Santiago, Buenos Aires, Montevideo, and Rio de Janeiro.

● **Panathenaea** ▶ In Greek religion, an annual Athenian summer festival consisting of rites, sacrifices, games, and contests in honour of ▷Athena. Its central feature, a procession up to the Parthenon with the goddess' new robe, is portrayed on the temple frieze.

● **Panay** ▶ An island in the central Philippines, in the Visayan Islands. Mountainous in the W, its central plain produces rice, maize, and sugar. It also has timber, fishing, and copper and coalmining industries. Area: 12 287 sq km (4744 sq mi). Population (latest est): 2 595 314. Chief town: Iloilo.

● **Panchen Lama** ▶ In ▷Tibetan Buddhism, the title of the chief abbot of Tashilhunpo monastery at Zhikatse, ranking second to the ▷Dalai Lama. He is said to be a reincarnation of Amitabha, the Buddha of Infinite Light. The last Panchen Lama, who was enthroned in 1952 at Tashilhunpo (where he remained despite Chinese occupation of Tibet), died in 1989. In 1995 Gendun Choekyi Nyima (1989–) was named as his reincarnation by the Dalai Lama. However, the boy was immediately seized by the Chinese authorities, who have attempted to impose their own candidate, Gyaincain Norbu (1989–).

● **pancreas** ▶ A gland, about 15 cm long, situated in the abdomen behind the stomach (*see* Plate II). When food passes into the intestine the pancreas secretes several digestive enzymes that drain into the intestine through the pancreatic duct. Small clusters of cells (called islets of Langerhans) scattered throughout the pancreas secrete the hormones ▷insulin and ▷glucagon, which control blood-sugar levels.

panda ▶ The elongated wrist bone of the giant panda acts like a thumb, enabling it to manipulate bamboo shoots.

● **panda** ▶ A bearlike mammal, (*Ailuropoda melanoleuca*), also called giant panda, that is very rare; its natural habitat is in the cold bamboo forests of central China, where it feeds on young bamboo shoots. Giant pandas, of which there are about 1000 left in the wild, are up to 1.6 m long, weigh 75–100 kg, and have black and white markings. Family *Ursidae* (*see* bear).

The unrelated red panda (*Ailurus fulgens*), also called the lesser panda, lives in the forests of the Himalayas and W China. 80–110 cm long including the bushy tail (30–50 cm), it is red-brown with black markings on its white face. Red pandas live in trees and feed on the ground at twilight on roots, nuts, lichens, and bamboo shoots. Family: *Procyonidae* (raccoons, kinkajous, etc.)

● **Pandanus** ▷*See* screw pine.

● **Pandarus** ▶ In Greek legend, a Trojan archer who wounded the Greek commander Menelaus and was killed by Diomedes. In the medieval story concerning Troilus and Cressida he is the lovers' go-between, giving rise to the English expressions "pander" (i.e. pimp) and "to pander to" (i.e. to exploit a weakness or craving).

● **Pandit, Vijaya Lakshmi** ▶ (1900–90) Indian diplomat; sister of Jawaharlal ▷Nehru. As a member of ▷Gandhi's movement of non-cooperation with the British she was imprisoned. Following independence she was ambassador to the Soviet Union (1947–49) and to the USA (1949–51); she then became president of the UN General Assembly (1953–54) and high commissioner to the UK (1955–61).

● **Pandora** ▶ In Greek mythology, the first woman, fashioned by ▷Hephaestus and invented by Zeus as his revenge on ▷Prometheus, who had stolen fire from heaven. She married Epimetheus, brother of Prometheus. Her dowry was a box, which, when opened, released all the varieties of evil and retained only hope.

● **Pangaea** ▷*See* continental drift.

● **pangolin** ▶ An armoured mammal belonging to the genus *Manis* and order *Pholidota* (7 species), of Africa and S Asia, also called scaly anteater. 30–80 cm long with long prehensile tails, pangolins are covered on their backs with overlapping horny scales. Toothless, with a long sticky tongue and strong claws, they sleep in deep burrows, emerging at night to feed on ants and termites. They can walk on their hind legs, climb trees, and curl up into a tight ball if attacked.

● **Pan Gu** ▶ (*or* P'an Ku) In Chinese Taoist mythology, the first man. His knowledge of ▷yin and yang enabled him to shape the world.

● **Pan Gu** ▶ (*or* P'an Ku; 32–92 AD) Chinese historian. He expanded the work of ▷Si-ma Qian to cover the history of the Han dynasty until his own time. His great work *The History of the Former Han* started the Chinese tradition of compiling dynastic histories.

● **panic disorder** ▶ An ▷anxiety disorder in which the sufferer experiences recurrent **panic attacks**, episodes of acute distress and fear, accompanied by rapid breathing, sweating, and a fast heart rate, in the absence of any realistic cause. The attacks are particularly common in those who suffer from agoraphobia (*see* phobia). Panic disorder is treated with antidepressants and by behaviour therapy.

● **panic grass** ▶ An annual or perennial ▷grass of the genus *Panicum* (500 species), mostly of the tropics and subtropics. The flowering stems, up to 80 cm high, have many branches, each bearing several slender-stalked spikelets (flower clusters). Some species are cultivated for their grain (*see* millet).

● **Panini** ▶ (6th or 5th century BC) Indian grammarian. Panini's analysis of Sanskrit, the *Ashtadhyayi*, is one of the earliest studies of a language and the most comprehensive grammatical work to appear before the 19th century. Although intended to regulate the use of Sanskrit rather than to teach it, the *Ashtadhyayi* is still used in some Brahman schools.

● **Pankhurst, Emmeline** ▶ (1858–1928) British suffragette, who founded, in Manchester, the Women's Social and Political Union (1903). She was imprisoned several times for destroying property, undergoing hunger strikes and forcible feeding. During World War I, she abandoned her militancy and encouraged the industrial recruitment of women. Her daughters **Dame Christabel Pankhurst** (1880–1958) and **Sylvia Pankhurst** (1882–1960) were also suffragettes. ▷*See* women's movement.

● **P'an Ku** ▷*See* Pan Gu.

● **panorama** ▶ A narrative scene or landscape painted on a large canvas, which was either hung up around the walls of a circular room or slowly unrolled before an audience. The first panorama was produced by the Scottish painter Robert Barker (1739–1806) in 1788. An antecedent of films, panoramas provided a popular form of entertainment as well as fulfilling an educational function in the 19th century.

● **panpipes** ▶ (*or* syrinx) An ancient musical instrument consisting of a row of small graduated pipes bound together. It is played by blowing across the holes. According to Greek legend it was invented by the deity Pan, who pursued the nymph Syrinx. When she was changed into a reed by Apollo, Pan made the instrument from the reed stem.

● **pansy** ▶ A popular annual or perennial garden plant that is a hybrid of the wild pansy (*Viola tricolor*), developed in the early 19th century. There are now many varieties, up to 20 cm high, with leafy stems and (usually) yellow, orange, purple, brown, or white flowers, up to 5 cm across. The wild pansy, or heartsease, found throughout Eurasia, has small flowers coloured purple, yellow, and white. Family: *Violaceae*. ▷*See also* violet.

● **Pantelleria Island** ▶ (ancient name: Cossyra) A volcanic island in Italy, in the Mediterranean Sea. Produce includes wine and raisins. Area: 83 sq km (32 sq mi). Population (latest est): 7860. Chief town: Pantelleria.

● **pantheism** ▶ Any belief or doctrine presenting the natural world, including man, as part of the divine. Pantheism is a predominant tendency in Hinduism but is frowned on by orthodox Christianity.

▷Spinoza's phrase equating God and Nature (*Deus sive natura*) was an influential formulation of the idea, which enjoyed some currency among 19th-century philosophers. The Romantic poets, particularly ▷Wordsworth, were also attracted to pantheism.

● **Pantheon** ▶ **1.** A temple dedicated to the worship of many gods. The most famous is that in Rome begun in 27 BC but rebuilt about 118 AD under Emperor Hadrian. It is a daring circular design built in concrete and topped by a huge concrete dome 43 m (142 ft) wide. In 609 AD it became the Church of Sta Maria Rotonda. **2.** A building honouring the famous. The best known is that in Paris designed by ▷Soufflot in 1759.

● **panther** ▶ A colour variety of leopard that has a great deal of black pigmentation, which sometimes extends to the tongue and gums. Panthers can occur among a litter of normally spotted leopards. The name "panther" is sometimes also applied to the ▷cougar.

● **pantomime** ▶ A British form of dramatic entertainment for children, traditionally performed at Christmas. Although the word also refers to other dramatic forms, such as mime plays, dumbshows, and 18th-century ballets on mythological themes, pantomime as a distinct genre developed during the 19th century from the English harlequinade (*see* Harlequin). Pantomime is now presented as an entertainment for children, especially at Christmas; it includes popular songs, slapstick comedy, and frequently acrobatics and other acts of skill. Pantomimes are based on fairy tales about such well-known characters as Cinderella and Aladdin. The principal boy is traditionally played by a girl in tights, and the dame, a comic old woman, by a man wearing a wig.

● **panzer** ▶ A mechanized division of the German army. The term panzer, meaning a coat of armour, has become widely used to denote armoured forces, tanks, self-propelled artillery, and armoured troop carriers.

● **paolo worm** ▷*See* palolo worm.

● **papacy** ▶ The office of the pope as temporal head of the Roman Catholic Church. Popes claim to be elected in direct line from St ▷Peter, to whom Christ deputed his authority on earth (Matthew 16.18–19) and who became the first bishop of Rome. The keys symbolizing this authority are still a papal emblem. The bishop of Rome, however, was not immediately recognized as pre-eminent and the title "Pope" was only formally reserved for him in 1073. In W Europe the papacy's political influence spread rapidly after 600 and Pope Leo III's coronation of ▷Charlemagne (800) marked the beginning of a relationship between the papacy and Holy Roman Empire that dominated Europe until the Reformation. In the East the papacy's attempt to assert its authority by excommunicating the Patriarch of Constantinople brought about the schism between the Roman Catholic and Orthodox Churches (1054; *see* East–West Schism; Filioque). Lesser and temporary schisms were caused by the election of antipopes, notably during the 14th century, when, after the popes had been in exile in Avignon (1309–77; *see* Avignon papacy), there was a period called the ▷Great Schism (1378–1417) during which there were rival popes in France and Rome. The Reformation seriously weakened the papacy's spiritual and temporal power, although papal territories in Italy remained under the pope's sovereignty. During the unification of Italy, these ▷papal states were appropriated (1870) and the pope's authority over the Vatican City was only formally acknowledged by the Italian state in the Lateran Treaty (1929). In 1870 the promulgation of the doctrine of papal ▷infallibility at the First Vatican Council (*see* Vatican Councils) caused further schism (*see* Old Catholics). This emphasis on papal supremacy was to some extent moderated by the Second Vatican Council (1962–65), which stressed the collegiate responsibility of the bishops and cardinals. In the 20th century the papacy resolutely opposed communism and is held to have contributed to its downfall; on the other hand its muted response to Nazism and Fascism was widely condemned as inadequate. The papacy has also maintained a ban on ▷contraception (formalized in Pope Paul VI's encyclical *Humanae Vitae*) in opposition to those who believe that poverty and hunger can only be controlled by population restraint (*see* overpopulation). Owing to air transport and modern media, the popes of the late 20th century were able to become more internationally visible than any of their predecessors: John Paul II became particularly well known for his global travels.

● **papain** ▶ A protein-digesting enzyme found in the fruit of the ▷papaw tree (*Carica papaya*). It is used in biochemical research and as a meat tenderizer.

● **papal states** ▶ The central Italian states under papal sovereignty between 756, when ▷Pepin the Short presented Ravenna to Pope Stephen II (reigned 752–57), and 1870. They included parts of Emilia-Romagna, Marche, Umbria, and Lazio. They were a major obstacle to the movement for Italian unification (*see* Risorgimento) but were finally annexed in 1870. The popes refused to recognize their loss of temporal power until the ▷Lateran Treaty (1929) established the Vatican City as an independent papal state.

● **Papandreou, Andreas George** ▶ (1919–96) Greek statesman; prime minister of Greece (1981–89, 1993–96). A socialist, he was imprisoned for political activities in 1967, but later emerged as leader of the opposition. In 1981 he became the first socialist prime minister of Greece; his liaison with a young woman (whom he later married) and allegations of corruption contributed to his electoral defeat in 1989. Cleared of the corruption charges in 1992, he was re-elected in 1993.

● **papaya** ▷*See* papaw.

● **papaw** ▶ (*or* papaya) A small tropical American tree, *Carica papaya*, cultivated throughout the tropics. About 7.5 m tall, it has lobed toothed leaves crowded at the tips of the branches and fragrant creamy-white flowers. The yellowish fruit resembles an elongated melon: its succulent pinkish or orange flesh encloses a mass of seeds. The fruits are eaten fresh, boiled, and in preserves or pickles. Family: *Caricaceae*. ▷*See also* papain.

● **Papeete** ▶ 17 32S 149 34W The capital of French Polynesia, in NW Tahiti. A tourist centre, it is a stop on many Pacific routes. Population (latest est): 78 814.

● **Papen, Franz von** ▶ (1879–1969) German statesman and diplomat; chancellor (1932). A Catholic Centre Party politician with extreme right-wing views, he resigned the chancellorship after six months and persuaded Hindenburg to appoint Hitler as chancellor (1933). Papen was ambassador to Austria (1934–38) and then to Turkey (1939–44). He was found not guilty at the Nuremberg war trials and only served three years of an eight-year prison sentence.

● **paper** ▶ A substance in sheet form made from the pulped cellulose fibres of wood, grass, cotton, etc., and used for writing and printing on, wrapping, cleaning, etc. The Chinese invented paper (c. 2nd

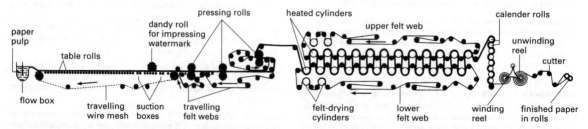

paper pulp · pressing rolls · dandy roll for impressing watermark · heated cylinders · upper felt web · calender rolls · table rolls · unwinding reel · cutter · flow box · travelling wire mesh · suction boxes · travelling felt webs · felt-drying cylinders · lower felt web · winding reel · finished paper in rolls

paper ▶ The Fourdrinier paper-making machine is one of the longest machines in use.

century BC) and the Arabs learnt the secret in 768 AD from Chinese prisoners of war at Samarkand. From Arab manufacture in the Middle East and Spain, paper spread to Byzantium (mid-11th century) and thence all over Europe. Foreign competition meant a slow start to British paper making, the first successful mill being set up about 1589.

All early paper was handmade: shallow wooden frames (moulds) with wire mesh bases (*see also* watermark) were dipped into vats of pulp and shaken until the pulp fibres felted together. The resulting sheets were dried, pressed, and, if necessary, sized (dipped in a gelatinous solution to render the surface less permeable). A machine for making paper in a continuous roll (or web) was not invented until 1798, in France. Brought to England in 1803 by Henry Fourdrinier (1766–1854), this machine, of which variants are still in use, picked up the pulp on a travelling wire mesh and shook it until the fibres interlaced and the water drained, before passing it to pressing and drying rollers.

The **pulp** for papermaking is obtained chiefly from wood, but also from esparto grass, rags, and increasingly from recycled wastepaper. Wood pulp may be produced by direct grinding of whole logs, as in making newsprint. For whiter higher quality paper, the wood undergoes a more complex chemical treatment. Esparto grass and rags are used for strong durable high-quality paper, such as bank notes and legal documents. Recycled wastepaper often requires careful sorting and de-inking and is usually mixed with fresh wood pulp.

● **paper mulberry** ► A shrub or small tree, *Broussonetia papyrifera*, native to E Asia and Polynesia but planted elsewhere as an ornamental, especially in the USA. Up to 15 m tall, it has oval pointed leaves, flowers in catkins, and round rough fruits, 2.5 cm across. Its bark is used in paper making and to produce tapa cloth in Polynesia. The bast fibres form the basis of coarse fabrics. Family: *Moraceae*.

● **papilionid butterfly** ► A butterfly belonging to the widely distributed mainly tropical family *Papilionidae* (about 800 species). Papilionids comprise the ▷swallowtail butterflies, with tail-like projections on the hindwings, the ▷bird-wing butterflies, with very large, often brightly coloured, wings, and the parnassians, which are mainly alpine.

● **papilloma** ► A harmless tumour that grows from the surface of the skin or from the lining of a hollow organ, for example the bladder, womb, or lungs. ▷Warts and ▷polyps are types of papilloma. If they bleed or undergo any other change they are best treated by removal.

● **papillon** ► A breed of toy dog, possibly of Spanish origin, associated with such illustrious owners as Mme de Pompadour and Marie Antoinette. Its name is derived from its large forward-facing ears, which resemble the wings of a butterfly (French word: *papillon*). The tail is held over the back and the long fine coat is white with coloured patches. Height: 20–28 cm.

● **Pappus of Alexandria** ► (4th century AD) Greek mathematician, who wrote an encyclopedia consisting of eight volumes, much of which survives.

● **paprika** ▷*See* Capsicum.

● **Papua New Guinea, State of** ► A country in the Pacific Ocean, E of Indonesia. It consists of the E part of ▷New Guinea and several islands, including the Bismarck Archipelago (including New Britain and New Ireland), the N part of the Solomon Islands (including Bougainville), and the Admiralty Islands. Most of the population are Melanesians.

Economy: subsistence agriculture and the growing of cash crops, such as coconuts, cocoa, coffee, and rubber, are the chief occupations. Livestock rearing is being developed and the country's dense rain forest provides timber. The chief mineral resource and export is copper; mining on Bougainville was halted by secessionist violence in 1989. Other exports include gold, coffee, cocoa, timber, and copra. Privatization and other economic reforms were introduced in the 1990s. In 1997 agriculture was devastated by drought, leading to a severe economic crisis. The country's massive external debt absorbs about a quarter of government spending.

History: the SE part of the island of New Guinea was annexed by

Queensland in 1883, becoming a British colony in 1888, known as the Territory of Papua. The NE part, formerly a German territory, came under Australian rule in 1914 as the Trust Territory of New Guinea. In 1921 the two territories including their islands were merged, later becoming a UN Trusteeship under Australia. This was renamed Papua New Guinea in 1971, achieved self-government within the Commonwealth in 1973, and became independent in 1975. In 1990 rebels on Bougainville declared independence, leading to a prolonged conflict in which at least 7000 people were killed. In 1997 an attempt to use foreign mercenaries to suppress the rebellion led to an army mutiny that forced the resignation of prime minister Sir Julius Chan: following elections, a government was formed under Bill Skate. A permanent ceasefire with the Bougainville rebels was signed in 1998, and a political settlement agreed in 2001. In 1997–98 Papua New Guinea suffered a series of natural disasters including severe drought and a massive tidal wave. In 1999 a new coalition was formed with Sir Mekere Morauta as prime minister.

State of Papua New Guinea

Head of state	Queen Elizabeth II, represented by the governor-general, Silas Atopare
Official languages	English, pidgin, and Motu
Official currency	kina of 100 toea
Area	462 840 sq km (178 656 sq mi)
Population (2001 est)	5 287 000
Capital and main port	Port Moresby

● **papyrus** ► An aquatic reedlike plant, *Cyperus papyrus*, up to 3 m tall, originally cultivated in the Nile delta and now growing wild in Africa and in Syria. The ancient Egyptians used it to make paper. It was also used for rope, mats, sails, and shoes, and the pith was a common food. Family: *Cyperaceae*.

● **parabola** ► The curve, formed by a ▷conic section, in which the distance from a fixed point (focus) and a fixed line (directrix) are equal. In Cartesian coordinates a standard form of its equation is $y^2 = 4ax$, for a parabola that is symmetrical about the *x*-axis and cuts it at the origin (vertex).

● **Paracel Islands** ► An archipelago of coral islands and reefs in the South China Sea, SE of Hainan Island. They lie above oil deposits and were seized by China from Vietnam in 1974.

● **Paracelsus** ► (Theophrastus Bombastus von Hohenheim; 1493–1541) Swiss physician, whose radical ideas influenced the development of medicine during the Renaissance. Paracelsus established a reputation for arrogance and aroused controversy by publicly burning the works of ▷Avicenna and ▷Galen, denouncing quack remedies, and clashing with the medical establishment. He stressed the importance of chemical compounds in treating disease, disputed that mental illness was caused by demons, and linked goitre with minerals in drinking water.

● **paracetamol** ► A mild analgesic that also reduces fever, widely used for headache, menstrual pain, children's infections, etc. Unlike ▷aspirin it causes no stomach irritation, but overdoses can cause liver damage.

● **parachuting** ► The use of a parachute (a fabric canopy) to float down to the ground, usually from an aircraft, either if the aircraft is about to crash, as a way of landing troops in an area, or as a form of sport. Parachutes were used for entertainment long before they were used for safety; the first successful parachute descent was made in 1797, when Jacques Garneria jumped from a balloon over Paris. In World War I, parachutes were first used by pilots of aircraft who were shot down. The first parachuting contest was held in 1926. In competitions contestants use vents in the parachute to steer onto a target area, a red cross with arms 5 m (16 ft) long and 1 m (3 ft) wide. In the middle is a red disc 10 cm (4 in) in diameter. Top-class parachutists land exactly on the disc. ▷*See also* skydiving.

● **paradox** ► An apparently self-contradictory statement that contains the seed of a valuable idea. Religious teachings are often expressed in paradoxes of this kind, for example "Love your enemies." In logic, a paradox is a proposition in which one or more of its premises are inconsistent with its conclusion. "All Cretans are liars" is the classical example. When made by the Cretan Epimenedes the statement is false, as he is a Cretan and therefore a liar; therefore all Cretans cannot be liars. Such paradoxical propositions were used by Bertrand ▷Russell in establishing the bases of mathematical logic.

● **paraffin** ▶ **1.** (*or* kerosene) A mixture of hydrocarbons that boil in the range 150–300°C and have a relative density of 0.78–0.83. It is obtained from crude ▷oil by distillation and is used as a fuel for heating and aircraft. **2.** ▷*See* alkanes.

● **paraffin wax** ▶ A wax obtained during the refining of crude ▷oil. Fully refined, it is a white tasteless solid (mp 50–60°C) consisting of higher ▷alkanes; it is extensively used in the manufacture of waxed papers, candles, and polishes (especially microcrystalline wax polishes).

● **para-gliding** ▷*See* hang-gliding.

● **Paraguay, Republic of** ▶ A landlocked country in the centre of South America. It is divided by the River Paraguay into two zones: an area of fertile plains and hills to the E and the semidesert of the Gran Chaco to the W. The great majority of the population is of mixed Spanish and Guarani Indian descent.
Economy: chiefly agricultural, with livestock rearing being of particular importance. Meat packing is one of the main industries, and meat remains one of the principal exports, although this has been reduced since the EC ban on meat imports. Other exports include cotton, oilseed, timber, and coffee. The main crops are cotton, soya beans, cassava, and sugar cane and there are extensive forests yielding many kinds of timber. Mineral resources are sparse, but some limestone, salt, and kaolin is produced. Hydroelectricity is a major source of power, the dam at Itaipú being the largest in the world. An economic liberalization programme was introduced in the 1990s and has had some success in attracting foreign investment. Paraguay's external debt has been reduced but remains large.
History: explored by the Spanish in the early 16th century, it subsequently became a Spanish colony, forming part of the viceroyalty of Peru and later (1776) of the new viceroyalty of Río de la Plata. It became independent of Spain in 1811, and in 1814 José Gaspar Rodríguez de Francia (1766–1840) was elected dictator, becoming dictator for life in 1817. From 1844 to 1870 Paraguay was dominated by the López family. The population suffered great losses in the War of the ▷Triple Alliance (1865–70) against Brazil, Argentina, and Uruguay and again in the ▷Chaco War (1932–35) with Bolivia. A period of political unrest was ended in 1954, when Gen Alfredo Stroessner (1912–   ) seized power and became president. During the 1970s Stroessner's government attracted criticism for human rights violations; it was overthrown in a coup (1989) led by Gen Andrés Rodríguez (1922–97), who became president. In 1993 Paraguay's first democratic elections were held and a civilian, Juan Carlos Wasmosy, was elected president. Presidential and legislative elections in 1998 resulted in victory for Raúl Cubas Grau and his Colorado Party. However, his action in freeing and pardoning his ally Gen Lino Oviedo, who had been imprisoned for leading a coup attempt in 1996, led parliament to begin impeachment proceedings in 1999. The crisis intensified in March, when Cubas's main opponent, Vice President Luis Maria Argana, was assassinated by supporters of the president. After a week of street violence, Cubas resigned and fled abroad to escape arrest; Gonzalez Macchi assumed the role of president. Paraguay is a member of the OAS and LAIA.

Republic of Paraguay

Head of state	President Gonzalez Macchi
Official language	Spanish; the majority speak Guaraní
Official currency	guaraní of 100 céntimos
Area	406 752 sq km (157 042 sq mi)
Population (1998 est)	5 223 000
Capital and main (river) port	Asunción

● **Paraguay, River** ▶ (Portuguese name: Rio Paraguai) A river in South America. Rising in Brazil in Mato Grosso state, it flows S to the Río Paraná in SW Paraguay. It is an important means of transport. Length: about 2400 km (1500 mi).

● **Paraguayan War** ▷*See* Triple Alliance, War of the.

● **parakeet** ▶ A small seed-eating ▷parrot characterized by a long tapering tail and a predominantly green plumage and found especially in SE Asia and Australia. Large flocks may damage crops; brightly coloured species are popular as cagebirds. ▷*See also* budgerigar; rosella.

● **parallax** ▶ The apparent displacement of an object against a distant background when viewed from different positions. In astronomy **diurnal parallax** is the angular displacement in the apparent position of a celestial body as a result of viewing it from the earth's surface rather than its centre. **Annual parallax** is caused by observations being made from the earth rather than the centre of the sun.

● **paralysis** ▶ Failure of a muscle or a group of muscles to work. This is commonly caused by damage to the nerve (and its connections) supplying the muscle, as resulting from injury or infection (*see* poliomyelitis), but it may also be due to failure of the nerve impulse to be transmitted to the muscle (as in myasthenia gravis) or by wasting of the muscle (as in ▷muscular dystrophy). In Western countries paralysis is most common following a ▷stroke: this causes damage to the part of the brain that controls movement and commonly results in **hemiplegia**, i.e. one half of the body and face becomes paralysed. ▷Multiple sclerosis also causes paralysis. **Paraplegia** (paralysed legs) results from injury to the spinal cord. **Quadriplegia** (paralysed legs and arms) results when the spinal cord is damaged close to the brain.

● **paramagnetism** ▶ A form of ▷magnetism occurring in materials that when placed in a ▷magnetic field have an internal field stronger than that outside. This is caused by the presence in atoms or molecules of electrons with unpaired spins. The atom or molecule therefore acts as a tiny magnet (*see* ferromagnetism). In the presence of an external magnetic field these magnets tend to align with the field, reinforcing it. The effect is destroyed by random thermal motion and, except at low temperatures and high field strengths, the ▷permeability is inversely proportional to the temperature.

● **Paramaribo** ▶ 5 52N 55 14W The capital and main port of Suriname, near the N coast on the River Suriname. Founded by the French in 1540, it was later under English and then Dutch rule. The University of Suriname was founded in 1968. Population (1993 est): 200 970.

● **Paramecium** ▶ A genus of microscopic single-celled organisms (⌐protozoa), sometimes called slipper animalcules, found in fresh water. They are slipper-shaped, 0.1–0.3 mm long, and covered with cilia, which are used for swimming and to waft bacteria and small protozoans into the gullet. They reproduce asexually by binary ▷fission and sexually by ▷conjugation. Phylum: ▷*Ciliophora*.

● **paramedical personnel** ▶ Trained staff who do not have a full medical qualification but who carry out medical duties in a relatively narrow field. In hospitals in the developed world radiographers, physiotherapists, dieticians, etc., are regarded as paramedical personnel. In the ambulance service paramedics are trained to use portable life-saving equipment at the site of an accident and to fulfil the role of a doctor until the patient can reach a hospital. In the developing world, nurses and others without full medical qualifications are used to provide primary health care, such as immunization, administration of certain medicines, and checking children for certain symptoms. In Africa and China paramedical personnel of this type (often called "barefoot doctors") are widely used.

● **Paraná** ▶ 31 45S 60 30W A city in E Argentina, on the Río Paraná. It is an outlet for agricultural produce (especially cattle, sheep, and grain). Notable buildings include the Cathedral of Paraná (1883). Population (1991): 277 338.

● **Paraná, Rio** ▶ (Spanish name: Río Paraná) A river in South America. Formed by the confluence of the Rio Grande and Rio Paranaíba in SE central Brazil, it flows generally S for 2900 km (1800 mi) to join the River Uruguay and form the Río de la Plata. The Itaipu Dam, which is sited at Foz do Iguaçu near the Paraguayan border, was opened in 1982.

● **paranoia** ▶ A mental disorder in which the patient is governed by a system of irrational beliefs (delusions). The sufferer may believe that he is being persecuted, or betrayed, or that he is overwhelmingly important. The condition, which can result from ▷schizophrenia, ▷alcoholism, or ▷manic-depressive psychosis, is treated according to the cause.

● **paraplegia** ▷*See* paralysis.

● **parapsychology** ▷*See* extrasensory perception.

● **Paraquat** ▶ ($C_9H_{20}N_2(SO_4)_2$) The trade name for a yellow water-soluble solid used as a weedkiller. It is highly toxic, concentrates in the lungs, and causes kidney damage. Treatment for Paraquat poisoning, by ▷activated charcoal or some other absorbing material, must be carried out immediately.

● **parasite** ▶ An organism living in or on another organism of a different species (called the host), from which it obtains food and protection: the relationship may or may not be harmful to the host. A facultative parasite is one that becomes parasitic only under certain conditions, while an obligate parasite must always live parasitically. Many parasites have complex life cycles, with one or more intermediate hosts (of different species) supporting the parasite in the larval stages of its development. The study of parasites—**parasitology**—is of great importance in medicine since many parasites either cause or transmit disease. Disease-causing parasites include bacteria, fungi, and other microorganisms (*see* infection) and tapeworms; mites, ticks, and fleas are examples of external parasites that transmit disease. Some plants are partly parasitic, usually on other plants; mistletoe is an example.

● **parasol mushroom** ▶ An edible mushroom, *Lepiota procera*, found in clearings and around the edges of deciduous woods. Its cap, 10–20 cm in diameter, is greyish brown with darker scales. The scales form rings on the stem, which has a double collar just below the cap. Phylum: ▷*Basidiomycota*.

● **parathyroid glands** ▶ Two pairs of small endocrine glands lying immediately behind the thyroid gland. These glands secrete **parathyroid hormone** in response to a reduction in the level of calcium in the blood. This hormone causes the release of calcium from the bones and its transfer to the blood. Deficiency of parathyroid hormone (and therefore lack of calcium in the blood) results in muscle spasms and cramps (tetany).

● **paratyphoid fever** ▶ Infection of the digestive tract caused by the bacterium *Salmonella paratyphi*. It is a mild form of ▷typhoid fever and can be treated by antibiotic drugs.

● **parchment** ▶ Animal skin, usually of the goat, sheep, or calf, treated for writing on but untanned. It derives its name from Pergamum, where in the 2nd century BC the development of improved methods of cleaning, stretching, and scraping skins enabled them to have writing on both sides. It was used for manuscripts and early bound books. More delicate skin from young animals is called **vellum**. Parchment now often describes high-grade paper manufactured from wood pulp and rag, treated with a special finish. ▷*See also* leather.

● **parchment worm** ▶ An ▷annelid worm, belonging to the genus *Chaetopterus*, that lives in a U-shaped tube made of parchment-like material on muddy shores of the Atlantic and Pacific Oceans. Up to 25 cm long, the worm draws in a current of water by beating its paddle-shaped appendages, trapping food particles in a bag of mucus. Parchment worms are strongly luminescent. Class: *Polychaeta*.

● **Pardubice** ▶ (German name: Pardubitz) 50 03N 15 45E A town in the Czech Republic, in E Bohemia on the River Elbe. It has an architecturally distinguished square containing a 16th-century gothic castle and the Green Gate (1507). Population (1993 est): 163 000.

● **Paré, Ambroise** ▶ (1510–90) French surgeon and one of the fathers of modern surgery. As barber-surgeon to the army, Paré discarded the practice of treating wounds with boiling oil and hot irons in favour of cleansing, the use of ointments, and surgery to tie off major arteries.

● **parenchyma** ▶ The general packing tissue of plants, consisting of simple undifferentiated cells. In young stems, parenchyma encloses the vascular (conducting) tissue and provides support for the plant.

● **Pareto, Vilfredo** ▶ (1848–1932) Italian economist and sociologist. Pareto's early work in economics culminated in Pareto's Law, which held that the distribution of incomes could be defined by a mathematical formula. His later sociological work *The Mind and Society* (1916) attacked political liberalism while supporting the free market economy. He is also known for his theory on the rise and fall of governing elites.

● **Paris** ▶ 48 52N 2 18E The capital of France and a department of the Paris Region, situated in the N of the country on the River Seine. One of Europe's greatest cities, Paris dominates France as the administrative, commercial, and cultural centre. It is also an important industrial base, and many international organizations, including UNESCO, have their headquarters here. The city is in turn dominated by its river, which contributes to the division of Paris into several distinct districts, each with its own characteristics. At the heart of the city, the Île de la Cité contains the cathedral of ▷Notre-Dame de Paris, the Palais de Justice, and the 13th-century Sainte Chapelle. On the Left Bank lie Montparnasse and the Latin Quarter, which is known for its associations with writers and artists and still contains some faculties of the university of the Sorbonne (founded in the 12th century) although much of it has now been moved to other sites. On the Right Bank stands the Palais du Louvre, one of the world's most important museums, and not far away is the avant-garde Pompidou Centre (1977), housing Paris's museum of modern art. Further W is a series of radiating boulevards meeting at the Place Charles de Gaulle (formerly Place de l'Étoile), which were laid out by Baron ▷Haussmann in the 19th century. The Champs Élysées runs from the ▷Arc de Triomphe at the centre of the Place Charles de Gaulle to the Place de la Concorde. Further N lies Montmartre (the artists' colony of Paris until the migration to Montparnasse in the 1920s), dominated by the Basilica of the Sacré Coeur (1919). The tunnels beneath Montmartre, created by quarrying, are now a major problem, causing subsidence and structural damage to buildings. To the S of the

Paris ▶ The Trocadéro gardens with the Palais de Chaillot (museums) beyond, as seen across the Seine from the Eiffel Tower. The Pont de l'Iéna (foreground) was built in 1813 to celebrate Napoleon's victory at the Battle of Jena.

Seine is the ▷Eiffel Tower, built for an exhibition in 1889. Nearby is the Hôtel des Invalides (1676), built by Louis XIV for wounded war veterans; at its centre is the Dôme Church, in which the body of Napoleon Bonaparte lies. To the W of the city, on the outskirts, lies La Défense, an enormous business centre begun in 1958 and now occupying 80 ha (198 acres). Some 32 km (20 mi) to the E of the city is the Euro Disney theme park, which opened in 1992.

History: the earliest known settlement was on the Île de la Cité in Roman times. According to legend, St Denis became the first bishop in the 3rd century AD and Ste Geneviève saved the city from sacking by German tribes in the 5th century. In the 6th century Clovis made it the capital of his Frankish kingdom but it later suffered attacks from Vikings. It regained importance as the capital under the ▷Capetians and from the 13th century its independence as a city increased. Since the storming of the Bastille (1789), heralding the beginning of the French Revolution, it has been the scene of many revolts, such as the ▷July Revolution and the ▷Revolution of 1848; the most recent disturbance was in May, 1968. Occupied by the Germans in World War II, it was liberated by the Allies in 1944. Population (1990): 2 152 000.

● **Paris** ▶ In Greek legend, a son of ▷Priam and Hecuba. He was brought up as a shepherd on Mount Ida. His abduction of ▷Helen with the help of Aphrodite caused the ▷Trojan War, during which he killed Achilles and was himself killed by Philoctetes. ▷*See also* Eris.

● **Paris, Matthew** ▶ (c. 1200–59) English chronicler. He became a monk of the Benedictine abbey of St Albans in 1217 and was a member of the court of Henry III. His careful coverage of the years 1235–59 form the second part of his major work, the *Chronica majora*, a history of the world from the Creation to 1259.

● **Paris, Treaties of** ▶ **1.** (1763) The treaty that ended the ▷Seven Years' War. France ceded its North American territories E of the Mississippi River to Britain and Louisiana to Spain, from which Britain acquired Florida. Britain also gained Minorca, Senegal, Grenada, St Vincent, Dominica, and Tobago. **2.** (1783) The treaty that ended the ▷American Revolution. US independence was recognized and Britain ceded Florida to Spain. **3.** (1814) The peace between France and the victorious allies (Prussia, Russia, Austria, Britain, Sweden, and Portugal) that confirmed Napoleon's abdication and limited France to its 1792 boundaries. **4.** (1815) The peace following Napoleon's final defeat at Waterloo that reduced France to its 1789 boundaries. **5.** (1856) The peace that ended the ▷Crimean War. Russia guaranteed the neutrality of the Black Sea and ceded S Bessarabia to Moldavia.

● **parish** ▶ In England, the smallest unit of local government and ecclesiastical administration. Defined as a district under the care of a priest or team of priests, parishes date from the 7th century, if not earlier. As more churches were built during the middle ages, parishes became smaller, until they usually consisted of a single large estate or village with its outlying communities. Parishes first became units of civil administration in the 16th century, when they became responsible for highways and (from 1601) the ▷Poor Laws. Authority generally rested in the hands of the local landowner. With the movements of populations in the late 18th and 19th centuries, the boundaries of civil and ecclesiastical parishes became increasingly divergent. Larger parishes (currently defined as those with over 200 electors) now have elected parish councils, whose functions include the maintenance of footpaths, bus shelters, open spaces, etc. The Welsh and Scottish equivalent of the (civil) parish is the **community**. Community councils are units of local government in Wales but in Scotland have only a consultative role.

● **Paris Peace Conference** ▶ (1919–20) A conference of representatives of the Allied and Associated Powers held after World War I. Proceedings were dominated by the USA (Woodrow Wilson), France (Clemenceau), the UK (Lloyd George), and Italy (Orlando). Five treaties arose from the conference: ▷Versailles with Germany (1919); Saint-Germain with Austria (1920); Neuilly with Bulgaria (1919); Trianon with Hungary (1920); and Sèvres with Turkey (1920). In addition the conference ratified the Covenant of the ▷League of Nations.

● **parity** ▶ In ▷particle physics, the concept of left- and right-handedness. According to the law of conservation of parity, no fundamental distinction exists between left and right and the laws of physics apply equally to left- and right-handed systems. In 1957 this principle was shown to be violated in ▷weak interactions between certain elementary particles. For example, when a neutron decays the electron produced is always left-polarized (i.e. spins in a direction opposite to that of its motion), whereas if parity was conserved there would be equal numbers of left- and right-polarized electrons. This lack of parity provides a fundamental distinction between left and right. The parity of elementary particles is expressed as a ▷quantum number.

● **Park, Mungo** ▶ (1771–c. 1806) Scottish explorer. A surgeon, he made two explorations of the River Niger. In 1795–96 he ascended the Niger from the mouth of the River Gambia, crossed the Sénégal Basin, and was imprisoned by Arabs. Escaping, he eventually returned to Pisania (now Karantaba, The Gambia). His *Travels in the Interior Districts of Africa* (1797) related his adventures. In 1805, with 40 companions, he resumed his exploration. The expedition was attacked by Africans and Park died.

● **Park Chung Hee** ▶ (1917–79) South Korean statesman and general; president from 1963 until his murder in 1979. He served in the Japanese army in World War II and then in the South Korean army. He led the coup that established a military regime in 1961. In 1972 he declared martial law and assumed quasi-dictatorial powers.

● **Parker, Charlie (Christopher)** ▶ (1920–55) US Black jazz saxophonist and composer, known as "Bird" or "Yardbird." With Dizzy ▷Gillespie he originated the ▷bop style of jazz and appeared with a number of bands. In the 1950s he made recordings with a band containing strings and wind and was regarded as one of the greatest of all jazz musicians.

● **Parker, Dorothy Rothschild** ▶ (1893–1967) US humorous writer. Famous as a wit and regular member of the ▷Algonquin Round Table, she established her reputation while drama critic for *Vanity Fair* and the *New Yorker* (1927–33). Her popular short stories and sketches were collected in *Here Lies* (1939), but she also wrote poems, collected in *Not So Deep As a Well* (1936), plays, and filmscripts.

● **Parker, Matthew** ▶ (1504–75) Anglican churchman. A moderate Protestant reformer, he was deprived of his preferments under Queen Mary. As Archbishop of Canterbury (1559–75) under Elizabeth I, he maintained a strongly independent Anglican position between Roman Catholicism and Puritanism and revised the ▷Thirty-Nine Articles.

● **Parkes** ▶ 33 10S 148 13E A market town in Australia, in New South Wales in the Lachlan River Valley. A 210-ft (64-m) dish radiotelescope, one of the largest in the world, is nearby. Population (latest est): 9047.

● **Parkes, Sir Henry** ▶ (1815–96) Australian statesman; prime minister of New South Wales (1872–75, 1877, 1878–83, 1887–89, 1889–91). Born in England, he emigrated to Australia in 1839. He campaigned (1849–52) against the British transportation of convicts to Australia and as prime minister worked for the federation of the Australian states and for compulsory free education.

● **Parkinson, (Cyril) Northcote** ▶ (1909–93) British author, historian, and journalist. While professor of history at the University of Malaya (1950–58), he wrote his well-known *Parkinson's Law* (1958), a study of business administration containing the aphorisms that work expands to fill the time allotted to it and that subordinates multiply at a fixed rate regardless of the amount of work produced. His other books include *Britain in the Far East* (1955), *The Law and the Profits* (1960), and *Big Business* (1974).

● **Parkinson's disease** ▶ A chronic disease affecting the part of the brain controlling voluntary movement, first described in 1817 by a British physician, James Parkinson (1755–1824). It occurs most commonly in older people, being associated with the ageing process. The symptoms are tremor of the hands and mouth, stiffness, and difficulty in initiating movements. Sometimes this group of symptoms, known as **parkinsonism**, may result from infection, side effects of drugs, or injury. The condition is treated with drugs, including ▷levodopa.

● **Parkman, Francis** ▶ (1823–93) US historian. *The Oregon Trail* (1849) records an adventurous expedition among the American Indians. Thenceforth he suffered from illness and blindness but completed a history of *France and England in North America* (9 vols, 1851–92). His other works include *History of the Conspiracy of Pontiac* (1851).

● **parlement** ▶ The supreme court of France until the French Revolution. The parlement of Paris developed in the 12th century out of the king's court. Membership was at first elective but by the 14th century seats could be bought and in 1614 became hereditable with the introduction of the *paulette* (annual right), which secured a seat by payment of an annual fee. From its duty, and right of refusal, to register royal edicts the parlement derived considerable political power and by the 17th century had become a bastion of reaction. It impeded government attempts to put its own house in order and in 1792, in the wake of the French Revolution, the parlement of Paris, together with its less influential provincial counterparts, was abolished.

● **parliament** ▶ The legislative assembly of a country. In the UK parliament is the supreme legislature; it consists of the sovereign, the House of Lords, and the House of Commons; its seat is the ▷Palace of Westminster. Parliament developed in the 13th century from the ▷Curia Regis (King's Court), in which the monarch consulted with his barons. In 1213, 1254, and 1258 representatives of the shires were also summoned to attend parliament and in 1265 the parliament summoned by Simon de ▷Montfort included borough representatives—the origins of the House of Commons. The **Model Parliament** (1295) established the Commons as a representative body, its members having full authority to act without further consultation on behalf of their constituents. By the reign of Edward III (1327–77) Lords and Commons, meeting separately, were recognized constituents of government. Parliament's power declined in the later middle ages but Thomas Cromwell's use of parliament in legislating the breach with Rome (*see* Reformation) gave it a new self-consciousness. Increasingly assertive under Elizabeth I (1559–1603), its conflict with James I and Charles I over the extent to which the Crown was answerable to parliament led to the Civil War (1642–51) and the establishment of republican government under Oliver Cromwell. Following the Restoration of the monarchy in 1660, the attempts of James II to rule arbitrarily led to the Glorious Revolution (1688), which achieved the beginning of parliamentary ascendancy over the Crown. The 18th century saw the emergence of party politics (*see* Whigs; Tories) and of a ▷prime minister and the development of ▷cabinet government. In the 19th century the ▷Reform Acts of 1832, 1867, and 1884 greatly reduced the influence of the House of Lords, which lost its veto power by the Parliament Act (1911).

Until the present government began its promised reform of the House of Lords in 1999 its membership comprised 26 bishops and archbishops, over 750 hereditary peers, and about 500 life peers (*see* peerage). In 1999 the hereditary peers were removed except for a rump of 92, who will remain until further reform has been completed. Although it is envisaged that the reformed house will have about 600 members, some of whom will be elected and some appointed, attempts to devise a precise formula have met with little agreement. MPs will be given a free vote on a series of options in 2002 and it is hoped that the reform will be complete by 2005. The House of Commons has (1999) 659 members of parliament (MPs), each representing a geographical constituency, and is regulated by the ▷Speaker of the House of Commons. Legislation is introduced in the form of private or public bills. Private bills originate outside parliament, for example with a local authority, which may wish to acquire certain powers. Public bills are sponsored by the government or a private member and may be introduced in either house. After a first reading a bill will be printed and then debated in a second reading. It is then referred to a committee by which it may be amended. (A private bill, when opposed, is considered by a committee, which hears both sides of the case.) Its amendments are considered by the whole house (in proceedings known as the report stage) and it then receives a third reading after which it is sent to the other house, where it goes through a similar procedure. The Lords may not veto a finance bill for longer than a month and may veto other public bills (private bills rarely cause controversy after the first hearing) for only one session. After passing both houses the bill receives the royal assent and becomes an Act of Parliament. Radio broadcasting of parliament began in 1978. Televising of the Lords began in 1986 and of the Commons in 1989.

● **parliamentary commissioner for administration** ▷*See* ombudsman.

● **Parma** ▶ 44 48N 10 19E A city in N Italy, in Emilia-Romagna. Dating from Roman times, it became an important cultural centre in the middle ages. Its university was established in 1222 and it has a romanesque cathedral and a 16th-century palace, damaged in 1944 during World War II. The centre of an agricultural district, Parma's industries include the manufacture of Parmesan cheese. Population (1998 est): 167 165.

● **Parmenides** ▶ (c. 510–c. 450 BC) Greek philosopher, born at Elea (S Italy). According to Parmenides, things either are or are not. Only "being" is real; "not-being" is illusory. For change to occur "being" must become "not-being," which is absurd. Therefore change does not occur. But our senses indicate that change does occur: therefore our senses are misleading, and "being," as apprehended by reason, is the only reality. Parmenides described "being" as finite, spherical, timeless, undifferentiated, and indivisible. His doctrines influenced ▷Plato. ▷*See also* Heraclitus; Zeno of Elea.

● **Parmigianino** ▶ (Girolamo Francesco Maria Mazzola; 1503–40) Italian painter, born in Parma (hence his nickname). After painting frescoes in S Giovanni Evangelista, Parma, he moved to Rome (1524) but was forced to flee to Bologna during the sack of Rome (1527). His ▯mannerism is evident in the *Madonna with the Long Neck* (Uffizi Gallery, Florence). His portraits include *Self-Portrait in a Convex Mirror* (Kunsthistorisches Museum, Vienna).

● **Parnassians** ▶ A group of French poets in the mid-19th century who reacted against the subjectivism of the Romantics and whose poetry was characterized by objective restraint and technical precision. They were led by ▷Leconte de Lisle, whose disciples included ▷Sully-Prudhomme, Théodore de Banville (1823–91), and J.-M. de Hérédia (1842–1905).

● **Parnassus, Mount** ▶ (Modern Greek name: Parnassós) 38 32N 22 41E A mountain in S central Greece, formerly held sacred to Apollo and the Muses. Height: 2457 m (8061 ft).

● **Parnell, Charles Stewart** ▶ (1846–91) Irish politician, who in 1880 became the leader of the ▷Home Rule party in the British House of Commons. Parnell, an MP from 1875, reconciled constitutional and radical forces and enjoyed widespread popular support in Ireland. He allied his party with the Liberals in 1886, when Gladstone introduced the Home Rule bill. Parnell remained a dominant political figure until 1890, when he fell from grace after being cited in a divorce suit brought against Katherine ▷O'Shea, whom he then married.

● **parole** ▶ The conditional release of a prisoner after a portion of the sentence has been served. In the UK, under the Criminal Justice Act (1991), a person sentenced to imprisonment for between 12 months and 4 years must be paroled after serving half the sentence. Those sentenced to 4 years or more may be considered for parole after serving half their sentence by local review committees, which advise the Home Secretary, who may release the prisoner or refer the case to the Parole Board. In such cases the Parole Board defines the conditions under which the prisoner may be released. Under the Crime (Sentences) Act (1997) responsibility for releasing juveniles convicted of murder is the responsibility of the Parole Board rather than the Home Secretary. All prisoners sentenced to more than 4 years' imprisonment must be paroled after serving two-thirds of their sentences. If a prisoner on parole commits an offence during the period of the original sentence he or she may have to serve the outstanding part of the original sentence.

● **Páros** ▶ A Greek island in the S Aegean Sea, in the Cyclades. Marble has been quarried here for sculpture since ancient times. Area: 195 sq km (75 sq mi). Population (latest est): 7881.

● **parquetry** ▶ The inlaying of geometrically shaped pieces of wood into the plane surfaces of furniture, floors, staircases, etc. The word is often now used to describe geometric ▷marquetry, particularly as used on 17th- and 18th-century furniture.

● **Parr, Catherine** ▶ (1512–48) The sixth wife (1543–47) of Henry VIII of England. She was noted for her kindness to her three stepchildren. After Henry's death, she married (1547) Thomas, Baron Seymour of Sudeley (d. 1549).

Parthenon ► Dominating the city of Athens for over 2400 years, this damaged triumph of classical Greek architecture remains a magnificent sight.

● **Parramatta ►** 33 10S 148 13E A city in Australia, in New South Wales on the Parramatta River comprising a suburb of Sydney. Founded in 1788, it is the second oldest European settlement in Australia. Its buildings include Elizabeth Farm House (1793), the nation's oldest existing farmhouse.

● **parrot ►** A bird belonging to the family (*Psittacidae*; 300 species) occurring worldwide in warm regions. 10–100 cm long, parrots have a compact body, a short neck, and strong rounded wings suited for fast flight over short distances. The plumage is typically brightly coloured and the short stout hooked bill is used to open nuts and to feed on fruits and seeds. Most are arboreal and excellent climbers, having clawed feet with rough scaly toes. They are gregarious and have a harsh screaming voice. Many species are classified as endangered. Order: *Psittaciformes*. ▷*See also* cockatoo; kakapo; lory; lovebird; macaw; parakeet.

● **parrot disease** ▷*See* psittacosis.

● **parrot fish ►** A fish, also called parrot wrasse, belonging to the family *Scaridae*, found among tropical reefs. Up to 1.2 m long, it has a deep often brilliantly coloured body and the teeth are fused to form a hard beak, which is used to feed on coral, molluscs, and seaweed. Order: *Perciformes*.

● **Parry, Sir (Charles) Hubert (Hastings) ►** (1848–1918) British composer. He composed many operatic, orchestral, choral, chamber, and solo works, the best known of which is the unison choral song *Jerusalem* (1916). He was the director of the Royal College of Music (1894–1918) and professor of music at Oxford University (1900–08).

● **Parry, Sir William Edward ►** (1790–1855) British navigator, who made three journeys in search of the ▷Northwest Passage (1819–20, 1821–23, 1824–25). In 1827 he tried to reach the Pole by sledge from Spitsbergen.

● **parsec ►** A unit of distance, used in astronomy, corresponding to a parallax of one second of arc. 1 parsec = 3.26 light-years or 3.084×10^{16} metres.

● **Parseeism ►** The religion of the descendants of Persians who fled their country in the 8th century AD to avoid persecution following the Arab conquest. Mostly located in Bombay, Madras, Calcutta, and Karachi, they practise ▷Zoroastrianism.

● **parsley ►** A fragrant biennial herb, *Petroselinum crispum*, native to the Mediterranean region but widely cultivated. The compound leaves have an aromatic flavour. They are used fresh or dried in fish and meat dishes, soups, garnishes, and bouquets garnis. The flowering stems, which grow up to 1 m high, bear yellowish flowers. Family: ▷*Umbelliferae*.

● **parsnip ►** A hairy strong-smelling biennial plant, *Pastinaca sativa*, native to Eurasia and cultivated in temperate regions for its large starchy white taproot, which is eaten as a vegetable or used as cattle feed. The leaves consist of paired lobed toothed leaflets on a long furrowed stalk; the tiny yellow flowers are borne on stems up to 150 cm high. Family: ▷*Umbelliferae*.

● **Parsons, Sir Charles Algernon ►** (1854–1931) British engineer, who invented the steam ▷turbine in 1884. His earliest machines were used to drive generators in power stations. Using his turbine to power his ship *Turbinia*, in 1897 he reached 35 knots.

● **Parsons, Talcott ►** (1902–78) US sociologist. His early theories are expounded in *The Structure of Social Action* (1937); he later adopted a functionalist (*see* functionalism) approach in *The Social System* (1951) and incorporated evolutionism and cybernetics. The consequences of such an approach are seen in his analysis of social stratification, in which he emphasized its integrative supportive role. His work has been criticized for obscurity and failure to deal with conflict, power, and deviance.

● **Pärt, Arvo ►** (1935–) Estonian composer, now settled in Germany. His earlier works include three symphonies. His later works, which became popular in the 1990s, show the influence of ▷minimal music and the Orthodox liturgy. His epic choral work *Kanon Pokajanen* was first performed in 1998.

● **parthenogenesis ►** A method of reproduction in which the egg develops without ▷fertilization to produce an individual usually identical to the parent. It occurs commonly among certain animals, particularly aphids, ants, bees, and wasps, principally to accelerate the production of individuals at certain times of the year. In many species, for example aphids, sexual reproduction does take place from time to time to provide genetic variation. Parthenogenesis also occurs sporadically among plants.

● **Parthenon ►** A temple on the Acropolis in Athens dedicated to the goddess Athena. Built 447–432 BC by ▷Ictinus and ▷Callicrates at the instigation of ▷Pericles, it represents the summit of classical Greek architecture. Its rectangular colonnaded exterior of Doric columns originally contained a walled chamber with ▷Phidias' gold and ivory statue of Athena. In the 5th century AD it became a church and in the 15th century a mosque. Used by the Turks as a magazine in the 17th century, it was blown up during the Venetian siege of Athens in 1687. Much sculpture was removed in the 19th century. ▷*See* Elgin Marbles.

● **Parthia ►** The region S of the Caspian Sea approximating to present-day Khorasan (NE Iran). Inhabited by seminomadic tribes, Parthia, once a feudal confederacy of vassal kingdoms under the Achaemenians and then the Seleucids, controlled a great empire from about 250 BC to 224 AD with its capital at ▷Ctesiphon. Parthia's famous cavalry and mounted archers harassed Rome's eastern frontiers, overwhelming Crassus' army in a humiliating defeat at ▷Carrhae in 53 BC. In 224 AD the Parthian empire was conquered by the ▷Sasanians.

● **particle physics ►** The study of elementary particles and their interactions. Until the discovery of the ▷electron (J. J. Thomson; 1897), the atom had been thought of as a minute indivisible "billiard ball." The existence of the electron and the discovery of the ▷proton (Rutherford; 1911) made it clear that the atom had an internal structure. When the ▷neutron was discovered (Chadwick; 1932), it appeared that the whole universe was constructed of these three particles. The outstanding problem was the nature of the force that held neutrons and protons together in the nucleus. The only fundamental forces known at that time were the gravitational force and the electromagnetic (em) force: the gravitational force was too weak to account for the stability of the nucleus and the em force had no effect on neutrons.

In 1935 ▷Yukawa suggested that there might be in nature a short-lived particle (later called the meson) that jumped between protons and neutrons and held them together. This concept of exchange forces and the subsequent discovery of short-lived particles led to intensive research into particle physics (*see* accelerators). By the 1960s some 200 "elementary" particles had been identified and it became clear that there were four basic types of force; in addition to gravitational and em forces there were ▷strong interactions (100 times more powerful than em forces) and ▷weak interactions (10^{10} weaker than em forces). In general, there are now believed to be two classes of elementary particles: leptons (the electron, muon, tau particle, and ▷neutrinos), which interact by the em or the weak forces and have no apparent internal structure; and hadrons (including the proton, neutron, pion, etc.), which interact by the strong interaction and have an internal structure.

The current model of hadrons is based on Murray Gell-Mann's concept of the quark, introduced in 1964. In this model, hadrons are divided into two classes: baryons, which decay into protons; and mesons, which decay into leptons and ▷photons or into proton pairs. Baryons consist of three quarks and mesons consist of a quark-antiquark pair. Thus all matter is now seen as being made of leptons and quarks.

Although a single quark has never been identified experimentally, there is now some evidence that they actually exist. Quarks have fractional electronic charges (+2/3 or −1/3 of the electronic charge) and come in six **flavours** called up (u; +2/3), down (d; −1/3), charmed (c; +2/3), strange (s; −1/3), top (t; +2/3), and bottom (b; −1/3). For each flavour there is an equivalent antiquark (ū, d̄, etc.). The proton consists of uud (2/3 + 2/3 − 1/3 = 1) and the neutron consists of udd (2/3 − 1/3 − 1/3 = 0).

In this form quark theory conflicted with the ▷Pauli exclusion principle and it therefore became necessary to introduce colour charge. Thus each flavour of quark can have one of the three colours red, green, or blue, with antiquarks having the corresponding anticolours. Colour charge has no connection with visual colour but the analogy is useful. All hadrons are regarded as white and baryons must consist of a red, a blue, and a green (since these visual colours produce white); mesons consist of a quark of any colour and its corresponding anticolour. This aspect of particle physics is known as **quantum chromodynamics** by analogy with quantum electrodynamics (*see* quantum theory). In this theory the strong interaction is thought to occur by the exchange of gauge bosons called gluons, just as the em interaction occurs by the exchange of photons. Gluons are massless and chargeless but they have a colour charge. There are eight types, each carrying one colour and an anticolour. In a strong interaction a quark can change its colour but all colour changes involve the emission of a gluon, which is absorbed by another quark and causes its colour to change. Thus quark colours move from point to point, the strong interaction being seen as the force that maintains hadrons white. This interpretation of the nature of matter is known as the **standard model**; the one missing particle required to complete the integration of the weak interaction into the model is the ▷Higgs boson (*see* CERN). ▷*See also* antimatter; charm; gauge theories; strangeness.

● **partnership** ▶ An association of two or more people formed to carry on a business; the partnership does not have a separate identity and the partners are not safeguarded by ▷limited liability. Partnerships are often formed by members of a profession, e.g. solicitors or accountants, and by commercial undertakings, such as banks or merchants. Partners share in the assets, expenses, and profits according to a written agreement.

● **partridge** ▶ A small gamebird native to the Old World but widely introduced elsewhere. Partridges are 25–40 cm long and have rounded bodies with short rounded wings and a low gliding flight. The European partridge (*Perdix perdix*) is a common farmland bird and has a greyish plumage with a red face and tail and a dark U-shaped marking on its belly. Family: *Phasianidae* (pheasants, quail, partridges). ▷*See also* francolin.

● **Partridge, Eric Honeywood** ▶ (1894–1979) British lexicographer, born in New Zealand. After World War I he settled in England, where he produced many witty, idiosyncratic, and learned works, including *A Dictionary of Slang and Unconventional English* and an etymological dictionary called *Origins*.

● **Parvati** ▷*See* Shiva; ⸆Cola.

● **Parzifal** ▷*See* Perceval.

● **Pasadena** ▶ 34 10N 118 09W A city in the USA, in California. It is a winter health resort and well-known residence for Los Angeles cinema stars. The annual Tournament of Roses and the Rose Bowl football game are held here. The California Institute of Technology was established here in 1891. Population (1998 est): 134 587.

● **Pasargadae** ▶ An ancient Persian city in Fars province, Iran. It was founded as the capital between 546 and 530 BC by ▷Cyrus (II) the Great, whose tomb still stands there. His successors abandoned it for ▷Persepolis in the 6th century BC.

● **pascal** ▶ (Pa) The ▷SI unit of pressure equal to one newton per square metre. Named after Blaise ▷Pascal.

● **Pascal** ▶ A computer-programming language, named after Blaise ▷Pascal. Designed in 1970 by Nicklaus Wirth at Zürich for teaching computer science, it is now widely used on ▷microcomputers.

● **Pascal, Blaise** ▶ (1623–62) French mathematician, physicist, and theologian. He made a study of conic sections when still in his teens; later he explored the mathematics of ▷probability with Pierre de Fermat and invented Pascal's triangle for calculating the coefficients of a binomial expansion. He also made discoveries in ▷fluid mechanics, notably that the pressure in a fluid is everywhere equal (**Pascal's principle**). In 1641 he invented the first calculating machine. At the age of 31 he had a mystical experience and from then on devoted his life to religion. He became a Jansenist and in his *Lettres provinciales* (1656–57) defended ▷Jansenism against the ▷Jesuits. His greatest work was *Pensées sur la religion* (1669), a metaphysical treatise on human nature.

● **pasha** ▶ An honorary title applied in the Ottoman Empire to military, naval, and civil commanders. It was abolished in Turkey in 1934 but lasted until 1952 in Egypt.

● **Pashto** ▶ The language of the Pathan people of N Pakistan and Afghanistan, which belongs to the ▷Iranian family. Pashto is the official language of Afghanistan. There are two main dialects, Pashto in Afghanistan and Pakhto in Pakistan. Both are written in a modified Arabic script.

● **Pashtuns** ▷*See* Pathans.

● **Pašić, Nicola** ▶ (1845–1926) Serbian statesman. Pašić was prime minister of Serbia (1891–92, 1904–05, 1906–08, 1909–11, 1912–18). After World War I he was a representative of the newly formed Yugoslavia at the Paris Peace Conference. As prime minister of Yugoslavia (1921–24, 1924–26), he advocated Serbian supremacy.

● **Pasionaria, La** ▷*See* Ibarruri, Dolores.

● **Pasmore, Victor** ▶ (1908–98) British artist. His early works included landscapes and figure studies, influenced by fauvism and cubism. After 1947 he dramatically changed direction, devoting himself to abstract paintings and reliefs. He held several teaching posts, including Master of Painting at Durham University (1954–61).

● **Pasolini, Pier Paolo** ▶ (1922–75) Italian film director and writer. His controversial films include original treatments of Greek legends, such as *Oedipus Rex* (1967) and *Medea* (1969), a highly acclaimed biblical film, *The Gospel according to St Matthew* (1964), Marxist allegories, such as *Theorem* (1968) and *Pigsty* (1969), and anthologies, such as *The Decameron* (1970). He was murdered.

● **passage rites** ▷*See* rites of passage.

● **Passau** ▶ 48 35N 13 28E A town in S Germany, in Bavaria at the confluence of the Rivers Danube, Inn, and Ilz. An important medieval trading centre and port, its notable buildings include a 13th-century castle, the cathedral (1668), and the 18th-century episcopal palace. Its university was established in 1972. Its manufactures include machinery and textiles. Population (1989 est): 49 140.

● **Passchendaele** ▷See World War I.

● **passenger pigeon** ▶ A slender long-winged ▷pigeon, *Ectopistes migratorius*, once common in deciduous woodlands of North America but extinct by the end of the 19th century. It was 32 cm long and had a pointed tail and a slate-grey plumage with a deep pink breast. It fed on beech nuts, acorns, and fruits and was highly migratory, able to fly long distances for food, and formed flocks numbering millions of birds. Harvesting of eggs, chicks, and adults and rapid deforestation led to its extinction.

● **passerine bird** ▶ A bird belonging to the order *Passeriformes*, which includes over half (about 5100) of all bird species. Passerines— the perching birds—are characterized by their feet, which are specialized for gripping branches, and stems. They are the most highly evolved birds and occur in large numbers in almost every habitat, although few live or feed in water. Most species are between 12 and 20 cm in length, although some are as small as 7.5 cm, with others reaching 117 cm. There are both migratory and sedentary species. Passerines are often of economic importance—as a source of food, for their ornamental plumage, or as cagebirds. Some species, such as the ▷quelea and ▷wood pigeon, are serious crop pests.

The order is divided into four major groups (suborders): *Eurylaimi* (broadbills); *Tyranni* (includes manakins, ovenbirds, pittas, and tyrant flycatchers); *Menurae* (lyrebirds and scrubbirds); and, the largest and most advanced group, *Oscines* (see songbird).

● **passionflower** ▶ A climbing plant of the genus *Passiflora* (500 species), native chiefly to tropical and subtropical America and cultivated for ornament. The leaves may be simple or deeply lobed; some are modified as tendrils. The distinctive flowers each consist of a cup-shaped base with five coloured sepals and petals at its upper edge surmounted by a coloured fringe. From the centre of this protrudes a stalk bearing the stamens and ovary. The fruit is a berry or capsule, which in some species (e.g. *P. quadrangularis*) is edible (passionfruits *or* granadillas). Family: *Passifloraceae*.

● **Passion plays** ▶ Religious dramas concerning the crucifixion and resurrection of Christ and often including other related religious episodes. They were performed on Good Friday throughout medieval Europe and survived after the Reformation in Switzerland, Austria, and Germany. The Passion play at ▷Oberammergau in W Germany, the best-known modern example, has been performed every ten years since 1634 in fulfilment of a vow made by the villagers during an epidemic of the plague.

● **passive resistance** ▷See civil disobedience.

● **Passover** ▶ (Hebrew word: *Pesach*) One of the three biblical pilgrimage festivals (the others are Weeks and Tabernacles) observed in the Jewish religion. Celebrated in March/April, it commemorates the Exodus from Egypt and also incorporates a spring harvest festival. It recalls the Lord "passing over" the houses of the Jews in Egypt, the doorposts of which were marked with the blood of a lamb, so that their first-born were not slaughtered. It is celebrated for seven or eight days, beginning on the eve of the first day with a formal meal called the *seder* (see also haggadah). Unleavened bread (*matzah*) is eaten, all leaven being removed from the house to commemorate the haste with which the Jews left their homes in the Exodus. In Christianity it has been replaced by ▷Easter.

● **Passy, Frédéric** ▶ (1822–1912) French economist and politician, whose efforts for peace were rewarded with the first Nobel Peace Prize (1901), which he won jointly with ▷Dunant. He established a peace arbitration society (Ligue international de la Paix, 1867) and helped found the International Parliamentary Union (1889), as well as arbitrating in international disputes.

● **pasta** ▶ An originally Italian dough made from semolina obtained from durum wheat and water, sometimes with the addition of eggs.

Among the many varieties of pasta are spaghetti (long thin rods), macaroni (short hollow thicker tubes), lasagne (flat rectangular pieces), ravioli (little squares of pasta stuffed with meat), and tagliatelle (long flat ribbons). Pasta is usually served with well-flavoured sauces.

● **Pasternak, Boris** ▶ (1890–1960) Russian poet and novelist. He was born into a cultured Jewish family and studied music and philosophy. He published several volumes of Symbolist poetry between 1917 and 1923 and many translations during the 1930s. His epic novel *Dr Zhivago* became an international bestseller after its publication in Italy (1957); it was unpublished in Russia until the cultural thaw of the mid-1980s. Under pressure Pasternak declined the 1958 Nobel Prize.

Louis Pasteur ▶ An unusual photograph of the inventor of vaccination (seated left) with a group of English children who had been bitten by dogs and sent to him for inoculation against rabies.

● **Pasteur, Louis** ▶ (1822–95) French chemist and microbiologist, who made great advances in the prevention and treatment of diseases caused by microorganisms. A tanner's son, Pasteur became a science master and pursued his interest in chemistry: in 1848 he discovered two different optically active forms of tartaric acid that had differing biological properties. In 1854 Pasteur was appointed dean of the faculty of sciences at Lille University. He found that fermentation was caused by microorganisms and that by excluding these, souring or decay could be prevented (see pasteurization). Although partially paralysed in 1868, Pasteur's interest in germs and disease directed his attention to anthrax (the life cycle of the causative bacillus in cattle had been studied by ▷Koch). By 1881 Pasteur had devised a means of safely inducing immunity to the disease by injecting a vaccine of heat-treated (attenuated) live anthrax bacilli. Pasteur also produced a vaccine for chicken cholera and—in 1885, his most spectacular achievement—an effective rabies vaccine. The Pasteur Institute was founded in 1888 to treat rabies and has since developed into a world centre for biological research.

● **pasteurization** ▶ Heat treatment used to destroy the microorganisms in milk. The method involves heating milk for 30 minutes at 60°C, which kills the tuberculosis bacteria without damaging the milk protein. This process is named after Louis ▷Pasteur, who demonstrated that heat could prevent the spoilage of wine and beer caused by fermentation of yeasts and other microorganisms.

● **Pasto** ▶ 1 12N 77 17W A city in SW Colombia, on a slope of the Pasto volcano. It is the commercial centre of an agricultural and cattle-rearing area. The University of Nariño was founded here in 1827. Population (1985): 252 115.

● **Paston Letters** ▶ Correspondence largely relating to the Norfolk family of Paston. Written between 1422 and 1509, they constitute an invaluable source for the history of that period, describing not only domestic and local affairs but also political events. The majority are preserved in the British Library.

● **Patagonia** ▶ A geographic area of S South America in Argentina and Chile, extending S of the River Colorado to the Strait of Magellan. It consists chiefly of an arid plateau rising to the Andes. Sheep raising is the principal economic activity. It contains the major oilfield of Comodoro Rivadavia, Argentina's chief source of oil, and the Río Turbio coalfield. Area: about 777 000 sq km (300 000 sq mi).

● **patas monkey** ▶ An ▷Old World monkey, *Erythrocebus patas*, of African grasslands. Patas monkeys are 110–160 cm long including the tail (50–75 cm) and are mainly terrestrial and omnivorous. They live in well-ordered troops (hence, their alternative name—military monkeys). A white-nosed eastern race is called the nisnas monkey.

● **patchouli** ▶ An aromatic herb, *Pogostemon patchouli*, native to Malaysia. It contains a fragrant essential oil used in perfumery in SE Asia. The dried leaves are used as an insect repellent. Family: ▷*Labiatae*.

● **Patenier, Joachim** ▷*See* Patinir, Joachim.

● **patent** ▶ A type of ▷intellectual property consisting of the sole right to make, use, and sell a new invention for a period of 20 years from the date of application for the patent. The privilege is conferred on the applicant (usually the inventor) by letters patent from the Crown. A patent will only be granted for a thing or process that is novel, capable of achieving the purpose intended by the inventor, and that has some practical use. Applications to the Patent Office in London must be accompanied by a written specification of the invention, appropriate drawings, formulas, or specimens. From the late 1980s there were moves towards allowing the issue of patents for new plants and animals created by genetic engineering.

● **Pater, Walter (Horatio)** ▶ (1839–94) British critic and essayist. He established his reputation with *Studies in the History of the Renaissance* (1873). His historical fiction *Marius the Epicurean* (1885) advanced his philosophical and aesthetic theories, which greatly influenced the ▷Aesthetic movement. His many critical essays on art and poetry are noted for their highly polished prose style.

● **Paterson** ▶ 40 55N 74 10W A city in the USA, in New Jersey, part of the Greater New York Metropolitan Area. Founded in 1791, it became known as the Silk City in the 19th century, because of its large silk industry. Its varied manufactures today include cotton, paper, and chemicals. Population (1996 est): 150 270.

● **Paterson, William** ▶ (1658–1719) Scottish merchant and banker, who founded the Bank of England (1694). He resigned from the Bank within a year because of disagreements in policy. His attempt to set up a rival bank failed.

● **Pathans** ▶ A large group of tribes of N Pakistan and SE Afghanistan who speak the ▷Pashto language. They are also known as Pashtuns. Each tribe is subdivided into a number of patrilineal clans, said to be descended from a common ancestor. Genealogical lines of many generations are remembered and determine land rights, succession, and inheritance. Devout Muslims, the Pathans are farmers and warriors, many entering into military service.

● **pathogen** ▶ Any parasitic microorganism that causes disease in its host (*see* infection). Pathogens may be bacteria, viruses, protozoa, or fungi. Normally harmless—or even beneficial—microbes that live within other organisms may become pathogenic under certain circumstances. For example, antibiotic treatment of bacterial infections may result in the overgrowth of the fungi that cause ▷candidiasis.

● **pathology** ▶ The branch of medicine concerned with the study of disease and disease processes in order to understand their causes and nature. The specialty originated in the mid-19th century, when ▷Virchow demonstrated that changes in the structure of cells and tissues were related to specific diseases. Cellular pathology advanced further with the work of Pasteur and Koch on the bacterial cause of disease, but it was not until the beginning of the 20th century that the knowledge gained in the laboratory was applied to the treatment and prevention of disease in patients. Examples of early work in the science of clinical pathology include Schick's test for diphtheria and Wassermann's test for syphilis. Chemical pathology developed from the observation of changes in the composition and structure of blood in disease, notably with the work of Banting and Best on the importance of insulin in diabetes and contributions from such haematologists as Landsteiner in the discovery of the blood groups. Today pathology includes studies of the chemistry of blood, urine, faeces, and diseased tissue, obtained by biopsy or at autopsy, together with the use of X-rays and many other investigative techniques.

● **Patinir, Joachim** ▶ (*or* Patenier; c. 1485–1524) Flemish painter, noted for his panoramic views, which dwarf the religious themes that were his ostensible subjects. His paintings include *St Christopher* and *St Jerome* (both Prado).

● **Patmore, Coventry** ▶ (1823–96) British poet. A friend of Tennyson and Ruskin and an associate of the ▷Pre-Raphaelite Brotherhood, his *The Angel in the House* (4 vols, 1854–62) is a poetic treatment of married love. After his conversion to Roman Catholicism in 1864 he wrote mostly on religious themes.

● **Pátmos** ▶ A Greek island in the E Aegean Sea, in the Dodecanese. St John the Divine is believed to have written the Book of Revelation here. Area: 34 sq km (13 sq mi). Population (latest est): 2534.

● **Patna** ▶ 25 37N 85 12E A city in India, the capital of Bihar on the River Ganges. It was founded in 1541 on the former site of Pataliputra, ancient capital of the Maurya and Gupta empires. Population (1991): 916 980.

● **pato** ▶ A four-a-side equestrian sport related to ▷polo and ▷basketball, played in Argentina. The mounted players try to throw a ball, to which are attached six leather handles, into a goal (a net attached to a post).

● **Paton, Alan** ▶ (1903–88) South African novelist. His best-known novel, *Cry, the Beloved Country* (1948), condemns injustice in South African society. His other works include *Too Late the Phalarope* (1953), *The Land and the People of South Africa* (1955), *Ah, But Your Land Is Beautiful* (1982), and a collection of short stories, *Debbie Go Home* (1961). He was national president of the Liberal Party from 1953 to 1960.

● **Patras** ▶ (*or* Pátrai) 38 14N 21 44E A port in W Greece, in the N Peloponnese on the Gulf of Patras. The War of Greek Independence began here in 1821. Exports include currants, sultanas, tobacco, and olive oil. Its university was established in 1966. Population (1991): 172 763.

● **patriarch** ▶ 1. In the Old Testament, ▷Adam and the other ancestors of the human race before the Flood, as well as the later forebears of the Hebrew nation: Abraham, Isaac, Jacob, and Jacob's 12 sons who gave their names to the 12 tribes of Israel. 2. In the Orthodox Church, the title of a bishop with jurisdiction over other bishops. At the Council of Chalcedon (451) five such sees were recognized: Alexandria, Antioch, Constantinople, Jerusalem, and Rome. The patriarch of Constantinople took the title Ecumenical Patriarch, despite Rome's objections (*see* papacy).

● **patricians** ▶ The hereditary aristocracy of ancient Rome. Originally the sole holders of political and religious offices, the patricians were gradually forced during Republican times to admit ▷plebeians to political offices and their privileged position was eroded.

● **Patrick, St** ▶ (c. 390–c. 460 AD) The patron saint of Ireland. Legend tells of his abduction from Britain by Irish marauders at the age of 16. A local chief's slave in Antrim, he later escaped to Gaul, finally returning to Ireland as a missionary. He established an archiepiscopal see at Armagh and by the time of his death had firmly established

Christianity in Ireland. His only certain works are a spiritual autobiography, the *Confession*, and the *Epistle to Coroticus*. Feast day: 17 March. Emblems: snakes and shamrock.

● **Patriotic Front ▶** (PF) A Black nationalist organization, founded in 1976, to oppose the government of Ian Smith in Rhodesia (now ▷Zimbabwe). Using guerrilla techniques, its two wings—the Zimbabwe African National Union (ZANU), led by Robert ▷Mugabe, and the Zimbabwe African People's Union (ZAPU), led by Joshua ▷Nkomo—were based in Mozambique and Zambia respectively. In the elections (1980) that followed the Lancaster House agreements, Mugabe became prime minister of Zimbabwe. In 1987 ZANU and ZAPU merged to create a new ruling party known as ZANU-PF, making Zimbabwe effectively a one-party state.

● **Patroclus ▶** In Homer's *Iliad*, the companion of Achilles. During the Trojan War he was killed by Hector while wearing the armour of Achilles.

● **Patti, Adelina ▶** (Adela Juana Maria; 1843–1919) Italian-born operatic soprano. She specialized in the Italian coloratura repertoire, singing both in the USA and Europe.

● **Patton, George S(mith) ▶** (1885–1945) US general. In World War II he commanded the Seventh Army in Sicily (1943) and then the Third Army in France. He breached the German defences in Normandy and led a spectacular advance to the Moselle. In the Ardennes he cleared the W bank of the Rhine, crossed it, and encircled the Ruhr.

● **Pau ▶** 43 18N 0 22W A town in SW France, the capital of the Pyrénées-Atlantique department. It was the former capital of Béarn and residence of the French Kings of Navarre. Pau is a tourist resort and trades in horses, wine, and leather. Population (1990): 83 928.

● **Paul I ▶** (1754–1801) Tsar of Russia (1796–1801). Paul reversed many of the enlightened policies of his mother, Catherine the Great, and pursued an inconsistent foreign policy that isolated Russia. His incompetence and despotism led to his assassination.

● **Paul I ▶** (1901–64) King of the Hellenes (1947–64). The third son of Constantine I, he lived mostly in exile from 1917 to 1935, and again during World War II, succeeding his brother George II (1890–1947; reigned 1922–23, 1935–47). In 1938 Paul married Frederika (1917–   ) of Brunswick.

● **Paul III ▶** (Alessandro Farnese; 1468–1549) Pope (1534–49). First of the ▷Counter-Reformation popes, Paul restored the ▷Inquisition, summoned the Council of ▷Trent, and actively supported the new orders, especially the ▷Jesuits. He was also a considerable patron of learning and the arts. However, he was noted for his nepotism and worldliness, creating the duchy of Parma for his illegitimate son Pier Luigi Farnese (1503–47). His great-grandson became Phillip II's general, Alessandro ▷Farnese, Duke of Parma.

● **Paul VI ▶** (Giovanni Battista Montini; 1897–1978) Pope (1963–78). Succeeding ▷John XXIII, Paul continued his predecessor's policies of reform, reconvening the second ▷Vatican Council after his election. While working for ecumenicism and administrative reform he maintained papal authority and traditional doctrines, notably in the encyclical *Humanae Vitae* (*Of Human Life*; 1968), which reiterated the Church's position on birth control.

● **Paul, St ▶** (c. 3–c. 64 AD) Christian Apostle, born Saul of Tarsus, who spread Christianity among the Gentiles; the 13 Epistles attributed to him form a major part of the New Testament. The son of a Pharisee and a Roman citizen, he was educated at Jerusalem and was initially anti-Christian, having participated in the martyrdom of St ▷Stephen. While travelling to Damascus, he had a vision that led to his conversion to Christianity. He began his activity as an Apostle in Damascus, later joining the other Apostles in Jerusalem. His important missionary work consisted of three journeys in which he travelled to Cyprus, Asia Minor, Macedonia, Greece, Ephesus, and elsewhere, establishing churches or bringing support to previously established Christian communities. After his third journey, he returned to Jerusalem and was arrested by Roman soldiers in order to protect him from the hostility of the mob, who attacked him for teaching transgression of the Mosaic Law. He eventually appealed to

Caesar and, as a Roman citizen, was taken to Rome for trial. He was imprisoned for two years; here the New Testament account (in Acts) ends. It appears that he may have been released, before being arrested and beheaded under Nero. Paul's influence was decisive in extending Christianity beyond the Jewish context of the Church at Jerusalem, and the Pauline Epistles formed the basis of all subsequent Christian theology. Feast day: 29 June.

● **Pauli, Wolfgang ▶** (1900–58) US physicist, born in Austria, who in 1925 formulated the ▷Pauli exclusion principle for which he received the 1945 Nobel Prize. In 1931 he postulated that some of the energy of a ▷beta decay was carried away by massless particles, which ▷Fermi named neutrinos.

● **Pauli exclusion principle ▶** The principle that no two ▷fermions may exist in the same state. It is most commonly applied to atomic electrons, which cannot have the same set of ▷quantum numbers. Named after Wolfgang ▷Pauli.

● **Pauling, Linus Carl ▶** (1901–94) US chemist, who originated and developed important concepts concerning the structure of molecules. Successfully using new analytical techniques, Pauling elucidated the nature of chemical bonding, publishing his highly influential book, *The Nature of the Chemical Bond*, in 1939. He received the Nobel Prize for Chemistry (1954) for his research and the Nobel Peace Prize (1962) for his pacifist stance against nuclear weapons.

● **Paulinus, St ▶** (c. 584–644 AD) Roman missionary, who assisted St ▷Augustine of Canterbury in the conversion of England to Christianity. Paulinus became the first bishop of York (627), having baptized the Northumbrian king ▷Edwin; in 634 he became archbishop of Rochester.

● **Paulinus of Nola, St ▶** (c. 353–431 AD) Christian Latin poet, born at Bordeaux. After a political career as a senator, consul, and governor of Campania, he became a Christian and was ordained in 394. Bishop of Nola from 409, he is famous for his poetic epistles. Feast day: 22 June.

● **Paulus, Friedrich ▶** (1890–1957) German field marshal in World War II. In command of the Sixth Army on the Eastern Front, he captured Stalingrad (1943) but his army was forced to surrender, thus ending the German offensive in the Soviet Union. ▷*See* Stalingrad, Battle of.

● **Pausanias ▶** (2nd century AD) Greek traveller, whose *Description of Greece* is an invaluable source for places and buildings now destroyed. His accuracy and judgment are attested by his description of those that survive.

● **Pau-t'ou** ▷*See* Baotou.

● **Pavarotti, Luciano ▶** (1935–   ) Italian operatic tenor. He made his debut at La Scala, Milan, in 1966. He specializes in the works of Bellini, Verdi, and Puccini. His rendering of "Nessun Dorma" became a bestseller in 1990 and he is now known worldwide for his recordings and performances as one of the "Three Tenors," the others being Placido ▷Domingo and José ▷Carreras.

● **Pavese, Cesare ▶** (1908–50) Italian novelist and poet. He was imprisoned for his antifascist journalism in 1935 and later joined the resistance movement. His best-known novels, which concern human isolation, include *Il compagno* (1947) and *La luna e i falò* (1950). He also published poetry and translations. Lonely throughout his life, he committed suicide. His diaries were published as *Il mestiere di vivere* (1952).

● **Pavia ▶** (ancient name: Ticinum) 45 12N 9 09E A town in Italy, in Lombardy on the River Ticino. Dating from Roman times, it has a 12th-century church, in which St Augustine is buried, a 15th-century cathedral, a monastery, palaces, and a university (1361). Pavia's 12th-century bell tower collapsed in 1989, killing three people. Pavia lies in an agricultural region and produces sewing machines, metal goods, textiles, and furniture. Population (1990): 80 650.

● **Pavia, Battle of ▶** (24 February, 1525) A major engagement in the Italian wars between ▷Francis I of France and the Habsburg emperor ▷Charles V. It marked the beginning of Habsburg ascendancy in Italy.

Some 23 000 Habsburg troops relieved the besieged city of Pavia, captured Francis, and virtually destroyed the French army of 28 000.

● **Pavlodar** ▶ 52 21N 76 59E A port in NE Kazakhstan on the River Irtysh. It was founded in 1720 but remained small until the mid-20th century, since when it has become an important industrial centre: food processing is the principal activity. Population (1995 est): 340 700.

● **Pavlov, Ivan Petrovich** ▶ (1849–1936) Russian physiologist, noted for his studies of digestion and his demonstration of the ▷conditioned reflex. Pavlov showed how heartbeat is regulated by the vagus nerve and how eating stimulates secretion of digestive juices by the stomach. Pavlov extended his theories of reflex behaviour to cover aspects of human behaviour, such as learning.

Pavlov was a persistent critic of the communist regime although it continued to provide him with facilities for research. He was awarded the 1907 Nobel Prize.

● **Pavlova, Anna** ▶ (1885–1931) Russian ballet dancer. She joined Diaghilev's company in Paris in 1909, and from 1914 she devoted her career to international tours with her own company. She created the chief role in *Les Sylphides* and was especially associated with *Le Cygne*, choreographed for her by ▷Fokine in 1907.

● **pawnbroking** ▶ The lending of money on the security of an item of personal property. An article pawned is pledged to the pawnbroker but can be redeemed within a specified time by the repayment of the loan plus ▷interest. In the UK, pawnbrokers require a licence and are governed by the Consumer Credit Act (1974), which replaced the Pawnbrokers Acts (1872, 1960). Articles unredeemed after six months (or an agreed period) after pawning become the pawnbroker's property if valued at £25 or less. If valued at more the pawnbroker may sell the article (after giving the original owner notice), any surplus raised being repayable to the original owner.

● **Pawnee** ▶ A confederation of Caddoan-speaking North American Indian tribes of the Platte River area, Nebraska. They were typical of the Eastern Plains Indian semiagricultural and buffalo-hunting culture. Their villages consisted of large circular earth-covered lodges. Shamans were important. The Pawnees worshipped the sun, had a star cult, and observed the morning-star ceremony in which a captured maiden was sacrificed by cutting out her heart.

● **Pawtucket** ▶ 41 53N 71 23W A city in the USA, in NE Rhode Island on the Blackstone River. The site of the first US cotton mill (1790), its industries include textiles, silks, machinery, and paper. Population (1990): 72 644.

● **Paxinou, Katina** ▶ (1900–72) Greek actress. As well as acting in classical Greek tragedies she translated and produced British and US plays for the Greek National Theatre. Her films include *For Whom the Bell Tolls* (1943) and *Mourning Becomes Electra* (1947).

● **Paxton, Sir Joseph** ▶ (1801–65) British architect. Initially a gardener, Paxton, under the patronage of the Duke of Devonshire, experimented with new techniques of construction employing iron and glass in building greenhouses at ▷Chatsworth. This experience culminated in the design of the revolutionary ▷Crystal Palace for the Great Exhibition of 1851. He also designed country houses, for example Mentmore, and practised landscape gardening.

● **PAYE** ▶ (Pay As You Earn) A system used for the collection of direct ▷taxation in the UK, introduced in 1944. Income tax is deducted from employees' wages before the employer distributes them; thus while the amount deducted appears on the employee's pay slip, the employee never actually receives the tax taken.

● **Paysandú** ▶ 32 21S 58 05W A port in W Uruguay, on the River Uruguay. Accessible to oceangoing vessels, its chief exports are cereals, flax, and livestock. It is a meat-processing centre and has tanning and sugar-refining industries. Population (latest est): 75 200.

● **Paz, Octavio** ▶ (1914–98) Mexican poet, critic, and diplomat, whose early poetry was influenced by Marxism and surrealism. His mature poetry is philosophical and deals with the problem of solitude; the collection *La estación violenta* (1958) contains his best-known poem, "Piedra del sol." He won a Nobel Prize in 1990.

● **Pazzi conspiracy** ▶ (1478) A plot to assassinate Lorenzo and Giuliano de' ▷Medici in Florence Cathedral. It was led by their political and business rivals, the Pazzi, and was supported by the papacy. Guiliano died but the Medici maintained control of the government and many of the conspirators were captured and killed. A war with the papacy followed but Lorenzo's dominance over Florence had been demonstrated.

● **PCBs** ▷*See* polychlorinated biphenyls.

● **pea** ▶ An annual herb of the genus *Pisum* (about 6 species), native to the Mediterranean area and W Asia, especially the widely cultivated *P. sativum*. The leaves consist of paired oval leaflets and have curling tendrils used for climbing. The white flowers have a large rear petal and two smaller wing petals enclosing a cuplike keel petal. The edible round seeds are contained in an elongated pod and are an important source of protein for man and livestock. Family: ▷*Leguminosae*.

● **Peace Corps** ▶ A US Government agency founded in 1961 by John F. Kennedy to provide the Third World with skilled manpower, especially teachers and agriculturalists. The Corps consists of volunteers, who must be US citizens and at least 18 years old.

● **Peace River** ▶ A river in W Canada, whose headstreams (Finlay and Parsnip Rivers) rise in the British Columbia Rockies. Flowing generally NE across the N Alberta plains, it empties into the Slave River. It is mostly navigable and is also tapped for hydroelectricity. Its valley is fertile farmland, with important oil and timber reserves. Length: 1923 km (1195 mi), including Finlay River.

● **peach** ▶ A small tree, ▷*Prunus persica*, probably native to China but widely cultivated in Mediterranean and warm temperate regions. Up to 6 m high, it has toothed glossy green leaves and pink flowers, borne singly or in groups in the leaf axils. The round fleshy fruit (a ▷drupe) has a distinct cleft and thin velvety skin, yellowish with a crimson tinge. The sweet white or yellow flesh encloses a wrinkled stone. Peaches are eaten fresh, canned, or in preserves. Nectarines (*P. persica* var. *nectarina*) are varieties with smooth-skinned fruits. Family: *Rosaceae*.

● **peacock** ▷*See* peafowl.

● **Peacock, Thomas Love** ▶ (1785–1866) British satirical novelist. He worked for the East India Company from 1819 to 1856 and was a close friend of Shelley. His seven novels, which include *Nightmare Abbey* (1818) and *Gryll Grange* (1860), satirize contemporary fashions and ideas through the conversation of stereotyped characters often based on real people, such as Shelley, Malthus, and Coleridge.

● **peacock butterfly** ▶ A common Eurasian ▷nymphalid butterfly, *Inachis io*. The adults are brownish purple with a bright eyespot on each wing. They fly from early spring well into summer. The black spiny caterpillars are gregarious and feed on stinging nettles.

● **pea crab** ▶ A small pea-shaped ▷crab belonging to the genus *Pinnotheres*. The female lives within the shell of certain bivalve molluscs, such as oysters and mussels, obtaining food and shelter but not harming its host (*see* commensalism). The larvae and usually the males are free-swimming. Tribe: *Brachyura*.

● **peafowl** ▶ An Old World gamebird belonging to a genus (*Pavo*; 2 species) native to lowland forests of India and SE Asia. Peafowl are 75 cm long and the female (peahen) has a green-brown plumage; males (peacocks) have elaborate lacy tails, 150 cm long, the feathers of which are tipped by blue-and-bronze markings and raised over the body during display. The blue (Indian) peacock (*P. cristatus*) is a metallic blue colour and has been domesticated as an ornamental bird. Family: *Phasianidae* (pheasants, partridges, etc.); order: *Galliformes* (pheasants, turkeys, etc.).

● **Peak District** ▶ A hilly area in N central England, mainly in Derbyshire, at the S end of the Pennines. It reaches 727 m (2088 ft) at Kinder Scout and contains many limestone caves, notably Peak Cavern, near Castleton. It was designated the UK's first national park in 1951.

● **Peake, Mervyn** ▶ (1911–68) British novelist. Born in China, he studied art and later illustrated his own books. His trilogy of novels,

Titus Groan (1946), *Gormenghast* (1950), and *Titus Alone* (1959), is a modern gothic fantasy whose bizarre horrors parallel those of the real world. *Selected Poems* (1972) was published posthumously.

● **peanut** ▷*See* groundnut.

● **pear** ▶ A tree of the genus *Pyrus* (about 20 species), native to temperate Eurasia. The numerous cultivated varieties of orchard and garden pears are derived from *P. communis*. Up to 13 m high, it has oval leaves and bears clusters of five-petalled white flowers. The fruit, which narrows towards the stalk, has freckled brownish-yellow or russet skin surrounding sweet gritty flesh and a core of pips; it is eaten fresh or canned and used to make an alcoholic drink, perry. The wood is used for furniture making. Family: ▷*Rosaceae*.

● **pearl** ▶ A natural calcareous concretion formed in certain bivalve molluscs popularly known as pearl oysters or pearl mussels. Used for jewellery since earliest times, pearls are usually white or bluish grey and of globular, oval, pear-shaped, or irregular form. A pearl is formed around a foreign body, such as a worm larva, either against the inner side of the shell (a blister pearl) or within the mollusc sealed off as a cyst. It consists of concentric films of nacre, consisting of aragonite, which also forms the smooth lustrous lining (mother-of-pearl) in the shells of pearl-bearing molluscs. Cultured pearls are beads of mother-of-pearl artificially inserted into the mollusc, where they are left for three to five years. Artificial pearls are usually glass beads with a coating prepared from fish scales. Birthstone for June.

● **pearlfish** ▶ An eel-like parasitic fish, also called fierasfer or cucumber fish, belonging to the family *Carapidae* (about 27 species), found in shallow tropical marine waters. About 15 cm long, it lives in the bodies of echinoderms and molluscs (including pearl oysters), feeding on their reproductive and respiratory organs. The larvae are components of ▷plankton. Order: *Perciformes*.

● **Pearl Harbor** ▶ An inlet of the Pacific Ocean in the USA, in Hawaii on Oahu Island. Following the annexation of Hawaii by the USA in 1900, it became a US naval base. On 7 December, 1941, the Japanese launched an air attack on US military installations in Hawaii. Four battleships were lost in Pearl Harbor and 3300 service personnel killed. This action precipitated US involvement in World War II. It is now a naval shipyard, supply centre, and submarine base.

● **pearlite** ▶ A constituent of ▷steel. It has a regular structure of alternate layers of ferrite (pure iron) and amentite. The name comes from its iridescent appearance under a microscope.

● **Pearl River** ▷*See* Zhu Jiang.

● **pearlwort** ▶ A small tufted or matted annual or perennial herb of the genus *Sagina* (about 20 species), native chiefly to N temperate regions. It has small narrow stalkless leaves and tiny four-petalled white flowers. The evergreen *S. subulata* is cultivated as a rock-garden or border plant. Family: *Caryophyllaceae*.

● **Pears, Sir Peter** ▶ (1910–86) British tenor. He was well known for his performances of Bach and Schubert and was closely associated with the music of his partner ▷Britten, who wrote many works and operatic roles for him, such as the role of Aschenbach in the opera *Death in Venice* (1973).

● **Pearse, Patrick Henry** ▶ (1879–1916) Irish nationalist, Gaelic enthusiast, and teacher. Pearse became a leader of the Irish Republican Brotherhood (*see* Fenians) and in the ▷Easter Rising of 1916 proclaimed an independent Irish republic with himself as president. The insurgents were defeated and Pearse and 14 others were executed. Pearse realized the military futility of the rising but believed a blood sacrifice was required for Irish nationalism.

● **Pearson, Lester B(owles)** ▶ (1897–1972) Canadian statesman and diplomat; Liberal prime minister (1963–68). Ambassador to the USA (1945–46), chairman of NATO (1951), and delegate to the UN, Pearson played a key role in settling the Suez crisis (1956), which earned him the Nobel Peace Prize in 1957. At home the Pearson government conciliated French separatists with a commission on means to establishing French-English equality.

● **Peary, Robert Edwin** ▶ (1856–1920) US explorer in the Arctic. In 1909, in the last of six expeditions, he became the first to reach the North Pole.

● **Peary Land** ▶ An area in N Greenland, between Victoria Fjord and the Greenland Sea. It is the most northerly land area in the world and was named after the Arctic explorer, Robert E. Peary, who first explored it in 1892.

Peasants' Revolt ▶ A manuscript illustration from Froissart's *Chronicles* (a history of the period 1326–1400) showing Richard II sailing down the Thames to meet the rebels.

● **Peasants' Revolt** ▶ (1381) The only major popular revolt in England during the middle ages. It was occasioned by heavy ▷poll taxes and reflected a general discontent with government policies. The rising, led by Wat ▷Tyler and John ▷Ball, was concentrated in East Anglia and the Home Counties. The peasants marched on London, where they were joined by disaffected craftsmen, artisans, and lesser clergy. They achieved initial success, taking the Tower of London, but the revolt soon collapsed and its supporters were ruthlessly suppressed.

● **Peasants' War** ▶ (1524–25) A peasant uprising in S Germany, precipitated by economic hardship. The revolt was condemned by Luther and crushed by the Swabian League. Some 100 000 peasants died.

● **peat** ▶ Partially decomposed dark-brown or black plant debris laid down in waterlogged conditions in temperate or cold climates. The remains of ▷*Sphagnum* (peat or bog moss) are important constituents. Peat is the starting point for the formation of coal and is itself used as a fuel. The more alkaline fen peat is used for horticultural purposes.

● **pecan** ▷*See* hickory.

● **peccary** ▶ A small gregarious hoofed mammal belonging to the genus *Tayassu* (2 species) of South and Central American forests. Resembling a pig, the collared peccary (*T. tajacu*) is dark grey with a light stripe from chest to shoulder and grows to a length of 90 cm. It has two pairs of short tusks. The white-lipped peccary (*T. albirostris*) is darker and larger and has a white patch on the snout. Both are omnivorous. Family: *Tayassuidae*.

● **Pechenga** ▶ (Finnish name: Petsamo) 69 28N 31 04E A port in NW Russia, on the Barents Sea. It was in Finnish possession between the World Wars (1919–40). Ice free, it supports a fishing fleet and other industries relate to the nearby mining (chiefly nickel, copper, and uranium) region. Population: about 3500.

● **Pechora, River** ▶ A river in N Russia. Rising in the Ural Mountains, it flows generally N to enter the Barents Sea and is navigable for much of its length. Length: 1814 km (1127 mi).

● **Peck, Gregory** ▶ (1916–) US film actor, who generally played dignified heroes. He made his debut in 1943 and went on to star in *The Keys of the Kingdom* (1944), *Spellbound* (1945), *Roman Holiday* (1953), *Moby Dick* (1956), and *To Kill a Mocking Bird* (1963), which earned him an Oscar. Later films include *The Omen* (1976) and *Old Gringo* (1989).

● **Peckinpah, Sam** ▶ (1926–84) US film director. His westerns, which include *Guns in the Afternoon* (1962) and *The Wild Bunch* (1969), include powerful scenes of violence. Other films include *Straw Dogs* (1971) and *The Getaway* (1973).

● **peck order** ▶ (or dominance hierarchy) A pattern of social structure found in certain animal groups that denotes the order of precedence of individuals, particularly in relation to feeding. It was first described—and is particularly well developed—in birds, in which the aggressive behaviour shown by members of the hierarchy to all those inferior to them takes the form of pecking. It can occur between different species competing for the same food or among a single-species population, especially under captive conditions.

● **Pecos River** ▶ A river of the S USA, rising in N New Mexico and flowing SSE through Texas, to join the Rio Grande. It is an important source of irrigation. Length: 1180 km (735 mi).

● **Pécs** ▶ (German name: Fünfkirchen) 46 04N 18 15E An industrial city in SW Hungary. An old trading centre, it became an important humanist centre (14th–15th centuries) and has the earliest established university in the country (1367; reopened 1922). Its rapid growth in the 19th and 20th centuries was based on nearby coalfields. Population (1999 est): 158 607.

● **pectin** ▶ A carbohydrate found combined with cellulose in the cell walls of plants. Ripening fruits change any other pectic compounds present into jelly-like pectin—an essential ingredient for the gelling of jam.

● **Pedro I** ▶ (1798–1834) Emperor of Brazil (1822–31). The son of John VI of Portugal, Pedro became regent in Brazil in 1821 and declared its independence in 1822. On John's death (1826) he refused the Portuguese Crown, which was granted to Pedro's daughter. Forced to abdicate in 1831, Pedro returned to Portugal.

● **Pedro II** ▶ (1825–91) Emperor of Brazil (1831–89), following the abdication of his father Pedro I. His reign saw an era of prosperity, in spite of wars against Argentina and Paraguay. His gradual abolition of slavery alienated the landowners, who joined the army in deposing him and declaring a republic in 1889.

● **Pedro the Cruel** ▶ (1334–69) King of Castile and León (1350–69). He ruled with great cruelty and his brother, Henry of Trastamara (1333–79; reigned, as Henry II, 1369–79), attempted, with French help, to depose him in 1367. England was drawn into the conflict on Pedro's side and Spain thus became a battlefield of the ▷Hundred Years' War between France and England. Pedro was killed by Henry after defeat at the battle of Montiel.

● **Peebles** ▶ (or Peeblesshire) A former county of SE Scotland. Under local government reorganization in 1975 it became part of the Borders Region (now Scottish Borders).

● **Peebles** ▶ 55 39N 3 12W A market town in SE Scotland, in Scottish Borders on the River Tweed. It is a woollen manufacturing town and health resort. Population (1991): 7065.

● **Peel** ▶ 54 14N 4 42W A town on the W coast of the Isle of Man. It has the remains of a cathedral (13th–14th centuries) and castle ruins.

Formerly an important fishing port, it is now principally a resort. Population (latest est): 3690.

● **Peel, Sir Robert** ▶ (1788–1850) British statesman; Conservative prime minister (1834–35, 1841–46). Elected to parliament in 1809, he was twice home secretary (1822–27, 1828–30), introducing prison and criminal-law reforms, founding the Metropolitan Police (1829), and securing the passage of the Catholic Emancipation Act (1829). In the Tamworth manifesto (1834), a speech to his constituents, he stated a programme of reform that clearly identified the ▷Conservative Party. His second ministry re-introduced income tax (1841), reduced duties on food and raw materials (1841, 1845), and introduced the Bank Charter Act (1844). He is best remembered, however, for the repeal of the ▷Corn Laws (1846), which caused his followers, the Peelites, to defect from the Conservative Party; they subsequently joined the Liberals.

● **Peele, George** ▶ (1556–96) English dramatist. In 1581 he moved from Oxford to London. His numerous works include the pastoral *The Arraignment of Paris* (1584), the chronicle play *Edward I* (1593), and the satirical *The Old Wives' Tale* (1595), as well as poems and pamphlets.

● **Peenemünde** ▶ 54 09N 13 46E A fishing village in E Germany, on the Baltic coast. The Rocket Test Centre was opened in 1937 and German rockets (V2) and flying bombs (V1) were developed here under Wernher ▷von Braun during World War II. Population (latest est): 826.

● **peepul** ▷See bo tree.

● **peerage** ▶ The nobility of the UK and Ireland, which originated in the tenants in chief of the Norman kings of England. The five ranks of the hereditary peerage are **dukes** (from Latin *duces*, the Roman and Saxon army leaders), **marquesses** (originally nobles who held fiefs on the marches, or borders), **earls** (from the Danish *jarl*, which replaced the ▷ealdorman, the chief Anglo-Saxon magistrate of a shire), **viscounts** (from *vicecomes*, the sheriff of a county court), and **barons** (who originally held land from the king *per baroniam*, i.e. directly). The wives of peers (or female peers in their own right) have the titles duchess, marchioness, countess, viscountess, or baroness, respectively. Dukes of the blood royal must be direct male descendants of the sovereign (e.g. the Duke of York), whereas members of the royal family not so descended (e.g. the Duke of Edinburgh) are sometimes called royal dukes.

Peerages, with two classes of exceptions, are hereditary titles usually descending to the eldest male son of the holder, but in certain cases they may descend through the female line. The first class of nonhereditary peers are the Lords of Appeal in Ordinary. These are lawyers raised to the peerage for life (since the 19th century) to enable them to act as judges in the House of Lords. The other class are the life peers created since the Life Peerages Act (1958) to reward those who have given outstanding service to their country. These peerages are given as baronies to both men and women.

Until recently peers had an automatic right to sit in the House of Lords (*see* parliament) but were not allowed to be MPs in the House of Commons (although from 1963 peers were able to disclaim their titles for life to enable them to sit in the Commons, without interfering with the rights of succession). In 1999 parliament approved legislation to deprive hereditary peers of the right to sit in the House of Lords. Under a White Paper published in 2001, newly created life peers would no longer have a seat in the Lords and the existing life peers would gradually be replaced with new appointees (who would have no title).

● **peewit** ▷See lapwing.

● **Pegasus** ▶ (astronomy) A large constellation in the N sky that contains the **Square of Pegasus**, formed from three 2nd- and 3rd-magnitude stars in the constellation together with the 2nd-magnitude star Alpheratz in Andromeda.

● **Pegasus** ▶ (Greek mythology) A winged horse that sprang from the blood of ▷Medusa. It carried the legendary hero Bellerophon in his battles but unseated him when he attempted to ride to heaven. It became a constellation and the bearer of thunderbolts for Zeus.

● **pegmatite** ▶ A coarse-grained igneous rock, usually occurring in veins in or around granite. Crystals over 10 metres across have been found. Most consist of alkali feldspar and quartz but many also contain otherwise rare minerals.

● **Pegu** ▶ 17 18N 96 31E A city in S Myanmar (Burma). The former capital of the Mon kingdoms, which dominated Burma at intervals from the 6th century AD until the 17th century, it has a vast reclining statue of Buddha, 55 m (181 ft) long. Population (latest est): 150 447.

● **Péguy, Charles** ▶ (1873–1914) French poet and essayist. From his socialist bookshop he published the journal *Cahiers de la quinzaine* (1900–14), which expressed the literary ideals of his generation. He was killed in World War I.

● **Pei, Ieoh Ming** ▶ (1917–) US architect, born in China. Having moved to the USA in 1935, he became a US citizen in 1954. His buildings, admired for their practical simplicity, include the John Hancock Tower (1973) in Boston, a new wing (1978) for the National Gallery of Art in Washington, DC, The Fragrant Hill Hotel (1983) in Beijing, a glass and steel pyramid at the ▷Louvre (1989), and the Rock and Roll Hall of Fame in Cleveland (1995).

● **Peipus, Lake** ▶ (Russian name: Ozero Chudskoye) A lake in E Europe, in Estonia and Russia. It is drained by the River Narva N into the Gulf of Finland. Area: 3512 sq km (1356 sq mi).

● **Peirce, Charles Sanders** ▶ (1839–1914) US philosopher and logician. He spent much of his career in government service, and his *Collected Papers* were only published posthumously (1931–58). Peirce believed that an idea could best be defined by examination of its consequences. This concept became known as ▷pragmatism, a name that he later changed to pragmaticism. His work on formal logic was also significant.

● **Peking** ▷*See* Beijing.

● **Pekingese** ▶ An ancient breed of toy □dog originating in China and brought to the West by British forces who sacked the Imperial Palace, Beijing, in 1860. The Pekingese has a long coat forming a mane on the shoulders and may be any colour. The face is always black. Height: 15–23 cm.

● **Peking man** ▶ A type of fossil ▷hominid belonging to the species *Homo erectus* and represented by skeletal remains found near Peking (Beijing). Formerly known as *Sinanthropus*, Peking man lived during the middle Pleistocene period (c. 500 000 years ago), used flint and bone tools, hunted, and could make fire.

● **Pelagius** ▶ (c. 360–c. 420 AD) The originator of the heretical Christian doctrine known as **Pelagianism**. Born in Britain, he settled in Rome (c. 380) and later preached in Africa and Palestine. He rejected the doctrines of ▷original sin and predestination, believing in man's free will and inherent capacity for good. These beliefs were hotly disputed by St ▷Augustine of Hippo and a series of synods. Pope Innocent I finally condemned them in 417 and excommunicated Pelagius.

● **Pelargonium** ▷*See* geranium.

● **Pelasgians** ▶ (*or* Pelasgi) The inhabitants of Greece before the 12th century BC. They spoke a non-Greek language and lived mainly in the N Aegean. They were scattered during Bronze Age infiltrations of Greek-speakers from the N.

● **Pelé** ▶ (Edson Arantes do Nascimento; 1940–) Brazilian footballer, who played for Santos (1955–74), the New York Cosmos (1975–77), and Brazil. The greatest inside forward of his time, he became a world star at 17 when Brazil first won the World Cup (1958). He scored over 1300 goals. In 1994 he was appointed special minister for sports and in 1997 he was awarded an honorary British knighthood.

● **Pelée, Mount** ▶ (French name: Montagne Pelée) 14 18N 61 10W An active volcano on the West Indian island of Martinique. In 1902 an eruption engulfed the town of St Pierre. Height: 1463 m (4800 ft).

● **Peleus** ▶ In Greek legend, a king of Phthia in Thessaly. He was married to ▷Thetis and was the father of Achilles.

● **Pelham, Henry** ▷*See* Newcastle, Thomas Pelham-Holles, 1st Duke of.

● **pelican** ▶ A large waterbird belonging to a family (*Pelecanidae*; 7 species) occurring on lakes, rivers, and coasts of temperate and tropical regions. 125–180 cm long, pelicans are typically white with dark wingtips and have short legs, strong feet, a short tail and very large wings. Their long straight pointed bills have a distensible pouch underneath, in which fish are held before being swallowed. Order: *Pelecaniformes* (gannets, pelicans, etc.).

● **Pella** ▶ The capital, about 39 km (24 mi) NW of Thessaloníki (N Greece), of Macedon (*see* Macedonia) from about 400 to 167 BC. Archelaus I (reigned 413–399) established his court here and it is the birthplace of Alexander the Great. Important finds of jewellery, sculpture, and other treasures were unearthed here in 2001.

● **pellagra** ▶ A disease caused by deficiency of nicotinic acid (*see* vitamin B complex). It occurs mainly in poor countries in people whose diet consists predominantly of maize. The disease causes dermatitis, diarrhoea, and delirium or depression. Health can be rapidly restored by giving nicotinic acid, nicotinamide, or a diet rich in milk, yeast, beans, or peas.

● **Pelletier, Pierre Joseph** ▶ (1788–1842) French chemist, who in 1817 isolated ▷chlorophyll. He also isolated a number of naturally occurring ▷alkaloids, including ▷quinine and ▷strychnine, which were later introduced into medical preparations by François ▷Magendie.

● **Peloponnese** ▶ (Modern Greek name: Pelopónnesos) The S peninsula of Greece, joined to central Greece by the Isthmus of Corinth. It includes the towns of Corinth, Patras (the chief port), and ▷Sparta. Area: 21 637 sq km (8354 sq mi). Population (1991): 605 663.

● **Peloponnesian War** ▶ (431–404 BC) The conflict between Athens and Sparta and their allies, in which Sparta was finally victorious. According to the historian Thucydides, the war was caused by Spartan fear of Athenian imperialism. Sparta's superior infantry invaded Athens in 431 while Athens, under Pericles, relying for security on walls connecting it to its seaport, attacked at sea. Lacking conclusive victories, both sides agreed to the peace of ▷Nicias (421). In 415, however, Athens led by ▷Alcibiades set out to conquer Sicily, which retaliated with Spartan help and destroyed the Athenian fleet (413). The war continued until Sparta under ▷Lysander captured the partially rebuilt Athenian fleet (405) and beseiged Athens, which surrendered (404).

● **Pelops** ▶ The legendary Greek founder of the Pelopid dynasty of Mycenae, a son of ▷Tantalus. He won his bride Hippodamia by winning a chariot race with the help of his driver Myrtilus. When Myrtilus demanded his reward, Pelops refused and instead drowned him. The curse pronounced by the dying Myrtilus was passed on to his son ▷Atreus and all his descendants until it was exorcized by the purification of ▷Orestes.

● **pelota** ▶ A generic name for a variety of court games played with a ball using the hand or a racket or bat. They derive from ▷real tennis and are widely played in the Basque provinces.

● **Pelotas** ▶ 31 45S 52 20W A seaport in S Brazil, in Rio Grande do Sul state on the São Gonçalo Canal. The chief exports of Pelotas are meat, wool, and hides. Population (1996): 282 713.

● **Peltier effect** ▷*See* thermoelectric effects.

● **Pelton wheel** ▷*See* □turbine.

● **pelvis** ▶ A basin-like structure composed of the hip bones and lower part of the spine. It protects the soft organs of the lower abdomen and provides attachment for the bones and muscles of the legs. The pelvis is larger in women to allow for the passage of a baby during childbirth. ▷*See* Plate II.

● **Pemba** ▶ 5 10S 39 45E An island in Tanzania, off the NE coast of the mainland. Its major industry is the growing of cloves, of which it is the world's largest producer. Area: 984 sq km (380 sq mi). Population (latest est): 265 039.

● **Pembroke** ▶ 51 41N 4 55W A market town in SW Wales, in Pembrokeshire on Milford Haven. It has a moated castle (dating from 1200 but much restored) and is the birthplace of Henry VII. Nearby is Pembroke Dock (the dockyard closed in 1926). Population (1991): 15 424.

● **Pembrokeshire** ▶ A county of SW Wales, on the Irish Sea and the Bristol Channel. Under local government reorganization in 1974 it became part of ▷Dyfed but was reinstated in 1996. It consists of a hilly peninsula with a spectacular indented coast, rising to the Prescilly Mountains in the N. Agriculture, fishing, and tourism are important. A major oil-refining area has developed around the Milford Haven estuary. Area: 1593 sq km (615 sq mi). Population (1996 est): 113 500. Administrative centre: Haverfordwest.

● **PEN** ▶ The acronym of the International Association of Poets, Playwrights, Editors, Essayists, and Novelists, an organization founded in 1921 by C. A. Dawson Scott to promote international fellowship between writers. Its presidents have included H. G. ▷Wells and Heinrich ▷Böll. Among its other concerns, PEN campaigns against censorship and the persecution of dissident writers worldwide.

● **Penal Laws** ▶ (1571, 1581, 1593) A series of Acts passed during the reign of Elizabeth I to punish those (recusants), especially Roman Catholics, who refused to attend Church of England services. Recusants were fined, imprisoned, banished, or executed and suffered civil disabilities, such as loss of property. The Laws were repealed in 1829 (*see* Catholic emancipation). ▷*See also* Test Acts.

● **penance** ▷*See* confession.

● **Penang** ▶ A state in NW Peninsular Malaysia, on the Strait of Malacca, consisting of Penang island and Province Wellesley on the mainland. Ceded to the East India Company in 1786, the island was the first British settlement in Malaya. The main products are rice, rubber, and tin. The third largest bridge in the world was opened here in 1985. Area: 1031 sq km (398 sq mi). Population (1993 est): 1 141 500. Capital: Georgetown.

● **Penates** ▷*See* Lares and Penates.

● **pencil cedar** ▶ A ▷juniper tree, *Juniperus virginiana*, native to E and central North America and quite widely cultivated for ornament. It has scalelike leaves and blue berry-like fruits, up to 6 mm long. Its aromatic wood has been used to line clothing chests and cupboards (it repels moths) and for making lead pencils. The tree usually grows to a height of 15 m.

● **Penda** ▶ (d. 655) King of Mercia (c. 634–55), who made Mercia one of the most powerful English kingdoms. He remained a heathen but permitted the conversion of his people to Christianity. He was killed in battle by Oswiu, King of Northumbria.

● **Penderecki, Krzysztof** ▶ (1933–   ) Polish composer. His music, for which he has devised a special system of notation, is characterized by note clusters and unusual sound effects. His works include *Threnody for the Victims of Hiroshima* (for strings; 1960), *De Natura Sonoris I* (for orchestra; 1966), five symphonies (1973, 1980, 1988, 1989, 1992), four operas, and the *Polish Requiem* (1983–84).

● **Pendlebury, John Devitt Stringfellow** ▶ (1904–41) British archaeologist. Pendlebury initially worked at Tell el-Amarna (Egypt) but in 1928 he transferred to Crete, the subject of his classic *Archaeology of Crete* (1939). He was killed organizing guerrilla resistance to the German invasion of Crete in World War II.

● **pendulum** ▶ A device in which a mass (the bob) swings freely about a fixed point with a constant period. In the ideal simple pendulum the bob is connected to the fixed point by a length (*l*) of weightless string, wire, etc. Its period is $2\pi(l/g)^{\frac{1}{2}}$, where *g* is the ▷acceleration of free fall, and is independent of the mass of the bob. A compound pendulum consists of a bob attached to the fixed point via two rigid rods. Pendulums are used to regulate a clock mechanism and in instruments that determine the value of *g*.

● **Penelope** ▶ In Homer's *Odyssey*, the wife of ▷Odysseus. During her husband's absence she put off her many suitors by saying that she must first make a shroud for her father-in-law Laertes. Each night she unravelled what she had woven by day. After 20 years Odysseus returned and killed the suitors.

● **Penghu Islands** ▶ (English name: Pescadores) A Taiwanese archipelago of about 64 small islands in Taiwan Strait. Area: 127 sq km (49 sq mi). Population (latest est): 100 927. Main island: Penghu.

● **penguin** ▶ A flightless black-and-white seabird belonging to a family (*Spheniscidae*; 14–18 species) occurring on cold coasts of the S hemisphere. Penguins are adapted for aquatic life, having wings reduced to narrow flippers giving fast propulsion when chasing fish and squid and escaping predators. 40–120 cm long, they have dense plumage enabling them to tolerate extreme cold. Penguins are highly gregarious and often migrate long distances inland to nest in "rookeries." Order: *Sphenisciformes*. ▷*See also* emperor penguin; fairy penguin.

● **penicillins** ▶ A group of ▷antibiotics. The first penicillin was discovered in the mould *Penicillium notatum*, in 1928, by Sir Alexander ▷Fleming but was not used to treat infections in humans until 1941, having been isolated and purified by ▷Chain and ▷Florey. Natural penicillins include benzylpenicillin (*or* penicillin G), which is usually administered by injection, and phenoxymethylpenicillin (*or* penicillin V), which is administered orally. Semisynthetic penicillins (e.g. flucloxacillin, methicillin) are effective against infections resistant to naturally occurring penicillins. Ampicillin is a broad-spectrum penicillin, i.e. it kills many species of bacteria. Penicillins can cause severe allergic reactions in susceptible patients.

● **Penicillium** ▶ A genus of fungi (about 250 species) that are common moulds in soil and on organic matter. The observation of the antibacterial action of *P. notatum* by Sir Alexander ▷Fleming led to the discovery of penicillin and other antibiotics. *P. camemberti* and *P. roqueforti* are important in cheese making. Family: *Eurotiaceae*; phylum: ▷Ascomycota.

● **Peninsular War** ▶ (1808–14) That part of the Napoleonic Wars fought in Spain and Portugal. The French took Portugal in 1807 and in 1808 Napoleon's brother, Joseph ▷Bonaparte, replaced Ferdinand VII as King of Spain. Popular revolts broke out and turned into a vicious ▷guerrilla war. The Spanish rebels managed an initial victory at Bailén but against crack French troops could do no more than resist the sieges of Gerona and Zaragoza. British troops under the command of the Duke of ▷Wellington eventually liberated the Peninsula. After their victory at Vitoria (1813) they invaded France, helping to force Napoleon's abdication (1814).

● **penis** ▶ The male copulatory organ of mammals, some reptiles, and a few birds. In humans (and other mammals) it contains a tube (urethra) through which both semen and urine can be discharged (*see* Plate II). Erectile tissue making up the bulk of the penis becomes engorged with blood during sexual excitement, enabling the penis to be inserted into the vagina. The corresponding part in women is the **clitoris**, a small erectile mass of tissue situated in front of the urinary opening.

● **Pen-ki** ▷*See* Benxi.

● **Penn, William** ▶ (1644–1718) English Quaker and founder of Pennsylvania, son of Admiral Sir William Penn (1621–70). Sent down from Oxford (1661) because of his refusal to conform to the restored Anglican Church, he joined the Quakers in 1664. In 1668 he was imprisoned in the Tower for his writings. Here he wrote *No Cross, No Crown* (1669), a classic of Quaker practice. From 1682 he was involved in the establishment of Quaker settlements in America, including Pennsylvania, for which he drew up a constitution, "The Frame of Government", allowing freedom of worship.

● **Penney, William George, Baron** ▶ (1909–91) British mathematician, who worked at Los Alamos on the first atom bomb. Knighted (1952) for designing the British atom bomb, he went on to develop the British hydrogen bomb. He was later chairman (1964–67) of the UK Atomic Energy Authority, becoming a life peer (1967) and member of the OM (1969).

● **Pennines** ▶ (*or* Pennine Chain) An upland range in N England. It extends from the Cheviot Hills in the N to the Trent valley in the S. Sometimes known as the "backbone of England" it is the watershed of the chief rivers in N England. It rises to 893 m (2930 ft) at Cross Fell. The **Pennine Way**, a 402 km (250 mi) long footpath, extends between Edale in Derbyshire and Kirk Yetholm in Scottish Borders.

● **Pennsylvania** ▶ A state in the E USA, it is dominated by the uplands of the Appalachian Plateau. Much of the land is under forest or farmed, although it is generally considered to be an urbanized industrial state, dominated by Philadelphia in the E and Pittsburgh in the W. It is a leading iron and steel producer and provides nearly all the country's hard coal. Oil has long been important and the world's first oil well was drilled near Titusville in 1859. Dairy farming predominates in the NE, while the fertile lands of the SE yield cereals, fruit, and vegetables. This latter area is associated with the Pennsylvania Dutch, whose decorated barns can be seen throughout the area.

History: one of the 13 original colonies, the first European settlers, the Swedes, were soon dispossessed by the Dutch (1655). In 1681 the area was given to William Penn by Charles II of England as a haven for Quakers. It became a state in 1787. Area: 117 412 sq km (45 333 sq mi). Population (1996 est): 12 056 112. Capital: Harrisburg.

● **Pennsylvanian period** ▷*See* Carboniferous period.

● **pennyroyal** ▶ A perennial herb, *Mentha pulegium*, native to wet places throughout Eurasia and naturalized in North America. 10–50 cm tall, it has small strongly scented hairy oval leaves and widely spaced whorls of tubular pink or lilac flowers. It is used as a flavouring and to scent soap. Family: ▷*Labiatae*.

● **Penrose, Sir Roger** ▶ (1931–) British mathematician and theoretical physicist. Penrose worked with Stephen ▷Hawking on the theory of black holes. He has also contributed to pure mathematics. A plane surface can be covered with simple symmetrical shapes (e.g. squares and hexagons), but not with other shapes, such as pentagons, which have a five-fold symmetry. Penrose showed that if the diagonal of a parallelogram is divided by a golden section, the two figures produced can cover a plane in a nonregular way. The resulting pattern, known as a **Penrose tiling**, has five-fold symmetry elements (*see also* quasicrystals). His books *The Emperor's New Mind* (1989) and *Shadows of the Mind* discuss artificial intelligence. He was appointed to the OM in 2000.

● **Pensacola** ▶ 30 26N 87 12W A city and port in the USA, in NW Florida. An important naval air base, Pensacola's industries include fish canning and the manufacture of furniture. Population (1994 est): 60 025.

● **pensions** ▶ Regular payments to people who cannot work because of age, sickness, war injury, etc., and to widows and dependents. In the UK, pensions can be broadly classified into government pensions (*see* National Insurance), occupational pensions, and personal pensions. Occupational pension schemes may be contributory (both employer and employee contributing) or noncontributory (only the employer contributing). Civil servants, local-government employees, teachers, doctors, and the employees of many industrial and commercial firms belong to occupational pension schemes. The Finance Act (1987) enables all classes of employed persons to arrange their own personal pensions, the cost of which can be deducted from taxable income (*see* annuity; assurance). In 2001 the government introduced a new class of "stakeholder pensions," designed to bridge the gap between government and personal provision. These are to be administered mainly by the private sector but regulated by government; they will be funded by personal contributions and rebates of National Insurance payments. Pension funds generate vast sums of money, which are available for investment; with insurance companies they are now the "institutions" that dominate stock markets.

● **Pentagon** ▶ The headquarters of the US Defense Department, a massive five-sided building in Virginia built (1941–43) during World War II. It houses all three services and is the largest office building in the world extending over 14 hectares (34 acres). The terrorist attack on ▷September 11, 2001 left some 180 workers dead and seriously damaged the building.

● **Pentateuch** ▶ (Greek: five books) The title used by biblical scholars for the first five books of the ▷Old Testament, traditionally ascribed to Moses. ▷*See also* Torah.

● **pentathlon** ▶ An athletic competition comprising five events, the winner being the competitor with the highest total. It originated in an Olympic contest of sprinting, long jumping, javelin throwing, discus throwing, and wrestling (instituted in 708 BC). The women's version, consisting of the 100 m hurdles, shot put, high jump, long jump, and 800 m run, has been replaced at Olympic level by the **heptathlon**, which has added javelin and 200 m run events. The men's pentathlon has been replaced in major competitions by the ▷decathlon. It has not been an Olympic event since 1924. It comprises the long jump, javelin throw, 200 m sprint, discus throw, and 1500 m run. The **modern pentathlon** is a sporting competition comprising five events: a 5000 m cross-country ride (on horseback), fencing, pistol shooting, a 300 m swim, and a 4000 m cross-country run. It was first included in the Olympics in 1912.

● **Pentecost** ▶ **1.** ▷*See* Whit Sunday. **2.** The harvest festival in the Jewish religion that is celebrated 50 days (Greek *pentēkostē*: fiftieth) after the second day of ▷Passover. Also called the Feast of Weeks or *Shavuot*, it also celebrates the giving of the ▷Ten Commandments to Moses.

● **Pentecostal Churches** ▶ A Christian movement originating in revivalist meetings in Los Angeles in 1906. In Pentecostal assemblies people seek spiritual renewal through baptism by the Holy Spirit, as took place on the first Pentecost (Acts 2.1–4; *see* Whit Sunday). Glossolalia (speaking in tongues, or making unintelligible utterances under the influence of intense religious experience) is an accompanying phenomenon in many cases. Pentecostalism emphasizes the spiritual gifts of healing and prophecy and gives a central role to charismatic preachers (often laymen). In the early 20th century

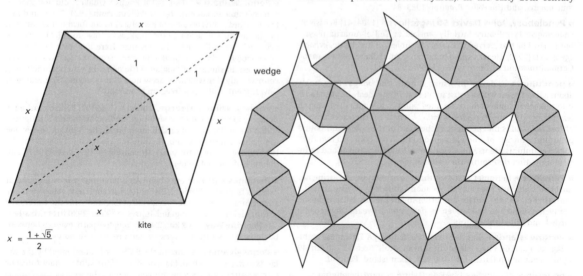

$$x = \frac{1 + \sqrt{5}}{2}$$

Roger Penrose ▶ He divided a parallelogram to produce two figures, a wedge and a kite, and showed how these figures tile a plane surface in a nonregular way. Parts of the pattern show five-fold symmetry.

Pentecostalism spread rapidly among the US poor, including Blacks (*see* gospel music). Many independent Churches were founded, most of which are now affiliated to the Assemblies of God (founded 1914). The movement spread to Europe and subsequently to the developing world—it is now especially important in Indonesia, South Korea, and parts of South America. Since the 1960s there has also been a ▷charismatic movement (sometimes referred to as neo-Pentecostalism or the Charismatic Renewal) within the mainstream Churches, including the Roman Catholic Church. Unlike the original movement, this is predominantly middle-class.

● **Pentland Firth** ▶ A channel separating the N Orkney Islands from the mainland of N Scotland. It is notorious for its rough seas and dangerous currents. Length: 32 km (20 mi). Width: 13 km (8 mi).

● **pentlandite** ▶ The principal ore mineral of nickel, (Ni,Fe)S, found in association with pyrrhotite and chalcopyrite in basic and ultrabasic igneous rocks. It is mined in Canada, Australia, and the republics of the former Soviet Union.

● **Penutian languages** ▶ A major family of North American Indian languages spoken along the NW Pacific coast, on the Columbia River plateau, and in California. There are four main divisions: ▷Chinook and Tsimshian; Coos, Takelma, and Kalapooia; the Sahaptin group, which includes ▷Nez Percé; and the Californian group.

● **Penza** ▶ 53 11N 45 00E A city in W Russia. Founded in 1666, it suffered repeated Tatar attacks. Long an agricultural centre, food processing remains important. Other industries include machine manufacturing and paper making. Population (1995 est): 534 000.

● **Penzance** ▶ 50 07N 5 33W A resort in SW England, in SW Cornwall. It is the sea and helicopter port for the Scilly Isles and is a market town, with early flowers, fruit, and vegetables grown locally. Population (1991): 19 709.

● **peony** ▶ A large perennial herb or shrub of the genus *Paeonia* (33 species) of N temperate regions, often cultivated for its showy flowers. The large glossy deeply cut leaves arise from underground stems or woody aerial shoots and the solitary white, pink, crimson, or yellow flowers are about 10 cm across, with incurving petals and a fleshy central disc supporting the stigma and numerous stamens. The fruit is a leathery pod containing black seeds. Family: *Paeoniaceae*.

● **People's Liberation Army** ▶ (PLA) The military forces of the People's Republic of China. The name was adopted by Chinese communist troops during the civil war of the 1930s and 1940s. Their aim was to liberate the people from the control of the ▷Guomindang. Since Liberation (1949) the PLA has exercised considerable power in Chinese communist politics with some 3.65 million personnel, it is today the largest army in the world, with a strength greater than that of US and Russian forces combined.

● **Peoria** ▶ 40 43N 89 38W A city in the USA, in Illinois on the Illinois River. The state's second largest city, it is the grain and livestock centre for an extensive agricultural area. Population (1996 est): 112 306.

● **PEP** ▷*See* personal equity plan.

● **Pepin (II) of Herstal** ▶ (d. 714 AD) Ruler of the Franks (687–714). He became mayor of the palace (viceroy) of ▷Austrasia in 679 and virtual ruler of all the Franks after defeating ▷Neustria at Tertry (687). The Merovingian kings remained nominal rulers until the overthrow of the dynasty by his grandson ▷Pepin the Short.

● **Pepin the Short** ▶ (d. 768 AD) King of the Franks (751–68) after overthrowing the ▷Merovingians. The son of ▷Charles Martel, Pepin founded the ▷Carolingian dynasty and was crowned king by St Boniface. He checked Lombard expansion and in 756 presented Pope Stephen II with the territories around Ravenna—the nucleus of the ▷papal states. His son ▷Charlemagne inherited the Frankish kingdom in 771.

● **pepper** ▶ A condiment derived from a perennial climbing vine, *Piper nigrum*, native to India. Up to 10 m high, it bears chains of up to 50 inconspicuous flowers that form berry-like fruits (or peppercorns), about 5 mm in diameter. Whole peppercorns yield black pepper while white pepper is obtained from peppercorns with the outer part of the fruit wall removed. Family: *Piperaceae*.

The fleshy red and green peppers are the fruits of ▷*Capsicum* species.

● **pepperbox** ▶ A 19th-century firearm, usually a pistol, with a cluster of barrels, each fired separately. Most bizarre was the *Mariette* design (1837) with 18 barrels, firing in groups of three.

● **peppered moth** ▶ A European ▷geometrid moth, *Biston betularia*, the typical form of which has a similar coloration to the lichen-encrusted tree bark on which it rests (*see* Plate I). During the past century a dark form, var. *carbonaria*, has become common in sooty industrial areas, where it is better camouflaged—and thus better protected from predators—than the typical form.

● **peppermint** ▶ A perennial herb, *Mentha × piperata*: a hybrid between water mint (*M. aquatica*) and ▷spearmint. It has smooth dark-green leaves and oblong clusters of reddish-lilac flowers and is the source of oil of peppermint, used as a flavouring.

● **pepsin** ▶ A protein-digesting enzyme found in gastric juice. The inactive form, pepsinogen, is secreted by glands in the stomach wall and converted to pepsin by the hydrochloric acid in the stomach. Pepsin is a powerful coagulant of milk.

● **peptic ulcer** ▶ An inflamed eroded area in the wall of the stomach (**gastric ulcer**) or, more commonly, the duodenum (**duodenal ulcer**). Ulcers are very common but it is not known exactly why they occur; they are more common in people who secrete excessive amounts of stomach acid. They may cause abdominal pain, nausea, and vomiting. Serious complications occur when the ulcer bleeds or perforates (bursts). In some patients ulcers disappear as quickly as they come; others require drugs, a special diet, or even surgery (especially if an ulcer perforates). There is now evidence that many ulcers are caused by infection with a bacterium, *Helicobacter pylori*, which must be controlled by antibiotics to prevent recurrence of ulceration.

● **peptide** ▶ A chemical compound comprising a chain of two or more ▷amino acids linked by peptide bonds (–NH–CO–) formed between the carboxyl and amino groups of adjacent amino acids. Polypeptides, containing between three and several hundred amino acids, are the constituents of ▷proteins. Some peptides are important as hormones (e.g. ▷ACTH, insulin) and as antibiotics (e.g. bacitracin, gramicidin).

Samuel Pepys ▶ From an original by Sir Godfrey Kneller. Pepys' original diary was written in code, which was deciphered by the Rev John Smith and first published in 1825.

● **Pepys, Samuel** ▶ (1633–1703) English diarist. His long career in naval administration culminated in his appointment as secretary to the Admiralty (1669–88). He was also an MP and president of the Royal Society. His *Diary* (1660 to 1669), which includes descriptions of the Restoration, the Plague, and the Fire of London, is the intimate record of a man for whom every detail of life held interest. He left the manuscript of his diary to Magdalene College, Cambridge.

● **Perak** ▶ A populous state in NW Peninsular Malaysia, on the Strait of Malacca. In the Kinta Valley are important tin mines, and rubber, coconuts, and rice are produced. Area: 20 668 sq km (7980 sq mi). Population (1993): 2 222 400. Capital: Ipoh.

● **Perceval** ▶ A hero of ▷Arthurian legend, who played a leading part in the quest of the ▷Holy Grail. In ▷Chrétien de Troyes' romance, *Conte du Graal*, and in ▷Wolfram von Eschenbach's *Parzival*, he succeeds in the quest, but in later romances ▷Galahad is the only Arthurian knight to succeed.

● **Perceval, Spencer** ▶ (1762–1812) British politician; prime minister (1809–12). He is remembered mainly for his assassination in the House of Commons by a mad and bankrupt broker, John Bellingham.

● **perch** ▶ One of two species of freshwater food and game fish belonging to the genus *Perca*. The common perch (*P. fluviatilis*) of Eurasia has a deep elongated body, usually about 25 cm long, and is greenish in colour, with dark vertical bars on its sides, reddish or orange lower fins, and a spiny first dorsal fin. The yellow perch (*P. flavescens*) is North American. Perch usually live in shoals, feeding on fish and invertebrates. Family: *Percidae*; order: *Perciformes*. ▷*See also* climbing perch; sea bass.

● **Percheron** ▶ A breed of heavy draught horse originating in the Perche district of France. It has a deep muscular body, powerful neck and shoulders, and a characteristically small refined head. Percherons are commonly black or grey. Height: 1.63–1.73 m (16–17 hands).

● **perching duck** ▶ A ▷duck belonging to a tribe (*Cairinini*) found chiefly in tropical woodlands. Perching ducks nest in treeholes and have long-clawed toes for gripping branches. Drakes are larger and have brighter colours than females. ▷*See* mandarin duck; Muscovy duck.

● **percussion cap** ▶ A device for igniting the charge in firearms, enabling breech-loading ▷muskets and ▷rifles to be developed. A Scot, A. J. Forsythe (1769–1843), first patented detonating pills of mercury fulminate in 1807. Joshua Shaw, perhaps in 1815, encased these in a waterproof copper container, which could be incorporated into cartridges. Percussion muskets with cartridge ammunition were soon widely adopted in place of flintlocks.

● **percussion instruments** ▶ Musical instruments that are struck by the hand or by a stick to produce sounds. The family includes the triangle, gong, rattle, block, cymbals and whip, as well as the pitched xylophone, glockenspiel, bells, celesta, and vibraphone. *Compare* drums; stringed instruments; wind instruments.

● **Percy, Sir Henry** ▶ (1364–1403) English rebel, called Hotspur. Together with his father, Henry, 1st Earl of Northumberland (1342–1408), he led the most serious revolt against Henry IV, whom they had helped to the throne in 1399. Headstrong and fearless (hence his nickname) Percy was defeated and killed at Shrewsbury.

● **Percy, Bishop Thomas** ▶ (1729–1811) British antiquary and poet, who became Bishop of Dromore in 1782. In 1765 Percy published *The Reliques of Ancient English Poetry*, known as *Percy's Reliques*. This was a manuscript of medieval ballads found by Percy in a house at Shifnal, Shropshire.

● **Pérec, Marie-José** ▶ (1968–) French sprinter, born in Guadeloupe. She won the 400 m at the world championships in 1991 and 1995 and at the Olympic Games in 1992. At the 1996 Olympic Games she won both the 200 m and 400 m.

● **Père David's deer** ▶ A rare Chinese deer, *Elaphurus davidianus*, now found only in parks and zoos. About 120 cm high at the shoulder, it has a long tail, splayed hooves, and a reddish-grey coat with a white ring round the eye. The male has long branching antlers. A French missionary, Père Armand David (1826–1900), described specimens in the Chinese emperor's hunting park in 1865.

● **peregrine falcon** ▶ A large powerful ▷falcon, *Falco peregrinus*, occurring in rocky coastal regions worldwide. It is 33–48 cm long and has long pointed wings and a long tail. The male is blue-grey with black-barred white underparts; females are browner. It feeds mainly on ducks, shorebirds, and mammals, soaring high and diving at great speed.

● **Pereira** ▶ 4 47N 75 46W A city in W Colombia. Notable buildings include the cathedral (1890) and the university (1961). An agricultural trading centre, it has brewing, coffee-processing, and clothing industries. Population (1997 est): 434 267.

● **Perelman, S(idney) J(oseph)** ▶ (1904–79) US humorous writer. After publishing his first book in 1929, he worked for a time as a Hollywood scriptwriter, notably on some Marx Brothers films. In the 1930s he began contributing to the *New Yorker*, in which he published most of his short stories and sketches. One of the leading American humorists, he published numerous collections of his pieces, including *Strictly From Hunger* (1937), *Crazy Like a Fox* (1944), *Baby, It's Cold Inside* (1970), and *Eastward, Ho!* (1977). In the 1970s he moved to London but had returned to the USA before his death.

● **perennials** ▶ Plants that can live for many years. In herbaceous perennials, such as the iris and daffodil, aerial parts die down each winter and the plants survive in the form of underground organs (rhizomes, bulbs, corms, etc.). Woody perennials—trees and shrubs—have hardy woody stems, which may or may not shed their leaves in winter.

● **Peres, Shimon** ▶ (1923–) Israeli statesman; Labour prime minister (1984–86, 1995–96), foreign minister (1986–88, 1992–95, 2001–), and finance minister (1988–90). Born in Poland, Peres emigrated to Palestine in 1934. He became head of the navy in 1948 and was defence minister from 1974 to 1977. In 1984 he became prime minister under a special power-sharing agreement with Yitzhak ▷Shamir of Likud. In 1994 he was awarded the Nobel Peace Prize with Yassir ▷Arafat and Yitzhak ▷Rabin. He took over as prime minister following Rabin's assassination in 1995 but was defeated by Binyamin ▷Netanyahu in the subsequent election.

● **perestroika** ▷*See* glasnost.

● **Pérez de Cuéllar, Javier** ▶ (1920–) Peruvian diplomat; UN secretary-general (1982–91). A respected negotiator, he worked unsuccessfully for peaceful solutions to the Falklands War and the ▷Gulf War.

● **Pérez Galdós, Benito** ▶ (1843–1920) Spanish novelist. He wrote 46 novels about 19th-century Spain, *Episodios nacionales* (1873–1912), and a second series about contemporary society, of which the best known is *Fortunata y Jacinta* (1886–87).

● **perfect competition** ▶ A theoretical market structure in economic theory in which no producer supplies a sufficiently large portion of the market to be able to influence prices or to make an exorbitant profit. *Compare* monopoly; oligopoly.

● **perfect number** ▶ An integer that is equal to the sum of all its factors (except itself); for example 28 = 1 + 2 + 4 + 7 + 14. If the sum of all the factors of n is greater or less than n, then n is called excessive or defective. ▷*See also* numbers.

● **perfume** ▶ A mixture of fragrant ▷essential oils, a fixative, and alcohol used to give the human body a long-lasting pleasant smell. The essential oils are obtained by distilling flowers, plants, grasses, etc., such as orange blossom, jasmine, and rose. Aromatic chemicals are also used. Fixatives, which bind the various fragrances together, include balsams, ambergris, and secretions from the scent glands of civets and musk deer (undiluted these have unpleasant smells but in alcoholic solution they act as preserving agents). The amount of alcohol added depends on whether perfumes, toilet waters, or colognes are required. The mixture is normally aged for one year. The art of making perfume began in ancient Egypt, was developed by the Romans and the Arabs, and came to Europe in the ▷Renaissance. By the 14th century flowers were being grown for perfume in France, which remains the centre of the European trade.

● **Perga** ▶ (modern name: Ihsaniye) 36 59N 30 46E An ancient city in SW Turkey, near Antalya. It was the starting point of St Paul's first missionary journey (Acts 13.13) and remains include a theatre, an agora, and basilicas.

● **Pergamum** ▶ An ancient city of W Asia Minor. After about 230 BC it became capital of a Hellenistic kingdom, allied with Egypt and Rome against the ▷Seleucids. Pergamum became rich from ▷parchment and textiles produced by slave labour. Pergamene sculptors led artistic fashion, its library rivalled that of ▷Alexandria, and the architecture of the upper city was magnificent. The last king bequeathed his realm to Rome (133 BC).

● **Pergolesi, Giovanni (Battista)** ▶ (1710–36) Italian composer from Naples. His comic intermezzo *La serva padrona* (1733) was influential in the development of ▷opera buffa. His last work was a *Stabat Mater* (for soprano, alto, and orchestra; 1736).

● **peri** ▶ In Persian myth, a beautiful female spirit. Originally peris had a demonic character and were ruled by Eblis, the leading evil spirit, but subsequently they became benign and graceful.

● **pericarp** ▷See drupe.

● **Pericles** ▶ (c. 495–429 BC) Athenian statesman, who presided over Athens' golden age. According to ▷Plutarch, Pericles became leader of the democratic party in 461 and secured power shortly afterwards, following the ostracism of his rival ▷Cimon. He dominated Athens until 430 by his outstanding oratory, leadership, and honesty. Under Pericles, Athens asserted its leadership of the ▷Delian League and suppressed revolts among its members: following the Thirty Years' Peace with Sparta, Pericles reduced Euboea (445) and then Samos (439). By 431, rivalry with Sparta had led to the ▷Peloponnesian War. The effectiveness of Pericles' strategy, which stressed Athenian naval power, was undermined by the plague of 430 and Pericles briefly lost office. He died shortly after his reinstatement. In 447 Pericles initiated great public works on the ▷acropolis. He also fostered the work of the playwright Sophocles, the philosopher Anaxagoras, and the sculptor Phidias.

● **peridotite** ▶ An ultrabasic coarse-grained igneous rock consisting mainly of olivine; some varieties contain other ferromagnesian minerals, but none contain feldspar. The earth's mantle is some-times called the peridotite shell. Peridotites occur beneath many mountains and islands.

● **perigee** ▶ The point in the orbit of the moon or of an artificial satellite around the earth at which the body is nearest the earth. *Compare* apogee.

● **Perigordian** ▶ A culture of the Upper ▷Palaeolithic. Perigordian is the preferred French designation for the pre-▷Solutrean industries in W Europe, excluding the typologically different ▷Aurignacian. Upper Perigordian is approximately equatable with ▷Gravettian.

● **Périgueux** ▶ 45 12N 0 44E A town in SW France, the capital of the Dordogne. It has Roman remains and a 12th-century cathedral and is renowned for its *pâté de foie gras*, truffles, and wine. Population (1990): 32 850.

● **perihelion** ▶ The point in the orbit of a body around the sun at which the body is nearest the sun. The earth is at perihelion on 3 Jan. *Compare* aphelion.

● **Perilla** ▶ A genus of herbs (4–6 species), native to India and SE Asia, with tubular lilac flowers. A fast-drying oil derived from the seeds is used in printing inks, paints, and varnishes. The leaves are used as a condiment. Family: ▷*Labiatae*.

● **Perim Island** ▶ 12 40N 43 24E A Yemeni island off the SW tip of the Arabian Peninsula. It belonged to Aden from 1857 to 1967. Area: 13 sq km (5 sq mi).

● **period** ▷See geological time scale; periodic table; simple harmonic motion.

● **periodic table** ▶ A tabular arrangement of the chemical ▷elements in order of increasing atomic number, such that physical and chemical similarities are displayed. The earliest version was devised

Group	1	2	3	4	5	6	7	8	9	10	11	12	13	14	15	16	17	18	n
1 H																		2 He	1
3 Li	4 Be												5 B	6 C	7 N	8 O	9 F	10 Ne	2
11 Na	12 Mg												13 Al	14 Si	15 P	16 S	17 Cl	18 Ar	3
19 K	20 Ca	21 Sc	22 Ti	23 V	24 Cr	25 Mn	26 Fe	27 Co	28 Ni	29 Cu	30 Zn	31 Gs	32 Ge	33 As	34 Se	35 Br	36 Kr	4
37 Rb	38 Sr	39 Y	40 Zr	41 Nb	42 Mo	43 Tc	44 Ru	45 Rh	46 Pd	47 Ag	48 Cd	49 In	50 Sn	51 Sb	52 Te	53 I	54 Xe	5
55 Cs	56 Ba	57–71 La–Lu	72 Hf	73 Ta	74 W	75 Re	76 Os	77 Ir	78 Pt	79 Au	80 Hg	81 Tl	82 Pb	83 Bi	84 Po	85 At	86 Rn	6
87 Fr	88 Ra	89–103 Ac–Lr	104 Rf	105 Db	106 Sg	107 Bh	108 Hs	109 Mt	110 Uun	111 Uuu	112 Uub							7

	57 La	58 Ce	59 Pr	60 Nd	61 Pm	62 Sm	63 Eu	64 Gd	65 Tb	66 Dy	67 Ho	68 Er	69 Tm	70 Yb	71 Lu	6
Lanthanoids																
Actinoids	89 Ac	90 Th	91 Pa	92 U	93 Np	94 Pu	95 Am	96 Cm	97 Bk	98 Cf	99 Fs	100 Fm	101 Md	102 No	103 Lr	7

(Period)

Correspondence of recommended group designations to other designations in recent use

IUPAC Recommendations 1990	1	2	3	4	5	6	7	8	9	10	11	12	13	14	15	16	17	18
Usual European Convention	IA	IIA	IIIA	IVA	VA	VIA	VIIA	VIII (or VIIIA)			IB	IIB	IIIB	IVB	VB	VIB	VIIB	0 (or VIIIB)
Usual US Convention	IA	IIA	IIIB	IVB	VB	VIB	VIIB	VIII			IB	IIB	IIIA	IVA	VA	VIA	VIIA	VIIIA (or 0)

periodic table

in 1869 by D. ▷Mendeleyev, who predicted several el-ements from gaps in the table. The rows across the table are known as periods and the columns as groups. The elements in a group have a similar config-uration of outer electrons in their atoms and therefore similar chem-ical behaviour. Across each period, atoms are electropositive (form positive ions) to the left and electronegative to the right. For exam-ple, in the first period fluorine (F) is the most electronegative ele-ment and lithium (Li) the most electropositive. ▷Atomic theory explains this behaviour using the concept of electron shells, corre-sponding to different energy levels of the atomic electrons. Atoms combine in order to form complete outer shells. The shells are built up by filling the lower energy states (inner shells) first. The first shell takes two electrons, the second, eight, and so on. In larger atoms, the inner electrons screen the outer electrons from the nucleus, result-ing in a more complex shell-filling sequence. This explains the partly filled shells of the ▷transition elements, forming the middle block of the table, in the long periods. The short periods are from lithium (Li) to neon (Ne) and from sodium (Na) to argon (Ar). The ▷noble gases in group 18 have complete outer shells and are generally chemically in-active.

● **periodontal disease** ▶ Disease of the gums and other structures surrounding the teeth, formerly known as pyorrhoea. Caused by the action of bacteria on food debris that forms a hard deposit (tartar) in the spaces between the gums and teeth, it results in swelling and bleeding of the gums: eventually the teeth become loose and fall out. Periodontal disease is the major cause of tooth loss in adults: it may be prevented (and treated) by regular brushing, scaling, and polish-ing, to remove tartar. Advanced cases require surgery.

● **Peripatus** ▶ A common genus of wormlike arthropods belonging to the tropical subphylum *Onychophora* (about 90 species; some biolo-gists regard the *Onychophora* as a distinct phylum). The soft unseg-mented body, about 50 mm long, bears 14–44 short stumpy legs. The animals live in moist dark places, under stones or logs, and feed on insects. The young develop within the mother and at birth resemble the adults.

● **periscope** ▶ An optical device consisting, typically, of a tube in which mirrors or prisms are arranged so that light passing through an aperture at right angles to the tube is reflected through the length of the tube to emerge at an aperture at the other end also at right angles to the tube. Periscopes in their simplest form are used to see over the heads of a crowd; in their more sophisticated form, they are extendible and used by submerged submarines to see above the sur-face of the water. In this form they may contain aiming devices for weapons, etc.

● **Perissodactyla** ▶ An order of hoofed mammals (16 species) that includes ▷horses, ▷tapirs, and ▷rhinoceroses. The name—meaning odd-toed—arose because the weight of the body is carried mainly by the central (third) digit of the foot. They are herbivorous but have evolved separately from other hoofed mammals and have a single stomach, which is less efficient than the digestive system of ▷rumi-nants. *Compare* Artiodactyla.

● **peristalsis** ▷*See* digestion; intestine.

● **peritonitis** ▶ Inflammation of the peritoneum—the membrane that lines the abdominal cavity. This is a serious condition that re-sults from the bursting of an abdominal organ (such as the appendix, gall bladder, or spleen) or of a peptic ulcer. Alternatively it may result from bacterial infection. The patient will be very ill, possibly in shock, with a painful and rigid belly. An immediate operation is es-sential to repair the perforated organ and to cleanse inside of the ab-domen; antibiotics are also administered.

● **periwinkle** ▶ (botany) An evergreen creeping shrub or perennial of the genus *Vinca* (5 species), native to Europe and W Asia. The soli-tary blue or white flowers are tubular with five lobes and the fruit is usually a long capsule. They thrive in shade and are cultivated as ornamentals; *V. major* is an important species. Family: *Apocynaceae*.

● **periwinkle** ▶ (zoology) A ▷gastropod mollusc belonging to the family *Littorinidae*, also called winkle. The common edible winkle (*Littorina littorea*) of European seashores is about 2 cm high and has a dark-green rounded shell with a pointed spire and grazes on algae.

The flat-sided periwinkle (*L. littoralis*) lacks the spire and occurs in many colours.

● **perjury** ▶ The offence of giving false evidence in judicial proceed-ings, on ▷oath or affirmation. It is punishable by up to seven years' imprisonment and a fine. The Perjury Act (1911) also creates the of-fence of making a false statement in nonjudicial proceedings (e.g. when registering a birth, marriage, or death), which is also punish-able by seven years' imprisonment.

● **Perkin, Sir William Henry** ▶ (1838–1907) British chemist, who in 1856 synthesized the first artificial dye, aniline purple. Perkin's dis-covery, when he was only 18, was made by accident while he was trying to synthesize quinine. The following year he built a factory to manufacture the dye but he later returned to chemical research and the synthesis of many compounds.

● **Perlis** ▶ The most northerly state in Peninsular Malaysia, border-ing on Thailand. Its well-watered plain produces rice, with some rubber and coconuts; tin is mined. Area: 803 sq km (310 sq mi). Popu-lation (1993 est): 187 600. Capital: Kangar.

● **Perm** ▶ (name from 1940 until 1957: Molotov) 58 01N 56 10E A port in W Russia, on the River Kama. Its varied industries include en-gineering, footwear and chemical manufacturing, and oil refining. The ▷Permian period was first identified here. Population (1995 est): 1 032 000.

● **permafrost** ▶ The permanent freezing of the ground, sometimes to great depths, in areas bordering on ice sheets. During the summer season the top layer of soil may thaw and become marshy, while the frozen ground below remains an impermeable barrier. Problems arise with construction of roads and buildings in permafrost areas due to the freeze-thaw processes. This seriously hindered the con-struction of the ▷Trans-Alaska Pipeline, completed in 1977.

● **Permalloy** ▶ An ▷alloy of one part iron to four parts nickel, often with other metals added. It has a high magnetic permeability, which makes it useful for parts of electrical machinery that are subjected to alternating magnetic fields.

● **permeability, magnetic** ▶ (μ) A measure of the response of a ma-terial to a ▷magnetic field equal to the ratio of the magnetic ▷flux in-duced in the material to the applied magnetic field strength. The relative permeability, μ_r, is the ratio of μ in the medium to that in a vacuum, μ_0 (*see* magnetic constant). Paramagnetic materials have a μ_r greater than unity because they reinforce the magnetic field. Ferro-magnetic materials can have a μ_r as high as 100 000. Diamagnetic ma-terials have a μ_r of less than one.

● **Permian period** ▶ The last geological period of the Palaeozoic era, between the Carboniferous and Triassic periods, lasting from about 280 to 240 million years ago. The period was marked by an in-creasingly dry climate that continued into the Triassic, and the two periods are often linked together as the Permo-Triassic, during which the New Red Sandstone was laid down.

● **permittivity** ▶ (ε) The absolute permittivity of a medium is the ratio of the electric displacement to the electric field at the same point. The absolute permittivity of free space is called the ▷electric constant. The relative permittivity (or dielectric constant) εr of a ca-pacitor is the ratio of its capacitance with a specified dielectric be-tween the plates to its capacitance with free space between the plates.

● **Pernambuco** ▷*See* Recife.

● **Pernik** ▶ 42 36N 23 03E A town in W Bulgaria, situated on the River Struma near Sofia. It has engineering and iron and steel indus-tries with coalmining nearby. Population (1990): 99 643.

● **Perón, Juan (Domingo)** ▶ (1895–1974) Argentine statesman; president (1946–55, 1973–74). Elected in 1946 after winning popular support as head of the labour secretariat, his position was strength-ened by the popularity of his second wife, **Evita Perón** (María Eva Duarte de P.; 1919–52), who was idolized by the poor for her chari-table work. After her death, support for Perón waned and he was de-posed. He went into exile but remained an influential political force in Argentina, returning in 1973, when he was re-elected president.

Juan Perón ► With his second wife Evita, photographed in 1950.

He died in office and was succeeded by his third wife **Isabel Perón** (María Estela Martínez de P.; 1931–   ), who was deposed by the army in 1976.

● **Pérotin** ► (Latin name: Perotinus Magnus; c. 1155–c. 1202) French composer, active in Paris. A leading exponent of ▷organum, he composed complex music in the ▷ars antiqua style.

● **Perpendicular** ► The style of [□]gothic architecture predominant in England between about 1370 and the mid-16th century. The name derives from the panel-like effect of the window design, with its pronounced vertical mullions broken regularly by horizontal divisions. Gloucester Cathedral choir (c. 1357) is an early example. The flat network effect was repeated in the late 14th-century development of fan vaulting for ceilings. Eton College chapel (begun 1441), King's College chapel, Cambridge (1446–1515), St George's chapel, Windsor (begun 1481), and the Henry VII chapel, Westminster Abbey (1503–19), are masterpieces of the Perpendicular style.

● **perpetual-motion machine** ► A hypothetical machine that produces continuous and unending motion without drawing energy from an outside source. Although such a machine would contravene the laws of ▷thermodynamics and therefore cannot be made, there have always been, and indeed still are, hopeful inventors who believe that it is possible to find loopholes in the laws of nature. A perpetual-motion machine would need to be frictionless (in contravention of the second law of thermodynamics) or would need to be able to create energy to overcome the friction (in contravention of the first law). Using the heat of the ocean to drive a ship (perpetual motion of the second kind) is also impossible, because it would contravene the second law. Applications for patents to cover perpetual-motion machines have not been accepted by the Patent Office in London since 1949.

● **Perpignan** ► 42 42N 2 54E A city in S France, the capital of the Pyrénées-Orientales department situated near the Spanish border. The capital of the former province of Roussillon in the 17th century, it has a gothic cathedral and a 13th-century castle (the former residence of the Kings of Majorca). Perpignan is a tourist and commercial centre, trading in wine, fruit, and vegetables. Population (1990): 108 049.

● **Perrault, Charles** ► (1628–1703) French poet and fairytale writer. As a member of the Académie Française he opposed ▷Boileau by championing the modern writers against the ancients. He is best known for his collection of fairytales, *Contes de ma mère l'Oye* (1697), translated into English in 1729 and best known by the English title, *Tales of Mother Goose*.

● **Perrin, Jean-Baptiste** ► (1870–1942) French physicist, who discovered that cathode rays carry a negative charge and therefore consist of particles and not waves, as many physicists then thought. He also used Einstein's equations for the Brownian movement to determine the approximate size of molecules.

● **Perry, Fred(erick John)** ► (1909–95) British tennis and table-tennis player. He was the world singles table-tennis champion in 1929 and in the three years 1934–36 he won the singles title at Wimbledon (a record beaten in 1979 by ▷Borg), as well as many other championships.

● **Perry, Matthew C(albraith)** ► (1794–1858) US naval officer. He led the naval expedition (1853–54) that forced Japan to open diplomatic relations with the USA, thus ending Japan's traditional isolation.

● **Perse, Saint-John** ► (Alexis Saint-Léger; 1887–1975) French poet. He was born in the West Indies, served as a diplomat in the Far East, and became secretary general of the Foreign Ministry in 1933. From 1940 to 1958 he lived in the USA. His poems, written in long free-verse lines, include *Anabase* (1922), translated by T. S. Eliot in 1930, and *Chronique* (1960). He won the Nobel Prize in 1960.

● **Persephone** ► (Roman name: Proserpine) Greek goddess of the underworld, daughter of Zeus and ▷Demeter. She was abducted by ▷Hades, who made her queen of the underworld. Zeus, moved by Demeter's sorrow for her daughter, allowed her to spend part of each year on earth, symbolizing the regeneration of natural life in the spring.

● **Persepolis** ► An ancient Persian city in Fars province, Iran. ▷Darius I (reigned 522–486 BC) planned it as the ceremonial capital of his empire and its wealth and splendour were legendary. Among the buildings on the vast central terrace were the apadana (royal audience hall), which was approached by stairways flanked by reliefs of tribute bearers, and ▷Xerxes' throne hall. The Achaemenian royal tombs are nearby. ▷Alexander the Great destroyed Persepolis in 330 BC.

● **Perseus** ► (astronomy) A constellation in the N sky near Cassiopeia, lying in the Milky Way. The brightest stars are the 2nd-magnitude Mirfak and the eclipsing binary ▷Algol.

● **Perseus** ► (Greek mythology) The son of Zeus and Danae. One of the greatest Greek heroes, he beheaded the ▷Medusa with the help of Athena, who gave him a mirror to avoid looking at the Gorgon and being turned to stone. He married **Andromeda**, daughter of the Ethiopian king. She had been chained to a rock as a sacrifice to a sea monster, which Perseus turned to stone by showing it the Medusa's head.

● **Pershing, John J(oseph)** ► (1860–1948) US general. After the US entry into World War I (1917), he commanded the American Expeditionary Force (AEF) in France, independently from Allied forces. He was chief of staff (1921–24).

● **Pershing missile** ► A US army two-stage solid-fuelled nuclear surface-to-surface missile launched from launcher vehicles and having a range of 740 km (460 mi). Several improved versions of the missile have been produced. It is named after Gen J. J. ▷Pershing.

● **Persia** ▷*See* Iran, Islamic Republic of.

● **Persian** ► A language of the ▷Iranian family. The official language of Iran, it is written in a modified Arabic script.

● **Persian art and architecture** ► The styles associated with the three principal phases of the Persian empire: ▷Achaemenian (550–331 BC), ▷Sasanian (224–651 AD), and Islamic. Achaemenian and Sasanian architecture are represented respectively by ▷Persepolis and ▷Ctesiphon. Sasanian kings commissioned monumental relief sculptures to commemorate victories and coronations. The Persian tradition of craftsmanship in metalwork, glassware, and ceramics dates from this period. After 651, Persian styles became an aspect of international trends in ▷Islamic art. Book illustration evolved into the renowned 15th–17th-century Persian miniature painting. The love of brilliant colours is epitomized in Persian carpets and in the architectural use of turquoise coloured tiles.

● **Persian cat** ► A domesticated cat, also called a Longhair, having a flowing coat with a ruff or frill around the neck. The 20 or so breeds are characterized by their short bodies and legs and bushy tails. The head has a snub nose, large round eyes, and small wide-set ears and the coat may be of any colour.

● **Persian Empire** ▷*See* Achaemenians.

● **Persian Gulf** ▸ An arm of the Arabian Sea, extending some 950 km (590 mi) NW beyond the Gulf of Oman. The large offshore oil deposits are exploited by the surrounding ▷Gulf States. Area: 233 000 sq km (89 942 sq mi).

● **Persian Wars** ▷*See* Greek-Persian Wars.

● **persicaria** ▷*See* Polygonum.

● **persimmon** ▸ A tree of the genus *Diospyros* that produces edible fruits. These are the Japanese persimmon (*D. kaki*), the American persimmon (*D. virginiana*), and the Asian date plum (*D. lotus*). Up to 30 m high, they have dark-green oval leaves. The round orange, yellow, or red fruits, 5–8 cm across, are eaten fresh, cooked, or candied. Family: *Ebenaceae*.

● **persistent vegetative state** ▸ (PVS) A condition resulting from brain damage usually caused by oxygen deprivation. The higher functions of the brain are destroyed, but reflex activities (including breathing) can continue. Thus the patient shows no awareness and cannot speak, think, feel, or move, but can survive indefinitely with artificial feeding. The first ruling by an English court that to discontinue treating such a patient would be lawful was made in November 1992.

● **personal equity plan** ▸ (PEP) A UK scheme to encourage individuals to invest in EU companies through an authorized plan manager, who buys securities on the investors' behalf. Investment decisions may be made by the manager (in **managed PEPs**) or by the investor (in **self-select PEPs**). Reinvested dividends are free of income tax and capital-gains tax is not incurred if investments are held for at least one year. Investors put in a lump sum or regular amounts up to an annual limit of £6000 for a **general PEP**, investing in more than one company, and an additional £3000 for a **single-company PEP**. **Corporate-bond PEPs** invest in fixed securities. PEPs were replaced by ▷ISAs on 6 April, 1999, but the arrangements for PEPs acquired before that date continue unchanged.

● **perspective** ▸ Any means of rendering objects or space in a picture to give an illusion of depth. The rules of linear perspective were formulated by ▷Brunelleschi and Leon Battista ▷Alberti in the 15th century and became one of the ▷Renaissance artists' most important scientific investigations. Objects are foreshortened by distance to an extent determined by guide lines that converge on one, two, or three points on the horizon line, known as vanishing points, according to whether the orientation of a scene is central, angular, or oblique.

● **Perspex** ▸ (polymethyl methacrylate) A colourless transparent thermoplastic material made by ▷polymerization of methyl methacrylate. It is used in light fittings, aircraft parts, and car parts. Resistant to ultraviolet radiation from fluorescent lights, it is widely used as a glass substitute.

● **perspiration** ▷*See* sweat.

● **Perth** ▸ 31 58S 115 49E The capital of Western Australia, on the Swan River. Founded in 1829, it expanded following the discovery of gold (1893) at Kalgoorlie. The University of Western Australia was founded in 1913 and there are two cathedrals. Its port, ▷Fremantle, and Kwinana, both to the S, are growing industrial centres. Population (1995 est): 1 262 600.

● **Perth** ▸ 56 24N 3 28W A city in E Scotland, the administrative centre of Perth and Kinross on the River Tay. An early capital of Scotland, it was the scene of the assassination of James I (1437). There are dyeing, textiles, whisky distilling, and carpet industries and it is a popular tourist centre. Population (1991): 41 453.

● **Perth and Kinross** ▸ A council area of central Scotland. Under local government reorganization in 1975 the historic county of Perthshire was abolished; the greater part combined with the small county of Kinross to form Perth and Kinross District in Tayside Region. In 1996 Tayside was abolished and Perth and Kinross became an independent ▷unitary authority. It is chiefly mountainous, with deep glens and lochs. Agriculture is concentrated in the SE lowlands. Other sources of income include tourism, forestry, and wool products. Area: 5231 sq km (2019 sq mi). Population (1999 est): 132 570. Administrative centre: Perth.

● **perturbations** ▸ Small departures of a celestial body from the orbital path it would follow if under the influence of a single central force. Short-term periodic disturbances arise from gravitational interactions with other bodies. Progressive disturbances or those of very long period can also occur.

● **Peru, Republic of** ▸ A country in the NW of South America, on the Pacific Ocean. Narrow coastal plains rise to the high peaks of the Andes, reaching heights of over 6500 m (21 000 ft). The land descends again through an area of forested plateaus to the tropical forests of the Amazon basin. Most of the population is of Indian or mixed Indian and European descent.
Economy: Peru is one of the world's leading fishing countries, the main product being fishmeal. Agriculture is important and the main crops include maize, rice, sugar cane, cotton, and coffee. Large-scale irrigation projects have been undertaken. The illegal cultivation of coca, which is sent to Colombia for processing into cocaine, is also widespread. Livestock is particularly important to the economy, especially the production of wool from sheep and llamas. Rich mineral resources include copper, silver, lead, zinc, and iron. In the 1970s oil was discovered, both in the jungles and offshore, but production is now declining. In recent years there have been considerable developments in industry and in communications. With its relics of ancient civilizations and its rain forests, Peru has a valuable tourist trade. The main exports include minerals and metals and fishmeal. Since the early 1990s the government has implemented a radical policy of privatization and other free-market reforms. This has been successful in curbing the hyperinflation of the 1980s and in attracting foreign investment, but social inequalities have grown. The country still has a large foreign debt.
History: Peru's precolonial history encompasses the civilization of the ▷Chimú and that of the ▷Incas, who were conquered by the Spanish under Pizarro in 1533. The viceroyalty of Peru, centred on Lima, enjoyed wealth in which the Indians had little share. A revolt in 1780 led by Tupac Amarú was suppressed. Peru was the last of Spain's American colonies to declare its independence (1821) and the Spanish were finally defeated in 1824. Political stability was achieved by Gen Ramón Castilla (1797–1867; president 1845–51, 1855–62), who developed Peru's economy, based on nitrates and phosphates from guano deposits. The country's prosperity was undermined by the War of the ▷Pacific (1879–83) in which Peru lost the nitrate-rich province of Tarapacà to Chile. After World War II, in which Peru declared war on Germany in 1945, the country depended on US aid. From the late 1960s there was a series of military coups, the last being in 1975, when Gen Francisco Bermúdez became president. In 1980, in Peru's first general election in 17 years, the former civilian president Fernando Beláunde Terry was re-elected; in 1985 he was replaced by Alan García Pérez. Since the late 1970s some 30 000 people have died in civil unrest, mostly owing to the activities of left-wing guerrillas, including the Maoist Sendero Luminoso (Shining Path) group. In 1990 Alberto Fujimori (1939–) was elected president. He suppressed guerrilla activity and pursued free-market policies; in 1992 opposition to his policies led him to dissolve Congress and suspend the 1979 constitution. A new constitution followed in 1993. In December, 1996 Marxist guerrillas took some 500 businessmen and politicians hostage in the Japanese embassy in Lima; the resulting siege ended when Peruvian forces stormed the building in April, 1997. Peru's long-standing border dispute with Ecuador, which led to war in 1941, 1981, and 1995, was finally settled in 1998. In 2000 Fujimori was elected to a third term amidst accusations of electoral fraud. Continuing protests and a corruption scandal led him to stand down later that year. In 2001 Alejandro Toledo was elected president, becoming the first Indian to hold the post. Peru is a member of the OAS and LAIA.

Republic of Peru

Head of state	President Alejandro Toledo
Official languages	Spanish and Quechua; Aymará is also widely spoken
Official currency	nuevo sol of 100 centavos
Area	1 285 215 sq km (496 093 sq mi)
Population (1999 est)	25 232 000
Capital	Lima
Main port	Callao

● **Peru Current** ▷*See* Humboldt Current.

● **Perugia** ▶ 43 07N 12 23E A city in Italy, the capital of Umbria. Originally an Etruscan city, it has 13th-century city walls, a 14th-century cathedral, an ancient fountain (the Maggiore Fountain), and a university (1200). Perugia is an agricultural trading centre and its manufactures include furniture and textiles. Population (1998 est): 154 566.

● **Perugino** ▶ (Pietro di Cristoforo Vannucci; c. 1450–1523) Italian Renaissance painter, born near Perugia. He worked on frescoes in the Sistine Chapel, including the *Giving of the Keys to St Peter* (1481–82). His spacious compositions and graceful figure style influenced his pupil ▷Raphael.

● **Perutz, Max Ferdinand** ▶ (1914–2002) British chemist, born in Austria, who developed ▷X-ray diffraction to determine the molecular structure of haemoglobin. For this work he shared a Nobel Prize (1962) with J. C. ▷Kendrew.

● **Pesaro** ▶ 43 54N 12 54E A town in Italy, in Marche on the Adriatic coast. It is the birthplace of Rossini, who established a school of music here. Population (1998 est): 88 210.

● **Pescadores** ▷*See* Penghu Islands.

● **Pescara** ▶ 42 27N 14 13E A seaport in Italy, in Abruzzi on the Adriatic coast. Its chief industries are tourism, shipbuilding, and fishing. Population (1998 est): 117 411.

● **Peshawar** ▶ 34 01N 71 40E A city in N Pakistan, situated at the E end of the Khyber Pass. One of the oldest cities in Pakistan, it has for centuries been a centre of trade between the Indian subcontinent, Afghanistan, and central Asia. Industries include textiles, shoes, and pottery and it has a university (1950). Population (1998): 988 055.

● **Pestalozzi, Johann Heinrich** ▶ (1746–1827) Swiss educationalist. A pioneer of mass education, Pestalozzi made several unsuccessful attempts to establish schools for poor children. His book *Wie Gertrud ihre Kinder lehrt* (1801) reflected his ideas on the intuitive method of education. Despite his apparent failures, his theories were of great importance to subsequent educational developments. Pestalozzi's work is commemorated in the **Pestalozzi International Children's Villages**, the first of which was established in 1946 for war orphans at Trogen (Switzerland). A second international village was established in 1958 at Sedlescombe, East Sussex, in the UK for the care and education of selected children from developing countries.

● **pesticides** ▶ Chemicals used to destroy plants, animals, or other organisms that interfere with agricultural or horticultural production or are harmful to humans. They include ▷herbicides, ▷insecticides, fungicides (which kill fungi), rodenticides (which kill rats and other rodents), and nematocides (which kill roundworms). In practice, pesticides are rarely specific in their actions, often harming or killing plants or animals that are not pests, and some may be toxic to humans in large quantities. In addition, pesticides that are not ▷biodegradable persist in the environment and accumulate in ▷food chains. For these reasons, alternative measures of pest control are being explored, including ▷biological control and—more recently—genetic modification of crop plants, using ▷genetic engineering techniques, to make them resistant to pesticides and/or disease-causing organisms.

● **Pétain, (Henri) Philippe** ▶ (1856–1951) French general and statesman. In World War I he distinguished himself at the defence of Verdun (1916), becoming marshal of France (1918). In World War II, when France was on the verge of defeat (1940), Pétain became prime minister. In June, 1940, he signed an armistice with Hitler that allowed for a third of France to remain unoccupied by Germany. His government of unoccupied France at Vichy was authoritarian and from 1942 was dominated by ▷Laval and the Germans. Pétain was sentenced to death in August, 1945, for collaboration but was then reprieved and imprisoned for life.

● **Peter (I) the Great** ▶ (1672–1725) Tsar (1682–1721) and then Emperor (1721–25) of Russia, who established Russia as a major European power. Peter ruled with his half-brother Ivan V (1666–96) until Ivan's death and under the regency of his half-sister ▷Sophia until

1689, when he became effective ruler. Peter travelled in W Europe in the late 1690s, acquiring knowledge of Western technology and returning to Russia with Western technicians, who were to implement the modernization programmes that marked his reign. He instituted many reforms in government and administration, trade and industry, and in the army. In the Great ▷Northern War (1700–21), he acquired Livonia, Estonia, and also Ingria, where in 1703 he founded St Petersburg. He campaigned less successfully against the Turks (1710–13) but gained territory in the Caspian region from war with Persia (1722–23). Peter's eldest son ▷Alexis died in prison, having been condemned to death for treason; Peter was succeeded by his wife, who became ▷Catherine I.

● **Peter I** ▶ (1844–1921) King of Serbia (1903–18) and then of Yugoslavia (1918–21). Brought up in exile, Peter was elected king after the assassination of the last Obrenović monarch. His rule was marked by its constitutionalism.

● **Peter, St** ▶ In the New Testament, one of the 12 Apostles. He was a fisherman on the Sea of Galilee until called by Jesus along with his brother ▷Andrew. He became the leader and spokesman for the disciples. Although his faith often wavered, notably at the crucifixion, when he denied Christ three times, Peter was named as the rock upon which the Church was to be built. He was entrusted with the "keys of the Kingdom of Heaven" (Matthew 16.19)—hence his symbol of two crossed keys. After Christ's death, he dominated the Christian community for 15 years, undertaking missionary work despite imprisonment. Whereas Paul had responsibility for the Gentiles, Peter's was to the Jews. He is believed to have been martyred and buried in Rome. Feast day: 29 June.

● **Peterborough** ▶ **1.** 52 35N 0 15W A city in E central England, in Peterborough unitary authority, Cambridgeshire, on the River Nene. The cathedral (begun in the 12th century) contains the tomb of Catherine of Aragon. Designated a new town in 1967, its industries include sugar-beet refining, foodstuffs, engineering, and brick making; it is a marketing centre for the surrounding agricultural area. Population (1991): 134 788. **2.** A unitary authority in E central England, in Cambridgeshire. Area: 402 sq km (155 sq mi). Population (1998 est): 156 000.

● **Peterborough** ▶ 44 19N 78 20W A city in SE Canada, in Ontario. It is an important manufacturing centre and the main commercial centre for central Ontario. The largest deposit of nepheline in the world (used in the manufacture of glass) is nearby. Population (1991): 68 371.

● **Peter Damian, St** ▶ (1007–72) Italian churchman; cardinal and Doctor of the Church. He is famous as a religious reformer who campaigned for clerical celibacy and attacked simony. Feast day: 23 Feb.

● **Peterhead** ▶ 57 30N 1 46W A port in NE Scotland, in Aberdeenshire. Scotland's most easterly town, built of locally quarried pink granite, Peterhead is a fishing port (formerly whaling) and servicing centre for North Sea oil rigs with engineering and fish-curing industries. Population (1991): 18 674.

● **Peter Lombard** ▶ (c. 1100–60) Italian theologian. He studied in Rheims and in Paris, where, between 1136 and 1150, he taught theology at the school of Notre Dame. He became Bishop of Paris in 1159. His most famous work, the *Books of Sentences* (1148–51), was an objective summary of the beliefs of earlier theologians. It was a standard text in the universities until the 16th century and many medieval scholars wrote commentaries on it, including Thomas ▷Aquinas.

● **Peterloo Massacre** ▶ (1819) The name given, by analogy with the battle of Waterloo, to the violent dispersal of a political meeting held in St Peter's Fields, Manchester. A peaceful crowd, numbering about 60 000, had gathered to hear Henry ▷Hunt speak on parliamentary reform. The magistrates, anxious about the size of the crowd, called in local troops. The cavalry were ordered to charge and in the ensuing panic 11 people were killed.

● **Peterson, Oscar Emmanuel** ▶ (1925–   ) Canadian Black jazz pianist, who has played with many leading jazz musicians as well as with his own trio. His many recordings include *The Gershwin Song Book* and *Peterson Plays Basie.*

● **Peter's pence** ► An annual contribution for the support of the papacy levied on all English householders from the 9th century. The one-penny tax continued to be raised, with some interruptions, until its abolition in 1534.

● **Peters' projection** ▷*See* map projection.

● **Peter the Hermit** ► (c. 1050–1115) French monk. A fervent supporter of the first ▷Crusade under Pope Urban II, he rallied over 20 000 peasants to follow him to the Holy Land, where many were massacred by the Turks. He later founded the monastery of Neufmoutier at Liège.

● **Petipa, Marius** ► (1819–1910) French dancer and choreographer. He exercised an important influence on the Russian imperial ballet in St Petersburg, where he worked from 1847 until 1903. He became its chief choreographer in 1862. His many ballets include *Don Quixote* (1869) and *The Sleeping Beauty* (1890), on which he collaborated with its composer, Tchaikovsky.

● **Petit, Roland** ► (1924–) French ballet dancer and choreographer. His innovatory ballets, characterized by elements of fantasy and contemporary realism, include *Carmen* (1949), *Kraanerg* (1969), and *The Blue Angel* (1985). He toured with his company in Europe and the USA and also choreographed for Hollywood films. Many of his productions starred his wife, the actress and dancer Zizi Jeanmaire (1924–).

● **petition of right** ► The procedure by which a person formerly petitioned against the English Crown for the restoration of property that the Crown had taken possession of, or for damages for breach of ▷contract. This method of claiming against the Crown, dating back to the reign of Edward I, has been replaced by ordinary court actions under the Crown Proceedings Act (1947). The **Petition of Right** (1628) was a parliamentary declaration accepted by Charles I. It made illegal imprisonment without trial, taxation without parliamentary approval, and the billeting of soldiers on private individuals.

● **petit mal** ▷*See* epilepsy.

● **Petöfi, Sándor** ► (1823–49) Hungarian poet. He came from a peasant background and elements of traditional folksong occur in his early poetry, notably in the narrative poem *Janós the Hero* (1845). His later poetry was chiefly concerned with the cause of nationalism. He disappeared during the battle of Segesvar (1849), in which the Hungarian revolutionary army was defeated by the Austrians and Russians.

● **Petra** ► An ancient town in S Jordan. It was the capital of the Nabataeans, nomadic Arabs who settled along the caravan routes from Arabia to the Mediterranean. Petra was a great trading centre from the 3rd century BC. It was incorporated in the Roman Empire in 106 AD and was superseded by ▷Palmyra in the 2nd century. Accessible only through a narrow gorge, Petra is renowned for its rock-cut temples and dwellings.

● **Petrarch** ► (Francesco Petrarca; 1304–74) Italian poet. He was born in Florence, but his family was banished and he lived mostly in Provence from 1312 to 1353, when he returned to Italy. He travelled widely in Europe and in 1341 was crowned as poet laureate in Rome. His humanist works of scholarship anticipated the Renaissance in their combination of classical learning and Christian faith. His other works include *Secretum meum*, his spiritual self-analysis, and *Africa*, a Latin verse epic on Scipio Africanus, but he is remembered chiefly for the *Canzoniere*, a series of love poems addressed to Laura. His work greatly influenced writers throughout Europe, including ▷Chaucer.

● **Petrea** ► A genus of tropical climbing plants (about 30 species), native to tropical America and the West Indies. Up to 9 m high, they have oblong leaves and sprays of bluish-purple flowers, each with five widely spaced strap-shaped petals and coloured sepals. Popular ornamental species include *P. volubilis* and *P. kohautiana*. Family: *Verbenaceae*.

● **petrel** ► A marine bird belonging to a widely distributed family (*Procellariidae*; 55 species) characterized by a musky smell, thick plumage, webbed feet, and a hooked bill with long tubular nostrils. 27–90 cm long, petrels are well adapted for oceanic life, feeding on fish and molluscs and only coming ashore to breed. Diving petrels belong to a family (*Pelecanoididae*; 5 species) occurring in the S hemisphere; they are 16–25 cm long, have short wings, and feed mostly on crustaceans. Order: *Procellariiformes*. ▷*See also* fulmar; prion; shearwater; storm petrel. ▫oceans.

● **Petrie, Sir (William Matthew) Flinders** ► (1853–1942) British archaeologist. After surveying British prehistoric sites, Petrie went to Egypt (1880), where his painstaking excavations and study of artefacts revolutionized and set new standards for archaeology. He excavated numerous sites, including ▷Naukratis, ▷Tell el-Amarna, and ▷Abydos, finally leaving Egypt for Palestine in 1926. He was the first professor of Egyptology at University College, London (1892–1933).

Petra ► The massive rock-cut temple of Ed Deir. The human figure in the central doorway shows the scale.

● **petrochemicals** ▷*See* oil.

● **Petrograd** ▷*See* St Petersburg.

● **petrol engine** ▷*See* car; internal-combustion engine.

● **petroleum** ▷*See* oil.

● **petrology** ► The study of rocks, including their formation, structure, texture, and mineral and chemical composition. **Petrogenesis** is the origin or mode of formation of rocks; **petrography** is the description and classification of rocks from hand specimens or thin sections.

● **Petronius Arbiter** ► (1st century AD) Roman satirist. He was appointed "Arbiter of Taste" at the court of Nero. The *Satyricon*, his picaresque novel of which only fragments survive, relates the scandalous adventures of the youths Encolpius and Ascyltos and includes the famous satirical portrait of a coarse and vulgar millionaire, Trimalchio. Petronius committed suicide after being falsely accused of conspiring against Nero.

● **Petropavlovsk** ▶ 54 53N 69 13E A city in N Kazakhstan, on the River Ishim. It is an important junction on the Trans-Siberian Railway and has varied industries. Population (1995 est): 239 000.

● **Petropavlovsk-Kamchatskii** ▶ 53 03N 158 43E A port in E Russia, on the Kamchatka Peninsula. Long a major naval base, it was attacked by the French and British during the Crimean War. Fishing, fish processing, and ship repairing are important. Population (1993 est): 265 000.

● **Petrópolis** ▶ 22 30S 43 06W A city and mountain resort in SE Brazil, in Rio de Janeiro state. Notable buildings include the Museum of the Empire (formerly the royal palace) and the gothic-style cathedral. Population (1991): 164 849.

● **Petrosian, Tigran Vartanovich** ▶ (1929–84) Soviet chess player, who was world champion from 1963 to 1969, when he lost the title to ▷Spassky. Despite his exhaustive preparations, as world champion his matches were often disappointing because his style of play tended to lead to draws.

● **Petrozavodsk** ▶ 61 46N 34 19E A city in NW Russia, the capital of the Karelian Republic on Lake Onega. It was founded (1703) by Peter the Great: engineering and timbering are important and there are many educational institutions. Population (1995 est): 280 000.

● **Petsamo** ▷See Pechenga.

● **Petunia** ▶ A genus of tropical American herbs (about 40 species), cultivated for their showy funnel-shaped flowers, which are sometimes frilled at the edges. Ornamental species include *P. integrifolia*, with pink, blue, or purple flowers, the white-flowered *P. axillaris*, which has a pleasant night fragrance, and hybrids between them. Family: ▷Solanaceae.

● **Pevensey** ▶ 50 49N 0 20E A village in SE England, in East Sussex. The landing place of William the Conqueror and an ancient Cinque Port (now inland), it has a ruined Norman castle built inside Roman walls. Population (1991): 2537.

● **Pevsner, Antoine** ▶ (1886–1962) Russian sculptor and painter, who worked in Paris from 1923. His early career was spent in W Europe but it was in Russia that he and his brother Naum ▷Gabo pioneered ▷constructivism in their *Realist Manifesto* (1920). His most characteristic works consist of curving shapes in striated metal.

● **Pevsner, Sir Nikolaus (Bernhard Leon)** ▶ (1902–83) British art historian, born in Germany. His best-known work was on architecture and included *An Outline of European Architecture* (1942) and his comprehensive survey *The Buildings of England* (1951–74).

● **pewter** ▶ An ▷alloy of tin (80–90%) and lead (20–10%) with small amounts of antimony to harden it or of copper to soften it. It was formerly used for plates, spoons, and other utensils but now only beer mugs are made from it.

● **peyote** ▶ A blue-green ▷cactus, *Lophophora williamsii*, also called mescal, native to Mexico and the SW USA. About 8 cm across and 5 cm high, it bears white to pink flowering heads, which, when dried, are known as "mescal buttons." They contain the alkaloid ▷mescaline, which produces hallucinations when chewed.

● **Pfeiffer, Michelle** ▶ (1957–   ) US film actress. After success in *Scarface* (1983) and *The Witches of Eastwick* (1987), she became a star in *Dangerous Liaisons* (1988) and *The Fabulous Baker Boys* (1989). Later films include *Batman Returns* (1992), *The Age of Innocence* (1993), *One Fine Day* (1997), and *What Lies Beneath* (2000).

● **Pforzheim** ▶ 48 53N 08 41E A city in SW Germany, in Baden-Württemberg. It was an important medieval trading centre and is the centre of the German watch and jewellery industry. Population (1996 est): 118 763.

● **pH** ▶ A measure of the acidity or alkalinity of a solution, equal to the logarithm to the base 10 of the reciprocal of the number of moles per litre of hydrogen ions it contains. Thus a solution containing 10^{-6} mole of hydrogen ions per litre has a pH of $\log_{10}(1/10^{-6}) = 6$. In pure water there is a small reversible dissociation into equal amounts of hydrogen and hydroxide ions: $H_2O \rightarrow H^+ + OH^-$. The product of the concentrations of these ions (moles/litre) is about 10^{-14}:

$[H^+][OH^-] = 10^{-14}$. In neutral solutions, therefore, the hydrogen ion concentration is 10^{-7} and the pH is consequently 7. In acid solutions the pH is less than 7; the lower the pH, the more acidic the solution. Conversely, alkaline solutions have pH values greater than 7. The pH scale is logarithmic; for example, a pH of 1 is ten times more acidic than a pH of 2. ▷See also acids and bases.

● **Phaedra** ▶ In Greek mythology, the daughter of ▷Minos and Pasiphaë and the wife of Theseus. She fell in love with her stepson ▷Hippolytus. When he rejected her, she hanged herself, having first written a letter to Theseus accusing Hippolytus of having seduced her.

● **Phaedrus** ▶ (1st century AD) Roman writer. Born a slave in Macedonia, he gained his freedom in the household of the emperor Augustus. He wrote poetic versions of the fables ascribed to ▷Aesop.

● **Phaethon** ▶ In Greek mythology, the son of the sun god Helios, who granted him his wish to drive the chariot of the sun for one day. Unable to control the horses, he was about to burn the earth when Zeus struck him down with a thunderbolt.

● **phaeton** ▶ A four-wheeled open carriage usually drawn by two horses. Various modifications of the phaeton (pony phaeton, Victoria phaeton, Stanhope phaeton, etc.) were fashionable in the 19th century for pleasure driving.

● **phagocyte** ▶ A cell that engulfs and then digests particles from its surroundings: this process is called **phagocytosis**. Many protozoans are phagocytic, but the word specifically refers to certain cells, especially ▷macrophages and monocytes (*see* leucocyte), that protect the body by engulfing bacteria and other foreign particles.

● **phalanger** ▶ A small herbivorous ▷marsupial of the family *Phalangeridae* (48 species), occurring in woodlands of Australia, (including Tasmania), and New Guinea. They range in length from 12 to 120 cm and are adapted for climbing trees, having strong claws and prehensile tails. The family includes the ▷cuscuses, ▷flying phalangers, ▷honey mouse, ▷koalas, and ▷possums.

● **Phalaris** ▶ (reigned c. 570–c. 554 BC) Tyrant of Agrigento in Sicily, who subjugated the indigenous Sicels and defied the Phoenicians. Phalaris was noted for his cruelty and was overthrown and executed.

● **phalarope** ▶ A lightly built migratory shorebird belonging to a family (*Phalaropodidae*; 3 species) in which the female fights for a territory and courts the male, which rears the young. 20–25 cm long, phalaropes have a slim neck and a grey and red-brown plumage. Two species breed in the Arctic and one in North America.

● **phallus** ▶ Any representation of the male sexual organ. A feature of primitive worship, especially as a symbol of fertility or creativity, in South America, among Australian aborigines, in India, and elsewhere, it also appeared in the Dionysiac festivals of ancient Greece and acquired significance in the early theatre, denoting farce.

● **phanerogam** ▶ In old classification systems, any plant that reproduces by means of flowers and seeds. Phanerogams comprised the flowering plants and the gymnosperms (conifers, etc.). *Compare* cryptogam.

● **Phanerozoic time** ▶ Geological time from the end of the Precambrian to the present day, about 590 million years. It refers to the eon of "evident life," when abundant recognizable fossils were laid down. *Compare* Cryptozoic time.

● **pharaoh** ▶ The title of ancient Egyptian rulers. The word derives via Hebrew from the Egyptian for great house. There were various symbols of kingship: the crook and flail and the white, red, or blue crown. The royal cobra, the sun god Ra's symbol, bound round the brow, signified divinity; pharaoh represented Ra reigning on earth. The first dynasty of pharaohs was founded about 3200 BC. □ p. 968.

● **Pharaoh hound** ▶ A breed of hunting dog whose ancestors are depicted in sculpture and friezes found in the tombs of the Egyptian pharaohs. The Pharaoh is a slender long-legged hound with a long muzzle and large ears. The short glossy coat is tan, with or without white markings. Height: 56–63 cm (dogs); 53–61 cm (bitches).

● **Pharisees** ▶ An ancient Jewish religious and political party. They stressed ritual purity and acknowledged a body of traditional laws not contained in the written ▷Torah. The party originated in the 2nd century BC and vied for political influence with the ▷Sadducees. In the ▷Gospels they are frequently criticized by Jesus, although his own teachings are very close to theirs. After the destruction of the ▷Temple of Jerusalem they ceased to exist, but many of their teachings were taken over into rabbinic Judaism.

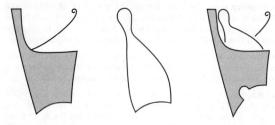

pharaoh ▶ The pharaoh's double crown, combining the red crown of Lower Egypt with the white crown of Upper Egypt, symbolized the unification of the two lands (c. 3100 BC).

● **pharmacology** ▶ The study of the action of drugs on living organisms. Pharmacologists examine the uptake of drugs after administration, the routes by which they reach their site of action, their subsequent effects, how drugs are destroyed by the body, their unwanted side effects, and the interaction between different drugs. Clinical pharmacology (or therapeutics) studies the effects of drugs in treating disease. **Pharmacy** is the science concerned with the preparation, manufacture, packaging, quality, and supply of medicinal drugs. The practice of pharmacy should conform to the standards laid down in the official **pharmacopoeia** of the country. This is a government-approved list giving details of the manufacture, dosage, uses, and characteristics of drugs. It is compiled by experts in pharmacy and pharmacology. The World Health Organization has issued the *Pharmacopoeia Internationalis* in an attempt to standardize drug preparations throughout the world.

● **Pharos of Alexandria** ▶ An ancient lighthouse, one of the ▷Seven Wonders of the World. Built in about 280 BC by Sostratus of Cnidos for Ptolemy II of Egypt, it was over 135 m (440 ft) high. It was demolished in the 13th century AD.

● **Pharsalus, Battle of** ▶ (48 BC) The decisive encounter near present-day Fársala (Greece) in the Roman civil war, in which Julius Caesar defeated Pompey. Pompey's defeat opened the way to Caesar's dictatorship.

● **pharynx** ▶ The muscular tract, lined with mucous membrane, between the back of the mouth and oesophagus (gullet) and larynx. It acts as a passageway for food between the mouth and gullet and it also conducts air from the nasal cavity (which opens into it) to the larynx and windpipe. The Eustachian tubes from the middle ▷ear also open into the pharynx. Inflammation of the pharynx (pharyngitis) is a common cause of a sore throat.

● **phase** ▶ (astronomy) The fraction of the face of the moon or a planet that is illuminated at a particular time in its orbit. Lunar phases vary from new moon (unilluminated) through a waxing crescent, first quarter (half illuminated), a waxing gibbous moon, to full moon (fully illuminated) followed by a waning gibbous moon, last quarter, a waning crescent, and the next new moon.

● **phase** ▶ (physics) **1.** The fraction of its whole cycle that a periodically varying system has completed. For example, two ▷alternating currents of the same frequency are **in phase** if they reach their maximum values at the same instant. If they are out of phase the angle between the ▷vectors representing the quantities is called the **phase angle**. In an electricity-supply system there are usually three phases, i.e. three separate alternating voltages having the same frequency but being displaced in phase relative to each other by one third of a cycle. **2.** Any portion of a system that is physically distinct, is homogeneous throughout, and can be mechanically separated from other phases. For example, a salt solution is a one-phase system, whereas a mixture of ice and water is a two-phase system. ▷See also phase rule.

● **phase rule** ▶ A rule stating the conditions of equilibrium for a heterogeneous system. It relates the number of degrees of freedom of a system f, the number of ▷phases p, and the number of components c, by the rule $f = c - p + 2$. It was proposed by J. W. ▷Gibbs in 1877 and is important in the study of metallurgy, mineralogy, and ceramics.

● **Phasmida** ▶ An order of generally flightless insects (2000 species), occurring mostly in tropical and oriental regions. They comprise the ▷leaf insects and ▷stick insects, both of which show a striking resemblance to the vegetation on which they live and feed.

● **pheasant** ▶ A long-tailed gamebird belonging to an Old World subfamily (*Phasianinae*; 50 species) occurring in open or woodland regions (see Plate III). 50–200 cm long, pheasants are heavily built and have short rounded wings, a short bill, and strong claws for scratching up grain, roots, and grubs. Males are larger than females and brightly coloured, with bright fleshy wattles, large leg spurs, and long tail feathers. They have been introduced to many regions for sport or ornament. Family: *Phasianidae* (pheasants, quail, partridges); order: *Galliformes* (pheasants, turkeys, etc.). ▷See also golden pheasant; tragopan.

● **phenobarbitone** ▷See barbiturates.

● **phenol-formaldehyde resins** ▷See plastics.

● **phenols** ▶ A class of organic compounds with the general formula ROH, in which the –OH group is linked directly to a carbon atom in an aromatic ring (see aromatic compound). Although formally similar to alcohols, the phenols have widely different properties; in particular, the aromatic ring confers acidic behaviour on the –OH group. The simplest example, phenol itself (or **carbolic acid**), C_6H_5OH, is a white deliquescent solid used as a disinfectant and in the production of drugs, weedkillers, and synthetic resins.

● **phenomenology** ▶ A philosophical enquiry into intellectual processes, which is characterized by the vigorous exclusion of any preconceptions about existence or causes. It is thus distinct from ▷psychology, the aim of which is causal explanations rather than pure description. ▷Husserl was the first to elevate this method into an independent philosophy.

● **phenothiazines** ▶ A group of powerful tranquillizing drugs, including chlorpromazine and fluphenazine. Used in the treatment of ▷schizophrenia and ▷manic-depressive psychosis, they are thought to act by inhibiting the action of a chemical (dopamine) in the brain. ▷See also antipsychotics.

● **phenotype** ▶ The characteristics of an individual, representing the sum total of the effects of the interaction of its inherited characteristics with its environment. A striking example of this occurs in the Himalayan rabbit, which grows either black or white fur according to the temperature. *Compare* genotype.

● **phenylamine** ▷See aniline.

● **phenylketonuria** ▶ A genetic disease that leads to mental deficiency if untreated. Patients are unable to metabolize the amino acid phenylalanine, which is a normal constituent of diet; the amino acid and its derivatives accumulate in the body and prevent proper mental development. Phenylketonuria can now be easily detected at birth by a routine test. Babies with the disease need a special diet that contains little phenylalanine, which should be maintained until adolescence.

● **pheromone** ▶ A chemical substance produced by animals to communicate with others of the same species. The best-known pheromones are the sex attractants secreted by moths to attract mates and the queen substance produced by queen honeybees, which controls the development and behaviour of worker bees. Pheromones are also used by ants to lay trails and by mammals to mark out territories.

● **Phidias** ▶ (c. 490–c. 417 BC) Athenian sculptor, one of the most influential artists of his time. Phidias designed and supervised the sculptures of the ▷Parthenon (see Elgin Marbles). His works included a bronze statue of ▷Athena on the Athenian ▷acropolis and two famous chryselephantine statues: Athena in the Parthenon and ▷Zeus at Olympia (where his workshop has been found).

● **Phidippides** ▶ (5th century BC) Greek runner who ran 241 km (150 mi) from Athens to Sparta in two days to ask for help against the Persians before the Battle of ▷Marathon in 490 BC.

● **Philadelphia** ▶ 40 00N 75 10W A city in the USA, situated on the Delaware River in Pennsylvania at the junction of the Schuylkill River. Founded in 1681 by the Quaker, William Penn, its religious tolerance attracted a large number of immigrants. It has many historic buildings, including Independence Hall (1732–59), where the Declaration of Independence was adopted and the ▷Liberty Bell is kept. Benjamin Franklin is buried here. A cultural centre, it is the site of the University of Pennsylvania (1779) and the Franklin Institute (1824) and has a famous symphony orchestra. It is the USA's fourth largest city and has the world's largest freshwater port. Its output of manufactured goods is exceeded only by four other US cities. Industries include oil refining, textiles, and shipbuilding. Population (1996 est): 1 478 002.

● **Philadelphus** ▷*See* mock orange.

● **Philae** ▶ 24 02N 32 59E A submerged islet in the River Nile, in SE Egypt just above Aswan. Flooding caused by the first Aswan Dam from 1902 onwards damaged the many ancient temples on the island. These were moved to a higher island before Philae was totally submerged by Lake Nasser after the construction of the ▷Aswan High Dam.

● **philately** ▶ (*or* stamp collecting) Collecting and studying postage stamps as a hobby, which began immediately following their introduction in England (1840). Catalogues were first issued in the early 1860s as collecting became increasingly concerned with such details as watermarks, perforations, and numberings. Collectors usually specialize in a particular theme, country, or type of issue. Rare stamps in good condition, which fetch extremely high auction prices, are a form of investment, while the market among collectors for commemorative stamps or first-day covers is an important source of revenue for post offices.

● **Philby, H(arry) St John (Bridge)** ▶ (1885–1960) British explorer and Arabist. He joined the Indian civil service in 1907 and in World War I undertook a political mission to central Arabia, where he crossed the Empty Quarter. He became a Muslim in 1930 and friend and adviser of Ibn Saud of Saudi Arabia. His son **Harold Adrian Russell Philby** (1912–88) was an intelligence officer and Soviet secret agent, known as Kim Philby. He became a Soviet agent in 1933 and entered the British intelligence service in 1940. From 1949 to 1951 he was liaison officer between the British and US intelligence services in Washington, DC. He defected to Russia in 1963.

● **Philemon** ▶ (c. 368–c. 264 BC) Greek dramatist. Born in Sicily, he became a citizen of Athens and also worked in Alexandria. His plays, of which only fragments survive, were frequently acclaimed by his contemporaries as superior to those of his rival, ▷Menander.

● **Philemon, Epistle of Paul to** ▶ A New Testament book written in about 60 AD that is the only strictly private letter of Paul to be preserved. In it he requests Philemon, a Christian friend in Colossae, to welcome and forgive Onesimus, his runaway slave, who had become a Christian after meeting Paul. Onesimus delivered the letter.

● **Philemon and Baucis** ▶ In Greek mythology, an old peasant couple who offered hospitality to Zeus and Hermes, who were disguised as mortals. They were subsequently spared from a flood that destroyed the land and their cottage was transformed into a temple. They were granted their wishes to serve as priest and priestess in the temple and finally to die together.

● **Philidor, André Danican** ▶ (d. 1730) French musician. As assistant librarian of the Royal Music Library at Versailles he made a large collection of instrumental court music. His youngest son **François André Danican Philidor** (1726–95) wrote several operas and was also a considerable chess player.

● **Philip (I) the Handsome** ▶ (1478–1506) King of Castile (1506). Son of Emperor Maximilian I and Mary of Burgundy he succeeded to his mother's possessions in 1482. In 1496 he married Joanna the Mad, who inherited the Castilian throne in 1504. Her insanity led Philip to assume sole control in 1506. Their son became Emperor ▷Charles V.

● **Philip (II) of Macedon** ▶ (382–336 BC) King of Macedon (359–336), who founded the Macedonian empire. Philip unified Macedonia, expanded the economy, and trained a professional army with which he gradually bore down on the Greek city states. Despite the resolute opposition of ▷Demosthenes at Athens, the Greeks were defeated at the battle of ▷Chaeronea (338). Philip planned to lead a combined force against Persia but he was assassinated and the plan was carried out by his son ▷Alexander (III) the Great.

● **Philip II Augustus** ▶ (1165–1223) King of France (1179–1223), who destroyed the ▷Angevin empire of the English kings. He waged war with Henry II (1187–89), Richard Lionheart (1194–99), and John; he took Normandy in 1204, followed by Maine, Touraine, and Anjou (1204–05), and in 1214 defeated an English-imperial alliance at ▷Bouvines. He participated in the third Crusade.

● **Philip II** ▶ (1527–98) King of Spain (1556–98). He inherited a vast empire from his father ▷Charles V, including Naples and Sicily, the Netherlands, and Spanish possessions in America; in 1580 he annexed Portugal. He married Mary I of England in 1554. Philip faced the ▷Revolt of the Netherlands and the Turkish threat in the Mediterranean, suppressed the ▷Moriscos, launched the Spanish ▷Armada against Protestant England (1588), and intervened in the French ▷Wars of Religion against the Huguenots. On his death Spain was bankrupt and its economy destroyed, largely as a result of the cost of these wars.

● **Philip (IV) the Fair** ▶ (1268–1314) King of France (1285–1314). Hostilities with England (1294–1303) were ended by the betrothal of Philip's daughter Isabella of France to Edward II. Conflict with Pope Boniface VIII over the right of lay rulers to tax clergy ended only with Boniface's death (1303) but his successor Clement V was more easily handled and in 1309 moved the papacy to Avignon. In 1306 Philip expelled the Jews from France and his reign also witnessed the suppression of the ▷Templars (1307–13).

● **Philip V** ▶ (1683–1746) The first Bourbon King of Spain (1700–24, 1724–46). The grandson of Louis XIV of France, his accession instigated the War of the ▷Spanish Succession. He abolished the self-

Philae ▶ The rising waters of Lake Nasser partially submerging the Kiosk of Trajan.

governing privileges of Aragon and centralized the administration. He abdicated in 1724 in favour of his son Luis (1707–24) but returned to the throne when Luis died.

● **Philip VI** ► (1293–1350) The first Valois King of France (1328–50), succeeding his cousin Charles IV. The failure of the rival claim of Edward III of England to the French throne contributed to the outbreak in 1337 of the ▷Hundred Years' War, in which Philip suffered severe defeats at Sluys (1340) and Crécy (1346).

● **Philip, Prince, Duke of Edinburgh** ► (1921–) The husband (from 1947) of Elizabeth II of the United Kingdom. A descendant of Queen Victoria and the son of Prince Andrew of Greece, he assumed the name Mountbatten in 1947, when he took British citizenship. He served in the Royal Navy during World War II. In 1956 he introduced the **Duke of Edinburgh's Award Scheme** to encourage the social awareness and personal development of young people aged 14–25.

● **Philip, St** ► In the New Testament, one of the 12 Apostles. He was a native of Bethsaida and was responsible for bringing Nathanael (probably Bartholomew) to Jesus. In medieval art he is symbolized by loaves because of his participation in the miracle of the loaves and fishes. He may have been martyred. Feast day: 11 May.

● **Philippeville** ▷See Skikda.

● **Philippi, Battle of** ► (42 BC) The battle in which Mark Antony and Octavian (later Emperor ▷Augustus) defeated ▷Brutus and ▷Cassius Longinus in the Roman civil war.

● **Philippians, Epistle of Paul to the** ► A New Testament book written by Paul in about 60 AD to the church at Philippi in Macedonia, the first church that he founded in Europe. He thanks the Philippians for the gifts they have sent to him in prison in Rome and tells how he has continued to spread Christianity while imprisoned. The epistle contains an important doctrinal passage on the nature of Christ and the Incarnation.

● **Philippine eagle** ► A rare ▷eagle, *Pithecophaga jefferyi*, occurring in tropical forests of the Philippines, formerly called monkey-eating eagle because it feeds mainly on macaque monkeys. It is 85–100 cm long and has a brown plumage with pale underparts, a shaggy crest, a huge bill, and very powerful talons.

● **Philippines, Republic of the** ► A country in SE Asia, consisting of an archipelago of over 7000 islands, of which some 880 are inhabited, between the Pacific Ocean and the South China Sea. Except for the central plain of Luzon (where most of the population is concentrated) there are few extensive lowlands, most of the larger islands, including Mindanao, being mountainous and volcanic and reaching heights of almost 3000 m (10 000 ft). Most of the inhabitants are Filipinos with small minorities of Chinese and others.
  Economy: based principally on agriculture, forestry, and fishing. The production of the staple crops of rice and maize and the main cash crops (sugar, coconuts, bananas, and pineapples) is concentrated around the central plain of Luzon although attempts are being made to develop economic activities elsewhere. The fastest-growing productive sector in recent decades has been mining, based on the country's wide range of metallic minerals, which include copper, gold, iron ore, manganese, molybdenum, zinc, lead, and silver. Forests cover over half the land, providing gums and resins, bamboo, and dyes in addition to good-quality hardwoods. The main industries are electronics, food processing, textiles, and wood processing. Tourism and manufacturing are expanding. In general, economic development has been hindered by the unstable political situation, massive government corruption during the Marcos years, and huge inequalities of land ownership. Some 70% of the population are estimated to live below the poverty line and there is a large foreign debt.
  History: colonized by Spain in 1565, the islands were ceded to the USA in 1898 following the Spanish-American War. Occupied (1942–45) by the Japanese during World War II, they became an independent republic in 1946. During the initial years of independence, a succession of presidents, US economic interests, and the Filipino landowning class did little to improve the standard of living of the peasant majority, but following the election of President ▷Marcos in 1965 rapid economic development and a greatly improved infrastructure brought increased prosperity to the Philippines. During

the early 1970s growing communist guerrilla activity in the N and a Muslim separatist movement in the S led to martial law (1972). In 1978 President Marcos was re-elected. In 1981 martial law was lifted but the assassination of the exiled opposition leader, Benigno S. Aquino (1983), rekindled unrest. Marcos was exiled to the USA in 1986 when Cory ▷Aquino (widow of Benigno) became president. Her reforms included a new constitution; several attempted coups by Marcos supporters failed and left-wing guerrillas kept up a continuing campaign. She was succeeded by her ally Fidel Ramos, who became president in 1992. In 1996 he signed a peace agreement with the Muslim rebels, involving the creation of an autonomous Muslim region in the S. Presidential elections in 1998 resulted in victory for the left-wing populist Joseph Estrada. In 2001 allegations that Estrada had amassed a fortune from bribes led to huge protests that forced his resignation; he was subsequently arrested.

Republic of the Philippines

Head of state	President Gloria Macapagal-Arroyo
Official languages	Filipino (a new language based on Tagalog) and English
Official currency	Philippine peso of 100 centavos
Area	300 000 sq km (115 830 sq mi)
Population (1999 est)	74 723 000
Capital and main port	Manila

● **Philippine Sea** ► A section of the W Pacific Ocean, N and E of the Philippines. It contains deep trenches, volcanic submarine mounts, and coral reefs and is particularly prone to hurricanes. Its warm currents provide important fishing grounds. Maximum depth: 10 540 m (34 580 ft).

● **Philippopoli** ▷See Plovdiv.

● **Philip the Bold** ► (1342–1404) Duke of Burgundy (1363–1404), so called because of his military courage, particularly at the battle of Poitiers (1356) in the Hundred Years' War. The youngest son of John the Good of France, during the minority of his nephew Charles the Well-Beloved he was one of the regents of France and later, when Charles became insane, virtual ruler. He was also a noted art patron.

● **Philip the Good** ► (1396–1467) Duke of Burgundy (1419–67). He recognized Henry V of England as heir to the French throne in 1420 but acknowledged Charles VII as King of France in 1435. In 1430 he founded the Order of the ▷Golden Fleece. He was a notable patron of artists.

● **Philip the Magnanimous** ► (1504–67) Landgrave of Hesse, an ally of ▷Luther. Converted to Protestantism in 1524, Philip led the suppression of the ▷Peasants' War in 1525. He attempted to reconcile Luther and ▷Zwingli, who became theologically divided over the Eucharist. In 1531 he helped establish the Schmalkaldic League of Protestant princes. However, in 1540 his bigamous marriage, approved by Luther, was used by Emperor Charles V to split the Protestants and in 1547 the League was defeated by Charles at the Battle of Mühlberg.

● **Philistines** ► A non-Semitic people, who were driven from Egypt about 1200 BC and settled in Canaan, resisting Israelite attacks so vigorously that the region took the name Palestine from its new settlers. Tradition holds they were originally one of the ▷Sea Peoples who left Crete as the Mycenaean world collapsed. A warlike seafaring people, without cultural pretensions (hence the derogatory word philistine), they were largely absorbed into the kingdom of Israel under King David about 1000 BC.

● **Phillip, Arthur** ► (1738–1814) British admiral, who founded New South Wales. After service in the Seven Years' War and the American Revolution he was appointed to found a penal settlement in New South Wales. Arriving in 1788, he chose the site of Sydney, administering the colony until 1792.

● **Phillips' curve** ► A relationship between the rate of wage increase and unemployment, plotted by the British economist A. W. Phillips (1914–75) in 1958. The Phillips' curve suggested that the UK Government had an option between unemployment and inflation, i.e. it could achieve a little less of one if it was prepared to accept a little more of the other. The monetarists (*see* monetarism) hold that the relationship is theoretically unsound and it has indeed broken down in practice since 1966.

● **Philoctetes** ▶ A legendary Greek hero, who had inherited from his father the bow and arrows of Heracles. On the way to Troy with the Greek expedition he was bitten by a snake. His cries and the stench of his wound forced the Greeks to leave him on Lesbos. Odysseus and Diomedes later returned to fetch him, needing the help of his bow and arrows. He then killed Paris and helped to bring about the fall of Troy.

● **Philodendron** ▶ A genus of woody, usually climbing, plants (275 species), native to tropical America. They have oval, oblong, arrow-shaped, or heart-shaped leaves, either deeply cut or coloured along the veins, and they cling to trees or other supports by means of aerial roots growing from their stems. Cultivated as ornamental house plants for their foliage, *P. andreanum* and *P. erubescens* are among the most popular species. Family: *Araceae*.

● **Philo Judaeus** ▶ (c. 30 BC–45 AD) Jewish philosopher from the ▷diaspora community in Alexandria, then the Greek capital of Roman Egypt. Philo's voluminous treatises, written in Greek, reinterpret Jewish religion in terms of Greek philosophy. Some were designed for sophisticated Jews; others defend Judaism against Greek scorn of Jewish culture. In old age Philo represented the Jews on a deputation to the Roman emperor following antisemitism in Alexandria. Most of his works have survived owing to their popularity with later Christian writers.

● **philology** ▶ The study of language in general, before the growth of modern ▷linguistics. It originally applied to the study of classical languages and literatures but came to be applied to what is now called comparative linguistics. Comparative studies were undertaken in the 19th century by many philologists, including Jacob ▷Grimm, who helped to identify and trace the relationships of the ▷Indo-European languages.

● **Philomela and Procne** ▶ In Greek legend, the daughters of an Athenian king. Procne married Tereus, King of Thrace. He fell in love with Philomela, raped her, and cut out her tongue to prevent her telling his secret. By means of an embroidery Philomela told Procne of the outrage and in revenge Procne killed her own son, Itys, and fed his flesh to Tereus. He then attempted to kill the sisters but was turned into a hoopoe and the sisters into a swallow and a nightingale.

● **philosopher's stone** ▶ A hypothetical substance sought by alchemists for its ability to turn less valuable minerals into gold. In alchemical literature it is also called the elixir, the tincture, and hundreds of other fanciful names. It was sometimes credited with the power of curing all diseases and of making its possessors immortal. ▷*See* alchemy.

● **Philosophes** ▶ A group of French philosophers and writers of the 18th century whose faith in the ultimate authority of reason was expressed in their active concern with social and political reform. They included ▷Montesquieu, ▷Voltaire, J.-J. ▷Rousseau, and ▷Diderot, the chief editor of their literary monument, the *Encyclopédie* (1751–72; *see* Encyclopedists).

● **philosophy** ▶ (Greek: love of wisdom) The field generally concerned with the study of ultimate reality and the first principles of thinking, knowledge, and truth. The main theoretical branches of modern Western philosophy are ▷epistemology, ▷ethics, and ▷metaphysics; ▷logic (now closely associated with mathematics) and ▷aesthetics are also traditionally included. Historically, philosophical as opposed to religious or magical speculation arose in Greece in the 6th century BC in the attempts of the school of Miletus (*see* Thales; Anaximander; Anaximenes) to discover the single element underlying all things. This line of enquiry was pursued further by later Presocratics, including Heraclitus, Pythagoras, Parmenides, and Democritus. The most important phase of ancient philosophy occurred with the teaching of Socrates, who developed the dialectical method and applied it to political and other problems. The works of his successors, Plato and Aristotle, not only shaped the future of European philosophy in most fundamental respects, but also deeply influenced Christian theology. Among later schools of classical philosophy were ▷Epicureanism, ▷Stoicism (which strongly appealed to Roman philosophers), and ▷Neoplatonism. Aristotelianism was preserved in the works of medieval Islamic philosophers, such as Avicenna and Averroes, and re-entered Christian Europe in the ▷scholasticism of Anselm, Abelard, and Aquinas. Although influenced by scholasticism, the work of Descartes, with its systematic doubt and emphasis on reason, signalled the end of the medieval synthesis and the beginning of the modern period and the dominance of science. Spinoza and Leibniz attempted to deal with problems raised by Descartes; their rationalist systems are usually contrasted with the empiricism of the English philosophers, especially Locke, Berkeley, and Hume. Kant, whose aim was to reconcile these approaches and relate the sensible and the intelligible, was one of the most significant thinkers of the 18th century and stimulated the development of German idealism in the works of Fichte, Schelling, and Hegel. Idealism was also stimulated by the writings of Rousseau, whose ideas were the major source of 19th-century Romanticism and influenced the work of Schopenhauer and Nietzsche. In England utilitarianism was developed by Bentham and J. S. Mill, dialectical materialism by Marx and Engels, and Hegelian idealism by F. H. Bradley. Pragmatism is particularly associated with the Americans William James and, later, John Dewey. Philosophy in the 20th century has been characterized by a marked difference in interests and emphases between most Continental philosophers and those working in English-speaking countries. The writings of Bergson and Croce had an influence on a number of writers (including prominent English men of letters) early in the century. The phenomenology of Husserl (and the works of Kierkegaard) led to the ▷existentialism of Heidegger and Sartre. Since the 1970s continental philosophy has been dominated by ▷structuralism and ▷poststructuralism (notably the deconstruction of Derrida). In contrast to their speculative approach to many of the large issues of traditional philosophy, the principal concern of English-speaking thinkers has been a critical approach that concentrates on logical analysis and the role of language—a development that may be traced in the works of Bertrand Russell, A. N. Whitehead, G. E. Moore, Wittgenstein, the logical positivists (the ▷Vienna Circle), and in the school of "ordinary language" philosophy centred at Oxford.

Indian and other eastern types of philosophical thought are closely bound to the religious or cultural framework in which they developed (e.g. ▷Taoism, ▷Vedanta, Zen Buddhism).

● **Phiz** ▷*See* Browne, Hablot Knight.

● **phlebitis** ▶ Inflammation of a vein, which is always accompanied by some ▷thrombosis in the vein. The inflammation may be caused by injury or infection or it may occur for no apparent reason: thrombosis of the vein then follows. Alternatively inflammation may develop after thrombosis. Treatment of superficial phlebitis is by rest and support.

● **phloem** ▶ Plant tissue specialized to transport synthesized foods, mainly sugars, around the plant. It consists principally of tubelike cells that lack nuclei, the end of one cell being linked to the next by means of a porous wall (sieve plate). The cells are controlled by small neighbouring cells, known as companion cells.

● **phlogiston theory** ▶ A theory of combustion introduced by Johann Becher (1635–82) and refined by Georg ▷Stahl in about 1700. It assumes that all combustible substances contain phlogiston, which is liberated when the substance is heated, leaving calx or ash. The theory was finally overthrown in the late 18th century by Antoine ▷Lavoisier, who correctly explained combustion in terms of oxidation.

● **phlogopite** ▶ A ▷mica mineral, $K_2(Mg,Fe^{2+})_6(Si_6Al_2O_{20})(OH,F)_4$. It is brown or bronze coloured and occurs in some peridotites and metamorphosed limestones. Phlogopite is used principally for making commutators.

● **Phlox** ▶ A genus of ornamental herbs (about 65 species), mostly native to North America. Growing to about 1 m high, they have terminal clusters of tubular flowers with five white, pink, red, or purple spreading petals. The creeping phlox, or moss pink (*P. subulata*), forms carpets of flowers in rock gardens. *P. drummondii* is the source of most garden varieties. Family: *Polemoniaceae*.

● **Phnom Penh** ▶ (*or* Pnom Penh; Cambodian name: Phnum Pénh) 11 35N 104 55E The capital of Cambodia a port at the head of the Mekong delta. The capital since about 1432, it is now the site of the royal palace and of many museums and pagodas. A cultural centre, it has several universities, including a Buddhist university (1954) and the University of Phnom Penh (1960). The country's commercial centre, its industries include textiles and food processing. Population (1994 est): 920 000.

● **phobia** ▶ A pathological fear of a situation or thing. The main kinds are agoraphobia (fear of public places and open spaces); claustrophobia (fear of enclosed places); specific phobias of individual things, such as knives; social phobias of encountering people; and animal phobias, as of spiders or snakes. Phobias are sometimes learned after a frightening incident, sometimes acquired in childhood from other people, and sometimes result from ▷depression. They are treated with ▷behaviour therapy, ▷psychotherapy, and drug treatment.

● **Phocis** ▶ A region of ancient Greece, N of the Gulf of Corinth. The Phocians were intermittently engaged in a struggle to retain control of Apollo's shrine at ▷Delphi. In the first Sacred War (c. 590 BC) the Phocians lost Delphi. The second confirmed their possession. Early in the 4th century they again lost it, retaking it in 356. In the third Sacred War (355–346) the Phocians were defeated by Philip of Macedon, who then conquered all Greece.

● **Phoenicia** ▶ A group of city states on the coastal plain of Syria N of ancient ▷Canaan. Semitic peoples settled here sometime before 1800 BC and after about 1000 BC they became outstanding navigators and merchants, establishing trading posts all over the E Mediterranean and beyond. Their major cities—▷Tyre, ▷Sidon, and ▷Byblos—were ports. The Phoenician alphabet, the ancestor of all Western alphabets, was the chief Phoenician contribution to cultural progress. Phoenicia fell successively under Egyptian, Babylonian, and Persian influence. It was attacked by ▷Alexander the Great (332 BC), becoming part of the Hellenistic and later the Roman Empires. Phoenicia's major colony in N Africa was ▷Carthage.

● **phoenix** ▶ A fabulous bird associated with sun worship, especially in Egypt, and representing resurrection and immortality. According to Herodotus, it was like an eagle in size, had red and golden plumage, and lived for 500 years. Only one bird existed at a time. The dying phoenix was consumed by fire and from its ashes a new bird arose.

● **Phoenix** ▶ 33 30N 112 03W A city in the USA, the capital of Arizona on the Salt River. The commercial centre for a cotton-growing and farming region, it manufactures aircraft and textiles. Its warm dry climate makes it a popular health resort. Population (1996 est): 1 159 014.

● **Phoenix Islands** ▶ An uninhabited group of coral atolls in the S Pacific Ocean. They comprise ▷Canton and Enderbury under joint US-British control and the Birnie, McKean, Phoenix, Hull, Sydney, and Gardner islands in Kiribati. Area: about 28 sq km (11 sq mi).

● **Phoenix Park Murders** ▶ (1882) The assassination in Phoenix Park, Dublin, of the new chief secretary for Ireland, Lord Frederick Cavendish (1836–82), and the permanent undersecretary, Thomas Burke (1829–82), by extreme Irish nationalists calling themselves the Invincibles. British public opinion forced ▷Gladstone to respond with a new Coercion Act for Ireland.

● **phon** ▶ A unit for measuring the loudness of sound equal to the intensity in ▷decibels of a sound of frequency 1000 hertz, which appears to the ear to be as loud as the sound to be measured.

● **phonetics** ▶ The study of the production and perception of sounds in languages. Sounds are classified in terms of the way in which they are produced by the speech organs. There is a wide range of possible speech sounds but each language uses only a selection of them. The study of the system of sounds within any given language is called **phonology** and the selected individual sounds are called phonemes. Phonetics also includes the study of stress and intonation.

● **phonology** ▷See phonetics.

● **phosphates** ▷See phosphorus.

● **phosgene** ▶ (*or* carbonyl chloride; $COCl_2$) A lethal war gas that attacks the respiratory system and causes death by asphyxiation. It was first used by the Germans in World War I. ▷See also chemical warfare.

● **phospholipid** ▶ Any of a group of ▷lipids that consist of a phosphate group and one or more fatty acids. They are major components of cell ▷membranes in plants and animals. Phospholipids possess a polar "head" (the phosphate group) and a hydrophobic hydrocarbon "tail"—a structure that lends itself to the formation of membrane-like formations in water.

● **phosphorescence** ▷See luminescence.

● **phosphorus** ▶ (P) A nonmetallic solid element discovered by H. Brand (died c. 1692) in 1669. It exists in at least four forms: white (α and β), red, and black. White phosphorus is a waxy solid, which ignites spontaneously in air to form the pentoxide (P_2O_5). Red phosphorus, a more stable allotrope, is formed when white phosphorus is heated to 400°C; it is used in matches. Black phosphorus is also stable and forms when white phosphorus is heated to 200–300°C. Phosphorus exists in nature chiefly as the mineral ▷apatite ($Ca_3(PO_4)_2$), from which the element is obtained, either by reduction with carbon or reaction with silica at high temperatures. Phosphates are used extensively as fertilizers (mainly as "superphosphate"—calcium hydrogen phosphate) but find other uses in detergents, water softeners, and specialist glasses. A wide range of compounds is formed including the hydride (phosphine; PH_3), numerous phosphates (for example Na_3PO_4), and phosphides (for example Na_3P). Phosphorus occurs in DNA and RNA molecules and is therefore essential to life; bones also contain phosphates (*see* apatite) but some organo-phosphorus com-

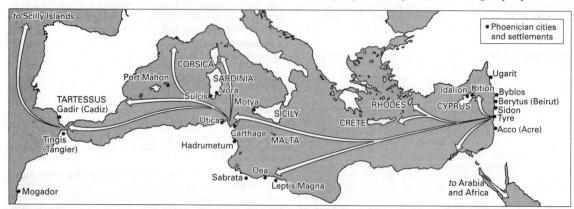

Phoenicia ▶ From their homeland along the E Mediterranean shore (modern Lebanon and Syria) the Phoenicians traded throughout the Mediterranean and beyond and established many settlements.

pounds are extremely toxic and are used as nerve gases. At no 15; at wt 30.9738; mp (white) 44.1°C; bp (white) 280°C.

● **Photius** ▶ (c. 810–c. 895 AD) Patriarch of Constantinople, whose condemnation of certain practices and doctrines of the Western Church contributed to the rift with the Eastern Church. A leading statesman at the Byzantine court, he was elected patriarch in 858 amid much controversy and before he had been ordained. In 867 he convened a council at Constantinople at which he excommunicated Pope ▷Nicholas I, who had earlier deposed him, and denounced the ▷Filioque clause in the creed. Several depositions and reinstatements followed until he was finally exiled to Armenia in 886. He is also famous for his scholarship and is a saint in the Orthodox Church.

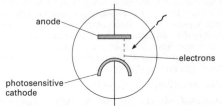

photoemissive cell Illumination releases electrons from the cathode.

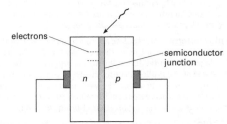

photovoltaic cell Illumination creates a potential difference at a p–n semiconductor junction.

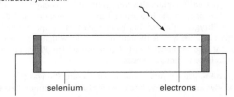

photoconductivity cell Illumination increases the conductivity of a semiconductor, such as selenium.

photocell

● **photocell** ▶ (or photoelectric cell) A device that makes use of a ▷photoelectric effect to measure or detect light or other electromagnetic radiation. In the photoemissive cell, a photosensitive cathode emits electrons when it is illuminated; these photoelectrons constitute a current when they flow to the positive anode of the cell. In solid-state devices the light changes the behaviour of a p–n junction (as in the photodiode), creating a potential difference by the ▷photovoltaic effect. In the conductivity cell, the resistance of a substance, such as selenium, changes when light falls on it as a result of ▷photoconductivity. Photocells are widely used in light-operated controls, such as automatic doors, fire alarms, and burglar alarms; they are also used in solar cells (see solar power) and photographic light meters. ▷See also selenium cell.

● **photochemistry** ▶ The branch of chemistry concerned with chemical reactions in which light or ultraviolet radiation causes the reaction to take place. The photons from the light are absorbed by reactant molecules to create reactive excited molecules (see excitation) or free radicals, which undergo further reactions. ▷Photosynthesis, ▷photography, and solar cells (see solar power) all involve photochemistry.

● **photoconductivity** ▶ The increase in the conductivity of certain semiconductors, such as selenium, when exposed to light. It occurs when photons excite electrons in the material from the valence band into the conduction band. ▷See energy bands; photocell.

● **photocopying machine** ▶ A device that prints black-and-white or coloured copies of documents, drawings, etc., from an optical image. The most common technique is a dry electrostatic process known as xerography. A pattern of electric charge is induced by light falling on a layer of ▷semiconductor material on a conducting surface. Toner powder is sprayed or rolled onto this material, so that it sticks to the highly charged areas. The image so formed is printed onto charged paper, where it is fixed by heating to produce the final copy. Xerography is also used for high-speed printing of computer output, with printing heads instead of a light image.

● **photoelectric cell** ▷See photocell.

● **photoelectric effects** ▶ A number of effects in which electromagnetic radiation interacts with matter, frequently with the emission of electrons. These effects include ▷photoconductivity, the ▷photovoltaic effect, and the ▷Compton effect and the ▷Auger effect. The frequency of the radiation (f) has to be such that the energy of the photon (hf, where h is the Planck constant) is sufficient to liberate the electron. For solids, the minimum energy required is called the work function; for free atoms or molecules it is equal to the first ▷ionization potential, the effect then being known as ▷photoionization. For most substances, an ultraviolet frequency is needed to eject an electron, but for some metals, such as caesium, visible light is sufficient. ▷See photocell.

● **Photofit** ▷See Identikit and Photofit.

● **photography** ▶ The recording of images on sensitized material, by means of visible light, X-rays, or other radiation, and the subsequent chemical processing. The first photograph was taken in 1826 by Joseph Nicéphore Niépce (d. 1833) using the action of light on asphalt solution. In 1839, ▷Daguerre introduced the daguerrotype, a positive image of milky white on a silver background, produced directly from silver iodide emulsion on plates exposed inside a simple ▷camera. Modern photography involves a negative made by the development of ▷film coated with silver salts. The positive picture is obtained by shining light through the negative onto light-sensitive paper with a coating similar to that on the original film. Lenses can be used to enlarge or reduce the size of the final image on the print. Transparencies, for use with a slide ▷projector, may also be made. Film is usually developed and printed in a darkroom by dipping it in baths of chemicals. Polaroid photography, however, produces positive pictures directly from the camera in one stage. This system was invented by Edwin Land in 1947 and is used for instant pictures for security passes, laboratory records, etc.

Photography as an art dates back almost to the origins of the technique. Portraiture was already established in the 1850s and was a prime interest of the Photographic Society (later the Royal Photographic Society) founded in London in 1853. The Crimean War in the 1850s and the US ▯Civil War in the 1860s provided the first opportunities for the true miseries of war to be realistically portrayed. However, during the last half of the 19th century photographic interest centred on the landscape, especially as horizons broadened with the growth of travel.

In the 1920s the collages of the cubist painters encouraged such photographers as László ▷Moholy-Nagy to experiment with photomontages. But by the 1930s the Frenchman Henri ▷Cartier-Bresson had led fashion back to a more realistic technique: using the camera as an extension of the eye, he captured transient scenes in revealing detail. Picture magazines were also a feature of this period, one of the best-known being Picture Post, started in London in 1938 by a German refugee from Hitler, Stephen Lorant. Postwar photography has developed many of these themes, using the new precision cameras and techniques, and many galleries now have permanent exhibitions of photography.

Photography has also had a profound effect on painting. Some art historians believe that the 20th-century trend towards abstract painting has been primarily a reaction to the camera's ability to do superbly what representationalist painters have often only been able to do indifferently. ▷*See also* colour photography; cinematography; digital photography.

● **photoionization** ▶ The ▷ionization of an atom when it is bombarded with electromagnetic radiation. The frequency of the radiation has to be such that the energy of its ▷photons exceeds the first ▷ionization potential of the atom.

● **photoluminescence** ▷*See* luminescence.

● **photolysis** ▶ The breaking of a chemical bond by absorbed electromagnetic radiation. The photon energy of the radiation must exceed the bond energy, and photolytic reactions can be produced by light, ultraviolet radiation, and X-rays. Examples occur in ▷photosynthesis, suntan, and photography. **Flash photolysis** is a technique for identifying and studying unstable reaction intermediates. The intermediates are produced in a gas by an intense brief flash of light, and their reactions are followed by spectroscopy.

● **photometry** ▶ The branch of physics concerned with measuring quantities related to the intensity of light. These quantities are measured in two ways. If the intensity is measured in terms of the energy of the light, they are known as radiant quantities. They may also be measured in terms of their visual effect, since the sensitivity of the eye varies with the wavelength of the light. They are then known as luminous quantities.

● **photomicrograph** ▷*See* microscope.

● **photomultiplier** ▶ An instrument that produces an amplified current when exposed to electromagnetic radiation. Photons striking a photocathode cause the emission of electrons by the ▷photoelectric effect. These electrons then strike another surface causing a greater number of electrons to be emitted, the process being repeated several times to produce a greatly amplified current. Photomultipliers are used in certain ▷scintillation counters.

● **photon** ▶ The quantum of ▷electromagnetic radiation, having an energy hf, where h is the ▷Planck constant, and f is the frequency of the radiation. It may also be regarded as an elementary particle with ▷spin 1 and zero mass that travels at the speed of ▷light.

● **photoperiodism** ▶ The response of an organism to the relative lengths of day and night, based either on a daily, seasonal, or yearly cycle. Flowering in plants, breeding in animals, and bird migration are examples of photoperiodic responses, which may be modified by such factors as temperature and availability of food. In general the response is a reaction to day length, but the flowering of plants actually depends on the length of the dark period. Thus, short-day plants (e.g. chrysanthemums) flower in response to a long night and long-day plants (e.g. certain cereals) flower when nights are short.

● **photosphere** ▶ The boundary between the atmosphere of a star and its much denser interior. The sun's photosphere is its visible surface, several hundred kilometres thick, lying between the opaque outer (convective) zone of the sun's interior and its transparent atmosphere. Almost all the energy emitted by the sun is radiated from the photosphere. Its temperature falls from about 6000°C at the convective zone to about 4000°C where the photosphere merges with the ▷chromosphere. ▷*See also* sunspots.

● **photosynthesis** ▶ The means by which plants and certain bacteria produce carbohydrates from carbon dioxide and a hydrogen source. The energy for the process is provided by light absorbed by the green pigment chlorophyll, which is contained in the ▷chloroplasts. Plants use water (H_2O) as the hydrogen source and release its oxygen as a by-product, thus replenishing the atmospheric oxygen that is used in respiration by all living organisms. Photosynthesis occurs in the chloroplasts and comprises two sets of reactions. One set, which requires light, produces energy-storing and reducing compounds; the other reactions, which may proceed in the light or dark, use these compounds to add hydrogen atoms to carbon dioxide and make carbohydrates. The overall reactions can be summarized by the equation $6CO_2 + 6H_2O \rightarrow C_6H_{12}O_6 + 6O_2$.

● **phototypesetting** ▷*See* typesetting.

● **photovoltaic effect** ▶ The production of a voltage when light falls on certain materials coated with another substance. The effect can be detected by connecting the two materials through an external circuit to generate a current. It occurs in copper (I) oxide on copper and in selenium on iron. ▷*See also* photocell.

● **phrenology** ▶ An obsolete approach to the study of the nervous system, first proposed by a Viennese doctor, F. J. Gall (1758–1828). The degree of mental development was supposed to be indicated by the shape of the skull, reflecting the development of the underlying parts of the brain in which the various mental processes were assumed to take place. Although discredited, it was important in developing ideas about the localization of brain function.

● **Phrygia** ▶ The central and W areas of Asia Minor inhabited after the Hittite empire collapsed (12th century BC) by Thracian migrants. The shortlived Phrygian kingdom, centred on its capital Gordium, reached its peak in the late 8th century. The legendary ▷Midas was King of Phrygia. In about 700 BC Phrygia was conquered by Lydia. Phrygia was a centre for the cult of ▷Cybele, which it passed on to Greece; it also influenced early Greek music. The Phrygians are reputed to have invented embroidery.

● **Phryne** ▶ (4th century BC) Greek courtesan. She was the lover of ▷Praxiteles and probably the model for his most famous statue, the

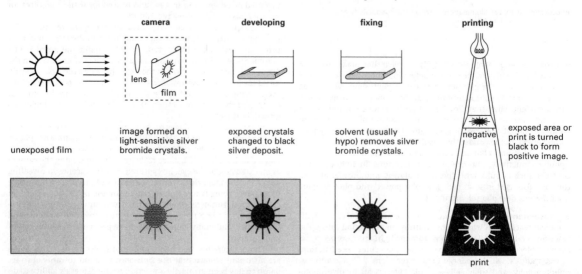

photography ▶ The stages in making a black and white photographic print.

Aphrodite of Cnidos, as well as for the painting of Aphrodite Anadyomene by Apelles.

● **Phyfe, Duncan** ▶ (*or* Fife; 1768–1854) US cabinetmaker and furniture designer, born in Scotland. His highly successful firm in New York produced furniture in the Sheraton, Regency, and French Empire styles.

● **phylacteries** ▶ (Hebrew word: *tefillin*) Two small black boxes attached by leather straps to the left arm and the forehead of adult male Orthodox Jews during morning prayers (except on the Sabbath or religious festivals). The boxes contain biblical texts, such as the *Shoma* (Deuteronomy 6.4–9), and their use reflects obedience to the biblical injunction that the law should be "a sign upon your arm and a frontlet between thine eyes" (Deuteronomy 6.8).

● **phyle** ▶ A tribal subdivision or clan in ancient Greek city states, its members being tied by descent from a common ancestor. The phyle upheld clan traditions, cults, and loyalties and encouraged aristocratic rule. By the 5th century BC Athens and Sparta had replaced the phylae with artificial district divisions for administrative and military purposes, engendering allegiance to the city rather than the clan.

● **Phyllanthus** ▶ A mostly tropical genus of trees, shrubs, herbs, and aquatic plants (600 species), including a few ornamental greenhouse plants. Many have flattened green stems resembling leaves, with yellow, red, or white flowers along their margins. *P. acidus* (Indian gooseberry) has round fleshy ribbed fruits used in pickles and preserves. Family: *Euphorbiaceae*.

● **phylloxera** ▶ A plant-eating insect belonging to the family *Phylloxeridae*, closely related to the ▷aphids. The grape, or vine, phylloxera (*Phylloxera vitifoliae* or *Viteus vitifolii*) is a notorious pest of grapevines. During a complex life cycle, the insect forms galls on the leaves and roots, which damage the plant. The grape phylloxera spread to Europe from North America in the 19th century and almost destroyed the wine industry in France.

● **phylogeny** ▶ The history of the ▷evolution of a species or other group of organisms. By studying the fossil record, comparative anatomy, embryology, biochemistry, and geographical distribution of the groups involved, one can establish the probable lines of descent and degrees of relationship between broad groups of plants or animals to produce a phylogenetic tree. For example, it is believed that whales and carnivorous land mammals developed from insectivorous mammals living more than 65 million years ago. Phylogeny forms the basis for the classification of organisms (*see* taxonomy). It should be distinguished from **ontogeny**, which is the succession of developmental stages through which an individual organism passes during its lifetime. ▷*See also* biogenetic law.

● **phylum** ▶ A major unit of classification for living organisms (*see* taxonomy). Organisms belonging to the same phylum share basic features but are divided into classes, orders, genera, and species according to their supposed degrees of relationship. For example, the phylum *Arthropoda* is a very diverse group including the insects, spiders, scorpions, crustaceans, etc., which all share the features of a tough segmented external skeleton and jointed limbs. In traditional plant-classification systems the equivalent term is division.

● **physical chemistry** ▷*See* chemistry.

● **physical medicine** ▶ The medical specialty concerned with the treatment of physical disabilities. Originally this was restricted to the diagnosis and management of rheumatic diseases, but it has now been extended to the treatment and rehabilitation of patients disabled by back injuries, polio, asthma, and many other disorders.

● **physics** ▶ The study of the interrelationship between matter and energy, without reference to chemical change. Traditionally the subject was divided into the study of mechanics, electricity and magnetism, heat and thermodynamics, optics, and acoustics. More modern aspects of the subject include quantum mechanics, relativity, nuclear physics, particle physics, solid-state physics, and astrophysics.

● **Physiocrats** ▶ A group of French 18th-century economists, led by François ▷Quesnay. The Physiocrats believed that the only real pro-

ductive sector in the economy was agriculture: industry and merchants were seen as mere processors. As mercantile interests (*see* mercantilism) were no longer identified with the wealth of the nation, ▷laissez-faire and ▷free trade were advocated.

● **physiology** ▶ The study of the functioning of living organisms and their constituent parts. Physiology is closely linked with both ▷anatomy (the study of structure) and ▷biochemistry (the chemical reactions that play a vital role in many physiological processes).

● **physiotherapy** ▶ The treatment of injuries or disabilities using physical methods, such as massage, manipulation, exercise, and heat. Physiotherapists play an important role in restoring mobility to patients confined for a long period to bed or a wheelchair; they also enable the rehabilitation of those handicapped by strokes, cerebral palsy, polio, etc., or immobilized by fractures. Physiotherapy is also useful in reducing the pain and stiffness of arthritis. In the UK student physiotherapists must undergo a three-year training period and pass an examination before qualifying as members of the Chartered Society of Physiotherapy (MCSP).

● **phytochrome** ▶ A pigment of plants that exists in two interchangeable forms, one absorbing red light and the other, far-red light. Day-length responses (*see* photoperiodism), greening of young leaves, and the breaking of dormancy in some seeds are among the processes controlled by phytochrome.

● **phytosaur** ▶ An extinct amphibious reptile, resembling a modern crocodile, having long pointed jaws with sharp teeth and protective bony plates beneath the skin. Phytosaurs lived during the late Triassic and Jurassic periods (210–135 million years ago) and probably fed on fish. The nostrils were set on a mound near the eyes and not at the end of the snout (as in crocodiles).

● **pi** ▶ In mathematics, the ratio of the circumference of a circle to its diameter, denoted by the Greek letter π. It was proved to be an irrational number by J. H. ▷Lambert and transcendental by F. Lindemann (1852–1939). Its value is 3.14159.... ▷*See also* numbers.

● **Piacenza** ▶ 45 03N 09 41E A city in N Italy, in Emilia-Romagna on the River Po. Dating from Roman times, it has several notable buildings, including a 12th-century cathedral and a 13th-century town hall. Piacenza is primarily an agricultural trading centre. Population (1994 est): 101 692.

Edith Piaf ▶ After the war Piaf came to represent the spirit of Paris. When she died the traffic in much of the city ground to a halt as the dejected Parisians flocked on to the streets to watch her funeral procession.

● **Piaf, Edith** ▶ (Edith Giovanna Gassion; 1915–63) French cabaret and music-hall singer. Originally a street singer, her small size earned her the nickname "piaf" (French slang: sparrow). Many of her songs, which include "Je m'en fou pas mal," "Je ne regrette rien," and "La Vie en rose," reflected the defiance and despair of her own tragic life, which was ended prematurely by her addiction to alcohol and drugs.

● **Piaget, Jean** ▶ (1896–1980) Swiss psychologist, noted for his studies of thought processes in children. He described the development of perception, judgment, reasoning, and logic during childhood, which had important consequences for children's education. His books include *The Origin of Intelligence in Children* (1954) and *The Early Growth of Logic in the Child* (1964).

● **piano** ► A ⬚musical instrument consisting of a number of wire strings stretched over a metal frame, which are hit by felt-covered wooden hammers operated by a keyboard. The piano was invented by ▷Cristofori in the early 18th century; the name derives from the Italian *pianoforte*, soft-loud, referring to the variation in volume obtainable on the piano in contrast to the earlier ▷clavichord and ▷harpsichord. In the modern instrument the frame is either horizontal, as in the **grand piano**, or vertical, as in the **upright piano**. Groups of two or three strings are tuned to each note. When a key is struck the escapement mechanism allows the hammer to fall away from the strings after they have been struck; when the key is released a felt damper stops the vibration of the strings. Two pedals allow a wide variation in volume. The right-hand pedal prevents the dampers from cutting off the sound; the left-hand pedal moves the hammers so that they are either closer to the strings (in the upright piano) or only able to strike one or two strings of each group (in the grand piano). The piano has a compass of seven and a quarter octaves; it has the largest repertory of any single instrument. Famous makers of pianos include J. B. Broadwood (1732–1812) and the firms of Bechstein, ▷Steinway, and Bösendorfer.

● **Piano, Renzo** ► (1937–) Italian architect. With Richard ▷Rogers he designed the Pompidou Centre, Paris (1971–77). Other projects include the De Menil Collection Museum in Houston, Texas (1981–86), a new international airport in Kansai, Japan (1990–), and a major redevelopment of the Potsdamer Platz in central Berlin (1992–).

● **pianola** ▷See player piano.

● **Piave, River** ► A river in NE Italy. It flows generally S from the Carnic Alps to the Adriatic Sea 32 km (20 mi) NE of Venice. It formed the main Italian line of defence in World War I after the Austro-German offensive in 1917. Length: 220 km (137 mi).

● **Picabia, Francis** ► (1879–1953) French painter and writer. Working chiefly in Paris but also in New York (1913–17), Barcelona, and Zürich, he was associated successively with ▷cubism, ▷dada, and ▷surrealism. He is known mainly for his periodical *391* (1917–24), containing his poems, essays, and satirical drawings of machinery.

● **Picardy** ► (French name: Picardie) A planning region and former province in N France. It was incorporated into France in 1477 by Louis XI of France. During World War I it was the scene of heavy fighting. Area: 19 411 sq km (7493 sq mi). Population (1995 est): 1 855 300.

● **picaresque novel** ► A type of narrative that recounts the adventures of a single protagonist in a loose episodic form. The term derives from the Spanish *pícaro*, a rogue. Early examples of the form include the Spanish *Lazarillo de Tormes* (1554) and the French *Gil Blas* (1715–35) by ▷Lesage. English examples include *Moll Flanders* (1722) by ▷Defoe, *Jonathan Wild* (1743) by ▷Fielding, and *Peregrine Pickle* (1751) by ▷Smollett. The form is usually characterized by comedy and social satire rather than by the development of ideas or characters; it was continued in the 19th century by ▷Thackeray in *Barry Lyndon* (1844) and in the 20th century by Thomas ▷Mann in *The Confessions of Felix Krull, Confidence Man* (1954).

● **Picasso, Pablo** ► (1881–1973) Spanish artist, born in Malaga. The most inventive and versatile of 20th-century painters and a precocious draughtsman, Picasso trained in Barcelona but worked chiefly in Paris after 1900. Although his most popular paintings are those of the beggars, acrobats, and harlequins of his blue (1901–04) and rose (1905–08) periods, his most original work began with *Les Demoiselles d'Avignon* (1907), influenced by Cézanne and African sculpture, and resulted in his development of ▷cubism with ▷Braque. In 1912 he made the first collage. He later began a series of classical paintings of colossal figures, followed by nightmarish distorted figure studies in the 1920s and 1930s, when he was loosely associated with ▷surrealism. One of his major works, *Guernica* (1937), is a horrific depiction of the destruction of the Basque capital during the Spanish Civil War. His later works include numerous reworkings of the Old Masters, paintings on the theme of the artist and model, and erotic etchings. The Pablo Picasso Museum in Paris, housing the largest collection of his works, opened in 1985.

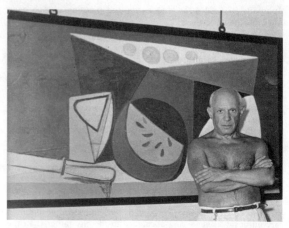

Pablo Picasso ► The artist photographed in his studio in the late 1940s.

● **Piccard** ► A family of Swiss scientists and explorers. **Auguste Piccard** (1884–1962) and his twin **Jean-Félix Piccard** (1884–1963) pioneered the scientific study of the stratosphere in balloons, reaching a height of 16 940 metres in 1932. In 1948 Auguste designed a **bathyscaphe**, using it to explore the sea depths, descending to over 3000 metres in 1953. His son **Jacques Piccard** (1927–) collaborated with his father in designing bathyscaphes and reached a depth of 10 917 metres in the vessel *Trieste* in 1960.

● **piccolo** ► A woodwind instrument, the smallest and shrillest member of the ▷flute family. It is pitched an octave higher than the flute and its music is written an octave lower than it sounds. It is used in the orchestra and in the military band.

● **picketing** ► The act of employees or their union representatives in attending at their place of work to persuade others not to work in furtherance of a trade dispute. **Primary picketing** (in which the employer is the immediate party to the dispute) is not wrongful if carried out peacefully. **Secondary picketing** (in which the employer is not directly concerned in the dispute) is not always wrong. Employees may, for example, picket their employer, who is a supplier of the employer in the dispute.

Flying pickets are pickets that are ready to move at a moment's notice to a plant at which they are not employed, and have no immunity from legal action.

● **Pickford, Mary** ► (Gladys Mary Smith; 1893–1979) Canadian-born US film actress. She played the roles of innocent young heroines in early silent films, such as *The Little American* (1917) and *Polyanna* (1919). In 1919 she cofounded United Artists with Charlie ▷Chaplin, D. W. ▷Griffith, and Douglas ▷Fairbanks, whom she married.

● **pick-up** ► A device that converts information stored in a gramophone record into an electrical signal. In a record player, the pick-up cartridge, usually a removable assembly, consists of a stylus and a ▷transducer. The stylus is forced to vibrate by the undulations in the record groove. The transducer responds electrically to these vibrations. The most common types of transducer use the ▷piezoelectric effect or ▷electromagnetic induction, but ▷capacitor, variable-resistance, and variable-reluctance pick-ups are also used. A stereo pick-up has one stylus that picks up vibrations from both sides of the V-shaped groove. The components of the resulting two-dimensional vibration contributed by each side are at right angles and are separated by two suitably oriented transducers. Since the advent of tape recorders and the compact disc, record players have become virtually obsolete.

● **Pico della Mirandola, Giovanni, Conte** ► (1463–94) Italian Renaissance philosopher. He was converted by ▷Ficino to ▷Neoplatonism and became interested in the Hermetic and Zoroastrian writings. Although Pico was concerned to prove the truth of Christianity, he was inevitably regarded with suspicion by the Church, which banned a proposed discussion (1486) by him of philosophical and theological topics. He wrote an important study of the ▷kabbalah.

● **picric acid** ► (*or* 2,4,6-trinitrophenol; $C_6H_2(NO_2)_3OH$) A yellow crystalline solid used as a dye and to make explosives.

● **pictographic writing systems** ► (*or* pictography) Writing systems in which each symbol represents a concept or word in the form of a sketch or diagram of the object it represents (the referent). Prehistoric pictographic records have been found throughout the world. It is a characteristic of primitive societies that a distinction is not maintained between an object, a word denoting the object, and a pictorial representation of it. Pictography is therefore often associated with magic rather than the recording of information. Disadvantages of pictography include the difficulty of representing any word except nouns having concrete referents. Pictographic systems therefore generally developed into ▷ideographic writing systems.

● **Picts** ► (painted people) The Roman name (referring to their tattoos) for Scottish tribes living N of the ▷Antonine Wall. The Picts' hostility forced the Romans to withdraw behind ▷Hadrian's Wall by 200 AD; they remained independent until Kenneth I MacAlpine unified S Scotland in the 9th century.

● **piddock** ► A burrowing ▷bivalve mollusc belonging to the family *Pholadidae*, of cold and temperate seas. Piddocks are adapted for boring into rock, having shells with serrated cutting edges, the largest being 10 cm long. They can damage concrete breakwaters, sea walls, and wharves.

● **pidgin** ► A form of English, used between Chinese and Europeans, having a greatly reduced vocabulary, simplified grammar, and modified sound system. The term may also be applied to ▷Neo-Melanesian and the Beach-la-Mer of the South Seas. *Compare* creole.

● **Pieck, Wilhelm** ► (1876–1960) German communist politician. He opposed both the Weimar Republic and Nazism and advocated their overthrow by violent revolution with the aid of Soviet troops. In 1946 he was elected joint chairman, with Otto Grotewohl, of the Socialist Unity Party in the postwar Soviet zone of Germany and was the first president of the German Democratic Republic (1949–60).

● **Piedmont** ► (Italian name: Piemonte) A region in NW Italy. Associated with the House of Savoy since the early 11th century, it became the nucleus of Italian unification in the mid-19th century. It consists of the upper Po Valley, bordered by the Alps in the N and W and the Apennines in the S. Manufacturing is important, with engineering and steel centred on Turin; other industries include textiles, chemicals, rubber, and food products. Agriculture produces rice, cereals, wine, and dairy products. Area: 25 400 sq km (9807 sq mi). Population (1994 est): 4 306 565. Capital: Turin.

● **Piepoudre, Court of** ► (Anglo-French: dusty feet, i.e. pedlars) A court that decided summarily and on the spot commercial disputes arising at a given fair or market. The last of these ancient courts sat at Bristol until it was abolished in 1972. The courthouse of the Piepoudre Court in Harrow-on-the-Hill can still be seen.

● **Piero della Francesca** ► (c. 1420–92) Italian Renaissance painter, born in Sansepolcro. He probably trained in Florence, where he worked on frescoes in Sant' Egidio in 1439. *The Baptism of Christ* (National Gallery, London) shows his monumental figure style and the influence of Florentine artists, particularly ▷Masaccio. He frequently worked at the court of Urbino, where he painted the double portrait of the duke and his wife in profile (Uffizi). His lifelong interest in perspective is reflected in his fresco cycle *The Legend of the True Cross*, painted for the church of S Francesco, Arezzo, and in his treatise *On Perspective in Painting*. After his death his work was neglected until it was reappraised in the 20th century.

● **Piero di Cosimo** ► (P. di Lorenzo; 1462–1521) Florentine Renaissance painter. He trained under the painter Cosimo Rosselli (1439–1507) and was chiefly influenced by ▷Leonardo da Vinci and ▷Signorelli. His mythological paintings and fantasies on the primitive life of mankind are highly original, one of the best examples being *The Death of Procris* (National Gallery, London).

● **Pierre** ► 44 22N 100 21W A city in the N central USA, the capital of

South Dakota on the Missouri River. First settled in 1880 as a railway terminus, it is now an administrative and agricultural centre. Population (1990): 12 900.

● **Pierrot** ► A stock character developed in the French theatre from **Pedrolino** in the commedia dell'arte. Usually a young and honest but not too bright valet, he is a butt for the jokes of his fellow male actors and an unsuccessful suitor for the hand of the female lead. Originally he wore a loose white jacket and had his face powdered white. In the 19th century he featured in French pantomime, becoming an increasingly melancholy and pathetic figure. In British pantomime, he gradually eclipsed the popularity of ▷Harlequin in the harlequinade.

● **pietà** ► (Italian: pity) A sculpture or painting of the dead Christ mourned by angels or holy men or women, especially his mother. The best known is the marble sculpture (c. 1499) by Michelangelo that stands in St Peter's, Rome, showing Christ lying in his mother's lap. This theme originated in Germany in the 14th century and was popular in France before it was taken up in Italy in the 16th century. It was revived by many artists in the 19th century.

● **Pietermaritzburg** ► 29 36S 30 24E A city in SE South Africa. It was founded by Boers (1838) and named after their leaders, Piet Retief and Gert Maritz, massacred by the Zulus. The Church of the Vow (1839), built to commemorate the subsequent Boer victory over the Zulus, now houses the Voortrekker Museum. It has a university (1910). Population (1986): 133 809.

● **Pietism** ► A movement for spiritual regeneration among Lutherans in 17th-century Germany. It was started by P. J. Spener (1635–1705), whose *Pia Desideria* (1675) proposed instilling new life into Lutheranism by concentrating on devotion instead of dogma. Pietism survived for over 200 years and influenced many subsequent Christian organizations.

● **Pietro da Cortona** ► (P. Berrettini; 1596–1669) Italian Renaissance painter and architect. He trained in Rome, where he was influenced by Raphael and executed frescoes for Sta Bibiena. His finest works included the church of SS Luca e Martina (1635–50) and the *Allegory of Divine Providence* (1633–39), a ceiling fresco in the Barberini Palace in a new Roman High Baroque style.

● **piezoelectric effect** ► The production of electric charges on the opposite faces of certain asymmetric crystals when they are compressed or expanded. The charges are of equal magnitude but opposite in sign on the two faces, the sign on each face depending on whether the crystal is expanded or compressed. Such piezoelectric crystals include quartz and Rochelle salt. In the converse effect a voltage applied across a piezoelectric crystal causes it to expand or contract. The effect is used in the piezoelectric oscillator, the crystal microphone, and the piezoelectric loudspeaker.

● **pig** ► A hoofed mammal belonging to the Old World family *Suidae* (8 species). Also called hogs or swine, pigs have a stocky body with short legs, a short neck, and a large head with a long cylindrical snout used for digging up roots, seeds, small animals, etc., from soil. Wild ▷boars were originally domesticated about 5000 years ago, probably in Asia, and used for meat and clearing vegetation. Modern breeds include the ▷Landrace and ▷Large White and are reared for pork and bacon (*see* livestock farming). ▷*See also* babirusa; peccary; wart hog.

● **pigeon** ► A bird belonging to a family (*Columbidae*; 300 species) occurring worldwide except in the coldest regions; the smaller long-tailed forms are called doves. 17–75 cm long, pigeons have a plump body, a small head, short bill and legs, and a cooing call. Pigeons feed mainly on seeds and other plant material and feed the young on "pigeons' milk"—the sloughed-off lining of the crop. Order: *Columbiformes* (pigeons and sandgrouse). ▷*See also* mourning dove; passenger pigeon; pigeon racing; wood pigeon.

● **pigeon racing** ► The sport of racing homing pigeons back to their home lofts (which they must enter). Pigeons were first, and still are, used for carrying messages; Genghis Khan had a system of pigeon post. The first race of over a hundred miles was held in Belgium (1818), where the sport is still very popular. Birds are banded for racing; their times of departure and arrival are then recorded. Pigeons can cover several thousand miles at speeds of more than 145 km per hour (90 mph).

● **pigeon wheat** ▷*See* Polytrichum.

● **Piggott, Lester Keith** ▶ (1935–) British jockey. Having ridden his first winner at the age of 12, he was champion jockey eleven times from 1960 and Derby winner a record nine times. He became a trainer in 1985 but returned as a jockey in 1990, winning his 30th classic race in 1992. He was imprisoned (1987–88) for a £3.25 million tax fraud and finally retired in 1995.

● **pig iron** ▶ The type of iron produced by ▷blast furnaces, and used as the first stage in ▷steel making. It has a high carbon content (about 4% by weight) and contains impurities, including some slag, which make it brittle. ▷*See also* cast iron.

● **pigments** ▶ Insoluble substances, in the form of fine particles, that give colour and opacity to ▷paints, ▷plastics, and ▷rubber. They can be broadly divided into naturally occurring pigments (such as red iron oxide), inorganic pigments manufactured from minerals, organic pigments, and ▷lakes.

● **pigmies** ▷*See* Pygmies.

● **Pigou, Arthur Cecil** ▶ (1877–1954) British economist. His books include *The Theory of Employment* (1933) and *Lapses from Full Employment* (1945). The latter describes the **Pigou effect** (1944), according to which unemployment brings about a fall in wages and prices, enabling holders of liquid money to increase their demand for goods and services, thus creating more employment.

● **pigweed** ▶ **1.** A stout leafy annual herb of the genus *Amaranthus* (about 50 species), found in tropical and temperate regions, often as a weed. Pigweeds have furrowed stems, up to 1 m high, with simple pale-green hairy leaves and long branching greenish-white flower spikes. Family: *Amaranthaceae*. **2.** ▷*See* goosefoot.

● **pika** ▶ A small mammal belonging to the genus *Ochotona* (14 species), of Asia and North America, also called mouse hare, cony, and rock rabbit. 12.5–30 cm long and resembling large short-tailed mice, pikas live in cold rocky areas above the tree line. They build stacks of sun-dried vegetation under sheltering ledges to feed on during the winter. Family: *Ochotonidae*; order: ▷Lagomorpha.

● **pike** ▶ (fish) A freshwater fish of the genus *Esox* found in temperate regions of Eurasia and America. It has an elongated body, up to about 1.4 m long, a broad flat snout, and a large mouth with strong teeth. It feeds voraciously on fish and other animals. The common pike (*E. lucius*) is olive-grey above with silvery underparts and pale spots. Family: *Esocidae*; order: *Salmoniformes*.

● **pike** ▶ (weapon) A pre-1800 infantry weapon with a wooden shaft 4–6 m (12–21 ft) long, a steel head on an iron sleeve, and an iron butt. Useless in the face of arrows or musketry, it was replaced by the ▷bayonet.

● **pikeperch** ▶ One of several food and game fish related to perch, especially members of the genera *Lucioperca* and *Stizostedion*, found in Europe and North America. The European pikeperch or zander (*L. lucioperca*) has a slender elongated body, 0.5–1 m long, with greenish or greyish mottling. It is carnivorous, feeding mainly on other fish.

● **Pikes Peak** ▶ A mountain in the USA, in central Colorado in the Rocky Mountains. It is popular with tourists for its views from the summit, which is reached by a cog railway and a road. Height: 4300 m (14 109 ft).

● **pilaster** ▷*See* orders of architecture.

● **Pilate, Pontius** ▶ (1st century AD) Roman governor. As procurator of Judaea and Samaria (26–36) he condemned Christ to death but, according to the New Testament Gospels, did so reluctantly, fearing the outcome of any other course. He came into frequent conflict with the Jews and was finally dismissed for his cruel suppression of a Samaritan rebellion. In one tradition he committed suicide, but in the Ethiopian Church he is regarded as a saint and martyr.

● **Pilbara** ▷*See* Western Australia.

● **pilchard** ▶ An important food fish, *Sardina pilchardus*, related to the herring and sprat, that occurs in abundance in the Mediterranean, E Atlantic, and English Channel. Its slender body, 25–35 cm long, is bluish green above and whitish below and it swims in large shoals feeding on crustaceans and fish eggs. Pilchards up to one year old are called ▷sardines and are fished extensively off the coast of Spain and Portugal. Pilchards are eaten fresh and tinned.

● **Pilcomayo, Río** ▶ A river in S central South America, rising in the Bolivian Andes and flowing generally SE, forming part of the Argentina–Paraguay border before joining the River Paraguay. Length: about 1600 km (1000 mi).

● **piles** ▷*See* haemorrhoids.

● **Pilgrimage of Grace** ▶ (1536) A revolt in N England against the government of Henry VIII. The rebels were united by their opposition to the recent ▷Reformation legislation and the ▷dissolution of the monasteries as well as by economic grievances. Under Robert Aske (c. 1500–37) they seized York but were persuaded by promises of pardon and a full hearing of their complaints to surrender. However, some 230 men, including Aske, were executed.

● **Pilgrim Fathers** ▶ The 102 English colonists who sailed in the ▷*Mayflower* from Plymouth in England, landed at Cape Cod in America in December, 1620, and established the first English settlement in Massachusetts, which they called New Plymouth. Of the 102 colonists, 35 were Puritans, who had earlier travelled to the Netherlands to escape persecution in England. These Puritans obtained the financial backing of a London stock company for their venture, the remaining 67 members of the party being hired to protect the company's interests. During their first winter, 47 of the colonists died, probably of the same epidemic that had decimated the native Indians a few years earlier. This encouraged the Indians and the colonists to collaborate in order to survive; after their successful autumn harvest of 1621 the first ▷Thanksgiving Day feast was held. The term "Pilgrim Fathers" was not coined until 1820 at a bicentennial celebration; before then they were known as the "Old Comers."

● **Pilgrim's Way** ▶ A prehistoric track following the ridge of the North Downs in Surrey and Kent. It probably originated as a trade route, although its name suggests its later use by pilgrims. In *The Old Road* (1904), Hilaire ▷Belloc identified the Way as a continuous track from Winchester to Canterbury, used by pilgrims to the tomb of Thomas Becket.

● **Pilgrim Trust** ▶ A British charity founded in 1930 by Edward Harkness (1874–1940), a US philanthropist. He wished to promote British education and social welfare and the conservation of Britain's national heritage, for which he donated £2 million.

● **Pill, the** ▷*See* oral contraceptive.

● **Pillars of Hercules** ▶ Two promontories at the entrance to the Mediterranean Sea, known in ancient times as Calpe (modern Gibraltar) and Abyla (modern Jebel Musa, at Ceuta, Morocco). According to one legend, the promontories were joined until Heracles tore them apart.

● **pilot fish** ▶ A fish, *Naucrates ductor*, that has a pale-blue elongated body, up to 60 cm long, marked with five to seven dark vertical bands. It is found in warm and tropical seas, accompanying ships and large fish, especially sharks, to feed on parasites and scraps of food. Family: *Carangidae*; order: *Perciformes*.

● **pilot whale** ▶ A gregarious toothed ▷whale, *Globicephala melaena*. Growing up to 6 m, pilot whales are black with a blunt head, narrow tapering flippers, and a broad dorsal fin. They were named by fishermen who found groups of them near herring shoals. Family: *Globicephalidae*.

● **Pilsen** ▷*See* Plzeň.

● **Piłsudski, Józef Klemens** ▶ (1867–1935) Polish statesman, who fought for Polish independence. Piłsudski formed three Polish legions, which fought against Russia in World War I. When Germany refused to guarantee Polish sovereignty, Piłsudski withdrew his support and was imprisoned. After Germany's defeat he declared Poland independent and served as head of state (1919–27). In 1926 he established a military dictatorship, remaining in power until his death.

● **Piltdown man** ▶ Skeletal remains once thought to be those of a fossil ▷hominid, found on Piltdown Common, near Lewes (England), in 1912. In 1953–54 the "find" was shown to be a hoax or fraud. Analysis showed the skull to be made up of a human cranium and an ape's jaw, stained to simulate age. Extinct animal bones and tools had also been placed in the site.

● **pimento** ▷See allspice.

● **pimpernel** ▶ A slender annual or perennial herb of the genus *Anagallis* (about 20 species), found in Eurasia, Africa, and America, especially the annual scarlet pimpernel (*A. arvensis*). Growing 5–30 cm tall, pimpernels have simple leaves and small red, pink, blue, or white bell-shaped flowers with five petals, borne individually on slender stalks. The fruit is a capsule, which opens by a round lid. The yellow pimpernel (*Lysimachia nemorum*) belongs to a closely related genus. Family: *Primulaceae*.

● **pinchbeck** ▶ A ▷brass containing between 10% and 15% zinc. It was formerly used in jewellery as a cheap substitute for gold. It was invented by the watchmaker Christopher Pinchbeck (d. 1732).

● **Pinckney, Charles** ▶ (1757–1824) US statesman. He represented South Carolina in the ▷Constitutional Convention (1787) and his proposals for the new US government—the Pinckney plan—were included in the constitution. His cousins were **Charles Cotesworth Pinckney** (1746–1825), who was minister to France (1796), and **Thomas Pinckney** (1750–1828), who negotiated **Pinckney's Treaty** (the Treaty of San Lorenzo) with Spain in 1795, determining the boundary between US and Spanish possessions in America at 31°N latitude.

● **Pindar** ▶ (518–438 BC) Greek poet. Born into an aristocratic family in Boeotia in central Greece, he was educated in Athens and lived in Sicily for two years from 476 BC. Of his 17 books of choral lyrics only 4 survive. These contain Epinician Odes written in honour of victors of athletic games and noted for their exalted style and religious feeling. He was acclaimed by the ancient Greeks as their greatest poet.

● **Pindus Mountains** ▶ (Modern Greek name: Píndhos Óros) A range of mountains extending some 500 km (311 mi) NW–SE across W Greece and S Albania and rising to 2637 m (8652 ft) at Mount Smólikas.

● **pine** ▶ A coniferous tree of the genus *Pinus* (about 80 species), widely distributed in the N hemisphere. Pines have long slender needles, usually in clusters of two, three, or five, and hanging cones, of variable shape, made up of overlapping woody scales. Pines are important softwoods: the timber is easily worked and yields turpentine, tar, pitch, and other resinous products. Commercially important and widely planted species include the Scots pine (*P. sylvestris*), of N and W Europe and Asia, up to 40 m high (☐tree); the Monterey pine (*P. radiata*), from Monterey, California, up to 35 m high; the shore pine (*P. contorta*), of N North America, up to 25 m high; the Corsican pine (*P. nigra* var *maritima*), up to 45 m high; and the maritime pine (*P. pinaster*), of W Mediterranean regions and N Africa, up to 35 m high. These and other species are also planted for shelter and ornament and some species have edible seeds (*see* stone pine). Family: *Pinaceae*. ▷See also bristlecone pine.

A number of other unrelated conifers are called pines, including species of ▷*Araucaria*, the ▷Cypress pine, and the ▷kauri pine.

● **pineal gland** ▶ A small gland within the brain. In the 18th century it was supposed to be the site of the soul. In amphibians and some reptiles, for example certain lizards, it is receptive to light and is visible externally as a third eye (pineal eye); in other vertebrates, including humans, it secretes a hormone, melatonin, that is involved in the regulation of biorhythms (*see* biological clock).

● **pineapple** ▶ A perennial herbaceous plant, *Ananas comosus*, native to tropical and subtropical America and cultivated in many warm and tropical regions for its fruit. It reaches a height of 1 m and bears a rosette of 30–40 stiff succulent toothed leaves on a thick fleshy stem. Purplish flowers occur at the centre of the rosette and—with their bracts—fuse to form the composite fruit, which ripens 5–6 months after flowering begins and can weigh up to 10 kg. It takes nearly two

years for a plant to bear its first marketable fruit. The major producing countries are the Hawaiian Islands, Brazil, Mexico, Cuba, and the Philippines. Family: *Bromeliaceae*.

● **pine marten** ▶ A European carnivorous mammal, *Martes martes*. About 70 cm long, it inhabits dense evergreen forests, preying on squirrels, birds, insects, and eggs. As with other ▷martens, the female has a litter (2–5 cubs) only every second year, a disadvantage for a species widely hunted for fur.

● **Pinero, Sir Arthur Wing** ▶ (1855–1934) British dramatist. He abandoned his law studies to become an actor. His early plays, which included *The Magistrate* (1885) and *Dandy Dick* (1887), were hugely successful farces that exploited his professional knowledge of stagecraft. His later plays, notably *The Second Mrs Tanqueray* (1893), were more serious treatments of contemporary social problems.

● **pink** ▶ One of several usually perennial herbaceous plants derived from ▷*Dianthus plumarius* and often grown as fragrant garden ornamentals. They have long slender leaves and showy white, pink, or red flowers, often with fringed petals. Family: *Caryophyllaceae*.

● **Pinkerton, Allan** ▶ (1819–84) US detective, born in Scotland. He emigrated to the USA in 1842. He founded the Pinkerton National Detective Agency in 1850 and organized an intelligence service for the Federal states during the Civil War.

● **pinkeye** ▷See conjunctivitis.

● **Pinkie, Battle of** ▶ (10 September, 1547) The battle near Musselburgh, Midlothian, in which the Scots were defeated by the English forces of the Duke of ▷Somerset.

● **pink salmon** ▶ A ▷salmon, *Oncorhynchus gorbuscha*, also called humpback salmon, found in the North Pacific. It is 40–50 cm long and marked with large irregular spots. It has the shortest migration of all the salmon and the male develops a hump on its back during the breeding season.

● **Pinochet, Augusto** ▶ (1915–) Chilean general and head of state (1973–90). He led a military coup that overthrew ▷Allende and became the head of a military junta. His regime has been accused of widespread human-rights abuses, including some 3000 political murders. After defeat in a plebiscite in 1988, he stepped down in favour of a civilian president in 1990; he remained head of the army until 1998, when he was made a senator for life. While visiting London in 1998 he was arrested pending extradition to Spain to answer charges of murder and torture of Spanish nationals during his presidency. There followed a protracted legal battle in the English courts, only resolved when the home secretary authorized Pinochet's release on medical grounds (2000). After his return to Chile he was charged with murder and kidnapping but eventually (2001) found mentally unfit to stand trial.

● **Pinsk** ▶ 52 08N 26 01E A port in Belarus, at the confluence of the Rivers Pina and Pripet. A medieval Russian principality, it came under Lithuania (13th century), Poland (16th century), Russia again (1793), and Poland again (1920–39); ceded then to the Soviet Union, it was occupied by the Germans in World War II. Timber, shipbuilding, and metalworking are the principal activities. Population (1998 est): 132 000.

● **pintail** ▶ A ▷duck, *Anas acuta*, occurring in the N hemisphere, that breeds on inland waters and winters in coastal areas. The male is 70 cm long and has a brown head and neck with a white band down the neck, grey flanks, and long black central tail feathers. Females have mottled brown plumage and both sexes have a blue-grey bill.

● **Pinter, Harold** ▶ (1930–) British dramatist. During the 1950s he was a professional actor. His first full-length play, *The Birthday Party* (1958), failed when it was first staged; it was successfully revived after he won praise with his second play, *The Caretaker* (1960), a study of suspicion between a tramp and two brothers. Later plays include *Betrayal* (1978), *Party Time* (1991), *Ashes to Ashes* (1996), and *Celebration* (2000). He uses elliptical dialogue to evoke tension and ambiguity. He has also written film scripts, including *Turtle Diary* (1985) and *The Trial* (1993), and directed plays.

● **pinto** ▶ A horse whose coat consists of sharply defined patches of white and a darker colour—either black (piebald pattern) or brown, bay, dun, or roan (skewbald pattern). A pinto may be white (tobiano pattern) or dark with white splashes (overo pattern). Pintos were commonly used by American Indians. Height: 1.42 m minimum (14 hands).

● **Pinturicchio** ► (Bernardino di Betto; c. 1454–1513) Italian Renaissance painter, born in Perugia. He was influenced chiefly by ▷Perugino, whom he probably assisted on frescoes for the Sistine Chapel in the Vatican, where he later decorated the Borgia apartments (1492–94). His other major fresco cycle (1503–08) is in the cathedral library, Siena.

● **pinworm** ► A slender parasitic ▷nematode worm, *Enterobius vermicularis*, also called seatworm or threadworm. Up to 1 cm long, pinworms are white and inhabit the human intestine; they are common in Europe and America. Female worms migrate to the anus to lay thousands of eggs, causing itching, especially at night. Pinworms are eradicated with anthelmintics.

● **pinyin** ▷*See* Chinese.

● **pion** ► A group of three elementary particles (*see* particle physics) classified as ▷mesons (symbol: π). The charged pions (π^+ and π^-) have a mass of 139.6 MeV, the neutral pion (π^0) a mass of 136 MeV. The ▷strong interaction can be represented by the exchange of virtual pions between particles (*see* virtual particle).

● **Pioneer probes** ► A series of US solar-system space probes, first launched in 1958. Pioneers 4 to 9 went into solar orbit, monitoring solar activity in the 1960s and early 1970s. Pioneers 10 and 11 flew past and studied Jupiter in 1973 and 1974. Pioneer 11 approached Saturn in 1979, while Pioneer 10 passed Neptune in 1983 and left the solar system; signals from them can still be detected. Two **Pioneer Venus** probes reached Venus in 1978.

● **Piozzi, Hester Lynch** ► (1741–1821) British writer and friend of Samuel ▷Johnson. Also known as Mrs Thrale, she was the wife of a wealthy brewer and a sympathetic confidante of Johnson from 1765 until her second marriage to Gabriel Piozzi, an Italian music master, in 1783. She published volumes of memoirs and letters relating to Dr Johnson.

● **p'i-p'a** ► An ancient Chinese ▷lute. It is short, with a shallow pear-shaped body and has four silk strings. It is held upright in the lap and played with a plectrum. Poets of the Tang dynasty (618–906 AD) played it to accompany their poems; it is still a popular instrument.

● **pipal** ▷*See* bo tree.

● **pipefish** ► One of several slender long-bodied fish belonging to the family *Syngnathidae* (*see also* sea horse). 2.5–50 cm long, it has a long tubular snout with a small mouth and lives among aquatic plants mainly in warm marine waters, feeding on small organisms. The males carry the young until they hatch. Order: *Gasterosteiformes*.

● **Piper, John** ► (1903–92) British painter and writer. He painted abstract works in the 1930s and was an official war artist in World War II. He is known for his watercolours and aquatints of architecture, such as Windsor Castle (1941–42), commissioned by Queen Elizabeth II. He designed stained glass, notably for Coventry Cathedral, and stage sets, including those for Benjamin Britten's *Death in Venice* (1973).

● **Pipe rolls** ► The earliest surviving account records of the Exchequer of England. Each Michaelmas (29 Sept), amounts paid into the royal treasury were recorded on long pieces of parchment, later rolled up into "pipes." The earliest of the pipe rolls dates from 1129–30 and they survive almost continuously from 1155 to 1831.

● **pipistrelle** ► A small insect-eating ▷bat belonging to the genus *Pipistrellus* (50 species) with a worldwide distribution. The Eurasian pipistrelle (*P. pipistrellus*) is about 3.5 cm long with a 20-cm wingspan. It often flies near houses where insects are attracted to light. Pipistrelles have a prehensile tail, used when crawling into crevices to roost. Family: *Vespertilionidae*.

● **pipit** ► A small insectivorous songbird of the genus *Anthus* (30 species), 14–16 cm long with a brown-streaked plumage and paler speckled underparts. The meadow pipit (*A. pratensis*) occurs on moors and

downs in Britain and is the chief prey of the ▷merlin. The water pipit (*A. spinoletta*) inhabits the high mountains of Eurasia and North America; it is also found in coastal regions, when it is known as the rock pipit. The Antarctic pipit (*A. antarcticus*) is the only passerine land bird in Antarctica. Family: *Motacillidae* (wagtails and pipits).

● **Piraeus** ► (Modern Greek name: Piraiévs) 37 57N 23 42E The chief port of Greece, SW of Athens on the Saronic Gulf. It was founded during the 5th century BC as the port of Athens. Following the bombings of World War II extensive industrial renewal has taken place; industries include shipbuilding, oil refining, and chemicals. Its exports include wine and olive oil. Population (1991): 169 622.

● **Pirandello, Luigi** ► (1867–1936) Italian dramatist and novelist. He was born in Sicily and studied philology in Germany. In 1903 his wife became insane, and his writing was greatly influenced by his life with her. He gained international success with his plays exploring the nature of reality and illusion, notably *Six Characters in Search of an Author* (1921) and *Henry IV* (1922). His other works include the novel *The Late Mattia Pascal* (1904) and the critical study *Humour* (1908). He won the Nobel Prize in 1934.

● **Piranesi, Giambattista** ► (1720–78) Italian etcher, born in Venice. Initially trained as an architect and stage designer, he achieved a wide reputation with his prints of Rome and its ruins. As an archaeologist and champion of the superiority of Roman architecture over Greek (*compare* Winckelmann, Johann Joachim), he was an important figure in early ▷neoclassicism, although his imaginative and dramatic style, particularly in the *Carceri d'invenzione* (*Imaginary Prisons*), anticipates ▷Romanticism.

● **piranha** ► A freshwater fish, also called caribe and piraya, belonging to a genus (*Serrasalmus*) found in South America. It has a deep body, up to 60 cm long, ranging from silver to black in colour, strong jaws, and razor-sharp teeth. Piranhas swim in groups and feed on other fish; they will also attack larger animals, including man. Family: *Characidae* (*see* characin).

● **Pirani gauge** ► A pressure gauge used for measuring low gas pressures. It consists of an electrically heated wire placed in the gas. The rate at which the gas conducts heat away from the wire depends on its pressure; the pressure is measured by observing the resistance of the wire at a fixed voltage or observing the voltage at a fixed resistance.

● **pirates** ▷*See* buccaneers.

● **Pisa** ► 43 43N 10 24E A city in Italy, in Tuscany on the River Arno. Dating from Etruscan times, it developed into a thriving maritime republic (11th–12th centuries) but declined in importance after it fell to the Florentines in 1509. It is the birthplace of Galileo, who taught at the university (founded in 1343). The most famous of its buildings is the Leaning Tower of Pisa, which is 59 m (194 ft) high and about 5 m (17 ft) out of perpendicular. From the late 1980s work was undertaken to prevent the Leaning Tower from falling over (completed in 2001). Other notable buildings include the cathedral (11th–12th centuries) and the baptistry (12th–13th centuries). It is a popular tourist centre. Machinery, textiles, bicycles, and glass are manufactured. Population (1998 est): 93 133.

● **Pisanello** ► (Antonio Pisano; c. 1395–c. 1455) Italian ▷international gothic painter, draughtsman, and medallist. He worked on frescoes, begun by ▷Gentile da Fabriano, in Venice and Rome. His portrait medals, influenced by Roman and Greek coins, were popular in court circles, particularly in Ferrara. In such paintings as the *Vision of St Eustace* (National Gallery, London) Pisanello recreated the world of chivalry.

● **Pisano, Andrea** ► (Andrea de Pontedera; c. 1290–1348) Italian sculptor. Unrelated to Nicola and Giovanni ▷Pisano, Andrea worked chiefly in Florence, where he succeeded Giotto as architect of the cathedral (1336). His most important works are the bronze reliefs of the life of St John for the south doors of the Baptistry.

● **Pisano, Nicola** ► (c. 1220–c. 1278) Italian sculptor. He initiated the revival of antique Roman forms that led eventually to Renaissance sculpture, beginning with his pulpit in the Baptistry, Pisa. Such later works as the pulpit in Siena Cathedral and the fountain in the main square of Perugia reveal the hand of his son **Giovanni Pisano** (c. 1250–1314). Giovanni introduced gothic elements into his sculptures for the façade of Siena Cathedral and his pulpit for S Andrea, Pistoia, returning to a more classical style in his pulpit for Pisa Cathedral.

● **Pisces** ▶ (Latin: Fish) A large inconspicuous constellation that lies on the ▷zodiac between Aries and Aquarius, mainly in the N sky. It contains the vernal ▷equinox.

● **Pishpek** ▷See Bishkek.

● **Pisistratus** ▶ (c. 600–c. 528 BC) Athenian tyrant. After several abortive attempts to seize power in Athens, Pisistratus succeeded in 546 with a mercenary army. As tyrant, he reduced the power of landed aristocrats by instituting circuit judges to adjudicate local cases. He encouraged agriculture and commerce and his benevolent tyranny promoted the national unity necessary for the later development of democracy.

● **Pissarro, Camille** ▶ (1830–1903) French impressionist painter, born in the West Indies. After running away to Venezuela to become an artist, he was sent by his parents to Paris (1855). He trained in the École des Beaux-Arts, and the Académie Suisse, where he met ▷Monet. Influenced by ▷Corot, he was more interested in landscape structure than the other impressionists. He participated in the impressionist exhibitions (1874–86) and is noted for his encouragement of younger painters, especially ▷Cézanne and ▷Gauguin. In the 1880s he experimented with ▷pointillism. His son **Lucien Pissarro** (1863–1944) was also a painter.

● **pistachio** ▶ A small aromatic tree, *Pistacia vera*, native to central Eurasia and widely cultivated in Mediterranean regions for its edible green kernels ("nuts"). Growing 7–10 m high, it has compound leaves with 1–5 pairs of leathery leaflets and drooping spikes of small male and female flowers, borne usually on separate trees. The oval white fruits, 1.5–2 cm long, often split to expose the kernels, which are used as dessert nuts and for decorating and flavouring confectionery, cakes, etc. Family: *Anacardiaceae*.

● **pistil** ▶ The part of a flower consisting of the female reproductive organs. It consists of one or more ▷carpels, which may be united into a single structure. Some plants, such as the cucumber, have separate male and female flowers: the latter are described as pistillate.

● **Pistoia** ▶ 43 56N 10 55E A town in N central Italy, in Tuscany. ▷Catiline was killed in battle near here (62 BC). The 12th-century cathedral contains a famous silver altar. Population (1990): 89 972.

● **pistol** ▶ A short-range ▷small arm that can be used with one hand. It evolved from a small cavalry matchlock in the 15th century, later improvements following those of the ▷musket. The need to make a weapon that would fire more than once without reloading led to the division of pistols into two classes: the ▷revolver and the automatic. The first revolver (c. 1540) had multiple barrels, which were rotated by hand past the lock. However, the first successful revolver was the ▷Colt of 1835, in which a magazine chamber revolves behind a single barrel. The first automatics (1893) combined a box magazine in the butt with a recoil loading action. The ▷Luger 9 mm automatic went into service with the German navy in 1904 and remained the standard weapon until 1938.

Both revolvers and automatics are still in military and police use throughout the world.

● **pit bull terrier** ▷See bull terrier.

● **Pitcairn Islands** ▶ A small island group in the central S Pacific Ocean, a United Kingdom overseas territory, consisting of Pitcairn Island and three uninhabited islands. Subsistence agriculture is the chief occupation; fruit, vegetables, and souvenirs are sold to passing ships.

History: Pitcairn Island was occupied in 1790 by mutineers from the *Bounty* and women from Tahiti (*see* Christian, Fletcher). By 1856 the island was overpopulated and the inhabitants were moved to Norfolk Island; some later returned. Area: 4.6 sq km (1.75 sq mi). Population (1995): 54. Sole town: Adamstown.

● **pitch** ▶ (chemistry) A black or dark-brown residue resulting from the partial evaporation or fractional distillation of coal tars or tar

products. The term is sometimes used for the resi-due obtained from petroleum distillation (bitumen) or for the naturally occurring petroleum residue (asphalt). Bitumen is a mixture of heavy hydrocarbons with a high proportion of free carbon. It is used as a binding agent (it is the main constituent of road tars), as a protective coating in bituminous paints, in roofing felts, and as a fuel.

● **pitch** ▶ (music) The highness or lowness of a note, depending on the frequency of the vibrations producing it. Standard pitch has varied through the centuries: Handel's still extant ▷tuning fork gives A as 422.5 Hz. Modern **concert pitch** was standardized by international agreement in 1939, and the frequency of the note A was fixed at 440 Hz. **Perfect pitch** is the ability to recognize and name notes by ear alone; since notes have no absolute pitch value, even this depends on relative frequencies. ▷*See also* temperament.

● **pitchblende** ▶ The chief ore of uranium, a massive form of uraninite, UO_2, a black radioactive mineral found in hydrothermal veins and as an accessory mineral in acid igneous rocks. It occurs in North America, Africa, Australia, and central Europe.

● **pitcher plant** ▶ Any ▷carnivorous plant with pitcher-shaped leaves, belonging mainly to the families *Nepenthaceae* and *Sarraceniaceae*. The pitcher is often brightly coloured and secretes nectar to attract insects, which often fall inside and drown in the digestive juices at the bottom of the pitcher. The *Nepenthaceae* comprises herbs and shrubs of the Old World, many of which are climbers. Their leaf tendrils are swollen to form the pitcher, 5–30 cm long. The *Sarraceniaceae* are perennial herbs of the New World with rosettes of pitchers arising from a swollen underground stem.

17th-century English wheellock pistol.

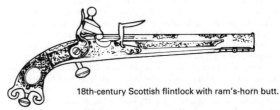

18th-century Scottish flintlock with ram's-horn butt.

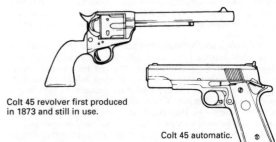

Colt 45 revolver first produced in 1873 and still in use.

Colt 45 automatic.

pistol

● **Pithecanthropus** ▶ A group of extinct Pleistocene ▷hominids, now regarded as specimens of *Homo erectus* (*see* Homo). The name *Pithecanthropus* (literally apeman) was coined by ▷Haeckel before any supporting fossil evidence was found for the evolutionary link.

● **Pitlochry** ▶ 56 43N 3 45W A town in central Scotland, in Perth and Kinross on the River Tummel. Set amid magnificent scenery, it is a popular tourist centre and site of the famous Pitlochry Festival Theatre. The Tummel-Garry hydroelectric scheme is nearby. Population (1991): 2541.

• **Pitman, Sir Isaac** ▷*See* shorthand.

• **pitot tube** ▶ A type of ▷anemometer for measuring the velocity of a fluid, invented by Henri Pitot (1695–1771). It consists of an L-shaped tube placed in the moving fluid; the vertical limb of the tube has an opening facing into the flow. The difference in pressure between the interior of the tube and the surroundings enables the velocity of the fluid to be calculated. The device is used to measure the velocity of liquids, aircraft airspeeds, etc.

• **Pittosporum** ▶ A genus of small evergreen trees (about 150 species), called parchment-bark or Australian laurels, native to Australia and New Zealand and often grown as ornamentals. They have long pale leathery leaves and blue, white, yellow, or red flowers. *P. tenuifolium* is popular in flower arrangements. Family: *Pittosporaceae.*

• **Pitt-Rivers, Augustus Henry Lane Fox** ▶ (1827–1900) British anthropologist and archaeologist. Pitt-Rivers formed a major anthropological collection, now in the Pitt-Rivers Museum, Oxford, in his pioneering work on establishing typological sequences for artefacts from different cultures and eras. After 1880 he excavated prehistoric and Romano-British remains in S England, becoming the first Inspector of Ancient Monuments (1882). His *Excavations in Cranborne Chase* (1887–98) testifies to his meticulous standards.

• **Pittsburgh** ▶ 40 26N 80 00W A city in the USA, in Pennsylvania at the confluence of the Allegheny and Monongahela Rivers, which here form the Ohio River. It was founded in 1764 around Fort Pitt, which was named after ▷Pitt the Elder because its site had been captured from the French in 1758 during the Seven Years' War, which Pitt masterminded. It is the site of several colleges and universities, including the University of Pittsburgh (1787) and the Carnegie Institute, which contains a two-million-volume library, museums, and the Carnegie Music Hall. Pittsburgh has grown as a centre of the steel industry and is the country's largest inland port. Other manufactures include machinery, petroleum, coal, glass, and chemicals. Population (1996 est): 350 363.

• **Pitt the Elder, William, 1st Earl of Chatham** ▶ (1708–78) British statesman, known as the Great Commoner. Entering parliament in 1735 as MP for the ▷pocket borough of Old Sarum, he established a reputation as an outstanding orator. He opposed the government of Sir Robert Walpole, who fell in 1742, and attacked Carteret's conduct (1742–44) of the War of the Spanish Succession. As paymaster general (1746–55) he was notable for his incorruptibility. In 1756 he became secretary of state and leader of the House of Commons but was dismissed in 1757 and then recalled to form a ministry with ▷Newcastle. In charge of foreign affairs, he was largely responsible for British victory in the ▷Seven Years' War, reorganizing the militia and navy and rallying public opinion. Forced to resign in 1761, he returned to form a new ministry in 1766 as Earl of Chatham. Plagued by ill health, he resigned in 1768. He died after collapsing while speaking in the House of Lords.

His second son, **William Pitt the Younger** (1759–1806), was twice prime minister (1783–1801, 1804–06), the youngest in British history. He entered parliament in 1781 and became Shelburne's chancellor of the exchequer in 1782. As prime minister (and at the same time chancellor and first lord of the treasury) he inherited an enormous public debt, which he reduced by a fiscal policy influenced by Adam ▷Smith. He introduced new taxes, overhauled customs duties, and introduced a new sinking fund. He also reformed the Indian administration (*see* Government of India Acts). Pitt negotiated the first (1793) and second (1798) coalitions against France (*see* Revolutionary and Napoleonic Wars) and resolved the crisis caused by the Irish rebellion in 1798 by union of Britain and Ireland in 1800. He resigned following George III's refusal to accept Catholic emancipation. His second ministry was marked by an alliance with Russia, Sweden, and Austria against Napoleon, which collapsed shortly before his death in office. Although he did not consider himself a Tory, Pitt's rivalry with the Whig leader, Charles James ▷Fox, contributed to the clearer identification of Whigs and Tories.

• **pituitary gland** ▶ A small ▷endocrine gland, about 12 mm by 8 mm, lying within the skull close to the centre of the head. The anterior (front) lobe produces ▷growth hormone, ▷prolactin, and hormones that regulate the function of other glands, notably the ▷thyroid and ▷adrenal glands and the ovary and testis. The posterior (back) lobe is a downgrowth from the ▷hypothalamus and stores various neurohormones, including antidiuretic hormone (*see* diabetes) and ▷oxytocin, that are synthesized in this part of the brain. The pituitary is therefore the master endocrine gland, from which neural control of the entire endocrine system is effected.

• **pit viper** ▶ A New World viper, belonging to the subfamily *Crotalinae*, that has a sensory pit between the eye and nostril used to detect the tiny changes in temperature caused by warm-blooded prey nearby. Pit vipers occur in habitats ranging from deserts to rain forests and are chiefly ground-dwellers. ▷*See also* bushmaster; copperhead; fer-de-lance; rattlesnake; sidewinder; water moccasin.

• **Pius II** ▶ (Enea Silvio (*or* Aeneas Silvius) de' Piccolomini; 1405–64) Pope (1458–64), who was also a notable humanist. He served Emperor Frederick III as both imperial poet and secretary before becoming a priest (1446). On his election he attempted to restore papal authority by condemning the view that general councils had supreme authority in the Church. His proclamation of a crusade against the Turks after the fall of Constantinople (1453) was ignored by the secular powers and he died shortly after resolving to lead it in person.

• **Pius IV** ▶ (Giovanni Angelo de' Medici; 1499–1565) Pope (1559–65). He continued papal support of the ▷Counter-Reformation, presiding over the last session of the Council of ▷Trent and reforming the Sacred College of cardinals.

• **Pius V, St** ▶ (Michele Ghislieri; 1504–72) Pope (1566–72). A Dominican friar and noted for his asceticism, he was the greatest of the 16th-century reformer popes. Pius re-edited a number of liturgical texts, including the breviary and missal, enforced the decrees of the Council of ▷Trent, and expanded the activities of the ▷Inquisition. He excommunicated the Protestant Elizabeth I of England in 1570. He was canonized in 1712. Feast day: 30 Apr.

• **Pius VI** ▶ (Giovanni Angelico Braschi; 1717–99) Pope (1775–99). His pontificate was marked by attempts to combat growing opposition to papal control from both national churches and states, especially in France, where he condemned the state church established during the French Revolution. Pius was captured in the Revolutionary Wars, during which the French attacked the papal states, and died a prisoner.

• **Pius VII** ▶ (Gregorio Barnaba Chiaramonti; 1740–1823) Pope (1800–23), who made several unsuccessful attempts to preserve papal privileges in the face of Napoleon's demands. In 1804, under duress, he consecrated Napoleon emperor and in 1809, after the French conquest of Rome, was taken prisoner and forced to make extensive concessions in the Concordat of Fontainebleu (1813). After Napoleon's fall in 1815 Pius gained the restoration of the papal states and negotiated concordats with many of the victorious powers.

• **Pius IX** ▶ (Giovanni Maria Mastai-Ferretti; 1792–1878) Pope (1846–78). At first sympathetic to liberal and nationalist movements, he abandoned radicalism for reaction after the Revolution of 1848, in which he fled Rome. He refused to acknowledge the newly established kingdom of Italy, into which Rome was incorporated in 1870. He defined the Immaculate Conception (1854) and papal infallibility (1869–70) and his encyclical *Quanta Cura* (1864), with its *Syllabus of Errors*, condemned modernism in theology and philosophy. He was beatified in 2000.

• **Pius X, St** ▶ (Giuseppe Sarto; 1835–1914) Pope (1903–14). His pontificate was marked by his defence of the Church's independence against encroachment by the state, support of social reforms (especially in the Catholic Action movement), reform of the liturgy, and a new codification of canon law. He condemned theological modernism and revolutionary political movements. He was canonized in 1954. Feast day: 3 Sept.

• **Pius XI** ▶ (Achille Ratti; 1857–1939) Pope (1922–39). He attempted to extend the educational and social work of the Church, supporting the role of the laity in the Catholic Action movement. He signed the ▷Lateran Treaty (1929), establishing the Vatican as a sovereign state.

• **Pius XII** ▶ (Eugenio Pacelli; 1876–1958) Pope (1939–58). Pius' failure to condemn fascism during World War II caused controversy, although he attempted to prevent the outbreak of war, to curb atrocities, and to relieve suffering. He was a staunch conservative both in politics and doctrine, condemning communism and modernist theology.

● **Pizarro, Francisco** ▶ (c. 1475–1541) Spanish conquistador. He accompanied Balboa on the expedition that discovered the Pacific (1513) and in the 1520s explored the NW coast of South America. In 1531 having gained Charles V's assent to the conquest of Peru and an assurance of the major part of the spoils, he crossed the Andes to Cajamarca. There he treacherously murdered the Inca king, Atahuallpa. He then consolidated the Spanish conquest of the Inca empire, founding Lima in 1535. He came into conflict with a fellow conquistador, Diego de Almagro (c. 1475–1538), who was defeated and put to death; his followers, subsequently murdered Pizzaro.

● **PK** ▷*See* telekinesis.

● **Place, Francis** ▶ (1771–1854) British radical, who campaigned for the repeal of the anti-union ▷Combination Acts (1799, 1800). With the help of Joseph ▷Hume he was successful by 1824.

● **placenta** ▶ **1.** An organ formed within the womb of mammals and other viviparous animals during pregnancy, composed of fetal and maternal tissues. Within the placenta the blood vessels of the fetus and mother come into close contact, enabling exchange of substances in the blood. Thus the fetus receives nutrients, oxygen, and antibodies from the mother's blood and its waste products are absorbed into the mother's circulation. The fetus is attached to the placenta by the umbilical cord. The placenta also secretes hormones that contribute to the control of pregnancy. The placenta is expelled (as the afterbirth) shortly after the baby is delivered. **2.** A tissue in plants that connects the ovules (later the seeds) to the ovary (later the fruit wall).

● **Placodermi** ▶ An extinct class of fish that lived from the Devonian to the Permian periods (415–240 million years ago). Their bodies, usually 10–40 cm long, were covered with bony scales, particularly over the head and front half, and had a bony skeleton, primitive jaws, gill covers (opercula), and median and paired fins. Many species were bottom-dwelling carnivores.

● **plagioclase** ▶ A group of ▷feldspar minerals with compositions varying between the two end-members albite ($NaAlSi_3O_8$) and anorthite ($CaAl_2Si_2O_8$). They are milky white or colourless, and occur both as phenocrysts and in the groundmass of most basic and intermediate igneous rocks and in many metamorphic rocks.

● **plague** ▶ An infectious disease caused by the bacterium *Yersinia pestis*, which is transmitted to man by rat fleas. There are three forms of the disease, the most common of which is bubonic plague, in which fever, vomiting, and headache are accompanied by swollen inflamed lymph nodes (buboes). The more severe pneumonic and septicaemic plagues develop when the bacteria enter the lungs and bloodstream respectively. Plague is treated with antibiotics. Epidemics of plague afflicted Europe throughout the middle ages, the

▷Black Death of 1348 being the most devastating. The **Great Plague of London** (1665–66) was the last of the epidemics from which England had suffered intermittently since the Black Death. It claimed an estimated 70 000 lives. Today plague is usually restricted to areas of poor sanitation in tropical countries.

● **plaice** ▶ A commercially important ▷flatfish, *Pleuronectes platessa*, that occurs in the N North Atlantic and British coastal waters. It is usually 25–40 cm long, occasionally up to 90 cm, and is coloured brown with bright-red or orange spots above and white beneath. There are four to seven bony warts running backwards from the eyes.

● **Plaid Cymru** ▶ A political party, founded in 1925, dedicated to the achievement of Welsh independence from the UK. The party benefited from the rise of nationalism in the 1960s and early 1970s, securing its first parliamentary seat in 1966 (in 2001 it won four seats). In the referendum of 1997 the Welsh electorate voted in favour of devolution and the establishment of a Welsh assembly. In the first elections to this body (May 1999) Plaid Cymru achieved its best-ever result, gaining 17 of the 60 seats and forming the main opposition to Labour.

● **plainchant** ▶ (*or* plainsong) The ritual music of the early Christian Church, as distinct from later polyphonic music. It consists of unaccompanied melodic lines deriving from natural intonation, with flexible rhythms to fit the Latin prose of the daily services. Probably initially influenced by Jewish liturgical chant, its melodic basis derived from the Greek system of ▷modes. At the end of the 6th century, during the papacy of Gregory I, it was codified as ▷Gregorian chant and flourished with few changes until the advent of harmonized melody in about 1000.

● **plains-wanderer** ▶ An Australian bird, *Pedionomus torquatus*, of dry grassland regions. 10–13 cm long, it has short rounded wings, a short tail, and a mottled red-brown plumage with a white throat and a collar of black spots. Largely ground-dwelling, it feeds on plant material and insects and is the only member of its family (*Pedionomidae*). Order: *Gruiformes* (cranes, rails, etc.).

● **planarian** ▶ A free-living ▷flatworm of the order *Tricladida*, occurring in marine and freshwater habitats of temperate regions. Flattened and symmetrical, with simple eyespots and olfactory organs, planarians range from 2 mm to 10 cm in length. They glide smoothly by means of beating cilia (hairs) and use a long retractable feeding tube (pharynx) to consume small invertebrates. Class: *Turbellaria*.

● **Planck, Max Karl Ernst Ludwig** ▶ (1858–1947) German physicist; the originator of ▷quantum theory, who was professor at Kiel University (1880–89) and then at the University of Berlin (1889–1926). Planck solved the problem of black-body radiation by assuming that the radiation was emitted in discrete amounts called quanta, the magnitude of a quanta being the product of the frequency of the radiation and a constant, now known as the ▷Planck constant. For this work he received the Nobel Prize in 1918. He remained in Germany during the Nazi period and attempted to intercede with Hitler on

plague ▶ A contemporary woodcut showing Londoners leaving the city to escape the Great Plague of 1665.

A simplified classification of the plant kingdom

broad category	major groups (phyla)	important classes	representative members
nonvascular plants (bryophytes)	Hepatophyta		liverworts (e.g. *Pellia*)
	Bryophyta		mosses (e.g. *Sphagnum*)
	Anthocerophyta		hornworts (e.g. *Anthoceros*)
vascular plants (tracheophytes)	Lycophyta		clubmosses (e.g. *Lycopodium*)
	Sphenophyta		horsetails (*Equisetum*)
	Filicinophyta		ferns (e.g. *Pteridium*)
	Coniferophyta (conifers)		pines, larches, spruces, firs, yews
	Anthophyta (flowering plants)	Monocotyledonae (monocotyledons)	grasses, palms, orchids, lilies
		Dicotyledonae (dicotyledons)	daisies, roses, buttercups, hardwood trees (oak, beech, etc.)

behalf of Jewish scientists. For this he was deprived of the presidency of the research institute that bears his name. His eldest son, **Erwin Planck** (1914–44), was executed for his involvement in the plot to assassinate Hitler.

● **Planck constant** ▶ (*h*) A fundamental constant that relates the quantum of energy (*E*) of a photon to the frequency (*f*) of the corresponding electromagnetic radiation by the equation $E = hf$. Its value is $6.626\ 196 \times 10^{-34}$ joule second. Named after Max ▷Planck.

● **Planck's radiation law** ▶ Electromagnetic radiation is emitted from and absorbed by matter in discrete amounts (quanta) known as ▷photons. The energy (*E*) of a photon is related to the frequency (*f*) of the radiation by the equation $E = hf$, where *h* is known as the ▷Planck constant. Max ▷Planck discovered the law (1900) while investigating the distribution of wavelengths of the radiation emitted by a ▷black body. It forms the basis of the ▷quantum theory.

● **planet** ▶ A celestial body that moves around a star and shines by light reflected from its surface. The only known planets are those orbiting the sun (□solar system): there are nine major planets and numerous ▷minor planets. The major planets in order from the sun are ▷Mercury, ▷Venus, ▷earth, and ▷Mars (the **terrestrial planets**), ▷Jupiter, ▷Saturn, ▷Uranus, and ▷Neptune (the **giant planets**) and, usually outermost, ▷Pluto. There is evidence of planets already formed or forming around other stars.

● **planetarium** ▶ **1.** A complex instrument that projects an artificial but accurate picture of the night sky, showing planets, stars, and other celestial bodies, on the interior of a hemispherical dome. The dome forms the upper part of an auditorium. The images of the celestial bodies are produced by a considerable number of small optical projectors in the instrument. By moving the individual projectors at the correct speed, the bodies are made to follow their natural paths through the sky. **2.** A building housing such an instrument. Famous planetariums include those in Moscow (1929) and London (1958); there are some 60 in the USA.

● **planetary nebula** ▶ A luminous cloud of gas cast off and expanding away from a dying star. It is a type of emission ▷nebula, being ionized by radiation from the hot central star.

● **planetary probe** ▶ An unmanned spacecraft that studies conditions on and near one or more planets and their satellites and in the interplanetary medium along the flight path. The information gathered is then transmitted to earth. The transmitters, TV cameras, and other instruments are powered by solar cells or, for deep-space probes, by thermoelectric generators, etc. Flight corrections can be made by rocket motors. ▷*See* Galileo probe; Mariner probes; Pioneer; Vega; Venera; Viking; Voyager probes.

● **plane tree** ▶ A large tree of the genus *Platanus* (10 species), native to the N hemisphere and often grown for shade and ornament. Up to 50 m tall, the trees have patchy peeling bark, large lobed leaves, and separate round clusters (catkins) of male and female flowers: the female flowers give rise to bristly round fruits. The London plane (*P.* × *acerifolia*) is a hybrid between the Oriental plane (*P. orientalis*) and North American buttonwood (*P. occidentalis*). The timber is a valuable hardwood used in carpentry. Family: *Platanaceae.*

● **planimeter** ▶ A device for measuring small irregular plane areas. A moving arm is traced around a closed curve. The enclosed area is calculated from the revolution of a small wheel attached to the arm.

● **plankton** ▶ Minute or microscopic animals (zooplankton) and algae (phytoplankton) that float and drift in the open waters of a sea or lake. The phytoplankton (diatoms and other algae) carry out ▷photosynthesis in the surface waters and so provide the basic food source for all aquatic animals. The zooplankton include protozoa as well as small crustaceans and larvae (e.g. barnacle and fish larvae). Plankton are of great ecological and economic importance as a food source for fish and whales and thus—indirectly—to man, whose fishing industry depends upon them. □oceans.

● **plant** ▶ A living organism belonging to the kingdom *Plantae*, of which there are some 280 000 or so species. Plants are typically immobile and most manufacture their own food from simple inorganic nutrients by ▷photosynthesis, trapping the energy required for the process in the green pigment chlorophyll. Plant cells have rigid cell walls, providing support, and growth occurs from specialized zones of tissue (*see* meristem), continuously or periodically throughout life. Plants lack specialized sense organs and a nervous system; response to external stimuli is usually slow and often permanent. Unlike animals, there is considerable variation in form between individuals of the same species. Green plants are the primary source of food and oxygen for all land animals.

Plants are broadly classified into vascular plants, which have specialized tissues for conducting water and foods; and nonvascular plants, which lack this tissue. Within these two broad groups plants are further divided into separate phyla (or divisions) and classes (see table). Algae, formerly regarded as plants, are now usually classified in the kingdom ▷*Protoctista*.

● **Plantagenet** ▶ The surname of the Angevin, Lancastrian, and Yorkist Kings of England (1154–1485). They were descended from Queen Matilda and Geoffrey Martel, Count of Anjou (d. 1151), who was nicknamed Plantagenet because he wore a sprig of broom (*plante genêt*) in his cap. The name was not formally adopted until the 15th century, when it was used by Richard Plantagenet, Duke of ▷York, to further his claim to the throne in the Wars of the Roses.

● **Plantagenet, Richard, Duke of York** ▷*See* York, Richard Plantagenet, Duke of.

● **plantain** ▶ **1.** An annual or perennial herb of the genus *Plantago* (about 50 species), occurring in temperate regions and on mountains in the tropics, often as a troublesome weed. Plantains have a basal rosette of simple leaves from which arises a stalk, 3–70 cm high, bearing a dense terminal head of inconspicuous green, white, yellow, or brown flowers with protruding stamens. The leaves of the greater plantain (*P. major*) of Eurasia are used to treat insect stings. Family: *Plantaginaceae.* **2.** ▷*See* banana.

● **Plantation of Ireland** ▶ (1556–1660) The government-sponsored settlement of British families in Ireland in the 16th and 17th centuries. Conceived as a method of subjugating the rebellious Irish, the first plantations were not noticeably successful but the Ulster plantation (1608–11), composed of English and Scots, survived and prospered. Under Charles I and Oliver Cromwell, there were further land

plant

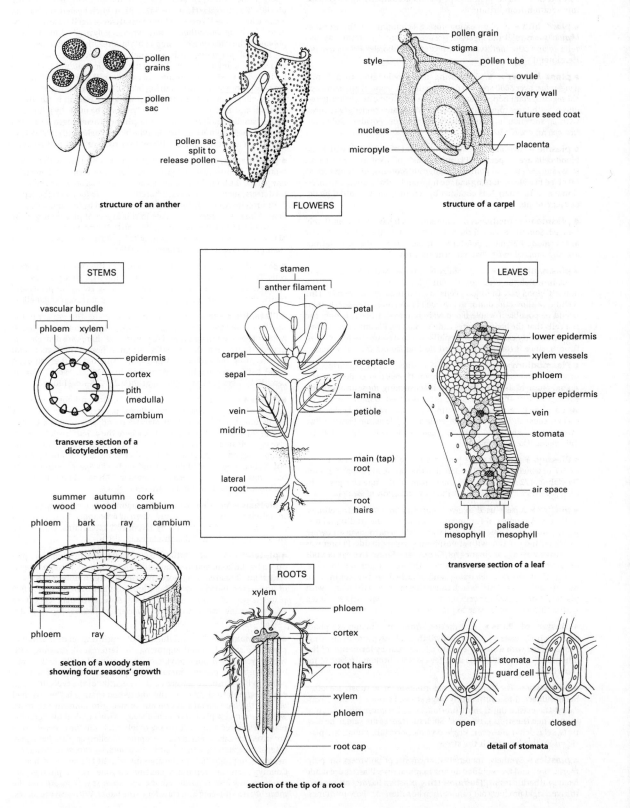

pollen grains

pollen sac

pollen sac split to release pollen

structure of an anther

FLOWERS

pollen grain
stigma
style
pollen tube
ovule
ovary wall
future seed coat
nucleus
micropyle
placenta

structure of a carpel

STEMS

vascular bundle
phloem   xylem

epidermis
cortex
pith (medulla)
cambium

transverse section of a
dicotyledon stem

summer wood   autumn wood   cork cambium
phloem   bark   ray   cambium

phloem   ray

section of a woody stem
showing four seasons' growth

stamen
anther filament

petal

carpel
sepal

receptacle

vein
midrib

lamina
petiole

main (tap) root

lateral root

root hairs

LEAVES

lower epidermis
xylem vessels
phloem
upper epidermis
vein
stomata

air space

spongy mesophyll   palisade mesophyll

transverse section of a leaf

ROOTS

xylem

phloem
cortex

root hairs

xylem
phloem

root cap

section of the tip of a root

stomata
guard cell

open   closed

detail of stomata

confiscations, called plantations, but no accompanying large-scale immigration from Britain.

● **plant bug** ► A plant-eating insect belonging to the families *Myridae* (*see* capsid) and *Lygaeidae* (*see* ground bug). The term may also refer to any other herbivorous insect of the suborder *Heteroptera* (*see* Hemiptera).

● **plant hopper** ► A plant-eating insect belonging to a family (*Fulgoridae*; over 5000 species) found mainly in tropical and subtropical regions. Plant hoppers are 10–50 mm long and often brightly coloured, with large unusually shaped heads. Some species are covered with a secretion of white waxy threads or powder. Suborder: *Homoptera*; order ▷*Hemiptera*.

● **plasma** ► (anatomy) The fluid constituent of ▷blood, in which the blood cells are suspended. Plasma consists of a solution of various salts, sugars, etc., and contains numerous proteins, including those involved in ▷blood clotting and the immunological response to infection (i.e. antibodies). It is obtained by centrifuging unclotted blood. *Compare* serum.

● **plasma** ► (physics) A gas the atoms of which have been completely ionized. Sometimes called the fourth state of matter, plasmas occur at enormously high temperatures, such as those in the sun. Plasmas are also created in ▷thermonuclear reactors.

● **plasmapheresis** ► A laboratory technique used in blood transfusions in which the fluid constituent (plasma) is separated from the donor's blood and the blood cells are returned to the donor. This technique allows the donor to provide plasma more frequently than would be possible if whole blood were removed, since it is only the red cells that the body requires time to replace. Plasma transfusions are particularly useful for haemophiliacs, who require frequent transfusions, since it contains the blood-clotting factors that they lack.

● **Plasmodium** ► A genus of parasitic single-celled organisms (*see* protozoa) that cause ▷malaria in man. *Plasmodium* undergoes the sexual phase of its development in bloodsucking mosquitoes of the genus *Anopheles*, through which it is transmitted to man. Asexual division of the parasite occurs in human liver and red blood cells. Four species cause different forms of malaria: *P. falciparum* (causing the most severe kind), *P. vivax*, *P. malariae*, and *P. ovale*. Phylum: Apicomplexa (*see* sporozoan).

● **Plassey, Battle of** ► (23 June, 1757) The battle in West Bengal (India) in which Robert ▷Clive defeated the Nawab of Bengal, Siraj-ud-Dawlah (c. 1728–57). Aided by the mutiny of the nawab's generals, Clive's victory made possible Britain's acquisition of Bengal.

● **plaster** ► A paste used to give a smooth hard coating to ceilings, walls, etc. A number of formulations are in use, the traditional one being a mixture of lime, sand, and water, which hardens in air owing to drying and reaction with atmospheric carbon dioxide. Plaster was extensively used in ancient Egypt, Greece, and Rome. In early periods ornate designs were executed *in situ* in the wet plaster, but more recently they are cast separately and attached to the ceilings. In modern buildings plasterboard, consisting of fibreboard coated with plaster, is often used for ceilings, which are subsequently skimmed with a thin layer of plaster to provide a smooth finish.

● **plaster of Paris** ► A hydrated form of calcium sulphate ($CaSO_4.\frac{1}{2}H_2O$) made by partial dehydration of ▷gypsum by heating. When mixed with water it sets into a hard mass by formation of the dihydrate ($CaSO_4.2H_2O$). It is used for casts for broken limbs and for modelling.

● **plasticity** ► The permanent deformation of a substance after being subjected to a sufficiently large stress. Below a certain stress, called the elastic limit, most substances will recover their original shape when the stress is removed. Such substances are said to be elastic (*see* elasticity). However, single crystals of certain metals are plastic no matter how small the stress.

● **plastics** ► Synthetic materials that consist of polymers (*see* polymerization) and are moulded during manufacture. Plastics are made from synthetic ▷resins. **Thermosetting plastics** harden on heating to give a rigid product that cannot then be softened. ▷Polyurethanes,

▷polyesters, ▷silicones, and ▷epoxy resins all form thermosetting plastics. **Thermoplastic materials** soften when heated and harden again when cooled. These include derivatives of ▷cellulose and polymers, such as ▷polythene, polystyrene, polyvinyl chloride, and polymethylmethacrylate, which contain a reactive double bond.

Natural polymers, such as ▷shellac and ▷rubber, have been known for many centuries. The first synthetic material was Celluloid, made in 1870 from cotton and camphor. This highly inflammable substance was replaced during World War I by cellulose acetate and casein products. These materials were all based on naturally occurring large molecules. The first polymers to be made by joining together smaller molecules were the **phenol-formaldehyde resins** (trade name Bakelite) invented in 1908 by Leo Baekeland (1863–1944). Since then a vast number of different resins have been synthesized.

● **plastic surgery** ► The branch of surgery concerned with the correction of deformities, disfigurements, or other forms of damage to any part of the body. This includes the reconstruction of developmental defects, such as cleft palate, harelip, and club foot, and the repair of injuries (particularly those of the face) caused by fire or traffic accidents. Great advances were made in this aspect of plastic surgery by Sir Archibald ▷McIndoe, during and after World War II. Cosmetic plastic surgery is performed simply to improve the appearance: an example is facelifting to remove wrinkles.

● **plastid** ► A small structure occurring in the cytoplasm of plant cells. The most important are the ▷chloroplasts. Other plastids contain red, orange, and yellow pigments, giving colour to petals and fruits, and some contain starch, oil, etc., acting as storage organelles.

● **Plata, Río de la** ► (English name: River Plate) The estuary of the Río Paraná and the River Uruguay, on the Atlantic coast of SE South America between Uruguay and Argentina. Its shores are densely populated; Montevideo, the capital of Uruguay, lies on the N shore and Buenos Aires, the capital of Argentina, is situated on the S shore. A naval battle was fought off its mouth in 1939 (*see* World War II). Length: 275 km (171 mi). Width (at mouth): 225 km (140 mi).

● **Plataea** ► An ancient city of Boeotia. Grateful for protection against Thebes, Plataea became Athens' permanent ally; Plataeans alone joined the Athenians at Marathon and they played a crucial role in the battle of Plataea (479 BC), where the allied Greek forces decisively defeated the Persians (*see* Greek-Persian Wars). During the Peloponnesian War Plataea suffered severely for its pro-Athenian policy, being besieged (429–427) and sacked by Sparta. Although rebuilt, it was again destroyed (by Thebes in 373) and then restored (by Philip of Macedon in the late 4th century BC).

● **plateau** ► An extensive area of comparatively level elevated land, sometimes known as a tableland where it is bounded by steep slopes or scarps. It may be crossed by rivers and mountains. One of the world's highest is the Tibetan plateau.

● **platelet** ► A small particle, 0.001–0.002 mm in diameter, produced by the bone marrow and found in the ▢blood. Platelets are essential for ▷blood clotting, accumulating in large numbers at the site of an injured blood vessel. There are normally 150 000 to 400 000 platelets per cubic millimetre of blood. Absence of platelets causes severe bleeding and may occur in a variety of illnesses (e.g. liver disease).

● **platemaking** ► The production of ▷printing plates. Original plates are made by hand engraving (for letterpress), drawing with wax crayons (for lithography), etc., or photographically. In one type of photographic process, metal with a photosensitive coating is exposed to light, usually through a film negative of the type, drawing, or photograph to be printed. The unexposed coating is then washed off and the bare metal underneath turned into nonprinting areas: with a letterpress plate it is etched away; with a typical lithographic plate it is wetted and made grease-repellent, while the exposed areas are inked to make them grease-receptive. A collotype plate has a photosensitive gelatin coating that is hardened, by exposure through a negative, in proportion to the amount of light falling on each area. Collotype can thus reproduce continuous tone, as in a photograph: the more any area is hardened, the less water it will absorb and the more ink it will accept and transfer to the paper. With gravure plates, the printing areas are etched away through an exposed gelatin layer. Continuous tone is simulated in letterpress and lithography by converting the image into a grid of dots of varying size called a half-tone and in gravure by varying the depth of the etched cells and thus the amount of ink that each transfers to the paper.

Duplicate (letterpress) plates are made from original plates by one of two methods. In **stereotyping**, a mould (*or* matrix) is made, in which the duplicate is cast in metal or moulded from rubber or plastic. In **electrotyping**, a thin layer of copper is deposited electrolytically in a matrix similar to that used in stereotyping and then itself filled with molten metal to make it rigid when the metal cools.

● **plate tectonics** ▶ The theory, developed mainly in the 1960s, that the earth's crust is divided into rigid plates (oceanic, continental, or a combination of both), which move about the earth's surface at rates of 1–9 cm per annum. The edges of the plates are called plate margins. At constructive plate margins new oceanic crust is created where two plates are moving apart and magma rises to fill the gap; this occurs at midocean ridges (*see* sea-floor spreading). At destructive plate margins two plates collide and one dips beneath the other into the earth's mantle. This process, known as **subduction**, creates a subduction zone associated with earthquakes, volcanic activity, and volcanic island arcs. Where two continental plates collide, mountain chains are formed. All the major structural features of the earth's surface and seismic and volcanic activity can be ascribed to plate movements.

● **Plath, Sylvia** ▶ (1932–63) US poet and writer. In 1956 she married the British poet Ted ▷Hughes, whom she had met at Cambridge University. The disciplined poems of her first volume, *The Colossus* (1960), contrast with the anguished poems of *Ariel* (1965), published after her suicide, as were a novel, *The Bell Jar* (1966), letters to her mother (*Letters Home*; 1975), and her journals (1982). Her *Collected Poems* (1981) won a Pulitzer Prize.

● **platinum** ▶ (Pt) A precious silver-white noble metal, known to the South American Indians. It is malleable, ductile, and has a high melting point. Platinum is found in nature in nickel ore, as about one part in two million of ore. It can absorb large quantities of hydrogen and is used as a catalyst, particularly in the contact process for making ▷sulphuric acid. It is also used in thermocouple wires and in jewellery. Although unreactive, platinum forms a few compounds, including the hexafluoride (PtF_6), one of the most powerful oxidizing agents known. At no 78; at wt 195.08; mp 1769°C; bp 3827 ± 100°C.

● **platinum-iridium** ▶ An alloy of platinum and iridium that is highly resistant to heat and is used in instruments for measuring high temperatures.

● **Plato** ▶ (429–347 BC) Greek philosopher. An Athenian nobleman, he was early disillusioned by both democrats and aristocrats. Seeing no hope for man unless rulers became philosophers or philosophers rulers, he became a devoted follower of ▷Socrates. After Socrates' death he travelled widely, apparently becoming acquainted with many distinguished thinkers. In 387 he returned to Athens and founded his ▷Academy. To this he devoted the rest of his life, except that in 367 and again soon afterwards, he visited Sicily to assist his friend, Dion, in his futile attempts to turn Dionysius II (*see* Dionysius (I) the Elder), the young and unstable tyrant of Syracuse, into a philosopher, and Syracuse into a Platonic state. Some of Plato's poetry and all his prose works survive. Apart from 13 possibly spurious letters and the *Apology*, which purports to be Socrates' defence of himself before his judges, they are dramatic dialogues of outstanding literary merit. The early ones illustrate Socrates' character and philosophical methods, focusing especially on the question of whether virtue can be taught. The *Phaedo*, *Symposium*, and *Republic* of Plato's middle period develop Plato's views on such topics as metaphysics, love, and government, notably his theory of ideas (Forms), the perfect spiritual entities of which the physical world is a feeble and imperfect copy. ▷*See also* Platonism.

● **Platonism** ▶ The philosophical tradition originating (c. 385 BC) in the Greek ▷Academy under ▷Plato. In the period of Middle Platonism (1st century BC–2nd century AD) interest centred on Plato's thought on God and the supersensible world. Subsequently the philosophers of Alexandria (*see* Plotinus) creatively systematized these and other

aspects of their forerunners' work in ▷Neoplatonism. Works of Platonic character produced by such writers as St ▷Augustine of Hippo, ▷Boethius, and Macrobius transmitted Platonism to the medieval West. The impact of ▷Aristotelianism in the 13th century brought a temporary eclipse, but at the Renaissance Platonism, promoted by such scholars as ▷Ficino and ▷Nicholas of Cusa, reasserted itself and exercised enormous influence on artists and writers, such as ▷Botticelli and ▷Spenser, as well as on philosophers and theologians (*see also* Cambridge Platonists). Elements of Platonism still permeate Western thought in areas as diverse as realist logic (*see* realism) and Christian ▷ethics.

● **Platte River** ▶ A river in the central USA. Formed by the confluence of the North Platte and South Platte Rivers at North Platte, Nebraska, it flows generally E to join the Missouri River. It is unnavigable but is a source of irrigation and hydroelectric power. Length: 499 km (310 mi).

● **Platyhelminthes** ▷*See* flatworm.

● **platypus** ▷*See* duck-billed platypus.

● **Plauen** ▶ 50 30N 12 07E A town in SE Germany, on the Weisse Elster River. Several old buildings remain despite damage done during World War II. Famous for lace making since the 15th century, Plauen is a centre for textile manufacture. Population (1991 est): 70 860.

● **Plautus, Titus Maccius** ▶ (c. 254–184 BC) Roman dramatist. He is traditionally believed to have worked as a craftsman in the theatre before beginning, in middle age, his career as a dramatist. His 21 surviving plays are all adapted from Greek ▷New Comedy writers, especially Menander and Philemon, and are noted for their robust humour and lively colloquial dialogue. His plays influenced the early development of comic drama by Shakespeare, Molière, and others.

● **player piano** ▶ (*or* pianola) A mechanical piano in which the hammers are operated by an airflow produced by pedals or electrically operated bellows and controlled by perforations on a rotating roll of paper. Rolls are either cut by a special machine attached to a piano and thus record an actual performance or they are produced mechanically. The player can control the volume and the speed by means of levers. Invented in the mid-19th century, its heyday was in the 1920s before the popularity of the gramophone. In the 1970s electronic player pianos appeared.

● **playing cards** ▶ Cards with pictures and symbols on one side, used in a wide variety of games, of which ▷bridge, ▷whist, ▷poker, ▷rummy, and ▷cribbage are the most popular. Modern cards derive from the ▷tarot pack; the 52-card French pack with suits of hearts, spades, diamonds, and clubs is now standard, the suits deriving from the tarot suits of cups, swords, money, and clubs respectively. Traditional German, Spanish, and Italian packs with variations in the number of cards and designs of the suits also derive from tarot cards. A connection has been suggested between the suits and the cup, sword, ring, and baton traditionally held by Hindu statues. Playing cards have long been used in divination and conjuring.

● **plea bargaining** ▶ In criminal proceedings, an agreement between the prosecution and the defence in which the accused changes a "not guilty" plea to "guilty" in return for some benefit. For example, the accused may plead guilty to a lesser charge provided that a more serious charge against him is dropped, or there may be an informal indication from the judge that the sentence will be minimized if the plea is changed to "guilty." Any negotiation taking place between a judge and the defence counsel must be in the presence of the prosecuting counsel; the accused does not take part in the discussions, but must be free to decide how to plead.

The practice is widespread in the USA and is sanctioned by the Supreme Court. In the UK it is regarded more cautiously but is sanctioned in certain cases according to principles laid down by the Court of Appeal. The advantages are that it can sometimes induce an accused person to plead guilty in a case that is difficult to prove, and that it shortens trials and thereby speeds up the administration of justice. On the other hand, it can cause more serious charges to be dropped by the prosecution, enabling some criminals to escape the punishments they deserve.

● **Pleasence, Donald** ▶ (1919–95) British actor. His best-known stage performance was in Pinter's *The Caretaker* (1959; film 1963). His films, in which he usually played villains or eccentrics, include *Dr Crippen* (1962), *Cul de Sac* (1966), *The Eagle Has Landed* (1976), and *The Hour of the Pig* (1994).

● **plebeians** ▶ Romans other than the privileged ▷patricians. At first without civil rights, excluded from state and religious offices, and forbidden to marry patricians, in 493–92 the plebeians forced the Senate to appoint their own tribunes and an assembly. During the subsequent two centuries of conflict, the plebeians gradually gained admission to all Roman offices and the wealthy and ambitious among them merged with the patricians. Thus, from later Republican times, the term plebeian implied low social class.

● **plebiscite** ▶ A vote by the whole electorate on a particular issue. The term is usually used to refer to those ▷referendums held to decide to which state an area should belong. A plebiscite was first held by France in 1790–91 concerning the papal territory of Avignon.

● **Pléiade, La** ▶ A group of seven French writers in the 16th century who sought to liberate French poetry from medieval tradition. Their principles, deriving from the study of Greek, Latin, and Italian literature, were expounded in *Défense et illustration de la langue française* (1549) by Joachim du ▷Bellay, and their innovations included the introduction of the sonnet, the ode, and the alexandrine. Led by Pierre de ▷Ronsard, the group included du Bellay, J.-A. de Baïf (1532–89), Étienne Jodelle (c. 1532–73), Rémy Belleau (c. 1528–77), Pontus de Tyard (c. 1522–1605), and Jacques Peletier (1517–82; for whom the name of Jean Dorat (1508–88) was occasionally substituted by contemporaries).

● **Pleiades** ▶ (*or* Seven Sisters) A young open ▷star cluster in the constellation Taurus that contains several hundred stars, of which six are clearly visible to the naked eye and another can sometimes be seen. The brighter stars are surrounded by reflection ▷nebula. They were named after the seven daughters of ▷Atlas, who were changed by the gods into stars while being pursued by Orion.

● **Pleistocene epoch** ▶ The epoch of geological time between the Pliocene and the Holocene, at the beginning of the Quaternary period. It lasted from about 1.8 million to 10 000 years ago. It is often called the ▷Ice Age because during this time the earth experienced great fluctuations in temperature: cold glacial periods, when the ice margins advanced towards the equator, separated by warmer interglacials, when temperatures at times were higher than today. Four main ice advances are recognized in the Pleistocene. Fossils from the Pleistocene include horses, pigs, and elephants.

● **Plekhanov, Georgi Valentinovich** ▶ (1857–1918) Russian revolutionary and Marxist philosopher. Known as the "father of Russian Marxism," Plekhanov was instrumental in the creation (1898) of the Russian Social Democratic Workers' Party. He believed that Russia must pass through industrialization and capitalism before reaching socialism and came to side with the ▷Mensheviks against Lenin. After the Bolshevik victory, he lived in Finland.

● **Plenty, Bay of** ▶ An inlet of the S Pacific Ocean, in New Zealand on the E coast of North Island. It was so named by Capt Cook, who received generous supplies of food and water from the Maoris here in 1769. Width: about 160 km (100 mi).

● **pleochroism** ▶ The ability of certain crystals to transmit light vibrations in one plane only while absorbing those vibrations in other planes. Pleochroic crystals thus produce plane-▷polarized light. If the effect occurs along only one axis of the crystal, the crystal is said to be dichroic. ▷Polaroid, for example, contains dichroic crystals. In trichroic crystals, the effect occurs along two axes perpendicular to each other.

● **plesiosaur** ▶ A widely distributed marine reptile of the Jurassic and Cretaceous periods (200–65 million years ago). Up to about 12 m long, plesiosaurs had broad turtle-like bodies with paddle-like limbs, a long flexible neck, and jaws armed with sharp teeth used to catch fish.

● **pleurisy** ▶ Inflammation of the **pleura**—the membrane that covers the lungs and lines the chest cavity. The commonest cause of pleurisy is bacterial or viral infection: pleurisy will often complicate ▷pneumonia. The patient will often have a fever, a pain in the chest that is worse on coughing or taking a deep breath, and a cough. Bacterial pleurisy is treated with antibiotics.

● **Pleurococcus** ▶ A genus of common unicellular ▷green algae forming thin green powdery incrustations on the windward side of walls and tree trunks, particularly in tropical regions. The spherical cells are either solitary or form small flat aggregations; reproduction is by cell division.

● **Pleven** ▶ 43 25N 24 40E A city in central N Bulgaria. The Russians and the Turks fought here in 1877. It has various industries and serves a mixed agricultural area. Population (1996 est): 125 029.

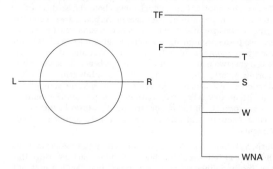

Plimsoll line ▶ The lines and letters mark the waterline under various conditions. TF = fresh water in the tropics; F = fresh water; T = salt water in the tropics; S = salt water in the summer; W = salt water in the winter; WNA = winter in the N Atlantic. LR represents Lloyd's Register.

● **Plimsoll line** ▶ A series of lines painted on the outside of a cargo ship's hull showing the various safe levels to which the ship can be loaded. Typically, the loading levels are marked for loaded and unloaded draught in sea and fresh water, winter and summer, and tropical or northern waters. The measure was introduced in the UK as a result of the Merchant Shipping Act (1876) at the instigation of the MP Samuel Plimsoll (1824–98).

● **Pliny the Elder** ▶ (Gaius Plinius Secundus; 23–79 AD) Roman scholar, whose universal encyclopedia, *Natural History*, was a major source of scientific knowledge until the 17th century. During his military career, Pliny assembled material from numerous sources on a wide range of disciplines, including astrology, geography, agriculture, medicine, precious stones, and—most notably—zoology and botany. Pliny did not discriminate fact from fiction and included much folklore and superstition. He finally completed this work of 37 volumes in 77 AD.

● **Pliny the Younger** ▶ (Gaius Plinius Caecilius Secundus; c. 61–c. 113 AD) Roman writer, nephew and adopted son of the encyclopedist Pliny the Elder. He held various administrative posts including that of consul in 100 AD and was a prominent legal orator. His ten volumes of private letters constitute an intimate unofficial history of his time.

● **Pliocene epoch** ▷*See* Tertiary period.

● **pliosaur** ▶ An extinct marine reptile that evolved from the ▷plesiosaurs but had a shorter neck and a longer head with stronger jaws, giving it a more streamlined appearance. It was a powerful swimmer and fed on cuttlefish, squid, etc.

● **PLO** ▷*See* Palestine Liberation Organization.

● **Płock** ▶ 52 32N 19 40E A town in central Poland, on the River Vistula. Its 12th-century cathedral contains the tombs of Polish kings. Industries include oil refining; it is served by pipeline from Russia. Population (1996 est): 126 900.

● **Ploieşti** ▶ 44 57N 26 01E A city in SE Romania, at the foot of the Transylvanian Alps. It is the centre for the country's oil production. Population (1994 est): 254 136.

● **Plomer, William** ▶ (1903–73) South African poet and novelist. He went to Japan in 1927 after the hostile reception to his first novel, *Turbott Wolfe* (1925), and came to England in 1929. His *Collected Poems* (1960) contain many satirical poems in ballad form. He also published short stories and memoirs and wrote the librettos for operatic works by Benjamin Britten.

● **Plotinus** ▶ (205–70 AD) Greek philosopher and founder of ▷Neoplatonism. Born in Egypt, he studied at Alexandria, visited Persia (242–43), and finally settled in Rome, becoming the focus of an intellectual circle. Developing ▷Plato's mysticism, he taught that the immaterial impersonal indescribable "One" is the ground of all existence and value. From it emanate successively mind, soul, and nature. Mind contemplates and organizes within itself the Platonic Forms; soul thinks less coherently, thus creating time and space; nature "dreams" the chaotic material world, the source of all evil. Man partakes of all these; by rejecting material nature and cultivating the intellect he may briefly become mystically united with the One.

● **Plough** ▶ A distinctively shaped group of the seven brightest stars in the constellation ▷Ursa Major. Two of the stars, Dubhe and Merak (the **Pointers**), point towards the pole star ▷Polaris.

● **Plovdiv** ▶ (former name: Philippopoli) 42 08N 24 45E A city in S central Bulgaria, on the River Maritsa. It is Bulgaria's second largest city and has the remains of the Roman walls. Its industries include food processing and carpet manufacture. Population (1996 est): 344 326.

● **plover** ▶ A bird belonging to a widely distributed family (*Charadriidae*; 56 species) occurring in open regions and along shores. 15–30 cm long, plovers have brown or grey plumage, often mottled, with white underparts, which become black in summer for some species. They feed on insects and other small invertebrates and nest on the ground (*see* Plate III). Order: *Charadriiformes* (gulls, plovers, etc.). ▷*See also* lapwing.

● **Plowright, Joan** ▶ (1929–   ) British actress. Her reputation is based on her performances in both classical and modern plays, the latter including the first productions of Osborne's *The Entertainer* (1957; filmed 1960) and Wesker's *Roots* (1959). She married Laurence ▷Olivier in 1961 and joined the National Theatre in 1963, remaining its leading actress until 1974. Other successful appearances include those in *Filumena* (1977) and Lorca's *Yerma* (1986); in 1988 she directed *Married Love*. Her films include *Surviving Picasso* (1997).

● **plum** ▶ A small tree, ▷*Prunus domestica*—a natural hybrid between the ▷blackthorn and the cherry plum (*P. cerasifera*), native to SW Asia and cultivated in most Mediterranean and N temperate regions for its □fruit. 6–10 m tall, it has oval toothed leaves and clusters of attractive white flowers. The fruit is round or oval and has a dark-red to blue-black skin (when ripe), enclosing a sweet greenish-yellow pulp and a central oval stony seed. Plums are eaten fresh, cooked in desserts, canned, or dried as prunes. Family: *Rosaceae*. ▷*See also* bullace; damson.

● **plumbago** ▷*See* graphite.

● **Plumbago** ▶ A genus of herbaceous plants, shrubs, and climbers (12 species), native to warm regions and including a number of ornamentals. They have simple leaves and terminal clusters of white, blue, violet, pink, or red flowers, with five petals arranged to form a narrow tube with spreading lobes. *P. auriculata*, with pale-blue flowers, and *P. rosea*, with red flowers, are popular greenhouse plants. Some species are used for medicinal purposes and some yield a juice that causes blistering. Family: *Plumbaginaceae*.

● **plumule** ▷*See* germination.

● **Plunket, St Oliver** ▶ (1629–81) Irish Roman Catholic martyr and churchman. He was educated in Rome and was a professor of theology there until appointed Archbishop of Armagh in 1669. He was falsely implicated in the ▷Popish Plot against Charles II and executed, the last Roman Catholic to be martyred in England. He was canonized in 1976.

● **pluralism** ▷*See* dualism.

● **Plutarch** ▶ (c. 46–c. 120 AD) Greek biographer and essayist. He was

a citizen of both Athens and Rome, a priest of Delphi, and director of a school in his native town of Chaeronea in Boeotia in central Greece. His *Parallel Lives* consists of biographies of 23 pairs of Greek and Roman statesmen and soldiers. The *Moralia* contain 83 essays on ethical, scientific, and literary topics. His works had a great influence in Europe in the 16th and 17th centuries. The English translation by Sir Thomas North of the *Lives* (1579) was the source of Shakespeare's Roman plays. The *Moralia* served as models for the essays of both Montaigne and Francis Bacon.

● **Pluto** ▶ (astronomy) The smallest and usually outermost planet, orbiting the sun every 248 years at a mean distance of 5900 million km. Its eccentric orbit has brought it inside Neptune's orbit for the period 1979–99. Pluto was discovered in 1930 but little was known about it until its satellite was discovered in 1978. It is a very cold low-density body about 3000 km in diameter.

● **Pluto** ▶ (mythology) ▷*See* Hades.

● **plutonic rock** ▷*See* igneous rock.

● **plutonium** ▶ (Pu) An important synthetic transuranic element discovered in 1940. Trace quantities exist in natural uranium ores. It is produced in large quantities in nuclear reactors by beta-decay from uranium-239. Plutonium is fissile and was used in the atomic bomb dropped on Nagasaki in 1945 (*see* nuclear weapons). It is absorbed into bone marrow and is one of the most toxic substances known. It forms oxides (PuO, PuO_2), halides (for example PuF_3), and other compounds. It is used in ▷fast reactors and small power units for spacecraft. At no 94; at wt (244); mp 640°C; bp 3230°C.

● **Plymouth** ▶ **1.** 50 23N 4 10W A port in SW England, in Plymouth unitary authority, Devon; it is situated on Plymouth Sound between the Tamar and Plym estuaries. Since 1914 it has included the adjacent towns of Devonport and Stonehouse. On Plymouth Hoe Drake is reputed to have finished his game of bowls while the Spanish Armada approached and the *Mayflower* embarked from here for America in 1620 (*see* Pilgrim Fathers). Severely damaged by bombing during World War II, much of the city centre has been rebuilt. Plymouth is an important naval base with associated marine industries. Shipping is guided into the harbour by the Eddystone Lighthouse (*see* Eddystone Rocks). More recent industries include the manufacture of clothing, radio equipment, and processed foods. Population (1991): 245 991. **2.** A unitary authority in SW England, in Devon. Area: 76 sq km (30 sq mi). Population (1996 est): 255 800.

● **Plymouth** ▶ 41 58N 70 40W A town in the USA, in Massachusetts on Plymouth Bay. The first European settlement in New England, it was founded by the ▷Pilgrim Fathers from the *Mayflower* (1620). Industries include fisheries, boatyards, and tourism. Population (1990): 45 608.

● **Plymouth Brethren** ▶ An austere Protestant sect founded at Plymouth in 1830 by a former Anglican priest, J. N. Darby (1800–82). The Brethren have strict standards of behaviour and shun many secular trades and professions. They insist on the spiritual priesthood of believers and celebrate communion weekly. Small groups exist throughout the world, often as active missionaries.

● **Plymouth Rock** ▶ A breed of domestic fowl developed in the USA and widely used for meat production. It has a deep compact body with large thighs. The plumage can be of various colours, including white with black bars and pure white. Weight: 4.3 kg (cocks); 3.4 kg (hens).

● **Plzeň** ▶ (German name: Pilsen) 49 45N 13 25E A city in the Czech Republic, in W Bohemia. It has been famous for its beer (Pilsener lager) since the middle ages. Local coal and iron ore resources have led to the development of heavy industry, including engineering and chemicals. Population (1996 est): 171 249.

● **pneumococcus** ▶ A spherical bacterium, ▷*Streptococcus pneumoniae*, that is commonly found in the throat and causes pneumonia if it infects the lungs. Pneumococci typically exist in pairs and often form capsules, the composition of which is used to identify different strains (pneumococcal typing).

● **pneumoconiosis** ▶ Chronic lung disease caused by inhaling dust, most commonly coal dust (causing coalworkers' pneumoconiosis) and silica (causing ▷silicosis). Considerable coal dust may be taken into the lungs without causing much damage, but later progressive massive fibrosis may develop and the coalworker is disabled by breathlessness. Lung cancer may also complicate pneumoconiosis. There is no effective treatment; therefore prevention is all important. ▷See also asbestosis; occupational disease.

● **pneumonia** ► Inflammation of the lungs, most commonly caused by infection. Pneumonia may arise in only one lobe of the lung (lobar pneumonia) or in patches in the small bronchi and both lungs (bronchopneumonia). The infective organisms may be streptococci, viruses (causing a mild disease), tubercle bacilli, mycoplasmas, or other organisms, such as the protozoan *Pneumocystis carinii* (which affects those whose immune systems are impaired, such as AIDS patients). The patient has a fever, cough, and pain in the chest and may be breathless. Treatment is with antibiotics and physiotherapy.

● **pneumothorax** ► The presence of air in the pleural cavity, which causes the lung to collapse. This may happen for no apparent reason or it may develop in ▷emphysema or after a penetrating injury of the chest. The patient has pain in the chest and may be breathless. The lung will slowly expand itself or a tube may be inserted into the pleural cavity to allow the trapped air to escape.

● **Pnom Penh** ▷See Phnom Penh.

● **Po, River** ► (Latin name: Padus) The longest river in Italy rising in the Cottian Alps and flowing mainly ENE through Turin to enter the Adriatic Sea by way of a large delta in the E. The Po Valley is the most fertile and economically important region in Italy. Length: 652 km (405 mi).

Pocahontas ► A contemporary engraving showing the Native American "princess" in European dress. Only 22 when she died, Pocahontas managed to establish for herself an enduring place in American history as a person of great integrity and goodwill.

● **Pocahontas** ► (c. 1595–1617) American Indian woman. Daughter of the Indian chief Powhatan, Pocahontas is said to have saved the life of Capt John ▷Smith from her father's warriors. She married the English colonist John Rolfe (1585–1622) and was entertained as a princess at the English court; she died of smallpox at Gravesend, while waiting for a ship back to America.

● **pochard** ► A large-headed ▷duck, *Aythya ferina*, occurring in temperate inland waters of Eurasia. It is 45 cm long and has grey legs and a grey-blue bill; males have a reddish head, black breast, and grey body; females are brown. It feeds on water plants and small aquatic invertebrates.

● **Po Chü-i** ▷See Bo Zhu Yi.

● **pocket borough** ► A British borough constituency that, before the ▷Reform Act of 1832, was controlled by a patron who, through money or influence, ensured the election of any candidate he put forward: the borough was thus "in the pocket" of the patron. ▷See also rotten borough.

● **pocket gopher** ► A ▷rodent belonging to the subfamily *Geomyinae* (39 species), of North and Central America. Pocket gophers are 10–25 cm in length and brownish in colour. They inhabit open dry country, where they dig extensive burrows, and feed on roots, seeds, insects, and mice. Their large cheek pouches have an outside opening like a pocket.

● **Podgorica** ► (name from 1948 until 1992: Titograd) 42 28N 19 17E A city in S Serbia and Montenegro, the capital of Montenegro. It was renamed in honour of Marshal Tito on being rebuilt following extensive damage during World War II. Its university was established in 1973. Population (2000 est): 130 875.

● **Podgorny, N(ikolai) V(iktorovich)** ► (1903–83) Soviet statesman. Podgorny was president of the Soviet Union from 1965 to 1977, when he resigned under pressure and was replaced by Brezhnev.

● **Podocarpus** ▷See yellowwood.

● **Podolsk** ► 55 23N 37 32E A city in W Russia, 42 km (26 mi) S of Moscow. Lenin and his Bolshevik colleagues often met here before the Russian Revolution. Industries include oil refining, machinery manufacturing, and railway engineering. Population (1997 est): 198 000.

● **podzol** ► A type of ▷soil typical of many cool temperate humid zones especially with coniferous vegetation, as in the taiga of Russia and North America. It is characterized by an ashen-coloured upper layer (A horizon) and an underlying layer (B horizon) of redeposition humus and iron, which may develop into an impermeable pan.

● **Poe, Edgar Allan** ► (1809–49) US poet, short-story writer, and critic. He was brought up by foster parents after the death of his mother in 1811. He briefly attended Virginia University and West Point Military Academy. After publishing two volumes of poetry (1827, 1829), he began to contribute to and work for literary magazines. Among his many prose tales and horror stories are "The Fall of the House of Usher" (1839), "The Purloined Letter" (1842), "The Black Cat" (1843), "The Cask of Amontillado" (1846), and the first ever detective story, "The Murders in the Rue Morgue" (1841). His best-known poems are "The Raven" (1845) and *The Bells* (1849) and his most influential critical work is "The Philosophy of Composition" (1846).

● **poet laureate** ► A title bestowed by the British monarch on a contemporary poet, whose traditional duties include the writing of commemorative odes on important public occasions. Although Ben Jonson received a royal stipend from 1616 and is therefore usually considered the first poet laureate, the first to hold the title officially was Dryden, who served from 1668 to 1688. Subsequent laureates included Wordsworth (1843–50) and Tennyson (1850–92), as well as many inferior versifiers. Their most recent successors have been John Betjeman (1972–84), Ted Hughes (1984–98), and Andrew Motion (1999–   ). Until 1999 the title was bestowed for life and the holder was rewarded with an annual present of wine; it is now a salaried post with a fixed tenure of 10 years.

● **poetry** ► A form of literature distinguished from prose by the use of ▷metre, rhythm, ▷rhyme, sound (e.g. alliteration and assonance), and figurative language. In general, the requirements of metre and rhyme have demanded a more compressed use of language, involving departures from normal prose syntax. Poetry probably originated as a form of language distinct from ordinary speech in religious ritual and is an earlier development than written prose. The earliest poetic landmarks in Western literature are Homer's *Odyssey* and *Iliad*, which developed out of a primitive oral tradition and became models for the epic poems of Virgil and later poets. Poetry was associated with ▷drama from its appearance in the dramatic choruses of ancient Greece until the 19th century; verse drama was revived by T. S. Eliot and others in the 20th century. The early forms of lyric poetry derived from the dithyrambic poetry of religious ritual; they are characterized by the repetition of songlike elements arranged in stanzas. The ▷sonnet, one of the most popular forms, evolved in Renaissance Italy. Narrative poetry, like the epic, derived from oral tradition; the ▷ballad combines lyrical and narrative qualities. A tradition of didactic verse, stretching from Hesiod to Cowper, employed rhyme or metre as an aid to the expression of ideas. Poetry has been a medium for satire (Pope), religious and philosophical statement (Lucretius and Wordsworth), and even for scientific classification (Erasmus Darwin). While the poetry of ancient Greece and Rome depended on the variation of fixed metrical patterns, the early poetry of N Europe was characterized by alliteration. ▷Blank verse was evolved by the Earl of Surrey and became the main medium for drama in the works of Shakespeare and his contemporaries and much subsequent poetry. In French poetry the 12-syllable alexandrine became the standard form for serious or elevated poetry, while English poets, from Dryden to Johnson, adopted the ▷heroic couplet. In the late 19th and 20th centuries some poets adopted free verse to avoid the constraints of regularity in metre or rhyme. The extent to which poetry requires a special vocabulary, distinct from that of speech or prose, has been a recurrent subject of literary dispute. In many periods poets have adopted a specialized form of diction characterized by archaisms ("yore"), compressions ("o'er"), conventional epithets and allusions ("Phoebus" for the sun), and dignified circumlocutions ("feathered tribes" for birds). Such periods have generally been followed by a reaction in favour of more natural language, such as that led by Wordsworth in the late 18th century or Eliot and Pound in the early 20th century.

● **Poggio Braccliolini, Giovanni Francesco** ▶ (1380–1459) Italian humanist. A pupil of Manuel ▷Chrysoloras, Poggio recovered the manuscripts of Lucretius, Quintilian, Silius, and other classical writers. His books include a *History of Florence* and the humorous tales, *Liber Facetiarum*.

● **Pogonophora** ▶ A phylum of deep-sea wormlike invertebrates (20 species)—the beardworms. Up to 30 cm long, beardworms live in tubes built in the mud of the ocean floor. Their head ends are crowned with tentacles, which protrude from the tubes and are believed to function in respiration and feeding (beardworms lack a digestive system).

● **pogrom** ▶ (Russian: devastation) An attack on Jews and Jewish property, especially in the Russian Empire. Russian pogroms, which were condoned by the government, were particularly common in the years immediately after the assassination of Alexander II in 1881 and again from 1903 to 1906, though mob persecution of Jews continued until the Russian Revolution (1917).

● **Po Hai** ▷*See* Chihli, Gulf of.

● **poikilothermy** ▶ The condition of being cold-blooded. Invertebrate animals, fishes, amphibians, and reptiles have no physiological mechanism for the control of their body temperature, which therefore fluctuates with that of the environment. They are therefore restricted to environments with a suitable temperature range. *Compare* homoiothermy.

● **Poincaré, Jules Henri** ▶ (1854–1912) French mathematician; cousin of Raymond ▷Poincaré. He is regarded by some as the last universal mathematician because he made important contributions to all fields of mathematics as well as to physics and astronomy. A gifted writer, Poincaré in later life wrote important treatises on the nature of mathematical creativity, emphasizing its intuitional aspects.

● **Poincaré, Raymond** ▶ (1860–1934) French statesman; president (1913–20) and prime minister (1912–13, 1922–24, 1926–29). His foreign policy aimed to prevent French isolation in the face of possible German aggression and when, after World War I, Germany delayed in the payment of reparations he ordered French troops to occupy the Ruhr. His postwar economic policy brought a period of stability to France.

● **poinciana** ▶ A tropical shrub or small tree of the genera *Caesalpinia* or *Delonix* (both formerly called *Poinciana*), often grown for ornament. Up to 15 m tall, they have large feathery compound leaves and clusters of showy orange or scarlet flowers. Popular species include the Barbados pride (*C. pulcherrima*) and the ▷flamboyant tree (*or* royal poinciana). Family: ▷*Leguminosae*.

● **poinsettia** ▶ An ornamental shrub, ▷*Euphorbia pulcherrima*, native to Mexico and tropical America and a popular pot plant. Growing 0.6–3 m tall, it has simple dark-green leaves and clusters of tiny greenish-yellow flowers surrounded by large scarlet bracts, up to 14 cm long, which resemble petals. Family: *Euphorbiaceae*.

● **point** ▶ **1.** A unit of weight for precious stones, especially diamonds, equal to two milligrams. **2.** A unit of type size equal to 0.0138 inch or 0.0148 inch in Europe.

● **Pointe-à-Pitre** ▶ 16 14N 61 32W The chief town and port of Guadeloupe. It possesses a good harbour and is the chief commercial centre for the island. Population (1990): 26 029.

● **Pointe-Noire** ▶ 4 46S 11 53E A port in Congo-Brazzaville, on the Atlantic coast. Its port was completed in 1939 and has a considerable entrepôt trade. Population (1995 est): 576 206.

● **pointer** ▶ A breed of sporting ▢dog originating in England and named after its habit of pointing its nose towards game. It is lithely built with a long tapering tail, a long slightly concave muzzle, and drooping ears. The short smooth coat is white combined with yellow, orange, liver, or black. Height: 63–68 cm (dogs); 61–66 cm (bitches).

● **pointillism** ▶ A style of painting in which primary colours are applied to the canvas in dots, allowing the colours to be mixed by the eye, thus achieving an intense luminosity. Also called divisionism and neoimpressionism, it was developed by ▷Seurat in France in the 1880s and carried into the 20th century by his disciple ▷Signac.

● **point-to-point** ▷*See* steeplechase.

● **poise** ▶ A unit of viscosity in the ▷c.g.s. system equal to the tangential force per unit area, in dynes per square centimetre, required to maintain unit difference in velocity, in centimetres per second, between two parallel planes in a fluid one centimetre apart. Named after J. L. M. ▷Poiseuille.

● **Poiseuille, Jean Louis Marie** ▶ (1799–1864) French physician and scientist. He is known for his work on blood circulation and the **Poiseuille formula**, giving the flow of fluid through a narrow tube (radius r, length l) as $\pi p r^4/8 l \eta$, where p is the pressure difference between the ends and η the viscosity of the fluid.

● **poison ivy** ▶ An extremely poisonous woody vine or shrub, *Rhus toxicodendron* (or *Toxicodendron radicans*), native to North America. It has compound leaves with three broad leaflets and small whitish-green flowers, which give rise to whitish berries. All parts contain a poison that causes severe skin inflammation on contact. Family: *Anacardiaceae*.

● **poisons** ▶ Substances that injure health or cause death when introduced into the body. The term is often restricted to those substances that are fatal in small doses (e.g. strychnine, cyanide) but can also be applied to those that are harmful when small doses are taken over long periods (cumulative poisons, e.g. lead) and to otherwise safe drugs taken in large doses. Poisons may be classified in various ways, one of which is according to use: i.e. agricultural (pesticides, herbicides, etc.); industrial (poisonous elements and gases, etc.); medicinal (dangerous drugs, e.g. opiates); and natural (bacterial toxins, poisonous plants, animal venoms, etc.). Another way is to group them according to activity: corrosives (acids, alkalis, etc.); blood poisons (e.g. carbon monoxide, warfarin); nerve poisons (e.g. strychnine, cocaine); poisons that interfere with cell function (e.g. cytotoxic drugs, nitrogen mustard); etc.

　　Toxicology is the study of poisons, which deals with their nature and origin, the pathological changes they induce, their recognition in a patient, and the determination of antidotes.

● **Poisson, Siméon-Denis** ▶ (1781–1840) French mathematician, who became professor at the École Polytechnique in 1806. He studied electricity, magnetism, and mechanics. His work on electricity led him in 1837 to discover Poisson's equation, which describes the electric field created by an arbitrary charge density. Poisson's distribution is widely used in probability calculations and **Poisson's ratio** (the ratio of the lateral strain to the longitudinal strain in a stretched wire) is used by engineers in studying the elongation of structural members.

● **Poitiers** ▶ (Latin name: Limonum) 46 35N 0 20E A town in W central France, the capital of the Vienne department. A Roman town and former capital of Poitou, it was the site of a battle (1356) in which the English under the Black Prince defeated the French. Notable buildings include the 4th-century baptistry of St John, the cathedral (11th–

12th centuries), and the university (1432). Metallurgy, textiles, and brewing are the chief industries. Population (1999): 83 448.

● **poker** ▶ A card game, usually for five to seven players, using a single pack of cards. There are many variants but in the standard game each player receives five cards, with an option to discard any of them and receive up to five more. The objective is to make the best hand or to bluff one's opponents into believing one has the best hand. The best hand is (in ascending order) the one containing the highest pair of cards of the same denomination (irrespective of suit); two pairs; three cards of the same denomination; a straight (a sequence of denominations irrespective of suit); a flush (all of the same suit, irrespective of denomination); a full house (a pair and three of the same denomination); four cards of the same denomination; or a straight flush. Each player makes bets on his hand before and after discarding and the betting continues until the limit (if there is one) is reached or until no one wishes to bet further. Although poker is a game of chance there is an element of skill in the opportunity it provides for bluffing one's opponents.

● **Pola** ▷See Pula.

● **Poland, Republic of** ▶ A country in N Europe, on the Baltic Sea. Extensive plains in the N rise to the Carpathian Mountains in the S, which reach heights of over 2500 m (8000 ft). Following the reorganization of the population after World War II, when Poles were transferred from the area ceded to the Soviet Union to that gained from Germany, forcing out the Germans, the majority of the inhabitants are now Polish. Approximately 90% are Roman Catholic.

Economy: since World War II there has been a significant shift in the balance of the economy from agriculture to industry, but Poland remains a leading agricultural nation. The chief crops are rye, wheat, oats, sugar beet, and potatoes. Its mineral wealth includes deposits of coal, copper, and sulphur, and natural gas has been found as well as some oil. Poland's industries include shipbuilding, textiles, engineering, steel, cement, chemicals, and food products. Tourism is an important source of revenue. The transition from a command to a free-market economy proved painful in Poland, with soaring unemployment and high food prices in the mid-1990s. The situation has since improved with rising productivity. Foreign debt remains high.

History: Poland first appeared as a separate state in the 10th century, which also saw the introduction of Christianity. From the 14th to 16th centuries its power was extended under the ▷Jagiellon dynasty, which was succeeded by elected kings. Poland declined in the 17th century, although it was able, under John III Sobieski, to defeat the Turks in 1683. Foreign intervention in the 18th century culminated in partition by Russia, Austria, and Prussia (in 1772, 1793, and 1795), and at the Congress of Vienna in 1815 the ▷Congress Kingdom of Poland was created under the Russian Crown. After the defeat of the Central Powers in World War I independence was declared under Józef Piłsudski. In 1939 Poland was invaded by Germany, precipitating World War II. Some six million Poles, including three million Jews, died during the occupation. Polish resistance to Germany, both within Poland and abroad, directed by Sikorski's government in exile, contributed to the Allied victory, and in 1945 Poland was occupied by the Russians. The ▷Oder-Neisse Line became its W frontier. The first postwar elections, in 1948, brought a communist-controlled government to power under ▷Gomułka. He was demoted in 1948 for asserting independence from the Soviet Union but returned to power after the ▷Poznań Riots. Further unrest in 1970 led to his enforced resignation and he was succeeded by Edward ▷Gierek. Gierek was dismissed in 1980 and succeeded by Stanisław Kania. The political and economic situation worsened and Kania resigned (1981) to be replaced by Gen Wojciech ▷Jaruzelski. In December 1981, the independent trade union ▷Solidarity, led by Lech ▷Wałęsa, was accused of attempting to overthrow the government, its leaders were detained, and a state of martial law was declared under a military council led by Jaruzelski. Martial law was lifted in 1983 but Solidarity remained banned until 1989. Popular pressure for liberal reform culminated in mass demonstrations and the first partly free elections for 40 years in 1989. Solidarity won all but two of the seats it was allowed to contest. A Communist-led government lasted just two weeks before being replaced by a noncommunist government, led by Solidarity. In 1990 Wałęsa replaced Jaruzelski as president. The early

1990s saw continuing economic crisis and a series of short-lived coalition governments. In 1993 the former Communist Party won parliamentary elections and in 1995 Aleksander Kwasniewski, a former communist, defeated ▷Wałęsa in presidential elections. Further parliamentary elections in 1997 resulted in the formation of a Solidarity-led coalition. That same year Poland adopted a new constitution that removed the last traces of communism. Poland joined NATO in 1999 and has been invited to join the EU in 2003. The former Communists returned to power in 2001.

Republic of Poland

Head of state	President Aleksander Kwasniewski
Official language	Polish
Official currency	złoty of 100 groszy
Area	312 677 sq km (120 624 sq mi)
Population (2000 est)	38 655 000
Capital	Warsaw
Main port	Gdańsk

● **Polanski, Roman** ▶ (1933–) Polish film director, born in Paris. After his first full-length film, *Knife in the Water* (1961), he worked in Britain and the USA. Subsequent films include *Repulsion* (1965), *Cul de Sac* (1966), *Rosemary's Baby* (1968), *The Tenant* (1976), *Tess* (1979), *Bitter Moon* (1992), and *Death and the Maiden* (1995).

● **polar bear** ▶ A white bear, *Thalarctos maritimus*, living on the shores of the Arctic Ocean. Up to 2.5 m long and weighing 500–700 kg (depending on the season), polar bears prey mainly on seals, also taking some fish and birds. Males move southwards in winter but females sleep in dens prior to the birth of their young in early Dec. □ p. 993.

● **polar coordinates** ▷See coordinate systems.

● **Polaris** ▶ (or North Star) A remote cream ▷supergiant, apparent magnitude 2.0 and about 650 light years distant, that is the brightest star in the constellation Ursa Minor. It is the present ▷pole star, lying about 1° from the N celestial pole; its position is found using the Pointers in the Plough. It is a ▷Cepheid variable and is the primary component of a ▷multiple star.

● **Polaris missile** ▶ A US navy two-stage solid-fuelled nuclear strategic missile launched from a submarine and having a range of 4500 km (2800 m). Travelling at mach 10, some versions (Poseidon) can deliver 10 separately guided 15-kiloton warheads. When fired from below the surface, the missile is ejected from the vessel by compressed gas, its rocket firing at the surface. Its inertial guidance system is programmed to the launching vessel's exact position. Firing is by two-key control, linked directly to Washington. In the UK they were replaced by ▷Trident missiles in the 1990s.

● **polarized light** ▶ Light in which the direction of vibration is restricted. In ordinary light (and other types of ▷electromagnetic radiation) the transverse vibrations of the electric and magnetic fields are at right angles to each other in all possible planes. In **plane-polarized light** the vibrations of the electric field are confined to one plane and the magnetic field to one at right angles to it. Plane-polarized light can be produced by reflection at a certain angle (*see* Brewster's law) or by passing light through such doubly refracting substances as ▷Polaroid. **Circularly** and **elliptically polarized light** occur when the electric vector describes a circle or an ellipse round the direction of the light beam.

● **Polaroid** ▶ **1.** A tradename for a plastic sheet impregnated with crystals of a dichroic substance (*see* pleochroism) orientated parallel to each other. Invented (1932) by Dr Erwin Land (1909–91), it is used to reduce glare. **2.** Dr Land used the same company to market his Polaroid Land Camera, which he invented in 1947. This produces finished prints in less than 1 minute by using a film in which the emulsion is enclosed in a pod of developer. Modern Polaroid cameras produce colour prints, the appropriate dyes being enclosed in the pod.

● **polder** ▶ An area of low-lying land reclaimed from the sea or other water, often for agricultural purposes. Polders are usually formed by constructing dykes around the area, which is then drained. Land lying below low-tide mark must be pumped clear of water, while that above may be drained by means of tide gates, which close as the tide rises. The most notable polders are those of Holland, next to the IJsselmeer.

● **Pole, Reginald, Cardinal** ▶ (1500–58) English Roman Catholic churchman; Archbishop of Canterbury. As Dean of Exeter (1527–32) he opposed Henry VIII's divorce and in 1532 went to Italy. He wrote *Pro ecclesiasticae unitatis defensione* (1536), attacking Henry's claims of supremacy over the English Church. He advocated reform within the Roman Catholic Church and presided at the Council of ▷Trent. Returning to England on Mary's accession, he became Archbishop of Canterbury in 1556.

● **polecat** ▶ A carnivorous mammal, *Mustela putorius*, found in woods and grassland throughout Europe, Asia, and N Africa. About 50 cm long, it has a dark-brown coat with yellowish patches on the face and ears. Polecats are nocturnal, foraging for rodents and insects. They eject a pungent fluid when alarmed. Family: *Mustelidae* (weasels, etc.). ▷*See also* ferret.

● **Poles, North and South** ▶ The most northerly and southerly points of the earth's surface and the ends of the earth's axis, about which it rotates. The magnetic north and south poles are the slowly changing points to which a magnetic compass needle points and where the lines of force of the earth's magnetic field are vertical. They do not coincide with the geographical poles. ▷*See also* Arctic Circle; Antarctica.

● **pole star** ▶ Either of two stars that are nearest the N or S celestial pole. The poles are not fixed in position but, owing to ▷precession of the earth's axis, trace out two circles in the sky over 25 800 years. Thus a sequence of stars slowly, in turn, become the N or S pole star. ▷*See also* Polaris.

● **pole vault** ▶ A field event for men in which competitors use a fibreglass pole to vault a horizontal bar. A competitor is allowed three tries at each height and is eliminated if he fails. The height is increased until one competitor is left. World record: 6.14 m (1994) by Sergei Bubka (Ukraine).

● **police** ▶ A force established to maintain law and order and to prevent and detect crime; in many countries police also have traffic-control duties. The earliest organized police force in Britain was the Bow Street Runners, formed by the writer Henry ▷Fielding, who was JP for Westminster (1748–53). These were merged in 1829 with the Metropolitan Police (newly established by Sir Robert ▷Peel), a force of one thousand blue-coated men, who patrolled the streets of London. In 1835 police forces were established in the boroughs and from 1839, in the counties where forces became compulsory in 1856. Conditions for police were standardized in 1919, when the Police Federation (a representative body) was established. Responsibility for police forces in the UK is now shared by the Home Office (responsible primarily for the Metropolitan Police with little power over provincial forces) and local police authorities. There is no central administration but common training facilities, forensic laboratories, and criminal-record offices have been set up. British police officers have authority throughout the country and are not normally armed (except with US-style batons), unlike their counterparts in many other countries. Decentralized police forces are found in the USA and Australia, centralized forces in France, Italy, Belgium, Spain, Scandinavia, and Japan. ▷*See also* Criminal Investigation Department; Interpol.

● **Polignac, Auguste Jules Armand Marie, Prince de** ▶ (1780–1847) French statesman. As chief minister to Charles X (1829–30) he supported the absolute authority assumed by the king, thus helping to bring about the ▷July Revolution. Imprisoned until 1836, he was then exiled until 1845.

● **poliomyelitis** ▶ A viral infection of the central nervous system that may result in muscle paralysis. It was known as infantile paralysis, because children were commonly affected. In most cases the infection is mild, with only a nonspecific fever, but sometimes a severe illness develops three to seven days later, which may lead to pain in the limbs followed by permanent paralysis. There is no specific treatment, but an Australian nurse, Elizabeth Kenny (1886–1952), developed the practice of exercising affected limbs rather than immobilizing them. An effective vaccine is available (*see* Sabin vaccine; Salk vaccine).

● **Polisario Front** ▷*See* Western Sahara.

● **Polish** ▶ (*or* Lekhitic) A West Slavonic language spoken in Poland and related to ▷Czech, ▷Slovak, and Sorbian. The Latin script is used; the standard form is based on the Poznań dialect.

● **Polish Corridor** ▶ A belt of land that separated E Prussia from the rest of Germany and was granted to Poland in the Treaty of Versailles (1919). It allowed Poland access to the sea at Danzig (now Gdańsk). It was annexed by Germany in 1939 and returned to Poland in 1945, after World War II.

● **Polish Succession, War of the** ▶ (1733–35) A European war precipitated by the election of rival claimants to the Polish throne in succession to Augustus the Strong: ▷Stanisław I Lesczyński, supported by France, Spain, and subsequently Sardinia, and Augustus' son, Frederick Augustus III (1696–1763), supported by Russia and Austria. After the fall of Danzig (1734) Stanisław fled and the Treaty of Vienna (1735) recognized Frederick Augustus as king.

● **Politburo** ▶ The Political Bureau of the Central Committee of the Communist Party in the Soviet Union. Its members were elected by the Central Committee. The highest organ of the party, it decided party and government policy. It was abolished in 1991.

polar bear ▶ Male polar bears in Hudson Bay, Canada, which is frozen over during winter. One of the animals is basking to keep cool. In the winter females usually remain in their dens.

● **Politian** ▷*See* Poliziano.

● **political asylum** ▶ Refuge granted by one country to immigrants fleeing persecution in another. To claim asylum, applicants must show that they have well-founded fears of persecution in their own country on the grounds of their race, religion, nationality, or political opinion. The right to such asylum was established by the United Nations Convention on the Status of Refugees (1951), which forbade member states from expelling, harrassing, or incarcerating political refugees. Owing to endemic instability and intractable ethnic conflicts in large parts of the world, together with the availability of modern forms of transport, the number of political refugees rose to unprecedented levels at the end of the 20th century (most estimates put the current figure at over 17 million). The great majority of these have fled from one developing country to another. Despite their clear obligations under the UN Convention, many countries have found ways of limiting their hospitality to asylum seekers, either because they fear to incur an economic burden or because of political factors, such as a wish not to offend other governments or to shelter undesirable ideological groups. There is also a reluctance for any country to appear to be operating a more liberal policy than its neighbours, for fear of becoming the first port of call.

In the UK applications for political asylum rose steadily in the 1990s, partly owing to ethnic conflicts in E Europe. In 1998 applications (which are decided by the Home Office) reached a new peak of 46 000, with an estimated backlog of over 70 000 unresolved cases. Largely in response to public opinion, recent British governments have taken steps to tighten asylum policy, despite concern from organizations dealing with the welfare of refugees. In particular, governments have sought to enforce a distinction between genuine asylum seekers and so-called "economic migrants," who are deemed to be fleeing poverty rather than political oppression. Genuine problems have arisen from the need to house and support asylum seekers while their cases are being heard and from the lengthy (and costly) appeals procedure, which is alleged to encourage claims by bogus applicants who simply wish to protract their stay in this country. In 1999 the government introduced a controversial bill replacing social security payments to asylum seekers with payments in kind, imposing new obligations on local authorities to make hostels and vacant housing available as necessary, and seeking to streamline the application and appeals system.

● **political correctness** ▶ A concept, originating in the USA, based on the observation that language contains words and phrases that express such prejudices as racism, sexism, and hostility to homosexuals; to avoid the slightest risk of giving offence, it is argued, extreme care must be taken to avoid all such phrases. Most reasonable people would accept that such words as "nigger," "yid," and "pansy" are offensive and should not be used. However, the extremes of political correctness can easily lend themselves to ridicule (e.g. by insisting on such terms as humankind and differently abled, to replace the traditional mankind and disabled). The term is now widely used in a pejorative sense to indicate overzealous liberal attitudes in general.

● **Poliziano** ▶ (or Politian; 1454–94) Italian poet and scholar, born Angelo Ambrogini. He gained the patronage of Lorenzo de' ▷Medici and later of Cardinal Francesco Gonzago in Mantua. His major work is *Stanze per la giostra* (1475–78), an unfinished poem expressing humanist ideals in classical style. His other works include *Orfeo* (1480), a dramatic court entertainment, and translations.

● **Polk, James K(nox)** ▶ (1795–1849) US statesman; Democratic president (1845–49). An expansionist, Polk set up an independent treasury; lowered tariffs between North and South; acquired California, giving access to the Pacific; and pushed the disputed boundary of Oregon up to the 49th parallel.

● **polka** ▶ A Bohemian folk dance in 2/4 time, which became a popular ballroom dance in 19th-century Europe, rivalling the ▷waltz. It is characterized by three steps and a hop.

● **pollack** ▶ A popular game fish, *Pollachius* (or *Gadus*) *pollachius*, related to cod, with a protruding lower jaw and no chin barbel. Its body, usually up to 1 m long, is brown or olive, sometimes with orange markings above. It occurs in European coastal waters down to 200 m.

● **Pollack, Sydney** ▶ (1934–) US film director. He directed *They Shoot Horses Don't They?* (1969), *Tootsie* (1982), the Oscar-winning *Out of Africa* (1986), and *The Firm* (1993).

● **Pollaiuolo, Antonio** ▶ (c. 1432–98) Florentine Renaissance artist. He and his brother **Piero Pollaiuolo** (c. 1441–96) trained as goldsmiths and often collaborated. Antonio is famous for his bronzes, the painting *Martyrdom of St Sebastian* (National Gallery, London), and the engraving *Battle of the Nudes* (Uffizi). He was reputedly the first artist to make anatomical dissections. Piero painted a series of *Virtues* (Uffizi) and *The Coronation of the Virgin* (Duomo, Florence).

● **pollarding** ▶ Pruning the young branches of a tree to encourage a round bushy head, usually above the heads of grazing animals. It is often done with willows, the year-old branches being used for fencing. In **coppicing** trees are pruned to ground level to produce firewood, etc.

pollen ▶ A scanning electron micrograph of hollyhock pollen grains (magnification × 202). The spikes on the outer surface of the grains may help to ensure that the pollen sticks to insect pollinators.

● **pollen** ▶ The male gametes of seed plants, which are produced in the ▷stamens of flowering plants and in the male ▷cones of conifers and other gymnosperms. To ensure fertilization, the pollen must be transferred to the stigma (in flowering plants) or the female cone (in conifers)—the process of **pollination**. Many flowers are cross-pollinated, i.e. the pollen from one plant is deposited on the stigma of another of the same species by animal carriers (usually insects), wind, or water. Some flowers are self-pollinated, the pollen being transferred from the anthers to the stigma of the same plant. After pollination, a pollen tube grows down from the pollen grain into the pistil of the pollinated flower until it reaches the ovule. Two pollen nuclei travel down this tube: one fertilizes the egg cell, which develops into the embryo plant in the seed; the other fuses with a nucleus in the ovule to become food for the seed.

● **pollen analysis** ▷*See also* palynology.

● **Pollock, Jackson** ▶ (1912–56) US painter, born in Wyoming. He trained in New York under Thomas Hart ▷Benton but his chief early influences were the muralist ▷Orozco and ▷surrealism. By 1947 he had developed the dynamic style of action painting that established his reputation as the leader of US ▷abstract expressionism. His later canvases, some of which were painted only in black and white, were very large. An alcoholic, he died in a car crash.

● **poll tax** ▶ A levy on individuals (*poll*, head) regardless of means. Levied in England occasionally between the 13th and 17th centuries, the imposition of 1380 was a cause of the ▷Peasants' Revolt (1381). A poll tax was revived by the Local Government Act (1988) in the form of the **community charge** to replace domestic ▷rates. Fixed by local authorities, this was paid by all residents over 18, by landlords of designated buildings whose occupants moved frequently, and by owners of unoccupied domestic properties. Public opposition to the tax contributed to the fall of Margaret ▷Thatcher in 1990. In 1993 it was replaced by the ▷council tax.

● **pollution** ▶ The addition to the environment of substances that cannot be rendered harmless by normal biological processes. Modern industrial and agricultural activities have led to the pollution of land, rivers, seas, and the atmosphere by either man-made toxic substances (such as ▷pesticides and ▷fertilizers) or by the overproduction of naturally occurring substances (such as carbon dioxide gas). Pesticides, such as ▷DDT, can build up in the environment and in the bodies of living organisms until they reach toxic levels. Other forms of pollution may have long-term effects on the health of living things, including humans. Current problems include the disposal of ▷radioactive wastes; atmospheric pollution by heavy metals (such as lead), carbon dioxide (*see* greenhouse effect), and sulphur dioxide and nitrogen oxides (*see* acid rain; smog); the disposal of human refuse and sewage (*see* waste disposal); ▷noise pollution; damage to the ▷ozone layer; and orbiting debris from spacecraft. In many cases a technical solution to these problems is available but cannot be implemented because the cost is too high or because of conflict with minority interests. ▷*See also* conservation; fluorocarbons.

● **Pollux** ▶ An orange ▷giant star, apparent magnitude 1.15 and 35 light years distant, that is the brightest star in Gemini.

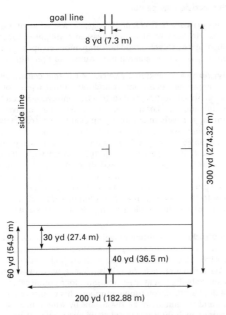

goal line

8 yd (7.3 m)

side line

300 yd (274.32 m)

60 yd (54.9 m)

30 yd (27.4 m)

40 yd (36.5 m)

200 yd (182.88 m)

polo ▶ The dimensions of the ground. If the side lines are boarded, the width is 160 yd (146.4 m) and there is a safety area extending 10 yd (9 m) beyond each side line and 30 yd (27 m) beyond each goal line.

● **polo** ▶ A four-a-side stick-and-ball game, in which the players are mounted on ponies (*see* polo pony). It was played in Persia by 600 BC and spread E but had almost died out when it was rediscovered by British officers in India in the 19th century. The riders use long sticks with mallet heads to hit a solid wooden ball, with the object of scoring goals. Several balls are worn out in a game. A game consists of up to eight seven-minute periods, or "chukkas," after each of which mounts are changed. After every goal the teams change ends. It is presided over by two mounted umpires and a referee. Since World War II Argentina has been the leading polo-playing nation but the game has long had a following in the UK.

● **Polo, Marco** ▶ (c. 1254–1324) Venetian traveller. His father Niccolò Polo and uncle Maffeo Polo undertook a trading expedition to Beijing (1260–69) and in 1271 they returned at the request of the Mongol emperor, ▷Kublai Khan, taking Marco with them. Having

learned Mongolian, he entered Kublai's service, conducting missions as far as S India, until leaving China in 1292. He subsequently fought for the Venetians against the Genoese and was captured. In prison (1296–98) he dictated an account of his travels, which remained almost the only source of information about the Far East until the 19th century.

● **polonaise** ▶ A Polish dance in triple time, with characteristic rhythmic stresses and cadences. Originally a processional folk dance, it evolved into a courtly dance in 18th century Europe; it also became a purely instrumental form, as in Chopin's polonaises for the piano.

● **polonium** ▶ (Po) A radioactive element discovered in 1898 by Marie Curie in minute amounts in pitchblende. It is 5000 times as radioactive as ▷radium and liberates considerable amounts of heat. With 27 isotopes, it has more than any other element. It is used in compact radiation and thermoelectric power sources. At no 84; at wt (209); mp 254°C; bp 962°C.

● **polo pony** ▶ A pony bred and selected as a mount for polo. Polo demands speed, agility, stamina, and courage and the ponies ideally have a strong back, broad deep chest, powerful shoulders and hindquarters, a long flexible neck, and hard legs and feet. Some of the best polo ponies come from Argentina. Height: 1.47–1.63 m (14½–16 hands).

● **Pol Pot** ▶ (1925–98) Cambodian politician; head of state of Democratic Kampuchea (1975–79). Head of the Communist Party from 1963, he launched an armed revolution in 1968 and commanded the victorious ▷Khmer Rouge movement in the ensuing civil war (1970–75). He then began a radical restructuring of Cambodian society, having thousands killed in labour camps (the so-called "killing fields"). In 1979 his regime fell. From Thailand he maintained influence over Khmer Rouge guerrillas in Cambodia and the exiled Coalition Government of Democratic Kampuchea, which returned to form part of the governing coalition in Cambodia in 1991. In 1997 he was sentenced to life imprisonment by former Khmer Rouge colleagues; his death is thought by some to have been suicide.

● **Poltava** ▶ 49 35N 34 35E A city in E Ukraine. The centre of a fertile agricultural region, it has food-processing industries and produces machinery, building materials, and consumer goods.

History: it dates back to the 8th century and was a Cossack centre in the 17th century. Peter the Great defeated Charles XII of Sweden here (1709) during the Great ▷Northern War. Population (1996 est): 321 000.

● **poltergeist** ▶ A noisy, mischievous, and destructive invisible agent that persecutes the occupants of a house, commonly by throwing or moving objects. Famous poltergeist hauntings were the 17th-century "demon drummer of Tedworth" and the 20th-century Borley Rectory phenomena.

● **polyandry** ▷*See* marriage.

● **polyanthus** ▶ A hardy perennial, *Primula × polyanthus*, derived from a cross between the common primrose and the cowslip. There are many varieties, with yellow, brown, blue, or red flowers, grown as ornamentals. ▷*See also* Primula.

● **Polybius** ▶ (c. 200–c. 120 BC) Greek historian. While he was a political hostage in Rome from 168 to 150 BC he became a friend of ▷Scipio Aemilianus. His major work was a history of Rome from 220 to 145 BC in 40 books; the first 5 survive intact.

● **Polycarp, St** ▶ (c. 69–c. 155) Greek martyr and Bishop of Smyrna. He was reputedly converted to Christianity and made a bishop by St John the Apostle. His *Epistle to the Philippians* explains St Paul's teachings and defends Christianity against contemporary heresies. The *Martyrdom of Polycarp* is an anonymous letter describing his death. Feast day: 23 Feb.

● **polychlorinated biphenyls** ▶ (PCBs) Compounds of biphenyl ($C_{12}H_{10}$) in which several hydrogen atoms are substituted by chlorine atoms. They are very stable, making them useful as flame retardants and as electrical insulators. However, they are highly toxic and constitute an environmental hazard as they and their degradation products can persist in the food chain. In 1973 their use was controlled by international agreement.

● **Polyclitus** ▶ (5th century BC) Greek sculptor, born at ▷Argos. A very popular and much copied artist, he sculpted athletes in relaxed poses, combining naturalism with beauty of proportion. His works, as known from later copies, seem less majestic and more individual than those of ▷Phidias.

● **Polycrates** ▶ (died c. 522) Tyrant of Samos, whose naval campaigns made Samos an important power in the eastern Mediterranean. Deceived into believing he was joining a revolt against the Persians, Polycrates was captured and crucified by the Persian governor of Lydia, Oroetes.

● **polycythaemia** ▶ An excessive accumulation of red cells in the blood. This may occur in response to a chronic shortage of oxygen (e.g. in people living at high altitudes) or for no obvious reason (polycythaemia vera). The blood becomes much thicker and both ▷thrombosis and haemorrhage are more common. Treatment is by radiotherapy or with cytotoxic drugs.

● **polyesters** ▶ Synthetic resins or ▷plastics that are polymers of ▷esters. Saturated polyesters (those with no double bonds), made by a condensation reaction, are widely used in such synthetic fibres as Dacron and Terylene. Unsaturated polyesters are used as resins to make thermosetting plastics.

● **polygamy** ▷See marriage.

● **polygon** ▶ A plane straight-sided geometrical figure with three or more sides; for example a pentagon, which has five sides. A regular polygon has all sides equal and all interior angles equal.

● **Polygonum** ▶ A genus of annual or perennial herbs (about 75 species), found worldwide, especially in temperate regions. Ranging usually from 10 to 200 cm in height, they bear simple leaves and clusters of small five-lobed white or pink flowers. Species include the ▷knotgrass, ▷bistort, and persicaria (*P. persicaria*)—a creeping weed. Several others are grown in gardens. Family: *Polygonaceae*.

● **polygraph** ▶ (or lie detector) An instrument designed to detect whether a person is lying by measuring such factors as blood pressure, respiration rate, skin conductivity, and pulse rate. A sudden change in these factors in a person being questioned is taken to indicate that he is under stress and may be telling a lie. Lie detectors are not usually accepted in a court of law.

● **polyhedron** ▶ A solid bounded by plane ▷polygons called the faces. Two faces intersect at an edge and three or more at a vertex. The five regular polyhedrons, the Platonic solids, in which all the faces are equal regular polygons, are the regular tetrahedron, hexahedron, octahedron, dodecahedron, and icosahedron with 4, 6, 8, 12, and 20 sides respectively.

● **polymerization** ▶ The chemical combination of simpler molecules (monomers) to form long chain molecules (**polymers**) of repeating units. In **addition polymerization**, the monomers simply add together and no other compound is formed. Polythene is made from ethylene in this way. In **condensation polymerization**, water, alcohol, or some other small molecule is formed in the reaction, as in the production of ▷nylon.

● **polymethyl methacrylate** ▷See Perspex.

● **polymorphism** ▶ In biology, the functional or structural variation between members of a species, determined by differences in either genetic constitution, environmental conditions, or both. In **transient polymorphism** two forms exist together temporarily, while one form is replacing the other. This occurs in industrial melanism in moths: with industrial pollution of the environment, the black variety has an advantage over the normal pale form. In **balanced polymorphism** the different forms continue to coexist, as in the ▷castes in social insects.

● **Polyneices** ▶ In Greek legend, a son of Oedipus. Having succeeded to the Theban throne, Polyneices and his brother Eteocles agreed to rule the city in alternate years. At the end of his term Eteocles refused to yield to Polyneices, who then laid siege to the city (*see* Seven Against Thebes). Eteocles and Polyneices killed each other in the war, fulfilling Oedipus' curse on his sons. ▷*See also* Antigone.

● **Polynesia** ▶ A division of Oceania in the S and central Pacific Ocean. The volcanic and coral islands include those of French Polynesia, Hawaii, Samoa, Tonga, Tuvalu, Kiribati, and the Line and Cook Islands. ▷*See also* Melanesia; Micronesia.

● **Polynesian** ▶ The people of the Pacific islands contained within the roughly triangular area between and including Hawaii, New Zealand, and Easter Island. They are seafarers, skilled in navigation. Fishing and cultivating are also important. There is considerable uniformity in culture throughout this huge area but social organization varies greatly. Kinship is important everywhere. The Polynesian languages belong to the Oceanic branch of the ▷Austronesian family and include Samoan, ▷Maori, Tongan, Tahitian, and Hawaiian.

● **polyp** ▶ (biology) A sedentary form of many ▷cnidarian animals. It has a cylindrical body attached at the base, with the mouth at the free end surrounded by tentacles bearing stinging cells (nematocysts). Polyps occur singly or in colonies; colonial polyps are modified for different functions, such as feeding, reproduction, and protection. Polyps can reproduce either asexually, to form new polyps or ▷medusae, or sexually, to form polyps.

● **polyp** ▶ (or polypus) (medicine) A growth that has a narrow base or stalk. Polyps may occur in the bowel, nose, womb, larynx, and other sites. They often cause obstruction or infection and some forms may become cancerous: for this reason they are best removed by surgery or cauterization. ▷*See also* papilloma.

● **polypeptide** ▷See peptide.

● **Polyphemus** ▶ In Greek mythology, a one-eyed giant, one of the ▷Cyclops. He lived in Sicily and was an unrequited lover of the nymph ▷Galatea. Odysseus and his companions escaped from imprisonment in his cave by making him drunk and then blinding him.

● **polyphony** ▶ (Greek: many voices) Music that consists of a horizontal combination of melodic strands rather than a series of vertical chords. In its earliest form (9th to 11th centuries) it consisted of voices moving in parallel fourths, fifths, and octaves, called ▷organum, a development of ▷plainchant. The true polyphonic period began when the voices became independent, moving in contrary motion and having different note values. The high point of the polyphonic style was reached in the 16th century with ▷Palestrina's church music, the Italian ▷madrigal, the compositions of the English madrigalists, and the church music of Tallis and Byrd. The music of later polyphonic composers completed the transition from modal polyphony to the system of major and minor keys and stands at the threshold of the harmonic period. ▷*See* counterpoint; harmony; modes.

● **polyploidy** ▶ A condition in which the number of sets of chromosomes in a cell is greater than normal. Most organisms have two representatives of each chromosome in their body cells—the diploid state. With three of each the cell is triploid, with four—tetraploid, and so on. Polyploidy may arise naturally, for example when a sterile hybrid doubles its chromosome number. This results in a fertile organism and is thought to be the means by which many species of plants arose, including wheat. Polyploid plants often show improved size and vigour, and the condition has been induced in crop plants by treating them with chemicals.

● **polypody** ▶ A ▷fern of the genus *Polypodium*, especially *P. vulgare*, which grows on walls, rocks, and trees in temperate regions. It has a creeping slender scaly rhizome with numerous roots, and the tapering branched fronds, 5–75 cm long, are made up of paired leaflets. The spore capsules are grouped in yellow or orange clusters (sori) and usually occur in two rows under the upper leaflets. Family: *Polypodiaceae*.

● **polypropylene** ▶ A thermoplastic material made by ▷polymerization of propylene ($CH_2{:}CHCH_3$). It is similar to high-density ▷polythene but stronger, lighter, and more rigid. Polypropylene products, such as beer crates, luggage, and hinges, are injection moulded. Fibres, which are used to make sacks and carpet backings, are made by extrusion.

● **polysaccharide** ▶ A carbohydrate comprising chains of between three and several thousand linked ▷monosaccharide units. Polysaccharides, such as ▷starch, ▷glycogen, and ▷cellulose, are important as energy reserves and structural components of plants and animals.

● **polystyrene** ▶ A clear glasslike thermoplastic made by polymerization of styrene (phenylethene; $C_6H_5CH{:}CH_2$). It is used for thermal and electrical insulation and as packing.

● **polytechnics** ▶ Institutes of further and higher education concentrating on courses with vocational relevance. The first polytechnic was established in Paris in 1794 to provide technical training for artillery and engineering officers. Polytechnics were established in Germany during the first half of the 19th century, while their development in the UK began largely through the initiative of Quintin Hogg, who in 1880 established the Regent Street Polytechnic (which later became the Polytechnic of Central London and is now part of the University of Westminster). Since then polytechnics have developed widely: most were maintained by LEAs (*see* education) until the Education Reform Act (1988) set up the Polytechnics and Colleges Funding Council, independent of the LEAs. Under the Higher and Further Education Act (1992) all 34 polytechnics in England and Wales became universities, awarding their own degrees.

● **polytetrafluoroethene** ▶ (PTFE) A synthetic material produced by the ▷polymerization of tetrafluoroethene ($F_2C{:}CF_2$). It can withstand temperatures of up to 400°C and has a very slippery surface. PTFE is used to coat nonstick cooking utensils and in gaskets, bearings, and electrical insulation. Tradenames include Teflon and Fluon.

● **polytheism** ▶ Belief in more than one god (*compare* monotheism). Polytheism characterized the religions of the ancient Indo-European peoples (*see* Greek religion; Roman religion) and survives today in ▷Hinduism.

● **polythene** ▶ (polyethylene) A white translucent thermoplastic material made by ▷polymerization of ▷ethene. **Low-density polythene** is made at high pressure and is a soft material used for flexible pipes, sheets, and bags. **High-density polythene,** made at lower pressures, is more rigid, softens at a higher temperature, and is used for mouldings.

● **Polytrichum** ▶ A genus of ▷mosses (over 100 species), known as pigeon wheat and hair-cap mosses, that form large mats in peat bogs, old fields, and acid soils. *P. commune* is the most widely distributed species and grows up to 15 cm high. *Polytrichum* has been used in brooms, baskets, and in stuffing mattresses. Family: *Polytrichaceae*.

● **polyunsaturated fats** ▷*See* fatty acid.

● **polyurethane** ▶ A synthetic polymer the molecules of which contain the –NH.CO.O– group. Some polyurethanes form thermosetting resins and others, thermoplastic resins. They have a wide range of properties and are used in paints, adhesives, moulded articles, rubbers, lacquers, and foams. Polyurethane foam is manufactured from ▷urethane and can be made flexible or rigid.

● **polyvinyl acetate** ▶ (PVA) A vinyl ▷resin produced by ▷polymerization of vinyl acetate ($CH_2{:}CHOOCCH_3$). It is a soft material, used in paints, adhesives, and as a substitute for ▷chicle in ▷chewing gum.

● **polyvinyl chloride** ▶ (PVC) A vinyl ▷resin or plastic produced by ▷polymerization of vinyl chloride (chloroethene; $CH_2{:}CHCl$), a toxic gas. Rigid PVC products are made by moulding. The addition of a plasticizer produces flexible PVC. PVC is tough, nonflammable, resistant to moisture, and a good electrical insulator. It is widely used in sheets, pipes, electrical insulators, and clothing.

● **Pombal, Sebastião José de Carvalho e Mello, Marquês de** ▶ (1699–1782) Portuguese statesman, who was the virtual ruler of Portugal from 1750 to 1777 as the chief minister of José I (1715–77; reigned 1750–77). A proponent of enlightened despotism (*see* Enlightenment), he reformed government administration, encouraged manufacturing, and modernized education. He also directed the rebuilding of Lisbon following the earthquake of 1755. His reforms did not last and his unpopular methods caused his downfall after José's death.

● **pomegranate** ▶ A shrub or small tree, *Punica granatum*, native to W Asia and widely cultivated in the tropics and subtropics for its fruit. 5–7 m tall, it has narrow pointed leaves, about 7.5 cm long, and orange-red flowers growing in the leaf axils. The large round fruit has a thick leathery yellowish-reddish skin and contains several chambers, each containing many seeds coated with a pinkish acid-sweet juicy pulp. Pomegranates are eaten fresh or used in beverages or wines. The seeds are used in preserves and syrups. Family: *Punicaceae*.

● **Pomerania** ▶ A region of NE Europe on the Baltic Sea between the Rivers Oder and Vistula. Pomerania was Polish territory until the 17th century, when the western and central regions were acquired by Brandenburg (later Prussia). Sweden gained W Pomerania in 1648 but by 1815 it had been reacquired by Prussia, which in 1772 had annexed E Pomerania. Territorial redistribution after World Wars I and II restored Pomerania E of the River Oder to Poland; W Pomerania became part of East Germany (now Germany).

● **Pomeranian** ▶ A breed of toy dog, developed in Pomerania, whose ancestors are thought to have been Scandinavian sledge dogs. The Pomeranian has a compact body and foxlike head with small erect ears. The short undercoat is covered by a long straight outercoat and the fluffy tail is held over the back. The coat may be any recognized colour, including white, black, brown, or reddish. Height: 14–18 cm.

● **Pomona** ▶ (mythology) A Roman goddess of fruit to whom a sacred precinct outside Rome was dedicated. She was married to Vertumnus, a god who controlled the change of seasons.

● **Pomona** ▶ (Orkneys) ▷*See* Mainland.

● **Pompadour, Mme de** ▶ (Jeanne Antoinette Poisson, Marquise de P.; 1721–64) The mistress of Louis XV, who exerted considerable political influence from 1745 until her death. She influenced the negotiation of an Austrian alliance against Prussia and was blamed for French defeats in the subsequent ▷Seven Years' War. She was a notable patron of artists and scholars.

● **pompano** ▶ A valuable food fish of the genus *Trachinotus*. It has a deep body, usually up to 50 cm long, coloured silvery blue or grey. Pompanos are carnivorous and live in fast-swimming groups, usually around rocks in warm coastal waters. Family: *Carangidae*; order: *Perciformes*.

● **Pompeii** ▶ An ancient city near Naples, in Italy. It was buried four to six metres deep under volcanic ash by the eruption of Mount ▷Vesuvius (79 AD). Its rediscovery (1748) stimulated general interest in classical archaeology. Pompeii, now about three-quarters excavated, provides unparalleled evidence for daily life in Roman times: buildings, often standing to the first floor and with extensive wall paintings and graffiti; normally perishable objects including food, wooden furniture, and paintings, preserved by the ash; and personal possessions abandoned by the fleeing inhabitants. □ p. 998.

● **Pompey** ▶ (Gnaeus Pompeius; 106–48 BC) Roman general and statesman, called Pompeius Magnus (Pompey the Great). Granted extraordinary powers (67–66) to destroy marauding pirates and then to wage war in Asia, Pompey returned a popular hero. In 60 he joined Julius Caesar and Crassus in the first ▷Triumvirate, marrying Caesar's daughter Julia (d. 54) in 59, but in 50 he supported the Senate's demand for Caesar to resign his armies. In the civil war that followed Pompey was defeated by Caesar at Pharsalus (48) and fled to Egypt, where he was murdered.

● **Pompidou, Georges (Jean Raymond)** ▶ (1911–74) French statesman; prime minister (1962, 1962–66, 1966–67, 1967–68) and president (1969–74). He served under de Gaulle during World War II and was his personal assistant in 1958–59, when he helped draft the constitution of the Fifth Republic. He negotiated a settlement with the Algerians (1961) and with the students in the revolt of May, 1968. He succeeded de Gaulle as president and reversed his policy of opposing the UK's bid to join the EC.

● **Ponce** ▶ 18 01N 66 36W A major city and port in S Puerto Rico, on the Caribbean Sea. Industries include iron processing, sugar refining, and canning. Population (1996 est): 189 988.

● **Ponce de Leon, Juan** ▶ (1460–1521) Spanish explorer. He accompanied Columbus on his second voyage to Central America (1493–96) and in 1508–09 founded the first settlement in Puerto Rico, of which

Pompeii ► A typical street with a raised pavement and stepping stones for pedestrians.

he became governor (1510). In 1512, searching for the legendary fountain of eternal youth, he discovered Florida. He died while attempting to colonize it, from a wound received from an Indian's poisoned arrow. The port of Ponce is named after him.

● **Pondicherry** ► A Union Territory in SE India, on the Coromandel Coast. Founded by the French in 1674, it was their chief settlement in India until transferred to Indian administration in 1954. Rice and millet are the chief products. Area: 479 sq km (185 sq mi). Population (1994 est): 894 000. Capital: Pondicherry.

● **pond skater** ► A ▷water bug belonging to the family *Gerridae* (about 350 species). Pond skaters, or water striders, have a dark slender body and long legs. They are found mainly in fresh water, running or skating across the surface and feeding on small insects.

● **pond turtle** ► Either of two species of turtle found in ponds and other still waters. The Pacific pond turtle (*Clemmys marmorata*), of the W coast of North America, is 15–18 cm long and brown with yellow spots; it is widely sold for food. The European pond turtle (*Emys orbicularis*) of Europe, N Africa, and W Asia, is 12–13 cm long and brown with yellow speckles. Family: *Emydidae*.

● **pondweed** ► A usually perennial aquatic herb of the genus *Potamogeton* (100 species), found worldwide in fresh water. It has submerged or floating oblong or pointed leaves, 2–20 cm long, and stalked heads of tiny four-lobed greenish flowers. Family: *Potamogetonaceae*.
  The Canadian pondweed (*Elodea canadensis*) has submerged stems, up to 3 m long, with whorls of narrow backward-curving dark-green leaves. Native to North America, it is naturalized in Europe. Family: *Hydrocharitaceae*.

● **Poniatowski, Józef** ► (1763–1813) Marshal of France, born in Austria, who served consecutively in the Austrian and Polish armies before becoming commander of the Duchy of Warsaw, established by Napoleon in 1807. He fought in Napoleon's Russian campaign (1812–13) and died at ▷Leipzig.

● **Ponta Delgada** ► 37 29N 25 40W A town in the Azores, the capital of São Miguel Island. Important since 1540, it is a tourist resort and the main commercial centre of the Azores. Population (latest est): 22 200.

● **Pontefract** ► 53 42N 1 18W A market town in N England, in West Yorkshire. Richard II was murdered in its 11th-century castle. Pontefract's licorice sweets (Pontefract or Pomfret cakes) are widely known. There is local coalmining and market gardening. Population (1991): 28 358.

● **Ponte Vecchio** ► A bridge over the River Arno in Florence. Topped by buildings, it was designed by Taddeo ▷Gaddi and finished in 1345. It was a highly advanced structure for its period.

● **Pontevedra** ► 42 25N 8 39W A port in NW Spain, in Galicia. It has a 16th-century cathedral and an episcopal palace. Its manufactures include cloth, leather, and pottery. Population (1991): 74 850.

● **Pontiac** ► (c. 1720–c. 1769) American Indian chief, who organized local tribes to resist White migration to the NW. In **Pontiac's Conspiracy** (1763–66) the Indians took all but three of the British fortified posts. Fighting continued until 1765, when the posts were all recaptured, and peace was signed at Oswego in 1766.

● **Pontianak** ► 0 05S 109 16E A port in Indonesia, in W Kalimantan on the Kapuas delta. Formerly Borneo's main gold town, its chief industries are shipbuilding and rubber, palm oil, sugar, and timber processing. Its university was established in 1963. Population (1995 est): 449 100.

● **Pontine Marshes** ► (Italian name: Agro Pontino) A reclaimed marshland area in S central Italy, bordering on the Tyrrhenian Sea. An extensive scheme to drain the marshes was begun in 1928; several towns including Littoria (now Latina) were established and it has become one of the most productive agricultural areas in Italy.

● **pontoon** ► (*or* vingt-et-un) A card game in which the objective is to score 21, counting court cards as 10 and the ace as 1 or 11. One card is dealt face down to each player, who puts up a stake accordingly. A second card is then dealt face down and the betting continues in some games. Players then have the option of "sticking" (keeping the cards they have), buying another card face down, or "twisting" (accepting another card face up at no cost). Hands scoring more than 21 after this procedure lose their stakes (go "bust"). The winner is the player with the score nearest to 21. Players scoring exactly 21 (a 10 and an ace) win double their stakes. ▷*See also* blackjack.

● **pontoon bridge** ► A type of temporary bridge in which the deck (or roadway) rests on floating flat-bottomed vessels (pontoons). Pontoons were often used in the earliest military campaigns as they could be preassembled, floated into position, and did not need to last for ever. Modern pontoon bridges often have a movable section to allow boats to pass; they are useful where the earth is unsuitable for heavy pier foundations or the traffic is too light to justify a piered bridge.

● **Pontormo, Jacopo da** ► (J. Carrucci; 1494–1557) Italian mannerist painter, born in Pontormo (*see* mannerism). He settled in Florence, where he trained under ▷Andrea del Sarto. He painted mythological scenes in the Medici villa at Poggio a Caiano (1521) and scenes of the Passion (1522–25) at the Certosa, near Florence, but his major work is the *Deposition* (Sta Felicità, Florence).

● **Pontus** ► The coastal region S of the Black Sea in NE Asia Minor. Pontus was a kingdom from the 4th century BC, becoming prominent in the 1st century BC under ▷Mithridates VI Eupator. Pompey conquered Pontus in 64, after which the region was administered by Rome.

● **Pontypool** ► 51 43N 3 02W A town in SE Wales, in Torfaen county borough. Glass and nylon are manufactured; coalmining was formerly important. The first successful tinplate in Britain was made here in 1703. Population (1991): 35 564.

● **Pontypridd** ► 51 37N 3 22W A town in South Wales, in Rhondda, Cynon, Taff county borough at the confluence of the Rivers Taff and Rhondda. Its heavy industry includes iron and brass founding and chemicals; coalmining was once important. There are light industries at a nearby trading estate. Population (1991): 28 487.

● **pony** ► A ▷horse that does not exceed 1.47 m (14½ hands) in height at maturity, measured from the top of the shoulders (withers). The many modern breeds of pony are thought to have developed from one or two original types, which may have resembled ▷Przewalski's horse and the ▷Exmoor pony. Ponies have traditionally been used by man as pack animals and for riding. Today, they are especially popular as children's mounts and for pony trekking.

● **Pony Club** ▶ An international organization founded in England in 1929 to promote sound horsemanship among people under 21. Branches were originally connected with various hunts (*see* foxhunting), but mounted games (*see* gymkhana), ▷showjumping, and ▷horse trials are also typical activities.

● **poodle** ▶ A breed of ▢dog of uncertain origins but long associated with France and Germany. The poodle is an active intelligent dog with a long straight muzzle, drooping ears, and a docked tail. The dense coat, which was originally clipped to enable them to swim and retrieve in water, may be any recognized colour, including grey, white, black, brown, or cream. The miniature poodle and toy poodle are derivative breeds of the standard poodle. Height: 38 cm minimum (standard); 28–38 cm (miniature); under 28 cm (toy).

● **pool** ▶ An American form of ▷billiards played on a table usually 1.4 × 2.7 m (4.5 × 9 ft) with six pockets. The object is to use a white cue ball to pot the 15 coloured balls into the pockets.

● **Poole** ▶ 50 43N 1 59W **1.** A resort in S England, in Poole unitary authority, Dorset; it stands on **Poole Harbour**, an almost landlocked inlet of the English Channel that serves as one of the world's largest natural harbours. Poole is a minor port, with boatbuilding, engineering, pottery (using local clays), and chemical industries. Population (1991): 138 479. **2.** A unitary authority in S England, in Dorset. Area: 37 sq km (14 sq mi). Population (1996 est): 139 200.

● **Poona** ▶ (*or* Pune) 18 34N 73 58E A city in India, in Maharashtra. Capital of the Marathas in the late 18th century, it was taken by the British in 1817. It is the site of a university (1949) and a renowned oriental research institute (1919). A commercial, manufacturing, and military centre, it has cotton textiles, rubber, paper, and munitions industries. Population (1991): 1 559 558.

● **Poor Laws** ▶ The laws that governed assistance to the poor in Britain. From the 16th century parishes were responsible for providing for their poor and from 1572 levied a rate for poor relief, which was further systematized by Acts of 1576, 1598, and 1601. The Poor Law Amendment Act of 1834 abolished such outdoor relief and those seeking assistance had to enter a ▷workhouse. The Poor Law system was not abolished until 1947. ▷*See also* Speenhamland system; social security.

● **pop art** ▶ A modern art movement dominant in the USA and UK in the 1960s. Pop art was strongly influenced by the mass media—television, comics, advertising, etc.—in its subject matter and techniques. Also characteristic is the use of silkscreen ▷printing, ▷collage, and the ▷ready-made. Pioneered in the 1950s by Jasper ▷Johns and Robert ▷Rauschenberg, it was influenced by the early-20th-century ▷dada movement and developed as a reaction to ▷abstract expressionism. Leading pop artists were Andy ▷Warhol, Roy ▷Lichtenstein, George Segal, Claes ▷Oldenburg, and, in the UK, Richard Hamilton and Peter ▷Blake.

● **pope** ▷*See* papacy.

● **Pope, Alexander** ▶ (1688–1744) British poet. A severe childhood illness left him a cripple for life. He established his reputation as a poet of biting wit and skill, especially in his masterly use of the ▷heroic couplet, with *An Essay on Criticism* (1711) and the mock epic *The Rape of the Lock* (1712–14). The financial gains from his translations of Homer's *Iliad* (1715–20) and *Odyssey* (1725–26) enabled him to move in 1719 to his comfortable house in Twickenham. Here he wrote the mock epic *The Dunciad* (1728; revised 1742–43), the philosophical poem *An Essay on Man* (1733–34), and poems modelled on the satires of Horace.

● **Popish Plot** ▶ (1678) A supposed conspiracy invented by Titus Oates (1649–1705) and Israel Tonge. They alleged the existence of a plot to assassinate Charles II and place his Roman Catholic brother, James, on the throne. The anti-Catholic passions Oates and Tonge thus aroused led to the execution of 35 suspects and the exclusion of Catholics from parliament (*see* Test Acts).

● **poplar** ▶ A shrub or tree of the genus *Populus* (about 30 species), native to N temperate regions and grown for wood pulp, shade, and ornament. Up to 40 m tall, the trees may have a broad spreading crown, as in the European black poplar (*P. nigra*), or a tall slender one, as in the Lombardy poplar (*P. nigra* var. *italica*). The oval, triangular, or heart-shaped leaves may have striking autumn colours and the drooping male and female catkins are usually borne on separate trees. The seeds have tufts of silky white hairs. Family: *Salicaceae*. ▷*See also* aspen.

● **pop music** ▶ Any music that is general in its appeal, especially among younger people; it includes folk, blues, gospel, country and western, and, predominantly, rock music. It is distinguished from classical music and jazz by its harmonic simplicity. Pop emerged as a distinct genre in the 1950s with the emergence of small groups using electronically amplified instruments, simple harmonies, and heavy rhythms (*see* rock and roll). Pop songs are generally about universal emotions, such as love and desire. The emergence of rebellious youth movements in the 1960s found expression in the life styles of pop musicians, the increasingly political and drug-influenced lyrics of pop songs, and unconventional styles of dress and performance. The multiplicity of styles since the early 1970s has included **disco**, music with a thumping beat designed for dancing, **progressive rock**, with long instrumental solos and complex rhythms, **punk rock** and **new wave**, which returned to a basic and aggressive style of performance, **heavy metal**, relying upon distorted guitars and high volume, **rap**, in which the vocal line consists of a fast rhythmic chant, ▷reggae and **ragga**, which originated in the Caribbean, **World music**, using ethnic styles from around the world, **acid house** (or house) music, characterized by a repetitive beat and synthesized sounds, and aggressive angst-ridden **grunge**. Developments in the 1980s included the increased use of synthesizers and computer technology and the making of short pop videos. The 1990s saw the continuing rise of electronic dance styles associated with drug culture. The term **popular music** usually refers to light romantic music.

● **Popocatépetl, Mount** ▶ 19 02N 93 38W A volcano in central Mexico, near Mexico City. Its crater contains sulphur deposits. An eruption in 1997 (the first since 1925) covered Mexico City in ash. Height: 5452 m (17 887 ft).

● **Popov, Aleksandr Stepanovich** ▶ (1859–1905) Russian physicist, who studied the transmission of radio waves. Popov's work preceded that of ▷Marconi and in 1897 he succeeded in transmitting over a distance of five kilometres. However, he failed to pursue the use of radio waves for communication.

● **Popov, Oleg Konstantinovich** ▶ (1930–) Russian clown. His act, influenced by Charlie Chaplin, incorporated his skills as acrobat and juggler. He toured with the Moscow Circus.

● **Popper, Sir Karl Raimund** ▶ (1902–94) Austrian-born philosopher. Forced by the Nazi threat to emigrate, Popper was a professor at the London School of Economics (1949–69). In *The Logic of Scientific Discovery* (1935) he cast doubt upon traditional methods of establishing scientific laws by observation and experiment: "all crows are black" is a generalization that can never be verified (we can never observe *all* crows), but it could be falsified by the observation of one white crow. Thus scientific theories should not be said to be true: at best they can survive attempts at falsification. *The Open Society and its Enemies* (1945) and *The Poverty of Historicism* (1957) promote "methodological individualism," the restoration of the historical importance of the individual against collective doctrinaire systems such as Marxism.

● **poppy** ▶ An annual, biennial, or perennial plant of the genus *Papaver* (about 120 species), native mainly to the N hemisphere and often grown for ornament. 15–100 cm high, it yields a milky sap (latex) and bears large lobed or divided leaves and white, pink, or red flowers, sometimes with a dark centre, with 4–6 petals around a whorl of stamens. The ▢fruit is a capsule with pores through which the seeds are dispersed. Species include the ▷corn poppy and ▷opium poppy. Family: *Papaveraceae*. ▷*See also* horned poppy; prickly poppy; Welsh poppy.

● **Popski's Private Army** ▶ A unit famous for its courageous missions (1942–45) behind enemy lines in N Africa and Italy in World

War II. It was named after its Belgian commander, Lieutenant Colonel Vladimir Peniakoff (known as Popski; 1897–1951), who had joined the British army in 1940.

● **popular front** ► A coalition of left-wing and moderate political groups. Increasingly concerned by the rise of fascism in the mid-1930s, many Communist Parties, with Soviet encouragement, sought political alliances with socialist and liberal groups. In 1936 a popular-front government was elected in France; but generally the different parties were too divided to oppose fascism effectively. ▷*See also* United Fronts.

● **population** ► In ecology, a group of individuals of the same species living as part of a ▷community in a defined area or habitat. The size of a population depends on the difference between the birth rate and the death rate and the difference between immigration and emigration. Populations grow when the birth rate exceeds the death rate, when immigration exceeds emigration, or when a combination of these factors occurs.

On a much larger scale, a population can be defined as the total number of individuals of the same species living within a defined area. The world population of human beings has increased enormously in the last 400 years. From the beginning of the Christian era to about 1600, the growth was slow but steady. Since then it has increased approximately tenfold. This rapid rise, especially in the last 150 years, has occurred as a result of improved agricultural techniques producing more food and improved public health facilities providing cleaner water and safer sanitation. At the same time medical services have become much more effective in combating disease and in preventing it by the identification and control of disease-causing organisms. As a result, ▷life expectancy in the UK during the 20th century increased from 52 years to 79 years for women (and a few years less for men). While these figures are typical of the industrialized world, in the developing world life expectancy is now only at the same level as it was in the UK in 1900. ▷*See* overpopulation.

The population of the world is not, of course, evenly distributed over the globe. **Population density** provides a useful measure of the number of people inhabiting a particular area. For example, in a large part of Australia the population density is less than 1 per sq km, while in parts of Europe, India, and China it is over 100 per sq km.

● **porbeagle** ► A ▷mackerel shark, *Lamna nasus*, commonly called the Atlantic mackerel shark, that lives mainly in N temperate shallow waters. It has a dark-blue robust body, 1.5–3 m long, with a white belly and may occur in small groups, feeding principally on fish, especially mackerel.

● **porcelain** ► White vitrified ceramic evolved by Chinese potters about 900 AD. It developed out of stoneware pottery. There are three kinds of porcelain: hard-paste or true porcelain, soft-paste or artificial, and English bone china. Hard-paste porcelain consists of china clay (kaolin) and fusible feldspathic rock (petuntse) finely mixed and fired to about 1400°C. This forms a translucent white resonant vitreous body, which is usually glazed with pure petuntse during the firing. Hard-paste porcelain was made in Japan about 1500 AD but the secret of its manufacture defied discovery elsewhere until the early 18th century when the alchemist Böttger (1682–1719) succeeded in making it at ▷Meissen. By the mid-18th century the smaller works at Plymouth and Bristol also succeeded. Soft-paste porcelain differs from hard-paste in that the clay or kaolin is mixed with an artificial flux. This might be sand with lime, or flint, soda, etc., depending on the factory. The mixture is fired at about 1100°C and the glaze, usually of glass, is applied in a second firing at about 1000°C. Bone porcelain is an 18th-century English invention using bone ash as a flux.

● **porcupine** ► A large herbivorous spiny ▷rodent belonging to either of the families *Erethizontidae* (New World porcupines; 11 species) or *Hystricidae* (Old World porcupines; 15 species). American porcupines tend to be arboreal and have prehensile tails. The North American porcupine (*Erethizon dorsatum*) is about 75 cm long and grows a soft winter coat that almost conceals its covering of quills. Old World porcupines are mainly ground-dwelling. The Indian crested porcupine (*Hystrix indica*) grows to 1 m in length and may have spines 35 cm long. Porcupines respond to a threat by turning their backs and raising their spines. □mammal.

● **porcupine fish** ► A fish, also called sea porcupine, of a family (*Diodontidae*) related to ▷puffers, found in tropical seas. It has a short broad body, up to about 90 cm long, which it inflates when provoked, erecting numerous spines.

● **porgy** ▷*See* sea bream.

● **Pori** ► (Swedish name: Björneborg) 61 28N 21 45E A seaport in S Finland, on the Gulf of Bothnia. Its industries include copper refining, textiles, wood processing, steel, and chemicals. Population (1994): 76 561.

● **pornography** ► Written or visual material depicting sexual activities in a manner that is intended to cause sexual arousal rather than artistic appreciation. Archaeological evidence suggests that pornography is among the most ancient of human artefacts; it has certainly existed throughout recorded history, adapting itself quickly to each new medium, be this the printed book, photography, cinema, video, or computers and the Internet. Since the liberalization of the 1960s, pornography has become a multimillion pound industry, especially in the form of magazines and videos for men (who appear to be more susceptible to visual stimulation than women). In the USA the "adult" film business now rivals Hollywood in its scale and productivity, with estimated earnings of around $10 billion annually.

The question of whether pornography is or may be harmful, either to individuals or to society as a whole, remains contentious. For most of modern history it was subject to legal controls of some strictness (*see* censorship), while continuing to flourish underground. In the later decades of the 20th century, the milder forms of pornography are openly available in most Western countries; moreover, material that would once have been considered blatantly pornographic now has a widely accepted place in both mainstream entertainment and serious art. This situation has not been welcomed by everybody. Some religious and other groups still regard any sexual material as unacceptable and agitate for it to be banned, while many feminists regard pornography as intrinsically demeaning to women because women are featured in it only as sex objects. Some feminists also maintain that pornography incites men to rape and other sexual crimes; although research suggests that sex offenders are very likely to be users of pornography, a causal connection has not been (and perhaps cannot be) demonstrated. Others take a more liberal view, making a distinction between so-called "soft porn," which is regarded as harmless or in any case not justifying the loss of freedom involved in banning it, and "hardcore porn," which is thought to require some form of control. Soft porn generally features nudity, simulated sex acts, or other material designed to satisfy mainstream tastes and fantasies. By contrast hardcore porn involves unsimulated sex acts shown in unsparing detail and often contains material catering to minority or deviant tastes. At the extreme end this may involve violence to women, child abuse, or other forms of sexual activity in which people (or animals) are physically or mentally damaged. Pornography of this kind is generally illegal and is defended by only the most radical libertarians.

In British law, pornography may incur legal action if it is thought to contravene the Obscene Publications Acts (1959 and 1964), which make it an offence to publish any material that "tends to deprave or corrupt." However, since 1959 the publisher has been able to claim a "public good" defence if the material can be shown to have artistic, educational, or scientific value. The importance of this defence was demonstrated in 1960, when Penguin Books were prosecuted for publishing the first unexpurgated UK edition of *Lady Chatterley's Lover* (1928) by D. H. Lawrence. At the trial 36 witnesses (including a bishop and several leading writers) testified to the book's artistic merit and the jury unanimously declared that it was not obscene. This verdict proved a watershed in the publication of sexually explicit material; subsequent prosecutions have been rare and largely unsuccessful.

● **porphyria** ► A group of genetic disorders in which there is an accumulation in the body of one or more porphyrins—precursors of the red blood pigment—due to an enzyme defect. The disease affects the digestive tract, causing abdominal pain, vomiting, and diarrhoea; the nervous system, causing psychotic disorder, epilepsy, and weakness; the circulatory system, causing high blood pressure; and the skin, causing photosensitivity. There is no specific treatment. One form of the disease, acute intermittent porphyria, was responsible for the insanity—at first episodic but later permanent—of George III.

● **porphyry** ► An igneous rock, usually hypabyssal, containing numerous large crystals called phenocrysts set in a finer-grained, or sometimes glassy, groundmass. The term porphyry is often given with the name of the porphyritic mineral, for example quartz porphyry.

● **Porphyry** ► (232–305 AD) Syrian-born philosopher and devoted disciple, editor, and biographer of ▷Plotinus. Among nearly 80 titles attributed to him are religious and philosophical works, including a *Treatise against Christians*, banned in 448 AD but still partly extant.

● **porpoise** ► A small toothed ▷whale belonging to the family *Phocoenidae* (7 species), of coastal waters. Porpoises are 1.5–2 m long and have no beak. The common, or harbour, porpoise (*Phocoena phocoena*) of the N Atlantic and Pacific, has a rounded body, tapering towards the tail, blue-grey above and pale grey beneath. It lives in large groups called schools, feeding on fish, squid, and crustaceans.

● **Porsche, Ferdinand** ► (1875–1951) German car designer. In 1937 he designed the Volkswagen "Beetle" (▷car) for the Nazis and in 1949, with his son Ferry, the first Porsche sports car.

● **port** ► A fortified dessert ▷wine from Oporto (N Portugal). The grapes grown on the Douro hillsides are trodden in stone presses. Fermentation is halted by adding brandy. The wine is later taken to lodges near Oporto, where it matures in wood. Port-type wines are made in other countries.

● **Port Adelaide** ► 34 52S 138 30E The chief port of South Australia, NW of ▷Adelaide on an inlet of Gulf St Vincent. It has a container and passenger terminal; the main exports are wool, fruit, flour and wheat. Population (latest est): 39 000.

● **Portadown** ► 54 26N 6 27W A market town in Northern Ireland, in Co Armagh. A centre for the surrounding rich farming region, it manufactures linen, carpets, and furniture. There are famous rose nurseries. Population (1991): 21 229.

● **Portal, Charles Frederick Algernon, Viscount Portal of Hungerford** ► (1893–1971) British air marshal. He joined the Royal Flying Corps in World War I and in 1937 became an air vice-marshal at the Air Ministry. In World War II he was head of Bomber Command (1940–41) before being appointed Chief of the Air Staff; he remained the head of the RAF until 1946. Created a baron in Churchill's resignation honours, he was subsequently made a viscount. From 1946 to 1951 he was Controller of Atomic Energy in the UK.

● **Port Arthur** ► 29 55N 93 56W A city in the USA, in Texas. Situated in an oil region known as the Golden Triangle, Port Arthur is a major shipping outlet for oil and has large petrochemical industries. Population (1990): 58 724.

● **Port Arthur** ▷See Lüda; Thunder Bay.

● **Port Augusta** ► 32 30S 137 48E A port in South Australia, on the Spencer Gulf. It is an important railway centre and has the state headquarters of the Royal Flying Doctor Service. Chief exports include wheat and wool. Population (1994 est): 14 561.

● **Port-au-Prince** ► 18 40N 72 20W The capital of Haiti, a port in the SW on the Gulf of Gonaïves. Its main exports are coffee and sugar. The University of Haiti was founded here in 1944. Population (1995 est): 846 247.

● **Port Elizabeth** ► 33 58S 25 36E A city in S South Africa, on Algoa Bay. It was founded in 1820 by British settlers. The university was founded in 1964. Nearby is the Addo Elephant National Park. It is a major port, ore being the chief export; industries include car assembly, fruit canning, and flour milling. Population (1991): 303 353.

● **Porter, Cole (Albert)** ► (1893–1964) US composer of musicals and popular songs. He wrote a series of musicals, including *The Gay Divorcee* (1932), *Anything Goes* (1934), *Kiss Me Kate* (1948), and *Can Can* (1953). His songs included "Night and Day" and "Begin the Beguine."

● **Porter, George, Baron Porter of Luddenham** ► (1920–) British physical chemist, who worked at Cambridge (1945–66) on fast gas reactions, developing with R. G. W. Norrish the technique of flash

▷photolysis, for which they shared a Nobel Prize (1967). He is a former director of the Royal Institution and former president of the Royal Society.

● **Porter, Katherine Anne** ► (1890–1980) US short-story writer and novelist. *Flowering Judas*, her first collection of stories, was published in 1930. Her stories, especially those in *Pale Horse, Pale Rider* (1939), are mostly delicate explorations of autobiographical material. Her only novel, *Ship of Fools* (1962), won a Pulitzer Prize.

● **Porter, Peter** ► (1929–) British poet, born in Australia. His poetry is noted for its wit and formal elegance. His volumes include *The Last of England* (1970), *The Automatic Oracle* (1987), and *Millennial Fables* (1995); his *Collected Poems* appeared in 1999.

● **portfolio theory** ► The theory, largely due to the US economist James ▷Tobin, that predicts how a rational investor will spread his wealth between the various types of asset available. The resulting portfolio of assets will, the theory assumes, give the maximum return for the minimum risk and the lowest possible risk for an acceptable rate of return. Different investors will build up different portfolios of assets, balancing expected income, capital gains, and risk according to the extent of their wealth and their personal temperament. A set of efficient portfolios can be set out, enabling investors to choose the one most appropriate to their needs and the risk they find acceptable.

The theory also covers the extent to which an investor will wish to incorporate **portfolio protection** into this strategy, by making use of ▷options and ▷futures markets.

● **Port-Gentil** ► 0 40S 20 35E A port in W Gabon, near the mouth of the River Ogooué. It is the nation's chief industrial centre having an oil-refining and a large timber industry. Population (1993): 80 841.

● **Port Glasgow** ► 55 56N 4 41W A town in W central Scotland, in Inverclyde council area, on the Clyde estuary. Formerly the outport for Glasgow with a thriving shipbuilding industry, it is now concerned chiefly with textiles and engineering. Population (1991): 19 693.

● **Port Harcourt** ► 4 43N 7 05E A port in S Nigeria. Founded in 1912, it developed as a port following the arrival of the railway (1916) from the Enugu coalfields. It exports coal, tin, and palm oil. It is the industrial centre of the Niger delta oilfields. It has a university (1975). Population (1996 est): 410 000.

● **Portillo, Michael (Denzil Xavier)** ► (1953–) British Conservative politician. First elected to parliament in 1984, he served in a series of cabinet posts under John ▷Major from 1992, notably as secretary of state for defence (1995–97). He lost his seat at the 1997 general election but was re-elected in 1999 and appointed shadow chancellor of the exchequer in 2000.

● **Port Jackson** ▷See Sydney.

● **Port Klang** ► (name until 1971: Port Swettenham) 3 01N 101 25E A port in W Peninsular Malaysia, on the Strait of Malacca. Exporting chiefly rubber, it serves the Klang Valley, Malaysia's chief industrial area. Population (1991): 243 698.

● **Portland** ► 45 32N 122 40W A city in the USA, in Oregon on the Willamette River. It was founded in 1829 and its growth was stimulated by several gold rushes along the Oregon Trail. The state's largest city, it is a deepwater port, with shipbuilding, timber, and metallurgical industries. It is the site of the University of Portland (1901). Population (1996 est): 480 824.

● **Portland** ► 43 41N 70 18W A city in the USA, in SW Maine on Casco Bay. Destroyed by Indians, French, and British, it was the state capital (1820–32). It is a major petroleum port and commercial centre. Industries include timber, textiles, and chemicals. Population (1992 est): 62 756.

● **Portland, Isle of** ► A rugged peninsula in S England, in Dorset, connected to the mainland by ▷Chesil Beach. It contains Portland Castle, built by Henry VIII (1520). The Portland stone (a type of limestone) quarried here has been used in many London buildings, notably St Paul's Cathedral. Portland Harbour, on the N side, is the UK's largest manmade harbour.

● **Portland, William Henry Cavendish Bentinck, 3rd Duke of** ► (1738–1809) British statesman; prime minister (1783, 1807–09). He was nominal head of the coalition between Lord North and Charles James Fox (1783) and was later home secretary (1794–1801) under Pitt the Younger. In his second ministry he was overshadowed by George Canning and Castlereagh. His second son **Lord William (Henry Cavendish) Bentinck** (1774–1839) was the first governor general of India (1828–35). He abolished ▷suttee (the burning alive of a widow on her husband's funeral pyre), enabled the ▷Thugs to be suppressed, and made it easier for Indians to obtain public posts.

● **Portland cement** ▷See cement.

● **Portland vase** ► A Roman vase (c. 1st century AD) of dark blue glass with a white glass relief of figures, discovered in Italy in 1644. It once belonged to the Duke of Portland but is now in the British Museum. It was restored in 1989.

● **Portlaoise** ► (Portlaoighise) 53 02N 7 17W A town in the Republic of Ireland, the county town of Co Laois. There are woollen, flour-milling, and malting industries. Population (1990 est): 9500.

● **Port Louis** ► 20 10S 57 30E The capital of Mauritius, in the NW of the island. Founded in about 1736, it is the site of two cathedrals. Sugar is exported. Population (1995 est): 145 584.

● **Port Lyautey** ▷See Kenitra.

● **Portmeirion** ► A holiday resort in Gwynedd, N Wales, built by Sir Clough ▷Williams-Ellis on his own land overlooking Tregmadog Bay. He incorporated many fragments of destroyed buildings into his fanciful design, which was loosely based on the fishing village of Portofino in NW Italy.

● **Port Moresby** ► 9 30S 147 07E The capital and main port of Papua New Guinea, on the Gulf of Papua. It was an important Allied base in World War II and since then the port has been considerably modernized. The University of Papua New Guinea was founded in 1965. Population (1990): 193 242.

● **Pôrto** ▷See Oporto.

● **Pôrto Alegre** ► 30 03S 51 10W A city in S Brazil, the capital of Rio Grande do Sul state on the Lagôa (Lagoon) dos Patos. It is a commercial and industrial centre; industries include meat processing, tanning, and the manufacture of textiles. It is the seat of two universities. Population (1991): 1 237 223.

● **Portobelo** ► 9 33N 79 37W A village in E central Panama, on the Caribbean Sea. Founded in 1597, it became an important transshipment point in the New World and was often attacked by English buccaneers. Sir Francis ▷Drake was buried at sea in the Bay of Portobelo.

It declined following the building of the Panama railway in the 1850s and the opening of the Panama Canal (1914). Population (1990 est): 3026.

● **Port-of-Spain** ► 10 38N 61 31W The capital and main port of Trinidad and Tobago since 1783, on the W coast of Trinidad. It was the capital of the short-lived Federation of the West Indies from 1958 until 1962. Notable buildings include the Anglican and Roman Catholic cathedrals. Petroleum products, sugar, and rum are among the main exports. Population (1995 est): 52 000.

● **Porto Novo** ► 6 30N 2 47E The de facto capital of Benin, on the Gulf of Guinea. A former centre of the slave trade with the Portuguese, it came under French rule in the late 19th century. Trade includes palm oil and cotton. Population (1994 est): 200 000.

● **Port Phillip Bay** ► An inlet of Bass Strait, in SE Australia with the port of Melbourne at its head and Geelong on its W shore. Length: 56 km (35 mi). Width: 64 km (40 mi).

● **Port Pirie** ► 33 11S 138 01E A port in South Australia, on the Spencer Gulf. It is important for metal smelting, using ores from Broken Hill. Population (1994 est): 14 671.

● **Port Royal** ► A former Cistercian nunnery originally situated SW of Paris; also called Port Royal des Champs. In the 17th century it became a centre of ▷Jansenism under Abbess Angélique Arnauld (1591–1661), sister of Antoine ▷Arnauld. After persecution the nuns were dispersed (1709).

● **Port Said** ► (or Bur Said) 31 17N 32 18E A major port in Egypt, situated at the Mediterranean entrance to the Suez Canal. Founded in 1859, it became an important fuelling point but suffered from the closure of the Suez Canal (1967–75) and Israeli occupation of the E bank. Population (1994 est): 460 000.

● **Portsmouth** ► **1.** 50 48N 1 05W A port in S England, in Portsmouth unitary authority, Hampshire, at the entrance to Portsmouth Harbour opposite ▷Gosport. Notable landmarks include Nelson's flagship HMS *Victory* and Charles Dickens' birthplace (now a museum). The chief naval base in the UK, Portsmouth is also a commercial and continental ferry port with shipbuilding, ship-maintenance, electronics, and aircraft-engineering industries. The resort of Southsea is within the district. Population (1991): 174 690. **2.** A unitary authority in S England, in Hampshire. Area: 37 sq km (14 sq mi). Population (1999 est): 190 400.

● **Portsmouth** ► 36 50N 76 20W A city and port in the USA, in Virginia on Hampton Roads. Founded in 1752, it is the site of the Norfolk Naval Yard, abandoned by Federal troops (1861) during the US Civil War and used by the Confederates to transform the scuttled USS

Portmeirion ► A Mediterranean fantasy in North Wales, designed and constructed by the Welsh architect Sir Clough Williams-Ellis.

Merrimack into the ▷ironclad *Virginia*. The main industry is shipbuilding and ship repairing. Population (1996 est): 101 380.

● **Portsmouth** ▶ 43 03N 70 47W A city in the USA, in New Hampshire on the Atlantic coast. It has several notable buildings, including the John Paul Jones House (1758). The state's only seaport, it is the site of the Portsmouth Naval Yard (established in 1800); it is an important submarine base. Population (latest est): 22 925.

● **Port Sudan** ▶ 19 38N 37 07E A port in the Sudan, on the Red Sea. It handles much of the country's trade; exports include cotton, gum arabic, and sesame seeds. It also has an important salt-panning industry. Population (1993): 305 385.

● **Port Sunlight** ▷*See* Bebington.

● **Port Swettenham** ▷*See* Port Klang.

● **Port Talbot** ▶ 51 36N 3 47W A town in South Wales, in Neath Port Talbot county borough on Swansea Bay, formed by the amalgamation of Aberavon and Margam in 1921. Steel-making is the major employer and the deepwater harbour is now used almost exclusively by bulk carriers of iron ore. Other industries include chemicals and the manufacture of motor-vehicle and electrical components. It is also a resort, mainly for day-trippers from the nearby industrial towns. Population (1991): 37 647.

● **Portugal, Republic of** ▶ A country in SW Europe, occupying the W section of the Iberian Peninsula and bordering on the Atlantic Ocean. The ▷Madeira Islands are an integral part of Portugal. Coastal plains rise to mountains, reaching 1935 m (6352 ft) in the N. The main rivers are the Douro, Miño, and Tagus.

Economy: traditionally agricultural, but now moderately industrialized. Agricultural products include wines, fruit and vegetables (including olives, figs, and almonds), and cereals. The extensive forests yield valuable timber. Portugal's principal exports include motor vehicles and components, textiles and clothing, cork, wood products, sardines, and fortified wines. Political upheavals, an inefficient farming system (made worse by drought), and loss of cheap raw materials following the independence of former colonies, led to many economic difficulties in the 1970s and 1980s. Since joining the EC in 1986, Portugal has benefited from generous development aid. Industries include shipbuilding, metalworking, pharmaceuticals, and manufacturing. Tourism is an important source of foreign currency. Rich mineral resources include coal, copper pyrites, kaolin, and haematite and hydroelectricity is a valuable source of power.

History: the early history of the region is that of the rest of the Iberian Peninsula (*see* Spain, Kingdom of). Portugal as a distinct Christian territory dates from 868. It became a kingdom in 1139 under Alfonso I (1112–85) and its position was consolidated in the 13th century by the conquest of Muslim territory. Portugal's long alliance with England began in the 14th century. From the 15th century Portuguese explorers opened up new trade routes, allowing for the establishment of an extensive overseas empire that included Angola, Mozambique, and Brazil. In 1580 Portugal came under Spanish domination, which lasted until 1640, when a nationalist revolt brought the Braganza dynasty to power. Thereafter the Portuguese monarchy became increasingly reactionary, a trend that ▷Pombal's reforms of the 1750s attempted to reverse. In 1807 Portugal was invaded by the French, who were defeated in the subsequent ▷Peninsular War. A revolution in 1910 overthrew the monarchy and established a republic. A long period of instability culminated in a military coup in 1926. A prominent role in the new government was played by ▷Salazar, who became prime minister in 1932 and established the corporatist New State. His long dictatorship also saw bitter colonial wars in Africa. In April 1974, Salazar's successor, Marcello Caetano (1906–80), was overthrown in a coup led by Gen Antonio de Spinola, who granted independence to Portugal's remaining colonies before falling from power later the same year. Constitutional government was restored in 1976. In 1986 the socialist Mario ▷Soares, who was prime minister from 1976 to 1979 and from 1983 to 1985, became president. In 1986 Portugal joined the EC. Parliamentary elections in 1995 resulted in a victory for the socialists under António Guterres: a socialist president, Jorge Sampaio, was elected in 1996. Portugal adopted the single European currency in 1999–2002. Following elections in 2002 a right-wing coalition was formed under Paulo Portas.

Republic of Portugal

Head of state	President Jorge Sampaio
Official language	Portuguese
Official religion	Roman Catholic
Official currency	euro of 100 cents
Area	91 631 sq km (34 861 sq mi)
Population (2000 est)	10 005 000
Capital and main port	Lisbon

● **Portuguese** ▶ A ▷Romance language spoken in Portugal, Galicia (Spain), Brazil, Madeira, and the Azores. It emerged as a distinct language during the early medieval period. The standard form is based on the dialect of Lisbon. Brazilian Portuguese differs slightly in grammar and sound system. A characteristic of Portuguese is the use of nasal vowel sounds.

● **Portuguese East Africa** ▷*See* Mozambique, Republic of.

● **Portuguese Guinea** ▷*See* Guinea-Bissau, Republic of.

● **Portuguese literature** ▶ Literature in the Portuguese language commences with the lyrics of a school of poets who flourished under the kings Alfonso III (1248–79) and Dinis (1279–1325) are preserved in three collections of *cancioneiros*. In a later collection, the *Cancioneiro Geral* (1516), the influence of Provençal poetry was replaced by that of Spanish and Italian models. During the 16th century, the golden age of Portuguese literature, Gil Vicente wrote pioneering works of drama, Sá de Miranda (c. 1481–1558) introduced many new poetic forms from Italy, and Luís de Camões composed the national epic poem, *Os Lusíadas* (1572). The subsequent period of decline lasted until the influence of Romanticism in the early 19th century inspired the works of João Baptista da Silva Leitão Almeida-Garrett (1799–1854) and Alexandre Herculano (1810–77). Further stimulation was provided by a reaction against the pseudoclassicism of Feliciano de Castilho led by Antero de Quental (1842–91) and by the influence of French Symbolism. Outstanding individual writers of the 20th century include the poet Fernando Pessoa (1888–1935), the novelist Manual Ribeiro (1879–1941), and the novelist and writer José ▷Saramago, who was awarded the Nobel Prize in 1998.

● **Portuguese man-of-war** ▶ A colonial marine invertebrate animal belonging to a genus (*Physalia*) of ▷cnidarians found mainly in warm seas. It has a translucent bladder-like float (pneumatophore), pink, blue, or violet in colour, which acts like a sail in the wind. Attached underneath are clusters of ▷polyps bearing stinging tentacles, up to 50 m long, used to paralyse fish and other prey. The sting can also have a serious effect on humans. Order: *Siphonophora*; class: ▷*Hydrozoa*. ▢oceans.

● **Portuguese West Africa** ▷*See* Angola, Republic of.

● **Porvoo** ▶ (Swedish name: Borgå) 60 24N 25 40E A city in S Finland. One of the country's oldest settlements, it has a 15th-century cathedral. Its industries include brewing and publishing. Population (latest est): 19 226.

● **Poseidon** ▶ The Greek god of the sea and earthquakes, son of Cronus and Rhea and brother of Zeus and Hades. He used his ability to change his form mainly to further his amorous desires, and his many offspring included Theseus, Polyphemus, and the winged horse Pegasus. He was usually portrayed with a trident and dolphin. He was identified with the Roman ▷Neptune.

● **Posen** ▷*See* Poznań.

● **Po-shan** ▷*See* Zibo.

● **positivism** ▶ The philosophical doctrine of ▷Comte and his successors. It asserts that knowledge of reality can be achieved *only* through the particular sciences and ordinary observation. Positivism rejects all metaphysical propositions, but it has been pointed out (with regard to later ▷logical positivism) that this rejection itself constitutes a metaphysical proposition. ▷Hobbes was an earlier positivist with regard to the status of the law. The only law is positive law, the law that is actually enforced; there is no "higher" law such as natural law. ▷Existentialism, especially in France, has been a reaction against positivism.

● **positron** ▶ The antiparticle of the ▷electron, having the same mass and ▷spin as the electron but opposite electric charge. A positron and an electron annihilate each other on collision, producing two gamma-ray photons.

● **positron emission tomography** ▶ (PET) ▷See tomography.

● **possum** ▶ The most common Australian ▷marsupial, *Trichosurus vulpecula*, also called brush-tailed phalanger. Nocturnal and arboreal, it is cat-sized and has a soft greyish coat and bushy tail. It feeds mainly on buds, leaves, and fruit, and occasionally fledgling birds. The name possum is often used for other members of the family *Phalangeridae*.

● **post** ▶ Letters, parcels, etc., that are carried from one place to another. In the UK the postal service developed from the medieval system of royal messengers employed to transport government documents around the country. In 1512 Henry VIII appointed a master of the post and the service came to include the carriage of private correspondence. Postal services became a government monopoly and William Dockwra (d. 1716), who established a private penny post in London in 1680, was prosecuted and his business closed in 1682. The postal service developed in the 18th century, when stagecoaches were used to carry post, and in 1830 the first railway mails were carried. In 1840—as a result of the efforts of Sir Rowland ▷Hill—uniform letter postage rates (of one penny), dependent on weight and regardless of distance carried, were introduced. Similar developments in other countries led to the establishment in 1875 of what became the Universal Postal Union, which greatly encouraged international mail services. In 1919 the first regular airmail service—between London and Paris—was introduced. Today post offices throughout the UK deal with other business besides the carriage of letters and parcels: the Post Office maintains close links with the national ▷giro system (although Girobank was privatized in 1988), a national savings bank, the payment of ▷social security, and the sale of vehicle and television licences. In 1968 the system of classifying letters into first- and second-class mail was introduced, the service for the former being faster than for the latter. Postal sorting is being mechanized but delivery remains labour-intensive, the Post Office being the biggest employer in the country. In 1981 control of ▷telecommunications passed from the Post Office to British Telecom, which was privatized in 1984; the Post Office finally lost its monopoly status in 1987. A government review in 1998 rejected privatization of the Post Office but recommended that it should be given greater commercial freedom and that certain restrictions on its competitors should be lifted. In 2001 the Post Office Group became a government-owned public limited company named Consignia.

● **poster art** ▶ The design of public notices for advertising and propaganda purposes. Poster design originated in the mid-19th century, the first major poster artist being the Frenchman Jules Chéret (1836–1933). Its development was facilitated by the use of lithography (*see* printing), an inexpensive and easy printing process. Leading painters of the period who designed posters included ▷Toulouse-Lautrec and Aubrey ▷Beardsley, while among specialists in the art were the "Beggarstaff Brothers"—William Nicholson (1872–1949) and James Pryde (1866–1941) as well as John ▷Hassall and the Czech Alphonse Mucha (1860–1939).

● **postimpressionism** ▶ The art of the late 19th-century French painters ▷Cézanne, ▷Seurat, ▷Van Gogh, ▷Gauguin, ▷Toulouse-Lautrec, and their followers whose work developed out of and, to some extent, in reaction to ▷impressionism. The term was coined by the British art critic, Roger ▷Fry. Many of them painted impressionist works early in their careers but later rejected the objectivity and fleeting light effects of impressionism. Cézanne was the forerunner of ▷cubism and Van Gogh of ▷expressionism, while Gauguin developed a style, known as ▷synthetism, and Seurat introduced ▷pointillism. The postimpressionists were not an organized group with a coherent style.

● **postmodernism** ▶ A movement in the arts of the late 20th century away from the assumptions and practices of ▷modernism. In architecture, the term came into use in the mid-1970s to describe the amalgam of styles employed by such architects as ▷Saarinen and Robert ▷Venturi, and in the UK includes buildings by Richard ▷Rogers and others. Although the term was very widely used by cultural commentators in the 1990s, the concept of postmodernism is less clear when applied to the other arts. In general terms, postmodern culture is thought to be characterized by an eclectic approach in which traditional distinctions between styles and genres and between high and low culture are dissolved. Pastiche, playful irony, and an easy familiarity with pop culture and the mass media are all thought to be characteristic of the postmodern style.

● **postmortem** ▷*See* autopsy.

● **postnatal depression** ▶ A state of depression that can afflict women a few days after they have given birth. In its mildest and least persistent form (often known as **baby blues**) it affects about half the women having their first babies and may also occur during pregnancy. It can manifest itself as unexplained tearfulness and short-lived sadness. More persistent is **puerperal depression**, in which the new mother is continuously depressed for up to two months. Family support is usually sufficient to see the mother through this bad period, although it can affect her desire to breastfeed her baby. If the depression is serious the sufferer may require admission to hospital as she may become suicidal or in extreme cases could endanger her baby.

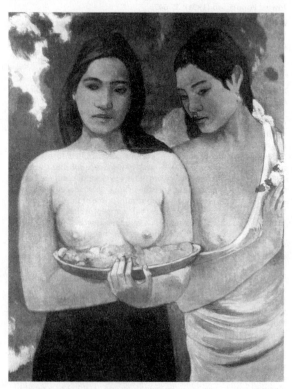

postimpressionism ▶ Gauguin's *Women with Mangoes* (Metropolitan Museum of Art, New York).

● **poststructuralism** ▶ The various intellectual tendencies that developed from French ▷structuralism in the late 1960s. The concept is a very general one, embracing a number of disparate thinkers who have extended the subversive tendency of structuralist analysis while rejecting its objective approach and reliance on fixed categories. The deconstruction of ▷Derrida, the psycholinguistics of ▷Lacan, the historical writings of ▷Foucault, and the feminist theory of Hélène Cixous (1937–) and Julia Kristeva (1941–) have all been characterized as poststructuralist in their rejection of fixed notions of meaning and identity.

● **post-traumatic stress disorder** ▶ (PTSD) An anxiety disorder that can arise if an individual is subject to a traumatic event, such as a road accident, rape, war experience (including shell shock), mugging, or assault, or witnesses a traumatic event in which there are serious casualties. The reaction may be immediate or delayed for several months. Typically sufferers have recurrent dreams, images, or thoughts based on the trauma, or may feel isolated, depressed, numbed to the extent of lacking involvement with their work or families, or guilty for having survived the event in which others perished. The condition usually fades with time, but skilled counselling can be helpful and in the worst cases some form of ▷psychotherapy may be indicated. An extreme and often protracted form of PTSD occurs with the victims of German concentration camps, in which "survivor-guilt" may be the overriding syndrome.

● **postviral fatigue syndrome** ▷*See* chronic fatigue syndrome.

● **potassium** ▶ (K) A reactive alkali metal discovered by Sir Humphry Davy in 1807. It is a common constituent of the earth's crust; forming ▷feldspars ($KAlSi_3O_8$), clays, and evaporite minerals (for example sylvite; KCl). The metal is prepared by electrolysis of the molten hydroxide. It is soft, easily cut with a knife, and reacts readily with water, catching fire and liberating hydrogen. It oxidizes rapidly in air and must therefore be stored under oil. The element is highly electropositive and its chemistry is dominated by its ability to form ionic salts (for example KCl, KNO_3, K_2CO_3, KBr, K_2SO_4, and KCN). Its largest use is in fertilizers, potassium being essential for plant growth. Alloys of potassium and sodium have been proposed as heat transfer media in nuclear reactors, since the lowest melting alloy melts at $-12.3°C$. One of the three isotopes (^{40}K) is radioactive with a half-life of 1.3×10^9 years and is used in ▷potassium-argon dating. The metal and its salts impart a lilac colour to flames. At no 19; at wt 39.0938; mp 63.71°C; bp 759°C.

● **potassium-argon dating** ▶ A method of ▷radiometric dating of geological specimens based on the decay of the radioactive isotope potassium-40, which is present to a small extent in all naturally occurring potassium. Its half-life is 1.3×10^9 years and it decays to argon-40; thus an estimate of the ratio of the two isotopes in a specimen of rock indicates its age.

● **potato** ▶ A perennial herbaceous plant, *Solanum tuberosum*, native to the Andes but cultivated throughout the world, especially in temperate regions, as an important vegetable crop. Potatoes were first introduced to England in the late 16th century by Sir Walter Raleigh; they reached Spain and Portugal earlier. The plants grow to a height of 50–100 cm, with compound leaves and clusters of white and purple flowers. The tubers (swollen tips of underground stems) have a thin brownish-white, white, yellow, or pinkish skin and are rich in starch; there are several varieties, up to 1.5 kg in weight, and they are eaten cooked or ground into flour. Commercial potatoes are grown from small tubers termed "seed" potatoes. Potatoes are vulnerable to a number of diseases, the most notorious being the potato ▷blight that ravished Ireland in 1845–47 (*see also* Irish famine). Family: ▷*Solanaceae*. ▷*See also* sweet potato.

● **Potchefstroom** ▶ 26 42S 27 06E A town in central South Africa. Founded by Voortrekkers (1838), it is the oldest town in the Transvaal. Gold mining and agriculture are important. Population (latest est): 77 560.

● **Potemkin, Grigori Aleksandrovich** ▶ (1739–91) Russian field marshal and favourite of ▷Catherine (II) the Great. Potemkin distinguished himself in Catherine's first Turkish War (1768–74) and became her lover for two years as well as her chief adviser. Potemkin retained his political influence, especially in foreign affairs, until his death.

● **potential, electric** ▶ A measure of electrical work. The potential at a point in an ▷electric field is one volt when one joule of energy is needed to bring a positive charge of one coulomb to that point from infinity. Usually the **potential difference** in volts between two points, rather than the absolute potential, is used. ▷*See also* electromotive force.

● **potential energy** ▶ ▷Energy stored in a body by virtue of its position or configuration. Thus a body, mass *m*, at a height *h* above the ground has a potential energy equal to *mgh*, where *g* is the ▷accelera-

tion of free fall, relative to the ground. A compressed spring and an electrically charged body also store potential energy.

● **Potentilla** ▶ A genus of mostly perennial herbs (500 species), found mainly in N temperate and arctic regions. It includes several species and hybrids grown as ornamentals. They have erect or creeping stems, 5–70 cm long, bearing compound leaves and yellow, white, or red four- or five-petalled flowers with many stamens. The fruit is a group of seedlike achenes. Family: ▷*Rosaceae*. ▷*See also* cinquefoil; tormentil.

● **potentiometer** ▶ A variable electrical ▷resistance in which a sliding contact can be adjusted to any position along its length so that a variable proportion of the resistance can be included in a circuit. Potentiometers are used for measuring unknown voltages and as a potential divider, producing a voltage output corresponding to calibrated positions of the sliding contact.

● **potholing** ▷*See* speleology.

● **potlatch** ▶ The ceremonial distribution of gifts, practised by the American Indians of the NW Pacific coast region, in order to affirm claims to rank and status at lavish feasts, to which rivals were invited. Gifts had to be returned with interest at subsequent potlatches to avoid humiliation. Among the ▷Kwakiutl, potlatching developed to an exaggerated extent often involving the destruction of property. The practice continued clandestinely after its prohibition by the Whites.

● **pot marigold** ▶ A herb, *Calendula officinalis*, native to S Europe and cultivated in temperate regions as an ornamental. About 30–35 cm tall, it bears simple oblong leaves and yellow or orange daisy-like flowers, often double. The fresh petals may be eaten in salads or puddings or are dried and used in medicines. Family: ▷*Compositae*.

● **Potomac River** ▶ A river in the E central USA, rising in the Appalachian Mountains of W Virginia and flowing generally NE through Washington, DC, to Chesapeake Bay. Length: 462 km (287 mi).

● **Potosí** ▶ 19 34S 65 45W A city in S Bolivia, at an altitude of 4066 m (13 340 ft). It is the chief industrial centre of Bolivia. Mining of tin, copper, and zinc is important. Its university was founded in 1892. Population (1993 est): 123 327.

● **Potsdam** ▶ 52 19N 13 15E A city in E Germany, on the River Havel adjoining Berlin. It was the residence of Prussian kings and German emperors. The city was severely damaged during World War II. Notable buildings include the Brandenburg Gate (1770) and the Sanssouci Palace (1745–47) built by Frederick II. An industrial city, Potsdam has many scientific institutes and is a centre of the German film industry. Population (1996 est): 136 619.

● **Potsdam Conference** ▶ (1945) The conference attended by Truman (USA), Stalin (Soviet Union), and Churchill (later Attlee; UK) after the conclusion of World War II in Europe. Its objectives were to confirm the conclusions of the ▷Yalta Conference, to establish a political and economic programme for Allied-occupied Germany, and to decide upon action towards Japan. The Conference was marked by the conflict of interests between the communist and noncommunist powers that developed into the ▷Cold War.

● **Potter, Beatrix** ▶ (1866–1943) British children's writer and illustrator. During a solitary childhood she became a skilled artist and observer of nature. *The Tale of Peter Rabbit* (1900) was the first of her famous children's books depicting such animals as Jemima Puddle-Duck and Mrs Tittlemouse.

● **Potter, Dennis Christopher George** ▶ (1935–94) British dramatist, noted for his plays for television. His successes include the serials *Pennies from Heaven* (1978), *The Singing Detective* (1986), and *Karaoke* (1995).

● **Potter, Paul** ▶ (1625–54) Dutch animal painter and etcher, born in Enkhuizen, the son and pupil of a landscape artist. Working successively in Delft, The Hague, and Amsterdam, he was painting as early as 1640. His best works, such as *The Bull* (The Hague), were executed in 1647.

● **Potter, Stephen** ▶ (1900–70) British humorist and critic. He wrote studies of D. H. Lawrence (1930) and Coleridge (1935) but is best remembered for his humorous books on the art of establishing personal superiority. These include *Gamesmanship* (1947) and *One-Upmanship* (1952).

● **Potteries** ▶ The Staffordshire towns of Burslem, Fenton, Hanley, Longton, and Tunstall, making up the modern city of ▷Stoke-on-Trent. They became the industrial centre of English pottery in the 19th century.

● **potter wasp** ▶ A solitary ▷wasp belonging to the genus *Eumerus*, common in North America and Europe. It constructs juglike nests of mud or clay, cemented by saliva and attached to plant stems. A single egg is laid in each nest and paralysed caterpillars are provided as food for the larva.

● **pottery** ▶ Generally, all ▷ceramics other than porcelain, but especially clay that has been shaped into containers (*compare* terracotta) and baked at varying temperatures over 400°C. Usually thrown on a potter's wheel, pottery can also be coiled and moulded. Being opaque and porous, it is often glazed with an impervious glassy layer. Pottery making is worldwide and of great antiquity. It was being made about 10 000 BC in Japan; from about 3500 BC the fast wheel was used in Mesopotamia. Pottery styles and decorative techniques are important aids to archaeologists in identifying and dating cultures. The ancient Greeks (*see* Greek art and architecture) and Renaissance Italians (*see* maiolica) raised pottery making to high aesthetic levels, but since the 18th-century advent of porcelain in Europe it has been mainly utilitarian until the art was revived by such potters as Bernard ▷Leach.

● **potto** ▶ A ▷loris, *Perodicticus potto*, of African forests. It is about 40 cm long with a short tail, a catlike face, stout legs, and strong grasping hands. Pottos have a row of spines on the neck and shoulders, used for butting in self-defence.

● **pouched rat** ▶ An African rodent characterized by cheek pouches used for carrying food. They range in size from the African giant pouched rat (*Cricetomys gambianus*), 24–45 cm long excluding the tail (36–46 cm), to the Cape pouched mouse (*Saccostomus campestris*), 12–15 cm long, excluding the tail (3–6 cm). All are vegetarians.

● **Poulenc, Francis** ▶ (1899–1963) French composer and pianist, a member of Les ▷Six. He was influenced by Ravel and Satie and produced a wide variety of compositions, including the song cycle *Le Bestiaire* (1919), a concerto for piano (1950) and one for two pianos (1932), the operas *Les Mamelles de Tirésias* (1944) and *Les Dialogues des Carmélites* (1953–56), and the ballet *Les Biches* (1923). As a pianist he frequently accompanied the French tenor Pierre Bernac (1899–1979).

● **poultry** ▶ Domesticated birds, especially fowls, turkeys, ducks, and geese, reared chiefly for their eggs and meat but also for their feathers and down. ▷*See* livestock farming.

● **Pound, Ezra** ▶ (1885–1972) US poet and critic. After studying Romance languages, he went to Europe in 1908 and became a dynamic propagandist for modernist literary and artistic movements in London (*see* Imagism; vorticism). His early poetry included *A Lume Spento* (1908), his first volume, and the long poems *Homage to Sextus Propertius* (1917) and *Hugh Selwyn Mauberly* (1920). He also produced many admired translations. He moved to Paris and, in 1924, to Italy, where he worked on the *Cantos* (1925–69). His support for Mussolini and his broadcasts of fascist propaganda during World War II led to his confinement in a mental hospital in the USA (1946–58), after which he returned to Italy.

● **Poussin, Nicolas** ▶ (1594–1665) French painter, regarded as one of the greatest exponents of ▷classicism. Poussin lived in Rome from 1624 until his death, apart from two years (1640–42) as painter to the French king Louis XIII. His representation of religious themes, such as *The Martyrdom of St Erasmus* (1628; Vatican), gave way in the 1630s to an interest in mythology and the Old Testament, for example *The Worship of the Golden Calf* (c. 1635; National Gallery, London). The pure classicism of his second Roman period is exemplified in such landscapes as *Landscape with Diogenes* (1648; Louvre).

● **Poverty Bay** ▶ An inlet of the SW Pacific Ocean, in New Zealand on the E coast of North Island. It was the site of Capt Cook's first landing in New Zealand (1769).

● **poverty trap** ▶ A failure in a tax and social benefit system causing the poor to find it difficult to escape from poverty. If social benefits are means tested and ▷taxation is progressive, a person may find that an increase in pay leaves him no better off, and perhaps worse off, because of the loss of benefits and increase in tax that his pay rise entails. Thus to be better off, a low-paid worker needs a substantial rise in pay to clear the trap.

● **powder metallurgy** ▶ The shaping of metals by pressing powdered metal into blocks, heating (*see* sintering), and then shaping it by stamping. Often pressing and sintering are done together in a mould to produce the finished article in one operation. The method is used for working metals, such as platinum and tungsten (used in light-bulb filaments) that are difficult to shape by other means. It has the advantages of leaving no scrap and being suitable for intricate shapes. Nonmetal additives can be easily included, such as the graphite lubricant in self-lubricating bearings.

● **Powell, Anthony** ▶ (1905–2000) British novelist. His novel sequence *A Dance to the Music of Time* comprises 12 social satires beginning with *A Question of Upbringing* (1951) and ending with *Hearing Secret Harmonies* (1975). He also published memoirs, diaries, and criticism.

● **Powell, Cecil Frank** ▶ (1903–69) British physicist, who became professor at Bristol University. Powell pioneered the technique of observing particles by the tracks that they leave on specially prepared photographic plates. In 1947 he exposed his plates to ▷cosmic rays high up in the Andes and discovered the ▷pion. He was awarded the 1950 Nobel Prize for this work.

● **Powell, (John) Enoch** ▶ (1912–98) British politician. He was professor of Greek at Sydney University, Australia (1937–39), served in the army throughout World War II, and became a Conservative MP in 1950. From 1960 to 1963 he was minister of health, his only cabinet post, and in 1968 he was dismissed from Heath's shadow cabinet following a controversial speech warning against the immigration of non-Whites. He did not stand in the February election of 1974 but from Oct 1974 until June 1987 was the United Ulster Unionist Council MP for South Down. Although his racial views came to seem anachronistic, Powell's free-market philosophy and hostility to European integration continued to influence Conservatives in the 1980s and 1990s.

● **Powell, Michael** ▶ (1905–90) British film director and screenwriter, who from 1942 to 1956 collaborated with the Hungarian screenwriter and director **Emeric Pressburger** (1902–88) on a series of highly original films. These included *49th Parallel* (1941), *The Life and Death of Colonel Blimp* (1943), *A Canterbury Tale* (1944), *A Matter of Life and Death* (1946), and the ballet films *The Red Shoes* (1948) and *The Tales of Hoffman* (1951). Powell's career was effectively ended by the reaction to *Peeping Tom* (1960), about a sadistic murderer.

● **power** ▶ The rate at which a body or system does work. It is measured in watts or horsepower. If a body of mass m is raised a height h in the earth's gravitational field in a time t, the power required is mgh/t, where g is the ▷acceleration of free fall. Thus if the mass is to be raised in half this time, i.e. $t/2$, the power required is doubled. The work done is unchanged but the rate at which the work must be done is increased.

● **power station** ▶ An electricity generating plant that forms part of the ▷electricity supply system. In **thermal power stations**, heat from the burning of fossil fuels (oil, coal, and gas) or from ▷thermal reactors is used to generate steam. The steam drives ▷turbines connected to alternating-current generators (turbo-alternators), thus converting heat via mechanical energy into electricity. Gas turbines are also used, missing out the steam-generation stage. They are easy to build and flexible to run, but have an efficiency of only about 25%. Sometimes the exhaust gas is used to help generate steam for a steam turbine, in order to increase overall efficiency. Usually in a steam-turbine thermal station about 30 to 40% of the heat is converted to electricity, most of the rest being lost when steam is condensed to water before it is returned to the boilers. ▷Hydroelectric power stations are more efficient (up to 90%) and provide about 0.2% of UK electricity supplies. ▷*See also* energy.

● **Powhatan** ▶ A confederation of Algonquian-speaking North American Indian tribes of Virginia. It was founded by the chief known to the European settlers as Powhatan (c.1550–1618), the father of ▷Pocahontas. The Powhatans were maize cultivators and hunters living in palisaded villages.

● **Powys** ▶ A county of E central Wales, bordering on England. It was formed in 1974 from Montgomeryshire, Radnorshire, and most of Breconshire. It is generally mountainous, rising to 886 m (2907 ft) in the Brecon Beacons in the S, and is drained by several rivers, including the Wye and Severn. The extensive moorlands of the W form one of the most remote and sparsely populated areas of the UK; several large reservoirs were created here in the 1960s, while subsequent developments include large-scale afforestation and the siting of windfarms. Agricultural activities include sheep, cattle, dairy, and arable farming; tourism is also important. Area: 5077 sq km (1960 sq mi). Population (1996): 124 000. Administrative centre: Llandrindod Wells.

● **Powys, John Cowper** ▶ (1872–1963) British novelist. He wrote poetry, philosophy, and criticism, but his best-known books are his long novels imbued with mystical feeling for the people and landscape of the West Country. These include *Wolf Solent* (1929) and *A Glastonbury Romance* (1932). In 1934 he moved to Wales, where he wrote the historical novels *Owen Glendower* (1940) and *Porius* (1951). His brother **Theodore Francis Powys** (1875–1953) was a novelist and short-story writer who lived a secluded life in Dorset. The best known of his idiosyncratic symbolic novels is *Mr Weston's Good Wine* (1927). His philosophical ideas are more directly expressed in *Soliloquies of a Hermit* (1916). A third brother, **Llewellyn Powys** (1884–1939), was known for his essays on rural life.

● **Poyang, Lake** ▶ An area of marsh and lakes in SE China, drained by the Yangtze River. In summer the whole area is flooded. Area (summer): about 2780 sq km (1073 sq mi).

● **Poynings' Law** ▶ (1495) A measure introduced by Sir Edward Poynings (1459–1521), Lord Deputy of Ireland, which ensured that the Irish parliament could only pass laws previously approved by the English Crown. A further act applied all English laws to Ireland.

● **Poznań** ▶ (German name: Posen) 52 55N 16 53E A city in W Poland, on the River Warta. One of the oldest cities in Poland, it became the first Polish bishopric in 968 AD. It possesses an 18th-century cathedral, rebuilt following extensive damage in World War II; its university was founded in 1919. An important industrial and commercial centre, its manufactures include railway rolling stock, chemicals, and glass. Population (1996 est): 581 800.

● **Poznań Riots** ▶ (1956) Labour disturbances in Poland. They began when workers at a steel plant in Poznań staged a strike to protest against the country's political restrictions and economic problems. The ensuing riots were ruthlessly suppressed, with the death of 53 people, but they forced the appointment of a reformist leader, Władysław Gomułka.

● **Pozsony** ▷*See* Bratislava.

● **Pozzuoli** ▶ (Greek name: Puteoli) 40 49N 14 07E A port in S Italy, in Campania on the Gulf of Pozzuoli. It is in an area of intense volcanic activity and the local volcanic ash is used to produce cement. Population (latest est): 65 025.

● **Prado** ▶ An art gallery in the Prado Avenue, Madrid. Designed originally as a natural-history museum by the neoclassical architect Juan de Villanueva (1739–1811), the art gallery was founded in 1818 by Ferdinand VII. Most of its collection consists of paintings collected by the Spanish monarchs from the 16th century onwards. Its works by ▷Velázquez, ▷Goya, ▷El Greco, ▷Titian, and Hieronymus ▷Bosch are among the finest in the world.

● **Praesepe** ▶ An open ▷star cluster in the constellation Cancer, just visible to the naked eye.

● **praetor** ▶ In ancient Rome, originally a consul as leader of an army and subsequently a magistrate responsible for the administration of justice. From about 242 BC a second praetor assisted with lawsuits involving foreigners. Later more praetors were appointed to administer the increasing number of provinces and numbered 18 under Emperor Nerva (96–98 AD).

● **Praetorian Guard** ▶ The official bodyguard of the Roman emperors created by Augustus in 27 BC. Composed of up to 16 long-serving cohorts (infantry divisions) each of 500–1000 men, and stationed as a single unit in Rome, the Guard developed great political influence; as senatorial power diminished emperors came to rely upon Praetorian support for election and in later imperial times the emperor's position and even his life depended on the Guard's favour.

● **Praetorius, Michael** ▶ (M. Schultheiss; 1571–1621) German composer. He studied the organ, worked in the service of Julius Heinrich, Duke of Brunswick (1564–1613), and was kapellmeister in Wolfsbüttel (1612–21). He composed a large number of motets, hymns, madrigals, and dance pieces, as well as writing *Syntagma musicum* (1615–20), a valuable account of the musical theory and instruments of the time.

● **pragmatic sanction** ▶ A royal edict establishing a fundamental principle of government. Historically the term is usually applied to the edict of Emperor Charles VI (1713) settling the succession to his Austrian territories in his daughter Maria Theresa. Disregard of this edict by European powers provoked the War of the ▷Austrian Succession (1740–48). The Edict of Bourges, issued by Charles VII of France in 1438 and limiting papal authority over the French Church, was also a pragmatic sanction.

● **pragmatism** ▶ A philosophical movement initiated by William James (*see* James, Henry) and C. S. ▷Peirce in the USA. It asserts that the truth of a theory can be judged only by its practical consequences, so the question is: what difference would it make if it were true? The comprehensive metaphysical schemes of European philosophers were thus found to have no meaning, since their truth or falsity did not affect human experience. In science, a theory was true if it "worked"—if its expected consequences occurred. In ethics and theology a principle or belief was true if it satisfied its holders. ▷*See also* Dewey, John.

● **Prague** ▶ (Czech name: Praha) 50 8N 14 25E The capital of the Czech Republic, in the centre of the country on the River Vltava. The industrial and commercial centre of the country, its various manufactures include machinery, cars, aircraft, food processing, clothing, and chemicals. A leading cultural centre, Prague possesses Charles University (1348) and a technical university (1707). Notable buildings include Hradčany Castle and the mainly gothic Cathedral of St Vitus.

History: in the middle ages it was the seat of the Přemyslid kings of Bohemia. Following rivalry between the Czechs and Germans, it became the centre of the religious reform movement of Jan ▷Hus. Under Habsburg rule from the 16th century, it was made the capital of newly independent Czechoslovakia in 1918. In 1968 the city was occupied by Soviet troops following Soviet opposition to the liberal Dubček government. In 1989 it was the scene of mass protests, leading to the fall of the Communists. Population (1996 est): 1 209 855.

● **Prague School** ▶ A group of language scholars based in Prague during the 1920s and 1930s, including N. S. Trubetskoy (1890–1938) and Roman Jakobson (1896–1982). Their work was chiefly in the field of Saussurean structural ▷linguistics. They originated aspects of modern phonological theory, drew sociolinguistic distinctions between various aspects of language use (for example, between everyday and poetic language), and devised the concept of analysing both speech sounds and word meanings into ultimate components transcending individual languages.

● **Praia** ▶ 15 5N 24 3E The capital of Cape Verde, a seaport on São Tiago, the largest of the country's islands. Agricultural products, chiefly bananas, coffee, and sugar cane, are exported. There is a submarine cable station. Population (1995 est): 68 000.

● **prairie dog** ▶ A large ▷ground squirrel, *Cynomys ludovicanis*, of North America, also called black-tailed prairie marmot. Heavily built animals, about 30 cm long, prairie dogs live in large colonies called "towns." They feed on grass and have been treated as pests by cattle ranchers. Prairie dogs raise a rim of soil round their burrows so that the surface water will not enter. ⌐mammal.

• **Prairie Provinces** ► The Canadian provinces of ▷Alberta, ▷Manitoba, and ▷Saskatchewan. They lie chiefly in the Great Plains and are major producers of wheat and oil.

• **prairies** ► The extensive grasslands of the interior of North America. They occupy a broad N–S belt extending from Alberta and Saskatchewan through the Midwest into Texas, reaching as far W as the Rocky Mountains. They are extensively ploughed for wheat production. ▷*See also* steppes.

• **prairie wolf** ▷*See* coyote.

• **Prakrit** ► Ancient ▷Indo-Aryan languages of N India, which were simpler than the standard written form of ▷Sanskrit. From these spoken forms are derived a number of literary styles and the modern languages of N India. ▷Pali, the language of the Jain scriptures, is among the Prakrits.

• **Prandtl, Ludwig** ► (1875–1953) German physicist, whose discovery of the boundary layer adjoining the surface of a solid over which a fluid flows led to the foundation of aerodynamics. His major studies were on the effects of streamlining and the properties of aircraft wings. He made important improvements to such constructions as wind tunnels; the **Prandtl number** is a dimensionless group used in the study of convection.

• **Prasad, Rajendra** ► (1884–1963) Indian statesman; the first president of India (1950–1962). He gave up his legal practice to join ▷Gandhi's movement of noncooperation with the British and was president of the ▷Indian National Congress (1934, 1939, 1947–48).

• **praseodymium** ► (Pr) A ▷lanthanide element, which was separated from its mixture with neodyminium by von Welsbach in 1885. It forms trihalides (e.g. $PrCl_3$) and an oxide (Pr_2O_3), which is used to give a yellow colour to glass. At no 59; at wt 140.9077; mp 931°C; bp 3520°C.

• **Pratchett, Terry** ► (1948–) British author, best known for his *Discworld* series of best-selling comic fantasy novels. Beginning with *The Colour of Magic* (1983) and including *Wyrd Sisters* (1988) and *The Last Hero* (2001), the series now numbers over 25. He has also written children's books, such as the *Bromeliad* trilogy (1989–90).

• **pratincole** ► A bird belonging to an Old World subfamily (*Glareolinae*; 6 species). 17–22 cm long, pratincoles have a forked tail, long pointed wings, and a small bill with a wide gape for catching insects. The common pratincole (*Glareola pratincola*) has red-brown underwings and a yellow throat. Family: *Glareolidae* (pratincoles and coursers); order: *Charadriiformes* (gulls, plovers, etc.).

• **Prato** ► (*or* Prato in Toscana) 43 53N 11 06E A city in central Italy, in Tuscany on the River Bisenzio. It has a cathedral, which dates from the 12th century, and the city is an important centre of the woollen industry. Population (1996 est): 169 927.

• **prawn** ► A large shrimplike ▷crustacean (up to 20 cm long), belonging to the suborder *Natantia*. The antennae are longer than the body and a forward projection of the carapace forms a spike (rostrum) between the eyes, bearing six or more teeth. The second pair of appendages are enlarged to form pincers (*compare* shrimp). The common edible prawn (*Leander serratus*) of temperate coastal waters is 5–8 cm long. ▷*See also* Dublin Bay prawn.

• **Praxiteles** ► (mid-4th century BC) Athenian sculptor, renowned for his handling of marble. His statue of Hermes, discovered at ▷Olympia in 1877, exemplifies the sensuous grace and repose of his work. Most of his statues have perished, but some, such as the famous Aphrodite of Cnidos, are known from Roman copies.

• **Precambrian** ► Geological time from the formation of the earth's crust, about 4500 million years ago, to about 590 million years ago when the Palaeozoic era began. Precambrian rocks lie below the Cambrian system and fossils are rare. They have been subjected to much alteration because of their great age. Most are metamorphosed and have undergone one or more Precambrian mountain-building periods as well as later ones. The largest areas of exposed Precambrian rocks are the ▷shield areas. Correlation of successive strata is done where possible by ▷radiometric dating. ▷*See also* Cryptozoic time.

• **precession** ► The rotation about an axis of a line that is itself the axis of a rotating body. The effect may be observed in a spinning top, of which the axis of rotation is initially vertical but, as the top slows down, begins to precess about its original position. ▷*See also* precession of the equinoxes.

• **precession of the equinoxes** ► The gradual westward motion of the ▷equinoxes around the ▷ecliptic in a period of about 25 800 years. It is caused by the ▷precession of the earth's axis of rotation, which results mainly from the gravitational pull of the sun and moon on the equatorial bulge of the nonspherical earth. As the axis precesses, slowly tracing out a cone in the sky, the celestial equator (lying in a plane perpendicular to the axis) moves relative to the ecliptic. The points of intersection, i.e. the equinoxes, thus continuously change.

• **pre-Columbian art and architecture** ► The painting, pottery, and building of the native Americans before the arrival of ▷Columbus, i.e. before the 16th century. Between 300 and 900 AD the palaces, temples, and pyramids of the ▷Maya showed great artistic achievements—which were subsequently developed by the ▷Toltecs and the ▷Aztecs. In Peru, the prolific ▷Chimú and ▷Inca cultures also predated the arrival of the Spaniards.

• **predestination** ► In Christian doctrine, God's foreordaining of salvation for certain people. The idea is propagated by St ▷Paul in the Epistles. It raises problems about the nature of divine justice and the role of the human will and endeavours. St ▷Augustine of Hippo, ▷Origen, and St Thomas ▷Aquinas were among those who produced influential approaches to the difficulties. An extreme form of predestination was integral to ▷Calvinism, with salvation for the elect and damnation for everyone else. Modern thinking tends to stress the universality of God's will to save mankind.

• **pre-eclampsia** ► (*or* pregnancy-induced hypertension, PIH) High blood pressure (*see* hypertension) in pregnant women, which may be accompanied by ▷oedema (fluid in the tissues) and protein in the urine. Unless treated (by bedrest), it may progress to the much more serious condition of **eclampsia**, which is marked by convulsions that usually lead to coma. Eclampsia is now rare, if proper care is given to patients with pre-eclampsia, but it can threaten the life of mother and baby if not treated immediately.

• **prefect** ► A high-ranking French government official. Created in 1800 by Napoleon's reorganization of provincial government, prefects are responsible for general administration, public law and order, and the enforcement of central government policies in their own departments. Although dependence on the government in power and a centralized bureaucracy weakens their position, prefects still have considerable civil authority.

• **preference shares** ► Shares that entitle their holders to prior rights over ordinary shareholders to ▷dividends and to capital repayment in the event of liquidation. They do not usually carry voting rights and they pay a fixed rate of interest. A cumulative preference shareholder is entitled to arrears of interest out of current profits before ordinary shareholders receive dividends.

• **pregnancy** ► The period during which a fetus develops within the womb, usually lasting for about 266 days from conception to delivery of the baby. Pregnancy is signalled by cessation of the menstrual periods, tenderness and discomfort in the breasts, and—sometimes—an increase in appetite, nausea, and vomiting. These changes are brought about by the activity of hormones, including ▷progesterone and human chorionic ▷gonadotrophin (HCG), secreted by the corpus luteum (in the ▷ovary) and ▷placenta. In the early weeks pregnancy can be definitely diagnosed only by pregnancy tests. A commonly used test is based on the detection of HCG in the urine. ▷*See also* childbirth; embryo; prenatal diagnosis.

Pregnancy in animals is usually called gestation, and the period varies between species. In elephants, for instance, it is 18 months and in rats 3 weeks.

• **prelude** ► A piece of instrumental music, originally one that served as an introduction to a ▷fugue, ▷suite, or operatic act. From the middle of the 17th century preludes formed the first movements of lute or harpsichord suites. In the 19th century Chopin used the name to describe 25 short piano pieces. Subsequently Scriabin, Debussy, Rachmaninov, and others wrote piano preludes, while

Shostakovich in the 20th century wrote three sets of piano preludes and fugues in the tradition of J. S. Bach.

● **premenstrual tension** ► (PMT) Symptoms of irritability, nervousness, headache, depression, etc., experienced by some women for up to 10 days before menstruation. Part of the **premenstrual syndrome**, PMT is associated with a build-up of salt and water in the tissues; the hormone progesterone and a deficiency of essential fatty acids have been postulated as causes. The symptoms disappear when menstruation begins.

● **Preminger, Otto (Ludwig)** ► (1906–86) US film director, born in Austria. His films range from literary adaptations to large-scale epics and include *Laura* (1944), *Anatomy of a Murder* (1959), *Exodus* (1960), and *The Human Factor* (1979).

● **premiss** ► One of the statements in an argument or chain of reasoning from which the conclusion follows or is said to follow. For example from the premisses "only dogs bark" and "Fido barks," the conclusion is that "Fido is a dog."

● **premium bond** ► A UK government ▷security, held in numbered units of one pound, the interest on which is put into a fund and allocated to bond holders by a monthly lottery, as tax-free prizes. The numbers of winning bonds are selected by Electronic Random Number Indicator Equipment (ERNIE). Premium bonds were introduced in 1956. The maximum holding for one person is £20,000.

● **Premonstratensians** ► A Roman Catholic order of monks, also called Norbertines after St Norbert (c. 1080–1134), who founded them in 1120 at Prémontré (N France). They originally followed an austere rule, which included abstinence from meat. They spread all over Europe but were nearly wiped out during the French Revolution. Belgium is now their base.

● **prenatal diagnosis** ► Tests on pregnant women to diagnose genetic or developmental abnormalities in the fetus. If these reveal severe malformation or malfunctioning in the fetus an ▷abortion is considered. The tests include ultrasound scanning (*see* ultrasonics); analysis of fetal cells obtained either by ▷amniocentesis or, at an earlier stage of pregnancy, by chorionic villus sampling (in which placental tissue is analysed); a maternal blood test to measure the level of alpha-fetoprotein (which is abnormally high or low in certain congenital conditions); and fetoscopy, in which a sample of fetal blood is examined for abnormal cells (indicating blood disorders, such as ▷thalassaemia). Ultrasound scanning is undertaken routinely; most of the other tests are only performed when there is a likelihood of abnormality (e.g. in older women).

● **prep school** ▷*See* independent schools.

● **Pre-Raphaelite Brotherhood** ► A group including the British painters Dante Gabriel ▷Rossetti, John Everett ▷Millais, and William Holman ▷Hunt, who joined together in 1848 in reaction to the banality of contemporary British painting and its enthusiasm for ▷Raphael. Signing all their works PRB, they sought to emulate Italian painters earlier than Raphael and to paint subjects of a moral or religious character, many of their subjects being drawn from medieval literature. Although initially attacked for their naturalism, particularly in religious subjects, by 1851 the PRB had won the support of the art critic John ▷Ruskin. Although the group disbanded soon afterwards (Hunt being the only member to remain faithful to PRB ideas), the PRB influenced such artists as William ▷Morris and Edward ▷Burne-Jones, as well as subsequent painting styles.

● **presbyopia** ▷*See* longsightedness.

● **Presbyterianism** ► A form of Protestant church organization based on government by elders (*compare* episcopacy). These comprise the ministers and certain laymen from each congregation and all have equal rank; they enforce a strict code of ethics and determine Church policy through a system of presbyteries, synods, and general assemblies. Presbyterianism originated with the 16th-century followers of ▷Calvin. In Scotland the tenets of Presbyterianism were formulated (1560) by ▷Knox and adopted by the established Church of Scotland in 1696; Scotland has several other Presbyterian bodies, notably the ultra-Calvinist Free Presbyterian Church of Scotland (known as the "Wee Frees"). Presbyterianism is the majority religion

in Northern Ireland (where it has strong links with political unionism) and also has a strong following in Wales. The Presbyterian Church of England merged with various Congregationalist bodies to form the ▷United Reformed Church in 1972. A pan-Presbyterian alliance (founded 1875) embraces the Presbyterian Churches in the UK, the USA, and elsewhere.

● **preschool education** ► Education for children below the age of compulsory school attendance (five in England, Scotland, and Wales; four in Northern Ireland), which generally takes the form of creative play rather than formal learning. Its importance in the social and mental development of young children was first recognized by ▷Froebel, who founded the first ▷kindergarten in 1837. In the UK **nursery education** is provided for children aged two upwards, either in nursery schools (about 50% of which are publicly maintained) or more frequently in nursery classes in primary schools (*see* primary education). In 1998 the government promised preschool places for all four-year-olds and a doubling of places for three-year-olds. Younger children often attend playgroups run by parents or voluntary bodies (notably the Pre-School Learning Alliance).

● **Prescott, John (Leslie)** ► (1938–) British Labour politician; deputy prime minister (1997–). Elected to parliament in 1970, he became deputy leader of the party in 1994. He was appointed secretary of state for the environment, transport, and the regions (1997–2001) and head of the cabinet office (2001–).

● **Prescott, William Hickling** ► (1796–1859) US historian. Prescott established his reputation with a major work, *The History of the Reign of Ferdinand and Isabella* (1837). There followed *The Conquest of Mexico* (1843), *The Conquest of Peru* (1847), and *The History of Philip II* (1855–58). Prescott combined factual accuracy with a vivid narrative style. His discursive memory compensated for his partial blindness.

● **present value** ► The current net value of an investment project, used to compare the net benefits and costs of investment projects, taking into account the rate of interest, to decide which will be the best to back. The present value is equal to the sum of the benefits in each year of the project, less the costs in each year, discounted back to the present time using the market rate of interest. If the present value is positive, the project will earn more than if the money were lent to a savings institution. By establishing present values of different projects, investors can ensure that projects that show a quick return will not necessarily be preferred to projects showing a larger return at a later date.

● **president** ► In most republics, the executive head of state. In the USA the president is the head of the executive branch of government, which was established together with the legislature (*see* Congress) and the judiciary (*see* Supreme Court of the United States) by the US constitution (1789). In modern times a member of the ▷Democratic Party or the ▷Republican Party, he is elected every four years; no one may hold the office for more than eight years. The president is head of the ▷cabinet. In some other countries (e.g. Germany and Italy) the president fulfils the nonexecutive function of a monarch.

● **Presley, Elvis (Aaron)** ► (1935–77) US popular singer, whose fusion of Black rhythm and blues and White country styles effectively created modern pop music. His first big hit, "Heartbreak Hotel" (1956), was followed by numerous others, including "Hound Dog," "Don't Be Cruel," and "Suspicious Minds," making him the most successful recording artist in history. Presley also appeared in numerous films. After his early death, which was accelerated by drug dependence, he became a cult figure. □ p. 1010.

● **Presocratics** ► Greek philosophers who lived in Ionia and S Italy (Magna Graecia) during the 6th and early 5th centuries BC, before the time of ▷Socrates. They were responsible for the earliest philosophical—as opposed to magical and religious—speculation about the universe. The Ionians were ▷Thales, ▷Anaximander, and ▷Anaximenes, all of Miletus, ▷Xenophanes of Colophon, and ▷Heraclitus of Ephesus. Notable figures in Italy were ▷Parmenides and ▷Zeno, both of Elea (*see* Eleatics), and ▷Pythagoras.

● **Pressburg** ▷*See* Bratislava.

● **Pressburg, Treaties of** ► **1.** (1491) The treaty in which Maximilian, Habsburg heir to the Holy Roman Empire, recognized Vladislav II of Bohemia (1456–1516) as King of Hungary, renouncing his own claim in return for Austria, Styria, and Carinthia, which had been annexed by Matthias I Corvinus in 1486. **2.** (1805) The treaty between Austria and France following Napoleon's defeat of Austria at Austerlitz. Austria surrendered territory and paid a large indemnity.

Elvis Presley ► The US pop star at his wedding in Las Vegas in May, 1967, cutting the cake with his bride Priscilla.

● **Press Complaints Commission ►** An organization founded in January 1991 to deal with complaints of unwarranted invasion of privacy and unfair treatment by the press and to ensure that the press maintains the highest professional standards. Funded by the press industry, it comprises both professional and nonprofessional members and an independent chairman. It changed its structure in 1993 in response to criticisms that it was ineffective. It replaced the **Press Council**, founded in 1953 to defend the freedom of the press. Chairman: Lord Wakeham.

● **press gang ►** A band of men employed to force paupers, vagabonds, or criminals into the army or navy. This system of impressment (recruits were paid imprest money), common throughout the world in the 18th century, ceased when improved pay and conditions in the army and navy increased voluntary recruitment.

● **pressure ►** Force per unit area. For a liquid, density d, the pressure at a depth h is hdg, where g is the ▷acceleration of free fall. Pressure is usually measured in pascals, millimetres of mercury, or millibars. ▷*See also* atmospheric pressure.

● **pressure gauge ►** An instrument for measuring the pressure of a fluid. Atmospheric pressure is measured with a mercury ▷barometer or an aneroid barometer. Pressures above atmospheric pressure are usually measured with a Bourdon gauge, which consists of a flattened curved tube that tends to straighten under pressure. As it straightens it moves a pointer round a scale. Low pressures are measured with such vacuum gauges as the ▷McLeod gauge or ▷Pirani gauge.

● **pressurized-water reactor ►** (PWR) ▷*See* nuclear energy; thermal reactor.

● **Prestel** ▷*See* viewdata.

● **Prester John ►** A legendary Christian priest king. First mentioned in 12th-century chronicles, he became famous as the hero destined to help the Crusaders against Islam. He was sometimes identified as a Chinese prince but more commonly as the King of Ethiopia.

● **Preston ►** 53 46N 2 42W A city and port in NW England, the administrative centre of Lancashire on the River Ribble. It was the site of a major battle in the ▷Civil War. It has plastics, chemical, motor-vehicle and aircraft construction, and electronics industries as well as the traditional cotton and engineering works. Preston was granted city status in 2002. Population (1991): 177 660.

● **Prestonpans ►** 55 57N 3 00W A town in E central Scotland, in East Lothian on the Firth of Forth. It owes its fame to the defeat here of the English by Bonnie Prince Charlie in 1745. Population (1991): 7014.

● **prestressed concrete** ▷*See* concrete.

● **Prestwick ►** 55 30N 4 37W A town and resort in SW Scotland, in South Ayrshire on the Firth of Clyde. It has an international airport. Population (1991): 13 705.

● **Pretender, Old** ▷*See* James Edward Stuart, the Old Pretender.

● **Pretender, Young** ▷*See* Charles Edward Stuart, the Young Pretender.

● **Pretoria ►** 25 36S 28 12E The administrative capital of South Africa, in the NE of the country. Founded in 1855, it became the capital of the Union of South Africa in 1910. The University of South Africa was founded here in 1873; other important institutions are the University of Pretoria (1930) and the Onderstepoort Veterinary Research Institute. Its industries include iron and steel processing, engineering, and food processing. Population (1991): 1 104 479.

● **Pretoria Convention ►** (1881) The peace treaty between Britain and the Transvaal that ended the first ▷Boer War. The Transvaal acquired self-government under the British Crown, which, however, retained control of foreign relations and the power to veto legislation regarding Africans.

● **Pretorius, Andries (Wilhelmus Jacobus) ►** (1799–1853) Afrikaner leader in the ▷Great Trek to Natal and then in the Transvaal. He defeated (1840) the Zulu King Dingane and fought the British in Natal (1842) and then in the Transvaal (1848), establishing Transvaal's independence as the South African Republic (1852). The city of Pretoria is named after him. His son **Marthinus Wessel Pretorius** (1819–1901) was president of the South African Republic (formerly and subsequently the Transvaal) from 1857 to 1871 and of the Orange Free State from 1859 to 1863. He returned to politics after Britain's annexation of the Transvaal, retiring after Afrikaner victory in the first ▷Boer War (1880–81).

● **Prévert, Jacques ►** (1900–77) French poet. He was associated with the surrealist movement in the 1920s. His best-known poems about the street life of Paris, written with anarchic humour, are collected in *Paroles* (1946); later volumes include *Spectacle* (1951) and *Hebromadaires* (1972). He also wrote film scripts, notably for *Les Enfants du paradis* (1944).

● **Previn, André ►** (Andreas Ludwig Priwin; 1929–) German-born conductor, pianist, and composer. He took US citizenship in 1943. He was conductor of the London Symphony Orchestra (1968–79) and its Conductor Laureate since 1992, conductor of the Pittsburgh Symphony Orchestra (1976–84), and musical director of the Royal Philharmonic Orchestra (1984–86), remaining as its principal conductor. He was also musical director of the Los Angeles Philharmonic Orchestra (1986–89). His first opera, *A Streetcar Named Desire*, was staged in 1998.

● **Prévost d'Exiles, Antoine François, Abbé ►** (1697–1763) French novelist. His unsettled career included periods of military service, of religious retreat as a Benedictine monk, and of exile in England and Holland. Of his many novels and translations, mostly written to pay off debts, the best known is *Manon Lescaut* (1731), the story of a young nobleman ruined by his love for a courtesan, which was used by both Massenet and Puccini as the basis for operas.

● **Priam ►** In Greek legend, the last king of Troy, husband of Hecuba. As an old man he witnessed the deaths of many of his 50 children in the ▷Trojan War and he pleaded with Achilles for the body of Hector. He was killed at the altar of Zeus by Neoptelemus.

● **Priapus ►** A Greek fertility god associated with gardens, son of Dionysus and Aphrodite. He was usually portrayed as a comic ugly figure with an enormous phallus. The donkey, symbol of lust, was sacrificed to him.

● **Pribilof Islands ►** Four US islands in the Bering Sea. They are the breeding ground of the northern fur seal. In 1911 agreements between the USA, Russia, Japan, and the UK protected the seals. Area: about 168 sq km (65 sq mi).

● **price index** ▶ A single figure used to measure the average percentage change in the price of a set of goods over a period of time, taking a base figure of 100 for a specified year. Thus if a particular price index, in January, 1990, stands at 156 (January, 1985 = 100), there has been a 56% increase in the average prices over the five-year period. The best-known indexes are the Wholesale Price Index and the Retail Price Index, the latter providing a reliable guide to the ▷cost of living. Some wages, salaries, and costs are **index-linked** (i.e. increase in proportion to a specified price index) to cover the devaluation of money as a result of ▷inflation. **Indexation** is commonly used in agreements that extend over a long period during which inflation is expected to be a significant factor.

● **prices and incomes policy** ▶ A policy designed to hold down prices and incomes in an attempt to stem ▷inflation. The policy's chances of success depend on the prime causes of the inflation. Only if inflation is caused by the pressure of costs does a prices and incomes policy have a fair chance of success. The chief drawback of such a policy is that it distorts markets by suppressing the gradual movement of prices and wages in response to ▷supply and demand. There are also great problems of enforcement, especially in controlling incomes. If legal enforcement of the policy is attempted and fails, the law is brought into disrepute.

● **prickly heat** ▶ A disorder that occurs most commonly in the tropics due to obstruction of the ducts of the sweat glands. It causes itching and a red rash and often leads to secondary infection.

● **prickly pear** ▶ A ▷cactus of the genus *Opuntia*, native to North and South America and sometimes cultivated for food or ornament. Introduced to Australia and South Africa, it has become a troublesome weed. It has flat jointed spiny stems bearing large orange or yellow flowers, which give rise to edible pear-shaped fruits. The seeds are used to produce an oil and the shoots are eaten as vegetables or used as animal feed.

● **prickly poppy** ▶ A plant of the genus *Argemone*, especially *A. mexicana*, also called devil's fig, native to North America and the West Indies and cultivated as a garden ornamental. Growing 30–90 cm tall, its blue-green bristly stems bear spiny lobed leaves and orange or pale-yellow flowers, with five pointed petals. Family: *Papaveraceae*.

● **Pride, Thomas** ▶ (d. 1658) English parliamentary soldier during the Civil War, famous for effecting **Pride's Purge** of the ▷Long Parliament in 1648. He excluded over a hundred Presbyterian MPs suspected of wanting to treat with Charles I, leaving the remaining members to sit as the Rump Parliament. He was a signatory of Charles' death warrant.

● **Priestley, J(ohn) B(oynton)** ▶ (1894–1984) British novelist and dramatist. He first won popular success with his picaresque novel *The Good Companions* (1929). His plays include *Dangerous Corner* (1932), *Laburnum Grove* (1933), *An Inspector Calls* (1946), and several mildly experimental expressionist dramas, including *The Glass Cage* (1957). A traditionalist by temperament and conviction, he published many volumes of criticism and memoirs and was a popular broadcaster during World War II.

● **Priestley, Joseph** ▶ (1733–1804) British chemist and one of the discoverers of oxygen (together with Carl ▷Scheele). Priestley, being a firm believer in the ▷phlogiston theory, named his gas dephlogisticated air and first prepared it in 1774 by heating mercuric oxide. In 1778–79 ▷Lavoisier demolished the phlogiston theory and named the gas oxygen. Priestley also produced and studied several other gases, including ammonia, sulphur dioxide, and hydrogen chloride. He invented the method of collecting them over mercury, since some of these gases dissolved in water. Priestley was a Presbyterian minister and strongly influenced Unitarianism. He held unpopular views, being a supporter of Revolutionary France. In 1794, no longer feeling safe in Britain, he left for America where he spent the rest of his life.

● **priest's hole** ▶ A secret room, found in some English country

houses, where Roman Catholic priests were hidden to escape persecution under Elizabeth I.

● **primary colours** ▶ The minimum number of ▷colours that, when mixed in the correct proportions, are capable of giving all the other colours in the visible spectrum. When light of three **primary additive colours** (usually red, green, and blue) is mixed in equal intensities, white light results. This principle is used in colour television and ▷colour photography. Any particular colour can also be obtained by subtracting from white light a mixture of three **primary subtractive colours**, usually cyan (blue-green), magenta (purplish red), and yellow, which are complementary to red, green, and blue. Adding pigments of these in equal proportions gives black pigment.

● **primary education** ▶ The education of children between the ages of 4 or 5 and 11 or 12. Primary education was introduced in England and Wales as a result of the Education Act (1944), to replace elementary education. Primary schools are often divided into infant and junior sections, the transfer taking place around seven years of age; the Education Act (1964) enabled local authorities to vary the age at which the break took place and to create "middle schools" between primary and secondary, with an age range from 8 to 14. Many primary schools offer nursery classes for children under five (*see* preschool education).

● **primate** ▶ A mammal belonging to the order *Primates* (about 195 species), which includes ▷prosimians, ▷monkeys, ▷apes, and humans. Primates probably evolved from insectivorous climbing creatures like ▷tree shrews and have many adaptations for climbing, including five fingers and five toes with opposable first digits (except in the hind feet of humans). They have well-developed sight and hearing and—most importantly—enlarged cerebral hemispheres of the brain, most marked in higher primates. Most forms are arboreal but the great apes and humans are largely terrestrial.

● **prime meridian** ▷*See* latitude and longitude.

● **prime minister** ▶ A head of government. In some countries (e.g. the UK) the prime minister is also the head of the executive, while in others (e.g. France) he or she is subordinate to an executive president. In the UK the post developed in the 18th century with the growth of the ▷cabinet. Sir Robert ▷Walpole is generally regarded as the first prime minister (1721–42) but the post was not formally recognized until 1905. The prime minister is customarily a member of the House of Commons and is head of government by virtue of being the leader of the dominant political party in the Commons. The monarch makes all governmental appointments on the advice of the prime minister, who receives a salary of £107,179 (1999) plus his or her salary as an MP. See table in Appendix.

● **prime number** ▶ An integer greater than one that has no integral factors except itself and one; for example 2, 3, 5, 7, 11, 13, 17. Every natural number can be expressed uniquely as a product of prime numbers; for example $1260 = 2^2 \times 3^2 \times 5 \times 7$. Prime numbers are of major interest in number theory.

● **primitivism** ▶ In art, the style of untrained artists who ignore or are ignorant of both traditional aesthetic standards and avantgarde trends. Its chief characteristics are meticulous detail, brilliant colours, childlike representation, and faulty perspective. Among the first primitives were 17th- and 18th-century American painters who developed in cultural isolation from European artistic trends, but the best known is the French painter Henri ▷Rousseau. More recent primitives include the Yugoslav peasants Ivan Generalič (1914–92) and Mijo Kovačič (1935–), the American Grandma ▷Moses, and the Cornish fisherman Alfred Wallis (1885–1942). The term is also sometimes applied to African and Polynesian indigenous art.

● **Primo de Rivera, Miguel** ▶ (1870–1930) Spanish general, who led a successful coup on 13 September, 1923, and was dictator of Spain until 1930. He brought the Moroccan War to a victorious end (1927) but dissatisfaction with his absolute rule, exacerbated by the Depression, caused his downfall. ▷Alfonso XIII's support of Primo de Rivera discredited the monarchy, which was overthrown a year later. His son **José Antonio Primo de Rivera** (1903–36) founded the Falange, the Spanish fascist party. Executed by the Republic shortly after the start of the Spanish Civil War, his memory was honoured by Franco's National Movement.

● **primrose** ► A perennial herbaceous plant, ▷*Primula vulgaris*, growing in woodlands and hedge banks in Europe and N Africa. It has a basal rosette of puckered spoon-shaped leaves, with solitary pale-yellow flowers on slender stalks, up to 10 cm high. Bird's-eye primrose (*P. farinosa*) has pale-purple flowers with yellow centres. Family: *Primulaceae*. ▷*See also* evening primrose.

● **Primrose League** ► A Conservative political organization founded in 1883 by Lord Randolph ▷Churchill and others to commemorate ▷Disraeli's ideals of Conservatism, including the preservation of the traditional freedoms of the British way of life. It also sought to develop his wish to improve the lot of the working people in the country. Its emblem, from which it takes its name, is the primrose, Disraeli's favourite flower.

● **Primula** ► A genus of perennial plants (about 500 species), native mainly to N temperate regions and often grown as ornamentals. They have a basal rosette of oval to spoon-shaped leaves and erect flower stalks bearing erect or nodding five-petalled flowers, red, pink, purple, blue, white, or yellow in colour and usually with a different coloured centre. The fruit is a capsule. The genus also includes the ▷cowslip and ▷primrose. Family: *Primulaceae*. ▷*See also* auricula.

● **Prince Edward Island** ► An island province of E Canada, in the S Gulf of St Lawrence. Its gentle rolling hills and mild climate support small farms producing potatoes, grains, dairy cattle, and other livestock. Tourism and fishing are also important.
  History: discovered (1534) and colonized (1720) by France, the island was captured (1758) and resettled by Britain. In 1873 it joined Canada. Area: 5657 sq km (2184 sq mi). Population (1991): 129 765. Capital: Charlottetown.

● **Prince of Wales** ► A title customarily conferred on the eldest son of the British sovereign. It was a native Welsh title until 1301, when Edward I, following his annexation of Wales, bestowed it on his son, the future Edward II. The present holder of the title is Prince ▷Charles.

● **Prince Rupert** ► 54 09N 130 20W A city and port in W Canada, in British Columbia at the head of Dixon Entrance on the Pacific Ocean. Founded as the terminus of a transcontinental railway (1906), it is an ice-free deepwater port. Forestry, pulp and paper, and fishing are also economically important. Population (1991): 16 620.

● **Princess Royal** ► A title sometimes conferred on the eldest daughter of the sovereign. In 1932, Princess Mary (1897–1965), daughter of George V, became the Princess Royal. In 1987 the title was conferred upon Princess ▷Anne.

● **Princeton** ► 40 21N 74 40W A town in the USA, in New Jersey. George Washington defeated the British here on 3 January, 1777. It is the site of **Princeton University** (1746), one of the oldest in the USA, and the Rockefeller Institute for Scientific Research. Population (1990): 12 016.

● **princewood** ► A dark wood with lighter veins, obtained from two tropical trees found in the West Indies, *Hamelia ventricosa*, also called Spanish elm (family *Rubiaceae*), and *Cordia gerascanthoides* (family *Ehretiaceae*). It is used for furniture, doors, boats, etc.

● **Príncipe Island** ▷*See* São Tomé and Príncipe.

● **printed circuit** ► An electronic circuit in which the connections between components are formed by a pattern of conducting film on a board, instead of by wires. The method greatly facilitates mass-production. An insulating board is coated with a conducting material, such as copper, and a protective pattern is deposited on it using photographic techniques. The unprotected metal is then etched away and components are soldered in place. In television receivers, the replacement of thermionic valves by plug-in printed-circuit boards has made maintenance easier. A faulty circuit board can be replaced without tracing the failed component.

● **printing** ► The production of multiple copies of text or pictures, usually on paper. The oldest method, in use in China and Japan before 800 AD, is **letterpress**, in which the raised surfaces of etched,

engraved, or cast material are inked and pressed onto the paper. This method was revolutionized by the invention of movable type (*see* typesetting) in the 15th century, but printing itself remained fundamentally unchanged for four centuries until other methods of mechanization were introduced. Early printing presses were of the hand-operated platen variety in which the type stands on a horizontal surface and the paper is pressed onto it from above. Faster production became possible on the power-driven presses of the 19th century: first the cylinder press, in which the paper is rolled by a cylinder over a flat printing surface, and later the rotary press, in which the printing surface is also a cylinder. Different types of rotary press print either on separate sheets or on a web (*see* paper), which makes for still faster printing—up to 35 000 impressions per hour.
  In **lithography**, a method invented by Aloys ▷Senefelder in 1798, the printing surface is smooth (originally a polished stone but now usually an aluminium sheet), the printing and nonprinting areas being made grease-receptive and grease-repellent respectively (*see* platemaking). Greasy ink is rolled over the entire area but is taken only by the grease-receptive areas; the ink is then transferred by rolling onto the paper. **Offset printing**, most commonly lithography, involves an intermediate rubber-covered cylinder that transfers the ink from plate to paper. In **gravure printing**, the small square etched holes (cells) in the copper printing plate are filled with a free-flowing ink, the rest of the plate is wiped clean, and the plate is rolled against the paper, which absorbs the ink out of the cells. Nearly all gravure and offset lithography is done on rotary presses.
  Letterpress and offset lithography are used for almost all types of printing job; because of the expensive copper plates gravure is limited to long runs, such as cheap illustrated magazines, postage stamps, and packaging. Direct lithography has been used almost exclusively by artists— ▷Goya and ▷Manet, for example—and was the principal medium for ▷poster art in the 19th century. **Flexography** is a widespread form of (usually rotary) letterpress printing using fluid volatile ink and a rubber printing surface. It is used for paperback books, packaging materials, and for printing on nonabsorbent surfaces, such as plastic foil. In **silk-screen printing** (screen-process printing *or* serigraphy), a piece of taut open-weave silk, metal, or synthetic fabric carries the negative of the desired image in an impervious substance, such as glue; ink is forced through the clear (printing) areas by a squeegee onto the paper, glass, fabric, or other material, behind. It is used for printing posters, electronic circuit boards, labelling on bottles, and anything that requires a thick layer of ink or other material. For example pop artists, such as Andy ▷Warhol, use it to make painted photographic transfers. **Collotype** is a method of printing short runs of high-quality illustrations from gelatin plates; it is not widely used but it is the only method by which continuous tone can be reproduced (*see* platemaking).
  Full-colour reproduction is achieved by **colour-process printing**, in which all colours can be produced from combinations of three primary colours—yellow, cyan (blue), and magenta. Four separate printing plates are made, one for each primary and one for black; each is printed in succession in exactly the same place. In letterpress and lithography, half-tones are used instead of printing plates (*see* platemaking). At the normal viewing distance for any colour-process printing, the dots are imperceptible.

● **prion** ► (bird) A ▷petrel belonging to a genus (*Pachyptila*; 4 species) found in Antarctica and nearby islands. 20–27 cm long, prions have blue-grey plumage with white underparts. The flattened bill has a fringe of strainers; the bird feeds by skimming over the sea and straining out small invertebrates.

● **prion** ► (protein) The agent thought to be responsible for a group of degenerative brain disorders, the transmissible spongiform encephalopathies, that includes ▷BSE in cattle and ▷Creutzfeldt-Jakob disease in humans; the name is a shortened and altered form of "*pro*teinaceous *in*fectious particle." Small amounts of prion protein occur normally in the brain, but the brains of affected individuals contain large amounts of an abnormal form of prion, resulting from a gene mutation or transmitted by accidental consumption or injection of infected tissue. Highly resistant to heat and radiation, this abnormal prion damages and destroys surrounding brain cells.

● **Prior, Matthew** ► (1664–1721) British poet. He became an MP in

1700 and served as a diplomat in France and Holland. He wrote philosophical poems but is best known for his witty verse in *Poems on Several Occasions* (1709).

● **Pripet, River** ► (Russian name: Pripyat) A river in E Europe. Rising in NW Ukraine, it flows mainly ENE through Belarus and joins the River Dnepr near Kiev. Extensive fighting in World War II occurred in the **Pripet Marshes** along its course. Length: 800 km (500 mi).

● **Priscian** ► (6th century AD) Latin grammarian, born at Caesarea (now Cherchell, Algeria). He taught at Constantinople. His *Institutiones Grammaticae*, in 18 books, which sum up the researches of all previous grammarians, remained a standard work throughout the middle ages.

● **prism** ► A piece of glass or other transparent material having parallel polygonal ends, with a number of rectangular surfaces meeting them at right angles. They are used in optical instruments, such as cameras and binoculars, for changing the direction of light, either by refraction or by reflection from its walls. They are also used for splitting light into its component colours by double refraction, once on entering the prism and again on leaving it.

● **prisoner of war** ► A soldier captured by a belligerent in war. Guerrillas are included if they have a commander, wear distinctive clothing, carry arms openly, and obey the laws of war. The rights of a prisoner of war, defined in the ▷Geneva Conventions of 1929 and 1949 and supervised by the International ▷Red Cross, include: withholding information except name, rank, and number; receiving food, drink, and medical care; engaging in correspondence and receiving parcels; and trying to escape without being punished. Prison camps must be open for inspection by the representatives of neutral powers.

● **prisons** ► Institutions for confining convicted criminals (*see* criminal law). In primitive societies, and throughout much of history, offenders were either banished, executed, or physically punished; prisons were places in which people were held until these punishments could be carried out. It was not until the 18th century that the main purpose of prisons became custodial. The appalling prison conditions at this time led to the reform movements of John ▷Howard

and Elizabeth ▷Fry. During the 19th century a massive prison-building programme was carried out in the UK, modelled on Pentonville (1842), the structure of which was based on the principle of solitary confinement. Reforms since the 19th century have changed the emphasis in penal institutions from retribution (the Criminal Justice Act, 1948, abolished hard labour and penal servitude) to correction and rehabilitation. The first "open prison," in which prisoners are permitted some personal freedom, was opened in 1936 and followed Scandinavian models. A further UK building programme was launched in the late 1950s, the most recent prisons consisting of self-contained units with work and leisure facilities. Overcrowding, however, has remained a feature of British prisons since World War II and has contributed to several prison riots, including the violent seizure of parts of Strangeways prison in Manchester by prisoners in 1990. A series of escapes in the early 1960s led to the Mountbatten Report (1966), with its emphasis on increased security. The policy of privatizing prisons in the UK was criticized in 1993 following a number of escapes. ▷*See also* community service; electronic tagging; young offender institution.

● **Priština** ► A city in S Serbia and Montenegro, the capital of the rebel province of ▷Kosovo. Although for most of its recent history the great majority of the population has been Albanian, Serbs regard the city as a focus of their history and culture; it was the medieval capital of Serbia and the site of a celebrated battle (1389) in which the Serbs were defeated by the Turks. In the 20th century Priština developed as an administrative and communications centre with various industries. In 1999 the city was virtually emptied of its population and very severely damaged by Serb forces engaged in "ethnic cleansing." Population (2000 est): 186 611.

● **Pritchett, Sir V(ictor) S(awden)** ► (1900–97) British short-story writer and critic. He travelled widely in Europe during the 1920s and wrote frequently about Spain. He published critical works, volumes of stories including *Complete Short Stories* (1992), and two autobiographical books, *A Cab at the Door* (1968) and *Midnight Oil* (1971).

● **private enterprise** ▷*See* capitalism.

● **privateering** ► The practice of permitting, under government

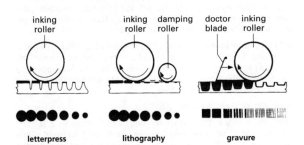

letterpress   lithography   gravure

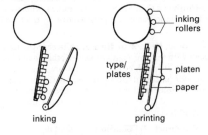

platen letterpress

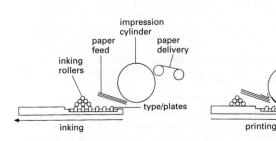

cylinder letterpress

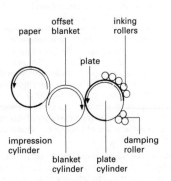

rotary offset lithography

printing ► Principles of three major printing processes and the three major designs of printing press.

licence, private individuals to equip ships to attack and capture enemy merchantmen. Such action constituted piracy without the privateers' official authorization—"letters of marque." Although a useful complement to regular navies in the 17th and 18th centuries, privateering frequently degenerated into piracy; all European countries, except Spain, renounced privateering in 1856. ▷*See also* buccaneers.

● **private medical insurance** ▶ ▷Insurance against the cost of illness, provided by an insurance company or association rather than a government. In some countries, such as the UK, private and public insurance schemes exist side by side, the citizen being free to pay to join a private scheme to enable him to choose a consultant, have a private room in a hospital, and avoid waiting for nonurgent treatment. In the USA, where no comprehensive government scheme exists, private medical insurance is widespread.

● **privatization** ▶ The sale of a public corporation to the private sector. The Conservative governments of the 1980s and 1990s sold interests in British Aerospace, Britoil, British Telecom, British Gas, British Airways, the sewage and water companies, electricity companies, and British Rail, etc., to private investors to increase the efficiency of these organizations and the number of shareholders in the community. Since the collapse of communism in 1989–91 similar policies have been implemented by the countries of E Europe and also by many developing countries in Africa and Asia. ▷*See* nationalization.

● **privet** ▶ An evergreen or deciduous shrub or small tree of the genus *Ligustrum* (40–50 species), native to Eurasia and Australia and widely used for ornamental hedges, especially the European common privet (*L. vulgare*). Growing up to about 5 m high, it has simple oval leaves and small creamy four-lobed flowers, and black berries. Family: *Oleaceae*.

● **Privy Council** ▶ A body advising the British monarch, now having chiefly formal functions. It grew out of the Curia Regis (King's Court), forming a distinct group of royal advisers in the 14th century. The emergence of the ▷cabinet system of government in the 18th century led to a lessening of its power. By convention, the Privy Council consists of all the cabinet ministers, the Archbishops of both Canterbury and York, the speaker of the House of Commons, and a number of senior British and Commonwealth statesmen, who are all addressed as the Right Honourable. It is presided over by the Lord President of the Council.

● **Privy Purse, Keeper of the** ▶ An officer of the royal household who deals with the sovereign's expenses, other than those covered by the ▷civil list, although he may make up any civil-list deficit. He is responsible for palace interiors, estates, salaries of royal officers and servants, Thoroughbred studs, etc. The modern counterpart of medieval monarchs' domestic financial officers, the office of Keeper dates from the 19th century.

● **Prix Goncourt** ▷*See* Goncourt, Edmond de.

● **probability** ▶ The mathematical concept concerned with the effects of chance on an event, experiment, or observation. It originated in 1654, when the mathematicians ▷Pascal and ▷Fermat worked on problems sent to them by a gambler.

If an event can occur in *n* ways and *r* is the number of ways it can occur in a specified way, then the **mathematical probability** of it occurring in the specified way is r/n. For example, the probability of the number 5 coming up on a six-faced dice in one throw is 1/6. The probability of a 5 coming up *x* times in *x* throws is obtained by multiplication, i.e. it is $(1/6)^x$. Probabilities are expressed as numbers between 1 (a certainty) and 0 (an impossibility).

If in a number of experiments an event has occurred *n* times and failed *m* times, the **empirical probability** of success in the next trial is $n/(n+m)$. Actuarial tables of life expectancy are based on empirical probabilities.

● **probate** ▶ A certificate issued by the UK High Court on the application of the executors of a will, stating that the will is valid and the executors are authorized to administer the estate. If the validity is unquestioned, probate is granted in **common form** on the executors' oath. In the case of a dispute, probate is granted in **solemn form** after the court has heard a probate action, dealing with a chal-

lenge on the grounds that the will was not properly executed or had been revoked or that the deceased lacked testamentary capacity.

● **probation** ▶ In English law, a court order, given instead of a sentence, requiring an offender of or over 17 years of age to be under the supervision and to comply with the directions of a probation officer for between 6 months and 3 years. The offender's consent is needed. Failure to comply with the order makes the offender liable to be sentenced for the original offence.

● **proboscis monkey** ▶ A large leaf-eating ▷Old World monkey, *Nasalis larvatus*, of Borneo. Up to 1.5 m tall, proboscis monkeys have a protruding nose and live in groups in forests, feeding on young palm leaves. They can swim as well as climb.

● **Proclus** ▶ (410–85 AD) Neoplatonist philosopher, head of ▷Plato's Academy at Athens. Indefatigable in commenting on, and explaining, earlier philosophers, Proclus integrated pagan religion, philosophy, and mathematics into a single system. His works, translated into Latin and Arabic, transmitted ▷Neoplatonism to the medieval world.

● **Procne** ▷*See* Philomela and Procne.

● **Proconsul** ▶ A genus of extinct apes whose remains have been found in E Africa. They lived 20 million years ago and were probably ground-dwellers but could not stand erect. *Proconsul* apes were ancestors of modern apes.

● **Procop** ▷*See* Prokop.

● **Procopius** ▶ (6th century AD) Byzantine historian. He accompanied the military commander Belisarius on several campaigns and worked in Constantinople from about 540 AD. His works include histories of the wars and of the public works undertaken during the reign of the Emperor Justinian I.

● **Procrustes** ▶ A legendary Greek robber. He tortured his victims by stretching them or cutting off their limbs to make them fit his bed. He was killed by Theseus.

● **procurator fiscal** ▷*See* coroner.

● **Procyon** ▶ A conspicuous star, apparent magnitude 0.35 and 11.4 light years distant, that is the brightest star in the constellation Canis Minor and one of the nearest stars to the sun. It is part of a ▷multiple star, forming a visual ▷binary star with a ▷white dwarf.

● **Prodi, Romano** ▶ (1939–) Italian politician; prime minister (1996–98). A former businessman and academic, he led a centre-left coalition to victory in the 1996 election. In 1999 he was appointed president of the European Commission, with a brief to implement reform and eradicate corruption.

● **producer gas** ▷*See* water gas.

● **productivity** ▶ The output of goods and services in a factory, country, etc., in relation to inputs (men, machines, land) used to produce them. It is difficult to produce a single measure of productivity, but output per manhour can be used as a rough approximation. Increases in productivity are largely responsible for the large increases in output in Western economies since World War II; these increases are probably largely due to increased ▷investment in new machines and the higher levels of education and skill in the workforce. Two causes of low productivity may be distinguished: overmanning, the use of too many men to produce a given level of output, and underproduction, a given number of men producing less output than they should. **Productivity bargaining** is a form of ▷collective bargaining in which wage increases are agreed subject to a corresponding increase in productivity.

● **profit and loss account** ▷*See* balance sheet.

● **profit sharing** ▶ Any scheme for sharing the profits of a firm between employees as well as shareholders. The aim is to give employees an interest in the profitability of a firm both as an incentive to productivity and to promote good ▷industrial relations. Profits may be shared in the form of bonuses or by making employees shareholders.

● **Profumo, John (Dennis)** ▶ (1915–99) British Conservative politician and social worker. While secretary of state for war (1960–63) his affair with Christine Keeler, who was also the mistress of a naval attaché at the Soviet embassy, caused a political scandal that threatened Macmillan's government and forced Profumo's resignation. He became president of ▷Toynbee Hall in 1985.

● **progesterone** ▶ A steroid hormone secreted mainly by the corpus luteum of the mammalian ▷ovary following ovulation. It prepares the womb for implantation of the embryo and maintains this state during pregnancy. Progestogens—synthetic steroids with progesterone-like actions—are constituents of ▷oral contraceptives; they are also used to treat menstrual disorders and (with oestogens) in ▷hormone replacement therapy. Progesterone preparations have been used in cattle breeding to suspend the oestrous cycle and to enable the mating of the whole herd to be synchronized.

● **program, computer** ▶ A series of instructions that controls the operation of a ▷computer. The programs executed by the computer are in a machine code, which has the form of a series of numbers that the device interprets as either instructions or data. These instructions perform very simple tasks and many thousands are required for all but the most rudimentary programs. Programming languages have been developed that simplify the programmer's task (for example by the use of English words and mathematical symbols), from which the machine code is generated automatically. Low-level languages are those that resemble closely the logic of the machine; high-level languages, such as ▷Basic, ▷Fortran, ▷Cobol, ▷Algol, and ▷Pascal, use abstract constructs more suited to human thought and are independent of any particular machine. ▷*See also* software.

● **programmed cell death** ▷*See* apoptosis.

● **programme music** ▶ Music that is based on a literary, descriptive, or emotional subject, in contrast to **abstract** (*or* absolute) **music**, which has no overt associations outside the music itself. Programmatic elements are found in music of almost all periods; one of the first major works of programme music was Vivaldi's set of violin concertos entitled *The Four Seasons* (1725), based on four sonnets by the composer. The development of the ▷symphonic poem and the concert ▷overture in the 19th century resulted in such well-known programmatic compositions as Mussorgsky's *Night on a Bare Mountain* (a depiction of a witches' sabbath), Liszt's *Les Préludes* (based on Lamartine's *Méditations poétiques*), and Richard Strauss's *Alpine Symphony* (a description of the ascent and descent of a mountain).

● **progressive taxation** ▷*See* taxation.

● **Prohibition** ▶ (1919–33) A period of "noble experiment," during which the manufacture, sale, and transportation of alcoholic drinks were prohibited in the USA by the 18th Amendment to the constitution. The ▷temperance movement, which attributed crime and poverty to alcohol, combined with the wartime need to divert grain from distilleries to food manufacture, led to national prohibition. It proved impossible to enforce, not least because prohibition agents were outnumbered by gangsters and others profiting from illicit alcohol, and in 1933 prohibition was repealed by the 21st Amendment. ▷*See* bootlegging.

● **projection** ▶ (geometry) A mapping of a figure in one plane onto its image in another, called the image plane or plane of projection. A map of the earth's surface is an example of a projection (*see* map projection). The image of each point in the figure is the intersection of a straight line (the projector) and the image plane. In central projection a projector is the straight line drawn through the point and a fixed point (the centre of projection). In orthogonal projection a projector is the perpendicular from the point to the image plane. The set of image points makes up the image figure.

● **projection** ▶ (psychology) The process of attributing one's own qualities to other people or things. In ▷psychoanalysis this is a ▷defence mechanism; people may cope with their own emotions by believing that other people have them. In projective tests, such as the ▷Rorschach test, a person's character is assessed from his descriptions of ambiguous objects.

● **projector, film** ▷*See* cinematography.

● **Prokofiev, Sergei** ▶ (1891–1953) Soviet composer and pianist. He studied at the St Petersburg conservatoire under Rimsky-Korsakov. He won the Anton Rubinstein Prize in 1914, playing his first piano concerto. He lived abroad from 1918 to 1933 and in 1948 was officially condemned for "undemocratic tendencies" in his music. His work includes seven symphonies (the first, the *Classical Symphony*; 1916–17), five piano concertos, two violin concertos, the operas *Love for Three Oranges* (1919) and *War and Peace* (1941; revised 1952), the ballet *Romeo and Juliet* (1935–36), music for the films *Lieutenant Kijé* (1934) and *Alexander Nevsky* (1938), and *Peter and the Wolf* (1936) for speaker and orchestra.

● **Prokop** ▶ (*or* Procop; c. 1380–1434) Bohemian priest. In the 1420s Prokop successfully led the ▷Hussites against the imperial armies detached to destroy them but, after joining the radical (Taborite) Hussites against the moderates (1434), he was killed in the ensuing battle of Lipany.

● **Prokopyevsk** ▶ 53 55N 86 45E A city in S Russia. Located in the Kuznetsk Basin, it is an important coalmining centre. Population (1995 est): 253 000.

● **prolactin** ▶ A protein hormone, produced by the pituitary gland, that initiates and maintains lactation in mammals. In other animals, it has a variety of functions, being involved in growth and the balance of water and salts, as well as in reproduction. ▷*See also* gonadotrophin.

● **proletariat** ▶ Originally, the lower class of Rome and other ancient states, the term was later used to refer to the lower class of any community. Karl ▷Marx defined the proletariat as the wage labourers of capitalist economies, who depended on the sale of their labour to live and who owned no property; the struggle between this class and the ▷bourgeoisie would eventually lead to revolution. ▷*See* Marxism.

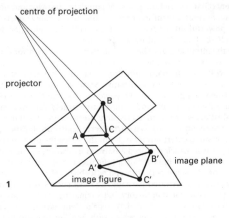

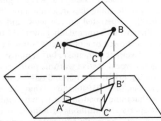

projection ▶ The mapping of a triangle by (1) central and (2) orthogonal projections.

● **promenade concerts** ▶ Concerts in which some of the audience can stand while listening to the music. The most famous are the BBC Promenade Concerts (the Proms), begun by Henry ▷Wood in 1895. They were held in the Queen's Hall until it was bombed in World War II and thereafter in the Royal Albert Hall. The "last night of the Proms" is a uniquely British occasion in which audience participation makes up for in enthusiasm what it lacks in musical skill.

● **Prometheus** ► (Greek: forethought) In Greek mythology, the son of a Titan and Themis who created man and endowed him with reason. He also stole fire from heaven to give to man. Zeus chained him to a rock in the Caucasus and sent an eagle each day to devour his liver, which grew again by night. After thousands of years he was rescued by Heracles.

● **promethium** ► (Pm) A radioactive element, not known on earth but identified by its spectrum in the light from stars, in which it is continuously being formed by nuclear reactions. The most stable isotope has a half-life of 17.7 years. Promethium salts exhibit bluish-green ▷luminescence and can be used in photoelectric cells. It is obtained from nuclear reactors. At no 61; at wt (145); mp 1042°C.

● **pronghorn** ► A hoofed mammal, *Antilocapra americana*, resembling an antelope and found in rocky deserts of the W USA. Up to 100 cm high at the shoulder, pronghorns are not true antelopes, shedding the horny sheath of their branched horns every year; the bony core is permanent. Brown above and white beneath with white chevrons under the neck, they have brilliant-white rump hairs used for signalling. They are the only surviving members of the family *Antilocapridae*.

● **proof spirit** ▷*See* alcohol strength.

● **propaganda** ► The dissemination of information (or misinformation) to promote a political, religious, or other cause. The term originated with the Sacra Congregatio de Propaganda Fide (Latin: Sacred Congregation for Propagating the Faith), a Roman Catholic organization responsible for directing the work of foreign missions and training their priests in the 18th century.

In the 20th century, especially with the advent of the cinema, radio, and other forms of mass media, propaganda became more widely diffused than ever before. It was during World War I that governments first realized the power of popular newsprint and the new medium of cinema to influence public opinion. *England Expects* (1914) was a powerful British recruiting film, while *The Kaiser, the Beast of Berlin* (1918) blatantly vilified the Germans.

In the interwar years, the ▷totalitarian regimes in Europe made a concerted use of all channels of communication to spread their ideologies, while also (perhaps more crucially) using the apparatus of repression to exclude any alternative view. In the Soviet Union a Department of Agitation and Propaganda was established in 1920 to spread Bolshevik propaganda among the largely illiterate masses. Special trains were organized to carry theatre and film shows to all parts of the country, giving rise to the term "agitprop" for such politically motivated entertainments. From the 1930s the doctrine of ▷socialist realism, which required a naive glorification of communism and its leaders, was imposed on all the literary and visual arts.

During the same period Joseph ▷Goebbels, Hitler's minister of propaganda, orchestrated perhaps the most successful and malign propaganda campaign in history, indoctrinating the German people with Nazi aspirations to achieve world domination for a bogus master race (*Herrenvolk*). Goebbels's skill and German gullibility resulted in the German people going to war, acquiescing in the most horrific atrocities being perpetrated on the Jews, and destroying their culture. Leni ▷Riefenstahl's undeniably powerful film *Triumph of the Will* (1934), which showed one of Hitler's Nuremberg Rallies, made her the regime's favourite film-maker but demolished her reputation in the rest of the world. British wartime propaganda largely concentrated on extolling British decency and self-sacrifice, notably in such films as *London Can Take It* (1940) and *In Which We Serve* (1941). It was during the war that radio broadcasting, with its ability to carry speeches and news reports into millions of homes, as well as its power to penetrate enemy and occupied territory, emerged as the main tool of propaganda on both sides. Radio remained important during the Cold War, with such stations as Radio Moscow and the Voice of America promoting rival interpretations of world events.

In the postwar world, propaganda has continued to be a vital part of most governments. In repressive regimes there are no safeguards, but countries with a free press are able to assume that government information has at least some relation to truth. Indeed, owing to the global nature of modern communications systems (most recently, the Internet), it is difficult for any but the most closed societies to achieve the total triumph of propaganda over truth characteristic of Nazi Germany or Stalinist Russia. Perhaps because of its association with these oppressive and manipulative regimes, the word propaganda has acquired a pejorative undertone. More recently, propagandists have become **spin doctors**, who are employed by political parties and governments to put a favourable gloss on news items or potentially unpopular policies. Spin doctors are, of course, propagandists by another name—they are expected to manipulate (spin) the facts to the advantage of their employers, but not to invent them.

● **propane** ► (C_3H_8) A colourless flammable gaseous ▷alkane found in crude oil. It is used as a bottled gas for fuel.

● **propanone** ► (*or* acetone; CH_3COCH_3) A colourless inflammable liquid used as a solvent, for example as a nail-polish remover, and in the manufacture of ▷rayon.

● **propellant** ► **1.** A solid or liquid substance used to provide thrust in a rocket engine or gun. Propellants utilize fast exothermic chemical reactions to produce large quantities of expanding gas quickly. Generally, they are explosive substances or mixtures. A single unstable substance (such as nitrocellulose) or mixture of combustible material and oxidant (such as alcohol and hydrogen peroxide) is a **monopropellant**. If the combustible material and oxidant are mixed in a combustion chamber the mixture forms a **bipropellant**. Generally, bipropellants are hypergolic, i.e. ignite spontaneously when mixed. **2.** The pressurized inert liquids used to drive an ▷aerosol from its container.

● **propeller** ► A device for converting the rotation of a shaft into thrust in the direction of its axis. A **marine propeller** is attached to a shaft connected to the ship's engine and has between two and six blades, shaped as part of a helical surface. It acts as a screw, accelerating a column of water rearwards. An **air propeller** (*or* airscrew), moving in a thinner medium, has longer thinner blades (usually two or four) and a higher rotational speed. It, too, accelerates a mass of air rearwards thrusting the aircraft forwards by reaction.

● **proper motion** ► The rate at which a star is observed to move on the ▷celestial sphere, i.e. perpendicular to the line of sight. Values are very small, often negligible.

● **Propertius, Sextus** ► (c. 50–c. 16 BC) Roman poet. Born in Assisi in Umbria, he went to Rome as a young man and established himself in literary circles. *Cynthia*, the first of his four surviving books, contains highly personal love poems addressed to his mistress Hostia. His later books contain poems on various topics, including the psychology of love, written in a style noted for its bold originality.

● **prophets** ► Ancient Israelite religious leaders and visionaries. The books of the prophets make up the second of the three divisions of the Hebrew ▷Bible and are grouped into the "Former Prophets" (Joshua, Judges, Samuel, and Kings) and the "Latter Prophets" (Isaiah, Jeremiah, Ezekiel, and the 12 Minor Prophets). Moses is regarded by Jews as the first and greatest of the prophets, and the gift of prophecy is thought to have ceased in the 5th century BC. In Islam Adam, Moses, and Jesus are regarded as prophets, while Mohammed is regarded as the greatest and the last prophet.

● **proportional representation** ► (PR) A voting system that aims accurately to reflect the wishes of the electorate and to ensure that votes for unsuccessful candidates are not wasted. Most democracies now employ some form of PR, the main exceptions being the UK, USA, and Canada, which adhere to a simple majoritarian ("first-past-the-post") system. In the system of PR known as the **single transferable vote** (used in the Republic of Ireland and for elections to the Northern Ireland Assembly), electors indicate their preferences among the candidates by numbering them on their ballot paper (1, 2, 3, etc.). Those candidates who obtain a required quota of first-choice votes are elected. First-choice votes for these candidates in excess of this quota are then redistributed to the next-preference candidates on a proportional basis, as are those cast for the least successful candidate, who is eliminated. The process continues until the requisite number of candidates has been elected (the system usually requires multimember constituencies). The **alternative vote** system is similar but takes place in smaller single-member constituencies. Voters number candidates in order of preference; if no candidate obtains more than 50% of the vote, the bottom candidate is eliminated and his or her votes redistributed according to preference until a clear winner emerges. Under the **additional member** system people vote separately for a candidate and a party. Parties are awarded additional members of parliament if the number of constituences they win does not reflect their share of the overall vote. In the **party-list system** (widely used on the Continent and introduced for the UK's elections to the European Parliament in 1999) electors vote for a party, which is then allocated seats in proportion to its total vote; the individuals who will occupy these seats are chosen by the parties, rather than the electorate. In the UK, PR has long been advocated by the ▷Liberal Democrats and has influential supporters in the current Labour government. In 1998 a commission on electoral reform, chaired by Lord Jenkins of Hillhead, recommended that the UK change to a new system combining the alternative vote with the additional member system. In May, 1999, the first elections to the devolved bodies in Scotland and Wales were held using a combination of first-past-the-post and the additional member system.

Advocates of PR claim that it is fairer (especially to minority parties), prevents long periods of dominance by a single party, and strengthens democracy by making every vote count. Opponents argue that it removes or weakens the link between voters and their local representatives, tends to produce unstable coalitions or weak governments without a working majority, and that the frequency of coalitions gives undue influence to small parties (often of the extreme right or left). ▷*See also* vote.

● **propositional calculus** ▶ A system of formal logic that assigns truth or falsehood to compound propositions or statements on the basis of the rules governing the connective words between them. Examples of such connective words are "and," "or," or "if...then...." For example, the rule for "and" is that a statement containing it is true only if both the simple statements it connects are true; for "or" it is sufficient that only one statement be true. Thus "pigs fly and birds sing" is false, while "either pigs fly or birds sing" is true.

● **propylaea** ▶ Ancient Greek monumental gateways, generally the ceremonial entrances to the ▷acropolis of a town. The best-preserved example is that on the Acropolis of Athens.

● **proscenium** ▶ The arch at the front of a ▢theatre stage through which the audience views the play. It became a standard feature of theatre architecture following its first use in Italy in the 17th century but has been dispensed with in many theatres built during the 20th century.

● **Proserpine** ▷*See* Persephone.

● **prosimian** ▶ A ▷primate of the suborder *Prosimii* (53 species), including the ▷lemurs, ▷indris, ▷sifakas, ▷lorises, ▷bushbabies, ▷tarsiers, and the ▷aye-aye. Prosimians are the most primitive of the primates and are mainly arboreal.

● **Prost, Alain** ▶ (1955–   ) French motor racing driver. His record of 51 Grand Prix victories stood until 2001, when it was beaten by Michael ▷Schumacher; he won the World Championship in 1985, 1986, 1989, and 1993. He retired in 1993.

● **prostaglandins** ▶ Compounds derived from long-chain (essential) fatty acids and found in mammalian body tissues. Their effects include stimulation of contraction in the womb, dilation of blood vessels, and modification of hormonal activity. They are released at sites of inflammation following tissue damage and the pain-relieving properties of such drugs as aspirin are due to their inhibition of prostaglandin synthesis. Synthetic prostaglandins are used to induce labour and abortion and to treat complications following childbirth, peptic ulcers, congenital heart disease, and impotence.

● **prostate gland** ▶ A gland in men, situated just beneath the bladder (*see* Plate II). It secretes an alkaline fluid during ejaculation that forms part of the semen. Enlargement of the prostate (benign prostatic hypertrophy, BPH) commonly occurs in elderly men, obstructing the bladder and preventing urination; it is usually treated by means of drugs or by transurethral resection (removal of part of the gland by passing an instrument through the urethra). In cases of prostate cancer the gland is removed surgically (prostatectomy).

● **prostitution** ▶ The practice of offering sexual gratification in return for money or other reward. It has always been common, especially in societies in which legitimate sexual relations are closely regulated. Attitudes to prostitution differ greatly in different societies. Sometimes a bride earns her dowry in this way with general approval. It was practised in ancient Mesopotamia by priestesses for religious reasons. In modern societies it is generally controlled by legislation, usually with the object of preventing the spread of ▷sexually transmitted diseases and of preventing pimps (men who live off the earnings of prostitutes) from introducing young girls into the profession. In the UK, since the enactment of the ▷Wolfenden Report (1957) as legislation (1959), prostitution has ceased to be illegal, but soliciting, procuring someone to be a prostitute, and living off a prostitute's earnings are punishable offences, as is kerb crawling. Although male prostitutes for women are not unknown, male prostitution is largely confined to homosexual relations.

● **protactinium** ▶ (Pa) A radioactive ▷actinide element, first identified by K. Fajans and O. H. Göhring in 1913. It is present in pitchblende as a member of the uranium decay series. The oxide (Pa_2O_5) and iodide (PaI_5) have been produced. The latter decomposes on heating to give the metal. At no 91; at wt (231); mp <1572°C.

● **Protagoras** ▶ (c. 485–415 BC) Greek ▷Sophist. He claimed to teach virtue (more accurately interpreted as "success") and was himself successful and respected for more than 40 years. His saying, "Man is the measure of all things," shows his subjectivist attitude to knowledge. His scepticism extended to religion, but not, apparently, to morality.

● **Protea** ▶ A genus of evergreen shrubs and trees (over 100 species), native to S and central Africa. They have broad simple leaves and small white, pink, yellow, or orange flowers that are grouped into showy cup-shaped clusters, up to 30 cm across, and surrounded by whorls of coloured bracts. The flowers are a national emblem of South Africa. Family: *Proteaceae.*

● **protected species** ▷*See* endangered species.

● **Protectorate** ▶ (1653–59) The period during which England was governed by Oliver ▷Cromwell. The Instrument of Government (1653) vested executive authority in the Lord Protector (Cromwell) and a state council and legislative authority in the Protector and a triennial parliament. The Instrument was modified by the Humble Petition and Advice (1657), which gave more power to parliament and less to the state council. Cromwell's relations with parliament subsequently deteriorated and he dismissed it in 1658. Following his death later in the year, his son Richard ▷Cromwell was Protector until his abdication in 1659.

● **protein** ▶ A complex organic compound that consists of one or more chains of ▷amino acids linked by ▷peptide bonds (–NH–CO–). These chains are variously coiled, wound, and cross-linked to form a three-dimensional molecular structure, revealed by such techniques as ▷X-ray diffraction, that determines the biological properties of the protein. This structure is irreversibly damaged at temperatures above 60°C. Proteins are manufactured within cells according to the genetic information carried in the chromosomes and the specific function of the cell (*see* DNA; RNA). Proteins fulfil many important biological roles: some proteins, including ▷collagen and ▷keratin, are important structural materials of body tissues, while the proteins of ▷muscle—actin and myosin—are responsible for its contractile properties. Proteins vital to the functioning of the body include enzymes—the biological catalysts of metabolic reactions; ▷antibodies—important in the body's defence mechanisms; and many ▷hormones—the chemical messengers of the body.

● **Protestantism** ▶ The movement for Church reform that arose in the Western Church in the 16th century and led to the establishment of the Reformed Churches. The word derives from the *protestatio* of the dissident reforming minority at the Diet of ▷Speyer (1529). The early leaders of the ▷Reformation—▷Luther, ▷Calvin, and ▷Zwingli—each promoted his own brand of Protestantism. Under Elizabeth I Protestantism finally became the established religion in England, although since the 19th century some Anglicans have objected to the

Protestant label and have emphasized the Catholic traditions of the Church of England (*see* Anglo-Catholicism).

There are many doctrinal divisions among Protestants, but all reject a varying number of tenets and practices retained in Catholicism. In general Protestants rely less upon ecclesiastical tradition, believing the Bible to be the sole source of truth. They deny papal authority and admit a variety of forms of Church government (*see* episcopacy; Presbyterianism); in some sects the spiritual priesthood of all the faithful is emphasized. ▷Transubstantiation, ▷purgatory, special veneration of the Virgin Mary, and invocation of saints are all repudiated. The importance of the sacraments is minimized, with only baptism and the ▷Eucharist being accorded widespread acceptance, and some groups, such as the ▷Quakers, reject even these. The preaching and studying of God's word in the Bible is conversely important. Church furnishings, vestments, and music are more austere than their Roman Catholic equivalents. The 20th-century ecumenical movement has gone some way towards reconciling the Roman Catholic and Protestant Churches, but there are still serious doctrinal and other differences, while fresh issues, such as the ordination of women, introduce new elements of divisiveness.

● **Proteus** ▶ (bacteria) A genus of motile rod-shaped bacteria found mainly in soil and sewage, where they decompose organic matter, but also in the wounds of animals and man. Some species cause enteritis and urinary-tract infections.

● **Proteus** ▶ (mythology) A Greek sea god who served Poseidon as a shepherd of seals. He is usually portrayed as an old man. He had prophetic powers but used his ability to change his form to avoid communicating his knowledge.

● **Protista** ▶ A kingdom that originally comprised all unicellular organisms (including bacteria); it was proposed by the German biologist Ernst ▷Haeckel in 1866. Bacteria were later excluded on the grounds that their cell structure differed fundamentally from that of other organisms. The kingdom is still used in some modern classifications and is usually held to comprise all eukaryotic organisms (*see* cell) consisting of single cells or aggregates of similar cells, including the protozoa, unicellular algae (such as diatoms), and slime moulds. *Compare* Protoctista.

● **Protoceratops** ▶ A dinosaur that lived during the late Cretaceous period (about 100–65 million years ago). It was a short-legged

squat quadruped, 2 m long and weighing 1.5 tonnes, and had long sharp teeth and huge jaw muscles attached to a bony neck frill. Its diet probably consisted of palm fronds. Order: ▷*Ornithischia*.

● **Protocols of Zion** ▶ A document published in 1903 purporting to contain Jewish plans to overthrow Christian civilization. Although conclusively proved a forgery in 1921, Hitler, like earlier antisemitic agitators, used it to justify his persecution of the Jews.

● **Protoctista** ▶ In the five-kingdoms classification system (*see* taxonomy), a kingdom that contains all organisms that cannot be classified as bacteria, fungi, plants, or animals. It includes the ▷algae (including multicellular forms, such as seaweeds), ▷protozoa, ▷slime moulds, and oomycetes (the last two are sometimes classified as fungi).

● **proton** ▶ A positively charged elementary particle classified as a baryon (*see* particle physics). It forms part of all atomic nuclei, a single proton being the nucleus of the hydrogen atom. It is a stable particle, 1836 times heavier than the electron. The **proton number** is the number of protons in an atom (*see* atomic number).

● **protostar** ▶ An embryonic star that has formed out of a contracting cloud of interstellar gas and dust. It continues to contract, the density and temperature at its centre rising slowly at first and then increasingly rapidly until they are sufficiently high to cause energy-releasing thermonuclear reactions to begin in the central core. The collapse is then halted, and the object becomes a luminous star.

● **protozoa** ▶ A large and diverse group of typically microscopic single-celled organisms, traditionally classified as simple animals but now assigned to a variety of phyla that are usually placed in the kingdom ▷*Protoctista*. Widely distributed in moist and watery places, including mud, soil, fresh waters, and oceans, protozoans range in size from 0.1 mm to several centimetres. They may have one or several nuclei and a variety of specialized structures, including a contractile vacuole for regulating the water content and cilia or flagella for movement and feeding. The cell may be fairly rigid, with a stiff cell wall (pellicle) or skeletal elements, or flexible and variable. Some protozoans contain pigment and obtain food by photosynthesis in the same way as plants. However, most forms take in dissolved nutrients or solid food particles (detritus, bacteria, etc.). Asexual reproduction is by means of simple division of the parent cell (binary fission) or by

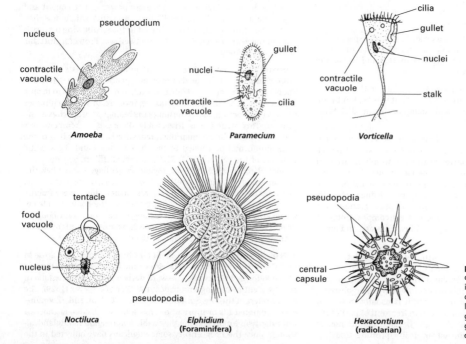

Amoeba

Paramecium

Vorticella

Noctiluca

Elphidium
(Foraminifera)

Hexacontium
(radiolarian)

protozoa ▶ Although consisting only of single cells, these organisms show a surprising complexity of structure. Many have organs of locomotion (pseudopodia, flagella, or cilia) and some have gullets, through which food is channelled.

budding to form new cells; various forms of sexual reproduction occur, including ▷conjugation. Protozoans can survive dry or adverse conditions by forming resistant cysts or spores. Some are important parasites of humans and animals, including species of ▷*Plasmodium*, which cause malaria, and trypanosomes, which cause sleeping sickness.

● **Protura** ▶ A worldwide order of primitive wingless insects (150 species) that live in humus and soil, feeding on decaying organic materials. They have a pale cylindrical body (0.5–2 mm long), which tapers to a simple tail (telson) and lacks eyes and antennae.

● **Proudhon, Pierre Joseph** ▶ (1809–65) French political theorist. In *Qu'est-ce que la propriété?* (1840) and the *Système des contradictions économiques ou philosophie de la misère* (1846), he argued that all property was theft and that in a just society orderly anarchy would replace oppressive government.

● **Proust, Joseph-Louis** ▶ (1754–1826) French chemist, who demonstrated by accurate analysis that compounds always contain fixed proportions of elements. This is now known as the law of definite proportion or sometimes as Proust's law. This work contributed to ▷Dalton's atomic theory.

● **Proust, Marcel** ▶ (1871–1922) French novelist. The son of rich bourgeois parents, he suffered from asthma from childhood and was devotedly cared for by his mother. He studied at the Lycée Condorcet and the Sorbonne and in the 1890s became a socialite in the most fashionable aristocratic circles in Paris. After the deaths of his parents (1903, 1905), he dedicated his life to writing and, because of asthma, lived as an invalid recluse in a cork-lined room in a flat on the Boulevard Haussmann. In 1912 he financed the publication of the first volume (*Swann's Way*) of what was to become his masterpiece, *In Search of Lost Time*. He then set to work expanding his original conception, realizing that his time was limited because of his ill health. The second volume, *Within a Budding Grove* (1919), won the Prix Goncourt; it was followed by *The Guermantes Way* (1920–21) and *Cities of the Plain* (1921–22). Proust managed to complete but not revise the final volumes, *The Captive* (1923), *The Sweet Cheat Gone* (1925), and *Time Regained* (1927), before his death. Written in an elaborate style and influenced by the philosophy of ▷Bergson, *In Search of Lost Time* is a detailed portrait of the society that Proust had abandoned, recreated through the involuntary workings of memory. There is a strong autobiographical element in the narration and in the theme of homosexuality that plays a large part in several sections.

● **Prout, William** ▶ (1785–1850) British chemist and physiologist, who in 1824 discovered the presence of hydrochloric acid in the stomach. He was also the first to classify foods in terms of what are now called proteins, fats, and carbohydrates. He also formulated the idea that atomic weights are all multiples of the atomic weight of hydrogen (Prout's hypothesis).

● **Provençal** ▶ A ▷Romance language, strictly the dialect of ▷Provence, but also used to refer to the dialects of various regions of S France and in this broad sense often called Occitan. These dialects are also collectively described as the *langue d'oc*, in contrast to the *langue d'oïl* spoken in northern and central areas of France (*oc* and *oïl* being the medieval forms for *yes* in these two dialect areas). The primary literary use of Provençal was by the ▷troubadours; it fell into disuse as a literary language during the later middle ages. About nine million people still speak it.

● **Provence** ▶ A former province in SE France, bordering on Italy and the Mediterranean Sea. A kingdom during the 9th century AD, it became part of France in 1481 and now forms the modern planning region of **Provence-Alpes-Côte-d'Azur**. Chiefly mountainous, its fertile river valleys produce grapes, olives, and mulberries. The perfume industry, centred on Grasse, is important. It contains the French ▷Riviera, a popular tourist area, along the S coast. Area: 31 435 sq km (12 134 sq mi). Population (1995 est): 4 428 200.

● **Proverbs** ▶ An Old Testament book that is a collection of moral and religious maxims, traditionally ascribed to Solomon. Its chief theme is the nature and value of wisdom, which is the result of "fear of the Lord." Also prominent are maxims relating to justice, self-control, purity, industry, friends and family, and life and death.

● **Providence** ▶ 41 50N 71 25W A city and seaport in the USA, the capital of Rhode Island on Narragansett Bay. Founded in 1636, it is the site of many historical buildings, including the First Baptist Church (1775), the First Unitarian Church, two cathedrals, and Brown University (founded in Warren in 1764 and moved to Providence in 1770). A major outlet for much of New England's oil, its manufactures include jewellery, machinery, and rubber goods. Population (1996 est): 152 558.

● **province** ▶ A territorial subdivision of the empire of ancient Rome administered by a Roman governor. Provincial governors, who in Republican times (510–27 BC) were appointed by the Senate, commanded the garrisons, levied taxes, administered justice, and in wartime recruited troops. Under the Empire (after 27 BC), the Senate continued to provide governors for the ten more peaceful provinces while the emperors through their legates controlled those provinces still requiring military occupation. ▷*See also* Roman Republic; Roman Empire.

● **Proxima Centauri** ▷*See* Alpha Centauri.

● **Prudhoe Bay** ▶ A small inlet of the Arctic Ocean in the USA, on the coast of N Alaska. Since the discovery of vast oil deposits in the area (1968) it has been a centre of drilling activity. A pipeline transfers oil from Prudhoe Bay to the S.

● **Prud'hon, Pierre Paul** ▶ (1758–1823) French painter and draughtsman, born at Cluny. He trained in the Dijon Academy and in Rome (1784–7), where he was influenced by the works of ▷Correggio and ▷Leonardo da Vinci. The style of his court portraits, for example *Empress Josephine* (Louvre), and his famous *Crime Pursued by Vengeance and Justice* (Saint-Omer, N France) display a romantic feeling distinctly different from the current neoclassical vogue (*see* neoclassicism).

● **Prunus** ▶ A genus of deciduous or evergreen shrubs and trees (over 200 species), mostly native to N temperate regions. It includes the ▷plums, ▷almonds, ▷apricots, ▷peaches, and ▷cherries as well as many ornamental species. They have oval toothed leaves, often rolled in the bud, and white or pink flowers, about 1 cm across, with five petals and many stamens. They produce stone fruits (*see* drupe), often with edible flesh or kernels. Family: *Rosaceae*.

● **Prussia** ▶ A former state in N Germany on the NE Baltic coast. Established in the 13th century by the Teutonic Knights, Prussia became a duchy in 1525 under ▷Hohenzollern rule. United with Brandenburg in 1618, under ▷Frederick William, the Great Elector, it became the most powerful N German state. In 1701 his son took the title King of Prussia. In the 18th century, under ▷Frederick (II) the Great, Prussia annexed Silesia and parts of Poland and became a major European power. Following Napoleon's defeat, it made important territorial gains at the Congress of Vienna (1815). Under ▷Bismarck's ambitious leadership, Prussia defeated Austria and Austria's German allies (1866), acquiring ▷Schleswig-Holstein and forming the ▷North German Confederation. Following victory in the ▷Franco-Prussian War (1870–71) the German Empire was proclaimed under Prussian leadership. In 1918 Prussia became a republic and was abolished after World War II.

● **prussic acid** ▷*See* hydrogen cyanide.

● **Prynne, William** ▶ (1600–69) English Puritan. He was imprisoned in 1633 for his book *Histrio Mastix: The Players Scourge, or Actors Tragedie* (1633), seen to contain an attack on the queen, and in 1634 his ears were cut off. Released (1640) by the ▷Long Parliament, he was imprisoned (1650–53) under the Commonwealth for nonpayment of taxes.

● **Przemyśl** ▶ 49 48N 22 48E A town in SE Poland. During World War I it withstood a five-month siege by Russian armies before surrendering. Its industries are varied and include flour milling, tanning, and the manufacture of machinery. Population (1989 est): 67 000.

● **Przewalski's horse** ▶ The single surviving species of wild horse, *Equus przewalskii*, discovered in Mongolia in about 1880 by the Russian explorer Nicolai Mikhailovich Przewalski (1839–88). Although now extinct in the wild, a small number survive in captivity. They are sturdily built with a relatively large head, a short erect dark-brown

Przewalski's horse ► Most of these horses are descendants of three pairs captured in the wild at the beginning of the 20th century.

mane, and a dark dorsal stripe. The coat is reddish brown, becoming paler in winter. Height: 1.22–1.42 m (12–14 hands).

● **Psalms** ► An Old Testament book, also known as the Psalter, containing 150 spiritual songs. They were formerly all attributed to David but are now generally believed to be by a number of different authors; some of them may date from the early period of the Jewish monarchy. They were intended to be sung with musical accompaniment and used in the liturgy of the Temple at Jerusalem; they continue to be used in both public and private worship by Jews and Christians. The majority are expressions of praise and worship of God and his works. A large number deal with aspects of a believer's experience, such as penitence, trust, doubt, fear, and suffering.

● **psaltery** ► A medieval musical instrument, a type of ▷zither. It was plucked by the fingers of both hands or by two plectra.

● **Psamtik I** ► King of Egypt (664–610 BC); the founder of the 26th dynasty. Appointed viceroy of Egypt by ▷Ashurbanipal of Assyria in 663, he took advantage of Assyria's weakness to repudiate its suzerainty, while remaining its ally. Psamtik encouraged trade with Greece and employed Greek mercenaries (the "brazen men"). During his reign Egyptian national sentiment revived the art and institutions of the pyramid age.

● **PSBR** ► (Public Sector Borrowing Requirement) ▷See public sector.

● **Pseudo-Dionysius the Areopagite** ► (early 6th century AD) Mystical theologian, probably born in Syria, whose real name is unknown. His fame rests on several Greek treatises and letters, which influenced medieval scholars. They attempt to combine Christianity with ▷Neoplatonism and include *The Celestial Hierarchy*, *The Ecclesiastical Hierarchy*, *The Divine Names*, and *The Mystical Theology*. They were formerly attributed to St ▷Dionysius the Areopagite.

● **pseudopodium** ► A temporary extension of the cytoplasm found in some ▷protozoa and used for locomotion and for engulfing food particles. In *Amoeba*, the pseudopodia are blunt lobular processes but in other protozoa they may be slender, filamentous, or branching.

● **Psilocybe** ► A genus of mushrooms growing in soil and dung. The Mexican species *P. mexicana* contains the hallucinogenic compounds

psilocin and psilocybin, which have effects similar to those of ▷LSD. It was regarded as a sacred mushroom in Mexico and eaten during religious ceremonies. Mushrooms of the liberty cap fungus (*P. semilanceolata*) are common in pastures and lawns, having greyish-brown or olive-green conical caps, 1–2 cm in diameter.

● **psi particle** ► An elementary particle discovered in 1974 and classified as a meson. Its unusually long lifetime led to the extension of the quark model (*see* particle physics) to include a quark (and its antiquark) having a new property called ▷charm. The psi particle itself is not charmed as it consists of a charmed quark and its antiquark.

● **psittacosis** ► (*or* parrot disease) An infectious illness caused by the virus-like bacterium *Chlamydia psittaci*, which is caught from birds, particularly parrots. The severity of the disease varies, but usually it causes pneumonia. Tetracycline antibiotics are used to treat the disease.

● **Pskov** ► 57 48N 28 26E A city in NW Russia, on the River Velikaya, SE of Lake Pskov. Nicholas II abdicated at the railway station here in 1917. Industries include food processing and tourism, Pskov having many historic buildings. Population (1995 est): 207 000.

● **Pskov school** ► A school of Russian ▷icon and mural painting that flourished in the city of Pskov between the late 12th and early 16th centuries. It developed in isolation from other cultural centres since most other parts of Russia were occupied by the Mongols during this period. Characteristics of the school's style were the influence of ▷Byzantine art, monumental forms, brilliant colours, emotional intensity, and the persistence of archaic methods of representation.

● **psoriasis** ► A chronic recurring skin disease marked by excessive scaling of the skin. It is very common and affects over 2% of the UK population. It begins with small red patches covered in scales and may spread extensively. The knees, elbows, lower back, scalp, and nails are most commonly affected, and it is often associated with arthritis (psoriatic arthritis). There is no known cure, but various creams (including steroids) and photochemotherapy (which uses ultraviolet light) are used to alleviate the condition.

● **Psyche** ► In Greek mythology, a personification of the soul, portrayed as a beautiful mortal girl. ▷Apuleius tells the allegorical story of how she lost her divine lover, Cupid, and of her subsequent quest and suffering before she was finally reunited with him in marriage in heaven.

● **psychedelic drugs** ▷*See* hallucinogens.

● **psychiatry** ► The study and treatment of mental disorders. A psychiatrist is a medically qualified physician specializing in mental illness. Modern psychiatry also involves those of other professional disciplines, including nurses, social workers, and psychologists. The range of mental disorders includes ▷psychosis, anxiety disorders (*see* neurosis), ▷psychosomatic disorders, ▷drug dependence, and ▷mental retardation. Within psychiatry there are several specialities, notably child psychiatry, forensic psychiatry (which deals with those who have broken the law), and geriatric psychiatry (psychogeriatrics), which cares for the mentally disordered elderly. Psychiatrists, being medically qualified, can prescribe psychoactive drugs.

● **psychical research** ► Scientific investigation into paranormal phenomena. Proper subjects for psychical research include ▷ghost and ▷poltergeist hauntings, ▷extrasensory perception, and ▷spiritualism. The London Society for Psychical Research (founded in 1882) was the first of numerous kindred organizations throughout the world, but mainstream science is still sceptical about their methodology and conclusions.

● **psychoanalysis** ► A school of ▷psychology and a method of treating mental disorders based upon the teachings of Sigmund ▷Freud (*see also* Adler, Alfred; Jung, Carl Gustav). Psychoanalysis stresses the interplay of unconscious mental forces and the way in which the adult personality is determined by sexual development in childhood. The chief techniques of psychoanalysis are free ▷association and the recall of ▷dreams, which usually requires several 50-minute sessions each week for up to three years. In the course of this treatment transference takes place, in which aspects of the patient's past experiences and relationships are transferred to the analyst, the object being to bring repressed conflicts into consciousness so that they can be resolved. Although analysis was originally intended as a treatment for neurosis, it has been extended to some psychotic conditions by W. R. Bion (1897–1979), Herbert Rosenfeld (1909–86), and others. The work of Melanie ▷Klein was devoted to exploring early infantile experiences on a Freudian basis; some of Freud's concepts were challenged by such analysts as W. ▷Reich, E. ▷Fromm, and others. Most analysts are medically qualified, but there are some lay analysts. Psychoanalysis is time-consuming and therefore expensive; analysts have been criticized for poor documentation of results and patient follow-up. ▷*See also* defence mechanisms; ego; id; Oedipus complex; repression; superego; unconscious.

● **psychokinesis** ▷*See* telekinesis.

● **psycholinguistics** ▷*See* linguistics.

● **psychology** ▶ The scientific study of the behaviour of humans and animals. Different schools of psychology use differing methods and theories. These include ▷behaviourism; experimental psychology, in which laboratory experiments are used to investigate factors influencing behaviour (particularly ▷memory, perception, and learning); ▷Gestalt psychology; associationist psychology (*see* association); ▷cognitive psychology; and ▷psychoanalysis. Clinical psychology applies these approaches to the understanding and treatment of mental illness (*see also* psychiatry). Educational psychology studies the ways in which children learn, in order to intervene as problems arise. Occupational psychology studies people in their working environment. ▷*See also* ethology.

● **psychoneurosis** ▷*See* neurosis.

● **psychopath** ▶ A person with a personality disorder who behaves violently or antisocially and shows neither guilt nor any feeling for others. Psychopathy can be caused by a constitutional abnormality or an emotionally deprived upbringing. Psychopaths are difficult to treat—some end up in prison as a result of the crimes they have committed—but psychiatric hospitals will not accept them because the chances of being able to help them are remote. In 1999 the government introduced legislation enabling the detention of people judged to be dangerous psychopaths, even if they have committed no crime.

● **psychosis** ▶ A severe mental illness in which the sufferer loses contact with reality. Organic psychoses are caused by diseases affecting the brain, such as epilepsy, alcoholism, and dementia; functional psychoses have no known physical cause. The major functional psychoses are ▷schizophrenia and ▷manic-depressive psychosis. All psychoses can cause ▷hallucinations, delusions, and altered thought processes. They are common and disabling illnesses that account for the occupation of more hospital beds than any other illness.

● **psychosomatic disorder** ▶ An illness in which physical symptoms are caused or exacerbated by mental factors. Certain physical illnesses, including asthma, eczema, and peptic ulcer, are thought to be partly a response to psychological ▷stress.

● **psychosurgery** ▶ Surgical operations performed on the brain in order to relieve psychological symptoms. The commonest operation is ▷leucotomy. In modern surgical procedures the area of the brain to be operated upon is located very accurately using three-dimensional measurements (stereotactic surgery). These are all irreversible treatments and are reserved for the most severe forms of mental illness that are resistant to other therapies.

● **psychotherapy** ▶ Psychological methods of treatment for mental disorders. There are many different approaches to psychotherapy, including ▷group therapy and family therapy, which involves several members of a family meeting together with a therapist to improve their relationships. These approaches share the goal of helping self-understanding and personal development, often with the therapist (who is usually not medically qualified) not giving direct advice. ▷*See also* aversion therapy; behaviour therapy; cognitive therapy; hypnosis.

● **Ptah** ▶ In ancient Egyptian mythology, the creator god. A local

deity of ▷Memphis, he was proclaimed the supreme god when Egypt was first unified (c. 3100 BC), but was later identified with ▷Osiris and became the patron of craftsmen. He is always shown in the form of a ▷mummy.

● **ptarmigan** ▶ A grouse, *Lagopus lagopus*, found in Arctic tundra and mountain regions. 35 cm long, it has white wings and a mottled blackish-brown body that changes to white in winter. Its feet are covered with feathers and it feeds on shoots and fruits in summer and on lichens and leaves dug from the snow in winter.

● **Pteranodon** ▶ An extinct flying reptile of the Cretaceous period (135–65 million years ago). 3 m long with a wingspan of 7.5 m, it had an enormous bony crest that balanced its large head. It lived around sea cliffs, clinging to them with its long hind claws and gliding over the sea to catch fish in its long toothless beak.

● **Pteraspis** ▶ An extinct genus of jawless fishlike vertebrates, belonging to the class *Ostracodermi*, that lived from the Ordovician to the Devonian periods (about 500–370 million years ago). The head and anterior part of the body were covered by a heavy bony shield, the remainder by small scales, and there was an upturned beaklike extension of the head (rostrum). Fins were placed singly, not in pairs. Subphylum: *Agnatha*.

● **pteridophyte** ▶ A flowerless perennial vascular plant that shows a distinct ▷alternation of generations with the asexual spore-bearing (sporophyte) generation predominating. The sporophyte plant consists typically of leaves, stems, and roots and bears spores in special capsules (sporangia), which are often arranged in clusters (sori) on the leaves. Pteridophytes were formerly classified together in the division *Pteridophyta*, but in most modern classification systems they are assigned to separate divisions (or phyla). They include the ▷clubmosses (*Lycophyta*), ▷horsetails (*Sphenophyta*), whisk ferns (*Psilophyta*; mostly extinct), and ▷ferns (*Filicinophyta*).

● **pterodactyl** ▷*See* pterosaur.

● **pterosaur** ▶ An extinct flying reptile, also called pterodactyl, that lived during the Jurassic and Cretaceous periods (200–65 million years ago). A thin wing membrane stretched from the elongated fourth finger of the fore limb along the body to the knee; a second membrane stretched to the neck. It had a compact body and long slender hind limbs, probably used to cling, batlike, to rocks and trees. Its light bones, toothless beaked jaw, large eyes, and large brain resembled those of modern birds. ⌐fossil.

● **PTFE** ▷*See* polytetrafluoroethene.

● **Ptolemaic system** ▶ A theory concerning the motions of the sun, moon, and planets that was originally advanced in Greece in the 3rd century BC and was completed by ▷Ptolemy in the 2nd century AD. It was a geocentric system in which the moon, Mercury, Venus, Sun, Mars, Jupiter, and Saturn moved around the earth. Prediction agreed reasonably well with observation. To achieve this Ptolemy had to propose that each orbiting body moved in a small circle (an epicycle) the centre of which moved in a larger circle (a deferent) around the earth. A sphere of stars lay beyond the seven deferents. The Ptolemaic system was finally abandoned when the ▷heliocentric system of ▷Copernicus was accepted.

● **Ptolemies** ▶ A Macedonian dynasty that ruled Egypt from 323 BC, when ▷Ptolemy I Soter became governor of Egypt, until 30 BC, when Ptolemy XV Caesar (or Caesarion; 47–30 BC; reigned 44–30 BC), the son of Cleopatra and, perhaps, Caesar, was executed by Octavian (later ▷Augustus).

● **Ptolemy** ▶ (*or* Claudius Ptolemaeus; 2nd century AD) Egyptian mathematician, astronomer, and geographer. Little is known of his life except that he lived and worked in Alexandria, probably publishing his major works between 127 and 145. The foremost of these outlines the ▷Ptolemaic system of astronomy and was originally known as *He mathematike syntaxis* (*The Mathematical Collection*) but it was known to Arab astronomers by the Greek superlative *Megiste*, which took the Arab form *Almagest*. His other works include *Analemma* and *Planisphaerium* on geometry, *Harmonica* on music, and *Geographike hyphegesis*, on geography.

● **Ptolemy I Soter** ▶ (?367–?283 BC) The first Macedonian King of

Egypt and founder of the dynasty of the ▷Ptolemies. He was a general of Alexander the Great, after whose death he became governor of Egypt. He conquered Palestine, Cyprus, and much of Asia Minor, taking the title of king in 304. He founded the library of Alexandria, his capital, and wrote a history of Alexander's campaigns.

● **Ptolemy II Philadelphus** ▶ (308–246 BC) King of Egypt (285–246); the son and successor of Ptolemy I. He and his second wife and sister ▷Arsinoe II fought unsuccessfully with Syria. He completed ▷Alexandria, restored the Nile–Red Sea canal, and introduced camels into Egypt.

● **Ptolemy XIII Theos Philopator** ▶ (63–47 BC) King of Egypt (51–47), ruling jointly with his sister and wife ▷Cleopatra VII until he and his advisers expelled her (48). He murdered ▷Pompey, hoping for ▷Caesar's favour, but when Caesar reinstated Cleopatra, Ptolemy opposed him and was killed.

● **ptomaines** ▶ Compounds formed during bacterial decomposition of proteins in animal and plant tissues. Most are amines, such as diethylamine, putrescine, and cadaverine; they may be poisonous, but the symptoms ascribed to "ptomaine poisoning" are usually due to bacterial toxins in contaminated food (*see* food poisoning).

● **puberty** ▶ The onset of sexual maturity. The age at which this occurs is very variable but is usually between 12 and 17 in boys and between 10 and 16 in girls. The sexual organs develop to their adult form and pubic hair starts to grow; in girls the menstrual periods begin (menarche). The secondary sexual characteristics develop: in girls the breasts enlarge and in boys the muscles enlarge, the voice deepens, and facial hair grows. Psychological changes include an increase in sexual drive and in anxiety and insecurity.

● **public examinations** ▶ In the UK (except Scotland), secondary school pupils take the ▷GCSE around the age of 16. They formerly took the A-level exam two years later. Advanced Supplementary level (AS-level) exams were introduced in 1989, covering half the syllabus of the full A-level. Since 2000 the AS-level (now called Advanced Subsidiary level) is taken as a one year course either on its own or as the first year of the full A-level, the second year of which is known as the A2-level. Most universities require three full A-levels as an entry qualification; some require an additional AS-level. National Vocational Qualifications (NVQs) recognize proficiency in a particular trade or profession; the General National Vocational Qualification (GNVQ), which was introduced in 1992, is for those wishing to explore a range of employment options. In Scotland pupils take examinations for the Scottish Certificate of Education (SCE) at Standard grade (16+). A new system of academic and vocational qualifications is currently (2000–2002) being phased in to replace the old SCE Higher grade (17+) and the Certificate of Sixth-Year Studies (CSYS). Degrees are awarded by ▷universities.

● **Public Record Office** ▶ (PRO) The UK government archives, established in 1838. Formerly archives were stored in over 50 different buildings, including the Tower of London and Westminster Abbey. Sir James Pennethorne's mock-Tudor building in Chancery Lane opened in 1860. In 1977 records of government departments from after 1782 were moved to a new building in Kew and by the early 1990s the remaining archives had also been transferred there. Records are not made publicly available until they are at least 30 years old.

● **public relations** ▶ Efforts by firms, organizations, individuals, etc., to present a good public image. Good public relations are achieved by prompt servicing of complaints and enquiries from the public, involvement in local affairs, sponsorship of charities, etc. A public relations officer (PRO) may be appointed to ensure that these tasks are carried out and to promote his employer in the media.

● **Public Safety, Committee of** ▶ A governing body during the French Revolution. It was established to meet the emergency when a coalition of European powers attacked France after the king's execution (1793). Under Robespierre, it conducted the ▷Reign of Terror. After Robespierre's fall in July 1794, its powers were curtailed.

● **public school** ▶ In the USA, a school that is not under private ownership or control; in the UK the name somewhat misleadingly refers to certain fee-paying ▷independent schools, usually boarding schools with a well-established reputation. Although traditionally

male preserves, most public schools now admit girls, especially at sixth-form level, and a number of well-known independent girls' schools were established in the 19th century; entrance is usually at 13. Although a few public schools date back to the 16th century, it was not until the reforms of Frederick Temple (1821–1902), Henry Montagu Butler (1833–1918), and Thomas ▷Arnold in the 19th century that the demand for public-school places grew; by the time of the Clarendon Commission (1864), only nine schools were considered to enjoy such status. Any school the headteacher of which is a member of the Headmasters' and Headmistresses' Conference, the Governing Bodies Association, or the Governing Bodies of Girls' Schools Association is now regarded as a public school, making the total number about 200, although this includes many of the former direct-grant schools (state-assisted schools that have either been incorporated into the state system or become independent). Although many of the schools maintain high academic standards they have been criticized for their divisive perpetuation of the class system.

● **public sector** ▶ Those parts of the economy that are financed out of taxation, are under state control, or both. It usually embraces central and local government, education, health and social services, police and armed forces, public institutions, and any nationalized industries. In the UK and many other countries certain businesses essential to the life of the community, such as the public utilities, were formerly nationalized but are now privately owned and administered (*see* privatization); state ownership of shares in others may also represent a form of ▷nationalization. The amount by which the receipts of the public sector, including ▷taxation, fall short of public expenditure constitutes the Public Sector Borrowing Requirement.

● **publishing** ▶ The commissioning, production, and distribution of ▷books, periodicals, and ▷newspapers. Before the invention of printing, reading matter was produced by hand in the form of papyrus rolls in ancient Egypt, Greece, and Rome, and later in the form of manuscripts copied by hand. With the invention of printing by ▷Gutenberg, early printed books (*see* incunabula) were sold by the printer, who also functioned as publisher and bookseller. During the 15th and 16th centuries these functions began to separate; the Netherlands was one of the earliest centres of book publishing and the house founded by Louis Elzevir (1540–1617) is still active in Haarlem. After the introduction of the Copyright Act (1709), book publishing, which had previously been financed largely by rich patrons, expanded in the UK and the USA as an independent industry.

The growth of libraries, the spread of literacy, and technical innovations in printing and papermaking during the 19th century enabled the independent publisher to flourish. In 1896 Sir Frederick Macmillan, son of the founder of the firm of Macmillan, combined with other British publishers to set up the Publishers Association, one of the first tasks of which was to negotiate the Net Book Agreement (1899), which controlled the prices at which booksellers could sell books. During the 1990s this was challenged by publishers and booksellers, despite fears that without it supermarkets could sell popular books at a discount, depriving bookshops of the profitable sales that enable them to stock slow-moving books. The Agreement was abandoned in 1995. During the 20th century the main innovation in the UK and the USA was the cheap paperback. The advent of book clubs also expanded the market, especially for nonfiction. ▷Electronic publishing is a more recent innovation. Many reference books are now available on ▷compact discs and on the Internet. In addition new viewing devices are available that allow whole books to be downloaded from Internet sites and viewed on a small portable "electronic book."

● **Puccini, Giacomo** ▶ (1858–1924) Italian opera composer. He was a church organist before studying at the Milan conservatoire with Amilcare Ponchielli (1834–86). His first success was *Manon Lescaut* (1893). The operas that followed established him as the master of *verismo* (Italian: realism): *La Bohème* (1896), *Tosca* (1900), and *Madame Butterfly* (1904). *La fanciulla del West* (1910) and the three one-act operas of *Il Trittico* (1918) were less successful. His final work, *Turandot* (produced in 1926), was completed by Franco Alfano (1876–1954).

● **Pucelle, Jean** ▶ (?1300–?1355) French miniature painter and manuscript illuminator. His best-known works are the *Belleville Bre-*

viary and *The Hours of Jeanne d'Évreux* (Metropolitan Museum, New York), the latter being a prayer book commissioned by the French queen.

● **puck** ▶ In English folklore, a household spirit, malicious fairy, or demon. The famous Puck of Shakespeare's *A Midsummer Night's Dream* is identified with the mischievous fairy Robin Goodfellow.

● **puddling process** ▶ A method of making pure iron from ▷pig iron. The pig iron is melted in a furnace and powdered iron oxide is stirred in to drive off the slag. As the iron becomes purer, its melting point increases and eventually it forms a pasty mass, which is removed and hammered or rolled into shape. Puddling superseded ▷wrought-iron working by hand and its introduction was an important contribution to the industrial revolution, although it is now little used.

● **Pudovkin, Vsevolod** ▶ (1893–1953) Russian film director. He is best known for his silent films, especially *Mother* (1926), *The End of St Petersburg* (1927), and *Storm Over Asia* (1928). He published influential lectures concerning the technique of montage.

● **Puebla** ▶ (*or* Puebla de Zaragoza) 19 03N 98 10W A city in S Mexico. Strategically situated on the route between Mexico City and Veracruz, it was an important fortress city for several centuries. Notable buildings include an ornate cathedral (1649) and the Teatro Principal (1790). A major agricultural and industrial centre, Puebla is famous for its onyx products. Population (1990): 1 454 526.

● **Pueblo** ▶ 38 17N 104 38W A city in the USA, in Colorado on the Arkansas River. Established in 1842, it developed on the arrival of the railway (1872) and has important steel industries, which use local coal. Other industrial activities include oil refining and meat packing. Population (1996 est): 99 406.

● **Pueblo Indians** ▶ North American Indian tribes of the SW region including the Tewa, Keres, ▷Hopi, and Zuni. Their collective name derives from the Spanish term for their villages—*pueblos*. They began to abandon their hunting existence and adopt their present farming economy about 1600 years ago. They were always extremely peaceful peoples, much given to ritual and ceremonial pursuits. Their villages are often constructed around a central courtyard; the buildings, made from mudbrick blocks, have several storeys, each set back from the one below. Communities were traditionally governed by a council of the heads of the various secret religious societies, which met in underground rooms called kivas. The diversity of Pueblo languages indicates different origins.

● **puerperal depression** ▷*See* postnatal depression.

● **puerperal fever** ▶ Persistent fever occurring in a woman soon after childbirth, most commonly caused by infection of the genital tract, particularly of the lining of the womb. The infection may be serious and progress to blood poisoning. Formerly many women died of puerperal fever, but with improved hygiene and antibiotics the disease is now rare and can be cured by prompt treatment with antibiotics.

● **Puerto de Mahón** ▷*See* Mahón.

● **Puerto Rico, Commonwealth of** ▶ (name from 1898 until 1932: Porto Rico) An island and self-governing commonwealth in association with the USA. It is in the West Indies, the smallest and most easterly island in the Greater Antilles. It is largely mountainous, rising over 1200 m (3937 ft) and supports one of the densest populations in the world.
Economy: rapid industrialization has taken place since the 1940s transforming the economy from a basically agricultural one to a mixed one. Manufacture (chemicals, textiles, plastics, food processing) is the main source of income, while in the agricultural sector income from dairy and livestock farming has overtaken that of sugar, the principal crop. Tourism is an important source of revenue.
History: inhabited by Arawak Indians when discovered by Columbus in 1493, it was under Spanish rule for nearly 400 years until ceded to the USA in 1898. Full US citizenship was granted in 1917 and it attained its present status in 1952, which was ratified by a plebiscite (1967). During the 1940s and 1950s emigration to the USA was high but later moderated. In 1976 the New Progressive Party regained

governorship and legislative control, led by Carlos Romero Barceló (1932–   ), who advocates Puerto Rico becoming a state of the USA. Since 1974 there has been militant pressure for the independence of Puerto Rico and in 1978 the UN special committee on decolonization reaffirmed the right of Puerto Ricans to self-determination. In 1993 and 1998 Puerto Ricans voted against US statehood and against independence, choosing to maintain their current status. Official language: Spanish; English is also widely spoken. Official currency: US dollar of 100 cents. Area: 8674 sq km (3349 sq mi). Population (1997 est): 3 809 000. Capital: San Juan.

● **Pufendorf, Samuel von** ▶ (1632–94) German jurist, philosopher, and historian, known for his contribution to natural and international law. A professor at Heidelberg and later at Lund, he became historiographer to the Swedish court in 1677 and to the Elector of Brandenburg in 1688. In his best-known work, *De Jure naturae et gentium* (1672), influenced by ▷Grotius and ▷Hobbes, he argued that all men are entitled to be free and equal and that international law is not restricted to Christendom but is common to all nationalities. His *De habitu religionis christianae ad vitam civilem* (1687) advocated state superiority over the church in civil affairs.

● **puff adder** ▶ A large stout-bodied highly venomous ▷adder belonging to the genus *Bitis* (8 species), occurring in semiarid areas of Africa and characterized by its habit of hissing loudly and inflating its body in a threatening posture. 0.3–2 m long, puff adders are brown or grey with yellow chevron patterning.

● **puffball** ▶ The globular or pear-shaped fruiting body of certain fungi. As it matures, the outer layer cracks and sloughs off; the spongy interior produces powdery spores, which are released either through a pore (genus *Lycoperdon*) or from the upper surface (genus *Calvatia*). The greyish-white giant puffball (*C. giganteum*) occurs in pastures, woodlands, and road verges and may reach over 1 m across. Phylum: ▷*Basidiomycota*.

● **puffer** ▶ A □fish, also called globe fish, belonging to the family *Tetraodontidae*, that inflates its body with air or water when disturbed. The tough spiny skin contains a highly toxic chemical (tetraodontoxin), which can be fatal. Up to 50 cm long, puffers live mainly in tropical and subtropical seas, feeding on corals, molluscs, and crustaceans using their beaklike snouts. They are edible if expertly prepared. Order: *Tetraodontiformes*.

● **puffin** ▶ A N Atlantic seabird, *Fratercula arctica*. 29 cm long, it is black with a white face and underparts, red legs, and a blue ring around the eye. Its large triangular bill is striped red, yellow, and blue in the breeding season. It feeds at sea on fish and molluscs and breeds in disused rabbit burrows. Family: *Alcidae* (auks). □ p. 1024.

● **pug** ▶ A breed of toy □dog originating in China and introduced to Britain from Holland in the 17th century. It is stockily built, with the tail curled over the back, and has a wrinkled skin and a large head with a short square muzzle. The short smooth coat can be silver, black, or apricot-fawn with a black mask on the face and a black line along the back. Height: 25–28 cm.

● **Pugachov, Yemelyan Ivanovich** ▶ (1726–75) The leader of a Cossack rebellion in Russia, the Pugachov Rebellion (1773–74). Claiming to be the assassinated Tsar Peter III (1728–62; reigned 1762), Pugachov raised a revolt against the government of ▷Catherine (II) the Great. The revolt collapsed and Pugachov was beheaded.

● **Pugin, Augustus Welby Northmore** ▶ (1812–52) British architect and theorist. Pugin was the most vocal exponent of the English ▷gothic revival, particularly in his most influential book, *Contrasts* (1836), which exalted the English ▷Decorated style (late 13th to early 14th centuries) above all other architectural forms. As an architect he was most accomplished at designing churches, such as Nottingham Cathedral (1842). However, he is best known for his collaboration with ▷Barry on the ▷Palace of Westminster, being responsible for the interior design.

● **Puglia** ▷*See* Apulia.

● **Pugwash Conferences** ▶ International conferences on science and world affairs, convened at the suggestion of, among others, Albert Einstein and Bertrand Russell, that discuss the problems of

▷disarmament and the social responsibility of scientists. The first conference was held in Pugwash, Nova Scotia (Canada), in 1957.

puffin ► The bill of this bird, which breeds in large colonies, is armed with serrations that enable it to carry 30–40 fish at a time. Puffins will continue to bring food to the nest even after the young have left.

● **P'u-i, Henry** ▷*See* Pu Yi, Henry.

● **Pula** ► (Italian name: Pola) 44 52N 13 52E A port in NW Croatia, on the Adriatic coast. An important Austrian naval base (1815–1918), it subsequently belonged to Italy before passing to Yugoslavia in 1947. There are many ancient buildings, including a Roman amphitheatre. Industries include shipbuilding. Population (1991): 62 300.

● **Pulci, Luigi** ► (1432–84) Italian poet. He lived mostly at the court of Lorenzo de' ▷Medici and wrote all his works in Italian. His major work is the epic poem *Morgante* (1483), a colloquial and irreverently comic treatment of French chivalric material concerning Roland (*see* Charlemagne).

● **puli** ► A Hungarian breed of sheepdog whose unique coat hangs to the ground in long tight cords. The puli is agile and lively; its tail is held over the back and its coat is usually black but may be bronze-black, grey, or white. Height: 41–46 cm (dogs); 36–41 cm (bitches).

● **Pulitzer Prizes** ► Annual awards endowed by the US publisher Joseph Pulitzer (1847–1911) for achievements in journalism and literature. The prizes for journalism, including awards for investigative reporting and criticism, and those for literature, including awards for fiction and poetry etc., were first awarded in 1917. Since 1943 a prize for musical composition has also been awarded.

● **Pullman, George Mortimer** ► (1831–97) US businessman, who invented the luxurious Pullman sleeping car for railways. His first such car, the Pioneer, was made in 1865.

● **Pullman, Philip** ► (1946–) British author. He writes primarily for older children, but has attracted readers of all ages. He is best known for *His Dark Materials*, a trilogy of fantasy novels comprising *Northern Lights* (1997), *The Subtle Knife* (1999), and *The Amber Spyglass* (2000). The last-named work won the Whitbread Prize in 2002.

● **pulsar** ► A celestial object that emits extremely regular pulses of radiation and is almost certainly a rotating ▷neutron star. Pulsars were originally discovered, in 1967, at radio wavelengths. The Crab and Vela pulsars also emit pulses at optical and gamma-ray wavelengths. The pulses arise when a beam of radio waves emitted by the rotating star sweeps past the earth, similar to the way in which lighthouse flashes are produced. The radiation (synchrotron radiation) is generated by electrons moving in the star's strong magnetic field; the emission site is still uncertain. The pulsation periods, ranging from less than 2 milliseconds to 4 seconds, are all very gradually increasing. Pulsars are thought to originate in ▷supernovae. X-ray pulsars also exist but apparently involve a neutron star as a component of a close binary star; their pulsation periods are much longer, up to several minutes, and are gradually decreasing.

● **pulsating stars** ▷*See* variable star.

● **pulse** ► The rhythmic contraction and expansion of the elastic walls of the arteries caused by the pressure of blood pumped from the heart. The pulse therefore reflects the heart rate and can be readily felt in arteries just beneath the skin: it is usually measured at the radial artery in the wrist. The average pulse rate of a resting adult is 60–80 per minute; it increases with exercise and emotion. The pulse also becomes faster during a fever and irregular in heart-rhythm disorders. A reduction in blood pressure (e.g. after haemorrhage) will cause a fast feeble pulse.

● **puma** ▷*See* cougar.

● **pumice** ► A volcanic rock derived from acidic lava. It resembles sponge in having many cavities produced by bubbles of gas trapped on rapid solidification. Pumice is light in colour and weight and often floats on water.

● **pumped storage** ▷*See* hydroelectric power.

● **pumpkin** ► The fruit of certain varieties of *Cucurbita pepo* and *C. maxima*, small bushes or trailing vines cultivated in North America and Europe. The fruit is large and round, up to 30 kg in weight with a lightly furrowed yellow rind surrounding an edible fleshy pulp and numerous seeds. It is cooked and eaten as a vegetable, in pies, puddings, and soups or used as animal feed. Family: *Cucurbitaceae*.

● **pumps** ► Machines designed to transfer mechanical energy to a fluid. This energy may be required to move the fluid from one place to another, raise its level, increase its pressure, or provide circulation. Pumps are of three kinds: reciprocating, centrifugal, and rotary displacement. The reciprocating pump consists of a piston moving to and fro; liquid is drawn in through one valve on the down stroke, and expelled through an exhaust valve on the upstroke. The centrifugal pump draws liquid into the centre of a rotating impeller, which thrusts it out of the exit. Rotating pumps consist of shaped gears or rotors, which move the liquid around a close-fitting chamber.

● **Punch and Judy** ► A British puppet show performed with glove puppets and featuring the violent quarrels of the heartless Punch and his wife Judy. The character of Punch, who wears a striped costume and has a hooked nose and a humped back, derives from the Italian ▷commedia dell'arte and was popularized in England by Italian puppeteers in the late 17th century.

● **Pune** ▷*See* Poona.

● **Punic Wars** ► Three wars between Rome and Carthage, which gave Rome control of the Mediterranean. The first Punic (from the Latin *Punicus*, Carthaginian) War (264–241 BC) was provoked by Roman intervention in Sicily and was marked by the emergence of Roman naval power: its newly built fleet was victorious off Mylae (260) and again off the Aegates Insulae (241), which brought the war to an end with Carthage's evacuation of Sicily. The second Punic War (218–201) was instigated by ▷Hannibal's capture (219) of Saguntum, a Roman ally in Spain. His advance into Italy was eventually checked, after disastrous Roman losses at Trebia (218), Trasimene (217), and ▷Cannae (216), by ▷Fabius Maximus and ▷Scipio Africanus, who defeated Hannibal at Zama (202). Carthage gave up its Spanish conquests and became a dependent ally of Rome. Roman fears of a resurgence of Carthaginian power caused the third Punic War (149–146), in which Carthage was destroyed and its territory became the Roman province of Africa.

● **Punjab** ► A region of the NW Indian subcontinent, in India and Pakistan below the Himalayan foothills on the flat alluvial plain of five Indus tributaries. Hot and dry, it produces grain surpluses with irrigation. Pulses, cotton, sugar cane, oilseeds, fruit, and vegetables are also grown. Industries include textiles, bicycles, electrical and metal goods, machinery, and food products. The region is comparatively urbanized. Its population is 60% Sikh in India's Punjab state, and almost entirely Muslim in Pakistan's Punjab province.

History: on the invasion route into India, the Punjab passed successively under different rulers. It was conquered by Muslims (11th century) but eventually became a Sikh stronghold until Britain established control (19th century). On the partition of India and Pakistan (1947), the Punjab was divided on a religious basis. This led to massacres and mass migration. The W section became the Pakistan province of West Punjab (renamed Punjab in 1949), with an area of 205 346 sq km (79 284 sq mi) and its capital at Lahore; its population in 1985 was 53 840 000. The Indian section was reorganized in 1956 and 1966 on a linguistic basis when the Punjabi-speaking state of Punjab was created, 50 376 sq km (19 445 sq mi), with its capital at Chandigarh; its population in 1994 was estimated at 21 695 000. From 1987 to 1992 the national government assumed direct control of the state after violence between Sikhs and Hindus.

● **Punjabi** ► An ▷Indo-Aryan language of the ▷Punjab. It is similar to ▷Hindi and written in the Devanagari script or in the Gumurki script of the Sikh scriptures.

● **punk rock** ▷*See* pop music.

● **Punt, land of** ► A country with which the ancient Egyptians traded from 2750 BC for gold, ivory, incense, and spices. It was probably situated on the Somali coast of NE Africa.

● **Punta Arenas** ► 53 10S 70 56W A port in S Chile, on the Strait of Magellan. It serves a large sheep-rearing area. Exports include hides, wool, mutton, lumber, and oil. Population (1990 est): 50 000.

● **pupa** ► A stage in the life cycle of certain insects, including flies, butterflies (in which it is the chrysalis), ants, bees, and beetles, during which ▷metamorphosis from larva to adult takes place. The adult emerges by cutting or digesting the pupal case after a few days or several months.

● **pupil** ▷*See* eye; iris.

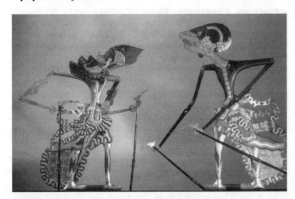

puppetry ► Javanese shadow puppets (18th century). The wooden puppets have movable arms and are manipulated from below with rods. They feature in popular all-night performances, usually based on ancient Hindu epics.

● **puppetry** ► The art of manipulating puppets or marionettes in a dramatic performance. Puppets were used in religious ritual and folk drama in many early civilizations and still have this function in Java and parts of India. In Japan, the form of puppet theatre known as *Bunraku* or *Joruri* and developed by Chikamatsu Monzaemon (1653–1724) is still actively maintained. Introduced into England from Italy in the late 17th century, puppet theatre flourished throughout Europe during the 18th century and enjoyed an artistic revival in the late 19th and early 20th centuries.

● **Purbeck, Isle of** ► A peninsula in S England, in Dorset between the English Channel and Poole Harbour. Purbeck marble, a limestone used in building, is quarried here.

● **Purcell, Edward Mills** ► (1912–97) US physicist, who shared the 1952 Nobel Prize with Felix ▷Bloch for their independent measurements of the magnetic moments of nuclei in solids and liquids. He

also worked in astronomy, discovering an important emission by interstellar hydrogen in the microwave region.

● **Purcell, Henry** ► (1659–95) English composer and organist. He was a choirboy at the Chapel Royal and a pupil of John Blow, whom he succeeded as organist of Westminster Abbey in 1679. In 1677 he was appointed composer to the orchestra of the Chapel Royal and, in 1682, organist there. He wrote keyboard pieces, sonatas, anthems, songs, cantatas, and much music for the stage, including incidental music for *King Arthur* (1691) and *The Fairy Queen* (1692) and one opera, *Dido and Aeneas* (1689).

● **Purchas, Samuel** ► (1577–1626) English clergyman and compiler of travel books. He continued the work of ▷Hakluyt, whose papers he inherited, in collecting accounts of voyages of trade and exploration. His major work is *Hakluytus Posthumus, or Purchas His Pilgrimes* (4 vols, 1625), which is now mainly known for having inspired Coleridge's *Kubla Khan*.

● **purchase tax** ► An indirect tax on goods calculated by adding a percentage to the wholesale price of the goods. The tax was introduced in the UK in 1940 for certain classes of consumer goods and was replaced by ▷value-added tax in 1973.

● **purdah** ► The custom in some Muslim and Hindu communities of keeping women secluded and insisting that they wear clothing that conceals them completely (*chuddar*) when they leave their homes. The word "purdah" comes from the Hindi *parda*, veil, and the Persian *pardah*, curtain. With the westernization of many Asian and Middle-Eastern communities purdah was dropped and women and men mixed on an equal basis. However, in the 1980s in Iran, the fundamentalist regime imposed the *chuddar* on women again and other Muslim states have followed this lead. The issue of whether or not Muslim and Hindu women should enjoy the complete equality encouraged by Western societies is still a hotly debated issue in Islamic and some Hindu communities.

● **Pure Land Buddhism** ► A popular E Asian devotional form of Mahayana Buddhism, originating in China in the 4th century AD. Its adherents, following the Sukhavativyuha sutras, believe that by reciting the name of Amitabha, the Buddha of Infinite Light, they will be reborn in the Pure Land in the West (Sukhavati), which he has created.

● **purgatives** ▷*See* laxatives.

● **purgatory** ► In Roman Catholic doctrine, the state in which souls are purified after death to make them fit for heaven. Masses or prayers for the dead are believed to shorten a soul's purgatorial sufferings. The doctrine of purgatory was officially adopted by the Church in the late 6th century, but at the Reformation the Protestants rejected the concept, holding that souls either go directly to heaven or hell or sleep until the Last Judgment.

● **Puri** ► 19 49N 85 54E A port in India, in Orissa on the Bay of Bengal. A major religious centre, it holds many festivals and has an exceptional 12th-century temple. Population (1991): 125 199.

● **Purim** ► A Jewish festival, commemorating the frustration of an attempt to exterminate the Jews of the Persian Empire (473 BC), as narrated in the book of Esther. It is celebrated on the 14th Adar (Feb–March), with lighthearted festivities and charitable gifts. The scroll (*megillah*) of Esther is read in synagogues.

● **purine** ► An organic nitrogenous base ($C_5H_4N_4$) consisting of a two-ringed molecule of carbon and nitrogen atoms. The derivatives adenine and guanine are constituents of the nucleic acids ▷DNA and ▷RNA. ▷Uric acid and ▷caffeine are also purines.

● **purism** ► An art movement launched in 1918 by the manifesto, *Après le Cubisme*, of the painter Amédée Ozenfant (1886–1966) and the architect and painter ▷Le Corbusier. Their aim was to purify ▷cubism by stripping it of its decorative features and basing their austere geometrical shapes on machine forms.

● **Puritanism** ► A movement among Protestants in 16th- and 17th-century England. The term originally denoted members of the Church of England in Elizabeth I's reign who wished to eliminate elements in the Church's liturgy and hierarchy that were reminiscent of

Roman Catholicism (*see* Marprelate Tracts). In the 17th century Puritan criticism of the Anglican episcopacy was intensified by ▷Laud's policies, and the Puritans, many of them now forming extremist sects (*see* Fifth Monarchy Men; Levellers), became associated with the parliamentarian side in the Civil War. After the Act of Uniformity (1662) the term ▷Nonconformists became generally applied to the sects of Puritan origin that survived, such as the ▷Quakers.

● **Purple Heart** ▶ US military decoration, established as the Badge of Military Merit by George Washington in 1782 and awarded during the American Revolution. Reinstituted in 1932, it is awarded to those wounded in battle. It is a purple heart of cloth, bordered by bronze.

● **purpura** ▶ Localized limited bleeding into the skin, causing a rash of purple spots. This is a common and harmless condition of the elderly (senile purpura). Purpura may also result from reactions to drugs and infections, scurvy, autoimmunity, and an allergic disease of childhood called Henoch-Schönlein purpura. A deficiency of blood platelets (important in clotting) also leads to purpura.

● **purslane** ▶ An annual herbaceous plant, *Portulaca oleracea*, with prostrate reddish stems bearing fleshy oval leaves and dense terminal clusters of tiny pink flowers. It is widespread as a weed and has been used as a culinary herb. Family: *Portulacaceae*.

Sea purslane (*Halimione portulacoides*) is a shrubby perennial of temperate salt marshes, with greyish oval leaves and heads of tiny golden flowers. Family: *Chenopodiaceae*. *Honkenya peploides*, also called sea purslane, is a creeping perennial of N temperate sandy beaches. It has pointed fleshy leaves and small five-petalled white flowers on short stalks, surrounded by fleshy sepals. Family: *Caryophyllaceae*.

● **Purus, Rio** ▶ A river in NW South America, rising in SE Peru and flowing generally NE through Brazil to the River Amazon. Length: about 3200 km (2000 mi).

● **pus** ▶ Thick yellow fluid that arises in infected areas and contains dead bacteria, dead white blood cells, serum, and damaged tissue. It is formed as a result of the body's defensive action against invading bacteria and other particles. Pus is present in boils and similar skin conditions but can be formed anywhere in the body (*see* abscess).

● **Pusan** ▶ 35 05N 129 02E A port in SE South Korea, on the Korea Strait, capital of South Kyongsang province and South Korea's second largest city. It is the site of a state and a private university. Its varied industries include shipbuilding. Population (1995): 3 813 814.

● **Pusey, Edward Bouverie** ▶ (1800–82) British leader of the ▷Oxford Movement. A Fellow of Oriel College, Pusey was ordained in 1828 and in the same year became professor of Hebrew at Oxford. In 1833 he joined the movement at Oriel to revive the Catholic tradition in the Anglican Church. He became its leader in 1841, when John Henry ▷Newman was converted to Roman Catholicism.

● **Pushkin** ▶ (name from 1708 until 1937: Tsarskoye Selo) 59 43N 30 22E A town in NW Russia, 24 km (14 mi) S of St Petersburg, with which it was joined by Russia's first railway (1837). Founded in 1708 by Peter the Great, it was the site of the imperial summer residence, and Catherine the Great's palace (1748–62) is still to be seen. In 1937 it was renamed after the Russian poet. It has manufacturing industries and a botanical institute. Population (latest est): 97 000.

● **Pushkin, Aleksandr** ▶ (1799–1837) Russian poet, novelist, and dramatist. In 1820 he was exiled to the south for his political verse. In exile he wrote two long Romantic poems strongly influenced by Byron and began the epic verse novel *Eugene Onegin* (1833), on which Tchaikovsky based his opera (1877–78). In 1824 he was transferred to NW Russia, where he wrote the historical drama *Boris Godunov* (1831), which became the basis of Mussorgsky's opera (1874). After his return to Moscow in 1826 he was still hindered by censorship, but during his last years he wrote the epic poem *The Bronze Horseman* (1837) as well as lyrical poetry and several prose works. He was killed in a duel. Pushkin was the most versatile and influential of Russian writers; he broke with artificial conventions, established new genres and themes, and made Russian a highly adaptable literary medium.

● **Pushtu** ▷*See* Pashto.

● **puss moth** ▶ A moth, *Cerura vinula*, of Europe, Asia, and N Africa. The adult has a fat white hairy body with black spots. The caterpillar

is green with black markings; when alarmed it raises its head and tail in a warning display. It feeds on sallow, willow, and poplar.

● **Putin, Vladimir (Vladimirovich)** ▶ (1952–) Russian statesman; president (2000–). A former KGB colonel, he became head of Russia's security services in 1998 and prime minister in 1999. Appointed acting president on ▷Yeltsin's resignation (31 December, 1999), he became full president following elections in March 2000. His crushing of the revolt in ▷Chechenia (1999–2000) was criticized in the West but highly popular in Russia.

● **Putrajaya** ▶ 2 80N 101 40E The new administrative capital (since 1999) of Malaysia, situated about 35 km (22 m) S of Kuala Lumpur in Selanghor province. The construction of this high-tech garden city began in 1995 and is expected to be complete by 2010, when it will provide housing for some 330 000 people.

● **putrefaction** ▶ The decomposition of organic matter, particularly of proteins by bacteria under anaerobic conditions (i.e. in the absence of oxygen). Putrefaction is associated with a characteristic bad smell, produced by the amines, ammonia, hydrogen sulphide, and other compounds that are formed.

● **Puttnam, David (Terence), Baron** ▶ (1941–) British film producer. His films of the 1980s did much to boost the British film industry; he was also chairman (1986–87) of Columbia Pictures in Hollywood. His films include *Midnight Express* (1978), *Chariots of Fire* (1981), *The Killing Fields* (1984), *The Mission* (1986), *Memphis Belle* (1990), and *Being Human* (1993). He was made a life peer in 1997.

● **putty** ▶ A mixture of boiled linseed oil and powdered calcium carbonate (whiting) used as a cement. Of doughlike consistency, it is used for cementing glass in windows.

● **Putumayo, Río** ▶ A river in South America. Rising in the Colombian Andes, it flows generally SE forming most of the border between Colombia and Peru. On entering Brazil it is known as the Rio Içá before joining the River Amazon. Length: 1578 km (980 mi).

● **Puvis de Chavannes, Pierre (Cécile)** ▶ (1824–98) French painter. He was an independent artistic figure but an important influence on ▷Seurat and ▷Gauguin. He is famous for his murals, notably *The Life of S Genevieve* (Panthéon, Paris), and for his painting *The Poor Fisherman* (Louvre). Imitating in oil the pale colours and simplified forms of frescoes, he chiefly painted allegorical subjects.

● **Pu Yi, Henry** ▶ (*or* H. P'u-i; 1906–67) The last emperor of China (1908–12) as Xuan-tong (*or* Hsuan-t'ung). He became emperor at the age of two and abdicated three years later after the republican revolution of 1911. He was allowed to live in the summer palace on a government pension until the Japanese made him ruler, as Kang-de (*or* K'ang-te), of ▷Manchukuo (1934–45).

● **PVC** ▷*See* polyvinyl chloride.

● **Pycnogonida** ▷*See* sea spider.

● **pyelitis** ▶ Infection of the central part of the kidney, where the urine collects before passing to the ureter. Infection may spread through the blood or up to the kidney from the bladder. The patient usually has a fever and loin pain and produces urine containing protein, white blood cells, and sometimes red blood cells. In some cases the infection spreads to the rest of the kidney (**pyelonephritis**). The infection will normally settle with antibiotics, but repeated infections may lead to kidney failure and ▷uraemia.

● **Pygmalion** ▶ In Greek mythology, a king of Cyprus who made an ivory statue (known as Galatea in modern versions) and fell in love with it. When he prayed for a wife who would be as beautiful as the statue, Aphrodite gave the statue life and Pygmalion married her.

● **Pygmies** ▶ Peoples of the tropical forest region of Africa, who are much smaller in stature than their Bantu neighbours. The males are less than 150 cm (4 ft 11 in) in height. They are nomadic hunters and gatherers, wandering in small and basically patrilineal exogamous bands of around 30 members. They use either the bow and arrow or, more usually, nets and spears. There are no chiefs, decisions being made by consensus. They speak Bantu languages.

● **pygmy hippopotamus** ▶ A small ▷hippopotamus, *Choeropsis liberiensis*, of West African forests. Up to 100 cm high at the shoulder and weighing about 200 kg, pygmy hippos are less aquatic and more solitary than their larger relatives. They frequent river banks, feeding in the forest at night.

● **pygmy owl** ▶ A very small ▷owl belonging to a widely distributed genus (*Glaucidium*; 12 species). About 16 cm long, pygmy owls hunt small mammals, birds, and insects, which may be larger than themselves.

● **Pylos** ▶ (Greek name: Pílos) 36 55N 21 42E A seaport (also called Navarino) in W Greece, on the Peloponnesian coast. It lies at the S end of Órmos Navarínou (Bay of Navarino), scene of two important battles: the Athenian victory over the Spartans during the Peloponnesian War (425 BC) and the decisive battle of ▷Navarino (1827) in the War of Greek Independence. The Mycenaean town associated with the legendary King ▷Nestor lies N of the modern town. Here excavations revealed a well-preserved palace and archive of ▷Linear B tablets.

● **Pym, John** ▶ (?1583–1643) English parliamentary opponent of Charles I; he sat in every parliament from 1621 until his death. In the ▷Long Parliament he helped to impeach ▷Strafford and to draw up the ▷Grand Remonstrance (1641) and was one of the five MPs whom Charles tried to arrest (1642). After the outbreak of the Civil War he organized supplies to the parliamentary forces.

● **Pynchon, Thomas** ▶ (1937–) US novelist. He was acclaimed as one of the most original and ambitious writers to emerge in the 1960s. A common theme of his five novels, *V* (1963), *The Crying of Lot 49* (1967), *Gravity's Rainbow* (1973), *Vineland* (1989), and *Mason and Dixon* (1997), is the protagonists' wandering quest through a bizarre and unpredictable landscape.

● **P'yŏngyang** ▶ 39 00N 125 47E The capital of the Democratic People's Republic of (North) Korea, in the NW on the River Taedong. Reputedly the oldest city in Korea, it suffered severely from successive Japanese and Chinese attacks over the centuries and was almost destroyed by US bombing in the Korean War (1950–53). It is a major industrial as well as administrative and commercial centre. Its three universities include the Kim Il Sung University, founded in 1946. Population (1996 est): 2 500 000.

● **pyorrhoea** ▷*See* periodontal disease.

● **Pyracantha** ▶ A genus of thorny evergreen shrubs (about 10 species), known as firethorns, native to SE Eurasia and widely cultivated as garden shrubs in hedges or against walls. A commonly grown species is *P. coccinea*. It has finely toothed leaves and flat-topped clusters of white or pinkish-yellow flowers. The scarlet berries may last all winter. Family: *Rosaceae*.

● **pyralid moth** ▶ A moth of the widespread family *Pyralidae*. The adults have generally narrow forewings and broader hindwings. Both pairs are fringed. The larvae feed on a variety of substances, including dried stored products. They can be serious economic pests, especially the ▷corn borer, ▷wax moth, and meal moth (*Pyralis farinalis*). Many larvae spin silken tunnels in which they live.

● **pyramids** ▶ Royal funerary monuments in ancient Egypt. The greatest are the pyramids of ▷Khufu, ▷Khafre, and Menkaura (Greek name: Mycerinus) at Giza (built c. 2600–2500 BC), the only survivors of the ▷Seven Wonders of the World. Their tombs were all robbed in antiquity but they nevertheless remain extraordinary feats of engineering. For over four millenniums the pyramid of Khufu, now 138 m (453 ft) high, was the highest building in the world. Pyramids were also built in ancient Mexico.

● **Pyramids, Battle of the** ▶ (21 July, 1798) The battle in which Napoleon with some 25 000 troops defeated about 40 000 Egyptians near Imbaba on the W bank of the Nile. The battle was followed by Napoleon's defeat of the Ottoman Turks at ▷Aboukir.

● **Pyramus and Thisbe** ▶ Legendary lovers in a Babylonian story retold by ▷Ovid. The couple were forbidden to marry by their parents but exchanged vows through a chink in the wall between their houses. They arranged a secret meeting. Thisbe arrived first at the meeting place, which was near a mulberry tree; but she was frightened by a lion and fled, dropping her veil. Pyramus, finding her veil and thinking her dead, stabbed himself, and when Thisbe returned she killed herself also. The mulberry tree has borne blood-red fruit ever since. The rustics' farce in Shakespeare's *A Midsummer Night's Dream* is based on this story.

● **Pyrenean mountain dog** ▶ (or Great Pyrenees) A breed of large dog, possibly of Asian origin, used in Europe for over 3000 years to guard shepherds and their flocks. They are massively built with drooping ears and an ambling gait. The long thick slightly wavy coat is white, with or without grey or brown patches. Height: 71 cm (dogs); 66 cm (bitches).

● **Pyrenees** ▶ (French name: Pyrénées; Spanish name: Pirineos) A mountain range in SW Europe. It extends between the Bay of Biscay in the W and the Mediterranean Sea in the E, forming a barrier between France and Spain. The entire republic of Andorra lies within the range, which rises to 3404 m (11 168 ft) at Pico de Aneto, close to the source of the River Garonne in the centre.

● **Pyrenees, Treaty of the** ▶ (1659) The treaty that ended the war of 1648–59 between France and Spain and marked the rise of French predominance in Europe. Spain lost Artois and the Catalan counties of Rousillon and Cerdana. Maria-Theresa, the daughter of Philip IV of Spain, was married to Louis XIV of France.

● **pyrethrum** ▶ A perennial plant, ▷*Chrysanthemum coccineum* (or *Pyrethrum roseum*), with finely divided leaves and showy red, pink, lilac, or white flowers. It is native to Persia and the Caucasus and widely cultivated for ornament in temperate regions. The name is also given to an insecticide prepared from the dried flower heads of this and related species. Family: ▷*Compositae*.

● **Pyrex** ▶ The trade name for a heat-resistant glass containing borosilicate. It is also resistant to many chemicals and is an electrical insulator. Pyrex is used in laboratory glassware, ovenware, and large telescopes.

● **pyridine** ▶ (C_6H_5N) A hygroscopic colourless liquid, with a strong odour, which boils at 115°C. It is a basic aromatic compound with a six-membered heterocyclic molecule, made by passing tetrahydrofurfuryl alcohol and ammonia over a catalyst at 500°C. It is used as an industrial solvent and in the manufacture of various drugs and pesticides.

● **pyridoxine** ▷*See* vitamin B complex.

● **pyrimidine** ▶ An organic base ($C_4H_4N_2$) consisting of a six-membered ring of carbon and nitrogen atoms. Its derivatives cytosine, thymine, and uracil are constituents of the nucleic acids ▷RNA and ▷DNA.

● **pyrite** ▶ (or iron pyrites) A pale brassy yellow mineral, FeS_2, the most common sulphide mineral. It occurs as an accessory mineral in igneous rocks, in hydrothermal veins, in contact metamorphic rocks, and in sediments laid down in anaerobic conditions. It is usually mined for its sulphur, used for the manufacture of sulphuric acid, or for the gold and copper found in association with it. Because of its colour it has been called fool's gold. The term is sometimes used for other sulphides, for example copper pyrites, but if used alone it refers to iron pyrites.

● **pyroclastic rock** ▶ Rock formed from fragments thrown out by volcanic explosions, in either the solid or molten state. Fragments less than 2 mm in diameter are known as ash or, when consolidated, tuff. Lapilli are larger fragments and bombs are even larger, often spindle-shaped. Blocks are large angular fragments ejected in the solid state.

● **pyroelectricity** ▶ The development of opposite electric charges on opposite faces of asymmetric crystals when they are heated. The charges occur on those faces that are responsible for the crystal's asymmetry. Quartz and tourmaline have pyroelectric properties. ▷*See also* piezoelectric effect.

● **pyrogallol** ▶ (or pyrogallic acid; $C_6H_3(OH)_3$) A white soluble crystalline solid. It is a powerful reducing agent, used in developing photographs and to absorb oxygen in gas analysis.

● **pyrolysis** ▶ A chemical reaction produced by high temperatures. Common examples include the charring of wood and firing of pottery. Pyrolysis has many industrial applications, a recent one being the recovery of hydrocarbon fuels from waste organic materials.

● **pyrometer** ▶ An instrument used for measuring high temperatures. The two most important types are the optical pyrometer and the radiation pyrometer. In the optical pyrometer a filament, heated to a known temperature, is viewed with the hot body in the background. The temperature of the filament is adjusted until it appears to vanish, at which point its temperature is the same as the temperature to be measured. In the radiation pyrometer, radiant heat from the hot body is focused into a thermopile (*see* thermocouple), which develops a potential difference proportional to the temperature.

● **pyrope** ▷*See* garnet.

● **pyroxenes** ▶ A group of ferromagnesian rock-forming silicate minerals. They usually occur in basic and ultrabasic igneous rocks but also in some metamorphosed rocks. Those of orthorhombic crystal structure are orthopyroxenes and those of monoclinic structure are clinopyroxenes. Orthopyroxenes vary in composition between the end-members enstatite ($MgSiO_3$) and orthoferrosilite ($FeSiO_3$). Clinopyroxenes, the larger group, include diopside, hedenbergite, augite, pigeonite, aegirine, jadeite, and spodumene (a source of lithium).

● **Pyrrhon** ▶ (*or* Pyrrho; c. 360–c. 270 BC) Greek philosopher, born at Elis, who was the founder of ▷scepticism. Pyrrhon believed that objective knowledge was impossible, the limitations of knowledge being explored by later sceptics. He sought a way of achieving mental tranquillity by suspension of judgment.

● **Pyrrhus** ▶ (319–272 BC) King of Epirus (307–303, 297–272). Having secured his throne (297), Pyrrhus pursued an adventurous policy of expansion but his empire was short-lived: in support of Tarentum against Rome he won victories that cost much in loss of life ("Pyrrhic" victories), especially at Asculum (279), and he was forced to withdraw.

● **pyruvic acid** ▶ An organic acid ($CH_3COCOOH$). Its anion, pyruvate (CH_3–CO–COO⁻), is an important intermediate compound in the carbohydrate metabolism of living organisms.

● **Pythagoras** ▶ (6th century BC) Greek philosopher and religious leader. Born at ▷Sámos, he migrated in about 530 BC to Crotone (S Italy), where he founded a religious society that governed Crotone for many years until its suppression (460–440 BC). Its members followed an ascetic regime of dietary taboos, self-examination, and study aimed at purifying the soul and releasing it from "entombment" in successive bodies. Pythagoras probably discovered the geometrical theorem named after him and certainly discovered the arithmetical ratios governing musical intervals, which led him to interpret the universe in terms of mathematics alone. Pythagoreans were pioneers in several branches of science. ▷*See also* Alcmaeon; Archytas; Pythagoreanism.

● **Pythagoreanism** ▶ The philosophy of the followers of ▷Pythagoras, who developed the two main strands in their master's thought: mysticism and mathematics. The former was fostered by an ascetic religious order founded by Pythagoras at Crotone, Italy, the rules of which included silence and vegetarianism. Other disciples extended Pythagoras' interpretation of the physical world through numbers and made substantial advances in geometry. In astronomy they evolved a model of the universe that anticipated the heliocentric system of ▷Copernicus. An eclectic form of Pythagoreanism, known as Neopythagoreanism, developed in Alexandria during the 1st century BC.

● **Pytheas** ▶ (4th century BC) Greek navigator. From Marseille he made a voyage along the coasts of Spain, France, and E Britain and seems to have reached as far N as Iceland. His narrative is lost but was later used by the Greek geographer ▷Strabo.

● **Pythian Games** ▶ The ancient Greek festival at Delphi in honour of Apollo. Second only to the Olympic Games in importance, the festival originally consisted of musical competitions but from 582 BC also included athletic and equestrian events, taking place every four years.

● **python** ▶ A large ▷constrictor snake belonging to the Old World subfamily *Pythoninae* (20–25 species), occurring in tropical and temperate regions. Pythons usually live near water and tend to be sluggish, catching prey—which may include goats, pigs, and deer—by ambush. The reticulated python (*Python reticulatus*) is the largest of all constrictors, reaching 10 m in length. Many pythons are killed for their meat and skin. Family: *Boidae*. □reptile.

Q

● **Qaboos ibn Sa'id ▶** (1940–) Sultan of Oman (1970–). He became sultan after deposing, with British support, his reactionary father Sa'id ibn Taymur. With Omani oil revenues Qaboos has initiated modernization programmes. His rule was threatened by Chinese-backed guerrillas in the 1970s.

● **Qaddafi, Moammar al-** ▷*See* Gaddafi, Moammar al-.

● **Qairouan** ▷*See* Kairouan.

● **Qajars** ▷*See* Agha Mohammad Khan.

● **Qandahar** ▷*See* Kandahar.

● **Qatar, State of ▶** A country in the Middle East, in ▷Arabia occupying a desert peninsula on the W coast of the Persian Gulf. The native population is mainly Arab and Wahhabi Sunnite Muslim, but over 80% of workers are immigrants from other countries, including Iran and Pakistan.
  Economy: despite a decline in oil revenues since the 1980s, oil extraction accounts for over 90% of the national income and has led to the development of other industries. Qatar is a member of OPEC. Natural gas has been produced since 1991. There is also some fishing. Despite the very small area of cultivable land, agriculture is being developed with the aim of the country becoming self-sufficient in food production.
  History: Qatar relied on Britain for most of the 19th and 20th centuries, becoming a protectorate in 1916; it became independent in 1971. Qatar is at present an absolute monarchy (there is a consultative council but no legislature). However, democratic municipal elections were held for the first time in 1999 and there are plans to create an elected national body early in the 21st century. In 1995 Sheikh Hamad bin Khalifa al-Thani became emir after ousting his father, Sheikh Khalifa bin Hamad al-Thani (1937–).

State of Qatar

Head of state	Emir Sheikh Hamad bin Khalifa al-Thani
Official language	Arabic
Official currency	Qatar riyal of 100 dirhams
Area	11 000 sq km (4246 sq mi)
Population (1997 est)	561 000
Capital	Doha

● **Qattara Depression ▶** An area in NE Egypt descending to 133 m (436 ft) below sea level. Its steep N side proved a defence for the S flank of the British army in the battle of El Alamein. Area: about 18 000 sq km (7000 sq mi).

● **Qazvin** ▷*See* Kazvin.

● **Q fever ▶** An infection with the microorganism *Coxiella burnetti* (*see* rickettsia), first described in Queensland (hence Q fever) in 1937. The disease affects cattle and sheep but can be transmitted to humans through contaminated milk or by inhalation of the organism. The incubation period is 2–4 weeks and the disease usually takes the form of a viral ▷pneumonia. Treatment is with tetracycline antibiotics.

● **Qian Long ▶** (*or* Ch'ien-lung; 1711–99) The title of Hong-li (*or* Hung-li), Chinese emperor (1736–96) of the Qing dynasty. During his reign the Chinese empire saw its greatest expansion through continuing wars of conquest, which, however, undermined China's econ-

omy. His government was further weakened by the corruption of his minister He-shen (*or* Ho-shen). Qian Long was a distinguished patron of the arts. He abdicated in favour of his son.

● **Qin ▶** (*or* Ch'in; 221–206 BC) The dynasty under which China became a unified empire. The first Qin emperor, Shi Huangdi (*or* Shih Huang Ti; c. 259–210 BC), consolidated his vast conquest by unifying weights, measures, and coinage and by creating one system of writing for the whole empire. He ordered the burning of all books in China, except for practical handbooks and the history of his own dynasty. Believing in the absolute power of the ruler, his government was so harsh that the dynasty outlasted him by only four years. It was during the Qin reign that much of the ▷Great Wall of China was built. Excavations in the vicinity of his tomb in the late 1970s revealed several thousand life-size terracotta men and horses. The remains of the Qin capital were discovered in 1985. ⌐China.

● **Qing ▶** (*or* Ch'ing; 1644–1911) A Manchu dynasty, founded by ▷Nurhachi, that ruled China from the fall of the Ming dynasty until the revolution of 1911. The Manchus, living on the borders of Chinese civilization, gradually conquered Chinese territory as the Ming government weakened. The Qing (pure) dynasty was declared in 1636 but Beijing was not captured until 1644. At its height in the 18th century under ▷Qian Long, the Qing ruled a vast empire that included Outer Mongolia, Tibet, and Turkistan. Trade and commerce flourished, as did cultural life and learning. In over two and a half centuries, however, there was little change in the social order with dangerous results. Bureaucratic conservatism resisted modernization, corruption became rife, and China suffered a series of defeats by foreign powers (e.g. ▷Opium Wars) as well as internal rebellions (e.g. the ▷Taiping Rebellion) that culminated in the overthrow of the Qing in 1911.

● **Qingdao ▶** (Ch'ing-tao *or* Tsingtao) 36 04N 120 22E A port in E China, in Shandong province on the Yellow Sea. From 1898 to 1922 it was under German and then Japanese control. It is a centre of heavy industry. Population (1993 est): 1 459 195.

● **Qinghai ▶** (Ch'ing-hai *or* Tsinghai) A mountainous province in NW China. Tibetan and Mongol nomadic herdsmen keep yaks, sheep, and cattle, and it is famed for its horses. The monastery near Xining is an important centre of Tibetan Buddhism. Salt, oil, coal, and iron are produced. Area: 721 000 sq km (278 400 sq mi). Population (1993 est): 4 610 000. Capital: Xining.

● **Qinghai, Lake ▶** (*or* Koko Nor) A shallow salt lake of N central China, in the mountains of Qinghai province, the largest lake in China. Area: about 4100 sq km (1600 sq mi).

● **Qom ▶** (*or* Qum) 34 39N 50 57E A city in central Iran, S of Tehran. It is the burial place of many Islamic saints and a pilgrimage centre. Population (1994 est): 780 453.

● **quadratic equation ▶** An algebraic ▷equation in which the greatest power of the ▷variable is two. It is usually written in the form $ax^2 + bx + c = 0$, in which the two ▷roots, or possible solutions, are given by $x = [-b \pm \sqrt{(b^2 - 4ac)}]/2a$. Both roots are real ▷numbers when the quantity under the square-root sign is greater than or equal to zero. They are equal when that quantity is zero. If it is less than zero the roots are complex numbers. The sum of the roots is $-b/a$ and their product is c/a.

● **quadrature ▶** The position of a celestial body in the solar system when its angular distance from the sun, as measured from earth (i.e. the angle body–earth–sun), is 90°.

● **quadriplegia** ▷*See* paralysis.

● **Quadruple Alliances** ► **1.** (1718) The alliance formed by Britain, France, the Holy Roman Emperor, and the Netherlands to maintain the Treaties of ▷Utrecht (1713-14), which had been repudiated by Spain. **2.** (1814) The alliance formed by Britain, Austria, Prussia, and Russia against Napoleon. It was confirmed at the Congress of ▷Vienna after Napoleon's fall. **3.** (1834) The alliance between Britain, France, Spain, and Portugal that sought to maintain constitutional monarchy in Spain and Portugal.

● **quaestors** ► Ancient Roman financial officers. Originally two were elected annually; more were appointed as Rome expanded. Two stayed in Rome in charge of the state treasury and records; others supervised Rome's corn supply and the financing of the provinces and military campaigns.

● **quagga** ► An extinct wild horse, *Equus quagga*, that lived on the plains of South Africa. Up to 180 cm high at the shoulder, quaggas had a neck and head striped like a zebra with sandy-coloured hindquarters and white legs and tail. The last quagga died in Amsterdam Zoo in 1883.

● **Quai d'Orsay** ► A street in Paris, on the Left Bank of the River Seine, on which the French Ministry of Foreign Affairs is situated.

● **quail** ► A round-bodied short-tailed gamebird of open grassland and farmland. Old World quail (subfamily *Perdicinae*; 95 species) are 13–20 cm long and characterized by a smooth-edged bill and leg spurs; they are stocky and usually sandy in colour. New World quail (subfamily *Odontophorinae*; 36 species) are up to 30 cm long and have a strong serrated bill, no leg spurs, and are brightly coloured and patterned, often with crests; males and females differ on seeds, berries, and leaves. Family: *Phasianidae* (pheasants, partridges, and quail).

● **Quakers** ► The Christian sect, formally known as the Religious Society of Friends, founded in England by George ▷Fox in the late 1640s. They suffered violent persecution for many years and in 1682 William ▷Penn led a colony of Friends to ▷Pennsylvania. In the USA they were leaders in the fight against ▷slavery, emancipating their own slaves. The early Quakers adopted an unostentatious dress and way of life. They were (and remain) pacifists, refused to take oaths, and rejected the use of titles. In speech they used the old singular form "thou" in preference to the plural form "you" for one person, as more suited to the truth. They rejected the ministry and sacraments of the established Church. They worship in meetings, which start with silence until one member is moved by the "inner light," which they believe to be their guide, to address the congregation or to pray. There are currently some 213 800 Quakers worldwide.

● **quaking grass** ► An annual or perennial ▷grass of the genus *Briza* (about 20 species), mostly native to South America. Their long slender flower stalks bear spikelets of open flower clusters, which quiver in the wind. *B. media* is native to temperate Eurasia and grows 20–50 cm high. It is sometimes planted for ornament.

● **quality control** ► The techniques used to ensure that the quality of goods and services delivered to customers by a supplier is consistently high and consistently meets the customers' expectations. It has been shown repeatedly that manufacturers and service providers who maintain high-quality standards combined with high levels of service will have satisfied customers, who will reward these suppliers with future purchases. This has resulted in two concepts, **servqual** and **total quality management** (TQM), that together aim to ensure customer satisfaction.

Servqual is an important marketing strategy that combines service and quality. It aims to provide tangible evidence of service to clients in an empathetic manner, to understand their needs, to respond promptly to their requirements, and to supply goods and services that reliably conform to the standards on which they are sold. If the actual level of service fails to match the consumers' expectations, a "negative gap" is created that can result in serious consumer dissatisfaction. Conversely, a "positive gap," in which the consumers' expectations are exceeded by the servqual provided, is the objective of all successful companies.

In TQM, management seeks to integrate all the resources of a company to meet the needs and expectations of its clients. The Japanese innovation of "quality circles" is an important tool in achieving this end, in which employees at all levels join to commit themselves to getting things right the first time, understanding the costs involved in providing the goods or services, and improving communications between staff and management. ▷*See also* just in time; kanban.

● **quandong** ► A small shrubby Australian tree, *Fusanus acuminatus*, with simple leaves and heads of small inconspicuous flowers. The fruit is fleshy and edible, with a hard stony pitted edible seed. Family: *Santalaceae*.

● **quango** ► (*quasi-autonomous national government organization*) A term that came into use in the UK in the 1970s to describe organizations, such as the Monopolies Commission and the Equal Opportunities Commission, which have been set up by the government as independent bodies but are dependent on the government for their existence. The Conservative governments of the 1980s and 1990s disbanded many quangos to save government funds but also found it

Quakers ► A meeting of Friends, from a 17th-century engraving. The broad-brimmed hats and long cloaks worn by the men became the distinctive garb of male Quakers. The decor of the meeting house is sternly plain, with no religious symbols of any kind.

necessary to establish new ones. In 1994 the number of quangos in the UK was estimated at over 1000. In the USA the acronym stands for "quasi-autonomous non-governmental organization."

● **Quant, Mary** ▶ (1934–　) British fashion designer, one of the first to become known for ready-to-wear rather than *haute couture* clothes. Her miniskirts, created especially for the young, made London a leading fashion centre in the 1960s. Her original boutique (Bazaar, opened in 1957) in the King's Road, London, soon expanded into an international business selling a wide range of fashion products.

● **quantity theory of money** ▶ A theory that seeks to explain how the money supply (*see* money) affects the economy. Originally put forward in the 17th century, it has been restated in its modern form by Milton ▷Friedman. It states that if there is a change in the money supply, either the price level will change or the supply of goods in the economy will alter. The monetarists (*see* monetarism) assert, on the basis of the quantity theory, that if there is full employment it is the price level that will be affected by altering the money supply.

● **quantum chromodynamics** ▷*See* particle physics.

● **quantum entanglement** ▷*See* EPR paradox; Bell's theorem.

● **quantum field theory** ▶ A ▷quantum theory in which particles have quantized normal modes of oscillation. Quantum electrodynamics (*see* particle physics) is a quantum field theory in which the photon is the quantum of the electromagnetic field. Relativistic quantum field theories are used to describe fundamental interactions between elementary particles. ▷*See also* string theory.

● **quantum mechanics** ▷*See* quantum theory.

● **quantum number** ▶ An integral or half-integral number (0, ½, 1, 1½, 2, ...) that gives the possible values of a property of a system according to the ▷quantum theory. For example, in Bohr's atomic theory the angular momentum of an electron moving in orbit round an atomic nucleus can only have the values $nh/2\pi$, where n is a quantum number specifying these values and h is Planck's constant. Bohr's theory has now been replaced by the more versatile ▷wave mechanics, but the concept of quantum numbers is useful in some contexts. It is also used to quantify the properties of elementary particles (*see* particle physics). For example spin is characterized by the quantum numbers $+\frac{1}{2}$ or $-\frac{1}{2}$ for an electron, depending on whether it is parallel or antiparallel to a specified direction. ▷Parity, ▷electric charge, ▷strangeness, ▷charm, ▷isotopic spin, etc., are other properties of elementary particles expressed by quantum numbers.

● **quantum theory** ▶ The theory first developed by Max ▷Planck in 1900 to explain the distribution of wavelengths of electromagnetic radiation emitted by a ▷black body. The experimental observations could only be explained when Planck assumed that the radiation was emitted and absorbed in discrete amounts, which he called quanta. The energy of each quantum has the value hf, where h is a universal constant (now known as the Planck constant) and f is the frequency of the radiation. Planck's quantum theory was used by ▷Einstein to explain the ▷photoelectric effect and in 1913 by Niels ▷Bohr to explain the spectrum of hydrogen. Quantum theory has since become an essential part of modern physics. **Quantum mechanics** is the application of quantum theory to the mechanics of atomic systems. In this form of mechanics a particle is treated as a wave that can either be extended over a significant distance or localized as a short pulse. The wave's amplitude at a point is a measure of the ▷probability that a particle exists at that point; the wavelength is a measure of its energy. Thus, in quantum mechanics particles with a finite energy cannot be said to be in a precisely defined position (*see* Heisenberg uncertainty principle). **Quantum electrodynamics** is the theory of ▷electromagnetic interactions between elementary particles. **Quantum statistics** is the application of statistical methods to many-particle quantum systems. ▷*See also* wave mechanics.

● **quarantine** ▶ The period during which a person or animal suspected of carrying an infectious disease is kept in isolation. The term was originally applied to the 40-day period (French: *quarantaine*) during which ships suspected of carrying infected people were prevented from communicating with the shore. The quarantine period is now slightly longer than the incubation period of the disease; if no

symptoms appear during quarantine the individual is considered free of the infection. Until 2000 all domestic animals entering the UK had to undergo a six-month quarantine to prevent the importation of rabies. Under the new "passports for pets" scheme, this quarantine requirement has been lifted for animals from rabies-free countries with proof of vaccination and a fitted microchip to identify them.

● **quarks** ▷*See* particle physics.

● **quarrying** ▷*See* mining and quarrying.

● **quarter days** ▶ In law, days in each quarter of the year on which rent and other dues on land were traditionally paid. In England they are 25 March (Lady Day), 24 June (Midsummer Day), 29 Sept (Michaelmas Day), and 25 Dec (Christmas Day).

● **Quarter horse** ▶ A breed of horse developed in colonial America from both local and English stock for racing over short distances, popularly a quarter of a mile. It has a deep compact muscular body and, with its speed and agility, is widely used for ranch work. Quarter horses may be any colour. Height: 1.45–1.57 m (14¼–15½ hands).

● **Quarter Sessions, Courts of** ▶ Courts presided over by two or more ▷justices of the peace in a county or a ▷recorder in a borough, which formerly sat four or more times a year to try certain offences or hear appeals from the inferior petty sessions courts. They originated in 1363 but were replaced by the Crown Court in 1972. In 1842 their power to try serious offences, including murder, was transferred to the assize courts, also abolished in 1972. ▷*See also* courts of law.

● **quartz** ▶ The commonest mineral, consisting of crystalline ▷silica. It occurs particularly in acid igneous rocks (such as granite), many metamorphic rocks (such as gneisses), and in sands and gravels, which form sandstones on consolidation. It is commonly milky white. Pure quartz (rock crystal) is colourless; it is used in glassmaking, jewellery, and (because of its piezoelectric properties) electrical oscillators. Such coloured varieties as amethyst (violet), rose quartz (pink), and citrine (yellow) are gemstones. As sand it is used as an abrasive and in cement.

● **quartzite** ▶ A resistant pale-coloured rock consisting almost wholly of quartz. It is formed by the metamorphism of a pure sandstone, the original quartz grains being recrystallized and interlocking.

● **quasar** ▶ (*quasi*-stellar object; *or* QSO) A class of celestial objects discovered in 1964–65, lying beyond our Galaxy. They appear as star-like points of light, each emitting more energy than several hundred giant galaxies. Quasar ▷redshifts are extremely large indicating that they are the most distant and the youngest extragalactic objects known. They must be highly luminous to be visible at such distances. About 3500 quasars are known. The energy-producing region is extremely compact; the prodigious energy could result from matter spiralling into a supermassive ▷black hole (maybe 10^9 solar masses) at the centre of a galaxy.

● **quasicrystals** ▶ Solid materials, similar to crystals, that have a semiregular arrangement of atoms, causing the appearance of five-fold symmetry elements (*see also* Penrose, Sir Roger). It was thought quasicrystals could not exist, but they were found in a rapidly cooled sample of an aluminium–manganese alloy in 1984.

● **Quasimodo, Salvatore** ▶ (1901–68) Italian poet. His early work, such as *And Suddenly It's Night* (1942), was evocative and private, but after World War II his poetry, as in *Il falso e vero verde* (1956), expressed his active concern for social issues. He won the Nobel Prize in 1959.

● **Quassia** ▶ A genus of tropical Asian trees and shrubs (40 species). Bitterwood (*Q. amara*) is an attractive shrub or small tree with trifoliate leaves and clusters of tubular red flowers. The heartwood is a source of quassiin, a bitter substance used in medicine. Family: *Simaroubaceae*.

● **Quaternary period** ▶ The most recent period of geological time, from the end of the ▷Tertiary (about 1.8 million years ago) to the present day. It includes the ▷Pleistocene (Ice Age) and ▷Holocene epochs. It is the period in which man became the dominant terrestrial species. Some authorities consider the Quaternary to be a division of the Tertiary.

● **Quathlamba** ▷*See* Drakensberg Mountains.

● **Quayle, Sir (John) Anthony** ► (1913–89) British actor and director, who funded his own touring company, Compass Productions, in 1984. His roles included Falstaff, Othello, and Marlowe's Tamburlaine and many film parts. He was also a cofounder of the ▷Royal Shakespeare Company.

● **Quebec** ► The largest province of Canada, stretching from the ▷St Lawrence River N to Hudson Bay and Strait. The rocky forested Canadian Shield covers the N nine-tenths. Most of the population lives in the St Lawrence valley. The SE strip of Quebec enters the fertile Appalachian Highlands. The province's highly industrialized economy is based on its abundant natural resources, especially forests, minerals, and water power. Quebec is a major source of the world's paper. Asbestos, the rich iron-ore deposits at Ungava, copper, zinc, gold, and other minerals are mined. Cheap hydroelectricity aids smelting, refining, food processing, and the manufacture of electronic and electrical products, textiles, aircraft, and motor vehicles. The service industries are also important.

History: claimed by France (1534), Quebec or New France was a French colony (1608–1763) until ceded to Britain. French-Canadian culture was preserved and nationalism increased steadily after the formation of Canada (1867). The Quiet Revolution (1960s) enlivened cultural life and led to the victory of the secessionist Parti Québecois in the 1976 provincial election. However, secession was rejected in a referendum in 1980. The Meech Lake Accord of 1987 recognized Quebec as a "distinct society" but lapsed when two other provinces failed to ratify it in 1990. Proposals to grant Quebec greater autonomy were rejected in a national referendum in 1992. In 1995 a proposal that Quebec should become a sovereign state was very narrowly rejected in a referendum within the province. Support for the Parti Québecois remains high. Area: 1 356 791 sq km (523 858 sq mi). Population (1995 est): 7 334 200; over 80% are French speaking. Capital: Quebec. ▷*See also* Montreal.

● **Quebec** ► 46 50N 71 15W A city and port in E Canada, the capital of Quebec. First settled in 1608, it is strategically located above a sudden narrowing of the St Lawrence River. Quebec was the key to New France until captured by Britain (1759). It remains a cultural centre of French-speaking Canada, housing Laval University. Most of the workforce is employed by government and service industries but textiles, leather goods, printing, publishing, and pulp and paper are also important. Quebec is a major tourist attraction, with its citadel and steep narrow streets. The Plains of ▷Abraham lie to the SW. Population (1991): 645 550 (metropolitan area).

● **quebracho** ► A tropical or subtropical tree of the genus *Schinopsis*, especially *S. lorentzii* and *S. balansae*. Their reddish-brown wood is a source of tannin, while *S. quebracho-colorado* produces timber. Family: *Anacardiaceae*.

● **Quechua** ► The language of the ▷Incas and of the present-day American Indian peoples of the central Andean highlands. These peoples, having now mainly lost their lands to Spanish settlers, form an impoverished peasantry. Crops are potatoes, corn, and quinoa. Llamas and alpacas are herded. The people are nominally Roman Catholic but many pagan beliefs and rituals survive.

● **Queen, Ellery** ► The pen name of the US cousins Frederic Dannay (1905–71) and Manfred Lee (1905–), who together wrote (from 1929) numerous stories featuring a detective also called Ellery Queen. The stories have inspired several films and television series.

● **Queen Anne style** ► An English architectural and decorative style with some baroque elements, dating from about 1700 to 1715. It was characterized by increasing restraint in the decorative elements. Beautiful walnut veneered furniture was made; it was curvilinear in outline, exhibiting wellchosen figured woods, and enhanced by the restrained use of herringbone inlays. Gilt and lacquer continued in vogue but in a less flamboyant manner. Chairs became lighter, more comfortable, and invariably had cabriole legs. Plateglass wall mirrors in gilt frames decorated panelled rooms.

● **Queen Charlotte Islands** ► An archipelago of W Canada, 160 km (100 mi) off British Columbia. Mountainous with lush vegetation (especially forests), the islands are inhabited by Haida Indians engaged in fishing and forestry. Area: 9596 sq km (3705 sq mi). Population (1991): 5316.

● **Queen Maud Land** ▷*See* Norwegian Antarctic Territory.

● **Queens** ► 40 45N 73 50W A borough of New York City, USA, on Long Island. It is both residential and industrial and is the site of La Guardia and John F. Kennedy airports. Area: 307 sq km (118 sq mi). Population (1990): 1 951 598.

● **Queen's Award** ► An award to industry in the UK, instituted in 1965 and made on the birthday (21 April) of Queen Elizabeth II. In 1976 it was divided into two classes, for export achievement and for technological achievement. Awarded to firms, rather than individuals, it entitles holders to use a special emblem for five years.

● **Queensberry Rules** ▷*See* boxing.

● **Queen's Counsel** ► (QC) A ▷barrister appointed to senior rank as counsel to the English queen on the recommendation of the Lord Chancellor. A Queen's Counsel is called a **King's Counsel** (KC) during the reign of a king. QCs have no special duties to the Crown; they wear a silk gown, sit within the Bar of the court, and take precedence over the "utter barristers" (i.e. the outer or junior barristers, who sit outside the Bar). Since reforms were introduced in the 1990s, some ▷solicitors have also been able to apply for the title of Queen's Counsel.

● **Queen's County** ▷*See* Laois.

● **Queensland** ► The second largest state of Australia, situated in the NE. The ▷Great Dividing Range separates the hilly coastlands from the vast inland plain and the ▷Great Barrier Reef runs parallel to the Pacific coast. It is Australia's most decentralized region, containing about a third of Australian urban centres. The area is rich in natural resources, which form the basis of Queensland's rapid economic progress. Coal is the most important mineral and over half the annual production is exported to Japan and Europe. Other minerals extracted include copper, bauxite, lead, silver, and zinc; oil was discovered at Moonie in 1961 and production began in 1964; natural gas mined at Roma and Rolliston is piped to Brisbane. Manufactures include metals, machinery, chemicals, motor vehicles, textiles, and food. Agricultural activities are also important; large quantities of sugar cane are produced in the E, while elsewhere bananas, pineapples, cotton, and tobacco are grown. Beef and wool are major industries. Another growing industry is tourism. Area: 1 728 000 sq km (667 000 sq mi). Population (1996 est): 3 339 000. Capital: Brisbane.

● **Queen's Proctor** ▷*See* Treasury Solicitor.

● **Queenstown** ▷*See* Cóbh.

● **quelea** ► A small brown African weaverbird, *Quelea quelea*, about 13 cm long, also called the red-billed dioch and labelled the most destructive bird in the world. Queleas live in vast colonies: they destroy grain crops, often causing famine, and damage the trees in which they roost by their combined weight. Attempts to control them by poisoning, introducing disease, and by dynamiting their colonies have failed.

● **Quemoy** ▷*See* Jinmen.

● **Queneau, Raymond** ► (1903–76) French novelist and poet. He was involved in the surrealist movement in the 1920s and subsequently wrote a series of parodies and other literary exercises the surface humour of which is founded on profound erudition. Notable among these is *Exercices du style* (1947), in which the same episode is rendered in many different styles. His novels include *Le Chien-dent* (1933), *Rude hiver* (1939), *Pierrot mon ami* (1942), and *Zazie dans le métro* (1959).

● **Quercia, Jacopo della** ▷*See* Jacopo della Quercia.

● **Querétaro** ► 30 38N 100 23W A city in central Mexico. The movement for Mexican independence was begun here (1810). There are many Spanish colonial buildings, notably the cathedral and federal palace. Industries include cotton textiles and potteries. Population (1990): 454 049.

● **Quesnay, François** ▶ (1694–1774) French economist. Originally the physician of Louis XV, Quesnay devoted himself to the study of economics after 1756. He was founder and leader of the ▷Physiocrats, a school of economic theorists. He contributed articles to Diderot's *Encyclopédie* and published such books as *Tableau économique* (1758).

● **Quesnel, Pasquier** ▶ (1634–1719) French Jansenist theologian (*see* Jansenism). He was a priest of the French Oratory (*see* Oratorians) until expelled in 1684 for his views. He settled in Brussels but was imprisoned in 1703 and finally escaped to Holland. His *Nouveau Testament en français avec des réflexions morales* (1692) was condemned by the pope in 1713.

● **Quetta** ▶ 30 15N 67 00E A city in W central Pakistan, at an altitude of 1650 m (5500 ft). The chief town of Baluchistan, it was badly damaged by an earthquake in 1935. Quetta is a trading centre and summer resort. The University of was established here in 1970. Population (latest est): 286 000.

● **quetzal** ▶ A Central American bird, *Pharomachus mocinno*, that lives in cloud forests and feeds on fruit, insects, tree frogs, and lizards. The male reaches 1.3 m in length, including its curved ornamental tail feathers; its plumage is iridescent green, red, and white and the long outer wing feathers curl over the flight feathers. Family: *Trogonidae* (trogons).

● **Quetzalcoatl** ▶ A Mexican wind and fertility god, usually portrayed as a feathered snake. During the Aztec period (14th–16th centuries) he was identified with the planet Venus, symbol of death and resurrection. He was also a creator god, having made humans by sprinkling blood on bones he brought from the underworld.

● **Quezon City** ▶ 14 39N 121 01E A city in the N Philippines, in S Luzon near to Manila. It was the nation's former capital (1948–76). The University of the Philippines was established here in 1908. Mainly residential, its chief industry is textiles. Population (1994 est): 1 676 644.

● **Quibdó** ▶ 5 40N 76 40W A town in NW Colombia. It is an important platinum- and gold-mining centre. Population (1997 est): 123 102.

● **Quiberon** ▶ 47 29N 3 07W A peninsula in NW France, on the S coast of Brittany. In 1759, during the Seven Years' War, a naval battle in which the French were defeated by the English was fought off its coast, in Quiberon Bay.

● **quicklime** ▷*See* calcium.

● **quicksand** ▶ A mass of soft unconsolidated sand that, when saturated with water, becomes semiliquid and unable to support any appreciable weight. Quicksands occur where conditions permit large amounts of water to remain in the sand.

● **Quietism** ▶ A form of mystical passivity that discounts all human effort of will or activity and sees perfection in total dependence upon God. Quietism is associated with certain 17th-century theologians, notably the Spanish priest Miguel de ▷Molinos, and the French mystic Jeanne-Marie Guyon (1648–1717). It was condemned by the pope (1687) on account of its practical and philosophical implications.

● **Quiller-Couch, Sir Arthur Thomas** ▶ (1863–1944) British critic and novelist who published under the pseudonym "Q." He wrote several adventure novels, many of them set in his native Cornwall, but is best known for his collections of Cambridge lectures and as compiler of the influential *Oxford Book of English Verse* (1900).

● **quillwort** ▶ A small perennial nonvascular flowerless plant of the genus *Isoetes* (about 60 species), which grows in water or on land, mainly in swampy cooler regions of N North America and Eurasia. Tufts of stiff spiky quill-like leaves, about 5–18 cm long, grow from a short stout rhizome that bears numerous roots. The spore capsules are embedded in the expanded bases of the leaves. The common Eurasian quillwort (*I. lacustris*) is aquatic. Order: *Isoetales*; phylum: *Lycophyta* (clubmosses, etc.).

● **Quimper** ▶ 48 00N 4 06W A town in NW France, the capital of the Finistère department. A tourist centre, it has a gothic cathedral and is famous for its Breton pottery. Industries include textiles and furniture. Population (1990 est): 62 000.

● **quince** ▶ A small tree or shrub, *Cydonia vulgaris*, probably native to W Asia but cultivated in temperate regions for its fruit. 4.5–6 m high, it has oval leaves (which are woolly beneath) and white or pink flowers, 5 cm across. The pear-shaped fruit is 7.5–10 cm long with a golden-yellow skin and many pips. When cooked, its flesh turns pink, giving a distinctive colour and flavour to preserves and jellies. Family: *Rosaceae*.

● **Quincy** ▶ 42 15N 71 00W A city in the USA, in Massachusetts on Boston Harbor. It is the birthplace of two US presidents, John Adams and his son John Quincy Adams. Industries include shipbuilding and the manufacture of machinery. Population (1996 est): 85 532.

● **Quine, Willard van Orman** ▶ (1908–) US philosopher. He became professor of philosophy at Harvard in 1955. His philosophy was largely concerned with language and logic. He argued that linguistic adjustments could make any statement valid. His works include *Word and Object* (1960), *Set Theory and Its Logic* (1963), *Philosophy of Logic* (1970), *The Roots of Reference* (1973), and *The Logic of Sequences* (1990).

● **Qui Nhon** ▶ 13 47N 109 11E A port in S Vietnam, on the South China Sea. The site of ancient ruins, it was a naval base during the Vietnam War. Its main industry is fishing. Population (1992 est): 163 385.

● **quinine** ▶ The first drug used to treat malaria. Quinine, which is obtained from the bark of ▷*Cinchona* trees, has now been largely replaced by other drugs (including ▷chloroquine), which have fewer side effects and are less toxic. Quinine-like compounds (e.g. quinidine) are used to treat abnormal heart rhythms. Quinine may produce allergic reactions in susceptible patients.

● **quinone** ▶ ($O{:}C_6H_4{:}O$) An ▷aromatic compound with two hydrogen atoms in the benzene ring replaced by two oxygen atoms. Quinones are used in photography and dye manufacture. They are also found in plants.

● **quinsy** ▶ An abscess in the tissue surrounding a tonsil. This arises from infection of the tonsils and may be a complication of tonsillitis. The patient has a sore throat and difficulty in swallowing. Quinsy is treated with antibiotics; some cases may require surgical draining of the abscess.

● **Quintero brothers** ▷*See* Álvarez Quintero brothers.

● **Quintilian** ▶ (Marcus Fabius Quintilianus; c. 35–c. 100 AD) Roman rhetorician. He was born in Spain and educated in Rome, where he worked as an advocate and teacher of rhetoric. The emperor Domitian appointed him tutor to his heirs. His *Institutio oratoria*, a practical treatise on rhetoric, includes a comparative survey of Greek and Latin literature and many original observations on the education of children.

● **Quisling, Vidkun (Abraham Lauritz Jonsson)** ▶ (1887–1945) Norwegian army officer and Nazi collaborator, whose name is a synonym for "traitor." After serving as minister of defence, Quisling formed (1933) the fascist National Union Party in Norway. He encouraged the Nazi occupation of Norway (1940), and as "minister president" in the occupation government, sent a thousand Jews to concentration camps. Arrested in 1945, he was found guilty of war crimes and executed.

● **Quito** ▶ 0 20S 78 45W The capital of Ecuador, on the slopes of the volcano Pichincha at an altitude of 2850 m (9350 ft). Originally settled by Quito Indians, it was the capital of the Inca kingdom of Quito until 1534, when it was captured by the Spanish. It contains Spanish-colonial churches with fine wooden sculptures and paintings; its two universities were founded in 1769 and 1946. Population (1997 est): 1 487 513.

● **Qum** ▷*See* Qom.

● **Qumeran, Khirbat** ▶ The site, on the NW shore of the Dead Sea in Israel, where a Jewish sect called the ▷Essenes lived from about 125

BC to 68 AD. The community produced the ▷Dead Sea Scrolls, which were concealed in nearby caves and found in 1947 by two Bedouin shepherds.

● **quotas, import** ▶ Limits set by a government to the quantity of specified goods that can be imported from abroad (or sometimes from a specified country) in a given period. Quotas are usually operated by a licensing system, importers being granted licences authorizing them to import a certain quantity of a product and to purchase the requisite amount of foreign exchange. Quotas are used to remedy a weak ▷balance of payments or to protect domestic manufacturers but must be used with discretion to avoid provoking retaliation from other countries. ▷*See also* free trade; tariffs.

● **Qu Qiu Bai** ▶ (*or* Ch'ü Ch'iu-pai; 1889–1935) Chinese communist leader. He was a leading literary figure in the communist movement and became general secretary of the Chinese Communist Party in 1927. He was captured and executed by ▷Guomindang (Nationalist) forces in Shanghai.

● **Quran** ▷*See* Koran.

● **Qwaqwa** ▷*See* Bantu Homelands.

Ra ► (*or* Re) The Egyptian sun god and lord of creation, usually portrayed with a falcon's head bearing a solar disc. He sailed across the sky by day in his sun boat and through the underworld by night. His centre of worship was at Heliopolis. During the 18th dynasty (1567–1320 BC) he became identified with the Theban god ▷Amon as Amon-Ra.

Rabat ► (Arabic name: Ribat) 34 00N 6 42W The capital of Morocco, near the Atlantic coast. Founded as a military post in the 12th century, it became the capital under the French protectorate in the early 20th century. It has a university (1957) and its notable buildings include the 12th-century Hassan Tower. It has an important textile industry. Population (1994 est): 623 457.

Rabaul ► 4 13S 152 11E A town in Papua New Guinea, the chief town on the island of New Britain. The capital until 1941 of the Territory of New Guinea, it was evacuated in 1937 because of a volcanic eruption and heavily bombed during World War II. Copra is exported. Population (1990): 17 022.

rabbi ► A Jewish scholar and religious authority. The term came into use in the 1st century AD, and the Judaism of the following centuries is often called "rabbinic Judaism." Originally, the rabbinate was not salaried; the title indicated scholarly and legal competence. Rabbis are not priests, either in the Christian sense of being ordained to act as a mediator between God and humanity or in the Jewish sense of being a descendent of the family of ▷Aaron. Modern rabbis are community leaders, teachers of the young, preachers, and pastoral workers. Reform Judaism and Liberal Judaism permit women to become rabbis, but this is not allowed in Orthodox Judaism.

rabbit ► A burrowing ▷mammal belonging to the family *Leporidae* (which also includes the ▷hares). The European rabbit (*Oryctolagus cuniculus*) grows to about 45 cm; it has long ears, a short tail, and soft grey-brown fur. Rabbits are gregarious, living in large warrens and feeding on grasses and vegetation. They mature at three months and females can produce a litter of up to ten young (kittens) every month. Rabbits can become a serious agricultural pest. Order: ▷*Lagomorpha*.

Rabelais, François ► (1483–1553) French humanist and satirist. He became a Franciscan and then a Benedictine monk, left the monastery to study and practise medicine, and visited Italy with his patron, Cardinal Jean du Bellay (1492–1560). His humanism is expressed in his works of inventive and often coarse satire, *Pantagruel* (1532), *Gargantua* (1534), *Tiers Livre* (1546), and *Quart Livre* (1552). The authenticity of the posthumous *Cinquiesme Livre* (1564) is uncertain. His attacks on superstition and scholasticism were condemned by theologians. The classic English translation of his works is by Sir Thomas Urquhart (1653).

Rabi, Isidor Isaac ► (1898–1988) US physicist, born in Austria, who invented a highly accurate technique for measuring the nuclear magnetic moments of atoms. For this work he was awarded the Nobel Prize in 1944. During World War II Rabi worked on the development of the atom bomb.

rabies ► An acute viral infection of the brain that can affect all warm-blooded animals and may be transmitted to humans through the bite of an infected animal (usually a dog). Symptoms, which appear after an incubation period of from ten days to two years, include painful spasms of the throat on swallowing. Later, the very sight of water induces convulsions and paralysis (hence the alternative name of the disease—hydrophobia, literally "fear of water") and the patient eventually dies in a coma. There is no treatment for the established disease, but antirabies vaccine and rabies antiserum given to patients immediately after they have been bitten may prevent the infection from developing. Rabies has spread across Europe in recent decades; to prevent the disease from reaching Britain, the UK has enforced strict ▷quarantine regulations for imported domestic animals, although these are due to be relaxed by 2001.

Rabin, Yitzhak ► (1922–95) Israeli politician; prime minister (1974–77, 1992–95) He was a chief of staff of the Israeli army (1964–68) and minister of defence (1984–90). Leader of the Labour Party from 1974 to 1977, he was recalled to the leadership in 1992. In 1993 he signed a peace agreement with Yassir ▷Arafat of the ▷Palestine Liberation Organization; he shared the Nobel Peace Prize in 1994 with Arafat and Shimon ▷Peres. He was assassinated by a right-wing Jewish extremist.

raccoon ► (*or* racoon) An omnivorous mammal belonging to the genus *Procyon* (7 species), of the Americas. About 1 m long, raccoons are stockily built, with long hind legs and short forelegs. A black patch across the eyes and a striped tail contrast with the thick grey coat. Raccoons forage at night for nuts, roots, snails, mammals, and birds and take aquatic prey, such as crustaceans, molluscs, and fish. Family: *Procyonidae*; order: *Carnivora*.

raccoon dog ► A short-legged wild ▷dog, *Nyctereutes procyonides*, of Asia. It is golden-brown, about 60 cm long, with black eye patches (like a raccoon). It lives near water and feeds on frogs. Its fur is known as Japanese fox.

race ► A hypothetical subspecies of *Homo sapiens* distinguished on the basis of genetically transmitted differences of skin colour, head shape, facial features, etc. Races, however, are not clearly defined, there are no fundamental differences of intellectual or physical ability, and all humans can and do interbreed. Members of so-called races have some but not all of the characteristics said to distinguish them. Since the end of the 19th century, largely as a result of the work of the anthropologist Franz ▷Boas, there has been no scientific agreement as to the validity of the concept. The traditional geographical classification into Ethiopian (including Negroid), Palaearctic (including Caucasoid and Mongoloid), and Oriental (including Australoid) is no longer regarded as genetically meaningful. The racial theories of the ▷Nazis were strongly opposed by the German-born Boas and are now regarded as totally spurious. The legacy of their attempt to eliminate Jews, Slavs, and Gipsies from Europe is that any racial theory is regarded as morally tainted and intellectually discredited. ▷*See also* racial discrimination.

Rachel ► (Élisa Félix; 1820–58) French actress. She made her debut at the Comédie-Française in 1838 and gained an international reputation as a tragic actress. She was particularly effective in plays by Racine and Corneille. She died of tuberculosis.

raceme ► (*or* racemose inflorescence) ▷*See* inflorescence.

Rachmaninov, Sergei ► (1873–1943) Russian composer, pianist, and conductor. He studied in St Petersburg and Moscow, where he became famous as a pianist, particularly in his own compositions. He left Russia in 1917 and spent most of the rest of his life in the USA. His works include four operas, three symphonies, four piano concertos (which he also recorded), the *Rhapsody on a Theme of Paganini* (for piano

Sergei Rachmaninov ► A photograph of the composer in about 1920, when he was living in the USA. A virtuoso pianist, he became known as a composer when he performed his sumptuously lyrical second piano concerto, which has remained a favourite with pianists and concert-goers all over the world.

and orchestra; 1934), and *The Bells* (for soloists, chorus, and orchestra; 1910). One of his most popular pieces for piano is the prelude in C sharp minor (1892).

● **racial discrimination ►** The practice of making unfavourable distinctions between the members of different ▷races. In South Africa (*see* apartheid) race relations were characterized by a tradition that led to the legal and economic separation of peoples on the basis of their ethnic backgrounds. A similar tradition characterized southern states of the USA (*see* civil-rights movement). The circumstances that lead to prejudice are many and diverse and much has been written attributing inferiority to particular races (*see* social Darwinism); however, no scientifically accepted work exists to support these contentions. In the UK the Race Relations Acts (1965, 1968, 1976) aimed to secure the integration of Commonwealth and other immigrants

(*see* migration, human) into what has become a multiracial society. Under the 1976 Act, the Commission for Racial Equality was established to investigate and help to eliminate racial discrimination. In British schools measures have been taken to combat any racial disadvantage. In 1999 measures to combat institutional racism, especially in the police, were recommended in a report on the murder of a Black student, Stephen ▷Lawrence, for which no-one was convicted. ▷*See also* antisemitism.

● **Racine, Jean ►** (1639–99) French dramatist. He received a Jansenist education at the convent of Port-Royal but was attracted by the Parisian theatre and began writing plays in 1664. His major classical verse tragedies, influenced by those of ▷Corneille but eventually surpassing them, include *Andromaque* (1667), *Britannicus* (1669), *Bérénice* (1670), and *Phèdre* (1677). In 1677 he retired from the theatre, married a young pious girl, and accepted a post at the court of Louis XIV. His final works were two dramas based on Old Testament subjects, *Esther* (1689) and *Athalie* (1691). Racine was the outstanding tragedian of the French classical period.

● **Rackham, Arthur ►** (1867–1939) British watercolourist and book illustrator. Using an ▷Art Nouveau style, he became famous for his representation of fairytale characters in such books as *Peter Pan* (1906), *Hans Andersen's Fairy Tales* (1932), and *The Arthur Rackham Fairy Book* (1933).

● **racoon** ▷*See* raccoon.

● **rad ►** The unit of absorbed dose of ionizing radiation in the ▷c.g.s. system equal to an energy absorption of 100 ergs per gram of irradiated material.

● **radar ►** (*radio detection and ranging*) A method of detecting distant objects based on the reflection of microwaves (10–1000 mm wavelength). It was developed during the years preceding World War II by a British team led by Sir Robert ▷Watson-Watt as a means of detecting enemy aircraft. In primary radar, a high-powered beam of pulses produced by a ▷magnetron thermionic valve is transmitted from a rotating aerial and reflected back to the same receiving aerial by any object it encounters. Various computerized techniques are

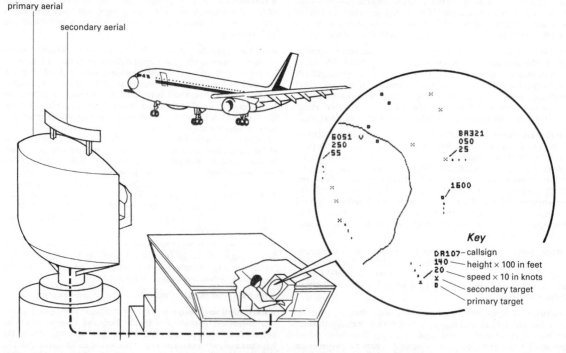

radar ► The high-frequency pulses sent out by the transmitting aerial are reflected back by the target and displayed on a screen. The typical air-traffic control picture seen here shows East Anglia (only a few of the targets are labelled, for clarity).

used to filter out unwanted reflections, an image of the target (aircraft, missile, etc.) being displayed on the screen of a ▷cathode-ray tube (CRT). The beam of the CRT scans the screen of the tube presenting a plot of the target area and any targets within it. Radar is the basis of air-traffic control and can detect targets at 450 km to an accuracy of about 100 metres. Primary radar is also carried on aircraft themselves for mapping and weather detection. It is used in sea navigation and by the police to detect speeding motorists (using the ▷Doppler effect).

In secondary radar, coded pulses from the ground are used to obtain a reply from a ▷transponder carried by aircraft, which signals back various information, including the aircraft's call sign and altitude. This information is displayed on the radar screen, together with an image of the target, using letters and numbers. Computer processing enables the display to include targets from several different radar transmitters.

● **Radcliffe, Ann (Ward)** ▶ (1764–1823) British novelist. Despite their technical clumsiness and lack of characterization, her gothic novels, such as *The Mysteries of Udolfo* (1794) and *The Italian* (1797), were important influences in the change of literary taste and the increasing interest in Romantic characters, description, etc.

● **Radcliffe-Brown, Alfred Reginald** ▶ (1881–1955) British anthropologist. A pioneer of social anthropology, Radcliffe-Brown held professorships at Chicago, Sydney, Cape Town, and Oxford Universities. His specific contribution to anthropology lies in his studies of ▷kinship and society, for which he did field work in Australia and the Andaman Islands.

● **Radek, Karl** ▶ (1885–?1939) Soviet politician and journalist. Radek participated in the Russian Revolutions of 1905 and 1917. In 1920 he became secretary of Comintern and served until 1924. Accused of being a Trotskyite, Radek was expelled from the Communist Party in 1927. After recanting in 1929, he wrote for the newspaper *Izvestia* and helped to draft the 1936 constitution. Accused of treason in 1937, he probably died in a Siberian labour camp.

● **Radhakrishnan, Sir Sarvepalli** ▶ (1888–1975) Indian statesman and philosopher; president of India (1962–67). After teaching philosophy at the universities of Mysore and Calcutta, he moved to Oxford University (1936–52), where he introduced Indian philosophy to Western philosophers in such works as *Eastern Religions and Western Thought* (1939). In 1949 he was appointed India's ambassador to the Soviet Union and also chairman of UNESCO. He became vice-president of India (under Nehru) in 1952 and was appointed president in 1962. He was knighted in 1931.

● **radial velocity** ▶ The velocity of a star, etc., along the line of sight, i.e. towards or away from the earth. It is calculated from the Doppler shift of the lines of the star's spectrum (*see* Doppler effect).

● **radian** ▶ (rad) The ▷SI unit of plane angle equal to the angle subtended at the centre of a circle by an arc equal in length to the radius of the circle.

● **radiation** ▶ The propagation of energy by electromagnetic waves, beams of particles, ions, etc. ▷*See* electromagnetic radiation; ionizing radiation; radiation sickness; radioactivity.

● **radiation sickness** ▶ Illness caused by exposure to ▷ionizing radiation, either naturally occurring or from nuclear weapons, X-ray machines, etc. The radiation affects the cells of the body in various ways. Early effects include nausea and diarrhoea (a dose equivalent exceeding 10^5 microsieverts), loss of hair and skin burns (over 10^6 μSv), and death (over 10^7 μSv). Late effects, including cancer (especially leukaemia), sterility, and genetic changes to germ cells that can affect unborn children, can be caused by any level of exposure; the natural background level (about 2000 μSv; *see* ionizing radiation) causes a very low risk, which increases with the exposure level.

● **radiation units** ▶ Units of measurement to express the activity of radioactive substances and the dose (energy per unit of mass) absorbed by matter exposed to ▷ionizing radiation. The ▷curie, ▷roentgen, and ▷rad have been replaced by the SI units ▷becquerel, ▷gray, and ▷sievert.

● **Radić, Stjepan** ▶ (1871–1928) Croatian statesman. Founder of the Croatian Peasant Party (1904), Radić advocated a federated Yugoslavia with Croatian autonomy and opposed ▷Pašić's centralized Yugoslav Government. In 1925, however, he became minister of education but resigned a year later. He was assassinated in parliament.

● **radical** ▶ A group of atoms in a chemical compound that behaves as a unit in chemical reactions. For example, the methanol molecule (CH_3OH) can be considered as a methyl radical (CH_3.) and a hydroxyl radical (.OH). In this sense, radicals are often simply referred to as groups, a functional group being one responsible for the characteristic reactions of a class of compounds. Thus, the hydroxyl group is the functional group of alcohols. **Free radicals** are groups existing independently. Because they have unpaired electrons they are usually extremely reactive transient species. They can be produced by ▷pyrolysis or ▷photolysis and are important intermediates in many reactions, particularly photochemical, combustion, and polymerization reactions. Oxygen free radicals are formed within the body during normal metabolic processes and as a response to infection and toxins. They can cause cell damage, which may be neutralized or prevented by ▷antioxidant nutrients.

● **Radiguet, Raymond** ▶ (1903–23) French novelist. His precocious talent was recognized by several prominent literary and artistic figures, especially Jean Cocteau. His two novels were *Le Diable au corps* (1923), a story of adolescent passion and cruelty, and *Le Bal du Comte d'Orgel* (1924).

● **radio** ▶ The transmission of information by radio-frequency (3 kilohertz to 300 gigahertz) electromagnetic waves. The use of radio waves for communication was pioneered by ▷Marconi in 1895, although their existence was postulated by ▷Maxwell in 1873 and demonstrated by ▷Hertz in 1888.

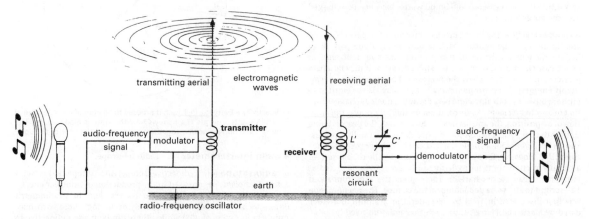

transmitting aerial   electromagnetic waves   receiving aerial

audio-frequency signal   modulator   **transmitter**   **receiver** L' C' demodulator   audio-frequency signal

resonant circuit   earth

radio-frequency oscillator

radio ▶ The transmission and reception of sound broadcasts.

A **radio transmitter** generates a radio-frequency electrical signal (carrier wave) in an oscillator and superimposes the sound signal on it by ▷modulation. The composite signal is then fed to an aerial, which transmits electromagnetic waves. Although the waves travel in straight lines, transmission beyond the horizon is made possible by the ionosphere, a layer of the upper atmosphere that reflects long and medium waves. Long-wave (30 to 300 kilohertz) and medium-wave (300 to 3000 kilohertz) radio is used for direct (ground-wave) transmission in amplitude-modulated (AM) sound broadcasting. Short-wave radio is used for AM broadcasting over longer distances using the ionosphere (sky waves) and for communication to ships and aircraft. VHF (very high frequency; 30 to 300 megahertz) is used for ▷stereophonic sound broadcasting in frequency modulated (FM) transmissions. Television uses mostly UHF (ultrahigh frequency). Neither VHF nor UHF are reflected by the ionosphere, but can be relayed by ▷communications satellites. All **radio receivers** consist of an ▷aerial, which detects the signal and converts it to an electrical current; a resonant circuit, which selects the required frequency band; a demodulator to retrieve the audio-frequency signal from the modulated carrier wave; an amplifier; and ▷loudspeakers to reproduce the sound.

● **radioactive isotope** ▷*See* radioisotope.

● **radioactive tracer** ► A radioactive ▷isotope used for following the course of a substance during a physical, biological, or chemical process. A nonradioactive isotope in the substance is replaced by a radioactive isotope of the same element, which can then be detected by observing its emitted radiation with, for example, a ▷Geiger counter. Substances containing such radioisotopes are called labelled compounds. Radioactive tracing is used in medical, scientific, and industrial research.

● **radioactive waste** ► Solid, liquid, and gaseous waste products from nuclear reactors, uranium processing plants, hospitals, etc., that are radioactive. Because the radioactivity of some materials will remain for thousands of years, their disposal must be undertaken with great care. High-level waste (spent nuclear fuel, etc.) needs artificial cooling and is therefore stored by its producers for several decades before disposal. Intermediate-level waste (reactor components, filters, sludges, etc., from processing plants) is solidified and stored mixed with concrete in steel drums in power stations prior to burial in deep mines or beneath the seabed in concrete chambers, where it cannot contaminate ground water. Low-level waste (solids and liquids contaminated by traces of radioactivity) presents fewer problems; in the UK, since 1988 it has been disposed of by a special company (Nirex Ltd), set up by the government and the nuclear industry, using steel drums in concrete-lined trenches at Driggs, Cumbria. There is a nuclear fuel reprocessing plant at Dounreay, and another opened in 1994 at ▷Sellafield. Other countries make similar arrangements. Until 1983, when it was suspended by international agreement, low- and intermediate-level wastes were disposed of in the deep Atlantic in steel drums cast in concrete. In addition some very dilute low-level gaseous and liquid wastes have been discharged into the air and the sea.

● **radioactivity** ► The spontaneous emission of a particle by an atomic nucleus. The emitted particle may be an alpha particle (a helium nucleus consisting of two protons and two neutrons), in which case the process is known as ▷alpha decay; or it may be a beta particle (an ▷electron), when the process is known as ▷beta decay. Highly energetic X-rays (*see* gamma radiation) may also be emitted simultaneously. In both alpha and beta decay the nucleus changes into that of another element. A less common method of decay is the emission of a ▷positron, the antiparticle of the electron, the process being similar to that of beta decay. Radioactive decay is a random process and its occurrence for a single nucleus can be neither predicted nor controlled. However, for a large number of nuclei the time taken for a certain fraction of nuclei to decay can be accurately predicted as either its ▷mean life or ▷half-life. These quantities vary from about 10^{-8} second to 10^{10} years depending on the isotope. The phenomenon was first discovered in 1898 by ▷Becquerel in uranium and elucidated by Marie and Pierre ▷Curie, ▷Rutherford, and ▷Soddy.

● **radio astronomy** ► The study of celestial objects (*see* radio

source) by means of the radio waves they emit (*see* radio telescope). This radio emission was first noticed by K. G. ▷Jansky in the USA in 1932 and developed in the UK during and after World War II, especially at ▷Jodrell Bank and Cambridge University. It now forms an important branch of ▷astronomy. Radio astronomy has enabled the evolution of the universe to be studied from its creation (*see* big-bang theory).

● **radio beacon** ► An automatic navigational beacon that broadcasts a coded radio signal. The angular position of the source of the signal can be determined by a vessel or aircraft carrying a radio direction finder or radio compass and can be identified by its code, usually given in Morse. Where two such radio beacons can be received, the exact position of the receiver can be determined by triangulation.

● **radiocarbon dating** ► A method of estimating the age of a material, such as wood, that was once living. Atmospheric carbon dioxide contains a small proportion of the radioisotope carbon-14. As all living things absorb carbon from atmospheric carbon dioxide, either directly or indirectly, they too contain a constant proportion of carbon-14. However, once dead, the level of carbon-14 falls as a result of ▷beta decay. By measuring the radioactivity of a material, the concentration of carbon-14 and hence its age can be estimated. The method is used to determine ages up to 70 000 years. Celebrated examples of its use include the testing of the ▷Shroud of Turin. ▷*See also* radiometric dating.

● **radiochemistry** ► The branch of chemistry concerned with compounds containing radioactive ▷isotopes. It includes chemical techniques for isotope separation, and the use of ▷radioactive tracers for investigating chemical reactions.

● **radio galaxy** ► A ▷radio source that lies beyond our Galaxy, is identified with an optical ▷galaxy, and the radio-power output of which greatly exceeds that of a normal galaxy. The size can be immense. A massive ▷black hole at the galaxy centre has been postulated as a possible energy source.

● **radiography** ► The technique of examining the internal structure of a solid body by passing ▷X-rays or ▷gamma radiation through it to produce an image on a photographic plate or fluorescent screen. Radiography is used in medicine (*see* radiology) and in industry to find structural defects. ▷*See also* ultrasonography.

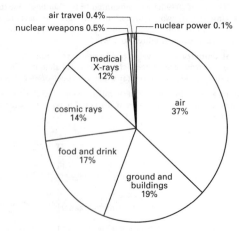

radioactivity ► Everyone in Britain is exposed to an annual average dose of 2.1 millisieverts. This pie chart shows how this dose is made up. Nuclear weapons and nuclear power, together, make up less than 1% of the dose.

● **radio interferometer** ▷*See* radio telescope.

● **radioisotope** ► (or radioactive isotope) An ▷isotope that is radioactive. Radioisotopes are used in the production of ▷nuclear energy, in ▷radiotherapy, as ▷radioactive tracers, and in ▷radiometric dating techniques. Some are naturally occurring (those with mass numbers in excess of 208) while others can be made radioactive by neutron bombardment.

● **radiolarian** ► Any one of a group of single-celled marine organisms (*see* protozoa), traditionally regarded as a class or order, *Radiolaria*, but now usually classified in several different classes, occurring chiefly as a component of plankton. Radiolarians are typically spherical, 0.1 mm to several millimetres in diameter, with a silicaceous skeleton of radiating spines from which long thin pseudopodia extend to capture food particles. The skeletal remains of dead radiolarians sink to the ocean floor to form a deposit called radiolarian ooze. Phylum: *Actinopoda*. ▯protozoa.

● **radiology** ► The branch of medicine concerned with the use of radiation in the diagnosis and treatment of disease. ▷Radiography is used to diagnose a wide range of disorders, including fractures, ulcers, cancer, and arterial disease (*see* arteriography): hollow organs are often visualized by injecting a fluid that is opaque to X-rays. Radiology also includes the use of computerized ▷tomography. A radiologist is a doctor specialized in the interpretation of radiological images. ▷*See also* radiotherapy.

● **radiometric dating** ► A method of dating rocks, developed mainly in the 1950s, by observing the extent to which a radioactive (parent) element in a rock has decayed to form a stable daughter element. Since the half-life or rate of decay of the radioactive element chosen is known, the age of the rock can be calculated from the ratio of parent to daughter isotopes present. The most frequently used methods are ▷radiocarbon dating, ▷potassium-argon dating, and ▷rubidium-strontium dating. Methods based on uranium-lead and thorium-lead decays are also sometimes used.

● **radio source** ► A celestial object that emits radio waves. The sun and Jupiter are solar-system sources. Other radio sources within our Galaxy are pulsars, supernova remnants, interstellar hydrogen clouds, and the galactic centre. Extragalactic sources include spiral galaxies, radio galaxies, and some quasars. The spatial distribution and intensity of the radio emission can be shown on a contour map.

● **radiotelephone** ▷*See* cellular network.

● **radio telescope** ► An instrument for detecting and measuring the radio emissions from celestial ▷radio sources. It consists of an antenna, or system of antennas, the radio-frequency signals of which are carried by wires or waveguides to one or more receivers. The receiver output signal is finally displayed on a graph, stored on magnetic tape, etc. The antenna may be a large metal parabolic or spherical dish, usually steerable, that brings radio waves from a radio source to a focus on a secondary antenna. Alternatively simple dipole antennas may be used. An antenna system may consist of two separate units the signals of which are fed to a common receiver. This **radio interferometer** has a very much greater resolving power than a single antenna; the greater the distance between antennas the finer the detail observed in a radio source. Varied scales of detail can be obtained by using a number of antenna pairs at different distances. In earth-rotation **aperture synthesis** a few small antennas can be made to simulate an enormous dish antenna, as the earth rotates. One of the best-known radio telescopes is the steerable dish instrument at ▷Jodrell Bank, which forms one component of a UK network of radio dishes. The largest single radio telescope dish in the world is that at Arecibo, Puerto Rico; it measures 305 m (1000 ft) across.

● **radiotherapy** ► The use of X-rays and other forms of ▷ionizing radiation, produced by machines or emitted by radioactive isotopes, for treating disease. The radiation may be directed at the target organ from a distance or radioactive needles, wires, pellets, etc., may be implanted in the body. Radiation is particularly destructive to rapidly dividing cells: it is therefore used in treating various forms of ▷cancer and certain other tumours as well as overactivity of the thyroid gland. The exact position of tumours can be identified by the use of computerized ▷tomography. Complementary computerized equipment can be used in planning the treatment of malignant tumours with multiple small doses of radiation to avoid damaging normal surrounding tissues.

● **radish** ► An annual or biennial herb, *Raphanus sativus*, grown for its hot-tasting root, which may be red, white, or purple. Spring variet-

ies are quick-growing while winter varieties may be stored. The plant bears white flowers. Family: ▷*Cruciferae*.

● **radium** ► (Ra) A metallic element, discovered in pitchblende in 1898 by Pierre and Marie Curie. It is a divalent alkaline-earth element, forming a number of simple salts, such as the chloride ($RaCl_2$). It decays to form the noble gas radon and is used in radiotherapy for the treatment of cancers. At no 88; at wt (226); mp 700°C; bp 1140°C.

● **Radium Hill** ► 32 30S 140 32E A mining settlement in E South Australia, where radium was mined until 1930 and uranium was extracted (1952–61).

● **radius** ▷*See* arm.

● **Radnorshire** ► A former county of E Wales. Under local government reorganization in 1974 it became part of ▷Powys.

● **Radom** ► 51 26N 21 10E An industrial town in SE central Poland. Founded in 1340, it was held successively by Austria and Russia before returning to Poland in 1918. Industries include leather, glass, and chemicals. Population (1996 est): 232 300.

● **radon** ► (Rn) The heaviest noble gas, produced by the decay of radium, thorium, and actinium. It is radioactive, the longest-lived isotope (^{222}Rn) having a half-life of 3.825 days. Like the other noble gases, Rn forms clathrates and fluorides. Increased radon levels have been noted in ground water shortly before earthquakes. At no 86; at wt (222); mp −71°C; bp −61.8°C.

● **Raeburn, Sir Henry** ► (1756–1823) Scottish portraitist. The leading Scottish painter of his generation, he was apprenticed to a goldsmith. Before painting his earliest known portrait in 1776, he produced miniatures. Although he visited London and Italy (1785–87), he worked chiefly in Edinburgh, where his sitters included lawyers, scholars, and such Highland lairds as *The MacNab* (The Collection of John Dewar and Sons, Ltd).

● **Raeder, Erich** ► (1876–1960) German admiral; commander in chief of the navy (1928–43). In contravention of the Treaty of Versailles, he rebuilt the German navy before World War II but was dismissed after disagreeing with Hitler. He was sentenced to life imprisonment for war crimes but released in 1955.

● **RAF** ▷*See* Royal Air Force.

● **raffia** ► (*or* raphia) A ▷palm tree of the genus *Raphia*, especially *R. pedunculata* (or *R. ruffia*), native to Madagascar and cultivated for its fibre. Its leaves, up to 20 m long, are composed of 80–100 leaflets from which the fibre is torn in thin strips and dried in the sun. Raffia is soft, strong, pliable, and resistant to shrinking; it is woven into mats and baskets, etc.

● **Raffles, Sir Thomas Stamford** ► (1781–1826) British colonial administrator and oriental scholar, who acquired Singapore for the East India Company (1819). He was lieutenant governor of Java (1811–16), while it was under British rule, and then of Bengkulu (1818–23) in W Sumatra.

● **Rafflesia** ► A genus of Malaysian parasitic herbs (12 species), the vegetative parts of which are reduced to fungus-like threads that extract food from the roots and stems of other plants. The monster plant (*R. arnoldii*) has the world's largest flower—up to 45 cm across and weighing up to 10 kg. It smells of rotten meat and attracts carrion flies, which act as pollinators. The genus was named after Sir Stamford ▷Raffles. Family: *Rafflesiaceae*.

● **Rafsanjani, Hojatoleslam Ali Akbar Hashemi** ► (1934–   ) Iranian politician; president (1989–97). Speaker of parliament under Ayatollah ▷Khomeini, he became president after Khomeini's death and set about improving Iran's international relations. He was reelected in 1992 but retired in 1997, when he was replaced by Ayatollah Khatami.

● **raga** ► (Sanskrit: colour) In Indian music, a type of ▷scale used as the basis for improvisation. There are many different ragas, some of which are associated with particular moods, feelings, times of day, etc.

● **ragged robin** ► A Eurasian perennial herb, *Lychnis flos-cuculi*. Growing to a height of 75 cm, it has rose-red flowers with five deeply divided ragged petals. It is common in damp places and has been introduced to North America. Family: *Caryophyllaceae*.

● **ragged schools** ► Institutions that provided such services as free education and clothing for deprived children in 19th-century Britain. The ragged schools, which were probably inspired by the Sunday School movement (*see* Raikes, Robert), formed the Ragged School Union in 1844 but were rendered obsolete after 1870, when free compulsory education was introduced.

● **Raglan, FitzRoy James Henry Somerset, 1st Baron** ► (1788–1855) British field marshal. After service in the Napoleonic Wars (in which he lost his sword arm at Waterloo), he became secretary to Wellington, whom he succeeded as master general of the ordnance in 1852. In 1854 he became commander in the ▷Crimean War and, in spite of success at ▷Inkerman, his strategy was much criticized (*see also* Balaclava, Battle of). The Raglan sleeve, extending to the neck without shoulder seams, is named after him.

Ragnarök ► *The Doomsday of the Teutons* by Johannes Gehrts. The gods struggle in vain against the evil progeny of Loki.

● **Ragnarök** ► In Norse mythology, doomsday, when a catastrophic battle between the gods and the forces of evil will occur. It will be preceded by warning signals: three years of perpetual winter will be followed by three years of moral decline among men. After the defeat of the gods by the forces of evil, led by ▷Loki, everyone will be destroyed except for ▷Lif and Lifthrasir.

● **ragtime** ► A precursor of ▷New Orleans style jazz. Ragtime developed from minstrel-band music, but many rags were published as piano compositions. Ragtime was characterized by syncopation in the melody against a regular marchlike accompaniment and was popular from the 1890s until around 1920. Famous rags include "Harlem Rag" (1895) and "Maple Leaf Rag" (1899), written by Scott ▷Joplin, the first ragtime composer to write down his music. The revival of ragtime in the 1970s was largely due to its use in the popular film *The Sting* (1973).

● **Ragusa** ► (ancient name: Hybla Heraca) 36 56N 14 44E A town in Italy, in Sicily on the River Irminio. It has an 18th-century cathedral. Oil production and asphalt mining are the chief industrial activities. Population (1990): 68 850.

● **ragworm** ► A marine ▷annelid worm, *Nereis cultrifera*, also called chainworm, of European coastal waters. 5–10 cm long, ragworms swim by means of paddle-like structures occurring in pairs on each body segment. Most ragworms live in burrows in sand or mud or among stones, feeding on dead organisms and detritus using a pair of horny jaws inside a protrudable mouth tube. Class: *Polychaeta*.

● **ragwort** ► A perennial or biennial herb, *Senecio jacobaea*, that grows up to 150 cm high and has much-divided leaves and dense flat-topped heads of yellow flowers. It is found on dunes, waste places, and pastures of Eurasia and N Africa and has been introduced to New

Zealand and North America. When eaten in large quantities it is poisonous to livestock. Family: ▷*Compositae*.

● **Raikes, Robert** ► (1735–1811) British journalist and philanthropist, who founded the Sunday School movement. In 1780 he opened a Sunday School in Gloucester devoted to teaching children Scripture and elementary school subjects. He publicized his project through his own newspaper, the *Gloucester Journal*, and it was soon imitated elsewhere in England, resulting in the establishment of the Sunday School Union (1803).

● **rail** ► A slender secretive ground-dwelling bird belonging to a widely distributed family (*Rallidae*; about 300 species), occurring mostly in swamps, marshes, and fresh waters. 11–45 cm long, rails have short rounded wings, a short tail, and typically a dull grey or brown plumage, often barred for camouflage. They feed on plant material, invertebrates, and birds' eggs. Order: *Gruiformes* (cranes, rails, etc.). ▷*See also* coot; corncrake; gallinule.

● **railway** ► A permanent track, consisting of parallel rails, on which □locomotives draw wagons or trucks for transporting goods or passengers. Wooden rails have been in use in mines since the 14th century, but flanged wheels running on cast-iron rails were not introduced until 1789. Thereafter they were quite widely used in the mining and metallurgical industries, although trucks were horse-drawn until the invention of the steam locomotive at the beginning of the 19th century. The first effective railway in the world opened in England in 1825 and ran between Stockton and Darlington, using ▷Stephenson's *Locomotion* as the locomotive. During the next 12 years some 2400 km (1500 mi) of track were laid in the UK; by 1885 this figure had increased to 26 900 km (16 700 mi) and by 1921 it was 31 120 km (19 300 mi). The Railways Act (1921) consolidated the 250 railway companies then operating into four companies: London Midland and Scottish Railway (LMS), London and North Eastern Railway (LNER), Great Western Railway (GWR), and Southern Railway (SR). In 1947 these four companies were amalgamated in the state-owned British Railways (which became British Rail in 1965). The privatization of British Rail, which involved franchising different routes to different companies, came into effect in 1996. The national rail infrastructure is now owned and managed by Railtrack, a private company that leases track and stations to the operating companies. A new Strategic Rail Authority was established to regulate the system in 1999.

Until the 1860s railways were an exclusively British expertise and any foreign railways that existed were British built and used British rolling stock. For example the earliest US line, between Boston and Albany (1842), used British locomotives and British rails. After the Civil War, however, US railways developed independently and by 1887 there were 140 000 km (87 000 mi) of rail. The USA now has more than any other nation, with 338 000 km (209 000 mi); what was formerly the Soviet Union has 136 800 km (85 000 mi), Canada 74 800 km (46 500 mi), India 60 200 km (37 400 mi), Australia 41 500 km (25 800 mi), and France 34 000 km (22 300 mi).

After World War II the growth of internal air services, the development of road-haulage services, and the spread of private motoring led to a reduction in railway services in industrial countries. However the introduction of high-speed trains, the continued use of the railways by postal services, increasing road congestion, and the advent of the ▷Channel tunnel have combined to give the railways new opportunities in Europe. ▷*See also* underground railways.

● **rain** ► A form of precipitation composed of liquid water drops ranging in size from about 0.5 to 5 mm diameter. Minute droplets of water in clouds may coalesce to form larger drops; if these are sufficiently heavy they will fall as rain. The amount of rain, together with other forms of precipitation, that falls in a specific time is usually measured with a **rain gauge**. This is a cylindrical container with a funnel of standard diameter into which the rain falls. The water collected is periodically measured and recorded in millimetres or inches; some rain gauges are designed to record automatically.

● **rainbow** ► An optical phenomenon consisting of an arc of light across the sky composed of the colours of the spectrum. It is caused by the refraction of sunlight through falling water drops; the larger the drops the stronger the colours.

● **Raine, Kathleen** ▶ (1908–) British poet. Her volumes of poetry, which include *Stone and Flower* (1943), *The Lost Country* (1971), and *Living with Mystery* (1991), are noted for their visionary lyricism. She has also published several studies of William Blake, notably *Blake and Tradition* (1969).

● **rain forest** ▷*See* forest.

● **Rainier, Mount** ▶ A mountain in the USA, the highest peak in Washington state and the Cascade Mountains. It is noted for its many glaciers. Height: 4392 m (14 408 ft).

● **Rainier III** ▶ (1923–) Prince of Monaco (1949–). He repudiated the principle of the ▷divine right of kings in a new constitution (1962). In 1956 he married Grace ▷Kelly. Their three children are Prince Albert (1958–), Princess Caroline (1957–), and Princess Stephanie (1965–).

● **Rais, Gilles de** ▶ (*or* G. de Retz; 1404–40) French marshal, who fought with ▷Joan of Arc. After her capture he retired to his estates in Brittany and dabbled in alchemy and witchcraft. In 1440 he was sentenced to death for the torture and murder of over 140 children. He was later associated with the story of Bluebeard, immortalized by Charles ▷Perrault.

● **Raj, British** ▷*See* British Raj.

● **Rajasthan** ▶ A state in NW India, extending from the Thar Desert along Pakistan's border SE into forested hills. The economy depends primarily on grain and livestock farming, as well as cotton, sugar cane, and pulses. Coal, phosphates, gypsum, marble, mica, and salt are mined. Industries include textiles, cement, and glass.
History: Rajasthan flourished in the Harappan period (3rd–2nd millenniums BC). ▷*See* Rajput. Area: 342 239 sq km (132 111 sq mi). Population (1994 est): 48 040 000. Capital: Jaipur.

● **Rajkot** ▶ 22 18N 70 53E A city in India, in Gujarat. A commercial and industrial centre, it produces textiles and chemicals. Population (1991): 556 137.

● **Rajput** ▶ A group of clans in N and central India, now numbering about 11 million people. They appeared in about the 5th century AD and are believed to have been descended from invading tribes from Central Asia, although they claim descent from more ancient Indian tribes. They were at some time included within the Ksatriya (warrior) caste of Hindu society. The Rajput states fought vigorously against the Muslim invaders, maintaining their independence in Rajasthan. They acknowledged the rule of the Moguls in the 16th century, the Marathas in the 18th century, and the British in 1808. Rajput dynasties were responsible for building many fine temples.

● **Raleigh** ▶ 35 46N 78 39W A city in the USA, the capital of North Carolina. Named after Sir Walter Raleigh, its industries include the manufacture of computers and textiles. North Carolina State University (1887) and Shaw University (1865) are situated here. Population (1996 est): 243 835.

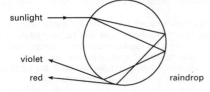

rainbow ▶ The refraction of light by a raindrop.

● **Raleigh, Sir Walter** ▶ (1554–1618) British explorer and writer; half-brother of Humphrey ▷Gilbert. He became a favourite of Elizabeth I, from whom he received a knighthood after serving in Ireland. He was unsuccessful in his attempts (1584–89) to found a colony in Virginia (now North Carolina) but brought back the potato and tobacco plant from America. In 1595–96 he led an expedition to South America, which he described in *The Discoverie of Guiana* (1596), and in 1596 took part in the sack of Cádiz. At James I's accession (1603) he stood trial for treason, but the death sentence was commuted to imprisonment; while in the Tower of London he wrote *The History of the*

Sir Walter Raleigh ▶ A 19th-century engraving.

World (1614). He was released in 1616 to search for gold along the Orinoco but his mission was a failure and after his return his death sentence was invoked and he was executed.

● **rally** ▶ **1.** A competitive motoring event, in which drivers have to reach checkpoints by certain times. The routes are normally over public roads, but rallies often also include speed or other tests after the route has been completed. Major events, such as the Monte Carlo Rally (first held in 1911), require extensively modified cars. **2.** A similar event for motorcycles, but usually with more emphasis on the social and touring aspects than the competitive.

● **Rama** ▶ The seventh incarnation of ▷Vishnu, appearing as a hero in the epics the ▷*Ramayana* and ▷*Mahabharata*. In the ▷*Upanishads* and elsewhere he appears as a god. Since about the 15th century he has been widely worshipped as the supreme deity, epitomizing reason and virtue. He is usually represented holding a bow and arrow and attended by his wife.

● **Ramadan** ▶ The ninth month of the Muslim year. It is a time of atonement, and every able-bodied Muslim is required to observe a strict fast daily from dawn to dusk until the new moon of the next month is visible.

● **Ramakrishna** ▶ (1836–86) Hindu saint and religious teacher. Son of an impoverished Brahmin family, he had little formal education, but he gathered a following throughout the world. He condemned greed, lust, and the caste system, teaching the essential unity and truth of all religions.

● **Raman, Sir Chandrasekhara Venkata** ▶ (1888–1970) Indian physicist, who was professor at Calcutta University. He won the Nobel Prize in 1930 for his discovery that there is a change in the wavelength of light or ultraviolet radiation when scattered by certain molecules (**Raman effect**). This discovery was used to determine some of the finer details of molecular structure.

● **Ramanuja** ▶ (11th century AD) Hindu philosopher and theologian, born in Kanchipuram (S India). He diverged sharply from the tradition in ▷Vedanta associated with ▷Sankara, insisting upon the value and reality of the physical world. In religion he provided an influential philosophical basis for devotional worship (*bhakti*), based upon his concept of a personal God epitomized by the god ▷Vishnu.

● **Ramapithecus** ▶ A genus of fossil ▷hominids that lived during the late Miocene and early Pliocene. It is represented by fossil remains found in India in 1934. They were about the size of a gibbon, possibly walked erect, and may represent the earliest ancestors of modern humans after the divergence of the hominid evolutionary line from the apes.

● **Ramat Gan** ▶ 32 04N 34 48E A city in central Israel, just E of Tel Aviv-Yafo. It has some manufacturing and is the seat of Bar-Ilan University. Population (1997): 121 700.

● **Ramayana** ▶ (Sanskrit: romance of Rama) Hindu epic poem in seven books. Probably composed in its present form after the 4th century BC, it tells the story of ▷Rama and his devoted wife Sita, her abduction by the demon king Ravana, and Rama's struggle to recover her with the aid of ▷Hanuman. The *Ramayana* and ▷*Mahabharata* are the two great classics of Sanskrit literature.

● **Rambert, Dame Marie** ▶ (Cyvia Rabbam, later Miriam Rambach; 1888–1982) British ballet dancer and choreographer, born in Poland. She worked with Diaghilev's Ballets Russes in 1913 and was naturalized as a British citizen in 1918. As director of the Carmargo Society, which in 1935 became the Ballet Rambert, she trained and encouraged many young British dancers and choreographers.

● **Ramblers' Association** ▶ A British organization founded in 1935 to promote love and care for the countryside. It campaigns for greater access to the countryside and organizes such activities as rambles and lectures. Director: Alan Mattingly.

● **Rambouillet** ▶ 48 39N 1 50E A town in N France, in the Yvelines department. Its chateau (14th–18th centuries) is now the summer residence of French presidents. Population (1990): 25 300.

● **rambutan** ▶ A Malaysian tree, *Nephelium lappaceum*, that grows 20 m high and produces edible plum-sized red or yellow spiny fruit. It is cultivated in moist tropical lowlands. Family: *Sapindaceae*.

● **Rameau, Jean Philippe** ▶ (1683–1764) French composer. He held several posts as organist and wrote a *Traité de l'harmonie* (1722), a significant contribution to modern musical theory, before beginning to compose. His works include chamber, keyboard, and vocal music, as well as 24 operas, including the opera *Hippolyte et Aricie* (1733), and opera-ballets, including *Les Indes galantes* (1735) and *Castor et Pollux* (1737). There was great rivalry between his adherents and those of Lully and Pergolesi.

● **Rameses (II) the Great** ▷*See* Ramses (II) the Great.

● **Rameses III** ▷*See* Ramses III.

● **ramie** ▶ A perennial plant, *Boehmeria nivea*, also called China grass, native to E Asia. Each plant produces several stalks, up to 2.4 m high, with clusters of greenish-white flowers in the leaf axils. Although strong and durable, ramie fibre is not widely used due to difficulties in extraction, spinning, and weaving. Family: *Urticaceae* (nettle family).

● **Ramillies, Battle of** ▶ (23 May, 1706) The battle in the War of the ▷Spanish Succession in which British, Dutch, and Danish forces under Marlborough defeated the French 21 km (13 mi) N of Namur. The victory gave much of the Spanish Netherlands to the allies.

● **ramjet** ▷*See* jet engine.

● **Ramón y Cajal, Santiago** ▶ (1852–1934) Spanish histologist, who established the neurone (nerve cell) as the basic unit of the nervous system. Ramón improved staining techniques to distinguish the complex connections between neurones in the brain, spinal tissue, and the retina of the eye. He was awarded the 1906 Nobel Prize with Camillo ▷Golgi.

● **Ramsay, Allan** ▶ (?1685–1758) Scottish poet and editor. He combined an admiration for English Augustan culture with an interest in traditional Scottish literature and life. He published poems by Henryson and Dunbar and made collections of Scottish ballads and proverbs, thus creating an awareness of native culture that helped to pave the way for ▷Burns and other later Scottish writers. His son **Allan Ramsay** (1713–84) was a portrait painter, who trained in London and in Italy (1736–38). His later paintings, such as the portrait of his wife Margaret Lindsay (National Gallery, Edinburgh), were influenced by the delicate draughtsmanship and intimacy of French portraiture. In 1767 he was appointed court painter to ▯George III.

● **Ramsay, Sir William** ▶ (1852–1916) Scottish chemist, whose work on the ▷noble gases earned him the 1904 Nobel Prize for Chemistry. His interest was kindled when ▷Rayleigh discovered that atmospheric nitrogen was slightly heavier than laboratory-prepared nitrogen. In 1894, Ramsay, working with Rayleigh, removed all known gases from some air and discovered a small residue, which they identified spectroscopically as a new element, naming it argon (inert). By fractionally distilling argon, Ramsay isolated neon, xenon, and krypton in 1898. In 1895 he had discovered the inert gas, helium, being given off by the mineral cleveite.

● **Ramses (II) the Great** ▶ King of Egypt (1304–1237 BC) of the 19th dynasty. He fortified the coast road to repel nomads and pirates. His more serious, though indecisive, warfare against the Hittites, whose success at Qadesh (c. 1300) unsettled Egypt's Palestinian subjects, ended in lasting peace around 1284. Ramses built, or enlarged, more temples than any other pharaoh and built the temple complex of ▷Abu Simbel. He is probably the pharaoh who oppressed the Israelites.

● **Ramses III** ▶ King of Egypt (1198–1166 BC) of the 20th dynasty, famous for two victories against the invading Sea Peoples. The first recorded strike in history occurred during his reign, when workers building a necropolis protested against the government's failure to deliver grain rations.

● **Ramsey, Sir Alf** ▶ (Sir Alfred Ernest R.; 1920–99) British Association footballer, who played for Southampton (1946–49) and Tottenham Hotspur (1949–55). He also played for England 32 times. Following his success as manager of Ipswich Town (1955–62), he was made national team manager. Under his control, England won the World Cup in 1966.

● **Ramsgate** ▶ 51 20N 1 25E A resort and port in SE England, in Kent. Formerly one of the Cinque Ports, it is now a fishing and yachting centre. St Augustine is said to have landed nearby in 597 AD. Population (1991): 37 895.

● **Ram Singh** ▶ (1816–85) Indian Sikh leader. He organized a new, severely puritanical, sect of Sikhs, the Kukas, and worked to oust the British from India. His men were brutally punished for their attacks on Muslims and Ram Singh died after a long exile in Burma (now Myanmar).

● **Ramus, Petrus** ▶ (Pierre de la Ramée; 1515–72) French humanist philosopher and logician. In *Aristotelicae Animadversiones* and *Dialecticae Institutiones* (both 1543), Ramus attacked ▷Aristotelianism mainly on the grounds that it falsified the logic of the human mind. An intellectual hero to Protestant Europe, Ramus was murdered in the ▷St Bartholomew's Day Massacre.

● **Rancagua** ▶ 34 10S 70 45W A city in N central Chile. Industries are chiefly related to processing agricultural produce and copper from the El Teniente mine. Population (1995 est): 193 755.

● **Rance, River** ▶ A river in NW France, rising in Brittany and flowing generally E and N to the Gulf of St Malo. It powers the world's first successful ▷tidal power station, opened in 1966. Length: 100 km (62 mi).

● **Rand, the** ▷*See* Witwatersrand.

● **Rangoon** ▶ (*or* Yangon) 16 47N 96 10E The capital of Myanmar (Burma), a port in the S on the River Rangoon. Industry has increased greatly since independence in 1948. Its university was founded in 1920.

History: a settlement grew up in very early times around the Shwe Dagon Pagoda, which is the focal point of Burmese religious life. King Alaungpaya made it his capital in the 18th century. Twice captured by the British in the 19th century, it became the capital of all Burma in 1886. It was badly damaged in World War II during the Japanese occupation (1942–45). Population (1995): 3 851 000.

● **Ranjit Singh, Maharaja** ▶ (1780–1839) Sikh ruler, known as the Lion of the Punjab. At the age of 20 he took control of Lahore and in 1802 seized Amritsar, the holy city of the Sikhs. With an enormous army based on the European model, he became master of a large part of the Punjab. In spite of uneasy relations with the British, he supported them against Afghanistan in 1838.

● **Ranjitsinhji Vibhaji, Kumar Shri, Maharajah Jam Sahib of Nawanagar** ▶ (1872–1933) Indian cricketer and statesman, who captained Sussex (1899–1903) and played for England. He was the first batsman to score 3000 runs in a season (1899). A progressive ruler (1907–33), he was a colonel in the British army during World War I and chancellor of the Indian Chamber of Princes from 1932.

● **Rank, J(oseph) Arthur, 1st Baron** ▶ (1888–1972) British industrialist and film executive. Before becoming chairman of his family's flour-milling business, Rank Hovis McDougall Ltd, he had developed an interest in religious films as aids in his activities as a leading Methodist layman. In 1935 he produced his first commercial film, and in 1946 he founded the Rank Organization, a film production, distribution, and exhibition company that controlled the leading British studios. When film production declined during the 1950s, the organization diversified its business interests.

● **Rank, Otto** ▶ (1884–1939) Austrian psychiatrist, noted for his theory that emotional disorders could stem from psychological trauma experienced during birth. Rank was a colleague of Sigmund ▷Freud and applied Freudian psychology to an analysis of many literary works, pointing especially to the ▷Oedipus complex as a recurrent theme.

● **Ranke, Leopold von** ▶ (1795–1886) German historian. A professor at Berlin University from 1825 to 1871, von Ranke published work on German, French, Spanish, Italian, and English history. His *History of the Latin and Teutonic Nations (1494–1535)* (1824) is generally regarded as the first critical historical work.

● **Ransom, John Crowe** ▶ (1888–1974) US poet and critic. In 1939 he founded the *Kenyon Review*, a literary organ for the school of criticism that took its name from his book *The New Criticism* (1941). He was also a cofounder of the Fugitives, a group of Agrarian poets. His formal ironic poetry is included in *Selected Poems* (1945) and other volumes.

● **Ransome, Arthur Mitchell** ▶ (1884–1967) British journalist and children's writer. He published critical works and travel books but is best known for his series of children's books beginning with *Swallows and Amazons* (1931).

● **Ranunculaceae** ▶ A family of herbaceous and woody plants (about 1300 species), found all over the world but most abundant in N temperate and Arctic regions. They are mainly bitter-tasting and sometimes poisonous. The family includes such garden flowers as ▷*Anemone*, ▷*Aquilegia*, ▷*Clematis*, and ▷*Delphinium*, as well as weeds, e.g. ▷buttercup.

● **Raoult, François Marie** ▶ (1830–1901) French chemist, who while working at the university in Grenoble discovered **Raoult's law**, relating the partial vapour pressure of a solvent to the number of molecules dissolved in it. This accounts for the elevation of the boiling point of a solvent by the addition of solute molecules and provides an important method of determining the relative molecular mass of the dissolved substance.

● **rap** ▷*See* pop music.

● **Rapallo** ▶ 44 21N 9 13E A port and resort in NW Italy, in Liguria on the Gulf of Genoa. It was the scene of the signing of two treaties after World War I, the first between Italy and Yugoslavia (1920) and the second between the Soviet Union and Germany (1922). Olive oil and cement are manufactured here. Population (1990 est): 30 000.

● **Rapanui** ▷*See* Easter Island.

● **rape** ▶ (botany) An annual or biennial herb, ▷*Brassica napus* var. *arvensis*, also called oilseed rape or coleseed, that grows to a height of 1 m and has deeply divided lobed leaves and yellow flowers. It is widely cultivated for its seeds, contained in pods, which yield an edible oil; the residue is used as a cattle feed. Family: ▷*Cruciferae*.

● **rape** ▶ (law) Sexual intercourse with a woman without her freely given and genuine consent. Intercourse with a married woman by impersonating her husband is thus rape. A genuine belief, however mistaken, that a woman has consented is a valid defence. In England, rape was previously punishable by death and now carries a maximum sentence of life imprisonment. The woman's accusation must be supported by other evidence: for example, of penetration. Since 1991 rape within marriage has been a criminal offence. In 1994 rape of a man by another man was recognized as a criminal offence.

● **Raphael** ▶ (Raffaello Sanzio; 1483–1520) Italian Renaissance painter and architect, born in Urbino, the son of a painter. He trained under ▷Perugino, in Perugia, where he painted *The Marriage of the*

Raphael ▶ Detail of an early self-portrait.

Virgin (Brera, Milan) before moving to Florence in 1504. There, influenced by ▷Leonardo and ▷Michelangelo, he painted numerous Madonnas and also the portraits of Angelo and Maddalena Doni (Palazzo Pitti, Florence). Settling in Rome in 1508, he decorated the papal apartments in the Vatican with frescoes, which include the *School of Athens* and the *Disputa*. He painted his patron Pope Julius II (Palazzo Pitti) and the *Sistine Madonna* (Dresden). In 1514 he succeeded Bramante as architect of St Peter's but only a few of his architectural projects were realized, for example the Chigi chapel in Sta Maria del Popolo. In 1515 he designed tapestries for the Sistine Chapel—seven of the cartoons for which are in the Victoria and Albert Museum. His last work, the *Transfiguration* (Vatican Museum), which was completed by Giulio Romano, anticipates ▷mannerism.

● **raphia** ▷*See* raffia.

● **rare-earth metals** ▷*See* lanthanides.

● **Rarotonga** ▶ 21 15S 159 45W A mountainous island in the SW Pacific Ocean, the administrative centre of the ▷Cook Islands. Copra and citrus fruit are exported. Area: 67 sq km (26 sq mi). Population (latest est): 9281. Chief town: Avarua.

● **Ras al-Khaimah** ▷*See* United Arab Emirates.

● **Rashi** ▶ (Solomon ben Isaac; 1040–1105) French rabbi, who established a school at Troyes. His most celebrated works are his commentaries (in Hebrew) on the Bible and the Babylonian ▷Talmud, which are remarkable for their simplicity.

● **Rashid** ▷*See* Rosetta Stone.

● **Rasht** ▶ (or Resht) 37 18N 49 38E A town in N Iran, near the Caspian Sea. It is an agricultural trading centre and has a university (1977). Population (1994 est): 374 475.

● **Rasmussen, Knud Johan Victor** ▶ (1879–1933) Danish explorer and ethnologist, who led Arctic expeditions from Thule in Greenland to study Inuit culture, which he said was akin to that of the North American Indians. In the longest recorded dog-sledge ride (1921–24) he reached the Bering Strait, describing the journey in *Across Arctic America* (1927).

● **raspberry** ▶ A prickly woody perennial plant, *Rubus idaeus*, native to woods and heaths of Eurasia and North America. Up to 1.5 m high, it bears five-petalled white flowers, which produce red (or occasionally yellow) sweet fruits. There are many cultivated varieties, fruiting in summer or autumn. Upright canes grow from basal buds and bear fruit in their first autumn or second summer. The old canes, which die after fruiting, should be removed and the young canes pruned. Family: ▷*Rosaceae*.

● **Rasputin, Grigori Yefimovich** ▶ (c. 1872–1916) Russian mystic, who was a favourite of Emperor ▷Nicholas II and ▷Alexandra. A Siberian peasant, Rasputin's apparent ability to ease the bleeding of the haemophiliac crown prince brought him considerable influence over the royal family and thus over the government: high offices were held by his hangers-on, who were invariably corrupt and incompetent. His unpopularity, aggravated by his debauchery, led to his murder by a group of nobles: his assassins attempted to poison him and when this inexplicably failed he was shot and thrown into the River Neva.

● **Rastafarians** ▶ Members of a religious and political movement that originated in Jamaica; they believe that Ras Tafari Makonnen (▷Haile Selassie) will arrange for the deliverance of the Black races by procuring for them a homeland in Ethiopia. Most Rastafarians wear their hair in dreadlocks (long matted curls).

● **rat** ▶ A ▷rodent belonging to the suborder *Myomorpha*, distributed worldwide. Typical rats belong to the Old World genus *Rattus* (137 species) and are among the most successful rodents. The black rat (*R. rattus*), originally Asian, has spread by travelling on ships to most regions of the world, living in human habitations and sewers. The brown rat (*R. norvegicus*), also called Norway rat, is larger, measuring 30–45 cm including its tail (15–20 cm), and tends to live outdoors in burrows. It has displaced the black rat in many places. Both species eat a variety of plant and animal materials, often causing serious damage to stored food, gnawing through pipes and cables, and transmitting such diseases as typhus and food poisoning. Rats are commonly bred for use as laboratory animals in research. ▷*See also* mouse.

● **ratel** ▶ An omnivorous mammal, *Mellivora capensis*, also called honey badger, of Africa and S Asia. About 70 cm long, grey above and black underneath, it lives in thick woods, eating almost anything from ants to young antelopes (especially honey). Family: ▷*Mustelidae*.

● **rates** ▶ In the UK, taxes raised by local authorities on properties. For domestic premises, rates were replaced by the community charge in 1989 in Scotland and 1990 in the rest of the UK, in accordance with the Local Government Finance Act (1988); the community charge was itself replaced by the ▷council tax in 1993. For nondomestic (business) premises the 1988 act empowers central government to fix a poundage to be paid on the rateable value of business premises (based on former rateable values). These business rates are collected by local authorities, paid into a central pool, and redistributed to local authorities on the basis of their adult population.

● **ratfish** ▷*See* chimaera.

● **Rathenau, Walther** ▶ (1867–1922) German industrialist and politician, who organized Germany's economy during and after World War I. As minister of reconstruction (1921–22), he recommended the prompt payment of German reparations. Becoming foreign minister in 1922, he concluded the Treaty of Rapallo with the Soviet Union shortly before being assassinated. In *The New Economy* (1918) he advocated industrial self-government with worker participation.

● **Rathlin Island** ▶ 55 17N 6 15W An island in Northern Ireland, off the N coast of Antrim in the North Channel. It was the refuge of Robert the Bruce (1306).

● **rationalism** ▶ A philosophical movement stemming from 17th-century attempts to study the universe using reason, in the form of deductive and mathematical methods, rather than sense-experience. ▷Descartes, for example, tried to deduce what God's world is like from the axioms of divine existence and goodness. The scientific interests of the early rationalists made use of their religious views, but conflict between the new sciences and religion developed, and is re-

flected in the work of ▷Spinoza, ▷Arnauld, and ▷Leibniz. By the 19th century a compromise evolved, allocating science and religion to their separate spheres. Kant was called a rationalist in so far as he believed in the possibility of synthetic ▷a priori propositions. Recent intuitionists (*see* intuitionism) have been sympathetic to rationalism.

● **Ratisbon** ▷*See* Regensburg.

● **ratite** ▶ A bird characterized by a smooth breastbone that lacks a keel for the attachment of flight muscles. Ratites are flightless and usually large and swift-running and include the cassowary, emu, kiwi, ostrich, and rhea and the extinct moa.

● **rat kangaroo** ▶ A ▷marsupial belonging to the subfamily *Potoroinae* (9 species), of Australia (including Tasmania). Two species are commonly known as boodies and two others as potoroos. Measuring 23–44 cm excluding the tail (15–38 cm), rat kangaroos are related to kangaroos and have a long narrow ratlike face. They have large canine teeth and long claws and forage at night for grubs and tubers. Family: *Macropodidae*.

● **rattan** ▶ The stems of climbing ▷palms of the genus *Calamus* (375 species), native to Old World tropical regions. Up to 130 m long, the stems are stripped of leaves and used in furniture, matting, baskets, brooms, etc.

● **Rattigan, Sir Terence** ▶ (1911–77) British dramatist. His highly successful plays include upper-class comedies (*French without Tears*, 1936), more ambitious studies of human relationships (*The Deep Blue Sea*, 1952), and studies of historical characters (*Ross*, 1960).

● **Rattle, Sir Simon** ▶ (1955–) British conductor. Born in Liverpool, he was principal conductor (1980–91) and musical director (1991–98) of the City of Birmingham Symphony Orchestra, and has been principal guest conductor of the Los Angeles Philharmonic since 1981. In 2002 he succeeded ▷Abbado as chief conductor of the Berlin Philharmonic. He was knighted in 1994.

● **rattlesnake** ▶ A ▷pit viper belonging to either of two genera, *Sisturus* (2 species) or *Crotalus* (28 species), and characterized by having a rattle composed of loosely connected horny tail segments, which is vibrated to produce a warning sound. Rattlesnakes occur in both North and South America, usually in dry regions, and are 0.3–2.5 m long with dark diamond, hexagonal, or spotted markings on a pale background. They feed on rabbits, rodents, lizards, etc., and bear live young. ▷*See also* diamondback; sidewinder.

● **Ratushinskaya, Irina** ▶ (1954–) Russian poet. Trained as a teacher, she was charged by the Soviet authorities with subversion in 1983 and sentenced to seven years hard labour. Released in 1986, she emigrated to the UK and has been acclaimed for such works as *No, I'm Not Afraid* (1986) and *Grey Is the Colour of Hope* (1988).

● **Rauschenberg, Robert** ▶ (1925–) US artist. A leading exponent of ▷pop art, he studied under Josef ▷Albers. In the early 1950s he produced collages and assemblages made from rusty nails, rags, Coca-Cola bottles, etc. His best-known works are probably those produced in the 1960s, when he adopted the silk-screen printing technique for transferring photographic images to canvases.

● **Rauwolfia** ▶ A tropical genus of trees and shrubs (50 species). The dried roots of some species, including *R. serpentina* of India and *R. vomitoria* of Africa, contain sedative alkaloids sometimes used to treat hypertension. Family: *Apocynaceae*.

● **Ravel, Maurice** ▶ (1875–1937) French composer of the impressionist school. A pupil of Fauré, he repeatedly entered compositions for the Prix de Rome, his failures provoking strong critical protest. His works include, for piano, *Pavane pour une infante défunte* (1899), *Valses nobles et sentimentales* (1911), and *Le Tombeau de Couperin* (1914–17), which were all later orchestrated, the suite *Gaspard de la nuit* (1908), and two piano concertos (one for left hand alone); for orchestra, *La Valse* (1920), *Boléro* (1927), and the ballet *Daphnis and Chloe* (1909–12); the opera *L'Enfant et les sortilèges* (1920–25); many songs; and an orchestration (1922) of Mussorgski's *Pictures at an Exhibition*.

● **raven** ▶ A large glossy black crow, *Corvus corax*, about 63 cm long with bristling feathers at the throat, a massive bill, and a wedge-shaped tail. It feeds on carrion, small animals, seeds, and fruits and often roosts in large colonies. Ravens occur in mountain and moorland regions of the N hemisphere; numbers are increasing after near extermination.

● **Ravenna** ▶ 44 25N 12 12E A city and port in N Italy, in Emilia-Romagna, connected to the Adriatic Sea by canal. Ravenna is said to have been founded by the Sabines. It was the capital of the western Roman Empire (402–76 AD), of the Ostrogothic kings (476–526), and of the Byzantine exarchate (military governorship) from 584 to 751. It is noted for its ancient mosaics. Today Ravenna is a growing industrial centre, based principally on oil and natural-gas refining. Population (1996 est): 137 216.

● **Ravi, River** ▶ A river in NW India and Pakistan, one of the five rivers of the Punjab. Rising in the Himalayas, it flows W and SW to join the River Chenab. Length: 724 km (450 mi).

● **Rawalpindi** ▶ 33 40N 73 08E A city in N Pakistan, 14 km (9 mi) SW of the national capital, Islamabad. From 1959 until 1969 it acted as the interim capital while the new capital at Islamabad was being built. Rawalpindi is an important military, commercial, and trading centre with varied industries, including oil refining, chemicals, and railway engineering. Population (1995 est): 1 290 000.

● **Rawlinson, Sir Henry Creswicke** ▶ (1810–95) British orientalist. As an army officer and later consul at Baghdad, Rawlinson tried for years (1835–46) to obtain a complete copy of the trilingual ▷cuneiform text carved (516 BC) by Darius I on the sheer rock face at Behistun (Iran). He eventually deciphered two of its three scripts: Old Persian (1847) and Babylonian (1857).

● **Rawsthorne, Alan** ▶ (1905–71) British composer. He studied in Manchester and Berlin and gained attention with his *Symphonic Studies* (1938) at a festival in Warsaw. His works include three symphonies, various concertos, a ballet, chamber music, and some film music.

● **ray** ▶ A predominantly marine ▷cartilaginous fish of the worldwide order *Batoidea* (or *Rajiformes*; about 350 species). Rays have a flattened head and body with greatly enlarged winglike pectoral fins; the tapering tail often bears sharp poison spines. The mouth and gill slits are ventral and a pair of openings (spiracles), located behind the dorsally situated eyes, are used to take in water for respiration. Rays are generally bottom-dwelling and move using their pectoral fins. They feed mainly on fish and invertebrates. Subclass: *Elasmobranchii.* □fish.

● **Ray, John** ▶ (1627–1705) English naturalist, who originated basic principles of plant classification. After compiling a survey of English plants, Ray's botanical studies culminated in his *Historia plantarum* (3 vols, 1686–1704). This was followed by works on birds, fishes, quadrupeds, and insects. Ray made the important taxonomic distinction between monocotyledonous and dicotyledonous plants and established the species as the basic taxonomic unit. He emphasized the importance of internal anatomy as a taxonomic criterion. The Ray Society was founded in 1844, in his memory.

● **Ray, Man** ▶ (Emmanuel Rudnitsky; 1890–1976) US artist and photographer. He first achieved prominence as cofounder with Marcel ▷Duchamp of the New York ▷dada movement (1917) and for his ▷ready-mades, notably his iron armed with nails and ironically called *The Gift* (1921). After moving to Paris (1921), where he was associated with ▷surrealism, he became a successful portrait photographer.

● **Ray, Satyajit** ▶ (1921–92) Indian film director. He achieved an international reputation with *Pather Panchali* (1955), *The Unvanquished* (1956), and *The World of Apu* (1959), a trilogy of films about social change in modern India. His other films, all characterized by an understanding of both Eastern and Western values, include *Charulata* (1964), *The Chess Players* (1977), *The Home and The World* (1984), *Branches of the Tree* (1990), and *The Stranger* (1992). He received an honorary Oscar in 1992.

● **Rayleigh, John William Strutt, 3rd Baron** ▶ (1842–1919) British physicist. Succeeding James Clerk ▷Maxwell as director of the Cavendish Laboratory, Cambridge (1879–84), he later became professor at the Royal Institution (1887–1905). His work on black-body radiation was upset by ▷Planck's discovery of the quantum theory but he did much valuable work in optics, hydrodynamics, and the theory of electrical units. He was awarded the 1904 Nobel Prize for his discovery of argon, in conjunction with Sir William ▷Ramsay. He was appointed to the OM in 1901. His son **Robert John Strutt, 4th Baron Rayleigh** (1875–1947) was also a physicist, who specialized in spectroscopy. He later worked on natural radioactivity, showing that the age of rocks can be estimated from their radioactivity.

● **Raynaud's disease** ▶ A disorder in which the arteries of the hands have spasms (sustained contractions) as a local response to cold. The fingers become pale and numb and in severe cases lack of blood to the fingertips can cause gangrene or ulceration. Named after a French physician, Maurice Raynaud (1834–81).

● **rayon** ▶ A textile fibre or fabric made from ▷cellulose. **Viscose rayon** is made by dissolving wood pulp in a mixture of sodium hydroxide and carbon disulphide. The fibres are reconstituted in an acid bath. **Acetate rayon** is made by mixing wood pulp with acetic anhydride, acetic acid, and sulphuric acid to form cellulose acetate, which is then dissolved in a solvent and forced through fine holes to form fibres.

● **Razi, ar-** ▶ (*or* Rhazes; c. 865–c. 928 AD) Persian physician and philosopher. In his *Comprehensive Book*, he surveyed the medical knowl-

Ravenna ▶ The church of San Vitale, begun under Queen Amalasuntha in 1535 and consecrated in 1547, is regarded as the masterpiece of Ravenna's Byzantine period.

edge of the Greeks, Syrians, and Arabs and he wrote works on alchemy, philosophy, and diseases, such as smallpox and measles.

• **Razin, Stenka ▶** (d. 1671) Cossack leader. From 1667 to 1669 he led a group of propertyless Cossacks in raids along the Volga and the Caspian Sea. In 1670 he was captured leading a revolt against the tsar and subsequently executed.

• **razorbill ▶** A black-and-white ▷auk, *Alca torda*, that breeds around N Atlantic coasts and winters in the Mediterranean. 40 cm long, it has a laterally compressed bill. The wings are used as paddles in diving to catch fish, shellfish, and worms.

• **razor shell ▶** A burrowing ▷bivalve mollusc of the family *Solenidae* (about 40 species), also called a jack-knife clam, of Atlantic and Pacific coasts. The common razor (*Ensis siliqua*), about 15 cm long, has a narrow ▯shell with squared ends; its curved foot is used to burrow up to 30 cm into sand.

• **Re** ▷*See* Ra.

• **reactance** ▷*See* impedance.

• **Read, Sir Herbert ▶** (1893–1968) British poet and critic. The son of a Yorkshire farmer, he served as an infantry officer in World War I, and his war poetry constitutes a large proportion of his *Collected Poems* (1966). His art criticism, written from the basis of a personal philosophy of anarchism, promoted the work of Henry ▷Moore and many other artists of his generation. His literary criticism was chiefly concerned with the Romantic poets.

• **Reade, Charles ▶** (1814–84) British novelist. His best-known novel is the historical romance *The Cloister and the Hearth* (1861), set in Europe during the Reformation. His other novels tackle such topical social issues as prison reform and trade unionism; he also wrote popular melodramas.

• **Reading ▶ 1.** 51 28N 0 59W A town in S England, in Reading unitary authority, Berkshire, on the River Thames. It has the remains of a 12th-century Benedictine abbey and a university (1892). An important railway junction, Reading has electronics works and is the headquarters of several international industries. Population (1991): 134 600. **2.** A unitary authority in S England, in Berkshire. Area: 37 sq km (14 sq mi). Population (1996 est): 142 900.

• **Reading ▶** 40 20N 75 55W A city in the USA, in Pennsylvania. It grew as an iron and steel centre, linked by canal and rail to nearby anthracite mines. Industries today include the manufacture of bricks, speciality steels, and textiles. Population (1996 est): 75 723.

• **Reading, Rufus Daniel Isaacs, 1st Marquess of ▶** (1860–1935) British lawyer, Liberal MP (1904–13), and diplomat. He became solicitor general and then attorney general in 1910. As Lord Chief Justice (1913–21) he presided over the trial of Sir Roger Casement (1916). He was subsequently ambassador to the USA (1918–19), viceroy of India (1921–26), and foreign secretary (1931).

• **ready-made ▶** An everyday manufactured object elevated to artistic status by the personal whim of the artist. The ▷dada painter Marcel ▷Duchamp produced the first ready-made, a bicycle wheel on a stool, in 1913; it was followed by his snow shovel (1915), and his notorious urinal (1917). The ready-made is also a feature of ▷surrealism, ▷pop art, and ▷conceptual art.

• **Reagan, Ronald ▶** (1911–) US statesman; Republican president (1981–89). He achieved fame as a film actor before entering politics. He was governor of California from 1966 until 1974. In 1981 he survived an assassination attempt. A conservative, as president he cut taxes, increased defence spending, and approved the US invasion of Grenada (1983) and CIA operations in Nicaragua, despite Congressional opposition. Re-elected by a landslide in 1984, he focused upon arms-control talks with the Soviet Union, resulting in the Intermediate Nuclear Forces (INF) Treaty (1987). Despite his early hostility towards the Soviet Union, he later responded to ▷Gorbachov's attempts to improve relations. A scandal over US arms sales to Iran provoked worldwide criticism late in his presidency. ▷*See also* disarmament; Strategic Defence Initiative.

• **realism ▶ 1.** The medieval philosophical theory that general terms (called universals) have a real existence, that is that there is some abstract entity that corresponds with the term. For example, blueness is not just one idea of the sum of all blue objects (called particulars), but a really existing entity. ▷Plato and ▷Aristotle were realists in believing that the universe contained universals in addition to particulars. The difference between them was that Plato thought universals, which he called Forms, merely could have corresponding particulars and were independent of them, while Aristotle thought that Forms must have particulars and could exist only as instantiated in things. ▷Aquinas and ▷Duns Scotus were leading realists. *Compare* nominalism. **2.** In modern philosophy, a stance opposed to ▷idealism. Realists, such as G. E. ▷Moore (*see also* common sense, philosophy of), assert that objects exist independently of being perceived. Mathematical realism implies that mathematical entities exist in this way and that mathematical truths are independent of our ability to prove them. **3.** ▷*See* Naturalism.

• **real number** ▷*See* complex numbers; numbers.

• **real tennis ▶** A racket-and-ball indoor court game, which originated in France in the 12th–13th centuries as *jeu de paume*. It was originally played with the bare hand, the strung racket being developed in about 1500. Many other handball and racket-and-ball court games developed from it. Its world championships are the oldest of any sport, dating back to about 1750, although it is now very much a minority sport. The stone or concrete floor area is approximately 29 × 10 m (96 × 32 ft). The cloth ball is hit over a central net, as in ▷tennis and ▷badminton, but it also bounces off the side walls, as in ▷squash rackets and ▷fives.

• **Réaumur, René-Antoine Ferchault de ▶** (1683–1757) French physicist, whose work on thermometers led him to devise the temperature scale that bears his name. On this scale water freezes at 0° and boils at 80°. He also carried out experiments on animals to show that digestion was a chemical process and not a mechanical one.

• **Reber, Grote ▶** (1911–) US astronomer, who, following Karl ▷Jansky's discovery, built the first radio telescope (1937) and used it to discover a number of radio sources that had no visible counterparts. It was largely as a result of his published observations that several large radio telescopes were built after World War II.

• **recall ▶** A political device designed to enable voters dissatisfied with an elected official to replace him before the expiry of his term of office. The recall originated in Switzerland and has been operative in a number of US states since 1903. The usual procedure is the securing of a petition stating the charges against the official, the holding of an election to determine whether the official shall be removed, and the choice of a successor. Usually the official is allowed space on the ballot or petition in which to state his defence.

• **Recamier, Jeanne Françoise Julie Adelaide ▶** (1777–1849) French society hostess. She was married to a wealthy Parisian banker from 1792 to 1830. Her salon was attended by influential statesmen and politicians opposed to Napoleon. Her close friends included Mme de ▷Staël and ▷Chateaubriand.

• **Received Pronunciation ▶** (RP) The pronunciation of English most generally accepted as standard or correct in England and to some extent elsewhere. The term was coined in 1926 by Daniel ▷Jones to describe the characteristic ▷accent of the public schools and universities and later extended to include that of the BBC. Historically, it is derived from the dialect of Middle English spoken in the London area.

• **recession ▶** A decline in the ▷trade cycle that, in a serious setback to the economy, becomes a transitory phase between ▷boom and ▷depression. In a recession, consumption demand falls off, investment (according to the ▷accelerator principle) declines, and business failures become common.

• **recessive gene ▶** The ▷allele of a gene the function of which is hidden when the organism concerned is crossed with one carrying a different allele (called the dominant allele) for the same gene. ▷*See* dominance.

• **Recife ▶** (or Pernambuco) 8 06S 34 53W A port in NE Brazil, the capital of Pernambuco state, on the Atlantic Ocean. It is a major port; the chief exports are sugar and cotton. Industries include sugar refining and spirit distilling and it has two universities. Population (1995): 3 168 000.

● **Recklinghausen** ▶ 51 37N 7 11E A city in NW Germany, in North Rhine-Westphalia in the ▷Ruhr. Notable buildings include the 13th-century church (founded 1276) and the castle (1702). A port on the Rhine-Herne Canal, its manufactures include iron and steel, machinery, and textiles. Population (1996 est): 127 216.

● **recombinant DNA technology** ▷*See* genetic engineering.

● **Reconstruction** ▶ (1865–77) The period after the US ▷Civil War in which the defeated Confederate states of the South were brought back into the Union. The southern states were readmitted to the Union after accepting the 14th (1866) or, subsequently, 15th Amendment, which guaranteed Black citizenship and franchise. The new state governments were dominated by Whites prepared to compromise, newly enfranchised Blacks, and northern carpetbaggers, but after the withdrawal of Federal troops in 1877 southerners dedicated to White supremacy were restored to power.

● **recorder** ▶ (law) ▷*See* judge.

● **recorder** ▶ (music) A woodwind instrument of medieval origin, much used in the 17th and 18th centuries and revived in the 20th century. In contrast to the side-blown ▷flute, the recorder is end-blown, through a whistle mouthpiece mounted in a block (*or* fipple). The holes are covered with the fingers; the tone is quieter than that of the flute.

● **recording of sound** ▶ A system for storing and reproducing sound. In music recording, the most common methods are tape recording, usually in ▷cassette form, and ▷compact discs, which had largely replaced gramophone records by the early 1990s. The gramophone record was made by converting the sound into an electrical signal, which was amplified and used to control a cutter that produced a spiral undulating groove in a master disc. Copies of this, originally on a shellac-based record and subsequently on a vinyl plastic record, were then mass-produced for sale. In a record-player, the stylus travelled along the groove and reproduced the mechanical vibrations of the cutter. The ▷pick-up then converted these to an electrical signal, which was amplified and fed to a loudspeaker. Many electronic devices were used to ensure that the system reproduced the original sound with a high fidelity, i.e. that sounds in the frequency range 80–12 000 hertz were reproduced without distortion. The ▷compact disc (CD) consists of a specially treated glass disc cut by a high-intensity laser beam and played back on a compact disc player. CDs are resistant to scratches and offer better quality sound reproduction than conventional gramophone records. **Digital audio tape** (DAT), which reproduces sound equal in quality to the compact disc and also permits home-recording to the same standard as cassettes, makes use of **digital recording** technology. In this the musical signal is sampled, up to 30 000 times per second, and the characteristics of the sampled signal are represented by digits (as information is represented in a computer). The digits are then transmitted or recorded and reconstituted in the receiver or player. In this way the actual signal suffers no interference or distortion during transmission or in the recording process. New developments involving digital technology include the **digital compact cassette** (DCC), which uses magnetic tape but produces high-quality sound. DCCs may supersede the old analogue cassettes; DCC players have been designed to play both types of cassette. The **minidisc** (MD) is a small version (about 5 cm in diameter) of the CD. It is possible to record over some MDs.

● **rectifier** ▶ A device that allows electric current to flow in one direction only; it is generally used to convert alternating current to direct current. ▷Semiconductor diodes have now replaced thermionic valves (diodes) for lower voltage applications. For power supplies of several megawatts, mercury-arc rectifiers are used.

● **rectum** ▷*See* intestine.

● **recycling** ▶ The repeated use of the same resources. Recycling involves the manufacture of a complex product followed by breakdown of the spent product to release its constituents for reuse. This process—a feature of most natural ▷ecosystems—is becoming an eco-nomic necessity in industry in order to conserve scarce raw materials and reduce pollution of the environment. ▷*See* waste disposal.

● **red admiral** ▶ A ▷nymphalid butterfly, *Vanessa atalanta*, found throughout Europe, Asia, and North America. The wings are black with red and white markings. Red admirals migrate to northern regions for the summer but do not survive the cold winters there; in warmer climates they hibernate. The caterpillars feed on stinging nettles.

● **red algae** ▶ ▷Algae of the phylum *Rhodophyta* (about 3000 species), which are usually red or blue due to the presence of the pigments phycoerythrin (red) or phycocyanin (blue), which mask the green chlorophyll. They range from small unicellular or filamentous forms to branching or sheetlike ▷seaweeds, found attached to other plants in deep warm seas or sometimes in rock pools. Reproduction is asexual or sexual.

● **Redbridge** ▶ A borough of NE Greater London, created in 1965 from the former municipal boroughs of Ilford, Wanstead, and Woodford and parts of Chigwell and Dagenham. Area: 56 sq km (22 sq mi). Population (1996 est): 230 600.

● **Red Brigades** ▶ (Italian name: Brigate Rosse) A group of Italian terrorists formed in 1969 and dedicated to the violent overthrow of capitalist society. They were responsible for the murder of the statesman Aldo ▷Moro in 1978. Most of their leading members had been captured and imprisoned by the mid-1980s.

● **Redcar and Cleveland** ▶ A unitary authority in NE England, in North Yorkshire; part of Cleveland county from 1974 to 1996. Area: 240 sq km (93 sq mi). Population (1996 est): 144 000.

● **Red Cross, International** ▶ An organization founded by the Geneva Convention of 1864 to provide care for the casualties of war. Inspired by Henri ▷Dunant, a Swiss philanthropist, its headquarters are in Geneva and its emblem, the red cross, represents the Swiss flag with its colours reversed. Most Muslim countries have adopted the crescent as their emblem. The International Red Cross, staffed mainly by volunteers, has twice won the Nobel Peace Prize (1917 and 1944). The **British Red Cross Society**, incorporated in 1908, undertakes first-aid and welfare duties throughout the world.

● **redcurrant** ▶ A shrub of the genus *Ribes* (*see* currant), cultivated for its clusters of small acid-tasting red fruits, which may be made into jellies, jams, etc. Cultivated redcurrants have been derived from *R. rubrum* of Eurasia, *R. sativum* of W Europe, and *R. petraeum* of central and S Europe. Whitecurrants are varieties that lack red pigment.

● **red deer** ▶ A large reddish-brown deer, *Cervus elaphus*, of European and Asian woodlands. Over 120 cm high at the shoulder, males have spreading branched antlers up to 125 cm long; females are more lightly built. Stags and hinds live apart in winter, spring, and summer, coming together in the autumn for the rut, when mature males compete to gather a harem of hinds. ▷*See also* wapiti.

● **Redditch** ▶ 52 19N 1 56W A town in the English Midlands, in Worcestershire. Designated for development as a new town in 1964, its manufactures include fishing tackle and springs. Population (1991): 73 372.

● **Red Duster** ▶ The popular name for the British Merchant Navy's Red Ensign—a red flag with the Union Flag in its upper corner nearest the flagstaff. It was authorized in 1674, amended in 1707 and 1801, and reconfirmed in 1894.

● **Redford, Robert** ▶ (1936–) US film actor and director. He costarred with Paul ▷Newman in *Butch Cassidy and the Sundance Kid* (1969) and *The Sting* (1973). Other films include *All the President's Men* (1976), *Out of Africa* (1986), and *Indecent Proposal* (1993). Films he has directed include *Ordinary People* (1980), *Quiz Show* (1994), and *The Horse Whisperer* (1998), in which he also starred. In 1980 he founded the Sundance Institute, which now hosts one of the USA's leading film festivals.

● **red fox** ▶ A ▷fox, *Vulpes vulpes*, found throughout the N hemisphere. It is about 100 cm long, including its bushy tail (50 cm). There are a number of local races and the North American red fox and its grey-black variety, the silver fox, were once thought to be a separate species (*V. fulva*).

● **red giant** ▶ A greatly distended cool but very luminous ▷giant star, often variable in nature. It is one of the final evolutionary stages of a normal ▷star, attained when its central hydrogen has been converted to helium. Hydrogen burning in a shell surrounding the inert helium core causes a rapid expansion and cooling of the outer atmosphere of the star. As it evolves it may change to a hotter more compact type of giant and then back to a red giant.

● **Redgrave, Sir Michael** ▶ (1908–85) British Shakespearean actor, who also performed in and directed modern plays. His films included *The Browning Version* (1951) and *The Go-Between* (1971). His daughter **Vanessa Redgrave** (1937–) has acted on stage in Shakespeare and Chekhov and in such films as *Isadora* (1968), *Julia* (1977), *Howards End* (1992), and *Mrs Dalloway* (1998). She is known for her left-wing political activities, as is her brother the actor **Corin Redgrave** (1939–). Their sister **Lynn Redgrave** (1943–) is also an actress. Vanessa Redgrave's daughters **Natasha Richardson** (1963–) and **Joely Richardson** (1965–) have also appeared on stage and in films.

● **Redgrave, Sir Steve(n)** ▶ (1962–) British oarsman, who won gold medals at five consecutive Olympic Games (1984, 1988, 1992, 1996, 2000). He has also won nine gold medals at the world championships. He was knighted in 2001.

● **red grouse** ▶ A ▷grouse, *Lagopus lagopus scoticus*, found on moorlands of Great Britain and Ireland, where it is managed as a gamebird. 34–37 cm long, it feeds chiefly on ling heather. The male is red-brown with red wattles above the eyes and the female is browner and heavily barred: both sexes have white underwing markings.

● **Red Guards** ▶ High-school and university students organized by Mao Tse-tung during the ▷Cultural Revolution (1966–68) to eliminate revisionism. The Red Guards destroyed property, humiliated foreign diplomats, and attacked officials opposed to Mao's policies.

● **red-hot poker** ▶ A plant of the African genus *Kniphofia*, especially *K. uvaria* and *K. rufa* (and their varieties), cultivated as garden plants. 45–120 cm tall, they have tubular flowers, usually scarlet and/or yellow. Family: ▷Liliaceae.

● **Red Indians** ▷*See* American Indians.

● **Redmond, John Edward** ▶ (1856–1918) Irish politician. An MP from 1881, in 1900 he reunited the pro- and anti-Parnellite factions under his leadership. In 1909 he allied his party with the Liberals to achieve ▷Home Rule. The rise of ▷Sinn Féin undermined the appeal of his moderate policies.

● **red mullet** ▶ A fish, also called surmullet or goatfish, belonging to the family *Mullidae* (about 50 species), found usually in shallow warm seas. They have a body up to 25 cm long, with two dorsal fins and two long flexible chin barbels. They feed on bottom-dwelling invertebrates; many species are valued food fish. Order: *Perciformes*.

● **Redon, Odilon** ▶ (1840–1916) French symbolist painter and lithographer; a forerunner of ▷surrealism. Working exclusively in black and white in charcoal drawings, lithographs, and etchings until the 1890s, he created a fantasy world of plants with human heads, mythical figures, etc. From the 1890s he turned to oil painting and pastel, producing a number of flower paintings in powdery colours and paintings inspired by literary subjects.

● **Redouté, Pierre Joseph** ▶ (1759–1840) French flower painter. He worked for all the French courts from Louis XV to Louis Philippe, painting his flowers, notably roses, chiefly in watercolours and after careful scientific study.

● **redox reactions** ▷*See* oxidation and reduction.

● **redpoll** ▶ A tiny finch, *Acanthis flammea*, about 12 cm long with a brown streaked plumage, a red crown, and a black chin. The male has a red breast in summer. It breeds in the Arctic tundra and high mountains of Europe, migrating to central Europe and the N USA in winter.

● **Red River** ▶ (Vietnamese name: Song Hong) The chief river of N Vietnam, rising in S China and flowing SE to enter the Gulf of Tonkin via an extensive delta. Length: 500 km (310 mi).

● **Red River of the North** ▶ (*or* Red River) A river in central North America, rising in W Minnesota and flowing N into Canada to empty into Lake Winnipeg. Although navigable, it is subject to severe floods that damage the farms of its fertile valley. Length: 1000 km (621 mi).

● **Red River Settlement** ▶ A colony of immigrants led by Thomas Douglas, 5th Earl of Selkirk (1771–1820), settled in 1811 on the banks of the Red River in present-day Manitoba. In 1836 it was bought by the Hudson's Bay Company. In 1869 Louis ▷Riel led an uprising against the proposed transfer of the colony to Canada (effected in 1870).

● **red salmon** ▷*See* sockeye salmon.

● **Red Sea** ▶ A long narrow arm of the Indian Ocean between Africa and Asia, extending some 2400 km (1491 mi) NNW beyond the Gulf of Aden and the Bab el-Mandeb. In the N, it is connected to the Mediterranean Sea by the Suez Canal, which has enormously increased shipping in the Red Sea. It is part of the ▷Great Rift Valley. Area: 438 000 sq km (169 076 sq mi).

● **redshank** ▶ An Old World ▷sandpiper, *Tringa totanus*, that breeds in cool marshy regions of Eurasia. 30 cm long, it has long reddish legs, a black-tipped red bill, and a brown-grey plumage with a white rump. It winters on mudflats of Africa and Asia, feeding on crustaceans, molluscs, and ragworms.

● **redshift** ▶ An overall displacement towards larger wavelengths of the spectral lines of a celestial object. Its astronomical significance was suggested by Edwin ▷Hubble in 1929, when it was used as the basis of the theory that the universe is expanding (*see* expanding universe). A redshift usually arises from the ▷Doppler effect, that is from recession of a celestial object. It increases as the object's radial velocity increases and for an extragalactic body can be used as a measure of distance. A **gravitational redshift** occurs whenever radiation is emitted by a body: it is generally negligible except when the gravitational field is very strong.

● **red squirrel** ▶ A tree ▷squirrel, *Sciurus vulgaris*, of Eurasia. About 20 cm long with a 20-cm tail, red squirrels have dark glossy red fur and tufted ears. They feed mainly on seeds and nuts but will eat buds and dried fungi in winter. They are less aggressive than the immigrant grey squirrels, which have displaced them in many areas.

● **redstart** ▶ A small Eurasian thrush of the genus *Phoenicurus*, about 14 cm long with a sharp fine bill. The male European redstart (*P. phoenicurus*) is grey with a russet breast, black throat and face with a white stripe, and a red tail, which it fans out in its courtship display to the yellow and brown female. It is found in woodland and heathland while the black redstart (*P. ochruros*) inhabits cliffs and buildings. Both of these species migrate to Africa for the winter.

● **reduction** ▷*See* oxidation and reduction.

● **reductionism** ▶ A 20th-century trend in philosophy prompted by scepticism. Reductionists argue that material objects are nothing but collections of sensations; other minds are nothing but the physical manifestations of their owners; statements about the past are nothing but aggregates of statements about the presently available evidence for them. Reduction of the meaning of a statement to statements of the evidence for it was popular among phenomenalists and logical positivists.

● **redundancy** ▶ An end to the immediate usefulness of labour or machines, caused by a decline in the demand for the product they produce or, technological change, or restructuring in the company or business concerned. Lump-sum redundancy payments to employees so displaced have been statutory in the UK since 1965, a portion of which was formerly recoverable from the Department of Employment. The Employments Rights Act (1996) gives employees dismissed for reasons of redundancy the right to statutory redundancy payments if they are under retirement age but over 18 and have been continuously employed by the company for at least two years. The statutory sum is now paid in full by the employer and is calculated on the basis of one and a half weeks' pay for each year of employment in which the employee was aged 41 or over, one week's pay for each year between 22 and 41, and half a week's pay between 18 and 22.

● **redwing** ▶ A European thrush, *Turdus iliacus*, resembling a small song thrush but having a white eyestripe, red underwings, and red patches on the flanks. It feeds on earthworms, snails, beetles, fruits, and berries. Redwings breed mainly in Scandinavia and occasionally in Scotland, migrating to W Europe for the winter.

● **redwood** ▶ A coniferous tree, *Sequoia sempervirens*, thought to be the tallest tree in the world and one of the longest lived: a specimen in California is over 111 m tall and some Californian trees are over 2000 years old. Also called coast redwood, it is native to the Pacific coast between Oregon and California and is an important timber tree in North America; in Europe it is planted mainly for ornament. It has brown-red fibrous bark, bladelike leaves, 1.5–2 cm long, and woody red-brown globular cones, about 2 cm long. Family: *Taxodiaceae*. ▷*See also* dawn redwood; sequoia.

● **reed** ▶ Any of several species of tall aquatic grasses, especially those of the genus *Phragmites* (2–3 species). The common reed (*P. communis*) has a creeping underground stem (rhizome) and grows worldwide along the margins of marshes, lakes, streams, and fens. 1.5–3 m tall, it has long flat leaves, 10–20 mm wide, a stiff smooth stem, and clusters of purple-brown flowers. Dried reed stems have been used for arrows, basketry, pens, and in musical instruments.

The name is also given to similar but unrelated plants, such as the paper reed, *Cyperus papyrus* (*see* papyrus).

● **Reed, Sir Carol** ▶ (1906–76) British film director. His best-known films include *The Fallen Idol* (1948) and *The Third Man* (1949), both with screenplays by Graham ▷Greene. His later, more commercial, films include *The Agony and the Ecstasy* (1965) and *Oliver!* (1968).

● **Reed, John** ▶ (1887–1920) US journalist. He helped found the Communist Party in the USA and was a personal friend of Lenin. *Ten Days that Shook the World* (1919) is an account of the 1917 Revolution in Russia, where he died.

● **Reed, Lou** ▶ (1943–   ) US rock singer, songwriter, and guitarist. After cult success with the Velvet Underground group in New York in the late 1960s, he embarked on a solo career after 1970; his solo albums include *Transformer* (1972), *The Blue Mask* (1982), *Magic and Loss* (1992), and *Set the Twilight Reeling* (1996).

● **Reed, Walter** ▶ (1851–1902) US physician. After serving as an army surgeon, Reed was appointed to investigate yellow fever in Cuba, where C. J. ▷Finlay had suggested that the mosquito was the agent responsible for spreading the disease. Reed and his team subjected themselves to the bites of infected mosquitoes, one of the team dying as a result, but proving that mosquitoes were responsible and enabling yellow fever to be eliminated from the region.

● **redbuck** ▶ An African antelope belonging to the genus *Redunca* (3 species). The common reedbuck (*R. arundinium*) grows to 90 cm and has a grey coat and ridged horns and inhabits grassland. The bohor reedbuck (*R. redunca*) is smaller and lives in swampy regions, while the gregarious mountain reedbuck (*R. fulvorufula*) lives in hilly areas.

● **reed instruments** ▶ Musical instruments in which a column of air is made to vibrate by a reed. The ▷clarinet family have a single (or beating) reed clamped to and vibrating against a slot in the mouthpiece. The ▷oboe and ▷bassoon use a double reed. The **reed organ** family contains such instruments as the ▷harmonium, ▷concertina, ▷accordion, and ▷harmonica, which have free reeds (sometimes made of some other substance, such as brass) that vibrate from side to side of the slot in which they are fixed.

● **reedling** ▶ A Eurasian bird, *Panurus biarmicus*, about 16 cm long, also called bearded tit. It lives in reedbeds, feeding on insects and seeds. The plumage is brown with pale underparts: the male has a grey head with a black moustache of feathers. Reedlings belong to the ▷babbler family.

● **reedmace** ▶ A widely distributed perennial herbaceous plant, *Typha latifolia*, also called bulrush or cat's-tail, growing in reed swamps. It has an erect stem, 1.5–2.5 m high, bearing a terminal spike of male and female flowers, the latter developing into the cylindrical fruit, which tapers into the stem at its base. There are several other reedmaces of the genus *Typha* (*see* elephant grass). Family: *Typhaceae*.

● **reed warbler** ▶ An acrobatic ▷warbler, *Acrocephalus scirpaeus*,

about 12 cm long with a reddish-brown plumage, pale underparts, and a pale eyestripe. It winters in SE Africa and breeds in European reedswamps, building a deep nest around the stems of several reeds and feeding on small marsh insects. It is frequently parasitized by cuckoos.

● **reef** ▶ A ridge of rock lying just above or near the surface of the sea, built mainly of the skeletons of ▷coral or other sedentary marine organisms. **Barrier reefs** lie parallel to the coast with a deep lagoon between; **fringing reefs** are attached to the coast; bioherms are dome-shaped reefs; apron reefs are tabular masses; atolls are circular with a central lagoon. Reef formation was much more widespread in the geological past.

● **Reeves, William Pember** ▶ (1857–1932) New Zealand politician. He was a progressive minister of education, labour, and justice (1891–96), originating among other labour reforms the influential Industrial Conciliation and Arbitration Act. He was subsequently high commissioner in London (1905–08) and then director of the London School of Economics (1908–19). Among his books is *The Long White Cloud: A History of New Zealand* (1898).

● **referendum and initiative** ▶ Votes on specific legislation by the whole electorate. Referendums are votes on particular political questions framed by parliament and put to the electorate. In the UK referendums have been held concerning membership of the EC (1975) and ▷devolution for Scotland and Wales (1979 and 1997). Initiatives are proposals, drafted by a citizen or group of citizens, that by virtue of attaining a requisite number of signatures on a petition are put to the electorate for acceptance or rejection. Initiatives are used in about half of the states of the USA to decide contentious matters of local government. ▷*See also* plebiscite.

● **reflection** ▶ The rebounding of a wave of light or other radiation when it strikes a surface. Reflected light obeys two laws: first, the normal (an imaginary line vertical to the surface at the point of impact), the incident ray, and the reflected rays all lie in the same plane; second, the angle of incidence (i.e. the angle between the incident ray and the normal) is equal to the angle of reflection. ▷*See also* mirrors.

● **reflex** ▶ An automatic and involuntary response by an organism to a change in the environment. An example is the rapid withdrawal of a finger in response to a pinprick, which occurs before the brain has had time to convey the necessary information to the muscles involved. The nervous circuit involved in a reflex response is called a reflex arc. In its simplest form this consists of a receptor (e.g. a pain receptor in the skin) linked to a sensory ▷neurone, which forms a ▷synapse with a motor neurone in the spinal cord or brain; the motor neurone typically supplies a muscle. ▷*See also* conditioned reflex.

● **reflexology** ▶ A traditional method of diagnosing and healing diseases of the body by foot massage. Practised for many thousands of years by the Chinese, Indians, and Egyptians, it was introduced to the Western world in 1913 by the US ear, nose, and throat surgeon William Fitzgerald. He divided the body into ten zones; pressure on one part of a zone could, he claimed, affect all parts of that zone. In the 1930s Eunice Ingham, a therapist, extended zone therapy by claiming that tension in one part of the foot is a reflection of tension in a corresponding part of the body. Practitioners of reflexology claim that massage can stimulate the blood supply and lymphatic system by dispersing the crystalline deposits that cause congestion, and that massaging the reflex areas of the feet helps to increase blood circulation and relax tensions.

● **Reform Acts** ▶ The legislation that reformed the British parliamentary system. The Reform Act of 1832 gave the vote in the boroughs to the occupants of houses worth £10 a year and in the counties to £10 copyholders and £50 leaseholders, in addition to the already enfranchised 40-shilling freeholders. It disenfranchised some ▷rotten and ▷pocket boroughs and gave parliamentary representation to new industrial towns, such as Birmingham and Manchester. However, it did not destroy the dominance over the electoral system of the landed classes. The 1867 Reform Act gave the vote to all householders and £10 rent payers in the towns, thus enfranchising many of the working class for the first time. It doubled the existing electorate to 2.4 million. The 1884 Reform Act made the county franchise the same as that in the towns, thus increasing the electorate to about five million. Adult male suffrage was achieved only in 1918 and women had to wait until 1928.

● **Reformation** ► A religious movement in 16th-century Europe that began as an attempt to reform the ▷Roman Catholic Church and ended with the establishment of independent Protestant Churches (*see* Protestantism). The Reformation, which was preceded by such reform movements as those led by John ▷Wycliffe (the ▷Lollards) and Jan ▷Hus (the ▷Hussites), was caused by the inability of the Catholic Church to put its own, increasingly worldly, house in order; the critical examination of the Bible emphasized by the humanists (*see* humanism) and its translation into the vernaculars; the development of printing, which disseminated new ideas more widely and more quickly; and the growth of nationalism, which sought to weaken papal jurisdiction within the states of W Europe.

The Reformation began on 31 October, 1517, when Martin ▷Luther nailed his 95 theses on the door of the castle church at Wittenburg. Luther's attack on the sale of ▷indulgences and, subsequently, on papal authority and the ▷sacraments (save baptism and the Eucharist) was condemned by the pope and the Holy Roman Emperor but gained the support of several German princes. The consequent conflict (*see* Charles V) was not resolved until 1555 (*see* Augsburg, Peace of).

In Switzerland, the Reformation was initiated by ▷Zwingli in Zurich in 1520, spreading to Basle, Berne, and also to Geneva, where it was led by John ▷Calvin. Calvinism was adopted in France, the Low Countries, England, Scotland, and subsequently in North America. In France, where Protestants were called Huguenots, the Reformation became involved in a political struggle for control of the Crown, giving rise to the ▷Wars of Religion, and in the Low Countries it fired the ▷Revolt of the Netherlands against Spanish rule.

In England, the Reformation had three stages. Under Henry VIII papal authority in England was destroyed. Thomas Cromwell's legislation (1529–36) attacked ecclesiastical abuses (1529–31) and clerical jurisdiction (1532) and abolished the payment of first fruits (annates) to the pope (1532, 1534) and, thereby enabling Henry to divorce Catherine of Aragon, the lodging of appeals to Rome (1533); the Act of Supremacy (1534) proclaimed the king as supreme head of the English Church and in 1536 the ▷dissolution of the monasteries was authorized. Under Edward VI Protestantism was established by the 1552 Book of ▷Common Prayer, the accompanying Acts of ▷Uniformity, and the 42 Articles (1553). Following the re-establishment of Roman Catholicism under Mary I, Protestantism finally became the established ▷Church of England under Elizabeth I and a new Act of Supremacy was passed (1559).

In Scotland, the Reformation was influenced by John ▷Knox and ▷Presbyterianism was established in 1592. Elsewhere Lutheranism was adopted by Sweden in 1527, by Denmark in 1546, and became the established religion of Norway, Finland, and Iceland. ▷*See also* Counter-Reformation.

● **Reformed Churches** ▷*See* Protestantism.

● **Reform Judaism** ► A religious movement attempting to adapt traditional Judaism to modern circumstances. It began in Germany in the early 19th century. The first Reform synagogue in England was established in 1840; **Liberal Judaism** (founded 1903) instituted more radical reforms typical of US Reform Judaism. The World Union for Progressive Judaism was founded in London in 1926 (it is now based in Jerusalem). The reforms include abolition of many of the ritual laws, acceptance of modern biblical criticism, vernacular services, and full equality for women.

● **refraction** ► The bending of a beam of radiation as it passes from one medium onto another. For a light ray the amount by which it is bent depends on the angle of the incident ray and on the refractive indices of the two media, the exact dependence being given by ▷Snell's law. Refraction is caused by the difference in the speed of the radiation in the two media. The ratio of the speed of light in the two media is known as the **refractive index**. If the first medium is a vacuum, the ratio is known as the absolute refractive index of the second medium. The refractive index of glass lies between 1.5 and 1.7, for diamond it is 2.1, and for water 1.33 (at 25°C).

● **refractories** ► Firebricks or other heat-resisting materials used for lining furnaces to retain the heat and protect the outer shell of the furnace. There are three types, characterized by their chemical interaction with the hot substances in the furnace: acid (e.g. silica); basic (e.g. dolomite); and neutral (e.g. Carborundum).

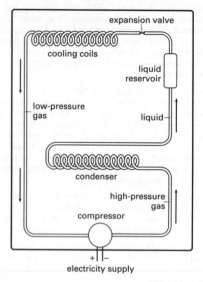

refrigeration ► The vapour–compression cycle commonly used in domestic refrigerators. The energy for the cycle is supplied by the mains electricity.

● **refrigeration** ► The process of lowering the temperature inside a closed insulated container. In the domestic refrigerator the method most commonly used is the vapour-compression cycle in which a liquid refrigerant, such as a ▷fluorocarbon, is pumped through cooling coils formed into the ice-making compartment. In these coils the refrigerant evaporates, taking the latent heat required to make it into a gas from the surroundings (i.e. the inside of the ice compartment). It is then passed to an electrically driven compressor; after compression it condenses back to liquid, when the absorbed heat is given out (usually at the back of the refrigerator). This cycle is repeated over and over again until the required temperature (about 1–2°C in the food chamber and −15°C in the deep-freeze compartment) is achieved. The compressor is then switched on and off by the thermostat. Other cycles (e.g. ammonia absorption) are also used, but in all of them the refrigerator functions as a heat engine in reverse: in order to transfer heat from the cold interior to the warmer surrounding air, work must be done. In the vapour-compression refrigerator this is supplied by the electricity that drives the compressor. ▷*See also* cold storage; freezing.

● **refugees** ▷*See* political asylum.

● **Regency** ► In the UK, the years 1811 to 1820, during which King ▷George III suffered a debilitating attack of madness, forcing parliament to appoint the Prince of Wales to act as regent for his father. The prince was known as the Prince Regent from 1811 until the death of his father in 1820, when he became ▷George IV.

The main political events of the Regency were the ▷War of 1812, the conclusion of the ▷Revolutionary and Napoleonic Wars, the Congress of ▷Vienna, and government repression of reform movements, culminating in the notorious ▷Peterloo Massacre. The period is also notable for its achievements in poetry (Byron, Shelley, and Keats) and its distinctive style of architecture and furniture design (*see* Regency style).

● **Regency style** ► An English architectural, furniture, and decorative style fashionable during the ▷Regency period and for some 10 years before and after it. In architecture, the main tendency was the ▷neoclassicism that can be seen in the terraced houses of Bath, the seaside squares of Brighton, and the elegant Regent's Park terraces in

London. In Brighton, too, a Regency interpretation of oriental styles dominates the Royal Pavilion, redesigned for the Prince Regent by John ▷Nash. Other prominent Regency architects were Robert ▷Smirke, John ▷Soane, and James ▷Wyatt (*see also* English art and architecture).

In furniture, dark exotic woods and veneers, such as rosewood, were popular and were set off by ormolu mounts and grilles for doors. Leading designers produced rather heavy furniture purporting to derive from antique Greek, Roman, and Egyptian models. Concurrently there was a vogue for oriental motifs (*see* chinoiserie) and some magnificent lacquer was produced, for example for the Royal Pavilion. Initially elegant, the style later became somewhat clumsy.

● **regeneration** ▶ In biology, the regrowth and development of tissues or organs lost through injury, as a normal process (e.g. during moulting), or by any other means. The ability to regenerate is present in all forms of life to some degree: it is particularly well developed in plants and simple animals. Thus, whole plants can regenerate from stem and leaf cuttings and simple animals, such as sponges and planarians, can develop from minute fragments. More complex animals, such as crustaceans, replace lost appendages, while lizards can grow new tails. In mammals regeneration is limited to wound healing and regrowth of peripheral nerve fibres.

● **Regensburg** ▶ (English name: Ratisbon) 49 01N 12 07E A city in SE Germany, in Bavaria at the confluence of the Rivers Danube and Regen. Many medieval buildings survived the bombing of World War II, including the gothic cathedral (1275–1524). Its university was established in 1962. It is a port and commercial and industrial centre.
History: originally a Celtic settlement, it became a Carolingian capital and a prosperous medieval trading centre. From 1663 until 1806 the imperial diets (assemblies) were held here. Population (1996 est): 125 836.

● **Regent's Park** ▷*See* London; Nash, John.

● **Reger, Max** ▶ (1873–1916) German composer, organist, and teacher. In Leipzig he was director of music at the university (1907–08) and professor of composition at the conservatoire. His vast output includes *Variations and Fugue on a Theme of Mozart* and a *Fantasy and Fugue on BACH*.

● **reggae** ▶ A style of popular music combining West Indian rhythms and US ▷rhythm and blues. It is characterized by a strong accent on the upbeat in each bar. Reggae emerged among the poor of Jamaica and became especially associated with ▷Rastafarians; it first became popular internationally in the 1970s through the work of such musicians as Bob ▷Marley.

● **Reggio di Calabria** ▶ 38 06N 15 39E A seaport in Italy, in Calabria on the Strait of Messina. It was founded by Greek colonists in the 8th century BC. Fruit, herbs, and oil are exported. Population (1996 est): 179 623.

● **Reggio nell'Emilia** ▶ 44 42N 10 37E A city in Italy, in Emilia-Romagna. Dating from Roman times, it was ruled by the Este family (15th–18th centuries) and has a cathedral (rebuilt in the 13th century). The centre of a rich agricultural area, its industries include agricultural engineering and meat canning. Population (1996 est): 135 406.

● **Regina** ▶ 50 30N 104 38W A city in W Canada, the capital of Saskatchewan. Founded in 1882, it has expanded rapidly since 1945 as a centre of agricultural industries, oil refining, and potash production. It houses the University of Regina (1917). Population (1991): 179 178.

● **Regiomontanus** ▶ (Johannes Müller; 1436-76) German astronomer and mathematician, who introduced algebra and trigonometry to Germany. He produced a table of trigonometric functions that was printed by Johann Gutenberg and widely used by navigators. He was an ardent follower of ▷Ptolemy, producing a new translation of his *Almagest*. He also drew up a table of planetary motions.

● **Regnier, Henri François Joseph de** ▶ (1864–1936) French poet. He published several early collections of Symbolist poetry written in *vers libre*, but in his later works, such as *Les Médailles d'argile* (1900), he reverted to classical forms.

● **Regulus, Marcus Attilus** ▶ (died c. 251 BC) Roman general of the

first ▷Punic War. In 256 he defeated the Carthaginian navy, invaded Africa, and overwhelmed the Carthaginians. Rejecting his peace terms, in 255 the Carthaginians utterly defeated Regulus, who was captured and sent to Rome to negotiate peace. Urging continued war, he returned to certain death in Carthage.

● **Rehoboam** ▶ King of Judah (c. 922–915 BC); the son of Solomon. His intransigent attitude to the northern tribes resulted in the secession of Israel under Jeroboam and the disintegration of Solomon's empire.

● **Reich** ▶ (German: kingdom) Any of three periods in German history. The ▷Holy Roman Empire is regarded as the First Reich, which lasted from 962 to 1806; the ▷Hohenzollern German Empire is the Second Reich (sometimes called the *Kaiserreich*), which lasted from 1871 to 1919; and the Nazi dictatorship aspired unsuccessfully to create a world-dominating ▷Third Reich (1933–45). ▷*See also* Germany, Federal Republic of.

● **Reich, Wilhelm** ▶ (1897–1957) US psychiatrist, born in Austria, noted for his controversial notion of a universal energy, which he called orgone, that is released during sexual intercourse. Failure to achieve regular release of this energy resulted, so he claimed, in both personal and social neuroses. Reich's "orgone box" was declared fraudulent and he was jailed for contempt of court in the USA in 1956. His works include *The Function of the Orgasm* (1948).

● **Reichenberg** ▷*See* Liberec.

● **Reichstag** ▶ (Imperial Diet) The legislative assembly of the German Empire (1871–1918) and the Weimar Republic (1919–33). Its origins lay in the diet of the Holy Roman Empire. It was divided into an electoral college (*see* electors), a college of princes, and a college of cities. The decline of imperial control over the German states after the Thirty Years' War brought a corresponding decline in the power of the diet until its revival by Bismarck in 1867 as the representative assembly of the ▷North German Confederation, then of the German Empire, and finally of the Weimar Republic. In 1933 the **Reichstag fire** reduced the Reichstag building in Berlin (built in 1894) to a burnt-out shell; Nazi allegations of communist responsibility provided an excuse to ban opposition parties, and the Reichstag became a mere puppet under Hitler. In the late 1990s the Reichstag building was radically restored (by Norman Foster) to provide a new seat for the German government, which was transferred from Bonn to Berlin in 1999.

● **Reid, Thomas** ▶ (1710–96) Scottish philosopher. He maintained that Hume, in his theory of ideas, had overlooked "common sense," which was to become the cornerstone of his own philosophy. In his *Enquiry into the Human Mind on the Principles of Common Sense* (1764), he discussed "common sense," in linguistic and metaphysical, as well as mundane, contexts.

● **Reigate** ▶ 51 14N 0 13W A town in SE England, in Surrey at the foot of the North Downs. It is a dormitory town for London and includes the adjacent newer town of Redhill. Population (1991): 47 602.

● **Reign of Terror** ▶ (1793–94) The most violent period of the French Revolution. Dominated by ▷Robespierre, the governing Committee of Public Safety authorized severe measures against the Revolution's opponents. Over 250 000 suspects were arrested and about 1400 were summarily guillotined. Public reaction caused Robespierre's downfall and execution in July, 1794, thus ending the Terror.

● **Reims** ▶ (*or* Rheims) 49 15N 4 02E A city in NE France, in the Marne department. An important Roman town, it was the scene of the coronations of most of the French kings. The magnificent gothic cathedral was badly damaged in World War I but it has gradually been restored. Its university was established in 1969. A centre for the marketing of Champagne wines, it has varied manufacturing industries. Population (1990): 185 164.

● **reincarnation** ▶ (*or* metempsychosis) The migration of the soul from one body at death and its re-entry into another (human or animal) body. Belief in reincarnation appears in many different cultures, partly because it offers an explanation for the perplexing differences between individuals' characters and destinies, these being ascribable to traces of previous characters and the rewards or punishments for actions in previous lives. The cycle of reincarnation (*samsara*) is fundamental to Hindu, Buddhist, and Jain conceptions of the world, all spiritual effort being directed towards release (*moksa*) from the cycle. ▷Plato and ▷Pythagoras also subscribed to reincarnation, but orthodox Christianity rejected it as contrary to belief in the resurrection of the body.

● **reindeer** ▸ A large deer, *Rangifer tarandus*, of European and North American tundra (in America it is called a caribou). About 125 cm high at the shoulder, reindeer have a grey-brown coat and spreading branched antlers—male antlers are larger with an extra forward point over the face. Reindeer feed mainly on lichens (reindeer moss) but also eat dwarf willow and other shrubs. The small summer groups gather into herds numbering several hundreds for their winter migration southwards, at which time their coat fades to a dull white. ▯mammal.

● **reindeer moss** ▸ A grey tufted ▷lichen, *Cladonia rangiferina*, that is very abundant in Arctic regions, especially Lapland. It has a stalked much-branched body, up to 8 cm high, and covers immense areas of tundra, serving as the major food source for reindeer, moose, musk oxen, etc.

● **reinforced concrete** ▷*See* concrete.

● **Reinhardt, Django** ▸ (Jean Baptiste R.; 1910–53) Belgian jazz guitarist of gipsy origin. He injured his hand in a fire at the age of 18 but developed an original guitar technique. From 1934 to 1939 he led the quintet of the Hot Club de France with Stephane ▷Grappelli.

● **Reinhardt, Max** ▸ (M. Goldmann; 1873–1943) Austrian theatre director. His large-scale productions, involving massed crowds and spectacular lighting and scenery, included *Oedipus Rex* in Berlin in 1910 and *The Miracle* in London in 1911. He also directed more conventional theatre productions, opera, and a film of *A Midsummer Night's Dream* (1935), and founded the Salzburg Festival in 1920. From 1938 he lived in the USA.

● **Reith, John Charles Walsham, 1st Baron** ▸ (1889–1971) British administrator. His severe moral principles greatly influenced the early development of the BBC, of which he was first general manager from 1922 and director general from 1927 to 1938. He subsequently held many other important administrative posts, including the chairmanship of the British Overseas Airways Corporation (BOAC), which he formed in 1939. The Reith lectures, broadcast annually, were established in 1947 and named in his honour.

● **relative aperture** ▷*See* f-number.

● **relative atomic mass** ▸ (A_r) The ratio of the average mass of the atoms of the naturally occurring form of an element to one-twelfth the mass of a carbon-12 atom. *Formerly called* atomic weight.

● **relative molecular mass** ▸ (M_r) The ratio of the average mass per molecule of the naturally occurring form of an element or compound to one-twelfth the mass of a carbon-12 atom. It is the sum of the ▷relative atomic masses of the atoms comprising a molecule. *Formerly called* molecular weight.

● **relativistic mass** ▸ The mass of a body that is moving at a speed comparable to the speed of ▷light. According to the theory of ▷relativity, if the speed of the body is *v* then its mass is $m_0(1 - v^2/c^2)^{-\frac{1}{2}}$, where *c* is the speed of light and m_0 the rest mass (the mass when stationary). The relativistic mass of an electron travelling at 99% of the speed of light is seven times its rest mass.

● **relativity** ▸ An important theory proposed by Albert ▷Einstein. The first part of the theory, published in 1905 and known as the special theory, applies only to motion in which there is no acceleration. The problem that Einstein set out to solve was concerned with the speed at which ▷light travels relative to an observer.

Up to this time it was thought that light travelled through a stationary medium, called the ether, at a constant speed and that its speed relative to an observer could be calculated in the same way as the relative speed of any two moving objects. For example, if one car (A) travelling at 90 mph on a motorway overtakes another (B) travelling at 70 mph, the speed of the two cars relative to each other is 20 mph. In talking about relative speeds it is necessary to be precise about what a particular speed is relative to. Car A's speed relative to

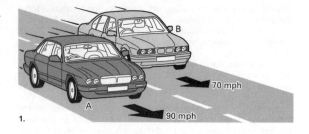

1.

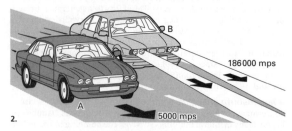

2.

relativity ▸ 1. Two cars, A and B, travelling along a motorway. The speed of car A relative to the earth is 90 mph. The speed of car B relative to the earth is 70 mph. The speed of car A relative to car B is 90–70 = 20 mph. 2. Car B is now stationary; its headlight beams are turned on as supercar A passes, travelling at 5000 miles per second. The speed of car B's headlight beam relative to car A is 186 000 miles per second (not 186 000–5000 miles per second). The speed of light is absolute.

car B is 20 mph, but relative to the earth it is 90 mph. Relative to the sun it is about 64 000 mph. Because two American scientists, Michelson and Morley (*see* Michelson-Morley experiment), had shown that light travelled at the same speed whether measured in the direction of the earth's rotation or at right angles to this direction, Einstein suggested that the restriction about relative motion does not apply to light. It always has the same speed of 2.998×10^8 metres per second (186 000 miles per second), irrespective of the motion of the observer. The speed of light is absolute.

This has far-reaching effects. In his special theory Einstein suggested that as bodies increase in speed they become shorter and heavier (*see* Lorentz, Hendrick Antoon). This effect is only noticeable as the speed of light is approached. Cars on the motorway do get heavier and shorter but the effect is minute. On the other hand, an electron travelling at 99% of the speed of light becomes seven times heavier than its mass at rest. Einstein also showed that no body could actually travel at the speed of light itself. If it did it would be infinitely heavy and have zero length.

The increase in mass and decrease in length that a body undergoes when moving at high speeds led Einstein to the conclusion that mass (*m*) and energy (*E*) are two different aspects of the same thing; they are related by the simple equation $E = mc^2$, where *c* is the speed of light. The atom bomb and ▷nuclear energy both depend on this equation. ▷*See also* time-dilation effect.

In the general theory of 1916, Einstein considered accelerated relative motion, especially as it is concerned with gravitation. In this theory, the gravitational force experienced by a body is treated as a property of space and time, which Einstein suggested was "curved" by the presence of the mass. The motion of the stars and planets is controlled by this curvature of space in the vicinity of matter. Light, too, is bent by the gravitational field of a massive body. The observed bending of light rays as they pass close to the sun and the shift of certain lines in the solar ▷spectrum have provided experimental verification of the theory.

● **relay, electric** ▸ An electrical switching device in which one circuit is controlled by a separate circuit, often to avoid the danger of direct contact with high-voltage supplies or to reduce the length of high-current cable needed. Relays may involve electromagnetic connection between the two circuits or be controlled by ▷solid-state devices.

● **relief sculpture** ▶ A form of sculpture in which figures are attached to a background of stone, bronze, or wood, in contrast to free-standing sculpture seen in the round. There are four main types of relief: high relief, in which the figures project almost as much as free-standing sculptures; middle relief; bas-relief, in which the image is only very slightly raised and of which ▷Donatello developed a variation in the 15th century; and sunken or coelanaglyphic relief, also called ▷intaglio, particularly associated with ancient Egyptian sculpture.

● **religion** ▷*See* God.

● **reluctance** ▶ (*or* magnetic resistance) The ratio of the ▷magneto-motive force in a material to the total ▷magnetic flux induced by it. It is analogous to electrical ▷resistance.

● **remand centres** ▷*See* prisons.

● **remanence** ▷*See* ferromagnetism.

● **Remarque, Erich Maria** ▶ (1898–1970) German novelist. After being wounded in World War I, he worked as a journalist until the publication of his immediately successful *All Quiet on the Western Front* (1929), describing life in the trenches. His books banned by the Nazis, he lived in America and Switzerland from 1932.

Rembrandt ▶ A self-portrait painted in about 1631, when the painter was in his mid-twenties.

● **Rembrandt (Harmenszoon) van Rijn** ▶ (1606–69) Dutch painter and etcher, born in Leiden, the son of a miller. After studying briefly at Leiden University, he became the pupil of Jacob van Swanenburgh (c. 1571–1638) and later in Amsterdam of Pieter Lastman (1583–1633), who trained him in the Italian ▷baroque style and had a lasting influence on him, for example in encouraging him to paint historical and religious subjects. Settling permanently in Amsterdam (1631), he made his name as a portrait painter with *The Anatomy Lesson of Dr Tulp* (1632; The Hague), a group portrait. It was followed by many other portraits, including those of his wife Saskia and culminating in the famous group portrait, *The Nightwatch* (1642; Rijksmuseum, Amsterdam). He also treated mythological and biblical subjects. Rembrandt was a popular teacher of painting and at the

height of his success was an avid collector of art. He eventually became bankrupt, spending the last 20 years of his life isolated from society. Many of his greatest works belong to this period. He concentrated on depicting the inner life of his sitters and the biblical characters he painted. He also excelled as a landscapist and an etcher.

● **Remembrance Sunday** ▶ The day on which the British remember the dead of World Wars I and II and subsequent conflicts. From 1919 to 1945 it was named Armistice Day and was observed on 11 November, the date of the Armistice in 1918. Renamed Remembrance Sunday in 1945, it has been observed on the second Sunday of November since 1956. A two-minute silence marks the time, 11 am, of the signing of the Armistice and wreaths of poppies are laid at the Cenotaph in Whitehall, London, and other war memorials. In 1996 the practice of observing silence on 11 November was revived.

● **Remington, Eliphalet** ▶ (1793–1863) US inventor and gun manufacturer. His innovations included a method of producing really straight gun barrels and the invention of a lathe for cutting gunstocks. In 1873 the business founded by Remington bought the patents of Christopher ▷Sholes' typewriter.

● **Remonstrants** ▶ The Dutch adherents of Arminianism (*see* Arminius, Jacobus) who rejected the Calvinist doctrine of ▷predestination in a statement known as the Remonstrance (1610). Condemned by the Synod of Dort (1618–19), they suffered persecution until 1630. They influenced many Protestant thinkers, including ▷Locke and ▷Wesley.

● **remora** ▶ A dark elongated fish, 30–90 cm long, of the family *Echeneidae* (8–10 species) found in warm marine waters. The dorsal fin is modified to form a flat oval sucking disc on its head by which it attaches itself to various marine animals (e.g. sharks and turtles) or ships to feed on scraps of food or the hosts' parasites. Order: *Perciformes*.

● **Remscheid** ▶ 51 10N 7 11E A city in NW Germany, in North Rhine-Westphalia on the River Wupper. An industrial centre, it specializes in tool manufacture. It is the birthplace of Roentgen. Population (1996 est): 122 260.

● **REM sleep** ▷*See* sleep.

● **Remus** ▷*See* Romulus and Remus.

● **Renaissance** ▶ (French: rebirth) An intellectual and cultural movement that began in Italy in the 14th century, spread to N Europe, and flourished until the mid-16th century. Fundamental to the Renaissance were the revival of classical learning, art, and architecture and the concept of the dignity of man, which characterized ▷humanism. Both were advocated by the 14th-century poet and classical scholar ▷Petrarch. Other great writers of the Italian Renaissance were ▷Dante, ▷Boccaccio, ▷Machiavelli, and ▷Ariosto.

The first painter to mirror these new ideals was ▷Giotto. He was followed in the 15th century by ▷Masaccio, ▷Uccello, ▷Piero della Francesca, ▷Mantegna, and others, who helped place art on a scientific basis through their concern with the structure and proportions of the human body. They also introduced into painting the use of linear ▷perspective, the laws of which were developed by the architect ▷Brunelleschi. Humanism was reflected in the development of portrait painting and the emphasis upon human feelings in religious painting. The High Renaissance denotes the period between about 1500 and about 1520, when the artists ▷Leonardo da Vinci, ▷Raphael, and ▷Michelangelo perfected the harmony and balance associated with classical art.

In sculpture the major figures were Nicola ▷Pisano, ▷Donatello, ▷Ghiberti, ▷Verrocchio, and Michelangelo. In building Brunelleschi was the first to revive the classical use of the ▷orders of architecture. Later architects, such as ▷Bramante, ▷Alberti, and ▷Palladio, also revived ancient temples and domed structures. ▷*See also* Italian art.

In the 16th century the Renaissance spread to N Europe, where it manifested itself in the art of ▷Dürer, the scholarship of ▷Erasmus, the plays of ▷Shakespeare, and particularly in the courts of such rulers as Elizabeth I of England, where the ideal of Renaissance civilization was epitomized in the lifestyle of such courtiers as Sir Philip ▷Sidney.

● **Renan, (Joseph) Ernest** ▶ (1823–92) French philosopher and theologian. Renan's famous *Life of Jesus* (1863) undermined the supernatural aspects of Christ's life but defended the moral nature of his teachings.

● **Rendell, Ruth (Barbara), Baroness** ▶ (1930–   ) British author of crime novels. Her books, several of which feature Chief Inspector Wexford, include *Wolf to the Slaughter* (1967), *Simisola* (1994), *Road Rage* (1997), *A Sight for Sore Eyes* (1998), and (published under the pseudonym Barbara Vine) *A Fatal Inversion* (1987), *The Brimstone Wedding* (1996), and *The Chimney Sweeper's Boy* (1998). She was made a life peer in 1997.

● **renewable energy sources** ▷*See* alternative energy.

● **Renfrew** ▶ 55 53N 4 24W A town in W central Scotland, in Renfrewshire on the River Clyde below Glasgow. Formerly an important port and shipbuilding town, it now has engineering and tyre-manufacturing industries. Renfrew has a commercial airport. Population (1991): 20 764.

● **Renfrewshire** ▶ A council area of W Scotland, on the Clyde Estuary W of Glasgow. Under local government reorganization in 1975 the historic county of Renfrewshire was absorbed into Strathclyde Region. In 1996 Strathclyde was abolished and the ▷unitary authorities of ▷Inverclyde, Renfrewshire, and ▷East Renfrewshire were established. It is mainly low lying, with much urban development in the E. The main economic activities are engineering, textiles, and agriculture. Area: 261 sq km (101 sq mi). Population (1996 est): 178 550. Administrative centre: Paisley.

● **Reni, Guido** ▶ (1575–1642) Italian painter, born in Bologna. He studied under the Flemish artist Denis Calvaert (c. 1575–1619) but was chiefly influenced by the ▷Carracci. In Rome (c. 1600–14) he painted his masterpiece, the ceiling fresco of *Aurora* (Palazzo Rospigliosi). Later, working in Bologna, his highly idealized style became somewhat sentimental.

● **renin** ▶ An enzyme, secreted by the kidneys, that breaks down a liver protein to form the peptide angiotensin I. This is converted to angiotensin II, which constricts blood vessels—causing a rise in blood pressure—and increases the secretion of ▷aldosterone from the adrenal glands.

● **Rennes** ▶ 48 06N 1 40W A city in NW France, in the Ille-et-Vilaine department. The capital of the old province of Brittany, it was badly damaged by fire in 1720 and most of its notable buildings, including the cathedral and university, were built after that date. The main commercial centre of W France, Rennes is an important railway junction and military headquarters and has textile, electrical, and pharmaceutical industries. Population (1990): 203 533.

● **rennet** ▶ An extract, prepared from cows' stomachs, that contains the milk-coagulating enzyme rennin. It is used in the manufacture of cheese and junket.

● **Rennie, John** ▶ (1761–1821) British civil engineer, who designed several of the 19th-century bridges over the Thames in London, all of which have been replaced. He also constructed or redeveloped docks throughout Britain, including the London and East India docks (c. 1800), which he built on the River Thames.

● **Reno** ▶ 39 32N 119 49W A city and resort in the USA, in W Nevada near the foot of the Sierra Nevada. Founded about 1860, it is known for its easily obtainable divorces and legalized gambling. The University of Nevada (1864) was moved here from Elko in 1886. Population (1996 est): 155 499.

● **Renoir, Pierre Auguste** ▶ (1841–1919) French impressionist painter, born in Limoges. He trained as a decorator of porcelain before entering (1861) the studio of Charles Gleyre (1808–74) and meeting ▷Monet, with whom he frequently painted on the banks of the Seine. He exhibited at the first three impressionist exhibitions but largely abandoned impressionism after studying Renaissance art in Italy (1881–82). Increasingly crippled by arthritis, he spent his last years in the south of France, painting many sensuous nudes. His best-known works include *Les Parapluies* (National Gallery, London) and *Le Moulin de la Galette* (Louvre). His son **Jean Renoir** (1894–1979) was a film director whose best-known films, *La Grande Illusion* (1937) and *La*

Règle du jeu (1939), are personal and subtle reflections of prewar French society. During World War II he went to Hollywood but returned to Europe to make *French Can-can* (1955), *Le Déjeuner sur l'herbe* (1959), and other films.

● **rent** ▷*See* landlord and tenant.

● **repertory theatres** ▶ Theatres in which a resident company presents plays from an extended repertoire of productions rather than putting on a single production for as long as the public will pay to see it. This was the system adopted in most theatres until the late 19th century, when the rising cost of productions encouraged the practice of staging each play for as long as it was commercially viable. At the same time the development of a national rail network made it attractive for companies to tour extensively with a single play. In the UK a repertory system was revived at the beginning of the 20th century by ▷Granville-Barker and other champions of the so-called repertory movement. The system was modified so that each play in the repertoire was given a run of one or two weeks. In this form there were some 100 repertory theatres (nearly all regional) operating in the early 1950s, although the number has now fallen to less than 60. Both the ▷Royal National Theatre and the ▷Royal Shakespeare Company are repertory theatres in the original sense.

In the USA, repertory companies are still known by the older British name of stock companies.

● **repetitive strain injury** ▶ (RSI) An ill-defined condition, characterized by arm or wrist pains, that can affect people who habitually perform awkward hand movements, including violinists, pianists, employees operating computer terminals, and children playing computer games. Also known as work-related upper-limb disorder (WRULD *or* ULD), it is exacerbated by awkward arm posture or hand grip while performing the movements. Some practitioners do not regard RSI as a clinical condition. ▷*See also* occupational disease.

● **Representatives, House of** ▷*See* Congress.

● **repression** ▶ In ▷psychoanalysis, the process of excluding unacceptable ideas from consciousness. Repressed wishes and thoughts continue to exist in the ▷unconscious mind and may give rise to symptoms. One of the goals of psychoanalysis is to bring repressed material into consciousness so that it can be coped with rationally. ▷*See also* defence mechanisms.

● **reproduction** ▶ In biology, the generation of new individuals of the same species. In **asexual reproduction** individuals are derived from one parent and no special reproductive structures are involved. The simplest form is ▷fission, occurring mostly in unicellular organisms. Simple multicellular organisms, such as sponges and cnidarians, reproduce by budding: a new individual arises as an outgrowth (bud) from the parent. In fragmentation, the individual breaks into two or more parts, each capable of growth to form a new individual: this is seen in flatworms and some algae. In plants a common form of asexual reproduction is **vegetative reproduction** (*or* vegetative propagation), in which new individuals develop from such structures as ▷bulbs, ▷corms, ▷rhizomes, and ▷tubers, which become detached from the parent plant. Most animals and plants, however, reproduce by a process involving specialized reproductive cells (*see* gamete)—typically male and female—that fuse to produce a new individual with a different genetic makeup. This process, **sexual reproduction**, occurs in its simplest form in ▷conjugation. In more complex organisms the gametes are produced in special organs, e.g. the ▷carpel and ▷stamen in flowering plants and the ▷ovary and ▷testis in animals. The importance of sexual reproduction is that it allows genetic variation in a population, enabling it to adapt to the changing environment.

● **reptile** ▶ A vertebrate animal belonging to the class *Reptilia* (about 6000 species), which includes ▷crocodiles, ▷turtles, ▷lizards, ▷snakes, and the ▷tuatara. Reptiles occur in terrestrial, freshwater, and marine habitats, chiefly in tropical regions. They have a covering of horny scales and are cold-blooded. Fertilization of the egg by sperm takes place within the female, unlike fish and most amphibians. The egg is large and yolky, has special membranes that nourish the embryo, and a protective leathery or calcareous shell, i.e. features that enable it to be laid on land. In some lizards and snakes the eggs

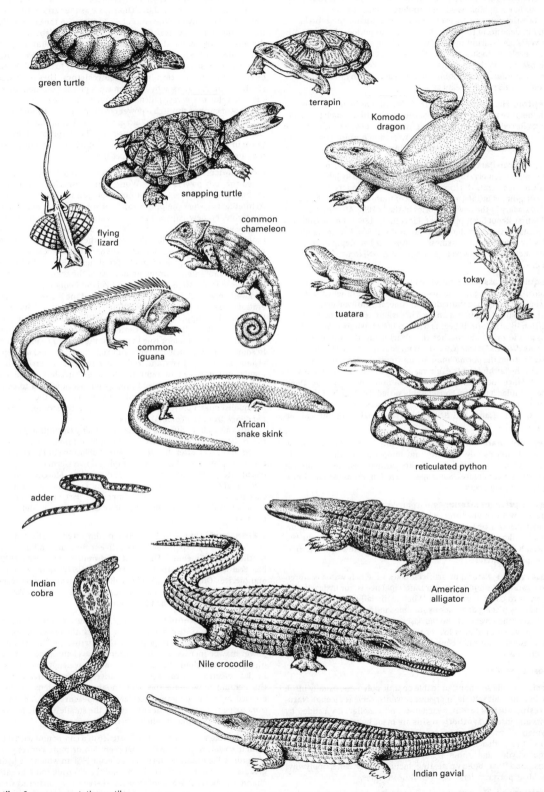

green turtle

terrapin

Komodo dragon

snapping turtle

flying lizard

common chameleon

tuatara

tokay

common iguana

African snake skink

reticulated python

adder

Indian cobra

American alligator

Nile crocodile

Indian gavial

reptile ▶ Some representative reptiles.

are retained inside the female and live young are born. Young reptiles—unlike amphibians—do not undergo metamorphosis.

The primitive reptiles evolved from amphibians: their fossils are found in deposits of the Upper Carboniferous period, about 300 million years ago. During the following 240 million years, a variety of forms evolved, including the fishlike ▷ichthyosaurs, the flying ▷pterosaurs, and the mammal-like ▷therapsids, culminating in the giant ▷dinosaurs, which dominated the earth during the Cretaceous period (136–65 million years ago).

● **Repton, Humphry** ▶ (1725–1818) British landscape gardener, a term he invented. A country gentleman until financial circumstances forced him to make a living from his hobby, he laid out some 200 parks and gardens. His gardens were much more formal than those of his predecessor, Capability ▷Brown.

● **Republican Party** ▶ One of the two major political parties of the USA (*compare* Democratic Party). The name was used by Jefferson's Republican Democrats (formed in 1792), but the modern Republican Party originated in 1854 as an alliance of those opposed to the extension of slavery in the new territories in the W USA. After the election of the first Republican president, Lincoln, in 1860, the Republicans were usually the ascendant party until the 1930s, becoming identified with conservative business interests. Other Republican presidents include T. ▷Roosevelt, ▷Eisenhower, ▷Nixon, ▷Reagan, and ▷Bush.

● **requiem mass** ▶ The mass (*see* Eucharist) for the dead (*Missa pro defunctis*) said or sung in Roman Catholic and some other churches. It may be said for named individuals at funerals, anniversaries, etc., or for the departed in general on such occasions as All Souls Day. In its traditional Latin form it begins with an Introit (short prayer said or sung as the priest approaches the altar) using the words *Requiem aeternam dona eis Domine* (Give them eternal rest, O Lord). The *Gloria* and *Credo* from the normal mass are omitted as these are expressions of joy by the faithful but the *Dies irae* (day of wrath) is traditionally included. Since the revision of Roman Catholic liturgy in the 1960s these formulae have been considerably varied. The words of the Latin requiem mass have inspired many composers, including Mozart, Berlioz, Verdi, Fauré, and Britten, to create elaborate musical settings.

● **requiem shark** ▶ A ▷shark of the family *Carcharhinidae* (over 60 species), found mainly in warm and temperate oceans. 1.5–5.5 m long, they have two dorsal fins and are carnivorous, feeding on fish and various invertebrates. Some species are dangerous to man, for example the ▷tiger shark.

● **resale price maintenance** ▶ (rpm) A ▷restrictive trade practice operated by a manufacturer, who prohibits retailers from selling a product below a certain price. This prevents price competition between retailers and keeps inefficient retailers in business. In the UK, the Resale Prices Act (1964) forbids rpm unless it can be proved to be in the public interest.

● **reservoirs** ▶ Natural or artificial lakes in which water is stored for irrigation, to supply water for municipal needs, for hydroelectric power, or to control water flow. When artificially constructed they are made by placing dams across suitable land formations. They may often combine several of the purposes above and are invaluable in areas in which rainfall is low or unpredictable. The water flowing into a reservoir must not contain too much sediment or its capacity will diminish.

● **Resht** ▷*See* Rasht.

● **resins** ▶ Adhesive nonflammable organic polymers, usually insoluble in water but soluble in organic solvents, such as alcohol. **Natural resins**, such as ▷rosin, ▷sandarac, and ▷shellac, are exuded by plants and insects. **Synthetic resins** are made by modifying natural polymers or by polymerization of petrochemicals. Thermosetting resins, those that harden on heating, include ▷epoxy, ▷urea-formaldehyde, and some ▷polyurethane resins. Thermoplastic resins, those that soften on heating, include ▷polythene, ▷polyvinyl chloride, ▷polypropylene, and cellulose acetates.

● **resistance** ▶ The property of all materials, except superconduc-

tors (*see* superconductivity), that reduces the flow of electricity through them. It is defined by ▷Ohm's law as the ratio of the potential difference between the ends of a conductor to the current flowing through it. The resistance of a conductor depends on its dimensions, the material of which it is made, its temperature, and in some cases the extent to which it is illuminated. Devices with a known fixed resistance used in electronic circuits to control the flow of current through a circuit are called **resistors**. They are usually small carbon cylinders with coloured rings painted on them to indicate the value of the resistance. A variable resistance used to control the flow of current through a power circuit is called a **rheostat**. This usually consists of a wire coil along which a sliding contact can be moved. The unit of resistance is the ▷ohm. The reciprocal of the resistance in a direct current circuit is the conductance. Conductance is measured in ▷siemens (*see also* impedance).

● **resistance movements** ▶ Underground organizations that resisted the Axis powers during World War II, especially in occupied Europe. Their activities ranged from sabotage and ▷guerrilla warfare to intelligence work, helping escaped prisoners-of-war, and publishing forbidden newspapers. In Germany itself, resistance to the Nazi regime was limited to a few idealistic Christian organizations (such as the Roman Catholic White Rose group), the communists, and a section of the traditional military elite (*see* Stauffenberg, Claus). Following the German conquest of much of continental Europe in 1939–41, resistance movements sprang up in most of the occupied countries, with those in France (*see* Maquis) and Poland being especially large and well organized. In 1940 Churchill formed the British Special Operations Executive (SOE) to coordinate resistance activity across Europe and to supply these movements with arms and other equipment. From June, 1941, when Germany invaded the Soviet Union, communists took a major role in most of the resistance movements. In some countries, such as Greece and Yugoslavia, this led to deep divisions between leftists and right-wing patriots. Guerrilla movements also emerged to fight the Japanese invaders in SE Asia, although here intelligence and propaganda work tended to be carried out separately by small US and British units. After the war, many nationalist guerrillas remained in arms to lead the struggle for independence from the colonial powers.

Historians have differed widely in assessing the military value of the resistance; although this was probably minimal in the earlier stages of the war, after the Allied invasion of Europe in 1944 guerrilla activities played a valuable role in tying down German troops and disrupting their communications and supplies. Moreover, the extraordinary courage shown by the resistance (who faced torture and execution if captured) played an important part in re-establishing national pride in many countries after the traumas of defeat and occupation.

● **Resnais, Alain** ▶ (1922–) French film director. His films are characterized by experimental narrative techniques and a concern for the theme of memory. The scripts for *Hiroshima, mon amour* (1959), *Last Year at Marienbad* (1961), and *Providence* (1977) were written by Marguerite ▷Duras, Alain ▷Robbe-Grillet, and David ▷Mercer respectively. His other films include *Mon oncle d'Amerique* (1980), *La Vie est un roman* (1983), and *On connait la chanson* (1998).

● **resolving power** ▶ **1.** The ability of a ▷microscope to produce separate images of two neighbouring points; the closer the points, the greater the resolving power of the microscope. The resolving power may be increased by using shorter wavelength radiation (e.g. ultraviolet radiation) or by using very short wavelength electrons (as in the ▷electron microscope). Alternatively the refractive index of the medium between the specimen and the objective lens may be increased, as in the ▷oil-immersion lens. **2.** A measure of the ability of a ▷telescope to distinguish detail, usually the smallest angle between two point objects that produces distinct images.

● **resonance** ▶ (chemistry) The existence of a compound with a molecular structure intermediate between two or more conventional structures. For example, the polar molecule HCl, in which the hydrogen atom has some positive charge and the chlorine some negative charge, can be regarded as intermediate between two structures. One form is the covalent molecule H–Cl and the other the ionic compound H⁺Cl⁻. The molecule is a **resonance hybrid** with contributions from the two forms, written $H-Cl \leftrightarrow H^+Cl^-$.

● **resonance** ▶ (physics) The sympathetic oscillation of a system in response to an external excitation. A wire under tension, for example, will not respond to an external vibration unless the vibration is at the natural frequency of oscillation of the wire, which depends on its length, tension, etc. It will then resonate at its natural frequency. Resonance also occurs in electrical, magnetic, and electromagnetic phenomena in which matter or energy is being changed periodically. A **resonant circuit** consists of a capacitance in parallel with an inductance. When the capacitor discharges through the inductor an induced emf is produced, which again charges the capacitor (in the opposite sense). The circuit will then continue to oscillate, provided that energy is supplied from an outside source, at a frequency determined by the values of the capacitor (which is usually a variable device) and the inductor. Such circuits, feeding an aerial, are used in ▷radio transmitters to generate radio-frequency oscillations and in receivers to detect incoming signals.

● **resonances** ▶ Elementary particles with extremely short lifetimes (about 10^{-23} seconds). They are formed when colliding particles react by the ▷strong interaction. Resonances are either ▷mesons or ▷baryons (see particle physics).

● **Respighi, Ottorino** ▶ (1879–1936) Italian composer. He became director of the Santa Cecilia in Rome (1923–25). He wrote several operas, the symphonic poems *The Fountains of Rome* (1917) and *The Pines of Rome* (1924), the orchestral suite *The Birds* (1927), and ballets, including *La Boutique fantasque* (1919), based on themes by Rossini.

● **respiration** ▶ The process by which an organism takes up oxygen from its environment and discharges carbon dioxide into it. In humans and most air-breathing animals the organs through which this takes place are the ▷lungs (aquatic animals use ▷gills; insects use ▷tracheae). Air is transported to and from the lungs by **breathing**, which involves movements of the muscular diaphragm and the rib cage. Oxygen-depleted blood is pumped from the ▷heart to the air sacs (alveoli) of the lungs, where it receives oxygen (from inhaled air) and releases carbon dioxide (which is exhaled). Oxygen in the blood is carried to the tissues and cells, where it oxidizes foodstuffs to produce energy, used for physiological processes, and carbon dioxide, which is transported in the blood to the lungs. This is called tissue, or cellular, respiration.

● **respirator** ▶ A machine used to maintain breathing in patients whose respiratory muscles are paralysed or not functioning for any other reason. The cabinet respirator (iron lung) encloses the patient in a sealed container from the neck down; by lowering the pressure in the cabinet the chest expands and draws air into the lungs. A positive-pressure respirator pumps air at regular intervals into the lungs through a tube placed in the windpipe; the air is exhaled naturally or removed by suction through the respirator.

● **rest mass** ▷*See* relativistic mass.

● **Restoration** ▶ (1660) The re-establishment of the monarchy in England following the fall of the ▷Protectorate. The Restoration of Charles II, whose father Charles I had been executed (1649) during the Civil War, was engineered by General ▷Monck. In April, 1660, the Convention Parliament accepted Charles' Declaration of Breda, in which he promised religious toleration and an amnesty to all but 57 of those who had fought the Crown in the Civil War; it also arranged for the restoration of confiscated royalist lands and an income for Charles. The subsequent Cavalier Parliament (1661–79) enacted a religious settlement in the form of the anti-Nonconformist ▷Clarendon Code.

● **Restoration literature** ▶ English literature written during the reigns of Charles II (1660–85) and James II (1685–88), following the Restoration of the monarchy in 1660 and the relaxation of restraints on literature imposed during the Puritan Interregnum. The period was especially distinguished by its drama, notably the witty comedies of manners of ▷Wycherley, ▷Etherege, and ▷Congreve; these are often called the **Restoration comedies**. In poetry, the period was characterized by the late work of ▷Milton and ▷Marvell, the sat-

ires of ▷Dryden, and the licentious verse of John Wilmot, Earl of ▷Rochester.

● **restrictive trade practices** ▶ Agreements between traders over price, conditions of supply, etc., that limit competition in an industry. In the UK, under the Fair Trading Act (1973), which replaced earlier legislation, restrictive practices are held to be against the public interest unless proved otherwise in the Restrictive Practices Court.

● **resurrection plant** ▷*See* rose of Jericho.

● **retail price index** ▶ (RPI) ▷*See* cost of living.

● **retina** ▶ The layer of tissue that forms the inner surface of the □eye. Light is focused by the lens onto the retina, the innermost part of which contains numerous interconnecting light-sensitive cells that send signals to the visual centre of the brain via the optic nerve. These cells are of two kinds: the rods, which are sensitive to light and dark and are responsible for vision in dim light; and the cones, which are sensitive to colour and visual detail. The greatest concentration of cones occurs at a small area at the back of the eye (the fovea), which is therefore the area of greatest visual acuity. The outer part of the retina, between the light-sensitive layer and the choroid, consists of pigmented cells. Separation of these two layers of the retina results in loss of vision (see detached retina).

● **retriever** ▶ One of several breeds of large strongly built sporting dogs characterized by a "soft" mouth and good swimming ability. All are descended from the ▷Labrador retriever crossed with other breeds. The flat-coated retriever has a fine dense black or liver-coloured coat while the curly-coated retriever has a coat of small tight curls, indicating possible poodle ancestry. The Chesapeake Bay retriever has a short thick coat and has been developed in the USA from British stock. Height: 56–68 cm. ▷*See also* golden retriever.

● **retrovirus** ▶ A virus in which the genetic material is RNA, which becomes integrated into the DNA of its host cell by means of the enzyme reverse transcriptase. Retroviruses include HIV (which causes AIDS) and several viruses causing cancer.

● **Retz, Gilles de** ▷*See* Rais, Gilles de.

● **Retz, Jean François Paul de Gondi, Cardinal de** ▶ (1613–79) French churchman, one of the leaders of the rebellion called the ▷Fronde (1648–53), which he used to further his own political ambitions at the expense of Cardinal ▷Mazarin. He was made a cardinal in 1652 but arrested soon after. Exiled until 1662 he returned to France to become Abbot of Saint-Denis until his death. He is best known for his *Mémoires*, which recall his role in the Fronde.

● **Reuben, tribe of** ▶ One of the 12 ▷tribes of Israel. It claimed descent from Reuben, the eldest son of ▷Jacob and Leah. The territory E of the Dead Sea was allocated to Reuben's people.

● **Réunion** ▶ A volcanic island and French overseas department in the W Indian Ocean, in the Mascarene Islands. It was settled in about 1642 by the French with their African and Indian slaves. Sugar, rum, and molasses are exported. Area: 2512 sq km (970 sq mi). Population (1996): 671 000. Capital: Saint-Denis.

● **Reuter, Paul Julius, Baron von** ▶ (Israel Josephat; 1816–99) British founder of the first news agency. Born in Germany, he adopted the name of Reuter in 1844. He went to London in 1851 and opened a telegraph office from which he supplied newspapers with international news. He was made a German baron in 1871.

● **Reval** ▷*See* Tallinn.

● **Revelation, Book of** ▶ A prophetic book, the last in the New Testament, written perhaps about 90–95 AD by "John the Divine," who is often identified with the apostle John. It consists of seven highly symbolic visions that trace the fortunes of the Christian Church from its inception to the end of the world. The only example of apocalyptic literature in the New Testament, the book may have been written in reaction to the persecutions of the emperor Domitian.

● **reverberatory furnace** ▶ A furnace designed for operations in which it is not desirable to mix the material being heated with the fuel. The flame is directed at the roof of the furnace and the heat radiated downwards. This type of furnace is used in the smelting of copper and nickel ores.

● **Revere, Paul** ▶ (1735–1818) American silversmith and revolutionary. Prominent in the colonial opposition to Britain, he became famous as the man who, on 18 April, 1775, rode out to warn the people of Massachusetts that the British troops were on the march. On the following morning the first shots of the American Revolution were fired on the British at Lexington. Revere's ride is celebrated in a poem by Longfellow.

● **Revolt of the Netherlands** ▶ The rebellion against Spanish rule in the Netherlands, inspired by political and economic grievances and resentment at the suppression of Protestantism. Revolt broke out in 1568 but only took fire in 1572, when the Dutch cause prospered in the strongly Protestant northern provinces under the leadership of ▷William the Silent. In 1576 the N was joined by the predominantly Roman Catholic provinces in the S but the union ended with the Spanish victory at Gembloux in 1578, when the S submitted once more to Spain. In the following year the seven northern provinces, by the Union of Utrecht, declared their independence from Spain. War continued, however, until the 12-year truce negotiated in 1609 by William's son and successor ▷Maurice of Nassau and was renewed in the Thirty Years' War (1618–48). By the Peace of Westphalia (1648) the independence of the United Provinces of the Netherlands was at last acknowledged.

● **Revolutionary and Napoleonic Wars** ▶ (1792–1815) A series of European wars precipitated by the ▷French Revolution and ▷Napoleon I's ambitions for the conquest of Europe. Revolutionary fervour within France and the hostile reaction of Austria and Prussia to the arrest of Louis XVI led to the outbreak of war. Initial French success prompted Britain, the Netherlands, and Spain to close ranks with Austria and Prussia in the first coalition (1793). Hard pressed, France was transformed into a nation at arms (see conscription) and its armies achieved a series of victories. In 1795 Prussia, the Netherlands, and Spain sued for peace and, following Napoleon's first Italian campaign (1796–97), Austria followed suit. French supremacy was thwarted only by Nelson's great victory of the ▷Nile (1798), which brought Britain control of the Mediterranean. The second coalition (1798–99) of Britain, the Ottoman Empire, Naples, Portugal, and Austria collapsed (1801) in the face of Napoleon's victories, especially at ▷Hohenlinden (1800); the Revolutionary Wars ended with the uneasy Treaty of Amiens (1802) between Britain and France.

Napoleon's aggression, including his imposition of the ▷Continental System against Britain, led to the resumption of naval war between Britain and France. In 1805 Pitt the Younger negotiated a third coalition against Napoleon, by now emperor, and Nelson (although mortally wounded) won the naval victory at ▷Trafalgar. Napoleon defeated Austria and Russia at ▷Ulm and Austerlitz (1805), Prussia at ▷Jena and Auerstädt (1806), and Russia again at ▷Friedland (1807). However, with the failure of the Continental System and Wellington's victories in the ▷Peninsular War, Napoleon's dominance diminished. Following his disastrous Russian campaign (1812) the allies were able to defeat him at ▷Leipzig (1813) and then, following his return from exile, at ▷Waterloo (1815). The post-Napoleonic settlement of Europe was decided at the Congress of ▷Vienna.

● **Revolution of 1905** ▶ An insurrection in Russia, an expression of the widespread discontent that culminated in the ▷Russian Revolution of 1917. It began on 22 January, 1905 (Bloody Sunday), when a group of striking workers marched peacefully on the Winter Palace in St Petersburg and were fired on by troops. The massacre precipitated nationwide strikes, uprisings, and mutinies (including the mutiny on the battleship *Potemkin*). By October Russia was gripped by a general strike, which with the establishment of the St Petersburg Soviet (workers' council), dominated by the ▷Mensheviks, including Trotsky, forced Nicholas II to promise constitutional government (see Duma). The Revolution was crushed by the end of December.

● **Revolutions of 1848** ▶ A series of revolutions in continental Europe caused by economic distress and liberal agitation against the conservatism that characterized the post-Napoleonic era. The first revolution broke out in France, where the insurgents overthrew the July Monarchy of Louis Philippe, but a split in their ranks between

moderates and socialists led to the suppression of the Left and the election of Louis Napoleon (later ▷Napoleon III) as president. In the Italian states the revolution had constitutional aims, in which it had some success in Piedmont, but also formed part of the movement against the Austrian presence in Italy (see Risorgimento). In the Austrian Empire revolts in Vienna secured the resignation of Metternich and the summoning of a constituent assembly. The revolution spread with short-lived success to Prague and Budapest before being suppressed by Schwarzenberg. In the German states the revolution began in Prussia, where Frederick William IV was forced to convene a constituent assembly. By December, however, the revolutions there and in other German states had been suppressed and in 1849 the Frankfurt Parliament, which had hoped to achieve a united Germany, was dissolved. The revolutions were all quelled but not without some concessions to liberal and nationalist movements, and 1848 is thus generally regarded as ending the post-1815 period of reaction that had been dominated by Metternich.

● **revolver** ▶ A short-range ▷small arm having a revolving cylinder containing the rounds behind the barrel. In single-action types, drawing back the hammer cocks the weapon and simultaneously rotates the cylinder; a slight pressure on the trigger then fires it. In double-action types pressing the trigger performs all these functions at once. Most double-action revolvers can also be used in single-action mode for greater accuracy. Calibres range from .21 inches to .455 inches. The first successful revolver was the ▷Colt, designed in 1835. ▷See also pistol.

● **revue** ▶ A theatrical entertainment consisting of a succession of songs, dances, and sketches of a topical and often satirical nature. Originating in France, revues attained great popularity in Britain and the USA during the early 20th century with such spectacular productions as the *Ziegfeld Follies* (1907). As competition from cinema and television increased, revues became more intimate in form, an early example being the British *Sweet and Low* (1943). The success of *Beyond the Fringe* (1961) led to a succession of sophisticated satirical revues during the 1960s.

● **rex** ▶ A breed of cat having a curly coat of very short fine hairs. Two types are recognized—the Cornish rex and the Devon rex, named after the counties in which they originated. They have long slender bodies and may be of any colour.

● **Reykjavík** ▶ 64 10N 21 53W The capital of Iceland, an important fishing port, on Faxa Fjord in the SW. Founded by the Vikings in 874 AD, it became the seat of parliament (the Althing) in 1843 and capital of Iceland in 1918. Its university was founded in 1911. Most of the city's heating comes locally from natural hot springs. Population (1996 est): 105 487.

● **Reynaud, Paul** ▶ (1878–1966) French politician, who was briefly prime minister before the German occupation of France in 1940. He was a forceful opponent of Nazism in the late 1930s and after the collapse of France was arrested by the Germans and held until 1945. After the war he again held ministerial posts and helped draft the constitution of the Fifth Republic (1959).

● **Reynolds, Albert** ▶ (1932–) Irish statesman; prime minister of Ireland (1992–94). He entered parliament in 1977 and succeeded Charles Haughey as president of the ▷Fianna Fáil party and prime minister in 1992. In 1993 he joined John Major in drafting the ▷Downing Street Declaration. In 1994 he lost the support of the Irish Labour Party, with which the Fianna Fáil had formed a coalition government, and had to resign.

● **Reynolds, Sir Joshua** ▶ (1723–92) British portrait painter, born in Plympton (Devon), where his father was headmaster of a school. He studied in London (1740–43) under the portraitist Thomas Hudson (1701–79). In 1749 he travelled to Italy, staying for two years in Rome before returning to London. Using the techniques of the Old Masters in such paintings as *Sarah Siddons as the Tragic Muse* (San Marino, California), Reynolds aimed to give portraits the prestige of history paintings. In 1768 he became the first president of the ▷Royal Academy, where he delivered the *Discourses*, which contain his artistic theories. His friends included Dr ▷Johnson and ▷Garrick, both of whom he painted.

● **Reynolds number** ▶ (*Re*) In fluid dynamics, a dimensionless quantity associated with the flow of a fluid. $Re = \rho v l/\eta$, where ρ and η are the ▷density and ▷viscosity of the fluid moving with velocity *v* through a system characterized by a length *l*. If the Reynolds number of the fluid is less than about 1500, the flow is streamlined; above this number it becomes turbulent. Named after the British engineer Osborne Reynolds (1842–1912).

● **Reza Shah Pahlavi** ▶ (1878–1944) Shah of Iran (1925–41). After leading an army coup in 1921, he deposed Ahmad Shah Qajar (1898–1930) in 1925. As shah himself, Reza aimed at the modernization of Iran, following the example of ▷Atatürk in Turkey. In 1941 Britain and the Soviet Union, fearing German influence in Iran, invaded the country and forced Reza Shah to abdicate in favour of his son ▷Mohammed Reza Pahlavi. He died in exile in Johannesburg.

● **rhapsody** ▶ A piece of music that has no fixed form (from Greek *rhapsōidia*, epic poem). In the 19th century it was generally based on folk tunes, as in Liszt's *Hungarian Rhapsodies* or Dvořák's *Slavonic Rhapsodies*. In the 20th century rhapsodies often feature a solo instrument in a free-form composition, such as Debussy's *Rhapsodie* for clarinet and orchestra, Gershwin's *Rhapsody in Blue* for piano and orchestra, and Rachmaninov's *Rhapsody on a Theme of Paganini*, also for piano and orchestra.

● **Rhazes** ▷*See* Razi, ar-.

● **rhea** ▶ A large flightless bird belonging to a family (*Rheidae*; 3 species) occurring in South America. 120 cm tall, rheas have a brownish plumage and long legs with three toes. They live in flocks, feeding on leaves, roots, seeds, insects, and small vertebrates. The male builds the nest and incubates the eggs. Order: *Rheiformes*.

● **Rhea** ▶ In Greek religion, a Titan, daughter of Uranus and Gaia. Her consort ▷Cronus swallowed her children, fearing that they would overthrow him. Rhea substituted a stone for one child, ▷Zeus, who eventually overthrew Cronus and forced him to disgorge the other children.

● **Rhee, Syngman** ▶ (1875–1965) Korean statesman; first president of South Korea (1948–60). He became leader of South Korea in 1945 and as president claimed his government's right to rule over all Korea. Popular unrest forced him to resign in 1960 and he went into exile.

● **Rheims** ▷*See* Reims.

● **rhenium** ▶ (Re) A dense (relative density 21.02) silvery-white transition metal with a very high melting point. The metal is very ductile and is used to alloy with tungsten. Alloys with molybdenum are superconducting. The metal is obtained as a by-product of molybdenum refining. At no 75; at wt 186.2; mp 3186°C; bp 5596°C.

● **rheostat** ▷*See* resistance.

● **rhesus factor** ▶ (Rh factor) A blood protein present on the red cells in 83% of the population: the presence or absence of the Rh factor is the basis of the Rh ▷blood group system, people with the factor being described as Rh positive and those without as Rh negative. If a Rh-negative woman has a Rh-positive baby she may produce anti-Rh antibodies that will react against subsequent Rh-positive pregnancies. The affected baby's blood cells may be destroyed by these antibodies, leading to the severe anaemia of haemolytic disease of the newborn. The incidence of this disease has been reduced by taking steps to prevent the formation of maternal anti-Rh antibodies soon after delivery of the first baby.

● **rhesus monkey** ▶ A ▷macaque monkey, *Macaca mulatta*, of S Asia, widely used in medical research. In the wild, rhesus monkeys live in large colonies in forests or on hillsides, sometimes stealing fruit from orchards.

● **Rheticus** ▶ (Georg Joachim von Lauchen; 1514–76) German mathematician, who was the first follower of ▷Copernicus. In 1540 Rheticus wrote a summary of Copernicus' ideas and then persuaded him to publish his own book, De Revolutionibus, in which he had originally expressed these ideas. Rheticus was the first mathematician to regard the trigonometric functions in terms of angles rather than arcs of a circle.

● **rhetoric** ▶ The art of using language for communicating information and for intellectual and emotional persuasion. Mastery of rhetoric by orators was considered essential training in ancient Greece and Rome. Influential textbooks were written by ▷Aristotle, ▷Quintilian, and ▷Cicero, and all classical literary criticism was based on rhetorical principles. Aristotle distinguished three modes of persuasion—logical, emotional, and ethical—and codified the rules for rhetorical composition under categories of invention, arrangement, and style. Together with logic and grammar, rhetoric formed the trivium, an essential part of the curriculum in medieval education, and its principles were adapted to medieval forms, such as sermons and legal documents. In the 20th century, the study of rhetoric forms part of the theoretical analysis of techniques of persuasion.

● **rheumatic fever** ▶ A disease of children that occurs (rarely) after infection with a streptococcus bacterium. The symptoms develop 10–14 days after the original infection (which is usually of the throat) and include fever, aching joints, chorea (involuntary movements), and inflammation of the heart, which—in a few cases—may lead to chronic heart disease. Treatment is with bed rest, penicillin, aspirin, and sometimes steroids.

● **rheumatism** ▶ Any condition involving pain in the joints. This may be caused by a simple strain or by rheumatoid ▷arthritis, ▷osteoarthritis, ▷gout, or ▷rheumatic fever.

● **Rheydt** ▶ 51 10N 6 27E A city in NW Germany, in North Rhine-Westphalia. Its fine Renaissance palace (1568–81) escaped the bombing of World War II. An industrial centre, its main manufacture is textiles. Population (latest est): 101 500.

● **Rhine, Joseph Banks** ▶ (1895–1980) US psychologist, noted for his experiments in parapsychology, especially extrasensory perception (ESP). Using packs of specially designed cards in scientifically objective tests, Rhine produced statistical evidence, which is not universally accepted, to support the occurrence of ESP.

● **Rhine, River** ▶ (German name: Rhein; Dutch name; Rijn) A river in central and W Europe. Rising in SE Switzerland, it flows N into Lake Constance, continuing W along the Swiss-German border to Basle. It then flows generally N along the Franco-German border and into Germany, turning NW past Bonn, Cologne, Düsseldorf, and Duisburg. It enters the Netherlands below Emmerich and splits into two major distributaries, the Lek and the Waal. The Lek continues W through Rotterdam and enters the North Sea at the Hook of Holland. The Waal joins the River Meuse and enters the North Sea by the Hollandsch Diep. The main tributaries are the Rivers Ruhr, Main, Moselle, and Neckar. It is W Europe's main navigable waterway and passes through one of the most highly industrialized regions on the continent. Length: 1320 km (820 mi).

● **Rhine-Herne Canal** ▶ An important waterway in W Germany, in the ▷Ruhr. Completed in 1914, it forms part of the ▷Mittelland Canal and extends from Duisburg to Herne. Length: 39 km (24 mi).

● **Rhineland Palatinate** ▶ (German name: Rheinland-Pfalz) A *Land* in W Germany, bordering on France, Luxembourg, and Belgium. It includes the historic cities of Mainz, Speyer, Trier, and Worms. Over 75% of Germany's wine is produced in the river valleys of the Rhine, Moselle, and Nahe. Potatoes and grain are grown and livestock is important in the mountainous SW. Industries include chemicals, engineering, and shoe manufacture. Area: 19 838 sq km (7658 sq mi). Population (1990 est): 3 700 000. Capital: Mainz. ▷*See also* Palatinate.

● **rhinoceros** ▶ A large hoofed mammal belonging to the family *Rhinocerotidae* (5 species), of Asia and Africa. Rhinos have a massive virtually naked dark-skinned body with short thick legs, a short neck, and a large head. The Indian rhinoceros (*Rhinoceros unicornis*) has a single horn composed of solid fibrous ▷keratin; all other rhinos have two horns. Rhinos range in size from the large ▷white rhinoceros to the Sumatran rhinoceros (*Didermocerus sumatrensis*), which is up to 150 cm high at the shoulder and weighs 500–1000 kg. Rhinos are generally solitary, grazing or browsing on grass and leaves, and are fond of wallowing in muddy pools. All are now endangered species. □ p. 1060.

● **rhinoceros beetle** ▶ A horned scarab beetle, up to 150 mm long (including the horn), so called because of the resemblance of its horn to that of a rhinoceros. The larvae of most rhinoceros beetles live in rotting wood, although some eat roots or burrow into the stems of palm trees. *Oryctes rhinoceros* is sometimes a serious pest in oriental coconut groves through its destruction of the leaf bases. ▷*See also* hercules beetle.

● **rhizome** ► An underground plant stem producing aerial leaves and shoots. It may extend some distance below ground and can be fleshy (as in the iris) or wiry (as in couch grass). Rhizomes can function both as organs of vegetative ▷reproduction and as overwintering structures. They usually grow horizontally; vertical rhizomes (e.g. of strawberry) are commonly called rootstocks.

● **Rhode Island** ► The smallest state in the USA, indented by Narragansett Bay. One of the New England states, it is the second most densely populated US state. It is highly industrialized, the once important cotton industry having been replaced by modern technological industries, such as electronics and the manufacture of machine tools. It also has important naval installations. Agriculture is limited by the rocky terrain; it is famous for its poultry.
History: one of the original 13 colonies, it was first settled in 1636 and was the first colony to declare its independence from Britain. Area: 3144 sq km (1214 sq mi). Population (1998 est): 988 480. Capital: Providence.

● **Rhode Island Red** ► A breed of domestic fowl developed from blackish-red Asiatic breeds kept on Rhode Island farms in the 19th century. It has a deep broad long body with a nearly horizontal back and a slightly curved beak. The plumage is red. It lays brown eggs and is used for both egg and meat production. Weight: 3.8 kg (cocks); 3.0 kg (hens).

● **Rhodes** ► (Modern Greek name: Ródhos) A Greek island in the SE Aegean Sea, the largest of the Dodecanese group. It has a mountainous interior with fertile coastal strips, producing cereals, fruit, and wine. Tourism is an important source of revenue.
History: colonized by Dorians before 1000 BC, Rhodes entered its period of greatest prosperity in the 3rd century BC. It suffered several earthquakes, one of which destroyed the ▷Colossus of Rhodes in 244 BC. It was occupied by the Knights ▷Hospitallers from 1282 until 1528, when it became part of the Ottoman Empire. Conquered by Italy in 1912, it was ceded to Greece in 1947. Area: 1400 sq km (540 sq mi). Population (latest est); 40 392. Capital: Rhodes.

● **Rhodes, Cecil (John)** ► (1853–1902) South African financier and statesman. Born in Britain, he went to Natal in 1870 and then to the Orange Free State to work in the Kimberley diamond mines. In 1881 he entered the Cape Colony parliament, helping to obtain Bechuanaland (now Botswana) in 1884. In 1888 his company, De Beers Consolidated Mines, bought up the Kimberley mines and in 1889 he gained a charter for the British South Africa Company to develop the territory that in 1895 was named Rhodesia in his honour.

He became prime minister of Cape Colony in 1890 but was forced to resign in 1896 over his involvement in ▷Jameson's abortive raid into the Transvaal. Rhodes endowed 170 Rhodes scholarships at Oxford University for students from the British Empire, the USA, and Germany.

● **Rhodes, Wilfred** ► (1877–1973) British cricketer, who played for England and Yorkshire. A great all-rounder, he took a record 4187 wickets and both scored 1000 runs and took 100 wickets in a record 16 seasons.

● **Rhodes, Zandra (Lindsey)** ► (1940–) British fashion designer, who founded her first dressmaking business in 1966 and a chain of shops in 1975. Many of her inventive and colourful designs feature screen printing on delicate fabrics, such as chiffon or taffeta.

● **Rhodesia** ▷*See* Zimbabwe, State of.

● **Rhodesia and Nyasaland, Federation of** ► (*or* Central African Federation) A former (1953–63) federation of the British colony of Southern Rhodesia (now Zimbabwe) and the British protectorates of Northern Rhodesia (now Zambia) and Nyasaland (now Malawi). It was opposed by Nyasaland nationalists on the grounds that it existed to further the economic interests of Southern Rhodesia, where most of the Whites lived. Violent unrest in 1959 led to its dissolution. Zambia and Malawi became independent in 1964; Zimbabwe gained independence in 1980.

● **Rhodesian ridgeback** ► A breed of hunting □dog originating in South Africa, characterized by a ridge of forward-growing hair along the back. The ridgeback is strongly built with a prominent muzzle and its short glossy coat is yellowish brown to reddish fawn. Height: 63–68 cm (dogs); 61–66 cm (bitches).

● **rhodium** ► (Rh) A metal of the platinum group, discovered in 1803 by W. H. Wollaston (1766–1828). It is alloyed with platinum and palladium to form thermocouples and crucibles and is used in equipment for the production of glass fibres. It is a very hard highly reflective metal and is used to plate jewellery and optical instruments. At no 45; at wt 102.905; mp 1963 ± 3°C; bp 3697 ± 100°C.

● **Rhododendron** ► A genus of small trees and shrubs (about 250 species), mainly of N temperate regions. They have leathery often evergreen leaves, large scaly winter buds, and terminal clusters of colourful fragrant bell- or funnel-shaped flowers. They occur in a variety of habitats and many, including ▷azaleas, are widely cultivated as ornamentals. Family: *Ericaceae*.

● **Rhondda** ► A town in South Wales, in Rhondda, Cynon, Taff county borough, built along the Rhondda Fawr and Rhondda Fach Valleys. Formerly important for coalmining, it now has varied industrial activities; much of the former industrial landscape has been afforested or developed as parkland to attract tourists. The last mine closed in 1990. Population (1991): 77 288.

rhinoceros ► A white rhinoceros (*Ceratotherium simum*) being dehorned in Zimbabwe. This measure is sometimes adopted in an attempt to deter poachers: rhinoceros horn is highly valued in the East as an aphrodisiac.

● **Rhondda, Cynon, Taff** ▶ A county borough in S Wales, created in 1996 from part of Mid Glamorgan. Area: 558 sq km (215 sq mi). Population (1996 est): 232 581. Administrative centre: Rhondda.

● **Rhône, River** ▶ A major river in W Europe. Rising in the Rhône Glacier in Switzerland, it flows through Lake Geneva to enter France, flowing generally SW between the Jura and the Alps. It merges with the River Saône at Lyon and flows S to enter the Gulf of Lions via la ▷Camargue. The Rhône-Saône Valley has historically been an important route and since 1976 the River Rhône has been canalized from Lyon to the Mediterranean Sea. This has provided improved navigation, hydroelectric power, and irrigation for agriculture and has encouraged industrial development along its length. Length 812 km (505 mi).

Cecil Rhodes ▶ A drawing of the statesman at his home at Groote Schuur in 1900. He used the wealth amassed from his mining concerns to found the Rhodes scholarships, which enable students from the Commonwealth, the USA, and Germany to study at Oxford.

● **rhubarb** ▶ A perennial plant, *Rheum rhaponticum*, possibly of Asian origin, widely cultivated for its juicy red or green leafstalks, up to 1 m high, which are cooked in sugar. Later in the season, a central flower stalk may be produced bearing small greenish-white flowers. The leaves are poisonous. Family: *Polygonaceae*.

● **Rhum** ▷*See* Rum.

● **rhyme** ▶ Similarity in sound between two or more words, a device used in poetry to reinforce the metrical pattern of a poem. Usually the rhyme is between words occurring at the ends of lines, but internal rhymes, where the rhyme is between a word within a line and a word at the end of or within another line, are also used. The rhyme scheme of a poem is shown by assigning a single letter to each rhyme; thus the scheme of lines rhyming *house/cat/mouse/rat* would be noted *abab*. Masculine rhyme refers to words having the same vowel sounds in their final syllables (*night/delight*). Feminine rhyme refers to words having similar sounds in the last accented syllable and following syllables (*joviality/morality*). ▷*See also* blank verse.

● **rhyming slang** ▷*See* slang.

● **rhyolite** ▶ A fine-grained or glassy acid igneous rock, mineralogically the volcanic equivalent of granite. It consists of alkali feldspars and quartz, with some ferromagnesian minerals; many rhyolites are porphyritic and display banding resulting from the flowing lava.

● **Rhys, Jean** ▶ (1894–1979) British novelist. Born in Dominica, she wrote five books, including the novels *Voyage in the Dark* (1934) and *Good Morning, Midnight* (1939), about bohemian life in Paris and London. After living in seclusion in the West Country for many years, she published a novel, *Wide Sargasso Sea* (1966), retelling the story of Charlotte Brontë's *Jane Eyre* from the point of view of Mr Rochester's mad wife, and two further collections of stories.

● **rhythm and blues** ▶ (R and B) A form of US popular music of the 1940s and 1950s, resulting from the fusion of blues, jazz, and gospel elements by Black musicians. The term was used fairly loosely by the White music industry to denote music by and for Blacks. Rhythm and blues musicians employed amplified instruments to produce powerful rhythms, especially in the form known as Chicago blues. One of the earliest rhythm and blues artists was Ray Brown (1926–81), who recorded "Good Rockin' Tonight" (1948). Other rhythm and blues musicians included Fats Domino (1928–), Little Richard (1935–), and Lloyd Price (1932–). The adoption of rhythm and blues by White musicians (notably Elvis ▷Presley) led to the emergence of ▷rock and roll in the mid-1950s.

● **rhythm method** ▷*See* contraception.

● **rib** ▶ A curved bone, 12 pairs of which make up the rib cage, enclosing and protecting the heart and lungs. Each rib forms a joint with the vertebrae of the ▷spine, permitting movement of the rib cage during breathing. The other ends of the upper seven ribs (the so-called true ribs) are fixed directly to the breastbone by means of a cartilage. Each of the next three pairs (the "false" ribs) is connected by the cartilage to the rib above it, and the two lowest ribs (the floating ribs) end in the body wall muscles. ▷*See* Plate II.

● **Ribbentrop, Joachim von** ▶ (1893–1946) German Nazi politician and diplomat. He joined the Nazi Party in 1932 and became Hitler's foreign-affairs adviser. From 1936 to 1938 he was ambassador to the UK and then became foreign minister. He secured the Nonaggression Pact with the Soviet Union in 1939 but thereafter his influence declined. He was arrested in 1945, found guilty of war crimes, and hanged.

● **ribbonfish** ▶ An offshore marine fish, of the family *Trachipteridae*, that has a long ribbon-like body. Species include the ▷oarfish. Order: *Lampridiformes*.

● **ribbonworm** ▶ A long flat wormlike animal, also called proboscis worm, belonging to the invertebrate phylum *Nemertina* (about 600 species). Ranging in length from 1 mm to 30 m, ribbonworms may be black, brown, or white but many are brightly patterned. Most live at the bottom of shallow seas, using a long sticky harpoon-like proboscis to capture annelid worms, molluscs, and crustaceans.

● **Ribeirão Prêto** ▶ 21 09S 47 48W A city in S Brazil, in São Paulo state. It is the centre of a coffee- and sugar-growing area. Population (1991): 430 805.

● **Ribera, José de** ▶ (*or* Jusepe R.; 1591–1652) Spanish-born painter and etcher. He settled in Naples (1616), where he was known as Lo Spagnoletto (Little Spaniard). Influenced by the realism and dramatic lighting of ▷Caravaggio, he painted chiefly religious subjects and some everyday life scenes and portraits, the best examples of which are *The Martyrdom of St Bartholomew* (Prado) and *Clubfooted Boy* (Louvre). After 1630 he painted in richer colours and chose less gruesome subjects, probably as a result of his study of Venetian art and ▷Velázquez.

● **riboflavin** ▷*See* vitamin B complex.

● **ribonucleic acid** ▷*See* RNA.

● **ribose** ▶ A simple sugar ($C_5H_{10}O_5$). Ribose and its derivative deoxyribose are important constituents of ▷RNA and ▷DNA respectively.

● **ribosome** ▶ A granular particle present in enormous numbers in the cytoplasm of nearly all ▷cells, either free or bound to the surface of membranes within the cell. Ribosomes are composed of ▷RNA and protein and are the site of protein synthesis. During synthesis they often link together in a chain (polyribosome or polysome).

● **Ricardo, David** ▶ (1772–1823) British political economist. Ricardo was the first economist to argue systematically from *a priori* assumptions. His main work, *Principles of Political Economy and Taxation* (1817), argued that exchange value is determined by the labour expended in production and put forward the theory of "comparative costs" as the determining factor in international exchange. As an MP (1819–23), he contributed greatly to the free-trade movement and to the eventual repeal of the ▷Corn Laws.

● **Ricci, Matteo** ▶ (1552–1610) Italian ▷Jesuit missionary and scholar. Working in China from 1583 until his death, he proselytized by methods that were later condemned by the Roman Catholic Church. He showed the converts European books, maps, and clocks and allowed them to retain some of their ancient religious traditions.

● **Ricci, Sebastiano** ▸ (1659–1734) Venetian painter. Influenced by ▹Veronese, he worked in Bologna, Rome, Vienna, and London (1712–16), where he painted the *Resurrection* in the apse of Chelsea Hospital chapel. His nephew **Marco Ricci** (1676–1730), a landscape artist, occasionally collaborated with him after about 1707.

● **Riccio, David** ▸ (or D. Rizzio; c. 1533–66) Italian secretary to ▹Mary, Queen of Scots. His close relationship with the queen aroused the jealousy of her husband, Lord ▹Darnley, and other nobles, who had him murdered.

● **rice** ▸ An annual cereal ▹grass, *Oryza sativa*, or its edible grain, probably native to India but widely cultivated throughout tropical, subtropical, and warm temperate regions. There are many varieties, growing up to 1 m high and bearing spikes of flower clusters. Seedlings are generally transplanted to flooded paddy fields, although varieties of upland rice do not require flooding. The field is drained to enable mechanical harvesting. Milling the grain removes either the outer husk alone, resulting in brown rice, or both the husk and the bran layer, resulting in vitamin-B-deficient white rice. Apart from being a major staple food, rice is used as a source of starch and for alcohol production.

● **Rich, Richard, 1st Baron** ▸ (c. 1496–1567) English lawyer, who was the chief prosecutor in the trial of Sir Thomas More. He subsequently assisted in the ▹dissolution of the monasteries, becoming a privy councillor (1540). As Lord Chancellor (1547–51) under Edward VI he helped oust the protector, ▹Somerset (1549).

● **Richard (I) the Lionheart** ▸ (1157–99) King of England (1189–99); a hero of medieval legend, he spent all but six months of his reign abroad. The third son of Henry II and ▹Eleanor of Aquitaine, he became Duke of Aquitaine in 1168 and of Poitiers in 1172. He joined the third Crusade in 1189 and conquered Messina and Cyprus before arriving in the Holy Land. His victory at Arsuf gained Joppa (1191). On his way home he was captured in Austria and was only released by Emperor Henry VI after payment of an enormous ransom (1194). He returned briefly to England but died campaigning in France.

● **Richard II** ▸ (1367–1400) King of England (1377–99). Succeeding his grandfather Edward III, as a minor, government was largely in the hands of his uncle ▹John of Gaunt. Richard provoked considerable baronial opposition by his autocratic rule, defence of the royal prerogative, and reliance upon favourites. Factional struggles culminated in the banishment in 1398 of Gaunt's son Henry Bolingbroke. He returned in 1399, while Richard was in Ireland, and seized the throne as Henry IV. Richard died shortly afterwards at Pontefract Castle in mysterious circumstances.

● **Richard III** ▸ (1452–85) King of England (1483–85). He was the youngest brother of Edward IV, on whose death in 1483 he became protector for Edward V, a minor. After destroying the power of the Woodville faction (*see* Woodville, Elizabeth), Richard imprisoned Edward and his brother, declared Edward illegitimate, and seized the throne. It was, and continues to be, alleged that Richard murdered the boys, who disappeared in August, 1483. As king, he made important administrative and financial reforms but faced considerable opposition, first from Henry Stafford, 2nd Duke of Buckingham (who was defeated and executed in October, 1483), and then from Henry Tudor (subsequently ▹Henry VII), by whom Richard was defeated and killed at Bosworth.

● **Richard, Sir Cliff** ▸ (Harry Rodger Webb; 1940–) British pop singer. With such records as "Livin' Doll" (1959) and "We Don't Talk Anymore" (1979), he has maintained his popularity for over 40 years. He starred in the films *The Young Ones* (1961) and *Summer Holiday* (1962) as well as the stage musicals *Time* (1986) and *Heathcliff* (1996). In the 1960s he became a born-again Christian and an active evangelist. He was knighted in 1995.

● **Richards, Frank** ▸ (Charles Hamilton; 1876–1961) British children's writer. He wrote for the boys' papers *Gem* (1907–39) and *Magnet* (1908–40), in which he created the character of Billy Bunter, the comic fat boy of Greyfriars School. Writing under many different pseudonyms he created nearly 50 fictional public schools.

● **Richards, Sir Gordon** ▸ (1904–86) British jockey, who was champion jockey a record 26 times (1925–53). He rode 4870 winners out of a total of 21 843 mounts (1920–54), his 269 wins in 1947 constituting a British record. He later became a trainer and finally retired in 1970.

● **Richards, I(vor) A(rmstrong)** ▸ (1893–1979) English literary critic, linguist, and poet. With C. K. ▹Ogden, Richards compiled ▹Basic English and wrote *The Meaning of Meaning* (1923). An emeritus professor of Harvard University, Richards' publications include *Principles of Literary Criticism* (1924), *Goodbye Earth and Other Poems* (1958), and *Tomorrow Morning Faustus!* (1962).

● **Richards, Viv** ▸ (Isaac Vivian Alexander R.; 1952–) West Indian cricketer. An outstanding batsman of the 1980s, he scored over 6000 Test runs and captained the West Indies from 1985 until his retirement in 1991.

Richard (I) the Lionheart ▸ A manuscript illustration (1195–96) from *Liber ad honorem Augusti*, by Petrus de Ebulo. It shows Richard's capture in Austria in 1194 and his subsequent homage to the Emperor Henry VI.

● **Richardson, Henry Handel** ▸ (Ethel Florence R.; 1870–1946) Australian novelist. She studied music in Leipzig and lived in England from 1903. Her trilogy *The Fortunes of Richard Mahoney* (1917–29) is a naturalistic study of an emigrant doctor in Australia based on the life of her father.

● **Richardson, Henry Hobson** ▸ (1838–86) US architect. The first stylistically independent US architect, Richardson graduated from

Harvard and studied architecture in Paris. He used a revived roman-esque style in different types of buildings, ranging from wholesale stores to railway stations. Some of his best work was done for Harvard in the 1870s.

● **Richardson, Sir Ralph** ► (1902–83) British actor. He established his reputation as an actor of Shakespearean and other classical roles while working with the Old Vic Company during the 1930s and 1940s. He also acted in modern plays, such as David Storey's *Home* (1970) and Harold Pinter's *No Man's Land* (1976) and made many films.

● **Richardson, Samuel** ► (1689–1761) British novelist. His pioneering novel *Pamela* (1740), written in the form of correspondence between the characters, evolved from a publisher's commission for a book of model letters for inexperienced writers. His acute psychological characterization was further developed in *Clarissa* (1748), and in *Sir Charles Grandison* (1753) he portrayed the ideal gentleman.

● **Richelieu, Armand Jean du Plessis, Cardinal de** ► (1585–1642) French statesman, who greatly increased the absolute authority of the Crown and France's power in Europe. He rose to prominence as adviser to Louis XIII's mother ▷Marie de Médicis, entering the king's employ in 1624 and officially becoming his chief minister in 1629. He ruthlessly suppressed the ▷Huguenots and by means of an extensive secret service thwarted a series of aristocratic conspiracies against himself. He directed France with brilliance in the Thirty Years' War, although he did not live to see the dominance of Spain over Europe replaced by that of France. A writer and patron of learning, he founded the French Academy.

● **Richler, Mordecai** ► (1931–) Canadian novelist. He settled in England during the 1950s. He explores the dilemmas of his Jewish protagonists in an exuberant and often bawdy style. His novels include *The Apprenticeship of Duddy Kravitz* (1959), *St Urbain's Horseman* (1971), *Joshua Then and Now* (1981), and *Solomon Gursky was Here* (1990). *Home Sweet Home* (1984) is a collection of essays about his native Canada.

● **Richmond** ► 37 34N 77 27W A city and port in the USA, the capital of Virginia on the James River. Richmond was the capital of the Confederate states during the US Civil War. It is an important educational centre and site of the University of Richmond (1882). The chief manufacture is tobacco. Population (1996 est): 198 267.

● **Richmond** ► 54 24N 1 44W A market town in N England, in North Yorkshire on the River Swale. It has one of the oldest theatres in England (1788). Population (1991): 7862.

● **Richmond-upon-Thames** ► A mainly residential borough of SW Greater London, on the River Thames. Created in 1965 from the former municipal boroughs of Richmond, Barnes, and ▷Twickenham, it contains Richmond Park, consisting of some 1018 ha (2500 acres) of parkland originally enclosed by Charles I to enhance the grounds of the 14th-century Richmond Palace, which fell into decay by the 18th century and has since disappeared. Hampton Court Palace and ▷Kew Gardens are also in the borough. Area: 55 sq km (21 sq mi). Population (1996 est): 179 900.

● **Richter, Hans** ► (1843–1916) Hungarian conductor. In 1866 he became an assistant to Wagner, of whose works he became the leading interpreter. He also conducted the Hallé Orchestra in Manchester and championed the works of Brahms.

● **Richter, Johann Paul Friedrich** ▷*See* Jean Paul.

● **Richter, Sviatoslav (Teofilovitch)** ► (1914–) Ukrainian pianist. The winner of the Stalin Prize in 1949, he is famous worldwide as a concert and recording artist. He is particularly noted for his performances of Beethoven, Schubert, Schumann, and Prokofiev.

● **Richter scale** ► A scale of earthquake magnitude devised in 1935 by the US geologist C. F. Richter (1900–85) in California and now in worldwide use. It is a logarithmic scale from 0 to 9, the largest earthquakes having the highest numbers. It is based on seismic recordings, taking into account distance from the epicentre. The strongest earthquake so far recorded had a Richter scale value of 8.6.

● **Richthofen, Manfred, Freiherr von** ► (1892–1918) German air ace of World War I, who shot down 80 Allied aircraft before being

killed himself in action. His nickname, the Red Baron, referred to the colour of his plane.

● **rickets** ► A disease of children affecting the bones and caused by ▷vitamin D deficiency. Vitamin D is derived from the diet and can be made in the skin in the presence of sunlight; with a poor diet and/or inadequate sunshine the bones become soft and do not grow properly and the child may be knock-kneed, bowlegged, or pigeon-chested. The disease is readily treated with vitamin D preparations or foods rich in vitamin D.

● **rickettsia** ► A minute organism belonging to a group of parasitic bacteria that—like viruses—cannot reproduce outside the bodies of their hosts. They infect arthropods (especially ticks and mites) and can be transmitted to humans, in whom they cause such diseases as ▷typhus, ▷Q fever, and Rocky Mountain spotted fever. All species live within the cytoplasm or nuclei of living cells. The name derives from the principal genus (*Rickettsia*), which was named after H. T. Ricketts (1871–1910), a US pathologist who died of typhus while investigating the cause of the disease.

● **Ridgeway** ► A prehistoric trackway in S England. It runs along the scarp of the Berkshire Downs, linking the ▷Avebury region with the Thames, whence the ▷Icknield Way continues northeastwards. Many prehistoric monuments lie along its route. The Ridgeway long-distance footpath extends from near Avebury to Ivinghoe Beacon in the Chilterns.

● **Ridley, Nicholas** ► (c. 1500–55) Anglican reformer and martyr. He became Master of Pembroke College, Cambridge, in 1540, Bishop of Rochester in 1547, and Bishop of London in 1550. Under Mary he was deprived of his see, tried for heresy at Oxford, and, with ▷Latimer, burnt at the stake.

● **Ridolfi, Roberto** ► (R. di Ridolfo; 1531–1612) Italian conspirator against Elizabeth I of England. A businessman in London, he organized a Roman Catholic plot supported by Spain to overthrow Elizabeth and place Mary, Queen of Scots, on the throne. The conspiracy was exposed while Ridolfi was abroad and he escaped punishment.

● **Riebeeck, Jan van** ► (1619–77) Dutch colonial administrator, who founded Cape Town in 1652. He was sent to the Cape by the Dutch East India Company to establish a provisioning port for ships. He became secretary to the Council of India in 1665.

● **Riefenstahl, Leni** ► (1902–) German film director and photographer. During the 1930s she produced ▷propaganda films for the Nazis, notably *Triumph of the Will* (1935), glorifying the Nuremberg rallies, and *Olympische Spiele* (1938), about the Berlin Olympics; these films effectively destroyed her reputation outside Germany. Her books include two photographic studies of Sudanese tribes, *People of Kau* (1976) and *Last of the Nuba* (1976).

● **Riel, Louis** ► (1844–85) Canadian rebel. Attempting to resist surveys that he believed would lead to the métis (offspring of Indian-White parents) being robbed of their land, Riel led a rebellion of métis and set up a provisional government at Winnipeg (1869–70). Defeated and outlawed, he later led a similar rebellion (1884–85) that ended in his execution.

● **Riemann, Georg Friedrich Bernhard** ► (1826–66) German mathematician, who, like ▷Lobachevski and ▷Bolyai before him, produced a ▷non-Euclidean geometry. **Riemannian geometry** involves the development of a generalized space (Riemannian space) of any dimensions in which measurements may vary from point to point. It was used by Einstein in his general theory of ▷relativity.

● **Rienzo, Cola di** ► (1313–54) Roman popular leader, who during the papacy's sojourn in Avignon gained the support of the people of Rome against the nobles. He was proclaimed tribune (1347) and attempted to restore Rome to its ancient greatness. He was driven out by the nobles and later killed in a popular uprising.

● **Riesman, David** ► (1909–) US social scientist and lawyer. Riesman's published work includes *The Lonely Crowd: A Study of the Changing American Character* (1950), *Individualism Reconsidered* (1954), and *The Perpetual Dream: Experiment and Reform in the American College* (1978). Riesman's insights into US society are as profound and disturbing as those of his friend Erich ▷Fromm.

● **Rif** ▶ A ▷Berber people of N Morocco. Most of the 19 tribes speak the Rif dialect of the Berber language but a few speak Arabic. Many are light skinned and have blue or grey eyes. The Rif are Muslims and are renowned for their warrior tradition. They are cereal cultivators, herdsmen, and, along the coast, sardine fishers.

● **Rifkind, Sir Malcolm (Leslie)** ▶ (1946–) British Conservative politician; foreign secretary (1995–97). He was previously secretary of state for Scotland (1986–90), transport (1990–92), and defence (1992–95). He was knighted in 1997.

● **rifle** ▶ A shoulder ▷small arm with a spiral groove inside its long barrel to make the projectile spin during its trajectory. Invented in the 15th century, rifles were widely used in America in the 18th century. In Europe the rifle superseded the ▷musket after the invention of the Minié system (by the French officer, Claude-Etienne Minié (1814–79) in 1849) based on an expanding lead bullet. This was made obsolete in 1865 by the introduction of breech-loaded metal cartridges. During the 1880s breech-loading rifles became capable of firing more than one cartridge without reloading. These were the immediate predecessors of the modern repeating rifle. ▷*See also* Mauser rifle; Browning Automatic Rifle.

● **riflebird** ▶ A large ▷bird of paradise having a black plumage with iridescent throat patches and small ornamental plumes. The magnificent riflebird (*Craspedophora magnifica*) is about 30 cm long with a slender curved bill, a glossy green crown, and a purplish throat. The male performs its courtship display on specially selected and fiercely defended perches.

● **rifleman** ▶ A tiny brown passerine bird, *Acanthisitta chloris*, occurring in forested regions of New Zealand. It feeds by creeping up and down tree trunks picking out insects from bark, crevices, and epiphytic plants with its fine pointed bill. Family: *Xenicidae* (New Zealand wrens).

● **rift valley** ▶ A steep-sided valley with a flat floor formed as a result of the valley floor subsiding between two roughly parallel faults. Volcanic activity often occurs along these faults. The most notable example of this feature is the vast ▷Great Rift Valley in Africa; others include the central lowlands of Scotland and the Rhône rift valley.

● **Riga** ▶ 56 53N 24 08E The capital of Latvia, a port on the Gulf of Riga in the Baltic Sea. It is an industrial and cultural centre, with shipbuilding, machine-building, and many manufacturing industries. The picturesque old town has many historic buildings.
History: the order of Livonian Knights was founded here in 1201, and in 1282 Riga became a member of the Hanseatic League. A major trading centre, after the demise of the Livonian Knights it passed to Poland (1581), to Sweden (1621), and then to Russia (1710). The capital of independent Latvia (1918–40 and from 1991) and of the Latvian SSR (1940–91), it was occupied by the Germans (1941–44) in World War II. Population (1996 est): 826 100.

● **Rigel** ▶ A remote yet very conspicuous blue ▷supergiant, apparent magnitude 0.1 and about 800 light years distant, that is the brightest star in the constellation ▷Orion.

● **right ascension** ▶ An angular distance, analogous to terrestrial longitude, that is used with **declination** to specify the position of an astronomical body on the ▷celestial sphere. It is measured eastwards along the celestial equator from the vernal ▷equinox. Declination, analogous to terrestrial latitude, is the angular distance of the body N or S of the celestial equator.

● **Rights of Man and of the Citizen, Declaration of the** ▶ (1789) The formal expression of the ideals of the ▷French Revolution. Comprising 17 articles, it was drafted by the National Assembly to preface the constitution of 1791. Incorporating ▷Enlightenment theories and both English and American precedents (*see* Bill of Rights), the Declaration asserted that "all men are born free and equal in rights," such as equality before the law, freedom of speech, and ownership of property. The Declaration was an inspiration to later revolutionary movements.

● **right whale** ▶ A whalebone ▷whale of the family *Balaenidae* (5 species), so called because they were the right whales to catch (by whalers). Up to 18 m long and weighing over 20 tonnes, they are large-headed slow-moving plankton feeders with very long baleen plates and a double-jetted blowhole.

● **Rigi** ▶ 47 04N 8 28E A mountain in N central Switzerland, between Lake Lucerne and Lake Zug. It is popular for the fine views from the summit. Height: 1800 m (5906 ft).

● **rigor mortis** ▶ The stiffening of a body after death caused by chemical changes in the muscle tissue. The time at which it appears depends on the external temperature and the circumstances of death. It usually passes after about 24 hours.

● **Rijeka** ▶ (Italian name: Fiume) 45 20N 14 27E The chief seaport in Croatia, on the Adriatic Sea. Made a free port in 1723, it was annexed by Hungary in 1779. In 1919, following claims by Italian ▷Irredentists and Yugoslavia, ▷D'Annunzio led a force to capture it for Italy. It again became a free port in 1920, reverted to Italy in 1924, came to Yugoslavia in 1947 as reparation after World War II, and subsequently (1991) fell within independent Croatia. It has a university (1973) and varied industries, including oil refineries and shipyards. Population (1994 est): 167 964.

● **Rijksmuseum** ▶ A museum and art gallery in Amsterdam, housing the national collection of the Netherlands. It originated in 1808 as the Royal Museum and became the Rijksmuseum in 1817. Its highlights are its paintings of the Dutch school, notably the celebrated *Night Watch* by ▷Rembrandt.

● **Rijswijk, Treaty of** ▶ (1697) The treaty that ended the War of the ▷Grand Alliance between France and England, Spain, Austria, and the Netherlands. Louis XIV of France surrendered most of the territories he had conquered (retaining Alsace), recognized William III as King of England, and granted trading concessions to the Dutch.

● **Riley, Bridget Louise** ▶ (1931–) British painter. She studied at Goldsmith's College (1949–53) and the Royal College of Art and in the early 1960s began her black and white all-over patterns of repeated wavy lines, squares, etc., which associate her with ▷Op art. Later works incorporate colour. She was appointed a Companion of Honour in 1998.

● **Rilke, Rainer Maria** ▶ (1875–1926) Austrian poet, born in Prague (then in Bohemia). After an unhappy childhood and a brief marriage, he travelled widely in Europe and Russia, becoming in Paris a friend of Rodin, and finally settled in Switzerland. Paris is the setting for the meditative prose of *Die Aufzeichnungen des Malte Laurids Brigge* (1910). In his poetry, the mysticism of his early devotional *Das Stunden-Buch* (1905) develops into a pantheistic celebration of life in the *Duino Elegies* (1923) and the *Sonnets to Orpheus* (1923).

● **Rimbaud, Arthur** ▶ (1854–91) French poet. After writing "Le Bateau Ivre" and other early precocious poems he was welcomed to Paris in 1871 by ▷Verlaine, with whom he formed a tempestuous relationship that eventually ended in a violent quarrel. His visionary theories about poetry were expressed in the prose poems of *Une Saison en enfer* (1873) and *Les Illuminations* (1886). At the age of 20 he renounced poetry and wandered in Europe and the Near East, eventually becoming a gun-runner in Ethiopia. He died in Marseille.

● **Rimini** ▶ (Latin name: Ariminium) 44 03N 12 24E A town and resort in Italy, in Emilia-Romagna on the N Adriatic coast. It has various Roman and medieval remains. There is a textile industry and flour mills; pasta is produced. Population (1996 est): 129 598.

● **Rimsky-Korsakov, Nikolai** ▶ (1844–1908) Russian composer. Largely self-taught, he started his career as a naval officer and was appointed professor of composition at the St Petersburg conservatoire in 1871. He was a member of the group of nationalist composers known as the Mighty Five, the others being Balakirev, Borodin, César Cui (1835–1918), and Mussorgski. He wrote 15 operas, including *The Snow Maiden* (1880–81) and *The Golden Cockerel* (1906–07), such orchestral works as *Scheherazade* (1888), chamber music, and songs. He also reharmonized Mussorgski's *A Night on the Bare Mountain*.

● **rinderpest** ▶ A contagious virus disease, also known as cattle plague, affecting cattle and certain wild animals in Asia and Africa. Symptoms arise three to nine days after infection and include loss of appetite, fever, mouth ulcers, dysentery, and emaciation. 90% of acute cases are fatal; in chronic cases, mortality is lower. Compulsory slaughter and vaccination are used to control outbreaks of the disease.

● **ringhals** ▷*See* cobra.

● **ringlet** ▶ A ▷satyrid butterfly characterized by brownish wings marked with small white rings. The larval food plants are mainly grasses. Chief genera: *Aphantopus, Cacnonympha, Erebia.*

● **ring ouzel** ▶ A shy songbird, *Turdus torquatus*, which replaces the closely related blackbird in mountainous regions. The male is black with a broad white crescent around the throat; the female is dark brown with less distinct marking. They migrate to S Europe and the Atlas mountains for the winter. Family: *Turdidae* (thrushes).

● **ringworm** ▶ A highly infectious disease of the skin, hair, and nails that is caused by various fungi: it is known medically as **tinea**. Ringworm is usually transmitted by direct contact. The affected area, commonly on the scalp, feet (athletes' foot), armpits, or groin, is usually inflamed, scaly, and itchy and may be ring-shaped (especially on the scalp). Infections are treated with a variety of antifungal drugs, which are applied locally or taken by mouth.

● **Río Bravo** ▷*See* Rio Grande.

Rio de Janeiro ▶ The giant statue of Christ on the peak of Corcovada, some 690 m (2264 ft) above the city.

● **Rio de Janeiro** ▶ 22 53S 43 17W The chief port in Brazil, the capital of Rio de Janeiro state situated on the SW shore of Guanabara Bay. Discovered by the Portuguese in 1502, it was the capital of Brazil from 1763 until 1960, when it was transferred to Brasilia. Many colonial buildings remain, notably the 17th-century Candelaria church. It is renowned for its spectacular setting backed by mountains, the most famous of which is the conical Sugar Loaf Mountain. Another famous landmark is the giant figure of Christ standing on the highest peak, Corcovado, which is 690 m (2264 ft) high. The city is the site of several universities, the Oswaldo Cruz Institute (specializing in experimental medicine), and the Brazilian Academy of Science. It is an important port and trading centre and has a fine natural harbour; exports include coffee, sugar, and iron ore. The chief industries include shipbuilding, sugar refining, and railway engineering. Population (1995): 9 888 000.

● **Río de la Plata** ▷*See* Plata, Río de la.

● **Rio Grande** ▶ (Spanish names: Río Bravo; Río Bravo del Norte) The fifth longest river of North America. Rising in the Rocky Mountains, in Colorado, it forms the entire border between Texas (USA) and Mexico before entering the Gulf of Mexico. Length: 2040 km (1885 mi).

● **Río Muni** ▷*See* Equatorial Guinea, Republic of.

● **Riot Act** ▶ (1715) The Act stipulating that a gathering of more than 12 people must disperse when asked by a magistrate (or, subsequently, a soldier) to do so. The Act reflected government fear of the ▷Jacobites.

● **Ríotinto, Minas de** ▶ (*or* Minas de Río Tinto) A mining centre in SW Spain, in Andalusia near the source of the Río Tinto. Worked since Roman times, its copper mines are among the most valuable in the world.

● **Ripon** ▶ 54 08N 1 31W A city in N England, in North Yorkshire on the River Ure. It is a market town and tourist centre and has a cathedral (begun in 1154) and a racecourse. The ruins of Fountains Abbey are nearby. Population (1991): 13 806.

● **Risorgimento** ▶ (Italian: resurgence) The nationalist movement in 19th-century Italy that achieved the country's independence and unification. Secret societies, such as the ▷Carbonari and ▷Mazzini's Young Italy, encouraged Italian patriotism after 1815, and abortive uprisings occurred in Naples and Sicily (1820) and the papal states, Modena, and Parma (1830–31). Piedmont's attempts in 1848–49 to oust the Austrians from Lombardy ended in defeat at Custozza (1848) and Novara (1849) and afterwards ▷Garibaldi's Roman Republic was suppressed by the French. In 1859, however, the Piedmontese prime minister ▷Cavour freed Lombardy and in 1860 Garibaldi surrendered to Piedmont the conquests made in the S by his Expedition of the ▷Thousand. In the same year Tuscany, Modena, Parma, Bologna, and Romagna formed an independent alliance, all accepting entry into the kingdom of Italy under the House of Piedmont, proclaimed in 1861. Unification was completed by Italy's annexation of Venetia in 1866 and of the papal states in 1870.

● **rites of passage** ▶ Rituals and ceremonies performed on a person's transition from one social status to another. The most common are those at birth, puberty, marriage, death, and succession to office. Practices vary greatly but a pattern consisting of three stages is common to many such rites. First, there is a rite of separation, removing the subject from his previous status; next, a transitional stage in which the person is suspended between statuses; and finally, a rite of aggregation, in which the new status is conferred. In many primitive societies such rites have a strong element of magic and are thought to be essential to ensure success in the new role. However, similar rituals persist in highly developed secular cultures, suggesting that they continue to have an important psychological and social function long after any belief in their magical efficacy has faded. It seems that rites of passage can help individuals to place the key events in their lives in a larger context—as part of the wider life and continuing history of the community (religious, ethnic, or social) to which they belong, and as part of the universal pattern of human birth, maturation, and death. ▷*See also* initiation rites.

● **river** ▶ A large body of water, confined within a channel by banks, that flows into the sea, a lake, or another river. Its source may be a spring, a lake, a number of rivulets, or a glacier. Rivers are sometimes classified according to their development, a youthful river having a narrow V-shaped valley with many rapids and a mature river having a broad flood plain, meanders, and oxbow lakes. Rivers are important in the processes of erosion and the transportation and deposition of material; they are thus responsible for many of the landforms in those parts of the world of which they are a feature. Throughout history rivers have attracted settlement by man; broad river valleys were the site of some of the earliest great civilizations, such as in the Nile valley, and many of the world's major cities are located on rivers. As important communications routes, rivers often provided the point of entry to the surrounding land for explorers, traders, and settlers. Other uses of rivers include irrigation, hydroelectric power generation, and fishing. ▷*See also* flood.

● **Rivera, Diego** ▶ (1886–1957) Mexican mural painter. In Mexico in the 1920s, with ▷Orozco and ▷Siqueiros, he revived the old techniques of ▷fresco and ▷encaustic painting in murals for educational institutions. His communist-inspired subject matter made him notorious in the USA, where his mural for the Rockefeller Center was removed because it included a portrait of Lenin. His wife **Frida Kahlo** (1907–54) was also an important painter, whose work shows the influence of Mexican folk art and surrealism.

● **river blindness** ▷*See* onchocerciasis.

● **Riverina** ▶ A district of Australia, in S New South Wales, between the Murray and Lachlan Rivers. It consists chiefly of flat alluvial plains; the Murrumbidgee Irrigation Area is of greatest economic importance producing rice, stone and citrus fruits, and grapes. Area: 68 658 sq km (26 509 sq mi).

● **Riverside** ▶ 33 59N 117 22W A city in the USA, in S California on the Santa Ana River, and a long-established citrus town. The state's first navel orange tree was introduced here in 1873. It is the site of the citrus experiment station (1907) of the University of California. Population (1996 est): 255 069.

● **Riviera** ▶ (French name: Rivière) The narrow Mediterranean coastal belt of France and Italy, extending roughly between Toulon (France) and La Spezia (Italy). Its climate, coastal scenery, and beaches have made it a long-standing resort. Panoramic roads follow the coast; the famous two-tiered Corniche roads extend along the French Riviera (also known as the Côte d'Azur) between Nice and Menton.

● **Riyadh** ▶ 24 39N 46 46E A city in Saudi Arabia, in the centre of the Arabian Peninsula. Riyadh and Mecca are joint capitals of the kingdom. The discovery of oil in Saudi Arabia in the 1930s has turned Riyadh into a thriving modern city, the commercial and communications centre of the country; it has two universities (1950 and 1957). Population (1996 est): 2 800 000.

● **Rizzio, David** ▷*See* Riccio, David.

● **rms value** ▷*See* root-mean-square value.

● **RNA** ▶ (or ribonucleic acid) A nucleic acid that is important in the synthesis of proteins by living organisms. In some viruses RNA is the genetic material. Structurally, it is similar to ▷DNA but usually occurs as a single-stranded molecule with the sugar ribose and the base uracil replacing the deoxyribose and thymine of DNA. There are three main types of RNA (most of which occurs in the cell cytoplasm): ribosomal (r) RNA, messenger (m) RNA, and transfer (t) RNA. mRNA contains the ▷genetic code necessary for protein synthesis. It is transcribed from DNA in the nucleus and then moves to the ribosomes (small cytoplasmic particles consisting of rRNA and protein), where the genetic information encoded within it is translated into a particular polypeptide chain. The amino acids making up the protein are brought to their correct positions in the chain by tRNA.

● **RNLI** ▷*See* Royal National Lifeboat Institution.

● **roach** ▶ One of several freshwater fish related to carp, especially *Rutilus rutilus*, a game fish found in N Europe. It has an elongated body, 15–45 cm long, olive-green to grey-green above and silvery white below with reddish fins and red eyes. It lives in shoals, feeding on small animals and plants.

● **Roach, Hal** ▶ (1892–1992) US film producer. His production company, founded in 1914, produced many of the films of Harold ▷Lloyd, ▷Laurel and Hardy, and other comedians of the silent cinema. His single serious film was *Of Mice and Men* (1939).

● **roadrunner** ▷*See* cuckoo.

● **roan antelope** ▶ A large African antelope, *Hippotragus equinus*. 130–150 cm high at the shoulder, it is roan or reddish grey with a black-and-white face, long tufted ears, and an erect mane. The horns are shorter than those of the related ▷sable antelope. Roan antelopes live in herds of up to 25 in scrub and woodland.

● **Roanoke** ▶ 37 15N 79 58W A city in the USA, in W Virginia on the Roanoke River. Settled in 1740, it is an industrial centre and railway junction. Manufactures include textiles and chemicals. Population (1996 est): 95 548.

● **Roaring Forties** ▷*See* Southern Ocean.

● **Robbe-Grillet, Alain** ▶ (1922–) French novelist and filmmaker. He trained as an agronomist and statistician. He is a leading theorist and practitioner of the ▷*nouveau roman. Instantanés* (1961) and *Pour un nouveau roman* (1963) contain a number of influential essays on the subject. As well as his novels, which include *Le Voyeur* (1955) and *Angélique ou l'enchantement* (1988), he has written film scripts, notably the scenario for *L'Année dernière à Marienbad* (1961), and directed a number of avant-garde films.

● **robber crab** ▶ (or coconut crab) A ▷crab, *Birgus latro*, found on the shores of the SW Pacific and Indian Oceans. It has an extremely large body (about 1 m from head to tail), ranging from violet to brown in colour. It lives in sand burrows during the day, emerging at night to feed on coconuts broken open by its two large pincers. Tribe: *Anomura*.

● **robber fly** ▶ A predatory fly, also called assassin fly, belonging to a worldwide family (*Asilidae*; over 4000 species) of insect eaters. Robber flies have prominent eyes and strong bristly legs. Many species have a humped thorax and a long slender abdomen, but some (e.g. *Asilis crabroniformis*) resemble bees and wasps. Most larvae are herbivorous and live in the soil.

● **Robbins, Frederick Chapman** ▶ (1916–) US microbiologist, who, working with John ▷Enders and Thomas Weller (1915–), first cultivated poliomyelitis virus outside living organisms, using cultures of living human tissue in nutrient solution. This technique enabled the development of the polio vaccine and the culture of other viruses. He shared the 1954 Nobel Prize.

● **Robbins, Jerome** ▶ (1918–98) US ballet dancer and choreographer. He choreographed the dances for many musicals, including *The King and I* (1951), *West Side Story* (1957), and *Fiddler on the Roof* (1964). He was choreographer for the New York City Ballet from 1949 until 1990.

● **Robert (I) the Bruce** ▶ (1274–1329) King of the Scots (1306–29). After a long career of rebellion against the English Crown Robert seized the Scottish throne in 1306. Although immediately forced into exile by Edward I of England, on the accession of Edward II he slowly recovered the kingdom, decisively defeating the English at Bannockburn (1314). A period of consolidation of his power followed, culminating in English recognition of Scottish independence in 1328.

● **Robert (II) the Pious** ▶ (c. 970–1031) King of France (996–1031), who conquered Burgundy (1015) after years of warfare with a rival claimant. His nickname reflects his encouragement of monasticism.

● **Robert II Curthose** ▶ (c. 1054–1134) Duke of Normandy (1087–1134); the eldest son of William the Conqueror. He twice rebelled against his father (1077, 1083) and came into conflict with his brother William II Rufus. After fighting in the first Crusade, he attempted to usurp the English throne from his youngest brother Henry I and following defeat at Tinchebrai was imprisoned (1106–34).

● **Robert II** ▶ (1316–90) The first ▷Stuart King of the Scots (1371–90). He was three times regent of Scotland (jointly 1334–35; alone 1338–41 and 1346–57) while his uncle ▷David II was imprisoned or in exile. His own rule, as an old man, was of little consequence.

● **Roberts, Frederick Sleigh, 1st Earl** ▶ (1832–1914) British field marshal. Born in India, he gave outstanding service during the ▷Indian Mutiny, for which he won the Victoria Cross (1858), and in the second Afghan War (1878–80). He crowned his career with victory as commander in chief (1899–1900) in the second ▷Boer War.

● **Roberts, Julia** ▶ (1967–) US film actress, who rose to stardom in *Pretty Woman* (1990). Her other films include *Steel Magnolias* (1989), *Sleeping With the Enemy* (1991), *My Best Friend's Wedding* (1997), *Notting Hill* (1999), and *Erin Brockovich* (2000), for which she won an Academy Award. By 2000 she was Hollywood's highest paid actress.

● **Roberts, Richard** ▷*See* Sharp, Phillip.

● **Roberts, Tom** ▶ (1856–1931) Australian painter, born in Britain. He launched ▷impressionism in Melbourne with an exhibition (1889) of Australian landscapes painted on cigar-box lids. Specializing chiefly in scenes of rural life, he also painted the opening of the first Commonwealth of Australia parliament (St James's Palace, London).

● **Robert the Wise** ▶ (1278–1343) King of Naples (1309–43), a leader of the Italian ▷Guelfs (papal party) against the Ghibellines (imperial party). He was an outstanding administrator (hence his nickname) and patron of scientists and writers, including Petrarch and Boccaccio.

● **Robeson, Paul** ▶ (1898–1976) US Black actor and singer. His best-known stage performances were in the title roles of *Othello* and Eugene O'Neill's *Emperor Jones*. He sang Negro spirituals, made several films, and actively campaigned for Black civil rights.

● **Robespierre, Maximilien François Marie Isidore de** ▶ (1758–94) French revolutionary. A lawyer, Robespierre was elected to the States General in 1789, on the eve of the ▷French Revolution, and became one of the leaders of the radical ▷Jacobins. He gained a wide following in Paris and after the execution of Louis XVI was instrumental in the overthrow of the Girondins (1793). He subsequently wielded supreme power on the Committee of ▷Public Safety, instituting the ▷Reign of Terror. In 1794 the tide turned against him and his cult of the Supreme Being: he was denounced in the Legislative Assembly and guillotined.

● **Robey, Sir George** ▶ (George Edward Wade; 1869–1954) British music-hall comedian. He began his stage career in 1891 and became known as "the prime minister of mirth." He also appeared in pantomimes, films, and plays, notably as Falstaff in Shakespeare's *Henry IV* (Part I).

● **robin** ▶ A small Eurasian songbird, *Erithacus rubecula*, adopted as Britain's national bird. About 13 cm long it has an olive-brown plumage with an orange-red breast, throat, and forehead and feeds on insects, earthworms, fruit, and seeds. In Britain, robins are common on farmland, in woodland, and in towns and gardens. A robin defends its territory fiercely, using its warbling song as a signal to warn off intruders. Family: *Turdidae* (thrushes).

Several other thrushes are also known as robins, including the American robin (*Turdus migratorius*), and the name is also applied to unrelated birds, such as the Australian robins (which are flycatchers).

● **Robin Hood** ▶ An English outlaw, probably legendary, who figures in a series of ballads dating from the 14th century. Traditionally, he stole from the rich to give to the poor and in some versions was the banished and disguised Earl of Huntingdon. According to the *Lytell Geste of Robyn Hoode* (c. 1495) he killed the evil sheriff of Nottingham, was visited in his forest home by the king, and was subsequently employed in the royal household. His mistress Maid Marian, his association with Sherwood Forest, and his friends and accomplices Friar Tuck, Little John, and Will Scarlet were later additions to the story.

● **Robinson, Edwin Arlington** ▶ (1869–1935) US poet. Troubled by poverty and alcoholism, he established his reputation with a novel in verse, *Captain Craig* (1902), and the poems in *The Town down the River* (1910) and *The Man against the Sky* (1916). He also wrote dramatic monologues and narrative poems, including *Tristram* (1927). Some of his best verse appeared in *The Children of Night* (revised 1897).

● **Robinson, Edward G.** ▶ (Emanuel Goldenberg; 1893–1972) US film actor, born in Romania. He was cast as a gangster in *Little Caesar* (1930) and other films during the 1930s but he played more varied roles in later films, such as *Double Indemnity* (1943) and *The Outrage* (1964). He was also a noted art collector.

● **Robinson, John** ▶ (1919–83) British bishop and theologian. A distinguished New Testament scholar, he was Suffragan Bishop of Woolwich (1959–69). His controversial *Honest to God* (1963) popularized radical theological discussion.

● **Robinson, Mary** ▶ (1944–) Irish politician; president of Ireland (1990–97). A lawyer, she was a member of the Seanad Eireann (Irish Senate) from 1969 to 1989. She was UN high commissioner for human rights from 1997 to 2001.

● **Robinson, Sir Robert** ▶ (1886–1975) British chemist, who investigated the structure of the alkaloids ▷morphine (1925) and ▷strychnine (1946). The latter work enabled Robert ▷Woodward to synthesize strychnine eight years later. Robinson received the Nobel Prize in 1947.

● **Robinson, Sugar Ray** ▶ (Walker Smith; 1921–89) US boxer, world welterweight champion (1946–51) and five times middle-weight champion (twice in 1951, 1955, 1957, 1958–60). He fought 202 professional bouts, of which he lost only 19.

● **Robinson, William Heath** ▶ (1872–1944) British cartoonist and book illustrator. Working for the *Sketch*, *Bystander*, and other journals, he became famous for his witty drawings of bizarre machines for performing everyday tasks.

● **robotics** ▶ The study of automatic machines that are capable of simulating and replacing human activities. Some robotic machines have sensory devices and can make decisions based on a sensory input and a self-programming facility. However, most robots in current industrial use carry out a fixed sequence of computer-controlled operations. Current research and development seeks to combine the concepts of ▷artificial intelligence with a mechanical robot capable of visual perception by means of a television camera. Such a robot could use a mechanical limb in response to its perception of a restricted number of events in its immediate vicinity. □ p. 1070.

● **Rob Roy** ▶ (Robert Macgregor; 1671–1734) Scottish outlaw, whose violent life was romanticized in Sir Walter Scott's novel *Rob Roy* (1818). He embarked on his career of banditry after losing his family fortunes in 1712. Arrested and sentenced to transportation, he was pardoned in 1727.

● **Robson, Dame Flora** ▶ (1902–84) British actress. She was successful in both comedy, as in *Captain Brassbound's Conversion* (1948), and in serious drama, such as Ibsen's *Ghosts* (1958) and *John Gabriel Borkman* (1963). In her many films she usually played character parts.

● **Rochdale** ▶ **1.** 53 38N 2 09W A town in N England, in Rochdale unitary authority, Greater Manchester. Formerly important for cotton spinning, its main industry is now engineering. The Cooperative Society was founded here in 1844 by the Rochdale Pioneers. Population (1991): 94 313. **2.** A unitary authority in N England, in Greater Manchester. Area: 159 sq km (61 sq mi). Population (1995 est): 207 600.

● **Rochefort-sur-Mer** ▶ 45 57N 0 58W A port in W France, in the Charente-Maritimes department on the River Charente. It has a naval museum and manufactures aircraft parts. Pierre Loti was born here. Population (latest est): 27 720.

Mary Robinson ▶ The former UN High Commissioner for Human Rights giving a news conference in Geneva in August, 1998, when she spoke on the plight of refugees from Kosovo.

● **Rochester** ▶ 43 12N 77 37W A city in the USA, in New York state on Lake Ontario and the Genesee River. Founded in 1789, it is the site of the University of Rochester (1850) and the Rochester Institute of Technology (1829). Its industries include horticulture and the manufacture of photographic and optical equipment. Population (1996 est): 221 594.

● **Rochester** ▶ 44 01N 92 27W A city in the USA, in Minnesota. It is the site of the Mayo Clinic (1889) and the Mayo Medical Centre. Manufactures include electronic and recording equipment. Population (1996 est): 75 638.

● **Rochester** ► 51 24N 0 30E A city and port in SE England, in Medway unitary authority, Kent. Rochester is situated on the Medway estuary, adjacent to Chatham. It was a Roman stronghold and has a 12th-century castle and a Norman cathedral. Population (1994 est): 146 200.

● **Rochester, John Wilmot, 2nd Earl of** ► (1647–80) British poet. A dissolute member of the court of Charles II, he wrote many short poems famous for their uninhibited bawdiness. His longer satirical poems include *A Satire against Mankind* and *Upon Nothing*.

robotics ► An arc-welding robot (MetaTorch) equipped with a combination of lasers and miniature cameras enabling it to locate the precise position of a joint and to cope with irregularities and imperfections in the components.

● **rock** ► (music) ▷*See* pop music; rock and roll.

● **rock** ► (petrology) A solid mixture of ▷minerals forming part of the earth's crust. The minerals are usually consolidated to form a hard compact mass, but geologists include unconsolidated material, such as sand, as rock. Rocks are classified according to their formation (*see* igneous rock; metamorphic rock; sedimentary rock), their age (*see* stratigraphy), and their composition. Individual rock types are much more varied in chemical composition than minerals, and most consist of several different minerals. Some minerals in rocks can be seen with the naked eye, such as the quartz, orthoclase, and biotite in granite, whereas the minerals in clay can only be seen under an electron microscope. The principal minerals in rocks are the silicates (including silica), carbonates, and oxides. The essential minerals in a rock are those that determine its classification; accessory minerals are those that do not affect its classification. ▷Petrology is the study of rocks.

● **Rockall** ► 57 40N 13 30W An uninhabited rocky British islet in the N Atlantic Ocean. Area: about 743 sq m (8000 sq ft).

● **rock and roll** ► A style of popular music dating from the mid-1950s, resulting from the fusion of rhythm and blues with country music. The name was originally applied to such songs as "Rock Around the Clock" (1955) by Bill Haley (1925–81) and the Comets and "Heartbreak Hotel" (1956) by Elvis ▷Presley, whose bands consisted of electric guitars, drums, and amplified vocalists. The development of rock and roll created a new teenaged audience and produced such stars as Jerry Lee Lewis, Gene Vincent, Eddie Cochran, Little Richard, Chuck Berry, Chubby Checker (best known for "The Twist"), Ray Charles, and Buddy Holly. Performers in the UK included Cliff ▷Richard (who based his early style upon Presley) and Lonnie Donegan, who played a derivative form of rock and roll called skiffle. Rock and roll lost its pre-eminence in the early 1960s but has influenced the development of modern rock and ▷pop music through the more sophisticated styles of such groups as the ▷Beatles.

● **rock crystal** ▷*See* quartz.

● **rock dove** ► A cliff-nesting dove, *Columba livia*, of S Europe, Asia, and N Africa. 32 cm long, it has a grey plumage with a green-and-purple neck patch, two black wing bars, and a white rump. A fast flier with excellent homing ability, it feeds on seeds, grain, shellfish, and seaweed.

● **Rockefeller, John D(avison)** ► (1839–1937) US industrialist, who founded the monopolistic oil-refining company, Standard Oil (1870). In 1881 he turned the company, based at Cleveland, Ohio, into a business trust, the first such in the USA. A philanthropist, he founded the University of Chicago in 1891 and, with his son **John D(avison) Rockefeller, Jr** (1874–1960), established the Rockefeller Institute for Medical Research (now Rockefeller University) in 1901. The latter's nephew **Nelson A(ldrich) Rockefeller** (1908–79) was Republican governer of New York (1959–74) and Gerald Ford's vice-president (1974–77).

● **rocket** ► Any of several annual or biennial herbaceous plants of the genus *Sisymbrium*, having yellow flowers. London rocket (*S. irio*), up to 60 cm high, is found on roadsides, walls, etc. in Europe, W Asia, North America, and N Africa. Its name results from its abundance after the Great Fire of London in 1666. The name is also given to plants of other related genera, notably *Eruca sativa* (also known as arugula, rucola, *or* Italian cress), a Mediterranean plant whose leaves are eaten raw in salads or cooked. Family: ▷*Cruciferae*.

● **rockets** ► Vehicles or missiles powered by jet propulsion that carry their own fuel and oxidizer and can therefore travel both in space and in the atmosphere. Rockets have no lift surfaces (*see* aeronautics), obtaining both lift and thrust from their propulsive jets. Solid-fuel firework rockets were known to the Chinese in the 13th century and have been used sporadically in war ever since. However, the first liquid-fuelled rocket to fly was designed by the American R. H. ▷Goddard in 1926. This achievement attracted little interest, except in Germany, where the ▷Peenemünde rocket research station was set up. It was here that Werner ▷von Braun produced the ▷V-2 rocket in World War II. Intercontinental ▷ballistic missiles (with nuclear warheads), developed by both the USA and Soviet Union from this model, came to form part of the armoury of all the principal nations. These rockets, in turn, led to the space rockets that carried man to the moon.

The **launch vehicles** for space satellites and space stations are rockets built in stages. A high-thrust vehicle provides lift-off and acceleration into the thinner atmosphere, where this first stage is jettisoned and the second stage takes over. The world's biggest space rocket, the US Saturn V, is a three-stage rocket weighing 3000 tonnes fully laden. The first stage burns kerosene and the second and third stages burn liquid hydrogen. Liquid oxygen (lox) is the oxidizer for all stages. This rocket can carry a load of 45 tonnes into space. Fuel economy is one of the most important factors in rocket design—the specific impulse of a rocket being its most significant characteristic. The specific impulse is the time in seconds to burn one kilogram of fuel while producing one newton of thrust. Typical values are 3400 s for a solid fuel, 4500 s for liquid hydrogen-lox, and over 10 000 s for an ion engine. In an ion-engine rocket an easily ionized substance, such as caesium, is heated to produce ions, which are accelerated by an electric field to produce thrust. These engines of the future could be powered by nuclear energy or solar energy to produce the necessary 50 kW of electricity for each newton of thrust.

● **Rockhampton** ► 23 22S 150 32E A city and port in Australia, in central Queensland on the Fitzroy River. It is a commercial centre for an extensive hinterland producing meat, gold, copper, and coal. Population (1993): 65 868.

● **Rockies** ▷*See* Rocky Mountains.

● **Rockingham, Charles Watson-Wentworth, 2nd Marquess of** ► (1730–82) British statesman; prime minister (1765–66, 1782). As leader of the so-called Rockingham Whigs, he supported the American colonies in their conflict with Britain. In 1765 he repealed the ▷Stamp Act and led the opposition to Lord North's government during the American Revolution.

● **rockrose** ► A small spreading shrub, *Helianthemum chamaecistus*, up to 30 cm high with bright-yellow five-petalled flowers; it is found in grassland and scrub of Europe and W Asia. Hybrids of this and similar species are cultivated as ornamentals, with many coloured varieties. Family: *Cistaceae*.

● **rock tripe** ► A leafy ▷lichen of the genus *Umbilicaria*, found in Arctic and temperate regions. It is rich in carbohydrates and is edible when boiled. In Japan it is considered a delicacy, being eaten in salads or deep fried. Some species are also used as dyes.

● **Rockwell, Norman** ► (1894–1978) US illustrator. His paintings depicting everyday small-town life in the USA reached an enormous audience as covers to leading US magazines.

● **Rocky Mountains** ► (*or* Rockies) The chief mountain system in North America. It extends roughly N–S for about 4800 km (3000 mi) between New Mexico (USA) and the Yukon (Canada), forming the ▷continental divide. It rises to 4399 m (14 431 ft) at Mount Elbert. Some geographers include the Yukon and Alaska ranges in the system, making Mount McKinley, at 6194 m (20 320 ft), the highest point.

● **rococo** ► A style dominant in the fine arts and decorative arts of France between about 1700 and 1750. Developing in reaction to the ▷baroque pomp of the Louis XIV period, it was characterized by curved forms, slender proportions, asymmetry, pastel colours, and a general effect of intimacy, gaiety, and delicacy. The rococo style was particularly manifest in the interior decoration of Parisian townhouses and furniture, porcelain, and metalwork. Famous rococo artists include the painters ▷Fragonard, ▷Boucher, and ▷Watteau and the sculptor ▷Clodion. The style spread to Austria and Germany, where the leading exponent was the architect Balthazar ▷Neumann. England remained largely untouched by it, although some rococo features appear in the work of ▷Hogarth and ▷Gainsborough. The rococo was supplanted by ▷neoclassicism.

● **Roddick, Anita** ► (*born* Perilli; 1942–) British businesswoman, founder (1976) and director of the Body Shop chain, which now has over 800 outlets worldwide. Her shops supply natural cosmetics and toiletries with an emphasis on care for the environment.

● **rodent** ► A mammal belonging to the order *Rodentia* (over 1700 species). Rodents are distributed worldwide and occupy a wide range of terrestrial and semiaquatic habitats. They range in size from about 7.5 cm (the smallest mice) to 130 cm (the capybara). Rodents have distinctive teeth. The single pairs of chisel-like incisors in each jaw continue to grow throughout life, as they are worn away by gnawing. There are no second incisor or canine teeth, leaving a gap between the front teeth and cheek teeth. When the rodent is gnawing, the cheeks are drawn into the gap and the lower jaw is moved forward so that the upper and lower incisors can meet. This prevents the rodent from swallowing gnawed material and from wearing out its cheek teeth.

Rodents are important as agricultural pests, fur animals, and for scientific research. They are divided into three suborders: *Hystricomorpha* (porcupines, cavies, chinchillas, etc.; 180 species); *Sciuromorpha* (squirrels, beavers, marmots, chipmunks, etc.; 366 species); and *Myomorpha* (rats, mice, lemmings, voles, etc.; 1183 species).

● **rodeo** ► A US sport that grew out of ranching skills after the Civil War, now controlled by the Rodeo Cowboys Association. A rodeo, or contest, includes six main events: bronco riding with and without a saddle, bull riding, calf roping, steer wrestling, and team roping. Professional rodeo riders are not hired to take part, but live on prize money.

● **Roderic** ▷*See* Rory O'Connor.

● **Rodgers, Richard Charles** ► (1902–79) US composer of musical comedies. With the lyricist Lorenz Hart (1895–1943) he wrote such works as *The Girl Friend* (1926) and *Pal Joey* (1940). After Hart's death he collaborated with Oscar ▷Hammerstein II on *Oklahoma!* (1943), *South Pacific* (1949), *The King and I* (1951), *The Sound of Music* (1959), and other musicals.

● **Rodin, Auguste** ► (1840–1917) French sculptor. He produced his first major work, *The Age of Bronze* (1877), after visiting Italy (1875), where he was influenced by ▷Michelangelo and ▷Donatello. Its controversial realism was a factor in the vicissitudes of his public commissions: *The Burghers of Calais* (1884–86), his nude monument of Victor Hugo, and his dressing-gowned Balzac were all initially rejected. Nevertheless, by 1900 Rodin had established an international reputation, his bronze portrait busts and his figures in marble, notably *The Kiss* (1886; Tate Gallery), being particularly admired. His most personal work, *The Gates of Hell*, a government commission of the 1880s, was left unfinished. Many of its symbolic figures, for example *The Thinker*, became well-known independent sculptures.

● **Rodney, George Brydges, 1st Baron** ► (1719–92) British admiral. He wrecked (1759–60) a French invasion fleet during the Seven Years' War and won victories (1780–82) against the powers that supported the American Revolution. His victory over the French off Dominica (1782) helped Britain at the concluding Peace of Versailles (1783).

● **Rodrigo, Joaquín** ► (1902–99) Spanish composer, blind from the age of three. His works include the *Concierto de Aranjuez* (for guitar and orchestra; 1940) and *Concierto Pastorale* (for flute and orchestra; 1978) commissioned by the flautist James ▷Galway.

● **rods and cones** ▷*See* retina.

● **Roebling, John Augustus** ► (1806–69) US engineer, who with his son **Washington Augustus Roebling** (1837–1926) designed Brooklyn Bridge in New York, which was opened in 1883. They also designed major suspension bridges, including those over the Niagara River and over the Ohio River. John Roebling died after an accident while supervising the construction of the Brooklyn Bridge.

● **roe deer** ► A small deer, *Capreolus capreolus*, of temperate Eurasian forests. About 70 cm high at the shoulder, roe deer have a dark-brown winter coat, a red-brown summer coat, and a large white rump patch; males have small three-pointed antlers. They feed at night on leaves, shoots, and berries and live in pairs or small family groups.

● **roentgen** ► A unit of dose of ionizing radiation equal to the dose that produces ions of one sign carrying a charge of 2.58×10^{-4} coulomb in air.

● **Roentgen, Wilhelm Konrad** ► (1845–1923) German physicist, who discovered ▷X-rays while professor at the University of Würzburg, Bavaria. In 1895 Roentgen was investigating the ▷luminescence that cathode rays produce in certain substances and discovered that the luminescence persisted when the cathode rays themselves were blocked by cardboard. He correctly concluded that some other type of radiation was coming from the cathode-ray tube. He named the radiation X-rays and his discovery that the rays pass through matter quickly led to their use in medical diagnosis. In 1901, he received the first Nobel Prize for Physics. The unit of X-ray dose (*see* roentgen) is named after him.

● **Roeselare** ► (French name: Roulers) 50 57N 3 08E A town in W Belgium. An important German base in World War I, it suffered much damage. Industries include textiles (particularly linen) and carpets. Population (1991): 52 825.

● **Roethke, Theodore** ► (1908–63) US poet. He examined his own subconscious in such collections as *The Lost Son and Other Poems* (1948) and *Words for the Wind* (1957). He won a Pulitzer Prize for *The Waking* (1953).

● **Rogation Days** ▶ Four days in the Christian calendar devoted to prayer and fasting. The Major Rogation is on 25 April and the Minor Rogations are on the three days before ▷Ascension Day. Rogation Day processions and prayers were successors of pagan rituals to ensure a good harvest and in England the traditional ceremony of ▷beating the bounds took place at Rogationtide.

● **Roger II** ▶ (1095–1154) Norman King of Sicily (1130–54). He became Count of Sicily in 1105 and created a strong kingdom augmented by the acquisition of Calabria (1122), Apulia (1127), Capua (1136), and Naples (1140) on the Italian mainland. He also attacked the Byzantine Empire, pillaging of Dalmatia and Epirus. His court was a great intellectual centre for both Christian and Muslim scholars.

● **Rogers, Ginger** ▶ (Virginia McMath; 1911–95) US actress and singer. During the 1930s she partnered Fred ▷Astaire in many popular film musicals, including *Top Hat* (1935), *Swing Time* (1936), and *Follow the Fleet* (1936).

● **Rogers, John** ▶ (c. 1500–55) English Protestant martyr. While a chaplain in Antwerp from 1534, he was converted to Protestantism by ▷Tyndale and edited a Bible translation—"Matthew's Bible" (1537). After returning to England in 1548 he was tried for heresy and burnt at the stake at Smithfield, the first martyr of Queen Mary's reign.

● **Rogers, Richard, Baron** ▶ (1933–) British architect, born in Italy. With his first wife Su he formed Team 4 with Norman and Wendy ▷Foster (1963–67). His buildings include the Pompidou Centre in Paris (1971–77; with Renzo ▷Piano), Lloyd's in London (1986), the European Court of Human Rights in Strasbourg (1989–95), and the ▷Millennium Dome in Greenwich. In recent years he has taken a leading role in schemes for urban regeneration in British cities. He was knighted in 1991 and made a life peer, Baron Rogers of Riverside, in 1996.

● **Roget, Peter Mark** ▶ (1779–1869) British physician and philologist. He was secretary of the Royal Society from 1827 to 1849. His well-known *Thesaurus of English Words and Phrases* (1852) is a dictionary of synonyms.

● **Röhm, Ernst** ▶ (1887–1934) German soldier, who organized Hitler's ▷Brownshirts. Röhm's ambition to increase the power of the Brownshirts led to his execution without trial.

● **Rokitansky, Karl, Freiherr von** ▶ (1804–78) Austrian pathologist, whose detailed anatomical studies of numerous autopsies helped establish pathological anatomy. Rokitansky is noted for describing the different kinds of pneumonia and a liver disease known as Rokitansky's disease.

● **Roland, Song of** ▷*See* chanson de geste.

● **Rolfe, Frederick William** ▶ (1860–1913) British novelist, also known by the pseudonym **Baron Corvo**. A Roman Catholic convert, he failed to persuade Church authorities that he had a priestly vocation, and his frustration and delusions were expressed in the fantasy *Hadrian the Seventh* (1904), which concerns a convert who becomes pope. His other works include *Stories Toto Told Me* (1898) and *The Desire and Pursuit of the Whole* (1934). Interest in his life and works was aroused by A. J. A. Symons' biography, *The Quest for Corvo* (1934).

● **Rolland, Romain** ▶ (1866–1944) French novelist, dramatist, and essayist. He was also a distinguished musicologist, and his best-known novel, *Jean Christophe* (1904–12), concerns a German composer. His philosophical idealism, much influenced by Tolstoy, was expressed in numerous volumes of essays and biographies. He won the Nobel Prize in 1915.

● **roller** ▶ A short-legged bird belonging to a family (*Coraciidae*; 12 species) occurring in warm regions of the Old World. 25–40 cm long, rollers are blue or violet and have a large head, a strong slightly hooked bill, and a long tail. They feed in flocks on ants, locusts, and lizards. Order: *Coraciiformes* (hornbills, kingfishers, etc.).

● **Rolling Stones, the** ▶ A British rock group, formed in 1962. Their early hits included "The Last Time" and "Satisfaction." They became famous for their notorious behaviour in public, made successful tours of the USA, and recorded such albums as *Beggar's Banquet* (1968), *Sticky Fingers* (1971), *Exile on Main Street* (1972), *Some Girls* (1978), and *Stripped* (1994). The original members of the group were Mick ▷Jagger, Keith Richard (1943–), Bill Wyman (1936–), Charlie Watts (1941–), and Brian Jones (1942–69).

● **Rollo** ▶ (c. 860–c. 931) Viking leader, who founded the duchy of Normandy. Having invaded NW France, Rollo was given the territory around Rouen by treaty (911) with Charles (III) the Simple (879–929; reigned 898–923), thus becoming the first Duke of Normandy.

● **Rolls, Charles Stewart** ▶ (1877–1910) British car manufacturer and aviator. A car dealer, in 1906 he went into partnership with Henry ▷Royce to found Rolls-Royce Ltd. Rolls was the first to fly non-stop across the English Channel and back (1910), dying shortly afterwards in an aircrash.

● **Romains, Jules** ▶ (Louis Farigoule; 1885–1972) French poet, novelist, and dramatist. He was a leading exponent of the philosophical theory of *unanimisme*, which emphasized collective as opposed to individual emotions and psychology. His best-known works are the satirical play *Knock* (1923) and the novel cycle *Les Hommes de bonne volonté* (1932–46).

Richard Rogers ▶ A view of his controversial Pompidou Centre for Art and Culture in central Paris (1971–77, with Renzo Piano). As with several of Rogers' high-tech designs of the 1970s and 1980s, the service ducts are provocatively displayed on the outside of the building. Although initially much criticized, the Centre is now one of Paris's most popular sights.

● **Roman art and architecture** ▶ The styles of art and architecture of the ancient Romans. Deriving principally from their Greek and Etruscan predecessors, Roman styles in the fine and applied arts have profoundly influenced Western traditions. The Romans' main contribution to classical architecture was the formal and structural development of the ⁰arch, ▷dome, and ▷vault and the introduction of new types of building, such as ▷thermae, ▷amphitheatres, and triumphal arches. Their advanced building techniques and use of concrete were unsurpassed until the 19th century. The Pantheon and the Colosseum (both in Rome) remain as fine examples of their monumental building techniques, while the ruins of Pompeii provide an insight into their domestic architecture and their skill in town planning. In the other arts their style was modelled on that of the Greeks, although their sculptures were less idealistic and more inclined to portraiture. Little painting has survived, but from the evidence of Pompeii and elsewhere ▷mosaics and murals seem to have been popular.

● **Roman Britain** ▶ (43–410 AD) The Romans first came to Britain when Julius ▷Caesar invaded in 55 and 54 BC during the ▷Gallic Wars. However, they did not stay, maintaining only trading links until 43 AD, when ▷Claudius I dispatched an expeditionary force of four legions under Aulus Plautius. The army, which landed at Rutupiae (Richborough) in Kent, encountered little resistance until it faced a force of Britons at Medway, led by ▷Caratacus, chief of the Catuvellauni. It took the Romans two days to defeat this force. Claudius subsequently arrived to accept the surrender of several other tribes at Camulodunum (Colchester). By 47 Roman Britain comprised all the land S of the ▷Fosse Way, from Exeter to the Humber; by 48 incursions had also been made into Wales. A major revolt took place in 61, when the Romans tried to annex the territory of ▷Boadicea, queen of the Iceni; her armies sacked Camulodunum, Verulamium (St Albans), and Londinium (London), the three main Roman centres in Britain, before being defeated. However, other kings and princes in Britain, such as Cogidubnus (mid-1st century AD), king of the Regni, allied themselves with the Romans and became important in the Roman government of the country. The Romans built a palace for Cogidubnus at modern Fishbourne, near his headquarters at Noviomagus (modern Chichester). The remains of Fishbourne Palace, as it is now called, were discovered in 1960. Subsequently, under the governorship (78–84) of ▷Agricola, the Roman conquest was extended well into the Scottish highlands. The construction (122–27) of ▷Hadrian's Wall, from the Solway Firth to the Tyne, established the northern frontier of assured Roman control; despite the subsequent building (140–42) of the ▷Antonine Wall, from the Forth to the Clyde, it was not considered to be worth the expense of occupying Scotland.

South of Hadrian's Wall, Roman Britain was divided into two zones (provinces from the 3rd century) along a line extending from the Mersey to the Humber. A northern military zone, Britannia Inferior, was sustained by legionary fortresses at Deva (Chester) and Eboracum (York), the northern capital, and numerous smaller fortresses, garrisoned with a total of some 15 000 legionaries and 40 000 auxiliaries. It was, however, in the southern province, Britannia Superior, with its capital at Londinium, that Roman civilization had the greatest impact. Roads were built, trade links improved, pottery and metalwork flourished, urbanization increased, and administration was centralized; in the country, agriculture benefited from new techniques and markets and villas began to appear. According to ▷Tacitus, as early as the time of Agricola Latin was becoming the language of communication, spreading down the social scale from Romanized aristocratic Britons.

The decline of Roman Britain began before 350, with the Picts breaching Hadrian's Wall and the Saxons raiding the SE coast. Thereafter successive governors gradually withdrew troops in order to stake their own claims to the imperial throne in Rome, leaving Britain poorly defended. In 410, requiring his legions to combat barbarian incursions in the northern empire, the emperor Honorius abandoned Britain for good.

● **Roman Catholic Church** ▶ The Christian Church of which the pope is the temporal leader (*see* papacy). After the schism with the Eastern ▷Orthodox Churches (1054; *see* East–West Schism), Roman Catholicism was the unchallenged spiritual authority in W Europe;

during the middle ages Church dignitaries possessed great political, as well as spiritual, power and ▷monasticism flourished. In the early 16th century the rising tide of ▷Protestantism demonstrated the need for urgent reforms within the Church. The Council of Trent (1545–63), convoked to discuss these reforms, has largely determined the present dogmatic, disciplinary, and liturgical character of Roman Catholicism (*see also* Counter-Reformation), although important reforms (the so-called aggiornamento) were initiated by the second ▷Vatican Council. In general, a higher reliance is placed by Roman Catholics upon tradition and authority, especially regarding interpretation of the Bible, than in most Protestant Churches. The Church organization is largely centralized and hierarchical (*see* cardinals, college of; Roman Curia), and the pope's decisions are reinforced by the doctrine of ▷infallibility promulgated in 1870. Other distinctive doctrines include ▷transubstantiation and ▷purgatory. The number of the ▷sacraments has been fixed at seven since the 12th century. The cult of the Virgin Mary, which flourished in the middle ages, underwent a major revival in the 19th century, and the veneration and invocation of ▷saints are encouraged. Church furnishings, music, and vestments are more elaborate than in Protestant Churches. Until the mid-20th century Latin was the sole language of the Mass. Roman Catholicism has spread worldwide due to strenuous missionary efforts since the 16th century (*see* Jesuits) and is the largest Christian denomination. In a world becoming progressively more disinclined to accept Christian authority, the Catholic Church has managed to maintain its strong following. However, some modernization has already taken place (the use of the vernacular in the Mass, changes in monastic dress, etc.), although the present pope has maintained the traditional policies on abortion, contraception, and divorce, as well as an exclusively male and celibate priesthood. The Vatican's reluctance to change its views on contraception, particularly, has damaged its reputation with liberals in its own Church as well as in other Christian denominations and in other religions. ▷Liberation theology, which became popular in South America in the 1970s, claims that the Church should support the poor in their political struggle against rich elites. The traditionalist archbishop Marcel Lefebvre was excommunicated in June, 1988, after conducting an illegal consecration of four bishops in Switzerland. The number of practising Roman Catholics is now estimated at some 1000 million worldwide.

● **romance** ▶ A term loosely applied to a medieval verse or prose narrative that dealt with nonhistorical material and first became popular in 12th-century France. Its central themes were courtly love, chivalry, and adventure, and it was distinguished from the earlier ▷chanson de geste by being less heroic and more sophisticated in tone. It was intended as entertainment rather than for any religious or political purpose. Romances are conventionally classified into three types: (1) the Matter of Britain—romances based on the ▷Arthurian legend, which was popular throughout Europe; (2) the Matter of Rome—romances about the Trojan War, Thebes, or Alexander the Great; and (3) the Matter of France—romances about Charlemagne and his knights. Among the most famous medieval romances are the five Arthurian romances of ▷Chrétien de Troyes; the *Parzival* (c. 1210) of Wolfram von Eschenbach; the *Tristan und Isolde* (c. 1210) of Gottfried von Strassburg; the anonymous Middle English *Gawain and the Green Knight* (c. 1400); and Sir Thomas Malory's *Morte d'Arthur* (c. 1470).

● **Romance languages** ▶ Descendants of the ▷Italic language group, in particular of the spoken form of ▷Latin, called Vulgar Latin. The group consists of modern ▷French, ▷Italian, ▷Spanish, ▷Portuguese, ▷Romanian, ▷Catalan, the Rhaetian (*see* Romansch) group of dialects, Sardinian, and the now extinct Dalmatian. As this list shows, many Romance languages are in fact regional dialects rather than national languages. They are classified as a group on the basis of a shared section of vocabulary, which originated in the influence of the language of the Roman conquerors of the Mediterranean area in which the languages of the group are clustered. Since 1500 their use has spread outside Europe to South America and Africa, as a result of French, Spanish, and Portuguese colonization.

● **Roman comedy** ▶ A dramatic genre that developed chiefly from Greek sources and flourished in the late 3rd and 2nd centuries BC.

The first Latin version of a Greek comedy was written by Livius Andronicus (c. 284–c. 204 BC) in 240 BC. His successors included Naevius (c. 270–c. 201 BC) and ▷Plautus, whose plays, based on those of Greek ▷New Comedy writers, especially Menander and Philemon, were enlivened by colloquial language and topical and bawdy humour. The plays of ▷Terence and Caecilius Statius (c. 219–168 BC) were more sophisticated in their plots and characterization. At the Renaissance the plays of Plautus and Terence, the only representatives of Roman comedy to survive complete, were revived and became the basis of modern ideas of comedy.

● **Roman Curia** ▶ (Latin: *Curia Romana*) The papal court, comprising the chief judicial and administrative bodies of the ▷Roman Catholic Church. Its powers are delegated by the pope, who takes responsibility for its acts. Extensively reformed in 1967 by Pope Paul VI, it consists of three tribunals, which are mainly concerned with judicial matters; five offices, including the Chancery, which issues papal bulls, and the offices of the Palatinate Secretaries, such as that of the Cardinal Secretary of State, which deals with political affairs; and nine Roman Congregations, which are permanent commissions of cardinals having specific tasks (regarding rites, missions, etc.).

● **Roman Empire** ▶ The imperial period of ancient Roman history from 27 BC, when Octavian became emperor as ▷Augustus, until 476 AD. Under imperial government many of the political institutions of the ▷Roman Republic, notably the Senate, continued to function, although Augustus and his successors enjoyed supreme power as *princeps* (chief citizen). Augustus, who created an efficient administrative system for the Empire, fostered peace and prosperity, which continued, despite outbreaks of rebellion, under the paternalistic rule of the Flavian emperors (69–96 AD; *see* Vespasian; Titus; Domitian, Titus Flavius) and the Antonine emperors (96–180; *see* Nerva, Marcus Cocceius; Trajan; Hadrian; Antoninus Pius; Marcus Aurelius). Trade and industry flourished throughout the Empire, new cities were founded, and frontiers, although little extended, were strengthened. Civil war, however, followed the death of

▷Commodus (193), with provincial armies nominating their own imperial candidates. Order was briefly restored by Lucius Septimius ▷Severus (reigned 193–211), who openly acknowledged his dependence on military might, increasing the powers of the ▷Praetorian Guard (imperial bodyguard). The 3rd century saw a rapid succession of army-nominated emperors, while Rome's frontiers were threatened by the aggression of the ▷Sasanians and the Goths. ▷Diocletian (reigned 284–305) countered these attacks with the reorganization of the Empire between East (*see* Eastern Roman Empire) and West (293). It was reunited (324) under ▷Constantine the Great, the first Christian emperor, who founded a new imperial capital at Constantinople (*see* Istanbul). His attempts to establish unity were, however, short lived: civil war and economic decline followed his death and the western Empire fell prey to barbarian invasions. The Visigoths sacked Rome in 410; Carthage was captured in 439 by the Vandals, who in 455 also sacked Rome; in 476 the last Roman emperor of the West, ▷Romulus Augustulus, was deposed by the German king Odoacer. The Eastern Roman, or Byzantine, Empire survived until 1453.

● **romanesque art and architecture** ▶ A style of art and architecture that flourished in Europe from the 11th century until the introduction of the ▷gothic in the mid-12th century. Its origins were mixed, being a combination of Carolingian, Roman, and Byzantine styles, and regional influences produced many variations between areas. Primarily an ecclesiastical art form, it was largely stimulated by the need for more churches, now possible on a large scale because of the arrival of relative peace after centuries of disturbance. The increasing complexity of Church ritual was reflected in the greater number of side chapels. The decline of building techniques since antiquity resulted in very solid buildings with thick walls, windows with semicircular arches, and simple stone vaulting. The other important branch of romanesque art was sculpture. It was primarily used to decorate churches, either with geometrical or plant and animal patterns on the fabric of the building, especially on the capitals, or statues of religious subjects inside the building. Many exam-

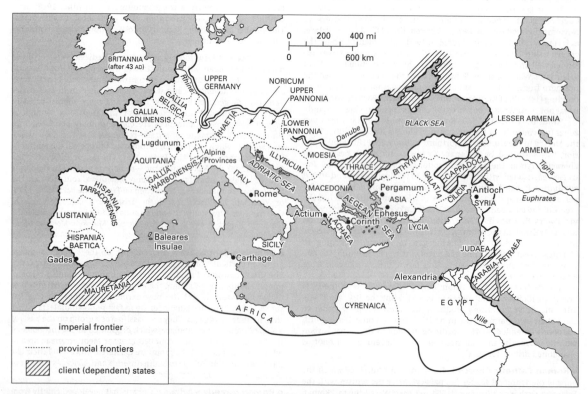

Roman Empire ▶ In 14 AD, at the death of Augustus, Roman rule or influence extended all the way round the Mediterranean.

ples of romanesque art still survive, one of the most notable being Pisa Cathedral. ▷*See also* Norman art and architecture. □arch.

● **Romania, Republic of** ▶ A country in SE Europe, with an E coastline on the Black Sea. The Carpathian Mountains and the Transylvanian Alps in the centre of the country separate the plains in the E and S from the Transylvanian plateau in the NW; the River Danube forms most of its S boundary. Most of the inhabitants are Romanians, who trace their ancestry back to the Latin settlers of the Roman province of ▷Dacia.

Economy: although there has been a pronounced shift in the balance of the economy towards industry since World War II, agriculture is still important and employs almost one third of the workforce. Much of the cultivable land was formerly organized in collectives and state farms, but since 1991 there has been a return of collectivized land to its former owners. The main crops are maize, wheat, potatoes, sugar beet, and fruit. Livestock is also important and there is a growing wine industry. Minerals include oil and gas, coal, lignite, iron, and uranium. Hydroelectricity is a valuable source of power. The industrial sector depends on heavy industries such as minerals and metals, oil, motor vehicles, machinery, and chemicals, and there is a general need for modernization. There is a considerable timber industry based on the extensive forests. Although one of the most fertile and mineral-rich regions of Europe, Romania has a long history of economic backwardness, made worse by the disastrous policies of the 1970s and 1980s. Many features of the centrally planned economy were retained until the mid-1990s, when soaring inflation and a depreciating currency obliged the government to introduce free-market reforms.

History: formed in 1861 from the principalities of ▷Moldavia and ▷Walachia, Romania gained independence from the Ottoman Empire in 1878 and in 1881 became a kingdom under Carol I. Romania joined (1916) the Allies in World War I and was occupied by the Germans. In 1918 it obtained ▷Bessarabia, ▷Bukovina, and ▷Transylvania; Bessarabia and part of Bukovina were subsequently (1940) ceded to the Soviet Union. In 1940 Carol II abdicated in favour of his son Michael and the fascist leader Ion Antonescu came to power. He gave Romanian military support to Germany until Soviet forces entered the country and he was overthrown (1944). After World War II a communist-dominated coalition was established (1945) and in 1947 Michael abdicated. Elections in 1948 resulted in a clear communist victory. From the 1960s Romania grew increasingly independent of the Soviet Union. Nicolae ▷Ceauşescu, president from 1974, repressed internal opposition, embarked on the destruction of many rural communities, and failed to rescue the impoverished economy. By December 1989 Romania stood virtually alone in its adherence to a hardline Stalinist approach; riots in Timişoara marked the start of a national revolution, in which at least 7000 died. Ceauşescu was overthrown and executed (with his wife Elena) and a new National Salvation Front government was installed, which won elections in 1990. A new constitution enshrining a multiparty system, human rights, and free-market reforms was approved in a referendum in late 1991. However, the government continued to be dominated by the ex-Communists and the president, Ion Iliescu, was accused of blocking reform. Popular demonstrations against the government were brutally repressed. In 1996 non-Communists were victorious in both presidential and parliamentary elections. Unrest continued, with a violent miners' strike in 1999 and racial attacks on the Hungarian and Gipsy minorities. Elections in 2000 saw the return of Iliescu to the presidency and the ex-Communists to government.

Republic of Romania

Head of state	President Ion Iliescu
Official language	Romanian
Official currency	leu of 100 bani
Area	237 500 sq km (91 699 sq mi)
Population (1999 est)	22 405 000
Capital	Bucharest
Main port	Constanţa

● **Romanian** ▶ A ▷Romance language, the main form of which (Daco-Romanian) is spoken in Romania and Moldova (where it is writ-

ten in the Cyrillic alphabet and known as Moldovan). Other forms are Aromanian or Macedo-Romanian (Greece, Macedonia, Serbia, Albania, and Bulgaria); Megleno-Romanian (N Greece); and Istro-Romanian (Istrian peninsula). Geographical proximity to the Slavonic languages has influenced Romanian's grammar, vocabulary, and phonology.

● **Roman law** ▶ The body of laws compiled by the Romans, which forms the basis of the ▷civil law of many modern countries. Although Roman law dates from the time of the kings (from c. 753 BC), the ▷Twelve Tables (450 BC) is regarded as the first major codification. Before about 150 BC these laws were elaborated as the *jus civile* (civil law), i.e. the law applicable exclusively to Roman citizens. With increasing territories, commercial interests, and foreign treaties, another system, the *jus gentium* (law of nations), was also applied by Roman courts. This system of international law derived from the philosophical concept of natural law (i.e. a law common to all men and to nature) and was used in cases involving provincial Roman subjects of different states and in suits between a foreigner or provincial and a Roman citizen. It gradually influenced the *jus civile*, and the two systems came to have many identical features. As Roman law developed, by judicial interpretation, by edict, and by legislation, there arose a number of anomalies, until the Byzantine emperor ▷Justinian I sponsored legal reforms embodied in the definitive codification of Roman law, the *Corpus Juris Civilis* (Body of Civil Law) or Justinian Code, published between 529 and 565 AD. This consisted of four parts: (1) the *Codex Constitutionum*, a chronological collection of the ordinances (*constitutiones*) of the emperors, with all contradictions, anomalies, etc., eliminated; (2) the *Digest*, a collection of statements by jurists on points of law; (3) the *Institutes*, a textbook for law students explaining legal institutions; and (4) the *Novellae* or *Novels*, the new ordinances issued by Justinian after the publication of the *Codex*. Roman law, with local variations, continued in use throughout medieval Europe and after the fall of the Byzantine Empire. The impetus for its spread outside Europe in the 19th century was given by the influential modern codification, the ▷*Code Napoléon*.

● **Roman literature** ▷*See* Latin literature.

● **Roman numerals** ▶ The system of numbers used by the Romans, based on letters of the alphabet: I=1, V=5, X=10, L=50, C=100, D=500, and M=1000. Intermediate numbers are given by the sum of a larger number and the smaller number that follows it (e.g. VI=6) or the difference between a larger number and the smaller number that precedes it (IV=4). By the 9th century the system had been replaced by ▷Arabic numerals.

● **Romanovs** ▶ The last ruling dynasty of Russia (1613–1917), noted for their absolutism and for transforming Russia into a large empire. The first Romanov tsar was ▷Michael, whose election ended the ▷Time of Troubles. His most famous successors were ▷Peter the Great, ▷Catherine the Great, ▷Alexander I, ▷Nicholas I, and ▷Alexander II. Romanov rule ended with the abdication of ▷Nicholas II (March, 1917).

● **Roman religion** ▶ The polytheistic religion of ancient Rome. The earliest cults worshipped local Italian deities of the fields, woods, springs, and hearth. As Rome grew to statehood its religion changed character: the gods of its Sabine and Etruscan neighbours (e.g. Quirinus and ▷Juno) were absorbed and ▷Mars, originally an agrarian spirit, became god of war. The state religion with its various priestly colleges (*see also* augury) centred on the temple of ▷Jupiter on the Capitoline hill (Rome). The influence of ▷Greek religion caused the identification of many Roman deities with Greek counterparts (Jupiter with ▷Zeus, ▷Vesta with ▷Hestia, etc.). In 204 BC the orgiastic cult of ▷Cybele reached Rome, followed soon afterwards by that of ▷Dionysus. The eastward expansion of Roman power brought contact with the esoteric cult of ▷Isis (*see also* mysteries) and ▷Mithraism. Emperor worship became an important part of official religion and a touchstone of loyalty. In the fringes of the Empire the Roman gods were often assimilated with local deities (e.g. at ▷Bath Minerva was equated with the resident goddess Sulis and worshipped as Sulis Minerva). Official toleration of Christianity under ▷Constantine the Great from 313 AD led to the gradual extinction of the old religion, despite attempts at revival (360–63) by ▷Julian the Apostate. ▷*See also* ancestor worship; Feriae.

● **Roman Republic** ▶ (510–27 BC) The period of ancient Roman history between the expulsion of ▷Tarquin the Proud and the proclamation as ▷Augustus of the first Roman emperor. Republican government comprised two chief magistrates (later ▷consuls) elected annually, an increasing number of subordinate magistrates, the ▷Senate, and popular assemblies (*see* comitia). Power lay in the hands of the ▷patricians until the ▷plebeians achieved access to all state offices.

Roman dominance over the rest of Italy was achieved by the early 3rd century: the tribes of Latium (the Latin League) were reduced by 338, victory against the Samnites of the S Apennines was attained by 290, and the Greek settlements in the S were conquered by 275. By the mid-2nd century Cisalpine ▷Gaul had been subdued and the ▷Punic Wars with Carthage brought control of the Mediterranean (146) and Rome's first overseas ▷provinces (Sicily, Sardinia, Spain, Africa). Concomitantly, dominance over Greece was achieved with the subjection of Illyria, Macedonia (*see* Macedonian Wars), and the Achaean League (*see* Achaea) and, following the acquisition of Pergamum in 133, control of much of Asia Minor. In the mid-1st century ▷Caesar completed the conquest of Transalpine Gaul.

The conquest of Italy was accompanied by the gradual extension of Roman citizenship (*see* civitas) and the construction of a network of roads, which brought Italy a degree of unity. The emergence, however, of a landowning elite who built up vast estates (*latifundia*) at the expense of small farmers resulted in serious unemployment. The attempts in the second half of the 2nd century of the ▷Gracchus brothers at agricultural reform aggravated the conflict between the Optimates (the aristocratic party) and the Populares (the popular party). The Republic was further undermined by provincial unrest, which, together with the military ineptness of the Senate in the late 2nd century, brought a series of ambitious army commanders to the fore.

The first of these, ▷Marius, emerged as a champion of the people but the popular party lost a bloody power struggle to the aristocrat, ▷Sulla, whose dictatorship (83–79) was marked by legislation to strengthen the Senate. This was revoked in 70 by ▷Pompey and ▷Crassus, who ten years later formed the so-called first ▷Triumvirate with Caesar. The death of Crassus (53) and Pompey's intrigues with Caesar's senatorial enemies brought civil war. Caesar's victory and subsequent short-lived dictatorship rang the knell of the Roman Republic, which was finally destroyed by Octavian's defeat of ▷Mark Antony and his assumption of absolute power as Augustus. ▷*See also* Roman Empire.

● **Romans, Epistle of Paul to the** ▶ A New Testament book written from Corinth by Paul in about 57 AD to the Christians at Rome. The first 11 chapters are a systematic explanation of Christian doctrine and explain the nature of salvation. The remaining chapters explain how believers are expected to live in the Church and in society.

● **Romansch** ▶ A ▷Romance language belonging to the Rhaetian group, spoken in N Italy and in the Rhine Valley in Switzerland. It is one of Switzerland's four national languages.

● **Romanticism** ▶ A fundamental development in Western art, literature, music, and their related fields of theory in the late 18th and early 19th centuries. Romanticism constituted a reaction against the unquestioned authority of reason and tradition (*see* classicism) and an affirmation of faith in the individual's innate powers of creativity. Its various manifestations included a passionate concern with the relationship between human beings and their natural environment, a new interest in the primitive and the irrational (including dreams, hallucinations, and madness), and an emphasis on emotional intensity. In literature, English Romanticism is usually dated from the publication of *Lyrical Ballads* by Wordsworth and Coleridge in 1798 and is associated with the poetry of Keats, Shelley, and Byron and the novels of Walter Scott. Major German Romantic writers included the Schlegel brothers, the young Goethe, and Schiller; romanticism also imbues the entire post-Kantian tradition of German philosophy from Schelling to Schopenhauer. In France, where the theories of Rousseau had anticipated many aspects of the movement, the important

writers included Chateaubriand and Victor Hugo. The influence of Romanticism is seen in the works of such painters as Turner, Friedrich, and Delacroix, and on musical composition from the time of Beethoven until the early 20th century.

In the theory of the arts, Romanticism was responsible for such widely accepted notions as the transcendence of the creative imagination, the superiority of organic form over more artificial structures, and the role of the tormented and misunderstood genius. In politics, it was initially influenced by the enthusiasm for liberty and impatience with social conventions that accompanied the French Revolution but later became identified with a mystical quietism and respect for tradition that can be seen as essentially conservative.

● **Romany** ▶ The language spoken by ▷Gipsies. It is related to ▷Sanskrit and the ▷Indo-Aryan languages of N India but diverged from these about 1000 AD, when the Gipsies began their nomadic way of life. Romany has been greatly influenced in vocabulary by the languages spoken in regions the Gipsies have passed through, resulting in many different dialects. There is little written literature in Romany but a rich oral tradition.

Rome ▶ The Arch of Constantine. Built in 315 by the Senate and people of Rome, it commemorates Constantine's victory over his enemy Maxentius.

● **Rome** ▶ (Italian name: Roma) 41 53N 12 33E The capital of Italy, on the River Tiber. It is mainly an administrative and cultural centre and, with the ▷Vatican City State within its boundaries, the focal point of the Roman Catholic Church. Known as the Eternal City, it is one of the world's greatest historical and art centres; tourism is an important source of revenue. The Italian film industry is centred here. Relics of classical times include the Forum, the ▷Pantheon, and the ▷Colosseum. There are many ancient churches the origins of which go back to the early Christian era; with the exception of Sta Maria Maggiore, the patriarchal basilicas (St Peter's in the Vatican City, S Giovanni in Laterano, S Lorenzo Fuori le Mura, and S Paolo Fuori le Muri) were built on the sites of martyrs' tombs. The Renaissance produced not only many outstanding buildings, such as St Peter's Basilica, but the paintings and sculpture of such artists as Michelangelo and Raphael. The 17th and 18th centuries brought more fine architecture, with squares, fountains, and façades designed by Borromini, Bernini, and others. The university was founded in 1303.

History: according to legend Rome was founded on the Palatine Hill in 753 BC by Romulus, its first king, later spreading to six other hills E of the Tiber: the Aventine, Capitoline, Quirinal, Viminal, Esquiline, and Caelian. Seven kings were followed by the ▷Roman Republic, and the ▷Roman Empire was founded in the 1st century BC. As the Empire declined in the 5th century AD Rome, no longer its centre, was sacked by Germanic tribes. From the time of Pope Gregory in the 6th century it regained importance, this time as an ecclesiastical power. In 800 Charlemagne was crowned emperor here. In succeeding centuries, it was sacked by Arabs and by Normans, and in the middle ages there was a continuing struggle between popes and emperors. It remained under papal control until 1871, when it became capital of the newly unified Italy. The popes however refused formally to relinquish their temporal power until the Lateran Treaty of 1929, when their jurisdiction was confined to the Vatican City. Mussolini's March on Rome in 1922 marked the beginning of his fascist rule; the city was occupied by the Allies in World War II. Population (1996): 2 654 187.

● **Rome, Treaties of** ▶ (1957) Two treaties signed in Rome by the representatives of Belgium, France, Italy, Luxembourg, the Netherlands, and West Germany, which led to the establishment of the ▷European Economic Community and the ▷European Atomic Energy Community.

● **Rommel, Erwin** ▶ (1891–1944) German general, known as the Desert Fox because of his victories in N Africa in World War II. In 1940 he became commander of the Seventh Panzer Division and, in 1941, of the Afrika Corps. In N Africa he was hailed as a liberator by the Arabs and gained the respect of the enemy but in 1943, after his defeat at Alamein (1942), he was recalled and became commander of the Channel defence. His involvement with the conspirators who attempted to assassinate Hitler in 1944 (*see* Stauffenberg, Claus, Graf von) led to his suicide, under pressure from Hitler, who wished to avoid a treason trial implicating his most popular general.

● **Romney, George** ▶ (1734–1802) British portrait painter, born in Lancashire. Although his training was limited, he attracted a fashionable clientele and rivalled Reynolds when he moved to London in 1762. He is best known for his numerous portraits of Lady Emma ▷Hamilton, whom he met in 1781.

● **Romney Marsh** ▶ An area of reclaimed marshland in SE England, on the Strait of Dover between Hythe in Kent and Winchelsea in East Sussex. Since reclamation was completed in the 17th century, sheep grazing has remained its chief use.

● **Romulus and Remus** ▶ The legendary founders of Rome, the sons of Mars and Rhea Silvia, daughter of Numitor, King of Alba Longa. Amulius, who had deposed Numitor, threw the twin babies into the Tiber. They were washed ashore and suckled by a she-wolf and later adopted by a shepherd. They eventually founded Rome at the place where they had been rescued. Romulus built the city on the Palatine hill and became the first king.

● **Romulus Augustulus** ▶ (b. ?461) The last Roman emperor in the West (475–76 AD). He was deposed by the German ruler ▷Odoacer.

● **Roncesvalles** ▶ (French name: Roncevaux) 43 01N 1 19W A village in N Spain, in the Pyrenees. Nearby is the Pass of Roncesvalles, where Charlemagne's rearguard, under Roland, was ambushed by the Saracens (788 AD) on his retreat to France.

● **Ronda** ▶ 35 46N 5 12W A mountain town in S Spain in the Andalusian province of Malaga. Perched high on steep rock faces, it overlooks the spectacular gorge of the River Guadalevin. It has a famous bullring and has long been a mountain resort for the British stationed in Gibraltar; it is now popular with tourists to the ▷Costa del Sol. Population (1995): 34 000.

● **rondeau** ▶ A short lyrical poem using an intricate verse form developed in 14th- and 15th-century France. Intended for singing, rondeaux were generally 10 or 13 lines long, used only two rhymes, and had an elaborate repetitive pattern of words and lines. Their subjects were the standard themes of the ▷courtly love tradition. The rondeau's virtuosity reached a peak in ▷Dufay's compositions.

● **rondo** ▶ A musical form in which a recurring theme alternates with contrasting episodes. In its simplest form it consists of the pattern ABACADA, A being the rondo theme and B, C, and D the episodes. In this form it was much used in the 18th century; Mozart, Beethoven, Schubert, and others developed the rondo by combining it with ▷sonata form.

● **ronin** ▶ A samurai (warrior) left masterless by the total defeat of his lord. In the 1860s, however, many patriotic samurai deliberately became *ronin* in order to engage in extremist political activities.

● **Ronsard, Pierre de** ▶ (1524–85) French poet. He turned to literature after deafness interrupted his career at court and became a leading member of the ▷Pléiade. His *Odes* (1550) and *Amours* (1552) gained him the patronage of Charles IX. His later works include *La Françiade* (1572), an unfinished national epic, and *Sonnets pour Hélène* (1578), which contains his best-known love poems.

● **Roodepoort** ▶ 26 10S 27 53E A town in NE South Africa. A W suburb of Johannesburg, it has developed manufacturing industries and is an important residential area. Population (1991): 162 632 (with Maraisburg).

● **rood screen** ▶ (*or* chancel screen) The screen of wood or stone, often elaborately carved, that separated the chancel from the nave in a medieval church. The name derives from the cross (Old English: rood) that surmounted the screen.

● **rook** ▶ A large blue-black Eurasian crow, *Corvus frugilegus*, about 45 cm long and having a narrow grey bill with pale patches of bare skin at its base. It is highly gregarious, breeding in large colonies and forming well-developed communities. Rooks feed on earthworms, larvae, carrion, and grain, sometimes damaging newly sown crops.

● **Roon, Albrecht, Graf von** ▶ (1803–79) Prussian general, who as war minister (1859–73) effected important military reforms. He introduced compulsory three-year service in the face of fierce opposition but his policies, which were supported by Bismarck, were vindicated by Prussian victory in the Austro-Prussian War (1866) and in the Franco-Prussian War (1870–71).

● **Rooney, Mickey** ▶ (Joe Yule Jnr; 1920–   ) US film star, who made his film debut at the age of six. Changing his name to Mickey Rooney in 1932, he made numerous comedies in the 1930s and 1940s, costarring in ten of them with Judy ▷Garland. In most of these he played Andy Hardy, a clean-living small-town boy (an image that Louis B. ▷Mayer tried to preserve by giving Rooney a minder to control his behaviour in public). He was married nine times, declared bankrupt, made a comeback in the Broadway musical *Sugar Babies* (1978), and was awarded an honorary Oscar in 1983.

● **Roosevelt, Franklin D(elano)** ▶ (1882–1945) US statesman; Democratic president (1933–45). He was paralysed from the waist down by poliomyelitis in 1921 but despite this disability became the only US president to be elected four times. He helped US recovery from the Depression with the ▷New Deal relief programmes and legislation to stimulate employment, industry, and agriculture. After the outbreak of World War II he introduced lend-lease aid to the Allies and, after the Japanese bombing of Pearl Harbor (1941), took the USA into the war. He attended the ▷Tehran and ▷Yalta Conferences with Churchill and Stalin but died in office before the conclusion of the war. His wife (from 1905) **Eleanor Roosevelt** (1884–1962) was the niece of Theodore ▷Roosevelt, to whom Franklin was distantly related. She supported minority groups and educational causes as US delegate to the UN (1945–53, 1961) and as chairman of the UN Commission on Human Rights (1946–51).

● **Roosevelt, Theodore** ▶ (1858–1919) US statesman; Republican president (1901–09). A rancher and big-game hunter, he led the Rough Riders (1st Volunteer Cavalry) in the 1898 war with Cuba. As president he introduced his ▷Square Deal programme for social reform. Roosevelt's foreign policy was to "speak softly and carry a big stick." He established US control over the building of the Panama Canal and made the USA a policing power in the Americas. Roosevelt ran again for president in 1912 but lost to Woodrow ▷Wilson.

● **root** ▶ (algebra) 1. One of the equal factors of a number. The square root is one of two equal factors; for example $\sqrt{9} = \pm3$; the rth root of a number n is the number that when raised to the rth power gives n. 2. The solution of an equation, i.e. the values of the variable that will satisfy the equation. ▷*See* quadratic equation.

● **root** ▶ (botany) The part of a ▢plant that provides anchorage and enables the uptake of water and nutrients from the soil. Roots contain vascular (conducting) tissue and just behind the tip is an area of root hairs, which increase the surface area for absorption. Some plants, such as the dandelion, have one main root with smaller branches—a tap root system; others, such as grasses, have a mass of similar-sized roots—a fibrous root system. Roots can act as food-storage organs, as in the carrot and turnip (tap roots); fibrous roots that become swollen with food are called tuberous roots, such as those of dahlias. Some roots grow in unusual positions and act as supports.

● **Root, Elihu** ▶ (1845–1937) US lawyer and statesman. A lawyer from 1867, he later became secretary of war (1899–1904) and secretary of state (1905–09). His achievements included reforms in the organization of the army, the improvement of relations with Latin America, and the Root-Takahira agreement with Japan (1908), committing the two nations to maintaining the status quo in the Pacific. A member of the Hague Tribunal (the Permanent Court of Arbitration), he received the Nobel Peace Prize in 1912.

● **root-mean-square value** ▶ (or rms value) The square root of the arithmetic ▷average of the squares of a set of numbers; for example the rms of 2, 4, 5, 6 is $[(2^2 + 4^2 + 5^2 + 6^2)/4]^{1/2} = 4.5$. The rms value is useful in continuous quantities, such as alternating electric current, in which the heating effect is proportional to the current squared. The rms value is therefore directly comparable to direct current.

● **ropes and cables** ▶ Flexible lengths of material made from strands of natural ▷fibres (e.g. hemp, jute, sisal, manila), synthetic fibres (e.g. nylon, polypropylene), or wire. In natural-fibre ropes, the material is spun into yarn and then formed into strands, which are twisted round each other in an opposite direction to that of the yarn. For many purposes nylon and polypropylene ropes, made by a similar method, are replacing natural-fibre ropes. A hawser consists of three strands, a cable consists of three hawsers wound together, and a shroud-laid rope has a central strand with three or four strands wound round it. Wire ropes are made by a similar process: high-tensile steel wires are twisted together to form strands, which are then wound round each other. In some cases the wires are preformed into helical strands to reduce internal stresses and are wound round a hemp core, for lubrication and flexibility.

● **Roque de los Muchachos Observatory** ▶ An international observatory on the island of La Palma in the Canaries at an altitude of 2400 m, set up in the 1980s by Britain, Denmark, Spain (who owns the site), and Sweden. UK telescopes (shared with the Netherlands and Republic of Ireland) include the new 4.2 m (165 in) William Herschel Telescope and the refurbished 2.5 m (100 in) Isaac Newton Telescope moved from the ▷Royal Greenwich Observatory.

● **Roquefort** ▶ 43 59N 2 58E A village in SE France, in the Aveyron department. Roquefort is famous for the ewes' milk cheese named after it. Population (latest est): 880.

● **Roraima, Mount** ▶ 5 14N 60 44W A mountain in South America, at the junction of the borders of Brazil, Guyana, and Venezuela. It is the highest peak in the Pacaraima Mountains. Height: 2810 m (9219 ft).

● **rorqual** ▶ A small-headed fast-moving whalebone ▷whale of the family Balaenopteridae (6 species). The common rorqual (Balaenoptera physalus), also called fin whale or razorback, grows up to 25 m long; it has a dark back, shading to white underneath, and a small dorsal fin that shows when it is blowing. Common rorquals are found in all oceans. ▷See also blue whale; humpback whale; sei whale.

● **Rorschach test** ▶ A psychological test intended to measure aspects of personality. Devised by the Swiss psychiatrist Hermann Rorschach (1884–1922), it consists of ten inkblots in complex shapes. The way in which the subject describes these pictures suggests his character. ▷See also projection.

● **Rory O'Connor** ▶ (or Roderic; ?1116–98) King of Connaught and last High King of Ireland. In 1171 he marched against ▷Dermot MacMurrough but was defeated at Dublin. Later he was forced to submit to Henry II of England.

● **Rosa, Salvator** ▶ (1615–73) Italian painter and etcher. Working in Naples, Rome (where he finally settled in 1649), and Florence (1640–49), he was also known as a poet, comic actor, and musician.

His reputation rests on his romantic landscapes, which were much admired in 18th-century England.

● **Rosaceae** ▶ A cosmopolitan family of trees, shrubs, and herbs (about 2000 species). Many are of economic value for their fruits, for example strawberries, raspberries, cherries, apricots, apples, and plums. Others are cultivated as ornamentals, including Spiraea, Potentilla, and roses.

● **Rosario** ▶ 33 00S 60 40W The second largest city in Argentina, on the Río Paraná. It is an industrial and commercial centre and the terminus of the pampas railways. Industries include sugar refining and food processing. Its university was founded in 1968. Population (1992 est): 1 157 372.

● **rosary** ▶ In the Roman Catholic Church, a religious devotion consisting of repeated prayers, particularly associated with the cult of the Virgin Mary. The recitation of a rosary is subdivided into 15 decades, each decade comprising an opening Paternoster, 10 Ave Marias, and a concluding Gloria. A subject of meditation, or Mystery, relating to the life of Christ or the Virgin is attached to each decade. By association the string of beads used to count the prayers is also called a rosary. The feast day established in 1716 in honour of the rosary is observed on 7 Oct.

● **Roscelin** ▶ (died c. 1125) French scholastic philosopher (see scholasticism). He was an early proponent of ▷nominalism, which he may even have originated. His philosophical belief that a being could have no parts led him to the Tritheist heresy, a deviant form of the doctrine of the Trinity. He was opposed by his famous pupil ▷Abelard.

● **Roscius, Quintus** ▶ (d. 62 BC) Roman comic actor. He was praised by Cicero, and his name has been applied as an epithet to many outstanding actors of the modern theatre.

● **Roscommon** ▶ (Irish name: Ros Comáin) A county in the N Republic of Ireland, in Connacht. It has many lakes and extensive bogs. Agriculture, especially cattle rearing, is the chief occupation. Area: 2463 sq km (951 sq mi). Population (1996 est): 52 000. County town: Roscommon.

● **rose** ▶ A prickly shrub or climber of the genus Rosa (200–250 species), native to N temperate regions but widely cultivated. The leaves are compound, with leaflets arranged in pairs. The five-petalled flowers are usually white, yellow, pink, or red and the fruits are red, yellow, or black hips, rich in vitamin C, containing many seeds. Wild species include ▷dog rose and ▷sweet briar. Family: Rosaceae.
   Modern hybrid roses—usually with double flowers—can be divided into several groups, the most important bedding varieties being the hybrid teas and floribundas. The former, derived from the tea rose (R. odorata), produce large shapely often fragrant blooms of good colour. The floribundas bear clusters of flowers and are usually grown for their colour effect rather than for the beauty of individual blooms. The climbers and ramblers are suitable for covering walls, fences, etc. Climbers include climbing forms of hybrid teas and floribundas as well as climbing species (such as R. banksiae). Ramblers include the wichuraiana group of hybrids.

● **Roseau** ▶ 1 15N 61 23W The capital of Dominica in the Windward Islands. A deep-water port at the mouth of the Roseau river, it was largely destroyed by a hurricane in 1997. It exports vegetables, spices, and limes. Population (1991): 15 853.

● **Rosebery, Archibald Philip Primrose, 5th Earl of** ▶ (1847–1929) British statesman; Liberal prime minister (1894–95). He was foreign secretary (1886, 1892–94) under Gladstone, whom he replaced. He resigned the Liberal leadership in 1896 and became well known as a biographer of British statesmen, and as a racehorse owner.

● **rosella** ▶ A brightly coloured ▷parakeet belonging to a genus (Platycercus; 7 species) occurring in Australia and New Zealand. 18 cm long, rosellas have a long broad tail, which is usually blue or green edged with white, black shoulders, and distinctive face and throat markings. They are largely ground-dwelling.

● **roselle** ▶ An annual or perennial fibrous plant, ▷Hibiscus sabdariffa, cultivated in tropical regions for its stem fibres, which are used for sacking and twine, and for its edible stalks, leaves, and flower parts. It grows up to 5 m high and bears solitary white or yellow flowers in the leaf axils. Family: *Malvaceae*.

● **rosemary** ▶ An evergreen shrub, *Rosmarinus officinalis*, native to the Mediterranean region and W Asia. Up to 2 m high, it has bluish flowers and small needle-like aromatic leaves, up to 5 cm long. It is widely cultivated for its oil, which is used in toiletries; for its leaves, used as a culinary herb; and for ornament. Family: ▷*Labiatae*.

● **Rosenberg, Isaac** ▶ (1890–1918) British poet and painter. The son of Jewish immigrants from Russia, Rosenberg has become well-known for his powerful descriptions of life in the trenches of World War I. He was killed in action.

● **Rosenberg, Julius** ▶ (1918–53) US spy, who with his wife **Ethel Rosenberg** (1915–53) was executed for espionage activities. They gained information about nuclear weapons from Ethel's brother and passed it on to the Russian vice consul. The severity of their sentences has since been criticized. Other members of the espionage ring were imprisoned.

● **rose of Jericho** ▶ A perennial herb, *Anastatica hierochuntica*, also called resurrection plant, native to W Asia. During the dry season the leaves are shed and the branches curve inwards so that the whole plant forms a wickerwork-like ball that is blown by the wind. When moistened, the plant regains its shape and produces tiny white flowers. Family: ▷*Cruciferae*.

● **rose of Sharon** ▷*See* Hibiscus; St John's wort.

● **Roses, Wars of the** ▶ (1455–85) The civil wars between the Houses of ▷Lancaster (the red rose) and ▷York (the white rose) for possession of the English Crown, which both claimed by right of descent from Edward III. The Lancastrian Henry VI's incompetent rule resulted in factional struggles led by the Lancastrian Beauforts and Richard Plantagenet, Duke of ▷York, and the Earl of ▷Warwick (the Kingmaker). Open warfare broke out in 1455. York was killed in 1460 and his son seized the Crown in 1461, becoming Edward IV, and crushed the Lancastrians. In 1470–71 Henry VI was briefly restored by disaffected Yorkists but Edward returned to the throne after his victory at ▷Tewkesbury. In 1483 he was succeeded by his young son ▷Edward V. The throne was then seized by Edward IV's brother Richard III, whose reign ended with his defeat by Henry Tudor (who

became Henry VII) at Bosworth (1485). The remaining Yorkists were finally overcome at Stoke in 1487.

● **Rose Theatre** ▶ An Elizabethan ▷theatre, in Southwark, in which William ▷Shakespeare may have acted. Built in 1587 and demolished in 1605, its foundations were rediscovered in 1989, and have been partly preserved.

● **Rosetta Stone** ▶ An inscribed stone slab discovered (1799) at Rosetta (Arabic name: Rashid), near Alexandria (Egypt). It carries a decree (196 BC) of Ptolemy V Epiphanes (reigned 205–180) in two languages and three scripts: Egyptian ▷hieroglyphic and ▷demotic, and Greek. The repetition of Ptolemy's name in the different scripts gave Thomas ▷Young the clue to deciphering hieroglyphs; his work was continued by ▷Champollion.

● **rose window** ▶ A decorative circular window in a medieval church. Rose windows, which were probably inspired by oriental models, had radiating tracery, usually glazed with ▷stained glass, and reached their apogee in 13th-century French ▷gothic architecture.

● **rosewood** ▶ An attractive hardwood, usually dark reddish and often rose-scented, derived from several tropical evergreen trees of the genus *Dalbergia* (family *Leguminosae*). These include Brazilian rosewood, or blackwood (*D. nigra*), used for veneers and cabinetwork; Honduras rosewood (*D. stevensoni*), used for musical instruments; and East Indian rosewood (*D. latifolia*), used mostly for small articles. Decreasing supplies have restrcited their use.

● **Rosh Hashana** ▶ (Hebrew: head of the year) The Jewish New Year festival, celebrated in September or October. Of biblical origin, by tradition the anniversary of the creation of the world, it is a time of penitence and preparation for ▷Yom Kippur. A ram's horn (*see* shofar) is blown in the synagogue.

● **Rosicrucianism** ▶ An esoteric movement for spiritual renewal that originated in Protestant Germany in the early 17th century and spread across Europe. Its manifesto traces its source to a fictitious brotherhood founded by a certain Christian Rosenkreuz in 1484. The philosophical programme propounded by its mainly anonymous adherents was a blend of theosophical and occult traditions, including ▷alchemy, ▷Hermeticism, and ▷Neoplatonism. ▷*See also* freemasonry.

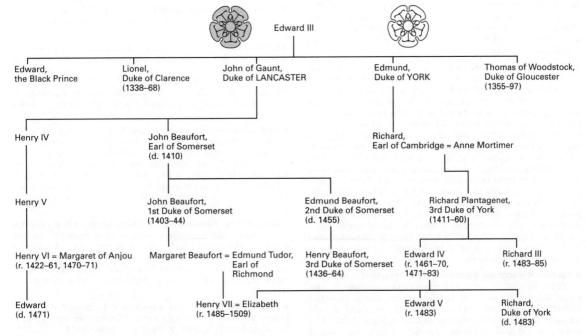

Wars of the Roses ▶ The rival Houses of Lancaster and York.

● **rosin** ► (*or* colophony) A yellowish ▷resin obtained as a residue from the distillation of ▷turpentine. It is used in varnishes, soaps, soldering ▷flux, and to rub on violin bows.

● **Roskilde** ► 55 39N 12 07E A seaport in Denmark, in Sjœlland. It was the Danish capital until 1443, and most of Denmark's kings are buried in the 13th-century cathedral. A university was established in 1970. Its industries include tanning, meat canning, distilling and agricultural engineering. Population (1990): 49 080.

● **Ross, Sir James Clark** ► (1800–62) British explorer. From 1819 to 1827 he accompanied Sir William ▷Parry on his Arctic expeditions and from 1829 to 1831 accompanied his uncle **Sir John Ross** (1777–1856). In this expedition Sir James discovered the North Magnetic Pole (1831). He later (1839–43) explored the Antarctic, discovering the area and sea named after him (*see* Ross Dependency; Ross Sea).

● **Ross, Sir Ronald** ► (1857–1932) British bacteriologist, who confirmed the theory of Sir Patrick Manson (1844–1922) that mosquitoes transmit malaria. While working in India, Ross discovered malaria parasites in the guts of *Anopheles* mosquitoes. In his honour was founded the Ross Institute and Hospital for Tropical Diseases (1926), incorporated into the London School of Hygiene and Tropical Medicine in 1933. Ross received the 1902 Nobel Prize.

● **Ross and Cromarty** ► A former county of N Scotland. Under local government reorganization in 1975 its boundaries were adjusted to form a district of the same name in the Highland Region. This was abolished in 1996.

● **Ross Dependency** ► An area in Antarctica claimed by New Zealand (since 1923), lying between longitudes 160°E and 150°W and including the ▷Ross Sea and islands S of latitude 60°S. The area and sea were named after their discoverer Sir James ▷Ross. Area: about 414 400 sq km (160 000 sq mi).

● **Rosse, William Parsons, 3rd Earl of** ► (1800–67) Irish MP (1821–34) and astronomer, who constructed a large 72-inch reflecting telescope. In 1848 he used it to study one of the blurred objects listed by ▷Messier and named it the Crab Nebula, because of its shape. He also discovered the first spiral galaxy in 1845.

● **Rossellini, Roberto** ► (1906–77) Italian film director. The neorealist style of *Rome, Open City* (1945), which included documentary film shot during the German occupation of Rome, greatly influenced postwar Italian cinema. His other films include *Paisà* (1946), also concerned with wartime Italy, *L'Amore* (1948), and *India* (1958), a documentary film. He subsequently worked mostly in television and the theatre.

● **Rossetti, Dante Gabriel** ► (Gabriel Charles Dante R.; 1828–82) British painter and poet. He was born in London, the son of a Neapolitan royalist exile who had fled to England in 1824 and who eventually became professor of Italian at King's College, London University. Rebelling against the conventional instruction he was given at the Royal Academy, in 1848 Rossetti joined with John Everett ▷Millais, William Holman ▷Hunt, and other artists to found the ▷Pre-Raphaelite Brotherhood. He founded the shortlived Pre-Raphaelite journal *The Germ* (1850–51), in which he began publishing his own verse. He later published several volumes of poetry and translations, including *Poems* (1870) and *Ballads and Sonnets* (1881). During his final years he lived virtually as a recluse, suffering from ill health. His sister **Christina Georgina Rossetti** (1830–74), a poet, was also born in London. Deeply influenced by the ▷Oxford Movement, she was a prolific writer much of whose work reflects her devotion to the Anglican faith. *Goblin Market and Other Poems* (1862), her first published volume, gave literary expression to Pre-Raphaelite ideals and contains perhaps her best work.

● **Rossini, Gioacchino Antonio** ► (1792–1868) Italian composer. His father was a trumpeter and his mother an opera singer. He studied at Bologna and wrote 36 highly successful operas, including *Tancredi* (1813), *The Italian Girl in Algiers* (1813), *The Barber of Seville* (1816), *La Cenerentola* (*Cinderella*) and *The Thieving Magpie* (both 1817), and *William Tell* (1829). At the age of 37 he gave up serious composition, although he did write a light-hearted *Petite Messe solennelle* (1863)

and pieces entitled "Sins of My Old Age." He invented a number of recipes, including Tournedos Rossini.

● **Ross Island** ► 77 40S 168 00E A volcanic island in the W ▷Ross Sea, at the edge of the **Ross Ice Shelf**, a vast mass of permanent ice. Mount Erebus is situated here. New Zealand established a base here in 1957.

● **Ross Sea** ► A large inlet of the S Pacific Ocean, in the Antarctic continent between Victoria Land and Byrd Land. Its S section is covered by the **Ross Ice Shelf**, a body of floating ice with an area approximately equal to that of France. The sea was discovered and explored by Sir James ▷Ross in 1841. ▷*See also* Ross Island.

● **Rostand, Edmond** ► (1868–1918) French dramatist. He gained international success with *Cyrano de Bergerac* (1897), a romantic comedy about a nobleman with an oversize nose. Sarah Bernhardt acted in many of his plays, notably *L'Aiglon* (1900).

● **Rostock** ► 54 03N 12 07E A city and Baltic port in NE Germany, on the River Warnow. Once an important Hanseatic port, its fine medieval buildings have been restored following damage during World War II. Its university was established in 1419. The main industries are shipbuilding and fisheries. Population (1996 est): 227 535.

● **Rostov-na-Donu** ► 47 15N 39 45E A port in S Russia, on the River Don near its mouth on the Sea of Azov. It produces agricultural machinery and has ship-repairing, food-processing, and textile industries. Its importance owes much to its position on the route from the W to the Caucasus. Population (1995 est): 1 026 000.

● **Rostropovich, Mstislav** ► (1927–) Soviet-born cellist. He became a US citizen after losing Soviet citizenship in 1978 (restored in 1990). He is also a conductor, notably of opera, and as a pianist frequently accompanied his wife the soprano Galina Vishnevskaya (1926–). Prokofiev, Britten, and Shostakovich wrote works for him.

● **Roth, Philip** ► (1933–) US novelist. Middle-class Jewish themes predominated in his early works including *Goodbye, Columbus* (1959) and *Portnoy's Complaint* (1969). In subsequent novels, such as *The Great American Novel* (1973), *The Ghost Writer* (1979), *Zukerman Unbound* (1981), and *Operation Shylock* (1993), the targets of his satire were more various. His most recent novels, *Sabbath's Theatre* (1995), *American Pastoral* (1997), and *I Married a Communist* (1998), show a further broadening of his range and are usually considered his best work.

● **Rothenburg ob der Tauber** ► 49 23N 10 13E A town in S Germany, in Bavaria. It is famed for its medieval town centre and town walls. Population (1989 est): 11 225.

● **Rotherham** ► **1.** 53 26N 1 20W A town in N England, in Rotherham unitary authority, South Yorkshire, on the River Don. Historically a centre for the coal, iron and steel, and glass industries, Rotherham now manufactures steel, steel products, and foodstuffs. Population (1991): 121 380. **2.** A unitary authority in N England, in South Yorkshire. Area: 283 sq km (109 sq mi). Population (1996 est): 255 300.

● **Rotherhithe** ► An area of E London S of the Thames in the borough of Southwark. The Surrey Commercial Docks here were, until their closure in 1970, an important part of the port of London. It was here that M. I. ▷Brunel built the first tunnel under the Thames, from Rotherhithe to Wapping. A very difficult operation at the time, it took from 1825 to 1843 to complete. Originally a road tunnel, it was converted to a railway tunnel in 1871. A new road tunnel was built in 1904–08 and is still in use.

● **Rothermere, Harold Sydney Harmsworth, 1st Viscount** ► (1868–1940) British newspaper proprietor. He partnered his brother (*see* Northcliffe, Alfred Charles William Harmsworth, 1st Viscount) in founding several newspapers, including the *Daily Mirror* (1903), and concentrated on the financial and advertising aspect of their business, Amalgamated Press. In World War I he was air minister (1917–18).

● **Rothesay** ► 55 51N 5 03W A town in W Scotland, in Argyll and Bute on the Isle of Bute. It is a resort and fishing town, with a ruined castle (founded 11th century). Population (1991): 5264.

● **Rothko, Mark** ► (Marcus Rothkovitch; 1903–70) Russian-born painter, who emigrated to the USA in 1913. In the late 1940s, with Barnett Newman (1905–70) and Clifford Still (1904–80), he pioneered colour-field painting (an abstract style using only colour) on mural-size canvases covered with horizontal bands of hazy colour.

● **Rothschild, Mayer Amschel** ► (1744–1812) German merchant and banker, whose business in Frankfurt prospered during the Napoleonic Wars, making loans to the various combatants and trading in high-demand goods, such as arms, wheat, and cotton. He was succeeded in Frankfurt by his son **Amschel Mayer Rothschild** (1773–1855). Four other sons established branches of the firm abroad. **Salomon Mayer Rothschild** (1774–1855) went to Vienna, **Nathan Mayer Rothschild** (1777–1836), to London, **Karl Mayer Rothschild** (1788–1855), to Naples, and **James Rothschild** (Jakob R.; 1792–1868), to Paris. In London, Nathan's son **Lionel Nathan Rothschild** (1808–79) was an MP (1858–68, 1869–79) as was (1865–85) his grandson **Nathan Mayer, 1st Baron Rothschild** (1840–1915). **Nathaniel Mayer Victor, 3rd Baron Rothschild** (1910–90) succeeded his uncle in 1937. A zoologist, he was research director of the Shell Oil Co (1963–70) before becoming director general of the Central Policy Review Staff (known as the think tank) from 1970 to 1974. The London merchant banking firm, N. M. Rothschild, is now headed by **Sir Evelyn de Rothschild** (1933–   ).

● **rotifer** ► A tiny invertebrate animal belonging to the phylum *Rotifera* (about 2000 species), also called wheel animalcule, found mainly in fresh water. Rotifers vary in shape from spherical to worm-like and range between 0.1 and 0.5 mm in length. Each has a ring of cilia (corona) around the mouth, beating in a wheel-like manner, for wafting food particles into the mouth and providing a means of locomotion in active species.

● **Rotorua** ► 38 07S 176 17E A spa city in New Zealand, in N North Island on SW Lake Rotorua. A Maori centre, situated within a volcanic area with hot springs, boiling mudpools, and □geysers, it has been developed as a health resort. Population (1990): 63 000.

● **rotten borough** ► A British borough constituency that, before the ▷Reform Act of 1832, continued to be represented in parliament although it had become depopulated. Examples of the 50 such boroughs were Gatton (a gentleman's park), Old Sarum (a green mound with a handful of electors), and Dunwich (most of which was submerged under the North Sea). ▷*See also* pocket borough.

● **Rotterdam** ► 51 55N 4 29E The chief port and second largest city in the Netherlands, in South Holland province on the New Meuse River. It became important during the 19th century, mainly with the opening of the 35 km (12 mi) long Nieuwe Waterweg (New Waterway) in 1872 linking it to the North Sea. During World War II the city centre was destroyed; this has since been rebuilt with an underground railway. Its notable buildings include the restored Groote Kerk (Great Church). The Erasmus University of Rotterdam was founded in 1973. The largest Atlantic port in Europe, Rotterdam handles considerable export trade from Germany, including Ruhr coal. Its dockyards extend W along the Nieuwe Waterweg and include Europoort, on the North Sea. Begun in 1958, Europoort's huge facilities handle chiefly oil importing and refining. Rotterdam's industries include oil refining, shipbuilding, brewing, distilling, and engineering. Population (1996 est): 592 745.

● **Rottweiler** ► A breed of working dog developed originally in Rottweil, Germany, as a guard dog and cattle drovers' dog. It is stockily built, having a broad round body, a strong neck, and a large head with a deep muzzle. The coarse short coat is black with tan markings. It has a reputation for aggression. Height: 63–68 cm (dogs); 58–63 cm (bitches).

● **Rouault, Georges (Henri)** ► (1871–1958) French artist. A major 20th-century religious artist, he was a largely independent figure, except for a brief and loose association with ▷fauvism. His favourite themes were clowns (sometimes modelled on himself or Christ) and prostitutes, expressing his sympathy with social outcasts. He was influenced by his early training as a stained-glass maker and was the favourite pupil of Gustave ▷Moreau. Until 1918 he worked chiefly in gouache and watercolour, using rich dark colours and heavy outlines. As a graphic artist his main achievement was his series of etch-

ings (1916–27), entitled *Miserere* and *Guerre*. He also designed tapestries and stained-glass windows.

● **Roubaix** ► 50 42N 3 10E A town in N France, in the Nord department on the Roubaix Canal. Famous for its cloth since the 15th century, it is (together with Tourcoing) the centre of the country's woollen industry. Population (1990): 98 179.

● **Roubillac, Louis François** ► (or L. F. Roubiliac; 1695–1762) French sculptor. He fled (1727) for religious reasons to England, where his statue of Handel, erected (1738) in Vauxhall Gardens, London, secured his reputation. His portrait bust of Pope and full-length statue of Newton are also outstanding. After a visit to Rome (1752) he executed the Nightingale and Hargreaves monuments in Westminster Abbey, reflecting some of Bernini's dramatic power and skill in composition.

● **Rouen** ► (Latin name: Rotomagus) 49 26N 1 05E A city and port in NW France, the capital of the Seine-Maritime department on the River Seine. The ancient capital of Normandy, it was here that Joan of Arc was tried and burned in 1431. Many of its notable buildings, including the cathedral (13th–16th centuries), survived the damage of World War II. Its university was established in 1966. The main industries are textiles, petrochemicals, engineering, paper, and electronics. Population (1990): 105 470.

● **Rouget de l'Isle, Claude Joseph** ► (1760–1836) French military engineer and composer. He composed the ▷Marseillaise in 1792 while stationed in Strasbourg at the outbreak of war between France and Austria. He was later imprisoned for a year for refusing to take the oath against the Crown; he was reinstated in 1795 and published a volume of 50 *Chants français* in 1825.

● **Roulers** ▷*See* Roeselare.

● **roulette** ► A game of chance played in most casinos. Of obscure origins, it was developed in the Monte Carlo casino. The principle of the game is that a small white ball is thrown in a clockwise direction into a horizontal wheel spinning in a counterclockwise direction. The rim of the wheel is divided into numbered compartments. Players bet (against the bank) on the number of the compartment into which they predict the ball will come to rest. There are two main varieties of roulette: French roulette and American roulette. In the French game there are 37 numbered compartments on the wheel (0–36), and the colour of the betting chips denotes their denomination. In the American game there are 38 compartments (00, 0–36), and each player has a distinctively coloured set of chips. In both games bets are placed on green baize tables on which the numbers of the compartments are laid out in groups of three. In the French game a successful bet on a single number pays 35–1 (and the stake is returned), giving the bank an advantage of 2.7%. In the American game, the bank's advantage is increased to 5.4%. There are also three types of even-money bets that the player can make: red or black, even or odd numbers, and 1–18 or 19–36. The red or black bet arises because alternate numbers on the wheel are coloured red and black. Between the extremes of even money odds and 35–1, the player can make virtually any odds he chooses by backing different groups of numbers.

● **rounders** ► A nine-a-side bat-and-ball field game, which is probably the prototype of ▷baseball. The two teams take turns at batting and fielding and a match consists of two innings per team. The hard ball is delivered underarm to each batsman in turn until all are out. The batsmen try to score rounders by hitting it and running round the four bases without being caught or run out. The batsman's square and first base, first base and second base, and second base and third base are 12 m (39.5 ft) apart, but third and fourth base are only 8.5 m (28 ft) apart.

● **Roundheads** ► The parliamentary party during the English ▷Civil War. The name referred originally to the short haircuts of the apprentices who demonstrated against the king at Westminster in 1640. It was later applied to all parliamentarians and referred to their drab appearance in contrast to the more flamboyant ▷Cavaliers.

● **Round Table Conference** ► (1930–32) Three meetings held in London to discuss a form of government acceptable to India. The meetings were attended by representatives of the British Government and of India's states and major political parties. Mahatma ▷Gandhi, representing the ▷Indian National Congress, boycotted the first meeting. The Conference led to the ▷Government of India Act of 1935.

● **roundworm** ▷See nematode.

● **Roussé** ▷See Ruse.

● **Rousseau, Henri** ▶ (1844–1910) French painter. Although known as Le Douanier (customs official) he was really a toll collector and as a painter was self-taught. From 1886 he exhibited at the Salon des Indépendants but his work, resembling folk art in technique (see primitivism), was ridiculed. After 1894, when he exhibited *War* (Louvre), followed by the *Sleeping Gypsy* (1897; New York), he received serious attention, particularly from ▷Picasso and ▷Apollinaire. The childlike quality and hallucinatory atmosphere of his portraits and jungle landscapes influenced the surrealists.

● **Rousseau, Jean Jacques** ▶ (1712–78) French philosopher and writer. Through his acquaintance with ▷Diderot, Rousseau joined the ▷Encyclopedists. In the *Discourse on the Origin and Foundations of Inequality amongst Men* (1754) he argued that man's perfect nature is spoiled by corrupt society. *Émile* (1762), a novel on education, expanded his views on ideal unfallen human nature. Rousseau's political influence was significant and many of the ideas embodied in such works as *Du contrat social* (1762) were taken up by revolutionaries. His fine style and romantic outlook inspired Shelley, Byron, and Wordsworth. His continued belief in a somewhat emasculated Christianity counterbalanced the atheism of Voltaire and the rationalists.

● **Rousseau, (Pierre Étienne) Théodore** ▶ (1812–67) French Romantic landscape painter and leader of the ▷Barbizon school. His melancholy scenes were influenced by ▷Constable and Richard ▷Bonington but his practice of open-air painting anticipated ▷impressionism. After permanently settling in Barbizon in the 1840s he received official recognition.

● **Roussel, Albert** ▶ (1869–1937) French composer. Serving in the French navy until 1894, he sailed to Indochina in 1890. Eastern culture became a source of inspiration although his later works are largely neoclassical. His compositions include the ballet *The Spider's Banquet* (1912), the opera-ballet *Pâdmâvatî* (1914–18), four symphonies, a piano concerto, chamber music, and songs.

● **Roussel, Raymond** ▶ (1877–1933) French writer and dramatist. His writings, constructed around elaborate puzzles and linguistic games, include *Impressions d'Afrique* (1910) and *Locus Solus* (1914) and three plays the first productions of which caused scandals. He is regarded as a precursor of both surrealism and the *nouveau roman*.

● **Roux, Pierre Paul Emile** ▶ (1853–1933) French bacteriologist, who, following the discovery of the Klebs-Loeffler (diphtheria) bacillus in 1884, showed that the disease symptoms were caused by a toxin released by the bacilli. Roux helped develop an antitoxin serum for diphtheria and—working with ▷Pasteur—discovered a vaccine for anthrax using attenuated bacilli. Roux was director of the Pasteur Institute (1904–33).

● **rove beetle** ▶ A beetle belonging to the worldwide family *Staphylinidae* (about 27 000 species), having short wing cases covering the folded hindwings. Rove beetles range from 0.7 to 32 mm in length although most are small. They are commonly found near dung and dead animal matter, preying upon insects and mites. Some species live in ant and termite nests. ▷See also devil's coach horse.

● **rowan** ▷See mountain ash.

● **Rowe, Nicholas** ▶ (1674–1718) British dramatist. He exploited the fashion for sentimentalism in his tragedies *The Fair Penitent* (1703) and *The Tragedy of Jane Shore* (1714). He produced the first critical edition of Shakespeare (1709) and became poet laureate in 1715.

● **rowing** ▶ A sport using narrow light boats (*or* shells) propelled by two, four, or eight people and often steered by a coxswain, usually on a river or lake. The oarsmen sit in line in sliding seats, bracing their feet against stretchers. Each controls one oar set in a rowlock, the oars being arranged on alternate sides. **Sculling** is a form of rowing for one, two, or four people per boat, each person controlling two

oars. The governing body is the Fédération internationale des Sociétés d'Aviron. ▷See also Boat Race.

● **Rowlandson, Thomas** ▶ (1756–1827) British caricaturist. A student at the Royal Academy and in Paris, he worked first as a portraitist but specialized in caricature after 1781. Using a reed pen and delicate washes of colour, he produced the popular satirical *Dr Syntax* series (1812–21) and the *English Dance of Death* (1815–16). He also illustrated books by Smollett, Goldsmith, and Sterne.

● **Rowley, Thomas** ▶ (c. 1585–c. 1642) English dramatist. He collaborated with other Jacobean dramatists, notably with Ford and Dekker on *The Witch of Edmonton* (1621) and with Thomas Middleton on *The Changeling* (1622). His own plays were mostly comedies.

● **Rowling, J(oanne) K(athleen)** ▶ (1965–) British children's writer, whose stories about the boy wizard Harry Potter—*The Philosopher's Stone* (1997), *The Chamber of Secrets* (1998), *The Prisoner of Azkaban* (1999), and *The Goblet of Fire* (2000)—became a publishing phenomenon; the last-named was the fastest selling book in history on first publication.

● **Rowntree, Benjamin Seebohm** ▶ (1871–1954) British businessman and sociologist, who in 1889 joined the family cocoa and chocolate business in York. He introduced pension plans, profit sharing, and other reforms on behalf of the employees and made influential studies of poverty in York. The chocolate business was founded by his uncle **Henry Rowntree** (1838–83), who was later joined by Henry's brother (Benjamin's father) **Joseph Rowntree** (1836–1925).

● **Rowse, A(lfred) L(eslie)** ▶ (1903–97) British historian and literary critic. Rowse was best known for his books on the Tudor period, including *The Elizabethan Renaissance* (1971), and on Shakespeare, whose Dark Lady of the sonnets he controversially identified as Emilia Lanier, daughter of a court musician.

● **Roxburgh** ▶ (or Roxburghshire) A former county of SE Scotland. Under local government reorganization in 1975 its boundaries were adjusted to form Roxburgh District in the Borders Region (now Scottish Borders). This district was abolished in 1996.

● **Royal Academy** ▶ An art society in Burlington House, London, that holds annual summer exhibitions of contemporary British art, as well as loan exhibitions of modern artists and the old masters. Founded in 1768, it originally had an important teaching function. It's first president was Sir Joshua ▷Reynolds. It moved to its present premises in 1867, after being housed at various stages in Pall Mall, Somerset House, and the National Gallery.

● **Royal Academy of Dramatic Art** ▶ (RADA) The leading British school of acting, founded in London in 1904 by Sir Herbert Beerbohm ▷Tree. It has received a government subsidy since 1924 and benefited from a legacy bequeathed by G. B. Shaw in 1950. It has three theatres, the Vanbrugh, the George Bernard Shaw, and a small studio theatre.

● **Royal Air Force** ▶ (RAF) A British armed service formed in 1918 by the amalgamation of the Royal Flying Corps (1912) with the Royal Naval Air Service (1914). It contributed to the final operations on the western front in World War I and played a decisive role in ▷World War II. It is now divided into Strike Command (the operational command), Maintenance Command, and Training Command and is administered by the Air Force Department of the Ministry of Defence. The **Women's Royal Air Force** was formed in 1949 in succession to the Women's Auxiliary Air Force (WAAF) of World War II and the Women's Royal Air Force (1918–20). ▷See also aircraft.

● **Royal and Ancient Golf Club of St Andrews** ▶ One of the World's major golf clubs (founded 1754). In 1919 it was officially accepted as the governing body of golf in Britain.

● **royal antelope** ▶ The world's smallest antelope, *Neotragus pygmaeus*, of West African forests. 25–30 cm high at the shoulder, it is red-brown with white underparts; males have spiky horns. They are nocturnal and occur singly or in pairs.

● **Royal Ballet** ▶ The leading British ballet company and school. Based at the Royal Opera House, Covent Garden, since 1946, it was known as the Sadler's Wells Ballet until 1956, when it was granted a royal charter. It was founded by Ninette ▷de Valois in 1931 and during the 1930s it performed at the Old Vic and the Sadler's Wells Theatres with such principal dancers as Margot ▷Fonteyn and Robert ▷Helpmann. De Valois was succeeded as director by Sir Frederick ▷Ashton in 1963, followed by Kenneth ▷MacMillan in 1970, Norman Morrice in 1977, and Anthony Dowell in 1986; Ross Stretton took over in 2001. In 1990 the Royal Ballet's supporting company moved to Birmingham and was renamed the Royal Birmingham Ballet.

● **Royal British Legion** ► An organization for ex-servicemen and women, founded in 1921 largely through the efforts of Douglas ▷Haig. It provides aid with housing or employment problems and runs homes for the sick and aged. It also makes the Flanders poppies sold before ▷Remembrance Sunday.

● **Royal Canadian Mounted Police** ► (*or* Mounties) Canadian police force. Founded in 1873 as the North West Mounted Police, it has become famous for the efficiency and discipline of its members, dressed in distinctive scarlet tunics, blue breeches, and wide-brimmed hats.

● **royal fern** ▷*See* Osmunda.

● **Royal Geographical Society** ► A British learned society, established in 1830 and incorporated in 1859, for the advancement of geographical knowledge. Among other functions it helps to finance expeditions; explorers who have benefited in this way include ▷Livingstone, ▷Scott, ▷Shackleton, and John ▷Hunt. Two Royal Medals are awarded annually to geographers recommended by the Society.

Royal Greenwich Observatory ► The original building in Greenwich, on a hill overlooking the River Thames. The ball above the turret (centre) is dropped at one o'clock precisely every day as a time signal.

● **Royal Greenwich Observatory** ► An observatory founded in 1675 by Charles II at Greenwich, London, in a building designed by Sir Christopher Wren. The meridian through Greenwich (0°) was internationally adopted as the prime meridian in 1884 and became the basis of Greenwich Mean Time and British Summer Time. In 1948–54 the observatory moved to Herstmonceux, Sussex. Its 2.5 m (100 in) reflecting telescope (the Isaac Newton Telescope) was moved to the new ▷Roque de los Muchachos Observatory in the Canary Islands in the 1980s. The observatory staff moved to Cambridge in 1990.

● **Royal Horticultural Society** ► A society in the UK that exists to further interest in vegetables and ornamental plants. Founded in 1804, it received its royal charter in 1809 and now has its headquarters in Vincent Square, London. The society maintains public gardens, notably at Wisley, Surrey, and organizes various shows, including the Chelsea Flower Show.

● **Royal Institute of British Architects** ► (RIBA) A British learned society founded in 1834 and granted a royal charter in 1837. It controls admission to the profession and provides architects with advice, information, and other support. It also aims to promote public awareness of architecture. It has some 28 000 members, membership being controlled by examination. Its prestigious Royal Gold Medal is awarded annually. President: David Rock.

● **Royal Institution** ► One of the first scientific research centres, founded by Benjamin Thompson, Count ▷Rumford, in 1799 (royal charter in 1800). Several famous scientists have worked here, including ▷Davy, ▷Faraday, and ▷Bragg. It has also been concerned to present scientific ideas to nonscientific audiences; its Christmas lectures for young people have long been a feature of London life.

● **royal jelly** ► A thick white mixture of proteins, carbohydrates, minerals, and vitamins that is secreted by worker bees and fed to the larvae. Larvae destined to become queens are fed entirely on royal jelly. ▷*See also* honeybee.

● **Royal Marines** ► A corps of troops, founded in England in 1664, which serves on land (as commandos), at sea, or in the air. Their ranks correspond to those of the army but they are administered by the Navy Board. They served in both World Wars, in the Korean War, and in Northern Ireland.

● **Royal Mint** ► The factory in which the UK's coins are made. Formerly in the Tower of London, it moved to Tower Hill in 1811 and to Llantrisant, South Wales, in 1968. Medals and decorations are also made, while foreign coins for export now make up about 65% of the 18 000 tonnes of coins produced each year by the Mint. In 1999 the government announced that it would be semiprivatized.

● **Royal National Lifeboat Institution** ► (RNLI) A voluntary organization, founded in 1824 by Sir William Hillary (1771–1847), that operates a 24-hour ▷lifeboat service around British coasts. Each lifeboat has a full-time mechanic but the other crew members are volunteers. Offshore lifeboats, usually 16 metres in length, are designed to right themselves in the event of a capsize. The RNLI also operates small inflatable craft powered by outboard motors.

● **Royal National Theatre Company** ► A British government-subsidized theatre company established as the National Theatre Company in 1963. Sir Laurence ▷Olivier, its first director, was succeeded by Peter ▷Hall in 1973, Richard Eyre in 1988, Trevor ▷Nunn in 1996, and Nicholas Hytner in 2002. The company's building (1976), designed by Sir Denys Lasdun, comprises an open-stage theatre called the Olivier, a proscenium-stage theatre called the Lyttelton, and a studio theatre for experimental plays called the Cottesloe.

● **Royal Navy** ► (RN) The senior of Britain's three armed services. Founded in the 9th century by Alfred the Great, the RN emerged as "the wooden walls of England" in the 16th century with such victories as that over the Spanish ▷Armada (1588) under Sir Francis ▷Drake. The 17th century saw further victories against the Dutch, but little improvement in the lot of the sailors ("Jack Tars") with harsh discipline, poor pay, and disease. Despite the efforts of such men as Samuel ▷Pepys and Captain ▷Cook to improve conditions, mutiny finally broke out at the Nore and Spithead (1797) even as the RN entered its greatest era with a series of victories under ▷Nelson against Napoleonic France, notably at the Nile (1798), Copenhagen (1801), and Trafalgar (1805). Now the supreme sea power, the RN became increasingly professional during the 19th century; living conditions improved, training schools were founded, and new iron-clad vessels, notably HMS *Dreadnought* (launched in 1905), replaced the traditional sailing ships. The RN fought its last set-piece battle at Jutland (1916) during World War I. However, during World War II it sunk 37 German submarines and escorted countless convoys across the Atlantic. After the war it was greatly reduced in size, though its three aircraft carriers have been important. The RN also has nuclear submarines and sophisticated helicopters.

● **Royal Opera** ► The leading British opera company, based at the Royal Opera House in ▷Covent Garden. The company acquired its present name in 1969. Conductors with the company have included Sir Thomas Beecham, Karl Rankl, and Sir Georg Solti. The Royal Opera House also houses the ▷Royal Ballet and under 1997 proposals would house the ▷English National Opera. The Royal Opera House closed for two years in 1997 for refurbishment. In recent years it has suffered from severe financial and organizational problems; the entire 1999 season was cancelled as part of a radical plan to avoid bankruptcy. Chairman: Sir Colin Southgate.

● **royal prerogative** ▷*See* monarchy.

● **Royal Shakespeare Company** ▶ (RSC) A British theatre company, founded in 1960 from the company at the Shakespeare Memorial Theatre in Stratford-upon-Avon. Peter ▷Hall, its first director, was succeeded in 1968 by Trevor ▷Nunn, who was joined by Terry Hands in 1978. Adrian Noble became director in 1991 but his plans to restructure the company and rebuild its main Stratford theatre caused opposition; he announced his resignation in 2002. The company performs Shakespeare and many other classics as well as modern plays and musicals at Stratford and elsewhere; it tours frequently and has a strong international reputation.

● **Royal Society** ▶ The oldest and most important scientific society in the UK. It originated in 1645 with a group of thinkers, including Robert ▷Boyle and John Wilkins, who met to discuss the "new or experimental philosophy" popularized by Francis Bacon. It was incorporated by royal charter from Charles II in 1662, early members including Sir Christopher ▷Wren and Samuel ▷Pepys; with the presidency from 1703–27 of Isaac ▷Newton, the Royal Society achieved great standing and financial security. The Society publishes scientific papers in the *Proceedings* and the *Philosophical Transactions*, maintains a large library, disburses grants for scientific research, and awards medals for scientific achievement. There are now some 800 fellows, who put the initials FRS after their names.

● **Royal Society for the Prevention of Cruelty to Animals** ▶ (RSPCA) A British charity founded in 1824 to investigate and act upon reports of cruelty to animals. It also runs animal clinics. Funded by voluntary contributions, it has branches in the Commonwealth and a Junior Movement.

● **Royal Society for the Protection of Birds** ▶ (RSPB) A British charity founded in 1889 to protest against the wholesale killing of birds for their plumage. Since then it has promoted the conservation of wild birds and their habitats and established reserves throughout Britain.

● **Royal Victorian Order** ▶ An order of ▷knighthood founded by Queen Victoria in 1896 to reward distinguished service to the sovereign and having five classes: Knights or Dames Grand Cross (GCVO); Knights or Dames Commanders (KCVO or DCVO); Commanders (CVO); Lieutenants (LVO); and Members (MVO).

● **Royal Warrant Holder** ▶ A UK tradesman or firm authorized by the royal household to display a crest indicating that it supplies goods or services to a member of the royal family.

● **Royce, Sir (Frederick) Henry** ▶ (1863–1933) British □car manufacturer, who founded, with Charles ▷Rolls, Rolls-Royce Ltd (1906). In 1884 Royce opened an engineering business in Manchester and in 1904 began to build cars, which much impressed Rolls and led to the merger of their businesses. Ill-health forced Royce to live in the south of France, where he set up a design team that later moved back to England. Here he designed some of his most famous cars and the aeroengine that became the Merlin (used in Spitfires and Hurricanes in World War II). In the 1970s the firm was split into two separate companies, the car manufacturers and the aeroengine business. The latter was taken into public ownership owing to the enormous cost of research and development, while Rolls-Royce (Cars) remained a private company. In 1987 the aeroengine company was privatised and in 1998 the car company was sold to the German car manufacturer Volkswagen. ▷*See* Schneider Trophy.

● **RR Lyrae stars** ▶ A class of short-period pulsating ▷variable stars that are old giant stars found in globular ▷star clusters, all with about the same mean ▷luminosity.

● **RSC** ▷*See* Royal Shakespeare Company.

● **RSPB** ▷*See* Royal Society for the Protection of Birds.

● **RSPCA** ▷*See* Royal Society for the Prevention of Cruelty to Animals.

● **Ruapehu, Mount** ▶ 39 18S 175 36E An active volcano in New Zea-

land, the highest peak in North Island. Having been dormant since 1946, it erupted again in 1995–96. Height: 2797 m (9175 ft).

● **Rub' al-Khali** ▶ The S part of the Arabian Desert, mainly in Saudi Arabia. It constitutes the largest continuous area of sand in the world. Area: about 800 000 sq km (308 815 sq mi).

● **rubber** ▶ A synthetic or natural organic polymer that is elastic and tough. The name comes from its ability to erase pencil marks. **Natural rubber**, which consists mainly of polyisoprene—$(CH_2CH:C.CH_3:CH_2)_n$—is made from latex, a milky fluid collected from the ▷rubber tree grown in SE Asia. The rubber is coagulated from latex (using acids) and pressed into sheets. ▷Vulcanization increases its durability. **Synthetic rubbers** are made from petrochemicals (*see* oil). Styrene-butadiene rubber (SBR), now the commonest synthetic rubber, was introduced during World War II. It is made by the emulsion process, in which styrene and butadiene are mixed in soapy water containing a catalyst. SBR is used in tyres, often mixed with natural rubber to improve its resilience. Butyl rubber is made by ▷polymerization of isobutylene. It is used for inner tubes. Neoprene (polychloroprene) is used for protective clothing and electrical insulation. Nitrile polyisoprene and polyurethane and silicone rubbers have specialist uses.

● **rubber plant** ▶ A tree, *Ficus elastica*, native to India and Malaysia, where it grows to a height of 35 m in forests. Its latex is the source of Assam or India rubber. It is also a popular house plant, grown for its shiny leaves. Family: *Moraceae*.

● **rubber tree** ▶ A Brazilian tree, *Hevea brasiliensis*, also called Pará rubber, widely cultivated in humid tropical regions, especially SE Asia. Its milky latex is the chief source of natural ▷rubber, which is obtained by making sloping cuts in the trunk. Trees yield latex from about the sixth year and reach full height, about 20 m, in eight years. *H. guianensis* and *H. pauciflora* are also sometimes cultivated for rubber. In 1876, some seeds of South American rubber trees were shipped to Kew Gardens by Sir Henry Wickham (1846–1928). Seedlings were subsequently exported to Ceylon and SE Asia to form the basis of the rubber industry. Family: *Euphorbiaceae*.

● **Rubbra, Edmund** ▶ (1901–86) British composer. He was self-taught until he took lessons at the Royal College of Music from Holst, John Ireland, Vaughan Williams, and others. His works include 11 symphonies, a piano concerto and a viola concerto, chamber music, madrigals and motets, and two masses.

● **rubella** ▷*See* German measles.

● **Rubens, Peter Paul** ▶ (1577–1640) Flemish painter, who was born in Seigen (Westphalia) but lived chiefly in Antwerp. The greatest of the ▷baroque artists and one of the finest European colourists, Rubens first worked for the Mantuan court in Italy (1600–08). Returning to Antwerp, he became court painter to the Archduke Albert and painted his first major works, *The Raising of the Cross* and *Descent from the Cross* (both Antwerp Cathedral). Many visits abroad, sometimes as a diplomatic envoy, and commissions followed, including a cycle for Marie de' Medici commemorating her marriage to Henry IV (Louvre) and the ceiling of the Banqueting House, Whitehall, for Charles I. Aided by a large workshop, he painted mythological, historical, and religious subjects but his most personal works are his portraits of his family, notably *Helena Fourment with a Fur Cloak* (Kunsthistorisches Museum, Vienna), and such landscapes as *The Château de Steen* (National Gallery, London). His Antwerp house is now a museum.

● **Rubicon** ▶ A stream in N central Italy flowing E into the Adriatic Sea, which formed the boundary between Italy and Cisalpine Gaul in the time of the Roman Republic. In 49 BC Julius Caesar, then provincial commander in Gaul, precipitated the civil war with Pompey by leading his army across the Rubicon into Italy. This action was tantamount to a declaration of war because it was forbidden for a general to lead an army outside the province in which he had been given command. Hence "crossing the Rubicon" has come to mean taking an irrevocable step.

● **rubidium** ▶ (Rb) A highly electropositive alkali metal, discovered spectroscopically by R. W. Bunsen and G. R. Kirchhoff in 1861. The element is soft and silvery-white. It ignites spontaneously in air and reacts violently with water, liberating hydrogen and then setting fire to it. The isotope ^{87}Rb is radioactive with a half-life of 5×10^{11} years and is used in ▷rubidium-strontium dating. Rubidium forms ionic salts and four oxides (Rb$_2$O, Rb$_2$O$_2$, Rb$_2$O$_3$, RbO$_2$). At no 37; at wt 85.47; mp 39.48°C; bp 688°C.

● **rubidium-strontium dating** ► A method of ▷radiometric dating, used mainly for rocks, fossils, etc. It utilizes the fact that naturally occurring rubidium contains about 28% of the radioactive isotope rubidium-87, which undergoes ▷beta decay to strontium-87 with a ▷half-life of 5×10^{11} years. Thus by measuring the ratio of rubidium-87 to strontium-87 in the sample, its age may be estimated. The method can date items several thousands of millions of years old.

● **Rubinstein, Anton** ► (1829–94) Russian pianist and composer. He started performing abroad at the age of 12 and founded the St Petersburg conservatoire in 1862. His works include 20 operas, 6 symphonies, 5 piano concertos, 2 cello concertos, and numerous other piano pieces, including the well-known "Melody in F."

● **Rubinstein, Artur** ► (1888–1982) Polish-born pianist. He became a US citizen in 1946. He studied in Warsaw and Berlin and soon acquired a worldwide reputation, particularly as a performer of Chopin. He wrote two autobiographies, *My Young Years* (1974) and *My Many Years* (1980).

● **Rublyov, Andrey** ► (or A. Rublev; c. 1370–1430) A leading Russian icon painter. He sometimes collaborated with the Greek painter Theophanes and late in life became a monk. In his masterpiece *The Old Testament Trinity* (Tretyakov Gallery, Moscow) the influence of ▷Byzantine art is modified by a distinctive gracefulness.

● **Rubus** ► A genus of prickly perennial herbs and shrubs (225 species), found mainly in N temperate regions. Many species, including the ▷blackberry, ▷loganberry, and ▷raspberry, are grown for their juicy fruits. Family: ▷Rosaceae.

● **ruby** ► A red transparent variety of ▷corundum, the colour being due to traces of chromium. It is used as a gemstone and in lasers, watches, and other precision instruments. Many fine rubies come from Mogok in Myanmar (Burma), where they occur in metamorphic limestones with other precious and semiprecious stones. Prior to the 14th century rubies were called carbuncles. Birthstone for July.

● **Ruda Śląska** ► 51 10N 16 39E A town in SW Poland. The first coalmine in Poland was opened here (1751). Population (1996 est): 166 300.

● **Rudbeckia** ▷*See* black-eyed Susan.

● **rudd** ► A game fish, *Scardinius erythrophthalmus*, found among vegetation in fresh waters of Europe and W Asia. It has a stout body, 35–40 cm long, coloured golden- or olive-brown above and silvery white below, deep-red fins, and golden eyes.

● **Rudolf, Lake** ▷*See* Turkana, Lake.

● **Rudolph** ► (1858–89) Archduke of Austria. His liberal views brought him into conflict with his father Emperor Francis Joseph. He and his mistress Baroness Marie Vetsera were found dead at his hunting lodge of Mayerling, having apparently committed suicide.

● **Rudolph I** ► (1218–91) The first ▷Habsburg Holy Roman Emperor (1273–91). His conquests in central Europe—Austria, Styria, Carinthia, and Carniola—formed the nucleus of future Habsburg territorial power.

● **Rudolph II** ► (1552–1612) Holy Roman Emperor (1576–1612). A dilatory ruler, he was forced to relinquish his powers in Hungary (1608) and Bohemia (1611) to his brother ▷Matthias.

● **rue** ► An evergreen shrub, *Ruta graveolens*, also known as herb of grace, native to S Europe. Growing up to 90 cm high, it has fleshy blue-green leaves and terminal clusters of yellow flowers. The leaves yield a bitter oil, once used as a spice and in medicines. Family: *Rutaceae*.

● **Rueil-Malmaison** ► 48 52N 2 11E A town in France, a suburb of Paris in the Hauts-de-Seine department. Its chateau was once a favourite residence of Napoleon I and the Empress Josephine is buried here. Population (latest est): 64 545.

● **ruff** ► An Old World ▷sandpiper, *Philomachus pugnax*, that breeds in coastal wetlands of N Eurasia and winters on mudflats of South Africa and S Asia. The female (called a reeve) is 25 cm long and has a grey-brown plumage; the larger male has a double crest and a multicoloured collar in the breeding season. ▷*See* Plate III.

● **Rugby** ► 52 23N 1 15W A town in the English Midlands, in Warwickshire. According to tradition the game of rugby football originated here in 1823 at the famous public school (1567), which was described in *Tom Brown's Schooldays*. Rugby's industries include engineering, cement, and the manufacture of lasers; it is also a major distribution centre. Population (1997 est): 87 500.

● **rugby football** ▷*See* football.

● **Rügen** ► A German island in the Baltic Sea, 2.5 km (1.5 mi) off

Rubens ► *Perseus and Andromeda* (The Hermitage, St Petersburg). This mythological subject shows Rubens' baroque style at its most sumptuous and elaborate.

Stralsund, to which it is connected by a road and rail causeway. Area: 926 sq km (358 sq mi). Population (latest est): 84 500.

● **Ruggles, Carl** ▶ (1876–1971) US composer. His works, although few, had considerable influence; they are generally dissonant and strident and include *Angels* (1939) for brass or strings and the orchestral works *Sun-Treader* (1932) and *Men and Mountains* (1924–36).

● **Ruhr, River** ▶ A river in W Germany, rising in the Sauerland and flowing NW and W past Essen to join the River Rhine at Duisburg. The Ruhr Valley (German name: Ruhrgebiet) is the centre of the German iron and steel industry. Length: 235 km (146 mi).

● **Ruisdael, Jacob van** ▶ (?1628–82) One of the greatest of Dutch landscape painters. Born in Haarlem, he studied under his father and probably also under his uncle, the landscape painter **Salomon van Ruysdael** (c. 1600–70). His baroque compositions, regularly framed by fantastic trees, are noted for their dramatic contrasts of light and shade. *The Jewish Cemetery* (c. 1660) is a striking evocation of human mortality.

● **Ruiz, Juan** ▶ (c. 1283–c. 1350) Spanish poet. Nothing is known of his life apart from the fact that he was Archpriest of Hita. His *Libro de buen amor* (1330) consists of a series of love stories interspersed with ironic didactic digressions.

● **rum** ▶ A ▷spirit distilled from molasses derived from sugar cane. Rum is colourless and is used in mixed drinks, especially punches, or with soda water, fruit juice, or Coca-Cola. Better-quality rums are aged in oak casks for several years. It is produced wherever sugar cane is grown, predominantly in the Caribbean region but also in the USA.

● **Rum** ▶ (or Rhum) An island in NW Scotland in the Inner Hebrides group. Acquired by the Nature Conservancy Council (1957), it is now managed as a nature reserve with restricted access in spring.

● **Rumania** ▷See Romania, Republic of.

● **Rumelia** ▶ The Balkan possessions of the Ottoman Empire from the 14th to 19th centuries. The Congress of ▷Berlin (1878) divided Rumelia into the state of Bulgaria under Ottoman suzerainty, the autonomous province of Eastern Rumelia, and the provinces of Edirne, Salonica, and Monastir. Eastern Rumelia was annexed by Bulgaria in 1885 and Monastir and Salonica were ceded to Serbia and Greece respectively in 1913.

● **Rumford, Benjamin Thompson, Count** ▶ (1753–1814) American-born scientist, who spied for the British in the American Revolution and was forced to flee America and abandon his wife to settle in England in 1776. There he carried out scientific research in ballistics and the theory of heat. Suspected of spying for the French, he left England in 1785 for Paris and then Bavaria, where he worked as an administrator for the elector, Karl Theodor (1724–99), who made him a count of the Holy Roman Empire in 1791 (he chose the title Rumford, his home town in America—now Concord). In 1795 he returned to England, where he helped to demolish the caloric theory and found the ▷Royal Institution (1799).

● **ruminant** ▶ A hoofed mammal belonging to the suborder *Ruminantia* (about 175 species), which includes deer, cattle, antelopes, sheep, and goats. Ruminants eat grass, leaves, and other vegetation and are characterized by possession of a four-chambered stomach. The first and largest chamber (rumen) contains bacteria and protozoa, which ferment the stomach contents and enable the animal to digest and utilize its food efficiently. Ruminants regurgitate their food periodically to "chew the cud," which helps to break up the plant cell walls.

● **rummy games** ▶ Various related card games, of which rummy is the basic form. Its object is to form melds (sets or sequences) composed of three or four cards of the same rank (such as four jacks) or sequences of three or more cards of the same suit (such as seven, eight, nine, and ten, of diamonds). In each turn a player takes a card from the pack and discards one. The first player to dispose of his cards wins, scoring points according to the cards left in his opponents' hands. In **gin rummy** (for two players) the object is to reach a certain score before one's opponent. No melds are laid down until a player's unmatched cards make a total of ten or less, when the player lays his whole hand down. It is a "gin" if he has no unmatched cards. **Canasta** itself has several variants but is usually a partnership game for four players. Two packs are used; the jokers and all the twos are "wild." The winners are the first to score 5000 by making melds and canastas (a meld of seven or more cards of the same value).

● **Rump Parliament** ▷See Long Parliament.

● **Rum Rebellion** ▶ (1808) A rebellion in Australia in which William ▷Bligh, governor of New South Wales, was ousted from his post and imprisoned by officers of the New South Wales Corps. It was incited by Bligh's suppression of the rum traffic. In 1810 the Corps was recalled.

● **Runcie, Robert Alexander Kennedy, Baron** ▶ (1921–2000) British churchman; Archbishop of Canterbury (1980–91). He was formerly bishop of St Albans (1970–80).

● **Runcorn** ▶ 53 20N 2 44W A town in NW England, in Halton unitary authority, Cheshire, on the River Mersey and Manchester Ship Canal. Designated a new town in 1964, it has chemical and brewing industries. Population (1991): 64 154.

● **Rundstedt, (Karl Rudolf) Gerd von** ▶ (1875–1953) German field marshal, who was recalled from retirement at the outbreak of World War II, becoming (1942) commander in chief in France. He held command in the battle of the Bulge (1944) and was a competent if uninspired general. He was captured in 1945 but his ill health secured his release.

● **Runeberg, Johan Ludvig** ▶ (1804–77) Finnish poet of Swedish origin, who wrote in Swedish and whose style was influenced by his study of Finnish folk poetry. His major works include the epic poem *Kung Fjalar* (*King Fialar*; 1844), in which he attempted a synthesis of Christian and classical pagan ideals, and *Fänrik Ståls sägner* (*Tales of Ensign Stål*; 1848–60), a collection of patriotic ballads, one of which became the Finnish national anthem.

● **runic alphabet** ▶ An alphabetical writing system used for Norse and certain other Germanic languages. It originated, probably as a modified version of the Etruscan or the Roman alphabet, in the 2nd or 3rd century AD, and went out of use gradually after the 14th century. The Gothic word *runa* means secret or mystery, and runes were always associated with magical powers. The runic alphabet, called the *futhark* from the names of the first six letters, consisted at first of 24 characters, extended in Old English to 28 and later 31.

● **runner bean** ▶ A climbing plant, *Phaseolus coccineus*, also known as scarlet runner, native to South America and widely cultivated as a vegetable crop, especially in Britain. Growing up to 3 m high, it bears usually red five-petalled flowers, which give rise to edible bean pods, 20–60 cm long, that are eaten cooked. Wild plants are perennial, but cultivated plants are treated as annuals. Family: ▷*Leguminosae*. ▷*See also* bean.

● **Runnymede** ▶ (or Runnimede) 51 26N 0 33W A meadow in SE England, near Egham in Surrey on the S bank of the River Thames. The Magna Carta was granted here by King John (1215).

● **Runyon, Damon** ▶ (1884–1946) US humorous writer. For his stories about New York characters, first collected in *Guys and Dolls* (1932) and notable for their lively slang, he drew on his long experience as a journalist and sports reporter. *Guys and Dolls* formed the bases of a highly successful musical (1950).

● **Rupert, Prince** ▶ (1619–82) Cavalry officer, who fought for the Royalists in the Civil War; he was the son of Frederick the Winter King of the Palatinate and Elizabeth, daughter of James I of England. Charismatic and able, he lacked the ability to keep control when battle commenced. He was defeated at ▷Marston Moor (1644) and ▷Naseby (1645) and after Charles' surrender he was banished from England. He returned at the Restoration (1660) and served as an admiral in the ▷Dutch Wars.

● **Rupert's Land** ▶ (or Prince Rupert's Land) A region in N and W Canada around Hudson Bay. In 1670 it was granted by Charles II to the ▷Hudson's Bay Company, the first governor of which was Prince ▷Rupert. It is now an ecclesiastical province of the Anglican Church of Canada.

● **Rurik** ▶ (died c. 879) The semilegendary founder of the Rurik dynasty of Russian princes (862–1598). A Varangian chieftain, Rurik was allegedly Prince of Novgorod from 862. His descendants ruled Kiev, Vladimir, and Muscovy.

● **Ruse** ▶ (Russe *or* Roussé) 43 05N 25 59E A city in central N Bulgaria. It is the site of the Friendship Bridge (1954) over the River Danube into Romania and is Bulgaria's principal river port. Population (1998 est): 166 416.

● **Rusedski, Greg** ▶ (1973–   ) Canadian-born British tennis player. In 1997–98 he was ranked Britain's top male tennis player and sixth in the world.

● **rush** ▶ A grasslike plant of the genus *Juncus* (over 300 species), found worldwide in damp temperate and cold regions. Rushes have slender rigid stalks, up to about 1 m high, bearing long flat leaves and clusters of small green or brown flowers, which produce many-seeded capsules. The leaves are used to make mats, baskets, etc. Family: *Juncaceae*.
　　The name is also applied to similar plants, including the ▷bulrush, ▷flowering rush, and ▷woodrush.

● **Rushdie, Salman** ▶ (1947–   ) British novelist, born in India, who now lives in the USA. His first novel, *Grimus* (1975), was followed by the Booker prizewinner *Midnight's Children* (1981), *Shame* (1983), and *The Satanic Verses* (1988), which many Muslims interpreted as blasphemous. After Ayatollah Khomeini's ▷fatwa offering a reward for killing the author, he went into hiding. Rushdie subsequently published *Imaginary Homelands* (1991), a collection of essays, and the novel *The Moor's Last Sigh* (1995). In the mid-1990s he gradually began to emerge from hiding and in 1998 the Iranian government formally dissociated itself from the fatwa, effectively ending his ordeal. His most recent novels are *The Ground Beneath Her Feet* (1999) and *Fury* (2001).

● **Rushmore, Mount** ▷*See* Mount Rushmore National Memorial.

● **Rusk, (David) Dean** ▶ (1909–94) US statesman. After World War II he held posts in the State Department and in 1950 became assistant secretary of state for Far Eastern affairs, influencing US policy in the Korean War. As secretary of state (1961–69) he defended US military involvement in Vietnam. In 1970 he became professor of international law at the University of Georgia.

● **Russe** ▷*See* Ruse.

● **Ruskin, John** ▶ (1819–1900) British art and social critic. He began to write his first work of art criticism, *Modern Painters* (1843–60), to defend the paintings of J. M. W. Turner. In *The Stones of Venice* (1851–53) he promoted the gothic style in architecture. In *Unto This Last* (1862) and other volumes of social criticism he denounced materialism and laissez-faire economics from a moral and aesthetic perspective. His sonorous prose style is most fully developed in his unfinished autobiography, *Praeterita* (1885–89). During his last years he suffered recurrent attacks of insanity.

● **Russell, Bertrand Arthur William, 3rd Earl** ▶ (1872–1970) British philosopher, grandson of Lord John ▷Russell. His first major philosophical work, *Principia Mathematica* (1910–13), written with A. N. ▷Whitehead, presented pure mathematics as a development of ▷logic. On a smaller logical basis *Our Knowledge of the External World* (1914) attempted a new approach to traditional problems in epistemology. From his pupil ▷Wittgenstein, he also acquired a lasting interest in language. His prolific writings on religion, politics, and morals always stimulated interest, often to his own detriment. He was imprisoned (1918) and deprived of his Cambridge lectureship for his outspoken pacifism. In 1940 a US court disqualified him from holding a professorship at New York University on account of his moral views. In 1961 he was again imprisoned for civil disobedience during the Campaign for Nuclear Disarmament. He was appointed to the OM in 1949 and awarded the Nobel Prize for Literature in 1950. He claimed that "longing for love, the search for knowledge, and unbearable pity for mankind" were the governing passions of his life.

● **Russell, John, 1st Earl** ▶ (1792–1878) British statesman; Whig (Liberal) prime minister (1846–52, 1865–66); the grandfather of Bertrand Russell. Elected an MP in 1813, he championed parliamentary reform in the 1820s and helped to draft the Reform Act (1832).

Under Melbourne he was home secretary (1835–39), introducing the Municipal Reform Act (1835), and then secretary for war (1839–41). His first ministry was dominated by his foreign secretary Palmerston. Russell was himself foreign secretary (1852–53) under Aberdeen and then colonial secretary (1855) under Palmerston with whom his relations were strained. He resigned as prime minister following defeat of the second parliamentary reform bill.

● **Russell, Ken** ▶ (1927–   ) British film director. His early work for the BBC included *A Song of Summer* (1968), about Delius. His films include *Women in Love* (1969), *Gothic* (1986), *The Rainbow* (1989), *Whore* (1991), and controversial biographical films, such as *The Music Lovers* (1970), about Tchaikovsky, *Mahler* (1974), and *Valentino* (1977).

● **Russell, Lord William** ▶ (1639–83) English Whig politician, who was beheaded for complicity in the ▷Rye House Plot against Charles II and the king's brother James, Duke of York. Russell had played a leading role in the movement to exclude the Roman Catholic James from the succession.

● **Russell, Sir William Howard** ▶ (1820–1907) British war correspondent. Working for *The Times*, he reported the Crimean War, exposing its mismanagement in dispatches later collected in *The War, 1855–56*. His description of the infantry at ▷Balaclava as a "thin red line" became well known.

● **Russell, Willie** ▶ (William Martin R.; 1947–   ) British playwright, born in Liverpool. Trained as a hairdresser, he won acclaim for such works as the musicals *John, Paul, George, Ringo and Bert* (1974) and *Blood Brothers* (1983) and the plays *Breezeblock Park* (1975), *One For the Road* (1976), *Educating Rita* (1979), and *Shirley Valentine* (1986).

● **Russell's viper** ▶ A common highly venomous viper, *Vipera russelli*, of SE Asia. Up to 1.5 m long, it is patterned with three rows of black-and-white ringed reddish spots. It is the cause of many snakebite deaths.

● **Russia** ▷*See* Russian Federation.

Bertrand Russell ▶ The 89-year-old philosopher (seated right) during a 1961 demonstration in London against the building of a US Polaris missile base in Scotland.

● **Russian** ▶ The main language of Russia, belonging to the East ▷Slavonic family. It is a highly inflected language with six cases and a notable feature is the frequency of clusters of consonants. It is written in the ▷Cyrillic alphabet. The standard form is based on the dialect of Moscow.

● **Russian Blue** ▶ A breed of short-haired cat, thought to have been introduced to the UK by Russian sailors. It has a slender body and a short flat head with large pointed ears and green eyes. The coat is lustrous and blue-grey.

● **Russian Federation** ▶ (*or* Russia) The world's largest country, covering N Eurasia and bordering on the Pacific and Arctic Oceans and the Baltic, Black, and Caspian Seas. It consists of 21 constituent republics, 11 national-territorial formations, 6 territorial formations, 49 regions, and 2 federal cities (Moscow and St Petersburg). Its climate ranges from Arctic to subtropical and its geographical zones include tundra, forest, steppe, and rich agricultural soil. The area W of the River Yenisei consists of vast plains and depressions, dissected by the Ural Mountains, while the E consists mainly of mountains and plateaus. Over 80% of the population are Russians, the remainder consisting of 38 national minorities.

Economy: Russia contains outstanding mineral resources including iron ore, coal, oil, gold, platinum, copper, zinc, lead, and tin. The major industrial region is around Moscow. It produces ships, lorries, machine tools, electronic equipment, textiles, and chemicals. Because of the extensive forests, timber and related occupations are important. The main agricultural products are wheat, cotton, fruit and vegetables, tobacco, and sugar beet. The new Russian state, which appeared in 1991, inherited the economic troubles created over many years under the ▷Soviet Union; immediate action was taken to reorganize the country's economy, including the abolition of state subsidies and central planning. Mass privatization began in 1992 and some 80% of the economy was in private hands by 1996. Reorganization of agriculture, previously run by a system of state and collective farms, also began. The initial results were instability, hyperinflation, and a serious decline in productivity. Although the economy began to stabilize in the later 1990s, this was undermined by the financial and currency crisis of 1998.

History: the area has been populated for three to four millenniums, although little is known of its history until the 8th century AD, when European and Middle Eastern traders began its exploration. Control of the area between the Baltic and Black Seas was established by Scandinavian adventurers by 1000. Dominated by Kiev from the mid-10th to mid-11th centuries, these Varangian principalities submitted (after 1223) to the overrule of the ▷Golden Horde. By the time of the Horde's collapse in the 14th century, Moscow, ruled by Rurik princes, had emerged as a powerful principality, becoming the capital of a united Russia under Ivan the Great in the 15th century. Contact with W Europe was established in the late 17th century by Peter the Great, who also established the Russian bureaucracy and educational system and built a new capital, St Petersburg. By the 19th century Russian territories had been greatly extended but, although a force to be reckoned with in the world, Russia was industrially far behind the UK, Germany, and the USA, its bureaucracy had grown unwieldy and oppressive, and its Romanov emperors (tsars) were opposed to any political change. Revolutionary activity began with the Dekabrists' conspiracy, uncovered in 1825, and, although serfdom was abolished in 1861, its abolition was achieved on terms unfavourable to the peasants and served to encourage revolutionaries, a group of whom assassinated Alexander II in 1881. Bloody Sunday (22 January, 1905), on which several hundred workers were killed during a demonstration in St Petersburg, was followed by great disorder (*see* Revolution of 1905). A parliament, the ▷Duma, was established in 1906, but political unrest continued and was aggravated during World War I by military defeat and food shortages. The February and October Revolutions (*see* Russian Revolution) were followed by a period of civil war (1918–22), after which communist control was complete. Russia itself became the Russian Soviet Federal Socialist Republic (RSFSR) and was joined with Ukraine, Belorussia, and Transcaucasia in 1922 to constitute the Soviet Union. The Soviet Union was dismantled in 1991 and the new Russian Federation was established with Boris ▷Yeltsin as its first president. In 1993 Yeltsin's

reforms were endorsed in a referendum, held in response to opposition from the Congress of People's Deputies. Further constitutional deadlock was only resolved when Yeltsin ordered the military to act against a defiant parliament (October, 1993). A referendum (December, 1993) endorsed a new constitution. In 1995 the Communists became the largest party in the Russian parliament. The republic of ▷Chechenia achieved de facto independence following a fierce struggle between separatists and Russian troops in 1994–96, but was reoccupied by Russian forces in 1999–2000. Despite failing health, Yeltsin was re-elected in 1996. In mid-1998 Russia suffered its worst financial crisis since the end of communism. There followed a further prolonged power struggle between president and parliament, in which Yeltsin sacked the entire government four times in 18 months. Vladimir ▷Putin succeeded Yeltsin as president in 2000.

Russian Federation

Head of state	President Vladimir Putin
Official language	Russian
Official currency	rouble of 100 kopeks
Area	17 074 984 sq km (6 592 658 sq mi)
Population (1998 est)	146 861 400
Capital	Moscow

● **Russian literature** ▶ Until the beginning of the 18th century Russian literature consisted chiefly of chronicles and religious works written in Old Slavonic. The outstanding early work is *The Song of Igor's Campaign* (c. 1187). The development of modern literature owed much to the political reforms of Peter the Great (reigned 1682–1725) and the artistic patronage of Catherine the Great (reigned 1762–96). Major writers of the 18th century included the poet and scholar M. V. Lomonosov (1711–65), the poet G. R. Derzhavin (1743–1816), and the fabulist I. A. Krylov (1768–1844). The first half of the 19th century was dominated by Pushkin and Lermontov and the second half, following the pioneering fiction of Gogol, by the novelists Tolstoy, Dostoievski, and Turgenev. They were followed by the dramatist and short-story writer Chekhov, whose detached compassion contrasted with the strong social commitment of Gorki. The political unrest of the early 20th century stimulated much artistic experimentation, but in the 1930s the Soviet authorities decreed that all literature must adhere to the official doctrine of ▷socialist realism. Writers whose works were banned in Russia include the poets Akhmatova, Mandelstam, and Tsvetaeva and the novelist Pasternak. The apparent liberalization of culture heralded by the publication of works by Solzhenitsyn, Yevtushenko, and Voznesenskii in the 1960s was short lived and in 1974 Solzhenitsyn joined the growing number of Russian writers living abroad. Several previously banned writers were subsequently rehabilitated and censorship relaxed as part of the liberal reforms which culminated in the break-up of the Soviet Union in 1991.

● **Russian Orthodox Church** ▶ An offshoot of the Greek ▷Orthodox Church, dating from the baptism of the emperor Vladimir (later St Vladimir) in 988. Since 1328 the metropolitan see has been at Moscow. During the 15th century connections with the Greek parent Church were severed. In the 18th century the Church fell increasingly under state control. After the 1917 Revolution it was intermittently persecuted until 1991, when the disintegration of the Soviet Union introduced a new age of religious toleration. ▷*See also* Old Believers.

● **Russian Revolution** ▶ (1917) The revolution between March and November (Old Style February and October), 1917, that overthrew the Russian monarchy and established the world's first communist state. It began with the February Revolution, when riots over shortage of bread and coal in Petrograd (now renamed St Petersburg) led to the establishment of the Petrograd Soviet of Workers' and Soldiers' Deputies, dominated by ▷Mensheviks and Social Revolutionaries, and of a provisional government of ▷Duma deputies, which forced ▷Nicholas II to abdicate. The failure of the provisional government, under Prince ▷Lvov and then ▷Kerenski, to end Russia's participation in World War I and to deal with food shortages led to the demand of the ▷Bolsheviks under ▷Lenin for "All power to the Soviets." The Bolsheviks, who had gained a majority in the Soviet by September, staged the October (*or* Bolshevik) Revolution, seizing power and establishing the Soviet of People's Commissars. The new government came to terms with Germany in early 1918 but almost immediately faced opposition at home. In the subsequent civil war (1918–21) the Red Army was victorious against the anticommunist White Russians but some 100 000 Russians died and two million emigrated.

● **Russo-Finnish War** ▶ (*or* Winter War; 1939–40) The war between the Soviet Union and Finland at the beginning of World War II. It was won by the Soviet Union, the aggressor, which gained part of the Karelian Isthmus.

● **Russo-Japanese War** ▶ (1904–05) A confrontation arising from conflicting Japanese and Russian interests in Manchuria, where Russia controlled Port Arthur (now Lüda). In 1904 Japan attacked Port Arthur, which fell in January, 1905. In May a Japanese fleet under ▷Togo Heihachiro destroyed Russia's Baltic Fleet in the Tsushima Straits, forcing Russia's surrender. In the peace conference at Portsmouth (New Hampshire, USA), over which Theodore Roosevelt presided, Japan gained the ascendancy in S Manchuria and Korea.

● **rust** ▶ A reddish-brown solid consisting of hydrated iron oxide. The mechanism of corrosion by rusting is complicated and still not fully understood but involves the setting up of a cell in which iron is the anode and a metal impurity the cathode. Both water and oxygen must be present for rust to form although the most serious damage, pitting, is always found in an oxygen-free portion of metal. Rust prevention involves protective coatings (paint, zinc plating, etc.) or alloying with chromium and other metals to produce stainless steels.

● **rust fungi** ▶ Fungi, belonging to the order *Uredinales*, that are parasites of plants, forming spots, blotches, and pustules on the stems and foliage of their hosts. Several are important pests of cereal crops, including black rust (*Puccinia graminis*) of wheat. This forms red pustules on wheat leaves, releasing spores that infect barberry (*Berberis vulgaris*)—the secondary host—in which the life cycle continues. Control therefore involves eradication of barberry in wheat-growing areas as well as developing resistant strains of wheat. Other important wheat rusts include yellow rust (*P. striiformis*) and brown rust (*P. recondita*). Phylum: ▷Basidiomycota.

● **Ruth** ▶ A Gentile from Moab who was an ancestress of David. The Old Testament **Book of Ruth**, set in the time of the ▷Judges (c. 1000 BC), records the events by which Ruth came to marry Boaz, a Hebrew.

● **Ruth, Babe** ▶ (George Herman R.; 1895–1948) US baseball player. Known as the "Sultan of Swat," he became the top player of the 1920s and revitalized the sport. His home run record of 714 stood until 1974.

● **Ruthenia** ▶ A region comprising the S slopes of the Carpathian Mountains, now part of Ukraine, which was part of Hungary until it was attached to Czechoslovakia in 1920. Following Hitler's seizure of Czechoslovakia in 1939, Ruthenia briefly proclaimed its independence, before being annexed by Hungary. After World War II it was ceded to the Soviet Union. It became part of newly independent Ukraine in 1991.

● **ruthenium** ▶ (Ru) A hard metal of the platinum group, first separated in 1844 by K. K. Klaus (1796–1864). It is used to harden platinum and palladium for use in electrical contacts and is a versatile catalyst. The tetroxide (RuO_4) is toxic. The element shows a wide range of ▷valence states. At no 44; at wt 101.07; mp 2334°C; bp 4150°C.

● **Rutherford, Ernest, 1st Baron** ▶ (1871–1937) English physicist, born in New Zealand, who was a professor at Montreal (1898–1907), Manchester (1907–19), and Cambridge (1919–37), where he was also director of the Cavendish Laboratory. He made fundamental discoveries concerning the nature of ▷radioactivity, distinguishing between the three types of radiation, which he named alpha, beta, and gamma rays. Working with Hans ▷Geiger he discovered that alpha radiation consisted of positively charged helium atoms. In 1906, while bombarding gold foil with alpha particles, he deduced the existence of a heavy positively charged core in the atom, which he called the ▷nucleus. In 1908, Rutherford received the Nobel Prize for Chemistry. He was knighted in 1914, appointed to the OM in 1925, and made a baron in 1931.

● **Rutherford, Dame Margaret** ▶ (1892–1972) British actress. She was particularly successful in comedies, such as *Blithe Spirit* (1941). In her films, which included *Murder She Said* (1962) and *The VIPs* (1963), she played elderly eccentrics.

● **Rutherford, Mark** ▶ (William Hale White; 1831–1913) British novelist. He left theological college because of his unorthodox opinions and became a civil servant. His religious doubts and convictions are the central theme of his novels and his *Autobiography of Mark Rutherford* (1881). *The Revolution in Tanner's Lane* (1887) is his best-known novel.

● **rutherfordium** ▷*See* kurchatovium.

● **Ruthwell cross** ▶ A stone cross, 5 m (18 ft) high, carved about 700 AD. It is now in Ruthwell church, Dumfries and Galloway. The cross bears reliefs depicting gospel scenes, Latin biblical inscriptions, and lines in the ▷runic alphabet from the Anglo-Saxon poem *The Dream of the Rood*.

● **rutile** ▶ A brown to black form of natural titanium dioxide, TiO_2. It is found as an accessory mineral in igneous and metamorphic rocks, in veins, and as fibres in quartz, known as Venus' hair.

● **Rutland** ▶ A historic county in the East Midlands of England. The smallest county in England, under local government reorganization in 1974 it became part of ▷Leicestershire. It was reinstated as an independent ▷unitary authority in 1997. It consists of gently rolling hills around Rutland Water, one of the largest artificial reservoirs in the UK. Area: 394 sq km (152 sq mi). Population (1996): 34 600. Administrative centre: Oakham.

● **Ruwenzori Mountains** ▶ A mountain range in East Africa, on the border between Uganda and the Democratic Republic of Congo between Lakes Albert and Edward, rising to 5119 m (16 795 ft) at Mount Stanley.

● **Ruyter, Michiel Adriaanszoon de** ▶ (1607–76) Dutch admiral, who served outstandingly in the ▷Dutch Wars (1652–54, 1665–67, 1672–78). In the battle of the Medway (1667) he destroyed most of the English fleet and his victories in 1672–73 saved the United Provinces from invasion. He was killed in action.

● **Rwanda, Republic of** ▶ A small landlocked country in E central Africa. Lake Kivu forms most of its W boundary and the land is chiefly mountainous and rugged. The majority of the inhabitants are Bantu-speaking ▷Hutu, the Nilotic Tutsi comprising less than 10% of the total.
Economy: chiefly subsistence agriculture, including livestock. The main food crops are beans, cassava, and maize, and the principal cash crops are coffee, tea, and sugar; these, together with cassiterite, animal hides, and quinine bark, form the main exports. Methane gas has been found under Lake Kivu. Some small-scale industry is being developed including food processing and textiles. The country has a massive foreign debt.
History: a Tutsi kingdom from the 16th century, the area (with present-day Burundi) came under German East Africa in 1890. From 1919, after World War I, it was administered by Belgium as the N part of Ruanda-Urundi, which under League of Nations mandate and then a UN trust territory. In 1959 the Tutsi kingdom was violently overthrown by the Hutu, who in 1961 declared Rwanda a republic; independence was recognized by Belgium in 1962. There were further massacres of the Tutsi by the Hutu in 1964. In 1973 the government was overthrown in a bloodless coup and the Hutu Maj Gen Juvénal Habyarimana (1937–94) became president. In 1990 Rwanda was invaded by Uganda-based Tutsi rebels, the Rwandan Patriotic Front (RPF), who were contained by troops from France, Belgium, and Zaïre (now Democratic Republic of Congo). In 1991 the government agreed to adopt a multiparty constitution and a peace treaty was signed in 1993. A transitional government was formed, but in April, 1994 Habyarimana was assassinated, apparently by Hutu extremists in the army. Over the next three months at least half a million people, mainly Tutsis, were massacred by the army and Hutu militias, leading to outright civil war. The RPF had gained control of most of the country by July, 1994 and some two million Hutus fled into exile. A broad-based government was established but sporadic ethnic violence continued. The late 1990s saw the repatriation of over a million

refugees and the establishment of a UN International Criminal Tribunal to prosecute those responsible for genocide.

Republic of Rwanda

Head of state	President Paul Kagame
Official languages	Kinyarwanda and French
Official currency	Rwanda franc of 100 centimes
Area	26 330 sq km (10 166 sq mi)
Population (1999 est)	8 155 000
Capital	Kigali

● **Ryazan** ▶ 54 37N 39 43E A city in W central Russia. Founded in 1095, it was the capital of a principality until annexed by Russia in 1521. Industries include oil refining, metalworking, and engineering. Population (1995 est): 536 900.

● **Rybinsk** ▶ (name from 1946 until 1958: Shcherbakov; name from 1984 until 1991: Andropov) 58 01N 38 52E A port in W central Russia, on the River Volga. It is situated below the **Rybinsk Reservoir**, an artificial lake of some 5200 sq km (2000 sq mi) created in 1941. Rybinsk has a hydroelectric station and shipbuilding, engineering, and food-processing industries. Population (1995 est): 248 000.

● **Ryder, Sue** ▷*See* Cheshire, (Geoffrey) Leonard, Baron.

● **Ryder Cup** ▶ A biennial golf tournament between teams from Europe and the USA. It was first played between members of the British and US Professional Golfers' Associations, in 1927. The cup was donated by Samuel Ryder, a British businessman. In 1979 the British team was opened to continental golfers. The cup was won by Europe in 1995 and 1997 and by the USA in 1999.

● **rye** ▶ A cereal ▷grass, *Secale cereale*, native to W Asia but widely cultivated in cool temperate and upland regions. 1–2 m high, it bears a terminal spike, 10–15 cm long, of numerous two- or three-flowered spikelets. The grain is milled to produce a dark-coloured flour, which is used in making black bread or for livestock feed. Rye may be sown in autumn to provide winter grazing or as a green manure crop.

● **Rye** ▶ 50 57N 0 44E A town in SE England, in East Sussex. Once a Cinque Port, it is now about 3 km (2 mi) inland from Rye Bay, on the Strait of Dover. Population (1991): 3708.

● **Rye House Plot** ▶ (1683) A failed plot to murder Charles II of England and his brother, the Duke of York (later James II), at Rye House, Hoddesdon, Herts, while on their way to London from Newmarket. The object was to prevent the Roman Catholic James from succeeding to the throne. Several leading Whigs, including Lord William ▷Russell and Algernon ▷Sidney, were found guilty of conspiracy and executed on flimsy evidence.

● **Rykov, Aleksei Ivanovich** ▶ (1881–1938) Soviet politician. After the ▷Russian Revolution Rykov was prominent in the Soviet Government until 1930, when he was expelled from the Communist Party for opposing the brutality of collectivization. He was forced to recant in 1929 and perished in Stalin's purges.

● **Ryle, Gilbert** ▶ (1900–76) British philosopher. He was Waynflete Professor of Metaphysical Philosophy at Oxford (1945–68) and editor of *Mind* (1947–71). His philosophy centred on detailed analysis of mental concepts. *The Concept of Mind* (1949) maintained that ▷Descartes' idea of the human being consisting of mind and body ("the ghost in the machine") was misleading.

● **Ryle, Sir Martin** ▶ (1918–84) British astronomer; professor at Cambridge University and astronomer royal (1972–84). A pioneer of radio telescopy, his most important work was the development of a technique for studying distant radio sources by using two radio telescopes placed a distance apart, thus increasing their effective aperture. In 1974 he shared the Nobel Prize for Physics with Antony Hewish (1924–).

● **Ryukyu Islands** ▶ A group of volcanic and coral islands in the W Pacific Ocean, extending almost 650 km (400 mi) from Kyushu to N Taiwan. An independent kingdom until the 14th century, the islands were dominated by the Chinese before becoming a part of Japan (1879). They were under US control (1945–72). The chief industries are agriculture and fishing. Area: 2196 sq km (849 sq mi). Population (1995): 1 273 508. Chief city: Naha (on Okinawa).

Rwanda ▶ Hutu refugees returning to Rwanda from Zaïre (now the Democratic Republic of Congo) in November, 1996. About one million Hutus had taken refuge in Zaïre to escape reprisals for the genocide of some half a million Tutsis in 1994.

● **Saale, River** ▶ A river in Germany, rising in NE Bavaria and flowing mainly N to join the River Rhine near Magdeburg. Length: 426 km (265 mi).

● **Saar, River** ▶ (French name: Sarre) A river in W Europe, rising in the Vosges Mountains in NE France and flowing generally N into W Germany, then NW through Saarland to join the River Moselle above Trier. The Saar Valley is noted for its wines. Length: 240 km (149 mi).

● **Saarbrücken** ▶ (French name: Sarrebruck) 49 15N 6 58E A city in SW Germany, the capital of Saarland on the River Saar near the French border. It was under French administration (1801–15, 1919–35, 1945–57). Some historic buildings, such as the gothic abbey church (1270–1330), survived World War II and it has a university (1948). It produces iron, steel, and machinery. Population (1996 est): 187 032.

● **Saarinen, Eero** ▶ (1910–61) US architect, born in Finland. One of the most innovative 20th-century architects, Saarinen emigrated (1923) to the USA with his father, the architect **Eliel Saarinen** (1873–1950). His first independent design was the General Motors Technical Center in Warren, Michigan (1948–56). His most famous building is the Trans World Airlines terminal at Kennedy Airport, New York (1956–62). Other works include the St Louis Arch (1964).

● **Saarland** ▶ A small *Land* in SW Germany, bordering on France. The area has often passed between France and Germany, but plebiscites (1935 and 1955) led to union with Germany. Rich in coal, it has a large steel industry. Area: 2569 sq km (992 sq mi). Population (1995 est): 1 084 200. Capital: Saarbrücken.

● **Sabadell** ▶ 41 33N 2 07E A city in NE Spain, in Catalonia. It has an important textile industry. Other industries include metallurgy and leather. Population (1995 est): 188 386.

● **Sabah** ▶ (former name: North Borneo) A state in Malaysia, in NE ▷Borneo on the South China and Sulu Seas. Forested and mountainous, it rises to 4125 m (13 533 ft) at Mount Kinabalu, the highest peak in Malaysia and Borneo. It is largely undeveloped, but on the western coastal plain rice and rubber are grown. Copper and oil resources are being exploited; timber, rubber, copra, and abaca are exported.
   History: until colonization, most contact was with the Philippines. North Borneo was first colonized by the British in 1877, becoming a protectorate in 1882. In 1963 it joined Malaysia under its present name. Tension between Muslims and the government led to violence in the 1980s. Area: 76 115 sq km (29 388 sq mi). Population (1993 est): 1 472 700. Capital: Kota Kinabalu.

● **Sabatier, Paul** ▶ (1854–1941) French chemist, who was professor at Toulouse University (1884–1941), where he discovered that nickel catalyses hydrogenation reactions. Since nickel is relatively cheap, this enabled similar reactions to be performed on an industrial scale, e.g. in the production of margarine. He shared the 1912 Nobel Prize with F. A. V. Grignard, the discoverer of ▷Grignard reagents.

● **sabbath** ▶ In Judaism, the seventh day of the week, ordained by God in the Pentateuch as a day of rest for the benefit of his people. It was reckoned from sunset on Friday to sunset on Saturday. For Orthodox Jews, the sabbath is a day on which no work or casual activity is allowed (including switching on the light—although time switches are permitted). The early Christian Church soon substituted Sunday as the Christian day of rest and worship because Christ's resurrection took place on the first day of the (Jewish) week.

● **Sabines** ▶ The peoples of the scattered hilltop communities NE of ancient Rome. The legendary abduction of the Sabine women by Roman settlers, a favourite theme in the history of art, indicates the early interbreeding of Sabines with Romans. Sabine influence on Roman religion was especially strong. They became Roman citizens in 268 BC.

● **Sabin vaccine** ▶ A vaccine that prevents poliomyelitis, developed by a US virologist, Albert B. Sabin (1906–93). It contains a weakened live polio virus that stimulates the body's defence against polio without causing the disease. Sabin vaccine is given by mouth (often on a sugar lump). It has replaced the ▷Salk vaccine, which used a killed virus and was injected.

● **sable** ▶ A carnivorous mammal, *Martes zibellina*, native to N Eurasia. It is less than 50 cm long and has thicker legs and longer ears than other ▷martens. Its coat is thick, soft, and glossy and is valued as fur (Siberian sable).

● **sable antelope** ▶ A large antelope, *Hippotragus niger*, of S African forests. 130 cm high at the shoulder, it has backward-curving ringed horns up to 170 cm long. The coat is black in males, lighter in females, with a white face, rump, and belly.

● **Sable Island** ▶ A sandy island in Canada, in the Atlantic Ocean off the coast of Nova Scotia. The scene of many shipwrecks, it is known as "the graveyard of the Atlantic."

● **sabre-toothed tiger** ▶ An extinct ▷cat that lived 30 million years ago and became extinct in the Pleistocene epoch (1 million years ago). *Smilodon*, a Pleistocene form, was about the size of a tiger, with very long upper canine teeth used to pierce the thick hide of its prey. □fossil.

● **saccharin** ▶ An organic compound ($C_7H_5NO_3S$) used as a sweetening agent in the food industry and as a sugar substitute by diabetics and others. It has about five hundred times the sweetening power of table sugar and passes through the body without being absorbed or changed.

● **saccharose** ▷*See* sucrose.

● **Sacco-Vanzetti case** ▶ The controversial trial (1921) of two US anarchists. Nicola Sacco and Bartolomeo Vanzetti were Italian-born immigrant workers convicted of murder on flimsy evidence. The verdict, which was reached largely because of their political activities and was influenced by current anti-alien and antiradical prejudice, aroused international protests. An investigative committee supported the sentence and Sacco and Vanzetti were executed in 1927, six years after being sentenced.

● **Sachs, Hans** ▶ (1494–1576) German poet and folk dramatist, most famous of the ▷Meistersingers of Nuremberg. He wrote thousands of works, including lively farces still performed at annual festivals throughout Germany, verse tales, religious poetry, and other works in support of ▷Luther. He is the central character, portrayed as wise and philosophic, of Wagner's opera *The Mastersingers of Nuremberg* (1868).

● **Sachs, Nelly (Leonie)** ▶ (1891–1970) German Jewish poet and dramatist. Helped by Selma ▷Lagerlöf, she escaped from Nazi Germany and settled in Sweden. Her best-known play is *Eli: Ein Mysterienspiel vom Leiden Israels* (1951). In 1966 she shared a Nobel Prize with Shmuel Yosef ▷Agnon.

• **sackbut** ▷*See* trombone.

• **Sacks, Jonathan (Henry)** ▶ (1948–) British rabbi. An academic philosopher by training, he became a rabbi in 1978 and Commonwealth chief rabbi in 1991. His books include *Tradition and Transition* (1986), *The Persistence of Faith* (Reith Lectures; 1991), and *The Politics of Hope* (1997).

• **Sackville, Thomas, 1st Earl of Dorset** ▶ (1536–1608) British poet and dramatist. He collaborated with Thomas Norton (1532–83) on *Gorbuduc* (1561), the first English play in blank verse, and planned and introduced *The Mirror for Magistrates* (1563), a collection of narrative poems based on the lives of eminent men.

• **Sackville-West, Vita** ▶ (Victoria Mary S-W; 1892–1962) British poet and novelist. A close friend of Virginia ▷Woolf, she married Sir Harold ▷Nicolson, with whom she settled at Sissinghurst Castle, Kent, where she laid out extensive gardens. Her writings include the novel *All Passion Spent* (1931) and the pastoral poem *The Land* (1931).

• **sacrament** ▶ In Christian theology, a ritual having a special significance as a visible sign of an inner grace in its participants. The ▷Roman Catholic Church and ▷Orthodox Churches accept seven sacraments: ▷baptism, ▷confirmation, penance (*see* confession), the ▷Eucharist, ▷marriage, ▷holy orders, and ▷anointing of the sick. Baptism and the Eucharist are the only commonly accepted Protestant sacraments (*see* Protestantism).

• **Sacramento** ▶ 38 32N 121 30W A city in the USA, the capital of California on the Sacramento River. Founded in 1839, it grew after the discovery of gold at nearby Sulter's Mill in 1848. Linked by canal (1963) to San Francisco Bay, it is a deepwater port and serves an extensive agricultural area. Industries include food processing, aerospace, and printing. Population (1996 est): 376 243.

• **sacred ibis** ▶ An African ibis, *Threskiornis aethiopica*, that was revered in ancient Egypt. 75 cm long, it is pure white except for dark ornamental plumes on its back, dark wing tips, and a black head and neck. It has a black bill and feeds in flocks along rivers, taking frogs and small aquatic animals.

• **Sadat, Anwar** ▶ (1918–81) Egyptian statesman; president (1970–81). A colleague of ▷Nasser in the Free Officers movement, Sadat was twice vice president (1964–66, 1969–70) before becoming president on Nasser's death. He moved Egypt away from the Soviet Union and towards the USA, under the influence of which he negotiated a peace agreement with Israel in 1979. For this initiative and his courage in visiting Israel in the face of some Arab opposition he was awarded the 1978 Nobel Peace Prize jointly with Begin. He was assassinated (1981) by Islamic extremists while watching a military display in Egypt.

• **saddleback** ▶ A very rare songbird, *Creadion carunculatus*, surviving only on small islands around New Zealand. It has a black plumage with a chestnut patch on its back and orange wattles at the base of the sharp pointed bill. A weak flier, it feeds in the undergrowth on larvae, insects, and fruits. Family: *Callaeidae* (wattlebirds).

• **Sadducees** ▶ An ancient Jewish religious and political party. They formed a conservative and aristocratic group centring on the priesthood in Jerusalem. With the destruction of the temple the party ceased to exist, but many of its ideas surfaced later in medieval Jewish sects. ▷*See also* Pharisees.

• **Sade, Donatien Alphonse François, Marquis de** ▶ (1740–1814) French novelist. Most of his works of sexual fantasy and perversion, which include *Justine*, *La Philosophie dans le boudoir*, and *Les 120 Journées de Sodome*, were written in the 1780s and 1790s, during his many years of imprisonment for sexual offences. During his last years he was confined to the mental asylum of Charenton. His moral nihilism has been seen as a stage in the development of ▷existentialism. The sexual perversion "sadism," in which sexual pleasure is derived from causing or observing pain, is named after him.

• **Sa'di** ▶ (Mosleh al-Din S.; c. 1215–92) Persian poet, who studied in Baghdad and subsequently spent much of his life wandering in Asia Minor and Egypt, claiming also to have visited India and central Asia. He settled in Shiraz in 1256. His major works are *Bustan* (*The Orchard*; 1257), a didactic poem illustrating the Islamic virtues of justice, con-

tentedness, and modesty, and *Galestan* (*The Rose Garden*; 1258), a collection of moralistic anecdotes. He also wrote a number of odes and popularized the *ghazal* form later used by ▷Hafiz.

• **Sadler's Wells Theatre** ▶ A theatre in London where Lilian ▷Baylis established an opera and ballet company in 1931. From the 1680s the medicinal wells on the site were exploited and its owner, Mr Sadler, later erected a music hall. In 1753 this became a theatre, where such actors as Sarah Siddons and Edmund Kean performed before it closed in 1878. Baylis restored the derelict building and here the Sadler's Wells Opera Company (now the ▷English National Opera) and the ▷Royal Ballet made their names. The Sadler's Wells Theatre Ballet was founded in 1946 as a touring company, later becoming the Sadler's Wells Royal Ballet, and (on transfer to Birmingham in 1990) the Birmingham Royal Ballet. In 1998 Sadler's Wells reopened as a high-tech "dance theatre for the millennium" after a multimillion-pound redevelopment. The spring water is still sold.

• **Sadowa** ▶ (Czech name: Sadorá) A village in the Czech Republic, in NE Bohemia. It was the scene of a battle in the Austro-Prussian War (1866) in which the Austrians were defeated by the Prussians.

• **Safavids** ▶ The ruling dynasty of Persia from 1502 to 1706. It was founded by Esmail I (1486–1524) and named after his ancestor Safi od-Din (1252–1334), a Muslim saint. Esmail established Shiism (*see* Shiites) as the state religion. Among his descendants was ▷Abbas the Great (reigned 1588–1628). The Safavids were overthrown by ▷Nader Shah.

• **safety lamp** ▶ A lamp developed for use in coalmines, where the atmosphere may be highly inflammable or lacking in oxygen. The most celebrated safety lamp was that developed by Sir Humphrey ▷Davy in 1815 in which the flame produced by burning oil was protected by an iron gauze to prevent the passage of the flame to the surrounding atmosphere. Flame lamps have now been almost entirely replaced by electric cap lamps and mains electric lighting.

• **safflower** ▶ An annual herbaceous plant, *Carthamus tinctorius*, native to Asia and Africa. 30–120 cm tall, it has red, orange, yellow, or white flowers. It is cultivated in India, the Middle East, North America, and Australia for its seeds, which yield safflower oil, used in paints, varnishes, cooking oils, and margarines. A red dye can be obtained from the dried flowers. Family: ▷*Compositae*.

• **saffron** ▶ The dried orange-yellow stigmas of the saffron crocus (*C. sativa*), used for flavouring and colouring foods and liqueurs and formerly as a dye for fabrics. The crocus, which has purple flowers, is probably native to the Mediterranean region and SW Asia and has been cultivated since ancient times; today the main producing areas are France, Spain, and Italy.

• **Safi** ▶ (ancient name: Asfi) 32 20N 9 17W A port in Morocco, on the Atlantic coast. Its artificial harbour serves Marrakech, and exports include phosphates. Besides its important fishing industry, it manufactures pottery and has a chemical complex. Population (1994 est): 364 648.

• **Sagan, Françoise** ▶ (Françoise Quoirez; 1935–) French writer. She made her name with the best-selling novel *Bonjour Tristesse* (1954), published when she was only 18. Subsequent novels, most of which concern brief affairs between wealthy characters, include *Aimez-Vous Brahms?* (1959), *With Fondest Regards* (1986), and *Evasion* (1993). Her plays include *Château en Suède* (1960) and *Zaphorie* (1973).

• **sagas** ▶ Heroic prose narratives in Old Norse, the best of which were written down in Iceland in the 12th and 13th centuries (*see* Icelandic literature). Translations of French ▷romances, Latin histories, and saints' lives were part of the saga tradition but its characteristic subject matter was drawn from ancient Scandinavian oral traditions: fictionalized accounts of the deeds of Norwegian kings (e.g. Snorri ▷Sturluson's *Heimskringla*), heroic legends of the pagan past (e.g. *Volsungasaga*), and the "family" sagas that mirrored contemporary Icelandic society (e.g. *Egilssaga, Laxdaelasaga, and Njálssaga*).

• **sage** ▶ A perennial herb or shrub, *Salvia officinalis*, native to the Mediterranean region and widely cultivated for its leaves, which are used for flavouring foods. It grows 45–60 cm high and has blue, pink, or white flowers. ▷*See also* Salvia.

● **sage grouse** ▶ A large grouse, *Centrocercus urophasianus*, occurring in sagebrush deserts of western USA. It is 75 cm long and the male has ornamental wattles and a long slender tail, which is fanned out during its courtship display.

● **Sagittarius** ▶ (Latin: Archer) A large constellation in the S sky, lying on the ▷zodiac between Capricornus and Scorpius. The brightest star is the 2nd-magnitude Kaus Australis. The constellation contains several notable ▷star clusters and emission ▷nebulae, including the **Lagoon nebula**. The centre of the ▷Galaxy lies in the direction of Sagittarius, located in the intense radio source Sagittarius A.

● **sago** ▶ A starchy food obtained from the Indonesian sago ▷palms (*Metoxylon sagu* and *M. rumphii*), cultivated in Malaysia. The palms, up to 9 m high, take 15 years to mature and are harvested just before flowering. The starchy pith in their stems is extracted, ground, and washed to make flour or pearl sago. The pithy stems of a tropical Asian ▷cycad, *Cycas circinalis*, also called sago palm, are used as a source of sago. The plant has ornamental fernlike leaves.

● **saguaro** ▶ A giant □cactus, *Cereus* (or *Carnegiea*) *gigantea*, native to the S USA and Mexico. It has a ribbed branched stem and is slow-growing, producing its white flowers from the age of 50–75 years; it may live for 200 years and reach a height of 12 m.

● **Saguenay River** ▶ A river in E Canada, in E Quebec flowing from Lac St Jean ESE into the St Lawrence estuary. Its upper reaches drop steeply, providing hydroelectric power, while the lower course flows between high cliffs, a popular tourist attraction. Length: 170 km (105 mi).

● **Sagunto** ▶ (Latin name: Saguntum) 39 40N 0 17W A town in E Spain, in Valencia. It was captured by Hannibal in 219 BC, precipitating the second Punic War. There are many fine Roman remains including a theatre and circus. It exports iron ore and citrus fruits. Population (1989): 57 300.

● **Sahara** ▶ The largest desert in the world, covering most of N Africa. The terrain consists chiefly of a plateau with central mountains rising to 3415 m (11 204 ft) and some areas of sand dunes, such as the Libyan Desert in the NE. The vegetation is sparse but sufficient in most parts for nomads to keep sheep and goats. Geological evidence shows that the Sahara was once well vegetated and that parts were formerly under the sea. There are large deposits of oil and gas in Algeria and Libya and phosphates in Morocco and Western Sahara. Rainfall is minimal and irregular, but there are numerous scattered oases watered from under ground that support small communities and are visited by nomads and travellers. The first European crossed the desert in 1822–24. Area: about 9 000 000 sq km (3 474 171 sq mi).

● **Sahel** ▶ An area in West Africa, mainly in Mauritania, Mali, Niger, and Chad. It forms a band of savanna between the Sahara desert to the N and tropical vegetation to the S and is used as pasture. The desert is gradually encroaching on the area and in recent years it has suffered severe droughts. □desertification.

● **Saida** ▷*See* Sidon.

● **saiga** ▶ A small antelope, *Saiga tatarica*, of Asian deserts and steppes. About 80 cm high at the shoulder, saigas are slightly built with a pale woolly coat and a remarkable swollen snout with convoluted nasal tracts, thought to be an adaptation for warming inhaled air or to be related to their keen sense of smell. Males have straight ridged horns up to 30 cm long. Saigas form large herds to migrate southwards in winter. □mammal.

● **Saigon** ▷*See* Ho Chi Minh City.

● **Saigo Takamori** ▶ (1828–77) Japanese samurai famous for his tragic role in the Meiji restoration. He played a major part in the overthrow of the ▷Tokugawa regime (1868) but was opposed to radical modernization and the complete abolition of feudalism. When his supporters clashed with the government in 1877, he was torn between competing loyalties but committed himself to the rebellion and was eventually forced to commit hara-kiri.

● **sailfish** ▶ A food and game fish, belonging to a genus (*Istiophorus*) related to marlins, that occurs in warm and temperate seas. Its slender body, deep blue above, silvery below, and up to 3.4 m long, has a long pointed snout, long pelvic fins, and a large sail-like dorsal fin. Sailfish feed mainly on other fish.

● **sailing** ▶ Cruising or racing in a boat fitted with one or more sails. Some smaller sailing boats are equipped with an outboard motor; larger boats have one or more inboard auxiliary engines, for use in calm weather and for navigating in and out of harbours. Craft used for recreation and sport range from dinghies of 2.3 m (7.5 ft) to ocean-going yachts of 23 m (75 ft) or more. All classes of boat can be used for racing but boats used primarily for racing have more complex sail plans requiring a relatively large crew, while the emphasis in a cruising boat is more on providing living accommodation. Racing, which became popular in the 19th century, is organized according to class of boat. Races are held either for yachts of the same design or for yachts of different designs competing with appropriate handicaps. Current Olympic classes (1980) are: Finn (4.5 m; single-handed), 470 (4.7 m; two-man), Flying Dutchman (6.05 m; two-man), Star (6.91 m; two-man), Soling (8.16 m; three-man), and Tornado (6.1 m catamaran; two-man). In the Olympic Games seven races are held for each class.

Until the invention of nylon and Terylene (Dacron), all sails were made of canvas. Modern sails, made of synthetic fabrics, are more durable, resist mildew (can be stored wet), and retain their shape better than canvas.

Many different types of rigging have been used for sailing vessels throughout history. Square sails, which are of little use except when a vessel is sailing away from the wind, were the type employed on square-riggers, a rig prevalent in Europe from the 14th to the 19th centuries. These were largely replaced by the quadrilateral sails of early schooner-rigged vessels. Called gaffsails because the upper part of the sail was supported by a gaff boom, these were succeeded by triangular sails, which are popular on yachts today. ▷Sloops, ▷ketches, ▷schooners, and ▷yawls now employ triangular sails. Gaff-rigged vessels have given way to marconi- or Bermuda-rigged sailing boats, i.e. those with triangular sails. Small boats—sailing dinghies, etc.—may have only one sail, usually a gunter-rigged triangular sail supported at the upper leading edge by a boom that fits onto the top of a stubby mast set well forward in the boat. This rig is a modern version of the traditional lateen rig, a native design from the Near East that also uses a triangular sail hung from a very long boom. In the late 19th century, yachtsmen enlarged jibs into foresails called genoas. They

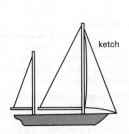
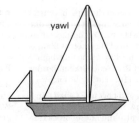
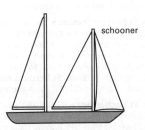

sloop　　ketch　　yawl　　schooner

sailing

also developed lightweight triangular foresails, called spinnakers, which often have a cross section like a part of the surface of a sphere. ▷*See also* ships.

● **Saimaa, Lake** ▶ A lake in SE Finland, the main lake in an extensive system. Area: about 1760 sq km (680 sq mi).

● **sainfoin** ▶ A perennial herb, *Onobrychis viciifolia*, native to temperate regions of Eurasia and found on chalky soils. Up to 50 cm tall, it has pale-pink flowers and has been cultivated as a forage plant. Family: ▷*Leguminosae*.

● **saint** ▶ In Christian belief, a person characterized by special holiness. In the early Church the term applied to all believers, and certain modern sects follow this practice in calling their adherents saints, for example the ▷Mormons. In the ▷Roman Catholic Church saints formally admitted to the calendar of saints by ▷canonization can be invoked as intercessors, although recently their numbers have been reduced in an effort to cut superstitious practices. ▷Protestantism rejects the invocation of saints, although the ▷Church of England's calendar recognizes a number of saints' days.

● **St Albans** ▶ 51 46N 0 21W A city in SE England, in Hertfordshire. Across the River Ver stood the important Romano-British town of Verulamium, where St Alban was martyred; Roman remains include a theatre and mosaic pavement. The Benedictine abbey, founded in honour of the saint in 793 AD, was made a cathedral in 1877 and has the second longest nave in Britain. The city now has various service and light industries. Population (1991): 80 376.

● **St Andrews** ▶ 56 20N 2 48W A resort in E Scotland, in Fife on St Andrews Bay. An ancient ecclesiastical centre, its university (1412) is the oldest in Scotland. The famous Royal and Ancient Golf Club was founded here in 1754. Population (1991): 11 136.

● **St Anthony's fire** ▷*See* ergot.

● **St Augustine** ▶ 29 54N 81 19W A city in the USA, in Florida. The oldest city in the USA, it was founded by the Spanish in 1565 and for most of the next two and a half centuries remained the most northerly outpost of the Spanish colonial empire. The Castillo de San Marcos (1672) stands as a reminder of Spanish rule. Tourism is the main source of revenue. Population (1990): 11 692.

● **St Austell** ▶ 50 20N 4 48W A market town in SW England, in Cornwall near St Austell Bay. It is a holiday resort and centre of the local china-clay industry (now in decline). The Eden Project, a rainforest environment in the world's largest greenhouse, is being created in a disused clay pit nearby. Population (1991): 21 622.

● **St Bartholomew's Day Massacre** ▶ The slaughter of ▷Huguenots that began on 24 August, 1572, in Paris. The massacre was ordered by Charles IX of France under the influence of his mother, Catherine de' Medici. Some 3000 Huguenots died in Paris and many more were murdered in the provinces.

● **St Basil's Cathedral** ▶ The cathedral of the Russian Orthodox Church in Moscow built between 1554 and 1560 for Ivan the Terrible. It is named after the Russian saint, who was buried there at the end of the 16th century.

● **St Bernard** ▶ A breed of large working dog developed in Europe from Asian ancestors and employed as a rescue dog by the hospice of St Bernard in the Swiss Alps since the 17th century. It is massively built, having a large head with drooping ears. The coat may be either short or of medium length and is white marked with red-brown or brindle. Height: 65 cm minimum.

● **St Bernard Passes** ▶ Two mountain passes in the Alps, in central Europe. The **Great St Bernard Pass** on the Swiss-Italian border is one of the highest alpine passes at 2433 m (8111 ft). The hospice at its summit, founded (11th century) by St Bernard of Menthon, is famous for the St Bernard dogs that were formerly used to rescue snowbound travellers. The **Little St Bernard Pass** on the French-Italian border reaches 2187 m (7177 ft) and also has an 11th-century hospice.

● **St Catherines** ▶ 43 10N 79 15W A city and port in E Canada, in S Ontario at the entrance to the ▷Welland Ship Canal. Founded in 1790, it is a fruit-farming and industrial centre and houses Brock University (1962). Population (1991): 129 300.

● **St Christopher-Nevis** ▷*See* St Kitts-Nevis, Federation of.

● **St Clair, Lake** ▶ A lake in E North America, on the US–Canadian border. It lies near Detroit, between Lakes Huron and Erie in the Great Lakes chain. Area: 1190 sq km (460 sq mi).

● **St-Cloud** ▶ 46 22N 5 50E A town in France, a W suburb of Paris. Mainly residential, it is the site of the Sèvres porcelain factory. Population (1990): 28 670.

● **St Croix** ▶ (*or* Santa Cruz) A West Indian island, the largest of the US Virgin Islands. The economy is based on tourism and agriculture. Area: 207 sq km (80 sq mi). Population (1990): 50 139. Chief town: Christiansted.

● **Saint-Cyr, École de** ▶ French military academy founded in 1803 and established in 1808 at Saint-Cyr-l'École, near Versailles. Its buildings were destroyed in World War II and it is now at Coëtquidan, Brittany.

● **St David's** ▶ (Welsh name: Tyddewi) 51 54N 5 16W A village in SW Wales in Pembrokeshire, the smallest cathedral city in Britain. The 12th-century cathedral, the largest in Wales, was an important medieval pilgrimage centre for the shrine of St David. Population (1991): 1627.

● **St-Denis** ▶ 20 52S 55 27E The capital of the French overseas region Réunion, on the W Indian Ocean. A port on the N of the island, its activities are mainly administrative, with some commerce. Population (1995): 207 158.

● **St-Denis** ▶ 48 56N 2 21E A town in France, an industrial suburb of Paris in the Seine-St Denis department on the River Seine. Its gothic abbey contains the tombs of many French kings. Population (1990): 90 806.

● **St Dunstan's** ▶ (for Men and Women Blinded on War Service) A British organization for the training, settlement, and lifelong care of those blinded in war. It was founded in 1915 by a blind newspaper proprietor, Sir Arthur Pearson (1866–1921).

● **Sainte-Beuve, Charles-Augustin** ▶ (1804–69) French literary historian and critic. He first studied medicine, but abandoned it to write poetry. After writing the novel *Volupté* (1834), based in part on his love affair with Victor Hugo's wife, he devoted himself to criticism. His literary journalism helped to establish many young writers of the Romantic movement. His major critical works include *Critiques et portraits littéraires* (1836–39) and *Port-Royal* (1840–59), a study of Jansenism.

● **St Elias Mountains** ▶ A mountain range in NW North America, running SE along the Alaska-Yukon border. Many summits surpass 5000 m (16 400 ft) and it reaches 6050 m (19 850 ft) at Mount Logan, its highest point. The range also includes the world's largest nonpolar ice cap.

● **St Elmo's fire** ▶ A small electrical discharge, with a luminous appearance, that is associated with stormy weather and seen around the extremities of tall objects, such as the tops of trees and mastheads. It is caused by ionization of the air in the electric field created around sharp projections. It is named after St Elmo (otherwise known as **St Erasmus**) who was, according to legend, martyred by having his intestines wound out of his body on a windlass or capstan. This vaguely nautical connection served to make him the patron saint of sailors; St Elmo's fire was taken as a sign that Elmo would protect any vessel that exhibited it.

● **St-Étienne** ▶ 45 27N 4 22E A city in S central France, the capital of the Loire department. It has produced firearms since the 16th century and was the site of France's first steel mill (1815). More recent manufactures include aero-engines, chemicals, and dyes. St-Étienne has a famous school of mining engineering (1816) and a university. Population (1990): 201 695.

● **Saint-Exupéry, Antoine de** ▶ (1900–44) French novelist and aviator. The themes of his novels, which include *Night Flight* (1931) and *Wind, Sand and Stars* (1939), derive from his experience as a pioneer of air-mail routes in N Africa and South America. He also wrote a fable for children, *The Little Prince* (1943), and an uncompleted philosophical book. He failed to return from a mission while on active service with the French air force in World War II.

● **St Gall** ► (German name: Sankt Gallen) 47 25N 9 23E A town in NE Switzerland, S of Lake Constance. The Celtic missionary St Gall established a hermitage here (612 AD), later to become a Benedictine abbey. Monastic buildings remaining include the cathedral (1755–72) and the library, which contains a fine collection of manuscripts. Population (1994): 75 541.

● **St George's** ► 12 04N 61 44W The capital of Grenada, on the SW coast. Founded by the French in the 17th century, it was capital of the British Windward Islands from 1885 to 1958. It is now a tourist resort as well as an important port. Population (1991): 4439.

● **St George's Channel** ► A channel between SE Ireland and Wales, linking the Irish Sea with the Atlantic Ocean. Length: about 160 km (100 mi). Maximum width: 145 km (90 mi).

● **St Gotthard Pass** ► 46 34N 8 31E A pass in the Alps, in S Switzerland linking central Europe and Italy by road. The St Gotthard railway tunnel (constructed 1872–80) below the pass is 15 km (9 mi) long and the second longest in the Alps. Height: 2114 m (6935 ft).

● **St Helena** ► 15 58S 5 43W A mountainous island in the S Atlantic Ocean, a UK overseas territory. Napoleon I was exiled here (1815–21). The economy declined when sailing ships stopped calling here following the opening of the Suez Canal (1869); it now depends on fishing, low-level agriculture, and the UK subsidies it receives. Area: 122 sq km (47 sq mi). Population (1994 est): 7000. Capital: Jamestown.

● **St Helens** ► **1.** 53 28N 2 44W A town in NW England, in St Helens unitary authority, Merseyside. It has an important glass industry, besides brick and tile manufacturing, engineering, and brewing. Population (1991): 106 293. **2.** A unitary authority in NW England, in Merseyside. Area: 130 sq km (50 sq mi). Population (1996 est): 179 500.

● **St Helens, Mount** ► 46 12N 122 11W A volcano in SW Washington, in the S Cascade Range, S of Seattle. Dormant since 1857, the mountain erupted in May, 1980, causing widespread destruction and more than 50 deaths. Further eruptions since 1980 have caused minor damage. Height: 2950 m (9677 ft).

● **St Helier** ► 49 12N 2 07W A market town and resort in the Channel Islands, on the S coast of Jersey. There is trade in early vegetables and Jersey cattle. Population (1996): 27 523.

● **St Ives** ► 50 12N 5 29W A resort in SW England, in Cornwall on St Ives Bay (an inlet on the N coast). It is a small fishing port and centre for water sports and artists. The **St Ives School** of artists established itself here after 1939, when Barbara ▷Hepworth and her husband Ben ▷Nicholson came to live and work in St Ives. In 1993 the ▷Tate Gallery opened a branch here, largely devoted to the work of the St Ives School. Population (1991): 16 510.

● **St James's Palace** ► A royal palace in Pall Mall, in London, built for Henry VIII on the site of an 11th-century hospital for leprous women. It was the principal London residence of the monarch from 1697, when Whitehall was burnt down, until superseded by Buckingham Palace in 1837, when Queen Victoria moved there. Much of the original building was destroyed by a fire in 1807. However, foreign ambassadors are still said to be accredited to the Court of St James.

● **Saint John** ► 45 16N 66 03W A city and port in E Canada, in New Brunswick at the mouth of the St John River. Originally a French fort (1631), it developed with the arrival of American Loyalists (1783) into the province's centre of heavy industry. Population (1991): 90 457.

● **St John River** ► A river in E North America. Rising in Maine, USA, it flows NE to New Brunswick, Canada, and then SE to the Bay of Fundy, where high tides cause the river to reverse its course at the famous Reversing Falls. Length: 673 km (418 mi).

● **St John's** ► 47 34N 52 41W A city in E Canada, the capital of Newfoundland. Settled in the 16th century, it is Canada's easternmost city, located beside a huge protected harbour. It was here in 1901 that Marconi received the first transatlantic radio message. St John's has two cathedrals (Roman Catholic and Anglican) and is the site of Memorial University (1925). Newfoundland's commercial centre, its industries include manufacturing, construction, and government services. Population (1991): 95 770.

● **St John's** ► 17 07N 61 51W The capital of Antigua and Barbuda. The chief port of Antigua, on the NW coast, it handles the island's produce. Population (1991): 21 514.

● **St John's wort** ► A perennial herb or shrub belonging to the genus *Hypericum* (400 species), found in temperate regions. They have yellow five-petalled flowers with many stamens and many species are cultivated for ornament, including *H. calycinum* (also known as rose of Sharon). The common European St John's wort (*H. perforatum*) reaches a height of 50 cm; an extract of this species is used as an antidepressant in alternative medicine and is being increasingly recommended for the treatment of mild depression by orthodox practitioners. Family: *Guttiferae*.

● **St Joseph** ► 39 45N 94 51W A city in the USA, in Missouri on the Missouri River. Often referred to as St Joe, it is an important grain and livestock centre, serving a large agricultural area. It was the home of Jesse ▷James. Population (1990): 71 852.

● **Saint-Just, Louis (Antoine Léon) de** ► (1767–94) French politician, who supported ▷Robespierre in the French Revolution. His pamphlet, *Esprit de la révolution et de la constitution de France* (1791), calling for a new moral order, brought him to public notice. He was a member of the Committee of ▷Public Safety, supervising military affairs, and led the attack on the Austrians at Fleurus (1794). He was arrested and guillotined with Robespierre.

● **St Kilda** ► 57 49N 8 34W A group of three small mountainous islands about 200 km (124 mi) W off the Scottish mainland, the most westerly of the Outer Hebrides. Populated from prehistoric times until evacuation in 1930, they are now a nature reserve. Area: about 16 sq km (6 sq mi).

● **St Kitts-Nevis, Federation of** ► (*or* St Christopher-Nevis) A country in the West Indies, in the Leeward Islands in the E Caribbean Sea.

Economy: primarily agricultural, sugar, molasses, cotton, and coconuts being the main products. Tourism has become of major importance and light industry (notably food-processing and electronics) is being developed.

History: the islands were visited by Columbus in 1473 and settled by English colonists in the early 17th century. In 1967 a UK associated state consisting of the three islands of St Kitts, Nevis, and ▷Anguilla was formed. Anguilla had its own constitution from 1976 and in 1980 became a separate British dependency. St Kitts-Nevis became fully independent within the British Commonwealth in 1983. Since 1995 the Federation has had a Labour Party government with Dr Denzil Douglas as prime minister. In 1997 the Nevis parliament announced plans to secede from the Federation. In 1998 a referendum on these plans was held on Nevis: although 60% of voters favoured secession, this fell short of the two-thirds majority required for independence.

Federation of St Kitts-Nevis

Head of state	Queen Elizabeth II, represented by the governor-general, Sir Cuthbert Montraville Sebastian
Official currency	East Caribbean dollar of 100 cents
Area	262 sq km (101 sq mi)
Population (1997 est)	41 800
Capital	Basseterre, on St Kitts

● **Saint-Laurent, Yves** ► (1936–) French fashion designer, who trained with ▷Dior and took over his fashion house (1957), opening his own in 1962. His creations for women have been predominantly influenced by male fashion; he has also designed clothes for men. He was the first to introduce ready-to-wear designer clothes on a mass basis. □ p. 1094.

● **St Lawrence, Gulf of** ► An arm of the Atlantic Ocean in E Canada, at the mouth of the St Lawrence River. Historically the gateway to Canada, it has always been an important fishing ground. Ice closes the gulf to navigation from early December until mid-April.

● **St Lawrence River** ► A river in North America. Although the river proper is fairly short, it belongs to one of the world's greatest water systems, draining the ▷Great Lakes into the Atlantic Ocean. From Lake Ontario it flows NE along the Canadian-US border as a broad stream through the Thousand Islands, a major tourist district. Above Montreal it enters Canada and passes through rapids where hydroelectricity is produced. At Quebec it broadens into a long estuary that gradually merges with the Gulf of ▷St Lawrence. The St Lawrence valley is an important agricultural and industrial belt as well as a rail, water, and road corridor. The upper reaches of the river become unnavigable during winter months. Length: Lake Ontario to Quebec 480 km (298 mi); St Louis River headwaters to Anticosti Island 3395 km (2110 mi). ▷*See also* St Lawrence Seaway.

Yves Saint-Laurent ▶ Working as artistic director at Dior (1962).

● **St Lawrence Seaway** ▶ A navigable waterway in North America through the St Lawrence River and the Great Lakes, completed in 1959. With a season of over eight months, it admits ships of up to 9000 tons, mainly carrying heavy nonperishables.

● **St Leger** ▶ A flat race for three-year-old horses, run in September at Doncaster over 2.9 km (1 mi 6½ furlongs). It was the earliest of the English ▷Classics to be established (1776).

● **St-Lô** ▶ 49 01N 1 05W A town in NW France, the capital of the Manche department. A market town famous for its horse breeding, it was virtually destroyed in ▷World War II. Population (1990): 22 819.

● **St Louis** ▶ 38 40N 90 15W A city and port in the USA, in Missouri on the Mississippi River. It was a major centre in the colonization of the West, outfitting such exploring parties as that of Lewis and Clark (1804–06), as well as pioneers using the Santa Fe, California, and Oregon Trails. It has four universities, including St Louis University (1818), which maintains a library built to house microfilms of Vatican Library treasures. The state's largest city, it is an important market, trading in livestock, wool, grain, and timber. Industries include aircraft, cars, chemicals, and iron and steel. Population (1996 est): 351 565.

● **St Louis** ▶ 16 00N 16 27W A port in W Senegal, on an island in the River Senegal estuary. It was the capital of Senegal until replaced by Dakar (1958). Population (1994 est): 132 444.

● **St Lucia** ▶ An island country in the West Indies, in the Windward Islands in the E Caribbean Sea. It is a mountainous island of volcanic origin. The population is mainly of African descent. *Economy*: mainly agricultural, the chief products being bananas and coconuts. Tourism is a growing industry and attempts are being made to develop the manufacturing sector (notably clothing and timber products). St Lucia's trade with the UK declined sharply in 1992, when trade barriers between EU countries disappeared; in 1993 banana growers rioted because of loss of earnings. It is a member of CARICOM. *History*: St Lucia was colonized by the French in the 17th century and ceded to Britain in 1814. It became internally self-governing in

1967 and attained full independence within the British Commonwealth in February, 1979. The country was governed by the United Workers' Party from independence until 1997, when the Labour Party was elected and Kenny Anthony became prime minister.

St Lucia

Head of state	Queen Elizabeth II, represented by the governor-general, Perlette Louis
Official language	English
Official currency	East Caribbean dollar of 100 cents
Area	616 sq km (238 sq mi)
Population (1997 est)	148 000
Capital	Castries

● **St-Malo** ▶ 49 39N 2 00W A port and resort in NW France, in the Ille-et-Vilaine department on the English Channel. Many of its old buildings were destroyed during World War II, although its ramparts (12th–18th centuries) remain. A flourishing trading, fishing, and passenger port, it has shipbuilding and electrical industries. Population (latest est): 47 500.

● **St Mark's Cathedral** ▶ The cathedral church of Venice since 1807. It was built in the 9th century to house the relics of St Mark but rebuilt in the 11th century after a fire. Designed as a Greek cross surmounted by five domes, it is strongly influenced by ▷Byzantine art and is famous for its opulent mosaic and sculptural decoration both inside and out.

● **St Martin** ▶ (Dutch name: Sint Maarten) 18 05N 63 05W A West Indian island in the Lesser Antilles, administratively divided between France and the Netherlands. The N part is a dependency of Guadeloupe, area 52 sq km (20 sq mi) with a population (1990) of 28 518; the S is part of the Netherlands Antilles, area 33 sq km (13 sq mi) with a population (1992 est) of 33 459. Salt is the main export.

● **St Marylebone** ▶ A district in the Greater London Borough of the City of Westminster. It contains Harley Street and Wimpole Street (noted for their doctors), Madame Tussaud's, the Planetarium, and Regent's Park. ▷Lord's cricket ground is situated in St John's Wood (London's first garden suburb). Its name derives from the parish church of St Mary by the Bourne (the local name for the River ▷Tyburn); the present building in Marylebone Road was designed by Thomas Hardwick in 1813.

● **St Moritz** ▶ (German name: Sankt Moritz) 46 30N 9 51E A resort in SE Switzerland, on St Moritz Lake. A renowned winter-sports centre at a height of 1822 m (5978 ft), its famous Cresta Run (for bobsleds) dates from 1885. Population (1990): 5335.

● **St-Nazaire** ▶ 47 17N 2 12W A major port in W France, in the Loire-Atlantique department on the Loire estuary. An important German submarine base in World War II, it was virtually destroyed by Allied bombing. Its main industries are shipbuilding, aircraft construction, chemicals, and oil refining. Population (1990): 66 087.

● **St Paul** ▶ 45 00N 93 10W A city in the USA, the capital of Minnesota on the Mississippi River, opposite Minneapolis. The Twin Cities comprise the commercial and industrial centre of an extensive grain and cattle area. St Paul's industries include oil refining, car assembly, and food processing. Population (1996 est): 259 606.

● **St Paul's Cathedral** ▶ The cathedral of the diocese of London; there have been five cathedrals on this site, the first three of which were Saxon. The Norman cathedral, begun in 1087 and one of the largest buildings in England, was destroyed in the ▷Fire of London and ▷Wren was appointed to rebuild it. His design (1672–1717), combining ▷classicism and the ▷baroque style, features a traditional cruciform plan, a two-tiered portico, a great dome, and flanking towers. The best contemporary artists decorated the interior, including the painter ▷Thornhill, the woodcarver Grinling ▷Gibbons, and the iron worker Jean Tijou (died c. 1711).

● **St Peter Port** ▶ 49 27N 2 32W A resort in the Channel Islands, the only town in Guernsey. It has a large protected harbour. Population (1991): 16 648.

● **St Peter's Basilica** ▶ The Catholic basilica in the ▢Vatican City

State, Rome. The original basilica, a huge gothic building, was pulled down by Pope Julius II in the early 16th century. Its replacement is the largest church in the world. Its general shape was determined by ▷Bramante, although it was designed together with its enormous dome by ▷Michelangelo. ▷Vignola continued the work and the nave and façade were added by ▷Maderna. ▷Bernini completed the building in the 17th century, adding the huge baldacchino and the colonnade to the piazza outside.

● **St Petersburg** ► 27 45N 82 40W A city in the USA, in Florida on Tampa Bay. It is primarily a tourist resort. Population (1996 est): 235 988.

St Paul's Cathedral ► An engraving of 1829 showing Sir Christopher Wren's masterpiece from the River Thames.

● **St Petersburg** ► (name from 1914 until 1924: Petrograd; name from 1924 until 1991: Leningrad) 59 55N 30 25E The second largest city in Russia, at the head of the Gulf of Finland on the River Neva. It is a major industrial and commercial centre and its port, although frozen between January and April, is one of the largest in the world. Industries include heavy engineering (particularly shipbuilding), metallurgy, electronics, chemicals, car manufacture, and light industries; the city is an important railway junction. St Petersburg is rich in baroque and neoclassical buildings and is noted for its broad boulevards and many bridges and canals. The most notable buildings include the Peter–Paul Fortress (St Petersburg's oldest building, founded in 1703), the Winter Palace (1754–62, rebuilt 1839), the Gostiny Dvor (1761–85), and Kazan cathedral (1801–11). The city is an important cultural centre; it has a university (1918) and many museums, of which the Hermitage Museum, founded by Catherine the Great in 1764, is the most famous with its fine collection of European paintings.

History: the city was founded (1703) by Peter the Great as a "window on Europe" and was the capital of Russia from 1712 until 1918, replacing Archangel as Russia's main seaport. In the late 19th century it developed as an important industrial centre and from its labour force emerged several revolutionary parties, later united by Lenin to form the St Petersburg Union for the Struggle for the Liberation of the Working Class. In 1905 a general strike took place and on Bloody Sunday (22 January, 1905) more than a thousand people were killed in a march on the Winter Palace. St Petersburg was also prominent in the 1917 revolution (*see* Russian Revolution). During World War II the city withstood a siege by the Germans (8 September, 1941–27 January, 1944), in which nearly a million people perished. In 1941 a road was constructed across frozen Lake Ladoga over which sup-

plies could be brought. The city was awarded the status of "Hero City" in recognition of its ordeal. Population (1995 est): 4 838 000.

● **St Pierre** ► 14 44N 61 11W A small port in Martinique, at the foot of the volcano Mount Pelée. In 1902 an eruption destroyed the town leaving only one survivor. It is now the centre of an area growing sugar cane. Population (1990): 3550.

● **St Pierre et Miquelon** ► A French overseas department, consisting of two neighbouring islands in the NW Atlantic Ocean S of Newfoundland. All that remained to France of its Canadian territories after 1763, they have traditionally been bases for fishing and smuggling. More recently tourism has been developed. Area: St Pierre 26 sq km (10 sq mi); Miquelon 215 sq km (83 sq mi). Population (1990): 6300.

● **St-Quentin** ► 49 51N 3 17E A town in NE France, in the Aisne department on the River Somme. It was the scene of French defeats by Spain (1557) and by Prussia (1871) in the Franco-Prussian War and was almost completely destroyed in ▷World War I. It has textile, electrical, and metallurgical industries. Population (latest est): 69 000.

● **Saint-Saëns, Camille** ► (1835–1921) French composer, conductor, pianist, and organist. He began to perform and compose while still a child. He studied with Halévy and Gounod and held various organ posts, including nearly 20 years at the Madeleine. His piano pupils included Messager and Fauré, and he championed the music of Liszt, Berlioz, and Wagner. He wrote 12 operas, five symphonies (the third with organ; 1886), *The Carnival of the Animals* (published posthumously; 1922) for two pianos and orchestra, five piano, three violin, and two cello concertos, chamber music, and choral works.

● **Saint-Simon, Claude Henri de Rouvroy, Comte de** ► (1760–1825) The founder of French socialism. Saint-Simon was educated by ▷d'Alembert. Having witnessed the horror and chaos of the French Revolution, Saint-Simon was concerned to reconstruct society and his writings have a positive and idealistic tone. In *Du système industriel* (1821) he declared his aim of achieving an industrial state in which poverty is eliminated and in which science replaces religion as the spiritual authority.

● **Saint-Simon, Louis de Rouvroy, Duc de** ► (1675–1755) French memoir writer. He lived at the court of Louis XIV and although he exercised some influence during the regency of Philippe, Duc d'Orléans (1715–23), his ambitions at court were never realized. His *Mémoires*, covering the years 1694–1723, are enlivened by his prejudices, his sharp observation of detail, and his brilliant portraits. The definitive edition was not published until 1879–1923.

● **St Sophia** ► **1.** (*or* Hagià Sophia) A museum in Istanbul. The original church on the site was built by Constantine the Great in 326 but replaced in 537 by a Byzantine building of great size and beauty, erected by Justinian I. In 1453, after the Turkish conquest of the city, it became a mosque with added minarets. In 1935 Kemal Atatürk converted it to its present use. □ p. 1096. **2.** The 6th-century church in Sofia, Bulgaria.

● **St Stephen's Crown** ► The crown of Hungary, which was reputedly first used by Stephen I. It was originally a Byzantine circlet made between 1074 and 1077 and converted into an emperor's crown by Hungarians in the 12th century. It fell into the hands of the US army in 1945 but was returned in 1978.

● **St Thomas** ► 18 22N 64 57W A West Indian island in the US Virgin Islands, in the Lesser Antilles. After 1680 it became a major Caribbean sugar producer and later, after 1764, the largest slave-trading port. Tourism is now of major importance. Area: 83 sq km (28 sq mi). Population (1990): 48 166. Capital: Charlotte Amalie.

● **St Vincent, Cape** ► (Portuguese name: Cabo de São Vicente) 37 01N 8 59W A promontory in the extreme SW of Portugal, in the Algarve on the Atlantic Ocean. A number of naval battles have been fought off the cape; in 1797 the Spanish fleet was defeated by the British under Admiral Jervis during the Napoleonic Wars.

● **Saint Vincent, Gulf** ► An inlet of the Indian Ocean, in S Australia E of Yorke Peninsula. It has an important salt industry on the E coast. Length: about 145 km (90 mi). Width: about 73 km (45 mi).

● **St Vincent and the Grenadines** ► A country in the E Caribbean

Sea, in the Windward Islands of the Lesser Antilles. It consists of the principal island of St Vincent and its dependencies of the Grenadine islets.

Economy: it is predominantly agricultural, the chief crops being bananas, taro, and sweet potatoes. The sugar industry closed down in 1985, although some sugar cane is still grown for rum production.

History: visited by Columbus in 1498, it became a British possession in 1763, attaining internal self-government in 1969 and full independence in 1979. The 2001 general election was won by the United Labour Party under Ralph Gonsalves.

St Vincent and the Grenadines

Head of state	Queen Elizabeth II, represented by the governor-general, Sir Charles Antrobus
Official language	English; local creole is widely spoken
Official currency	East Caribbean dollar of 100 cents
Area	390 sq km (150 sq mi)
Population (2001 est)	113 000
Capital	Kingstown

● **St Vitus's dance** ► The old name for Sydenham's ▷chorea, so called because of the uncontrolled movements characteristic of the disease and because sufferers in the middle ages prayed for a cure at the shrine of St Vitus (the patron saint of dancers).

● **Saipan** ► 15 12N 145 43E One of the Northern Mariana Islands, in the W Pacific Ocean. It was the administrative centre of the UN Trust Territory of the Pacific Islands (1947–75). Area: 180 sq km (70 sq mi). Population (latest est): 38 896. Chief town: Susupe.

● **saithe** ► A food fish, *Pollachius* (or *Gadus*) *virens*, also called coalfish or coley, that is related to cod and lives in shoals in the North Atlantic. Its elongated body, up to about 120 cm long, is greenish brown above and silvery white below.

● **Sakai** ► 34 35N 135 28E A city in Japan, in S Honshu on the Yamato delta. Formerly an important port (15th–17th centuries), it is part of the Osaka-Kobe industrial complex. Population (1995): 802 965.

● **saké** ► (or *rice wine*) An alcoholic drink made in Japan from steamed rice, to which a special yeast is added, and slowly fermented. It resembles a light sherry in taste and is served warm.

● **Sakhalin** ► (Japanese name: Karafuto) An island in Russia, off the SE coast between the Sea of Okhotsk and the Sea of Japan. It comprises two parallel mountain ranges on either side of a central valley and is heavily forested. Timber, coal- and iron-mining, and paper milling are important industrial activities, and there are oilfields in the NE. Agriculture, principally the cultivation of vegetables and dairy farming, is pursued in the S.

History: a Russo-Japanese condominium from 1855 until 1875, it then passed to Russia but in 1905 was again divided between the two countries. In 1945 the Soviet Union acquired the whole island and expelled its Japanese population (about 400 000); the island reverted to Russia in 1991. Area: about 76 000 sq km (29 300 sq mi). Population (1995 est): 673 000.

● **Sakha Republic** ▷*See* Yakutia.

● **Sakharov, Andrei Dimitrievich** ► (1921–89) Soviet physicist and politician. After helping to develop the Soviet hydrogen bomb during the 1940s and 1950s he spoke out against nuclear weapons in the 1960s and argued for freedom of speech in the Soviet Union. He was awarded the Nobel Peace Prize in 1975. His exile to Gorkii (Nizhnii Novgorod) in 1980 aroused international protest. He was finally released in 1986 and in 1988 was allowed to travel abroad. In 1989, a few months before his death, he became a member of the new Congress of People's Deputies. His wife, the physician Yelena Bonner (1923–), shared in many of his struggles.

● **saki** ► A South American monkey belonging to the genus *Pithecia* (3 species), found in forests. Sakis are 55–125 cm long including the tail (25–55 cm) and have a thick shaggy coat and hairy hood. Wholly arboreal, they feed on berries, honey, leaves, and small animals. Family: *Cebidae*.

● **Saki** ► (H(ector) H(ugh) Munro; 1870–1916) British humorous short-story writer. Born in Burma (now Myanmar), he worked as a foreign correspondent before settling in London in 1908. He published several volumes of humorous stories many of which were based on the outrageous activities of his fastidious and snobbish heroes Clovis and Reginald. He also wrote a novel, *The Unbearable Bassington* (1912). He was killed in action in World War I.

● **Saladin** ► (Arabic name: Salah ad-Din; ?1137–93) The leader of the Muslims against the Crusaders in Syria. Of Kurdish descent, he obtained control over the Muslim lands in Egypt, of which he became sultan in 1175, and Syria. He then captured the Kingdom of Jerusalem following his great victory over the Crusaders at the battle of Hattin (1187). The last years of his life were spent fighting the third ▷Crusade, during which he won his legendary reputation as a chivalrous warrior.

● **Salado, Río** ► The name of several South American rivers, meaning salty river. **1.** A river in N Argentina, rising in the Andes and flowing SE to join the Río Paraná. Length: 2012 km (1250 mi). **2.** A river in W Argentina, rising near the Chilean border and flowing S to join the Río Colorado. Length: about 1365 km (850 mi).

● **Salam, Abdus** ► (1926–96) Pakistani physicist, who became professor of physics at Imperial College, London, in 1957. He was also director of the International Centre for Theoretical Physics in Trieste.

St Sophia ► Istanbul's greatest Byzantine building photographed from the south. The main structure dates chiefly from the 6th century, when an earlier church was rebuilt on a massive scale by Justinian I. The central dome has a diameter of 32 m (105 ft). The four flanking minarets were added in the 15th century, when the building became a mosque.

In 1979 he shared the Nobel Prize with the US physicists Sheldon ▷Glashow and Steven ▷Weinberg for their **Glashow-Weinberg-Salam theory** unifying ▷weak and electromagnetic interactions.

● **Salamanca** ► 40 58N 5 40W A city in central Spain, in Salamanca province. During the Peninsular War the battle of Salamanca was fought here on 22 July, 1812, in which Wellington secured a decisive victory over the French. An intellectual centre of Renaissance Europe, Salamanca remains an important cultural centre with a university (founded 1218). Its notable buildings include two cathedrals and it has a fine Roman bridge. Population (1995 est): 167 316.

● **salamander** ► A tailed ▷amphibian belonging to a widely distributed order (*Urodela* or *Caudata*; about 225 species). Salamanders have short legs and long bodies and move by bending the body from side to side to give as wide a movement as possible for their feet. They usually hide in damp places when not hunting small worms and insects. Their habits range from the wholly aquatic Japanese giant salamander (*Megalobatrachus japonicus*), 1.5 cm long, to the American woodland salamanders (genus *Plethodon*) that live entirely on land. ▷*See also* congo eel; hellbender; mudpuppy; olm; newt; siren.

● **Salamis** ► A Greek island in the Aegean Sea. It was the scene of a Greek naval victory over the Persians in 480 BC. Area: 95 sq km (37 sq mi). Population (latest est): 20 000. Chief town: Salamis.

● **sal ammoniac** ► (*or* ammonium chloride; NH₄Cl) A white crystalline solid, used in batteries and as a pickling agent in zinc coating and tinning.

● **Salazar, António de Oliveira** ► (1889–1970) Portuguese dictator. Salazar became prime minister in 1932 and ruled until suffering a stroke in 1968. His New State imposed his corporatist ideas on Portugal. It repressed opposition and fought long colonial wars in Africa, which gravely impeded the country's economic development.

● **Salé** ► 34 04N 6 50W A port in NW Morocco, on the Atlantic coast opposite Rabat. It was an important medieval port and during the 17th century was the base for the Sallee Rovers, a notorious group of Barbary pirates. Population (1994 est): 504 420.

● **Sale** ► 38 06S 147 06E A city in Australia, in S Victoria on the Thomson River. It is a centre for the irrigated East Gippsland area; tourism is also important. Population (1991): 13 858.

● **Salem** ► 11 38N 78 08E A city in India, in Tamil Nadu. A developing industrial centre, it has large-scale textile manufacturing. Population (1991): 363 934.

● **Salem** ► 42 32N 70 53W A town in the USA, in Massachusetts on Salem Bay. Founded in 1626, it was the scene of notorious witchcraft trials in 1692, when a number of young girls made accusations of witchcraft against more than 300. 20 people were executed before the hysteria faded. Population (1990): 38 091.

● **Salem** ► 44 57N 123 01W A city in the USA, the capital of Oregon on the Willamette River. Founded in 1840, it is a food-processing centre. Willamette University was founded in 1844. Population (1996 est): 122 566.

● **Salerno** ► 40 40N 14 46E A port in Italy, in Campania on the Gulf of Salerno. Founded by the Romans in 197 BC, Salerno is best known for its medical school, which flourished here in the middle ages. It was the scene of heavy fighting during World War II, following major Allied troop landings here in 1943. Notable buildings include the 11th-century cathedral, where Gregory VII is buried. The chief industries are engineering, flour milling, textiles, and cement. Population (1996 est): 143 863.

● **Salford** ► **1.** 53 30N 2 16W A city in NW England, in Salford unitary authority, Greater Manchester, on the River Irwell and the Manchester Ship Canal. The docks for Manchester are here. Formerly a centre of the cotton industry, Salford now has engineering and manufacturing industries. There is a Roman Catholic cathedral (1848) and a university (1967). The Lowry, a major art gallery and cultural centre named in honour of L. S. ▷Lowry, opened in 2000. Population (1991): 227 400. **2.** A unitary authority in NW England, in Greater Manchester. Area: 97 sq km (37 sq mi). Population (1999 est): 220 463.

● **Salic Law** ► The law of the Salian ▷Franks issued under Clovis in the early 6th century. Owing little to other contemporary law codes or to Roman law, it is concerned with both criminal and civil law. Its importance for later periods lies in its prohibition against women inheriting land. This canon was invoked in France in 1316 and 1321 to prevent a woman from succeeding to the throne and, in 1328, Edward III's claim to the French Crown was rejected on the grounds that his claim was by female descent.

● **Salicornia** ▷*See* glasswort.

● **salicylic acid** ► An antiseptic compound (OHC₆H₄COOH) that causes the skin to peel. It is used to treat certain skin conditions, including psoriasis, eczema, warts, and corns. Acetylsalicylic acid (*see* aspirin) is a derivative.

● **Salieri, Antonio** ► (1750–1825) Italian composer and conductor. He studied and worked in Vienna from 1766. His pupils included Beethoven, Schubert, and Liszt. Because of his rivalry with Mozart, he was fancifully credited with having poisoned him.

● **Salinger, J(erome) D(avid)** ► (1919–) US novelist. After contributing stories to the *New Yorker* he achieved success with his novel of adolescent alienation *The Catcher in the Rye* (1951). Later works include *Franny and Zooey* (1961), *Raise High the Roof Beam, Carpenters* (1963), and *Seymour, An Introduction* (1963), but he subsequently became a recluse and published very little. *Hapworth 16, 1924* appeared in 1997.

● **Salisbury** ▷*See* Harare.

● **Salisbury** ► 51 05N 1 48W A city in S England, in Wiltshire at the confluence of the Rivers Avon and Wylye. Its 13th-century cathedral has the highest spire in the country, 123 m (403 ft) high. Salisbury's industries include light engineering, research and development, and tourism. Nearby is Old Sarum, the site of an Iron Age hill fort with extensive earthworks; settlement here continued until the 13th century, when the cathedral was moved to New Sarum (Salisbury). Old Sarum was the most notorious of the pre-1832 ▷rotten boroughs. Population (1996): 39 431.

● **Salisbury, Robert Cecil, 1st Earl of** ▷*See* Burghley, William Cecil, Lord.

● **Salisbury, Robert Arthur Talbot Gascoyne-Cecil, 3rd Marquess of** ► (1830–1903) British statesman; Conservative prime minister (1885–86, 1886–92, 1895–1902). Elected an MP in 1853, he was twice secretary for India (1866–67, 1874–78) before becoming Disraeli's foreign secretary (1878). As prime minister he served as his own foreign secretary (except in 1886 and 1900–02) and his policy has been characterized as one of "splendid isolation." Although he negotiated the Mediterranean Agreements with Italy and Austria-Hungary in 1887, under Salisbury Britain had no formal ally until an alliance was concluded with Japan in 1902.

● **Salisbury Plain** ► An area of open chalk downs in S England, in Wiltshire. It contains many prehistoric remains, notably ▷Stonehenge. It is extensively used as a military training ground; the first permanent camp was established at Tidworth (1902). Area: about 518 sq km (200 sq mi).

● **saliva** ► The fluid secreted by three pairs of **salivary glands** around the mouth in response to the sight, smell, taste, or thought of food. Although saliva contains ▷amylase, which aids the digestion of starch, its major role is to bind the food particles and to lubricate the mouth and gullet.

● **Salk vaccine** ► The first successful antipolio vaccine. It was developed by the US virologist J. E. Salk (1914–95) and first used in 1954. The vaccine, which contains killed polio viruses that stimulate the defence mechanisms of the body, is given by subcutaneous injections. It has been replaced by the ▷Sabin vaccine in many countries.

● **sallow** ▷*See* willow.

● **Sallust** ► (Gaius Sallustius Crispus; c. 86–c. 34 BC) Roman politican and historian. Expelled from the Senate for alleged immorality, he supported Julius Caesar in the war against Pompey and became governor of Numidia. He was accused of corruption and extortion and retired from politics in about 44 BC. His best-known works are *Bellum Catilinae* and *Bellum Jugurthinum*, noted for their forceful style.

● **salmon** ► One of several fish of the genera *Oncorhynchus* or *Salmo*, especially the Atlantic salmon (*S. salar*)—a valuable food and game fish. It has an elongated body, up to 150 cm long, and two dorsal fins. Salmon live mainly in the sea, feeding on other fish, especially herrings. However, they migrate into fresh water to spawn, at which time they change from silvery-blue or green to become brownish or greenish with orange markings. The spawned fish (kelts) either die or return to the sea and spawn in successive years. On hatching the young fish are known as alevins, although when they start feeding they are called parr. At about two years the coat becomes silver and the fish (smolt) migrate to the sea to reach maturity. After about two to three years they return to their native spawning waters as grilse, guided upstream by their sense of smell. Salmon is eaten freshly cooked (and canned) or smoked (Scotch salmon being regarded as the best). Family: *Salmonidae*; order: *Salmoniformes*.

● **Salmonella** ► A genus of rod-shaped bacteria that are parasites of animals and humans and cause several diseases: in humans, *S. typhi* causes ▷typhoid fever, *S. paratyphi* can cause ▷paratyphoid fever, while *S. typhimurium* is a common cause of ▷food poisoning. Both diseases and poisoning occur as a result of consuming contaminated foods, such as undercooked meat, meat products, poultry, the eggs of infected hens, and raw milk. Food can be contaminated during preparation if standards of hygiene are so low that the food comes into contact with bacteria from human or animal excretions, sewage, etc. Salmonella survives freezing but is destroyed by thorough cooking.

● **Salò, Republic of** ► (1943–45) The fascist government established by ▷Mussolini after Italy's surrender in World War II. Mussolini, rescued from prison by German parachute troops, set up his government at Salò on Lake Garda in German-controlled N Italy. Partisan opposition, Mussolini's death, and Germany's surrender caused its collapse.

● **Salome** ► The daughter of Herodias by her first husband, Herod Philip. The Jewish historian Josephus identifies her with the unnamed girl in the Gospels who requested the head of ▷John the Baptist from her stepfather, ▷Herod Antipas, as a reward for her dancing. According to the Gospels, Salome made this ruthless request on the prompting of her mother, because John the Baptist had criticized Herod Antipas for marrying Herodias, his half-brother's ex-wife, as contrary to Mosaic law.

● **Salon** ► The annual exhibition held by the French Royal Academy, which was founded in 1648. Housed in the Salon d'Apollon, in the Louvre, it became a bulwark of conservative art in the 19th century. The **Salon des Refusés** (1863) was a special exhibition held at the instigation of Napoleon III to exhibit the enormous number of paintings rejected by the Salon jury that year. Its contributors included ▷Manet, ▷Pissarro, and ▷Whistler.

● **Salon des Indépendants** ► The annual exhibition of the Société des Artistes Indépendants in Paris. The Société was founded in 1884 to enable such avantgarde painters as ▷Cézanne and ▷Seurat to exhibit works that had been or would have been rejected by the French Royal Academy's ▷Salon. Unlike the Salon, the Salon des Indépendants had no jury.

● **Salonika** ▷*See* Thessaloníki.

● **salp** ▷*See* tunicate.

● **salsify** ► A biennial herb, *Tragopogon porrifolius*, native to the Mediterranean region, also called vegetable oyster or oyster plant. It is cultivated in temperate regions for its fleshy white root, supposed to taste like oysters when cooked. The plant has long narrow leaves and a head of purple flowers surrounded by stiff pointed green sepals. The leaves may be eaten in salads. Family: ▷*Compositae*.

● **salt** ► 1. (sodium chloride; NaCl) The crystalline solid that is used for seasoning and preserving food and is present in sea water and **halite** (a crystalline form of sodium chloride found in deposits in Germany, the USA, etc.), which is its chief sources (naturally occurring sodium chloride is often called rock salt). NaCl forms cubic crystals. It has an important function in the human body and is used in the manufacture of many chemicals, such as soap, fertilizer, and ceramics. 2. Any similar compound formed, together with water, when

an acid reacts with a base, for example the salt potassium sulphate is formed when sulphuric acid reacts with potassium hydroxide: $H_2SO_4 + 2KOH \rightarrow K_2SO_4 + 2H_2O$.

● **SALT** ► (Strategic Arms Limitation Talks) ▷*See* disarmament.

● **Salta** ► 24 46S 65 28W A city in N Argentina. It is a commercial centre on the Trans-Andean Railway and trades with Bolivia and Chile. Population (1991): 373 857.

● **saltbush** ► A salt-tolerant herb or shrub, especially one belonging to either of the genera *Atriplex* or *Chenopodium*. They have inconspicuous flowers and are used as forage plants in dry salty regions of Australia and North America. Family: *Chenopodiaceae*.

● **Saltillo** ► 25 30N 101 00W A city in NE Mexico. The focal point of road and rail routes, it is the commercial centre for an agricultural region. Its university (1867) was refounded in 1957. Population (1990): 440 845.

● **Salt Lake City** ► 40 45N 111 55W A city in the USA, the capital of Utah near Great Salt Lake. Founded in 1847 by Mormons under the leadership of Brigham Young, it is the world headquarters of the Mormon Church. The Mormon tabernacle (1867) and the University of Utah (1850) are here. It is a commercial centre for nearby mining operations and industries include food processing, textiles, oil refining, and printing and publishing. Population (1996 est): 172 575.

● **salt marsh** ► A tract of land that is subjected to periodic flooding by the tides. It supports a type of vegetation that is adapted to grow in soil containing a high concentration of salt; typical salt-marsh plants include ▷*Spartina* (cord grasses) and sea rocket (*Cakile maritima*). Wading birds and ducks feed on an abundance of burrowing molluscs and crustaceans. Salt marshes usually form on the muddy or sandy shores of sheltered river estuaries, from deposits of mud and silt carried by the incoming tide; they may be divided into hummocks and small islands of vegetation surrounded by creeks and drainage channels. Notable examples are the salt marshes of East Anglia, on the E coast of England.

● **Salto** ► 31 27S 57 50W A port in NW Uruguay, on the River Uruguay. It is an important meat-packing centre; other products include wine and soft drinks. Population (latest est): 77 400.

● **saltpetre** ► (potassium nitrate *or* nitre; KNO_3) A white crystalline solid used as a fertilizer, a food preservative, and in ▷gunpowder and fireworks.

● **saltwort** ► An annual or perennial herb belonging to the widely distributed genus *Salsola* (50 species), found on seashores and salt marshes. They have fleshy spiked leaves and small flowers. The European saltwort (*S. kali*) grows up to 60 cm tall. Family: *Chenopodiaceae*.

● **saluki** ► A breed of hunting dog dating back over 8000 years in Egypt and used by Arabs for hunting gazelle. It has a slender streamlined body with long legs, giving speed and agility, and a small head with a long narrow muzzle. The smooth soft coat can be white, brownish, reddish, or black, tan, and white. Height: 50–70 cm.

● **Salvador** ► (*or* Bahia) 12 58S 38 29W A port in NE Brazil, the capital of Bahia state on the Atlantic Ocean. It has a fine natural harbour; exports include cocoa, sugar, tobacco, and diamonds. The chief industries are food and tobacco processing. It has two universities. Population (1991): 2 070 296.

● **Salvador** ▷*See* El Salvador, Republic of.

● **salvage** ► In law, the compensation allowed to persons (salvors) who have voluntarily assisted in saving a ship and its cargo or passengers from shipwreck, capture by an enemy, or similar damage or loss at sea. Salvors have a retaining lien (right to hold the salvaged property as security) on the salvaged vessel, etc., that takes priority over other claims. The amount payable as salvage is assessed by the Admiralty Court (*see* maritime law).

● **Salvarsan** ▷*See* Ehrlich, Paul.

● **Salvation Army** ► The international Christian organization founded in 1865 in London by William ▷Booth. Run on strictly military lines, it exacts absolute obedience from its members, who wear a characteristic uniform on public occasions. Morality in practical

Christian living is more esteemed than doctrinal niceties and the Army rejects the sacraments. It is famous for its social and evangelistic work. It also operates a successful missing persons investigation service.

● **Salvia** ▶ A genus of perennial herbs and shrubs (about 700 species), widely distributed in temperate and tropical regions. Many are cultivated for ornament, including the Brazilian scarlet sage (*S. splendens*) and the blue-flowered *S. patens*. Common ▷sage is the culinary herb. Family: ▷*Labiatae*.

● **sal volatile** ▶ (*or* ammonium carbonate) A mixture of ammonium salts, or their solution in alcohol, that is used in smelling salts. It smells of ammonia and is made by heating ammonium chloride (*or* sal ammoniac) with calcium sulphate.

● **Salween River** ▶ (Chinese name: Nu Jiang *or* Nu Chiang) A river in SE China and E Myanmar (Burma), rising in Tibet and flowing E then S to the Andaman Sea. Little of its length is navigable but it supplies hydroelectric power. Length: 2400 km (1500 mi).

● **Salyut** ▶ A series of manned Soviet space stations first launched into earth orbit in 1971. Cosmonauts from E Europe were conveyed to and from the orbiting laboratory by Soyuz spacecraft, there being two docking ports. They remained on the space station for either short or very long periods, in weightless conditions, conducting a variety of experiments and observations. Salyut stations were smaller than the US ▷Skylab space station and were eventually superseded by the ▷Mir space stations.

● **Salzburg** ▶ 47 54N 13 03E A city in central Austria, the capital of Salzburg. Its many fine buildings include the fortress of Hohensalzburg and the cathedral (1614–28). Salzburg University was refounded in 1962. Mozart was born here and the Salzburg Festival is held annually. Industries include textiles and leather. Population (2001): 144 816.

● **Salzgitter** ▶ 52 02N 10 22E A city in N Germany, in Lower Saxony formed in 1942 from 29 separate towns. The area is rich in iron ore, which is used in the manufacture of steel products. Population (1999 est): 113 700.

● **samadhi** ▶ The state of perfect concentration attained in deep ▷meditation. In Hinduism it is taken to be union with ▷Brahman or with a deity. In Buddhism it refers to transcending the distinction between subject and object. Its attainment is a precondition of spiritual liberation.

● **Samar** ▶ The third largest island in the Philippines, in the Visayan Islands linked by bridge to Leyte. Its frequent typhoons restrict agriculture; the chief products are rice, coconuts, and hemp. Copper and iron ore are mined. Area: 13 415 sq km (5181 sq mi). Population (latest est): 1 300 000. Chief town: Catbalogan.

● **Samara** ▶ (name from 1935 until 1991: Kuibyshev) 53 10N 50 10E A port in SW Russia, on the River Volga. Oil refining is a major industrial activity and market gardening is also important. Population (1999 est): 1 168 000.

● **Samaria** ▶ **1.** The central region of ancient Palestine, which became part of the northern kingdom of Israel in the 10th century BC. ▷*See also* Samaritans. **2.** 32 17N 35 12E The capital from the 9th century until its destruction by the Assyrians in about 721 BC of the kingdom of Israel. Occupied from the 4th millennium BC, the site was excavated in 1908–10, 1931–33, and 1935. Among the discoveries unearthed were a collection of 9th-century BC ivory carvings. The city was rebuilt in the 1st century AD under Herod the Great and renamed Sebaste (modern name: Sebastiyah, in Jordan).

● **Samaritans** ▶ **1.** A people of ancient Samaria (now in N Israel), with a religion closely akin to Judaism. Numerous in Roman and Byzantine times and much disliked by the Jews, they declined under Muslim rule. They now number only a few hundred. They have a conservative religious tradition and many distinctive beliefs and customs. **2.** A British telephone and e-mail service for the suicidal and despairing. Started in 1953 by the Rev Chad Varah (1911–) in a London church (St Stephen Walbrook) with one telephone, it now has over 200 branches in the UK, operated by some 22 000 trained volunteers, in which telephones are manned 24 hours per day and callers

are welcomed for personal visits. A nonreligious charity, it offers a nonprofessional, confidential, and anonymous service to anyone in distress. Samaritans offer little advice, believing that their callers will be helped to make their own decisions by talking to someone who cares. They receive some 4 million calls each year in Great Britain and Ireland. Many overseas branches are affiliated to the associated organization Befrienders International.

● **samarium** ▶ (Sm) A ▷lanthanide element discovered spectroscopically by Lecoq de Boisbaudran in 1879. It occurs naturally, with other lanthanides, in monazite (CePO$_4$). The oxide (Sm$_2$O$_3$) is used in glasses that absorb infrared radiation and the element is used in lasers as a dopant in calcium fluoride. At no 62; at wt 150.36; mp 1074 ± 5°C; bp 1794°C.

● **Samarkand** ▶ 39 40N 66 57E A city in E Uzbekistan. The principal industrial activities are cotton and silk manufacturing, winemaking, and metalworking but its interest lies chiefly in its past.
History: it was the chief junction of the ancient ▷Silk Road between China and the Mediterranean and, conquered by the Arabs in the 8th century, became the Abbasids' capital (9th–10th centuries) and a great Islamic centre. In the 14th century it became the capital of Timur's mighty empire, coming later under the rule of the Uzbek people (16th–19th centuries). The city's historic buildings include Timur's mausoleum. Population (1998 est): 388 000.

● **Samarra'** ▶ 34 13N 43 52E A city in central Iraq, N of Baghdad. It is a Shiite Muslim pilgrimage centre with a 17th-century mosque and many ruins dating from the 9th century, when Samarra' was the capital of the Abbasid caliphs (Islamic leaders). Population (latest est): 62 008.

● **Sami** ▷*See* Lapps.

● **samizdat** ▶ (Russian: self-publication) The underground system of distributing prohibited literature within the former Soviet Union. Literature circulated in this way, usually in the form of typewritten copies, included work by such writers as ▷Solzhenitsyn and ▷Sakharov.

● **Samoa, American** ▶ An unincorporated US territory in the S central Pacific, consisting of Tutuila and several smaller islands in the Samoan archipelago (*see* Samoa Islands). Agriculture is the main occupation; canned tuna is an important export. The E islands of the Samoa chain were annexed by the USA in 1899. Swain's Island, which lies some 336 km (210 mi) to the N, was added to American Samoa in 1925. An elected legislature with limited law-making powers was established under the constitutions of 1960 and 1967. Area: 197 sq km (76 sq mi). Population (2001 est): 58 000. Capital: Pago Pago.

● **Samoa, Independent State of** ▶ (name until 1997: Western Samoa) A country in the S central Pacific, consisting of the islands of Savai'i and Upolu and several smaller islands.
Economy: subsistence agriculture is the main occupation and exports include copra, bananas, and cocoa. The government has taken steps to encourage industry (principally food processing), fishing, and tourism.
History: following the division of the Samoa Islands in 1899, Western Samoa became a German protectorate. It was under New Zealand control from 1914 until 1962, when it became independent. The following year chief Susuga Malietoa Tanumafili II (1913–) became head of state for life. Universal adult suffrage was introduced in 1990. The Human Rights Protection Party under Tofilau Eti Alesana has played the leading role in government since 1996.

Independent State of Samoa

Head of state	Susuga Malietoa Tanumafili II
Official languages	Samoan and English
Official currency	tala (Samoan dollar) of 100 sene
Area	2842 sq km (1097 sq mi)
Population (2001 est)	179 000
Capital	Apia

● **Samoa Islands** ▶ A chain of volcanic islands in the S central Pacific Ocean. The islands are fringed with coral reefs and covered with evergreen rain forest; their unique ecology supports a number of species not found elsewhere. Discovered by the Dutch in the 18th century, the islands were politically divided in 1899 between the USA and Germany. The German islands subsequently became independent as Western Samoa, which changed its name to ▷Samoa in 1997. American Samoa, comprising the E islands of the chain, is an unincorporated US territory. Area: 2679 sq km (1034 sq mi).

● **Sámos** ▶ A Greek island in the SE Aegean Sea, lying close to the mainland of Turkey. Already one of the principal commercial centres of Greece by the 7th century BC, it achieved its greatest prosperity under the tyrant Polycrates in the 6th century. It is the birthplace of ▷Pythagoras. Area: 492 sq km (190 sq mi). Population (1991): 41 965.

● **Samothrace** ▶ (Modern Greek name: Samothráki) A Greek island in the N Aegean Sea. The statue of the Winged Victory (now in the Louvre) was discovered here in 1863. Area: 181 sq km (70 sq mi). Population (latest est): 4000.

● **Samoyed** ▶ (dog) A breed of dog developed in Siberia and used by the Samoyed tribesmen as a sledge dog. It is robustly built with husky-like features; the white or cream coat consists of a short soft undercoat and a long coarse outer coat. Height: 51–56 cm (dogs); 46–51 cm (bitches).

● **Samoyed** ▶ (people) A group of Siberian peoples of the tundra and N forest region of central Russia. They were traditionally nomadic reindeer hunters and fishers until settled by Soviet collectivization as reindeer breeders. ▷Shamanism dominates their religious life. Of the five Samoyed languages, which, with the ▷Finno-Ugric languages, comprise the ▷Uralic family, only Nenets (or Yurak) has a large number of speakers.

● **samphire** ▶ A perennial herb, *Crithmum maritimum*, native to rocky coasts of W Europe, also called rock samphire. Up to 30 cm high, it has small white or yellowish flowers, a succulent stem, and slender fleshy leaves, which are edible. Family: ▷*Umbelliferae*.
  The unrelated golden samphire (*Inula crithmoides*), native to coasts of Europe and W Asia, grows to 80 cm and has broader leaves and larger yellow flowers. Family: ▷*Compositae*. ▷*See also* glasswort (marsh samphire).

● **sampler** ▶ A sample piece of embroidery to provide a pattern or model for other work or an example of a needleworker's skill. Samplers dating back to the mid-17th century are well preserved in museums. From the 18th century it was common practice for children to embroider samplers showing the alphabet, biblical texts, or snatches of verse.

● **Sampras, Pete** ▶ (1971–) US tennis player, who was Wimbledon singles champion in 1993, 1994, 1995, 1997, 1998, 1999, and 2000. He has also won the US Open (1990, 1993, 1995, 1996).

● **Samson** ▶ In the Old Testament, an Israelite hero who led the resistance against the Philistines. He was deprived of his great strength when **Delilah**, his Philistine lover, had his long hair cut. Captured, blinded, and enslaved, he destroyed both his enemies and himself after his hair had regrown, by pulling down the Philistine temple at Gaza.

● **Samsun** ▶ 41 17N 36 22E A port in central N Turkey, on the Black Sea. It exports cereals, copper, and tobacco and has a university (1975). Population (1995 est): 330 360.

● **Samudra Gupta** ▶ (died c. 380 AD) Emperor of India (c. 330–c. 380) of the ▷Gupta dynasty and grandson of ▷Chandra Gupta I. He strove to expand and consolidate his empire, making many conquests, and kings of neighbouring dynasties paid him tribute.

● **Samuel** ▶ In the Old Testament, the first of the Hebrew prophets and the last of the "judges," who led the Israelites before the establishment of the monarchy in Palestine. The two **Books of Samuel** appear to be compiled from various sources. They are the principal written sources for the history of the Israelites in the 11th and 10th centuries BC and describe events in the reigns of ▷Saul and ▷David, whom Samuel anointed as the first two kings of Israel.

● **Samuel, Herbert Louis, 1st Viscount** ▶ (1870–1963) British politician. A Liberal MP from 1905, he was postmaster general (1910, 1915), high commissioner for Palestine (1920–25), and twice home secretary (1916, 1931). The president of the British Institute of Philos-

ophy, he published *Philosophy and the Ordinary Man* (1932) and *Belief and Action* (1937).

● **samurai** ▶ The provincial warriors (also known as *bushi; see* Bushido), who rose to power in Japan in the 11th century. The term originally referred to the armed retainers employed by court nobles from the late 8th century. The samurai mostly became the vassals of ▷*daimyo* and after 1600, when they comprised about 6% of the population, they were generally forced to reside in their lord's castle town. The samurai class was divided from other classes by its superior status and distinctions existed within its own ranks. After the Meiji restoration (1868) the samurai lost their status.

● **Sana'a** ▶ 15 23N 44 14E The capital of Yemen, in the west of the country. Until the formation of the state of Israel, there was a large Jewish ghetto in the city. Notable buildings include the Great Mosque, where there is a sacred Muslim shrine, and the Liberty Gate. A university was founded here in 1970. The city was damaged during the civil war in 1994. Population (1995): 972 000.

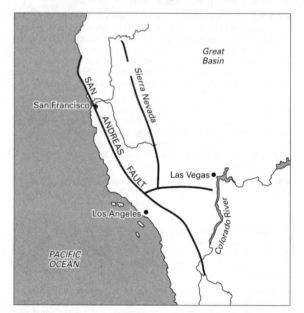

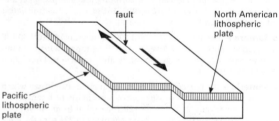

San Andreas Fault ▶ An example of a tear fault in which the rocks are being displaced horizontally.

● **San Andreas Fault** ▶ A fault in the earth's crust, 1200 km (750 mi) in length, running along the margin between the Pacific tectonic plate (*see* plate tectonics) and the North American plate in NW California. In 1906 a horizontal displacement between the plates of about 6 metres and a lateral displacement of 1 metre caused an earthquake that devastated San Francisco; in 1989 and 1994 earthquakes caused further damage to the city. The fault is named after San Andreas Lake, through which it passes.

● **San Antonio** ▶ 29 25N 98 30W A city in the USA, in Texas. Founded in 1718, it was the scene of the Mexican attack on the ▷Alamo (1836) during the Texan revolution. San Antonio has several military bases and is a commercial and industrial centre for a large agricultural region. The mild climate has attracted many tourists and retired people. Population (1996 est): 1 067 816.

● **San Bernardino** ▶ 34 07N 117 18W A city in the USA, in California. Situated in a fruit-growing area, it is the site of the annual National Orange Show but industrial developments in aerospace and steel are now the main economic activities. Population (1996 est): 183 474.

● **San Cristóbal** ▶ 7 46N 72 15W A city in W Venezuela. It is the commercial centre for an area producing maize, cassava, sugar cane, and coffee. Its university was founded in 1962. Population (1990 est): 230 000.

● **sanctions** ▶ Penalties imposed for breaking a law, especially international law. They were first imposed by the ▷League of Nations on Italy following its invasion of Ethiopia. Recent examples of economic sanctions are those imposed by Britain and other members of the UN against Rhodesia (now ▷Zimbabwe), following its unilateral declaration of independence in 1965; those against South Africa (1985–94); those against Iraq following its invasion of Kuwait in 1990 and subsequent failure to abide by UN peace terms; and those against Serbia following its involvement in the war in Bosnia-Hercegovina (1992–95) and subsequent policy in Kosovo (1998–   ).

● **sanctuary** ▶ The holiest part of a church or temple, where the main altar stands. During the middle ages criminals could claim right of sanctuary, i.e. they took refuge in a church and were thus immune from prosecution for 40 days, during which time they could opt to accept a safe conduct out of the country. In England this right was abolished for criminals in 1623 and for civil offenders in 1723.

● **sand** ▶ Unconsolidated grains of rock, varying in size from 0.06 to 2.00 mm in diameter. Consolidated sands form ▷sandstones; grits are coarse sandstones with angular grains. Most sands consist principally of quartz, derived from the weathering of quartz-bearing rocks. Sand is used in glass and cement production, and as an abrasive.

● **Sand, George** ▶ (Aurore Dupin, Baronne Dudevant; 1804–76) French novelist. In 1831 she left her husband and went to Paris to write her first novel, *Indiana* (1832), a plea for women's right to independence, the first of an enormous number of successful novels. Among her many lovers were Alfred de Musset and Frédéric Chopin.

● **Sandage, Allan Rex** ▶ (1926–   ) US astronomer, who in 1961 discovered the first ▷quasar, which he originally named a "quasi-stellar radio object" since it emitted radio waves. Using the 200-inch reflecting telescope at Mt Palomar, California, he went on to discover a number of other quasars, including some that were not radio sources.

● **sandalwood** ▶ An evergreen tree belonging to the genus *Santalum* (about 25 species), native to SE Asia and the Pacific Islands. The true sandalwood (*S. album*) grows to a height of about 10 m and is partially parasitic on the roots of other trees. Its white wood is used to make boxes and furniture and, when distilled, yields sweet-scented sandalwood oil, used in perfumes, incense, candles, etc. Family: *Santalaceae*.

● **sandarac** ▶ The ▷resin of a N African conifer, *Tetraclinis articulata*, used in making varnishes.

● **Sandburg, Carl** ▶ (1878–1967) US poet. His idiomatic free verse, especially in *The People, Yes* (1936), expressed hope for an ideal socialist society. His works include a biography of Abraham Lincoln in six volumes: *The Prairie Years* (two vols.; 1926) and *The War Years* (four vols.; 1939).

● **sand dollar** ▶ A marine invertebrate animal, also called cake urchin, belonging to an order (*Clypeastroida*) of ▷echinoderms. Its round flat rigid body is covered with small spines and saclike organs (tube feet). Sand dollars live on the sea bed and sift minute food particles from the sand in which they burrow. Class: ▷*Echinoidea*.

● **sand dune** ▶ The accumulation of wind-blown sand into a mound. Sand dunes are characteristic of desert areas where there is a plentiful sand supply and of coastal areas. They are unvegetated and two main forms occur in desert areas: the barchan, or crescent-shaped dune, and the seif, or longitudinal dune. In coastal areas dunes generally become "fixed" by vegetation.

● **sanderling** ▶ A bird, *Calidris alba*, that nests on Arctic coasts and winters on shores worldwide. 20 cm long, it has a rust-coloured upper plumage, changing to pale-brown in winter, and a long white wing stripe. It feeds on shrimps, sandhoppers, and molluscs with its straight slender bill. Family: *Scolopacidae* (sandpipers).

● **sand flea** ▷*See* sand hopper.

● **sandfly** ▶ A small fly belonging to the widely distributed genus *Phlebotomus*. Sandflies are among the worst pests of the tropics: the bloodsucking females can give a painful bite and several species are carriers of serious human diseases, including infections caused by the parasite *Leishmania* (*see* leishmaniasis).

The name has also been used for many bloodsucking ▷gnats and ▷midges of sandy places.

● **sandgrouse** ▶ A bird belonging to a family (*Pteroclidae*; 16 species) occurring in warm arid regions of Europe and Africa. 22–40 cm long, sandgrouse have camouflaging plumage, long pointed wings, short legs, feathered feet, and a very tough skin. They are gregarious and feed on plant material, flying long distances to water at dawn and dusk. Although resembling grouse, they belong to the order *Columbiformes* (pigeons).

● **sand hopper** ▶ A small terrestrial jumping ▷crustacean, also called beach hopper and sand or beach flea, belonging to the family *Talitridae*. Its body, 10–25 mm long, is laterally flattened and lacks a carapace. During the day it is buried in sand but at night it emerges to feed on organic debris under stones or among seaweed. Order: *Amphipoda*.

● **Sandhurst** ▶ 51 02N 0 34E A village in SE England, in Berkshire. The Royal Military Academy has been situated in the nearby town of Camberley since 1946, when the Royal Military College at Sandhurst (founded 1799) and the Royal Military Academy at Woolwich (1741) amalgamated. Population (1991): 19 153.

● **San Diego** ▶ 32 45N 117 10W A city in the USA, in California on San Diego Bay. It has a US naval base and large naval air service facilities. Employment is mainly dependent on the aircraft and aerospace industries. San Diego is also an important centre of scientific research and it is the site of the Scripps Institute of Oceanography (1903). Population (1996 est): 1 171 121.

● **Sandinista National Liberation Front** ▶ (Spanish: Frente Sandinista de Liberacion Nacional) A left-wing guerrilla movement and subsequently a political party in Nicaragua; it was formed in 1961, taking its name from the revolutionary martyr César Augusto Sandino (1898–1934). The Sandinista campaign attracted growing support from the landless peasantry and in 1976 escalated into all-out civil war. This ended with the overthrow of the corrupt Somoza regime in 1979 and the formation of a Sandinista government under Daniel ▷Ortega. In power the Sandinistas ended the worst abuses of the Somoza era and embarked on a radical programme of land distribution; however, their regime failed to find international recognition and was fatally undermined by right-wing Contra rebels backed by the USA. In the elections of 1990 the Sandinistas were defeated by a centre-right coalition led by Violeta Chamorro. They remain the chief opposition party and have retained considerable influence owing to their strength in the armed forces and trade unions.

● **sand lizard** ▶ A slender long-tailed European lizard, *Lacerta agilis*, occurring in sandy regions. Up to 20 cm long, it is pale-brown or grey with whitish underparts and three rows of white-centred dark spots along its back. It feeds on insects and spiders. Family: *Lacertidae*.

● **sandpiper** ▶ A wading bird belonging to a family (*Scolopacidae*; 82 species) occurring chiefly in the N hemisphere, breeding in northerly latitudes and migrating south to winter. 12–60 cm long, sandpipers typically have long legs, long wings, a mottled brown or grey plumage, which commonly changes colour seasonally, and a long slender bill. They nest in marshy regions or on mud flats and feed on small invertebrates. Order: *Charadriiformes* (gulls, plovers, etc.).

● **Sandringham** ▶ 52 49N 0 30E A village in E England, in Norfolk. The Sandringham estate was bought by Queen Victoria for the Prince of Wales (later Edward VII) in 1861. Sandringham House, a 19th-century Tudor-style building, remains a royal residence. It was the birthplace of George VI, who also died there. Population (latest est): 440.

● **Sand River Convention** ▶ (1852) An agreement between Great Britain and the Afrikaners of South Africa, which granted the Transvaal self-government. The **Bloemfontein Convention** (1854) gave autonomy to the Afrikaners of the Orange River Sovereignty, which became the Orange Free State.

● **sandstone** ▶ A sedimentary rock consisting of consolidated ▷sand, cemented mainly by calcareous, siliceous, or ferruginous minerals. They may be deposited by wind action in deserts or in shallow seas, estuaries and deltas, and along low-lying coasts by water. Sandstones vary in colour from red to yellow to white according to the presence of other minerals (feldspar, mica, glauconite, iron oxides, etc.) in addition to the quartz.

● **Sandwell** ▶ A unitary authority in W central England, in West Midlands. Area: 86 sq km (33 sq mi). Population (1999 est): 290 091.

● **Sandwich** ▶ 51 17N 1 20E A market town in SE England, on the River Stour near the coast of Kent. It was once an important Cinque Port, but the harbour silted up by the 16th century. Sandwich is a holiday and golfing resort. Population (1991): 4164.

● **Sandwich, John Montagu, 4th Earl of** ▶ (1718–92) British politician; first lord of the admiralty (1748–51, 1771–82). He was notorious for his part in the prosecution of his former friend ▷Wilkes and the inadequacy of the navy during the American Revolution was attributed to his corrupt practices. He gave his name to the sandwich, a snack devised to sustain him through round-the-clock gaming.

● **Sandwich Islands** ▷*See* Hawaii; South Sandwich Islands.

● **San Fernando** ▶ 10 16N 61 28W A port in Trinidad, on the Gulf of Taria. It is the centre of an area containing rich oilfields (discovered 1900). Population (1990): 30 100.

● **San Francisco** ▶ 37 40N 122 25W A city in the USA, in California situated on a peninsula between San Francisco Bay and the Pacific Ocean. A major seaport, San Francisco serves a large agricultural and mining area and is a financial and insurance centre. Industries include food processing, shipbuilding, and petroleum refining. Among its many famous landmarks are the San Francisco–Oakland Bay Bridge (1936), the Golden Gate Bridge (1937), Chinatown, and the city's cable cars. A major cultural and educational centre, it is the site of several universities and colleges.

History: founded by the Spanish in 1776, it was still a village when captured by the USA (1846) during the Mexican War. It expanded rapidly following the discovery of gold in California (1848) and it was during this period that the first Chinese settled in the city. In 1906 movement in the ▷San Andreas Fault led to devastation of the city by an earthquake and a three-day fire. A further earthquake in 1989 caused about 70 deaths. Population (2000): 776 733.

● **Sanger, Frederick** ▶ (1918–) British biochemist. Working at Cambridge, he had determined the order of ▷amino acids in insulin by 1955 and the sequence of ▷nucleotides in a strand of viral DNA by 1977. The latter involved synthesizing a new strand of DNA from a single strand of the DNA to be sequenced, and stopping the synthesis, in turn, at each of the four nucleotides (*see* gene sequencing). He was awarded Nobel Prizes in 1958 and 1980 and appointed to the OM in 1986.

● **sangha** ▶ The Buddhist monastic order. Together with the ▷Buddha and ▷dharma, it forms the third of the ▷tri-ratna of Buddhism. An individual may become a monk temporarily or for life.

● **Sanhedrin** ▶ The highest court of the Jews, which met in Jerusalem. Its development is unclear; in early New Testament times the Greeks allowed the establishment of a senate and later forms became known as the Sanhedrin. Its composition and its jurisdiction varied with its history. In New Testament times, the high priest was president and its functions were administrative, judicial, and religious.

● **sanicle** ▶ A perennial herb belonging to the widely distributed genus *Sanicula* (37 species). The common European sanicle (*S. europaea*) grows to a height of 50 cm and has several broad lobed leaves and clusters of small pinkish flowers. Family: ▷*Umbelliferae*.

● **San Ildefonso** ▶ (*or* La Granja) 40 53N 4 01W A town in central Spain. It has a magnificent royal palace built by Philip V of Spain (18th century); the palace chapel contains his tomb. Population (latest est): 4588.

● **San José** ▶ 37 20N 121 55W A city in the USA, in California on the S arm of San Francisco Bay. Founded in 1777, it was the first city in California and state capital (1849–51). Situated in the fertile Santa Clara Valley, it has many food-processing plants and wineries as well as aerospace and electronics industries. Population (2000): 894 943.

● **San José** ▶ 9 50N 84 02W The capital of Costa Rica, situated in the centre of the country in a high fertile valley. Founded in 1736, it became a centre of the tobacco trade and later of coffee production. The University of Costa Rica was founded in 1843. Population (2000 est): 344 349.

● **San Juan** ▶ 18 29N 66 08W The capital and main port of Puerto Rico, in the N. Founded by the Spanish in 1508, it was captured by the US navy in 1898. It expanded considerably in the 20th century and is now also an industrial and tourist centre. The chief exports are coffee, sugar, and tobacco. The Inter-American University of Puerto Rico was founded in 1912 and a campus of the University of Puerto Rico in 1950. Population (2000 est): 421 958.

● **San Juan** ▶ 31 33S 68 31W A city in W Argentina. Severely damaged by an earthquake (1944), it is the commercial centre of a wine-producing area. Domingo Sarmiento (1811–88), an educationalist and statesman, was born here. Population (1999 est): 120 000.

● **Sankara** ▶ (*or* Shankara; 8th century AD) Hindu philosopher. Sankara left his native Kerala to become a wandering holy man. It was popularly believed that he was an incarnation of ▷Shiva. He wrote commentaries on the *Brahmasutras*, the *Bhagavadgita*, and the *Upanishads* and founded the Smarta Brahmin sect and several monasteries. He made major contributions to the ▷Vedanta philosophical tradition, believing that the physical world relates to the ultimate reality as a state of ignorance does to knowledge.

● **San Lorenzo, Treaty of** ▷*See* Pinckney, Charles.

● **San Luis Potosí** ▶ 22 10N 101 00W A city in NE Mexico. It is the industrial centre for a rich agricultural and silver-mining area and has a fine baroque cathedral and a university (founded 1826). Population (1990): 525 819.

● **San Marino, Republic of** ▶ A small independent republic, an enclave in Italian territory, situated on the slopes of the Apennine mountain range, SW of Rimini.

Economy: farming, winemaking, tourism, and the sale of postage stamps are the main sources of income. Textiles and metal goods are manufactured. There is very high unemployment.

History: dating from the 4th century AD, it was an independent commune by the 12th century. In 1862 the newly established kingdom of Italy guaranteed San Marino's independence and established a customs union. Executive power lies in the Congress of State and two regents elected by the Great and General Council.

Republic of San Marino

Heads of state	two regents elected at six-monthly intervals
Official language	Italian
Official currency	euro of 100 cents; San Marino also issues its own coins
Area	61 sq km (24 sq mi)
Population (2001 est)	27 200
Capital	San Marino

● **San Martín, José de** ▶ (1778–1850) South American soldier and statesman; the national hero of Argentina. After participating in the struggle of Buenos Aires against the Spanish, he raised and trained an army in Argentina (1814–16), which he led heroically across the Andes, and, with Bernardo ▷O'Higgins, defeated the Spanish at Chacabuco (1817) and Maipo (1818), achieving the liberation of Chile. In 1821, after creating a Chilean navy, he entered Lima, proclaimed the independence of Peru, and became its "protector." He resigned in 1822, after differences with Bolívar, and retired to France.

● **San Miguel de Tucumán** ▶ (*or* Tucumán) 26 47S 65 15W A city in

NW Argentina, at the foot of the E Andes. It has a cathedral and a university (1914) and is an important sugar-refining centre. Population (1991): 473 014.

● **San Pedro Sula** ▶ 15 26N 88 01W A city in NW Honduras. It serves an agricultural area producing bananas and sugar cane and is the chief industrial centre of the country. Population (1995 est): 383 900.

● **San Remo** ▶ 43 48N 7 46E A port and resort in Italy, in Liguria near the French border. It has a 12th-century romanesque cathedral. There is a market in flowers and fruit. Population (latest est): 60 800.

● **San Salvador** ▶ 13 59N 89 18W The capital of El Salvador, situated in the centre of the country. Founded by the Spanish in 1525, it was capital of the Central American Federation from 1831 until 1838, becoming capital of El Salvador in 1839. It has suffered several severe earthquakes. Industries include textiles and food processing. The University of El Salvador was founded in 1841. In 1989 over 1000 people died in fighting between government forces and rebels when the latter occupied parts of the city. Population (1992): 422 570.

● **San Salvador Island** ▶ (former name: Watling Island) 24 00N 74 32W A West Indian island in the central Bahamas. It was Columbus' first sight of land (1492) in the New World. Area: 156 sq km (60 sq mi). Population (1990): 465.

● **sans-culottes** ▶ (French: without knee breeches) The violent extremists of the French Revolution, so called because they wore trousers rather than the knee breeches of the aristocracy. The original sans-culottes were the Paris workers who stormed the Bastille and led the food riots in 1789. Later radical extremists, such as Marat and Danton, were also called sans-culottes.

● **San Sebastián** ▶ 43 19N 1 59W A seaside resort in N Spain, in the Basque Provinces on the Bay of Biscay. It possesses a cathedral and a palace. The La Concha beaches attract many tourists. Population (1991): 169 933.

● **Sansevieria** ▶ A genus of herbaceous perennial plants (60 species) native to tropical and S Africa and S Asia. They have a basal rosette of stiff swordlike leaves arising from thick creeping underground stems (rhizomes). *S. trifasciata* var. *laurentii* (mother-in-law's tongue) is a popular house plant with ornamental leaves, striped green and yellow, up to 90 cm long. The leaves of several species (e.g. *S. zeylanica*) yield a fibre (bowstring hemp) used for ropes, mats, etc. Family: ▷*Liliaceae*.

● **Sanskrit** ▶ The classical literary language of the Hindu scriptures, belonging to the ▷Indo-Aryan family. From it the ▷Prakrits and modern N Indian languages developed. It was spoken in NW India from 1500 BC, became a scholarly language when the grammarian ▷Panini standardized it (5th century BC), and is still used as a sacred language. It is highly complex and is written in the ▷Devanagari script.

● **Sansovino, Jacopo** ▶ (Jacopo Tatti; 1486–1570) Florentine sculptor and architect. His work shows the influence of classical Roman architecture, ▷Michelangelo, and his teacher Andrea Sansovino (c. 1467–1529), whose name he took. He was active in Florence (1511–17) and then in Rome (1517–27), where his work includes the *Madonna del parto* in S Agostino. From 1527 he introduced the High Renaissance style to Venice, serving as the city's chief architect until his death. His major Venetian works include the library of St Mark's Cathedral (from 1537), the bronze doors for the cathedral sacristy (from 1546), and the gigantic statues of *Neptune* and *Mars* in the Doge's Palace (from 1554).

● **San Stefano, Treaty of** ▶ (1878) The treaty that concluded the war between the Ottoman Empire and Russia (1877–78). The defeated Ottomans recognized the independence of Serbia, Romania, and Montenegro and the autonomy of Bosnia-Hercegovina and Bulgaria. At the Congress of ▷Berlin (1878), the other great powers, fearing that the Balkans would fall under the dominance of Russia, modified the treaty.

● **Santa Ana** ▶ 14 00N 79 31W The second largest city in El Salvador. It is a major coffee centre and has one of the largest coffee mills in the world. Population (1992): 202 337.

● **Santa Anna, Antonio López de** ▶ (1794–1876) Mexican soldier and statesman; president (1833–36) and dictator (1839, 1841–45).

After engineering ▷Itúrbide's downfall in 1823, Santa Anna dominated Mexican politics for the next 20 years. He is best known for his defeat of Texan forces at the ▷Alamo (1836). Subsequently taken prisoner by the Americans, he was forced to retire but twice returned to power before being driven into exile (1845–74).

● **Santa Clara** ▶ 22 25N 79 58W A city in central Cuba. It is the commercial centre for an agricultural area producing sugar and tobacco. Population (1994 est): 205 400.

● **Santa Claus** ▷*See* Nicholas, St.

● **Santa Cruz** ▷*See* St Croix.

● **Santa Cruz** ▶ 17 45S 63 14W A city in SE Bolivia. It is the commercial centre for an area producing chiefly sugar cane, rice, and coffee. Industries include the manufacture of cigarettes and sugar refining. It is the site of a university (1880). Population (1993 est): 767 260.

● **Santa Cruz de Tenerife** ▶ 28 28N 16 15W A city in the Canary Islands, in NE Tenerife. An uprising that began the Spanish Civil War took place here (1936). It is a major fuelling station with an oil refinery. Population (1995 est): 204 948.

● **Santa Fe** ▶ 35 41N 105 57W A city and resort in the USA, the capital of New Mexico on the Santa Fe River. Following Mexico's attainment of independence from Spain in 1821, Santa Fe developed a commercial route (the **Santa Fe Trail**) with the USA. Population (1994 est): 62 514.

● **Santa Fé** ▶ 31 38S 60 43W A port in E Argentina, the furthest point accessible to oceangoing vessels on the Río Paraná. Founded in 1573, it has a cathedral (1685) and a university (1919) and is the centre of a grain-growing and stock-rearing area. Population (1991): 442 214.

● **Santa Isabel** ▷*See* Malabo.

● **Santa Marta** ▶ 11 18N 74 10W A port in N Colombia, on the Caribbean Sea. The chief exports are bananas, coffee, and cocoa. Simón ▷Bolívar, leader of the South American independence movement, died here (1830). Population (1997 est): 343 038.

● **Santander** ▶ 43 28N 3 48W A city and port in N Spain, in Old Castile on Cape Mayor. Part of the city was rebuilt after being burnt in 1941. It possesses a gothic cathedral. Its industries include fishing and shipbuilding. Population (1995 est): 194 837.

● **Santayana, George** ▶ (1863–1952) Spanish-born US philosopher and poet. He taught at Harvard (1889–1911) and then moved to Oxford before eventually settling in Rome (1924). He believed that the mind was largely governed by physical and biological considerations, a view set out in *Realms of Being* (1927–40). His witty and urbane works include *The Sense of Beauty* (1896), *The Life of Reason* (1905–06), *Scepticism and Animal Faith* (1923), and *The Last Puritan* (1935).

● **Santer, Jacques** ▶ (1937–   ) Luxembourg politician. A former prime minister of Luxembourg (1984–95), he was subsequently president of the European Commission (1994–99). He resigned in March, 1999, following a critical report that detailed corruption and mismanagement in the Commission.

● **Santiago** ▶ (or Santiago de Chile) 33 35S 70 40W The capital of Chile, situated in the centre of the country at the foot of the Andes. It was founded by the Spanish in 1541. About half of Chile's industry is centred here, including food processing, textiles, and metallurgy. There are three universities. Population (1995 est): 5 076 808.

● **Santiago de Compostela** ▶ 42 52N 8 33W A city in NW Spain, in Galicia. Since the 9th century AD it has been a famous place of pilgrimage reputedly containing the tomb of St James, the patron saint of Spain. Its romanesque cathedral (1078–1211) was built on the site of the tomb. The university was founded in 1532. Population (1991): 87 472.

● **Santiago de Cuba** ▶ 20 00N 75 49W A port in Cuba, on the Caribbean Sea. It was the scene of Fidel ▷Castro's 26 July revolt (1953). Exports include metal ores, sugar, coffee, and tobacco. It is the site of the University of Oriente (1947) and has a large cathedral. Population (1994 est): 440 084.

● **Santiago de Guayaquil** ▷*See* Guayaquil.

● **Santiago del Estero** ▸ 27 48S 64 15W A city in N Argentina. It is a commercial centre serving an agricultural area producing wheat, cotton, maize, and livestock. The chief industry is food processing. Population (1999 est): 202 876.

● **Santiago de los Caballeros** ▸ 19 30N 70 42W A city in the N Dominican Republic. The commercial centre for a fertile agricultural region, its industries include the manufacture of cigarettes, pharmaceuticals, and furniture. Population (1993 est): 690 000.

● **Santo Domingo** ▸ 18 32N 69 50W The capital of the Dominican Republic, a port on the S coast. Founded by Bartolomeo Columbus in 1496, it became the capital of the first Spanish colony in the Americas. It was under French rule (1795–1809), and later under that of Haiti, becoming capital of the new Dominican Republic in 1844. During the rule of the dictator ▷Trujillo, it was known for a time (1936–61) as Ciudad Trujillo. It is the site of the first cathedral (1521) and the first university (1538) in the New World. A second university was established in 1966. Population (1993): 1 555 656.

● **Santoríni** ▷*See* Thera.

● **Santos** ▸ 23 56S 46 22W A city in SE Brazil, in São Paulo state on the Atlantic Ocean. It is the leading coffee port of the world. Population (2000): 415 553.

● **São Luís** ▸ 2 34S 44 16W A port in N Brazil, the capital of Maranhão state. The chief exports are babaçu palm products, cotton, sugar, and balsam. It is the site of the University of Maranhão (1966). Population (2000): 834 968 (metropolitan area).

● **Saône, River** ▸ A river in E France, rising in Lorraine and flowing mainly S to join the River Rhône at Lyons. It is linked by canal to the Rivers Moselle, Rhine, Loire, Seine, and Meuse. Length: 480 km (298 mi).

● **São Paulo** ▸ 23 33S 46 39W The largest city in Brazil, the capital of São Paulo state. Founded in 1554, it grew rapidly after 1880 with the development of coffee plantations. Coffee remains important but there has been considerable diversification of industry and it is now the fastest-growing city in Brazil. Industries include food processing and the manufacture of textiles, electrical appliances, and chemicals. It has several universities, including the University of São Paulo (1934). It also contains the Butantan Institute, a scientific research establishment with a famous snake farm. Population (2000): 9 785 640.

● **São Tomé and Príncipe, Democratic Republic of** ▸ A small island country off the coast of West Africa, in the Gulf of Guinea. An archipelago, it comprises the two main islands with coastal plains rising to volcanic mountains in their interiors, together with the islets of Pedras Tinhosas and Rolas. Most of the population is descended from African slaves and southern Europeans, with comparatively recent influxes from Mozambique and Angola.

Economy: chiefly agricultural, the main crops being cocoa, copra (which is the main export), palm oil and kernels, and coffee. Rice is being developed and livestock is also important. Tourism is a major source of revenue.

History: discovered by the Portuguese in 1471, the islands came under Portuguese rule in 1522. They became an overseas province in 1951 and gained independence in 1975. A multiparty constitution was adopted in 1990 and the following year an independent, Miguel Trovoada, was elected president. The 1990s saw an ongoing power struggle between parliament and President Trovoada; Fradique de Menezes was elected president in 2001.

Democratic Republic of São Tomé and Príncipe

Head of state	President Fradique de Menezes
Official language	Portuguese
Official currency	dobra of 100 cêntimos
Area	964 sq km (372 sq mi)
Population (2001 est)	147 000
Capital and main port	São Tomé

● **sap** ▸ The fluid found in the vascular (conducting) system of plants. It consists of water and minerals, absorbed from the soil and transported through the plant in the ▷xylem, and sugars, made in the leaves and distributed in the ▷phloem.

● **Sapir, Edward** ▸ (1884–1939) US linguist and anthropologist, born in Germany. Much of his work was done on American-Indian languages and cultures. His book *Language* (1921) is notably lucid. He was interested in all aspects of communication and in the role played by language in determining the personality of the individual in relation to society. ▷*See also* Whorf, Benjamin Lee.

● **sapodilla** ▸ An evergreen tree, *Achras sapota*, native to Central America but cultivated elsewhere in the tropics. Up to 20 m tall, it produces edible brown rounded fruits, up to 10 cm across, with a juicy pulp surrounding black seeds. It tastes of pears and brown sugar. Milky latex from the bark is a source of chicle gum, used in chewing gum. Family: *Sapotaceae*.

● **saponins** ▸ Plant glycosides (sugar compounds) that form lathery emulsions in water. The saponins are extremely potent in destroying red blood cells. They are used as foam producers in fire extinguishers and as emulsifiers, ▷detergents, etc.

● **sappan** ▸ A tree, *Caesalpinia sappan*, native to SE Asia. The wood (sappanwood) is used in making furniture and yields a red dye. An extract of the bark produces a black dye when mixed with iron salts. Family: ▷*Leguminosae*.

● **Sapper** ▸ (H(erman) C(yril) McNeile; 1888–1937) British novelist. After distinguished service in World War I he achieved literary success with his popular thriller *Bulldog Drummond* (1920), about an adventure-seeking ex-officer, and its sequels.

● **sapphire** ▸ A transparent variety of ▷corundum that may be any colour except red (*see* ruby) due to traces of iron and titanium. It is used as a gemstone and in record-player styluses. Sapphires occur in igneous and metamorphic rocks but most are obtained from detrital gravels. Many sapphires come from Sri Lanka, Kashmir, Myanmar (Burma), East Africa, the USA, and Australia. Artificial sapphires are manufactured from ammonium alum. Birthstone for September.

● **Sappho** ▸ (c. 612–c. 580 BC) Greek poet. She and her contemporary ▷Alcaeus pioneered the form of the brief subjective lyric. Her passionate poetry, which has survived in fragments, was written for her group of female admirers on the island of Lesbos (from which the term "lesbianism" is derived). She appears to have been married and had one child; according to a romantic and unreliable legend, she committed suicide by throwing herself from a rock off the coast of Epirus because of an unhappy love affair.

● **Sapporo** ▸ 43 5N 141 21E A city in Japan, in SW Hokkaido. It is the island's main administrative and educational centre; Hokkaido University was established in 1918. It is also a ski resort famed for its annual festival of snow sculpture and was the site of the 1972 winter Olympics. Industries include flour and timber milling, printing, and machinery manufacture. Population (1995): 1 756 968.

● **saprotroph** ▸ (*or* saprophyte) An organism that obtains its energy by feeding on dead or decaying tissue. Bacteria and fungi are important saprotrophs, using enzymes to break down organic material and release nutrients into the soil, which can be used by plants (*see* decomposition).

● **Saqqarah** ▸ A mortuary area near ancient ▷Memphis. The most famous monument here is the stone-built Step Pyramid, designed (c. 2630 BC) for Pharaoh ▷Djoser by ▷Imhotep. It is architecturally the forerunner of the Giza ▷pyramids. The bulls sacred to ▷Apis were buried in the Sarapeum.

● **Saracens** ▸ Before Islam, the term used by the non-Arab peoples of the Middle East to refer to the Arabs. After the establishment of Islam, Saracen was usually synonymous with Muslim. The origin of the word is unknown.

● **Saragossa** ▷*See* Zaragoza.

● **Sarah** ▷*See* Abraham.

● **Sarajevo** ▸ 43 52N 18 26E The capital of Bosnia-Hercegovina. Formerly a centre of resistance to Austrian domination, it was here that the heir apparent to the Dual Monarchy of Austria-Hungary, ▷Francis

Ferdinand, was assassinated (28 June, 1914), precipitating World War I. In 1992 fierce fighting broke out in the city between Bosnian Serbs and Muslims following the republic's declaration of independence from Yugoslavia. From April 1992 Sarajevo was besieged and bombarded by Bosnian Serb forces; their grip on the city was finally broken by NATO airstrikes on their positions in 1995. Following the signing of the Bosnian peace accord in Dec 1995, Sarajevo was reunited under Bosnian government control. Sarajevo has two cathedrals, several mosques, and a university (1946). An industrial centre, it manufactures carpets, pottery, sugar, and beer. Population (1991): 525 980.

● **Saramago, José** ▶ (1922–) Portuguese novelist and writer. His earlier publications were poetry and essays but he first found international success with the love story *Baltasar and Blimunda* (1982). Subsequent novels have included *The Year of the Death of Ricardo Reis* (1984) and *The Gospel According to Jesus Christ* (1991). He was awarded the Nobel Prize in 1997.

● **Saransk** ▶ 54 12N 45 10E A city in W central Russia, the capital of the Mordvinian Republic. It is an industrial centre, producing machinery, electrical goods, and food. Population (1995 est): 320 000.

● **Saratoga, Battles of** ▶ (19 September and 7 October, 1777) Two battles fought near Saratoga, New York, which formed the turning point of the ▷American Revolution. The first saw the defeat of the British attempt to open a route to Albany. The second ended with the surrender of Gen Burgoyne to the Americans. The outcome of the battles helped persuade the French to recognize and support the USA.

● **Saratov** ▶ 51 30N 45 55E A city in W Russia, on the River Volga. Baku oil is transported from here and a natural-gas pipeline supplies Moscow. Other industrial activities include ship repairing and the manufacture of precision instruments. Population (1993 est): 904 000.

Saqqarah ▶ The Step Pyramid. At the time of its construction in about 2630 BC, it was the largest stone structure ever built.

● **Sarawak** ▶ A state in Malaysia, in NW ▷Borneo on the South China Sea. It has a mountainous forested interior with a swampy coastal plain, where rubber, pepper, sago, and rice are grown. Oil production is of prime importance; crude oil, petroleum products, timber, and pepper are the chief exports.
    History: it was given in 1841 by the sultan of Brunei to the Englishman James Brooke, who as "white rajah" tried to suppress piracy and headhunting. Although it became a British protectorate in 1888, it was ruled by the Brooke family until World War II, when it was occupied by the Japanese. Ceded to Britain in 1946, it joined Malaysia in 1963. Area: 124 970 sq km (48 250 sq mi). Population (1991): 1 648 217. Capital: Kuching.

● **sarcoma** ▷*See* cancer.

● **sarcophagus** ▶ A stone or terracotta coffin, often elaborately dec-

orated with ritual motifs. Sarcophagi evolved in ancient Egypt to protect mummies, and Minoan, Greek, Roman, and early Christian examples survive.

● **sardine** ▶ A young ▷pilchard or any of several species of food fish of the family *Clupeidae*, especially members of the genera *Sardina*, *Sardinops*, and *Sardinella*. They are tinned in oil, an industry centred on Portugal and Spain.

● **Sardinia** ▶ (Italian name: Sardegna) The second largest island in the Mediterranean Sea, comprising an autonomous region of Italy. It is largely mountainous. Agriculture is important, especially on the fertile Campidano (a broad alluvial plain in the SW) where cereals, vines, and olives are cultivated. Sheep are raised on the hills. Its major industry is mineral production, especially lead, zinc, coal, fluorspar, and sea salt. Modern industries, especially petrochemicals, chemicals, and food processing, are being developed. Tourism is a growing source of revenue.
    History: first settled by the Phoenicians, it was ceded to Savoy by Austria (1720) in exchange for Sicily and formed the kingdom of Sardinia with Piedmont, which formed the basis of a unified Italy. Area: 23 813 sq km (9194 sq mi). Population (1994 est): 1 657 375. Capital: Cagliari.

● **Sardis** ▶ 38 28N 28 02E The capital of ancient Lydia, 56 km (35 mi) NE of present-day Izmir (Turkey), famous for its coinage and craftwork. After Persia conquered Lydia, overthrowing Croesus about 550 BC, its strategic position made Sardis Asia Minor's political centre until Hellenistic times.

● **sardonyx** ▷*See* onyx.

● **Sardou, Victorien** ▶ (1831–1908) French dramatist. His many successful comedies and historical dramas include *Les Pattes de mouche* (1860) and *Tosca* (1887), a melodrama on which Puccini's opera is based. Sarah Bernhardt acted in many of his plays.

● **Sargasso Sea** ▶ An elliptical section of the N Atlantic Ocean between latitudes 20°N and 35°N and longitudes 30°W and 70°W. Contained within a current system, it is still and warm. It takes its name from the floating brown seaweed of the genus *Sargassum* (gulfweed), found in it.

● **Sargent, John Singer** ▶ (1856–1925) US portrait painter, born in Florence. Working in Paris, London, and the USA, he achieved success with his portraits of such celebrities as Ellen Terry, R. L. Stevenson, and John D. Rockefeller. In watercolour, he produced remarkable landscape studies of World War I.

● **Sargent, Sir Malcolm** ▶ (1895–1967) British conductor. A notable organist, he first conducted in 1921 at the London Promenade Concerts, of which he was chief conductor from 1948 to 1967. He was also conductor of the BBC Symphony Orchestra (1950–57).

● **Sargon II** ▶ (d. 705 BC) King of Assyria (722–705). Perhaps a usurper (Sargon means "legitimate king"), he deliberately named himself after the legendary ▷Sargon of Akkad. He was constantly occupied in warfare to maintain Assyrian power in Elam, Urartu, Babylonia, Syria, and Palestine, where he captured and depopulated Samaria. He was succeeded by ▷Sennacherib.

● **Sargon of Akkad** ▶ The semilegendary Semitic ruler (c. 2334–c. 2279 BC) of territories extending from the Mediterranean to the Persian Gulf. According to tradition, he was brought up by a gardener, who retrieved his cradle adrift in the River Euphrates. After usurping kingly power, he founded ▷Akkad and an empire that lasted a century.

● **Sark** ▶ (French name: Sercq) 49 26N 2 22W The smallest of the four main Channel Islands. It consists of Great Sark and Little Sark, connected by a narrow isthmus, the Coupée. It is governed by a hereditary seigneur or dame in a semifeudal system. Cars are prohibited here. Area: 5 sq km (2 sq mi). Population (1991): 575.

● **Sarnia** ▶ 42 57N 82 24W A city and port in E Canada, in SW Ontario at the S end of Lake Huron. With the discovery of local oil (1858) and the completion of the oil pipeline from Alberta, it grew into a major refining and petrochemical centre. Steel and salt are also important. Population (1991): 74 167.

● **Saronic Gulf** ► (*or* Gulf of Aegina) An inlet of the W Aegean Sea between the Attic Peninsula (on which lie Athens and its port Piraeus) and the Peloponnese. It contains the island of Salamis.

● **saros** ► The period of about 18 years (6585.3 days) at which ▷eclipses of the sun and moon repeat in the same order and with nearly the same time intervals.

● **Saroyan, William** ► (1908–81) US dramatist and fiction writer. *The Daring Young Man on the Flying Trapeze* (1934) was his first success. His other works include the plays *The Time of Your Life* (1939) and *My Heart's in the Highlands* (1939), a novel, *The Human Comedy* (1943), and the autobiographical *My Name is Aram* (1940) and *Obituaries* (1979).

● **Sarraute, Nathalie** ► (1902–99) French novelist, born in Russia. She practised as a lawyer until 1939. Her work includes *Tropismes* (1939), a collection of sketches analysing human behaviour in great psychological detail, *Le Planétarium* (1959), *Les Fruits d'or* (1963), *C'est Beau* (1973), and *Tu ne t'aimes pas* (1989). She was a leading exponent of the ▷*nouveau roman*; *L'Ère du soupçon* (1956) is a collection of essays on the novel.

● **sarsaparilla** ► An extract of the roots of several perennial climbing or trailing vines of the genus ▷*Smilax*, especially *S. aristolochiaefolia*, cultivated in Central and South America. The roots are harvested and dried for use as a tonic and as flavouring for medicines and beverages. Family: *Smilacaceae*.

● **Sartre, Jean-Paul** ► (1905–80) French philosopher, novelist, dramatist, and critic. After World War II, during which he was an active member of the resistance, he founded the journal *Les Temps modernes* and became a leading public exponent of ▷existentialism. His major works of philosophy include *Being and Nothingness* (1943) and *Critique de la raison dialectique* (1960). His novels include *Nausea* (1938) and the trilogy *The Roads to Freedom* (1945–49). Among his several plays are *The Flies* (1943), *In Camera* (1944), *The Respectable Prostitute* (1946), and *Lucifer and the Lord* (1951). He also wrote literary criticism and autobiographical works. In 1964 he refused the Nobel Prize. He had a close association with Simone de ▷Beauvoir, whom he met while a student. He was an adherent of Marxism and supported left-wing groups.

● **Sarum** ▷*See* Salisbury.

● **SAS** ▷*See* Special Air Service.

● **Sasanians** ► (*or* Sassanids) The dynasty that ruled Persia from 224 AD until overthrown by the Arabs about 636. Ardashir I (reigned 224–41) founded the dynasty (named after his grandfather Sasan), overthrowing the Parthian empire (*see* Parthia) and seizing its capital ▷Ctesiphon. His most notable successors were ▷Shapur II (reigned 309–79), ▷Khosrow I (reigned 531–79), and ▷Khosrow II (reigned 590–628). The Sasanian empire, which at its greatest extent stretched from Syria to India, saw the establishment of Zoroastrianism as the state religion and a resurgence of art and architecture (*see* Persian art and architecture).

● **Sasebo** ► 33 10N 129 42E A port in Japan, in W Kyushu on the East China Sea. It was a village until the late 19th century, when it became a naval base. Sasebo's main industries are shipbuilding and engineering. Population (1995): 244 879.

● **Saskatchewan** ► A province of W Canada, on the Great Plains. The N is covered by forest, mostly noncommercial, with lakes and swamps. The S is open prairie, now chiefly comprising large highly mechanized farms, and is one of the world's most important wheatlands; the province normally produces about two-thirds of Canada's wheat. There are highly developed marketing cooperatives, begun in the early 20th century. Saskatchewan is rich in minerals, including uranium, oil, natural gas, potash, zinc, and copper; associated industries are important.
  History: explored in the 17th and 18th centuries, Saskatchewan was first exploited for furs. Agricultural settlement began slowly (1870s) but sped up in the decade before 1914. The area became a province in 1905 and was the first part of North America to elect a socialist government (1944–64, 1971–82). Area: 570 269 sq km (220 181 sq mi). Population (1997 est): 1 023 500. Capital: Regina.

● **Saskatchewan River** ► A river in W Canada, rising in two separate branches in the Rocky Mountains and flowing generally E through prairie grainlands to unite in central Saskatchewan. The river then continues to Lake Winnipeg. Length: 1940 km (1205 mi).

● **Saskatoon** ► 52 10N 106 40W A city in W Canada, in central Saskatchewan. Founded in 1883, it is the distribution centre of a vast grain area, with numerous agricultural industries. Other industries include potash, metals, clothing, and chemicals. Saskatoon houses the University of Saskatchewan (1907). Population (1991): 186 058.

● **sassafras** ► A tree, *Sassafras albidum*, native to North America. Up to 20 m high, it bears clusters of yellow flowers and dark-blue berries. The aromatic roots are dried for use in medicines and also yield oil of sassafras, which is used in perfumes and as flavouring for beverages. Family: *Lauraceae*.

● **Sassanids** ▷*See* Sasanians.

● **Sassari** ► 40 43N 8 34E A town in Italy, near the N coast of Sardinia. It has a cathedral (12th–18th centuries) and a university (1562). It is the agricultural trading centre of N Sardinia. Population (1996 est): 121 639.

● **Sassetta** ► (Stefano di Giovanni; c. 1392–c. 1450) A leading painter of the Sienese school. Some of his work reflects his admiration of Florentine art, for example *Madonna of the Snow*, painted for Siena Cathedral (Contini Bonacossi collection, Florence); his later work, however, typifies the ▷international gothic style. He painted many altarpieces, for example a now dismembered altarpiece, originally painted for the church of S Francesco in Sansepolcro, notable for its scenes from the life of St Francis of Assisi.

● **Sassoon, Siegfried** ► (1886–1967) British poet and writer. In 1917 his disgust with World War I led him to make a public refusal to continue serving; having been seriously wounded, he was sent to a military hospital where he met Wilfred ▷Owen. His antiwar poetry appeared in *The Old Huntsman* (1917) and *Counterattack* (1918), and he wrote several volumes of war memoirs as well as *The Memoirs of a Foxhunting Man* (1928), a semiautobiographical record of his love for the English countryside.

● **Satan** ▷*See* Devil.

● **satanism** ► Worship of the forces of evil. Formerly a synonym for atheism or certain heresies, the term now generally applies to beliefs and practices, such as the ▷black mass, that parody Christian equivalents. Evolving in this form in late-19th-century France, satanism is usually a blend of magic, religion, and bizarre sexual practices. Aleister Crowley (1875–1947) was a notorious modern exponent.

● **satellite** ► **1.** A celestial body orbiting a ▷planet. The planets of the solar system have at least 50 known satellites, ranging greatly in size. The rings of Saturn, Uranus, and Jupiter may also be regarded as satellites. Mercury and Venus have no satellites. The earth's satellite is the ▷moon. The two small heavily cratered Martian satellites, Phobos and Deimos, have been extensively studied by Mariner and Viking planetary probes. Saturn has at least 23 satellites, the largest, Titan, having a nitrogen atmosphere. The largest of Neptune's satellites, Triton and Nereid, were photographed in 1989 by ▷Voyager 2. **2.** A spacecraft that is launched into orbit around the earth or enters an orbit around some other solar-system body. It may be a ▷communications satellite, retransmitting radio signals from one location on earth to another. Alternatively, its instruments may gather information from earth or from other celestial objects and transmit it, by radio signals, to ground-based receiving stations. This information is used in weather forecasting, ▷navigation, scientific research, and for military purposes. Since the late 1980s several satellites have been launched to monitor damage to the ▷ozone layer. ▷*See also* Global Positioning System.

● **satellite broadcasting** ▷*See* communications satellite; television.

● **satisficing behaviour** ► In economics, behaviour by a firm that is aimed at achieving satisfactory profits and satisfactory growth rather than maximum profits. This is often a more rational approach than always seeking optimum profitability. For example, in pricing a product, maximum profits would be obtained by asking the highest price the market would stand without loss of sales to a competitor.

Planetary satellites

planet & satellite	diameter (km)	distance from primary (1000 km)	year of discovery
EARTH			
Moon	3476	384.40	—
MARS			
Phobos	22	9.38	1877
Deimos	13	23.46	1877
JUPITER			
Metis	40	128	1979
Adrastea	20	129	1979
Amalthea	190	181	1892
Thebe	100	222	1979
Io	3630	422	1610
Europa	3138	671	1610
Ganymede	5262	1070	1610
Callisto	4800	1883	1610
Leda	16	11 094	1974
Himalia	185	11 480	1904
Lysithea	36	11 720	1938
Elara	76	11 737	1905
Ananke	30	21 200	1951
Carme	40	22 600	1938
Pasiphae	50	23 500	1908
Sinope	36	23 700	1914
SATURN			
Pan	20	134	1991
Atlas	30	138	1980
Prometheus	105	139	1980
Pandora	90	142	1980
Janus	90	151	1966
Epimetheus	120	151	1966
Mimas	390	186	1789
Enceladus	500	238	1789
Tethys	1050	295	1684
Telesto	30	295	1980
Calypso	25	295	1980
Dione	1120	377	1684
Helene	30	377	1980
Rhea	1530	527	1672
Titan	5150	1222	1655
Hyperion	290	1481	1848
Iapetus	1440	3561	1671
Phoebe	220	12 952	1898
URANUS			
Cordelia	26	50	1986
Ophelia	30	54	1986
Bianca	42	59	1986
Cressida	62	62	1986
Desdemona	54	63	1986
Juliet	84	64	1986
Portia	108	66	1986
Rosalind	54	70	1986
Belinda	66	75	1986
Puck	154	86	1985
Miranda	472	129	1948
Ariel	1158	191	1851
Umbriel	1172	266	1851
Titania	1580	436	1787
Oberon	1524	584	1787
NEPTUNE			
Naiad	54	48	1989
Thalassa	80	50	1989
Despina	150	53	1989
Galatea	160	62	1989
Larissa	200	74	1989
Proteus	420	118	1989
Triton	2700	354	1846
Nereid	340	5511	1949
PLUTO			
Charon	1186	19	1978

However, this information is never available and the aim of maximum profitability might result in a price that is too high for the market. A more intelligent approach would be to set a price that gives satisfactory profits and growth, with the possibility of edging it upwards as the market develops, carefully watching the effect on sales resulting after each incremental increase has been made.

● **Satie, Erik** ▶ (1866–1925) French composer. He studied briefly at the Paris conservatoire and, aged 39, at the Schola Cantorum with Roussel and d'Indy. Satie was known for his eccentricity and influenced such composers as Milhaud and Poulenc. His works include the ballet *Parade* (1916), piano pieces, including *Trois Gymnopédies* (1888), *Pièces froides* (1897), and *Trois morceaux en forme de poire* (1903).

● **satinwood** ▶ A tree, *Chloroxylon swietenia*, native to S India and Sri Lanka. Its wood is valued in cabinetmaking for its fine golden-yellow finish; it was used in particular by Thomas ▷Sheraton. The wood of certain West Indian species is also known as satinwood. Family: *Meliaceae*.

● **satire** ▶ A literary or dramatic work that ridicules human or social pretensions. Among the earliest satirists were the Roman poets ▷Juvenal and ▷Horace. In Europe satire became a dominant literary form during the late-17th and 18th centuries through ▷Dryden, ▷Pope, and ▷Swift in England and ▷Voltaire in France. During the 19th century ▷Byron continued the tradition of verse satire, but prose fiction became the usual medium, as in the works of Samuel ▷Butler. In the 20th century novelists have been the dominant practitioners, for example Evelyn ▷Waugh in England and Joseph ▷Heller in the USA. The English magazine *Private Eye* (founded 1962) is an example of political satire in journalism.

● **satsuma** ▷*See* tangerine.

● **Saturn** ▶ (astronomy) The second largest planet, orbiting the sun every 29.5 years at a mean distance of 1427 million km. It is the most oblate planet (equatorial diameter 120 000 km, polar diameter 108 000 km) and has the lowest mean density (0.7 g cm^{-3}). In a telescope dark and light yellowish cloud bands are visible, running parallel to the equator. The dominant feature is **Saturn's rings**, lying in the equatorial plane and tilted at 27° to the orbital plane. There are seven rings, labelled D, C, B, A, F, G, and E in order of distance from Saturn. They differ considerably in brightness and width but are all composed of small icy chunks. The overall diameter is almost 600 000 km but the thickness is only a few hundred metres. The main rings, C, B, and A, were discovered in the 17th century. The outermost, A, extends to 73 000 km above Saturn's clouds. Ring A and the brightest ring, B, are separated by the Cassini division. Saturn also has at least 22 ▷satellites. Saturn is made up primarily of hydrogen and helium, possibly with a central rocky core surrounded by liquid hydrogen. ▷*See also* planetary probe.

● **Saturn** ▶ (mythology) The Roman god of agriculture and father of the gods, identified with the Greek ▷Cronus. His consort was Ops, identified with the Greek ▷Rhea. Various aspects of the Saturnalia, his annual festival held in December, at which presents were exchanged, were taken over by the Christian festival of Christmas. His name survives in *Saturday*.

● **saturniid moth** ▶ A moth belonging to the mainly tropical family *Saturniidae* (about 800 species). They are usually large with a transparent eyespot on each wing. Their cocoons can be a source of silk (*see* silkworm) and the larvae are typically green, feeding chiefly on tree foliage. ▷*See also* cecropia moth; emperor moth; hercules moth.

● **satyagraha** ▶ The Sanskrit expression referring to ▷Gandhi's policy of nonviolent resistance to British rule in India. ▷*See* civil disobedience.

● **satyrid butterfly** ▶ A butterfly of the worldwide family *Satyridae*. The wings are mainly brownish with a few or numerous eyespots. The forelegs are rudimentary and the flight weak and fluttering. Satyrids hide when alarmed, folding the forewings inside the camouflaged hindwings. The striped pale-green or brown caterpillars feed on grasses.

● **Satyrs and Sileni** ▶ In Greek mythology, male fertility spirits of the woods and fields, usually portrayed with goats' legs and pointed ears or horns. Associated with ▷Dionysus, they were typically drunk and lustful. The Roman equivalents were the fauns. ▷*See also* Silenus.

● **sauce** ▶ A thickened savoury or sweet liquid accompanying a dish and enhancing its flavour. Many classical dishes are named after the sauce served with them (e.g. spaghetti bolognese, poulet chasseur, sole bonne femme). Sauces often require a liaison, which binds together the liquids and other ingredients, the commonest being a *roux* (a paste of melted butter and flour). Other liaisons are egg yolks and butter kneaded with flour (*beurre manié*). Flour-based sauces include béchamel (white sauce), mornay (cheese sauce), soubise (onion sauce), and parsley sauce. Hollandaise and béarnaise sauces are made with wine vinegar, spices, and egg yolks. Other well-known sauces are mint sauce (with lamb), apple sauce (with pork), cranberry sauce (with turkey), horseradish sauce (with beef), tartare sauce (with fish), and tomato sauce. Among sweet sauces are butterscotch sauce (made with golden syrup and sugar), chocolate sauce, and melba sauce (puréed raspberries and icing sugar).

● **Saud** ▷*See* Saudi Arabia.

● **Saudi Arabia, Kingdom of** ▶ A country in the Middle East comprising most of ▷Arabia, bordering on the Red Sea and the Persian Gulf. In the W a line of mountains runs close to the Red Sea, while the ▷Najd, the central plateau, slopes downwards W–E. In the N and SE are large areas of desert. The population, densest in the SW, is mainly Arab Muslim, the majority being Sunnite with some Shiites in the E. About 27% are nomads. There are also many foreign workers, chiefly unskilled Yemenis and skilled Americans and Europeans.
Economy: based on oil, discovered in 1936 in the Persian Gulf and exploited since 1938; an increasing proportion of this is now refined locally. The country, a member of OPEC, is the world's greatest exporter of oil, the revenues being used to diversify the economy and provide education and health services. Recent industries include petrochemicals, fertilizers, construction materials, and machinery; considerable mineral resources have also been discovered and are now being exploited. Income is also derived from pilgrims visiting Mecca, Medina, and Jiddah. Owing to successful irrigation and desalination programmes, agricultural production has increased greatly since the 1970s; livestock is kept on the extensive pasture land. Consumer and capital goods and foodstuffs (particularly cereals) are imported, mainly from Japan, the USA, Germany, and the UK. In the 1990s the economy contracted owing to falling oil prices and the cost of the ▷Gulf War of 1991.
History: the establishment of Saudi Arabia (1932) under ▷Ibn Saud followed the 19th-century struggle by the Saud family to dominate the warring tribes of the peninsula and take overall control from Turkey. Asir was incorporated in 1934. Saudi Arabia became a founding member of the Arab League (1945). Under Ibn Saud's son, Saud (1902–69), conflict with Egypt developed, especially during the North Yemen civil war, in which Saudi Arabia supported the royalists and Egypt the republicans. Saud's brother, Faisal Ibn Abdul Aziz (1905–

75), who replaced him (1964), restored relations with Egypt and also used the oil crisis of the early 1970s to increase Saudi holdings in oil operations. On Faisal's apparently motiveless assassination (1975) by one of his nephews he was replaced as king by his brother, Khalid Ibn Abdul Aziz (1913–82). On Khalid's death his brother, ▷Fahd Ibn Abdul Aziz, became king. Iraq's invasion of Kuwait in 1990 precipitated the arrival of a multinational force in Saudi Arabia, which quickly routed Iraq's army in the Gulf War, but not before Saudi cities had come under Iraqi rocket attack. Saudi Arabia is a hereditary monarchy with a constitution and legal system based on the Koran and Islamic law. An appointed consultative council was established in 1993.

Kingdom of Saudi Arabia

Head of state	King Fahd ibn Abdul Aziz al Saud
Official language	Arabic
Official currency	riyal of 100 halalah
Area	2 400 000 sq km (927 000 sq mi)
Population (1997 est)	19 072 000
Capital	Riyadh
Chief port	Jiddah

● **Saul** ▶ **1.** In the Old Testament, the first King of Israel, who reigned in the 11th century BC. Son of Kish, he was anointed king by ▷Samuel. After victory over the Ammonites he fought against the Philistines. Following an act of disobedience during the Israelite destruction of the ▷Amalekites, Saul, according to the Old Testament, lost divine favour; his last years were marked by resentment towards his son Jonathan's friendship with ▷David. After Saul's three sons, including Jonathan, were killed by the Philistines at the Battle of Mount Gilboa, Saul, who was himself seriously wounded, killed himself. **2.** In the New Testament, Saul of Tarsus, the original name of St ▷Paul.

● **Sault Ste Marie** ▶ 46 32N 84 20W A city in E Canada, in NW Ontario on the St Mary's River opposite Sault Ste Marie, USA. Its canal allows ships to bypass local rapids that provide hydroelectricity for steel and other heavy industry. Population (1991): 84 476.

● **Sault Ste Marie** ▶ 46 29N 84 22W A city in the USA, in Michigan, on the St Mary's River opposite Sault Ste Marie, Canada. Founded in 1668, it became part of the USA in 1820. It serves the traffic of the St Lawrence Seaway by way of the Soo locks, which attract tourists. Population (1990): 14 689.

● **Saumur** ▶ 47 16N 0 05W A town in W France, in the Maine-et-Loire department on the River Loire. A former Huguenot stronghold, it is famous for its cavalry school (1768) and its sparkling white wines. Population (latest est): 34 000.

● **Saunders, Dame Cicely Mary Strode** ▶ (1918–   ) British philanthropist. After training as a nurse, in 1967 Cicely Saunders founded St Christopher's Hospice in London for the care of the terminally ill, which specializes in the relief of pain and support for the

Saudi Arabia ▶ Saudi law, which adheres closely to traditional Islamic teaching, requires women to veil themselves from head to foot in public places. The sexes are strictly segregated and women's freedom is severely circumscribed.

families. She is also the author of such books as *Care of the Dying* (1960), *Living with Dying* (1983), and *Beyond the Horizon* (1990). ▷*See also* hospice movement.

● **Saurischia** ► An order of ▷dinosaurs dominant in the Jurassic period (about 195–130 million years ago). They had hip bones like those of modern lizards (the name means "lizard hips") and most of them were bipedal carnivores, although some were quadrupedal herbivores. ▷*See also* Allosaurus; Apatosaurus; Ornitholestes; Tyrannosaurus.

● **saury** ► A marine fish, also called skipper, belonging to the family *Scomberesocidae* (about 4 species). It has a long slim body, up to 50 cm long, blue or olive above and golden or silvery below, with beaklike jaws and finlets behind the dorsal and anal fins. Sauries occur in large shoals in tropical and temperate surface waters, feeding on crustaceans and small fish. They are often seen leaping or skipping over the surface to escape predators. Order: *Atheriniformes*.

● **Saussure, Ferdinand de** ► (1857–1913) Swiss linguist. His great influence on 20th-century linguistics is due to the posthumously published *Course in General Linguistics* (1916), compiled by his pupils from lecture notes. It offers an integrated picture of all aspects of language. De Saussure's distinction between *parole* (the utterance of the individual) and *langue* (the common language of a community) was of great importance to both sociolinguistics and structural linguistics (see linguistics; structuralism). He also drew influential distinctions between diachronic (historical) and synchronic linguistics and between syntagmatic (collocational) and paradigmatic (organizational) relations in language.

● **Savage, Richard** ► (c. 1696–1743) British poet. Although he claimed to be the illegitimate son of an earl, he was of humble origin. He led a bohemian life and was convicted of murder in 1727 but received a royal pardon. He died in a debtors' prison. His works, which are now largely forgotten, include *The Wanderer* (1729). He was the subject of a sympathetic biography (1744) by his friend Dr Johnson.

● **Savai'i** ► 13 44S 172 18W The largest island of Samoa. Lava from a volcanic eruption in 1905 laid waste a large area. Copra, bananas, and cocoa are exported. Area: 1174 sq km (662 sq mi). Population (latest est): 44 930. Chief town: Tuasivi.

● **savanna** ► (or savannah) The extensive tropical grasslands, bordering on the equatorial rain forests in both the N and S hemispheres. They cover extensive areas in N Australia, Africa, and South America (where they are known as the ▷llanos in Venezuela and Colombia and the campos in Brazil). The vegetation of savannas is dominated by tall grasses, such as elephant grass, interspersed with low often flat-topped trees and bushes. They are ideal cattle-rearing areas.

● **Savannah** ► 32 04N 81 07W A city in the USA, in Georgia on the Savannah River. Established by James Oglethorpe in 1733, it was an important colonial port. The first Atlantic steamship crossing was from here to Liverpool in 1819. A major tourist centre and seaport, its industries include shipbuilding and chemicals. Population (2000): 131 510.

● **Savery, Thomas** ► (c. 1650–1715) English engineer, who in 1698 constructed the first practical steam engine. Savery's engine, which was dangerous because it utilized high-pressure steam, was superseded by ▷Newcomen's engine.

● **Save The Children Fund** ► A charity founded in 1919 to provide for the care of children throughout the world, especially in developing countries. Its headquarters are in London and its patron, the Princess Royal, works actively for it.

● **Savimbi, Jonas** ► (1934–2002) Angolan nationalist leader; president of the UNITA movement from 1966. He led UNITA forces against the Portuguese until independence (1975) and then declared himself president of the People's Democratic Republic of Angola. From 1976 until 1994 he conducted a guerrilla war against the internationally recognized MPLA government; this was renewed in 1999, following the breakdown of peace agreements. His death, in a skirmish with government troops, was followed by a new ceasefire.

● **savin** ► A low-growing ▷juniper shrub, *Juniperus sabina*, native to mountainous regions of S and central Europe. It has scalelike leaves

and blue-black berry-like cones, 4–6 mm long. The shrub has a strong unpleasant smell and yields a poisonous oil used in medicine and veterinary work.

● **savings banks** ► Banks, managed by trustees, that grew up in the UK in the 19th century to encourage thrift amongst workers. Their role has now been taken over by the ▷commercial banks, the ▷building societies, and the National Savings Bank (formerly the Post Office Savings Bank), which is operated by the Department for National Savings through the agency of the Post Office. Set up in 1861, it now offers ordinary accounts (maximum £10,000) and investment accounts (£25,000). The Trustee Savings Banks were originally non-profit-making organizations. They have gradually evolved into a single commercial bank, floated in 1986 as the TSB Group plc.

● **Savitskaya, Svetlana** ► (1949–) Soviet cosmonaut, who on 25 July, 1984, became the first woman to walk in space. She also held world records in parachuting and flying, and became the first woman to make two space trips. In 1989 she was elected to the Soviet parliament.

● **Savona** ► 44 18N 8 28E A port in NW Italy, in Liguria on the Gulf of Genoa. It rivalled Genoa in the middle ages but was subjugated by the Genoese in 1528. It has a 16th-century cathedral. Savona is an important centre of the Italian iron and steel industry. Population (latest est): 69 806.

● **Savonarola, Girolamo** ► (1452–98) Italian religious reformer. Joining the Dominicans in 1474, he became a lecturer in the Convent of San Marco, Florence, and later its prior (1491). His crusade against religious and political corruption focused on the papacy and the Medici. His fervent preaching attracted a large following, and he became the virtual ruler of Florence when the Medici were expelled by the populace in 1494. Excommunicated by Alexander VI in 1497, he was imprisoned, hanged, and burned for heresy by his political rivals.

● **savory** ► A herb belonging to the genus *Satureja*, of warm and temperate regions. Summer savory (*S. hortensis*) is an annual, native to central Europe and Asia. Both the dried leaves and the oil extract are used for flavouring foods. The perennial winter savory (*S. montana*) grows up to 40 cm high, has small white flowers, and is also a culinary herb. Family: *Labiatae*.

● **Savoy** ► An Alpine frontier region of SE France corresponding to the present-day departments of Savoie and Haute-Savoie. Strategically important for its mountain passes, the county of Savoy was founded in 1034 by Umberto Biancomano (Umberto I). He and his successors extended Savoyard territory, acquiring Piedmont in the 14th century. In 1416 ▷Amadeus the Peaceful became a duke and was subsequently elected antipope as Felix V. After acquiring Sardinia in 1720, Savoyard dukes took the title King of Sardinia, which in 1748 became the kingdom of Piedmont-Sardinia. Savoy (but not Sardinia) was annexed by France during the Revolutionary Wars but restored in 1815 and Piedmont-Sardinia became the leading spirit in the movement for Italian unification (see Risorgimento). Savoy became part of France in 1860 in return for Napoleon III's assistance against Austria but the House of Savoy ruled the newly formed kingdom of Italy (1861–1946).

● **sawfish** ► A ▷ray fish of the family *Pristidae* that occurs in salt and brackish waters of tropical and subtropical regions. Its sharklike body, up to 7 m long, bears a long snout edged with teeth and is used to forage along the bottom or to catch prey.

● **sawfly** ► An insect belonging to the widely distributed suborder *Symphyta* and so named because the female possesses a needle-like tubular ovipositor, which is used as a saw or drill to insert eggs into foliage and timber. Adults are 5–50 mm long and the larvae, resembling caterpillars, damage trees. Chief families: *Argidae*, *Siricidae*, *Cimbicidae*, *Diprionidae*, *Tenthredinidae*; order: ▷Hymenoptera.

● **Saxe, Maurice, Comte de** ► (1696–1750) Marshal of France, the illegitimate son of Augustus the Strong of Poland. He fought in the French army, outstandingly in the War of the ▷Austrian Succession (1740–48), and wrote *Mes Rêveries* (1757) on warfare.

● **Saxe-Coburg-Gotha** ► The ruling dynasty of a German duchy.

The children of Duke Francis Frederick (1750–1806) included Victoria Mary Louisa (1786–1861), who married (1818) Edward, Duke of Kent (their daughter was Queen Victoria); and Leopold, who became ▷Leopold I of Belgium. Francis' son Ernest I (1806–44) was the father of Prince Albert, who married Queen Victoria in 1840. The UK royal house was called Saxe-Coburg-Gotha from 1901 until 1917, when the name ▷Windsor was adopted.

● **saxhorn** ▶ A valved wind instrument of the bugle type, patented by the Belgian Adolphe Sax (1814–94) in Paris in 1845. The tenor saxhorn (or tenor horn) is used in the military and brass bands and occasionally in the orchestra, as in Mahler's seventh symphony.

● **saxifrage** ▶ A perennial herb belonging to certain genera of the family *Saxifragaceae*, found in cold and temperate regions. The leaves may either form a basal rosette or occur in pairs along the stem and the flowers are white, yellow, purple, or red. The European meadow saxifrage (*Saxifraga granulata*) may reach 45 cm. ▷*See also* London pride.

● **Saxo Grammaticus** ▶ (c. 1150–c. 1206) Danish chronicler. Little is known of his life, except that he served as secretary to the Archbishop of Roskilde. He was the author of *Gesta Danorum*, a Latin history of the Danes, the first part of which is based on mythological and legendary material.

● **Saxons** ▶ A Germanic people who, during the 5th century AD, expanded from their Baltic coastal homelands to other areas of N Germany, the coast of Gaul (France), and (with the ▷Angles and ▷Jutes) to Britain. Charlemagne eventually defeated the continental Saxons and converted them to Christianity, incorporating their lands into his empire after a long period of warfare (772–804 AD). ▷*See also* Anglo-Saxons.

● **Saxony** ▶ (German name: Sachsen) **1.** An ancient NW German duchy. Named after its original inhabitants, the ▷Saxons (who expanded to Britain in the 5th century), it was conquered by Charlemagne in the 8th century and subsequently became a duchy. In 919 AD Henry, Duke of Saxony, became German king and his son ▷Otto (I) the Great, the first Saxon Holy Roman Emperor. In 1142 Saxony passed to ▷Henry the Lion but in 1180 the duchy was broken up, to be reformed in various territorial combinations in following centuries. In the 13th century Saxony became an electorate and in the 16th and 17th centuries a leading German Protestant state. In 1697 Elector Frederick Augustus I (1670–1733) became King of Poland and Saxony's subsequent involvement in Polish affairs kept it apart from German power struggles until the 19th century. Conquered by Napoleon in 1806, N Saxony was annexed by Prussia in 1815 and in 1866 joined the Prussian-dominated ▷North German Confederation. The remainder of Saxony joined the German Empire in 1871. **2.** A *Land* in E Germany, formerly part of East Germany. Population (1995 est): 4 584 300.

● **Saxony-Anhalt** ▶ A *Land* in E Germany, created as a state of East Germany in 1947 from Anhalt and the parts of Prussia previously ruled by Saxony. It was reinstated upon reunification in 1990. Population (1995 est): 2 759 200.

● **saxophone** ▶ A woodwind instrument with a brass body, keys, and a single reed mouthpiece similar to that of a ▷clarinet. It was invented by the Belgian Adolphe Sax (1814–94) and patented in France in the 1840s. The most common sizes of saxophone are the soprano, alto, tenor, and baritone. They are most commonly used as solo instruments in jazz; they are sometimes used in classical music.

● **Sayan Mountains** ▶ A mountain range in S central Russia, on the Mongolian border. It extends some 800 km (497 mi) E–W, rising to 3491 m (11 453 ft) in Munku Sardyk in the SE. The River Yenisei and many of its tributaries rise here.

● **Sayers, Dorothy L(eigh)** ▶ (1893–1957) British writer, educated at Oxford, who is best known for her series of detective novels, beginning with *Whose Body?* (1923), featuring the erudite detective Lord Peter Wimsey. She also wrote plays on Christian themes and a translation of Dante's *Divine Comedy*.

● **scabies** ▶ A contagious skin infection caused by the ▷itch mite, which tunnels and breeds in the skin, causing intense itching. The burrows of the mites are seen between the fingers, on the side of the hands, in the armpits, and on the groin, nipples, and buttocks. Treatment is by application of a scabicide, such as permethrin or malathion lotions, and clothing and bedding should be disinfested.

● **scabious** ▶ An annual or perennial herb belonging to the genus *Scabiosa* (80–100 species), native to the Mediterranean region and temperate parts of Eurasia and Africa. The small scabious (*S. columbaria*) is widely distributed on chalky soils. 15–70 cm high, it has a cluster of small bluish-lilac flowers borne on a long stalk. The field scabious, *S.* (or *Knautia*) *arvensis*, is very similar and may reach a height of 1 m. Family: *Dipsacaceae*.

● **Scafell Pike** ▶ 54 28N 3 12W The highest peak in England, in Cumbria, in the Lake District. It is popular for walking and rock climbing. Height: 978 m (3210 ft).

● **scalar quantity** ▶ A quantity that is represented by magnitude only. Unlike a ▷vector quantity, a scalar quantity has no direction. Examples include mass, time, and speed.

● **scale** ▶ (music) An ascending or descending succession of notes, characterized by a fixed succession of intervals between the notes that constitute it. Many thousands of different scales exist; all the major musical traditions of the world are based upon them.

In Western music there are three **diatonic scales**, which derive from the ancient Greek ▷modes: the major scale, the harmonic minor scale, and the melodic minor scale. The octave is divided into 12 notes (*see* temperament) and any of these scales may be constructed on any of these notes. The version of the scale produced is associated with a particular ▷tonality. The **chromatic scale** includes all 12 semitones of the octave. The **pentatonic scale**, consisting of only 5 notes, is common in Chinese and Scottish music.

● **scale** ▶ (zoology) A platelike structure that generally forms part of a protective body covering in many vertebrate animals. Fish and certain reptiles have an overlapping series of bony scales, derived from the deep layers of the skin (dermis). The periodic growth of fish scales gives rise to annual rings, by which the age of the fish may be estimated. In reptiles the scales are periodically renewed and may be modified and enlarged as spines.

● **scale insect** ▶ An insect belonging to the superfamily *Coccoidea* (about 4000 species), abundant in warm and tropical regions. Scale insects are usually small (on average 1–15 mm long) and the females are often legless, wingless, and eyeless and covered by a waxy scale or mass of threads. They become encrusted on plants and suck the juices, often becoming serious pests. Other species are of value by producing ▷shellac, ▷cochineal, and various waxes. Suborder: *Homoptera*; order: ▷*Hemiptera*.

● **Scaliger, Julius Caesar** ▶ (1484–1558) Italian humanist scholar. He engaged in controversy with ▷Erasmus and wrote several commentaries on classical writers. Aristotle's theories of tragedy became known to the French 17th-century dramatists through his discussion of them in the *Poetice* (1561). His son **Joseph Justus Scaliger** (1540–1609), born in France, was an outstanding classical scholar and published many works of historical scholarship, notably the *Opus de emendatione tempore* (1583), a scientific study of chronology.

● **scallion** ▶ Any ▷onion or related plant that produces small white-skinned mild-flavoured bulbs, with a long neck and stiff leaves. Examples are spring onions and ▷shallots, used in salads. Leeks and chives may also be called scallions.

● **scallop** ▶ A ▷bivalve mollusc belonging to the family *Pectinidae* (about 400 species), of warm and temperate seas. 2–20 cm across, the valves of the shell are broad, flattened, and fluted; the animal swims by flapping them with a powerful muscle. Scallops are important as seafood.

● **scaly-tailed squirrel** ▶ An African arboreal ▷rodent belonging to the family *Anomaluridae* (9 species). They range in size from 8 to 45 cm and most species have a gliding membrane like that of the ▷flying squirrel. Their name refers to the backward-pointing scales under the tail that grip the tree trunk when the squirrel is clinging to it.

● **scampi** ▷*See* Dublin Bay prawn.

● **Scandinavia** ▶ Geographically, a peninsula in NW Europe, comprising Norway and Sweden. Culturally and historically, it includes Denmark, Iceland, the Faeroes, and Finland.

● **Scandinavian languages** ▶ A subgroup of the ▷Germanic languages consisting of ▷Swedish, ▷Norwegian, ▷Danish, ▷Icelandic, and Faeroese. The first three are similar enough to be mutually intelligible. They all developed from a common Scandinavian ancestor, which originally used the ▷runic alphabet (*see also* Old Norse). This language spread with the Vikings to Iceland, the Faeroes, and elsewhere.

● **scandium** ▶ (Sc) The first transition metal, predicted by Mendeleyev and discovered in 1879 by L. F. Nilson (1840–99). It is trivalent, forming an oxide (Sc_2O_3), halides (for example ScF_3), and other compounds. It is light (relative density 2.989) and has a much higher melting point than aluminium, making it of interest as a possible spacecraft material. At no 21; at wt 44.956; mp 1541°C; bp 2836°C.

● **Scania** ▷*See* Skåne.

● **scanner** ▶ (medicine) ▷*See* tomography; ultrasonography.

● **scanning tunnelling microscope** ▶ A type of high-resolution microscope in which a small conducting probe is scanned slowly across the surface of a specimen. An electrical signal is produced as a result of electrons moving be-tween the sample and the probe by the ▷tunnel effect. The probe is raised or lowered to keep the signal constant, enabling a computer-generated contour map of the surface to be produced. The technique, which is used on conducting specimens, can resolve individual atoms. ▷*See also* atomic force microscope.

● **Scapa Flow** ▶ A section of the Atlantic Ocean off the N coast of Scotland, enclosed by the Orkney Islands. It was the main base of the British Grand Fleet in World War I. Following its surrender, the German fleet scuttled itself here (1919). The naval base closed in 1957. Scapa Flow is now a major centre for the oil industry. Length: about 24 km (15 mi). Width: 13 km (8 mi).

● **scapegoat** ▶ An animal, person, or object chosen as the symbolic bearer of the sins or misfortunes of an individual or group. At the ancient Jewish ritual of the Day of Atonement, a goat was chosen to bear the sins of the people and driven off a cliff. Similar rituals were practised in ancient Greece and Rome.

● **scapula** ▷*See* shoulder.

● **scarab** ▶ An ancient Egyptian seal or amulet made of stone or faience in the shape of a dung beetle. Associated with the sun's regenerative powers, scarabs were often buried with the dead.

● **scarab beetle** ▶ A beetle belonging to the worldwide family *Scarabaeidae* (over 19 000 species). The largest beetles—the ▷goliath and ▷hercules beetles—are scarabs, while other species have developed extraordinary horns (*see* rhinoceros beetle). The family has two main groups—the ▷dung beetles and ▷chafers. Certain dung-rolling beetles, especially *Scarabaeus sacer*, were the sacred scarabs of the ancient Egyptians.

● **Scarborough** ▶ 54 17N 0 24W A resort in NE England, on the North Yorkshire coast. The promontory separating the North and South Bays is the site of a prehistoric settlement, a Roman signal station, and a 12th-century castle. The town is best known as a fishing and tourist centre but now has a growing manufacturing base. Population (1995): 44 930.

● **Scarfe, Gerald** ▶ (1936–) British cartoonist. Working for such journals as *Private Eye*, *Punch*, and the *Sunday Times*, he is noted for his scathing caricatures of public figures.

● **Scargill, Arthur** ▶ (1941–) British trades union leader; president of the National Union of Mineworkers (1981–). A charismatic speaker, he led the NUM in a long and unsuccessful strike (1984–85) against proposed pit closures. In 1991 he was cleared of making improper use of NUM funds and in 1992 he led a further unsuccessful campaign against pit closures. He launched a new political party, the Socialist Labour Party, in 1996.

● **Scarlatti, Domenico** ▶ (1685–1757) Italian composer and noted harpsichordist and organist. After studying in Venice and holding court posts in Rome and Naples, he was engaged by Princess Maria Barbara of Portugal in Lisbon in 1720. When she married into the Spanish royal family in 1729 he moved with her to Madrid, where he stayed until his death. Besides some operas and church music, he wrote over 600 harpsichord sonatas, many of which were highly innovative. His father **Alessandro Scarlatti** (1660–1725) was also a composer. He worked chiefly in Rome and Naples. His works include over a hundred operas, 600 chamber cantatas, 200 masses, 12 chamber symphonies, and 14 oratorios.

● **scarlet fever** ▶ A highly infectious disease of children caused by toxin-producing streptococcus bacteria. After an incubation period of 2–4 days the child develops a sore throat, fever, and headache; 24–48 hours later a red rash spreads from the chest over the whole body. Before antibiotics scarlet fever killed many children or left them disabled with ▷rheumatic fever, kidney disease, or ear infections.

● **Scarron, Paul** ▶ (1610–60) French poet, dramatist, and satirist. His best-known work is the picaresque novel *Le Roman comique* (1651–57). From the age of 30 he suffered from paralysis. In 1652 he married Françoise d'Aubigné, who later became, as Madame de ▷Maintenon, the wife of Louis XIV.

● **scattering** ▶ The deflection of waves or particles by the atoms or molecules of the medium through which they are passing or by other particles. The scattering of waves is due to either ▷reflection or ▷diffraction. For particles, the scattering is described as inelastic if the scattered particles gain or lose energy (as in the ▷Raman effect). Otherwise it is elastic.

● **scaup** ▶ A ▷diving duck, *Aythya marila*, that breeds in northern latitudes and winters on more southerly coasts. 40–45 cm long, it dives deeply to feed on mussels and small crabs. The male has green-black fore parts, a grey back, white flanks, and a brown rump and tail; females are dark brown with a white patch around the bill.

● **scepticism** ▶ The philosophical tradition that absolute certainty or knowledge cannot be attained. It began perhaps with ancient Greek scepticism about the senses (*see* Pyrrhon). Sometimes the sceptic's claim was that any knowledge attained must go unrecognized; sometimes he systematically suspected certain subjects, such as reality, religious beliefs, or moral principles, on the grounds, for example, of the relativity or subjectivity of such beliefs.

● **Schacht, Hjalmar** ▶ (1877–1970) German financier and politician. As president of the Reichsbank (1923–30), he checked Germany's rampant inflation. He was reappointed by Hitler in 1933 but was dismissed in 1939. From 1934 to 1937 he served as minister of economics. He was acquitted at Nuremberg of war crimes.

● **Schaffhausen** ▶ (French name: Schaffhouse) 47 42N 8 38E A town in N Switzerland, on the River Rhine. Its notable buildings include the Munot fort and the romanesque cathedral (11th–12th centuries). Industries include aluminium smelting; hydroelectric power is obtained from the falls on the River Rhine. Population (latest est): 35 000.

● **Scheel, Walter** ▶ (1919–) German statesman; president of West Germany (1974–79). He served in the Luftwaffe during World War II and was minister for economic cooperation (1961–66) and foreign minister (1969–74).

● **Scheele, Carl Wilhelm** ▶ (1742–86) Swedish chemist, who discovered a number of compounds and elements. His greatest work in this field was the discovery of oxygen (c. 1771), but as his results were not published until 1777 ▷Priestley is usually credited with the discovery. Scheele was also the first to isolate and prepare the gases hydrogen sulphide, hydrogen cyanide, and hydrogen fluoride.

● **scheelite** ▶ A tungsten ore mineral, $CaWO_4$, occurring in veins and contact-metamorphic rocks. It is yellowish white or brown. ▷*See also* wolframite.

● **Scheldt, River** ▶ (French name: Escaut; Flemish and Dutch name: Schelde) A river in W Europe. Rising in NE France, it flows generally NNE through W Belgium to Antwerp, then NW to the North Sea in the SW Netherlands. Canals connect it to the Rivers Somme, Seine, Sambre, Meuse, and Rhine. Length: 435 km (270 mi).

● **Schelling, Friedrich** ▶ (1775–1854) German philosopher. Schelling was first influenced by the writings of ▷Fichte and ▷Kant. Later, he became convinced that knowledge could not be confined to phenomena and argued that there was "a secret wonderful faculty which dwells in us all." His *System of Transcendental Idealism* (1800) contains his metaphysical philosophy, which, with his insistence that human consciousness is fulfilled by art, influenced ▷Romanticism and in particular ▷Coleridge.

● **Schenectady** ▶ 42 48N 73 57W A city in the USA, in New York state on the Mohawk River. In 1886 the Thomas Edison Machine Works was moved here, later becoming the General Electric Company, which dominates the city today. Population (1990): 65 566.

● **scherzo** ▶ (Italian: joke) **1.** An early 17th-century Italian vocal or instrumental piece of music, such as a light-hearted madrigal. Monteverdi's *Scherzi musicali* (1607) is a collection of such pieces. **2.** A lively movement in a sonata or symphony (commonly the third movement); it evolved in the 18th century from the slower minuet. In the symphonies of Beethoven, Schubert, and others it has a fast tempo in 3/4 time and often includes a contrasting slower section (the trio). **3.** A fast piece for piano, such as any of Chopin's four scherzi, that combines lyricism and intensity with humour. In the 20th century, scherzi for orchestra, such as Stravinsky's *Scherzo fantastique*, have been quite common.

● **Scheveningen** ▷*See* Hague, The.

● **Schiaparelli, Elsa** ▶ (1896–1973) Italian-born fashion designer, who opened fashion houses in Paris (late 1920s) and New York (1949). Her flamboyant designs were particularly associated with the padded shoulder and "shocking pink."

● **Schick test** ▶ A skin test for the presence of antibodies to ▷diphtheria. Injection of small amounts of diphtheria toxin causes a localized inflammation of the skin in those who have not been vaccinated or have not had diphtheria. The test was devised in 1913 by an Austrian paediatrician, Bela Schick (1877–1967).

● **Schiedam** ▶ 51 55N 4 25E A town in the W Netherlands, in South Holland province. It has famous gin distilleries. Population (1994): 72 515.

● **Schiele, Egon** ▶ (1890–1918) Austrian expressionist painter. Influenced by the French impressionists and by ▷Klimt, Schiele painted portraits and nudes having a disturbing anguished quality and eroticism through a distorted use of line. With ▷Kokoschka he was a leader of Austrian expressionism until his death from influenza.

● **Schiller, (Johann Christoph) Friedrich (von)** ▶ (1759–1805) German dramatist, poet, and writer. His first, anonymously published, play, *Die Räuber* (1781), typifies the ▷*Sturm und Drang* call for political freedom. His next important play and his first in blank verse was the tragedy *Don Carlos* (1787), set in the time of Philip II of Spain. With Goethe's friendly encouragement from 1794, Schiller turned from the historical and academic studies with which he had been involved and produced the brilliant dramas of the last decade of his life: the trilogy *Wallenstein* (1798–99), *Maria Stuart* (1800), based on the life of Mary, Queen of Scots, *Die Jungfrau von Orleans* (1801), concerned with Joan of Arc, and *Wilhelm Tell* (1804). His nondramatic works include poems, the important essay on aesthetics, *Über naive und sentimentalische Dichtung* (1795–96), and a history of the Thirty Years' War (1793).

● **Schindler, Oskar** ▶ (1908–74) German businessman who saved the lives of some 1200 Jews from the Kraków ghetto in Poland. The Jews were originally employed as forced labour in his factory. When the Germans cleared the ghetto in 1943, Schindler drew up his list of 1200 Jews, whom the Nazis would have sent to concentration camps, and used his influence to have them transferred to a new armaments factory in Czechoslovakia. Steven Spielberg's film *Schindler's List* (1993), based on Thomas Keneally's novel *Schindler's Ark* (1982), commemorates Schindler's bravery in defying the Nazi regime.

● **Schinkel, Karl Friedrich** ▶ (1781–1841) German architect, painter, and stage designer. His Berlin buildings, including the Royal Theatre (1821) and the Old Museum (1830), are classical but later works include the neogothic Werdersche Kirche (1831) and the unadorned functional Academy of Architecture (1837).

● **schipperke** ▶ A breed of ⬚dog originating in Flanders and used as a guard dog on barges. It has a stocky tailless body with short legs and a foxlike head with erect ears. The dense coat is usually black and forms a mane. Height: 30.5–33 cm.

● **schism** ▶ **1.** ▷*See* East–West Schism. **2.** *See* Great Schism.

● **schist** ▶ A coarse-grained ▷metamorphic rock with a pronounced banded structure, in which the minerals show parallel alignment at right angles to the direction of stress, leaving no trace of the original bedding. The minerals are segregated into alternate thin layers rich in mica and quartz/feldspar, and the rock readily splits along these schistosity planes. Schists are named according to the dominant minerals, e.g. mica-schist.

● **schistosomiasis** ▶ (*or* bilharziasis) A widespread disease of the tropics caused by blood flukes of the genus *Schistosoma* (or *Bilharzia*). The disease is contracted by bathing in water contaminated by snails, which harbour the larvae of the parasite. The larvae penetrate the skin and—when mature—settle in the blood vessels of the intestine or bladder. Symptoms, caused by the release of eggs by adult flukes, include anaemia, inflammation, and diarrhoea and dysentery (from an intestinal infection), or cystitis and blood in the urine (from a bladder infection). The disease is treated by drugs that destroy the parasite.

● **schizophrenia** ▶ A severe mental disorder characterized by disintegration of the processes of thinking, contact with reality, and emotional responsiveness. Delusions and ▷hallucinations are common, especially those that produce the feeling of a loss of personal identity. Schizophrenics often become withdrawn and apathetic. The condition tends to get worse (in about half of all cases) unless treatment is given. Modern treatment has improved the outlook: it consists of ▷antipsychotic drugs and vigorous psychological and social rehabilitation. Schizophrenia is believed to be caused by genetic factors, but environmental stress can trigger an episode of illness. ▷*See also* paranoia; psychosis.

● **Schlegel, August Wilhelm von** ▶ (1767–1845) German critic, poet, and translator. With his brother, he exerted a powerful influence on the early Romantics through critical works, such as *Über dramatische Kunst und Literatur* (3 vols, 1809–11), and translations, especially of Shakespeare. His brother **(Carl Wilhelm) Friedrich von Schlegel** (1772–1829) was a writer and critic. The chief influence on the German Romantic movement, his literary and philosophical works appeared first in *Das Athenäum*, a periodical published by him and his brother. He later published the first study in comparative philology (1808).

● **Schleiden, Matthias Jakob** ▶ (1804–81) German botanist, who first formulated the theory that plants are composed of ▷cells (this was later extended to animals by Theodor ▷Schwann). Schleiden also recognized the importance of the cell nucleus, although he mistakenly believed that new cells budded from its surface.

● **Schlesinger, John** ▶ (1926–   ) British film and theatre director. His first major films, *A Kind of Loving* (1962) and *Billy Liar* (1963), concerned working-class life in N England. His later films, most of which have been made in the USA, included the Oscar-winning *Midnight Cowboy* (1969), *Sunday Bloody Sunday* (1971), *The Believers* (1987), *Pacific Heights* (1990), and *Eye for an Eye* (1995). He was an associate director of the National Theatre Company (1973–88).

● **Schleswig** ▶ A breed of draught horse originating in the Danish duchy of Schleswig. It has a long body with short legs and a fairly large head. The coat is chestnut, bay, or grey. Height: about 1.60 m (15¾ hands).

● **Schleswig-Holstein** ▶ A low-lying *Land* in N Germany bordering on the North Sea, the Baltic Sea, and Denmark. Grain and potatoes are grown and cattle reared; industries include shipbuilding and engineering.

History: during the 19th century the **Schleswig-Holstein question** arose when Denmark and the Austrian-led German confederacy both laid claim to the two duchies of Schleswig and Holstein. War broke out in 1863 and the duchies were annexed to Prussia in 1866. In 1949 the *Land* of Schleswig-Holstein was formed. Area: 15 696 sq km (6059 sq mi). Population (1995 est): 2 708 400. Capital: Kiel.

● **Schlick, Moritz** ▶ (1882–1936) German philosopher. Schlick was professor of philosophy at Vienna University (1922–36). The leader of the ▷Vienna Circle (*see also* logical positivism), he approached philosophy in a basically experimental way and concerned himself with problems of truth and verifiability. His published work includes the *General Theory of Knowledge* (1918) and *Problems of Ethics* (1930).

● **Schlieffen, Alfred, Graf von** ▶ (1833–1913) German general, who, as chief of the general staff (1891–1905) devised the **Schlieffen Plan**, on which German strategy at the outbreak of World War I was unsuccessfully based. The plan provided for a concentration of German forces on the Western Front, which would rapidly defeat France in a flanking movement through the Low Countries, while a smaller army held off Russia in the east.

● **Schliemann, Heinrich** ▶ (1822–90) German archaeologist. After a successful business career, Schliemann retired (1863) to pursue his childhood ambition of discovering Homeric ▷Troy. Ignoring scholarly derision, he excavated Hissarlik on the Asia Minor coast of Turkey, finding ruins of nine consecutive cities. The second oldest (Troy II), which he wrongly identified with Homer's city, yielded a hoard that Schliemann romantically called "Priam's Treasure." His spectacular finds at ▷Mycenae (1874–76), Orchomenos in Boeotia (1880), and ▷Tiryns (1884–85) established him as the discoverer of ▷Mycenaean civilization.

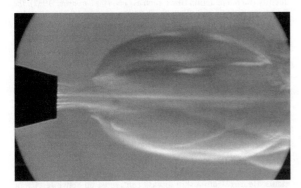

Schlieren photography ▶ A Schlieren photograph showing turbulence in the exhaust gases from a jet engine.

● **Schlieren photography** ▶ A method of observing differences of density in a transparent medium, such as air. Light from a spark is photographed as it passes through the medium; any differences in density present cause local variations in the refractive index, which show up as streaks (German: *Schlieren*) in the photograph. The method is used for observing sound waves, shock waves, and flaws in glass.

● **Schmeling, Max** ▶ (1905–) German boxer, the first European to win the world heavyweight title in the 20th century (1930). In 1936 he beat Joe ▷Louis but Louis took his revenge in two minutes in 1938.

● **Schmidt, Helmut** ▶ (1918–) German statesman; Social Democratic chancellor of West Germany (1974–82). He became minister for domestic affairs in Hamburg (1961–65) and was then Federal minister of defence (1969–72) and for finance (1972–74) before becoming chancellor. He has written several books, mainly on foreign affairs.

● **Schmidt telescope** ▶ A ▷telescope developed by Bernard Voldemar Schmidt (1879–1935). It produces very sharp photographic images of celestial objects over a very wide angle of sky. The incoming light passes through a thin correcting plate, is reflected by a large short-focus spherical mirror, and focused on a curved photographic plate.

● **Schnabel, Artur** ▶ (1882–1951) Austrian pianist, especially famous for his performances of Beethoven. He studied in Vienna and in Berlin, where he later taught until 1933, after which he lived

mainly in Switzerland and the USA. He also composed three symphonies and a piano concerto.

● **schnauzer** ▶ A breed of dog originating in Germany and used as a guard dog. Strongly built with a docked tail, it has a characteristic square muzzle with long sidewhiskers. The wiry coat is black or light grey and brown. The giant schnauzer has been bred for farm and police work and the miniature schnauzer as a pet. Height: 33–35 cm (miniature); 45–48 cm (standard); 54–65 cm (giant).

● **Schneider Trophy** ▶ A cup awarded in international competitions for ▷seaplanes between 1913 and 1931, presented by the French patron of aviation Jacques Schneider. Combining seaworthiness and speed trials, it was eventually won outright by the UK; the Spitfire and its Rolls Royce Merlin engine of World War II were derived from the Supermarine S6B seaplane that won the competition at a speed of 655 kph (407 mph) in 1931.

● **Schnittke, Alfred** ▶ (1934–98) Russian composer and musicologist, living in Germany from 1979. His works, which are highly eclectic in style, include nine symphonies (1972–98), four violin concertos, numerous chamber works, and the opera *Life with an Idiot* (1992).

● **Schnitzler, Arthur** ▶ (1862–1931) Austrian Jewish dramatist and novelist. A physician, he was especially interested in psychiatry and his works are notable for their psychological observation. They include the witty dramatic cycles *Anatol* (1893) and *Reigen* (1900; filmed as *La Ronde,* 1950) and his prose masterpiece, *Leutnant Gustl* (1901).

● **Schoenberg, Arnold** ▶ (1874–1951) Austrian-born composer. He studied in Vienna with Alexander von Zemlinsky (1872–1942) and began his career by orchestrating theatre music. In 1910 he became a teacher at the Vienna Academy; his students included Berg and Webern. Mahler became a champion of his music. In 1933 Schoenberg, as a Jew, was forced to leave Berlin; he became a US citizen in 1941 and was professor at the University of California (1936–44). His early compositions, in a late Romantic style, include two string quartets, *Verklärte Nacht* (for string sextet; 1899), and the symphonic poem *Pelleas und Melisande* (1902–03). His subsequent works were characterized by ▷atonality; they include the melodrama *Pierrot Lunaire* (1912) in which the voice part is noted in *Sprechgesang* (German: speech song). Schoenberg subsequently developed ▷serialism (1924), which he employed in most of his later works, including a violin concerto (1936), a piano concerto (1942), and the unfinished opera *Moses und Aaron* (1932–51).

● **scholasticism** ▶ The intellectual discipline comprising all the philosophical and theological activities pursued in the medieval universities (schools). As the international philosophy of Christendom it respected orthodoxy and was concerned with the philosophies of ▷Plato and ▷Aristotle as assimilated over centuries of Christian thought. For scholastics religion was predominant and in their method philosophy was the servant of theology. It was by theology that the selection of problems for study and the scope of scientific enquiry were to be decided. ▷Anselm of Canterbury was an early scholastic, and ▷Abelard perfected its method. After ▷Aquinas, ▷Aristotelianism developed until, in the Renaissance, it was virtually synonymous with scholasticism.

● **schooner** ▶ A □sailing vessel with at least two masts, a shorter one set near the bows, a taller one at some distance behind it. Schooners, being quite fast and efficient when sailing off the wind, were widely used before the advent of steam and motor vessels in both coastal and long-distance commercial trade, especially fishing. Because they do not sail well into the wind, they are not a favoured rig in racing.

● **Schopenhauer, Arthur** ▶ (1788–1860) German philosopher. His main contribution to philosophy is the emphasis that he placed upon the human will as a means to understanding. *The World as Will and Idea* (1818) sets out his principal ideas and pessimistic conclusions. Distrustful of rationalism and the scientific method, he was instead concerned with intuitive cognition. He saw the ideal state of man as one of contemplative freedom, achieved through art.

● **Schreiner, Olive** ▶ (1855–1920) South African novelist. She went to England in 1881 and won literary and social success with her autobiographical *The Story of an African Farm* (1883). She returned to South

Africa in 1889. Her other books include the short allegorical *Dreams* (1891) and the feminist *Women and Labour* (1911).

● **Schröder, Gerhard** ► (1944–) German politician; chancellor (1998–). A Social Democrat, he was a member of the Bundestag (1980–86) and prime minister of Lower Saxony (1990–98) before defeating Helmut ▷Kohl and the CDU in the elections of 1998. During his chancellorship Germany adopted the single European currency (1999–2002).

● **Schrödinger, Erwin** ► (1887–1961) Austrian physicist. He shared the 1933 Nobel Prize with ▷Dirac for his development of the form of the ▷quantum theory known as ▷wave mechanics, which is based on the **Schrödinger equation**. This equation enables wavefunctions to be calculated, giving the probability of finding an electron at a particular place. Although not Jewish, he was an ardent anti-Nazi and came to England when Hitler took Austria. He was professor at the School for Advanced Studies in Dublin (1940–56), returning to Vienna after his retirement.

● **Schubert, Franz (Peter)** ► (1797–1828) Austrian composer, who had a musical upbringing but little formal training, other than at the imperial choir school in Vienna. He made a precarious living as a composer and teacher and achieved little recognition. He died from typhoid fever at the age of 31. Schubert's melodic genius is perhaps most evident in his 600 *Lieder*, which include "Erlkönig," "Death and the Maiden," and "The Trout." Some of his greatest songs are to be found in the song-cycles *Die Schöne Müllerin* (1823) and *Die Winterreise* (1827). His other works demonstrate his mastery of large-scale composition. They include nine symphonies (of which one is lost and the eighth is unfinished), string quartets, piano trios, an octet, two quintets, piano sonatas and pieces, and much choral music. He also wrote several less successful operas.

● **Schumacher, Michael** ► (1969–) German motor-racing driver. He was Formula One world champion in 1994, 1995, 2000, and 2001. He has won more Grand Prix races than any other driver.

● **Schuman, Robert** ► (1886–1963) French statesman. He held several ministerial posts from 1946 to 1956 and was briefly prime minister (1947–48). As foreign minister (1948–52), he proposed the **Schuman Plan** (1950) for European unity, which advocated the establishment (achieved in 1952) of the ▷European Coal and Steel Community. He was president of the EEC assembly (1958–60).

● **Schuman, William (Howard)** ► (1910–91) US composer. He taught at Sarah Lawrence College in New York (1935–45) and was president of the Juilliard School of Music (1945–61). His compositions included a ballet, *The Undertow* (1945), choral works, nine symphonies, an opera about baseball, entitled *The Mighty Casey* (1953), *Song of Orpheus* (for cello and orchestra; 1962), and a cantata, *A Free Song* (1943), which won a Pulitzer Prize.

● **Schumann, Elisabeth** ► (1885–1952) German-born soprano. She settled in the USA in 1938, becoming a US citizen in 1944. She performed in operas, concerts, and recitals, excelling in the music of Mozart and Richard Strauss.

● **Schumann, Robert (Alexander)** ► (1810–56) German composer. He played and composed music from an early age and at Leipzig University devoted more time to it than to his law studies. Almost all his musical compositions up to 1840 were for the piano; he was also a critic, editing (1835–44) the journal *Die Neue Zeitschrift für Musik*, which he had founded. Gradual insanity in later life culminated in his attempt to drown himself and he died in an asylum. His compositions include four symphonies, the opera *Genoveva* (1847–50), songs, including the cycles *Dichterliebe* (1840) and *Frauenliebe und Leben* (1840), violin, piano, and cello concertos, and piano pieces, including the *Davidsbündlertänze* (1837) and *Kreisleriana* (1838).

His wife **Clara Schumann** (1819–96), whom he married in 1840, was the daughter of Friedrich Wieck (1788–1873), with whom he had studied the piano in Leipzig (1830–32). She was a famous pianist, teacher, and composer, and became a great interpreter and editor of her husband's works.

● **Schuschnigg, Kurt von** ► (1897–1977) Austrian statesman; chancellor (1934–38). He tried in vain to prevent the Nazi ▷*Anschluss*

and was forced to resign, being imprisoned by Hitler throughout World War II. On his release he taught in the USA until 1967, when he returned to Austria.

● **Schütz, Heinrich** ► (1585–1672) German composer. He sang in the choir of the royal chapel at Kassel and studied with Giovanni Gabrieli in Venice (1609–12). He was court kapellmeister in Dresden after 1615. He composed much sacred music, including Passions and *The Seven Words of Christ on the Cross* (c. 1645), as well as madrigals and the first German opera, *Dafne* (1627), which is now lost.

● **Schwann, Theodor** ► (1810–82) German physiologist, who applied ▷Schleiden's cell theory to animals—an important conceptual advance in biology. Schwann pointed out that egg cells develop by successive divisions and he identified the **Schwann cells** that surround nerve fibres. He was the first person to isolate a digestive enzyme (pepsin) from animal tissue and he also coined the term metabolism for the chemical changes that take place in living tissues.

● **Schwarzenberg, Felix, Fürst zu** ► (1800–52) Austrian statesman. He served in the diplomatic corps before becoming first minister during the Revolution of 1848. He restored order in the Habsburg Empire, issuing a new constitution (1849) that strengthened the absolute power of the emperor. He also frustrated Prussia's attempts to establish a Prussian-dominated union of German states.

● **Schwarzenegger, Arnold** ► (1947–) US film actor, born in Austria. A former Mr Universe, he first became widely known for his role in the bodybuilding documentary *Pumping Iron* (1977). He subsequently starred in action films, such as *Conan the Barbarian* (1982), *The Terminator* (1984), and *Total Recall* (1990), becoming one of Hollywood's highest paid stars. In the 1990s he successfully extended his range in comedies such as *Kindergarten Cop* (1992) and *Junior* (1994).

● **Schwarzkopf, Dame Elisabeth** ► (1915–) German-born British soprano. She studied and made her debut (1938) in Berlin and then sang in Vienna, London, Milan, and the USA. She was especially noted for her interpretation of Mozart and Richard Strauss.

● **Schwarzkopf, Norman** ► (1934–) US army officer, known as "Stormin' Norman." Trained at West Point, he served in Vietnam and rose through the ranks to become a general. As supreme commander of the allied forces in the ▷Gulf War (1991), he planned the "Desert Storm" campaign, which liberated Kuwait from its Iraqi invaders.

● **Schwarzschild, Karl** ► (1873–1916) German astronomer, who developed photographic techniques for making astronomical measurements. He died from a skin disease contracted on active service in World War I. In 1916 he defined the **Schwarzschild radius** (SR), the radius of a contracting star at which nothing, including light, can escape from it. It then becomes a ▷black hole. The SR for the sun is 3 km (actual radius 7×10^8 m).

● **Schwarzwald** ▷*See* Black Forest.

● **Schweitzer, Albert** ► (1875–1965) Alsatian-born theologian, medical missionary, and organist. A theologian in the liberal Protestant tradition, Schweitzer wrote *The Quest of the Historical Jesus* (1906), emphasizing Christ's humanity. His writings on Bach and his recitals of Bach's organ music were highly acclaimed. From 1913 until his death, Schweitzer practised as a doctor in the hospital he founded in Gabon at the jungle village of Lambaréné. His philosophy is best summarized in his ethic of "reverence for life." In 1952 he received the Nobel Peace Prize.

● **Schwerin** ► 53 38N 11 25E A city in N Germany, on Lake Schwerin; the capital of Mecklenburg–West Pomerania. Largely destroyed by fire in the 16th and 17th centuries, the city was rebuilt with squares and wide streets. Schwerin has machinery and chemical industries. Population (1999 est): 104 200.

● **Schwitters, Kurt** ► (1887–1958) German artist and poet, born in Hanover. Associated with the ▷dada art movement, he became famous for his poems of meaningless sounds and his invention of elaborate structures and collages of tram tickets, broken glass, etc., which he salvaged from gutters and dustbins and labelled *Merz* (trash) constructions. He worked in Britain from 1940 until his death.

● **Schwyz** ► 47 02N 8 34E A town in Switzerland. It is a popular summer resort in a picturesque setting. Population (latest est): 12 534.

● **sciatica** ▶ Severe pain that starts in a buttock and spreads down the back of the leg. It is caused by pressure on the roots of the sciatic nerve—the longest nerve in the body. The commonest cause is pressure from a slipped disc in the backbone. Other kinds of injury to the back may also lead to sciatica. Treatment is by bed rest and pain killers.

● **science fiction** ▶ A literary genre in which scientific knowledge is used as a basis for imaginative fiction. The chief precursors of modern science fiction were Jules ▷Verne, who made use of speculative developments in engineering in such works as *Twenty Thousand Leagues Under the Sea* (1869) and *Propeller Island* (1895), and H. G. ▷Wells, who dealt with time travel, space travel, and alien invasion in *The Time Machine* (1895), *The First Men in the Moon* (1901), and *The War of the Worlds* (1898). In the 20th century such magazines as *Amazing Stories* (founded 1926) and *Astounding Science Fiction* reflected a growing popular interest in the science fiction inspired by advances in the fields of rocketry, electronics, and computers. Notable works of science fiction have been written by such scientists as Fred ▷Hoyle and Isaac ▷Asimov. Among writers who have written imaginative accounts of the origin, evolution, and destiny of the human race are Olaf Stapledon (1886–1950), author of *Last and First Men* (1931), and Arthur C. ▷Clarke, author of *The City and the Stars* (1956). Other leading writers of science fiction include Edgar Rice ▷Burroughs, John ▷Wyndham, Aldous ▷Huxley, Brian ▷Aldiss, Ray ▷Bradbury, Kurt ▷Vonnegut, J. G. ▷Ballard, Michael Moorcock (1939–), and Iain M. Banks (1954–). Since the 1970s science fiction has overlapped to some extent with the fantasy genre created by ▷Tolkien. Science fiction has also had an important place in the cinema, owing largely to the scope that film technology gives for spectacular special effects. Cinematic science fiction extends from such pioneering works as Fritz ▷Lang's *Metropolis* (1927), through such acknowledged classics as ▷Kubrick's *2001: A Space Odyssey* (1967; scripted with Arthur C. Clarke), to such contemporary blockbusters as *The Terminator* (1984) and *Independence Day* (1996).

● **Science Museum** ▶ A museum in South Kensington, London, devoted to the history of science, engineering, and industry. Its full name is the British National Museum of Science and Industry. It originally formed part of the South Kensington Museum (founded 1857), which became the Victoria and Albert Museum in 1899; the Science Museum was separated in 1909. The National Railway Museum, York, (opened 1975) is an outstation of the Science Museum.

● **Scientology** ▶ A tradename for a religious philosophy followed by the Church of Scientology, founded in 1954 in California by L(afayette) Ron(ald) Hubbard (1911–86). Originally a version of this doctrine was presented as a method of psychotherapy in Hubbard's *Dianetics: The Modern Science of Mental Health* (1950). It was later presented as a religious philosophy by which an adherent passes through many rigidly structured levels, increasing his IQ, creativity, etc., until he is finally "not on the body level" at all and has realized his full spiritual potential. In 1959 the Church's headquarters moved to East Grinstead in East Sussex (England); they are now in Hollywood, Los Angeles. The Church's methods of recruiting and controlling adherents have been widely criticized.

● **Scilla** ▶ A genus of bulbous plants native to Europe, Asia, and Africa, including the spring squill (*S. verna*), with small blue flowers. Family: ▷Liliaceae.

● **Scilly, Isles of** ▶ (or Scillies) A group of about 140 islands and islets in the Atlantic Ocean, off the extreme SW coast of England. Only five are inhabited, namely St Mary's (the largest), Tresco, St Martin's, St Agnes, and Bryher. Their mild climate has been exploited to produce early spring flowers for the UK market, their major source of income. Agriculture is intensive with dairy farming and the production of vegetables. Tourism is also an important source of revenue. Area: 16 sq km (6 sq mi). Population (latest est): 2628. Chief town: Hugh Town.

● **scintillation counter** ▶ An instrument that measures the number of radioactive atoms that decay in a certain time. The emit-

ted radiation strikes a scintillation crystal causing it to emit a flash of light. The light then activates a ▷photomultiplier, producing a pulse of electrons, which are counted to enable the activity of the source to be calculated. A **scintillation spectrometer** is used to show the energy distribution of a source.

● **Scipio Aemilianus Africanus** ▶ (c. 185–129 BC) Roman general, politician, and literary patron; the grandson by adoption of Scipio Africanus. After military successes in Greece and Spain, he blockaded and destroyed Carthage in 146 (*see* Punic Wars), becoming a national hero. After subduing Spain with the destruction of Numantia in 133, he lost support by attacking the reforms of his murdered brother-in-law, Tiberius ▷Gracchus. Scipio died during the subsequent political upheaval.

● **Scipio Africanus** ▶ (236–183 BC) Roman general of the second ▷Punic War. After defeating the Carthaginians in Spain, he won permission, despite ▷Fabius Maximus' opposition, to invade Africa. After crushing Hannibal at the battle of Zama in 202, he became a national hero, receiving the title Africanus. Subsequent pro-Greek policies provoked political hostility and he retired from public life. His son was the adoptive father of Scipio Aemilianus Africanus.

● **scirocco** ▷See sirocco.

● **sclerosis** ▶ Stiffening and hardening of the tissues. This is a feature of many diseases: it can affect the brain and spinal cord, causing ▷multiple sclerosis, and the walls of the arteries, causing ▷arteriosclerosis or ▷atherosclerosis.

● **Scofield, (David) Paul** ▶ (1922–) British actor. His major roles have included Hamlet (1948, 1955), Lear (1962), Othello (1980), and John Gabriel Borkman (1996). His best-known film performance was as Sir Thomas More in *A Man for All Seasons* (1966).

● **Scone** ▶ 56 25N 3 24W A parish in E central Scotland, in Perth and Kinross. It consists of the villages of New Scone and Old Scone, the Pictish and later Scottish capital where most Scottish kings were crowned. The coronation stone was taken from here by Edward I in 1296 and placed in Westminster Abbey. It was removed by Scottish nationalists in 1950 but later recovered. The stone was returned to Scotland in 1996 and placed in Edinburgh Castle on St Andrew's Day. Population (latest est): 4897.

● **scopolamine** ▷See hyoscine.

● **scops owl** ▶ A small ▷owl of the mainly tropical genus *Otus*, also called screech owl because of its call. 20–30 cm long and mostly arboreal, with camouflaging plumage, scops owls feed on insects, birds, and small mammals.

● **Scorpio** ▶ (astrology) ▷See zodiac.

● **scorpion** ▶ An ▷arachnid of the order *Scorpionida* (about 800 species), found in warm dry regions. Scorpions are 13–175 mm long; the second pair of appendages (pedipalps) form large pincers and the long abdomen curls upwards and bears a poisonous sting, which can be fatal to man. They live under stones or in burrows in soil during the day and prey at night, mainly on insects and spiders. The female produces live young, which ride on her back for several days. □ p. 1116.

● **scorpion fish** ▶ A carnivorous fish, often called rockfish or zebra fish, belonging to the family *Scorpaenidae*, found mainly on rocky beds of tropical and temperate coastal waters. It has a stout body, up to 1 m long, a large spiny head, and strong fin spines, which can inflict painful wounds and may be venomous. Order: *Scorpaeniformes*.

● **scorpion fly** ▶ An □insect of the order *Mecoptera* (400 species), so called because the males of many species curl the abdomen over the body, like a scorpion. 12–25 mm long, scorpion flies have long legs and antennae and, typically, two similar pairs of net-veined wings. The larvae develop in soil, feeding—like the adults—on dead animals and plants.

● **Scorpius** ▶ (Latin: Scorpion) A conspicuous constellation in the S sky, lying on the ▷zodiac between Sagittarius and Libra. The brightest star is ▷Antares. The constellation contains several notable open and globular ▷star clusters and the intense X-ray binary star **Scorpius X-1**.

scorpion

● **Scorsese, Martin** ▶ (1942–) US film director. He established his reputation with such films as *Mean Streets* (1973), *Taxi Driver* (1976), and *Raging Bull* (1980); subsequent work has included *GoodFellas* (1990), *Casino* (1995), and *Bringing Out the Dead* (1999).

● **Scotland** ▶ A country occupying the N part of Great Britain and comprising a political division of the ▷United Kingdom. Most of the population lives in a narrow lowland belt, which runs E–W across the country and separates the lower hills of the S (including the Tweedsmuir and Cheviot Hills) from the higher mountains of the N (including the Grampian and Cairngorm Mountains). Ben Nevis near Fort William in the W is the highest point in the British Isles at 1343 m (4406 ft). There are many islands off the N and W coasts, including the Hebrides to the W and the Orkneys and Shetlands to the N. The principal rivers are the Clyde, which flows into the North Channel, and the Forth, Tay, and Spey, which flow into the North Sea. There are many lochs in the northern mountains, and Lochs Ness and Lochy form the Great Glen (valley) between Fort William and Inverness. Administratively, Scotland is divided into 32 council areas.

Economy: the central belt of the country is highly industrialized. However, the traditional industries of coalmining and shipbuilding are now almost extinct, while steelmaking is largely based on Ravenscraig near Motherwell. Whisky, for which Scotland is internationally famous, is produced in Highland, Moray, and Aberdeenshire. The discovery of oil in the North Sea has led to a boom on the E coast of the country, and this has emphasized the problems of the Glasgow region in the W, with its outdated industrial structure and high unemployment. Agriculture remains important and includes sheep farming (especially in the border hills, where there is a famous textile industry), dairying in the SW (from whence the Ayrshire breed of cattle originated), beef production in the E and NE lowlands (famous for the Aberdeen-Angus cattle breed), and market gardening. Forestry has grown in importance. Fishing is a major source of revenue, especially on the E coast at such ports as Aberdeen and Fraserburgh, but there is concern over levels of stock. Salmon farming is a growing industry in the sea lochs of the W coast.

History: Scotland was never completely subdued by the Romans, but the barbaric northern tribes were kept N of ▷Hadrian's Wall and, for some 40 years, the more northerly ▷Antonine Wall (from the Forth to the Clyde). The diverse peoples (Picts, Scots, Britons, and Angles) of Scotland gradually united, helped by the spread of Christianity, and Kenneth I MacAlpine (died c. 858) is regarded as their first king. During the middle ages there was recurrent war between England and Scotland. In 1296 Edward I of England declared himself King of Scotland but after his death Robert the Bruce reasserted Scot-

tish independence, which was recognized by England in 1328. The 14th century saw the establishment of a long-standing alliance between France and Scotland and the succession of the ▷Stuart dynasty. Under the influence of John ▷Knox the Scottish Church became Presbyterian (*see* Church of Scotland) during the reign of Mary, Queen of Scots. In 1603 her son James VI succeeded as James I to the throne of England but political union between the two countries was not established until 1707 (*see* Union, Acts of). After the Hanoverian succession the Stuart cause was kept alive by the ▷Jacobites, who staged two unsuccessful rebellions (1715, 1745). Rapid industrialization in the 19th century encouraged considerable Irish immigration, while the ▷Highland Clearances caused many Scots to emigrate. Following the parliamentary Reform Act (1832) a tradition for Liberalism was established in Scotland but Labour gained political dominance in the 20th century. Improved economic prospects following the discovery of North Sea oil boosted the ▷Scottish National Party but ▷devolution plans failed to attract sufficient support in a referendum (1979). In 1997, however, 74.3% of voters backed government proposals to establish a Scottish parliament, with 63.5% voting to give the body tax-varying powers. Elections for the parliament took place in May, 1999, and power was transferred to the new body in July. The current first minister is Labour's Jack ▷McConnell. Area: 78 769 sq km (30 405 sq mi). Population (1999 est): 5 119 200. Capital: Edinburgh.

● **Scotland Yard** ▶ A street off Whitehall, London (UK), which gave its name to the headquarters of the Metropolitan Police, situated there until 1890. When the headquarters then moved to the Victoria Embankment its name became New Scotland Yard, which was kept in a subsequent move (1966) to Broadway, Westminster.

● **Scots law** ▶ Originally Scots law differed little from English law, but from the beginning of the 16th century there was a tendency to introduce elements of ▷Roman law, as embodied in the ▷civil law of France and the Netherlands. This resulted in marked differences from English law, the preservation of which was guaranteed by the Treaty of Union with England in 1707. An example is the Scots law of ▷contract, in which "consideration" does not have the importance it has in English law, where no contract is binding without consideration. Modern statutes have, however, introduced many new laws that are the same for both countries.

● **Scott, Sir George Gilbert** ▶ (1811–78) British architect. An advocate of the ▷gothic revival, Scott was a noted restorer of medieval buildings who renovated Westminster Abbey. His original buildings include the Albert Memorial (1864), St Pancras station (1865), and government offices in Whitehall (1861), built in the Renaissance style under pressure from Palmerston, who rejected Scott's earlier gothic scheme. His grandson **Sir Giles Gilbert Scott** (1880–1960) was also an architect, who won the competition for the design of the Anglican Cathedral in Liverpool in 1903. His other buildings include Cambridge University Library (1931–34), the new Bodleian Library, Oxford (1936–46), and the new Waterloo Bridge (1939–45).

● **Scott, Paul (Mark)** ▶ (1920–78) British novelist. He is known for the "Raj Quartet," a series of novels dealing with the end of British rule in India. They are *The Jewel in the Crown* (1966), *The Day of the Scorpion* (1968), *The Towers of Silence* (1972), and *A Division of the Spoils* (1975). His last novel, *Staying On* (1977), won the Booker Prize.

● **Scott, Ridley** ▶ (1937–) British film director. After work in television, he established himself in the cinema with the science-fiction films *Alien* (1979) and *Blade Runner* (1982). Later films include the feminist road movie *Thelma and Louise* (1991), the epic *Gladiator* (2000), which won five Academy Awards, and the highly successful *Hannibal* (2001). His brother **Tony Scott** (1944–) directed the films *Top Gun* (1986) and *True Romance* (1993).

● **Scott, Captain Robert Falcon** ▶ (1868–1912) British explorer and naval officer. He led two expeditions to the Antarctic, the first in the *Discovery* (1900–04) and the second (1910–12) in the *Terra Nova*. With a party of four (including L. E. G. Oates) he reached the South Pole by sledge on 17 January, 1912, only to find that ▷Amundsen had preceded them. Delayed by illness and blizzards they perished on the return journey. Their bodies and Scott's diaries were found in November that year. His son **Sir Peter Markham Scott** (1909–89) was an ornithologist and wildlife painter. In 1946 he founded the Wild-

Captain Scott ► Officers on Scott's last journey to the South Pole hauling sledges full of fodder that they have unloaded from the *Terra Nova*.

fowl Trust (now the Wildfowl and Wetlands Trust) at Slimbridge, Gloucestershire.

● **Scott, Sir Walter** ► (1771–1832) Scottish novelist. His early works included a collection of border ballads (1802–03) and the narrative poem *The Lay of the Last Minstrel* (1805). *Waverley* (1814) was the first of a series of historical novels that included *Old Mortality* (1816) and *The Heart of Midlothian* (1818). His last years were spent in frantic literary activity to pay off his creditors after his bankruptcy in 1826.

● **Scottish Borders** ► A council area in SE Scotland, bordering on England. Created in 1996, it has the same boundaries as the former Borders Region. Consisting chiefly of uplands descending E to the Merse lowlands, it is mainly agricultural; sheep farming and the manufacture of tweed and knitwear are the chief economic activities. Forestry is also important. Area: 4734 sq km (1827 sq mi). Population (1996 est): 106 100. Administrative centre: Newtown St Boswells.

● **Scottish literature** ► The literature of Scotland comprises a diversity of works in Scottish Gaelic, Lowland Scots (Lallans), English, and combinations of these. Literary Gaelic as practised by the ▷bards continued in use up to the 18th century and drew upon the same traditions as ▷Irish literature (especially the Ulster cycle and the ▷Fenian cycle). The 16th-century Book of the Dean of Lismore is an example of this heritage, although it was James Macpherson's alleged translation of ▷Ossian that popularized these Gaelic stories throughout Europe. In the Scots (non-Gaelic) vernacular, the first important work is John ▷Barbour's 14th-century epic *The Bruce*. In the 15th and 16th centuries were produced the greatest works of early Scottish literature, the poetry of the *makaris* or Scottish Chaucerians, including ▷Henryson, ▷Dunbar, Gavin ▷Douglas, Sir David Lindsay (1490–1555), the author of *Ane Satyre of the thrie Estatis* (1540), and ▷James I, King of Scots. In the 17th century, by contrast, there was little outstanding literary production. It was during this century that standard English became the main written language in Scotland and Scots became a spoken dialect. Robert ▷Burns' evocative use of the Lowlands dialect in the 18th century had a lasting effect on Scottish literature and national consciousness and influenced later poets, for example Hugh ▷MacDiarmid, who have written in Lallans. Since the 17th century, however, most Scottish writers have written in a variant of standard English with dialect passages introduced as appropriate: the works of ▷Boswell, ▷Smollett, Sir Walter ▷Scott, ▷Carlyle, Robert Louis ▷Stevenson, and many others form an essential part of the literature of English. Contemporary Scottish writers include Alasdair Gray (1934–), James Kelman (1946–), Iain Banks (1954–), and Irvine Welsh (1959–). The leading Gaelic poet of modern times was Sorley Maclean (1911–96).

● **Scottish National Party** ► (SNP) A political party, founded in 1928, dedicated to the achievement of Scottish independence from the UK. The party achieved growing popularity with the rise of nationalist sentiment in the 1960s and 1970s and secured 11 seats and 30.4% of the Scottish vote in the parliamentary election of October, 1974. The indecisive result of the ▷devolution referendum in 1979 was a setback and after the subsequent general election the SNP held only two seats. However, its fortunes rose again in the 1980s and 1990s and after the 1997 election it held six seats (five from 2001), thereby becoming the main opposition in Scotland. It also forms the official opposition in the Scottish parliament set up in 1999, with 35 of the 129 seats.

● **Scottish terrier** ► A breed of dog, originally called Aberdeen terrier, used to chase foxes from earth. It is thickset with short legs, a short erect tail, and pricked ears. The long muzzle has characteristically long whiskers and the wiry coat can be black, brindle, grey, or yellow-brown. Height: 25–28 cm.

● **Scout Association** ► An association founded by Robert ▷Baden-Powell in 1908 to encourage boys to become enterprising members of society. The Scouts' motto is "Be Prepared." The Scout Association classifies its members into Cub Scouts (for boys aged between 8 and 11), Scouts (11–16), and Venture Scouts (16–29). There are 14 million Scouts throughout the world, of whom 600 000 are in the UK. In Britain the first Girl Scouts were admitted in 1990. ▷*See also* Guides Association.

● **SCP** ▷*See* single-cell protein.

● **Scranton** ► 41 25N 75 40W A city in the USA, in Pennsylvania. It had a thriving anthracite industry and iron and steel operations until the 1950s. Since then it has shown great initiative in attracting many light industries to the city. It is the site of the University of Scranton (1888). Population (2000): 76 415.

● **scrapie** ► A fatal disease of sheep and goats characterized by progressive degeneration of the brain and spinal cord. After an incubation period of 18 months to 5 years, the affected animal appears excitable, and intense irritation of the skin causes it to seek relief by scraping itself against any surface (hence the name) or even by self-mutilation. These initial symptoms are followed by uncoordinated movements, collapse, and death. Like ▷BSE and ▷Creutzfeldt-Jakob disease, scrapie belongs to a group of diseases called transmissible spongiform encephalopathies and is believed to be caused by an abnormal ▷prion protein. However, although it is endemic in the UK, there is no evidence to suggest that it can be transmitted to humans or other species.

● **screamer** ► A marsh-dwelling bird belonging to a family (*Anhimidae*; 3 species) occurring in tropical and subtropical South America. 75 cm long, screamers have dark plumage, a short hook-tipped bill, two paired wing spurs, and either a crest or a horny protuberance on the head. They feed on water plants and the skin contains air sacs that can produce crackling noises. Order: *Anseriformes* (ducks, geese, etc.).

● **scree** ▷*See* talus.

● **screech owl** ▷*See* scops owl.

● **screw pine** ► A treelike plant of the genus *Pandanus* (about 150 species), native to the Old World tropics. The name derives from the spiral arrangement of the leaves, which leave scars in a corkscrew spiral when they fall. Stout aerial prop roots grow down from the stem into the ground: the part of the stem below these roots decays, so that the plant is supported entirely by the prop roots. The leaves, which are long and stiff with parallel sides, are used for matting and weaving. The flowers grow in large heads enclosed in leafy structures (spathes) and the fruits of some species are edible. Several species are grown as house plants. Family: *Pandanaceae*.

● **screwworm** ▷*See* blowfly.

● **Scriabin, Alexander** ► (1872–1915) Russian composer and pianist. His mature compositions were characterized by chords built on the interval of the fourth. His works include three symphonies—the third entitled *The Divine Poem* (1903)—a piano concerto (1894), ten piano sonatas, and *Prometheus* or *The Poem of Fire* (1909–10), intended to be accompanied by a sequence of coloured lights projected onto a screen.

● **scribes** ▶ (Hebrew: *sofrim*) Ancient Jewish biblical scholars. They preserved the textual tradition of the ▷Torah and cultivated its study and interpretation. In the Gospels they are frequently linked with the ▷Pharisees. In later Jewish usage the term applies to copyists of the Torah and other sacred texts.

● **Scriblerus Club** ▶ An English literary club founded in about 1713. Its members included ▷Pope, ▷Swift, ▷Gay, and John ▷Arbuthnot. In their collaborative *Memoirs of Martinus Scriblerus* (1741) they ridiculed literary pretentiousness.

● **scrofula** ▶ Ulceration of a lymph node infected with ▷tuberculosis, seen most commonly in the neck. This form of tuberculosis is now uncommon in developed countries but is still seen in poorer countries. Treatment is with antibiotic drugs and surgery. It was formerly known as king's evil, as it was believed that the touch of the sovereign would cure it.

● **scrub** ▶ Vegetation consisting mainly of short evergreen often aromatic shrubs, typically found in coastal regions with hot dry summers: the Mediterranean maquis and the Californian chaparral are examples. This type of vegetation is transitional between grasslands and forests. The shrubs are adapted to survive dry summers and usually flower and fruit in the spring.

● **scrub bird** ▶ A rare Australian passerine bird belonging to a primitive family (*Atrichornithidae*; 2 species). Scrub birds are brown with long pointed tails and loud voices, and are poor fliers, feeding on insects and nesting on the ground. The noisy scrub bird (*Atrichornis clamosus*) is about 22 cm long and occurs in SW Australia, where it was thought to be extinct until 1961. The smaller rufous scrub bird (*A. rufescens*) is found in the forests of New South Wales.

● **Scruton, Roger (Vernon)** ▶ (1944–) British philosopher and cultural historian. Professor of aesthetics at London's Birkbeck College (1985–92) and of philosophy at Boston University, Massachussetts (1992–94), he is now an author and editor of the right-wing journal *Salisbury Review*. His books include *Art and Imagination* (1974), *The Meaning of Conservatism* (1980), *Thinkers of the New Left* (1985), *Modern Philosophy* (1994), and *An Intelligent Person's Guide to Modern Culture* (1998).

● **Scudamore, Peter** ▶ (1958–) British jockey. A steeplechase rider, he passed Jonjo O'Neill's record of 149 wins in a season in 1989. He retired in 1993.

● **Scud missile** ▶ A Soviet ground-to-ground missile. The Scud-B, using a mobile launcher and having a range of 650 km (404 mi) as modified by Iraq, was used in the ▷Gulf War to attack Israel and Saudi Arabia.

● **Scullin, James Henry** ▶ (1876–1953) Australian statesman; Labor prime minister (1929–1931). The problems of the Depression plagued his administration, his deflationary measures bringing electoral defeat in 1931. He was opposition leader from 1932 to 1935.

● **sculpin** ▷*See* bullhead.

● **sculpture** ▶ The art of shaping or modelling such materials as stone, wood, ivory (*see* netsuke), clay, and metal either in relief (*see* relief sculpture) or in the round. Stone, particularly marble, has been most popular with sculptors since it is the most durable material for outdoor sculptures. Wood is principally associated with ▷African art and medieval indoor sculptures (*see also* wood carving). Clay is most often employed in preliminary models for sculptures later cast in metal. Bronze has been the most favoured metal for casting, although in the 20th century aluminium, iron, and sheet metal have been increasingly used.

Most civilizations have left a legacy of sculpture, the earliest known work being Palaeolithic representations of human and animal figures, believed to be of religious significance. More detailed figures, indicating the hierarchy of the social organization, appeared in Egypt in the 3rd millennium BC. The 5th and 4th centuries BC saw the rise of classical Greek sculpture with the work of ▷Praxiteles, ▷Phidias, and others. The Romans subsequently developed these clas-

sical themes, introducing more personalized portrait sculpture. In India from the 2nd century BC, Japan from the 6th century AD, and China from the 7th century AD, sculpture was devoted primarily to representations of the Buddha and his life. In medieval Europe, sculpture became largely an embellishment of architecture, until the revival of classical ideals in the Italian Renaissance with the works of such major sculptors as ▷Donatello and ▷Michelangelo. The spread of Renaissance ideas throughout the rest of Europe led to the work of Jean ▷Goujon in France and Grinling ▷Gibbons in England, while baroque sculpture attained its finest expression in the virtuosity of ▷Bernini. The neoclassicism of the 18th century saw a new respect for ancient Greek models. Outstanding among the sculptors of 19th-century Romanticism was ▷Rodin. Although the figural tradition was continued into the 20th century by such sculptors as Marino ▷Marini and Ernst ▷Barlach, semiabstract and abstract sculpture, influenced by African and other primitive carving, became the principal forms of sculptural expression. Semiabstract sculptures include the innovative work of ▷Modigliani, ▷Epstein, and Henry ▷Moore, as well as the geometricized forms of Jacques ▷Lipchitz and the simplified shapes of Constantin ▷Brancusi. Abstract or nonrepresentative sculpture includes the organic forms of such sculptors as ▷Arp and the geometric constructions of Naum ▷Gabo (*see also* constructivism). Kinetic and environmental sculpture were also specifically 20th-century developments. Kinetic sculptures, i.e. sculptures that move either by motor, magnetism, or air currents, were pioneered by Gabo and Alexander ▷Calder. Environmental sculpture is the re-creation of an environment as in Claes ▷Oldenburg's pop art work of the 1960s. The principal uses of sculpture have been architectural and commemorative.

● **Scunthorpe** ▶ 53 36N 0 38W A town in NE England, in North Lincolnshire unitary authority, Lincolnshire. The traditional iron and steel industries have declined and the service sector has risen in importance. Population (1991): 75 982.

● **scurvy** ▶ A disease caused by deficiency of ▷vitamin C (which is present in most fresh fruits and vegetables). In the past scurvy was common among sailors on long voyages, but it is now rarely seen except in old debilitated people and vagrants. The symptoms are weakness and aching joints and muscles, progressing to bleeding of the gums and—later—other organs. Scurvy can be readily treated by giving vitamin C or fresh fruit.

● **scurvy grass** ▶ An annual, biennial, or perennial herb of the genus *Cochlearia* (about 25 species), occurring in temperate regions, especially near coasts. Up to 50 cm tall, it has simple often heart-shaped leaves and the white or mauve flowers, each with four petals, are in small clusters. Family: ▷*Cruciferae*.

● **Scutari** ▷*See* Shkodër (Albania); Üsküdar (Turkey).

● **Scylla and Charybdis** ▶ In Greek mythology, two sea monsters on opposite sides of the Strait of Messina who menaced ▷Odysseus, the ▷Argonauts, and other legendary heroes. Scylla was a monster with six heads and a pack of baying hounds, while Charybdis was a raging whirlpool.

● **Scyphozoa** ▷*See* jellyfish.

● **Scythians** ▶ An Indo-European people who temporarily settled in Asia Minor before settling in what is now S Russia in the 6th century BC. The true Scythians, called Royal Scyths, established a kingdom N of the Black Sea and traded wheat for luxury goods with the Greek colonies there. Their skill as horsemen and archers halted Persian and Macedonian invasions but they remained a nomadic people until their disappearance during the Gothic onslaughts of the 3rd century AD. Objects recovered from their royal tombs demonstrate their metalworking skill and, especially in the animal designs that predominate as decorations, their artistry.

● **SDI** ▷*See* Strategic Defence Initiative.

● **sea anemone** ▶ A sedentary marine invertebrate animal belonging to a worldwide order (*Actiniaria*; over 1000 species) of ▷cnidarians. It has a soft columnar body (*see* polyp) of a few millimetres to about 1.5 m in diameter, with a mouth at the top surrounded by rings of tentacles, which—when expanded—give the animal a flower-like appearance. Sea anemones are usually blue, green, or yellow and are found attached to rocks and weeds or associated with other invertebrates. They feed mainly on fish and other animals. Class: *Anthozoa*.

● **sea bass** ▶ A carnivorous fish, also called sea perch, of the family *Serranidae* (about 400 species), found mainly in coastal waters of tropical and temperate seas. Its elongated body ranges up to 3.75 m long and varies in colour with the species. They may be active or sedentary and certain species are ▷hermaphrodite while others, such as ▷groupers, are able to change sex. Many are valued food and game fish. Order: *Perciformes*. ▷*See also* bass.

● **Seaborg, Glenn Theodore** ▶ (1912–99) US physicist, who as professor at the University of California led the search for ▷transuranic elements. Working with Edwin ▷McMillan, he produced plutonium in 1940 by bombarding neptunium with neutrons. Working with another group of researchers, Seaborg prepared samples of all the transuranic elements with atomic numbers from 95 to 105 by similar methods. For this work he shared the Nobel Prize with McMillan in 1951.

● **seaborgium** ▶ A synthetic transuranic element, synthesized and identified in 1974 and formerly known as element 106. It was the first element to be named after a living scientist (Glenn ▷Seaborg). At no 106.

● **sea bream** ▶ A fish, also called porgy, belonging to a family (*Sparidae*; about 400 species) found mainly in shallow waters of tropical and subtropical seas. It has a deep laterally flattened body covered with large scales, a single long dorsal fin, and well-developed teeth. It lives in shoals and feeds by scraping algae and small animals off rocks.

● **sea butterfly** ▶ A ▷gastropod mollusc belonging to the subclass *Opisthobranchia*, also called pteropod. Some sea butterflies (order *Thecosomata*) have a shell, are filter feeders, and swim by means of winglike appendages (parapodia). Others (order *Gymnosomata*) are naked, with only small parapodia, and prey on small animals.

● **sea cow** ▷*See* dugong.

● **sea cucumber** ▶ A marine invertebrate animal belonging to a worldwide class (*Holothuroidea*; 1100 species) of ▷echinoderms. Its cucumber-shaped body, 2–200 cm long, is covered with leathery skin containing small calcareous plates or spicules. There is a mouth at one end surrounded by a ring of tentacles, which are used for feeding on detritus and plankton. It crawls sluggishly on the sea bottom or burrows in sand or mud. □oceans.

● **sea eagle** ▶ An ▷eagle belonging to the widely distributed genus *Haliaeetus* (8 species). 70–120 cm long, sea eagles have a wedge-shaped tail and are typically brown with white markings. The smaller species feed mostly on fish but the larger species eat carrion, large birds, and mammals.

● **sea fan** ▶ A colonial ▷coral of the genus *Gorgonia*, in which the tiny cylindrical ▷polyps have a horny internal skeleton and grow upon one another to produce a fanlike structure. Sea fans are commonly yellow, pink, brown, or purple and occur mainly in shallow tropical waters.

● **sea-floor spreading** ▶ A concept developed in the 1960s that provides a mechanism for ▷continental drift. Magma rises from the earth's mantle to the surface along midocean ridges (constructive plate margins; *see* plate tectonics), cools to form new oceanic crust, and displaces the older material sideways at an average rate of 4 cm per year. Magnetic reversals recorded in the rocks in approximately symmetrical strips at each side of the midocean ridges provide strong evidence for sea-floor spreading.

● **sea gooseberry** ▷*See* ctenophore.

● **seagull** ▷*See* gull.

● **sea hare** ▶ A marine ▷gastropod mollusc belonging to the family *Aplysiidae*. Growing up to 35 cm long, sea hares are often green or yellow in colour; they have a pair of tentacles (resembling a hare's ears) and a much-reduced shell. When disturbed, they eject a cloud of purple ink into the water. Subclass: *Opisthobranchia*.

● **sea holly** ▶ A perennial herb, *Eryngium maritimum*, found on sandy and shingly European shores. Growing to a height of 30–60 cm, it has spiked holly-like leaves and bears clusters of purplish-blue flowers. Family: ▷*Umbelliferae*.

sea horse ▶ A female yellow sea horse (*Hippocampus kuda*). This species, which grows to a length of 28 cm (10 in), occurs in the Indo-Pacific region.

● **sea horse** ▶ One of several small bony-plated marine □fish of the family *Syngnathidae* (*see also* pipefish), especially the genus *Hippocampus*, that lives in shallow warm waters. They are 4–30 cm long and the horselike head with its long tubular snout is set at an angle to the body. They use the prehensile tail to cling to seaweed and swim in a vertical position by undulating the dorsal fin. The males have a brood pouch in which the young are hatched. Order: *Gasterosteiformes*.

● **Sea Islands** ▶ A chain of islands in the USA, off the coasts of South Carolina, Georgia, and Florida. Production of long-stapled Sea Island cotton was important until infestation by the boll weevil in the 1920s.

● **sea kale** ▶ A bushy perennial herb, *Crambe maritima*, found on Atlantic coasts of Europe. Growing to a height of 40–60 cm, it has cabbage-like leaves and bears clusters of small white flowers. It may be cultivated for its tender young edible shoots. Family: ▷*Cruciferae*.

● **seal** ▶ (sigillography) A stone, metal, or wooden stamp and its impression in wax or lead used to authenticate documents. The engraved surface of a seal is usually rock crystal or other hard stone but bronze and gold are also used. The impression cut into the seal generally consists of a central device of a heraldic or personal motif, surrounded by a legend. Officials' seals are practical in design but other seals, such as desk seals and fob seals (worn as jewels), enable jewellers and goldsmiths to exhibit their skills. **Sigillography** is the study of seals.

● **seal** ▸ (zoology) A carnivorous marine mammal belonging to the order *Pinnipedia* (34 species). Seals have a streamlined body with a smooth rounded head and an insulating layer of blubber under the sleek-coated skin. Both pairs of limbs flatten into flippers. They feed mainly on fish and breed on land or ice. There are two main families: the *Otariidae* (eared seals; 14 species) including fur seals and ▷sealions, which have external ears and can turn their hind flippers forward for walking on land; and the *Phocidae* (true seals; 19 species), which lack external ears and have trailing hind flippers. The ▷walrus is the only member of its family, *Odobenidae*.

● **sea lavender** ▸ A perennial or annual herb of the genus *Limonium* (about 300 species), found on coasts and salt marshes of W Asia, Europe, and North America. The common sea lavender (*L. vulgare*) has a basal rosette of slender leaves and a branched flower stem, 8–30 cm high, bearing clusters of purple-blue flowers. Family: *Plumbaginaceae*.

● **sea lettuce** ▸ A green ▷seaweed of the genus *Ulva*, found mainly between high and low tide levels on most rocky shores. It has broad flat translucent fronds, which resemble lettuce leaves, and grows in bunches up to about 30 cm long. It is rich in iodine and vitamins and is sometimes used in salads and soups.

● **sea lily** ▷*See* crinoid.

● **sealion** ▸ A large ▷seal belonging to the family *Otariidae* (14 species). Californian sealions (*Zalophus californianus*) of the Californian coast are popular circus animals. They grow to 2 m and live in groups with a definite social hierarchy. Steller's sealion (*Eumetopias jubatus*) is the largest species, growing to over 3 m.

● **Sealyham terrier** ▸ A breed of ⌐dog developed between 1850 and 1891 on the Sealyham estate, Haverfordwest, Wales, for hunting foxes and badgers. It is sturdily built with short legs, drooping ears, and a short thin tail. White with darker markings, Sealyhams have a soft under coat and a wiry outer coat. Height: 27–30 cm.

● **sea mouse** ▸ A marine ▷annelid worm belonging to a family (*Aphroditidae*) found in North Atlantic coastal waters. Sea mice grow up to 18 cm long and 7 cm wide with 15 pairs of scales buried in a dense covering of irridescent hairs. They are foraging carnivores and are generally found buried in fine sand or mud with only the hind end protruding. Class: *Polychaeta*.

● **sea otter** ▸ A marine ▷otter, *Enhydra lutris*, of the N Pacific. 1.2 m long and weighing 35 kg, it floats in colonies of up to 90 individuals. The cubs, well-furred and with open eyes and sharp teeth, are born in the sea. Sea otters feed on molluscs, crustaceans, and fish and can crack open shells using a pebble balanced on the chest. Once hunted for their valuable fur, they are now a protected species.

● **sea pen** ▸ A fleshy colonial marine invertebrate animal belonging to an order (*Pennatulacea*; 300 species) of ▷cnidarians, especially one forming a feather-like colony (e.g. *Leioptilus*). A central stalklike individual—the primary ▷polyp—is anchored into mud or sand and secondary polyps branch from it. Class: *Anthozoa*.

● **Sea Peoples** ▸ The seafaring tribes who colonized Asia Minor, the Aegean, and N Africa in the 13th and 12th centuries BC, destroying the ▷Hittite empire. About 1170 they were almost annihilated by Rameses III of Egypt and those that survived scattered—to Palestine, the Aegean, and perhaps to the W Mediterranean. They have been variously and uncertainly identified and may have been Achaeans, Etruscans, or Philistines.

● **sea perch** ▷*See* sea bass.

● **seaplane** ▸ An aircraft designed to take off and land on the sea (or other expanse of water). The two types are the **float plane**, which has a conventional fuselage with floats in the place of landing wheels, and the **flying boat**, which has a floating hull instead of a fuselage (and often floats at its wingtips). Because both types need a calm sea from which to take off and upon which to land they are now rarely used. However, between World War I and World War II, the development of seaplanes was encouraged by the ▷Schneider Trophy competitions, and in both wars flying boats (especially the Sunderland

flying boats of World War II) were used. In 1939 the first commercial transatlantic service made use of Short flying boats, capable of being fuelled in flight (*see* aircraft).

● **Searle, Ronald William Fordham** ▸ (1920–) British cartoonist. He worked for such journals as the *Sunday Express* and *Punch* but is best known for his cartoon creation of the outrageous schoolgirls of St Trinian's, who subsequently featured in four films.

● **sea robin** ▷*See* gurnard.

● **sea sickness** ▷*See* travel sickness.

● **sea slug** ▸ A marine ▷gastropod mollusc of the order *Nudibranchia*. Sea slugs have exposed feathery gills, two pairs of tentacles, and no shell. They browse on sponges, sea anemones, and corals and are often brightly coloured. Some sea slugs retain the stinging cells of their prey for their own defence.

● **sea snake** ▸ A venomous fish-eating snake belonging to the family *Hydrophiidae* (50 species) occurring mainly in coastal waters of Australasia and SE Asia. Sea snakes are adapted to an underwater life by having a flattened body with an oarlike tail and valvelike closures in the nostrils. Most produce live young (rather than eggs).

● **sea spider** ▸ A spider-like marine arthropod of the class *Pycnogonida* (or *Pantopoda*; over 600 species). Its short thin body, 3–500 mm long, usually bears four pairs of long walking legs and a long sucking proboscis. Sea spiders occur up to depths of 3600 m, feeding on soft-bodied invertebrate animals. Fertilized eggs are carried by the males and many larvae are parasitic on polyps or molluscs.

● **sea squirt** ▷*See* tunicate.

● **SEATO** ▷*See* South East Asia Treaty Organization.

● **Seattle** ▸ 47 35N 122 20W A city in the USA, in Washington state between the Puget Sound and Lake Washington. A port of entry to the Klondike, it became a boom town with the 1897 Alaska Gold Rush. Educational institutions include the University of Washington (1861) and Seattle University (1852). It is Alaska's main supply port. There are large timber mills and various forest-based industries. Other industries include the manufacture of aircraft, shipbuilding, ship repair, and food processing. Population (1996 est): 524 704.

● **sea urchin** ▸ A marine invertebrate animal, belonging to the class ▷*Echinoidea*, with a typically spherical rigid body covered by long movable spines. Sea urchins live on shores and ocean floors and use a complex feeding apparatus—Aristotle's lantern—to masticate algae and other organic material scraped off rocks. Phylum: *Echinodermata* (*see* echinoderm).

● **sea water** ▸ The water constituting the world's oceans and seas. It is usually saline, average salinity being about 35 g per kg of sea water. The principal dissolved salts are sodium chloride (2.8%), magnesium chloride (0.4%), and magnesium sulphate (0.2%). Where evaporation is high, salinity is increased, as in the Red Sea. Sea water is desalinated (*see* desalination) in some areas, e.g. Saudi Arabia, to obtain fresh water, although the process is costly. The properties of sea water, including its chemical composition, temperature, and movements (waves and tides) are studied in ▷oceanography.

● **seaweed** ▸ Large multicellular red, brown, or green marine ▷algae that are generally found attached to the sea bed, rocks, or other solid structures by rootlike structures called holdfasts. They have stemlike stalks and fronds, which may be flat and undivided, threadlike, or branched, sometimes with small air bladders for buoyancy. Seaweeds often occur in dense aggregations along shores but are also found to depths of about 200 m. Many are of commercial importance as food (e.g. ▷carrageen, ▷laver, and ▷sea lettuce), as fertilizers, in chemical and pharmaceutical products, etc. ▷*See also* kelp; wrack.

● **sebaceous glands** ▷*See* skin.

● **Sebastian, St** ▸ (3rd century AD) Roman martyr. According to tradition, he was an officer of the Praetorian Guards until his Christianity was discovered by Diocletian. His martyrdom at the hands of archers is a frequent subject of painting. Feast day: 20 Jan. Emblem: an arrow.

● **Sebastiano del Piombo** ▶ (S. Luciano; c. 1485–1547) Venetian painter. Although he was a pupil of Giovanni Bellini, his early works, notably *St John Chrysostom* (c. 1509; S Giovanni Crisostomo, Venice), were influenced by Giorgione. Moving to Rome in 1511, he painted decorations in the Farnesina with ▷Raphael, whose *Transfiguration* he directly challenged with his *Raising of Lazarus* (1517–19; National Gallery, London). He was also known as a portraitist; his sitters included Christopher Columbus and Pope Clement VII, who appointed him keeper of the papal seals (*piombi*) in 1531—hence his nickname.

● **Sebastopol** ▷*See* Sevastopol.

● **second** ▶ **1.** (s) The ▷SI unit of time equal to the duration of 9 192 631 770 periods of the radiation corresponding to a specified transition of the caesium-133 atom. The unit was formerly defined by astronomical measurement. ▷*See also* caesium clock; time. **2.** A unit of angle equal to one-sixtieth of a minute.

● **secondary education** ▶ Education for adolescent children, aged approximately from 11 to 18. Although found in ancient Greece and Rome, secondary education is a relatively recent creation in its present form. In the UK the Education Act (1944) introduced universal secondary education (compulsory to the age of 15, extended to 16 in 1972) to give greater scope to the terminal formal education of the majority of the population, hitherto carried on in elementary (extended primary) schools. Initially a tripartite system (comprising ▷grammar schools, ▷secondary modern schools, and technical schools) was implemented in England and Wales, selection being based upon the ▷eleven-plus examination. Although this exam has now been largely phased out and a widespread system of ▷comprehensive schools introduced, the extent to which pupils should be segregated on the basis of ability at secondary-school level remains controversial. Following legislation introduced by the Conservative governments of the 1990s, state secondary schools can now choose to specialize in certain subjects and to select a proportion of their pupils by aptitude. ▷*See also* City Technology Colleges; independent school.

● **secondary emission** ▶ The ejection of electrons from the surface of a metal when it is bombarded with charged particles of sufficient energy. Secondary emission is best observed when the bombarding particles are themselves electrons (primary electrons); the ejected electrons are called secondary electrons. In certain metals, up to ten secondary electrons can be emitted by one primary electron. The effect is used in such devices as the electron multiplier.

● **secondary modern school** ▶ A nonselective secondary school set up in the UK following the Education Act (1944). Secondary modern schools were for those "who deal more easily with concrete things than with ideas." Since the 1970s they have been largely replaced by ▷comprehensive schools.

● **secretary bird** ▶ A long-legged bird of prey, *Sagittarius serpen-*

tarius, that lives in dry uplands of Africa. 120 cm tall with a 200 cm wingspan, it has a hawklike face and a grey plumage with a long pair of tail feathers and a black crest of quills behind its head—hence its name. It feeds on snakes and lizards and is the only member of its family (*Sagittaridae*). Order: *Falconiformes* (falcons, etc.).

● **secret service** ▷*See* intelligence service.

● **securities** ▶ Documents that represent title to an investment, for example ▷stocks and shares, ▷bonds, ▷bills of exchange, and assurance policies. The list of securities owned by an investor is called a portfolio.

● **Securities and Exchange Commission** ▶ A US government agency created in 1934 to protect investors in ▷securities. It ensures that the information given to the public about new issues is complete and accurate.

● **Securities and Investment Board** ▶ (SIB) A UK body set up in 1986 to protect the interests of investors, especially on ▷stock exchanges and other self-regulating organizations.

● **Sedan** ▶ 49 42N 4 57E A town in NE France, in the Ardennes department on the River Meuse. It was the site of the Battle of Sedan. Its industries include textiles, metallurgy, and food processing. Population (1990): 22 400.

● **Sedan, Battle of** ▶ (1 September, 1870) The battle in the ▷Franco-Prussian War in which German forces, invading France, surrounded the army of Napoleon III and forced him to surrender with 100 000 men. The French defeat precipitated revolution in Paris (*see* Commune of Paris) and marked the end of the Second Empire.

● **sedan chair** ▶ An enclosed single-seater chair carried on poles by two men, one in front and one behind. Sedans probably originated in Italy, came to England in 1634, and were used for short journeys in town until after 1800. *Compare* palanquin.

● **sedatives** ▶ (*or* anxiolytics) Drugs that relieve restlessness, anxiety, and tension. Most drugs that depress the activity of the nervous system have this effect (including barbiturates and narcotics), but the most widely used sedatives are the ▷benzodiazepines, as they are less dangerous in overdosage than barbiturates. Sedatives are also used to induce sleep (*see* hypnotics) and to relieve muscular aches associated with tension and stress.

● **Seddon, Richard John** ▶ (1845–1906) New Zealand statesman, born in England; prime minister (1893–1906). His government implemented labour-protection measures and introduced old-age pensions and women's suffrage. He sent troops to support the British in the second Boer War (1899–1902) and opposed Asian immigration.

● **sedge** ▶ A perennial herbaceous grasslike plant of the genus *Carex* (about 2000 species), growing throughout the world, mainly in swampy places. Sedges have solid stems, triangular in cross section,

sedan chair ▶ Featured in this satirical engraving, entitled *Morning Frolick* (1747), showing a scene in front of St Paul's Church in Covent Garden, London.

with long narrow leaves and small male and female flowers usually grouped into separate clusters (spikes). The sand sedge (*C. arenaria*), found on the coasts of Europe and North America, has been used to bond sand dunes. Family: *Cyperaceae*.

● **Sedgemoor, Battle of** ▶ (6 July, 1685) The battle, fought on marshland at Westonzoyland, E of Bridgwater, Somerset, in which the forces of James II of England defeated the rebellion of his nephew, the Duke of ▷Monmouth. It was the last battle fought on English soil.

● **sedimentary rock** ▶ One of the three major categories into which rocks are divided (*compare* igneous rock; metamorphic rock). Sedimentary rocks are deposited mainly under water, usually in approximately horizontal layers (beds). **Clastic sedimentary rocks** are formed from the erosion and deposition of pre-existing rocks and are classified according to the size of the particles. Arenaceous rocks have sand-grade particles and include the sandstones; argillaceous rocks have silt- or clay-grade particles and include siltstones and mudstones; rudaceous rocks, with gravel-grade and larger fragments, include the breccias, conglomerates, etc. Organically formed sedimentary rocks are derived from the remains of plants and animals, for example limestone and coal. Chemically formed sedimentary rocks result from natural chemical processes and include sedimentary iron ores. Many sedimentary rocks show complex internal structures, formed during or after deposition.

● **Sedum** ▷*See* stonecrop.

● **Seebeck effect** ▷*See* thermoelectric effects.

● **seed** ▶ The reproductive structure formed after pollination and fertilization in higher plants. In flowering plants the seed begins to develop after the ▷pollen nucleus has fused with the egg. In gymnosperms (conifers and related plants) the ovule begins dividing before pollination. All seeds contain an embryo and usually a food store, which is mobilized on germination. Seeds of flowering plants are surrounded by a seed coat (testa) and contained within a ▷fruit; gymnosperm seeds are naked (*see* cone). The development of the "seed habit" has given the higher plants a marked advantage over the ferns and mosses. Water is not needed for fertilization, and therefore the plants can colonize arid habitats. In addition, seeds—unlike the spores of lower plants—can survive adverse conditions and may remain viable for many years before germinating.

● **seed fern** ▶ A ▷gymnosperm plant belonging to the extinct order *Cycadofilicales* (or *Pteridospermales*), abundant during the Carboniferous and Permian periods (370–240 million years ago). Seed ferns had large fernlike fronds but—unlike ferns—produced seeds, in cuplike structures.

● **Seeger, Pete** ▶ (1919–) US folksinger, banjo player, and songwriter, who was a member of the Almanac Singers (1940–45) and the Weavers (1948–58) before beginning a solo career. With Woody ▷Guthrie he was the main influence on the US folksong revival in the 1960s. He wrote such songs as "Where Have All the Flowers Gone" and "Kisses Sweeter than Wine." Blacklisted for his left-wing views in the 1950s, he later became prominent as an environmentalist campaigner.

● **Seferis, George** ▶ (Georgios Seferiadis; 1900–71) Greek poet and diplomat, who was ambassador to London (1957–62). He was influenced by the French Symbolists and by T. S. ▷Eliot, whose poetry he translated into Greek. His lyrical poetry was published in a number of collections, including *Strophe* (1931) and *Poiimata* (1940). He won the Nobel Prize in 1963.

● **Sefton** ▶ A unitary authority in NW England, in Merseyside. Area: 150 sq km (58 sq mi). Population (1996 est): 289 700.

● **Seghers, Hercules Pieterzoon** ▶ (c. 1589–c. 1638) Dutch landscape painter and etcher. His desolate and dramatically lit mountain landscapes influenced ▷Rembrandt, who owned some of Seghers' works. He is also known for his novel method of etching with coloured paper and inks.

● **Ségou** ▶ 13 28N 6 18W A town in central Mali, on the River Niger. It is an important trade centre serving an agricultural area. Population (1987): 88 877.

● **Segovia** ▶ 40 57N 4 07W A city in central Spain, in Old Castile. It has a fine Roman aqueduct that still supplies the city with water, a 16th-century cathedral, and the restored alcázar (citadel). Industries include potteries and flour milling. Population (1991): 58 060.

● **Segovia, Andrés** ▶ (1893–1987) Spanish guitarist. Playing all over the world, he revived the popularity of the guitar as a concert instrument and inspired composers to write works for it. In 1981 he became Marquis of Salobreña.

● **Segrè, Emilio** ▶ (1905–89) US physicist, born in Italy, who shared the 1959 Nobel Prize with Owen ▷Chamberlain for discovering (1955) the antiproton (*see* antimatter). Segrè was the first physicist to produce an artificial element, ▷technetium, by bombarding molybdenum with deuterium.

● **Seikan tunnel** ▷*See* Hokkaido.

● **Seine, River** ▶ A river in N France. Rising on the Plateau de Langres, it flows mainly NW through Paris to the English Channel, S of Le Havre. It is the second longest river in France, linked by canal with the Rivers Somme, Scheldt, Meuse, Rhine, Saône, and Loire. Length: 776 km (482 mi).

● **seismic belts** ▶ (or seismic zones) The narrow distinct belts on the earth's surface that are subject to frequent earthquakes. They usually follow the line of plate boundaries (*see* plate tectonics), especially along midocean ridges, near young orogenic belts, along island arc systems, and along major ▷faults.

● **seismic wave** ▶ An elastic shock wave emanating from the focus of an ▷earthquake or explosion. When seismic activity is recorded, several types of wave can be identified: longitudinal P (*primae*) waves and transverse S (*secundae*) waves are small rapid vibrations that come through the earth's interior. They form the first and second parts of the preliminary tremor of an earthquake. The main earthquake consists of large slow L (*longae*) waves travelling along the surface. This type of wave is limited to a narrow depth range and can also occur along deeper strata. Its components are Rayleigh waves (after R. J. S. Rayleigh), which are vertical vibrations in the plane of propagation, and Love waves (after A. E. H. Love; 1863–1940), which are horizontal and transverse. ▷*See* seismology.

● **seismology** ▶ The branch of geophysics concerned with the study of ▷earthquakes: their origin, the waves they produce (*see* seismic wave), their effects, and their distribution. The instruments used are the **seismograph**, which records the magnitude of the oscillations during an earthquake, and the **seismometer**, which detects and records the motions of the earth in a particular direction (usually used in sets of three). The study of nuclear explosions has also concerned seismologists, since they resemble earthquakes. Seismological data has provided the bulk of our knowledge of the earth's interior. It is estimated that earthquakes cause some 14 000 deaths per annum.

● **sei whale** ▶ A widely distributed ▷rorqual, *Balaenopteris borealis*, also called sardine whale. Up to 18 m long, it has a dark back, a white belly, and a large dorsal fin.

● **Sekhmet** ▶ An Egyptian war goddess, consort of the creator-god Ptah and destroyer of the enemies of Ra. She was usually portrayed as a lioness or with a lion's head.

● **Sekondi-Takoradi** ▶ 4 59N 1 43W A port in Ghana, on the Gulf of Guinea. Formerly two separate towns, Sekondi and Takoradi were linked in 1946. Bauxite is exported and industries include food processing. Population (latest est): 103 653.

● **Selaginella** ▶ A genus of mosslike vascular plants (700 species), also called spike mosses, found mainly in tropical forests. They are similar to the related ▷clubmosses but differ in having scales (ligules) at the bases of the leaves and two kinds of spore capsules (male and female). The prickly clubmoss (*S. selaginoides*) occurs in arctic and N regions. Order: *Selaginellales*; phylum: *Lycophyta*.

● **Selangor** ▶ A state in W Peninsular Malaysia, on the Strait of Malacca. It became a British protectorate in 1874. It is the economic centre of Malaysia with industry concentrated between Kuala Lumpur and Port Klang; the chief products are tin and rubber. Area:

8202 sq km (3167 sq mi). Population (1993 est): 1 981 090. Capital: Shah Alam.

● **Selby** ▶ 53 48N 1 04W A market town in N England, in North Yorkshire on the River Ouse. It has a 12th-century abbey church. Industries include paper, chemicals, glass, electricity generation, and those associated with the Selby coalfield. Population (1991): 17 696.

● **Selden, John** ▶ (1584–1654) English jurist, antiquary, and orientalist. Selden's work includes *Analecton Anglo-Britannicon* (1615), on the civil administration of England, *De Diis Syrris* (1617), and *Table Talk*, published posthumously in 1689. His opposition to tithes and the divine right of kings angered the clergy and monarchy. Elected to parliament in 1623, Selden helped to draft the Petition of Right (1628) concerning the privileges of the House of Commons, which resulted in his imprisonment (1629–34).

● **select committee** ▶ A committee of members of the House of Commons or House of Lords, or of both Houses jointly, that supervises or reviews government actions or other matters of public interest. Usually comprising between 10 and 15 members, of all parties, such select committees as each House's Committee of Privileges have a long history. In 1979 the system was adapted to establish 12 Commons' select committees to scrutinize government departments; by 1999 there were 16 departmental select committees.

● **Selene** ▶ The Greek moon-goddess, daughter of the Titan Hyperion and sister of Helios (the sun) and Eos (dawn). She became identified with the later Greek goddess ▷Artemis and with the Roman ▷Diana.

● **selenium** ▶ (Se) A chemical element of the sulphur family obtained from sludges produced during electrolytic copper refining. It exists in several forms, including deep-red crystals, but the commonest allotrope is grey. The element has photovoltaic properties and is used in photocells, light meters, and in photocopying machines. As a semiconductor it is used in rectifiers. The hydride (H₂Se) has a noxious smell and, like other selenium compounds, is toxic. Selenium is a ▷trace element with anti-oxidant properties. At no 34; at wt 78.96; mp 221°C; bp 685°C. ▷*See also* selenium cell.

● **selenium cell** ▶ A ▷photocell based on the ▷photovoltaic effect. It consists of a metal disc coated with selenium on which is placed a layer of gold or platinum thin enough to transmit light. When light falls on the disc a small current is generated. They are used in exposure meters in cameras, etc.

● **Seles, Monica** ▶ (1973–) US tennis player, born in Yugoslavia. She won the US Open in 1991 and 1992. She was unable to play for two years after being stabbed on court by a demented spectator in 1993 but made a full comeback by winning the Australian Open in 1996. She became a US citizen in 1994.

● **Seleucids** ▶ A Middle Eastern dynasty of the Hellenistic age (323–27 BC) founded by ▷Seleucus I Nicator, the Macedonian general who, after Alexander the Great's death, became governor and then ruler (312) of Babylonia. He extended his kingdom to the frontiers of India in the east and Syria in the west but his successors, faced with Egyptian aggression and internal unrest, failed to maintain his conquests. ▷Antiochus the Great (reigned 223–187) restored Seleucid power in the east but could not prevent Rome's expansion. Under ▷Antiochus IV Epiphanes (175–163) the empire was weakened by the revolt of the ▷Maccabees and although they were repressed by ▷Antiochus VII Sidetes (139–129) his failure to push back the Parthians anticipated the disintegration of the empire. In 64 BC Pompey annexed what was left to form the Roman province of Syria.

● **Seleucus I Nicator** ▶ (c. 356–280 BC) Macedonian general, who founded the ▷Seleucid dynasty. After Alexander the Great's death (323) Seleucus became governor and then ruler (312) of Babylonia, taking the title of king in 305. He subsequently conquered Syria, which brought him into conflict with the Ptolemies of Egypt, Asia Minor, and Macedonia before being murdered by Ptolemy Ceraunus (d. 279 BC), the son of Ptolemy I Soter.

● **self-heal** ▶ A perennial herb, *Prunella vulgaris*, common in temperate Eurasia, N Africa, North America, and Australia. 5–30 cm high, it has tapering leaves and terminal clusters of small, usually violet,

flowers. Extracts were formerly used to treat various illnesses. Family: *Labiatae*.

● **Seljuqs** ▶ A Turkish dynasty that ruled in E Islam from 1055. During the 10th century the Seljuqs (descended from Seljuq, chief of the Oguz tribes) led bands of migrating Turks into the Islamic world and in 1055 their head, ▷Toghril Beg, captured Baghdad. The dynasty was at its peak under Toghril Beg and his successors ▷Alp Arslan and ▷Malik-Shah, under whom the great vizier ▷Nizam al-Mulk administered the empire. After the death of Malik-Shah the empire disintegrated into rival kingdoms. His successors in Persia maintained a nominal suzerainty over the other kingdoms until defeated by invaders from central Asia in 1153. In Anatolia the Seljuqs of Rum ruled an important independent kingdom until coming under the domination of the Mongols in 1243.

● **Selkirk** ▶ (*or* Selkirkshire) A former county of SE Scotland. In 1975 it became part of the Borders Region (now Scottish Borders).

● **Selkirk, Alexander** ▶ (1676–1721) Scottish sailor. He joined the South Sea buccaneers in 1703 and in 1704, after quarrelling with his captain, was voluntarily left on one of the uninhabited Juan Fernández Islands. He was discovered in 1709 by a ship piloted by ▷Dampier. His experience inspired Defoe's *Robinson Crusoe* (1719).

● **Sellafield** ▶ (former name: Windscale) An atomic power station in W Cumbria, NW England. Several accidents, together with a high incidence of cancer among local inhabitants, have made Sellafield a focus for the nuclear power debate. A nuclear fuel reprocessing plant (THORP) opened here in 1994. In 2000 concerns over marine pollution led Ireland and Denmark to press for the station's closure, while safety worries led other countries to suspend processing contracts.

● **Sellers, Peter** ▶ (1925–80) British comic actor. He made his name in the 1950s with the BBC radio comedy series *The Goon Show*. His films include *I'm All Right, Jack* (1959), *The Millionairess* (1961), *Dr Strangelove* (1963), *The Pink Panther* series (1963–77), and *Being There* (1980).

● **Selwyn Lloyd, John, Baron** ▶ (1904–78) British Conservative politician. He was foreign secretary (1955–60), supporting Eden (*see* Avon, Anthony Eden, 1st Earl of) during the Suez crisis, and then chancellor of the exchequer (1960–62). He resigned over his unpopular wage-restraint policy and was speaker of the Commons (1971–76).

● **Selznick, David O(liver)** ▶ (1902–65) US film producer. In 1936 he formed his own production company and produced *A Star Is Born* (1937) and *Gone with the Wind* (1939) among other films. Many of his films, including *A Farewell to Arms* (1957), starred Jennifer Jones (1919–), his second wife.

● **semantics** ▶ Broadly, the branch of philology concerned with the study of the relationship between words and meanings. The study of signs and their relationships to the things or concepts that they signify has application both in mathematical logic and in the philosophy of language. Semantics as the study of meaning in individual words is part of ▷linguistics, but there are philosophical problems involved in trying to account for the relationship between words and the objects they refer to, particularly when a theory is extended to cover words that have no concrete referent (e.g. "honesty"). A distinction is often made between literal (or cognitive) meaning and associative meaning, and many linguists believe that the meaning of words can be broken into constituents by means of analyses similar to those used by ▷Chomsky to derive the surface structure of sentences from their deep structure. Some linguistic philosophers, such as ▷Wittgenstein in his later period and J. L. ▷Austin, account for word meaning not in terms of logical structures but rather according to the speaker's intention in using a word or utterance. However, logical analysis is widely accepted in explaining the aspect of meaning that is a function of grammatical structure, i.e. sentence meaning is seen as a matter of internal relationships among the words, word particles, and phrases involved. ▷*See also* semiotics.

● **semaphore** ▶ **1.** A visual method of communication between ships at sea, used mainly by warships wishing to maintain radio silence, and consisting of a pattern of signalling by the use of two flags, held by a signalman, their relative positions symbolizing an alphabetical or numerical character. **2.** A mechanical railway signalling

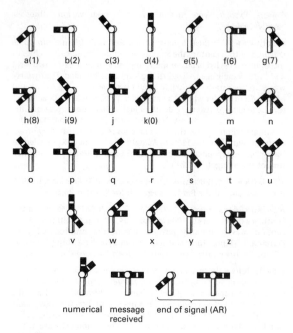

a(1) b(2) c(3) d(4) e(5) f(6) g(7)

h(8) i(9) j k(0) l m n

o p q r s t u

v w x y z

numerical message received end of signal (AR)

semaphore

device, consisting of a steel arm the position of which is changed by a signalman or by the tripping of a release by a passing train.

● **Semarang** ▶ 6 58S 110 29E A port in Indonesia, in central Java on the Java Sea. A commercial centre with textile and shipbuilding industries, it exports sugar, rubber, coffee, kapok, and copra. The port is sometimes disrupted by the monsoon. Its university was established in 1960. Population (1995 est): 1 366 500.

● **Semele** ▶ In Greek mythology, the daughter of ▷Cadmus, King of Thebes. She was killed by lightning when her lover Zeus appeared to her in his divine form but her unborn child, the god ▷Dionysus, was saved.

● **semen** ▷*See* sperm; testis.

● **semiconductor** ▶ A crystalline material in which the electrical conductivity increases with temperature and is between that of a conductor and an ▷insulator. The conductivity is also sensitive to minute quantities of impurities in the crystal lattice (□energy band). Some (donor) impurities increase the number of negative charge carriers (electrons), creating what is known as an n-type semiconductor. Other (acceptor) impurities increase the number of positive charge carriers (holes), creating a p-type semiconductor. The introduction of these impurities is called doping. ▷Solid-state devices, such as diodes, ▷transistors, and ▷integrated circuits, depend on the properties of junctions between p-type and n-type regions in the same piece of semiconductor crystal (p-n junctions). Metal oxide semiconductor (MOS) devices also use the properties of a thin layer of insulating oxide on the semiconductor surface. The element silicon is now the most widely used semiconducting material. Others are germanium, now used only for special applications, and gallium arsenide, which is used in high-speed logic circuits and microwave equipment.

● **semiconductor diode** ▶ A ▷solid-state device with two electrodes. It consists of a single p-n junction (*see* semiconductor). When the p-region is at a more positive voltage than the n-region (forward bias), the current flow increases exponentially as the voltage rises. In reverse bias, very little current flows until a sufficiently high reverse voltage has built up to cause breakdown; the current then increases sharply. The diode is, therefore, commonly used as a rectifier. The **Zener diode** is designed to break down at a specific reverse bias voltage, above which the voltage across it remains effectively constant.

The higher the doping levels on both sides of the junction, the lower the breakdown voltage. It is used as a voltage regulator.

Semiconductor diodes, which have largely replaced thermionic diodes, are also used to generate microwaves by the ▷Gunn effect, to detect light in ▷photocells, and to emit light in low-voltage displays. The latter, called **light-emitting diodes** (LEDs), are widely used in calculators and digital watches. They emit radiation (light) when holes and electrons combine, the colour of the light depending on the material of the crystal.

● **Seminole** ▶ A group of North American Indians related to the ▷Creeks, who speak a Muskogean language. In the late 18th century they migrated from Georgia to Florida, where, in several wars, they resisted domination by the government. They developed a simple hunting and fishing culture suited to the conditions of the region.

● **semiotics** ▶ (*or* semiology) The study of signs (i.e. basic elements of communication, verbal or nonverbal) and of the ways in which meanings are produced within particular sign systems. Semiotics differs from ▷semantics principally in its concern with nonlinguistic signs (e.g. gestures, clothing, any form of visual imagery). It is also less concerned with the philosophical and logical questions raised by the relationships of signs to the things or concepts signified, and more with the actual ways in which signs generate meaning in specific cultures and contexts. Although the discipline was first named and formulated by the US philosopher C. S. Peirce (1839–1914), the main influence on modern semiotic enquiry has been the linguistic theory of ▷Saussure. Because contemporary semiotics takes as its starting point Saussure's view that signs can have no meaning outside a structure of relationships to other signs, it has developed in close conjunction with ▷structuralism. In practice, semioticians will study a particular cultural product (anything from an epic poem to an advertisement or a hairstyle) in an attempt to make explicit the various, usually unstated, conventions by which it achieves significance. This approach has proved widely influential in the study of popular culture.

● **Semipalatinsk** ▶ 50 26N 80 16E A city in NE Kazakhstan, on the River Irtysh. Its name means "seven palaces" and refers to the nearby remains of seven ancient stone structures. Meat packing, food processing, and metalworking are among its industrial activities, and it is a communications centre. Population (1995 est): 320 200.

● **semipermeable membrane** ▶ A material that allows certain molecules in a fluid to pass through it but not others. It will usually permit solvent particles to pass but not the solute molecules. It thus creates ▷osmosis when placed in a suitable fluid. Semipermeable membranes include cell walls and parchment. The term "partially permeable membrane" is preferred when referring to biological membranes.

● **Semiramis** ▶ A legendary queen of Assyria, who, with her husband Ninus, was the alleged builder of ▷Babylon and, after his death, ruler of a vast empire extending to India. The legend derives from the historical queen Sammuramat, who ruled in Assyria during the 9th century BC.

● **Semites** ▶ A group of peoples, including the ▷Jews and ▷Arabs, said in the Bible to be descended from Shem, Noah's eldest son. The Babylonians, Assyrians, Canaanites, and Phoenicians were ancient Semitic peoples.

● **Semitic alphabets** ▶ The earliest known truly alphabetic writing systems, developed among the Semitic peoples of the E Mediterranean about 2000 BC. From them all the major ▷alphabets of today are derived: the south Semitic version gave rise to the modern Amharic script of Ethiopia; from North Semitic were derived Greek (and from Greek came the Roman, ▷Cyrillic, ▷runic, and other alphabets), Phoenician, and Aramaic (from which came the scripts of Hebrew, Arabic, and ▷Devanagari in India). The earliest records in North Semitic date from around 1300 BC and indicate that it was a purely consonantal system of 22 letters, generally written from left to right.

● **Semitic languages** ▶ A subgroup of the ▷Hamito-Semitic language family spoken in a large area of N Africa, extending through Palestine to the SW corner of Asia. The Semitic languages originated in Mesopotamia in the 3rd millennium BC and are recorded in Sumerian ▷cuneiform inscriptions. There are three subgroups recognized by language scholars, although these are very similar. NW Semitic consisted of Ugaritic, Canaanite, and ▷Aramaic, all extinct. From these are descended Phoenician and ▷Hebrew, the only living language of this subgroup. NE Semitic, the second subgroup, consisted of Assyrian and Babylonian, both extinct. The third group, S Semitic, is that from which modern ▷Arabic and Maltese are descended, as well as Amharic (*see* Amhara) and Tigrinya, a language of Eritrea.

● **semolina** ► Fine grains of durum wheat used in the manufacture of ▷pasta and couscous and also for making milk puddings.

● **Semtex** ► Tradename for a plastic explosive manufactured in the Czech Republic. Because it is odourless it is difficult to trace and therefore widely used by terrorists. Nitrogen-based, it is safe to handle and requires a detonator to ignite it.

● **Senanayake, D(on) S(tephen)** ► (1884–1952) Ceylonese statesman; the first prime minister (1947–52) of Ceylon (now Sri Lanka). His son **Dudley Senanayake** (1911–73) was prime minister (1952–53, 1960, 1965–70).

● **Senate** ► In ancient Rome, the state council. During Republican times it was largely composed of ex-magistrates and, although its role was primarily to advise the magistrates, it carried much weight, especially in foreign policy, finance, and religion. Under the Empire membership of the Senate became largely hereditary and its chief function was to ratify imperial decisions. ▷*See also* curia.

● **Senate, US** ▷*See* Congress.

● **Sendak, Maurice** ► (1928–) US writer and artist, best known for his illustrated children's books, including *Where the Wild Things Are* (1963) and *I Saw Esau* (1992). He has also designed sets for operas.

● **Sendai** ► 38 16N 140 52E A city in Japan, in NE Honshu. It is the largest city of N Japan. Tohoku University was established here in 1907. Population (1995): 971 297.

● **Seneca the Elder** ► (Marcus Annaeus Seneca; c. 55 BC–c. 41 AD) Roman rhetorician, born at Córdoba (Spain). Parts of his work on oratory, addressed to his sons, have survived: the *Suasoriae* (a compendium of styles and themes of earlier rhetoricians) and the *Controversiae* (imaginary court cases). One of his sons, **Seneca the Younger** (Lucius Annaeus Seneca; c. 4 BC–65 AD), was an author and politician. His career at court, interrupted by exile (41–49 AD), culminated in his appointment as tutor and later chief minister to ▷Nero. Retiring in 64 AD as a millionaire, he was accused of treason and forced to commit suicide. 13 philosophical treatises and numerous essays advocate ▷Stoicism in a highly rhetorical style. His nine tragedies, which influenced the Elizabethan dramatists, also survive.

● **Senefelder, Aloys** ► (1771–1834) German playwright and engraver, born in Prague, who invented (1798) lithography (*see* printing) after accidentally discovering (1796) the possibilities of drawing with greasy chalk on wet stone.

● **Senegal, Republic of** ► A country in West Africa, on the Atlantic Ocean. The River Senegal forms its N boundary and the River Gambia flows E–W through the country to the border of The Gambia, which forms an enclave within Senegalese territory. Senegal consists chiefly of level plains rising to a dissected plateau in the SE. Most of the population are Wolof, Serer, and Tukulor.
Economy: chiefly agricultural, the production of groundnuts being dominant. Other crops include millet, rice, and maize; livestock is important and fishing has been developed with foreign aid. Phosphates, iron ore, and offshore oil and natural gas have been found in significant quantities. Hydroelectricity is a valuable source of power. Industry, mainly concentrated on Dakar, includes cement, food processing, and textiles; tourism is expanding. The main exports are fish, phosphates, and groundnuts. The economy suffered badly from the instability of the 1990s. There is a large foreign debt.
History: in the 14th and 15th centuries the area was part of the Mali empire. St Louis was founded in 1659 by the French, who extended their control in the mid-19th century over most of the region. The country achieved self-government in 1958 as a member of the French Community and in 1959–60 briefly formed the Federation of Mali with Sudan. Senegal became a separate independent republic in

1960, with Léopold Senghor as its first president. From 1982 until 1989 it formed the Senegambia Confederation with The Gambia, with each country retaining its independence but having joint defence, foreign, and monetary policies. Abdou Diouf (1935–) succeeded Senghor as president in 1981 and was re-elected in 1988 and 1993. The 1990s saw rising ethnic tensions, a virtual frontier war with Mauritania (1989–92), and insurgency by separatists in the southern Casamance region. In 2000 President Diouf was defeated at the polls by Abdoulaye Wade, ending 40 years of socialist rule.

Republic of Senegal

Head of state	President Abdoulaye Wade
Official language	French
Official currency	CFA (Communauté financière africaine) franc of 100 centimes
Area	197 722 sq km (76 320 sq mi)
Population (2001 est)	10 285 000
Capital and main port	Dakar

● **Senegal, River** ► A river in West Africa. Rising in highlands in N Guinea, it flows mainly NW to the Atlantic Ocean forming part of the Mauritania–Senegal border. Length: 1690 km (1050 mi).

● **senescence** ▷*See* ageing.

● **Senghor, Léopold Sédar** ► (1906–2002) Senegalese statesman; president (1960–80). He formed the Senegalese Progressive Union, which took Senegal to independence in 1960. He also wrote books of poetry, including *Chants d'ombres* (1945) and *Nocturnes* (1961).

● **senna** ▷*See* Cassia.

● **Senna, Ayrton** ► (1960–94) Brazilian motor racing driver. Noted for his tempestuous character, he won the Formula One World Championship in 1988, 1990, and 1991, winning a record eight Grand Prix races in 1988. He was killed in a crash during the San Marino Grand Prix.

● **Sennacherib** ► (d. 681 BC) King of Assyria (704–681); the son and successor of ▷Sargon II. After 16 years of leniency towards the constantly rebellious Babylonians he sacked the city of Babylon in 689. He also crushed an Egyptian-inspired revolt of Palestine led by ▷Hezekiah. A patron of art and learning, he restored ▷Nineveh. Murdered by one of his sons, probably incited by Babylonian rebels, he was succeeded by ▷Esarhaddon.

● **Sennar** ► 13 31N 33 38E A town in the SE Sudan, on the Blue Nile River. The Makwar Dam (completed 1925) is part of the ▷Gezira irrigation scheme. Population (latest est): 8000.

● **Sennett, Mack** ► (Michael Sinott; 1884–1960) US film producer and director, born in Canada. In 1912 he joined the Keystone Company, for which he produced numerous short slapstick films featuring the ▷Keystone Kops, Charlie Chaplin, and Harold Lloyd.

● **Sens** ► 48 12N 3 18E A town in central France, in the Yonne department on the River Yonne. The site of one of the earliest gothic cathedrals in France, its manufactures include agricultural implements, electrical products, and chemicals. Population (latest est): 26 960.

● **sensitive plants** ▷*See* Mimosa.

● **sentimental novel** ► A type of fiction popular in 18th-century England and France in which scenes of emotional distress were intended to arouse the reader's pity and compassion. Examples include *Manon Lescaut* (1731) by the Abbé ▷Prévost and *Pamela* (1740) by Samuel ▷Richardson.

● **Seoul** ► 37 30N 127 00E The capital of the Republic of (South) Korea, in the NW on the River Han near the coast. The capital of Korea since 1394, the city served as the centre of Japanese-occupied Korea (1910–45). It suffered considerable damage in the Korean War (1950–53). It is a rapidly developing industrial as well as administrative and commercial centre. Its 16 universities include the Seoul National University (1946). Population (1995): 10 229 262.

● **separation of powers** ► The division of governmental powers between a legislature, executive, and judiciary that are distinct from, and indepedent of, each other. Such separation is most clearly seen in the institutions established by the US ▷constitution, in the drafting of which separation of powers was seen as the best way to safeguard liberty and the risk of ineffective government seemed preferable to governmental despotism. These institutions are the Congress (legislature), presidency (executive), and Supreme Court (judiciary). The separation is not complete (for instance, the president may veto legislation that does not have a two-thirds majority in each house of Congress) but is more distinct than in most other countries, such as the UK, where both legislature and executive are largely in the hands of the same individuals (e.g. the party with a majority in the House of Commons).

● **separation order** ► A court order, under the Family Law Act (1996), that does not end a marriage but frees the parties of their marital obligations. Under the Matrimonial Causes Act (1973), which was replaced by the 1996 Act, it was known as a **judicial separation order**. It is appropriate if the parties have religious objections to ▷divorce or as a step towards divorce. The court has the same power regarding financial orders and the custody of children as in a divorce. The grounds are the same as for divorce but irreconcilable breakdown of the marriage does not have to be proved.

● **Sephardim** ► (Hebrew *Sepharad*: Spain) Jews who went to Spain and Portugal in the ▷diaspora. When the Jews were expelled from Spain in 1492 they spread to many parts of the world, preserving their customs and their language, ▷Ladino. The first Jewish settlers in England were ▷Marranos from Spain. A few came secretly in the 16th century but more came from Holland in the 17th century. Granted permission by Cromwell to hold services, they opened their first synagogue in 1657, which was replaced in 1701 by a synagogue in Bevis Marks in the city of London, which is still in use as the principal Sephardi synagogue in the UK. The term is now sometimes applied, especially in Israel, to all non-▷Ashkenazim.

● **September 11** ► The day in 2001 that saw the worst terrorist atrocity in history, directed at targets in New York and Washington. Four airliners laden with passengers, crew, and fuel, were hijacked by Islamic terrorists: two were flown into the twin towers of the ▷World Trade Center in New York, causing their collapse, a third was crashed into the ▷Pentagon, while the fourth hit the ground near Pittsburgh, apparently as a result of a fight-back by passengers.

A total of 265 people (including 19 terrorists) died in the hijacked aeroplanes, over 2600 died in the collapse of the World Trade Center, and a further 180 were killed in the Pentagon, bringing the total death toll to about 3195. After the loss of life, it was perhaps the combination of precision planning with suicidal fanaticism that most shocked the world. Evidence was soon found to confirm suspicions that the ▷al-Qaida terrorist network led by Osama ▷Bin Laden was involved. In October, America launched its so-called ▷war on terrorism with air strikes against al-Qaida and ▷Taleban targets in Afghanistan.

● **septicaemia** ▷*See* blood poisoning.

● **septic tank** ► A large tank of steel or concrete sunk in the ground to provide ▷sewage disposal for isolated buildings or small communities. Effluent flows into the tank, the settled sludge being decomposed to a certain extent by bacterial action. The tank must be large enough (minimum 2.7 cu m in the UK) to store the sludge for several months, before emptying.

● **Sept Îles** ► 50 13N 66 22W A town and port in E Canada, in Quebec on the Gulf of St Lawrence. Founded in 1650, it developed with the construction of a railway to large iron-ore mines in the interior (1950). Population (latest est): 26 800.

● **Septuagint** ► (Latin: seventy) A Greek translation of the ▷Old Testament and ▷Apocrypha made for the use of Greek-speaking Jews in Egypt and improved and completed in stages between the 3rd century BC and the 1st century AD. It derives its name and symbol (LXX) from the legend that 72 Jewish scholars completed the work in 72 days.

● **sequence** ► An ordered set of numbers, generally denoted by a_1, a_2,...a_r,..., in which the rth term a_r can be expressed as a function of r. ▷*See also* series.

● **sequoia** ► Either of two Californian coniferous trees, the ▷redwood (*Sequoia sempervirens*), which is the world's tallest tree, or the giant sequoia, *Sequoiadendron giganteum* (formerly *Sequoia gigantea*),

also called Wellingtonia and big tree. The giant sequoia forms natural forests in California's Sierra Nevada, where some trees are over 3000 years old, over 80 m in height, and over 24 m in girth. In Europe it is grown as an ornamental. The red-brown bark is soft and fibrous and the shoots are covered with pointed leaves. The egg-shaped cones are 5–8 cm long. Family: *Taxodiaceae*.

● **Serang** ▷*See* Ceram.

● **seraphim** ▷*See* cherubim and seraphim.

● **Serapis** ► A god combining Greek and Egyptian elements, introduced into Egypt by ▷Ptolemy I in order to unite the worship of the two peoples. He was identical with ▷Osiris, with characteristics borrowed from ▷Zeus and ▷Asclepius.

● **Serbia** ► (Serbo-Croat name: Srbija) A constituent republic of the Union of ▷Serbia and Montenegro, incorporating the autonomous regions of ▷Vojvodina and ▷Kosovo. It is mountainous in the S, descending in the N to the Danube basin. Agriculture is important, especially stock raising and the growing of wheat, maize, and vines. Mineral deposits include copper (at Bor), antimony, coal, and chrome. In the 1990s the economy was devastated by the imposition of economic sanctions and NATO bombing (1999).

History: first settled by the Serbs in the 7th century AD, it accepted the Eastern Orthodox faith in the early middle ages. Following military defeat in 1389, Serbia came under Turkish control; repeated insurrections from 1804 led to its regaining its independence in 1878. Serbia played a major role in the ▷Balkan Wars and the events leading up to World War I: in 1914 Austria accused Serbia of involvement in the assassination of Archduke Francis Ferdinand and declared war. Serbia suffered badly during the war, losing about 23% of the population. In 1918 it became the leading partner in the kingdom of Serbs, Croats, and Slovenes, later renamed ▷Yugoslavia. In 1991 Serbia under Slobodan ▷Milošević attempted unsuccessfully to prevent the break-up of Yugoslavia by military action against Slovenia and Croatia. Serbia was also condemned for its involvement in the civil war in Bosnia-Hercegovina (1992–95). In 1992 Serbia and Montenegro formed a new Federal Republic of Yugoslavia. Serbia's attempt to suppress ethnic Albanian separatists in Kosovo through a campaign of "ethnic cleansing" led to NATO airstrikes in 1999. Serbia finally withdrew its forces from Kosovo in June 1999. Popular discontent with the authoritarian rule of Milošević culminated (October 2000) in a bloodless revolution in which he was ousted. He was replaced by the opposition leader, Vojislav Kostunica. A new agreement with Montenegro, establishing the Union of Serbia and Montenegro, was signed in March 2002. Area: 88 361 sq km (34 107 sq mi). Population (1997 est): 9 845 128. Capital: Belgrade.

● **Serbia and Montenegro, Union of** ► A country in SE Europe, consisting of the republics of ▷Serbia and its much smaller neighbour ▷Montenegro. It is chiefly mountainous, with fertile plains in the N. There is a short Adriatic coastline in Montenegro.

Economy: The country is self-sufficient in food production, livestock raising and the growing of cereals being the main agricultural activities. Forestry and wine-making are also important. Mineral resources include copper, antimony, and coal. The economy is only slowly beginning to recover from Serbia's international isolation in the 1990s and damage caused by NATO bombing during the ▷Kosovo war of 1999.

History: Following the break-up of ▷Yugoslavia in 1991–92, Serbia and Montenegro announced the formation of a new Federal Republic of Yugoslavia (not recognized by the UN until 2000). The Serbian leader Slobodan ▷Milošević became president of this "rump" Yugoslavia in 1997. His nationalist and authoritarian policies, together with the deepening economic crisis, led to a growing movement for separatism in Montenegro in the late 1990s. Following Serbia's defeat in the Kosovo war, Milošević was deposed in a mass uprising in Belgrade (2000). His successor, Vojislav Kostunica, moved to restore relations with both the West and Serbia's Balkan neighbours, including Montenegro. In March 2002 an EU-sponsored accord was signed in Belgrade, replacing the existing federation with a new Union of Serbia and Montenegro. The two republics now have a joint foreign and defence policy but virtual autonomy in domestic and economic matters. The status of Kosovo is unresolved; it remains nominally part of Serbia but is administered separately by the UN.

Union of Serbia and Montenegro

Head of state	President Vojislav Kostunica
Official language	Serbo-Croatian
Official currency	new dinar of 100 paras in Serbia; euro of 100 cents in Montenegro and Kosovo
Area	102 173 sq km (39 449 sq mi)
Population (2001 est)	10 677 000
Capital and main port	Belgrade

● **Serbo-Croat** ▶ The language of the Serbs and Croats of the former Yugoslavia. Serbian and Croatian differ only marginally in terms of vocabulary and not at all in grammar but Serbian is written in ▷Cyrillic and Croatian in Latin script. The standard literary form is based on a central dialect known as Shtokavian.

● **Serengeti National Park** ▶ A park in Tanzania, established in 1951 to protect wildlife, especially wildebeestes, gazelles, giraffes, elephants, and lions. It is now a World Heritage Site. Area: 14 763 sq km (5698 sq mi).

● **serf** ▶ An unfree peasant of the middle ages. Serfdom was characteristic of the manorial economic system (*see* manor). A serf was bound to the soil he tilled, paying his lord a fee and providing service in return for the use of his land. Serfs had their own homes, plots, and livestock and enjoyed customary rights that distinguished them from slaves (*see* slavery). Serfdom declined in W Europe in the late middle ages but continued in E Europe until the 19th century.

● **Sergius of Radonezh, St** ▶ (1314–92) Russian monk, who founded the monastery of the Holy Trinity at Sergiyev in the forest of Radonezh. It became a spiritual centre, helping to re-establish monasticism after the Tatar invasion. Feast day: 25 Sept.

● **Sergiyev** ▶ (name from 1930 until 1994: Zagorsk) 56 20N 38 10E A city in W Russia, 72 km (45 mi) NE of Moscow. It grew around and is named after the famous Trinity-St Sergius monastery (1337–40); the Trinity Cathedral (1422–23) and the Cathedral of the Assumption (1559–85) may still be seen. Population (1999 est): 111 800.

● **serialism** ▶ (*or* twelve-tone music) A method of composing music using all 12 notes of the chromatic scale equally, invented by Arnold Schoenberg in the 1920s. Schoenberg sought an alternative to ▷chromaticism and ▷atonality by using a fixed sequence of 12 notes (called a **series** or tone row). The series could be transposed so as to begin on any degree of the scale and could also be inverted and used in a retrograde form. In strict serialism no single note of the row could be repeated until the other 11 had occurred. In place of traditional ▷harmony he developed chords built on fourths. Schoenberg's pupils (Webern, Berg, and others) adopted serialism, although sometimes in a modified form. In **total serialism** musical elements, such as rhythm, dynamics, and tone colour, are classified in strict serial form. Such composers as Berio and Boulez have used this technique.

● **seriema** ▶ A bird belonging to a family (*Cariamidae*; 2 species) occurring in dry grassland regions of South America. The crested seriema (*Cariama cristata*) is 60 cm tall and has a brown plumage with pale underparts and a red bill and legs. Seriemas feed on insects, snails, reptiles, and berries. Order: *Gruiformes* (cranes, rails, etc.).

● **series** ▶ The sum of the terms in a ▷sequence, written as $a_1 + a_2 + a_3 + ...a_r + ...$. The partial sum to the nth term is denoted by S_n. A series is convergent if S_n approaches a particular value as n increases and divergent if it increases without limit. A geometric series has the general form $a + an + an^2 + ...$, where a and n are constant. It is convergent if n is less than one, divergent if n is greater than or equal to one. A power series has the general form $a_0 + a_1 x + a_2 x^2 + a_3 x^3 + ...$, where x is a ▷variable. ▷*See also* arithmetic progression.

● **serin** ▶ The smallest European ▷finch, *Serinus serinus*, closely related to the canary and having a sweet trilling song. Serins have a streaked olive-coloured plumage with a bright-yellow rump and, in the male, a yellow head and breast. Although a southern species, its range extends to N Europe.

● **Seringapatam** ▶ 12 25N 76 41E A town in India, in Karnataka on Seringapatam Island in the River Cauvery. It was the capital of

Mysore from 1610 until 1799, when it was captured by the British. Population (1991 est): 21 902.

● **Serlio, Sebastiano** ▶ (1475–1554) Italian architect and painter. Born in Bologna, he trained under Peruzzi in Rome and worked on the palace at Fontainebleau; he is best known for his treatises on architecture, notably *Tutte l'opere d'architettura e prospettiva* (1537–75).

● **serotine bat** ▶ An insect-eating ▷bat, *Eptesicus serotinus*, of Eurasia. It is about 12 cm long including the tail and has a 35 cm wingspan. Dark brown in colour, it flies at early dusk and dawn. Family: *Vespertilionidae*.

● **serotonin** ▶ (*or* 5-hydroxytryptamine) A compound, synthesized from the amino acid tryptophan, that occurs in certain nerve endings of the ▷hypothalamus (in the brain) and the autonomic nervous system. It is involved in the regulation of emotion; such drugs as ▷LSD and ▷ecstasy affect mood and behaviour by altering serotonin levels in the brain. Certain ▷antidepressant drugs act by inhibiting the reuptake of serotonin in the brain.

● **serow** ▶ A hoofed mammal, *Capricornis sumatraensis*, inhabiting wooded mountainous regions of S Asia. About 90 cm high at the shoulder, serows have short wrinkled horns and a coarse black or reddish-grey coat with white patches. Serows and ▷gorals are also called goat antelopes. Family: ▷*Bovidae*.

● **Serowe** ▶ 22 25S 26 44E A town in E Botswana. It is the headquarters of the Bamangwato tribe. The main industry is agriculture. Population (latest est): 95 041.

● **serpent** ▶ A curved bass wind instrument, 2 m (7 ft) long, in the shape of a coiled snake that was developed from the ▷cornett in the 16th century by Edmé Guillaume in France. It was used in church music and later in military bands (often with added keys). Like the cornett, it was made of wood and had finger holes of the woodwind type, with a cup-shaped mouthpiece. The serpent was largely replaced by the ▷tuba in the 19th century.

● **serpentine** ▶ A group of minerals consisting mainly of hydrous magnesium silicates, with a layered structure. They are usually green or white, and often streaked or mottled like a snake's skin. The two main varieties are chrysotile (fibrous, used in the manufacture of asbestos) and antigorite (platy). They occur in basic and ultrabasic igneous rocks from the breakdown of olivines and pyroxenes. **Serpentinite** is a rock consisting mainly of serpentine, formed by the hydrothermal alteration of ultramafic rocks; some are quarried for ornamental stone.

● **SERPS** ▶ (State Earnings-Related Pension Scheme) ▷*See* National Insurance.

● **serpulid** ▶ A small marine ▷annelid worm belonging to the family *Serpulidae*. Serpulids build limy tubes on stones and seaweed and extend a crown of tentacles to feed in the same way as the related ▷fanworms. Class: *Polychaeta*.

● **serum** ▶ The fluid that remains after blood has been allowed to clot. It can be obtained by centrifuging clotted blood and is similar in composition to plasma, except that it lacks the factors, such as fibrinogen, that are involved in blood clotting.

● **serum sickness** ▶ Illness resulting from an allergic reaction to injected serum or antiserum. It is seen most commonly following the injection of horse tetanus antitoxin. 6 to 12 days after the injection the patient develops fever, a rash, and painful joints. Treatment is with steroids.

● **serval** ▶ A slender long-legged ▷cat, *Felis serval*, of the African bush. It is about 1.25 m long including the tail (30 cm) and has large ears and a spotted coat. Servals hunt birds and small mammals, such as hares and duikers, mainly at night.

● **Servetus, Michael** ▶ (Spanish name: Miguel Serveto; 1511–53) Spanish theologian and physician, who discovered that the blood circulates to the lungs from the right chamber of the heart. Working chiefly in France, he published treatises attacking the orthodox doctrine of the Trinity. These incurred the hostility of both Roman Catholics and Protestants and, while hiding from the Inquisition in Geneva, he was arrested by Calvin and burnt as a heretic.

● **service tree** ▶ A tree, *Sorbus domestica*, about 15 m high, native to S Europe, W Asia, and N Africa and commonly grown for ornament. Related to the ▷mountain ash, it has compound leaves of 11–21 leaflets and its small green fruits are used for making wine. The wild service tree (*S. torminalis*) has simple lobed leaves, while the bastard service tree is an ornamental hybrid between the mountain ash and the ▷whitebeam. Family: *Rosaceae*.

● **servomechanism** ▶ A mechanical or electrical system that controls a mechanism requiring considerable power, using a low-power command device, often with feedback. For example, the rudder and other control surfaces of a large aircraft are moved by the pilot using rudder bars and a joystick, which vary the current to a set of electric motors that actually move the rudder, flaps, and ailerons. Feedback of the actual positions of those control surfaces to the control circuits enables the system to set the aircraft on a predetermined course without manual intervention.

The power-assisted brakes and steering in a road vehicle also use servomechanisms to amplify the power, without feedback but often using a hydraulic system in which a pump rather than an electric motor is used to provide the power amplification. Three-dimensional servomechanisms are used, with feedback, in tracking spacecraft and satellites and in the control and operation of automated machinery in factories.

● **servqual** ▷*See* quality control.

● **sesame** ▶ An annual herb, *Sesamum indicum*, cultivated in Central and South America, the Middle East, and SE Asia. Several varieties are known, growing 50–250 cm high and bearing small purplish flowers. The seeds are used in confectionery and as food flavouring. Oil extracted from the seeds is used as a cooking and salad oil and in margarines and other products; the residue (sesame cake) is used as cattle feed. Family: *Pedaliaceae*.

● **Sesostris I** ▶ King of Egypt (c. 1918–1875 BC) of the 12th dynasty. He extended Egyptian rule into Nubia, exploiting its mineral resources. His ambitious building projects include a magnificent funerary complex at Lisht.

● **Sesostris II** ▶ King of Egypt (c. 1844–37 BC) of the 12th dynasty. He began the land-reclamation works in El ▷Faiyum continued by ▷Amenemhet III. Excavations at the town he founded, al-Lahun, have produced much valuable evidence about this period.

● **Sesostris III** ▶ King of Egypt (1836–18 BC) of the 12th dynasty. The sudden cessation of the construction of the nobles' extravagant tombs and an evident rise in middle-class prosperity indicate great changes in Egyptian society during his reign. Sesostris extended his control of Nubia as far south as Wadi Halfa.

● **Sesshu** ▶ (1420–1506) Japanese landscape painter, also called Sesshu Toyo. After a visit to China (c. 1467) he introduced into Japan the Chinese techniques of monochrome ink painting on long scrolls.

● **Sessions, Roger** ▶ (1896–1985) US composer. A pupil of Ernest Bloch, he held several teaching posts in the USA. From 1925 to 1933 he lived mainly in Germany and Italy. His works include two operas, *The Trial of Lucullus* (1947) and *Montezuma* (1962), eight symphonies, a violin concerto, a piano concerto, and chamber music.

● **Set** ▶ An Egyptian deity. Originally a sun and sky god, he murdered his brother ▷Osiris and so came to represent all evil. Killed by ▷Horus, son of Osiris, he is usually portrayed as a composite figure with various animal features.

● **Sète** ▶ (former name: Cette) 43 25N 3 43E A major port in S France, in the Hérault department on the Gulf of Lions. Established in 1666, it developed as the terminus of the Canal du Midi and today has shipbuilding, oil-refining, metallurgical, and fishing industries. It is the birthplace of Paul Valéry. Population (latest est): 40 446.

● **Seth, Vikram** ▶ (1952–) Indian writer in English. His books include *The Golden Gate* (1986), a novel in verse, the novels *A Suitable Boy* (1993) and *An Equal Music* (1999), and four volumes of poetry.

● **Seton, Ernest Thompson** ▶ (1860–1946) US naturalist and writer, born in England. His experiences as a hunter in Canada were the foundation for his books about animals, notably *Wild Animals I Have Known* (1898). He was concerned with conservation and was a founder of the Boy Scouts of America.

● **Seto-Naikai** ▷*See* Inland Sea.

● **setter** ▶ One of three breeds of sporting ▢dog with a lean deep-chested body and drooping ears. Setters are named after their habit of squatting flat ("setting") after finding game. The English setter has a long white silky coat flecked with darker markings. The heavier Gordon setter, first bred at Gordon Castle, Scotland, is black with chestnut markings, while the Irish, or red, setter has a flat silky chestnut coat. Height: 61–69 cm.

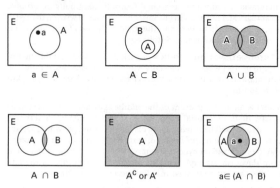

set theory ▶ Venn diagrams.

● **set theory** ▶ The study, founded by Georg ▷Cantor, of the logical and mathematical laws of sets. A set is a defined collection of objects or elements; for example the set of odd integers between 0 and 10 is $\{1, 3, 5, 7, 9\}$. The empty or null set, denoted by the symbol 0, has no elements. All sets are contained in the universal set E. The relationships between sets can be illustrated in a Venn diagram, named after the British logician John Venn (1834–1923), or shown by symbols. $a \in A$ means the element a is a member of the set A. $A \subset B$ means set A is contained in set B. $A \cup B$ means the union of A and B. $A \cap B$ means the intersection of A and B, i.e. those elements in both. A^c or A' is the complement of A, all elements in E but not in A.

● **Settlement, Act of** ▶ (1701) The Act that established the Hanoverian succession to the English throne. In the absence of heirs to William III or Anne, the Crown was to pass to James I's granddaughter ▷Sophia, Electress of Hanover, or to her Protestant descendants. The Act stipulated that the monarch must be a Protestant and that foreigners must not hold public office or enter parliament. Anne was succeeded by the first Hanoverian king, George I, in 1714.

● **Setúbal** ▶ 38 31N 8 54W A port in SW Portugal, on the Bay of Setúbal. It is an important centre for sardine fishing with associated fish-curing industries. Exports include oranges and muscatel wine and grapes. Population (1991): 83 550.

● **Seurat, Georges** ▶ (1859–91) French painter, famous for developing neoimpressionism, popularly called ▷pointillism. Influenced by writings on aesthetics and the colour theories of ▷Delacroix and the chemist Michel-Eugène Chevreul (1786–1889), he based his dots of pure colour and static compositions on scientific study. Although he finished only seven paintings in this demanding style, for example the famous *Sunday Afternoon on the Island of the Grande Jatte* (1884–86; Art Institute of Chicago) and *Le Cirque* (1890–91; Louvre), his work was very influential, one disciple being Paul ▷Signac.

● **Sevastopol** ▶ (English name: Sebastopol) 44 36N 33 31E A port in S Ukraine, in the Crimean *oblast* (region) on the Black Sea. It is a popular seaside resort.

History: founded in 1783, after Russia's annexation of the Crimea it became an important naval base and, later, a commercial port. It was besieged by the British and French during the Crimean War, falling after 11 months. Population (1996 est): 365 000.

● **Seven Against Thebes** ▶ In Greek legend, seven champions who fought against Eteocles, who had gained the throne of Thebes after the death of his father Oedipus and refused to relinquish it to his brother ▷Polyneices when his term as ruler had ended. The seven champions, led by Polyneices, attacked the seven gates of Thebes. Eteocles and Polyneices died at each other's hand. The story is the subject of a play by ▷Aeschylus.

● **Seven Deadly Sins** ▶ Pride, covetousness, lust, envy, gluttony, anger, and sloth. The traditional Christian list was already established by the 6th century and during the middle ages representations of the Seven Deadly Sins were a common feature of art and literature.

● **Seven Sisters** ▷*See* Pleiades.

● **Seven Sleepers of Ephesus** ▶ A legend of seven Christian soldiers who were entombed in a cave while hiding to escape religious persecution under the Emperor Decius in the 3rd century. They slept until the reign of Theodosius II (408–50), who, on hearing their miraculous experience, was converted to belief in the resurrection.

● **seventeenth parallel** ▶ The latitude of 17°N and the line of demarcation between North and South Vietnam established by the ▷Geneva Conference (1954).

● **Seventh Day Adventists** ▷*See* adventists.

● **Seven Weeks' War** ▷*See* Austro-Prussian War.

● **Seven Wonders of the World** ▶ The supreme man-made structures of the ancient world. They were the ▷Pyramids of Egypt, the ▷Colossus of Rhodes, the ▷Hanging Gardens of Babylon, the ▷Mausoleum of Halicarnassus, the statue of ▷Zeus at Olympia, the temple of ▷Artemis at Ephesus, and the ▷Pharos of Alexandria. Only the Pyramids have survived.

● **Seven Years' War** ▶ (1756–63) The war between Prussia, Britain, and Hanover on one side and France, Austria, Russia, and Spain on the other. The war had two main aspects: the rivalry between Austria and Prussia for domination of Germany and the struggle between France and Britain for overseas supremacy. The war was precipitated by Austria's desire to regain Silesia, lost to Frederick the Great of Prussia in the War of the ▷Austrian Succession, and began with Frederick's invasion of Saxony. Russia's defection (1762) to Prussia enabled Frederick ultimately to emerge victorious and Prussian ascendancy was confirmed by the Peace of Hubertusberg. Overseas, the British won a series of spectacular victories in India (by ▷Clive) and Canada (by ▷Wolfe). By the Treaty of ▷Paris (1763) Britain was confirmed as the supreme world power.

● **Severini, Gino** ▶ (1883–1966) Italian painter, born in Cortona. After training under ▷Balla, he moved to Paris (1906), where he became a pointillist. In 1910 he signed the futurist manifesto and thereafter combined ▷futurism and ▷cubism, especially in his nightclub scenes. He later returned to painting conventional landscapes and figure studies.

● **Severn, River** ▶ (Welsh name: Hafren) The longest river in the UK, rising in central Wales and flowing NE and E into England, then S to the Bristol Channel. It passes through Welshpool, Shrewsbury, Worcester, Tewkesbury, and Gloucester. It is linked by canal to the Rivers Thames and Trent and is spanned near its estuary by the **Severn Bridges**. The first of these, a suspension bridge 988 m (3240 ft) long, was constructed between 1961 and 1966 to carry motorway traffic between S England and S Wales. This elegant white-painted structure is now recognized as a design classic and achieved listed status in 1998. However, its vulnerability to high winds led to frequent closure. As a result a second, mainly cantilevered, bridge with much greater wind resistance was built slightly down-river and opened in 1996; this now takes the great majority of the traffic. A tidal-power barrier in the Severn Estuary has long been planned. Length: 365 km (227 mi).

● **Severus, Lucius Septimius** ▶ (c. 145–211 AD) Roman emperor (193–211). Severus was governor of Upper Pannonia (S of the Danube) before being proclaimed emperor. He defeated his rival Pescennius Niger in 194 and embarked on a punitive campaign against Pescennius' supporters. He introduced administrative and military reforms at Rome before embarking on a campaign in Britain, where he died.

● **Severus Alexander** ▶ (?208–35 AD) Roman emperor (222–35); the adopted son of his predecessor Elagabalus. Severus' mother, Julia Mamaea, murdered Elagabalus to secure Severus' accession. Severus depended upon the army, which saw his attempt to prevent war on the German frontier as cowardice, and murdered him and his mother.

● **Seveso** ▶ 45 38N 9 08E A town in N Italy, situated N of Milan. In July, 1976, a poisonous gas cloud (▷dioxin) escaped from a factory here contaminating a wide radius of land. Crops and animals were destroyed and people evacuated.

● **Sévigné, Marie de Rabutin-Chantal, Marquise de** ▶ (1626–96) French letter writer. In over 1500 letters, mostly written to her two children after the death of her husband in 1651, she described the pleasures and intellectual diversions of Parisian society—and life at her country house in Brittany—in a style that became a model for letter writing.

● **Seville** ▶ (Spanish name: Sevilla) 37 24N 5 59W A city and port in SW Spain, in Andalusia on the River Guadalquivir. Important during Roman times, it also thrived under the Moors (711–1248) as a cultural centre and became a major port with a monopoly of trade with the West Indies in the 16th century. The painters Velázquez and Murillo were born here. There is a university (founded 1502) and one of the world's largest cathedrals (1401–1591). The Easter festival with its procession of floats bearing religious subjects is a notable event. It is an important industrial centre, with textiles and engineering; exports include wine, fruit (especially oranges), and olive oil. Population (1995 est): 719 588.

● **Sèvres porcelain** ▶ The finest French porcelain, first produced in 1738. Originally at Vincennes, the Sèvres factory moved to Sèvres, near ▷Versailles, in 1756. It always enjoyed royal patronage and by 1759 Louis XV was proprietor. The early products were soft-paste porcelain but from 1768 hard-paste was made. Products were figures, vases, ornaments, and table services with blue, rose Pompadour, yellow, or green grounds richly gilded for royal taste. Now the national porcelain factory, it continues its fine output.

● **sewage disposal** ▶ The collection, treatment, and eventual discharge of domestic sewage and industrial waste. Sewers, systems of underground piping, channel the effluent to a sewage-treatment plant. There it is screened to remove solid objects before passing to a primary sedimentation tank, where suspended solids settle out. The liquid then passes through aeration tanks, where the oxygen content is increased by blowing air through it, and a final sedimentation tank before being discharged into rivers, etc. The solids meanwhile enter a sludge digester, a tank in which bacterial action partially eats away the organic material. Following thickening and drying the solid residue is incinerated, spread on the land, or sold as fertilizer. In some coastal areas raw sewage is pumped into the sea untreated, contributing to pollution; in 1990 the UK promised to cease this practice within 10 years. ▷*See also* waste disposal.

● **Sewell, Anna** ▶ (1820–78) British children's writer. A childhood accident left her an invalid for life. Her only book, *Black Beauty* (1877), is a protest against the cruel treatment of horses, told from the horse's point of view.

● **sewellel** ▶ A burrowing rodent, *Aplodontia rufa*, of W North America, also called mountain beaver. About 30 cm long and resembling a tailless muskrat, it is named after the North American Indian garment made from its pelts. Family: *Aplodontidae*.

● **sewing machine** ▶ A device for sewing together pieces of material. The lockstitch machine was invented in the USA by Elias Howe in 1846 and patented by Isaac Merrit Singer in 1851. In this machine, a needle with a thread passing through its eye penetrates the cloth from above, a loop being formed below the cloth either by passing a separate thread from a bobbin through the loop or by a rotary hook carrying the loop around a stationary bobbin. A toothed platform moves the material forwards for the next stitch. Sewing machines are powered by hand, treddle, or electric motor and modern machines have facilities for hemming, buttonholing, etc.

● **sex chromosome** ▶ A ▷chromosome that carries the genes for determining the sex of an individual. In humans there are two types of sex chromosomes, called X and Y. The body cells of normal males possess one X and one Y chromosome while those of normal females have two X chromosomes. Human sperm is therefore either "male" or "female" depending on whether it carries an X or a Y chromosome. The sex of the embryo is determined by which type fertilizes the female egg (which always carries an X chromosome). Abnormal numbers or combinations of sex chromosomes cause a range of disabilities, including physical abnormalities, mental retardation, and sterility.

● **sex hormones** ► Hormones that regulate the growth, development, and functioning of the reproductive organs and determine external sexual characteristics. The major female sex hormones are the ▷oestrogens, ▷progesterone, and ▷prolactin while the ▷androgens (including ▷testosterone and androsterone) are the principal male ones. Their production is regulated by ▷gonadotrophins from the pituitary gland.

● **sexism** ▷*See* women's movement.

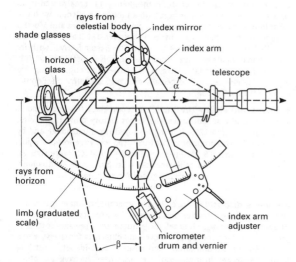

rays from celestial body
index mirror
shade glasses
index arm
horizon glass
telescope
α
rays from horizon
limb (graduated scale)
index arm adjuster
β
micrometer drum and vernier

sextant ► Angle α measures the angle between horizon and reference arm; β is the angle between index mirror and horizon glass, marked by the angular movement of the index arm along the limb. α = 2β, therefore the graduations marked on the scale are twice the actual angular movement.

● **sextant** ► An instrument used primarily in navigation for determining latitudes by measuring the angle subtended by some celestial body to the horizon. Thomas Godfrey of Philadelphia and John Hadley of London, working independently, discovered the sextant's principle in 1730. The graduated metal strip, shaped in an arc of the sixth part of a circle, gave the instrument its name. In use the movable index arm is slid along the scale until the image of the reference star as viewed in the half-silvered index mirror is aligned with the horizon. The reading on the scale then indicates the angle subtended.

● **sexton beetle** ▷*See* burying beetle.

● **sexually transmitted disease** ► (STD) Any disease transmitted predominantly by sexual intercourse, also known as venereal disease (VD). Among the most prevalent STDs are genital ▷herpes, nonspecific ▷urethritis (NSU; caused by *Chlamydia*), and ▷AIDS; ▷syphilis and ▷gonorrhoea—the former scourges—are now treatable with antibiotics.

● **Seychelles, Republic of** ► A country consisting of 87 widely scattered islands in the W Indian Ocean, NE of Madagascar. The main island is Mahé and others include Praslin, Silhouette, and La Digue; the islands of Aldabra, Farquhar, and Desroches were returned to the Seychelles in 1976. Most of the population is of mixed African and European descent.

Economy: the chief products and exports are fish, copra, and cinnamon bark. Industry remains limited but includes tobacco, brewing, and tuna canning. Tourism expanded rapidly in the 1970s and 1980s and now accounts for a large proportion of government revenue. The government has also taken steps to promote the Seychelles as an offshore financial centre.

History: the uninhabited islands became a French colony in the mid-18th century as a spice plantation. Captured by the British in 1794, they became a dependency of Mauritius from 1814 until 1903, when they became a British crown colony. In 1976 the country became an independent republic within the British Commonwealth, with James Mancham (1940–) as its first president. While attending the Commonwealth conference in London in 1977, he was overthrown and superseded as president by his prime minister, Albert René (1935–). In 1981 a mercenary force backed by South Africa attempted a coup. It was the third such attempt by forces from outside the country to seize power. In 1993 the first multiparty elections since 1977 resulted in victory for René and his ruling party; he was re-elected in 2002.

Republic of Seychelles	
Head of state	President Albert René
Official languages	English and French; the majority speak Creole
Official currency	Seychelles rupee of 100 cents
Area	444 sq km (171 sq mi)
Population (2001 est)	80 600
Capital and main port	Victoria

● **Seyfert galaxy** ► A class of galaxies with exceptionally bright central regions the majority of which are otherwise normal spiral galaxies. Intense radiation is emitted from the centre at infrared, visible, ultraviolet, and X-ray wavelengths, the source of this energy being relatively small. This type of galaxy was first described by the US astronomer C. K. Seyfert (1911–60). ▷*See also* active galaxy.

● **Seymour, Jane** ► (c. 1509–37) The third wife (1536–37) of Henry VIII of England. A lady in waiting to both his former wives, Catherine of Aragon and Anne Boleyn, she married Henry 11 days after Anne's execution. Jane died shortly after the birth of a son, Edward VI.

● **Sfax** ► 34 45N 10 43E The second largest city in Tunisia and a major port on the Gulf of Gabes. It developed as an early trade centre and still fulfils that role today, exporting phosphates, olive oil, cotton and woollen goods, and sponges. Population (1994): 230 900.

● **Sforza** ► An Italian family that ruled Milan from 1450 to 1499, 1512 to 1515, and 1522 to 1535. Originating in Romagna as the Attendoli, its name was changed to Sforza (Italian: force) by the condottiere **Muzio Attendoli** (1369–1424). His son **Francesco Sforza** (1401–66) obtained Milan by his marriage (1441) to Bianca Maria, the only child of Filippo Maria ▷Visconti. Francesco was succeeded by **Galeazzo Maria Sforza** (1444–76), a notable patron of the arts. Soon after his assassination his brother **Lodovico Sforza** (1452–1508), known as Lodovico il Moro (the Moor), seized power (1480) from Galeazzo's son **Gian Galeazzo Sforza** (1469–94). Lodovico made Milan one of the most powerful Italian states and was also an outstanding patron of artists, including Leonardo da Vinci. He was expelled from the duchy in 1499 by Louis XII of France. After a brief restoration (1512–15), the Sforza were again ousted by the French but in 1522 Lodovico's son **Francesco Maria Sforza** (1495–1535) was re-established by Emperor Charles V. With the failure of the line at Francesco's death, Milan passed to Charles.

● **SGML** ► (Standard Generalized Markup Language) A coding system for marking up a text so that different types of information are identified. For instance, in an encyclopedia the headwords, main text, and cross references can be tagged in a standard way, irrespective of how they may be typeset in printed material or displayed in electronic form. **Hypertext Markup Language** (HTML) is a particular application of SGML used in ▷electronic publishing. **Xtensible Markup Language** (XML) is a simplified version designed for use on the ▷Internet.

● **'s Gravenhage** ▷*See* Hague, The.

● **Shaba** ▶ (former name: Katanga) A province in SE Democratic Republic of Congo (formerly Zaïre), bordering on Zambia. Economically and politically the most advanced of the provinces, it was embroiled in civil war following decolonization by Belgium in 1960. In 1993 it again declared itself independent of Zaïre. It is an extremely important mining area (especially of copper, cobalt, and zinc) centred on Kolwezi. Area: 496 964 sq km (191 878 sq mi). Population (1998 est): 4 125 000. Capital: Lubumbashi.

● **Shache** ▶ (So-ch'e *or* Yarkand) 38 27N 77 16E A town in NW China, in Xinjiang Uygur AR on a fertile oasis in the ▷Tarim Basin. It is an agricultural and trading centre on the ▷Silk Road to Europe. Population (latest est): 25 000.

● **Shackleton, Sir Ernest Henry** ▶ (1874–1922) British explorer. He accompanied ▷Scott's expedition of 1901–04 and on his own expedition in 1908–09 nearly reached the South Pole. In an expedition of 1914–16 his ship, the *Endurance*, was marooned but he and his men reached Elephant Island by sledge and boats. With five others he then journeyed 1300 km (800 mi) to find relief. He died on his fourth expedition.

● **shad** ▶ A food fish, belonging to a genus (*Alosa*) related to herrings, that occurs in the N Atlantic, Mediterranean, and North Sea. It has one or a succession of black spots along each side and a notch in the upper jaw. They migrate in large shoals to spawn in fresh waters. The allis shad (*A. alosa*), about 75 cm long, and the smaller twaite shad (*A. fallax*) are European species.

● **shaddock** ▶ An evergreen tree, *Citrus grandis*, also called pomelo, native to SE Asia and cultivated in tropical regions of the Old and New Worlds. Growing 6–13 m high, it bears pale-yellow oval fruits, with coarse thick pulp and bitter-tasting pulp, which are sometimes eaten or used to make liqueurs. Family: *Rutaceae*. ▷*See also* Citrus.

● **shadoof** ▶ An ancient water-raising device still used, especially in Egypt and S India, for irrigation. It consists of a pole mounted on a pivot with a bucket at one end and a counterbalancing weight at the other.

● **Shadwell, Thomas** ▶ (c. 1642–92) British dramatist. His varied dramatic works included the comedies *Epsom Wells* (1672) and *The Virtuoso* (1676). He sustained a lengthy political and literary feud with ▷Dryden, who satirized him in *Absalom and Achitophel* (1681) and *MacFlecknoe* (1682). He succeeded Dryden as poet laureate in 1688.

● **Shaffer, Sir Peter** ▶ (1926–) British dramatist. He established his reputation with *Five-Finger Exercise* (1958). His epic treatment of the Spanish conquest of Peru, *The Royal Hunt of the Sun* (1964), was filmed and made into an opera. His later plays include *Equus* (1973), *Amadeus* (1979), *Lettice and Lovage* (1987), and *The Gift of the Gorgon* (1992). He was knighted in 2000. His twin brother **Anthony Shaffer** (1926–2001) was also a playwright, best known for the thriller *Sleuth* (1970).

● **Shaftesbury, Anthony Ashley Cooper, 1st Earl of** ▶ (1621–83) English statesman. Initially a royalist in the Civil War he came to support the parliamentarians and in the 1650s sat in Oliver Cromwell's parliaments. He gained Cromwell's distrust and participated in the Restoration of Charles II (1660), becoming chancellor of the exchequer (1661–72), lord chancellor (1672–73), and a member of the political group called the ▷Cabal. Dismissed in 1673 he led the movement to exclude the Roman Catholic James, Duke of York (later James II), from the succession. Charged with treason in 1681, the case was dismissed but Shaftesbury fled to Amsterdam, where he died. He was satirized as the Achitophel in Dryden's *Absalom and Achitophel* (1681). His grandson **Anthony Ashley Cooper, 3rd Earl of Shaftesbury** (1671–1713) was educated under the guidance of ▷Locke and is best known for his *Characteristics of Men, Manners, Opinions, Times* (1711) on a variety of philosophical and other topics. In opposition to ▷Hobbes, he held that men were born with a natural love of virtue.

Anthony Ashley Cooper, 7th Earl of Shaftesbury (1801–85) was a reformer and philanthropist. He became an MP in 1826 and as chairman of the lunacy commission from 1834 obtained reform of the lunacy laws (1845). His great work for factory reform achieved the ten-hour day for factory workers (1847) and his Coal Mines Act (1842) abolished the system of child apprenticeship and the employment in mines of women and of children under 13. With the Climbing Boys Act (1840) he ended the employment of children as chimney sweeps.

He also established lodging houses for the poor and was prominent in the ▷ragged schools movement.

● **shag** ▶ A small ▷cormorant, *Phalacrocorax aristotelis*, confined to rocky coasts and offshore islands of Europe and North Africa. It is 75 cm long and has a glossy green-black plumage with a distinct crest in the breeding season. It feeds on fish.

● **Shah Jahan** ▶ (1592–1666) Emperor of India (1628–58) of the Mogul dynasty; the son of ▷Jahangir. His reign was as ruthless as his means of attaining it; he put his nearest relatives to death in 1628. His passion for architecture produced such monuments as the ▷Taj Mahal and the Delhi Red Fort. He was deposed by his son ▷Aurangzeb.

● **Shahn, Ben** ▶ (1898–1969) Lithuanian-born artist, who lived in New York from 1906. He is best known for his social realist and political paintings, notably the series (1931–32) on the Italian anarchists Nicola Sacco and Bartolomeo Vanzetti (*see* Sacco-Vanzetti case).

● **Shah of Iran** ▷*See* Mohammed Reza Pahlavi; Reza Shah Pahlavi.

● **Shaka** ▶ (c. 1787–1828) Zulu chief, who made the Zulu nation the strongest in S Africa and began the period of warfare called the ▷Mfecane. Shaka claimed the chieftainship in about 1816, introduced military reforms, and ruthlessly expanded his possessions. He was stabbed to death by his half-brothers Dingane and Mhlangana.

● **Shakers** ▶ An austere sect originating in England as an offshoot of the ▷Quakers (1747). Led by Ann Lee (Mother Ann; d. 1784), in whose person they believed the Second Coming of Christ to be accomplished (*see* millenarianism), the Shakers founded a colony in the USA (1774), where they flourished until the 20th century. Celibacy, faith healing, common ownership of property, prescribed modes of dress, separation from the world in self-regulating communities, and abstinence from tobacco and alcohol characterized their way of life. Known more formally as the Millennial Church, they received their popular name from their practice of violent trembling in religious ecstasies during their meetings. They are also noted for their austere wooden furniture, which became highly fashionable in the 1980s.

● **Shakespeare, William** ▶ (1564–1616) English dramatist, universally recognized as the greatest English writer. The son of a tradesman who became high bailiff (mayor) of Stratford-upon-Avon in 1568, he was educated at the local grammar school and in 1582 married a local girl, Anne Hathaway, by whom he had three children. Soon afterwards he went to London, where he became an actor in the leading theatrical company, the Lord Chamberlain's Men (called the King's Men after 1603). The historical tetralogy comprising the three parts of *Henry VI* and *Richard III* were his first plays (1589–92). His dramatic poems *Venus and Adonis* (1593) and *The Rape of Lucrece* (1594) were dedicated to his patron Henry Wriothesley, 3rd Earl of ▷Southampton. His *Sonnets* (1609), probably written at this time, betray nothing of his private life despite their themes of love and friendship. His early comedies (1593–95) were *Love's Labour's Lost*, *The Two Gentlemen of Verona*, and *The Taming of the Shrew*. These were followed (1595–1600) by *A Midsummer Night's Dream*, *The Merchant of Venice*, *Much Ado About Nothing*, *Twelfth Night*, and *As You Like It*. During this period he also wrote his first significant tragedy, *Romeo and Juliet*, as well as *Richard II* and *Julius Caesar*. In 1597 he bought New Place, a large house in Stratford, and later became a shareholder in the ▷Globe Theatre in London and bought other property in London and Stratford. The two parts of *Henry IV* were completed before *Hamlet*, *Othello*, *King Lear*, and *Macbeth*, his major tragedies, which were written between 1600 and 1606. His final experimental plays, including *The Winter's Tale* (c. 1610) and *The Tempest* (c. 1611), were written for the educated audience of the indoor theatre at Blackfriars, which the King's Men had acquired in 1608. In about 1611 he retired to Stratford, where he died. His other plays were: *The Comedy of Errors*, *Titus Andronicus*, *King John*, *Henry V*, *The Merry Wives of Windsor*, *Antony and Cleopatra*, *Coriolanus*, *Troilus and Cressida*, *Measure for Measure*, *All's Well That Ends Well*, *Timon of Athens*, *Pericles*, *Cymbeline*, and (with John ▷Fletcher) *Henry VIII* and *The Two Noble Kinsmen*. Many scholars now believe that Shakespeare also wrote some scenes in the chronicle plays *Sir Thomas More* (1592–93) and *Edward III* (1596). The first collected edition of his works, known as the First Folio and containing 36 plays, was published in 1623. □ p. 1132.

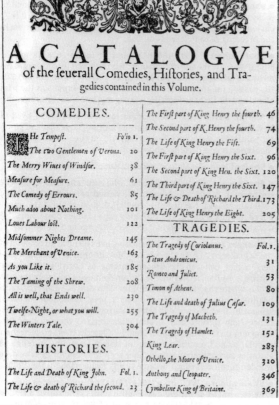

William Shakespeare ▶ The title page of the First Folio (1623).

● **Shakhty** ▶ 47 43N 40 16E A city in W Russia. Situated in the E Donets Basin, it is a major coalmining centre. Population (1991 est): 227 700.

● **shale** ▶ A fine-grained ▷sedimentary rock that splits easily along the closely spaced bedding planes as a result of the alignment of the clay mineral particles parallel to the bedding planes. Shales may disintegrate in water but do not become plastic. They are softer and lighter than slate, which is a fine-grained ▷metamorphic rock. **Oil shales** contain a considerable amount of decayed organic matter. The **shale oil** so formed can be extracted from the oil shales by destructive distillation and used as a source of petroleum. Shale oil is extracted on a commercial basis in Canada from the large deposits there. However, when the price of oil from wells falls, shale oil can become uncompetitive.

● **shallot** ▶ A hardy perennial herbaceous plant, ▷*Allium ascalonium*, probably of Asiatic origin. Its small hollow cylindrical leaves are often used for dressing food and in salads. Its small angular bulbs occur in garlic-like clusters and are used for flavouring and pickling. Family: *Liliaceae*.

● **shamanism** ▶ The religious beliefs and practices common in certain tribal societies of Asia, such as the ▷Samoyed. The term is also applied to North American Indian practices. The shaman is a tribal priest generally felt to be possessed by a spirit or deity and hence to have supernatural powers. He is liable to trances or ecstasies, may diagnose and cure disease, find lost or stolen goods, or foretell the future. He is usually a source of beneficial (white) magic. As an intermediary with the spirit world, he may act as the tribal ruler and judge. The office may be hereditary or there may be a long training.

● **Shamir, Yitzhak** ▶ (1915–   ) Israeli statesman, born in Poland;

prime minister (1983–84, 1986–92). He led the Israeli Freedom Fighters (1940–41), served in Israel's secret service (1955–65), and was foreign minister (1980–83; 1984–86). When a coalition was formed in 1984, he became deputy prime minister under a special power-sharing agreement with Shimon ▷Peres. He formed new coalitions in 1988 and 1990. In 1992 his government collapsed when right-wing groups withdrew in protest at Israel's participation in peace talks with Palestinian leaders.

● **shamrock** ▶ Any of several plants bearing leaves with three leaflets, especially various ▷clovers, black ▷medick (*Medicago lupulina*), and ▷wood sorrel (*Oxalis acetosella*). St Patrick is said to have adopted it as a symbol of the Holy Trinity and it is worn on St Patrick's Day.

● **Shandong** ▶ (or Shantung) A province in NE China, on the Yellow Sea, with central mountains. Densely populated, its fertile farmland produces chiefly wheat and cotton. From early times it has been an important trading area. Floods and famine in the 19th and 20th centuries have led to much emigration northwards. Area: 153 300 sq km (59 189 sq mi). Population (1997 est): 87 850 000. Capital: Jinan.

● **Shandong Peninsula** ▶ (or Shantung Peninsula) A hilly peninsula in E China. Together with the ▷Liaodong Peninsula opposite, it forms the mouth of the Gulf of Chihli.

● **Shanghai** ▶ 31 13N 121 25E An administratively autonomous port in E China, on the Yangtze estuary. The largest city in China, it is its chief port and industrial city. Its many educational establishments include two universities. It grew rapidly after it was opened to foreign trade in 1842, coming under British, US, and French rule until World War II. Industries include steel, textiles, chemicals, shipbuilding, engineering, and publishing. Following the liberalization of China's economy in the 1980s, it has also emerged as a major financial centre. Redevelopment in the 1990s included the construction of the World Financial Centre, one of the world's tallest buildings. Population (1997 est): 14 570 000.

● **Shan-hsi** ▷*See* Shanxi.

● **Shankara** ▷*See* Sankara.

● **Shankar, Ravi** ▶ (1920–   ) Indian ▷sitar player. He influenced the Beatles, performed with Yehudi Menuhin, and inspired André Previn to write a sitar concerto.

● **Shannon, River** ▶ The longest river in the Republic of Ireland. Rising in NW Co Cavan, it flows S to Limerick and then W into an estuary 113 km (70 mi) long, before entering the Atlantic Ocean. It powers Ireland's main hydroelectric plant. Length: 386 km (240 mi).

● **Shansi** ▷*See* Shanxi.

● **Shantou** ▶ (or Swatow) 23 23N 116 39E A port in SE China, in Guangdong province on the South China Sea. It has developed greatly since 1949 and its industries include food processing and shipbuilding. Population (1990): 578 630.

● **Shantung** ▷*See* Shandong.

● **Shantung Peninsula** ▷*See* Shandong Peninsula.

● **Shanxi** ▶ (Shan-hsi or Shansi) A province in NE China. It is mainly a high hilly plateau, prone to drought. It is important for its coal and iron reserves and the industry they supply. Its relatively sparse Chinese population lives chiefly by keeping animals and growing cotton and cereals. It is famous for its opera, metalwork, and pottery.

History: a buffer zone between the settled Chinese and the nomadic tribes of the N and W in the middle ages, it became politically stable in about the 14th century. An earthquake in 1556 was the worst recorded, killing 830 000 people. In the 18th and 19th centuries it was famous for its merchants and bankers. Opposition to foreigners was strong and the ▷Boxer Rising broke out here (1900). Its industry was established by the warlord Yan Xi-shan (or Yen Hsi-shan; ruled 1911–49). Area: 157 099 sq km (60 656 sq mi). Population (1997 est): 31 410 000. Capital: Taiyuan.

● **Shapur II** ▶ (309–79 AD) King of Persia (309–79) of the Sasanian dynasty; the posthumous son of his father and predecessor. During his long and successful wars to recover lost territory in Armenia and Mesopotamia from Rome, the emperor ▷Julian the Apostate was killed and Christians, suspected as followers of Rome's official religion, were persecuted.

● **shares** ▷*See* stocks and shares.

● **Shari, River** ▷*See* Chari, River.

● **shari'ah** ▷*See* Islamic law.

● **Sharjah** ▷*See* United Arab Emirates.

● **shark** ▶ A ▷cartilaginous fish belonging to the worldwide order *Selachii* (about 250 species). Ranging in size from the smallest ▷dogfish to the enormous ▷whale shark, they have a torpedo-shaped body with a muscular tail used in swimming, five to seven pairs of gill slits on the sides of the head, and numerous sharp teeth. They are chiefly marine and carnivorous, feeding on fish and invertebrates but in some cases, plankton, carrion, and other vertebrates. They produce live young or lay eggs. Subclass: *Elasmobranchii*.

● **Sharon, Ariel** ▶ (1928–) Israeli soldier and politician; prime minister (2001–). An Israeli army officer from 1948, he became a national hero for his brilliant tactics as a commander in the Yom Kippur War (1973). He then entered politics, serving in a series of Likud governments from 1977. As defence minister he organized Israel's invasion of Lebanon in 1982 but was removed from office (1983) when it was found that he had connived in the massacre of Palestinian refugees by right-wing Lebanese forces. In the 1990s he emerged as a leading critic of the Palestinian peace process and served as foreign minister (1998–99). He became leader of Likud in 2000, taking the party to a landslide victory in the elections of 2001.

● **Sharon, Plain of** ▶ A coastal plain in Israel, extending 80 km (50 mi) between Haifa and Tel Aviv-Yafo. It is noted for the production of citrus fruit.

● **Sharp, Cecil (James)** ▶ (1859–1924) British musician. He practised law in Australia, then turned to music and held several posts as an organist, returning to England in 1892. From then on he systematically collected, edited, and published English folksongs, for which he is best remembered.

● **Sharp, Phillip Allen** ▶ (1944–) US molecular biologist. Sharp discovered the existence, in eukaryotic ▷cells, of DNA sequences (later called "introns") that do not encode proteins or other gene products (*see* genetic code); these sequences lie within normal coding sequences ("exons"), resulting in so-called "split genes." His work was confirmed independently by the British biologist Richard Roberts (1943–) and they shared the 1993 Nobel Prize.

● **Sharpeville** ▶ A town in NE South Africa, near Vereeniging. It was the scene of a riot on 21 March, 1960, in which a crowd of Black African demonstrators were fired on by the police. Sixty-nine of the demonstrators were killed and many others wounded. A riot in 1984 led to the sentencing to death of six Black demonstrators for murder; this was commuted to 25 years' imprisonment in 1988 after international protests. A further riot in 1985 led to another 19 deaths.

● **Shastri, Shri Lal Bahadur** ▶ (1904–66) Indian statesman; prime minister (1964–66). As a young man he was imprisoned by the British while a member of Gandhi's noncooperation movement. He held four ministerial positions before becoming prime minister. His greatest achievement was in negotiating the ceasefire agreement with ▷Ayub Khan after the India-Pakistan war. He died the next day.

● **Shatt al-Arab** ▶ A river in SE Iraq, formed by the confluence of the Rivers Tigris and Euphrates. It enters the Persian Gulf via a delta in Kuwait, Iraq, and Iran, passing Basra and Abadan along its course. Length: 190 km (118 mi).

● **Shaw, Artie** ▶ (Arthur Arshawsky; 1910–) US jazz clarinetist and band leader, who introduced strings into his swing band in 1935. His version of Cole Porter's "Begin the Beguine" (1938) was a great success. After 1955 he gave up his band to write and compose.

● **Shaw, George Bernard** ▶ (1856–1950) Irish dramatist, critic, and man of letters, born in Dublin. He went to London in 1876 and after writing five novels, which were unsuccessful, he became a music and drama critic, an active socialist, and one of the founding members of the Fabian Society. He soon made a reputation with his

George Bernard Shaw ▶ At work on his 90th birthday. The photograph shows him in "The Wilderness," the garden hut at his Hertfordshire home that he used as a study.

brilliant speeches and pamphlets supporting the Fabian cause. He popularized the works of Wagner (*The Perfect Wagnerite*, 1898) and Ibsen, finding in the work of the latter a remedy for the current intellectual poverty of the London theatre. His views were summed up in *The Quintessence of Ibsenism* (1891). At first finding no large commercial audience for his plays, Shaw wrote extensive explanations (and stage directions) for the printed editions of his works. The Prefaces to his plays are consequently elaborate commentaries on the social and moral issues involved. He wrote more than 40 plays, the first of which, *Widowers' Houses* (1892), an attack on slum landlords, was printed in *Plays Pleasant and Unpleasant* (1898), which included *The Philanderer*, *Mrs Warren's Profession* (on prostitution), and the "pleasant" comedies *Arms and the Man*, *You Never Can Tell*, *Candida*, and *The Man of Destiny*. With *Three Plays for Puritans* (published 1901), which comprised *The Devil's Disciple*, *Caesar and Cleopatra*, and *Captain Brassbound's Conversion*, Shaw achieved a certain popularity. The epic comedy of ideas, *Man and Superman* (1903), was based on the Don Juan legend and developed Shaw's ideas on the "life force" and social evolution; it was followed by *John Bull's Other Island* (1904) and *Major Barbara* (1905). His next plays were *The Doctor's Dilemma* (1906), *Getting Married* (1908), *Misalliance* (1910), and *Androcles and the Lion* (1913). *Pygmalion* (1913) was a great commercial success and became a perennial favourite (and the basis of the musical *My Fair Lady*, 1955). It was followed by *Heartbreak House* (1917) and the series of plays entitled *Back to Methuselah* (1921). The historical drama *St Joan* (1924), on Joan of Arc, is often regarded as his greatest work. His late plays (from 1929 onwards) include *The Apple Cart*, *The Village Wooing*, and *In Good King Charles's Golden Days*. In 1925 he was awarded the Nobel Prize for Literature. Among his prose works are *The Intelligent Woman's Guide to Socialism and Capitalism* (1928) and *The Black Girl in Search of God* (1932).

● **Shaw, (Richard) Norman** ▶ (1831–1912) British architect. Principally known as a domestic architect, Shaw, in partnership with W. E. Nesfield (1835–88), broke the hold of the ▷gothic revival on English architecture. Using a variety of styles, including gothic, Tudor, Queen Anne, and later ▷classicism, Shaw produced buildings, such as Swan House, Chelsea (1876), which were less impressive, but more comfortable, than those of his predecessors. His works continue to influence British architecture.

● **Shawinigan** ▶ 46 33N 72 45W A city in E Canada, in Quebec on the St Maurice River near waterfalls 46 m (150 ft) high. Developed around 1900 to utilize their hydroelectric potential, Shawinigan is a centre for pulp and paper, chemicals (especially calcium carbide), and other heavy industries. Population (1991): 19 931.

● **Shcherbakov** ▷*See* Rybinsk.

● **shear stress** ▶ A form of ▷stress in which the applied force acts tangentially to the surface of the body. Thus a shear stress applied to the top of a pack of cards would cause the cards to slide over each other.

• **shearwater** ► One of a group of birds (about 15 species) of the oceanic family *Procellariidae*. 27–90 cm long, shearwaters have a dark plumage (some species have white underparts), long narrow wings, and slender bills; they feed on fish from the sea surface. The great shearwater (*Puffinus gravis*) breeds in the South Atlantic, migrating to spend summer and autumn in the North Atlantic. The Manx shearwater (*P. puffinus*) breeds off British and Mediterranean coasts and winters in E South America and Australia. Order: *Procellariiformes*. ▷*See also* petrel.

• **sheathbill** ► A small compact scavenging bird belonging to a family (*Chionidae*; 2 species) occurring on coasts near Antarctica. Sheathbills are 40 cm long and have a thick white plumage, shortish wings, and a horny sheath covering the nostrils at the base of the bill. Order: *Charadriiformes* (gulls, plovers, etc.).

• **Sheba** ► In the Bible, a land corresponding to Sabaea in present-day Yemen (SW Arabia). It was known for its trade in spices and gold. Its most famous monarch was the Queen of Sheba who visited King Solomon in Jerusalem (I Kings 10.1–13). According to Ethiopian tradition, she bore him a son, the first King of Ethiopia.

• **Shechem** ▷*See* Nablus.

• **sheep** ► A hoofed ▷ruminant mammal belonging to the genus *Ovis* (7 species), native to mountainous regions of Eurasia and North America. Related to goats, sheep are generally 75–100 cm tall at the shoulder and weigh 50–150 kg. They have a compact body with slender legs and a short tail and the coat ranges from white to brown in colour. Males (rams) have large spiralled horns; females (ewes) have smaller less curved horns. There are over 200 breeds of domestic sheep (*O. aries*), probably descended from the Asian red sheep (*O. orientalis*), which are reared worldwide for meat, wool, and milk (*see* livestock farming). They typically have a long woolly coat, unlike the coarser coat of wild sheep. Family: ▷*Bovidae*. ▷*See also* aoudad; argali; bighorn; mouflon.

• **sheepdog** ► A dog used for handling sheep. Many breeds are used for this purpose, including the ▷collie, ▷German shepherd dog, ▷Old English sheepdog, and ▷Shetland sheepdog, as well as crossbred derivatives. Sheepdog trials are held in the UK, in which teams of dog and handler are awarded points for driving, dividing, and penning a group of sheep over a marked course.

• **sheep ked** ► A flat wingless fly, *Melophagus ovinus*, also called sheep tick, that is parasitic upon sheep. Both sexes are bloodsuckers and are attached to the fleece, often causing serious skin irritations. The larvae are retained within the body of the female until they reach maturity, when they are deposited on the ground. Family: *Hippoboscidae*.

• **Sheerness** ► 51 27N 0 45E A town in SE England, in Kent at the mouth of the River Medway on the Isle of Sheppey. Sheerness is a port with modern cargo-handling facilities and a holiday resort. The former naval dockyard in Sheerness, founded about 1665, is now an industrial estate. Population (1991): 11 653.

• **Sheffield** ► **1.** 52 23N 1 30W A city in N England, in Sheffield unitary authority, South Yorkshire, situated on the River Don at the edge of the Pennines. It is world famous for steel, produced here since the mid-18th century, although Sheffield knives were known in Chaucer's day. Special and alloy steels are now more important than the traditional cutlery and tool-making trades, although these still survive. Sheffield also produces silverware and plate, glass, and engineering products, including medical instruments. Media and culture are increasingly important to the city's economy; a major centre for the visual arts, the Millennium Galleries, opened in 2000. There is a cathedral (partly 15th century) and two universities. In 1989 95 people were crushed to death in an accident at the city's ▷Hillsborough football stadium. Population (1991): 431 607. **2.** A unitary authority in N England, in South Yorkshire. Area: 368 sq km (142 sq mi). Population (1999 est): 501 202.

• **Sheffield plate** ► Articles that are made by fusing a silver coat

onto copper. The process was discovered (c. 1742) by Thomas Boulsover (1704–88), a Sheffield cutler. Used as a substitute for solid silver, Sheffield-plated articles, usually tableware, followed contemporary silver designs and were of the highest quality. By 1770 both sides of the copper were silvered and exposed copper on cut edges was concealed by silver borders. Sheffield plate became obsolete after the introduction of electroplating in the mid-19th century, but Sheffield-plated articles are now much sought after.

• **Shelburne, William Petty Fitzmaurice, 2nd Earl of** ► (1737–1805) British statesman; prime minister (1782–83). An advocate of conciliation towards the American colonies, his ministry negotiated the Treaty of Paris (1783), which ended the American Revolution.

• **shelduck** ► A large ▷duck, *Tadorna tadorna*, found around coasts of W and central Eurasia. It is 65 cm long and has black-and-white plumage with a green head, chestnut shoulders, and a red bill, which in the male has a red knob at the base. It feeds chiefly on molluscs and nests in disused rabbit burrows.

• **shellac** ► A natural thermoplastic ▷resin made from the secretions of the lac insect, *Laccifer lacca*, which is parasitic on certain trees in India and Thailand. It was formerly used for moulding records but was replaced by vinyl resins, which have, in turn, largely been replaced by compact discs. Its solution in alcohol is used as a varnish in French polishing and in lacquers. It is also used in sealing wax, printing inks, and electrical insulation.

• **Shelley, Percy Bysshe** ► (1792–1822) British poet. Expelled from Oxford University for publishing a pamphlet defending atheism in 1811, he married Harriet Westbrook and lived a nomadic life while completing the revolutionary poem *Queen Mab* (1813). In 1816 he met and befriended Byron in Switzerland. From 1818 until his death he lived in Italy, where he wrote the verse dramas *The Cenci* (1819) and *Prometheus Unbound* (1818–19), the elegy *Adonais* (1821) prompted by the death of Keats, and much lyrical poetry. He was drowned in a sailing accident off the Italian coast. His second wife, **Mary Wollstonecraft Shelley** (*born* Godwin; 1797–1851), British novelist, was the daughter of William ▷Godwin and Mary ▷Wollstonecraft. She eloped to the Continent with Shelley in 1814 and married him after Harriet's suicide in 1816. In addition to her best-known book, *Frankenstein: the Modern Prometheus* (1818), she wrote romances and travel books and edited Shelley's *Poetical Works* (1839).

• **shellfish** ► Edible aquatic invertebrates (not fish) whose bodies are covered with a shell or carapace. They include crustaceans, such as crabs, lobsters, prawns, and shrimps; and bivalve molluscs, such as oysters, scallops, mussels, cockles, winkles, and clams. They are exploited commercially, and shellfish farming forms an important part of the ▷fishing industry.

• **shells** ► The hard casings secreted by some animals to protect themselves or their eggs. The term usually refers to the shells of molluscs, which consist largely of calcium carbonate and come in a wide variety of shapes and sizes. They may be spiralled or flat, with one valve (in gastropods, such as snails) or two (in bivalves, such as mussels). A single valve of a giant clam may weigh up to 90 kg. The pearly nautilus has a many chambered shell, which provides buoyancy, while the female paper nautilus (*Argonauta*) secretes a shell-like cradle to transport its eggs and young. The shells of marine molluscs, particularly gastropods, are prized by collectors.

• **Shelter** ► (National Campaign for the Homeless) A British organization, founded in 1966, to raise funds for housing projects and housing aid centres for the homeless and to campaign for more and better housing. Its 300 voluntary groups also give advice on tenancy matters. Director: Ms S. McKechnie.

• **Sheltie** ▷*See* Shetland sheepdog.

• **Shenandoah River** ► A river in the E USA, flowing mainly NE through Virginia to join the Potomac River as its main tributary. It was a major ▷Civil War battleground (*see also* Sheridan, Philip H.). The **Shenandoah National Park**, in the Blue Ridge section of the Appalachian Mountains, lies to the S of the river. Length: 88 km (55 mi).

• **Shensi** ► (or Shen-hsi) ▷*See* Shenxi.

• **Shenstone, William** ► (1714–63) British poet. His best-known poem is *The Schoolmistress* (1737), influenced by Spenser. He was a contemporary of Samuel Johnson at Oxford, helped to renew interest in traditional ballads, and developed his pioneering ideas about landscape gardening on his Worcestershire estate.

● **Shenxi** ► (Shen-hsi *or* Shensi) A mountainous province in central China. In the Wei He (River) and Han River valleys wheat, millet, and cotton are grown. Coal, iron, and oil are also produced.

History: the Wei He valley was the centre of successive Chinese dynasties from 1122 BC. Its economy rested on an impressive irrigation system from about 300 BC until about 600 AD, when it began to deteriorate. From about 1860 until 1928 the N suffered from famines, epidemics, and civil wars. Following the ▷Long March, it was the communist base (1936–1949). Area: 195 800 sq km (75 598 sq mi). Population (1990): 32 882 403. Capital: Xi An.

● **Shenyang** ► (former name: Mukden) 41 50N 123 26E A city in NE China, on the River Hun, the capital of Liaoning province and the site of its university. China's fourth largest city, it is a major industrial centre. The **Mukden Incident** (1931), an explosion on the Japanese-controlled South Manchurian Railway, was the pretext for the Japanese occupation of Manchuria (*see* Manchukuo). Population (1991 est): 4 540 000.

● **she oak** ▷*See* Casuarina.

● **Shepard, Ernest Howard** ► (1879–1976) British artist. A cartoonist for *Punch*, he is best remembered for his illustrations for *Winnie the Pooh* (1926), *Wind in the Willows* (1931), and many other children's books.

● **Shepard, Jr, Alan Bartlett** ► (1923–   ) US astronaut, who on 5 May, 1961, became the first American in space. His flight, which came 23 days after ▷Gagarin's flight, lasted 15 minutes and reached a height of 185 km. He also commanded the Apollo 14 flight to the moon in 1971.

● **shepherd's purse** ► An annual or biennial herb, *Caspella bursa-pastoris*, found growing as a weed throughout the world. It has a basal rosette of leaves and a branching leafy stem, 3–40 cm high, bearing tiny white flowers that produce small purse-shaped fruits. Its ability to self-pollinate produces distinctive local populations. Family: ▷Cruciferae.

● **Sheppard, Jack** ► (1702–24) British criminal. He became famous for his many daring and ingenious escapes from Newgate and other prisons. His adventures were celebrated in contemporary ballads and plays.

● **Shepparton** ► A city in Australia, in N Victoria. It is within the Goulborn Valley Irrigation Area and is a major centre for the soft-fruit industry. Population (1989): 27 000.

● **Sheppey, Isle of** ► 51 25N 0 50E An island in SE England, off the N coast of Kent in the River Thames estuary. It is agriculturally important, producing cereals and vegetables; sheep (from which its name derives) are also raised.

● **sheradizing** ► A process for galvanizing iron or steel (i.e. protecting the metal from corrosion by coating it with zinc) by placing it in a rotating drum with zinc dust and heating to about 260°C. At this temperature the iron and zinc amalgamate forming an internal layer of zinc-iron alloys and an external layer of pure zinc. Named after the British inventor Sherard Cowper-Coles (d. 1935).

● **Sheraton, Thomas** ► (1751–1806) British furniture designer. Settling in London (c. 1790), he made his name with the designs in his *Cabinet-Maker and Upholsterer's Drawing Book* (1791–94). Influenced by ▷Adam and contemporary French styles, these designs were characterized by elegance, delicacy, straight lines, and inlaid decoration. Ordained in 1800, he also wrote religious works.

● **Sherbrooke** ► 45 24N 71 54W A city in E Canada, in S Quebec. Founded in 1794, it is the farming, transportation, commercial, and

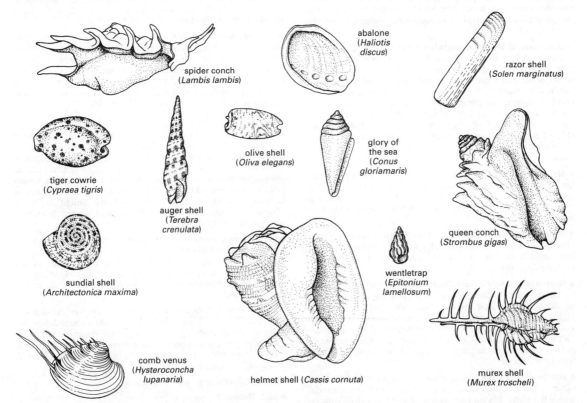

spider conch
(*Lambis lambis*)

abalone
(*Haliotis
discus*)

razor shell
(*Solen marginatus*)

tiger cowrie
(*Cypraea tigris*)

olive shell
(*Oliva elegans*)

auger shell
(*Terebra
crenulata*)

glory of
the sea
(*Conus
gloriamaris*)

sundial shell
(*Architectonica maxima*)

queen conch
(*Strombus gigas*)

wentletrap
(*Epitonium
lamellosum*)

comb venus
(*Hysteroconcha
lupanaria*)

helmet shell (*Cassis cornuta*)

murex shell
(*Murex troscheli*)

shells ► A selection of mollusc shells, drawn to scale (the largest, the helmet shell, is 35 cm long). All these species are marine and several, including the glory of the sea, are collectors' items.

cultural centre of the ▷Eastern Townships. Its manufactures include textiles, machinery, paper, and dairy produce. Sherbrooke houses the French-speaking University of Sherbrooke (founded 1954). Population (1991): 76 429.

● **Sheridan, Philip H(enry)** ▶ (1831–88) Union general in the US ▷Civil War. A regular soldier, he saw Civil War action in Tennessee and Georgia (1862). Appointed to command the Army of the Shenandoah, he led a number of destructive raids into Confederate territory, laying waste the Shenandoah Valley itself. His deployments in April, 1865, forced General Robert Lee to surrender at Appomattox.

● **Sheridan, Richard Brinsley** ▶ (1751–1816) Anglo-Irish dramatist. Born in Dublin, he lived in England from childhood. In 1772 he eloped with a fashionable singer. He wrote witty comedies of manners, of which the best known are *The Rivals* (1775), in which his most famous character, Mrs Malaprop, appears, and *School for Scandal* (1777). He was a manager of the Drury Lane Theatre and a Whig MP from 1780 to 1812, during which time he was recognized as being one of the great parliamentary orators. His last years were clouded by financial problems and the disappointment of his political ambitions.

● **sheriff** ▶ An official with administrative and judicial responsibilities in England, Scotland, and the USA. Originating in the 10th century as the shire reeve, the king's representative in the ▷shire and at the shire court, the sheriff continued in this role under the Normans, who expanded his judicial competence. Powerful and often corrupt, the sheriffs' powers were reduced by Henry II (reigned 1154–89) and succeeding kings and became little more than ceremonial in the 16th century. Sheriffs in England and Scotland are appointed by the Crown to each county; the City of London, however, has two sheriffs, elected by the Corporation. In England their duties under the Sheriffs Act (1887) include executing writs, attending judges, and responsibility for returns at parliamentary elections and for the safe custody of prisoners. In Scotland sheriffs are also the chief county judges. In the USA they are elected and are the principal law enforcement officers in a county.

● **Sherman, William Tecumseh** ▶ (1820–91) Federal general in the US ▷Civil War. Serving in the West, he captured Atlanta, Georgia (September, 1864), and then executed the March to the Sea—Atlanta to Savannah, thus dividing the Confederacy. In 1865 he turned and resumed his march through the Carolinas towards Raleigh, North Carolina. These campaigns contributed enormously to the Confederate defeat. His strategic planning, tactical skill, and leadership made him one of the great Civil War generals. His brother **John Sherman** (1823–1900) was a Congressman (1855–77, 1881–97) with a specialist interest in finance. The Sherman Anti-Trust Act (1890) was largely his work.

● **Sherpa** ▶ A people of Nepal who speak a dialect of Tibetan. They are farmers, cattle breeders, and traders and also spin and weave woollen cloth. They often act as porters for Himalayan expeditions. With Edmund Hillary, the Sherpa ▷Tenzing Norgay reached the summit of Everest in 1953.

● **Sherriff, R(obert) C(edric)** ▶ (1896–1975) British dramatist and novelist. He is best known for the play *Journey's End* (1928), set in the trenches of World War I; other plays include *Home at Seven* (1950) and *The Long Sunset* (1955).

● **Sherrington, Sir Charles Scott** ▶ (1857–1952) British physiologist, whose work provided the basis for present-day understanding of the nervous system. Sherrington demonstrated that reflex actions in higher animals and man are integrated with the rest of the nervous system. He proposed the terms neurone for a nerve cell and synapse for the point at which an impulse is transmitted between nerve cells. He was appointed to the OM (1924) and shared a Nobel Prize (1932) with Lord ▷Adrian.

● **sherry** ▶ A fortified ▷wine, made around Jerez de la Frontera (whence its name) in S Spain; similar wine is now also made elsewhere. It is blended by the *solera* system: sherry is drawn off from several different casks to make a blend and those casks are then topped up with younger sherry, maintaining its future character. There are

two basic types of sherry: fino is a pale dry wine on which the *flor* (flower or yeast) has developed fully; oloroso is a rich full-bodied wine on which the *flor* is little developed. Other types of sherry are related to these two, for example amontillado is a strong dark derivative of a fino; cream sherry is a sweetened oloroso.

● **'s Hertogenbosch** ▶ (or Den Bosch) 51 41N 5 19E A town in the S central Netherlands, the capital of North Brabant province. It has a famous gothic cathedral (rebuilt 1419–1520). Hieronymus Bosch was born here. Population (1996 est): 125 044.

● **Sherwood Forest** ▶ An ancient forest in the Midlands of England, in Nottinghamshire. Once an extensive royal hunting ground, it is famous for its associations with ▷Robin Hood.

● **Shetland Islands** ▶ (or Shetland; official name until 1974: Zetland) A group of about 100 islands in the North Sea, off the N coast of Scotland. It became an island authority under local government reorganization in 1975. The largest islands include Mainland, Yell, and Unst. Agriculture chiefly produces wool; Shetland ponies are also bred. Herring fishing, centred on Lerwick, and salmon farming are important. Industries include fish curing and knitting (especially in the Shetland and Fair Isle patterns). The islands are a base for North Sea oil exploitation with a pipeline from the Brent field. Area: 1427 sq km (551 sq mi). Population (1999 est): 22 910. Administrative centre: Lerwick.

● **Shetland pony** ▶ The smallest British pony breed, native to the Shetland Islands. It has a sturdy compact body with short legs and a relatively large head. The mane and tail are profuse and the coat becomes thick in winter. Formerly used as pack and pit ponies, Shetlands are now popular pets for children. Height: up to 1.05 m (10½ hands).

● **Shetland sheepdog** ▶ (or Sheltie) A breed of dog developed in the Shetland Islands for working sheep. Related to and resembling the ▷collie, it has a soft undercoat and a long outer coat and may be black, brown, or blue-grey, with white and tan markings. Height: 36 cm (dogs); 35 cm (bitches).

● **Shevardnadze, Eduard** ▶ (1928–) Georgian statesman; president (1992–). As the Soviet minister for foreign affairs (1985–90, 1991) he played a key role in arms negotiations with the USA but resigned in 1990 following disagreements with Gorbachov. He was briefly reinstated following the failed coup of 1991. As president of the Georgian state council he faced internal conflicts and a collapsing economy. He was re-elected in 1995 and 2000.

● **Shiah** ▷See Shiites.

● **shield** ▶ An extensive rigid block of Precambrian rocks unaffected by later periods of mountain building. Shields are the oldest continental regions, frequently of igneous granite or metamorphic gneiss. The shields were once the site of Precambrian mountain belts, although the mountains have been completely eroded. The **Canadian** (or Laurentian) **Shield** is the largest, covering several million square kilometres of NE North America. The **Baltic Shield** (or Fennoscandia), reaching the surface in Finland and Sweden, is another well-known example.

● **shield bug** ▶ A ▷plant bug, also called stink bug, belonging to the families *Acanthosomidae, Cydnidae, Scutelleridae*, or *Pentatomidae*. Shield bugs have heavy shieldlike bodies, 5–50 mm long, and are usually green or brown. They suck insect or plant juices, often becoming agricultural pests. Some species also foul plants with an evil-smelling secretion. *insect.

● **shield fern** ▶ A tufted ▷fern of the widely distributed genus *Polystichum* (about 135 species). It has a scaly stem and tapering branched fronds made up of toothed pointed leaflets. Small round clusters of spore capsules (sori) occur in rows on the undersides of the leaflets. The soft shield fern (*P. setiferum*) and the hard shield fern (*P. aculeatum*) are common species. Family: *Aspidiaceae*.

● **Shih-chia-chuang** ▷See Shijiazhuang.

● **Shih Huang Ti** ▷See Qin.

● **Shih tzu** ▶ A breed of small dog originating in Tibet and introduced to the UK in the 1930s. It has a long body with short legs, a short muzzle, and drooping ears. The long straight coat can be of various colours and the plumed tail is held over the back. Height: about 26 cm.

● **Shiites** ▶ (or Shiah) The general term applied to a number of different Muslim sects, the main body of which is dominant in Iran. They comprise about one-fifth of Muslims worldwide. The distinctive belief of the Shiites, which differentiates them from the other major Muslim group, the ▷Sunnites, is that ▷Ali, the fourth caliph, is the only legitimate successor of Mohammed. The leader of Islam, the ▷imam, must be a descendant of Ali and has exclusive authority in secular and religious matters. The Shiites differ among themselves as to the true line of imams. Some, known as "the twelvers," expect the return of the 12th imam (d. 9th century AD) at the end of time, while others recognize a different line from the seventh imam.

● **Shijiazhuang** ▶ (or Shih-chia-chuang) 38 04N 114 28E A city in NE China, the capital of Hebei province and the site of its university. Its industries include coalmining, textiles, chemicals, and engineering. Population (1990): 1 068 439.

● **Shikoku** ▶ The smallest of the four main islands of Japan, separated from Honshu and Kyushu by the Inland Sea. It is now joined to Honshu by several bridges, notably the Akashi Kaikyo bridge (1998), which at 2057 m (6750 ft) is the longest suspension bridge in the world. Shikoku is mountainous and forested. Its population is concentrated on the coastal plains, with industry mainly in the N. Copper is mined at Besshi; other products are fish, rice, grain, tobacco, mulberry, and camphor. Area: 17 759 sq km (6857 sq mi). Population (1995): 4 183 000. Chief cities: Matsuyama and Takamatsu.

● **Shillong** ▶ 25 34N 91 53E A city in India, the capital of Meghalaya. Rebuilt following an earthquake in 1897, Shillong is a military base and agricultural trading centre and has a university (1973). Population (1991): 130 691.

● **Shiloh** ▶ 32 03N 35 18E A city of Samaria in ancient N Palestine, now in Jordan. Hannah brought her son Samuel to this Israelite religious centre to dedicate him to God in the temple where Eli was priest of the ▷Ark of the Covenant. Shiloh was the traditional sanctuary of the Ark until the Philistines destroyed the city and captured the Ark in the mid-11th century BC.

● **Shimonoseki** ▶ 33 59N 130 58E A seaport in Japan, in SW Honshu, linked to ▷Kitakyushu by tunnels under the Shimonoseki Strait. The treaty ending the first Sino-Japanese War was signed here (1895). Industries include engineering, shipbuilding, chemicals, and fishing. Population (1995): 259 791.

● **shingles** ▶ An infection caused by the ▷herpes zoster virus, which lodges in nerve cells in the spinal cord. Shingles affects adults who have had chickenpox as children. It usually starts with pain along the course of a sensory nerve, followed by a band of blisters round half of the body or face. The rash usually eventually disappears but the patient may be left with severe neuralgia. Shingles can be treated with antiviral drugs, such as acyclovir.

● **Shinto** ▶ The native religion of Japan. Shinto is primarily an attitude of nationalistic and aesthetic reverence towards familiar places and traditions, rather than a set of religious beliefs. However, the central themes are the belief in numerous usually amoral *kamis* or nature spirits, together with ancestor worship and an ideal of military chivalry. The two principal *kamis* are the sun-goddess (reputedly mother of the emperor) and her brother the storm-god. The conflict between them expresses the creative and destructive forces of nature. The scriptures of Shinto, the *Ko ji ki* and the *Nihon Shoki*, are both semimythological histories of Japan, written around 720 AD. The hereditary priesthood officiates at ceremonies of birth, marriage, and death, ensuring ritual purification. State Shinto, which developed during the 19th century, required unquestioning obedience to the emperor, who was seen as divine, and encouraged an attitude of militaristic nationalism. After World War II, Shinto was disestablished as the state religion.

● **shinty** ▶ (or camanachd) A Scottish 12-a-side stick-and-ball field game deriving from ▷hurling and similar to ▷hockey. A standard pitch is 146 × 73 m (160 × 80 yd). The stick is called the "caman" and a goal, a "hail."

● **Shipley, Jenny** ▶ (1952–) New Zealand politician; prime minister (1997–99). She served in several positions in National Party cabinets (from 1990) before becoming New Zealand's first woman prime minister. In 1999 she led her party to defeat in the general election.

● **ship money** ▶ A tax raised by English monarchs in times of emergency for the defence of the coast. It gained notoriety under Charles I, who levied it indiscriminately between 1634 and 1639. In 1637 John ▷Hampden was tried for refusing to pay ship money, which became a focus of resistance to Charles I and was pronounced illegal by the ▷Long Parliament.

● **ships** ▶ Man's earliest sea voyages were probably made on rafts and in hollowed-out tree trunks. Larger and more stable vessels were certainly known to the ancient Egyptians, whose rock carvings and paintings depict ships that were made of planks and were propelled both by oars and sails. Other early mariners included the Chinese and the Phoenicians; the short broad 13th-century Phoenician merchant ships (known as round ships) were propelled by oars and a single square sail to catch the prevailing wind (see sailing). The Greeks developed biremes (with two banks of oars) and triremes (with three banks) as warships, especially strengthened for ramming enemy vessels. The Romans also relied on oars, but their larger grain ships, capable of carrying up to 300 tonnes of cargo, had a number of square

Shinto ▶ A *gagaku* performance in the shrine at Ise in Japan, one of Shinto's most sacred sites. *Gagaku* (literally, "elegant music") is the ancient court music of Japan, dating from the 5th century. It is important in Shinto rituals, when it is performed to delight the *kamis* (spirits) rather than to offer praise, as in Western religious traditions.

ships

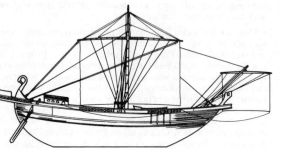

Roman merchantman (c. 100 AD) The Romans' need to transport grain from N Africa to Europe encouraged the building of imposing ships up to 55 m (180 ft) long.

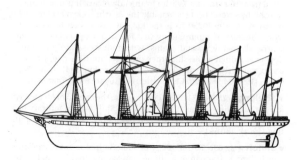

Portuguese caravel (c. 1450) Although it was only a little longer than a large rowing boat, the caravel took part in most of the 15th-century voyages of discovery. The lateen sail, derived from Arab examples, enabled it to sail against the prevailing winds.

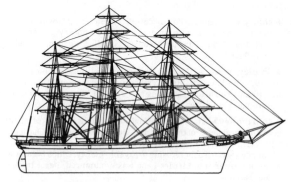

Cutty Sark (1869) The 19th-century clippers were renowned for their speed and grace. The *Cutty Sark*, built to bring tea from China, was one of the fastest and most consistent sailing ships of its time. It is now permanently moored at Greenwich.

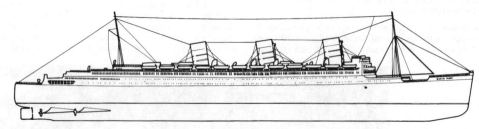

Great Britain (1843) The second steam ship designed by I. K. Brunel, the *Great Britain* was the first all-iron propeller-driven ship to cross the Atlantic, taking 15 days between Liverpool and New York. Wrecked off the Falkland Islands in 1937, it was restored in the 1970s in Bristol, where it is kept in dry dock.

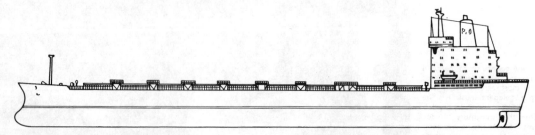

Queen Mary (1934) In 1938 this British passenger liner captured the Blue Riband for the fastest Atlantic crossing with a time of 3 days 20 hours 42 minutes. In 1967 it was anchored off Long Beach, California, as a tourist centre.

oil tanker (1968) The largest vessels afloat today, some of these giant ships have a deadweight capacity of over 300 000 tonnes.

warships

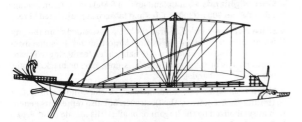

Greek bireme (c. 500 BC) Propelled during an attack by its two ranks of oars, the bireme was strongly built round a keel to support the strain of the ram attached to its bows.

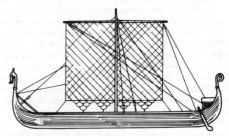

Viking longship (c. 1000 AD) The clinker-built, double-ended longship, propelled by oars and sail, was used mainly to transport fighting men.

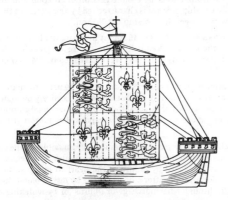

medieval nef (c. 1400) This single-masted vessel had platforms (castles) for fighting men at either end and one on the mast (topcastle) from which missiles could be hurled.

Victory (1759–65) Nelson's flagship at the battle of Trafalgar (1805), the *Victory* carried 100 guns and a crew of 850. It is now preserved at Portsmouth.

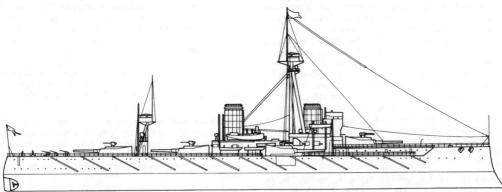

Dreadnought (1906) The design of the British *Dreadnought* became the model for battleships in a period in which a country's naval strength was reckoned in terms of how many battleships it possessed. The *Dreadnought* carried ten 12-inch guns, 27 smaller guns, and five underwater torpedo tubes.

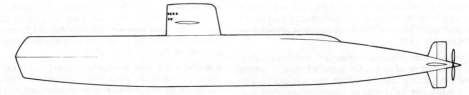

Nautilus (1954) The first nuclear-powered warship, the US *Nautilus* heralded an era in which naval strength is reckoned in terms of nuclear submarines. They are armed with torpedoes and long- and short-range missiles carrying nuclear warheads, all of which can be fired while the vessel is submerged.

sails. In the N the longships of the Vikings were double-ended and rose high out of the water to cope with the rough and windy North Sea; they still relied on oarsmen but the holes for the oars were fitted with shutters that could be closed when the ship was under sail. Developed in the 8th century AD, ships of this kind brought William the Conqueror to England. Ships with sails that also relied on banks of oarsmen were called **galleys**. Very often the oarsmen were slaves (hence **galley slaves**) or convicted criminals. It was not until the 12th century and the stimulus of the Crusades that the art of using sails was sufficiently developed for oars to be dispensed with. Sailing into the wind was originally pioneered by the Chinese in their junks, but it was the Arabs who perfected the lateen sail, which made it a reliable means of propulsion for large ships. By the 14th century sailing ships were commonplace. The warships of the period had "castles" built at each end to house fighting men, and guns were usually carried on the forecastle. However, muzzle-loading cannons were too heavy to be mounted on the forecastle and by the end of the 15th century they were carried in gun ports low in the hull. During this period, too, the single-master with one large heavy sail gave way to the three-master with more manageable small sails and full rigging. The first warship of the English navy, the *Henri Grâce à Dieu*, was built for Henry VIII in 1514 (*see also* Mary Rose). During the next 300 years sailing ships developed in many ways, usually with the merchantmen following the innovations in hull design and rigging made by the designers of warships. Sailing ships reached their zenith in the 19th-century ▷clipper ships, which remained supreme until Newcomen's ▷steam engine revolutionized seafaring. The first steamer to cross the Atlantic (in April, 1827) was the Dutch *Curaçao* (built 1826), the first British ship to do so (in April, 1838) being Brunel's *Great Western*, a wooden paddle steamer, which achieved recognition for steam by arriving in New York on the same day as a clipper that had left Cork three days before the *Great Western* had left Bristol. For the next century the N Atlantic crossing continued to be a proving ground for great ships. The propeller completely replaced the paddle and Parson's steam ▷turbine largely replaced the reciprocating engine. The ▷Blue Riband of the Atlantic is awarded for the fastest Atlantic crossing by a passenger ship in regular Atlantic service. Passenger travel across the Atlantic has now been almost entirely captured by the airlines; modern shipbuilding concentrates on cargo vessels, especially oil ▷tankers, and short-distance ferries. For ferries ▷hydrofoils and ▷hovercraft have been used to remove the hull from the water in order to reduce drag, although in the 1990s Hovercraft car ferries were largely replaced by high-speed (35-knot) catamarans.

Warships in the age of steam were largely modelled on the turbine-driven ▷battleship *Dreadnought* (1906), which together with the ▷cruiser, ▷destroyer, ▷frigate, and ▷submarine dominated naval warfare in World War I. By World War II the ▷aircraft carrier had evolved and with its long-range striking power became the supreme weapon of the war at sea. However, since the middle of the 20th century the importance of the surface warship has diminished and the strength of navies is now reckoned in terms of their missile- and aircraft-carrying capabilities, as well as in numbers of nuclear-powered submarines.

● **shipworm ►** A ▷bivalve mollusc belonging to the family *Teredidae*, also called pileworm. The shell plates of a shipworm are small with sharp ridges used for boring into wooden structures. The resulting burrow is lined with a limy material, encasing the long body (up to 180 cm). Shipworms can damage wooden ships, piers, etc.

● **Shiraz ►** 29 38N 52 34E A town in S central Iran. It is a trading centre for the surrounding region and is connected by road to the port of Bushire; Pahlavi University was established here in 1945. Population (1994 est): 1 042 801.

● **shire ►** The main unit of local government in Anglo-Saxon England. Shires were introduced in Wessex in the 8th century, where they replaced the Roman provinces, and subsequently extended to the rest of England. The units were of various origin: some (e.g. Sussex, Essex) were based on early Anglo-Saxon kingdoms, whereas others were areas dependent on a particular town (e.g. Bedfordshire, Hertfordshire, etc.). The king was represented in each shire by an ▷ealdorman (later, by a ▷sheriff), who presided over the shire court

(*or* moot) and dealt with administrative and legal matters. The shires were renamed ▷counties after the Norman Conquest.

● **Shiré Highlands ►** An upland area in S Malawi, with an average height of about 900 m (3000 ft). Tea and tobacco are cultivated here.

● **Shire horse ►** A breed of draught horse descended from the English warhorse and one of the world's largest horses. It is massively built with characteristic long white hair (called feathering) covering the lower parts of the legs. The coat is grey, bay, or black. Height: about 1.73 m (17 hands).

● **Shiva ►** (*or* Siva) The third member of the Hindu trinity, the ▷Trimurti. He is known as the Destroyer, but also represents generation as symbolized by the lingam or phallus. His female counterpart is **Parvati**, also known in her more ominous aspects as Kali and Durga. He is often portrayed in human form with four arms, a third eye in the centre of the forehead, and sometimes wearing a necklace of skulls. His most famous depiction is as *Nataraja* (king of dancing), his dance symbolizing the cosmic rhythm of creation and destruction. The worship of Shiva is characterized by an asceticism that contrasts with the gentler worship of ▷Vishnu.

● **Shizuoka ►** 34 59N 138 24E A port in Japan, in SE Honshu on an inlet of the Pacific Ocean. It is the centre of Japan's chief tea-producing region. Its university was established in 1949. Population (1995): 474 089.

● **Shkodër ►** (Italian name: Scutari) 42 03N 19 01E A town in NW Albania, on Lake Scutari. It has been ruled successively by many peoples, including the Turks. Local industries include food canning and the manufacture of cement and weapons. Population (1991 est): 83 700.

● **shock ► 1.** A severe condition resulting from failure of the circulatory system, when the blood supply to the tissues is inadequate. The shock may be caused by failure of the heart to pump sufficiently strongly, for example after a heart attack; by loss of blood fluid, for example through ▷haemorrhage or ▷burns; or by widening of the blood vessels so that there is not enough blood to fill them, for example after injury or during a very severe infection. The patient is in a state of collapse (possibly unconscious)—pale, sweaty, and nauseated, with low blood pressure and a weak fast pulse. Shock due to haemorrhage is treated with blood transfusions while that due to infection is treated with antibiotics and also often with fluid transfusions. There is no adequate treatment for shock caused by a failing heart. **2.** Injury resulting from electrocution. The extent of the injury depends on the current passing through the body, which is related to the voltage and the skin resistance. As skin resistance is greatly reduced when it is wet, mains voltage (240 V) can cause a lethal current (about 15 milliamps) to flow through the body if live terminals are touched with wet hands.

● **Shockley, William Bradfield ►** (1910–89) US physicist, born in England, who shared the 1956 Nobel Prize with John ▷Bardeen and Walter ▷Brattain for their discovery of the ▷transistor while working at the Bell Telephone laboratories in 1948. He was also known for his controversial views on the relationship between race and intelligence.

● **shock wave ►** A narrow region of a high pressure in a fluid, created when a fast-moving body passes through the fluid. The waves are propagated outwards from the body and occur, for example, when an aircraft passes through the ▷sound barrier.

● **shoebill ►** A large bird, *Balaeniceps rex*, occurring in papyrus swamps of E Africa. 120 cm tall, it has pale-grey plumage, long legs, and a large head with a broad shoe-shaped bill used to probe for lungfish. It is the only member of its family (*Balaenicipitridae*). Order: *Ciconiiformes* (herons, storks, etc.).

● **shofar ►** A Jewish ceremonial trumpet that is used in the synagogue. It is made of a ram's horn, flattened and bent by a steaming process. Its use as a prelude to proclamations and to sound the alarm is recorded in the Old Testament. It is blown in synagogues at the end of the fast on the Day of Atonement (*see* Yom Kippur) and to herald the Jewish New Year on ▷Rosh Hashana.

● **shogi ►** A board game for two players, a Japanese form of chess.

Each player starts with 20 flat pieces distinguished by size and markings. As in chess the pieces have prescribed moves and the object is to checkmate the enemy king, but unlike chess captured pieces may be used in the game by the player who captures them.

● **shogun** ▶ A military title held hereditarily by the heads of three families; they were successively the actual rulers of Japan, although the emperors retained formal sovereignty. The shogunate was secured for the Minamoto from the emperor in 1192 after ▷Minamoto Yoritomo's victory over the Taira league. From 1338 to 1573 the Ashikaga family held the title and in 1603 ▷Tokugawa Ieyasu, who claimed Minamoto ancestry, revived it. The last shogun was Tokugawa Keiki (1827–1913; ruled 1867–68).

● **Sholapur** ▶ 17 43N 75 56E A city in India, in Maharashtra. Sholapur is a major cotton textile centre. Population (1991): 603 870.

● **Sholes, Christopher Latham** ▶ (1819–90) US inventor of the typewriter, which was patented in 1868. He sold the patent to Eliphalet ▷Remington's company in 1873.

● **Sholokhov, Mikhail** ▶ (1905–84) Soviet novelist. After service with the Red Army during the Civil War he returned to his native village in the Don Cossack region, the setting for his first major novel (1928–40), translated in two parts as *And Quiet Flows the Don* and *The Don Flows Home to the Sea*. His authorship of this novel has been questioned by Solzhenitsyn and others. He won the Nobel Prize in 1965.

● **shooting** ▶ Discharging a weapon at a target or at game. The two main categories of **target shooting** for rifles are small bore (.22 calibre) at ranges of 25–200 m (27–219 yd), and full bore (7.62 calibre) at ranges of 200–1200 yd (183–1097 m); full-bore courses are fired from standing, sitting, kneeling, and prone (lying down) positions. Weapons for pistol shooting range from the .177 air pistol to the .45 pistol, with ranges between 10 and 50 yd (9–45 m). In **clay-pigeon shooting** (or trapshooting) clay discs are mechanically flung into the air and fired at with shotguns. In **grouse shooting** (in the UK grouse shooting is only permitted from 12 Aug to 10 Dec), **pheasant shooting** (1 Oct to 1 Feb), and **partridge shooting** (1 Sept to 1 Feb) the birds are either driven by a semicircle of beaters towards the shooters in butts (hides) or are flushed out by hunting dogs and beaters for a moving party of shooters. Dogs are also used in **rough shooting** for wildfowl, rabbits, etc.

● **shop stewards** ▶ Part-time ▷trade-union officials, who represent the union members with whom they work in negotiations with management and in talks with other union officials. In the UK, in the absence of a works' council system, shop stewards have often had a more influential role than full-time union officials.

● **shorthand** ▶ Any form of writing designed to be written quickly to transcribe the spoken language. Most forms are based on recording only as many letters or sounds as are necessary for accurate reading back, generally in simplified characters that are fast to write. In the Pitman System, for example, the characters are based on segments of a circle or straight lines; vowels are indicated only where the writer thinks it necessary, by a system of dots in descending order; voicing of consonants is indicated by thickening of strokes (thus, *b* is represented by \, *p* by \. This system is the most popular in Britain and was devised by Sir Isaac Pitman (1813–97). The most popular US system is that invented by John Robert Gregg (1867–1948). In these systems speeds of up to 300 words per minute can be achieved. **Speedwriting**, devised in the USA in the 1920s, uses ordinary Roman alphabet characters, omitting all but the essential ones. **Stenotypy** is a form of machine shorthand, employing a limited keyboard, used in the USA for reporting court proceedings. Shorthand is of great antiquity; for example, Cicero's secretary Tiro had devised a Latin shorthand system in the 1st century BC.

● **Shorthorn** ▶ A breed of cattle originating in NE England and formerly popular for both beef and dairy purposes. Stocky, with short legs, Shorthorns range from red to white with various mottled mixtures. They have been replaced by specialist beef and dairy breeds.

● **Short Parliament** ▶ The ▷parliament summoned (1640) by Charles I because he needed money for the ▷Bishops' Wars. The first parliament summoned since 1629, it refused to make a grant before

obtaining redress for its grievances and Charles I dissolved it after 23 days.

● **shortsightedness** ▶ (or myopia) Inability to focus on distant objects. The commonest kind of visual defect, it often runs in families and is due to a slightly misshapen eyeball, in which the light rays are focused in front of the retina (light-sensitive layer). It is corrected by wearing glasses with concave lenses or contact lenses or occasionally by laser surgery.

● **Shoshoni** ▶ A group of North American Indian tribes of the Great Basin region who spoke a language of the Uto-Aztecan family. They lived on wild fruits and insects and by trapping small game. Some acquired horses and moved onto the Plains to hunt buffalo and adopted much of the culture of this region. One such group was the ▷Comanche.

● **Shostakovich, Dmitri** ▶ (1906–75) Russian composer. He was a pupil of Glazunov at the St Petersburg conservatoire. His first symphony, written when he was 18, was very successful. Subsequent works, especially the operas *The Nose* (1927–28) and *Lady Macbeth of Mtsenk* (1930–32), brought allegations of formalism from the Soviet press. Shostakovich regained official favour with his fifth symphony (1937), subtitled "A Soviet artist's reply to just criticism." His compositions also include ten subsequent symphonies, including the wartime seventh symphony (*The Leningrad*; 1941), two concertos each for piano, violin, and cello, and 15 string quartets. His son **Maxim Shostakovich** (1938–), conductor and pianist, defected to the West in 1981. He became musical director of the New Orleans Symphony Orchestra in 1987 and of the Los Angeles Philharmonic in 1993.

● **shotgun** ▶ A smoothbore firearm with pump or automatic-repeating action. It may have one or two barrels and fires shot (small pellets) into a pattern covering a broad target. Guns with tapered barrels gain range but reduce the pattern area. Shot is used against small game, while lead slugs and balls are used against deer.

● **shot put** ▶ (or putting the shot) A field event in athletics, in which an iron or brass sphere is thrown as far as possible. It weighs 7.26 kg (16 lb) for men and 4 kg (8.8 lb) for women. It is thrown, or put, one-handed from in front of the shoulder and the putter must stay within a circle 2.1 m (7 ft) in diameter. World records: men: 23.12 m (1990) by Eric Randolph Barnes (USA); women: 22.63 m (1987) by Natalya Lisovskaya (USSR).

● **shoulder** ▶ The part of the body to which the ▷arm is attached. The skeleton of the shoulder consists of the scapula (shoulder blade), which forms a ball-and-socket joint with the humerus, permitting free movement of the arm. It is also the site of attachment of muscles of the arm and back. It is braced by the clavicle. ▷*See* Plate II.

● **shoveler duck** ▶ A ▷duck, *Spatula clypeata*, found in the N hemisphere, having a large bill specialized for feeding on water plants and invertebrates on the surface of fresh water. 50 cm long, it has a pale-blue wing flash; the male has a dark-green head, white breast, and chestnut underparts and the female is speckled brown.

● **Shovell, Sir Cloudesley** ▶ (1650–1707) English admiral. He captained the *Edgar* against the French at Bantry Bay (1689) and in the War of the Spanish Succession he helped take Gibraltar (1704). He was murdered by islanders for his rings when he was washed ashore after his ship went down off the Scillies.

● **showjumping** ▶ Competitive jumping of horses, often against the clock, over a series of artificial obstacles of varying severity. Penalties are given for knocking down or refusing fences. Since World War II it has become a major international sport.

● **Shrapnel, Henry** ▶ (1761–1842) British army officer, who invented the shrapnel shell. First used in 1804, the shell comprised a projectile that sprayed bullets when activated by a timing device.

● **Shreveport** ▶ 32 30N 93 40W A city in the USA, in Louisiana on the Red River. It is the industrial centre of a large oil and natural-gas region. Timber, cotton, and metal are also important products. Population (1996 est): 191 558.

● **shrew** ▶ A small insectivorous mammal belonging to the family

Soricidae (265 species), found all over the world except Australasia and the Polar regions. The dwarf shrew (*Suncus etruscus*) is the smallest mammal in the world, weighing only 2 g and measuring 7–8 cm. Shrews are very active: the common shrew (*Sorex araneus*) eats its own weight in food every 24 hours in order to meet its energy requirements. Order: ▷*Insectivora*.

● **Shrewsbury** ► 52 43N 2 45W A town in W central England, the administrative centre of Shropshire on the River Severn. It achieved importance as a gateway to Wales, and a castle was built in 1070. The famous boys' public school was founded here in 1552 and there are many half-timbered Tudor buildings. Charles Darwin was born here. Shrewsbury is a market town for the surrounding agricultural area, with various light industries; market gardening and tourism are also important. Population (1996 est): 97 371.

● **shrike** ► A fierce predatory songbird belonging to a family (*Laniidae*; 74 species) occurring in Eurasia, Africa, and North America and also called butcherbird. Shrikes range from 15 to 36 cm in length and have soft black, grey, or brown plumage. They dive on insects and small vertebrates from the air, killing them with their hooked bills, often impaling prey on thorns.

● **shrimp** ► A ▷crustacean, usually 4–8 cm long, belonging to a worldwide suborder (*Natantia*; about 2000 species) that occurs in fresh and salt water. Shrimps have a semitransparent body with long slender legs (the first pair pincer-like), a fanlike tail, and whiplike antennae, nearly as long as the body. Shrimps swim backwards by rapid flexions of the abdomen and tail and they feed on small animals or plants. Many species, including the European *Crangon vulgaris*, are commercially important as food. Order: ▷*Decapoda*.

● **shrimp plant** ► A popular ornamental plant, *Beloperone guttata*, native to warm regions of the Americas. Growing about 45 cm high, it has inconspicuous white flowers enclosed by reddish-brown leaflike bracts, so that the whole flower cluster resembles a shrimp. Family: *Acanthaceae*.

● **Shropshire** ► (name from 1974 until 1980: Salop) A county in the W Midlands of England, bordering on Wales. The River Severn separates the lowlands in the N and E from the uplands in the S and W. During the 18th century it became the main iron-producing county in England; the world's first cast-iron bridge was built at Ironbridge in 1779. It is now chiefly agricultural, with dairy farming in the N and cattle and sheep in the S. Principal arable crops are cereals and sugar beet. The rapidly developing area around Telford new town became an independent ▷unitary authority (as Telford and Wrekin) in 1998. Area (excluding Telford and Wrekin): 3201 sq km (1236 sq mi). Population (1996 est, excluding Telford and Wrekin): 277 100. Administrative centre: Shrewsbury.

● **Shroud of Turin** ► A relic formerly believed to be the cloth used to wrap Christ's body for burial. It bears impressions of a human body marked with wounds consonant with Christ's at the crucifixion. It has been kept in Turin since 1578, but there are gaps in its history prior to the 14th century. Carbon dating tests in 1988 indicated that it had been woven from flax gathered after 1260 but this conclusion has been called into question by further tests (including pollen tests).

● **Shrove Tuesday** ► In the Christian liturgical calendar, the day before the beginning of Lent (*see* Ash Wednesday), so called from the "shriving" (i.e. confession and absolution) of the faithful that was customary before the Lenten season. In many countries carnivals are held and in England pancakes are traditionally eaten—hence the popular name Pancake Day.

● **shrub** ▷*See* tree.

● **Shumen** ▷*See* Kolarovgrad.

● **Shushan** ▷*See* Susa.

● **Shute, Nevil** ► (Nevil Shute Norway; 1899–1960) British novelist. He combined novel writing with his professional career as an aeronautical engineer. He settled in Australia after World War II. His many popular novels include *A Town Like Alice* (1950) and *On the Beach* (1957), which concerns the destruction of mankind in an atomic war.

● **sial** ► The earth's continental crust, which is composed of granitic

rocks rich in silicon (Si) and aluminium (Al). It is less dense than the underlying layer of ▷sima and much thicker.

● **Sialkot** ► 32 29N 74 35E A city in Pakistan. The shrine of the first Sikh guru, Nanak, is situated here. Industries include textiles, surgical instruments, and sporting goods. Population (latest est): 296 000.

● **Siam** ▷*See* Thailand.

● **Siam, Gulf of** ► An arm of the South China Sea, about 500 km (310 mi) wide and 700 km (435 mi) long, bordering on Thailand, Cambodia, and Vietnam.

● **siamang** ► The largest of the ▷gibbons, *Hylobates syndactylus*, found in Malaya and Sumatra. Up to 90 cm tall, with arms spanning 150 cm, siamangs have a large naked vocal sac on the throat, which expands to give volume to their cries.

● **Siamese cat** ► A breed of short-haired cat, originating from SE Asia. The Siamese has a graceful slender body, a wedge-shaped head with slanted blue eyes and large pointed ears, and a long slim tapering tail. The fur on the body is cream-coloured or off-white, shading into one of several colours (seal-brown, blue-grey, chocolate, lilac, tabby, or red) on the ears, mask, paws, and tail (the "points"). The seal-pointed and blue-pointed varieties are probably the most popular.

● **Siamese twins** ► Identical twins who are fused together, usually at the head or along the trunk, more correctly known as conjoined twins. They may have developed equally or unequally; in the latter case, one baby is fairly normal but is attached to a wasted remnant of a fetus. Siamese twins can sometimes be surgically separated, providing that vital organs are not involved in the point of union. The original Siamese twins, Chang and Eng (1811–74), were born in Siam; they were joined at the hip and remained fused, despite which they each married and fathered children.

● **Sian** ▷*See* Xi An.

● **Sian incident** ▷*See* Xi An incident.

● **SIB** ▷*See* Securities and Investment Board.

● **Sibelius, Jean** ► (Johan Julius Christian S.; 1865–1957) Finnish composer. He began to compose as a child and studied at the Helsinki conservatoire and in Berlin and Vienna. In 1897 the government made him a grant for ten years to enable him to compose full time. Many of his works have Finnish associations and many were inspired by the epic poem, the *Kalevala*. His works include seven symphonies, the symphonic poems *Kullervo* (choral; 1892), *En Saga* (1892), *The Swan of Tuonela* (1893), *Finlandia* (1899–1900), and *Tapiola* (1925), a violin concerto, a string quartet ("Voces Intimae"), and many songs.

● **Siberia** ► A region chiefly in Russia, extending into N Kazakhstan. Corresponding to N Asia, it is bordered on the W by the Ural Mountains, on the N by the Arctic Ocean, on the E by the Pacific Ocean, and on the S by Mongolia and China. Parts of the extreme W, E, and S are excluded from Siberia for administrative purposes. Siberia comprises three geographical areas—the West Siberian Plain, the Central Siberian Plateau, and the Russian Far East. It is notorious for its long harsh winters, during which the lowest temperatures anywhere in the world have been recorded. Its outstandingly rich mineral resources include coal, especially in the ▷Kuznetsk Basin, petroleum, diamonds, and gold. Forestry is also important and Siberia's many rivers (notably the Ob, Yenisei, and Lena) are harnessed for hydroelectric power. The Russian settlement of Siberia began in 1581 but was intermittent until the building (1891–1905) of the Trans-Siberian Railway. Siberia has long been a place of exile for Russian criminals and political prisoners. Area: about 13 807 037 sq km (5 330 896 sq mi).

● **Sibiu** ► 45 46N 24 09E A city in central Romania. An important centre for Transylvania in the 15th century, it possesses the Brukenthal Museum and many medieval buildings. An industrial centre, it manufactures machinery, textiles, and food products. Population (1994 est): 170 528.

● **Sibyl** ► In Greek and Roman mythology, any of various divinely inspired prophetesses, the most famous of which was the Sibyl of Cumae, near Naples. Three books of these Sibylline prophecies were preserved in the Temple of Jupiter on the Capitoline hill at Rome and were consulted in national emergencies.

● **Sica, Vittorio De** ▷*See* De Sica, Vittorio.

● **Sichuan** ▶ (Ssu-ch'uan *or* Szechwan) A province in central China, on the Yangtze River, surrounded by mountains. The centre is a plateau and the E a fertile plain. Warm and humid and China's most productive rice area, it is prosperous and densely populated, with several ethnic groups. Besides rice, produce includes maize, sugar cane, wheat, cotton, and forest products. The W is good grazing land, exporting pig bristles. Salt, gas, oil, coal, and other minerals are produced. Despite great difficulties with transport because of its mountainous surroundings, it has flourishing industries. It is also known for its crafts.

History: it was among the first areas settled by the Chinese, important from the 3rd century BC, when China's oldest irrigation system was constructed here. A kingdom in the 3rd century AD, separatism often flourished because of the area's self-sufficiency and impenetrable position; it became the centre of the Nationalist government during the Sino-Japanese War (1937–45). Economic development was stimulated at this time by migration from the coasts and has again speeded up since the 1950s. Area: about 569 800 sq km (220 000 sq mi). Population (1995 est): 112 140 000. Capital: Chengdu.

● **Sicilian Vespers** ▶ (1282) The massacre of 2000 French residents of Palermo that began the Sicilian revolt, backed by Pedro III of Aragon (1236–85; reigned 1276–85), against the oppressive regime of the Angevin ▷Charles I. General war ensued between the Aragonese, Sicilians, and Italian Ghibellines on one side and the Angevins, French, and Italian Guelfs, supported by the papacy, on the other. Aragonese control was finally established in 1302 under Pedro's son Frederick II (1272–1337). ▷*See also* Guelfs and Ghibellines.

● **Sicily** ▶ The largest island in the Mediterranean Sea, which together with adjacent islands comprises an autonomous region of Italy. It is separated from the mainland by the Strait of Messina. Sicily is largely mountainous, rising to over 1800 m with its highest point at Mount Etna. Although most of the population is concentrated in urban centres, the region is underdeveloped and there is much poverty. The service sector is important, as is the mining industry, especially oil. The region's farmers produce citrus fruits, vegetables, wheat, rye, olives, and wine. Manufacturing industries include oil refining, petrochemicals, chemicals, pharmaceuticals, and food processing.

History: settled by the Greeks in the 8th century BC, it was later occupied by the Carthaginians and between 241 and 211 BC it became a Roman province. It was conquered by the Arabs in the 9th century AD and in 1060 the Norman conquest of Sicily began. In 1266 Charles I became the first Angevin King of Sicily, which was conquered by Aragon in 1284 following the revolt called the ▷Sicilian Vespers. In 1734 Don Carlos of Bourbon became Charles IV of Naples and Sicily (*see* Charles III of Spain), which formally became the Kingdom of the Two Sicilies in 1815 under ▷Ferdinand I. After conquest by Garibaldi (1860), Sicily was united with the rest of Italy. Since then Sicily's history has been one of trouble and discontent as a result of an ailing economy and the persistence of widespread poverty, which has not been helped by the island's social structure, the ▷Mafia, and other conservative forces on the island presenting an obstacle to reform. Area: 25 710 sq km (9927 sq mi), with adjacent islands. Population (1994 est): 5 025 280. Capital: Palermo.

● **Sickert, Walter Richard** ▶ (1860–1942) British impressionist painter and etcher, born in Munich of Danish and Irish parentage. He studied at the Slade School and under ▷Whistler and ▷Degas. His paintings of Venice and Dieppe (1895–1905) and scenes from the music hall and domestic life are distinguishable from French ▷impressionism chiefly by their sombre colours. Although well known on the Continent and among the British artists who formed the ▷Camden Town group (1911), he did not achieve widespread recognition in the UK until the 1920s.

● **sickle-cell disease** ▶ A condition resulting from the production of an abnormal form of haemoglobin (the pigment of red blood cells). The disease is hereditary and most commonly affects those of African and Mediterranean ancestry. When the blood is deprived of oxygen the abnormal haemoglobin crystallizes and distorts the red cells into a sickle shape: these sickle cells are removed from the blood by the spleen, which leads to ▷anaemia. Children affected with the severest form of the disease do not usually survive until adulthood; those less severely affected do survive and even tend to have some built-in resistance to malaria, which may partly explain the persistence of this harmful gene in the population.

● **Siddons, Sarah** ▶ (*born* ▷Kemble; 1755–1831) British actress. She acted in the provinces until 1782, when at her London debut at Drury Lane she was immediately acclaimed as the leading tragic actress of her time. Her most notable role was Lady Macbeth.

● **side drum** ▷*See* snare drum.

● **sidereal period** ▶ The ▷time taken by a planet or satellite to return to the same point in its orbit, i.e. to complete one revolution, with reference to the background stars. It can be determined from the body's ▷synodic period.

● **sidewinder** ▶ A small nocturnal ▷rattlesnake, *Crotalus cerastes*, occurring in deserts of the S USA and Mexico, that has a sideways looping method of locomotion enabling it to move quickly over loose sand. 45–75 cm long, it is usually pale brown or grey with indistinct darker spotting and a hornlike scale above each eye.

● **Sidgwick, Henry** ▶ (1838–1900) British moral philosopher. Sidgwick's major academic work, *The Methods of Ethics* (1874), was a comparative study of moral philosophy, which focused on ▷hedonism and ▷utilitarianism. As a university teacher, he worked for the abolition of religious tests at Cambridge and the admission of women students. He was the first president of the Society for Psychical Research (1882–85).

● **Sidi-Bel-Abbès** ▶ 35 12N 0 42W A town in NW Algeria. An old Moorish town, it was the headquarters of the French Foreign Legion until 1962. It lies in a fertile area renowned for its wine. Population (latest est): 152 778.

● **Siding Spring Mountain** ▶ 31 27S 149 10E A mountain in Australia, in New South Wales in the Warrumbungle Range. It is the site of the **Siding Spring Observatory**, with a 3.8 m (150 in) Anglo-Australian telescope and a British 1.2 m (48 in) Schmidt telescope. Height: 859 m (2817 ft).

● **Sidmouth, Henry Addington, 1st Viscount** ▷*See* Addington, Henry, 1st Viscount Sidmouth.

● **Sidney, Algernon** ▶ (1622–83) English Whig politician, who was beheaded for alleged complicity in the ▷Rye House Plot against Charles II and the king's brother James, Duke of York. In exile after the Restoration of Charles in 1660, he returned in 1677 and became prominent in attempts to exclude the Roman Catholic James from the succession. His involvement in the Rye House Plot was never proved.

● **Sidney, Sir Philip** ▶ (1554–86) English poet and courtier. A man of letters and man of action, he typified the Renaissance ideal of the complete gentleman. His works include the prose romance *Arcadia* (1580), the sequence of Petrarchan sonnets, *Astrophel and Stella* (1591), and an important work of critical theory, *The Defence of Poesy* (1595). A gifted linguist, he served as a diplomat in Europe and was killed while fighting the Spanish in the Netherlands.

● **Sidon** ▶ (*or* Saida) 33 32N 35 22E A small seaport in S Lebanon. An important Phoenician city, several references are made to it in the Bible and it was greatly damaged during the Crusades. It is now the terminus of an oil pipeline from Saudi Arabia. Population (1990 est): 24 740.

● **SIDS** ▶ (sudden infant death syndrome) ▷*See* cot death.

● **Siegen** ▶ 50 52N 8 02E A city in NW Germany, in North Rhine-Westphalia. A former centre for the mining of iron ore, its manufactures now include office equipment and computers. It is the birthplace of Rubens and has a university (1972). Population (1996 est): 111 398.

● **Siegfried** ▶ A hero of Germanic legend, who also appears in early Scandinavian legend as Sigurd. The two best-known versions of his story are the Germanic ▷*Nibelungenlied* and the Old Norse *Volsungasaga*. In the former, Siegfried wins ▷Brunhild for his brother-in-law Gunther, but a quarrel between Brunhild and Siegfried's wife Kriemhild leads to Siegfried's death by treachery. In the *Volsungasaga*, Sigurd is betrothed to Brynhild (the Old Norse version of her name) but is tricked (by a magic potion) into forgetting her and marries Gudrun. He then wins Brynhild for his brother-in-law Gunnar; later Brynhild incites Gunnar to kill him. Siegfried is the hero of the last two operas of ▷Wagner's *The Ring of the Nibelung*.

● **Siegfried line** ▶ The defensive line of pill boxes, minefields, etc., set up by the Germans in the 1930s along their western frontier in response to France's ▷Maginot line. It provided a slight respite for the German army in retreat in 1944 but was breached by Canadian troops in 1945 and dismantled after World War II. It was named by the Allies after the legendary Germanic hero ▷Siegfried.

● **siemens** ▶ (S) The ▷SI unit of conductance equal to the conductance between two points on a conductor when a potential difference of one volt between the points causes a current of one ampere to flow. Named after Ernst Werner von ▷Siemens.

● **Siemens, Ernst Werner von** ▶ (1816–92) German electrical engineer, who opened a telegraph factory in 1847 and, a year later, laid a government telegraph line from Berlin to Frankfurt. Together with his brother **Karl Siemens** (1829–1906), he established telegraph factories in a number of European cities. A third brother **Sir William Siemens** (Karl Wilhelm S.; 1823–83) moved to England in 1844. He invented the open-hearth steel process in 1861, based on the principle of heat regeneration previously patented by a fourth brother **Friedrich Siemens** (1826–1904).

Siena ▶ A view of the Tuscan city, dominated by the belfry of its 13th-century cathedral.

● **Siena** ▶ 43 19N 11 19E A city in central Italy, in Tuscany. Founded by the Etruscans, it was an important commercial and artistic centre in the middle ages. Its many fine buildings include a 13th-century gothic-romanesque cathedral, a university (1240), and several palaces, especially the Palazzo Pubblico (1297–1310). There are horse races through the main square of the city during the annual Palio festival. Tourism is Siena's main source of revenue. Population (1990): 58 728.

● **Sienkiewicz, Henryk** ▶ (1846–1916) Polish novelist. His only novel generally known outside Poland is *Quo Vadis* (1896), a frequently filmed epic of Nero's Rome. He also wrote a trilogy celebrating Poland's military struggles during the 17th century. He won the Nobel Prize in 1905.

● **Sierra Leone, Republic of** ▶ A country in West Africa, on the

Gulf of Guinea. Coastal plains, fringed by mangrove swamps, rise to higher land in the interior reaching heights of almost 2000 m (6500 ft). The main ethnic groups are Mende and Temne.

Economy: chiefly agricultural, organized mainly in smallholdings. The principal food crop is rice and cash crops include palm kernels, cocoa, coffee, and ginger. Livestock is important, particularly cattle in the N, and there has been considerable development in the fishing industry and in forestry. Minerals, including diamonds, iron ore, and bauxite, are the main exports; the country also has important deposits of rutile. The economy has been severely disrupted by the recent political instability. There is a large external debt.

History: in 1787 local chiefs ceded to Britain a piece of land along the coast for the settlement of slaves freed in the colonies. In 1896 the region became a British protectorate, gaining independence within the Commonwealth in 1961. In 1967 a military coup and counter-coup took place; civilian rule was restored in 1968. In 1971 Sierra Leone became a republic. In 1978 one-party government (by the All-People's Congress) was introduced. Plans to introduce multiparty democracy were approved in a referendum in 1991. The following year Capt Valentine E. M. Strasser took over in a military coup and the left-wing Revolutionary United Front (RUF) began a guerrilla campaign against his government. In 1996 he was ousted by his deputy, Capt Julius Maada Bio. Later that year free presidential elections resulted in victory for Ahmad Tejan Kabbah. In 1997 the civilian government was removed in a military coup: following an invasion by Nigerian-led forces, President Kabbah was restored in 1998. However, savage fighting recurred in late 1998, when members of the deposed military junta joined with RUF rebels to attack Freetown. The rebels caused massive destruction before being routed once more by Nigerian troops (January 1999). Following peace talks, a power-sharing government was established in late 1999 and a UN peacekeeping force deployed. When rebel violence erupted once more in 2000, British troops were sent in to provide support for the UN forces. Elections in 2002 resulted in a landslide for President Kabbah.

Republic of Sierra Leone

Head of state	President Ahmad Tejan Kabbah
Official language	English; Krio is widely spoken
Official currency	leone of 100 cents
Area	73 326 sq km (27 925 sq mi)
Population (2001 est)	5 427 000
Capital and main port	Freetown

● **Sierra Madre** ▶ The chief mountain system of Mexico. It extends for about 2500 km (1500 mi) SE from the US border, reaching 5699 m (18 697 ft) at Citlaltépetl. It comprises the Sierra Madre Oriental (E), the Sierra Madre del Sur (S), and the Sierra Madre Occidental (W).

● **Sierra Maestra** ▶ A mountain range in Cuba. It extends along the SE coast reaching 1974 m (6476 ft) at Pico Turquino. Fidel ▷Castro had his guerrilla base here in the 1950s.

● **Sierra Morena** ▶ A mountain range in S Spain, extending about 400 km (249 mi) E–W between the Rivers Guadiana and Guadalquivir.

● **Sierra Nevada** ▶ A mountain range in the USA. It extends NW–SE through California, reaching 4418 m (14 495 ft) at Mount Whitney. It contains Yosemite National Park.

● **Sierra Nevada** ▶ A mountain range in S Spain. It rises to 3481 m (11 421 ft) at Mulhacén, the highest point in Spain.

● **sievert** ▶ (Sv) The SI unit of dose equivalent being that arising when the absorbed dose of ▷ionizing radiation is 1 J/kg, taking into account the dimensionless factors required to compensate for different types of radiation having different biological effects.

● **Sieyès, Emmanuel Joseph** ▶ (1748–1836) French politician and churchman. His pamphlet *Qu'est-ce que le tiers état?* (*What Is the Third Estate?*, 1789) influenced the revolt of the Third Estate at the start of the ▷French Revolution. He voted for the execution of the king but withdrew from politics during the Jacobins' rule. In 1799 he helped to bring Napoleon to power. His influence thereafter declined.

● **sifaka** ▶ A ▷prosimian primate belonging to the genus *Propithecus* (2 species), of Madagascar. About 50 cm long, with a tail the same length, sifakas have long white fur with red or orange and black markings. They have long hind legs and are mainly arboreal. Family: *Indriidae*.

● **Siger of Brabant** ▶ (c. 1240–c. 1284) French theologian. A teacher at Paris University, Siger was accused of heresy (1276) on account of his criticisms of Aristotle, in which he cast doubt on the afterlife. ▷Aquinas wrote a treatise against him, but Dante placed him among the 12 sages.

● **Sigismund** ▶ (1368–1437) Holy Roman Emperor (1411–37; crowned 1433) and King of Hungary (1387–1437) and of Bohemia (1419–37). He conducted two unsuccessful crusades against the Turks (1396; 1428) and was largely responsible for the summoning of the Council of ▷Constance to heal the Great Schism. Implicated in the treacherous burning of Jan ▷Hus in 1415, he fought the ▷Hussites throughout the 1420s.

● **Sigismund (I) the Old** ▶ (1467–1548) King of Poland (1506–48). Sigismund gained control of E Prussia (1525) after defeating the ▷Teutonic Knights. He encouraged the development of the Renaissance in Poland.

● **Sigismund II Augustus** ▶ (1520–72) King of Poland (1548–72); the last of the Jagiellon dynasty. Sigismund's reign saw the Union of ▷Lublin (1569), which united Poland with Lithuania, and the expansion of the Polish Reforma-tion.

● **Sigismund III Vasa** ▶ (1566–1632) King of Poland (1587–1632) and Sweden (1592–99). Sigismund was deposed from the Swedish throne by his uncle, later ▷Charles IX of Sweden, and failed in his subsequent attempts to regain the Crown. Charles' son ▷Gustavus II Adolphus conquered Poland's Livonian territory (1621). Sigismund had some success against Russia, capturing and holding Moscow (1610–12).

● **Siglo de Oro** ▶ The Golden Age of Spanish literature that lasted from about 1550 to 1650. The literature of this period was characterized by patriotism and new attitudes of critical realism. Leading writers included Lope de Vega and Cervantes.

● **Signac, Paul** ▶ (1863–1935) French painter and art theorist associated with ▷pointillism. A disciple of ▷Seurat, he is known chiefly for his mosaic-like paintings of European harbours and his influential treatise *D'Eugène Delacroix au Néo-impressionisme* (1899).

● **sign language** ▶ A method of communication in which hand signs are used to replace normal spoken or written language. It is used mainly by deaf people. Many such systems based on the main spoken languages of the world are in use. In English the most widely used is the American Sign Language (ASL). Alternatives are cued speech, which is designed to assist lipreading, and several systems, such as Seeing Essential English, which are designed to assist those with a language handicap.

● **Signorelli, Luca** ▶ (c. 1441–1523) Italian Renaissance painter, born in Cortona. Probably the pupil of ▷Piero della Francesca, he worked in Florence, Perugia, and in the Vatican, where he painted a fresco for the Sistine Chapel (c. 1481). He completed frescoes in Orvieto Cathedral begun by Fra ▷Angelico and painted his masterpiece, *The Last Judgment*, there (1499). His studies of muscular nudes were admired by Michelangelo.

● **signoria** ▶ (Italian: lordship) A form of government in late medieval Italian city states following the collapse of communal government caused by factional struggles. Control was given (sometimes voluntarily) to a *signore* (lord), who formed a more or less despotic government. *Signori* established dynasties, especially in N Italy (e.g. the ▷Visconti and ▷Este), which often gained reputations for good government and artistic patronage.

● **Sigurdsson** ▷See Sverrir.

● **Sihanouk, Norodom** ▶ (1923–) King (1941–55, 1993–) of Cambodia; head of state (1975–76, 1991–93). When the Japanese occupation ended in 1945, Sihanouk achieved Cambodia's independence from France (1953). Abdicating in 1955, he dominated Cambodian politics as prime minister until 1970, when his regime was overthrown by a military coup and he went into exile in China. After the

victory of the Khmer Rouge guerrillas (1975) he again became head of state but was forced to resign in 1976. He headed the government in exile from 1982 until 1991, when he returned to Cambodia. He participated in peace negotiations as head of state and in 1993 a new monarchist constitution made him king once more.

● **sika** ▶ A deer, *Cervus nippon*, also called Japanese deer, native to S Asia, Japan, and Taiwan and introduced to New Zealand and Europe. Grey-brown in winter and chestnut with white spots in summer, its shoulder height is 70–100 cm. Stags have slender eight-pointed antlers about 80 cm long.

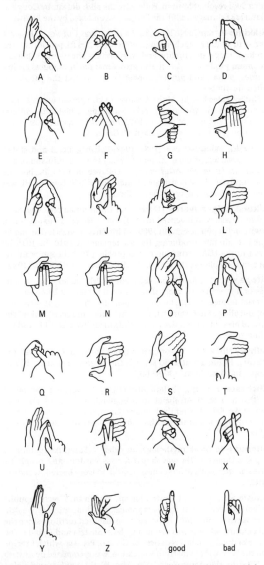

sign language ▶ The American Sign Language (ASL)—the most widely used sign language in English.

● **Sikhism** ▶ The religion of some nine million Indians, mostly inhabiting the Punjab. Founded in the 15th century by the Guru ▷Nanak, Sikhism combines Hindu and Islamic ideas. The Hindu concepts of ▷karma and rebirth are accepted, but the caste system is rejected. Sikhs believe that god is the only reality and that spiritual release can be obtained by taming the ego through devotional singing, recitation of the divine name, meditation, and service. The guidance of the ▷guru is essential. The concept of Khalsa, a chosen race of warrior-saints, is central, as are the so-called five Ks: *kangha* (comb); *kacch* (shorts); *kirpan* (sword); *kara* (steel bracelet); and *kes* (uncut hair and beard). The occupation of the Sikh Golden Temple at Amritsar by Indian troops in 1984 led to the assassination a few months later of the Indian prime minister Indira ▷Gandhi by Sikh members of her bodyguard. Violent reprisals against Sikhs followed throughout India. ▷*See also* 'Adi Granth; Gobind Singh.

● **Sikh Wars ▶ 1.** (1845–46) The war caused by the invasion of British India by Sikhs from the Punjab. The Sikh defeat resulted in the loss of territory that included Kashmir. **2.** (1848–49) The war that developed from a Sikh revolt at Multan. Following the Sikh defeat, by Gough at Gujarat (22 February, 1849), the Punjab was annexed by the British.

● **Sikkim ▶** A state in NE India, in the Himalayas E of Nepal. Low valleys rise to Mount Kangchenjunga, 8598 m (28 208 ft), providing a tremendous range in climate and vegetation. The world's biggest cardamom producer, Sikkim also grows mandarin oranges, grains, potatoes, pulses, and ginger. Copper is mined and the jungle exploited for timber.
History: ruled by a Buddhist dynasty, Sikkim passed under British and then Indian protection (1947). Following a plebiscite Sikkim became the 22nd state of India in 1975. Area: 7096 sq km (2739 sq mi). Population (1994 est): 444 000. Capital: Gangtok.

● **Sikorski, Władysław ▶** (1881–1943) Polish general and statesman. Sikorski was prime minister (1922–23) and then minister of military affairs (1924–25). After Poland's collapse in 1939, he became prime minister of the Polish government-in-exile in London. He was killed in an aeroplane crash near Gibraltar.

● **Sikorsky, Igor Ivan ▶** (1889–1972) US aeronautical engineer, born in Russia, who invented the helicopter. He began experimenting with helicopter designs in 1909 but his early models failed and he turned to aircraft, producing the S-1 biplane in 1910. In 1919 he moved to the USA, returning to the problem of helicopters in the 1930s and completing the first successful model, the VS-300, in 1939.

● **silage ▶** A cattle food produced from a fresh fodder crop, usually grass or a green cereal crop, that has been preserved by controlled bacterial fermentation. The crop is placed in an airtight structure (silo) and allowed to ferment; the organic acids produced "pickle" the crop and prevent further decay, resulting in highly digestible and nutritious food.

● **Silbury Hill ▶** A prehistoric mound in S England, near ▷Avebury, Wiltshire. Begun about 2150 BC, it is the largest man-made hill in Europe, standing 40 m (130 ft) high.

● **Silchester ▶** (Latin: Calleva Atrebatum) An ancient capital of the British tribe of Atrebates in S England, 11 km (18 mi) N of Basingstoke. Rebuilt after the Roman conquest, Silchester was inhabited until the 6th century AD. The Roman town wall (c. 200 AD) is still visible.

● **Silenus ▶** In Greek mythology, an elderly ▷Satyr, companion of the god ▷Dionysus. He was famed for his wisdom and prophetic powers as well as his drunkenness. The Sileni were his fellow nature spirits.

● **Silesia ▶** A region of E central Europe now in the Czech Republic and Poland. Because of its geographical position, mineral wealth, and industrial potential, Silesia has been disputed territory since the 17th century, when it was claimed by both Austria and Prussia. The seizure of much of it by Frederick the Great of Prussia, which precipitated the War of the ▷Austrian Succession, was recognized by Austria in 1763, after the ▷Seven Years' War. After World War I it was divided between Czechoslovakia, Germany, and Poland and after World War II, between Czechoslovakia and Poland.

● **silhouette ▶** In art, a profile image or portrait in black on a white background or vice versa. Named after the French finance minister Étienne de Silhouette (1709–67), who made paper cut-outs of silhouettes, this type of portrait was very popular in the late 18th and early 19th centuries until it was supplanted by photography.

● **silica ▶** The mineral silicon dioxide, SiO_2, the most abundant of all minerals. There are three main forms of silica: ▷quartz, tridymite, and cristobalite, the last two occurring in acidic volcanic rocks.

Cryptocrystalline silica is ▷chalcedony; amorphous silica is ▷opal. Creosite is a high-pressure variety, found near meteorite craters. Lechatelierite is a natural silica glass. Silica content is used to classify igneous rocks into acidic (over 65% silica), intermediate (52–66% silica), basic (45–52% silica), and ultrabasic (under 45% silica) varieties. Since these terms do not reflect pH value, another classification based on silica content is also frequently used; in this igneous rocks are classified as oversaturated (containing free silica), saturated (all silica combined with no unsaturated minerals, e.g. feldspathoids), or undersaturated (containing unsaturated minerals). ▷*See also* silicate minerals.

● **silicate minerals ▶** A group of minerals that constitute about 90% of the earth's crust and one-third of all minerals. They consist of silicates of calcium, magnesium, aluminium, or other metals, in varying degrees of complexity. They are classified according to their atomic structure; all are based on the tetrahedral unit SiO_4. ▷Feldspar and ▷quartz (which is chemically an oxide but resembles the silicates more closely in many properties and is usually included in this group) are the most common. ▷*See also* amphiboles; clay; garnet; micas; olivine; pyroxene.

● **silicon ▶** (Si) The second most abundant element in the earth's crust, after oxygen. It is a major constituent of almost all rock-forming minerals (*see* silicate minerals). The element was discovered by J. J. Berzelius in 1824 and is extracted by reduction of the oxide (silica; SiO_2) with carbon in an electric furnace. Pure silicon is now of great importance in the electronics industry as a semiconductor. It is prepared by decomposition of trichlorosilane ($SiCl_3H$). Silicates have been important for centuries as the main constituents of pottery, glasses, and many building materials. Silicon carbide (*see* carborundum) is a widely used abrasive, refractory, and semiconductor. Organic silicon compounds are known as ▷silicones. At no 14; at wt 28.086; mp 1414°C; bp 3267°C.

● **silicon chip ▶** *See* integrated circuit.

● **silicones ▶** Synthetic polymers consisting of chains of alternating silicon and oxygen atoms, with organic groups attached to the former. The chains can be cross-linked to varying degrees. Silicones include fluids, greases, rubbers, and resins. All have similar chemical properties: stability to heat, oxidation, many chemicals, and oils. The main applications are in adhesives, paints, elastomers, and waterproofing agents.

● **Silicon Valley ▶** The industrial area in Santa Clara County between Palo Alto and San José in California, USA, so called because it is an international centre for the manufacture of electronics, computers, etc., based on silicon chips. The name has sometimes been applied to other districts noted for the growth of high-tech industries (in the UK, for example, the Thames valley area between W Greater London and Reading).

● **silicosis ▶** A lung disease caused by prolonged inhalation of silica dust: an ▷occupational disease of stone cutters, quarry workers, etc. Silica causes more damage than an equivalent amount of coaldust: the air sacs of the lungs become thickened and scarred, causing breathlessness and coughing in the patients. There is no specific treatment and prevention by use of masks and other safety measures is essential. ▷*See also* pneumoconiosis.

● **silk ▶** The thread produced by the caterpillar of the ▷silkworm moth and the fabric woven from it. The cocoons are unravelled and the filaments from several twisted together; processing this raw silk includes combining these strands, washing away the sticky sericin secretion, and sometimes adding metallic salts for weight. China, where silk production was first practised, and Japan are the leading producers of pure silk; wild silk, produced by silkworms that feed on leaves other than mulberry or by uncultivated silkworms, includes a coarser brown Indian silk. Lustrous, elastic, absorbent, and very strong, silk remains a luxury fabric considerably superior to its synthetic imitations.

● **silk-cotton tree ▶** *See* kapok.

● **Silk Road ▶** A trade route, 6400 km (4000 mi) long, that connected China with the Mediterranean. It was most used in antiquity, when silk was taken westwards and wool and precious metals eastwards, but was again travelled in the later middle ages, notably by Marco Polo. Although it was superseded by E–W sea routes in the 15th century, it has remained important for communications in S central Asia. An oil pipeline some 3017 km (1875 mi) long is currently being constructed along the Silk Road from China to Kazakhstan.

● **silk-screen printing** ▷*See* printing.

● **silkworm** ▶ A caterpillar that spins a silken cocoon, especially one that is suitable for commercial silk production. The commonest is the Chinese silkworm (*Bombyx mori*), which feeds on mulberry leaves. The pupae are killed by heat and the silken thread, up to 900 m long, is then unwound. 50 000 cocoons are needed to produce 1 kg of silk. The Japanese oak silkmoth (*Antherea yamanai*) and the Chinese species *A. pernyi* are also used. Some American moths, such as the ▷cecropia and ▷io moths, also produce silk.

● **silky oak** ▶ One of two species of Australian trees. *Grevillea robusta*, found in forests of E Australia, grows to 35 m and has fernlike leaves. It is widely cultivated in the tropics as an ornamental or shade tree. The northern silky oak (*Cardwellia sublimis*) is an important timber tree, its pinkish soft wood being used in furniture and for building.

● **silky terrier** ▶ A breed of toy dog developed in Australia by crossing the Australian terrier with the Yorkshire terrier. Formerly called the Sydney silky, it has a compact body with short legs. The long fine glossy coat is blue and tan or grey-blue and tan. Height: 23–25 cm.

● **sill** ▶ A horizontal or near-horizontal sheetlike mass of intrusive igneous rock, lying parallel to the layering of the rock into which it is intruded. Most sills consist of medium-grained hypabyssal rock, the commonest being dolerite. *Compare* dyke.

● **Sillitoe, Alan** ▶ (1928–) British novelist. He began writing in Majorca, where he settled after World War II. He won immediate success with his first novel, *Saturday Night and Sunday Morning* (1958), about the violent and alienated life of a Nottingham factory worker. This was followed by a book of short stories, *The Loneliness of the Long Distance Runner* (1959). His many later books include the semi-autobiographical *Raw Material* (1972), *Her Victory* (1982), and *Snowstop* (1993).

● **Sills, Beverley** ▶ (Belle Silverman; 1929–) US soprano. A child prodigy, she made her operatic debut with the Philadelphia Civil Opera in 1948, since when she has sung major roles in more than 50 operas. She was director of the New York City Opera (1979–88) and became director of the New York Metropolitan Opera in 1991.

● **Silone, Ignazio** ▶ (Secondo Tranquilli; 1900–78) Italian novelist. He helped found the Italian Communist Party in 1921, lived in exile in Switzerland from 1930 until after World War II, and then returned to Italy to lead the Democratic Socialist Party until 1950. He became disillusioned with communism, but his novels, especially *Fontamara* (1930) and *Bread and Wine* (1937), express his socialist concern for the peasants of S Italy.

● **silt** ▶ A fine-grained sedimentary deposit, the rock particles of which range from 0.002 to 0.06 mm in diameter. Silts consist mainly of clay minerals, with iron oxides and hydroxides and silica. They collect in sheltered marine environments, such as estuaries, making dredging necessary. Consolidated silts form siltstones.

● **Silurian period** ▶ A geological period of the Lower Palaeozoic era between the Ordovician and Devonian periods, lasting from about 445 to 415 million years ago. Conditions were mainly marine and the first true fish appeared. The first evidence of land plants also comes from Silurian rocks. The Caledonian period of mountain building reached its peak towards the end of the period.

● **Silvanus** ▶ A Roman woodland god, sometimes identified with the Greek ▷Pan. He was usually portrayed as an old countryman. He was worshipped at sacred groves or trees.

● **silver** ▶ (Ag) A metallic element, known since ancient times. It occurs in nature as the metal, as argentite (Ag_2S), and in lead, zinc, and copper ores. Pure silver has the highest electrical and thermal conductivity known and is used in some printed electrical circuits. In air, silver tarnishes forming a coating of the black sulphide (Ag_2S). Alloys of silver are used as solders and sterling silver (92.5% pure) is used for jewellery. Although not a reactive metal, silver forms many compounds including the oxide (Ag_2O), the nitrate ($AgNO_3$), and halides (for example AgCl, AgBr). Silver salts are of great importance in photography since they are light sensitive, and some 30% of the silver produced is used in this way. Silver iodide (AgI) has been used in attempts to seed clouds to induce rainfall. At no 47; at wt 107.868; mp 961.93; bp 2163°C.

● **Silver Age, Latin** ▶ The period (18–c. 130 AD) succeeding the ▷Golden Age of ▷Latin literature. During this time rhetorical brilliance and ornamentation became prized for its own sake. Major writers include the satirist ▷Juvenal, the epigrammatist ▷Martial, the historians ▷Tacitus and ▷Suetonius, and the philosopher and dramatist ▷Seneca.

● **silverfish** ▶ A widely distributed primitive wingless ▢insect, *Lepisma saccharina*, also called fish moth. One of the three-pronged ▷bristletails, it is covered with silvery scales and is common in buildings, feeding on starchy materials, including books and fabrics. Family: *Lepismatidae*.

● **silverplate** ▶ Any object that is plated with silver rather than being solid silver. The first substitute for pure silver for tableware, etc., was the invention of ▷Sheffield plate in 1742. In 1840 the advent

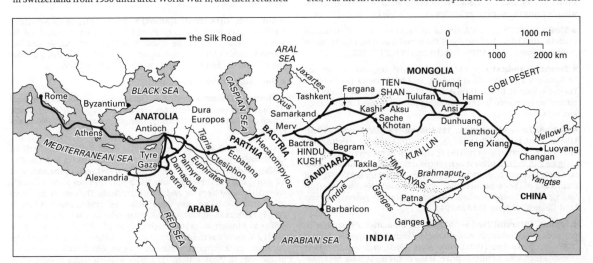

Silk Road ▶ Between the 1st century BC and the 3rd century AD Chinese silks travelled westwards to the Mediterranean in exchange for precious metals.

of ▷electroplating brought silverplated domestic articles to a much wider public and Sheffield plate is now of considerable value. Many silverplated articles are marked EPNS (electroplated nickel silver)—nickel silver itself is an alloy of copper, nickel, and zinc and contains no silver; in this process a layer of silver is electroplated onto the nickel-silver base.

● **silverside** ► A fish, also called sand smelt or whitebait, belonging to a family (*Atherinidae*) found in fresh and coastal waters of warm and temperate regions. Its small slim body, up to 70 cm long, bears a silvery band along each side and two dorsal fins. Order: *Atheriniformes*.

● **sima** ► The earth's oceanic crust, which is composed of basaltic rocks rich in silica (Si) and magnesium (Mg). It is denser than the ▷sial of the continental crust and is believed to continue beneath it.

● **Si-ma Qian** ► (*or* Ssu-ma Ch'ien; c. 145–c. 85 BC) Chinese historian, astronomer, and calendar reformer. He succeeded his father as historian to the Han Emperor Wu, but he offended the emperor and was castrated and imprisoned. He later became palace secretary. His *Records of the Historian*, the first major Chinese historical work, included the entire documented history of China to that date.

● **Simbirsk** ► (former name: Ulyanovsk) 54 19N 48 22E A port in W central Russia, on the River Volga. Industries include food processing, vodka distilling, and motor-vehicle manufacture. In 1924 it was renamed in honour of Lenin (originally V. I. Ulyanov), who was born here. Population (1996 est): 678 000.

● **Simenon, Georges** ► (1903–89) Belgian novelist. The best known of his several hundred novels are his detective stories featuring the Parisian *commissaire de police*, Maigret, who first appeared in 1931. His other novels, written in a brisk colloquial style and with intuitive psychological perception, include *La Neige était sale* (1948), the semiautobiographical *Pedigree* (1948), and *Destinées* (1981).

● **Simeon, tribe of** ► One of the 12 ▷tribes of Israel. It claimed descent from Simeon, the son of Jacob and Leah. The territory allocated to the tribe was S of that of Judah, W and SW of the Dead Sea. It was later assimilated into Judah.

● **Simeon Stylites, St** ► (c. 390–459 AD) Syrian monk and hermit, who lived for over 35 years on a small platform on top of a tall pillar (Greek, *stylos*). His many imitators were known as stylites. Feast day: 5 Jan.

● **Simferopol** ► 44 57N 34 05E A city in S Ukraine, the capital of Crimea. It has food-processing, engineering, and consumer-goods industries. Population (1996 est): 348 000.

● **simile** ► A figure of speech in which two things are compared in order to emphasize a particular feature or quality they share. A simile differs from a ▷metaphor in being an explicit comparison, usually using the words *as* or *like*, for example "He fought like a lion."

● **Simla** ► 31 07N 77 09E A city in India, the capital of Himachal Pradesh situated in the foothills of the Himalayas. It was the summer capital of India (1865–1939). Population (1991): 109 860.

● **Simnel, Lambert** ► (c. 1475–1535) English impostor whom the Yorkists tried to pass off as Edward, Earl of Warwick (1475–99), a Yorkist claimant to the throne, in a plot to overthrow Henry VII. Simnel was captured in 1487 and subsequently worked in the king's kitchens.

● **Simon, John Allsebrook, 1st Viscount** ► (1873–1954) British Liberal politician. An MP (1906–18, 1922–40) he became solicitor general (1910), attorney general (1913), and then home secretary (1915), resigning in 1916 in protest against conscription in World War I. He was later foreign secretary (1931–35), home secretary (1935–37), and chancellor of the exchequer (1937–40), supporting Neville Chamberlain's policy of ▷appeasement towards the fascist powers. He was Lord Chancellor from 1940 to 1945.

● **Simon, (Marvin) Neil** ► (1927–) US dramatist. His studies of personal relationships in modern society include *Barefoot in the Park* (1963), *California Suite* (1976), *Biloxi Blues* (1985), and *Lost in Yonkers* (1990), which won a Pulitzer prize. Many of his plays have been successfully filmed.

● **Simon, Paul** ► (1942–) US pop singer and songwriter. With **Art Garfunkel** (1942–) he wrote and performed for the film *The Graduate* (1967) and such albums as *Bridge over Troubled Water* (1970). His solo albums include *Graceland* (1986) and *The Rhythm of the Saints* (1990).

● **Simon, St** ► In the New Testament, one of the 12 Apostles. He is surnamed the Canaanite or Zelotes, which may mean that he was one of the ▷Zealots. He preached in Egypt and joined St ▷Jude in Persia, where, according to one tradition, he was cut in half with a saw. Feast day: 28 Oct.

● **Simonov, Konstantin** ► (1915–79) Soviet writer and journalist. His writings on World War II include the poem "Wait for Me" and the novels *Days and Nights* (1945), on the defence of Stalingrad, and *Victims and Heroes* (1959).

● **Simon's Town** ► 34 12S 18 26E A naval base in SW South Africa, on the Atlantic coast. An important naval base from 1741, it was used by the British navy (1814–1975) and is the base of the South African navy. As well as having dry-dock and harbour facilities, it is an important fishing port. Population (latest est): 6500.

● **simple harmonic motion** ► Any oscillation performed by a body about some reference point so that the restraining force is directly proportional to its displacement from that point. Examples of simple harmonic motion include a ▷pendulum swinging through a small angle and a vibrating string. The maximum displacement of the system is known as the amplitude and the time taken for one complete oscillation, the period. This displacement, x, at a time t is simply represented by the equation $x = A\sin\omega t$, where A is the amplitude and ω the angular frequency, which is related to the period T by $\omega = 2\pi/T$. Thus a graph of x plotted against t has the shape of a sine wave, i.e. it is sinusoidal.

● **Simplon Pass** ► An alpine pass linking Brig in Switzerland with Iselle in Italy. A road was built between 1800 and 1807 on Napoleon's orders and reaches a height of 2009 m (6590 ft). The **Simplon Tunnel** to the NE was, at 20 km (12 mi), the longest rail tunnel in the world until 1979. Built in 1890 by Alfred Brandt (1846–99), it was opened in 1906.

● **Simpson, Sir James Young** ► (1811–70) Scottish physician. Professor of obstetrics at Edinburgh University, he was the first to use ether (1847), and later that year, chloroform, in childbirth (in spite of both church and medical opposition). He also developed long obstetric forceps.

● **Simpson, N(orman) F(rederick)** ► (1919–) British dramatist. *A Resounding Tinkle* (1956) and *One Way Pendulum* (1959) are comedies in which the mixture of fantasy and logic is influenced by the ▷Theatre of the Absurd.

● **Simpson, O(renthal) J(ames)** ► (1947–) US Black American football player and film actor. After a long televised criminal trial, he was acquitted (1995) of the murders of his ex-wife Nicole and her friend Ronald Goldman. A subsequent civil trial found him liable for the two deaths and imposed damages of some $33.5M.

● **Simpson, Wallis** ▷*See* Edward VIII.

● **Simpson Desert** ► (*or* Arunta Desert) A desert of central Australia, mainly in Northern Territory. It is covered by parallel sand dunes, which extend to 160 km (100 mi) in length. Area: about 77 000 sq km (29 723 sq mi).

● **sin** ► A moral and theological concept that has a central role in Christianity, Judaism, and Islam; in these religions sin is defined as deliberate disobedience to the will of God and seen as the source of all moral evil. All three religions teach that sin is an abuse of man's free will, caused by pride and self-centredness. The results are alienation from God and inevitable suffering. This understanding is clearly distinct from that of the Eastern religions, which tend to see evil as an illusion, from the Greek philosophical tradition, which regards evil merely as the absence of good and attributes it mainly to ignorance, and from modern humanist views, which tend to see moral blame only in those actions that cause evident harm to others.

The monotheistic understanding of sin is encapsulated in the story of Adam and Eve in the Old Testament. Here Adam, the first and archetypal man, commits the first and archetypal sin by freely choosing to eat the expressly forbidden fruit of the tree of knowledge. Traditionally, this story has also been used to teach the doctrine of ▷original sin—the idea that since Adam's fall human beings are sinful both by nature and predisposition. Christian theology, which gives far greater prominence to this idea than either Judaism or Islam, makes a formal distinction between original sin, as a collective inheritance, and actual sin, which is evil performed by individuals in thought, word, or deed. Roman Catholic teaching also distinguishes between **mortal sins**, which incur a total loss of the grace of God, and **venial sins**, which involve only a partial loss of grace. In Christianity, the **seven deadly sins**—anger, avarice, envy, gluttony, lust, pride, and sloth—are held to be fundamental to all others.

While the monotheistic religions all stress the gravity of sin, they also emphasize the forgiving nature of God and teach that sincere repentance will always be accepted. For Jews, the traditional season for repentance is the ten days culminating in ▷Yom Kippur. Repentance may involve restitution to anybody wronged by the sin and physical penances, such as fasting. In Islam, in which the concept of sin is less developed than in Christianity or Judaism, the one unforgivable sin is to deny that Allah is the one and only God. Other sins may be atoned for by repentance and observance of the various duties enjoined on the faithful (notably fasting in ▷Ramadan). Christianity also demands repentance but sees this as effective only through the atoning sacrifice of Jesus on the cross. Most Christian Churches make use of some form of private or general ▷confession of sins as part of a ritual of absolution.

● **Sinai** ▶ A desert peninsula in Egypt, bounded by Israel and the Gulf of Aqaba to the E and the Gulf of Suez and mainland Egypt to the W. Mount Sinai, 2285 m (7497 ft) high, is in the mountain range in the S. According to the Old Testament it was on this mountain that Moses received the tablets of the law from Jehovah (Exodus 24). The N half of the desert is plateau. The chief resources of the region are manganese and the oil deposits in the W, based on Sudr; agriculture is practised on the Mediterranean coast. Sinai was occupied by Israel in the 1956 and again in the 1967 Arab-Israeli Wars and following the 1973 war Egyptian and Israeli lines were established on either side of a UN buffer zone. Under the 1979 Egyptian-Israeli agreement a large proportion of the area was returned to Egypt with Israeli withdrawal completed in 1982.

● **Sinatra, Frank** ▶ (Francis Albert S.; 1915–98) US singer and film actor, who recorded his first hit, "All or Nothing at All," in 1943. His nonsinging role in the film *From Here to Eternity* (1953) earned him an Oscar; he subsequently appeared in such films as *Guys and Dolls* (1955) and *The Manchurian Candidate* (1962). His later hits include "Strangers in the Night" (1966) and "My Way" (1969).

Frank Sinatra ▶ A photograph of the young crooner in the early 1940s, when he began his recording career with the big bands of Harry James (1916–82) and Tommy Dorsey (1904–57). He later claimed to have modelled his immaculate phrasing on Dorsey's trombone technique.

● **Sinclair, Upton** ▶ (1878–1968) US novelist. A committed socialist, he used the profits from *The Jungle* (1906), a novel of social protest, to establish a cooperative for left-wing writers and to finance several unsuccessful political campaigns. The best known of his many polemical novels are the 11-volume Lanny Budd series known as *World's End* (1940–53).

● **Sind** ▶ A province in SE Pakistan, on the Arabian Sea. From the broad Indus lowland it extends E into the Thar Desert and W into rocky hills. Grains, other crops, and livestock are raised. Important industries include textiles, chemicals, and cement.

History: Sind's history goes back 5000 years. Islam was introduced in 711–12 AD and British rule established in 1843. Ethnic unrest and tension with India brought Sind to the verge of civil war in 1990. Area: 140 914 sq km (54 407 sq mi). Population (latest est): 21 682 000. Capital: Karachi.

● **Singapore, Republic of** ▶ A republic in SE Asia, off the S tip of the Malay Peninsula, consisting of the island of Singapore and over 58 islets. The city of Singapore occupies much of the island's area. The majority of the population is Chinese with minorities of Malays, Indians, and others.

Economy: Singapore is one of the world's busiest ports and lies on a major sea route. It is a major commercial centre and in recent decades industry has been expanded and diversified. The chief industries include electronics, telecommunications, shipbuilding and repairs, oil refining, transport equipment, chemicals, and machinery. The fishing industry is well developed. The main exports are office machinery, oil and oil products, and electronic equipment. Singapore is also an important financial centre with a stock exchange, foreign-exchange markets, and numerous commercial and merchant banks.

History: although a prosperous commercial centre in the middle ages, the island was largely uninhabited in 1819, when Sir Stamford Raffles established a station of the British East India Company here. In 1824 it was ceded to Britain, later becoming part of the ▷Straits Settlements. During World War II it was occupied by the Japanese, the British defence forces having surrendered in 1942. It became a British crown colony in 1946 and a self-governing state within the Commonwealth in 1959. It joined the Federation of Malaysia on its formation (1963) but broke away in 1965 and formed an independent republic. The British military presence was phased out after 1967. The People's Action Party has governed continuously since 1965, and its leader Lee Kuan Yew was prime minister from that date until 1990; he was succeeded by Goh Chok Tung.

Republic of Singapore

Head of state	President Ong Teng Cheong
Official languages	Chinese, English, Malay, and Tamil
Official currency	Singapore dollar of 100 cents
Area	639 sq km (247 sq mi)
Population (1998 est)	3 164 000
Capital	Singapore

● **Singer, Isaac Bashevis** ▶ (1904–91) US novelist and short-story writer. Born into a rabbinical Jewish family in Poland, he emigrated to the USA in 1935. His novels and collections of stories, written in Yiddish and frequently dramatizing Jewish life in Poland, include *Gimpel the Fool* (1957), *The Slave* (1960), *Shosha* (1978), *Old Love* (1979), and *The King of the Fields* (1989). He won the Nobel Prize in 1978.

● **Singer, Isaac Merrit** ▶ (1811–75) US inventor, who in 1857 designed and built the first commercially successful domestic sewing machine. It was a great improvement on Elias ▷Howe's machine and incorporated a number of innovations, such as continuous stitching, that remain the basis of all modern sewing machines.

● **singing** ▷*See* alto; baritone; bass; bel canto; contralto; countertenor; soprano; tenor.

● **single-cell protein** ▶ (SCP) Protein derived from microorganisms, usually bacteria or yeasts, that are cultivated on a suitable medium and then harvested and processed for use as a food for livestock or humans. For example, the blue-green bacterium *Spirulina* is processed and sold as a protein-rich health food. Using similar technology, the mould *Fusarium graminearum* is cultured and processed to produce mycoprotein, marketed as Quorn (a meat substitute).

● **single-lens reflex** ▶ (SLR) ▷*See* camera, photographic.

● **single-parent families** ▶ Families consisting of one or more children under 16 residing with one parent only. Of all the families in the UK in 1997, 22% were single-parent families, most of which were headed by a mother. This percentage is roughly three times the equivalent in 1971. In 1995–97 some 38% of the mothers heading single families had never married, 57% were separated or divorced, and 6% had been widowed. In the period 1971–86 most of the increase in single-parent families resulted from marriage breakdowns (separation and divorce). Between 1987 and 1997, however, most of the increase was accounted for by children born to mothers who were not in a stable relationship (*see also* illegitimacy).

The lone mother without financial support from a former partner has considerable problems in combining parenting with earning a living. In 1993 some 70% of lone mothers were on income support and in 1996–97 households with one adult and one or more children had an average disposable income only slightly more than one-third of that of the average two-parent families (*see also* marriage). The problems of single-parent families, however, are not restricted to shortage of money. Without the support of a partner, many single parents lack the time and ability to provide their children with the stable and supportive background that appears to be necessary to enable them to cope resourcefully with the vicissitudes of adult life.

● **singularity** ▶ A point in the ▷space-time continuum at which the curvature of space (*see* relativity) is infinite and therefore the known laws of physics do not operate. A singularity is always concealed within an **event horizon**, from which no matter or energy can escape. Whatever happens within that event horizon must remain unknown to an observer in the universe outside it. Calculations predict that a ▷black hole must contain a singularity. Any matter falling into such a black hole will be compressed to an infinite density at a single point to which the laws of physics cannot apply. According to some theories, the big-bang model of the origin of the universe (*see* big-bang theory) is based on a singularity.

● **Sing Sing** ▷*See* Ossining.

● **Sinhalese** ▶ The major ethnic group in Sri Lanka. They speak an ▷Indo-Aryan language that has been much influenced by ▷Pali and the Dravidian languages, particularly ▷Tamil. They are descended from migrants from Bengal who colonized Sri Lanka during the 5th century BC. An agricultural people, they base their social organization on caste and practise Theravada Buddhism.

● **sinkhole** ▶ (*or* sink) A saucer-like hollow in the ground surface, typical of chalk and limestone areas. It may form through the solvent action on limestone of rain containing dissolved carbon dioxide; alternatively it may be due to a rock collapse. Sinkholes often act as channels down which water seeps into underground drainage systems.

● **Sinkiang Uigur** ▷*See* Xinjiang Uygur Autonomous Region.

● **sinking fund** ▶ A fund set up to reduce a debt: it is maintained by regular payments and accumulated interest. Such funds have been established at intervals to reduce the ▷national debt.

● **Sinn Féin** ▶ (Irish: We Ourselves) An Irish political party committed to the establishment of an Irish republic to include Northern Ireland. Founded in 1905 by Arthur ▷Griffith, the party became prominent after the ▷Easter Rising (1916). In 1918, under Eamon ▷De Valera, Sinn Féin won 75% of the Irish seats in the British parliament but declined to sit at Westminster. Meeting in Dublin (1919), they declared an Irish Republic, initiating a campaign of guerrilla warfare through their newly formed military wing, the ▷Irish Republican Army (IRA). The establishment of the Irish Free State (negotiated by Griffith in 1921), which entailed the partition of Ireland and fell short of complete independence, was rejected by De Valera, leading to the Irish Civil War of 1921–23. Following the military defeat of the Republicans, De Valera founded a new constitutional party, Fianna Fáil, in 1926. With the advent of the Northern Irish "Troubles" in

1968, Sinn Féin became prominent again as the political wing of the IRA; from 1986 it was also involved in constitutional politics. Following the ▷Downing Street Declaration, two IRA ceasefires (1994–96, 1997–) were announced by Sinn Féin president Gerry ▷Adams. Subsequently Sinn Féin voted to back the Good Friday Agreement of 1998 and its representatives were included in the assembly and the power-sharing executive established under the agreement. These institutions were suspended in February 2000, owing to lack of progress on the decommissioning of IRA arms, but re-established in May, after the IRA agreed to put its weapons "beyond use."

● **Sino-Japanese Wars** ▶ **1.** (1894–95) The war between China and Japan resulting from rivalry in Korea. War was declared after the Japanese sank the *Kowshing*, which was transporting Chinese reinforcements to aid the Korean king in suppressing the Tonghak uprising. Japan inflicted a crushing defeat on China, which was forced to pay a large indemnity and cede Taiwan, the Pescadores, and the Liaodong peninsula. **2.** (1937–45) The war between China and Japan brought about by Japanese expansion into China in the 1930s. The Japanese had established a puppet state in Manchuria (*see* Manchukuo) in 1932 but only after the negotiation of a Nationalist-Communist ▷United Front against Japan did full war break out. The Japanese took Shanghai and Nanchang in 1937 and Wuhan and Canton in 1938. Their position remained strong until the USA entered World War II (1941) and gave China assistance. After Japan's surrender (1945) China regained Manchuria, Taiwan, and the Pescadores.

● **Sinop** ▶ 42 02N 35 09E A port in central N Turkey, on the Black Sea. Ancient Sinope was the most important Greek colony on the Euxine (Black) Sea and flourished under Mithridates the Great, during whose reign fine buildings and a harbour were constructed. It became part of the Ottoman Empire in 1458. Population (latest est): 25 025.

● **Sino-Tibetan languages** ▶ A group of languages spoken in E Asia. It includes all the ▷Chinese dialects (which use the same alphabet but differ substantially in sound), the Tibeto-Burman languages (Tibetan, Burmese, and many related languages spoken in the valleys of the Himalayas), and probably the Tai languages, such as Siamese, Laotian, and Shan. The main characteristic that justifies this large grouping is the monosyllabic nature of the vocabulary of all these languages and their use of tonality to differentiate otherwise similar words. They are all isolating languages, that is they use word order, not inflection, to determine grammatical relations.

● **sintering** ▶ The heating without melting of powdered substance, usually metal or plastic, so that it becomes a solid mass. ▷*See also* powder metallurgy.

● **Sintra** ▶ (former name: Cintra) 38 48N 9 22W A town in central Portugal. Its beauty has been celebrated by several literary figures, including Byron in his *Childe Harolde*. The many notable buildings include the royal palace (14th–15th centuries) in Moorish and gothic styles. It is a tourist and agricultural centre. Population (latest est): 20 574.

● **Sinŭiju** ▶ 40 04N 124 25E A port in North Korea, on the River Yalu opposite Andong, China. Its industrial development began during the Japanese occupation (1910–45) and its principal industries include sawmilling and the manufacture of paper. Population (latest est): 289 000.

● **sinus** ▶ A hollow cavity, especially one in a bone. The term usually refers to the air sinuses of the head, which are cavities in the facial bones; all have connections with the nasal cavity and they are susceptible to infection (*see* sinusitis). The term is also used for a pus-filled channel leading from an infected organ or tissue to a surface (usually the skin).

● **sinusitis** ▶ Inflammation of the sinuses—the spaces in the skull that are connected to the nose. They commonly become infected when a patient has a cold or similar infection, causing pain in the face and prolonging the original illness. Sinusitis can also be caused by an allergic reaction. If the inflammation persists the affected sinuses may need to be surgically drained or washed out.

● **Siouan languages** ▶ A family of North American Indian languages including Dakota ▷Sioux, ▷Crow, and several others. Most are spoken by Plains tribes. Some experts classify the Siouan languages as a branch of a larger family called Macro-Siouan, which includes the Iroquoian and Caddoan languages.

Sioux ▶ A hide painting depicting a battle between the Sioux and the Blackfoot.

● **Sioux** ▶ A confederation of North American Plains Indian tribes, also known as the Dakota. They fought fiercely against White encroachments upon their territories and defeated Gen Custer at the battle of the ▷Little Bighorn (1876) under their leaders Sitting Bull and Crazy Horse. They were ultimately subdued, one group making a last stand at ▷Wounded Knee (1890).

● **Sioux City** ▶ 42 30N 96 28W A city in the USA, in Iowa on the Missouri River. An agricultural trading centre, it has a large livestock market and many food-processing plants. Population (1996 est): 83 791.

● **Sioux Falls** ▶ 43 34N 96 42W A city in the USA, in South Dakota on the Big Sioux River. Founded in 1857, it has one of the country's largest sheep and cattle markets and is an important wheat centre. Manufactures include farm machinery and electrical components. Population (1996 est): 113 223.

● **Siqueiros, David Alfaro** ▶ (1896–1974) Mexican painter, one of the leaders in the Mexican Revolution of 1910 and one of the founders of modern Mexican art. A committed socialist from the start of his career, Siqueiros is best remembered for his monumental murals that reflected his intimate knowledge of the Mexican people. His first major murals were painted in collaboration with ▷Rivera and ▷Orozco in the National Preparatory School, Mexico City; perhaps the most impressive is *The March of Humanity*, measuring 4600 sq m (50 000 sq ft), which Siqueiros painted while he was in prison for his political activities. After the 1950s he was internationally recognized as one of Mexico's greatest artists.

● **siren** ▶ An eel-like ▷salamander belonging to a North American family (*Sirenidae*; 3 species). Sirens have no hind legs, very small forelegs, and permanent gills. They hunt for worms, snails, etc., in ponds and swamps. The largest species is the 60-cm mud-coloured great siren (*Siren lacertina*) and the smallest is the grey mud siren (*Pseudobranchus striatus*), about 20 cm long.

● **Sirens** ▶ In Greek mythology, female creatures, sometimes portrayed with birdlike features, who lured sailors to their island by their singing and then destroyed them. ▷Odysseus saved himself by tying himself to the mast of his ship and filling the ears of his crew with wax. The ▷Argonauts were protected by the superior singing of ▷Orpheus.

● **Sirius** ▶ (*or* Dog Star) The brightest star in the sky, with an apparent magnitude of −1.47. It occurs in the constellation Canis Major

and can be found by following the descending line of Orion's Belt. It is also one of the nearest stars, lying 8.7 light years away. It forms a visual ▷binary star with **Sirius B**, the first ▷white dwarf to be detected (1915).

● **sirocco** ▶ (*or* scirocco) A southerly wind occurring in N Africa, Sicily, and S Italy. Hot and dry on the N African coast, it picks up moisture as it crosses the Mediterranean Sea bringing extensive cloud to S Italy.

● **Sirte, Gulf of** ▶ 30 20N 10 70W A gulf of the Mediterranean Sea, indenting the coast of Libya. It extends 443 km (275 mi) between Misratuh and Benghazi. In the 1980s Libya's attempts to close the Gulf to Western shipping led to friction with the USA.

● **sisal** ▶ A perennial plant, ▷*Agave sisalana*, native to central America and cultivated throughout the tropics for its fibre. The plant, the stem of which grows to a height of only 90 cm, matures three to five years after planting and yields fibre for seven to eight years. Sisal fibre is obtained by crushing the leaves to a pulp and then scraping the pulp from the fibre, which is washed and dried. It is used in shipping, general industry, and agriculture.

● **siskin** ▶ A Eurasian ▷finch, *Carduelis spinus*, occurring in N forests and at high altitudes in the south. It is about 12 cm long with a dark yellow-green plumage, paler streaked underparts, bright-yellow wingbars, and in the male a black chin and crown. Siskins feed on small seeds, particularly those extracted from alder cones.

● **Sisley, Alfred** ▶ (1839–99) Impressionist painter, born in Paris of British parents. In 1862, while training under Charles Gleyre (1808–74), he met ▷Monet and ▷Renoir and later exhibited with them. In the 1870s he produced some of his best landscapes, for example *Misty Morning* (Louvre), and three pictures of the *Floods at Port-Marly*. Unable to sell his works, he spent his last years in poverty.

● **Sistine Chapel** ▶ The principal chapel of the Vatican, so called because it was built for Pope Sixtus V (1473) by Giovanni dei Dolci. It is the meeting place for the College of Cardinals but is chiefly famous for its Renaissance interior decoration, with murals by ▷Perugino, ▷Botticelli, and ▷Ghirlandaio and the roof and ceiling by ▷Michelangelo (restored in the 1980s).

● **Sisyphus** ▶ A legendary Greek king of Corinth. For various offences he was condemned in the underworld eternally to roll a boulder to the top of a hill, from whence it always rolled down again.

● **sitar** ▶ An Indian long-necked ▷lute with a resonating body made from a large gourd, seven metal strings stopped against movable arched frets, and a series of sympathetic strings. The distinctive pitch distortions of sitar music are achieved by pulling and easing the strings over the raised frets. ▯musical instruments.

● **sitatunga** ▶ A spiral-horned antelope, *Tragelaphus spekei*, of central African swamplands, also called marshbuck or water kodoe. Long-legged and up to 120 cm high at the shoulder, it is deep brown with white markings on the face, chest, and back. The female lacks horns. Sitatungas feed on shrubs and aquatic plants.

● **Sitka** ▶ 57 05N 135 20W A port in the USA, in Alaska on Baranof Island. Founded in 1799, it was the capital of Russian America until 1867 and is the site of a Russian Orthodox cathedral (1848). It was an important US naval base during World War II. The main industries are fishing and timber. Population (1990): 8588.

● **Sitting Bull** ▶ (c. 1834–93) American Sioux Indian chief. Resisting US expansion into the Plains, Sitting Bull led the massacre of Gen Custer and his men at the ▷Little Bighorn (1876). After an amnesty he settled on a Dakota reservation but was killed during further hostilities in the 1890s.

● **Sitwell, Dame Edith** ▶ (1887–1964) British poet and writer. The eldest child of an aristocratic family, she and her brother Osbert played the roles of highly publicized rebels against bourgeois philistinism. A lighthearted aestheticism characterizes her early experimental poetry, especially *Façade* (1923), for which Sir William Walton wrote a musical accompaniment, and *Gold Coast Customs* (1929). Her brother **Sir Osbert Sitwell** (1892–1969) wrote poems, short stories, and novels, notably *Before the Bombardment* (1926), but his best-known works are his nostalgic autobiographical memoirs. Both he and his sister gave encouragement to a number of writers, artists, and musicians. The youngest brother, **Sir Sacheverell Sitwell** (1897–1988), was best known as an art critic and travel-book writer.

● **SI units** ► (Système International d'Unités) An international system of units, based on the ▷m.k.s. system, used for all scientific purposes. It has seven base units (metre, kilogram, second, ampere, kelvin, candela, and mole) and two supplementary units (radian and steradian). All physical quantities are expressed in these units or in derived units consisting of combinations of these units, 17 of which have special names and agreed symbols. Decimal multiples of all units are expressed by a set of prefixes. Where possible a prefix representing 10 raised to a power that is a multiple of 3 is used. See Appendix (Units of Measurement).

● **Siva** ▷See Shiva.

● **Sivaji** ► (1627–80) Emperor of India (1647–80), who founded the Maratha dynasty. Born and reared in Poona (later the Maratha capital), he raised a guerrilla force and soon took control of a large part of Maharashtra. A strong opponent of the Mogul Empire, he was crowned as independent king in 1647 and spread his dominion into S India, leaving a powerful legacy for his successors.

● **Sivas** ► 39 44N 37 01E A town in central Turkey. It is a trading centre for grain, wine, and minerals and has 13th-century Seljuq buildings and a university (1973). Population (1995 est): 243 342.

● **Six, Les** ► Six French composers: Auric, Louis Durey (1888–1979), Honegger, Milhaud, Poulenc, and Germaine Tailleferre (1892–1983). These composers, who were briefly under the influence of Cocteau and Satie in the 1920s, united in protest against lingering Romanticism and impressionism in French music. They each developed an individual style, however, and did not long remain a group.

● **Six Articles** ▷See Thirty-Nine Articles.

● **Six Counties** ► The historic counties of Antrim, Down, Armagh, Londonderry (Derry), Tyrone, and Fermanagh, which together constitute Northern ▷Ireland.

● **Six Day War** ▷See Israel, State of.

● **Sixtus IV** ► (Francesco della Rovere; 1414–84) Pope (1471–84), notorious for his nepotism, especially in his support of his nephew, the future ▷Julius II, and for political intrigue, especially against the Medici in Florence. A patron of arts and learning, he instigated the building of the Sistine Chapel and founded its choir.

● **Sixtus V** ► (Felice Peretti; 1521–90) Pope (1585–90), who reformed papal administration and taxation. He issued a revised version of the Vulgate and was a notable patron of the arts, instigating the building of the Vatican Library and Lateran Palace.

● **Sjælland** ► (English name: Zealand; German name: Seeland) The largest of the Danish islands, bounded by the Kattegat, the Sound, the Baltic Sea, and the Great Belt. Predominantly low lying and undulating, its fertile soil is important for both arable and dairy farming. Area: 7016 sq km (2709 sq mi). Population (latest est): 1 987 549. Chief town: Copenhagen.

● **Skagerrak** ► A channel in N Europe, lying between Denmark and Norway and connecting the Kattegat to the North Sea.

● **skaldic poetry** ► Old Norse poetry originally recited by skalds (professional bards generally attached to a princely or noble retinue). In contrast to the heroic poetry of the Eddaic tradition (*see* Eddas), it was descriptive and occasional, characterized by elaborate alliteration, internal rhyming, convoluted word order, and highly allusive, often riddling phrases called "kennings." It apparently originated in 9th-century Norway, but its outstanding practitioners were Icelanders (*see* Icelandic literature).

● **Skalkottas, Nikos** ► (1904–49) Greek composer. He was a pupil of Kurt Weill and Schoenberg. His works include two piano concertos, 36 Greek dances for orchestra, four string quartets, and a ballet suite *La Mer grecque* (1948).

● **skanda** ► (Kumara *or* Karttikeya) In Hindu mythology, a battle god. In one account he is the son of ▷Shiva, born to defend the gods against the demons. He is represented with 6 heads and 12 arms and rides on a peacock.

● **Skanderbeg** ► (George Kastrioti; c. 1404–68) Albanian national hero. Brought up in Islam as a hostage of the Turkish sultan, Skanderbeg led (1444–68) the Albanian resistance movement against Turkey. The use of guerrilla tactics aided by Albania's mountainous topography and a series of alliances with the great powers of Europe ensured his success but after his death the movement collapsed.

● **Skåne** ► (or Scania) A peninsular area in S Sweden, on the Baltic Sea and the Sound. It is known as the "granary of Sweden," its fertile plains producing wheat, rye, barley, oats, potatoes, and sugar beet. Area: 10 957 sq km (4230 sq mi).

● **Skara Brae** ► A late Neolithic village in Scotland, in Mainland, Orkney, dating to about 2000 BC. The houses were built of dry stone with stone slabs for furniture, all very well preserved. An artificial mound of refuse was heaped over the entire settlement, probably as protection against the weather.

● **skate** ► A large ▷ray fish belonging to the family *Rajidae* (over 100 species), especially the genus *Raja*. 50–200 cm long, skates have a diamond-shaped flattened body with spiny or thorny structures on the upper surface and often an extremely long snout. They lay eggs and some have weak ▷electric organs on the tail.

● **skateboarding** ► The recreation and competitive sport of riding on a board about 70 cm (2.3 ft) long to which two pairs of roller-skate wheels are attached. The sport began in about 1960 in California and combines surfing, skiing, and roller-skating techniques. Speeds of up to 107 km per hour (66 mph) have been attained. The first world championships were staged in 1966.

● **Skegness** ► 53 10N 0 21E A resort in E England, on the Lincolnshire coast, one of the nearest to the industrial centres of the Midlands. Light engineering is also important. Population (1991): 15 149.

● **skeleton** ► The rigid supporting framework of an animal's body. In such animals as arthropods it lies outside the body (exoskeleton) and must be shed periodically during growth. Vertebrates, including humans, have a skeleton (endoskeleton) of ▷bones and cartilage that is entirely within the body and grows with age. The human skeleton is made up of over 200 bones, which are connected to each other at ▷joints and held together by ligaments. The skeleton protects and supports the soft tissues of the body and provides a firm surface for the attachment of muscles and a system of levers that are essential for movement. ▷See Plate II.

● **Skelmersdale** ► 53 33N 2 48W A town in NW England, in S Lancashire. Designated for development as a new town in 1961 to relieve overcrowding in Merseyside, industries include engineering. Population (1991): 42 104.

● **Skelton, John** ► (c. 1460–1529) English poet. He was court poet to Henry VII and tutor to the future Henry VIII. His poems include *Speke Parot* (1521), *Colin Clout* (1522), and other satires, several of them attacks on Cardinal ▷Wolsey. Essentially medieval in form and theme, the most interesting of his poems are often written in short rhyming lines of doggerel verse, known as Skeltonics.

● **Skiddaw** ► 54 40N 3 08W A mountain in NW England, in Cumbria, in the Lake District. Height: 931 m (3054 ft).

● **skiing** ► A means of locomotion, a recreation, and a sport consisting of sliding over snow on a pair of specially shaped runners (skis) attached to the feet. Skis have been used in Scandinavia since the Stone Age, but skiing for pleasure did not develop until the late 19th century. It is divided into **Alpine** (*or* downhill) **skiing**, which includes the events of "downhill" (straightforward racing), slalom (a winding course through "gates"), and giant slalom (faster and less winding than slalom) and **Nordic skiing**, comprising cross-country (or *langlauf*) skiing, which involves self-propulsion and requires lighter equipment than Alpine skiing, and ski-jumping. Alpine and Nordic competitions are controlled by the International Ski Federation. There is also freestyle skiing (downhill skiing that is both balletic and gymnastic), skijoring (being towed on skis by a horse or vehicle), and ski-flying, which is ▷hang-gliding on skis. Recreational skiing has become a vast holiday industry, the most notable skiing areas of the world being the Alps and the Rockies.

● **Skikda** ▶ (former name: Philippeville) 36 58N 6 51E A port in NE Algeria, on the Mediterranean Sea. Occupying the site of the Roman port of Rusicade, it has the remains of a Roman theatre. It receives natural gas from the Sahara and exports iron ore. Population (latest est): 128 747.

● **skimmer** ▶ A black-and-white bird belonging to a family (*Rhynchopidae*; 3 species) occurring chiefly around western Atlantic coasts and African and Asian rivers. The skimmer fishes by flying close to the water, shearing the surface with the lower mandible and snapping the bill shut as soon as a fish is caught. ▷*See Plate III.*

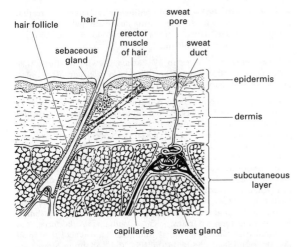

skin ▶ A vertical section through the human skin shows its microscopical structure. The subcutaneous layer of fat cells provides insulation.

● **skin** ▶ The tissue that covers the body. The outer layer (epidermis) consists of several layers of cells: the outermost layer contains dead cells made of keratin, which are constantly sloughed off and replaced by the deeper layers of continuously dividing cells. The inner layer of skin (dermis) contains ▷connective tissue with blood vessels, sensory nerve endings, ▷sweat glands, sebaceous glands (which secrete an oily substance, sebum, that protects the skin surface), and ▷hair follicles. The skin has several important functions. It protects the body from external injury and desiccation; it assists in regulating body temperature (e.g. by sweating); and it is sensitive to touch, temperature, and pain. The branch of medicine concerned with the diagnosis and treatment of skin disorders is called **dermatology**. Skin grafting is one of the most important and successful ▷transplantation operations.

● **skink** ▶ A lizard belonging to the family *Scincidae* (600 species), occurring throughout the tropics and in temperate North America. Skinks are well adapted for burrowing: up to 50 cm long, they have cylindrical streamlined bodies with smooth scales, internal eardrums, a transparent covering over the eye, and often reduced limbs. Many skinks have an elongated tail and move with sideways undulations of the body. They feed on insects or plant material and many bear live young. ⌐reptile.

● **Skinner, Burrhus Frederic** ▶ (1904–90) US psychologist and advocate of ▷behaviourism. Many of Skinner's experiments involved teaching animals (such as rats and pigeons) by reinforcing the desired action, when achieved, with rewards of food. He developed equipment, including the Skinner box, in order to standardize the teaching of simple actions to small animals and applied his principles to human educational aids. His novel *Walden Two* (1948) describes a utopian society based on his behaviourist principles. His other works include *The Behaviour of Organisms* (1938), *Science and Human Behaviour* (1953), and *Beyond Freedom and Dignity* (1971).

● **skipjack** ▶ A ▷tuna fish, *Euthynnus pelamis*, also called ocean bonito, found in all warm seas. It has four to seven dark horizontal stripes along its belly and grows to about 70 cm long.

● **skipper** ▶ A butterfly belonging to the widely distributed family *Hesperiidae* (about 3000 species). The adults are small and have a stout body and head resembling a moth and a swift darting flight. The caterpillars feed on plants and pupate in cocoons made of silk and leaves.

● **Skipton** ▶ 53 58N 2 01W A market town in N England, in North Yorkshire. It is also a tourist centre, with a castle (dating from the 11th century), and has a textile industry. Population (1991): 13 583.

● **Skopje** ▶ (Turkish name: Usküb) 42 00N 21 28E The capital of the Former Yugoslav Republic of Macedonia, on the River Vardar. It became the capital of Serbia in the 14th century and was occupied by the Turks (1392). It was burned down in 1689 to stop a cholera epidemic and almost completely destroyed by an earthquake in 1963. It has a university (1949) and varied industries, including cement, brick, glass, and steel. Population (1994): 541 280.

● **skua** ▶ A large hook-billed seabird belonging to a family (*Stercorariidae*; 4 species), also called jaeger, breeding in Arctic and Antarctic regions and wintering in warmer latitudes. 52–58 cm long, skuas are strong fliers and have a dark plumage with two long central tail feathers. They scavenge around seabird colonies, feeding on eggs, chicks, and food scraps. Order: *Charadriiformes* (gulls, plovers, etc.).

● **skull** ▶ The skeleton of the head, made up of 22 bones of varying shapes and sizes. The cranium consists of eight flat platelike bones that surround and protect the brain. Some of these contribute to the formation of the facial skeleton. The remaining 14 bones, including the mandible (*see* jaw), form the face: the mandible is the only movable bone in the skull; the rest are connected by immovable joints called sutures. Numerous holes puncture the skull to allow blood vessels and nerves to pass to and from the brain. The largest of these is the foramen magnum at the base of the skull, through which the spinal cord passes. ▷*See* Plate II.

● **skunk** ▶ A black and white carnivorous mammal of the family ▷*Mustelidae* known for ejecting a foul-smelling fluid as a defence. The nine species are found in the Americas. The North American striped skunk (*Mephitis mephitis*) inhabits woodland, feeding at night on insects, mice, and fruit.

● **sky** ▶ (blueness of) ▷*See* Tyndall, John.

● **skydiving** ▶ (*or* freefalling) The sport of jumping from an aeroplane with a parachute and performing manoeuvres before opening it. During this period of "free fall" the parachutist glides or performs rolls, turns, or other stunts. In a team event divers pass a baton to each other or form a star pattern by joining hands. ▷*See also* parachuting.

● **Skye** ▶ The largest and most northerly island of the Inner Hebrides group, off the W coast of Scotland. It is chiefly mountainous, with the Cuillin Hills in the S rising to 1009 m (3310 ft). The island's economy is based chiefly on crofting and tourism; sheep and cattle are also raised. A toll bridge linking Skye with the mainland was opened in 1996. Area: 1735 sq km (670 sq mi). Population (1994 est): 8139. Chief town: Portree.

● **Skye terrier** ▶ A breed of dog originating on the island of Skye and used to flush foxes and badgers from cover. It has a long body, short legs, and a large head. The soft undercoat is covered by a long outer coat which may reach the ground. Colours are grey, fawn, cream, or black. Height: 25 cm.

● **Skylab** ▶ A US manned space station launched into earth orbit in May, 1973. Three groups of three US astronauts were conveyed to and from the orbiting laboratory by modified Apollo spacecraft (*see* Apollo moon programme). They remained on board for 513 man days during May, 1973, to February, 1974, conducting experiments and observations. Skylab eventually crash-landed in July, 1979, in the Indian Ocean.

● **skylark** ▶ A ▷lark, *Alauda arvensis*, occurring in Eurasia and N

Africa and noted for its sustained warbling flight song. It is about 17 cm long, with brown plumage, a small crest and a white stripe above the eye. Skylarks were a delicacy in the 19th century and are still trapped in parts of Europe.

● **Skyros** ▶ (Modern Greek name: Skíros) A Greek island in the central Aegean Sea, the largest of the Northern Sporades. Area: 205 sq km (79 sq mi). Population (latest est): 2757.

● **skyscraper** ▶ A building with many floors built in cities in which the cost of land is high. The first skyscraper, the Equitable Life Assurance Society, was built in New York in 1868. Architecturally it was made possible by the development of high-speed lifts in the 1850s and the introduction of a metal frame in Chicago in the 1880s. The Empire State Building (1930–32) in New York was the tallest in the world until the completion in the 1970s, in the same city, of the ▷World Trade Center. The world's tallest skyscraper (450 m; 1476 ft) is currently Petronas Towers (1996) in Kuala Lumpur, Malaysia. However, it will soon be eclipsed by two buildings now under construction, a 120-storey office block in Melbourne, Australia (564 m; 1850 ft), and the Centre of India Tower in Karonda, India (677 m; 2222 ft).

● **Slade, Felix** ▶ (1790–1868) British art collector, who bequeathed his collection to the British Museum. He also endowed professorships of art at the Universities of Oxford and Cambridge and at University College, London. The Slade School of Fine Art is named after him.

● **slander** ▷*See* defamation.

● **slang** ▶ Words, senses, or idioms, mostly confined to the spoken language, that do not form part of the standard written language, (although they are found in most up-to-date dictionaries). In English, slang may be either widely used and understood colloquial and taboo words or the clandestine jargon of a particular group. *Bonkers* (mad) and *bonking* (having sexual intercourse) are examples of the first group, while *smack* (drug users' name for heroin) and *filth* (criminals' name for the police) are examples of the second.

Cockneys (working-class Londoners, traditionally defined as those born within the sound of Bow bells—the church bells of St Mary-le-Bow in Cheapside) have developed two kinds of slang, probably originally as underworld codes unintelligible to outsiders. **Rhyming slang**, which developed in the late 18th century, replaces a key word with another word or phrase that rhymes with it. *Half-inch* (pinch, i.e. steal), *apples and pears* (stairs), and *butcher's hook* (look) are common examples. Rhyming slang is made more obscure to outsiders when the rhyming word itself is omitted, as in the phrase *let's have a butcher's* meaning "let's have a look." **Back slang** is another variety of clandestine slang that probably originated in London's underworld. In this form of slang words are pronounced backwards: "evig eth dlo reggub eth elats elos" might be a message from one fishmonger to another, which the unfortunate customer would not understand. Back slang

is often a skill that the young agile minds of schoolchildren can quickly master.

Although it is sometimes deprecated, slang of all kinds adds exuberance and variety to a language.

● **Slánský, Rudolf** ▶ (1901–52) Czechoslovak statesman, secretary general of the Communist Party in Czechoslovakia's postwar government. He and nine other Jews were executed for espionage. He was posthumously absolved in 1963.

● **slate** ▶ A fine-grained rock produced by the low-grade metamorphism of mudstone, siltstone, or other argillaceous sediments. Its perfect cleavage is due to the parallel alignment of platy crystals of mica and chlorite. Slate is used as a constructional material, formerly for roofs.

● **slave-making ant** ▶ An ▷ant, confined to the N hemisphere, that raids colonies of other ants to capture larvae and pupae, which develop into worker "slaves." Genera: *Harpagoxenus, Formica, Polyergus, Anergates*. ▷*See also* Amazon ant.

● **Slave River** ▶ A river in W Canada, flowing N from Lake Athabasca (Alberta) to Great Slave Lake (Mackenzie); part of the ▷Mackenzie River system. Length: 415 km (258 mi).

● **slavery** ▶ The condition in which human beings are owned by others as chattels. Slavery existed from earliest times. In ancient Greece and early Rome captives from conquered lands were the chief source of slaves, who often had special skills, were well treated, and might be freed (manumission). In later Roman times conditions worsened until the deteriorating economy led to the virtual disappearance of slaves and the emergence of ▷serfs in the middle ages. Slaving became a lucrative business in the 16th century, with European traders transporting Africans to the Americas. By the early 19th century over 9 million slaves had been transported to work the plantations of the southern states of the USA and the Caribbean islands. By this time humanitarians, such as William ▷Wilberforce, had begun to attack slavery on moral grounds and it was abolished in all British territories by 1834. In the USA, the ▷Abolition Movement campaigned against slavery in the South and the issue became one of the causes of the Civil War. In 1863 Abraham Lincoln issued the ▷Emancipation Proclamation, officially liberating all slaves. This was not, however, the end of slavery. In World War II the Germans used Jews, Russians, and others as slave labour, often in worse conditions than those of African slaves. Moreover, the UN estimates that there are still some 200 million slaves (defined as persons who cannot voluntarily withdraw their labour) in Asia, Africa, and South America, where child slavery and bonded labour (workers who bind themselves to an employer to whom they are in debt) are still widespread.

● **Slavonic languages** ▶ A subgroup of the ▷Indo-European lan-

skyscraper ▶ A view of the skyscrapers of Manhattan, dominated by the World Trade Center before its destruction by terrorists on ▷September 11, 2001.

guage family, native to E Europe and NW Asia. There are three groups: South Slavonic (including ▷Serbo-Croat, Slovene, ▷Bulgarian, and Macedonian); West Slavonic (including Czech, ▷Slovak, Sorbian, and Polish); and East Slavonic (Russian, Belarussian, and Ukrainian). This division is not, however, as clearcut as the geographical classification suggests. All the dialects are linked historically and all developed from a common ancestor, Proto-Slavonic. Most Slavs speak Russian, many learning it as a second language.

● **Slavs** ▶ Peoples of E Europe and parts of W Asia. There are three groups: Eastern Slavs (including Russians, Ukrainians, and Belarussians); Western Slavs (including Poles, Czechs, and Slovaks); and Southern Slavs (including Serbs, Croats, Slovenes, Macedonians, and Bulgarians). Migrating from Asia, they moved westward during the second or third millennium BC, the present Slav nations emerging around the 5th and 6th centuries AD. ▷See also Slavonic languages.

● **sleep** ▶ A naturally occurring state of unconsciousness. Sleep occurs in various stages, which vary in depth and can be recognized by characteristic patterns on an EEG (see electroencephalography). The electrical activity of the brain continues but is more rhythmical than when awake and reacts less to outside stimuli. Drowsiness, distinguished by short irregular EEG waves, is followed by deeper sleep, when the waves become slower and larger. This slow-wave sleep is periodically interrupted by **REM sleep** (rapid-eye-movement *or* paradoxical sleep), in which the eyes move rapidly and the brain is more active, but the muscles are especially relaxed. REM sleep is marked by an EEG pattern similar to that when awake and is associated with ▷dreams. Cycles of slow-wave and REM sleep alternate throughout the sleeping period. Between 3 and 10 hours of sleep per day is biologically necessary for physical and mental health. Insomnia can be caused by changes of routine, ▷anxiety, ▷depression, and by many drugs. Disorders of sleep include ▷sleepwalking and ▷nightmares.

● **sleeping pills** ▷See hypnotics.

● **sleeping sickness** ▶ A disease caused by infection with a protozoan of the genus *Trypanosoma*, which is transmitted by the tsetse fly and occurs only in East, central, and West Africa: it is the African form of ▷trypanosomiasis. Initial symptoms are swelling of the lymph nodes and fever, which persists for several months. The brain is then infected, causing lethargy, weakness, and depression: without treatment the patient dies. The drugs pentamidine and suramin can be used to treat the early stages of the disease; arsenic-based compounds are needed when the brain is affected. Attempts to prevent the disease by eradicating the fly have not yet proved successful.

● **sleepwalking** ▶ (*or* somnambulism) A disorder of ▷sleep in which the sleeper walks about and performs complex activities automatically and without regaining consciousness. It is quite common in children and not a sign of illness. In adults it can indicate immaturity or ▷neurosis.

● **sleepy sickness** ▶ A highly infectious viral disease of the brain. Known medically as ▷encephalitis lethargica, it is marked by drowsiness leading eventually to coma. A worldwide epidemic of the disease occurred between 1917 and 1924.

● **slide rule** ▶ A mathematical instrument for performing multiplication and division, invented by the English mathematician William Oughtred (1575–1660) in 1622. It consists of a rule that slides along a groove in another rule. Both rules are marked with logarithmic scales so that products and quotients can be calculated by effectively adding and subtracting ▷logarithms in the form of lengths of rule. Slide rules have now been replaced by pocket ▷calculators.

● **Sligo** ▶ (Irish name: Contae Shligigh) A county in the NW Republic of Ireland, in Connacht bordering on the Atlantic Ocean. Chiefly hilly, much of the land is devoted to pasture; cattle rearing and dairy farming are important. It possesses some coal, lead, and copper. The county has many associations with the poetry of W. B. Yeats. Area: 1795 sq km (693 sq mi). Population (1996 est): 56 000. County town: Sligo.

● **Slim, William Joseph, 1st Viscount** ▶ (1891–1970) British field marshal. He joined the army at the outbreak of World War I and subsequently served in the Indian Army. In World War II he became com-

mander of the 14th Army (the "forgotten army") in Burma (1943). After successful operations against the Japanese he became commander in chief of Allied land forces in SE Asia. In 1948 he became chief of the imperial general staff and was then governor general of Australia (1953–60).

● **slime moulds** ▶ Organisms traditionally regarded as fungi (since they produce fruiting bodies) but having affinities with the protozoa; they are now usually classified in the kingdom ▷Protoctista. The so-called true (*or* plasmodial) slime moulds (*Myxomycota*) are found beneath logs and in other damp places. They consist of slimy sheets of protoplasm that engulf bacteria, wood particles, etc. The cellular slime moulds (*Acrasiomycota*) are single-celled amoeba-like organisms found in soil. The parasitic slime moulds (*Plasmodiophora*) live in the tissues of plants; the species *Plasmodiophora brassicae* causes ▷clubroot in cabbages.

● **slipper orchid** ▶ A terrestrial ▷orchid of the tropical Asian genus *Paphiopedilum* (about 50 species) and the related genera *Cypripedium* and *Phragmipedium*. They are characterized by their flowers, which have a pouched slipper-shaped lip and are usually borne singly or in clusters of two or three. *Paphiopedilum* flowers are usually a mixture of white, brown, and green, often with darker markings; the leaves may also be mottled or otherwise marked. Slipper orchids are popular greenhouse ornamentals.

● **slippery elm** ▶ Either of two North American trees, *Fremontodendron californica* (family *Bombacaceae*) or *Ulmus fulva* (family *Ulmaceae*). Mucilage extracted from the bark has been used in poultices and to treat diarrhoea, dysentery, and other conditions.

● **Sliven** ▶ 42 40N 26 19E A town in E central Bulgaria. Its main industry is textiles, the first mill in Bulgaria having been opened here in 1834. Population (1992 est): 114 596.

● **Sloane, Sir Hans** ▶ (1660–1753) British physician and naturalist, whose collection of books, manuscripts, pictures, etc., formed the nucleus of the ▷British Museum. A keen botanist, Sloane collected over 800 new plants while in Jamaica. He succeeded Newton as president of the Royal Society (1727–41).

● **sloe** ▷See blackthorn.

● **sloop** ▶ A sailing vessel with a single mast set approximately one-third of the boat's length from the bows. Formerly used extensively in coastal fishing, sloops are now a favoured rig for yacht racing, since they are the most efficient design for sailing towards the wind. Older sloops were gaff-rigged; more modern vessels are marconi-rigged or Bermuda-rigged. Sloops more than 20 m (60 ft) long are rare because of the number of crew required to handle the large sails. ▷See also ketch; yawl.

● **sloth** ▶ A primitive arboreal ▷mammal belonging to the family *Bradypodidae* (7 species) of Central and South America, also called ai or unau. 50–65 cm long sloths are slow-moving and hang upside down from branches, feeding on leaves and fruit. Their greyish-brown fur lies so that rain runs off easily and is often greenish from algae living there, which helps to camouflage them. They cannot walk on the ground. Order: *Edentata*.

● **sloth bear** ▶ A shaggy black ▷bear, *Melursus ursinus*, of S India and Sri Lanka. 1.5 m long and weighing about 100 kg, it feeds on bees or termites by tearing open nests with its long claws and sucking up the insects using its long snout.

● **Slough** ▶ 1. 51 31N 0 36W A town in SE England, in Slough unitary authority, Berkshire. It grew rapidly after a large trading and industrial estate was built here in the 1920s and has a great variety of light industries, including the manufacture of confectionary, food products, and paints. Since the 1980s Slough has been a centre for high-tech industries, including computer software, telecommunications, and biotechnology. Population (1998 est): 108 000. 2. A unitary authority in SE England, in Berkshire. Area: 28 sq km (11 sq mi). Population (1996 est): 110 500.

● **Slovak** ▶ A Western Slavonic language, closely related to ▷Czech. It is spoken mainly in Slovakia, where it is the official language, and is written in the Latin alphabet. There are three distinct dialects.

● **Slovakia, Republic of** ▶ A republic in central Europe. Lying mainly within the Carpathian Mountains, it descends SW to the plains of the Danube Valley.

Economy: chiefly agricultural, producing cereals, wine, fruit, and tobacco. Mineral resources include coal, iron ore, and antimony, and there is heavy industry in most of the larger towns and cities. Reform of the state-subsidized and centrally planned economic system was slower than in most of E Europe, but has now gathered pace. Having experienced considerable economic difficulties for most of the 1990s, the country is now becoming relatively prosperous.

History: settled by Slavic Slovaks (6th–7th centuries AD), the region was incorporated into Great ▷Moravia in the 9th century and conquered by the Magyars in the 10th century. Despite rising nationalism in the 18th and 19th centuries, Slovakia remained part of the Austro-Hungarian empire until 1918, when it became a province of the new republic of ▷Czechoslovakia. It became nominally independent under the Nazis immediately before and during World War II. Czechoslovakia was under communist control from 1948 until 1990. In the 1990s growing demands for independence led to the dissolution of Czechoslovakia, and on 1 January, 1993, Slovakia became an independent republic with the nationalist leader Vladimir Meciar (1942–) as prime minister. The 1990s saw Meciar's government adopting increasingly authoritarian policies, including attempts to control the media and judiciary. This resulted in conflict with the liberal president Michael Kovac. In 1997 Slovakia was refused EU membership owing to concerns about government corruption and human-rights abuses (including the treatment of the Hungarian and Gipsy minorities). Meciar's government was unexpectedly ousted in the 1998 elections and a coalition was formed under Mikulas Dzurinda, who promised major reforms. In 1999 presidential elections Meciar was defeated by the reformist Rudolf Schuster.

Republic of Slovakia

Head of state	Rudolf Schuster
Official language	Slovak
Official currency	koruna of 100 halérů
Area	49 039 sq km (18 934 sq mi)
Population (1999 est)	5 398 000
Capital	Bratislava

● **Slovenia, Republic of** ▶ (Serbo-Croat name: Slovenija) A republic in S central Europe. It is mountainous and drained mainly by the Rivers Sava and Drava.

Economy: agriculture includes livestock raising; potatoes, cereals, and vegetables are grown. The republic has deposits of coal, mercury, and zinc. Manufacturing has expanded and diversified, with metal goods, electronics, and textiles among the main products. There has been rapid privatization since 1992 and Slovenia now has one of the most successful of the ex-communist economies. Tourism was badly affected by the Balkan conflicts of the earlier 1990s but is now recovering.

History: the region was chiefly under Habsburg rule from the 14th century until 1918, when it was incorporated into the kingdom of Serbs, Croats, and Slovenes, later renamed Yugoslavia. It was divided between Germany, Italy, and Hungary in World War II but reincorporated into Yugoslavia (now under communism) in 1945. Nationalist feeling grew from the late 1980s and in 1991 Slovenia declared itself a sovereign state. A brief war between armed nationalists and the Serb-dominated Yugoslav army ended with the latter's withdrawal in July. Slovenia was recognized internationally as an independent state in 1992. The Liberal Democracy Party of Janez Drnovšek won election victories in 1996 and 2000.

Republic of Slovenia

Head of state	President Milan Kučan
Official language	Slovenian (Hungarian and Italian are also official languages in some regions)
Official currency	tolar of 100 stotin
Area	20 251 sq km (7819 sq mi)
Population (1999 est)	1 997 000
Capital	Ljubljana

● **slowworm** ▶ A legless lizard, *Anguis fragilis*, also called blindworm, occurring in heaths and open woodlands of Europe. It is about 30 cm long, usually brown, grey, or reddish, and feeds on snails, slugs, and other soft-bodied invertebrates. Family: *Anguidae* (glass snakes and slowworms).

● **slug** ▶ A ▷gastropod mollusc of the order *Stylommatophora*, widely distributed in moist terrestrial habitats. Slugs have slimy soft bodies with the shell vestigial or absent. They may reach 20 cm in length, and range in colour from yellow to black. Some are carnivorous or scavenging; others feed on plant tissues. Subclass: *Pulmonata. Compare* sea slug.

● **slump** ▷*See* depression.

● **Sluter, Claus** ▶ (c. 1345–1406) Dutch sculptor. Working in Dijon under the patronage of Philip the Bold, Duke of Burgundy, he produced his most famous works for the ducal mausoleum in the monastery of Champmol. These included the portal sculptures, the *Well of Moses*, and figures on the duke's tomb. Breaking away from the ▷international gothic style, Sluter developed a bold realism, which influenced many European sculptors and painters of the 15th century.

● **Sluys, Battle of** ▶ (24 June, 1340) A naval battle in the ▷Hundred Years' War, off the coast of Flanders, in which the French fleet was destroyed by the skilful use of archers by ▷Edward III's army. The victory gave the English crucial strategic control over the Channel.

● **smallage** ▷*See* celery.

● **small arms** ▶ Short-range ▷firearms, originally defined as capable of being handled by one individual: they included pistols, submachine guns, rifles, grenades, and shotguns. An artificial calibre ceiling of .60 in, or 20 mm, was abandoned with the introduction of small rocket antitank guided missiles.

● **smallpox** ▶ A highly infectious virus disease marked by a skin rash that leaves permanent pitted scars. Smallpox is transmitted by direct contact; secondary infection with staphylococci is often fatal. In 1967 the disease caused two million deaths. After a worldwide vaccination programme sponsored by the World Health Organization smallpox was declared to have been eradicated in 1979.

● **Smart, Christopher** ▶ (1722–71) British poet. He worked as a hack writer and received little recognition for his poetry in his lifetime. He suffered from religious obsessions and while confined to an asylum wrote *Rejoice in the Lamb* (or *Jubilate Agno*; published 1939). His *A Song to David* (1763) is now regarded as one of the best long poems of the 18th century.

● **smartcard** ▶ A plastic card containing a microchip that stores and updates information. Smartcard readers can read the data on the card and transmit signals back to the card to adjust the data. Smartcards can be used to make and record financial transactions, to store a person's medical records, etc.

● **smart materials** ▶ Structural materials that respond to their environment, compensating for unusual or dangerous stresses. In high buildings and bridges, for example, engineers are exploring the use of optical fibres to monitor exceptional stresses, using a computer-controlled compensating response to reduce vibrations, dampen oscillations, etc. Concrete structures with the capability of "self-healing" are also being investigated; these materials contain small reservoirs of strong adhesive material that break open under stress, repairing cracks as they appear.

● **smell, sense of** ▷*See* nose.

● **smelt** ▶ A slender food fish of the genus *Osmerus* and family *Osmeridae*, occurring in coastal and estuarine waters of Europe and North America. It migrates to fresh water to spawn. The European smelt (*O. eperlanus*), up to 30 cm long, is greenish above and silvery below. Order: *Salmoniformes*.

● **smelting** ▶ The extraction of a metal from its ore by heating. The method used depends on the metal, the type of ore, and the melting points of both. The smelting takes place either in a ▷blast furnace (e.g. to extract iron) or a ▷reverberatory furnace (e.g. to extract copper).

● **Smetana, Bedřich** ► (1824–84) Bohemian composer. He studied in Prague. In 1859 he left Sweden (where he had been conducting) and returned to Prague, joining a group of composers who established a national opera. *The Brandenburgers in Bohemia* (1862–63) and *The Bartered Bride* (1863–66) were composed for it. In 1874 he became deaf but continued to compose, writing the four symphonic poems *Má Vlast* (1874–79) and a string quartet "From My Life" (1876). He died insane.

● **smew** ► A sawbilled ▷duck, *Mergus albellus*, that breeds in N Eurasia and winters south in the Mediterranean. It is 40–44 cm long, has a short bill, and feeds on fish and crustaceans. Drakes are white with black markings; females are grey with a chestnut head and white throat and cheeks.

● **Smilax** ► A genus of shrubs and vines (about 300 species), also called catbriers, native to warm temperate and tropical regions. Many have prickly stems and the white or yellowish-green flowers produce red or bluish-black berries. Family: *Smilacaceae*. ▷See also sarsaparilla.

● **Smiles, Samuel** ► (1812–1904) British writer. He worked as a journalist and a railway administrator. His best-known work is the didactic *Self-Help* (1859). He also wrote biographies of Josiah Wedgwood and George Stephenson.

● **Smirke, Sir Robert** ► (1780–1867) British architect. His works in the Greek revival style included the Covent Garden Theatre (1808; destroyed 1850) and the ▷British Museum (1847). He was articled to Sir John ▷Soane and in 1813 joined him and ▷Nash as architects to the Board of Works.

● **Smith, Adam** ► (1723–90) Scottish moral philosopher and political economist. At Glasgow University (1751–63), he lectured and wrote on moral philosophy. In 1776, he published *An Enquiry into the Nature and Causes of the Wealth of Nations*, an attack on ▷mercantilism that became the bible of the free-trade movement. He held that employment, trade, production, and distribution are part of a nation's wealth. An individual promoting his own interests freely within the law often promotes the interests of society as a whole.

● **Smith, Bessie** ► (1894–1937) US Black jazz singer and songwriter, known as "Empress of the Blues," who began her career in travelling shows. In the 1920s she made records with Louis Armstrong and Fletcher Henderson (1898–1952). Her popularity declined in the 1930s. She died in a car crash.

● **Smith, F. E.** ▷See Birkenhead, F. E. Smith, 1st Earl of.

● **Smith, Harvey** ► (1938–) British showjumper, who represented Britain in the Olympic Games in 1968 and 1972 and won numerous British championships, including the British Grand Prix five times. He became a professional in 1972.

● **Smith, Ian (Douglas)** ► (1919–) Prime minister (1964–79) of Rhodesia (now ▷Zimbabwe). An advocate of White supremacy, he demanded full independence for Southern Rhodesia in 1964 but opposed Britain's stipulation that Black majority rule be prepared for. In 1965 he made a unilateral declaration of independence (UDI), which he maintained in spite of UN and UK sanctions until 1976, when he agreed to the principle of Black majority rule. He was a minister in the transitional government of Bishop Muzorewa (1979–80) and remained a member of the House of Assembly until 1988.

● **Smith, John** ► (c. 1580–1631) English colonist. In 1606, he invested in the new Virginia Company, which was granted a charter to settle in North America. On arrival at what became Jamestown, Virginia, he explored and charted the region. In 1607 he was saved from death at the hands of Indians by ▷Pocahontas. He returned to England in 1609 and wrote valuable accounts of his experiences.

● **Smith, John** ► (1938–94) British politician; leader of the Labour Party (1992–94). A barrister, he entered parliament in 1970, becoming shadow chancellor (1987–92). He died of a heart attack and was succeeded by Tony ▷Blair.

● **Smith, Joseph** ► (1805–44) US founder of the ▷Mormons. Smith announced in 1827 his discovery of the sacred *Book of Mormon*, which he claimed he had translated from two gold tablets written by a prophet named Mormon. His new church, founded in Fayette, New York (1830), grew rapidly but attracted opposition because of its doctrines. Smith encouraged westward migration and the group established itself in Nauvoo, Illinois (1840). While in jail on charges of conspiracy, Smith was killed by an angry mob. The Mormons continued westward to Utah under Brigham ▷Young.

● **Smith, Sir Keith Macpherson** ► (1890–1955) Australian aviator, who with his brother **Sir Ross Macpherson Smith** (1892–1922) made the first flight from England to Australia (1919). It took 28 days. The brothers were subsequently knighted and awarded a prize of £10,000.

Maggie Smith ► Photographed in 1994 in academic dress, prior to receiving her honorary Doctorate of Letters at Cambridge University.

● **Smith, Dame Maggie** ► (1934–) British actress. A performer with a talent for comedy, she appeared with Kenneth Williams in the revue *Share my Lettuce* (1957) and subsequently played in many productions of both modern and classical plays, including *Virginia* (1981) in which she appeared alone as Virginia Woolf. Her many films include *The VIPs* (1963), *The Honey Pot* (1967), *The Prime of Miss Jean Brodie* (1969), *A Room with a View* (1986), *The Secret Garden* (1993), and *Tea with Mussolini* (1999).

● **Smith, Michael** ► (1932–) Canadian biochemist. Smith demonstrated a method of introducing specific mutations into genes, a technique known as site-specific mutagenesis. This technique enables the function of a particular protein or gene to be established by observing the effects of the mutation. He was awarded the Nobel Prize in 1993.

● **Smith, Stevie** ► (Florence Margaret S.; 1902–71) British poet. She published highly original and deceptively simple poetry, the characteristic tone of which was a blend of tenderness, toughness, and humour. The best known of her idiosyncratic novels is *Novel on Yellow Paper* (1936). Her *Collected Poems* (1975) were published posthumously, and she was the subject of a play (1977) and a film (1978).

● **Smithfield** ► A district in the Greater London borough of Islington. It is noted for Smithfield Market, which handles meat and poultry. Originally a "smooth field" just outside the City walls, it became a horse market in the middle ages. Bartholomew Fair (originally a cloth fair) received a royal charter to be held here in 1133. By the 17th century the entertainments provided were more important than the cloth and in 1855 it was closed for its debauchery and rowdiness. It was replaced by the meat market in 1866.

● **Smithson** ► Two British architects in partnership. **Peter Smithson** (1923–) and his wife **Alison Smithson** (1928–93) were among the first in the UK to absorb the ▷international style of architecture. The ▷brutalism of their first major work, a school at Hunstanton, Norfolk (1954), caused considerable controversy, but their later designs, notably the *Economist* offices in London (1962–64), have been admired.

• **Smithsonian Institution** ▸ A research institution in Washington, DC. The Institution was founded in 1846 with a bequest from the Englishman James Smithson (1765–1829) as "an establishment for the increase and diffusion of knowledge." It has carried out important scientific work and explorations throughout the world, and administers several museums, including the National Air and Space Museum and the National Collection of Fine Arts.

• **smog** ▸ A fog containing a high proportion of smoke (its name is abbreviated from smoke fog) occurring chiefly in urban and industrial areas. Occasionally it may be particularly dense, as in London in 1952 when smog resulted in many deaths. Since the Clean Air Act (1956) in the UK, which introduced smokeless zones in towns and cities and controlled the gases emitted by industries, smogs have been virtually eliminated. However, photochemical smog, produced by the action of ultraviolet light from the sun on nitrous oxides and hydrocarbons from car exhausts, can be a problem in urban areas. In 1989 smog in Mexico City was declared to have reached irreversible levels, largely as a result of the burning of low-quality petrol.

• **smoke tree** ▸ (or smoke bush) One of several species of trees and shrubs having a whitish cloudy appearance at some stage of the season. The American smoke tree (*Cotinus obovatus*) grows to a height of 9 m and has a smokelike mass of whitish flower heads, as does the Australian smoke bush (*Conospermum stoechadis*). *Rhus cotinus* is the common smoke bush native to the Mediterranean and parts of Asia.

• **smoking** ▷*See* cigarette; tobacco.

• **Smolensk** ▸ 54 49N 32 04E A city in W Russia, on the River Dnepr. It has engineering, textile, and consumer-goods industries and several educational institutions.
  History: dating to at least the 9th century, it was sacked by the Tatars (13th century) and was subsequently disputed between Lithuania (and later Poland) and Russia, falling finally to the latter in 1654. It is on the route of Napoleon's retreat from Moscow in 1812 and was damaged in World War II. Population (1995 est): 353 000.

• **Smollett, Tobias (George)** ▸ (1721–71) British novelist. Born and educated in Scotland, he enlisted in the navy and married a Jamaican heiress before settling in London in 1744. His picaresque novels, lively in style and unsophisticated and rambling in structure, include *Roderick Random* (1748), *Peregrine Pickle* (1751), and *Humphry Clinker* (1771). He was also a journalist and translator. He died in Italy.

• **smooth snake** ▸ A widespread Eurasian snake, *Coronella austriaca*, that has smooth glossy scales and is brown or reddish with a pale belly and dark spots along its back and tail. Up to 65 cm long, it favours sandy heathlands and feeds on lizards, small snakes, and rodents. Family: *Colubridae*.

• **smuggling** ▸ The illegal import or export of goods to evade payment of duties or official restrictions. Trading countries often impose bans, limitations, or taxes on certain goods, the evasion of which provides an incentive for smugglers. Smuggling has flourished from the time of the Greek city states until the present day, especially in Britain during the Napoleonic Wars. After World War II smuggling of guns, narcotics, gold, diamonds, and illegal immigrants became rife, particularly through international airlines and remote frontier towns. In recent years one of the primary concerns of world customs authorities, the function of which is to detect and prevent smuggling, has been the breaking of international narcotic smuggling networks.

• **smut** ▸ A disease affecting flowering plants, particularly the cereals and grasses, caused by various basidiomycete fungi of the genus *Ustilago*. Infection is not usually apparent until spore formation, when dark powdery masses of spores are released over the flower head. Stinking smuts, or bunts, are caused by fungi belonging to the related genus *Tilletia*. Both types of smut cause reduced yields of grain and are controlled by spraying crops with fungicide and by treating seed before sowing.

• **Smuts, Jan (Christian)** ▸ (1870–1950) South African statesman and general; prime minister (1919–24, 1939–48). Following a brilliant undergraduate career at Cambridge University he was called to the Bar in London, returning to Cape Town in 1895. He was a commando

Jan Smuts ▸ The prime minister in field marshal's uniform, inspecting a contingent of the Westminster Home Guard in 1942.

leader in the second ▷Boer War (1899–1902) but thereafter worked for reconciliation with Britain. He played an important part in the achievement of responsible government for the Transvaal (1906) and the Union of South Africa (1910), becoming a minister in Louis ▷Botha's government (1910–19). He was a member of Lloyd George's imperial war cabinet in World War I and helped establish the League of Nations. He succeeded Botha as prime minister in 1919 but was defeated in 1924. Out of office until 1933 (when he became deputy prime minister to Hertzog), he had time to elaborate his philosophical concept of holism and to publish *Holism and Evolution* (1926). In 1939 he succeeded Hertzog as prime minister, advocating South Africa's entry into World War II. His desire to maintain South Africa's links with the British Commonwealth made him unpopular among some Afrikaners.

• **Smyrna** ▷*See* Izmir.

• **Smythe, Dame Ethel (Mary)** ▸ (1858–1944) British composer. Having studied in Leipzig, she wrote numerous works, notably such operas as *The Wreckers* (1906). She was imprisoned for her support of the suffragette movement.

• **snail** ▸ A ▷gastropod mollusc with a spirally coiled shell, including terrestrial, freshwater, and marine forms. The common garden snail (*Helix aspersa*) grows to about 3 cm and is active at night, feeding on vegetation and sheltering by day in crevices. In dry weather, a temporary covering is secreted over the shell aperture to prevent desiccation. The giant African land snail (*Achatina fulica*) grows up to 12 cm long.

• **snake** ▸ A legless ▷reptile belonging to the suborder *Serpentes* (about 3000 species), occurring worldwide but especially common in the tropics. Snakes are long and slender: they range from 0.12–10 m in length and grow throughout their lives, periodically shedding the skin in one piece. They feed chiefly on other vertebrates and are adapted to swallowing prey whole, having flexible ligaments and joints allowing the two parts of the lower jaw to move apart during swallowing. Prey may be killed by constriction, by engulfing it alive, or by the injection of a potent neurotoxic or haemorrhagic venom by means of hollow or grooved fangs. The major families are the *Boidae* (pythons, boas, etc.), the *Colubridae* (typical snakes, e.g. the grass snake), the *Elapidae* (cobras, coral snakes, etc.), and the *Viperidae* (vipers, etc.). Order: *Squamata* (lizards and snakes).

• **snakebird** ▷*See* darter.

• **snakefly** ▸ An insect of the family *Raphidiidae* (about 80 species), so called because its small head and long slender thorax ("neck") resemble a snake about to strike. It is found in woodland areas of every continent except Australia and uses chewing mouthparts to feed on small insects. Eggs are laid beneath bark. Order: ▷Neuroptera.

● **snake gourd** ▶ An annual or perennial vine of the genus *Trichosanthes* (about 15 species), especially *T. anguina*, native to tropical SE Asia and Australia. It is widely cultivated for its long tapering green edible fruits, which often exceed 1 m in length. Family: *Cucurbitaceae*.

● **snake-necked turtle** ▶ A freshwater turtle belonging to the family *Chelyidae* (35 species), found in South America, Australia, and New Guinea. They have a long snakelike neck that is extended to catch prey and breathe air at the surface. It cannot be retracted into the shell but is tucked sideways into a fold of shoulder skin. A South American species, the matamata (*Chelys fimbriata*), has a jagged well-camouflaged shell, 30–40 cm long, and a pointed head.

● **Snake River** ▶ A river in the NW USA. Rising in the Yellowstone National Park in Wyoming, it flows W through Idaho to join the Columbia River in Washington State. Length: 1670 km (1038 mi).

● **snakeroot** ▶ Any of various plants the roots of which were formerly reputed to cure snakebites. Snakeroots include the ▷bistort and several North American species, such as the herbs *Cimicifuga racemosa*, *Aristolochia reticulata*, and *Eupatorium urticoefolium*.

● **snapdragon** ▷*See* Antirrhinum.

● **snapper** ▶ A carnivorous shoaling fish of the family *Lutjanidae* (about 250 species), found in tropical seas. It has an elongated body, usually 60–90 cm long, a large mouth, and sharp teeth. Some are valuable food fish, especially the red snapper (*Lutjanus blackford*); others are poisonous.

● **snare drum** ▶ (*or* side drum) A small drum with gut strings (snares) stretched across the lower skin. These make a rattling sound when the drum is played. It is used in the orchestra in the military band, and in popular music.

● **sneeze** ▶ A reflex violent expulsion of air and droplets through the mouth and nose caused by irritation of the lining of the nasal cavity. The irritation may be due to inflammation of the nasal passages, such as occurs with a cold and hay fever. Sneezing is the principal means by which colds and similar infections are spread.

● **Snefru** ▶ King of Egypt (c. 2600 BC); founder of the 4th dynasty traditionally noted for his kindliness, in contrast with his son ▷Khufu. He encouraged shipping to facilitate communications within Egypt and to import materials from abroad. Two pyramids at Dashur are attributed to him.

● **Snell's law** ▶ When a ray of light passes from one medium to another the angle (*r*) between the refracted ray and a line normal to the interface between the media is related to the angle (*i*) of the incident ray, also taken to the normal, by the equation $\sin i / \sin r = n$, where *n* is the relative refractive index of the media (*see* refraction). It is named after the Dutch astronomer Willebrord Snell (1591–1626), who discovered it in 1621. It was not published until 1638, when Descartes announced it without crediting Snell.

● **snipe** ▶ A ▷sandpiper belonging to a subfamily (*Scolopacinae*; 10 species) occurring in wet areas of warm and temperate regions. Snipe have a long flexible bill used to probe for worms, and a barred and striped brown, black, and white plumage. The common snipe (*Gallinago gallinago*) is 30 cm long and a popular gamebird.

● **snooker** ▶ A game, deriving from ▷billiards, that arose among British officers in India (1875). It is played by two players or pairs of players on a billiards table. There are 22 balls: 1 white cue ball, 15 red balls (value 1 point each), and 6 coloured balls—yellow (2 points), green (3), brown (4), blue (5), pink (6), black (7). The object is to pocket a red ball and a coloured ball alternately, each time returning the coloured ball to its prescribed spot on the table. The red balls are not replaced. When all the red balls have been potted the colours are potted in order of numerical value. Championships were instituted in 1916 and the world professional championship in 1927. Television coverage greatly increased the game's popularity in the 1970s and 1980s.

Joe Davis (1901–78) was the supreme player for many years. Leading players of recent years include Steve ▷Davis and Stephen ▷Hendry.

● **snoring** ▶ Noisy breathing occurring during sleep, caused by vibration of the soft palate at the back of the mouth. Snoring generally occurs when sleeping on the back with the mouth open. It is most liable to occur when the nose is blocked (e.g. by a cold) and breathing is through the mouth. Loud snoring may be caused by enlarged tonsils or adenoids or abnormalities of the pharynx that obstruct normal breathing. This can lead to a condition called sleep apnoea, in which the concentration of oxygen in the blood falls, which can lead to heart failure. Corrective surgery to the soft palate or pharynx may be required.

● **snow** ▶ A solid form of precipitation composed of ice crystals or snowflakes. Ice crystals occur when temperatures are well below freezing point; with temperatures nearer to 0°C (32°F) snowflakes develop through the clustering together of crystals. Snow is usually measured with a graduated ruler, which is inserted into the flat surface of undrifted snow. Approximately 0.3 m (1 ft) of snow is equivalent to 25 mm (1 in) of rainfall.

● **Snow, C(harles) P(ercy), Baron** ▶ (1905–80) British novelist and scientist. The moral problems of politics and power are a recurrent theme of his series of novels beginning with *Strangers and Brothers* (1940) and ending with *Last Things* (1970). His lecture *The Two Cultures and the Scientific Revolution* (1959) prompted a lively controversy with the critic F. R. ▷Leavis. He was married to the writer Pamela Hansford Johnson (1912–81).

● **snowball tree** ▷*See* guelder rose.

● **snow bunting** ▶ A short-billed ▷bunting, *Plectrophenax nivalis*, of Arctic snowfields, that visits Britain in winter. It is about 16 cm long and has a brownish plumage with white underparts and black wingtips. In summer the male is white with an orange bill and black markings. It nests in rock crevices and feeds on seeds and insects.

● **Snowdon** ▶ (Welsh name: Eryri) 53 04N 4 05W The highest mountain in Wales, in Gwynedd. A rack railway runs from Llanberis to its main peak, Y Wyddfa. The surrounding area, **Snowdonia**, is popular for hill walking, rock climbing, and mountaineering; it was designated a National Park in 1951. Height: 1085 m (3560 ft).

● **Snowdon, Antony Armstrong-Jones, Earl of** ▶ (1930–) British photographer. His work includes several television documentaries, photographic books, such as *Sittings* (1983), and the design of the Snowdon Aviary, London Zoo (1965). His marriage (1960–78) to Princess Margaret ended in divorce.

● **snowdrop** ▶ A small early spring-blooming herbaceous plant of the genus *Galanthus* (about 10 species) native to Europe and W Asia. They grow from bulbs to produce grasslike leaves and slender stems bearing solitary nodding white flowers, tipped with green or yellow. There are over 50 cultivated varieties, which are easily grown in gardens and survive for years without attention. *G. nivalis* is the common European snowdrop; *G. elwesi* is the giant snowdrop of SW Asia. Family: *Amaryllidaceae*.

● **snow goose** ▶ An Arctic ▷goose, *Anser caerulescens*. It is 70–78 cm long and is either pure white with black wingtips, pink legs, and a red bill or blue-grey with a white head. Snow geese winter in the southern USA, Japan, and China.

● **snow leopard** ▶ A big ▷cat, *Panthera* (or *Uncia*) *uncia*, also called ounce, found in the mountains of central Asia. It is 1.9 m long, with a thick ash-grey coat marked with dark rosettes. It hunts mountain goats, sheep, and marmots, catching its prey by stalking.

● **snow-on-the-mountain** ▶ A hardy annual plant, ▷*Euphorbia marginata*, native to North America and widely cultivated as a garden foliage plant. Up to 60 cm high, it has pale-green pointed leaves, 3–8 cm long, with white margins (sometimes the whole leaf is white). Family: *Euphorbiaceae*.

● **snowshoe hare** ▶ A ▷hare, *Lepus americanus*, of N North America, also called varying hare. Up to 70 cm long, it has a white winter coat and leaves tracks similar to snowshoes. Populations of snowshoe hares can vary greatly from year to year; similar fluctuations occur in the populations of lynxes—their chief predator.

● **Snowy Mountains** ▶ A mountain range in Australia. It lies within the ▷Australian Alps, in New South Wales, and contains Australia's highest mountain, Mount ▷Kosciusko. The Snowy Mountains Hydroelectric Authority, which was established in 1949, has diverted rivers and constructed dams and reservoirs for irrigation and hydroelectric purposes.

● **snowy owl** ▶ A large ▷owl, *Nyctea scandiaca*, occurring chiefly in Arctic tundra regions. 52–65 cm long, it has broad wings, a round head, and a snow-white plumage with black barring. It nests on open ground and feeds on lemmings, hares, and birds.

● **snuff** ▶ A preparation of tobacco and other ingredients that is sniffed rather than smoked. The character of a particular variety of snuff depends on the coarseness of the tobacco used, the moisture content, and the added ingredients, such as lavender and menthol, which introduce flavour and scent to the mixture.

Spaniards discovered snuff-taking among the natives of the Americas in the 16th century. The habit was fashionable in England from the 17th century until the early 19th century, when it was largely replaced by the ▷cigar. Highly decorated snuffboxes were made as valuable items of jewellery.

● **Snyders, Frans** ▶ (1579–1657) Flemish animal painter, born in Antwerp. He studied under Pieter ▷Brueghel the Younger. At first a still-life painter, he later specialized in hunting scenes, working under ▷Rubens and for Archduke Albert.

● **Soames, (Arthur) Christopher (John), Baron** ▶ (1920–87) British Conservative politician and diplomat. An MP from 1950 to 1966, he was minister of agriculture (1960–64). Subsequently he was ambassador to France (1968–72), a vice president of the EC Commission (1973–77), and governor (1980) of Zimbabwe before it attained independence.

● **Soane, Sir John** ▶ (1753–1837) British architect, who developed ▷neoclassicism into a highly original style. He trained under George ▷Dance and on the Continent. He rebuilt the Bank of England (1788–1833; now destroyed), the striking austerity of which was relieved only by simplified classical motifs. Later designs include Dulwich College Art Gallery (1811–14) and his own house in Lincoln's Inn Fields, London (1812–13), which is now the Sir John Soane Museum, containing his collection of antiques, paintings, etc.

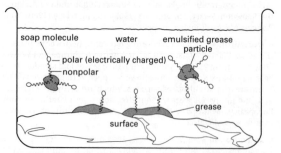

soaps ▶ The action of soap in emulsifying grease. The nonpolar hydrocarbon end of the soap molecule attaches itself to the grease. The attraction of the polar end to water breaks up the grease and distributes it throughout the solution.

● **soaps** ▶ Salts of ▷fatty acids. Household soap (**hard soap**) is a mixture of sodium stearate, oleate, and palmitate. It is made by the ▷hydrolysis of ▷fats with sodium hydroxide, converting the glycerides of stearic, oleic, and palmitic acids into sodium salts and glycerol. **Soft soap** is made with potassium hydroxide. Soaps cleanse because they contain negative ions composed of a long hydrocarbon chain attached to a carboxyl group. The hydrocarbon chain has an affinity for grease and oil, and the carboxyl group has an affinity for water. Grease or oil is therefore emulsified in soapy water. Insoluble salts of other metals with fatty acids are used as fillers and waterproofing agents and are also called soaps. ▷*See also* detergents.

● **soapstone** ▷*See* talc.

● **soapwort** ▶ A perennial herb, *Saponaria officinalis*, native to Europe and temperate Asia and introduced to North America. It grows to a height of 30–90 cm and bears pink flowers. The leaves and roots contain a lathering agent (saponin), formerly used for washing clothes. Family: *Caryophyllaceae*.

● **Soares, Mario** ▶ (1924–) Portuguese statesman; prime minister (1976–79, 1983–85) and president (1986–96). He was a critic of ▷Salazar and lived in exile from 1970 to 1974, when he became foreign minister. He became prime minister as leader of the Portuguese Socialist Party.

● **Sobers, Garry** ▶ (Sir Garfield Saint Auburn S.; 1936–) West Indian cricketer, who captained the West Indies and Nottinghamshire and also played for Barbados and South Australia. One of the greatest all-rounders, he played in 93 Test matches, scoring 8032 runs, including 26 centuries, and taking 235 wickets and 110 catches.

● **So-ch'e** ▷*See* Shache.

● **Sochi** ▶ 43 35N 39 46E A city in SW Russia, on the Black Sea. It is a resort, where, since 1977, smoking has been forbidden. Population (1995 est): 355 000.

● **Social and Liberal Democrats** ▶ (SLD) ▷*See* Liberal Democrats.

● **social class** ▶ Any of the main divisions into which a population can be divided according to wealth, education, birth, occupation, or lifestyle. In 19th-century Britain there were rigid class barriers between the aristocracy, gentry, middle class, and working class. During the following century these barriers were largely eroded as a result of universal suffrage, the rise of the labour movement, the spread of education, and two world wars. In 1962 the Institute of Practitioners in Advertising issued a classification that has been widely used for commercial and social purposes: (A) higher managerial and professional; (B) administrative and professional; (C1) supervisory and clerical; (C2) skilled manual workers; (D) semiskilled and unskilled workers; (E) pensioners and casual workers.

In 1998 a new form of classification was issued by the Office for National Statistics. In this classification, which takes into account the importance of women in the workforce, there are seven classes for those in work and an eighth class for those on benefit, etc. Class 1A includes large employers and managers, senior police and military officers, restaurateurs, and football managers; class 1B covers professional people, including teachers and airline pilots; class 2 includes journalists, nurses, actors, musicians, lower managers and police officers, and NCOs; class 3 covers professional sportspeople, secretaries, air stewards, etc.; class 4 has small employers and the nonprofessional self-employed (e.g. plumbers and publicans); class 5 covers skilled workers, foremen, train drivers, etc.; class 6 is for semiroutine occupations, such as caretakers, gardeners, assembly-line workers; class 7 includes routine occupations, such as cleaners, waiters, waitresses, dockers, road workers, and messengers; while class 8 is for the long-term unemployed and sick and those who have never worked.

In the USA, where almost everyone attends the same type of school, social stratification depends largely on wealth.

The economically active population (percentages) of the UK by social class in 1996–97

social class	men (16–64)	women (16–64)
Professional	8	3
Intermediate	29	28
Skilled (nonmanual)	12	37
Skilled (manual)	32	8
Partly skilled	15	19
Unskilled	5	6

● **social contract** ▶ 1. An agreement under which people consent to surrender liberties in return for the guarantee of responsible government. Hobbes saw the contract as one in which citizens surrender the freedom inherent in a state of nature to an absolute sovereign;

Locke, however, argued that the sovereign is limited by the obligation to preserve certain fundamental liberties; and Rousseau, the third of the chief theorists of the social contract, believed that governments require the support of the general will of the people. 2. (*or* social compact) The agreement (1974) between the Labour government of the UK and the trades unions, which undertook to moderate their wage demands in exchange for certain social and industrial reforms. In 1975 it was replaced by specific limits on wage increases.

● **social Darwinism** ▶ The theory that the principles governing the evolution of biological species by natural selection also govern social evolution. Either relations in society are held to be determined by a "struggle for existence" between individuals and groups or history is interpreted as a series of conflicts in which only the "fittest" social systems thrive.

● **Social Democratic and Labour Party** ▶ (SDLP) A British political party, active in Northern Ireland. Founded by John ▷Hume and others in 1970, it supports peaceful union with Ireland. Its parliamentary leader at Westminster and its principal representative in the Northern Ireland assembly is Mark Durkan (1960–   ).

● **Social Democratic Party** ▶ (SDP) A British political party of the centre, formed on 26 March, 1981, by the "gang of four" Labour dissidents: Roy ▷Jenkins, Shirley ▷Williams, David ▷Owen (leader 1983–87), and William Rodgers. The SDP formed a political alliance with the Liberal Party in 1981; in 1987, after poor results in the general election, the SDP voted to merge with the Liberals and Owen was replaced by Robert Maclennan. After the formation of the Social and Liberal Democrats (subsequently renamed the ▷Liberal Democrats) in 1988, a reduced SDP was relaunched under Owen but was wound up by him in 1990.

● **socialism** ▶ A political and economic concept that has various meanings, resulting in diverse political movements, but one that generally emphasizes the establishment of cooperation rather than competition as the basis of human society. The word was first used in the early 19th century to describe the followers of Robert ▷Owen in England and François Fourier and ▷Saint-Simon in France. Two main senses of the word soon emerged. The first sense was in effect a continuation of liberalism, the emphasis being on reform of the social system to develop liberal values, such as political freedom, and the ending of class privileges. Socialism in the second sense was explicitly contrasted with a competitive individualist form of society; practical cooperation, it was claimed, could not be achieved until a society based on private property was replaced by one based on social ownership and control. The resulting controversy between reformists and revolutionaries was often bitter and violent.

In 1848 Marx and Engels laid down the principles of scientific socialism in *The Communist Manifesto* and ▷Marxism became the theoretical basis for most socialist thought. The British ▷Fabian Society (founded 1884) revived a variant of the first sense of the term, which later found political expression in the ▷Labour Party. It was the split in Russia, however, between the revolutionary ▷Bolsheviks and the reformist ▷Mensheviks that led to the decisive distinction between the terms ▷communism and socialism as they are now generally understood, socialists being those who seek change by peaceful reform and communists being those dedicated to change by revolution. In the late 20th century socialist parties in many countries abandoned or revised traditional socialist teachings in response to the collapse of Marxist systems worldwide and the apparent triumph of global capitalism.

● **socialist realism** ▶ A theory of creative composition decreed by the Soviet authorities in Russia in 1932 to be the official doctrine to which all communist writers and artists must adhere. It defined the purpose of literature as the promotion of socialism and resulted in the production of much literature that was little more than political ▷propaganda. The liberalization of Soviet society in the 1980s signalled that artists would no longer have to comply with such principles.

● **social science** ▷*See* sociology.

● **social security** ▶ State provision of financial aid to alleviate deprivation and poverty. In the UK the establishment of a ▷welfare

state was based initially on government insurance schemes, which were extended after World War II to cover almost all the population (*see* National Insurance). Family allowances and the provision of subsidized local-authority accommodation, however, were not based on contributions. The policy was later modified by the introduction of other noncontributory benefits (such as income support, which is claimed by over 5 million people) for those in need and the replacement (1988) of family allowances with a new system of child benefits and family credits. By the 1990s, the increasing longevity of the population, the rise in the number of ▷single-parent families, and the growth of long-term unemployment, together with the disinclination of the electorate to pay higher taxes, had forced many governments, including those in the UK, to cut back on the extent to which they were prepared to safeguard the poorest members of society.

● **Society Islands** ▶ An archipelago in French Polynesia. It consists of two island groups, the **Windward Islands** (including Tahiti and Moorea) and the **Leeward Islands** (including Raiatea and Huahine). The capital of French Polynesia, Papeete, is on Tahiti. Discovered in 1767, they are mountainous and the site of ruined temples. Copra, vanilla, phosphates, and mother-of-pearl are produced. Area: 1595 sq km (616 sq mi). Population (latest est): 162 573.

● **Society of Friends** ▷*See* Quakers.

● **Society of Jesus** ▷*See* Jesuits.

● **Socinus, Laelius** ▶ (Italian name: Lelio Francesco Maria Sozini; 1525–62) Italian Protestant reformer. He travelled widely in N Europe, meeting other leading Protestant reformers. His anti-Trinitarian beliefs and his desire to reconcile Christianity with humanism deeply influenced his nephew **Faustus Socinus** (Fausto Paolo Sozini; 1539–1604). He settled in Poland in 1579, where he led an anti-Trinitarian branch of the Reformed Church. Its doctrine, known as Socinanism, contributed to Unitarianism (*see* Unitarians).

● **sociobiology** ▶ The study of social behaviour in animals and humans. Sociobiologists believe that such aspects of behaviour as aggression, male dominance, and the roles of the sexes have developed through evolution in the same way as structural features. The study was developed in the 1970s.

● **sociology** ▶ The systematic study of the development, organization, functioning, and classification of human societies. Its growth was stimulated by the rapid industrial and social change in Europe in the early 19th century, Auguste ▷Comte (the first to use the term "sociology"), Emile ▷Durkheim, and Max ▷Weber being among the founding fathers of the discipline. Established in several universities in the USA by the early 20th century, it became widely established in British universities during the 1960s. Precluded from experimental methods, the discipline has employed techniques of participant observation, the systematic comparison of different societies, and surveys of social conditions, attitudes, and behaviour. Contemporary sociology is divided into several specialized subdisciplines including demography, political, educational, and urban sociology as well as sociological studies of deviance, religion, and culture.

● **sockeye salmon** ▶ A ▷salmon, *Oncorhynchus nerka*, also called red salmon or blueback, that lives in the N Pacific and spawns in Canadian fresh waters.

● **Socotra** ▶ A Yemeni island in the Indian Ocean, off Somalia. It is generally barren, rising to 1503 m (4931 ft), but in some valleys such crops as dates are grown and livestock is raised. It came under British protection in 1886 but belonged to South Yemen from 1967 to 1990. Area: 3100 sq km (1197 sq mi). Chief town: Tamrida.

● **Socrates** ▶ (c. 469–399 BC) Athenian philosopher. He wrote nothing himself but his disciples ▷Plato and ▷Xenophon stress his intellect, integrity, courage, humour, and sense of divine guidance. ▷Aristophanes caricatured him in *The Clouds* as an eccentric intellectual. Socrates diverted philosophy from the physical speculations of the ▷Presocratics towards ▷ethics. His insistence upon thorough critical analysis of ethical concepts also marked the beginning of ▷logic. The "Socratic method" of teaching was by eliciting answers from interlocutors to reveal inconsistencies in accepted opinions, a method particularly effective against the ▷Sophists. His resolute stance against tyranny, whether exercised by the mob or oligarchs, brought about his trial on charges of atheism and "corrupting the youth," and he was condemned to die by drinking hemlock. Plato's *Phaedo* is an eloquent account of his death.

● **Soddy, Frederick** ▶ (1877–1956) British chemist, who worked under ▷Rutherford and ▷Ramsay and went on to win the 1921 Nobel Prize for his discovery of ▷isotopes. His scientific books included *The Interpretation of the Atom* (1932); he also wrote on economics, his main work being *Cartesian Economics* (1922).

● **Söderblom, Nathan** ▶ (1866–1931) Swedish churchman; Archbishop of Uppsala (1914–31). A pioneer of the modern ecumenical movement, he made new contacts with Anglican and Eastern Orthodox Churches and was a chief initiator of conferences on "Faith and Order" (Uppsala, 1919) and "Life and Work" (Stockholm, 1925). He received the Nobel Peace Prize in 1930.

● **sodium** ▶ (Na) A highly reactive alkali metal, long-recognized in compounds but first isolated as the element by Sir Humphry Davy in 1807 by electrolysis of the molten hydroxide (NaOH; caustic soda). It is now obtained commercially by electrolysis of common ▷salt (NaCl). It occurs naturally in some silicate minerals (for example ▷feldspars; $NaAlSi_3O_8$), as well as in salt deposits and in the oceans. The metal is soft, bright, and less dense (relative density 0.97) than water, with which it reacts violently, liberating hydrogen. For safety, it has to be stored in mineral oil. It is used in organic chemistry as a reducing agent and in the production of ▷tetraethyl lead. Sodium forms a low-melting-point (–12.3°C) alloy with potassium, but liquid sodium itself is used as the coolant in fast-breeder nuclear reactors. It is a highly electropositive element, forming many ionic salts of great importance, such as the chloride (common salt; NaCl), the carbonate (soda ash; Na_2CO_3), the bicarbonate (baking soda; $NaHCO_3$), various phosphates, the nitrate ($NaNO_3$), and many others. ▷Soap is usually the sodium salt of fatty acids (e.g. sodium stearate). Sodium gives a strong yellow colour to flames. At no 11; at wt 22.9898; mp 97.8°C; bp 882.9°C.

● **sodium bicarbonate** ▶ (sodium hydrogen carbonate *or* bicarbonate of soda; $NaHCO_3$) The white soluble powder that is a constituent of ▷baking powder and is used to make fizzy drinks and as an antacid in medicine. It is made from ▷sodium carbonate by passing ▷carbon dioxide through a saturated solution.

● **sodium carbonate** ▶ (Na_2CO_3) A white soluble salt. The commercial form (**soda ash**) is a white anhydrous powder and is used in making glass, soap, paper, as well as other chemicals. **Washing soda**, its hydrated form ($Na_2CO_3.10H_2O$), is a white crystalline solid used as a domestic cleanser and water softener.

● **sodium hydroxide** ▶ (*or* caustic soda; NaOH) A white solid that is strongly alkaline in aqueous solution and is very corrosive to organic tissue. It is made by electrolysis of salt solution and is used in making rayon, paper, detergents, and other chemicals.

● **Sodom and Gomorrah** ▶ In the Old Testament, two cities of Palestine, known as the "cities of the plain," S of the Dead Sea in the area in which Lot, the nephew of Abraham, settled. According to Genesis (18, 19), they were destroyed by fire and brimstone from heaven because of the utter depravity of their inhabitants.

● **Sofia** ▶ (Bulgarian name: Sofiya) 42 40N 23 18E The capital of Bulgaria, situated on a plateau in the W of the country. Industries include engineering, metals, textiles, and food processing. It contains some ancient churches, including that of St Sofia (6th century), as well as two mosques. The university was founded in 1888.
History: a Roman town (known as Serdica) from the 1st to the 4th centuries AD, it was destroyed by the Huns in 447. Sofia came under the Byzantine Empire in the 6th century and was taken over by the Bulgars in the 9th century. Under Turkish rule from 1382, the city was liberated by the Russians in 1878 and became the national capital (1879). Population (1996 est): 1 116 823.

● **soft-shelled turtle** ▶ A freshwater turtle belonging to the family *Trionychidae* (20–25 species), occurring in North America, Africa, and Asia. They have a flat almost circular shell covered by a leathery skin instead of horny plates, a long neck with a small head, and webbed feet. They are carnivorous and often lie buried in mud but can be fast-moving and aggressive. Chief genus: *Trionyx*.

● **software** ▶ The suite of ▷programs that sets up a ▷computer system for operation, as distinct from the physical equipment (hardware). Computer manufacturers generally supply machines complete with most of the basic software, which is regarded as an integral part of the computer. This controls various parts of the system and provides facilities for further programming. Supplementary programs to perform specific tasks are purchased separately or written by the user.

● **Sogne Fjord** ▶ The longest and deepest fjord in Norway, extending 204 km (127 mi) inland N of Bergen. It is flanked by spectacular mountain scenery. Depth: about 1220 m (4000 ft).

● **Soho** ▶ A district in the Greater London borough of the City of Westminster. Its name derives from the old hunting cry "So-Ho," as hunting took place in the area when Henry VIII made it into a royal park for Whitehall Palace (burnt down in 1698). It possesses many restaurants, theatres, and nightclubs and a large cosmopolitan population, including a Chinese community in and around Gerard Street. During the 1960s Soho became notorious for its stripclubs, brothels, and sex shops. However, by the 1990s strict licensing and a number of corruption trials (in which several police officers were gaoled) resulted in a sharp fall in the number of premises devoted to the sex industry.

● **soil** ▶ The mixture of unconsolidated mineral particles, derived from weathered rock, and organic matter (humus), derived from the breakdown of plant tissue by living organisms, that covers much of the earth's land surface and provides a medium for plant growth. Soil formation (pedogenesis) depends on the nature of the parent material, the climate and topography of the region, the organisms present in the soil, and the time that has elapsed since pedogenesis began on a bare surface. Soils are characterized by their texture, which depends on particle sizes (*see* sand; silt; clay), and their structure, which depends on the way the particles are bound into aggregates (e.g. crumbs, granules, flakes, etc.). These are important factors in determining the fertility of the soil, particularly its moisture and air content, susceptibility to leaching (the removal of nutrients to deeper levels by percolating water), and ease of cultivation. Soils are also classified according to their profiles—the arrangement of the layers (horizons) between the ground surface and the bedrock. ▷*See also* chernozem; loam; podzol.

● **Soissons** ▶ 49 23N 3 20E A town in France, in the Aisne department on the River Aisne. Strategically situated on the NE approaches to Paris, it has been sacked many times. It has a fine 13th-century cathedral. Soissons is a market town and has metallurgical industries. Population (latest est): 32 236.

● **Sokoto** ▶ 13 02N 5 15E A city in NW Nigeria. It is a major trade centre for livestock and agricultural products. The University of Sokoto was founded in 1975. Population (1996 est): 204 900.

● **sol** ▷*See* colloid.

● **Solanaceae** ▶ A family of herbaceous plants and shrubs (about 2000 species), widely distributed but chiefly tropical. Their flowers have five fused sepals and petals and are usually pollinated by insects. The family includes several commercially important species (e.g. the potato, tomato, pepper, and tobacco) and some ornamentals (e.g. *Petunia*); various other members are poisonous (e.g. the nightshades).

● **solar cell** ▷*See* solar power.

● **solar constant** ▶ The total amount of solar energy passing perpendicularly through unit area per unit time at a particular distance from the sun. It is about 1.36 kW m^{-2} at the earth's mean orbital distance.

● **solar flare** ▶ A sudden brightening, within minutes, of areas in the sun's atmosphere, resulting from an explosive release of energetic particles and radiation. Flares occur in regions of intense localized magnetic field, often above ▷sunspot groups, and take up to an hour to fade. Large flares affect radio transmission on earth and produce ▷auroras.

solar power ▶ A television set operated by solar power in the Republic of Niger, W Africa.

● **solar power** ▶ The use of the sun's energy to provide heating or to generate electricity. A vast amount of solar energy (about 3×10^{24} joules) falls on the earth every year. This energy can be converted into heat, the commonest method being by heating water flowing through special **solar panels** on the roof of a building. The temperature rise produced is small but it reduces the energy required from other sources for hot water and space heating. As some 45% of energy is used in space heating buildings in the UK, solar heating could make a considerable contribution to UK energy needs. Higher temperatures, to raise steam for electricity generation, are possible using mirrors to focus the sun's rays in a **solar furnace**. It is estimated that 7000 square metres of mirror are required to generate 1 megawatt by boiling water to drive a turbogenerator. Direct conversion of solar radiation into electrical energy is possible with **solar cells**. These consist of semiconductor junctions in silicon crystals that are sensitive to the ▷photovoltaic effect. The method is used mainly in small-scale applications, for example powering remote monitoring equipment, spacecraft, marine beacons, etc. For this method to have wider commercial applications the cost of solar cells would need to be reduced.

● **solar prominences** ▶ Immense clouds of gas in the solar atmosphere, denser and cooler than their surroundings and visible, usually only spectroscopically, as flamelike projections beyond the sun's limb. They show great diversity in structure. **Quiescent prominences** persist for possibly several months at high solar latitudes, reaching, typically, a height and length of 40 000 km and 200 000 km. **Active prominences** are short lived in comparison and may alter their shape in minutes.

● **solar system** ▶ A system comprising the ▷sun and the astronomical bodies gravitationally bound to the sun, that is the nine major ▷planets, their ▷satellites, and the immense numbers of ▷minor planets, ▷comets, and meteoroids (*see* meteor). Almost all the mass of the solar system (99.86%) resides in the sun. The planets orbit the sun in the same direction and, with the exception of Pluto, move in paths close to the earth's orbit (i.e. close to the ▷ecliptic) and the sun's equator. This and other information is taken as evidence of the common origin of the sun and planets, some 4600 million years ago, following the contraction and subsequent flattening of a rotating cloud of interstellar gas and dust. □ p. 1164.

● **solar time** ▷*See* time.

● **solar wind** ▶ An almost radial outflow of charged particles discharged from the sun's corona into interplanetary space. The particles, mainly protons and electrons, are moving at speeds between 200 and 900 km per second in the vicinity of the earth's orbit and although low in density (about 8 per cubic centimetre) can still interact with the earth's ▷magnetosphere.

● **solder** ▶ An ▷alloy that is melted to form a joint between other metals or, occasionally, nonmetals. The surfaces to be joined are heated by a soldering iron or by a flame, but are not melted. **Soft solder** is usually made of lead and tin and melts in the range 200–250°C. Because the solder itself is not very strong, it is not used for joints that have to stand up to stress or heat, but is used for making secure electrical connections. **Brazing**, also called **hard soldering**, uses a harder alloy with a higher melting temperature (850–900°C), usually a ▷brass with 60% zinc and 40% copper. **Silver solder** originally contained silver and was used for jewellery. It has a slightly lower melting point (630–830°C) than brass, and often contains antimony or other metals but no silver. Like brazing, its strength makes it useful in engineering applications. A flux of zinc chloride or a resin is applied to the hot surfaces before soldering to clean them and to enable the solder to flow. In some solders (resin-cored) the flux is contained inside the solder.

● **soldier beetle** ▶ A slender soft-bodied beetle with hairy wing cases, belonging to a small but widely distributed family (*Cantharidae*; 3500 species). Brightly coloured and 5–15 mm long, the adults are attracted to flowers, particularly those of the parsley family (*Umbelliferae*), although most feed on small insects. The larvae are found in soil and moss.

● **sole** ▶ An elongated ▷flatfish of the family *Soleidae* (over 100 species), found in temperate and tropical seas. The common European sole (*Solea solea*), also called Dover sole, is a valuable food fish and has a blotchy brown body, up to 50 cm long, with a black spot on each pectoral fin. ▷*See also* lemon sole.

● **Solemn League and Covenant** ▶ (1643) An agreement between the parliamentarians and the Scots during the English ▷Civil War. Presbyterianism was to be established in England and Ireland and the Scots undertook to supply parliament with forces against Charles I in return for a monthly payment of £30,000.

● **solenodon** ▶ A shrewlike mammal of the family *Solenodontidae* (2 species) found in Cuba and Haiti. Solenodons measure 28–32 cm and have a long naked tail and a long snout with large upper incisor teeth. They feed chiefly on insects, using their long claws to tear open rotten wood. Order: ▷*Insectivora*.

● **solenoid** ▶ A coil of wire usually forming a long cylinder. When electric current flows through it a ▷magnetic field is created. This field can be used to move an iron rod placed on its axis. Solenoids are often used to operate mechanical valves attached to the iron rod by switching on or off the current. In most cars a solenoid is used to operate the heavy-current switch that supplies energy to the starter motor.

● **Solent, the** ▶ A channel between the coast of Hampshire in S England and the Isle of Wight. It is an important shipping route between Southampton and the English Channel and is famous for its yacht races. Maximum width: 6 km (4 mi).

● **solfeggio** ▷*See* solmization.

● **Solferino, Battle of** ▶ (24 June, 1859) An indecisive battle between Austria on one side and Sardinia-Piedmont and France on the other. As the Austrians withdrew, Solferino was technically a French victory but the French emperor Napoleon III, alarmed by unrest in Paris and the strength of the Austrians, made peace at Villafranca less than three weeks after the battle. The heavy casualties (about 30 000 dead) led an eyewitness, Henri ▷Dunant, to campaign for the ▷Red Cross.

● **solicitor** ▶ In the UK, a member of the legal profession qualified to give legal advice to clients, to present his clients' cases in court, and to undertake other legal work, such as the transfer of property (conveyancing). A person qualifies as a solicitor by completing a one-year legal practice course and passing examinations conducted by the Law Society, which issues certificates to practise, and then by serving two years as an employee under a training contract with a practising solicitor. Before 1971 solicitors could represent clients only in Magistrates' Courts and County Courts; they now have rights of audience in all the higher courts provided that they have obtained the necessary advocacy qualification. Qualification for higher advocacy rights is not currently part of a solicitor's training and must be obtained after qualification as a solicitor. However, in 1998 the Lord Chancellor's Department published proposals to include higher advocacy training in the solicitor's three-year prequalification period, so that a newly qualified solicitor will, like a barrister, have full rights of audience. They are eligible for appointment as circuit judges and recorders, but are not eligible for the higher judiciary. A ▷barrister must always be instructed through a solicitor. The **solicitor general** is a law officer of the crown with ministerial rank, who acts as a deputy to the ▷attorney general. ▷*See also* Treasury Solicitor.

● **Solidarity** ► (Polish name: Solidarnosc) A Polish trade union. Formed in Gdańsk (1980) and led by Lech ▷Wałęsa, Solidarity became a focus of resistance to ▷Jaruzelski's Soviet-dominated government. Internal unrest and pressure from the USSR forced the government to suspend Solidarity in 1982. However, Solidarity continued underground and was legalized in 1989. Its campaign for liberal reform culminated in the same year in multiparty parliamentary elections, which Solidarity won. By 1993, however, the movement had split into several political groupings, only one of which retained the name Solidarity, and was out of power. Following the elections of 1997 a Solidarity-led coalition was formed.

● **solid state** ► One of the four states of matter and that to which all substances, except helium, revert at sufficiently low temperatures. It is the only one in which matter retains its shape, as a result of the stronger intermolecular forces.

● **solid-state devices** ► Electronic devices made with solid ▷semiconductor components. They have no moving parts and depend for their operation on the movement of charges within a crystalline solid. Solid-state devices are smaller, lighter, physically more robust, and can be more easily mass-produced than ▷thermionic valve equipment. ▷*See also* semiconductor diode; thyristor; transistor.

● **solifluction** ► A process of mass movement of soil and rock debris, associated with areas bordering on ice sheets in which ▷permafrost is a feature. During the summer season the top layer of soil thaws but as the ground below remains frozen the water is unable to drain away. The soil therefore becomes saturated and on slopes will flow downhill.

● **Solihull** ► **1.** 52 25N 1 4SW A town in central England, in West Midlands. It developed as a residential area for Birmingham in the 19th century. Motor vehicles are manufactured and there are various light industries. Birmingham International airport is nearby. Population (1991): 94 531. **2.** A unitary authority in central England, in West Midlands. Area: 180 sq km (70 sq mi). Population (1996 est): 203 900.

● **Solingen** ► 51 10N 7 05E A city in NW Germany, in North Rhine-Westphalia. Its reputation for blades and cutlery dates to the middle ages. It was severely damaged in World War II. Population (1996 est): 165 735.

● **solipsism** ► The philosophical view that the human mind has no logical justification for believing in the existence of anything other than itself. It is thus an extreme form of ▷idealism in which the outside world exists only in the mind of the observer. Critics, including ▷Wittgenstein, regard it as incompatible with the existence of a language capable of expressing the view.

● **solmization** ► A method of teaching singing that eliminates learning to read music notation. The tonic sol-fa system derived from the hexachord invented by ▷Guido d'Arezzo. It was systematized in the 1840s by John ▷Curwen: the notes of the rising major scale are represented by the syllables doh, ray, me, fah, soh, lah, ti, and doh. The system can be applied in any key; modulation simply involves shifting doh to another pitch. Vocal exercises on solmization syllables are known by the Italian word solfeggio.

● **Solo** ▷*See* Surakarta.

● **Solomon** ► In the Old Testament, the third King of Israel, son of ▷David and Bathsheba, who reigned in the 10th century BC. During his peaceful reign foreign alliances were formed (notably with Phoenicia and Egypt), trade and commerce were expanded, and the ▷Temple of Jerusalem and many palaces were built. To realize his

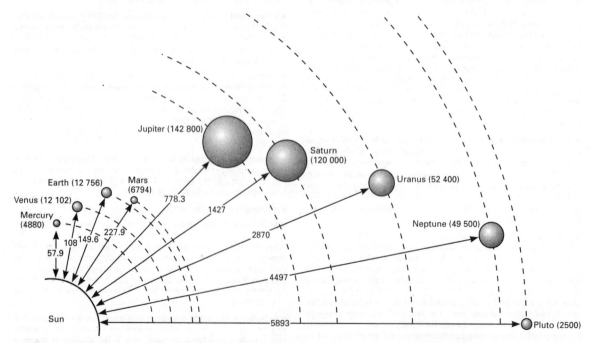

solar system ► The planets with their equatorial diameters in kilometres (in brackets after the planet's name) and their distance from the sun in millions of kilometres (not to scale).

schemes he had to impose heavy taxes and use compulsory labour, resulting in the revolt of N Israel. He was famous for his wisdom, and much of the "wisdom" literature of the Old Testament, such as the ▷Song of Solomon, Proverbs, and Ecclesiastes, is attributed to him.

● **Solomon** ▶ (S. Cutner; 1902–88) British pianist. He made his debut at the age of eight. He later studied in Paris and began his professional career in 1923. Paralysis ended his career in 1955.

● **Solomon Islands** ▶ A country in the Pacific Ocean, E of New Guinea. It consists of numerous small islands, the largest being ▷Guadalcanal, Malaita, San Cristobal, New Georgia, Santa Isabel, and Choiseul. ▷Bougainville, within the Solomon Islands archipelago, is part of Papua New Guinea. The islands are mainly forested and mountainous, with some active volcanoes. Most of the population are Melanesian, with Polynesian and Micronesian minorities.

Economy: the chief exports are copra, timber, and palm oil, and fishing is also important. Most foodstuffs and consumer goods have to be imported.

History: the first Europeans to discover the islands were the Spanish in 1568. The four main islands became a British protectorate in 1893 and others were added in 1898–99. During World War II they were the scene of fighting between the Japanese and Allied forces. They achieved self-government in 1976 and became independent within the Commonwealth in 1978. Following elections in 1997 Bartholomew Ulufa'alu became prime minister. Ethnic fighting between Malaitans and Isatabus (natives of Guadalcanal) erupted in 1999. This led to the ousting (2000) of Ulufa'ulu by a Malaitan militia; Manasseh Sogavare became prime minister and a peace deal was signed (Oct 2000).

Solomon Islands

Head of state	Queen Elizabeth II, represented by the governor-general, Sir Moses Pitakaka
Official language	English
Official currency	Solomon Islands dollar of 100 cents
Area	29 785 sq km (11 500 sq mi)
Population (1999 est)	442 000
Capital and main port	Honiara

● **Solomon's seal** ▶ A hardy perennial herbaceous plant of the genus *Polygonatum* (about 25 species), native to moist shady woods of the N hemisphere, especially *P. multiflorum*. Its arching stem, 30–80 cm long, bears two rows of broad spindle-shaped leaves, 5–12 cm long, in the axils of which grow clusters of 2–5 greenish-white tubular flowers followed by red berries. Family ▷Liliaceae.

● **Solon** ▶ (6th century BC) Athenian statesman, who laid the foundations of Athenian democracy. As archon (c. 594–593), Solon cancelled debts for which land or liberty was the security and introduced a new coinage and weights and measures. He also instituted a new constitution, dividing the citizens into four classes, and a more lenient legal code.

● **Solothurn** ▶ (French name: Soleure) 47 13N 7 32E A town in NW Switzerland. It has a cathedral (1762–73) and a former arsenal containing an excellent collection of armour and old weapons. Industries include watchmaking and precision instruments. Population (1990): 15 429.

● **Soloviov, Vladimir Sergevich** ▶ (1853–1900) Russian philosopher and poet. A friend of Dostoievski, Soloviov was influenced by ▷Hegel and Jakob ▷Böhme. He held that there was a female principle, Sophia, the world-soul.

● **solstice** ▶ Either of two points on the ▷ecliptic, midway between the ▷equinoxes, at which the sun reaches its greatest angular distance above or below the celestial equator (*see* celestial sphere). In the N hemisphere the sun's northernmost position occurs at the **summer solstice**, usually on 21 June, when daylight hours are at a maximum. Its southernmost position occurs at the **winter solstice**, usually on 22 December, when daylight hours are minimal.

● **Solti, Sir Georg** ▶ (1912–97) Hungarian-born naturalized British conductor and pianist. He studied in Budapest with Kodály and Dohnányi, serving as musical director of the Royal Opera, Covent Garden (1961–71), the Orchestre de Paris (1972–75), and the Chicago

Symphony Orchestra (1969–91). He was conductor of the London Philharmonic Orchestra (1979–83).

● **solution** ▶ A homogenous liquid mixture of two or more substances. Solutions, unlike ▷colloids, contain no identifiable particles of different substances. The components mix as single molecules, ions, or atoms. When a solid or gas is dissolved in a liquid, the liquid is known as the **solvent** and the dissolved material the **solute**. If the components are all liquid, the one in excess is the solvent. In a **solid solution**, molecules, atoms, or ions of one component occupy positions in the crystal structure of the other. The **solubility** of a substance is the maximum quantity of it that will dissolve in a given quantity of solvent (usually in kg m^{-3} or mol kg^{-1}) to form a saturated solution at a given temperature.

● **Solutrean** ▶ A culture of the Upper ▷Palaeolithic succeeding ▷Gravettian. Named after the site of Solutré near Mâcon (E France), it existed in W Europe from about 18000 to 15000 BC in the warmer climate that followed the last of the four main ▷Pleistocene glaciations. It is characterized by symmetrical pressure-flaked flint and other stone points of laurel- and willow-leaf (foliate) shape, which foreshadow the concern for aesthetic expression in the subsequent ▷Magdalenian culture.

● **Solvay process** ▶ A process for the production of sodium carbonate. Limestone is heated to produce calcium oxide and carbon dioxide: $CaCO_3 \rightarrow CaO + CO_2$. The carbon dioxide is passed through brine saturated with ammonia, precipitating sodium hydrogencarbonate ($NaHCO_3$). This, on heating, yields sodium carbonate and carbon dioxide, which is recycled. The ammonia is recovered from the second step, by the lime produced in the first step. Named after the Belgian chemist Ernest Solvay (1833–1922).

● **solvent abuse** ▶ The sniffing of organic solvents in glue, cleaning fluids, aerosols, etc., especially by adolescents. An offshoot of the drug culture, the practice is highly dangerous. In the UK the sale of materials containing solvents to children is restricted.

● **Solway Firth** ▶ An inlet of the Irish Sea between Dumfries and Galloway in SW Scotland and Cumbria in NW England. Length: about 56 km (35 mi).

● **Solzhenitsyn, Aleksandr** ▶ (1918–   ) Russian novelist. After distinguished service in World War II, he was held in prison camps until rehabilitated in 1956. The cultural liberalization heralded by the publication of *A Day in the Life of Ivan Denisovich* (1962), dealing with life in the Stalinist labour camps, was short lived and in 1974 he left the Soviet Union to live in the USA. His major works include *Cancer Ward* (1968), *The First Circle* (1968), *The Gulag Archipelago* (1974–78), and *October 1916* (1985). He won the Nobel Prize in 1970. His memoirs, *The Oak and the Calf*, appeared in 1975. In 1991 the Soviet authorities dropped all charges against him and he returned to Russia in 1994.

● **soma** ▶ A plant of uncertain identity. In the Vedic religion of India its intoxicating or hallucinogenic juice was used in sacrifices, especially to ▷Indra. It is also personified as a god in a number of hymns in the *Rigveda*.

● **Somali** ▶ An E African people occupying Somalia, Djibouti (where they are called Issas), Ethiopia, and NW Kenya. There are many tribes, which are divided into patrilineal clans headed by a chief chosen by the senior men. Among the nomadic herdsmen of the interior blood feud is common. Dwellers in towns and along the coast are traders and farmers. All are at least nominally Muslims. Their language belongs to the Cushitic branch of the ▷Hamito-Semitic family.

● **Somalia** ▶ (official name: Somali Democratic Republic) A country in East Africa, occupying most of the Horn of Africa between the Gulf of Aden and the Indian Ocean. Coastal plains rise in the N to a plateau reaching heights of over 1800 m (6000 ft). Most of the inhabitants are nomadic ▷Somalis with minorities of Sab, Bantu, and others.

Economy: chiefly agricultural, livestock raising, including sheep, goats, cattle, and camels, being especially important. There is some crop growing in the S, including sugar, maize, sorghum, bananas, and other fruit. The limited mineral resources include tin, iron ore, gypsum, and uranium. Fishing has been encouraged, and industry concentrates mainly on leather and food processing. The main exports are livestock, hides and skins, and fruit (especially bananas). Agricultural production has improved since the famine of 1991–92 but remains at about 50% of pre-civil war levels.

History: see Somaliland. In 1969, after a military coup, a Supreme Revolutionary Council was established in Somalia under Gen Mohammed Siad Barré. The country has had serious territorial disputes with Ethiopia (*see* Ogaden, the), which has a considerable Somali population. Barré was replaced as president in a coup in 1991 by Ali Mahdi Mohammed. Ali Mahdi's rule was rejected by rival factions, and in May, 1991 the Somali National Movement (SNM) declared independence for the N of the country, calling it the Somaliland Republic. Fighting in the S, between supporters of Ali Mahdi and those of Gen Mohammed Farah Aidid, escalated into civil war, which exacerbated famine in the country, leading to mass starvation and thousands of civilian deaths. In 1992 UN troops intervened to secure the distribution of food aid. During 1993 and 1994 attempts by a massive UN peacekeeping force failed to maintain a ceasefire: the rival leaders signed a peace agreement but fighting continued, and UN troops were withdrawn by March, 1995. In the subsequent power struggle Gen Aidid declared himself president but this was not generally accepted and he was assassinated in July, 1996. Confused factional fighting continued until December, 1997, when 26 of the warring militias signed an agreement in Cairo, proposing the establishment of an all-party transitional government pending elections. A new national assembly was finally inaugurated in 2000 and Abdiqassim Salad Hassan became Somalia's first president since 1991.

Somalia

Head of state	President Abdiqassim Salad Hassan
Official language	Somali; Arabic, Italian, and English are used extensively
Official religion	Islam
Official currency	Somali shilling of 100 centesemi
Area	700 000 sq km (270 000 sq mi)
Population (1999 est)	7 141 000
Capital and main port	Mogadishu

● **Somaliland** ▶ A region now occupied by Somalia and Djibouti. Between the 7th and 12th centuries AD the coastal region was occupied by Muslim traders while the N was settled from the 10th century by Somalis. During the 19th century it was divided between France, Britain, and Italy. Italian Somaliland was united with Ethiopia by Mussolini to form Italian East Africa (1935) and after World War II became an Italian trust territory. British and Italian Somaliland united to become independent as Somalia (1960) and the French territory, Afars and Issas, as Djibouti (1977).

● **somatotrophin** ▷*See* growth hormone.

● **Somers, John, Baron** ▶ (1651–1716) English statesman. He became an MP (1689) after the ▷Glorious Revolution and chaired the committee that drafted the ▷Bill of Rights. He was attorney general (1692), Lord Keeper of the Great Seal (1693), Lord Chancellor (1697–1700), and Lord President of the Privy Council (1708–10).

● **Somerset** ▶ A county of SW England, on the Bristol Channel. In 1974 it lost the NE part to ▷Avon; when Avon was abolished in 1996 administration of this area passed to two ▷unitary authorities, ▷Bath and North East Somerset and ▷North Somerset, which are considered part of Somerset for ceremonial purposes. Somerset consists mainly of a flat plain enclosed by the Quantock Hills and Exmoor in the W, the Blackdown Hills in the S, and the Mendip Hills (containing Cheddar Gorge) in the N. It is chiefly agricultural; dairy farming is important with over half the county under permanent pasture and there is the traditional cider making. Industries include food processing and textiles. Tourism is also important. Area (excluding unitary authorities): 3452 sq km (1332 sq mi). Population (1996 est, excluding unitary authorities): 482 700. Administrative centre: Taunton.

● **Somerset, Edward Seymour, 1st Duke of** ▶ (c. 1500–52) English statesman, who was ruler of England (1547–49) during the minority of Edward VI. Seymour's advancement was facilitated by the marriage of his sister Jane Seymour to Henry VIII, on whose death he became Protector of England and a duke. He defeated the Scots at Pinkie in 1547 and furthered the Protestant ▷Reformation with the first Book of Common Prayer (1549). He fell from power in 1549 and was subsequently executed by the Earl of Warwick (later Duke of ▷Northumberland).

● **Somerset, Robert Carr, Earl of** ▶ (c. 1590–1645) A favourite of James I of England from 1607 to 1615, when he was imprisoned for the murder of Sir Thomas Overbury. Overbury was poisoned in 1613 after opposing the divorce of Robert Devereux, 3rd Earl of ▷Essex, and Frances Howard, whom Somerset wished to marry. James' influence secured the divorce and in 1613 Somerset and Howard were married. Their subsequent conviction and imprisonment caused a scandal. They were released in 1621 and pardoned in 1624.

● **Somerset House** ▶ A building in the Strand, London (UK), built between 1776 and 1786 to a design by Sir William ▷Chambers. It occupies the site of a palace that the Duke of ▷Somerset ordered to be built in the mid-16th century. It formerly housed the General Register Office of births, marriages, and deaths, which has since been moved to the Family Records Centre in Myddleton Street, but the Board of Inland Revenue still occupies parts of the building. Its later E wing is part of King's College, London University; the Courtauld Institute took over another part of the building in 1990. A new complex of museums, restaurants, and shops opened in 2000, and open-air events are staged in the central Great Court.

● **Somme, River** ▶ A river in N France, rising in the Aisne department and flowing mainly W through Amiens and Abbeville to the English Channel. It was the scene of fighting in ▷World War I (1916). Length: 245 km (152 mi).

● **Sommerfeld, Arnold Johannes Wilhelm** ▶ (1868–1951) German physicist, who did his work on atomic structure while he was professor at Munich (1906–31). His modifications of the ▷Bohr atom included the introduction of elliptical orbits for the electrons and azimuthal and magnetic ▷quantum numbers. He also worked on ▷wave mechanics and the theory of electrons in metals.

● **somnambulism** ▷*See* sleepwalking.

● **sonar** ▷*See* echo sounding.

● **sonata** ▶ (Italian: sounded, as opposed to *cantata*, sung) A piece of music for one or more instruments. The name has been used of a variety of abstract musical forms, including baroque works for one or more instruments and continuo, the one-movement keyboard sonatas of Scarlatti, and the piano sonatas of Haydn and Mozart. **Sonata form**, the normal structure of the first movement of the classical sonata, was based on the exposition, development, and recapitulation of two contrasting themes. It was applied to the first movement of the ▷symphony and of ▷chamber music compositions as well as the sonata proper. Beethoven and his successors enlarged the formal boundaries of the sonata; Liszt evolved a single-movement form out of the three or four movements of the classical sonata. In the 20th century sonata form was adapted in a variety of ways and new formal patterns have been evolved by such composers as Bartók, Hindemith, Stravinsky, and Tippett.

● **Sondheim, Stephen (Joshua)** ▶ (1930–) US composer, who studied lyric writing with Oscar Hammerstein II and composition with Milton Babbitt. He wrote the lyrics for *West Side Story* (1957) and both words and music for *A Little Night Music* (1973), *Sweeney Todd* (1979), *Sunday In the Park with George* (1989), and *Assassins* (1992). The revue *Side by Side by Sondheim* (1976) contains many of his songs. In 1989 he became the first visiting professor of drama and musical theatre at Oxford University.

● **son et lumière** ▶ (French: sound and light) A nighttime, open-air dramatization of the history of a building, town, etc., using theatrical lighting effects with a synchronized sound track of music and speech. It was developed in 1952 at the Château de Chambord, France, by the Château's curator, Paul Robert-Houdin.

● **song** ▶ A short composition for one or more singers, with or without accompaniment. Song is usually regarded as the foundation of music and is certainly the oldest form of musical expression. Besides the folksong traditions of every race, solo song has been a significant part of established musical tradition. In Western music the French chansons of the 15th century, the Italian ▷frottola, the lute songs of the Elizabethans, operatic ▷arias, German *Lieder* (as treated by Schubert, Schumann, and Wolf), and the French tradition of *mélodies* (as treated by Duparc and Fauré) are all of great importance. A **song cycle** is a group of songs intended to be performed in sequence: the texts are either thematically related, or are all by the same poet.

● **Song** ► (*or* Sung) (960–1279) A Chinese dynasty that may be divided into the Northern and Southern Song periods. It was founded in N China by Zhao Guang Yin (*or* Chao K'uang Yin; 927–76), who reunited the war-torn country but, despite a strong administration, was never able to control the ▷Juchen. These tribes forced the Song south in 1127 and founded their own dynasty in the N. The Southern Song established a new capital at Hangzhou, where a great flourishing of Chinese poetry, painting, and pottery occurred. The Song were overthrown by the Mongols under Kublai Khan in 1279.

● **Song, T. V.** ► (*or* T. V. Sung; 1894–1971) Chinese banker and politician. He was finance minister (1925–31) and foreign minister (1942–45) in the Chinese Nationalist Government. After 1949 he lived in the USA. His elder sister **Song Qing-ling** (*or* Sung Ch'ing-ling; 1892–1981) married (1914) ▷Sun Yat-sen, who in 1923 became the first president of the Chinese Republic. She later became a revolutionary leader and remained a prominent member of the Chinese Communist Party until her death. Her younger sister **Song Mei-ling** (*or* Sung Mei-ling; 1900–) married (1927) the Nationalist leader ▷Chiang Kai-shek, fleeing with him to Taiwan following the Communist victory in 1949.

● **songbird** ► A ▷passerine bird belonging to the suborder *Oscines* (about 4000 species), in which the vocal organ (syrinx), at the junction of the trachea (windpipe) and bronchi, is highly developed. The flow of air vibrates the vocal membranes; muscles alter their tension and so produce the different notes. ▷Bird song communicates the identity and whereabouts of an individual to other birds and also signals alarm and sexual intentions; it is especially important in birds that feed or migrate in flocks.

● **Songhai** ► A West African people inhabiting the region of the Middle Niger River S of Timbuktu. Adopting the Islamic religion in the 11th century AD and influenced by Muslim traders from Africa, the Songhai became prosperous and cultured traders. Between about 1350 and 1600 their kings developed a vast commercial empire, based on the gold and salt trade, which extended from the West African coast to Lake Chad and absorbed the earlier empire of Mali. After the Moroccan invasion of 1591, the Songhai empire collapsed.

● **Songhua River** ► (*or* Sungari R.) A river in NE China, rising in ▷Jilin province and flowing roughly NE to the Heilong (*or* Amur) River on the border with Russia. Length: over 1300 km (800 mi).

● **Song of Solomon** ► An Old Testament book, also known as the Song of Songs or Canticles. It was traditionally ascribed to ▷Solomon but was probably written in the 2nd century BC. Written in extravagantly erotic language, it is a series of oriental love poems concerning a bridegroom and his bride, "the Shulamite." Both Jews and Christians interpreted the work allegorically as describing the relation between God and Israel or, for Christian commentators, between Christ and the Church.

● **song thrush** ► A Eurasian thrush, *Turdus philomelos*, about 22 cm long and having a brown back, pale breast streaked with brown, and orange underwings (*see* Plate III). Its song is loud and distinctive, each phrase being repeated several times. It feeds on invertebrates and smashes snails against a stone before eating them.

● **sonic boom** ▷*See* sound barrier.

● **sonnet** ► A poem of 14 lines originating in Italy in the 13th century and introduced into England in the 16th century by Sir Thomas ▷Wyatt. Its two principal variations are the Petrarchan sonnet, usually divided into an octet rhyming *abbaabba* and a sestet rhyming *cdecde*, and the Shakespearean sonnet, usually rhyming *abab cdcd efef gg*. Sonnets have been written by Milton, Wordsworth, and G. M. Hopkins and it remains one of the few traditional forms still employed by major 20th-century poets. ▷*See also* rhymes.

● **Soochow** ▷*See* Suzhou.

● **Soper, Donald Oliver, Baron** ► (1903–98) British Methodist minister and campaigner; he was made a life peer in 1965. A noted preacher and orator, he was known for his campaigns against war, homelessness, and field sports, among other causes; in his late eighties he was a leader in the pacifist opposition to the ▷Gulf War (1991). His books include *All His Grace* (1953) and *Calling for Action* (1984).

● **Sophia** ► (1657–1704) Regent of Russia (1682–89) for her brother Ivan V (1666–96) and half-brother ▷Peter the Great. She was overthrown by Peter and forced to retire to a convent.

● **Sophia** ► (1630–1714) Electress of Hanover (1658–1714), in whom the Act of ▷Settlement (1701) vested the English Crown. Wife of Elector Ernest Augustus (1629–98; ruled 1692–98), she was the granddaughter of James I of England and daughter of Frederick the Winter King, of the Palatinate. Her son became king of England as George I.

● **Sophists** ► The Greek sages of the 5th and early 4th centuries BC who were itinerant experts on various subjects including public speaking, grammar, ethics, literature, mathematics, and elementary physics. They were not a clearly defined school, but they did have certain interests in common. In philosophy they attacked the ▷Eleatics' account of reality and tried to explain the phenomenal world. Their educational programme centred on the belief that virtue can be taught. From their opponent ▷Plato, they acquired a bad name as philosophical tricksters, more interested in money and prestige than in truth. In Roman times the term "sophist" came to mean simply a teacher of rhetoric.

● **Sophocles** ► (c. 496–406 BC) Greek dramatist; with Aeschylus and Euripides, one of the three great Athenian tragic dramatists. He developed the more static drama of Aeschylus by introducing a third actor and reducing the role of the chorus. Of his 123 plays, 7 survive: *Ajax*, *Women of Trachis*, *Electra*, *Philoctetes*, and his three most famous plays dealing with Thebes, *Oedipus Rex*, *Oedipus at Colonus*, and *Antigone*. A friend of Pericles, he held several important civil and military administrative posts.

● **soprano** ► (Italian: upper) The highest female singing voice. Range: two octaves from middle C. The **mezzo-soprano** voice lies between the soprano and the contralto. Range: A below middle C to F an octave and a sixth above.

● **Sopwith, Sir Thomas Octave Murdoch** ► (1888–1989) British aircraft designer, best known for the World War I biplane, the Sopwith Camel, which he designed and built. He learned to fly in 1910 and founded the Sopwith Aviation Company Ltd in 1912. He was chairman of the Hawker Siddeley Group (1935–63), which developed the Hurricane fighter.

● **Soranus of Ephesus** ► (2nd century AD) Greek physician, whose works were a major influence on gynaecology and obstetrics until the 17th century. He described contraception, abortion, and procedures during childbirth and also wrote about fractures and diseases.

● **Sorbonne** ► One of the oldest parts of the university in Paris, France, founded by the theologian Robert de Sorbon (1201–74) in about 1257. The present site of the Sorbonne, off the Boulevard Saint-Michel, dates from 1627.

● **Sorel, Georges** ► (1847–1922) French social philosopher. As a political activist, Sorel believed that socialism could only come about through a general strike (*see* syndicalism). His theory of the "social myth," which held that the proletariat could be manipulated by propaganda, was, ironically, most successfully proved by the fascist dictators.

● **Sorghum** ► A genus of annual or perennial ▷grasses (about 30 species), native to Africa, especially *S. vulgare*, of which there are several varieties, such as sweet sorghum, ▷durra, and ▷kaffir corn, widely cultivated as cereal crops. Usually growing up to 2.5 m high, they have rigid stalks, sometimes containing a sweet sap, long flat leaves, and terminal flower clusters bearing 800–3000 starch-rich seeds. The seeds are used as grain for making bread, etc., and as a source of edible oil, starch, and sugar. The stalks are used as fodder or sometimes for syrup manufacture. □ p. 1168.

Sorghum ▶ A woman bringing in the harvest in Silmiougou village, Burkina Faso.

● **Sorocaba ▶** 23 30S 47 32W A city in S Brazil, in São Paulo state on the Rio Sorocaba. It is a major industrial centre; manufactures include textiles, fertilizers, and wine. Population (1991): 348 952.

● **sorrel ▶** A perennial herb, *Rumex acetosa*, common throughout temperate Eurasia and North America. It grows to a height of 1 m and bears numerous small red flowers. The tangy-tasting leaves are used as a culinary flavouring and in salads. Family: *Polygonaceae*. ▷*See also* wood sorrel.

● **Sorrento ▶** 40 37N 14 23E A seaport in SW Italy, in Campania. A resort since Roman times, it is the birthplace of the poet Tasso. Oranges and lemons are grown. Population (1990): 17 500.

● **Sosigenes of Alexandria ▶** (1st century BC) Greek astronomer, about whom little is known except that, on his advice, Julius Caesar reformed the calendar and added an extra day every four years to produce the modern system of leap years. This system is known as the Julian ▷calendar.

● **Sosnowiec ▶** 50 16N 19 07E A town in S Poland. It is a metallurgical centre; other industries include engineering, chemicals, and the manufacture of textiles. Population (1996 est): 249 000.

● **Sotho ▶** A large group of Bantu-speaking peoples of S Africa. The term applies in a general sense to the peoples of Botswana, Lesotho, and parts of NE South Africa, but, more specifically, to one of the four main divisions of these peoples, the Sotho of Lesotho. The other branches are the Tswana, Pedi, and Venda, each with many tribes. All live by combined agriculture and animal husbandry and have a broadly similar culture, now disintegrating under the impact of urbanization.

● **Soto ▶** The largest Japanese school of Zen Buddhism, founded in China in the 9th century AD and brought to Japan by ▷Dogen in 1227. Soto emphasizes meditation and morality. Adherents strive to live as what they hope to become, perfect Buddhas.

● **Soto, Hernando de ▶** (?1496–1542) Spanish explorer. After exploration in Central America, he set out in 1539 to conquer Florida. He landed with 600 men at Tampa Bay and journeyed circuitously through what became the S USA in search of gold. In 1541 he crossed the Mississippi, the first White man to do so, but died on the return journey.

● **Soufflot, Jacques Germain ▶** (1713–80) French architect. After training in Italy (1731–38), Soufflot became the leading French exponent of ▷neoclassicism. Apart from the Hôtel Dieu in Lyons (1841–48), his most famous building is the Church of St Geneviève in Paris (begun in 1757), now called the Panthéon.

● **soul music ▶** A style of popular music that emerged among US Blacks in the early 1960s; it combined the energy of ▷rhythm and blues and the fervour of ▷gospel music with elements of both jazz and popular White styles to create a fusion of wide appeal. Its main characteristic is an emotional and semi-improvised vocal style, in which the melody is interrupted by cries, shouts, etc., to convey passion. Famous soul singers include Aretha Franklin (1942–   ), Otis Redding (1941–67), and James Brown (1933–   ). Unlike earlier Black styles, soul music achieved popularity across racial barriers, particularly in the more commercial and melodic style developed by the Tamla Motown company of Detroit. Other varieties emphasized heavy dance rhythms, leading to the funk and disco styles of the 1970s.

● **Soult, Nicolas Jean de Dieu, Duc de Dalmatie ▶** (1769–1851) French general in the Revolutionary and Napoleonic Wars. A sergeant at the outbreak of the French Revolution, he rose to the rank of general in 1794 and later commanded in the Peninsular War. He became president of the council (1832–34, 1839–40, 1840–47) under Louis Philippe.

● **sound ▶** A disturbance propagated through a medium by longitudinal waves. Strictly the term applies only to those waves that are audible to the human ear, i.e. with frequencies between about 20 and 20 000 hertz, those with frequencies above 20 000 hertz being called ultrasound and those below 20 hertz infrasound. Sound is propagated by vibrations of molecules in the medium, producing fronts of compression and rarefaction. Sound waves are longitudinal as the molecules vibrate in the direction of propagation; the speed of sound in air at 0°C is about 332 metres per second (760 mph). The three principal characteristics of a sound are its pitch (the frequency of the wave), loudness (the amplitude of the wave), and ▷timbre (the extent to which it contains harmonics of the fundamental frequency). However, there is a relationship between pitch and loudness (*see* sound intensity). ▷*See also* acoustics; recording of sound.

● **Sound, the ▶** (Danish name: Øresund; Norwegian name: Öresund) A sea channel in N Europe, between Denmark (Sjælland) and Sweden, linking the Kattegat and the Baltic Sea. A bridge linking Denmark and Sweden was completed in 2000. Length: 113 km (70 mi). Narrowest point: 4 km (2.5 mi).

● **sound barrier ▶** An obstacle experienced by subsonic ▷aircraft attempting to fly at or above the speed of sound. Drag increases sharply, lift falls off, and the aircraft becomes difficult to control (*see* aeronautics). At subsonic speeds the pressure waves created by the aircraft as it flies through the air are able to move ahead of the aircraft; at supersonic speeds they cannot escape in a forward direction as the source is moving faster than the pressure waves themselves. Thus shock waves build up on the aircraft's wings and fuselage, creating an apparent barrier to supersonic flight. The barrier was overcome for the first time by the US Bell X1 rocket aircraft in 1947. Since then many aircraft capable of supersonic flight have been built (including Concorde) by greater streamlining, sweptback wings, and more powerful engines. As these aircraft cross the sound barrier a **sonic boom** is heard. This is created by a shock-wave cone with the nose of the aircraft at its vertex. In level flight the intersection of this cone with the ground produces a hyperbola at all points along which the boom is heard. The sound barrier on land was first broken by the British car ▷Thrust SSC in 1997.

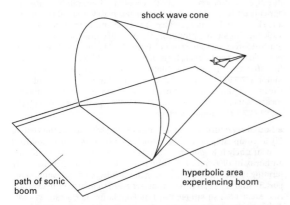

shock wave cone

path of sonic boom

hyperbolic area experiencing boom

sound barrier ▶ As an aircraft passes through the sound barrier the sonic boom is heard along a hyperbolic area on the ground.

● **sound intensity ▶** The rate at which sound energy is propagated through a unit area perpendicular to the direction of propagation. It is measured in watts per square metre. The intensities of two sound levels are compared by a unit called the ▷decibel. The intensity of sound is not the same as its loudness, the latter being the magnitude of the sensation produced by the human ear, which is dependent on the frequency of the sound.

● **Souphanouvong, Prince ▶** (1902–95) Laotian statesman; president (1975–86). In the civil war in Laos (1953–73) he led the revolutionary Pathet Lao and, on its conclusion, joined the coalition government established in 1974. In 1975, however, Pathet Lao forces seized complete control and Souphanouvong became president.

● **soursop ▶** An evergreen tree belonging to the tropical American genus *Annona*, especially *A. muricata*, widely cultivated in the Old World tropics. It grows to a height of 8 m and produces large oval spiny green fruit, the flesh of which can be eaten or used as an ingredient of soft drinks, ice cream, etc. Family: *Annonaceae*.

● **Sousa, John Philip ▶** (1854–1933) US composer and bandmaster. In 1880 he was appointed leader of the US Marine Corps Band and in 1892 formed his own band, which toured the world. He wrote military marches including "The Stars and Stripes Forever," "The Washington Post," "Semper Fidelis," and "Liberty Bell" and invented the **sousaphone**, a tuba-like band instrument with a forward-facing bell.

● **souslik ▶** (or suslik) A nocturnal ▷ground squirrel belonging to the genus *Citellus* (34 species), of E Europe, Asia, and North America (where it is sometimes called a gopher). The European souslik (*C. citellus*) is yellowish brown with large eyes and small ears and lives in burrows in dry open country, feeding on seeds, nuts, and bulbs. ▷*See also* chipmunk.

● **Sousse ▶** 35 50N 10 38E A port in central Tunisia, on the Mediterranean coast. It was founded by the Phoenicians as a port and trade centre. Its industries include sardine fishing and canning and olive-oil manufacture. Population (1994 est): 125 000.

● **Soustelle, Jacques (Émile) ▶** (1912–90) French anthropologist and politician. A member of the ▷Free French during World War II, he became secretary general of de Gaulle's Rassemblement du Peuple français in 1947. He was governor general of Algeria (1955–56) and subsequently opposed the policies of successive French governments towards Algeria, living in exile from 1961 to 1968. He then became director of the École pratique des hautes Études. His books include *Arts of Ancient Mexico* (1967).

● **South Africa, Republic of ▶** (Afrikaans name: Suid-Afrika) A country occupying the S tip of Africa. Narrow coastal plains rise to plateaus in the interior, with the Drakensberg mountains in the E reaching 3299 m (10 822 ft). The N is mainly desert. The Limpopo, Molopo, and Orange Rivers mark the N boundary. The Vaal, a tributary of the Orange, is another important river. The majority of the inhabitants are Africans (71%) with White, Coloured, and Asian (mostly Indian) minorities.

Economy: although South Africa is highly industrialized, agriculture is still important, with cereals, fruit growing, and cotton, as well as livestock. Fishing is a valuable source of income and whaling continues although efforts at conservation have reduced its scale. Mining is a major employer and the chief source of foreign exchange. South Africa is the world's biggest producer of gold, diamonds, platinum, and chrome; its exceptionally rich and varied mineral resources also include uranium, coal, manganese, vanadium, phosphates, and iron. Hydroelectricity is a valuable source of power. Industry is well developed but concentrated in the major cities and ports; it includes metals, machinery, chemicals, food processing, and textiles. Main exports include metals (especially gold), citrus fruits, sugar, wines, and textiles. Since the ending of ▷apartheid the economy has benefited from the lifting of international sanctions and embargoes but suffered from falling gold prices and foreign disinvestment. The government aims to repay the country's large foreign debt by 2002.

History: originally inhabited by ▷Khoisan peoples. Bantu-speaking tribes arrived from the north between 1000 and 1500. The Portuguese under ▷Dias first sighted the Cape of Good Hope (1488) but made no permanent settlement there. The Dutch East India Company settlement (1652) at Table Bay (Cape Town) expanded into a colony that spread into the interior. After Louis XIV revoked the Edict of Nantes (1685) Huguenot refugees augmented the White settlers. During the Napoleonic Wars Britain acquired the Cape Colony for strategic reasons, a possession confirmed in 1814. In the 1830s increasing numbers of Dutch farmers (or Boers, forebears of the modern Afrikaners) moved E and N to escape British rule, clashing with the ▷Bantu peoples who were then migrating southwards (*see* Great Trek). The Boers founded two independent republics, the Orange Free State and the Transvaal (*see* Sand River Convention), but their republic in Natal was soon annexed by the British (1843), who were also expanding the eastern boundaries of the Cape Colony (*see* Cape Frontier Wars). ▷Kruger's assertion of Boer independence led to war (1880–81), which broke out again between the Boers and the British after the discovery of gold (1886) in the Transvaal had led to hostility between the Boers and the immigrant gold-diggers (*see* Boer Wars). The need for cooperation led the two former Boer republics and the two British colonies to combine in the Union of South Africa (1910). In both World Wars South Africa, under J. C. ▷Smuts, enthusiastically supported Britain, but in 1948 Smuts was ousted by the anti-British Afrikaner National Party and in 1961 South Africa became a republic outside the Commonwealth. From 1910 until 1994 the treatment of the non-White majority was the crucial political issue; the system of apartheid, or religious segregation, was codified in 1948. In 1976 the ▷Transkei became the first independent ▷Bantu Homeland (Homelands were abolished in 1994). South Africa intervened in Angola (1976) and ▷Namibia and supported the White minorities in ▷Zimbabwe and ▷Mozambique. Some non-Whites received limited parliamentary power under a new tricameral constitution (1984). In 1985 the USA and EC imposed economic sanctions in protest against apartheid. In the face of increasing internal unrest, a state of emergency was declared in 1985. In 1989 P. W. ▷Botha was replaced as president by F. W. ▷de Klerk, who released Nelson ▷Mandela and other ANC leaders. The state of emergency was lifted in 1990 and de Klerk began to dismantle the apartheid system. In 1991 classification by race was ended and constitutional talks between the government and Black leaders began. In 1993 the government was replaced by a multiracial multiparty Transitional Executive Council, which devised an interim constitution establishing South Africa as a democratic multiparty state. Multiracial elections were held peacefully in April, 1994 and won by the ANC: Nelson ▷Mandela became president and de Klerk a deputy president. South Africa rejoined the Commonwealth in 1994. A permanent constitution was adopted in May, 1996; later that month, tensions in the ruling coalition led de Klerk's National Party to withdraw from government. Mandela's deputy, Thabo ▷Mbeki, was mainly responsible for the executive functions of government from late 1997. Mandela retired in 1999: the ANC won elections that year and Mbeki became president.

Republic of South Africa

Head of state	President Thabo Mbeki
Official languages	Afrikaans, English, and African languages
Official currency	rand of 100 cents
Area	1 221 042 sq km (472 359 sq mi)
Population (1998 est)	42 835 000
Capitals	Pretoria (administrative), Bloemfontein (judicial), Cape Town (legislative)

● **South America** ► The fourth largest continent, lying chiefly in the S of the W hemisphere between the Pacific and Atlantic Oceans. Roughly triangular in shape and tapering in the S, it is linked to the continent of North America by the Isthmus of Panama. An ancient shield occupies much of the NE part of the continent and forms the Brazilian and Guiana Highlands. These are separated by the vast basins of the Orinoco, Amazon, and Paraná–Paraguay river systems. In the extreme W, beyond a series of plains, rise the mountains and high plateaus of the ▷Andes, the world's longest mountain system. The Andes rise to their highest point at Mount ▷Aconcagua and contain Lake ▷Titicaca, the continent's highest lake. South America's climate varies considerably, largely because of its length, but much is tropical with vast areas of tropical rainforest (selva). The population consists chiefly of the indigenous Indians, Europeans (especially Spanish and Portuguese), and mestizos together with large numbers of Negroids.

History: archaeological evidence remains of the kingdoms of South America (such as those of the ▷Incas and ▷Chibchas), which were vanquished by the Spanish conquistadors. The entire continent was divided—Portugal taking the NE portion (now Brazil) and Spain the remainder—during the 16th century. With the collapse of the Spanish Empire during the early 19th century, there followed struggles for independence under national leaders, who included ▷Bolívar and ▷San Martín. Large-scale European immigration (including German and Italian) occurred in the 19th century. During the 20th century the constituent nations became increasingly industrialized and saw rapid rises in their populations. Although political and economic instability remained endemic for most of the century, democratic government is now in place everywhere except Ecuador, and several countries (notably Chile and Brazil) have achieved prosperity. Regional economic organizations now include the Latin American Integration Organization (*see* Latin America) and ▷Mercosur. Area: 17 767 331 sq km (6 858 527 sq mi). Population (1996 est): 317 846 000.

● **South American languages** ► The indigenous languages of South America, the Antilles, and parts of Central America, many of which are now extinct. Brought originally from North America by migrating Indians, the 600 documented languages are extremely diverse in nature. The number of speakers is currently estimated at 11 200 000, the majority of whom are to be found in the central Andes. The languages probably shared a common source.

● **Southampton** ► **1.** 50 55N 1 25W A city in S England, in Southampton unitary authority, Hampshire, on Southampton Water (an inlet of the English Channel). It is the UK's principal passenger port and has four tides daily. Southampton's industries include marine technology and research and yachtbuilding; at Fawley on Southampton Water is a large oil refinery. The University of Southampton was established in 1952. Population (1991): 210 138. **2.** A unitary authority in S England, in Hampshire. Area: 49 sq km (19 sq mi). Population (1999 est): 214 859.

● **Southampton, Henry Wriothesley, 3rd Earl of** ► (1573–1624) English courtier, famous as the patron of Shakespeare: *Venus and Adonis* (1593) and *The Rape of Lucrece* (1594) were dedicated to him. He was involved in the Earl of Essex's conspiracy against Elizabeth I (1600), persuading the players of the Globe Theatre to perform Shakespeare's *Richard II* (about the deposition of a king) to encourage revolt. His death sentence was commuted to life imprisonment; he was released by James I (1603).

● **South Australia** ► A state of S central Australia, bordering on the Indian Ocean and Great Australian Bight. It consists chiefly of low-lying plains with the ▷Great Victoria Desert in the W, rising in the NW to the Musgrave Ranges and in the SE to the Flinders Range. The only major river is the Murray. The rivers lying in the N exist only during a rainy season and Lake Eyre is often a huge salt flat. Intensive agriculture is restricted to the S; wheat, barley, vegetables, grapes, and sheep are the chief products. The vineyards of the fertile Barossa Valley are important, producing almost half of Australia's wine. Mineral resources include iron ore from the Middleback Ranges, low-grade coal at Leigh Creek, large natural gas fields in the N, and opals. Industry, concentrated in Adelaide, includes the manufacture of motor vehicles, textiles, and chemicals. There are iron and steel works and shipyards at Whyalla; Woomera has an experimental rocket range. Area: 984 377 sq km (380 070 sq mi). Population (1996 est): 1 477 700. Capital: Adelaide.

● **South Ayrshire** ► A council area of SW Scotland, on the Firth of Clyde, comprising part of the historic county of ▷Ayrshire. Absorbed into Strathclyde Region in 1975, it became an independent ▷unitary authority in 1996. South Ayrshire is mainly agricultural, with arable farming in the N and sheep raising in the hills to the S. Fishing is important and the coastal resorts of Ayr and Troon attract many tourists. Area: 1202 sq km (464 sq mi). Population (1999 est): 114 440. Administrative centre: Ayr.

● **South Bend** ► 41 40N 86 15W A city in the USA, in Indiana on the St Joseph River. Industries include the manufacture of aircraft, motor-vehicle parts, and machinery. The University of Notre Dame is here. Population (1996 est): 102 100.

● **South Carolina** ► A state in the SE USA, on the Atlantic coast. Lowlands make up two-thirds of the state rising to uplands in the NW. Although the state is mainly rural, industry is being developed. The large areas of woodland supply the furniture industries and the large textile and clothing industries are based on the region's cotton crop. Other leading manufactures include chemicals, machinery, and food products.

History: one of the 13 original colonies, it became separate from North Carolina in 1713 and was the first state to secede from the Union (1860). Area: 80 432 sq km (31 055 sq mi). Population (1997 est): 3 760 181. Capital: Columbia.

● **South Caucasian languages** ► A group of languages, also known as the Kartvelian languages, spoken by the people of W Transcaucasia and adjacent regions. It includes ▷Georgian, Svan, Mingrelian, and Laz. Only Georgian possesses a literary tradition.

● **South China Sea** ▷*See* China Sea.

● **Southcott, Joanna** ► (1750–1814) British religious fanatic. A domestic servant, she began prophesying in 1792, claiming to be the woman in Revelation 12 who would give birth to the second Messiah. She died of a brain disease. Her following lasted into the 20th century.

● **South Dakota** ► One of the Plains states in N central USA. The Missouri River separates the arid Badlands, the Black Hills, and the Great Plains in the W from the flat fertile prairie in the E, which forms the basis of South Dakota's predominantly agrarian economy. Livestock and livestock products are the chief source of revenue. Although it has the largest gold mine in the USA, mineral extraction is minimal.

History: part of the Louisiana Purchase (1803), the gold rush and land boom of the 1880s brought many settlers and South Dakota became a state in 1889. Area: 199 551 sq km (77 047 sq mi). Population (1997 est): 737 973. Capital: Pierre.

● **South East Asia Treaty Organization** ► (SEATO) An organization formed to protect SE Asia from possible communist aggression. It was analogous to the ▷North Atlantic Treaty Organization. The treaty was signed in Manila in 1954 by Australia, France, New Zealand, Pakistan, the Philippines, Thailand, the UK, and the USA. Pakistan withdrew in 1973 and the organization was formally ended in 1977. ▷*See also* Association of South-East Asian Nations.

● **Southend-on-Sea** ► **1.** 51 33N 0 43E A resort in SE England, in Southend-on-Sea unitary authority, Essex, on the lower Thames estuary. It is the nearest seaside resort to London and has the world's longest pleasure pier. Population (1991): 158 517. **2.** A unitary authority in SE England, in Essex. Area: 42 sq km (16 sq mi). Population (1997 est): 175 500.

● **Southern Alps** ► The highest range of mountains in New Zealand. It extends SW–NE through South Island and contains many peaks over 3000 m (10 000 ft), including Mount ▷Cook. Glaciers, fed by the central snowfields, flank the mountains and include Tasman Glacier. It is an important winter-sports area.

● **Southern and Antarctic Territories** ▷*See* Terre Adélie.

● **Southern Cross** ▷*See* Crux.

● **Southern Ocean** ► The name sometimes given to the S parts of the Atlantic, Pacific, and Indian Oceans. It lies S of the **Roaring Forties**, i.e. at latitudes between 40° and 50° S, where strong westerly winds predominate, making it the stormiest of the world's oceans. Inside the Antarctic Circle the sea is sometimes called the **Antarctic Ocean**, which is covered with drifting pack ice except in late February and early March.

● **Southern Rhodesia** ▷*See* Zimbabwe, State of.

● **southernwood** ► A perennial herb, *Artemisia abrotanum*, also called lad's love, native to S Europe and Asia and cultivated for ornament and for its aromatic leaves, which can be used to make a beverage. Family: ▷*Compositae.* ▷*See also* wormwood.

● **Southey, Robert** ► (1774–1843) British poet and writer. He was a close associate of ▷Wordsworth and ▷Coleridge and in 1803 settled in the Lake District. His early political radicalism was short lived, and he became a leading contributor to the Tory *Quarterly Review*. He became poet laureate in 1813. His poetry lacks originality and was overshadowed by the work of his greater contemporaries. He wrote several historical books, notably *The Life of Nelson* (1813).

● **South Georgia** ► An island in the S Atlantic Ocean, a United Kingdom overseas territory (with the South Sandwich Islands). There is no permanent population but the British Antarctic Survey has a base here; the British military garrison was withdrawn in 2001. Until 1985 South Georgia was a dependency of the Falkland Islands. With the Falkland Islands, it was invaded by Argentina in 1982, but was recaptured by British forces. Area: 3755 sq km (1450 sq mi).

● **South Glamorgan** ► A former county of SE Wales, bordering on the Bristol Channel. It was created in 1974 from S Glamorgan, including Cardiff, and SW Monmouthshire. In 1996 it was replaced by two new ▷unitary authorities, the county boroughs of Cardiff and Vale of Glamorgan.

● **South Gloucestershire** ► A unitary authority of SW England, in Gloucestershire; it was part of Avon county from 1974 to 1996. Area: 510 sq km (197 sq mi). Population (1996 est): 235 100.

● **South Holland** ► (Dutch name: Zuid-Holland) A province in the W central Netherlands, on the North Sea. Its S part consists of several islands. It is densely populated and agriculture, especially cattle raising and flower bulbs, is the chief occupation. The extensive trading and shipping industry is centred on the port of Rotterdam. Tourism is also important. Area: 3333 sq km (1287 sq mi). Population (1997 est): 3 334 700. Capital: The Hague.

● **South Island** ► The larger of the two principal islands of New Zealand, separated from North Island by Cook Strait. It is generally mountainous, rising over 3500 m (11 483 ft) in the ▷Southern Alps in the W, with coastal plains. Area: 153 947 sq km (684 sq mi).

● **South Korea** ▷*See* Korea.

● **South Lanarkshire** ► A council area of S Scotland, consisting of the S part of the historic county of Lanarkshire. Absorbed into Strathclyde Region in 1975, it became an independent ▷unitary authority in 1996. It consists of the valley of the River Clyde, running from the Lowther Hills in the S to the edges of the Glasgow conurbation in the NW. It is mainly agricultural, with sheep farming in the S uplands and fruitgrowing in the lower Clyde valley; forestry is also important. There are various industries in Hamilton and East Kilbride. Area: 1771 sq km (684 sq mi). Population (1996 est): 307 450. Administrative centre: Hamilton.

● **Southland Plain** ► A low-lying area of New Zealand, on SE South Island bordering on the Pacific Ocean. Sheep rearing and dairying are important.

● **South Orkney Islands** ► A group of islands within the British Antarctic Territory, in the S Atlantic Ocean. A dependency of the Falkland Islands until 1962, they were a whaling base. They are also claimed by Argentina.

● **South Ossetia** ► (official name since 1996: Tskhinvali) A disputed region in Georgia. Its inhabitants comprise chiefly Orthodox Christian Ossetians, a Caucasian people. Timber is produced and its many rivers are used to generate hydroelectric power. Livestock are raised in the higher regions. In 1990 South Ossetia voted to join Russia, leading to armed conflict with Georgian state forces. The situation stabilized following the deployment of joint Russian and Georgian peacekeeping forces in 1992 but a permanent settlement has not been found. Area: 3900 sq km (1500 sq mi). Population (1990 est): 100 000. Capital: Tskhinvali.

● **South Pole** ▷*See* Antarctica.

● **Southport** ► 53 39N 3 01W A town and resort in NW England, in Sefton unitary authority, Merseyside, on the Irish Sea. Its annual flower show is famous and there is a well-known golf course at nearby Birkdale. Population (1991): 90 959.

● **South Sandwich Islands** ► A group of islands in the S Atlantic Ocean, about 750 km (470 mi) SE of South Georgia. The islands, which are uninhabited and have an Antarctic climate, form part of the United Kingdom overseas territory of South Georgia. Area: 285 sq km (130 sq mi).

● **South Sea Bubble** ► (1720) The collapse of the British market in South Sea stocks that had far-reaching political repercussions. The South Sea Company was founded in 1711 to trade with Spanish America and in 1718 George I became its governor. A boom in South Sea stock was followed by collapse; a subsequent inquiry revealed corruption among ministers and even touched the king. The day was saved by Sir Robert ▷Walpole, who transferred the South Sea stocks to the Bank of England and the East India Company.

● **South Shetland Islands** ► An uninhabited archipelago within the British Antarctic Territory, in the S Atlantic Ocean. Until 1962 they were a dependency of the British Falkland Islands.

● **South Shields** ► 55 00N 1 25W A port in NE England, in South Tyneside unitary authority, Tyne and Wear; it is situated on the Tyne estuary opposite North Shields. Petrochemicals and paint manufacture are important, but shipbuilding has declined. The first lifeboat was built here (1790). Population (1991): 83 704.

● **South Tyneside** ► A unitary authority in NE England, in Tyne and Wear. Area 64 sq mi (25 sq mi). Population (1996 est): 156 100.

● **Southwark** ► A borough of S central Greater London, on the River Thames. Created in 1965 from the former metropolitan boroughs of Bermondsey, Camberwell, and Southwark, it is famous for its historic inns, its 12th-century cathedral, and the sites of the ▷Globe and ▷Rose Theatres. Area: 29 sq km (11 sq mi). Population (1996 est): 229 900.

● **South West Africa** ▷*See* Namibia, Republic of.

● **South Yorkshire** ► A metropolitan county of N England, created in 1974 from the S part of the West Riding of Yorkshire and a small part of NE Derbyshire. In 1986 the county council was abolished and administrative powers were devolved to the districts of Sheffield, Rotherham, Doncaster, and Barnsley. Agriculture is varied with sheep farming in the W on the Pennines, dairy farming on the lower slopes, and arable farming on the lowlands in the E. Industry includes iron and steel, and engineering. Area: 1562 sq km (603 sq mi).

● **Soutine, Chaim** ► (1893–1943) Lithuanian-born painter, who emigrated to Paris in 1913. Influenced by ▷expressionism, he achieved recognition in the 1920s despite his reluctance to exhibit his work. Using thickly applied paint, intense colour, and distorted forms, he was, with ▷Chagall, the leading representative of French expressionism.

● **sovereignty** ► The supreme power of a nation or state to rule over its territory. It is recognized by other nations or states either *de jure* (by the right of law) or *de facto* (because it exists in fact rather than by law). Although sovereignty theoretically implies that the nation or state has total power within its territory to do what it wants, in practice ▷international law can impose some restrictions if ▷human rights are endangered or infringed.

Internally, sovereignty within a nation or state lies with a monarch (the **sovereign**), a legislature or executive, or the people of the state. In the UK sovereignty lies with parliament, but in the USA the constitution places restrictions on the government's powers, ultimate responsibility residing with the people.

● **Sovetsk** ▶ (name until 1945: Tilsit) 55 02N 21 50E A town in W Russia, on the River Nemen. Founded by the Teutonic Knights in 1288, it was here that the Treaties of ▷Tilsit were signed (1807) between Napoleon and, respectively, Prussia (which held the town until 1945) and Russia. Industries include food processing and the manufacture of pulp. Population (latest est): 43 000.

● **soviet** ▶ A government council in the Soviet Union. Soviets originated as committees of workers' deputies in the ▷Revolution of 1905 and were again established in the ▷Russian Revolution of 1917, which established the ▷Soviet Union. The Supreme Soviet was in theory the supreme organ of government in the Soviet Union; soviets were also elected at the local, provincial, and republican levels. Candidates, one for each deputy, were selected by the Communist Party.

● **Soviet Union** ▶ (official name: Union of Soviet Socialist Republics) A former country in E Europe and Asia, covering N Eurasia and bordering on the Pacific and Arctic Oceans and the Baltic, Black, Caspian, and Aral Seas. It was a federal state comprising 15 constituent republics: the Armenian, Azerbaidzhan, Belarussian, Estonian, Georgian, Kazakh, Kirgiz, Latvian, Lithuanian, Moldavian, Russian Soviet Federal, Tadzhik, Turkmen, Ukrainian, and Uzbek Soviet Socialist Republics. Administrative subdivisions included 20 Autonomous Soviet Socialist Republics and, within some of these, 8 autonomous regions (Russian *oblast*, region). The population included over a hundred national groups, for whom many of the country's subdivisions were established. Chief among these were the Russians, Ukrainians, Uzbeks, Belarussians, Tatars, and Kazakhs.

Economy: formerly based on state ownership and controlled through Gosplan (the State Planning Commission) and Gosbank (the State Bank), it began a programme of liberalization in the late 1980s, with plans to adopt a free-market economy and to permit privatization of state monopolies, the establishment of a stock exchange, and new pricing policies. Such a system was designed to replace the ▷five-year plans, under which the economy had been directed since 1928. With vast natural resources, the Soviet Union was the world's leading producer of oil, coal, iron ore, cement, and steel; manganese, gold, natural gas, and other minerals were also of major importance. Industry was concentrated after 1928 on the production of capital goods through metalworking, machine manufacture, and the chemical industry, and relatively few consumer goods were produced. In the 1980s the latter received much more emphasis. Agriculture, organized in a system of state and collective farms, was on a large scale and highly mechanized but not highly productive, hampered in many areas by the climate and by a shortage of resources. The Soviet Union was one of the world's greatest producers of cereals, although bad harvests in the 1970s and 1980s necessitated imports and hampered the economy. Fishing, forestry, and dependent industries were also important; the country was the world's greatest producer of timber.

History: The February and October revolutions in Russia (*see* Russian Revolution) were followed by a period of civil war after which communist control was complete. The Soviet Union was created in 1922 from the union of Russia, Ukraine, Belarussia and Transcaucasia. After ▷Lenin's death (1924), ▷Stalin had emerged as leader by 1928, having ousted Trotsky. Under Stalin, who replaced Lenin's New Economic Policy with five-year plans and collective farms, the Soviet Union became a major industrial power but a totalitarian state, with effective political opposition eliminated during the 1930s by purges. The end of World War II established the Soviet Union as one of the two major world powers, with effective control over much

of E Europe (*see* Warsaw Pact). Relations with the other superpower, the USA, became tense during the ▷Cold War and again following the Soviet invasion of Afghanistan (1979). The Soviet Government used military force to crush the Hungarian Revolution (1956) and the Czechoslovakian liberalization programme (1968). In 1982 the Soviet leadership directed the suppression of the ▷Solidarity trade union in Poland. Internal dissent was similarly suppressed until the mid-1980s, when more liberal policies were adopted under ▷Gorbachov (*see* glasnost). A limited parliament of approved elected representatives called the Congress of People's Deputies was established in 1989 and in 1990 the Communists voted to give up their guaranteed right to rule, to create a strong new executive presidency, and to allow private property ownership. Relations with the West improved greatly with important agreements on ▷disarmament. In 1989 the Soviet Union did not intervene when Communist regimes throughout E Europe were replaced by multiparty systems. The 1980s also saw growing separatist movements in many of the Soviet Union's constituent republics. In 1991 Communist Party rule in the Soviet Union collapsed following the failure of an anti-Gorbachov coup by Communist hardliners. The constituent republics asserted their independence and the Soviet Union ceased to exist in December, 1991. In the same month the ▷Commonwealth of Independent States, a looser organization with responsibility for economic and military cooperation, was formed.

● **Soweto** ▶ 26 10S 28 02E A large urban area in South Africa, forming a suburb of Johannesburg. It is inhabited solely by Black Africans and comprises 36 townships, divided into tribal areas. In June, 1976, it was the scene of serious rioting during which over a hundred people died. There were further riots in 1985. Population (1991): 596 632.

● **sow thistle** ▶ A herb of the genus *Sonchus*, especially *S. oleraceus*, occurring as a weed in Europe, W Asia, and N Africa. Growing to 20–150 cm, its oval leaves have prickly edges; it produces yellow flowers. Family: ▷*Compositae*.

● **soya** ▶ (or soya bean, soy, or soybean) An annual plant, *Glycine max*, widely cultivated for its seeds. The many commercial varieties grow to heights of 20–200 cm and produce clusters of pods, each containing two or three seeds. The ripe seeds contain 35% protein. Soya-bean oil is extracted for use in making margarines, cooking oils, and many other foods, resins, paints, chemicals, and textiles. The meal residue is an important protein food for livestock and a meat substitute for humans. The beans are also eaten whole, ground into flour, made into soy sauce and soya milk, and form the basis of a variety of other foods. Genetically modified soya products are now used in the food industry (*see* genetic engineering). Family: ▷*Leguminosae*.

● **Soyinka, Wole** ▶ (1934–) Nigerian dramatist and writer. His works include the plays *The Lion and the Jewel* (1963) and *A Scourge of Hyacinths* (1992), the novels *The Interpreters* (1965) and *The Man Died* (1973), and *The Burden of Memory, the Muse of Forgiveness* (1998), a collection of essays. He edited the literary journal *Black Orpheus* (1960–64) and was imprisoned during the Nigerian civil war (1967–69). In the mid-1990s he became a leading critic of the military regime and was obliged to flee abroad: he was charged with treason in 1997 but the charges were dropped in 1998 and he returned to Nigeria. He was awarded the 1986 Nobel Prize.

● **Soyuz** ▷*See* Salyut.

● **Spa** ▶ 50 29N 5 52E A town in SE Belgium. It is a tourist resort, renowned since the 14th century for its mineral springs. Population (1991): 10 140.

● **spacecraft** ▶ A vehicle designed to be launched into space and to function effectively for a considerable period in the hostile conditions of space. Due to the immense expense and the difficulties involved in prolonged space travel, most spacecraft are unmanned. Their instruments are powered by arrays of solar cells (*see* solar power), for craft out to about Mars' orbit, and can be controlled by ground stations. Their information is sent back to earth as radio transmissions. Some 75 unmanned spacecraft were launched into orbit in 1992. ▷*See also* planetary probe; space shuttle; space station.

● **space exploration** ▶ The space age began with the launching of the Soviet satellite Sputnik 1 on 4 October, 1957. The first manned flight, one earth orbit, was made by the Soviet cosmonaut Yuri ▷Gagarin on 12 April, 1961. Man first flew round the moon in December, 1968, aboard the US Apollo 8 and first landed on the lunar surface in the lunar module of Apollo 11 in July, 1969 (see Apollo moon programme). Although manned exploration of space has at present gone no further than the moon, unmanned ▷planetary probes have been sent to every planet as far as Neptune. Pioneer 10 (launched in 1972) passed Jupiter in 1973 and is now 5 billion miles away but is still detecting the solar wind; Pioneer 11 reached Saturn in September, 1979; Voyager 2 flew past Uranus sending back photographs in 1986 and passed Neptune in 1989. Most probes have made a close fly-by of targeted planets; the Mariner 9, Viking, Vega, and Pioneer Venus spacecraft orbiting both Mars and Venus were able to make more extensive observations, as was the Pathfinder spacecraft that landed on Mars in 1997.

space shuttle ► The US shuttle *Atlantis* as seen from the Russian space station *Mir*, during docking operations in 1995.

● **space shuttle ►** One of a series of manned reusable space transportation systems. The first series was developed by ▷NASA and was in operational use by 1982. It consists of a delta-wing Orbiter that has three powerful rocket engines, a large cargo bay, and living space. It is launched into low earth orbit by rocket propulsion. Although its two externally mounted rocket boosters can be recovered after they detach shortly after launch, the huge external propellant tank is discarded. Satellites, probes, and manned space laboratories such as Spacelab can be launched from the cargo bay and have also been brought into the bay for on-site repair and redeployment or return to earth. Scientific, technological, and medical experiments are also performed. Having completed its mission (7–30 days), the shuttle enters the earth's atmosphere in a shallow dive and makes an unpowered landing. The series began with the first successful test flight of *Columbia* (1981) and ended with the explosion of *Challenger* (1986) two minutes after blast-off, with the death of the seven crew; flights were resumed in 1988. The Soviet Union first launched the *Buran* space shuttle in 1988. In 1993 the US shuttle *Endeavour* was used to take a team of scientists to repair the ▷Hubble space telescope.

● **space station ►** A large orbiting spacecraft on which people can live and work in weightless conditions. Crews are ferried to and from the station, remaining on board for up to several months. The first space station was the Soviet ▷Salyut–1, launched in 1971; America's ▷Skylab was orbited in 1973. In 1986 the USSR put into orbit its giant space station ▷Mir and in 1994 NASA announced plans for Alpha, an international space station. The project started in 1998 in collaboration with 14 other nations.

● **space-time continuum ►** (or Minkowski space) A coordinate system that has four dimensions, three representing physical space and the fourth time. The four-dimensional space-time continuum was suggested by Herman ▷Minkowski and is used in ▷relativity to define an event. For example, an event occurring on the sun would be observed at different times on earth and on Jupiter, as light from the sun takes some 35 minutes longer to reach Jupiter than to reach the earth. Thus the concept of simultaneity requires a four-dimensional coordinate system to define events without ambiguity.

● **space warfare** ▷See Strategic Defence Initiative.

● **spadefoot toad ►** A nocturnal burrowing ▷toad belonging to a widely distributed family (*Pelobatidae*). Spadefoot toads survive in arid regions by digging themselves deep holes in sand or mud with a special horny structure on the foot. The European spadefoot (*Pelobates fuscus*) exudes a garlic-smelling secretion when harmed.

● **Spain, Kingdom of ►** A country in SW Europe, occupying over four-fifths of the Iberian Peninsula. The Balearic and Canary Islands are also part of Spain and there are several tiny enclaves on the N African coast. It consists mainly of a high plateau, rising over 3000 m (10 000 ft) in the Pyrenees in the NE.

Economy: although Spain retained a traditional agricultural economy for much longer than most of W Europe, the industrial sector had begun to predominate by the early 1970s. After many years of economic stagnation, there was a remarkable improvement in the 1960s with the development of the motor-vehicle, machine-tool, shipbuilding, and chemical industries. Tourism, an important source of foreign currency, has flourished since the 1970s. There is both livestock and crop farming and varied crops include wheat, barley, citrus fruit, olives, and vegetables (especially potatoes, onions, and tomatoes). There is a thriving wine industry and sherry is produced in the SW. Forestry is important, and fishing (sardines, tuna, and cod) has been developed as a major industry. Rich mineral resources include coal, lignite, anthracite, and iron ore. Hydroelectricity is a valuable source of power. A major privatization programme was inaugurated in 1996.

History: remains of Neanderthal man have been found at Gibraltar, Valencia, and Gerona, and Spain was subsequently inhabited by Iberians, Celts, Phoenicians, and Greeks. In the 3rd century BC the Carthaginians under Hamilcar Barca conquered most of the Iberian peninsula but were expelled by the Romans in the second ▷Punic War (218–201 BC). Christianity was introduced in the 1st century AD and by the 5th century the Romans had given way to German tribes, including the Vandals and then the Visigoths. The Visigothic kingdom collapsed (711) in the face of Muslim invaders, who dominated most of the central and S parts of the peninsula under a series of powerful dynasties (see Umayyads; Abbadids; Almoravids; Almohads). The reconquest of Muslim Spain was pursued throughout the middle ages by the Christian kingdoms in the N and was completed in 1492 with the conquest of Granada by Ferdinand of Aragon and Isabella of Castile. The union of Spain, begun by the union of Aragon and Castile following the marriage (1469) of Ferdinand and Isabella, was now complete. The year 1492 also saw the expulsion from Spain of the Jews, who were followed after much persecution (1609) by the Muslims; the influence of both peoples on Spanish culture was enormous. The 16th century was Spain's golden age. Overseas exploration led to the formation of an empire in the New World, which brought great wealth to Spain. The country's prestige and power, as well as its possessions, in Europe were furthered by the Habsburg kings Charles I (who as ▷Charles V was also Holy Roman Emperor) and his son Philip II but the latter's reign witnessed the beginnings of decline. The ▷Revolt of the Netherlands against Spanish rule led to the secession (1581) of the northern Dutch provinces and in 1588 Spain suffered the humiliating defeat of the Armada by the English. Following the Thirty Years' War Spain lost to France its position as the leading European power (1659). The death in 1700 of the last Habsburg king (Charles II), without an heir, led to the War of the ▷Spanish Succession (1701–14). This confirmed the succession of the Bourbon Philip V but deprived Spain of the Spanish Netherlands, Milan, Naples, Sardinia, and Sicily. In the second half of the 18th century Spain's decline was arrested by reform, especially under ▷Charles III, but in 1808 Napoleon invaded and established his brother Joseph Bonaparte on the Spanish throne. The Spanish resistance to their French conquerors contributed to the defeat of Napoleon (see Peninsular War) and in 1814 the Bourbon Ferdinand VII was restored.

▷Carlism and conflict between monarchists and republicans (the latter achieved short-lived victory in 1873–74) dominated the 19th century, during which Spain also lost its last American possessions. It was neutral in World War I, following which ▷Primo de Rivera established a military dictatorship that undermined the position of the monarchy. In 1931 Alfonso XIII abdicated and the Second Republic was established. The electoral victory of the Popular Front under Azaña in 1936 precipitated a military revolt led by Gen ▷Franco that became the ▷Spanish Civil War (1936–39). Franco's victory initiated over three decades of Nationalist dictatorship. Following Franco's death in 1975, the monarchy was restored and Juan Carlos de Borbón became king and head of state. After widespread demonstrations and industrial conflict Carlos Arias Navarro was replaced as prime minister by Adolfo Suárez and the return to a democratic form of government proceeded more rapidly. In 1978 provisional regional self-government was granted to Catalonia, Valencia, the Canary Islands, Aragon, Galicia, and the Basque provinces, although terrorist activities by Basque separatists have continued. The remaining regions of Spain have also been granted limited autonomy. Spain's first Socialist government in nearly 50 years was elected in 1982 under Felipe González. He was re-elected in 1993 but without an overall majority, forcing him to form a coalition. In 1996 José María Aznar led the right-wing Popular Party to victory in general elections. He was re-elected with a large majority in 2000. Spain joined the North Atlantic Treaty Organization (NATO) in 1982 and became a member of the EC (now the EU) in 1986. It adopted the European single currency in 1999–2002.

Kingdom of Spain

Head of state	King Juan Carlos I
Official language	Spanish; Basque, Catalan, and Galician also have official status in the appropriate regions
Official religion	Roman Catholic
Official currency	euro of 100 cents
Area	504 879 sq km (194 883 sq mi)
Population (2001 est)	40 144 000
Capital	Madrid
Main port	Barcelona

● **Spalato** ▷See Split.

● **Spalding** ► 52 47N 0 10W A market town in E England, in S Lincolnshire on the River Welland. It is well known for bulb growing (especially its tulips). Population (1991): 18 731.

● **Spallanzani, Lazzaro** ► (1729–99) Italian physiologist, noted for his studies of microscopic life. Spallanzani demonstrated that microorganisms arose not by spontaneous generation but from spores in the air. He also studied regeneration, digestion, and spermatozoa. He showed that contact by semen was necessary for development of the egg and he achieved the first successful artificial insemination of a dog.

● **Spandau** ► 52 32N 13 13E An industrial district of Berlin, Germany. Nazi war criminals were imprisoned in the 16th-century fortress after 1946. After the suicide of the last inmate, Rudolf Hess, in 1987 the prison was demolished. Population (latest est): 193 700.

● **spaniel** ► One of several breeds of sporting dogs developed in Britain and thought to have originated in Spain. The English springer spaniel is typical, having a lean compact body, long muzzle, and long drooping ears. It is longer in the leg than the similar ▷cocker spaniel but has the same flat wavy weather-resistant coat. It is generally black and white or liver and white, while the smaller Welsh springer spaniel is always red and white. The white Clumber spaniel, bred at Clumber Park, Nottinghamshire, England, is the heaviest breed. The Irish water spaniel has a distinctive curly dark-brown coat and is a strong swimmer. Height: 51 cm (English springer); 53–61 cm (Irish water); 46–48 cm (Welsh springer). ▷See also King Charles spaniel.

● **Spanish** ► A ▷Romance language spoken in Spain, Latin America, the Philippines, and elsewhere by about 308 million people. The standard form is based on the Castilian dialect, originally spoken in the Burgos region, which was the official language of Spain in the late 15th century.

● **Spanish Armada** ▷See Armada, Spanish.

● **Spanish Civil War** ► (1936–39) The civil war in Spain precipitated by a military revolt on 18 July, 1936, led by the Nationalist Gen ▷Franco, against the Republican Government of ▷Azaña. By the end of 1936 the Nationalists had gained control of most of W and S Spain, while the Republicans held the urban areas of the E and N, including Madrid, Valencia, Barcelona, and Bilbao. During 1937 the Nationalists, with Italian and German help, failed in their attempt to take Madrid but captured Bilbao; in April occurred the indiscriminate bombing by German planes of the town of Guernica, an event commemorated in a famous painting by Picasso. In 1938, however, in spite of the assistance of the ▷International Brigade and the Soviet Union, the Republican front was broken and early in 1939 Barcelona, Valencia, and then Madrid fell. The war, which claimed some 750 000 Spanish lives, rallied liberals throughout Europe against fascism.

● **Spanish fly** ► A golden-green European ▷blister beetle, *Lytta vesicatoria*, that is the chief source of cantharidin. This chemical can be extracted from its dried body—especially the wing cases—and was formerly used as a blistering agent and diuretic (it was also reputedly an aphrodisiac).

● **Spanish Guinea** ▷See Equatorial Guinea, Republic of.

● **Spanish Inquisition** ▷See Inquisition.

● **Spanish literature** ► The earliest major work of Spanish literature is the heroic epic *Poema de mío Cid*, dating from the 12th century and written in the Castilian vernacular. Catalan poetry flourished during the 15th century, but after the union of Aragon and Castile in 1479, the Castilian language became dominant throughout Spain. Major writers of the ▷Siglo de Oro, which lasted from about 1550 to 1650, include ▷Cervantes and Lope de ▷Vega. After the death of ▷Calderón de la Barca, little literature of major importance was produced until the regional novels of Juan Valera (1824–1905) and ▷Pérez Galdós appeared in the late 19th century. A dominant influence during the early 20th century was the philosopher and novelist Miguel de ▷Unamuno. The major poets were Rubén ▷Darío, who introduced modernist theories to Spain from his native Nicaragua, ▷Jiménez, and ▷García Lorca. Many writers went into exile during the Civil War and Franco dictatorship; partly as a consequence, most of the best literature in Spanish in recent decades has been produced in Latin America by such writers as ▷Borges, ▷Neruda, ▷Paz, ▷García Márquez, and ▷Vargas Llosa. In Spain itself the leading writers of the postwar era have included the poet Vicente Aleixandre (1898–1984) and the novelists Camilo José ▷Cela and Juan Goytisolo (1931–).

● **Spanish moss** ► **1.** An epiphytic plant, *Tillandsia usneoides* (or *Dendropogon usneoides*), also known as black moss, long moss, and vegetable horsehair, which is found in warm regions of America. Its seeds are windblown to trees, where they germinate and grow downwards in silvery-grey masses, 6–7.5 m long. It is covered in hairlike scales, which absorb water from the air. When dried it can be used as packing material or upholstery. Family: *Bromeliaceae*. **2.** A tropical lichen, *Usnea longissima*, which resembles *T. usneoides*.

● **Spanish Riding School** ► (full name: Imperial Spanish Riding School of Vienna) A centre for classical horsemanship in Vienna. Founded in the Habsburg imperial palace, prob-ably in the late 16th century, it was moved to its present building, designed by ▷Fischer von Erlach, in about 1730. Here the purest *haute école* ▷dressage of the 16th and 17th centuries is practised. The white ▷Lipizzaner stallions used here have been bred from horses imported from Spain in the 16th century—hence the title "Spanish."

● **Spanish Sahara** ▷*See* Western Sahara.

● **Spanish Succession, War of the** ► (1701–14) The third of the European wars caused by Louis XIV's attempts to increase French power. The immediate cause of conflict was the dispute over the succession to the Spanish throne. Following the death of the childless Charles II, Louis proclaimed the succession of his grandson as Philip V. England felt menaced by the prospect of a union of French and Spanish dominions and by French commercial expansion. England, the Dutch Republic, and the Holy Roman Emperor formed an alliance against France in 1701 and were joined by most German states upon the outbreak of general hostilities (1702). Spain, Bavaria, Portugal, and Savoy supported France. The English won a series of brilliant victories under the Duke of ▷Marlborough but pressed for peace in 1712, when a Spanish-Austrian union threatened. The Treaties of ▷Utrecht (1713–14) concluded the war, which marked the end of French expansionism under Louis.

● **Spanish Town** ► 17 59N 76 58W A town in SE Jamaica, on the Rio Cobre. Founded in 1525, it was the capital of Jamaica until 1871. Population (1982): 89 097.

● **Spark, Dame Muriel** ► (1918–) British novelist, born in Edinburgh. She achieved success with satirical novels such as *Memento Mori* (1959), *The Prime of Miss Jean Brodie* (1961), *The Abbess of Crewe* (1974), *Territorial Rights* (1979), *The Only Problem* (1984), *A Far Cry From Kensington* (1988), *Symposium* (1990), and *Reality and Dreams* (1996). *Curriculum Vitae*, an account of her early years, appeared in 1992.

● **spark chamber** ► A device that detects charged particles. It consists of a gas-filled chamber containing a number of thin parallel wires or plates separated by a few centimetres and held at a high voltage. An incoming particle causes a spark to jump from plate to plate across the chamber, enabling the progress of the particle to be photographed.

● **sparrow** ► A small thick-billed member of the ▷weaverbird family. Sparrows range from 10–17 cm in length and are generally brown and grey in colour, often with black or bright yellow patches. They are mostly tropical Old World species but also occur in Eurasia and have been introduced to North America where the ▷house sparrow is a pest. Sparrows eat seeds, feeding on the ground and nesting in holes in banks and buildings. Subfamily: *Passerinae*.

The name "sparrow" is also given to various other unrelated birds, including the American chipping sparrow (*Spizella passerina*), which is a bunting, and the hedge sparrow (*see* dunnock).

● **sparrowhawk** ► A small woodland ▷hawk, *Accipiter nisus*, occurring in Eurasia and NW Africa. It has a long tail and short rounded wings and the male (27 cm long) is grey with brown-barred white underparts; females (38 cm long) are brown above. It hunts small birds.

● **Sparta** ► 37 05N 22 25E In ancient Greece, the capital of Laconia on the River Eurotas in the S Peloponnese. Developing from Dorian settlements during the 10th century BC, Sparta controlled much of Laconia and Messenia by 700 BC. The indigenous peoples became ▷helot serfs or semi-independent half-citizens (*perioeci*) and were subject to the governing class of Spartiates. Two hereditary kings ruled, with a powerful body of magistrates (*ephors*) and a council of elders (*gerousia*); there was also a citizen assembly (*apella*). Sparta became an austere militaristic state, where weaker boys were abandoned at birth and those that survived were subjected from the age of seven to a rigid military training. Its military strength brought conflict in the 5th century with Athens, and ultimate victory (404) in the consequent ▷Peloponnesian War: defeat by the Thebans at ▷Leuctra (371) marked the beginning of Spartan decline. The ancient city was destroyed by the Visigoths in 396 AD and the modern town (population (latest est): 15 915) S of its ruins dates from 1834.

● **Spartacus** ► Thracian gladiator, who led a revolt against Rome in 73 BC. After defeating the Romans in five separate engagements in Italy, he moved N to Cisalpine ▷Gaul. When his followers refused to disperse, Spartacus marched S again and was defeated by Marcus Licinius ▷Crassus (71). He and his followers were crucified.

● **Spartacus League** ► A German socialist group, founded during World War I, that adopted the name of the leader of a slave revolt in ancient Rome, ▷Spartacus. Its leaders were Rosa ▷Luxemburg and Karl ▷Liebknecht, both of whom were murdered after an attempted rising in 1919. The German Communist Party was largely formed by members of the Spartacus League.

● **Spartina** ► A genus of ▷grasses (16 species), known as cordgrass, found on salt marshes and tidal flats of North America, Europe, and Africa. They have stiff erect stems, 0.3–3 m tall and yellowish flower spikes. Rice grass (*S. anglia*), a natural hybrid, has been used extensively to help reclaim coastal land.

● **Spassky, Boris** ► (1937–) Russian chess player. He was world champion from 1969 to 1972, when he lost the title to ▷Fischer at Reykjavík.

● **Speaker of the House of Commons** ► The presiding officer of the lower chamber of the British parliament. A Speaker was first appointed in 1377. Elected by each new parliament, the Speaker, or the Speaker's deputy regulates with impartiality all the debates and proceedings of the House, except for proceedings in committee. Sanctions open to the Speaker include "naming" a member for an offence and indefinite suspension from the House. The equivalent officer in the House of Lords is the Lord (High) ▷Chancellor. The first woman to hold the office (1992–2000) was Betty Boothroyd (1929–). She was succeeded by Michael Martin.

● **Spearman, Charles Edward** ► (1863–1945) US psychologist, whose statistical studies of the results from various intelligence tests led him to postulate a factor of intelligence, G, common to all aspects of intelligence. His work pointed to factorial analysis as an important statistical method.

sparrowhawk ► This bird of prey can be seen cruising through woodlands and over hedges, hunting small birds and other animals.

● **spearmint** ► An aromatic perennial herb, *Mentha spicata*, native to central and S Europe and widely cultivated as a culinary herb. It grows to a height of 30–90 cm and has spikes of small lilac flowers. The oil extract from the leaves is used to flavour sweets, etc. Family: ▷*Labiatae*.

● **Special Air Service** ► (SAS) A specialist division of the British army. Formed in 1942 in North Africa by Col (later Sir) David Stirling (1916–90), the unit is highly trained in operations behind enemy lines and is the most secretive of the British forces. In recent years the SAS has seen action against terrorists in Malaya, Aden, and Northern Ireland; in 1980 it spearheaded an assault upon the Iranian embassy in London. Its motto is "Who dares wins."

● **Special Drawing Rights** ► (SDRs) The rights of member countries of the ▷International Monetary Fund to draw on the fund to finance ▷balance-of-payments deficits. First instituted in 1970, SDRs (unlike normal drawings) do not have to be repaid and therefore form a permanent addition to the drawing country's reserves, functioning as an international reserve currency and supplementing its holdings of gold and convertible currencies. The value of SDRs is computed as a weighted average of 16 currencies. Their advantage over gold and other reserve currencies is that their supply can be controlled and does not depend either on mineral deposits or on the US balance of payments.

● **special education** ► A wide range of facilities that aim to provide suitable education for children who, for various reasons, would be ill-served by the mainstream provision. In the UK this is mainly children with physical or mental disabilities, while in the USA it is mainly exceptionally gifted children. Although special education in the UK dates back to the 18th century, it was not until the Education Act (1944) that children with mental or physical difficulties were regarded like other children as needing an education appropriate to age, aptitude, and ability. Special education is provided either within ordinary schools or in special schools.

● **species** ► The fundamental unit of classification of living organisms. Individuals of the same species usually resemble one another closely and can breed among themselves to produce fertile offspring that resemble the parents. Examples of species are the domestic cat, the dogrose, and the field mushroom.

Some species are subdivided into subspecies and varieties. Breeds of domestic animals and cultivated varieties of plants have been specially developed by man for economic or other purposes and are all derived from a few wild species. Those originating from the same species can interbreed, despite obvious differences in character. All breeds of domestic dog, for instance, belong to the same species— *Canis familiaris*—and types as diverse as the poodle, corgi, and greyhound can breed together. There are internationally recognized rules for the naming of species (*see* binomial nomenclature).

● **specific gravity** ▷*See* density.

● **specific heat capacity** ► (*c*) The quantity of heat needed to raise a unit mass of substance by 1 °C. It is measured in joules per kelvin per kilogram. For gases, the specific heat capacity at constant pressure (c_p) exceeds that at constant volume (c_v) as heat is required to do work against the surroundings during the expansion. The ratio c_p/c_v (symbol: γ) is 1.66 for monatomic gases, 1.4 for diatomic gases, and about 1 for other gases.

● **spectacled bear** ► The only South American ▷bear, *Tremarctos ornatus*, also called Andean bear. Up to 1.5 m long, it is brownish-black with white circles around the eyes and climbs trees to feed on leaves, nuts, and fruit.

● **spectacles** ► Lenses worn in frames in front of the eyes to correct defective vision. Convex lenses bend parallel light rays inward; they are used by those unable to focus on close objects (*see* longsightedness). Concave lenses have the opposite effect and are used by those unable to focus on distant objects (*see* shortsightedness). ▷Astigmatism is treated by wearing lenses that produce a compensating distortion of the light rays. **Bifocals** have convex lenses consisting of upper and lower parts of different curvatures, for focusing on distant and near objects, respectively: they are worn for presbyopia. **Varifocals** have lenses in which the curvature is graduated to accommodate any length of vision between distant and near. ▷*See also* contact lenses.

● **spectral type** ▷*See* Harvard classification system.

● **spectroscopy** ▷*See* spectrum.

● **spectrum** ► In general, the way in which a particular property of a system is distributed over its components. The visible spectrum, for example, is observed in a ▷rainbow, which shows the distribution of frequencies when sunlight is split up into its components by raindrops. The visible spectrum, however, is only a small part of the electromagnetic spectrum, which ranges from X-rays to radio waves (*see* electromagnetic radiation). **Spectroscopy** is concerned with analysing the emission and absorption of electromagnetic energy by atoms and molecules.

According to the ▷quantum theory, atoms and molecules can only emit or absorb energy in discrete amounts, called quanta. When an atom or molecule is heated, bombarded with electrons, etc., it absorbs energy (becomes excited); on falling back to its lower state it emits a photon (a quantum of radiation energy). The energy of this photon is equal to hf, where f is the frequency of the radiation and h is ▷Planck's constant. Each atom or molecule can only make specific energy transitions. This means that as well as the continuous ▷blackbody radiation produced by thermal agitation, atoms can emit and absorb radiation at particular frequencies, which show up as coloured lines in their spectrum. These **line spectra** can be used to identify particular elements. The spectrum formed by atoms or molecules that are emitting radiation is called an **emission spectrum**. As atoms absorb energy at the same frequency as they emit it, if a substance lies in the path of radiation its atoms will absorb certain of the energy quanta in the radiation, producing dark lines in the spectrum. These dark lines are **absorption spectra**.

For example, the sun's spectrum contains many dark lines (called Fraunhofer lines). These are caused by atoms of hydrogen, helium, etc., in the sun's atmosphere absorbing energy from the radiation produced in the centre of the sun.

Spectroscopes (*or* spectrometers) are instruments for analysing a spectrum. They usually consist of a collimator to collect the radiation from the source, a grating or prism to split it into its components and a telescope to view the refracted radiation. A means of recording the spectrum photographically is needed for ultraviolet and infrared radiation.

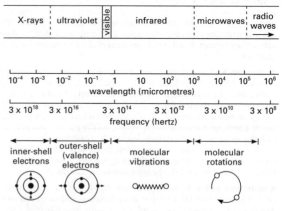

spectrum ► Energetic photons in the X-ray region of the spectrum alter the excitation of atomic inner-shell electrons. The ultraviolet and visible photons interact with the outer-shell electrons that participate in chemical reactions. Infrared photons alter the vibrational states of molecules and microwave photons affect molecular rotation.

● **speech therapy** ► Treatment aimed at assisting patients whose speech is incoherent as a result of speech disorders (e.g. ▷stammering), illness (especially strokes), or accidents. Measures include introducing new techniques of speech production (e.g. teaching the patient to speak very slowly) and the use by the patient of acoustic devices to increase fluency. Speech therapists (called speech pathologists in the USA) have a recognized training but are not medically qualified.

● **speed of light** ▷*See* light.

● **speed of sound** ▷*See* sound.

● **speedway** ► A form of professional ▷motorcycle racing, which originated in Australia in the late 1920s. Races are held on dirt tracks in heats of four laps between four riders. 500 cc motorcycles with no brakes are used. In the UK, where teams compete in a two-division league, speedway is second in popularity only to Association football as a spectator sport.

● **speedwell** ▶ An annual or perennial herbaceous plant of the genus *Veronica* (about 200 species), up to 60 cm high, occurring throughout temperate regions. The flowers are usually blue, sometimes white or pinkish, with four unequal petals. The fruit is a flattened heart-shaped capsule. Two common species are *V. officinalis* and the germander speedwell (*V. chamaedrys*). Family: *Scrophulariaceae*.

● **Speedwriting** ▷*See* shorthand.

● **Speenhamland system** ▶ A system of poor relief started by the Speenhamland magistrates in Berkshire in 1795. Allowances were given from the parish rates to men unable to support their families themselves due to unemployment or low wages. It was unsuccessful in alleviating rural poverty and was very expensive for the parish. It was abolished by the ▷Poor Law Amendment Act (1834).

● **Speke, John Hanning** ▶ (1827–64) British explorer. He accompanied Richard ▷Burton on the expeditions (1855, 1857–58) to locate the source of the Nile. They were the first Europeans to discover Lake Tanganyika and then Speke went on alone to discover Lake Victoria, which on a second visit in 1860, accompanied by J. A. Grant (1827–92), he established to be the source of the Nile. Burton disputed Speke's claim and Speke accidentally shot himself just before an engagement to defend himself before the British Association.

● **speleology** ▶ (*or* spelaeology) The study and exploration of ▷caves and underground water courses. This includes the survey of caves and the study of their formation, plant and animal life (past and present), and geology. Potholing—or descending through potholes into underground drainage passages in order to follow the course of underground streams—is an increasingly popular although relatively dangerous activity.

● **spelling** ▶ The conventional representation of spoken words in an alphabetic writing system. The underlying principle of alphabetic writing is that there should be a consistent one-for-one relationship between speech sounds and written letters but this is rarely fully realized in practice. Inconsistencies arise partly because a change in pronunciation is not always matched by a corresponding spelling change. In English, for example, an extensive change in the value of vowels took place in the 15th century (*see* Great Vowel Shift), *-e* at the end of a word ceased to be pronounced, and the sound represented by *-gh-* (the sound of *-ch* in Scottish *loch*) dropped out or changed to *-f-*. Another cause of spelling inconsistencies is that English has evolved during the last 1500 or more years from Anglo-Saxon, Old Norse, Latin, Norman French, and some Greek. This diversity of sources has probably made it the most versatile language in the world. However, each language that has contributed to it has its own conventions in spelling, which has made for lack of homogeneity in the spelling conventions of modern English. Since the early days of printing many reformers (including George Bernard ▷Shaw) have offered more rational systems for spelling the language. However, once the conventions of a language are entrenched and standardized it becomes too unpopular, costly, and impractical to change them. Pressure towards a standardized form of spelling began with the printing of the first English books, was accelerated by the rise of a literate middle class anxious to write "correctly," and consolidated by the publication of dictionaries that offered an authoritative standard of correctness. Indeed, before dictionaries were commonplace in the home and workplace, spelling remained to some extent a matter of personal whim. To change the rules and conventions by which this hard-won standardization has been achieved does not seem to most native English speakers a desirable enterprise.

● **Spence, Sir Basil** ▶ (1907–76) British architect. Originally a designer of country houses in Scotland, he became internationally known with his design for rebuilding Coventry Cathedral (consecrated 1962). Later buildings included Sussex University and the British Embassy in Rome (completed 1971).

● **Spencer, Herbert** ▶ (1820–1903) British philosopher. As subeditor of the *Economist* (1843–53), Spencer was an influential exponent of ▷laissez-faire. His early book *Social Statics* (1851) was strongly tinged with an individualistic outlook, as was his multi-volume *System of Synthetic Philosophy* (1860–96), of which the most important volume was *First Principles* (1862). He believed that state intervention limited progress and he developed this idea fully in his popular *The Man versus the State* (1884). Spencer's other writings include works on psychology, ethics, and sociology. He supported Charles ▷Darwin's theory of evolution by natural selection, coining the phrase "survival of the fittest," and applied evolutionary ideas to social development.

● **Spencer, Sir Stanley** ▶ (1891–1959) British painter. He is known for his religious subjects, often depicted in the everyday setting of his native village of Cookham, Berkshire. He studied at the Slade School (1910–14) and first became known for his murals of army life for Sandham Memorial Chapel, Burghclere (1926–1932), and for *The Resurrection: Cookham* (1922–27; Tate Gallery). He was knighted in 1959.

● **Spencer Gulf** ▶ An inlet of the Indian Ocean, in S Australia situated between Eyre Peninsula and Yorke Peninsula, with Port Augusta, Port Pirie, and Whyalla located on its shores. Length: about 320 km (200 mi). Width: about 120 km (75 mi).

● **Spender, Sir Stephen** ▶ (1909–95) British poet and critic. A friend of W. H. Auden, he published left-wing poetry during the 1930s and was briefly a member of the Communist Party. His later poetry, included in *Collected Poems* (1954), *The Generous Days* (1971), *Collected Poems 1930–1985* (1985), and *Dolphins* (1994), is more personal and lyrical. Other works include an autobiography, *World within World* (1951), *Journals 1939–1983* (1985), the novel *The Temple* (1988), and books of criticism.

● **Spengler, Oswald** ▶ (1880–1936) German philosopher. His most famous work, *The Decline of the West* (1918), argued that nations and cultures have a natural lifespan and their rise is inevitably followed by their eclipse. Spengler's ideas appealed to the German fascists, as he emphasized the individual's duty of obedience to the state.

● **Spenser, Edmund** ▶ (c. 1552–99) English poet. He dedicated *The Shepheardes Calendar* (1579), pastoral poems arranged by the months of the year, to Sir Philip Sidney, nephew of his patron the Earl of Leicester. In 1580 he was appointed secretary to the Lord Deputy of Ireland, where he became a prominent landowner. His major work, *The Faerie Queene*, a long moral allegory in nine-line "Spenserian" stanzas, was dedicated to Elizabeth I and published in six books in 1590 and 1596. His other works include the sonnet sequence *Amoretti* (1595) and the *Epithalamion* (1595), celebrating his second marriage.

● **Speranski, Mikhail Mikhailovich** ▶ (1772–1839) Russian statesman, described by Napoleon as "the only clear head in Russia." Speranski, as Alexander I's chief adviser (1807–12), presented proposals for the reform of the administration and for the drafting of a new constitution. His unpopularity with colleagues led to his exile until 1816. In 1826 he began his greatest achievement, the codification of Russian law.

● **sperm** ▶ (*or* spermatozoon) The reproductive cell of male animals, which is formed in the ▷testis and fertilizes an egg cell during sexual ▷reproduction. In humans and other mammals, at ejaculation they are mixed with secretions from various glands (including the ▷prostate gland) to form semen. A sperm usually has a head region, containing the genetic material, and a tail, by means of which it swims to the egg. The head region contains an acrosome, a caplike structure that releases enzymes allowing the sperm to penetrate the egg at fertilization.

● **spermaceti** ▶ A ▷wax obtained from the head cavity and from the oils of whales, dolphins, and porpoises. It is liquid at room temperature and is separated from the oil by chilling. Spermaceti is used in ointments, cosmetics, fine candles, and textile finishing.

● **spermatophyte** ▶ Any plant that reproduces by ▷seeds rather than spores. Spermatophytes include the ▷gymnosperms (conifers, etc.) and the ▷angiosperms (flowering plants), which were formerly classified together in the division *Spermatophyta* but are now assigned to separate phyla (or divisions).

● **sperm banks** ▷*See* artificial insemination.

● **sperm whale** ▶ A large toothed ▷whale, *Physeter cathodon*, also called cachalot. It is 18 m long, grey-blue above and pale beneath, with tiny flippers and large tail flukes. The blowhole is near the tip of the snout and it can dive up to 1 km in search of octopus and squid, sometimes staying under water for over one hour. Family: *Physeteridae*.

● **Spey, River** ▶ A fast-flowing river in NE Scotland, flowing mainly NE through the Grampian Mountains to Spey Bay. It is known for its salmon fishing. Length: 172 km (107 mi).

● **Speyer** ▶ (English name: Spires) 49 18N 8 26E A city in SW Germany, in Rhineland-Palatinate on the River Rhine. The cathedral (1030) contains the tombs of eight emperors. An important diet (assembly) was held here in 1529 (*see* Protestantism). It is a port and industrial centre. Population (1991): 47 450.

● **Sphagnum** ▶ A widely distributed genus of mosses (over 300 species), called bog or peat moss, forming dense raised clumps in bogs and other waterlogged places. Green to dark red in colour and up to 30 cm high, the fine stems bear clusters of threadlike branches, densely clothed with tiny leaves, and globular spore capsules. The ability of the stems and leaves to retain water (up to 20 times the weight of the plant) is responsible for the outstanding ability of these mosses to drain very wet ground and form bogs. The dead remains of the plants accumulate to form ▷peat—an important fuel and ingredient of horticultural composts. Family: *Sphagnaceae*.

● **sphalerite** ▶ (or zinc blende) The principal ore of zinc, a sulphide, usually brown or black in colour. It frequently occurs with ▷galena in metasomatic deposits, and in hydrothermal veins and replacement deposits.

● **spherical coordinates** ▷*See* coordinate systems.

● **sphinx** ▶ A mythological creature with a lion's body and a human head, occurring in the art and legends of most ancient Near and Middle Eastern civilizations. The most famous representation is the Great Sphinx at Giza, Egypt, dating from the 3rd millennium BC. In Greek legend, the Sphinx was a female monster that preyed on travellers going to Thebes. She killed those who could not answer her riddle, which was finally solved by ▷Oedipus.

● **sphygmomanometer** ▶ A device for measuring arterial ▷blood pressure. It consists of an inflatable arm cuff connected via a rubber tube to a column of mercury with a graduated scale or an aneroid device. The cuff is inflated until the pulse cannot be detected (using a stethoscope) and then slowly deflated until the systolic and then the diastolic pressure can be recorded as the pulse returns. In recent years electronic devices have been used to measure blood pressure.

● **Spica** ▶ A conspicuous blue star, apparent magnitude 0.97 and about 215 light years distant, that is the brightest star in the constellation Virgo. It is an eclipsing ▷binary star.

● **Spice Islands** ▷*See* Moluccas.

● **spices** ▷*See* herbs and spices.

● **spider** ▶ An ▷arachnid belonging to the worldwide order *Araneae* (or *Araneida*; over 30 000 species). 1–90 mm long, the body of a spider consists of a cephalothorax abdomen separated by a narrow "waist." There are eight walking legs, up to eight eyes, and several pairs of spinnerets, which produce silk used for making webs, egg cocoons, etc. Spiders are predominantly terrestrial and prey mainly on insects, hunting them or trapping them in their webs. The victims are killed with poison-bearing fangs; in a few species the poison is harmful to humans. The female is generally larger than the male, which she sometimes kills and eats after mating. She then deposits the eggs on or near the web, among leaves or twigs, etc., or carries them until they hatch. The young go through a series of moults to reach the adult stage. ▷*See also* black widow; tarantula; water spider; wolf spider.

● **spider crab** ▶ A marine ▷crab belonging to the widely distributed family *Maiidae*, especially one of the genus *Libinia*. It has a thick rounded body, with long spindly legs and generally moves slowly. Most spider crabs are scavengers, especially of dead animals.

● **spider mite** ▶ A red or yellow ▷mite, 0.5 mm long, also called red spider mite, belonging to the family *Tetranychidae*. It sucks plant juices from foliage and fruits and is a serious pest of orchard trees, crops, and house plants.

● **spider monkey** ▶ A monkey belonging to the genus *Ateles* (4 species), of Central and South American forests. Spider monkeys have very long legs and are 88–150 cm long including the prehensile tail (50–90 cm), which is capable of supporting their weight. They live in family groups in thick forest, feeding on seeds and leaves. Family: *Cebidae*.

● **spider plant** ▶ A plant of the genus *Chlorophytum*, especially *C. elatum*, native to South Africa and widely grown as a house plant. It has narrow green and white striped leaves, 60–90 cm long, and periodically produces a stem bearing small white flowers or young plantlets. Family: *Liliaceae*.

● **spider wasp** ▶ A solitary ▷wasp belonging to a family (*Pompilidae*) of worldwide distribution. It preys chiefly on spiders, which are also paralysed and stored in underground nests as food for the larvae. Spider wasps have dark slender bodies (5–75 mm long), long legs, and usually smoky or amber-coloured wings.

● **spiderwort** ▷*See* Tradescantia.

● **Spielberg, Steven** ▶ (1946–) US film director and producer, whose fantasy and adventure films have made him the most commercially successful director in cinema history. He first achieved major box-office success with *Jaws* (1975) and *Close Encounters of the Third Kind* (1977); *ET* (1982) and *Jurassic Park* (1993) also drew recordbreaking audiences. *The Color Purple* (1986), *Empire of the Sun* (1988), *Schindler's List* (1994), *Amistad* (1997), and *Saving Private Ryan* (1998), are more serious. In 1996 he set up Dream Works, his own Hollywood studio. He was awarded an honorary knighthood in 2000.

● **spikenard** ▶ A perennial Himalayan herb, *Nardostachys jatamansi*, growing to a height of 60 cm and bearing tiny purple flower clusters. It is cultivated for an essential oil derived from its roots, used for perfumes. Family: *Valerianaceae*.
　　Ploughman's spikenard (*Inula conyza*) is a perennial herb of Europe and N Africa with yellow flowers and fragrant roots. Family: ▷*Compositae*.

● **Spillane, Mickey** ▶ (Frank Morrison S.; 1918–) US detective-story writer. His numerous crime novels featuring the detective Mike Hammer, the popular success of which was due to the uninhibited description of sex and violence, include *I, the Jury* (1947) and *The Twisted Thing* (1966).

● **spin** ▶ A property possessed by elementary particles as a result of which they possess a constant angular momentum that is independent of their motion. The spin is quantized and labelled by a spin ▷quantum number (symbol: s), which may be integral or half-integral.

● **spina bifida** ▶ A defect, present at birth, in which the backbone fails to fuse properly, leaving the spinal cord and its coverings exposed. Commonly the child has paralysed legs and disordered bladder and bowel function. The degree of the handicap varies: children who survive and are severely affected require crutches or wheelchairs and need special surgical procedures to help their bladder function. The intelligence of children with spina bifida is often normal, but the condition is frequently associated with ▷hydrocephalus. Spina bifida can be diagnosed during pregnancy (*see* amniocentesis), and is less likely to occur if pregnant women take extra folic acid.

● **spinach** ▶ An annual herbaceous plant, *Spinacia oleracea*, native to Asia and widely cultivated as a vegetable. Its edible leaves are rich in iron and vitamins A and C and are boiled as a vegetable and used in salads, soups, soufflés, etc. Family: *Chenopodiaceae*.
　　Much spinach grown in gardens and allotments is spinach ▷beet, which has a milder flavour. It is also known as perpetual spinach, as cutting the stems stimulates new leaf growth.

● **spinal cord** ▶ An elongated part of the central ▷nervous system, running downwards from the base of the brain and consisting of a core of grey matter (nerve cell bodies) surrounded by white matter (nerve fibres). It is surrounded and protected by the ▷spine and is enclosed in membranes (meninges). It gives off spinal nerves, usually in pairs, and ends in a bundle of nerves supplying the legs and lower part of the body. Through it run the nerve fibres between the brain and the body; injury can therefore cause paralysis and loss of sensation. ▷*See* Plate II.

● **spindle tree** ▶ A Eurasian tree or shrub, *Euonymus europaeus*, that grows to a height of about 6 m. It produces small white flowers and pink and orange fleshy fruits, 10–15 mm across, which yield a yellow food dye. The fine-grained wood has been used to make spindles and clothes pegs. The winged spindle tree (*E. alatus*) occurs in China. Family: *Celastraceae*. ▷*See also* Euonymus.

● **spin doctor** ▷*See* propaganda.

● **spine** ▶ In anatomy, the backbone, or vertebral column: a series of small bones (vertebrae) that runs up the centre of the back. The spine encloses and protects the ▷spinal cord, articulates with the skull, ribs, and pelvis, and provides attachment for muscles of the back. There are 26 vertebrae in the adult spine, which are subdivided as follows: 7 cervical, in the neck; 12 thoracic, in the chest region attached to the ribs; 5 lumbar, in the lower back; 5 sacral, attached to the hip bone (fused into a single bone—the sacrum); and 4 coccygeal (fused into a single bone—the coccyx). The vertebrae are connected by tough discs of cartilage (intervertebral discs), which absorb the shock produced by running and other movements. ▷*See* Plate II.

● **spinel** ▶ A group of oxide minerals, usually occurring as octahedral crystals. The spinel minerals form a compositional series between true spinel ($MgAl_2O_4$) and hercynite ($Fe^{2+}Al_2O_4$). Magnetite ($Fe^{2+}Fe_2^{3+}O_4$) is the most common and is an important iron ore. Chromite, a source of chromium, is $Fe^{2+}Cr_2O_4$. Spinels occur mostly in metamorphic rocks, especially limestones, and in basic and ultrabasic igneous rocks.

● **spinet** ▶ A plucked keyboard instrument of the ▷harpsichord family that superseded the ▷virginals in the 17th century. It is wing shaped, the strings (one to each note) being at an angle of 45° to the keyboard.

● **Spinifex** ▶ A genus of ▷grasses (3 species), native to S and E Asia and Australia. They grow on sand dunes and form long underground stems (rhizomes), which stabilize the dunes. The heads of spiny one-flowered spikelets break off and are blown about by wind. The name is also used for other Australian grasses that form spiny hummocks, especially *Triodia hirsuta* and *T. irritans*, also called porcupine grass.

● **spinning** ▶ The process of converting cleaned and straightened fibres into yarn by twisting overlapping fibres together; until the 18th century this was a household task. Yarn was made originally by drawing out a length of fibre from the mass and attaching it to a vertically hanging stick (spindle) that was weighted to help it spin round; as it spun, the fibre wound onto it. This process was mechanized first by the spinning wheel (in Europe not until the 14th century, although it was used in India long before). The 16th-century Saxony wheel was an improved version, which could be operated continuously. The inventions of James ▷Hargreaves, Richard ▷Arkwright, and Samuel ▷Crompton in the late 18th century industrialized the process. Modern spinning machines produce thousands of metres of yarn every hour. As applied to synthetic fibres, spinning is the extrusion of viscous solutions to form continuous filaments.

● **Spinoza, Benedict** ▶ (or Baruch de S.; 1632–77) Dutch philosopher, theologian, and scientist of Jewish parentage. Influenced by the writings of ▷Descartes, ▷Hobbes, and ▷Bruno, Spinoza rejected the concepts of the personal nature of God and the immortality of the soul. The Jewish community of his native Amsterdam expelled him in 1656 on account of his unorthodoxy and his *Tractatus Theologico-Politicus* (1670) was furiously attacked by Christian scholars. The idea of God as the basis of all things (*Deus sive Natura*...God or Nature—in his phrase) was, however, central to his philosophy. For this reason he is often cited as the herald of modern ▷pantheism. He maintained that man's highest good is his "knowledge of the union existing between the mind and the whole of Nature." His major work, the *Ethica ordine geometrico demonstrata*, generally known as the *Ethics*, could

only be published posthumously in 1677. Both ▷Hegel and Friedrich Schleiermacher (1768–1834) were greatly influenced by his writings.

● **spiny lobster** ▶ A ▷lobster, also called sea crayfish or crawfish, belonging to the mainly tropical family *Palinuridae*. Its carapace is covered with spines and it lacks pincers, but the antennae are strongly developed.

● **spiracle** ▶ The external opening of a respiratory tubule (trachea) of insects and spiders. The term is also used for the paired gill openings of cartilaginous fishes, such as sharks, and for the respiratory openings of tadpoles and whales.

● **Spiraea** ▶ A genus of shrubs (about 100 species), widely distributed in N temperate regions. Many are cultivated as ornamentals, including the willow spiraea (*S. salcifolia*), which grows to a height of 1–2 m and bears dense clusters of small pink flowers. Other species and hybrids may have white or crimson flowers. Family: ▷*Rosaceae*.

● **Spires** ▷*See* Speyer.

● **spirits** ▶ Distilled liquor defined in the UK as having an alcohol content of at least 40%. Spirits are derived from fermented liquids, for example wine (giving brandy); fruit wines (giving fruit brandies, such as slivovitz from plums and ▷kirsch from cherries); cider (giving calvados or applejack); grain or potatoes (giving ▷whisky, ▷gin, ▷vodka, or ▷aquavit). These liquids are distilled, i.e. some of the water is removed by vaporization to increase the alcohol content of the remaining liquid. Distillation often takes place in an onion-shaped potstill.

● **spiritual** ▶ A type of religious song developed by plantation slaves in the USA, with texts adapted from the Bible. The spiritual was often extemporized, with a lead singer relating the story in stanzas and a chorus singing the refrain. Harmonized arrangements of spirituals have eliminated the improvisational quality. Famous spirituals include "Steal Away," "Go Down, Moses," and "Deep River."

● **spiritualism** ▶ Any theory that emphasizes the direct intervention of spiritual and supernatural forces in the everyday world. The term can cover phenomena as disparate as ▷extrasensory perception, ▷telekinesis, and various states associated with religious ecstasy, such as glossolalia (speaking in tongues, or making unintelligible utterances). In Western societies, spiritualism commonly means the practice of communicating with the spirits of the dead through a medium in seances or with a ouija board. Organizations devoted to ▷psychical research have amassed considerable evidence for spiritualist phenomena, some occurring under rigidly controlled conditions to preclude fraud, although much of it is not the reproducible kind of evidence that scientists seek. Advocates of spiritualism include William ▷Crookes, Lord ▷Dowding, Conan ▷Doyle, and Oliver ▷Lodge.

● **spirochaete** ▶ A bacterium belonging to the order *Spirochaetales*. Spirochaetes are corkscrew-shaped, flexible, and up to 0.5 mm long: they swim by means of bending and looping motions, achieved by contraction of a bundle of fibrils (the axial filament) within the cell. Some spirochaetes cause diseases, including syphilis and yaws in humans.

● **Spirogyra** ▶ A genus of ▷green algae, also called mermaid's tresses or pond scum, in the form of threadlike strands of connected cells up to about 30 cm long. Large masses may be found floating near the surface of quiet fresh waters. Reproduction is asexual (by fragmentation) or sexual (*see* conjugation).

● **spit** ▶ A linear deposit of sand or shingle extending from a coastline. It often occurs where the coastline changes direction sharply and is deposited by the movement of beach material by wave action.

● **Spitalfields** ▶ A district in the Greater London borough of Tower Hamlets. It was noted for silk weaving, which was introduced by Huguenot refugees in the 17th century. Many European Jews settled here in the late 19th century and there is now a substantial Bangladeshi community.

● **Spithead** ▶ 50 43N 0 56W An extensive roadstead between the mainland of England and the Isle of Wight, off Portsmouth. In April,

1797 sailors based here mutinied against the appalling working conditions then prevalent in ships of the ▷Royal Navy. Most of their demands were met, which encouraged the leaders of the ▷Nore mutiny to take action the following month.

● **Spitsbergen** ▷*See* Svalbard.

● **spittlebug** ▷*See* froghopper.

● **spitz** ▶ One of a group of dog breeds originating in N Eurasia and having a thick coat, small pricked ears, and a brushlike tail carried over the back. The Finnish spitz, bred in Finland as a hunting and guard dog, has a reddish-brown or yellowish-red coat while the Lapland spitz is either white, brown and black, or blackish brown. ▷Husky breeds also show spitz characteristics. Height (Finnish spitz): 44 cm (dogs); 39 cm (bitches).

● **Spitz, Mark (Andrew)** ▶ (1950–) US swimmer, who won a record seven gold medals in the Munich Olympic Games (1972). In the period 1967–72 he won altogether nine Olympic golds and set 27 individual world records for freestyle and butterfly. Following the 1972 Olympics he retired from swimming and became an actor.

● **spleen** ▶ A rubbery dark-red organ, about 14 cm long, situated in the abdomen just beneath the lower border of the left side of the rib cage. The spleen assists in the body's defence mechanisms by producing lymphocytes in newborn babies and by absorbing and digesting bacteria in the bloodstream. It also removes worn-out and abnormal red blood cells and other particles from the circulation. The spleen becomes enlarged in some diseases, including liver disease and severe infections. The spleen can be removed in adults without any ill effects.

● **spleenwort** ▶ A tufted ▷fern of the genus *Asplenium* (about 700 species), growing on walls and rocks throughout the world. The tapering branched fronds are about 5–30 cm long, with triangular lobed leaflets bearing oval or spindle-shaped clusters of spore capsules. The name derives from the former use of some species to treat disorders of the spleen and liver. Family: *Aspleniaceae.* ▷*See also* bird's nest fern.

● **Split** ▶ (Italian name: Spalato) 43 31N 16 28N A port in SE Croatia on the Adriatic Sea. The vast 3rd-century AD Palace of Diocletian contains the present-day city centre, including the cathedral, which was Diocletian's mausoleum. It has a university (1974) and diverse industries. Population (1991): 206 559.

● **Spock, Benjamin McLane** ▶ (1903–98) US physician and paediatrician, whose books on child care, which advocated a permissive approach (later somewhat modified), became bestsellers, especially his *Common Sense Book of Baby and Child Care* (1946). He was a prominent opponent of US policy during the Vietnam War and stood for the US Presidency in 1972.

● **Spode porcelain** ▶ Fine tableware and other porcelain made in the Staffordshire (England) factory started by Josiah Spode I in 1770. Josiah Spode II (1754–1827) introduced "Feldspar" porcelain and "Stone China" as well as using ▷creamware. The meticulous decoration used transfer printing and painted Japan patterns enhanced by careful gilding.

● **Spohr, Louis** ▶ (Ludwig S.; 1784–1859) German violinist and composer. His works include operas, oratorios, symphonies, violin concertos, a concerto for string quartet and orchestra, and a nonet for strings and wind.

● **Spokane** ▶ 47 40N 117 25W A city in the USA, in Washington state. It is a shipping centre for a four-state area called the Inland Empire, which has mineral deposits and farms producing cattle, wheat, and fruit. Industries include timber and food processing. Population (1996 est): 186 562.

● **Spoleto** ▶ 42 44N 12 44E A town in Italy, in Umbria. Dating from Etruscan times, it has Roman remains and a 12th-century cathedral. Its annual festival of music and drama was founded in 1958 by Gian Carlo ▷Menotti. There is a textile industry. Population (latest est): 22 100.

● **spondee** ▷*See* metre (poetry).

● **sponge** ▶ An aquatic invertebrate animal belonging to the phylum *Porifera* (about 5000 species). Most sponges are marine, found attached to rocks or the sea bed, and measure up to several metres across: they may be treelike, cylindrical (*see* Venus's flower basket), or flat irregular masses. Sponges have an internal skeleton of lime, silica, or a fibrous protein (spongin). Bath sponges are spongin skeletons without the living animals. The simplest type of sponge has a vase-shaped body with a pore at the top and smaller pores in the sides. The inside is lined with flagellated collar cells, which maintain a flow of water in through the side pores and out at the top. Food particles in the water are extracted by the collar cells; other cells in the body wall digest food, secrete the skeleton, and produce eggs and sperm. Fertilized eggs are dispersed in the water and the free-swimming larvae settle and become new sponges. The animals can also reproduce asexually, by budding or fragmentation.

● **spontaneous generation** ▶ (*or* abiogenesis) The theory that living organisms arise from nonliving materials. It was widely upheld for many centuries, based on such observations as the appearance of tadpoles from mud and maggots in decaying meat. Belief in the spontaneous development of microorganisms continued until the 19th century, when Louis ▷Pasteur proved that, like higher organisms, they were capable of reproduction.

● **spoonbill** ▶ A long-legged wading bird belonging to a subfamily (*Plataleinae;* 6 species) occurring around estuaries and lakes in tropical and subtropical regions worldwide. 60–80 cm long, spoonbills are usually entirely white, often with a naked head. They feed on fish and crustaceans picked up by sweeping the large spatulate bill from side to side in mud or shallow water. Family: *Threskiornithidae* (ibises and spoonbills); order: *Ciconiiformes* (herons, storks, etc.).

● **Spooner, William Archibald** ▶ (1844–1930) British clergyman and academic. A somewhat eccentric Oxford don, Spooner became famous for his frequent transposition of the first letters of words, for example "a well-oiled bicycle" became "a well-boiled icicle." Such a transposition became known as a **Spoonerism.**

● **Sporades** ▶ Two groups of Greek islands in the Aegean Sea, the **Northern Sporades,** which include Skyros, and the **Southern Sporades,** which, with the exception of Sámos and Ikaría, constitute the ▷Dodecanese.

● **spore** ▶ The small, often single-celled, reproductive unit of plants, algae, fungi, protozoa, and bacteria, which may serve either as a rapid means of propagation or as a dormant stage in the life cycle. Spores may be produced sexually or asexually, i.e. fusion of sex cells (gametes) may or may not occur before their formation. In plants exhibiting an ▷alternation of generations spores are formed by the sporophyte following meiosis and give rise to the gametophyte, which produces the sex cells. In some algae and fungi spores are produced following cell division (*see* mitosis) and thus give rise to an exact replica of the parent.

● **sporophyte** ▷*See* alternation of generations.

● **sporozoan** ▶ A microscopic single-celled organism of the phylum *Apicomplexa* (formerly *Sporozoa; see* protozoa), all of which are parasites with complex life cycles involving asexual and sexual forms of reproduction. They are often found in the intestinal tracts or blood of animals and form resistant spores or cysts, which can remain dormant until entering a suitable host. The phylum includes the malaria parasite (*see* Plasmodium).

● **Sports, Book of** ▶ (1618) The list of those amusements that were permitted (e.g. dancing, May Games, archery) and forbidden (e.g. bear- and bull-baiting, bowling) on Sundays under James I and Charles I of England. It was strongly opposed by the Puritans, who wished to forbid all such amusements.

● **sprat** ▶ A small food fish, *Clupea* (*Sprattus*) *sprattus,* also called brisling, that is similar and related to the herring. Up to 17 cm long, it lives in shoals in the E Atlantic, N Mediterranean, and British coastal waters. The young are known as ▷whitebait.

● **Spratly Islands** ▶ 8 45N 111 54E An archipelago in the South China Sea, consisting of low-lying islets and reefs. Claimed by China, Malaysia, the Philippines, Taiwan, and Vietnam for their strategic importance, they became a focus of international tension in the late 1980s.

● **spring** ▶ An emission of water from the ground. Springs occur where the water table intersects the surface or where a subsurface stream flowing over an impermeable rock stratum reaches the ground surface. Small outflows of water (seepages) may create a small localized marsh or bog. ▷*See also* hot spring.

● **spring balance** ▶ A device for measuring weights. The simplest form consists of a helical spring fixed at its upper end; from the lower end the load is suspended, extending the spring in direct proportion to its weight (according to ▷Hooke's law).

● **springbok** ▶ A rare antelope, *Antidorcas marsupialis*, inhabiting arid regions of S Africa. About 80 cm high at the shoulder, the springbok has a white face with a black line along each side of the muzzle, a fawn body with dark flank hairs, and a patch of white hairs on the rump, which can be flashed as an alarm signal. It is the national emblem of South Africa. □*mammal*.

● **Springfield** ▶ 39 49N 89 39W A city in the USA, the capital of Illinois on the Sangamon River. Abraham Lincoln lived here from 1837 until 1861 and is buried nearby; his home is preserved. Situated in an agricultural area, Springfield is an administrative, commercial, and medical centre with varied industries. Population (1996 est): 112 921.

● **Springfield** ▶ 42 07N 72 35W A city in the USA, in Massachusetts on the Connecticut River. The arsenal operating here from 1794 until 1966 developed the Springfield and Garand rifles. Industries include chemicals and plastic. Population (1996 est): 149 948.

● **Springfield** ▶ 37 11N 93 19W A city in the USA, in Missouri in the Ozark Mountains. The commercial centre for an agricultural region, its industries include railway engineering and the manufacture of furniture and textiles. Population (1996 est): 143 407.

● **springhaas** ▶ A nocturnal kangaroo-like rodent, *Pedetes capensis*, inhabiting the grasslands of eastern and southern Africa. Also called the Cape jumping hare, it is about 35 cm long with yellowish-brown fur and a long bushy black-tipped tail. The springhaas uses the long claws on its forelimbs for excavating burrows and digging up the roots and tubers on which it feeds.

● **Springs** ▶ 26 15S 28 26E A city in E South Africa. Founded in 1885, it became the centre of goldfields and today is a mining and manufacturing centre producing gold and uranium. Population (latest est): 68 235.

● **Springsteen, Bruce** ▶ (1949–) US rock singer and guitarist. Born in New Jersey, he built up a huge following with songs describing modern industrial US society and with his energetic live performances; his albums include *Born to Run* (1975), *The River* (1980), *Born in the USA* (1984), *Lucky Town* (1992), and *The Ghost of Tom Joad* (1995).

● **springtail** ▶ An eyeless wingless □insect of the worldwide order *Collembola* (about 3500 species). 3–10 mm long, it has a forked appendage on the abdomen, which is used for jumping. Springtails crawl about in moist soil and leaf litter or on water or snow and feed on decaying vegetable material, sometimes becoming minor pests of garden crops.

● **spring tide** ▶ A □tide of relatively large range that occurs near the times of full and new moon. Low tides are lower and high tides higher than normal, and flooding may occur if strong onshore winds coincide with high water. *Compare* neap tide.

● **sprinkler system** ▶ A safety system often installed in hotels, warehouses, factories, etc., for ▷fire prevention. It consists of a set of sprinkler valves connected to a water supply and an initiating alarm mechanism sensitive to heat or smoke. This may be a thin alloy bar in each sprinkler that bends at a low temperature or a sophisticated electronic sensor.

● **spruce** ▶ A coniferous □tree of the genus *Picea* (about 50 species), widely distributed in the N hemisphere. Its needles grow in spirals and leave peglike projections on the shoots when they fall. The woody cones, 5–15 cm long, hang down from the branches. An important and widely grown timber tree is the Norway spruce (*Picea abies*), from N and central Europe, of which the timber—known as white

wood or deal—is used for paper pulp, roofing, barrels, boxes, etc. This conifer can reach a height of 40 m, but young specimens are used as Christmas trees in Britain. Family: *Pinaceae*.

● **sprue** ▶ A disease of the lining of the small intestine in which food is not properly absorbed. It is common in the tropics, often affecting people who have moved from temperate regions. Symptoms include diarrhoea, anaemia, and weight loss, and patients are treated with antibiotics, vitamin preparations, and a special diet.

● **spurge** ▶ An annual or perennial herb of the genus ▷*Euphorbia*, especially the hardier temperate species, which have been used as purgatives. Many are weeds but some are cultivated as ornamentals, including the Cypress spurge (*E. cyparissias*). Family: *Euphorbiaceae*.

● **Spurs, Battle of the** ▶ (16 August, 1513) The battle in which Henry VIII of England defeated the French at Guinegate, near Thérouanne (N France). The battle was so called because of the speed of the French retreat. The English victory led to the capture of Tournai.

● **Sputnik** ▶ A series of Soviet unmanned satellites, the first of which was the first spacecraft to be launched (4 October, 1957). It burnt up in the atmosphere after 92 days. Sputnik 2, launched 3 November, 1957, carried the first animal, the dog Laika, into space.

● **Square Deal** ▶ A programme of economic and social reform intended by Theodore ▷Roosevelt (president 1901–09) to benefit the "plain man" in the USA. It sponsored improved labour conditions, regulations regarding the quality of food, and antimonopoly legislation.

● **square root** ▷*See* root.

● **squash** ▶ The fruit of certain plants belonging to the genus *Cucurbita* (15 species), especially *C. maxima*. Native to the New World, squash plants are widely cultivated and form erect bushes, 45–75 cm high, producing fleshy edible fruits, which are variable in shape, texture, and size. They are usually served as a cooked vegetable. Family: *Cucurbitaceae*.

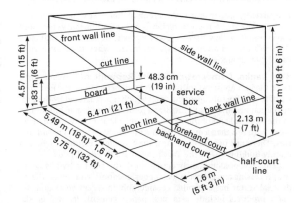

squash rackets ▶ The dimensions of the court.

● **squash rackets** ▶ A racket-and-ball game played in a fourwalled court. It originated from an older game (rackets) played at Harrow School, London, in the mid-19th century. Players hit a small ball of synthetic rubber with the object of making a shot that the opponent cannot return. (When the ball is played it must hit the front wall of the court and may hit any other wall.) The service each time goes to the winner of the previous point. The British version is a singles game going to nine or sometimes more points and only the server may score; the US version is a singles or doubles game going to 15 points and either side may score.

● **squatting** ▶ **1.** In 19th-century Australia, the unauthorized settlement of Crown lands. Awarded licences in the 1840s, many squatters prospered, forming a politically powerful "squattocracy." **2.** In the UK, the occupation of an empty and often condemned building without authority. Owing to the housing shortage, especially in urban areas, squatting in unoccupied buildings scheduled for demolition is often sanctioned by local authorities for those in need. New laws restricting the rights of squatters were introduced in 1993.

● **squid** ▶ A ▷cephalopod mollusc of the order *Decapoda*. Surrounding the mouth, squids have ten arms bearing suckers; two arms are long retractile tentacles used for capturing prey. Their cylindrical tapering bodies have fins on either side and a reduced internal stiffening shell. Squids feed on fish and molluscs, using a siphon to produce a jet of water to dart forwards. The giant squid (genus *Architeuthis*) can reach 20 m in length. □oceans.

● **squill** ▶ A perennial herbaceous plant of the genus *Scilla* (100 species), native to temperate Europe and Asia. Growing from bulbs, they produce long narrow leaves and clusters of blue, white, or purple flowers on a leafless stalk. Some species, including *S. nonscripta* and *S. sibirica*, are cultivated as ornamentals. Family: ▷Liliaceae.

● **squint** ▶ (or strabismus) A condition in which both the eyes cannot focus on the same object at the same time. This may be caused by paralysis of one of the nerves moving the eye, in which case the squint is often temporary. Nonparalytic squints are often seen in children and may be corrected by special lenses, eye exercises, or surgery.

● **squirrel** ▶ A ▷rodent belonging to the family *Sciuridae*, which includes ▷ground squirrels, ▷flying squirrels, and tree squirrels, distributed worldwide. The grey squirrel (*Sciurus carolinensis*) native to North America but now found in most parts of the world, is an agile climber with a long bushy balancing tail and grasping hands. Grey squirrels feed chiefly on nuts, berries, and buds and have become a pest of orchards and gardens. They do not hibernate, but store food for the winter. ▷See also red squirrel.

● **squirrel monkey** ▶ A long-tailed monkey, *Saimiri sciureus*, common in Amazonian forests. Squirrel monkeys are 60–80 cm long including the tail (35–43 cm) and live in large troops, feeding on flowers, fruits, and small animals. They have tufted ears and white rings round their eyes with greenish fur and orange feet. Family: *Cebidae*.

● **squirting cucumber** ▶ A perennial herb, *Ecballium elaterium*, native to the Mediterranean region. It has spreading hairy stems and leaves and its yellow flowers produce elastic-walled fruits that eject the seeds up to a distance of several metres when the fruit is ripe. Family: *Cucurbitaceae*.

● **Sri Lanka, Democratic Socialist Republic of** ▶ (name until 1972: Ceylon) An island country in the Indian Ocean, to the E of the S tip of the Indian subcontinent, from which it is separated by the Gulf of Mannar and the Palk Strait. Broad coastal plains rise to mountains in the S central part of the island. Sri Lanka is primarily a land of villages, with less than a quarter of the inhabitants living in urban centres. There are two main groups: the Sinhalese majority, who are mainly Buddhists, and the Tamils, who are chiefly Hindus.

Economy: predominantly agricultural, the chief activities being the processing and export of tea, rubber, coconuts, and spices. The industrial sector has expanded considerably in recent years and the main products include ceramics, paper, cement, leather goods, chemicals, textiles, fertilizers, and jewellery. There is little mineral wealth, the most valuable deposits being gemstones and ilmenite.

History: according to tradition an Indian prince, Vijaya, conquered the island in the 6th century AD and became the first King of the Sinhalese. In 1505 the Portuguese established settlements in the W and S, which passed to the Dutch in the mid-17th century and to the British in 1798. In 1802 the island was made a separate crown colony. Following World War II Ceylon became a dominion (1948) within the British Commonwealth, with the nationalist S. W. R. D. Bandaranaike as prime minister. In 1972 Sri Lanka became a republic under the leadership of his widow, Sirimavo R. D. Bandaranaike. Following the general election of 1977, in which the United National Party (UNP) was victorious, the Tamil United Liberation Front (TULF) emerged as the main parliamentary opposition. Tension between the Sinhalese and Tamil communities erupted into violent conflict in 1983, when the so-called ▷Tamil Tigers, a separatist militia, began to take control of Tamil-dominated areas in the N and E. An Indian peacekeeping force arrived in 1987 but withdrew in 1990 when its presence threatened war between the two states. Separatist violence intensified and claimed thousands of lives, including that of the president, R. Premadasa (1924–93), who was assassinated. Abortive peace talks in 1994–95 were followed by an all-out military offensive against the rebels, who were heavily defeated in their main northern stronghold. A renewed Tamil insurgence in 1996 led to fierce fighting once more. In 1994 Chandrika Kumaratunga was elected president and reinstated her mother, Sirimavo Bandaranaike, as prime minister. In 1999 Kumaratunga survived an assassination attempt. Ramasiri Wickremanayake became prime minister following elections in 2000. A long-term ceasefire with the Tamil Tigers was agreed in 2002 and peace talks began.

Democratic Socialist Republic of Sri Lanka	
Head of state	President Chandrika Kumaratunga
Official language	Sinhala
Official currency	Sri Lanka rupee of 100 cents
Area	65 610 sq km (25 332 sq mi)
Population (2001 est)	19 399 000
Capital	Colombo

Sri Lanka ▶ Tamil tea pickers on a tea plantation.

● **Srinagar** ▶ 34 08N 74 50E A city in India, the summer capital of Jammu and Kashmir on the River Jhelum. It has museums, palaces, mosques, and a fortress, and is the site of the University of Jammu and Kashmir (1948). Industries include carpets, silver, silk, and leather. Population (1991): 586 038.

● **SS** ▶ (German: Schutzstaffel, Defence Squad) The infamous Nazi military corps, created in 1925 as Hitler's bodyguard and commanded by Heinrich Himmler from 1929. The SS, or Blackshirts, by the mid-1930s controlled the Nazis' security system, including the ▷Gestapo, ▷concentration camp guards, and the Waffen SS, an elite corps of combat troops in World War II. After the German defeat Himmler committed suicide and the activities of the SS were condemned at the Nuremburg trials (1946).

● **SSSI** ▶ (Site of Special Scientific Interest) ▷*See* nature conservation.

● **Ssu-ch'uan** ▷*See* Sichuan.

● **Ssu-ma Ch'ien** ▷*See* Si-ma Qian.

● **St** ▶ Names beginning St are listed under Saint.

● **stabilizers** ▶ (shipbuilding) Adjustable finlike devices, projecting from the hull of a vessel, that reduce the vessel's motion in a heavy sea. They are operated automatically by a heavy gyroscope and are often called gyrostabilizers.

● **stabilizers** ▶ (economics) Factors that temper the booms and recessions of the ▷trade cycle. They may be actions taken as a result of either government ▷monetary or ▷fiscal policy or "built-in" stabilizers that work automatically, e.g. the increase in money paid out in unemployment benefit during a recession, which helps to maintain consumption.

● **stadholder** ▶ (or stadtholder) The ruler of the United Provinces of the Netherlands. Originally a provincial governor responsible to the central government of the Netherlands' Burgundian and then Spanish rulers, following the ▷Revolt of the Netherlands in the 16th century the secessionist United Provinces elected ▷William the Silent as their stadholder. The office was traditionally held by the House of Orange until the fall of the republic in 1795.

● **Staël, Anne Louise Germaine Necker, Madame de** ▶ (1766–1817) French writer, daughter of the financier ▷Necker. Her Paris salon became a centre of liberal intellectual opposition to Napoleon, with whom she quarrelled and consequently, after 1803, was forced to live in exile, mostly at her chateau on Lake Geneva. She travelled widely in Europe, studied with Schiller and Goethe in Weimar, and returned to Paris after the Bourbon restoration in 1814. Her most important work was *De l'Allemagne* (1810), which introduced German literature to France. She also wrote two novels featuring unconventional young heroines, *Delphine* (1802) and *Corinne* (1807).

● **Staffa** ▶ 56 26N 6 21W An uninhabited island off the W coast of Scotland, in the Inner Hebrides. Composed largely of basalt columns, it is famous for its spectacular coast and caves, including ▷Fingal's Cave.

● **Stafford** ▶ 52 48N 2 07W A market town in the English Midlands, the administrative centre of Staffordshire. The ruined castle occupies the site of a Saxon fortress. Footwear, chemicals, and electrical goods are manufactured. Population (1991): 61 885.

● **Staffordshire** ▶ A county in the English Midlands. It consists mainly of undulating lowlands rising to moorland in the N, with the River Trent flowing SE. Agriculture is important, especially dairy farming. Industries include the manufacture of pottery, which became famous during the 18th century through the work of Josiah ▷Wedgwood. Coalmining was formerly important. In 1974 the industrial area in the S (the Black Country) passed to the new metropolitan county of the West Midlands. Stoke-on-Trent became an independent ▷unitary authority in 1997. Area (excluding Stoke-on-Trent): 2716 sq km (1049 sq mi). Population (1996 est, excluding Stoke-on-Trent): 801 300. Administrative centre: Stafford.

● **Staffordshire bull terrier** ▶ A breed of dog developed from a bulldog-terrier cross as a pit dog. It is stockily built with a broad deep head and a short smooth coat that is pure white; red, fawn, black, or blue; or any of these colours in combination with white. Height: 35–40 cm (English); 43–48 cm (American).

● **stag beetle** ▶ A beetle of a family (*Lucanidae*; about 900 species) occurring mostly in the tropical regions. The males have well-developed mandibles that in many species resemble antlers—sometimes equal to the length of the body (which is about 8–40 mm long). They are used during combat with other males. Most stag beetles are black or brown, although tropical species are often more colourful. The scavenging larvae develop from eggs laid in rotten wood.

● **stagecoach** ▶ A large four-wheeled carriage drawn by four or six horses and used for scheduled long-distance transport services in England from the mid-17th century until the advent of rail travel. The journey was divided into stages; horses, kept at strategically sited coaching inns, were changed after each stage. The coach usually had seats for six inside and poorer passengers rode on the roof. After 1784 mails were carried by coach. In the USA and Australia stagecoaches remained important auxiliaries to the developing railway systems throughout the 19th century.

● **staghorn fern** ▶ A ▷fern of the genus *Platycerium*, which grows upon other plants but is not a parasite. The fronds fork repeatedly into long pointed leaflets, resembling antlers, and the spore capsules are borne on their undersides. The fern, which is native to most warm regions, is cultivated as a pot plant. Family: *Polypodiaceae*.

● **staghound** ▶ A ▷foxhound used for hunting wild deer. ▷*See also* deerhound.

● **Stahl, Georg Ernst** ▶ (1660–1734) German physician and chemist, who in about 1700 formulated the ▷phlogiston theory of combustion. Stahl had an alchemical disregard for quantitative measurement and consequently the phlogiston theory does not take changes of mass on combustion into account. Stahl's work in physiology was equally unscientific in modern terms, relying on a vitalist approach.

● **stained glass** ▶ Coloured glass panels formed of fragments of glass cut to shape according to a pictorial or abstract design and held together by "H" section lead strips. The earliest surviving stained-glass windows date from the 12th century AD, but this principle of embellishing buildings was known much earlier. The glass used was either coloured throughout by the addition of metallic oxides (e.g. copper oxide (CuO) for ruby red) while molten or dipped into molten coloured glass to obtain a fine film of colour on both sides (flashed glass). From the 16th century painted glass displaced the more expensive coloured glass. The 12th century saw considerable production of religious stained glass windows in N Europe. Much survives in France. Less exuberant colours and a classical restraint marked the post-Renaissance use of stained glass until leading designers (e.g. William ▷Morris, ▷Burne-Jones) exploited its decorative potential in the 19th century. Modern stained glass employs abstract patterns in secular as well as ecclesiastical surroundings.

● **Stainer, Sir John** ▶ (1840–1901) British composer and organist. He wrote much sacred music, including the oratorio *The Crucifixion* (1887).

● **stainless steel** ▶ An alloy ▷steel containing up to 20% chromium and 10% nickel. It is corrosion resistant because the oxide that forms on the surface remains intact and protects the metal, unlike other steels in which it flakes off. Stainless steel is used in a wide variety of engineering applications where this property is important, as well as in kitchen utensils. It is more expensive to produce than ordinary carbon steel and more difficult to machine.

stag beetle ▶ A male of the European species *Lucanus cervus*.

● **Stakhanovite** ▶ A member of a Soviet movement that strove to increase industrial production. Named after Aleksei Grigorievich Stakhanov (1906–77), a coalminer who in 1935 reorganized his gang to increase its production sevenfold, the movement failed because quality could not be maintained.

● **stalactites and stalagmites** ▶ Deposits of calcium carbonate in limestone caves; stalactites are conical or cylindrical projections from the cave roof, while stalagmites grow upwards from the floor and are generally more stumpy. They sometimes meet to form a continuous column. They are gradually formed from water containing calcium bicarbonate dripping from the roof. When the water evaporates a solid residue of calcium carbonate is left.

● **Stalin, Joseph** ▶ (J. Dzhugashvili; 1879–1953) Soviet statesman.

Born in Georgia, Stalin (whose adopted name means "man of steel") became a Marxist in the 1890s and was expelled from a theological college for his revolutionary activity (1899). In 1903 he joined the ▷Bolsheviks under Lenin and in the years preceding the Russian Revolution (1917) was repeatedly imprisoned and exiled. In 1921 he became commissar for nationalities and in 1922 general secretary of the Communist Party. After Lenin's death in 1924 Stalin struggled to eliminate his rivals, above all ▷Trotsky, and emerged as supreme dictator in 1929. He abandoned Lenin's ▷New Economic Policy, initiating a series of five-year plans to enforce, with great brutality, the collectivization of industry and agriculture. The 1930s saw the reign of terror, culminating in the great purge, in which Stalin sought to enhance his power by the removal of his real, or imagined, rivals. In World War II, Stalin became chairman of the Council of People's Commissars and, following Hitler's invasion of the Soviet Union (1941), reversed the German alliance of 1939. He attended Allied conferences at ▷Tehran (1943) and at ▷Yalta and Potsdam (1945), where his negotiating skills were noted by Roosevelt and Churchill. In the postwar years, when Stalin's autocracy intensified, he pursued a foreign policy of imperialism towards the communist countries of E Europe together with unremitting hostility towards the noncommunist world. After his death many of Stalin's policies were denounced by the Soviet regime.

● **Stalinabad** ▷*See* Dushanbe.

● **Stalingrad** ▷*See* Volgograd.

● **Stalingrad, Battle of** ▶ (1942–43) A battle in World War II, in which the German 6th Army under ▷Paulus, having entered Stalingrad (now Volgograd), surrendered to the Russians under ▷Zhukov. The Germans lost 200 000 men.

● **Stalinsk** ▷*See* Novokuznetsk.

● **Stamboul** ▷*See* Istanbul.

● **stamen** ▶ The part of a flower that produces the ▷pollen (male gametes). It comprises an anther, a lobed structure consisting of four pollen sacs, borne on a stalk (filament). The pollen develops within the sacs, which split open to release it. In self-pollinated flowers, the stamens open inwards, towards the pistil, but in cross-pollinated flowers they open outwards. ▷*See also* flower. ⬚plant.

● **Stamford Bridge** ▶ 53 59N 0 55W A village in N England, in the East Riding of Yorkshire on the River Derwent. Here King Harold defeated his brother Tostig and King Harald of Norway in 1066, three weeks before his own defeat at Hastings. Population (1991): 3099.

● **Stamitz, Johann** ▶ (Jan Stamic; 1717–57) Bohemian composer and director of the Mannheim court orchestra. His composition helped to establish ▷sonata form and he introduced the controlled crescendo into his symphonies.

● **stammering** ▶ A disorder of the rhythm of speech, known medically as dysphemia. The normal flow of speech is interrupted by hesitations, repetitions of syllables, and sometimes by grimaces. Stammering is common in children, especially if speech is slow to develop, and does not indicate any illness. It is often made worse by anxiety and can become persistent; it usually improves with ▷speech therapy.

● **Stamp Act** ▶ (1765) The first British Act that imposed direct taxes on documents, newspapers, and dice in the American colonies. Parliament was forced by colonial hostility to repeal the Act but asserted its right to impose laws on the colonies (Declaratory Act, 1766), thus aggravating the opposition that led to the ▷American Revolution.

● **stamp collecting** ▷*See* philately.

● **standard deviation** ▷*See* variance.

● **standard form** ▶ The writing of large and small numbers as a number between 1 and 10 multiplied by a power of ten; for example, 1 350 000 in standard form is written 1.35×10^6 and 0.0006234 is written 6.234×10^{-4}. See also Appendix (Units of Measurement)

● **standard model** ▷*See* particle physics.

● **standardwing** ▶ A ▷bird of paradise, *Semioptera wallacei*, discovered in 1858 in the Moluccan Islands. The male is about 25 cm long and has two long white ribbon-like feathers at each shoulder, which are erected over the back during its courtship display.

● **Standish, Myles** ▶ (c. 1584–1656) English colonist in America. He sailed to America on the ▷*Mayflower*, becoming military leader of the first settlement in New England, at Plymouth.

● **Stanford, Sir Charles (Villiers)** ▶ (1852–1924) Irish composer. He became professor of composition at the Royal College of Music in 1883. Among his compositions are six operas, seven symphonies, concertos, chamber music, songs, and Anglican church music.

● **Stanhope, James, 1st Earl** ▶ (1673–1721) British soldier and statesman; George I's chief minister (1717–21). He served under Marlborough in the War of the Spanish Succession (1701–14) and helped suppress the ▷Jacobite uprising (1715). He was in charge of foreign affairs before becoming chief minister. His grandson **Charles, 3rd Earl Stanhope** (1753–1816) was a politician and scientist. Becoming an MP in 1780, he urged parliamentary reform and supported the French Revolution. His inventions included two calculating machines, a microscope lens, and a stereotyping machine that was acquired (1805) by the Clarendon Press at Oxford. He also experimented with electricity.

● **Stanislavsky, Konstantin** ▶ (K. Alekseyev; 1863–1938) Russian actor and theatre director. As director of the Moscow Art Theatre, which he founded in 1898 with Nemirovich Danchenko (1859–1943), he developed an innovatory style of naturalistic production that was ideally suited to the plays of Chekhov and Gorki. His theories about acting, published in *My Life in Art* (1924) and *An Actor Prepares* (1926) and later developed in the USA as "method" acting at the ▷Actors' Studio, emphasized the value of ensemble playing and of the actor's complete identification with the character he played.

● **Stanisław I Leszczyński** ▶ (1677–1766) King of Poland (1704–09, 1733–35) and Duke of Lorraine (1735–66). Stanisław was placed on the throne by ▷Charles XII of Sweden, after whose defeat Stanisław was deposed. He regained the throne by election but lost the subsequent War of the Polish Succession and became Duke of Lorraine.

● **Stanisław II Poniatowski** ▶ (1732–98) The last King of Poland (1764–95). Stanisław became a favourite of Catherine the Great of Russia, who secured his election to the throne and dominated his reign. In 1772 parts of Poland were annexed by Russia, Prussia, and Austria; in 1793 it was again partitioned (by Russia and Prussia). After ▷Kosciuszko's rebellion and a third partition Stanisław abdicated.

● **Stanisław, St** ▶ (or Stanislaus; 1030–79) The patron saint of Poland. Of noble birth, he was elected Bishop of Cracow in 1072. He was implicated in a plot against Bolesław II and murdered in mysterious circumstances. Feast day: 7 May.

● **Stanley** ▶ 51 45S 57 56W The capital of the Falkland Islands, in NE East Falkland Island on the Atlantic Ocean. A whaling base, it exports wool, skin, tallow, and seal oil. It was the focus of the Falklands War of 1982. Population (1991): 1643.

● **Stanley, Sir Henry Morton** ▶ (1841–1904) British explorer and journalist. He went to the USA in 1859, joined the *New York Herald*, and in 1871 was sent by James Gordon ▷Bennett to search for David ▷Livingstone in Africa. Having found him at Ujiji, the two men explored Lake Tanganyika together. On a second expedition (1874–77) Stanley followed the Congo River to its mouth. By obtaining Belgian sponsorship for exploration in the Congo he was instrumental in securing Belgian sovereignty over the Congo Free State. His last African expedition (1886–89) relieved ▷Emin Paşa in the S Sudan.

● **Stanley Falls** ▷*See* Boyoma Falls.

● **Stanley Pool** ▷*See* Malebo Pool.

● **Stanleyville** ▷*See* Kisangani.

● **Stannaries** ▶ The tinmining district of Cornwall and Devon. Until 1897 the Stannaries held its own courts, which had jurisdiction over tinminers except in murder or land disputes. A so-called Stannaries parliament was unofficially established by Cornish nationalists in 1974.

● **Stanovoi Range** ▶ A mountain range in SE Russia extending about 800 km (497 mi) E–W. It rises to 2482 m (8143 ft) and forms part of the watershed between the Arctic and Pacific Oceans.

● **Stansted** ▶ 51 54N 0 12E A village in SE England, E of London in Essex. It is the site of London's third airport. Population (1991): 4943.

● **Staphylococcus** ▶ A genus of spherical bacteria. *S. aureus* is responsible for boils and abscesses, *S. pyogenes* infects wounds, and certain strains cause acute food poisoning.

● **star** ▶ A luminous celestial body that is composed of gas and that derives its energy from thermonuclear reactions in its hot dense core. The sun is a typical star: stellar mass usually ranges from about 0.05 to 60 times the sun's mass. A star's mass determines its ▷luminosity, surface temperature, size, and other properties as well as its evolutionary path and lifetime: the higher the mass, the brighter, hotter, and larger the star and the shorter its life. During the course of their history stars evolve, a process called stellar evolution. Young stars evolve from the ▷protostar stage when they begin to generate energy by the thermonuclear fusion of hydrogen to form helium. This continues for some 10^{10} years for stars of solar mass but for only a few million years for the most massive stars. When the hydrogen is exhausted, stars evolve into ▷giant stars, those of near solar mass becoming ▷red giants. Further thermonuclear reactions occur involving fusion of helium and possibly the heavier elements in more massive stars. A low-mass star finally evolves to a ▷white dwarf. More massive stars explode as ▷supernovae, the surviving cores possibly forming ▷neutron stars or ▷black holes depending on mass. Stars are not distributed uniformly throughout the ▷universe, but are grouped into enormous assemblies, called ▷galaxies, as a result of gravitational forces. The sun forms part of the ▷Galaxy (written with a capital G), often known as the Milky Way system. The nearest star to the sun is 4.3 light years away.

● **star apple** ▶ An evergreen tree, *Chrysophyllum cainito*, native to the West Indies and Central America. Growing to a height of 15 m, it has purplish-white flowers and bears sweet-tasting smooth-skinned fruits that resemble apples, red to yellow in colour with star-shaped cores. Family: *Sapotaceae*.

● **Stara Zagora** ▶ 42 25N 25 37E A city in central Bulgaria. The city was rebuilt after its destruction by the Turks in the late 19th century. Fruit, in particular, is grown in the surrounding area. Population (1996 est): 149 666.

● **starch** ▶ A carbohydrate that is an important storage product of many plants. Chemically it consists of linked glucose units in the form of two polysaccharides, amylose and amylopectin, which are present in varying proportions. Starch occurs naturally as white powdery granules that are insoluble in cold water but form a gelatinous solution in hot water. Plants manufacture starch by photosynthesis and it is a major constituent of seeds, fruits, roots, and tubers and a major source of dietary energy for animals and humans. It is also used in the paper and textile industries.

● **Star Chamber, Court of** ▶ A court, originating in the king's council of medieval England, that met in the Star Chamber at Westminster Palace. It was concerned chiefly with breaches of the peace. Its misuse by Charles I to enforce his unpopular policies led to its abolition (1641) by the ▷Long Parliament on the eve of the Civil War.

● **star cluster** ▶ A group of stars that are associated by gravitational effects and that shared a common origin. **Open clusters** are loosely bound asymmetrical groupings of up to a few hundred stars and occur in the disc of our ▷Galaxy. **Globular clusters** are compact spherical groupings containing many thousands of very old stars and occur in the Galactic halo.

● **starfish** ▶ A marine invertebrate animal, also called sea star, belonging to a worldwide class (*Asteroidea*; 1800 species) of ▷echinoderms. Its fleshy star-shaped body is covered with a spiny skin and has five or more radiating arms. Starfish occur on shores and ocean floors and move slowly, using saclike tube feet on the underside of the arms. They feed mainly on molluscs, crustaceans, and other invertebrates.

● **stargazer** ▶ A fish belonging to either of the families *Uranoscopidae* (electric stargazers; about 25 species) or *Dactyloscopidae*

(sand stargazers; about 24 species), found in tropical and temperate seas. Stargazers have a tapering body, up to 30 cm long, a vertically slanting mouth, and eyes on top of the head. They lie buried in sand awaiting prey. Order: *Perciformes*.

● **Stark, Dame Freya (Madeline)** ▶ (1893–1993) British travel writer. Born in Paris and educated in Italy and London, she began her travels in the Arab countries in the late 1920s. Her many books include *The Southern Gates of Arabia* (1936), *Beyond Euphrates* (1951), and *The Journey's Echo* (1963).

● **starling** ▶ A noisy sharp-winged songbird, *Sturnus vulgaris*, having a black plumage speckled with iridescent purple, green, and white. It is a versatile bird, common on farmland, where it probes the soil for insects, and also in cities, where it is a scavenger. It is gregarious and commonly nests in flocks in buildings and trees, sometimes becoming a serious crop pest. Family: *Sturnidae*.

● **star-of-Bethlehem** ▶ A spring-blooming perennial plant, *Ornithogalum umbellatum*, native to the Mediterranean and grown in gardens. Growing from a bulb, it has grasslike basal leaves and a slender stalk, up to 30 cm tall, bearing clusters of star-shaped white flowers striped with green. Family: *Liliaceae*.

● **star of David** ▶ (Hebrew *magen David*: shield of David) A six-pointed star or hexagram, composed of two equilateral triangles. Widely used from antiquity as an ornament or magical sign, it has been regarded since the 17th century as a Jewish symbol, and was imposed on the Jews as a "badge of shame" by the Nazis. In 1897 it was officially adopted as an emblem of Zionism and it now appears on the flag of Israel.

● **Starr, Ringo** ▶ (Richard Starkey; 1940–) British rock musician, former drummer of the ▷Beatles. His solo albums include *Ringo* (1973), *Goodnight Vienna* (1974), and *A Vertical Man* (1998). He has also appeared in films and is popular as a broadcaster on children's television.

● **START** ▶ (STrategic Arms Reduction Talks) ▷*See* disarmament.

● **star wars** ▷*See* Strategic Defence Initiative.

● **Stassfurt** ▶ 51 51N 11 35E A town in central Germany, on the River Bode. The Stassfurt deposits consist of several strata, some 1100 m thick, providing since 1861 a valuable source of sodium and potassium compounds, magnesium bromide, and rock salt.

● **Staten Island** ▶ An island in the USA coextensive with Richmond, one of the five boroughs of New York City. Largely residential, it is the least densely populated of the city's boroughs. Area: 148 sq km (57 sq mi). Population (1990): 378 977.

● **States General** ▶ **1.** In France, the assembly of representatives of the three estates—clergy, nobility, and the Third Estate or commons. First summoned by Philip the Fair in 1302, the States General did not meet after 1614 until summoned by Louis XVI in 1789 on the eve of the ▷French Revolution. The Third Estate declared itself a National Assembly, which replaced the States General. **2.** In the Netherlands, the assembly of provincial representatives created by its Burgundian rulers in the 15th century. Following the ▷Revolt of the Netherlands against Spain, it became (1579) the chief organ of the United Provinces' central government.

● **states of matter** ▶ Any of three distinct physical states: solid, liquid, and gas. A fourth state, ▷plasma, is often added. The different states are distinguished by the strength of the intermolecular forces compared to their random thermal motion. For example, in a solid the intermolecular forces are sufficiently strong to hold the molecules to an approximately fixed position, whereas in a gas the intermolecular forces have hardly any effect on the random movements of the atoms and molecules. Liquids represent an intermediate state.

● **states' rights** ▶ In the USA, the rights of the individual states of the USA in relation to the power of the federal government. The issue arose in debates over the ▷constitution (1789), which established a strong federal government. Assertion of states' rights, especially that of secession from the Union, led eventually to the ▷Civil War.

● **static electricity** ▶ The effects created by electrical charges at rest. Current electricity is an effect resulting from a flow of electrons; in static electricity electrons from one object are pulled onto another object, usually by rubbing them together, but they do not flow. The effect can be observed with many nonconducting materials, for example a comb passing through dry hair or a leather sole on a nylon carpet. A force exists between two charged bodies (*see* electric field), attractive if they have opposite charges, repulsive if the charges are similar; the magnitude of the force is given by ▷Coulomb's law. Static electricity can often cause problems (*see* lightning) but can be useful in electrostatic precipitators. ▷*See also* electroscope; electrostatic generators.

● **statics** ▷*See* mechanics.

● **Stationery Office, The** ► (TSO) A UK company that supplies all the stationery, office supplies, office machinery, and printing and binding needed for use in the civil service. It also publishes and sells government publications, producing more titles (ranging from high-quality books to free leaflets) than any other publishing organization in the country. Formerly known as Her Majesty's Stationery Office (HMSO), it was privatized in 1996. The Stationery Office is based in Norwich and London.

● **Stations of the Cross** ► A series of 14 pictures or images depicting the final events of the life of Christ, beginning at Pontius ▷Pilate's house, where he was condemned to death, and concluding at the sepulchre. They are usually arranged on the walls of a church and form the basis of a devotion in which prayers are recited as each station is visited in turn. The devotion was popularized in the middle ages by the Franciscans but derived from the early custom of pilgrims who followed the Way of the Cross in Jerusalem.

● **statistical mechanics** ► A branch of physics in which statistics is used to predict the macroscopic properties of a system from its microscopic constituents. In **classical statistical mechanics**, particles are assumed to occupy an exact position and to have an exact momentum at any instant. The Maxwell-Boltzmann law (*see* Boltzmann, Ludwig Eduard; Maxwell, James Clerk) is then used to give the most probable distribution of the particles. In **quantum statistics**, a particle cannot be assigned an exact position and momentum simultaneously (*see* Heisenberg uncertainty principle) and quantum considerations have to be applied. This led to ▷Bose-Einstein statistics and, for particles that obey the ▷Pauli exclusion principle, to ▷Fermi-Dirac statistics.

● **statistics** ► The study of methods for collecting and analysing quantitative data. The data measure certain characteristics of a group of people or objects, called the population; usually the whole population cannot be observed, often because it is too large, so data are collected from a representative sample of the population (random sampling). The sample is analysed and conclusions are inferred about the whole population, using ▷probability theory because the inferences cannot be certain. A population that has what is called a normal or Gaussian distribution (named after Karl ▷Gauss) varies randomly about a mean value. The standard deviation, the root-mean-square deviation from the mean value, is a measure of the spread in the population. The higher the standard deviation, the larger the sample size needed to be representative of the population. In binomial distributions the population consists of only two possible outcomes, as in tossing a coin, and in this case different statistical methods are used. In descriptive (*or* deductive) statistics data for a group are collected and analysed without conclusions being drawn about a larger group.

● **Statue of Liberty** ► A statue of a woman 46 m (152 ft) high holding a torch in her raised right hand, on Liberty Island in New York harbour. Designed by the French architect ▷Bartholdi, it was given to the Americans by the French in 1884 to commemorate the French and American Revolutions. Unveiled and dedicated in 1886, it has been a US national monument since 1924. It underwent complete renovation in the 1980s.

● **Staudinger, Hermann** ► (1881-1965) German chemist, who was professor at Freiburg University. He won the 1953 Nobel Prize for his work on the molecular structure of polymers. Staudinger showed that polymer molecules consisted of chains of repeated units and not a random distribution of such units as was previously thought. His work was crucial to the developing plastics industry.

● **Stauffenberg, Claus, Graf von** ► (1907-44) German army officer, who attempted to assassinate Hitler on 20 July, 1944 (known as the **July Plot**). Stauffenberg served in N Africa, where he was badly wounded. He tried to eliminate Hitler by planting a bomb under his conference table at his headquarters at Rastenburg. Although the bomb exploded, Hitler was only slightly wounded. Stauffenberg and his fellow conspirators were executed.

● **Stavanger** ► 61 32N 5 12E A seaport in SW Norway. Its 12th-century cathedral was built by Bishop Reinald from Winchester. Its industries include fish canning and shipbuilding. Stavanger is also the centre of Norway's North Sea oil industry. Population (1996 est): 105 573.

● **Stavisky affair** ► A French political scandal. In 1933 the fraudulent dealings of a financier Serge Alexandre Stavisky (c. 1866-1934) were revealed and shortly afterwards he was found dead. Attempts by the government to hush up the affair encouraged rumours that Stavisky had been murdered to prevent him from exposing the involvement of public figures in his affairs. Consequent right-wing riots led to the replacement of the left-wing government with a broad-based coalition.

● **Stavropol** ► **1.** 45 03N 41 59E A city in SW Russia. The centre of a fertile agricultural region, it has food-processing industries. It possesses several educational institutions. Population (1995 est): 342 000. **2.** ▷*See* Togliatti.

● **steady-state theory** ► A cosmological theory (*see* cosmology) proposed in 1948 by ▷Bondi, ▷Hoyle, and T. Gold (1920–) in which the universe is regarded as having always existed in a steady state. The ▷expansion of the universe is compensated by the continuous creation of new matter. On the present evidence this theory has largely been discredited in favour of the ▷big-bang theory.

● **steam distillation** ▷*See* distillation.

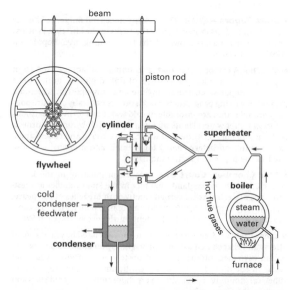

steam engine ► The principle of a double-action beam engine of the kind patented by James Watt. During the first half of the cycle, valve A opens, steam flows in and pushes the cylinder down, and steam flows out to the condenser through valve C. During the second half of the cycle, B opens and the steam pushes the piston the other way.

● **steam engine** ► A ⬜heat engine in which heat from a furnace is used to raise steam, the expansion of which forces a piston to move up and down in a cylinder to provide mechanical energy. A primitive steam engine was invented in 1698 by a Capt Savery to pump water from mines. In 1711 ▷Newcomen improved on this design but still relied on cooling the cylinder with a jet of water after each stroke. ▷Watt's single-acting steam engine, patented in 1769, was the first to use a separate condenser. Watt went on to invent the double-acting engine, the crank and crosshead mechanism, and the governor. Thus by the end of the 18th century man had, for the first time, a reliable source of power that did not rely on muscles or the wind. It was largely this engine that created the ▷industrial revolution. In 1808 Richard ▷Trevithick made the first use of a steam engine to drive a carriage, but it was not until the end of the century that steam cars were in use—and they were quickly replaced by cars using Otto's petrol engine. The steam engine, however, was the supreme prime mover of ▷railways throughout the world from 1829 (when ▷Stephenson built his first ▷locomotive) until after World War II, when steam was largely replaced by electric and Diesel-electric trains. From the beginning of the 19th century steam engines were also widely used in place of sails in ▷ships. Moreover, it was the steam engine that drove the first electricity generators for public supply. However, the more compact and efficient steam ▷turbine has now replaced the steam engine for this purpose.

● **steam turbine** ▷See turbine.

● **steatite** ▷See talc.

● **steel** ▶ An ▷alloy of iron containing a small carefully controlled proportion of carbon, usually less than 1%. Carbon steels contain principally iron and carbon. Alloy steels have other metals added. Steel products form the basis of modern technology and steel production is therefore a key factor in the world economy. Annual world trading in iron ore amounts to about US$5 billion, and that in scrap iron and steel about US$1.5 billion. About 312 thousand tonnes of steel are produced every week in the UK, over half of this from recycled scrap steel. The uses of steel range from steel girders in bridges and buildings to kitchen utensils. For many engineering products the starting material is **mild steel**, a carbon steel with between 0.2% and 0.8% carbon and sometimes a little manganese or silicon. It can be further improved by ▷heat treatment. Alloy steels, such as ▷stainless steel, are usually more expensive to produce. They are used where special hardness, strength, or corrosion resistance are needed. Steel is made by ▷smelting iron ore in a blast furnace to produce pig iron, which is added to melted down scrap iron before being converted by the ▷basic-oxygen process, the ▷open-hearth process, or the ▷electric-arc furnace.

● **Steel, David (Martin Scott), Baron** ▶ (1938–) British politician; leader of the Liberal Party (1976–88). He entered parliament in 1964 and succeeded Jeremy Thorpe as Liberal leader. In 1977 he negotiated a pact between the Liberal Party and the minority Labour government. From 1981 to 1987 he headed the SDP-Liberal Alliance alongside the SDP leader, David Owen. He was knighted in 1990 and raised to the peerage in 1997. In 1999 he was elected speaker of the new Scottish parliament.

● **steel guitar** ▷See Hawaiian guitar.

● **Steele, Sir Richard** ▶ (1672–1729) British essayist and dramatist. Born in Dublin, he served in the English army from 1692 to 1705 and wrote a number of successful sentimental comedies, beginning with *The Funeral* (1701). He edited the *London Gazette* (1707–10), the official government journal. He is best remembered for his essays in *The Tatler* (1709–11) and the *Spectator* (1711–12), periodicals that he founded and on which he collaborated with Joseph ▷Addison.

● **Steen, Jan** ▶ (c. 1626–79) Dutch painter. After training under Adriaen Van ▷Ostade and Jan van ▷Goyen, whose daughter he married, he worked in The Hague, Delft, and Haarlem, but principally in Leiden, where he kept a tavern. Although he painted some landscapes and biblical and mythological subjects, he is best known for his humorous and sometimes bawdy tavern and domestic scenes. Representative works are *The Feast of St Nicholas* (Rijksmuseum, Amsterdam), *Merry Company* (Mauritshuis, The Hague), and *The Morning Toilet* (Buckingham Palace).

● **steeplechase** ▶ **1.** A form of horse race that grew out of ▷foxhunting, in which horses jump artificial hedges and ditches. The severity of the obstacles varies between courses and between countries. Hurdling is a less taxing version over lower lighter fences and

shorter distances. Both are governed in England by National Hunt rules. The horses used are either trained for the purpose or turn to steeplechasing after their ▷flat-racing careers are over. Point-to-points are steeplechases for amateur riders, run by the local hunts. ▷*See also* Grand National Steeplechase. **2.** A track event for men in athletics over a 3000 m course that includes 28 hurdles 91 cm (3 ft) high and seven water jumps 3.66 m (12 ft) across. World record: 7 minutes 1.8 seconds (1995) by Moses Kiptanui (Kenya).

● **Stefan-Boltzmann law** ▶ The total energy emitted per unit time and per unit area by a ▷black body at an absolute temperature T is proportional to T^4. The constant of proportionality, known as Stefan's constant, is equal to 5.6697×10^{-8} W m^{-2} K^{-4}. The law is named after the Austrian physicist Joseph Stefan (1835–93), who first discovered it, and Ludwig ▷Boltzmann, who derived it thermodynamically.

● **Stefan Dušan** ▶ (1308–55) King of Serbia (1331–55). Serbia's foremost medieval ruler, Stefan Dušan established Serbian supremacy in the Balkans by conquering Macedonia, Albania, and parts of Greece; in 1346 he was crowned Emperor of the Serbs and Greeks. He introduced a new legal code.

● **Stegodon** ▶ A genus of long-legged extinct ▷elephants that lived in Asia and Africa between 12 and 1 million years ago. The first of the true elephants, it gave rise to the now extinct ▷mammoths and to the Indian and African elephants.

Stegosaurus ▶ It was originally thought that the plates on the back of this dinosaur were erect and probably functioned as weapons. Recent theories, however, postulate a horizontal arrangement of plates, which acted as heat exchangers.

● **Stegosaurus** ▶ A dinosaur of the late Jurassic period (about 150–135 million years ago). 7 m long and weighing 1.75 tonnes, it had a double row of large triangular plates arranged in pairs along its back and two pairs of spikes at the end of its tail. *Stegosaurus* had a small head and fed on soft plants. Order: ▷*Ornithischia*.

● **Stein, Sir (Marc) Aurel** ▶ (1862–1943) British explorer and archaeologist of Hungarian birth. Stein made expeditions to India, Persia, Turkistan, and the Far East, which resulted in many discoveries, including the Cave of the Thousand Buddhas near Dun-Huang (W China), with its paintings and documents. His books include *Ancient Khotan* (1907) and *Innermost Asia* (1928).

● **Stein, Gertrude** ▶ (1874–1946) US writer. From 1903 she lived in Paris, where she presided over the American expatriate literary community. Her experiments in prose, which include *Three Lives* (1909) and *Tender Buttons* (1914), were influenced by the cubist theories of Picasso, Braque, and other painters whom she helped. Her most accessible work is *The Autobiography of Alice B. Toklas* (1933).

● **Stein, Karl, Freiherr vom** ▶ (1757–1831) Prussian statesman. He became first minister to Frederick William III in 1807, after serving as finance minister (1804–07), and introduced major administrative and economic reforms that helped Prussia to recover from its defeat by Napoleon. Dismissed in 1808, he then became adviser to Alexander I of Russia.

● **Steinbeck, John** ▶ (1902–68) US novelist. The majority of his novels, notably *Of Mice and Men* (1937) and *The Grapes of Wrath* (1939), an epic account of migrant farm workers, deal with the social and economic conditions of his native California. *East of Eden* (1952) is the most ambitious of his later novels. He won the Nobel Prize in 1962.

● **steinbok** ▶ A small solitary African antelope, *Raphicerus campestris*, inhabiting long grass or thinly forested areas. Steinboks are about 50 cm high at the shoulder with a reddish-brown coat; males have small horns.

● **Steiner, George** ▶ (1929–) French-born British academic and critic, who taught comparative literature at Cambridge and in Geneva. His books include *The Death of Tragedy* (1960), *After Babel* (1975), *Antigones* (1984), *Real Presences* (1989), and the largely autobiographical collection of essays *Errata* (1998).

● **Steiner, Rudolf** ▶ (1861–1925) Austrian-born founder of ▷anthroposophy. Steiner rejected the oriental associations of ▷theosophy, with which he was originally associated, and aimed in his system to reintegrate man with the world of the spirit. He founded his first school in 1919; there are now over 70 Rudolf Steiner schools, which aim to develop the child's whole personality. Some Steiner schools concentrate on teaching children with learning difficulties.

● **Steinmetz, Charles Proteus** ▶ (1865–1923) US electrical engineer, born in Germany, who developed the mathematical theory of ▷alternating current, introducing both real and imaginary components. This work greatly stimulated the development of devices running on alternating current. Steinmetz also discovered the law of ▷hysteresis and made some 200 inventions in electrical engineering, including a high-voltage generator.

● **Steinway, Henry (Engelhard)** ▶ (Heinrich Steinweg; 1797–1871) German-born US piano maker. He had a piano factory in Brunswick but emigrated to the USA in 1849 and founded Steinway and Sons in New York, branches of which were opened in London (1875) and Hamburg (1880).

● **stela** ▶ (*or* stele) A free-standing oblong slab, used in ancient Greece and the Near East as a grave or boundary marker. The Greek grave stelae were usually inscribed and ornamented with relief sculptures of the dead. The ▷Maya of Central America set up stelae with calendrical information.

● **stellar evolution** ▷*See* star.

● **Stellenbosch** ▶ 33 56S 18 51E A town in SW South Africa. Founded in 1679, it is the second oldest White settlement in the country. Its university was incorporated in 1918. It is an important wine-producing centre. Population (latest est): 55 914.

● **stem cells** ▶ Simple cells in the body that give rise to specialized tissue cells when stimulated by growth factors and other chemical signals produed by the body. Stem cells occur in the embryo, where they continually divide to produce all the many different tissues required by the developing embryo. They are also found at various sites in the adult body (including skin, bone, muscle, and intestine) to provide replacement cells for the repair of tissues at those sites. For example, stem cells in the bone marrow are active throughout life, providing a continual supply of new blood cells as the old ones wear out. Much interest now focuses on the potential of stem cells to treat disease or repair injured tissue. Adult stem cells, such as bone marrow cells, are already used in treating leukemia and other diseases of blood cells by forming new healthy cells to replace the defective ones, as are tissue-matched cord-blood stem cells, taken from the umbilical cord of a newborn baby. Other disorders that might benefit from stem-cell therapy include diabetes, Parkinson's disease, and spinal injury. Embryonic stem cells are particularly attractive since they can produce many different types of cells (i.e. they are pluripotent) and—triggered by the appropriate chemical signals—begin producing the required tissue cells wherever they are inserted. Human embryos cloned from a person's cells could, in theory, provide genetically identical therapeutic stem cells that would not be rejected by that person's immune system. But technical hurdles and ethical objections lie in the way of attaining this goal. In 2002 the UK became one of the first countries to license stem-cell research, subject to strict guidelines. This would include the use of spare embryos generated by IVF techniques as well as—if there is an exceptional need—embryos produced by therapeutic cloning.

● **Stendhal** ▶ (Henri Beyle; 1783–1842) French novelist. Between 1799 and 1813 he became acquainted with social life in Paris and also served with Napoleon's armies in Italy, Germany, Russia, and Austria. From 1814 to 1821 he lived in Italy and returned there as consul in 1830. His two major novels, *Le Rouge et le noir* (1830) and *La Chartreuse de Parme* (1839), are notable for their blend of romantic vigour with dispassionate and often ironical psychological analysis. He also wrote works of literary and musical appreciation.

● **sten gun** ▶ A 9 mm submachine gun designed by Sheppard and Turpin during World War II. Some four million of these simple weapons were produced at a cost of £1.50 each. They were dangerously short and sometimes unreliable but some are still used by terrorists.

● **Steno, Nicolaus** ▶ (*or* Niels Stensen; 1638–86) Danish anatomist and geologist, who established that fossils were the petrified remains of ancient living organisms and that the layers (strata) of rocks represented stages in their deposition. Originally a physician (he discovered the duct of the parotid salivary gland), he later became a bishop.

● **Stentor** ▶ A genus of tiny single-celled organisms (*see* protozoa) occurring in fresh water. Up to 2 mm long, they are trumpet-shaped, with tracts of hairlike cilia over the body surface, and are often attached by a stalk to the substrate. They feed by wafting currents of water containing bacteria, algae, and protozoans into the funnel-shaped gullet entrance. Phylum: ▷*Ciliophora*.

● **Stephanotis** ▶ A genus of evergreen climbing shrubs (5 species), also called Madagascar jasmine, native to Madagascar, and including some ornamental species. *S. floribunda* is a popular greenhouse plant with small fragrant white waxy flowers. Family: *Asclepiadaceae*.

● **Stephen** ▶ (c. 1097–1154) King of England (1135–54); grandson of William the Conqueror. Stephen seized the throne from Henry I's daughter Matilda, who invaded England in 1139. The civil war that followed proved Stephen a brave soldier but lacking in political sense. In 1152, after much of the country had been ravaged in factional fighting and the royal administration had broken down, Stephen recognized Matilda's son Henry (later Henry II) as heir to the throne.

● **Stephen, Sir Leslie** ▶ (1832–1904) British man of letters and critic, who coedited the *Dictionary of National Biography*. His best-known book is the *History of English Thought in the Eighteenth Century* (1876). The novelist Virginia ▷Woolf was his daughter.

● **Stephen I, St** ▶ (?975–1038) The first King of Hungary (997–1038). Stephen was crowned in 1000, allegedly with a crown sent by Pope ▷Sylvester II—the St Stephen's Crown. Stephen's promotion of Christianity led to his canonization in 1083. Feast day: 16 Aug.

● **Stephen, St** ▶ In the New Testament, the first Christian martyr. According to Acts 6, he was one of seven deacons appointed by the Apostles to provide charity for the Greek-speaking widows in the Christian community. Also a preacher and miracle worker, he was accused of blasphemy and stoned to death by the Jews. Feast day: 26 Dec.

● **Stephen Báthory** ▶ (1533–86) King of Poland (1575–86). Stephen defeated ▷Ivan the Terrible of Muscovy in the ▷Livonian War but his plan to conquer Muscovy was cut short by his death.

● **Stephenson, George** ▶ (1781–1848) British engineer, who developed a greatly improved steam □locomotive. Stephenson became interested in locomotives in 1813, when he saw John ▷Blenkinsop's model. Two years later he built the *Blucher*, a steam locomotive that could draw 30 tons of coal at 4 mph. Subsequently he assisted his son, **Robert Stephenson** (1803–59), in constructing a number of improved models, culminating in Robert's most famous locomotive, the *Rocket*, built in 1829. It carried passengers at a speed of 36 mph on the new Liverpool–Manchester line and stimulated railway development throughout Europe and in North America. Robert also designed a number of important railway bridges; he was appointed chief engineer of the London and Birmingham Railway in 1833. His best-known bridges are the tubular Britannia Bridge over the Menai Strait in Wales and the six-arch bridge over the River Tyne at Newcastle.

● **Stepney** ▶ A district in the Greater London borough of Tower

Hamlets, on the N bank of the River Thames. It contains the ▷Tower of London and Petticoat Lane (noted for its Sunday morning market).

● **steppes** ▶ The midlatitude grasslands of Eurasia extending in a broad belt from Ukraine to SW Siberia. They consist chiefly of level, virtually treeless, plains.

● **steradian** ▶ (sr) The ▷SI unit of solid angle equal to a solid angle that encloses a surface on a sphere equal to the square of its radius.

● **stere** ▶ A metric unit of volume equal to one cubic metre.

● **stereochemistry** ▷See isomers.

● **stereophonic sound** ▶ Sound reproduction in which two signals are used to give a directional quality. It results in more realistic reproduction than a single signal system (monophonic sound) because the brain distinguishes the direction by assessing the difference between the sound in each ear. For recording, either two directional ▷microphones at right angles in one place or two separated microphones are needed. Playing back requires at least two ▷loudspeakers, one for each signal.

● **sterility** ▶ (or infertility) Inability to produce offspring by sexual reproduction. Sterility in men may be caused by various conditions in which the sperms are deficient in numbers or defective in quality. It may also result from psychological problems causing ▷impotence. In women sterility may be due to disease of the womb, blockage of the Fallopian tubes leading from the ovaries to the womb, or failure of the ovaries to produce egg cells. Generalized illness can also affect fertility. Numerous methods of treatment are possible depending on the cause; if the underlying condition cannot be treated, the couple may consider undergoing one of the procedures of assisted reproduction that are now available, such as ▷artificial insemination, *in vitro* fertilization (*see* test-tube baby), or ▷GIFT. Sterility can also be deliberately induced (*see* sterilization).

● **sterilization** ▶ The surgical technique or any other means used to induce ▷sterility. Surgical sterilization may be performed for contraceptive purposes or when pregnancy would damage the health of the woman. For men, the operation—vasectomy—involves cutting and tying the duct (vas deferens) that conveys sperm from the testicle. In women the Fallopian tubes are clipped or tied (tubal ligation), which prevents the passage of the egg cells to the womb. This operation is now performed, using a fibreoptic laparoscope, through a minute incision in the abdominal wall. Neither operation affects sexual desire or the ability to satisfy it. Sterilization should be considered as irreversible. ▷See also castration.

● **sterling** ▶ 1. The currency of the UK. The pound sterling is named after the Norman *steorling*, a coin with a star (*steorra*) on one face. Coins of the realm that comply with the standards laid down from time to time are called sterling. 2. Sterling silver is a silver alloy containing at least 92.5% silver.

● **Stern, Isaac** ▶ (1920–2001) Russian-born US violinist. He was taken to the USA as a young child and studied and made his debut in San Francisco. He was a world-famous soloist and toured extensively.

● **Sternberg, Josef von** ▶ (J. Stern; 1894–1969) US film director, born in Austria. He directed films noted for their pictorial quality, notably a series starring Marlene ▷Dietrich, including *The Blue Angel* (1930), *Blonde Venus* (1932), *Shanghai Express* (1932), and *The Scarlet Empress* (1934). He also wrote the scripts for most of his films.

● **Stern Gang** ▶ (Fighters for the Freedom of Israel) A militant Zionist organization founded in 1940 by Abraham Stern (1907–42) to attack British targets in Palestine. Stern was killed by the British and the movement was banned on the creation of Israel (1948), although some units were incorporated into the Israeli army.

● **Sterne, Laurence** ▶ (1713–68) British novelist. Born in Ireland, he was educated at Cambridge and became a clergyman in Yorkshire. After the publication of the first two volumes of *Tristram Shandy* (1759), an eccentric comic novel consisting largely of sentimental rhetoric and witty digressions, he was lionized by London society. His second novel, *A Sentimental Journey* (1768), was based on his travels on the Continent undertaken for health reasons.

● **sternum** ▷See thorax.

● **steroids** ▶ A class of organic chemical compounds with a basic structure of three six-membered carbon rings joined to a five-membered ring. Steroids and their hydroxy derivatives (**sterols**) fulfil many biological roles in plants and animals and include the ▷sex hormones, ▷corticosteroids, ▷bile acids, ▷vitamin D, and moulting hormones in insects. ▷Cholesterol is an important precursor in the synthesis of many steroids.

● **stethoscope** ▶ An instrument widely used by doctors to listen to sounds within the body (*see* auscultation). The first stethoscope was invented by R. T. H. ▷Laënnec. Modern instruments consist of two earpieces joined by two tubes to a head, which is placed on the body. The head usually has a diaphragm (for high-pitched sounds) and a bell (for low-pitched sounds). More sophisticated stethoscopes are fitted with electronic amplification devices.

● **Stettin** ▷See Szczecin.

● **Stevenage** ▶ 51 55N 0 14W A town in SE England, in Hertfordshire. The first of the new towns (1946) to be developed after World War II, it is now an important centre for electrical and aerospace industries and for pharmaceutical research. Population (1997 est): 78 114.

● **Stevens, Wallace** ▶ (1879–1955) US poet. He worked as an insurance executive and wrote most of his poetry after the age of 50. In many of his best-known poems, such as "The Man with the Blue Guitar," he explores the relationship between reality and imagination. His poems are collected in *Collected Poems* (1954) and *Opus Posthumus* (1957) and his essays in *The Necessary Angel* (1951).

● **Stevenson, Adlai E(wing)** ▶ (1900–65) US Democratic politician. As governor of Illinois (1949–53) Stevenson achieved reforms in the civil service, police, and public education. He twice ran for the presidency (1952, 1956) but was defeated on both occasions by Eisenhower. He was an adviser at the San Francisco Conference (1945), helping to found the UN, to which he was later US delegate (1961–65).

● **Stevenson, Robert Louis** ▶ (1850–94) British novelist, born in Edinburgh. He studied law at Edinburgh University. In 1880 he married Fanny Osbourne, whom he had met in France and followed to her native California. Returning to Scotland, he published several books, which established his reputation and which remain among the best-known works of fiction in the language: the classic adventure tale *Treasure Island* (1883), *Kidnapped* (1886), set in Scotland after the 1745 Jacobite rebellion, and *The Strange Case of Dr Jekyll and Mr Hyde* (1886). Constantly troubled by respiratory disease, he returned to the USA in 1887 and finally settled on the island of Samoa in 1890. His other works include the novel *The Master of Ballantrae* (1889) and the unfinished *Weir of Hermiston* (1896).

● **Stewart, Sir Jackie** ▶ (John Young S.; 1939–) British motorracing driver, who won a record 27 Grand Prix and was world champion in 1969, 1971, and 1973. He retired in 1973 and was knighted in 2001.

● **Stewart, James (Maitland)** ▶ (1908–97) US film actor. He began his Hollywood career in 1935 and established himself as a vulnerable idealist with a distinctive drawl in such films as *Mr Smith Goes to Washington* (1939), *Destry Rides Again* (1939), *The Philadelphia Story* (1940), *It's a Wonderful Life* (1946), and *Vertigo* (1958).

● **Stewart Island** ▶ (Maori name: Rakiura) 47 00S 168 00E A volcanic island of New Zealand, separated from S South Island by Foveaux Strait. Area: 1735 sq km (670 sq mi). Population (1989 est): 450.

● **Stewarts** ▷See Stuarts.

● **Steyr** ▶ 48 04N 14 25E A town in NE central Austria, in Upper Austria. It is an iron and steel centre; other products include motor vehicles, bicycles, and ball bearings. Population (1991): 39 542.

● **stibnite** ▶ An ore mineral of antimony, SbS_3. It is a lead-grey colour with a metallic lustre and often occurs as distinctive radiating crystals. It is found in low-temperature hydrothermal veins and in replacement deposits.

● **stick insect** ▶ An □insect, also called walking stick, belonging to the family *Phasmidae*. Up to 320 mm long, it has a twiglike body and long spindly legs and the wings are reduced or absent. Males are rare; the females live in trees or shrubs, producing eggs that develop without fertilization (*see* parthenogenesis). Order ▷*Phasmida*.

● **stickleback** ► A fish of the family *Gasterosteidae* (about 12 species), found in both fresh and salt water in temperate regions of the N hemisphere. Up to 17 cm long, sticklebacks have a row of spines along the back. The male builds a nest for the eggs and guards the young. Order: *Gasterosteiformes*.

● **Stieglitz, Alfred** ► (1864–1946) US photographer. He is famous for his promotion of modern art in the USA and his technical innovations in photography. His Photo-Secession gallery in New York (1905–17), known as 291, put on exhibitions of Matisse (1908), children's art (1912), and ▷Brancusi (1914). Among his most admired photographs are those of his wife, Georgia ▷O'Keeffe.

● **Stiernhielm, Georg Olofson** ► (1598–1672) Swedish poet and scholar, known as the father of Swedish poetry. Believing that Swedish was man's original language, he tried to purify it by excluding loan words. His greatest work is the epic poem *Hercules* (c. 1647).

● **stigma** ► The part of the pistil of a flower that is specialized to receive ▷pollen. In insect-pollinated flowers the stigma is sticky, whereas wind-pollinated flowers have large feathery stigmas.

● **stigmata** ► (Greek: marks) Marks appearing on the body of a living person that resemble the five wounds (in the hands, feet, and side) that Christ received at the crucifixion. There have been more than 300 reported cases, typically involving devoutly religious persons. The stigmata are unknown before the 13th century, St ▷Francis of Assisi being the first saint to receive them. A number of natural explanations have been advanced, and the Roman Catholic Church takes a cautious view of the phenomenon.

● **Stijl, de** ► (Dutch: the Style) A group of 20th-century Dutch artists and architects, who launched the art periodical *De Stijl* (1917–1928). Prominent members were the painters ▷Mondrian and Theo van Doesburg (1883–1931) and the architects J. J. P. Oud (1890–1963) and Gerrit Rietveld (1888–1964). The group adhered to the principles of Mondrian's neoplasticism, an abstract style that sought a harmonious and universal means of expression applicable to all branches of art. This would be achieved by reducing form to horizontals and verticals and colours to the three ▷primary colours and black, white, and grey. In architecture and design neoplasticism was seen at its purest in Rietveld's Schröder house at Utrecht (1924) and in his furniture. Many of its principles were influential at the ▷Bauhaus.

● **Stilicho, Flavius** ► (d. 408 AD) Roman general under ▷Theodosius I, who appointed him guardian of his son Honorius (384–423). On Theodosius' death in 395, Honorius was proclaimed western emperor but Stilicho ruled in effect, ruthlessly removing opposition. He repulsed invasions by the Visigoths under Alaric and by the Ostrogoths but his political intrigues with Alaric and others eventually brought about his execution on Honorius' orders.

● **still-life** ► A branch of painting concerned with the representation of inanimate objects. Although still-life was used in religious paintings and portraits, it did not appear as an art form until the 16th century and then only in the Netherlands. Particularly popular were still-lifes of objects symbolizing the transience of life—skulls, guttering candles, etc. Still-lifes of food and drink became the favourite subjects of ▷Zurbarán, ▷Chardin, ▷Cézanne, and ▷Braque; specialists in flowerpieces have included Pierre ▷Redouté.

● **stilt** ► A wading bird belonging to the family *Recurvirostridae* (avocets and stilts). 35–45 cm long, stilts occur in warm wet regions, where they probe in mud for small aquatic animals. The common stilt (*Himantopus himantopus*) has black-and-white plumage, pink legs, and red eyes.

● **Stilwell, Joseph W(arren)** ► (1883–1946) US general, known as Vinegar Joe. A Chinese linguist, in World War II he was appointed (1941) ▷Chiang Kai-shek's chief of staff and to the command of all US forces in China, Burma (now Myanmar), and India. His dislike of the British and his differences with Chiang forced his recall in 1944. In 1945 he became commander of the US Tenth Army in the Pacific.

● **stimulants** ► A large group of drugs that stimulate activity of the nervous system. Caffeine (in tea and coffee) and nicotine (in cigarettes) are stimulants used widely to reduce feelings of tiredness and to improve concentration. ▷Hallucinogens, ▷amphetamine, and ▷co-caine are also stimulants. Stimulants may affect other parts of the body, particularly the heart.

● **stimulated emission** ▷See laser.

● **stingray** ► A round or diamond-shaped ▷ray fish belonging to a family (*Dasyatidae*; 89 species) found mainly in warm shallow ocean waters. Most species have a whiplike tail armed with one or more saw-edged venomous spines, which can inflict an intensely painful wound causing paralysis and occasionally death. Live young are born.

● **stink bug** ▷See shield bug.

● **stinkhorn** ► A fungus of the order *Phallales*, producing a phallus-shaped fruiting body. This consists of a stout whitish stalk arising from a basal egg-shaped structure and bearing a thimble-shaped cap containing spores. When the spores are ripe the cap produces a strong-smelling secretion that attracts flies, which disperse the spores. The common stinkhorn (*Phallus impudicus*) reaches a height of 10–20 cm. Phylum: ▷Basidiomycota.

● **stinkwood** ► One of several species of trees with unpleasant-smelling timber, including *Gustavia augusta* of tropical America and the African species *Celtis kraussiana* and *Ocotea bullata* (black stinkwood). The wood can be used in furniture making.

● **Stirling** ► A council area of central Scotland. In 1975 the historic county of Stirling was abolished, most of it being incorporated into a new Stirling District in Central Region. In 1996 this district became an independent ▷unitary authority. The valley of the River Forth separates the Breadalbane Mountains in the NW from the southern hills. Agriculture is important, with some arable farming in the SE. Manufacturing is mainly concentrated around Stirling; coal is no longer mined near Fallin. The main economic activities are now administration, finance, and tourism, with Loch Lomond and the Trossachs among the principal attractions. Area: 2173 sq km (839 sq mi). Population (1999 est): 84 700. Administrative centre: Stirling.

● **Stirling** ► 56 07N 3 57W A city in Scotland, the administrative centre of Stirling council area on the River Forth. It was once a residence of the Scottish kings and the first Scottish parliament was held here in 1326. The castle occupies a prominent position on a dolerite outcrop. Stirling is an important market town with varied industries; the economy is now based mainly on public administration, financial services, retail, and tourism. The university was founded in 1967. Stirling was granted city status in 2002. Population (1997 est): 30 791.

still-life ► A still-life of fruits and a goblet by the 19th-century German painter Hermann Koch.

● **Stirling, James** ► (1692–1770) Scottish mathematician, best known for the mathematical formula named after him. Stirling's formula gives the approximate value for the factorial of a large number. It was in fact first derived by Abraham de Moivre (1667–1754).

● **Stirling, Sir James** ► (1926–92) British architect. His engineering department for Leicester University (1959–63) epitomizes ▷brutalism, while the Neue Staatsgalerie in Stuttgart (1977–84) is an example of ▷postmodernism.

● **Stirling engine** ► A ▷heat engine invented by Robert Stirling (1790–1878), a Scottish Presbyterian minister, and his brother in 1816. It is an external combustion engine consisting of a hot cylinder and a cold cylinder separated by a regenerator that functions as a heat exchanger. The cylinders enclose oscillating linked pistons. Heat applied externally to the hot cylinder causes the working fluid in it to expand and drive the piston. The fluid then passes to the regenerator, where it gives up its heat before passing to the cold cylinder to be compressed by its piston. The fluid is then heated in the regenerator before starting the cycle again in the hot cylinder. Although expensive to make, these engines are quiet and efficient. They had a modest success in the 1890s and were revived in the 1960s, using helium as a working fluid. They have not, however, found a practical use.

● **stitchwort** ► A perennial herb belonging to the widely distributed genus *Stellaria* (85 species), having white starlike flowers. The greater stitchwort (*S. holostea*) is a common woodland and roadside plant of Europe, N Africa, and W Asia, growing to a height of 15–60 cm. Family: *Caryophyllaceae*.

● **STM** ▷*See* scanning tunnelling microscope.

● **stoat** ► A small carnivorous mammal, *Mustela erminea*, of Europe, Asia, and North America. About 35 cm long, with a long sinuous body, flattish head, and short legs, it can be distinguished from a ▷weasel by its black-tipped tail. Stoats prey mainly on rabbits. ▷*See also* ermine.

● **stock** ► One of several herbaceous plants of the genus *Matthiola* that are cultivated as ornamentals. Many garden varieties, including ten-week stocks and Brompton stocks, are derived from the European biennial *M. incana*, which grows to a height of 30–60 cm and has clusters of purple flowers. The night-scented stock (*M. bicornis*) has small lilac flowers that emit their fragrance at night. Family: ▷*Cruciferae*.

● **stock-car racing** ► A form of ▷motor racing that originated in the USA in the 1920s, when cars were modified for transporting illegally made whiskey, for which speed was all-important. Stock cars are specially built steel-bodied saloon cars weighing around 2000 kg; they withstand frequent accidents. They are raced on oval tracks at speeds up to about 320 km per hour (200 mph).

● **stock exchange** ► A market in which securities are bought and sold. It has two main functions—to enable companies to raise long-term capital and to provide individuals and institutions with an opportunity to invest in commercial enterprises. The London Stock Exchange, founded in 1773 to replace coffee-house dealings, was until the "Big Bang" (October, 1986) divided into brokers (who dealt with the public) and jobbers (who bought and sold securities for their own account and dealt with the public through brokers). After the "Big Bang" this distinction was abolished, brokers' commissions became negotiable, and dealings were computerized to such an extent that

personal contact on the floor of the Exchange became unnecessary. The main market deals in shares of large well-established companies. The **Alternative Investment Market** (AIM), established in 1995, deals with smaller and newer company shares. ▷*See also* stocks and shares.

● **Stockhausen, Karlheinz** ► (1928–　) German composer, a pupil of Messiaen and Milhaud. From 1953 he worked at the West German Radio Studio for electronic music in Cologne. His early works employed serialism but he later rejected traditional forms and techniques, developing a concept of music as a sequence of sound "events" in such works as *Gruppen* (for three orchestras; 1955–57), *Zyklus* (for solo percussionist; 1959) and *Kontra-Punkte* (for ten instruments; 1962). *Stimmung* (for six singers; 1968) and *Mantra* (for two pianos and percussion; 1970) were influenced by Indian mysticism. Later works include the operas *Donnerstag* (1980), *Samstag* (1984), *Montag* (1988), *Dienstag* (1991), and *Freitag* (1996).

● **Stockholm** ► 59 20N 18 95E The capital of Sweden, built on several islands between Lake Mälar and the Baltic Sea. It is the country's second largest port and its varied industries include shipbuilding, engineering, sugar refining, and brewing. The old town contains many buildings erected in the middle ages and in the 16th and 17th centuries, including the Royal Palace and Storkyrkan, Stockholm's cathedral. Its university was established in 1877.
History: a settlement from very early times, it developed in the 13th century around a fortress erected to protect the entrance to the trading centres of Lake Mälar. It became the capital in 1436 and enjoyed great prestige in the 17th century. Population (1997 est): 718 462.

● **Stockport** ► **1.** 53 25N 2 10W A town in N England, in Stockport unitary authority, Greater Manchester, on the River Mersey. Traditionally a textile town (particularly for cotton and silk), Stockport now has a diverse economy that includes engineering (including aerospace), electronics, high technology (including semiconductors), and chemicals, as well as financial and business services. Population (1991): 132 813. **2.** A unitary authority in N England, in Greater Manchester. Area 126 sq km (49 sq mi). Population (1998 est): 290 567.

● **stocks and shares** ► Documents representing money invested in industrial and commercial corporations or loaned to a government. In the UK stocks represent fixed-interest loans made to the government (*see* gilt-edged security), foreign governments, local authorities, or companies (*see* debenture stock). Shares represent equal amounts of capital subscribed to a company in return for membership rights. The total assets of a company are known as its equity; shares in companies are known as equities. Ordinary shareholders are the last to receive their ▷dividends, which fluctuate according to the level of profits. They usually have voting rights in the company (*compare* preference shares). Listed companies, in which the assets of a company exceed a specified value, have shares that can be bought and sold on the main market of the London ▷Stock Exchange. The **Alternative Investment Market** (AIM) of the London Stock Exchange opened in

stingray ► A blue-spotted ribbon-tail ray (*Taeniura lymma*) from the Red Sea. This species, which has bright blue spots on a sand-coloured background and measures 95 cm (3 ft) across the wings, is well camouflaged in the sandy areas of coral reefs in which it lives. It has two venomous barbs near the base of the tail.

1995 to enable smaller companies to have access to a trading market, without the expense of a full listing. In the USA ordinary shares are called common stock.

• **Stockton** ▶ 37 59N 121 20W A city and port in the USA, in California on the San Joaquin River. It accommodates oceangoing vessels and is a distributing and processing centre for the fertile San Joaquin Valley. Population (1996 est): 232 660.

• **Stockton, 1st Earl of** ▷See Macmillan, (Maurice) Harold, 1st Earl of Stockton.

• **Stockton-on-Tees** ▶ **1.** 53 34N 1 19W A market town in NE England, in Stockton-on-Tees unitary authority, Co Durham, on the River Tees. The world's first passenger railway was built from here to ▷Darlington in 1825. It was once a port, exporting coal carried by the railway, with engineering and ship-repairing industries but is now mainly residential with retail and services as the chief employers. Population (1996 est): 82 800. **2.** A unitary authority in NE England, in Co Durham and North Yorkshire; from 1974 to 1996 it was part of the county of Cleveland. Area: 195 sq km (75 sq mi). Population (1996 est): 179 000.

• **Stoicism** ▶ The philosophical school founded about 300 BC in the Painted Porch (Greek: Stoa Poikile) at Athens by ▷Zeno of Citium. Stoics believed that God (identified with reason) was the basis of the universe, that human souls were sparks of the divine fire, and that the wise man lived "in harmony with nature." Knowledge of virtue was all-important. Stoicism was later modified to stress active virtue and duty. ▷Epictetus (55–135 AD) taught that all men were brothers. Stoicism appealed to such prominent Romans as Marcus ▷Brutus and ▷Marcus Aurelius and influenced later thinkers.

• **Stoke-on-Trent** ▶ **1.** 53 00N 2 10W A city in N central England, in Stoke-on-Trent unitary authority, Staffordshire, on the River Trent. Formed in 1910 by the amalgamation of five towns, the area is known as the Potteries and is the centre of the British ceramic industry. Josiah Wedgwood and Arnold Bennett were born here. There are also engineering and manufacturing industries. Nearby is Keele University (1962). Population (1991): 266 543. **2.** A unitary authority in N central England, in Staffordshire. Area 93 sq km (36 sq mi). Population (1996 est): 254 400.

• **Stoke Poges** ▶ A village in SE England, in Buckinghamshire near Slough. The poet Thomas Gray is buried in the churchyard, believed to be the setting of his famous "Elegy Written in a Country Churchyard" (1751). Population (1991): 4851.

• **Stoker, Bram** ▶ (Abraham S.; 1847–1912) Irish novelist. He worked as a civil servant (1867–77), wrote drama criticism, and became secretary and manager to the actor Henry ▷Irving in 1878. Stoker is chiefly remembered as the author of *Dracula* (1897), a horror story in the ▷gothic novel tradition. ▷See also Dracula, Count; vampires.

• **Stokes, Sir George Gabriel** ▶ (1819–1903) British physicist and mathematician, who was professor of mathematics at Cambridge University. He discovered the law concerning the terminal velocity of a sphere falling through a viscous fluid (see Stokes' law). He also attempted to deduce a mathematical model of the luminiferous ether, the medium in which light was at that time thought to vibrate.

• **Stokes' law** ▶ The resisting force acting on a sphere, radius r, moving through a fluid under gravity with velocity v is $6\pi r \eta v$, where η is the ▷viscosity of the fluid. Named after Sir George ▷Stokes.

• **Stokowski, Leopold** ▶ (1882–1977) British-born conductor. He became a US citizen in 1915. A keen supporter of modern music, Stokowski also became well known for his orchestral transcriptions of Bach's organ music. He conducted such leading US orchestras as the Philadelphia Orchestra (1912–38). In 1940 he arranged the music for Walt Disney's film *Fantasia*, which used cartoons to bring classical music to a wide range of cinema-goers. Stokowski also appeared in the film as conductor of the orchestra.

• **Stolypin, Petr Arkadievich** ▶ (1863–1911) Russian statesman. Tsarist Russia's last gifted politician, he became prime minister in 1906. He promoted many reforms, outstandingly the land reforms that enabled many peasants to be economically independent. He

became unpopular with both Right and Left owing to his disregard of the Duma and his harsh treatment of revolutionaries; he was assassinated in Kiev.

• **STOL** ▶ (short take-off and landing) Aircraft capable of taking off and landing on short runways. This is usually achieved by extending the wing area by means of flaps, etc., to increase the lift for take-off and landing. The need for such aircraft arises when an airport is unable to provide a runway of the usual length or if an aircraft is required to fly well at lower speeds than usual, especially for observational duties. The De Havilland DHC-7 is a STOL airliner used on the restricted runway at London's Dockland airport. ▷See also VTOL.

• **stomach** ▶ A muscular sac, just beneath the diaphragm, that opens from the oesophagus (gullet) and leads to the duodenum (part of the small intestine). It secretes gastric juice, containing hydrochloric acid and the enzyme ▷pepsin, which continue the digestion of food that started in the mouth. Release of acid is triggered by the ▷vagus nerve and by a hormone (gastrin) secreted by the stomach in response to the presence of food. The stomach's churning action ensures constant mixing of food and its secretions. ▷See Plate II.

• **Stone Age** ▶ The cultural phase during which humans relied on stone, supplemented by wood, bone, or antler, as material for weapons and tools. It is the earliest phase in the system devised (1816) by Christian Thomsen (1788–1865) for classifying human technological progress (*compare* Bronze Age; Iron Age). The Stone Age is subdivided into Old (*see* Palaeolithic), Middle (*see* Mesolithic), and New (*see* Neolithic).

• **stone bass** ▷See wreckfish.

• **stonechat** ▶ A small ▷chat, *Saxicola torquata*, occurring in Eurasia and N Africa and feeding chiefly on insects and their larvae. About 12 cm long, the male has a dark-brown head and back, chestnut underparts, and white rump; the female is a drabber brown. Stonechats favour dry heathland and are declining in Britain with the destruction of these habitats.

• **stonecrop** ▶ An annual or perennial herb belonging to the genus *Sedum* (600 species), found chiefly in warm N temperate regions and also in Central and South America. They have small thick fleshy leaves and clusters of white, pink, or yellow flowers. Some are popular ornamentals, including autumn glory (*S. spectabile*), which grows to a height of 30–45 cm. Family: *Crassulaceae*.

• **stone curlew** ▶ A ground-nesting bird belonging to a widely distributed family (*Burhinidae*; 9 species) characterized by thickened tarsal joints, also called thickknee. They are typically nocturnal, living in stony barren regions and feeding on beetles, worms, and other small animals. Order: *Charadriiformes* (gulls, plovers, etc.).

• **stonefish** ▶ A fish, belonging to the genus *Synanceja*, that occurs in shallow waters of the Indian and Pacific Oceans. It has a robust body, up to 35 cm long, covered with wartlike lumps and fleshy flaps, a large head, and poisonous dorsal fins. It lies camouflaged and motionless among rocks or coral to await its prey. Family: *Synancejidae*.

• **stonefly** ▶ An insect of the order *Plecoptera* (3000 species), 6–60 mm long with long antennae and two pairs of membranous wings. The short-lived adults rarely feed and are found near fresh water. The aquatic ▷nymphs, which favour fast-flowing streams with stony bottoms, feed on plants, decaying organic material, or other insects.

• **Stonehenge** ▶ A famous megalithic structure, the focus of a cluster of ceremonial sites on Salisbury Plain in Wiltshire (England). Scientific study and excavation over many years have revealed a complex history with three main phases of modification (c. 3000–1600 BC) contributing to the Stonehenge seen today. Sarsens and bluestones, the latter probably brought from S Wales, are set upright in concentric circles and horseshoes the orientation of which suggests one purpose as being sun and moon observation. The alleged "Druid" connection is entirely spurious, dating only from the 18th century AD. In 1998 English Heritage announced a £125 M scheme to improve the site and its surroundings, the condition of which has provoked much criticism in recent years; this will involve rerouting two main roads, increasing pedestrian access to the stones, and removing the car park and visitors centre from view. ▷See also megalith.

● **stone pine** ► A ▷pine tree, *Pinus pinea*, native to SW Europe and Asia but planted throughout Mediterranean regions since Roman times for its edible seeds. Up to 30 m high, it has spreading branches and an umbrella-shaped crown, needles grouped in pairs, and cones about 12.5 cm long. The oily seeds are eaten raw or roasted or are used to flavour stews, etc.

● **stoneworts** ► ▷Green algae of the class *Charophyceae*, many of which contain stony deposits of calcium carbonate. The plants have an erect stemlike axis with whorls of branches and rootlike threads (rhizoids), by which they are anchored to muddy bottoms of fresh or brackish waters.

● **Stopes, Marie Charlotte Carmichael** ► (1880–1958) British birth-control campaigner. A botanist, she worked at Manchester University and Imperial College in London until the failure of her first marriage (1916) turned her attention to the study of marital problems. In 1921 she opened the first birth-control clinic in Britain—in Holloway, London. Among her books are *Married Love* (1918) and *Con-*

traception: Its Theory, History, and Practice (1923). In 1918 she married H. V. Roe (1878–1949), an aircraft manufacturer.

● **Stoppard, Sir Tom** ► (Thomas Straussler; 1937–) British dramatist, born in Czechoslovakia and educated in Britain. After working as a journalist in Bristol, he achieved international success with his play *Rosencrantz and Guildenstern Are Dead* (1967), using characters from Shakespeare's *Hamlet*. In his later plays, such as *Jumpers* (1972), *Travesties* (1975), *Night and Day* (1978), *The Real Thing* (1982), and *Hapgood* (1988), he explored philosophical and political ideas with great verbal facility. His most recent plays are *Arcadia* (1993), *Indian Ink* (1995), and *The Invention of Love* (1997), about A. E. ▷Housman. He has also written television and radio plays and film scripts, including the inventive *Shakespeare in Love* (1999; with Marc Norman), which won seven Academy Awards. Stoppard was knighted in 1997 and in 1998 was paid the unique honour by the ▷Comédie-Française in Paris of having a French translation of his *Arcadia* added to its repertoire. He thus became the first foreign playwright to see his work staged in the Salle Richelieu. He was appointed to the OM in 2000.

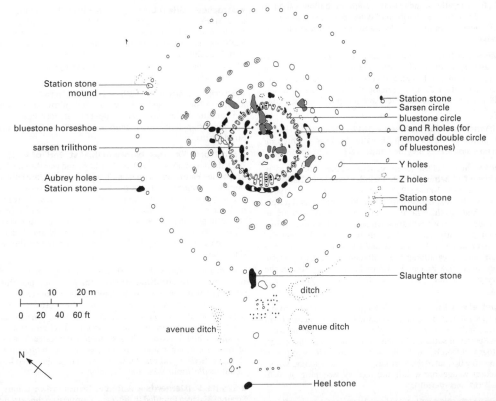

Station stone mound
Station stone
Sarsen circle
bluestone circle
Q and R holes (for removed double circle of bluestones)
bluestone horseshoe
sarsen trilithons
Y holes
Z holes
Aubrey holes
Station stone
Station stone mound
Slaughter stone
ditch
avenue ditch
avenue ditch
Heel stone

0   10   20 m
0   20   40   60 ft

N

Stonehenge ► The plan reveals features of consecutive building phases that may no longer be visible to the visitor to the site.

● **storax** ► A tree or shrub belonging to the genus Styrax (130 species), occurring in tropical regions. They have small white flowers and several species are cultivated as ornamentals, including the Japanese snowbell (*S. japonicum*), which grows to a height of 9 m, and *S. officinalis*, from which the vanilla-scented resin known as storax was formerly obtained. The storax used today in cough mixtures, pastilles, etc., is extracted from trees of the genus *Liquidambar*. The Sumatran species *S. benzoin* is a source of ▷benzoin. Family: *Styracaceae*.

● **Store Bælt** ▷*See* Great Belt.

● **Storey, David** ► (1933–) British novelist and dramatist. He was an art student and professional Rugby League player before achieving literary success with his novel *This Sporting Life* (1960). His later novels include *Pasmore* (1972), *Present Times* (1984), and *A Serious Man* (1998), and his plays include *In Celebration* (1969), *Home* (1970), and *Stages* (1992).

● **stork** ► A large bird of a widely distributed family (*Ciconiidae*; 17 species) occurring in temperate regions. 60–150 cm tall, storks have long necks, legs, and bill and are white with black markings. They feed on fish, frogs, molluscs, and insects—caught in shallow waters or grasslands—and build a nest platform of twigs in a tree or on a rooftop. Order: *Ciconiiformes* (herons, storks, flamingos). ▷*See also* adjutant stork; marabou.

● **storksbill** ► A herb of the genus *Erodium* (about 90 species) occurring in Eurasia, Australia, and South America. The seeds have a beaklike projection (hence the name) that is spirally twisted at maturity and unwinds when damp to release the seeds. The common storksbill (*E. cicutarium*) grows to 60 cm and has purplish-pink flowers. Family: *Geraniaceae*.

● **Storm, (Hans) Theodor Woldsen** ► (1817–88) German writer. A lawyer, he spent most of his life in his native Schleswig, which inspired such novellas as *Immensee* (1849) and *Der Schimmelreiter* (1888).

● **Stormont** ► The seat of the government of Northern Ireland, situated in parkland E of Belfast; the site includes Stormont Castle, the neoclassical Parliament House (1932), and Dundonald House (1963). For many years it housed the parliament of Northern Ireland (established in 1921) and was the official residence of the province's prime minister; as such Stormont became a symbol of Protestant domination. Following the outbreak of violence in the province in 1969, the UK Government suspended Stormont and reinstituted direct rule from London (1972). The buildings were subsequently used as government offices. Since 1998 Parliament House has been the seat of the Northern Ireland Assembly, set up under the Good Friday Agreement of that year.

● **storm petrel** ► A small seabird belonging to a family (*Hydrobatidae*; 20 species) occurring in all oceans. 13–25 cm long, storm petrels have dark-grey or brown plumage, often with paler underparts. Species of southern oceans have square tails, long legs, and short toes and feed by "walking" on the water with wings outstretched, picking up plankton. Northern species have longer wings and a forked or wedge-shaped tail and feed by swooping on fish. Order: *Procellariiformes* (petrels).

● **Stornoway** ► 58 12N 6 23W A port in NW Scotland, in the Outer Hebrides, on the Isle of Lewis. It is the administrative centre of the Western Isles Islands Area and the largest town of the Outer Hebrides. Fishing, tourism, tweed manufacture, and industries related to offshore oil are the main economic activities. Population (1991): 5975.

● **Stoss, Veit** ► (c. 1445–1533) German gothic sculptor and woodcarver. Working chiefly in Nuremberg but also in Poland, Hungary, and Bohemia, Stoss developed a style that combined Flemish realism with swirling draperies and expressive gestures and faces. His most important work is the altar of the *Life of the Virgin* for the Church of St Mary, Cracow.

● **Stourbridge** ► 52 27N 2 09W A town in central England, in West Midlands on the River Stour. Dr Johnson attended the grammar school (founded 1552). There are glass-manufacturing and iron-working industries here. Population (1991): 55 624.

● **stout** ▷*See* beer and brewing.

● **Stowe, Harriet Beecher** ▷*See* Beecher, Lyman.

● **STP** ► (standard temperature and pressure) The standard conditions used to compare the properties of gases; i.e. 273.15 K (0°C) and 101 325 Pa (760 mm Hg).

● **Strabane** ► A district in Northern Ireland, in Co Tyrone. Area: 861 sq km (332 sq mi). Population (1995): 36 100.

● **strabismus** ▷*See* squint.

● **Strabo** ► (c. 64 BC–c. 21 AD) Greek geographer, born at Amaseia (now Amasya, Turkey). His *Geography*, in 17 books, is an invaluable source of information about the ancient world. After a survey of previous geographers and a discussion of mathematical geography and maps, Strabo describes the Europe-Asia-Africa land mass clockwise round the Mediterranean, from Spain to N Africa. He marshals the evidence of other writers and his own observations into a comprehensive account, and is a master of historical and political geography, notably when describing the growth of the Roman Empire.

● **Strachey, (Giles) Lytton** ► (1880–1932) British biographer and essayist. He was a leading member of the ▷Bloomsbury group. His irreverent attitude towards his subjects (Thomas Arnold, Florence Nightingale, Cardinal Manning, and others) in *Eminent Victorians* (1918) revolutionized the ponderous Victorian tradition of biography. His other biographical studies include *Queen Victoria* (1921) and *Elizabeth and Essex* (1928).

● **Stradivari, Antonio** ► (?1644–1737) Italian violin maker. He was a pupil of Niccolò ▷Amati. From 1666 he and two of his sons made outstanding violins, violas, and cellos at their workshop in Cremona. Stradivari signed his instruments with the Latin form of his name, Stradivarius.

● **Strafford, Thomas Wentworth, 1st Earl of** ► (1593–1641) English statesman, who with Archbishop Laud was the chief executor of Charles I's unpopular personal rule (1629–40). Initially a parliamentary opponent of the king, he became a supporter of Charles when appointed Lord President of the north (1628). As Lord Deputy of Ireland (1633–39) his policy of "thorough," which ruthlessly strengthened royal power, and his attempt to suppress the ▷Bishops' Wars (1639–40) in Scotland made him extremely unpopular. He was impeached by the ▷Long Parliament and executed on the eve of the Civil War.

● **strain** ► In physics, the deformation of a body when it is subjected to a ▷stress. **Longitudinal strain** is the extension per unit length when a body is stretched; **bulk strain** is the volume change per unit volume when a body is compressed; and **shear strain** is an angular measure of deformation. Strain is measured using a **strain gauge**, in which a fine wire forming part of an electric circuit is attached to backing, which is fixed to the specimen being tested. The extension of the wire brought about as the specimen is subjected to stress changes its electrical resistance, which can be shown to be proportional to the strain. ▷*See also* elasticity.

● **Straits Settlements** ► A former British crown colony on the Strait of Malacca founded in 1867 and comprising the settlements of Penang, Singapore, Malacca, and Labuan. In 1946 Singapore became a separate crown colony, Labuan was incorporated in North Borneo, and Penang and Malacca joined the Malayan Union. In 1963 all became part of Malaysia, Singapore becoming independent in 1965.

● **Stralsund** ► 54 18N 12 58E A town and port in NE Germany, on an inlet of the Baltic Sea. Founded in 1209, it became an important Hanseatic port. Industries include shipbuilding, fish processing, and the manufacture of machinery. Population (1991): 71 620.

● **strangeness** ► A property of matter, expressed as a ▷quantum number (*s*), postulated to account for the unusually long lifetime of some ▷hadrons. In the quark model (*see* particle physics) strange hadrons contain the strange quark or its antiquark. Strangeness is conserved in ▷strong interactions and ▷electromagnetic interactions.

● **Stranraer** ► 54 54N 5 02W A port in SW Scotland, on the W coast of Dumfries and Galloway at the head of Loch Ryan. There are ferry services to Belfast and Larne, Northern Ireland. Population (1991): 11 348.

● **Strasberg, Lee** ▶ (1901–82) US theatre director and drama teacher, born in Austria, who formulated the system known as "method" acting. In 1931 he cofounded the Group Theatre in New York and from 1950 he directed the famous ▷Actors' Studio, where many Hollywood stars were schooled in the naturalistic techniques of the "method."

● **Strasbourg** ▶ (German name: Strassburg) 48 35N 7 45E A city in NE France, the capital of the Bas-Rhin department on the River Ill. It is the seat of the European Parliament and of the ▷Council of Europe. An important inland port, it trades in wine, iron ore, and potash; it has varied industries, including chemicals, oil refining, and textiles. It is famous for its *pâté de foie gras*. Notable buildings include the cathedral (11th–15th centuries) and the university (1538).

History: made a free imperial city in the 13th century, it was ceded to France in 1697. Captured by the Germans (1871), it was returned to France after World War I. Population (1990): 255 937.

● **Strategic Arms Limitation Talks** ▶ (SALT) ▷*See* disarmament.

● **Strategic Arms Reduction Talks** ▶ (START) ▷*See* disarmament.

● **Strategic Defence Initiative** ▶ (SDI) A US research project, also known as "star wars," which aimed to destroy incoming nuclear missiles in space. Announced by President Reagan in March, 1983, the programme included tests of various systems, of which ground-based or satellite-mounted lasers were favoured. The project was abandoned in 1993 amid allegations that test results had been falsified. The SDI department has been renamed the Ballistic Missile Defence Organization and is now working on ways of destroying incoming missiles nearer the ground.

● **Stratford** ▶ 43 22N 81 00W A city in E Canada, in SW Ontario. Founded in 1831, its annual Shakespearean Festival began in 1953. Stratford is also a centre for light industry and dairying. Population (1991): 27 666.

● **Stratford-on-Avon** ▶ 52 12N 1 41W A town in central England, in Warwickshire on the River Avon. It is famous as the birthplace of William Shakespeare. The Royal Shakespeare Theatre (opened in 1932) is devoted mainly to Shakespeare's plays. Tourists visit Shakespeare's birthplace, Holy Trinity Church (where he and his wife Anne Hathaway are buried), Anne Hathaway's cottage nearby, and many other buildings associated with the playwright. Stratford is also a market town with canning, aluminium ware, and boatbuilding industries. Population (1991): 22 231.

● **Strathclyde Region** ▶ A former administrative region in W Scotland, on the Atlantic Ocean. It was created in 1975 from the counties of Ayrshire, Bute, Dunbarton, Lanarkshire (including Glasgow), Renfrewshire, and parts of Argyll and Stirling. In 1996 administration passed to 12 ▷unitary authorities: ▷Argyll and Bute, ▷West Dunbartonshire, ▷East Dunbartonshire, ▷Inverclyde, ▷Renfrewshire, ▷East Renfrewshire, ▷North Ayrshire, ▷South Ayrshire, ▷East Ayrshire, ▷Glasgow, ▷North Lanarkshire, and ▷South Lanarkshire.

● **stratification** ▶ The layering of sedimentary rocks and certain volcanic deposits in horizontal beds, known as strata. The bed is the smallest division of stratified sedimentary rocks, being a single sheetlike layer of sediment separated from overlying and underlying beds by a surface (the bedding plane), which marks a break in sedimentation. An unconformity is a surface representing a gap in the stratigraphic succession caused by changing conditions; it shows a period of erosion or nondeposition.

● **stratigraphy** ▶ The branch of geology concerned with the formation, composition, sequence in time, and spatial correlation of the stratified rocks. **Lithostratigraphy** involves the lithological and spatial relations of rock units. **Biostratigraphy** utilizes fossils in calibrating rock successions. **Chronostratigraphy** studies rock bodies according to the time of their formation (*see* geological time scale).

● **stratocumulus cloud** ▶ (Sc) A low type of ▷cloud composed of dark grey globular masses, often forming extensive sheets.

● **stratosphere** ▷*See* atmosphere.

● **Stratton, Charles** ▷*See* Tom Thumb.

● **stratus cloud** ▶ A low type of ▷cloud forming below 2400 m (7874 ft), having a grey uniform appearance; it may actually occur at ground level as hill fog. Precipitation, if any, is usually no more than a fine drizzle.

● **Strauss, Richard** ▶ (1864–1949) German composer and conductor. He studied in Munich and Berlin and conducted opera at Munich, Bayreuth, and Vienna. He was much influenced by Wagner, whose use of ▷leitmotifs he adopted. From 1887 to 1899 Strauss wrote a series of symphonic poems, including *Death and Transfiguration* (1889), *Till Eulenspiegels lustige Streiche* (1894–95), *Also sprach Zarathustra* (1895–96), *Don Quixote* (1897), and *Ein Heldenleben* (1898). He then turned to opera, writing 15 works, including *Salome* (1905), *Elektra* (1906–08), *Der Rosenkavalier* (1909–10), and *Ariadne auf Naxos* (1912). His works also include two concertos for horn, one for oboe and one for violin, many songs, and *Metamorphosen* for strings (1944–45).

● **Strauss the Younger, Johann** ▶ (1825–99) Austrian violinist, conductor, and composer. He led his own dance ensemble from the age of 18 and was conductor of the Vienna court balls (1863–70). He wrote a great many waltzes, such as "The Blue Danube," "Vienna

Strasbourg ▶ The Palais de l'Europe (top right) and associated offices. Henry Bernard's fortress-like building (1972–77) is the seat of the Council of Europe and also hosted meetings of the European Parliament until 1999, when this body acquired its own seat on the other side of the river.

Blood," and "Tales from the Vienna Woods," as well as polkas and marches. He also wrote 16 operettas, including *Die Fledermaus* (1874), *A Night in Venice* (1883), and *The Gipsy Baron* (1885). His father **Johann Strauss the Elder** (1804–49) played in the orchestra of the composer Joseph Lanner (1801–43), before forming his own. He was made conductor of the Vienna court balls in 1845, and composed 152 waltzes as well as quadrilles, marches (including the "Radetzky March"), galops, etc. Strauss and Lanner created the Viennese waltz.

● **Stravinsky, Igor** ▶ (1882–1971) Russian-born composer. He became a US citizen in 1945. His father was an opera singer and Stravinsky was a pupil of Rimsky-Korsakov in St Petersburg. He became famous with the series of ballet scores commissioned by Diaghilev for the Ballets Russes, including *The Firebird* (1910), *Petrushka* (1911), and *The Rite of Spring* (1913), which was extremely modern in its use of rhythm and dissonance; it provoked demonstrations at its premiere and had a strong influence on 20th-century music. Stravinsky subsequently developed a neoclassical style in which he attempted to revive baroque and classical composition in a modern form. His works in this style include a piano concerto (1924), the oratorio *Oedipus Rex* (1927), and the opera *The Rake's Progress* (1951). Towards the end of his life Stravinsky adopted ▷serialism in such works as *Canticum Sacrum* (1955).

● **Straw, Jack** ▶ (John Whitaker S.; 1946–) British Labour politician; home secretary (1997–2001) and foreign secretary (2001–). He entered parliament in 1979 and from 1987 held several front-bench posts, including shadow home secretary (1994–97).

● **strawberry** ▶ A perennial herb belonging to the genus *Fragaria* (15 species), native to N temperate regions and widely cultivated for its edible □fruit. Most of the commercial varieties are hybrids derived from the European hautbois strawberry (*F. moschata*), the Chilean strawberry (*F. chiloensis*), and the North American scarlet strawberry (*F. virginiana*). The plants are low growing, with creeping stems and small clusters of usually white flowers. It is the flower base (receptacle) that develops into the red fleshy "fruit": the true fruits (achenes) appear as "seeds" embedded in its surface. Strawberries are consumed fresh or used for canning, freezing, and jam making. Family: ▷*Rosaceae*.

● **Strawberry Hill** ▶ A house in Twickenham, London, built for and partially designed by Horace ▷Walpole between 1748 and 1777. It is one of the earliest examples of the ▷gothic revival style, for which Walpole was an enthusiast.

● **strawberry tree** ▷*See* Arbutus.

● **strawflower** ▷*See* everlasting flowers.

● **Strawson, Sir Peter Frederick** ▶ (1919–) British philosopher. He became Waynflete Professor of Metaphysical Philosophy at Oxford in 1968. Strawson's early philosophy centres around the relationship between language and logic. His later work in descriptive metaphysics revived the popularity of this field. His books include *The Bounds of Sense* (1966) and *Freedom and Resentment* (1974).

● **streamlining** ▶ The process of shaping the contours of a body so that it presents the least resistance to motion through a fluid. The mathematical study of these contours is part of ▷aerodynamics and ▷hydrodynamics. Streamlining must take into account drag forces, which are always present in real fluids, and is important in the design of aircraft, especially for supersonic flight (*see* sound barrier). ▷*See also* turbulence.

● **stream of consciousness** ▶ A technique used by novelists in which the flow of impressions, thoughts, and feelings are recorded as they pass through a character's mind. The term was first used by William ▷James in *Principles of Psychology* (1890). The technique was used by James ▷Joyce in *Ulysses* (1922) and also by Virginia ▷Woolf and William ▷Faulkner.

● **Streep, Meryl** ▶ (Mary Louise S.; 1949–) US film actress. She achieved fame in *The Deerhunter* (1978) and *Kramer vs. Kramer* (1980). Subsequent films have included *The French Lieutenant's Woman* (1981), *Sophie's Choice* (1982), which earned her an Academy Award, *Out of Africa* (1986), *A Cry in the Dark* (1989), *She-Devil* (1990), *The River Wild* (1994), and *One True Thing* (1998).

● **Streicher, Julius** ▶ (1885–1946) German Nazi journalist, who spread antisemitic propaganda. A collaborator in Hitler's Munich Putsch (1923), he was then editor of *Der Stürmer* (1923–45). He was hanged as a war criminal.

● **Streisand, Barbra** ▶ (1942–) US singer and actress. She has performed on stage, as a recording artist, and in film musicals including *Funny Girl* (1968), *Hello Dolly!* (1969), *A Star is Born* (1976), and *Yentl* (1983), which she wrote, produced, directed, and starred in. Her other films, several of which she has also directed, include *What's Up, Doc?* (1972), *The Way We Were* (1973), *Nuts* (1987), *The Prince of Tides* (1991), and *The Mirror Has Two Faces* (1996).

● **Streptococcus** ▶ A genus of spherical anaerobic bacteria many of which live as parasites in the respiratory and digestive systems of animals and humans. *S. pyogenes* causes scarlet fever in humans, *S. agalactiae* is responsible for bovine mastitis, and *S. lactis* produces lactic acid and causes souring of milk. ▷*See also* pneumococcus.

● **streptomycin** ▶ An ▷antibiotic, obtained from the bacterium *Streptomyces griseus*, that revolutionized the treatment of tuberculosis. This disease is now treated by a combination of drugs, including isoniazid. Streptomycin (given by injection) may still be used, but because in some patients it may cause serious side effects it is usually reserved for cases in which the tuberculosis bacteria are resistant to isoniazid.

● **Stresemann, Gustav** ▶ (1878–1929) German statesman; chancellor (1923) and foreign minister (1923–29) of the Weimar Republic. After World War I he negotiated the ▷Locarno Pact and secured the admittance (1926) of Germany to the League of Nations. He shared the Nobel Peace Prize with Briand in 1926.

● **stress** ▶ (physics) The force per unit area that causes a deformation (or ▷strain) in a body. **Tensile stress** tends to stretch a body; **bulk stress** tends to compress it; and **shear stress**, which acts tangentially, tends to twist it. ▷*See also* elasticity.

● **stress** ▶ (psychology) The condition of individuals under more physical or emotional pressure than they can cope with. It can become an issue of considerable importance in modern industrial societies. Common causes are excessive demands or anxieties in the workplace (which can include schools and universities, because stress can afflict people of all ages) as well as in the family, where financial problems, bereavement, divorce, and poor relationships are often the triggers.

Like mechanical stress, if psychological stress is neither too severe nor too prolonged, no damage is sustained (*see* elasticity). However, if the stress builds up to a level that is beyond the resources of the sufferer, and if it persists, permanent damage can result. This damage can take the form of ▷psychosomatic disorders, such as skin diseases (particularly psoriasis), gastric ulcers, hormonal imbalances, and heart disease. Alternatively, and sometimes in addition, if the stress is sufficiently serious, clinical depression and other mental disorders may arise, which can even lead to ▷suicide or parasuicide.

The only remedy for stress, apart from treating the conditions it causes, is to be aware of the factors causing it and, where possible, to change the circumstances in which they occur. ▷*See also* post-traumatic stress disorder.

● **strike** ▶ A form of industrial action in which a group of employees, usually organized in a trade union (or unions), withdraws its labour in order to achieve its demands. A strike is the last resort in the process of ▷collective bargaining: it may prompt a settlement either because it proves that neither side is bluffing or because the costs involved (in terms of lost pay and profits) force a compromise. As future orders and job security may be jeopardized by a strike, responsible unions only resort to the measure in extreme cases.

An official strike is one that is recognized by a trade union, whereas an unofficial (or wildcat) strike is a walkout organized by shopfloor workers without official union backing. The Trade Union Act (1984) provides for compulsory ballots in connection with strikes and other industrial actions ▷*See also* picketing; *compare* lockout.

● **Strindberg, August** ▶ (1849–1912) Swedish dramatist and writer, born in Stockholm. After 1883 he lived chiefly in Berlin and Paris. His unhappy childhood and three unsuccessful marriages gave rise to mental instability and a violent hatred of women. This is reflected in the plays *The Father* (1887) and *Miss Julie* (1888), the autobiographical prose work *Confessions of a Fool* (1912), and a study of mental illness entitled *Inferno* (1897). Returning to Sweden in 1898, Strindberg began work on a cycle of history plays and the dramatic religious trilogy *To Damascus* (1904). The other major works of this period are *The Dance of Death* (1900), on marital tensions, the symbolistic *Easter* (1901), and *A Dream Play* (1901), in which Strindberg abandoned the naturalism that had figured in his earlier plays. His late chamber plays, such as *The Ghost Sonata* (1907), combine irrational elements with realistic settings; they anticipated many of the later innovations of 20th-century drama.

● **stringed instruments** ► Musical instruments in which notes are produced by the vibration of stretched strings. The strings may be plucked, as in the guitar, lyre, harp, lute, balalaika, zither, banjo, and ukulele; bowed, as in the violin family and viol family; plucked mechanically, as in the harpsichord; struck mechanically, as in the clavichord and piano; or played with hammers, as in the dulcimer and cimbalom. *Compare* drums; percussion instruments; wind instruments.

● **string theory** ► A theory used in ▷particle physics and cosmology that makes use of a one-dimensional object in the form of a line or loop (closed string) to replace the concept of a pointlike elementary particle. The states of a particle may be seen as standing waves along this string. By combining this theory with the idea of **supersymmetry**, the **superstring theory** has emerged. Supersymmetry introduces a hypothetical symmetry between ▷fermions and ▷bosons, with new bosonic partners for existing fermions and new fermionic partners for known bosons. Although there is no evidence for this doubling of particles, the concept has been more successful than ▷quantum field theory in approaching a ▷unified field theory involving all four fundamental interactions, as it appears to avoid the infinities that the gravitational interaction creates in other field theories. Superstring theory makes use of a ten-dimensional space in which particles appear to have energies far above those attainable in current accelerators. It has not, therefore, been possible to provide direct evidence for the superstring concepts.

● **stroboscope** ► An instrument used to study periodic motion using a flashing light of known frequency. For example, if a disc revolving at 50 revolutions per second is illuminated by 50 hertz alternating-current mains lighting, it will appear to be stationary. This is because the eye, for any particular flash, sees the disc in exactly the same position as it was for the previous flash. Strobe lighting is used in discotheques to accentuate the music's beat, with which it flashes in time.

● **Stroheim, Erich von** ► (Hans Erich Maria Stroheim von Nordenwall; 1885–1957) US film director and actor, born in Austria. His films as director include the classic *Greed* (1923), *The Wedding March* (1927), and the unfinished *Queen Kelly* (1928). As an actor, he specialized in the roles of villains and German officers, as in *La Grande Illusion* (1937). In *Sunset Boulevard* (1950) he played a director from Hollywood's past.

● **stroke** ► (*or* apoplexy) Sudden loss of consciousness with weakness or paralysis of one side of the body, caused by interruption of the blood supply to the brain. This may be due to a blood clot in one of the arteries of the brain (*see* embolism; thrombosis) or to the rupture of a blood vessel in the brain (cerebral haemorrhage). The underlying causes include untreated atherosclerosis and hypertension (high blood pressure) and diseases affecting the valves of the heart. With careful nursing and physiotherapy to restore the function of paralysed limbs many patients recover completely.

● **Stromboli** ► An Italian island in the Tyrrhenian Sea, in the ▷Lipari Islands. Its active volcano produces a stream of lava.

● **Strong, Sir Roy (Colin)** ► (1935–) British art critic and historian. He was director of the National Portrait Gallery (1967–73) and of the Victoria and Albert Museum (1974–87). A specialist in Tudor and Jacobean art, Strong has published *Nicholas Hilliard* (1975), *The Cult of Elizabeth* (1977), and *The English Renaissance Miniature* (1983), as well as his indiscreet *Diaries* (1997).

● **strong interaction** ► One of the four basic forces in the universe; it occurs between the class of elementary particles called hadrons. It is the strongest of the four (being 100 times stronger than the electromotive interaction) but is effective only over a very short range of about 10^{-15} metre. It is the force that holds the protons and neutrons together in the nucleus and is thought to occur as the result of the exchange of gluons between quarks. ▷*See* particle physics.

● **strontium** ► (Sr) A reactive ▷alkaline-earth metal, discovered by Sir Humphry Davy in 1808 and named after Strontian, a town in Scotland where the carbonate ($SrCO_3$) is found. It also occurs as the sulphate, celestine ($SrSO_4$). It is a highly reactive metal, being more electropositive than calcium and reacting vigorously with water to liberate hydrogen. It imparts a strong red colour to flames and is used in fireworks. The isotope ^{90}Sr is produced in nuclear fallout. It emits high-energy beta-rays and has a half-life of 28 years; it presents a serious health hazard as owing to its chemical similarity to calcium it can become incorporated into bone. At no 38; at wt 87.62; mp 769°C; bp 1384°C.

● **Strophanthus** ► A genus of trees, shrubs, and vines (about 60 species), native to tropical regions of Africa and SE Asia. The petals of some species have long threadlike extensions. The bark and seeds yield the drug strophanthin, which resembles ▷digitalis and is used medicinally as a heart stimulant. Family: *Apocynaceae*.

Stromboli ► The volcano erupting.

● **structuralism** ► An approach to the study of culture and society that seeks to uncover underlying patterns and structures and the basic elements from which such patterns are constructed. The leading figure of this school was the French social anthropologist Claude ▷Lévi-Strauss, whose work on kinship, art, myth, ritual, and religion has been concerned also with the elucidation of universal laws of human thought through the analysis of its underlying structure. This approach was stimulated by the structural school in ▷linguistics, as originated by ▷Saussure, which maintains that linguistic signs are in themselves completely arbitrary and achieve meaning only through their structural relationships with other signs in the same system. In the 1960s a structuralist approach to literary criticism and popular culture was pioneered by French critics, such as Roland ▷Barthes, and became widely influential in the humanities and social sciences (*see also* semiotics). During the 1970s structuralism evolved into so-called ▷poststructuralism in the work of ▷Derrida and others.

● **Struve, Otto** ► (1897–1963) US astronomer, born in Russia, who discovered the existence of interstellar clouds and observed that they contain hydrogen and calcium. He also noticed that certain stars, including our own sun, rotate much more slowly than others and suggested that this is because they possess planetary systems.

● **strychnine** ▶ An alkaloid poison derived from plants of the genus *Strychnos*. It acts on the central nervous system, causing convulsions and ultimately death. Strychnine has been used in "tonics" and is still used as a poison for pests (such as moles).

● **Stuart, John McDouall** ▶ (1815–66) Scottish explorer. He emigrated to Australia in 1838 and in 1844 joined ▷Sturt's expedition into central Australia. In 1860, following two unsuccessful attempts, he crossed Australia from S to N. The **Stuart Highway**, constructed between Alice Springs and Darwin in 1943, was named after him.

● **Stuarts** ▶ (*or* Stewarts) The ruling dynasty of Scotland from 1371 to 1714 and of England from 1603 to 1714. The family originated in the 11th century in Brittany and in the 12th century entered Scottish royal service with the appointment of Walter (d. 1177) as steward to David I. The sixth steward, Walter (1293–1326), married (1315) Marjory, the daughter of Robert the Bruce, and their son became Robert II in 1371. The direct male line ended with the death of James V in 1542, when the throne passed to his daughter Mary, Queen of Scots, and following her abdication (1567) to her son James VI, who inherited the English Crown (1603) as James I. He was succeeded by Charles I (executed 1649), Charles II, James II, Mary II (and her husband William III), and Anne (d. 1714). The Crown then passed to the Hanoverians (*see* Settlement, Act of) but the Stuart claim was kept alive by ▷James Edward Stuart the Old Pretender, and his son, ▷Charles Edward Stuart the Young Pretender. The last royal Stuart was Henry Stuart, Cardinal York (d. 1807), the younger son of the Old Pretender.

● **Stubbs, George** ▶ (1724–1806) British animal painter. Largely self-taught as an artist, Stubbs studied anatomy and his earliest works included illustrations for a midwifery textbook (1751) and *The Anatomy of the Horse* (1766), for which he made dissections. He is best known for his horse paintings, such as *Mares and Foals in a Landscape* (Tate Gallery), but he also painted portraits and farming scenes. His meticulous observation of nature reflects his maxim that nature is always superior to art.

● **Stubbs, William** ▶ (1825–1901) British historian and churchman. He was Regius Professor of Modern History at Oxford (1866–1901) and Bishop of Chester (1884–89) and of Oxford (1889–1901). A good palaeographer and textual critic, Stubbs is best known for his *Constitutional History of England* (1874–78).

● **stupa** ▶ A Buddhist shrine in the form of a mound or dome with a central projection. An early example (c. 100 AD) at Sanchi in N central India is a solid brickwork mound surrounded by a carved stone railing. Some fine later stupas survive in Sri Lanka. When modified to become a reliquary the stupa evolved into the ▷pagoda.

● **sturgeon** ▶ A ▷bony fish belonging to a family (*Acipenseridae*; about 24 species) and found in N temperate fresh and salt waters. Sturgeons have a large sharklike body, up to 8.4 m long, with five longitudinal rows of sharp bony plates, a small ventral mouth, and four sensory barbels. They feed near the bottom on small animals and plants. Eggs are laid in fresh water and are commercially important as caviar. ▷*See also* beluga. ⁰fish.

● **Sturluson, Snorri** ▶ (1178–1241) Icelandic poet, who was also the author of the *Prose Edda* (*see* Eddas). A leading Icelandic nobleman, Sturluson visited Norway (1218, 1237) and intrigued against King Haakon, who intended to invade Iceland. Haakon had Sturluson murdered in 1241. His work includes a life of St Olaf and the *Heimskringla* (1223–35), a series of sagas about the Norse kings.

● **Sturm und Drang** ▶ (German: Storm and Stress) A German literary movement of the 1770s that anticipated many aspects of Romanticism. Its influence is most notable in the drama, where it is characterized by epic scale, violent emotions, and the rejection of neoclassical conventions. Goethe and Schiller were leading writers of this movement during their early careers.

● **Sturt, Charles** ▶ (1795–1869) British explorer. An army captain, he went to Australia in 1827 and led three expeditions into the interior. He discovered the Darling River (1828) and in 1829 in a whale-boat explored the Murrumbidgee to its confluence with the Murray. In 1844, believing in the existence of an inland sea, he tried unsuccessfully to cross the Simpson Desert.

● **Stuttgart** ▶ 48 47N 9 12E A city in SW Germany, the capital of Baden-Württemberg on the River Neckar. It became the capital of Württemberg in 1482. It was largely destroyed in World War II. One of Germany's main industrial centres, its manufactures include electrical goods, cars, and metallurgical goods. It is also a centre for banking, exhibitions, and publishing. It has a university (1967). Population (1996 est): 585 604.

● **Stuyvesant, Peter** ▶ (c. 1610–72) Dutch colonial administrator; governor of New Netherland (1647–64). His unpopular autocratic rule, which denied religious and political freedom, ended when the British forcibly took over the colony, dividing it into New York and New Jersey.

● **stye** ▶ A small abscess at the root of an eyelash. Styes, which commonly occur in crops, are usually treated with warm compresses to drain the pus.

● **stylops** ▶ A minute insect of the order *Strepsiptera* (about 400 species), which is parasitic on bees and other insects, affecting their reproductive systems and secondary sexual characteristics. The grublike female lives permanently inside the host's body; the winged male, often less than 4 mm long, leaves its host to find and fertilize a female. After hatching, the larvae complete their development in a larval host.

● **Styria** ▶ (German name: Steiermark) A federal state in SE Austria, bordering on Slovenia. It possesses important mineral resources and the Erzberg is Austria's chief source of iron ore; other minerals include lignite and magnesite. Area: 16 384 sq km (6326 sq mi). Population (1994 est): 1 203 993. Capital: Graz.

● **Styx** ▶ In Greek mythology, the main river of Hades across which the souls of the dead were ferried by ▷Charon. It was sometimes personified as the daughter of Oceanus. After she helped Zeus in his war against the Titans, oaths sworn in her name were held to be inviolable.

● **Suárez (Gonzalez), Adolfo, Duke of** ▶ (1932–) Spanish statesman; prime minister (1976–81). He was appointed by King Juan Carlos to guide Spain into democracy.

● **Súarez, Francisco de** ▶ (1548–1617) Spanish Jesuit theologian. He is known for his synthesis of Thomist and Aristotelian philosophy. He developed the theological system of congruism, the reconciliation of grace and free will. In *De legibus* (1612), he expounded the principles of natural and divine law.

● **subconscious** ▷*See* unconscious.

● **subduction** ▷*See* plate tectonics.

● **sublimation** ▶ In chemistry, the evaporation of a solid without melting. For any substance the liquid phase only occurs within certain limits of temperature and pressure—if the pressure is low enough, heating a solid will result in sublimation. Substances that sublime at atmospheric pressure include carbon dioxide (dry ice) and iodine.

● **submachine gun** ▶ A light short-range ▷small arm developed from the infantry light machine gun. Submachine guns became militarily popular after 1918, filling the gap between the pistol and the rifle, by offering greater fire-power than either. They are also more accurate than the pistol and smaller than the rifle. The first successful type was the ▷tommy gun, but now all major armies have their own designs. Almost all use 9 mm ammunition, fire automatically, and depend on blowback action (i.e. use the expanding gas of the ammunition to activate the reloading mechanism).

● **submarine** ▶ A warship designed for sustained operation under water. The earliest record of a submarine craft is that developed by Cornelis Drebbel (1572–1634) of Holland in 1620, demonstrated before James I in 1624 in the Thames estuary. A more practical model, the "Turtle," was invented by David Bushnell (1742–1824) of Connecticut in 1776, and saw limited use in the American Revolution. Submarines, called **U-boats** (German name: *Unterseeboot*, undersea boat), were first used extensively by the German navy in World War I. They became an important armament in World War II, when the German navy sank millions of tons of Allied ships, especially supply ships in convoy from the USA to the UK and the Soviet Union. The US navy used submarines to advantage against the Japanese, when 63% of all Japanese merchant shipping exceeding 1000 tons of cargo weight was sunk and 276 war vessels of various kinds were destroyed. Modern submarines may be powered by nuclear reactors, which require no air for recharging batteries and, hence, can remain submerged for months at a time. These vessels also carry guns mounted on deck, torpedoes for firing under water, and surface-to-air or surface-to-surface missiles that can be launched when the submarine is submerged.

● **Subotica** ▶ 46 04N 19 41E A town in N Serbia and Montenegro, in Serbia near the Hungarian border. It has a large Hungarian minority and is an agricultural trading centre. Its manufactures include metal goods, chemicals, and food products. Population (1991): 150 666.

● **subsidence** ▶ The sinking of part of the earth's surface relative to the surrounding area. On a large scale it may result from crustal movements (e.g. rift valleys). On a small scale it may result from collapsed mining excavations, collapsed roofs of limestone caves, etc. Subsidence involves vertical movement and lacks the horizontal component of landslides, etc.

● **substitution reaction** ▶ A type of chemical reaction in which one atom or group of atoms is displaced by another. An example is the reaction of methyl chloride (CH_3Cl) with hydroxide ions (OH^-) to give methanol (CH_3OH) and chloride ions (Cl^-). The hydroxide ion, in this case, is referred to as the substituent. ▷*See also* addition reaction.

● **succession** ▶ In ecology, the process of continual change that takes place in the composition of a ▷community of organisms occupying a particular habitat from the time of its initial colonization to the establishment of a stable ▷climax community. Succession is influenced by many factors, principally the nature of the habitat, climatic changes, and the effects of colonization on the habitat.

● **succubus** ▷*See* incubus.

● **succulent** ▶ A plant that has fleshy leaves or stems, which contain specialized ▷parenchyma cells in which water is stored. In this way succulents are specialized for growing in dry regions, such as deserts, subject to prolonged periods of drought, or in areas, such as salt marshes, in which fresh water is difficult to obtain. Many such plants are adapted in other ways to conserve water (*see* xerophyte). Succulents include the ▷cactuses, which have fleshy stems, and species of ▷*Agave*, ▷*Aloe*, and *Sedum* (*see* stonecrop), which have fleshy leaves.

● **Su-chou** ▷*See* Suzhou.

● **Suckling, Sir John** ▶ (1609–42) English poet and dramatist. From 1632 he spent his time as a courtier and was famous for his wit, generosity, and his taste for gambling. A loyal supporter of Charles I at the beginning of the Civil War, he was later discovered to be involved in a plot (1641) to free the imprisoned Earl of ▷Strafford and was forced to flee to Paris, where, according to John ▷Aubrey, he committed suicide. He wrote four plays and many elegant short lyrics.

● **Sucre** ▶ 19 00S 65 15W The capital of Bolivia, in the S at an altitude of 2790 m (9153 ft). It was founded by the Spanish in 1538 on the site of an Indian settlement. The centre of the revolutionary movement against Spain, it became the capital in 1859. The seat of government was moved to La Paz in 1898. The St Francis Xavier University was established in 1624. Population (2000 est): 192 238.

● **Sucre, Antonio José de** ▶ (1795–1830) South American revolutionary, born in Venezuela. The most able of ▷Bolívar's generals, Sucre defeated the Spaniards at Ayacucho (1824) and established the republic of Bolivia. He was its president from 1826 to 1828, when he resigned after a rebellion. The capital city, Sucre, is named after him.

● **sucrose** ▶ (cane sugar *or* beet sugar *or* saccharose) A carbohydrate consisting of ▷glucose and ▷fructose linked together. The most widely used ▷sugar, it is used as a sweetener in foods and drinks. When heated to 160°C it forms barley sugar and at 200°C becomes caramel.

● **Sudan, Democratic Republic of the** ▶ A large country in NE Africa, bordering on the Red Sea. It consists chiefly of a vast plateau rising to mountains in the S and W, reaching heights of over 3000 m (10 000 ft). The main rivers are the Blue Nile and White Nile, which join at Khartoum and provide the country's main source of water. About half the population are Arabs, and there are minorities of ▷Dinka, Nubians, and others.
Economy: chiefly agricultural, the main cash crop and export being cotton; other crops include sugar, wheat, millet, sorghum, and groundnuts, production having been increased by means of irrigation schemes, such as the ▷Gezira irrigation scheme. Livestock rearing is also important. Forest products include gum arabic, of which the Sudan is the world's main producer. Mineral resources, which remain largely unexploited, include iron ore, gold, and manganese. Since the mid-1980s the poorly developed Sudanese economy has been devastated by drought, famine, US sanctions (1996–99), and continuous civil war. There is a large foreign debt.
History: the NE was part of ancient ▷Nubia, which dominated Egypt (c. 730–670 BC). The region was Christianized in the 6th century and resisted invasion from the N until the 13th century, after which it was converted to Islam. In 1821 it was conquered by the Egyptians, against whom a revolt under the Mahdi (*see* Mahdi, al-) took place in 1881. In 1898 an Anglo-Egyptian force under Kitchener subdued his followers and in 1899 an Anglo-Egyptian condominium was established. In 1956 the Sudan became an independent republic. After a coup in 1958 it was ruled by a military government until 1964, when civilian rule was restored. Another coup in 1969 brought Col Jaafar al Nimeiry (1929–) to power. In 1972 Nimeiry negotiated an end to the civil war between the Muslim N and the animist and Christian S, which had raged since independence. However, new violence erupted in the S in 1983, with the rebel Sudanese People's Liberation Army (SPLA) taking control of large areas. In the midst of widespread famine in 1985, Nimeiry was overthrown. In 1989 the civilian government of Sadiq al-Mahdi was ousted in a military coup led by Lt Gen Omar Hassan Ahmad al-Bashir, who established an Islamic state. The new government's abuse of human rights and alleged support for Islamic terrorism led to its international isolation in the 1990s. In 1996 al-Bashir and his supporters were victorious in parliamentary and presidential elections, although these were widely considered to be unfair. During the 1990s the military situation was further complicated by tribal infighting within the SPLA. Although the government initiated talks to end the civil war, fighting broke out again in 1997. Talks were renewed in 1998, as the threat of famine loomed once more. Altogether war and war-related food shortages are thought to have claimed about 1.5 million lives since 1983 and to have left about twice that number homeless; in early 1999 President al-Bashir announced that he was ready to let the S secede if this would end the conflict.

Democratic Republic of the Sudan

Head of state	President Omar Hassan Ahmad al-Bashir
Official language	Arabic; English is widely spoken
Official currency	Sudanese dinar of 10 pounds
Area	2 500 000 sq km (967 500 sq mi)
Population (2001 est)	36 080 000
Capital	Khartoum
Main port	Port Sudan

● **Sudbury** ▶ 46 30N 81 01W A city in E Canada, in Ontario. Established in 1883, it is one of the world's great mining cities, especially for nickel and copper. A distribution and commercial centre for NE Ontario, Sudbury has important timber and tool industries. It houses the bilingual Laurentian University (1960). Population (1996): 92 059.

● **sudden infant death syndrome** ▶ (SIDS) ▷*See* cot death.

● **Sudetenland** ▶ A mountainous region in the Czech Republic. Incorporated in Czechoslovakia in 1919, it formed a defensible frontier with Germany, with which its mainly German population wanted reunion. Nazi pressure resulted in the ▷Munich Agreement of 1938, which permitted German reoccupation of the area. After World War II Czechoslovakia regained the region and expelled many thousands of Sudeten Germans. Considerable bitterness remained on both sides until 1997, when the German and Czech governments signed a new agreement and apologized for their past actions.

● **Su Dong Po** ▶ (or Su Tung-p'o; 1036–1101) Chinese poet, essayist, and painter, whose father Su Hsün (or Su Xun; 1009–66) and brother Su Tse-yu (or Su Ze-yu; 1039–1112) were also famous writers. An imperial official, he was imprisoned and exiled on several occasions for his criticisms of government policy. His poems introduced more varied metres and subjects into the traditional verse forms of his period.

● **Sue, Eugène** ▶ (Joseph Marie S.; 1804–57) French novelist. He worked as a ship's doctor until 1829. He achieved popular success with his novels about the Parisian underworld, notably *Les Mystères de Paris* (1842–43). *Le Juif errant* (1844–45) expressed his socialist views.

● **Suetonius** ▶ (Gaius Suetonius Tranquillius; c. 69–c. 140 AD) Roman historian and biographer. He was a friend of Pliny the Younger and served as secretary to the emperor Hadrian. Of his many works only *Lives of the Twelve Caesars* and fragments of *Lives of Famous Men* survive. His work is especially informative about the private lives of his subjects.

● **Suez** ▶ (Arabic name: As-Suways) 29 59N 32 33E A port in Egypt, on the Gulf of Suez near the mouth of the Suez Canal. An important refuelling station, it was virtually deserted following the Arab-Israeli War of 1967 and its oil refineries were damaged. Since the reopening of the Suez Canal (1975), rebuilding has taken place. Population (1994 est): 458 000.

● **Suez Canal** ▶ A canal in Egypt connecting the Mediterranean Sea and the Red Sea. Running between Port Said in the N and Suez in the S (via the Great and Little Bitter Lakes), it is 165 km (103 mi) long. It is of great importance to much of the world's shipping. It was designed by the French engineer Ferdinand de Lesseps and was opened in 1869. In 1888 it became a neutral zone, with Britain the guarantor of its status. In 1956, following the withdrawal of British troops, President Nasser nationalized the canal, ostensibly to pay for the building of the ▷Aswan High Dam, for which US support had been withdrawn. This provoked Britain and France to appeal to the International Court to declare the nationalization illegal. However, the Court declared the move to be within the sovereign rights of Egypt. In the ensuing **Suez War**, Britain and France secretly connived with Israel in an Israeli attack on Sinai, giving joint Anglo-French forces a pretext to bomb Egyptian bases and to attack Port Said on the dubious grounds that they were separating the combatants (Israel and Egypt). Under international pressure, led by the USA and the Soviet Union, the Anglo-French forces were withdrawn and Israel gave up Sinai. Anthony Eden (*see* Avon, Anthony Eden, 1st Earl of), the British prime minister, who was largely responsible for this unsuccessful duplicity, resigned shortly afterwards. The canal was closed from 1967 to 1975 because of Arab-Israeli hostilities and was not opened to Israeli ships until 1979.

● **Suffolk** ▶ A county in E England, in ▷East Anglia bordering on the North Sea. It consists of undulating lowlands. The principal rivers are the Little Ouse, Wavensey, Orwell, Deber, and Stour. It is mainly agricultural, producing cereals and sugar beet, and is noted for its horse breeding (Suffolk Punches). Industries are generally related to agriculture. Fishing is centred on Lowestoft. Under local government reorganization in 1974, it lost small parts to Norfolk and Cambridgeshire. Area: 3800 sq km (1467 sq mi). Population (1996 est): 661 600. Administrative centre: Ipswich.

● **Suffolk Punch** ▶ A breed of draught horse originating in Suffolk, England. It has a powerful round body and short thick neck and legs and is always chestnut. Hardy and docile, Suffolks are still employed for local haulage by some breweries. Height: about 1.63 m (16 hands).

● **suffragettes** ▷*See* women's movement.

● **Sufism** ▶ (Arabic *sufi*: wearer of a woollen cloak, mystic) A mystical movement arising within Islam in the 8th and 9th centuries AD. The goal of the Sufis was mystical union with God achieved by fervent worship. Later Sufism shows the influence of Neoplatonism and some devotional practices, such as rhythmical body movements, may

derive from Hindu asceticism. Sufi thought has influenced Arabic and Persian poets. As it evolved, Sufism divided into different orders or brotherhoods, some of which survive. ▷*See also* dervishes.

● **sugar beet** ▶ A biennial herb derived from the European sea ▷beet (*Beta vulgaris*). Sugar beet is widely cultivated for the sucrose content of its large roots, which is over 20% by weight in modern commercial varieties. Sugar was first extracted from beet in the 18th century and the plant is now a major source of sugar, especially in Europe and the former Soviet Union. Family: *Chenopodiaceae*.

● **sugar cane** ▶ A perennial grass of the tropical genus *Saccharum* (5 species), especially *S. officinarum*, which is cultivated in tropical and subtropical regions for its sugar content. The clumps of stalks (canes), 3–8 m high, have lance-shaped leaves and may bear dense woolly clusters of female flowers. Usually, the canes are cut before flowering and crushed between rollers to extract the sugary liquid. This is concentrated and refined to produce sucrose crystals for table sugar, etc. The remaining liquor (molasses) is used for animal feedstuffs, industrial alcohol, etc., and is fermented to make rum. The fibrous residue (bagasse) is used as fuel and for paper making, cattle feed, etc.

● **sugars** ▶ A class of sweet-tasting ▷carbohydrates, classified chemically as ▷monosaccharides or ▷disaccharides. The sugar widely used to sweeten food, drinks, and confectionery is the disaccharide ▷sucrose, some 70–80 million tonnes of which are produced annually. Half of this total is derived from the stems of sugar cane (11–15% sucrose) and half from the roots of sugar beet (17% sucrose).

Sugar manufacture is believed to have originated in India (Sanskrit *sarkara*, sand) around 3000 BC, the method travelling westwards through Arab countries (*sukkar*), Greece (*sákharon*), Italy (*zucchero*), and France (*sucre*). It was taken to the New World by Christopher Columbus in 1493. Until the mid-18th century it was an expensive luxury, used primarily as a medicinal sedative.

Sucrose is extracted from raw sugar cane by pressure, the extract being crystallized by evaporation. It is extracted from beet by hot water. Raw cane sugar and beet sugar are further refined to produce the granulated, caster, icing, and cube sugars. By-products from sugar processing include molasses and sugar-beet pulp, which are used in animal feedstuffs.

● **Suger of Saint-Denis** ▶ (1081–1151) French abbot and statesman. Suger was educated at the Abbey of Saint-Denis, becoming abbot in 1122. He introduced reforms based on the example of St ▷Bernard of Clairvaux. As adviser to both Louis VI (reigned 1108–37) and Louis VII (reigned 1137–80), Suger wielded considerable political influence.

● **Suharto** ▶ (1921–) Indonesian statesman and general; president (1967–98). He gained prominence in the struggle for Indonesian independence, becoming chief of the army staff in 1965. He came to power in the gradual overthrow (1965–67) of Sukarno. His rule was marked by economic growth and the repression of political opponents. Following the collapse of Indonesia's economy in 1997, there were mass protests leading to his resignation (1998). He went on trial for corruption in 2000.

● **suicide** ▶ Intentional self-destruction. Condemned by Christianity, Judaism, and Islam, suicide is a criminal offence in some societies. In the UK until the 19th century suicides were not permitted burial in consecrated ground but were interred in public highways with a stake through the heart. Only in 1961 did suicide cease to be a criminal offence under English law. In many traditional societies suicide, whether voluntary or an honourable obligation, is an accepted practice. Compulsory suicide may be performed out of loyalty to a dead master or spouse, derived from the once widespread custom of immolating wives and servants, or in the interest of the group as a whole, such as self-murder by elderly people no longer able to provide for their own subsistence. In certain instances suicide might be offered to a privileged few as an alternative to execution, as among the Greeks (*see* Socrates), the Roman nobility, and the Japanese aristocracy. With the breakdown of traditional practices, especially in industrial societies, the causes of suicide become less clear. Since Durkheim's classic statistical study *Suicide* (1897) sociologists have sought to relate the incidence of suicide to social pressures and the lack of social integration (*see* anomie). Psychologists have emphasized the importance of guilt, anxiety, and loneliness (*see also* stress); they have also distinguished between attempted suicide (when death is intended but averted) and parasuicide (when self-injury but not death is intended). ▷*See also* Samaritans.

Suicides in the UK by age and gender (1996)

age	15–24	25–44	45–64	over 65
Males	547	2030	1152	645
Females	152	533	430	376
Total	699	2563	1582	1021

● **suite** ► A sequence of musical dance movements in the same key, much used in keyboard and instrumental music in the 17th century and the first half of the 18th century. Usually a suite then consisted of an allemande, courante, sarabande, and gigue (jig). A prelude and optional dances (such as the minuet or gavotte) were later added and featured in the music of J. S. Bach. In the second half of the 18th century the form declined, but it re-emerged at the end of the 19th century as a selection of excerpts from ballets or operas, as for example in Tchaikovsky's *Nutcracker Suite* (1892).

● **Sukarnapura** ▷*See* Jayapura.

● **Sukarno** ► (1901–70) Indonesian statesman, the first president of Indonesia (1945–67). He helped to found the Indonesian Nationalist Party in 1927 and was Indonesia's main resistance leader during the Japanese occupation (1942–45). When Indonesia was declared independent he became president. In 1957 with popular and military support, he introduced so-called Guided Democracy. From 1965 he effectively lost power to the army under ▷Suharto, who formally deposed him in 1967.

● **Sukhumi** ► 43 01N 41 01E A port in W Georgia, on the Black Sea, the capital of Abkhazia. It is the site of the ancient Greek colony of Dioscurias and is a popular resort. Population (1993): 112 000.

● **Sukkur** ► 27 42N 68 54E A city in Pakistan, on the River Indus. Nearby is the major irrigation project, the Sukkur (or Lloyd) Barrage (1923–32). Industries include textiles and cement. Population (latest est): 191 000.

● **Sulawesi** ► (former name: Celebes) An island in Indonesia, off E Borneo. Irregularly shaped, it is mountainous and forested, with rich mineral deposits. It is Indonesia's chief producer of copra and nickel. Area, including adjacent islands: 189 033 sq km (72 986 sq mi). Population (1995 est): 13 771 600. Chief towns: Ujung Pandang and Menado.

● **Suleiman (I) the Magnificent** ► (?1494–1566) Ottoman sultan (1520–66), under whom the Ottoman Empire reached its peak. Suleiman captured Belgrade in 1521 and Rhodes in 1522. In 1526 he defeated the Hungarians at ▷Mohács and annexed large parts of Hungary. In 1529 he besieged Vienna. In campaigns against Persia he made many conquests, including Baghdad (1534), and the Ottoman navy, under ▷Barbarossa and others, controlled the E Mediterranean. To the Turks Suleiman is known as the Lawgiver because of the many regulations issued during his reign.

● **sulky** ► A two-wheeled vehicle drawn by a horse, consisting of a light springy frame bearing a single seat for the driver and supported on wheels like bicycle wheels. Used now in ▷harness racing, this type of cart was used in the 19th century by doctors and others needing to travel alone and was so called supposedly because of the inventor's temperament.

● **Sulla, Lucius Cornelius** ► (c. 138–78 BC) Roman dictator, associated with the aristocratic party; an opponent of ▷Marius and ▷Cinna. Nicknamed Felix (Lucky), he enjoyed early success. Enraged because his command against ▷Mithridates was transferred to Marius, he stormed Rome (87), forcing Marius and Cinna to flee. Although outlawed when his rivals returned, he successfully concluded the campaign against Mithridates and in 83 invaded Italy and took Rome. Elected dictator, Sulla butchered his political opponents. After restoring the Senate's constitutional powers, he retired (79).

● **Sullivan, Sir Arthur** ► (1842–1900) British composer. He is best known for his collaboration with W. S. ▷Gilbert in such comic operas as *The Pirates of Penzance* (1879), *The Mikado* (1885), and *The Yeomen of the Guard* (1888). He also composed the grand opera *Ivanhoe* (1891) and popular songs and hymns (including "Onward Christian Soldiers").

● **Sullivan, Louis Henry** ► (1856–1924) US architect of the ▷Chicago School. His work, begun in the classical style, was modified by ▷Art Nouveau, and developed into a form of ▷functionalism. He was among the first to design skyscrapers, such as the Wainwright building, St Louis (1890), and the Carson store, Chicago (1899), in both of which the structural framework is clearly visible.

● **Sully, Maximilien de Béthune, Duc de** ► (1560–1641) French statesman; chief minister to ▷Henry IV. Sully's financial reforms were fundamental in restoring prosperity after the ▷Wars of Religion. He retired (1611) following Henry's assassination.

● **Sully-Prudhomme, René François Armand** ► (1839–1907) French poet. His early verse was lyrical and subjective, but his involvement with the ▷Parnassians, who favoured greater impersonality, led to his attempts in *La Justice* (1878) and other works to write epical philosophic verse. He won the Nobel Prize in 1901.

● **sulphonamides** ► (or sulpha drugs) A group of drugs, derived from sulphanilamide, that prevent the growth of bacteria and were first used in 1936, to treat infections associated with childbirth. Sulphonamides are now used mainly to treat infections of the urinary tract and certain other serious infections (*see* co-trimoxazole). Since sulphonamides may cause severe allergic disorders and other adverse effects, and because bacteria are becoming increasingly resistant to them, these drugs are less widely used now than they were formerly.

● **sulphur** ► (S) A yellow nonmetallic solid element, occurring in various crystalline and amorphous forms. Sulphur was known in ancient times as brimstone. It is found near volcanoes and in large deposits associated with oil trapped against salt domes, from which it is extracted commercially. Extraction is by the **Frasch process**, in which the sulphur is melted with superheated steam and pumped to the surface. Sulphur reacts readily with many elements to form sulphides, sulphates, and oxides. Common compounds include sodium sulphide (Na_2S), zinc sulphide (ZnS), the poisonous gas hydrogen sulphide (H_2S), copper sulphate ($CuSO_4$), and calcium sulphate ($CaSO_4$). The oxides SO_2 and SO_3 are acidic gases that dissolve in water to form sulphurous acid (H_2SO_3) and ▷sulphuric acid (H_2SO_4). At no 16; at wt 32.06; mp 115.22°C; bp 444.674°C.

● **sulphuric acid** ► (H_2SO_4) A colourless oily liquid that has a great affinity for water and is used as a drying agent. Mixing with water must be carried out carefully because of the heat produced. H_2SO_4 is made by the contact process, in which sulphur dioxide is heated and passed through columns of platinized asbestos catalyst to produce sulphur trioxide (SO_3). The SO_3 is then dissolved in water to form H_2SO_4. Adding further SO_3 to H_2SO_4 produces fuming sulphuric acid (**oleum**; $H_2S_2O_7$), a fuming liquid that forms a crystalline solid on cooling.

Sulphuric acid is one of the most important industrial chemicals, being used in the manufacture of fertilizers, paints, rayon, explosives, and many other products, as well as in oil refining and car batteries.

● **Sulu Archipelago** ► An island group in the SW Philippines, between Borneo and Mindanao. The most important of its 400 volcanic and coral islands are Basilan and Jolo. Area: 2815 sq km (1087 sq mi). Population (latest est): 555 239. Chief town: Jolo.

● **sumach** ► (or sumac) A tree or shrub of the genus *Rhus* (250 species), native to warm temperate and subtropical regions. The leaves of the Sicilian sumach (*R. coraria*) yield a substance used in tanning and dyeing. Several species are cultivated as garden ornamentals: the stag's-horn sumach (*R. typhina*) of North America grows to a height of 7–12 m and has a crimson or orange autumn foliage. Some species are poisonous and irritate the skin on contact, particularly the American ▷poison ivy and poison sumach (*R. vernix*). Family: *Anacardiaceae*. ▷*See also* lacquer tree.

● **Sumatra** ▶ (or Sumatera) The second largest Indonesian island, separated from Peninsular Malaysia by the Strait of Malacca. The mountainous volcanic spine descends in the NE to swamps. Producing over 75% of the country's exports, it is Indonesia's chief rubber and oil producer and also possesses large natural gas deposits and other minerals. Crops include coffee, tea, and pepper.

History: the Buddhist kingdom of Sri Vijaya (7th–13th centuries) was based in Palembang, spreading through Indonesia and the Malay Peninsula. During the 15th century the Islamic influence became dominant, resisting Dutch domination in the N until 1908. Since 1949 there has been considerable separatist activity directed against the Java-based government. The island suffered a devastating earthquake in 1995. Area: 524 097 sq km (202 311 sq mi). Population (1990): 21 280 900. Chief towns: Palembang and Medan.

● **Sumer** ▶ The area in S Mesopotamia in which the earliest civilization evolved during the 4th millennium BC. The fertile natural environment encouraged settlements that grew into such cities as ▷Ur and ▷Eridu with all the prerequisites of civilized life: a writing system (*see* cuneiform), accumulation of wealth through trade, specialist organization of labour, and sophisticated crafts and architecture. Politically Sumer was a collection of independent city states, each with its own patron deity. Centralized control was temporarily asserted by neighbouring ▷Akkad (c. 2300 BC) and after 2000 BC Sumer was gradually absorbed into ▷Babylonia.

● **summer cypress** ▶ Either of two annual herbaceous plants, *Kochia scoparia* or *K. trichophylla*, native to temperate Eurasia and cultivated as ornamentals. They form compact bushes, 1–1.5 m high, and the foliage assumes an attractive red-bronze colour in autumn. Family: *Chenopodiaceae*.

● **summer time** ▶ A time system in which one hour, usually, is added to local (clock) time, i.e. to Greenwich Mean Time in the UK, so prolonging useful daylight hours. Summer time is used in temperate latitudes in spring, summer, and early autumn.

● **sumo** ▷*See* wrestling.

● **sun** ▶ The nearest star, lying at an average distance of 149.6 million km from earth at the centre of the ▷solar system. It has a diameter of 1 392 000 km, a mass of 1.99×10^{30} kg, and rotates on its axis in a mean period of 25.38 days (lengthening as solar latitude increases). It is a typical yellow (G2) main-sequence star and is composed primarily (99%) of hydrogen and helium in the approximate ratio 3:1 by mass.

In its hot central core, about 400 000 km in diameter, energy is generated by nuclear fusion reactions. This energy is transported to the sun's surface, from where it is radiated into space, mainly as heat and light. The surface, called the ▷photosphere, is the boundary between the opaque outer (convective) zone of the sun's interior and its transparent atmosphere. The atmosphere comprises the ▷chromosphere and the inner and outer ▷corona. The corona extends many millions of kilometres into interplanetary space. There are regions of intense localized magnetic fields on the sun, extending from the photosphere through the chromosphere to the corona. A variety of phenomena occur in these active regions, including ▷sunspots, ▷solar prominences, and ▷solar flares. ▷*See also* solar wind.

● **sun bear** ▶ A ▷bear, *Helarctos malayanus*, of tropical forests of Asia, Sumatra, and Borneo. It is the smallest bear (110–140 cm long) and climbs well, hunting in tall trees for small vertebrates, fruit, and its favourite food, honey.

● **sunbird** ▶ An arboreal bird belonging to a tropical family (*Nectariniidae*; 104 species) ranging from Africa to Australasia. Sunbirds are 9–15 cm long and have a brilliant metallic plumage, slender down-curved bills, and long extensible tongues for feeding on nectar. Sunbirds are similar to New World hummingbirds but perch on flowers to feed rather than hovering in front of them.

● **sun bittern** ▶ A Central American ground-dwelling bird, *Eurypyga helias*, that occurs in wet forests. 43 cm long, it has a brown, yellow, black, and white spotted plumage and feeds on insects with its sharp bill. It is the only member of its family (*Eurypygidae*). Order: *Gruiformes* (cranes, rails, etc.).

● **Sunda Islands** ▶ An Indonesian group of islands, the W part of the Malay Archipelago between the Indian Ocean and South China Sea. It consists of the **Greater Sunda Islands** including Sumatra, Java, Borneo, and Sulawesi and ▷Nusa Tenggara (formerly the Lesser Sunda Islands).

● **Sunderland** ▶ **1.** 54 55N 1 23W A port in NE England, in Sunderland unitary authority, Tyne and Wear, at the mouth of the River Wear. Sunderland exported coal from the Durham coalfield from the 14th century until the 1990s, when the last deep pits closed. Shipbuilding and the traditional glass making have also ceased. The main industries are now car manufacture (Nissan), engineering, and chemicals. Sunderland was given city status in 1992. Population (1991): 183 310. **2.** A unitary authority in NE England, in Tyne and Wear. Area: 138 sq km (53 sq mi). Population (1999 est): 289 040.

● **Sunderland, Robert Spencer, 2nd Earl of** ▶ (1641–1702) English statesman under Charles II, James II, and William III. He was secretary of state (1679–81) but was dismissed for supporting attempts to exclude the Roman Catholic James from the succession. He subsequently served James, becoming a Catholic in 1688. He fled England after James' deposition but returned in 1690 after renouncing Catholicism. He persuaded William to initiate a policy of selecting his ministers from the dominant party in the House of Commons.

● **sundew** ▶ A perennial or annual ▷carnivorous plant of the genus *Drosera* (about 100 species), of temperate and tropical regions. Sundews have a basal rosette of leaves covered in sticky reddish gland-tipped hairs, used to trap insects. The cup-shaped flowers are usually borne in a group on a stalk 6–35 cm long and are white, red, or purple. The fruit is a capsule. Family: *Droseraceae*.

● **sundial** ▶ An instrument that indicates the time by the direction or length of the shadow cast by an indicator (gnomon) mounted on a calibrated hour scale. Sundials may be fixed (mounted perpendicularly or horizontally) or portable (in which case they incorporate a device for direction finding) and come in a wide range of shapes. Known from ancient Egypt, Greece, and Rome, sundials reached the peak of their popularity between about 1500 and 1800, being used as a check on the accuracy of mechanical ▷clocks, which eventually superseded them.

● **Sundsvall** ▶ 62 22N 17 20E A port in E Sweden, on the Gulf of Bothnia. It is icebound in winter. Industries include timber processing and timber and wood pulp are the main exports. Population (1994): 94 815.

● **sunfish** ▶ An omnivorous fish of the family *Molidae*, especially *Mola mola*, found in all tropical and temperate seas. It has a disc-shaped laterally flattened body, up to 3 m long, with the tail fin reduced to a wavy frill attached to the triangular dorsal and anal fins. Order: *Tetraodontiformes*.

The name is also applied to several carnivorous freshwater food and game fish of the North American family *Centrarchidae*. They have deep laterally flattened bodies, 2.5–80 cm long, and a single long dorsal fin. Order: *Perciformes*.

● **sunflower** ▶ A herbaceous plant of the genus *Helianthus*, native to North and South America but widely cultivated for its showy flowers. A popular annual sunflower is the giant *H. annuus*, about 3 m high with rough hairy leaves and yellow flower heads, up to 35 cm in diameter. It is cultivated both for ornament and for its seeds, from which oil is obtained. Perennial sunflowers include *H. salicifolius* and *H. decapetalus*. Family: ▷*Compositae*.

● **Sung** ▷*See* Song.

● **Sungari River** ▷*See* Songhua River.

● **sunn** ▶ An annual herb, *Crotalaria juncea*, cultivated in India for its stem fibres—called sunn hemp or sann hemp. It grows to a height of 2–3 m and produces small yellow flowers that give rise to seed pods, at which stage the crop is cut. The fibres, comparable in strength to true ▷hemp, are used for netting, canvas, yarns, and in certain paper products. Family: ▷*Leguminosae*.

● **Sunnites** ▶ (or Sunni; Arabic *sunna*: custom) The name of the larger of the two main Muslim Sects. In contrast to the ▷Shiite Muslims, the Sunnites accept the first three caliphs as Mohammed's legitimate successors. They are strictly orthodox in their obedience to the Koran and in the emphasis they place on following the deeds and utterances of the Prophet. They form the majority party in most Islamic countries except Iran.

● **sun spider** ▶ A large ▷arachnid (10–50 mm long), also called sun scorpion, belonging to an order (*Solpugida* or *Solifugae*; 800 species) found in tropical and semitropical deserts. It has a hairy spider-like body, usually golden in colour, and a large powerful pair of pincers. Sun spiders are voracious carnivores.

● **sunspots** ▶ Comparatively dark markings on the sun's ▷photosphere, typically a few thousand kilometres across with the central region being darkest and coolest. They tend to occur in groups and can influence the climate on earth. They are centres of intense localized magnetic fields, the majority forming and disappearing within two weeks. The number of sunspots seen in a year, and their mean solar latitude, varies in a cycle of about 11 years, known as the **sunspot cycle**.

● **sunstroke** ▶ A form of ▷heatstroke caused by overexposure to the sun. **Sunburn** is damage to the skin resulting from overexposure to the sun. This may vary from slight reddening to large painful blisters: fair-skinned people are more susceptible to sunburn due to lack of the protective pigment melanin in the surface layers of the skin. ▷*See also* melanoma.

● **Sun Yat-sen** ▶ (*or* Sun Zhong Shan; 1866–1925) Chinese revolutionary. He qualified as a doctor but abandoned a medical career to pursue his political interests. After an abortive attempt to overthrow the Qing dynasty in 1895, he lived in exile and, while in Britain, was briefly imprisoned in the Chinese legation (1896). After establishing various revolutionary groups in Europe, he founded the Alliance Society in Japan (1905). Following the 1911 Chinese Revolution he returned to China, became president of the new republic but resigned almost immediately in favour of ▷Yuan Shi Kai. In 1913 Sun led an unsuccessful revolt against Yuan's dictatorial government and again left China. He returned after Yuan's death (1916) and in 1923 became president of a government based at Canton. Coming under Soviet influence he reorganized the ▷Guomindang (Nationalist People's Party), cooperated with the communists, and formulated Three Principles of the People—nationalism, democracy, and social reform. He remains a hero of both the Nationalist (i.e. Taiwan) and communist Chinese governments.

● **supercharger** ▷*See* turbocharger.

● **superconductivity** ▶ The disappearance of electrical resistance when certain substances are cooled to very low temperatures. First discovered in 1911 in mercury, it has now been observed in many elements, alloys, and compounds. The temperature below which it occurs, called the transition temperature, depends on the substance. Originally, the transition temperature was close to 0 K, but with "high temperature" superconductivity transition temperatures of 127 K and even 250 K have been claimed. The ultimate aim is room-temperature superconductivity. According to the BCS theory (1957), named after J. ▷Bardeen, L. N. Cooper (1930–   ), and J. R. Schrieffer (1931–   ), an electron moving through a crystal lattice creates a slight lattice distortion, which can persist long enough to affect a second passing electron. In superconductors current is carried by these pairs of electrons, called Cooper pairs; because the total momentum of the pair is unchanged by any interaction between one of the electrons and the lattice, the electron flow continues indefinitely. Superconducting coils create strong magnetic fields and are used in particle ▷accelerators. In recent years materials that will be superconducting up to 90 K have been developed (*see* Bednorz, Johannes Georg).

● **supercooling** ▶ The reduction in the temperature of a liquid below its freezing point without its solidification. The effect can only be achieved by slow and continuous cooling with pure liquids, since any solid matter would cause the liquid to solidify around it. A supercooled liquid is in a metastable state and any disturbance will cause solidification.

● **superego** ▶ In ▷psychoanalysis, the part of the mind that acts as a moral conscience. It was believed by ▷Freud to result from the incorporation of the parent's instructions into a child's mind. ▷*See also* ego; id.

● **superfluid** ▶ A fluid that exhibits a very high thermal conductivity and virtually no friction at temperatures close to absolute zero. Such a fluid will flow up the sides and out of an open container. Liquid helium becomes a superfluid at 2.19 kelvins, called the lambda point.

● **supergiant** ▶ The largest and most luminous type of star, bright enough to be visible in nearby galaxies. They evolve from massive but more compact stars and are rare. ▷Rigel, ▷Betelgeuse, and ▷Antares are examples. ▷*See also* giant star.

● **superheated steam** ▶ Dry steam that has been heated to a temperature above 100°C. It is widely used as a working medium for converting heat into mechanical energy, for which purpose it is more efficient than normal steam.

● **superheterodyne** ▶ A system widely used in radio receivers; the incoming radio-frequency signal is combined with a locally generated carrier wave to give an intermediate frequency between radio- and audio-frequency (*see* modulation). The intermediate frequency is easier to amplify than radio-frequency, giving less noisy reception and better tuning.

● **Superior, Lake** ▶ The largest of the Great Lakes in North America and one of the largest freshwater lakes in the world, situated between the USA and Canada. It is important for shipping. Area: 82 362 sq km (31 800 sq mi).

● **supernova** ▶ A cataclysmic stellar explosion, seen as a sudden increase in a ▷star's brightness by a million times or more. It occurs late in the evolution of certain stars, one type almost certainly involving massive ▷supergiant stars, another type disrupting ▷white dwarfs. Most of the star's substance is blown off at high velocity, forming an expanding gas shell—the **supernova remnant**. If the star's core survives, it probably ends up as a ▷neutron star or ▷black hole. ▷*See also* Crab nebula.

● **superphosphates** ▶ Highly active phosphorus-containing fertilizers. Single superphosphate is made by reacting sulphuric acid with insoluble calcium phosphate rock to form calcium sulphate and soluble calcium hydrogen phosphate $Ca(H_2PO_4)_2$. Often the process is carried out under pressure. The product also contains sulphates and impurities. Triple superphosphate is more concentrated, since phosphoric acid is used instead of sulphuric.

● **supersonic speed** ▷*See* sound barrier.

● **superstring theory** ▷*See* string theory.

● **supersymmetry** ▷*See* string theory.

● **Suppiluliumas I** ▶ King of the ▷Hittites (c. 1375–c. 1335 BC); founder of the Hittite empire. He subdued the Mitanni kingdom and conquered N Syria, displacing the Egyptians, then ruled by Akhenaton (*see also* Ankhesenamen). Suppiluliumas rebuilt the Hittite capital ▷Hattusas.

● **supply and demand** ▶ Two concepts fundamental to economics. Supply is the amount of a commodity that producers are willing and able to sell, while demand is that amount that consumers wish to and are able to buy. These amounts vary with price: as the price rises, producers wish to sell more, while consumers wish to buy less, and vice versa as the price goes down. There is one price (the equilibrium price) at which producers wish to sell the same amount as consumers wish to buy (i.e. the market clears). The **market forces** of supply and demand in a free economy control the market price. However, they are almost completely suppressed in controlled economies and in ▷mixed economies they may have only a restricted effect, depending on the extent to which government policy influences supply, demand, or price through, for example, a ▷prices and incomes policy, controlling interest rates, or ▷fiscal policy. Since the 1980s most governments have tended to avoid the more direct forms of intervention.

● **Supremacy, Acts of** ▷*See* Reformation.

● **suprematism** ► An abstract Russian art movement founded (c. 1913) by the painter ▷Malevich. It was the first and one of the most austere geometrical styles of the 20th century. Although Malevich declared in 1919 that suprematism was over, it continued to be influential in the 1920s, particularly at the ▷Bauhaus (*see also* Kandinsky, Wassily).

● **Supreme Court of the United States** ► The highest law court in the USA, comprising the chief justice and eight associate justices appointed for life by the president. Its main functions include interpreting and safeguarding the constitution through the power to declare as unconstitutional laws passed by ▷Congress or the state legislatures. Other actions of the government, the president, and the judiciary are subject to review by the court. It also decides disputes between states and between one state and the citizens of another and hears appeals from state and federal courts. In the 20th century it has played an important role in abolishing racially discriminatory laws and in desegregating the public schools.

● **Sur** ▷*See* Tyre.

● **Surabaja** ► 7 14S 112 45E A port in Indonesia, in E Java on the Mas estuary. It was bombed by the British in 1945 during the struggle for the Indonesian Republic. It is Indonesia's second largest city and chief naval base, with a naval college and university (1954). Its industries include shipbuilding, oil refining, and rubber processing. Population (1990): 2 027 913.

● **Surakarta** ► (*or* Solo) 7 32S 110 50E A city in Indonesia, in central Java on the River Solo. A cultural centre noted for its shadow plays, it is the site of a sultan's palace (1745). Batiks, musical instruments, and gold objects are produced. Population (1995 est): 516 500.

● **Surat** ► 21 10N 72 54E A city in India, in Gujarat on the River Tapti. It was the Mogul Empire's chief port (16th–17th centuries). The first British trading post was established here (1612) and it was the headquarters of the East India Company until 1687. It has textile industries. Population (1991): 1 496 943.

● **surface tension** ► A force occurring on the surface of a liquid that makes it behave as if the surface has an elastic skin. It is caused by forces between the molecules of the liquid: only those at the surface experience forces from below, whereas those in the interior are acted on by intermolecular forces from all sides. Surface tension causes a meniscus to form, liquids to rise up capillary tubes, paper to absorb water, and droplets and bubbles to form. It is defined as the force acting tangentially to the surface on one side of a line of unit length (newtons per metre) or as the work required to produce unit increase in surface area (joules per square metre).

● **surfactant** ► A substance that lowers the surface tension of a liquid: allowing easier penetration and spreading, they are often known as **wetting agents**. Surfactants active in water are usually organic substances, e.g. ▷alcohols, and ▷soaps, the molecules of which contain both a water-soluble and a water-repelling portion; the latter forces the molecules to the surface. Surfactants are used in ▷detergents, emulsifiers, paints, adhesives, inks, etc.

● **surgeonfish** ► A tropical marine fish, also called tang, belonging to the family *Acanthuridae* (about 100 species). Its deep laterally flattened body, up to about 50 cm long, is often brightly coloured, with a single long dorsal fin, and a sharp bladelike spine on each side of the tail. They feed mainly on algae. Order: *Perciformes*.

● **surgery** ► The branch of medicine in which disorders and injuries are treated by operation, usually with the patient in a state of ▷anaesthesia. Amputations and some elementary surgical operations have been performed since ancient times in Egypt, Greece, India, and China; the skills required were transmitted by Arab surgeons to Europe, where they were mostly practised in monasteries. Bloodletting—regarded as an antidote for most ailments—was widely practised. In England, however, in the 12th century, monks were forbidden to perform surgery and the practice passed to barbers until 1540. The two arts were then separated, although they continued to be controlled by the Company of Barbers and Surgeons until 1745. In this year the Company of Surgeons was formed, which became the Royal College of Surgeons in 1800.

The 19th century saw the foundation of modern surgery, with the introduction of anaesthetics, ▷Lister's discovery of antisepsis, and a greater knowledge of anatomy and physiology. In the 20th century the advent of antibiotics has made surgery safe from infection, the use of blood transfusions, intravenous drips, and electrolyte control have overcome problems of shock, and better knowledge of anaesthetics and relaxant drugs has made surgery a less hurried procedure. Moreover, specialization (e.g. gastrointestinal surgery, neurosurgery, ophthalmological surgery) and great ingenuity in the design of surgical instruments have made surgery an extremely safe and usually successful procedure. ▷*See also* plastic surgery.

Recent advances include techniques in ▷transplantation surgery; operations on the exposed heart; the use of extreme cold to destroy tissues (cryosurgery); the use of ▷lasers and ultrasound (*see* ultrasonics); and the development of microsurgery, in which surgeons operate through a special microscope using miniaturized instruments, and minimally invasive (or "keyhole") surgery, in which operations are performed through tiny incisions using endoscopes (*see* endoscopy).

● **Suriname, Republic of** ► (name until 1948: Dutch Guiana) A country on the N coast of South America, on the Atlantic Ocean. Much of the land is covered by tropical forest, with coastal plains rising to higher land in the interior. The population is ethnically extremely diverse, owing to the importation of African slave labour from the 17th century and of East Indian plantation workers in the 19th century.
Economy: based on bauxite, the chief industry being aluminium processing; alumina and aluminium comprise the main exports, although in the late 1980s production was disrupted by guerrilla activity. Agriculture remains underdeveloped, the rice industry being the only fully developed sector. The vast forests are largely unexploited. Fishing is important, especially for shrimps. Hydroelectricity is a valuable source of power.
History: Suriname was sighted by Columbus in 1498 and the first permanent settlement was established by the English in 1650. It was ceded to the Netherlands in 1667. During the Revolutionary and Napoleonic Wars it was again (1799–1802, 1804–16) under British rule. In 1949 it gained a certain measure of self-government as Dutch Guiana, subsequently becoming an autonomous part of the Netherlands (1954) and then an independent republic (1975). At independence some 40 000 Surinamers emigrated to the Netherlands, to the detriment of Suriname's economy. The early years of independence also saw deepening ethnic and party strife. Following a coup in 1980, the National Military Council took power with Lt Col Désiré Bouterse as the effective leader. Civilian rule was outwardly restored in 1988 but the military remained the main source of power. The civilian president Ramsewak Shankar (1937–) was ousted in 1990 in a coup staged by Bouterse, who installed a caretaker president. After free elections in 1991 the opposition leader Runaldo Venetiaan became president and took steps to limit the power of the army. Maroon rebels (descended from African slaves) waged a guerrilla campaign from 1986 until a peace settlement was made in 1992. In 1996 Venetiaan was succeeded as president by Jules Wijdenbosch. Suriname is a member of the OAS and the Caribbean Community.

Republic of Suriname

Head of state	President Jules Wijdenbosch
Official language	Dutch; English, Hindustani, and Javanese are widely spoken; Surinamese (Sranang Tongo) is used as a lingua franca
Official currency	Suriname guilder of 100 cents
Area	163 265 sq km (63 020 sq mi)
Population (1997 est)	424 000
Capital and main port	Paramaribo

● **surrealism** ► A European movement in art and literature of the 1920s and 1930s. It began as a literary movement, when its leader, the poet André ▷Breton, published the surrealist manifesto in Paris (1924). It aimed, under the influence of ▷Freud, to embody in art and poetry the irrational forces of dreams and the subconscious mind. To achieve this, such techniques as automatic drawing and writing were employed, which allowed the subconscious mind to produce an unpremeditated design or poem. The leading surrealists were the poets ▷Aragon and ▷Éluard and the painters ▷Ernst, ▷Miró, ▷Dali, ▷Magritte, ▷Delvaux, and ▷Tanguy.

● **Surrey** ▶ A county in SE England, bordering on Greater London. Under local government reorganization in 1974 it lost part of the SE to West Sussex. It is mainly low lying with the North Downs running E–W across the middle of the county. Although it has developed primarily as a residential and recreational area, agriculture is important in the S. Industry is mainly concentrated in the NE. Area: 1679 sq km (648 sq mi). Population (1996 est): 1 047 100. Administrative centre: Kingston-upon-Thames.

● **Surrey, Henry Howard, Earl of** ▶ (1517–47) English poet. The son of the Duke of Norfolk, he led a precarious life in the service of Henry VIII, and was finally executed on a charge of treason lodged by his enemies at court. He pioneered the use of blank verse in his translation of Virgil's *Aeneid* (1557), and, with Sir Thomas ▷Wyatt, was responsible for introducing Italian forms and metres into English poetry.

● **surrogate motherhood** ▷*See* artificial insemination.

● **Surtees, John** ▶ (1934–) British racing motorcyclist and motor-racing driver. He won seven world championships as a motorcyclist (350 cc in 1958–60 and 500 cc in 1956, 1958–60) and later became world champion motor-racing driver (1964), the only man to have held both titles.

● **Surtees, Robert Smith** ▶ (1803–64) British journalist and novelist. From 1831 to 1836 he edited the *New Sporting Magazine*, to which he contributed stories about the sporting life of English country gentry later collected in *Jorrocks's Jaunts and Jollities* (1838) and other volumes.

● **Surtsey** ▶ 63 18N 20 37W An island in the N Atlantic Ocean off S Iceland. It was formed by an underwater volcanic eruption (1963). Many scientific studies have been made here, especially of the colonization of flora and fauna.

● **surveying** ▶ The measurement of distances, levels, angles, etc., on, above, or below the earth's surface. It is necessary for the delineation of property lines (**boundary surveying**) and for planning the construction of almost any building or structure. **Plane surveying** is suitable for smaller areas as it neglects the earth's curvature, whereas **geodetic surveying** does not. Topographic surveys locate natural features and elevations for map making, dam planning, etc.

● **Surya** ▶ In Hindu mythology, the sun-god. He appears as a major deity in the ▷*Vedas* and remained prominent as patron of numerous Hindu royal dynasties. Like his Greek counterpart ▷Apollo, he is represented as a charioteer.

● **Susa** ▶ (*or* Shushan) An ancient city in SW Iran. Occupied since the 4th millennium BC, it was a capital of ▷Elam, whose rulers made successful forays against ▷Ur and ▷Babylon during the 2nd millennium. Susa's heyday was as administrative capital of the ▷Achaemenian kings of Persia (521–331). It continued to be important under Seleucid, Parthian, and Sassanian rule.

● **suslik** ▷*See* souslik.

● **Suslov, Mikhail** ▶ (1902–82) Soviet politician. A Communist Party member from 1921, Suslov rose in the Party hierarchy during the 1930s and 1940s. He fought all deviation from Soviet policy, especially that of Yugoslavia in 1948. In 1964 he helped to oust ▷Khrushchev.

● **Susquehanna River** ▶ A river in the E USA. It rises in Otzego Lake in central New York State and flows mainly S through Pennsylvania before entering Chesapeake Bay. It caused serious flooding in 1972 to several cities, especially ▷Harrisburg. Length: 715 km (444 mi).

● **Sussex** ▶ A historic county of S England. Under local government reorganization in 1974 it was divided into the counties of ▷West Sussex and ▷East Sussex. West Sussex gained part of S Surrey together with part of the former administrative area of East Sussex.

● **Sutcliffe, Herbert** ▶ (1894–1978) British cricketer, who played for Yorkshire and England. An opening batsman, known especially

for his partnerships with ▷Hobbs, he scored 16 Test centuries and during his career (1919–45) totalled 50 135 runs and 149 centuries.

● **Sutherland** ▶ A former county of N Scotland. Under local government reorganization in 1975 it became part of the Highland Region. Sutherland District, which partly corresponded with the former county, was abolished in 1996.

● **Sutherland, Graham Vivian** ▶ (1903–80) British artist. After working as an etcher and engraver he turned to painting in 1935, specializing in disturbing landscapes, usually magnifying insect and plant forms, and (while official war artist in World War II) scenes of war desolation. Also well known are his *Crucifixion* (1946; St Matthew's, Northampton), his tapestry for Coventry Cathedral, and his portraits, e.g. of Somerset Maugham (Tate Gallery) and his controversial portrait of Winston Churchill (destroyed on the orders of Lady Churchill).

● **Sutherland, Dame Joan** ▶ (1926–) Australian operatic soprano. She established her reputation at Covent Garden in 1959 in the title role of Donizetti's *Lucia di Lammermoor*. She specialized in coloratura roles and is married to the conductor Richard Bonynge (1930–). She was made a DBE in 1977 and appointed to the OM in 1991: she retired in 1990.

● **Sutlej, River** ▶ A river in India and Pakistan, the longest of the five rivers of the Punjab. Rising in SW Tibet, it flows mainly SW across the Punjab plain into Pakistan, where it joins the River Chenab. It is a source of irrigation and hydroelectric power. Length: 1368 km (850 mi).

● **suttee** ▶ An ancient Hindu custom of self-immolation of widows on their husbands' funeral pyres. It was officially abolished in India by the British in 1829.

● **Sutton** ▶ A mainly residential borough of S Greater London, created in 1965 from parts of N Surrey. Area: 43 sq km (17 sq mi). Population (1996 est): 175 500.

● **Sutton, Walter Stanborough** ▶ (1877–1916) US geneticist, who linked observations of chromosome behaviour during cell division with ▷Mendel's observations of inheritance of physical characteristics. Sutton postulated that chromosomes carried the units of inheritance (genes) and that their behaviour during sex cell formation (meiosis) explained some of Mendel's findings.

● **Sutton Coldfield** ▶ 52 34N 1 48W A town in England, in Birmingham unitary authority, West Midlands. A mainly residential suburb of Birmingham, it contains Sutton Park, a large area of woodland, lakes, and heathland, which was given to the people of the town in the 16th century. Population (1992 est): 103 097.

● **Sutton Hoo** ▶ The site of a Saxon ship burial near Woodbridge, in Suffolk (E England). Excavations in 1939 revealed the remnants of a 38-oar boat containing a treasure hoard: gilt bronze helmet, sword decorated with gold and garnets, royal sceptre, silver dishes, drinking vessels, and jewellery. The mound is thought to be a cenotaph (as it contained no body) to King Raedwald (died c. 625 AD).

● **Sutton-in-Ashfield** ▶ 53 08N 1 15W A town in central England, in E Nottinghamshire. It lies in a coalmining district and manufactures hosiery and metal boxes. Population (1991): 37 890.

● **Su Tung-p'o** ▷*See* Su Dung Po.

● **Suu Kyi, Aung San** ▷*See* Aung San.

● **Suva** ▶ 18 08S 178 25E The capital of Fiji, on the S coast of Viti Levu. Its industries include tourism and the production of coconut oil and soap. The University of the South Pacific was established here in 1968. Population (1996 est): 167 421.

● **Suvorov, Aleksandr Vasilievich, Count** ▶ (1729–1800) Russian field marshal. Following outstanding victories against the French revolutionary armies in Italy (1799), the defeat of a Russian force at Zurich forced his withdrawal. The winter retreat, achieved against desperate odds, assured Suvorov's reputation as a brilliant tactician.

● **Suwannee River** ▶ (*or* Swannee R.) A river in the SE USA, flowing from the Okefenokee Swamp in SE Georgia across Florida to the Gulf of Mexico. It is the Swannee River of the song by Stephen Foster. Length: 400 km (200 mi).

● **Suzhou** ► (Su-chou *or* Soochow) 31 21N 120 40E A city in E China, in Jiangsu province on the Yangtze delta and the ▷Grand Canal. Famed for its beautiful canals and gardens, it is a centre of culture and handicrafts. Founded in 484 BC, it prospered, especially in the 14th to 19th centuries, as a result of its silk industry. The chief industry is still textiles. Population (1990 est): 706 459.

● **Suzman, Helen** ► (Helen Gavronsky; 1917–) South African White politician and human-rights campaigner. A member of the South African legislature (1961–1989), she campaigned against ▷apartheid for over 30 years. She was made an honorary DBE in 1989. Her niece **Janet Suzman** (1939–) is an actress noted for both classical and modern roles. A member of the Royal Shakespeare Company in the 1960s, she was married to Trevor ▷Nunn from 1969 to 1986.

● **Suzuki method** ► A method for teaching young children to play musical instruments, devised by the Japanese violinist Shinichi Suzuki (1898–1998). He believed that any child can be trained to develop musical ability, just as any child can learn to speak its mother tongue. Suzuki's Mother-Tongue Approach for teaching the violin is based on a sequential repertoire presenting musical and technical points in a logical order. Later teachers adapted the method to teaching the cello, piano, and flute. The method is ideally begun with children aged 3–4 years, although it is never too late to start.

● **Svalbard** ► (*or* Spitsbergen) A Norwegian archipelago in the Arctic Ocean, the chief islands being Spitsbergen (formerly Vestspitsbergen), Edgeøya, Nordaustlandet, Barentsøya, and Prins Karls Forland. Following disputes over their sovereignty, the islands were granted to Norway in 1920. Mountainous and covered largely by icefields and glaciers their major importance is as a source of coal; other minerals include asbestos and copper. Area: 62 050 sq km (23 958 sq mi). Population (latest est): 3544. Chief town: Longyearbyen.

● **Sverdlovsk** ▷*See* Ekaterinburg.

● **Sverrir** ► (*or* Sigurdsson; c. 1149–1202) King of Norway (1177–1202). He claimed the throne after being informed by his mother that he was the son of a former king, but did not defeat his predecessor, Magnus V (1156–84; reigned 1162–84), until 1184. His story is told in the Icelandic *Sverris Saga*.

● **Svevo, Italo** ► (Ettore Schmitz; 1861–1928) Italian novelist. His first two novels, *A Life* (1892) and *As a Man Grows Older* (1898), were unsuccessful, but he was encouraged by James ▷Joyce, who taught him English in Trieste in 1907 and later publicized his work. His best-known novel is *Confessions of Zeno* (1923), a portrait of an introspective ineffectual hero.

● **Swabia** ► (German name: Schwaben) A former region in SW Germany now divided between Germany, Switzerland, and France. Swabia became one of the leading German duchies in the middle ages, passing in 1079 to the ▷Hohenstaufen. When the dynasty died out in 1268 Swabia was divided among local noble families. A series of Swabian leagues culminated in that of 1488–1534, which foundered on religious differences during the Reformation. When Napoleon reconstructed Europe in 1807, Swabia was partitioned among neighbouring states; its distinguishing dialect still survives.

● **Swahili** ► (*or* Kiswahili) A Bantu language of East Africa and the lingua franca of Tanzania, Kenya, Congo, and Uganda. There are three main dialects but standard Swahili is based on the Zanzibari form known as Kiunguja. It has been much influenced by Arabic.

● **swallow** ► A songbird belonging to a cosmopolitan family (*Hirundidae*; 78 species) of acrobatic fliers that catch insects on the wing. Swallows are 10–22 cm long, with short necks, long pointed wings, short legs, and often forked tails. All temperate swallows migrate to hot climates for the winter. The barn swallow (*Hirundo rustica*) visits Europe and North America in summer and has a glossy blue-black upper plumage with a red forehead and throat, a blue breast band, and white underparts. ▷*See also* martin.

● **swallowtail butterfly** ► A ▷papilionid butterfly having long swallow-like tails on the hindwings. Many species are tropical and brightly coloured, with the sexes often of different colours. The cater-

pillars feed on a variety of plants and possess scent organs behind the head, giving off a strong odour if the caterpillar is disturbed. ⁰insect.

● **Swammerdam, Jan** ► (1637–80) Dutch naturalist and microscopist, who first observed red blood cells. However, much of his work was concerned with collecting insects, describing their anatomy and life histories, and classifying them: three of his groupings are still used in modern classification systems. He discovered the Swammerdam valves in lymphatic vessels and showed that muscles do not change in volume during contraction.

● **swamp** ► An area of permanently water-saturated land, usually covered with reeds or mangroves. It is an intermediate stage between an entirely aquatic environment and a temporarily saturated marsh. Once drained, swamps produce fertile soils with a high humus content.

● **swamp cypress** ► A deciduous conifer, *Taxodium distichum*, also called bald cypress, native to swampy regions of the SE USA. It is grown for its timber and as an ornamental. In waterlogged soils its roots produce "knees," which protrude above the water and may help in respiration. Up to 45 m high, it has soft needles arranged in two rows and globular cones, 2.5 cm across. Family: *Taxodiaceae*.

● **swamp eel** ► A slim eel-like bony fish of the order *Synbranchiformes*, unrelated to true eels and found in fresh and brackish tropical waters. 20–50 cm long, they have no pectoral fins and the gills often have only one opening. Oxygen is sometimes absorbed through the throat or intestine. Swamp eels are used for food in Asia.

● **swan** ► A large waterbird belonging to a genus (*Cygnus*; 7–8 species) occurring worldwide on fresh waters or sheltered coasts and estuaries. 100–160 cm long, swans are usually white with black legs and have large feet, a long neck, and a powerful spatulate bill, which they use to feed on underwater plants. Immature swans have a mottled brown plumage until about two years old. ▷*See also* black swan; mute swan; trumpeter. Family: *Anatidae* (ducks, geese, swans).

● **Swan, Sir Joseph Wilson** ► (1828–1914) British physicist, who in 1860 invented a lightbulb, consisting of a carbon filament in an evacuated glass bulb. Its practical use was limited by its short life. Swan also introduced the dry photographic plate and, in 1879, he developed bromide paper, now widely used in photographic prints.

● **Swannee, River** ▷*See* Suwannee, River.

● **Swanscombe skull** ► Fossil cranial remains of a ▷hominid, fragments of which were found at Swanscombe in Kent (England) in River Thames gravels (1935, 1936). It seems to be an early example of *Homo sapiens* dating from about 200 000 years ago. ▷*See also* Homo.

● **Swansea** ► (Welsh name: Abertawe) A county of S Wales on the Bristol Channel, created in 1996 from part of West Glamorgan. It includes the Swansea conurbation, the ▷Gower Peninsula, and some hillier country in the N. The economy is based on heavy industry and port facilities in Swansea and tourism in the Gower; there are also varied agricultural activities. Area: 378 sq km (146 sq mi). Population (1996 est): 230 600. Administrative centre: Swansea.

● **Swansea** ► (Welsh name: Abertawe) 51 38N 3 57W A city and port in Swansea county, on Swansea Bay. It is the second largest city in Wales and a major industrial and trading centre with metals, chemicals, and oil refining. Exports were formerly dominated by coal and steel rails but are now more diversified, including metal products, oil, petrochemicals, and containerized goods. Swansea University opened in 1920. Part of the maritime quarter has been redeveloped as a marina and recreational area. Population (1991): 181 906.

● **SWAPO** ► (South West African People's Organization) ▷*See* Namibia, Republic of.

● **swastika** ► An ancient symbol of uncertain origin, generally held to signify prosperity and creativity (the word derives from the Sanskrit *svasti*, prosperity). It is a cross, the four arms of which are deflected at right angles either clockwise or anticlockwise. It has been revered by Buddhists, Hindus, Celts, and Amerindians. The Nazis adopted the symbol, mistakenly believing it to be of Aryan origin, following the guidance of an earlier German poet, Guido von List, who promoted it as a symbol of antisemitism. As the feature of the German flag (1935–45) it has become a symbol of evil.

● **Swatow** ▷*See* Shantou.

● **Swazi** ▶ A Bantu-speaking people who occupy Swaziland and adjacent areas of E South Africa. They are an agricultural and pastoral people, traditionally ruled by a hereditary paramount chief together with his mother. Descent, inheritance, and group membership are patrilineal. Polygyny is practised by senior men, the chief taking many wives who are dispersed in a number of royal villages throughout the territory. ▷Age-set organization was the basis of military service. Traditionally ▷ancestor worship, witchcraft, and magic were prominent features of religious life.

● **Swaziland, Kingdom of** ▶ A small country in SE Africa between South Africa and Mozambique. It consists of three distinct regions extending N–S: the Highveld in the W, the Middleveld in the centre, and the Lowveld in the E (*see* veld).

Economy: agriculture is important, the main food crop being maize. The chief cash crop is sugar; other crops include rice, citrus fruit, and cotton, and livestock raising is also important. Rich mineral resources include iron ore, asbestos, and coal, and hydroelectric schemes provide irrigation as well as power. Manufacturing has developed rapidly and overtook agriculture as the most important sector of the economy in the late 1980s. Products include timber and wood pulp, food products, textiles, and footwear.

History: the ▷Swazi occupied the area in the late 18th century. It became a South African protectorate in 1894 and in 1902, after the Boer War, it came under British rule. Swaziland attained internal self-government in 1967 and became an independent kingdom within the Commonwealth in 1968. In 1973 King Sobhuza II (1899–1982) increased his personal power and under a new constitution (1978) political parties were banned. There is a partially elected House of Assembly. In 1986 Prince Makhosetive (1969–) was inaugurated as King Mswati III. Pro-democracy activism grew in the late 1990s, leading to a number of violent incidents. Following elections in 1998 Dr Barnabas Sibusiso Dlamini was reappointed as prime minister.

Kingdom of Swaziland

Head of state	King Mswati III
Official languages	Siswati and English
Official currency	lilangeni of 100 cents; South African currency is also legal tender
Area	17 400 sq km (6705 sq mi)
Population (1997 est)	1 032 000
Capital	Mbabane

● **sweat** ▶ (*or* perspiration) A watery fluid, consisting mainly of sodium chloride and urea in solution, that is secreted by the sweat glands in the ⬚skin. Sweating is a means of excreting nitrogenous waste products, but it is also, and more importantly, a means of temperature regulation. Evaporation of sweat from the skin surface has a cooling effect; therefore in hot weather, or when the individual feels hot through exercise, more sweat is produced. Sweating is increased by nervousness and nausea and decreased by colds.

● **sweating sickness** ▶ An illness that devastated Renaissance Europe in several epidemics. It was characterized by copious sweating, high fever, pains in the extremities and over the heart, and breathlessness and was often fatal. It may have been a severe form of ▷influenza.

● **swede** ▶ An annual or biennial herbaceous plant, ▷*Brassica napus napobrassica*, growing to a height of 1 m, with deeply lobed leaves and yellow flowers. It is cultivated for its fleshy edible taproot, which is yellow, white, or purplish; this is eaten as a vegetable and also fed to livestock. The yellow variety is called rutabaga. Family: *Cruciferae*.

● **Sweden, Kingdom of** ▶ (Swedish name: Sverige) A country in N Europe occupying the E part of the Scandinavian peninsula. It borders on the Gulf of Bothnia and the Baltic Sea in the E and S and on the Kattegat and Skagerrak in the SW. Undulating land in the S rises to mountains in the N. There are numerous lakes and approximately half the country is forested.

Economy: Sweden is rich in mineral resources, notably iron ore,

which forms the basis of the country's heavy industry (metalworking, steel, machinery, motor vehicles, and aircraft) and is a major export. Other minerals include lead and zinc. Hydroelectric sources supply a large proportion of Sweden's energy needs but oil, coal, and gas have to be imported. Nuclear power is an important source of energy but owing to environmental concerns it is to be phased out by 2010. The large forests support important pulp and paper industries as well as shipbuilding. There is a thriving fishing industry. Agricultural activities are concentrated in the S, the principal crops being barley, wheat, oats, and potatoes, although there is some livestock raising in the N. Other exports include electrical goods, plastics, pharmaceuticals, and chemicals. Since the recession of the early 1990s governments have cut back Sweden's highly developed welfare state and introduced privatization and other free-market reforms.

History: the area was inhabited from early times by German tribes, the Swedes in the N and the Goths in the S, and its people participated in the exploits of the Vikings. Christianity was introduced in the 9th century but not established until the 12th century. Finland was acquired in the 13th century and the 14th century witnessed the Kalmar Union of Sweden with Denmark and Norway. Independence was achieved in 1523 under Gustavus I Vasa, during whose reign Lutheranism was introduced. In the 17th century, under Gustavus Adolphus, Sweden emerged from the ▷Thirty Years' War as a major European power, a position undermined by the Great ▷Northern War (1700–21). In 1809, during the Napoleonic Wars, Finland was surrendered to Russia. In 1814 Norway was ceded to Sweden, the two countries remaining united until 1905, and in 1818, with the extinction of the ▷Vasa dynasty, a Frenchman, ▷Bernadotte, became Charles XIV John. Sweden remained neutral in both World Wars, and for four decades (1932–76) was dominated politically by the Social Democrats, who created a mixed economy and a comprehensive welfare state. On the accession of Carl XVI Gustaf in 1975 a new constitution reduced the power of the monarchy. In 1976 a centre-right government led by Thorbjörn Fälldin (1926–) came to power. The Social Democrats led by Olof ▷Palme won the 1982 elections; after Palme's assassination in 1986 Ingvar Carlsson became prime minister. In 1991 a centre-right government was formed under Carl Bildt and began a process of reforming the economy and welfare state. Following elections in 1994, Carlsson again became prime minister; he was succeeded by Göran Persson in 1996. In 1995 Sweden joined the EU. A further Social Democrat-led coalition was formed after elections in 1998.

Kingdom of Sweden

Head of state	King Carl XVI Gustaf
Official language	Swedish
Official currency	krona of 100 øre
Area	449 964 sq km (173 732 sq mi)
Population (1997 est)	8 863 000
Capital and main port	Stockholm

● **Swedenborg, Emanuel** ▶ (1688–1772) Swedish scientist, mystic, and philosopher. As an official on the Swedish Board of Mines (1716–47) he did pioneering work in magnetic theory and crystallography but later tried to show by scientific and logical analysis that the universe was of spiritual origin. After 1743 his ideas became more mystical in accordance with visions that he claimed to have had. His work includes *Arcana Coelestia* (1756), *The New Jerusalem and Its Heavenly Doctrine* (1758), and *Divine Love and Wisdom* (1763). The sect called the New Jerusalem Church (*or* Swedenborgians) was founded by his followers in London in 1787.

● **Swedish** ▶ A language belonging to the ▷Scandinavian branch of the North ▷Germanic group. It is the official language of Sweden and is spoken by a minority of the population of Finland, where it is also officially recognized. The standard literary form is based mainly on the dialect of Stockholm known as Svea.

● **sweet briar** ▶ A stiffly branched prickly fragrant ▷rose, *Rosa rubiginosa* (or *R. eglanteria*), also called eglantine. Found in scrub and chalk grassland across the N hemisphere, it grows to a height of 2 m and has bright-pink flowers.

● **sweet corn** ▷*See* maize.

● **sweeteners** ▶ Substances other than sugar used as ▷food additives, usually for diabetics, weight-watchers, etc., who need or wish to avoid sucrose products. Most are several hundred times sweeter than sucrose and provide no energy or bulk. The most widely used is ▷saccharin; others include aspartame (aspartyl-phenylalanine methyl ester), which is used in drinks, etc., and under the tradename Canderel, and thaumatin (a protein from the African fruit *Thaumatococcus danielli*). ▷Cyclamates were formally used for this purpose but are now banned because of their side-effects, while acesulphame-K is still in use in some countries but is banned in the USA. Many artificial sweeteners are banned from baby foods and some people have allergies to specific sweeteners.

● **sweet gale** ▶ A widely distributed shrub, *Myrica gale*, also called bog myrtle, that grows to a height of 60–250 cm in bogs and wet heaths. It produces reddish-brown catkins and the leaves yield an aromatic resin used in medicines. Family: *Myricaceae*.

● **sweet gum** ▶ A tree, *Liquidambar styraciflua*, native to E North America. Up to 45 m high, it has triangular-lobed leaves, small greenish flowers, and spiky fruits and yields a useful timber (satin walnut). The oriental sweet gum (*L. orientalis*), of SW Asia, is the chief source of ▷storax, a fragrant balsam. Family: *Hamamelidaceae*.

● **sweet pea** ▶ An annual climbing herb, *Lathyrus odoratus*, native to Sicily and widely cultivated as a garden ornamental. The scented flower consists of a large petal (the standard) with two lateral wing petals and a front keel petal. Many colour varieties have been developed. The fruit is a hairy pod, about 5 cm long. Family: ▷*Leguminosae*.

● **sweet potato** ▶ An annual herb, *Ipomoea batatas*, native to tropical America and widely cultivated for its starchy edible tubers (swollen roots), which are reddish-brown with white or orange flesh. The trailing stems bear pinkish flowers and, after a growing season of 4–5 months, the tubers are lifted and cooked like potatoes or yams. Family: *Convolvulaceae*.

● **sweetsop** ▶ A small tree, *Annona squamosa*, also called sugar apple, native to tropical America and cultivated for its yellowish-green edible fruits. The yellow flesh is soft and sweet and makes a tasty dessert. Family: *Annonaceae*.

● **sweet william** ▶ A usually biennial herb, *Dianthus barbatus*, native to S Europe and widely cultivated as a garden ornamental. Growing to a height of 30–70 cm, sweet williams produce dense flower heads, coloured red or pink in the wild but of various shades and patterns in cultivated varieties. Family: *Caryophyllaceae*.

● **Sweyn I Forkbeard** ▶ (d. 1014) King of Denmark (c. 986–1014). After conquering Norway in 1000, Sweyn's regular raids on SE England to avenge Ethelred's massacre of Danes in 1002 culminated in an invasion in the course of which he died. He was the father of ▷Canute II.

● **swift** ▶ A bird belonging to a widely distributed family (*Apodidae*; 75 species). 9–23 cm long, swifts have grey or brown plumage with white markings; a wide slightly curved bill, and forked tail. With scimitar-shaped wings and a high-speed flight that may reach 110 km per hour (nearly 70 mph), they spend much of their time flying, capturing insects and even mating and sleeping on the wing. Order: *Apodiformes* (swifts, hummingbirds, etc.).

● **Swift, Graham** ▶ (1946–) British novelist and short-story writer. His novels include *The Sweet Shop Owner* (1980), *Waterland* (1983), *Out of this World* (1988), and *Last Orders* (1995), which won the 1996 Booker Prize.

● **Swift, Jonathan** ▶ (1667–1745) Anglo-Irish clergyman, poet, and satirist. Born in Dublin, he became an Anglican priest in 1695 and served as secretary to Sir William Temple in England, where he met Hester Johnson (1681–1728), the "Stella" of his letters recounting his life in London and later collected as *Journal to Stella* (1710–13). He was also close to Esther Vanhomrigh (1690–1723), whom he called "Vanessa" in his writings. While in England, he wrote the satire *A Tale of a Tub* (1704) and became the leading Tory political journalist from about 1710. After the accession of George I in 1714 and the fall of the Tories, he returned to Dublin, where he had been appointed dean of

Jonathan Swift ▶ An 18th-century engraving showing the great satirist as dean of St Patrick's Cathedral in Dublin. Swift spent the last 30 years of his life in Ireland, where he became a popular hero for his savage attacks on English misrule in such pamphlets as *A Modest Proposal* (1729).

St Patrick's Cathedral. During this period he concerned himself with Irish affairs and wrote his satirical masterpiece, *Gulliver's Travels* (1726), the story of an imaginary voyage. His last years were clouded by illness and mental decay.

● **swiftlet** ▶ A small ▷swift belonging to a genus (*Collocalia*; 15–20 species) occurring in SE Asia and Australia. 9–15 cm long, swiftlets use echolocation to navigate in the caves where they nest; their nests, made chiefly of saliva, are the main ingredient of bird's nest soup.

● **swift moth** ▶ A moth belonging to the widely distributed family *Hepialidae* (about 300 species), also called ghost moth. The adults lack a proboscis and are unable to feed. The caterpillars feed underground on roots, and the pupae move to the surface before the adults emerge.

● **swim bladder** ▶ (gas bladder *or* air bladder) A gas-filled sac by means of which the buoyancy of most ▷bony fishes can be regulated. Air can be taken into the bladder, which lies above the gut, through a duct leading from the pharynx; alternatively gas can be extracted from capillary blood vessels. By these means the pressure in the bladder and hence the relative density of the fish can be adjusted according to the depth at which it is swimming. The lungs of air-breathing vertebrates and the swim bladder of fish evolved from a common structure; in ▷lungfish the swim bladder is modifed as a lung.

● **swimming** ▶ Moving through water by means of leg and arm strokes, popular for recreation and sport. Major competitive events, held in pools 50 m (55 yd) long, include freestyle races (the crawl—invented in Australia—is invariably used) over 100, 200, 400, 800, and 1500 m and the 4 × 100 m and 4 × 200 m relay; breaststroke, butterfly, and backstroke races over 100 and 200 m; and medley races over 200 and 400 m and 4 × 100 m relay. The most popular marathon swim is across the English Channel (first swum in 1875).

● **Swinburne, Algernon Charles** ▶ (1837–1909) British poet. His poetry, especially in the first volume of *Poems and Ballads* (1866), is characterized by sensuous flowing rhythms and imagery. He supported republican movements in Europe and rebelled against conventional British morality. His alcoholism led to the collapse of his health, and from 1879 he was cared for by his friend, the critic Theodore Watts-Dunton (1832–1914).

● **Swindon** ▶ 1. 51 34N 1 47W A town in S England, in Swindon unitary authority, Wiltshire. It developed around the workshops of the former Great Western Railway and has a railway museum. Considerable expansion has taken place since the 1960s: in the 1980s and 1990s Swindon was one of the fastest growing towns in Europe. Railway engineering is still a major employer but there are now various industries (including high technology and motor vehicles) as well as financial and other services. Population (1991): 145 236. 2. A unitary authority in S England, in Wiltshire. Area: 230 sq km (89 sq mi). Population (1996 est): 174 600.

● **swine fever** ► An infectious virus disease of pigs. In young pigs the disease is usually acute, with fever, loss of appetite, lethargy, diarrhoea, and distressed breathing, resulting in death. In older pigs the symptoms are less plain. Animals are treated with antiserum and antibiotics to combat secondary infection. Thorough boiling of swill is essential to prevent contamination. In the UK outbreaks must be reported to the authorities and infected animals are slaughtered.

● **swing** ► A style of ▷jazz popular in the 1930s. The original jazz band was expanded to include the saxophone and additional cornets and trombones, making an average swing band of 15 players. Colourful orchestrations replaced the improvisational qualities of early jazz, and the swing bands of Benny Goodman, Duke Ellington, and Glenn Miller functioned chiefly as dance bands.

● **swing wing** ► A hinged aircraft wing that provides a traditional configuration for take-off and landing but folds in to form a delta wing for supersonic flight. Technically known as a **variable geometry wing**, it was invented by Sir Barnes ▷Wallis and first used on the F111. □aircraft (military).

● **switch grass** ► A perennial pasture ▷grass, *Panicum virgatum*, which is a major component of the North American prairie flora. It forms clumps, 1–2 m tall, and is sometimes used to control erosion because of its penetrating underground stems.

● **Swithin, St** ► (d. 862) English churchman. A counsellor to Kings Egbert and Ethelwulf, he was appointed Bishop of Winchester in 852. His tomb in Winchester Cathedral has become a famous shrine and according to legend the weather conditions on his feast day, 15 July, continue for 40 days.

● **Switzerland, Confederation of** ► (French name: Suisse; German name: Schweiz; Italian name: Svizzera) A small landlocked country in central Europe. Undulating land in the N rises to the Jura Mountains in the W and the high peaks of the Alps in the S, reaching heights of over 4500 m (14 500 ft). The River Rhine and Lake Constance form most of the N and E boundaries, while in the S the River Rhône flows through Lake Geneva to the French border. The majority of the population is German, with large French and Italian minorities; there is a very small Romansch population.
Economy: although lacking in mineral wealth, Switzerland owes much of its prosperity to its terrain and central European position. The latter (together with Switzerland's tradition of political and military neutrality) has led to its development as a centre for trade, banking, and insurance, while the magnificent scenery has long been a major tourist attraction. The fast-flowing rivers of the Alps provide abundant hydroelectric power and heavy industries, such as engineering and chemicals, have been developed as well as the smaller traditional industries (watches and clocks, precision instruments, and jewellery). Electronics, pharmaceuticals, and publishing are also important. Agricultural products include dairy goods, grains, and fruit and vegetables, and there is an important wine industry. The principal exports are machinery, watches, chemicals, and textiles.
History: its Celtic inhabitants (the Helvetii) were conquered by the Romans in the 1st century BC; the region was overrun by German tribes in the 5th century AD and became part of the Holy Roman Empire in the 10th century. In 1291 Uri, Schwyz, and Nidwalden formed the Everlasting League, which is traditionally regarded as the origin of the Swiss Federation. By 1499 the Federation had achieved virtual independence of the Empire and in the 16th century it became an important centre of the Reformation, notably under Zwingli in Zürich. In 1648, at the conclusion of the Thirty Years' War, its independence was formally recognized by the European powers. The French conquered Switzerland in 1798, establishing the Helvetian Republic, but after Napoleon's fall (1815) the Congress of Vienna guaranteed Swiss neutrality. Religious conflict led to war between Protestant and Roman Catholic cantons and a modified constitution (1848) by which Switzerland became a unified federal state. It maintained its neutrality through both World Wars and has become the headquarters of many international organizations. Switzerland's postwar prosperity has been assisted by migrant workers (*see* migration, human) the repatriation of whom was rejected in a referendum in 1975. Another controversial issue was the enfranchisement of women, which was finally achieved in 1971. Switzerland is a member of the ▷European Free Trade Association but the electorate rejected membership of the European Economic Area in 1992 and voted against joining the EU in 2001. Following intense international pressure, the Swiss banks admitted holding the property of Jews murdered in the Holocaust and agreed (1998) to pay some $1.25 billion in reparations. Switzerland is governed by a federal council of seven councillors, elected for four years, from whom a president and vice president are elected yearly. In 2002 Switzerland ended its long tradition of isolationism by deciding to join the UN.

Confederation of Switzerland

Head of state	President Moritz Leuenberger
Official languages	French, German, Italian, and Romansch
Official currency	Swiss franc of 100 centimes
Area	41 288 sq km (15 941 sq mi)
Population (2001 est)	7 222 000
Capital	Bern

● **sword** ► A weapon consisting of a cutting or stabbing blade on a short handle, used in hand-to-hand fighting. Of uncertain origin, the sword evolved in the Bronze Age. The Roman soldier's principal weapon was a short, two-edged, iron-bladed sword (*gladius*). In the middle ages heavier and longer swords, some needing to be wielded with two hands, developed in response to heavier armour. The advent of gunpowder forced foot soldiers gradually to abandon swords, but cavalry units until the 20th century fought with long often curved blades. ▷*See also* fencing.

● **swordfish** ► A food and game fish, *Xiphias gladius*, related to tuna and found in all tropical and temperate seas. It has an elongated body, up to 4.6 m long, a triangular front dorsal fin, no pelvic fins, and an elongated swordlike snout used to slash at shoaling fish on which it feeds. It is the only member of its family (*Xiphiidae*).

● **swordtail** ► A tropical freshwater fish of the genus *Xiphophorus*, especially *X. helleri*. It has an elongated body, up to 13 cm long; males have a swordlike extension of the lower lobe of the tail fin. Swordtails are green with a red stripe on each side, but have been bred in other colours for aquaria. Family: *Poeciliidae*; order: *Atheriniformes*.

● **Sybaris** ► 39 39N 16 20E A Greek settlement founded about 700 BC near present-day Terranova di Sibari in S Italy. Territorial expansion and a monopoly of Etruscan trade brought prosperity and Sybarites were famous for their luxurious lives (hence the word sybaritic, meaning pleasure seeking). In 510 and again in 457 Sybaris was destroyed by its neighbour Croton. Rebuilt a third time, its inhabitants were subsequently exiled by the Athenians.

● **sycamore** ► A large ▷maple tree, *Acer pseudoplatanus*, native to central and S Europe and widely grown elsewhere. Up to 30 m tall, it has five-lobed leaves and produces clusters of winged □fruits. The wood is used for violin cases, carvings, and furniture.

● **Sydenham's chorea** ▷*See* chorea.

● **Sydney** ► 33 55S 151 10E The oldest and largest city in Australia, the capital of New South Wales, situated on Port Jackson inlet. It is essentially a commercial, cultural, and financial centre dependent on its port for its prosperity. The N side of Port Jackson is predominantly residential, industry being located to the S. The two shores are connected by Sydney Harbour Bridge (1932), the second largest single span bridge in the world, and Glebe Island Bridge (1995), the longest suspension bridge in Australia. Industry is diverse and includes shipbuilding, chemicals, and the manufacture of consumer goods; Botany Bay is developing as the main industrial area. The chief exports are wheat and wool. A cultural centre, Sydney possesses three universities, including Sydney University (1850), and the world-famous Sydney Opera House (opened 1973; □architecture), designed by Jørn Utzon as the result of an international competition in 1955. There are abundant sports facilities, including many nearby beaches.
History: a penal settlement (Sydney Cove) was established by Capt Arthur ▷Phillip at Port Jackson (in 1788). Under the governorship of Lachlan ▷Macquarie (1810–21), aided by a convict-architect, Francis Greenway, it developed into a thriving town and grew rapidly be-

tween 1850 and 1890. In 1994 bush fires caused extensive damage to the suburbs. Area: 1735 sq km (670 sq mi). Population (1995 est): 3 772 000.

● **Sydney** ▶ 46 10N 60 10W A city and port in SE Canada, in Nova Scotia on Cape Breton Island. Founded in 1785, it is located on a major coalfield and has an important steel industry. Population (1992 est): 26 063.

● **syenite** ▶ A range of coarse-grained intrusive rocks (*see* igneous rock) consisting mainly of alkali feldspar or feldspathoids, together with hornblende and biotite.

● **Sykes-Picot Agreement** ▶ (1916) A secret agreement between the UK and France, negotiated by Sir Mark Sykes (1879–1919) and François Georges-Picot. It arranged, with Russian approval, for the post-World War I partition of the Ottoman (Turkish) Empire between the Allied powers. The agreement was eventually shelved but disclosure of the scheme by the Russian revolutionary government caused considerable controversy.

● **Syktyvkar** ▶ 61 42N 50 45E A city in NW Russia, the capital of the Komi Republic. Founded in the 16th century, it became a place of exile for criminals and political prisoners. Notable industries are timber and paper and pulp manufacturing. Population (1995 est): 229 000.

● **Sylhet** ▶ 24 53N 91 51E A town in NE Bangladesh, in the Surma Valley. The former capital of a Hindu kingdom conquered by Muslims in 1384, it is the chief town of a tea-growing region and has large natural-gas reserves. Population (1991): 114 284.

● **syllabaries** ▶ Writing systems in which each symbol represents a syllable in the language rather than a concept (*compare* ideographic writing systems). The only major language using a syllabary today is Japanese. However, the North ▷Semitic alphabet, from which all the world's major alphabets are derived, almost certainly developed out of a syllabary, in which the symbols came to represent speech sounds rather than concepts as in ideography.

● **syllogism** ▶ A form of deductive argument, rules for the validity of which were developed by ▷Aristotle. Each syllogism must be composed of three propositions—two premises and a conclusion—and one of its forms may thus be schematically represented: "All As are Bs. All Cs are As. Therefore all Cs are Bs." Since the conclusion that all Cs are Bs "follows" from the premises, one cannot without self-contradiction assert the premises and deny the conclusion, and this is true of all forms of valid syllogism.

● **Sylvanus** ▷*See* Pan.

● **Sylvester II** ▶ (Gerbert of Aurillac; c. 940–1003) Pope (999–1033), who was also a mathematician and astronomer. He attempted to reform abuses and organized the Churches of Poland and Hungary. His learning was popularly credited to have been acquired by magic.

● **symbiosis** ▶ Any close relationship between individuals of two different species of organisms. The term can therefore include parasitism (*see* parasite), ▷commensalism, and ▷inquilinism but is often restricted to—and used synonymously with—**mutualism**, in which both partners (symbionts) benefit from the association. An example of such a symbiotic relationship is provided by a sea anemone (*Adamsia paliata*), which lives attached to the snail shell inhabited by the hermit crab (*Eupagurus prideauxii*). The anemone protects and camouflages the crab, from which it receives food and transport.

● **Symbolists** ▶ A group of French poets in the late 19th century whose poetry, which they regarded as a means of transcending reality, was determined by their belief in the power of words and images to evoke responses in the subconscious mind. They included ▷Mallarmé, ▷Verlaine, and ▷Rimbaud, and acknowledged the influence of ▷Baudelaire. They were precursors of the Surrealist movement and had a profound influence on poets in Russia and many other countries.

● **Symonds, John Addington** ▶ (1840–93) British art historian and critic. He suffered from tuberculosis, and from 1877 lived mostly in Switzerland. His major work is *The Renaissance in Italy* (7 vols, 1875–86). He also wrote poetry, travel books, and literary biographies.

● **Symons, Arthur (William)** ▶ (1865–1945) British poet and critic. He coedited the literary journal *Savoy* (1896) with Aubrey Beardsley and wrote lyrical poetry, the best of which he published in *Poems* (2 vols, 1902). A disciple of Walter ▷Pater, he wrote the influential study *The Symbolist Movement in Literature* (1899).

● **symphonic poem** ▶ (or tone poem) A one-movement orchestral composition based on a literary, dramatic, or pictorial theme. The symphonic poem was invented by ▷Liszt, who composed a series of such works, the most famous of which is *Les Préludes* (1854), after Lamartine's poem *Méditations Poétiques*. Smetana, Richard Strauss, Tchaikovsky, Sibelius, Respighi, and Elgar, among others, composed notable works in this genre.

● **symphony** ▶ An orchestral composition, usually in four movements. The classical symphony evolved in the mid-18th century and was perfected by Haydn and Mozart: the fast first movement was generally in ▷sonata form, the second was slow and expressive, the third a ▷minuet and trio, and the fourth fast. Beethoven extended the formal and emotional range of the symphony, introducing a chorus and soloists in the last movement of his ninth symphony. In the 19th century Schubert, Schumann, Mendelssohn, Brahms, Dvořák, and Tchaikovsky all wrote symphonies broadly in this tradition. In the hands of such composers as Bruckner and Mahler the symphony underwent further enlargement: Mahler's eighth symphony (1907) requires a thousand performers. Sibelius developed a concentrated approach to symphonic writing: his seventh symphony (1924) is in one movement. In the 20th century Nielsen, Shostakovich, Vaughan Williams, Henze, Schnittke, and others all developed the symphony in differing ways.

● **synagogue** ▶ A Jewish place of worship. The synagogue probably originated during the ▷Babylonian exile as a substitute for the Temple at Jerusalem. In antiquity it was a public meeting place, devoted mainly to the reading and exposition of the ▷Torah. It is now primarily a house of prayer, but often has a communal centre attached. The principal feature is the cupboard (Ark) containing the Torah scrolls. A synagogue service requires a quorum (*minyan*) of ten adult males. In Orthodox synagogues the men sit downstairs and the women sit upstairs behind a screen; singing and chanting are unaccompanied by musical instruments. In non-Orthodox synagogues the sexes are not separated and musical accompaniment is allowed. Continental and US Reform Judaism prefer the term "temple."

● **synapse** ▶ The meeting point between one nerve cell and another (*see* neurone). The nerve impulse, as it arrives at the end of one nerve process, causes a chemical neurotransmitter (e.g. ▷acetylcholine or noradrenaline) to be released. This reaches receptors on the opposite neurone and produces a new nerve impulse.

● **synchrocyclotron** ▶ A type of ▷cyclotron in which the frequency of the accelerating electric field can be varied to compensate for the relativistic increase in the mass of the accelerated particles. This enables energies of up to 500 MeV to be obtained.

● **synchrotron** ▶ A particle ▷accelerator, similar to the ▷cyclotron, in which protons or electrons are accelerated in a circular path by an alternating electric field. The frequency of the field is synchronized with the energy of the particles to counteract their relativistic increase in the mass. Proton energies of several hundred GeV have been attained in these devices. ▷*See also* bevatron.

● **synchrotron radiation** ▶ Electromagnetic radiation emitted in certain directions by a charged particle when the presence of a magnetic field confines its motion to a circle. The particle has to be moving at speeds comparable to that of light for a noticeable amount of radiation to be emitted. Therefore a high magnetic field is needed. Such fields are used in ▷synchrotrons, a type of particle ▷accelerator. The emission of radio-frequency radiation also occurs from interstellar gas clouds in radio galaxies and, by analogy, is also known as synchrotron radiation.

● **syncline** ▶ A trough-shaped fold or downfold in folded rock strata, the strata dipping towards a central axis (*compare* anticline). The youngest rocks occur in the core unless very complex deformation has occurred. Where the strata dip inwards from all directions the resulting feature is called a structural basin.

● **syndicalism** ▶ A type of ▷socialism, advocated by ▷Sorel, under which the workers, not the state, would take over the productive resources of industry. Syndicalists were widely influential in Europe from the late 19th century until World War I. They worked through industrial action, rather than political or parliamentary means, to substitute for the state a federation of functional economic units (syndicats).

● **Synge, John Millington** ▶ (1871–1909) Anglo-Irish dramatist. Most of his plays, the realism and poetic intensity of which contributed greatly to the ▷Irish Literary Renaissance, were inspired by his experience of life in an isolated Irish community, recorded in *The Aran Islands* (1907). His best-known play, *The Playboy of the Western World* (1907), caused riots at its first performance at the Abbey Theatre, Dublin.

● **synodic period** ▶ The average time taken by a planet or satellite to return to the same point in its orbit, relative to the sun, as seen from earth or from the satellite's primary (i.e. the body it orbits). It is therefore the interval between ▷oppositions or between identical ▷phases.

● **Synoptic Gospels** ▷*See* Gospels.

● **synovitis** ▶ Inflammation of the synovium—the membrane lining the joints. This usually results from mild injuries to joints and causes pain and swelling.

● **syntax** ▷*See* grammar.

● **synthesizer** ▶ A device that can reproduce the sounds of conventional instruments electronically or produce a variety of artificial tones. Electronic oscillators produce a range of signals, which after amplification and appropriate filtering are converted to sound waves, of which some have the characteristic resonances of musical instruments, some are pure tones, and some are arbitrary combinations of sounds. Individual circuits can be plugged in and out by the player, enabling a wide range of sounds to be produced. The **Moog synthesizer**, invented by Robert Moog (1934–) in 1965, can play one note at a time and is controlled by a keyboard. More recent **polyphonic synthesizers** can be programmed to produce any number of different tones simultaneously.

● **synthetism** ▶ A style of painting developed by ▷Gauguin and Émile Bernard (1868–1941) in Brittany in 1888. The visual arts' counterpart to the Symbolist literary movement, synthetism sought to express an idea or emotion through formal correspondences of line and colour. It was also known as cloisonnisme, since its use of rich unmodulated colour contained within thick black contours resembled ▷cloisonné enamelwork, as well as Japanese prints. Synthetism greatly influenced the art of the ▷Nabis.

● **syphilis** ▶ A sexually transmitted disease caused by the ▷spirochaete bacterium *Treponema pallidum*, which in nearly all cases is transmitted during sexual intercourse. The effects of the disease occur in three stages. In primary syphilis chancres (hard ulcers) appear after about 25 days at the site of infection (usually the genitals). The chancre disappears after about eight weeks, but weeks or months later the rash of secondary syphilis occurs. Arthritis, meningitis, and hepatitis may also occur at this stage. Without treatment the tertiary stage of syphilis may appear up to 30 years later and give rise to a variety of symptoms, including large tumour-like masses (gummas) in many organs, heart disease, blindness, and madness and paralysis (general paralysis of the insane). The disease can be passed on to an unborn child by an infected mother (congenital syphilis). Syphilis can be treated with penicillin. Several blood tests are available for diagnosing the disease (*see also* Wassermann, August von).

● **Syracuse** ▶ (Italian name: Siracusa) 37 04N 15 18E A seaport in Italy, in SE Sicily on the Ionian Sea. Founded by Greeks from Corinth in 734 BC, it became an important cultural centre in the 5th century. The Greek poet Theocritus and the Greek mathematician and scientist Archimedes were born here. In 212 BC Syracuse fell to the Romans after a three-year siege. There are many ancient remains, including a Greek temple, a Roman amphitheatre, and a fortress built by Dionysius I. Today Syracuse is a processing centre for agricultural produce, with some light industry. Population (1994 est): 127 496.

● **Syracuse** ▶ 43 03N 76 10W A city in the USA, in New York state. Founded in 1788, it had a thriving saltmaking industry until after the US Civil War. In 1819 the Erie Canal was opened and the railways followed, attracting many industries. Today its many manufactures include aircraft parts, typewriters, and chemicals. Syracuse University was established here in 1849. Population (1996 est): 155 865.

● **Syr Darya, River** ▶ (ancient name: Jaxartes) A river in central Asia rising in the Tian Shan and flowing mainly W through Uzbekistan and Kazakhstan to the Aral Sea. It is the longest river in Central Asia. Length: 2900 km (1800 mi).

Syria ▶ Traditional houses near Aleppo.

● **Syria** ▶ (official name: Syrian Arab Republic) A country in the Middle East, bordering on the Mediterranean Sea. In the W the Ghab depression (an extension of the ▷Great Rift Valley) runs N–S, separated from the coast by a mountain range. To the E of this is plateau of steppe and desert with some mountains. The main fertile areas, in which the population is concentrated, are the coastal strip and the basin of the River Euphrates (*see* Fertile Crescent). Nomads live in the centre and E; ethnic minorities include Kurds (in the NE), Turks, Armenians, Assyrians, Circassians, and Jews. The population is predominantly Muslim (mainly Sunnites with some Shiites).
Economy: largely agricultural; cotton and grain are the main crops and livestock are kept. Tobacco is also grown. The area of cultivable land has been greatly extended by government irrigation projects. Natural resources include oil, natural gas, phosphates, and salt. Industries, mainly developed since the 1940s, include food processing, oil refining, and the manufacture of textiles, leather goods, clothing, plastics, and chemicals. Syria has a planned socialist economy; much of its industry is nationalized, and much land has been redistributed in favour of the peasants (1958, 1963, and 1966).
History: before the 20th century Syria extended over the area that is now Lebanon, Israel, Jordan, W Iraq, and N Saudi Arabia. In ancient times the ▷Amorites settled here and later ▷Phoenicia flourished. It was frequently conquered; Islam was introduced by conquering Arabs (c. 640 AD) and the ▷Umayyads established the caliphate at Damascus. Subsequent conquerors included the ▷Fatimids and the Crusaders (many of whose fortresses remain). From 1517 until World War I it was part of the Ottoman Empire. In 1920 it became part of a French mandate, from which Lebanon was separated in 1926. Demands for Syrian independence were finally satisfied in 1946. From the late 1940s until the early 1970s Syria's history was marked by economic growth, political instability with many coups, and militant participation in the Arab-Israeli Wars. It united briefly with Egypt in the United Arab Republic (1958–61) but withdrew because of Egyptian domination. In 1971 Syria, Libya, and Egypt united loosely in the Federation of Arab Republics but disagreement with Egypt developed

over its attitude towards Israel. Lt Gen Hafiz al-▷Assad came to power following a military coup in 1970 and created a one-party state. A rising of Muslim extremists in 1979–82 was suppressed with great brutality. From 1976 Syria intervened in the civil war in Lebanon, at first as a mediator but later, after the Israeli invasion of 1982, as an active supporter of certain Muslim factions. Syria's military presence in Lebanon was formalized by treaty in 1991. During the 1970s and 1980s Syria's foreign policy was characterized by friendliness to the Soviet Union and other communist states and implacable hostility to Israel. However, after the collapse of communism in 1989–90 Assad improved relations with the West, notably by participating on the Allied side in the 1991 Gulf War. A tentative rapprochement with Israel also began. Assad died in 2000 and was succeeded by his son Bashar al-Assad. Syria is a member of the Arab League.

Syria

Head of state	President Bashar al-Assad
Official language	Arabic
Official currency	Syrian pound of 100 piastres
Area	185 680 sq km (71 772 sq mi)
Population (1999 est)	15 727 000
Capital	Damascus

● **Syriac** ▶ A ▷Semitic language based on the dialect of ▷Aramaic spoken in Edessa (now Urfa, SE Turkey). It became an important literary and liturgical language in which many scriptures, biblical commentaries, hymns, etc., were written during the 3rd to the 7th centuries AD when Edessa was an important Christian centre.

● **syringa** ▷See lilac; mock orange.

● **syrinx** ▶ The vocal organ of birds, located at the base of the windpipe. Air from the lungs vibrates membranes within a resonating chamber. Muscular tension alters pitch, and the two halves of the syrinx can produce different notes simultaneously. ▷See also bird song.

● **Syros** ▶ (Modern Greek name: Síros) A Greek island in the S Aegean Sea, in the Cyclades. The chief town, Hermopolis, is the capital of the Cyclades. Area: 85 sq km (33 sq mi). Population (1991 est): 16 008.

● **systole** ▷See blood pressure; heart.

● **Szabó, Istvan** ▶ (1938–) Hungarian film director. In *The Age of Illusions* (1964) and *25 Fireman's Street* (1973) he addressed the problems of postwar Hungary. Later films include *Mephisto* (1981), *Colonel Redl* (1985), *Sweet Emma, Dear Böbe* (1991), and *Meeting Venus* (1992).

● **Szczecin** ▶ (German name: Stettin) 53 25N 14 32E A city in the extreme NW of Poland, on the River Oder 65 km (40 mi) upstream from the Baltic Sea. It is a major port, the chief export being coal. Shipbuilding is the principal industry; others include engineering, chemicals, and the manufacture of textiles.

History: it became a member of the Hanseatic League in 1360. Seized by the Swedes (1648) it passed to Prussia in 1720, remaining under German control until being ceded to Poland (1945). It suffered severe damage during World War II but has since been rebuilt. Population (1996 est): 419 300.

● **Szechwan** ▷See Sichuan.

● **Szeged** ▶ 46 15N 20 09E A city in S Hungary, on the River Tisza. Replanned with concentric and radiating streets after a flood in 1879, it has a university (1872) and considerable industry. Population (1997 est): 166 000.

● **Székesfehérvár** ▶ 47 11N 18 22E A town in W central Hungary. It was the capital of the Hungarian kingdom from the 10th until the 16th century. It was almost totally destroyed in World War II. Population (1997 est): 106 000.

● **Szell, George** ▶ (1897–1970) Hungarian conductor. He studied in Vienna, conducted in various German opera houses, and went to the USA in 1942. In 1946 he became permanent conductor of the Cleveland Orchestra, a post he held until his death.

● **Szent-Györgyi, Albert (von Nagyrapolt)** ▶ (1893–1986) US biochemist, born in Hungary. He identified the role of ascorbic acid in living cells and later showed it to be ▷vitamin C. Szent-Györgyi determined certain organic compounds involved in the breakdown of carbohydrates by cells to produce energy—a prelude to ▷Krebs' major discoveries in this field. He also found that the proteins actin and myosin, working in conjunction with ATP, formed the basis of the contractile apparatus of muscles. Szent-Györgyi was awarded a Nobel Prize (1937).

● **Szewinska, Irena** ▶ (1946–) Polish sprinter. At 18 she won two silver medals in the 1964 Olympics, in the 1968 Olympics she won the 200 metres, and in the 1976 Olympics she set a world record in the 400 metres.

● **Szilard, Leo** ▶ (1898–1964) US physicist, born in Hungary, who in 1934, while working in England, conceived the idea of a self-sustaining nuclear chain reaction. Szilard emigrated to the USA in 1937 and when he heard of ▷Hahn and ▷Meitner's work on the fission of uranium, recognized its significance in terms of nuclear weapons. He joined ▷Teller in persuading Einstein to write to Roosevelt to warn him of the possibility that Germany might make an atom bomb first. During World War II he actually worked on the atom bomb, but later regretted its development and pressed for the abolition of all nuclear weapons.

● **Szymanowski, Karol** ▶ (1882–1937) Polish composer. He studied at the Warsaw conservatoire, where in 1926 he became director. The influences on his music include Chopin, Liszt, Scriabin, Debussy, and Polish folk music. His works include three symphonies, a *Symphonie Concertante* (for piano and orchestra; 1931–32) two violin concertos, the ballet *Harnasie* (1926), the opera *King Roger* (1920–24), and *Mythes* (for violin and piano; 1915).

T

● **Tabari, Muhammad ibn Jarir al-** ▶ (838–923 AD) Arab historian. His works include an important commentary on the Koran and the *Annals*, a history of the world from the Creation to the year 915 AD.

● **tabasco** ▶ A hot red pepper or sauce made from the entire fruits of a variety of the South American plant ▷*Capsicum frutescens* and used to flavour soups, stews, curries, etc. Family: *Solanaceae*.

● **tabernacle** ▶ **1.** The portable sanctuary or "tent of meeting" used by the Israelites in the wilderness (Exodus 25–31, 33, 35–40). **2.** The English name of the *sukkah*, a hut made of greenery, used by Jews in homes and synagogues during the autumn **Feast of Tabernacles** (*sukkot*), which celebrates God's deliverance of the Israelites from Egypt and his care of them in the wilderness. For seven days it is customary to eat in the *sukkah*.

● **Table Bay** ▶ 33 50S 18 25E An inlet, some 10 km (6 mi) long, of the Atlantic Ocean, in SW Africa. The Dutch settled here in 1652, founding Cape Town on the S shore. The bay and Cape Town itself are overlooked by the flat-topped **Table Mountain** (1082 m; 3550 ft). The cloud that frequently hangs above the mountain is called the "Table-cloth."

● **table tennis** ▶ (*or* Ping-Pong) An indoor game for two or four players that originated in England in the late 19th century from ▷real tennis. It is played on a table 2.74 m (9 ft) long and 1.52 m (5 ft) wide, divided across its width by a net 15.25 cm (6 in) high and along its length by a line separating right-hand from left-hand half courts for doubles play. The players hit a resilient small hollow plastic ball with a rubber-faced wooden bat. A point is scored when the opponent fails to return the ball after it has bounced once. Each player serves five consecutive points and the winner is the first to reach 21 points with a two-point lead.

● **taboo** ▶ A ritual prohibition relating to things that are considered either sacred, powerful, and dangerous (*see also* totemism) or unclean and polluting. The term is derived from Polynesian *tapu*, forbidden, and may apply to things, animals, plants, people, places, words and names, or actions. Customs of this kind are widespread in all societies, but actual practices vary greatly. Certain things may be taboo for all people in a society (as eating pig is for Jews). Other things are taboo for only certain categories of persons (*see* incest). Some things are taboo for particular people at particular times (e.g. in many societies menstruating women are subject to restrictions as to what they may touch).

● **Tabora** ▶ 5 02S 32 50E A town in W central Tanzania. It was an important centre for trade in ivory and slaves; today trade remains significant and includes groundnuts and sunflower seeds. Population (1992 est): 214 000.

● **Tabriz** ▶ 38 05N 46 18E A city in NW Iran, close to the borders of Turkey, Armenia, and Azerbaidzhan. It has several times suffered earthquakes. The most notable buildings are the Blue Mosque (15th century) and the citadel, and Tabriz is famous for its carpets; it is connected by rail to Tehran and Russia and has an airport. Tabriz University was opened in 1949. Population (1994 est): 1 166 203.

● **tachometer** ▶ An instrument for measuring the speed of rotation of a shaft, such as a revolution counter in a car. Centrifugal tachometers measure the force experienced by rotating masses. Others are electrical or magnetic, measuring electrical current or force generated by a small generator in the instrument. The **tachograph** mea-

sures a vehicle's speed and the time for which it is moving, recording these details on a card, disc, or tape. Tacographs are used to record the length of time the driver of a goods vehicle, bus, or coach has been working.

● **tachyon** ▶ A hypothetical particle that travels faster than the speed of light. Such a particle would have either an imaginary rest mass or an imaginary energy and no such particle has ever been detected.

● **Tacitus, Cornelius** ▶ (c. 55–c. 120 AD) Roman historian. After holding various provincial administrative posts he made his reputation as a public orator in Rome and became consul in 97 AD; in 112–13 he was governor of Asia. In 98 he wrote two historical monographs, *Germania* and *Agricola*, the latter an account of his father-in-law's career. His major works, the *Histories* and the *Annals*, survey Roman history during the periods 69–96 AD and 14–68 AD and are noted for their terse style and acute understanding of the men and issues involved. Although claiming impartiality, Tacitus appears to stress the evils of imperial government.

● **Tacna** ▶ 18 00S 70 15W A town in S Peru. It was under Chilean occupation (1883–1929). It serves an agricultural area producing tobacco, cotton, and sugar cane. Population (1993): 172 393.

● **Tacoma** ▶ 47 16N 122 30W A city in the USA, in Washington state on Puget Sound. Founded in 1868, it grew as the terminus of the North Pacific Railroad (1873). The University of Puget Sound was established here in 1888. It is an important port; its industries include timber processing, meat packing, railway workshops, and foundries. Population (1996 est): 179 114.

● **tadpole** ▶ The aquatic larva of frogs and toads. The newly hatched tadpole feeds on vegetation but later becomes carnivorous. The external gills are gradually replaced by internal gills, and after about ten weeks the limbs start to appear, the tail degenerates, the lungs develop, and the circulatory system changes to enable the adult to lead a terrestrial life. Metamorphosis is complete after about three months, depending on the external temperature and available food.

● **tadpole shrimp** ▶ A freshwater crustacean belonging to an order (*Notostraca*) that occurs in North America and the Arctic. Up to 30 mm long, it has a shieldlike carapace, short antennae, 35–70 pairs of appendages, and two long tail filaments. Class: ▷*Branchiopoda*.

● **Tadzhikistan, Republic of** ▶ (*or* Tajikistan) A republic in central Asia. Largely mountainous, it contains the Pamir and Altai ranges in the E and centre; over half the country is above 4000 m (13 124 ft). Below the treeline there are large forests and alpine meadows. Some 59% of the population are ▷Tadzhiks; there are Uzbek (23%) and Russian (10.4%) minorities. *Economy:* mainly agricultural, with livestock and cotton growing. Substantial mineral deposits (including mercury, lead, zinc, and gold) support a mining industry; engineering and textiles are also important. Health resorts have grown up around the country's mineral springs. The economy suffered badly from the civil war of the early 1990s and was only saved from collapse by monetary union with Russia (1994) and substantial foreign loans. A programme of privatization and other reforms is now in place.
History: the region was conquered by Arabs in the 7th century and converted to Islam. Subsequently ruled by the Persians (9th century) and the Uzbeks (from the 15th century), it was taken by Russia in the 1860s. It was a constituent republic of the Soviet Union from 1929

until 1991, when it declared independence. In 1992 violent unrest led to the forced removal of President Rakhmon Nabiyev by an alliance of Islamists and democrats. However, procommunist forces (backed by the Russian army) regained control of the country in 1993. A ceasefire between the ex-communist government and Muslim rebels was signed in 1994 but subsequent elections were boycotted by the opposition and fighting recurred. Peace was secured by a further agreement (1997), which involved a degree of power sharing with the opposition.

Republic of Tadzhikistan

Head of state	President Imamali Rakhmanov
Official language	Tadzhik
Official currency	Tadzhik rouble of 100 tanga
Area	143 100 sq km (55 240 sq mi)
Population (1999 est)	6 213 000
Capital	Dushanbe

● **Tadzhiks** ► An Iranian people of Afghanistan and parts of Turkistan. Muslims, they practise agriculture using irrigation to grow cereals and fruit trees. Trade has also been important traditionally because of their position on the caravan routes between China, India, and Persia. They speak Tadzhik, a form of Persian that is the official language of Tadzhikistan.

● **Taegu** ► 35 52N 128 36E A city in SE South Korea, the capital of North Kyongsang province. An old cultural centre, it is the site of a university (1946). It has an important textile industry. Population (1995): 2 449 139.

● **Taejon** ► 36 20N 127 26E A city in SE South Korea, capital of South Chungchong province. It is an agricultural and industrial centre, with a university (1952). Some 70% of the city was destroyed during the Korean War (1950–53). Population (1995): 1 272 143.

● **taekwondo** ► An oriental form of unarmed combat that originated in Korea. Similar to ▷karate, it includes both kicking and punching.

● **Tafilalt** ► (or Tafilelt) An oasis in SE Morocco, in the Sahara. It stretches for about 50 km (31 mi) along the River Ziz and includes the towns of Erfoud and Rissani.

● **Taft, William Howard** ► (1857–1930) US statesman; Republican president (1909–13). Taft's conservative presidency was characterized by the ▷antitrust acts and high protective tariffs, which cost him Theodore Roosevelt's support, split the Republican vote, and lost the 1912 election to the Democrats. Taft's rulings as chief justice (1921–30) reinforced federal powers. His son **Robert Alphonso Taft** (1889–1953), a senator from 1939, was an unsuccessful candidate for the Republican presidential nomination on four occasions (1940, 1944, 1948, 1952). He introduced the Taft-Hartley Act (1947), which restricted trade unions.

● **Tagalog** ► A people of Luzon and Mindanao islands in the Philippines who speak an ▷Austronesian language. Although less numerous than the speakers of the related language of Cebuano, they tend to dominate in the economic, professional, and political spheres. Tagalog is the basis of the national language and is spoken by the population of the capital, Manila. The rural Tagalog are mainly rice farmers.

● **Taganrog** ► 47 14N 38 55E A port in SW Russia on the Gulf of Taganrog in the Sea of Azov. Its port serves the coalmines of the Donets Basin and industries include steel making. The playwright Chekhov was born here. Population (1995 est): 292 000.

● **Taglioni, Marie** ► (1804–84) Italian ballet dancer. Daughter of a choreographer, she was much admired in such ballets as her father's *La Sylphide* (1832), notably for being the first to dance extensively upon the tips of her toes.

● **Tagore, Rabindranath** ► (1861–1941) Indian poet, philosopher, and teacher. Knighted in 1915, he resigned the honour in 1919 as a protest against the Amritsar massacre. He wrote poetry, drama, and fiction in the Bengali language and was also a celebrated artist and musician. He advocated cultural links between the East and the West

and won the Nobel Prize for Literature in 1913 after the publication in English of *Gitanjali* (1912), a volume of spiritual poetry. His father **Debendranath Tagore** (1817–1905) was a radical religious reformer and teacher. In 1886 he established the "Abode of Peace," a retreat in Bengal made famous by his son as an educational centre.

● **Tagus, River** ► (Portuguese name: Tejo; Spanish name: Tajo) A river in SW Europe. Rising in E central Spain, it flows NW and then SW across Spain and Portugal to Lisbon, where it is crossed by a suspension bridge. Length: 1007 km (626 mi).

● **Tahiti** ► The largest of the Society Islands in the S central Pacific Ocean, in French Polynesia. Mountainous and famous for its beauty, it was Gauguin's home for two years (1891–93). Settled by Polynesians in the 14th century, it was first visited by Europeans in 1767. The London Missionary Society christianized the island by helping the Pomare family to power. It became French in 1842. Tourism is important, and copra, sugar cane, vanilla, and coffee are exported. Area: 1005 sq km (388 sq mi). Population (latest est): 116 000. Chief town: Papeete.

● **tahr** ► A wild goat belonging to the genus *Hemitragus* (3 species), inhabiting forested mountain slopes of S Asia. 60–100 cm high at the shoulder, the large Himalayan tahr (*H. jemlahicus*) and the smaller Nilgiri tahr (*H. hylocrius*) have long coarse shaggy brownish hair; the Arabian tahr (*H. jayakari*) is slender and sandy-coloured.

● **Tai** ► Peoples of SE Asia and China who speak a group of related languages probably belonging to the ▷Sino-Tibetan family. They are traditionally rice cultivators dwelling in villages with elected headmen. The nuclear family is the basic social unit and women have high status. They are mainly Theravada Buddhists, the monks having considerable influence and authority. Major groupings are the Thai or Siamese, the Lao, Shan, and Lu. ▷*See also* Austro-Asiatic languages.

● **Taibei** ▷*See* Taipei.

● **tai chi** ▷*See* Taoism.

● **taiga** ► The coniferous forests, composed chiefly of spruces, pines, and firs, in the N hemisphere in subpolar latitudes. It extends from Norway across Sweden, Finland, and Russia (including Siberia). The coniferous forests of North America, Canada, and Alaska, are also known as taiga.

● **Taika** ► (Japanese: great change; 645–50 AD) The period associated with the first major upheaval in Japanese history. Influenced by the Tang dynasty of China, Japanese leaders introduced a Chinese-style system of government, including land nationalization and the establishment of a centralized bureaucracy. Their programme was not completed, however, until the erection of a permanent capital at Nara in 710.

● **taille** ► An income and property tax in France before the Revolution. Originally levied for royal expenses and paid in lieu of military service, the taille was a major source of grievance as clergy and nobility were exempt. It was abolished in 1789.

● **tailorbird** ► A S Asian ▷warbler belonging to the genus *Orthotomus* (9 species), named after its habit of sewing the edges of a large leaf together with plant fibres or gossamer to form a bag in which the nest is built.

● **Taimyr Peninsula** ► (or Taymyr Peninsula) A promontory in central N Russia, between the Kara Sea and the Laptev Sea with Cape ▷Chelyuskin at its extremity.

● **Tainan** ► 23 01N 120 14E A city in SW Taiwan, the island's third largest. It is the island's former capital (1683–1891). The National University was established in 1971. An agricultural and fish market, it has varied industries and handicrafts. Population (1997 est): 712 172.

● **Taine, Hippolyte Adolphe** ► (1828–93) French writer and critic. In contrast to the prevailing ▷Romanticism, Taine was intensely logical and positivist in his approach. In works such as the *Philosophy of Art* (1865–69), his analysis is conducted in scientific, mathematical, physiological, or environmental terms.

● **taipan** ► A small-headed ▷cobra, *Oxyuranus scutellatus*, that occurs in NE Australia and New Guinea. Up to 3.3 m long, it has a ridged brown back and a yellow belly. Its venom contains a blood-clotting agent that is fatal within a few minutes.

● **Taipei** ▶ (*or* Taibei) 25 00N 121 32E The capital of Taiwan, in the N of the island. Founded in the 18th century, it was under Japanese occupation (1895–1945) and became the seat of the Nationalist Government (*see* Guomindang) in 1949. It is an important industrial centre, especially for textiles, food processing, and machinery. The National University was founded in 1928. Population (1997 est): 2 595 669.

● **Taiping Rebellion** ▶ (1851–64) A peasant rebellion in China that seriously undermined the Qing dynasty. In 1851 a Hakka peasant, ▷Hong Xiu Quan, claiming he was the brother of Christ come to save his people from their Qing rulers, proclaimed himself "Heavenly King of the Taiping (Heavenly Peace) Kingdom." He soon won converts among the southern peasantry and anti-Qing secret societies. The rebels marched N, capturing Nanjing in 1853. They then marched on Beijing but imperial forces, and cold weather, drove them back. The rebellion, which devastated 17 provinces, was weakened by internal division and finally crushed. When Nanjing fell, Hong and his followers committed mass suicide.

● **Taira** ▶ An important Japanese military clan of imperial descent. After gaining many vassals in the provinces, the Taira became involved in politics in the capital, Kyoto, in the 12th century and under the leadership of Taira Kiyomori (1118–81) came to dominate the imperial government. Shortly before Kiyomori's death, Taira power was challenged by the leaders of a rival clan, the Minamoto (*see* Minamoto Yoritomo), and destroyed in the Gempei War (1180–85).

● **Taiwan** ▶ (official name: Republic of China) An island some 145 km (90 mi) E of the SE coast of mainland China. Together with several nearby islands, including the Penghu Islands and the islands of ▷Jinmen and ▷Mazu, it comprises the so-called Republic of China. Taiwan island is largely mountainous, apart from narrow plains along the W coast, and two-thirds of the land is under forest. The people are predominantly Chinese, but there is friction between the island Chinese (the majority of the population) and those from the mainland.

Economy: since 1945 the economy has shifted from agriculture to industry and services, a trend that began under the Japanese and accelerated in the 1960s. Iron and steel are important and the large volume of exports includes electronic and electrical goods, television and radio sets, mass-produced plastic goods, chemicals, textiles, sugar, and vegetables. As well as coal, gold, and other minerals, oil, and natural gas have been found, although timber remains the main natural resource. The chief agricultural products are sugar cane, rice, and sweet potatoes. Fishing and fish farming are also important.

History: the island, named Formosa ("beautiful") by the Portuguese, who discovered it in 1590, was ceded by China to Japan in 1897. It surrendered to Gen ▷Chiang Kai-shek in 1945 and after the defeat of his Nationalist (▷Guomindang) Government by the Chinese communists he fled here in 1949. Following threats by the People's Republic of China the USA undertook in 1955 to protect Taiwan from outside attacks. However, Taiwan's importance in international affairs has diminished, as the People's Republic has gained recognition by the major powers: in 1971 it lost its seat at the UN to the People's Republic and in 1979 the USA, on establishing diplomatic relations with mainland China, severed those with Taiwan. Taiwan is recognized by less than 40 countries. Chiang Kai-shek died in 1975 and was succeeded by his son Gen Jiang Jing Guo (Chiang Ching-kuo; 1910–88). Relations with mainland China improved in the early 1990s but declined in 1995–96, when Taiwan embarked on democratic elections and China carried out military exercises in the Taiwan Strait. The elections were won by the incumbent president, Lee Teng-hui. The Guomindang's 50-year domination of Taiwanese politics ended in 2000, when Chen Shui-bian of the Democratic Progressive Party was elected president.

Taiwan

Head of state	President Chen Shui-bian
Official language	Mandarin Chinese; Taiwanese is the most widely spoken language
Official currency	new Taiwan dollar of 100 cents
Area	35 981 sq km (13 892 sq mi
Population (1998)	21 843 000
Capital	Taipei
Main port	Gaoxiong

● **Taiyuan** ▶ 37 50N 112 30E A city in NE China, the capital of Shanxi province. An ancient fortified city, it is a centre of technology, coal-mining, and heavy industry. Population (1991 est): 1 960 000.

● **Taizé** ▶ A Protestant religious community based in Taizé, in SE France. Founded in 1940 by Roger Schutz (1915–), its members accept celibacy, obedience, and community of goods. It is an international ecumenical centre, which attracts many young people for short stays. The style of liturgical music originated by the community, which is characterized by simple meditative chants, is now widely used by Christian denominations.

● **Tajikistan** ▷*See* Tadzhikistan.

Taj Mahal ▶ Over 20 000 workmen were employed in the building of the mausoleum (1631–53). The pure white Makrana marble with which it is faced was chosen to reflect changing conditions of light and weather, an effect reinforced by the water landscaping.

● **Taj Mahal** ▶ The mausoleum in Agra (N India) built (1631–53) for Mumtaz-i-Mahal, wife of the Mogul emperor, ▷Shah Jahan, who is also buried here. Set in formal gardens, the Taj Mahal is built mainly of white marble, delicately carved and inlaid with precious stones. Its symmetrical design reflects Persian influence. ▷*See also* Mogul art and architecture.

● **Tajo, River** ▷*See* Tagus, River.

● **takahe** ▶ A rare flightless New Zealand bird, *Notornis mantelli*, thought to be extinct but rediscovered on South Island in 1948. 60 cm tall, it has blue-and-green plumage and a heavy red conical bill surmounted by a red frontal shield. Takahes feed on seeds. Family: *Rallidae* (rails).

● **Takao** ▷*See* Gaoxiong.

● **Takoradi** ▷*See* Sekondi-Takoradi.

● **Talaing** ▷*See* Mon.

● **talapoin** ▶ The smallest ▷guenon monkey, *Cercopithecus talapoin*, of central West Africa, also called pygmy guenon. With head and body only 30 cm long, it has slightly webbed fingers and inhabits swampy forests. It has olive-green fur and conspicuously swollen genitals.

● **talaq** ▶ An Islamic extra-judicial law of divorce enabling a husband to unilaterally divorce his wife by repudiating her three times. The marriage is then dissolved, unless the husband revokes the pronouncement during the next three months or, if the wife is pregnant, before the child is born.

● **Talbot, William Henry Fox** ▶ (1800–77) British botanist and physicist, who pioneered many techniques of photography. In 1841 he invented the calotype, which for the first time used photographic negatives and was a great improvement on the earlier daguerrotype. He also introduced prints on paper treated with silver chloride.

● **talc** ▶ A white or green mineral of hydrated magnesium silicate, $Mg_3(Si_4O_{10})(OH)_2$, with a layered structure. It is soft (hardness 1 on ▷Mohs' scale) and greasy. Soapstone (steatite) is a rock consisting almost wholly of talc. Talc is formed by the hydrothermal alteration of basic and ultrabasic igneous rocks and by the low-grade thermal metamorphism of siliceous dolomites. Besides its use as talcum powder, it is used as a filler, lubricant, and soft abrasive.

● **Talca** ▶ 35 28S 71 40W A city in central Chile. The site of the declaration of Chile's independence (1815), it was rebuilt following an earthquake in 1928. Talca serves a rich wine-producing area. Population (1999 est): 174 858.

● **Talcahuano** ▶ 36 40S 73 10W A major port in S Chile, on Concepción Bay. It serves as an outlet for Concepción and is Chile's chief naval base. Population (1999 est): 269 265.

● **Taleban** ▶ (Pashto: seeker) A militant Sunni Muslim organization that controlled most of Afghanistan from 1996 until late 2001. Initially consisting largely of theological students, it captured Kabul (1996) and imposed strict Islamic law. Although forces loyal to the ousted government continued to resist in the N, the Taleban controlled the great majority of the country by 1999. Almost all Western influences were proscribed and women were denied access to education or paid work. The regime was also criticized for destroying most of Afghanistan's ancient Buddhist remains. In October 2001 the Taleban's links with the ▷al-Qaida terrorist organization prompted massive US air strikes on its command centres (*see* war on terrorism). The regime crumbled within weeks.

● **Ta-lien** ▷*See* Lüda.

● **Taliesin** ▶ (6th century AD) Welsh poet. The poems attributed to him in the manuscript *Book of Taliesin* (c. 1275) include odes eulogizing the Welsh king Urien Rheged and lamenting the death of his son Owain.

● **talipot palm** ▶ A ▷palm tree, *Corypha umbraculifera*, cultivated in India and Myanmar (Burma). Its trunk, up to 26 m high, bears fan-shaped leaves up to 5 m in diameter. Trees may be 80 years old before flowering, after which they die. The pyramid-shaped flower cluster, more than 7 m tall, is the largest in the plant kingdom. The seeds are used for buttons and ornaments and the leaves for matting, fans, and thatching.

● **Tallahassee** ▶ 30 26N 84 19W A city in the USA, the capital of Florida. It is the site of Florida State University (1857) and an agricultural and mechanical university (1887). A trade centre for timber, cotton, and livestock, industries include metal and concrete. Population (2000 est): 150 624.

● **Talleyrand** ▶ (Charles Maurice de Talleyrand-Périgord; 1754–1838) French politician and diplomat. He took holy orders in 1775 but was excommunicated for his reform of the church during the ▷French Revolution. He was foreign minister from 1797 until 1807, when he quarrelled with Napoleon, and again under the restored Louis XVIII. He represented France at the ▷Congress of Vienna.

● **Tallien, Jean Lambert** ▶ (1767–1820) French politician in the ▷French Revolution. He helped overthrow Robespierre in 1774 and was a member of the Council of Five Hundred. He subsequently served in Napoleon's Egyptian campaign.

● **Tallinn** ▶ (German name: Reval) 59 22N 24 48E The capital of Estonia, a port on Tallinn Bay in the Gulf of Finland. Its varied industries include shipbuilding and it possesses many educational institutions and historic buildings.

History: it occupies the site of an ancient settlement and was ruled by Denmark and then Sweden before being captured (1710) by Peter the Great. A member of the Hanseatic League, it was a prominent trading centre in the middle ages. It was independent Estonia's capital (1918–40) and, following annexation by the Soviet Union, was occupied by the Germans in World War II; it reverted to Estonia in 1991. Population (2000 est): 404 000.

● **Tallis, Thomas** ▶ (c. 1505–85) English composer. He was appointed a gentleman of the Chapel Royal and became joint organist there with his pupil Byrd. In 1575 he and Byrd were granted a monopoly for printing music and music paper. They produced *Cantiones Sacrae*, a collection of their motets, in the same year. Tallis' most famous works are *The Lamentations of Jeremiah* and the 40-part motet *Spem in Alium*.

● **Talmud** ▶ Two of the most important works of Jewish religious literature: the Babylonian and the Palestinian (or Jerusalem) Talmud. The Babylonian Talmud is more than three times as long as the Palestinian and enjoys greater authority. Both Talmuds are written in a mixture of Hebrew and Aramaic and are presented as a commentary (the **Gemara**) on the ▷Mishnah. They contain records of rabbinic discussions on a wide range of subjects, but concentrating especially on ▷halakhah. The rabbis mentioned in the Talmuds are called *Amoraim* (as opposed to *Tannaim*, the rabbis of the Mishnah, and *Savoraim*, later rabbis thought to have edited the Babylonian Talmud). The Palestinian *Amoraim* flourished in the 3rd and 4th centuries AD; the Babylonian *Amoraim* continued to about 500.

● **talus** ▶ (*or* scree) The accumulation of weathered debris at the foot of a cliff that has originated from erosion of the rock face above.

● **Tamale** ▶ 9 26N 0 49W A town in N Ghana. It is an educational centre and has a trade in cotton and groundnuts. Population (1998): 229 000.

● **tamandua** ▶ An insect-eating mammal, *Tamandua tetradactyla*, of Central and South American forests, also called lesser ▷anteater. Almost 1 m long including the long prehensile tail, it is pale in colour and has a shorter snout than the giant anteater. It feeds on termites using its long sticky tongue. Family: *Myrmecophagidae*; order: *Edentata*.

● **tamarin** ▶ A South American monkey found in open woodland and forests, closely related to ▷marmosets. Tamarins are 39–88 cm long including the tail (20–42 cm), have tusklike lower canine teeth, and feed on fruit, insects, eggs, etc. Chief genera: *Leontocebus* (21 species), *Leontideus* (3 species); family: *Callithricidae*.

● **tamarind** ▶ An evergreen tree, *Tamarindus indica*, probably native to tropical Africa and cultivated in tropical regions for its fruit. It grows to a height of 24 m and bears clusters of yellow flowers. The fruit is a plump pod containing seeds and a bitter-sweet pulp, which is used in chutneys, curries, and medicines. Family: ▷*Leguminosae*.

● **tamarisk** ▶ A tree or shrub belonging to the genus *Tamarix* (90 species), native to W and S Europe, central Asia, and India. Tamarisks have small scalelike leaves and produce feathery clusters of small pink flowers. Their deep roots enable them to grow on arid salt flats and sand dunes and they have been widely planted to stabilize sand dunes. *T. mannifera* of the Middle East and central Asia exudes a sweet white edible substance (manna) when the stems are punctured by certain insects. The false tamarisks (genus *Myricaria*; 10 species), native to temperate Eurasia, are similar to the true tamarisks. Family: *Tamaricaceae*.

● **tamarou** ▶ (*or* tamarau) A rare hoofed mammal, *Anoa mindorensis*, of lowland forests of the Philippines. A little larger than the related anoa (*A. depressicornis*), which stands 1 m high at the shoulder, it is similarly dark brown or black with short horns and it feeds at night on sugar cane and water plants.

● **Tamatave** ▷*See* Toamasina.

● **Tambo, Oliver** ▶ (1917–93) South African politician; president of the African National Congress (1977–91). A lawyer, he was arrested with Nelson ▷Mandela in 1956, but released a year later. From 1960 to 1990 he directed ANC activities from outside South Africa.

● **tambourine** ▶ A drum with a single head and loose metal discs fitted into its shallow frame. Held in the hand, the drum is struck with the knuckles and shaken to obtain a jingling sound from the metal discs. Of Middle Eastern origin, it came to Europe during the Crusades, being originally known as the **timbrel** in English (the French name, *tambourin*, was adopted later). Long used by Gipsies and in the 19th century by military bands, the tambourine is now often included in the orchestra, especially to impart a Turkish or Spanish flavour.

● **Tambov** ▶ 52 44N 41 28E A city in W Russia. It is an important engineering centre. Population (1995 est): 316 000.

● **Tamerlane** ▷*See* Timur.

● **Tameside** ▶ A unitary authority of NW England, in Greater Manchester. Area: 103 sq km (40 sq mi). Population (1996 est): 220 700.

● **Tamil** ▶ A ▷Dravidian language of S India and Sri Lanka. It is the official language of the state of Tamil Nadu. There are a number of regional dialects as well as those associated with different caste groups, such as Brahmins and non-Brahmins. It is written in a script known as Vattelluttu and there are marked differences between the written and spoken forms. Tamil society is highly stratified into caste groups and based on descent in the male line. They are mainly Hindu, and devotional (*bhakti*) cults are prevalent.

● **Tamil Nadu** ▶ (name until 1968: Madras) A state in SE India, at the tip of the peninsula. From the Western ▷Ghats it slopes E over lower plateaus and the Eastern Ghats to the Bay of Bengal. Important crops include rice, cotton, and coffee. One of India's more urbanized states, it produces cotton textiles, machinery, and electrical and leather goods. Tamil literature, music, and dance continue to thrive.
History: flourishing Hindu dynasties extended Tamil influence into medieval SE Asia until Muslims conquered Tamil Nadu (1565). British power was established in the 17th century. The present state was formed in 1956. Area: 130 058 sq km (50 204 sq mi). Population (1994 est): 58 840 000. Capital: Madras.

● **Tamil Tigers** ▶ (Liberation Tigers of Tamil Eelam *or* LTTE) A Sri Lankan guerrilla group that has been fighting government forces since 1983. The Tigers claim to represent the Tamil minority in Sri Lanka, who comprise about 18% of the population as a whole but up to 80% in certain areas of the NE. Longstanding tensions between the Sinhalese and Tamil communities erupted into violent conflict in the 1980s and the Tamil Tigers took effective control of the Tamil-majority areas. A ceasefire in 1987 and abortive peace talks in 1989–90 were followed by intensified conflict, in which thousands were killed. Further talks broke down in 1995 and the government launched major offensives (1996, 1997) in an attempt to regain control of the Jaffna peninsula, the rebels' main power base. Despite recent defeats the Tamil Tigers remain a powerful force, with some 10 000 men in arms.

● **Tammany Hall** ▶ The Democratic Party organization in New York City, which became notorious for its political corruption. It maintained power by the use of bribes and patronage. Its power was largely curtailed by the reforming mayor ▷La Guardia and disintegrated during the administration (1966–73) of John V(liet) Lindsay.

● **Tammuz** ▶ A Mesopotamian fertility god identified with the Greek ▷Adonis. Originally a pastoral god, he became an agricultural god of Assyria. The annual seasonal cycle was symbolized in the myth of his descent to the underworld, from whence he was recovered by the goddess ▷Ishtar.

● **tamoxifen** ▶ A drug that is used for the treatment of breast cancer: it acts by opposing the action of ▷oestrogen, which stimulates the growth of the tumour. Side-effects are uncommon but may include hot flushes, vaginal bleeding, and nausea.

● **Tampa** ▶ 28 10N 82 20W A city and port in the USA, in Florida on Tampa Bay. It is a major resort and phosphate-mining centre. Manufactures include cigars, cement, and fertilizers. Two universities are situated here. Population (1996 est): 285 206.

● **Tampere** ▶ (Swedish name: Tammerfors) 61 32N 23 45E The second largest city in Finland. It has a 20th-century cathedral and a university (1925). It is the country's main industrial centre, being well provided with hydroelectric power from the Tammerkoski Rapids. Its manufactures include railway rolling stock, textiles, wood pulp, paper, and footwear. Population (1997 est): 186 026.

● **Tampico** ▶ 22 18N 97 52W A port and winter resort in SE Mexico, on the Río Panuco. Oil refining is the chief industry. Population (1990): 271 636.

● **Tamralipti** ▶ An ancient town in NE India; its site is now occupied by the village of Tamluk. From about 250 BC it was the principal port of the Ganges basin; it was from here that the famous Chinese traveller ▷Fa Xian sailed for home in the early 5th century AD.

● **tam-tam** ▷*See* gong.

● **Tamworth** ▶ 52 39N 1 40W A town in central England, in S Staffordshire. It is an expanded market town with a diverse economy, including engineering, retail, warehousing, and leisure. It was the ancient capital of Mercia and has a Saxon castle. In 1834 Sir Robert ▷Peel issued the Tamworth manifesto here. Population (1997 est): 73 100.

● **Tamworth** ▶ 31 07S 150 57E A city in Australia, in E New South Wales on the Peel River. It is a market centre serving an agricultural region. Population (1991 est): 33 830.

● **Tana, Lake** ▶ (*or* Lake Tsana) 12 00N 37 20E A lake in NW Ethiopia. Its surface is 1830 m (6004 ft) above sea level and it is the source of the Blue Nile River. Area: about 3100 sq km (1197 sq mi).

● **tanager** ▶ A brightly coloured songbird belonging to a family (*Thraupidae*; 222 species) occurring in tropical and subtropical America. Tanagers are 10–20 cm long, plumpish, with a short neck and a conical bill. They live mainly in forests and feed on fruit, nectar, and insects.

● **Tanagra figurines** ▶ In Greek art, moulded terracotta statuettes of about 300 BC found at Tanagra (Boeotia) in 1874. These charming and technically excellent figures represent everyday subjects, usually women in quiet poses.

● **Tananarive** ▷*See* Antananarivo.

● **Tancred** ▶ (c. 1078–1112) Norman Crusader, prominent at the siege of Antioch and the conquest of Jerusalem (1099; *see* Crusades), who was regent of Antioch (1101–03, 1104–12) for Bohemond I. He is portrayed in ▷Tasso's *Gerusalemme liberata* (1575).

● **Tang** ▶ (*or* T'ang; 618–906 AD) A Chinese dynasty that established an empire extending over much of central Asia and Korea. In Tang times foreign trade was encouraged and many Chinese scientific ideas, such as gunpowder, which was invented under the Tang for fireworks, spread to the West. Arts, especially poetry, flourished, Neo-Confucianism was revived, printing was invented (the world's first known book, the Buddhist *Diamond sutra*, was printed in 868), and paper money was used for the first time. In 751 Arab forces recaptured Turkestan and the Tang empire began to disintegrate. Disastrous revolts and invasions decimated the population and two great rebellions finally led to the collapse of the dynasty and the division of China into many kingdoms.

● **Tanga** ► 5 07S 39 05E A port in Tanzania, in NE Zanzibar. It became an important port under German colonial rule but has since declined in importance. Population (latest est): 187 634.

● **Tanganyika** ▷*See* Tanzania, United Republic of.

● **Tanganyika, Lake** ► A lake in E central Africa, in Democratic Republic of Congo, Burundi, Tanzania, and Zambia. Discovered for Europeans by Burton and Speke in 1858, it is drained intermittently to the W by the River Lukuga. Area: about 33 000 sq km (12 738 sq mi).

● **Tange Kenzo** ► (1913–) Japanese architect. The most famous modern Japanese architect, Tange combined the influence of ▷Le Corbusier with traditional Japanese architecture. He built many civic buildings in Japan, notably the Kurashiki city hall (1960). Other designs include the National Gymnasium (1961–64) for the 1964 Tokyo Olympics, St Mary's Cathedral (1962–64) in Tokyo, and the New Tokyo City Hall (1986). As a town planner he produced schemes for Tokyo (1960) and Skopje, Macedonia (1965).

● **tangent** ► A straight line that touches a curve at only one point, known as the point of contact. A tangent plane is one that touches a curved surface at one point. ▷*See also* trigonometry; calculus.

● **tangerine** ► The fruit of a tree, ▷*Citrus reticulata*, also called mandarin, native to SE Asia and cultivated in the S USA and the Mediterranean region. The orange fruit, which peels easily and readily splits into segments, is usually eaten fresh. Many varieties have been developed, including the satsuma and clementine. The temple orange is a hybrid between the ▷orange and the tangerine.

● **Tangier** ► (or Tangiers) 35 48N 5 45W A port in N Morocco, on a bay on the Strait of Gibraltar. An important Roman town, it was held successively by many powers until it was established as an international zone in 1923. During World War II it was under Spanish occupation (1940–45) and its international status was abolished on Moroccan independence (1956). It has a university (1971). Its industries include cigarette and textile manufacture, fishing, market gardening, and tourism; it is also a commercial and financial centre. Population (1994 est): 521 735.

● **tango** ► 1. A Spanish flamenco dance. 2. A ballroom dance in 2/4 time, first performed in a fast form in the 1880s in the poor quarters of Buenos Aires. In the 1920s it spread to the USA and Europe, where it developed melancholic musical rhythms and a stylized elegance. By the 1950s it had become a showpiece for enthusiasts of ballroom dancing, but a revival of its wider popularity occurred in the 1990s, when an Argentinian dance troupe toured Europe and in 1999, when Prince Charles, on a state visit to Argentina, danced the tango in public.

● **Tangshan** ► 39 37N 118 05E A city in NE China, in Hebei province. A centre of heavy industry, its coalmines were under British control until 1952. China's first railway began here (1882). The city was levelled and 240 000 people died in an earthquake in 1976. Population (1991 est): 1 500 000.

● **Tanguy, Yves** ► (1900–55) French surrealist painter. Entirely self-taught, in 1927 he began to paint bizarre forms, partly organic and partly mechanical, which he situated in barren landscapes. He continued to explore this unique vision after emigrating to the USA in 1939.

● **Tanizaki Jun-ichiro** ► (1886–1965) Japanese novelist. His first short stories of the early 1900s were a brilliant success. Their sensuous and grotesque themes are reminiscent of Edgar Allan Poe's work. In the 1930s, while updating *The Tale of Genji* by ▷Murasaki, he became strongly influenced by early Japanese literature. Such later novels as *The Makioka Sisters* (1943–48) show appreciation for the traditional Japanese way of life.

● **Tanjore** ▷*See* Thanjavur.

● **tank** ► An armour-plated military vehicle, self-propelled on caterpillar tracks and typically armed with a ▷gun (usually turret-

mounted) and machine guns. Tanks are classified as main battle tanks (MBTs), for independent operation, and light tanks, for reconnaissance and other specialized uses. Based on a design of Sir Ernest Swinton (1868–1951) and first used during the Somme offensive in September, 1916, their true value became evident at Cambrai in November, 1917. In World War II the Germans initially achieved great success by using their Panzer divisions as an independent force rather than as infantry support or cavalry replacement. Tank battles across Europe and N Africa replaced the static trench warfare of World War I. In the Arab-Israeli War of 1973 guided missiles caused heavy Israeli tank losses. Modern tank development has concentrated on improving weapons, armour, and computer-aided navigation and fire control. ▷*See also* armoured car.

● **tanker** ► A seagoing vessel equipped with a large cargo tank for transporting liquids, especially oil. The forerunner of the modern tanker, the *Gluckauf* (2307 tonnes) was built in 1885; modern **supertankers** with a carrying capacity of 75 000 tonnes were developed after World War II in response to the increased world demand for oil. Ultra-Large Crude Carriers (ULCCs) have deadweights of up to nearly half a million tonnes. Size is not always an advantage, however, as such vessels can only enter certain ports, cannot negotiate the Suez Canal, and can cause ecological disasters if they are wrecked and spill their enormous cargoes into the sea.

● **Tannenberg, Battles of** ► 1. (5 July, 1410) The battle in which Polish and Lithuanian troops defeated the ▷Teutonic Knights, whose drive into E Europe was thereby arrested. 2. (26–30 August, 1914) The battle early in World War I in which Germany defeated Russia, thus thwarting the Russian invasion of Prussia. Some 100 000 Russians were captured.

● **Tannhäuser** ► (c. 1200–c. 1270) German poet. A Minnesinger several of whose lyrics survive, he travelled widely, serving in various courts. Wagner's opera of this name (1845) is based on the legend of his seduction by Venus, his life of sensuality at her court, and his pilgrimage to seek papal forgiveness.

● **tannin** ► (or tannic acid) One of a group of phenol derivatives present in the bark, leaves, fruits, and galls of many plants. Tannins are used as mordants for many dyes, in tanning leather, and in making ink.

● **tanning** ▷*See* leather.

● **Tannu-Tuva** ▷*See* Tuva Republic.

● **tansy** ► A perennial herb, *Tanacetum* (or *Chrysanthemum*) *vulgare*, native to temperate Eurasia. Growing to a height of 30–100 cm, it has flat-topped clusters of yellow flowers and was formerly cultivated for its aromatic leaves, used for cooking and medicinal purposes. Family: ▷*Compositae*.

● **Tanta** ► 30 48N 31 00E A city in Egypt, on the Nile Delta. It is noted for its fairs and Muslim festivals and is an important commercial centre with cotton and tobacco industries. Population (1992 est): 380 000.

● **tantalum** ► (Ta) A very hard grey dense metallic element, discovered in 1802 by A. K. Ekeberg (1767–1813). It occurs (with niobium from which it is difficult to separate) in the ore columbite $(Fe(Nb,Ta)_2O_6)$. It is resistant to chemical attack and is used in alloys, for example in surgical materials for implantation in the body and in incandescent filaments. The oxide (Ta_2O_5) is used in special glass, with high refractive index, for camera lenses. At no 73; at wt 180.948; mp 3020°C; bp 5458 ± 100°C.

● **Tantalus** ► A legendary Greek king of Lydia, son of Zeus and Pluto and father of ▷Niobe and ▷Pelops. In Hades he was punished for certain offences against the gods by being made to stand within reach of water and fruits that moved away whenever he tried to drink or eat.

● **Tantras** ► A group of Sanskrit religious texts written in India in the 5th century AD. The contents are miscellaneous but they form the basis of esoteric systems of ▷meditation in both Hinduism and Buddhism. In the **Tantric yoga** of Hinduism, two principles are postulated: Shiva and Shakti, male and female, mind and creative energy, situated in the head and at the base of the spine, respectively. The

tank

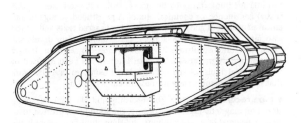

Mark IV British Tanks were first successfully used during World War I in the battle of Cambrai in November, 1917. They were designed to be able to cross trenches.

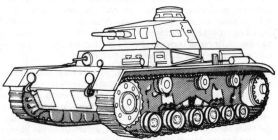

German Pz III At the beginning of World War II the German Panzer divisions were based on Pz III tanks, armed with a 50-mm gun and having a maximum speed of 30 mph (48 km per hour).

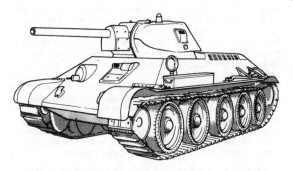

Soviet T-34 The German invasion of the Soviet Union (1941) met resistance from the T-34, then probably the best design in the world. It had a 76.2-mm gun and a top speed of 32 mph (51 km per hour).

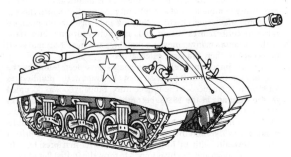

US M-4 A US design used extensively in World War II was the M-4, known as the "General Sherman." Introduced in 1942, it had a 75-mm gun and a top speed of 24 mph (38 km per hour).

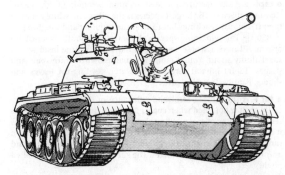

Soviet T-54 This main battle tank, with its 100-mm gun, effective use of armour, and road speed of 34 mph (54 km per hour) was the most advanced tank in the world when it appeared in 1954.

British Challenger Introduced during the 1980s, this main battle tank is heavily armed with a 120-mm gun, has a top speed of 35 mph (56 km per hour), and is protected by Chobham armour.

object of tantric practices is to arouse the female element, which can be focused in various centres of the body, and ultimately to unite it with the male principle. **Tantric Buddhism** involves an elaborate system of meditation by means of mudras (gestures), mantras (symbolic sounds; *see* Om), and mandalas (diagrams). The imagery of sexual union is the distinctive feature of both systems, which emphasize the fulfilment of bodily desires rather than the ascetic practices that are more typical of Hinduism and Buddhism.

● **Tanzania, United Republic of** ▸ A country in East Africa, on the Indian Ocean. It consists of a mainland area (formerly the republic of Tanganyika) and the islands of ▷Zanzibar and ▷Pemba, as well as some smaller islands. On the mainland its boundaries are formed partly by Lakes Victoria, Tanganyika, and Malawi. The land rises from the coast through plateaus to mountains, especially in the N, with Mount Kilimanjaro at 5950 m (19 520 ft). The majority of the population is African, mainly of Bantu origin.

Economy: the vast majority of the workforce is employed in agriculture, chiefly subsistence farming. In mainland Tanzania the chief crops are coffee, cotton, sugar cane, and cassava. Sisal, once important, has now declined; there are plans for diversification of crops as well as development in forestry and livestock. Agricultural production suffered badly from droughts in the late 1990s. Zanzibar (with Pemba) is the world's largest producer of cloves, with coconuts as the second cash crop. Food crops include rice, bananas, and cassava. Minerals extracted in Tanzania include diamonds, gold, tin, and salt; coal and iron have been found, as well as offshore gas. Hydroelectricity is a valuable source of power. Industry is mainly limited to the processing of minerals and agricultural products for export; there is some manufacturing, chiefly of clothing and footwear. The main exports are coffee, cloves, cotton, and diamonds. Tourism is important with Tanzania's many game parks (notably ▷Serengeti National Park) and beaches. There is a large external debt.

History: important prehistoric remains have been found by the ▷Leakey family. The area was visited by the Arabs in the middle ages and by the Portuguese in the 16th century. Tanganyika was occupied by the Germans in the 1880s, becoming a German protectorate in 1891. After World War I it was under British rule, first under League of Nations mandate and then as a UN trust territory. It gained independence in 1961 and in 1962 became a republic within the British Commonwealth with Dr Julius K. Nyerere as its first president. In 1964 Tanganyika and Zanzibar joined to form the United Republic of Tanganyika and Zanzibar, now known as Tanzania. In 1977 the official political parties of the two countries merged to form the Revolutionary Party, which became the only legal party. In the Arusha Declaration (1967) Nyerere launched a policy of decentralization, which involved the division of rural areas into cooperative communities (Ujamaas). Tanzania was instrumental in the overthrow in Uganda of President Idi ▷Amin. Relations with Zambia are close, particularly since the opening of the Tanzam Railway (1975). Plans to introduce a multiparty system were endorsed in 1992. In 1995 elections resulted in victory for the ruling Party of the Revolution and Benjamin Mkapa became president.

United Republic of Tanzania

Head of state	President Benjamin Mkapa
Official languages	Swahili and English
Official currency	Tanzanian shilling of 100 cents
Area	945 087 sq km (364 900 sq mi)
Population (1997 est)	29 461 000
Capital	Dodoma
Main port	Dar es Salaam

● **Taoism** ▸ Emerging in the 6th century BC, Taoism is one of the two great native Chinese religio-philosophical systems (the other is ▷Confucianism) and a major influence in the development of Chinese culture. The goal of Taoism as a philosophy, as expressed in the *Tao Te Ching* of ▷Lao Zi, the *Chuang Tzu*, and the *Lieh Tzu*, is profound, joyful, mystical, and practical harmony with the universe. In politics and livelihood, the Taoist seeks the effective path of least resistance and of inconspicuousness. All extreme positions revert to their opposites. All is in flux except Tao (the Way) itself. *Yin* (the feminine) balances

yang (the masculine). Meditation, spontaneity, and simplicity are stressed. *Te* (virtue) and *ch'i* (energy) represent the power of effortless action accessible to the Taoist. As a religion Taoism emphasizes the alchemical relations between macrocosm and microcosm, seeking a formula for immortality by breath control, diet, exercises (*tai chi*), sexual continence, or chemical elixirs. A priesthood, a huge hierarchical pantheon of gods, and a multitude of sacred texts and rituals associated with various sects arose. Later monasticism developed. Since the Chinese Cultural Revolution (1966–68) religious Taoism survives mainly in Taiwan. Western interest has been aroused by philosophical Taoism, especially by the ▷*I Ching*, an oracular work that claims to demonstrate purpose in chance events.

● **tape recorder** ▸ A device for recording and playing back sound stored on magnetic tape. In recording, the sound is converted to an electrical signal by a ▷microphone and then amplified before being fed to an electromagnet in the recording head. The varying field of the magnet leaves a pattern of magnetization in the iron (or sometimes chromium) oxide coating of the tape as it passes through the machine. To play back, the magnetized tape induces a current in a coil as it passes the reproducing head. The coil current is then amplified and fed to loudspeakers. Tape recorders provide a compact and portable means of recording sounds of all kinds; the tapes are usually wound into ▷cassettes. However, while music centres and (especially) personal and car stereos still play cassette tapes, ▷compact discs have now largely replaced them in the home.

● **tapestry** ▸ A decorative or pictorial woven textile, used as wall hangings, furniture covers, etc. Tapestry weaving has been practised since antiquity but it only flourished in Europe from the 14th century, the major centres of production being Arras, Tournai, and Brussels in Flanders, and Beauvais and the ▷Gobelins factory in France. Medieval tapestries, often of floral and leaf patterns, were used as portable draught screens; others showing religious scenes were made for churches. From the 16th century painters, notably ▷Raphael and ▷Boucher, were commissioned to design tapestries. In the 19th century machine-made tapestries were introduced, but hand weaving in England was kept alive by William ▷Morris, who established the Merton Abbey looms (1877). A major revival of tapestry design was led by Jean ▷Lurçat in the 1930s. One of the most spectacular tapestries of the 20th century, "Christ in Glory" (1962), was designed by Graham ▷Sutherland for Coventry Cathedral.

● **tapeworm** ▸ A parasitic hermaphrodite ▷flatworm of the class *Cestoda* (about 3000 species). Tapeworms range from 20 mm to 15 m in length and anchor themselves inside the intestine of their host by means of hooks and suckers on the head. They have no gut or sense organs, the body consisting of a chain of progressively large segments through which food is absorbed. The terminal segments—full of eggs—are regularly shed, passing out of the host's body to infect a secondary host, where larvae invade muscle tissue. Species infecting humans include the beef tapeworm (*Taenia saginata*) and the pork tapeworm (*T. solium*).

● **tapioca** ▷*See* cassava.

● **tapir** ▸ A shy nocturnal hoofed mammal belonging to the genus *Tapirus* (4 species). The largest species is the black and white Malayan tapir (*T. indicus*), reaching about 1 m at the shoulder and weighing up to 350 kg. The remaining species of Central and South America are brown. All have a sparse covering of hairs and a large head with a short fleshy snout. Young tapirs are marked with white spots and stripes. Tapirs inhabit forests near water, feeding on leaves and shoots. Family: *Tapiridae*; order: ▷Perissodactyla.

● **tar** ▸ A thick black semisolid substance of organic origin, especially coaltar obtained when coal is heated to over 1000°C in the absence of air (1 kg of coal yielding about 50 g of tar). Tar can be used as it is, e.g. for the production of roofing felt, or distilled to produce a range of organic chemicals including benzene, naphthalene, and anthracene and their derivatives. The substance remaining is called pitch.

● **Tara** ▸ 53 34N 6 35W A village in the Republic of Ireland, in Co Meath. The Hill of Tara was the ancient religious and political centre of Ireland and here the early Irish Kings lived and were crowned. The original coronation stone is reputed to have been taken to Scone, Scotland.

● **Taranaki** ▶ A district of New Zealand, on W North Island. It is important for dairy farming, especially on the volcanic ring plain encircling Mount ▷Egmont. Area: 9713 sq km (3750 sq mi). Population (1993 est): 107 500. Chief town: New Plymouth.

● **Tarantino, Quentin** ▶ (1963–) US film director and screenwriter, noted for his violent stylish crime dramas. He directed *Reservoir Dogs* (1993), *Pulp Fiction* (1994), and *Jackie Brown* (1998) and wrote the screenplay for *True Romance* (1993).

● **Taranto** ▶ 40 28N 17 15E A seaport in Italy, in Apulia on the Gulf of Taranto. Founded by the Greeks in the 8th century BC, it has an 11th-century cathedral. It is an important naval base, with shipyards. Its large iron and steel works were established in 1965. Population (1996 est): 212 650.

● **tarantula** ▶ A large dark hairy spider (up to 75 mm long) of the family *Theraphosidae*, found in tropical America. Many tarantulas live on trees or in burrows in the soil, feeding mainly at night on insects and occasionally frogs, toads, mice, and small birds. Their poisonous bite is painful but not fatal to man.
   The name was originally given to a ▷wolf spider (*Lycosa tarentula*) of Taranto (Italy). In the middle ages it was believed that the poisonous effects of the bite of this spider could be eliminated by dancing (the dance came to be known as the tarantella).

● **Tarbes** ▶ 43 14N 0 05E A town in SW France, the capital of the Hautes-Pyrénées department. A Huguenot stronghold (16th–17th centuries), it has a 13th-century cathedral and trades in horses and agricultural produce. Population (1990): 50 228.

● **Tardigrada** ▶ A phylum of tiny invertebrate animals (about 350 species), known as water bears, that are probably related to arthropods. About 1 mm long, they are almost transparent, with four pairs of short legs ending in claws. Tardigrades are found in terrestrial, freshwater, and marine habitats, feeding on the sap of mosses and other plants.

● **tare** ▶ One of several annual herbs of the genus *Vicia* (which also includes ▷vetches) that grow as weeds on cultivated land throughout the world. Tares have slender trailing stems, which grow up to 60 cm long, and branches with paired leaflets and terminal climbing tendrils. The tiny white or bluish flowers give rise to seed pods. Family: ▷*Leguminosae*.

● **Taree** ▶ 31 54S 152 26E A town in Australia, in NE New South Wales. It is the principal town of the Manning River district, specializing in dairy products; tourism is important. Population (1989): 18 000.

● **targum** ▶ (Aramaic: translation) An Aramaic translation of part of the Bible. There are several targumim, notably those of Onkelos (of the Torah) and Pseudo-Jonathan (of the Prophets). They were produced in Palestine and Babylonia in the Talmudic and gaonic periods, and include a great deal of ▷Midrash.

● **tariffs** ▶ A surcharge imposed by a government on imported goods. Several arguments are used to justify tariffs. The "infant industry" argument is that tariffs are needed to protect a domestic industry while it becomes established. Other arguments include the need to protect employment in domestic industries, the need to provide a counter to "dumping" (foreign industries selling goods at a lower price abroad than at home), and the benefit of the revenue that will accrue from tariffs. The ▷General Agreement on Tariffs and Trade served as a centre for negotiating tariff agreements until 1996, when it was replaced by the ▷World Trade Organization. ▷*See also* customs unions.

● **Tarim Basin** ▶ A great depression in NW China, covering the area between the ▷Tian Shan in the N and the ▷Kunlun Mountains in the S. Drained by the Dalimu (or Tarim) River, it consists of the Takelamagan (or Takla Makan) Desert with the salt lake of ▷Lop Nor in the E, where nuclear tests have been held. There are oasis towns but the region is largely undeveloped. Area: about 906 500 sq km (350 000 sq mi).

● **Tarkington, (Newton) Booth** ▶ (1869–1946) US novelist. Born in Indiana, he enjoyed success with his portrayal of the Midwest in such novels as *The Magnificent Ambersons* (1918); other novels included *Monsieur Beaucaire* (1900) and *Alice Adams* (1921).

● **taro** ▶ A perennial herbaceous plant, *Colocasia esculenta*, also known as eddo, dasheen, and elephant's ear, native to tropical Asia and widely cultivated in tropical and subtropical areas for its edible tubers. The tubers, which are large, starchy, and spherical, contain more protein than potatoes and are eaten cooked as vegetables or made into puddings or bread. Family: *Araceae*.

tarot ▶ The 13th card (The Grim Reaper) and the 6th card (The Lovers) of the Greater Arcana from a pack of French tarot cards of c. 1460.

● **tarot** ▶ A pack of 78 cards used primarily in fortune telling, although they are also the forerunners of modern ▷playing cards, and games are still played with them. They originated in 14th-century Italy, although their symbolism probably draws on a far older tradition. The original pack is now known as the Greater Arcana; this consists of 22 cards (believed to correspond to the letters of the Hebrew alphabet), 21 numbered cards representing natural elements, vices, and virtues and a "Fool" (the original joker). During the 14th century these were combined with 56 number cards of the Asian kind then also beginning to be used. Now known as the Lesser Arcana, these 56 are in 4 suits: cups, swords, money, and clubs or rods, representing clergy, nobility, merchants, and peasants. Each suit consists of number cards from one to ten and four court cards: king, queen, knave, and knight.

● **tarpan** ▶ A Eurasian wild horse, *Equus caballus*, that became extinct in the early 20th century. Small and dun-coloured, it had a long flowing mane. Attempts have been made to reconstitute the tarpan by crossing various modern breeds that are thought to be related to it.

● **Tarpeia** ▶ In Roman legend, a Roman commander's daughter who offered to betray Rome to the attacking Sabines in return for what they wore on their left arms, meaning their golden bracelets. When the Sabines overran the citadel, they literally obeyed her wish by crushing her to death with their shields.

● **tarpon** ▶ A marine game fish belonging to the family *Elopidae*. It has a slender body covered by large thick silvery scales. The Atlantic tarpon, *Tarpon* (or *Megalops*) *atlanticus*, reaches up to 2 m in length and occurs inshore in warm waters. Order: *Elopiformes*.

● **Tarquin the Proud** ▶ (Tarquinius Superbus) The last King of Rome, who ruled, according to Roman tradition, from 534 to 510 BC. Tarquin is probably a historical figure but many myths evolved to account for the nickname Superbus; he was expelled from Rome and brought monarchy into permanent disrepute there.

● **tarragon** ▶ A perennial herb, *Artemisia dracunculus*, native to central Asia and widely cultivated. It grows to a height of about 60 cm and has slender leaves and flowers, which are often dried and used in salads, sauces, pickles, etc. It also yields an essential oil used in cooking and perfumery. Family: ▷*Compositae*.

● **Tarragona** ▶ (Latin name: Tarraco) 41 07N 1 15E A port in NE Spain, in Catalonia on the Mediterranean Sea. It was a major Roman port and has many Roman ruins, including an aqueduct; it also possesses a cathedral (12th–13th centuries). An agricultural centre, it also has a petrochemicals industry. Population (1995 est): 114 931.

● **Tarrasa** ▶ 41 38N 2 00E A town in NE Spain, in Catalonia. An important industrial centre, it is famous for its woollen textiles; other industries include glass and fertilizers. Population (1995 est): 162 327.

● **tarsier** ▶ A small nocturnal ▷prosimian primate belonging to the genus *Tarsius* (3 species), of Sumatra, Borneo, Celebes, and the Philippines. 22–43 cm long including the naked tail (13–27 cm), tarsiers have enormous eyes, large hairless ears, and gripping pads at the end of their digits. They are mainly arboreal, using both hands to seize small insects and lizards. Family: *Tarsiidae*. ▯mammal.

● **Tarsus** ▶ 36 52N 34 52E A town in central S Turkey, near Adana. The first known settlement here was Neolithic; it was Assyrian for many centuries and an important town in the Roman and Byzantine Empires. St Paul was born here. Population (1995 est): 229 518.

● **tartan** ▷*See* Highland dress.

● **tartaric acid** ▶ (HOOC(CHOH)₂COOH) A white crystalline powder with an acid taste; it is a constituent of ▷baking powder.

● **Tartarus** ▶ In Greek religion, the place of punishment and perpetual torment in the underworld. The ▷Titans were imprisoned there after their defeat by the gods.

● **tartrazine** ▶ A yellow food-colouring dye made from petroleum and permitted to be used for this purpose as E-102 (*see* food additives). It has, however, been implicated as having an adverse effect on hyperactive children and in causing allergic reactions in hypersensitive people.

● **Tartu** ▶ (German and Swedish name: Dorpat) 58 20N 26 44E A city in SE Estonia. Although an industrial centre, it is best known for its university founded (1632) by Gustavus II Adolphus of Sweden, Tartu being held successively by Sweden, Poland, and Russia to which it was ceded in 1704. Population (1996 est): 103 400.

● **Tashkent** ▶ 41 16N 69 13E The capital of Uzbekistan, in the E of the country. It is the oldest and largest city of central Asia, being a major communications, industrial, and cultural centre. Textiles (based on cotton from the surrounding oasis), food- and tobacco-processing, and chemical industries are important.
  History: dating from at least the 1st century BC, it fell successively to the Arabs (7th century) and the Turks (12th century), becoming a great commercial centre under Timur. It was captured by Russia in 1865. Tashkent was severely damaged by earthquake in 1966. Population (1994 est): 2 106 000.

● **Tasman, Abel Janszoon** ▶ (c. 1603–c. 1659) Dutch navigator. Commissioned in 1642 by van ▷Diemen to explore the S Pacific, Tasman sighted present-day Tasmania (which he named Van Diemen's Land, after his patron), New Zealand, and in 1643 Tonga and Fiji. In 1644 he sailed along the N coast of Australia, thus proving it continuous.

● **Tasmania** ▶ An island and the smallest state of Australia, separated from the SE corner of the mainland by Bass Strait. Sighted by Abel ▷Tasman in 1642, it was called Van Diemen's Land until 1856. It is the most mountainous of the Australian states and is dominated by the Central Plateau. Agriculture is important with mixed and dairy farming, sheep rearing, and the cultivation of apples and hops. More than 40% of the island is covered by forest and the export of wood chips to Japan is a significant industry. Large mineral deposits include tin, iron ore, zinc, lead, and copper; King Island, off the NW coast, is Australia's main producer of tungsten. Area: 68 332 sq km (26 383 sq mi). Population (1996): 459 659. Capital: Hobart.

● **Tasmanian devil** ▶ A carnivorous marsupial, *Sarcophilus harrisi*, formerly found on the Australian mainland but now restricted to Tasmania. About 1 m long, it is black with a large head and wide jaws containing doglike teeth. Strong and heavily built, it feeds on wallabies, birds, and lizards and fights ferociously when cornered. Family: *Dasyuridae* (dasyures).

● **Tasmanian wolf** ▷*See* thylacine.

● **Tasman Sea** ▶ A section of the SW Pacific Ocean, lying between SE Australia and Tasmania on the W and New Zealand on the E. Area: about 2 300 000 sq km (900 000 sq mi).

● **Tass** ▷*See* news agency.

● **Tassili-n-Ajjer** ▶ A sandstone massif in the central Sahara containing numerous caves decorated with rock paintings of people and animals (c. 8000–c. 100 BC). Depictions of hippopotamuses and vast herds of cattle indicate a far damper climate than at present.

● **Tasso, Torquato** ▶ (1544–95) Italian poet. After studying law at Padua and publishing his epic *Rinaldo* (1562) he joined the court of the Este family at Ferrara, where he wrote the pastoral drama *Aminta* (1573) and his major work, the romantic epic *Gerusalemme liberata* (1575). For the rest of his life he suffered from mental instability but continued to write lyrics, religious poems, philosophical dialogues, and a tragedy, *Re Torrismondo* (1587).

● **taste** ▷*See* tongue.

● **Tatar Republic** ▶ (Tataria *or* Republic of Tatarstan) A constituent republic of Russia, in the W. The ▷Tatars, who comprise some 50% of the population, were conquered by Ivan the Terrible in the 16th century. The region was an autonomous Soviet republic from 1920 to 1991. The Tatar Republic is Russia's main producer of oil and natural gas and also has deposits of coal and other minerals. There are highly developed engineering, oil, and chemical industries, and the timber, textile, and food industries are now also expanding. Agricultural products include fodder crops and cereals. The Tatar Republic declared independence in 1992. Area: 68 000 sq km (26 250 sq mi). Population (1996 est): 3 760 000. Capital: Kazan.

● **Tatars** ▶ A people, mainly living in the Tatar Republic of Russia, who belong to the NW division of the Turkic-speaking peoples. They traditionally lived by farming and herding. There are many Tatar dialects, one of which, Kazan Tatar, is a literary language that goes back to the 13th century. The Tatars are descended from peoples associated with the various states of the Mongol empire and the name was often used to refer to all the nomadic Turkic and Mongol peoples of the steppes. Their society was traditionally divided into noble and commoner groups ruled by khans. They are mainly Muslim. ▷*See also* Golden Horde.

● **Tate, Allen** ▶ (1899–1979) US poet and critic, a founder-member of the ▷Fugitives. The Civil War is the main subject of his novel *The Fathers* (1938) and his best-known poem "Ode to the Confederate Dead" (1926). He published much criticism, including *On The Limits of Poetry* (1948), and his verse is collected in *Collected Poems* (1978).

● **Tate, Harry** ▶ (Ronald Hutchinson; 1874–1940) British music-hall comedian. His best-known sketches concerned golf, fishing, and unreliable cars.

● **Tate, Nahum** ▶ (1652–1715) British poet. Born in Dublin, he is notorious for his version of Shakespeare's *King Lear*, which ended happily with Cordelia marrying Edgar. He was coauthor of the second part of Dryden's *Absalom and Achitophel* (1681). He became poet laureate in 1692.

● **Tate Galleries** ▶ Two art galleries in London, housing paintings of the British school and modern work. The original Tate Gallery was built on Millbank in 1897 with the financial support of the sugar merchant and philanthropist Sir Henry Tate (1819–99), who donated his collection of British paintings to the nation in 1890. Highlights are its Pre-Raphaelite works and paintings by ▷Turner, housed in the Clore Gallery since 1987. New branches were opened in Liverpool's Albert docks (1988) and in St Ives, Cornwall (1993). In 1999–2000 the former Bankside power station, on the S bank of the Thames, was converted into Tate Modern by Herzog and de Meuron;

this now holds the collection of international modern art, leaving the Millbank gallery (Tate Britain) as a showcase for British works.

● **Tati, Jacques** ▶ (J. Tatischeff; 1908–82) French film actor and director. He was a music-hall performer before he turned to films. He wrote, directed, and acted in a number of popular award-winning comedies, such as *Jour de Fête* (1947), *Monsieur Hulot's Holiday* (1952), *Mon Oncle* (1958), and *Playtime* (1968), which rely on Tati's talent for pantomime.

● **Tatra Mountains** ▶ Two mountain ranges in central E Europe: the **High Tatras** (Polish name: Tatry Wysokie; Czech name: Vysoké Tatry), which extend 90 km (56 mi) E–W along the Polish-Slovakian border and constitute the highest area of the ▷Carpathian Mountains, and, to the S, the **Low Tatras** (Czech name: Nízké Tatry), which run parallel for some 150 km (93 mi) and rise to 2043 m (6703 ft).

● **Tattersall, Richard** ▶ (1724–95) British racehorse owner, who established auctions for horses in London in 1766. The company of Tattersall's still holds bloodstock auctions at Newmarket, Suffolk.

● **tattooing** ▶ Making pictures or designs on the skin by pricking and staining with indelible dyes. Although the word was introduced into English and other European languages from the Tahitian *tatau*, as a result of James ▷Cook's expedition of 1768, the practice itself is of much greater antiquity. Egyptian mummies from around 2000 BC provide evidence that tattooing was practised then and it appears to have been widespread in classical times; for example, the Romans tattooed slaves and criminals for purposes of identification. Other early civilizations have been adept at tattooing, although for obvious reasons it is much less prevalent with dark-skinned peoples. It was forbidden in early Christian Europe, perhaps because of the injunction in the Old Testament "Ye shall not make any cuttings in your flesh for the dead, nor print any marks upon you" (Leviticus 19.28). Tattooing was not reintroduced into Europe until it became popular among sailors during the explorations of America, where it was commonly practised by native Americans.

Over the ages tattoos have been used for a wide variety of purposes, including identification of individuals or members of a group (class, clan, club), for ritual, religious, or magical reasons, or for pure decoration. Its most nefarious practice in the 20th century was its use by the Germans to identify by tattooed number the prisoners held in concentration camps. In Britain and the USA it is still performed (by tattoo artists using electric needles in hygienic tattoo studios), especially on working-class men for whom it seems to represent some kind of symbol of virility, perhaps connected to withstanding the pain of the tattooist's needle.

In recent years, both sexes of the middle classes have shown an interest in tattooing, with girls favouring small discreet tattooes in imitation of some female pop stars. Some girls prefer their tattooes to be visible to all, while others use them to decorate parts of the body only seen by lovers.

● **Tatum, Art(hur)** ▶ (1910–56) US Black jazz pianist, who began playing as a child when already blind. A soloist in the 1930s, he formed his own trio in 1943. His superb technique and advanced sense of harmony earned him a high reputation among both jazz and classical musicians.

● **Tatum, Edward Lawrie** ▶ (1909–75) US geneticist, who (working with G. W. ▷Beadle on mutant strains of bread mould) provided evidence that specific genes determine the structure of specified enzymes. In 1946 Tatum and J. ▷Lederberg discovered the phenomenon of genetic recombination in certain bacteria. Tatum shared a Nobel Prize (1958) with Beadle and Lederberg.

● **Taunton** ▶ 51 01N 3 06W A market town in SW England, the administrative centre of Somerset. The 12th-century castle was the scene of Judge Jeffreys' Bloody Assizes (1685) after the failed Monmouth Rebellion. Service industries predominate, with strong retailing and financial sectors. Precision engineering is well represented and traditional products include cider. Population (1996): 60 300.

● **tau particle** ▶ An elementary particle with a very short lifetime (5×10^{-12} second) and a mass about 3500 times that of the ▷electron. It

is classified as a lepton (*see* particle physics). It reacts by the ▷weak interaction.

● **Taupo, Lake** ▶ (*or* Taupomoana) The largest lake in New Zealand. It lies on the volcanic plateau of central North Island and is drained by the Waikato River. Area: 616 sq km (238 sq mi).

● **Tauranga** ▶ 37 42S 176 11E A city and port in New Zealand, in North Island on the Bay of Plenty. Tauranga's chief exports are dairy produce, meat, and fruit. Population (1994): 76 100.

● **Taurus** ▶ (Latin: Bull) A large constellation in the N sky near Orion, lying on the ▷zodiac between Gemini and Aries. The brightest star is ▷Aldebaran. The constellation contains the ▷Hyades and ▷Pleiades star clusters and the ▷Crab nebula with its associated pulsar.

● **Taurus Mountains** ▶ A mountain range in S Turkey. It extends 560 km (348 mi) parallel to the Mediterranean coast and rises to 3734 m (12 251 ft) at Ala Dağ, or to 3916 m (12 848 ft) at Erciyas Daği if the Anti-Taurus range (an extension to the NE) is included.

● **tautology** ▶ A statement that is always true and therefore gives no information. For example, "It is either raining or it is not raining."

● **tautomerism** ▷*See* isomers.

● **Tavener, Sir John** ▶ (1944–) British composer. His earlier compositions include the cantata *The Whale* (1966) and the opera *Thérèse* (1979). Later works, such as *The Protecting Veil* (1989) and *Mary of Egypt* (1992), are influenced by the liturgy of the Russian Orthodox Church. His choral work *Song for Athene* achieved wide popularity after being performed at the funeral of ▷Diana, Princess of Wales. He was knighted in 2000.

● **Taverner, John** ▶ (c. 1495–1545) English composer. He became choirmaster at Cardinal College (later renamed Christ Church) Oxford, in 1526. In 1528 he was imprisoned for heresy and left Oxford in 1530. He became an agent of Thomas Cromwell and gave up music. He left 28 motets, a *Te Deum*, 8 masses, and some instrumental music.

● **Tawney, R(ichard) H(enry)** ▶ (1880–1962) British economic historian. Influenced by the theories of Max ▷Weber, Tawney wrote on capitalism, his most famous book being *Religion and the Rise of Capitalism* (1926). A professor at London University (1931–49), he was a formative influence on the British Labour Party.

● **tawny owl** ▶ A common ▷owl, *Strix aluco*, occurring in Europe and SE Asia. 38 cm long, it has short rounded wings, dark-brown eyes, a mottled brown plumage, and lacks ear tufts.

● **taxation** ▶ The means by which a government raises funds to finance its spending and, to some extent, by which it regulates the economy (*see* fiscal policy) or achieves its social and political aims (e.g. the equal distribution of wealth). Direct taxes are paid by individuals (e.g. ▷income tax, ▷capital-gains tax, ▷inheritance tax) or by companies (*see* corporation tax) directly to the tax authorities; indirect taxes are levied on goods and services (e.g. ▷value-added tax). In most cases taxation is levied when funds change hands, but in a wealth tax this is not the case. Progressive taxation, in which those with higher incomes or greater wealth pay more in proportion than those with lower incomes or less wealth, is a means of achieving social or political objectives. ▷*See also* council tax; customs and excise duties; tax-credit system.

● **tax-credit system** ▶ A system that combines taxation and social-benefit payments; the state fixes a level of income above which taxation (income tax) is levied and below which benefits (negative income tax) are paid. The advantages claimed are: each individual is guaranteed a fixed minimum income, there is a positive incentive to work as after-tax income always increases with earnings (*compare* poverty trap), there is less opportunity for unscrupulous people to make fraudulent claims on the welfare system, and there is a great saving in costs by combining the administration of taxation with the welfare system.

● **tax exempt special savings account** ▷*See* TESSA.

● **tax haven** ▶ (*or* tax shelter) A country or area with low taxes that can offer advantages to foreign individuals or companies that pay high taxes in their own countries. Individuals have to take up residence in these countries, giving up their domiciliary rights in their own countries; companies can open subsidiary companies in the haven countries, through which they can put part of their business.

● **taxi** ▷*See* cab.

● **taxidermy** ► The art of making lifelike zoological models of creatures by preserving their skins and mounting them on suitable dummies. Taxidermy dates from the 17th century but improved technology and the use of plastic body forms have resulted in greater degrees of realism.

● **Taxila** ► The site of an ▷Achaemenian and Greek city near Rawalpindi (N Pakistan). Occupied from the 5th century BC, it was a famous centre of learning. Excavations revealed a blend of Greek and Buddhist elements, typical of the ▷Gandhara culture. The ▷Huns destroyed Taxila in 460 AD.

● **taxis** ► The movement of a living organism or cell in response to an external stimulus: the movement is either towards or away from the stimulus, i.e. a positive or negative taxis. Taxes are specified according to the type of stimulus. For example, **chemotaxis** is the response to a change in the concentration of a chemical. Many insects, for example, respond chemotactically to the scents emitted by the opposite sex. **Phototaxis** is the response to light: cockroaches are negatively phototactic. *Compare* tropism.

● **taxonomy** ► The study of the classification and nomenclature of organisms. The principles of taxonomy were established in the 18th century by the work of ▷Linnaeus (*see also* binomial nomenclature). As far as possible, organisms are arranged into a hierarchy of groups (called taxa) based on degrees of relationship (*see* phylogeny). When knowledge of the evolution of a group is lacking taxonomy is based on structural and other similarities. The basic unit of classification is the ▷species. Related species are grouped into genera, genera into orders, orders into classes, and classes into phyla (*see* phylum). Related phyla are regarded as belonging to the same kingdom. Traditionally two kingdoms were recognized: *Animalia* (*see* animal) and *Plantae* (*see* plant). In most modern classifications the number of kingdoms has been increased to five with the addition of the *Fungi* (*see* fungi), *Bacteria* (or *Prokaryotae*; *see* bacteria; cell), and ▷*Protoctista* (*see also* Protista). Some modern classification systems recognize a category in the taxonomic hierarchy that is higher than the kingdom—the domain. According to such systems there are three domains: *Archaea* (*see* archaebacteria), *Bacteria*, and *Eukarya* (eukaryotes; *see* cell). Other authorities, however, regard these as superkingdoms. The two main methods used in determining taxonomic positions are classical taxonomy, which is based on morphological and biochemical data, and numerical taxonomy, in which mathematical and statistical methods are used to assess similarities and differences. ▷*See also* cladistics.

● **Tay, River** ► The longest river in Scotland, rising in the Grampian Mountains and flowing generally NE through Loch Tay before flowing SE to enter the North Sea through the Firth of Tay. Length: 193 km (120 mi).

● **Taylor, A(lan) J(ohn) P(ercivale)** ► (1906–90) British historian, who specialized in modern European political history. Among his many books are *The Origins of the Second World War* (1961) and *English History 1914–45* (1965); his television broadcasts made him well known.

● **Taylor, Brook** ► (1685–1737) English mathematician, best known for the Taylor series in calculus. He also made contributions to the mathematics of perspective. Taylor, educated at Cambridge, was secretary of the Royal Society between 1714 and 1719.

● **Taylor, Dame Elizabeth** ► (1932–) US film actress, born in England. She began her career as a child star, notably in *National Velvet* (1944). Her adult films include *Raintree County* (1957), *Cat on a Hot Tin Roof* (1958), *Butterfield 8* (1960), and *Winter Kills* (1985). In *Cleopatra* (1962), *Who's Afraid of Virginia Woolf?* (1966), and several other films she costarred with Richard ▷Burton, whom she married twice; she has had six other husbands. She was created DBE in 2000.

● **Taylor, Frederick Winslow** ► (1856–1915) US engineer, who pioneered the techniques of scientific management. In 1881, while working for the Midvale Steel Company, he introduced time and motion study as a means of increasing efficiency, incurring considerable resentment from those affected by it. He later became a management consultant.

● **Taylor, Jeremy** ► (1613–67) English Anglican churchman. Chaplain to Archbishop Laud and Charles I, he was imprisoned by parliamentary forces in 1645 and forced to live in seclusion during the Interregnum. At the Restoration he was made Bishop of Down and Connor (1660) and vice chancellor of Dublin University. His works, which include *The Liberty of Prophesying* (1647), *Holy Living* (1650), *Holy Dying* (1651), and *The Rule of Conscience* (1660), have earned him the title of the "Shakespeare of the pulpit."

● **Taylor, Joseph Hooton** ► (1941–) US astrophysicist. Taylor, working with Russell Hulse (1950–), discovered a binary pulsar and showed how an analysis of its orbital period demonstrated the existence of gravitational waves. Taylor and Hulse were awarded the Nobel Prize in 1993.

● **Taylor, Zachary** ► (1784–1850) US statesman and general; president (1849–50). In the ▷Mexican War (1846–48), he won at Buena Vista although his forces were outnumbered by four to one. As president he offered little leadership in the extension of slavery to the states acquired from Mexico.

● **Taymyr Peninsula** ▷*See* Taimyr Peninsula.

● **Tay-Sachs disease** ► An inherited disorder of lipid metabolism leading to blindness, mental retardation, and death in infancy. Occurring mostly in Jews from Eastern Europe, the disease can be detected by ▷amniocentesis. Named after the British ophthalmologist W. Tay (1843–1927) and the US neurologist B. B. Sachs (1858–1944).

● **Tayside Region** ► A former administrative region in SE Scotland, bordering on the North Sea. It was created under local government reorganization in 1975 from the counties of ▷Angus, most of Perth, and Kinross. In 1996 it was abolished and replaced by three ▷unitary authorities: Angus, Dundee, and ▷Perth and Kinross.

● **Tbilisi** ► (former name: Tiflis) 41 43N 44 48E The capital city of Georgia (Asia), on the River Kura. It is a major industrial centre, engineering and the manufacture of textiles, wine, and food being the principal economic activities; Tbilisi also has a lively cultural life.

History: founded in the mid-5th century, it fell successively to the Persians, Byzantines, Arabs, Mongols, Turks, and (in 1801) to the Russians. Its name was changed to Tbilisi in 1936. In 1991 it was the scene of fighting between opponents and supporters of President Gamsakhurdia. Population (1994): 1 253 100.

● ▷**Tchaikovsky, Peter Ilich** ► (1840–93) Russian composer. He studied under Anton Rubinstein in St Petersburg and became professor at the Moscow conservatoire in 1866. After the success of his first piano concerto, Tchaikovsky was offered financial support from Nadezhda von Meck (1831–94), a wealthy widow, whom he never met. Unhappy with his homosexuality, in 1877 he made a disastrous marriage, which led to depression and a suicide attempt, although much of his work was now successful. Officially, his death was attributed to cholera although some believe he committed suicide to avoid further homosexual scandals. Among his compositions are six symphonies, including the last known as the *Pathétique* (1893), three piano concertos (one unfinished), a violin concerto, string quartets, the opera *Eugene Onegin* (1877–78), and the ballets *Swan Lake* (1876–77) and the *Nutcracker* (1891–92).

● **tea** ► The dried leaves and shoots of the evergreen shrub or tree, *Camellia sinensis*, which yield a beverage when infused with water. Native to parts of India and China, the tea plant has three major varieties—China, Assam, and Cambodia—and numerous hybrids, ranging from 2.75 to 18 m in height. The shoots and young leaves are picked by hand and left to wilt before being lightly rolled and dried. Before drying, the leaves may be allowed to ferment, producing either black tea or, if only partially fermented, oolong tea. Leaves that are not fermented produce green tea. The major tea exporters are India and Sri Lanka; most of China's production goes for home consumption. Tea is also produced in SE Asia and parts of Africa and South America. Tea is sold in the form of chopped leaves—loose or contained in small porous paper bags (tea bags)—or as a soluble powdered extract (instant tea). Its stimulating effect is due to the caffeine content (about 3.5%); flavour depends on the presence of volatile oils, and tannins are responsible for its colour. Family: *Theaceae*.

● **tea ceremony** ▷*See* cha-no-yu.

● **Teach, Edward** ► (d. 1718) British pirate, nicknamed Blackbeard, who molested shipping in the Atlantic from his headquarters in N Carolina. In 1718 he was killed by a punitive force sent from Virginia.

● **teacher training** ► Vocational training for entrants to the teaching profession. In England and Wales Qualified Teacher Status (QTS) is mandatory for those aiming to teach in state-maintained schools, but this can now be acquired in a variety of ways. The traditional route is either a Bachelor of Education (BEd) degree or, for those who already have a first degree, a one-year Postgraduate Certificate of Education (PGCE); both qualifications combine an academic element with teaching practice in schools. In the late 1990s, however, reforms were introduced to make teacher training less academic and more school-based. The Graduate Teacher Programme (introduced 1998) enables graduates to undertake a period of practical training in school rather than a PGCE, while the Registered Teacher Scheme (introduced 1998) permits mature entrants to the profession with relevant employment-based experience to become teachers without a formal teaching qualification. Since 1998 trainee teachers in all subjects have been required to demonstrate basic competence in maths, English, science, and computer technology. Teacher training in England and Wales is funded by the Teacher Training Agency (TTA), which also accredits all courses and the institutions providing them.

● **teak** ► A tropical □tree, *Tectonia grandis*, native to SE Asia and cultivated for its timber. Growing to a height of 45 m in its natural state, it has small white flowers and fleshy fruits. The aromatic golden-yellow heartwood becomes darker when seasoned and is very hard and durable, being used for furniture, construction purposes, etc. Myanmar (Burma) is the major teak exporter. Family: *Verbenaceae*.

● **teal** ► A small ▷dabbling duck, *Anas crecca*, of the N hemisphere, nesting on marshes and wintering on mudflats and estuaries. 35 cm long, it feeds on water plants and aquatic invertebrates. Drakes are grey and have a chestnut head with a cream-edged green eye stripe and a white wing stripe; females are mottled brown and both sexes have a green-and-black wing patch.

● **tear gas** ► (or lachrymator) A substance, generally an atomized liquid rather than a gas, that is used to control crowds by causing acute eye irritation with temporary blindness and copious flow of tears. Side effects include lasting damage to the eyes and nasal and lung tissues and dermatitis. Chloroacetophenone (Mace) is the best-known example. ▷*See also* chemical warfare.

● **teasel** ► A biennial herb, *Dipsacus fullonum*, native to Europe, W Asia, and N Africa. The prickly stems grow to 2 m and bear conical heads of blue, purple, or white flowers with stiff hooked bracts. Fuller's teasel (*D. fullonum sativus*) was formerly cultivated for its flower heads, which were used to tease fabrics and raise a nap. Family: *Dipsacaceae*.

● **Tebaldi, Renata** ► (1922–) Italian soprano. Having made her debut in Boito's *Mefistofele* at Rovigo (1944), she established a reputation for her interpretation of roles in the operas of Puccini.

● **Tebbit, Norman (Beresford), Baron** ► (1931–) British Conservative politician; chairman of the Conservative Party (1985–87) and Chancellor of the Duchy of Lancaster (1985–87). A former airline pilot, he subsequently served as secretary of state for employment (1981–83) and trade and industry (1983–85). In 1984 he and his wife Margaret were injured by an IRA bomb in Brighton; in 1992 he became a life peer.

● **technetium** ► (Tc) A silvery-grey radioactive element that was the first to be produced artificially. It does not occur naturally on earth but has been observed spectroscopically in a number of stars, where it is being continuously formed by nuclear reactions. It is chemically similar to rhenium and the compound $KTcO_4$ is a remarkable corrosion inhibitor in steels. At no 43; at wt (98); mp 2204°C; bp 4265°C.

● **technology** ► The application of scientific principles and engineering techniques to building, communications, healthcare, industry, agriculture, warfare, etc. Some technological processes, such as extracting metals from their ores (smelting), weaving fabrics, and the making of primitive weapons, predated science. But with the development of civilizations in China and the Middle East, especially in Egypt, in the third millennium BC, the technology of building (for example, the pyramids), the ▷wheel and axle, and the first roads to accommodate wheeled vehicles demonstrated the beginnings of scientific engineering. The classical civilizations of Greece and Rome produced enhanced building skills, resulting in edifices that have lasted for over two thousand years, and irrigation systems, some of which remain in working order. The Arab world became the centre of technological advance after the decline of the classical civilizations, and in the New World Mayan and Aztec cultures developed technologies that paralleled some of those that had emerged in the Old World.

Industrial technology in Britain in the 18th century was based largely on the ▷steam engine, which for the first time in human history provided a source of power that was not reliant on muscles, wind, or the water mill. The ▷agricultural revolution and the subsequent ▷industrial revolution transformed the economies first of Britain, then of the rest of Europe, and eventually of North America and other parts of the world. The steam engine brought technology to mining and the textile and many other industries, the ▷railways developed to allow the movement of goods and people without relying on canals and the horse, and by the end of the 19th century the civilized world was beginning to generate and transmit the electrical power that has revolutionized the energy industry and brought technological advances to the home as well as to the workplace. The beginning of the 20th century saw the invention of the ▷internal-combustion engine and the ▷oil industry needed to fuel it. Powering motor vehicles (*see* car) and agricultural machinery (*see* tractor), the internal-combustion engine also provided the means for manned flight (*see* aeronautics). In the two World Wars of the first half of the 20th century engineers and scientists harnessed all these new technologies to the demands of the military.

In the second half of the century the age of ▷nuclear power dawned. However, the promise of cheap and plentiful energy that it once seemed to herald has not been fulfilled. Although nuclear power has found a place in the energy industry, its potential dangers and the problem of disposing of its waste products have unexpectedly curbed its use. In addition, the threat posed by nuclear weapons continues to hang ominously over the world. The atom bomb brought World War II to an end, but the prospect that it might one day bring the Armageddon of World War III is always present. The technology of weapons, especially of the intercontinental ▷rocket, was also responsible for the dawn of the space age in the late 1950s (*see* space exploration). The second half of the 20th century has witnessed yet another technological upheaval based on electronics. ▷Telecommunications and the ▷computer have together provided an explosion in human knowledge, enabling information to flow around the world with an unprecedented facility.

The price the world has had to pay for the enormous benefits that technology has brought is ▷pollution, depletion of the ozone layer, and the consequent ▷greenhouse effect and global warming. The relentless demands of consumerism and automated factory processes are also denuding the world of its natural resources. Human beings have yet to learn how to strike the appropriate balance between the benefits and the dangers of technology.

● **tectonics** ► The study of the major structural features of the earth's crust and the processes by which they are constructed. Thus a feature described as tectonic is formed by deformational movements of the earth's crust or by volcanic action rather than by geomorphological processes. The most modern theory of global tectonics is that of ▷plate tectonics.

● **Tecumseh** ► (c. 1768–1813) American Shawnee Indian chief, who led an Indian confederacy against the advance of White settlement in the NW. After his tribe was surprised at the battle of Tippecanoe (1811) he swore eternal war on the settlers. The conviction among frontiersmen that the British in Canada were helping Tecumseh led to a demand among the so-called war hawks in the US Congress for war with Britain, the ▷War of 1812, in which Tecumseh was killed.

● **Tedder, Arthur William, 1st Baron** ▸ (1890–1967) British air marshal. He joined the Royal Flying Corps in 1916 after army service. In World War II he was appointed (1940) to command the RAF in the Middle East and then (1943) in the Mediterranean. He became Eisenhower's deputy in 1944 and contributed greatly to the success of the Normandy landings.

● **Tees, River** ▸ A river in N England. Rising in the Pennines in Cumbria, it flows mainly E through Co Durham into the Teesmouth estuary at Middlesbrough to join the North Sea. The valley above Darlington, known as **Teesdale**, contains High Force, England's highest waterfall, and Cross Fell, at 893 m (2954 ft) the highest point in the Pennines. Length: 113 km (70 mi).

● **Teesside** ▸ An industrial district in NE England, on the River Tees estuary. The chief towns are Stockton-on-Tees in Durham and Middlesbrough in North Yorkshire.

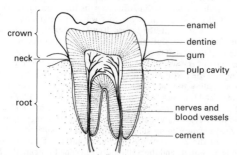

molar tooth The root of the tooth is anchored into the socket by a bonelike substance, cement.

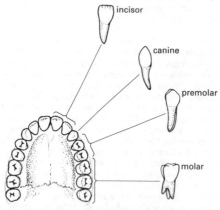

teeth in the adult upper jaw The incisors and canines are used principally for biting; the premolars and molars are used for grinding and chewing. The lower jaw contains the same number and type of teeth.

teeth

● **teeth** ▸ Hard structures in the mouth, embedded in the jaws, used for biting and chewing food. The human adult (permanent) dentition consists of 32 teeth, including incisors (8), canines (4), premolars (8), and molars (12). Young children have a milk (deciduous) dentition of 20 teeth (incisors, canines, and molars), which are replaced by the permanent teeth between the ages of 6 and 12. The third molar (wisdom tooth) on each side of both jaws does not normally appear until the age of about 20 (sometimes later). The crown of a tooth consists of dense hard enamel (largely ▷apatite) overlying the yellow bonelike dentine, which is slightly spongy and sensitive to touch, temperature, and pain. The pulp at the centre contains blood vessels and nerve fibres. The principal disorders of teeth are ▷caries and ▷periodontal disease. ▷*See also* dentistry.

● **tefillin** ▷*See* phylacteries.

● **Teflon** ▷*See* polytetrafluoroethene.

● **Tegucigalpa** ▸ 14 20N 87 12W The capital of Honduras, situated in the centre of the country in a high valley. Founded in 1579, it was an important centre of gold and silver mining. It became the capital in 1824. The University of Honduras was founded in 1847. In late 1998 it was utterly devastated by floods and mudslides in the wake of Hurricane Mitch. Population (1995 est): 813 900.

● **Tehran** ▸ (*or* Teheran) 35 40N 51 26E The capital of Iran, in the N centre of the country at the foot of the Elburz Mountains. Most of its buildings are modern, but the Gulistan Palace is a notable older structure. Tehran is the commercial, industrial, administrative, and cultural centre of the country, with six universities (oldest 1934). It became the capital in 1788 and was greatly enlarged during the 20th century. Fierce rioting here preceded the overthrow (1979) of the Shah of Iran. Population (1994 est): 6 750 043.

● **Tehran Conference** ▸ (1943) The conference in World War II attended by F. D. Roosevelt (USA), Stalin (Soviet Union), and Churchill (UK). Its chief purpose was to coordinate Allied strategy in W and E Europe.

● **Tehuantepec, Isthmus of** ▸ An isthmus in S Mexico, between the Gulf of Campeche and the Gulf of Tehuantepec.

● **Teilhard de Chardin, Pierre** ▸ (1881–1955) French Jesuit theologian and palaeontologist. His philosophical books were suppressed by the Roman Catholic Church during his lifetime. He is best known for his synthesis of natural science and religion and his Christian metaphysical philosophy. In his books *The Phenomenon of Man* (1955) and *Le Milieu divin* (1957), he maintained that the universe and mankind are in constant evolution towards a perfect state.

● **Tejo, River** ▷*See* Tagus, River.

● **Te Kanawa, Dame Kiri** ▸ (1944–) New Zealand soprano. She studied in England at the London Opera Centre and made her major debut in the role of Countess Almaviva in the *The Marriage of Figaro* at Covent Garden in 1971. In 1981 she sang at the wedding of the Prince and Princess of Wales. She was made a DBE in 1982.

● **tektite** ▸ A glassy object (2–3 cm in diameter) found in certain areas, including Australia (called australites) and the former Czechoslovakia (moldavites). They are thought to have been formed by the fusion of terrestrial material during the impact of meteorites (*see* meteor), although some may have arisen from terrestrial or lunar volcanoes.

● **Telanaipura** ▷*See* Jambi.

● **Tel Aviv-Jaffa** ▸ 32 05N 34 46E A city in central Israel, on the Mediterranean coast. Most of the buildings in the city are modern, but some old streets have been restored. It is the largest city in Israel, and its commercial, industrial, and cultural centre. Israel's stock exchange is here, and there are two universities (1953 and 1974). The city's port is at Ashdod, to the S.
   History: Tel Aviv was originally a suburb of Jaffa (ancient name: Joppa; Arabic name: Yafa), founded in 1909 to relieve overpopulation of the Jewish quarter in an Arab town. Following tension between Arabs and Jews, the towns were separated in 1921, and, as Jewish immigration increased, Tel Aviv expanded rapidly. Almost the entire Arab population fled Jaffa on its capture by Jewish forces in 1948, and the two cities were reunited in 1950 as Tel Aviv-Jaffa. Population (1997 est): 355 900.

● **telecommunications** ▸ The transfer of information by any electromagnetic means, such as wire or radio waves. Telecommunications includes telephones, telegraphy, ▷radio, ▷televison, etc. Generally, a telecommunications system consists of a transmitter, a transmission channel, and a receiver. The input to the transmitter is usually coded in some way and then fed to a modulator, in which it is combined with a carrier signal (*see* modulation).
   The transmission channel may be a wire, an optical fibre, or radio waves within a specified frequency range (the bandwidth). A single channel may carry several signals if a ▷multiplexer is used. The receiver demodulates the signal and decodes it, converting it into the desired form of output, which may be sound, an electrical signal to a

computer, a teleprinter printout, etc. Distortion may occur in the transmission because the signal has taken two different paths (shadowing) or because the channel may not respond equally to all the frequencies being transmitted. Noise (spurious signals) may arise at any stage of the transmission and reception process.

The **telephone**, which was invented by Alexander Graham Bell in 1875, carries speech in the form of electrical signals along a wire. A carbon ▷microphone in the mouthpiece produces an electrical signal that passes through a network of exchanges and relays to the receiving earpiece, where it is converted back into sound by a small diaphragm ▷loudspeaker. Telephone connections are now normally made automatically, first going through a local exchange and then, for long-distance calls, through the trunk network. All the switching operations are activated by the caller and controlled and monitored electronically. Telephone connections exist to almost all parts of the world through undersea cables and ▷communications satellites. **Telegraphy** is the transmission of written or printed messages by electrical signals and was developed before the telephone, in 1837. The >Morse code was used in the first commercial recording telegraph, between England and France in 1851. Now telegrams, ▷Telex, and >fax messages are carried along the same wires as telephone conversations, using different frequency ranges. Radiotelegraphy uses radio waves instead of a wire to carry the message. Like long-distance telephone links it may be relayed by communications satellites. Optical fibres transmitting beams of laser light are now in use and can carry considerably more information than an electric cable of the same thickness. New developments include the widespread use of >mobile phones based on a ▷cellular network and video telephones that send and receive images as well as sound. Both use digital technology based on the Integrated-Services Digital Network (ISDN). ▷*See also* electronic mail; Internet; teletext; viewdata; WAP.

● **telekinesis** ▶ Apparent change in or movement of material objects, caused by mental effort alone. It is also called psychokinesis (PK). The claims of Uri Geller (1946–), an Israeli, to break metal objects merely by concentrating on them have received great publicity. Telekinesis has been evoked to explain levitation and certain ▷poltergeist manifestations.

● **Telemachus** ▷*See* Odysseus.

● **Telemann, Georg Philipp** ▶ (1681–1767) German composer, born in Magdeburg. Whilst studying law at Leipzig University he taught himself to play various instruments and to compose, obtaining a post in 1704 as organist at the New Church. He held other musical posts in various cities, including Frankfurt and Hamburg (1721). His output was very large and included operas, oratorios, church music, and much chamber music.

● **teleology** ▶ The philosophical study of ends, goals, and the ultimate good. It has application in both ethics (*see* utilitarianism) and >metaphysics. Teleology was studied by ▷Kant who used it to provide a proof of the existence of God in terms of the purposiveness of the universe.

● **teleost** ▶ Any ▷bony fish belonging to the infraclass *Teleostei* (over 20 000 species), which includes nearly all the important food and game fish and many aquarium fish. Teleosts have a symmetrically divided (homocercal) tail fin and an air-filled ▷swim bladder, which is emptied or filled to regulate buoyancy and give great manoeuvrability. They are solitary or shoaling fish and most lay eggs on rocks or plants, or freely in the water, although some bear live young. Males or sometimes the females may guard the young. Chief orders: *Clupeiformes* (see herring; anchovy), *Salmoniformes* (see salmon; trout; pike), *Cypriniformes* (see carp), *Gadiformes* (see cod; hake), *Perciformes* (see perch; mackerel), *Pleuronectiformes* (see flatfish); subclass: *Actinopterygii*.

● **telepathy** ▷*See* extrasensory perception.

● **telephone** ▷*See* cellular network; telecommunications.

● **telephoto lens** ▶ A camera lens that gives a bigger image than a normal lens without moving the camera closer to the subject or extending the camera. It consists of two groups of lenses. The front unit converges the light rays and the rear unit partially corrects this. The light reaching the film appears to converge from a point some dis-

tance in front of the camera. Telephoto lenses tend to result in a slightly flattened perspective in the final picture.

● **telescope** ▶ An optical instrument that produces a magnified image of distant objects. It is used on land and as a major research tool in astronomy. The first **reflecting telescope** was produced by

refractors

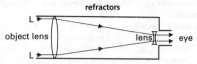

Galilean The simplest practical form of refracting telescope was developed by Galileo in about 1609 from Lippershey's invention.

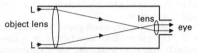

Keplerian Kepler's arrangement produces an inverted image but was much used for astronomical observations in which the inversion did not matter.

reflectors

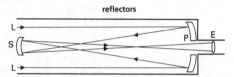

Gregorian James Gregory proposed this design in 1663 but it has had little general application.

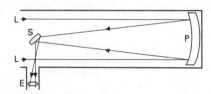

Newtonian In Newton's 1671 design the secondary mirror is placed at an angle of 45° to the axis of the beam.

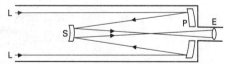

Cassegrain Widely used, this form was invented by the obscure French astronomer N. Cassegrain in 1672.

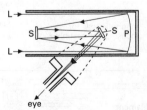

coudé (French: angled) This arrangement is valuable in larger telescopes as it increases their focal length.

L = light rays   P = primary mirror
E = eyepiece   S = secondary mirror

telescope

▷Newton in 1668. In the reflecting telescope the light from an object is collected by a concave, usually paraboloid, mirror of long focal length. This primary mirror reflects the light into a secondary optical system, which in turn reflects it into a short-focus eyepiece. The eyepiece lenses produce a magnified image that can be viewed by eye, photographed, or otherwise analysed. Depending on the secondary optics, reflectors are called **Gregorian**, **Newtonian**, **Cassegrain**, or **coudé telescopes**.

The **refracting telescope** was invented in 1608 by ▷Lippershey in Holland and developed by ▷Galileo as an astronomical instrument a year later. The light in the refracting telescope falls on a converging long-focus objective lens. The resulting image is then magnified by the short-focus eyepiece to produce the final image. An example is the **Keplerian telescope**, which was the first major improvement on Galileo's original design. Refractors are also used as terrestrial telescopes, usually containing an additional lens or a prism to cause the inverted image to be seen erect.

A telescope's light-gathering power depends on the area of the primary mirror or the objective lens. Since large mirrors are easier to fashion and mount than large lenses, the major astronomical telescopes are reflectors. In addition, unlike the objective in refractors, the reflector's mirror suffers no chromatic ▷aberration and its spherical aberration and coma are minimal. The Hubble space telescope, launched in 1990, is 350 times more powerful than other earth-based telescopes. ▷*See also* Schmidt telescope; radio telescope.

● **Telesio, Bernardino** ▶ (1509–88) Italian humanist. His philosophy was influenced by the ancient Greeks and was strongly empirical and opposed to ▷Aristotelianism. He founded a scientific society (1566) to propagate his approach and among those he influenced were ▷Campanella and Giordano ▷Bruno.

● **teletext** ▶ An information service in which pages of text are transmitted together with normal television broadcasts for display on a modified domestic television set. The system utilizes two of the unused lines between picture frames. All the stored information, which may be weather reports, news flashes, sports results, etc., is sent out continuously in a cycle at a rate of 50 lines per second (2 per picture frame). The required pages are selected for display by keyboard, and the user may have to wait a few minutes for them to come up on the screen if the cycle is a long one containing a large number of transmissions. The two systems in use in the UK are **Ceefax**, run by the BBC, and **Oracle**, run by the Independent Broadcasting Authority. ▷*See also* videotex.

● **television** ▶ (TV) The broadcasting of pictures and sound by ▷radio waves or electric cable. Television was invented by John Logie ▷Baird in 1926. At a TV studio or outside-broadcast unit, a television

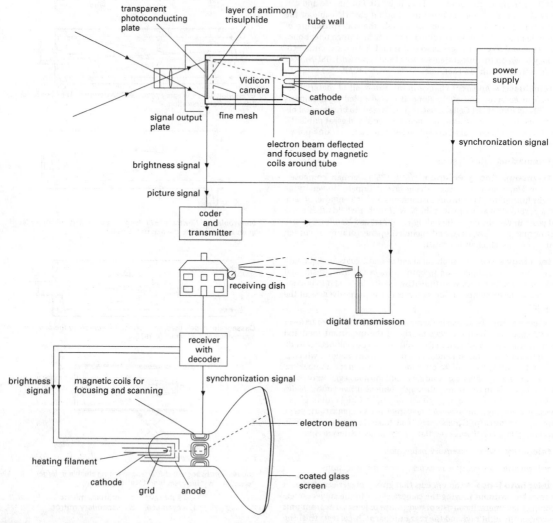

television

▷camera converts the picture into electrical signals, which are modulated and transmitted. In most of Europe the picture consists of 625 lines made by an electron beam scanning the screen of a ▷cathode-ray tube, 25 such pictures being formed every second. In the USA and Japan, 525 lines and 30 frames per second are used. High-definition television (HDTV) employs pictures with up to 1125 lines in a wide-screen format. A brightness signal and a synchronization signal (to form the lines and frames of the picture) make up the picture signal, which is used to modulate (*see* modulation) a VHF or UHF carrier wave and is broadcast with the modulated sound carrier wave (which has a slightly different frequency). In colour TV, a colour signal is added to the picture signal. Since the late 1990s there has been a growing use of digital systems in which the signal is sampled up to 30 000 times per second and the characteristics of the sampled signal are represented by digits (in the same way as information is represented in a computer). The digits are then transmitted and reconstituted in the receiver. The digital process ensures that no distortion or interference occurs, as it can in analog systems. In the UK there are plans to complete the switch to digital by 2010, when all viewers will require a set-top decoder or an integrated digital TV.

TV is transmitted in one of three ways: by direct ground waves, by means of a satellite in earth orbit (*see* communications satellite), or by cable. High-frequency ground waves operate only over line-of-sight distances (usually up to 80 km) from the transmitter. **Satellite broadcasting**, using microwave frequencies, enables intercontinental broadcasts to be made and provides additional channels for domestic TV. Coaxial cables are used for closed-circuit television (CCTV), usually for surveillance and conferencing, and for pay TV. Commercial cable TV (CATV) may alternatively use ▷fibre-optic cables, which carry dozens of channels simultaneously.

The aerial of the TV receiver detects the broadcast radio waves and the picture and sound signals are separated within the receiver. The picture signal is demodulated, and the resulting current is used to control the electron beam in a cathode-ray tube so that the picture is reconstructed, the scanning being fast enough to appear as a continuous moving picture. A dish aerial is used for receiving digital and satellite broadcasts.

In a **colour television** camera light from the scene to be televised is filtered into three primary colour components: red, green, and blue. Light of each colour goes to a separate image tube. There are three systems in use for encoding colour picture information for transmission: the US system, also used in Canada, Mexico, and Japan; the PAL (phase alteration line) system used in the UK and most other W European countries; and SECAM (système électronique couleur avec mémoire), used in France, E Europe, and Russia. All of these combine colour and intensity information with sound and synchronization. The colour television receiver splits the signal into red, green, and blue components and applies these to three separate electron guns. The beam from each gun activates a set of phosphor dots of that colour on the screen, thus reconstructing the red, green, and blue components of the picture.

Many televisions now produce high-quality stereo sound; in addition, miniature televisions are available, and a flat high-resolution wall-mounted set has been developed.

● **Telex** ▶ A telegraphy system using telephone lines to transmit printed messages from one terminal (the teleprinter) to another. The message is typed onto a keyboard transmitter, which converts the characters into a coded electrical signal for transmission. A printing receiver (combined with the transmitter) carries out the reverse process, typing out messages as they arrive. Telex messages are directed through the telephone lines by the subscribers' numbers, each subscriber also being identified by his call sign. The system is used by commercial organizations, because it provides both parties with a written copy of the messages. For many purposes it has been replaced by ▷fax and by ▷electronic mail.

● **Telford** ▶ 52 35N 2 35W A town in W central England, in Telford and Wrekin unitary authority, Shropshire. Created as a new town in 1963 (originally called Dawley New Town), it has grown rapidly as a site for modern technological industries. It is named after Thomas ▷Telford. Population (1991): 119 340.

● **Telford, Thomas** ▶ (1757–1834) British civil engineer, best known for his construction of the suspension bridge over the Menai Strait. The bridge, which was completed in 1825, is 177 metres long. Telford also designed and constructed some 1500 kilometres of roads, many bridges and aqueducts, and such canals as the Caledonian Canal and the Göta Canal in Sweden. He also designed St Katherine's Dock in London.

● **Telford and Wrekin** ▶ A unitary authority in W central England, in Shropshire. Area: 289 sq km (112 sq mi). Population (1999 est): 149 900.

● **Tell, William** ▶ A Swiss national hero who is first mentioned in a 15th-century chronicle and who, in Schiller's play *Wilhelm Tell* (1804), embodies the Swiss struggle for independence. After refusing to do homage as required by Gessler, the Austrian governor, Tell was ordered to shoot an apple from his son's head with a crossbow at 80 paces. He passed this test and later killed Gessler.

● **Tell el-Amarna** ▶ The site of Akhetaten, the capital founded (c. 1375 BC) by the heretic Egyptian pharaoh ▷Akhenaton. It was to have been the centre of Akhenaton's new religion but was abandoned shortly after his death (c. 1360). Amarna is associated with a naturalistic art style and a diplomatic correspondence (the ▷Amarna Tablets) showing the decline of Egyptian prestige in W Asia.

● **Teller, Edward** ▶ (1908–) US physicist, born in Hungary. After studying in Germany he left in 1933, going first to London and then to Washington, DC. He worked on the fission bomb during World War II and subsequently on the fusion bomb making a significant contribution to its development. He is sometimes known as "the father of the H-bomb." Teller's unfavourable evidence in the Robert ▷Oppenheimer security-clearance hearing lost him some respect amongst scientists.

● **tellurium** ▶ (Te) A silvery-white semiconductor of the sulphur group, discovered by Müller von Reichenstein in 1782. The hydride (H_2Te) is volatile and toxic, with a powerful smell of bad eggs. Bismuth telluride (BiTe) is used as an effective thermoelectric cooler. The metal is used in some special alloys and in some semiconducting devices. At no 52; at wt 127.60; mp 449.5 ± 0.3°C; bp 988°C.

● **Telstar** ▷*See* communications satellite.

● **Telukbetung** ▶ 5 28S 105 16E A port in Indonesia, in S Sumatra on the Sunda Strait. It was devastated by the eruption of ▷Krakatoa in 1883. Exports include rubber, coffee, and cinchona. Population (latest est): 284 275.

● **Tema** ▶ 5 41N 0 00E A port in Ghana, on the Atlantic coast. It has Africa's largest man-made harbour (opened 1962). Industries include oil refining, chemicals, and fishing. Population (1998): 300 000.

● **temazepam** ▷*See* benzodiazepines.

● **tempera** ▶ A method of painting, using ground pigment and a water-soluble gelatinous base, usually egg yolk. It was a very common medium for murals and easel paintings until it was supplanted by oils during the 15th century. It has lately been revived by German and US artists for its strong pure colours.

● **temperament** ▶ The method of tuning the notes of the scale to allow music in all ▷tonalities to sound in tune. The necessity arises because of the way scales are constructed in Western countries; systems of temperament sharpen or flatten certain notes to compensate for the slight discrepancy that arises in the interval between C and the C seven octaves higher. This interval should be (on the basis of seven octaves) $2^7 = 128$. However, in passing through the cycle of 12 keys, each using as its fundamental the fifth of its predecessor, the interval between Cs becomes $(3/2)^{12} = 129.75$. This difference, known as the comma of Pythagoras, can be compensated in several ways. From the 16th to the early 18th centuries, **meantone temperament** prevailed, in which the interval of a fifth was reduced to $\sqrt[4]{5} = 1.495$, enabling music written in tonalities with few sharps or flats to sound acceptably in tune. This was succeeded by **equal temperament**, in which the interval between each of 12 semitones of the octave is equal; the advantages of this system were demonstrated by Bach in *The Well-Tempered Clavichord* (1722), a collection of keyboard preludes and fugues in all keys. This system prevails today.

● **temperance movement** ▶ The promotion of abstinence or moderation in the consumption of alcohol. The earliest temperance societies were in the 19th century in the USA, which by 1833 had 6000 local groups (*see also* Prohibition). The Ulster Temperance Society, founded in 1829, was the first in Europe. The movement then spread to Scandinavia, where societies were established in Norway (1836) and Sweden (1837). The Church of England Temperance Society was founded in 1862.

● **temperature** ▶ A physical quantity that is a measure of the average ▷kinetic energy of the constituent particles of a body. It determines the direction in which ▷heat flows when two bodies are in contact, the body with the higher temperature losing heat to that with the lower. The temperature of a body may be measured using a scale between two or more fixed points, e.g. the ▷Celsius scale or ▷Fahrenheit scale. For scientific purposes the International Practical Temperature Scale (1990) is used; this has 16 fixed points and is designed to conform closely with **thermodynamic temperature**, which is measured in kelvins and is defined by one fixed point, the ▷triple point of water taken as 273.16 kelvins. The thermodynamic temperature was originally devised by Lord ▷Kelvin as the absolute scale based on the ▷Carnot cycle.

The normal **body temperature** of a human being is 36.9° Celsius or 98.4° Fahrenheit. A temperature in excess of normal is marked by fever and is often due to an infection. A temperature consistently lower than normal results in ▷hypothermia. Body temperature is controlled by the ▷hypothalamus of the brain.

● **Templars** ▶ (Poor Knights of Christ and of the Temple of Solomon) A religious order of knighthood founded (c. 1120) in Jerusalem, by a group of French knights, to protect pilgrims travelling to that city. The Templars were, with the ▷Hospitallers, the most important military order of the ▷Crusades. After the fall of Jerusalem (1187) they moved with the Hospitallers to Acre, where considerable rivalry and mutual distrust arose between the two orders. When Acre fell in 1291, both orders moved to Cyprus, where the wealth of the Templars enabled them to act as bankers for much of European nobility. Their power and influence attracted considerable hostility, especially from Philip IV of France. Accused of heresy and immorality by Philip, the Templars were suppressed by the papacy in 1312 with great cruelty, the Grand Master and many others being burnt at the stake.

● **Temple, Shirley** ▶ (1928–   ) US film actress and diplomat. She featured as a child star in many films during the 1930s, including *Little Miss Marker* (1934) and *Heidi* (1937). She won a special Academy Award in 1934. During the 1960s she went into politics and was appointed US ambassador to Ghana in 1974 under her married name, Shirley Temple Black. From 1989 to 1992 she was US ambassador to Czechoslovakia.

● **Temple, Sir William** ▶ (1628–99) English diplomat, who negotiated the Triple Alliance (1668) with the United Provinces and Sweden and the treaty that ended the third ▷Dutch War (1674). He also arranged the marriage of Charles II's niece Mary to William of Orange. The author of *Observations upon the United Provinces* (1673), he employed Jonathan Swift as his secretary in the 1690s.

● **Temple, William** ▶ (1881–1944) British churchman; Bishop of Manchester (1921–29), Archbishop of York (1929–42), and Archbishop of Canterbury (1942–44). Noted as a preacher, writer, a reformer of Church structures, and pioneer of the ecumenical movement, he is best remembered for *Nature, Man, and God* (1934), an influential theological work. His father **Frederick Temple** (1821–1902) was also Archbishop of Canterbury (1896–1902).

● **Temple Bar** ▶ A former gateway in London, between the Cities of London and Westminster. A barrier, which existed in medieval times, was replaced by an archway (1670–72) designed by Sir Christopher Wren and it became customary for the heads of executed criminals to be displayed here. In 1878 the Temple Bar Memorial replaced the archway, which is now in Theobalds Park, Herts, although there is a movement to restore it to a City site. The sovereign still continues an ancient tradition by seeking the Lord Mayor's permission here before entering the City.

● **Temple of Jerusalem** ▶ The ancient centre of Jewish religious

life, and traditionally the site of Jacob's dream of angels ascending a ladder to heaven. The first Temple was built by King Solomon (c. 950 BC) and destroyed by Nebuchadnezzar in 586 BC. The second Temple was built in the later 6th century BC, restored by the ▷Maccabees and later by Herod the Great, and destroyed by the Romans in 70 AD. Both temples were built on the same walled platform, known as the **Temple Mount**; part of the western retaining wall of this structure is the Wailing (Western) Wall, still a holy site for Jews. Since 691 the Muslim ▷Dome of the Rock has stood on the Temple Mount. ▷*See also* high priest; Holy of Holies.

● **temples** ▶ In ancient Greece and Rome, the sanctuaries of the gods. The first Greek temples were built of timber or brick but by the 6th century BC stone and marble were being used. They were rectangular buildings surrounded by a colonnade, with an inner sanctum containing the altar and a sculpture of the deity to whom they were dedicated. The best known is the ▷Parthenon.

Roman temples were raised on pedestals and usually had solid walls and a deep central portico. The Maison Carrée at Nîmes, France (1st century BC), and the domed ▷Pantheon in Rome are famous surviving examples.

● **Temuco** ▶ 38 45S 72 40W A city in S Chile and the gateway to Chile's lake district. It serves an area producing chiefly cereals, apples, and timber. Population (1995 est): 239 340.

● **tenant farming** ▶ A farming system in which a tenant has the use of agricultural land in return for the payment of rent to the landowner. The terms of the tenancy are usually legally laid down; in the UK, where tenant farming is commonly practised, the Agricultural Holdings Act (1948) confers security of tenure and certain rights to compensation for capital improvements made by the tenant and for disturbance when forced to quit.

● **tench** ▶ An elongated food and game fish, *Tinca tinca*, that is related to ▷carp and occurs in European fresh waters. Its slimy body, 18–45 cm long, is greenish or blackish above with lighter undersides. It lives in quiet waters that are rich in vegetation, feeding on small animals and plants.

● **Ten Commandments** ▶ The ▷covenant, also called the Decalogue, that was delivered by Jehovah to Moses on two stone tablets at Mount Sinai (Exodus 20.1–17; Deuteronomy 5.6–21). According to Exodus, Moses broke the original tablets when he descended from Mount Sinai and discovered the idolatry of the Israelites; they were replaced by two others, which were kept in the ▷Ark of the Covenant. Jews, Roman Catholics, and Protestants are not agreed as to the exact numbering of the commandments. The New Testament insists that unlike many other Old Testament laws they are binding on all mankind.

Although the numbering varies the Ten Commandments are: (1) The God of Israel is unique; (2) Jews must have no other gods and must not make idols; (3) God's name must never be taken in vain (misused); (4) the Sabbath must be respected as a holy day; (5) one must honour one's parents; (6) one must not commit murder; (7) adultery is forbidden; (8) one must not steal; (9) one must not give false evidence against another; (10) one must not covet another's possessions.

● **tendon** ▶ A strong fibrous cord that joins a muscle to a bone. The tendon fibres merge with the muscle fibres and extend to the fibrous tissue lining the bone, serving to concentrate the pull of the muscle on a small part of the bone. Inflammation of a tendon, called **tendinitis**, usually occurs through overuse, as in tennis elbow.

● **Tenerife** ▶ 28 15N 16 35W A Spanish island in the Atlantic Ocean, the largest of the Canary Islands. Its Pico de Teide mountain is, at 3710 m (12 172 ft), the highest in Spain. Early fruit and vegetables, such as bananas and tomatoes, are produced and the island is popular for holidays. Area: 2020 sq km (780 sq mi). Population (1990): 771 000. Chief town: Santa Cruz de Tenerife.

● **Teng Hsiao-p'ing** ▷*See* Deng Xiao Ping.

● **Teniers the Younger, David** ▶ (1610–90) Flemish painter. Known chiefly for his peasant scenes, he also made historically valuable copies of the paintings in the collection of Archduke Leopold

Wilhelm, whose court painter he became in Brussels in 1651. His father **David Teniers the Elder** (1582–1649) was a painter of religious subjects.

● **Ten Lost Tribes of Israel** ▶ The Hebrew tribes that rebelled against ▷Solomon's successor, Rehoboam, and formed a separate kingdom. This kingdom, which they called Israel, lay to the N of the territory occupied by the two remaining tribes of ▷Judah and of ▷Benjamin, which together constituted the southern kingdom of Judah. In 722 BC the northern kingdom was conquered by the Assyrians, many of its inhabitants deported, and their ethnic identity lost. The disappearance of the ten tribes from history has inspired many fanciful theories and conjectures.

● **Tennant Creek** ▶ 19 31S 134 11E A mining town in Australia, in central Northern Territory. Minerals extracted include gold (discovered in 1930) and copper and silver (discovered in 1955). Population (1986): 3503.

● **Tennessee** ▶ A state in the S central USA. It can be divided into East, Middle, and West Tennessee. In the E there is an upland region of thickly wooded mountains and in Middle Tennessee, in the loop of the Tennessee River, an area of upland plateau and rolling hills gives way in the W to an area of lowland plains and swamps situated between the Tennessee and Mississippi Rivers. An agriculturally poor state, its major crops are tobacco, soya beans, and cotton. Beef and dairy products are also important. Manufacturing is being encouraged especially by the Tennessee Valley Authority (*see* Tennessee River) and the leading industries produce chemicals, food products, electrical and nonelectrical machinery, and textiles. The state is an important hardwood producer in the S. It is the USA's largest producer of zinc and the extraction of stone is a major source of revenue.

History: disputed by the English and French in the 17th century, it was under British rule during the American Revolution. In 1790 the area was declared a territory and it became a state in 1796. Tennessee was a supporter of the Confederate cause in the US Civil War. Martin Luther ▷King, Jr was assassinated in Memphis in 1968. Area: 109 411 sq km (42 244 sq mi). Population (1996 est): 5 319 654. Capital: Nashville.

● **Tennessee River** ▶ A river in SE USA. It follows a U-shaped course from E Tennessee, flowing through NE Alabama before returning across Tennessee to join the Ohio River as its main tributary at Paducah, Kentucky. **The Tennessee Valley Authority**, created in 1933, built dams along the river to control floods and arrest soil erosion as well as to generate electricity. Length: 1049 km (652 mi).

● **Tennessee Walking Horse** ▶ A breed of horse developed in Tennessee and used by plantation owners for its characteristic running walk, which gives a smooth ride. It is solidly built with a thick neck and full mane and tail. The coat may be black, brown, bay, chestnut, or roan. Height: 1.57–1.63 m (15½–16 hands).

● **Tenniel, Sir John** ▶ (1820–1914) British cartoonist and book illustrator. He worked for *Punch* from 1851 to 1901 and specialized in humorous political cartoons, the best known being *Dropping the Pilot* (1890), inspired by Bismarck's resignation from the German chancellorship. His illustrations for *Alice in Wonderland* are his most famous works.

● **tennis** ▶ (*or* lawn tennis) A game for two or four players using rackets to hit a cloth-covered rubber ball on a grass or composition (hard) court. It originated in England in the mid-19th century and was highly popular by 1877, when the first Wimbledon championships were staged. It derives from the earlier French game of ▷real tennis. A modern tennis match lasts a maximum of five sets for men and three for women and the minimum number of games per set is six. A lead of two games is needed to win a set. However, if the score reaches six games each a tiebreaker is played (a game in which each side serves twice alternately). The scoring system derives from ▷real tennis and a minimum of four points is needed for a game: 15, 30, 40, and game; a lead of two points is also needed to win a game. A score of 40 on both sides is called "deuce"; the side that wins the next point then has the "advantage," which can either be clinched to win the game with a further point or nullified by the opposing side winning a point, in which case the score returns to deuce. Players take turns to serve for a

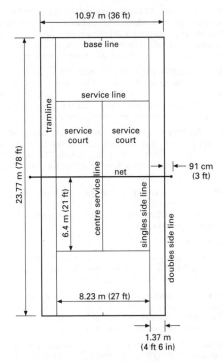

tennis ▶ The dimensions of the court. For singles games the posts holding the net are moved to inside the doubles sidelines. The net is 3 ft (91.4 cm) high at the centre.

game. A player is allowed two attempts to serve into the service court diagonally opposite, alternating courts between points. To win points players must return the ball over the net either before it bounces (volley) or after the first bounce, trying to position it so that their opponents cannot return it. The game is immensely popular at all levels of play, from the local club to the All England Championships at Wimbledon, which has admitted professional players since 1968. Other highly prized trophies are the US, Australian, and French Championships and the ▷Davis Cup and the ▷Wightman Cup for national teams.

● **Tennis Court Oath** ▶ (1789) The oath taken by the Third Estate of the ▷States General of France at the start of the French Revolution. After declaring itself a National Assembly, the Third Estate was excluded from its meeting place at Versailles. Adjourning to a nearby tennis court, the Assembly defiantly swore not to disband until the French kingdom had a written constitution.

● **Tennyson, Alfred, Lord** ▶ (1809–92) British poet. He began writing as a child at his father's rectory in Lincolnshire and at Cambridge University. He published two volumes in 1830 and 1832, but he gained general acclaim only with his 1842 volume, which included "Morte d'Arthur." In 1850 he married, became poet laureate, and published *In Memoriam*, a sequence of elegaic lyrics mourning the death of his close friend Arthur Hallam (1811–33). Now established as the national poet of the Victorian age, he reinforced his popularity with the Arthurian sequence *Idylls of the King* (1859) and other poems. He accepted a peerage in 1884.

● **Tenochtitlán** ▷*See* Mexico, United States of; Mexico City.

● **tenor** ▶ A high adult male singing voice. The word comes from the Latin *tenere*, to hold; in Renaissance polyphonic music the tenor part held the melody on which the music was based. Range: C on the bass stave to C two octaves above.

● **tenpin bowling** ▷*See* bowling.

● **tenrec** ▶ An insect-eating mammal belonging to the family *Tenrecidae* (30 species), found only in Madagascar and the Comoro Islands. Tenrecs measure 5–40 cm, some with long tails and some tailless, and generally have a brownish coat of bristly hairs or spines. Most tenrecs live in burrows and are nocturnal, feeding mainly on small invertebrates with some plant material. They are prolific breeders, producing litters of over 20. Order: ▷Insectivora.

● **tensile strength** ▶ The ability of a material to withstand a "pulling" stress (**tensile stress**). It is usually measured by taking a bar of the material and stretching it to destruction. The ultimate tensile strength is the maximum load divided by the bar's cross-sectional area and is measured in newtons per square metre.

● **Tenzing Norgay** ▶ (c. 1914–86) Sherpa mountaineer, who, with Sir Edmund ▷Hillary, was the first man to reach the summit of Mount Everest (1953), after working as a porter in 19 Himalayan expeditions from 1935. He became a director at the Himalayan Mountaineering Institute, Darjeeling.

● **Teotihuacán** ▶ An ancient city in central Mexico. Between 300 and 650 AD Teotihuacán controlled a wide area. It was destroyed about 750. The pyramid temples of the sun, moon, and ▷Quetzalcoatl are the most impressive remains.

● **tepee** ▷See wigwam.

● **Teplice** ▶ (or Teplice Šarnov) 50 40N 13 50E An industrial town and spa in the Czech Republic, in N Bohemia. Industries include paper, glass, and potteries. Population (1990 est): 55 000.

● **tequila** ▶ A Mexican spirit made of the fermented juice of an agave plant (see Agave), water, and, sometimes, sulphuric acid and yeast. The spirit is distilled twice in potstills then may be aged in casks. It is produced near the town of Tequila.

● **terbium** ▶ (Tb) A ▷lanthanide element, discovered in 1843 by C. G. Mosander (1797–1858) and named after the village Ytterby in Sweden. It is obtained from monazite ($CePO_4$), and the brown oxide (Tb_2O_3) is used as a phosphor in colour-television tubes. The metal is silvery-grey and can be cut with a knife. At no 65; at wt 158.92; mp 1356°C; bp 3230°C.

● **Terborch, Gerard** ▶ (1617–81) Dutch painter. He visited England (1635), Rome (1640), and Westphalia, where he painted the Dutch and Spanish diplomats signing the Peace of Münster (1648; National Gallery, London). His portraits and his family and guardroom scenes are remarkable for their skilled rendering of expression and textures.

● **Terbrugghen, Hendrik** ▶ (1588–1629) Dutch painter of the Utrecht school. After studying under the mannerist painter Abraham Bloemaert (1564–1651), he went to Italy in 1604, returning to Utrecht in 1614, where he specialized in religious and musical subjects in the style of ▷Caravaggio.

● **terebinth** ▶ A small tree, Pistacia terebinthus, native to the Mediterranean region. It has small flowers producing purple fruit and was formerly an important source of turpentine. Family: Pistaciaceae.

● **Terence** ▶ (Publius Terentius Afer; c. 185–c. 159 BC) Roman dramatist. Born in Carthage, he was taken to Rome as a slave by a senator who educated and later freed him. His six plays were all adapted from Greek New Comedy writers, especially Menander. He achieved popular success only with The Eunuch (161 BC), his style being more refined and sophisticated than that of his rival ▷Plautus. His work influenced several 17th- and 18th-century European writers.

● **Teresa, Mother** ▶ (Agnes Gonxha Bejaxhui; 1910–97) Indian nun born in Yugoslavia of Albanian parents, who founded the Order of the Missionaries of Charity (Calcutta; 1948) to help lepers, cripples, and the dying throughout the world. She received the first Pope John XXIII Peace Prize (1971), the 1979 Nobel Peace Prize, and honorary membership of the OM (1983).

● **Teresa of Ávila, St** ▶ (1515–82) Spanish Carmelite nun and mystic, who dedicated her life to reforming the Carmelite order. Of noble birth, she joined the Carmelites at Ávila in 1533 and in 1555 experienced a spiritual awakening followed by several visions. To restore the original Carmelite rule she founded the Convent of St Joseph in Ávila in 1562 and later other religious houses with the help of St ▷John of the Cross. Her books include Life (1562–65), The Way of Perfection (after 1565), and The Interior Castle (1577), which are regarded as classics of mysticism.

● **Tereshkova, Valentina Vladimirovna** ▶ (1937–) Soviet cosmonaut. In 1963, aboard Vostok 6, she became the first woman in space, completing 48 orbits of the Earth.

● **Teresina** ▶ 5 09S 42 46W A city in NE Brazil, the capital of Piauí state on the Rio Parnaíba. Its exports include cattle, hides, cotton, rice, and manioc. Its university was founded in 1968. Population (1991): 556 073.

● **Terman, Lewis Madison** ▶ (1877–1956) US psychologist, who published the first widely used intelligence test in the USA. Developed at Stanford University, his Stanford–Binet test was scored on an ▷intelligence quotient (IQ) rating based on both chronological and mental ages. In 1921 Terman established a long-term study of gifted children and he also estimated the IQs of famous people, rating Goethe at 210 and Darwin at 165.

● **terminal velocity** ▶ The maximum velocity attained by a body falling through a fluid. It occurs when the drag balances the gravitational force on the body; until the terminal velocity is reached the falling body accelerates; thereafter the velocity remains constant. According to ▷Stokes' law the terminal velocity of a sphere (radius r) falling through a fluid with a coefficient of viscosity η is $2\phi r^2 g/9\eta$, where ϕ is the difference between the body and fluid densities and g is the acceleration of free fall.

● **termite** ▶ A social ⬚insect, also called white ant (although unrelated to the ants), belonging to the mainly tropical order Isoptera (2000 species). Termite colonies nest in tunnels and galleries in wood, soil, or earth mounds (termitaria). There are three major castes: winged reproductives, workers, and soldiers. The reproductives swarm to found new colonies, a single pair (king and queen) producing huge numbers of offspring. The workers construct galleries, feed the colony, and care for the young, while the soldiers are concerned with defence. Termites eat cellulose and are very destructive when they invade houses and attack wood products.

● **tern** ▶ A seabird belonging to a subfamily (Sterninae; 35–40 species) occurring around coasts and inland waters worldwide and often called sea swallow or noddy. 20–55 cm long, terns have long wings, short legs, usually a forked tail, and their plumage is white, black-and-white, or almost totally black. They feed on fish and crustaceans and often migrate long distances (see Arctic tern). Family: Laridae (gulls and terns). ▷See Plate III.

● **Terni** ▶ 42 34N 12 39E A town in Italy, in Umbria on the River Nera. Industries include the manufacture of iron and steel, machinery, firearms, soap, and textiles. It is reputed to be the birthplace of Tacitus. Population (1996 est): 108 435.

● **terpenes** ▶ Naturally occurring hydrocarbons found in the ▷essential oils. Typically they are volatile compounds with pleasant odours and are used in flavouring foods and in perfumes. Their molecules are made up of isoprene units (C_5H_8). ▷Rubber is an example of a polyterpene.

● **Terpsichore** ▷See Muses.

● **terracotta** ▶ (Italian: baked earth) A fired clay, usually reddish in colour, used to make sculpture, tiles, bricks, containers, etc. It is principally associated with sculpture. Terracotta figurines, often painted, were very common in ancient Greece and Rome, a famous Greek type being the ▷Tanagra figurines. The art was revived during the ▷Renaissance, when the ▷Della Robbia family in Florence specialized in enamelled terracotta Madonnas. Later sculptors in terracotta include the Frenchman ▷Clodion.

● **terrapin** ▶ A small edible turtle belonging to the family Emydidae, occurring chiefly in the New World. The diamondback terrapin (Malaclemys terrapin), which occurs in coastal waters and salt marshes of North America, has diamond-shaped patterns on its dark carapace and is yellow with black speckles underneath. ⬚reptile.

● **terrarium** ▶ A transparent receptacle for land plants, used for propagation, decoration, or scientific study. The plants grow in a bottom layer usually consisting of sand or pebbles mixed with some charcoal and covered by topsoil.

● **Terre Adélie** ► (*or* Adélie Land) The only French territory in Antarctica, in the French Southern and Antarctic Territories on the coast of the Indian Ocean between longitudes 136°E and 142°E. It is the site of a French research station.

● **terrier** ► One of about 20 breeds of ▯dog characterized by their small sturdy build and traditionally used for hunting vermin, foxes, badgers, etc. The Scottish breeds, such as the ▷cairn terrier, ▷Scottish terrier, ▷Skye terrier, and ▷West Highland white terrier, tend to be smaller and longer haired than others, which are descended from the hunting terrier and other breeds.

● **Territorial Army** ► A British force of volunteers, created as the Territorial Force in 1907 and renamed in 1922. Between 1967 and 1979 it was known as the Territorial Army Volunteer Reserve. Its 84 000 men constitute a pool of trained and equipped reinforcements for the regular army.

● **territory** ► In ecology, a defined area defended by an animal against intrusion by another animal, usually of the same species. Territories can either reduce competition for food or serve to protect mates and young from interference. They vary in size according to their function, the fitness of the defending animal, and the population density of the species.

● **terrorism** ► The use of violence and intimidation to achieve an objective that is usually, but not always, political. This may involve the capture or assassination of members of a government or organization who are known to be antagonistic to the terrorists' cause; alternatively, the targets may be members of the public, who have no connection with the cause involved. In the latter case the motive is usually an attempt to generate publicity through outrage, or to put pressure on governments by arousing public alarm and concern. Indiscriminate shooting, bombing, hostage-taking, kidnapping, and ▷hijacking of public vehicles or aircraft are all part of the terrorist's armoury. Such acts may range from cowardly shootings-in-the-back, involving the perpetrators in little or no risk, to the activities of suicide bombers. The psychology of terrorists clearly varies widely; while in some cases their behaviour defies rational understanding (e.g. the ▷Baader-Meinhof Gang), other groups can be seen to have made a calculating use of terrorist methods as part of a political strategy and to have disbanded when these objectives were achieved (e.g. ▷EOKA, ▷Irgun Zvai Leumi). A third category of terrorists, it may be argued, are those for whom violence has become a way of life that cannot easily be given up, even when this would be in their political interests (e.g. the ▷Irish Republican Army). Terrorist groups whose motivation is not strictly or wholly political include those motivated by racism (e.g. the Nazi ▷Brown- shirts, the US ▷Ku Klux Klan), a religious belief (e.g. ▷Hamas, ▷al-Qaida) or an extreme minority cause (e.g. militant ▷animal rights movements).

The containment of terrorism is usually extremely difficult, not least because many of the organizations involved are financed, abetted, and protected by sympathetic governments. International collaboration against terrorism has rarely proved effective, owing to the different interests of the governments and police authorities involved. Following the terrorist attacks on America on ▷September11, 2001 (the most murderous and spectacular in history), President George W. Bush announced a concerted ▷war on terrorism in which US military force would be used against international terrorist networks and those regimes found to be harbouring them. This policy is supported by the UK government with British troops working alongside those of the USA. ▷*See also* guerrilla warfare; resistance movements.

● **Terry, Dame Ellen (Alice)** ► (1847–1928) British actress. A member of a large and talented family of actors, from 1878 to 1898 she acted with Sir Henry ▷Irving at the Lyceum Theatre, achieving particular success in the major Shakespearean roles. She later managed the Imperial Theatre, toured extensively, and gave lectures on Shakespeare. Her correspondence with G. B. ▷Shaw was published in 1931. Her son **(Edward Henry) Gordon Craig** (1872–1966) was an actor, designer, and producer. He joined Irving's company at the Lyceum as a child actor, but eventually devoted himself exclusively to design and production. He published *The Mask*, a theatre journal, and opened a school of acting after settling in Florence in 1908. His ideas on stage production have been very influential.

● **tertiary education** ► All vocational and nonvocational courses for school leavers and adults (*see* adult education). In the UK, **higher education** refers to academic education above A-level and its Scottish equivalent, as provided mainly by ▷universities and ▷colleges of higher education. In 1996–97 some 1 194 600 students were in full-time higher education in the UK. **Further education** consists of all post-secondary education other than higher education. In England and Wales it is funded by Further Education Funding Councils. The courses, provided in a range of general and specialist institutions, are mostly in technical, professional, and vocational training (e.g. National Vocational Qualifications), with part-time or full-time courses for GCSE and A-level exams also provided. Sixth-form or tertiary colleges offer normal sixth-form school courses and some vocational courses. Almost all the UK's 543 institutions of further education are now controlled by autonomous corporations. In 1997–98 some 775 941 students were in full-time further education in the UK, with a further 1 148 917 following part-time courses. Since the 1992 Further and Higher Education Act, which enabled the former polytechnics and other colleges of further education to designate themselves universities, many institutions have offered a mixture of higher and further education courses.

● **Tertiary period** ► The first geological period of the Cenozoic era, following the Cretaceous period and preceding the Quaternary (which is sometimes considered a continuation of the Tertiary). It lasted from about 65 to 1.8 million years ago and contains the Palaeocene, Eocene, Oligocene, Miocene, and Pliocene epochs, in ascending order. Most of the rocks of the period were laid down in shallow water. Modern invertebrates and mammals evolved and became increasingly abundant; the modern angiosperms became the dominant plants. The Alpine period of mountain formation extended through the period and reached its peak in the Miocene. The climate began to deteriorate in the Oligocene, leading to the Ice Age of the Pleistocene.

● **Tertullian(us), Quintus Septimius Florens** ► (c. 160–225 AD) African Father of the Church, born in Carthage. Educated in law, he was converted to Christianity by 197. He strongly defended the Montanists (*see* Montanism), whom he joined in 213. His writings, which include *Apologeticum*, *Ad nationes*, and *De praescriptione haereticorum*, were the first major Christian works in Latin.

● **Terylene** ▷*See* polyesters.

● **terza rima** ► A verse form consisting of a series of three-line stanzas the second line of which rhyme with the first and third lines of the preceding stanza (aba/cac/dcd/ede/...). It originated in Italy and was used by ▷Dante in the *Divine Comedy*. It was introduced into England by Sir Thomas ▷Wyatt in the 16th century. ▷*See also* rhyme.

● **tesla** ► (T) The ▷SI unit of magnetic flux density equal to one weber per square metre. Named after Nikola ▷Tesla.

● **Tesla, Nikola** ► (1856–1943) US electrical engineer, born in Croatia, who recognized the advantages of distributing electricity as alternating current rather than direct current. He fought a long battle with ▷Edison over this principle. The unit of magnetic flux density (*see* tesla) is named after him.

● **TESSA** ► (*or* tax exempt special savings account) A UK savings account at a bank or building society containing not more than £9000 (£3000 in the first year and £1800 increments in subsequent years) on which interest is tax free provided the capital and 25% of the interest remains in the account for five years. TESSAs were introduced in 1991 and replaced by ▷ISAs in 1999; however, TESSAs entered into before 6 April, 1999, continue until their term expires.

● **Test Acts** ► 1. In England, the Acts stipulating that public office holders must take Holy Communion in the Church of England (1673) and excluding all Roman Catholics except the Duke of York (later James II) from parliament (1678). It was repealed in the mid-19th century. **2.** In Scotland, the Act (1681) forcing public office holders to declare their belief in Protestantism; it was repealed in 1889.

● **testis** ► The organ of male animals in which ▷sperm is produced. In men a pair of testes, or testicles, produce sperm and sex hormones (*see* androgens). Before birth the testicles descend into the scrotum—a sac of skin outside the abdominal cavity—since sperms require a lower than body temperature to mature. The sperms complete their development in a convoluted tube (epididymis) outside the testis. At ejaculation they pass through a duct (vas deferens) to the urethra and out through the penis. ▷See Plate II.

• **testosterone** ▶ A steroid hormone—the most important of the ▷androgens. First isolated from bull testes in 1935, testosterone is now manufactured for medical uses, including the treatment of forms of sterility in men that are caused by underdevelopment of the testes. Its use to promote muscular development among athletes is illegal.

• **test-tube baby** ▶ A baby produced by fertilizing the mother's egg cell with sperm from the father in a test tube (*in vitro* fertilization): the fertilized egg is then implanted surgically into the mother's womb and allowed to come to term in the normal way. It is a means of overcoming sterility in a woman due to blocked Fallopian tubes or any similar defect. The technique was developed in Britain by Dr Patrick Steptoe and Robert Edwards and the first test-tube baby was born in 1978. The first baby developed from a frozen embryo was delivered in 1988. In this process a donor's egg is fertilized *in vitro* by the prospective father's sperm, the zygote is frozen, and later implanted into his wife's (or partner's) womb (zygote intra-Fallopian transfer). ▷See also artificial insemination; GIFT.

• **tetanus** ▶ A serious disease caused by the bacterium *Clostridium tetani* entering wounds and producing a powerful poison that irritates the nerves supplying muscles. The organism is prevalent in soil contaminated with animal droppings. After incubation for seven–ten days spasm and rigidity of the muscles affects the jaw (hence the popular name—lockjaw) and spreads to other muscles. In severe cases the whole body is seized with spasms and the patient may die from asphyxia. The disease is treated with tetanus antitoxin and penicillin; it can be prevented by antitetanus immunization.

• **tetra** ▶ One of several small brightly coloured freshwater fish of the family *Characidae* (*see* characin), found in South America and Africa and popular for aquaria. Well-known species include black tetra (*Gymnocorymbus ternetzi*), glowlight tetra (*Hemigrammus erythrozonus*), neon tetra (*Hyphessobrycon innesi*), and silver tetra (*Ctenobrycon spilurus*).

• **tetrachloromethane** ▶ (*or* carbon tetrachloride; CCl_4) A colourless nonflammable liquid that gives off toxic fumes. Formerly used as a fire extinguisher and in dry cleaning, it has been replaced for these purposes by other compounds on account of its toxicity. It is still used as a solvent for fats on a restricted basis.

• **tetracyclines** ▶ A group of ▷antibiotics derived from *Streptomyces* bacteria. Active against a large number of different bacteria, they are frequently the first choice of antibiotic for unidentified infections. Tetracyclines, which are taken by mouth, may cause the side effects of diarrhoea, nausea, and discoloration of teeth and bones.

• **tetraethyl lead** ▶ ($Pb(C_2H_5)_4$) A colourless poisonous oily liquid. It is made by treating lead-sodium alloys with chloroethane or by electrolysis and is added to petrol to prevent ▷knocking in engines. A source of air pollution, its use is being phased out; in recent years lead-free petrol has been introduced and, in the UK, given a lower excise duty. All new cars will shortly be able to run on unleaded fuel in which methyl tert-butyl ether (MTBE) is used as the antiknock agent.

• **Tetrazzini, Luisa** ▶ (1871–1940) Italian coloratura soprano. Born in Florence, she attended the Liceo Musicale there with her sister Eva, making her debut in Meyerbeer's opera *L'Africaine* in 1895. She toured with great success.

• **Tetuán** ▶ 35 34N 5 22W A city in N Morocco. Its port, on the Mediterranean coast, handles livestock and agricultural produce. The city produces textiles and light manufactured products. Population (1994 est): 277 516.

• **Tetzel, Johann** ▶ (c. 1465–1519) German Dominican friar, a preacher of ▷indulgences. His attempt to sell indulgences, which had been authorized to raise funds for the renovation of St Peter's in

Rome, provoked Luther's publication of the 95 theses and a famous debate between the two men.

• **Teutonic Knights** ▶ (Knights of the Teutonic Order) A religious order of knighthood founded (c. 1190) at Acre. In 1211 they moved from Palestine to E Europe, where they campaigned against pagan peoples, notably the Prussians, whom they had conquered by the end of the 13th century. They colonized Prussia and established their headquarters at Marienburg in 1309. They also gained control over much of the E Baltic region, as well as parts of Germany. During the 15th century they were defeated by the Poles, of whose king the order's grand master became a vassal. At the Reformation the order was dissolved except for one branch, which survived in Germany until its abolition by Napoleon (1809).

• **Tewkesbury** ▶ 51 59N 2 09W A market town in SW England, in Gloucestershire at the confluence of the Rivers Avon and Severn. The famous abbey church is Norman. In 1471 the Yorkists finally defeated the Lancastrians at the **Battle of Tewkesbury** in the Wars of the ▷Roses. Population (1991): 9488.

• **Texas** ▶ The second largest and the third most populous state in the USA, situated in the SW of the country. It consists of four main physical regions: the West Gulf Coastal Plain in the SE covering more than two-fifths of the state; the Central Lowland; the Great Plains, which extend mainly W from the Central Lowland into New Mexico; and the Trans-Pecos or mountainous area in the W. The chief producer of minerals since 1935, it leads the nation in the production of oil and natural gas; it is also a major producer of sulphur. Oil-related industries dominate the manufacturing sector, the most important being the chemical industry, especially along the Gulf Coast. There is also an important space centre at Houston and Dallas is a major commercial and industrial centre. Texas is a major agricultural region and has more farmed land than any other US state. It produces a variety of crops, especially cotton, sorghum grains, rice, and peanuts and it is a leading livestock producer.
History: colonized by the Spanish in 1682, the first permanent Anglo-American settlement was established by Stephen F. Austin in 1821. In 1836 the Texans set up a provisional government in opposition to the Mexican dictatorship of Antonio López de Santa Anna and following the heroic defence of the ▷Alamo, the revolutionary army under Sam Houston finally defeated Mexican forces in April of the same year. A republic was established and Texas remained independent for almost a decade until annexation by the USA was agreed upon and Texas became a state. It was a supporter of the Confederate cause during the US Civil War. Changes in the course of the Rio Grande, which forms part of the Texas–Mexico border, has led to several border disputes between the USA and Mexico and in 1970 the two countries agreed on plans to prevent any further substantial changes in the river's course. Area: 692 402 sq km (267 338 sq mi). Population (1996 est): 19 128 261. Capital: Austin.

• **Texas Rangers** ▶ A US paramilitary force whose exploits in the mid-19th century became part of the mythology of the Wild West. They were first organized in the 1830s to protect US settlers in Texas (then part of Mexico) from Indians and other marauders. Following the creation of the independent republic of Texas in 1836, they were reorganized as an elite mounted force to patrol the lawless Mexican border. In later decades their main function was to protect herders on the great cattle trails. They merged with the Texas state police in the 1930s.

• **textiles** ▶ Fabrics made from natural or synthetic ▷fibres. Textiles can either be made directly from these fibres, as in felt and bonded fabrics, or be woven or knitted from yarn spun from the fibres. Braiding, netting, and lace making are less common ways of producing textiles from yarn. The fibres used include animal fibres, such as ▷wool, hair, and ▷silk; vegetable fibres, such as ▷cotton, ▷flax, and ▷hemp; and synthetic fibres, such as rayon, nylon, and acrylic. Wool and hair were used in prehistoric times; ▷linen, derived from flax, was an early discovery, which declined when mass-produced cotton textiles became available cheaply. The invention of synthetic fibres and their combination with natural fibres has enormously increased the textile industry's range. ▷See also spinning; weaving.

• **texturized vegetable protein** ▶ (TVP) Vegetable protein, usually derived from soya beans, that has been processed for use as a meat substitute. Ground soya beans from which the oil has been removed are bound into a mixture and extruded into fibres. These are mixed with flavourings and other additives and consolidated into a protein-rich food with the fibrous texture of meat.

● **Tezcatlipoca** ▶ The Aztec god of the night sky, identified with the constellation Ursa Major and associated with witchcraft and evil. He was a creator-god and was usually portrayed with an obsidian mirror as a foot.

● **TGV** ▶ (Train à Grande Vitesse) A French train that averages over 130 mph (210 km/hr), which was initially used on the route from Paris to Lyons. It has since been developed to link Paris with other destinations, including the Channel Tunnel, Brussels, Cologne, Switzerland, and the Mediterranean. Electrically powered from overhead lines and running on continuously welded rails, it has a top speed of 236 mph (370 km/hr); since its introduction in 1981 it has been the fastest train in service.

● **Thackeray, William Makepeace** ▶ (1811–63) British novelist. Born in Calcutta, the son of an East India Company official, he was educated at Cambridge University and became a journalist. After publishing several novels in magazines under pseudonyms, he won fame with *Vanity Fair* (1847–48), which he followed with the semiautobiographical *The History of Pendennis* (1848–50) and the historical novel *Henry Esmond* (1852). In his last years he travelled widely and edited the *Cornhill Magazine* (1860–62).

● **Thailand, Kingdom of** ▶ (name until 1939: Siam) A country in SE Asia, on the Gulf of Thailand. Fertile plains and hills in the S rise to mountains in the N. The main river is the Chao Phraya and the Mekong forms part of the E boundary. Most of the population is Thai, with Chinese and Malay minorities.
Economy: the chief food crop is rice, which is also the main export. Production has been increased by irrigation schemes, such as the Chao Phraya Dam. Other crops include sugar, maize, sorghum, and cassava. Livestock and fishing are of growing importance. Forests cover 60% of the land, but hardwood export is now banned. Oil and gas were found in the 1970s and the petrochemical industry is being encouraged. Mineral resources include tin, tungsten, manganese, antimony, and zinc. The cement, textile, and motor vehicle industries are important; other manufactures include electrical equipment and computers. Tourism has been the main source of foreign revenue since the early 1980s. Rapid economic growth in the 1990s came to a sudden end with the collapse of the currency and the stock market in mid-1997; this proved a major factor in fomenting the general economic and financial crisis in SE Asia in the late 1990s.
History: there are indications of human settlement from very early times, and by the 6th century AD the Thais had reached the area from the N. They conquered the Mons to the S and in succeeding centuries were involved in frequent struggles with the Burmese and Khmers. In the 19th century they lost some territory to the French and the British but remained independent—the only country in the region never to be colonized by a European power. In 1932 the long-standing absolute monarchy was replaced by a constitutional monarchy. Civil and military governments alternated thereafter, often through violent upheavals. The country was occupied by the Japanese in World War II. In the 1970s it developed closer links with its communist neighbours, although relations with Vietnam deteriorated to a virtual state of war in the 1980s. In 1988 there were also border clashes with Laos. In 1992 protests against the political influence of the military led to the resignation of prime minister Gen Suchinda Kraprayoon. Following free elections Chuan Leekpai became prime minister of a reformist coalition. In the mid-1990s

Kingdom of Thailand

Head of state	King Bhumibol Adulyadej
Official language	Thai
Official religion	Hinayana Buddhism
Official currency	baht of 100 satang
Area	514 000 sq km (198 250 sq mi)
Population (1999 est)	61 806 000
Capital and main port	Bangkok

Thailand had the fastest growing economy in the world. However, in 1997 the financial crisis, caused by reckless lending by Thai banks, led to the virtual collapse of the economy and the fall of prime minister Chavalit Yongchaiyudh. The telecommunications tycoon Thaksin Shinawatra was elected prime minister in 2001.

● **Thais** ▶ (4th century BC) Greek courtesan, who accompanied ▷Alexander the Great's army during its invasion of Persia. According to tradition, she instigated the burning of the palace of Xerxes in Persepolis in 331 BC.

● **Thakin Nu** ▷*See* Nu, U.

● **thalassaemia** ▶ A form of ▷anaemia caused by an inherited abnormality of the haemoglobin molecule (the pigment of red blood cells). The disease is seen most commonly around the Mediterranean but can also affect any people of Mediterranean origin. Patients inheriting the abnormality from both parents suffer from the major form of the disease, which requires repeated blood transfusions. Those inheriting the disease from one parent are often free of symptoms.

● **Thales** ▶ (c. 624–547 BC) The first of the Greek speculative scientists, born at ▷Miletus. He used Babylonian astronomers' data to predict the solar eclipse of 28 May, 585 BC, advised on stellar navigation, and introduced Egyptian land measurements into Greece. He held that all things derive from water and set the ▷Presocratics on their quest for the basic substance of the universe.

● **Thalia** ▶ In Greek religion, one of the nine ▷Muses, the patron of comedy. She was the mother, by Apollo, of the ▷Corybantes.

● **thalidomide** ▶ A sedative drug found to cause severe developmental defects in the fetus when taken during pregnancy. The most common thalidomide-induced abnormality is phocomelia, in which the feet and hands develop normally without corresponding growth of the bones of the arms and legs. Between 1959 and 1962 some 500 deformed babies were born in the UK and over 2000 in West Germany.

● **thallium** ▶ (Tl) A metallic element, discovered spectroscopically by Sir William Crookes in 1861 and named after the Greek *thallos*, a green shoot, because of its bright-green spectral line. It is malleable and reacts to form numerous salts. The sulphate (Tl_2SO_4) is used as a rat poison. It occurs naturally in sulphide ores of lead and zinc and in iron pyrites (FeS_2). At no 81; at wt 204.38; mp 304°C; bp 1473 ± 10°C.

● **Thallophyta** ▶ In traditional plant classification systems, a subkingdom containing all those plants that lack true stems, leaves, and roots, i.e. the algae, fungi, and lichens. The plant body is a **thallus** and lacks the vascular (conducting) tissue of higher plants. Although this subkingdom is no longer used in modern classifications, the term "thallus" is still used for the body of algae and some lower plants.

● **Thames, River** ▶ The longest river in England. Rising in the Cotswold Hills near Cirencester, it flows mainly ESE through Oxford (as the Isis), Reading, and ▷London to enter the North Sea at the Nore. It is tidal as far as Teddington, and Tilbury can dock the largest oceangoing vessels. A tidal barrier has been constructed (1973–83) below London to reduce the danger of flooding. There have been successful attempts to combat pollution; whereas only eels could survive in the river in the early 1960s, many different species of fish can now be caught. Length: 346 km (215 mi).

● **Thanet, Isle of** ▶ 51 22N 1 15E An island in SE England, separated from the Kent mainland by two channels of the River Stour. It contains the resorts of Ramsgate and Margate. Area: 109 sq km (42 sq mi).

● **Thanjavur** ▶ (former name: Tanjore) 10 46N 79 09E A city in India, in Tamil Nadu. It has an 11th-century Hindu temple and a 16th-century raja's palace. Industries include textiles and jewellery. Population (1991): 200 216.

● **Thanksgiving Day** ▶ A national holiday in the USA, celebrated on the fourth Thursday in November. Thanksgiving Day was originally observed by the Pilgrim Fathers, who in 1621 celebrated their first harvest in North America. It became a national holiday in 1863, with roast turkey and pumpkin pie being eaten. It is also celebrated in Canada, on the second Monday in October.

● **Thant, U** ► (1909–74) Burmese diplomat who became secretary-general of the United Nations (1961–72). Having served in the independence movement during World War II, he became Burma's director of broadcasting (1948–52) before becoming his country's delegate to the UN. As secretary-general he dealt impressively with a series of testing international crises, including the Cuban missile crisis (1962), the civil war in Cyprus (1964), and the Arab-Israeli Six-Day War (1967).

● **Thapsus, Battle of** ► (46 BC) The battle in which Julius Caesar crushed ▷Pompey's supporters in North Africa. The battle was part of Caesar's campaign to retain control of Rome.

● **Thar Desert** ► (*or* Great Indian Desert) A large arid area lying along the central 800 km (497 mi) of the India-Pakistan border, mostly in India. Area: about 250 000 sq km (96 504 sq mi).

● **Tharp, Twyla** ► (1941–) US choreographer, whose work combines elements of classical ballet and modern dance. After training under Martha ▷Graham she founded her own company in 1965. Her best-known works include *Eight Jelly Rolls* (1971), *Push Comes to Shove* (1976), and several collaborations with Mikhail ▷Baryshnikov. She has choreographed films and Broadway musicals.

● **Thásos** ► A Greek island in the N Aegean Sea. It is the site of archaeological excavations and zinc is mined. Area: 399 sq km (154 sq mi). Population (latest est): 1311.

Margaret Thatcher ►
The UK's first woman prime minister. Made a life peeress in 1992 and has continued to oppose Britain's closer integration with the European Union.

● **Thatcher, Margaret (Hilda), Baroness** ► (1925–), British stateswoman; Conservative prime minister (1979–90). After working as a research chemist and then a barrister, she entered parliament in 1959 and was appointed minister of pensions and national insurance in 1961. In 1969 she became opposition spokesman on education and was secretary of state for education and science from 1970 to 1974. In 1975 she succeeded Edward Heath as Conservative leader and in 1979 became the first woman prime minister of the UK. In 1980–81 her anti-inflationary policies of monetarism and curbs on government spending led to high unemployment and some social unrest. However, following the successful Falklands Islands campaign (1982) and faced by a divided opposition she gained a landslide victory in 1983. Her second term was characterized by policies of privatization, curbs on union power, and reduced taxation implemented by her chancellor, Nigel ▷Lawson. Abroad she gained a reputation as either a formidable opponent or a loyal ally, both views being reflected in the (originally Russian) epithet "Iron Lady." Signs of economic recovery led to a third election victory in 1987 and Thatcher became the longest serving UK prime minister of the century. However, discontent with her personal style of leadership and her apparent reluctance to commit the UK to full participation in the EC led to the resignations of Lawson in 1989 and Sir Geoffrey (now Lord) ▷Howe in 1990. Implementation of the ▷poll tax and an economic downturn contributed to disaffection within the Tory party and failing popularity with the

electorate. In 1990 she resigned after failing to win an outright victory over Michael ▷Heseltine in a ballot for the leadership of the party. She entered the House of Lords as a life peer in 1992 and has continued to attack moves towards greater EU integration. She has published two volumes of memoirs, *The Downing Street Years* (1993) and *The Path to Power* (1995).

● **Theatre of Cruelty** ► A theatrical genre originated by Antonin ▷Artaud, who believed that drama should destroy the superficial restraints of civilized life and liberate repressed emotions. *Les Cenci* (1935), his chief experimental production, was a failure, but his theories influenced many later writers and directors, including ▷Barrault, ▷Camus, and ▷Genet.

● **Theatre of the Absurd** ► A theatrical genre ("the Absurd" being borrowed from the existentialist philosophy of Albert ▷Camus) popularized in the 1950s and 1960s in which the human condition is presented as absurd. It includes the plays of Eugene ▷Ionesco, Samuel ▷Beckett, Arthur ▷Adamov, and others, which reject established theatrical conventions and use comic effects in developing pessimistic philosophical themes.

● **theatres and stages** ► The design of buildings specifically for the staging of plays has been governed by the shifting religious and social significance of the ▷drama and the type of illusion or effect intended by different sorts of play. Another factor has been the attempt to provide optimum acoustics and visibility using the technical means available at the time. Ancient Greek theatres were large outdoor structures built to adjoin such religious centres as ▷Athens, ▷Epidauros, and ▷Delphi. The secularized theatres that were a feature of most Roman towns were similar but particularly adapted to the production of ▷Roman comedy, notably in their use of curtains and scenic devices. Christian drama evolved from the liturgy but in late medieval Europe moved outside the churches as the craft guilds presented ▷miracle plays. Renaissance court theatres mainly imitated indoor Roman models, while the open-air Elizabethan theatre represented a more popular tradition. During the 17th century elaboration of stage machinery (*see* masque), demands for illusionistic settings (often involving complex perspective scenery), and the development of ▷opera and ▷ballet stimulated the spread of the proscenium arch stage design, in which an opening (with retractable curtain) provides a picture-frame setting for the action. With the rise of realism the proscenium arch remained virtually universal in the 18th and 19th centuries. The modern drama's tendency towards abstraction and evocation of mood, together with nonrealistic scenery and stage lighting, has fostered renewed interest in theatre-in-the-round (seats round a central acting arena) and the Elizabethan apron stage. ▷*See also* repertory theatres.

● **Thebes** ► An ancient city in Upper Egypt and capital of all Egypt (c. 1570–c. 1085 BC). Thebes' power was linked with the supremacy of its god ▷Amon. With its associated sites of ▷Karnak, ▷Luxor, and the ▷Valley of the Kings, Thebes testifies to the splendour of ancient Egyptian civilization.

● **Thebes** ► 88 19N 23 19E A town in Boeotia, in central Greece. It was founded in Mycenaean times and its legends were favourite themes in Greek drama. Predominant among its Boeotian neighbours, Thebes lost influence supporting the Persians in 480 BC, but became the leading Greek state after defeating the Spartans at Leuctra (371). Opposition to Macedonia led to destruction (336). Population (latest est): 18 712.

● **theft** ► The offence of dishonestly appropriating property belonging to another with the intention of permanently depriving the other person of it. The property need not be tangible. The earlier offence of larceny involved "taking and carrying away" the goods and was until 1827 divided into Grand Larceny, which originally carried the death penalty or ▷transportation, and Petty Larceny, when the value of the stolen property was less than a shilling. It was replaced by theft as defined by the Theft Act (1968).

● **thegn** ► A person in Anglo-Saxon England who held land from his lord in return for service. The status of thegn (meaning one who serves) was hereditary. The king's thegns had military and administrative duties and also attended the ▷witan (king's council). Their im-

An engraving of the classical Greek theatre at Aspendus, Pamphylia.

Medieval miracle and mystery plays were performed on large wagons in public places. Different wagons were used for different scenes.

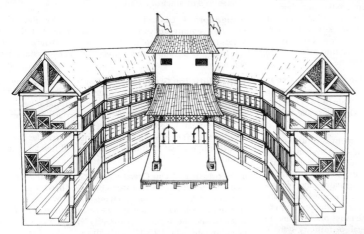

Spectators in the Elizabethan theatre sat in galleries or stood in the open pit. The acting area comprised the main stage, a rear stage, and a balcony. The Globe Theatre in London (opened 1996) is an almost exact replica of the Elizabethan theatre shown here, except that the seating galleries form a circle round the pit.

The proscenium arch allowed the audience to view a scene as if through a window. This engraving is of the Olympic Theatre, near London's Drury Lane.

The theatre-in-the-round design of the Chichester Festival Theatre (1962) recreates a primary feature of Elizabethan theatre — close contact between actors and audience.

portance declined in the early 11th century, when the Danish kings introduced their ▷housecarls, and the thegns died out as a clan after the Norman conquest.

● **theism** ▶ The belief in a personal God as creator and preserver of the universe, who intervenes in his creation and reveals himself by supernatural means to his creatures. Apparently coined (1678) by ▷Cudworth as an opposite to ▷atheism, theism excludes both ▷pantheism and ▷deism. It is central to Christian, Judaic, and Islamic belief.

● **theme park** ▶ An amusement park, usually catering primarily for children, in which a central theme determines the character of the attractions provided. The first was Disneyland, which opened in 1955 in Anaheim, California, and was based on the cartoon characters of Walt ▷Disney. The success of this venture encouraged the Disney organization to open similar parks in Florida (1971), Tokyo (1983), and Paris (1992). In the UK there are some 15 theme parks, including Alton Towers, Staffordshire (1979), Chessington World of Adventure, Surrey (1987), and Legoland, Windsor, Berkshire (1996).

● **Themis** ▶ The Greek goddess of justice and wisdom, often portrayed carrying a pair of scales. She was a Titan, the daughter of Uranus and Gaia and the second wife of Zeus. As the wife of the Titan Iapetus, she was also the mother of ▷Prometheus.

● **Themistocles** ▶ (c. 528–462 BC) Athenian statesman, who built Athens' naval power. Themistocles persuaded Athens to expand its navy (483) and to transfer its port from Phaleron to the more defensible Piraeus. These policies, and his leadership at the battle of ▷Salamis, saved Greece from Persia (480) (*see* Greek-Persian Wars). Themistocles argued successfully for the fortification of Athens, despite Spartan opposition, but his opponents had him ostracized in about 471. He subsequently fled to Asia, where he died.

● **Thenard, Louis-Jacques** ▶ (1777–1857) French chemist, who in 1808 was the first to isolate the element ▷boron in collaboration with ▷Gay-Lussac. He also discovered hydrogen peroxide in 1813 and produced a pigment known as Thenard's blue, which is stable at high temperatures and so can be used in porcelain.

● **theocracy** ▶ A society in which the government is controlled by the priesthood or in which the political and legal system is conducted in strict accordance with religious belief. Pure theocracy has been rare in human history, with John ▷Calvin's Geneva as perhaps the only true European example. This may be explained by the obvious difficulties involved in translating religious teachings (which are often deliberately paradoxical and extreme) into workable human laws; it is, for instance, arguable that the teachings of Christ are incompatible with any realistic economic, legal, or military system. Nevertheless, many societies (e.g. those of medieval Europe) have combined elements of theocracy with more secular arrangements. The early modern period saw the ascendancy of the secular power over that of the Church in most European countries, a process that was accelerated by the ▷Enlightenment, which taught that religion was a private matter that should be separated from public life. This separation is enshrined in the First Amendment to the US Constitution (1791) and for all essential and practical purposes acknowledged in nearly all Western societies today. The theocratic principle has not, however, disappeared entirely from the modern world. Tibet under the ▷Dalai Lama was a theocracy until the country was occupied by China (1951), while a contemporary example of a near-theocracy, in which the government was controlled by a religious leader, was Iran under Ayatollah ▷Khomeini (1978–89). The term is sometimes extended to mean any society in which religious organizations or doctrines are accorded an official role in the political or legal system; this would include many modern Muslim states and, until very recently, the Republic of Ireland. The State of Israel presents a more complex case, as ▷Zionism can be seen as a secular movement based on an essentially religious belief (i.e. that ancient Palestine was promised to the Jews by God). Nevertheless the secular governments of Israel frequently have to contend with an Orthodox Jewish faction in the ruling coalition.

● **Theocritus** ▶ (c. 310–250 BC) Greek poet. Born in Sicily, he worked for part of his life on the island of Cos and at Alexandria. His surviving poems, the *Idylls*, include six poems cast in the dramatic form of dialogues or contests between countrymen. These poems on Sicilian rural life are unsurpassed examples of the pastoral, a form which Theocritus originated and which influenced many later works, such as Milton's *Lycidas*.

● **theodolite** ▶ An instrument used in ▷surveying to measure horizontal and vertical angles. It consists of a telescope, with crosshairs in the eyepiece for focusing on the target, that can swivel on horizontal and vertical axes, which pass through two circular scales. It has a spirit level to indicate when the instrument is horizontal and is mounted on a tripod with adjustable legs.

● **Theodora** ▶ (c. 500–48 AD) Byzantine empress (527–48); the wife of ▷Justinian I. Theodora was the daughter of a circus bearkeeper and had been an actress before she married Justinian in 525 and became one of the most influential women in the history of the Eastern Roman Empire. Justinian consulted her on all affairs of state and his reign achieved little of consequence after her death. She was noted for her early championship of the rights of women.

● **Theodorakis, Mikis** ▶ (1925–) Greek composer, who led a revival of Greek folk music in the 1960s and has incorporated elements of it into his compositions, which include music for the film *Zorba the Greek* (1964). He has also been politically active in Greece and in 1967 was imprisoned by the military government for his left-wing activities. After international protests, he was released in 1970 and re-elected to parliament in 1981.

● **Theodore I Lascaris** ▶ (c. 1175–1222) The founder of the Byzantine empire at Nicaea after Constantinople fell to the Crusaders (1204). In 1214, following a period of warfare, Theodore and the Latins determined the borders between Constantinople and Nicaea.

● **Theodoric the Great** ▶ (c. 445–526) King of the Ostrogoths (471–526), who ruled Italy (493–526). He defeated ▷Odoacer in 493 and established an Ostrogothic kingdom with its capital at Ravenna, ensuring peace by religious toleration and marriage alliances with the other barbarian kingdoms. His chief minister was ▷Boethius. However, territorial expansion brought conflict with the Frankish king ▷Clovis and his death left Italy leaderless and ripe for Byzantine annexation.

● **Theodosius (I) the Great** ▶ (347–95 AD) Roman emperor in the East (379–94) and sole emperor (394–95). Theodosius allowed the Visigoths independence on Roman territory by a treaty in 382 and they undertook to supplement the Roman army. A devout and orthodox Christian, he imposed Christianity on the Empire in 391, closing pagan temples and forbidding sacrifices.

● **Theodosius II** ▶ (401–50 AD) Eastern Roman emperor (408–50). He was strongly influenced by his sister, his wife, and a series of advisers. He sponsored the compilation of the **Theodosian Code** (438), a collection of laws that had been issued since 312.

● **theology** ▶ Literally, the study of ▷God. Each of the higher religions has its own theology. Christian theology includes within its scope the nature of God, his relationship with the universe, his providence regarding man, and the teachings of the Church. Different traditions exist within the Roman Catholic, Orthodox, and Protestant communions, but typical subdivisions of theology are dogmatic, historical, and pastoral theology. Until the emergence of Renaissance ▷humanism, theology was accounted the highest science (*see* scholasticism) but from the 18th century onwards its findings came under hostile scrutiny from nonbelievers. In the 20th century theology has been influenced by new historical understandings of the Bible and by such movements as ▷existentialism and Marxism (*see* liberation theology).

● **Theophilus** ▶ (d. 842 AD) Byzantine emperor (829–42). He was a man of great learning and, despite frequent attacks by the Muslims, stimulated a resurgence of cultural activity. He was the last emperor to uphold ▷iconoclasm.

● **Theophrastus** ▶ (c. 370–286 BC) Greek philosopher and scientist. He studied under ▷Plato and became ▷Aristotle's closest friend, succeeding him as head of the ▷Lyceum. He established botany as a science and lectured and wrote on a vast number of subjects.

● **theorbo** ► A large double-necked ▷lute having two sets of strings. One set could be stopped against a fingerboard, the other plucked as open strings.

● **theosophy** ► Speculation tending towards a mystical understanding of the divine. The term originated in ▷Neoplatonism but is now mainly applied to the blend of Hindu and Neoplatonic doctrines propounded by the Theosophical Society, which was founded by Helena ▷Blavatsky in 1875. *Compare* anthroposophy.

● **Thera** ► (or Santoríni; Modern Greek name: Thíra) A Greek island in the Aegean Sea, the southernmost of the Cyclades group. The present island is the E side of a volcano the catastrophic explosion of which (some time between 1645 BC and 1450 BC) precipitated the decline of ▷Minoan civilization on Crete, 110 km (70 mi) to the S (*see also* Atlantis). In 1966 a well-preserved Minoan town was found on Thera. Population (latest est): 7083. Area: 75 sq km (29 sq mi).

● **therapsid** ► An extinct reptile of the order *Therapsida*, which lived during the Permian and Triassic periods (280–200 million years ago). The ancestors of mammals, they had a number of mammal-like features: the limbs were positioned under the body to carry it well off the ground; the skull was deep with a fairly large braincase; and the teeth were specialized for different functions. There were both carnivorous and herbivorous forms.

● **Theravada** ► The old conservative school of ▷Buddhism, also called Hinayana (Pali: lesser vehicle) by its detractors. Prevalent in Myanmar (Burma), Cambodia, Laos, Sri Lanka, and Thailand, it emphasizes the ideal of the *arhat*—one who, as a monk, achieves enlightenment by his own efforts. In Theravada, the ▷Buddha is revered but not the Bodhisattvas, and only the Pali canon is considered orthodox.

● **Thérèse, St** ► (Marie Françoise Thérèse Martin; 1873–97) French Carmelite nun, known as the Little Flower of Jesus. She entered the Carmelite convent at Lisieux when only 15 and died there 9 years later of tuberculosis. Her fame rests on her spiritual autobiography, *Histoire d'une âme* (1898), showing that spiritual perfection could be attained through childlike humbleness and goodness. She was canonized in 1925 and declared a doctor of the church in 1997. Feast day: 1 Oct.

● **therm** ► An obsolete unit of energy equal to 100 000 Btu (1.055 06 $\times 10^8$ joules); it was formerly used by British Gas to charge for gas consumed, but has now been replaced by the kilowatt hour (0.0341 therm).

● **thermae** ► Ancient Roman public baths. They reached their height of architectural sophistication under the Empire, being equipped with libraries and other amenities for relaxation. The best surviving examples include the baths of Titus (81 AD) and Caracalla (217).

● **thermal** ▷*See* gliders.

● **thermal reactor** ► A nuclear reactor (*see* nuclear energy) in which natural or enriched uranium is used with a moderator, in most cases to generate heat for a ▷power station. The moderator slows down the neutrons emitted during the fission of uranium-235, so that their velocities are comparable to the thermal velocities of gas molecules. In a thermal reactor, fuel rods made of uranium metal or oxide are surrounded by a moderator (together forming the reactor core), the heat of the reaction being removed by a coolant. After leaving the core, the coolant passes to a heat exchanger in which steam is raised. The rate of reaction is controlled by control rods, moved in and out of the core: these contain a neutron-absorbing element, e.g. boron or cadmium.

The first nuclear reactor was built by ▷Fermi in 1942, using natural uranium, a graphite moderator, and a water coolant. Early British thermal reactors were the Magnox type, using natural uranium; 18 were built, the earliest of which are now being decommissioned. The next generation of British reactors were the advanced gas-cooled reactors (AGR), using enriched uranium dioxide pellets, each about the size of a thimble and equivalent to 1.25 tons of coal. However, thermal reactors are now usually based on the US-designed pressurized-

water reactors (PWR), using ordinary water as both moderator and coolant. These are now considered the most economical and efficient; they also power all nuclear submarines. ▷*See also* fast reactor; □nuclear energy.

● **thermic lance** ► A device used for cutting through steel, concrete, etc.; it consists of a steel tube filled with steel wool or steel rods, through which oxygen is fed. The iron burns in the oxygen, producing a temperature of over 3000°C. It is used by safebreakers as well as for legitimate purposes.

● **Thermidorian Reaction** ▷*See* French Revolution.

● **thermionic valve** ► A device consisting of a sealed glass or metal tube, either evacuated or containing gas at low pressure, into which two or more electrodes are inserted. One heated electrode, the cathode, emits free electrons, which are attracted to the positively charged anode, forming an electric current. This current flows in one direction only and can be controlled by the voltage applied at one or more other electrodes (called grids). The **diode** was invented in 1904 by Sir John Ambrose Fleming. It has two electrodes and functions as a simple ▷rectifier. The **triode** with one grid was invented in 1910 by Lee De Forest; it was the first to function as an amplifier. The weak signal fed to the grid produces a stronger signal in the anode circuit. The **thyratron** is a gas-filled triode that functions as a relay, as it continues to pass current once the discharge has been initiated. It was widely used as an electronic switch. Diodes and triodes made possible the development of radio and all electronic devices made use of valves—diodes, triodes, and pentodes (with five electrodes)—until they were replaced in the 1950s by ▷semiconductor diodes and ▷transistors. These devices are cheaper, smaller, and more reliable than thermionic valves; they also consume less power. However, for some special purposes thermionic valves are still used (*see* cathode-ray tube; klystron; magnetron).

● **thermistor** ► A ▷semiconductor device with an electrical resistance that decreases sharply as temperature increases. It is used in temperature-control circuits and as a thermometer.

● **thermite** ► A mixture of powdered aluminium and iron oxide. When ignited, aluminium oxide and iron are produced. The reaction is exothermic, yielding iron at a temperature of over 2000°C. It is used in welding steel and in incendiary bombs.

● **thermocline** ► A layer some 100–200 m below the surface of the ocean, in which there is a marked increase in temperature with depth. Above and for some distance below it, there is little vertical temperature gradient.

● **thermocouple** ► A type of thermometer consisting of an electric circuit formed by two dissimilar metals joined at each end. One junction is exposed to the temperature to be measured, a voltage being generated between it and the other (reference) junction as a result of the temperature difference between them (*see* thermoelectric effects). The output is usually displayed on a ▷galvanometer. Copper-constantan junctions are used up to 500°C and platinum-rhodium alloy up to 1500°C. A **thermopile** consists of several thermocouples in series to increase the voltage output for a particular temperature difference.

● **thermodynamics** ► The study of ▷heat and its relationship with other forms of energy. Thermodynamics is primarily a statistical subject, thermodynamic quantities, such as ▷temperature and ▷entropy, being dependent on the statistical behaviour of the particles that comprise a system. There are three fundamental **laws of thermodynamics**. The first law, largely due to J. P. ▷Joule and H. L. F. von ▷Helmholtz, states that the energy of a closed system remains constant during any process. This law is a restatement of the law of ▷conservation of mass and energy. The second law states that heat cannot flow from a cold body to a hot body without the expenditure of external work. Another way of stating this law, due to R. J. E. ▷Clausius in 1854, is to say that the entropy of a closed system can never decrease. If the entropy change is zero then the process is said to be reversible. The third law, due to W. H. ▷Nernst in 1906, states that as the thermodynamic temperature of a system aproaches ▷absolute zero, its entropy approaches zero. All three laws of thermodynamics depend on the statement that if two bodies are each in thermal equilibrium with a third body, then all three bodies are in thermal equilibrium with each other. This is sometimes known as the **zeroth law of thermodynamics**. Thermodynamics has proved most valuable in studying ▷heat engines and chemical reactions, but it also has wider implications in other statistical sciences. ▷*See* heat death of the universe.

● **thermodynamic temperature** ▷*See* temperature.

● **thermoelectric effects** ▶ The effects of changes of temperature on electric circuits or devices. The **Seebeck effect**, named after Johann Seebeck (1770–1831), provides the basis for the ▷thermocouple; it occurs when a circuit has two junctions between dissimilar metals. If the junctions are maintained at different temperatures, a voltage is generated between them. The **Peltier effect**, named after Jean Peltier (1785–1845), is the converse of this. One junction heats up and the other cools down when a steady current flows through such a circuit. In the **Thomson effect** (*or* Kelvin effect), named after Lord ▷Kelvin, a temperature gradient along a single metal conductor causes a current to flow through it.

● **thermography** ▶ A diagnostic technique for measuring heat produced by different parts of the body, using photographic film sensitive to infrared radiation; the record is a **thermogram**. Regions of poor circulation produce less heat, while tumours, having an increased blood supply, generate more heat and are recorded as "hot spots" on the thermogram. Thermography to diagnose breast tumours is called **mammothermography**.

● **thermoluminescence** ▶ ▷Luminescence caused by heating a substance and thus liberating electrons trapped in its crystal defects. The phenomenon is used as a dating technique, especially for pottery. The number of trapped electrons is assumed to be related to the quantity of ▷ionizing radiation to which the specimen has been exposed since firing (as the crystal defects are caused by ionizing radiation) and therefore to its age. Thus, by measuring the amount of light emitted on heating, an estimate of its age can be made.

● **thermometer** ▶ An instrument for measuring temperature. Thermometers use a property of a substance that varies uniformly with temperature, commonly the expansion of liquid mercury. The first mercury thermometer was invented by G. D. Fahrenheit (*see* Fahrenheit scale). It consists of a glass bulb filled with mercury and attached to a closed evacuated capillary tube on which the temperature scale is marked. As the temperature increases, the mercury from the bulb expands and rises up the capillary, indicating the temperature on the scale. A clinical thermometer is a typical mercury-in-glass thermometer in which a constriction above the bulb ensures that the mercury remains at its maximum level until it has been shaken back into the bulb. More accurate thermometers use the expansion of a gas, which is greater than that of a liquid. Other thermometers include the resistance thermometer, which depends on the variation in the resistance of a wire (usually platinum); the bimetallic strip in which the unequal expansion of two metals welded together causes a pointer to move round a dial; and the ▷thermistor. High temperatures are measured by a ▷pyrometer and very low temperatures (cryogenic temperatures) in the range of 0.2 K to 20 K are measured by semiconductor devices.

● **thermonuclear reactor** ▶ A reactor in which a fusion reaction (*see* nuclear energy) takes place with the controlled release of energy. It is now accepted that a thermonuclear reactor is unlikely to be in commission in the forseeable future. The most readily achieved fusion reaction is the combination of deuterium and tritium to form helium ($^2_1H + ^3_1H = ^4_2He + n + 17.6$ MeV). To overcome the electrostatic repulsion (*see* Coulomb's law) between nuclei a temperature of about 40 million °C is needed. Containing the ▷plasma is the central problem. To produce useful power gain at this temperature, the product of the plasma density and the containment time must exceed 10^{14} particle seconds per cm^3. In magnetic containment the plasma is kept away from the containing walls by magnetic fields (of a few tesla) generated by electric currents flowing through external coils as well as the plasma itself. Toroidal tokamak devices, which originated in the Soviet Union, have approached this figure but problems of magnetic instabilities and impurity control have not yet been solved. Other possible techniques include inertial confinement in

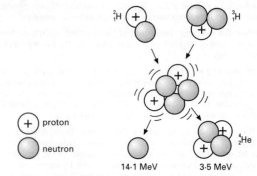

+ proton

◯ neutron

14·1 MeV   3·5 MeV

deuterium-tritium fusion reaction

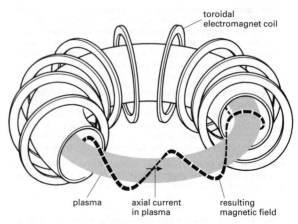

toroidal
electromagnet coil

plasma   axial current   resulting
                in plasma   magnetic field

fusion reactor experiment

thermonuclear reactor ▶ The combination of deuterium ($^2_1$H) and tritium ($^3_1$H) in a fusion reaction that forms helium. This is being attempted using a toroidal electromagnet to contain plasma consisting of deuterium and tritium nuclei.

which a pellet of fuel is exposed to ▷laser or particle beams to produce ▷adiabatic compression (to 100 times solid density), which causes ignition. The outstanding problems relate to the efficient generation of high-power beams (ultraviolet, X-ray, or proton) and to maintaining symmetry during compression. The virtually inexhaustible supply of thermonuclear fuel (hydrogen and its isotopes) makes the fusion reactor extremely attractive.

● **thermopile** ▷*See* thermocouple.

● **thermoplastic materials** ▷*See* plastics.

● **Thermopylae, Battle of** ▶ (480 BC) The battle in which the Greeks under the Spartan king, ▷Leonidas, attempted for three days to hold the pass of Thermopylae in E central Greece against the Persians. After the main Greek force had retreated the Spartans and Thespians, surrounded and outnumbered, fought to the death. Their heroic stand inspired continued Greek resistance to Persia (*see* Greek-Persian Wars).

● **thermosetting plastics** ▷*See* plastics.

● **Thermos flask** ▷*See* Dewar flask.

● **thermostat** ▶ A device for maintaining a constant temperature, by cutting off the energy supply when the required temperature is reached and restoring it when the temperature falls. On-off thermostats of this kind usually consist of a bimetallic strip that bends when it expands and contracts, thus opening and closing an electrical circuit or a gas or liquid flow valve. "Regulo" thermostats, which provide continuous temperature control, as used in domestic gas ovens, consist of a metal rod of low thermal expansion attached to a brass rod that expands as the temperature rises. This expansion moves the rod of low expansion so that it operates a valve to reduce the gas flow to the burner.

● **Theroux, Paul Edward** ► (1941–) US writer. His novels include *Picture Palace* (1978), *The Mosquito Coast* (1981), *Chicago Loop* (1990), and *Millroy the Magician* (1993); he has also won acclaim for such travel books as *The Great Railway Bazaar* (1975), and *The Pillars of Hercules* (1995).

● **thesaurus** ▷*See* Roget, Peter Mark.

● **Theseus** ► A legendary Greek hero, son of Aegeus, King of Athens, or of Poseidon. He freed the Athenians from their annual tribute to ▷Minos by killing the ▷Minotaur of Crete with the help of ▷Ariadne, who escaped with him. He extended the rule of Athens and was the subject of many legends. He was father of ▷Hippolytus by Hippolyte, Queen of the Amazons, and he married ▷Phaedra, sister of Ariadne.

● **Thespiae** ► An ancient city of Boeotia at the foot of Mount Helicon, the Muses' traditional home. ▷Praxiteles' famous statue of Eros was at Thespiae. Thespians were the only Boeotians to resist the Persian invasion (*see* Greek-Persian Wars) and fought alongside the Spartans at ▷Thermopylae (480 BC). It retained its importance under the Romans.

● **Thespis** ► (6th century BC) Semilegendary Greek poet. He won a prize for tragedy at Athens in about 534 BC. Traditionally held to be the inventor of tragedy, he was said to have introduced a single actor (a thespian) in dramatic performances that had hitherto been exclusively choral. He was also believed to have introduced the wearing of linen masks.

● **Thessalonians, Epistles of Paul to the** ► Two New Testament books written by Paul to new converts in Thessalonica in about 51 AD. They are therefore among the earliest books of the New Testament. The first letter is filled with reminiscences, thanksgiving, and instruction but gives special prominence to the second coming of Christ. The second letter is a sequel, warning against the neglect of everyday duties caused by an overenthusiastic expectation of the second coming.

● **Thessaloníki** ► (English name: Salonika) 40 38N 22 58E The second largest port in Greece, in Macedonia on the Gulf of Salonika. Founded in 315 BC as Thessalonica, it became the capital of Macedonia. It was captured by the Turks (1430) and remained in the Ottoman Empire until ceded to Greece (1913). During World War I it was a base for Allied operations. Notable Byzantine architecture includes the Panaghia Chalkeon (1028). Its university was founded in 1925. The port handles about one-third of Greek exports, including chrome, manganese, and agricultural produce. Industries include textiles and food processing. Population (1991): 377 951.

● **Thessaly** ► (Modern Greek name: Thessalía) A region of E central Greece, bordering on the Aegean Sea. In the 4th century BC it was briefly a strong and united state before falling to Philip of Macedon. Freed from Macedonian rule by Rome in 196 BC, it was incorporated in the Roman province of Macedonia in 148 BC. It subsequently formed part of the Byzantine Empire, falling to Turkey in the late 14th century AD. It was annexed by Greece in 1881. Population (1991): 734 846.

● **Thetford** ► 52 25N 0 45E A market town in E England, in Norfolk. An important Saxon town, it once had 20 churches and 8 monasteries. There has been considerable industrial expansion since the early 1960s. Population (1991): 20 058.

● **Thetford Mines** ► 46 06N 71 18W A city in E Canada, in SE Quebec. Founded in 1876, it is located by the world's largest asbestos mines. Other mining and light industry are also important. Population (1991): 17 273.

● **Thetis** ► In Greek mythology, one of the ▷nereids. She was courted by Zeus and Poseidon, but after hearing that she was fated to bear a son greater than its father they married her to the mortal Peleus, to whom she bore ▷Achilles.

● **thiamine** ▷*See* vitamin B complex.

● **thiazine** ► An organic compound that has a molecular structure containing a ring of four carbon atoms and two sulphur atoms. Thiazine derivatives are used in such drugs as tranquillizers, antihistamines, and antibiotics, as well as in various dyes.

● **thiazole** ► (C_3H_3NS) An organic compound that has a molecular structure containing a ring of three carbon atoms, one sulphur atom, and one nitrogen atom. Thiazole derivatives occur in thiamine (vitamin B_1), penicillin, and in numerous synthetic drugs, dyes, and chemicals.

● **thickhead** ► An insectivorous songbird belonging to a family (*Pachycephalidae*; 35 species) occurring in mangrove swamps, scrub, and open forests in S Asia and Australasia. Thickheads are 15–18 cm long and have large heavy heads and a loud whistling song. Male birds of the chief genus, *Pachycephalus*, are typically yellow and green with black, white, or brown markings.

● **Thiers, Louis Adolphe** ► (1797–1877) French statesman and historian; the first president of the Third Republic (1870–73). He served Louis Philippe in various ministerial posts and was a critic of Napoleon III, after whose fall during the Franco-Prussian War Thiers became president. He negotiated peace with Prussia and his economic policies facilitated France's economic recovery. He was responsible for the suppression of the Commune of Paris (1871). His publications include *Histoire de la Révolution française* (10 vols, 1823–27).

● **Thimphu** ► (*or* Thimbu) 27 29N 89 40E The capital of Bhutan since 1962, situated in the foothills of the E Himalayas. Population (1993 est): 30 340.

● **Thíra** ▷*See* Thera.

● **Third Reich** ► (1933–45) The period during which Germany was ruled by the Nazis; it refers to the Nazi ambition to revive the medieval Holy Roman Empire (the first ▷Reich) and the German Empire (the second Reich; 1871–1918). The Third Reich succeeded the Weimar Republic and ended with Germany's defeat in World War II.

● **third stream** ► A type of music created by the fusion of jazz and classical music. The name was coined by the composer Gunther Schuller (1925–), who encouraged classically trained jazz musicians, such as Charlie Mingus and John Coltrane (1926–67), and composers interested in jazz, such as Milton Babbitt, to work together.

● **Third World** ▷*See* developing countries.

● **Thirteen Colonies** ► The 13 North American colonies that became the United States of America in 1776 (*see* American Revolution). They were Connecticut, Delaware, Georgia, Maryland, Massachusetts, New Hampshire, New Jersey, New York, North Carolina, Pennsylvania, Rhode Island, South Carolina, and Virginia.

● **thirty-eighth parallel** ► The latitude of 38°N that approximates to the border between North and South Korea. It was the line, agreed at the ▷Yalta Conference at the end of World War II, N of which Soviet troops accepted the Japanese surrender and S of which US troops did so. Hostility between the Soviet-dominated North Korea and the US-dominated South Korea led to the ▷Korean War, after which the thirty-eighth parallel was confirmed as the border.

● **Thirty-Nine Articles** ► (1563) The doctrine, together with the Book of ▷Common Prayer, of the ▷Church of England. They were derived from Thomas Cranmer's 42 Articles (1553), which replaced the Six Articles of 1539 and had been revoked by Mary I in re-establishing Roman Catholicism in England. The Articles do not represent a creed; rather they give the Anglican position with regard to certain controversial points, especially as distinguished from the Roman Catholic, Calvinist, or Anabaptist views. They were probably written to permit differing interpretations (e.g. ▷transubstantiation is rejected although the same Article appears to support the doctrine of the Real Presence of Christ in the Eucharist). The clergy of the Church of England are no longer required to subscribe formally to the Articles but only to promise not to contradict them.

● **Thirty Years' War** ► (1618–48) The conflict between rival dynastic and religious interests in the Holy Roman Empire that escalated into a major European war. It was caused by the revolt of Protestants in Bohemia against the Counter-Reformation policies of the imperial government at Prague. Although imperial forces defeated the Bohemians in 1620, the revolt spread, with the German Protestants under Ernst von Mansfeld (1580–1626) receiving sporadic support from the English, Dutch, and Danes. With the Edict of Restitution (1629) Emperor Ferdinand II, helped by the armies of ▷Wallenstein and ▷Tilly, dispossessed many German Protestants, who were only saved by the intervention in 1630 of Sweden under ▷Gustavus II Adolphus. In 1635 France, hoping to contain the power of Spain and the Empire, entered the conflict. The war ended with the Peace of ▷Westphalia (1648), although the Franco-Spanish conflict continued until 1659 (see Pyrenees, Treaty of the). The war caused serious economic and demographic reverses in Germany.

● **Thisbe** ▷See Pyramus and Thisbe.

● **thistle** ► A prickly-leaved herb of several genera of the family ▷Compositae, especially Carduus (120 species), Cirsium (120 species), Carlinus (20 species), and Onopordum (20 species), found throughout the N hemisphere. Thistles have purple flower heads and spiny stems. The perennial creeping thistle (Cirsium arvense) is a weed, having spreading roots that give rise to new plants. ▷See also globe thistle; sow thistle.

● **Thistle, Order of the** ► A Scottish order of knighthood, probably founded by James III (1451–88); it was revived by James VII (II of England) in 1687. It comprises the sovereign and 16 knights and its motto is Nemo me impune lacessit (vernacular: Wha daur meddle wi' me?).

● **Thistlewood, Arthur** ▷See Cato Street Conspiracy.

● **thixotropy** ► A property possessed by certain gels as a result of which they become liquid when stirred and return to a gel-like state when left to stand. Thixotropic gels are used in nondrip paints as they prevent the various components from settling out during storage without affecting the fluid properties of the paint when applied. Certain types of quicksand are naturally thixotropic.

● **Thomas, Dylan** ► (1914–53) Welsh poet. Born in Swansea, Wales, he moved to London after the publication of 18 Poems in 1934 and worked for the BBC. Deaths and Entrances (1946) contains many of his best-known poems. In 1949 he returned to Wales, where he wrote his radio play Under Milk Wood (1954). Alcoholism precipitated his death, while on tour in the USA.

● **Thomas, Edward** ► (1878–1917) British poet and writer. Most of his work consists of nature studies and literary biographies. His poetry, written after encouragement from Robert Frost, is chiefly concerned with his love of the English countryside. He was killed in action in World War I.

● **Thomas, R(onald) S(tuart)** ► (1913–   ) Welsh poet. His earlier volumes, which include The Stones of the Field (1947) and Song at the Year's Turning (1955), draw on his work as a clergyman in rural Wales. Later volumes include Pieta (1966), Laboratories of the Spirit (1975), and Counterpoint (1990). His Collected Poems appeared in 1993. He is known as a militant nationalist and supporter of the Welsh language (although he writes in English).

● **Thomas, St** ► In the New Testament, one of the 12 Apostles. He is known as "Doubting Thomas" because he refused to believe in the resurrection until he had seen and touched Christ. Feast day: 21 Dec.

● **Thomas à Kempis** ► (Thomas Hemmerken; c. 1380–1471) German spiritual writer and monk. He spent most of his life writing and teaching novices at the Augustinian convent of Agnietenberg near Zwolle (Netherlands). His fame rests on his devotional treatise, The Imitation of Christ, although his authorship has been doubted by some scholars.

● **Thomas of Erceldoune** ► (13th century) English poet and prophet. Traditionally thought to be the author of a 14th-century romance, Sir Tristram, and of a 15th-century collection of prophecies, this semilegendary poet is best known from the ballad "Thomas the Rhymer."

● **Thomism** ▷See Aquinas, St Thomas.

● **Thompson, Benjamin** ▷See Rumford, Benjamin Thompson, Count.

● **Thompson, Daley** ► (Francis Morgan T.; 1958–   ) British decathlete. He won the decathlon in the Commonwealth Games in 1978. Unbeaten until 1987, he won two Olympic gold medals (1980 and 1984), and three European championships. He retired in 1992.

● **Thompson, Emma** ► (1959–   ) British actress. Her film appearances include Henry V (1989), Howards End (1992), for which she won an Oscar, and Sense and Sensibility (1995), for which she also wrote the Oscar-winning screenplay. Her subsequent films include The Winter Guest (1997) and Primary Colors (1998). She was formerly married (1989–95) to Kenneth ▷Branagh.

● **Thompson, Francis** ► (1859–1907) British poet. He began writing while an impoverished opium addict. A Roman Catholic, he wrote frequently on religious themes. "The Hound of Heaven," his best-known poem, is included in Poems (1893).

● **Thomson, James** ► (1700–48) British poet. Born in Scotland, he went to London in 1725. His works include The Seasons (1730), a poem that foreshadowed the Romantic movement, the patriotic song "Rule Britannia" (1740), and the moral allegory The Castle of Indolence (1748).

● **Thomson, Sir Joseph John** ► (1856–1940) British physicist, who discovered the ▷electron. After becoming director of the Cavendish Laboratory in Cambridge, Thomson studied ▷cathode rays, the nature of which was then unknown. In 1897 he succeeded in deflecting cathode rays by an electric field, thus showing that they consisted of negatively charged particles. He measured the ratio of their charge to mass and, using the known figure for the minimum charge on an ion, deduced that electrons were about 2000 times lighter than the hydrogen atom. Thomson thought that atoms consist of electrons embedded in a positively charged sphere, a concept that was superseded by ▷Rutherford's model. He was awarded the Nobel Prize in 1906. His son **Sir George Paget Thomson** (1892–1975) discovered the effect of electron diffraction (1927). He shared the 1937 Nobel Prize with Clinton Davisson (1881–1958), who had independently discovered the same effect. He was professor of physics at Imperial College, London (1930–52), and Master of Corpus Christi, Cambridge (1952–62).

● **Thomson, Roy Herbert, 1st Baron Thomson of Fleet** ► (1894–1976) British newspaper proprietor, born in Canada. After starting and acquiring radio stations and newspapers in North America, he moved to Edinburgh and bought The Scotsman (1953). In 1959 he bought Kemsley Newspapers, which included the Sunday Times, and in 1966 he acquired The Times. His son **Kenneth Roy, 2nd Baron Thomson** (1923–   ) succeeded him as chairman of the Thomson Organization.

● **Thomson, Virgil** ► (1896–1989) US composer, music critic, and conductor. He studied composition with Nadia Boulanger in Paris. His compositions include two operas with libretti by Gertrude Stein: Four Saints in Three Acts (1928) and The Mother of Us All (1947). He composed a variety of other vocal and instrumental music, including music for the film Louisiana Story (1948). His writings include The Art of Judging Music (1948) and American Music Since 1910 (1971).

● **Thomson, William** ▷See Kelvin, William Thomson, 1st Baron.

● **Thomson effect** ► (or Kelvin effect) ▷See thermoelectric effects.

● **Thonburi** ► 13 43N 100 27E A city in central Thailand, part of Bangkok Metropolis on the River Chao Phraya. It is noted for the Wat Arun temple. Industries include rice and timber milling. Population (latest est): 627 989.

● **Thor** ► The Teutonic god of thunder, in some legends the son of ▷Odin. He presided over the home and controlled the weather and crops; he was also worshipped as a god of war. Armed with a magic hammer and a belt, which increased his strength, he battled frequently against giants and monsters. His name survives in Thursday.

● **thorax** ► In mammals (including humans), the region of the body between the ▷diaphragm and the neck, which contains the lungs and heart and their associated vessels. The skeleton of the thorax is formed by the breastbone at the front, the spine at the back, and the ribs at the sides. In arthropods the thorax is between the head and abdomen.

● **Thoreau, Henry David** ▶ (1817–62) US naturalist and writer. Thoreau is best known for his Walden experiment (1845–46) during which he lived as a recluse in the woods of Walden near his native Concord (Massachusetts). He developed a great love and intuitive knowledge of animals. *Walden* was published in 1854. Influenced by ▷Emerson and ▷Hawthorne, Thoreau also wrote poems and essays, many about his homeland. His best-known essay, "Civil Disobedience," grew out of his opposition to the Mexican War. ▷*See also* Transcendentalists, New England.

● **thorium** ▶ (Th) A naturally occurring radioactive metal. It is possible that thorium-fuelled nuclear reactors may be developed in the future, since it is more abundant than uranium and does not produce plutonium-239 in appreciable quantities (*see* uranium). Thorium oxide (ThO$_2$) has one of the highest known melting points (3300°C), which led to its use in gas mantles, as it glows white when heated. At no 90; at wt 232.038; mp 1755°C; bp 4788°C.

● **thorium series** ▶ One of three naturally occurring series of radioactive decays. The thorium series is headed by thorium-232, which undergoes a series of alpha and beta decays ending with the stable isotope lead-208. ▷*See also* actinium series; uranium series.

● **thorn apple** ▶ An annual herb, *Datura stramonium*, also called jimsonweed, occurring in N temperate and subtropical regions. Growing to a height of 1 m, it has white trumpet-shaped flowers producing a fruit with a spiny capsule that splits to release the black seeds. All parts of the plant are very poisonous, containing the alkaloids hyoscyamine, hyoscine, and scopolamine. Family: ▷*Solanaceae*.

● **thornbill** ▶ A drab-coloured Australian bird belonging to one of three genera, especially *Acanthiza*. The yellow-tailed thornbill (*A. chrysorrhoea*) builds a very long oval nest with several nest chambers, the upper being used to rear young and the lower providing accommodation for the male. Family: *Muscicapidae* (*see* flycatcher).

● **Thorndike, Dame Sybil** ▶ (1882–1976) British actress. She acted many Shakespearean roles at the Old Vic between 1914 and 1918 and played the title role in the first production of Shaw's *St Joan* (1924). She also acted in several films. She toured during and after World War II with her husband, the distinguished actor **Sir Lewis Casson** (1875–1969).

● **Thornhill, Sir James** ▶ (1675–1734) English ▷baroque decorative painter. One of the first English painters to earn an international reputation, Thornhill is best remembered for his decoration of the Painted Hall at Greenwich Hospital (1704), the interior of the dome of ▷St Paul's Cathedral (1707), and the hall at Blenheim Palace. He was the teacher and father-in-law of ▷Hogarth.

● **Thoroughbred** ▶ A breed of horse descended from three Arab stallions brought to England between 1689 and 1728. Thoroughbreds have a refined streamlined build and a sensitive temperament and are noted for speed and stamina, being used worldwide for racing and as bloodstock to improve other breeds. They may be any solid colour. Height: 1.52–1.73 m (15–17 hands).

● **Thorpe, (John) Jeremy** ▶ (1929–　) British Liberal politician; leader of the Liberal Party (1967–76). MP for North Devon (1959–79), he was charged with, but acquitted of, conspiracy and incitement to murder Norman Scott, with whom he was alleged to have had a homosexual relationship.

● **Thorvaldsen, Bertel** ▶ (*or* B. Thorwaldsen; 1768–1844) Danish sculptor. His highly successful career began in Rome, where he worked from 1797 until his return to Copenhagen in 1838. Reviving the tradition of ancient Greek sculpture in his mythological and religious statues, he became one of the leading figures in ▷neoclassicism.

● **Thoth** ▶ The Egyptian god of learning, the scribe and arbiter of the gods, usually portrayed with the head of an ibis. He was the inventor of writing, arithmetic, and geometry and the keeper of various magic formulae. ▷*See also* Hermes Trismegistos.

● **Thousand, Expedition of the** ▶ (1860) The expedition of about a thousand volunteers, led by Giuseppe ▷Garibaldi, which embarked from Genoa and, after landing in Sicily, overthrew the Kingdom of the Two Sicilies, enabling S Italy to be united with the N. ▷*See also* Risorgimento.

● **Thousand Islands** ▶ A group of about 1700 small islands and islets in North America, in the St Lawrence River. They are chiefly in Ontario (Canada) with a few in New York state (USA) and are a popular resort area.

● **Thrace** ▶ The Balkan region bordered by the Black Sea, the Aegean, Macedonia, and the River Danube. From the 8th century BC Greek cities colonized the coasts, while the inland tribes were an easy target for invaders—the Persians in about 516 BC and then Philip II of Macedon in the mid-4th century. After Alexander the Great's death (323) it passed to his general Lysimachus (c. 355–c. 281 BC) and then to Macedonia before coming under the influence of Rome in 168 BC; it became a Roman province in 46 AD. Famous for its horses and horsemen, and for ecstatic religious rituals, Thrace was traditionally the birthplace of the mysteries associated with the worship of Dionysus. It is now divided between Turkey, Greece, and Bulgaria.

● **Thrale, Hester Lynch** ▷*See* Piozzi, Hester Lynch.

● **threadfin** ▶ A fish, also called threadfish, belonging to the family *Polynemidae* (about 24 species), that is found along warm seashores. It has a silvery elongated body, usually 30–60 cm long, two dorsal fins, and four to seven long threadlike pectoral fin rays. Order: *Perciformes*.

● **threadworm** ▷*See* pinworm.

● **Three Rivers** ▷*See* Trois-Rivières.

● **Three Wise Men** ▷*See* Magi.

● **thresher shark** ▶ A ▷shark of the family *Alopiidae* (5 species), found usually in offshore waters of tropical and temperate seas. About 6 m long, it has a long scythelike extension of the upper tail lobe, which it uses to thrash the water while circling its prey (squid and schooling fish), forcing them into tighter groups, which it then attacks. ⬜fish.

● **thrift** ▶ A perennial herb, *Armeria maritima*, also called sea pink, native to mountains, salt marshes, and coastal regions of N Europe. The flower stem, up to 30 cm high, rises from a basal tuft of grasslike leaves and bears a cluster of pink or white flowers. The Jersey thrift (*A. arenaria*) is taller with a denser tuft of broader leaves and grows on sand dunes in central and S Europe. Family: *Plumbaginaceae*.

● **thrips** ▶ A minute insect, also called thunder fly, belonging to the order *Thysanoptera* (about 3000 species). Thrips have dark slender bodies, 0.5–5 mm long, and usually two pairs of narrow fringed wings. Many species suck the juices of flowering plants, often causing serious damage and spreading plant diseases. Others eat fungi, decaying organic material, mites, and small insects. In some species there are no males and the larvae develop by ▷parthenogenesis.

● **Throckmorton, Sir Nicholas** ▶ (*or* Throgmorton; 1515–71) English diplomat. He fought at the battle of Pinkie (1547) and was ambassador to France and, during the 1560s, to Scotland. He was imprisoned (1569) by Elizabeth for his friendship with Mary, Queen of Scots. Throgmorton Street, the site in London of the Stock Exchange, is named after him. His nephew **Francis Throckmorton** (1554–84) organized (1583) a plot supported by France and Spain to overthrow Elizabeth I in favour of Mary, Queen of Scots. The conspiracy was discovered by Walsingham and Throckmorton was arrested, tortured, and executed.

● **thrombosis** ▶ The formation of a blood clot inside a blood vessel, which often obstructs the flow of blood. Thrombosis is more likely to occur if the blood vessel is damaged, if the blood flow is very slow, or if the blood is in a condition in which it is more likely to clot. The commonest site of thrombosis is in the veins of the legs. This is particularly likely to occur if a person is bedridden for a long time and it is often accompanied by inflammation of the vein (*see* phlebitis). The clot may become detached and carried to the lungs, causing pulmonary ▷embolism. The patient is treated with ▷anticoagulants. Thrombosis can also occur in the arteries supplying the heart (coronary thrombosis), causing a heart attack (*see* myocardial infarction), or the brain, causing ▷stroke.

● **thrush** ▶ (bird) A songbird belonging to a family (*Turdidae*; 300 species) found throughout the world but predominantly in Old World regions. Thrushes are slender billed, 13–30 cm long, and usually brown—often with speckling or patches of red, yellow, or blue. Terrestrial or arboreal, they feed chiefly on insects and fruit and often have melodious songs. Northern species are migratory. ▷*See also* blackbird; fieldfare; mistle thrush; redwing; ring ouzel; song thrush.

● **thrush** ▶ (disease) ▷*See* candidiasis.

● **Thrust SSC** ▶ A British-engineered "super car" that took the world land-speed record beyond the sound barrier in October 1997. Driven by Andy Green (1964–   ), one of a British team led by Richard Noble, the jet-powered car reached a top speed of 766.109 mph (1232.93 km per hour) during trials in the Nevada Desert, USA.

● **Thucydides** ▶ (c. 460–c. 400 BC) Greek historian. He served as an Athenian general in the Peloponnesian War but was banished in 424 BC for allowing the Spartan general Brasidas to capture the colony of Amphipolis. He remained in exile until 404 BC. His eight-volume *History of the Peloponnesian War*, written in a plain narrative style, is notable for its political, moral, and psychological analysis of the issues and leaders involved.

● **Thugs** ▶ (Sanskrit word: *sthaga*, deceiver) A Hindu sect, members of which worked in small gangs, murdering (usually by strangulation), robbing, and burying travellers in India. They worshipped Kali, the Hindu goddess of death, and observed strict rules, employing a private language amongst themselves. They were suppressed by Captain William Sleeman (1788–1856) in the 1830s.

● **Thuja** ▷*See* arbor vitae.

● **Thule** ▶ **1.** A far northern land first described in the 4th century BC by ▷Pytheas. It is tentatively identified with Norway or Iceland. **2.** An Inuit culture of the Arctic region, dating from between about 500 and 1300 AD.

● **thulium** ▶ (Tm) The least abundant of the ▷lanthanide elements, discovered in 1879 by P. T. Cleve (1840–1905). It forms the oxide Tm_2O_3. Radioactive ^{169}Tm is used in portable X-ray generators. At no 69; at wt 168.934; mp 1545°C; bp 1950°C.

● **Thun** ▶ (French name: Thoune) 46 46N 7 38E A town in central Switzerland, on Lake Thun. It is the centre of the Bernese Oberland; industries include cheese production and watchmaking. Population (1990): 37 700.

● **Thunder Bay** ▶ 48 20N 89 23W A city and port in E Canada, in Ontario on Lake Superior. Settled after 1800, it consists of Fort William and Port Arthur, which amalgamated in 1970. A major wheat-exporting port, it is also a transportation centre. Pulp and paper, timber, aircraft, buses, and shipbuilding are economically important. Lakehead University (1965) is situated here. Population (1991): 124 427 (metropolitan area).

● **thunderstorm** ▶ A storm of rain, hail, or snow, accompanied by thunder and ▷lightning. A lightning flash is an electrical discharge causing sudden heating and expansion of air as the flash passes through the atmosphere, resulting in the sound of thunder. Although both occur simultaneously, thunder is heard later than lightning is seen, as light travels faster than sound. An approximate measure of distance from a storm is 1.6 km (1 mi) for every 5 seconds between flash and thunder.

● **Thurber, James** ▶ (1894–1961) US humorous writer and cartoonist. A contributor to the *New Yorker* and a leading member of the ▷Algonquin Round Table, he satirized intellectual fashions and domestic habits. His writings are collected in *The Thurber Carnival* (1945) and other volumes.

● **Thuringia** ▶ A *Land* and historic region of central Germany, N of Bavaria and W of Saxony. Dominated by the Thuringian forests and strategically positioned, Thuringia became a buffer state against invaders from the E. Frequently partitioned during the middle ages, it passed to the Wettin family in 1265. It was part of East Germany from 1949 to 1990. Population (1995 est): 2 517 800. Capital: Erfurt.

● **Thurrock** ▶ A unitary authority in SE England, in Essex. Area: 163 sq km (63 sq mi). Population (1996 est): 132 300.

● **Thursday Island** ▶ 10 37S 142 10E An Australian island in Torres Strait, off the N coast of Queensland. Pearl fishing is the main industry. Area: 4 sq km (1.5 sq mi). Population (latest est): 2283. Chief town: Port Kennedy.

● **Thutmose I** ▶ King of Egypt (c. 1512–c. 1504 BC) of the 18th dynasty. He conquered Nubia beyond the Fourth Nile Cataract and Syria as far as the River Euphrates. He enlarged and embellished the temple of Amon at ▷Karnak.

● **Thutmose II** ▶ King of Egypt (c. 1525–c. 1512 BC) of the 18th dynasty, the son of ▷Thutmose I and the brother and husband of ▷Hatshepsut. He crushed a rebellion in Nubia before dying young.

● **Thutmose III** ▶ (d. 1450 BC) King of Egypt (c. 1504–1450) of the 18th dynasty, who ruled Egypt at its most powerful and prosperous. In his first year of independent rule, after the death of his half-sister ▷Hatshepsut (1468), he defeated Syrian rebels at Megiddo and in later campaigns advanced beyond the River Euphrates. He organized and supervised the country's complicated administration and was an outstanding athlete and big-game hunter. A patron of art and architecture, he collected foreign plants, birds, and beasts on campaign. His mummy is to be seen in Cairo.

● **Thutmose IV** ▶ King of Egypt (1425–1417 BC) of the 18th dynasty. He cultivated the alliance of Babylonia and the Mitanni kingdom against the Hittites and built extensively at ▷Karnak.

● **thylacine** ▶ The largest carnivorous ▷marsupial, *Thylacinus cynocephalus*, also called Tasmanian wolf or tiger. About 1.5 m long, it resembles a dog with dark stripes across its grey-brown back. Its teeth—adapted for eating meat—include pointed canines and shearing premolars. The dingo has exterminated thylacines on the Australian mainland, but a few may have survived in Tasmania. Family: *Dasyuridae*.

● **thyme** ▶ A small shrub belonging to the genus *Thymus* (about 50 species), native to temperate Eurasia. Garden thyme (*T. vulgaris*) is cultivated for its fragrant leaves and small mauve flowers, which are dried and used as a culinary herb. An oil extract is used in perfumes and medicines. The common wild thyme (*T. drucei*) has a branching creeping stem up to 7 cm long and clusters of rose-purple flowers. Family: ▷*Labiatae*.

● **thymus** ▶ An organ situated at the base of the neck, above the heart. The thymus is well developed at birth and grows until puberty, after which it shrinks and ceases to function. During infancy T-lymphocytes (a type of white blood cell), which form the ▷antibodies associated with allergic responses and the rejection of transplanted tissues and organs, mature in the thymus. ▷*See also* immunity.

● **thyratron** ▷*See* thermionic valve.

● **thyristor** ▶ A solid-state electronic device, also called a semiconductor or silicon-controlled rectifier; it consists of four layers of ▷semiconductor forming three p-n junctions. It acts as a switch, blocking the current through two terminals until it has been turned on by a pulse applied to the third terminal. This pulse can be initiated by light or a temperature change. Thyristors are used in a wide range of power-switching and control-circuit applications. They can pass currents ranging from milliamperes to several hundred amperes and have replaced the thyratron (*see* thermionic valve).

● **thyroid gland** ▶ An ▷endocrine gland situated at the base of the neck, in front and on either side of the windpipe. It secretes two **thyroid hormones**, the most important of which is thyroxine, which controls the basal metabolism of the body; thyroxine secretion is regulated by thyroid-stimulating hormone, released from the ▷pituitary gland. Because thyroxine production requires iodine, deficiency of iodine causes the thyroid to enlarge in an attempt to produce adequate amounts of the hormone (*see* goitre). The thyroid gland also secretes another hormone, ▷calcitonin. ▷*See also* cretinism; hyperthyroidism; myxoedema.

● **Tiahuanaco** ▶ A ruined city at an altitude of nearly 4000 m (13 000 ft) in the Andes in Bolivia. Occupied by up to 30 000 people between 500 and 1200 AD, it predated the ▷Inca civilization. Remains of its stone architecture and carving provide evidence of a highly developed civilization. It is thought to have been a lake port on Lake ▷Titicaca, which formerly may have extended to this site.

● **Tiananmen Square** ▷*See* Beijing.

● **Tianjin** ▶ (T'ien-ching *or* Tientsin) 39 08N 117 12E An administratively autonomous port in NE China, the third largest city in the country, on the ▷Grand Canal. A prosperous city for centuries, it was the scene of much friction between Chinese and Europeans in the late 19th century. It is the site of two universities. Industries include chemicals, machinery, and textiles, notably carpets. Population (1991 est): 5 770 000.

● **Tian Shan** ▶ (*or* Tien Shan) A mountain system of central Asia. It extends about 2500 km (1500 mi) NE from the ▷Pamirs in Tadzhikistan, through NW China to the Mongolian border, reaching 7439 m (24 406 ft) at Pobeda Peak.

● **Tibaldi, Pellegrino** ▶ (1527–96) Italian architect and painter, a leading exponent of ▷mannerism. In Spain (1587–96), at the invitation of Philip II, he oversaw the construction and decoration of the ▷Escorial.

● **Tiber, River** ▶ (Italian name: Tevere; Latin name: Tiberis) A river in central Italy, rising in the Apennines of Tuscany and flowing mainly S through Rome to the Tyrrhenian Sea near Ostia. Length: 405 km (252 mi).

● **Tiberias** ▶ 32 48N 35 32E A town in N Israel, on the W shore of the Sea of Galilee. Founded by Herod Antipas in about AD 20 and named after the Roman Emperor Tiberius, it became the centre of Jewry in Palestine after the Roman destruction of Jerusalem. It is now a resort. Population (latest est): 29 000.

● **Tiberias, Sea of** ▷*See* Galilee, Sea of.

● **Tiberius** ▶ (42 BC–37 AD) Roman emperor (14–37 AD). Tiberius, who was ▷Livia Drusilla's son by her first husband, was recognized by his stepfather, Emperor Augustus, as his successor in 4 AD. As emperor his policies were unambitious though sound but he faced the Senate's hostility, family intrigue, and military rebellion. Tiberius' reign saw a series of treason prosecutions before his retirement to Capri in 26 AD, where he gained a reputation for depravity.

● **Tibesti Mountains** ▶ A mountain range in N Africa, in the central Sahara. It lies chiefly in NW Chad but extends NE into Libya and rises to 3415 m (11 204 ft) at Emi Koussi, the highest peak in the Sahara.

● **Tibet** ▶ (Chinese name: Xizang Autonomous Region) An administrative region in W China, bordering on India, Nepal, Bhutan, and Myanmar (Burma). It consists of a high plateau and is surrounded by mountains, including the Himalayas and the Kunlun Mountains. Most agriculture and the country's cities are in the river valleys, while nomads herd such animals as yaks on the plateau. The area is rich in minerals, not mined until the 1950s because of religious proscription. Tibet is famous for its Buddhist-inspired art and its handicrafts.
History: Buddhism, introduced in the 7th century AD, has exerted a profound influence on Tibetan history. The lamas (priests) of ▷Tibetan Buddhism attained political power in the 13th century, when Kublai Khan gave the government of his conquests in E Tibet to the Sa-skya lama. Subsequent disunity was brought to an end in 1642, when the fifth ▷Dalai Lama became ruler of all Tibet. In 1720 the Chinese Qing dynasty established a control over Tibet lasting until the Qing's overthrow in 1911. Independence was declared, but in 1950 Tibet again fell to the Chinese. An uprising in 1959 was suppressed and the Dalai Lama, with thousands of refugees, fled. Tibet was subsequently subjected to Chinese influence; demands for independence led in the late 1980s and early 1990s to riots in Lhasa and elsewhere and the imposition (1989–90) of martial law. China has been widely accused of violating Tibetans' human and religious rights. In 1997 the International Commission of Jurists denounced Chinese rule as an alien occupation and called for a UN-monitored referendum to decide Tibet's future. Area: 1 221 601 sq km (471 660 sq mi). Population (1995 est): 2 360 000. Capital: Lhasa.

● **Tibetan Buddhism** ▶ (*or* lamaism) A form of Mahayana Buddhism practised in Tibet and Mongolia. Introduced to Tibet in the 7th

century AD, it has a symbolic literature and monastic discipline, with surviving features of ▷Bon shamanism. The esoteric aspects of Buddhism are explored, hence the array of deities, ▷mandalas, etc. The ▷guru is of prime importance; some are held to be reincarnations of previous lamas. Until 1959, the ▷Dalai Lama was both temporal and spiritual head of the state. ▷*See also* Panchen Lama.

● **tibia** ▷*See* leg.

● **Tibullus, Albius** ▶ (c. 55–c. 19 BC) Roman poet. He lived quietly on his estate near Rome and was a friend of Horace and Ovid. His elegiac poetry is mostly addressed to his patron, M. Valerius Messalla. Two books of his poems were published during his lifetime and were known as "Delia" and "Nemesis" after the pseudonyms of his women subjects.

● **Tichborne claimant** ▶ A former butcher, Arthur Orton (1834–98), who claimed in 1866 to be Sir Roger Tichborne, the eldest son of the 10th baronet, who was presumed lost at sea. Having emigrated to Australia at the age of 18, Orton returned to Britain, where he convinced some members of the Tichborne family that he was the heir to the Tichborne fortune. However, after a long trial in 1872 he lost his claim; two years later he was convicted and imprisoned for perjury.

● **Ticino, River** ▶ A river in Switzerland and Italy. It flows mainly S from the Leopontine Alps to the River Po near Pavia in Italy. Length: 248 km (154 mi).

● **tick** ▶ A parasitic ▷arachnid of the worldwide suborder *Metastigmata* (850 species), which sucks the blood of birds and mammals and may transmit such diseases as ▷typhus. Its round unsegmented body, up to 30 mm long, bears eight bristly legs and may be covered by a dorsal shield. After feeding, the adults drop off the host and lay eggs on the ground. The larvae attach themselves to a victim, feed, then drop off and moult into nymphs. Order: *Acarina* (or *Acari*). *Compare* mite.

● **tidal power** ▶ Power used to generate electricity by using the ▷tides to collect water behind a barrage and releasing it to turn a turbogenerator. The Severn estuary, with its tidal rise of 8.8 m, could generate 7% of the UK's electricity demand; however, the capital cost, estimated as £8 billion, is regarded as prohibitive, although French experience with their tidal power station on the River ▷Rance indicates a payback period of only 16 years. It is estimated that 34 UK sites could generate 100 MW each, but the Severn barrage is the one currently most likely to be built. Russia also has a tidal power station on the White Sea and others are planned.

● **tides** ▶ The regular rising and falling of seawater resulting from the gravitational attraction between the earth, sun, and moon. Variations in their relative positions produce variations in tidal range (*see* spring tide; neap tide). Most parts of the world experience semidiurnal tides (occurring twice per tidal day—24 hours 50 minutes). Tidal currents are periodic horizontal flows of water resulting from the tides. Near the coast they are usually perpendicular to it and reversing, but in the ocean they rotate around a series of nodal points; water level remains constant at these points, tidal range increasing concentrically outwards. □ p. 1246.

● **Tieck, (Johann) Ludwig** ▶ (1773–1853) German writer. Associated with ▷Novalis, the ▷Schlegels, and other Romantic writers centred in Jena, Tieck was highly versatile, writing novels, and plays, translating, and publishing medieval lyrics. His works include the fairytale, *Der blonde Eckbert* (1797) and the comedy, *Der gestiefette Kater* (1797).

● **Tien Shan** ▷*See* Tian Shan.

● **Tientsin** ▶ (*or* T'ien-ching) ▷*See* Tianjin.

● **Tiepolo, Giovanni Battista** ▶ (1696–1770) Venetian ▷rococo painter. Influenced by ▷Veronese, his early sombre style evolved into the exuberance of his first major frescoes, for the Archbishop's Palace at Udine (1725–29). These were followed by decorations for many N Italian palaces and churches. Abroad he decorated the Residenz Palace, Würzburg, built by the architect ▷Neumann, and the Royal Palace in Madrid (1762–66). His son **Giovanni Domenico Tiepolo** (1727–1804) is best known for his paintings of clowns and acrobats.

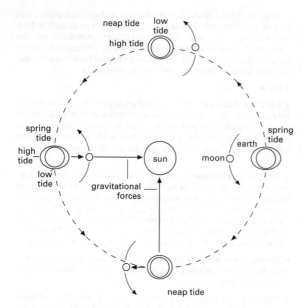

neap tide
low tide
high tide

spring tide
high tide
low tide
spring tide
earth
sun
moon
gravitational forces

neap tide

tides ► The force of gravity between the earth and the moon pulls the waters of the seas towards the moon, creating high tides once a day. The second daily high tide occurs because the moon pulls the earth itself away from the water on the far side of the moon. Exceptionally high spring tides occur twice monthly when the gravitational force of the moon is in line with that of the sun. The lower neap tides occur when these two forces are at right angles.

● **Tierra del Fuego** ► An archipelago separated from the mainland of S South America by the Strait of Magellan. The W and S belong to Chile, the E to Argentina. Sheep farming and oil production are the principal economic activities. Chief towns: Punta Arenas (Chile); Ushuaia (Argentina).

● **Tiffany, Louis Comfort** ► (1848–1933) US glassmaker and craftsman. A leading proponent of ▷Art Nouveau, he created the iridescent *Favrile* style of stained glass, used in lampshades and screens. He was also admired as an artist.

● **Tiflis** ▷*See* Tbilisi.

● **tiger** ► A large ▷cat, *Panthera tigris*. Tigers are usually about 3 m long, but the race of Siberian tigers can reach 4 m. Tigers evolved in Siberia and have spread south to most of Asia; they shed their coat seasonally and shelter from hot sun during the day. They hunt at night, stalking their prey (mainly antelope). A fully grown tiger will eat up to 25 kg of meat at one feed.

● **tiger beetle** ► A long-legged beetle, with pointed mandibles, belonging to a family (*Cicindelidae*; 2000 species) occurring mainly in the tropics and subtropics. Tiger beetles range from 6 to 70 mm in length; although most are black or brown some are brilliantly coloured. Both adults and larvae are predatory.

● **tigerfish** ► Any fish that resembles a tiger, especially members of the genus *Hydrocynus*, family *Characidae* (see characin), found in fresh waters of Africa and South America. They have horizontally striped elongated bodies, reaching 1 m in length, and feed voraciously on other fish. Tigerfish of the family *Theraponidae* (order *Perciformes*) occur in Indo-Pacific marine and fresh waters and include the three-striped tigerfish (*Therapon jarbua*), also called saltwater zebra fish.

● **tiger moth** ► A moth belonging to the family *Arctiidae*, occurring in Eurasia, N Africa, and North America. The adults have a stout body and are brightly coloured, often orange and black. The hairy larvae, which are commonly called woolly bears, incorporate their hairs into the cocoon and are seldom destructive, eating various wild plants.

● **tiger shark** ► A large ▷requiem shark, *Galeocerdo cuvieri*, that lives mainly in tropical seas. It has a greyish-brown body, up to about 5.5 m

long, patterned with vertical bars and a lighter underside. It is a voracious omnivore and eats virtually anything, including mammals, birds, fish, invertebrates, refuse, and man.

● **Tiglath-pileser I** ► King of Assyria (c. 1120–1074 BC), who greatly extended Assyrian territory, reaching the Mediterranean coast in the W. He patronized art and architecture and collected one of the oldest surviving libraries.

● **Tiglath-pileser III** ► King of Assyria (c. 745–727 BC). Probably a usurper, he restored Assyrian military power in Babylonia, Syria, and against Urartu in the N. He also improved the efficiency of Assyrian administration, appointing provincial governors.

● **tigon** ► A sterile hybrid cat, resulting from the mating of a lion and a tiger, also called a liger. This can only happen in captivity, because lions and tigers naturally inhabit different continents.

● **Tigré** ► (*or* Tigray) An autonomous region in N Ethiopia. An arid semi-desert region, it relies upon agriculture; products include cereals, coffee, and cotton. Failure of these crops caused by drought and ▷desertification led to widespread famine and migration of its inhabitants in 1984, 1987, and 1989. Poor transport routes and civil war severely hampered massive relief programmes launched with foreign aid. In 1991 Tigreans formed the basis of the Ethiopian People's Revolutionary Democratic Front, which joined forces with the Eritrean People's Liberation Front to bring about this overthrow of President Mengistu's government. Area: 65 900 sq km (25 439 sq mi). Population (1993 est): 2 299 948.

● **Tigris, River** ► A river in SW Asia, rising in SE Turkey and flowing SE through Diyarbakir, along the Turkish-Syrian border, and into Iraq. 190 km (118 mi) from the Persian Gulf it joins the River Euphrates to form the Shatt al-Arab. Length: 1850 km (1150 mi).

● **Tihwa** ▷*See* Ürümqi.

● **Tijuana** ► 39 29N 117 10W A city in NW Mexico, on the US border. Tijuana is the main entry point to Mexico from California and is a popular tourist resort. Population (1990): 742 686.

● **Tikal** ► An ancient ▷Maya city in N Guatemala. After about 300 AD it grew into the largest Maya ceremonial centre, with imposing pyramid temples. It was mysteriously abandoned about 900.

● **Tilak, Bal Gangadhar** ► (*or* Lokamanya; 1856–1920) Indian nationalist leader. Joining the ▷Indian National Congress (1885) he changed its policy to one of resistance to British rule, advocating Indian independence. Also active as an educationalist, he founded new schools and societies in Poona and was the first leader to propose the adoption of Hindi as the national language. He was twice arrested and imprisoned on charges of sedition.

● **Tilburg** ► 51 34N 5 05E A city in the S Netherlands, in North Brabant province. A major industrial centre, it produces textiles. Population (1996 est): 164 380.

● **Tilbury** ► An area in SE England, in Essex on the River Thames. It is the chief dock complex of the Port of London Authority, having a passenger landing stage and roll-on-roll-off facilities for cargo vessels.

● **till** ► (*or* boulder clay) The unstratified material that ranges from clay to angular stones and boulders, deposited by glaciers and ice sheets. Its form depends on the rock from which it originated. Large areas of N Europe are covered by till remaining from the Ice Age.

● **Tillett, Benjamin** ► (1860–1943) British trade unionist. As secretary (1887–1922) of the Dock, Wharf, Riverside, and General Workers' Union he directed the dock strikes of 1889 and 1911. He was also a Labour MP (1917–24, 1929–31).

● **Tilley, Vesta** ► (Matilda Alice Powles; 1864–1952) British music-hall entertainer, who specialized in male impersonations. She also acted in pantomime and toured in the USA. She retired from the stage in 1920.

● **Tillich, Paul (Johannes)** ► (1886–1965) US Protestant theologian of German birth. A Lutheran pastor and later a professor at several German universities, he moved to the USA in 1933, when Hitler came to power. He lectured in New York and at Harvard and Chicago Universities. In *Systematic Theology* (3 vols, 1950–63) he attempted to demonstrate Christianity's relevance to contemporary life.

● **Tilly, Johan Tserclaes, Graf von** ▶ (1559–1632) Bavarian general, who commanded the Catholic League in the ▷Thirty Years' War. He won the battle of the White Mountain (1620) and went on to gain control of NW Germany. He defeated the Swedes at Lutter (1626) and, in command of imperial forces, as well as the League's, razed Magdeburg (1631), gaining a reputation for brutality. He was killed in action after being defeated (1631) by the Swedes at Breitenfeld.

● **Tilsit** ▷*See* Sovetsk.

● **Tilsit, Treaties of** ▶ (1807) The two treaties that France signed at Tilsit (now Sovetsk, Russia) with Russia and Prussia respectively after Napoleon's defeat of the Prussians at ▷Jena and Auerstädt and the Russians at ▷Friedland. Russia became an ally of France and Prussia, its territory considerably reduced, was occupied by French troops. Both Russia and Prussia joined the ▷Continental System of blockade against British trade.

● **Timaru** ▶ 44 23S 171 14E A port and resort in New Zealand, in E South Island on Canterbury Bight. It serves an agricultural district and exports include grain, wool, and frozen meat. Population (1995 est): 15 350.

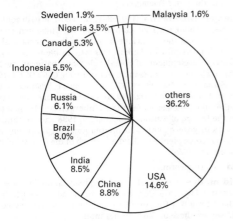

timber ▶ World production of timber in the mid-1990s; coniferous and nonconiferous roundwood.

● **timber** ▶ Sawn wood used for purposes other than fuel. Timber is divided into hardwoods (derived from broad-leaved trees) and softwoods (derived from conifers). The bulk of the world's softwoods are derived from Russia, Canada, the USA, and Scandinavia. Hardwoods, which take longer to grow, are not confined to one specific climate zone. Uses for timber include furniture manufacture (usually hardwoods), building construction, and paper manufacture (largely softwoods).

● **timber wolf** ▶ A large shaggy-coated ▷wolf of North America, also called the grey wolf. A Texan variety with a rufous coat is called the red wolf.

● **timbre** ▶ A quality in the sound of a musical instrument, voice, etc., that distinguishes it from others. Thus a violin and a clarinet sound different even when they are playing the same note. The difference arises because each type of instrument produces different ▷harmonics (or overtones) in different strengths when a note is played. The production of harmonics is controlled by the way the note is produced (plucking, blowing, etc.) and by the characteristics of the individual instrument.

● **Timbuktu** ▶ (French name: Tombouctou) 16 49N 2 59W A town in E central Mali, on the River Niger. It was an important centre on the trans-Saharan caravan route and an Islamic cultural centre (1400–1600). It declined after conquest by Morocco (1591). Population (latest est): 31 925.

● **time** ▶ A concept that measures the duration of events and the periods that separate them. It is a fundamental parameter of all changes, measuring the rates at which they occur; it provides a scale of measurement enabling events that have occurred to be distinguished from those that are occurring and those that will occur. It appears, intuitively, to be flowing at a constant rate in one direction only, for all observers. However, according to Einstein's theory of ▷relativity this is not the case. The rate at which time passes (as measured by a clock) is not the same for observers in different frames of reference that are moving at a constant velocity with respect to each other. Thus, according to the ▷time-dilation effect, if two observers are moving at a constant velocity relative to each other it appears to each that the other's time processes are slowed down. This means that events that appear to be simultaneous to observers in the same frame of reference would not be simultaneous to observers in different frames of reference. In order to pinpoint an event in the universe, its position in a four-dimensional space-time continuum must be specified. This continuum has three space dimensions and one time dimension.

Historically, the measurement of time on earth has been based on astronomical observations—the time taken for the earth to revolve on its axis (the day) or for it to complete its orbit round the sun (the year). **Sidereal time** is defined with respect to the stars; for example, the sidereal day is the time taken for one revolution of the ▷celestial sphere. **Solar time** is defined in relation to the position of the sun in the sky and is therefore related to both the earth's rotation and its orbital motion (*see* universal time). **Ephemeris time** is a modified form of solar time in which variations in the earth's time of rotation are corrected. However, in modern science the basis of time measurement is the ▷second (*see* International Atomic Time), which is defined in terms of the frequency of the radiation emitted in a specified transition of an isotope of caesium (*see* caesium clock).

Timbuktu ▶ This street in Timbuktu, a former Islamic cultural centre, is dominated by the mosque.

● **time and motion study** ▶ A study of a machine and its operator in a factory, measuring the time taken to complete each action and the sequence of the operator's movements. The study is then used to recommend methods of speeding up the operation and reducing the effort involved in order to utilize labour as economically as possible.

● **time-dilation effect** ▶ An effect predicted by Einstein's special theory of ▷relativity. If two observers, A and B, are moving at a velocity v relative to each other, it will appear to A that B's clock will show that ▷time is running more slowly; thus a time t measured on A's clock will be $t(1 - v^2/c^2)^{1/2}$ on B's clock, where c is the speed of light. The effect has been observed in some particles moving at high velocities, which appear to have an anomalously long lifetime.

● **Time of Troubles** ▶ A period of confusion in Russia following the death of Boris ▷Godunov (1605). Godunov was succeeded by a Polish-supported pretender, the False Dimitrii, who claimed to be the son of Ivan the Terrible. The False Dimitrii was assassinated in 1606 by Muscovite nobles, who raised Vasilii Shuiski (1552–1612) to the throne. His rule was threatened by a second False Dimitrii, who established a court at Tushino in 1608. Shuiski was deposed and the second False Dimitrii murdered in 1610, following a successful Polish invasion. A third False Dimitrii asserted his claim in 1611–12 but a successful rebellion against the Poles brought ▷Michael (Romanov) to the throne in 1613, ending the Time of Troubles.

● **Timişoara** ▶ (Hungarian name: Temesvár) 45 45N 21 15E A city in W Romania, near the border with Serbia. It is a commercial and cultural centre with a university (1945) and has two cathedrals. The uprising (1989) against Ceauşescu began here, resulting in many deaths. Population (1997 est): 334 098.

● **Timor** ▶ The largest island of the ▷Nusa Tenggara group. Mountainous and dry, it is largely undeveloped. Crops include coffee, coconut, and sandalwood.

History: in 1859 it was divided between Portugal and Holland. West (Dutch) Timor was included in independent Indonesia (1949), becoming part of the province of East Nusa Tenggara. When ▷East Timor declared independence from Portugal in 1975, this provoked an invasion by Indonesia followed by wholesale massacres of the population. Indonesia formally annexed East Timor in 1976, but this was not accepted by the UN. Demonstrations against Indonesian rule in the 1990s were severely repressed. In 1999 a referendum on the territory's future status was held in East Timor, resulting in a large vote in favour of independence. There followed a campaign of terror by anti-independence militias, with apparent backing from government forces, before Indonesia withdrew its troops. East Timor remained under UN administration from October 1999 until May 2002, when it finally became an independent nation. Area: 39 775 sq km (11 883 sq mi). Chief towns: Kupang and Dili.

● **Timoshenko, Semyon Konstantinovich** ▶ (1895–1970) Soviet marshal, who rebuilt the army after its defeats in the ▷Russo-Finnish War. He commanded at ▷Stalingrad in World War II but failed to stem a German advance (1942–43) and was reassigned to the staff.

● **timothy** ▶ A perennial ▷grass, *Phleum pratense*, also called herd's grass or cat's tail, native to Europe. It forms large clumps, 0.5–1 m tall, with swollen bulblike bases and dense cylindrical flower clusters. It is widely cultivated as a hay and pasture grass, especially as part of a mixture with other grasses.

● **Timothy, St** ▶ In the New Testament, a disciple of ▷Paul, whom he accompanied on many missions. According to tradition he was martyred in Ephesus. Feast day: 6 Feb.

The Epistles of Paul to Timothy, in the New Testament, consist of advice and directions concerning Timothy's personal conduct and public responsibilities. The second letter contains Paul's last known words before his martyrdom under Nero.

● **timpani** ▶ (*or* kettledrums) Tuned percussion instruments consisting of a large copper bowl or "kettle" with parchment or plastic stretched across the top. The pitch can be altered by means either of metal keys round the circumference or a pedal mechanism. The sound also depends on the type of sticks used and where they strike the head; a glissando can be obtained by use of the pedals. □musical instruments.

● **Timur** ▶ (*or* Tamerlane; c. 1336–1405) Mongol conqueror, a descendant of Genghis Khan. After winning control of Turkestan in central Asia, Timur left his capital Samarkand to conquer the world. Ruthlessly sweeping through Mongolia, Persia, Turkey, Russia, and India, leaving death and destruction behind him, he sought conquest rather than a permanent empire. Paradoxically, he spared and encouraged all kinds of artists.

● **tin** ▶ (Sn) A silvery-white metal known to the ancients. Its principal ore is the oxide cassiterite (SnO_2), often found in alluvial concentrations. The element exists as at least two allotropes—the grey alpha-tin, and beta-tin, which is the common form above 13.2°C. At low temperature beta-tin slowly changes into alpha-tin causing **tin plague**. It is obtained by reduction with coal in a reverberatory furnace. In addition to the oxide, compounds include tin chloride ($SnCl_2$), which is used as a reducing agent and in the dyeing industry. The major use of tin is in ▷tinplate. It alloys with copper to form ▷bronzes and with niobium to give a superconducting composition, which is used in electromagnets. Some organic compounds of tin are toxic. At no 50; at wt 118.710; mp 231.9°C; bp 2603°C.

● **tinamou** ▶ A solitary ground-dwelling bird belonging to a family (*Tinamidae*; 50 species) occurring in Central and South America. 23–38 cm long, tinamous are well camouflaged with a mottled grey or brown plumage. They have small wings and a very short tail and are poor fliers. They feed on seeds, fruit, and insects and are the only members of the order *Tinamiformes*.

● **Tinbergen, Niko(laas)** ▶ (1907–88) Dutch-born British zoologist and pioneer ethologist. Like Konrad ▷Lorenz, Tinbergen concentrated on studying the behaviour of animals in their natural surroundings. Tinbergen, with Lorenz, was responsible for tracing the evolutionary development of social behaviour patterns, such as courtship displays. His works include *The Herring Gull's World* (1953), *Social Behaviour in Animals* (1953), and *Animal Behaviour* (1965). Tinbergen shared a Nobel Prize (1973) with Lorenz and von ▷Frisch. His brother, the Dutch economist **Jan Tinbergen** (1903–94), was adviser to the League of Nations from 1936 to 1938 and continued to advise various governments and international organizations from 1955. He was corecipient with Ragnar ▷Frisch of the first Nobel Prize for Economics (1969).

● **tinea** ▷*See* ringworm.

● **tineid moth** ▶ A moth of the widespread family *Tineidae*. The adults are small with a golden or silvery sheen and frequently do not feed. The caterpillars feed on plant and animal matter; especially well known are those of the ▷clothes moth.

● **tinnitus** ▶ A continuing noise in the ear; causes include wax, damage to the eardrum, ▷Ménière's disease, diseases of the inner ear, and the side effects of some drugs (e.g. aspirin and quinine). If no curable cause can be diagnosed, some alleviation may be provided by external sound sources that are more acceptable than the tinnitus.

● **tinplate** ▶ A mild ▷steel sheet coated with a very thin film of tin, usually deposited by ▷electrolysis. Tinplate combines the strength and rigidity of steel with the attractive appearance and corrosion resistance of tin. It began to be used in the 19th century for cans in which to preserve food, still its widest use, although it was used for decorative purposes in the 13th century.

● **Tintagel** ▶ 50 40N 4 45W A village in SW England, on the N coast of Cornwall. On the rugged promontory of Tintagel Head are the ruins of Tintagel Castle, reputedly the birthplace of King Arthur.

● **Tintern Abbey** ▷*See* Chepstow.

● **Tintoretto** ▶ (Jacopo Robusti; 1518–94) Venetian painter, whose nickname, meaning "little dyer," derived from his father's profession of silk dyeing. His three paintings of the *Miracles of St Mark* (1562–66) for the Confraternity of S Marco were followed by his series of the life of Christ (1564–87; Scuola di S Rocco) and his paintings for the Doge's Palace, including the enormous *Paradise*. He combines Michelangelo's figure style and Titian's rich colour with dramatic movement. He was particularly adept at painting old men, for example *Bearded Man with Fur* (Kunsthistorisches Museum, Vienna).

● **Tipperary** ▶ (Irish name: Contae Tiobraid Árann) A county in the S Republic of Ireland, in Munster. Mountainous in parts, it contains part of the Golden Vale (one of the most fertile areas in Ireland). It is predominantly agricultural with industries mainly related to processing agricultural produce. The largest county in Ireland, it is divided for administrative purposes into a North Riding and a South Riding. Area: 4255 sq km (1643 sq mi). Population (1996): 133 000. County town: Clonmel.

● **Tippett, Sir Michael** ▶ (1905–98) British composer. He studied at the Royal College of Music and was musical director of Morley College (1940–51). He wrote five operas: *The Midsummer Marriage* (1947–52), *King Priam* (1958–61), *The Knot Garden* (1966–70), *The Ice Break* (1977), and *New Year* (1989), acting as his own librettist. Other works include four symphonies, five string quartets, four piano sonatas, the oratorios *A Child of Our Time* (1940) and *The Mask of Time* (1982), and the cantata *The Vision of St Augustine* (1965). President of the London College of Music, he was appointed to the OM in 1983.

● **Tipu Sahib** ▶ (1749–99) Sultan of Mysore (1782–99); the son of ▷Hyder Ali. A good administrator in his own state, he was an opponent of British power in India and entered into a tentative alliance with the French. Defeated by ▷Cornwallis in 1792, he continued his opposition and was killed by the British while defending his capital Seringapatam.

● **Tirana** ▶ (Albanian name: Tiranë) 41 20N 19 49E The capital of Albania, situated on a fertile plain in the centre of the country. Founded in the 17th century by a Turkish general, it became the capital in 1920. There has been considerable industrial expansion since World War II. The university was founded in 1957. Population (1995 est): 270 000.

● **Tiresias** ▶ In Greek legend, a blind Theban soothsayer, who lived for seven generations. For part of his life he had been transformed into a woman, after coming upon a pair of snakes and killing the female. ▷Oedipus learned from him of his own patricide and incest and ▷Odysseus consulted him in the underworld, where he retained his prophetic powers. According to one of various legends, he was struck blind by Hera after supporting Zeus' opinion in an argument, namely that love was more enjoyable for women than men. In compensation Zeus granted him longevity and the gift of prophecy.

● **Tirich Mir, Mount** ▶ 36 18N 71 55E A mountain in NW Pakistan, the highest in the Hindu Kush. Height: 7692 m (25 236 ft).

● **Tirol** ▶ (or Tyrol) A mountainous federal state in W Austria, bordering on Germany and Italy. It is alpine in character having an international reputation for winter sports, especially at Kitzbühel, and tourism is important throughout the year. The chief occupations are agriculture and forestry, with some mining and manufacturing industries. Recent years have seen tension between the German and Italian communities. Area: 12 648 sq km (4883 sq mi). Population (1994 est): 654 753. Capital: Innsbruck.

● **Tirpitz, Alfred von** ▶ (1849–1930) German admiral, who as secretary of state for the navy (1897–1916) rebuilt the German fleet to rival Britain's naval supremacy. His advocacy of intensive submarine warfare in World War I was opposed by the chancellor, Bethmann-Hollweg, and Tirpitz resigned.

● **Tirso de Molina** ▶ (Gabriel Téllez; c. 1584–1648) Spanish dramatist, a disciple of Lope de ▷Vega, who wrote over 300 comedies and historical plays. His tragedy *El Burlador de Sevilla* (1635) is the earliest portrayal of ▷Don Juan.

● **Tirthankara** ▶ In Jainism, one who has attained liberation from rebirth and serves as a guide for others. Every aeon is said to produce 24 Tirthankaras, each associated with a particular symbol and colour. ▷Mahavira is the last of the present series.

● **Tiruchirappalli** ▶ (or Trichinopoly) 10 50N 78 43E A city in India, in Tamil Nadu on the River Cauvery. The city is dominated by the Rock of Trichinopoly with its fort and temple. It is an important rail centre. Population (1991): 386 628.

● **Tiryns** ▶ A ▷Mycenaean citadel near Mycenae (S Greece). First excavated (1884–85) by ▷Schliemann, Tiryns was occupied from Neolithic times. The Bronze Age Mycenaean palace, first built in the early 14th century BC and sacked about 1200 BC, possessed frescoes showing ▷Minoan influence and massive defensive walls, much of which still stand.

● **Tissot, James Joseph Jacques** ▶ (1836–1902) French painter and etcher. In Paris he was influenced by ▷Degas and Japanese prints but after settling in England in the 1870s he became known for his charming scenes of Victorian life, notably *The Ball on Shipboard* (Tate Gallery).

● **tissue** ▶ In anatomy, a group of cells specialized to perform a particular function. The cells may be of the same type (e.g. the muscle cells of muscles) or of different types (as in connective tissue). Combinations of tissues make up organs. The study of tissues is ▷histology.

● **Tisza, River** ▶ (Slavonic and Romanian name: Tisa) A river in S central Europe. Rising in W Ukraine, it flows generally W and S across the Hungarian Plain to join the River Danube below Novi Sad in Serbia. It is a source of irrigation and power, especially in NE Hungary. Length: 980 km (610 mi).

● **tit** ▶ A small acrobatic songbird (also called titmouse) belonging to a family (*Paridae*; 65 species) occurring in Eurasia, North America, and Africa. Tits are versatile birds and frequent woodlands and gardens, feeding chiefly on insects. They are 7–20 cm long with soft plumage, usually grey or black and often with blue and yellow markings. ▷*See also* bluetit; coal tit; great tit; long-tailed tit.

● **Titan** ▶ The largest ▷satellite of the planet Saturn and the second largest in the solar system. It has a nitrogen atmosphere of a reddish or orange colour.

Titanic ▶ The "unsinkable" cruise ship, dropping anchor at Queenstown (now Cóbh, in the Irish Republic), two days before it went down.

● **Titanic** ▶ A luxury liner that on 14–15 April, 1912, struck an iceberg near Newfoundland on its maiden voyage and sank with the loss of 1513 lives. Thought to be unsinkable, it carried enough lifeboats for only half the passengers. As a result of the disaster safety rules for ships at sea were drawn up by the International Convention for Safety of Life at Sea (1913) and the International Ice Patrol was established. The wreck of the *Titanic* was located and photographed in 1985. The disaster has been the subject of several films, most notably James ▷Cameron's epic *Titanic* (1997).

● **titanium** ▶ (Ti) A relatively light strong transition metal discovered in 1791 by W. Gregor (1761–1817). It occurs in nature in the minerals rutile (TiO_2), ilmenite ($FeTiO_3$), sphene ($CaTiO_3$), and in some iron ores. Rutile and ilmenite beach sands are mined as a source of titanium. The dioxide (TiO_2) is used in white paint as it has excellent opacity. The metal is as strong as steel but 45% lighter (relative density 4.54) and 60% heavier than aluminium but twice as strong. It is used in alloys for missiles and aircraft. At no 22; at wt 47.88; mp 1670°C; bp 3289°C.

● **titanothere** ▶ An extinct North American mammal, related to horses and rhinoceroses, that lived between 45 and 20 million years ago. Later Oligocene forms were 4.5 m long and 2.5 m high at the shoulder. They fed on soft vegetation and became extinct possibly because their simple teeth were unable to cope with a change in the vegetation.

● **Titans** ▶ In Greek mythology, 12 primeval gods and goddesses, the children of ▷Uranus and ▷Gaia. They were Oceanus, Coeus, Crius, Hyperion, Iapetus, Cronus, Thea, Rhea, Themis, Mnemosyne, Phoebe, and Tethys. They were overthrown by Zeus and the Olympian deities.

● **tithes** ▶ The tenth part of an income allotted to religious purposes. Originating in the offering of the "first fruits" as a divine sacrifice, tithes were decreed by Mosaic law, which demanded payment in kind from all agricultural produce. Christian ecclesiastical law also enjoined tithes to maintain churches and clergy. Gradually exemptions were made, money payments replaced payments in kind, and as organized religion declined the tithe laws were repealed. Tithes, which were abolished in Britain in 1936, are still voluntarily paid by individuals according to conscience.

● **titi** ▶ A small monkey belonging to the genus *Callicebus* (8 species), of the Amazonian jungle. Titis are 50–115 cm long including the tail (25–55 cm) and live in treetops in family groups. They have soft thick fur, often brightly coloured. Family: *Cebidae*.

● **Titian** ▶ (Tiziano Vecellio; c. 1488–1576) Venetian painter of the High Renaissance, born in Pieve di Cadore, in the Dolomites. His earliest influences were Giovanni Bellini, his teacher, and Giorgione, with whom he collaborated on frescoes for the façade of the German Exchange (1508). In his *Assumption of the Virgin* (Sta Maria dei Frari) his more monumental style links him with such Florentine painters as Raphael. His greatest works for the Habsburgs, who patronized him from 1530 onwards, were the equestrian portrait of Emperor Charles V at Mühlberg (1548; Prado) and *Philip II* (1550–51; Prado). He painted Pope Paul III twice, in Bologna (1543) and in Rome with his grandsons (1546). Both portraits are in Naples. His mythological works include *Bacchus and Ariadne* (National Gallery, London). His last religious paintings, such as the *Pietà* (Accademia, Venice), seem to be inspired by a new emotional intensity.

● **Titicaca, Lake** ▶ A lake in South America, between Peru and Bolivia, in the Andes. At an altitude of 3809 m (12 497 ft) it is the world's highest lake navigable to large vessels (*see also* Tiahuanaco). It is fed by 25 rivers but has only one outlet, the River Desaguadero. Area: 8135 sq km (3141 sq mi). Depth: 370 m (1214 ft).

● **titmouse** ▷See tit.

● **Tito** ▶ (Josip Broz; 1892–1980) Yugoslav statesman; president 1953–80. Tito was captured by the Russians in World War I and subsequently fought with the Red Army in the Russian civil war. He returned to Yugoslavia in 1920, joined the Communist Party, and was briefly imprisoned (1928–29); in 1937 he became secretary general of the Party. In World War II he led the partisans in resistance to the German occupation, becoming a marshal in 1943, when he also gained Allied recognition, previously given to the ▷Chetniks. He became Yugoslavia's postwar leader. After Yugoslavia's expulsion (1948) from the ▷Cominform, Tito introduced the policy of decentralization to workers' councils that distinguished Yugoslav socialism and successfully maintained his country's independence from Soviet interference, pursuing a foreign policy of nonalignment. Tito succeeded in holding together the component parts of Yugoslavia. Twelve years after his death the country was torn apart by separatist movements.

● **Titograd** ▷See Podgorica.

● **Titus (Flavius Vespasianus)** ▶ (39–81 AD) Roman emperor (79–81). He fought with his father Vespasian in Judaea and ended the Jewish revolt (70) by capturing Jerusalem. Proclaimed emperor after Vespasian's death, Titus proved a popular ruler; when Vesuvius erupted (79), he aided the victims generously. At his death he was called "darling of the human race" and deified.

● **Titus, St** ▶ In the New Testament, a disciple and assistant of Paul. He organized the collection of alms for poor Christians in Judaea and replaced Timothy as Paul's commissioner at Corinth. Feast day: 6 Feb.

In the **Epistle of Paul to Titus**, written between 60 and 64 AD, Paul tells Titus how to organize and superintend the new churches of Crete.

● **Tivoli** ▶ 41 58N 12 48E A town in central Italy, in Lazio. A summer resort in Roman times, it possesses the remains of Hadrian's villa and the Renaissance Villa d'Este. Paper and wine are produced. Population (1990): 55 030.

● **Tiw** ▷See Tyr.

● **Tizard, Sir Henry (Thomas)** ▶ (1885–1959) British chemist. After working on bomb sights and new aircraft in World War I, he specialized in the application of science for military purposes. He was rector of the ▷Imperial College of Science and Technology (1929–42). In 1935 he won backing for the development of radar against the arguments of Frederick ▷Lindemann. He clashed again with Lindemann in World War II, over bombing policy, but it was Tizard who supported Frank ▷Whittle in his development of the jet engine and Barnes ▷Wallis in his bouncing bomb device.

● **Tjirebon** ▶ (*or* Cheribon) 6 46S 108 33E A port in Indonesia, in N Java on the Java Sea. The **Tjirebon Agreement** of Indonesian independence was signed here (1946) by the Dutch. It is an agricultural and manufacturing centre. Population (1980): 223 776.

● **Tlaloc** ▶ An Aztec rain god, ranking with the sun and war god ▷Huitzilopochtli. He possessed both creative and destructive powers and children were ritually sacrificed to him.

● **Tlaxcala** ▶ (*or* Tlaxcala de Xicohténcatl) 19 20N 98 12W A city in Mexico, on the central plateau. One of the oldest cities in Mexico, it is the site of the Church of San Francisco, which was founded by ▷Cortés (1521) and is the oldest in the Americas. Population (1980): 13 000.

● **Tlemcen** ▶ (Latin name: Pomaria) 34 55N 1 20W A town in NW Algeria, near the Moroccan border. It became an important Islamic religious centre, flourishing until the 16th century; many old buildings remain, notably the 12th-century Great Mosque. Industries include leatherwork and carpets; blankets and olive oil are exported. Population (latest est): 107 632.

Tito ▶ The president of Yugoslavia taking the salute at a military parade in Belgrade in September, 1975, on the 30th anniversary of the defeat of Germany in World War II.

● **Tlingit** ▶ A North American Indian people of the NW Pacific coast in SE Alaska. There were 14 tribes divided into independent matrilineal clans, each headed by a chief. They lived by salmon fishing and hunting, built wooden houses, and practised the ▷potlatch at the death of a chief. Their language belongs to the ▷Na-Dené group.

● **T-lymphocytes** ▷See immunity.

● **TMV** ▷*See* tobacco mosaic virus.

● **TNT** ▶ (trinitrotoluene; $C_6H_2(NO_2)_3CH_3$) A highly explosive pale yellow crystalline solid. It is prepared from toluene treated with concentrated sulphuric and nitric acids and is used in shells, bombs, etc., and blasting explosives. ▷*See also* amatol.

● **toad** ▶ A tail-less amphibian belonging to a widely distributed order (*Anura*; about 2600 species). Toads have long hind legs and short forelegs; they swim by means of partially webbed feet. They have a long sticky tongue, attached at the front of their mouth, that can extend very rapidly to capture flying insects. Some species use the throat as a resonating chamber to amplify their mating calls. ▷*See also* clawed frog; midwife toad; natterjack; tree frog; spadefoot toad.

● **toadfish** ▶ A bottom-dwelling carnivorous ▷bony fish of the order *Batachoidiformes* (about 45 species), found mainly in tropical and subtropical seas. It has a heavy brownish body, up to 30 cm long, and makes grunting or croaking sounds resembling a toad. ▷*See also* midshipman.

● **toadflax** ▶ An annual or perennial herb belonging to the genus *Linaria* (about 150 species), especially *L. vulgaris*, found in the Mediterranean area, temperate Eurasia, and North America. It grows to a height of 30–80 cm and has an elongated terminal cluster of yellow snapdragon-like flowers (*see* Antirrhinum). Purple toadflax (*L. purpurea*) is cultivated in gardens. Family: *Scrophulariaceae*.

● **toadstool** ▷*See* mushroom.

● **Toamasina** ▶ (name until 1979: Tamatave) 18 10S 49 23E The chief port of Madagascar, on the Indian Ocean. It was destroyed by a hurricane in 1927. Since rebuilt, it is the country's major commercial centre; industries include rum distilling. Population (1993): 127 441.

● **tobacco** ▶ A plant belonging to the genus *Nicotiana*, especially *N. tabacum* and *N. rustica*, which are cultivated for their leaves, used to make ▷cigarettes, ▷cigars, ▷snuff, etc. Commercial tobacco plants grow to a height of 1–3 m and bear pink, white, or greenish flowers. After harvesting, their large sticky leaves are slowly dried in the sun, hot air, or smoke for up to two months and then fermented for another four–six weeks. The main growing regions are the USA, China, India, the republics of the former Soviet Union, E Europe, South America, SE Asia, and S Africa.
    Tobacco contains about 2–4% nicotine, which produces its stimulant and addictive properties when smoked as cigars and cigarettes, and in pipes. Smoking tobacco is now known to be an important cause of lung cancer and other diseases. Family: *Solanaceae*.

● **tobacco mosaic virus** ▶ (TMV) A virus that causes mosaic disease in tobacco and related plants; it is a rod-shaped virus in which the genetic material is RNA. TMV was the first virus to be discovered. In 1892 the Russian botanist Dmitri Ivanovsky (1864–1920) found that sap from tobacco plants infected with mosaic caused the disease in healthy plants: since the sap had been filtered to exclude bacteria, he concluded that the infective agent was a "filterable virus" (the term virus originally meant any infective or noxious substance). In 1935 TMV was crystallized by the US biochemist Wendell Stanley (1904–71), enabling early studies to be carried out on its structure, which was finally elucidated with the development of electron microscopy.

● **Tobago Island** ▷*See* Trinidad and Tobago, Republic of.

● **Tobata** ▷*See* Kitakyushu.

● **Tobey, Mark** ▶ (1890–1976) US painter. He is known for paintings in which coloured forms are overlaid by white brush strokes. He adopted this so-called "white writing" technique after he visited Japan and China (1934), where he was influenced by oriental calligraphy.

● **Tobin, James** ▶ (1918–   ) US economist, who has taught at both Harvard and Yale universities. He is best known for his work on ▷portfolio theory; he was awarded the Nobel Prize in 1981. His books include *The American Business Creed* (1956), *National Economic Policy* (1966), and *Policies for Prosperity* (1987).

● **tobogganing** ▶ The recreation and sport of sliding down snow or ice on a toboggan, a low platform on steel runners, of which there are two competitive types: the luge, for one or two riders lying almost flat on their backs, and the skeleton or Cresta (named after the Cresta Run at St Moritz, Switzerland), for one rider lying prone. Like ▷bobsledding, both were developed mainly by British sportsmen at St Moritz and other Swiss resorts in the late 19th century. In races competitors slide, one vehicle at a time, down a narrow icy chute some 1000 m (1094 yd) long with high banked turns, at more than 130 km per hour (81 mph) and steering only by shifts of weight and touching with either foot.

● **Tobolsk** ▶ 58 15N 68 12E A port in central Russia, at the confluence of the Rivers Irtysh and Tobol. Founded by the Cossacks in 1587, it has shipbuilding, timber, and food-processing industries. Population (latest est): 83 000.

● **Tobruk** ▶ A port in NE Libya, on the Mediterranean coast. During World War II it was the scene of heavy fighting and changed hands five times before being finally recaptured by the British in 1942. Population (latest est): 34 200.

● **Toby jug** ▶ An English pottery jug in the shape of a seated middle-aged man in 18th-century dress, holding a tankard and pipe. Toby jugs, which were first made in the 1760s in Staffordshire by Ralph Wood (1715–72) and his son (also called Ralph Wood; 1748–95), depict various characters, e.g. Squire Toby and Sailor Toby.

● **Toc H** ▶ An interdenominational Christian fellowship open to anyone over the age of 16 and devoted to social service. It was founded in 1915 in Belgium by the Rev P. B. Clayton (1885–1972), a Church of England chaplain, as a military chapel and club; it was named Talbot House in memory of Gilbert Talbot (1891–1915), a British lieutenant, killed in action, who was a member of a prominent Anglican family. Its name derives from army signallers' designations of the initials *T H*.

● **Tocharian** ▶ An extinct ▷Indo-European language of the Tarim Basin region of Chinese Turkistan. It is mainly known from Buddhist scriptures written between about 500 and 1000 AD in the N Indian Brahmi script. Its relationship to the other Indo-European languages is highly debatable.

● **tocopherol** ▷*See* vitamin E.

● **Tocqueville, Alexis de** ▶ (1805–59) French political scientist, historian, and politician. After visiting the USA (1831–32) Tocqueville wrote *Démocratie en Amérique*, a study of US democracy that also dealt with the constitutions of France and Europe. Tocqueville argued that the French Revolution had not achieved a break with the past, since an egalitarian society required greater centralization and thus sacrificed liberty. Elected to the Chamber of Deputies in 1839, he became vice president of the Constituent Assembly and briefly minister of foreign affairs in 1849. After Louis Napoleon's coup d'état he retired to write *L'Ancien Régime et la révolution* (1856).

● **Todd, Alexander Robertus, Baron** ▶ (1907–97) British biochemist, who helped determine the molecular basis of genetics through his work on nucleic acids (DNA and RNA). In 1949 Todd synthesized ADP and ▷ATP, substances vital to energy utilization by living cells. He received a Nobel Prize (1957) and was created a life peer in 1962.

● **tog** ▶ A unit of thermal insulation used in textiles, bedding, etc. The value of the insulation in togs is ten times the difference in temperature in degrees Celsius between the two surfaces of textile, blanket, duvet, etc., when 1 joule of heat energy flows between the surfaces per second per square metre.

● **toga** ▶ The outer garment worn by the ancient Romans, originally by both sexes and all classes but finally only by male patricians on formal occasions. It consisted of a semicircular piece of cloth draped intricately around the body; colour and markings were prescribed according to status.

● **Toghril Beg** ▶ (c. 990–1063) Sultan of Turkey (1055–63), who founded the Seljuq dynasty. His conquests in central Asia culminated in the conquest of Baghdad (1055). An uprising forced his expulsion in 1058 but by 1060 he had suppressed it.

● **Togliatti** ▶ (name until 1964: Stavropol) 53 32N 49 24E A city in W central Russia, on the River Volga. It was renamed in honour of the

Italian communist leader, Palmiro Togliatti. Industries include ship repairing, engineering, and food processing. Population (1995 est): 702 000.

● **Togliatti, Palmiro** ► (1893-1964) Italian politician, the leader of the Italian Communist Party (1926-64). In exile from 1926 to 1944, after Mussolini's fall he became a minister (1944) and then vice premier (1945). He was the author of *Italian Road to Socialism* and his ideas greatly influenced communism in Italy.

● **Togo, Republic of** ► (French name: République Togolaise) A small narrow country in West Africa, on the Gulf of Guinea between Ghana and Benin. Coastal swamps rise to higher land in the interior. The majority of the population is African, mainly Ewe in the S.
   Economy: chiefly agricultural, with food crops consisting mainly of cassava, maize, and rice and cash crops including cocoa, coffee, and cotton. Forests produce not only timber but also oil palms and dyewoods. There are rich deposits of phosphates, which are the main export. Bauxite was found in the 1950s and there is some, as yet unexploited, limestone and iron ore. Industry is being developed, concentrating mainly on food processing, but there is also a large cement plant and an oil refinery.
   History: settled by the Ewe in the 12th and 13th centuries, the area was raided for slaves from the 17th to 19th centuries. From 1884 to 1914 Togoland was a German protectorate and after World War I it was divided between France and the UK, first (1922) under League of Nations mandate and then (1946) as a UN trustee territory. The French territory became an autonomous republic within the French Union in 1956 and gained full independence in 1960. (The British part joined Ghana in 1957.) Togo's first president, Sylvanus Olympio, was assassinated in 1963 and a military coup in 1967 brought Lt Col (later Gen) Etienne Gnassingbé Eyadéma (1937-   ) to power. Following prodemocracy riots, Eyadéma was stripped of his powers by a constitutional conference in 1991, provoking several rebellions by his supporters in the military. In 1992 a multiparty constitution was approved but Eyadéma contrived to regain his position as head of state. He subsequently won presidential elections in 1993 and 1998 but these polls were condemned by international observers. Opposition parties gained a majority in the legislative elections of 1994 but the government continued to be dominated by supporters of Eyadéma. Further elections in 1999 were boycotted by the opposition.

Republic of Togo

Head of state	President Etienne Gnassingbé Eyadéma
Official language	French
Official currency	CFA (Communauté financière africaine) franc of 100 centimes
Area	56 000 sq km (21 616 sq mi)
Population (1998 est)	4 906 000
Capital and main port	Lomé

● **Togo Heihachiro** ► (1847-1934) Japanese admiral. His destruction of the Russian fleet in the battle of Tsushima Strait in May, 1905, ensured Japan's victory in the ▷Russo-Japanese War (1904-05).

● **Tojo Hideki** ► (1884-1948) Japanese general, who was war minister (1940-44) and also prime minister (1941-44) during World War II. After Japan's defeat he was executed as a war criminal.

● **Tokaj** ► (*or* Tokay) 48 08N 21 23E A small town in NE Hungary, at the confluence of the Rivers Bodrog and Tisza. It has given its name to the famous wine produced in the area. Population (latest est): 5778.

● **tokamak** ▷*See* thermonuclear reactor.

● **tokay** ▷*See* gecko.

● **Tokelau Islands** ► A group of three coral atolls in the SW Pacific Ocean, an overseas territory of New Zealand. Chief exports are copra and woven goods. Area: 10 sq km (4 sq mi). Population (1991): 1578.

● **Tokugawa** ► The military family that controlled Japan from 1603 to 1867. ▷Tokugawa Ieyasu secured the title of ▷shogun (military overlord) from the emperor in 1603 and established his capital at Edo (Tokyo). Ieyasu's immediate successors were responsible for isolating Japan from the outside world, a policy that established domestic peace but ultimately led to political stagnation and technological

backwardness. After Japan's reopening under Western pressure in the 1850s the reluctance of the family to abandon its monopoly of power brought about the overthrow of the last shogun, Tokugawa Keiki (1827-1913; ruled 1867-68).

● **Tokugawa Ieyasu** ► (1542-1616) Japanese ▷shogun (military overlord), who completed the re-establishment of central authority in feudal Japan. A vassal of both Oda Nobunaga and Hideyoshi, he steadily increased his domain and in 1600 was able to defeat his rivals in the decisive battle of Sekigahara. In 1603, having confiscated much enemy territory, he acquired from the emperor the title of shogun. He passed this to his son in 1605 but continued to supervise the ▷Tokugawa administration.

● **Tokyo** ► 35 40N 139 45E The capital of Japan, in E central ▷Honshu on Tokyo Bay (an inlet of the Pacific). Administratively joined to its port Yokohama and to the industrial centre of Kawasaki, Greater Tokyo is the world's largest city. It has over 100 universities, including the University of Tokyo (1877) and is a major economic and cultural centre.
   History: site of human settlements from very early times, the village of Edo was founded in the 12th century, growing in importance as a city by the 17th century. As Tokyo, it replaced Kyoto as imperial capital in 1868. It was badly damaged by an earthquake in 1923 and by bombing during World War II, since when its industrial growth has been spectacular. Population (1995): 7 966 195.

● **Toledo** ► 41 40N 83 35W A city in the USA, in Ohio on Lake Erie at the mouth of the River Maumee. The development of the coalfields and the discovery of oil and gas in the late 19th century stimulated its growth and today it is a major Great Lakes port, shipping oil, coal, and farm products. Industrial activities include shipbuilding and oil refining. Population (1996 est): 317 606.

● **Toledo** ► 39 52N 4 02W A city in central Spain, in New Castile on the River Tagus. It was formerly the capital of Spain. It has a magnificent cathedral (13th-17th centuries). Famous for its swords and knives, it produces metalwork engraved in the Moorish tradition. Population (1991): 63 560.

● **Tolkien, J(ohn) R(onald) R(euel)** ► (1892-1973) British scholar and writer, born in Bloemfontein (South Africa). He was professor of Anglo-Saxon (1925-45) and of English language and literature (1945-59) at Oxford University. His trilogy *The Lord of the Rings* (1954-55), in which he created a richly detailed fantasy world, became an international bestseller. Related works include *The Hobbit* (1937) and *The Silmarillion* (1977).

● **Toller, Ernst** ► (1893-1939) German playwright and poet. After being wounded in World War I, he became committed to revolutionary politics and in 1919 was imprisoned for five years for his activities. His reputation was established soon after his release by experimental expressionist plays, such as *Die Wandlung* (1919) and *Masse Mensch* (1920). Driven into exile in 1932, he committed suicide in New York.

● **Tolpuddle Martyrs** ► Six members of the Friendly Society of Agricultural Labourers of Tolpuddle, Dorset. This union was founded in 1833 to secure fair wages for its members. Its leader, George Loveless, and five others were unfairly charged with administering unlawful oaths and transported to Australia. They were pardoned in 1836. The Tolpuddle Martyrs are regarded as among the founders of English trades unionism.

● **Tolstoy, Leo (Nikolaevich), Count** ► (1828-1910) Russian writer and moralist. After active service in the Crimean War, he travelled in Europe and then returned to his family estate of Yasnaya Polyana, where he devoted much energy to the education of his peasants. Following his marriage in 1862 he wrote two novels, *War and Peace* (1865-69), concerning the Napoleonic War, and *Anna Karenina* (1875-77), both acknowledged masterpieces of Russian literature. Around 1879 he underwent a spiritual crisis from which he emerged with a faith in an extreme form of Christian anarchism. He worked and dressed as a peasant, became a vegetarian, espoused total pacifism, repudiated his former literary works, and divided his property among the members of his family. His numerous moral tracts and stories gained him an international discipleship, but his family relationships suffered. He died at 82 of pneumonia a few days after secretly leaving his home in order to live in solitude. Tolstoy was one of the most prolific of writers, his literary work filling 45 volumes. His other works include the story "The Death of Ivan Ilyich" (1884–86) and the novel *Resurrection* (1899).

● **Toltecs** ▶ An Indian people who dominated much of central Mexico between the 10th and 12th centuries AD. Their language, ▷Nahuatl, was also spoken by the Aztecs. A militaristic people, they sacked the city of ▷Teotihuacán (c. 750) and eventually fused the many small states of the area into an empire. They introduced the cult of ▷Quetzalcoatl and were accomplished temple builders. The ▷Aztecs destroyed their capital of ▷Tula in the mid-12th century.

● **Toluca** ▶ (or Toluca de Lerdo) 19 20N 99 40W A city in central Mexico. The centre of a stock-raising area, its industries include the processing of agricultural products. Population (1990): 827 339.

● **toluene** ▶ (or methylbenzene; $C_6H_5CH_3$) A colourless flammable liquid obtained by catalytic reforming of ▷oil. It is used in aviation fuels, as a solvent, and to produce ▷phenol and ▷TNT.

● **tolu tree** ▶ A tree, *Myroxylon balsamum*, native to South America. Growing to a height of over 20 m, it has whitish flowers and yields a ▷balsam from its trunk, used in cough mixtures and perfumery. Family: ▷*Leguminosae*.

● **tomato** ▶ An annual plant, *Lycopersicon esculentum*, native to South America and widely cultivated for its fleshy red ⁰fruit. In warm temperate regions, tomatoes are grown in fields and are low branching and spreading plants; the hothouse tomatoes of cooler regions are often trained to grow a single erect fruiting stem. The clusters of yellow flowers produce rounded or pear-shaped fruits, 2–10 cm in diameter, which are eaten fresh or canned and made into purée, pickles, etc. Family: ▷*Solanaceae*.

● **Tombouctou** ▷*See* Timbuktu.

● **Tombstone** ▶ 31 44N 110 04W A town in the USA, in Arizona. Scene of a silver rush from 1877, it is famous for the gunfight (1881) that took place at the OK Corral between the Clanton gang and Wyatt ▷Earp, his brother Virgil, and Doc Holliday. Population (1990): 1220.

● **tommy gun** ▶ A light US .45 calibre submachine gun invented by General John Thompson (1860–1940) in 1918. Widely used in World War II in various models, especially the M1 and the M3 "blowbacks," some are still in use today.

● **tomography** ▶ The technique, widely used in medicine for diagnostic purposes, of producing an image of a selected plane of the body using X-rays or other forms of radiation.

In **computerized tomography** (CT), a ring-shaped X-ray machine, called a CT scanner (or, formerly, a CAT scanner), is rotated around the patient and records different planes of the body. The information thus obtained is assembled by the scanner's built-in computer into a three-dimensional representation of the body, from which images of selected planes can be extracted. The patient is not at risk as the dose of X-rays used is only about 20% of that used in normal X-ray examination. The technique is useful for imaging soft structures of the body and revealing tumours and other abnormalities.

Positron emission tomography (PET) was originally used specifically for scanning the brain, revealing the presence of tiny blood clots (which might cause strokes), tumours, etc. It is now also used to scan the chest and abdomen. The patient is injected with a form of glucose that has been radioactively labelled and emits positrons. This is absorbed by cells and metabolized. In damaged or diseased areas of tissue metabolism is reduced therefore positron emission is either reduced or absent: this is recorded by the PET scanner.

In **nuclear magnetic resonance (NMR) tomography** (or magnetic resonance imaging; MRI), similar images are obtained utilizing the phenomenon of ▷nuclear magnetic resonance.

● **Tomsk** ▶ 56 30N 85 05E A port in central Russia, on the River Tom. Industries include engineering; it has a university (1888) and other educational institutions. In 1993 an explosion at a nuclear reprocessing plant nearby resulted in radioactive contamination of the surrounding region. Population (1995 est): 470 000.

● **Tom Thumb** ▶ (Charles Stratton; 1838–83) US midget, who was publicly exhibited by the circus impresario P. T. ▷Barnum. He grew to a height of only 40 in. In 1863 he married another midget, Lavinia Warren (1841–1919).

● **ton** ▶ An Imperial unit of weight equal to 2240 lb (long ton) or 1016 kilograms. In the USA a unit equal to 2000 lb (short ton) is also used. The metric ton (or **tonne**) is equal to 1000 kilograms.

● **tonality** ▶ The presence of a tonal centre or **key** in a musical composition. Musical compositions from at least the early 17th century to about 1900 are in distinct keys. These are based on individual scales, in which certain notes (the tonic and dominant degrees) form tonal centres to which the music periodically returns. Once such a centre has been established, the music can modulate into other keys and return to the home key (or underlying tonality). Music in which tonal centres are deliberately avoided exhibits ▷atonality; this is characteristic of some music written after 1900. ▷*See also* serialism.

● **Tone, (Theobald) Wolfe** ▶ (1763–98) Irish nationalist, who was inspired by the French Revolution to work for an independent Irish republic. In 1791 he founded the Society of United Irishmen and unsuccessfully sought French aid for a revolt against British rule. He was captured and sentenced to death, but committed suicide before the sentence could be carried out.

● **tone poem** ▷*See* symphonic poem.

● **Tonga, Kingdom of** ▶ (or Friendly Islands) A country in the SW Pacific Ocean, E of Fiji. It consists of 169 small islands (36 inhabited), the largest of which is Tongatapu, 40 × 16 km (25 × 10 mi); the E islands are low lying, while those to the W are hilly and volcanic.
Economy: chiefly agricultural, the main products and exports being copra, vanilla beans, and fruit. Fishing remains important but has declined. Apart from foodstuffs, manufactures include clothing, leather goods, and boats. Tourism is an important source of revenue.
History: the islands were visited in 1773 by Captain Cook, who named them the Friendly Islands. Under King Taufa'ahau Tupou (George I; 1797–1893) Tonga became a united kingdom and converted to Christianity. The country became a British protectorate in 1900, and in 1970 became an independent state within the British Commonwealth. There is a legislative assembly comprising elected, appointed, and hereditary members, but considerable power remains with the monarch; the present king, Taufa'ahau Tupou IV (1918–), came to the throne in 1965.

Kingdom of Tonga	
Head of state	King Taufa'ahau Tupou IV
Official languages	Tongan and English
Official currency	pa'anga of 100 seniti
Area	700 sq km (270 sq mi)
Population (1997 est)	101 300
Capital and main port	Nuku'alofa (on Tongatapu)

● **tongue** ▶ A muscular organ situated in the floor of the mouth. The root of the tongue is attached by muscles to the U-shaped hyoid bone in the neck. The tongue is the main organ of taste: its surface is covered by minute projections (giving it a rough appearance) around which the taste buds are grouped, detecting sweet, sour, salt, and bitter tastes. It also manipulates food during chewing and swallowing and helps in the articulation of speech. Furring of the tongue is a symptom of fever; a smooth and sore tongue may indicate anaemia.

● **Tong Zhi** ▶ (or T'ung-chih; 1856–75) The title of Cai-chun (or Tsai-ch'un), Chinese emperor (1862–75); the son of ▷Zi Xi, who acted as regent until he was 17. The Tong Zhi Restoration (his title means Union for Order) aimed to repair the upheaval of the ▷Taiping Rebellion but was thwarted by the corrupt court, which dominated the young emperor.

● **tonic sol-fa** ▷*See* solmization.

● **tonka bean** ▶ The seed of the tonka tree, *Coumarouna odorata*, native to N South America. Coumarin, a fragrant edible extract of the black almond-shaped seeds, has been used as a flavouring and in perfumes and snuff. Family: ▷*Leguminosae*.

● **Tonkin** ▶ (*or* Tongking) A region in N Vietnam, long ruled from Hanoi. The Chinese, who had occupied it in 111 BC, were driven out in 939 AD, and from then until 1802 it was an independent state. Following the dissolution of the Vietnamese empire it became a French protectorate (1884). In 1949 it became part of independent Vietnam.

● **Tonkin, Gulf of** ▶ (Chinese name: Beibu Gulf) An inlet of the South China Sea between China, N Vietnam, and Hainan Island.

● **Tonle Sap** ▶ A lake in W central Cambodia. For most of the year it is drained by the River Tonle Sap into the Mekong, but in the monsoon season the swollen Mekong reverses the flow, and the lake roughly quadruples in depth and area to about 10 000 sq km (3860 sq mi). Carp are fished here.

● **tonnage and poundage** ▶ Revenues granted by parliament to the Crown in England (1373–1787). Tonnage (*or* tunnage) was a duty on each imported cask (tun) of wine. Poundage was a duty on each pound's worth of imported and exported goods. They were generally granted for life to each monarch but in 1625 were granted for only a year to Charles I. His subsequent levy of tonnage and poundage without parliamentary consent provoked much opposition.

● **tonsillitis** ▶ Inflammation of the ▷tonsils due to infection of the upper respiratory tract. Symptoms include fever, a sore throat, and difficulty in swallowing. If the tonsils become chronically infected, causing recurrent sore throats, they can be removed.

● **tonsils** ▶ Patches of tissue situated on each side at the back of the mouth and below the tongue that produce lymphocytes: a type of white blood cell that protects the body against infection. ▷*See also* tonsillitis.

● **tontine** ▶ A financial scheme to provide life ▷annuities to a group of subscribers; when a member dies his share is divided amongst the others until the last survivor enjoys the whole income. The idea of an Italian banker (Lorenzo Tonti) in 1653, it was popular in the 18th century.

● **Tonton Macoutes** ▷*See* Duvalier, François.

● **Tooke, John Horne** ▶ (1736–1812) British radical. In 1769 he and John Wilkes founded the Society of the Supporters of the Bill of Rights but the two quarrelled and Tooke established (1771) his own Constitutional Society to campaign for parliamentary reform. In 1778 he was imprisoned for seditious libel and in 1794 was again arrested but acquitted of treason. He was elected an MP in 1801. He was also a philologist, the author of *The Diversions of Purley* (1786).

● **toothed whale** ▷*See* whale.

● **Toowoomba** ▶ 27 34S 151 54E A city in Australia, in SE Queensland. It is a centre for an agricultural region specializing in sheep and dairy farming. It is the site of the Perseverance Creek Water Supply Scheme. Population (1991 est): 83 776.

● **topaz** ▶ A mineral consisting of a hydrous fluosilicate of aluminium, $Al_2SiO_4(OH,F)_2$. It occurs in acidic igneous rocks, in pegmatites and veins. It is usually colourless or yellow, and when cut and polished is used as a gemstone. The finest specimens come mainly from the Urals, Brazil, and Sri Lanka. All yellow gemstones were formerly known as topaz. Birthstone for November.

● **tope** ▶ A slender ▷requiem shark, *Galeorhinus galeus*, that is up to 2 m long with a dark-grey body and a white belly. It lives in shallow tropical and temperate seas and feeds on bottom-dwelling fish and invertebrates.

● **Topeka** ▶ 39 02N 95 41W A city in the USA, the capital of Kansas on the Kansas River. An agricultural trading and processing centre, Topeka is famous as a centre for psychiatric research. Population (1996 est): 119 658.

● **top minnow** ▷*See* killifish.

● **topology** ▶ The branch of ▷geometry concerned with the properties of an object that do not change under ▷homeomorphisms, i.e. when the object is bent, stretched, or shrunk but not torn or deformed so that several points on it are fused. The hole in a doughnut is such a property; for example if a rubber doughnut is distorted to the shape of a cup the hole is still there in the handle. Topology is often called rubber-sheet geometry because rubber objects can be suitably distorted. It was formerly called analysis situs. One application is in networks (e.g. an electricity-distribution network) in which the topological properties depend on the so-called Euler characteristic (named after Leonhard ▷Euler) $V - E + F$, where V is the number of vertices in the network, E the number of edges, and F the number of areas enclosed by the edges.

● **Topolski, Feliks** ▶ (1907–89) British painter, born in Poland. He is best known for his large-scale murals, which have included a depiction of the coronation of Elizabeth II for Buckingham Palace (1958–60) and the huge *Memoir of the Century* painted on viaduct arches on London's South Bank, upon which he worked from 1975 until his death.

● **Torah** ▶ (Hebrew: instruction) The five books of Moses (Genesis, Exodus, Leviticus, Numbers, and Deuteronomy), which constitute the first of the three divisions of the Hebrew ▷Bible. In Judaism, the term is also applied more widely to the whole body of religious teachings, viewed as the revealed word of God and including both the written Torah (traditionally revealed to Moses on Mount Sinai) and the oral Torah (*see also* Mishnah). The reading of the Torah, from a manuscript scroll (*sepher Torah*), occupies a central place in ▷synagogue services.

● **Torbay** ▶ A unitary authority in SW England, in Devon on the S coast: it consists of the three resorts of Torquay, Paignton, and Brixham. Area: 63 sq km (24 sq mi). Population (1997 est): 122 900.

● **Torfaen** ▶ A county borough in SE Wales, created in 1996 from part of Gwent. Area: 290 sq km (112 sq mi). Population (1996 est): 90 527. Administrative centre: Pontypool.

● **Torgau** ▶ 51 35N 12 58E A town and port in E Germany, on the River Elbe. A league of Protestant princes was formed here in 1526. In 1760 a battle was fought nearby, in which the Austrians were defeated by Frederick II of Prussia. Population (latest est): 21 301.

● **Tories** ▶ A British political group that became the ▷Conservative Party under Robert ▷Peel in the 1830s; Tory is still used synonymously with Conservative. Originally an Irish name for a Roman Catholic outlaw, it was applied in 1679 to a supporter, in opposition to the ▷Whigs, of the succession to the throne of the Roman Catholic Duke of York (later James II). The Tories were later associated with the rebellious Jacobites and were excluded from politics until the 1780s, when they re-emerged, led by William ▷Pitt the Younger. They represented the interests of the country gentry, merchants, and Anglicans.

● **Torino** ▷*See* Turin.

● **tormentil** ▶ A perennial herb, *Potentilla erecta*, native to Europe, W Asia, and N Africa. Its slender stems, 10–30 cm long, bear yellow flowers and grow from a woody rootstock, which has astringent properties. The trailing tormentil (*P. anglica*) has creeping flower stems up to 70 cm long and larger flowers. Family: ▷Rosaceae.

● **tornado** ▶ A violently rotating column of air, small in diameter, characterized by a funnel-shaped cloud, which may reach ground surface. Wind speeds of up to 200 knots (100 m per second) have been experienced. Occurring over land, tornadoes cause large-scale destruction and are a considerable problem in the central USA and Australia.

● **Toronto** ▶ 43 42N 79 25W A city and port in E Canada, the capital of Ontario on Lake Ontario. A centre of finance, it houses a stock exchange and many business headquarters. With Canada's busiest airport, Toronto is also a water, road, and rail hub. Its diversified industries include heavy engineering, the manufacture of electrical, chemical, and wood products, foods, clothing, sporting goods, publishing, and films. With theatres, orchestras, museums, opera, ballet, and three universities, Toronto is the cultural centre of English-speaking Canada.

History: established as Upper Canada's capital and military centre (1793), Toronto was burned by American troops (1813) and was the scene of the Mackenzie Rebellion (1837) against oligarchic government. It evolved into an industrial and commercial centre with the development of railways (1850s). Population (1991): 3 431 981 (metropolitan area).

● **torpedo** ► (armament) A self-propelled guided underwater missile carrying a high-explosive warhead. They can be launched by ships or aircraft but have been used most successfully by submarines. Designed in 1866 by a British engineer, Robert Whitehead (1823–1905), they were used to sink 25 million tons of Allied shipping in World Wars I and II. Modern torpedos are driven by steam turbines or by battery-powered electric motors and have sophisticated active or passive acoustic homing systems (active devices send out sounds and are guided by the echo from the target; passive devices are guided by sounds from the target).

● **torpedo** ► (fish) ▷*See* electric ray.

● **Torquay** ► 50 28N 3 30W A coastal resort in SW England, in Torbay unitary authority, S Devon. Its attractions include the mild climate, Torre Abbey (1196), and Kent's Cavern (where prehistoric remains have been discovered).

● **torque** ► The turning effect of a force; it is equal to the product of the force and the perpendicular distance between the line of action of the force and the axis of rotation. In SI units it is measured in newton metres. The power generated by an engine is given by the product of the torque on its drive shaft and the angular velocity of the shaft.

● **Torquemada, Tomás de** ► (1420–98) Spanish Dominican friar and Grand Inquisitor. Confessor to Ferdinand and Isabella, he was appointed head of the Spanish ▷Inquisition in 1483. His sentences were extremely harsh and he was responsible for the expulsion of the Jews from Spain in 1492.

● **torr** ► A unit of pressure used in high vacuum technology, equal to 1 mm of mercury or 133.322 pascals.

● **Torrens, Lake** ► A salt lake in E South Australia. It is a mud flat except during the rainy season. Lowest point: about 8 m (25 ft) below sea level. Area: 5776 sq km (2230 sq mi).

● **Torreón** ► 25 34N 103 25W A city in NE Mexico. It is the centre of La Laguna, a vast agricultural cooperative producing cotton and wheat. Population (1990): 459 809.

● **Torres Strait** ► A channel between New Guinea and Cape York Peninsula, N Australia, linking the Arafura Sea and Coral Sea. It was discovered (1606) by the Spaniard, Luis Vaez de Torres. Width: 145 km (90 mi).

● **Torres Vedras** ► 39 05N 9 15W A town in central Portugal. During the Peninsular War (1808–14) Wellington constructed his famous defence system—the Lines of Torres Vedras—near here, successfully defending Lisbon against the French. Population (1981): 10 997.

● **Torricelli, Evangelista** ► (1608–47) Italian physicist, who succeeded ▷Galileo as professor of mathematics at Florence University. He discovered that the atmosphere exerts a pressure and demonstrated it by showing that it could support a column of mercury in a tube, thus inventing the mercury barometer (1643). He also created the first man-made vacuum in his simple barometer, the space above the mercury still being callid a Torricellean vacuum.

● **tort** ► In law, a civil wrong that constitutes a breach of a duty established by law rather than by ▷contract. It is distinguished from a crime in that it affects the interests of the injured person rather than of the state. Thus in tort the offender may be sued for damages in a civil court. The law of tort is concerned mainly with providing an opportunity for compensation to be obtained in cases involving personal injury or damage to property as a result of ▷negligence. It also offers protection of one's reputation (*see* defamation), personal freedom (*see* assault and battery), title to and enjoyment of property (*see* nuisance), and commercial interests (*see* intellectual property). Although the main remedy for a tort is an action for damages, ▷injunctions can also be obtained to prevent repetition of an injury.

Torts are distinguished from crimes and breaches of contract, although some torts are also crimes (e.g. assault) and some are both torts of negligence and breaches of contract. For example, a taxi driver may cause injury to a passenger, which in addition to being a tort of negligence is also a breach of the contract to carry passengers safely to their destination.

A person who commits a tort is called a **tortfeasor**. The word "tort" comes from Latin *tortum*, twisted, through Old French.

● **Tortelier, Paul** ► (1914–90) French cellist. He won first prize at the Paris conservatoire at the age of 16. After playing in orchestras in the USA he began a career as a soloist, composer, and teacher. He made many recordings and wrote a book on cello playing.

● **tortoise** ► A slow-moving herbivorous reptile belonging to the family *Testudinidae* (40 species), occurring in both Old and New Worlds, especially in Africa. Tortoises have a protective hard-domed shell, tough scaly legs, and range in size from about 10 cm to 1.5 m (*see* Galápagos giant tortoise). Tortoises lay eggs and have long lifespans, reputedly up to 150 years. The common Mediterranean tortoise (*Testudo graeca*) is a popular pet; in colder climates, it must hibernate during the winter. *Compare* turtle; terrapin.

● **tortoise beetle** ► A ▷leaf beetle with a carapace-like shield. Tortoise beetles are 9–12 mm long and many tropical species are brilliantly coloured (the South American species *Desmonota variolosa* is emerald green). The flat spiny larvae have a forked appendage at the rear end of the body to which they attach excrement for camouflage.

● **tortoiseshell butterfly** ► A ▷nymphalid butterfly whose wings are mainly orange with black markings. Tortoiseshells are found in Europe, Asia, and North America. The caterpillars feed mainly on nettles and willows. The adults hibernate. Chief genera: *Aglais, Nymphalis*.

● **Tortoiseshell cat** ► A breed of cat whose coat consists of distinct evenly spread patches of black, red, and cream. All Tortoiseshells are female (any males produced are sterile); they have compact bodies, short legs, and yellow or orange eyes. There are both long- and short-haired breeds.

● **Tortuga Island** ► (French name: Île de la Tortue) 1 00S 90 55W A West Indian island, N of Haiti in the Greater Antilles. It was a haunt of buccaneers during the 17th century. Area: 180 sq km (70 sq mi). Population (latest est): 22 080.

● **torture** ► The deliberate infliction of extreme physical or mental pain by one person on another to humiliate, intimidate, punish, or obtain information or a confession from that person. Torture may also be used by depraved people to gratify their sadistic appetites or to further their enhancement of human physiology or powers of endurance. Despite condemnation by all civilized people and nations, it seems to be an ineradicable feature of human behaviour. In classical Greece it was legal to torture slaves; later freemen could be tortured if they committed acts of treason. The later Roman emperors were particularly infamous for elaborate, arbitrary, and sadistic acts of cruelty. In the medieval and early modern period torture was an accepted part of the judicial process, especially in cases of alleged treason. Religious authorities, most notoriously the ▷Inquisition of the Roman Catholic Church, also used it to obtain confessions of heresy and witchcraft or to force heretics to recant or incriminate others.

Torture was officially banned in Britain in the 17th century, in France during the ▷Enlightenment, and in the USA by the 8th Amendment to the Constitution. However, it is safe to assume that throughout human history someone somewhere has been or is being tortured. The 20th century was certainly no exception. In the first half of the century Nazi Germany, imperialist Japan, and Stalin's Soviet Union dragged human standards of conduct down to unprecedented levels of barbarity. In the German concentration camps and Japanese prisoner-of-war compounds qualified doctors refined the techniques of torture into a medical science, both devising new methods of dehumanizing their victims and carrying them out. In the Soviet gulags, psychiatrists abused psychoactive drugs to disorientate and brainwash their victims. In the second half of the century the regimes of Pol Pot in Cambodia, Pinochet in Chile, the French in Algeria, and the advocates of ▷apartheid in South Africa are only some of those who have made use of torture and murder to establish and maintain their power. In the 1990s ethnic and religious differences in Africa and the Balkans resulted in renewed outbreaks of brutality and torture. In Northern Ireland, beatings and shootings by both Republican and loyalist paramilitary groups have continued in spite of the peace process.

The best one can say for the 20th century is that at least attempts have been made to outlaw torture. In 1984 the UN adopted the Convention against Torture and Other Cruel, Inhuman, or Degrading Treatment or Punishment, making torture a punishable offence and providing for the compensation of victims. Many countries (including the UK) have also passed laws making torture an extraterritorial offence, with the aim of denying its perpetrators the security of exile. ▷Amnesty International, a London-based charity founded in 1961, has also campaigned vociferously against torture and the infringement of human rights. In 1985 Helen Bamber set up the Medical Foundation for the Care of Victims of Torture to help overcome the shame and degradation that victims so often experience. In 1997 they helped 2000 people come to terms with their ordeal. It remains to be seen how effective these and other measures will be in eliminating torture in the new millennium.

● **Toruń** ▶ (German name: Thorn) 53 01N 18 35E A town in N central Poland, on the River Vistula. Copernicus, the Polish astronomer, was born here (1473). Its university was founded in 1945. Industries include precision engineering and chemicals. Population (1995 est): 203 800.

● **Torvill and Dean** ▶ British ice-skaters. In 1975 **Jayne Torvill** (1957–), a British junior pairs champion (1970), teamed up with **Christopher Dean** (1958–), who won his first national title in 1972. They became the British ice-dance champions (1977–84), their celebrated "Barnum" and "Bolero" routines bringing them European and World championships and, in 1984, an Olympic gold medal with perfect marks, before they turned professional. They returned to competition in 1993 but withdrew again after winning the bronze medal at the 1994 Winter Olympics.

● **Toscanini, Arturo** ▶ (1867–1957) Italian conductor. He began his career as a cellist. He made his debut in Rio de Janeiro in 1886 in Verdi's *Aida* and subsequently conducted at La Scala, Milan, and at the Metropolitan Opera in New York. From 1937 until his death he conducted the NBC (National Broadcasting Company) Symphony Orchestra.

● **Tosks** ▶ One of the two divisions of the Albanian people living in the S of the country. ▷*See also* Ghegs.

● **Tostig** ▶ (d. 1066) Earl of Northumbria from 1055 until his exile in 1065 following a revolt against his misrule. He allied with Harold III Hardraade of Norway and invaded N England but was killed by his brother, Harold II, at Stamford Bridge.

● **totalitarianism** ▶ A form of authoritarian government characterized by a one-party system (often dominated by a single dictator), central control of all aspects of political, social, legal, military, and economic life, brutal suppression of opposition by a secret police, and a forcefully promoted ideology from which no deviation is permitted. Modern totalitarianism is defined by four regimes established between the 1920s and 1940s: Stalin's Soviet Union, Mussolini's Italy, Mao's China, and above all Hitler's Germany. Italian facism and German Nazism were destroyed during World War II, while the Soviet Union persisted as a totalitarian state until Gorbachov's reforms of the 1980s; despite considerable economic liberalization, the present-day People's Republic of China retains many totalitarian features.

Why did the 20th century see these totalitarian states flourish and some of their worst features reappear in the regimes that have emerged in developing countries since World War II? Many answers have been given, but most commentators would point to such elements of modern life as the breakdown of religious and traditional values, economic and social dislocation caused by rapid change, and the fragmentation of families. Disorientating change of this kind, it is suggested, makes people vulnerable to those offering easy certainties and a sense of belonging, especially when this involves the scapegoating of traditional enemies or ethnic minorities. Moreover, the claims of democracy to offer a superior system have often been undermined by its inability to provide solutions to such problems as poverty and unemployment. Totalitarian regimes are able to provide irresponsible short-term solutions by undertaking programmes of grandiose public works, building up massive armament industries and large armies of state police, and embarking on expansionist for-

eign policies. Totalitarian control has also been made possible by 20th-century technology; the growth of the mass media has enabled ▷propaganda to be disseminated in an unprecedented way, while modern communications have allowed totalitarian states to create systems of surveillance and suppression that could only be dreamt of by earlier tyrants.

● **Totalizator** ▶ (or Tote) A system of betting on horse and greyhound races in which all the stake money is pooled, the pool being shared among winners (after deducting taxes and operating costs). The system was invented in France in 1872, where it is known as the *pari-mutuel*, but was not used there until 1929. It was introduced into the UK and the USA in 1930.

● **total quality management** ▶ (TQM) ▷*See* quality control.

● **totemism** ▶ In primitive societies, the common occurrence of a special relationship of ritual significance between certain animal and plant species or other natural phenomena and certain social groups or individuals. Features of this relationship are belief in descent from the totem species (which may include animal worship), a ▷taboo on killing or eating it except at special ritual feasts, and clan exogamy, but only among Australian aborigines do all these occur together. The Indians of the NW Pacific coast of America also practise totemism, as did the ancient Indo-European peoples.

● **totem pole** ▶ Among the Indians of the NW Pacific coast, a carved and painted pole used to commemorate important events, as a house post, or to mark or contain funerary remains. The carvings are largely of animals associated with particular families and their histories and legends.

● **Totila** ▶ (d. 552 AD) King of the Ostrogoths (541–52), who temporarily recovered much of central and S Italy from the Eastern Roman Empire. He took Rome in 546, lost it to ▷Belisarius, and then recaptured it. He was finally defeated and killed by ▷Narses.

● **toucan** ▶ A noisy forest-dwelling bird belonging to a family (*Ramphastidae*; 37 species) occurring in tropical America. 25–60 cm long, toucans have huge brightly coloured bills and typically black plumage with a brightly coloured breast. They feed on fruit. Order: *Piciformes* (woodpeckers, etc.).

● **touch-me-not** ▶ A European annual herbaceous plant, ▷*Impatiens noli-tangere*, 20–100 cm high. It has narrow leaves and bright-yellow tubular flowers, each with a large lower lip and a long curled spur, borne on slender drooping stalks. The ripe fruits split open at the slightest touch to expel the seeds explosively. Family: *Balsaminaceae*.

● **touchstone** ▶ A black or grey flintlike stone, formerly used for testing the purity of gold and silver. The metal to be tested and one of known purity are both rubbed with the touchstone and compared. The colour of the marks left indicates the impurities present. Treatment with nitric acid highlights the marks. The method is still sometimes used to test the purity of gold.

● **Toulon** ▶ 43 07N 5 55E A port in SE France, in the Var department on the Mediterranean Sea. In 1942 most of the French fleet was scuttled here to prevent its capture by the Germans. Toulon is one of France's principal naval bases and has marine engineering, chemical, oil, and textile industries. Population (1990): 170 167.

● **Toulouse** ▶ 43 33N 1 24E A city in S France, the capital of the Haute-Garonne department on the River Garonne. A major commercial and industrial centre, it has aircraft, armaments, chemical, and textile industries. It is also an important agricultural trading centre. Notable buildings include the basilica (11th–13th centuries), the gothic cathedral, and the university (1230).

History: capital of the Visigoths and later of the kingdom of Aquitaine, it passed to France in 1271. It suffered badly during the campaign against the Albigenses. Population (1990): 608 000.

● **Toulouse-Lautrec, Henri (Marie Raymond) de** ▶ (1864–1901) French artist, born in Albi of aristocratic descent. Stunted in growth by a childhood accident, he settled in Paris, where he trained under two conservative artists in the early 1880s and led an unconventional life among the music halls and cafés of Montmartre. His comic but sympathetic studies of popular entertainers (for example Jane Avril

Henri Toulouse-Lautrec ▶ An 1894 gouache, *Yvette Guilbert sings Linger Longer Loo* (Pushkin Museum, Moscow).

and Aristide Bruant), circus life, and prostitutes in posters, lithographs, and paintings were influenced by ▷Degas and Japanese prints. Characteristic paintings are *At the Moulin Rouge* (Art Institute of Chicago) and *La Toilette* (Louvre).

● **touraco** ▷*See* turaco.

● **Touraine** ▶ A former province of central France. Centred on its capital city, Tours, it now largely occupies the Indre-et-Loire department. Once independent, later under Angevin control, and in 1641 incorporated into the French kingdom, Touraine was famous until the late 17th century for its Huguenot silk weavers. The region is noted for its royal chateaux.

● **Tourcoing** ▶ 50 44N 3 10E A town in N France, in the Nord department. Together with its twin town, Roubaix, it forms the centre of the French woollen industry. Population (1990): 93 765.

● **Tour de France** ▶ The main Continental professional cycling race. Founded in 1903, the road race, of some 20 stages, lasts three weeks or more and has a maximum length of approximately 4000 km (2480 mi). The race starts in a different town each year but always ends in Paris. The teams are commercially sponsored. The 1998 race nearly had to be abandoned after almost half the riders withdrew protesting at zealous enforcement of the rules against drug use.

● **Touré, (Ahmed) Sékou** ▶ (1922–84) Guinean statesman; president (1958–84). Active in trades unionism in French West Africa, in 1956 Touré was elected to the French National Assembly. He opposed de Gaulle's plan of federalism in French West Africa and lost French support on independence (1958), when he became head of state.

● **Tourette's syndrome** ▶ A condition of unknown cause in which the patient has severe tics and indulges involuntarily in obscene speech. Named after the French physician Georges Gilles de la Tourette (1859–1904), it usually starts in early childhood and is most common in males. Treatment with such drugs as pimozide is sometimes helpful.

● **tourmaline** ▶ A group of minerals composed of complex cyclosilicates containing boron. There are numerous varieties, some being used as gemstones and some for their piezoelectric and polarizing properties. Tourmalines are found in veins and pegmatites, in granite rocks.

● **Tournai** ▶ (Flemish name: Doornik) 50 36N 3 24E A town in W central Belgium, on the River Scheldt. It has a notable cathedral (11th–14th centuries). Industries include carpets, textiles, and leather. Population (1995 est): 68 086.

● **tournament** ▶ In medieval Europe, a festival at which knights competed in various tests of skill and courage. The best-known example was jousting, in which mounted knights charged each other with lances. Usually, combatants were members of noble families and weapons were blunt. Tournaments originated in France in the 11th century and had died out by the end of the 16th century. In modern times, the word refers to military displays and sporting competitions.

● **Tournefort, Joseph Pitton de** ▶ (1656–1708) French botanist, who proposed a system of plant classification that used a single Latin name to distinguish a particular genus. This was later incorporated in the binomial system of nomenclature developed by ▷Linnaeus.

● **Tourneur, Cyril** ▶ (c. 1575–1626) English dramatist. He published several poems, including the satire *The Transformed Metamorphosis* (1600), and is the presumed author of *The Atheist's Tragedy* (1611) and *The Revenger's Tragedy* (1607). The latter play has also been attributed to Thomas ▷Middleton. He died in Ireland after taking part in an expedition to Cádiz.

● **Tournier, Michel** ▶ (1924–) French writer. His novels, which show the influence of his philosophical studies, include *Friday and Robinson* (1967), *Erlking* (1970), and *The Golden Droplet* (1985).

● **Tours** ▶ 47 23N 0 42E A city in central France, the capital of the Indre-et-Loire department situated between the Rivers Loire and Cher. It was formerly the capital of the province of ▷Touraine. Its silk industry declined following the revocation of the Edict of Nantes (1685) and the exodus of the Huguenot weavers. Notable buildings include the gothic cathedral, the archiepiscopal palace (17th–18th centuries), and the university (1970). Tours is a tourist centre for the Loire Valley. Population (1990): 133 403.

● **Toussaint-L'Ouverture, François Dominique** ▶ (c. 1743–1803) Haitian slave, who led a slave rebellion in Haiti that achieved self-government under French protection. L'Ouverture became lieutenant governor of Haiti in 1794 and established a free society, expelling the Spanish and British landowners. He became governor general in 1801 but the French, afraid of his power, forcibly retired him in 1802. He was then arrested for plotting a rebellion and imprisoned.

● **Tower Bridge** ▶ A bridge over the River Thames in London. Opened in 1894 and designed in the gothic style by John Wolfe-Barry (engineer) and Sir Horace Jones (architect) to complement the nearby ▷Tower of London, it has a central portion that lifts to allow large ships to pass through it into the Pool of London. The original hydraulic mechanism for opening the bridge was electrified in 1976.

● **Tower Hamlets** ▶ A borough of E Greater London, created in 1965 from the former metropolitan boroughs of Bethnal Green, Stepney, and Poplar. The name was in use in the 16th century; by 1720 it designated 21 hamlets, covering an area that became the parliamentary borough of Tower Hamlets in 1832. The name was not used between 1918 and 1965. Area: 20 sq km (8 sq mi). Population (1996): 176 600.

● **Tower of London** ▶ A royal fortress on the N bank of the River Thames, E of the City of London. It was begun in the 11th century on the orders of ▷William (I) the Conqueror soon after the Battle of Hastings. Originally a temporary fort, it became permanent with the addition of the stone White Tower (1078), designed by the Norman monk Gundulf, who became Bishop of Rochester. It was a royal palace until the 17th century and a state prison, which held such famous prisoners as Lady Jane ▷Grey and Anne ▷Boleyn. It is now a barracks, armoury, and museum, containing the British crown jewels, which makes it a leading London tourist attraction.

● **Townes, Charles Hard** ▶ (1915–) US physicist, who constructed the first ▷maser (1953). For this work he shared the 1964 Nobel Prize with Nikolai Basov (1922–) and Aleksandr Prokhorov (1916–), two Soviet physicists, who independently worked out the theory of the maser.

● **town planning** ▶ The designing of urban areas with a view to providing adequate public amenities, healthy and pleasant surroundings, and good communications. Among the first town planners were the Romans, who evolved a grid plan for many of their towns. Interest in the subject revived during the ▷Renaissance but it only became of major importance during the 19th-century urban expansion, when the need for an assured supply of housing and services became urgent. As a branch of the social sciences town planning has become highly sophisticated in the 20th century, now having to deal not only with unprecedented concentrations of people but also with heavy traffic.

● **Townsend, Sue** ▶ (1946–) British writer. Her novel *The Secret Diary of Adrian Mole, aged 13¾* (1982) and its sequels were immensely popular. Other works include the play *The Great Celestial Cow* (1984) and the novels *The Queen and I* (1992) and *Ghost Children* (1997).

● **Townshend, Charles, 2nd Viscount** ▶ (1674–1738) British politician; secretary of state for the north (1714–16, 1721–30). He was dismissed in 1716 after a dispute with the 1st Earl Stanhope but was restored to power in 1721 and was responsible for foreign affairs in the 1720s. He was overshadowed by his brother-in-law Sir Robert Walpole and resigned. He was nicknamed Turnip Townshend for improving the cultivation of turnips.

● **Townshend Acts** ▶ (or American Import Duties Act; 1767) Four acts passed by Britain to assert its authority over the American colonies by imposing revenue duties on tea, paper, glass, and painters' colours. They were named after Charles Townshend (1725–67), chancellor of the exchequer (1766–67). The acts, the uses to which the resulting revenues were put, and their repressive enforcement contributed to the outbreak of the ▷American Revolution.

● **Townsville** ▶ 19 13S 146 48E A port in Australia, in NE Queensland on Cleveland Bay. It is the commercial centre for N Queensland; industries include sugar processing, copper refining, and meat packing. It is the site of the James Cook University of North Queensland (1970). Population (1998 est): 87 235.

● **toxaemia** ▶ The presence of bacterial toxins, such as those of diphtheria and tetanus, in the blood. The condition of ▷pre-eclampsia was formerly described as toxaemia of pregnancy as it was thought to be caused by toxins.

● **toxicology** ▷*See* poisons.

● **toxic shock syndrome** ▶ A state of shock caused by ▷blood poisoning, often due to a retained foreign body, such as a tampon or contraceptive device, combined with infection by staphylococci or streptococci. The condition can be dangerous if not treated promptly by antibiotics, fluid replacement, etc.

● **toxin** ▶ A poison produced by an organism. Many microorganisms, including bacteria and fungi, produce toxins. In diphtheria and tetanus the toxin is produced by the bacteria within the patient's body; in botulism the toxin is produced in contaminated food ingested by the patient. Some toxins are useful: penicillin is a toxin, produced by fungi, that kills bacteria.

● **Toyama** ▶ 36 42N 137 14E A city in Japan, in central Honshu on the Sea of Japan. It has been known since the 17th century for its pharmaceutical industry. Population (1995): 325 375.

● **Toynbee, Arnold** ▶ (1852–83) British economist and philanthropist. Author of *Lectures on the Industrial Revolution* (1984), he also worked amongst the poor of London's East End (*see* Toynbee Hall. His nephew, **Arnold (Joseph) Toynbee** (1889–1975), was a historian. After holding several university posts, he was director of studies at the Royal Institute of International Affairs (1925–55). His major work, *A Study of History* (12 vols, 1934–61), structured according to the rise and fall of civilizations, embodies his theory of historical progress. His son, the journalist **(Theodore) Philip Toynbee** (1916–81), wrote a number of novels, including *Tea with Mrs Goodman* (1947) and *Pantaloon* (1961). Philip Toynbee's daughter **Polly Toynbee** (1946–) is also a well-known journalist and broadcaster.

● **Toynbee Hall** ▶ (The Universities' Settlement in East London) A residential settlement for men and women, founded in 1885 and named after Arnold ▷Toynbee. It houses many welfare services, including playgroups, a legal advice centre, adult literacy courses, and care for the mentally handicapped.

● **Trabzon** ▶ (former name: Trebizond) 41 00N 39 43E A port in NE Turkey, on the Black Sea. It was the capital of the Comnenian empire (1204–1461) and has a university (1963). Population (1997): 182 552.

● **trace element** ▶ A chemical element required by an organism for healthy growth but only in minute amounts. For example, mammals (including humans) require traces of such elements as copper, zinc, manganese, cobalt, chromium, fluorine, and iodine. Many trace elements are constituents of vitamins and enzymes. ▷*See also* nutrient.

● **tracer bullet** ▶ A bullet that when ignited by the propellant emits light or smoke. In flight, its path appears as a continuous streak enabling the gunner to correct his aim. Mixed with other types of bullets during loading, tracer bullets are used in aircraft and by ground troops.

● **tracery** ▶ In ▷gothic architecture, decorative stonework supporting the glass in windows. Moulded stone bars were introduced as an ornamental element in 13th-century France and England. Designs were at first geometric (*see* Early English), but later became curvilinear (*see* Decorated; Flamboyant). In England the regular rectangular tracery of the ▷Perpendicular style resulted in some enormous windows.

● **trachea** ▶ **1.** The windpipe: a tube that conducts air from the larynx to the left and right bronchi, which continue to the ▷lungs. The trachea is lined by ▷mucous membrane and supported by hoops of cartilage in its wall. ▷*See* Plate II. **2.** One of the air passages in insects, which lead directly to the tissues. Each trachea has an external opening (spiracle).

● **trachoma** ▶ An eye disease that occurs in dry poor parts of the world and is caused by a large virus-like bacterium of the genus *Chlamydia*. It is a severe form of ▷conjunctivitis in which the membrane lining the eyelids and covering the cornea becomes scarred and shrunken and the eyelids become deformed. Trachoma is the world's most common cause of blindness; it is treated with antibiotics.

● **Tractarianism** ▷*See* Oxford Movement.

● **tractor** ▶ A self-propelled vehicle designed to provide high power and traction at relatively low speeds for use in agriculture, construction, etc. Tractors were developed from mobile versions of the steam engines used in the 19th century. The American Burger tractor of 1889 was the first to use an internal-combustion engine. The modern tractor is usually powered by a Diesel engine and equipped with a cab that insulates the driver from weather and noise. A power take-off (PTO) and hydraulically operated fittings enable powerful and versatile implements to be operated by the tractor, including shovels, mowing machines, muck spreaders, and cultivators.

● **Tracy, Spencer** ▶ (1900–67) US film actor. He began his film career in the 1930s by playing gangsters, but later costarred with Katherine ▷Hepburn in nine films, including *Woman of the Year* (1942), *Adam's Rib* (1949), and *Guess Who's Coming to Dinner* (1967). He earned Academy Awards for *Captains Courageous* (1937) and *Boys' Town* (1938). Other notable films include *Inherit the Wind* (1960) and *Judgment at Nuremberg* (1961).

● **trade cycle** ▶ The repeated cycle of ▷boom, ▷recession, ▷depression, recovery, and boom in an economy. In the 19th century, the UK's trade cycle displayed remarkable regularity and stability; in the 20th century, it fluctuated more. The ▷Depression of the 1930s was a severe and protracted world slump followed, after World War II, by a period of boom, interrupted by only minor recessions; this persisted until another depression was entered in the 1970s. The subsequent boom was interrupted by depression in the early 1990s. The causes of the cycle are uncertain, but it may result from the regular cycles of electoral politics as well as erratic shocks to the economy, such as wars, rises in the prices of essential commodities (such as oil), etc. Governments have sometimes tried to temper the effects of the trade cycle through ▷deficit financing, but this is not favoured by most contemporary economists.

● **trademarks** ▶ A type of ▷intellectual property consisting of distinctive emblems owned by a manufacturer or trader and applied to his goods to identify them. The owner of a trademark has the right to its exclusive use in connection with the goods associated with it. In the UK most trademarks are registered at the Patent Office. Any trademark can be protected against infringement by legal action and registered trademarks enjoy additional statutory protection.

● **Tradescant, John** ► (1570–1638) English gardener and botanist. Gardener to Charles I, he introduced numerous plants to Britain; his work was developed by his son **John Tradescant** (1608–62), who collected plants from Virginia and elsewhere; the genus ▷*Tradescantia* was named after him.

● **Tradescantia** ► A genus of flowering plants (about 60 species), native to North and Central America. Varieties of the wandering jew (*T. fluminensis*) are popular house plants, having oval green leaves, tinged with pink or mauve or with silver stripes. Spiderworts, derived from *T. virginiana*, have three-petalled blue, purple, red, or white flowers and grasslike leaves. Family: *Commelinaceae.*

● **trade union** ► An organization of employees joined together to present a collective front in negotiations with an employer and to provide a measure of security for its members. The origins of trade unions lie in the local clubs of skilled craftsmen in 18th-century Britain. These were suppressed by the ▷Combination Acts until 1824; although the right of workers to form unions was then acknowledged they continued to suffer restrictions. Robert Owen's Grand National Consolidated Trades Union (1834), the first attempt to unite skilled and unskilled workers, collapsed following the transportation of the ▷Tolpuddle Martyrs. In 1851 the first successful national trade union, the Amalgamated Society of Engineers, was formed and in 1868 the Trades Union Congress (TUC) met for the first time. Granted legal status in 1871, trade unions began to be formed by unskilled workers, who were encouraged by the successful London Dockers' strike (1889) for a wage of 6d an hour. During the 1890s the trades union movement supported the formation of the ▷Labour Party. Unions in the UK finally became secure with the passing of the Trade Disputes Act (1906), which prevented employers from suing unions for damages after a ▷strike. The failure of the ▷General Strike (1926) was a blow to the trades union movement in Britain and the consequent Trade Disputes Act (1927) made general strikes illegal. This was repealed by the postwar Labour Government, during whose term unions became increasingly powerful. The Industrial Relations Act (1971), introducing strike ballots and a cooling-off period, was brought in by a Conservative Government and repealed in 1974 by the next Labour Government, who in the following year set up ▷ACAS to assist in settling industrial disputes. The power of the unions was greatly diminished by the restrictions imposed by the Thatcher governments in the Employments Acts (1980, 1982, and 1988). These restricted secondary picketing, the closed shop, and unfair disciplining of members. The Trade Union Act (1984) made secret ballots before a strike compulsory. The law relating to the regulation of trade unions is now codified in the Trade Union and Labour Relations (Consolidation) Act 1992. The Labour Party has loosened its traditional links with the Trade Unions since the mid-1990s and the advent of New Labour.

Craft unions consist of members possessing a particular skill; **industrial unions** are restricted to those in a particular industry; and **general unions** have members from any industry. Compared to the USA and W Europe, the UK has a multiplicity of craft unions, a situation thought by some analysts to be one of the main causes of its industrial relations problems. In the UK, membership of unions reached a peak of 13.29 million in 1979, but declined to 10 million in 1991. The number of unions was 519 in 1973, but had declined to 302 in 1992.

Unions are often affiliated to national organizations, such as the TUC in the UK. These national organizations vary in character; some are tight-knit groups (as in Scandinavia), some are loose federations (e.g. the TUC), some (e.g. the ▷American Federation of Labor) act as pressure groups within the political system, while others have political aims. The first international trade union was the first ▷International (1864); the international trades union movement is now represented by the ▷World Federation of Trade Unions and the ▷International Confederation of Free Trade Unions.

● **trade winds** ► (or tropical easterlies) The predominantly easterly

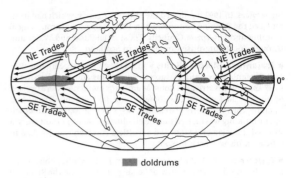

◼ doldrums

trade winds

winds that blow in the tropics. They blow generally from the NE in the N hemisphere and from the SE in the S hemisphere, converging towards the equator. They are noted for their constancy of direction and speed.

● **Trafalgar, Battle of** ► (21 October, 1805) The naval battle in the Napoleonic Wars in which the British under Nelson (in the *Victory*; □ships) defeated the French W of Cape Trafalgar, between Cádiz and Gibraltar. Nelson's tactic of attacking enemy lines at right angles was an important element in the British success, which was marred by Nelson's death. It ended the threat of a French invasion of Britain and established British naval supremacy. It was at Trafalgar that Nelson signalled "England expects that every man will do his duty."

● **Trafford** ► A unitary authority in NW England, in Greater Manchester. Area: 106 sq km (41 sq mi). Population (1996 est): 218 900.

● **tragacanth** ▷*See* gums.

● **tragedy** ► A form of ▷drama recounting the fall (usually, the death) of a noble protagonist. It evolved in ancient Greece from the ▷dithyramb, a choral song, and was developed in the plays of Aeschylus, Sophocles, and Euripides. Little was then written until the Elizabethan period of English literature, when Marlowe prepared the way for the tragedies of Shakespeare and his followers. In 17th-century France the neoclassical tragedies of Racine and Corneille were based on principles derived from Aristotle's *Poetics* (*see* unities). During the 19th century the elements of tragedy were more apparent in the novel than drama. Ibsen and Strindberg in Europe and Eugene O'Neill in the USA contributed to the development of tragic drama, but few 20th-century dramatists have attempted to write tragedies in the classical or Elizabethan sense.

● **tragicomedy** ► A genre of ▷drama developed in Europe in the late 16th and early 17th centuries. Its combination of tragic and romantic elements was pioneered by the Italian dramatist ▷Guarini in *Il pastor fido* (c. 1583) and was further developed in France and by several Jacobean and Restoration dramatists in England. The term is also used more generally to mean any play containing both tragic and comic elements.

● **tragopan** ► A short-tailed ▷pheasant belonging to a genus (*Tragopan*) occurring in wet forests of the Himalayas. Male tragopans have vivid plumage, including long crown feathers, and two erectile blue fleshy "horns" on the head; a fold of skin beneath the bill forms a large bib during display.

● **Traherne, Thomas** ► (c. 1637–74) English poet. The discovery of manuscripts on a London bookstall in 1896 led to the publication of his *Poetical Works* (1903) and *Centuries of Meditation* (1908), a series of mystical and religious meditations written in an exalted prose style.

● **Trail** ► 49 04N 117 39W A city in W Canada, in British Columbia. Founded in 1865, it has a huge smelter to exploit local lead, zinc, iron, and other mineral deposits. Steel, metal products, and chemicals are manufactured here. Population (latest est): 9600.

● **Training, Enterprise and Education Directorate** ► A statutory body that organizes British government employment and training services. In 1992 it replaced the Training Agency, which had itself replaced the Training Commission in 1989. It operates through local Training and Enterprise Councils (TECs) in England and Wales and through Local Enterprise Companies in Scotland.

● **Trajan(us), Marcus Ulpius** ► (53–117 AD) Roman emperor (98–117). Trajan's early military successes led to his adoption by ▷Nerva in 97 AD. After his arrival in Rome as emperor his virtues were praised by Pliny in the *Panegyric*. His domestic policies were munificent and humane: corn was freely distributed, taxes were lessened, and much public building was carried out. He conducted two important wars: a successful Dacian campaign and a fruitless Parthian war. He died in Cilicia on his way back to Rome.

● **Tralee** ► 51 16N 9 42 W A town and port in the SW Republic of Ireland, the administrative centre of Co Kerry. It stands on the River Lee just inland from Tralee Bay, a picturesque inlet of the Atlantic. Tralee is a tourist centre for the nearby Dingle Peninsula and the headquarters of the Folk Theatre of Ireland. Population (1991): 17 200.

● **tranquillizers** ► Drugs used to relieve ▷anxiety and tension, also called anxiolytic drugs, they include the ▷benzodiazepines (*see also* sedatives). The drugs, formerly known as major tranquillizers, which are used in the treatment of schizophrenia and other mental disorders, have been renamed ▷antipsychotic drugs.

● **Trans-Alaska Pipeline** ► A 1.2 metre-diameter oil pipeline that runs the 1285 km (798 miles) from Prudhoe Bay on the Arctic Ocean to the ice-free port of Valdez in the Gulf of Alaska. It carries crude oil from the Alaskan North Shores (the largest oil field in the USA) to the tanker terminal at Valdez. It opened in 1977 and cost $8 billion.

● **Transcaucasia** ► A region in central Asia, in Georgia, Azerbaidzhan, and Armenia. The Great ▷Caucasus range is in the N and the Little Caucasus, in the S. Its resources include oil and it is an important agricultural region. In 1918 Georgia, Azerbaidzhan, and Armenia formed the short-lived Transcaucasian Federative Republic, the basis of the Transcaucasian Soviet Federated Republic (1922–36).

● **transcendentalism** ► A philosophy that emphasizes thought and apprehension beyond the world of experience. In the philosophy of ▷Kant, everything beyond man's limited experience is transcendental and essentially unknowable. Human intuitions about time and space and understanding of quality and quantity are vital for experience, but are transcendent as they do not come from that experience. ▷*See also* Transcendentalists, New England.

● **Transcendentalists, New England** ► A group of mid-19th century US writers and philosophers united by their philosophic idealism and their trust in the moral value of intuition. Their beliefs derived from the philosophy of ▷Kant, especially as interpreted by Carlyle and Coleridge. The group included ▷Emerson and ▷Thoreau. Many of their writings advocating social, political, and religious reforms were published in the periodical *The Dial* (1840–44).

● **transcendental meditation** ► (TM) A form of ▷meditation taught by the Indian-born guru Maharishi Mahesh Yogi. Based loosely on Hindu meditation techniques and the use of a ▷mantra to concentrate the mind, it is believed by its followers to promote self-knowledge, relieve stress, and produce relaxation. Its practice first became popular in the 1960s when the Beatles became advocates.

● **transducer** ► Any device that changes a signal or physical quantity into another form. ▷Microphones, ▷loudspeakers, and ▷thermocouples are examples. It is also usually the primary sensor in a measurement or sensing system.

● **trans-fatty acids** ▷*See* fatty acid.

● **transformational grammar** ▷*See* grammar.

● **transformer** ► A device for converting alternating current from one voltage to another. The input is fed to a primary winding, a coil of wire round a soft iron core, creating an oscillating magnetic field in the core. This field induces a secondary current of the same frequency in the secondary winding wound on the same core. The ratio of primary to secondary voltage is equal to the ratio of the number of turns in the secondary coil to that in the primary. The device is

widely used both in electronic circuits and in the transmission and distribution of electricity (*see* electricity supply).

● **transhumance** ► A form of pastoral nomadism in which livestock are moved seasonally between mountain summer pastures and lower lying winter pastures, or between northern and southern or wet and dry season grazing areas.

● **transistor** ► A ▷semiconductor device with three or more electrodes. Transistors form the basic elements of electronic ▷amplifiers and logic circuits, often combined with other components in ▷integrated circuits. They were first developed in 1948 by William ▷Shockley and his coworkers at the Bell Telephone Co and now replace ▷thermionic valves in most applications. The term transistor usually refers to the **bipolar junction transistor**, which consists of two junctions between p-type and n-type semiconductors forming either a p-n-p or n-p-n structure. Current is carried across these junctions by both negative and positive charge carriers (electrons and holes). The current between the emitter and the collector electrodes varies not only with the voltage drop across them, but also with the voltage or current level at the base (the third electrode). Depending on how it is connected into a circuit, the junction transistor can act as a voltage or current amplifier in much the same way as a triode valve. Transistors, however, work at a much lower voltage than valves, are more compact and robust, emit less heat, and are cheaper.

Originally, junction transistors were made by alloying the impurity metal onto the semiconductor crystal or by adding impurities as the crystal was being grown. Now the doping is diffused in as a gas, introduced by ion implantation, or, more commonly, achieved by a combined process of etching and diffusion, known as the planar process.

The **field effect transistor** (FET) is a unipolar device, in which current is carried by only one type of charge. There are two types: the junction FET (JFET) has a region of semiconductor of one doping type flanked by two highly doped layers of the opposite type. Current flows parallel to the junctions, between the so-called source and drain electrodes, through a narrow channel between the highly doped regions (the gate); it is controlled by the electric field arising from the gate input voltage, which alters the width of the conducting channel. The JFET is used as a separate component in amplifiers and switches. In the insulated-gate FET (IGFET) the source and drain electrodes are highly doped regions in a substrate of the opposite type. The gate electrode is a conductor separated from the substrate by a thin insulating layer across the surface. The electric field caused by the gate voltage controls the source-drain current on the other side of the insulator. The IGFET is used mainly in metal-oxide semiconductor (MOS) integrated circuits. It is smaller than the equivalent bipolar junction transistor and uses less power. The first plastic transistor was built in 1988.

● **transit circle** ▷*See* meridian circle.

● **transit instrument** ► A telescope theodolite, or similar device, that is used to measure angular position. In astronomy, for instance, transit telescopes measure the vertical angles of stars or planets.

● **transition elements** ► A large group of metallic elements, including most of the commonly used metals, the inner electron shells of which are incomplete. The ▷lanthanides and the ▷actinides are sometimes included in this definition. The elements show considerable similarities to their horizontal neighbours in the ▷periodic table. In general, they are hard, brittle, high-melting, and excellent conductors of heat and electricity. Their chemistry is complicated; they have multiple valencies and tend to form coloured compounds.

● **Transjordan** ▷*See* Jordan, Hashemite Kingdom of.

● **Transkei, Republic of** ► A former Bantu Homeland in South Africa, consisting of three separate areas. Most of the population was ▷Xhosa. Created in 1963, as the first of the Bantu Homelands, it became independent in 1976. All Black Africans of Transkeian origin became its citizens, simultaneously losing their South African citizenship. Its independence was, however, recognized only by South Africa. In 1978 it broke off diplomatic relations with South Africa, in spite of economic dependence on the country. In 1987 intertribal disputes threatened civil war. In 1994, following the adoption of a

Germanium is a typical semiconductor. The four outer electrons in each of its atoms form covalent bonds with adjacent atoms. In the pure state it acts as an insulator as no electrons are available to carry current.

Arsenic atoms have five outer electrons. Germanium containing arsenic atoms as an impurity can carry current because the fifth electron is available as a carrier. This is an n-type semiconductor because current is carried by negative electrons.

Indium atoms have three outer electrons. Germanium doped with indium therefore has holes in its electronic structure. These can be filled by electrons from neighbouring atoms, creating new holes; this has the effect of positive charge moving through the crystal in the opposite direction to electrons. This is p-type germanium.

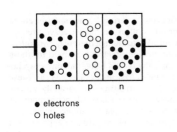

● electrons
○ holes

In the bipolar junction transistor a piece of p-type material is sandwiched between two n-type pieces, making an n-p-n structure (p-n-p transistors are also used).

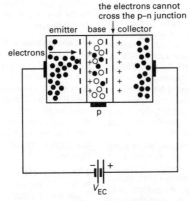

In an n-p-n transistor, a negative voltage is applied to one end (the emitter) and a positive to the other (the collector). No current flows, however, because a potential barrier forms at the junction between the emitter and the central region (the base).

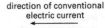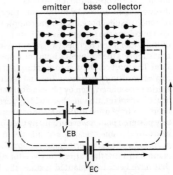

If the base region is positively biased, the free electrons in the emitter are attracted to the p-type base and current flows through the thin base to the collector. As the collector current depends on the amount of bias to the base, the device can be used as an amplifier.

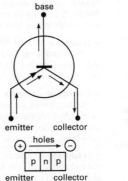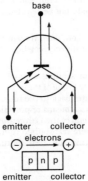

In the symbolic representation of a transistor, the directon of the arrow on the emitter indicates the direction of the current and the type of transistor (n-p-n or p-n-p).

transistor ► The operation of the bipolar junction transistor.

multiracial constitution, the Bantu Homelands were reintegrated into South Africa and South African citizenship was granted to their inhabitants.

● **translucence** ► One of the degrees of transparency used by geologists for classifying minerals. A mineral is translucent if it transmits light but not sufficiently so to enable the outline of an object to be seen.

● **transmigration of souls** ▷*See* reincarnation.

● **transmutation** ► The conversion of one element into another. It was originally the (unfulfilled) aim of alchemists to bring about the transmutation of base metals into gold (*see* alchemy). Transmutations were achieved in the 20th century by bombarding elements with ▷alpha particles or ▷neutrons. An example is the production of oxygen-17 when nitrogen-14 is bombarded with alpha particles.

● **transpiration** ► The loss of water vapour from the surface of a plant, which occurs primarily through small pores (stomata) in the leaves but also (slowly) through the cuticle of the ▷epidermis. The rate of water loss is controlled by the opening and closing of the stomata, greater loss occurring during the day than at night.

● **transplantation** ► The surgical implantation of a tissue or organ derived either from another part of the body of the patient or from another individual (the donor). Skin grafting is an example of the former type of operation: it is used particularly to repair damage and disfigurement caused by burns and other injuries. Transplantation of donor tissues or organs is more complex since the body's immune system rejects the foreign tissue. These operations require matching of the donor's and recipient's tissues together with the use of drugs that suppress the recipient's immune responses (*see* immunosuppression). The most common type of transplantation using donor tissue is corneal grafting (*see* cornea). The first successful heart transplant operation was undertaken by Christiaan ▷Barnard in 1967, since when heart transplantation has been widely performed. The first artificial heart was implanted in 1988. Made of titanium and plastic, these battery-powered pumps were originally used only to support an existing heart until a donor heart was available. In the UK, the first artificial heart to be used as a permanent support for a diseased heart was implanted in 1994; the patient survived for nine months. Other organs that have been transplanted include the kidneys, lung, liver, pancreas, and bowel, of which kidney transplants have been the most successful. The first heart, lung, and liver transplant took place in 1989. Transplantation of bone marrow, heart valves, and pieces of bone have also been attempted with some success. The main problem in transplantation surgery is shortage of organs. The UK code requires two independent doctors to certify that a donor is brain dead (*see* death) before organs are used. Because of the shortage of human donors, the possibility of using animal organs in human transplants (**xenotransplantation**) is being explored. To this end experimental work is being done to produce pigs that have been genetically modifed in such a way that their organs would not be rejected in a human recipient.

● **transponder** ► In telecommunications, a combined transmitter and receiver that sends out a signal automatically on receiving a predetermined trigger signal.

● **transportation** ► In law, the practice of sending a convicted criminal to some place outside Britain, usually to one of the colonies, to be kept in hard labour. Transportation dates back to the reign of Elizabeth I, becoming increasingly popular as a means of providing labour in the American colonies towards the end of the 17th century. After the ▷American Revolution, convicts were transported to Australia. Transportation was phased out during the 19th century, ending altogether in 1868.

● **transputer** ▷*See* computer.

● **transsexualism** ▷*See* transvestism.

● **Trans-Siberian Railway** ► The world's longest railway, running 9335 km (5800 mi) from Moscow to Vladivostok, known as Siberia's lifeline. Double track, largely electrified, has replaced the single track line built between 1891 and 1905.

● **transubstantiation** ► In Roman Catholic theology, the doctrine

that the substance of the elements of bread and wine in the ▷Eucharist is changed at consecration into the substance of the body and blood of Christ. Only the accidents (i.e. the qualities apparent to the senses) of the bread and wine remain. *Compare* consubstantiation.

● **transuranic elements** ► Elements with higher atomic number than uranium. Apart from traces of neptunium and plutonium, none of them has ever been detected in nature, since no isotopes of sufficient ▷half-life exist; they have been created since 1940, usually in minute amounts, in nuclear reactions. Over a dozen are known. ▷*See also* actinides.

● **Transvaal** ► A former province in South Africa. Much of the area is plateau with rolling country and high ridges, including the Witwatersrand. Heavily populated in the S, it is very prosperous and contains the country's main industrial area, centred on the Witwatersrand; iron, steel, and chemicals are produced. Mineral deposits include gold, diamonds, uranium, coal, chromite, tin, and platinum. It has a well-developed agriculture producing maize, wheat, peanuts, citrus fruit, cotton, and tobacco; sheep and cattle are raised. Forestry is also important.
  History: originally an Afrikaner republic, it fought in the ▷Boer Wars against Britain (1880–81, 1899–1902). It became a province in the Union of South Africa in 1910. In 1994 the province was replaced by the new regions of **Gauteng**, **Mpumalanga**, **Northern**, and parts of **Northwest**.

● **transvestism** ► The practice of wearing clothes appropriate to the opposite sex, usually for sexual pleasure. Many transvestites are heterosexual males and do not wish to change their sex. Psychotherapy and aversion therapy can provide effective treatment for those requiring it. **Transsexualism** is the settled belief that one's psychological gender is opposite to one's physical sex, and this can cause considerable suffering. Psychological treatments are usually unhelpful. Some transsexuals manage to pass successfully as members of the opposite sex; hormone therapy and plastic surgery on genitals and breasts can help this adjustment by effecting an apparent sex change.

● **Transylvania** ► A region of SE Europe, bounded by the Carpathian Mountains and the Transylvanian Alps, now in Romania. Transylvania retained its distinctive character under successive Roman, Magyar, and Hungarian rulers; during the 16th and 17th centuries, it was a self-governing princedom within the Ottoman Empire. Restored to Hungary, within the Holy Roman Empire, in 1687, Transylvania became part of Romania after World War I. In 1996 a new treaty was signed under which Hungary renounced any claim to Transylvania, while Romania guaranteed the rights of ethnic Hungarians.

● **Transylvanian Alps** ► (*or* Southern Carpathian Mountains; Romanian name: Carpaţii Meridionali) A mountain range extending 360 km (227 mi) E–W across S central Romania and rising to 2543 m (8343 ft) at Mount Moldoveanu.

● **Trapani** ► 38 02N 12 32E A seaport in Italy, in NW Sicily. A Carthaginian naval base, it was ceded to Rome after the first Punic War. Its industries include fishing, salt production, and marbleworking. Population (1990) 72 840.

● **trap-door spider** ► A ▷spider, especially one of the family *Ctenizidae*, that constructs a silk-lined burrow in the ground covered by a tight-fitting silk-hinged door. Ctenizids are dull brown, with short stout legs. They occur in tropical and subtropical regions and only leave their burrows to hunt.

● **Trappists** ► A Roman Catholic monastic order, officially known as the ▷Cistercians of the Strict Observance. It was founded in 1664 at the abbey of La Trappe in Normandy by D. A. J. le B. de Rancé (1626–1700). When the monks were expelled during the French Revolution, the order established houses in other countries; there are now monasteries in Britain, Ireland, North America, and elsewhere. The order is notable for its austerity, which includes the observance of strict silence, manual labour, and a simple vegetarian diet.

● **Trasimeno, Lake** ► (*or* Lake Perugia) A lake in central Italy. It is drained via an artificial tunnel by the River Tiber. Area: 129 sq km (50 sq mi).

● **traveller's tree** ▶ A palmlike tree, *Ravenala madagascariensis*, native to Madagascar. It grows over 27 m tall and bears a crown of banana-like leaves, 120–180 cm long, on long stalks (2–4 m long). Each leaf base, shaped like a huge cup, holds about one litre of water, which can provide a drink for thirsty passers-by (hence the name). Family: *Strelitziaceae*.

● **travel sickness** ▶ (*or* motion sickness) Nausea and sometimes vomiting caused by travelling in cars, buses, trains, planes, boats (sea sickness), or on roundabouts and fairground machines. It arises when the constant movement disturbs the organs of balance in the inner ear, which causes nausea. Travel sickness is especially common in children and many of them grow out of it. It is treated with drugs to stop the nausea, particularly sedative ▷antihistamines. As many of these cause sleepiness as well, a person driving should not take them.

● **Traven, B(en)** ▶ (Berick Traven Torsvan; 1890–1969) US novelist. Despite much speculation, his identity remained uncertain until after his death. He was probably born in Chicago of German ancestry, worked in Germany in 1918–19, and lived in Mexico from the 1920s. His allegorical novels include *The Death Ship* (1926) and *The Treasure of the Sierra Madre* (1927).

● **Travers, Ben(jamin)** ▶ (1886–1980) British dramatist, who established his reputation with farces played at the Aldwych Theatre between 1925 and 1933. These include *Rookery Nook* (1926), *Thark* (1927), and *Plunder* (1928). He wrote *The Bed before Yesterday* (1976) at the age of 90.

● **trawler** ▶ A vessel equipped for catching fish by towing nets. Such vessels are often designed with cold storage facilities for the catch for extended voyages at sea.

● **treachery** ▶ In English law, during World War II, assisting, or conspiring or attempting to assist, the naval, military, or air operations of the enemy. Punishable by death, treachery was defined in the Treachery Act (1940), which expired in 1946. ▷*See also* treason.

● **treadmill** ▶ A penal device used in 19th-century prisons. It consisted of a hollow cylinder with a series of steps. A prisoner treading on the steps would set the cylinder in motion, which could then be used for grinding corn, etc. It was invented in 1818 by the British civil engineer Sir William Cubitt (1785–1861).

● **treason** ▶ The violation by a citizen of his allegiance to the sovereign or the state. In England, the Statute of Treasons (1352) defined two kinds of treason: high treason, now the only kind of treason, and petty treason, abolished in 1828, which was where a servant killed his master, a wife killed her husband, or an ecclesiastic killed his superior (i.e. the violation of private allegiance). (High) treason, as defined in 1352 and in subsequent Acts, is: (1) to plot to kill or maim the sovereign; (2) to wage war against him in his realm or to join his enemies; (3) to kill his eldest son or heir; (4) to violate his wife, eldest daughter (if unmarried), or heir's wife; (5) to kill the chancellor, or any judge while he or she is performing his or her office. Until 1999 conviction for all forms of treason carried the death penalty, but this is now abolished except for treason in times of war or imminent threat of war. ▷*See also* treachery.

● **treasure trove** ▶ Formerly, gold or silver items of unknown ownership found hidden in a concealed place. Under English law it belonged to the Crown provided it could be shown that the items had been deliberately concealed, rather than abandoned or lost (in which case the finder had the first claim). Objects buried with no intention of recovery were the property of the owner of the land. The finder of treasure trove received the value of the property, unless he concealed it, in which case he was liable to imprisonment. The Treasure Act (1996) redefined treasure as any item at least 300 years old and containing more than 5% precious metal (not including single coins). All treasure now belongs to the Crown, which will pay a reward to the finder.

● **Treasury** ▶ The UK government department, established in 1653, that is responsible, with the ▷Bank of England, for the management of the economy (*see* fiscal policy; monetary policy) and the allocation

of the available government money between the spending departments. The prime minister is the first lord of the treasury, but it is run by the ▷chancellor of the exchequer, assisted by the chief secretary to the Treasury and the financial secretary.

● **treasury bill** ▶ A government stock providing a source of short-term borrowing (usually three months) for a government. Bills are in denominations of £5,000 upwards in the UK and are offered at a discount, which influences the Bank of England's lending rate. Treasury bills were first used in the UK in 1877 and in the USA in 1929. ▷*See also* open-market operations.

● **Treasury Solicitor** ▶ (full name: Her Majesty's Procurator General and Treasury Solicitor) A solicitor who advises the ▷Treasury on legal matters, instruct barristers appearing for the Crown on Treasury issues in civil cases, instructs parliamentary barristers on bills, and acts as the **Queen's Proctor** (King's Proctor if the sovereign is a king). As Queen's Proctor the Treasury Solicitor, under the direction of the attorney general, advises the courts on legal problems involving divorce and has the power to intervene to prevent a divorce order from being made if there is a suspicion that not all the facts were presented to the court.

Between 1883 and 1908 the Treasury Solicitor was also the Director of Public Prosecutions (*see* Crown Prosecution Service).

● **treaty ports** ▶ The five Chinese ports that were opened to British consuls and merchants in 1842 at the end of the first ▷Opium War. They were Canton, Amoy, Fuzhou, Ningbo, and Shanghai.

● **Trebizond** ▷*See* Trabzon.

● **Treblinka** ▶ A German ▷concentration camp opened in 1942 at a railway junction on the Bug River some 72 km (45 mi) NE of ▷Warsaw in Poland. The purpose of the camp was to exterminate the Jews of Poland (*see* Wannsee conference), including the 350 000 survivors of the Warsaw ghetto. It is estimated that the Germans murdered some 850 000 Jews in Treblinka; it was closed in October, 1943, after some 700 Jewish forced-labourers rose in revolt, killing 15 guards. All but 12 of the insurgents, who escaped, were shot.

● **tree** ▶ A tall perennial woody plant, usually with a single main stem (the trunk) and secondary stems (the branches) arising some distance above ground level. (Shrubs are smaller bushier woody perennials without a distinct trunk.) Most tree species are either ▷dicotyledons (angiosperms)—the broad-leaved trees—or ▷conifers (gymnosperms). These are the only trees that form true ▷wood and they are of economic importance as producers of hardwoods and softwoods, respectively. Other groups containing trees are the cycads (gymnosperms), monocotyledons (notably the ▷palms), and the ferns. Trees grow wherever the annual rainfall exceeds 76 cm (30 in) but a few have adapted to desert conditions. The conifers and tropical trees are mostly ▷evergreen plants, while broad-leaved trees growing in regions with marked seasonal changes in climate are typically deciduous. □ p. 1264.

The tallest existing tree on record is a Californian redwood, which has attained a height of 111 m (364 ft). The study of the ecology and classification of trees is called **dendrology**. ▷*See also* forest.

● **Tree, Sir Herbert (Draper) Beerbohm** ▶ (1853–1917) British actor and theatre manager, halfbrother of Max ▷Beerbohm. He was manager of the Haymarket Theatre from 1887 to 1899 and then of Her Majesty's Theatre, where he staged many lavish Shakespearean productions. In 1904 he founded the ▷Royal Academy of Dramatic Art.

● **treecreeper** ▶ A small songbird belonging to a family (*Certhiidae*; 5 species) occurring in Europe, Asia, and North America. It has a brownish streaked plumage with pale silvery underparts, long claws, and a slender down-curved bill. The European treecreeper (*Certhia familiaris*), 12.5 cm long, occurs mainly in coniferous woods, where it creeps up tree trunks to probe for small beetles, spiders, woodlice, etc.

● **tree fern** ▶ A tropical ▷fern belonging to the genus *Cyathea* (600 species), found mainly in moist mountainous regions. It has a trunklike stem, 3–25 m high, and a crown of large tapering branched fronds. Family: *Cyatheaceae*.

tree

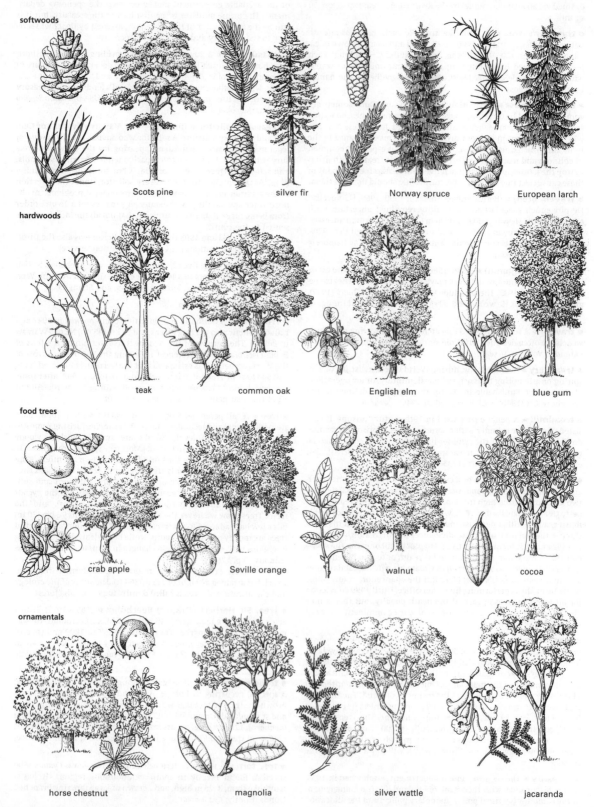

softwoods

Scots pine   silver fir   Norway spruce   European larch

hardwoods

teak   common oak   English elm   blue gum

food trees

crab apple   Seville orange   walnut   cocoa

ornamentals

horse chestnut   magnolia   silver wattle   jacaranda

● **tree frog** ▶ A small toad belonging to a widely distributed family (*Hylidae*; about 500 species). They have adapted to living in trees and have adhesive pads on their toes that enable them to cling to leaves and branches, leaping acrobatically to capture insects. Most species breed in water although some carry the developing eggs on their backs.

● **treehopper** ▶ A winged insect, less than 13 mm long, belonging to the mainly tropical family *Membracidae* (2600 species). An enlargement of the thorax extends over the body to form a "hood," which varies in colour and shape to camouflage the insects against the background vegetation on which they live and feed. Suborder: *Homoptera*; order ▷*Hemiptera*.

● **tree kangaroo** ▶ A ▷wallaby of the genus *Dendrolagus* (9 species) of Australia and New Guinea. The black tree kangaroo (*D. ursinus*) is an agile climber that feeds at night on the ground and sleeps during the day in trees.

● **tree of heaven** ▶ A tree, *Ailanthus altissima*, native to central Asia and planted elsewhere as an ornamental. Growing to a height of 30 m, it has compound leaves, up to 1 m long, composed of paired leaflets. Male and female flowers appear on separate trees, forming greenish-white clusters; the female flowers produce winged fruits. The trees are resistant to pollution and hence popular in urban areas. Family: *Simaroubaceae*.

● **tree-ring dating** ▷*See* dendrochronology.

● **tree shrew** ▶ A mammal belonging to the order *Scandentia* (19 species), found in Java, Borneo, Sumatra, the Philippines, and S Asia. The common tree shrew (*Tupaia glis*) is 30–45 cm long including the tail (15–23 cm) and has a slender pointed face. It darts among the branches, feeding on insects, fruit, and seeds. Tree shrews were formerly classified as a family of primitive primates.

● **tree snake** ▶ Any of a number of slender tree-dwelling snakes that hunt birds, frogs, and lizards in tropical forests. The blunt-headed tree snake (*Imantodes cenchoa*) of Central and South America can stiffen most of its 60–90 cm body length to reach another branch while supported by only a single coil of the tail. ▷*See also* flying snake; vine snake.

● **trefoil** ▶ One of several annual herbs of the genus *Trifolium* (which also includes the ▷clovers), characterized by leaves consisting of three leaflets. The hop trefoil (*T. campestre*), found on grassland and road verges of Europe, W Asia, N Africa, and North America, grows to a height of 35 cm and has compact globular heads of yellow flowers. The birdsfoot trefoils belong to the genus *Lotus* (about 70 species), of temperate Eurasia, Africa, and Australia. The leaves have five leaflets and the yellow or reddish flowers have a prominent keel resembling a lip. A common species is *L. corniculatus*, a perennial grassland herb growing to a height of 10–40 cm. Family: ▷*Leguminosae*.

● **Trematoda** ▷*See* fluke.

● **Trenchard, Hugh Montague, 1st Viscount** ▶ (1873–1956) The first British air marshal. In World War I, as commander of the Royal Flying Corps, he advocated the separation of air and army forces and was chiefly responsible for the establishment of the RAF (1918). He founded the police college at Hendon while commissioner of the Metropolitan Police (1931–35).

● **Trengganu** ▶ A state in NE Peninsular Malaysia, on the South China Sea. Mountainous and forested inland, it is settled mainly along the coast, with fish, rice, rubber, and copra being the chief products. Area: 12 955 sq km (5002 sq mi). Population (1993 est): 752 030. Capital: Kuala Trengganu.

● **Trent, Council of** ▶ (1545–63) The 19th general council of the Roman Catholic Church, an expression of the ▷Counter-Reformation, which was summoned by Pope Paul III to strengthen the Church in its confrontation with Protestantism. It was held in Trento (N Italy). There were three sessions (1545–47, 1551–52, 1562–63), which clarified doctrine and instituted reforms: the Council condemned Luther's doctrine of justification by faith alone and defined ▷transubstantiation. It also strengthened episcopal authority and issued decrees on clerical abuses and education. The Council effectively determined the structures, doctrines, and liturgy of the Church until the Second ▷Vatican Council 400 years later.

● **Trent, River** ▶ A river in central England. Flowing mainly NE from Staffordshire through Nottingham, it joins the River Ouse to form the Humber estuary. The Midlands' main river, it is linked to the Mersey by the Trent, Mersey, and Grand Union Canals. Length: 270 km (170 mi).

● **Trentino-Alto Adige** ▶ (Former name: Venetia Tridentina) An autonomous region in N Italy. Formerly part of Austria, it passed to Italy after World War I and has a large German-speaking population. It is a mountainous forested region, situated entirely within the Alps. The fertile valleys of the River Adige and its tributaries produce wine, fruit, and dairy products. Timber is an important industry. Numerous hydroelectric plants have encouraged the development of manufacturing industry. Tourism is an important source of revenue. Area: 13 613 sq km (5256 sq mi). Population (1994 est): 903 598. Capital: Trento.

● **Trento** ▶ (German name: Trent) 46 04N 11 08E A city in N Italy, the capital of Trentino-Alto Adige on the River Adige. A pre-Roman city, it has a romanesque cathedral (12th century) and the 16th-century Church of Sta Maria Maggiore, where the Council of ▷Trent met. Its products include chemicals, electrical goods, and silk. Population (1996 est): 103 181.

● **Trenton** ▶ 40 15N 74 43W A city in the USA, the capital of New Jersey. George Washington defeated the British here in 1776. Industries include the manufacture of pottery, cable, rope, and metal. Population (1996 est): 85 437.

● **trepang** ▶ (or bêche-de-mer) The boiled, dried, and smoked body wall of certain ▷sea cucumbers, used to make soup in the East. It is produced mainly from the genera *Holothuria*, *Stichopus*, and *Thelonota*, found on coral reefs of the SW Pacific.

● **trephine** ▶ A surgical saw used to remove a circular section of the skull in order to release pressure caused by bleeding within the skull or to provide access to the brain. The use of trephines dates from ancient times, when it was thought that the procedure released evil spirits causing madness.

● **Trevelyan, Sir George Otto** ▶ (1838–1928) British statesman and historian, nephew and biographer of Lord Macaulay. He was an MP from 1868 to 1897. His son **George Macaulay Trevelyan** (1876–1962), was Regius Professor of History at Cambridge University (1927–40). His works aimed at a popular audience included *English Social History* (1942).

● **Trèves** ▷*See* Trier.

● **Trevino, Lee** ▶ (1939–　) US golfer, who was US Open champion (1968, 1971), British Open champion (1971, 1972), and US Professional Golfers Association champion (1974).

● **Treviso** ▶ 45 40N 12 15E A city in Italy, in Veneto. Dating from Roman times, it has an 11th-century cathedral and other historic buildings. Its manufactures include ceramics and agricultural machinery. Population (1990): 84 066.

● **Trevithick, Richard** ▶ (1771–1833) British engineer, who developed high-pressure steam engines. He built the first steam-driven carriage to carry passengers (1801) and the first locomotive to run on smooth wheels on smooth rails (1804). In 1816 he went to Peru, where his engines were being used in mines. He died in London, penniless.

● **Trevor-Roper, Hugh Redwald, Baron Dacre** ▶ (1914–　) British historian. Trevor-Roper's many books include *Archbishop Laud* (1940), *The Last Days of Hitler* (1947), and *Catholics, Anglicans, and Puritans* (1987). He was Regius Professor of Modern History at Oxford (1957–80).

● **Triad** ▶ A criminal organization that originated as a Buddhist cult in China in 36 AD. Venerating the triangle as a symbol in its rituals, it later became a political force, being active against the ▷Qing dynasty, in the ▷Taiping Rebellion, and in support of ▷Sun Yat-sen. In recent times, however, it has become widely known for involvement in crime (including drug-dealing) outside China, probably directed from Hong Kong.

● **triage** ► The principle, mainly important in ▷medical ethics but applicable in other fields, that if one's ability to help the suffering is limited, aid should be concentrated on those most likely to benefit from it rather than those in greatest need. Deriving from the Old French *trier*, to sift or pick out, the word triage originally (in the 18th century) meant the sorting of samples of a commodity according to quality. Its modern meaning dates from the battlefields of World War I, when the hard-pressed medical corps developed a technique (which they called triage) for sorting those casualties considered treatable in the circumstances from those thought unlikely to benefit from any attention they could provide; in order to be sure of saving the former, the latter were usually left to die. This medical usage has found another context, in the crowded accident and emergency departments of British National Health hospitals. A specially trained triage nurse (*see* nursing) is now routinely assigned the task of deciding the order in which patients are seen by a doctor. Here the objective is to make sure that patients with conditions that *may* worsen dangerously without prompt attention are seen first; this may mean leaving those with painful but stable conditions to wait for considerable periods.

Ideally, triage should achieve a balance of humanity and common sense; in practice, however, it may mean suspending one's natural humanitarian instincts in the name of a ruthless pragmatism. For example, aid may be withdrawn from a desperately poor country on the grounds that the limited resources available could do more good if deployed in a country whose economy is not so close to collapse. One might call this the dark side of triage.

● **trial by ordeal** ► The most ancient form of trial. It was practised by Anglo-Saxons and based on the belief that God would intervene to protect an innocent person and hence involved a *judicium Dei* (judgment of God). There were four kinds: (1) by fire, which was reserved for persons of rank and involved walking over red-hot ploughshares or carrying a piece of red-hot iron; (2) by hot water, involving plunging the arm in boiling water; (3) by cold water, whereby the accused, thrown into a river or pond, was judged innocent if he sank; and (4) by combat, fought before judges. Ordeal was replaced in the reign (1216–72) of Henry III by compurgation, whereby 12 men had to swear that they believed the accused (*see* jury).

● **triangle** ► A percussion instrument consisting of a steel rod bent into the shape of a triangle. The triangle was first used in late 18th-century orchestral works to provide a "Turkish" atmosphere. □musical instruments.

● **Trianon, Grand and Petit** ► Two villas in the grounds of the Palace of Versailles, near Paris. The Grand Trianon was built (1687) for Louis XIV by ▷Mansart and the Petit Trianon (1762–1768) for Louis XV by Jacques Ange Gabriel (1698–1782).

● **Triassic period** ► (*or* Trias) A period of geological time during the early Mesozoic era, lasting from about 240 to 200 million years ago. The rocks of the period, laid down mainly under continental conditions, are sometimes considered together with those of the ▷Permian period as the Permo-Trias(sic). The dinosaurs, ichthyosaurs, and plesiosaurs appeared in the Triassic.

● **tribes of Israel** ► In the Bible, the Hebrew people. The 12 tribes, descended from the sons and grandsons of ▷Jacob, were ▷Reuben, ▷Simeon, ▷Judah, ▷Issachar, ▷Zebulun, ▷Benjamin, ▷Dan, ▷Naphtali, ▷Gad, ▷Asher, Levi (*see* Levites), and ▷Ephraim and ▷Manasseh. These last two were counted as one, except in parts of the Bible where the tribal lists omit either Levi or Simeon. After the death of Solomon, ten of the tribes broke away from Benjamin and Judah to form the northern kingdom of Israel (*see* Ten Lost Tribes of Israel).

● **tribology** ► The study of ▷friction and such allied topics as lubrication, abrasives, surface wear, etc. It includes such effects of friction as triboluminescence and frictional electricity.

● **tribune** ► In ancient Rome, a plebeian magistrate appointed to protect ▷plebeians' rights. Instituted during the 5th-century struggles between ▷patricians and plebeians, the tribunes, first two, later ten, in number, could veto legislative proposals of the Senate or popular assemblies and could propose legislation without senatorial approval. This power considerably influenced Roman politics from the

Gracchi's revolutionary times (*see* Gracchus, Tiberius Sempronius) to Augustus' assumption of tribunicial power in the late 1st century BC.

● **Triceratops** ► A three-horned dinosaur of the late Cretaceous period (about 100–65 million years ago). 8 m long and weighing 8.5 tonnes, it had an enormous head with one horn on the snout and one (up to 1 m long) over each eye. It also had a large bony neck frill and short limbs with hoofed feet and browsed on tough plants. Order: ▷Ornithischia. □fossil.

● **Trichinopoly** ▷See Tiruchirappalli.

● **Trident missile** ► A US navy three-stage solid-fuelled nuclear strategic missile launched from a submarine and having a range of 7800 km (4800 mi). Designed as a replacement for the Poseidon missile, Trident missiles, first deployed in the early 1980s, are capable of great accuracy at increased distances and carry a new stellar-inertial guidance system. They replaced the UK's Polaris systems in 1994–96. The UK launched its fourth and last Trident submarine in 1998.

● **Trier** ► (French name: Trèves) 49 45N 6 39E A city in SW Germany, in Rhineland-Palatinate on the River Moselle. Founded by the Emperor Augustus, it has important Roman remains. The cathedral (11th–12th centuries) is built around the 4th-century basilica. It shares a university with Kaiserslautern (1970) and is the birthplace of Karl Marx. It is a wine-trading and industrial centre. Population (1991): 98 750

● **Trieste** ► (Serbo-Croat name: Trst) 45 39N 13 47E A seaport in Italy, the capital of Friuli-Venezia Giulia, situated on the Gulf of Trieste at the head of the Adriatic Sea. An important transit port for central Europe, it has shipyards, oil refineries, and a steel industry. It has a 14th-century cathedral and a university (1938).

History: an important Roman port in the 1st century AD, it passed to Austria in 1382. It expanded rapidly in the 19th century as an outlet for Austrian goods and in 1920 was ceded to Italy. Following World War II it became the capital of the Free Territory of Trieste, which was established by the UN (1947). In 1954 most of the N of the Territory (including Trieste) passed to Italy and the remainder to Yugoslavia. Population (1996 est): 223 611.

● **triggerfish** ► A shallow-water fish, belonging to a family (*Balistidae*) related to ▷puffers, that occurs in tropical seas. Its deep laterally flattened body, up to 60 cm long, is covered with large scales. The strong spine of the first dorsal fin is erected and locked into position by the second dorsal fin, forming a "trigger" that wedges the fish into crevices. It feeds on molluscs and crustaceans.

● **trigonometry** ► A branch of mathematics founded by Hipparchus in the mid-2nd century BC, concerned originally with the measurement of triangles. The ratios of the lengths of the sides of a right-angled triangle are used to define the sine, cosine, and tangent of one of the angles of the triangle. Trigonometry deals with the properties of these and related functions. The two basic rules of trigonometry, applying to any plane triangle ABC, are the **cosine rule**, $a^2 = b^2 + c^2 - 2bc \cos A$ (where a is the length of the side opposite angle A, etc.), and the **sine rule**, $a/\sin A = b/\sin B = c/\sin C$. Its study is essential to most branches of physics and mathematics. In spherical trigo-

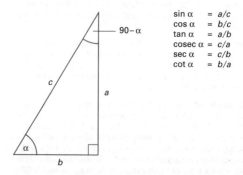

$\sin \alpha$	$= a/c$
$\cos \alpha$	$= b/c$
$\tan \alpha$	$= a/b$
$\csc \alpha$	$= c/a$
$\sec \alpha$	$= c/b$
$\cot \alpha$	$= b/a$

trigonometry ► Definitions of the trigonometric functions sine, cosine, and tangent and of their reciprocals cosecant, secant, and cotangent.

nometry, triangles formed on the surface of a sphere are considered. These, important in navigation and astronomy, present more complex problems.

● **Trilling, Lionel** ▶ (1905–75) US literary critic. In *The Liberal Imagination* (1950), *Sincerity and Authenticity* (1974), and his novel *The Middle of the Journey* (1947) he expressed a moral concern with all aspects of modern culture.

● **trilobite** ▶ An extinct marine ▷arthropod belonging to a subphylum (*Trilobita*; over 4000 species) that flourished between Cambrian and Permian times, i.e. 500–200 million years ago. Trilobite ⁰fossils are abundant in rocks of this period. Its flattened oval body, 10–675 mm long, was divided by two longitudinal furrows into three lobes. The head bore a pair of antennae and usually a pair of compound eyes and each segment of the thorax and tail region carried a pair of forked appendages. Many trilobites burrowed in sand or mud, preying on other animals or scavenging.

● **trimaran** ▶ A modern sailing vessel with three parallel hulls, a larger central one and two smaller ones used as stabilizers or outriggers. Trimarans are usually rigged as sloops. It is modelled on the outrigger canoe, or **proa**, of the SW Pacific. ▷*See also* catamaran.

● **Trimble, (William) David** ▶ (1944–　) Northern Irish politician, leader of the Ulster Unionist Party (1995–　). A university lecturer in law, he became an MP in 1990. He was a leading participant in the multiparty talks that led to the Good Friday Agreement of 1998 and became Northern Ireland's first minister later that year. In 1998 he was awarded the Nobel Peace Prize jointly with John ▷Hume.

● **Trimurti** ▶ The Hindu triad of gods, ▷Brahma, ▷Vishnu, and ▷Shiva, representing the creative, sustaining, and destructive aspects of reality respectively, sometimes portrayed as one body with three heads.

● **Trincomalee** ▶ 8 34N 81 13E A seaport in NE Sri Lanka. It has an excellent natural harbour and was much fought over in colonial times. It was a major British base in World War II. Population (latest est): 51 000

● **Trinidad and Tobago, Republic of** ▶ A country off the N coast of South America, consisting of the islands of Trinidad and Tobago. The most southerly of the Caribbean islands, both are hilly and wooded with a tropical climate. Most of the population is of African and East Indian descent.
Economy: oil has replaced cocoa and sugar as the main source of the country's wealth and reserves of offshore gas have also been discovered. Other industrial developments include aluminium smelting, plastics, iron and steel, and chemicals. Motor vehicles, electrical goods, and other domestic appliances are assembled from imported parts; local manufactures include fertilizers, clothing, and foodstuffs. Tourism is a growing industry. The republic is a member of CARICOM.
History: Trinidad was inhabited by Arawak and Carib Indians when it was discovered by Columbus in 1498. It was a Spanish colony from the 16th century until 1802, when it was ceded to Britain; it joined with Tobago in 1888. During World War II naval bases here were leased to the USA but most have since been given up. The country was a member of the Federation of the West Indies from 1958 to 1961 and became an independent state within the Commonwealth in 1962. In 1976 it became a republic with the former governor general, Ellis Clarke (1917–　), as its first president; his successors have been Noor Mohammed Hassanali (1987–97) and Arthur N. Robinson (1997–　). A coup attempt in 1990 failed. Legislative elections in late 2001 produced a straight tie between the two main parties, causing a constitutional crisis.

Republic of Trinidad and Tobago

Head of state	President Arthur N. Robinson
Official language	English
Official currency	Trinidad and Tobago dollar of 100 cents
Area	5128 sq km (1980 sq mi)
Population (2001 est)	1 298 000
Capital and main port	Port-of-Spain

● **Trinity, the** ▶ A central doctrine of Christian theology, stating that God is one substance but with three distinct, coequal, and coeternal "persons," the Father, the Son, and the ▷Holy Spirit. The belief is based on several passages in the New Testament. It was first formally defined by the Council of ▷Nicaea (325), which asserted that the Son was "of the same essence (*homoousios*) as the Father." In the West, St Augustine and St Thomas Aquinas developed the doctrine. The Eastern Church rejects the so-called "double procession" of the Holy Spirit from the Father and the Son, which is accepted by the Western Church (*see* East–West Schism; Filioque).

● **Trinity House, Corporation of** ▶ The UK marine authority, responsible for the maintenance of lighthouses and the granting of pilots' licences. It also has a charitable function relieving distressed mariners and their dependants.

● **triode** ▷*See* thermionic valve.

● **Triple Alliance** ▶ (1882) An alliance between Germany, Austria-Hungary, and Italy, which with the opposing ▷Triple Entente shaped European diplomacy in the decades before World War I. At the outbreak of war (1914) Italy declared its neutrality, thus breaking the alliance.

● **Triple Alliance, War of the** ▶ (*or* Paraguayan War; 1865–70) The war between Paraguay and a coalition of Argentina, Brazil, and Uruguay. Conflict was precipitated by the belligerent diplomacy of Paraguay's dictator, F. S. ▷López, towards Argentina, which with Brazil and Uruguay invaded Paraguay. López refused to surrender and following the capture of Asunción in 1868 waged a guerrilla war in the N until taken prisoner in 1870. The war shattered the economy of Paraguay, which lost about half its population.

● **Triple Crown** ▶ The three major races for three-year-old horses in the USA: the Kentucky Derby, the Preakness Stakes, and the Belmont Stakes.

● **Triple Entente** ▶ An informal combination of France, Russia, and Britain resulting from the Franco-Russian alliance (1893), the Franco-British ▷Entente Cordiale (1904), and the Anglo-Russian agreement (1907). It was formed in opposition to the ▷Triple Alliance.

● **triple jump** ▶ (former name: hop, step, and jump) A field event for men in athletics, similar to the ▷long jump but executed as a continuous series of three jumps. The jumper lands first on the takeoff foot and then on the other, which becomes the takeoff foot for the final jump. World record: 18.29 m (1995) Jonathan Edwards (UK).

● **triple point** ▶ The temperature and pressure at which the gaseous, liquid, and solid phases of a substance are in equilibrium. Water has its triple point at 273.16 ▷kelvins and 611.2 pascals. This value forms the basis of the definition of the kelvin and the thermodynamic ▷temperature scale.

● **Tripoli** ▶ (Arabic name: Tarabulus al-Gharb) 32 58N 13 12E The capital and main port of Libya, on the Mediterranean Sea. Originally founded as Oea by the Phoenicians, it has come under the rule of many different countries through the ages. It became the capital of Libya on independence in 1951. Its notable buildings include a Spanish fortress and it has a university (1973). Exports include fruit and olive oil and it is a transshipment centre. Population (1995 est): 1 140 000.

● **Tripoli** ▶ (Arabic name: Tarabulus ash-sham) 34 27N 35 50E A port in NW Lebanon, on the Mediterranean Sea. It was the capital of a Phoenician federation of three other cities (hence its name, from Greek *tripolis*). Iraqi oil is brought by pipeline to the refinery here. The city was heavily damaged in 1983 in fighting between Syrian and Palestine Liberation Organization forces. Population (1998 est): 160 000.

● **Tripolitania** ▶ A region of N Africa, between Tunisia and Cyrenaica. Colonized in the 7th century BC by the Phoenicians, who founded three cities, including Tripoli, the coast was controlled by a succession of foreign powers, including Romans, Arabs, Ottoman Turks, and Italians, while the nomadic Berbers of the interior remained generally unaffected. Since 1951 Tripolitania has been part of Libya.

● **Tripura** ▶ A state in NE India, in tropical jungle and plains E of

Bangladesh. Rice, jute, tea, and bamboo are produced. Local cottage industries are flourishing.

History: the Moguls ended 1000 years of Hindu monarchy (18th century) before Britain won Tripura. In 1949 it entered the Indian Union. Area: 10 486 sq km (4048 sq mi). Population (1994 est): 3 055 000. Capital: Agartala.

● **triptych** ▶ A painting consisting of three distinct scenes or parts, the central part usually being larger than the two sidepieces. A development of the earlier two-part diptych, the triptych was widely used in medieval and Renaissance churches as an altarpiece. Triptychs were often executed on three hinged panels, so that the two wing panels could be closed over the central painting; in such cases the reverse sides of the wings were often painted as well. The most famous modern example of a triptych is probably Francis Bacon's *Three Studies for Figures at the Base of a Crucifixion* (1945).

● **tri-ratna** ▶ (Sanskrit: three jewels) In Buddhism, the ▷Buddha, ▷dharma, and ▷sangha, that is, the spiritual ideal, the truth regarding the means to its attainment, and the monastic order of those who strive towards it.

● **trireme** ▷*See* ships.

● **Tristan** ▶ The tragic hero of several medieval romances. After accidentally drinking a magic love potion, he becomes the lover of the Irish princess Iseult (Isolde), who is betrothed to his uncle, King Mark of Cornwall. He later renounces Iseult and goes to Brittany, where he marries the duke's daughter. Dying from a wound, he sends a ship to bring back Iseult to nurse him. By his wife's treachery, she arrives too late and dies of grief at his side. Of Celtic origin, the legend appeared in a French poem, written in about 1150 (now lost). Other old versions include one by an Anglo-Norman poet, Thomas, and ▷Gottfried von Strassburg's *Tristan und Isolde*, the source of Wagner's opera. In a 13th-century prose romance the story was incorporated into the ▷Arthurian legend.

● **Tristan da Cunha** ▶ 37 15S 12 30W A group of four small islands in the S Atlantic Ocean, a dependency of the UK overseas territory of St Helena (some 2333 km or 1449 mi to the N). The only settlement, Edinburgh, which is on Tristan (the largest island), grew from a British garrison (established 1816). Situated on a main sailing route, it originally flourished but became isolated when steam replaced sail. Its community is now perhaps the most isolated in the world, being some 3033 km (1882 mi) from Cape Town, South Africa, whence there is an annual passenger service. In 1961 the inhabitants were evacuated to the UK to escape a volcanic eruption but most chose to return in 1963. The economy is based on crawfish canning and postage stamps. Area: about 100 sq km (40 sq mi). Population (latest est): 313.

● **tritium** ▶ (T *or* ^{3}H) A radioactive isotope of hydrogen, the nucleus of which contains one ▷proton and two ▷neutrons. It does not occur naturally but is produced in nuclear reactors and is used as a radioactive tracer and in nuclear weapons. Tritium decays with a half-life of 12.3 years, emitting beta-rays.

● **Triton** ▶ In Greek mythology, a sea deity, the son of Poseidon and Amphitrite. He is usually portrayed as human above the waist and as a dolphin below; he blows a shell in order to control the waves.

● **triton shell** ▶ A ▷gastropod mollusc of the family *Cymatiidae* (about 100 species), occurring mainly in tropical seas. Triton trumpets (genus *Charonia*) grow to 40 cm and have ribbed shells, often with prominent knobs. They are carnivorous, feeding on molluscs and echinoderms. Hairy tritons have a rough hairy shell.

● **triumvirate** ▶ In Roman affairs, a board of three men officially appointed for special administrative duties. The so-called first Triumvirate (60 BC) of Caesar, Pompey, and Crassus was merely a private arrangement for mutual convenience. The triumvirate, or triple dictatorship, of Mark Antony, Lepidus, and Octavian was unique; appointed in 43 BC to maintain public order in Rome, they held office with absolute powers until Lepidus was ousted in 36 and power was divided between Mark Antony and Octavian.

● **Trivandrum** ▶ (official name from 2000: Thiruvanthapuram) 8 41N 76 57E A city in India, the capital of Kerala. A cultural, commercial, and communications centre, it processes minerals and is the site of the University of Kerala (1937). Population (1991): 523 733.

● **Trobriand Islands** ▶ A group of coral islands in the SW Pacific Ocean, in Papua New Guinea. The largest is Kiriwana (Trobriand). It produces yams, mother-of-pearl, and trepang (edible sea cucumber). The islands became famous through the studies of the anthropologist, Bronisław Malinowski. Area: about 440 sq km (170 sq mi).

● **trochee** ▷*See* metre (poetry).

● **trogon** ▶ An insectivorous bird belonging to a family (*Trogonidae*; 35 species) occurring in forested regions of Africa, Asia, and America. 24–46 cm long, trogons have iridescent plumage, which in males is usually dark with a bright red or yellow belly. They have rounded wings, a short curved bill, and a long tail and are the sole family of the order *Trogoniformes*. ▷*See also* quetzal.

● **Troilus** ▶ In Greek mythology, a son of King Priam of Troy who was killed by Achilles. The story of his love for Cressida, who deserted him for the Greek Diomedes, first appeared in the *Roman de Troie* by the 12th-century French poet Benoît de Sainte-Maure.

● **Trois-Rivières** ▶ 46 21N 72 34W A city and deepwater port in E Canada, in Quebec on the St Lawrence River. Founded in 1610, it is a transport and industrial centre, producing a large proportion of the world's newsprint. Population (1991): 136 303.

● **Trojan group** ▶ ▷Minor planets that lie close to either of two points in Jupiter's orbit. Each point forms an equilateral triangle with Jupiter and the sun.

● **Trojan Horse** ▶ In Greek legend, a gigantic hollow wooden horse devised by Odysseus or by its builder, Epeius, in the ▷Trojan War. The Trojans hauled it inside their city, believing it to be a gift to Athena, and Greek warriors then emerged from it to open the gates to their army.

● **Trojan War** ▶ In Greek legend, a ten years' war waged by the Greeks against ▷Troy after the abduction of ▷Helen, wife of King Menelaus of Sparta, by Paris, a Trojan prince. Its history, probably based on an actual war fought in the 12th century BC, is related in Homer's *Iliad*. The Greeks were led by ▷Agamemnon and their champions included ▷Achilles, ▷Diomedes, and ▷Odysseus. The chief Trojan warriors were ▷Hector and ▷Paris, sons of King Priam. Most of the action in the *Iliad* is concentrated in the final year of the war and culminates in the capture of Troy by the stratagem of the ▷Trojan Horse.

● **troll** ▶ In Scandinavian folklore, originally a gigantic ogre-like creature imagined as guarding treasure, inhabiting a castle, and stalking through the forest only at night since they are destroyed or turned to stone if they see the sun. In later folklore, trolls were conceived as dwarflike cave- and mountain-dwellers who were skilled craftsmen.

● **Trollope, Anthony** ▶ (1815–82) British novelist. He worked for the General Post Office from 1834 until he retired in 1867. He established his reputation with a series of novels set in the imaginary county of Barsetshire with a cast of predominantly clerical characters. These books include *The Warden* (1855), *Barchester Towers* (1857), and *The Last Chronicle of Barset* (1867). A second series of novels, set against a political background, includes *Phineas Finn* (1869) and *The Eustace Diamonds* (1873).

● **trombone** ▶ A brass musical instrument, consisting of a cylindrical tube, about 3 m (9 ft) long, turned back upon itself, a cup-shaped mouthpiece, and a flaring bell. By means of a slide that is used in seven positions and by varying lip pressure, seven different harmonic series can be produced, covering a chromatic range of almost three octaves above E below the bass stave in the tenor trombone. A bass instrument also exists. The trombone has been part of the symphony orchestra since the late 18th century and is frequently used in jazz. The old English name for the trombone was the **sackbut**.

● **Tromp, Maarten (Harpertszoon)** ▶ (1598–1653) Dutch admiral. Tromp defeated a numerically superior Spanish fleet at the Battle of the Downs (1639). His encounter with the English (1652) began the first ▷Dutch War, during which he defeated the English off Dungeness (1652). He died in action. His son **Cornelis (Martenszoon) Tromp** (1629–91) was an admiral in the second and third ▷Dutch Wars and was briefly commander in chief of the Dutch fleet (1665), being replaced by de ▷Ruyter.

● **trompe l'oeil** ► (French: fool the eye) A method of painting figures and objects to create the illusion that they are real rather than painted. The elaborate arches, vistas, doors, etc., painted on walls in Pompeii are an example of this visual trickery. It is also associated with Italian ▷baroque art.

● **Tromsø** ► 69 42N 19 00E A seaport in N Norway, on an island just off the mainland. The largest town N of the Arctic Circle, it has fishing, sealing, and fish-processing industries. Its university was established in 1968. Population (1990): 50 563.

● **Trondheim** ► 63 36N 10 23E A city and seaport in W Norway on Trondheim Fjord. It has a famous cathedral (12th–14th centuries) where Norwegian sovereigns have been crowned since early times. The Technical University of Norway was established here in 1900 and the University of Trondheim in 1968. Its industries include shipbuilding and fishing; the main exports are timber, wood pulp, fish, and metal goods. Population (1997 est): 144 599.

● **trooping the Colour** ► Traditionally, the parade of the British sovereign's flag, or Colour, displayed so that foreign mercenaries would recognize it in battle. It is now a military parade held on the Horse Guards parade ground in Whitehall, London, on the sovereign's official birthday.

● **tropic bird** ► A white seabird belonging to a family (*Phaethontidae*; 3 species) occurring in tropical and subtropical waters. Tropic birds have black eye and wing markings and are up to 50 cm long excluding the long streamer-like tail feathers. Tropic birds spend most of their lives at sea. Order: *Pelecaniformes* (cormorants, pelicans, etc.).

● **tropics** ► The area of the earth's surface lying roughly between the Tropic of Cancer on the 23°30′N parallel of latitude and the Tropic of Capricorn on the 23°30′S parallel.

● **tropism** ► The growth of a plant or sedentary animal in response to a directional external stimulus: a growth movement towards the stimulus is a positive tropism; the opposite response is a negative tropism. Different forms of tropism are named according to the type of stimulus. For example, positive **hydrotropism** is growth towards water, observed in plant roots; negative **geotropism** (or gravitropism) is growth away from the pull of gravity, which occurs in plant stems.

● **troposphere** ▷*See* atmosphere.

● **Trossachs, the** ► 56 13N 4 23W A picturesque glen in central Scotland, in Stirling between Loch Katrine and Loch Achray. It was popularized by Sir Walter Scott in his poem *The Lady of the Lake*.

● **Trotsky, Leon** ► (Lev Bronstein; 1879–1940) Russian revolutionary and Marxist theorist. Trotsky became a Marxist in the 1890s and was imprisoned and exiled for participating in revolutionary activities. He lived in W Europe from 1902 until the Revolution of 1905. Again imprisoned and exiled, he escaped abroad (1907), where he remained until 1917. On the outbreak of the Russian Revolution, he returned to Russia and abandoned his previous ▷Menshevik loyalities to become a ▷Bolshevik. He played a major role in the October Revolution, which brought the Bolsheviks to power, and as war commissar during the civil war (1918–20) directed the Red Army to victory. Under Lenin, Trotsky was Russia's second most powerful man but lost to Stalin the power struggle that followed Lenin's death and was banished from the Soviet Union. He moved eventually to Mexico, where he was murdered, probably by a Soviet agent. ▷*See also* Trotskyism.

● **Trotskyism** ► The form of Marxism developed by Leon ▷Trotsky, who advocated world revolution in opposition to the view that socialism could be achieved in one country in isolation. Stalin sought to secure the Soviet Union against the counter-revolutionary forces of capitalism, primarily by military and economic means. Trotskyists believed that the revolution could only be maintained and capitalism defeated by developing the strength and solidarity of the work-

ing class throughout the world, since the main struggle was against the capitalist class and not between states. To this end Trotsky and his supporters founded the Fourth International in 1937, after what they saw as the degeneration of the Third International under the influence of Stalinism. Despite Trotsky's murder in 1940 and various subsequent internal splits, in 1979 the Fourth International had functioning sections in over 60 countries. These and other revolutionary groups with Trotskyist aims were regarded as dangerous and counter-revolutionary by the leaders of the Soviet Union and other communist states.

troubadours ► An equestrian portrait of Bernard de Ventadour, a 12th-century troubadour, taken from a 13th-century French book.

● **troubadours** ► Provençal poets of the 12th to 14th centuries whose lyric poetry had a profound influence on both the subject matter and form of subsequent European verse. A number of the troubadours were of noble birth and were enthusiastically patronized by several European courts. Both poets and composers, the troubadours wrote songs introducing a new concept of love, later labelled ▷courtly love (although they were also noted for their satires and poems on political subjects). They developed several poetic genres and verse forms, including the *canso d'amor* (a love song in five or six stanzas), the *pastorela* (a narrative relating a meeting between a knight and a shepherdess), the *alba* (a song of lovers parting at dawn), the *tenso* or *partimen* (a debate on love), and the *sestina* (a poem of six stanzas with the same end-words repeated in each stanza according to a shifting pattern). The earliest troubadour was Guillaume, 9th Duc d'Aquitaine (1071–1127). Other famous troubadours were Marcabru (mid-12th century); Bertrand de Born, Vicomte de Hautefort (c. 1140–c. 1207), whose patron was Henry Curtmantle, son of Henry II of England and whom Dante places in hell in the *Inferno* for sowing political discord; Arnaut Daniel (c. 1180), who was credited with inventing the *sestina* and was considered the greatest craftsman by Dante; and Bernard de Ventadour (late 12th century), in whose lyrics the conventions of courtly love were most clearly developed. ▷*See also* trouvères.

● **Troubles, Council of** ▷*See* Blood, Council of.

● **trout** ► One of several predatory fish belonging to the family *Salmonidae*, especially the genus *Salmo*, that are native to the N hemisphere but introduced elsewhere as food and game fish. It has a stout body with a blunt head and varies in colour from blackish to light olive with characteristic black or red spots or X-shaped markings. Trout occur mainly in fresh water but in some cases the young migrate to the sea to mature and return annually to streams to spawn. The common European brown trout (*S. trutta*), up to 140 cm long, has a migratory variety called the sea trout. The North American rainbow trout (*S. gairdneri*), up to 70 cm long, is distinguished by a broad purple band along its sides. Order: *Salmoniformes*.

● **trouvères** ► Medieval poets of N France, especially Picardy, who were contemporary with, and influenced in subject matter and style by, the ▷troubadours. Notable trouvères include Conon de Béthune (d. 1224), Thibaud (IV) de Champagne, King of Navarre (d. 1253), ▷Adam de la Halle, and Rutebeuf (13th century).

● **Trowbridge** ► 51 20N 2 13W A market town in S England, the administrative centre of Wiltshire. It has woollen manufacturing, bacon and ham curing, and brewing industries. Population (1991): 29 334.

● **Troy** ► An ancient city in Asia Minor, near the Dardanelles. According to legend, when the Trojan prince ▷Paris abducted ▷Helen, her husband's brother, ▷Agamemnon, led a Greek force to recover her, captured Troy by the stratagem of the wooden horse after ten years' fighting, and destroyed it (traditional date: 1184 BC). ▷Schliemann's excavations (1870) identified Troy at Hissarlik. Excavations have revealed nine superimposed cities, the seventh of which (not the second, as Schliemann thought) was contemporary with the legendary siege and had met a violent end. ▷*See also* Homer; Trojan War.

● **Troyes** ► 48 18N 4 05E A town in NE France, the capital of the Aube department on the River Seine. The capital of the old province of Champagne, it has a cathedral (13th–16th centuries). Manufactures include textiles, machinery, and food products. Population (1990): 60 755.

● **Troy weight** ▷*See* units of measurement.

● **Trucial States** ▷*See* United Arab Emirates.

● **Truck Acts** ► A series of 19th-century British acts of parliament prohibiting employers from paying their workers in goods or in tokens that could only be exchanged at shops (known as **tommy shops**) owned by the employers. The original act of 1831 listed those trades in which payment had to be made in coins. It was extended in 1887 to include most manual workers. Certain sections had to be repealed in 1960, however, to permit payments by cheque.

The **truck system**, which those acts abolished, took its name from the archaic verb "to truck," meaning to barter or exchange. The attractiveness of the system to employers was that they made a profit on their tommy shops by buying on a wholesale basis and forcing employees to pay full retail prices.

● **Trudeau, Pierre Elliott** ► (1919–2000) Canadian statesman; Liberal prime minister (1968–79, 1980–84). A French Canadian, he nevertheless opposed French separatism and in 1970 briefly introduced martial law to deal with separatist agitation in Quebec. In the same year his government recognized the People's Republic of China. Trudeau's dashing image was reinforced by his young wife, Margaret Trudeau, but the couple finally separated in 1977 after a series of much publicized estrangements. Defeated in 1979 by Joseph ▷Clark, he was re-elected in 1980. He retired from office in 1984, and his Liberal party lost the subsequent general election.

● **Trueman, Freddy** ► (Frederick Sewards T.; 1931–) British cricketer, who played for Yorkshire and England. A great fast bowler, he was the first bowler to take 300 Test wickets.

● **Truffaut, François** ► (1932–84) French film director. He wrote for the magazine *Cahiers du Cinéma* during the 1950s and was an influential member of the ▷New Wave. His films, noted for their visual charm and elegance, include *Les Quatre Cent Coups* (1959), *Shoot the Pianist* (1960), *Jules et Jim* (1961), *L'Enfant sauvage* (1970), *Day for Night* (1973), *L'Histoire d'Adèle H.* (1975), *Love on the Run* (1978), and *Le Dernier Métro* (1980).

● **truffle** ► A fungus belonging to the order *Tuberales*. Up to 10 cm across, truffles are rounded and occur in chalky soils, usually in association with tree roots. Having a strong smell and taste, they are unearthed and eaten by squirrels, rabbits, etc., which disperse the spores in their faeces. Several species are regarded as delicacies, including the black Périgord truffle (*Tuber melanosporum*) and the white Piedmont truffle (*T. magnatum*), both of France. They are collected in

oak woods using trained pigs or dogs. The bluish-black English truffle (*T. aestivum*) is found mainly in beech woods. Phylum: ▷*Ascomycota*.

● **Trujillo** ► 8 06S 79 00W A city in Peru, situated 13 km (8 mi) from its port, Salaverry, on the Pacific coast. Founded in 1535, it has a university (established in 1824 by Simón Bolívar). Trujillo is the commercial centre for an area producing sugar cane and rice. Population (1995 est): 627 553.

● **Trujillo (Molina), Rafael (Leónidas)** ► (1891–1961) Dominican dictator, who governed the Dominican Republic, directly or indirectly, from 1930 to 1961, aided by a powerful police force. His tyranny led to his assassination.

● **Truman, Harry S.** ► (1884–1972) US statesman; Democratic president (1945–53). He became president on the death in office of F. D. Roosevelt and one of his earliest acts was to order the atomic bombing of Hiroshima and Nagasaki to end the war with Japan. In the **Truman Doctrine** he announced economic and military aid to countries threatened by interference from other states. His administration introduced the Marshall Plan (*see* Marshall, George) of postwar economic aid to Europe (1948) and saw the establishment of the ▷North Atlantic Treaty Organization (1949). In domestic politics his ▷Fair Deal programme promised social reform.

● **trumpet** ► A brass □musical instrument. The modern trumpet consists of a cylindrical tube, 1.5 m (5 ft) long, turned back on itself, a cup-shaped mouthpiece, and a flaring bell. Three valves alter the effective length of the tube, allowing the notes of the harmonic series on six successive semitones to be played. With varying lip pressure the B flat trumpet has a chromatic range of two and a half octaves below E below middle C. The early trumpet (from the Renaissance to the early 19th century) could only produce the notes of its natural harmonic series. The upper notes of the series were known as the *clarino* (Italian: clarinet) register, used for brilliant effects by such composers as Bach.

● **trumpet creeper** ► A vine of the genus *Campsis*. The American trumpet creeper (*C. radicans*) is native to the S USA and the Chinese trumpet creeper (*C. grandiflora*) is of Asian origin. Both produce trumpet-shaped orange flowers and are cultivated as ornamentals. Family: *Bignoniaceae*.

● **trumpeter** ► A long-legged ground-dwelling bird belonging to a family (*Psophiidae*; 3 species) occurring in forests of N South America. 50 cm long, trumpeters have a small head, soft dark plumage, and short bills, feeding on insects and berries. They travel in small flocks and have a loud trumpeting call. Order: *Gruiformes* (cranes, rails, etc.).

● **trunkfish** ► A tropical fish, also called boxfish or cowfish, belonging to a family (*Ostraciidae*) related to ▷puffers, that occurs in the Atlantic and Pacific Oceans. Its body is often brightly coloured and encased in a boxlike shell of fused bony plates with spaces for the fins, etc.

● **Truro** ► 50 16N 5 03W A cathedral city in SW England, the administrative centre of Cornwall. It is a small port and market town, with pottery and biscuit manufacturing. The cathedral was begun in 1880. Population (1991): 18 966.

● **trust** ► In law, a binding arrangement under which one person (the trustee, who may be an individual or a corporation) has control of property (the trust property), which he administers for the benefit of the other (the beneficiary). The trustee may himself be one of the beneficiaries. Trusts developed in the middle ages when certain parties, such as religious orders, had the use or benefit of property that they were not allowed to own. Such rights were enforced by the Court of ▷Chancery but not recognized by the common law courts (*see* equity). Trusts are of two types: (1) **express trusts** are intentionally created in clear words, as in a will or deed; and (2) **implied** (or constructive) **trusts**, as when a court may rule that as a matter of equity the legal owner of a property should be compelled to hold it as a trustee for another. The powers and duties of trustees are strictly defined and are contained mainly in the Trustee Act (1925). On the death of a trustee, trust property is exempt from taxation provided the deceased was not in any way a beneficiary of the trust. ▷*See also* investment company; unit trust.

● **trust territory** ▶ A territory being prepared for self-government, the administration of which is supervised by the Trusteeship Council of the UN. The trust territories replaced the ▷mandates of the League of Nations. The last remaining trust territory, the Republic of ▷Belau (formerly part of the Trust Territory of the Pacific Islands), gained independence in 1994.

● **trypanosomiasis** ▶ Any infection caused by parasitic protozoa of the genus *Trypanosoma*. In Africa the species *T. brucei* is transmitted by the tsetse fly and causes ▷sleeping sickness. In South America the species *T. cruzi* is transmitted by ▷assassin bugs—bloodsucking bugs of the family *Reduviidae*—and causes ▷Chagas' disease.

● **trypsin** ▶ A digestive enzyme, secreted by the pancreas, that breaks down dietary proteins in the small intestine. It is secreted in an inactive form, which is converted to trypsin by the enzyme enterokinase in the intestine.

● **Tsana, Lake** ▷*See* Tana, Lake.

● **Ts'ao Chan** ▷*See* Cao Chan.

● **tsar** ▶ The title (derived from the Latin, Caesar) of the rulers of Russia from 1547 to 1721. It was first adopted by Ivan the Terrible and, though commonly used until 1917, was officially replaced with the title Emperor by Peter the Great.

● **Tsaritsyn** ▷*See* Volgograd.

● **Tselinograd** ▷*See* Astana.

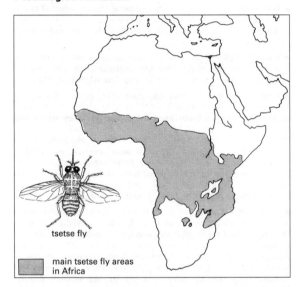

tsetse fly

main tsetse fly areas in Africa

tsetse fly ▶ Several species of tsetse fly carry the parasites causing sleeping sickness in humans and cattle. The tsetse areas in Africa correspond to the areas where sleeping sickness is endemic.

● **tsetse fly** ▶ A fly, 6–16 mm long, belonging to a genus (*Glossina*; 22 species) restricted to tropical Africa. Both sexes bite and suck the blood of mammals, transmitting trypanosomes to man and domestic animals. Thus *G. palpalis* carries human sleeping sickness and *G. morsitans* transmits nagana in cattle. The larvae develop to maturity within the female before being deposited in the soil to pupate. Family: *Muscidae*.

● **Tshombe, Moise (Kapenda)** ▶ (1919–69) Congolese statesman; prime minister (1964–65) of the Congo (named Zaïre between 1971 and 1997). He led the secession of the copper-rich Katanga (now Shaba) province of the Congo in 1960, which for three years maintained its independence under Tshombe's presidency. On its collapse Tshombe fled to Spain but was recalled briefly to become the Congo's prime minister. Dismissed by President Kasavubu in 1965, he returned to Spain and died of a heart attack in Algeria.

● **Tsinan** ▷*See* Jinan.

● **Tsinghai** ▷*See* Qinghai.

● **Tsingtao** ▷*See* Qingdao.

● **Tsiolkovski, Konstantin Eduardovich** ▶ (1857–1935) Russian aeronautical engineer, who pioneered space and rocket research. Becoming deaf as a child he studied mathematics and physics. In 1892 he built the first wind tunnel in Russia, which he used for testing his designs of dirigibles. He then went on to investigate the use of rockets in space travel and anticipated many of the ideas that Robert ▷Goddard was later to develop, especially liquid-fuelled rockets.

● **Tskhinvali** ▷*See* South Ossetia.

● **tsunami** ▶ (Japanese: harbour wave) An ocean wave produced as a result of a vertical movement of the sea floor. It is usually caused by an earthquake, a volcanic eruption, or a landslide. When a tsunami reaches coastal shallows it slows down but builds up enormous waves, which when they strike the coast can cause appalling devastation. Tsunamis have killed many thousands of people living in coastal regions of the Pacific Ocean.

● **Tsushima** ▶ A group of five Japanese islands, in the Korea Strait. During the Russo-Japanese War, Russia suffered a major naval defeat near here (1905). Fishing is the chief industry. Area: 698 sq km (269 sq mi). Population (latest est): 50 810. Capital: Izuhara.

● **Tsvetaeva, Marina** ▶ (1892–1941) Russian poet. Her highly original and emotionally powerful poetry was praised by Akhmatova, Pasternak, and other contemporaries. She opposed the Revolution and left Russia in 1922 to live in Prague, Berlin, and Paris. In 1939 she followed her husband back to Russia. He was shot, and she later committed suicide.

● **Tuamotu Archipelago** ▶ A chain of about 80 coral atolls in the S Pacific Ocean, in French Polynesia. Rangiroa is the largest island and Fakarava, the most important economically. French nuclear tests were held here during the 1960s. Mother-of-pearl, phosphate, and copra are produced. Area: 860 sq km (332 sq mi). Population (1988): 12 374. Administrative centre: Apataki atoll.

● **tuatara** ▶ A lizard-like reptile, *Sphenodon punctatus*, that is the only living representative of the primitive order *Rhynchocephalia*, which flourished 200 million years ago. It is found only on islands off the North Island of New Zealand and has a brown-black to greenish body with a crest of spines running from head to tail; up to 70 cm long, it may live 100 years. Tuataras live in burrows during the day and emerge at night to feed on spiders, insects, and birds' eggs. The clutch of 8–14 eggs is incubated for 13–14 months before hatching.

● **Tuareg** ▶ A ▷Berber nomad people of NW Africa. Traditionally they travelled vast distances across the Sahara with their caravans and livestock, trading between the Sahel zone and the Mediterranean. Their society is hierarchical, with a strongly defined caste structure, and the men have traditionally worn veils. In recent decades their way of life has been threatened by droughts and national trading restrictions and their numbers are now depleted (less than 900 000). The 1990s saw uprisings by militant Tuaregs in Mali (1990–93) and Niger (1991–95).

● **Tuatha Dé Danann** ▶ (Old Irish: people of the goddess ▷Danu) In Old Irish mythology, a divine race, one of the several mythological groups believed to have invaded and settled in Ireland. According to the *Book of Invasions*, they came from the east in the mid-15th century BC and were learned in science and the arts of the Druids. Sometimes they are portrayed as mortal men but exceptionally strong, beautiful, learned, etc.

● **tuba** ▶ A valved brass instrument with a conical bore and low pitch, derived originally from the ▷saxhorn. Various types of tuba exist under a variety of names; the instrument is used in the symphony orchestra as well as in the military band. The **Wagner tuba** is not a true tuba but a bass version of the ▷French horn.

● **tuber** ▶ A swollen underground plant stem in which carbohydrates (often in the form of starch) are stored. Some tubers, for example potatoes and yams, are important human foods. Tuber-bearing plants may reproduce vegetatively from buds on the tuber, and tuber crops are usually grown from tubers rather than seed.

● **tuberculin** ► A protein derived from tuberculosis bacilli that have been killed. In the Mantoux test tuberculin is injected into the skin to test whether a person has been in contact with tuberculosis. The appearance of an inflamed patch (a positive reaction) indicates previous exposure to the bacilli (and therefore some immunity) but not necessarily active infection.

● **tuberculosis** ► An infectious disease caused by the bacillus *Mycobacterium tuberculosis* (which was first recognized by Robert ▷Koch in 1882). In pulmonary tuberculosis the bacillus is inhaled into the lungs, where it forms a primary tubercle that usually heals without trouble. Alternatively the disease may smoulder for months without showing any symptoms: affected people can act as carriers without being aware that they are infected. Reactivation of the primary disease, or reinfection, may lead to active tuberculosis (formerly called "consumption"), characterized by a cough (often producing some blood), fever, lassitude, weight loss, and breathlessness. The infection may also spread to other organs. The TB bacillus can also enter the body through drinking infected cows' milk, setting up a primary tubercle in the abdominal lymph nodes. Improved environmental conditions, pasteurization of milk, X-ray screening, and ▷BCG vaccinations all reduce the incidence of TB. Treatment consists of rest, isolation, and combinations of antibiotics, including ethambutol, isoniazid (INH), and rifampicin.

● **tuberose** ► A perennial summer-flowering garden plant, *Polianthes tuberosa*, native to SW North America. It has tuberous roots, long bright-green leaves clustered at the base of the stem, and smaller clasping leaves along the stem. Its fragrant white flowers are in pairs on a terminal spike and are used to manufacture perfume. Family: *Amaryllidaceae*.

● **tubifex** ► A freshwater ▷annelid worm, also called bloodworm, belonging to the widely distributed family *Tubificidae*. Found along muddy rivers and estuaries, the most common species is the bright-red extremely active *Tubifex tubifex*, up to 85 mm long. Class: *Oligochaeta*.

● **Tübingen** ► 48 32N 9 04E A town in SW Germany, in Baden-Württemberg on the River Neckar. The university (1477) is famed for its theological faculty established in the 19th century. Industries include publishing and textile manufacture. Population (latest est): 76 040.

● **Tubman, William V(acanarat) S(hadrach)** ► (1895–1971) Liberian statesman; president (1943–71). He was largely responsible for welding together modern Liberia.

● **Tubuai Islands** ► (*or* Austral Is) 23 23S 149 27W A group of seven islands in S French Polynesia, including Tubuai and Rurutu. Coffee, copra, and arrowroot are produced. Area: 173 sq km (67 sq mi). Population (latest est): 6509.

● **tubular bells** ► A tuned percussion instrument consisting of a row of metal tubes, graduated in length, hung on a frame and struck with a leather-covered hammer.

● **TUC** ▷*See* trade union.

● **Tucson** ► 32 15N 110 57W A city and health resort in the USA, in Arizona. Its growth came with the arrival of the Southern Pacific Railroad (1880) and the discovery of silver at nearby Tombstone. Tucson is an industrial centre for an agricultural and mining district and site of the University of Arizona (1885). Population (1996 est): 449 002.

● **Tucumán** ▷*See* San Miguel de Tucumán.

● **Tudjman, Franjo** ► (1922–99) Croatian soldier and politician, president of Croatia (as a federal republic of Yugoslavia 1990–92, as an independent state 1992–99). He was imprisoned in the 1970s and 1980s for advocating Croatian independence. In 1991–92 he led the Croatian struggle against the Serb-led Yugoslav army and in 1992–95 he involved his country's forces in the civil war in ▷Bosnia-Hercegovina. His regime was nationalistic and authoritarian.

● **Tudors** ► The ruling dynasty of England from 1485 to 1603. Owen Tudor (c. 1400–61), a Welshman, entered the service of Henry V and married (1422) his widow Catherine of Valois (1401–37). Their eldest son Edmund, Earl of Richmond (c. 1430–56), married Margaret ▷Beaufort, the great-great-granddaughter of Edward III, and their son became the first Tudor monarch, Henry VII. Subsequent Tudor monarchs were Henry VIII, Edward VI, Mary I, and Elizabeth I.

● **Tudor style** ► The style of ▷English art and architecture prevalent from about 1485 to 1600, i.e. during the reigns of the ▷Tudors. In large houses it encompassed the transition from ▷gothic architecture to the ▷Renaissance, making use of ▷half-timber work, mullioned windows, and tall chimneys (as in ▷Hampton Court), with warm interior panelling and more comfortable furnishings. ▷*See also* Elizabethan style.

● **tuff** ▷*See* pyroclastic rock.

● **Tu Fu** ▷*See* Du Fu.

● **Tugela River** ► A river in South Africa, flowing generally E from the Drakensberg Mountains, where it forms the **Tugela Falls**, 856 m (2810 ft) high, to the Indian Ocean. Length: about 500 km (312 mi).

● **tui** ► A black ▷honeyeater, *Prosthemadera novaeseelandiae*, occurring in mountain forests of New Zealand. It is about 27 cm long and has a white tufted throat. Once common, it has been extensively captured for its ability to mimic human speech and is now very rare.

● **Tuigamala, Va'aiga** ► (1969–) Samoan rugby player. Tuigamala made his name playing Rugby Union for New Zealand (1989–92) before switching to Rugby League to sign with the English side Wigan. Since 1996 he has also played the Union game for Samoa.

● **Tula** ► An ancient ▷Toltec city in central Mexico. Adopted as the Toltec capital around 980 AD, Tula was destroyed in 1168. Distinctive Toltec features here include a terraced pyramid, colonnaded buildings, and relief sculptures.

● **Tula** ► 54 11N 37 38E A city in W central Russia, 169 km (105 mi) S of Moscow. An important ironworking centre since the 17th century, it also has food-processing industries. Population (1995 est): 532 000.

● **tulip** ► A perennial herbaceous plant of the genus *Tulipa* (about 100 species), native to the Old World but widely cultivated for ornament. Growing from bulbs, most tulips have a solitary bell-shaped flower, with bluish-green leaves clustered at the base of the plant. There are nearly 4000 varieties of garden tulips, which show enormous variation in colour and type: the older varieties are descended from *T. gesneriana* and *T. suaveolens*; the newer ones often have *T. kaufmanniana*, *T. greigi*, or *T. fosteriana* as one of the parent species. The Netherlands, the Channel Islands, and Lincolnshire (England) are main commercial growing areas. Family: *Liliaceae*.

● **tulip tree** ► A tree, *Liriodendron tulipifera*, native to E North America and widely planted for ornament. Reaching a height of 58 m in the wild, it has three-lobed leaves, which turn golden in autumn. The flowers are large and tulip-like, greenish white or yellow, and produce papery cones containing winged fruits. The wood, known as white wood, is used for furniture, plywood, paper, and boxes. The Chinese tulip tree (*L. chinense*) is similar but smaller. Family: *Magnoliaceae*.

● **Tull, Jethro** ► (1674–1741) English agriculturalist, best known for his invention in 1701 of the seed drill. The drill planted seeds in straight lines, thus facilitating weeding, and covered them with soil to protect them from birds.

● **Tulsa** ► 36 07N 95 58W A city in the USA, in Oklahoma on the Arkansas River. Oil was discovered in 1901 and today over 800 oil companies have established plants here. It has also developed as a port since the opening of a waterway (1971) linking Tulsa to the Gulf of Mexico. Population (1996 est): 378 491.

● **Tulsidas** ► (c. 1532–1623) Indian poet. He was a brahmin and lived at Benares. His best-known work is the *Ramcaritmanas* (c. 1574–77), a Hindi version of a Sanskrit epic.

● **Tulufan Depression** ► (Turpan Depression *or* Turfan Depression) A mountain basin in NW China. Known for its fruit, it was the centre of an Indian-Persian civilization (3rd–4th centuries AD). Lowest point: 154 m (505 ft) below sea level.

● **tumour** ► Any swelling in the body caused by the abnormal proliferation of cells. Tumours that do not spread to other parts of the body (i.e. are noncancerous) are described as **benign**. They are usually harmless but may become very large, exerting pressure on neighbouring tissues: in such cases they are often surgically removed. Tumours that destroy the tissue in which they arise and spread to other parts of the body are described as **malignant** (see cancer).

● **tuna** ▶ A carnivorous food and game fish, sometimes called tunny, belonging to a family (*Scombridae*) found in warm seas. Its elongated robust body is generally dark above and silvery below, with a keeled tail base and finlets behind the anal and dorsal fins. The large bluefin tuna (*Thunnus thynnus*) reaches 4.3 m in length. Large quantities of tinned tuna are consumed throughout the world. Order: *Perciformes.* ▷See also albacore; skipjack; yellowfin tuna. □oceans.

● **Tunbridge Wells** ▶ (or Royal Tunbridge Wells) 51 08N 0 16E A town in SE England, in Kent. Visited for its medicinal (iron-rich) waters since the 17th century, it became a fashionable health resort. In 1909 Queen Victoria visited the town, since when it has the right to the "Royal" prefix. It is mainly residential. Population (1991): 45 155.

● **tundra** ▶ The level, virtually treeless, areas in the N hemisphere (in Eurasia and North America) lying between the most northerly region in which trees grow and the polar regions of perpetual snow and ice. Winters are long and severe with brief summers in which temperatures remain below 10°C (50°F); ▷permafrost is a feature. Vegetation is able to grow in summer and includes mosses, lichens, dwarf shrubs, herbaceous perennials, and a few stunted trees, such as willows and birches. Through freeze-thaw processes on the ground a variety of patterns can form, such as stone polygons and soil circles.

● **T'ung-chih** ▷See Tong Zhi.

● **tung oil** ▶ (or wood oil) A pale-yellow oil obtained from the seeds of the tung tree (*Aleurites fordii*; family *Euphorbiaceae*), found in China. It polymerizes spontaneously (and on heating) to a hard gel and is used in paints and varnishes.

● **tungsten** ▶ (or wolfram; W) A grey brittle metal with the highest melting point of any element. It was discovered in 1779 and is obtained from the ores wolframite ($FeWO_4$) and scheelite ($CaWO_4$) by reduction with hydrogen or carbon. It oxidizes readily when heated, forming the oxide WO_3. The metal is used extensively as filaments in electric light bulbs, as well as in television tubes, contact breakers, and X-ray tubes. It is also used in many hard alloys for high-speed cutting tools. Tungsten carbide (WC) is very hard and is used for tipping drill bits. At no 74; at wt 183.85; mp 3422 ± 20°C; bp 5555°C.

● **Tung-t'ing, Lake** ▷See Dongting, Lake.

● **Tunguska, River** ▶ Three rivers in Russia, in Siberia, comprising tributaries of the River Yenisei. These are the **Lower** (Nizhnyaya) **Tunguska**, 2690 km (1670 mi) long, the **Stony** (Podkammenaya) **Tunguska**, 1550 km (960 mi) long, and the **Upper** (Verkhnyaya) **Tunguska**, the lower course of the River Angara. In June, 1908, in the Tunguska Valley an enormous explosion occurred, known as the **Tunguska Event**. Equivalent to the explosion of an atomic bomb, it was thought to have been caused by the impact of the nucleus of a comet or an asteroid. It caused widespread devastation and a massive shock wave.

● **tunicate** ▶ A small marine animal belonging to the phylum (or subphylum) *Urochordata* (or *Tunicata*; about 2000 species). Tunicates are cylindrical, spherical, or irregular in shape, ranging from several millimetres to over 30 cm in size. They have a saclike cellulose tunic covering the body; water is drawn in through a siphon at the top and expelled through a second siphon. Food particles are filtered out and propelled along flagellated grooves to the mouth. Individuals are hermaphrodite and produce free-swimming tadpole-like larvae that show the major characteristics of all ▷chordates. They subsequently undergo metamorphosis, losing their chordate features and becoming adults. The class *Larvacea* retain their larval characteristics throughout life. Sea squirts (class *Ascidacea*) live attached to rocks, etc., singly or in colonies, while the salps (class *Thaliacea*) float in the sea, sometimes as chains of several hundred individuals.

● **tuning fork** ▶ A two-pronged metal fork that vibrates at a fixed frequency when struck. It is used by musicians to verify ▷pitch. Elec-

trically maintained tuning forks, operated by an electromagnet, are also used in scientific experiments.

● **Tunis** ▶ (Arabic name: Tunus) 36 48N 10 13E The capital of Tunisia, on the Gulf of Tunis. It was developed by the Arabs in the 7th century AD. It came under French rule in the late 19th century, and became the capital on independence in 1956. The Islamic university was founded in 1960. Industries include chemicals, lead smelting, and textiles. Population (1994): 674 100.

● **Tunisia, Republic of** ▶ (Arabic name: al-Jumhuriyah at-Tunisiyah) A small country in N Africa, bordering on the Mediterranean Sea. Its narrow coastal zone, where over half the total population live, extends into desert in the S and rises to uplands in the N. The population is largely Arabic with a Berber minority.

Economy: predominantly agricultural, with wheat, olive oil, citrus fruits, dates, and wine among the chief products; livestock, including sheep, cattle, and goats, is also important. Mining is a major source of revenue and Tunisia is one of the world's largest producers of phosphates. Oil reserves were discovered in 1964 and exploitation began in 1972; iron ore and lead are also mined. Manufacturing industry is based largely on processing the local raw materials and includes oil refining, cement, and steel processing. Fine beaches and notable architecture contribute to Tunisia's popularity with tourists. There is a large foreign debt.

History: first settled by the Phoenicians, the region developed into the empire of Carthage and was later absorbed into the Roman Empire, becoming "the granary of Rome." Under the dynasty of the Berber Hafsids (1207–1574) it became powerful. During the 19th century Tunisia's strategic importance aroused European interest and in 1883 it became a French protectorate. It was the scene of fierce fighting in World War II and gained independence from France (1956) following nationalist agitation. Habib ▷Bourguiba became Tunisia's first president the following year; in 1987 he was replaced in a bloodless coup by Zine al-Abidine Ben Ali. Elections in 1989 and 1994 were won by President Ben Ali and his supporters.

Republic of Tunisia

Head of state	President Zine al-Abidine Ben Ali
Official religion	Islam
Official language	Arabic; French is widely spoken
Official currency	Tunisian dinar of 1000 millimes
Area	164 150 sq km (63 362 sq mi)
Population (1997 est)	9 218 000
Capital	Tunis

● **tunnel effect** ▶ The passage of an electron or other particle through a potential barrier when, according to classical mechanics, it has insufficient energy to do so. It is explained by ▷wave mechanics on the basis that the electron is not completely localized in space, part of the energy of the associated wave being able to tunnel through the barrier. The effect has a negligible probability in large-scale systems, but a finite probability in microscopic systems. It is the basis of some radioactive decay processes and is made use of in the **tunnel diode**, a semiconductor device that has a negative resistance over part of its operating range. It was invented by Leo ▷Esaki.

● **tunnels** ▶ Underground passages for roads, railways, sewers, or aqueducts for power stations. Tunnels through rock are formed by first drilling holes for explosive, blasting out the rock, removing the debris, and then lining the inside of the tunnel. Tunnelling through softer substances requires special techniques: a tunnelling shield with a diameter slightly larger than that of the finished tunnel is forced into the ground by hydraulic piston jacks, the earth inside the shield is removed, and the tunnel is then lined, often with concrete sections. ▷See also Channel tunnel; Simplon Pass; Mont Blanc.

● **Tunney, Gene** ▶ (James Joseph T.; 1897–1978) US boxer, who was world heavyweight champion from 1926 to 1928, when he retired. He lost only 1 of his 77 professional bouts, in 1922.

● **tunny** ▷See tuna.

● **Tupac Amarú** ▶ (José Gabriel Condorcanqui; ?1742–81) Peruvian revolutionary. A direct descendant of the last Inca emperor, he led an unsuccessful Indian revolt against Spanish rule in 1780 and was executed. The Tupamaros, the 20th-century South American urban guerrillas, derived their name from his.

● **tupelo** ▸ A tree of the genus *Nyssa* (c. 10 species), native to swampy regions of E North America, the Himalayas, and E Asia. The North American black tupelo (*N. sylvatica*), also called black gum, sour gum, or pepperidge, is grown as an ornamental, having scarlet autumn foliage, and also yields a useful wood. The sour tupelo, or ogeeche lime (*N. ogeche*), also of E North America, produces edible fruits and its flowers are a good source of honey. The water tupelo, or cotton gum (*N. aquatica*), grows in swamps of the SE USA. Family: *Nyssaceae*.

● **Tupi** ▸ A group of South American Indian peoples and languages including the ▷Guarani. They are mainly a tropical rainforest people who practise slash and burn agriculture. They also fish in the rivers and off the coast where their villages are located. In some areas, these were fortified against warfare. Cannibalism was common. Culture varied according to region. Religion emphasized nature spirits and the "Grandfather Cult," associated with thunder, often led to migrations in search of a promised paradise.

● **Tupolev, Andrei Nikolaievich** ▸ (1888–1972) Soviet designer of the first supersonic passenger aircraft, the TU-144, tested in 1969. He also designed supersonic bombers, such as the TU-22, and swing-wing bombers. His TU-104, first produced in 1955, was one of the first passenger jet aircraft.

● **turaco** ▸ (*or* touraco) A brightly coloured arboreal bird belonging to a family (*Musophagidae*; 18 species) occurring in Africa. 35–70 cm long, turacos have short rounded wings, a short down-curved bill, and are often crested. Most species have a greenish plumage. They feed on fruit and insects. Order: *Cuculiformes* (cuckoos and turacos).

● **turbine** ▸ A device in which a moving fluid drives a wheel or motor, converting the kinetic energy of the fluid into mechanical energy. In its simplest form it is known as a **water wheel**, which has been in use since ancient times to drive mills, pumps, etc. The principle of the water wheel forms the basis of the hydraulic turbine, used in the generation of ▷hydroelectric power. The most widely used types are the Pelton wheel, patented in 1889 by Lester Allen Pelton (1829–1918), the radial Francis turbine, designed in 1849 by J. B. Francis (1815–92), and the Kaplan turbine, designed by Viktor Kaplan

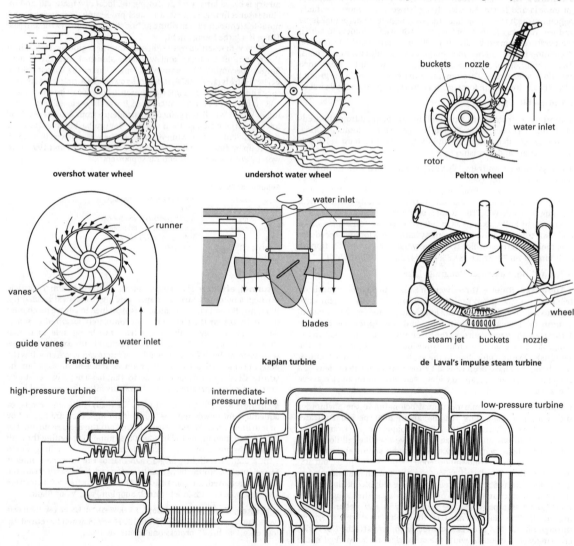

overshot water wheel

undershot water wheel

buckets nozzle

water inlet

rotor

Pelton wheel

runner

vanes

guide vanes   water inlet

Francis turbine

water inlet

blades

Kaplan turbine

wheel

steam jet   buckets   nozzle

de Laval's impulse steam turbine

high-pressure turbine

intermediate-pressure turbine

low-pressure turbine

multistage steam turbine

turbine

(1876–1937). The Pelton wheel, consisting of a ring of buckets or bucket-shaped vanes arranged around the periphery of a wheel, is known as an **impulse turbine** as it is only the impulse of the water that makes the wheel turn. The Francis turbine, with its outer ring of stationary guide vanes and inner ring of curved vanes on the surface of one side of the wheel, is a **reaction turbine**; part of the energy is derived from the impulse of the water and part from the reaction between the water and the blades.

The **steam turbine** was invented in the 1st century AD by ▷Hero of Alexandria. However, the first practical turbine to be driven by steam was a reaction device with several rows of turbine wheels (enabling the energy of the expanding steam to be utilized in stages) invented in 1884 by Sir Charles ▷Parsons. An impulse turbine using several steam nozzles was invented by Carl de Laval (1845–1913) in the 1890s. Since the beginning of the 20th century steam turbines based on these designs have replaced the ▷steam engine as the prime mover in ▷power stations. ▷*See also* gas turbine.

● **turbocharger** ► A device that raises the pressure of the air fed to an internal-combustion engine to increase the power delivered. If it is driven by the engine or an electric motor it is known as a **supercharger**. If it is driven by a turbine in the exhaust-gas stream, it is a turbocharger.

● **turbofan** ▷*See* □jet engine.

● **turbot** ► A ▷flatfish, *Scophthalmus maximus*, that occurs off European shores down to 70 m and sometimes in brackish water. It has a broad circular body, up to 1 m long, which is usually grey-brown on the upper (left) side and whitish underneath. It is a valuable food fish. Family: *Bothidae*.

● **turbulence** ► Any random irregularity in the distribution of velocity or pressure in a fluid. Most flows of rivers and winds are turbulent and turbulence in the atmosphere affects aircraft. Turbulence also causes the laminar layers of flow around an irregular object, or a smooth object at high velocities, to be disturbed, creating a sharp increase in drag. It is to avoid turbulent flow that such objects as aerofoils are streamlined (*see* streamlining; aerodynamics). In some cases turbulence is desirable; in the combustion chamber of a petrol or Diesel engine the designer seeks to create turbulence to improve mixing of the fuel and air.

● **Turenne, Henri de la Tour d'Auvergne, Vicomte de** ► (1611–75) French marshal, who made his name in the ▷Thirty Years' War. At the outbreak (1649) of the rebellion against Mazarin (*see* Fronde) he supported the rebels, who were led by his rival ▷Condé, but in 1652, after transferring his loyalties to the crown, he received a royal command and by 1653 had brilliantly suppressed the revolt. In 1658, at the battle of the Dunes, he again defeated Condé, who now held a Spanish command. He subsequently fought in the War of ▷Devolution (1667–68) and the third ▷Dutch War (1672–75), dying at Sasbach. He was admired by Napoleon.

● **Turfan Depression** ▷*See* Tulufan Depression.

● **Turgenev, Ivan** ► (1818–83) Russian novelist. His criticism of the Russian social system in his *Sportsman's Sketches* (1852) led indirectly to his brief imprisonment and confinement to his family estate at Spasskoye. His later works, of which the best known are the novel *Fathers and Sons* (1862) and the long story *The Torrents of Spring* (1872), are noted for their analysis of social trends. He also wrote poetry and plays, notably *A Month in the Country* (published 1870). A lifelong admirer of Western society, he went into self-imposed exile in Baden Baden (1862–70) and Paris (1871–83), where he was befriended by many European writers.

● **Turgot, Anne Robert Jacques, Baron de l'Aulne** ► (1727–81) French economist, who served under Louis XV and XVI. Educated at the Sorbonne, he was one of the ▷Physiocrats and an advocate of ▷laissez-faire. He became comptroller general in 1774. There was great opposition to his reforms, especially the Six Edicts, which included the abolition of forced labour, and he was dismissed in 1776.

● **Turin** ► (Italian name: Torino) 45 04N 7 40E A city in NW Italy, the capital of Piedmont on the River Po. Dating from Roman times, it was associated with the House of Savoy during the middle ages. It was the first capital (1861–65) of united Italy. Turin has an ancient university (1404), a 15th-century cathedral, a 17th-century palace, and other notable buildings. It is a centre of commerce and industry and is important for the production of motor vehicles. Other industries include engineering, publishing, and the manufacture of textiles, paper, and leather goods. Chocolate and wine are also produced. ▷*See also* Shroud of Turin. Population (1996 est): 923 106.

● **Turing machine** ► A hypothetical computing machine used to determine whether a particular mathematical problem can be solved by a computation procedure (algorithm). It is postulated that the machine has an infinite tape that stores characters in a number of discrete locations. The machine goes through a procedure of scanning and altering the characters, regarded as a series of active states. If the problem is soluble, the machine settles in a passive state, in which the tape contains the solution. The concept was developed in 1936 by Alan Mathison Turing (1912–54) and others and represented an important advance in computer logic.

● **Turishcheva, Ludmilla** ► (1952–　) Soviet gymnast, who was world champion in 1970 and won the combined exercises competition in the 1972 Olympic Games.

● **Turkana, Lake** ► (name until 1979: Lake Rudolf) A lake in Kenya and Ethiopia. Fish and birds abound here and, since it has no outlet, it has become increasingly saline through evaporation. Significant fossil finds have been made here by Richard Leakey. Area: about 6405 sq km (2473 sq mi).

● **Turkestan** ▷*See* Turkistan.

● **turkey** ► A large terrestrial bird belonging to a family (*Meleagrididae*; 2 species) native to North and Central American woodlands. Wild turkeys reach 130 cm in length and have green-bronze plumage, a warty red neck, and a long fleshy bill ornament and throat wattle. They feed on seeds and insects. The common turkey (*Meleagra gallopavo*), first domesticated by Mexican Indians, was brought to Europe in the 16th century and is now farmed for its flesh. Order: *Galliformes* (pheasants, turkeys, etc.).

● **Turkey, Republic of** ► A country in the Middle East. The large Asian area, Anatolia, lies between the Mediterranean Sea and the Black Sea. The small European area, Thrace (part of ancient ▷Thrace), is bordered by Greece and Bulgaria. Anatolia consists of a central plateau surrounded by mountains, the Pontic Mountains in the N and the ▷Taurus Mountains in the S. The plateau is semiarid and contains several shallow salt lakes. The high E range contains Mount ▷Ararat. The coastal areas are the most populous. Minority population groups include Kurds, Arabs, Greeks, Circassians, Georgians, Armenians, Lazes, and Jews; 98% of the population is Muslim.

Economy: mainly agricultural. Wheat, barley, sugar beet, potatoes, and rice are grown in the interior, and cotton, tobacco, and citrus fruit are grown for export around the coast. Cattle, sheep, and goats are kept for skins, wool, and mohair, which are exported. Copper, chromium, borax, coal, bauxite, and oil are produced, although the country's large mineral deposits are not greatly exploited. The main industries are motor vehicles, iron and steel, cement, glass, textiles, and pharmaceuticals. Machinery, oil and petroleum products, and electrical goods are imported, chiefly from W Europe and the USA. Turkey is an associate member of the EU. Many Turks work in Europe, mainly in Germany, for long periods at a time.

History: Anatolia, formerly known as ▷Asia Minor, was dominated by the ▷Seljuqs (1055–1243) and later became the core of the ▷Ottoman Empire (c. 1300–1922). Under Kemal ▷Atatürk, who ruled as a virtual dictator, the new Republic of Turkey (declared 1923) was rapidly westernized; religious orders were abolished and Islam was disestablished; polygamy was forbidden and women were enfranchised; the Arabic alphabet was replaced by the Roman; and relations with W Europe became closer. Economic problems were tackled by the establishment of new industries under state ownership. After the death of Kemal (1938) and World War II, in which Turkey was neutral until finally siding with the Allies in 1945, it became less stable politically, although more democratic. Turkey became a member of NATO in 1952. The Democratic Party, previously in opposition, came to power in 1950 but grew increasingly reactionary; unrest increased until a military coup took place in 1960. The army again intervened in 1971, when martial law was imposed (until 1973). Troubles between Kurds and Turks led to the reimposition of martial law in several provinces. Relations with Greece have been a further problem; apart from rivalry over Cyprus, which almost resulted in war in 1974, when the island was invaded by Turkish troops, there has been friction since 1976 over Turkey's exploration for oil in the Aegean Sea. There has also been tension with Bulgaria over the latter's treatment of ethnic Turks. A military coup in 1980, led by Gen Kenan Evren, overthrew the government of Suleiman Demirel (1924–). Evren became head of state and a new constitution was introduced in 1982. Turgut Özal (1927–93) was elected prime minister in 1983 and became president in 1989. With the end of the state of emergency Demirel returned to power in 1991; he became president in 1993, on the election of Tansu Çiller as Turkey's first woman prime minister. The 1990s saw a growing challenge to Turkey's secular constitution from Muslim fundamentalists; in 1996 an alliance of Islamists and conservatives came to power, led by Necmettin Erbakan. When this government resigned under military pressure in 1997 Mesult Yilmaz formed a secularist coalition. Following the collapse (1999) of this coalition, the veteran leftist Bulent Ecevit formed a government. In 1987 Turkey applied to join the EC (now the EU), but this application has been frozen since 1989, owing to concern over Turkey's human-rights record. There has been fighting in the SE between Kurdish separatist guerrillas and government troops since 1984. In August, 1999 the NW was hit by Turkey's worst earthquake for 60 years; over 17 000 died and 200 000 were made homeless.

Republic of Turkey

Head of state	President Suleiman Demirel
Official language	Turkish; Kurdish and Arabic are also spoken
Official currency	Turkish lira of 100 kurus
Area	779 452 sq km (330 883 sq mi)
Population (1998 est)	64 567 000
Capital	Ankara

● **Turkic languages** ▶ A group of languages of the ▷Altaic language family, related to ▷Mongolian and ▷Manchu-Tungus. Spoken by over 66 million people, the languages are spread over a geographical area extending from Turkey to Siberia. Originally written in the Arabic script in the 9th century, the languages are now written in the ▷Cyrillic alphabet in the republics of the former Soviet Union and in Latin script in Turkey. Phonological processes are characterized by vowel harmony and morphological processes by agglutination.

● **Turkish** ▶ A ▷Turkic language, spoken mainly in Turkey. Since 1929 it has been written in a modified Latin alphabet, replacing Arabic script. Its grammatical system is based on the use of suffixes.

● **Turkish cat** ▶ A breed of long-haired cat originating from Turkey. They have long bodies, white coats with auburn markings on the face and an auburn tail, and amber-coloured eyes. Unusually for cats, they are fond of swimming.

● **Turkistan** ▶ (or Turkestan) A region of central Asia, now comprising the Xinjiang Uygur AR of China, Kazakhstan, Turkmenistan, Tadzhikistan, Kirgizstan, and Uzbekistan. It is a historic route of travel, migration, and invasion between Asia and Europe. The W was ruled by the Persians from the 6th century BC, Islam from the 7th century AD, and the Russians from the 18th century; the E was long disputed between Chinese dynasties and nomadic tribes.

● **Turkmen** ▶ (or Turkoman) A people of SW Asia speaking a language of the ▷Turkic language group (it is the official language of Turkmenistan). The majority live as settled farmers in Turkmenistan, but groups in Iran, Afghanistan, E Turkey, N Syria, and N Iraq retain their traditional nomadic existence. Rug making is still an important craft. The main social division is between those engaged in agriculture and the more prestigious livestock farming. They are Sunni Muslims.

● **Turkmenistan, Republic of** ▶ A republic in central Asia, lying E of the Caspian Sea. It is low lying and mainly comprises deserts, including the ▷Kara Kum, and semi desert plains. Most of the population (66% of which are Turkmen) are concentrated around oases.

There is a large ethnic Russian minority, most of whom have dual citizenship.

Economy: the country is economically viable owing to the large deposits of oil and natural gas in the Caspian plains. Gas is now exported by pipeline to Europe and Turkey. Other mineral resources include coal, sulphur, and lead. Agriculture is the main occupation; cotton, maize, and fruit are grown in the oases and irrigated areas, while livestock, including camels and karakul sheep, are raised in the arid regions. There is some heavy industry, including metals and chemicals. Other products include textiles, carpets, and the traditional silk.

History: Turkmenistan did not exist as a unified state prior to its gradual conquest by Russia during the 19th century. Resistance to Russian rule culminated in full-scale rebellions in 1916 and 1918–19 but the Red Army had gained control by 1920. The Turkmen SSR was established in 1924 and became part of the Soviet Union the following year. With the collapse of the Soviet Union the republic became independent as Turkmenistan in 1991. Power has remained in the hands of the former Communist Party and President Saparmurad Niyazov, whose executive powers were extended to the point of virtual dictatorship by the new constitution of 1992. State harrassment has prevented the emergence of an effective opposition or a free press. Turkmenistan is a member of the Commonwealth of Independent States and continues to have a close relationship with Russia, with which it maintains joint armed forces.

Republic of Turkmenistan

Head of state	President Saparmurad Niyazov
Official language	Turkmen
Official currency	manat of 100 tenesi
Area	488 100 sq km (186 400 sq mi)
Population (1998 est)	4 731 000
Capital	Ashkhabad

● **Turks and Caicos Islands** ▶ A UK overseas territory consisting of a series of over 30 islands in the Atlantic Ocean, to the SE of the Bahamas. The most important are Grand Turk, Grand Caicos, and Salt Cay. Most of the inhabitants are of African descent.

Economy: mainly based on fishing and offshore finance; exports include conchs, conch shells, crawfish, salt, and fishmeal. Tourism is now an important source of revenue.

History: the islands were discovered by the Spanish in 1512, but remained uninhabited until 1678, when a Bermudan salt-panning industry was set up. A dependency of Jamaica (1874–1959), they became a crown colony after the dissolution of the Federation of the West Indies in 1962, and gained internal self-government in 1976. Allegations of corruption led to power being transferred to the governor and an advisory council from 1986 to 1988. Official language: English. Official currency: US dollar of 100 cents. Area: 430 sq km (192 sq mi). Population (1999 est): 23 000. Capital: Grand Turk.

● **Turku** ▶ (Swedish name: Åbo) 60 27N 22 15E A seaport and third largest city in Finland, on the Gulf of Bothnia. Capital of Finland until 1812, it has Finnish (1920) and Swedish (1917) universities. Population (1997 est): 166 929.

● **turmeric** ▶ A perennial herbaceous plant, *Curcuma longa*, native to S India and Indonesia and cultivated for its underground rhizomes. It has narrow leaves, 30–45 cm long, and bears yellow flowers in dense heads, 10–18 cm long. The rhizomes are boiled and dried in the sun for 5–7 days, then polished and usually sold in ground form. Turmeric is used as a spice and as a yellow dye. Family: *Zingiberaceae*.

● **Turner, Joseph Mallord William** ▶ (1775–1851) British landscape and marine painter, born in London, the son of a barber. After studying at the Royal Academy schools and painting many watercolours, he achieved success in the late 1790s with his landscapes in oil. In 1802 he made the first of several continental tours, which provided him with such scenic subjects as the Alps, Venice, and Rome. While supervising the publication of his *Liber Studiorum* (1807–19), a series of engravings based on his works, his style evolved from the Dutch landscape tradition and the classicism of the landscapists ▷Poussin and ▷Claude Lorraine into a romantic vision of colour,

Joseph Mallord William Turner ▶ Lithograph of the painter after a drawing (1800) by George Dance.

light, and weather: such late paintings as *Rain, Steam, and Speed* (National Gallery) and *Interior at Petworth* (Tate Gallery) anticipate French ▷impressionism. He bequeathed most of his works to the nation.

● **Turner, Nat** ▶ (1800–31) US rebel slave, who led the only substantial US slave revolt. The so-called **Turner's Insurrection** was an attempt by 75 slaves to capture a Virginian armoury. More than 50 whites died before the rebels were captured and executed. The resulting uneasiness in the South led to repressive antislave legislation.

● **Turner, Tina** ▶ (Annie Mae Bullock; 1938–　) US rock and soul singer. Born in Nutbush, Tennessee, she married Ike Turner in 1956 and with him recorded such hits as "River Deep, Mountain High" (1966) and "Nutbush City Limits" (1973). After the collapse of this marriage in 1976 her career stalled until the 1980s, when she achieved huge success with such solo albums as *Private Dancer* (1984).

● **Turner Prize** ▶ An annual prize of £20,000 for work in the visual arts by a British artist under the age of 50. First presented in 1984, it is administered by the Patrons of New Art in association with the Tate Galleries and sponsored by Channel 4 television. Past winners have included Gilbert and George (1986) and Damien Hirst (1995).

● **turnip** ▶ A biennial plant, ▷*Brassica rapa*, probably native to Asia and widely cultivated for its thick fleshy root, which is used as a vegetable. An erect branching stem, up to 1 m high, grows out of the basal leaf rosette in the plant's second season and produces bright-yellow flowers. Turnips are usually harvested in the first season. Family: ▷*Cruciferae*.

● **turnover tax** ▶ A tax levied whenever goods are exchanged or services provided, according to the increased value of the goods or services at each stage. The consumer pays the accumulated tax. Value-added tax is an example.

● **turnstone** ▶ A small ▷plover, *Arenaria interpres*, that breeds around Arctic coasts and migrates to the S hemisphere to winter. 20 cm long, it has a black-and-brown upper plumage, becoming tortoise-shell in summer, and white underparts. Turnstones have short black bills used to turn over pebbles and shells in search of molluscs, small fish, and sandhoppers.

● **turpentine** ▶ An oily liquid extracted from pine resin. Its main constituent is pinene ($C_{10}H_{16}$); it is used as a solvent for paints.

● **turpentine tree** ▶ One of several trees yielding a viscous resin. The Australian turpentine tree (*Syncarpia glomuliferae*) grows to about 45 m and has deeply furrowed bark. The timber, which is durable and resistant to fire and wood-boring ▷shipworms, is used to construct piers, ships, etc. The brush turpentine tree (*S. leptopetala*) is smaller. Family: *Myrtaceae*. The tropical African tree *Copaifera mopane* (family *Leguminosae*) is also called turpentine tree.

● **Turpin, Dick** ▶ (1706–39) British highwayman. He was hanged at York for murder and horse stealing. The story of his ride from London

to York on his horse Black Bess, popularized in Harrison Ainsworth's novel *Rookwood* (1834), is probably based on a much older legend.

● **turquoise** ▶ An opaque greenish-blue mineral used as a gem. It consists of a basic aluminium phosphate, traces of copper providing the colour. Birthstone for December.

● **turtle** ▶ An aquatic reptile belonging to the order ▷Chelonia, which also includes ▷tortoises and ▷terrapins. 10–200 cm long, turtles have broad paddle-like flippers and a streamlined body and occur in most seas, often migrating long distances to lay eggs on traditional nesting beaches. They are graceful and swift swimmers but clumsy on land. Their diet consists of worms, snails, crustaceans, and fish. Some turtles live in fresh water. ▷*See also* green turtle; leatherback turtle; snake-necked turtle; soft-shelled turtle.

● **turtle dove** ▶ A small slender dove, *Streptopelia turtur*, occurring in S Europe and N Africa, visiting N Europe in the summer. 26 cm long, it has a chequered red-brown back, grey wings, a pink breast, a black-and-white striped neck patch, and a long white-tipped tail. It feeds on seeds. Family: *Columbidae* (pigeons).

● **Tuscan order** ▷*See* orders of architecture.

● **Tuscany** ▶ (Italian name: Toscana) A region in N central Italy, consisting of hills and mountains with coastal lowlands in the W. It is a mainly agricultural region producing cereals, wines (Chianti), olives, and fruit. Tourists are attracted by the scenery and the cultural centres of Florence, Siena, and Pisa. The major manufacturing industries are iron, steel, and shipbuilding. Lignite, iron, mercury, salt, borax, and marble are mined. Area: 22 989 sq km (8876 sq mi). Population (1996 est): 3 523 238. Capital: Florence.

● **Tusculum** ▶ An ancient city of central Italy, near modern Frascati. A rival of ▷Rome before about 480 BC but later a staunch ally, Tusculum was granted Roman citizenship in 381 BC. In the 1st century BC it became a fashionable resort: ▷Lucullus, ▷Maecenas, and ▷Cicero owned villas nearby.

● **tusk** ▶ In certain mammals, a greatly elongated incisor or canine tooth that is made of ▷ivory. It may be used as a weapon but in some animals has no obvious function. Elephants have a pair of tusks developed from the upper incisors: they are present in both sexes of the African elephant but only in male Indian elephants. In the walrus both sexes have a pair of tusks, developed from the upper canines, which may function as ice picks. Two pairs of tusks develop from the upper incisors and canines in members of the pig family, most conspicuously in the males; they are especially prominent in the ▷babirusa and ▷warthog. Narwhals have a single straight spirally twisted tusk that develops from the left upper tooth (this whale has only two teeth) and is usually present only in males.

● **tusk shell** ▶ A marine ▷mollusc of the class *Scaphopoda* (about 200 species), also called tooth shell. The common tusk shell (*Dentalium entale*) grows to 5 cm; its shell is tusk-shaped and open at both ends and it lives partly buried in sand. The mollusc has a digging foot and tentacles around the mouth for collecting microscopic plants and animals.

● **Tussaud, Marie** ▶ (Marie Grosholtz; 1761–1850) Swiss wax modeller. Born in Strasbourg, she grew up in Bern before moving to Paris, where she learnt modelling from her uncle, Philip Curtius. After he was guillotined (1794), she inherited his business and during the French Revolution was forced to model the severed heads of Louis XVI and Marie Antoinette. Her marriage (1795) to François Tussaud, a French engineer, failed and in 1802 she fled to London. There, in 1835, she established a permanent exhibition of her work, which remains a major tourist attraction. It moved to its present premises in 1884. Features include the "Chamber of Horrors," which Mme Tussaud initiated, and the panoramic "Spirit of London" (1993).

● **tussock moth** ▶ A moth belonging to the family *Lymantriidae*, occurring in both the Old and New Worlds and including the vapourers, tussocks, and ▷gypsy moths. The caterpillars, cocoons, and adults are typically hairy, frequently causing skin irritation and swelling if handled. Some can be economic pests.

● **Tutankhamen** ▶ King of Egypt (c. 1361–1352 BC) of the 18th dynasty. Tutankhamen, perhaps Akhenaton's son, became king at the

Tutankhamen ▶ The gold coffer of the Egyptian king discovered in 1922.

age of 11 after the brief reign of ▷Akhenaton's immediate successor. He abandoned Akhenaton's worship of the sun-god Aton, reinstating that of ▷Amon and transferring the capital once more to Thebes. His splendid and elaborate tomb, discovered by Howard ▷Carter in 1922, is the only Egyptian royal tomb to remain substantially intact to modern times. The beauty and craftsmanship of its contents have continued to fascinate the world.

● **Tutsi** ▷See Hutu.

● **Tutu, Desmond** ▶ (1931–) South African clergyman, noted for his tireless opposition to ▷apartheid. Ordained in 1960, he became the first Black general secretary of the South African Council of Churches (1979), Anglican Bishop of Johannesburg (1984), and Archbishop of Cape Town (1986). In 1996 he retired and was appointed head of the Truth and Reconciliation Commission set up to investigate crimes of apartheid, which presented its report in 1998. He won the Nobel Peace Prize in 1984.

● **Tutuola, Amos** ▶ (1920–) Nigerian writer. Drawing on Yoruba tribal myths and legends, he created vivid fantasies in which the real and the supernatural coexist. His works include *The Palm-Wine Drinkard* (1952), *Pauper, Brawler and Slanderer* (1987), and the short-story collection *Feather Woman of the Jungle* (1962).

● **Tuva Republic** ▶ (*or* Tyva; name until 1944: Tannu-Tuva Republic) A constituent republic of Russia. The region, in the S of the country, is mostly mountainous. Some 50% of the population comprise Tuvinians, a Turkic-speaking people, who are mainly livestock farmers. Industry is rapidly developing. Area: 170 500 sq km (65 800 sq mi). Population (2000 est): 311 000. Capital: Kizyl.

● **Tuvalu** ▶ (name until 1976: Ellice Islands) A small country in the SW Pacific Ocean. It consists of a group of nine coral islands, the main one being Funafuti. Most of the population is Polynesian.
Economy: coconut growing and fishing are the chief occupations. The only export is copra. Most foodstuffs have to be imported and the country is heavily reliant on foreign aid. About 15% of the population works abroad or at sea. Since 1993 the main source of revenue has been a multimillion-dollar deal whereby Tuvalu allows its national Internet suffix (.tv) to be used by a US television company.
History: formerly part of the Gilbert and Ellice Islands colony, it became a separate colony after a referendum in 1974 and gained independence in 1978. Tuvalu is a member of the Commonwealth of Nations. The current prime minister (from 2001) is Koloa Talake. As few of the islands rise more than 3m (11.5 ft) above sea level, their future is threatened by predicted rises in sea levels.

Tuvalu	
Head of state	Queen Elizabeth II, represented by the governor-general, Sir Tulaga Manvella
Official language	Tuvalu
Official currency	Australian dollar of 100 cents; the Tuvalu dollar is also used
Area	24 sq km (9.5 sq mi)
Population (2001 est)	11 000
Capital	Fongafale

● **Tver** ▶ (name from 1931 until 1991: Kalinin) 56 49N 35 57E A port in central Russia, on the River Volga. The city was renamed in 1931 in honour of M. I. ▷Kalinin. It is a major industrial and administrative centre, with industries that include engineering and textiles. Population (1999 est): 457 100.

● **TVP** ▷*See* texturized vegetable protein.

● **Twain, Mark** ▶ (Samuel Langhorne Clemens; 1835–1910) US novelist. He worked for four years as a steamboat pilot on the Mississippi before gaining a national reputation for his humorous journalism. After marrying and settling in Connecticut in 1870 he wrote several works based on his early life, notably *Life on the Mississippi* (1883) and his masterpiece *The Adventures of Huckleberry Finn* (1884). He became an internationally successful public lecturer, but bankruptcy and the deaths of his wife and daughter caused him much private suffering.

● **twayblade** ▶ The most common European orchid, *Listera ovata*, which grows in damp woods, meadows, etc. Up to 60 cm high, it has a pair of rounded leaves situated about half way down the stem. The flowering stalk, which is sticky with glands, carries a long head of small greenish flowers.

● **tweed** ▶ A woollen fabric, more closely woven than ▷cheviot. Hardwearing, often with a roughened surface texture, tweed is manufactured in weave patterns, such as checks, stripes, flecks, and herringbones. Coats, skirts, and suits are made from famous traditional tweeds, such as Harris and Donegal cloth. It derives its name from "tweel" a Scottish word for ▷twill.

● **Tweed, River** ▶ A river in SE Scotland and NE England. Flowing E from the Tweedsmuir Hills to the North Sea at Berwick, it forms part of the border between England and Scotland. Length: 156 km (97 mi).

● **Twelfth Day** ▷*See* Epiphany.

● **Twelve Tables** ▶ (450 BC) The earliest codification of ▷Roman law, in full known as the Law of the Twelve Tables (*Lex duodecim tabularum*). The laws were engraved on bronze tablets, which were permanently displayed in public. None of the original text survives, although fragments have been preserved in quotations. The tablets dealt with (1) proceedings preliminary to trial; (2) trial; (3) enforcing judgments; (4) rights of fathers; (5) inheritance; (6) ownership of property; (7) land law; (8) ▷trusts; (9) public law; (10) sacred law (burials etc.); (11 and 12) supplementary matters.

● **twelve-tone music** ▷*See* serialism.

● **Twickenham** ▶ A residential district in the Greater London borough of Richmond-upon-Thames, on the N bank of the River Thames. It contains the English Rugby Football Union ground and ▷Hampton Court Palace.

● **Twiggy** ▶ (Lesley Hornby; 1949–   ) British model and occasional actress and singer. Her sticklike figure, accentuated by the miniskirts and other fashions of the era, made her an icon of "Swinging Sixties" London in the later 1960s. Her films include *The Boy Friend* (1971). Having married Leigh Lawson in 1988, she is now known as Twiggy (or Lesley) Lawson.

● **twill** ▶ Any woven fabric with a diagonal rib, produced by varying the regular weave of plain cloth (*see* weaving); herringbone is a common variation. Twilled fabrics are much used for making suits and trousers. ▷*See also* tweed.

● **twins** ▶ Two individuals born from the same pregnancy: 1 in 83 human pregnancies results in twins. **Identical** (monozygotic) **twins** are produced when a fertilized egg splits into two and develops as two fetuses of the same sex; such twins are difficult to tell apart and often have an emotional affinity. Because they are genetically identical, studies of monozygotic twins have provided much valuable information on the relative effects of inheritance and environment on human development. More commonly, **fraternal** (dizygotic) **twins** are produced when two eggs are fertilized at the same time; they may be of different sexes and are no more alike than other siblings. ▷*See also* Siamese twins.

● **Two Thousand Guineas** ▶ A flat race for three-year-old horses, run each spring at Newmarket over the Rowley Mile course. An English ▷Classic, it was instituted in 1809.

● **Tyburn** ▶ A stream in SE England, in London. It now flows underground for its entire length from South Hampstead to the River Thames at Vauxhall. The London gallows, known as the Tyburn Tree (1571–1759), stood at the W end of Oxford Street (formerly Tyburn Road) on the site now occupied by Marble Arch. The present Park Lane, which runs from Marble Arch to Hyde Park Corner, was formerly called Tyburn Lane.

● **Tyche** ▶ A Greek goddess personifying fortune, daughter of Oceanus or Zeus and Tethys. She is identical with the Roman ▷Fortuna.

● **Tyler, John** ▶ (1790–1862) US statesman; president (1841–45). A planter from Virginia, he had proslavery sympathies and defended ▷states' rights, which lost him the support of his cabinet. His government annexed Texas in 1844.

● **Tyler, Wat** ▶ (d. 1381) English rebel, who led the Kentish peasants during the ▷Peasants' Revolt (1381). He was the peasants' most influential spokesman until his murder by the (Lord) Mayor of London and other royalists, during negotiations with Richard II at Smithfield.

● **Tylor, Sir Edward Burnett** ▶ (1832–1917) British anthropologist. The first professor of anthropology at Oxford (1896) and the foremost 19th-century British anthropologist, Tylor developed his interest in the subject when he visited Mexico with the US ethnologist Henry Chrysty. His *Primitive Culture: Researches into the Development of Mythology, Philosophy, Religion, Language, Art, and Custom* (1871) became the standard work on anthropology.

● **Tyndale, William** ▶ (c. 1494–1536) English biblical translator. His influential translation of the New Testament, begun at Cologne in 1525 and completed at Worms, was a major source of the later Authorized or King James Version. In 1520 he published a translation of the Pentateuch. Accused of heresy, he was taken by imperial officers at Antwerp in 1535 and strangled and burned at Vilvorde, Belgium.

● **Tyndall, John** ▶ (1820–93) Irish physicist, who in 1869 discovered the scattering of light by microscopic particles, such as those in dust and colloids. Because the scattered intensity is related to the fourth power of the wavelength, blue light is more strongly scattered than red (**Tyndall effect**), which explains why the sky appears blue. Tyndall also showed that the air contains microorganisms, which helped to refute the theory of spontaneous generation of fungi, etc.

● **Tyne, River** ▶ A river in N England. Flowing E from the SW Cheviot Hills to the North Sea at Tynemouth, it passes through Newcastle, Gateshead, and Jarrow. Length: 48 km (30 mi).

● **Tyne and Wear** ▶ A metropolitan county of NE England, created in 1974 from SE Northumberland and NE Durham. In 1986 the county council was abolished and administrative powers passed to the unitary authorities of Newcastle upon Tyne, North Tyneside, Gateshead, South Tyneside, and Sunderland. It was the first major industrial region in Great Britain, developing long before the industrial revolution. Industries grew up along the River Tyne allied to the large coalfields. In the 19th century most of the region became industrialized; the development of the shipyards was especially important. During the Depression of the 1930s and the recession of the 1980s it suffered severely due to its dependence on heavy industry. The whole county is now designated a special development area with government financial assistance for firms; over the past 15 years there has been considerable diversification of industry. Area: 540 sq km (208 sq mi).

● **Tynemouth** ▶ 55 01N 1 24W A town in NE England, in North Tyneside unitary authority, Tyne and Wear, at the mouth of the River Tyne. It includes the port of North Shields and is itself a resort. Population (1991): 20 716.

● **Tynwald** ▷*See* Man, Isle of.

● **typesetting** ▶ The process by which type is assembled for ▷printing. Until the 15th century, type was cut or engraved, a page at a time, in blocks of wood or metal; with **movable type**, invented by ▷Gutenberg, each character is cast on a separate piece of metal for assembling by hand and is reusable. This was the only method available until 1884, when the American, Ottmar Mergenthaler (1854–99), invented the **Linotype** machine, on which the compositor operates a keyboard to assemble character matrices from a magazine; when a line is complete, molten type metal is pumped into the matrices to form a solid line of type. The **Monotype** system, invented in 1885 by the American, Tolbert Lanston (1844–1913), comprises separate keyboard and casting machines: as the compositor operates the keyboard, a punched paper tape is produced; when this is fed through the caster, the punched codes select characters in a matrix into which type metal is pumped to form pieces of type, which are accumulated in the correct sequence.

Since the 1950s **phototypesetting** (photosetting *or* filmsetting) has been used. In this technique images of characters are created on photographic paper or film, which is then used for ▷platemaking. The compositor operates a keyboard to produce a tape that drives the phototypesetter. In computer typesetting the data is keyboarded and automatically formatted by program into a form suitable for driving the phototypesetter. Typesetting machines are of various kinds. In some, light is flashed through a negative image of each character onto the film or paper. Modern machines produce the image by a ▷cathode-ray screen. In the 1990s the process of typesetting changed and the making of printing plates from film was superseded by ▷desk-top publishing, in which text and digitized illustrations are sent to the printer as PostScript computer files, from which the printer makes printing plates directly.

● **typewriter** ▶ A hand-operated machine for producing printed symbols. The first machine was invented in the USA in 1867 but the commercial success of the typewriter began in 1874 with the machines produced by the arms manufacturers Remington and Sons. With minor modifications this design, with the paper held in a moving platen, remained the basis of the typewriter until the advent of electric golf-ball machines, with a stationary platen, in the 1960s. These golf balls consist of rotatable spheres carrying the type in circles round their surface. Typewriters have now been virtually replaced by computer-controlled ▷word processors producing copy of print quality.

● **typhoid fever** ▶ An infectious disease of the digestive tract caused by the bacterium *Salmonella typhi*. This disease (and paratyphoid fever) are usually contracted by drinking infected water and occur predominantly in places without a clean water supply. The symptoms, which begin 10–14 days after ingesting the bacterium, include fever, headache, cough, loss of appetite, and constipation; a characteristic red rash may appear. If untreated, the patient may develop bowel haemorrhage or perforations. Treatment is by administration of fluids and the antibiotic chloramphenicol. A vaccine provides temporary immunity.

● **Typhon** ▶ In Greek mythology, a monster with a hundred heads, the son of Tartarus and Gaia. He was conquered by Zeus and buried under a volcano, usually identified as Mount Etna. His monstrous children included the ▷Chimera, the ▷Hydra, and ▷Cerberus.

● **typhoon** ► A tropical cyclone or ▷hurricane with winds above force 12 on the ▷Beaufort scale occurring in the China Sea and the W Pacific Ocean. The name is derived from a Chinese word meaning great wind.

● **typhus** ► An infection caused by certain bacteria (*see* rickettsia), which are transmitted to man by lice, fleas, mites, or ticks. There are many different forms of typhus, caused by different species of rickettsiae, but they share the symptoms of fever, headache, pains in muscles and joints, delirium, and a rash. These symptoms may be very mild throughout the disease. Treatment is with tetracycline antibiotics or chloramphenicol. Epidemic (or classical) typhus is carried by lice and was formerly very prevalent in overcrowded unhygienic conditions, with a high mortality rate. A vaccine against it is now available.

● **typography** ► 1. The art of ▷printing from movable type. 2. The aspect of printing concerned with the design and composition of printing type. Early typefaces, which imitated handwriting, belonged to three main groups: gothic (or black-letter), used by N European printers such as ▷Gutenberg and ▷Caxton; roman, introduced at Venice about 1470; and ▷italic, also Venetian, first used in 1501 (*see* incunabula). Holland dominated typefounding for most of the 16th and 17th centuries but England produced two outstanding typographers in the 18th century: William Caslon (1692–1766) and John Baskerville (1706–75). Between 1800 and 1850 the so-called modernface type designs predominated; they differed from the preceding old-face designs by their pronouncedly upright appearance and horizontal serifs (short finishing strokes on the ends of the main lines of letters). Sanserif (i.e. without serifs) typefaces originated in early 19th-century designs but only came into their own in the 1920s and 1930s through the work of the German ▷Bauhaus typographers. In England, William ▷Morris revitalized book design at the end of the 19th century, producing several archaizing but handsome typefaces for his Kelmscott Press. Influential 20th-century typographers include the Dutchman Jan van Krimpen (1892–1958), the Englishmen Eric ▷Gill and Stanley ▷Morison, and the American F. W. Goudy (1865–1947).

● **Tyr** ► (*or*, in Old English, Tiw) In Teutonic mythology, the god of war; with ▷Odin and ▷Thor, he is one of the three main Germanic gods. His name is linguistically related to *Zeus* (although Latin writers, beginning with Tacitus, identified him with Mars) and survives in *Tuesday*.

● **Tyrannosaurus** ► A huge bipedal dinosaur that lived in North America during the late Cretaceous period (about 100–65 million years ago). This animal was 15 m long, stood 6.5 m tall, and weighed up to 10 tonnes. It had a massive body with a short thick neck supporting a large head, large muscular hind limbs with clawed feet, and tiny fore legs. It was a carnivore with long dagger-like teeth but was probably quite rare and fed infrequently. Order: ▷*Saurischia*.

● **tyrant** ► In antiquity, a ruler who obtained absolute power without election or right of succession. In the Greek city states tyrants were often leading members of oligarchies who obtained popular support. Generally they ruled benevolently, conforming to established institutions, and were often significant patrons of the arts. Famous tyrants include ▷Aristagoras of Miletus, ▷Agathocles and ▷Dionysius (I) the Elder of Syracuse, ▷Phalaris of Agrigento, and ▷Pisistratus of Athens.

● **tyrant flycatcher** ► A passerine bird belonging to the New World family *Tyrannidae* (365 species), ranging from 9–27 cm in length, often with a long tail, and generally grey, brown, or olive-coloured with paler underparts. They are typically arboreal and seize flying insects. Tyrant flycatchers are very aggressive and will attack large birds that enter their breeding territories. *Compare* flycatcher.

● **Tyre** ► (modern name: Sur) 33 12N 35 11E A port in SW Lebanon, on the Mediterranean Sea. It was important to the Phoenicians for several centuries and was taken by Alexander the Great after a siege in 322 BC and by the Romans in 68 BC. The city was long held by the Crusaders but fell to Muslim forces in 1291. Population (1991 est): 70 000.

● **Tyrol** ▷*See* Tirol.

● **Tyrone** ► A historic county of W Northern Ireland, bordering on the Republic of Ireland. Its administrative powers were devolved to new district councils in 1973. It is predominantly hilly descending in the E to Lough Neagh. The Sperrin Mountains are in the N. Agriculture is important with cattle and sheep farming and the production of barley, potatoes, flax, and turnips. Small-scale manufacturing is carried out. Area: 3263 sq km (1260 sq mi).

● **Tyson, Mike** ► (1966–   ) US boxer. Born into poverty in New York City, he became the youngest ever world heavyweight champion in 1986 when he won the World Boxing Championship title. He added the World Boxing Association's title (1986) and the International Boxing Federation's title (1988) before defeat (1990) by James Douglas. In 1992 he was gaoled for rape. Following his release on parole in 1995, he regained both the WBC and WBA titles but then lost the latter to Evander Holyfield (1996). In a further contest against Holyfield (1997) he bit off part of his opponent's ear, was disqualified, and banned from the ring until 1998. In 1999 he was gaoled once more for a violent "road rage" incident, before being released on parole and under supervision.

● **Tyumen** ► 57 11N 65 29E A port in S central Russia, on the River Tura. It is a transport centre for oil and natural gas. Population (1995 est): 494 000.

● **Tyuratum** ▷*See* Baikonur.

● **Tyva** ▷*See* Tuva Republic.

● **Tzu-ch'eng** ▷*See* Zibo.

● **Tz'u-hsi** ▷*See* Zi Xi.

● **Tzu-po** ▷*See* Zibo.

● **Ubangi-Shari** ▷*See* Central African Republic.

● **Uccello, Paolo** ▶ (P. di Dono; 1397–1475) Florentine painter and craftsman. He trained in the ▷Ghiberti workshop. From 1425 to 1431 he worked in St Mark's, Venice, as master mosaicist. His frescoes for Sta Maria Novella, Florence, include the famous *Flood*, which shows his preoccupation with perspective and foreshortening. In the three paintings of the battle of San Romano, commissioned by the Medici, he combines a geometric structure with the rich decoration of the ▷international gothic style.

Paolo Uccello ▶ Detail from *The Battle of San Romano*, fought between Florence and Siena in 1432. This panel is one of a three-part series (c. 1456; Louvre, Paris).

● **Udaipur** ▶ 24 36N 73 47E A city in India, in Rajasthan. It was formerly the capital of Udaipur (*or* Mewar) princely state; its lake contains an island with a marble palace. Udaipur has chemical, asbestos, and zinc-smelting industries and a university (1962). Population (1991): 307 682.

● **Udall, Nicholas** ▶ (1505–56) English dramatist. He was headmaster of Eton College and later of Westminster School. *Ralph Roister Doister* (c. 1553), influenced by classical Roman drama, was the first full-length English comedy.

● **Udine** ▶ 46 04N 13 14E A city in NE Italy, in Friuli-Venezia Giulia. It was damaged in an earthquake in 1976. There are textile and leather industries. Population (1990): 98 322.

● **Udmurt Republic** ▶ (*or* Udmurtia) An administrative division in W central Russia. The Udmurts (formerly called Votyaks), comprising about 50% of the population, speak a Finno-Ugric language. The region has rich oil, shale, timber, and peat resources and manufactures engineering products. Cereals, flax, and some vegetables are grown. Area: 42 100 sq km (16 250 sq mi). Population (1995 est): 1 641 000. Capital: Izhevsk.

● **UEFA** ▶ (Union of European Football Associations) An Association ▷football organization founded in 1954 by the sport's governing bodies in 30 European countries; it now has 51 members. Each year UEFA organizes three major tournaments for club sides from the affiliated nations: the European Champion Clubs' Cup, a knock-out competition for the league champions of each country; the European Cup-Winners' Cup, for the winners of major cup competitions in each country; and the UEFA Cup, for leading sides not eligible for either of the other tournaments. It also organizes the European Championship, a competition for national sides held every four years.

● **Ufa** ▶ 54 45N 55 58E A city in W central Russia, the capital of the Bashkir Republic. Situated in the Ural Mountains, it has oil refineries and a large chemical industry; its university was founded in 1957. Population (1995 est): 1 094 000.

● **Uffizi** ▶ An art gallery in Florence, containing the art treasures of the Medici. Built by ▷Vasari in the 16th century to house government offices, the Uffizi was opened as a museum in 1765. The major part of its collection comprises Italian Renaissance paintings; it also includes sculpture and Flemish, Dutch, German, and French paintings.

● **UFOs** ▷*See* unidentified flying objects.

● **Uganda, Republic of** ▶ A landlocked country in East Africa. It consists chiefly of a high plateau rising to mountains, including the Ruwenzori Mountains in the W and Mount Elgon in the E, and a considerable proportion of the total area is occupied by lakes, notably Lake Victoria. The majority of the population is African, especially ▷Ganda.

Economy: chiefly agricultural, the main food crops being plantains, sugar cane, maize, millet, bananas, yams, and other tropical plants. Cash crops include coffee (the main export), tea, tobacco, and cotton; livestock is also important. There has been an increase in forestry production, almost all hardwood. Uganda's freshwater fishing industry is one of the largest in the world, and fish farming is being developed. The chief mineral resource is copper, much of which is exported to Japan. Hydroelectricity is a valuable source of power and there is some industry, including food processing, textiles, and cement. Since the late 1980s there has been steady economic growth, owing largely to an IMF recovery programme and increased foreign investment. Measures to relieve Uganda's large foreign debt were agreed in 1998.

History: the area was dominated by the kingdom of ▷Buganda from the 18th to the late 19th centuries, becoming a British protectorate in 1894. Uganda became an independent state within the British Commonwealth in 1962 and the following year a republic was established with ▷Obote as prime minister. In 1971 a military coup brought Gen Idi ▷Amin to power. His repressive regime was overthrown in 1979 by Ugandan exiles aided by Tanzanian troops. The subsequent provisional government fell in a military coup in 1980 and Obote was re-elected president. In 1985 a further military coup brought Lt Gen Tito Okello to power as head of a military council. In 1986, following virtual civil war, he was overthrown and replaced by Yoweri Museveni. A referendum in 2000 resulted in a large vote against returning to multiparty politics; however, this poll was boycotted by most opposition supporters. Rebel insurgency continues in N Uganda.

Republic of Uganda

Head of state	President Yoweri Museveni
Official language	English; Swahili and the local language Luganda are widely spoken
Official currency	Ugandan shilling of 100 cents
Area	236 860 sq km (91 343 sq mi)
Population (2001 est)	23 986 000
Capital	Kampala

● **Uganda Martyrs** ▶ A group of 22 Roman Catholic Ugandans who were executed between 1885 and 1897 on the orders of King Mwanga of Uganda; his victims included 12 pageboys who had rejected his homosexual advances. They were canonized in 1964, becoming the first African saints. Feast day: 3 June.

● **Ugarit** ▶ An ancient town on the Syrian coast (now Ras Shamra). Repeatedly destroyed and rebuilt from Neolithic times, Ugarit became a great international port between 1500 BC and its ultimate destruction about 1200. Pottery, carvings, and diplomatic correspondence recovered here bear witness to strong Mycenaean, Hittite, and Egyptian links. There were temples to ▷Baal and his father Dagon, and a set of religious texts, written in a type of alphabetic ▷cuneiform unique to Ugarit, throw light on religious cults in ancient ▷Canaan.

● **ugli** ▶ A hybrid cross between a ▷grapefruit and a ▷tangerine. The fruit resembles a small grapefruit with brownish-yellow warty skin and orange flesh. It is grown in the West Indies.

● **Uhland, (Johann) Ludwig** ▶ (1787–1862) German poet. A lawyer, he was also an active democrat. He collected folk songs, wrote historical dramas, and is noted for his popular ballads.

● **UHT** ▷See milk.

● **Uist** ▶ Two islands in NW Scotland, in the Outer Hebrides. North Uist is separated from South Uist by the island of Benbecula. Seaweed production and crofting are important.

● **Ujiji** ▶ 4 55S 29 39E A port in W Tanzania, on Lake Tanganyika. A former centre for trade in ivory and slaves, it was here Stanley found Livingstone (1871). Population (latest est): 14 000.

● **Ujjain** ▶ 23 11N 75 50E A city in India, in Madhya Pradesh. An ancient city, it was the capital of the Avanti kingdom (6th–4th centuries BC). One of the seven sacred Hindu cities, it is the scene of the 12-yearly bathing festival (Kumbh Mela). It is an agricultural trading centre with textile industries and has a university, founded in 1957. Population (1991): 366 787.

● **Ujung Pandang** ▶ (Makassar or Macassar) 5 09S 119 08E A port in central Indonesia, in SW Sulawesi. Already a flourishing port when the Portuguese arrived in the 16th century, its exports now include coffee, copra, resins, and vegetable oils. There is some manufacturing industry. Its university was established in 1956. Population (1995 est): 1 091 800.

● **UKAEA** ▷See Atomic Energy Authority.

● **ukiyo-e** ▶ (Japanese: pictures of the floating world) A Japanese art style concerned with the depiction of everyday life. It was popular among the middle classes in the 17th and 18th centuries. Favourite subjects included prostitutes, women engaged in domestic tasks, actors, etc. Ukiyo-e began as a style of painting but it is most closely associated with Japanese colour woodblock prints. The first ukiyo-e printmaker was probably Hishikawa Moronobu (c. 1618–94). The art culminated in the landscapes of ▷Hokusai and ▷Hiroshige, which influenced ▷impressionism, ▷postimpressionism, and the ▷Nabis.

● **Ukraine** ▶ A republic in SE Europe, on the Black Sea. It is a very fertile wooded region and was second only to Russia as the economically

most important of the Soviet republics. Some 96% of the population comprises Slavs, mostly Ukrainians.

Economy: there are major coalfields and iron-ore mines (including the ▷Donets Basin), resulting in the development of a large ferrous metallurgical industry. The machine-building, chemical, consumer-goods, and food industries are also important. Crops grown include wheat, sugar beet, flax, cotton, and tobacco. Ukraine's dependence on Russia for oil and raw materials contributed to its economic problems on independence. These were aggravated by reluctance to adopt reforms and severe mismanagement in the period 1991–94, which brought the economy to the brink of collapse, necessitating two changes of currency. The situation subsequently improved, owing to privatization and other reforms, foreign aid and investment, and a treaty of economic cooperation with Russia (1998).

History: the region was dominated by the Khazars from the 7th to the 9th centuries and then by the Rurik princes of Kiev. In the 13th century the Golden Horde overran the region, which subsequently came under the rule of Lithuania and, in the 16th century, Poland. In the 17th century many Ukrainians fled the harsh Polish government, becoming ▷Cossacks. Polish domination was followed by Russian rule during the later 18th century. After a national and cultural revival in the late 19th century, Ukraine declared independence in 1918 but subsequently became (1922) a constituent republic of the Soviet Union. It achieved independence following the break-up of the Soviet Union in 1991. Relations with Russia remained tense for some years, owing mainly to disputes over the possession of nuclear weapons on Ukrainian soil and the division of the Soviet Black Sea fleet. Further tensions arose over the largely Russian region of Crimea, which declared itself independent of Ukraine in 1992; Crimeans voted for dual citizenship of Russia and Ukraine in 1994. Ukraine's first postindependence governments were dominated by former communists and by the authoritarian president, Leonid Kravchuk. In 1994, however, Kravchuk was defeated in elections by the reformist Leonid Kuchma and in 1996 a new constitution consolidating democracy was adopted. Until 2002 the legislature was dominated by ex-communists, leading to persistent conflict with the presidency. In 2001 Kuchma faced demands for his resignation following allegations that he had ordered the murder of a hostile journalist.

Ukraine

Head of state	President Leonid Kuchma
Official language	Ukrainian; Russian is an official language in some regions
Official currency	hyrvna of 100 kopiykas
Area	603 700 sq km (231 990 sq mi)
Population (2001 est)	48 767 000
Capital	Kiev

● **ukulele** ▶ A small guitar, patented in Hawaii in 1917. The fingerboard of a ukulele is fretted; the four gut or nylon strings are strummed with fingers or a small plectrum. Originally used to accompany folksongs, it became popular in US jazz.

● **Ulan Bator** ▶ (or Ulaanbaatar; former name: Urga) 47 54N 106 52E The capital of the Republic of Mongolia, situated on a plateau in the N of the country. Built around a monastery, in the 17th century it developed as a centre of trade between China and Japan. It became the capital when Outer Mongolia declared its independence in 1911. It is Mongolia's main centre of industry. The Mongolian State University was founded in 1942. Population (2000 est): 691 000.

● **Ulanova, Galina** ▶ (1910–98) Russian ballet dancer. From 1928 she danced with the Leningrad Kirov Ballet, excelling in classical ballets, such as *Swan Lake* and *Giselle*, and from 1944 with the Moscow Bolshoi Ballet. She retired in 1962.

● **Ulan Ude** ▶ 51 55N 107 40E A city in SE Russia, the capital of the Buryat Republic, on the River Selenga. It is a transport centre and has boatbuilding, ship-repairing, and machinery-manufacturing industries. Population (1999 est): 371 400.

● **Ulbricht, Walter** ▶ (1893–1973) East German statesman. A Stalinist, Ulbricht rose rapidly in the Communist Party ranks. He lived in the Soviet Union during the Nazi period and after World War II was the main architect of the German Democratic Republic. He was general secretary of the Socialist Unity Party from 1950 and in 1960 became chairman of the council of state. In 1961 he erected the Berlin Wall.

● **ulcer** ▶ An inflamed eroded area of skin or mucous membrane. ▷Peptic ulcers, which occur in the digestive tract and most commonly affect the stomach and duodenum, are one of the most prevalent forms of ulcer. Ulcers also occur in the mouth—as small fungal infections—and in the intestine in inflammatory bowel disease (see colitis). Venous leg ulcers may develop in the skin, particularly around the ankles, of patients with chronic ▷varicose veins.

● **Uleåborg** ▷See Oulu.

● **Ullswater** ▶ The second largest lake in England, in central Cumbria in the Lake District. Length: 12 km (7.5 mi).

● **Ulm** ▶ 48 24N 10 00E An industrial city and port in SW Germany, in Baden-Württemberg on the River Danube. Its gothic cathedral (1377) escaped the damage of World War II. Napoleon defeated the Austrian army here in 1805 and it is the birthplace of Einstein. Population (1996 est): 115 721.

● **Ulm, Battle of** ▶ (25 September–20 October, 1805) A battle in which Napoleon with 210 000 men defeated 72 000 Austrians in Bavaria. The Austrians were taken by surprise in the rear and capitulated. Napoleon thus prevented a union between Austrian and Russian forces.

● **ulna** ▷See arm.

● **Ulster** ▶ A province and former kingdom of N Ireland. The earldom of Ulster passed to the English Crown in 1461 and during the 17th century most of the land was confiscated and given to English and Scottish settlers (see Plantation of Ireland). It was partitioned in 1921, six counties forming Northern ▷Ireland and the counties of Cavan, Donegal, and Monaghan forming the province of Ulster in the Republic of Ireland. Area (province in Irish Republic): 8013 sq km (3094 sq mi). Population (province in Irish Republic, 1996): 234 000.

● **Ulster Democratic Unionist Party** ▶ A British political party, active in Northern Ireland. A Protestant loyalist organization, it was founded in 1969 and vigorously opposes any attempt to weaken Northern Ireland's constitutional links to the UK. Parliamentary leader: Ian ▷Paisley.

● **Ulster Unionist Party** ▶ A British political party, active in Northern Ireland. A Protestant loyalist organization, it was reformed in 1974 as the Official Unionist Party. In April 1998 the party's leader David ▷Trimble was a chief architect of the Good Friday Agreement for the province, which was subsequently backed by the party's membership. It is the leading Unionist group in Northern Ireland and the largest party in the Northern Ireland Assembly elected in 1998.

● **ultramicroscope** ▶ A type of microscope, invented by ▷Zsigmondy in 1902, used to study colloidal particles in a liquid medium. A beam of light illuminates the particles from the side, the scattered light enabling the movements of the particles to be observed as flashes against a dark background (dark-field illumination).

● **Ultramontanism** ▶ (Latin: beyond the mountains, i.e. within Italy) A tendency within the Roman Catholic Church that supports the centralized power of the pope and the ▷Roman Curia as against nationalist movements, such as ▷Gallicanism, or greater independence at the diocesan level. The peak of Ultramontanism was the promulgation of papal ▷infallibility (1870).

● **ultrasonics** ▶ The study of ▷sound waves inaudible to the human ear, i.e. above about 20 000 hertz. Such waves are known as **ultrasound** and may be produced by ▷magnetostriction or by applying a rapidly alternating voltage across a ▷piezoelectric crystal. Ultrasound is used, for example, to destroy bacteria in milk, break up large molecules, and clean surfaces. In medicine, ultrasound is used both therapeutically, for example to break up kidney stones, and for diagnostic purposes (see ultrasonography).

● **ultrasonography** ▶ The use of ultrasound (see ultrasonics) to produce images of parts of the human body in medicine. An ultrasound scanner both transmits pulses of ultrasound and detects the waves as they are reflected from interior body surfaces. The information pro-

vided by the reflected ultrasound is converted into images on a cathode-ray tube. These images can be seen on a TV screen and subsequently transferred to photographic film. Ultrasonography is based on detecting the reflected waves occurring at interfaces within organs following a short pulse of ultrasound; a complete picture is built up from many such reflections. Because the procedure has no known adverse effects (unlike X-rays), it is widely used in obstetrics to detect fetal abnormalities and wrongly positioned fetuses. It is also used routinely to follow the course of a pregnancy. Wide use is also made of the technique to study the urinary tract, the bile ducts, and the vascular system. More specialized studies include **echocardiography**, in which ultrasound waves are used to monitor the heart as it beats to assess the severity of heart disease.

● **ultraviolet radiation** ▶ (UV) ▷Electromagnetic radiation the frequency of which lies between that of the violet end of the visible spectrum and ▷X-rays, i.e. between about 380 and 5 nanometres. Ultraviolet radiation is produced during arc discharges and by gas-discharge tubes (e.g. the mercury-vapour lamp). It is also produced in large quantities by the sun, although the radiation below 200 nm is absorbed by the ▷ozone layer of the atmosphere. **Ultraviolet astronomy** is concerned with the detection and analysis of UV from the sun and other celestial sources. Below 200 nm this can only be observed from rockets and satellites. For example, the International Ultraviolet Explorer (IUE), which was launched in 1978, has recorded UV from the solar system, the stars, and the galaxies and continues to do so.

● **Ulugh Beg** ▶ (1394–1449) Grandson of ▷Timur, who succeeded his father Shah Rokh as ruler of Turkistan. He made Samarkand a centre of Muslim culture and the site of a famous observatory, where he produced an important star catalogue. He was killed by his son Abd al-Latif.

● **Ulyanov, Vladimir Ilich** ▷See Lenin.

● **Ulyanovsk** ▷See Simbirsk.

● **Ulysses** ▷See Odysseus.

● **Umar** ▷See Omar.

● **Umayyads** ▶ (or Omayyads) The first dynasty of ▷caliphs, which ruled Islam from 661 to 750 AD. Their capital was Damascus. After reluctantly accepting Islam, the family obtained leading positions in the state and one of them, ▷Mu'awiyah, became caliph (661) on the death of his rival ▷Ali. The dynasty reached its peak with ▷'Abd al-Malik (reigned 685–705). The Umayyads were overthrown by a rebellion of Arabs and pious Muslims and were replaced by the ▷'Abbasids, a rival family. In Muslim Spain, an Umayyad, ▷'Abd ar-Rahman, seized power in 756 and established a dynasty that ruled until 1030.

● **Umbelliferae** ▶ (or Apiaceae) A widely distributed family of plants (2850 species), most abundant in N temperate regions. Most species are herbaceous, with much-divided leaves and umbrella-shaped heads (umbels) of tiny flowers, each usually with five petals and five sepals. The fruits are ridged, splitting into two parts when ripe. The family includes vegetables, such as the carrot, celery, and parsnip, and many culinary herbs and spices, such as angelica, caraway, chervil, coriander, dill, fennel, and parsley.

● **Umberto I** ▶ (1844–1900) King of Italy (1878–1900). He commanded with distinction in the war against the Austrians (1866). As king he led Italy into the ▷Triple Alliance with Germany and Austria (1882) and encouraged Italian colonialism in Africa. Defeat by the Ethiopians at Adowa (1896) and economic difficulties led to unrest at home and the imposition of martial law in 1898. Umberto was assassinated at Monza.

● **Umberto II** ▶ (1904–83) The last King of Italy (1946), following the abdication of his father Victor Emmanuel III. He himself was forced to abdicate after a referendum approved the establishment of republican government and he retired to Portugal as the Count of Sarre.

● **umbilical cord** ▶ The structure in mammals that connects an embryo to the ▷placenta in the womb. In humans it is about 50 cm long and contains three blood vessels (two arteries and one vein) that convey blood to and from the placenta. At birth the umbilical cord is tied off and cut; the part connected to the baby subsequently degenerates, leaving a scar on the abdomen (see navel).

● **umbrella bird** ► A fruit-eating passerine bird of the genus *Cephalopterus* of tropical American forests. Male birds have a large umbrella-shaped crest that is raised over the head during display. They also have fleshy wattles hanging from the chest—ranging from the short naked red wattle of the bare-necked umbrella bird (*C. glabriollis*) to the feather-covered pendulous wattle of the ornate umbrella bird (*C. ornatus*). Family: *Cotingidae* (*see* cotinga).

● **umbrella tree** ► A small North American tree, ▷*Magnolia tripetala*, up to 12 m high, that has umbrella-like clusters of large leaves (40 cm long) at the ends of the branches. The large flowers are creamy white with a strong scent and the fruits are scarlet. Family: *Magnoliaceae*.

● **Umbria** ► A landlocked mountainous region in central Italy. It produces cereals, vines, and olives. Hydroelectricity powers modern industries producing iron, steel, chemicals, engineering, and food products. Tourism is important. The Umbrian school of painting, which included Perugino and Raphael, was established here during the Renaissance. Area: 8456 sq km (3265 sq mi). Population (2000 est): 835 488. Capital: Perugia.

● **Umm al-Qaiwain** ▷*See* United Arab Emirates.

● **Umtali** ▷*See* Mutare.

● **Umtata** ► 31 35S 28 47E A town in SE South Africa, formerly the capital of the Transkei Republic. It has an Anglican cathedral. Population (latest est): 80 000.

● **Un-American Activities Committee** ► US House of Representatives committee established in 1935 to investigate subversive organizations in the USA. Headed by Martin Dies, the committee investigated Nazis and Fascists as well as liberals thought to have communist connections. Spurred on by Senator ▷McCarthy, it blacklisted Hollywood writers and directors and investigated government officials, notably Alger ▷Hiss. Its influence declined after 1954 and it was finally abolished in 1975.

● **Unamuno y Jugo, Miguel de** ► (1864–1936) Spanish writer and philosopher, of Basque parentage. Unamuno's chief philosophical work, *The Tragic Sense of Life* (1913), reflects the influence of ▷Kant, ▷Hegel, and ▷Kierkegaard. His works tackle the themes of faith, free will, the immortality of the soul, and the struggle for moral integrity.

● **uncertainty principle** ▷*See* Heisenberg uncertainty principle.

● **Uncle Sam** ► A personification of the people or government of the USA, usually portrayed as a lean figure with white hair and whiskers, wearing a tall hat, swallow-tail coat, and striped trousers. The name is associated with a certain meat inspector, Samuel Wilson (1766–1854), who confused the initials of the United States with those of his own nickname.

● **unconscious** ► In ▷psychoanalysis, the part of the mind that includes ideas and impulses of which the individual is unaware and which cannot readily be brought back into awareness. (It is distinguished from the **subconscious**, which comprises ideas and impulses that can readily be recalled to consciousness.) The unconscious mental processes are unacceptable to the conscious mind and are kept unconscious by the process of ▷repression. Psychoanalytic ▷psychotherapy attempts to bring these processes back into consciousness by overcoming the resistances to them.

● **Underground Railroad** ► In the USA, a secret network of abolitionists who aided the escape of fugitive slaves from the Southern States to freedom in the North. It was at its height in the years immediately before the American Civil War (1861–65), when perhaps 1000 slaves a year were smuggled to freedom. One of its leading heroines was Harriet Tubman (1821–1913), an escaped slave herself, who helped some 300 slaves to freedom, including her own parents. Although the numbers it helped were relatively small, the Underground Railroad was a potent symbol of the determination of the abolitionists and provoked intense anger in the South.

● **underground railways** ► Apart from short sections of tunnel on main-line railways, the world's first urban underground railway (1863) was built in London between Paddington and Farringdon Street, using the cut and cover method (cutting a trench from above and filling in over the railway) and steam trains. The first "tube" railway (1890), cut by boring through the earth with a Greathead shield (a steel ring forced forwards with a hydraulic ram), ran from the City to Stockwell and used electric trains. The network of London tubes and metropolitan railways is now some 415 km (257 mi) long, the more recent additions including the Victoria line (opened 1971), the extension of the Piccadilly line to London Airport (1977), the Jubilee line (1979), and its extension to Stratford via Greenwich (whose opening is timed to coincide with the opening of the ▷Millennium Dome). Other major cities to have an underground railway include New York (subway), Paris and Marseille (*métro*), Moscow, Tokyo, Buenos Aires, Madrid, Glasgow, and Hong Kong.

● **underwing moth** ► A moth whose brightly coloured hindwings are hidden by the camouflaged forewings when at rest. When disturbed the moth flies off flashing its bright colours, which startles and confuses predators. Underwings belong to several families and are found in Europe, Asia, and North America.

● **underwriting** ▷*See* insurance; Lloyd's.

● **Undset, Sigrid** ► (1882–1949) Norwegian novelist, best known for *Kristin Lavransdatter* (1920–22), a trilogy of historical novels set in 14th-century Norway. She wrote a number of other novels, most of them dealing with themes that reflect her conversion to Roman Catholicism in 1924. She also wrote essays and lives of the Norwegian saints.

● **undulant fever** ▷*See* brucellosis.

● **unemployment** ► The total number of people unable to find work at a given time. A certain amount of **frictional unemployment**, i.e. unemployment due to people changing jobs, etc., is inevitable. **Structural unemployment** is due to people having the wrong skills, living in different areas from vacancies, etc. The proportion of the workforce unemployed also increases with a downturn in the ▷trade cycle (this is **demand-deficient unemployment**); in the ▷Depression of the 1930s it reached nearly 3 million in the UK, a figure surpassed in July 1986, when it exceeded 3.25 million. While it is accepted that even with "full" employment up to about 3% of the workforce may be out of work (as a result of frictional and structural unemployment) considerable controversy remains as to the extent of structural unemployment as compared to demand-deficient unemployment. Monetarists (*see* monetarism) believe that, provided the ▷money supply is adequate, unemployment is largely due to structural problems and they advocate such measures as mobility allowances and retraining schemes. They claim that attempts to boost the economy by ▷deficit financing, as advocated by ▷Keynesianism, will not help the problem and will merely have the effect of fuelling ▷inflation. In the earlier 1990s there was a worldwide trade recession causing increased unemployment, which in the UK reached 3 million. The current figure is about 1.47 million (2000). The table below gives international unemployment figures.

Percentage of the total workforce unemployed

	1992	1996	2000
UK	10.1	8.2	5.5
USA	7.4	5.4	4.2
Japan	2.2	3.4	5.0
Italy	9.0	12.0	10.4
France	6.6	9.0	9.7
Germany	10.4	9.0	9.2

● **UNESCO** ▷*See* United Nations Educational, Scientific and Cultural Organization.

● **Ungaretti, Giuseppe** ► (1888–1970) Italian poet. He was born in Egypt and studied in Paris, where he met ▷Apollinaire, ▷Valéry, and other avantgarde writers and artists. He taught in Brazil from 1936 to 1942. His poetry, beginning with the war poems of *Il porto sepolto* (1916) and *L'allegria* (1919), was highly experimental, dispensing with rhyme and other conventions. The difficult language and symbolism of a later volume, *Sentimento del tempo* (1933), led a critic to describe Ungaretti's verse as *ermetico* (obscure), a term that was soon applied to the style of ▷Montale and ▷Quasimodo as well, the three being the leading practitioners of *La poesie ermetica*. Ungaretti's later volumes include *La terra promessa* (1950) and *Morte delle stagioni* (1967).

● **Ungava** ▶ A region in E Canada, in N Quebec E of Hudson Bay. A rocky plateau with many lakes, it is rich in minerals (especially iron ore) but sparsely populated. Area: 911 110 sq km (351 780 sq mi).

● **ungulate** ▶ A hoofed mammal. The term is not used in modern scientific classifications, the hoofed mammals being grouped into the orders ▷Perissodactyla (horses, tapirs, and rhinoceroses) and ▷Artiodactyla, which includes pigs, camels, deer, cattle, etc.

● **uniat churches** ▶ Various churches of Eastern Orthodox Christianity that are in full communion with the Roman Catholic Church. Although completely Catholic in faith and doctrine, they retain their own traditional liturgies and canon law. Generally they differ from Rome in giving communion under both kinds (i.e. the congregation receive both bread and wine), practising baptism by immersion, and allowing marriage of the clergy.

● **UNICEF** ▷See United Nations International Children's Emergency Fund.

● **Unicode** ▷See character set.

● **unicorn** ▶ A mythical animal described by classical writers as living in India and resembling a white horse, but with one long straight horn on its forehead. In the middle ages it was symbolically associated with chastity or virginity (and thus could be captured only by a virgin) and also with Christ's love of mankind. Its horn was supposed to reveal the presence of poison in food or drink. In heraldry it figured in the arms of Scotland and was combined with the lion in the arms of the British Crown after the accession of James I.

● **unidentified flying objects** ▶ (UFOs) Objects reported to have been seen in the sky (usually at night) that have not been identified as aircraft, satellites, or known astronomical bodies. Often described as saucer shaped (and known as "flying saucers"), they have been taken by some to be spacecraft from extraterrestrial sources—a view for which there is little credible evidence. They have, however, provided a source of considerable speculation and excitement among those who believe that they have witnessed an event that has passed unnoticed by the rest of mankind.

● **Unification Church** ▶ A religious sect that was founded in South Korea in 1954 by a millionaire Korean businessman, Sun Myung Moon (1920–). In the early 1960s it was introduced into the USA as a right-wing Christian Youth Crusade and is now also active in Britain, Australia, and elsewhere. The ideology of the cult is summarized in Moon's book, *Divine Principle*, which he claims was revealed to him by Christ in 1936. Moon is presented as the Second Messiah, the head of a family of perfect children (i.e. his followers, the Moonies), who will succeed in redeeming mankind from Satan. Absolute obedience is demanded of members, who spend most of their waking hours earning money for the organization by selling such items as artificial flowers in the streets. The large sums realized in this way enabled Moon to build an extensive property and business empire in the USA, where he has lived since 1972. He was imprisoned for tax evasion in 1984 and released in 1985.

● **unified field theory** ▶ A theory that encompasses the four fundamental interactions—▷strong, ▷weak, ▷electromagnetic, and ▷gravitational—in terms of a single field, analogous to the electromagnetic or gravitational fields. Einstein failed to unify gravitation and electromagnetism, although the Glashow-Weinberg-Salam theory (*see* Salam, Abdus) achieves unification of the weak and electromagnetic fields. ▷See also grand unified theory.

● **UNIFIL** ▶ (United Nations Interim Force In Lebanon) ▷See Lebanon, Republic of.

● **uniformitarianism** ▶ The theory that all geological changes have occurred through gradual processes although not at the same rate or intensity. *Compare* catastrophism.

● **Uniformity, Acts of** ▶ A series of Acts (1549, 1552, 1559, 1562) that enforced the use of the Book of ▷Common Prayer in England during the ▷Reformation.

● **Union, Acts of** ▶ **1.** The Acts (1536–43) uniting England and Wales. They imposed English law and administration on Wales, made English the language of officialdom, and provided for Welsh representation in parliament. **2.** The Act (1707) uniting England and Scotland to form Great Britain. Scotland retained its legal system and Presbyterian Church and was to be represented in parliament by 16 peers and 45 MPs. **3.** The Act (1800) that united Great Britain and Ireland to form (1801) the United Kingdom. It provided for Irish representation in parliament (4 spiritual peers, 28 life peers, 100 MPs). After the establishment of the Irish Free State (1921), the Act united Britain with Northern Ireland.

● **Union Movement** ▷See Mosley, Sir Oswald Ernald.

● **Union of European Football Associations** ▷See UEFA.

● **Union of Soviet Socialist Republics** ▷See Soviet Union.

● **Unitarians** ▶ A group of Christians who reject the doctrine of the Trinity and the divinity of Christ, believing instead in the single personality of God and regarding Christ as a religious teacher. They have no formal creeds but stress reason and conscience as the bases of religion and view human nature as essentially good; they therefore also reject orthodox Christian teaching on ▷original sin and atonement. Modern Unitarian thought dates from the Reformation, when it was propagated by ▷Socinus; congregations were first formed in Britain and the USA in the 18th century. These are now associated in the General Assembly of Unitarian and Free Christian Churches.

● **unitary authority** ▶ In the United Kingdom, a district administered by a single tier of ▷local government. In Scotland and Wales unitary authorities replaced the two-tier system (in which administrative powers were divided between ▷county or regional councils and district authorities) in April 1996. The new authorities are known as council areas in Scotland and as counties or county boroughs in Wales. Although most of England retains a two-tier system, 42 unitary authorities were created there between 1995 and 1998. Single-tier local government had already been introduced to Northern Ireland (1973), the Scottish island areas (1975), and Greater London and the metropolitan counties of England (1986).

● **unitary symmetry** ▶ A method of classifying ▷hadrons. It is found that by plotting ▷isotopic spin against hypercharge (the sum of ▷strangeness and ▷baryon number) on a graph for particular values of ▷spin and ▷parity, a symmetric pattern of hadrons is obtained. In this way families of hadrons can be constructed. The theory was used to predict the existence and properties of the omega-minus particle.

● **United Arab Emirates** ▶ (UAE; former name: Trucial States) A federation of seven sheikdoms in the Middle East, in ▷Arabia on the S coast of the Persian Gulf and the Gulf of Oman, comprising Abu Dhabi, Ajman, Dubai, Fujairah, Ras al-Khaimah, Sharjah, and Umm al-Qaiwain. Abu Dhabi occupies 87% of the total area and Abu Dhabi and Dubai each have about one-third of the population, which is mainly Arab and Sunnite Muslim. The terrain is flat sandy desert, below 200 m (656 ft) except for a slight rise to the NE.
Economy: fishing and pearls are still important, but the oil of Abu Dhabi and Dubai, both underground and offshore, is the chief product and export: it has made Abu Dhabi one of the richest per capita political units in the world. Financial and insurance services are important, as are transport and communications. The government has launched an afforestation programme and has achieved some success in encouraging horticulture (made possible by large-scale irrigation schemes). Tourism is expanding.

United Arab Emirates

Head of state	President Sheikh Zayed bin Sultan al-Nahayan of Abu Dhabi
Official language	Arabic
Official currency	dirham of 100 fils
Area	83 650 sq km (32 290 sq mi)
Population (1997 est)	2 580 000
Provisional capital	Abu Dhabi
Chief port	Dubai

History: the sheikdoms signed several common treaties with Britain from 1820; that of 1892 made them protectorates—the Trucial States—and British troops were stationed there until independence. The federation was formed in 1971 (Ras al-Khaimah joined in 1972) and is a member of OPEC. The country is governed by a Supreme Council consisting of the seven ruling sheikhs; there is also an appointed Federal National Council.

● **United Arab Republic** ► (UAR) The state created by the union of Egypt and Syria in 1958. Joined by North Yemen in the same year, it collapsed in 1961, when Syria withdrew, but Egypt retained the name until 1971.

● **United Fronts** ► In China, two periods of cooperation between the Chinese Communist Party and its opponent, the ▷Guomindang. The first United Front (1924–27) was brought about, under Soviet influence, to defeat the ▷warlords and dissolved as relations between the two parties declined into civil war. The second United Front (1937–45) was formed following the ▷Xi An incident, which forced ▷Chiang Kai-shek to ally with the communists against the Japanese invasion (*see* Sino-Japanese Wars).

● **United Irishmen, Society of** ► An Irish Protestant secret society established in Belfast in 1791 by Wolfe ▷Tone to press for an independent Irish republic. Hopes of French aid were frustrated but in 1798 the United Irishmen rose in Ulster and Wexford, being suppressed with some difficulty.

● **United Kingdom** ► (UK) A country in N Europe, consisting of ▷England, ▷Scotland, ▷Wales, and the province of Northern Ireland (*see* Ireland). The UK does not include the Channel Isles and the Isle of Man, which are direct dependencies of the Crown with their own legislatures and taxation systems.

History: The United Kingdom of Great Britain and Ireland was formed in 1801 (*see* Union, Acts of), since when the histories of the member countries have been inextricably linked (for history prior to 1801, and for geographical and economic information, *see* England; Scotland; Wales). With the ▷industrial revolution the UK evolved from an agricultural to an industrial economy, a development reflected during the long reign of Victoria in agitation for an extension of the franchise (*see* Reform Acts) and a shift in political influence from the landowners to the urban middle class. The growing labour movement (*see* trade unions) led to the formation in 1900 of the ▷Labour Party, which subsequently replaced the Liberals as one of the two chief political parties. The 19th century also saw the heyday of the British ▷Empire and colonial rivalry with Germany, which was a factor in the outbreak of ▷World War I. In 1922, following the creation of the Irish Free State, the UK was retitled the United Kingdom of Great Britain and Northern Ireland. The interwar years were dominated by the Depression and the growing threat of fascism abroad, which culminated in ▷World War II. Following Labour's landslide victory in 1945, the government established a welfare state and initiated a programme of nationalization. The ▷Conservatives subsequently returned to power (1951–64) before the return of Labour (1964–70; 1974–79). From 1979 until 1997 the Conservatives presided over extensive ▷privatization and rising unemployment: recessions in the early 1980s and early 1990s were followed by economic recovery. In 1997 Labour enjoyed a landslide victory and Tony ▷Blair became prime minister. Legislation to set up devolved bodies in Wales and Scotland was enacted in 1997 and put into effect in 1999 while hopes for a solution to the long-running problem of Northern Ireland were raised by the Good Friday Agreement of 1998.

United Kingdom

Head of state	Queen Elizabeth II
Official languages	English, with Gaelic and Welsh minority languages
Official currency	pound of 100 pence
Area	244 014 sq km (94 214 sq mi)
Population (2001 est)	59 953 000
Capital	London

● **United Kingdom Overseas Territories** ► (former names: British Dependent Territories *or* Crown dependencies) Overseas territories for which constitutional responsibility rests with the UK Foreign and Commonwealth Office. There are currently 13 such territories: Anguilla, Bermuda, British Antarctic Territory, British Indian Ocean Territory, British Virgin Islands, Cayman Islands, Falkland Islands, Gibraltar, Montserrat, Pitcairn Islands, St Helena and Dependencies, South Georgia and South Sandwich Islands, and Turks and Caicos Islands. With the exception of Gibraltar and the British Antarctic Territory, they are all small islands in the Caribbean, the Indian Ocean, the South Pacific, and the South Atlantic. These scattered territories, which have a combined population of about 200 000 (several have no permanent inhabitants), are the last remains of the UK's overseas empire. Although the Crown (advised by the Foreign Office) still appoints a governor or commissioner, who may have considerable executive powers, all the inhabited territories now have some degree of internal self-government. In 2002 full ▷British citizenship (which had been revoked in the 1980s for all but Gibraltar and the Falkland Islands) was restored to the inhabitants, giving them the right to live, work, and vote in the UK. In return, the territorial governments were instructed to improve their human rights records (e.g. by abolishing capital and corporal punishment), to clamp down on smuggling, and to take steps to prevent money laundering, tax evasion, and other abuses of their liberal financial regimes.

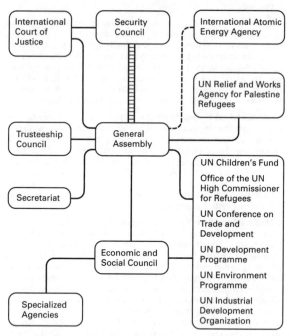

United Nations ► The structure of the organization.

● **United Nations** ► (UN) An organization established to maintain international peace and to foster international cooperation in the resolution of economic, social, cultural, and humanitarian problems. The UN was founded on 24 October, 1945 (United Nations Day), when the major powers ratified a charter that had been drawn up earlier in the year in San Francisco. There were 51 founder members, including the USA, which thus abandoned the isolationist stance it had taken to the UN's predecessor, the ▷League of Nations. Most countries are members of the UN, the chief exception being ▷Taiwan, which lost its seat to ▷China in 1971. Monaco and Eritrea joined in 1993 and Switzerland in 2002.

The headquarters of the UN are in New York. The organization's main deliberative organ is the **General Assembly**, which meets for three months every year. Each member state has one equal vote in the Assembly, which can only adopt recommendations: as a body of independent sovereign states, it cannot impose its will upon members. The **Security Council** bears the chief responsibility for maintaining international peace. Its permanent members are China, France, Russia (before 1991 the Soviet Union), the UK, and the USA; a further ten members are elected by the General Assembly for two-year terms. Decisions, except on procedure, must be agreed by nine members, including all the permanent members (the so-called veto privilege). In the event of a breach of international peace the Council may commit military forces to an attempt to re-establish peace, as for example during the ▷Korean War. The ▷Gulf War of 1991 was prosecuted to enforce a United Nations resolution demanding Iraq's withdrawal from Kuwait. The **Economic and Social Council** (ECOSOC) coordinates the economic and social work of the UN. The principal judicial organ of the UN is the ▷International Court of Justice. The **Secretariat**, headed by the secretary general (currently Kofi ▷Annan), is responsible for administration.

Other UN bodies include the **United Nations Development Programme** (UNDP), which fosters the economic growth of the ▷developing countries; its headquarters are in New York; the **United Nations Conference on Trade and Development** (UNCTAD), which encourages international trade, especially that of developing countries; its headquarters are in Geneva; the **United Nations Industrial Development Organization** (UNIDO), which promotes industrial development in the developing countries; its headquarters are in Vienna; and the **United Nations Environment Programme** (UNEP), which is concerned with international cooperation in the protection of the environment; its headquarters are in Nairobi. Specialized agencies charged with a specific function include the ▷Food and Agriculture Organization, ▷International Civil Aviation Organization, ▷International Labour Organisation, ▷International Monetary Fund, ▷International Telecommunication Union, ▷United Nations Educational, Scientific and Cultural Organization, ▷International Bank for Reconstruction and Development, ▷World Health Organization, and the ▷World Meteorological Organization.

● **United Nations Educational, Scientific and Cultural Organization** ► (UNESCO) A ▷United Nations agency established in 1945 to promote international cooperation in education, science, and culture. It collects and distributes information, provides assistance (e.g. funds for teacher training) to ▷developing countries, and funds research. Its headquarters are in Paris. Objecting to alleged inefficiency and political bias, the USA withdrew in 1984 and the UK in 1985–97.

● **United Nations High Commissioner for Refugees, Office of the** ► (UNHCR) A ▷United Nations body established in 1950 to provide international protection for refugees. It promotes voluntary repatriation, resettlement in other countries, or integration into the country of present residence. The UNHCR has recently been concerned with refugees from Chile, Cyprus, Angola, and Vietnam. Its headquarters are in Geneva. It won the Nobel Peace Prize in 1981.

● **United Nations International Children's Emergency Fund** ► (UNICEF) A ▷United Nations body established in 1946 to carry out postwar relief work in Europe. It is now chiefly concerned with providing health care, education, and improved nutrition to ▷developing countries. Most of UNICEF's funds come from voluntary government contributions. Its headquarters are in Geneva. It won the Nobel Peace Prize in 1965.

● **United Nations Relief and Works Agency for Palestine Refugees in the Near East** ► (UNRWA) A ▷United Nations body founded in 1950 to provide relief, health, education, and welfare services for Palestinian refugees in the Middle East (*see* Palestine). Its headquarters are in Beirut (Lebanon).

● **United Provinces of the Netherlands** ► The northern provinces of the Netherlands, which united (1579) during the ▷Revolt of the Netherlands against Spain and formed (1581) a self-governing independent federation. The so-called Dutch Republic survived until conquered by the French (1795).

● **United Reformed Church** ► (URC) A Protestant body formed in 1972 by the union of most of the Congregational Churches in England and Wales (*see* Congregationalism) and the Presbyterian Church in England (*see* Presbyterianism). In 1981 the Reformed Association of the Churches of Christ also joined the URC. The Church is governed by a General Assembly but allows local congregations considerable independence. It currently has about 750 full-time ministers and 100 000 lay members in the UK.

● **United States of America** ► (USA) A country in North America, the third most populous and fourth largest in the world. It is a federal republic of 50 states, including two separated from the others: Alaska, in the extreme NW of the continent, and Hawaii, in the central Pacific Ocean. The USA borders on Canada in the N and Mexico in the S. The Pacific mountain system and the Rocky Mountains, the watershed of the country, extend N–S in the W with an arid area between, while the Appalachian Mountains extend N–S in the E. In the centre lie vast plains. The population is of mixed ethnic stock, the majority being of European descent; other groups include Blacks, Chinese, Japanese, and ▷North American Indians (mostly living on reservations).

Economy: the USA is the world's greatest industrial producer, with a highly diversified economy. Its wealth of minerals and fuels make it the leading producer of natural gas, lead, copper, aluminium, and sulphur and of electrical and nuclear energy. It is almost self-sufficient in raw materials, although as its mineral resources are depleted it is having to increase its imports, notably of petroleum. The chief manufactures are steel, motor vehicles, chemicals, electronic equipment, and consumer goods. Although only 4% of the workforce are employed in agriculture, 15% of all exports are agricultural products. Farming is highly mechanized, with efficient control of disease and pests. Cereals, soya beans, cotton, tobacco, potatoes, and fruit are the main crops. Main exports include motor vehicles, aircraft, machinery, computers, electrical components, grain, and chemicals, while main imports include petroleum and petroleum products, chemicals, metals, machinery, cars, and newsprint. Finance, insurance, and real estate are also important sectors of the economy.

History: the first inhabitants probably came from Asia about 30 000 years ago. The ▷Vikings visited the N of the continent, but it was not until after the voyage of Columbus in 1492 that America was settled by Europeans, chiefly the Spanish, French, and British. The British colonies, in the E, had the greatest religious and economic freedom and were therefore the most attractive and successful. However, during the 18th century conflict developed between local colonial assemblies and their British governors, particularly over taxation. The colonists' confidence in themselves was strengthened by their success against the French in the ▷French and Indian War (1754–63) and the 13 colonies finally won independence in the ▷American Revolution (1775–83), having proclaimed their independence in 1776 (*see* Declaration of Independence). The USA was rapidly expanding W at this time and through the ▷Mexican War (1846–48) acquired California; the discovery of gold there (1848) further encouraged settlement in the W. By 1820 conflict was developing between the cotton-growing states of the South (where African slaves had worked since the late 17th century) and the commercial North (where the industrial revolution was under way and slavery was opposed). As the new states of the West aligned themselves with the North, the South felt increasingly threatened. This led to the ▷Civil War (1861–65), which ended in victory for the North and the abolition of slavery. It was followed by industrial and economic expansion, while territorial expansion continued with the purchase of Alaska (1867), the annexation of Hawaii (1898), and the Spanish-American War (1898), in which the USA acquired the Philippines, Puerto Rico, Guam, and some control over Cuba.

Intervention in Colombia led to the construction of the Panama Canal (opened 1914). Economic and territorial expansion made the USA a world power, a status confirmed by its role in World War I, which it entered reluctantly (1917) because of its policy of isolationism. The 1920s saw another industrial and commercial boom, which ended in the ▷Depression that followed the Crash of 1929. The USA was again reluctant to enter World War II but was forced to do so by the Japanese bombing of Pearl Harbor in Hawaii (December, 1941). US troops and weapons played a major part in defeating the Axis Powers in Europe and its development and use of the atom bomb ended the war against Japan. The part played by the USA in the establishment of the United Nations (1945) involved it inextricably in international affairs, in which it has since played a leading role. Postwar fear of Soviet expansion resulted in the Marshall Plan (1947), designed to render Europe less susceptible to communism by bolstering it economically, in the USA's involvement in the ▷Cold War, and in the harassment of supposed communists at home (*see also* McCarthy, Joseph R.; Un-American Activities Committee). Fear of the spread of communism led also to intervention in Korea (1950–53), Cuba (1961–62), and Vietnam (1961–75), and the use of foreign aid to maintain the status quo in developing countries. After 1963 relations with the Soviet Union improved, with arms limitation talks (see disarmament), and diplomatic relations were established with China in 1979. Interventionist policy continued, however, with the role of the CIA in foreign affairs being criticized and investigated in 1975–76. Domestic problems of the 1960s and 1970s included the difficulties of effecting racial integration and extensive opposition to the ▷Vietnam War. The ▷Watergate affair of 1972–74 was a major crisis that undermined confidence in US institutions. The postwar economic boom was followed by decline in the early 1970s, with continuing inflation. With its increasing dependence on petroleum imports the country suffered through the drying up of supplies from Iran (1978–79) and rises in world petroleum prices. In 1979 Iranian students took 52 US diplomats hostage in the American Embassy, Tehran, only releasing them in January 1981. Elsewhere, US troops intervened in Lebanon (1982), Grenada (1983), in covert operations against Nicaragua, and in Panama (1989). In 1986 US planes bombed Libyan cities in retaliation for terrorist attacks. Relations with the USSR deteriorated once more following the Soviet invasion of Afghanistan (1980), the deployment of US nuclear missiles in W Europe, and Ronald ▷Reagan's ▷Strategic Defence Initiative. Relations improved with the arrival of the reformist Soviet leader Mikhail Gorbachov and the signing of major treaties on nuclear weapons (1987, 1990) that effectively ended the Cold War. The subsequent collapse (1991) of the Soviet Union left the USA as the world's only superpower. In 1991 George ▷Bush responded to the Iraqi invasion of Kuwait (1990) by ordering an attack on Iraq (see Gulf War). The 1990s saw US airstrikes against targets in Iraq (1996, 1998) and Yugoslavia (1999) during the presidency of Bill ▷Clinton; there was also a prolonged economic boom. In 2001 George W. Bush became president following a disputed election that was only resolved by a Supreme Court ruling. Following the terrorist attacks on America on ▷September 11, 2001, Bush declared a ▷war on terrorism and sent US forces into action in Afghanistan.

United States of America

Head of state	President George W. Bush
Official language	English
Official currency	US dollar of 100 cents
Area	9 363 123 sq km (3 614 343 sq mi)
Population (2001 est)	286 067 000
Capital	Washington, DC

● **unities** ► Three principles concerning the representation in ▷drama of action, time, and space. According to the interpretation of Aristotle's *Poetics* by 16th- and 17th-century neoclassical critics, a play must represent a single action occurring in a single setting during the course of a single day. The unities were strictly observed in 17th-century France, notably by ▷Racine and ▷Corneille, but were largely ignored in England.

● **units of measurement** ► Standard measures that enable a physical quantity (such as a mass, length, or time) to be given a numerical magnitude. To express a physical quantity (Q) it is necessary to define a unit (u) in which to measure that quantity and to state the number (n) of such units required; i.e. $Q = n \times u$. Units of measurement have to be defined in terms of a standard. The standard may be a physical object, such as the platinum-iridium bar formerly used as a standard for the ▷metre, or a reproducible measurement, such as the distance travelled by a ray of light in a specified time, as used to define the metre since 1983.

For most of history humans have struggled with a bewildering diversity of systems of units. Only since the 1970s has a coherent system of units been used throughout the world in science and technology (but not in everyday life or in many trades). In the ancient world, units were often based on human parameters. For example, the Egyptians in about 3000 BC defined the unit of length, the cubit, in terms of the average length of a man's arm from the elbow to the fingertips. This was subdivided into 28 digits (finger widths). The Greeks adopted a mixture of Egyptian, Babylonian, and Hebrew units,

adding the foot, which the Romans later divided into 12 inches (*unciae*). The Romans also defined the pound (*libra*, which persists in the abbreviation lb) and the mile (*mille passus*, a thousand double paces).

During the middle ages the classical units continued to be used with regional variations and additions from Scandinavia and Arabia. The complicated hotchpotch of units making up the English system began to develop after ▷Magna Carta, influenced by the European trade fairs of the 12th and 13th centuries. Two particularly persistent and anachronistic units were the **troy** pound for weighing gold and silver, derived from Troyes (one of the principal Champagne Fair cities), and the **avoirdupois** pound, used at trade fairs for such goods as salt and grain, which had to be weighed (from *aver de peis*, goods of weight). Various attempts at standardization failed to clear up the medieval multiplicity of units. However, the UK Weights and Measures Acts of 1824 and 1878 established the gallon and the yard, respectively, as units backed by effective standards.

In the meantime, in France after the Revolution, Napoleon actively encouraged the establishment of the ▷metric system, based on decimal arithmetic. Given formal acceptance in France in 1795, this sensible system had become widespread in Europe by the 1830s. However, its patent merits were not finally accepted in the UK until 1963, when an Act of Parliament defined English weights and measures using the metric system. Metrication in the UK has, since then, progressed slowly and inconsistently (petrol prices are quoted in pence per litre, but some vehicle petrol gauges still register gallons). However, in science and technology, worldwide acceptance of ▷SI units, based on the ▷m.k.s. system, has at last brought order to one aspect of measurement, in which consistency and uniformity are essential (see Appendix). ▷*See also* mass and weight; metrology; time.

● **unit trust** ► An organization that uses funds raised by selling "units" to the public to buy and sell ▷securities in order to make profits for distribution to unit holders. Securities are held in the names of trustees, usually banks. The units can be resold to the managers at any time at their market value. The small investor thus has the advantages of a professionally managed widespread portfolio. *Compare* investment company.

● **Universal Decimal Classification** ► (*or* Brussels Classification) A system of library classification developed in 1895 at the International Institute of Bibliography in Brussels. It extends the ▷Dewey Decimal Classification, on which it is based, by using various symbols as well as Arabic numerals.

● **universal time** ► (UT) An internationally agreed basis for timekeeping, formerly related to ▷Greenwich Mean Time and based on the diurnal motion of the stars. **Coordinated universal time** (UTC), introduced in 1972, is based on ▷International Atomic Time, the SI unit of which is the ▷second. This is independent of the place of observation and variations in the earth's motion.

● **universe** ► The sum of all potentially knowable objects—the earth, sun, stars and other members of our ▷Galaxy, countless millions of other ▷galaxies, and the matter between these objects. Its unimaginable vastness in both space (about 10^{10} light years across and still expanding; see big-bang theory) and time (about 10^{10} years old) was only accepted in the 20th century. The possibility of life elsewhere in the universe is fairly high (i.e. there is a high probability that there are millions of stars similar to the solar system). ▷*See* cosmology.

● **universities** ► Independent degree-awarding institutions of higher education. They evolved in Europe in the middle ages from the *studia generalia*, schools open to scholars from all parts of Europe, and by the end of the 14th century consisted of communities of teachers and scholars, recognized by civil or ecclesiastical authorities. Among the earliest were Bologna (1088), Paris (c. 1150), Prague (1348), Vienna (1365), and Heidelberg (1386). The first universities in England were established at ▷Oxford and ▷Cambridge in the 12th century, while St Andrews (the first Scottish university) was founded in 1411 and Trinity College, Dublin, in 1591. In the USA the first universities evolved from institutions established prior to the American Revolution, such as ▷Harvard, ▷Yale, and ▷Princeton. Following industrialization during the 19th century, several new universities were established in the UK (including London University in 1836; see

London), a process that continued into the 20th century, especially after World War II. Increasing emphasis was placed upon the development of technical studies and following the Robbins Report of 1963 the colleges of advanced technology (CATs) were granted university status. The ▷Open University was established in 1969. Under the Higher and Further Education Act (1992) 34 ▷polytechnics in England and Wales became universities. There are now 71 universities in England, 13 in Scotland, and 2 each in Wales and Northern Ireland. ▷*See also* college; tertiary education.

● **University of the Third Age** ▶ (U3A) A learning programme for retired people, founded in Toulouse in 1973 by Pierre Vellus and introduced into the UK by Peter Laslett in 1983 (there are now over 100 branches in the UK). No qualifications are required or given, learning being for pleasure. There are no age limits; teaching and organization are given on a voluntary basis.

● **Unknown Warrior** ▶ (*or* Unknown Soldier) An unidentified soldier killed in World War I, whose grave serves as a permanent memorial to all those killed in both World Wars. Britain's tomb for an Unknown Warrior is in Westminster Abbey and France's lies below the Arc de Triomphe.

● **unleaded petrol** ▷*See* tetraethyl lead.

● **Upanishads** ▶ About 200 prose and verse treatises on metaphysical philosophy, commenting on the ▷*Vedas* and dating from around 400 BC. They deal with the nature of ▷Brahman and the soul and are reputedly divinely inspired.

● **upas** ▶ An evergreen tropical tree, *Antiaris toxicana*, native to SE Asia. Up to 30 m high, it has a crown of short spreading branches and long simple leaves; the flowers give rise to fleshy red pear-shaped fruits. The milky latex is a source of arrow poison. Family: *Moraceae*.

● **Updike, John (Hoyer)** ▶ (1932–) US novelist and short-story writer. Until 1959 he worked for the *New Yorker* magazine. In such novels as *Rabbit, Run* (1960), *Couples* (1968), *Rabbit Redux* (1972), and *Marry Me* (1976) he explored the moral confusions of contemporary US society. He moved beyond the suburban scene in *The Coup* (1979), a novel set in Africa. *Rabbit is Rich* (1981) and *Rabbit at Rest* (1990) won Pulitzer Prizes (1982, 1991). Later novels include *Memories of the Ford Administration* (1993), *Brazil* (1994), and *Bech at Bay* (1998).

● **Upolu** ▶ The most populous island in Samoa. It is fertile and copra, cacao, bananas, and rubber are produced. Area: 1114 sq km (430 sq mi). Population (latest est): 112 228. Chief town: Apia.

● **Upper Volta, Republic of** ▷*See* Burkina Faso.

● **Uppsala** ▶ 59 55N 17 38E A city in E central Sweden. It is a historic and cultural centre, with a famous library, a gothic cathedral, and Sweden's oldest university (1477), where ▷Linnaeus taught. It has light industries. Population (1997 est): 184 507.

● **Ur** ▶ An ancient city of ▷Sumer (S Iraq). Mentioned in Genesis as ▷Abraham's homeland, its site remained unidentified until 1854. Sir Leonard ▷Woolley's excavations (1922–34) made famous the spectacularly rich royal burials of about 2500 BC and seemed to provide historical evidence for ▷Noah's flood. The leading city in Sumer when it was sacked by barbarians about 2000 BC, Ur was superseded by ▷Babylon. Ur remained a centre for the worship of the moon god Nanna until changes in the course of the Euphrates forced its remaining inhabitants away (5th century BC).

● **uraemia** ▶ The accumulation of ▷urea in the blood due to kidney failure. Kidney failure can occur suddenly due to shock, obstruction of both ureters, injury, or acute kidney disease or it may arise slowly due to ▷nephritis or other diseases. In acute kidney failure the kidneys will often recover after ▷dialysis with a kidney machine. In chronic conditions, requiring long-term dialysis, a kidney transplant (if available) is preferred.

● **Ural, River** ▶ A river in central Russia and W Kazakhstan, rising in the S Ural Mountains, and flowing mainly S to the Caspian Sea near Guryev. Length: 2534 km (1575 mi).

● **Uralic languages** ▶ A major language family comprising two related groups of languages, the ▷Finno-Ugric and the Samoyedic (*see* Samoyed). Originating from a common source over 10 000 years ago

in an area N of the Ural Mountains, the two branches of the Uralic language family have developed into multiple forms covering an extensive geographical area in Europe, Scandinavia, and Asia.

● **Ural Mountains** ▶ A mountain range in W central Russia. It extends 2000 km (1243 mi) N–S from the Kara Sea to the steppes NE of the Caspian Sea and traditionally divides Europe from Asia. The highest point is Mount Narodnaya, in the N, at 1894 m (6214 ft). Most industrial metals are obtained here, as well as some precious stones, such as emerald and amethyst, and the S part is an important industrial area, including the towns of Ekaterinburg and Magnitogorsk.

● **Urania** ▶ In Greek mythology, one of the nine ▷Muses, the patron of astronomy, often portrayed with a globe and compass.

Ur ▶ Detail from the "Standard of Ur" (c. 2500 BC; British Museum, London), a carved stone box, the sides of which depict a king's campaign. The figures are composed of engraved shell on a background of lapis lazuli and red limestone; this panel shows a banquet, perhaps after a victory, with animals taken to be killed for it.

● **uranium** ▶ (U) The radioactive metallic element used as a fuel for nuclear reactors (*see* nuclear energy). Uranium is a silvery-white metal, almost as hard as steel and very dense (relative density 18.95). Before the development of nuclear power, one of its major uses was in making yellow glass. Uranium has the highest atomic number of the naturally occurring elements. It was first isolated in 1841 by E. Péligot (1811–90), although it had been identified before this in pitchblende. It is also found in the ores uranite, carnotite, and monazite; it is mined primarily in Canada, Australia, S Africa, and the republics of the former Soviet Union. Natural uranium contains three isotopes: ^{238}U (99.283%), ^{235}U (0.711%), and ^{234}U (0.006%). ^{238}U has a half-life of 4.51×10^9 years and is useful in dating rocks, as well as in fuel for fast reactors. The most important isotope in the nuclear industry is ^{235}U, which is used in ▷thermal reactors. Some reactors use metallic fuel, others uranium dioxide (UO_2). Other oxides include U_3O_8 and UO_3. The volatile gas uranium hexafluoride (UF_6) is used to separate uranium isotopes by gaseous diffusion. At no 92; at wt 238.0289; mp 1135°C; bp 4134°C.

● **uranium-lead dating** ▶ A group of methods of ▷radiometric dating certain rocks, depending on the decay of the radioactive isotope uranium-238 to lead-206 or of uranium-235 to lead-207. One method relies on measuring the amount of helium trapped in the rocks (eight helium nuclei are released in the U-238 decay), another depends on the ratio of radiogenic lead present to nonradiogenic lead (Pb-204). The methods are reliable for ages of between 10^7 and 10^9 years.

● **uranium series** ► One of three naturally occurring series of radioactive decays. The uranium series is headed by uranium-238, which undergoes a series of alpha and beta decays ending with the stable isotope lead-206. ▷*See also* actinium series; thorium series.

● **Uranus** ► (astronomy) A giant planet, orbiting the sun every 84 years (between Saturn and Neptune) at a mean distance of 2870 million km. Its axis of rotation is close to its orbital plane. It is somewhat larger (50 800 km in diameter) than Neptune and exhibits a similar greenish featureless disc in a telescope. In its equatorial plane lie some 15 ▷satellites and a system of about 20 narrow rings, some discovered in 1977, the rest observed in ▷Voyager 2 photographs (1986). Composed predominantly of hydrogen and helium, with cloud layers of methane and possibly ammonia, its atmospheric and interior structure are thought to be almost identical to those of Neptune. Uranus was discovered in 1781 by William ▷Herschel.

● **Uranus** ► (Greek mythology) The personification of Heaven. He was the son of Gaia (Earth), and his children by her included the ▷Titans and the ▷Cyclops. He was castrated by his son Cronus and his genitals were thrown into the sea, which gave birth to ▷Aphrodite.

● **Urartu** ► (biblical name: Ararat) A kingdom flourishing between about 850 and 650 BC in E Turkey. The inhabitants, of ▷Hurrian stock, made their capital at Van (ancient Tushpa). Their metalwork was famous, examples even reaching Etruscan Italy. Urartu was frequently at war with neighbouring Assyria.

● **Urban II** ► (Odo of Lagery; c. 1042–99) Pope (1088–99). Until 1094 his rule was challenged by Guibert of Ravenna (d. 1100), the antipope set up by Emperor Henry IV. A Cluniac monk, he was made a cardinal by ▷Gregory VII, whose reform policies he continued. Councils at Melfi (1089) and at Piacenza and Clermont (1095) condemned simony, lay investiture, and clerical marriage. At Clermont he also proclaimed the first ▷Crusade. He was beatified in 1881. Feast day: 29 or 30 July.

● **Urban VI** ► (Bartolommeo Prignano; c. 1318–89) Pope (1378–89). His anti-French policies and dictatorial behaviour inspired the French cardinals to declare his election void and to elect an antipope, thereby beginning the ▷Great Schism.

● **Urban VIII** ► (Maffeo Barberini; 1568–1644) Pope (1623–44) during the ▷Thirty Years' War, in which he supported Richelieu against the Habsburgs. A great scholar, Urban supported new religious orders and reforms, including the revision of the Missal and new canonization procedures. He promulgated several measures against heresy and condemned the writings of Galileo and Jansen.

● **Urbino** ► 43 43N 12 38E A town in Italy, in Marche. The birthplace of Raphael, Urbino possesses a 15th-century ducal palace and a university (1506). Its manufactures include textiles and maiolica. Population (latest est): 15 918.

● **Urdu** ► An ▷Indo-Aryan language of N India and Pakistan, where it is an official language. Like ▷Hindi it arose from ▷Hindustani, but since it was used largely by Muslims in this region, while Hindi has been progressively influenced by ▷Sanskrit, the two now differ considerably. It is written in a modified Arabic script.

● **urea** ► (or carbamide) A white crystalline compound $(CO(NH_2)_2)$ derived from ammonia and carbon dioxide. It is widely used as a nitrogen fertilizer, a feed supplement for ruminant animals, and in the plastics and pharmaceutical industries. Urea is the excretory product of nitrogen metabolism in mammals and is present in ▷urine.

● **urea-formaldehyde resins** ► Synthetic thermosetting resins that are made by the condensation in aqueous solution of urea and formaldehyde with an ammonia catalyst. Cellulose filler is added to the colourless syrupy solution produced and a moulding powder forms when it dries. This powder can be coloured and used to make cups, fittings, etc.

● **urethane** ► A white crystalline solid, $CO(NH_2)(OC_2H_5)$, made by heating ethanol with urea nitrate. It is soluble in water and alcohol and is used to manufacture ▷polyurethane foam.

● **urethritis** ► Inflammation of the urethra—the duct that carries urine from the bladder to the outside. Nonspecific urethritis (NSU),

usually caused by infection with the bacterium *Chlamydia trachomatis*, is one of the most common sexually transmitted diseases.

● **Urey, Harold Clayton** ► (1893–1981) US physicist, who received the Nobel Prize in 1934 for his discovery of deuterium. He also did valuable work on the separation of isotopes, which was useful in the manufacture of the hydrogen bomb. In postwar years, as professor at Chicago University (1945–52) and then at the University of California, he turned to geophysics.

● **Urfa** ► (ancient name: Edessa) 37 08N 38 45E A town in S Turkey, near the Syrian border. It was the birthplace of Abraham. It has changed hands frequently, being occupied by Crusaders from 1098 to 1637. Population (1995 est): 362 598.

● **Urfé, Honoré d'** ► (1568–1625) French novelist. His major work was the prose romance, *L'Astrée* (1607–27), which is set in his native Lyonnais in the 5th century and is considered to be the first French novel. He also wrote the pastoral dramas *Sireine* and *Sylvanire* (1627).

● **Urga** ▷*See* Ulan Bator.

● **uric acid** ► A compound $(C_5H_4N_4O_3)$ formed during the nitrogen metabolism of animals: it is the chief nitrogenous excretory product of reptiles and birds. In humans, raised levels of uric acid in the blood are associated with gout.

● **urine** ► The fluid that is formed by the kidneys and contains the waste products of metabolism and surplus water and salts. The human kidneys normally produce 0.9–1.5 l of urine per day, containing some 50–70 g of solids—mostly urea, creatine, uric acid, and inorganic salts.

● **Urmia, Lake** ► A shallow lake in NW Iran, the largest in the country, lying 1300 m (4265 ft) above sea level. It has no outlet and consequently is salty and varies in size. Average area: 5000 sq km (1930 sq mi).

● **Urnfield** ► A group of Bronze Age cultures originating in central Europe. Urnfield peoples characteristically cremated their dead and buried the ashes in cemeteries of pottery urns. Their culture spread to most of Europe before being displaced by Iron Age ▷Hallstatt or Roman influence. Urnfields are commonly associated with groups who later became identifiable as the ▷Celts.

● **Ursa Major** ► (Latin: Great Bear) A large conspicuous constellation in the N sky. The brightest stars, all of 2nd magnitude, are Alioth, Alcaid, and Dubhe. The seven brightest stars form the ▷Plough.

● **Ursa Minor** ► (Latin: Little Bear) A constellation in the N sky that contains the N celestial pole. The brightest star is ▷Polaris, the present pole star.

● **Ursula, St** ► A legendary British martyr. According to tradition, she and 11 000 virgins were murdered by the Huns at Cologne while returning from a pilgrimage to Rome in the 3rd or 5th century. She is first mentioned in the 10th century. She has given her name to numerous religious establishments, including the ▷Ursulines. Feast day: 21 Oct.

● **Ursulines** ► A Roman Catholic religious order for women, named after its patron St ▷Ursula, founded in Brescia in 1535 by St Angela Merici (1474–1540). It is devoted to educational work and is the oldest teaching order of women.

● **urticaria** ► (or hives) An acute or chronic disorder in which itching white raised patches surrounded by red areas appear on the skin: they resemble nettle stings (hence the alternative name—nettle rash). Acute urticaria usually arises from allergy to food or drugs and usually disappears quickly if the cause is removed. Chronic urticaria occurs in young people and its cause is not certain. Urticaria is treated with ▷antihistamines.

● **Uruguay, Oriental Republic of** ► A country in the SE of South America, on the Atlantic Ocean and the Río de la Plata. Coastal plains rise to higher ground, especially in the N. The River Uruguay forms its W boundary and the other main river is the Negro. Most of the population is of Spanish and Italian descent.
Economy: the traditional livestock industry was badly affected by

the 1974 EC ban on meat imports, although new markets have subsequently been found. The cultivation of the principal crops (wheat, barley, rice) has been intensified and the fishing industry has been expanded with government assistance. Citrus fruits and winemaking are also important. The principal industries include textiles, food processing, hides and leather, construction, metallurgy, and rubber. Hydroelectricity is a valuable source of power.

History: Charrúa and Chaná Indians inhabited Uruguay before its exploration by the Spanish in the 16th century; its subsequent history was one of rivalry between Spanish and Portuguese settlements. In the 18th century Spain established its control of Uruguay, which in 1776 became part of the viceroyalty of the Río de la Plata. Under the leadership of Artigas, Uruguay joined Argentina in the movement for independence against Spain but was subsequently fought over by Argentina and Brazil. In 1828, with British help, Uruguay achieved independence, since when politics have been dominated by two parties, the Colorados (liberals) and the Blancos (conservatives). The late 19th century saw considerable immigration from Europe, encouraged by the establishment in the first decades of the 20th century of Latin America's first welfare state. In the late 1960s there was considerable unrest caused partly by the Tupamaro urban guerrillas. In 1973 they were crushed by the army, which subsequently assumed power and imposed repressive measures that led to international protests. Elections took place in 1984 and military rule officially ended in early 1985, when the Colorado candidate Julio Sanguinetti became president; he was replaced after elections in 1989 by Luis Alberto Lacalle of the Blanco party. Sanguinetti was re-elected in 1995. Legislative elections in 2000 resulted in victory for a new left-wing grouping, while Jorge Battle of the Blancos was elected president. Uruguay is a member of the OAS and LAIA.

Oriental Republic of Uruguay

Head of state	President Jorge Battle
Official language	Spanish
Official currency	new Uruguayan peso of 100 centésimos
Area	186 926 sq km (72 172 sq mi)
Population (1998 est)	3 216 000
Capital and main port	Montevideo

● **Uruguay, River** ▶ (Portuguese name: Rio Uruguai; Spanish name: Río Uruguay) A river in South America. Rising in S Brazil, it flows generally SW forming the Argentina–Brazil and Argentina–Uruguay borders before joining the Rio Paraná to form the Río de la Plata. Length: about 1600 km (1000 mi).

● **Uruk** ▶ (biblical name: Erech; modern name: Warka) An ancient city in S Mesopotamia. The site testifies to the beginnings of Sumerian civilization in the 4th millennium BC; significant finds include pictographic writing and pottery made on a wheel. In the 3rd millennium, Uruk was a centre for the worship of the god ▷Anu. ▷Gilgamesh was one of its rulers. Supplanted by ▷Ur (c. 2100), Uruk nevertheless remained inhabited until the early Christian era.

● **Ürümqi** ▶ (or Urumchi; former name: Tihwa) 43 43N 87 38E A city in NW China, the capital of Xinjiang Uygur AR, and the site of its university. Industries include iron and steel and machine building. Population (1991 est): 1 160 000.

● **ushabti** ▶ A figurine of faience, wood, or stone placed in an ancient Egyptian tomb to serve the deceased in the afterlife. Called "answerers," they carried inscriptions asserting their readiness to answer the gods' summons to work.

● **Ushant** ▶ (French name: Ouessant) 48 28N 5 05W A French island off the W coast of Brittany. Two naval battles (1778 and 1794) between the British and the French were fought off its coast. Area: about 16 sq km (6 sq mi).

● **Usküb** ▷*See* Skopje.

● **Üsküdar** ▶ (former name: Scutari) 41 02N 29 02E A town in NW Turkey, a suburb of Istanbul on the opposite side of the Bosporus. The British military base here during the Crimean War included the hospital in which Florence Nightingale worked. Population (latest est): 261 141.

● **Uspallata** ▶ 32 43S 69 24W A pass through the Andes, in S South America at the foot of Mount Aconcagua, linking Santiago (Chile) with Mendoza (Argentina). The statue *Christ of the Andes* was erected here (1904). Height: 3840 m (12 600 ft).

● **Ussher, James** ▶ (1581–1656) Irish Protestant churchman, who drew up the articles of doctrine for the Irish Protestant Church in 1615. As Archbishop of Armagh from 1625, he frequently visited England, eventually settling there after the Irish Rebellion (1641). He is best remembered for dating the creation at 4004 BC.

● **USSR** ▷*See* Soviet Union.

● **Ussuri River** ▶ A river in E Asia, rising in the extreme E of Russia and forming part of the border with China as it flows N to the River Amur at Khabarovsk. Border fighting between Soviet and Chinese forces occurred here (1964, 1972). Length: about 800 km (500 mi).

● **Ustinov, Sir Peter (Alexander)** ▶ (1921–) British actor, director, and dramatist of Russian descent. In the theatre he acted mostly in his own plays, which include *The Love of Four Colonels* (1951), *Romanoff and Juliet* (1956), and *Beethoven's Tenth* (1983); his films include *Death on the Nile* (1978) and *Lorenzo's Oil* (1992). He has written novels and an autobiography; he is also known as an impersonator, television personality, and for his work for UNICEF.

● **Ust-Kamenogorsk** ▶ 49 58N 82 36E A port in E Kazakhstan, on the River Irtysh. It is the centre of a zinc-, copper-, and lead-mining region. Population (1995 est): 326 300.

● **Ustyurt Plateau** ▶ (or Ust Urt Plateau) A desert upland in central Asia, lying between the Caspian and Aral Seas in Kazakhstan and Uzbekistan at an average height of about 200 m (656 ft). Area: about 200 000 sq km (77 204 sq mi).

● **Usumbura** ▷*See* Bujumbura.

● **usury** ▶ In medieval canon law, the charging of interest for the loan of money. Although Christians were debarred from being moneylenders, the profession was permitted to Jews by the fourth Lateran Council (1215). Since Jews were allowed by the Pentateuch to lend money at interest to strangers, and were excluded from many alternative occupations, they comprised the majority of moneylenders. By the late middle ages, however, with growing demand for credit to meet the needs of trade, many Christians, notably at Cahors and in Lombardy, ignored canonical prohibition and became moneylenders and usury came to mean the charging of extortionate interest. Usury is expressly forbidden by Islam, a prohibition that has led Muslim governments and businessmen to devise various alternative arrangements for the supply of credit.

● **Utagawa Kuniyoshi** ▶ (Igusa Magosaburo; 1797–1861) Japanese painter and printmaker of the ▷ukiyo-e movement. He is known for his warrior and landscape prints.

● **Utah** ▶ One of the mountain states in the SW USA. The Wasatch Range of the Rocky Mountains divides the state into two arid regions: the Great Basin, which includes the Great Salt Lake, and the Great Salt Lake Desert in the W and the Colorado Plateau in the E. The raising of livestock is the principal agricultural activity but further growth in this sector is limited by the lack of irrigation and by soil erosion. Manufacturing is increasing in importance, especially food products, fabricated steel, spacecraft and, more recently, electronics equipment. There are significant deposits of copper, oil, natural gas, and uranium. Scenic attractions, such as Bryce Canyon and Zion National Park, make it a popular tourist area. □ p. 1292.

History: the persecuted Mormons, who had emigrated from New York, began major settlements here in 1847 and their religion continues to exert a dominating influence over the life of the state. Ceded to the USA by Mexico in 1848, Utah was finally admitted to the Union in 1896. Area: 219 931 sq km (84 916 sq mi). Population (1997 est): 2 059 148. Capital: Salt Lake City.

● **Utamaro** ▷*See* Kitagawa Utamaro.

● **uterus** ▷*See* womb.

● **Utica** ▶ 43 06N 75 15W A city in the USA, in New York state on the Mohawk River. F. W. Woolworth opened his first shop here in 1879. There is an annual Utica Eisteddfod, sponsored by its many Welsh inhabitants. Industries include dairy farming and textiles. Population (1990): 68 637.

● **utilitarianism** ▶ An ethical doctrine holding that the best action is the one that will result in the greatest happiness and least pain for the greatest number of people. Utilitarianism flourished in Britain from the mid-18th century to the mid-19th century. ▷Hume, ▷Bentham, and James ▷Mill propounded it and John Stuart Mill defended it. It influenced all thought in politics and morals and was the most widespread British contribution to such thought. Both ▷intuitionism and ▷idealism have developed critiques of the doctrine, based on its inherent unfairness, the difficulty of assessing consequences, and the belief that some acts are intrinsically good or intrinsically bad, regardless of outcome.

● **utopianism** ▶ A programme of total social and political reform with the object of establishing a perfect society. The term derives from the imaginary state depicted in Thomas ▷More's *Utopia* (1516). Utopian schemes have sometimes found practical expression in social experiment, such as Robert ▷Owen's New Lanark community. Others, such as *Utopia* itself, are literary satires attacking existing institutions by comparing them unfavourably with imaginary ideals. Utopianism advocates a communistic organization of society, but the concomitant authoritarianism reveals that no way has been found of reconciling individual freedom with social justice.

● **Utrecht** ▶ 52 06N 5 07E A city in the central Netherlands, the capital of Utrecht province. The Union of Utrecht (1579) united the northern provinces of the Netherlands against Spain. The Treaties of ▷Utrecht (1713–14) were concluded here. Its notable buildings include the gothic cathedral (14th century) and its famous university (founded 1636). An important railway centre, its industries include textiles, chemicals, and metallurgy. An annual trade fair is held here. Population (1996 est): 234 254.

● **Utrecht, Treaties of** ▶ (1713–14) A series of treaties between France and, respectively, Britain, the Netherlands, Prussia, Portugal, and Savoy that concluded the War of the ▷Spanish Succession. Further treaties arranged settlements with Spain and the Holy Roman Empire. The effect of the treaties was to end Louis XIV's attempts at European expansion.

● **Utrillo, Maurice** ▶ (1883–1955) French painter, the illegitimate son of Suzanne Valadon (1867–1938), an artist's model and later herself an artist. For almost his entire life, he suffered from alcoholism and drug addiction. He specialized in painting often deserted street scenes, notably of Montmartre, distinguished by their near-monochrome colours and precise drawing. These were often based on picture-postcards and after 1916 became somewhat repetitive.

● **Uttar Pradesh** ▶ A state in N India, stretching from highlands N across the Ganges plain into the Himalayas. The most populous state, it produces grains, pulses, and sugar cane. Forestry is important but there is little industry.
History: the centre of N Indian culture, Uttar Pradesh was also the core of the Mogul Empire. It was the centre of the Indian Mutiny (1857–59) against British rule and of Indian nationalism. Area:

294 413 sq km (113 649 sq mi). Population (1991): 139 031 130. Capital: Lucknow.

● **Utzon, Jørn** ▶ (1918–) Danish architect, whose design for the Sydney Opera House (⌐architecture) won the competition for the building in 1957. Controversy led to Utzon's resignation in 1966 and the interior was not completed to his design. His other buildings include the Bagsvaerd Church in Copenhagen (1974–76) and the Kuwait Houses of Parliament.

● **uvula** ▷*See* palate.

● **Uzbekistan, Republic of** ▶ A republic in central Asia, formerly a constituent republic of the Soviet Union. It is mainly low lying, extending SE from the plains of the Aral Sea region to the mountainous borders of Afghanistan and Tadzhikistan. The NW comprises desert, including part of the Kara Kum, but fertile land is found in the SE. The Uzbeks, who are Turkic-speaking Sunnite Muslims, make up two-thirds of the population.
Economy: based on intensive agriculture on large state farms, made possible by the major irrigation schemes of the Soviet era. Cotton is the chief crop; rice and fruit are also grown. However, the excessive use of chemical pesticides and pollution from heavy industry have caused serious environmental problems, which have affected production in recent decades. Uzbekistan is rich in mineral deposits, including oil, coal, copper, and gold, and has more than 20 hydroelectric plants and 3 natural gas pipelines in operation. Heavy industry includes mining, chemicals, and metals. Since the mid-1990s the government has followed a programme of abolishing or reducing subsidies and enlarging the private sector. Economic cooperation agreements were signed with Russia and Kazakhstan in 1994.
History: the region was invaded by the Persians under Darius I, the Macedonians under Alexander the Great, and then by the Arabs (8th century AD) and the Mongols under Genghis Khan (13th century). In the 14th century it became the centre of the empire of Timur, who established his capital at Samarkand. In the 16th century the Uzbeks dominated the region, which was annexed by Russia in the 19th century. The Uzbek SSR was formed in 1924. There were violent riots in 1989 over ethnic issues; Uzbekistan declared sovereignty in 1990 and achieved independence on the break-up of the Soviet Union in 1991. The Communist Party has remained in power, as the People's Democratic Party, with Islam Karimov as president. Despite the introduction of a multiparty constitution in 1992, political opposition and press criticism are effectively banned. Opponents of the regime have adopted increasingly violent means, including a bombing campaign in 1999. There have also been ethnic clashes between Uzbeks and Tadzhiks and tensions involving ethnic Russians.

Republic of Uzbekistan

Head of state	President Islam Karimov
Official language	Uzbek
Official currency	som
Area	449 600 sq km (173 546 sq mi)
Population (1997 est)	23 664 000
Capital	Tashkent

Utah ▶ Bryce Canyon, designated a National Park in 1928. It contains columns of orange limestone and sandstone, laid down when the entire area was a shallow sea and sculptured since then by erosion.

● **V-1** ▶ A German World War II unguided missile, also called a flying bomb or a buzz bomb. Powered by an air-breathing type of ramjet, it carried about 2000 pounds (900 kg) of high explosive. Some 8000 missiles were launched against London between June 1944 and March 1945, killing over 5500 civilians. Many were shot down before reaching their target. The "V" stands for the German *Vergeltungswaffe*, retaliation weapon.

● **V-2** ▶ A German World War II ▷ballistic missile powered by a rocket engine using alcohol and liquid oxygen as fuel. It carried about 2000 pounds (900 kg) of high explosive and had a preset guidance system with no in-flight corrections. Some 4000 were used against Britain and the Low Countries in 1944 and 1945. Under ▷von Braun, who was responsible for its design at the German Rocket Test Centre at Peenemünde, it became the basis for US and Soviet postwar rockets.

● **Vaal River** ▶ A river in South Africa, rising in the SE. It flows generally W and SW, to join the Orange River. The **Vaal Dam**, near Vereeniging, supplies water to the mines of the Witwatersrand. Length: 1210 km (750 mi).

● **Vaasa** ▶ (Swedish name: Vasa) 63 06N 21 36E A seaport in W Finland, on the Gulf of Bothnia. Founded in 1606, it was rebuilt following a fire in 1852. Its industries include ship repairing and food processing. Population (1994): 55 089.

● **vaccination** ▶ (*or* inoculation) The introduction of inactivated or dead disease-causing microorganisms (vaccine) into the body to stimulate the formation of ▷antibodies to these agents without producing the disease (*see also* immunity). The first vaccination (against smallpox) was performed by Edward ▷Jenner in 1798. In the UK vaccination is now routinely used to prevent such life-threatening infections as poliomyelitis, diphtheria, tetanus, and tuberculosis. It is also used to protect visitors to areas where such infections as yellow fever, cholera, and typhoid fever are endemic, and vaccination against hepatitis A and B is available for those considered to be at risk of developing these diseases. In addition vaccination against certain strains of influenza (especially A and B) is now routinely given to the older members of a population in many countries, especially those who suffer from respiratory and heart diseases, etc. Vaccines are usually given by injection but some can be administered through skin scratches and some are taken by mouth. Vaccination against German measles (rubella) may be given to nonpregnant women of childbearing age, if they have not been vaccinated in childhood with the MMR (measles, mumps, rubella) vaccine, in order to prevent the malformations in the fetus that this disease can cause. Suggestions of a link between MMR vaccination and autism led to a decline in childhood immunizations with this vaccine in the late 1990s. The use of the whooping cough vaccine is also controversial as in very rare cases it has caused brain damage. The Hib vaccine, against a common (but not the most serious) form of bacterial ▷meningitis in children, is now part of the routine immunization schedule for children.

● **vacuum** ▶ A region of space that contains no matter. A perfect vacuum is impossible to obtain and any region in which the pressure is less than about 1 mmHg may be considered a vacuum. A soft (*or* low) vacuum goes down to a pressure of 10^{-2} pascal, a hard (*or* high) vacuum is between 10^{-2} and 10^{-7} pascal, and an ultrahigh vacuum is below 10^{-7} pascal. Vacuum technology is used in making cathode-ray tubes, light bulbs, etc., and in certain forms of food preservation. **Vacuum gauges** include the ▷McLeod gauge and ▷Pirani gauge.

● **vacuum distillation** ▷*See* distillation.

● **vacuum flask** ▷*See* Dewar flask.

● **Vadodara** ▶ (name until 1976: Baroda) 22 19N 73 14E A city in India, in Gujarat. The siting of an oil refinery at nearby Kouali has helped to promote Vadodara's industrial growth and its chief products include petrochemicals, cotton textiles, wood, and tobacco. Population (1991): 1 021 084.

● **Vaduz** ▶ 47 08N 9 32E The capital of the principality of Liechtenstein. It is a tourist centre and its castle (restored 1905–16) is the residence of the ruling prince. Population (1997 est): 5017.

● **vagina** ▶ The part of the reproductive tract of women and other female mammals into which the ▷penis is inserted during sexual intercourse. It connects the womb to the exterior and is readily distensible to enable the baby to emerge in childbirth.

● **vagus nerve** ▶ An important nerve that connects the brain with the throat, larynx, heart, lungs, stomach, and gut. Surgical cutting of a branch of the vagus nerve (**vagotomy**) is sometimes carried out to reduce the secretion of acid by the stomach in the treatment of a peptic ulcer.

● **Valdemar I** ▶ (*or* Waldemar; 1131–82) King of Denmark (1157–82). His defeat of rival claimants to the throne ended a prolonged civil war. His campaigns against the Wends (1159–69), assisted by ▷Absalon, ended in victory with the seizure of Rügen. He subsequently repressed internal unrest.

● **Valdemar II** ▶ (*or* Waldemar; 1170–1241) King of Denmark (1202–41); the son of Valdemar I. Before becoming king he conquered Holstein and Hamburg (1200–01) and later conducted successful campaigns in the E Baltic region. In 1219 he conquered Estonia but from 1223 to 1225 was imprisoned by a German vassal. At home he introduced military and legal reforms, issuing a revised legal code, the Law of Jutland (1241).

● **Valdemar IV Atterdag** ▶ (*or* Waldemar; c. 1320–75) King of Denmark (1340–75). He was brought up at the court of Emperor Louis IV. Recognized as king in 1340, his reunification of Danish territories was completed by the recovery of Skåne from Sweden in 1360. His conquest of Gotland in the Baltic (1361) brought opposition from the Hanseatic League, which defeated Valdemar (1368) and forced him to accept the unfavourable Treaty of Stralsund (1370). His daughter ▷Margaret became Queen of Denmark, Norway, and Sweden.

● **Valdivia** ▶ 39 46S 73 15W A port in S Chile, on the Río Valdivia near the Pacific coast. It was badly damaged by earthquake (1960). Industries include tanning, shipbuilding, and sugar refining. It contains the Southern University of Chile (1954). Population (1995 est): 119 431.

● **valence** ▶ (*or* valency) The combining power of an atom, ion, or radical. It is equal to the number of hydrogen atoms that the atom, ion, or radical can combine with or replace in forming compounds, i.e. it is the number of single covalent or electrovalent bonds (*see* chemical bond) that an atom, etc., can make. Many elements have more than one valence, for example phosphorus has valences of three and five. A **valence electron** is an electron in the outer shell of an atom that participates in forming chemical (valence) bonds. ▷*See also* energy band.

● **Valence** ▶ 44 56N 4 54E A town in SE France, the capital of the Drôme department on the River Rhône. It has a cathedral (11th–12th centuries) and is a commercial centre for agricultural produce. Population (1990): 65 026.

● **Valencia** ▶ 39 29N 0 24W The third largest city in Spain, on the Guadalaviar estuary. In 1021 it became the capital of the Moorish kingdom of Valencia. El Cid, the legendary Spanish hero, took the city from the Moors and held it from 1094 until his death in 1099. Its many notable buildings include the cathedral (1262–1482); the university was founded in 1500. The centre of a productive agricultural area, Valencia has an important trade in oranges, rice, and silk. Population (1995 est): 763 299.

● **Valencia** ▶ 10 14N 67 59W The third largest city in Venezuela. It is the focus of the country's most productive agricultural area and is a major industrial centre. The University of Carabobo was founded here in 1852. Population (1990 est): 903 000.

● **Valencia** ▶ A former kingdom in E Spain, corresponding approximately to the present-day autonomous region of Valencia. It was taken from the Moors by El Cid during the 11th century and came under the rule of Aragon in 1238.

● **Valenciennes** ▶ 50 22N 3 32E A town in N France, in the Nord department. It has metallurgical and textile industries and an oil refinery. Its once famous lace industry is being revived. Population (latest est): 40 881.

● **valency** ▷*See* valence.

● **Valens** ▶ (d. 378 AD) Eastern Roman emperor (364–78). Valens owed his accession to his brother ▷Valentinian I, emperor in the West. During Valens' reign the Visigoths crossed the Danube and killed Valens at the battle of ▷Adrianople.

● **valentine** ▶ A greeting card sent anonymously on 14 February as a declaration of affection. In ancient Rome boys drew girls' names from a love urn on 15 February and the early Christian Church transferred this popular pagan custom to St Valentine's feast day rather than abolish it. Paper valentines date from the 16th century.

● **Valentine, St** ▶ (died c. 269) Roman priest and martyr, known as the patron of lovers. The customs practised on his feast day (14 Feb) have no connection with his life (*see* valentine).

● **Valentinian I** ▶ (d. 375 AD) Western Roman emperor (364–75). Valentinian became emperor by the acclamation of the army at Nicaea and shortly afterwards made his brother ▷Valens emperor in the East. Reputedly of cruel disposition, he fought campaigns in the north of the Empire, restoring the Rhine frontier and Hadrian's Wall.

● **Valentino, Rudolf** ▶ (Rodolpho Gugliemi di Valentina d'Antonguolla; 1895–1926) US film actor, born in Italy. He held various labouring jobs between arriving in the USA in 1913 and going to Hollywood in 1918. His performances in *The Sheik* (1921), *Blood and Sand* (1922), *Son of the Sheik* (1926), and other silent romantic dramas established him as the leading cinema idol of the 1920s.

● **Vale of Glamorgan** ▶ A county borough of S Wales, created in 1996 from parts of Mid Glamorgan and South Glamorgan. Area: 295 sq km (114 sq mi). Population (1996 est): 119 200. Administrative centre: Barry.

● **Valera, Eamon De** ▷*See* De Valera, Eamon.

● **valerian** ▶ A perennial or (rarely) annual herb of either of the genera *Valeriana* (200 species) or *Centranthus* (12 species), native to the N hemisphere. Up to about 1 m high, the plants usually have lobed leaves and small fragrant pink, red, or white five-lobed funnel-shaped flowers clustered into terminal heads. The root of the common valerian (*V. officinalis*), of Eurasia, has sedative properties. Family: *Valerianaceae*.

● **Valéry, Paul** ▶ (1871–1945) French poet, essayist, and critic. After publishing some early Symbolist verse he devoted himself for many years to abstract metaphysical study. *Cahiers* (29 vols, 1957–60) is a record of his daily speculations from 1894 until his death. His later poetry in *La Jeune Parque* (1917) and *Charmes* (1922) combines sensuous lyricism with intellectual force. He published many collections of essays on literary, scientific, and political topics.

● **Valhalla** ▶ In Teutonic mythology, one of the three homes of ▷Odin, imagined as an enormous hall the rafters of which are spears and the walls shields. Half of the warriors who die in battle are brought by the ▷Valkyries to Valhalla, where they spend their days in battle and their nights in feasting and listening to songs of their heroic exploits.

● **Valium** ▷*See* benzodiazepines.

● **Valkyries** ▶ In Teutonic mythology, beautiful maidens, between 3 and 27 in number, who are the personal attendants of ▷Odin. They wear helmets and armour, carry spears and, led by ▷Freyja, ride on horseback over battlefields in order to find and carry away the slain warriors whom Odin has chosen to live with him in ▷Valhalla.

● **Valla, Lorenzo** ▶ (1405–57) Italian Renaissance humanist. He was a violent opponent of ▷scholasticism and an able scholar. In his *De voluptate* (*On Pleasure*; 1431), he argued that the pleasures of the senses were the greatest good. Valla's iconoclastic views had a considerable influence upon later Renaissance thought.

● **Valladolid** ▶ 41 39N 4 45W A city in central Spain, in Old Castile. It was formerly the capital of Castile and León (14th–15th centuries). It has a 16th-century cathedral and contains Cervantes' house; its university was founded in 1346. Christopher Columbus died here (1506). An industrial centre, its industries include brewing and textiles. Population (1995 est): 334 820.

● **Valle d'Aosta** ▶ An autonomous region in NW Italy, consisting of the upper basin of the River Dora Baltea. Created in 1945, it has a large French-speaking population. Industry has replaced agriculture as the main activity and there are valuable hydroelectric resources. Tourism is important. Area: 3262 sq km (1260 sq mi). Population (1994 est): 118 239. Capital: Aosta.

● **Valletta** ▶ 35 54N 14 32E The capital of Malta, a port on the N coast with one of the finest harbours in the world. Founded in 1566 by the Knights of St John, its main buildings include the 16th-century St John's Co-Cathedral and the University of Malta (1769). Formerly an important British naval base, its dockyards have been converted to commercial use and it is now an important transit centre for Mediterranean shipping. Population (1996 est): 9129.

Rudolf Valentino ▶ In one of his most popular films, *The Son of the Sheik*, with Vilma Banky swooning in his arms.

● **valley** ▶ An elongated depression in the earth's surface. It is usually occupied by a river or stream at its base and terminates on joining another river, a lake, or the ocean. Valleys have various origins but the common **V-shaped valley** is formed as the result of erosion by a river. Those that originated through glacial erosion are **U-shaped valleys**, with steep sides and broad floors, often occupied by deep lakes (*see* fjord). ▷*See also* rift valley.

● **Valley Forge** ► The site, 35 km (22 mi) NW of Philadelphia, of the winter camp of Gen Washington's army in the winter of 1777–78 during the American Revolution. The patient endurance of his hungry, ill, and badly clothed men, who nevertheless emerged ready for the spring offensive against the British, became legendary.

● **Valley of Ten Thousand Smokes** ► A volcanic area in the USA, in S Alaska. Its name derives from the many fissures spouting smoke, gas, and steam.

● **Valley of the Kings** ► The cemetery of the Egyptian pharaohs from about 1580 to about 1085 BC, W of the Nile, near ▷Thebes. Tombs were tunnelled in the limestone cliffs while mortuary temples were built in the valley below. All the tombs were robbed, except that of ▷Tutankhamen.

● **Valois** ► The royal dynasty of France from 1328 to 1589, succeeding the ▷Capetians. The ▷Hundred Years' War (1337–1453) nearly destroyed Valois power, which was saved by ▷Charles VII (reigned 1422–61). He and his son ▷Louis XI vigorously extended royal authority. Their successors, ▷Charles VIII and ▷Louis XII, waged disastrous wars in Italy, where they opposed the ▷Habsburgs. The last Valois were the victims of rival religious factions at court (*see* Wars of Religion) and were succeeded by the ▷Bourbons.

● **Valois, Dame Ninette de** ▷*See* de Valois, Dame Ninette.

● **Valona** ▷*See* Vlora.

● **Valparaíso** ► 33 05S 71 40W The second largest city in Chile, on the Pacific Ocean. Founded by the Spanish (1536), it has suffered several earthquakes. Notable surviving buildings include the cathedral. It is the site of two universities (1926 and 1928). Valparaíso is a major port, handling most Chilean imports, and is an important industrial and commercial centre. Manufactures include chemicals, textiles, and vegetable oils. Population (1999 est): 283 489.

● **value-added tax** ► (VAT) An indirect tax on goods calculated by adding a percentage to the value of a product as it increases at each stage of production; the whole cost of the tax is eventually passed on to the consumer. The tax was introduced in the UK in 1973 to replace ▷purchase tax and to achieve compatibility with the EC taxation system. It is collected by the Board of Customs and Excise. It is charged at a rate of 17.5% on all goods and services except those that are zero-rated, exempt, or taxed at a special reduced rate. Basic food, children's clothes, and books are zero-rated. VAT has been charged on domestic fuel (which was formerly zero-rated) at a rate of 8% since April, 1994.

● **valve** ► 1. A device that controls the flow of a fluid. An inlet valve in an □internal-combustion engine permits the explosive mixture to enter the combustion chamber; the outlet valve allows the burnt gases to leave the combustion chamber. These mushroom-shaped valves are either open or closed. Other valves, such as needle valves or butterfly valves, permit controlled quantities of fluids to flow (usually in one direction). A domestic tap is such a valve. Yet other valves control only the direction of flow; these include the valves that occur

in the ▷hearts, ▷veins, and lymphatic systems of animals. They are usually cusp valves. Pocket-like cusps are attached to the walls of the vessel, so that a flow of blood or lymph in the desired direction flattens the cusps against the walls without impeding the flow; if the flow is reversed, the cusps are pushed out into the centre of the vessel, thus blocking a backflow. 2. ▷*See* thermionic valve.

● **vampire** ► In folklore, a soulless or "undead" corpse that rises from its coffin at night, sometimes taking the form of a vampire bat, and sucks the blood of living victims (who are thus also transformed into vampires). The vampire cannot rest but must continually find new victims. It attacks only at night and is repelled by crucifixes, garlic, and the light of day. The body of a vampire can be destroyed by being beheaded, burnt, having a stake driven through its heart, or exposure to sunlight. Although appearing in many cultures, the vampire legend is particularly associated with E Europe; it was popularized by Bram Stoker's *Dracula* (1897), the source of many vampire films.

● **vampire bat** ► A bat of the family *Desmodontidae* (3 species), of Central and South America. The most common species is *Desmodus rotundus*, 7.5–9 cm long. Vampire bats feed on the blood of mammals or birds. They make a small incision in the skin with their sharp incisor teeth and lap up the blood of their sleeping victim with a grooved tongue. Vampire bats are too small to cause serious blood loss to their host but they may transmit dangerous diseases, including rabies.

● **Van, Lake** ► A lake in SW Turkey. It has no outlet and is therefore salty; sodium carbonate is extracted by evaporation, and the lake is fished for darekh. Area: 3738 sq km (1443 sq mi).

● **vanadium** ► (V) A transition metal, named after the Norse goddess Vanadis. The metal is isolated by reduction of the trichloride (VCl_3) with magnesium or of the pentoxide (V_2O_5) with calcium. It is an important additive to rust-resistant ▷steels and high-speed tool steels. The pentoxide is a useful catalyst in the oil industry. Complex vanadate ions (for example VO_4^{3-}) exist in solution. At no 23; at wt 50.9415; mp 1910 ± 10°C; bp 3409°C.

● **Van Allen, James Alfred** ► (1914–   ) US physicist, who during World War II developed a proximity fuse for anti-aircraft shells. After the war he used rockets for research into the upper atmosphere, being especially interested in cosmic rays. In 1958, while professor of physics at Iowa University, he used the results of the Explorer satellites to deduce the existence of belts of charged particles (*see* Van Allen radiation belts) above the earth.

● **Van Allen radiation belts** ► Two regions of charged particles in the earth's ▷magnetosphere. The toroidal inner belt lies 1000–5000 km above the equator and contains protons and electrons captured from the ▷solar wind or derived from cosmic-ray interactions. The outer belt lies 15 000–25 000 km above the equator, curving down towards the earth's magnetic poles, and contains mainly electrons from the solar wind. The belts were discovered in 1958 by James ▷Van Allen on his analysis of observations by early Explorer satellites.

● **Vanbrugh, Sir John** ► (1664–1726) English architect. After a varied life as a soldier and fashionable playwright—his plays included *The Relapse* (1697) and *The Provok'd Wife* (1697)—Vanbrugh became England's most successful ▷baroque architect. Although he held a position in the Office of Works, most of his work was for private patrons.

(a)   (b)   (c)   (d)

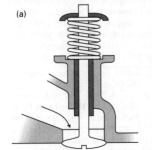
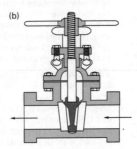
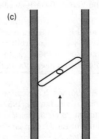
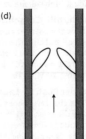

valves ► (a) A mushroom (*or* poppet) valve as used in a petrol engine. (b) A wedge-gate valve as used in a pipe. (c) A simple butterfly valve. (d) A cusp valve as occurring in a blood vessel to prevent backflow.

His most impressive buildings were Castle Howard (1699–1726), ▷Blenheim Palace (begun 1705), on which he collaborated with ▷Hawksmoor, and Seton Delaval (begun 1720). Highly imaginative and extravagant in his designs and costs, Vanbrugh rarely finished buildings and at Blenheim was dismissed by the dissatisfied Duchess of Marlborough.

● **Van Buren, Martin** ▶ (1782–1862) US statesman; Democratic president (1837–41) and a founder of the Democratic Party. He came to power during the panic of 1837, the country's first great economic depression, which was caused largely by a wave of land speculation in the West. His refusal of government aid, on a laissez-faire principle, led to his defeat in the 1840 election.

● **Vance, Cyrus** ▶ (1917–2002) US statesman; secretary of state (1977–80). He represented President Johnson in Cyprus (1967) and Korea (1968) and was US negotiator at the Paris peace talks on Vietnam (1968–69). He resigned as secretary of state in opposition to President Carter's attempt to rescue the US hostages held in Tehran (Iran). In 1992–93 he led (with Lord ▷Owen) attempts to negotiate a peace agreement in Bosnia-Hercegovina.

● **Vancouver** ▶ 49 13N 123 06W A city and port in W Canada, in British Columbia on Burrard Inlet and the Fraser River delta. Established in 1862 on a beautiful site at the S end of the Coast Mountains, it has developed a rich tourist industry. Vancouver is Canada's largest Pacific port and railhead. With a large airport, it is a centre for international trade and warehousing. It is the commercial and industrial centre of British Columbia, important especially for its timber, paper, and associated industries. Other industries include food processing, ship repairing, and fishing. Vancouver has two universities and a thriving cultural life. Population (1996): 514 008.

● **Vancouver, George** ▶ (c. 1758–98) British navigator. He served his apprenticeship under Capt ▷Cook and in 1791 set out on a long voyage in the Pacific. He visited Australia and then proceeded NW, charting the W coast of America and circumnavigating the island named after him.

● **Vancouver Island** ▶ A Canadian island off the Pacific coast of British Columbia. Its E coastal plain rises to glaciers and forested mountains. The economy depends on timber, mining, fishing, and tourism; it is also a popular retirement area. Area: 32 137 sq km (12 408 sq mi). Population (latest est): 461 573. Chief town: Victoria.

● **Vandals** ▶ A Germanic tribe that during the first four centuries AD migrated southwards from Scandinavia and the S Baltic coast through Europe to Spain and Africa. There, in 429, they established a kingdom under Genseric and in 455 sacked Rome. The devastation they caused gave rise to the term vandalism. In 534, however, their kingdom was destroyed by the Byzantine general, ▷Belisarius.

● **Van de Graaff generator** ▶ A type of ▷electrostatic generator, invented by the US physicist Robert Jemison Van de Graaff (1901–67), that produces static potentials of millions of volts. Charge from an external source is fed onto a continuously moving belt, which transfers it to the inside of a large hollow conducting sphere. The charge moves to the outer surface of the sphere, leaving the inside neutral and able to collect more charge. This type of generator can be used to provide a high-voltage source for the Van de Graaff ▷accelerator.

● **Vanderbilt, Cornelius** ▶ (1794–1877) US businessman. He built up a fleet of passenger and cargo steamships, a business that became very successful after the 1849 Gold Rush, when Vanderbilt provided a fast service from New York to San Francisco. In 1862 he sold his ships and bought several railway companies. He endowed Vanderbilt University in Nashville, Tennessee (1873).

● **Van der Post, Sir Laurens** ▶ (1906–96) South African writer and traveller. His travel books include *Venture to the Interior* (1952), *The Lost World of the Kalahari* (1958), and *Testament to the Bushmen* (1984). His novels, often imbued with deep feeling for the African landscape, include *The Hunter and the Whale* (1967), *A Story Like the Wind* (1972), and *About Blady* (1991). He was knighted in 1981.

● **Van der Waals, Johannes Diderik** ▶ (1837–1923) Dutch physicist, who was professor at Amsterdam University (1877–1907). He was

awarded the 1910 Nobel Prize for his work on the intermolecular forces (Van der Waals' forces) and his equation of state (*see* Van der Waals' equation).

● **Van der Waals' equation** ▶ A modification of the ideal gas equation, $pV = RT$, where p is the pressure exerted by a gas with volume V and absolute temperature T. R is the ▷gas constant. Van der Waals adjusted V to $(V − b)$ to take account of the volume occupied by the gas molecules. He also assumed that forces of attraction exist between the gas molecules and therefore adjusted the pressure term to $(p − a/V^2)$. Both a and b are constant for a particular gas. The intermolecular forces are known as **Van der Waals' forces** and are caused by molecules inducing electric ▷dipole moments in neighbouring molecules.

● **van de Velde** ▶ A family of 17th-century Dutch painters. **Willem van de Velde the Elder** (1611–93) and his eldest son **Willem van de Velde the Younger** (1633–1707) were both marine artists, who lived in England after 1672 in the service of Charles II. His younger son **Adriaen van de Velde** (1636–72) was a landscape painter, who was often employed by such artists as ▷Ruisdael and ▷Hobbema to paint the figures in their landscapes. **Esaias van de Velde** (c. 1591–1630), the landscape painter, was probably the brother of Willem van de Velde the Elder. He is best known as the teacher of the landscape painter Jan van ▷Goyen and for such works as *Winter Scene* (National Gallery, London), which herald the realistic landscapes of the later 17th-century Dutch school.

● **van de Velde, Henry** ▶ (1863–1957) Belgian ▷Art Nouveau architect and interior designer. A painter until about 1890, he took up design under the influence of William ▷Morris and the ▷Arts and Crafts movement. In 1901, after working in Paris and Berlin, he settled in Weimar, where he directed (1901–14) its School of Arts and Crafts, later part of the ▷Bauhaus.

● **Van Diemen's Land** ▷*See* Tasmania.

● **van Diemen, Anthony** ▷*See* Diemen, Anthony van.

● **Van Dyck, Sir Anthony** ▶ (*or* Vandyke; 1599–1641) Flemish ▷baroque painter, born in Antwerp. Early in his career, he was assistant to ▷Rubens, who greatly influenced his work. After working in England for James I, he visited Italy (1621–27). In 1632 he returned to England as painter to ⊓Charles I. Although he painted many religious and mythological subjects, such as *Cupid and Psyche* (Buckingham Palace), his reputation rests largely on his portraits of the English court. *Charles I on Horseback* (National Gallery, London) and *Thomas Killigrew and Lord Croft* (Windsor Castle) demonstrate the elegance and grandeur of his style. He had a profound influence on the development of British portraiture.

● **Vänern, Lake** ▶ The largest lake in Sweden. It drains into the Kattegat via the River Göta, a major source of hydroelectric power. Area: 5546 sq km (2141 sq mi).

● **Vane the Elder, Sir Henry** ▶ (1589–1655) English politician. He represented Charles I in negotiations with parliament (1640) but fought against the king in the Civil War. His son **Sir Henry Vane the Younger** (1613–62), a staunch Puritan, emigrated to New England in 1635 but returned to England in 1637 and was prominent in the opposition of the ▷Long Parliament to the king. During the Civil War he negotiated the ▷Solemn League and Covenant with the Scots (1643). A member of the state council during the Commonwealth (1649–53) he opposed the Protectorate and retired (1653). In 1655 he published the *Retired Man's Meditations*. He participated in the overthrow of Richard Cromwell (1659) but was executed after the Restoration.

● **van Eyck, Jan** ▶ (c. 1390–1441) Flemish painter, who also served as diplomatic envoy of Philip the Good, Duke of Burgundy. The controversial *Adoration of the Lamb* altarpiece (Cathedral of S Bavon, Ghent) was probably begun by his elder brother **Hubert van Eyck** (d. 1426) and completed by Jan after Hubert's death. Jan is noted for his realistic portraits, particularly *The Arnolfini Marriage* and *Man in a Red Turban* (both National Gallery, London). He certainly perfected and possibly invented the Flemish technique of oil painting, in which the pigment is mixed with oil and turpentine and applied in thin glazes.

Vincent Van Gogh ▶ His famous *Sunflowers*, painted in 1888.

● **Van Gogh, Vincent** ▶ (1853–90) Dutch postimpressionist painter, born at Zundert, the son of a pastor. He worked as an art dealer, a teacher in England, and a missionary among coalminers before taking up painting in about 1880. His early works were chiefly drawings of peasants. After a limited training in The Hague and in Antwerp, where he studied the works of ▷Rubens and Japanese prints, he moved to Paris (1886). Here he briefly adopted the style of ▷impressionism and later of ▷pointillism. In Arles in 1888 he painted his best-known works—orchards, sunflowers, and the local postman and his family—but only one painting was sold during his lifetime. The visit of his friend ▷Gauguin ended in a quarrel during which Van Gogh cut off part of his own left ear. In 1889 he entered a mental asylum at Saint-Rémy. The ominous *Wheatfield with Crows* (Stedelijk Museum, Amsterdam) was painted shortly before his suicide, in Auvers. His letters to his brother (Theo) contain the best account of his life and work. ▷*See* expressionism.

● **Vanilla** ▶ A genus of climbing ▷orchids (about 90 species), native to tropical Asia and America. They have long fleshy stems attached to trees by aerial roots and produce large white and yellow flowers. Several species are cultivated commercially for the flavouring agent vanilla, the most important being *V. planifolia*, which is cultivated in Madagascar, Mexico, and Indonesia. The fruit—a pod—contains an oily pulp and minute seeds and reaches a length of 20 cm. The aroma of vanilla is due to vanillin, a volatile oil resulting from curing and fermentation of the pods.

● **Vannes** ▶ 47 40N 2 44W A port in W France, the capital of the Morbihan department on the Gulf of Morbihan. An important Celtic settlement, it has a cathedral with a 16th-century chapel. Industries include shipbuilding and textiles. Population (latest est): 45 397.

● **Van't Hoff, Jacobus Henricus** ▶ (1852–1911) Dutch chemist, who pioneered the field of stereoisomerism, showing that the bonds of a carbon atom are arranged in a tetrahedron. This enabled him to explain ▷optical activity in terms of molecular structure. He contributed to chemical thermodynamics and to the theory of solutions, winning the 1901 Nobel Prize.

● **Vanua Levu** ▶ A volcanic island in the S Pacific Ocean, the second largest in Fiji. Sugar, copra, and gold are exported. Area: 5535 sq km (2137 sq mi). Population (latest est): 909. Chief town: Lambasa.

● **Vanuatu, Republic of** ▶ (name until 1980: New Hebrides) A country in the SW Pacific Ocean comprising a chain of about 80 forested volcanic islands, the largest of which is Espíritu Santo.
　Economy: chiefly agricultural. Copra, cocoa, and coffee are grown for export on commercial plantations; subsistence crops include yams, taro, and sweet potato. Beef and timber are also exported. The other main economic activities include tourism, fishing, and manganese mining. Vanuatu is also developing as a centre for financial services, owing to the lack of direct taxation.
　History: sighted by the Portuguese (1606), the islands were later (1774) charted by James Cook, who named them the New Hebrides. In the 19th century the population was decimated when thousands of indigenous inhabitants were removed to work on sugar plantations in Australia. From 1906 the islands were jointly administered as a condominium by France and the UK. In 1978 the islands became partially self-governing as a preliminary to their independence as the Vanuatu Republic in 1980. In 1989 President Ati George Sokomanu was deposed after illegally attempting to remove his prime minister, Maxime Carlot Korman. The current prime minister, Edward Natapei, took office in 2001.

Republic of Vanuatu

Head of state	President John Bernard Bani
Official languages	English, French, and Bislama
Official currency	vatu of 100 centimes
Area	about 14 760 sq km (5700 sq mi)
Population (2001 est)	195 000
Capital	Vila, on Efate

● **vapour pressure** ▶ The pressure of the vapour given off by a liquid or solid. The vapour pressure increases with temperature. If the liquid or solid is in an enclosed space the number of molecules leaving it eventually reaches an equilibrium with the number of molecules returning to it. At this point the vapour is saturated and the pressure is the **saturated vapour pressure**.

● **Varah, Chad** ▷*See* Samaritans.

● **Varanasi** ▶ (or Benares) 25 20N 82 00E A city in India, in Uttar Pradesh on the River Ganges. A major place of pilgrimage for Hindus, Jains, Sikhs, and Buddhists, it has 5 km (3 mi) of ghats (steps), from which Hindus bathe in the sacred river. There are also burning ghats, from which the ashes of the cremated are scattered over the water. The city contains 1500 temples and two universities. Population (1991): 925 962.

● **Varèse, Edgard** ▶ (1883–1965) French composer, who settled in the USA in 1915. He composed music characterized by dissonance, the use of unpitched sounds, and complex rhythms. His works include *Ionisation* (for 41 percussion instruments and two sirens; 1931) and *Density 21.5* (for solo flute; 1935).

● **Vargas, Getúlio** ▶ (1883–1954) Brazilian statesman; president (1930–45, 1951–54). Seizing power in the revolution of 1930 after losing the presidential election, he announced (1937) the fascist New State, modelled on Portugal. He was overthrown in 1945 and re-elected in 1950 but, threatened with a military coup, he committed suicide.

● **Vargas Llosa, (Jorge) Mario (Pedro)** ▶ (1936–　) Peruvian novelist and politician. Earlier novels, such as *The City and the Dogs* (1963) and *Conversation in the Cathedral* (1969), deal with the corruption and decay of Peruvian society under dictatorship. Later works include *The War of the End of the World* (1981), *The Writer's Reality* (1992), and *The Notebooks of Don Rigoberto* (1998). In 1990 he was an unsuccessful candidate for the presidency of Peru.

● **variable** ► A mathematical symbol for a quantity that can take any value from a set of values called the range. A variable that can take any value between two given values is called continuous; otherwise it is discrete. A quantity that can only take one value is called a constant.

● **variable star** ► A star whose brightness varies with time, the variations being regular, irregular, or a mixture of the two. In regular variables the brightness completes a cycle in a period ranging from minutes to years. The brightness variation can be several ▷magnitudes. The three major groups are: eclipsing ▷binary stars, which include ▷Algol variables; cataclysmic variables, such as ▷novae; and pulsating stars, which periodically brighten and fade as their surface layers expand and contract and which include ▷Cepheid variables, ▷RR Lyrae stars, and Mira stars (*see* Mira Ceti).

● **variance** ► In a set of numbers, usually measurements, the quantity obtained by summing the squares of the differences between each number and the average value of the set and then dividing by the number of members of the set. Variance and, more often, its square root, called the **standard deviation**, are used to estimate scatter or random error in experimental results.

● **varicose veins** ► Swollen tortuous veins in the legs caused by malfunctioning of the valves in the veins obstructing blood flow. Varicose veins tend to run in families and are commoner in older and overweight people, women, and those who are constantly standing. They often ache and may later cause thrombosis or infection. The veins may be surgically stripped or removed or injected with a substance that makes them shrivel up.

● **Varna** ► 43 12N 27 57E A city and port in E Bulgaria, on the Black Sea. Founded in the 6th century BC, it finally passed to Bulgaria in 1878. Processed foods and livestock are exported and it has engineering and boatbuilding industries. Population (1996 est): 301 421.

● **Varna, Battle of** ► (10 November, 1444) The battle in which the Hungarians were decisively defeated by the Turks. It enabled the Turks to expand further into the Balkans and ultimately to capture Constantinople (1453).

● **varnish** ► A resinous solution in oil or a solvent that dries to form a hard transparent coating on wood, metal, etc. The ▷resins may be natural, synthetic, or mixed. The natural resins used include ▷shellac, copal, dammar, and congo. **French polishing** consists of varnishing wood with a solution of shellac in alcohol (traditionally industrial methylated spirits). This is the varnish used on antique furniture. However, synthetic resins are now widely used on modern furniture; ▷polyurethane is a particularly durable synthetic resin used for protecting surfaces in harsh environments. Polyesters and alkyds are also used, for example for coating paper containers or as a protective finish for ink.

● **varnish tree** ▷*See* lacquer tree.

● **Varro, Marcus Terentius** ► (116–27 BC) Roman scholar and poet. After a varied public career he was appointed public librarian by Julius Caesar in 47 BC. Only *On Agriculture* and parts of a 25-volume work, *On the Latin Language*, survive.

● **varve dating** ► A technique used in geology and archaeology to give the age of a sediment and to provide information about the climate during which it was formed. Varves are layers of claylike sediment deposited from a melting glacier into a lake. Each varve represents a single year's deposition; a thick varve indicates that the sediment was deposited during a hot summer (since the glacier would melt more quickly and therefore deposit more material). Varves are particularly well developed in Scandinavia and in some regions their formation has continued from the Pleistocene Ice Age to the present: by counting the varves the absolute age of a particular sediment is calculated.

● **Vasa** ► The ruling dynasty of Sweden (1523–1818) and of Poland (1587–1668) founded by ▷Gustavus I Vasa. John III (1537–92; reigned 1568–92) married into the Polish royal house and his son Sigismund III (1566–1632) became King of both Poland (1587) and Sweden (1592). Sigismund was deposed (1599) in Sweden, where he was succeeded by his uncle ▷Charles IX, and the Vasa split into two competing lines.

The best-known Vasa monarchs in Sweden were ▷Gustavus II Adolphus and ▷Christina.

● **Vasarely, Victor** ► (1908–97) Hungarian-born painter. After training in Budapest, he moved to Paris (1930), where his abstract paintings of geometric forms were initially influenced by ▷constructivism. By the 1950s and 1960s he was painting dazzling patterns that appear to move; these works are regarded as leading examples of ▷Op art.

● **Vasari, Giorgio** ► (1511–74) Italian painter, architect, and writer. In Florence, under Medici patronage, he painted fresco cycles in the Palazzo Vecchio and built the ▷Uffizi, both works showing his respect for ▷mannerism. However he is best known for his *Lives of the Most Eminent Italian Architects, Painters, and Sculptors*, tracing the history of Renaissance art from Giotto to Michelangelo. First published in 1550, it is still popular and useful, despite some inaccuracies.

● **vascular plant** ▷*See* plant.

● **vasectomy** ▷*See* sterilization.

● **Västerås** ► 59 36N 16 32E A city in central Sweden, on Lake Mälar. An important city in medieval times, it has a 12th-century castle and a gothic cathedral. It is a major centre of the electrical industry. Population (1997 est): 124 084.

● **VAT** ▷*See* value-added tax.

● **Vatican City State** ► A small independent state within the city of Rome, the seat of government of the Roman Catholic Church. St Peter's Square, St Peter's Basilica, the Vatican Palace, and Papal Gardens are within its area, and it includes 12 buildings outside its boundary, notably several churches and the pope's summer palace at Castel Gandolfo. It has its own army, police, diplomatic service, coinage,

Vatican City State ► The dome of St Peter's Basilica towering above the Bridge of St Angelo across the Tiber.

postal facilities, and radio station (Radio Vaticano, which provides an all-day service in 31 languages giving information on the Church).

History: it came into being in 1929, when Pius XI signed the ▷Lateran Treaty with Mussolini, thereby ending a dispute between church and state dating from the incorporation of the ▷papal states into newly unified Italy in 1870. The state is governed by a commission appointed by the pope.

Vatican City State

Supreme pontiff	Pope John Paul II
Official language	Italian
Official currency	Italian lira
Area	44 hectares (109 acres)
Population (1997 est)	1000

● **Vatican Councils** ▶ The 20th and 21st ecumenical councils of the Roman Catholic Church, held at Rome. **1.** (1869–70) The council that was convoked by ▷Pius IX resulted in the promulgation of the doctrine of papal ▷infallibility. The council was suspended because of the Franco-Prussian War. **2.** (1962–65) The council that was convoked by ▷John XXIII and continued by ▷Paul VI. Its main purpose, in Pope John's words, was *aggiornamento*, a bringing-up-to-date of the Church. It promulgated no dogmas but instead initiated fundamental changes, including reform of the liturgy and commitment to the ▷ecumenical movement and to greater collegiality in Church government. It established an atmosphere in which progressive critics could freely express their views (a freedom subsequently curtailed under John Paul II).

● **Vatnajökull** ▶ An icefield in SE Iceland. Several peaks protrude above the ice level rising to 2119 m (6952 ft) at Öræfajökull, the highest point on the island. Area: 8133 sq km (3139 sq mi).

● **Vauban, Sébastien Le Prestre de** ▶ (1633–1707) French military engineer, who revolutionized siege warfare. Appointed engineer to Louis XIV of France in 1655, he directed sieges at Gravelines (1658), Maastricht (1673), and Luxembourg (1684).

● **vaudeville** ▷*See* music hall.

● **Vaudois** ▷*See* Waldenses.

● **Vaughan, Henry** ▶ (c. 1622–95) Welsh poet. After producing two volumes of secular verse, he turned to Metaphysical poetry, expressing a mystical religious awareness in vivid colloquial language. His best-known volumes are *Silex Scintillans* (1650; enlarged 1655) and *The Mount of Olives* (1652), a book of prose meditations.

● **Vaughan Williams, Ralph** ▶ (1872–1958) British composer. He studied at the Royal College of Music and had lessons from Ravel. Influenced by English folksong and Tudor music, he developed a modal style that found its first full expression in *Fantasia on a Theme by Tallis* (for string orchestra; 1910). His works include nine symphonies of which the first, *A Sea Symphony* (1903–09), is choral; the seventh, *Sinfonia Antarctica* (1951–52), is based on his music for the film *Scott of the Antarctic*. He also wrote the ballet *Job* (1931), the opera *The Pilgrim's Progress* (1951), and much other orchestral, chamber, and choral music.

● **vault** ▶ An arched roof usually in brick or stone and first developed in ancient Egypt. The simplest and oldest type is the barrel or tunnel vault, a single continuous arch, which originally had to be supported by very thick walls. A more complicated type is the groin vault of the Roman and medieval periods, using a series of mutually supporting interlocking arches, which could span greater distances. The rib vault, consisting of a skeleton of diagonal ribs to support the interlocking arches, was developed by gothic builders. Its decorative counterpart is the fan vault with its multiplication of radiating ribs, a principal feature of the ▷Perpendicular style. With the invention of reinforced concrete, vaulting can now cover huge distances without much support.

● **Vavilov, Nikolai Ivanovich** ▶ (1887–1943) Soviet plant geneticist. He travelled widely, amassing a vast collection of plant varieties, particularly varieties of wheat. His researches into the origins of cultivated plants led him to propose 12 world centres of plant origin.

Vavilov's views brought him into conflict with ▷Lysenko and Stalinist ideology. He was arrested and imprisoned in 1940.

● **VDU** ▷*See* visual display unit.

● **vector** ▶ (biology) **1.** An animal (often an insect) capable of transmitting a disease-causing microorganism (*see* pathogen) from one organism to another. For example, mosquitoes are vectors of the malarial parasite, which spends part of its life cycle in the mosquito before being transmitted to humans when the mosquito sucks blood. **2.** (*or* cloning vector) ▷*See* genetic engineering.

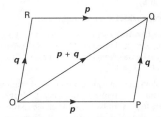

vectors ▶ The two vectors OP (*p*) and PQ (*q*) add to give the resultant vector OQ (*p* + *q*). OR = PQ = *q*; OP = RQ = *p*. OQP is a vector triangle and ORQP is a parallelogram of vectors.

● **vector** ▶ (mathematics) A quantity that has both magnitude and direction. Examples of vectors include velocity, force, magnetic flux density, etc. A vector needs three numbers (called components) to be defined, each number representing its magnitude in one of three mutually perpendicular directions. Two vectors are added by adding the corresponding components and may be multiplied to give either a ▷scalar quantity or another vector.

● **Vedanta** ▶ The various philosophical schools of Hinduism, which derive from the commentaries on the *Vedas*, especially the ▷*Upanishads*, the *Brahmasutras*, and the ▷*Bhagavadgita*. The schools differ in their views on the nature of ▷Brahman and the individual soul, but have in common the belief in reincarnation, the truth of the *Vedas*, the law of ▷karma, and the need for spiritual release. Believing Brahman to be the cause of the world, they condemn Buddhism and Jainism.

● **Vedas** ▶ (Sanskrit: divine knowledge) The basic Hindu scriptures, written in archaic Sanskrit (Vedic) around 1500 BC. It comprises hymns, invocations, mantras, spells, and rituals, mostly concerning the sacrificial worship of gods representing various natural forces. The canon comprises the *Rigveda*, the *Samaveda*, the *Yajurveda*, and the *Atharvaveda*. The *Brahmanas*, the *Aranyakas*, and the ▷*Upanishads*, which are later commentaries, may also be considered canonical.

● **veduta** ▶ (Italian: view) A painting, drawing, or print of a view of a town or city. Examples of vedute are ▷Piranesi's engravings of Rome and ▷Canaletto's paintings of Venice. The **capriccio** is a specialized form of veduta consisting of various architectural elements combined to produce an imaginary setting. A famous capriccio is the etching of *St Paul's Cathedral in London with the Grand Canal of Venice* by William Marlow (1740–1813).

● **Vega** ▶ A conspicuous white star, apparent magnitude 0.03 and 26.5 light years distant, that is the brightest star in the constellation Lyra.

● **Vega (Carpio), Lope Félix de** ▶ (1562–1635) Spanish poet and dramatist. After serving with the Spanish Armada (1588) he became secretary to the Duke of Alba in Toledo, settling in Madrid in 1610. His numerous love affairs continued after his ordination in 1614, but his later years were saddened by the deaths of his wife, children, and mistresses. Most of his numerous plays, such as *Fuenteovejuna* (1612–14) and *El caballero de Olmeda* (1615–26), were based on Spanish history.

● **Vega probe** ▶ An international spaceprobe launched in 1984. Sponsored by the USSR and several other countries, the probe dropped a helium balloon and land module on Venus in 1985 and intercepted Halley's comet in March l986, sending back remarkable photographs of the phenomenon.

● **vegetarianism** ▶ The practice of abstaining from eating animal flesh for ethical, religious, or nutritional reasons. Some vegetarians will not eat any animal products, including milk, cheese, eggs, etc., and are called **vegans**. Vegetarianism occurs in many religious traditions, including Buddhism, Jainism, and Hinduism, and it was advocated by ▷Pythagoras, ▷Plato, and many other thinkers. The first vegetarian society was founded in Manchester in 1847. Vegetarians, especially vegans, can suffer from anaemia unless their diet includes sufficient vitamin B$_{12}$.

● **vegetative reproduction** ▷*See* reproduction.

● **Veil, Simone (Annie)** ▶ (1927–) French stateswoman; president of the European Parliament (1979–82). A survivor of Nazi concentration camps, she was France's minister for health (1974–79) and for social affairs (1993–95).

● **vein** ▶ (physiology) A thin-walled blood vessel that carries oxygen-depleted blood from the tissues to the ▷heart. Most of the smaller veins have $^\square$valves to prevent backflow. Damage to these valves leads to ▷varicose veins. The veins opening directly into the heart are the superior and inferior **vena cavae** and the pulmonary veins from the lungs, which are unique in carrying oxygenated blood. ▷*See* Plate II.

● **Velázquez, Diego Rodriguez de Silva** ▶ (1599–1660) Spanish painter, born in Seville. He trained under Francisco de ▷Herrera the Elder and Francisco Pacheco (1564–1654), his father-in-law, but was most strongly influenced by ▷Titian. He specialized in religious subjects and scenes from everyday life with still-lifes, before becoming (1623) court painter to Philip IV (1605–65; reigned 1621–65) and thereafter painting chiefly portraits of the royal family. Other works include *Pope Innocent X* (Rome) and the *Rokeby Venus* (National Gallery, London), painted during his second visit to Italy (1649–51). *Las Meninas* (c. 1656; Prado) typifies the informality of his late portraits.

● **Velcro** ▶ The tradename for a fabric fastener invented in Switzerland in 1957 by Georges de Mestral (1902–90). It consists of two nylon strips, one covered with tiny hooks and the other with tiny loops into which the hooks fit when the two are pressed together. The name comes from *velours* + *crotchet*, from the velvety appearance of the strips.

● **veld** ▶ (or veldt) A tract of open grassland on the plateau of S Africa. It includes the Highveld (over 1500 m), Middleveld (1500–900 m), and Lowveld (below 900 m).

● **vellum** ▷*See* parchment.

● **velocity** ▶ (*v*) The speed of a body in a specified direction, i.e. its rate of displacement (*s*) in a specified direction is given by $v = ds/dt$. Velocity is a ▷vector quantity, whereas speed is a ▷scalar quantity. In SI units it is measured in metres per second. **Relative velocity** is the velocity of one body relative to another. **Angular velocity** (ω) is the rate of change of angular displacement (θ), i.e. $\omega = d\theta/dt$; it is measured in radians per second.

● **velocity ratio** ▷*See* mechanical advantage.

● **vena cava** ▷*See* vein.

● **Venda, Republic of** ▶ A former ▷Bantu Homeland in South Africa. Most of the population was Venda. It was the third Bantu Homeland to be granted notional independence from South Africa (1979), but this was not recognized elsewhere. In 1990 President Frank Ravhele was deposed by supporters of reintegration with South Africa, led by Col Gabriel Ramushwana. In 1994 Venda was reintegrated into South Africa and South African citizenship was granted to its inhabitants.

● **Vendée** ▶ A department in W France, in Pays de la Loire region. A series of peasant-royalist insurrections, the **Wars of the Vendée**, took place here (1793–1832). The first rebellion, catalysed by the Republican government's introduction of conscription, was also fuelled by loyalty to the Roman Catholic Church. The rebels were defeated at Savenay (December, 1793) and subsequent uprisings (1796, 1815, and 1832) were abortive. Area: 7016 sq km (2709 sq mi). Population (1999): 539 664. Capital: La Roche-sur-Yon.

● **Vendôme, Louis Joseph, Duc de** ▶ (1654–1712) French marshal under Louis XIV. He fought in the Wars of the ▷Grand Alliance (1689–97) and of the Spanish Succession (1701–14). He was victorious at Luzzara (1702) and Cassano (1705) but was defeated by Marlborough at Oudenaarde (1708) and was then recalled. From 1710 until his death he campaigned successfully in Spain.

● **Venera probes** ▶ A series of Soviet ▷planetary probes to Venus, first launched in 1961. Veneras 4 to 8 sent capsules into the hostile atmosphere, those of 7 and 8 surviving to reach the surface (1970, 1972). The Lander sections of Veneras 9 and 10 (1975), 11 and 12 (1978), and 13 and 14 (1982) all successfully reached the surface, relaying information and photographs back to earth. Veneras 15 and 16 orbited the planet in 1983 and mapped features of most of its northern hemisphere.

● **venereal disease** ▷*See* sexually transmitted disease.

● **Venetia** ▶ A region of NE Italy between the River Po, the Alps, and the Adriatic Sea. The mainland territory of the Republic of Venice until 1797, Venetia then came under French and from 1815 Austrian control (as part of the new kingdom of Lombardy-Venetia). Venetia was incorporated into the kingdom of Italy in 1866 and after World War I formed the "Three Venices"—Venezia Tridentina, Venezia Euganea, and Venezia Giulio. Most of the latter was lost to Yugoslavia after World War II and Italian Venetia was divided into the regions of Friuli-Venezia Giulia, Veneto, and Trentino-Alto-Adige.

● **Venezuela, Bolivaran Republic of** ▶ A country on the N coast of South America. The plains of the Orinoco basin in the N rise to the Guiana Highlands in the SE, and in the NW the N end of the Andean chain reaches heights of over 5000 m (16 000 ft). Also in the NW is Lake Maracaibo. Most of the population is of mixed European and Indian descent.

Economy: based chiefly on oil, first discovered in 1917, and petroleum products. Venezuela remains one of the world's largest oil producers and exporters, although production has declined steadily since the early 1970s. The industry was nationalized in 1976. Efforts are being made to diversify the economy, including development of the country's vast iron-ore deposits to increase steel production. Venezuela is a large exporter of both bauxite and aluminium; it is also rich in diamonds, gold, zinc, copper, lead, silver, phosphates, manganese, and titanium. The agricultural sector remains relatively underdeveloped, although a large share of the oil revenues has been spent in attempts to develop this area. A large proportion of the country's food has to be imported. Crop growing in the N includes cereals, bananas, coffee, cocoa, and sugar, while further S stock raising is the main agricultural activity. The vast forests remain largely unexploited but produce some rubber, timber, and gums. Severe and prolonged recessions in the 1980s and early 1990s led the governments of the day to introduce radical free-market reforms. Venezuela has a very large external debt.

History: sighted by Columbus in 1498, it was visited in 1499 by Vespucci, who named it Venezuela ("Little Venice") on seeing Indian villages built on stilts over Lake Maracaibo. Spanish settlement began in 1520 and Venezuela remained under Spanish rule until liberated by Bolívar in 1821. It then formed part of Colombia until 1830. Independent Venezuela was ruled by a series of dictators, notably ▷Guzmán Blanco and ▷Gómez, until the post-World War II period, which has seen more democratic and stable government, made possible in part by oil revenues. In the 1980s oil revenues declined, foreign debt increased, and an economic crisis ensued. Free-market reforms introduced under President Carlos Andrés Perez (from 1989) had some success but caused serious social unrest. Price rises provoked serious rioting in 1989, and there were two abortive coup attempts in 1992. President Carlos Pérez was removed from office and charged with corruption in 1993. He was replaced by a former president, Rafael Caldera Rodríguez. The 1998 presidential election resulted in victory for the radical populist Lt Col Hugo Chávez Frias, leader of a coup attempt in 1992. Chávez introduced a new constitution in 1999. That same year Venezuela suffered its worst natural disaster of the century, when at least 30 000 died in flooding and mudslides. The period 2001–02 saw deepening economic crisis, rising unrest, and an abortive military coup (April 2002). Venezuela is a member of the OAS, LAIA, and OPEC.

Bolivaran Republic of Venezuela

Head of state	President Hugo Chávez Frias
Official language	Spanish
Official currency	bolívar of 100 céntimos
Area	912 050 sq km (352 143 sq mi)
Population (1999 est)	23 707 000
Capital	Caracas
Main port	Maracaibo

● **Vengerov, Maxim** ▶ (1974–) Russian violinist, living in Holland. A childhood prodigy, he studied under Zakhar Bron in Moscow becoming known for his recitals in his teens. He has recorded acclaimed versions of the concertos by Prokofiev and Shostakovich (1995, 1997).

● **Venice** ▶ (Italian name: Venezia) 45 26N 12 20E A city in NE Italy, the capital of Veneto. It is a seaport built on over 100 islands in the Lagoon of Venice (an inlet of the Gulf of Venice at the head of the Adriatic Sea). Venice is a centre of commerce and tourism; its manufactures include glassware, textiles, and lace. The rise of the industrial suburbs of Mestre and Marghera on the mainland has led to the economic decline of the old city. The Grand Canal and about 170 smaller canals provide waterways for the city transport, which includes water buses (*vaporetti*) and gondolas. Famous bridges include the Rialto Bridge and the ▷Bridge of Sighs. St Mark's Square (Piazza San Marco) is overlooked by ▷St Mark's Cathedral, the 15th-century Clock Tower, the Campanile, and the Doge's Palace. An outstanding collection of Venetian paintings, including works by Bellini, Canaletto, and Titian, is housed in the Accademia. The seaside resort, the Lido, is situated 3 km (2 mi) to the SE, on the edge of the lagoon. *History*: originally settled by refugees fleeing the barbarian invasions

Venice ▶ The Bridge of Sighs.

on the mainland (5th century AD onwards), Venice was united under the first ▷doge in 697. Strategically positioned between Europe and the East, it became an independent republic and a great commercial and maritime power, defeating its rival Genoa in 1380. It declined in the 16th century following the discovery of the Cape route to India. With ▷Venetia it came under Austrian control in 1797 and was incorporated into the Kingdom of Italy in 1866. It has in recent years been endangered by floods, pollution, and subsidence. Population (1996 est): 298 215.

● **Venizélos, Eleuthérios** ▶ (1864–1936) Greek statesman; prime minister (1910–15, 1917–20, 1924, 1928–32, 1933). During the ▷Balkan Wars (1912–13), Venizélos acquired the Aegean islands and Crete for Greece. His unsuccessful attempt to instigate a revolt in Crete led to his exile in 1935.

● **Venn diagram** ▷See set theory.

● **ventricle** ▷See brain; heart.

● **Ventris, Michael** ▶ (1922–56) British architect and scholar, who deciphered ▷Linear B. Inspired by Sir Arthur ▷Evans' lecture in 1936, Ventris studied tablets from ▷Knossos and ▷Pylos. After his death his results were consolidated by his collaborator, John Chadwick (1920–).

● **Venturi, Robert** ▶ (1925–) US architect whose books *Complexity and Contradiction in Architecture* (1966) and *Learning from Las Vegas* (1972; with his wife Denise Scott Brown and S. Izenour) have been influential in ▷postmodernism. His buildings include the Guild House Retirement Home (1963) and Franklin Court (1975), both in Philadelphia, and an extension of the National Gallery, London (1991).

● **Venturi tube** ▶ A device consisting of an open-ended tube with a central constriction, used to measure the rate of flow of a fluid, which can be calculated from the pressure difference between the centre and the ends. It is used to measure airspeed of aircraft. Invented by G. B. Venturi (1746–1822).

● **Venus** ▶ (goddess) A Roman goddess originally of gardens and fertility who became identified with the Greek ▷Aphrodite as goddess of love. This identification followed the introduction into Rome of the cult of Aphrodite of Eryx in Sicily and was further established by the Julian family, including the emperors from Augustus to Nero who claimed descent from ▷Aeneas, son of Aphrodite. Having no myths of her own, she assumed those of Aphrodite.

● **Venus** ▶ (planet) The second planet in order from the sun, which it orbits every 225 days at an average distance of 108 million km. It is 12 102 km in diameter and has a long period of rotation (243 days). One of the most brilliant objects in the sky, reaching a ▷magnitude of −4.4, it exhibits ▷phases. Its surface is totally obscured by dense swirling yellowish clouds of sulphuric acid droplets and sulphur particles. The atmosphere is primarily (98%) carbon dioxide. ▷Planetary probes have shown that the surface temperature is 470°C and the atmospheric pressure is about 90 times that of earth. The surface has been mapped by the Pioneer Venus Orbiter and the ▷Venera probes, revealing rolling plains covering 70% of the area, plateaus in two main areas rising to more than 10 000 m, and depressions, including a rift valley. In 1990 the Magellan probe found evidence of volcanic activity.

● **Venus flytrap** ▶ A ▷carnivorous plant, *Dionaea muscipula*, native to the E USA. The upper part of each leaf is hinged; an insect triggers the leaf to snap shut, with its spined margins interlocking, trapping the prey. A cluster of white flowers is borne on a long stalk. Family: *Droseraceae*. □ p. 1302.

● **Venus's flower basket** ▶ A ▷sponge of the genus *Euplectella*, found in parts of the Pacific and Indian Oceans. They form enclosed cylindrical colonies, up to 30 cm long, with a delicate skeletal lattice of silica.

● **Venus's girdle** ▶ A marine invertebrate animal, *Cestum veneris*, belonging to an order (*Cestida*) of ▷ctenophores. Its transparent ribbon-like body is about 5 cm wide and 1 m or more long. It occurs in the Mediterranean and Atlantic.

● **Veracruz** ▶ (or Veracruz Llave) 19 11N 96 10W A port in E Mexico, on the Gulf of Mexico. Industries include iron and steel and sugar refining; the chief exports are coffee, chicle, and tobacco. It contains the Regional Technical Institute of Veracruz (1957). Population (1990): 327 522.

Venus flytrap ► Some of the hinged leaves are closed, trapping insects inside. The long stalk bears a flower bud at its tip.

● **Verbena** ► A genus of herbaceous plants or dwarf shrubs (about 250 species), chiefly native to North and South America. The leaves are simple, often with narrow lobes, and the funnel-shaped flowers form dense elongated or flat-topped clusters. Several species are grown as ornamentals, especially *V. × hybrida* from South America. Lemon verbena (*Lippia citriodora*) is a related shrub from tropical America, the lemon-scented leaves of which yield an oil used in perfumery. Family: *Verbenaceae*. ▷*See also* vervain.

● **Vercelli** ► 45 19N 8 26E A town in NW Italy, in Piedmont. An ancient Ligurian and later a Roman city, it has an outstanding library of manuscripts (notably the *Codex Vercellensis*, a 10th-century English manuscript which contains several poems and other literature). Vercelli lies in Europe's main rice-producing area. Population (1990): 50 313.

● **Vercingetorix** ► (d. 46 BC) Gallic chieftain, who led the revolt of the tribes of Gaul against Julius Caesar in 52. After early successes Vercingetorix was besieged at Alesia and his capture ended Gallic resistance to Rome. He was subsequently executed.

● **Verde, Cape** ▷*See* Cape Verde, Republic of.

● **Verdi, Giuseppe** ► (1813–1901) Italian composer of operas. He studied privately in Milan before beginning a career as a composer. He had an early success with *Nabucco* (1842) but his first mature work was *Rigoletto* (1851); this was quickly followed in 1853 with *La Traviata* and *Il Trovatore*. In 1869 he was commissioned to write an opera for the opening of the Suez Canal; the result was *Aida* (1871). His last works were the *Requiem* (in memory of Alessandro Manzoni; 1874) and the operas *Otello* (1887) and *Falstaff* (1893), with librettos, based on Shakespeare's plays, by Arrigo ▷Boito.

● **verdigris** ► A green copper acetate used as a paint pigment. The term is also applied to the green coating, consisting of copper sulphate or carbonate, that forms on copper roofs, etc.

● **Verdun** ► 49 10N 5 24E A town in NE France, in the Meuse department on the River Meuse. Strategically positioned on the E approach to the Paris Basin, Verdun has long been an important fortress. It was the scene of a major battle in 1916 (*see* World War I). It has brewing, textile, and metallurgical industries. Population (1990): 23 430.

● **Vereeniging** ► 26 41S 27 56E A town in NE South Africa, on the Vaal River. Founded in 1892, it was the venue for negotiations to end the second Boer War (1902). It is an important coalmining centre with iron and steel industries. Population (1990): 23 430.

● **Verhaeren, Émile** ► (1855–1916) The chief Belgian poet associated with Symbolism (*see* Symbolists). Beginning with the realistic verse of *Les Flamandes* (1883), he published many volumes of poetry the themes of which included his patriotism, his socialism, and his love for his wife. He was also a distinguished art critic.

● **Verlaine, Paul** ► (1844–96) French poet. His early poetry, notably *Fêtes galantes* (1869), reflects his association with the ▷Parnassians. His tempestuous relationship with ▷Rimbaud, who influenced his more experimental *Romances sans paroles* (1874), resulted in the breakup of his marriage, and in 1873 he was imprisoned for shooting and wounding Rimbaud. His later poetry concerned the conflicts inherent in his attempts to lead a reformed life. After the publication of *Les Poètes maudits* (1884), which included studies of Corbière, Mallarmé, Rimbaud, and "Pauvre Lelian" (Verlaine's anagram for himself) among others, Verlaine was the acknowledged leader of the Symbolist poets.

● **Vermeer, Jan** ► (1632–75) Dutch painter, who spent his entire life in Delft and whose importance was only established in the 19th century after centuries of obscurity. Despite his everyday subject matter, favourite themes being women reading or writing letters and playing musical instruments, his works are remarkable for their motionless figures, technical finish; and skilful use of light. His best-known paintings include *The Milkmaid* (Rijksmuseum, Amsterdam), *The Lacemaker* (Louvre), and *Allegory of Painting* (Kunsthistorisches Museum, Vienna), showing himself at work.

Jan Vermeer ► *A Geographer or Astronomer in his Study* (1669; Kunstinstitut, Frankfurt).

● **vermiculite** ► A ▷clay mineral with the property of expanding up to 22 times its original thickness on heating, when the water molecules between the silicate layers are driven off. In this form it is light and water-absorbent, and is used as a heat- or sound-insulating material, packaging material, fire extinguisher, and a growing medium for plants. Vermiculite results from the hydrothermal alteration of biotite and the intrusion of acid magma into basic rock.

● **vermilion** ▶ Red mercuric sulphide (HgS). It sublimes readily on heating and occurs naturally as the mineral cinnabar. It is used as a pigment, often mixed with red lead and ferric oxide.

● **Vermont** ▶ A state in the NE USA, in New England. The extensively forested Green Mountains run N–S through the centre of the state, with the lowlands of the Champlain Valley in the NW and the Connecticut Valley in the E. Small manufacturing industries and tourism are the main sectors of the economy and a variety of goods are produced, particularly wood and paper products. Mining is important, especially the extraction of stone, asbestos, sand, and gravel. The state's farmers produce dairy products, hay, potatoes, corn, and maple syrup.

History: settled by the British in 1724, it declared its independence in 1777 and joined the Union in 1791. Area: 24 887 sq km (9609 sq mi). Population (1996 est): 588 654. Capital: Montpelier.

● **vermouth** ▶ An alcoholic drink made from white wine distilled with herbs. The best-known vermouths are French and Italian and are drunk as aperitifs either neat, with soda or tonic water, or with ▷gin.

● **Verne, Jules** ▶ (1828–1905) French writer. He studied law in Paris but chose to follow a literary career. Verne's *Voyages extraordinaires*, beginning with *Five Weeks in a Balloon* (1863), introduced such scientific and technological marvels as the submarine, space travel, and television. They included *Journey to the Centre of the Earth* (1864), *From the Earth to the Moon* (1865), and *Twenty Thousand Leagues Under the Sea* (1873). One of the precursors of ▷science fiction, Verne wrote over 100 adventure stories, including *Around the World in Eighty Days* (1873).

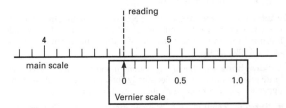

Vernier scale ▶ An auxiliary scale used to measure accurately to two places of decimals.

● **Vernier scale** ▶ A device for measuring subdivisions of a scale, such as those on a pair of calipers. The auxiliary Vernier scale is divided so that ten of its subdivisions correspond to nine of those on the main scale. If the reading falls between two main-scale divisions, say between 4.6 and 4.7, the zero mark on the Vernier scale is slid along so that its zero is lined up with the reading. By noting the division on the Vernier scale that is exactly in line with a main-scale division, the second decimal place of the measurement is obtained. If the fourth Vernier division is in line with a main-scale division, the reading would be 4.64. Named after Pierre Vernier (1580–1637).

● **Vernon, Edward** ▶ (1684–1757) British admiral. He was a hero of the War of ▷Jenkins' Ear, capturing Portobello (1739). His nickname Old Grog (referring to his grogram cloak) was given to the grog (diluted rum) that he introduced to the navy.

● **Verona** ▶ 45 26N 11 00E A city in N Italy, in Veneto on the River Adige. Strategically situated on major routes to N Europe, it possesses a Roman amphitheatre, a 12th-century cathedral, and the medieval Castelvecchio. A tourist centre, its manufactures include textiles, paper, furniture, and leather goods. Population (1996 est): 254 145.

● **Veronese, Paolo** ▶ (P. Caliari; 1528–88) Italian painter of the Venetian school, born in Verona. After training for his father's trade of stonecutter, he studied under minor artists but was chiefly influ-

enced by ▷Titian. In 1553 he settled in Venice, where he worked on decorations in the Ducal Palace and S Sebastiano. In the Villa Barbaro at Maser, designed by ▷Palladio, he painted illusionistic landscapes, mythological scenes, and portraits. His religious works, for example *Marriage at Cana* (Louvre), were often pretexts for depicting contemporary banquets in impressive architectural settings. Thus the *Last Supper* was condemned by the Inquisition for its irreverence; Veronese thereupon retitled the painting *Feast in the House of Levi* (Accademia, Venice).

● **Veronica** ▷*See* speedwell.

● **Veronica, St** ▶ In the New Testament, the woman who offered Jesus a cloth to wipe his face while carrying the cross to the Crucifixion. According to legend, the cloth became imprinted with an image of Jesus' face; a relic purporting to be this cloth is kept in St Peter's, Rome. Feast day: 12 July.

● **Verrocchio, Andrea del** ▶ (Andrea del Cione; c. 1435–88) Florentine Renaissance sculptor, painter, and goldsmith. His only known painting is the *Baptism of Christ* (Uffizi), in which his famous pupil ▷Leonardo da Vinci reputedly assisted. Verrocchio's major sculptures are *Doubting Thomas* (c. 1481; Orsanmichele, Florence), *David* (Bargello, Florence), and the equestrian monument of Bartolommeo Colleoni in the Campo SS Giovanni e Paolo, Venice.

● **verruca** ▷*See* wart.

● **Versailles** ▶ 48 48N 2 08E A town in N central France, in the Yvelines department. Versailles is chiefly famed for its baroque palace, the residence of the French kings from 1678 to 1769. It was built for Louis XIV between 1676 and 1708 on the site of a hunting lodge; the design includes architecture by J. H. Mansart (1646–1708), interior decoration by ▷Le Brun, and formal gardens by ▷Le Nôtre. In addition to the Grand Château, there are two smaller chateaux: the Grand Trianon and the Petit Trianon (a favourite residence of Marie Antoinette). Historic events enacted at the palace include Britain's recognition of American independence (1783), the crowning (1871) of William I as German emperor, and the signing of the Treaty of ▷Versailles (1919). Population (1990): 91 029.

● **Versailles, Treaty of** ▶ (1919) The treaty, signed at the ▷Paris Peace Conference after World War I, between the Allied and Associated Powers and defeated Germany. Versailles declared Germany guilty of causing the war, imposed heavy reparations payments, and limited the German army and navy to nominal strength. Territorial provisions included the return of Alsace and Lorraine to France, the cession of parts of Germany to Poland, and the Allied occupation of the Rhineland. Further, most of Germany's colonies were to become ▷mandates of the ▷League of Nations, which was established by the treaty. The USA refused to ratify the treaty and did not make peace with Germany until 1921.

● **vertebra** ▷*See* spine.

● **Vertebrata** ▶ (or Craniata) A subphylum (or phylum) of animals that includes the fish, amphibians, reptiles, birds, and mammals. They are characterized by a backbone consisting of interlocking vertebrae, which forms the main support for the body and protects the nerve cord (spinal cord). The skeleton may be of cartilage or bone and includes two pairs of fin or limb elements that articulate with girdles attached to the backbone. The brain is large and housed in a protective skull. Their highly versatile skeleton has enabled vertebrates to adapt to a wide variety of lifestyles in water, on land, and in the air. ▷*See also* chordate.

● **Verulamium** ▷*See* St Albans.

● **vervain** ▶ A slender erect branching perennial herb, ▷*Verbena officinalis*, found on waste ground throughout Eurasia and N Africa. 30–75 cm high, it has deeply lobed leaves and spikes of tiny pinkish flowers. The fruit splits into four nutlets. Cultivated forms of *Verbena* may also be called vervain.

● **vervet** ▷*See* grass monkey.

● **Verwoerd, Hendrik Frensch** ▶ (1901–66) South African statesman; prime minister (1958–66). Verwoerd's commitment to the ▷apartheid system, of which he was the chief architect, occasioned demonstrations among Blacks, including one at ▷Sharpeville during which the police fired on the crowd. He took South Africa out of the Commonwealth in 1960. He was assassinated in parliament in Cape Town.

● **Very light** ▶ A flare fired from a pistol, devised by the US naval officer Edward W. Very (1847–1910). It is used to provide a temporary light or to draw attention to the presence of a lifeboat, etc. The colour of the light can be varied by adding different salts to the chemical mixture.

● **Vesalius, Andreas** ▶ (1514–64) Flemish anatomist, whose major work, *The Seven Books on the Structure of the Human Body* (1543), contained some of the first accurate descriptions of human anatomy together with illustrations. Vesalius' observations challenged the prevailing theories of ▷Galen, opening up a new era of scientific investigation.

● **Vespasian** ▶ (9–79 AD) Roman emperor (69–79). He was acclaimed emperor by the army in Egypt (July, 69) but he was not recognized at Rome until the death in December of his rival Vitellius (15–69). Vespasian's decisive policies brought an end to civil war and he increased taxes and reformed the army. He was deified after his death.

● **Vespucci, Amerigo** ▶ (1454–1512) Italian navigator, after whom America is named. In 1499 he explored the NE coast of South America, finding the mouths of the Amazon, and in 1501, under Portuguese auspices, he explored the E coast and was the first European to reach Rió de La Plata.

● **Vesta** ▶ (goddess) The Roman goddess of the hearth, identified with the Greek ▷Hestia. She was worshipped in private households, and her annual festival, the Vestalia, was held in June. The **Vestal Virgins**, her priestesses, tended the eternal fire at her shrine in Rome. They served for periods of 30 years under strict vows of chastity.

● **Vesta** ▶ (planet) The third largest ▷minor planet, 538 km in diameter, and the only one occasionally visible with the naked eye. Its orbit lies between those of Mars and Jupiter.

● **vestibular apparatus** ▷*See* ear.

● **Vestmannaeyjar** ▶ (or Westman Islands) A group of rocky islands off the S coast of Iceland. In 1963 the volcanic island of Surtsey emerged from the ocean and the volcano, Helgafell, erupted in 1974 destroying part of the chief settlement of Vestmannaeyjar on Heimaey. Population (1994): 4888.

● **vestments** ▶ Distinctive garments worn by those in holy orders when performing the liturgy or other offices of the Church. In the early centuries of Christianity, clergy wore the ordinary male attire of the Greco-Roman world—an ankle-length tunic with an outer mantle or cloak. This form of dress was retained by the Church long after secular fashions had changed and was formalized for liturgical use in the early middle ages. By the 10th century standard liturgical costume in the West consisted of the alb (a white linen garment reaching from neck to ankle) and the chasuble or cope (a sleeveless overgarment for the upper body, sometimes highly decorated); with additions and variations, this forms the basis of the vestments still used in the Roman Catholic and Orthodox Churches and by most Anglican priests. During the middle ages the symbolism of church vestments became more elaborate, with different colours being appointed for the various liturgical seasons (purple for Advent and Lent, red for Pentecost, etc.). Additional vestments and insignia were bestowed on bishops, most notably the mitre, a tall cleft headpiece.

With the advent of Protestantism, most reformed Churches adopted a much simplified style of dress; in the Church of England this generally took the form of a white surplice (a loose wide-sleeved version of the alb, formerly associated with the lower clergy) and a black gown. Even this, however, was rejected by Puritans, who saw any distinctive liturgical dress as a sign of popery; the matter remained a subject of fierce dispute in the 16th and 17th centuries. The earlier tradition of elaborate liturgical wear was revived by the ▷Oxford Movement in the 19th century, with much initial opposition (including riots and legal actions). The Anglican Churches now permit considerable diversity of practice.

The vestments of the Eastern Orthodox Churches are similar to those developed in the West, but more elaborate and splendid; the chief additions are the *epimankion*, or embroidered cuffs, and the *epigonation*, a stiff lozenge-shaped vestment worn hanging from the right side by senior clergy. Bishops wear a crown-shaped mitre decorated with medallions.

● **Vesuvius** ▶ 40 49N 14 26E A volcano in S central Italy, in Campania region near Naples. It was presumed to be extinct until it erupted in 79 AD engulfing the towns of ▷Herculaneum and ▷Pompeii; the last eruption was in 1944. Wine is made from the grapes grown on its exceptionally fertile slopes. Average height: 1220 m (4003 ft).

● **vetch** ▶ A climbing or trailing annual or perennial herb of the genus *Vicia* (about 150 species), native to N temperate regions and South America. The leaves comprise several pairs of leaflets, often modified into tendrils, and the blue, purple, yellow, or white flowers are borne either in long spikes or singly in the leaf axils. Some species are grown as fodder crops or for green manure. Family: ▷*Leguminosae*.

● **veterinary science** ▶ The scientific discipline concerned with animal health and welfare. Some of the earliest descriptions of animal diseases were made by ▷Aristotle and, by the middle ages, veterinary practice was an established trade. The Royal College of Veterinary Surgeons was founded in London in 1844 and today all British veterinary practitioners must be qualified members. Control and eradication of livestock diseases have enabled improved productivity and the introduction of modern intensive farming methods. The care of domestic pets utilizes many of the diagnostic and surgical techniques of human medicine.

● **vetiver** ▶ A perennial ▷grass, *Vetiveria zizanioides*, also known as khus-khus, native to tropical Asia and introduced to South Africa. Its thick fragrant roots contain an oil used in perfumes.

● **Viagra** ▷*See* impotence.

● **Viareggio** ▶ 43 52N 10 15E A town and resort in Italy, in Tuscany on the Ligurian Sea. Shelley was cremated in Viareggio and Puccini is buried here. Population (latest est): 50 310.

● **Viborg** ▶ 56 28N 9 25E A town in N central Denmark, in Jutland. It has a 12th-century cathedral and its industries include iron founding, distilling, and the manufacture of textiles and machinery. Population (1990): 29 455.

● **vibraphone** ▶ A type of ▷xylophone in which a characteristic vibrato effect is produced by electrically operated fans installed at the upper ends of the resonator tubes. ⬚musical instruments.

● **Vibrio** ▶ A genus of freshwater and marine bacteria. They are rod-shaped, either straight or curved, and swim by means of whiplike flagella at one end of the cell. *V. cholerae* causes ▷cholera in humans and other types may cause gastroenteritis.

● **Viburnum** ▶ A genus of shrubs and small trees (about 200 species), mostly native to N temperate regions. They have rounded heads of small funnel-shaped white or pink flowers, each with five spreading white lobes. Many species and varieties are grown as garden shrubs and pot plants, including the snowball tree (*see* guelder rose) and ▷laurustinus. Family: *Caprifoliaceae*. ▷*See also* wayfaring tree.

● **Vicente, Gil** ▶ (c. 1465–1536) Portuguese dramatist. He wrote court entertainments, plays based on religious and chivalric stories, and comedies satirizing the clergy and nobility, including *Comedia de Rubena* (1521) and *Auto da Mofina Mendes* (1534). He wrote in both Portuguese and Spanish, and has been identified with a goldsmith of the same name. His plays were published by his son and daughter in 1562.

● **Vicenza** ▶ 45 33N 11 33E A city in NE Italy, in Veneto. It was the home of the 16th-century architect Andrea Palladio and many of his finest works are sited here and nearby. Vicenza has iron, steel, and textile industries. Population (1996 est): 107 786.

● **Vichy** ▶ 46 07N 3 25E A spa in central France, in the Allier department on the River Allier. Its waters, which were known to the Romans, are bottled and exported worldwide. Population (latest est): 30 554. ▷*See also* Vichy government.

● **Vichy government** ▶ The pro-German puppet government set up in Vichy after the fall of France (1940) during World War II. Its autonomy extended over unoccupied (i.e. central and southern) France and the French colonies. Established by the Franco-German armistice, with Marshal ▷Pétain as head of government, it was run on authoritarian lines from 1942 by Pierre ▷Laval. After the Allied liberation of France in 1945 the Vichy government fled to Germany and France was reunited. The Vichy regime deported over 70 000 Jews to their deaths in Germany and some 650 000 workers to Germany to help their war effort. The French prefer to regard the Free French government set up in exile under de Gaulle as the true representative of the defeated France, rather than the Vichy government under Pétain.

● **Vicksburg** ▶ 32 21N 90 51W A city in the USA, in Mississippi on the Mississippi River. During the US Civil War it was the site of the Vicksburg campaign, a 47-day siege in 1863 in which Gen Grant successfully gained control of the Mississippi River after the city fell. Vicksburg is an important distribution centre for cotton, timber, and livestock. Population (1990): 20 908.

● **Vicky** ▶ (Victor Weisz; 1913–66) British cartoonist, born in Berlin, of Hungarian parents. Working in England from 1935, he made his name in the *New Statesman* and *Evening Standard* with his political cartoons.

● **Vico, Giambattista** ▶ (*or* Giovanni Battista Vico; 1668–1744) Italian historical philosopher. Vico was one of the first philosophers to attempt a critical philosophy of history. He rejected Descartes' negative attitude to the study of history and argued that philosophers had underrated "the study of the world of nations, which since men made it, men should come to know." Language, ritual, and myth were, he maintained, essential clues to an understanding to the past. His ideas were particularly influential in the later 18th century.

● **Victor Emmanuel II** ▶ (1820–78) King of Italy (1861–78). He succeeded to the throne of Sardinia-Piedmont in 1849, following the abdication of his father Charles Albert. His appointment (1852) of ▷Cavour as prime minister was crucial to the achievement of Italian unification (*see* Risorgimento). Victor Emmanuel fought at Magenta and Solferino against the Austrians, freeing Lombardy, and coordinated with ▷Garibaldi in the campaign that freed S Italy. After becoming King of Italy he completed its unification by acquiring Venetia (1866) and Rome (1870), which he made the Italian capital.

● **Victor Emmanuel III** ▶ (1869–1947) King of Italy (1900–46) following the assassination of his father Umberto I. He acquiesced in Mussolini's seizure of power (1922) and after Mussolini's fall (1943) relinquished his powers to his son Umberto II. He formally abdicated in 1946, shortly before Italy became a republic.

● **Victoria** ▶ A state of SE Australia, bordering on the Tasman Sea, Bass Strait, and the Indian Ocean. It consists of central uplands, an extension of the ▷Great Dividing Range, descending to plains in the N and S. Agriculture is diverse with fruit and vineyards in the Murray Basin and wheat and sheep farming to the SW. Gippsland is a noted dairying area, where production has intensified in recent years as a result of a reorganization of the industry; 50% of the country's cattle and over half of the production are now concentrated in S Victoria. Brown coal, the mainstay of Victoria's thermal electricity industry, is mined in Central Gippsland and gas and oil are piped from fields in the Bass Strait. Industry, concentrated on Melbourne, includes engineering, oil refining, and the manufacture of cars and textiles. Area: 227 600 sq km (87 884 sq mi). Population (1996 est): 4 533 300. Capital: Melbourne.

● **Victoria** ▶ 22 16N 114 13E An urban district in S China, the administrative centre of Hong Kong, situated on the N of the island. The University of Hong Kong was established here in 1911. Population (latest est): 590 771.

● **Victoria** ▶ 48 26N 123 20W A city and port in W Canada, the capital of British Columbia on S Vancouver Island. Founded in 1843, it is a commercial and distribution centre. Victoria's mild climate attracts tourists and retired people. The provincial government and federal dockyards are the main employers. Victoria University (1963) is situated here. Population (1991): 287 897 (metropolitan area).

● **Victoria** ▶ (1819–1901) Queen of the United Kingdom (1837–1901), whose sense of duty and strict moral code came to symbolize the ethos of 19th-century Britain. The daughter of George III's fourth son Edward, Duke of Kent (1767–1820), and Victoria of Saxe-Coburg-Gotha (1786–1861), Victoria succeeded her uncle William IV. In 1840 she married her cousin Prince ▷Albert of Saxe-Coburg-Gotha, who exerted considerable, and generally beneficial, influence over her. They had nine children: Victoria (1840–1901), who became Empress of Germany as the wife of Frederick III (1831–88; reigned 1888); Edward, later Edward VII; Alice (1843–78), Grand Duchess of Hesse; Alfred (1844–1900), Duke of Edinburgh and Saxe-Coburg-Gotha; Helena (1846–1923), Princess of Schleswig-Holstein; Louise (1848–1914), Duchess of Argyll; Arthur (1850–1917), Duke of Connaught; Leopold (1853–84), Duke of Albany; and Beatrice (1857–1944), Princess of Battenberg. Albert's death in 1861 was a severe blow to Victoria and she resolved thereafter to act exactly as he would have wished.

She had an exalted view of the monarch's role in government, failing to appreciate the limitations of constitutional monarchy. Her refusal to dismiss her Whig ladies of the bedchamber when the Tory, Robert Peel, was attempting to form a ministry caused the ▷Bedchamber Crisis (1839) and to ▷Palmerston she insisted that no policy should be modified once she had approved it. Her close friendship with ▷Disraeli, who made her Empress of India (1876), contrasted with her strained relations with his rival ▷Gladstone. In the last years of her reign, especially after her Golden Jubilee (1887), she enjoyed enormous popularity.

● **Victoria, Lake** ▶ (*or* Victoria Nyanza) The largest lake in Africa, in Uganda, Tanzania, and Kenya. The second largest freshwater lake in the world (after Lake Superior), it was discovered for Europeans in 1858 by Speke in his search for the source of the River Nile, of which Lake Victoria is the chief reservoir. The level was raised by the construction of the ▷Owen Falls Dam. The main ports are Jinja, Kisumu, Mwanza, and Bukoba. Area: 69 485 sq km (26 826 sq mi).

● **Victoria, Tomás Luis de** ▶ (c. 1548–1611) Spanish composer. He studied in Rome and in 1571 succeeded Palestrina as maestro di cappella at the Roman Seminary. In about 1582 he returned to Spain as chaplain to the dowager Empress Maria, the sister of ▷Philip II. He composed many motets and more than 20 masses in the polyphonic style.

● **Victoria and Albert Museum** ▶ A London museum founded in 1853 to house and collect examples of applied arts of all periods and cultures. Originally at Marlborough House and called the Museum of Ornamental Art, it moved to South Kensington in 1857 and was given its present name in 1899 at the request of Queen Victoria, when she laid the foundation stone for a new building, designed by Aston ▷Webb, to house the collection. This building was opened in 1909. A controversial futuristic extension designed by Daniel Libeskind was approved in 1998.

● **Victoria Cross** ▶ (VC) The highest British military decoration, for "bravery...in the presence of the enemy." Instituted by Queen Victoria in 1856, VCs were until 1942 cast from the metal of Russian guns taken during the Crimean War (1854–56). A bronze Maltese cross on a crimson ribbon, it is superscribed *For Valour. Compare* George Cross.

● **Victoria Falls** ▶ 17 55S 25 52E A waterfall in the Zambezi River on the border of Zimbabwe and Zambia. The river flows over an abrupt rock edge 1.6 km (1 mi) wide, dropping as much as 128 m (420 ft), and then through a narrow gorge known as the **Boiling Pot**. A major tourist attraction, the falls also provide hydroelectric power.

● **Victoria Island** ▶ A Canadian island in the Arctic Ocean, in Nunavut and Northwest Territories. The third largest island in Canada, its lowlands rise to high cliffs in the NW. The scanty population is clustered in a few settlements. Area: 212 199 sq km (81 930 sq mi).

● **vicuna** ▶ A hoofed mammal, *Vicugna vicugna*, of high Andean plateaus. Resembling a small camel, the vicuna is 75 cm at the shoulder and has a tawny-brown coat with a white bib and underparts. They are highly valued for their wool and wild herds are rounded up for shearing. Family: *Camelidae* (camels, etc.).

● **Vidal, Gore** ▶ (1925–   ) US novelist and essayist. His moral concern with contemporary society is expressed with wit and elegance in his works, which range from historical novels, such as *Burr* (1974), *1876* (1976), *Lincoln* (1984), and *Live from Golgotha* (1992), to satires such as *Myra Breckinridge* (1968), and *Hollywood* (1989), a study of modern US society.

● **Vidal de la Blache, Paul** ▶ (1845–1918) French geographer. A professor at the Sorbonne, Paris (1898–1918), Vidal was the most eminent French human geographer of his day. His work includes *États et nations de l'Europe* (1889) and *Principes de géographie humaine* (1922). He was the founding editor of *Annales de géographie* in 1891.

● **video camera** ▶ (or camcorder) A hand-held camera used (largely by amateurs) to record moving pictures on video-tape cassettes for playing back on a television set. In a video camera the standard optical lenses focus the scene to be recorded onto an electronic camera tube, as in a television camera. The digital electronic data so obtained is recorded on video tape within the camcorder. At the same time, sound is picked up by a microphone attached to the camcorder, and recorded as a sound track along the edge of the video tape. The contents of the tape can usually be viewed on a miniscreen in the camcorder or played back through a television screen. The camcorder has completely replaced the ciné camera, formerly used to make home movies. The principle is also used in ▷digital photography. The relatively low cost of video, together with recent improvements in picture definition, have encouraged its growing use by makers of low-budget films for commercial release.

● **videogames** ▶ Electronic and computer games that have become increasingly sophisticated in recent years. The first videogames were simple versions of bat and ball games, such as tennis, and were operated by a control unit that plugged into a television set. Modern videogames, played on arcade machines, units attached to TVs, personal computers, or hand-held devices, use elaborate computer programs and can have high-quality graphics and sound (*see* computer graphics). Some games use digitized film for added realism. Almost any type of game, from shooting games to fantasy role-playing games and board games, can now be computerized.

● **video recording** ▶ The storage of a ▷television programme or prerecorded film on magnetic tape. Because the demodulated video (vision) signal can have frequencies in the megahertz range, a video tape cannot be used like a sound tape in which the highest frequencies will be less than 20 kilohertz. It would not be practical to run the tape one thousand times faster than a sound tape; instead the signal is recorded diagonally on the tape (each diagonal line representing one line of the picture) and the tape is run slowly over a drum on which the recording and reading heads rotate at high speeds. Such devices are available for use with domestic television sets and home ▷video cameras (camcorders), with which to make recordings. Video discs for the storage of television pictures include those in which the signal can be retrieved by a laser system.

● **videotex** ▶ A general name for ▷teletext (broadcast textual information) or ▷viewdata (which is generally sent from a host computer to a user along telephone lines). To the recipient the two types of display look much the same: alphanumeric characters on a screen, usually transmitted as ASCII codes. The user accesses a page in teletext by keying in its number, using a computer keyboard or a television set's remote control keypad. In viewdata, the user contacts the host computer by telephone line (often using an autodialler) and requests pages using a keypad. The user can then interact with the host computer (to book a hotel, for example).

● **Vienna** ▶ (German name: Wien) 48 12N 16 20E The capital of Austria, in the NE at the foot of the Vienna Woods (Wienerwald) on the River Danube. With its musical and theatrical life, its museums, and parks, it is a popular tourist attraction. Trade and industry, however, form the basis of the economy, the major industrial products being machinery, textiles, chemicals, and furniture. Most of the chief buildings lie on or within the Ringstrasse, the boulevard built in 1857 to replace the old city ramparts. These include the Cathedral of St Stephen (begun about 1135); the Hofburg (the former imperial palace); the Rathaus (1873–83); the parliament buildings (1883); the Opera House and Burgtheater; and the university (1365).
History: seat of the Habsburgs (1278–1918) and residence of the

Holy Roman Emperor (1558–1806), Vienna became an important political and cultural centre in the 18th and 19th centuries, having associations with many composers, including Haydn, Mozart, Beethoven, Schubert, and the Strauss family. At the end of World War I it became the capital of the small republic of Austria. It suffered considerable damage during World War II and was jointly occupied by the Allied Powers (1945–55). Population (1995 est): 1 593 000.

● **Vienna, Congress of** ▶ (1814–15) A conference of European powers that met following the fall of Napoleon. The chief countries represented were Austria (by ▷Metternich), Britain (by ▷Castlereagh and Wellington), Russia, Prussia, France (by ▷Talleyrand), and the papacy. Its Final Act created a kingdom of the Netherlands, a German confederation of 39 states, Lombardy-Venetia subject to Austria, and the ▷Congress Kingdom of Poland. Legitimate monarchs were restored in Spain, Naples, Piedmont, Tuscany, and Modena, and Louis XVIII was confirmed as King of France.

● **Vienna Circle** ▶ The group of scientific philosophers who developed the doctrine of ▷logical positivism (or logical empiricism). Founded by ▷Schlick in 1924, the Vienna Circle flourished until 1939. Philosophers and scientists cooperated to analyse and clarify both philosophical and scientific concepts and to set up criteria of meaningfulness for propositions other than the truths of logic. Members included ▷Carnap, ▷Gödel, and Otto Neurath (1882–1945). They did not consciously set out radically to revise traditional views about philosophy, but they had this effect, notably in America and Britain. ▷*See also* Ayer, Sir Alfred (Jules).

● **Vienne, River** ▶ A river in W central France, flowing mainly NNW from the Correè department to the River Loire. Length: 354 km (220 mi).

● **Vientiane** ▶ 18 06N 102 30E The capital of Laos, a port on the River Mekong on the border with Thailand (formerly Siam). Founded in the 13th century, it came under Siamese control in the 18th century and was destroyed (1828) following a revolt against Siamese rule. It became capital of the French protectorate of Laos in the late 19th century. The Université Sisavangvong was founded here in 1958. Population (1990 est): 442 000.

● **Vierwaldstättersee** ▷*See* Lucerne, Lake.

● **Viet Cong** ▶ Communist guerrillas who fought the government of South Vietnam during the ▷Vietnam War (1954–75). Dedicated to the union of North and South, in 1960 they established a political organization, the National Liberation Front, which amalgamated the various groups committed to the overthrow of the South Vietnamese Government.

● **Viet Minh** ▶ The Vietnam League for Independence, formed in 1941 by ▷Ho Chi Minh to overthrow French rule and to create an independent Vietnamese republic. Officially a multiparty movement, the Viet Minh was dominated by the communists and opposed by many nationalist leaders. Following the refusal of the French to recognize Vietnamese independence after World War II, the Viet Minh played a prominent role in the ▷Indochina war against France.

● **Vietnam, Socialist Republic of** ▶ A country in SE Asia, occupying the E part of the Indochina peninsula on the South China Sea. Fertile coastal lowlands rise to forested plateaus and mountains, the most populated areas being around the Mekong delta in the S and the Red River delta in the N. The inhabitants are mainly Vietnamese, with minorities of Chinese and others.
Economy: although seriously affected by the prolonged war of 1954–75 and subsequent political turmoil, the economy is now beginning to recover. Agriculture remains the most important sector, and the loosening of state control since the mid-1980s has greatly increased production. Rice is grown extensively and is now a major export. Other important crops include sugar cane, tea, maize, coffee, and rubber. Teak and bamboo are the chief forest products and fishing is also important. Industry, including steel, has traditionally been concentrated in the N, based on the coal, tin, zinc, and other metals to be found there. However, recent years have seen more general industrial development in such fields as construction, chemicals, food processing, and manufactures. This has been aided by increasing oil production from offshore fields. A radical programme

to convert the economy to a free-market basis began in 1986 and has had notable success. The USA ended its damaging embargo on aid and investment in 1995. The principal exports include coal, rubber, wood, tea, spices, and coffee. There is a large foreign debt.

History: the northern kingdom of Nam Viet was conquered in 111 BC by the Chinese. In 939 AD it broke free and resisted further Chinese invasions until the 15th century, when it was again briefly occupied. Its southward expansion culminated in the establishment (1802) of a united Vietnamese empire, which incorporated the three historic regions of Annam, Cochinchina, and Tonkin. The subsequent French conquest resulted in the institution of protectorates over Cochinchina, Tonkin, and Annam, which were joined with Cambodia (and later Laos) to form (1887) the Union of ▷Indochina. Vietnam was occupied by the Japanese in World War II, during which Ho Chi Minh formed the Viet Minh league to fight for independence. France's refusal in 1945 to recognize his government led to war (1946–54) after which, following defeat at Dien Bien Phu, the French withdrew. The Geneva Conference (1954) divided Vietnam along the seventeenth parallel into communist North Vietnam and noncommunist South Vietnam, between which civil war ensued. In 1961 the USA extended assistance to the South and remained involved in the conflict until 1973 (*see* Vietnam War). The civil war continued until 1975, when the North emerged victorious, proclaiming (1976) the reunited Socialist Republic of Vietnam. Attempts at reconstruction were hindered by further political developments. A deterioration of Sino-Vietnamese relations led to the withdrawal of all Chinese aid in 1978, and following Vietnam's invasion of Cambodia (December, 1978–January, 1979) many other nations suspended aid leading to an increased reliance on the Soviet Union. The Chinese invasion of Vietnam (February–March, 1979) led to a massive increase in the number of refugees attempting to leave Vietnam by small craft across the South China Sea. Many of these refugees, known as the Boat People, died by drowning or from disease, and failed to find a new country that would accept them; many spent years in camps in Hong Kong. In the mid-1980s there were armed clashes with Thailand. In 1989 Vietnamese troops withdrew from Cambodia. A new constitution was adopted in 1992, reaffirming the role of the Communist Party but endorsing the free-market reforms introduced in the previous decade.

Socialist Republic of Vietnam

Head of state	President Tran Duc Luong
Official language	Vietnamese
Official currency	dong of 100 hào
Area	329 466 sq km (127 180 sq mi)
Population (1997 est)	72 124 000
Capital	Hanoi
Main port	Haiphong

● **Vietnam War** ▶ (1954–75) The war between communist North Vietnam and South Vietnam, the latter aided from 1961 by the USA. It resulted in communist victory and the union (1976) of North and South Vietnam. From 1954 guerrilla warfare was waged against South Vietnam by the communist ▷Viet Cong, who were reinforced by North Vietnamese troops in 1959. In 1961 the USA, seeking to halt the spread of communism in SE Asia, dispatched troops (numbering 550 000 by 1969) in support of the beleaguered South; in 1965 US air raids on the North had begun. US participation was lessened after peace negotiations were initiated in 1969, but the war again took fire following the US-South Vietnamese invasion of Cambodia in 1970. A massive communist offensive in 1972, together with the strength of domestic opposition to US involvement in the war, prompted the USA to reopen negotiations for peace. These led to the Paris Agreement (January, 1973) and the withdrawal of US troops. By 1975 the North had emerged victorious. Some 900 000 Viet Cong and North Vietnamese, 50 000 Americans, and some 400 000 South Vietnamese died in the war. ▷*See also* Indochina.

● **viewdata** ▶ An interactive service provided by ▷videotex. Various countries have their own systems. In France, for example, it is called **Télétel**; in Germany, **Viewdata**; and in Britain, **Prestel**.

● **Vignola, Giacomo da** ▶ (1507–73) Roman mannerist architect (*see* mannerism). Vignola was the leading architect of his day in Rome, carrying on the building of ▷St Peter's Basilica after the death of ▷Michelangelo. Among his other works were the Palazzo Farnese (1564) in Piacenza and the influential church of Il Gesù, Rome (begun 1568). He was also the author of a popular architectural treatise.

● **Vigny, Alfred de** ▶ (1797–1863) French poet, novelist, and dramatist. He associated with many Romantic writers while serving as an army officer from 1814 to 1827. His fiction includes the historical novel *Cinq-Mars* (1826) and his plays include *Chatterton* (1835), his masterpiece, and several adaptions from Shakespeare. His poetry, especially in *Les Destinées* (1867), expresses through impersonal symbolic techniques his philosophy of stoical pessimism.

● **Vigo** ▶ 42 15N 8 44W A port and naval base in NW Spain, in Galicia on the Atlantic coast. In 1702 an English-Dutch fleet sank a Spanish treasure fleet here. Population (1995 est): 290 582.

● **Viipuri** ▷*See* Vyborg.

● **Vijayanagar** ▶ A Hindu empire established from the town of that name in S India during the first half of the 14th century. It enjoyed a reputation for trade, opulence, and cultural and artistic distinction. Its Muslim neighbours, with whom it had always had uneasy relations, defeated Vijayanagar at the battle of Talikota in 1565 and totally destroyed the city.

● **Vijayawada** ▶ (former name: Bezwada) 16 34N 80 40E A city in India, in Andhra Pradesh on the River Krishna. Industries include engineering and rice milling. Population (1994 est): 288 573.

● **Viking probes** ▶ Two identical US spacecraft that went into orbit around Mars in 1976. The Lander sections landed on the surface in July and September and performed various experiments, including tests for possible microorganisms; none were found. The Orbiter sections took measurements and photographs of Mars' surface and two satellites.

Vietnam ▶ Nung tribespeople puddling the rice paddies close to the Chinese border. Rice forms the staple diet of many Vietnamese and in recent years has been increasingly grown for export.

● **Vikings** ► Scandinavian sea warriors active from the late 8th to the mid-11th centuries. They established important settlements in the British Isles (especially at York and Dublin), where an Anglo-Danish dynasty was founded (1016) by ▷Canute, and in Normandy. Swedish Vikings raided, and then settled, in the E Baltic, established the Russian Kievan state, and traded with Constantinople, where they provided the imperial guard. They also established settlements in ▷Vinland and Greenland. Viking literature (the sagas) and art are noted for their dynamic vitality.

● **villa** ► A country house in Italy or the South of France. Villas date back to Roman times, when they were used as holiday retreats or as farmhouses. The Emperor Hadrian's Villa at Tivoli (123 AD) was built on a palatial scale with extensive parks. During the Renaissance the villa with its substantial estate was revived, particularly in Venetia in N Italy, where ▷Palladio designed them to combine farming and pleasure purposes. Gardens with grottoes, fountains, and sculptures became an integral part of such Renaissance villas as the Villa d'Este (1550) at Tivoli, built by Pirro Ligorio (c. 1500–83). Since the 19th century English detached or semidetached suburban houses and Mediterranean holiday houses are often referred to as villas.

● **Villa, Pancho** ► (Francesco V.; 1878–1923) Mexican revolutionary. An outlaw, Villa supported successive revolts against Mexican governments and came to dominate the north with an irregular army. In 1916 he raided Texas and New Mexico and a US force was sent into Mexico to capture him. It failed to do so but, after an agreement with the Mexican Government in 1920, he disbanded his army. He was later assassinated.

● **Villa-Lobos, Heitor** ► (1887–1959) Brazilian composer. He toured Brazil collecting folksongs and in 1945 founded the Brazilian Academy of Music. His music is characterized by native rhythms and exotic tone colours. His vast output includes 12 symphonies, *Bachianas Brasileiras* (1930–45), a series of pieces inspired by Bach, concertos for cello, guitar, and harp, 15 string quartets, guitar music, *Rudepoema* (1921–26) for piano, and the ballet *Uirapurú* (1917).

● **Villanovan** ► The earliest Iron Age culture of N Italy, named after the site of Villanova near Bologna. Emerging in the 9th century BC Villanovan culture is characterized by sophisticated metalworking, using local mineral resources. The dead were cremated and their bronze or pottery urns were often shaped like wattle and daub huts. Villanovan settlements preceded most of the important towns of the ▷Etruscans.

● **Villars, Claude Louis Hector, Duc de** ► (1653–1734) French marshal under Louis XIV. He fought in the third ▷Dutch War (1672–78) but his greatest achievements came in the War of ▷Spanish Succession (1701–14). He rallied France's flagging fortunes after Marlborough's victory at ▷Blenheim (1704) and imposed devastating losses on the allies at ▷Malplaquet (1709). He last saw active service when well into his 80s in the War of the ▷Polish Succession (1733–38).

● **Villehardouin, Geoffroi de** ► (c. 1150–c. 1213) French medieval chronicler. A participant in the fourth Crusade and witness of the fall of Constantinople (1204), Villehardouin wrote the best source description of these events in his *Conquête de Constantinople*. However, his bias towards the Latins possibly distorts the account.

● **villein** ► The unfree peasant of medieval Europe, holding land from the lord of the ▷manor in return for labour. Villeins were the most numerous class in England from the 11th to late 14th centuries, when many acquired written titles to their holdings following the ▷Peasants' Revolt.

● **Villeneuve, Jacques** ► (1971–) Canadian motor-racing driver. He won the Indycar world championship in 1995 and became Formula One world champion in 1997.

● **Villeneuve, Pierre** ► (1763–1806) French admiral during the Napoleonic Wars. He commanded the fleet that was unsuccessful in attempting to invade England and was defeated by Nelson at Trafalgar (1805) and taken prisoner. After his release he committed suicide.

● **Villiers de l'Isle-Adam, Philippe Auguste, Comte de** ► (1838–89) French poet, novelist, and dramatist. He was the impover-

ished descendant of an ancient aristocratic family. His best-known works are *Contes cruels* (1883) and the symbolist drama *Axël* (1886).

● **Villon, François** ► (1431–?1463) French poet. He studied at the University of Paris but thereafter led a life of vagrancy and crime. He was condemned to be hanged in 1463 but was banished from Paris instead, and nothing is known of him after that date. Only about 3000 lines of his work survive. The ballades and other poems in his *Lais* and *Grand Testament* are characterized by compassion, irony, and a fascination with death and decay. Among the best known of his poems are the *Ballade des dames du temps jadis* and his epitaph, the *Ballade des pendus*.

● **Vilnius** ► (Polish name: Wilno) 54 40N 25 19E The capital of Lithuania, on the River Neris in the E of the country. A commercial, industrial, and educational centre, it is a railway junction and has a wide range of manufacturing industries and a university founded (1579) by Stephen Báthory.
History: it dates back to the 14th century, when it became Gediminas' capital but declined following Lithuania's union with Poland. It was ceded to Russia in 1795. After World War I it was given to newly independent Lithuania but was seized by Poland in 1922. Restored to Lithuania in 1940, it then became part of the Soviet Union. The Germans occupied Vilnius in World War II, when its large Jewish population was virtually exterminated. In 1991 there were violent clashes as Soviet troops fired on demonstrators for Lithuanian independence, which was achieved later that year. Population (1996 est): 573 200.

● **Vimy** ▷*See* World War I.

● **Viña del Mar** ► 33 02S 71 35W A seaside resort in W central Chile, a suburb of Valparaíso on the Pacific Ocean. Its attractions include a casino, beaches, hotels, and a racecourse. Population (1995 est): 322 220.

● **Vincent de Paul, St** ► (c. 1580–1660) French priest, known for his work among the poor and sick. Captured by Barbary pirates on his way to Marseille (1605), he escaped and in 1625 founded the Congregation of the Mission Priests (*see* Lazarists). In 1633 he founded the Daughters of Charity. Feast day: 27 Sept.

● **Vincent of Beauvais** ► (c. 1190–1264) French Dominican friar, scholar, and encyclopedist. His greatest achievement was a Latin encyclopedia, the *Speculum maius*, which he compiled from the whole range of knowledge available to him. In three parts, it dealt with natural history, theological doctrine, and history.

● **vine** ► Any climbing or trailing plant that requires a support for upward growth. The term is often restricted to the grapevine (*Vitis vinifera*; *see* grape) and other plants of the genus *Vitis*, which climb by means of tendrils.

● **vinegar** ► A dilute solution of ▷ethanoic (acetic) acid, produced from soured wine, beer (malt vinegar), or other dilute alcoholic liquids. It is used in salad dressings, preserving, etc.

● **vinegar eel** ► A ▷nematode worm, *Anguillula* (or *Turbatrix*) *aceti*, that lives in fermenting vinegar. It feeds on the microorganisms that convert alcohol to acetic acid in the formation of vinegar.

● **vine snake** ► One of several species of slender venomous tree-dwelling snakes belonging to the family Colubridae. The South American green vine snake (*Oxybelis fulgidus*), up to 120 cm long, is well camouflaged, and preys on small lizards, which it paralyses before eating.

● **vingt-et-un** ▷*See* pontoon.

● **Vinland** ► The Viking name for the area of NE America, probably Newfoundland, discovered, explored, and briefly settled by ▷Leif Eriksson (c. 1000). It is possible that the area was visited a decade earlier by Bjarni Herjolfsson. Eriksson's achievement is celebrated in an important saga.

● **Vinnitsa** ► 49 11N 28 30E A city in central Ukraine. Originally Polish, it was ceded to Russia in 1793. It is the centre of a sugar-beet region and food processing is the principal industrial activity. Population (1996 est): 388 000.

● **Vinson Massif** ▶ 78 O2S 22 00W The highest peak in Antarctica, in the Ellsworth Mountains in Ellsworth Land. It was discovered in 1935. Height: 5140 m (16 864 ft).

● **vinyl resins** ▷*See* polyvinyl chloride; polyvinyl acetate.

● **viol** ▶ A bowed stringed instrument, common from the 15th until the early 18th centuries, when it was eclipsed by the ▷violin. Viols differ from violins in that they have six strings, tuned mainly in fourths, a shallower bridge, gut frets on the fingerboard, sloping shoulders, and flatter backs. They are held between the knees when played and the bow is held in an underhand grip. A consort of viols comprises treble, alto, tenor, and bass instruments; there is also a **violine** pitched an octave lower than the bass. The bass viol acquired the name **viola da gamba** from the Italian *gamba*, leg.

● **viola** ▶ A □musical instrument of the ▷violin family. It is similar to the violin, although larger in size, having thicker strings and a heavier bow. It has a range of over four octaves from the C below middle C; its strings are tuned C, G, D, A. It is a member of the orchestra and the string quartet.

● **violet** ▶ A perennial herb of the genus *Viola*, up to 40 cm tall, whose solitary flowers, usually blue, purple, or white, have two upright petals, two horizontally spreading ones, and a lower central one with guidelines for pollinating insects seeking nectar. The toothed leaves are oval or heart-shaped, often in a basal rosette, and the seeds are released explosively from a three-valved capsule. The sweet-scented garden violets are derived from the Eurasian sweet violet (*V. odorata*). The dog violet (*V. canina*) is another common species, and the genus also includes the ▷pansies. Family: *Violaceae*.

● **violin** ▶ A bowed string instrument, the soprano member of the family that includes the viola, cello, and double bass. It has four strings tuned in fifths (G, D, A, E), an arched bridge, and a smooth fingerboard. It has a range of over four octaves from the G below middle C. Early violins used gut strings; modern strings are steel or gut-covered steel. The violin is played with a bow strung with horsehair; the strings can also be plucked. The design of the violin was perfected by the Amati, Guarneri, and Stradivari families in Italy between the mid-16th and early 18th centuries. It is widely used as a solo concerto instrument, in the orchestra, in the string quartet, and in folk music. □musical instruments.

● **Viollet-le-Duc, Eugène Emmanuel** ▶ (1814–79) French architect and author. He began his career as a restorer of medieval buildings, working on the Ste Chapelle and ▷Notre-Dame de Paris. Viollet was the champion of both the revived gothic style and contemporary developments in architecture, his *Dictionnaire raisoné de l'architecture française* (1854–68) and later books indicating similarities between gothic and contemporary industrial methods of construction.

● **violoncello** ▷*See* cello.

● **viper** ▶ A venomous snake, belonging to the family *Viperidae* (150 species), that has long erectile fangs, which are folded back when not in use. 0.3–3 m long, vipers feed on small animals, which are injected with venom and then trailed until they die. Most give birth to live young. Old World vipers (subfamily *Viperinae*) are stout-bodied and broad-headed and mostly ground-dwelling, although some are burrowers and some arboreal. New World vipers (subfamily *Crotalinae*) are known as ▷pit vipers.

● **Virchow, Rudolf** ▶ (1821–1902) German pathologist and statesman. He originated the concept that disease arises in the individual cells of a tissue and—with publication of his *Cellular Pathology* (1858)—founded the science of cellular pathology. Virchow held public office, supervising improvements in standards of public health, and he also helped develop the science of anthropology in Germany.

● **Viren, Lasse Artturi** ▶ (1949–) Finnish middle-distance and long-distance runner. At the Munich Olympics (1972) he won the gold medals in the 5000 and 10 000 metres; at the Montreal Olympics (1976) he retained both titles.

● **Virgil** ▶ (Publius Vergilius Maro; 70–19 BC) Roman poet. He was born into a farming family near Mantua in N Italy. He completed his education in Rome, where he became a friend of Horace and ▷Maecenas. Reacting against the troubled political background of

civil war, he described in his *Eclogues* (42–37 BC) an idealized pastoral landscape. His more practical vision of Italy in the *Georgics* (36–29 BC) is informed by his passionate interest in agriculture. During his final years he worked on the *Aeneid*, a national epic in 12 books describing the wanderings of Aeneas, the founding of Rome, and extolling the Julian dynasty and Augustus, who claimed descent from Aeneas. He died of fever after returning from a voyage to Greece. The supreme poet of imperial Rome, Virgil became the object of superstitious reverence to later generations. The *Aeneid* was used for divination and its author was imagined to be a magician with supernatural power. In the middle ages, Virgil was treated almost as a Christian prophet because of a passage in the fourth *Eclogue* that seems to predict the birth of Christ.

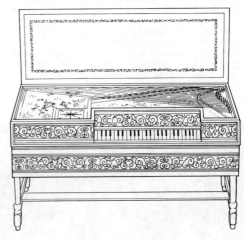

virginals

● **virginals** ▶ A keyboard instrument of the 16th and 17th centuries, the earliest and simplest form of the ▷harpsichord. Often made in the form of a box, which could be set on the table, the strings (one to each note) run parallel to the keyboard.

● **Virginia** ▶ A state on the mid-Atlantic coast of the USA. The low-lying coastal plain is separated from the forested Appalachian Mountains in the W by a region of rolling upland. Manufacturing is very important and the principal industries are chemicals and tobacco processing. Fishing and mining (especially of coal) are also significant sectors of the economy and there is a thriving tourist industry. The state's farmers produce tobacco, hay, corn, apples, and peaches. Timber is also important.
    History: one of the 13 original colonies, it was named after Elizabeth I of England, the Virgin Queen. A period of expansion followed the establishment of the first permanent English settlement in the New World by the Virginia Company (1607) and demands for self-government grew. It provided many leaders for the American Revolution, becoming a state in 1788. Four of the first five US presidents came from Virginia, and during the US Civil War Richmond was the capital of the Confederacy. Area: 105 716 sq km (40 817 sq mi). Population (1996 est): 6 675 451. Capital: Richmond.

● **Virginia creeper** ▶ A climbing shrub, also called woodbine, of the genus *Parthenocissus*, especially *P. tricuspidata* of SE Asia and *P. quinquefolia* of North America. It clings by means of branched tendrils with suckers and is often grown as an ornamental for its attractive red autumn foliage. The compound leaves have five pointed oval toothed leaflets and the tiny clustered flowers have five petals. Family: *Vitaceae*.

● **Virgin Islands** ▶ A West Indian group of approximately one hundred small islands and cays in the Lesser Antilles, administratively divided between the UK and the USA. **The British Virgin Islands** consist of about 40 islands, the largest being Tortola. They became a British crown colony following the defederation of the Leeward Islands colony in 1956 and are now a United Kingdom overseas territory. Tourism is replacing agriculture as the chief source of wealth. Area: 153 sq km (59 sq mi). Population (1997 est): 19 107. Capital: Road Town. **The Virgin Islands of the United States** consist of three main islands, the largest being ▷St Croix, and about 50 smaller ones. They were purchased from Denmark in 1917 for their strategic importance. Industries include tourism, rum distilling, and textiles. Area: 344 sq km (133 sq mi). Population (1992 est): 103 000. Capital: Charlotte Amalie.

● **Virgo** ▶ (Latin: Virgin) A large equatorial constellation that lies on the ▷zodiac between Libra and Leo. The brightest star is ▷Spica. The constellation contains the **Virgo cluster** of galaxies, which contains over 2500 members, the majority of which are spiral galaxies.

● **virtual particle** ▶ A short-lived particle that is used in quantum mechanics to represent the interaction between stable particles. For example, in classical physics two electrically charged particles are represented as interacting by the overlapping of the two fields that surround them; in quantum mechanics this interaction would be represented by the exchange of virtual photons between them. The ▷strong interaction is represented by the exchange of virtual pions, the ▷weak interaction by the exchange of intermediate vector bosons, and the ▷gravitational interaction by the exchange of virtual gravitons.

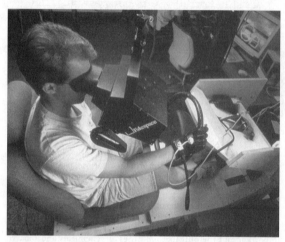

virtual reality ▶ A virtual reality machine being used in car design. The operator is sitting in a seating buck (a mock-up of the driver's seat and controls). A simulated road environment is viewed through the headset; these images are also shown on the screen at top right.

● **virtual reality** ▶ A computer-generated environment that simulates the real world or creates realistic fantasy worlds. Virtual reality machines provide sounds and images of the invented world, often referred to as **cyberspace**, usually through eyescreens and headphones. These are linked to movement sensors and other, often manual, controls, so that the images on the eyescreens and sounds from the headphones change in response to the movements of the user, giving the impression of a three-dimensional environment. Virtual reality technology has been developed for such military uses as training pilots in flight simulators, but it can be used for games, and as a means of remote control. ▷See computer graphics.

● **virus** ▶ A minute noncellular particle that can reproduce only in living cells. The first virus to be discovered was the ▷tobacco mosaic virus. Viruses consist of a core of nucleic acid (either ▷DNA or ▷RNA), surrounded by a protein coat (capsule) and, in some types, a lipid-containing envelope. Some bacterial viruses have tails (*see also* bacteriophage). They may be spherical, ellipsoid, rod-shaped, or polyhedral, with sizes in the range 20–450 nanometres (nm; *see* SI units), although some tailed forms may reach 800 nm. Viruses alternate between an inert virion stage and an infective stage, in which the capsule binds to the host cell and the viral nucleic acid (containing its

genes) enters the cell and directs the components of the host cell to assemble replica viruses. These are finally liberated, often with damage to or death of the host cell.

Viruses cause a wide range of diseases in plants and animals, including influenza, measles, rabies, and AIDS. They can also cause tumours. ▷*See also* retrovirus.

● **Visby** ▶ 57 37N 18 20E A port and resort in SE Sweden, on the W coast of Gotland Island. It was an early member of the Hanseatic League and a major commercial centre in the middle ages. Its industries include sugar refining and metal working. Population (1990): 57 110.

● **viscacha** ▶ A gregarious South American ▷rodent, *Lagostomus maximus*, related to ▷chinchillas. Over 50 cm in length, viscachas live in warrens of 12–15 burrows often with piles of earth outside. They are nocturnal and feed on grasses, roots, and seeds. Family: *Chinchillidae*.

● **Visconti** ▶ An Italian family that established (1310) lordship over Milan under **Matteo I Visconti** (1250–1322) and then, in spite of papal opposition, gained control over many Lombard cities. Skilful marriage alliances both within Italy and outside expanded their influence. By 1400, under **Gian Galeazzo Visconti** (1351–1402), the family's most brilliant representative, they controlled most of N Italy, centred on Milan and Pavia. Temporary reverses under his son **Giovanni Maria Visconti** (1388–1412) were arrested but the death of his brother **Filippo Maria Visconti** (1392–1447) without heirs led to the establishment of ▷Sforza control over the duchy.

● **Visconti, Luchino** ▶ (1906–76) Italian film director. Born into a noble family, he became a committed Marxist. His first film, *Obsession* (1942), is seen as a forerunner of cinematic ▷Neorealism. Later films especially are characterized by elaborate and formal visual composition. They include *The Leopard* (1963), *The Damned* (1970), and *Death in Venice* (1971). He also directed many opera and drama productions.

● **viscosity** ▶ A measure of the degree to which a fluid resists a deforming force. Viscosity is defined by Newton's law of viscosity: if two layers of a fluid, area A and distance x apart, flow with a relative velocity v, there is a force between them equal to $\eta Av/x$. η is called the coefficient of viscosity. Viscosity is measured in newton seconds per square metre. The **kinematic viscosity** is the coefficient of viscosity divided by the density of the fluid.

● **viscount** ▷*See* peerage.

● **Vishakhapatnam** ▶ 17 42N 83 24E A city in India, in Andhra Pradesh on the Bay of Bengal. It is an important port; India's first steamer was launched here in 1948. Industries include shipbuilding and oil refining. Population (1991): 750 024.

● **Vishnu** ▶ The second member of the Hindu trinity, the ▷Trimurti. Known as the Preserver, he complements ▷Brahma the Creator and ▷Shiva the Destroyer, and is married to ▷Lakshmi. He has ten avatars or manifestations, including ▷Rama and ▷Krishna, and is often portrayed asleep on a seven-headed snake in the intervals between his appearances in successive universes. His devotees are the Vaishnavas, a sect founded by the scholar Chaitanya (1486–c. 1534 AD), who stressed devotion to the god regardless of ▷caste.

● **Visigoths** ▶ A branch of the ▷Goths. Forced by the ▷Huns across the Danube (376 AD), they destroyed a Roman army at ▷Adrianople (378) and established themselves in the Balkans, expanding southwards and, under ▷Alaric I, sacking Rome in 410. Moving into France and Spain, they ruled first as Roman subjects and then independently until defeated by the ▷Franks (507) and in Spain by the Muslims (711).

● **Vislinsky Zaliv** ▷*See* Vistula Lagoon.

● **Vistula, River** ▶ (Polish name: Wisła) The longest river of Poland, rising in the S of the country, in the Carpathian Mountains, and flowing generally N and NW through Warsaw and Toruń, then NE to enter the Baltic Sea via an extensive delta region near Gdańsk. It provides an important economic link in the transportation system of eastern Europe. Length: 1090 km (677 mi).

● **Vistula Lagoon** ▶ (German name: Frisches Haff; Polish name:

Wiślany Zalew; Russian name: Vislinsky Zaliv) An inlet of the Baltic Sea on the coast of Poland and Russia (the Kaliningrad exclave), almost totally enclosed by a narrow spit. Area: 855 sq km (330 sq mi).

● **visual display unit** ▶ (VDU) A ▷cathode-ray tube used to display data held in a ▷computer. It is usually associated with a keyboard, enabling new data to be entered or existing data to be changed, and sometimes with a copying device to provide a permanent record of the display.

● **vitalism** ▶ The theory that organisms contain a vital force (*élan vital*) that distinguishes them from nonliving things. It was proposed by the French philosopher Henri ▷Bergson, who believed that the *élan vital* controlled the form, development, and activities of organisms.

● **vitamin** ▶ An organic compound, other than a protein, fat or carbohydrate, that is required in small amounts by living organisms for normal growth and maintenance of life (*see* nutrient). For animals vitamins must be supplied in the diet, although some group B vitamins may be produced by microorganisms present in the digestive tract. Vitamins function as ▷coenzymes in many metabolic reactions; they are involved in the formation and maintenance of ▷membranes, in the absorption and metabolism of calcium and phosphorus, and in many other essential processes. Many can now be synthesized commercially but some are easily destroyed by light or heat, e.g. in storage or cooking.

● **vitamin A** ▶ (*or* retinol) A fat-soluble vitamin and an essential constituent of the visual pigments of the eyes. It also functions in the maintenance of healthy mucous membranes. Vitamin A deficiency leads to dryness of membranes lining the mouth and respiratory tract, blindness, and defective growth. Sources include liver, fish-liver oils, and egg yolk, while precursors of vitamin A, such as beta-carotene, occur in green plants and vegetables (e.g. carrots).

● **vitamin B complex** ▶ A group of water-soluble vitamins that are all constituents of ▷coenzymes involved in metabolic reactions. Thiamine (**vitamin B$_1$**) is important in carbohydrate metabolism: it occurs in cereal grains, beans, peas, and pork. Deficiency leads to ▷beriberi. Riboflavin (**vitamin B$_2$**) is involved in carbohydrate and amino acid metabolism and sources include yeast, liver, milk, and green leafy plants. Nicotinamide (nicotinic acid *or* niacin) can be synthesized from the amino acid tryptophan; liver is a rich source of the vitamin and milk and eggs of tryptophan. **Vitamin B$_6$** (pyridoxine) is essential for amino acid metabolism and is widely distributed in yeast, liver, milk, beans, and cereal grains. Also common in many foods are pantothenic acid, a constituent of coenzyme A; biotin, which is synthesized by intestinal bacteria; and choline, a precursor of ▷acetylcholine (which transmits nervous impulses). Folic acid and **vitamin B$_{12}$** (cyanocobalamin) can be synthesized by intestinal bacteria: deficiency of either causes megaloblastic or pernicious ▷anaemia. Liver is a good source of vitamin B$_{12}$.

● **vitamin C** ▶ (*or* ascorbic acid) A water-soluble compound that is required for several metabolic processes, especially for the maintenance of healthy connective tissue. It cannot be synthesized by man and certain animals, in whom it must form part of the diet. Fruit and vegetables, especially citrus fruits, are good sources. Deficiency of vitamin C leads to ▷scurvy. Claims that large doses of the vitamin prevent colds have not been scientifically accepted.

● **vitamin D** ▶ A fat-soluble vitamin consisting of related compounds (sterols), principally cholecalciferol (D$_3$) and ergocalciferol (D$_2$). Vitamin D is important in calcium and phosphorus metabolism, especially in the absorption of calcium from the gut and the deposition and resorption of bone minerals. Vitamin D$_3$ is produced by sunlight on skin, which normally meets all the body's requirements. Fish and fish-liver oils are the main sources, while vitamin D$_2$ is added to margarine. Deficiency causes ▷rickets in children and ▷osteomalacia in adults.

● **vitamin E** ▶ A vitamin consisting of a group of related compounds that function as biological ▷antioxidants, inhibiting the oxidation of unsaturated fatty acids. The most potent form of vitamin E is alpha-tocopherol, found in green leafy plants, cereal grains, and eggs. Deficiency (which is rare) may lead to anaemia.

● **vitamin K** ▶ A vitamin consisting of a group of quinone-based compounds that are necessary for the formation of prothrombin, important in blood clotting. Vitamin K occurs in vegetables, cereals, and egg yolk and can be synthesized by intestinal bacteria. Deficiency is rare.

● **Vitebsk** ▶ 55 10N 30 14E A port in E Belarus, on the Western Dvina River. It serves as the transport centre of an agricultural region; industries include food processing. Population (1996 est): 365 600.

● **Viterbo** ▶ 42 24N 12 06E A town in Italy, in Lazio. A favourite papal residence in the 13th century, it has a 12th-century gothic cathedral. Its manufactures include pottery, furniture, and textiles. Population (latest est): 58 009.

● **Viti Levu** ▶ The largest Fijian island, in the S Pacific Ocean. Mount Victoria, the highest mountain in Fiji, rises to 1302 m (4341 ft). Sugar, pineapples, cotton, and rice are produced and gold is mined. Area: 10 386 sq km (4010 sq mi). Population (latest est): 340 561. Chief settlement: Suva.

● **Vitória** ▶ 20 19S 40 21W A port in E Brazil, the capital of Espírito Santo state. It serves the coffee-growing and mining areas of the state of Minas Gerais. Its university was founded in 1961. Population (1991): 258 243.

● **Vitoria** ▶ 42 51N 2 40W A city in N Spain, in the Basque Provinces. During the Peninsular War Wellington defeated the French under Joseph Bonaparte here (1813). A manufacturing and commercial centre, it has a trade in cereals and wine. Population (1995 est): 215 049.

● **Vitruvius** ▶ (Marcus Vitruvius Pollio; 1st century BC) Roman architect and military engineer, famous as the author of the only complete architectural treatise to survive from antiquity. In the ten books of *De architectura* he describes all the main aspects of Roman architecture—public and domestic buildings, temples, the ▷orders of architecture, interior decoration, town planning, engineering, etc. Rediscovered in Renaissance Italy, it strongly influenced such architects as ▷Alberti and ▷Palladio.

● **Vittorini, Elio** ▶ (1908–66) Italian novelist. An outspoken critic of fascism, he was imprisoned in 1943 following the publication of his novel *Conversation in Sicily* (1941). Released after the German occupation of Italy, he joined the resistance. He translated the works of many US writers and in postwar Italy had great influence as a literary critic.

● **Vittorino da Feltre** ▶ (V. Ramboldini; 1378–1446) Italian Renaissance humanist and educationalist. At his school in Mantua Vittorino educated the children of both the aristocracy and the poor. He developed a broad curriculum, including classics, gymnastics, drawing, and science.

● **Vittorio Veneto** ▶ 45 59N 12 18E A town and resort in N Italy, in Veneto. The Italians decisively defeated the Austrians here (1918) at the end of World War I. Population (latest est): 29 600.

● **Vivaldi, Antonio** ▶ (1678–1741) Italian composer and violinist. He was ordained priest in 1703 and taught music at the Ospedale della Pietà in Venice, for whose orchestra many of his works were written. Towards the end of his life he toured Europe and died in poverty in Vienna. Besides operas and sacred music, Vivaldi wrote over 450 concertos for a wide range of solo instruments, including a set of four violin concertos entitled *The Four Seasons*, which are musical illustrations of four sonnets by the composer.

● **Vivekananda, Swami** ▶ (1862–1902) Hindu philosopher. Born in Bengal, he studied Western science, which he realized was required to improve conditions in India. He dedicated himself to social reforms and to amalgamating Western scientific materialism with Eastern spirituality. He founded the Vedanta movement in the West, where, as the best-known disciple of ▷Ramakrishna, he was well received and where his teaching has had a continuing influence.

● **Viverridae** ▶ A family of mammals of the order ▷*Carnivora*. The 82 species include the genets, civets, linsangs, and mongooses. Viverrids typically have a long body and tail and short legs.

● **Vivés, Juan Luis** ▶ (1492–1540) Spanish humanist and writer. He visited England (1523, 1527–28) but lived mainly at Bruges. His *De anima et vita* (1538) is a psychological work of some depth. He also wrote a treatise on educational theory, *De disciplinis* (1531).

● **viviparity** ► A reproductive process in animals in which the embryo develops within the maternal body, from which it obtains continuous nourishment. Viviparity occurs in most mammals—the embryos being nourished through the placenta—and in some snakes, lizards, and sharks. In **ovoviviparity** the embryo develops within the mother but is surrounded by egg membranes and derives its food from the yolk. It occurs in certain snakes and fish. It should be distinguished from **oviparity**, occurring in birds and many other animals, in which fertilized eggs are laid or spawned by the mother.

● **vivisection** ► The use of live animals for experiments. Many animals, especially rats, mice, rabbits, guinea pigs, and monkeys, are used worldwide to determine the effects of drugs, cosmetics, food additives, and other chemicals on living organisms, often as an indication of their likely effects on humans. They are also used in medical and biological research and for many standard biological tests and assays. In many countries vivisection is controlled by legislation. In the UK experiments on vertebrates (animals with backbones) are controlled by the Cruelty to Animals Act of 1876 and experimenters are licensed by the Home Office. Alternatives to live animals include the use of test-tube (*in vitro*) techniques, tissue cultures, and computer-based mathematical models.

● **Vlaardingen** ► 51 55N 4 20E A major port in the SW Netherlands, in South Holland province on the Nieuwe Waterweg (New Waterway). It has the largest shipyard in Holland; other industries include herring fishing. Population (1994): 73 820.

● **Vladikavkas** ► (name from 1944 until 1954: Dzaudzhikau; name from 1954 until 1991: Ordzhonikidze) 43 02N 44 43E A city in S Russia, the capital of the North Ossetian Republic. An important road and rail junction, it has a variety of industries, including metallurgy and food processing. Population (1999 est): 310 600.

● **Vladimir** ► 56 08N 40 25E A city in W central Russia, 185 km (115 mi) NE of Moscow. It is a rail junction and a manufacturing and tourist centre. Its fine medieval buildings include the Cathedral of St Dimitrii (1197).
  History: founded in the early 12th century, it was the capital (c. 1157–1238) of the grand duchy of Vladimir. It was then virtually destroyed by the Tatars and in 1364 passed under the rule of Moscow. Population (1999 est): 339 200.

● **Vladimir I, St** ► (c. 956–1015) Prince of Novgorod (970–80) and Grand Prince of Kiev (980–1015). In about 987 Vladimir became a Christian and introduced the Byzantine rite to Kiev and Novgorod.

● **Vladivostok** ► 43 09N 131 53E A port in SE Russia, on the Sea of Japan. It is the terminus of the Trans-Siberian Railway and a major Russian naval base, also supporting fishing and whaling fleets. Ice breakers are employed to keep its harbour open in winter. Industries include shipbuilding and food processing. Population (1999 est): 613 100.

● **Vlaminck, Maurice de** ► (1876-1958) French painter. Self-taught, he worked with ▷Derain from 1899 and from 1901 was strongly influenced by ▷Van Gogh. He became a leading exponent of ▷fauvism, painted under the influence of ▷Cézanne from 1908, but returned after 1915 to a style expressing his aggressive temperament in numerous stormy landscapes, which hold a minor place in 20th-century ▷expressionism.

● **Vlissingen** ▷*See* Flushing.

● **Vlora** ► (or Vlorë; Italian name: Valona) 40 29N 19 29E An important seaport in SW Albania, on the Adriatic Sea. After centuries of foreign domination, the independence of Albania was proclaimed here on 28 November, 1912. Industries include fishing and an olive-oil refinery. Population (1991 est): 76 000.

● **Vltava, River** ► A river in the Czech Republic, rising in the Forest of Bohemia and flowing mainly SE then N to join the River Elbe near Melnik. It is an important source of hydroelectric power. Length: 434 km (270 mi).

● **vocal cords** ▷*See* larynx.

● **vodka** ► A ▷spirit distilled from potatoes, rye, barley, or malt, usually in E Europe. Colourless and without a distinctive flavour, it is used in mixed drinks, such as Screwdriver (vodka and orange juice) and Bloody Mary (vodka and tomato juice). It is also made in Warrington, Cheshire.

● **voiceprint** ► A graphic record of the sounds produced during speech. The record shows the range of frequencies and harmonics produced and can be used to identify any individual voice. Although there are certain standards in articulation, which are recorded on the voiceprint, individual timbre and harmonics are produced by the shape and flexibility of the larynx and the oral cavity. Voiceprints are used in phonetics and in forensic science.

● **Vojvodina** ► An autonomous province of NE Serbia and Montenegro, in N Serbia. Low lying and fertile, it produces cereals, fruit, and vegetables. With a large Hungarian minority, it became a focus of ethnic unrest in the late 1980s; in 1990 it was stripped of its autonomous status but this was restored in 2002. Area: 22 489 sq km (8683 sq mi). Population (1997 est): 1 954 432. Capital: Novi Sad.

● **volcanoes** ► Vents or fissures in the earth's surface, either on land or under the sea, through which magma rises from the earth's interior and erupts lava, gases, and pyroclastic material. Many volcanoes have cones consisting of ash, pyroclastic deposits, and lava. Basaltic lava tends to produce gently sloping cones, the lava flowing over a wide area, whereas the more viscous acid lava produces a steeper-sided cone. Volcanic cones are often topped by craters, created by volcanic explosions, and craters of over 1 km in diameter (calderas) sometimes occur through the collapse or explosive removal of the top of a volcano. Volcanoes may be active, quiescent (dormant), or extinct. The world's highest volcano (extinct) is Aconcagua (6959 m; 22 826 ft) in the Andes. Volcanoes frequently occur along plate boundaries (*see* plate tectonics).

● **Volcano Islands** ► A group of three small volcanic Japanese islands in the W Pacific Ocean. Claimed in 1891, they were under US administration (1951–68). Sulphur and sugar are produced. Area: about 28 sq km (11 sq mi).

● **vole** ► A small short-tailed ▷rodent belonging to the subfamily *Microtinae* (which also includes lemmings). Voles are found in Europe, Asia, and North America and range in size from 7 to 35 cm. They have blunt noses and their cheek teeth grow continuously. The common field voles (genus *Microtus*; 42 species) live under surface vegetation of meadowland, eating nearly their own weight in seeds, roots, and leaves every 24 hours. Family: *Cricetidae*.

● **Volga, River** ► A river in W Russia, the longest river in Europe. Rising in the Valdai Range, it flows mainly E and S through Volgograd to the Caspian Sea. It drains most of W Russia and its many large reservoirs provide important irrigation and hydroelectric power. The Moscow–Volga Canal, the Volga–Don Canal, and the Mariinsk Canal system form navigable waterways from the capital to the White Sea, the Baltic Sea, the Caspian Sea, the Black Sea, and the Sea of Azov. High levels of chemical pollution are causing concern. Length: 3690 km (2293 mi).

● **Volgograd** ► (name until 1925: Tsaritsyn; name from 1925 until 1961: Stalingrad) 48 45N 44 30E A city in SW Russia, on the River Volga. It has been rapidly redeveloped since its virtual destruction in World War II (*see* Stalingrad, Battle of) and it is now a major industrial city, having steel plants and factories manufacturing especially machinery, footwear, and food. Population (1995 est): 1 003 000.

● **volleyball** ► A six-a-side court game invented in the USA in 1895, in which an inflated ball is hit with the hands or arms. After the service each team is allowed to hit the ball three times before it crosses the net. A rally ends when the ball touches the ground or is not returned correctly. Only the serving side can score; if the receiving side wins a rally, it serves next. Players rotate on the court so that each has an opportunity of serving. A game goes to 15 points and a 2-point lead is required to win.

● **volt** ► (V) The ▷SI unit of potential, potential difference, or electromotive force equal to the potential difference between two points on a conductor carrying a steady current of one ampere when the power dissipated is one watt. Named after Alessandro ▷Volta.

● **Volta, Alessandro Giuseppe Antonio Anastasio, Count** ▶ (1745–1827) Italian physicist, who invented the electrophorus (1775), a device used to accumulate electric charge and the forerunner of the modern capacitor. His greatest invention, the Voltaic pile or cell, was the first practical battery and led to a number of important discoveries in electricity. He was professor of physics at Pavia University (1779–1815) and was made a count by Napoleon in 1801. The unit of potential difference is named after him.

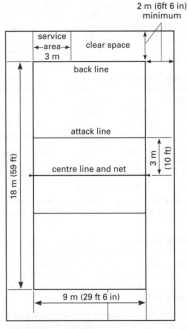

volleyball ▶ The dimensions of the court. The height of the ceiling is a minimum of 7 m (23 ft). The top of the centre of the net is 2.43 m (8 ft) above the floor for men or 2.24 m (7 ft 4 in) for women.

● **Volta, River** ▶ A river in West Africa. Its headstreams, the Black Volta and White Volta Rivers, join in N central Ghana to form the River Volta, which then flows S to enter the Bight of Benin. The Akosombo Dam, completed in 1965 as part of the River Volta scheme, provides Ghana's hydroelectric-power requirements and powers its important aluminium smelter. Length: 480 km (300 mi).

● **Voltaire** ▶ (François-Marie Arouet; 1694–1778) French man of letters, philosopher, scientist, and moralist, whose versatile work epitomizes the age of Enlightenment. He conducted a lifelong campaign against injustice and intolerance. For offending the Duc de Rohan, he was briefly imprisoned in the Bastille (1717) and then went into exile in England (1726–29). After the publication of his *Lettres philosophiques* (1734), which advocated political and religious toleration, he fled to Cirey in Champagne, where he lived with his mistress, Madame de Châtelet. He subsequently lived in Germany (1750–53) having earlier been on friendly terms with Frederick the Great through their correspondence, and in Switzerland (from 1754), chiefly at Ferney near Geneva. His voluminous writings cover history, science, philosophy, and verse drama (for which he was most popular among his contemporaries), and include the satirical and philosophical fable *Candide* (1759), *Traité de la tolérance* (1763), the *Dictionnaire philosophique* (1764), and histories of Peter the Great and Louis XV.

● **Volta Redonda** ▶ 22 31S 44 05W A city in S Brazil, in Rio de Janeiro state on the Rio Paraíba. It has the largest steelworks in South America. Population (1991): 219 988.

● **voltmeter** ▶ A device for measuring voltage. A voltmeter should

draw as little current as possible from the circuit and therefore requires a high input impedance. In the direct-current moving-coil voltmeter the magnetic force on a coil in a magnetic field is used to deflect a needle, the high impedance being provided by a high resistance in series with the coil. ▷Cathode-ray oscilloscopes and digital voltmeters, used for both direct and alternating current, have high internal impedances.

● **Volturno, River** ▶ A river in S central Italy, flowing SE and SW to the Tyrrhenian Sea. In 1860 it was the scene of a battle in which Garibaldi defeated the Neapolitans during the wars for Italian unity (*see* Risorgimento). It was the German line of defence during World War II. Length: 175 km (109 mi).

● **Voluntary Service Overseas** ▶ (VSO) A British organization founded in 1958 by Alexander Dickson (1914–) to send skilled volunteers at the request of overseas governments to work as teachers and doctors or on agricultural, industrial, or business schemes. A volunteer is employed for two years by a government, which provides accommodation and a living allowance. VSO provides the volunteer's air fare and a grant. Director: David Green.

● **Volvox** ▶ A genus of freshwater single-celled organisms that live in hollow spherical colonies of 500–50 000 individuals, which are linked together by fine strands of cytoplasm; the centre of the sphere contains a gelatinous mass. New colonies are formed asexually by division of certain cells or by sexual reproduction, in which the fertilized eggs become dormant cysts that subsequently form new colonies. *Volvox* is regarded by most authorities as a ▷green alga (it contains the green pigment chlorophyll).

● **von Braun, Wernher** ▶ (1912–77) US rocket engineer, born in Germany. Beginning his research into the design of rocket engines in 1932, he was director of the German Rocket Test Centre at Peenemünde during World War II. It was here that the ▷V-2 rocket was finally perfected, being launched on London in 1944. After the war von Braun was taken to the USA where he worked on US space rockets, including the Saturn launch vehicles (*see* rockets).

● **Vondel, Joost van den** ▶ (1587–1679) Dutch dramatist and poet. His works, which adhere to classical models, reflect his deep involvement in contemporary political and religious disputes and his gradual change from Calvinist to Catholic views. His three masterpieces, *Lucifer* (1654), *Adam in Ballingschap* (1664), and *Jephtha* (1659), treat biblical themes.

● **Vonnegut, Kurt** ▶ (1922–) US novelist. His novels and stories are noted for their satirical use of science-fiction techniques. *Slaughterhouse Five* (1969) is based on his experience as a prisoner of war during the fire-bombing of Dresden in 1945. His other works include *Cat's Cradle* (1963), *Breakfast of Champions* (1973), *Jailbird* (1979), *Deadeye Dick* (1982), *Galapagos* (1985), *Hocus Pocus* (1990), and *Timequake* (1997).

● **voodoo** ▶ Magical and animistic cults of West African origin taken by slaves to the Caribbean, where they are still practised by Blacks, especially in Haiti. Voodoo is also practised in parts of South America. Trances induced by spirit possession are central to voodoo ritual. Other elements in the nocturnal rites are animal sacrifice, drum beating, dancing, ancestor worship, and debased elements of Roman Catholic liturgy. The word comes from *Vodun*, god in the language of the Fon people of Benin. ▷*See also* zombie.

● **Voronezh** ▶ 51 40N 39 13E A city in W Russia. It is at the centre of an agricultural region and food processing is an important economic activity. Its educational institutions include a university that was transferred here from Tartu in 1918. Population (1995 est): 908 000.

● **Voroshilov, Kliment Yefremovich** ▶ (1881–1969) Soviet marshal and statesman. Voroshilov was a Red Army commander in the civil war (1918–20) and then commissar for defence (1925–40). He lost his command of the NW armies in 1941 for failing to raise the German siege of Leningrad (St Petersburg). He was president of the Soviet Union from 1953 to 1960.

● **Voroshilovgrad** ▷*See* Lugansk.

● **Vorster, Balthazar Johannes** ▶ (1915–83) South African statesman; prime minister (1966–78) and briefly president (1978). A lawyer, Vorster became minister of justice and police in 1960 and was known for his extreme right-wing views and strict enforcement of racial policies. Becoming prime minister after Verwoerd's assassination, he attempted to improve South Africa's relations with Black Africa. He retired during investigations of financial irregularities in his term as prime minister.

● **vortex** ▶ The circular motion of a fluid about a vertical axis. Examples include whirlpools, hurricanes, and cyclones. A vortex may be formed in a fluid at a point just behind a blunt obstacle past which it is flowing. The direction of rotation of a naturally occurring vortex is often determined by the direction in which the ▷Coriolis force is acting.

● **Vorticella** ▶ A genus of microscopic aquatic single-celled organisms found in dense clusters or singly. 0.05–0.15 mm long, they are bell-shaped and attached to the substrate by a long coiled contractile stalk. Cilia around the mouth of the "bell" create currents that carry food particles into the mouth. Phylum: ▷*Ciliophora*. □protozoa.

● **vorticism** ▶ A British art movement inaugurated in 1913 by the writer and painter Wyndham ▷Lewis. Influenced by ▷cubism and ▷futurism, it called for an art expressing the advanced technology and pace of modern life. Its journal, *Blast*, included contributions from Ezra ▷Pound and T. S. ▷Eliot. The sculptors ▷Gaudier-Brzeska and ▷Epstein were also associated with the movement.

● **Vosges** ▶ A range of mountains in NE France. It extends roughly N–S to the W of the River Rhine between Basle and Karlsruhe, rising to 1423 m (4672 ft) at Ballon de Guebwiller, close to the source of the River Moselle.

● **vote** ▶ The expression of a choice or opinion, by ballot or viva voce, especially for the purpose of electing members to representative assemblies. In the UK all British citizens over the age of 18 who are registered as electors may now vote in local government, devolved body, Westminster (UK parliament), and European elections, except the insane, prisoners, and those who have been found guilty of corrupt election practices within the previous five years. In 1999 the government introduced bills extending full voting rights to peers in their own right (previously barred from voting in parliamentary elections), prisoners on remand, the homeless, and certain classes of psychiatric patient. Commonwealth and Irish citizens living in the UK may also register to vote. Citizens of the European Union may vote in local, EU, and devolved body elections but not in elections to the Westminster parliament. Voting has been by secret ballot since 1872. For elections to the Westminster parliament the UK is divided into single-member constituencies in which the successful candidate is the one obtaining the most votes (this is known as the **first past the post system**). Critics of this system argue that it virtually disenfranchises supporters of the less popular party in nonmarginal seats, and of minority parties everywhere, and that it may elect to power a government not having the support of the majority of the electorate. For these reasons the various systems of ▷proportional representation have many advocates and wholesale reform of the UK system is under discussion.

● **vowel** ▶ In ▷phonetics, a voiced speech sound that is produced when the breath flows freely through the vocal tract without any obstruction from the pharynx, tongue, or lips. The quality of a vowel is determined chiefly by the position of the tongue and the shape of the lips. All other speech sounds fall into the category of **consonants**. A vowel or a vowel substitute (e.g. certain nasal sounds in English) forms the sonorous element or nucleus in every syllable; unlike consonants, a vowel can form a syllable by itself. ▷*See also* accent; Great Vowel Shift.

● **Voyager probes** ▶ Two highly successful US ▷planetary probes launched in 1977 towards the outer planets. Voyager 1 approached Jupiter in March, 1979, then flew towards Saturn, which it reached in November, 1980. Voyager 2 flew past Jupiter in July, 1979, Saturn in August, 1981, Uranus in January, 1986, and Neptune in August, 1989.

● **Voysey, Charles Francis Annesley** ▶ (1857–1941) British architect and designer. Influenced by William ▷Morris, Voysey began by designing wallpaper and furniture. Later he designed houses, gener-

ally small, comfortable, and practical, of which the best were Moor Crag, Windermere (1898), and The Orchard, Chorley Wood (1899).

● **Voznesenskii, Andrei** ▶ (1933–) Soviet poet. He has travelled in the USA and Europe and is, with ▷Yevtushenko, the best-known contemporary Soviet poet. His poems are noted for their lively originality and inventiveness. His translated poetry includes *Selected Poems* (1964), *Antiworlds* (1967), and *Nostalgia for the Present* (1978). More recent volumes include *Videomes* (1992).

● **VSO** ▷*See* Voluntary Service Overseas.

● **VTOL** ▶ (vertical take-off and landing) Denoting an □aircraft that can take off vertically without a runway. Although ▷helicopters can achieve this they are not usually called VTOL aircraft, a term reserved for fixed-wing aircraft that have jets that can be directed downwards for take-off and landing and swing into horizontal positions for level flight. The British Harrier jump jet was the first such aircraft to go into service (1969). ▷*See also* STOL.

● **Vuillard, (Jean) Édouard** ▶ (1868–1940) French artist. He was a member of the ▷Nabis in Paris and his work was influenced chiefly by Japanese prints. His intimate domestic scenes in paintings and lithographs featured large expanses of patterned wallpapers and textiles and became labelled intimist. After 1900 he concentrated on society portraiture but also produced murals for public buildings.

● **Vulcan** ▶ The Roman god of fire. Originally associated with purely destructive manifestations, such as volcanoes, he became patron of smiths and metalworkers after his identification with the Greek ▷Hephaestus, whose myths he assumed.

● **Vulcanite** ▶ (or Ebonite) A hard black insulating material made by heating rubber with sulphur (which makes up about 30% of the product).

● **vulcanization** ▶ A process in which sticky natural rubber is made into a harder useful material by heating it with sulphur. Rubber consists of polymer chains with frequent double bonds; the vulcanization process involves the formation of sulphur bridges (–S–S–) between the chains. An inert filler, such as carbon black, is incorporated at the same time.

● **Vulgate** ▶ The Latin translation of the Bible made by St Jerome in the 4th century AD. It is the oldest surviving translation of the whole Bible and differs from earlier Latin versions in translating the ▷Old Testament direct from Hebrew rather than from Greek. It was adopted by the Council of Trent (1546) as the official version of the Roman Catholic Church and is the basis of later English versions, such as the ▷Douai Bible and the version of Mgr Ronald Knox (1949).

● **vulture** ▶ A large carrion-eating bird belonging to the order *Falconiformes*. 60–100 cm long with a wingspan of up to 270 cm, vultures have a fleshy naked head, a large crop, and a graceful soaring flight. New World vultures (family *Cathartidae*; 6 species) have a slender hooked bill, large feet, and are voiceless. ▷*See also* condor.

Old World vultures (subfamily *Aegypiinae*; 20 species) are widely distributed in open temperate and tropical regions except Australia. They have heavy chopping bills, strong grasping feet, and a feathered ruff at the base of the neck. Family: *Accipitridae* (hawks and eagles). *See also* griffon vulture; lammergeier.

● **Vyborg** ▶ (Finnish name: Viipuri; Swedish name: Viborg) 60 45N 28 41E A port in NW Russia, on Vyborg Bay in the Gulf of Finland 113 km (70 mi) NW of St Petersburg. It supports a fishing fleet, and shipbuilding and lumbering are important industries.

History: founded (1293) by the Swedes as a fortress, it was taken by Peter the Great in 1710 but belonged to Finland from 1918 to 1940. It passed to the Soviet Union in 1944. Population (latest est): 80 000.

● **Vyshinskii, Andrei Yanuareevich** ▶ (1883–1954) Soviet diplomat and lawyer. Vyshinskii was a professor of law and chief prosecutor in Stalin's purge trials (1934–38). He became foreign minister in 1949 and remained in office until Stalin's death, when he was demoted to deputy foreign minister and permanent delegate to the UN.

● **Wabash River** ▶ A river of the E central USA, flowing from W Ohio through Indiana to join the Ohio River. Length: 764 km (475 mi).

● **Wace** ▶ (c. 1100–c. 1175) Anglo-Norman poet. He was made a canon of Bayeux by Henry II of England. His major works are the *Roman de Rou* (1160–74), concerning the history of Normandy, and the *Roman de Brut* (1155), which contained much new material relating to the ▷Arthurian legend.

● **Waco, Siege of** ▶ (February–April, 1993) The 51-day siege of a compound occupied by the Branch Dravidian religious cult in Waco, Texas, by the FBI. It began after members of the cult, led by self-styled Messiah David Koresh, shot dead four federal officials who attempted to serve search warrants. The siege ended with the mass suicide by fire of 72 cult members, including Koresh.

● **Waddenzee** ▷See Zuider Zee.

● **Waddington, Conrad Hal** ▶ (1905–75) British geneticist and embryologist, who proposed the theory of genetic assimilation to explain how characteristics apparently acquired by an organism during its evolutionary development could be brought under genetic control. His books include *Principles of Embryology* (1956).

● **Wade, Virginia** ▶ (1945–) British tennis player. She won her first national singles championship (US) in 1968, later also winning the Italian and Australian titles (1971 and 1972). In 1977 she won the Wimbledon singles.

● **Wade-Giles system** ▷See Chinese.

● **wader** ▷See wading bird.

● **wadi** ▶ A normally dry valley in a desert or semidesert area. It will occasionally contain water following the infrequent violent downpours of rain that occur in these areas.

● **Wadi Halfa** ▶ 21 55N 31 20E A town in the N Sudan, near the Egyptian border. Part of the town was flooded when the ▷Aswan High Dam was completed (1970). Agriculture and commerce are important and it is the terminus of railway and steamship services. Population (latest est): 11 000.

● **Wadi Medani** ▶ 14 24N 33 30E A town in the E central Sudan, on the Blue Nile River. Its recent growth has been due to its central position in the ▷Gezira irrigation scheme. Population (1993): 218 714.

● **wading bird** ▶ (wader *or* shorebird) A bird belonging to the suborder *Charadrii* (of the order *Charadriiformes*), which includes the sandpipers, curlews, avocets, stilts, oystercatchers, phalaropes, and pratincoles. Waders live close to water, either inland—on marshes, moors, etc.—or on the coast—on seashores, mudflats, sand beaches, etc. Most of them are ground nesting and inhabit fairly open ground; they tend to have brownish or otherwise cryptically coloured (camouflaging) plumage and are swift runners, which enables them to escape the attention of predators. The bills of waders are variously adapted for probing mud, sand, or soft ground for the molluscs, worms, crustaceans, insect larvae, etc., on which they feed.

● **Wafd** ▶ (Wafd al-Misri; Arabic: Egyptian Delegation) An Egyptian nationalist party. It was founded by Saad ▷Zaghlul and others in 1918 to demand an end to the British protectorate. After the British granted Egypt nominal independence in 1922, the Wafd campaigned for full autonomy, civil rights, and Egyptian control of the Sudan and the Suez Canal. The party won a victory in the election of 1924 but came into frequent conflict with King Fuad I, who suspended parliament in 1930. It returned to power under his successor, King Farouk, leading to further constitutional conflicts in the 1940s and 1950s. The Wafd was dissolved when ▷Nasser seized power in 1952.

● **Wagga Wagga** ▶ 35 07S 147 24E A city in Australia, in SE New South Wales on the Murrumbidgee River. It is a service centre for the Riverina district. Population (1991 est): 50 930.

● **Wagner, (Wilhelm) Richard** ▶ (1813–83) German composer. He studied at the Thomasschule in Leipzig. His early attempts at composition were unsuccessful but productions of his operas *Rienzi* (1842) and *The Flying Dutchman* (1843) led to his appointment as conductor at the Dresden opera house. In 1845 his opera *Tannhäuser* was successfully performed there but in 1848, after the failure of the May uprising, Wagner fled to Zürich, where he began the composition of the operatic cycle *Der Ring des Nibelungen*, an epic treatment of German mythology. Wagner developed the use of composition with ▷leitmotifs in order to achieve an integration of music and drama in opera, having as an ideal that of the *Gesamtkunstwerk* (German: complete work of art). During the composition of the *Ring*, he fell in love with Mathilde Wesendonck (1828–1902), who inspired the opera *Tristan und Isolde*. Wagner continued to face financial difficulties until, in 1864, King Ludwig II of Bavaria befriended him, financing the first performance of *Tristan* in 1865. Shortly afterwards Wagner eloped with Cosima von Bülow (1837–1930), Liszt's daughter, whom he married in 1870. In 1868 he produced his comic opera *Die Meistersinger von Nürnberg* and continued work on the *Ring*, raising money to build a theatre in Bayreuth for the first performance of the cycle (1876). His last opera, *Parsifal*, was produced in Bayreuth in 1882. Wagner was also a prolific writer on music, the theory of music drama (*see* opera), art, and other subjects. His son **Siegfried Wagner** (1869–1930) and grandson **Wieland Wagner** (1917–66) directed annual productions of Wagner's music dramas at Bayreuth after his death.

● **Wagner von Jauregg, Julius** ▶ (1857–1940) Austrian psychiatrist who, as professor of psychiatry and neurology at Vienna University, successfully treated patients suffering from progressive syphilitic brain disease by means of a controlled malarial infection. His work led to the introduction of fever therapy for various mental disorders and he was awarded the 1927 Nobel Prize.

● **Wagram, Battle of** ▶ (5–6 July, 1809) The battle in which Napoleon won a major victory over the Austrians. Fought NE of Vienna, it forced Austria to concede general defeat to the French. Wagram witnessed the largest concentration of field artillery in recorded history.

● **wagtail** ▶ A slender fine-billed songbird noted for its constantly bobbing tail. The pied wagtail (*Motacilla alba*) is black, grey, and white, about 18 cm long, and commonly occurs near houses. The larger grey wagtail (*M. cinerea*) lives near streams, catching flying insects. In summer the male has a bright-yellow breast, black throat, and bluish upper parts. The yellow wagtail (*M. flava*) visits Britain in the summer. Family: *Motacillidae* (wagtails and pipits).

● **Wahhabiyah** ▶ A Muslim sect founded in central Arabia by Muhammad ibn Abd al-Wahhab (1691–1787). It stresses the need for a Muslim state based on strict adherence to the literal authority of the ▷Koran and ▷Hadith. In 1744 these tenets were adopted by the powerful Saud family, who established a Wahhabiyah empire in the 19th century and the kingdom of Saudi Arabia in 1932.

● **Waikato River** ► The longest river in New Zealand, in North Island. Rising in Mount Ruapehu, it flows NW through Lake Taupo to the Tasman Sea near Auckland. It is a source of hydroelectric power. Length: 350 km (220 mi).

● **Wailing Wall** ► (*or* Western Wall) ▷*See* Temple of Jerusalem.

● **Wain, John** ► (1925–94) British novelist, poet, and critic. His first novel, the satirical *Hurry on Down* (1953), was followed by the novels *The Contenders* (1958), *The Pardoner's Tale* (1978), and *Comedies* (1990), and the biographical *Samuel Johnson* (1974). He also published books of poetry, criticism, and memoirs.

● **Wairarapa Plain** ► A low-lying sedimentary area in New Zealand, on SE North Island. Sheep and dairy farming are important. Area: about 830 sq km (320 sq mi).

● **Waitangi, Treaty of** ► (1840) A treaty between the British government and 46 Maori chiefs in New Zealand, which gave the Maori rights and confirmed their possession of their lands. Its infringement by settlers led to the ▷Maori Wars. The signing of the treaty on 6 Feb is celebrated as a national holiday in New Zealand (**Waitangi Day**).

● **Wajda, Andrzej** ► (1926–) Polish film director. He established his international reputation with *A Generation* (1954), *Kanal* (1957), and *Ashes and Diamonds* (1958), a trilogy of films concerning Poland during and after World War II. Later films include *The Wedding* (1972), *Man of Iron* (1981), *Danton* (1982), and *Holy Week* (1996).

● **Wakamatsu** ▷*See* Kitakyushu.

● **Wakashan languages** ► A group of ▷North American Indian languages of the NW Pacific coast, including ▷Nootka and ▷Kwakiutl.

● **Wakefield** ► **1.** 53 42N 1 29W A cathedral city in N England, in Wakefield unitary authority, West Yorkshire, on the River Calder. A battle was fought here in 1460 during the Wars of the Roses, in which Richard, Duke of York, was defeated and killed by the Lancastrians. A former centre for the coalmining industry, it is now home to the National Coalmining Museum. The chief manufactures are clothing, food and drink, and engineering products. Population (1995 est): 75 900. **2.** A unitary authority in N England, in West Yorkshire. Area: 333 sq km (129 sq mi). Population (1999 est): 310 915.

● **Wakefield, Edward Gibbon** ► (1796–1862) British colonist. After imprisonment for tricking an heiress into marrying him, he helped to found the New Zealand Association (1837; New Zealand Company from 1838). In 1839 he was a major influence on Lord ▷Durham's report on Canada. He emigrated to New Zealand in 1853.

● **Wake Island** ► 19 18N 166 36E A coral atoll in the central Pacific Ocean, a US air base. It was taken by the Japanese following the Pearl Harbor attack (December, 1941). Area: 8 sq km (3 sq mi).

● **Waksman, Selman Abraham** ► (1888–1973) US microbiologist, born in Russia. Waksman coined the term antibiotic for naturally occurring antibacterial substances. His search for these among soil microorganisms led to the discovery of actinomycin (1940) and ▷streptomycin (1943), the first effective agent for the treatment of tuberculosis. Waksman was awarded a Nobel Prize (1952).

● **Walachia** ► (*or* Wallachia) A principality in SE Europe between the lower River Danube in the E and the Transylvanian Alps in the N and NE. Founded in 1290, it was a Hungarian fief until 1330. In the late 14th century it came under Turkish domination, which lasted until the 19th century. In 1859 it united with ▷Moldavia to form Romania, the independence of which was recognized in 1878.

● **Walafrid Strabo** ► (c. 808–49 AD) German scholar and poet. He became Abbot of Reichenau in 838. His fame rests on such poems as *Visio Wettini*, which describes the hereafter, and a handbook on liturgical and archaeological subjects.

● **Wałbrzych** ► (German name: Waldenburg) 50 48N 16 19E An industrial town in SW Poland, in the Sudeten Mountains. It is a coalmining centre and has engineering and chemical industries. Population (1996 est): 139 600.

● **Walburga, St** ► (*or* St Walpurgis; c. 710–79 AD) English nun and missionary to Germany; the sister of the English missionary St Willibald (700–86), Bishop of Eichstätt. She worked with St ▷Boniface in Germany, where she became abbess of Heidenheim, an important cultural centre. It is not certain why *Walpurgisnacht* (Walpurgis Night; 1 May), the traditional German witches' sabbath, is associated with her name. Feast day: 25 Feb.

● **Walcheren** ► An island in the SW Netherlands, in Zeeland province in the Scheldt estuary. Protected from the sea by dykes, its fertile land produces sugar beet and vegetables. The disastrous Walcheren expedition (1809) during the Napoleonic Wars resulted in the loss of many British lives. Area: 212 sq km (82 sq mi). Chief towns: Flushing and Middelburg.

● **Walcott, Derek** ► (1930–) St Lucia poet and playwright. His works include the long poem *Omeros* (1990), *Collected Poems* (1986), *The Odyssey* (1993), and *The Bounty* (1997). He was awarded the Nobel Prize in 1992.

● **Waldemar** ▷*See* Valdemar I; Valdemar II.

● **Waldenburg** ▷*See* Wałbrzych.

● **Waldenses** ► (*or* Vaudois) A Christian group founded in the 12th century by Peter Waldes (d. 1217), a wealthy merchant of Lyons, who apparently gave his wealth to the poor and formed a community known as "the poor men of Lyons." The first settlements were in the French Alps, but religious persecution, which continued sporadically to the 18th century, scattered the Waldenses to Italy, Bohemia, Germany, Spain, and eventually North America. They were supported at the Reformation by other Protestant groups. They reject many Roman doctrines (e.g. transubstantiation, purgatory, celibacy of the clergy); at present they number about 20 000.

● **Waldheim, Kurt** ► (1918–) Austrian diplomat and statesman; president (1986–92). He was Austria's permanent representative to the UN (1964–68, 1970–71) before becoming secretary general (1972–81). He was elected president of Austria despite evidence of his war record with the Wehrmacht in the Balkans uncovered by the opposition. He was subsequently cleared of involvement in war crimes.

● **Waler** ► An Australian horse developed in the early 19th century by settlers using imported Thoroughbred and Arab stallions crossed with various mares. Named after New South Wales, Walers typically have a deep round body with a strong back and legs. Height: 1.47–1.63 m (14½–16 hands).

● **Wales** ► (Welsh name: Cymru) A principality in the W of Great Britain, comprising a political division of the ▷United Kingdom. It is bordered by England to the E, the Irish Sea to the N, St George's Channel to the W, and the Bristol Channel to the S. Much of the country is covered by hills and mountains, including the Brecon Beacons to the S, the Cambrian Mountains in central Wales, and the mountains of Snowdonia in the NW. The Isle of Anglesey lies off the NW coast. The principal rivers are the Usk, Rhymney, Taff, Neath, Towy, and Dovey. The principality is administered by 22 ▷unitary authorities (10 counties and 12 county boroughs), which replaced the two-tier system of county and district councils in April 1996. Central Wales is sparsely populated, most of the population living in the valleys and coastal plains of the S and along the coastal strip in the N.
Economy: the valleys and coastal plain in the S are highly industrialized, based originally on the coal found there. In the 19th century South Wales produced some of the best steam coal in the world and coal continued to be important, especially in the S, until the 1980s: there is now only one working pit. Steelmaking has long been associated with these coalfields, and Wales accounts for about half the UK's production of steel sheet and almost all its production of tinplate. Steelmaking is now concentrated on large plants near Port Talbot and Neath. The high unemployment in South Wales in the 1930s, associated with the concentration of traditional industries, led the government to take steps to direct light industry to the area. The Royal Mint is now situated at Llantrisant. Since the decline of traditional industries in the 1980s, South Wales has become one of Europe's chief centres for the manufacture of electrical goods and components (mainly for Japanese and Korean-owned companies). Milford Haven, in the far SW, is famous for its deep-water port, used for the importing of oil, which has given rise to oil refining and associated petrochemical industries here and at Llandarcy near Swansea. Towns on the coast of North Wales derive an important revenue from tour-

Wales ► Raglan Castle in Monmouthshire.

ism. Upland Wales is the source of an important water supply, much of which is used in England. Forestry is also important in the upland areas, as is sheep rearing. Dairying and beef production are important in the valleys and lowland areas.

History: the Celtic inhabitants of Wales were little affected by the Roman occupation and were christianized in the 3rd century AD. King ▷Offa of Mercia built a great dyke (8th century) stretching from sea to sea, providing a frontier behind which the Welsh kingdoms were contained. Temporary unity was achieved by Hywel the Good (d. 950) but the country's subsequent disunity enabled Edward I of England to defeat ▷Llywelyn ap Gruffudd (d. 1282) and establish English supremacy in Wales. Owen ▷Glendower's revolt in the early 14th century was also crushed and English rule was formalized with the Acts of ▷Union (1536–43). In common with England, Wales adopted Protestantism in the 16th century and has been a centre of Nonconformity since the 18th century. The early 19th century was characterized by rural overpopulation and near famine, which was alleviated by industrialization in the S and NE; Wales also suffered during the Depression of the 1930s. Politically, the Liberals were in the ascendant from 1867 until after World War I, when the Labour Party gained increasing support. Welsh nationalism became a growing force in the 1960s and 1970s (*see* Plaid Cymru) but ▷devolution plans were rejected in a referendum in 1979. Subsequent manifestations of nationalist feeling included the fire-bombing of houses owned by English people in Wales. In 1997 a further referendum resulted in a small majority in favour of a Welsh assembly. This was established following elections in May, 1999; Labour's Rhodri ▷Morgan is the current first secretary. Area: 20 767 sq km (8016 sq mi). Population (1996 est): 2 921 000. Capital: Cardiff.

● **Wałęsa, Lech** ► (1943–) Polish statesman and trade unionist; president of Poland (1990–95). An electrician at Gdańsk shipyard, he became leader of the independent trade union ▷Solidarity from its

establishment (1980). He was awarded the 1983 Nobel Peace Prize for his efforts to ensure workers' rights to establish their own unions. As president he was faced with economic crisis and political instability. In 1995 he was defeated in presidential elections.

● **Waley, Arthur** ► (1889–1966) British translator and poet. His translations of Chinese and Japanese poetry influenced many Western poets, notably Ezra Pound. He also translated novels and plays and wrote studies of oriental literature and art.

● **Walker, Alice** ► (1944–) US Black novelist, poet, and writer. Born into a poor family in Georgia, she was active in the civil-rights movement and worked as a social worker and an academic before becoming a full-time writer. Her novels, most of which concern Black women's struggle for fulfilment, include *The Third Life of Grange Copeland* (1970), *The Color Purple* (1982; filmed 1985), and *Possessing the Secret of Joy* (1992). Volumes of poetry include *Once* (1958) and *Horses Make a Landscape More Beautiful* (1984). She has also published essays and short stories.

● **walking** ► (*or* race walking) In athletics, a form of racing in which the advancing foot must touch the ground before the other leaves it. Races are held on a track or on roads. World records (track): 20 km: 1 hour 17 minutes 25.6 seconds (1994) by Bernardo Segura (Mexico); 50 km: 3 hours 40 minutes 57.9 seconds (1996) by Thierry Toutain (France).

● **wallaby** ► A herbivorous marsupial belonging to the ▷kangaroo family (*Macropodidae*). Wallabies are smaller than kangaroos. Hare wallabies (genus *Lagorchestes*; 3 species) are the smallest, measuring up to 90 cm in length. Rock wallabies (genus *Petrogale*; 6 species) have a squarish tail and rough-soled feet for negotiating rocky ground. Scrub wallabies (genus *Protemnodon*; about 11 species) inhabit brush or open forest, browsing on leaves and grass.

● **Wallace, Alfred Russel** ► (1823–1913) British naturalist, who formulated a theory of evolution by natural selection independently of Charles ▷Darwin. Wallace spent eight years (1854–62) assembling evidence in the Malay Archipelago, sending his conclusions to Darwin in England. Their findings were presented to the Linnaean Society in 1858. Wallace found that Australian species were more primitive, in evolutionary terms, than those of Asia, and that this reflected the stage at which the two continents had become separated. He proposed an imaginary line (now known as **Wallace's line**) dividing the fauna of the two regions.

● **Wallace, Edgar** ► (1875–1932) British novelist, the prolific and enormously successful author of over 170 popular novels and detective stories. He died in Hollywood, where he was working as a scriptwriter.

● **Wallace, Lew(is)** ► (1827–1905) US soldier, diplomat, and author. He served in the ▷Mexican War (1846–47), the ▷Civil War (on the Federal side), as governor of New Mexico (1878–81), and minister to Turkey (1881–85). He wrote the bestseller *Ben Hur* (1880), which has been filmed several times.

● **Wallace, Sir William** ► (c. 1270–1305) Scottish hero of the resistance to English rule in the 1290s. In 1297 he captured Stirling Castle and was proclaimed warden of Scotland. In 1298, however, he was defeated by Edward I at Falkirk and was eventually captured and hanged.

● **Wallace Collection** ► An art museum in Manchester Square, London. The collection, which was given to the nation in 1897, was formed by the 4th Marquess of Hertford and his half-brother Sir Richard Wallace (1818–90). It includes 18th-century French paintings and furniture, medieval armour, and such famous paintings as *The Laughing Cavalier* by ▷Hals. A large extension opened in 2000.

● **Wallachia** ▷*See* Walachia.

● **wallaroo** ► An Australian ▷kangaroo, *Macropus robustus*. Smaller than red or grey kangaroos, wallaroos are heavy-set and have long thick dark-grey fur. They are found mainly in Queensland and New South Wales.

● **Wallasey** ► 53 26N 3 03W A town in NW England, in Wirral unitary authority, Merseyside; it is situated on the Wirral Peninsula opposite Liverpool. It is a residential suburb and includes New Brighton (a resort), Egremont, and Seacombe. Population (1991): 60 895.

● **wallcreeper** ▶ A Eurasian songbird, *Tichodroma muraria*, about 17 cm long and having a grey plumage with broad black wings patched with red. It climbs rock faces at high altitudes, clinging with its sharp claws and square tail and probing crevices for insects with its long curved bill. Family: *Sittidae* (nuthatches).

● **Wallenberg, Raoul** ▶ (1912–?1947) Swedish diplomat. Sent to Hungary in 1944 as a special envoy, he helped many thousands of Jews to escape the Nazis, chiefly by issuing them with Swedish passports. In 1945 he was arrested by the Soviet authorities and disappeared. Although the Russians claimed that he died in 1947 in prison, there is considerable uncertainty as to his fate. He was made an honorary US citizen in 1981.

● **Wallenstein, Albrecht Wenzel von** ▶ (1583–1634) Bohemian-born general, who commanded the imperial forces (1625–30, 1632–34) in the ▷Thirty Years' War. He raised an army of 24 000 men for the emperor Ferdinand I, with which he won a series of victories, acquiring considerable territories for himself. His growing independence led Ferdinand to dismiss him in 1630 but he was recalled to deal with the Swedish threat in 1632. He subsequently betrayed Ferdinand and was murdered by a group of British officers.

● **Waller, Edmund** ▶ (1606–87) British poet. Banished for his part in a royalist conspiracy in 1643, he later managed to gain the favour of Oliver Cromwell and subsequently of Charles II. He wrote much occasional verse and many short elegant lyrics, such as the famous "Go, Lovely Rose."

● **Waller, Fats** ▶ (Thomas W.; 1904–43) US Black jazz musician and songwriter. Fats Waller played the piano in cabarets and accompanied such singers as Bessie Smith. In the 1930s he organized small bands and recorded many of his own compositions, including "Honeysuckle Rose" (1929) and "Ain't Misbehavin'" (1929). Many of his recordings have been reissued on tapes and discs, preserving for posterity the brilliant "stride" piano playing of this talented and witty artiste.

● **wallflower** ▶ An annual or perennial herb of either of the genera *Cheiranthus* (about 10 species), native to Eurasia and North America, or *Erysimum* (about 80 species), native to Eurasia. Wallflowers have narrow leaves and four-petalled flowers, usually orange, yellow, red, or brown. Many varieties of *C. cheiri* are cultivated as garden ornamentals. The Siberian wallflower (*E. × marshallii*) has brilliant orange or yellow flowers. Family: ▷*Cruciferae*.

● **Wallis, Sir Barnes (Neville)** ▶ (1887–1979) British aeronautical engineer, who made many notable contributions to aircraft design. He designed the airship R100 and geodetic constructions, which he used in his Wellington bomber. He also invented the swing-wing aircraft but is best known for his invention in 1943 of the bouncing bomb used to destroy the Ruhr dams in Germany in World War II.

● **Wallis and Futuna** ▶ A French overseas territory in the SW Pacific Ocean comprising two small groups of islands. Formerly a French protectorate, its status was changed following a referendum (1959). The chief of the **Wallis Islands** is Uvéa, while the **Futuna Islands** (or Îles de Horne) consist of Futuna and Alofi. Copra and timber are produced. Area: 275 sq km (106 sq mi). Population (1990): 13 705. Capital: Matautu, on Uvéa.

● **Walloons** ▶ The French-speaking inhabitants of Belgium, who live mainly in the S and E of the country (Wallonia). They are descended from the northernmost group of ▷Franks who adopted the Romance speech. From 1977 a series of amendments to the Belgian constitution have given Wallonia considerable autonomy. *Compare* Flemings.

● **Wall Street** ▶ The centre of the financial district in New York City, in which the New York Stock Exchange is situated. Wall Street, often known as the Street, is synonymous with the stock exchange.

● **walnut** ▶ A ⁰tree of the genus *Juglans* (about 17 species), especially the Eurasian species *J. regia*, which produces the best quality nuts. Up to 30 m tall, it has grey deeply furrowed bark and its leaves comprise

seven oblong leaflets grouped in opposite pairs. Separate male and female catkins occur on the same tree, and the plum-sized green fruits each contain a kernel enclosed in a wrinkled pale-brown shell. The kernels are eaten as dessert nuts or used in baking and confectionery, and the whole fruits may be eaten pickled. The timber of this species and of the American black walnut (*J. nigra*) is valued for furniture. Family: *Juglandaceae*.

● **Walpole, Sir Hugh (Seymour)** ▶ (1884–1941) British novelist. Born in New Zealand, he worked as a teacher before becoming a full-time writer. His novels include *The Dark Forest* (1916), *The Cathedral* (1922), and a four-volume family saga, *The Herries Chronicle* (1930–33).

● **Walpole, Sir Robert, 1st Earl of Orford** ▶ (1676–1745) British statesman, regarded as the first prime minister (1721–42). He became a Whig MP in 1700 and was secretary for war (1708–10) and treasurer of the navy (1710–11). In 1712 he was impeached for corruption but came back into the government in 1715 as first lord of the treasury and chancellor of the exchequer. Again losing office in 1717, he was restored in 1720, becoming paymaster general, and after his effective handling of the ▷South Sea Bubble again became (1721) first lord of the treasury and chancellor of the exchequer. His power was supreme after he had secured the dismissal of Carteret (later Earl ▷Granville) in 1724 and the resignation of ▷Townshend in 1730. He maintained his position by adroit patronage and skilful management of the House of Commons but his government was weakened by the failure of his excise bill (1733), which would have imposed taxes on wine and tobacco, and by his unpopular foreign policy. Conflict with Spain led to the War of ▷Jenkins' Ear and Walpole was forced to resign.

His fourth son, **Horace Walpole, 4th Earl of Orford** (1717–97), was a writer. Strawberry Hill, his villa at Twickenham, became a showpiece of the gothic architectural revival. He published memoirs, antiquarian works, and one of the most popular of gothic novels, *The Castle of Otranto* (1765). His vast private correspondence is of historical and literary interest.

● **Walpurgis, St** ▷*See* Walburga, St.

● **walrus** ▶ A large ▷seal, *Odobenus rosmarus*, of coastal Arctic waters. Males are up to 3.7 m long and weigh about 1400 kg. Walruses have tusks—elongated upper canine teeth up to 1 m long—used in digging for molluscs on the sea bed and for fighting and display. They have an inflatable bag of skin on each side of the neck, used for buoyancy when sleeping in the sea. Family: *Odobenidae*. ⁰mammal.

● **Walsall** ▶ **1.** 52 35N 1 58W An industrial town in central England, in Walsall unitary authority, West Midlands. Industries include engineering, machine tools, aircraft components, electronics, leather goods, hardware, and chemicals. A new multimillion-pound art gallery opened in 2000. Population (1991): 174 739. **2.** A unitary authority in W central England, in West Midlands. Area: 106 sq km (41 sq mi). Population (1999): 259 488.

● **Walsingham** ▶ 52 54N 0 52E A village in E England, in Norfolk. The shrine of Our Lady of Walsingham, with which many miracles have been associated, was built here in the 11th century and was a major place of pilgrimage in the middle ages; it was destroyed in 1538. Parts of its medieval priory remain. There is also an Anglican shrine.

● **Walsingham, Sir Francis** ▶ (c. 1532–90) English statesman; secretary of state (1573–90) under Elizabeth I after serving as ambassador to France (1570–73). He is best remembered for his activities against spies and conspirators and was responsible for unmasking the plots of Francis ▷Throckmorton and Anthony ▷Babington against the queen.

● **Walter, Bruno** ▶ (B. W. Schlesinger; 1876–1962) German conductor. He became conductor of the Leipzig Gewandhaus Orchestra in 1929 but went to the USA after the outbreak of World War II. He was famous as an interpreter of Mahler and conducted the first performance of *Das Lied von der Erde* in 1911.

● **Walter, Hubert** ▶ (d. 1205) English churchman and statesman. He became Bishop of Salisbury in 1189 and Archbishop of Canterbury in 1193. As chief justiciar (1193–98) and thus virtual ruler of England during Richard I's absence on the Crusades, he introduced administrative and tax reforms and created the post of justice of the peace.

● **Walter I, John** ► (1739–1812) British newspaper editor, who founded *The Times*. He acquired a printing press in Blackfriars, London, and began (1785) to publish the *Daily Universal Register*. He renamed it *The Times* for the edition of 1 January 1788. The newspaper remained in his family for nearly 125 years. His son **John Walter II** (1776–1847) managed *The Times* from 1802 to 1847. **John Walter III** (1818–1894) succeeded his father, John Walter II, in 1847.

● **Waltham Forest** ► A borough of NE Greater London, created in 1965 from the former municipal boroughs of Chingford, Leyton, and Walthamstow. Area: 40 sq km (15 sq mi). Population (1999 est): 212 033.

● **Walther von der Vogelweide** ► (c. 1170–c. 1230) German poet. After studying under the court poet of Vienna, he earned a precarious living as a Minnesinger at various courts until he was granted a fief by the Emperor Frederick II. His finest works are love poems and poems inspired by his loyalty to the Holy Roman Empire.

● **Walton, Ernest Thomas Sinton** ► (1903–95) Irish physicist, who shared the 1951 Nobel Prize with Sir John ▷Cockcroft for their invention in 1929 of the first particle accelerator. He was professor of physics at Dublin from 1934 until 1947.

● **Walton, Izaak** ► (1593–1683) English writer. His best-known work is *The Compleat Angler* (1653), an entertaining treatise on fishing. He also wrote short biographies of John Donne (1640), George Herbert (1670), and other churchmen.

● **Walton, Sir William (Turner)** ► (1902–83) British composer. He first became well known through *Façade* (1922), a setting of poems by Edith Sitwell for reciter and instrumental group. Later works include two symphonies (1932–35, 1960), the opera *Troilus and Cressida* (1954), concertos for viola (1929), violin (1939), and cello (1957), the oratorio *Belshazzar's Feast* (1931), and music for Laurence Olivier's films of Shakespeare's *Hamlet*, *Henry V*, and *Richard III*.

● **waltz** ► A ballroom dance in 3/4 time in which couples revolve round the room with gliding steps. It originated in Austria and Germany in the late 18th century from a popular folk dance, the *Ländler*. Although many considered it indecorous, it quickly spread to France and reached England in about 1812. Its variations include the skipping French waltz in 6/8 time, the slow Boston waltz, and the galloping Viennese waltz, for which the Strauss family composed their most famous music.

● **Walvis Bay** ► A port on the Atlantic coast of Namibia. Annexed to the Cape Colony in 1884, it was administered by South Africa as part of South West Africa (now Namibia) from 1922 until 1977, when it came under South African jurisdiction. South Africa retained control of the port after Namibian independence (1990) until 1994, when it was transferred to Namibia. It is a major port, handling most Namibian imports, and has important fishing industries. Area: 1124 sq km (434 sq mi). Population (1992 est): 23 000.

● **wampum** ► Strings, belts, or ornaments of shell-beads, made by Indians of the NE regions of the USA and used by them originally as a record of a treaty or agreement and later, after contact with Europeans, as a form of money.

● **wandering Jew** ▷*See* Tradescantia.

● **Wandering Jew** ► In legend, a Jew who rebuked Christ as he was carrying the cross to Calvary and told him to go faster; he was condemned to wander the earth until Christ's second coming. A version of the story was given by the 13th-century English chronicler Matthew ▷Paris; however, its popularity dates from a 1602 pamphlet containing the story of a bishop of Schleswig who had met a certain Ahasuerus, who claimed to be the Wandering Jew.

● **Wandsworth** ► A borough of S central Greater London. It was created in 1965 from most of the former metropolitan borough together with ▷Battersea and parts of Putney, Balham, and Tooting. Area: 35 sq km (13 sq mi). Population (1999 est): 252 425.

● **Wang** ▷*See* Koryŏ.

● **Wang An Shi** ► (or Wang An-shih; 1021–86) Chinese statesman and writer. As a leading minister (1069–76) during the Song dynasty,

he introduced wide-ranging economic reforms known as the New Policies. Conservative opposition led to his retirement, after which he devoted himself to scholarship and poetry.

● **Wanganui** ► 39 56S 175 00E A port in New Zealand, in SW North Island on the Wanganui River. It is a service centre for the ▷Taranaki district. Population (1995 est): 42 200.

● **Wang Jing Wei** ► (or Wang Ching-wei; 1883–1944) Chinese revolutionary, who attempted unsuccessfully to assassinate the Qing prime minister (1910). Wang later became a rival of ▷Chiang Kai-shek for the leadership of the ▷Guomindang and in 1927, in opposition to Chiang, he established a short-lived government at Wuhan. Reconciled with Chiang in 1932, Wang subsequently became prime minister of a Japanese puppet government in Nanjing and died in disgrace.

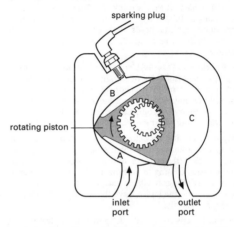

Wankel engine ► The rotary piston draws the fuel mixture through the inlet port into chamber A. At the same time the gas drawn into chamber B in the previous third of a cycle is compressed and ignited to drive the piston round. Meanwhile, the gas in chamber C is discharged through the outlet port.

● **Wankel engine** ► A four-stroke rotary ▷internal-combustion engine. It consists of a triangular-shaped rotating piston, with outward curved sides and rounded corners. This rotates in an oval-shaped chamber, which has inlet and exhaust ports and a sparking plug. The piston has an inner toothed annulus, which rotates about a central stationary gear, the whole piston being connected via gears to an output shaft. The small number of moving parts and the lack of vibration are the chief advantages of this engine, but gas leakage around the seals between the piston ends and the cylinder has restricted its use. It was invented by the German engineer Felix Wankel (1902–88).

● **Wankie** ▷*See* Hwange.

● **Wannsee conference** ► The conference held in Wannsee, near Berlin, early in 1942, at which the Germans formulated their plan to exterminate all European Jews. The euphemism used at the conference was the **Final Solution** (German *Endlösung*). Chaired at Hitler's insistence by Reinhard ▷Heydrich, who was well known for his brutality towards Jews, the conference appointed Adolf ▷Eichmann to formulate the logistics of the plan. Thirty copies of the minutes of this ghoulish meeting were circulated but conveniently lost by the end of the war. However, one copy (known as the **Wansee Protocol**) came to light in 1947 at the German Foreign Office. Described as "the most shameful document of modern history", it was used in evidence at the Jerusalem and ▷Nuremberg Trials of German war criminals. The exact nature of the Final Solution was not widely known in Germany in 1942. However, by the time Eichmann had organized his programme for identifying, arresting, and transporting the Jews to the death camps not many Germans could have remained ignorant of what was happening. ▷*See also* genocide; holocaust.

● **WAP** ► (*wireless application protocol*) A standard protocol for data transmission used in connecting ▷mobile phones to the ▷Internet. WAP phones are capable of sending and receiving e-mails and accessing a limited range of Internet services.

● **wapentake** ► Any of the medieval administrative subdivisions into which the parts of England settled by the Danes (*see* Danelaw) were divided. They corresponded to the ▷hundreds found in the rest of England. Derived from the Old Norse words for *weapon* and *take*, the term probably refers to the Scandinavian custom of brandishing weapons in an assembly as a gesture of assent.

● **wapiti** ▶ A large ▷red deer of North America, sometimes regarded as a separate species (*Cervus canadensis*). Males may exceed 1.5 m at the shoulder and have antlers up to 1.2 m high.

● **Wapping** ▶ A former dockland area in E London, in Tower Hamlets, the site of several national newspaper offices. Transfer of operations from Fleet Street to high-tech offices in Wapping in the mid-1980s led to job losses and labour unrest.

● **waratah** ▶ A much-branched Australian shrub, *Telopea speciosissima*: the floral emblem of New South Wales. Up to 2 m tall, it has leathery sometimes toothed leaves and crimson or scarlet flowers borne in large round terminal heads surrounded by ribbon-like red bracts. The fruit is a leathery capsule containing winged seeds. Family: *Proteaceae*.

● **Warbeck, Perkin** ▶ (c. 1474–99) Flemish-born impostor, the focus of a Yorkist plot against Henry VII of England. Pretending to be the Duke of York (presumed murdered with his brother Edward V in 1483) he landed in Cornwall in 1497 but he and his 6000 followers fled in the face of Henry's troops. Captured at Beaulieu, he was hanged after twice trying to escape from the Tower of London.

● **warble fly** ▶ A parasitic fly belonging to the family *Oestridae*, which is widespread in Europe and North America. *Hypoderma boris* and *H. lineatum* attack cattle: eggs are laid on the legs and the larvae burrow into the tissue, coming to lie beneath the hide of the back. There they produce swellings (warbles), each pierced with a hole for breathing. When mature the larvae leave the warble and pupate in the ground. ▷*See also* gad fly.

● **warbler** ▶ A small active songbird belonging to a family (*Sylviidae*; 400 species) widely distributed in Old World regions. Ranging from 9–25 cm in length, warblers have slender bills, soft thick plumage, and feed on insects and berries. They are usually drab brown or olive in colour and many have beautiful songs. ▷*See* blackcap; chiffchaff; reed warbler; whitethroat; willow warbler.

● **war crimes** ▶ Acts contrary to rules of ▷international law governing the conduct of war, mainly contained in the Hague Convention (1907) and the Geneva Convention (1949). Persons suspected of war crimes may be tried and punished by the state that obtains custody of them. The ▷Nuremberg Trials established the most important principle regarding war crimes, that "the fact that the defendant acted pursuant to the order of his government or of a superior shall not free him from responsibility...." The War Crimes Act (1991) enables people suspected of crimes committed in German-held territory during World War II to be tried in UK courts; the first trial (and conviction) of a Nazi war criminal in Britain took place in 1999, when Anthony Sawoniuk, aged 78, was found guilty of murdering 18 Jews while serving as a police officer in German-occupied Belarus. He was sentenced to life imprisonment. Although 376 cases have been investigated under the War Crimes Act, this is the only prosecution to have resulted from it and it is likely that this trial will be the last under the Act. The failure of the other cases has been due mainly to the incapacity or death during investigation of the suspects and lack of evidence. In 1993 the International Court of Justice, the main judicial body of the United Nations, convened an International War Crimes Tribunal for the former Yugoslavia, to investigate and try cases of alleged "ethnic cleansing" in Bosnia-Hercegovina; this has led to several successful prosecutions. In 1999 the tribunal indicted Yugoslav president Slobodan Milošević, who became the first head of state to stand trial (2002) for war crimes.

● **Ward, Artemus** ▶ (Charles Farrar Browne; 1834–67) US humorous writer. While working as a journalist for the Cleveland *Plain Dealer*, he wrote comic letters, the supposed author of which was an itinerant showman, Artemus Ward. He gained national fame as a lecturer using this pseudonym.

● **Ward, Barbara, Baroness Jackson** ▶ (1914–81) British economist and conservationist. She wrote several books on ecology and po-

litical economy, including *Spaceship Earth* (1966) and *Only One Earth* (1972; with René Dubos). She became president of the Institute for Environment and Development in 1973.

● **Ward, Mrs Humphry** ▶ (1851–1920) British novelist, niece of Matthew Arnold. Born in Tasmania, she moved to England in 1856 and married Humphry Ward, an Oxford don, in 1872. *Robert Elsmere* (1888) and her other novels are chiefly concerned with topical religious and social issues.

● **Ward, Sir Joseph George** ▶ (1856–1930) New Zealand statesman; Liberal (1906–12) and United Party (1928–30) prime minister. He entered parliament in 1887, becoming postmaster general (1891) and colonial treasurer (1893); he introduced the penny post to New Zealand in 1901. He advocated greater unity within the British Empire in foreign affairs and led the Liberals in the coalition government (1915–19) under W. F. Massey, before becoming leader of the Liberal Party's successor, the United Party.

● **Ward, Sir Leslie** ▶ (1851–1922) British caricaturist. After studying architecture and painting, he worked for *Vanity Fair* from 1873 under the pseudonym of Spy and became known for his caricatures of contemporary politicians, authors, musicians, and others.

● **Wardrobe** ▶ A royal administrative department in medieval England. Originally the room in which the king kept his clothes and jewels, it became a government department in the late 12th century owing to the king's need for immediate cash supplies while travelling. Closely controlled by the king, it was used by Henry III to counterbalance the Exchequer, which was controlled by the magnates, occasioning much hostility. It declined in importance during the 14th century, becoming again a mere household department.

● **warfarin** ▶ (or 3-(alpha-acetonylbenzyl)-4-hydroxycoumarin) An ▷anticoagulant that is used in medicine for the prevention and treatment of deep-vein ▷thrombosis and pulmonary ▷embolism. It is taken by mouth and bleeding is the main adverse effect. Lethal doses of warfarin are used as a rodenticide (*see* pesticides).

● **war games** ▶ Simulations in miniature of military manoeuvres and combat, using models and rules that enable authentic situations to be reproduced on the playing table. They originated in German states in the late 18th century and were developed by the Prussian army for training purposes during the 19th century. By World War I the military staffs of many countries were using them to assist in the preparation of plans and the training of commanders. War games, especially ▷videogames based on war, are still popular.

● **Warhol, Andy** ▶ (Andrew Warhola; 1926–87) US ▷pop artist and film producer. Originally a commercial artist, he achieved notoriety in the early 1960s with paintings of soup cans and portraits of film stars, notably Marilyn Monroe, made with the silk-screen ▷printing technique. His films include *Sleep* (1963) and *The Chelsea Girls* (1966).

Andy Warhol ▶ Sitting beside a late self-portrait.

● **Warlock, Peter** ▶ (Philip Heseltine; 1894–1930) British composer, critic, and music scholar. Largely self-taught, he was noted for his scholarly editions of early English music. His compositions include *The Curlew* (for voice, cor anglais, flute, and string quartet; 1920–22) and the *Capriol Suite* (for strings; 1926).

● **warlords** ▶ Local despots who seized control of China following the death of the first president of Republican China, ▷Yuan Shi Kai, in 1916. These local tyrants, with their own private armies, attempted to increase their personal power by engaging in civil war, which was only ended by Chiang Kai-shek's Northern Expedition against them in 1926. They continued to exert power in China until Liberation (1949).

● **warm-bloodedness** ▷*See* homoiothermy.

● **Warm Springs** ▶ 32 53N 84 42W A village in the USA, in Georgia. Its water, popular as a health cure since the 19th century, was used by Franklin D. Roosevelt after his attack of poliomyelitis and he subsequently established a foundation (1927) to help other victims of the disease. He died here in 1945. Population (latest est): 468.

● **War of 1812** ▶ (1812–14) The war declared on Britain by the USA in response to Britain's impressment of sailors from US ships and its blockade on US shipping during the Napoleonic Wars. The USA was also incensed by British assistance to Indians harassing NW settlements (*see* Tecumseh). The war was entirely inconclusive but helped forge unity and patriotism in the new US nation.

● **War of Independence, American** ▷*See* American Revolution.

● **war on terrorism** ▶ The "war" against international terrorism announced by President George W. ▷Bush in the wake of the attacks on the USA on ▷September 11, 2001. Bush declared that the USA would use military force to destroy international terrorist networks and any regimes found to be harbouring them. Several countries, including the UK, offered military assistance while others pledged operational support. In the days after September 11 suspicion alighted on the ▷al-Qaida terrorist network controlled by Osama ▷Bin Laden. This was based in Afghanistan and was known to have links with the ▷Taleban regime. After the Taleban refused to surrender Bin Laden, the USA launched cruise missiles against Afghan cities on 7 October 2001. Air strikes continued for several weeks before Taleban power crumbled, enabling their old enemies in the Northern Alliance to take control of Kabul (13 November) and other cities. US forces then concentrated on the Tora Bora, a cave complex in the S Afghan mountains believed to be the chief stronghold of Bin Laden. This resulted in the death or capture of many al-Qaida fighters but the fate of Bin Laden is unknown. Although sporadic fighting has recurred, al-Qaida's Afghan operation had been effectively destroyed by the end of 2001. Meanwhile, Bush has made it clear that further phases of the war on terrorism are planned—most probably in Iraq.

● **Warren, Earl** ▶ (1891–1974) US jurist. He was attorney general of California (1939–43) and its governor from 1943 to 1953, when Eisenhower appointed him chief justice of the Supreme Court. A champion of civil rights, he limited police malpractice and, in 1954, ended racial segregation in US schools. From 1963 to 1964 he chaired the investigation into the Kennedy assassination.

● **Warrington** ▶ **1.** 53 24N 2 37W A town in NW England, in Warrington unitary authority, Cheshire, on the River Mersey and the Manchester Ship Canal. Designated a new town in 1968, it has engineering, chemical, and high-technology industries. Population (1991): 81 812. **2.** A unitary authority in NW England, in Cheshire. Area: 176 sq km (68 sq mi). Population (1999 est): 187 000.

● **Warrnambool** ▶ 38 23S 142 03E A seaport and resort in Australia, in SW Victoria on Lady Bay. It is the centre of an important dairy-farming and sheep-rearing region. Population (latest est): 24 000.

● **Warrumbungle Range** ▶ A mountain range of Australia. It lies in N New South Wales, reaching 1228 m (4028 ft) at Mount Exmouth, and contains the Breadknife, a rock 90 m (300 ft) high but only 1.5 m (5 ft) wide.

● **Warsaw** ▶ (Polish name: Warszawa) 52 15N 21 00W The capital of Poland, in the E on the River Vistula. Settlements in the early middle ages developed into a city by the end of the 15th century, which became the capital in 1611. Thereafter it suffered a decline but it rose to power again in the 18th century. It was occupied by Russia in 1794 and later by France and Prussia. It played an important role in the Polish struggles for independence in the 19th century and, after German occupation in World War I, became the capital again in 1918. During the German occupation in World War II, a ghetto was established (1940) for 400 000 Jews; in February, 1943 the survivors (about 100 000) staged the first **Warsaw uprising**, after which they were put to death. In August, 1944 a second Warsaw uprising gained control of most of the city, overcoming a weak German garrison. Air-raids preceded a successful German counterattack, following which the Germans deported Warsaw's population and destroyed the city. The Russian army, already on the city's outskirts, failed to support the uprising in order to prevent the emergence of an organized alternative to Soviet domination. After the war much of the old town was reconstructed. It is now an important industrial and communications centre. The University of Warsaw was founded in 1818 and the Technical University in 1826. Population (1999 est): 1 618 468.

● **Warsaw Pact** ▶ (*or* Warsaw Treaty Organization) A military treaty signed in 1955 by the Soviet Union, Albania (until 1968), Bulgaria, Czechoslovakia, East Germany, Hungary, Poland, and Romania. It was formed as a communist counterpart to NATO. Following the demise of communism in Eastern Europe, East Germany left the Pact in 1990; the remaining members dissolved the organization in 1991.

● **warships** ▷*See* ships; aircraft carrier; battleship; corvette; cruiser; destroyer; frigate; submarine.

● **Wars of Religion** ▶ (1562–98) French civil wars arising out of the struggle of the Huguenots (French Protestants) for religious liberty and the rivalry between Protestants and Roman Catholic nobles for control of the Crown. The main parties were the Catholic ▷Guise family and successive Huguenot leaders, the Dukes of ▷Condé, Gaspard de ▷Coligny, and Henry of Navarre. The wars, comprising eight distinct conflicts, were exacerbated by the weakness of the monarchy under Charles IX and Henry III. They ended in the victory of Henry of Navarre, who after becoming a Catholic ascended the throne as ▷Henry IV. In 1598 he issued the Edict of ▷Nantes, granting the Huguenots religious freedom.

● **wart** ▶ A small leathery growth on the skin, caused by human papillomaviruses. Warts are most common in children and usually appear on the hands and on the soles of the feet (plantar warts *or* verrucae). Genital warts are often associated with other infections of the genital area. Warts appear suddenly and may disappear without treatment. Persistent warts can be treated by freezing or by the application of drugs, such as salicylic acid.

● **warthog** ▶ A wild pig, *Phocochoerus aethiopicus*, of tropical African woodland. Short-legged, with a large head, bulging eyes, and long curved tusks, warthogs grow to about 75 cm high at the shoulder. They are grey-brown with sparse body hair except on the shoulders and along the spine and they feed during the day on roots, grass, etc.

● **wart snake** ▶ A thick-bodied fish-eating aquatic snake belonging to the family *Acrochordidae* (2 species). The brown Javan wart snake (*Acrochordus javanicus*), also known as the elephant's-trunk snake, is 1.2 m long and occurs in rivers and coastal waters of Australia and SE Asia.

● **Warwick** ▶ 52 17N 1 34W A town in central England, the administrative centre of Warwickshire on the River Avon. It is a historic town with a 14th-century castle and two medieval gateways. Industries include engineering and tourism. Population (1994): 22 600.

● **Warwick, Richard Neville, Earl of** ▶ (1428–71) English statesman, known as the Kingmaker. He was the most prominent English magnate during the Wars of the ▷Roses. A supporter of the Yorkists from 1453, he was responsible for the seizure of the Crown in 1461 by Edward, Duke of York (Edward IV). In 1470, losing influence at court, he changed sides and briefly restored Henry VI to the throne. After the Lancastrians were routed (1471), he was killed, at Barnet.

● **Warwickshire** ▶ A county in the Midlands of England. It consists mainly of undulating countryside, drained to the SW by the River Avon. It is predominantly agricultural, dairy farming being especially important. There is also arable farming and market gardening.

Some light industry exists around the towns but it lost its more industrial NW area, including Birmingham, Coventry, and Solihull, to the West Midlands under local government reorganization in 1974. Area: 1981 sq km (765 sq mi). Population (1996 est): 500 600. Administrative centre: Warwick.

● **Wash, the** ► A shallow inlet of the North Sea, in E England between Lincolnshire and Norfolk, into which the Rivers Witham, Welland, Nene, and Great Ouse flow. In 1992 it became Britain's largest nature reserve. Length: about 30 km (19 mi). Width: 24 km (15 mi).

● **Washington** ► One of the Pacific states in NW USA. Mountains ring the state, including Mount ▷St Helens, and the Columbia Basin covers much of the central area, cut by the Columbia and Snake Rivers. The lowland around the Puget Sound in the W is highly populated, urbanized, and industrialized, while the E is predominantly rural and sparsely populated. The state's major manufacturing industry is the construction of aircraft. Washington is also a leader in nuclear research and timber production, although in 1983 construction of two nuclear power plants was halted, terminating the most costly public works project ever undertaken. Attempts to diversify the economy have led to a concentration on the growing tourist industry and there is significant mineral extraction, especially of gold, silver, and uranium. Fishing is important as is foreign trade. Wheat, potatoes, and fruit (especially apples) are grown and dairy farming is important.
History: the British Hudson Bay Company dominated the area until the 1840s. In 1846 the boundary between Washington and Canada was agreed and the state (1889) was named after George Washington. Area: 176 616 sq km (68 192 sq mi). Population (1996 est): 5 532 939. Capital: Olympia.

● **Washington** ► 54 54N 1 31W A town in NE England, in Sunderland unitary authority, Tyne and Wear. Designated for development as a new town in 1964, it was the home of the ancestors of George ▷Washington before they moved to Northamptonshire and then to Virginia, USA (1657). Population (1991): 56 848.

● **Washington, Booker T(aliaferro)** ► (1856–1915) US Black teacher and reformer. As first principal of the Tuskegee Institute (Alabama) for Blacks, Washington supported civil rights by encouraging Blacks to pursue industrial education rather than political agitation. His autobiography, *Up from Slavery* (1901), stressed the need for racial understanding.

● **Washington, DC** ► 38 55N 77 00W The capital of the USA, in the E of the country on the Potomac River. Coextensive with the District of Columbia, it is the centre of the government of the USA and most of its inhabitants are government employees. Its many notable landmarks include the Washington Monument, the Lincoln Memorial, the Capitol, the ▷White House, the ▷Pentagon, the National Gallery of Art, the Library of Congress, the Smithsonian Institution, the Arlington National Cemetery, the Vietnam Veterans Memorial, Washington National Cathedral, and the National Shrine of the Immaculate Conception. There are five universities and many cultural organizations have their headquarters here.
History: its location as the nation's capital was chosen by George Washington and approved by Congress in 1790. Planned by the French engineer, Pierre L'Enfant (1754–1825), its first constructions date from 1793. In recent years it has acquired a reputation as the USA's most violent city. Population (1996 est): 543 213.

● **Washington, George** ► (1732–99) US statesman and general; the first president of the USA (1789–97). Washington, who came from a wealthy Virginian family, was a surveyor before gaining a high military reputation in the ▷French and Indian War. From 1759 to 1774 he was a member of Virginia's House of Burgesses, becoming a leading opponent of British rule. On the outbreak of the ▷American Revolution (1775–83) he was appointed commander in chief of the American forces. After winning the final victory at Yorktown (1781), Washington presided over the ▷Constitutional Convention (1787) and was unanimously elected president of the new republic. Despite the development of party politics during his presidency, he remained neutral, as he was in foreign relations.

● **wasp** ► A stinging insect, 6–40 mm long, belonging to the order

▷*Hymenoptera*. The common European wasps (genus *Vespula*) are typical social wasps, forming colonies that consist of a queen, males, and workers. The nests are built under ground, in bushes, or in hollow trees. The adults feed on nectar, ripe fruit, insects, etc.; the larvae are usually fed on insects and insect larvae. Fertilized eggs produce queens or workers and unfertilized eggs produce the males. New colonies are established by young fertilized queens—the only individuals to survive the winter. Certain parasitic wasps lay their eggs in the nests of other wasps. Solitary wasps (family *Sphecidae*) lay their eggs in individual nests that are stocked with food and sealed by the parent. ▷*See also* digger wasp; gall wasp; hornet; potter wasp; spider wasp.

● **Wassermann, August von** ► (1866–1925) German bacteriologist, who invented the **Wassermann test** for detecting ▷syphilis, based on the complement-fixation studies of ▷Bordet. For many years this test was widely used for diagnosing the disease, but it has now been superseded by newer tests. Wassermann made many other contributions to immunology, including a test for tuberculosis and an antitoxin against diphtheria.

● **waste disposal** ► Increasing populations, higher standards of living, the widespread use of packaging, and the growth of throwaway consumer products have created enormous problems in waste disposal in the 20th century, especially in Western societies. Household, agricultural, and some industrial waste is disposed of by incineration, burial in landfill sites, dumping at sea, or briquetting into a refuse-derived fuel (RDF). ▷Radioactive waste and ▷sewage disposal are dealt with separately.
Waste disposal is generally considered a serious ecological problem, especially when waste is dumped in the sea. Conservationists, such as ▷Friends of the Earth, advocate greater use of ▷recycling of waste materials (mainly glass, paper, and aluminium), although in practice it has been hard to set up and maintain such schemes on a sufficiently large scale. On the other hand, waste products are beginning to make a useful contribution to energy conservation. Some incineration of waste materials makes use of the energy released for power generation, often in district heating schemes, while combustible materials are increasingly being used as RDF in power stations. The most widely used of the waste disposal options is landfill burial, because it is usually the most economical, although the scarcity of suitable sites in urban areas has tended to increase costs. The decay of organic wastes in landfill sites produces considerable volumes of methane and other combustible gases, which can be recovered as **landfill gas** (*see* biomass energy) and used as a commercial energy source.

George Washington ► An engraving after Gilbert Stuart Spencer's *History of the United States*. Washington's reputation for truthfulness gave rise to a probably apocryphal story of the young lad who was given an axe, which he tried out on a variety of objects on his father's farm—including a young cherry tree. When confronted by his angry father he confessed to killing the tree, protesting that he was unable to tell a lie. The story was immensely influential with adult Americans, but less popular with their sons.

● **watch** ► A timepiece small enough to be worn by a person. Watches, as small clocks, first came into use at the beginning of the 16th century with the invention by Peter Henlein (1480–1542) of the mainspring as the energy store in place of the earlier falling weight. Based on a verge escapement, watches were then bulky devices, often cylindrical, worn on the girdle. The invention of the balance spring (claimed by both Hooke and ▷Huygens) in 1675 converted the watch from a highly decorated ornament into a more functional article that could be concealed in the pocket. By the 18th century pocket watches had attained a high degree of accuracy as a result of the work of such master watchmakers as Thomas Tompion (1639–1713) and George Graham (1675–1751). At the beginning of the 20th century wrist watches were introduced and with World War I their advantages to men in uniform made them overwhelmingly popular. Between the wars wrist watches became smaller and cheaper or boasted such features as rust and shock resistance, luminous dials, or self-winding mechanisms. In the early 1950s the first electromagnetic watches were developed (powered by tiny batteries), but it was not until the late 1960s that the first electronic watch appeared. This used the piezoelectric oscillations of a quartz crystal as the time source and an electronic circuit to reduce the frequency to that required to drive the hands. In the 1970s quartz watches were developed without moving parts: this is the solid-state digital watch in which the dial and hands are replaced by a digital display. This can be made so small that some digital wrist watches incorporate several additional functions (e.g. date, stop-watch, alarm, reminder) as well as a tiny calculator.

● **water** ▶ (H_2O) A colourless odourless tasteless liquid consisting of eight parts of oxygen to two parts of hydrogen by weight. Water covers 72% of the earth's surface and is found in all living matter, in minerals, and as a small but important constituent of the atmosphere. The solid form of water (ice) is less dense (916.8 kg/m^3) than the liquid at $0°C$ (999.84 kg/m^3), which is why ice floats and frozen water pipes burst. The maximum density (999.97 kg/m^3) occurs at $3.98°C$, unlike most liquids in which the maximum density occurs at the melting point. The molecules of water are polar, i.e. they have a positive electric charge at one end and a negative at the other. This makes it an excellent solvent.

Water supplies: an adequate supply of clean water is a prerequisite of all communities. Rain is the prime source, although in arid areas ▷desalination of ▷sea water may be necessary. Rain water for distribution is collected in reservoirs, which may also be fed by rivers, streams, etc. The stored water is purified by filtration, usually through a deep bed of sand. Most of the impurities are trapped in the top 5–6 cm, which are periodically replaced. In fast filtration processes the addition of a coagulant (e.g. aluminium sulphate) is used to cause most particle impurities to fall to the bottom. The water then passes through several tanks of coarse sand. Disinfectants, usually chlorine, are added to kill microorganisms. Sufficient chlorine is added to leave about 0.2 mg/litre of uncombined chlorine after 30 minutes. In superchlorination larger quantities are added, followed by subsequent dechlorination with sulphur dioxide.

In the UK, water supply was delegated to nine Regional Water Authorities by the Water Act (1973). The industry was privatized (under public regulation) in 1989 and the functions of the Regional Water Authorities were taken over by ten holding companies. The Water Act (1989), which authorized this change, also set up the Office of Water Services (Ofwat) as the independent regulator of the water and sewerage companies. ▷*See also* fluoridation; water softening.

● **water beetle** ▶ A beetle of the family *Dytiscidae* (see diving beetle)—the so-called true water beetles. The name is also used loosely for any aquatic beetle, including the ▷whirligig beetles (family *Cyrinidae*); the water scavenging beetles (family *Hydrophilidae*), which resemble diving beetles but feed on algae or decaying organic matter; and the crawling water beetles (family *Haliplidae*), which crawl and feed on algae.

● **water boatman** ▶ A ▷water bug belonging to the cosmopolitan family *Corixidae* (over 300 species). It has a flattened boat-shaped body with fringed oarlike hind legs and feeds on plant debris and algae, scooped up by the spoon-shaped front legs. It is normally attached to

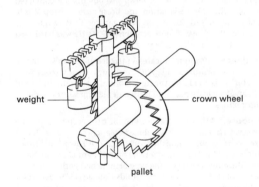

verge escapement

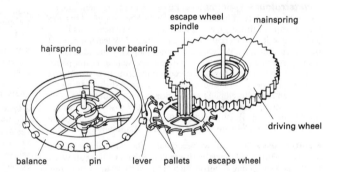

balance wheel and lever escapement

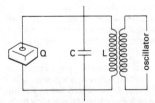

quartz-crystal watch A crystal of quartz (Q) uses the piezoelectric effect accurately to control the frequency of an oscillating electronic circuit consisting of a capacitor (C) and inductance (L).

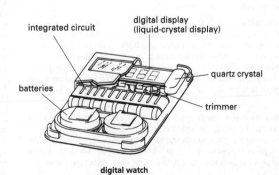

digital watch

watch ▶ Early watches used the verge escapement of clocks. The balance wheel and lever escapement dominated watch design until the quartz crystal and digital watch emerged in the 20th century.

bottom vegetation of fresh and brackish waters, rising only to replenish its air store.

● **waterbuck** ▶ A large African antelope, *Kobus ellipsiprymnus*. About 130 cm high at the shoulder, waterbucks have a long wiry brown coat with a white rump patch and long spreading horns. Small groups spend the night in riverside cover and graze on the plains during the day.

● **water buffalo** ▶ A large buffalo, *Bubalus bubalis*, also called Asiatic buffalo or carabao, found wild in swampy land of SE Asia and widely domesticated throughout Asia. Up to 180 cm at the shoulder and heavily built, water buffaloes are grey-black with long backward-curving horns and can be dangerous. Domestic breeds are more docile and have shorter horns: they are used for milk and as draught animals.

● **water bug** ▶ An insect of the suborder *Heteroptera* (*see* Hemiptera) that lives in or on fresh or brackish water. True water bugs include the ▷backswimmer, ▷giant water bug, ▷water boatman, and ▷water scorpion. The surface water bugs include the ▷pond skater, water cricket (*Vellidae*), and water measurer (*Hydrometridae*).

● **Waterbury** ▶ 41 33N 73 03W A city in the USA, in Connecticut. It was the nation's largest producer of brass products in the 19th century. Other manufactures include watches, clocks, and electronic parts. Population (1996 est): 106 412.

● **water chestnut** ▶ An annual aquatic plant of the genus *Trapa*, especially the Eurasian species *T. natans*, which has a rosette of diamond-shaped toothed floating leaves, feathery submerged leaves, and small white flowers. The hard spiny dark-grey fruit, up to 5 cm across, contains edible seeds that are eaten raw, roasted, boiled, or in porridge. Family: *Trapaceae*.

The Chinese water chestnut is the tuber of an E Asian sedge, *Eleocharis tuberosa*: it is cooked and eaten in various Chinese dishes. Family: *Cyperaceae*.

● **watercolour** ▶ A painting medium consisting of pigments bound with gum, which are diluted with water before being applied to a surface of white or tinted paper. Its special characteristics are its transparency and its white accents, which are created by leaving parts of the paper unpainted. Watercolour made opaque by the addition of white pigment and more glue is known as gouache or poster paint. Practised since ancient times, watercolour painting in postmedieval Europe was chiefly of a monochrome variety until the late 18th century, when it was developed to perfection by a series of British landscape artists, notably Paul Sandby (c. 1725–1809), ▷Girtin, ▷Cotman, ▷Blake, and ▷Turner. Outstanding 19th-century watercolourists included ▷Palmer, ▷Sargent, ▷Delacroix, and ▷Daumier.

● **watercress** ▶ Either of two perennial herbs, *Nasturtium officinale* or *N. microphyllum* × *officinale*, native to Eurasia and widely cultivated for the peppery young shoots, which are used in salads. Watercress grows submerged or floating in streams or on mud; it has compound leaves, with roundish or oval leaflets, and bears clusters of four-petalled white flowers. Family: ▷Cruciferae.

● **water cycle** ▷*See* hydrology.

● **waterfall** ▶ A steep fall of water along the course of a river or stream. It may be produced by the river crossing a band of hard rock; where the rock strata are horizontal the fall is likely to be steep. Falls also occur at the edges of plateaus or where faulting has taken place. The waterfall will continually retreat upstream through erosion. Large waterfalls and series of falls are also known as **cataracts**. The energy of a waterfall can be harnessed to provide hydroelectric power.

● **water flea** ▶ A small freshwater ▷crustacean of the suborder *Cladocera* (about 430 species). Its body, 1–3 mm long, is covered, behind the head, by a laterally flattened transparent carapace enclosing 4–6 pairs of appendages. It swims by means of two large forked antennae. Common genera: *Daphnia*, *Leptodora*; subclass: ▷Branchiopoda.

● **Waterford** ▶ (Irish name: Port Lairge) 52 15N 7 06W A city and port in the SE Republic of Ireland, the county town of Co Waterford.

It has Protestant and Roman Catholic cathedrals. It is an important trading and distribution centre; industries include light engineering, paper making, and glass making, for which it is famous. Population (1991 est): 40 345.

● **Waterford** ▶ (Irish name: Contae Port Lairge) A county in the S Republic of Ireland, in Munster bordering on the Atlantic Ocean. Chiefly hilly, it is drained by the Rivers Blackwater and Suir. Agriculture is the main occupation with dairy farming and cattle rearing. The traditional glass-making industry is of note. Area: 1838 sq km (710 sq mi). Population (1996 est): 95 000. County town: Waterford.

● **water gas** ▶ A mixture of equal amounts of hydrogen and carbon monoxide made by passing steam over red hot coke: $H_2O + C = H_2 + CO$. The mixture is a useful fuel gas but the reaction producing it is endothermic and heat must be supplied to the coke. One way of doing this is to make water gas in conjunction with an exothermic reaction—that between air and carbon: $O_2 + 4N_2 + 2C = 2CO + 4N_2$. The mixture of carbon monoxide and nitrogen is called **producer gas**. Although it has a lower calorific value than water gas the products are hot as a result of the high temperature of the reaction. The heating value of water gas can be improved by passing it through petroleum while hot, thus cracking liquid hydrocarbons to gaseous ones, which escape with the water gas. The process, known as carburetting, can almost double the calorific value. Water gas, however, is not as effective a fuel gas as ▷natural gas and its use is mainly as a raw material for chemical-manufacturing processes, such as the ▷Haber-Bosch process.

● **Watergate** ▶ A building complex in Washington, DC, that gave its name to a political scandal leading to the resignation of the Republican president, Richard Nixon. Amid growing suspicion of corruption among presidential officials, the *Washington Post* exposed their involvement during the 1972 presidential election in a burglary of the headquarters of the Democratic Party at the Watergate, and in subsequent arrangements (the "coverup") to buy off the convicted burglars. Following the resignation and prosecution of top White House staff, who alleged that Nixon had connived in Watergate, he resigned under the threat of impeachment (1974). He was pardoned by Gerald Ford later in the same year.

● **water glass** ▶ (or sodium silicate) A mixture of silicates with the general chemical formula $xNa_2O.ySiO_2$, forming a clear viscous solution in water. It is made by fusing ▷sodium carbonate and sand (▷silica) in an electric furnace and is used in making silica gel, detergents, and textiles.

● **Waterhouse, Alfred** ▶ (1830–1905) British architect of the ▷gothic revival. His early work was done in Manchester and included the Assize Court (1859; demolished 1959) and the Town Hall (1868). Thereafter he came to London, where he built the romanesque Natural History Museum (1881) and the now demolished gothic redbrick St Paul's School (1885) and City and Guilds College (1879). He was a prolific designer of scholastic institutions using redbrick and terracotta; it is his buildings (and those of his imitators) that inspired the term "redbrick university."

● **water hyacinth** ▶ An aquatic plant of the genus *Eichhornia* (about 5 species), native to tropical America. They have slender creeping rhizomes, rosettes of leaves, and clusters of flowers in the leaf axils. Some species float in shallow water; others are rooted in mud. *E. crassipes* is the most widely distributed species; it is used as an ornamental plant and has become a troublesome weed in the S USA, Australia, and Africa. Family: *Pontederiaceae*.

● **water lily** ▶ An annual or perennial freshwater plant of the family *Nymphaeaceae* (75 species), native to temperate and tropical regions. Water lilies have round wax-coated leaves floating on the water surface and borne on long central stalks arising from creeping stems buried in the mud below. The large showy flowers, whose stalks may rise above the water surface, are cup-shaped, with several whorls of oval pointed petals, usually white, yellow, pink, red, blue, or purple in colour. Most cultivated water lilies are hybrids and varieties derived from species of *Nymphaea*. ▷*See also* lotus.

● **Waterloo** ▶ 43 27N 80 30W A city in E Canada, in SW Ontario on the N side of ▷Kitchener. Founded by Mennonites (1806), it houses several insurance companies and two universities and is a musical centre. Its varied industries include distilling, brewing, furniture, and farm machinery. Population (1991): 71 181.

● **Waterloo** ▶ 50 43N 04 24E A village in central Belgium, 13 km (8 mi) S of Brussels. It was the site of the battle of ▷Waterloo, which ended the Napoleonic Wars. Population (latest est): 17 800.

● **Waterloo, Battle of** ▶ (18 June, 1815) The battle in which ▷Napoleon I was finally defeated by British, Dutch, Belgian, and German forces commanded by Wellington and the Prussians under von Blücher. Napoleon caught Wellington 5 km (3 mi) S of Waterloo (Belgium) in isolation from the Prussians and attempted to smash his army by a direct offensive. The British lines held the French columns until the Prussians arrived. A concerted charge brought victory and four days later Napoleon's second, and final, abdication.

● **water louse** ▶ A freshwater crustacean of the genus *Asellus*, related to the ▷woodlouse. It is found on submerged plants or the bottom of weedy streams and ponds. Order: *Isopoda*.

● **watermark** ▶ A distinctive mark produced in ▷paper during manufacture by making it slightly thinner in some places than in others. In handmade paper, the watermark is formed by the wires in the bottom of the mould. In machine-made paper the mark is put in by the dandy roll, a roller that has the mark in a raised form on its surface.

● **watermelon** ▶ The fruit of an annual climbing plant, *Citrullus vulgaris*, native to Africa but widely cultivated. The plant has hairy deeply lobed leaves and the yellow flowers produce large oval fruits, up to 25 cm across, with a shiny dark-green rind and red, yellow, or white flesh, which is juicy and sweet-flavoured. The seeds are also edible. Family: *Cucurbitaceae*. ▷*See also* melon.

● **water milfoil** ▶ A submerged or floating perennial freshwater aquatic plant of the worldwide genus *Myriophyllum* (about 45 species). It has whorls of feathery leaves and the green, white, or red flowers are borne in aerial spikes. A few species are grown in aquaria. Family: *Haloragaceae*.

● **water moccasin** ▶ A heavy-bodied venomous ▷pit viper, *Agkistrodon piscivorus*, occurring in marshes of the S USA and also called cottonmouth because it shows the white inside of its mouth when threatened. Up to 1.5 m long, it is brown with dark bands and hunts fish, turtles, and birds.

● **water polo** ▶ A ball game played seven-a-side (with four substitutes), usually in a swimming pool. It originated in England in the 1870s, with players riding floating barrels to resemble horses and hitting the ball with paddles; in the modern game players swim. The object is to score goals with an inflated ball that is passed between players by throwing. Except for the goalkeepers, players may not walk, jump, punch the ball, or touch it with both hands together.

● **water rat** ▶ A large aquatic ▷rodent belonging to the subfamily *Hydromyinae* (13 species) found in Australia, New Guinea, and the Philippines. The Australian water rat (*Hydromys chrysogaster*) is about 35 cm long and has otter-like fur and a white-tipped tail. Family: *Muridae*.
   ▷Water voles and ▷muskrats are also known as water rats.

● **water scorpion** ▶ A ▷water bug of the worldwide family *Nepidae* (about 200 species). Its scorpion-like "tail" is actually a breathing tube (siphon), which protrudes from the water while the insect hangs upside down from aquatic vegetation or the surface film of water. Water scorpions prey on small arthropods, tadpoles, and small fish.

● **watershed** ▶ (or divide) The dividing line, usually a ridge, between the ▷catchment areas of two separate river systems. In the USA the term is used for the entire catchment area of the drainage basin. ▷*See also* continental divide.

● **water shrew** ▶ A long-snouted Eurasian aquatic ▷shrew, *Neomys fodiens*. About 10 cm from nose to tail, water shrews feed chiefly on aquatic invertebrates, aided by their venomous saliva. Their hair-fringed toes assist in swimming.

● **water skiing** ▶ Planing on water on wooden skis (or a single ski for slalom competitions), often with fins attached for stability. It

originated in the 1920s. The skier is towed by a rope usually 23 m (75 ft) long attached to a powerboat travelling at a minimum of about 25 km per hour (15 mph). Competitions are held for jumping, slalom (through a course of buoys), and trick riding. Barefoot water skiing is also practised, requiring speeds of 55–65 km per hour (35–40 mph).

● **water snake** ▷*See* grass snake.

● **water softening** ▶ The process of removing calcium and magnesium ions from water, which cause scum to form with soap and prevent proper lathering. The main cause of **temporary hardness** in water is dissolved calcium hydrogen carbonate, $Ca(HCO_3)_2$, which is removed by boiling (causing fur, $CaCO_3$, to be deposited in kettles, etc.). **Permanent hardness** is mainly due to calcium sulphate, $CaSO_4$, which is removed by replacing the calcium ions by sodium ions (ion-exchange method) using ▷zeolites, or by locking up the calcium and magnesium ions using polyphosphates or other sequestration agents.

● **water spider** ▶ A European freshwater ▷spider, *Argyroneta aquatica*, that lives under water in a bell-shaped structure constructed from silk and plant material and filled with bubbles of air brought down in its body hairs. It feeds inside on small animals taken from the water surface. The male (15 mm long) is larger than the female (10 mm long).

● **waterspout** ▶ A funnel-shaped cloud extending from the base of a cumulonimbus cloud to the surface of the sea. It is a small-scale intense low-pressure system, the equivalent of a ▷tornado on land, characterized by intense rotating winds, which create violent agitation of the water surface and lift drops up into the cloud.

● **water strider** ▷*See* pond skater.

● **water table** ▶ The upper level of the water that has percolated into the ground and become trapped within pores, cracks, and fissures in permeable rocks. The level of the water table varies with the topography and local rainfall. ▷*See also* artesian well. □ p. 1326.

● **water vole** ▶ A large ▷vole, *Arvicola terrestris*, of Europe and Asia. 15–20 cm long, they have light-brown to black fur and burrow into river banks, feeding on aquatic vegetation.

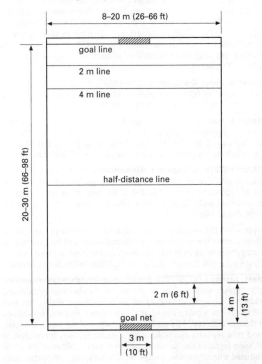

water polo ▶ The dimensions of the field of play. The water must be at least 1 m deep.

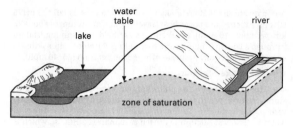

water table

● **water wheel** ▷*See* turbine.

● **Watford** ▶ 51 40N 0 25W A town in SE England, in Hertfordshire. It is a business, transport, and retail centre with industries that include printing, light engineering, electronics, computer software, and financial services. Watford is also the base for the National Lottery and a dormitory town for London. Population (1998 est): 80 000.

● **Watling Island** ▷*See* San Salvador Island.

● **Watling Street** ▶ The Roman road that traversed Britain from its commercial centre, London, via St Albans to the strategically sited Roman town near Wroxeter, with a branch to the legionary fortress at Chester. It left London by way of present-day Oxford Street and Edgware Road.

● **Watson, James Dewey** ▶ (1928–) US geneticist, who (with Francis ▷Crick) proposed a model for the molecular structure of ▷DNA (1953). Following this fundamental breakthrough, Watson investigated the ▷genetic code and the way in which it is "read" by the cell. His *Molecular Biology of the Gene* (1965) has become an influential text, and *The Double Helix* (1968) gave a popular account of his work on DNA. He received a Nobel Prize (1962) with Crick and Maurice ▷Wilkins.

● **Watson, John Broadus** ▶ (1878–1958) US psychologist and founder of the US school of psychology known as ▷behaviourism. Watson declared that speculations about animal behaviour should be based entirely on observations made under laboratory conditions. In *Psychology from the Standpoint of the Behaviourist* (1919), Watson applied his principles to human behaviour, which he regarded in terms of conditioned responses, excluding the possible contributions of reasoning and original thought. One of his most notable followers was B. F. ▷Skinner.

● **Watson, John Christian** ▶ (1867–1941) Australian statesman, born in Chile; the first Labor prime minister of Australia (1904). He was leader of the Labor Party from 1901 to 1907.

● **Watson, Tom** ▶ (Thomas Sturges W.; 1949–) US golfer; he was the world's highest earning player in the late 1970s. His victories include one US and five British Open championships and two Masters championships. He has also won the World Series of Golf three times.

● **Watson-Watt, Sir Robert Alexander** ▶ (1892–1973) Scottish physicist, who during the 1920s and 1930s pioneered the development of ▷radar. In 1935 the British Government set up a research team working under Watson-Watt, who put it into military operation by World War II.

● **watt** ▶ (W) The ▷SI unit of power equal to one joule per second. In electrical terms it is the energy per second expended by a current of one ampere flowing between points on a conductor between which there is a potential difference of one volt. Named after James ▷Watt.

● **Watt, James** ▶ (1736–1819) British engineer, whose development of the ▯steam engine contributed to the ▷industrial revolution. Working at Glasgow University as an instrument maker, he was asked in 1764 to repair a model of a ▷Newcomen engine. He realized that the machine could be made more efficient if the steam was condensed in a separate chamber. Watt's steam engine, completed in 1769, soon replaced the Newcomen engine, especially after Watt had introduced a double-acting model. In 1774 he went into partnership with Matthew Boulton (1728–1809), to manufacture steam engines and by 1800 some 500 stationary Watt engines were in use. He later

invented the centrifugal governor. Watt devised the unit "horsepower" and the metric unit of power is named after him.

● **Watteau, Jean-Antoine** ▶ (1684–1721) French rococo painter. Settling in Paris (1702), he trained under a painter of theatrical scenery and under the curator of the Luxembourg Palace, where he studied ▷Rubens. Despite his early death from tuberculosis, he achieved fame both in Paris and London (which he visited in 1719) with his charming *fêtes galantes* (scenes of gallantry) and paintings of comedians. His best-known works are *L'Embarquement pour l'île de Cythère* and the portrait of the clown *Gilles* (both Louvre).

● **wattle** ▶ Any of various Australian ▯trees and shrubs, especially those of the genus ▷*Acacia*, used for fencing, turnery, etc., and formerly employed in the wattle and daub construction of houses. The commonest are the black wattle (*A. binervata*), the golden or green wattle (*A. pycnantha*), and the silver wattle (*A. dealbata*), which has silvery fernlike leaves and fluffy globular yellow flower heads and is used by florists under the name of mimosa. Wattles are used as shade trees, ornamentals, and livestock fodder.

● **wattmeter** ▶ An instrument for measuring electrical power. The most common type has two conducting coils connected in series, one fixed and one movable. The magnetic forces between them produce a deflection of the movable coil proportional to the square of the current, which is in turn proportional to the power.

● **Watts, George Frederick** ▶ (1817–1904) British artist. After studying at the Royal Academy, he achieved early success with designs for frescoes for the Houses of Parliament (1843, 1847). He specialized in allegorical paintings, notably *Hope* (Tate Gallery) and portraits, including one of his first wife *Ellen Terry*. As a sculptor he is best known for *Physical Energy* (Kensington Gardens).

● **Waugh, Evelyn (Arthur St John)** ▶ (1903–66) British novelist. With *Decline and Fall* (1928) and other novels, including *Vile Bodies* (1930), *A Handful of Dust* (1934), and *The Loved One* (1948), he established his reputation as the most brilliant social satirist of his generation. After his conversion to Roman Catholicism in 1930, religious themes played an increasing part in his novels, especially in *Brideshead Revisited* (1945). Later novels include his war trilogy—*Men at Arms* (1952), *Officers and Gentlemen* (1955), and *Unconditional Surrender* (1961)—and the semiautobiographical *The Ordeal of Gilbert Pinfold* (1957). His elder brother **Alec (Raban) Waugh** (1898–1981), a novelist and travel writer, made his name with the controversial *The Loom of Youth* (1917), a story of public-school life. Many later novels, such as *Island in the Sun* (1956), deal with life in tropical countries. Evelyn's son **Auberon Waugh** (1939–2001) was a novelist and journalist, best known for his satirical "Diary" in the magazine *Private Eye*. His novels include *Consider the Lilies* (1968); *Another Voice* (1986) contains a selection of his writings. His autobiography *Will This Do?* was published in 1991.

● **wave** ▶ Any periodic change in a property of a system that is propagated through a medium (or through space). Waves are classified according to the curve produced when their magnitude is plotted against time on a graph. If the wave is shaped like a sine curve, it is known as a sine (*or* sinusoidal) wave. Examples of sine waves include electromagnetic waves and sound waves. A wave is characterized by three parameters: amplitude, the maximum displacement of the wave; ▷wavelength; and ▷frequency. The wave may propagate energy, in which case it is known as a travelling wave, or it may not, when it is known as a standing or stationary wave. For travelling waves the displacement may be either perpendicular to the direction of the propagation of the wave (a transverse wave) or in the direction of propagation (a longitudinal wave). Waves on water and electromagnetic waves are transverse, while sound waves are longitudinal. ▷*See also* electromagnetic radiation.

● **wave functions** ▷*See* wave mechanics.

● **waveguide** ▶ A hollow conductor for transmitting microwaves over short distances. The ▷electromagnetic radiation is guided along the tube, being reflected from the internal walls. The waveguide is usually filled with air but occasionally some other ▷dielectric is used.

● **wavelength** ▶ The distance between successive peaks (or troughs) of a wave. It is equal to the velocity of the wave divided by its frequency. For ▷electromagnetic radiation it is a parameter specifying the part of the electromagnetic spectrum to which the radiation belongs.

● **Wavell, Archibald Percival, 1st Earl** ▶ (1883–1950) British field marshal. After service in World War I he became ▷Allenby's chief of staff in Palestine. In World War II, as commander in chief in the Middle East, he defeated the Italians in N and East Africa. After the failure of his offensive against Rommel in June, 1941, he was transferred to SE Asia, where he was again replaced after failing to halt the Japanese advance. He was viceroy of India from 1943 to 1947. Also a writer, he edited a volume of poetry, *Other Men's Flowers* (1944).

● **wave mechanics** ▶ A branch of ▷quantum theory in which elementary particles are treated as ▷de Broglie waves. Systems of particles are described by a wave equation, known as the ▷Schrödinger equation. The solutions of this equation give the allowed values of the energy of each particle (eigenvalues) and the associated **wave functions** (eigenfunctions); the wave functions provide a measure of the probability that each particle will appear at different points in space. The theory, first proposed by de Broglie, was developed by Erwin Schrödinger.

● **wave number** ▶ The inverse of ▷wavelength, i.e. the number of cycles executed by a wave in a unit length.

● **wave-particle duality** ▷*See* complementarity principle; de Broglie wave.

● **wave power** ▶ The use of the energy of wave motion in the sea to generate electricity. Wave-power generators of various types have been developed, the best known being the "nodding-duck" type, which consists of a string of floats that bob up and down in the waves. The bobbing motion turns a generator. It is estimated that there are between 50 and 100 kilowatts of power per metre in the waves off the coast of Britain, a total of 120 gigawatts over all the suitable sites. However only a fraction of this would become electricity. One of the disadvantages of wave power is that it is variable and unpredictable although, like ▷wind power, its peak output is likely to coincide with peak demand. Another is that since it is sited off the coast it may be obstructive to shipping and difficult to maintain. In addition, the design and construction of generators and transmission lines to work at sea presents a formidable engineering problem. Nevertheless, research into wave power has been intensified in the UK as a result of the renewables obligation (*see* alternative energy).

● **wax** ▶ A smooth substance of low melting point (40–80°C) obtained from plants (e.g. ▷carnauba wax) or animals (e.g. ▷beeswax, ▷lanolin) or made synthetically. They consist of esters of higher fatty acids than are found in fats, usually with monohydric alcohols. Mineral waxes also exist, the most common being paraffin wax, which is a mixture of the higher hydrocarbons obtained from the distillation of petroleum. Waxes are used in making polishes, candles, mouldings, etc., and in modelling.

● **waxbill** ▶ A bird of the ▷weaverfinch family having a stout waxy-red bill. Most waxbills inhabit open grassy regions of Africa. They are 7.5 to 15 cm long and typically grey or brown with red, yellow, or brown markings and fine barring on the wings. Many rear the nestlings of the ▷whydahs, which lay their eggs in waxbills' nests.

● **wax moth** ▶ A moth whose caterpillars live in the nests of bees and wasps, where they eat refuse, honeycomb, and young host insects. Some are cannibalistic. The bee moth (*Galleria mellonella*) is the best-known species, having spread to many parts of the world. Chief genera: *Galleria, Achroea*.

● **waxplant** ▶ An evergreen climbing plant, *Hoya carnosa*, native to China and Australia. It produces clusters of large fragrant waxy white flowers with pink centres and is cultivated as an ornamental. Other cultivated species include *H. bella*, a dwarf shrub with crimson- or violet-centred waxy white flowers. Family: *Asclepiadaceae*.

● **waxwing** ▶ A broad-billed fruit-eating songbird, *Bombycilla garrulus*, occurring in N coniferous forests and birch woods, sometimes migrating south in hard winters. It has a soft plumage, liver-coloured above with a reddish crest, a yellow-banded tail, and a black throat and eyestripe. The red tips of the flight feathers resemble sealing wax. Family: *Bombycillidae* (9 species).

● **wayfaring tree** ▶ A deciduous shrub, ▷*Viburnum lantana*, growing in woodlands and hedges over much of Europe. Up to 6 m tall, it has oval to heart-shaped toothed leaves and flat-topped clusters of small creamy-white funnel-shaped flowers. The oval fruits ripen from red to black. Family: *Caprifoliaceae*.

● **Wayland** ▶ (or Weland) In Teutonic mythology, a skilled smith. He was captured and lamed by a Swedish king, Nidudr, who kept him on an island, where he was forced to practise his metalworking for the king. Wayland secretly murdered the king's sons, made ornaments of their skulls, eyes, and teeth, raped the king's daughter, and then revealed all to Nidudr before escaping. In England his forge, "Wayland's Smithy," is associated with an ancient site near White Horse Hill on the Berkshire Downs.

● **Wayne, John** ▶ (Marion Michael Morrison; 1907–79) US film actor. Following his success in *Stagecoach* (1939) he played the tough hero of numerous classic westerns including *Red River* (1948), *Rio Bravo* (1959), and *True Grit* (1969). He played similar roles in occasional war films, such as *The Green Berets* (1968). He was awarded a special Academy Award shortly before his death from cancer.

● **Waziristan** ▶ A mountainous area in Pakistan, bordering on Afghanistan. The Waziris, a ▷Pathan tribe who inhabit the area, are noted for their warlike behaviour.

● **weak interaction** ▶ One of the four fundamental interactions between elementary particles (*see* particle physics), the others being the ▷strong, ▷electromagnetic, and ▷gravitational interactions. The weak interaction is about 10^{10} times weaker than the electromagnetic interaction. The electroweak theory, proposed by S. L. ▷Glashow, S. ▷Weinberg, and A. ▷Salam (sometimes known as the GWS model), unifies the weak and electromagnetic interactions in a ▷gauge theory, mediated by photons and intermediate vector bosons (the W-boson and the Z-boson).

● **weakly interacting massive particles** ▶ (WIMPS) ▷*See* dark matter.

● **Weald, the** ▶ An area of raised land in SE England, in Kent, Surrey, and East and West Sussex, between the North and South Downs. Formerly an extensive forest, it is now a mixture of woodland, heath, and agricultural land.

● **weasel** ▶ A small carnivorous mammal, *Mustela nivalis*, of Europe, Asia, and N Africa, recently introduced into New Zealand. Growing to about 25 cm long, it is long-bodied and short-legged, bright red-brown above with white underparts. Weasels feed on rats, mice, and voles, hunting along hedgerows and ditches and entering burrows. They swim well but do not climb. Family: ▷*Mustelidae*.

● **weather** ▷*See* meteorology.

● **weathering** ▶ The physical and chemical disintegration of the rocks of the earth's crust on exposure to the atmosphere. Most rocks were formed under conditions in which temperatures and pressures were higher than those to which they are now exposed; weathering is largely a response to lower temperatures and pressures and the effects of air and water.

● **weaverbird** ▶ A small songbird belonging to a mainly tropical Old World family (Ploceidae; 132 species) noted for its nest-building activities. Most species build domed nests with long entrance tunnels, often elaborately woven with loops and knots to form a durable structure. Some species build huge communal nests—the nest of the sociable weaver (*Philetairus socius*) reaches about 2 m across and houses 20–30 pairs of birds. Weavers are seed eaters with stout conical bills and variously coloured plumage. ▷*See also* sparrow; quelea. □ p. 1328.

● **weaverfinch** ▶ A small finchlike seed-eating songbird belonging to a family (Estrildidae; 108 species) occurring in tropical regions of Africa, SE Asia, and Australasia. Weaverfinches have large conical bills and are usually brightly coloured. ▷*See* avadavat; grassfinch; mannikin; waxbill; zebra finch.

● **weaving** ▶ The process of interlacing two or more yarns at right angles to produce a fabric. The equipment used is called a loom, which is first set up with a series of longitudinal threads (warp). In plain weave, alternate warp threads are raised and lowered by means of wires or cords (heddles) to allow the crosswire threads (weft), wound onto a bobbin (shuttle), to pass between them. Different kinds of weave, such as ▷twill and herringbone, are made by altering the pattern of interlacing. Hand looms have been in use all over the world since ancient times and are still used on a cottage-industry basis in parts of the UK. Power looms, in which the shuttle is moved across the warp automatically, were invented by Edmund ▷Cartwright in 1786, since when many improvements have been made to increase the speed of travel of the shuttle and to enable more complicated designs to be woven.

weaverbird ▶ A male Jackson's weaver (*Ploceus jacksoni*) at Lake Baringo, Kenya, sitting on its nest.

● **Webb, Sir Aston** ▶ (1849–1930) British architect, who built many public buildings in a variety of classical styles, including the University of Edgbaston (1900) and, in London, the Royal College of Science (1906), the Victoria and Albert Museum (1909), and the new façade for Buckingham Palace (1913), as well as the Victoria Memorial, the Mall, and Admiralty Arch (1911).

● **Webb, Mary** ▶ (1881–1927) British novelist. She wrote tragic novels set in her native Shropshire and gained wide recognition when the prime minister Stanley Baldwin publicly praised her best-known novel, *Precious Bane* (1924).

● **Webb, Sidney (James), Baron Passfield** ▶ (1859–1947) British economist and socialist. He helped to organize the ▷Fabian Society in 1884 and was one of the founders of the London School of Economics (1895), where he served as professor of public administration (1912–27). He initiated many educational reforms while he was a member of the London County Council (1892–1910) and, after entering parliament in 1922, held several important government posts. His wife **Beatrice (Potter) Webb** (1858–1943), whom he married in 1892, collaborated with him on a number of books, including *The History of Trade Unionism* (1894) and *Industrial Democracy* (1897). Their work and writings had a lasting influence on the development of social policies within and outside the Labour Party.

● **weber** ▶ (Wb) The ▷SI unit of magnetic flux equal to the flux linking a circuit of one turn that produces an electromotive force of one volt when reduced uniformly to zero in one second. Named after Wilhelm Weber (1804–91).

● **Weber, Carl Maria von** ▶ (1786–1826) German composer, a pupil of Michael Haydn (1737–1806) and Abbé Vogler (1749–1814). His most successful opera, *Der Freischütz* (1821), based on a German fairy story, was the first opera in the German Romantic tradition. The operas *Euryanthe* (1823) and *Oberon* (1826) were less successful. Weber also composed a large number of orchestral works and much piano music.

● **Weber, Ernst Heinrich** ▶ (1795–1878) German physiologist, who became professor at Leipzig University in 1818. He is remembered for his discovery that the experience of differences in the intensity of human sensations (pressure, temperature, light, sound) depends on percentage differences in the stimuli rather than absolute differences. This is called the Weber-Fechner Law because Weber's discovery was popularized by Gustav Fechner (1801–87). His brother **Wilhelm Eduard Weber** (1804–91) was professor of physics at Göttingen University. He worked with ▷Gauss on magnetism and introduced a logical system of electrical units. The SI unit of magnetic flux is named after him.

● **Weber, Max** ▶ (1864–1920) German sociologist, who was one of the founders of modern ▷sociology. His best-known work, *The Protestant Ethic and the Spirit of Capitalism* (1904), relates the emergence of a particular type of economic system to the effects of religious values. In attempting to explain why capitalism developed first in Europe, he produced extensive studies in comparative sociology. His *Methodology of the Social Sciences* (1904) remains a major text, as does his account of social and economic organization, *Wirtschaft und Gesellschaft* (1922). He was politically active during the last years of his life and served on the committee that drafted the constitution of the ▷Weimar Republic.

● **Webern, Anton von** ▶ (1883–1945) Austrian composer. He studied with Schoenberg and earned his living as a conductor and teacher. He was killed by an American soldier during the occupation of Vienna. Webern adopted the technique of ▷serialism, as defined by Schoenberg in 1924. His compositions, which are characterized by great brevity, extreme dynamic contrast, and dissonant counterpoint, include a concerto for nine instruments (1934) and a string quartet (1938). His music has greatly influenced Boulez, Stravinsky, and many other composers.

● **webspinner** ▶ A brownish soft-bodied insect, 4–7 mm long, belonging to the mainly tropical order *Embioptera* (150 species). Biting jaws are used by the wingless females to feed on dead plant material; the males, which are mostly winged, are carnivores. Webspinners live in communities and make silken webs and tunnels under stones or in soil. The young are cared for by the females.

● **Webster, John** ▶ (c. 1580–c. 1625) English dramatist. Little is known of his life. He collaborated with Thomas Dekker and other dramatists. His own major plays are *The White Devil* (1612) and *The Duchess of Malfi* (c. 1613). Despite their typically Jacobean preoccupation with lust and violence, the plays are distinguished by their poetic intensity and psychological insight.

● **Webster, Noah** ▶ (1758–1843) US lexicographer and author of books on American English. His *American Dictionary of the English Language* (1828) took over 20 years to compile and was the most influential American dictionary. Webster also helped to standardize American spelling.

● **Weddell Sea** ▶ A large inlet of the S Atlantic Ocean in Antarctica, between the Antarctic Peninsula and Coats Land. Its S section is covered by the Ronne and Filchner Ice Shelves. It is named after the British explorer and seal hunter James Weddell (1787–1834).

● **Wedekind, Frank** ▶ (1864–1918) German dramatist, also an actor, singer, poet, and essayist. His tragedy *Frühlings Erwachen* (1891), produced by Max ▷Reinhardt (1905), caused a scandal by criticizing the bourgeois attitude to sex. Berg's opera *Lulu* (1937) is based on his plays *Erdgeist* (1895) and *Die Büchse der Pandora* (1904).

● **Wedgwood, Dame C(icely) V(eronica)** ▶ (1910–97) British historian, who specialized in the early modern history of Britain and Europe. Her books include *The Thirty Years' War* (1930), *William the Silent* (1944), *The Political Career of Rubens* (1975), and a trilogy of works about the English Civil War (1955–64). She was appointed DBE in 1968.

● **Wedgwood, Josiah** ▶ (1730–95) British potter, industrialist, and writer, who came from a family of potters. Trained under his brother Thomas, he partnered Thomas Whieldon (1719–95) from 1754 until 1759, when he opened his own factory at Burslem, Staffordshire (England). In 1769 he opened a new factory (Etruria), where he also built a village for his workmen, displaying his interest in social welfare. Employing such leading designers and artists as John ▷Flaxman, Wedgwood popularized the neoclassical taste in pottery and was a leading exporter to the Continent. His high-quality ceramics, **Wedgwood ware**, perfected ▷creamware and developed black basalt ware and typically blue jasperware, unglazed stoneware pieces with white embossed decoration. They also brought transfer printing to Staffordshire. Wedgwood ware is still made—since 1940 in Barlaston, Staffordshire.

● **weed** ▶ Any plant growing where it is not wanted, especially in cultivated areas. Weeds are most important in agriculture, competing with crop plants for space, light, and nutrients, reducing yields, and contaminating the crop. The major weeds of temperate regions include docks, thistles, nettles, shepherd's purse, groundsel, dandelions, couch grass, and wild oats. Some, such as ragwort, may be toxic to grazing livestock. Weeds may also damage paths and buildings and choke waterways. Weed control has traditionally relied on soil cultivation and crop rotation; modern methods involve selective and nonselective ▷herbicides (weedkillers) and, in a few cases, ▷biological control.

● **weedkiller** ▷See herbicide.

● **Weelkes, Thomas** ▶ (c. 1575–1623) English composer. He published his first book of madrigals in 1597 and became organist of Chichester Cathedral in 1603. His hundred surviving madrigals include "As Vesta Was from Latmos Hill Descending."

● **weever** ▶ A slender carnivorous fish of the genus *Trachinus*, found in sandy bottoms of European coastal waters. Up to 4.6 cm long, it has an upward slanting mouth, eyes near the top of its head, and venomous spines on the gill covers and first dorsal fin, which can inflict painful wounds. Family: *Trachinidae*; order: *Perciformes*.

● **weevil** ▶ A beetle, also called a snout beetle, belonging to the largest family (*Curculionidae*; about 60 000 species) in the animal kingdom. Most weevils are small (less than 6 mm) and their mouthparts are at the tip of a beaklike rostrum, which can exceed the body length. Many species are pests of gardens, crops, and stored grains and cereals, e.g. the ▷boll weevil (which attacks cotton seed pods), the grain weevil (*Sitophilus granarius*), and the rice weevil (*S. oryzae*). The larvae are particularly destructive, burrowing into all parts of the plant but especially into wood, fruit, and seeds.

● **Wegener, Alfred Lothar** ▶ (1880–1930) German geologist, who (in 1912) proposed the theory of ▷continental drift to account for his observations of the movements of land masses. Wegener also demonstrated how bombardment by meteors could have caused lunar craters. He died while on his fourth expedition to Greenland.

● **Weigela** ▶ A genus of E Asian flowering shrubs (12 species), including several ornamentals, often called Japanese honeysuckles. Up to 4 m high, they have simple leaves and small clusters of funnel-shaped white to red flowers, about 3.5 cm long, with four or five spreading lobes. The fruit is a long narrow seed pod. Family: *Caprifoliaceae*.

● **weight** ▷See mass and weight.

● **weightlessness** ▶ The condition in which a body possesses no weight. Such a body still possesses mass but its weight (*see* mass and weight) can become negligible when the gravitational field is extremely weak, as for example in space. It can also be produced artificially by creating a force that is equal and opposite to gravity. The physiological effects of weightlessness are important in long space flights and are countered by pressure suits, exercise routines, and correct control of cabin pressure, temperature, and humidity.

● **weight lifting** ▶ A sport in which men and women compete to lift weighted barbells. In the most common form of competition contestants make three attempts in each of two styles, the snatch and the clean and jerk. The weights, of their own choice, can be increased

but not reduced. Power lifting requires different styles, the squat, dead lift, and bench press.

● **weights and measures** ▷See units of measurement.

● **Weihai** ▶ 37 30N 122 04E A port in E China, in Shandong province on the Gulf of Chihli. A naval base in the 1880s and again in 1949, it was leased to Britain (1898–1930). It has fishing and textile industries. Population (1990 est): 128 888.

● **Weil, Simone** ▶ (1909–43) French mystic and philosopher. An active socialist in the 1930s, she worked briefly in a car factory to gain insight into working-class problems and served in a nonmilitary capacity on the Republican side in the Spanish Civil War. She also taught philosophy until 1938. After a mystical experience she became a convinced Roman Catholic, although she refused baptism. During World War II she worked for the Free French in London until her early death, which was brought on by her refusal to eat more than the official ration in Occupied France. Her writings on spiritual and social themes, published posthumously, include *Waiting for God* (1951) and *The Need for Roots* (1952).

● **Weill, Kurt** ▶ (1900–50) German composer. He studied under Busoni in Berlin. His collaboration with Bertolt ▷Brecht began with the opera *The Rise and Fall of the City of Mahagonny* (1927), a satirical portrayal of American life. Their most famous work was *The Threepenny Opera* (1928), an updating of *The Beggar's Opera* (*see* Gay, John). The rise of Nazism forced Weill to leave Germany; he settled in the USA in 1935 and wrote successfully for Broadway musicals. His wife, the singer Lotte ▷Lenya, frequently performed in his works.

● **Weil's disease** ▶ (leptospirosis) An infectious disease of rats, dogs, etc., caused by *Leptospira* bacteria. Humans may be affected by contact with water containing urine from an infected animal, causing jaundice and meningitis; responding poorly to antibiotics it has a mortality of about 20%. Named after Adolf Weil (1848–1916), German physician.

● **Weimar** ▶ 50 59N 11 15E A city in central Germany, on the River Ilm near Erfurt. Weimar has associations with Goethe, Schiller, and Liszt and was the cultural centre of Germany in the late 18th and early 19th centuries. It was the capital of the grand duchy of Saxe-Weimar-Eisenach (1815–1918). In 1919 the German National Assembly met in the city and drew up the constitution of the new ▷Weimar Republic. Population (1991): 59 100.

● **Weimar Republic** ▶ The government of Germany from 1919 to 1933. Named after the town in which the new German constitution was formulated, it faced constant political and economic crises and was overthrown by Hitler.

● **Weinberg, Steven** ▶ (1933–) US physicist and professor at Texas University. The Glashow–Weinberg–Salam theory, unifying the ▷weak and electromagnetic interactions, which he arrived at independently of ▷Salam and ▷Glashow, won them jointly the 1979 Nobel Prize.

● **Weir, Peter (Lindsay)** ▶ (1944–) Australian film director, who did much to bring Australian cinema to a world audience in the 1970s; since 1985 he has worked in Hollywood. His films include *Picnic at Hanging Rock* (1975), *Gallipoli* (1980), *Dead Poets Society* (1989), *Fearless* (1993), and *The Truman Show* (1998).

● **Weismann, August Friedrich Leopold** ▶ (1834–1914) German biologist, who (in 1883) proposed that heredity was based upon the transfer, from generation to generation, of a substance—germ plasm—with a definite molecular constitution. Weismann also predicted that germ plasm must undergo a special nuclear division to produce gametes for the next generation. Weismann's ideas have since been generally accepted and he is regarded as one of the founders of modern genetics.

● **Weiss, Peter** ▶ (1916–82) German dramatist and novelist. After leaving Nazi Germany, he settled in Sweden (1939). His plays include the highly successful *Marat/Sade* (short title; 1964), set in a lunatic asylum, and *The Investigation* (1965), recreating the Auschwitz trials.

● **Weissmuller, Johnny** ▶ (1904–84) US swimmer, who won five Olympic gold medals (three in 1924 and two in 1928) and set 24 world records. He was the first man to swim 100 m in less than a minute (1922). He later became the first Tarzan of sound films, starring in *Tarzan the Ape Man* (1932) and a subsequent series of Tarzan films, which ended with *Tarzan and the Mermaids* (1948).

● **Weizmann, Chaim (Azriel)** ▶ (1874–1952) Israeli statesman; the first president of Israel (1949–52). Born in Russia, he settled in England in 1904 and worked as a chemist at Manchester University. A leader of the English Zionist movement, his discovery (1916) of a manufacturing process for the production of acetone, which contributed to the British war effort, facilitated the Zionist negotiations with the British Government that led to the ▷Balfour Declaration (1917). His moderate policies as president (1920–31, 1935–46) of the World Zionist Movement brought the hostility of Zionist extremists but he played an important part in the establishment of Israel in 1948.

● **Weland** ▷*See* Wayland.

● **welding** ▶ A method of joining metals by melting the two parts together, pressing them together, or both (*see also* solder). In forge welding, which is used to make steel chains, the two parts are heated and then hammered together. Electrical methods use an electric current passed through two metal surfaces in close contact. The temperature rises at the interface because of the high electrical resistance and welds the surfaces together. In spot welding, point contact electrodes press the metal surfaces together. In seam welding, the electrodes are in the form of rollers. Both these methods are used in mass production. Gas welding uses an oxy-acetylene flame to heat the metal and a rod of metallic filler material. Molten filler material runs between the two heated edges and solidifies to form the joint. Another method, similar to gas welding, is electric-arc welding. The filler rod forms one electrode and the metal itself another. Current passes by arcing or sparking across the gap between them, melting the rod and the metal edges. Arc welding is generally used for thicker pieces of metal and higher temperatures than gas welding and for small delicate jobs ▷lasers have been used. A great deal of skill is required to produce a strong reliable weld.

● **Weldon, Fay** ▶ (1931–) British writer. Her novels include *The Fat Woman's Joke* (1967), *The Life and Loves of a She-Devil* (1983), *The Shrapnel Academy* (1986), *The Heart of the Country* (1987), *Darcy's Utopia* (1990), *Life Force* (1992), *Affliction* (1994), and *Big Women* (1998). She has also written plays, including many for radio and television.

● **Welensky, Sir Roy** ▶ (1907–92) Rhodesian statesman; prime minister of the Federation of ▷Rhodesia and Nyasaland (1956–63). A professional boxer, he was chairman (1953–63) of the Railway Workers Union in Northern Rhodesia. Welensky was largely responsible for the creation of the Federation but failed to establish a harmonious multiracial society.

● **welfare state** ▶ A state that provides a minimum level of wellbeing for all its members, especially the most vulnerable: the young, the old, the unemployed, and the sick. In the UK the 19th-century ▷Poor Laws were superseded by Lloyd George's National Insurance Act (1911), which provided unemployment and health insurance (*see* National Insurance). The setting up of the ▷National Health Service and the National Insurance Acts by the postwar Labour government, in consequence of the ▷Beveridge Report (1942), established the welfare state. However, since 1979 escalating costs and the electorate's unwillingness to accept higher taxation have resulted in a marked attenuation of the scope of the NHS and a series of measures restricting welfare payments. The post-1997 Labour government has promised further sweeping reforms to the system; a Welfare Reform Bill introduced in 1999 proposes tougher criteria for social-security claimants, a crackdown on fraud, and measures to encourage the unemployed back into work. ▷*See also* means test; social security.

● **Welkom** ▶ 27 59S 26 44E A town in central South Africa. It was founded in 1947 and rapidly developed after the discovery of gold. Population (latest est): 228 000.

● **Welland Ship Canal** ▶ A canal in S central Canada, in S Ontario bypassing Niagara Falls. Part of the St Lawrence Seaway, it links Lake Erie to Lake Ontario and has a total lift of 99 m (326 ft). Length: 45 km (28 mi).

● **Welles, (George) Orson** ▶ (1915–85) US film actor and director. After establishing his reputation as a theatre and radio producer he went to Hollywood in 1940. His first film, *Citizen Kane* (1941), became one of the most famous of all time. His other films include *The Magnificent Ambersons* (1942), *Macbeth* (1948), *The Third Man* (1949; as actor only), *The Trial* (1962), and *Chimes at Midnight* (1966).

● **Wellesley, Richard Colley, Marquess** ▷*See* Wellington, Arthur Wellesley, 1st Duke of.

● **Wellesz, Egon** ▶ (1885–1974) Austrian composer and musicologist. He studied in Vienna under Schoenberg and became reader in Byzantine music at Oxford University in 1948. His complex compositions employed ▷serialism.

● **Wellington** ▶ 41 17S 174 47E The capital of New Zealand, a port in S North Island on Cook Strait. It became the seat of central government in 1865 and is now the commercial and communications centre of New Zealand. Notable buildings include the Government Building (1876), one of the world's largest wooden structures, and Victoria University (1897). It has engineering, food-processing, and textile industries; the chief exports are wool, meat, dairy products, and fruit. Population (1996): 158 275.

● **Wellington, Arthur Wellesley, 1st Duke of** ▶ (1769–1852) British general and statesman, known as the Iron Duke; prime minister (1828–30). Born in Dublin, in 1787 he entered the army and in 1799 went to India, where he held command against ▷Tipu Sahib and became governor of Mysore. In the Napoleonic Wars he was responsible for victory (1814) against the French in the ▷Peninsular War, for which he was made a duke and given £500,000. He commanded British, German, and Dutch forces at Waterloo (1815), where he and the Prussian general ▷Blücher finally defeated Napoleon. He served in Lord Liverpool's Tory government as master general of the ordnance (1818–27) and represented Britain at the Congresses of ▷Aix-la-Chapelle (1818) and Verona (1822). As prime minister he came to support ▷Catholic emancipation and persuaded George IV to accept the bill of 1829. Wellington's opposition to parliamentary reform remained firm and brought about his resignation under pressure. Under Peel he served as foreign secretary (1834–35) and supported the repeal of the ▷Corn Laws; he was commander in chief of the British army (1827–28; 1842–52). His home at Apsley House, Piccadilly (London) is now the Wellington Museum.

His eldest brother **Richard Colley, Marquess Wellesley** (1760–1842) was simultaneously governor of Madras and governor general of Bengal (1797–1805). He greatly extended British power and territory in India by defeating (1799) Tipu Sahib, Sultan of Mysore, in a campaign in which his brother participated, and (1805) the Maratha states. He was subsequently foreign secretary (1809–12) and lord lieutenant of Ireland (1821–28, 1833–34). Increasingly jealous of his brother's success, he had an exaggerated sense of his own importance and was said to wear his medals in bed.

● **Wellingtonia** ▷*See* sequoia.

● **Wells** ▶ 51 13N 2 39W A city in SW England, in Somerset. It is famous for its cathedral (12th–13th centuries), with its 386 carved figures on the W front. Paper, cheese, and textiles are manufactured. Population (1991): 9763.

● **Wells, Henry** ▶ (1805–78) US businessman, who with **William Fargo** (1818–81) and others founded Wells, Fargo and Company (1852). An express business, it carried mail to and from the newly developed West. It also controlled banks and later ran a stagecoach service.

● **Wells, H(erbert) G(eorge)** ▶ (1866–1946) British novelist. After working as a shopkeeper's apprentice and a teacher, he studied biology with T. H. Huxley at the College of Science in South Kensington, graduating in 1890. He won literary success with *The Time Machine* (1895) and other science-fiction novels and increased his popularity with a series of comic social novels, including *Kipps* (1905) and *The History of Mr Polly* (1910). A member of the Fabian Society, he engaged in frequent controversy with G. B. Shaw and others concerning social and political issues. He wrote distinguished theoretical works, including *The Outline of History* (1920) and *The Shape of Things to Come* (1933).

● **wels** ▶ A large nocturnal predatory ▷catfish, *Silurus glanis*, found in fresh waters of Europe and W Asia. Up to 4.5 m long, it has three pairs of barbels, a long anal fin, and is mottled olive-green to blue-black with a paler belly.

● **Wels** ▶ 48 10N 14 02E A town in N central Austria, in Upper Austria. It has a castle in which Emperor Maximilian I died. Industries include agricultural machinery, textiles, and food processing. Population (1991): 52 594.

● **Welsh** ▶ A ▷Celtic language of the Brythonic group, known in Wales as *Cymraeg*. Some 19% of the Welsh population (about 600 000 people) speak Welsh as their first or favoured language, although virtually all Welsh speakers also speak English. Welsh is taught as a compulsory part of the National Curriculum in Welsh schools and is the general teaching language in some schools in Welsh-speaking areas (and a supplementary teaching language in many others). Modern Welsh is not highly inflected and for convenience Welsh speakers usually use English words and phrases for modern concepts. Road signs and other public notices throughout Wales are provided in both English and Welsh, as are such official documents as tax forms, driving licences, etc. ▷*See also* Welsh literature.

● **Welsh literature** ▶ The most important literature in the ▷Welsh language is poetry belonging to the early and medieval periods prior to the anglicization that began in the 16th century. Much of the poetry of the *Cynfeirdd*, or early poets of the 6th century, is anonymous, but the outstanding names associated with this early heroic, gnomic, and nature verse are Aneirin and Taliesin. The works of the period are preserved in the "Four Ancient Books of Wales," manuscripts dating from the 12th, 13th, and 14th centuries. The *Gogynfeirdd*, or medieval poets, belong to the Norman period (up to the loss of independence in 1282). These poets were ▷bards, who held important offices in the courts of Welsh princes; Cynddelw (12th century) is regarded as the greatest of them. The bardic order was reorganized in some uncertain way at this time, and a number of versified treatises on the poetic art were written. The ▷*Mabinogion* was written during this period. The 14th century was dominated by Wales' greatest poet, ▷Dafydd ap Gwilym, who introduced techniques and metaphors that influenced all subsequent Welsh poetry. The first record of an ▷eisteddfod dates from the 15th century, although it is believed that such bardic contests must date from a much earlier period. The accentual metre of English (of which there was nothing in the "strict" metres of Welsh verse) was introduced in the 16th century, which marks the beginning of a decline in the use of Welsh, although the language has recently been revived and continues to be used as a literary medium. Among the more important writers from the 17th century onwards are the poet Huw Morus (1622-1709), the prose writer Ellis Wynne (1671-1734), author of *Gweledigaetheu y Bardd Cwsc* (*Visions of the Sleeping Bard*; 1703), the hymnwriter William Williams Pantycelyn (1717-91), the poet and scholar Lewis Morris (1701-65), the poets Sir John Morris-Jones (1864-1929), Thomas Gwynn Jones (1871-1949), William John Gruffydd (1881-1954), and T. H. Parry-Williams (1887-1975), and the poet and playwright Saunders Lewis (1893-1985).

● **Welsh Nationalist Party** ▷*See* Plaid Cymru.

● **Welsh pony** ▶ One of two breeds of pony originating in Wales. The Welsh Mountain pony, used for riding and draught work, has a compact muscular body with short strong legs and a profuse mane and tail. It has been used to develop the larger Welsh riding pony, which is a popular children's mount. Both may be any solid colour. Height: Mountain pony: up to 1.22 m (12 hands); riding pony: up to 1.37 m (13½ hands).

● **Welsh poppy** ▶ A perennial herbaceous European plant, *Mecanopsis cambrica*, up to 38 cm tall. It has fernlike deeply lobed leaves and yellow flowers, up to 7.5 cm across. Cultivated forms may have single or double flowers.

● **welwitschia** ▶ An unusual ▷gymnosperm plant, *Welwitschia mirabilis*, confined to the deserts of SW Africa. The very short stem bears two strap-shaped waxy leaves, which grow continuously and are up to 1 m long. The long taproot absorbs water from the desert subsoil, and small conelike flowers produce winged seeds. Individual plants may live for more than a hundred years. Phylum: *Gnetophyta*.

● **Welwyn Garden City** ▶ 51 48N 0 13W A town in SE England, in Hertfordshire. Founded as a garden city in 1919 by Sir Ebenezer ▷Howard, it became a new town in 1948. Economic activities include food processing, high technology, electronics, and health care. Population (1991): 41 710.

● **Wembley** ▶ A district in the Greater London borough of Brent. Wembley Stadium, one of the many buildings erected in the early 1920s in connection with the British Empire Exhibition (1924-25), was the site of the 1948 Olympic Games and is the home of English national soccer. The stadium closed for major redevelopment in 2000. However, government-financed plans to replace it with a general sports stadium failed, leaving the Football Association to raise redevelopment funds. Wembley Conference Centre was opened in 1977.

● **Wenceslas** ▶ (1361-1419) King of Bohemia (1363-1402, 1404-19) and German king and Holy Roman Emperor (1376-1400). An extremely weak king, in Bohemia he was twice imprisoned by rebellious nobles (1393-94, 1402) and briefly deposed. In Germany, princes deposed him in 1400.

● **Wenceslas, St** ▶ (d. 929 AD) Duke of Bohemia (?924-29), famous for his piety. Wenceslas' unpopular submission to the German king Henry the Fowler gave rise to a conspiracy of nobles, who incited Wenceslas' brother to assassinate him. He became Bohemia's patron saint.

● **Wenchow** ▶ (or Wen-chou) ▷*See* Wenzhou.

● **wentletrap** ▶ A ▷gastropod mollusc of the worldwide family *Epitoniidae* (about 200 species), often found in association with sea anemones and corals. 2-10 cm long, wentletraps have □shells with long spires, usually white but sometimes tinged with brown (that of the precious wentletrap (*Epitonium scalare*) has long been prized by collectors). They can produce a purple substance used as a dye.

● **Wentworth, Thomas** ▷*See* Strafford, Thomas Wentworth, 1st Earl of.

● **Wentworth, William Charles** ▶ (1793-1872) Australian politician; the first Australian citizen to attain a political reputation. Son of a transported convict, he was a fervent federalist and, early in his career, a radical. He helped win (1855) self-government for New South Wales.

● **Wenzhou** ▶ (Wen-chou *or* Wenchow) 28 02N 120 40E A port in SE China, in Zhejiang province on the Ou Jiang (River). It is the site of many historic buildings. A trading centre, it has processed food, paper, and handicraft industries. Population (1999 est): 512 523.

● **werewolf** ▶ In folklore, a man who becomes a wolf by night and preys on humans. Some werewolves, who have no power over their condition because it is hereditary or the result of a spell or another werewolf's bite, only change form during a full moon, a transformation known as lycanthropy. In countries where wolves are rare, some men are believed to turn into other fierce animals. □ p. 1332.

● **Werfel, Franz** ▶ (1890-1945) Austrian Jewish poet, dramatist, and novelist. His pacifism and desire for human brotherhood are reflected in his poetry and plays, including *Der Spiegelmensch* (1920). His later novels include *The Song of Bernadette* (1941).

● **Wergeland, Henrik Arnold** ▶ (1808-45) Norwegian poet, known as the "uncrowned king" of Norway because of his involvement in nationalist politics. He is best known for his lyric poetry and for an epic on the Creation, entitled *Skabelsen, Mennesket, og Messias* (*Creation, Humanity, and Messiah*; 1830).

● **wergild** ▶ The sum payable as compensation in Anglo-Saxon England to the family of a slain man by his assassin or the latter's kin. The amount was regulated by law according to the status and nationality of the victim and varied in different regions.

● **Weser, River** ▶ A river in NW Germany. It flows NW from Münden, through Bremen, to the North Sea at Bremerhaven. The

Mittelland Canal connects it to the Rivers Rhine and Elbe. Length: 477 km (296 mi).

werewolf ► A woodcut from the *World Chronicle* (1493) by Hartman Schedel.

● **Wesker, Arnold** ► (1932–) British dramatist. Born into a poor Jewish family in London, he wrote a successful trilogy of plays reflecting his socialist beliefs: *Chicken Soup with Barley* (1958), *Roots* (1959), and *I'm Talking about Jerusalem* (1960). Later plays include *Chips with Everything* (1962), *The Friends* (1970), *The Merchant* (1976), *Shoeshine* (1988), *Blood Libel* (1991), and *Break My Heart* (1997).

● **Wesley, John** ► (1703–91) British religious leader, founder of ▷Methodism. As a student at Oxford and later as a Fellow of Lincoln College, Wesley was one of a group nicknamed "Methodists," who sought to live disciplined religious lives. His younger brother **Charles Wesley** (1707–88) was also a member. The brothers, both ordained, sailed to Georgia as missionaries in 1735, but returned disillusioned in 1738. In the same year both experienced a spiritual awakening while attending meetings of the ▷Moravian Brethren as a result of which they toured the country preaching a message of repentance, faith, and love. Anglican opposition forced them out of the churches into open-air meetings; they were also obliged to organize societies for their many working-class converts, whose spiritual needs had been neglected by the Established Church. They did not intend to form a new denomination, the Wesleyan Methodist Church being organized only after their death. John was a tireless writer and administrator, who travelled the country on horseback preaching thousands of sermons. Charles was the author of many well-known hymns. His son **Samuel Wesley** (1766–1837) was a composer and organist, who composed the oratorio *Ruth* at the age of eight. He was in-

strumental in reviving the music of Bach in England. His illegitimate son **Samuel Sebastian Wesley** (1810–76), also an organist, studied under his father and held posts at English cathedrals. He became professor of organ at the Royal Academy of Music in 1850.

● **Wessex** ► The kingdom of the West ▷Saxons, under which Anglo-Saxon England was united in the 9th century. Wessex centred on the upper Thames basin and from the late 6th century expanded southwestwards. Its expansion northwards was frustrated by the power of Mercia, which was supreme until Egbert, King of Wessex (802–39), destroyed Mercian ascendancy in 825 and made possible the subsequent union of England under the leadership of the Wessex king, Alfred the Great.

● **West, Benjamin** ► (1738–1820) British painter of American birth. Acclaimed as a portraitist in New York, he visited Italy (1760–63), where he was influenced by ▷neoclassicism, before settling permanently in England. There, patronized by George III and exhibiting at the Royal Academy of which he became president in 1792, he made his name as a history painter, particularly with his controversially realistic *Death of General Wolfe* (Kensington Palace, London).

● **West, Mae** ► (1892–1980) US actress. Her unashamedly sensual performances in vaudeville, the theatre, and films established her as an international sex symbol during the 1930s, although she is perhaps best known for her comic talent. Her early stage successes included *Sex* (1926) and *Diamond Lil* (1928). Her films, many of which she wrote, include *She Done Him Wrong* (1933), *I'm No Angel* (1933), and *My Little Chickadee* (1939).

● **West, Nathanael** ► (Nathan Weinstein; 1903–40) US novelist. The best known of his four short novels are *Miss Lonely-Hearts* (1933), about an advice columnist, and *The Day of the Locust* (1939), a satire of the grotesque world of Hollywood, where he worked as a scriptwriter. He was killed in a car accident.

● **West, Dame Rebecca** ► (Cicely Isabel Fairfield, 1892–1983) British novelist and journalist. She was the author of several novels, including *The Thinking Reed* (1936) and *The Birds Fall Down* (1966). Among a number of books of political journalism are *The Meaning of Treason* (1949) and *A Train of Powder* (1955), which includes her reports on the Nuremberg trials.

● **West, the** ► The area in the USA between the Mississippi River and the Rocky Mountains acquired by the ▷Louisiana Purchase (1803). Settled by migrants from the E in search of land and independence, it was associated with the hardship, self-reliance, and lawlessness that characterized the lives of pioneers.

● **West Atlantic languages** ► A subgroup of the ▷Niger-Congo family, spoken in Guinea and Senegal. It includes the languages Wolof and ▷Fulani, and, despite being a small group, is found over a wide area since the speakers of West Atlantic languages are mainly nomadic.

● **West Bank** ► A territory in the Middle East, on the W bank of the River Jordan. It comprises the hills of Judaea and Samaria and part of the city of ▷Jerusalem. Formerly part of ▷Palestine, it was left in Arab hands after partition (1948), became part of Jordan following the ceasefire of 1949, and was occupied by Israeli forces in 1967 after the Six Day War. In the Camp David agreement (1978) proposals were put forward for negotiations leading to the setting up of a self-governing West Bank. In 1988 Jordan relinquished claims to the area and the PLO declared a Palestinian state; pressure subsequently increased upon Israel to enter negotiations (*see* intifada). In 1993 Israel agreed to withdraw its troops from certain areas of the West Bank as part of a peace settlement with the PLO. The Palestinian National Authority assumed control of the Jericho area in 1994–95 but Israel subsequently postponed further withdrawals on security grounds. In 1998 Israel and the PLO signed an agreement under which security cooperation from the Palestine Authority would be rewarded with further territorial grants. However, the peace process then stalled, leading to mounting frustration on the West Bank that erupted into open violence in 2000. This escalated sharply during 2001–02, provoking Israel to reoccupy large parts of the West Bank. Area: about 6000 sq km (2320 sq mi). Population (2000 est): 1 949 000.

● **West Bengal** ► A state in NE India, stretching along the Bangladeshi W border from the Ganges delta N into the Himalayan foothills. Rice, jute, tea, and other crops are farmed. Fishing, forestry, and mining are important, as is industry. The Gurkhas, pressing for their own state, have caused unrest (1987). Area: 88 752 sq km (34 260 sq mi). Population (1991): 67 982 732. Capital: Calcutta. *▷See also* Bengal.

● **West Berkshire** ► A unitary authority of S England, in Berkshire. Area: 705 sq km (272 sq mi). Population (1996 est): 143 700.

● **West Bromwich** ► 52 31N 1 59W An industrial town in central England, in Sandwell unitary authority, West Midlands. Metal goods (kitchenware, springs, nails) are manufactured, as well as chemicals and paint. Population (1992 est): 154 531.

● **West Dunbartonshire** ► A council area of W central Scotland, between Loch Lomond and the Clyde estuary, comprising part of the historic county of ▷Dunbarton. Absorbed into Strathclyde Region in 1975, it became a ▷unitary authority in 1996. It is hilly in the SE and low-lying in the N, with extensive urbanization on the Clyde and Leven estuaries. The main economic activities are engineering, whisky distilling, and agriculture; shipbuilding is no more but there is still marine engineering in Clydebank. Area: 162 sq km (63 sq mi). Population (1996 est): 95 760.

● **westerlies** ► The chief winds blowing between 30° and 70° latitude. Their name derives from the prevailing wind direction; in the N hemisphere winds blow mainly from the SW and in the S hemisphere, from the NW.

● **Western Australia** ► The largest state of Australia, bordering on the Indian Ocean, Timor Sea, and Great Australian Bight. It is mainly an arid undulating plateau with the Great Sandy Desert, the Gibson Desert, and the Great Victoria Desert in the interior. In the SW is the Darling Range, a scarp behind the city of Perth (where most of the population is concentrated). In the N the broken edge of the plateau is marked by the Kimberleys, where the Ord River Project, completed in the early 1970s, has increased the acreage under irrigation. Other agricultural activities include dairy farming, lumbering, and the cultivation of citrus fruits, wheat, and vines in the extreme SW. The state is rich in mineral resources: bauxite in the Darling Range, nickel in the S central part, oil near Barrow Island off the NW coast, gold in the SW around Kalgoorlie, and huge deposits of ferrous minerals in the NW, in the Ashburton and Pilbara districts. Industry, located chiefly around Perth, includes iron and steel, chemicals, textiles, and oil refining. Area: 2 527 621 sq km (975 920 sq mi). Population (1996 est): 1 755 500. Capital: Perth.

● **Western Cape** ▷*See* Cape Province.

● **Western European Union** ► An organization formed in 1955 by the UK, Belgium, France, Italy, Luxembourg, the Netherlands, and West Germany to coordinate defence policy and equipment and to cooperate in other spheres. It succeeded the European Defence Community (formed in 1952) and collaborates closely with the ▷North Atlantic Treaty Organization. Portugal and Spain joined in 1988 and the former East Germany was included when Germany reunited (1990).

● **Western Isles Islands Area** ► An administrative area of NW Scotland since 1975, consisting of the Outer Hebrides (*see* Hebrides, the). Area: 2901 sq km (1120 sq mi). Population (1996 est): 28 880. Administrative centre: Stornoway.

● **Western Province** ▷*See* Hejaz.

● **westerns** ► A US genre of popular novels and films set in the American West during that region's development in the 19th century. It invested the struggles of pioneers and the battles between lawmen and outlaws with mythical significance. Notable writers include Owen Wister (1860–1938), the prolific Zane Grey (1872–1939), and Louis L'Amour (1908–). The first film western was *The Great Train Robbery* (1903). Other notable films include *Stagecoach* (1939), *Red River* (1948), *High Noon* (1952), *Once Upon a Time in the West* (1969), *Dances with Wolves* (1990), and *Unforgiven* (1992). Directors who have specialized in this genre include John ▷Ford, Howard Hawks (1896–1978), and Sergio Leone (1921–89), while its stars include John ▷Wayne, Gary ▷Cooper, and Clint ▷Eastwood.

● **Western Sahara** ► (name until 1975: Spanish Sahara) A disputed territory in NW Africa, bordering on the Atlantic Ocean, Mauritania, and Morocco. It consists chiefly of desert and has phosphate deposits (the chief export) SE of El Aaiún.
  History: in 1884 Spain claimed a protectorate over the S coastal zone of Río de Oro and in 1958 Spanish Sahara became a province of Spain with its capital at El Aaiún. In 1976 Spain withdrew from the province and it was partitioned between Mauritania and Morocco. Since then the Polisario Front, an organization engaged in guerrilla activities to establish Western Sahara as the independent Saharan Arab Democratic Republic, has been supported by Algeria. Mauritania withdrew from the S Western Sahara in 1979 and it came under Moroccan occupation with active opposition from the Polisario Front and Algeria. Conflict continued throughout the 1980s and a UN peacekeeping force has been in occupation since 1991. In 1988 it was agreed that the future status of the territory should be decided by a referendum, but no agreement could be reached on its terms and the plan was abandoned in 1996. Area: 266 000 sq km (102 680 sq mi). Population (1993 est): 214 000.

John Wesley ► During his preaching tours he often faced hostile demonstrations. This painting depicts him being taunted by a mob in Wednesbury in the English Midlands.

● **Western Samoa** ▷*See* Samoa.

● **Western Wall** ▶ (*or* Wailing Wall) ▷*See* Temple of Jerusalem.

● **West Germany** ▷*See* Germany, Federal Republic of.

● **West Glamorgan** ▶ A former county of South Wales, created in 1974 from W Glamorgan. In April 1996 it was abolished and replaced with two ▷unitary authorities, the new county of Swansea and the county borough of Neath and Port Talbot.

● **West Highland white terrier** ▶ A breed of dog thought to have originated in Argyll, Scotland. Known affectionately as the westie, it is compact and alert-looking with short legs and a long double-layered pure white coat. Height: about 28 cm.

● **West Indies** ▶ An archipelago extending in a curved chain for over 2400 km (1500 mi) from the Florida peninsula in North America to the coast of Venezuela enclosing the Caribbean Sea. It is often subdivided into the ▷Greater Antilles, the ▷Lesser Antilles, and the ▷Bahamas. The islands are chiefly of volcanic origin but some, including the Bahamas and Antigua, are composed largely of coral. Hurricanes occur frequently, often causing serious damage. The West Indian people are of mixed origin but the descendants of African slaves form the largest group. The original Arawak and Carib Indians have virtually disappeared, although some Caribs remain on Dominica.
Economy: sugar-cane cultivation has been of importance throughout the West Indies since the beginning of colonization. Many islands also grow a major subsidiary crop, such as tobacco, bananas, spices, or coffee. The few mineral deposits include asphalt from Trinidad's unique Pitch Lake and bauxite from Hispaniola and Jamaica.
History: Columbus discovered the archipelago for Europeans in 1492 and named it in the belief that he had found the west route to India. The Spanish, who were the first Europeans to settle, introduced the cultivation of sugar and imported African slaves to work the plantations. The slave trade was maintained until its abolition during the 19th century, by which time most of the islands were under British rule. In 1958, believing that the islands were untenable as independent countries, Britain created the Federation of the West Indies, comprising Antigua, Barbados, Dominica, Grenada, Jamaica, Montserrat, St Kitts with Nevis and Anguilla, St Lucia, St Vincent, and Trinidad and Tobago. A federal parliament was set up at Port-of-Spain, Trinidad, but the federation collapsed in 1962; Jamaica and Trinidad and Tobago then became independent nations within the Commonwealth, with Barbados following suit in 1966. The status of British associated state was adopted by Antigua, Dominica, Grenada, St Kitts-Nevis-Anguilla, and St Lucia in 1967, and by St Vincent in 1969. Grenada became independent in 1974, Dominica in 1978, St Lucia and St Vincent in 1979, Antigua (and Barbuda) in 1981, and St Kitts-Nevis in 1983. Further attempts at regional economic integration have been pursued by the ▷Caribbean Community. Area: over 235 000 sq km (91 000 sq mi).

● **West Irian** ▷*See* Irian Jaya.

● **West Lothian** ▶ A council area of SE Scotland, on the Firth of Forth. Under local government reorganization in 1975 the historic county of West Lothian was abolished; its boundaries were adjusted to form a district of the same name, in Lothian Region. In 1996 this district became an independent ▷unitary authority. It comprises arable plains in the N and hillier sheep-rearing country to the S. Oil refining is an important industry. Area: 425 sq km (164 sq mi). Population (1993 est): 146 730. Administrative centre: Livingston.

● **Westman Islands** ▷*See* Vestmannaeyjar.

● **Westmeath** ▶ (Irish name: Contae Na Hiarmhidhe) A county in the central Republic of Ireland, in Leinster. Predominantly low lying with areas of bog, much of the land is under pasture. Agriculture consists chiefly of cattle fattening and dairy farming. Area: 1764 sq km (681 sq mi). Population (1996 est): 63 000. County town: Mullingar.

● **West Midlands** ▶ A metropolitan county in the W Midlands of England, created in 1974 from SE Staffordshire, NW Warwickshire, and part of NE Worcestershire. In 1986 the county council was abolished and administrative power devolved to the districts of Wolverhampton, Walsall, Dudley, Sandwell, Birmingham, Solihull, and Coventry, which became ▷unitary authorites. Area: 899 sq km (347 sq mi).

● **Westminster, City of** ▶ A borough of central Greater London, on the N bank of the River Thames. It was created in 1965 from the former metropolitan boroughs of Westminster, Paddington, and ▷St Marylebone. The heart of London's West End, it contains many famous theatres, restaurants, and shops. Included among its historic buildings are ▷Buckingham Palace, Westminster Hall adjoining the Houses of Parliament (*see* Palace of Westminster), ▷Westminster Abbey, and ▷Westminster Cathedral. Westminster School is one of the oldest English public schools. The ▷National Gallery overlooks Trafalgar Square (containing Nelson's Column) and Whitehall is the site of the main government offices; ▷Downing Street is nearby. It contains St James's Park, Green Park, Hyde Park, and Regent's Park (containing London Zoo). Area: 22 sq km (8 sq mi). Population (1996 est): 204 100.

● **Westminster, Statutes of** ▶ **1.** (1275, 1285, 1290) Legislation initiated by Edward I of England. The first Statute dealt principally with criminal law and procedures for the improvement of royal justice while the second dealt with rights of inheritance, attempting to restrict the alienation of land from the main line of the family. The Statute of 1290 prohibited subinfeudation of land (i.e. the granting of portions of a knight's estate), which had occasioned loss of feudal dues to the king and magnates. **2.** (1931) The Statute that established the ▷Commonwealth of Nations.

● **Westminster Abbey** ▶ A historic abbey church at Westminster, London. The present building, begun (1245) in the French style by Henry III, replaces one dedicated (1065) by Edward the Confessor, whose shrine the abbey still houses. Since William I, every English monarch (with two exceptions—Edward V and Edward VIII) has been crowned in Westminster Abbey and many are buried there in magnificent tombs. The Coronation Chair, first used in 1307, incorporated the Stone of Scone, captured by Edward I from the Scots in 1296, until the Stone was returned to Scotland in 1996. Other notable features include Henry VII's chapel, the 13th-century chapter house (used for parliamentary sessions until 1547), and Poets' Corner, where Chaucer, Spenser, Dryden, Tennyson, Dickens, Browning, Kipling, and many others are buried or have memorials. The western towers of the abbey (1745) were designed by Christopher Wren and modified by Nicholas Hawksmoor.

● **Westminster Assembly** ▶ (1643–52) A body of 30 laymen and 121 clergy summoned by the ▷Long Parliament after the outbreak of the English Civil War to reform the Church of England along Calvinist lines.

● **Westminster Cathedral** ▶ A cathedral in ▷Westminster, London, which is the seat of the Roman Catholic archbishopric of Westminster. Founded in 1895, it was designed by J. F. Bentley in Byzantine style with an Italianate campanile 87 m (284 ft) high. It has the widest nave in England and is ornamented with over 100 different kinds of marble.

● **Westmorland** ▶ A former county of NW England. Under local government reorganization in 1974 it became part of the new county of ▷Cumbria.

● **Weston-super-Mare** ▶ 51 21N 2 59W A resort in SW England, North Somerset unitary authority, Somerset, on the Bristol Channel. Originally a fishing village, it developed as a resort in the 19th century. Population (1991): 69 372.

● **Westphalia** ▶ A region of NW Germany, approximating to present-day Nordrhein-Westfalen. By the 12th century Westphalia comprised many small principalities and in the 18th century came largely under Prussian control. During the period 1807–13 Prussian Westphalian territories became the kingdom of Westphalia, which Napoleon placed under the rule of his brother Jérôme Bonaparte. The Congress of Vienna (1815) dissolved the kingdom and restored most of Westphalia to Prussia.

● **Westphalia, Peace of** ▶ (1648) The agreements, negotiated in Osnabrück and Münster (Westphalia), that ended the ▷Thirty Years' War. It marked the end of the supremacy of the Holy Roman Empire and the emergence of France (which gained the bishoprics of Metz, Toul, Verdun, and Alsace) as a dominant power (*see also* Pyrenees, Treaty of). It recognized the sovereignty of the German states, the Swiss Confederation, and the Netherlands, previously subject to the Empire, and granted W Pomerania to Sweden. Lutherans, Calvinists, and Roman Catholics were given equal rights.

● **West Point** ► 41 23N 73 58W A military reservation in the USA, in New York state. It is the site of the United States Military Academy (1802).

● **West Riding** ▷*See* Yorkshire.

● **West Sussex** ► A county of S England, formerly part of ▷Sussex, bordering on the English Channel. It is mainly low lying, rising in the S to the South Downs, and drained by the Rivers Arun and Adur. It is predominantly agricultural, the chief products being cereals, root crops, and dairy produce. Tourism is important in the coastal resorts, notably Bognor Regis and Worthing. Area: 1989 sq km (768 sq mi). Population (1996 est): 737 300. Administrative centre: Chichester.

● **West Virginia** ► A state in the E central USA. It consists of the Appalachian Plateau and a ridge and valley region (the Great Appalachian Valley) in the E. Most of the larger cities lie on the Ohio River in the W. Although predominantly a rural state, manufacturing and mining (especially of coal) are important. The principal manufactures are chemicals, primary metals, and stone and clay products. The state's farmers concentrate on livestock products.
History: originally part of Virginia, it refused to secede with the state, and became West Virginia on joining the Union as a separate State in 1863. Area: 62 628 sq km (24 181 sq mi). Population (1996 est): 1 825 754. Capital: Charleston.

● **Westwood, Vivienne** ► (1941–) British fashion designer. With Malcolm McLaren (1941–) she pioneered the punk look in the late 1970s. Her highly original designs won her the Designer of the Year award in both 1990 and 1991.

● **West Yorkshire** ► A metropolitan county of NE England, created in 1974 from the W part of the West Riding of Yorkshire. In 1986 the county council was abolished and administrative power devolved to the districts of Bradford, Leeds, Calderdale, Kirklees, and Wakefield, which became ▷unitary authorities. Coalmining was formerly important but has declined. West Yorkshire remains the centre of the English wool textile industry. Area: 2039 sq km (787 sq mi).

● **wet rot** ► The decay that affects timber with a relatively high moisture content, caused by the cellar fungus (*Coniophora cerebella*) and characterized by the formation of a dark surface mass. Treatment is by drying affected timbers, and wet rot is prevented by the application of tar-based preservatives, such as creosote. *Compare* dry rot.

● **Wexford** ► (Irish name: Loch Garman) 52 20N 6 27W A port in the Republic of Ireland, the county town of Co Wexford on the River Slaney estuary. Industries include the manufacture of agricultural machinery and food processing. Population (1991): 9540.

● **Wexford** ► (Irish name: Contae Loch Garman) A county in the SE Republic of Ireland, in Leinster. It was the first Irish county to be colonized from England (1169). Consisting chiefly of lowlands, it rises to mountains in the W. Cattle rearing is important. Area: 2352 sq km (908 sq mi). Population (1996 est): 104 000. County town: Wexford.

● **Weyden, Rogier van der** ► (c. 1400–64) Flemish painter of portraits and religious altarpieces. Almost nothing is known of his early life, but he was probably the pupil of the Master of ▷Flémalle, whose influence is evident in *The Deposition* (Prado). From 1436 until his death he was city painter of Brussels and frequently worked for the Burgundian court. In 1450 he visited Italy and paintings from this period, for example the *Entombment* (Uffizi), show Italian influences. His work became widely known in Europe during his lifetime.

● **Weygand, Maxime** ► (1867–1965) French general; commander-in-chief of the French army at the time of the German invasion in 1940. He advised surrender and was imprisoned (1942–45) by the Germans; he was acquitted of collaboration in 1948.

● **Weymouth** ► 50 36N 2 28W A town in S England, on the coast of Dorset. It is a resort and working port. Industries include light engi-

neering, electronics, high-tech research, and quarrying (on the Isle of ▷Portland). It is also an international sailing centre. Population (1991): 46 065.

● **whale** ► A large marine mammal belonging to the order *Cetacea*. Whales have no hind limbs; their forelimbs are flippers and their tails are horizontally flattened to form a pair of flukes. They breathe through a blowhole on top of the head, which is closed when they are submerged. Whales are virtually hairless and insulated by a thick layer of blubber under the skin. They bear their young and suckle them at sea.
There are two suborders. The **whalebone whales** (*Mysticetae*; 12 species)—including the ▷rorquals, ▷blue whale, and ▷right whales—are large and slow-moving and feed on krill, which they filter from the water using a sieve of whalebone (*see* baleen) plates. They have a double blowhole. **Toothed whales** (*Odontocetae*; 80 species)—including the ▷dolphins, ▷narwhal, and ▷sperm whale—are smaller and more agile. They feed on fish and squid and are often gregarious, communicating by underwater sounds. ▷*See also* whaling.

● **whalebone** ▷*See* baleen.

● **whale shark** ► A gigantic but harmless ▷shark, *Rhincodon typus*, that has a grey or brown spotted body with pale undersides, ridges along its sides, and a terminal mouth. Up to 18 m long, it is found mainly in tropical waters, feeding on small fish, invertebrates, and plankton. Family: *Rhincodontidae*.

● **whaling** ► The hunting and slaughter of whales for their carcasses. Traditionally, whales were hunted offshore and processed on land, but modern commercial whaling fleets comprise a mother factory ship for processing the carcasses at sea and a fleet of small hunter vessels equipped with harpoon guns and winches. The car-

whaling ► A slaughtered minke whale (*Balaenoptera acutorostrata*) being hoisted onto a Norwegian whaler.

casses are a source of meat, fats, oils, and other chemicals used in many industries. Whaling has depleted whale populations to the point that some spe-cies, such as the blue whale and bowhead whale, are in danger of extinction. Many conservationists are campaigning for a complete ban on whaling, especially since substitutes for most whale products are available. Most countries have now agreed to suspend commercial whaling under pressure from the International Whaling Commission; Japan and Norway have continued to hunt minke whales, Japan claiming to do so for scientific purposes, Norway for commercial reasons.

● **Whangarei** ► 35 43S 174 20E A city in New Zealand, in North Island on Whangarei Harbour (a large sheltered inlet of the Pacific Ocean). It is the site of New Zealand's only oil refinery (1964). Population (1994): 44 800.

● **whangee** ► A hard white-skinned tropical ▷bamboo of the genus *Phyllostachys*, from SE Asia, the stems of which are used as canes or walking sticks. The woody jointed stems arise from a creeping underground stem; whorls of slender shoots with narrow leaves are produced from each joint.

● **Wharton, Edith (Newbold)** ► (1862–1937) US novelist. Her novels about New York society, such as *The House of Mirth* (1905) and *The Age of Innocence* (1920), were influenced by her friend Henry ▷James. From 1907 she lived in Paris. Her short fiction was printed in *Collected Short Stories* (2 vols, 1968). *Ethan Frome* (1911), a short novel set in New England, remains her best-known work.

● **wheat** ► A cereal ▷grass belonging to the genus *Triticum*, native to W Asia but widely cultivated in subtropical and temperate regions. With the exception of einkorn (*T. monococcum*), most commercial wheats are hybrids with the genus *Aegilops*. Many different varieties have been developed; winter wheats, sown in autumn, are hardier than spring wheats. The stems, up to 1 m high, each bear a cylindrical head of up to a hundred flower clusters, grouped in vertical rows and sometimes bearing bristles (awns) up to 10 cm long. The grain of bread wheat (*T. aestivum*) is milled to produce flour for bread, cakes, biscuits, etc. Hard or durum wheat (*T. durum*) is used to make pasta and semolina. Surplus grain, bran, etc., is fed to livestock. Wheat is also a commercial source of alcohol, dextrose, gluten, malt, and starch.

Leading wheat producers and consumers (millions of tonnes) in the mid-1990s

country	production	consumption
China	109	95
India	66	54
USA	59	23
Russia	30	21
Turkey	18	12
Pakistan	17	17

● **wheatear** ► A migratory songbird, *Oenanthe oenanthe*, that winters in tropical Africa and Eurasia, and breeds in N tundra regions, nesting in holes in the ground. It is about 15 cm long and in summer the male has a blue-grey back, white rump, and a black mask and wings. In winter, males resemble females, having a brown mask, back, and wings. Family: *Turdidae* (thrushes).

● **Wheatstone, Sir Charles** ► (1802–75) British physicist, who was originally a musical-instrument maker, reputedly inventing the harmonica (mouth organ) and the concertina. He was the first to patent the electrical telegraph and recognized the value of the network used to measure resistances now called the ▷Wheatstone bridge (invented by Samuel Hunter Christie; 1784–1865). He became professor of physics at King's College, London, in 1832 and was knighted in 1868.

● **Wheatstone bridge** ► An arrangement of four resistances used to measure the value of one of the resistances when the other three are known. The resistances are arranged to form a square with a voltage applied across two opposite junctions and a galvanometer connected across the other two opposite junctions. When the galva-

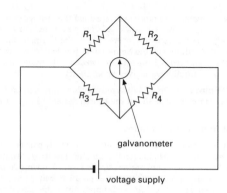

galvanometer

voltage supply

Wheatstone bridge

nometer indicates that no current is flowing the bridge is balanced and $R_1/R_2 = R_3/R_4$.

● **wheel** ► A solid circular disc revolving on an axle to interconvert rotary and linear motion. The invention of this device, which does not appear in nature, gave human beings access to an enormous range of technologies. Very few mechanical devices do not make use of wheels in one form or another.

It is thought that a rudimentary wheel was invented some 5000 or 6000 years ago, although such devices may have consisted of no more than rollers made from suitable logs or stones. The first true wheels, made from a section of a tree trunk or from two or more shaped planks held together, have been found in graves in the Middle East and dated to about 3500 BC. The first known illustration of a wheeled cart, from the Euphrates valley, appeared about 3000 BC. By 2000 BC spoked wheels were used on chariots in ancient Egypt and China. Later developments included a metal tyre to hold the wheel together and provide a more durable contact with the surface over which it ran.

The earliest wheels were fixed to an axle, which rotated with the wheel, and were supported by housings on the vehicle to which they were attached. The iron hub turning on a greased, but stationary, axle was a later development. In the 19th century wrought-iron wheels for the railways and light wire-spoked wheels for bicycles made their appearance. In the 20th century the ubiquitous motor car made use of cast aluminium or pressed steel wheels encircled by pneumatic tyres.

The industrial use of the wheel probably began with the millstone for grinding grain. The heavy stone had a fixed vertical shaft to which a long horizontal arm was attached. This arm was pushed either by manpower or animal power. Later mechanisms were devised to enable millstones to be rotated by treadmills, waterwheels, or windmills—all of which make use of the **wheel and axle** mechanism. A rope wound round a wheel can provide a ▷mechanical advantage in lifting a weight attached to a rope wound round the axle. The mechanical advantage is equal to the ratio of the diameter of the wheel to the diameter of the axle.

● **wheel animalcule** ▷*See* rotifer.

● **Wheeler, Sir (Robert Eric) Mortimer** ► (1890–1976) British archaeologist. Wheeler's skill in excavating, recording, and interpreting archaeological strata was renowned. He excavated Romano-British sites (e.g. ▷Maiden Castle) and was influential as director of the Archaeological Survey of India (1944–48).

● **wheel of life** ▷*See* Bhavachakra.

● **whelk** ► A ▷gastropod mollusc of the family *Buccinidae* (over 400 species), of warm and cold seas. 4–12 cm long, whelks feed on molluscs and worms. The common northern whelk (*Buccinum undatum*), 5 cm long, has a drab yellow-brown shell and edible flesh. Tropical species are more colourful.

● **whidah** ▷*See* whydah.

● **Whigs** ► Members of a British political group that became the

▷Liberal Party after about 1868. Originally an abusive Scottish name for a horsethief, the term "whiggamore" or "whig" was later applied to Scottish Presbyterians and from 1679 to those who, in opposition to the ▷Tories, wished to exclude the Roman Catholic Duke of York (later James II) from the succession. The Whigs dominated politics in the first half of the 18th century, forming rival aristocratic groups. When in the late 18th century the Tories re-emerged, the Whigs formed a more united group under Charles James ▷Fox. In the 1830s they returned to power after a long absence to pass the Great Reform Act of 1832 (*see* Reform Acts). Identifying with industrialist, Nonconformist, and reforming interests, they became the Liberal Party under ▷Gladstone.

● **whimbrel** ▶ A ▷curlew, *Numenius phaeopus*, that breeds on Arctic tundra and winters in Africa, South America, and S Asia. 40 cm long, it has a streaked brown plumage and a dark crown with a pale central stripe. It feeds on insects, spiders, worms, and snails.

● **whinchat** ▶ A migratory ▷chat, *Saxicola rubetra*, common on open farmland. It winters in Africa and breeds in Eurasia, nesting in rough vegetation and feeding on flies and moths. The male has a streaked brown plumage, pale chestnut breast, white wingbars, and a white eyestripe; the female is duller.

● **whip** ▶ In the UK, an official of a political party responsible for ensuring that the party's MPs vote according to its leadership's policies and for communicating MPs' views to the leadership. The term also refers to the summons to vote sent by whips to MPs, a crucial summons being underlined three times (three-line whip). In the USA, whips are not as influential as in Britain, where MPs seldom disobey directions.

● **whipbird** ▶ A shy songbird belonging to the Australian genus *Psophodes* (2 species). They are about 25 cm long with a dark-green plumage, and feed on insects among scrub and undergrowth. The eastern whipbird (*P. olivaceus*) has a long whistling call ended by a whipcrack sound. Family: *Muscicapidae*.

● **whippet** ▶ A breed of dog developed in England during the 19th century from terrier and greyhound stock and used for coursing and racing. It has a slender streamlined build with a smooth whiplike tail and long tapering muzzle. The fine short coat can be any mixture of colours. Height: 46 cm (dogs); 43 cm (bitches).

● **whippoorwill** ▶ A North American ▷nightjar, *Caprimulgus vociferus*, named after its distinctive call. About 24 cm long, it has a mottled brown plumage; the male has a white collar and tail markings. It lives in woodland and feeds on insects.

● **whip scorpion** ▶ A nocturnal ▷arachnid, sometimes called vinegarroon, belonging to a suborder (*Uropygi*; about 75 species) found in tropical and subtropical regions. Up to 13 cm long, it has large spiny pincers and a whiplike tail and it secretes acetic acid for defence. Order: *Pedipalpi*.

● **Whipsnade Wild Animal Park** ▶ A large zoological park, belonging to the London Zoological Society, situated in Bedfordshire, some 45 km (30 mi) NW of London, 5 km (3 mi) S of Dunstable. It covers some 2 sq km (500 acres) and was opened in 1931. Animals are kept in large enclosures that resemble their natural habitats.

● **whip snake** ▶ A slender arboreal snake belonging to the genus *Zamenis* (5 species). The common European speckled grey whip snake (*Z. gemonensis*) reaches a length of 1.8 m and feeds on other snakes and lizards. The green whip snakes (genus *Dryophis*; 8 species) occur in tropical Asia and Australasia and grow to a length of 1 m. Family: *Colubridae*.

● **whirligig** ▶ A dark shiny ▷water beetle belonging to the widely distributed family *Gyrinidae* (about 700 species). It spins around on the surface of still or slow-moving fresh water, feeding on insects or other small animals that have fallen in. The aquatic larvae prey on mayfly or dragonfly nymphs. If disturbed, whirligig beetles dive from the surface and exude a foul-smelling milky liquid.

● **whirlpool** ▶ A violent circular eddy in the sea or a large river, caused by opposing currents or winds or where a strong current is impeded by some obstacle. Large-scale whirlpools are rare. ▷*See also* Maelstrom.

● **whirlwind** ▶ A small revolving column of air, which whirls around a low-pressure centre produced by local heating and convectional uprising. It may pick up small pieces of debris and dust and in desert areas may cause sandstorms.

● **whisky** ▶ A ▷spirit distilled from malted barley or other grain. The word comes from the Gaelic *uisgebeatha*, water of life. The milled grain is mixed with water to form a mash, which must be converted to sugar before fermentation; the resulting alcoholic liquid is distilled and then aged in the cask for at least three years. Whisky is classified according to where it is produced, e.g. Scotch whisky, Irish whiskey (spelt with an e), or, as in the USA, by type. Most US whiskey is either rye or bourbon (named after the county in Kentucky where it was first produced).

● **whist** ▶ A card game for two pairs of partners; it originated in the 17th century and was popularized by ▷Hoyle. A pack of 52 cards is dealt out, the last card determining the trump suit. The object of the game is to win the highest number of tricks by playing the highest card of a suit (the cards ranking from ace high) or by trumping (one may also discard a nontrump when one cannot follow suit). The winner of a trick leads the next card. Each trick over the first six (the "book") scores a point to the partners; five or (in long whist) ten points make a game and two out of three games win the rubber. In **solo whist** each player makes a call indicating that he will play the hand for a certain number of tricks; the player with the highest call plays alone, or solo, against the other three. ▷*See also* bridge.

● **Whistler, James (Abbott) McNeill** ▶ (1834–1903) US painter. After briefly attending West Point, from which he was dismissed, he settled in Paris (1855), where he was particularly influenced by oriental art, especially Japanese prints. Moving to England (1859), he specialized in portraits and landscapes dominated by one or two colours, the best known being *The Artist's Mother* (Louvre) and *Nocturne in Blue and Gold* (Tate Gallery). In 1877 ▷Ruskin described one of Whistler's works as "flinging a pot of paint in the public's face" and was sued for libel (1878); although Whistler won the case his legal costs ruined him. Whistler was also famous as a wit and as the author of *The Gentle Art of Making Enemies* (1890).

● **Whistler, Rex** ▶ (1905–44) British artist. After training at the Slade School he became known for his illustrations for such books as *Gulliver's Travels* and his murals for the Tate Gallery restaurant. He was killed in World War II. His brother **Laurence Whistler** (1912–   ) is a glass engraver, writer, and poet.

● **whistling duck** ▶ A long-legged long-necked ▷duck belonging to a tribe (*Dendrocygnini*; 8 species), also called tree duck, ranging throughout tropical regions. They have a distinctive whistling cry. The fulvous tree duck (*Dendrocygnus bicolor*) is 55 cm long and has a red-brown plumage with cream stripes on the flanks.

● **Whitbread Book of the Year Award** ▶ An annual literary award of £23,000. Announced in 1985 and sponsored by the brewers Whitbread, it is open to authors who live in the British Isles. The prize is administered by the Booksellers Association of Great Britain. The judges choose a winner in each of five categories (novel, first novel, biography, poetry, and children's fiction) and then meet to choose an overall winner. The prize was won in 1997 and 1998 by Ted Hughes for *Tales from Ovid* and *Birthday Letters*, respectively, in 1999 by Seamus Heaney for *Beowulf*, in 2000 by Matthew Kneale for *English Passengers*, and in 2001 by Philip Pullman for *The Amber Spyglass*.

● **Whitby** ▶ 54 29N 0 37W A town in N England, on the North Yorkshire coast at the mouth of the River Esk. A monastery was founded here in 657 AD by St Hilda; only the ruins of a later abbey remain. Whitby has associations with Capt Cook, who lived here. It is a resort and fishing port with boatbuilding and fish-curing industries. Population (1991): 13 640.

● **Whitby, Synod of** ▶ (664 AD) A council convened at Whitby by King Oswy of Northumbria to decide whether to adopt Roman or ▷Celtic Church usages. The major source of controversy between the Roman party, led by St ▷Wilfrid, and the Celtic party led by St Colman (d. 676), was the dating of Easter. The Roman view triumphed.

● **White, Gilbert** ▶ (1720–93) English naturalist. Following his ordination in the Anglican Church in 1751, White began making observations of the natural history around his home at Selborne, Hampshire. He published *The Natural History and Antiquities of Selborne* (1789), a collection of his correspondence with fellow naturalists, still widely read and admired for its keen observation and charming style.

● **White, Patrick** ▶ (1912–90) Australian novelist. Born in England and educated at Cambridge University, he settled in Australia after World War II and explored the national consciousness in his epic novels *The Tree of Man* (1955) and *Voss* (1957). His other works include *The Vivisector* (1970), *A Fringe of Leaves* (1976), *The Twyborn Affair* (1980), and *Netherwood* (1983). He won the Nobel Prize in 1973.

● **White, T(erence) H(anbury)** ▶ (1906–64) British novelist. He lived as a recluse in Ireland and in the Channel Isles. His books include a retelling of the Arthurian legend, *The Once and Future King* (1958), and works of social history.

● **white ant** ▷*See* termite.

● **whitebait** ▶ The young of ▷herrings, ▷sprats, and sometimes ▷silversides. They are highly valued as food.

● **whitebeam** ▶ A tree, *Sorbus aria*, up to 15 m tall found mainly in S and central Europe. The young leaves are covered in white down; the white five-petalled flowers are borne in branched clusters and produce red berries. Swedish whitebeam (*S. × intermedia*), a hybrid between whitebeam and ▷mountain ash, is often planted in parks. Family: *Rosaceae*.

● **white blood cell** ▷*See* leucocyte.

● **white dwarf** ▶ A very small faint low-mass star (less than 1.44 solar masses) that has undergone ▷gravitational collapse following exhaustion of its nuclear fuel. Electrons are stripped from the constituent atoms, and it is the pressure exerted by these densely packed electrons that eventually halts the star's contraction. The density is then 10^7–10^{11} kg m^{-3}. As they cool, their colours change from white (for the brightest) through yellow and red until they become cold black objects.

● **white-eye** ▶ A small long-tailed songbird belonging to a family (*Zosteropidae*; 85 species) occurring in Old World tropical regions. White-eyes are less than 15 cm long, typically yellow-green with white underparts, and have characteristic white rings around the eyes. Arboreal, with brush-tipped tongues for feeding on nectar, they also eat insects and fruits.

● **Whitefield, George** ▶ (1714–70) British Methodist preacher. An associate of the Wesleys at Oxford, Whitefield was not allowed to preach in Anglican churches and began open-air preaching in England in 1739; in 1740, during one of his seven visits to America, he became associated with the ▷Great Awakening in New England. His preaching was strongly Calvinist, in contrast to the Wesleys' Arminianism.

● **whitefish** ▶ A slender fish, belonging to a genus (*Coregonus*) related to trout, that occurs mainly in deep northern lakes and rivers of Europe, Asia, and North America. It has a small mouth, minute teeth, and a covering of large silvery scales. Whitefish feed on insects and other small animals and most are food and game fish.

● **white fly** ▶ A small winged insect of the mainly tropical family *Aleyrodidae*. 2–3 mm long, it is covered with a mealy white powder and resembles a minute moth. White flies suck plant juices and exude honeydew on which a sooty black mould grows, often damaging crops. The larvae go through a sedentary stage, in which they are scalelike and covered with a cottony wax. Suborder: *Homoptera*; order ▷*Hemiptera*.

● **Whitehall** ▶ A street in Westminster, London, where many government offices are located; the name is often applied to the civil service. The ▷Cenotaph is also in Whitehall.

● **Whitehaven** ▶ 54 33N 3 35W A town in NW England, in Cumbria on the Irish Sea. It is a port with textile, chemical, and food-processing industries. Nearby is Calder Hill, the site of Britain's first nuclear power station. Population (1991): 26 542.

● **Whitehead, A(lfred) N(orth)** ▶ (1861–1947) British philosopher and mathematician. Whitehead's first major work, the *Principia Mathematica* (1910–13), was written in collaboration with Bertrand ▷Russell. In later books, such as the *Principles of Natural Knowledge* (1919) and *The Concept of Nature* (1920), he explored the relationships that exist between concepts and sense perception. Thereafter, his philosophy became more metaphysical. He was appointed to the OM in 1945.

● **Whitehorse** ▶ 60 40N 135 08W A city in NW Canada, the capital of the ▷Yukon. Founded in 1900, at the time of the Klondike gold rush, it is now a centre for distribution, administration, and tourism. Population (1995): 22 884.

● **White Horse, Vale of the** ▶ A valley in S England, in Oxfordshire drained by the River Ock. Its name derives from the Uffington White Horse, the figure of a horse 110 m (361 ft) long cut in the chalk of the Berkshire Downs. There are several theories concerning its origin but the general opinion is that it was a cult object of the Belgae, a tribe that occupied much of SE England from about 50 BC to 50 AD.

● **White House** ▶ The official residence of the president of the USA. In Washington, DC, on Pennsylvania Avenue, the building was designed by James Hoban (c. 1762–1831) in 1792. It was burnt (1814) by the British during the ▷War of 1812 but was subsequently restored under Hoban's supervision, being painted white to hide the smoke stains (its name, however, had been adopted earlier). It was partly rebuilt (1949–52).

● **Whitelaw, William (Stephen Ian), 1st Viscount** ▶ (1918–99) British Conservative politician. He entered parliament in 1955 and was leader of the House of Commons (1970–72), secretary of state for Northern Ireland (1972–73), and secretary of state for employment (1973–74); he became chairman of the Conservative Party in 1974 and home secretary (1979–83). In 1983 he became a viscount and was appointed lord president of the Council and leader of the House of Lords, resigning due to ill health in 1988.

● **Whiteman, Paul** ▶ (1891–1967) US big-band leader of the 1920s and 1930s, known as the King of Jazz. He commissioned ▷Gershwin's *Rhapsody in Blue*.

● **white rhinoceros** ▶ The largest species of ▯rhinoceros, *Ceratotherium simum*, of South Africa. It is greyish brown and has a broad square upper lip. Up to 2 m high at the shoulder and weighing up to 3.5 tonnes, white rhinos are now very rare.

● **White Russia** ▷*See* Belarus, Republic of.

● **White Russians** ▶ The Russians who fought against the Soviet Red Army in the civil war (1917–21) that followed the ▷Russian Revolution. The name derives from that of the royalist opponents to the French Revolution, called Whites because they adopted the white flag of the French Bourbon dynasty.

● **White Sea** ▶ (Russian name: Beloye More) A gulf of the Arctic Ocean in NW Russia, to the S and E of the Kola Peninsula. It gives access to Archangel and the fishing port and aluminium works of Kandalaksha and is connected by inland waterways to the Gulf of Finland.

● **white shark** ▶ A dangerous man-eating ▷mackerel shark, *Carcharodon carcharias*, that occurs singly or in groups, mainly in tropical and temperate seas. Its heavy body, up to 11 m long, is grey-brown to slate-blue with light-grey undersides and it feeds voraciously on fish, turtles, seals, ships' refuse, etc.

● **whitethroat** ▶ An Old World ▷warbler, *Sylvia communis*, that breeds in N Eurasia and winters in central Africa. It is about 14 cm long including its long slender tail. The male is russet brown with a greyish head and white throat and performs a tumbling courtship display in flight. The female is a duller brown.

● **white whale** ▶ A small Arctic toothed ▷whale, *Delphinapterus leucas*, also called beluga. Young white whales are blue-grey, but change to white as they mature. About 4.5 m long, with a rounded head and large flukes and flippers, they feed mainly on fish. Family: *Monodontidae*.

● **Whitgift, John** ▶ (c. 1530–1604) Anglican churchman. He became a professor at Cambridge in 1567 and Bishop of Worcester in 1577. As Archbishop of Canterbury (1583–1604) he opposed Puritan teaching and enforced Queen Elizabeth's policy of uniformity in the Church of England. He founded Whitgift School at Croydon (1595).

● **whiting** ▶ A marine food and game fish belonging to the genus *Gadus* (or *Merlangius*) related to cod, especially *M. merlangus* found in European waters down to 200 m. It has a slender body, up to 70 cm long, which is olive, sandy, or bluish above and silvery white below, a black blotch on each pectoral fin, and three dorsal and two anal fins.

● **Whitlam, (Edward) Gough** ▶ (1916–　) Australian statesman; Labor prime minister (1972–75). He became Labor leader in 1967. As prime minister following 18 years of Liberal rule, he ended conscription, relaxed rules on non-White immigration, and tried to lessen US influence in Australia. In 1975, after Malcolm ▷Fraser had blocked government finance bills, Whitlam was dismissed by the governor, Sir John Kerr (1914–91), for refusing to call a general election. Whitlam lost the election called by Fraser and resigned the party leadership (1977). His books include *The Whitlam Government 1972–1975* (1986) and *National and International Maturity* (1991).

● **Whitman, Walt** ▶ (1819–92) US poet. As a young man he worked as a printer, teacher, journalist, and property speculator and contributed unoriginal poems to various magazines. He expressed his democratic idealism and passionate love of life in the revolutionary free-verse poems of *Leaves of Grass* (1855), which was revised in nine editions during his lifetime. During the Civil War he nursed wounded soliders, and subsequently suffered from illness himself. His later works include the prose *Democratic Vistas* (1871).

● **Whitney, Eli** ▶ (1765–1825) American inventor, best known for his invention of the cotton gin, a machine that separated cotton fibre from the seeds. The device, patented in 1793, greatly stimulated cotton growing in the southern USA. Whitney subsequently turned to firearms manufacture, into which he introduced the notion of interchangeable parts.

● **Whit Sunday** ▶ The seventh Sunday after Easter, a Christian festival commemorating the descent of the Holy Spirit on the Apostles on the 50th day after Easter (Acts 2.1). Also called ▷Pentecost, it was originally a Jewish festival. In the Christian Church, Whit Sunday became a time for baptisms ("White" Sunday, referring to the white baptismal robes).

● **Whittier, John Greenleaf** ▶ (1807–92) US poet. An active Quaker and humanitarian, he championed the antislavery cause in both his journalism and his early poetry. His later and better-known poetry includes the narrative *Snow-Bound* (1866) and many shorter poems and ballads including "Barbara Frietchie" (1863), an epic of the Civil War, featuring "Stonewall" Jackson.

● **Whittington, Dick** ▶ (Richard W.; d. 1423) English merchant, who was three times Lord Mayor of London (1397–98, 1406–07, 1419–20). He traded with, and made loans to, both Henry IV and Henry V. The legend of Dick Whittington, the poor lad from Gloucestershire who came to London with his cat, believing the streets there to be paved with gold, dates from the early 17th century. Of the many embellishments of this legend, the most persistent is that, finding London streets less opulent than he expected, he set off back to Gloucestershire, still accompanied by his long-suffering cat. However, at the foot of Highgate Hill in N London, where a stone still stands to commemorate the event, he heard Bow Bells (some 5 miles away!), which seemed to be chiming "Turn again Whittington, Lord Mayor of London." The legendary Whittington, answering this call, returned to become a rich and successful mercer, who did indeed become Lord Mayor.

● **Whittle, Sir Frank** ▶ (1907–96) British aeronautical engineer and RAF officer, who designed and flew the first British jet aircraft. The engine was fitted into a specially constructed Gloster E28/39; its maiden flight took place on 15 May, 1941. His achievement was recognized by a government award of £100,000 and he was appointed to the OM in 1986.

● **WHO** ▷*See* World Health Organization.

● **whooping cough** ▶ A respiratory infection of children caused by the bacterium *Bordetella pertussis*. After an incubation period of 7–14 days, the child develops a cough, a nasal discharge, and fever, followed a week or two later by paroxysms of coughing accompanied by a characteristic whooping sound. The disease may persist for months and it may be complicated by pneumonia or convulsions. A vaccine is available but very rare cases of brain damage have been attributed to it.

● **whooping crane** ▶ A rare bird, *Grus americana*, that breeds in NW Canada and winters in the swamps of SE Texas: 150 cm tall with a wingspan of 210 cm, it has a white plumage with black-tipped wings, black legs, and a bare red face and has a loud whooping call. Captive breeding programmes may prevent its extinction. Family: *Gruidae* (cranes).

● **Whorf, Benjamin Lee** ▶ (1897–1941) US linguist. An insurance inspector by profession, he studied languages as a hobby. In *Language, Thought, and Reality* (1956) he argued that human conceptual systems are dependent upon individual languages and that comparison of different languages reveals that different peoples analyse the world in very different ways. This controversial form of linguistic relativism was also argued by ▷Sapir and has been influential in psycholinguistics (*see* linguistics).

● **whortleberry** ▷*See* bilberry.

● **Whyalla** ▶ 33 04S 137 34E A city and port in South Australia, on the E coast of Eyre Peninsula. It is an important industrial centre with the largest shipyards in Australia and major steelworks. Population (1991): 25 562.

● **whydah** ▶ (or whidah) A small ▷weaverbird belonging to the genus *Vidua* (11 species), also called widowbird and occurring in open grassy regions of Africa. The males have long ornamental tail feathers used in the courtship display and the females lay their eggs in the nests of closely related ▷waxbills, which rear their young. The young whydahs closely resemble the offspring of their host species.

● **Whymper, Edward** ▶ (1840–1911) British mountaineer, explorer, artist, and author. He led the first ascent of the Matterhorn (1865), in which four members of the team died on the descent. He also explored Greenland, the Andes, and Canada.

● **Wichita** ▶ 37 43N 97 20W A city in the USA, in Kansas on the Arkansas River. Founded in 1864, it had developed into an important agricultural trading centre by the late 19th century. Today Wichita is the state's largest city and the principal commercial and industrial centre of S Kansas with railway workshops, oil refineries, and an aircraft industry. It is the site of two universities, including Wichita State University (1895). Population (1994 est): 310 236.

● **Wick** ▶ 58 26N 3 06W A town in N Scotland, in the Highland Region. It is a fishing port with boatbuilding, distilling, and knitwear industries. There are air services to the Orkneys and Shetlands. Population (1991): 7681.

● **Wicklow** ▶ (Irish name: Contae Chill Mhantáin) A county in the E Republic of Ireland, in Leinster bordering on the Irish Sea. Fertile lowlands rise to the central Wicklow Mountains. Agriculture is the chief occupation; coastal resorts include Bray. Area: 2025 sq km (782 sq mi). Population (1996): 102 000. County town: Wicklow.

● **Widnes** ▶ 53 22N 2 44W A town in NW England, in Hatton unitary authority, Cheshire; it is situated on the River Mersey opposite Runcorn. It has an important chemical industry. Population (1991): 57 162.

● **Widor, Charles Marie** ▶ (1844–1937) French organist and composer. He was organist of Saint-Sulpice in Paris for over 60 years. His compositions include eight symphonies for the organ, concertos, chamber music, and choral music.

● **Wieland, Christoph Martin** ▶ (1733–1813) German novelist and poet. His first major work is the romance *Agathon* (1766–67), while his translations of Shakespeare influenced the ▷Sturm und Drang movement. The verse epic *Oberon* (1780) introduced exotic Middle Eastern matter into European literature.

● **Wiener, Norbert** ▶ (1894–1964) US mathematician. A child prodigy, Wiener entered university at the age of 11 and was awarded his doctorate at 18. During World War II he worked on the problem of aiming an anti-aircraft gun by computing such factors as the speed and direction of the aircraft, wind speed, etc. He thus developed an interest in the mathematics of information and communication, which he called ▷cybernetics. After the war Wiener, refusing to do any more military research, spent the rest of his life writing about the social problems resulting from automation.

● **Wiesbaden** ▶ 50 05N 8 15E A spa city in SW Germany, the capital of Hesse on the River Rhine. Its hot saline springs have made it a popular resort since Roman times. A centre of the wine industry, its manufactures include chemicals and plastics. Population (1999 est): 268 200.

● **Wiesel, Elie** ▶ (1928–) US author and human rights activist, born in Romania. A survivor of Buchenwald concentration camp in World War II, in his novels and other works he records crimes committed by the Nazis against the Jews. He won the Nobel Peace Prize in 1986.

● **Wiesenthal, Simon** ▶ (1908–) Austrian investigator of Nazi crimes against the Jews. Since World War II, during which he spent three years in concentration camps, he has helped to track down over 1000 Nazi war criminals, including ▷Eichmann. He has been head of the Jewish Documentation Centre (*or* Wiesenthal Centre) in Vienna since 1961.

● **Wigan** ▶ **1.** 53 33N 2 38W A town in NW England, in Wigan unitary authority, Greater Manchester. It is an industrial and market town, made famous by George Orwell's *Road to Wigan Pier*. The major industries include food processing, engineering, paper products, and distribution. Population (1991): 85 819. **2.** A unitary authority in NW England, in Greater Manchester. Area: 199 sq km (77 sq mi). Population (1999 est): 306 521.

● **wigeon** ▶ A fast-flying ▷duck, *Anas penelope*, that breeds on tundra and moorland of N Eurasia and winters on mudflats, estuaries, and lakes as far south as Africa and S Asia. 45 cm long, it has a pale-grey black-tipped bill; males have a chestnut head with a yellowish crown and grey back, while females are brown with a white belly and white shoulders.

● **Wight, Isle of** ▶ (Latin name: Vectis) 50 40N 1 15W An island and county in S England, separated from the mainland by the Solent and Spithead. It became a ▷unitary authority in 1995. It consists chiefly of undulating chalk downs with the ▷Needles off the W coast. Tourism and yachting (with the annual Cowes Regatta) are important, especially in the coastal resorts, including Ryde, Shanklin, and Ventnor. Other occupations include agriculture and shipbuilding. Area: 380 sq km (147 sq mi). Population (1999 est): 128 300. Administrative centre: Newport.

● **Wightman Cup** ▶ An annual tennis competition between British and US women's teams, instituted in 1923. The match consists of five singles and two doubles rubbers (matches). The USA have won 51 victories compared to Great Britain's 10. The trophy was donated by the US player Hazel Hotchkiss (later Mrs George Wightman; 1886–1974). The competition was suspended in 1990, owing to its increasingly unequal nature (the USA having won the last four tournaments 7-0).

● **Wigner, Eugene Paul** ▶ (1902–95) US physicist, born in Hungary, who worked out the theory of neutron absorption by nuclei and discovered that solids change their size under radiation (Wigner effect). Wigner helped persuade ▷Einstein to warn Roosevelt of the dangers of an atomic bomb being made by the Germans, and he worked with Fermi on the first atomic pile. He shared the 1963 Nobel Prize.

● **Wigtown** ▶ (*or* Wigtownshire) A former county of SW Scotland. Under local government reorganization in 1975 its boundaries were adjusted to form Wigtown District, in Dumfries and Galloway Region. This district was abolished in 1996.

● **Wigtown** ▶ 54 52N 4 26W A town in SW Scotland, in Dumfries and Galloway on Wigtown Bay. It is a market town and small port. Population (1991): 1117.

● **wigwam** ▶ **1.** Strictly, a square dome-roofed hut made of saplings covered with bark or rush matting used by some North American Indian peoples. **2.** (*or* tepee) A conical tent supported by poles tied together at the top and covered with decorated buffalo skins, used by the Plains tribes.

● **Wilberforce, Samuel** ▶ (1805–73) British churchman. He became Bishop of Oxford (1845) and Winchester (1869). His books include *Agathos* (1840), but he is best remembered for asking T. H. Huxley in a debate (1860) on Darwinism whether he was descended from an ape on his grandmother's or grandfather's side and for being demolished by Huxley's reply.

● **Wilberforce, William** ▶ (1759–1833) British philanthropist, who played a major part in the antislavery movement. As an MP (1780–1825) he led the parliamentary campaign to abolish the slave trade (achieved in 1807) and then to emancipate existing slaves (achieved a month after his death). A founder of the Society for the Abolition of the Slave Trade (1787) and of the Antislavery Society (1823), he was also a leading member of the ▷Clapham Sect.

● **wildcat** ▶ A ▷cat, *Felis sylvestris sylvestris*, of Europe and W Asia. About 75 cm long, it has a bushy rounded tail and thick striped coat. The African wildcat, (*F. sylvestris libyca*), of North Africa, is similar. Wildcats inhabit dense woodland and breed once a year, in a den in a hollow log or tree.

Oscar Wilde ▶ Well known for his repartee, Wilde was once asked to change a line in one of his plays. "Who am I to tamper with a masterpiece?" he snapped.

● **Wilde, Oscar (Fingal O'Flahertie Wills)** ▶ (1854–1900) British dramatist and poet, born in Dublin. He dazzled London literary society with his wit and became a leading figure of the ▷Aesthetic movement. His works include *Poems* (1881), a novel *The Picture of Dorian Gray* (1891), and a series of brilliant social comedies: *Lady Windermere's Fan* (1892), *A Woman of No Importance* (1893), *An Ideal Husband* (1895), and *The Importance of Being Earnest* (1895). Socially and financially ruined by a trial in 1895 arising from his homosexual relationship with **Lord Alfred Douglas** (1870–1945), he was imprisoned for two years, after which he lived in exile in France until his death. While in prison he wrote a long letter on his relationship with Douglas, parts of which were published as *De profundis* (1905). In exile he produced his poem *The Ballad of Reading Gaol* (1898).

● **wildebeest** ▷See gnu.

● **Wilder, Billy** ▶ (Samuel W.; 1906–2002) US film director, born in Austria. He went to Hollywood in 1934. His films include *The Lost Weekend* (1945), *Sunset Boulevard* (1950), *Some Like It Hot* (1959), *Front Page* (1974), and *Buddy, Buddy* (1981).

● **Wilder, Thornton** ▶ (1897–1975) US novelist and dramatist. His best-known plays are *Our Town* (1938) and *The Skin of Our Teeth* (1942), while his novels include *The Bridge of San Luis Rey* (1927). All of these works received Pulitzer Prizes.

● **wildfowl** ▶ Waterbirds, usually those shot for sport, especially ducks and geese but also coots, rails, and grebes.

● **Wildfowl and Wetlands Trust** ▷See Scott, Robert Falcon.

● **Wilfrid, St** ▶ (634–709 AD) English churchman; Bishop of York (c. 663–c. 703). He campaigned for the replacement of Celtic usages in Britain by Roman liturgy and practice at the Synod of ▷Whitby (664). Feast day: 12 Oct.

● **Wilhelm I** ▶ (King of Prussia) ▷*See* William I.

● **Wilhelm II** ▶ (German emperor) ▷*See* William II.

● **Wilhelmina** ▶ (1880–1962) Queen of the Netherlands (1890–1948), who encouraged Dutch resistance to the German occupation in World War II, making radio broadcasts from London. She abdicated in favour of her daughter Juliana.

● **Wilhelmshaven** ▶ 53 32N 8 07E A seaport in NW Germany, in Lower Saxony on the North Sea. It was founded in 1869 as the main Prussian (later German) naval base. Now also a popular resort and an oil port, its manufactures include machinery and electrical goods. Population (1989 est): 89 900.

● **Wilkes, John** ▶ (1725–97) British journalist and politician. He was a member of the Hellfire Club of debauchees (*see* High Wycombe). In 1757 he became an MP and in 1762 founded the weekly *North Briton*, in which he attacked George III's ministers. The famous issue No 45 (1763) accused the government of lying in the king's speech and Wilkes was arrested for libel. Although released, in 1764 while in Paris he was expelled from the House of Commons and outlawed. In 1768 he returned to England and was twice elected MP for Middlesex and twice expelled from parliament. He became the focus of the Society of the Supporters of the Bill of Rights and after serving as lord mayor of London (1774) was re-elected to parliament and at last permitted to take his seat (1774–90).

● **Wilkie, Sir David** ▶ (1785–1841) Scottish painter, acclaimed for his scenes of everyday life in the Dutch 17th-century tradition. He became painter to William IV in 1830. He travelled extensively and ▷Turner commemorated his death at sea in *Peace: Burial at Sea* (Tate Gallery).

● **Wilkins, Sir George Hubert** ▶ (1888–1958) British explorer, born in Australia. After experience with Vilhjalmur Stefansson (1879–1962) in the Arctic (1913–18) and ▷Shackleton in the Antarctic (1921–22), he flew over the North Pole from Alaska to Spitsbergen (1928). In 1931 he failed to reach it in the submarine *Nautilus*.

● **Wilkins, Maurice Hugh Frederick** ▶ (1916–   ) New Zealand physicist, who worked on the atom bomb during World War II. After the war, uneasy about nuclear weapons, he developed a method of using X-ray diffraction, which assisted James ▷Watson and Francis ▷Crick in determining the structure of DNA. These three scientists were awarded the 1962 Nobel Prize for this work.

● **Wilkins, William** ▶ (1778–1839) British architect. After visiting Greece and Italy he published *Antiquities of Magna Graecia* (1807) and pioneered the Greek revival style in his Downing College, Cambridge (1821), University College, London (1828), St George's Hospital, London (1829), and the National Gallery, London (1838).

● **will** ▶ In law, the written declaration of a person's wishes in relation to the disposal of his property after his death. Two witnesses are required to authenticate the will, neither of whom may be a beneficiary. Dependants of the deceased inadequately provided for may challenge the will, the provisions of which are carried out by one or more executors, who are responsible for obtaining ▷probate. Legacies are subject to ▷inheritance tax in the UK.

● **Willemstad** ▶ 12 12N 68 56W The capital and main port of the ▷Netherlands Antilles, on the SE coast of Curaçao. It is an important free port and a refining centre for Venezuelan oil. Population (1995 est): 119 000.

● **William (I) the Conqueror** ▶ (c. 1028–1087) Duke of Normandy (1035–87) and the first Norman King of England (1066–87). He claimed to have been named by Edward the Confessor as heir to the English throne. When Harold II succeeded Edward, William invaded England, killed his rival at the Battle of Hastings, and became king. The ▷Norman conquest of England was completed by 1072, aided by the establishment of ▷feudalism, under which his followers were granted land in return for pledges of service and loyalty. As king, Wil-

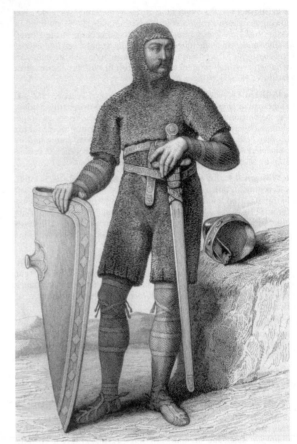

William (I) the Conqueror ▶ A copper engraving after a drawing by Armand Guilleminot.

liam was efficient, if harsh. His administration relied upon Norman and other foreign personnel, especially ▷Lanfranc, Archbishop of Canterbury. In 1085 William initiated the compilation of ▷Domesday Book.

● **William (I) the Bad** ▶ (1120–66) Norman King of Sicily (1154–66). In 1155 he reconquered Apulia from the Byzantines and in 1156 (the Concordat of Benevento) gained papal acknowledgement of his possessions. His attempts to reduce the power of the barons incited a revolt, which he was able to suppress. An outstanding patron of learning, he welcomed many Muslim scholars to his court.

● **William (I) the Lion** ▶ (1143–1214) King of the Scots (1165–1214). After his capture in a revolt against ▷Henry II of England in 1174, he became a vassal of the English throne. On Henry's death in 1189 he regained independence for his kingdom in return for a payment to Richard I.

● **William (I) the Silent** ▶ (1533–84) The leader of the ▷Revolt of the Netherlands against Spanish rule. The son of the Count of Nassau, in 1544 he became Prince of Orange, in 1555 a member of the Council of State, and in 1559 governor of Holland, Zeeland, and Utrecht. He opposed the Spanish Government and its persecution of Protestants (he became a Protestant in 1573), withdrawing with Egmont and Horn from the Council of State in 1563. When revolt broke out in 1568, William emerged as its leader and in 1576 succeeded in uniting the Catholic provinces in the south with the Protestant north. This union was short lived, however, and in 1579 the northern provinces declared their independence of Spain, with William as first stadholder (chief magistrate). He was assassinated by a Spanish agent.

● **William I** ▶ (1772–1843) King of the Netherlands (1815–40). Following Napoleon's conquest of the Netherlands (1795), he lived in exile until Napoleon's defeat (1813), becoming King of the United Netherlands, which included Belgium and Luxembourg. He fostered the Netherlands' economic recovery but antagonized the Belgians, who achieved independence (1831) by revolt. William abdicated in favour of his son William II.

● **William I** ▶ (or Wilhelm I; 1797–1888) King of Prussia (1861–88) and German emperor (1871–88). His advocacy of using arms against the Revolution of 1848 brought him the nickname Prince of Grapeshot and he was forced into exile (1848–49). He became regent for his brother Frederick William IV in 1858. His reign was dominated by ▷Bismarck, who achieved German unification under Prussian leadership in 1871, when William became German emperor.

● **William II Rufus** ▶ (c. 1056–1100) King of England (1087–1100), succeeding his father William the Conqueror. His harsh rule aroused baronial and ecclesiastical opposition, notably from ▷Anselm of Canterbury. He made several attempts to recover Normandy from his elder brother Robert (d. 1134) and was killed by an arrow while hunting in the New Forest. He may have been assassinated by order of his younger brother, who became Henry I.

● **William (II) the Good** ▶ (1154–89) The last Norman King of Sicily (1166–89). He ruled in person from 1171, engaging in intermittent war against the Byzantine Empire until final defeat near Constantinople in 1185. In 1177 he married Joan (1165–99), the daughter of Henry II of England.

● **William II** ▶ (1792–1849) King of the Netherlands (1840–49), following the abdication of his father William I. His authorization of a liberal constitution (1848) prevented the spread of the ▷Revolutions of 1848 to the Netherlands.

● **William II** ▶ (or Wilhelm II; 1859–1941) German emperor (1888–1918); grandson of Queen Victoria of the UK. After securing Bismarck's resignation as chancellor, William encouraged policies regarded abroad as warmongering. The German navy was built up under ▷Tirpitz, overtures were made to Turkey and to Kruger of the Transvaal (whom William congratulated on foiling the British ▷Jameson Raid), and Germany interfered against France in the Morocco crises (1905, 1911). William supported Austria-Hungary's ultimatum to Serbia and then tried to prevent the conflict escalating into a world war. Following Germany's defeat, he abdicated, retiring to Doorn, in the Netherlands.

● **William III** ▶ (1650–1702) King of England (1689–1702) and Stadholder (chief magistrate) of the United Provinces (1672–1702), known as William of Orange. Grandson of Charles I of England and son of William II, Prince of Orange (1626–50), in 1677 he married James II of England's daughter Mary. In 1688 he was invited by the opposition to his father-in-law to invade England and in 1689 was proclaimed joint sovereign with his wife, Mary II (see Glorious Revolution). William defeated the former king at the ▷Boyne in Ireland in 1690. On the Continent he was successful in the War of the ▷Grand Alliance (1689–97) against Louis XIV of France, leaving a strong army that, under the Duke of Marlborough, was to crush France after his death.

● **William IV** ▶ (1765–1837) King of England and Hanover (1830–37), known as the Sailor King or Silly Billy. He served in the Royal Navy from 1778 to 1790. He had ten illegitimate children by the Irish actress Dorothea Jordan before marrying (1818) Adelaide of Saxe-Meiningen (1792–1849). Their two daughters died in infancy and William was succeeded in England by his niece Victoria and in Hanover by his brother Ernest Augustus (1771–1851).

● **William and Mary style** ▶ An English derivative (1689–1702) of the ▷Louis XIV style of furniture. The Huguenot artisans patronized by William III were trained in France and their tastes and techniques predominated. The cabriole leg was a typical innovation replacing the preceding twist turned legs. Rich gilding was common and some important furniture was made of cast silver. Cabinet furniture was finely veneered with ▷marquetry or lacquered and gilded.

● **William of Malmesbury** ▶ (c. 1090–c. 1143) English Benedictine monk and historian. William's work, although lucid, is sometimes chronologically unsound. It includes the *Gesta Regum Anglorum*, a history of kings of England from the Saxon invasion to 1126, and the *Gesta Pontificum Anglorum* (1125), on English ecclesiastical history.

● **William of Ockham** ▶ (c. 1285–1349) English scholastic philosopher (see scholasticism). A pupil of ▷Duns Scotus and later his rival, Ockham is best known for his revival of ▷nominalism. He systematized the theories on the meaning of universals and linked them with logical principles. ▷See also Ockham's Razor.

● **William of Orange** ▷See William III (King of England).

● **William of Tyre** ▶ (c. 1130–85) French historian and churchman, born in the Latin kingdom of Jerusalem. He became chancellor of the kingdom in 1174 and Archbishop of Tyre in 1175. His only extant work is *Historia rerum in partibus transmarinis gestarum*, a history of medieval Palestine and a valuable source of information on the early Crusades.

● **William of Wykeham** ▶ (1324–1404) English churchman and statesman. Bishop of Winchester from 1366 and Lord Chancellor (1367–71, 1389–91), he founded New College, Oxford (1379), and Winchester College (1382).

● **Williams, John** ▶ (1941–) Australian guitarist, living in the UK. He studied at the Royal College of Music and with Segovia. A virtuoso of the classical guitar, he also composes and performs music influenced by pop and jazz.

● **Williams, J(ohn) P(eter) R(hys)** ▶ (1949–) Welsh Rugby Union footballer, who played for London Welsh, Bridgend, Wales, and the British Lions. A brilliant attacking full back of legendary courage, he won 52 international caps (up to 1979) and captained Wales in the 1978–79 season.

● **Williams, Roger** ▶ (c. 1604–83) English colonizer, who founded the colony of Rhode Island. A Puritan, Williams settled in Boston in 1631 but was banished in 1635 because he disagreed with the theocratic government of Massachusetts, advocating the separation of church and state. He founded (1636) a new settlement at Providence, Rhode Island, the patent of which allowed full religious freedom. There he established the first Baptist Church in America.

● **Williams, Shirley (Vivien Teresa Brittain), Baroness** ▶ (1930–) British Social Democrat politician, daughter of the writer Vera ▷Brittain and ex-wife of the philosopher Bernard Williams (1929–). She entered parliament in 1964 as a Labour member and was secretary of state for prices and consumer protection (1974–76). As secretary of state for education and science (1976–79) she championed comprehensive education. She was a cofounder of the ▷Social Democratic Party in 1981 and its president from 1982, but lost her parliamentary seat in the 1983 general election. She was made a life peer in 1992.

● **Williams, Tennessee** ▶ (1911–83) US dramatist. *The Glass Menagerie* (1945), his first major success, was partly autobiographical and introduced his recurrent themes of family tensions and sexual frustration, which were treated with increasing violence in *A Streetcar Named Desire* (1947) and *Cat on a Hot Tin Roof* (1955), both set in the South. After recovering from a mental and physical breakdown, he continued to write plays, including *Vieux Carré* (1978).

● **Williams, Venus** ▶ (1980–) US tennis player, whose titles include the Australian Open (1998), the US Open (2000), and Wimbledon (2000). Her sister **Serena Williams** (1981–), also a tennis player, won the US Open in 1999. The sisters won the Wimbledon Ladies Doubles title in 2000.

● **Williams, William Carlos** ▶ (1883–1963) US poet. The influences of ▷Imagism and of Ezra ▷Pound, whom he met while studying medicine at the University of Pennsylvania, are apparent in his early poetry, and he continued to develop a style noted for its clarity, directness, and use of natural speech rhythms. His volumes of poetry include *Collected Poems* (1934) and *Pictures from Brueghel* (1963), which won a Pulitzer Prize. *Paterson* (5 vols, 1946–58) is an ambitious epic poem employing various experimental techniques.

● **Williamsburg** ▶ 37 17N 76 43W A city in the USA, in Virginia. Once the state capital (1699–1779), many of its colonial buildings have been renovated or completely rebuilt, attracting many tourists to the city. One of the country's oldest colleges, the College of William and Mary (1693), is also situated here. Population (1980): 9870.

● **Williams-Ellis, Sir Clough** ► (1883–1978) Welsh architect. He designed several schools, churches, hotels, etc., but is best remembered for the resort of □Portmeirion (begun 1926).

● **Williamson, Henry** ► (1895–1977) British novelist. He is best known for his realistic animal stories, especially *Tarka the Otter* (1927) and *Salar the Salmon* (1935). He also wrote a series of 15 historical novels, *A Chronicle of Ancient Sunlight* (1951–69).

● **Williamson, Malcolm** ► (1931–) Australian composer, living in the UK since 1953. In 1975 he was appointed Master of the Queen's Music. His works include eight symphonies, an organ concerto (1961), the operas *Our Man in Havana* (1963) and *The Violins of St Jacques* (1966), and *Mass of Christ the King* (1977), written for the 25th jubilee of Queen Elizabeth II.

● **Willis, Ted** ► (Edward Henry, Baron Willis of Chislehurst; 1918–92) British author. His plays include *Hot Summer Night* (1959) and his novels include *Death May Surprise Us* (1974). He also wrote for television, notably the police series *Dixon of Dock Green*.

● **will-o'-the-wisp** ▷*See* ignis fatuus.

● **willow** ► A tree or shrub of the genus *Salix* (about 300 species), native to temperate and arctic regions. Most willows have long narrow leaves (an exception is the Eurasian goat willow (*S. caprea*), also called sallow and pussy willow, which has oval pointed leaves). Male and female catkins are borne on separate trees and open before the leaves; the seeds have long silky hairs. Willows are common in wet places and some are grown as ornamentals, especially the weeping willow (*S. babylonica*), with its slender drooping branches, and the bay willow (*S. pentandra*). Cricket bats are made from the wood of the cricket bat willow (*S. alba* var. *coerulea*). Family: *Salicaceae*. ▷*See also* osier.

● **willowherb** ► A perennial herb of either of the genera *Epilobium* (160 species) or *Chamaenerion* (about 8 species), of temperate and arctic regions. Rosebay willowherb, or fireweed (*E. angustifolium*), 30–120 cm high, is a common and fast-growing weed. It has showy spikes of purple flowers and white fluffy seeds. Family: *Onagraceae*.

● **willow pattern** ► A ▷chinoiserie pattern attributed to Thomas Minton (*see* Minton ware) and introduced about 1780. It was extensively used on 19th-century English ceramics. The elements are a willow tree, pagoda, figures on a river bridge, and two flying birds in an elaborate border.

● **willow warbler** ► A ▷warbler, *Phylloscopus trochilus*, very similar to the ▷chiffchaff. It occurs in European woodlands in summer and winters in Africa.

● **Wills (Moody), Helen** ► (Helen W. Roark; 1905–98) US tennis player, who won the singles title at Wimbledon a record eight times between 1927 and 1938. She also won the US singles title seven times and the French title four times.

● **Wilmington** ► **1.** 39 46N 75 31W A city in the USA, in N Delaware on the Delaware River. It was founded by Swedish settlers as Fort Christina in 1638 and now has chemical and engineering industries. Population (1994 est): 72 799. **2.** 34 14N 77 55W A city in the USA, in North Carolina on the Cape Fear River. The first armed resistance against the Stamp Act occurred here in November, 1765. The state's chief seaport, Wilmington is also a resort and has varied manufactures. Population (1994 est): 62 651.

● **Wilson, Sir Angus** ► (1913–91) British novelist and short-story writer. He worked at the British Museum until 1955 and later taught at the University of East Anglia. His fiction includes *Hemlock and After* (1952), *Anglo-Saxon Attitudes* (1956), *No Laughing Matter* (1967), *As If By Magic* (1973), *Setting the World on Fire* (1980), and *The Collected Stories of Angus Wilson* (1987). He also published criticism.

● **Wilson, Charles Thomson Rees** ► (1869–1959) British physicist, who won the 1927 Nobel Prize for his invention of the Wilson ▷cloud chamber. During the 1890s Wilson was experimenting on cloud formation and supersaturated air. He discovered that moisture condensed in the presence of ions and, when X-rays and radioactivity

were discovered, applied his discoveries to invent the cloud chamber for detecting ionizing radiation. It was perfected in 1911. Wilson was professor of natural philosophy at Cambridge University (1925–34).

● **Wilson, Colin** ► (1931–) British writer and novelist. He won immediate fame with *The Outsider* (1956), a study of alienated heroes in modern fiction. He has written many books on extrasensory phenomena, including *The Occult* (1971) and *Beyond the Occult* (1988).

● **Wilson, Edmund** ► (1895–1972) US critic and essayist. He gave valuable encouragement to young writers in his journalism from the 1920s to the 1940s. His books include *Axel's Castle* (1931), a study of symbolist writers, *To the Finland Station* (1940), on the origins of the Russian Revolution, and *The Scrolls from the Dead Sea* (1955).

● **Wilson, Edmund Beecher** ► (1856–1939) US biologist, who proposed that sex is determined by the presence or absence of certain chromosomes. Wilson's *Cell in Development and Inheritance* (1896) was a major influence in genetics.

● **Wilson, (James) Harold, Baron** ► (1916–95) British statesman; Labour prime minister (1964–70, 1974–76). An economist, he was economic assistant to the war cabinet secretariat (1940–41) and to the mines department (1941–43) and then director of economics and statistics at the ministry of fuel and power (1943–44). After World War II he became an MP (1945) and president of the Board of Trade in 1947, resigning in 1951 because of the government's proposed cuts in social-services expenditure. He succeeded Gaitskill as Labour leader in 1963 and achieved electoral victory in 1964. His statutory incomes policy and plans for industrial-relations reform were unpopular within the Labour Party and among trades unionists and he lost the 1970 election. His second ministry saw the renegotiation of the UK's terms of membership to the EC (now the EU), which was confirmed by a referendum in 1975. In 1976 Wilson unexpectedly resigned. His publications include *The Labour Government 1964–70* (1971) and *The Governance of Britain* (1976). He was made a life peer, Baron Wilson of Rievaulx, in 1983.

● **Wilson, Sir Henry Hughes** ► (1864–1922) British field marshal. He was director of military operations (1910–14) and in World War I held command in France before becoming chief of the imperial general staff (1918). Conservative MP (1922) for North Down (Ulster), he was assassinated by the IRA.

● **Wilson, Henry Maitland, 1st Baron** ► (1881–1964) British field marshal, nicknamed Jumbo. He served in the second Boer War and in World War I. In World War II he held command (under ▷Wavell) in the successful operations against the Italians in N Africa. However, he failed against the Germans in mainland Greece (1941) and the Dodecanese Islands (1943). He was chief of the British joint staff mission in Washington, DC (1943–45).

● **Wilson, Richard** ► (1714–82) British landscape painter, born in Wales. He worked as a portraitist in London before visiting Italy (1750–c. 1757), where, influenced by ▷Claude Lorraine and ▷Poussin, he gave up portraiture for landscape painting. After his return to England, he continued to paint Italian scenes as well as scenes of English country houses and their parks and scenes of the Welsh mountains. In their feeling for atmosphere and light these paintings established him as the first great British landscapist and an important influence on ▷Turner and ▷Constable.

● **Wilson, (Thomas) Woodrow** ► (1856–1924) US statesman; Democratic president (1913–21). In his first term as president he introduced progressive reforms. In World War I, despite a pledge of neutrality, Wilson declared war on Germany (1917) in response to its unrestricted submarine campaign. Wilson's ▷Fourteen Points (1918) proposed a basis on which peace might be settled and contained a plan for a League of Nations that was incorporated into the Treaty of Versailles. However, Wilson failed to obtain the US Senate's acceptance of the treaty. Severely disappointed, he suffered a heart attack and his administration achieved little more.

● **Wilton** ► 51 05N 1 52W A town in S England, in Wiltshire. It has been famous for carpet manufacturing since the 16th century and for its sheep fairs. Wilton House has Elizabethan literary associations. Population (1991): 3717.

● **Wiltshire** ▶ A county of S England. It consists of a rolling chalk plateau, which includes the Marlborough Downs and Salisbury Plain, bordered by lowlands in the NW and SE. It is predominantly agricultural; the chief crops are wheat, oats, and barley, and pig and sheep farming are important. There are many remaining features of prehistoric times, notably the Neolithic ▷Stonehenge and ▷Avebury. The fast-growing town of Swindon became an independent ▷unitary authority in 1997. Area (excluding Swindon): 3479 sq km (1343 sq mi). Population (1999 est, excluding Swindon): 429 100. Administrative centre: Trowbridge.

● **Wimbledon** ▶ A district in the Greater London Borough of Merton. It contains Wimbledon Common and the headquarters of the All England Tennis Club (since 1877), famous for the annual Championships.

● **WIMPS** ▶ (or weakly interacting massive particles) ▷See dark matter.

● **Winchester** ▶ 51 04N 1 19W A city in S England, the administrative centre of Hampshire. As capital of Saxon Wessex and residence of the Saxon kings, it rivalled the supremacy of London. The cathedral, built in the 11th century on earlier Saxon foundations, is the longest in England and contains many royal tombs. Winchester College (1382), founded by ▷William of Wykeham, is England's oldest public school. Population (1991): 36 121.

● **Winckelmann, Johann Joachim** ▶ (1717–68) German art historian, who worked mainly in Rome. His promotion of the critical study of Greek and Roman art was encouraged by contemporary discoveries at ▷Pompeii and ▷Herculaneum. His *History of Ancient Art* (1764), which exalted Greek art of the 5th and 4th centuries BC and denigrated Roman art in comparison, pioneered modern art historiography.

● **wind** ▶ The horizontal movement of air over the earth's surface and one of the basic elements of weather. Thermal differences throughout the world produce variations in air pressure and air will flow generally from high-pressure to low-pressure areas. A wind is classified according to the direction from which it blows, i.e. a wind blowing from the S is a southerly wind. Its speed is usually measured in knots or in metres per second, actual velocities being measured by an anemometer, and it may be classified according to the ▷Beaufort scale. The major wind systems in the world include the trade winds and ▷westerlies. □trade winds; □meteorology.

● **Windermere** ▶ The largest lake in England, in Cumbria in the Lake District. It drains into Morecambe Bay through the River Leven. The lake is extensively used for watersports and the small town of Windermere on its NE shore is a popular holiday centre. Length: 17 km (10.5 mi).

● **wind farm** ▷See wind power.

● **Windhoek** ▶ 22 34S 17 06E The capital of Namibia. It is the centre of the world's karakul (Persian lamb) skin industry; other industries include meat canning and bone-meal production. Population (1997 est): 169 000.

● **wind instruments** ▶ Musical instruments in which notes are produced by a vibrating column of air. ▷Brass instruments are activated by lip pressure; ▷reed instruments employ double or single reed mouthpieces; the ▷flute is side blown; the ▷recorder has a mouthpiece and fipple (whistle hole); ▷organ pipes have air blown into them by mechanically activated bellows. *Compare* drums; percussion instruments; stringed instruments.

● **windmills** ▶ Machines in which the energy of the wind turns a set of vanes or sails mounted on a horizontal shaft, the rotation of which is transmitted by gearing to working machinery. Windmills had appeared by 1150 in NE Europe and were used for grinding corn, pumping water, and powering light industry, until they were superseded by steam engines in the 19th century. Two common designs were the Dutch mill, in which only the sails and the conical roof moved to catch the wind, and the German post mill, in which the whole millhouse with sails attached rotated around a central supporting pole. The modern metal windmill with multiple-bladed sails is found

all over the world in rural areas, pumping water or powering small electric generators. ▷See wind power.

● **windpipe** ▷See trachea.

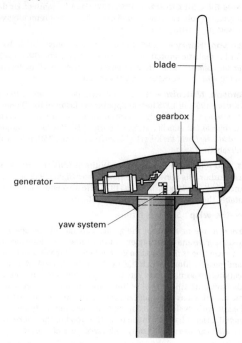

wind power ▶ A typical aerogenerator with a horizontal axis. The blades, rotated by the wind, drive the gearbox, which increases the number of revolutions to an efficient rate for the production of electricity by the generator. The yaw system turns the top of the structure to obtain the maximum amount of energy from the wind.

● **wind power** ▶ The use of wind energy to generate electricity. Because of the world shortage of conventional energy resources, wind turbines (aerogenerators), like other ▷alternative energy sources, have now become more attractive economically. Advantages of wind power are that it is free from pollution and uses no fuel. Disadvantages are that it must usually be supplemented by other schemes, including electricity storage, and the best sites are on open ground rather than in the cities, where most power is needed. Moreover, **wind farms** (groups of a few hundred wind turbines) occupy large areas of the countryside. For example, to produce 1 gigawatt of power (a modern nuclear power station produces about 1.2 GW) a farm would need to occupy nearly 400 sq km (150 sq mi).

There are several designs of aerogenerator: some with a horizontal axis and blades like the ▷windmill; some with specially shaped blades rotating on a vertical axis. In either case the power output is given by $\frac{1}{2}C\rho Av^3$, where C is a machine efficiency factor (usually 0.1–0.5), ρ is the air density, A is the area swept by the blades, and v is the wind speed. A considerable number of wind farms are now supplying the grid in the UK, USA, and elsewhere. California, for example, has a capacity of 1200 MW from wind energy. In the UK the renewables obligation (*see* alternative energy) will require a major increase in the number of wind farms. Small aerogenerators can be useful for isolated dwellings.

● **Windscale** ▷See Sellafield.

● **Windsor** ▶ 42 18N 83 00W A city and port in E Canada, in SW Ontario on the Detroit River opposite ▷Detroit. Settled in the 18th century by French colonists, it is a transportation and manufacturing centre, producing motor vehicles, foods, pharmaceuticals, machinery, and metals. Windsor is the centre of a rich farming district. The University of Windsor (1963) is situated here. Population (1991): 262 075 (metropolitan area).

● **Windsor** ▶ 51 29N 0 38W A town in SE England, in Windsor and

Maidenhead unitary authority, Berkshire; it is situated on the River Thames, opposite Eton. ▷Windsor Castle, a royal residence, dominates the town. Population (1991): 31 225.

● **Windsor, Duke and Duchess of** ▷See Edward VIII.

● **Windsor, House of** ► The name of Britain's royal family from 1917, when it replaced that of House of Saxe-Coburg-Gotha, of which Prince ▷Albert had been a member. In 1960 Elizabeth II declared that those of her descendants in the male line who were not princes or princesses would take the surname Mountbatten-Windsor, Mountbatten being Prince ▷Philip's surname.

● **Windsor and Maidenhead** ► A unitary authority in SE England, in Berkshire. Area: 197 sq km (76 sq mi). Population (1996 est): 141 500.

● **Windsor Castle** ► A royal residence in Windsor, Berkshire. It was begun by William the Conqueror as a stockaded earthwork. Many additions were made by subsequent monarchs, notably the keep by Henry III, St George's Chapel, an example of the ▷Perpendicular style, by Edward IV, and the Albert Memorial Chapel (so called by Queen Victoria) by Henry VII. Many monarchs are buried in these chapels. In the 16th and 17th centuries it began to be altered from a fortress to a palace, notably under Hugh May (1622–84) for Charles II, and later under Sir Jeffrey Wyatville (1766–1840) in the 19th century. It was damaged by fire in 1992.

● **windsurfing** ► A watersport in which the participant sails on a narrow board (resembling a surfboard) equipped with a mast and sail. The windsurfer steers the board with a hand-held crossbar, by which the sail is manoeuvred to catch the wind. Unlike surfing, successful windsurfing requires a calm expanse of water with no large waves.

● **wind tunnel** ► A device for testing the flow of air around an object, for example an aerofoil or aircraft, with a view to studying the lift, drag, streamlining, onset of ▷turbulence, etc. It consists of a duct with an electrically driven fan, usually with water-cooling systems to maintain the air at the correct temperature. ▷See also aerodynamics; aeronautics.

● **Windward Islands** ► (Spanish name: Islas de Barlovento) A West Indian group of islands forming part of the S Lesser Antilles. They comprise the islands of Martinique, St Lucia, St Vincent, the N Grenadines, and Grenada.

● **wine** ► An alcoholic drink made from fermented grape juice. The grapes are first crushed, traditionally by treading, now generally by machine. This process brings the yeast on the grapeskins, visible as the "bloom," into contact with the sugar in the juice, which it then converts into ethanol (ethyl alcohol). Depending upon whether the fermentation is stopped when all, part, or only a little of the sugar has been converted, the resulting wine is dry, medium, or sweet. Table wines contain about 9–13% alcohol. Fortified wines (e.g. ▷port, ▷sherry), to which a spirit is added at some stage in production, contain about 16–23% alcohol. The bubbles in sparkling wines are caused by a secondary fermentation in the bottle (see also champagne).

Wines may be red, white, or rosé. Red wines are made from whole grapes; for white wines the grapeskins are removed at an early stage in production. True rosé wines are made from the grenache grape, from which the skins are removed before the juice is deeply stained by them. Favoured varieties of wine grapes include Pinot, Cabernet, Hermitage, Riesling, and Sylvaner. The variety of grape, the soil of the vineyard, and the local climate govern a wine's quality. The appellation "vintage" is now used by wine producers under strictly regulated conditions to designate a wine of a particular year that shows outstanding quality.

French wines are famous for their quality and diversity, espcially those produced in Burgundy and the chateaux of the Bordeaux area (the red varieties of which are called clarets). Germany produces fine white wines (hocks). Italian wines are very diverse, including red Lambrusco, red or white Chianti, red Valpolicella, and sweet Marsala. Spain and other European countries produce notable wines. Wine is also made in South Africa (since 1688), Australia (first commercial vineyard established in 1827), California, Chile, and elsewhere. □ p. 1346.

● **Wingate, Orde Charles** ► (1903–44) British soldier, who led the ▷Chindits. A Zionist, he organized Jewish guerrillas in Palestine (1936–39). In World War II, after taking Addis Ababa from the Italians (1941), he formed the Chindits to disrupt communications behind the Japanese lines in Burma (now Myanmar). He was killed in an aircrash.

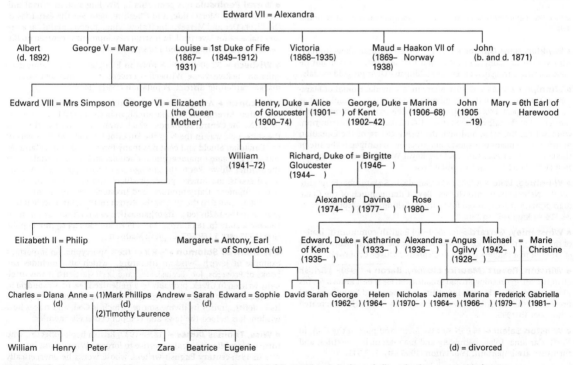

House of Windsor ► Members of the royal family who are descendants of Queen Victoria in the male line take the surname Windsor.

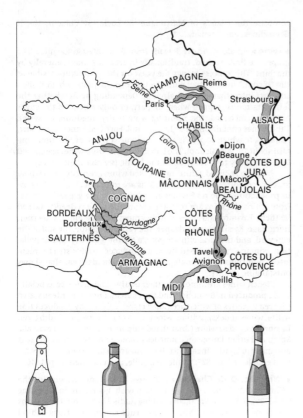

Champagne   Bordeaux   Burgundy   Alsatian white

wine ► The major French wine-producing regions and some standard bottle shapes.

● **Winkler, Hans Günter ►** (1926–) West German show jumper, who was world champion in 1954 and 1955 and won every major individual title during his career, also taking five Olympic gold medals.

● **Winnipeg ►** 49 53N 97 10W A city in W Canada, capital of Manitoba at the junction of the Assiniboine and Red Rivers. Established as a fur-trading post (1806), it expanded with the growth of farming and the arrival of the railway (1881) from E Canada. It is the distribution, wholesaling, financial, and manufacturing centre of the Canadian prairies and a major transportation junction. Winnipeg is the site of the University of Manitoba and the Royal Winnipeg Ballet. Population (1991): 652 354 (metropolitan area).

● **Winnipeg, Lake ►** A lake in W Canada, in S Manitoba. Emptying via the Nebon Rivers into Hudson Bay, it drains much of the Canadian prairies. It is exploited for tourism, fishing, and shipping. Area: 24 514 sq km (9465 sq mi).

● **Winstanley, Gerrard ►** (c. 1609–60) English communist, leader of the ▷Diggers (1649–50). He was the author of the pamphlet *The Law of Freedom in a Platform* (1652), dedicated to Oliver Cromwell.

● **Winston, Robert (Maurice Lipson), Baron ►** (1940–) British obstetrician, gynaecologist, and broadcaster. He is best known for his pioneering work on human infertility treatment and for writing and presenting the television series *The Human Body* (1998). He was created a life peer in 1995.

● **Winston Salem ►** 36 05N 80 18W A city and port in the USA, in North Carolina. Tobacco-growing and manufacturing, textiles, and furniture are important. Population (1996 est): 153 541.

● **winter aconite ►** An early-flowering perennial herb of the genus

Eranthis (7 species), native to temperate Europe, especially *E. hyemalis*, which is often grown in gardens. The flowers are cup-shaped, with six golden-yellow petals, and appear before the leaves. Family: ▷*Ranunculaceae*.

● **wintergreen ►** An evergreen creeping perennial herb or small shrub of the family *Pyrolaceae* (about 35 species), found in N temperate and arctic regions. The leaves are simple and the flowers are borne singly or in a terminal spike. They are white or pale-pink with five petals and the fruit is a capsule. **Oil of wintergreen** (methyl salicylate), used as a liniment to relieve muscular and rheumatic pain, comes from the leaves of the winterberry (*Gaultheria procumbens*), a North American shrub; the common wintergreen (*Pyrola minor*) is a herb of Eurasia and North America. Also in the family are the North American pipsissewas (genus *Chimaphila*), woodland herbs with leathery leaves and fragrant flowers.

● **Winterhalter, Franz Xavier ►** (1806–73) German painter and lithographer, famous for his portraits of European royalty. His sitters included Napoleon III and Queen Victoria and her family.

● **Winterthur ►** 47 30N 8 45E A city in N Switzerland. It is an industrial centre with heavy engineering and cotton textiles. Population (1994): 88 168.

● **Winter War** ▷*See* Russo-Finnish War.

● **Winthrop, John ►** (1588–1649) English colonizer; the first governor of the ▷Massachusetts Bay Colony (1629–33, 1637–39, 1642–43, 1646–48). His son, **John Winthrop** (1606–76), was one of the founders of Agawan (now Ipswich), Massachusetts. In 1662 he effected Massachusetts' union with Connecticut and New Haven. His scientific interests gained him a fellowship of the Royal Society in 1663.

● **wirehaired pointing griffon ►** A breed of hunting dog developed in France during the late 19th century. It is strongly built with a short tail and a square muzzle. The bristly coat is a mixture of grey, white, and brown. Height: 54–59 cm (dogs); 49–54 cm (bitches).

● **wireworm** ▷*See* click beetle.

● **Wirral ►** A unitary authority in NW England, in Merseyside. Area: 158 sq km (61 sq mi). Population (1999 est): 330 795.

● **Wirral Peninsula ►** A peninsula in NW England, in Wirral unitary authority (Merseyside) and Cheshire, between the estuaries of the Rivers Dee and Mersey. Chiefly low-lying, it serves mainly as a residential area for Liverpool. Industrial development is centred on Birkenhead, Port Sunlight, and Ellesmere Port.

● **Wisbech ►** 52 40N 0 10E A town in E England, in N Cambridgeshire on the River Nene. Wisbech is a river port and market town in a market-gardening district. Population (1991): 24 981.

● **Wisconsin ►** A state in the N central USA, situated between the Mississippi River in the W, Lake Michigan in the E, and Lake Superior in the N. The Central Lowlands, which cover the lower two-thirds of the state, give way in the N to the Superior Upland, which is part of the Canadian Shield and contains many forests and lakes. Manufacturing is the state's major economic activity and its industrial belt in the SE links Milwaukee to the Chicago area. Leading products include metal goods, machinery, paper products, and electrical and transport equipment. Dairy products and livestock are important.

History: ceded to the USA by the British in 1783, large-scale immigration in the 1820s led to its organization as a territory (1836) and it became a state in 1848. Area: 145 438 sq km (56 154 sq mi). Population (1997 est): 5 169 677. Capital: Madison.

● **Wisdom of Solomon ►** Book of the ▷Apocrypha, an important example of Jewish "wisdom literature," which also includes the books of Proverbs, Job, Ecclesiastes, and Ecclesiasticus. It was originally written in Greek, probably by a Hellenized Jew of Alexandria in the 2nd century BC. In encouraging a search for wisdom, it describes its benefits, praises its divine source, which is God, and traces how wisdom has helped the Jews and confounded their enemies.

● **Wise, Thomas James ►** (1859–1937) British book collector, who turned his bibliographical expertise to forgery. Wise's main interest was in 19th-century English writers, whose works he energetically collected. He issued numerous catalogues and received academic honours, but in 1934 his forgeries of certain rare pamphlets were exposed.

● **Wiseman, Nicholas Patrick Stephen ►** (1802–65) British Roman Catholic prelate, born in Seville of Irish parents. Appointed rector of the English College in Rome in 1828, he later devoted himself to reviving Roman Catholicism in England. In 1850 he was made a cardinal and the first Archbishop of Westminster.

● **wisent** ▷*See* bison.

● **Wishart, George ►** (c. 1513–46) Scottish Protestant reformer and martyr. Charged with heresy in 1538, he fled to England and in 1539 to the Continent, where he translated into Scots the *First Helvetic Confession*. He later preached in many Scottish towns, converting, among others, John ▷Knox. At the instigation of Cardinal Beaton he was tried for heresy and burnt at the stake at St Andrews, in 1546.

● **Wiślany Zalew** ▷*See* Vistula Lagoon.

● **Wismar ►** 53 54N 11 23E A town and Baltic port in N Germany. Once a Hanseatic port, it passed to Sweden under the Peace of ▷Westphalia (1648). Although pledged to Mecklenburg-Schwerin in 1803, Sweden did not renounce all rights to the city until 1903. Its industries include shipbuilding, fishing, and sugar refining. Population (1991): 54 470.

● **Wissler, Clark ►** (1870–1947) US anthropologist. Professor of anthropology at Yale University (1924–40), Wissler was famous for his research on the geographical and regional aspects of race and culture. His best-known book is *The American Indian* (1917).

● **Wisteria ►** A genus of twining usually woody vines (10 species), native to E Asia and North America and grown as ornamentals, especially *W. floribunda* from Japan, which may reach a height of 30 m. The compound leaves have paired pointed leaflets and the flowers, usually purple, are borne in large hanging clusters, up to 90 cm long. Family: ▷*Leguminosae*.

● **witan ►** A body of 30 to 40 high-ranking laymen and ecclesiastics, which advised Anglo-Saxon kings on such major policy matters as foreign policy and taxation. It met only at the king's will and had no fixed procedure. As a court, it decided on cases affecting the king and other important persons.

● **Witbank ►** 25 53S 29 13E A town in NE South Africa, the centre of an important coalmining area. Population (latest est): 83 400.

● **witchcraft ►** The supposed manipulation of natural events by persons using supernatural means. In Europe the biblical injunction "Thou shalt not suffer a witch to live" (Exodus 22.18) sanctioned widespread persecution. Social and religious upheavals in the 16th and 17th centuries brought an upsurge in witch hunts; the famous outbreak at Salem, Massachusetts (1692), is a paradigm case of witch hysteria. Witches were accused of worshipping the devil at nocturnal orgies (sabbaths), of keeping evil spirits (familiars), and of killing livestock, wrecking crops, and causing barrenness, impotence, and fits. Many traditional African communities hold witchcraft accountable for a similar range of inexplicable misfortunes. It is countered by witch-doctors who identify witches and suggest means of neutralizing their malign psychic powers. ▷*See also* magic.

● **witch hazel ►** A shrub or small tree of the genus *Hamamelis* (6 species), native to E Asia and North America, especially the American *H. virginiana*, which is the source of witch-hazel lotion used in pharmacy. This and several other species are often grown as ornamentals, having small clusters of attractive yellow flowers, each with four strap-shaped petals. The fruit is a woody capsule surrounded by a yellow cuplike calyx. Family: *Hamamelidaceae*.

● **witchweed ►** A parasitic herb of the genus *Striga* (about 10 species), native to the Old World tropics. Up to 75 cm tall, it has rough narrow sometimes scalelike leaves and solitary blue, purple, red, yellow, or white two-lipped flowers. The roots derive nutrients from the roots of other plants, including many crop plants. Family: *Scrophulariaceae*.

● **Witt, Johan de ►** (1625–72) Dutch statesman, chief minister of the United Provinces of the Netherlands (1653–72). He ended the first ▷Dutch War and then improved the Dutch navy, which performed

well in the second Dutch War. However, he lost his struggle to limit the executive power of the stadholder (William III of Orange and later of England) and resigned in 1672. He was killed by a rioting mob.

● **Witte, Sergei Yulievich ►** (1849–1915) Russian statesman. As finance minister (1892–1903) Witte initiated the Russian industrial revolution, making capital available to industry and obtaining foreign loans. He greatly encouraged railway construction. As prime minister (1905–06), he was instrumental in founding the ▷Duma following the Revolution of 1905.

● **Wittelsbach ►** The ruling dynasty of Bavaria and the Rhine Palatinate. Wittelsbachs ruled these German states from the late 12th century until deposed in 1918 in a republican coup.

● **Wittenberg ►** 53 00N 11 41E A town in E Germany, on the River ▷Elbe. The Reformation began here on 31 October, 1517, when Martin Luther nailed his 95 theses to the door of All Saints Church. The town is an important industrial centre. Population (1991): 87 000.

● **Wittgenstein, Ludwig ►** (1889–1951) Austrian philosopher. After studying engineering in Vienna he turned to philosophy, studying under Bertrand ▷Russell at Cambridge (1912–13), where he eventually succeeded G. E. ▷Moore as professor. His two major works are the *Tractatus Logico-philosophicus* (1921) and the posthumously published *Philosophical Investigations* (1953). Wittgenstein's abiding preoccupation was with language, particularly with the problems that language's relationship to things poses for the philosopher. In his earlier work he developed the "picture theory" of language—words represent things by established conventions—but later he developed the more sophisticated "game" or "toolkit" models, in which actual usage is more important than set convention. This approach to language as a predominantly social phenomenon has been enormously influential among English-speaking philosophers.

● **Witwatersrand ►** (or the Rand) A ridge of hills in NE South Africa. It extends about 160 km (99 mi) chiefly W of Johannesburg, forming the watershed between the Limpopo and Orange river systems. It has been worked for gold since the 1880s and now produces about one-third of the world's gold output.

● **WMO** ▷*See* World Meteorological Organization.

● **woad ►** A branching perennial or biennial herb, *Isatis tinctoria*, native to central and S Europe. Formerly cultivated for the blue dye extracted from its crushed leaves, it is now rare. Up to 120 cm tall, it has narrow leaves and terminal branching clusters of tiny four-petalled yellow flowers. Family: ▷*Cruciferae*.

● **Wodehouse, Sir P(elham) G(renville) ►** (1881–1975) British-born humorous writer, who became a US citizen in 1955. After 1909 he lived mostly abroad. In his many comic novels featuring Bertie Wooster and his manservant Jeeves, including *The Inimitable Jeeves* (1923) and *The Code of the Woosters* (1938), he portrayed an English upper-class society fixed forever in the 1920s.

● **Woden** ▷*See* Odin.

● **Woffington, Peg ►** (Margaret W.; c. 1714–60) Irish actress. She acted in many Restoration comedies at Covent Garden, often taking male parts. She became the mistress and leading lady of David ▷Garrick.

● **Wöhler, Friedrich ►** (1800–82) German chemist, who, while professor of chemistry at Göttingen University, synthesized urea from ammonium cyanate (1828). This was the first organic compound to have been derived from an inorganic compound, providing evidence against the theory that organic compounds contained a "vital force" absent in inorganic compounds. He also succeeded in isolating the elements aluminium, beryllium, and titanium.

● **Wokingham ►** A unitary authority in SE England, in Berkshire. Area: 179 sq km (69 sq mi). Population (1996 est): 142 400.

● **wolf ►** A wild ▷dog, *Canis lupus*, of Eurasia and North America. Wolves are 140–190 cm long including the tail (30–55 cm). They live in packs of 5–30 animals—which patrol their own territories—and feed mainly on mice, fish, and carrion but also attack deer. Mating is often for life and both parents may share in rearing the pups. Wolves in colder climate are generally larger and shaggier and form bigger packs. There is an almost white N Siberian race, while the Indian pale-footed wolf is small and grey. ▷See also timber wolf. □mammal.

• **Wolf, Hugo** ▶ (1860–1903) Austrian composer. He studied briefly at the Vienna conservatoire and earned his living as a teacher, conductor, and critic. He died insane in an asylum. He wrote 300 *Lieder* (many of which were settings of poems by Goethe and Mörike), the opera *Der Corregidor* (1895), and an *Italian Serenade* for string quartet.

• **Wolfe, Charles** ▶ (1791–1823) Irish poet and clergyman. He is remembered for a single poem, "The Burial of Sir John Moore at Corunna," commemorating the British general who died in the Peninsular War.

• **Wolfe, James** ▶ (1727–59) British soldier. He distinguished himself against the Jacobites in the 1740s and after the outbreak of the Seven Years' War was sent to Canada. He excelled, under ▷Amherst, in the capture of Louisberg from the French (1758) and in the following year he besieged ▷Montcalm in Quebec. His forces scaled the undefended Heights of Abraham from the St Lawrence and a pitched battle ensued in which both commanders were killed. The British victory established their supremacy in Canada.

• **Wolfe, Thomas** ▶ (1900–38) US novelist. After abandoning an attempt to become a dramatist, he wrote four long and lyrically powerful novels, beginning with *Look Homeward, Angel* (1929), all based on autobiographical material. The final two were published posthumously.

• **Wolfenden, John Frederick, Baron** ▶ (1906–85) British educationalist and government offical. Vice chancellor of Reading University (1950–63) and director of the British Museum (1969–73), Wolfenden chaired the Committee on Homosexual Offences and Prostitution; the **Wolfenden Report** (1957) recommended that private homosexual acts between consenting adults be legalized.

• **Wolf-Ferrari, Ermanno** ▶ (1876–1948) Italian composer of German-Italian parentage. He spent most of his life in Venice, composing such operas as *The School for Fathers* (1906) and *Susanna's Secret* (1909).

• **wolf fish** ▶ A slender marine fish, *Anarhichas lupus*, also called catfish, found in the N Atlantic and North Sea, down to 300 m. It has a blue-green or greenish body up to 120 cm long, with dark vertical bars, a long blunt head, doglike teeth, long dorsal and anal fins, and no pelvic fins. It feeds on bottom-dwelling hard-shelled animals. Family: *Anarhichadidae*; order: *Perciformes*.

• **Wölfflin, Heinrich** ▶ (1864–1945) Swiss art historian. A pupil of Jakob Burckhardt (1818–97), Wölfflin wrote chiefly on baroque and classical art. He was the principal exponent of the formal school of art historians, which analyses style by changes of form in art.

• **wolfhound** ▷See borzoi; Irish wolfhound.

• **Wolfit, Sir Donald** ▶ (1902–68) British actor and manager. He acted all the major Shakespearean roles, receiving especial acclaim for his Lear, first performed in 1943. In 1937 he founded his own touring company. He was knighted in 1957.

• **wolfram** ▷See tungsten.

• **wolframite** ▶ The principal ore of tungsten, consisting of ferrous tungstate, $(Fe,Mn)WO_4$. It is brown, black, grey, or reddish in colour and is found particularly in quartz veins associated with granitic rocks. ▷See also scheelite.

• **Wolfram von Eschenbach** ▶ (c. 1170–c. 1220) German poet. A knight, he served at several courts. His great romance, *Parzifal* (c. 1212), is the first German work to use the story of the Holy Grail and is the basis of Wagner's opera. Allegorizing man's spiritual development, it tells how the innocent fool becomes the wise keeper of the Grail.

• **wolfsbane** ▷See aconite.

• **Wolfsburg** ▶ 52 27N 10 49E A city in N Germany, in Lower Saxony on the Mittelland Canal. Founded in 1938, it grew around the Volkswagen car factory. Population (1996 est): 126 331.

• **Wolfson, Sir Isaac** ▶ (1897–1991) British businessman, who founded (1946) Great Universal Stores Ltd. A philanthropist, he endowed the Wolfson Foundation in 1955 for the advancement of health, education, and youth in the UK and the Commonwealth. University College, Cambridge, was renamed Wolfson College in 1973 after a grant from the Wolfson Foundation; Wolfson College, Oxford, was founded in 1966 with grants from the Wolfson and Ford Foundations. Both colleges are for graduate students.

• **wolf spider** ▶ A ▷spider, also called hunting spider, belonging to a widespread family (*Lycosidae*; over 175 species). Wolf spiders, up to 25 mm long, are dark brown with long stout legs and live on or in the ground, often in specially constructed tubes. They are usually active at night, hunting prey rather than trapping it in webs. The female carries the eggs and young.

• **Wollongong, Greater** ▶ 34 25S 150 52E A city in Australia, in New South Wales. It comprises an extensive urban area, extending 48 km (30 mi) along the coast and including the towns of Wollongong, Bulli, and Port Kembla. Many industries are based on the rich Bulli coal deposits, including metal processing, engineering, and chemicals. A university was established in 1975. Population (1991): 236 010.

• **Wollstonecraft, Mary** ▶ (1759–97) British writer. She was a member of a group of political radicals that included Tom Paine and her husband, the social philosopher William ▷Godwin. Her best-known work is *A Vindication of the Rights of Woman* (1792), which argued for equal opportunities for all in education. She died from blood poisoning after giving birth to her daughter, who became Mary ▷Shelley.

• **Wolseley, Garnet Joseph, 1st Viscount** ▶ (1833–1913) British field marshal. He fought in the Crimean War and against the Indian Mutiny in the 1850s and suppressed an Egyptian rebellion with his victory at Tall-all Kabir (1882). In 1884 he led the expedition to rescue Gordon in Khartoum. His chief importance lies in his army reforms, which completed ▷Cardwell's work.

• **Wolsey, Thomas, Cardinal** ▶ (c. 1475–1530) English churchman and statesman; Lord Chancellor (1515–29) under Henry VIII. He entered Henry's service in 1509 and became (1514) Bishop of Lincoln and then Archbishop of York and (1515) a cardinal. He used his position to amass a huge personal fortune that did much on the eve of the Reformation to bring the Church into disrepute. As chancellor he attempted to make England a significant European power and interfered unsuccessfully in the conflict between Francis I of France and Emperor ▷Charles V. Wolsey's attempts to raise taxes to pay for his foreign policy encountered violent opposition. He fell from power after failing to persuade the pope to annul Henry's marriage to Catherine of Aragon and died on his way to face trial in London. He founded Cardinal's College (later Christ Church) at Oxford.

• **Wolverhampton** ▶ 1. 52 36N 2 08W A city in central England, in Wolverhampton unitary authority, West Midlands. Metalworking and engineering are the principal industries. Traditionally known for locks and keys, it also produces bicycles, tools, hardware, and chemicals. It was granted city status in 2000. Population (1996 est): 244 500. 2. A unitary authority in W central England, in West Midlands. Area: 69 sq km (27 sq mi). Population (1996 est): 244 500.

• **wolverine** ▶ A carnivorous mammal, *Gulo gulo*, also called glutton, inhabiting northern evergreen forests of Europe, Asia, and America. It is heavily built, about 1 m long and weighing about 25 kg, and hunts alone, typically ambushing lemmings and hares (although it can overcome an old or unfit reindeer). Family: ▷Mustelidae.

• **womb** ▶ (or uterus) The part of the reproductive tract of female mammals (including women) in which the embryo or fetus develops (see Plate II). The womb is a hollow muscular organ, about 7.5 cm long in the absence of pregnancy. It is connected by the vagina to the outside and to the ovaries by the Fallopian tubes. In a nonpregnant woman the lining of the womb is shed at monthly intervals (see menstruation). During ▷childbirth the womb, which is greatly enlarged (about 30 cm long), undergoes strong contractions to expel the baby. ▷See also cervix.

• **wombat** ▶ A bearlike ▷marsupial belonging to the family

Phascolomidae (2–3 species), of Australia (including Tasmania). The coarse-haired wombat (*Phascolomis ursinus*) is about 1 m long and has short powerful legs with strong claws, which it uses for tunnelling underground. It feeds on grass, roots, and tree bark.

● **Women's Institutes, National Federation of** ▶ A British organization founded in 1915 to develop the quality, chiefly through further education, of rural life for women. The British women's institutes were closely modelled on those established in Canada by Adelaide Hoodless (from 1897). Local institutes meet monthly to hear talks on a wide range of subjects. The Federation has a residential college, where short courses are organized, and its members run some 300 cooperative markets throughout the UK.

● **Women's Land Army** ▶ An organization of women set up in Britain in 1916 to provide agricultural workers to replace the men who had joined the services in World War I. Disbanded after the Armistice in 1918, it reformed in 1939 to provide (by 1943) an army of some 87 000 "land girls" (as they were called) to work on farms. With food imports drastically reduced and the great majority of young farm workers in the services, the supply of food in Britain during the war could not have been maintained without them.

women's movement ▶ A demonstration by suffragettes in 1905 to promote their magazine *Votes for Women*.

● **women's movement** ▶ The social movement towards changing the subordinate role of women in society. Mary ▷Wollstonecraft, author of *A Vindication of the Rights of Woman* (1792), was a pioneer of the movement. In the USA the early feminist movement was closely associated with antislavery agitation, while in 19th-century Europe the analysis and criticism of the position of women in the family grew alongside emerging concepts of ▷socialism. In the UK the suffragist movement encompassed both those who sought votes for women on the limited property qualifications then applied to men and those, such as Sylvia ▷Pankhurst and Keir ▷Hardie, who sought universal adult suffrage. From 1903 the Women's Social and Political Union (WSPU), led by Emmeline and Christabel Pankhurst, was at the forefront of the movement. Its militant members, known as **suffragettes**, attacked property, refused to pay taxes, and staged public demonstrations, for which they were repeatedly imprisoned. The notorious "Cat and Mouse Act" (1913) allowed for the temporary release of suffragettes whose health was endangered by hunger striking and forcible feeding.

During World War I the women's organizations directed themselves to supporting the war effort and in 1918 the vote was granted to women aged 30 and over, subject to educational and property qualifications that were removed in 1928, making men and women politically equal. The present women's movement emerged in the 1960s; in the USA small "consciousness-raising" groups were formed and, in the UK, the **Women's Liberation Workshop** was established in London (1969) as a coordinating centre for local women's groups. In 1971 the first four basic demands of the movement (equal pay, equal educational and job opportunities, free contraception and abortion on demand, and 24-hour nurseries) were launched. Several legal reforms have been achieved in the UK, notably the Equal Pay Act (1970) and the Sex Discrimination Acts (1975 and 1986), which included setting up the Equal Opportunities Commission to promote equality of opportunity between men and women. The 1970s saw the establishment of refuges for battered wives, rape crisis centres, women's health clinics, etc. Women's groups in the UK now range from self-help groups for victims of sexual abuse to societies for successful businesswomen. Worldwide, there are women's movements campaigning against female infanticide, forced prostitution, and poor maternity care.

● **Women's Royal Voluntary Service** ▶ A British organization founded in 1938 as the Women's Voluntary Service (WVS). Its members work for local authorities or on national government schemes and perform many voluntary welfare services, including Meals on Wheels, which provides for the delivery of meals to those unable to shop and cook for themselves.

● **Wŏnsan** ▶ 39 20N 127 25E A port in SE North Korea, on the Sea of Japan. Badly damaged during the Korean War (1950–53), its industries have since been rebuilt and include oil refining, shipbuilding, railway engineering, and chemicals. Population (latest est): 274 000.

● **wood** ▶ The hard tissue of the stems and branches of trees and shrubs, beneath the bark, consisting of ▷xylem cells strengthened with deposits of lignin. The newest xylem—sapwood—is essential for transport of water and nutrients up the tree. As the xylem ages lignin is deposited within the cells, which eventually die. The central part of the trunk—heartwood—consists of dead xylem, which is darker than sapwood due to deposits of tannins and resins. Conifers are referred to as softwoods because the xylem is porous; broad-leaved (angiosperm) trees, which are called hardwoods, contain more fibres and are therefore stronger (*see* timber). □plant.

● **Wood** ▶ A family of English potters working in Staffordshire (England) in the 18th and 19th centuries. Related by marriage to Josiah ▷Wedgwood, the most famous member **Ralph Wood I** (1715–72) trained under John ▷Astbury; he established a factory at Burslem, where he specialized in earthenware figure groups and made the first ▷Toby jug (1762). His cousin **Aaron Wood** (1717–85) was employed by many Staffordshire potters as a modeller. Ralph's business was carried on by his son **Ralph Wood II** (1748–95) and later by his nephew **Enoch Wood** (1759–1840), who was famous for his pottery busts of Shakespeare, Wesley, Handel, etc. The business closed down in 1846.

● **Wood** ▶ A family of English architects, known for their contribution to town planning and urban classical architecture. They mainly worked in Bath, which **John Wood the Elder** (1704–54) began to develop in the late 1720s. In residential streets, such as Queen Square (1729–36) and the Circus (begun in 1754) he extended the classical form to link many buildings into one architectural block. His work was continued by his son **John Wood the Younger** (1728–81), who designed the famous Royal Crescent (1767–75) and the Assembly Rooms (1769–71).

● **Wood, Sir Henry (Joseph)** ▶ (1869–1944) British conductor. He was an organist and composer but is remembered for the London Promenade concerts, which he established at the Queen's Hall, London, and which continued at the Albert Hall after the Queen's Hall was bombed in World War II.

● **Wood, Mrs Henry** ▶ (1814–87) British novelist. The most famous of her popular melodramatic novels is *East Lynne* (1861), concerning an upper-class wife who returns in disguise to her family after an unhappy love affair; it was repeatedly dramatized. From 1867 she edited the magazine *Argosy*.

● **wood alcohol** ▷*See* methanol.

● **woodbine** ▷*See* honeysuckle; Virginia creeper.

● **wood carving** ► The art of carving sculptures or architectural and furniture decoration in wood. It has been practised universally since ancient times. ▷African art principally consists of wood carving. In Europe some of the finest decorative wood carving was achieved in medieval churches. The best-known British decorative carver was Grinling ▷Gibbons. In the 20th century sculptors, such as ▷Brancusi and Henry ▷Moore, have exploited the special characteristics of wood—its vertical graining and organic nature—in the trend towards retaining the inherent characteristics of materials in finished sculptures.

● **woodchat** ► A small ▷shrike, *Lanius senator*, occurring in wooded Mediterranean regions. The male has dark wings, back, and tail patches, white underparts, a chestnut neck and cap, and a broad black band across the forehead; the female is duller.

● **woodchuck** ▷*See* marmot.

● **woodcock** ► A Eurasian gamebird, *Scolopax rusticola*, occurring in dense damp woodland and generally active at night. It has a stocky body, 34 cm long, and a russet plumage with a dark-barred head and underparts and a white-tipped tail. Woodcocks have long bills and feed on worms and insect larvae. Males perform a display flight during courtship. Family: *Scolopacidae* (sandpipers, snipe).

● **woodcreeper** ► An arboreal passerine bird belonging to a family (*Dendrocolaptidae*; 48 species) ranging through Central and South America. Woodcreepers are typically 20–30 cm long and have stout bills, powerful feet with long claws, and an olive-brown plumage with pale stripes on the head and underparts. The tail is stiff, providing support when it climbs spirally up trees, prising off bark and probing in crevices for insects and spiders.

● **woodcut** ► A relief ▷printing technique. The design is drawn on the surface of a block of wood, all the undrawn parts being cut away to produce the white areas of the print. The design is then transferred to paper by pressing the inked block onto the paper. The woodcut was used in China (c. 5th century AD) for textile design but its history in Europe dates from the 14th century and is closely connected with the early printed book. Its special qualities—cheapness, boldness, and simplicity—made it particularly suitable for popular book illustration. Leading 16th-century German artists, such as ▷Dürer and ▷Holbein the Younger, used the medium to supreme effect. Although subsequently used for book illustration, it was only revived as an art form in the late 19th century by ▷Gauguin and ▷Munch.

● **wood engraving** ► A technique of printing images, refined in the 18th century by Thomas Bewick and used extensively during the 19th century for reproductive engraving. Original modern practitioners include Eric ▷Gill. The surface of the woodblock is cut away to leave raised areas which, when treated with ink, will appear dark when printed, in contrast to the white line of the incised areas. Boxwood is used for its fine grain, the block being cut transversely. Wood engraving produces a more subtle effect than ▷woodcut.

● **woodlouse** ► A terrestrial crustacean of the suborder *Oniscoidea*, found in damp shady places under stones, logs, etc. Woodlice have a body covering of armour-like plates: they can breathe air (through specially modified gills) but require damp surroundings to avoid desiccation. A common species is the pill bug or woodlouse (*Armadillidium vulgare*), about 17 mm long, which rolls into a ball when disturbed. It has spread from Europe to occur in leaf litter in wooded areas all over the world. Common genera: *Oniscus*, *Porcellio*; order: ▷*Isopoda*.

● **wood oil** ▷*See* tung oil.

● **woodpecker** ► A bird belonging to a family (*Picidae*; about 220 species) occurring worldwide except Madagascar, Australia, and New Zealand (*see* Plate III). 9–57 cm long, woodpeckers have multicoloured plumage, often barred or spotted. Most are exclusively arboreal, chiselling through bark with their long straight bills in search of insects, which are extracted with a long sticky protrusible tongue. Their short strong feet with large claws and the stiff wedge-shaped tail are adaptations for climbing. ▷*See also* ivory-billed woodpecker; wryneck.

● **wood pigeon** ► A large Eurasian ▷pigeon, *Columba palumbus*, which is a serious pest on farmland, eating grain and other crops. 40 cm long, it has a predominantly grey plumage with a black-tipped

tail, brownish back and wings, white wing patches, and a green, purple, and white neck patch.

● **woodrush** ► A grasslike perennial plant of the genus *Luzula* (about 80 species), occurring chiefly in cold N temperate regions. The Eurasian great woodrush (*L. sylvatica*) has leaves up to 30 cm long and 2 cm wide, which are fringed with colourless hairs. Family: *Juncaceae* (rush family).

● **Woods, Tiger** ► (Eldrick W.; 1975–) US golfer. He was three times US amateur champion before turning professional in 1996. In 1997 he became the youngest Masters champion and the first Black golfer to win a major championship. In 2000 he became the youngest player to win the Grand Slam of all four major competitions and in 2001 the only player to hold all four titles at once.

● **wood sorrel** ► A herbaceous plant of the genus *Oxalis* (about 800 species), of temperate and tropical regions, especially *O. acetosella*, of Europe. This species has compound three-part leaves (made up of heart-shaped leaflets) and solitary white five-petalled flowers. Many species are ornamentals and some, including the vegetable oca (*O. tuberosa*), have edible tubers. Family: *Oxalidaceae*.

● **Woodstock** ► 51 52N 1 21W A small market town in S central England, in Oxfordshire. Nearby is ▷Blenheim Palace; an earlier royal palace at Woodstock was destroyed after the Civil War. Population (1991): 2898.

● **Woodstock** ► 42 02N 74 08W A town in the NE USA, in New York state in the Catskill Mountains. It has been an artists' colony since 1906. The Woodstock Music and Art Fair (1969), a free rock festival attended by some 400 000 people, was held nearby. Population (1990): 1870.

woodpecker ► A green woodpecker (*Picus viridis*) at its nest hole with a chick demanding food.

● **Woodville, Elizabeth** ▶ (c. 1437–92) The wife from 1464 of Edward IV of England. Royal patronage of her family caused dissensions among Edward's Yorkist supporters and on his death (1483) the power of the Woodvilles was undermined by the Duke of Gloucester, who deposed Elizabeth's son Edward V and became Richard III. Elizabeth was retired to a convent.

● **Woodward, Robert Burns** ▶ (1917–79) US chemist, who, while working at Harvard, won the 1965 Nobel Prize for his syntheses of a number of organic compounds. His first success was his synthesis of quinine in 1944. He then went on to synthesize strychnine, cortisone, cholesterol, and chlorophyll as well as an antibiotic.

● **woodwasp** ▶ A ▷sawfly belonging to the families *Xiphydriidae* (Europe and North America), *Sytexidae* (North America), or *Orussidae* (worldwide). *Xiphydriidae* larvae bore into deciduous trees, such as alder, birch, and maple. *Sytexidae* are restricted to the incense cedar tree. *Orussidae* larvae are external parasites on wood-dwelling beetle larvae. ▷*See also* horntail.

● **woodwind instruments** ▶ Blown musical instruments in which a column of air is made to vibrate either by blowing across a mouth hole, as in the flute, or by making a single or a double reed vibrate, as in the oboe, bassoon, clarinet, and saxophone. The length of the vibrating column is varied by opening and closing holes, either with the finger or by means of keys.

● **woodworm** ▶ A wood-boring beetle of the genus *Anobium*, especially the furniture beetle (*A. punctatum*), 5 mm long, which damages furniture and old buildings. The larvae bore into wood and emerge when adult, leaving large numbers of holes. Family: *Anobiidae*.

● **Wookey Hole** ▶ A village named after a nearby limestone cavern in the Mendip Hills near Wells in Somerset. Bones of Palaeolithic man and animals, together with flint implements, show that the cave was inhabited over a long period. Population (latest est): 1000.

● **wool** ▶ Fibres obtained from the fleeces of domestic sheep. Elastic, resilient, and absorbent, it is also an excellent insulator because of its bulk, the result of its curliness (crimp). The fleeces of different breeds vary widely. ▷Merino wool is the best in quality; it is short, fine, soft, and the most crimpy. It now comes chiefly from Australia, South Africa, South America, and the USA. Garments labelled "Pure New Wool" are 100% merino. Wools from the 26 British breeds vary widely, while New Zealand sheep are crossbreeds of merino and British; durable and resilient, British and New Zealand wools are used, for example, in ▷tweeds and blankets. Being coarse and strong, the wool of Asian sheep and mountain breeds is used chiefly for carpets. Since World War II synthetic fibres have been mixed with wool.

● **Woolf, (Adeline) Virginia** ▶ (*born* Stephen; 1882–1941) British novelist. A central figure of the ▷Bloomsbury group, she developed an impressionistic style in which she attempted to express the essential fluidity of existence. Her novels include *Mrs Dalloway* (1925), *To the Lighthouse* (1927), and *The Waves* (1931). She also wrote biographies and criticism, including a series of essays entitled *The Common Reader* (1925–32). She committed suicide by drowning after the recurrence of a mental illness. Her husband **Leonard (Sidney) Woolf** (1880–1969), whom she married in 1912 and with whom she founded the Hogarth Press in 1917, was literary editor of the *Nation* (1923–30) and wrote five volumes of autobiography (1960–69).

● **Woollcott, Alexander** ▶ (1887–1943) US writer, critic, and broadcaster. A leading wit of the ▷Algonquin Round Table, he was theatre critic (1914–22) of the *New York Times* and a regular contributor to the *New Yorker* magazine. His book *While Rome Burns* (1934) became a bestseller.

● **Woollett, William** ▶ (1735–85) British engraver. He engraved topographical plates and after 1760 paintings by Claude. He achieved a wide reputation with his engraving (1776) after Benjamin ▷West's *Death of General Wolfe*.

● **Woolley, Sir Leonard** ▶ (1880–1960) British archaeologist. He worked at ▷Carchemish and ▷Tell el-Amarna but is famous chiefly for his excavations at ▷Ur (1922–34), his popular accounts of which stimulated widespread interest in the archaeology of the biblical lands.

● **woolly bear** ▷*See* tiger moth.

● **woolly monkey** ▶ A large long-tailed monkey belonging to the genus *Lagothrix* (3 species), of South America. The smoky woolly monkey (*L. cana*) has short pale hair and dark head, arms, legs, and tail. Males may grow to 120 cm long including the tail (60–70 cm). They have strong teeth and jaws and feed on fruit, leaves and unripe nuts. Family: *Cebidae*.

● **woolly rhinoceros** ▶ A rhinoceros belonging to the extinct genus *Coelodonta*, which inhabited Eurasia and North Africa during the Pleistocene epoch (2.5 million to 10 000 years ago). Well-preserved specimens show that it was a large shaggy-coated animal with two horns, the front one very long and sharp.

● **woolly spider monkey** ▶ A rare monkey, *Brachyteles arachnoides*, of SE Brazil. It has long legs, short woolly fur, and a prehensile tail and is thought to be arboreal and vegetarian. Family: *Cebidae*.

● **woolsack** ▶ A large red cushion, stuffed with wool, that is the seat of the Lord Chancellor when acting as speaker of the House of Lords. It is supposed to have been placed there in the middle ages, when the wool trade was important.

● **Woolwich** ▶ A district mainly in the Greater London borough of Greenwich, on the River Thames. It was an important Tudor dockyard and naval base. It contains the Royal Arsenal (founded in 1805).

● **Woolworth, F(rank) W(infield)** ▶ (1852–1919) US businessman, who created a chain of over a thousand shops across the USA selling low-priced goods. The first was opened in 1879 in Utica, New York. The Woolworth Building in New York, which he commissioned, was the world's tallest building (1913–30). He also opened stores in many other countries, including the UK.

● **Woomera** ▶ 31 11S 136 54E A town in central South Australia. The site of the Long Range Weapons Establishment, it has been used as a launching base for space satellites. Population (latest est): 1805.

● **Wootton, Barbara, Baroness** ▶ (1897–1988) British educationalist and economist. She worked in the fields of politics, social welfare, and penal reform and was the author of such books as *Social Science and Social Pathology* (1959).

● **Worcester** ▶ 42 17N 71 48W A city in the USA, in Massachusetts on the Blackstone River. Settled in 1673, textile manufacturing began in 1789 and the country's first corduroy cloth was produced here. The Free-Soil Party, opposing the extension of slavery, developed from a meeting here in 1848. A cultural and educational centre, it is the site of Clark University (1887). Manufactures include precision instruments and chemicals. Population (2000): 172 648.

● **Worcester** ▶ 52 11N 2 13W A city in W central England, the administrative centre of Worcestershire on the River Severn. The cathedral, begun in 1084, is mainly 14th-century. At the Battle of Worcester (1651) Charles II was defeated by Cromwell. It is traditionally associated with porcelain, sauce, gloves, and engineering but now has a diverse service-based economy. Population (1997): 93 500.

● **Worcester porcelain** ▶ A soft-paste English porcelain of first rank made in Worcester, England, from about 1751. Early wares derive from contemporary silver shapes and oriental porcelain. The factory is famous for fine transfer printing, painting, and gilding.

● **Worcestershire** ▶ A county of W central England. In 1974 it was absorbed into the new county of ▷Hereford and Worcester and lost part of the N to West Midlands: it was reinstated as a county in 1998. It consists of a broad plain watered by the rivers Severn and Avon, rising to the Cotswold Hills in the SE, the Malvern Hills in the W, and the Clent Hills in the N. It is mainly agricultural, with cattle breeding and fruit growing. Industries include engineering, chemicals, and food processing. The NE is a residential area for Birmingham. Area: 1742 sq km (674 sq mi). Population (1999 est): 539 800. Administrative centre: Worcester.

● **word processor** ▶ A software package for a computer enabling documents, letters, etc., to be created, edited, printed, and stored. Modern word processors enable text to be justified and correctly hyphenated, a variety of fonts and weights of typefaces to be used, tables and footnotes to be automatically generated, and graphics to be incorporated. Most word processors are now capable of producing print-quality documents. ▷*See also* desk-top publishing.

William Wordsworth ►
A drawing of the elderly poet by Miss M. Gillies. By this time the young radical and literary iconoclast had long settled into conservatism, becoming a revered figure in the nation's cultural life.

● **Wordsworth, William** ► (1770-1850) British poet. Born in Cumberland, he attended Cambridge University and became an enthusiastic republican during a visit to Revolutionary France (1791–92), where he fathered a child by a French girl, Annette Vallon. In 1795 he met S. T. ▷Coleridge, with whom he collaborated on *Lyrical Ballads* (1798), a seminal work of the Romantic movement, which includes the well-known "Tintern Abbey." In 1799 he settled in the Lake District, where, cared for devotedly by his wife Mary and his sister Dorothy, he completed his masterpiece, a verse autobiography entitled *The Prelude* (completed 1805; published 1850). In this and other poems he described his feelings of mystical union with nature. Dorothy's journals provide details of their life in the Lake District.

● **work** ► The product of a force and the distance through which it causes a body to move in the direction of the force. Work, like energy, is measured in ▷joules.

● **Workers' Educational Association** ▷*See* adult education.

● **work hardening** ► The strengthening of metal by hammering or rolling it without heating. Metal consists of small crystals (grains). Softness or ductility is caused by irregularities (dislocations) in the grains that are able to move and change the crystal shape under stress. Movement of dislocations is blocked at the boundaries between grains. Continued working makes the dislocations collect at the grain boundaries, thus making the metal harder.

● **workhouses** ► Institutions set up in the 17th century in Britain, and also found elsewhere in Europe, to provide employment and shelter for paupers. The 1834 Poor Law Amendment Act made it necessary for anyone seeking assistance to enter a workhouse, which because of their inhuman rules soon became dreaded places.

● **Working Men's Club and Institute Union** ► A club founded by the Rev Henry Solly in 1862 and now having over 4000 affiliated clubs throughout the UK. The Working Men's Clubs are nonpolitical and provide educational and recreational facilities.

● **World Bank** ▷*See* International Bank for Reconstruction and Development.

● **World Council of Churches** ► An organization of more than 200 Protestant and Orthodox churches. A product of the ▷ecumenical movement, it was founded at Amsterdam in 1948, with headquarters at Geneva. Membership includes almost all Christian Churches except the Roman Catholic, which sends observers and cooperates with it.

● **World Cup** ► An international association football competition first held in 1930 and thereafter every four years, except during World War II. It is organized by the ▷Fédération internationale de Football association. The winners have been Uruguay (1930, 1950), Italy (1934, 1938, 1982), West Germany (1954, 1974, 1990), Brazil (1958, 1962, 1970, 1994), England (1966), Argentina (1978, 1986), and France (1998).

● **World Federation of Trade Unions** ► An international association of national federations of trades unions, founded in 1945. A number of Western trades-union federations withdrew in 1949 to establish the ▷International Confederation of Free Trade Unions.

● **World Health Organization** ► (WHO) A specialized agency of the ▷United Nations established in 1948 to facilitate "the attainment by all peoples of the highest possible level of health." It supports programmes to eradicate diseases, carries out and finances epidemiological research, trains health workers, strengthens national health services, establishes international health regulations, and provides aid in emergencies and disasters. Its headquarters are in Geneva.

● **World Meterological Organization** ► (WMO) A specialized agency of the ▷United Nations set up in 1951 with the aim of standardizing international meteorological observations and improving the exchange of information. Its chief activities are the World Weather Watch programme, which coordinates facilities provided by member states, and a programme that aims to extend knowledge of the natural and human-induced variability of climate. Its headquarters are in Geneva.

● **World Trade Center** ► (WTC) A building complex, designed by Minotu Yamasaki, that formerly stood in New York's Manhattan district (□ skyscraper). When the building opened in 1974, its 417 m (1368 ft) and 415 m (1362 ft) towers were the tallest in the world. In the infamous terrorist attack of ▷September 11, 2001, each of the towers was struck by a hijacked airliner, caught fire, and collapsed from the top downward. Around 2800 people were killed, including at least 2034 workers and tourists in the WTC, several hundred emergency workers, and all 156 passengers and crew on the aircraft.

● **World Trade Organization** ► (WTO) An organization set up in 1995 to succeed the General Agreement on Tariffs and Trade (GATT) from 1 January, 1996. Its objective is to raise standards of living worldwide by liberalizing international trade; it also acts as a final tribunal in trade disputes. There are currently 108 member states. The secretariat is based in Geneva. Recent meetings of the WTO have provoked violent anticapitalist demonstrations in several countries.

● **World War I** ► (1914–18) The Great War between the ▷Allied Powers, including the UK, with countries of the British Empire, France, Russia, Belgium, Japan, Serbia, Italy (from May, 1915), Portugal (from March, 1916), Romania (from August, 1916), the USA (from April, 1917), and Greece (from July, 1917) on one side, and the ▷Central Powers, including Germany, Austria-Hungary, Turkey (from November, 1914), and Bulgaria (from October, 1915) on the other. Its causes included fear of the German Empire's European and colonial ambitions since its defeat of France in the Franco-Prussian War (1870–71). Tensions among European powers were expressed by the formation of the ▷Triple Alliance of Germany and Austria-Hungary (1879) and Italy (1882) and of the ▷Triple Entente between France and Russia (1893) and France and the UK (1904; *see* Entente Cordiale). Rivalries surfaced in the crises in Morocco in 1905–06 and 1911 and in Bosnia in 1909; the immediate cause of the war lay in the conflict of interests between Russia and Austria-Hungary in the Balkans. On 28 June, 1914, the heir to the Austro-Hungarian throne, Archduke Francis Ferdinand, was assassinated at Sarajevo in Bosnia by a Serbian nationalist and on 28 July Austria-Hungary, with German support, declared war on Serbia. On 29 July Russia mobilized its forces in support of Serbia; on 1 August Germany declared war on Russia and on 3 August, upon France. Germany's invasion of Belgium brought the UK into the war at midnight on 4 August. The main theatres of war were the Western and Eastern Fronts, the Middle East, Italy, and the German colonies in Africa and the Pacific.

Western Front: German strategy at the start of the war was based on the ▷Schlieffen plan, which envisaged a rapid flanking movement through the Low Countries. The German forces under von Moltke advanced rapidly through Belgium until they were forced by the British Expeditionary Force (BEF) and the French under Joffre, at the first Battle of the Marne (5–9 Sept), to retreat across the River Aisne. Germany's effort to reach the Channel was thwarted at the first Battle of Ypres (12 Oct–11 Nov) and the combatants settled, on either side of a line from Ostend to Switzerland, to the futile trench warfare for which World War I is notorious. The year 1915 saw a series of inconclusive battles with huge loss of life–at Neuve-Chapelle (March), again at Ypres (April–May), where the Germans used poison gas for the first time, and at Loos (Sept). On 21 February, 1916, the Germans launched a crippling attack on the French at Verdun but on 1 July Haig, who had succeeded Sir John French as commander of the BEF, opened the Battle of the Somme, during which ▷tanks were used (by the British) for the first time; the Allies lost some 600 000 men and the Germans, about 650 000. In early 1917 the Germans under Ludendorff withdrew behind the ▷Hindenburg line; in April Haig took Vimy Ridge (with the loss of 132 000 men); but the French campaign in Champagne was disastrous and in mid-May Gen R. G. Nivelle was replaced by Pétain. With the USA (incensed by German ▷submarine warfare) now participating, on 31 July Britain launched the third Battle of Ypres and by 6 November had taken Passchendaele (with 245 000 British losses). In the spring of 1918 Germany thrust a bulge in the Allied line, which the Allied commander in chief, ▷Foch, wiped out at the second Battle of the Marne. Ludendorff was forced back to the Hindenburg line, which in September was broken by Haig between Saint Quentin and Cambrai. By October Germany was suing for peace.

World War I ▶ The Eastern Front.

Eastern Front and Balkans: in August, 1914, Russia advanced into E Prussia but was defeated at ▷Tannenberg. When late in 1914 Turkey attacked Russia in the Caucasus, the Allies launched the **Gallipoli campaign**, at first a naval (Feb–March) and then a military operation in which Australian and New Zealand forces played a major part (*see* ANZAC). It failed to break through the Dardanelles and by January, 1916, the Allies had withdrawn. Germany's offensive on the Eastern Front in summer 1915 forced Russia back and after the Central Powers had overcome Poland, most of Lithuania, and Serbia the Allies landed at Salonika; the ensuing **Macedonian campaign** continued without progress until Bulgaria capitulated in September, 1918. Russia collapsed following the outbreak of the Russian Revolution (March, 1917) and signed the Treaties of ▷Brest-Litovsk.

Middle East: the **Mesopotamian campaign**, intended to protect oil installations, was launched with the landing of an Indian force at Abadan on 6 November, 1914. Early advances were halted when the Allies failed to take Baghdad (November, 1915) and in April, 1916, they lost Kut al-Amara to the Turks. In February, 1917, it was retaken and, in March, Baghdad fell. Meanwhile the Allies had invaded Palestine and, aided by the Arab revolt, Allenby took Jerusalem in December, 1917; his victory at Megiddo (September, 1918) and capture of Damascus and Aleppo finally crushed the Turks.

Italy: the Italian front was maintained along the River Isonzo through 11 battles until 1917, when the Italians were forced by Austria-Hungary to retreat from Caporetto (Oct–Nov) in an overwhelming defeat. In October, 1918, however, Austria-Hungary was defeated at Vittorio-Veneto and in November finally capitulated.

War at sea and in the air: at sea the larger British navy was dominant in the North Sea. German raids on the English coast began in December, 1914, but were repudiated by Beatty's victory at Dogger Bank in January, 1915. The indecisive Battle of Jutland (31 May, 1916) was the only engagement between the main fleets; the British sustained the greater losses, but remained numerically superior. The real threat to the Allies at sea came from the German U-boats, which sunk some 6000 ships, including the ▷*Lusitania*, in the course of the war. At their most active in 1917, their effectiveness was reduced following the introduction by Lloyd George of the convoy system. British superiority was more effective away from Europe. Although defeated off Coronel in November, 1914, victory in December off the Falkland Islands enabled Britain, with Australia, New Zealand, and Japan, to take the German colonies in Africa and the Pacific by September, 1916. World War I was the first war in which aircraft were used: in 1915 the German Zeppelins began to attack British cities and in 1917 German aircraft were also thus employed. Some air combat took place on the Western and Eastern Fronts and towards the end of the war the newly established ▷Royal Air Force was bombing German cities.

Conclusion: with the defeat of the Turks and Bulgarians in September, 1918, and of Germany on the Western Front and Austria-Hungary in Italy in October, revolt broke out in Germany. On 9 November the German emperor, William II, fled and on 11 November Germany signed the armistice. On 18 January, 1919, the Allies met at the ▷Paris Peace Conference to determine the peace settlement, which was signed by Germany (the Treaty of Versailles) on 28 June. The Allies lost some 5 million lives (3 million French and Russian) in the war and the Central Powers, some 3.5 million (3 million German and Austro-Hungarian). A further 21 million combatants were wounded.

● **World War II** ▶ (1939–45) The war between the Allied Powers, including the UK and countries of the Commonwealth, France (until June 1940; thereafter the Free French), the Soviet Union (from June, 1941), the USA (from December, 1941), and China (from December, 1941) on one side, and the ▷Axis Powers, including Germany, Italy (from June, 1940), and Japan (from December, 1941) on the other. The war was caused by the failure of the ▷Paris Peace Conference to provide for the maintenance of international security after World War I and by the territorial ambitions of Nazi Germany under Adolf Hitler. In March, 1938, Germany annexed Austria (*see* Anschluss) and in September, following the ▷Munich Agreement, the ▷Sudetenland. In March, 1939, Hitler occupied the rest of Czechoslovakia and Britain and France guaranteed to support Poland—Hitler's next objective—against German aggression. On 23 May Hitler came to an agreement with Mussolini's Italy, which in April had conquered Albania. Hitler's and Stalin's nonaggression pact followed on 23 August and Britain, France, and Poland made an agreement of mutual assistance on 25 Aug. On 1 September Germany invaded Poland and two days later Britain and France declared war.

Western Europe (1939–41): by 27 September Poland had succumbed to the German ▷Blitzkrieg. The Soviet invasion of Finland (*see* Russo-Finnish War) brought Finnish capitulation by March, 1940, and in April Germany invaded Denmark and Norway. The Allied failure in Scandinavia led to Neville Chamberlain's resignation and on 10 May, the day that Germany invaded Belgium and the Netherlands, Churchill became Britain's prime minister. The German advance across the River Meuse to the coast outflanked the ▷Maginot line and separated the main French force from the French First Army, the Belgian army, and the British Expeditionary Force; on 26 May an Allied evacuation from the Continent was ordered. Between 29 May and 4 June, in operation Dynamo, some 338 226 Allied troops were rescued from Dunkirk by the Royal Navy, and a fleet of small boats manned by their private owners, supported by the RAF Fighter Command. On 22 June Pétain signed the French armistice with Germany, following which French resistance to the Axis Powers was directed by de Gaulle from London, where he organized the ▷Free French (see also Maquis).

Britain now faced an imminent German invasion. In August and September, 1940, the German ▷Luftwaffe attacked SE England and then London in a series of daytime raids. In October German bombing was carried out at night and extended to other British cities in the following months. The Luftwaffe failed to cripple the RAF or to terrorize the British people and by the end of October the so-called ▷Battle of Britain had been won by the RAF Fighter Command under ▷Dowding.

Africa and the Middle East (1940–43): in September, 1940, Italy advanced from Libya into Egypt but the Italians were forced to retreat in the face of Wavell's troops. By 6 February, 1941, the Allies had captured 113 000 Italian soldiers but their success was undermined by the arrival in N Africa of Rommel and the German Afrika Corps. In March Wavell's force was weakened by the dispatch of troops to aid Greece against an imminent German invasion (Yugoslavia and

Greece were to fall in April and Crete, in May) and Rommel forced an Allied retreat to the Egyptian border.

In November Auchinleck (who had replaced Wavell in July) launched an Allied offensive against Rommel but by January, 1942, had again been forced to withdraw, taking up a defensive position at El-Alamein, inside the Egyptian frontier. In August Auchinleck was replaced by Alexander and Montgomery became commander of the Eighth Army. In the decisive Battle of Alamein (23 Oct–4 Nov) Montgomery defeated Rommel, forcing his retreat along the N African coast. On 8 November an Anglo-US force under Eisenhower landed on the coast of French N Africa. The French under Darlan surrendered and the Allies advanced through Tunisia to make contact (7 April, 1943) with Montgomery's Eighth Army, which was moving N from Alamein. On 7 May the Allies took Bizerta and Tunis and on 13 May the Axis forces surrendered; some 248 000 German and Italian troops were captured.

In East Africa, Wavell had taken Addis Ababa from the Italians in April, 1941, and was in control of Ethiopia, as well as British Somaliland (captured by Italy in August, 1940), by May. In the Middle East, in April Britain occupied Iraq, by June Lebanon and Syria were in Allied hands, and in August the Allies gained control of Iran.

Italy (1943–45): on 10 July, 1943, Alexander's army group (the Eighth under Montgomery and the US Fifth Army), under the supreme command of Eisenhower, landed in Sicily. On 25 July Musso-

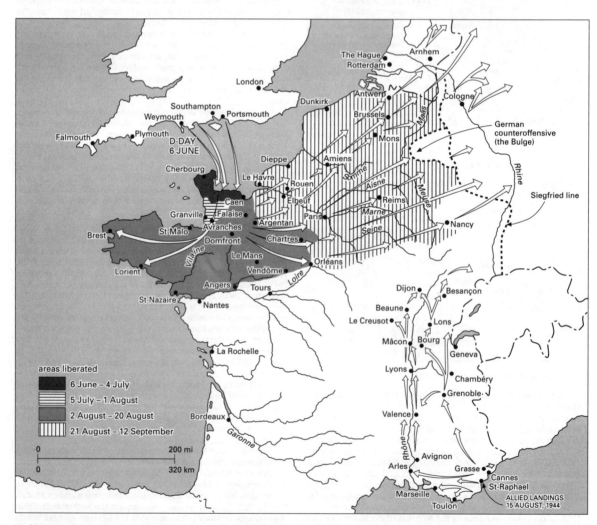

World War II ▶ The development of the Western Front after the Allied D-Day invasion of Normandy.

lini fell and on 3 Sept the Italian armistice was signed and the Allies landed on the Italian mainland. The Germans held back the Allies at the Ortona-Garigliano line until an Allied offensive, launched on 12 May, 1944, succeeded in breaking through to Rome (4 June). In the following months the Allied forces made their way northwards; Bologna and then Milan were taken in April, 1945, and on 2 May, shortly before the final German collapse, Trieste fell.

Eastern Front (1941–45): Germany, with Finland, Hungary, and Romania, invaded the Soviet Union on 22 June, 1941. The Axis forces took the Crimea and Ukraine in the S, besieged Leningrad (St Petersburg) in the N, and by November were in sight of Moscow. The Soviets staged an effective counterattack in the winter of 1941–42 but Germany retaliated in June with a new offensive and by August the famous Battle of ▷Stalingrad had begun. This heroic Soviet victory resulted in a decimated German Sixth Army and the capture (January, 1943) of its commander Paulus. The Germans launched a new offensive in July but were gradually forced back until expelled from Soviet soil in August, 1944. On 23 August the Soviet Union secured a Romanian armistice and on 19 Sept, a Finnish armistice. Also in September Bulgaria declared war on Germany and the Germans evacuated Greece. On 5 October Belgrade fell following collaboration between the Red Army and Tito's Partisans. In October Soviet troops invaded Germany and in January, 1945, launched a final offensive, taking Poland, Austria, and Hungary and entering Czechoslovakia. Berlin fell on 2 May, shortly after Hitler's suicide.

Western Front (1944–45): on 6 June, 1944 (*see* D-Day), the Allied invasion of Normandy began under the supreme command of Eisenhower. The RAF Bomber Command had prepared the way with heavy strategic bombing, including the bombing of German cities. This reached a peak in 1944, with the RAF dropping a greater bomb load in the last 11 months of war than in the previous 4¾ years. By 2 July one million US and British troops had landed in Normandy. The British under Montgomery took Caen and US troops, after capturing St Lô (July), invaded Brittany. The Canadians took Falaise on 17 August, shortly after US and French troops had landed in the South of France from the Mediterranean. On 25 August Paris fell to the Allies, who now pursued Montgomery's plan for advancing into the Ruhr from Belgium and the Zuider Zee.

At the Battle of Arnhem in September airborne troops were dropped to secure bridges but were withdrawn after ground forces were delayed in breaking through the German defence. In December the Germans launched a counteroffensive (the Battle of the Bulge), driving a bulge, or salient, into Allied lines in the Ardennes region of S Belgium. US troops forced the Germans to retreat in January, 1945, and the final Allied offensive was launched. The Rhine was crossed, with air support, in March and by 1 April the Ruhr was encircled. On 4 May, two days after the fall of Berlin to Soviet troops, Montgomery accepted the surrender of German forces in NW Germany, Holland, and Denmark at Lüneburg Heath. On 7 May the Germans signed a general surrender at Reims, which was ratified two days later in Berlin.

War at sea: The battle for control of the sea routes, known as the **Battle of the Atlantic**, was fought from December, 1939, when the German *Graf Spee* inflicted considerable damage on HMS *Exeter* in the Battle of the River Plate in the S Atlantic. In November, 1940, a successful naval air attack was launched on Taranto and in March, 1941, at Cape Matapan the British Mediterranean fleet thwarted an Italian attempt to prevent the transfer of British troops from Egypt to Greece. In May *Hood* was sunk by the *Bismarck* and, three days later, *Dorsetshire* sank the *Bismarck*. However, as in World War I, the major threat to Allied supremacy in western waters was posed by the German U-boats. These were most effective early in 1943 but by the summer, partly owing to the introduction of Allied escort carriers, 37 U-boats had been sunk and the Battle of the Atlantic was over.

Asia (1941–45): the Japanese attack on Pearl Harbor on 7 December, 1941, initiated a truly "world" war. On 10 December Germany and Italy declared war on the USA and the second ▷Sino-Japanese War became part of the wider conflict.

Japan invaded Malaya on 8 December and captured Hong Kong (25 Dec), Manila (3 January, 1942), and Singapore (15 Feb) together with 90 000 British and Commonwealth troops. The Dutch East Indies (Sumatra, Java, and parts of New Guinea) fell on 10 March and

the Philippines and Burma in May. The Japanese seemed within reach of India and Australia when the US naval and air victories of the ▷Coral Sea (4–8 May), ▷Midway Islands (4–6 June), and ▷Guadalcanal (Aug) halted Japan's eastward expansion. In October, 1944, the Japanese fleet was decisively defeated at ▷Leyte Gulf and the Allied conquest of Manila (February, 1945), the Philippines (June), and Borneo (May–June) followed. Burma, where Mountbatten had become supreme commander, SE Asia, in August, 1943, was reconquered by the 14th ("forgotten") Army under Slim (January–May, 1945). Japanese resistance was ended by the atomic bombing on 6 and 9 August respectively of Hiroshima and Nagasaki; Japan formally surrendered on 14 August.

Conclusion: in May, 1945, with the fall of Berlin and the German collapse in Italy and on the Western Front, the war in Europe was over. The postwar settlement was decided at the ▷Potsdam Conference, held near Berlin, in July and August (*see also* Tehran Conference; Yalta Conference).

In the course of the war Germany lost some 3.5 million combatants and 780 000 civilians (of which 593 000 were the victims of RAF bombs). In contrast the UK lost 92 673 civilians, of which 61 000 died in air raids; some 264 443 combatants died. The Soviet Union lost 11 million combatants and 7 million civilians; the Japanese 1.3 million and 672 000 respectively; and the USA, 292 131 and 6000. In addition some 5.7 million Jews died in Nazi ▷concentration camps; of these 3.2 millions were Poles.

● **World Wide Fund for Nature** ▶ An international organization dedicated to the conservation of endangered species and their natural habitats. Founded in 1961 as the World Wildlife Fund, it has financed projects both in Britain and abroad, protecting species as diverse as the rare bee orchid and the Arabian oryx. The international president is HRH the Duke of Edinburgh. Director: Dr R. Pellew.

● **World Wide Web** ▶ (WWW) A part of the ▷Internet in which documents may be accessed and viewed on-line. Web documents held on numerous sites worldwide typically make use of typographic design, special effects, diagrams, pictures, and sometimes also sounds and video. A feature of the World Wide Web is the inclusion of hypertext links in documents, which enable the user to jump easily to related documents on other sites. The Web is used for education and increasingly for entertainment, advertising, and commerce. It was originally developed in the 1980s at ▷CERN.

● **worm** ▶ Any of various soft-bodied elongated invertebrates, especially ▷earthworms and various parasitic species, and sometimes the larvae of insects. ▷*See also* annelid worm; flatworm; nematode; Pogonophora (beardworms); ribbon worm.

● **worm lizard** ▷*See* amphisbaena.

● **Worms** ▶ 49 38N 8 23E A town in SW Germany, in Rhineland-Palatinate on the River Rhine. Heavily bombed during World War II, it has an 11th-century cathedral and synagogue (1034). It is an industrial centre and is famed for its local wine, *Liebfraumilch*.

History: in the 5th century AD it was the capital of Burgundy. Among the imperial diets (assemblies) held here was that of 1521 at which Luther refused to recant. It was annexed by France in 1797 and passed to Hesse-Darmstadt in 1815. Population (1991): 77 430.

● **wormwood** ▶ An aromatic herb or shrub of the worldwide genus *Artemisia* (about 200 species), especially *A. absinthium*, which is found chiefly in grasslands of the N hemisphere and is the source of ▷absinthe. Up to 80 cm high, it has deeply divided leaves and small yellow flowers grouped into long loose spikes. Family: ▷*Compositae*. ▷*See also* southernwood.

● **worsted** ▶ A type of woollen yarn or cloth. It was manufactured originally only from the long wool fibres but shorter ones are now also used. The fibres are combed parallel so that spinning produces a smooth fine thread. The woven fabrics, which include gabardine and serge, are smooth and strong.

● **Worthing** ▶ 50 48N 0 23W A resort in S England, on the West Sussex coast; it is a centre for business and services. Nearby on the South Downs is the Neolithic and Iron Age site, Cissbury Ring. Population (1991): 95 732.

• **Wotan** ▷*See* Odin.

• **Wotton, Sir Henry** ► (1568–1639) English poet. A friend of Donne, he was a foreign diplomat before becoming provost of Eton (1624). His works include *The Elements of Architecture* (1624) and a posthumous volume of verse.

• **Wounded Knee** ► The site in SW South Dakota (USA) of the last confrontation (29 December, 1890) between the Indians and US troops. Fearing that the anti-White Ghost Dance cult (whose popularity was a response to the wretchedness of life on reservations) would cause an uprising among the Sioux, troops killed over 200 men, women, and children here. In 1973 some 200 members of the American Indian Movement occupied the village of Wounded Knee in protest against government Indian policies. After a 69-day siege, in which two Indians died, they were forced to surrender.

• **woundwort** ► An annual or perennial herb of the widely distributed genus *Stachys* (about 200 species). It has square stems and lance-shaped or heart-shaped toothed leaves. Whorls of two-lipped tubular flowers, yellowish-white, pink, deep-red, or purple, are borne in the leaf axils and the fruit is a small nutlet. Family: ▷*Labiatae*.

• **Wouwerman, Philips** ► (1619–68) Dutch painter, born in Haarlem. Influenced by the Dutch painter Bamboccio (Pieter van Laer; c. 1592–1642), he specialized in camp and battle scenes. Some of his output is attributed to his brothers **Pieter** (1623–82) and **Jan Wouwerman** (1629–66).

• **wrack** ► A large brown ▷seaweed of the order *Fucales*, found almost worldwide on rocky shores and prominent in colder regions. Leathery straplike branching fronds arise from a circular rootlike anchor (holdfast), often bearing air bladders to aid flotation. Examples are bladderwrack (*Fucus vesiculosus*) and serrated wrack (*F. serratus*).

• **Wrangel, Ferdinand Petrovich, Baron von** ► (1794–1870) Russian explorer. He led a Russian expedition to the Arctic (1820–24). The Wrangell Mountains and Wrangel Island are named after him. As governor of Russian territories in Alaska (1829–35), he opposed its sale to the USA.

• **Wrangel, Peter Nikolaievich, Baron** ► (1878–1928) Russian general. Following the Russian Revolution he joined the White armies against the Bolsheviks, distinguishing himself at Tsaritsyn (now Volgograd; 1919). Succeeding ▷Denikin as commander, he lost Sevastopol and was forced to evacuate his armies from the Crimea (1920).

• **Wrangel Island** ► (Russian name: Ostrov Vrangelya) A Russian island in the Arctic Ocean, between the East Siberian Sea and the Chukchi Sea. Since 1926 there has been a small Chukchi and Inuit population. Area: about 7300 sq km (2818 sq mi).

• **wrasse** ► A fish of the family *Labridae* (300 species) found near rocks or coral reefs in shallow tropical and temperate seas. It has a slender often brilliantly coloured body, 5–200 cm long, long dorsal and anal fins, and thick lips. They are known for their elaborate courtship and nesting behaviour and many species can change their sex and colouring. They feed on marine invertebrates and the external parasites of other fish. Order: *Perciformes*. ▷*See also* hogfish.

• **wreckfish** ► A carnivorous fish, *Polyprion americanus*, also called stone bass, found in Mediterranean and Atlantic offshore waters, often associated with floating wreckage and seaweed. It has a deep heavy body, up to 2 m long, dark brown above and yellowish below, a large head, and a jutting lower jaw. Family: *Serranidae*; order: *Perciformes*.

• **wren** ► A small brown bird belonging to a family (*Troglodytidae*; 63 species) found chiefly in South America. Wrens are 9–22 cm long with sharp slender bills and short cocked tails. The only Eurasian species, *Troglodytes troglodytes*, is about 10 cm long and has a reddish-brown plumage with barring on the wings and tail. It lives mainly in undergrowth, feeding on small insects and spiders.

The name is also given to small songbirds of the families *Maluridae* (Australian wrens, e.g. the ▷emu wren) and *Xenicidae* (New Zealand wrens, e.g. the rifleman).

• **Wren, Sir Christopher** ► (1632–1723) English architect and scientist. After studying science and mathematics at Oxford he became professor of astronomy first at Gresham College, London (1657–61), and then at Oxford (1661–73). He was also a founder member of the Royal Society and later its president (1680–82). His first architectural designs were for Pembroke College chapel, Cambridge (1663), and the Sheldonian Theatre, Oxford (1664). Following a short trip to Paris (1665–66), the architecture of which led him to adopt his typically baroque style, he abandoned astronomy and joined the Office of Works. Within days of the ▷Fire of London Wren produced a new plan for the whole City, incorporating spacious avenues and piazzas. The plan was rejected on the grounds that it would have involved vast sums in compensation and crippling damage to trade, but Wren was commissioned to rebuild 51 City churches and some 36 company halls. Basing many of his designs for the churches on ▷Vitruvius' Roman basilica, Wren showed enormous ingenuity in fitting his buildings into the old irregular sites. His design for ⬚St Paul's Cathedral was accepted, after many modifications, in 1675. His later buildings include the Greenwich Hospital (begun in 1694) and additions to Hampton Court (1698). Wren was also an MP (1685–87, 1701–02). He was buried in St Paul's, where his epitaph reads: *Si monumentum requiris, circumspice* (If you seek a monument, look around you).

• **Wren, P(ercival) C(hristopher)** ► (1885–1941) British novelist. He spent his early life wandering the world, working mostly as a soldier. The best known of his many popular adventure novels are those concerning the French Foreign Legion, especially *Beau Geste* (1924).

• **wren babbler** ► An insect-eating bird belonging to one of several genera of the family *Timaliidae* (*see* babbler), occurring chiefly in S Asia. 10–15 cm long, wren babblers have a shortish upturned tail and short straight bill. They usually live on the ground, feeding in small flocks beneath bushes and forest undergrowth.

• **wrestling** ► A form of unarmed combat, one of the most ancient sports, in which two people attempt to throw and hold each other down. It first became an Olympic sport in 704 BC. Modern wrestling became an organized sport in the 18th century. There are two main international styles. **Graeco-Roman wrestling** is the most popular style on the European continent; holds on the body below the waist and the use of legs to hold or trip are not allowed. They are, however, allowed in **freestyle wrestling** (which developed from the Anglo-American **catch-as-catch-can** form). In both styles a wrestler wins a match by securing a fall (throwing his opponent onto his back and pinning both shoulders to the mat for one second) or by accumulating the most points according to a complex scoring system. If neither wrestler achieves a fall or is disqualified the bout lasts for three three-minute rounds. There are ten weight categories. **Sambo wrestling** is the third recognized style, created in the 1930s from styles found in the Soviet Union. **Sumo** is the highly popular Japanese style in which the wrestlers, usually weighing around 130 kg (20 stone), attempt to force each other out of the ring. British variations include **Cumberland and Westmoreland wrestling** and **Devon and Cornwall wrestling**. The international governing body is the Fédération internationale des Luttes amateurs. ▷*See also* judo.

• **Wrexham** ► **1.** 53 03N 3 00W A town in NE Wales, in Wrexham county borough. It is a market town, manufacturing chemicals, cables, and metal goods. Elihu Yale, founder of Yale University, is buried here. Population (1991): 40 614. **2.** A county borough in N Wales, created in 1996 from part of Clwyd. Area: 500 sq km (193 sq mi). Population (1996 est): 123 400.

• **Wright, Frank Lloyd** ► (1869–1959) US architect of international fame, whose style was among the most individual of the modern movement. A pupil of Louis ▷Sullivan from 1888 to 1893, he first demonstrated his originality in a series of Chicago houses between 1900 and 1909, the most famous being the Robie house (1909). These long low spacious designs have proved very influential. Later buildings include the Johnson Wax factory at Racine, Wisconsin (1936–39), and Taliesin West (1938), his winter home in the Arizona desert, where he established an architectural community, and the Guggenheim Museum (1959). ⬚architecture.

• **Wright, Judith** ► (1915–2000) Australian poet and writer. Her volumes of poetry, mostly written in rural S Queensland, include *Woman to Man* (1949), *The Other Half* (1966), and *Journeys* (1982); her *Collected Poems* appeared in 1994. She also wrote children's books, critical and historical studies, and works supporting Aboriginal rights and environmental campaigns.

● **Wright, Orville** ▶ (1871–1948) US aviator, who with his brother **Wilbur Wright** (1867–1912) is usually regarded as having made the first powered and controlled flights on 17 December, 1903. They took place near Kitty Hawk, North Carolina, and in the second, lasting about a minute, the aircraft covered a distance of 250 metres. The flight failed to interest either the US public or the government but the brothers continued to make improvements to their machine, eventually succeeding in staying airborne for an hour. In 1908 Wilbur Wright shipped the aircraft to France, where it was enthusiastically received, and in 1909 Orville secured a US army contract. □aircraft.

● **Wright, Richard** ▶ (1908–60) US novelist and critic. He was born into a poor Black family. His works include *Native Son* (1940), a seminal novel of social protest, and the autobiographical *Black Boy* (1945). From 1946 he lived in Paris.

● **writing systems** ▶ The recording of human communication using signs or symbols to represent spoken words or concepts. The earliest known writing systems were all originally ▷pictographic; if they survived at all they developed into ▷ideographic writing systems (*see also* Chinese). True alphabetic writing, representing the sounds of the language, developed around the E Mediterranean about 2000 BC (*see* Semitic alphabets). An intermediate stage is the use of ▷syllabaries.

● **Wrocław** ▶ (German name: Breslau) 51 05N 17 00E A city in SW Poland, on the River Oder. Founded during the 10th century, it developed as an important centre on the amber trade route between the Roman Empire and the Baltic Sea. During World War II it suffered severe damage under siege from the Soviet armies (1945). Old buildings that have been reconstructed include the 13th-century cathedral. Its university was founded in 1945. It is now an important industrial and communications centre; industries include electronics, engineering, and food processing. Population (1996 est): 642 700.

● **wrought iron** ▶ An almost pure form of iron, often with less than 0.1% carbon. It was originally produced by a laborious process of repeatedly hammering and folding hot ▷pig iron to squeeze out the impurities. The ▷puddling process has now superseded hand working.

● **wrybill** ▶ A New Zealand ▷plover, *Anarhynchus frontalis*. 15 cm long, it has a grey plumage with white underparts and a black breast band. The bill, which is curved to the right, is used to probe for insects under stones and in shallow water.

● **wryneck** ▶ A small ▷woodpecker belonging to a subfamily (*Jynginae*; 2 species) occurring in Eurasia. 16 cm long, wrynecks have a grey-brown mottled plumage and a small bill. They do not drill holes but feed mostly on ants and pupae and nest in empty holes.

● **WTO** ▷*See* World Trade Organization.

● **Wuchow** ▶ (*or* Wu-chou) ▷*See* Wuzhou.

● **Wuhan** ▶ 30 35N 114 19E A port in E central China, the capital of Hubei province at the confluence of the Yangtze and Han Rivers. Formed by the amalgamation (1950) of the ancient cities of Hankou (*or* Hankow), Hanyang, and Wuchang, it is the commercial and industrial centre of central China. The university was established in 1913. It was a centre of both the Taiping Rebellion (1851–64) and 1911 revolution. Its chief industry is iron and steel. Population (1990): 3 284 229.

● **Wu Hou** ▶ (625–705 AD) A Chinese empress of the Tang dynasty. Following the death of her husband, the emperor, she ruled through two puppet emperors until 690 when she seized the throne and the imperial title. Although a capable ruler, she was forced to abdicate shortly before her death.

● **Wu-hsi** ▷*See* Wuxi.

● **Wu-hsing** ▷*See* Wuxing.

● **Wundt, Wilhelm** ▶ (1832–1920) German physiologist and pioneer of modern experimental psychology. His *Principles of Physiological Psychology* (2 vols, 1873–74) was one of the first scientific approaches to the study of the conscious mind. Wundt also wrote works on human physiology and perception.

● **Wuppertal** ▶ 51 05N 7 10E A city in NW Germany, in North Rhine-Westphalia in the ▷Ruhr. It was formed in 1929 from six towns, including Elberfeld, and was heavily bombed in World War II. It is a textile-producing centre. Population (1996 est): 381 884.

● **Württemberg** ▶ A former kingdom in W Europe. It became a duchy in 1495 and a kingdom in 1806. Divided into two West German *Länder* following World War II, these became part of the *Land* of ▷Baden-Württemberg (1952).

● **Würzburg** ▶ 49 48N 9 57E A city in SW Germany, in Bavaria on the River Main. The former episcopal residence (1720–44), containing frescoes by Tiepolo, was damaged in World War II but later restored, as was the cathedral (1034). Roentgen taught at the university (founded 1582). A wine-producing centre, its manufactures include machine tools and chemicals. Population (1996 est): 127 295.

● **Wuxi** ▶ (*or* Wu-hsi) 31 35N 120 19E A city in E China, in Jiangsu province on the ▷Grand Canal. A major grain market since the 7th century AD, it is also an industrial centre. Population (1990): 826 833.

● **Wuxing** ▶ (*or* Wu-hsing) 30 56N 120 04E A town in E China, in Zhejiang province. The ancient centre of an intensely farmed area, it suffered badly during the ▷Taiping Rebellion. Silk is the main industry. Population (latest est): 184 900.

● **Wuzhou** ▶ (Wu-chou *or* Wuchow) 23 30N 111 21E A city in S China, in Guangxi Zhuang AR. An old garrison town, it is now a commercial centre. Industries include silk textiles, chemicals, and engineering. Population (1990): 210 452.

● **Wyatt, James** ▶ (1747–1813) British architect. Wyatt rose to fame in 1770 with his design for the Pantheon, London (now destroyed), a neoclassical interpretation of Hagia Sophia, Istanbul. Subsequently he designed country houses, notably Heaton House, Lancashire (1772), and made essential restorations to Salisbury and Durham cathedrals, which were subsequently criticized for their doubtful taste. His most dramatic work, ▷Fonthill Abbey (1796–1807), designed in the ▷gothic revival style, collapsed in the 1820s, possibly as a result of shoddy workmanship.

● **Wyatt, Sir Thomas** ▶ (1503–42) English poet. A member of the court of Henry VIII, he served on various foreign diplomatic missions. With the Earl of ▷Surrey he introduced Italian verse forms and metres, notably the Petrarchan sonnet, into English poetry. 96 of his poems, together with 40 by Surrey, were included in *Tottel's Miscellany* (1557). His son **Sir Thomas Wyatt the Younger** (1521–54) led a rebellion, known as **Wyatt's Rebellion** (1553–54), against the marriage of Mary I to Philip II of Spain. He entered London with about 3000 men but was forced to surrender on finding that he could not count on the support of Londoners, most of whom were loyal to Mary. He, and some 100 of his supporters, were executed.

● **Wycherley, William** ▶ (1640–1716) English dramatist. After studying in France and at Oxford he became a member of the Inner Temple and enjoyed the favour of both Charles II and James II. He wrote four comedies, notably *The Country Wife* (1675) and *The Plain Dealer* (1676), adapted from Molière's *Le Misanthrope*. His plays are more fiercely satirical than those of his fellow Restoration dramatists.

● **Wycliffe, John** ▶ (c. 1329–84) English religious reformer. Wycliffe spent most of his life at Oxford, first as a student and then as lecturer in philosophy. Although initially protected by friends at court, he made increasingly radical criticisms of the Church, resulting in his enforced retirement to Lutterworth and his condemnation as a heretic. He attacked the doctrine of transubstantiation and emphasized the importance of the Bible, of which he supervised the first English translation from the Latin. Wycliffe's adherents, the ▷Lollards, were forerunners of English Protestantism.

● **Wye, River** ▶ A river in E Wales and W England. Flowing mainly

SE from Plynlimmon through Builth Wells and Monmouth, it joins the River Severn near Chepstow. It is noted for its beautiful scenery and has valuable salmon fisheries. Length: 210 km (130 mi).

● **Wyndham, John** ► (J. Wyndham Parkes Lucas Beynon Harris; 1903–69) British science-fiction writer. His best-known novel *The Day of the Triffids* (1951), which featured lethal mobile hybrid plants, was followed by the equally fantastic *The Kraken Wakes* (1953), *The Chrysalids* (1955), *The Midwich Cuckoos* (1957), and *Trouble with Lichen* (1960). His interest in feminine issues was revealed in a collection of short stories, *Consider Her Ways* (1961).

● **Wyoming** ► One of the mountain states in the NW USA. The topography is one of forested mountains and grassy plains. Its natural resources include oil, natural gas, uranium, coal, trona, bentonite clay, and iron ore. Livestock production dominates farming. There is very little manufacturing; the main activities are oil refining, food processing, and printing and publishing. Tourism is significant with such attractions as the Yellowstone National Park.

History: part of the territory acquired from France by the Louisiana Purchase (1803), the arrival of the Union Pacific Railway (1867–69) brought settlement in the S and the area became a state in 1890. Area: 253 596 sq km (97 914 sq mi). Population (1996 est): 481 400. Capital: Cheyenne.

● **Wyss, Johann Rudolph** ► (1782–1830) Swiss writer. A professor of philosophy, he collected and published Swiss folk tales and folklore. He also completed his father's manuscript of the successful novel *The Swiss Family Robinson* (1812–27) and wrote the Swiss national anthem.

● **Wyszyński, Stefan, Cardinal** ► (1901–81) Polish Roman Catholic churchman. Ordained in 1924, he became Bishop of Lublin in 1946, and Archbishop of Gniezno and Warsaw and Primate of Poland in 1953. He was imprisoned in 1953 for condemning communist opposition to the Church. On release (1956) he enjoyed considerable pastoral liberty, serving as president of the Second Vatican Council in 1962.

X

● **Xanthus** ▶ A city of ancient Lycia in Asia Minor famous for its heroic resistance to the Persians about 540 BC and to Brutus' Roman forces in about 43 BC.

● **Xenakis, Yannis** ▶ (1922–2001) Greek composer, who studied engineering and architecture before turning to music. He developed a method of composition based on mathematical studies of probability. His compositions include *Duel* (for 54 instruments and 2 conductors; 1959), *Terretektorh* (1966), and *Dox-orkh* (1991).

● **xenon** ▶ (Xe) A noble gas, present in the atmosphere and discovered in 1898 by Sir William Ramsay and M. W. Travers (1872–1961), in the residue of distilled liquid air. The first noble gas compounds were discovered by Neil Bartlett (1932–), by reacting xenon with dioxygenyl platinum hexafluoride $(O_2^+PtF_6^-)$ to form $Xe^+PtF_6^-$, which is a white solid. Several compounds are now known. Xenon is used in special lamps and the radioactive isotope ^{133}Xe is produced in nuclear reactors. It is a "poison," i.e. a neutron absorber, and is a crucial factor in the control of the chain reaction (*see* nuclear energy), building up to a constant level during steady operation and decaying with a half-life of a few days on shutdown. At no 54; at wt 131.3; mp −111.76°C; bp −108°C.

● **Xenophanes** ▶ (6th century BC) Greek poet. Born in Ionia, he travelled extensively in the Mediterranean countries and lived mostly in Sicily and S Italy. Only a few fragments survive of a philosophical poem on nature and of some elegies. He was a monotheist, rejecting Homeric mythology and traditional Greek religious beliefs.

● **Xenophon** ▶ (c. 430–c. 354 BC) Greek historian and soldier. He was born in Athens and, although he had little talent for philosophy, made the acquaintance of Socrates and became his devoted disciple. In 410 he joined a group of Greek mercenaries serving under the Persian prince Cyrus, who was leading an expedition against his brother, Artaxerxes II, King of Persia. Cyrus was killed in battle, the Asiatic army fled, and the force of 10 000 Greeks was left isolated. Xenophon as commander successfully led the mercenaries in a heroic retreat through the hostile Persian Empire to the Black Sea, a feat that formed the subject of his best-known work, the *Anabasis*. He later served in the Spartan army under King Aegesilaus. He wrote numerous other works, including *Memorabilia*, *Apology*, and *Symposium*, which deal with Socrates.

● **Xenopus** ▷*See* clawed frog.

● **xenotransplantation** ▷*See* transplantation.

● **Xerography** ▷*See* photocopying machine.

● **xerophyte** ▶ A plant that lives in a hot dry climate, such as a desert, and is adapted for conserving water. Cacti, for example, often have spiny leaves (to prevent water loss) and green fleshy stems (in which water is stored). A **xeromorph** is a plant that shows some of the features of xerophytes but may not live in desert areas. ▷*See also* succulent.

● **Xerxes I** ▶ (d. 465 BC) King of Persia (486–465). Having brutally repressed revolts in Egypt, he invaded Greece (*see* Greek-Persian Wars) with huge forces (480), at first successfully. However, defeat at ▷Salamis (480), ▷Plataea and Mycale (479), and the consequent revolt of the Asiatic Greeks forced him to withdraw. This tyrannous ruler and compulsive builder was assassinated in a court intrigue.

● **Xhosa** ▶ A Bantu people of S South Africa, especially the former Homeland of ▷Transkei. They are primarily cultivators, with some cattle. Today many Xhosa are migrant labourers in other areas of South Africa. Their language employs click sounds borrowed from the ▷Khoisan languages.

● **Xia Gui** ▶ (*or* Hsia Kuei; c. 1180–c. 1230) Chinese landscape painter, who worked for the Song emperors. His lyrical and mystical interpretations of landscape, in which human figures are dwarfed by mist-swathed mountains and dramatically poised trees, influenced later Chinese and Japanese artists.

● **Xiamen** ▶ (Hsia-men *or* Amoy) 24 26N 118 07E A city in SE China on the island of Xiamen, in Fujian province, situated on Taiwan Strait. It is linked to the mainland by a causeway. The university was established in 1921. Industries include shipbuilding, engineering, fishing, and food processing.
   History: Xiamen has traded intermittently with Europeans since 1544. After its capture by the British during the Opium War (1841) it became a major tea-exporting port, through which many Chinese emigrants passed. Population (1990): 368 786.

● **Xi An** ▶ (Hsi-an *or* Sian) 34 16N 108 54E A city in central China, the capital of Shenxi province on the Wei Ho (River). It contains many Tang pagodas and a noted museum. It is an important industrial centre, its industries including steel, chemicals, textiles, and electronics.
   History: as a Tang capital (618–906 AD) it attracted many Buddhist, Muslim, and Christian missionaries. After 1935 it was a Guomindang (Nationalist) base (*see* Xi An incident). Population (1991 est): 2 760 000.

● **Xiangtan** ▶ (*or* Hsiang-t'an) 27 55N 112 47E A port in SE China, in Hunan province on the Xiang Jiang (River; *or* Hsiang Chiang). The commercial centre of an agricultural area, its products include textiles, iron and steel, and pig bristles. Population (1990): 441 968.

● **Xi An incident** ▶ (1936) The kidnapping of Chiang Kai-shek by his mutinous army in Manchuria. Chiang was captured by two young marshals, who demanded an end to fighting between Chinese Nationalists (Guomindang) and communists in the face of the Japanese invasion. Chiang was released when the communists announced that they would cooperate with the Guomindang in opposing Japan (*see* United Fronts).

● **Xi Jiang** ▶ (*or* Hsi Chiang) The most important river in S China, rising in Yunnan province and flowing E to form the densely populated Canton delta and the ▷Zhu Jiang. Most of its length is navigable by large ships. Length: about 1900 km (1200 mi).

● **Xingu, River** ▶ (Portuguese name: Rio Xingu) A river in central Brazil, rising on the Mato Grosso plateau and flowing generally N to enter the Amazon delta. Length: 1932 km (1200 mi).

● **Xining** ▶ (*or* Hsi-ning) 36 35N 101 55E A city in N central China, the capital of Qinghai province. Formerly on the W Chinese border, it was strategically important. Industries include chemicals, metals, wool, and leather. Population (1990): 551 776.

● **Xinjiang Uygur Autonomous Region** ▶ (*or* Sinkiang Uigur AR) An administrative region in NW China, the largest of such regions, covering one-sixth of the country. It borders on Tadzhikistan, Kirgizstan, Kazakhstan, Russia, Mongolia, Kashmir, and Tibet. Very dry with extreme temperatures, it consists of mountains in the centre with the Junggar Pendi in the N and the mainly desert Tarim Basin in the S. The Muslim Uigurs and the Chinese are the largest ethnic groups. Nomads in the N herd livestock, and wheat, cotton, and fruit are grown in oases and valleys. Oil and minerals are produced.

History: from 206 BC to 1756 AD, Chinese rule alternated with rule by Uigurs, Tibetans, and Mongols, and rebellions against Chinese government continued until 1949. It has recently been greatly developed by the central government. The scene of border clashes with the Soviet Union in 1969, it has considerable strategic importance. The 1990s saw growing pressure for independence among Muslim Uighurs and a crackdown by the Chinese authorities. Area: 1 646 799 sq km (635 829 sq mi). Population (1995 est): 16 320 000. Capital: Ürümqi.

● **Xiong Nu** ▶ (*or* Hsiung-nu) Turkish and Mongol tribes on the N and NW borders of China, which threatened Chinese security from about 500 BC. They depended on herding animals for their livelihood and, skilled horseback warriors, conducted raids in times of hardship to plunder the settled Chinese farming communities. The Chinese attempted to control the Xiong Nu by building the frontier walls that eventually became the Great Wall of China, marrying their daughters to Xiong Nu leaders, and trading with them.

● **Xochimilco** ▶ 19 08N 99 09W A town in central Mexico, on Lake Xochimilco. It is famous for its chinamoas (floating gardens), which originated as soil covered rafts on which fruit and vegetables were grown and have since become islands. Population (1990): 271 020.

● **X-ray astronomy** ▶ The study of celestial objects by the X-rays they emit. As X-rays are absorbed by the earth's atmosphere, observations have to be made above 150 km by rocket or satellite. The first X-ray source, ▷Scorpius X-1, was discovered in 1962, since when many sources have been observed, only some of which have been identified optically. ▷*See also* astronomy.

● **X-ray diffraction** ▶ The ▷diffraction of ▷X-rays when they strike a crystal. The angle through which the X-rays are diffracted depends on the spacing between the different planes in the crystal in a manner given by ▷Bragg's law. The technique is used in studying crystal structure and is often called **X-ray crystallography**. This method was responsible for Dorothy Hodgkin's elucidation of the structure of vitamin B_{12}, Perutz's determination of the structure of haemoglobin, and Watson and Crick's model for the double helix of DNA.

● **X-rays** ▶ ▷Electromagnetic radiation lying between ultraviolet radiation and gamma rays in the electromagnetic spectrum. X-rays may have wavelengths between 10^{-9} metre and 10^{-11} metre, the shorter wavelengths being known as hard X-rays and the longer wavelengths as soft X-rays. Discovered by Wilhelm ▷Roentgen (and formerly called Roentgen rays) in 1895, they are produced when heavy metal atoms (usually tungsten) are struck by sufficiently energetic electrons, as in an **X-ray tube**. The electrons in an X-ray tube are produced by a heated cathode in an evacuated tube and accelerated to the heavy-metal anode by an electric field. The collisions knock inner electrons from the atoms, X-rays being emitted when the va-

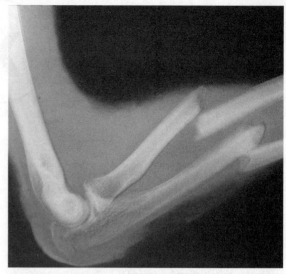

X-rays ▶ An X-ray of an arm with both the radius and the ulna broken in the lower arm.

cancy is filled by outer electrons. X-rays cause ionization in gases and penetrate matter. X-rays have many uses including the examination of internal organs and structures in medical diagnosis, the killing of cancer cells in ▷radiotherapy, investigating structures for flaws, and in ▷X-ray diffraction by crystals in order to study their structure.

● **Xuan Zang** ▶ (*or* Hsuan-tsang; 602–64 AD) Chinese Buddhist monk. He travelled alone to India and after studying there for about 10 years returned with Buddhist texts, 75 of which he translated. He also left a record of his travels, of great historical value.

● **xylem** ▶ A plant tissue specialized for the transport of water and salts. The main cells are tubelike, with their walls strengthened by deposits of ▷lignin in a spinal arrangement, which aids upward movement of materials by capillary action. In trees and shrubs the lignin deposits eventually block the tubes completely: this tissue forms ▷wood, and new secondary xylem is produced to transport water.

● **xylene** ▶ (*or* dimethyl benzene; $C_6H_4(CH_3)_2$) A colourless toxic flammable liquid consisting of a mixture of three isomers. It is obtained by fractional distillation of petroleum and is used as an aviation fuel and as a solvent.

● **xylophone** ▶ A pitched percussion instrument, consisting of a frame on which wooden bars in the pattern of a keyboard are fixed, each with a tubular metal resonator beneath it. It is played with two sticks. Orchestral xylophones usually have a compass of three octaves. *See also* vibraphone.

Y

● **yacht** ▶ A small vessel propelled by its sails, which may be used for pleasure cruising or racing. Olympic racing yachts are manned by one, two, or three persons (*see* sailing). The word comes from the obsolete Dutch *jaghtschip*, a chase ship, in commemoration of the *Mary*, a 100-ton vessel presented by the Dutch to Charles II in 1660, at the end of his exile on the continent.

Much larger power-driven pleasure boats with a paid crew are also called yachts. They are often the prized possessions of the wealthy, who wish to cruise between resorts in great comfort and style. The most lavish of such vessels was the Royal Yacht *Britannia*, the pleasure cruiser of the British royal family, until it was decommissioned in 1998.

● **Yacoub, Sir Magdi (Habib)** ▶ (1935–) Egyptian-born British cardiac surgeon. Working at the National Heart Hospital in London and Harefield Hospital, Greater London, he pioneered operating techniques in heart-valve surgery and heart and lung transplantation. He also devised techniques for the repair of complex congenital heart disease.

● **Yagi aerial** ▶ A VHF television and radio aerial consisting of a dipole aerial with a reflector and a number of parallel director aerials that focus the signal onto the dipole. It is more selective and less prone to interference than a simple dipole. It was devised in 1926 by the Japanese electrical engineer Hidetsugu Yagi (1886–1976).

● **Yahweh** ▶ The conjectural pronunciation of one of the Hebrew names of God. The name YHWH (the Tetragrammaton or "four-letter" name) occurs often in the Bible; out of reverence it was traditionally not pronounced, but replaced by *Adonai* (Lord) or *Hashem* (the Name), except by the ▷high priest when he entered the ▷Holy of Holies. "Jehovah" represents a largely Christian attempt to pronounce this name.

● **yak** ▶ A shaggy-coated wild ox, *Bos grunniens*, inhabiting mountain pastures of central Asia. Yaks have long been domesticated for draught purposes and milk. Wild yaks, up to 2 m high at the shoulder with long upcurved horns, are larger than domestic yaks and are always black; they live in large herds, feeding on coarse grasses, and are expert climbers.

● **Yakutia** ▶ (*or* Sakha Republic) The largest constituent republic of Russia. The Yakuts, a Mongoloid people, are traditionally nomadic herdsmen but have become sedentary. In NE Siberia, Yakutia (which was an autonomous Soviet republic from 1922 until 1991) is one of the world's coldest inhabited regions, and agriculture is only possible in the S. Mining for diamonds, gold, tin, and coal is the main occupation, with trapping for fur. Area: 3 103 000 sq km (1 197 760 sq mi). Population (1996 est): 1 198 200. Capital: Yakutsk.

● **yakuza** ▶ (Japanese: worthless) A Japanese gangster involved in gambling, pornography, prostitution, protection rackets, etc. Yakuza have a long history of involvement in organized crime and are divided into a number of syndicates (*boryokudan*) between which there is fierce rivalry. Members are loyal to their syndicates and have a somewhat misguided pride in their activities. Because yakuza are able to wield considerable political power they have managed to survive.

● **Yale University** ▶ One of the oldest universities in the USA, founded in 1701 by a group of Congregational clergymen as a collegiate school. After moving to New Haven, Connecticut, in 1716, it was named after Elihu Yale (1648–1721), who donated his books to the college. Yale has educated women since 1869.

● **Yalta** ▶ 44 30N 34 09E A port in S Ukraine, on the Black Sea. It is the Crimea's chief resort and was the site of the ▷Yalta Conference in 1945. Population (latest est): 89 000.

Yalta Conference ▶ Churchill (left), Roosevelt, and Stalin, with their advisers.

● **Yalta Conference** ▶ (February, 1945) The conference held at Yalta in the Crimea towards the end of World War II attended by F. D. Roosevelt (USA), Stalin (Soviet Union), and Churchill (UK). They agreed upon the postwar occupation of Germany by the USA, Soviet Union, UK, and France and that German surrender must be unconditional. Stalin also gave assurances (subsequently broken) that Poland and other countries of E Europe then occupied by the Red Army would not be subjected to communist control without their free democratic consent.

● **yam** ▶ A twining herbaceous plant of the genus *Dioscorea*, cultivated in wet tropical regions for its tubers, which are eaten like potatoes. Yams have long slender climbing stems, bearing entire or lobed leaves, and unisexual flowers in long clusters. Tubers can reach a length of 2.6 m and a weight of 45 kg; species commonly cultivated are *D. alata* (white yam), *D. rotundata* (white guinea yam), *D. batatas* (Chinese yam), and *D. cayenensis* (yellow yam). Family: *Dioscoreaceae*.

● **Yamagata Aritomo** ▶ (1838–1922) Japanese soldier and statesman. As commander of the Imperial Guard, he created a modern conscript army and while home minister (1885–89) he shaped Japan's modern local government. Twice prime minister (1890–91, 1898–1900), he oversaw Japan's victories against China (1894–95) and Russia (1904–05).

● **Yamasaki, Minoru** ▶ (1912–86) US architect. His earliest buildings, such as Missouri's St Louis airport (1953–55), were remarkable for their simple elegance. Later works, such as the Woodrow Wilson building in Princeton (1965) and the twin towers of the World Trade Center in New York (1970–77), employed pseudo-Gothic elements.

● **Yamato** ► The ruling dynasty of Japan under which the country was united in the 4th century AD. All subsequent Japanese emperors have claimed descent from the Yamato, under whom Buddhism was introduced in the 6th century.

● **Yamoussoukro** ► 6 49N 5 17W The capital of Côte d'Ivoire. Yamoussoukro was chosen as an inland replacement for the old capital of Abidjan in 1983. It includes a presidential palace, three universities, and the Our Lady of Peace basilica, the largest in the world. Population (1995 est): 110 000.

● **Yamuna, River** ▷*See* Jumna, River.

● **Yang, Chen Ning** ► (1922–) US physicist, born in China, who shared the 1957 Nobel Prize with his countryman Tsung-Dao ▷Lee for their theoretical work suggesting that parity would not be conserved in the ▷weak interaction. This was quickly confirmed by observations of beta decay.

● **Yangon** ▷*See* Rangoon.

● **Yangtze Incident** ► An attack by Chinese Communist forces on the British frigate *Amethyst* in the Yangtze River, during a routine visit to Nanjing in 1949. After 17 of the crew, including the captain, had been killed the ship remained imprisoned for three months, until a naval attaché, Commander Kerans, boarded it and under the noses of the shore batteries brought it out into the open sea without further loss of life.

● **Yangtze River** ► (Chinese name: Chang Jiang *or* Ch'ang Chiang) The longest river in China and the third longest in the world. Rising on the borders of Tibet and Qinghai province, it flows roughly E to enter the East China Sea via an extensive delta. The Yangtze is a major transport route and its densely populated basin is China's most productive agricultural region. Severe floods in 1998 are thought to have destroyed about 6 million homes with some 4000 fatalities. In 1994 work began on the **Yangtze dam**, a massive hydroelectric and flood-control project near Yichang, due to be completed in 2010. This £20-billion project, China's most spectacular public work since the Great Wall, will involve the creation of a giant reservoir some 595 km (370 mi) long and the relocation of some 1.8 million people. There are also plans to divert some 10% of the Yangtze's waters to desert areas thousands of miles to the N; if achieved, this will be the world's biggest infrastructure project. Length: 6380 km (3964 mi).

● **Yankee** ► A sometimes disparaging name for any citizen of the USA. Inside the USA it refers specifically to an inhabitant of New England and the northern states. During the US Civil War, the southern troops referred to the Federal soldiers as Yankees. The word is said to have come from the Dutch nickname *Jan Kees* ("John Cheese"), used derisively by Dutch settlers of English colonists in the New York area. In some contexts "real Yankees" are still New Englanders who can trace their ancestors back to British colonists.

● **Yannina** ▷*See* Ioánnina.

● **Yanomami** ► An Amazonian tribe of American Indians living on tribal lands in S Venezuela and N Brazil. In 1987 mineral deposits on their lands attracted the interest of speculative miners, and the Yanomami were threatened with dispossession; in 1991 the Brazilian government granted the Yanomami possession of some 58 000 sq km (36 000 sq mi) of their original land.

● **Yantai** ► (Yentai *or* Chefoo) 37 30N 121 22E A port in E China, on the Shandong Peninsula. Following the Chefoo Convention, signed in 1876 by Britain and China, many foreign traders lived here. The chief industries are fishing and food processing. Population (1999 est): 818 646.

● **Yaoundé** ► (or Yaunde) 3 51N 11 31E The capital of Cameroon. Founded under the German protectorate of Kamerun in 1888, it was capital of French Cameroon from 1922. The Federal University of Cameroon was founded in 1962. Population (1992 est): 800 000.

● **yard** ► An Imperial unit of length originally defined as the dis-

tance between two gold plugs on a bronze bar. In 1963 the yard was redefined as 0.9144 metre (*see* metric system).

● **Yarkand** ▷*See* Shache.

● **Yarmouth** ▷*See* Great Yarmouth.

● **Yaroslavl** ► 57 34N 39 52E A city in W Russia, on the River Volga. It has been a textile centre since the 18th century. Population (1995 est): 629 000.

● **yarrow** ► A perennial herb, *Achillea millefolium*, also called milfoil, native to pastures of Europe and W Asia. Up to 45 cm high, it has feathery strongly scented leaves and small white daisy-like flowers borne. Family: ▷Compositae.

● **Yawata** ▷*See* Kitakyushu.

● **yawl** ► A □sailing vessel with two masts, a tall one set one-third of the boat's length from the bows and a very short one just behind the rudder post. Yawls, like ▷ketches, are a favoured rig for yachts, for the split rig reduces the area of each sail, making handling easier. Yawls do not sail as well towards the wind as sloops do. ▷*See also* sloop.

● **yaws** ► A chronic tropical disease caused by a ▷spirochaete bacterium, *Treponema pertenue*. It occurs mostly among poor children and is spread by skin contact. After an incubation period of three to four weeks a growth appears on the thighs or buttocks; later, multiple growths that look like squashed raspberries appear all over the skin. Bones may also be affected and if not treated the disease can be very disfiguring. Treatment with penicillin is highly effective.

● **Yazd** ► (or Yezd) 31 55N 54 22E A town in central Iran. It has several mosques, some built in the 11th century, and produces silk fabrics. Population (1996): 326 776.

● **year** ► The time taken by the earth to complete one revolution around the sun. This is equal to the period of the sun's apparent motion around the ▷ecliptic. The **tropical year**, of 365.2422 days, is the interval between two successive passages of the sun through the vernal ▷equinox. The **sidereal year**, of 365.2564 days, refers to successive passages of the sun through a point relative to the background stars. These periods differ because of the ▷precession of the equinoxes. ▷*See also* calendar.

● **yeast** ► A fungus that is capable of fermenting carbohydrates and that reproduces asexually by budding new cells from its surface. Yeasts consist of individual cells that occur singly or in groups or chains of several cells. Some yeasts show sexual reproduction. Strains of *Saccharomyces cerevisiae*, the cells of which are 0.004–0.02 mm in diameter, are widely used to cause ▷fermentation in baking, brewing, and the manufacture of wines and spirits. Yeast extracts are used as a food for their high vitamin B content. Yeasts are also used as tools in genetic research, as cloning vectors in ▷genetic engineering, and as a source of protein (*see* single-cell protein). Some yeasts, including *Candida albicans* (*see* candidiasis), cause disease in humans. Phylum: ▷Ascomycota.

● **Yeats, William Butler** ► (1865–1939) Irish poet and dramatist. During the 1890s he helped found the Rhymers' Club in London, pursued his lifelong interest in the occult, and published several volumes of symbolist verse on Irish mythological and nationalist subjects. His best-known poems, many of which appeared in *The Tower* (1928) and *The Winding Stair* (1929), are mainly tragic meditations on personal and political themes. Among them are "Easter, 1916," "The Second Coming," and "Sailing to Byzantium." He was an admirer of Maud Gonne (1866–1953), Irish actress and nationalist who inspired many of his love poems, and with Lady ▷Gregory in 1904 he founded the Abbey Theatre, Dublin, for which he wrote a number of plays. He was a senator of the Irish Free State (1922–28) and won the Nobel Prize in 1923. His brother **Jack Butler Yeats** (1871–1957) was a noted Irish painter, born in London. After a childhood in Sligo he returned to London to study, but his paintings were essentially Irish, depicting life in bars, racecourses, etc., in dark colours, often shot with bright explosions of colour applied with a palette knife.

● **yellow fever** ► An acute viral infection transmitted by female mosquitoes of the genus *Aëdes*, which occur in areas of tropical rain forest. After an incubation period of 3–14 days the patient develops a fever with aching muscles. In severe cases the virus affects the liver causing jaundice (hence the name), the kidneys, and the heart; death may result from liver or heart failure. There is no specific treatment but two kinds of vaccine can prevent it.

● **yellowfin tuna** ▶ A large tuna fish, *Thunnus albacares*, with yellow fins and a golden stripe along its sides. It is found worldwide and is a valued food and game fish.

● **yellow-green algae** ▶ ▷Algae of the phylum *Chrysophyta* (about 6000 species), which are yellow-green to brown in colour depending on the proportion of green chlorophyll masked by the pigments fucoxanthin or diadinoxanthin. Most are unicellular or colonial and they form a major constituent of plankton (*see also* diatoms). Most reproduce asexually by spores.

● **yellowhammer** ▶ A Eurasian ▷bunting, *Emberiza citrinella*, that occurs on farmland and roadsides, where it feeds on grain and seeds. About 16 cm long, the male has a bright-yellow head and underparts, chestnut rump, and a brown-streaked back; females are less colourful. ▷*See* Plate III.

● **Yellowknife** ▶ 62 30N 114 29W A city in N Canada, the capital of the Northwest Territories. Founded in 1935, it is the commercial and administrative centre of the territory, with an airport and gold mines. Population (1990): 13 698.

● **Yellow River** ▶ (Chinese name: Huang He *or* Huang Ho) A river in China, rising in the W and flowing roughly E to enter the Gulf of Chihli via a fertile delta. Its summer floods have resulted in frequent disasters and changes of course. Its diversion as a measure against the Japanese invasion (1938) resulted in the death of 900 000 people. Length: about 4350 km (2700 mi).

● **Yellow Sea** ▶ (Chinese name: Huang Hai) A large shallow inlet of the W Pacific Ocean, bordered by China and Korea. It is so called because of the yellowish silt deposited by the Chinese rivers. It is rich in fish.

● **Yellowstone National Park** ▶ The largest national park in the USA, chiefly in NW Wyoming but extending into S Montana and E Idaho. Established in 1872, it consists mainly of forested volcanic plateaus. Its many active geysers include Old Faithful, which erupts at hourly intervals. Area: 8956 sq km (3458 sq mi).

● **Yellowstone River** ▶ A river in the W USA, rising in NW Wyoming and flowing N through the ▷Yellowstone National Park then E to the Missouri River. Length: 1080 km (671 mi).

● **yellowwood** ▶ An evergreen coniferous tree of the genus *Podocarpus* (over 100 species), mostly of warm temperate and tropical regions of the S hemisphere. The hard leathery leaves are strap-shaped and the green berry-like fruits are borne on fleshy stalks. The light elastic nonresinous wood is used for building, furniture, carving, and ships. Family: *Podocarpaceae*.

W. B. Yeats ▶ A drawing (1925) by Kathleen Shackleton. As he entered his sixties Yeats was in the throes of his greatest creative period, the years that saw the composition of most of the poems in *The Tower* (1928) and *The Winding Stair* (1929).

● **Yeltsin, Boris** ▶ (1931–) Russian politician; president of the Russian Federation (1991–99). He was first secretary of the Moscow Communist Party from 1985 until his removal by Gorbachov in 1987. In 1990 he was elected president of the Russian SFSR and left the Communist Party, becoming the chief rival to Gorbachov, whom he criticized for slowness in implementing reform. In 1991 he led resistance to the anti-Gorbachov coup by Communist hardliners, emerging with increased stature when the coup failed. Following the breakup of the Soviet Union he became president of independent Russia and played a leading role in creating the ▷Commonwealth of Independent States. In 1991–92 he began to implement free-market reforms despite opposition from parliament. This led to a brief military confrontation (1993) in which Yeltsin gained the upper hand. However, his handling of the crisis in ▷Chechenia (1994–96) led to international criticism. From 1995 he faced a parliament dominated by his Communist opponents. He was re-elected in 1996 but his authority was already in decline owing to ill health. A grave financial crisis in 1998 led to further constitutional conflicts, during which many of Yeltsin's powers were effectively transferred to parliament. However, Yeltsin reasserted himself by sacking the whole government four times in 1998–99. An attempt to impeach him by parliament subsequently failed (May, 1999). He finally resigned in favour of Vladimir ▷Putin on 31 December, 1999.

● **Yemen Republic** ▶ A country in the Middle East, in S ▷Arabia bordering on the Red Sea, the Gulf of Aden, and the Arabian Sea. It includes the islands of Kamaran in the Red Sea, ▷Perim Island, ▷Socotra, and the ▷Kuria Muria Islands. It consists of narrow dry coastal plains rising to upland valleys and mountains in the W (the wettest and most fertile in Arabia) and to the barren Hadhramaut plateau in the SE. The N and E are desert. The predominantly Arab population is chiefly Sunnite with Shiites and some Zaidi, the Jews having mostly emigrated after 1918. There are nomadic tribes in the N and E.
Economy: agriculture was the basis of the economy until oil production began in 1986. Subsistence farming remains the chief occupation with the cultivation of cash crops mainly confined to the more fertile W. Cotton is the main crop: others include cereals, coffee, fruit and vegetables, tobacco, and the narcotic qat. Livestock are kept. Sardine fishing is important. Apart from oil production and refining, industry is very limited but includes textiles, soft drinks, and cigarette factories: salt is mined and handicrafts are important. The S and E have almost no industry outside Aden. Refined oil, cotton, fish products, hides, and incense are exported. The economy, which is one of the poorest in the world, relies on foreign aid and money received from the large proportion of Yemenis who work abroad, mainly in Saudi Arabia. The greater part of Yemen's large foreign debt was written off by the IMF in 1997.
History: ruled by Muslim imams (priest-kings) from the 9th century, Yemen (excluding Aden) was nominally part of the Ottoman Empire from the 16th century to 1918. Aden was captured from the Turks in 1839 and occupied by the British East India Company. The British made protectorate treaties with other local rulers (1886–1914) to safeguard Aden and its trade routes; these 24 sultanates, emirates, and sheikdoms were called the Aden Protectorate (1937). The state of North Yemen, in the NW of present-day Yemen and with its capital at Sana'a, was established in 1934 by treaty with Saudi Arabia and the UK, although clashes with the British over the control of Aden continued. It joined the Arab League (1945) and the UN (1947) and was loosely allied with Egypt and Syria (1958–61) in the United Arab Republic. In 1963 the Aden Protectorate and adjoining sheikdoms formed the Federation of South Arabia. This collapsed in 1967, when anti-British nationalist groups in Aden took control (although the British had already agreed to withdraw), and the communist Peoples' Republic of South Yemen was established, with its capital at Aden. The history of North Yemen was marked by internal disorders, culminating in civil war (1962–70), which ended with the recognition of a republican regime. Another coup took place in 1974 and successive heads of state were assassinated in 1977 and 1978. Moves were made towards uniting the two Yemens following border clashes in 1967–72. However, allegations of South Yemeni involvement in the 1978 assassination were followed by increased border fighting. The history of South Yemen was dominated by border disputes with

North Yemen and with Oman (until 1976). Its underdeveloped economy was further damaged by the closure of the Suez Canal (1967–75). In 1986 foreign nationals were evacuated during a military coup; in the ensuing elections Haider Abu Bakr al Attas became president. Plans for union between the two Yemens were announced in 1989 and implemented in 1990. However, tensions soon recurred, leading to a civil war (1994) in which northern forces defeated southern secessionists. Policies of economic and constitutional reform have been adopted by subsequent governments. Multiparty elections were held in 1997; Yemen's first direct presidential elections, held in 1999, were won by the incumbent, President Saleh.

Yemen Republic

Head of state	President Ali Abdullah Saleh
Official language	Arabic
Official currency	riyal of 100 fils
Area	531 870 sq km (205 311 sq mi)
Population (1998 est)	16 388 000
Capitals	Sana'a (administrative) and Aden (commercial)

● **Yenisei, River** ▶ A river in central Russia, rising in the Sayan Mountains and flowing N to **Yenisei Bay** on the Kara Sea. There is a hydroelectric power station at Krasnoyarsk. Length: about 4000 km (2485 mi).

● **Yentai** ▷See Yantai.

● **yeoman** ▶ In medieval England, a person of common birth owning free land with an annual value of at least 40 shillings, who was thereby entitled to serve on juries and vote for the knight of the shire. A yeoman was originally a servant of a royal or noble household, but after the decline of ▷feudalism the term came to mean the freehold owner of a small estate. He would not, however, be regarded as a member of the **gentry**; to be a gentleman in medieval times was to be of good birth (and therefore entitled to bear arms) but not a member of the nobility.

More widely, from the 15th century, a yeoman was understood to be a respectable countryman of some means; the more affluent members of the yeomanry aspired to become members of the gentry, who by this time were defined as men of independent means who had no need to rely on a trade or profession.

● **Yeomanry** ▶ A volunteer cavalry force raised in Britain between 1794 and 1908. First organized as part of the country's defences following the French Revolution, it was eventually superseded by such forces as the ▷Territorial Army.

● **Yeomen of the Guard** ▶ The bodyguard of the British sovereign established by Henry VII for his coronation in 1485. Their last appearance in battle—and the last by a British monarch—was with George II at Dettingen in 1743. They are now a ceremonial guard. Although often confused with the Yeomen Warders at the Tower of London, who wear a similar red and gold uniform, the two bodies are quite distinct. The nickname Beefeaters (of disputed origin) is popularly applied to both but disliked by the Yeomen of the Guard.

● **Yerevan** ▶ (Russian name: Erevan) 40 10N 44 31E The capital of Armenia, situated in the W of the country. A commercial centre, it has chemical, textile, and food-processing industries.
History: the site of an ancient fortress, the city dates from at least the 7th century AD. Disputed by Persia and Turkey, it was ceded to Russia in 1828. In 1990 it became a focus of ethnic unrest. Population (1995 est): 1 248 700.

● **Yerkes Observatory** ▶ An observatory owned by the University of Chicago at Williams Bay, Wisconsin, USA. It was founded in 1892 by the businessman Charles Tyson Yerkes (1837–1905). Its 40-inch (1.02-metre) refractor, erected in 1897, is still the world's largest refracting telescope.

● **Yerwa** ▷See Maiduguri.

● **Yesenin, Sergei Aleksandrovich** ▶ (1895–1925) Russian poet. He emerged from a peasant background into Moscow society during the revolution. He travelled in the USA and Europe, was briefly married to Isadora ▷Duncan, suffered from alcoholism and drug addiction, and finally committed suicide. His volumes include *Confessions of a Hooligan* (1924).

● **Yeti** ▷See Abominable Snowman.

● **Yevtushenko, Yevgenii** ▶ (1933–) Russian poet. His implicit criticism of the Soviet authorities in such poems as *Babi Yar* (1961) gained him wide popularity and he has given many poetry readings in Europe and the USA. He was a member of the Congress of People's Deputies (1989–91). His more recent publications include his *Collected Poems* (1991), as well as several novels and books of photographs.

● **yew** ▶ A coniferous tree or shrub of the genus *Taxus* (10 species), native to the N hemisphere. Yews have dark-green leaves and the male and female flowers grow on separate trees. The female flowers produce bright-red fruits, each containing a single seed. The berries are sweet-tasting and attractive to birds, but the seeds and leaves are poisonous. The most widespread species is the common yew (*T. baccata*), of Europe, SW Asia, and N Africa; it grows to a height of 25 m but cultivated forms—grown for shelter, ornament, and topiary work—are often smaller. Family: *Taxaceae*.

● **Yezd** ▷See Yazd.

● **Yezidis** ▶ The name of a Kurd tribe of Iraq and their tribal religion, which was largely inspired by the 12th-century Sufi Sheikh Adi Ibn Musafir. The sect, the centre of which is in Mosul, combines Islamic, Christian, Judaic, and other ancient elements (including circumcision and baptism).

● **Yezo** ▷See Hokkaido.

● **Yggdrasill** ▶ In Norse mythology, an evergreen ash tree embracing the whole universe. Its three roots join the underworld, the land of giants, and the home of the gods (Asgard). Demons threaten its existence; the serpent Nidhögg constantly chews at one of its roots, while four stags eat its buds. However, it is preserved by the ▷Norns (the Fates), who water it from one of the three fountains at its base. The maypole and the Christmas tree are possibly symbolic derivatives of Yggdrasill.

● **Yibin** ▶ (or I-pin) 28 50N 104 35E A port and commercial centre in S central China, in Sichuan province at the confluence of the Yangtze and Min Rivers. Salt is mined here and chemicals and paper are manufactured. Population (1990): 241 019.

● **Yichang** ▶ (or I-ch'ang) 30 43N 111 22E A port in E central China, in Hubei province on the Yangtze River. An old commercial centre, it marked the limit of the Japanese advance during the Sino-Japanese War (1937–45). The Yangtze dam, the world's largest hydroelectricity project, is currently under construction some 65 km (40 mi) upstream. Population (1990): 371 601.

● **Yiddish** ▶ A language used by ▷Ashkenazim (East European) Jews and based on a dialect of High German. It emerged during the 11th century and has absorbed many Slavonic and other influences. It is written in the ▷Hebrew alphabet. Yiddish literature flourished in the 19th and early 20th centuries and includes the works of the US Nobel laureate Isaac Bashevis ▷Singer. However, after the ▷holocaust Yiddish yielded its place as the principal literary language of the Jews to Hebrew. Yiddish was taken to the USA by European Jews at the beginning of the 20th century and over the last hundred years many Yiddish words have entered the American language, especially as spoken in New York and California. From the USA, some have been introduced into British English.

● **yield** ▶ (stocks and shares) ▷See dividend; gilt-edged security.

● **yield point** ▶ The point at which a body becomes permanently deformed when subjected to a sufficiently large stress. Below the yield point the body is elastic, above the yield point it becomes plastic. ▷See also elasticity; plasticity.

● **yin and yang** ▶ Contrasting but complementary principles at the root of traditional Chinese cosmology. Yin is the negative feminine mode, associated with the earth, darkness, and passivity. Yang is the positive dynamic principle of masculine energy associated with heaven and light. The principles antedate ▷Confucius and are important in ▷Taoism, serving, for example, to explain the cycle of the seasons. ▷See also I Ching.

● **Yinchuan** ▶ 38 30N 106 19E A city in N central China, capital of Ningxia Hui AR. It is the ancient commercial centre of a fertile agricultural region. Its chief industries are coalmining and wool. Population (1999 est): 469 180.

● **Yingkou** ▶ (*or* Newchang) 40 40N 122 17E A port in NE China, in Liaoning province on the Hun estuary. Manchuria's chief port in the late 19th century, it has fishing, engineering, and oil-refining industries. Population (1999 est): 498 300.

● **ylang-ylang** ▶ A slender evergreen tropical Asian tree, *Cananga odorata*, also called perfume tree. It has pointed oval leaves, up to 20 cm long, and bears drooping clusters of fragrant stalked greenish-yellow flowers throughout the year. An oil distilled from the flowers is used in perfumery, cosmetics, and soaps. Family: *Annonaceae*.

● **YMCA** ▷*See* Young Men's Christian Association.

● **yoga** ▶ The principles and practice of self-training that permeates all Indian philosophical traditions. Traces of it exist from the ▷Indus Valley civilization before the Aryan invasion (1500 BC). The methods used are generally austere and ascetic and include physical control and meditative techniques (*see* meditation). Physical control is stressed in Hindu yoga; in the Buddhist practice contemplative methods predominate; in Jainism asceticism is emphasized. Usually the aim is a state of release and liberation from the material world. The yoga so fashionable in the West frequently takes the form of hatha-yoga, which involves physical exercises to bring peace and insight.

● **yogurt** ▷*See* dairy products.

● **Yogyakarta** ▷*See* Jogjakarta.

● **Yokohama** ▶ 35 28N 139 28E A port and second largest city of Japan, in SE Honshu on Tokyo Bay. Together with Tokyo it forms Japan's greatest urban and industrial area and handles 30% of foreign trade. Its industries include shipbuilding, oil refining, chemicals, steel, and textiles. Its two universities were both established in 1949.

History: It grew rapidly after 1859 as a second port for Tokyo, with which it was linked by Japan's first railway (1872). It was almost destroyed by the 1923 earthquake and badly bombed during World War II. A new port terminal is currently being constructed to a futuristic design. Population (1995): 3 307 408.

● **Yokosuka** ▶ 35 18N 139 39E A port in Japan, in SE Honshu on Tokyo Bay. William Adams (d. 1620), the first Englishman to visit Japan (1600), is buried here. A major naval base, its chief industry is shipbuilding. Population (1995): 432 202.

● **Yom Kippur** ▶ (Hebrew: Day of Atonement) A Jewish holy day, falling nine days after ▷Rosh Hashana. The holiest day of the year, it is a day of penitence and cleansing from sin and is marked by 24 hours' total fast and sexual abstinence. Traditionally Jewish families, on the eve of Yom Kippur (called Kol Nidre), eat a meal together before attending synagogue. The following day is also spent in synagogue, before a second family meal at which the fast is broken. ▷*See also* Holy of Holies.

● **Yom Kippur War** ▷*See* Israel, State of.

● **Yonge, Charlotte** ▶ (1823–1901) British novelist. Her novels and children's books are chiefly concerned with religious ideals, especially those of the ▷Oxford Movement. Her books include *The Heir of Redclyffe* (1853) and *Heartsease* (1854).

yin and yang ▶ The symbols are interlocked and each contains a tiny portion of the other.

● **Yong Lo** ▶ (*or* Yung-lo; 1360–1424) The title of Ch'eng-tsu, Chinese emperor (1402–24), after usurping the throne. He vigorously ex-

panded the ▷Ming dynasty, dispatching fleets to SE Asia and personally leading military expeditions. He transferred the capital to Beijing from Nanjing.

● **Yonkers** ▶ 40 56N 73 54W A city in the USA, in New York state on the Hudson River. Industries include elevators, carpets, chemicals, and clothing. Population (2000): 196 086.

● **York** ▶ 1. (Latin name: Eboracum) 53 58N 1 05W A city in N England, in York unitary authority, North Yorkshire on the River Ouse. It was the principal Roman garrison in Britain (Constantine was proclaimed emperor here in 306 AD) and from 866 was the capital of the Viking kingdom of Jorvik. During the middle ages it became the centre of the wool trade and was regarded as England's northern capital. The cathedral (Minster), seat of the Archbishop of York, was begun in 1154 and dominates the city. The south transept was damaged by fire in 1984. The medieval walls and four city gateways remain. Industries include chocolate manufacturing, sugar, and the production of scientific instruments. The National Railway Museum opened in 1975 and the Jorvik Viking Centre in 1984. York is a tourist centre as well as a market town and educational centre; the university was founded in 1963. Population (1994 est): 104 100. 2. A unitary authority in N England. Area: 272 sq km (105 sq mi). Population (1999 est): 175 925.

● **York** ▶ A ruling dynasty of England descended from Edmund, Duke of York (1342–1402), the fourth son of Edward III. Richard Plantagenet, Duke of ▷York, led the Yorkist opposition to Henry VI's Lancastrian government in the Wars of the ⌐Roses (1455–85), in which the Yorkist emblem was the white rose. His son Edward IV, established the royal dynasty. After the brief rule of his son Edward V and the overthrow of Richard III (1485) the Crown passed to Henry VII, the first ▷Tudor monarch, who married Edward IV's daughter Elizabeth.

● **York, Archbishop of** ▶ The second of the two archbishops of England and head of the northern province of the Church of England. York became an archiepiscopal see in 735 AD under Egbert (d. 766), brother of the Northumbrian king. Controversy between Canterbury and York regarding primacy was settled by Pope Innocent II (1352–62), with precedence given to the Archbishop of ▷Canterbury, called Primate of All England, while the Archbishop of York was styled Primate of England. He ranks next to the Lord Chancellor and before all other peers except the royal princes. He signs himself with his Christian name followed by the Latin abbreviation of York, for example "John Ebor." Recent archbishops are: (94th) Stuart (Yarworth), Baron Blanch (1974–83); (95th) John Habgood (1983–95); (96th) David Hope (1995–).

● **York, Prince Andrew, Duke of** ▶ (1960–) Second son of Elizabeth II and fourth in succession to the throne. A former helicopter pilot in the Royal Navy, he married Sarah Ferguson in 1986. Their daughters are Princess Beatrice (1988–) and Princess Eugenie (1990–). The couple separated in 1992 and divorced in 1996.

● **York, Frederick Augustus, Duke of** ▶ (1763–1827) British soldier, commander-in-chief of the British army (1798–1809). The second son of George III, he led two unsuccessful campaigns in the French Revolutionary Wars. He also opposed Roman Catholic emancipation and is remembered in a well-known nursery rhyme as "the grand old duke of York."

● **York, Richard Plantagenet, Duke of** ▶ (1411–60) English magnate, who was descended from the fourth son of Edward III and the second son in the female line. His claim to the throne against Henry VI (descended from Edward III's third son) resulted in the outbreak of the Wars of the ▷Roses in 1455. He was killed in a skirmish at Wakefield. His sons became Edward IV (1461) and Richard III (1483).

● **Yorke Peninsula** ▶ A peninsula of SE South Australia, situated between Spencer Gulf and Gulf St Vincent. It is an important wheat-growing and sheep-rearing area.

● **York mystery plays** ▶ A cycle of 48 plays originating in the 14th century and performed by the trade guilds of York on the feast of Corpus Christi. The most extensive cycle of medieval plays in England, the York cycle covered the whole of history from a Christian viewpoint, from the creation of the angels to the last judgment, concentrating on the fall of man and his redemption by Christ. They were all performed in chronological order in the course of one day. The series of 14 plays devoted to Christ's Passion were revised into alliterative verse at one stage and are notable for their disturbing realism. ▷*See* miracle plays.

● **Yorkshire** ▶ A historic county of NE England, bordering on the North Sea. The largest county in England, it was traditionally divided into North, West, and East Ridings (thirds). From the late middle ages onwards it was a centre of the wool industry. It was reorganized in 1974 to form the counties of ▷North Yorkshire, ▷West Yorkshire, and ▷South Yorkshire, and parts of ▷Humberside and ▷Cleveland. When Humberside and Cleveland were abolished in 1996, the ▷East Riding was reinstated as a ▷unitary authority and parts of the NE were returned to North Yorkshire for ceremonial and related purposes.

● **Yorkshire Dales** ▷*See* Dales, the.

● **Yorkshire terrier** ▶ A breed of toy □dog developed from several terrier breeds in N England during the 19th century. It is small and compact with a very long straight coat that trails on the ground. This is black at birth but matures to steel-blue with tan on the head and chest. Height: 20–23 cm.

● **Yorktown** ▶ 37 14N 76 32W A village in the USA, in Virginia on the York River. The last important battle of the American Revolution was fought here in 1781.

● **Yoruba** ▶ A people of W Nigeria, with groups in Benin and Togo, numbering in all about nine million. They speak a ▷Kwa language and many are now Christians or Muslims, although their traditional religion included sky gods and worship of ancestral spirits. Their city, ▷Ife, was the seat of their first independent kingdom (12th century). Many are now farmers, others are artisans and traders.

● **Yosemite National Park** ▶ A national park in the USA, in central California. The scenic Yosemite Valley, which lies within the park, contains the world's three largest monoliths of exposed granite. There are also many lakes, rivers, and waterfalls including the Yosemite Falls, which are the highest in North America with a drop in two segments of 739 m (2425 ft). Area: 3061 sq km (1182 sq mi).

● **Young, Arthur** ▶ (1741–1820) British writer. He published *Annals of Agriculture* (47 vols, 1784–1809) and several accounts of his tours throughout England. In *Travels in France* (1792) he was notably sympathetic to the Revolution. He became first secretary of the Board of Agriculture in 1793.

● **Young, Brigham** ▶ (1801–77) US Mormon leader, who succeeded Joseph ▷Smith. A former Methodist, Young joined the new church in 1832 and for a time supervised the Mormon Mission in England. After Smith's death he led the migration to Salt Lake City, Utah (1846–47). He became president of the Church and later governor of Utah Territory (1851).

● **Young, Thomas** ▶ (1773–1829) British physician and physicist, who spoke 12 languages at the age of 20. After studying in Germany and at Cambridge he practised medicine in London (1799–1814), becoming professor at the Royal Institution (1801–03). He identified astigmatism and described the ciliary muscles of the eye. He demonstrated the interference of light and used this observation to suggest a wave theory of light in opposition to ▷Newton's corpuscular theory. As a result of his work on the elasticity of materials, the ratio of stress to strain is known as Young's modulus. Also an Egyptologist, he helped decipher the ▷Rosetta Stone.

● **Young England** ▶ A Tory political movement of the 1840s that sought to unite the aristocracy and the working classes in an attempt to end the growing domination of politics by the middle class. Its leaders were John Manners (1818–1906; later Duke of Rutland) and George Smythe (1818–57; later Viscount Strangford). The movement acquired some credibility when the young ▷Disraeli became a member and used his novel *Coningsby* (1844) to promote its romantic ideals. However, the movement broke up in 1845 over the disputed issue of ▷free trade.

● **Younghusband, Sir Francis Edward** ▶ (1863–1942) British explorer and mountaineer. He explored Manchuria in 1886 and discovered the route from Kashgar into India via the Mustagh Pass. In 1902 he visited Tibet to make a treaty with the Dalai Lama and to open up the country to Western trade.

● **Young Ireland** ▶ An Irish nationalist movement formed by young Protestant radicals in the 1840s. Its rising in 1848 under William Smith ▷O'Brien was a humiliating failure.

● **Young Italy** ▶ A movement, founded by Giuseppe ▷Mazzini in 1831, that sought to establish a united republican Italy. After the failure of Mazzini's invasion of Savoy and other risings in the 1830s and 1840s it declined. ▷*See also* Risorgimento.

● **Young Men's Christian Association** ▶ (YMCA) A Christian organization for young men and, since 1971, for young women, founded in 1844 by George Williams (1821–1905), a British draper. Its aim is to encourage Christian morality and qualities of leadership. The World Alliance of YMCAs, formed in 1855 in Geneva, consists of 20 million members in 84 countries.

● **young offender institution** ▶ A British penal institution for confining offenders aged 15 or over but under 21. Offering a regime aimed to promote self-discipline and a sense of responsibility, they house offenders who would have been imprisoned for their offences if they were over 21 or who are considered to constitute a danger to the public. The minimum detention period is 21 days and the maximum is 2 years. ▷*See* criminal law.

● **Young's modulus** ▷*See* elastic modulus.

● **Youngstown** ▶ 41 05N 80 40W A city in the USA, in Ohio. A centre of iron and steel industry, it produces aluminium, office furniture, and aircraft. Youngstown State University was established here in 1908. Population (1996 est): 87 405.

● **Young Turks** ▶ A Turkish revolutionary group. In 1908 the Young Turks, officially named the Committee of Union and Progress, led the revolution that resulted in Sultan ▷Abdulhamid's abdication. Under ▷Enver Pasha and Talaat Pasha (1872–1921), they were the dominant force in Turkish politics until 1918.

● **Young Women's Christian Association** ▶ (YWCA) A Christian organization for women (to which men may now also belong). Founded in 1855 by Emma Robarts and Mary Jane Kinnaird to promote unity among Christians and understanding between those of different faiths, it provides social welfare, education, and recreational facilities, as well as accommodation in hostels. It is a member of the world movement of the YWCA, formed in 1894 and having branches in over 80 countries.

● **Youth Hostels Association** ▶ (YHA) A British organization, founded in 1930, to promote a greater understanding of the countryside, especially by providing hostels where young people of limited means may stay inexpensively. There are over 250 hostels in England and Wales and the Association's 250 000 members may also use hostels run by similar organizations abroad.

● **Ypres** ▶ (Flemish name: Ieper) 50 51N 2 53E A town in W Belgium, on the River Yperlee. A textile centre in the middle ages, its many medieval buildings, including the Cloth Hall (13th–14th centuries) and the cathedral, were destroyed during ▷World War I. It was later rebuilt, many buildings in their original style, and a memorial was erected to British troops killed here. Population (1991 est): 21 400.

● **Ypsilanti** ▶ A Greek family prominent in Balkan revolts against the Ottoman Empire. **Alexander Ypsilanti** (c. 1725–c. 1807), governor of Walachia (1774–82, 1796–97) and of Moldavia (1786–88), was executed for allegedly conspiring against the sultan. His son **Constantine Ypsilanti** (1760–1816), governor of Walachia (1802–06, 1807), participated in a Serbian revolt against the Turks. His elder son **Alexander Ypsilanti** (1792–1828) led an uprising in Moldavia and proclaimed Greek independence (1821). Defeated, he fled to Austria, where he was imprisoned (1821–27). Alexander's brother **Demetrios Ypsilanti** (1793–1832) played a prominent part in the War of ▷Greek Independence.

● **Ysselmeer** ▷*See* IJsselmeer.

● **ytterbium** ▶ (Yb) A ▷lanthanide element, named, like yttrium, erbium, and terbium, after the village of Ytterby in Sweden. It forms trivalent compounds, including the oxide (Yb_2O_3) and trihalides (for example $YbCl_3$). At no 70; at wt 173.04; mp 819°C; bp 1196°C.

● **yttrium** ► (Y) A ▷lanthanide element, discovered in 1794 by J. Gadolin (1760–1852). It is widely used as the oxide (Y_2O_3) to make red television-tube phosphors. At no 39; at wt 88.906; mp 1522°C; bp 3338°C.

● **Yuan** ► (1279–1368) A Mongol dynasty that ruled China after overthrowing the ▷Song dynasty. The first and strongest Mongol ruler was ▷Kublai Khan, who held the empire together by military force. Later, revolts broke out and the Mongols were eventually driven out of their capital, Beijing, following 27 years of fighting.

● **Yuan Shi Kai** ► (or Yüan Shih-k'ai; 1859–1916) Chinese general, who became president of the new Chinese republic in 1912 after the downfall of the ▷Qing dynasty. His attempts to rule dictatorially and to found a new dynasty brought about civil war with the followers of ▷Sun Yat-sen. Yuan died suddenly, leaving China in chaos.

Ypres ► Trenches from World War I are preserved in the Sanctuary Wood Museum, near Ypres.

● **Yucatán** ► A peninsula of Central America, chiefly in SE Mexico but extending into Belize and Guatemala, separating the Gulf of Mexico from the Caribbean Sea. Many relics of the civilization of the ▷Maya remain, notably at Uxmal and Chichén Itzá. Area: about 181 300 sq km (70 00 sq mi).

● **Yucca** ► A genus of ▷succulent plants (about 40 species), native to S North America and varying in height from small shrubs to 15-m-high trees. Most are stemless and have a rosette of stiff sword-shaped leaves crowded on a stout trunk. The waxy white bell-shaped flowers are borne in a dense terminal cluster and are pollinated by female yucca moths (genus *Pronuba*) when they lay their eggs inside the flowers. Several species are cultivated as ornamentals, including Adam's needle (*Y. filamentosa*) and Spanish dagger (*Y. gloriosa*). Family: Agavaceae. ▷See also Joshua tree.

● **Yugoslavia** ► A former country in SE Europe, on the Adriatic Sea. Yugoslavia was originally created in 1918 as a homeland for the South (Jugo) Slavic peoples (Serbs, Croats, Slovenes, and Macedonians), while also containing substantial numbers of Albanians, Hungarians, and other nationalities. Until its violent breakup in 1991–92 it comprised the area now occupied by the nations of ▷Croatia, ▷Slovenia, ▷Bosnia-Hercegovina, the Former Yugoslav Republic of ▷Macedonia, and the Union of ▷Serbia and Montenegro (including the autonomous provinces of ▷Kosovo and ▷Vojvodina).

Economy: agriculture was important, especially livestock raising and the growing of cereals. Forestry and wine-making were also major sources of revenue. Rich mineral resources included copper, antimony, and coal. Development of heavy and light industry was rapid in the decades after World War II, which also saw a growth in tourism. In the 1990s the economy was devastated by civil war, UN sanctions against Serbia because of its policy in Bosnia-Hercegovina, and NATO bombing during the Kosovo war of 1999.

History: Yugoslavia was so named in 1927, having been originally formed in 1918 as the Kingdom of Serbs, Croats, and Slovenes by the fusion of the Kingdoms of Serbia and Montenegro with the former Austro-Hungarian provinces of Croatia, Slovenia, and Bosnia-Hercegovina. The Serbian king, Alexander I (1888–1934), assumed the crown in the new country and Belgrade became its capital. The king assumed absolute power in 1929, only to be assassinated by extreme nationalistic Croatians (Ustashi) in 1934. In 1941 Yugoslavia was attacked and occupied by the Germans and Italians. Croatia was put under the rule of the Ustashi, who pursued a policy of genocidal atrocities against Serbs, Jews, and others. Internal resistance was divided between the ▷Chetniks and the communist Partisans under ▷Tito, the latter gaining Allied support in 1943. After the war Tito and the Partisans established a communist dictatorship, which became known as the Socialist Federal Republic of Yugoslavia. In 1948 Tito broke with Stalin, and although relations with the Soviet Union became closer after Stalin's death, Yugoslavia became a leader of the nonaligned countries in foreign affairs. Domestically, Tito pursued a less centralized form of communism from 1952 with fewer restrictions on personal freedom than in other communist countries. After Tito's death in 1980, the country struggled with economic and political crises, an excessively decentralized constitution, and lack of leadership. Growing nationalism in Serbia under Slobodan ▷Milošević and dissatisfaction in Croatia and Slovenia, together with the influence of developments elsewhere in E Europe, led to free elections in the two western republics in 1990 and to their declaring independence a year later. Military action by the Serb-led Yugoslav Army failed to subdue Slovenia, as did attempts to crush nationalism in Croatia. A Serb crackdown (1990) on separatists in the mainly Albanian province of Kosovo was, however, brutally successful. The independence of Slovenia and Croatia was recognized by EC and other states in January, 1992, and that of Bosnia-Hercegovina in March. The latter descended into savage civil war (1992–95) between ethnic Serbs, Muslims, and Croats, in which the national forces of Serbia and Croatia also became involved. In April 1992 Macedonia declared its independence, but this was not recognized until 1993. Also in April 1992, the Belgrade government announced the formation of a new Federal Republic of Yugoslavia, comprising Serbia and Montenegro; this was not recognized by many other countries until 2000. Milošević became president of this rump Yugoslavia in 1997. From 1998 Serbian forces made a further attempt to crush separatism in Kosovo, involving large-scale "ethnic cleansing." In response NATO bombed military and economic targets throughout Serbia in 1999. Over 1.5 million ethnic Albanians were forcibly displaced and thousands massacred before Serbia effectively surrendered and withdrew its forces (June 1999). Following elections in September 2000, Milošević refused to accept his defeat by the opposition candidate Vojislav Kostunica. He was subsequently deposed by a mass uprising in Belgrade and Kostunica became president. The name Yugoslavia was finally consigned to history in March 2002, when the Federal Republic of Yugoslavia was replaced by a new Union of Serbia and Montenegro.

● **Yukawa, Hideki** ▶ (1907–81) Japanese physicist, who, while working at Kyoto University, postulated (1935) that the ▷strong interaction could be accounted for by the exchange of ▷virtual particles. He calculated the mass of the particle involved, but at that time no such particle was known. Carl ▷Anderson's discovery of the muon was thought to have confirmed Yukawa's prediction. But in fact the confirmation did not come until 1947, when Cecil ▷Powell discovered the pion. Yukawa was awarded a Nobel Prize in 1949.

● **Yukon** ▶ A territory of NW Canada, on the Beaufort Sea. Mostly high mountains and plateaus of the Cordillera, it is covered by tundra in the N. Poor soils and low precipitation produce only sparse vegetation, except in S valleys. The population lives mainly on the central plateau, where silver, lead, zinc, copper, and asbestos are mined. There is some lumbering and tourism. The Yukon is a frontier region that was first opened up by the ▷Klondike gold rush (1897–99) and military projects (since 1939). Area: 531 844 sq km (205 345 sq mi). Population (2001 est): 29 900. Capital: Whitehorse.

● **Yukon River** ▶ A river in NW North America. Rising in NW Canada on the border between the Yukon and British Columbia, it flows N through Alaska, USA, then SW into the Bering Sea. Its great potential as a source of hydroelectricity has yet to be fully exploited. Length: 3185 km (1979 mi).

● **Yung-lo** ▷*See* Yong Lo.

● **Yunnan** ▶ A mountainous province in S China, bordering on Myanmar (Burma), Laos, and North Vietnam. The ethnically varied population includes aboriginal groups in the mountains. It is China's greatest tin-producing area and rice and timber are grown.

History: part of China since the 13th century, it was for long rebellious and little developed. It became industrialized during the Sino-Japanese War (1937–45), when many industries moved here from the coast. The province is prone to earthquakes (most recently in 1988 and 1997). Area: 436 200 sq km (168 400 sq mi). Population (2000 est): 42 880 000. Capital: Kunming.

● **Yupik** ▷*See* Inuit.

● **YWCA** ▷*See* Young Women's Christian Association.

Z

● **Zaanstad** ► 52 27N 4 49E A port in the W Netherlands, in North Holland province, formed in 1974 from Zaandam, Koog a/d Zaan, Zaandijk, Wormerveer, Krommenie, Westzaan, and Assendelft. Peter the Great of Russia studied shipbuilding at Zaandam in 1697. The main products are food and machinery. Population (1999 est): 135 126.

● **Zabaleta, Nicanor** ► (1907–93) Spanish harpist. He studied in Paris with Marcel Tournier (1879–1951). He commissioned many new works for the harp as well as reviving forgotten compositions.

● **Zabrze** ► (German name: Hindenburg) 50 18N 18 47E A town in SW Poland. It is a coalmining centre; industries include steel processing, engineering, and chemicals. Population (1999 est): 200 177.

● **Zacynthus** ► (or Zante; Modern Greek name: Zákinthos) A Greek island in the SE Ionian Sea, the southernmost of the Ionian Islands. The island is fertile and currants are produced. Area: 406 sq km (157 sq mi). Population (latest est): 33 000.

● **Zadar** ► (Italian name: Zara) 44 07N 15 14E A port in S Croatia, on the Adriatic Sea. It has a natural deepwater harbour and was once the most heavily fortified Adriatic town. There are many old churches and a Roman forum. Local industries produce maraschino liqueur, cigarettes, rope, and glass. Population (1991): 76 343.

● **Zadkine, Ossip** ► (1890–1967) French sculptor of Russian birth. He settled in Paris (1909), where he developed a cubist style in his figure sculptures. His best-known work is the war memorial in Rotterdam, *The Destroyed City* (1954).

● **Zagazig** ► (or az-Zaqaziq) 30 36N 31 30E A city in N Egypt, on the Nile Delta. The ruins of ▷Bubastis are nearby. It has a major trade in cotton and cereals. Population (1992 est): 287 000.

● **Zaghlul, Saad** ► (1857–1927) Egyptian nationalist politician; prime minister (1924). In 1918 he helped to found the nationalist ▷Wafd party. He was arrested by the British but after the granting of limited independence in 1922 he became prime minister. He was soon forced by the British to resign but was active behind the scenes until his death.

● **Zagorsk** ▷See Sergiyev.

● **Zagreb** ► 45 48N 15 58E The capital of Croatia, situated in the N of the country on the River Sava. A cultural centre of the Croats since the 16th century, it possesses a university (1669) and a gothic cathedral. Industries include textiles, machinery, and paper manufacture. Population (2001): 682 598.

● **Zagros Mountains** ► A mountain system in W Iran, extending 1600 km (994 mi) NW–SE between the Turkish border and the Strait of Hormuz. It consists of many parallel ranges and rises to 4811 m (15 784 ft) in the N at Sabalan.

● **Zaharoff, Sir Basil** ► (1849–1936) British financier and arms dealer, born in Turkey of Greek parents. In 1888 he became the representative in eastern Europe of Maxim-Nordenfelt, the armaments company. During World War I he was an Allied agent, for which he received a knighthood.

● **Zahir-ud-din Muhammad** ▷See Babur.

● **Zaïre, Republic of** ▷See Congo, Democratic Republic of.

● **Zaïre River** ▷See Congo River.

● **zaltys** ► A green snake that was a symbol of wealth and fertility in the Baltic region in ancient times. Households often kept a zaltys and it was believed that misfortune would befall anyone who killed one.

● **Zambezi River** ► A river in S Africa. Rising in NW Zambia, it flows generally S through E Angola before re-entering Zambia and curving E along the frontier of Namibia. It then forms the Zambia–Zimbabwe border, the ▷Victoria Falls and Kariba Dam (see Kariba, Lake) being located along this course, before flowing SE through Mozambique to enter the Indian Ocean via an extensive delta. It has the fourth largest drainage area in Africa with an area of about 1 347 000 sq km (520 000 sq mi). Length: 2740 km (1700 mi).

● **Zambia, Republic of** ► (name until 1964: Northern Rhodesia) A landlocked country in S central Africa. It consists chiefly of low undulating plateaus and is drained along its southern border by the Zambezi River; other main rivers are the Kafue and Luangwa. The swampy Lake Bangweulu lies in the N. The population is virtually all African, largely Bantu, with small minorities of Europeans, Asians, and Chinese.
Economy: the mining sector is responsible for producing most of Zambia's wealth from the rich mineral resources. Copper accounts for about 96% of the total mineral production and comes mainly from the ▷Copperbelt. Lead and zinc from Kabwe are also important, some coal is mined, and there are extensive iron-ore deposits, as yet unexploited. Agriculture is a major occupation; the chief subsistence crop is maize. Cash crops include cotton and tobacco, but commercial agriculture has declined since the 1970s. Livestock and forestry are also important. Since 1991 the government has taken steps to liberalize the economy. The abolition of food subsidies has caused considerable hardship. There is a large foreign debt.
History: the area had already been occupied by Bantu peoples when it was raided by Arab slave traders in the 18th century. In the 19th century British missionaries, notably ▷Livingstone, paved the way for Cecil ▷Rhodes, who incorporated the region into a territory named Rhodesia and administered by the British South Africa Company. Constituted as Northern Rhodesia in 1911, it became a British protectorate in 1924. It formed part of the Federation of Rhodesia and Nyasaland (1953–63), obtaining self-government and then full independence within the Commonwealth as the Republic of Zambia (1964). Kenneth ▷Kaunda became president on independence. In 1972 a new constitution led to one-party (the United National Independence Party) rule. Zambia supported the Zimbabwe nationalist movement, providing a base for the Patriotic Front, and its border with Rhodesia (now Zimbabwe) was closed from 1973 until 1980. In 1990 violent protests and an attempted coup led to the legalization of opposition parties. Kaunda was defeated in free elections in 1991 and Frederick Chiluba became president. In 1996 Chiluba was re-elected but accusations of fraud led to widespread protests. An attempted coup led the government to impose a state of emergency in 1997–98. Presidential elections in 2001 resulted in victory for Chiluba's chosen successor, Levy Mwanawasa, although opposition groups claimed widespread fraud.

Republic of Zambia

Head of state	President Levy Mwanawasa
Official language	English
Official currency	kwacha of 100 ngwee
Area	752 262 sq km (290 586 sq mi)
Population (2001 est)	9 770 000
Capital	Lusaka

● **Zamboanga** ► 6 55N 122 05E A port in the S Philippines, in SW Mindanao. A resort, it is noted for its picturesque setting and tropical flowers and has a 17th-century Spanish fort. Brass and bronzeware are produced and it exports copra, hardwoods, and hemp. Population (1994 est): 464 466.

● **Zamenhof, Lazarus Ludwig** ▷*See* Esperanto.

● **Zamoyski** ► A prominent Polish family, which became powerful under **Jan Zamoyski** (1542–1605), who was advisor to Sigismund II Augustus (*see* Jagiellons) and to ▷Stephen Báthory. **Andrzej Zamoyski** (1716–92) worked for parliamentary reform and the abolition of serfdom, freeing his own serfs. Andrzej's son **Stanisław Zamoyski** (1775–1856) played an important role in the November Insurrection against Russian dominance, as did Stanisław's son **Andrzej Zamoyski** (1800–74), who also participated in the January Insurrection, for which he was exiled (*see* Congress Kingdom of Poland).

● **Zamyatin, Yevgenii Ivanovich** ► (1884–1937) Russian novelist. His works include satirical studies of life in provincial Russia and England, where he worked during World War I. He was severely criticized after the Western publication of his novel *We* (1924), a bleak prophecy of a totalitarian future; from 1931 he lived in Paris.

● **Zante** ▷*See* Zacynthus.

● **ZANU** ► (Zimbabwe African National Union) ▷*See* Zimbabwe.

● **Zanzibar** ► An island in Tanzania, off the NE coast of the mainland. It came under Arab influence early on in its history and was, together with ▷Pemba, a sultanate from 1856 to 1964. It was under British rule from 1890 until it became independent within the British Commonwealth in 1963. In 1964 the Sultan was exiled and Zanzibar united with Tanganyika to form Tanzania. It exports mainly cloves and copra. Recent years have seen a growing movement for independence. Area: 1658 sq km (640 sq mi). Population (1994 est): 444 000. Chief town: Zanzibar.

● **Zao Zhan** ▷*See* Cao Chan.

Emiliano Zapata ► Photographed with his brother, Emilio (left).

● **Zapata, Emiliano** ► (?1877–1919) Mexican revolutionary, who championed the cause of agrarian reform against Porfirio ▷Díaz and succeeding governments. By late 1911 he controlled the state of Morelos, where he carried out land reforms, chasing out the estate owners and dividing their land amongst the peasants. In 1919 he was tricked into an ambush and assassinated.

● **Zaporozhye** ► (name until 1921: Aleksandrovsk) 47 50N 35 10E A city in E Ukraine, on the River Dnepr. A large hydroelectric station, built here in the years 1927–32, was destroyed in World War II but

subsequently rebuilt. There is an important iron and steel industry and a variety of engineering activities. Population (1996 est): 882 000.

● **Zapotecs** ► An American Indian people of the Oaxaca valleys (S Mexico). Their traditional culture, emerging about 300 AD, developed into one of the classic Mesoamerican Indian civilizations. Monte Alban, their chief city, declined under pressure from the ▷Mixtecs (c. 900–50).

● **Zappa, Frank** ► (1940–93) US musician and composer. Having formed the avant-garde rock band the Mothers of Invention in 1964, he released a series of albums noted for their eclectic style and satirical lyrics; these included *Lumpy Gravy* (1967), *Uncle Meat* (1969), and *Sheik Yerbouti* (1979). From the 1980s he also wrote complex experimental works for orchestra and became a leading campaigner against censorship.

● **ZAPU** ► (Zimbabwe African People's Union) ▷*See* Zimbabwe.

● **Zara** ▷*See* Zadar.

● **Zaragoza** ► (English name: Saragossa) 41 39N 0 54W A city in NE Spain, in Aragon on the River Ebro. During the Peninsular War it heroically resisted a French siege until about 50 000 of its defenders had died (1808–09). It has two cathedrals and a university (founded 1533). An industrial centre, Zaragoza produces paper and wine. Population (1995 est): 607 899.

● **Zarathustra** ▷*See* Zoroaster.

● **Zaria** ► 11 01N 7 44E A city in Nigeria. Founded in the 16th century, it became the capital of the emirate of Zaria. It has textile, cosmetics, and cigarette industries. Nearby is the Ahmadu Bello University (1962). Population (1996 est): 379 200.

● **Zátopek, Emil** ► (1922–2000) Czech long-distance runner. In 1948 he won his first Olympic gold medal, for the 10 000 metres. At the Helsinki Olympics (1952) he won gold medals for the 5000 metres, 10 000 metres, and the marathon.

● **Zawiyat al-Bayda'** ► (or Beida) 32 49N 21 45E A new town in NE Libya. Its construction was started in the 1950s as the future capital for the country, but in the mid-1980s had not become so. Population (latest est): 38 800.

● **Zealand** ▷*See* Sjælland.

● **Zealots** ► A Jewish political party of the 1st century AD. They were bitterly opposed to Roman rule in Judaea, and played a leading part in the revolt of 66 AD. Their last stronghold, ▷Masada, fell in 73. After the war their influence in Judaea was minimal but they may have been responsible for the further revolts in Egypt, Libya, and Cyprus in 115 AD.

● **Zeami Motokiyo** ► (1363–c. 1443) Japanese playwright, son of the dramatist Kanami Kiyotsugu (1333–84). He achieved fame first as an actor but later became a leading theorist of ▷No drama, his best-known treatise being *Kadensho*. He wrote over 150 plays.

● **zebra** ► An African wild horse having characteristic black and white stripes covering part or all of the body. There are three races of the plains zebra (*Equus burchelli*), distinguished by the extent and nature of their stripes. The mountain zebra (*E. zebra*) has very bold stripes and a dewlap on the throat, while Grévy's zebra (*E. grevyi*) is the largest species, standing over 1.5 m at the shoulder with narrow stripes.

● **zebra finch** ► An Australian ▷grassfinch, *Taeniopyga castanotis*, occurring in large flocks in the interior grasslands. It has a red bill and the males are grey above with white underparts, reddish flanks, red-brown ear patches, and black-and-white barred throat, breast, and tail. Zebra finches are popular cagebirds and have been selectively bred to produce a white form with the black-and-white barring.

● **zebra fish** ► A tropical freshwater fish, *Brachydanio rerio*, also called zebra danio, found in E India and popular in aquaria. It has a shiny blue body, up to 4.5 cm long, with four longitudinal yellowish gold stripes along its sides. ▷*See also* scorpion fish; tigerfish.

● **zebra wood** ► Any of several tropical trees that yield hard striped timber, used in furniture, especially *Connarus guianensis*, of Guyana. It has compound leaves with paired oval leaflets and clusters of five-petalled flowers. Family: *Connaraceae*.

● **zebu** ► The domestic ▷cattle of Asia and Africa, *Bos indicus*, also called Brahmin (*or* Brahman). Larger and leaner than Western cattle, zebus have a distinctive hump over the shoulders, a large dewlap under the throat, and long horns. They are generally grey or red, but a number of other colour varieties exist. Zebus are no longer found in the wild state and have been exported to many hot countries to confer their qualities of heat tolerance and insect resistance in crosses with beef breeds.

● **Zebulun, tribe of** ► One of the 12 ▷tribes of Israel. It claimed descent from Zebulun, the son of Jacob and Leah. Its people lived to the W and SW of the Sea of Galilee.

● **Zechariah** ► An Old Testament prophet of Judah, who flourished about 520 BC. **The Book of Zechariah** relates eight visions calculated to inspire the people to rebuild the Temple at Jerusalem. The book also deals with questions concerning fasting and predicts the coming of a kingly messiah and the end of the Diaspora.

● **Zedekiah** ► The last king of Judah (597–586 BC). Having rebelled against ▷Nebuchadnezzar, Zedekiah was forced to witness his sons' execution and was then blinded and removed to ▷Babylon, as described by ▷Jeremiah.

● **Zeebrugge** ► 51 20N 3 13E A small port in NW Belgium, on the North Sea, connected by ship canal (1907) to Bruges. A German submarine base in World War I, the canal was blocked by British naval forces in 1918. In 1987 the British ferry *Herald of Free Enterprise* capsized outside the harbour here with the loss of 193 lives.

● **Zeeland** ► A province in the SW Netherlands, on the Scheldt delta. It consists mainly of islands, including Walcheren. Severe flooding in 1953 necessitated the Delta Plan, under which several major dams have been constructed and dykes strengthened. The important mussel and oyster fisheries of the Oosterschelde estuary have been preserved. Agricultural produce includes wheat, sugar beet, fruit, and dairy products. Area: 2746 sq km (1060 sq mi). Population (1995): 365 846. Capital: Middelburg.

● **Zeeman, Pieter** ► (1865–1943) Dutch physicist, who, while working at Leiden University, discovered (1886) the splitting of the spectral lines of a substance when placed in a magnetic field (**Zeeman effect**). It is caused by changes in the energy levels of the electrons of the emitting atoms as a result of interaction between the magnetic moment of the orbit and the external field. For this discovery he shared the 1902 Nobel Prize with Hendrik ▷Lorentz.

● **Zeffirelli, G. Franco** ► (1923–) Italian director and stage designer. He was an actor under the direction of ▷Visconti and has directed film versions of *The Taming of the Shrew* (1966) and *Romeo and Juliet* (1968). Other films include *Jesus of Nazareth* (1975), *La Traviata* (1983), *Hamlet* (1990), and *Tea with Mussolini* (1999). He has worked on operas at Covent Garden, Glyndebourne, and the Metropolitan, New York. His stage productions include *Othello* (1961), *Hamlet* (1964), and *Six Characters in Search of an Author* (1992).

● **Zeiss, Carl** ► (1816–88) German industrialist and manufacturer of optical instruments. Zeiss opened his first workshop in Jena (1846) and later employed Ernst Abbe (1840–1905) to advise him on theoretical advances in optics.

● **Zen Buddhism** ► (Japanese *Zen*, meditation) In China and Japan, a Buddhist school emphasizing the transmission of enlightenment from master to disciple without reliance on the scriptures. It derives from the teaching of ▷Bodhidharma, who came to China in 520 AD. The two major sects, ▷Soto and Rinzai, stress meditation and the use of logical paradoxes (*koans*) respectively, in order to confound the rational mind so that transcendental wisdom can arise and the disciple can realize his own Buddha-nature. Much of Japanese and Chinese art, music, and literature, as well as calligraphy, the tea ceremony (*see* cha-no-yu), the martial arts, etc., express the spontaneous Zen attitude to life. Recently Zen has gained followers in the West, where its opposition to rationalism has popular appeal.

● **Zener diode** ▷*See* semiconductor diode.

● **zenith** ► The point in the sky lying directly above an observer and 90° from all points on his horizon. The (unobservable) point diametrically opposite the zenith is the **nadir**. □celestial sphere.

● **Zenobia** ► (3rd century AD) The wife of Odaenathus of Palmyra, whom she may have murdered (267) and whom she succeeded as regent for their son. Zenobia occupied Syria, Egypt, and much of Asia Minor before ▷Aurelian defeated and captured her in 272. She enjoyed a reputation for beauty and intelligence.

● **Zeno of Citium** ► (c. 335–262 BC) Greek philosopher, who was born in Cyprus of Phoenician stock, came to Athens in 313 BC, and attended lectures at ▷Plato's Academy. He was influenced by various philosophical schools, including the ▷Cynics, before evolving his own doctrine of ▷Stoicism.

● **Zeno of Elea** ► (born c. 490 BC) Greek philosopher. Zeno's paradoxes, supporting ▷Parmenides' doctrines that reality is indivisible and reason is at variance with the senses, are the first dialectic arguments, eliciting contradictory conclusions from an opponent's hypotheses. These paradoxes include: Achilles and the tortoise—if space is infinitely divisible, once Achilles has given the tortoise a start he cannot overtake it, for whenever he arrives where the tortoise was it has already moved on; the flying arrow—if space is divisible into finite parts, a moving arrow at each moment of its flight is opposite a particular piece of ground and therefore stationary.

● **zeolites** ► A group of complex silicate minerals containing loosely held water. They are divided into three groups: fibrous (natrolite, mesolite, scolecite), platy (heulandite, stilbite), and equant (harmatome, chabazite). Most occur in cavities in basic volcanic rocks. They are usually colourless or white and are relatively soft. Because of their property of ion exchange they were used as water softeners before the introduction of artificial substitutes. They are also used as molecular sieves in the petroleum industry and as drying agents.

● **Zephaniah** ► (late 7th century BC) An Old Testament prophet of

zebra ► A group of plains zebras. These horses are usually found in family groups of up to six mares with their offspring and a mature dominant stallion. Mutual grooming helps to reinforce bonding.

Judah. **The Book of Zephaniah** records his condemnation of those who continued as idolaters despite the reforms carried out by Josiah (d. 608 BC) and predicts universal judgment from which few will escape.

● **Zeppelins** ▷See airships.

● **Zermatt** ▶ 46 01N 7 45E A village in S Switzerland, at the foot of the Matterhorn. A popular resort, it is also a famous mountaineering and winter-sports centre, at a height of 1620 m (5315 ft). Population (1989 est): 4200.

● **Zernicke, Frits** ▶ (1888–1966) Dutch physicist, who was awarded the 1953 Nobel Prize for his invention of the phase-contrast microscope (1934). This invention enabled the parts of a cell to be seen without staining.

● **zero-point energy** ▶ The energy that remains in a substance at the ▷absolute zero of temperature. In ▷classical physics it was assumed that at absolute zero all particles would be at rest and that therefore they would contain no kinetic energy. However, ▷quantum theory has shown that the lowest energy state of a system is often not zero. According to the ▷Heisenberg uncertainty principle a particle cannot have zero momentum unless the uncertainty in its position is infinite. This means that the translational kinetic energy of molecules can only be zero for an ▷ideal gas.

● **Zetkin, Clara** ▶ (1857–1933) German communist and feminist leader. Zetkin founded the International Socialist Women's Congress in 1907 and joined the German Communist Party in 1919. She was a leader of the pro-Soviet wing of the Party and spent much time in the Soviet Union.

● **Zetland** ▷See Shetland Islands.

● **Zeus** ▶ The Greek sky and weather god, the supreme deity, identified with the Roman ▷Jupiter. He was the son of Cronus and Rhea, and brother of Poseidon and Hades. His defeat of Cronus and the ▷Titans represents the triumph of the Olympian deities over their predecessors. His offspring included ▷Athena, ▷Apollo, and ▷Dionysus and from his many love affairs, which excited the jealousy of his wife, ▷Hera, were produced numerous other divine and semidivine children. He was usually portrayed as a bearded man, with thunderbolts and the eagle as his attributes.

● **Zeus, statue of** ▶ The chryselephantine statue designed by the Greek sculptor ▷Phidias in about 430 BC for the temple of Zeus at Olympia. One of the ▷Seven Wonders of the World, it was 12 m (40 ft) high and covered with jewels and gold. It was destroyed in the 5th century AD.

● **Zeuxis** ▶ (late 5th century BC) Greek painter, born at Heracleia (S Italy). Zeuxis improved the contemporary use of perspective, shading, and mixed colours. His *trompe l'oeil* effect, it is said, induced birds to peck at grapes painted by him. He specialized in mythological subjects.

● **Zhangjiakou** ▶ (*or* Chang-chia-k'ou; Mongolian name: Kalgan) 40 51N 114 59E A city in NE China, in Hebei province near the ▷Great Wall of China. It was historically important for defence against and trade with the Mongols and is the site of two forts (1429, 1613). Industries include textiles and machinery. Population (1990): 529 136.

● **Zhao Guang Yin** ▷See Song.

● **Zhdanov** ▷See Mariupol.

● **Zhejiang** ▶ (Che-chiang *or* Chekiang) A mountainous province in E China, on the East China Sea. Densely populated, it has been a cultural centre since the Southern ▷Song dynasty was centred here (12th–13th centuries). It is a highly productive agricultural area and silk and fishing are important. Area: 102 000 sq km (39 780 sq mi). Population (1990 est): 41 680 000. Capital: Hangzhou.

● **Zheng Cheng Gong** ▶ (*or* Cheng Ch'eng-kung; 1624–62) Chinese pirate also known as Koxinga, who controlled most of the Fujian coast from his base in Amoy. He led the Ming resistance to the new Qing rulers and attempted to recapture Nanjing. This failed but he seized Formosa (now Taiwan) from the Dutch in 1661, which became the last Ming stronghold.

● **Zheng He** ▶ (*or* Cheng Ho; died c. 1433) A Chinese eunuch of the Ming dynasty, who in 1405 built a fleet and set out on a famous mission to Indochina. Further expeditions to Indochina and the Middle East re-established trade links that had been severed on the collapse of Yuan rule in 1368.

● **Zhengzhou** ▶ (*or* Cheng-chou) 34 35N 113 38E A city in E China, the capital of Henan province. An old administrative centre, it has many industries developed since 1949. Population (1990): 1 159 679.

● **Zhitomir** ▶ 50 18N 28 40E A city in central Ukraine. Dating from at least the 13th century, it was subsequently held by Lithuania and then Poland before being restored to Russia in 1793. A communications centre, it processes the produce of the surrounding agricultural region. Population (1996 est): 301 000.

● **Zhivkov, Todor** ▶ (1911–) Bulgarian statesman; head of state (1954–89). A partisan leader in World War II, Zhivkov led the communist overthrow of the monarchy in 1944. He became first secretary of the Bulgarian Communist Party in 1954 and was prime minister (1962–71) before becoming president (1971). Pressure for reform forced him to resign (1989). He was indicted on corruption charges in 1990 and convicted in 1993.

● **Zhou** ▶ (?1027–221 BC) The earliest Chinese dynasty of which there is accurate knowledge. The dynasty was founded in the area now called Shenxi after the Zhou ruler, Wu Wang, had annihilated the armies of the preceding Shang dynasty and set up a system of government under feudal rulers. These undermined Zhou authority in the so-called Warring States period (481–221), after which the ▷Qin emerged to unite China. Under the Zhou human sacrifice was abolished and the Chinese idea of ▷ancestor worship came into being. The late Zhou was also the great period of Chinese philosophy, when Taoist and Confucian thought (*see* Taoism; Confucianism) first emerged.

● **Zhou En Lai** ▷See Chou En-lai.

● **Zhuangzi** ▶ (*or* Chuang-tzu; c. 369–286 BC) Chinese philosopher. He is known only through the book to which he gave his name, a work of Taoist philosophy containing allegories, anecdotes, and satires on Confucius. The book, which greatly influenced the development of Chinese Buddhism, advocated spiritual harmony with Tao, the essential principle of the universe, through liberation from all worldly circumstances.

● **Zhu De** ▶ (*or* Chu Teh; 1886–1976) Chinese marshal. He joined the Chinese Communist Party while a student in Germany and after his return helped organize the Nanchang communist uprising against the ▷Guomindang (Nationalists; 1927). He joined Mao Tse-tung in 1928 and became commander of the Fourth Red Army (later the People's Liberation Army), a post he retained until 1954. He served with Mao throughout the period leading to the establishment of the People's Republic of ▷China (1949), during which his kindness to his troops became legendary.

● **Zhu Jiang** ▶ (*or* Chu Chiang; English name: Pearl River) A river in S China, formed by the confluence of the ▷Xi Jiang and Bei River near Canton and flowing into an estuary that is used by oceangoing ships. Since the mid-1980s the delta region has been rapidly urbanized; it is set to become the world's largest conurbation by 2000. Length: 177 km (110 mi).

● **Zhukov, Georgi Konstantinovich** ▶ (1896–1974) Soviet marshal. An armoured-warfare expert, he became chief of the army general staff (1941). He planned or commanded almost every major Soviet military operation in World War II, including the Soviet occupation force in Germany. Under Khrushchev he became defence minister and then a member of the presidium of the Communist Party.

● **Zia ul-Haq, Gen Mohammad** ▶ (1924–88) Pakistani statesman; president (1978–88). In 1976 he was appointed chief of the army staff and in the following year led the coup that overthrew Zulfikar Ali ▷Bhutto, becoming chief martial law administrator (1977). In 1979 Zia refused worldwide appeals to commute Bhutto's death sentence for conspiracy to murder. He died in an aircrash, possibly as a result of sabotage.

● **Ziaur Rahman** ▶ (1936–81) Bangladeshi statesman and army officer; president (1977–81). He fought in the war against Pakistan in 1971 and became chief of staff of the armed forces in 1975. He became chief martial law administrator in 1976, after ▷Mujibur Rahman's assassination (1975), and president following a referendum. He was himself assassinated during the military coup led by Gen ▷Ershad. His widow **Khaleda Zia** (1944–   ) became prime minister following the collapse of Ershad's regime in 1991; however, her attempts to impose radical privatization policies caused political crisis and she resigned in 1996.

● **Zibo** ► (or Tzu-po) 36 32N 117 47E A city in E China, in Shandong province, formed by the amalgamation of Zi-cheng (or Tzu-ch'eng) and Bo-shan (or Po-shan). It has coalmining, chemical, electrical, and machine-building industries. Population (1999 est): 1 458 060.

● **zidovudine** ▷See AIDS.

● **Ziegfeld, Florenz** ► (1867–1932) US theatrical producer. His lavish revues were modelled on the ▷Folies-Bergère. *The Ziegfeld Follies* appeared annually from 1907 until his death. He created such hits as *Show Boat* (1927) and *Bitter Sweet* (1929), while also launching such stars as Will Rogers and W. C. Fields.

● **Ziegler, Karl** ► (1898–1973) German chemist, who shared the 1963 Nobel Prize with Giulio Natta (1903–79) for their work on plastics and polymers. Ziegler showed that certain organometallic compounds (**Ziegler catalysts**) would catalyse the ▷polymerization of ethylene giving unbranched polymers that were tougher and had a higher melting point than those previously obtainable.

● **ziggurat** ► An ancient Mesopotamian brick-built temple tower. Ziggurats were constructed of rectangular terraces of diminishing size, generally with a shrine for the god on top. They existed in every major Sumerian, Babylonian, and Assyrian centre, the one at Babylon being the probable original of the Tower of ▷Babel.

● **Zimbabwe, State of** ► (name until 1979: Rhodesia) A landlocked country in SE Africa. It is bounded in the N by the Zambezi River and in the S by the Limpopo River. Much of the land consists of plateau, generally over 1000 m (3300 ft), with extensive areas of savanna. The majority of the population is Bantu with small minorities of Europeans, Asians, and others.

Economy: agriculture employs more than half the workforce. Tobacco production has fallen since the colonial period, when it dominated the economy, but Zimbabwe remains a major exporter. Diversification to cotton and beef cattle took place in the 1960s and 1970s; other cash crops include sugar, vegetables, and citrus fruit. The chief subsistence crops are maize, millet, and groundnuts. Forestry and fishing are important. Zimbabwe has gold, copper, asbestos, chrome, diamond, and nickel resources, but no oil reserves. Industry is mainly limited to the processing of food and minerals, although there are also some engineering and textile plants. The main exports are tobacco, nickel, and copper. The imposition of central planning in the years after independence, together with several years of drought, caused an economic growth crisis in the late 1980s and 1990s. By 1998–99 the financial sector was also in crisis, leading to the virtual collapse of the economy in the early 2000s. Commercial food production has dropped sharply, leaving some 70% of the population below the bread-line in 2002.

History: ruins at ▷Great Zimbabwe attest the existence of a medieval Bantu civilization in the region. In 1837 its Mashona inhabitants were conquered by the Matabele and later in the 19th century it was explored by European missionaries, notably David ▷Livingstone. In 1889 Cecil ▷Rhodes obtained a charter for the British South Africa Company, which conquered the Matabele and their territory, named Rhodesia (1895) in Rhodes' honour. In 1911 it was divided into Northern Rhodesia (now ▷Zambia) and Southern Rhodesia, the latter becoming a self-governing British colony in 1922. In 1953 the two parts of Rhodesia were reunited in the Federation of ▷Rhodesia and Nyasaland, and after its dissolution in 1963 the Whites demanded independence for Southern Rhodesia (Rhodesia from 1964). The UK's refusal to permit independence without a guarantee of majority rule within a specific period led the Rhodesian prime minister Ian ▷Smith to issue a unilateral declaration of independence (UDI) in 1965. Both the UK and the UN imposed economic sanctions on Rhodesia but these and further talks in 1966 and 1968 proved fruitless. In 1970 Rhodesia declared itself

a republic. In 1974 the Rhodesian government opened negotiations with the Zimbabwe African People's Union (ZAPU) and the Zimbabwe African National Union (ZANU), which had pursued guerrilla activities since the 1960s. Smith failed to negotiate an agreement with the Black nationalists, who remained seriously divided under the nominal umbrella of the Patriotic Front. In 1978, following the intervention of Henry ▷Kissinger (1976) and the UK (1977), agreement was reached on a transitional government leading to Black majority rule. However, when this government under Muzorewa failed to obtain the support of the Patriotic Front, an all-party conference was called at Lancaster House, London (1979–80). Here Lord ▷Soames was appointed governor to oversee the disarming of guerrillas, the holding of elections (which brought Robert ▷Mugabe, leader of ZANU (PF), to power), and the granting of independence to Zimbabwe as a member of the Commonwealth (1980). In 1987 White representation in parliament was no longer guaranteed and ZAPU and ZANU united to form a single party under Mugabe. The ruling party dropped its adherence to Marxist-Leninism in 1991. Since 1997 Mugabe has faced protests over food prices, corruption, and the lack of political reform. The government has responded with authoritarian measures. With Mugabe's collusion, a campaign of violent seizure of White farms by squatters began in 2000, leading to Western protests. Despite widespread intimidation, elections in June 2000 resulted in massive gains for the opposition. Although Mugabe won presidential elections in March 2002, the result was condemned as a fraud by foreign observers. State violence and repression during the election campaign led to Zimbabwe's suspension from the Commonwealth in 2002.

State of Zimbabwe	
Head of state	President Robert Mugabe
Official language	English; the most important African languages are Ndebele and Shona
Official currency	Zimbabwe dollar of 100 cents
Area	390 622 sq km (150 820 sq mi)
Population (2001 est)	11 365 000
Capital	Harare

● **zinc** ► (Zn) A bluish-white metal known in antiquity in India and the Middle East and rediscovered in Europe in 1846 by A. S. Marggraf (1709–82). It occurs in nature principally in the ores calamine ($ZnCO_3$), zincite (ZnO), and zinc blende (ZnS). It is extracted by reduction of the oxide (ZnO) with carbon. The metal is more electropositive than iron and is widely used to make ▷galvanized steel. Zinc forms a number of useful low-melting alloys, including ▷brass and type metal, and is also used to make castings. The sulphide (ZnS) is a phosphor and is used in making television screens and fluorescent tubes. Zinc oxide (ZnO) is widely used as a paint pigment and in medicines, batteries, cosmetics, plastics, and other products. Trace amounts of zinc are important for growth in animals, including humans. At no 30; at wt 65.37; mp 419.58°C; bp 907°C.

● **zinc blende** ▷See sphalerite.

● **zincite** ► A minor ore of zinc, consisting of zinc oxide. It is often found in association with ▷sphalerite and probably results from the alteration of sphalerite. It usually contains some manganese.

● **zinc yellow** ► A greenish yellow pigment, usually made by reaction of zinc oxide, potassium dichromate, and sulphuric acid. It is light fast, inhibits rusting, and is resistant to sulphides.

● **Zinder** ► 13 46N 8 58E A town in S central Niger. Once a centre for Saharan trade, it is now an important trade and processing centre for groundnuts. Population (1994 est): 100 000.

● **Zinjanthropus** ▷See Australopithecus.

● **Zinnemann, Fred** ► (1907–98) Austrian-born US film director. Trained as a lawyer in Vienna, he attended the School of Cinematography in Paris before moving to Hollywood in 1929. His films include the Oscar-winning documentaries *That Others Might Live* (1938) and *Benjy* (1951), as well as the features *High Noon* (1952), *From Here to Eternity* (1953), *A Man For All Seasons* (1966), and *Julia* (1977).

● **Zinnia** ► A genus of herbs and shrubs (about 15 species), mostly native to North America. They have stiff hairy stems, oval to heart-shaped leaves, and daisy-like flower heads with yellow or brownish central disc florets and variously coloured ray florets. Cultivated zinnias are hybrids derived from the Mexican species *Z. elegans*. They have double flowers, about 11 cm across, and most are half-hardy annuals. Family: ▷*Compositae*.

● **Zinoviev, Grigori Yevseevich** ▶ (1883–1936) Soviet politician. Zinoviev became a member of the politburo (1918) and chairman of the Comintern (1919) but was expelled from the Communist Party in 1927. In 1935 he was accused of complicity in the murder of ▷Kirov and was executed. A letter allegedly written by Zinoviev, in which the British Communist Party was urged to revolt, was leaked to the press by British Intelligence and contributed to the defeat of the Labour Government in 1924; this has now been shown to be a forgery, probably by White Russian exiles.

● **Zinzendorf, Nikolaus Ludwig, Graf von** ▶ (1700–60) German nobleman and churchman, who re-formed the ▷Moravian Brethren by settling Hussite refugees from Moravia on his estate in Saxony. Exiled from Saxony (1736–47), he became a bishop of the Moravian Church in 1737, spreading its beliefs in England, America, and elsewhere.

● **Zion** ▶ (*or* Sion) A stronghold (II Samuel 5.6–7) on the SE hill of Jerusalem, captured by David, who made it the centre of his capital (Jerusalem). Another name for Jerusalem, it is also described throughout the Old Testament as the place in which God dwells and reigns. In the New Testament and in later Christian writings, it symbolizes heaven.

● **Zionism** ▶ A Jewish nationalist movement. It emerged during the 19th century on a tide of European antisemitism and was formally established at the First Zionist Congress (Basle, 1897). The Congress defined its political aim as the establishment of a Jewish national home in Palestine; the World Zionist Organization was set up, with Theodor ▷Herzl as its first president. Jewish immigration into Palestine (*aliyah*) was encouraged, especially through the Jewish National Fund (founded 1901) and the Jewish Agency for Palestine (1929). It was also supported by the ▷Balfour Declaration, facilitated by Chaim Weizmann's relationship with the British government. Breakaway groups included the Territorialists, who sought a land outside Palestine, and the Revisionists, who were opposed to collectivism and collaboration with the British. After World War II, the holocaust provided Zionism with an unanswerable case, and with strong US support the State of Israel was created in 1948. Zionism has contin-

ued to be a strong domestic influence in Israel, maintaining the principle that all Jews have a right to live in Israel as Israeli citizens; the World Zionist Congress continues to promote Jewish immigration to Israel. The conflict between this principle and the rights of Palestinians has not, however, been resolved.

● **zip** ▶ A device for fastening clothes, bags, etc., consisting of two parallel tapes to which interlocking teeth are attached; the teeth are opened and closed by a small sliding clip. The teeth and clip may be made of metal or plastic. The device was invented by Whitcomb Judson, a Chicago engineer, in 1891, but the name "zip fastener" did not appear until the 1920s, when a US shoe company, B. F. Goodrich, marketed its "zipper boot." This effective device is now used on virtually all men's trousers and most women's dresses, skirts, etc.

● **zircon** ▶ A mineral consisting of zirconium silicate, found as an accessory mineral in intermediate and acid igneous rocks. It is usually colourless or yellowish. Gem varieties include hyacinth (red) and jargoon (colourless or smoky grey). It is the chief ore of zirconium and is used as a refractory material.

● **zirconium** ▶ (Zr) A grey high-melting transition metal, isolated by J. J. Berzelius in 1824. It occurs in nature as zircon (zirconium silicate; $ZrSiO_4$), which is used as a gem. The dioxide (zirconia; ZrO_2) has a high melting point (2715°C) and is used as a refractory in crucibles. The metal is used in cladding fuel elements in nuclear reactors. At no 40; at wt 91.22; mp 1855 ± 2°C; bp 4409°C.

● **zither** ▶ A plucked stringed instrument of ancient origin, consisting of a flat resonating box fitted with 30 to 40 strings, approximately 5 of which lie across a fretted fingerboard for playing the melody. The rest are used for playing accompanying chords. It is particularly popular in Bavaria and the Tirol.

● **Zi Xi** ▶ (*or* Tz'u-hsi; 1835–1908) Chinese empress. The daughter of a middle-class Manchu family, she became an imperial concubine. She was made empress on the birth of her son ▷Tong Zhi, becoming his regent and, after his death, regent for her young nephew ▷Guang Xu. She thus wielded enormous power over state affairs, her reactionary policies being largely responsible for the fall of imperial China.

● **Žižka, Jan, Count** ▶ (c. 1370–1424) Bohemian military leader, who was head of the ▷Hussite military community at Tabar. He was victorious against the Holy Roman Emperor Sigismund, using armoured farm wagons in tanklike warfare.

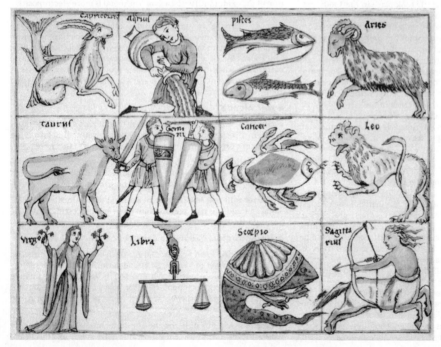

zodiac ▶ A drawing of the signs of the zodiac after an original from *Hortus delicarum* (Garden of Delights; 1170), by Herrad von Landsperg (d. 1195), who was abbess of the convent of Hohenburg from 1167.

● **Zlatoust** ▶ 55 10N 59 38E A city in W Russia. It has been the largest metallurgical centre in the Urals since the 18th century. Population (1995 est): 203 000.

● **zodiac** ▶ A zone of the heavens extending about 8° on either side of the ▷ecliptic. Within it lies the apparent annual path of the sun, as seen from the earth, and the orbits of the moon, and major planets, apart from Pluto. The 12 constellations in the zodiac are known as "signs" or "houses" to astrologers, who believe them capable of stamping their individual dispositions upon those born under their influence (*see* astrology). The 12 signs and their astrologically effective dates (different from their astronomical periods on account of ▷precession) are: Aries, the Ram 21 Mar–19 Apr; Taurus, the Bull 20 Apr–20 May; Gemini, the Twins 21 May–21 June; Cancer, the Crab 22 June–22 July; Leo, the Lion 23 July–22 Aug; Virgo, the Virgin 23 Aug–22 Sept; Libra, the Scales 23 Sept–23 Oct; Scorpio, the Scorpion 24 Oct–21 Nov; Sagittarius, the Archer 22 Nov–21 Dec; Capricornus, the Goat 22 Dec–19 Jan; Aquarius, the Water-carrier 20 Jan–18 Feb; and Pisces, the Fish 19 Feb–20 Mar.

● **zodiacal light** ▶ A faint glow that is visible in the western sky just after sunset and the eastern sky just before sunrise, especially in the tropics. It can be seen along the direction of the ▷ecliptic, tapering upwards from the horizon to an altitude of perhaps 20°. It is sunlight reflected from interplanetary dust particles.

● **Zoffany, Johann** ▶ (c. 1733–1810) German-born painter. He worked chiefly in England after about 1761, with visits to Italy (1772–79) and India (1783–89). He became known for paintings of theatrical scenes, notably several showing Garrick in certain roles. He also painted some distinguished portraits, for example that of George III and his family.

● **Zog I** ▶ (1895–1961) King of Albania (1928–39). Zog was proclaimed king after serving as prime minister (1922–24) and president (1925–28). He let Albania fall under Italian economic domination and when Mussolini invaded Albania (1939), he fled into exile.

● **Zohar** ▶ (Hebrew: splendour) The classical text of the ▷kabbalah. Written in Aramaic, it purports to be a mystical commentary on the ▷Torah and a collection of theosophical discussions dating from the time of the ▷Mishnah. It was written about 1280 by the Spanish kabbalist Moses de Leon, although it contains some later additions.

● **Zola, Émile** ▶ (1840–1902) French novelist. He went to Paris in 1858 and lived in poverty, working as a journalist and as a clerk in a publishing firm until the success of his first major novel, *Thérèse Raquin* (1867). He then dedicated himself to a literary career, conceiving the plan for the series of 20 novels entitled *Les Rougon-Macquart* (1871–93), which concern a family during the Second Empire (1852–70). Despite the pseudoscientific theory of Naturalism that first motivated his fiction, his talent for detailed realism produced powerful exposés of social problems. *L'Assommoir* (1877) describes the effects of drink on the disintegration of a working-class family. *Nana* (1880), concerning a girl from the slums, *Germinal* (1885), about a mining community, and *La Terre* (1887), concerning the life of peasants, are among his novels. He fled to England after defending ▷Dreyfus in an open letter, *J'accuse* (1898), but was welcomed back as a hero after Dreyfus had been cleared.

● **Zollverein** ▶ A customs union of 18 German states formed under Prussian dominance in 1834. By 1867 all German states except Hamburg and Bremen had joined. This commercial union helped pave the way for German unification under Prussian leadership (1871).

● **Zomba** ▶ 15 23S 35 19E A town in Malawi, in the Shire Highlands. It was the capital of Malawi until 1975 and has the University of Malawi (1964). It is the centre of a tobacco-growing and dairy-farming area. Population (1994 est): 62 700.

● **zombie** ▶ In ▷voodoo belief, especially in Haiti, a body without a soul that acts as the slave of a magician. The zombie may be either a living person whose soul has been removed or a revitalized corpse. In so far as zombies have any reality, their trancelike state probably derived from the use of the ▷puffer fish poison, tetraodontoxin, by voodoo priests (bocors). This substance creates a state that mimics death, although the victim later recovers.

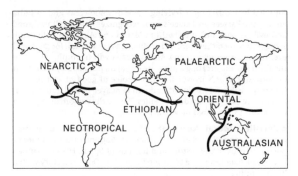

zoogeography ▶ The world can be divided into six regions according to the distribution of its animals. Since some animals are less fixed in their habitats than others and may be found in more than one region, the divisions between the regions are somewhat arbitrary. For example, Wallace's line, separating the Oriental and Australasian regions, has been modified since Wallace proposed it.

● **zoogeography** ▶ The study of the geographical distribution of animals. It is based mainly on the work of A. R. ▷Wallace (with later modifications), who divided the world into a number of zoogeographical regions, each with a distinctive fauna. The present-day distribution of animals reflects both their evolutionary history and past movements of the land masses (*see* continental drift). Thus the concentration of marsupials in the Australasian region is explained by the separation of Australia from the Asian mainland, which coincided with the evolutionary radiation of this group. The Australian marsupials therefore avoided competing with the more efficient placental mammals, which subsequently evolved on the mainland.

● **zoological gardens** ▶ Places in which wild animals are housed in captivity for scientific study or display. Private zoos were maintained by many rulers in the past, probably including King Solomon and Emperor Charlemagne. The royal menagerie started by Henry I at Woodstock, Oxfordshire, was later moved to the Tower of London, where it remained until about 1828. The Zoological Society of London founded its zoo in Regent's Park in 1828 and now houses about 7000 specimens of 1500 species. Zoos have contributed to knowledge of animals and in many cases have helped save endangered species through establishing breeding colonies. ▷Whipsnade started the trend towards open-range zoos, allowing animals to roam freely over large areas.

● **zoology** ▶ The branch of ▷biological sciences specializing in the study of animals. This includes their classification, anatomy, physiology, ecology, behaviour, evolution, etc. The importance of animals as food producers, pests, etc., makes many aspects of zoology economically significant. ▷*See also* entomology; ornithology.

● **zorilla** ▶ An African carnivorous mammal, *Ictonyx striatus*, also called striped weasel. It is 50–70 cm long including the tail (20–30 cm) with distinct longitudinal black and white stripes. It hunts at night, preying on small reptiles and birds. When attacked, it ejects a vile-smelling fluid from anal glands. Family: ▷*Mustelidae*.

● **Zorn, Anders (Leonard)** ▶ (1860–1920) Swedish artist, best known as an etcher. Travelling in Europe and the USA until 1896, he then returned to his native Mora in Sweden. He is noted for his impressionist landscapes and scenes of peasant girls bathing. He also produced portraits and some sculpture.

● **Zoroaster** ▶ (*or* Zarathustra; c. 628–c. 551 BC) Iranian prophet, founder of ▷Zoroastrianism. Probably born near Tehran, he is believed to have been a priest in the ancient polytheistic religion when he received a vision of ▷Ahura Mazda, who exhorted him to preach a new faith based on his worship. Zoroaster introduced reforms, abolishing orgiastic rituals, although animal sacrifice and the ancient fire cult continued to be practised. The teachings attributed to him are preserved in the Gathas (hymns) in the ▷Avesta.

● **Zoroastrianism** ▶ The pre-Islamic dualistic religion of Persia founded by ▷Zoroaster, surviving there in some areas and in India among the Parsees (*see* Parseeism). It recognizes two principles, good and evil, as personified by ▷Ahura Mazda and Ahriman. Life is the struggle between these forces. The dualism is not equal, for good will eventually outweigh evil and Ahura Mazda will triumph, resurrecting the dead and creating a paradise on earth, presaged by the return of Zoroaster. Man's irreversible free choice of good or evil renders him responsible for his fate after death in heaven or hell. Procreation and life are extolled, but death defiles—hence the custom of exposing corpses to be devoured by vultures.

● **Zorrilla y Moral, José ►** (1817–93) Spanish poet and dramatist. In *Cantos del trovador* (1840–41), *Granada* (1852), and other volumes of poetry he evoked the history and legends of Spain. His best-known play is *Don Juan Tenorio* (1844), a version of the ▷Don Juan story with a happy ending.

● **Zoser** ▷*See* Djoser.

● **Zouaves ►** Members of a French infantry corps, originally recruited from the Algerian Zwawa tribe following the French conquest of Algeria (1830). The Algerians were replaced after 1840 with French soldiers. The Zouaves' colourful uniforms, with their baggy red trousers, have been copied by others.

● **Zsigmondy, Richard Adolph ►** (1865–1929) Austrian chemist, whose interest in colloids led him to use the Tyndall effect to devise the ▷ultramicroscope (1902). In 1908 he was appointed professor at Göttingen University and was awarded the Nobel Prize in 1925.

● **Zuccarelli, Francesco ►** (1702–88) Italian painter. He worked chiefly in Venice (after 1732) and in England (1752–62, 1765–71). A founding member of the Royal Academy and a favourite painter of George III, he specialized in picturesque landscapes.

● **Zuccari ►** Two Italian painters, born at Sant' Angelo in Vado. Both leading figures in Roman ▷mannerism, **Taddeo Zuccari** (1529–66) is known for his frescoes, while his brother and pupil **Federico Zuccari** (c. 1540–1609) was also an art theorist. Federico painted Elizabeth I in England (1575) and decorated the dome of the Duomo, Florence, and the high altar in the ▷Escorial.

● **zucchini** ▷*See* courgette.

● **Zuckerman, Solly, Baron ►** (1903–93) British anatomist, born in South Africa, who was chief scientific adviser to the British Government from 1964 to 1971. His books include *The Social Life of Monkeys* (1932), *Beyond the Ivory Tower* (1970), and the autobiography *From Apes to Warlords* (1978). He was appointed to the OM in 1968.

● **Zug ►** (French name: Zoug) 47 10N 8 31E A town in N central Switzerland. It has a notable clock tower (1480). Industries include electrical equipment, metal products, and textiles. Population (1990): 84 009.

● **Zugspitze ►** 47 25N 11 00E The highest mountain in Germany, in the S on the Austrian border. Height: 2963 m (9721 ft).

● **Zuider Zee ►** A former inlet of the SE North Sea, within the Netherlands. The N part, the Waddenzee, is separated from the S part (now the ▷IJsselmeer) by a huge dam (completed 1932).

● **Zululand ►** An area of SE South Africa. The home of the ▷Zulu people, it became a powerful state during the 1820s under their king ▷Shaka. Following conflict with the Boers the Zulus, under ▷Cetshwayo, were defeated by the British (1879) and Zululand was incorporated into the former province of Natal in 1897. It comprised part of the ▷Bantu Homeland of KwaZulu and is now part of the KwaZulu/Natal region, which was created in 1994.

● **Zulus ►** A Bantu people of SE South Africa. They are traditionally cattle herders and cattle are still a prestige possession. Polygyny is practised by important men. In the 19th century under ▷Shaka, the Zulu conquered an extensive empire until eventually defeated in wars with the Europeans. Their highly efficient military organization was based on the age-set system; warriors could not marry until they attained a certain grade. ▷Ancestor worship and witchcraft

were prominent in their beliefs and the king had important ritual functions. Many Zulus are now migrant labourers. In the early 1990s there was much violence between Zulu ▷Inkatha supporters and Xhosa supporters of the ▷African National Congress. In 1994 the status of the Zulu king was enshrined in South Africa's constitution.

● **Zurbarán, Francisco de ►** (1598–1664) Spanish painter. Working chiefly in Seville, where he was appointed the city painter, and for religious orders, he specialized in scenes from the lives of the saints, in the manner of ▷Caravaggio, portraits, and still-lifes. In Madrid (1634) he painted historical and mythological subjects for the Buen Retiro Palace and settled there permanently in 1658. The paintings of the last few years of his life are characterized by a sentimental piety and lack the austere realism of his greatest works.

● **Zürich ►** 47 23N 8 33E The largest city in Switzerland, on Lake Zürich. It is the commercial and industrial centre of Switzerland; heavy engineering and machine production are the chief industries; banking and insurance are of international importance. Zürich's Alpine setting has contributed to the rise of its tourist industry. It has a notable romanesque cathedral, a university (1833), and the Federal Institute of Technology (1854).

History: the Romans occupied the site in the 1st century BC. During the middle ages it became the most important Swiss town, joining the Swiss confederation in 1351. A leading centre of the Reformation under Ulrich Zwingli, Zürich became a refuge for those persecuted in the Counter-Reformation. Population (1996 est): 343 869.

● **Zweig, Arnold ►** (1887–1968) East German Jewish novelist. After exile in Palestine, he returned to Germany in 1948. His pacifism and social criticism are reflected in such novels as *The Case of Sergeant Grischa* (1927).

● **Zweig, Stefan ►** (1881–1942) Austrian Jewish writer. After studying in Austria, France, and Germany, he settled in Salzburg. Exiled in 1934, he later committed suicide with his wife in Brazil. His interest in Freud is reflected in historical and biographical analyses of a number of European writers. *The Tide of Fortune* (1927) deals with European culture in crisis. He also wrote poetry, novels, and translations.

● **Zwickau ►** 50 42N 12 25E A city in E Germany, on the Zwickauer Mulde River. The birthplace of Robert Schumann, it has fine medieval and Renaissance buildings. Its industries include coalmining and the manufacture of automobiles, chemicals, and machinery. Population (1996 est): 102 563.

● **Zwingli, Ulrich ►** (1484–1531) Swiss Protestant reformer. A Roman Catholic priest and a chaplain to Swiss mercenaries, he became people's vicar at the Grossmünster in Zürich in 1518. There he emerged as a reformer, welcoming the writings of ▷Luther and preaching the doctrine of salvation by faith. He opposed his bishop, supported by the civil authorities, and by 1525 had established a reformed church. He separated from Luther over the theology of the Eucharist, regarding Luther's views as a persistence of Roman doctrine. Zwingli was killed during fighting between Roman Catholic and Protestant cantons.

● **zwitterion ►** An ▷ion that has both positive and negative charges on the same group of atoms. Zwitterions can be formed under suitable conditions from molecules that have both basic and acidic groups attached. ▷Amino acids, for instance, can form zwitterions by transfer of a proton from the carboxyl group to the amino group.

● **Zwolle ►** 52 31N 6 06E A town in the central Netherlands, the capital of Overijssel province. Thomas à Kempis lived at a nearby monastery. A trading centre, its industries include chemicals and shipbuilding. Population (1996 est): 100 835.

● **Zworykin, Vladimir Kosma ►** (1889–1982) US physicist, born in Russia, who went to the USA in 1919, eventually becoming a vice president of the Radio Corporation of America. He invented the form of television camera called the iconoscope (1938) and a year later produced the first ▷electron microscope.

● **zygote** ▷*See* fertilization.

A Brief History of the World Since 1000

Year	History	Science, Technology, and Exploration	Arts and Culture	Year
1000		Magnifying glass discovered by Arabs		1000
1014	Byzantine Empire reaching the height of its power under Basil II			1014
1045		Printing by movable type invented in China		1045
1050	Holy Roman Empire reaching the height of its power			1050
	Toltec civilization flourishing in Mexico			
1053			Building of Westminster Abbey (London) begun	1053
1054	East–West Schism within Christian Church			1054
1066	Norman Conquest of England			1066
1070			Building of York Cathedral begun	1070
			Bayeux tapestry thought to have been completed	
1086	Domesday Book in England begun	Magnetic compass invented in China	Omar Khayyam active in Persia	1086
1090		Water-driven clock invented in China		1090
1094			St Mark's Cathedral (Venice) completed	1094
1099	First Crusade (began 1096) culminated in the capture of Jerusalem			1099
1100	Feudalism established throughout W Europe		Chanson de Roland written at about this time	1100
1136			Abelard's Historia calamitatum mearum, his history of his love for Heloïse, written	1136
1138	Conflict between the Guelphs (pro-pope) and the Ghibellines (pro-Holy Roman Emperor) began		Beginning of Gothic architecture in W Europe	1138
1147	Second Crusade began			1147
1163			Notre-Dame Cathedral (Paris) begun	1163
1166	Trial by jury established in England		Chrétien de Troyes' Lancelot written about this time	1166
	Aztecs destroyed Toltec empire in Mexico		Troubadour poetry in Provence	
1167			Oxford University founded	1167
1169	Saladin drove Christians from Acre and Jerusalem			1169
1170	Becket murdered in Canterbury Cathedral		University of Paris founded	1170
1186	Kamakura era in Japan began			1186
1189	Third Crusade began: Acre retaken			1189
1193	Zen Buddhism established in Japan			1193
1194			Chartres Cathedral rebuilt in Gothic style	1194
1202	Fourth Crusade began, culminating in the sacking of Constantinople (1204)		Carmina Burana, German religious and erotic songs, collected	1202
1206	Genghis Khan established Mongol empire			1206
1209	St Francis of Assissi founded Franciscan order		Cambridge University founded	1209
1212	Children's Crusade			1212
1215	King John of England accepted Magna Carta			1215
	Mongols under Genghis Khan sacked Beijing			
	Islam spread to India and SE Asia			
1218	Genghis Khan conquered Persia			1218
1223	Mongols invaded Russia and (1237) captured Moscow			1223
1241	Hanseatic League formed			1241
	Batu, grandson of Genghis Khan, established the Golden Horde			
1248			Alhambra Palace in Granada begun	1248
1250	Mameluke dynasty established in Egypt			1250
1259	Kublai Khan became Mongol ruler and (1279) Emperor of China			1259
1271	Marco Polo travelled to China (dictated account of experiences in 1298)			1271
1273			Aquinas' Summa theologica completed	1273
1284	England completed subjugation of Wales			1284
1285	Inca Empire expanding into Peru			1285
1290	Jews expelled from England		Duccio painting in Sienna	1290
			Giotto painting in Florence	
1296			Florence Cathedral begun	1296
1303		Spectacles invented		1303
1307	Italian city states flourishing		Dante's Divine Comedy begun	1307
1309	Papacy moved to Avignon (to 1377)		Doge's Palace in Venice begun	1309
1314	Robert (I) the Bruce defeated English at Bannockburn			1314
1328	Ivan I made Moscow capital of Russia			1328
1337	Hundred Years' War between France and England began when Edward III claimed French throne			1337
1346	English defeated French at Crécy			1346
1348	Black Death devastated Europe (to 1349), killing a third of the population of England		Charles University in Prague founded	1348
1353			Petrarch's Canzoniere written	1353
			Boccaccio's Decameron completed	
1364	Aztecs established Tenochtitlán as their capital in Mexico			1364

Year	History	Science, Technology, and Exploration	Arts and Culture	Year
1378	The Great Schism in the Western Church began (to 1417)		Langland's *Piers Plowman* written at about this time	1378
1381	Peasants' Revolt in England under Wat Tyler defeated			1381
1386			Milan Cathedral begun	1386
1387			Chaucer's *Canterbury Tales* written	1387
1402	Timur defeated Ottomans at Ankara, having previously conquered Persia, Mongolia, and most of India Ming dynasty founded in China		Seville Cathedral begun	1402
1404	Owen Glendower became ruler of most of Wales (to 1408)			1404
1415	Henry V of England defeated French at Agincourt			1415
1425			Masaccio active in Florence	1425
1429	Joan of Arc relieved siege of Orleans (burnt at stake in 1431)			1429
1435	Cosimo de' Medici ruling in Florence		Donatello's *David* sculpted Van Eyck's *The Arnolfini Marriage* painted	1435
1453	Constantinople fell to Ottoman Turks Hundred Years' War between France and England ended Wars of the Roses in England began (to 1485)			1453
1455		Gutenberg, pioneer of movable-type printing, produced the Gutenberg Bible	Uccello's *Battle of San Romano* painted	1455
1456	Athens fell to the Ottoman Turks			1456
1460			Winchester Cathedral completed Piero della Francesca working on Arezzo frescoes	1460
1469	Aragon and Castile united under Ferdinand and Isabella I		Malory's *Morte d'Arthur* written (printed by Caxton in 1485)	1469
1476	Incas conquered Chimú kingdom			1476
1477		Caxton printed Chaucer's *Canterbury Tales*	Botticelli's *Primavera* painted	1477
1478	Spanish Inquisition established			1478
1480	Ivan III of Russia defeated Mongol Golden Horde			1480
1484			Botticelli's *Birth of Venus* painted	1484
1485	Battle of Bosworth: Henry VII established Tudor dynasty in England			1485
1492	Spanish defeated Moors at Granada, consolidating rule of Ferdinand and Isabella	Christopher Colombus reached the New World		1492
1498	Nanak founded Sikhism	Vasco da Gama sailed round the Cape, discovering sea route to India	Leonardo's *The Last Supper* painted	1498
1500			Approximate start of High Renaissance (lasted about 20 years)	1500
1503			Canterbury Cathedral completed	1503
1504			Michelangelo's *David* sculpted	1504
1506			Leonardo's *Mona Lisa* painted	1506
1509	Henry VIII became king of England	Watch invented in Germany	Erasmus' *Enconium Moriae* written	1509
1510	Portuguese acquired Goa		Raphael's *The School of Athens* painted	1510
1512			Michelangelo's Sistine Chapel ceiling completed	1512
1514			Dürer's *Melancholia* engraved	1514
1516			More's *Utopia* published Ariosto's *Orlando furioso* published	1516
1517	Ottoman Turks conquered Egypt and Syria Luther's 95 theses: start of the Reformation in Germany			1517
1519	Cortés began Spanish conquest of the Aztecs	Magellan crossed the Pacific		1519
1523			Titian's *Bacchus and Ariadne* painted	1523
1533	Jesuits founded by St Ignatius Loyola Pizarro conquered the Incas in Peru		Holbein's *The Ambassadors* painted	1533
1534	Act of Supremacy in England by which Henry VIII broke with the pope Ottoman Turks conquered Persia		Rabelais' *Gargantua* published Luther's German Bible published Calvin's *Institutes* published	1534
1536	Henry VIII dissolved the monasteries			1536
1540	Henry VIII excommunicated by pope			1540
1543		Copernicus' heliocentric *De Revolutionibus Orbium Coelestium* published Versalius published first accurate anatomy book		1543
1545	Council of Trent (to 1563) established the Counter-Reformation			1545
1547	Ivan (IV) the Terrible became tsar of Russia Portuguese began settling Brazil		Michelangelo drew up design for St Peter's Basilica, Rome	1547
1554	Mary I persecuting English Protestants		Palestrina's first book of masses published	1554
1555	Peace of Augsburg permitted Roman Catholicism and Lutheranism to coexist in Germany		Michelangelo's *Pietà* sculpted	1555
1556	Philip II became king of Spain Akbar expanding the Mogul empire in India			1556
1558	France recaptured Calais from the English Elizabeth I became Queen of England Knox active in Scotland			1558
1562	French Wars of Religion began			1562

Year	History	Science, Technology, and Exploration	Arts and Culture	Year
1566			Palladio's S Giorgio Maggiore (Venice) begun P. Brueghel's *Peasant Wedding* painted	1566
1567	Dutch revolt against Spanish rule			1567
1569		Mercator invented his map projection		1569
1570		Ortelius' first world atlas, *Theatrum orbis terrarum*, published		1570
1571	The Holy League routed the Ottoman navy at the Battle of Lepanto			1571
1574			Tintoretto's *Paradise* painted for Doge's Palace in Venice	1574
1575			Tasso's *Gerusalemme liberata* published	1575
1580	Spain annexed Portugal	Drake completed his circumnavigation of the world	Montaigne's Essais published Sidney's *Arcadia* published	1580
1582	Hideyoshi united Japan, becoming its dictator (1585)			1582
1585	England and Spain at war (to 1604)			1585
1587	Mary, Queen of Scots executed		Monteverdi's first book of madrigals published	1587
1588	Defeat of the Spanish Armada		Marlowe's *Tamburlaine the Great* acted Byrd's *Psalms, Sonnets, and Songs* published El Greco's *The Burial of Count Orgaz* painted	1588
1589	Henry IV became the first Bourbon king of France			1589
1590			Spenser's *The Faerie Queene* (Books I–III) published	1590
1592			Marlowe's *Doctor Faustus* acted Shakespeare active in the London theatre (early histories and comedies)	1592
1593		Microscope invented Thermometer invented		1593
1598	Edict of Nantes ended the Wars of Religion Boris Godunov became tsar of Russia		Jonson's *Every Man in His Humour* acted	1598
1601	Elizabeth I surveyed the achievements of her reign in her "Golden Speech" to parliament		Shakespeare's *Hamlet* acted	1601
1603	Elizabeth I died: James VI of Scotland became James I of England			1603
1605	Gunpowder Plot to blow up English parliament foiled	Bacon's *The Advancement of Learning* published		1605
1606			Jonson's *Volpone* acted Shakespeare's *King Lear* acted	1606
1607	Virginia settled by English		Monteverdi's *Orfeo* performed	1607
1608	Quebec settled by French Plantation of Ulster by English and Scottish Protestants began	Lippershey invented telescope in the Netherlands	Caravaggio's *The Beheading of St John the Baptist* painted	1608
1609		Galileo constructed his astronomical telescope Kepler's laws of planetary motion announced	Shakespeare's *Sonnets* published	1609
1610	Louis XIII became king of France		Rubens' *The Raising of the Cross* painted	1610
1611	Authorized Version of the Bible (King James Bible) published		Shakespeare's *The Tempest* acted	1611
1614		Napier invented logarithms	Lope de Vega active in the Spanish theatre	1614
1615			Cervantes' *Don Quixote* completed	1615
1618	Thirty Years' War in Europe began			1618
1619	First African slaves arrived in America (Virginia)			1619
1620	Pilgrim Fathers reached Cape Cod	Bacon's *Novum Organum* published, defining experimental method		1620
1622			Inigo Jones' Banqueting Hall (London) completed Rubens' *Le Chapeau de Paille* painted	1622
1623			Shakespeare's First Folio of 36 plays published posthumously	1623
1624	Richelieu came to power in France		Hals' *Laughing Cavalier* painted	1624
1628		Harvey described circulation of blood		1628
1629	Charles I of England dissolved parliament and ruled without one (to 1640)			1629
1630	English emigration to Massachusetts began		Calderón active in the Spanish theatre	1630
1632	Gustavus Adolphus of Sweden killed at Battle of Lutzen	Galileo expounded Copernican system of Universe	Milton's *L'Allegro* and *Il Penseroso* written	1632
1633		Galileo recants before the Inquisition	Donne's *Poems* published posthumously (written c. 1590–1615)	1633
1634			Richelieu founded the Académie Française	1634
1636		Descartes introduced coordinate geometry	Van Dyck's *Charles I on Horseback* painted Corneille's *Le Cid* acted	1636
1637	Japan closed to Europeans		Descartes' *Discourse on Method* published	1637
1641		Pascal's calculating machine	Descartes' *Meditations* published	1641
1642	Charles I failed to arrest five MPs in English parliament English Civil War began	Tasman explored Australia, discovered Tasmania and New Zealand	Rembrandt's *Night Watch* painted Puritans closed the London theatres (to 1660)	1642
1643	Louis XIV became king of France	Torricelli invented the barometer		1643
1644	France occupied Rhineland Qing dynasty founded in China			1644

Year	History	Science, Technology, and Exploration	Arts and Culture	Year
1648	Peace of Westphalia ended Thirty Years' War Dutch independence recognized		Poussin's *Landscape with Diogenes* painted	1648
1649	Charles I of England executed and Commonwealth established (to 1653) Cromwell invaded Ireland, sacking Drogheda and Wexford		Velázquez's *Rokeby Venus* painted	1649
1651	Cromwell defeated Scots at Worcester		Hobbes' *Leviathan* published	1651
1652	Dutch founded Cape Colony in S Africa		Bernini sculpted *The Ecstasy of St Teresa*	1652
1653	Cromwell became Lord Protector of England (to 1658)		Taj Mahal completed	1653
1654		Guericke demonstrated atmospheric pressure with the Magdeburg hemispheres		1654
1655	Cromwell readmitted Jews to England			1655
1656			Bernini completed St Peter's Basilica, Rome Velázquez's *Las Meninas* painted	1656
1657		Huygens invented pendulum clock		1657
1658	Aurangzeb became Mogul emperor of India	Hooke invented balance spring		1658
1660	Restoration of the English monarchy: Charles II became king		Pepys' *Diary* begun (to 1669)	1660
1661		Boyle's *Skeptical Chymist* published		1661
1662		Boyle's law stated Royal Society incorporated in London		1662
1663		Newton derived binomial theorem		1663
1664			Vermeer's *The Lacemaker* painted Molière's *Tartuffe* acted	1664
1665	London decimated by the Great Plague	Newton worked on gravitation; invented calculus	La Rochefoucauld's *Maximes* published	1665
1666	Great Fire of London		Molière's *Le Misanthrope* acted	1666
1667			Milton's *Paradise Lost* published Racine's *Andromaque* acted	1667
1668		Newton invented reflecting telescope		1668
1669			Pascal's *Pensées* published	1669
1671	Ottoman Turks declared war on Poland		Paris Opera opened	1671
1672		Newton's theory of light and colour announced		1672
1675			Wren began rebuilding of St Paul's Cathedral, London (to 1710)	1675
1676		Royal Greenwich Observatory, London, opened	Rebuilding of Versailles begun (to 1708)	1676
1677			Racine's *Phèdre* acted	1677
1678		Huygens' wave theory of light announced	Bunyan's *Pilgrim's Progress* published	1678
1680			Comédie-Française founded in Paris	1680
1681			Dryden's *Absalom and Achitophel* published	1681
1682	Pennsylvania founded Peter (I) the Great became tsar of Russia	Halley observed comet now named after him		1682
1683	Turks laid seige to Vienna			1683
1685	Monmouth Rebellion defeated in England Chinese ports opened to foreign travel			1685
1687		Newton's *Principia Mathematica* published		1687
1688	Glorious Revolution in England overthrew James II			1688
1689			Purcell's *Dido and Aeneas* performed	1689
1690	Battle of the Boyne in Ireland: James II defeated by William III	Locke's *Essay Concerning Human Understanding* and *Of Government* published		1690
1692	Macdonald clan massacred by Campbells in Glencoe Witch trials in Salem, Massachusetts		Purcell's music for *The Fairy Queen*	1692
1697	China conquered Mongolia			1697
1698		Savery's steam engine patented		1698
1700			Congreve's *The Way of the World* acted Kabuki theatre developing in Japan	1700
1701	War of the Spanish Succession (1701–14) began with Britain, the Netherlands, and the Holy Roman Empire against France			1701
1704	Britain captured Gibraltar (ratified by Treaty of Utrecht, 1713) Marlborough victorious in the Battle of Blenheim	Newton's *Opticks* published	Swift's *A Tale of a Tub* published	1704
1707	Act of Union between England and Scotland	Papin invented high-pressure boiler		1707
1709	Marlborough victorious in the Battle of Malplaquet	Newcomen's piston steam engine invented	Cristofori invented the piano	1709
1710			Berkeley's *Principles of Human Knowledge* published Leibniz's *Theodicy* published	1710
1712			Pope's *The Rape of the Lock* published	1712
1713	Treaties of Utrecht (1713–14) ended War of the Spanish Succession			1713
1714	George I became the first Hanoverian king of Great Britain	Fahrenheit's temperature scale published		1714
1715	First Jacobite rebellion suppressed			1715
1717			Handel's *Water Music* played on the Thames Watteau's *L'Embarquement pour l'île de Cythère* painted	1717
1719			Defoe's *Robinson Crusoe* published	1719

Year	History	Science, Technology, and Exploration	Arts and Culture	Year
1720	China invaded Tibet South Sea Bubble (financial crisis) in Britain			1720
1721	Walpole became Britain's first prime minister		J. S. Bach's *Brandenburg Concertos* composed	1721
1725			Vivaldi's *The Four Seasons* composed Vanbrugh's Blenheim Palace completed	1725
1726	Famine in Ireland (to 1729)		Swift's *Gulliver's Travels* published	1726
1727	Quakers began campaign for abolition of slavery			1727
1728		Bering discovered strait between Russia and Alaska	Gay's *Beggar's Opera* performed	1728
1729			J. S. Bach's *St Matthew's Passion* composed	1729
1730			Thomson's *The Seasons* published	1730
1733	War of the Polish Succession began	Kay's flying shuttle loom introduced		1733
1734			Voltaire's *Lettres philosophiques*, advocating religious toleration, published Pope's *Essay on Man* published	1734
1735		Linnaeus introduced systematic classification of plants and animals	Hogarth's *The Rake's Progress* completed Richardson's *Pamela* published	1735
1738			J. S. Bach's *Mass in B minor* performed	1738
1739	Wesley began Methodist movement	Hume's *A Treatise of Human Nature* published		1739
1740	Frederick (II) the Great became king of Prussia Maria Theresa became ruler of Austria and Hungary War of the Austrian Succession began (to 1748)			1740
1741		Bering discovered Alaska		1741
1742		Celsius introduced centigrade temperature scale	Handel's *Messiah* performed	1742
1745	Jacobite rebellion in support of Bonnie Prince Charlie			1745
1746	Battle of Culloden Moor in which the Jacobites were defeated by the Duke of Cumberland: the last battle on British soil	Pompeii excavated		1746
1748			Richardson's *Clarissa* published	1748
1749		Buffon began publishing his *Historie naturelle* (to 1788)	Fielding's *Tom Jones* published	1749
1751			Gray's *Elegy Written in a Country Churchyard* published Diderot began publishing the *Encyclopédie*	1751
1752	Britain adopted Gregorian calendar	Franklin invented lightning conductor		1752
1755	Lisbon earthquake killed 30,000		Johnson's *Dictionary* published Lessing's *Miss Sara Sampson* acted	1755
1756	Start of the Seven Years' War (to 1763) Pitt the Elder became prime minister of Great Britain			1756
1757	Clive captured Calcutta			1757
1759	Wolfe captured Quebec and Montreal		Voltaire's *Candide* published Sterne began publishing *Tristram Shandy* (to 1767)	1759
1760	George III became king of Great Britain		Haydn's symphonies two to five published	1760
1762	Catherine (II) the Great became empress of Russia		Rousseau's *Émile* and *Du contrat social* published	1762
1764		Cavendish isolated hydrogen	Voltaire's *Philosophical Dictionary* published	1764
1766	Mason–Dixon line drawn to separate Pennsylvania and Maryland		Goldsmith's *The Vicar of Wakefield* published Fragonard's *The Swing* painted	1766
1769		Watt invented steam engine with condenser Arkwright patented spinning machine		1769
1770		Cook charted New Zealand and E Australia	Gainsborough's *Blue Boy* painted	1770
1771	Russia conquered the Crimea	Galvani discovered nerve impulses to be electrical		1771
1773	Boston Tea Party: Americans dumped a cargo of tea in Boston harbour as act of colonial hostility			1773
1774	Louis XVI became king of France	Priestley isolated oxygen	Goethe's *The Sorrows of Young Werther* published	1774
1775	War of American Independence began		Sheridan's *The Rivals* acted	1775
1776	Declaration of Independence signed in America		Adam Smith's *The Wealth of Nations* published	1776
1778		Lavoisier explained the role of oxygen in combustion	Beaumarchais' *The Marriage of Figaro* acted	1778
1779	Spain declared war on Britain: Gibraltar besieged	Spallanzani proved that semen required to fertilize ova		1779
1780	Serfdom abolished in Bohemia and Hungary		Haydn's *Toy Symphony* composed	1780
1781		Cavendish established the composition of water Herschel discovered Uranus	Kant's *Critique of Pure Reason* published Schiller's *Die Rauber* acted (*Sturm und Drang* movement) Mozart's *Idomeneo* performed	1781
1783	War of American Independence ended with defeat of Britain	First flight in Montgolfier's hot-air balloon		1783

Year	History	Science, Technology, and Exploration	Arts and Culture	Year
1783	Pitt the Younger became prime minister of Great Britain			1783
1785			Cowper's *The Task* published	1785
1787	US constitution written British settlement of Australia began	Charles's law stated	Mozart's *Don Giovanni* performed Burns' *Poems in the Scottish Dialect* published Reynolds' *Duchess of Devonshire* painted Schiller's *Don Carlos* performed	1787
1788			Gibbon's *Decline and Fall of the Roman Empire* completed	1788
1789	French Revolution began with the storming of the Bastille: Declaration of the Rights of Man drafted Washington became first US president	First cotton factory powered by steam in Britain: beginning of the Industrial Revolution	Blake's *Songs of Innocence* written Bentham's *Principles of Morals and Legislation* published	1789
1790			Mozart's *Così fan tutte* performed Burke's *Reflections on the Revolution in France* published Kant's *Critique of Judgement* published	1790
1791	France abolished feudalism		Paine's *The Rights of Man* published Boswell's *Life of Johnson* published	1791
1792	French National Convention declared a republic Austria and Prussia at war with revolutionary France Denmark became the first country to abolish the slave trade		Mary Wollstonecraft's *A Vindication of the Rights of Woman* published	1792
1793	Louis XVI of France executed: the Reign of Terror began under Robespierre Britain and Spain joined the war on France			1793
1794	Robespierre executed Slave trade abolished in France and USA			1794
1796	Napoleon's Italian campaigns begun	Jenner first used cowpox vaccination		1796
1797			Coleridge's *Kubla Khan* written and *Ancient Mariner* begun	1797
1798	Nelson destroyed French fleet in the Battle of the Nile	Malthus' *Essay on Population* published	Wordsworth and Coleridge's *Lyrical Ballads* published Haydn's *The Creation* performed	1798
1799	Napoleon seized power in Paris	Lighting by coal gas patented	David's *Rape of the Sabine Women* painted	1799
1800	Napoleon defeated Austrians at Marengo	Volta's electric cell produced Dalton's law of partial pressures stated	Beethoven's first symphony performed	1800
1801	Act of Union of Great Britain and Ireland Jefferson became US president		Goya's *The Two Majas* painted	1801
1802		First steamship launched	Chateaubriand's *Le Génie du Christianisme* published	1802
1803	Jefferson purchased Louisiana from France	Dalton's atomic theory proposed Young's wave theory of light proposed		1803
1804	Napoleon crowned emperor by the pope	Trevithick's steam train ran	Beethoven's third symphony ("Eroica") performed	1804
1805	Nelson defeated the French at Trafalgar Napoleon victorious at Austerlitz		Scott's *The Lay of the Last Minstrel* published	1805
1806	Holy Roman Empire dissolved	Beaufort's wind scale published		1806
1807	Slave trade abolished in Britain	Fulton's steam-driven paddle boat entered service on the Hudson River	Hegel's *The Phenomenology of Mind* published	1807
1808	Madrid capitulated to Napoleon: Spanish uprising and Peninsular War began		Goethe's *Faust* (Part I) published Ingres' *La Grande Baigneuse* painted	1808
1809	Napoleon annexed the Papal States and imprisoned the pope	Gas lighting introduced in London street (Pall Mall)	Beethoven's *Emperor* piano concerto composed	1809
1810	Napoleon annexed the Netherlands		Goya's *The Disasters of War* painted	1810
1811	George III's mental illness: Prince Regent installed Luddites destroyed machinery in defence of their jobs	Avogadro's hypothesis stated		1811
1812	Napoleon's retreat from Moscow Lord Liverpool became British prime minister War between Britain and the USA		Byron's *Childe Harold's Pilgrimage* (I and II) published	1812
1813	Mexico declared independence from Spain		Austen's *Pride and Prejudice* published	1813
1814	Napoleon abdicated and banished to Elba	Stephenson invented his first locomotive	Beethoven's *Fidelio* performed Scott's *Waverley* published Wordsworth's *The Excursion* published	1814
1815	Napoleon returned to France, was defeated at Waterloo, and banished to St Helena Congress of Vienna settled European boundaries and restored monarchs	Davy invented miner's lamp Macadam invented crushed-stone road surfaces		1815
1816	Argentina declared independence		Rossini's *Barber of Seville* performed Austen's *Emma* published P. B. Shelley's *Alastor* published	1816
1817	Habeas corpus suspended in Britain		Constable's *Flatford Mill* painted Coleridge's *Biographia Literaria* published	1817
1818	Chile declared independence		M. Shelley's *Frankenstein* published Keats' *Endymion* published Byron began publishing *Don Juan* Schopenhauer's *The World as Will and Idea* published	1818
1819	British settlement in Singapore established	Oersted discovered electromagnetism	Schubert's *Trout* quintet composed	1819

Year	History	Science, Technology, and Exploration	Arts and Culture	Year
1819	Peterloo Massacre in Manchester Bolívar achieved the independence of Colombia	*Savannah* became the first steamship to cross the Atlantic	Gericault's *Raft of the Medusa* painted	1819
1820	Peru declared independence		P. B. Shelley's *Prometheus Unbound* published Scott's *Ivanhoe* published Keats' odes and *Hyperion* published Blake's *Jerusalem* written	1820
1821	Greek War of Independence from Ottoman empire began	Faraday invented simple electric motor	Constable's *The Haywain* painted Saint-Simon's *Du Système Industriel* published	1821
1822	Brazil declared independence		Schubert's *Unfinished Symphony* composed	1822
1823	Monroe Doctrine excluded Europe from the Americas	Babbage invented first computer Mackintosh invented waterproof material	Nash completed Brighton Pavilion Ingres' *La Source* painted	1823
1824	Trade unions decriminalized in Britain	Carnot described his thermodynamic cycle	Beethoven's ninth symphony performed Delacroix's *Massacre at Chios* painted Death of Byron at Missolonghi	1824
1825	Bolivia and Uruguay declared independence Dekabrist revolt suppressed in Russia	Stockton-Darlington Railway opened Ampère described forces between current carriers		1825
1826		Olber's paradox stated Ampère's *Electrodynamics* published	Weber's *Oberon* performed	1826
1827	Turkish and Egyptian fleets destroyed by French, Russian, and British navies at Battle of Navarino	Ohm's law stated Brownian motion discovered	Turner's *Ulysses Deriding Polyphemus* painted Schubert's *Die Winterreise* composed	1827
1828		Wöhler synthesized urea	Webster's *American Dictionary* published	1828
1829	Catholic emancipation in Britain and Ireland Peel founded the Metropolitan Police	Stephenson's *Rocket* built Graham's law of diffusion stated	Balzac's *Les Chouans* published	1829
1830	Charles X deposed in July Revolution in Paris France captured Algiers		Berlioz's *Symphonie Fantastique* performed Stendhal's *Le Rouge et le noir* published	1830
1831	Belgium separated from Netherlands Greece gained independence	Darwin's voyage on the *Beagle* began (to 1836) Faraday discovered electromagnetic induction	Bellini's *Norma* performed Hugo's *Hernani* acted	1831
1832	Great Reform Act passed in UK Britain occupied the Falkland Islands			1832
1833	First effective Factory Act in UK (child labour regulated)		Pushkin's *Eugene Onegin* published Chopin's *Etudes* published Beginning of Oxford Movement in Anglican Church	1833
1834	Abolition of slavery in British Empire Tolpuddle Martyrs transported (pardoned 1836) Peel founded the modern Conservative party in UK	Faraday's laws of electrolysis stated Braille's alphabet for the blind published	Hugo's *Hunchback of Notre Dame* published	1834
1835	Afrikaners began the Great Trek from British Cape Colony		Donizetti's *Lucia di Lammermoor* performed	1835
1836	Texas declared independence from Mexico			1836
1837	Victoria became queen of the UK Beginning of Chartist agitation	Pitman's shorthand invented	Dickens' *Pickwick Papers* completed	1837
1838	Boers defeated Zulus in Natal		Dickens' *Oliver Twist* published	1838
1839	Opium Wars between China and Britain began Boers founded independent Natal	Darwin's *Voyage of the Beagle* published Daguerrotype photograph	Turner's *Fighting Téméraire* painted Chopin's *Preludes* published	1839
1840	Penny post started in UK Treaty of Waitangi established New Zealand as a British colony	Macmillan invented pedal bicycle	Schumann's *Dichterliebe* composed	1840
1841	British announced sovereignty over Hong Kong		Rossini's *Stabat Mater* performed	1841
1842	Chinese ports opened to British trade	Ether first used as an anaesthetic	Mendelssohn's *Scottish Symphony* performed Gogol's *Dead Souls* published	1842
1843	Natal claimed as a British colony	M. I. Brunel's tunnel under the Thames completed I. K. Brunel's *Great Britain* became the first screw-driven steamer to cross Atlantic	Wagner's *The Flying Dutchman* performed Kierkegaard's *Either-Or* published	1843
1844		Planet Neptune discovered	Dumas' *Count of Monte Cristo* published	1844
1845	Potato famine in Ireland Anglo-Sikh wars began Texas became a US state	Kirchhoff's laws stated First submarine cable laid across English Channel	Wagner's *Tannhäuser* performed	1845
1846	Corn Laws repealed in UK US-Mexican War began		Mendelssohn's *Elijah* performed Balzac's *La Cousine Bette* published	1846
1847	UK Factory Act restricted working day to 10 hours Risorgimento in Italy began	Chloroform used as anaesthetic in surgery Helmholtz law of conservation of energy published	Verdi's *Macbeth* performed C. Brontë's *Jane Eyre* published E. Brontë's *Wuthering Heights* published	1847
1848	Revolutions in many European cities (Paris, Vienna, Venice, Berlin, etc.) Marx and Engels published *The Communist Manifesto*		J. S. Mill's *Principles of Political Economy* published Dumas' *La Dame aux Camélias* published Thackeray's *Vanity Fair* completed Pre-Raphaelite Brotherhood founded	1848
1849	Revolutions in Europe suppressed Britain annexed Punjab after suppressing Sikhs	Discovery of gold in California starts gold rush	Dickens' *David Copperfield* published	1849
1850	War between British and Kaffirs in S Africa (Cape Frontier Wars)	Bunsen burner invented Clausius stated 2nd law of thermodynamics Fizeau measured speed of light Paxton's Crystal Palace completed	Tennyson's *In Memoriam* published E. B. Browning's *Sonnets from the Portuguese* published Turgenev's *A Month in the Country* acted	1850

Year	History	Science, Technology, and Exploration	Arts and Culture	Year
1850			Hawthorne's *The Scarlet Letter* published Wordsworth's *The Prelude* published posthumously (written mainly 1799–1805) Courbet's *A Burial at Ornans* painted	1850
1851	Louis Napoleon led coup d'état in France Taiping Rebellion began in China	Great Exhibition held in London Foucault's pendulum demonstrated earth's rotation	Melville's *Moby Dick* published	1851
1852	Second French Empire founded under Napoleon III Cavour became premier of Piedmont	Frankland's theory of valency originated Joule-Thomson (Kelvin) effect discovered	Millais' *Ophelia* painted Beecher Stowe's *Uncle Tom's Cabin* published	1852
1853	Crimean War between Turkey and Russia began	First railway across the Alps (Vienna-Trieste) Vaccination against smallpox compulsory in UK	Verdi's *La Traviata* performed	1853
1854	Britain and France joined Turkey in Crimean War Battle of Balaclava an Allied victory but the Charge of the Light Brigade caused heavy British losses	Riemann's *Geometry* published Nightingale active at Scutari	Thoreau's *Walden* published	1854
1855		Rayon patented	Whitman's *Leaves of Grass* published Longfellow's *The Song of Hiawatha* published R. Browning's *Men and Women* published Tennyson's *Maud* published	1855
1856	Treaty of Paris ended Crimean War Natal became a British Crown Colony Transvaal established as an Afrikaner republic	Bessemer's steel-making process invented Perkins' first synthetic aniline dye developed	Flaubert's *Madame Bovary* published	1856
1857	Indian Mutiny against British rule began Unification of Italy by Garibaldi began	Pasteur proved that fermentation requires living organisms	Trollope's *Barchester Towers* published Baudelaire's *Fleurs du Mal* published Millet's *The Gleaners* painted	1857
1858	British Crown takes over government of India from the East India Company	Darwin and Wallace outlined theory of evolution Kekulé's theory of carbon bonding published		1858
1859		Darwin's *Origin of Species* published Bunsen and Kirchhoff developed spectral analysis	Gounod's *Faust* performed Tennyson's *Idylls of the King* published J. S. Mill's *On Liberty* published	1859
1860	Garibaldi proclaimed Victor Emmanuel as king of Italy Conflict between Maoris and White settlers in New Zealand		Eliot's *The Mill on the Floss* published Ruskin's *Modern Painters* completed	1860
1861	Lincoln became US president American Civil War began (to 1865) Russian serfs emancipated	Pasteur developed theory of germs in disease	Brahms' first piano concerto performed	1861
1862	Bismarck became prime minister of Prussia		Hugo's *Les Miserables* published Spencer's *First Principles* published C. Rossetti's *Goblin Market* published	1862
1863	Union forces victorious at the Battle of Gettysburg Lincoln emancipated US slaves French rule in Indo-China established	T. H. Huxley's *Man's Place in Nature* published	Manet's *Dejeuner sur l'herbe* and *Olympia* painted Kingsley's *The Water Babies* published Whistler's *Symphony in White* painted	1863
1864	First International founded Red Cross founded	Maxwell's *Theory of Electromagnetism* published Pasteurization of wine invented	Dickens' *Our Mutual Friend* published Newman's *Apologia pro vita sua* published Mallarmé's *Hérodiade* published	1864
1865	Confederate surrender ended American Civil War Lincoln assassinated	Atlantic submarine cable completed Kekulé proposed ring structure for benzene Lister used antiseptic spray in surgery Mendel's laws of heredity stated Clausius introduced entropy into thermodynamics	Carroll's *Alice in Wonderland* published Wagner's *Tristan and Isolde* performed	1865
1866	Venetian plebiscite endorsed union with Italy Reconstruction policy in US South	Nobel invented dynamite Leclanché cell invented	Dostoievski's *Crime and Punishment* published Smetana's *The Bartered Bride* performed Swinburne's *Poems and Ballads* published	1866
1867	Canada became a British Dominion Dual monarchy of Austria-Hungary established (to 1918) Second Reform Act extended franchise in UK	Livingstone explored Congo Railway through Brenner Pass completed Diamonds discovered in South Africa	J. Strauss' *Blue Danube* composed Marx began publication of *Das Kapital* Zola's *Thérèse Raquin* published Ibsen's *Peer Gynt* acted	1867
1868	Gladstone became prime minister of UK Isabella II of Spain deposed after revolution Japanese Shogunate abolished	Lockyer identified helium in solar spectrum	Degas' *l'Orchestre* painted Tchaikovsky's first piano concerto performed Grieg's piano concerto performed Brahms' *A German Requiem* performed	1868
1869	Suez Canal opened	Mendeleyev's periodic law stated Andrews established critical temperature in gas liquefaction	Dostoievski's *The Idiot* published Tolstoy's *War and Peace* completed R. Browning's *The Ring and the Book* completed	1869
1870	Napoleon III dethroned and exiled following defeat in the Franco-Prussian War Doctrine of papal infallibility proclaimed at the first Vatican Council	Meyer's periodic classification of the elements established	D. G. Rossetti's *Poems* published	1870
1871	William I proclaimed first emperor of German Reich	Darwin's *The Descent of Man* published	Whistler's *The Artist's Mother* painted Verdi's *Aida* performed	1871

Year	History	Science, Technology, and Exploration	Arts and Culture	Year
1871	Trade unions granted full legal status in UK			1871
1872	Voting by secret ballot introduced in UK	Dewar invented vacuum flask Westinghouse patented air brakes	Eliot's *Middlemarch* completed Butler's *Erewhon* published Monet's *Impression: Sunrise* painted	1872
1873	Spain declared a republic (to 1875)	Gibbs developed chemical thermo-dynamics	First impressionist exhibition in Paris Cezanne's *The Suicide's House* painted Rimbaud's *Une Saison en enfer* published	1873
1874	Disraeli became prime minister of UK	Osler discovered blood platelets	Bizet's *Carmen* performed Verdi's *Requiem* performed	1874
1875	Britain purchased control of Suez Canal			1875
1876	Victoria proclaimed Empress of India Custer defeated and killed by Sioux Indians at the Battle of Little Bighorn	Bell patented telephone Otto developed 4-stroke internal-combustion engine Edison invented phonograph Gibbs introduced phase rule	Renoir's *Le Moulin de la Galette* painted Wagner's complete *Ring* cycle performed at Bayreuth Degas' *The Glass of Absinthe* painted Tchaikovsky's *Swan Lake* performed	1876
1877	Russia declared war on Turkey Britain annexed the Transvaal	Stanley explored the Congo to its mouth	Saint-Saëns' *Samson and Delilah* performed Rodin's *The Age of Bronze* sculpted Tolstoy's *Anna Karenina* completed	1877
1878	Montenegro, Romania, and Serbia became independent of the Ottoman empire		Tchaikovsky's fourth symphony performed Gilbert and Sullivan's *H.M.S. Pinafore* performed	1878
1879	British fought Zulu War in S Africa	Telephone exchange established in London	Ibsen's *A Doll's House* acted Smetana's *Má Vlast* completed	1879
1880	Kruger declared Transvaal a republic, provoking the first Boer War (to 1881) Parnell leading Irish Home Rule movement	Edison and Swann independently invented electric lighting	Dostoievski's *Brothers Karamazov* published Zola's *Nana* published Rodin's *The Thinker* sculpted	1880
1881	Tsar Alexander II assassinated by Russian revolutionaries Political parties founded in Japan	St Gotthard Tunnel completed	James' *The Portrait of a Lady* published Offenbach's *Tales of Hoffman* performed posthumously	1881
1882	Britain occupied Egypt Triple alliance formed by Germany, Austria-Hungary, and Italy	Koch discovered tuberculosis bacillus	Ibsen's *An Enemy of the People* acted	1882
1883	Kruger became president of Republic of South Africa	Daimler built petrol engine First skyscraper built in Chicago	Stevenson's *Treasure Island* published Renoir's *Les Parapluies* painted	1883
1884	Germany occupied SW Africa Fabian Society founded in London	Parsons invented steam turbine Cocaine used as anaesthetic Eastman patented coated photographic paper	Twain's *Huckleberry Finn* published Massenet's *Manon* performed *Oxford English Dictionary* began publication Bruckner's seventh symphony performed Verlaine's *Les Poètes maudits* published	1884
1885	Khartoum fell to the Mahdi: General Gordon murdered Salisbury became prime minister of UK Congo became a possession of the Belgian crown Germany annexed Tanganyika and Zanzibar	Daimler patented internal-combustion engine	Brahms' fourth symphony performed Zola's *Germinal* published *Dictionary of National Biography* began publication	1885
1886	Chinese accepted Burma as part of British India	Gas mantles invented Severn Tunnel opened Benz patented 3-wheeled automobile	Millais' *Bubbles* painted Hardy's *The Mayor of Casterbridge* published Stevenson's *Dr Jekyll and Mr Hyde* published	1886
1887	Britain annexed Zululand	Hertz discovered photoelectricity Michelson–Morley experiment disproved existence of ether Arrhenius' theory of ionic dissociation published Tesla invented AC motor	Borodin's *Prince Igor* composed Conan-Doyle's *A Study in Scarlet* published Faure's *Requiem* composed	1887
1888	Wilhelm II became German emperor County councils established in UK	Hertz demonstrated propagation of radio waves Dunlop invented pneumatic tyres	Van Gogh's *Sunflowers* painted Strindberg's *Miss Julie* acted Kipling's *Plain Tales from the Hills* published	1888
1889	Ivory Coast became a French protectorate Japanese granted constitution, with emperor retaining extensive powers	Pavlov demonstrated conditioned reflexes Eastman patented celluloid roll film Lilienthal built a model glider	Eiffel Tower in Paris completed Ruskin's *Praeterita* published Mascagni's *Cavalleria Rusticana* performed	1889
1890	Bismarck forced to resign as German chancellor		Morris established the Kelmscott Press Ibsen's *Hedda Gabler* acted Dickinson's poems published posthumously	1890
1891	Japanese earthquake killed 10 000		Hardy's *Tess of the D'Urbervilles* published Wilde's *The Portrait of Dorian Gray* published Gauguin painting in Tahiti	1891
1892	Serious famine in Russia	Diesel patented his compression-ignition engine Johannesburg-Cape railway opened	Toulouse-Lautrec's *At the Moulin Rouge* painted Nietzsche's *Thus Spake Zarathustra* completed Tchaikovsky's *Nutcracker* performed Leoncavallo's *I Pagliacci* performed	1892
1893	Natal granted self-government	Poynting calculated value of gravitational constant Benz's 4-wheeled car produced	Tchaikovsky's sixth symphony ("Pathetique") performed Dvořák's ninth symphony ("New World") composed Munch's *The Scream* painted	1893

Year	History	Science, Technology, and Exploration	Arts and Culture	Year
1894	Japan declared war on China over Korea Dreyfus case began in France	Manchester Ship Canal opened	Aesthetic movement in British art and literature Degas' *Femme à sa toilette* painted Kipling's *Jungle Book* published Debussy's *Après-midi d'un faune* composed Mahler's second symphony ("Resurrection") performed	1894
1895		Roentgen discovered X-rays Marconi invented wireless telegraphy Lumière brothers invented cinematography	Wilde's *The Importance of Being Earnest* acted: his trial and imprisonment for homosexual acts Yeats' *Poems* published Wells' *The Time Machine* published	1895
1896	Russia and China signed defensive alliance	Nobel prizes founded Niagara hydroelectric plant opened Becquerel discovered radioactivity	Housman's *A Shropshire Lad* published Chekhov's *The Seagull* acted Puccini's *La Bohème* performed R. Strauss' *Also Sprach Zarathustra* performed	1896
1897	Turkey declared war on Greece Queen Victoria celebrated diamond jubilee Klondike gold rush began	J. J. Thomson discovered the electron Yerkes Observatory opened	Stoker's *Dracula* published	1897
1898	Spanish-American War	The Curies discovered radium Zeppelin built first airship Golgi apparatus described	Shaw's *Plays Pleasant and Unpleasant* published James' *The Turn of the Screw* published	1898
1899	Dreyfus pardoned after forgeries disclosed Second Boer War began (to 1902)	Rutherford distinguished between alpha and beta rays Marconi made first international radio transmission Aspirin developed Freud's *The Interpretation of Dreams* laid the foundation of psychoanalysis	Tolstoy's *Resurrection* published Elgar's *Enigma Variations* performed Monet began to paint his water lilies sequence (to 1926) Ragtime craze in the USA	1899
1900	Commonwealth of Australia created Boxer Rising in China Siege of Mafeking relieved	Rutherford discovered gamma radiation Planck's quantum theory introduced Evans excavated Minoan culture in Crete	Sibelius' *Finlandia* performed Conrad's *Lord Jim* published Elgar's *Dream of Gerontius* performed Puccini's *Tosca* performed Mahler's fourth symphony performed	1900
1901	T. Roosevelt became president of USA following assassination of President McKinley Death of Queen Victoria: Edward VII became king-emperor	Adrenaline isolated Nernst stated 3rd law of thermodynamics	Gorki's *The Lower Depths* published Mann's *Buddenbrooks* published Kipling's *Kim* published Rachmaninov's second piano concerto performed	1901
1902	USA acquired control over Panama Canal Zone Portugal declared national bankruptcy	Heaviside–Kennedy layer discovered Aswan Dam opened	Conrad's "Heart of Darkness" published Gide's *The Immoralist* published	1902
1903	Suffragette movement began in UK Bolsheviks and Mensheviks split in Russia	Wright brothers flew a powered aircraft	Butler's *The Way of All Flesh* published James' *The Ambassadors* published Picasso's *La Vie* painted ("Blue" period) Shaw's *Man and Superman* acted Bruckner's ninth symphony performed	1903
1904	Entente Cordiale established between Britain and France War between Russia and Japan declared (to 1905)	Photoelectric cell developed Fleming developed thermionic valve for radiotransmission Lorentz-Fitzgerald contraction postulated	Chekhov's *The Cherry Orchard* acted Conrad's *Nostromo* published Barrie's *Peter Pan* acted Janáček's *Jenufa* performed	1904
1905	Revolution of 1905 in Russia: insurrection in Moscow, general strike, and mutiny on the battleship *Potemkin* failed to create lasting change Norway voted in plebiscite to separate from Sweden	Einstein's special theory of relativity stated Rutherford and Soddy's theory of nuclear transformation published	Cezanne's *Grandes Baigneuses* painted R. Strauss' *Salomé* performed Lehár's *Merry Widow* performed	1905
1906	Labour Party formed in UK Aga Khan founded Muslim League in India Earthquake in San Francisco killed 700	Role of vitamins in diet discovered Amundsen determined position of magnetic North Pole Zuider Zee drainage scheme began	Galsworthy's *The Man of Property* published	1906
1907	New Zealand became a British Dominion	Lumières developed colour photography Minkowski suggested a 4-dimensional space-time continuum Alzheimer's disease described	Picasso's *Les Demoiselles d'Avignon* painted: beginning of cubist style Synge's *The Playboy of the Western World* performed R. Strauss' *Elektra* performed Mahler's eighth symphony performed Strindberg's *The Ghost Sonata* performed	1907
1908	Asquith became prime minister of UK Union of South Africa established Young Turks revolution in Turkey Earthquake in S Italy killed 150 000 Baden-Powell began Scout movement Bulgaria achieved independence from Turkey	Baekland invented Bakelite Haber process for synthesizing ammonia invented Ford began production of Model T car	Elgar's first symphony performed Forster's *A Room with a View* published Grahame's *The Wind in the Willows* published	1908
1909	Lloyd George's "people's budget" provoked constitutional crisis in UK	Blériot flew the English Channel Mohorovičić discontinuity discovered	Matisse's *The Dance* painted Diaghilev's *Ballets Russes* company opened in Paris	1909
1910	Japan annexed Korea China abolished slavery	100 inch telescope at Mount Wilson completed Roller bearings invented	Forster's *Howards End* published First postimpressionist exhibition in London Stravinsky's *The Firebird* performed	1910
1911	Chinese revolution established Republic of China under Sun Yat-sen Suffragette riots in London	Rutherford's theory of atomic structure announced Superconductivity discovered in mercury	Braque's *Man with Guitar* painted Kandinsky created the first abstract paintings	1911

Year	History	Science, Technology, and Exploration	Arts and Culture	Year
1911		Wilson invented Cloud Chamber Amundsen reached South Pole Hertzsprung-Russell diagram of stellar evolution devised	Chagall's *Me and the Village* painted Vaughan Williams' *Fantasia on a Theme by Tallis* performed Mahler's *Das Lied von der Erde* performed posthumously Stravinsky's *Petrushka* performed	1911
1912	Turkey declared war on Bulgaria and Serbia (first Balkan War)	Von Laue discovered X-ray diffraction Bragg's law of X-ray diffraction stated Deficiency diseases discovered Jung's *Psychology of the Unconscious* published *Titanic* sunk on maiden voyage Parachute jump from an aircraft successful	Picasso's *The Violin* painted Lutyens' Viceroy's House, New Delhi, built Tagore's *Gitanjali* published Proust began publishing *In Search of Lost Time* (to 1927) Schoenberg's *Pierrot Lunaire* performed	1912
1913	Under the Treaty of London Turkey lost virtually all its European possessions: second Balkan War between Serbia, Bulgaria, and Greece followed Panama Canal opened Wilson became president of USA	Bohr's theory of atomic structure stated Soddy discovered isotopes Chlorophyll's composition discovered Vitamin A isolated Bergius process for making motor fuel from coal invented Geological time scale proposed Russell and Whitehead's *Principia Mathematica* completed	Shaw's *Pygmalion* acted Sickert's *Ennui* painted D. H. Lawrence's *Sons and Lovers* published Stravinsky's *The Rite of Spring* performed Mann's *Death in Venice* published Debussy's *Jeux* performed First Chaplin films shown	1913
1914	Archduke Francis Ferdinand assassinated in Sarajevo: outbreak of World War I Trench warfare on Western Front began	Goddard began to experiment with rockets Stellar parallax used to measure stellar distances	Kokoschka's *The Vortex* painted Frost's *North of Boston* published Joyce's *Dubliners* published Epstein's *Rock Drill* sculpted	1914
1915	London attacked by Zeppelins Germans used poison gas on Western Front German submarine sunk Lusitania; 1198 civilians drowned Gallipoli campaign	Einstein's general theory of relativity stated Wegener proposed theory of continental drift	Picasso's *Harlequin* painted Buchan's *The Thirty-Nine Steps* published Holst's *The Planets* performed Sibelius' fifth symphony performed Griffith's *The Birth of a Nation* screened	1915
1916	Battles of the Somme and Verdun British used tanks on Western Front Cavell executed in Belgium Lloyd George became prime minister of UK UK lost over 1m tons of merchant ships Easter Rising in Dublin	Lewis' theory of valency stated	Dada movement began in Zürich Matisse's *Three Sisters* painted Griffith's *Intolerance* screened Joyce's *A Portrait of the Artist as a Young Man* published	1916
1917	USA entered war in Europe First Russian Revolution (March) forced abdication of Tsar Nicholas II Second Russian Revolution (November) installed the Bolsheviks under Lenin Balfour Declaration on Palestine made		Eliot's *Prufrock* published Feuchtwanger's *Jew Süss* published Bonnard's *Nude at the Fireplace* painted First jazz recordings made in USA	1917
1918	Armistice signed ending World War I, in which 8.5 million people died and 21 million were wounded Weimar Republic proclaimed in Germany Czechoslovakia and Yugoslavia (as the kingdom of the Serbs, Croats, and Slovenes) became independent Female suffrage and adult male suffrage granted in UK Civil war began in Russia (to 1922)	Mount Wilson Observatory completed	Kokoschka's *Friends* painted Klee's *Gartenplan* painted Les Six group of composers formed Hopkins' *Poems* published posthumously (written 1876–89) Strachey's *Eminent Victorians* published	1918
1919	Germany signed Versailles Peace Treaty League of Nations formed Mussolini founded Italian Fascist party Amritsar massacre: 1000 Indians killed by troops under British control Gandhi began policy of noncooperation in India Armed rebellion in Ireland (to 1921)	Rutherford achieved transformation of elements Aston's mass-spectrograph built Total eclipse of sun proved Einstein's general relativity theory Alcock and Brown flew the Atlantic	Klee's *Dream Birds* painted Modigliani's *Reclining Nude* painted Shaw's *Heartbreak House* acted Elgar's cello concerto performed Falla's *The Three Cornered Hat* performed Prokofiev's *Love for Three Oranges* performed The Bauhaus founded in Dresden	1919
1920	USA voted not to join League of Nations UK accepted Palestine Mandate Prohibition introduced in USA (to 1933)	Staudinger explained polymerization in formation of plastics	Picasso's *Three Musicians* painted Wharton's *The Age of Innocence* published Colette's *Chéri* published Owen's *Poems* published posthumously Pound's *Hugh Selwyn Mauberley* published	1920
1921	Irish Free State formed: civil war broke out (to 1923) Mao founded Chinese Communist Party Germany failed to pay reparations: state of emergency declared owing to economic crisis	Banting and Best isolated insulin and showed its importance in diabetes Public broadcasting began in USA Stopes opened first birth control clinic in UK	Munch's *The Kiss* painted D. H. Lawrence's *Women in Love* published Berg's *Wozzeck* performed Pirandello's *Six Characters in Search of an Author* performed Wittgenstein's *Tractatus* published	1921
1922	Mussolini marched on Rome and formed fascist government Soviet Union formed Kemal proclaimed Turkey a republic Egypt became independent	Friedmann's theory of the expanding universe published BBC began broadcasting	Eliot's *The Waste Land* published Joyce's *Ulysses* published in Paris Gorki's *My Universities* published Walton and Sitwell's *Façade* performed	1922
1923	German mark fell to four marks to the US dollar: uncontrollable inflation Hitler's Beer Hall Putsch failed	Lowry-Brønsted's theory of acids and bases published Compton scattering discovered	Wodehouse's *The Inimitable Jeeves* published Gershwin's *Rhapsody in Blue* performed Rilke's *Duino Elegies* published	1923

Year	History	Science, Technology, and Exploration	Arts and Culture	Year
1924	First Labour government in UK Lenin's death led to power struggle in Soviet Union New Reichsmark introduced in Germany Greece proclaimed a republic Albanian Republic formed	de Broglie's wave-particle theory stated Svedberg's ultracentrifuge invented	Forster's *A Passage to India* published Mann's *The Magic Mountain* published Shaw's *St Joan* acted O'Casey's *Juno and the Paycock* acted Surrealist manifesto published in Paris Puccini's *Turandot* composed Schoenberg devised serialist technique of composition	1924
1925	Locarno Pact guaranteed borders between France, Belgium, and Germany Hitler's Mein Kampf published	Pauli's exclusion principle stated Auger effect discovered Bosch process invented Fischer-Tropsch process developed Baird transmitted rudimentary TV images	Pound began publishing the *Cantos* (to 1970) Fitzgerald's *The Great Gatsby* published Kafka's *The Trial* published posthumously Woolf's *Mrs Dalloway* published Shostakovich's first symphony performed Eisenstein's *Battleship Potemkin* screened	1925
1926	General Strike called in UK Germany admitted to the League of Nations	Hubble's classification of galaxies published Müller discovered that X-rays can cause genetic mutations Goddard launched first liquid-fuelled rocket	Keaton's *The General* screened T. E. Lawrence's *Seven Pillars of Wisdom* published Kafka's *The Castle* published posthumously Hemingway's *The Sun Also Rises* published Heidegger's *Sein und Zeit* published Gropius' Bauhaus building in Breslau completed Gide's *The Counterfeiters* published Janáček's *Glagolithic Mass* performed	1926
1927	Stalin won control over Soviet Union Trotsky expelled from the Communist Party	Heisenberg formulated matrix mechanics and the uncertainty principle Thomson discovered electron diffraction Bohr stated complementarity principle Lindbergh flew solo from New York to Paris	Woolf's *To the Lighthouse* published Hesse's *Steppenwolf* published Kern's *Show Boat* performed Lang's *Metropolis* screened *The Jazz Singer*: era of sound cinema began Spencer's *The Resurrection: Cookham* completed	1927
1928	Women given equal voting rights to men in UK Soviet Union's first five-year plan announced Chiang Kai-shek united most of China under Nationalist government	Fleming discovered penicillin Ramon scattering discovered First electron microscope built Geiger-Müller counter invented	Yeats' *The Tower* published Huxley's *Point Counter Point* published D. H. Lawrence's *Lady Chatterley's Lover* published Ravel's *Boléro* performed Brecht and Weil's *The Threepenny Opera* produced	1928
1929	Great Depression began with Wall Street Crash	Hubble's law announced *Graf Zeppelin* flew round the world Quartz-crystal clock invented	Epstein's *Night and Day* sculpted Graves' *Goodbye to All That* published Hemingway's *A Farewell to Arms* published Remarque's *All Quiet on the Western Front* published Cocteau's *Les Enfants Terribles* published Faulkner's *The Sound and The Fury* published Dali and Buñuel's *Un Chien Andalou* screened	1929
1930	Last Allied troops left Rhineland France began to build the Maginot line Vargas seized power in Brazil Haile Selassie became emperor of Abyssinia	Planet Pluto discovered Pauli postulated the existence of the neutrino Dirac's discovery of negative energy suggested antimatter Amy Johnson flew solo from London to Australia	Waugh's *Vile Bodies* published Auden's *Poems* published Coward's *Private Lives* acted Hašek's *The Good Soldier Schweik* published Ellington's "Mood Indigo" recorded	1930
1931	National government formed in UK Spanish republic declared Australia and New Zealand became fully independent British Commonwealth established	Neoprene (synthetic rubber) produced Urey discovered heavy water Van de Graaff generator built	Bonnard's *The Breakfast Room* painted *Frankenstein* and *Dracula* screened Epstein's *Genesis* sculpted O'Neill's *Mourning Becomes Electra* acted Chaplin's *City Lights* screened Empire State Building in New York completed Hepworth's *Pierced Form* sculpted	1931
1932	Geneva disarmament conference held: 60 states attended, Germany subsequently left Hindenberg defeated Hitler in presidential elections: Hitler refused vice-chancellorship Salazar became dictator of Portugal Mosley formed British Union of Fascists Saudi Arabia established Iraq became an independent state	Chadwick discovered the neutron Anderson discovered the positron Jansky's discovery of radio waves in space led to radio astronomy Nuclear transformations achieved Zuider Zee drainage scheme completed	Huxley's *Brave New World* published Céline's *Journey to the End of the Night* published Spencer's Sandham Memorial Chapel completed	1932
1933	Nazis victorious in German elections: Hitler became chancellor Reichstag fire denounced by Hitler as communist plot Japanese occupied China north of the Great Wall F. D. Roosevelt became president of USA: New Deal introduced	Vitamin C synthesized Polythene discovered	Malraux's *La Condition Humaine* published Orwell's *Down and Out in Paris and London* published García Lorca's *Blood Wedding* acted	1933
1934	Hitler became German Führer "Night of the Long Knives" in Germany Dollfuss, Austrian Chancellor, assassinated by Nazis Soviet Union joined League of Nations	Curies discovered induced radioactivity Cherenkov radiation discovered Popper's *The Logic of Scientific Discovery* published	Dali's *William Tell* painted Graves' *I, Claudius* published Fitzgerald's *Tender is the Night* published Rachmaninov's *Rhapsody on a Theme of Paganini* performed	1934

Year	History	Science, Technology, and Exploration	Arts and Culture	Year
1934	The Long March of Chinese Communists began (to 1935)		Mandelstam arrested in Soviet Union	1934
1935	The Saar incorporated into Germany after plebiscite Nazis repudiated Versailles Treaty and introduced conscription Nuremberg laws deprived Jews of German nationality Mussolini invaded Abyssinia	Carothers invented nylon Richter earthquake scale introduced Watson Watt developed radar to detect aircraft First sulpha drugs developed	Isherwood's *Mr Norris Changes Trains* published Eliot's *Murder in the Cathedral* performed Gershwin's *Porgy and Bess* performed Berg's *Lulu* performed	1935
1936	Germany occupied Rhineland Italy annexed Abyssinia Rome–Berlin Axis proclaimed Germany began to build Siegfried line Spanish Civil War began (to 1939) Abdication Crisis in UK: Edward VIII succeeded by George VI Mosley led anti-Jewish march in London	Field-emission microscope developed Hoover Dam completed Dirigible airship *Hindenberg* crossed Atlantic Keynes' *General Theory of Employment* published	Huxley's *Eyeless in Gaza* published Canetti's *Auto da fé* published Auden's *Look, Stranger!* published Prokofiev's *Romeo and Juliet* and *Peter and the Wolf* performed Ayer's *Language, Truth, and Logic* published	1936
1937	N. Chamberlain became prime minister of UK: appeasement of Hitler began with visit of Lord Halifax to Germany Italy left League of Nations Sino-Japanese War began (to 1945): Japan took Beijing, Shanghai, and Nanking Irish Free State became the Republic of Ireland under De Valera	Kapitza discovered superfluidity of helium Whittle's first jet engine built Xerographic copier invented The *Hindenberg* airship destroyed by fire	Picasso's *Guernica* painted Orff's *Carmina Burana* performed Orwell's *The Road to Wigan Pier* published Steinbeck's *Of Mice and Men* published Disney's *Snow White and the Seven Dwarfs* screened Buber's *I and Thou* published Shostakovich's fifth symphony performed Renoir's *La Grande Illusion* screened	1937
1938	Germany annexed Austria (the Anschluss accepted by plebiscite) and occupied Sudetenland Chamberlain visited Hitler three times claiming to have achieved "Peace in our time" with the Munich Agreement, which ratified Germany's acquisition of the Sudetenland Germany mobilized for war Stalin's show trials in the Soviet Union eliminated his opponents	Hahn discovered nuclear fission Biró invented the ball-point pen	Sartre's *Nausea* published Greene's *Brighton Rock* published du Maurier's *Rebecca* published Bartók's violin concerto performed	1938
1939	Spanish civil war ended; UK and France recognized Franco's government Italy invaded Albania Soviet–German nonaggression pact signed UK and Poland signed mutual-assistance pact Germany invaded Poland: UK and France declared war on Germany starting World War II Soviet Union invaded Poland	Florey and Chain extracted penicillin Florey developed penicillin to cure bacterial infections Rhesus factor discovered First jet-powered flight made Sikorsky invented helicopter Armstrong invented frequency-modulation broadcasting Television broadcasting began in USA	Joyce's *Finnegans Wake* published Steinbeck's *The Grapes of Wrath* published Isherwood's *Goodbye to Berlin* published Renoir's *La Règle du jeu* screened *Gone With the Wind* screened Rodrigo's *Concierto de Aranjuez* composed	1939
1940	Germany invaded Norway, Denmark, the Netherlands, Belgium, France, and Luxembourg Churchill became prime minister of the UK British forces evacuated from Dunkirk in disarray Pétain signed armistice with Germany and was appointed head of Vichy government Free French set up under de Gaulle in London RAF defeated Luftwaffe in Battle of Britain: London Blitz began North African campaign started Trotsky assassinated in Mexico	Large cyclotron built DDT patented Feynmann developed quantum electrodynamics	Kandinsky's *Sky Blue* painted Greene's *The Power and the Glory* published Hemingway's *For Whom the Bell Tolls* published Chaplin's *The Great Dictator* screened Koestler's *Darkness at Noon* published Disney's *Fantasia* screened	1940
1941	Germany invaded Soviet Union Hess flew to Scotland with peace proposals North Africa campaign spread to western desert Roosevelt and Churchill signed the Atlantic Charter Japan bombed Pearl Harbor: USA entered the war Hong Kong and Burma fell to Japan	Manhattan Project to build atom bomb began Bailey bridge developed Whittle's jet engine successfully powered aircraft Terylene invented	Nash's *Totes Meer* painted Moore's *Shelter Sketchbook* published Welles' *Citizen Kane* screened Brecht's *Mother Courage* acted Coward's *Blithe Spirit* acted Tippett's *A Child of Our Time* performed	1941
1942	Rommel retreated in North Africa following Allied victory at El Alamein Battle of Stalingrad began Murder of millions of Jews in gas chambers by Germans began Singapore fell to Japan Gandhi demanded Indian independence Germans destroyed Lidice as reprisal for murder of Heydrich	Fermi initiated controlled nuclear chain reaction Recording on magnetic tape invented	Moore's *Madonna and Child* sculpted Chagall's *Juggler* painted Eliot's *Four Quartets* published Camus' *The Outsider* published Shostakovich's seventh symphony ("Leningrad") performed Vaughan Williams' fifth symphony performed Cela's *The Family of Pascal Duarte* published	1942
1943	Churchill and Roosevelt met in Casablanca to agree strategy German army defeated at Stalingrad Germans massacred Jews in Warsaw ghetto Allies invaded Italy: Mussolini deposed Italy declared war on Germany Churchill, Roosevelt, and Stalin met in Tehran	Seyfert galaxies discovered First electronic computer built in USA Streptomycin discovered	*Casablanca* screened Sartre's *Being and Nothingness* published Brecht's *Galileo* performed Bartók's concerto for orchestra performed Rodgers and Hammerstein's *Oklahoma!* performed	1943

Year	History	Science, Technology, and Exploration	Arts and Culture	Year
1944	Leningrad relieved D-Day landings in Normandy Flying bomb (V1) attacked London Paris liberated V2 rockets fell on Britain Battle of the Bulge began Attempt to assassinate Hitler by German officers failed	Synchrocyclotron invented Uranium pile to manufacture plutonium for atom bomb completed	Anouilh's *Antigone* acted Hayek's *The Road to Serfdom* published T. Williams' *The Glass Menagerie* acted Borges' *Fictions* published Parker and Gillespie pioneered bop style of jazz in New York Eisenstein's *Ivan the Terrible* (Part I) screened	1944
1945	Churchill, Roosevelt, and Stalin met at Yalta Allied bombing campaign culminated in destruction of Dresden Mussolini killed by partisans Hitler committed suicide Berlin surrendered to the Russians Germany capitulated and divided into four zones by Allies Churchill, Truman, and Stalin meet at Potsdam Conference Attlee became UK prime minister following landslide Labour victory Atom bombs dropped on Hiroshima and Nagasaki: Japan surrendered World War II ended with over 25 million killed plus 6 million Jews murdered by the Germans United Nations founded: formed World Bank Nuremberg Trials began	Vitamin A synthesized First atomic bomb tested one-gene, one-enzyme hypothesis stated	Moore's *Family Group* sculpted Andrić's *The Bridge on the Drina* published Wright's Guggenheim Museum, New York, designed (completed 1959) Orwell's *Animal Farm* published Waugh's *Brideshead Revisited* published Britten's *Peter Grimes* performed Carné's *Les Enfants du Paradis* screened Lean's *Brief Encounter* screened	1945
1946	Churchill's "Iron Curtain" speech marked beginning of Cold War 12 German leaders sentenced to death at Nuremberg Political power in Japan taken from emperor and given to elected assembly Perón became president of Argentina Civil War between Nationalists and Communists in China (to 1949)	Nuclear magnetic resonance invented	Sutherland's *Crucifixion* painted Miller's *All My Sons* acted O'Neill's *The Iceman Cometh* acted Bacon's *Three Studies* painted Lowell's *Lord Weary's Castle* published	1946
1947	British proposals to divide Palestine rejected by Jews and Arabs Burma proclaimed independence India became independent with Pakistan as a separate state Kashmir's admittance into India provoked crisis with Pakistan Cominform founded Attlee government nationalized major utilities in UK	Transistor invented Lamb shift discovered Radiocarbon dating discovered First supersonic flight (in USA) Heyerdahl's *Kon-Tiki* expedition	Genet's *The Maids* acted *Diary of Anne Frank* published Pollock developed action painting T. Williams' *A Streetcar Named Desire* acted Camus' *The Plague* published Miller's *Death of a Salesman* acted P. Levi's *If This Is a Man* published C. Levi's *Christ Stopped at Eboli* published	1947
1948	National Health Service and Welfare State founded in UK Gandhi assassinated Communism established in most of E Europe Apartheid established in South Africa Soviet Union blockaded Berlin: Berlin Airlift began (to 1949) Marshall Aid from USA to Europe agreed Korea proclaimed a republic State of Israel formed after UK passed mandate of Palestine to UN Arab forces attacked Israel	Alpher, Bethe, Gamow theory of origin of elements published Vitamin B_{12} discovered Gabor invented holography Mount Palomar observatory became operational Cortisone discovered Kinsey's *Sexual Behaviour in the Human Male* published	Greene's *The Heart of the Matter* published Mailer's *The Naked and the Dead* published Brecht's *The Caucasian Chalk Circle* acted Paton's *Cry, the Beloved Country* published De Sica's *Bicycle Thieves* screened R. Strauss' *Four Last Songs* composed Messiaen's *Turangalîla* symphony completed	1948
1949	Soviet Union tested atom bomb North Atlantic Treaty signed: NATO created People's Republic of China established Israel admitted to UN: occupied Jerusalem Republic of Ireland left the Commonwealth Indonesia became independent	Flash photolysis invented Feynmann diagrams introduced	Borges' *The Aleph* published Orwell's *1984* published de Beauvoir's *The Second Sex* published Brecht founded the Berliner Ensemble in East Berlin Reed's *The Third Man* screened	1949
1950	China occupied Tibet Korean War began (to 1953) McCarthy's anti-communist witch hunt in the USA began	Tokamak device for nuclear fusion invented in Soviet Union First successful kidney transplant performed Antihistamines developed against allergies	Chagall's *King David* painted Kurasawa's *Rashomon* screened Ionesco's *The Bald Prima Donna* performed: inaugurated the Theatre of the Absurd	1950
1951	Schuman Plan setting up single European coal and steel authority agreed Burgess and Maclean escaped to the Soviet Union Peace Treaty with Japan signed by 49 nations Festival of Britain celebrated	Heart-lung machine developed Colour television introduced in the USA First breeder reactor built	Matisse completed work on Vence chapel Picasso's *Massacre in Korea* painted W. C. Williams' *Paterson* completed Salinger's *Catcher in the Rye* published Bacon's *Study after Velázquez* painted Beckett's *Molloy* published Stravinsky's *The Rake's Progress* performed Britten's *Billy Budd* performed	1951
1952	Churchill announced British atom bomb Truman announced US hydrogen bomb Elizabeth II became queen of UK Mau Mau disturbances in Kenya caused state of emergency	Glaser invented bubble chamber CERN set up for joint nuclear research in Europe Contraceptive pill developed Comet jet airliner went into service	Zinnemann's *High Noon* screened D. Thomas' *Collected Poems* published Le Corbusier's Unité d'Habitation in Marseille completed Anouilh's *Waltz of the Toreadors* acted	1952

Year	History	Science, Technology, and Exploration	Arts and Culture	Year
1952			Beckett's *Waiting for Godot* acted (in French) Hemingway's *The Old Man and the Sea* published	1952
1953	Death of Stalin Eisenhower became US president Soviet Union exploded hydrogen bomb Rosenbergs executed in USA	Watson and Crick demonstrated 3-dimensional structure of DNA Strangeness concept in particle physics introduced Connection between smoking and lung cancer reported Hilary and Tensing reached summit of Everest	Miller's *The Crucible* performed Fleming's *Casino Royale* published Britten's *Gloriana* performed Baldwin's *Go Tell it on the Mountain* published	1953
1954	Nasser became head of state in Egypt War of Independence began in Algeria (to 1962) War between North and South Vietnam began	US hydrogen bomb exploded at Bikini US submarine *Nautilus* converted to nuclear power Series of Comet airliner disasters caused concern First commercial TV station opened in Britain	Sutherland's *Sir Winston Churchill* painted K. Amis' *Lucky Jim* published Golding's *Lord of the Flies* published Stevens' *Collected Poems* published D. Thomas' *Under Milk Wood* performed Hitchcock's *Rear Window* screened Kazan's *On the Waterfront* screened	1954
1955	West Germany admitted to NATO Warsaw Pact founded Treaty of Vienna restored Austrian independence State of emergency declared in Cyprus	Salk antipolio vaccine used Sanger established the structure of insulin Maser developed	Larkin's *The Less Deceived* published Le Corbusier's chapel at Ronchamp completed Nabokov's *Lolita* published Tolkien's *Lord of the Rings* completed Tippett's *The Midsummer Marriages* performed *Rebel Without a Cause* screened T. Williams' *Cat on a Hot Tin Roof* acted	1955
1956	Khrushchev denounced Stalin in Soviet Union Nasser seized Suez Canal, provoking international crisis Israel invaded Sinai Anglo-French troops attacked Egypt but withdrew under international pressure Soviet troops intervened in uprising in Hungary	Neutrino and antineutron identified Britain opened world's first nuclear power station Hodgkin established structure of vitamin B_{12} Non-conservation of parity established in weak interactions	Genet's *The Balcony* acted Lampedusa's *The Leopard* published posthumously Osborne's *Look Back in Anger* performed O'Neill's *Long Day's Journey Into Night* acted posthumously Ginsberg's *Howl* published Presley's "Heartbreak Hotel" released	1956
1957	Macmillan became prime minister of UK Israel withdrew from Sinai and handed the Gaza Strip to UN Treaty of Rome established the European Economic Community Ghana became independent	British hydrogen bomb test Soviet Union launched Sputnik 1 into space BSC theory of superconductivity formulated Mössbauer effect discovered Isaacs discovered interferon	White's *Voss* published Beckett's *Endgame* acted Hughes' *The Hawk in the Rain* published Osborne's *The Entertainer* acted Barthes' *Mythologies* published Kerouac's *On the Road* published Bergman's *Wild Strawberries* screened Bernstein's *West Side Story* performed	1957
1958	Egypt and Sudan formed United Arab Republic Great Leap Forward in China began	US launched first moon rocket (unsuccessful) US launched Explorer 1 satellite, which discovered the Van Allen belts Silicon chip invented in USA Esaki discovered tunnel effect	Achebe's *Things Fall Apart* published Pasternak's *Doctor Zhivago* published Lévi-Strauss' *Structural Anthropology* published Pinter's *The Birthday Party* performed Mies van der Rohe's Seagram building, New York, completed Wajda's *Ashes and Diamonds* screened	1958
1959	Cuban revolution ended with Castro assuming control Cyprus became a republic with Makarios as president De Gaulle became president of French Fifth Republic	Sabin's antipolio vaccine announced Soviet Union's Lunik reached moon Hovercraft crossed the English Channel North Sea gas discovered	Burroughs' *The Naked Lunch* published Ionesco's *Rhinoceros* acted Grass' *The Tin Drum* published Davis' *Kind of Blue* recorded Wesker's *Roots* acted Lowell's *Life Studies* published Ray's *Apu* trilogy of films completed	1959
1960	US U2 reconnaissance plane shot down over Soviet Union EFTA formed Belgian Congo gained independence Nigeria became independent Sharpeville massacre in South Africa	Optical laser constructed Leakey discovered *Homo erectus* remains at Olduvai Oral contraceptives marketed	Calvino's *Our Forefathers* published Bolt's *A Man for All Seasons* acted Pinter's *The Caretaker* acted Fellini's *La Dolce Vita* screened Godard's *A bout de souffle* screened Updike's *Rabbit, Run* published Stockhausen's *Kontakte* performed	1960
1961	Kennedy became US president Bay of Pigs, US-inspired invasion of Cuba, failed USA began military support of South Vietnam in Vietnam War Berlin wall constructed South Africa became a republic outside the Commonwealth	Gagarin orbited the earth in Soviet satellite Shepard made first US space flight The triplet basis of the genetic code discovered	Heller's *Catch 22* published Murdoch's *A Severed Head* published Spark's *The Prime of Miss Jean Brodie* published Truffaut's *Jules et Jim* screened Yevtushenko's *Babi Yar* published	1961
1962	Soviet Union sent arms to Cuba and installed missile base USA blockaded Cuba Soviet Union dismantled Cuban bases ending the Cuban Missile Crisis Algeria became independent with Ben Bella as prime minister Uganda and Tanganyika became independent US and Soviet Union signed agreement to cooperate in space Pope John XXIII convened the Second Vatican Council (to 1965)	US launched John Glenn into earth orbit Sea-floor spreading hypothesis formulated Telstar artificial satellite launched Josephson effect described Thalidomide identified as cause of deformed babies	Spence's Coventry Cathedral consecrated Albee's *Who's Afraid of Virginia Woolf?* acted Hochhuth's *The Representative* acted Warhol's *100 Soup Cans* exhibited Lessing's *The Golden Notebook* published Britten's *A War Requiem* performed Solzhenitsyn's *A Day in the Life of Ivan Denisovich* published Lean's *Lawrence of Arabia* screened	1962

Year	History	Science, Technology, and Exploration	Arts and Culture	Year
1963	Britain's application to join EEC rejected by de Gaulle (and again in 1967) US-Soviet "hot line" set up Nuclear Test Ban Treaty signed Kennedy assassinated: Johnson became US president Profumo, British war minister, resigned after lying to parliament about his relationship with Christine Keeler Kenya became independent.	Quarks discovered Soviet Union put Valentina Tereshkova into space—the first woman	Kubrick's *Dr Strangelove* screened "Beatlemania" in UK (and subsequently in USA) Plath's *The Bell Jar* published Friedan's *The Feminine Mystique* published Fellini's *8½* screened Lichtenstein's *Wham* painted Hitchcock's *The Birds* screened	1963
1964	Fighting between Greeks and Turks in Cyprus Zambia became independent under Kaunda Mandela sentenced to life imprisonment in South Africa China exploded its first atom bomb Civil Rights legislation in USA Brezhnev ousted Khrushchev in Soviet Union Wilson became Labour prime minister of UK	Cosmic microwave background discovered Word processors developed Aswan High Dam opened	Birmingham's Bull Ring completed Bellow's *Herzog* published Golding's *The Spire* published Larkin's *The Whitsun Weddings* published Schaffer's *Royal Hunt of the Sun* acted Britten's *Curlew River* performed	1964
1965	US air raids on North Vietnam began Revolution in Algeria deposed Ben Bella Rhodesia made unilateral declaration of independence (UDI): Britain imposed sanctions Military takeover in Indonesia Fighting between India and Pakistan over Kashmir	First spacewalks by both Soviet and US astronauts Mariner 4 flew past Mars sending back photographs Early Bird communication satellite launched	Plath's *Ariel* published posthumously London's Post Office Tower opened Mailer's *An American Dream* published Robbe-Grillet's *Pour un nouveau roman* published The Rolling Stones' "Satisfaction" released Dylan's *Highway 61 Revisited* released	1965
1966	Coup in Ghana removed Nkrumah Cultural Revolution in China began Indira Ghandi became prime minister of India	Soviet Union's Luna 9 and US Surveyor 1 made soft landings on moon Colour TV became widespread	Malamud's *The Fixer* published Heaney's *Death of a Naturalist* published Orton's *Loot* acted Buñuel's *Belle de jour* screened	1966
1967	Abortion and homosexuality legalized in the UK Six-Day War between Israel and Arab states left Jerusalem a united city under Israeli rule Biafran war began (to 1970) Che Guevara killed in Bolivia	Pulsars discovered Barnard performed first heart transplant Electroweak theory formulated	The Beatles' *Sergeant Pepper's Lonely Hearts Club Band* released Stoppard's *Rosencrantz and Guildenstern are Dead* acted Derrida's *Writing and Difference* published García Márquez's *One Hundred Years of Solitude* published	1967
1968	Martin Luther King assassinated in Memphis Robert Kennedy assassinated in Los Angeles Soviet Union invaded Czechoslovakia, crushing the "Prague Spring" Student riots in Paris	Mascons discovered on the moon Theory of plate tectonics became established	Stockhausen's *Stimmung* performed Kubrick's *2001: A Space Odyssey* screened Solzhenitsyn's *Cancer Ward* published	1968
1969	Violence between Catholics and Protestants in Northern Ireland: British troops sent to restore order De Gaulle resigned as French president Nixon became US president Gaddafi seized power in Libya	US Apollo II landed lunar module on moon: Armstrong and Aldrin became first men on moon Concorde made successful test flight Use of DDT banned in USA Open University founded in Britain	Nabokov's *Ada* published Roth's *Portnoy's Complaint* published Mailer's *Armies of the Night* published Messiaen's *Transfiguration* performed Shostakovich's 14th symphony performed Woodstock pop festival in USA	1969
1970	Biafra capitulated to federal Nigeria Assad came to power in Syria	Soviet Luna 16 brought back lunar material to earth Reverse transcriptase discovered First artificial gene synthesized Charm and string theory introduced in physics Major oil fields discovered in North Sea	Altman's *M*A*S*H* screened Greer's *The Female Eunuch* published Storey's *Home* acted Hughes' *Crow* published Fo's *Accidental Death of an Anarchist* acted	1970
1971	Internment without trial introduced in Northern Ireland Decimal currency introduced in UK Amin seized power in Uganda Bangladesh became an independent state Tidal wave in Bengal killed 10,000 people	US Mariner 9 orbited Mars Soviet Union landed unmanned capsule on Mars	Malamud's *The Tenants* published Visconti's *Death in Venice* screened Hockney's *Mr and Mrs Clark and Percy* painted Kubrick's *A Clockwork Orange* screened	1971
1972	US Watergate scandal began with arrests of intruders in headquarters of Democratic Party Escalating violence in Northern Ireland: direct rule from Westminster imposed 11 Israeli athletes killed at Munich Olympics by Palestinian terrorists Nixon visited China	Soviet Venus 8 made soft landing on Venus *Homo habilis* discovered Polaroid Land Camera and video cassette recorder introduced	Coppola's *The Godfather* screened Bertolucci's *Last Tango in Paris* screened	1972
1973	UK, Ireland, and Denmark joined the EC Vietnam peace agreement signed: US troops withdrawn Yom Kippur War between Arab states and Israel ended in unstable ceasefire Pinochet deposed Allende in Chilean coup Energy crisis and miners' strike in UK led to state of emergency and three-day week	US Skylab II enabled astronauts to spend 28 days in space CT scanner introduced		1973
1974	Democratic reform in Portugal began with Caetano's overthrow Nixon resigned US presidency under threat of impeachment for Watergate Cyprus invaded by Turks Northern Ireland Assembly and power-	CFCs discovered to deplete ozone layer US Air Force jet flew from New York to London in less than 56 minutes	Le Carré's *Tinker, Tailor, Soldier, Spy* published Larkin's *High Windows* published Gordimer's *The Conservationist* published	1974

Year	History	Science, Technology, and Exploration	Arts and Culture	Year
1974	sharing executive failed India exploded atom bomb			1974
1975	Vietnam War ended in victory for the North Monarchy restored in Spain after death of Franco Khmer Rouge took over Cambodia Civil war broke out in Lebanon Egypt reopened Suez Canal Angola and Mozambique became independent	USA and Soviet Union cooperated in docking their spacecrafts in orbit Milstein produced monoclonal antibodies	Heaney's *North* published Schaffer's *Equus* acted Boll's *The Lost Honour of Katharina Blum* published Forman's *One Flew Over the Cuckoo's Nest* screened Powell's *A Dance to the Music of Time* completed	1975
1976	North and South Vietnam reunited Rioting against apartheid in Soweto led to massacre of 100 Blacks: unrest spread to Johannesburg and Cape Town Civil war began in Angola Death of Mao Tse-tung led to power struggle in China Indonesia annexed East Timor	US Viking spacecraft landed on Mars and sent back photos 450 GeV Super proton synchrotron installed at CERN Concorde began commercial flights Legionnaire's disease diagnosed Dawkins' *The Selfish Gene* published	Bellow's *Humboldt's Gift* published Scorsese's *Taxi Driver* screened Stoppard's *Travesties* performed Ayckbourn's *The Norman Conquests* acted	1976
1977	Martial law declared in Pakistan Egypt's President Sadat made first visit of Arab leader to Israel Death of Biko in police custody in South Africa	Fairbank announced evidence for isolated quark US space shuttle *Enterprise* made first manned flight	Rogers and Piano's Pompidou Centre opened in Paris Allen's *Annie Hall* screened Grass' *The Flounder* published Lucas' *Star Wars* screened Punk rock in UK and USA	1977
1978	Begin and Sadat met President Carter at Camp David to draft peace treaty between Israel and Egypt Shah of Iran imposed martial law Ayatollah Khomeini in exile appealed for uprising to depose Shah Aldo Moro, former Italian premier, assassinated by Red Brigade John Paul II elected pope	Edwards and Steptoe produced first baby by fertilizing egg *in vitro* Moon of Pluto discovered	Murdoch's *The Sea, The Sea* published Solzhenitsyn's *Gulag Archipelago* completed Pinter's *Betrayal* acted Hare's *Plenty* acted	1978
1979	Islamic Revolution in Iran: Shah exiled and Khomeini became head of fundamentalist government Pol Pot regime deposed by Vietnamese invasion: mass graves of some three million victims of Khmer Rouge discovered Amin in Uganda overthrown Camp David Peace Treaty agreed but Egypt expelled from Arab League Soviet invasion of Afghanistan caused renewed East-West tension Thatcher became first woman prime minister of UK IRA bombs killed Earl Mountbatten and Airey Neave Sandinistas overthrew Somoza in Nicaragua	Nuclear accident at Three Mile Island in USA caused contamination	Coppola's *Apocalypse Now* screened Naipaul's *A Bend In the River* published Schaffer's *Amadeus* acted Tippett's *The Ice Break* performed Górecki's third symphony performed	1979
1980	Zimbabwe became independent Terrorists seized Iranian Embassy in London: SAS stormed building Solidarity movement began in Poland Iran-Iraq War began (to 1988)	WHO announced eradication of smallpox worldwide Pictures of Saturn's rings sent back to earth by Voyager 2	Golding's *Rites of Passage* published Burgess' *Earthly Powers* published Beckett's *Company* published Eco's *The Name of the Rose* published Scorsese's *Raging Bull* screened	1980
1981	Reagan became US president Mitterrand became president of France Greece joined EC Israel annexed Golan Heights, destroyed Iraqi nuclear plant Social Democratic Party formed in UK Sadat assassinated in Egypt Martial law imposed in Poland	AIDS first described Personal computers introduced by IBM	Rushdie's *Midnight's Children* published Updike's *Rabbit is Rich* published	1981
1982	Argentinian forces invaded Falkland Islands Thatcher sent task force that fought Falklands War and forced Argentinian surrender Israel returned Sinai to Egypt, invaded Lebanon Famine caused many deaths in Ethiopia Kohl became chancellor of West Germany	Soviet Venera 13 landed on Venus Oncogenes (causing cancer) discovered Dutch elm disease killed 20 million elm trees in Britain Tudor warship *Mary Rose* raised from seabed	Keneally's *Schindler's Ark* published Walker's *The Color Purple* published Attenborough's *Gandhi* screened Carter's *Nights at the Circus* published P. Levi's *If Not Now, When?* published Spielberg's *E.T.* screened	1982
1983	Deng Xiao Ping began to liberalize Chinese economy Fighting broke out in Sri Lanka between Sinhalese and Tamils Syria opposed peace treaty between Lebanon and Israel Cruise missiles installed at US base at Greenham Common in UK; women peace campaigners set up permanent picket Ethiopia appealed for help for its four million drought victims US troops invaded Grenada	France tested neutron bomb Compact discs launched	Mailer's *Ancient Evenings* published Coetzee's *Life and Times of Michael K* published M. Amis' *Money* published Wajda's *Danton* screened Bergman's *Fanny and Alexander* screened	1983
1984	Sikh extremists occupied Golden Temple in Amritsar, India; 250 killed when Indian army reoccupied Temple Indira Gandhi assassinated by her Sikh bodyguard as reprisal for the Golden	HIV identified as causative agent of AIDS Technique of genetic fingerprinting devised Thames flood barrier opened Royal Greenwich Observatory's Isaac	Brookner's *Hotel du Lac* published Kundera's *The Unbearable Lightness of Being* published Weldon's *The Life and Loves of a She Devil* published	1984

Year	History	Science, Technology, and Exploration	Arts and Culture	Year
1984	Temple killings Miners' strike began in UK (to 1985) Britain agreed to return Hong Kong to China in 1997 IRA bombed Grand Hotel, Brighton, during Conservative Party conference killing five people	Newton telescope moved from Herstmonceux to the Canary Islands	Mamet's *Glengarry Glen Ross* acted	1984
1985	UK and Ireland signed Anglo-Irish Agreement giving the Republic a consultative role in Northern Ireland Gorbachov became Soviet leader Italian cruise ship *Achille Lauro* hijacked by Palestinians	Hole discovered in ozone layer over Antarctica – thought to be due to CFCs All blood donors in UK screened for HIV Buckminsterfullerene (C_{60}) discovered Wreck of *Titanic* photographed on ocean bed	P. Levi's *The Periodic Table* published Lessing's *The Good Terrorist* published Live Aid rock concert raised $60 million for famine relief in Africa Kurosawa's *Ran* screened	1985
1986	Spain and Portugal joined EC Nuclear accident at Chernobyl in Soviet Union caused fallout over Europe USA bombed Libya in reprisal for terrorist incidents Liberalization of UK stock exchange ("Big Bang") Marcos deposed in the Philippines: C. Aquino became president	Voyager 2 flew by Uranus discovering 10 more moons Challenger space shuttle exploded on take-off killing 7 people Human Genome Project inaugurated	K. Amis' *The Old Devils* published Atwood's *The Handmaid's Tale* published Birtwistle's *The Mask of Orpheus* performed	1986
1987	Gorbachov introduced glasnost and perestroika in Soviet Union Intifada revolt by Palestinians in Israeli occupied territories IRA bomb at Eniskillin Remembrance Day parade killed 11 people Gorbachov and Reagan signed INF disarmament agreement	Superstring theory introduced Excavations for Channel Tunnel began	Drabble's *The Radiant Way* published Naipaul's *The Enigma of Arrival* published	1987
1988	Iran and Iraq accepted UN peace plan to end war B. Bhutto elected prime minister of Pakistan Strikes in Poland by Solidarity forced government to hold talks with Wałęsa Soviet troops began withdrawal from Afghanistan UK Liberal Party merged with Social Democrats US passenger plane destroyed by bomb over Lockerbie, Scotland, killing 270 people	Hawking's *A Brief History of Time* published Claim to have achieved cold nuclear fusion not supported	Rushdie's *The Satanic Verses* published Carey's *Oscar and Lucinda* published Hare's *The Secret Rapture* acted Davies' *Resurrection* performed Larkin's *Collected Poems* published posthumously	1988
1989	Khomeini announced fatwa on Rushdie for alleged blasphemy in Satanic Verses: UK protested and Rushdie went into hiding Berlin Wall demolished Communist regimes collapsed in Hungary, Poland, East Germany, Czechoslovakia, Bulgaria, and Romania Massacre of students in Tiananmen Square, Beijing De Klerk became president of South Africa	80 nations agreed to restrict production of CFCs owing to damage to ozone layer Cystic fibrosis gene located	Pei's glass pyramid erected in Louvre courtyard in Paris Ishiguro's *The Remains of the Day* published Kiéslowski's *Decalogue* series of TV films completed Tavener's *The Protecting Veil* performed	1989
1990	De Klerk lifted restrictions on ANC and released Mandela from prison Iraq invaded Kuwait and refused to comply with UN resolution demanding its withdrawal Thatcher failed to defeat Heseltine in leadership ballot and resigned: Major became prime minister East and West Germany reunited Cold War ended UK joined ERM	Hubble Space Telescope launched into space but fault in mirror limited its performance 18th moon of Saturn discovered	Byatt's *Possession* published Hare's *Racing Demon* acted Friel's *Dancing at Lughnasa* acted	1990
1991	Gulf War between US-led coalition and Iraq: Iraq defeated and Kuwait liberated but Saddam Hussein remained in power Attempted coup by antireformists in Soviet Union failed: led to end of Communist Party rule Soviet Union disintegrated: Yeltsin became President of Russian Federation Croatia and Slovenia broke away from Yugoslavia: invasions by Serb-led Yugoslav army resulted in civil war Warsaw Pact dissolved Presidents Bush and Yeltsin sign START disarmament agreement Rajiv Gandhi assassinated in India		Heaney's *Seeing Things* published Okri's *The Famished Road* published	1991
1992	Maastricht Treaty signed: EC became European Union (EU) Bosnia-Hercegovina declared independence: savage ethnic war broke out and Serb forces besieged Sarajevo Macedonia declared independence UK withdrew from ERM		Ondaatje's *The English Patient* published Morrison's *Jazz* published Mamet's *Oleanna* acted	1992
1993	Czechoslovakia split into the Czech Republic and Slovakia	NASA space shuttle launched to repair Hubble Space Telescope	R. S. Thomas' *Collected Poems* published Altman's *Short Cuts* screened	1993

Year	History	Science, Technology, and Exploration	Arts and Culture	Year
1993	Israel and the PLO signed peace accord Clinton became US president UK and Irish governments issued the Downing Street Declaration regarding Northern Ireland Eritrea became independent	Wiles claimed to have proved Fermat's last theorem (later making some changes to the proof)	Campion's *The Piano* screened Stoppard's *Arcadia* acted	1993
1994	IRA announced ceasefire (suspended 1995, resumed 1997) ANC won multiracial election in South Africa: Mandela became president Russia invaded rebel republic of Chechenia Genocide of Tutsis by Hutus in Rwanda	Channel Tunnel opened Yangtze dam project begun in China	Spielberg's *Schindler's List* screened Kiéslowski's *Three Colours* series of films completed Tarantino's *Pulp Fiction* screened	1994
1995	Wałęsa defeated in Polish presidential elections Chirac became French president Austria, Sweden, and Finland join EU Nigeria suspended from Commonwealth after hanging of Saro-Wiwa and others (to 1999) Peace agreement in Bosnia-Hercegovina Palestine National Authority established in Israeli occupied territories: Yitzhak Rabin assassinated	Global warming confirmed by panel on climate changes	M. Amis' *The Information* published Roth's *Sabbath's Theater* published	1995
1996	British beef banned worldwide after BSE outbreak Handguns banned in UK after massacre of children in Dunblane, Scotland Taleban militia gained control in Kabul Russian army forced to withdraw from Chechenia	Birth of Dolly, the sheep, the first animal to be cloned Link discovered between BSE and Creutzfeldt-Jakob disease in humans: agent believed to be a prion	A replica of Shakespeare's Globe Theatre opened in Southwark, London *Trainspotting* screened	1996
1997	Hong Kong became a special administrative area of China Death of Deng Xiao Ping in China Milošević became president of Yugoslavia (Serbia and Montenegro) Financial crisis throughout SE Asia Labour Party's electoral victory brought Tony Blair to power in UK after 18 years of Conservative rule Mobutu overthrown in Zaïre (Democratic Republic of Congo) Diana, Princess of Wales, widely mourned after death in car crash	US *Mars Pathfinder* made soft landing on Mars, releasing a 6-wheeled vehicle to explore the terrain World Wide Web in general use	Cameron's *Titanic* screened Hare's *Amy's View* acted Roth's *American Pastoral* published Hughes' *Tales from Ovid* published McEwan's *Enduring Love* published Gehry's Guggenheim Museum in Bilbao opened	1997
1998	Serbia sent troops to Kosovo to crush Albanian separatists UN Security Council voted to impose arms embargo on Yugoslavia to restrain Serbian violence in Kosovo Fall of Suharto in Indonesia Northern Ireland Peace terms agreed (Good Friday Agreement)	Hubble Space Telescope discovered planet orbiting Proxima Centauri Dolly, the cloned sheep, gave birth to normal female lamb	Hughes' *Birthday Letters* published Frayn's *Copenhagen* acted	1998
1999	Impeachment proceedings against Clinton for perjury failed NATO bombed Yugoslavia in attempt to stop "ethnic cleansing" by Serbs in Kosovo Some 1 600 000 Kosovo ethnic Albanians driven from their homes Elections to Scottish parliament and Welsh assembly took place Single European currency (the euro) launched (transition completed 2002) Yeltsin resigned: Putin became acting president of Russia (full president in 2000)		Coetzee's *Disgrace* published Mendes' *American Beauty* screened Spielberg's *Saving Private Ryan* screened Libeskind's Jewish Museum in Berlin opened	1999
2000	Russian troops reoccupied Chechenia Friendship agreement between North and South Korea signed Milošević overthrown in Yugoslavia Renewed violence in Israeli-occupied territories Disputed presidential election in US: Bush eventually declared victorious over Gore	First draft of map of the human genome completed (published in 2001) Øresund Bridge linking Denmark and Sweden completed	Tate Modern art gallery opened in London Rowling's *Harry Potter and the Goblet of Fire* became the fastest-selling book in publishing history Pullman's *His Dark Materials* trilogy completed	2000
2001	Bush became US president Massacre of the Nepalese royal family IRA began to put its weapons 'beyond use' September 11 terrorist attacks on New York and Washington US-led attack on Afghanistan to destroy al-Qaida and the Taleban		McEwan's *Atonement* published	2001
2002	Palestinian suicide bombings provoked Israel to reoccupy much of the West Bank East Timor became independent			2002

Prime Ministers of Great Britain (from 1721)

Name	Term	Name	Term	Name	Term
Robert Walpole	1721–42	George Canning	1827	Archibald Philip Primrose, Earl of Rosebery	1894–95
Spencer Compton, Earl of Wilmington	1742–43	Frederick John Robinson, Viscount Goderich	1827–28	Robert Gascoyne-Cecil, Marquis of Salisbury	1895–1902
Henry Pelham	1743–54	Arthur Wellesley, Duke of Wellington	1828–30		
Thomas Pelham-Holles, Duke of Newcastle	1754–56	Charles Grey, Earl Grey	1830–34	Arthur James Balfour	1902–05
William Cavendish, Duke of Devonshire	1756–57	William Lamb, Viscount Melbourne	1834	Henry Campbell-Bannerman	1905–08
		Robert Peel	1834–35	Herbert Henry Asquith	1908–16
Thomas Pelham-Holles, Duke of Newcastle	1757–62	William Lamb, Viscount Melbourne	1835–41	David Lloyd George	1916–22
		Robert Peel	1841–46	Andrew Bonar Law	1922–23
John Stuart, Earl of Bute	1762–63	John Russell	1846–52	Stanley Baldwin	1923–24
George Granville	1763–65	Edward George Geoffrey Smith Stanley, Earl of Derby	1852	James Ramsay MacDonald	1924
Charles Watson-Wentworth, Marquis of Rockingham	1765–66	George Hamilton Gordon, Earl of Aberdeen	1852–55	Stanley Baldwin	1924–29
				James Ramsay MacDonald	1929–35
William Pitt, Earl of Chatham	1766–68	Henry John Temple, Viscount Palmerston	1855–58	Stanley Baldwin	1935–37
Augustus Henry Fitzroy, Duke of Grafton	1768–70			Neville Chamberlain	1937–40
		Edward Stanley, Earl of Derby	1858–59	Winston Churchill	1940–45
Frederick North	1770–82	Henry Temple, Viscount Palmerston	1859–65	Clement Richard Attlee	1945–51
Charles Watson-Wentworth, Marquis of Rockingham	1782	John Russell, Earl Russell	1865–66	Winston Churchill	1951–55
William Petty, Earl of Shelburne	1782–83	Edward Stanley, Earl of Derby	1866–68	Anthony Eden	1955–57
William Henry Cavendish Bentinck, Duke of Portland	1783	Benjamin Disraeli	1868	Harold Macmillan	1957–63
		William Ewart Gladstone	1868–74	Alec Douglas-Home	1963–64
William Pitt (son of Earl of Chatham)	1783–1801	Benjamin Disraeli, Earl (1876) of Beaconsfield	1874–80	Harold Wilson	1964–70
Henry Addington	1801–04			Edward Heath	1970–74
William Pitt	1804–06	William Ewart Gladstone	1880–85	Harold Wilson	1974–76
William Wyndham Grenville, Baron Grenville	1806–07	Robert Gascoyne-Cecil, Marquis of Salisbury	1885–86	James Callaghan	1976–79
				Margaret Thatcher	1979–90
William Bentinck, Duke of Portland	1807–09	William Ewart Gladstone	1886	John Major	1990–97
Spencer Perceval	1809–12	Robert Gascoyne-Cecil, Marquis of Salisbury	1886–92	Tony Blair	1997–
Robert Banks Jenkinson, Earl of Liverpool	1812–27	William Ewart Gladstone	1892–94		

Prime Ministers of Australia

Name	Term	Name	Term	Name	Term
Edmund Barion	1901–03	Andrew Fisher	1914–15	Robert Gordon Menzies	1949–66
Alfred Deakin	1903–04	William M. Hughes	1915–23	Harold Edward Holt	1966–67
John C. Watson	1904	Stanley M. Bruce	1923–29	John Grey Gorton	1968–71
George Houstoun Reid	1904–05	James H. Scullin	1929–31	William McMahon	1971–72
Alfred Deakin	1905–08	Joseph A. Lyons	1932–39	Gough Whitlam	1972–75
Andrew Fisher	1908–09	Robert Gordon-Menzies	1939–41	J. Malcolm Fraser	1975–83
Alfred Deakin	1909–10	Arthur William Fadden	1941	Robert Hawke	1983–91
Andrew Fisher	1910–13	John Curtin	1941–45	Paul Keating	1991–96
Joseph Cook	1913–14	Joseph Benedict Chifley	1945–49	John Howard	1996–

Prime Ministers of Canada

Name	Term	Name	Term	Name	Term
John A. Macdonald	1867–73	Arthur Meighen	1920–21	Pierre Elliott Trudeau	1968–79
Alexander Mackenzie	1873–78	W. L. Mackenzie King	1921–26	Joseph Clark	1979–80
John A. Macdonald	1878–91	Arthur Meighen	1926	Pierre Elliott Trudeau	1980–84
John J. C. Abbott	1891–92	W. L. Mackenzie King	1926–30	John Turner	1984
John S. D. Thompson	1892–94	Richard B. Bennett	1930–35	Brian Mulroney	1984–93
Mackenzie Bowell	1894–96	W. L. Mackenzie King	1935–48	Kim Campbell	1993
Charles Tupper	1896	Louis Stephen St. Laurent	1948–57	Jean Chrétien	1993–
Wilfrid Laurier	1896–1911	John George Diefenbaker	1957–63		
Robert L. Borden	1911–20	Lester B. Pearson	1963–68		

Prime Ministers of New Zealand

Name	Term	Name	Term	Name	Term
Henry Sewell	1856	John Hall	1879–82	Michael J. Savage	1935–40
William Fox	1856	Frederick Whitaker	1882–83	Peter Fraser	1940–49
Edward William Stafford	1856–61	Harry Albert Atkinson	1883–84	Sidney G. Holland	1949–57
William Fox	1861–62	Robert Stout	1884	Walter Nash	1957–60
Alfred Domett	1862–63	Harry Albert Atkinson	1884	Keith J. Holyoake	1960–72
Frederick Whitaker	1863–64	Robert Stout	1884–87	John R. Marshall	1972
Frederick Aloysius Weld	1864–65	Harry Albert Atkinson	1887–91	Norman Kirk	1972–74
Edward William Stafford	1865–69	John Ballance	1891–93	Wallace Rowling	1974–75
William Fox	1869–72	Richard John Seddon	1893–1906	Robert D. Muldoon	1975–84
Edward William Stafford	1872	William Hall-Jones	1906	David Lange	1984–89
George Marsden Waterhouse	1872–73	Joseph George Ward	1906–12	Geoffrey Palmer	1989–90
William Fox	1873	Thomas Mackenzie	1912	Michael Moore	1990
Julius Vogel	1873–75	William Ferguson Massey	1912–25	James Bolger	1990–97
Daniel Pollen	1875–76	Francis Henry Dillon Bell	1925	Jenny Shipley	1997–99
Julius Vogel	1876	Joseph Gordon Coates	1925–28	Helen Clark	1999–
Harry Albert Atkinson	1876–77	Joseph George Ward	1928–30		
George Grey	1877–79	George William Forbes	1930–35		

Physics

1901	W. Roentgen (Ger)	1934	no award	1963	M. G. Mayer (USA)	1983	S. Chandrasekhar (USA)
1902	H. A. Lorentz (Neth)	1935	Sir J. Chadwick (UK)		E. P. Wigner (USA)		W. Fowler (USA)
	P. Zeeman (Neth)	1936	V. Hess (Austria)	1964	C. H. Townes (USA)	1984	C. Rubbia (It)
1903	A. Becquerel (Fr)		C. Anderson (USA)		N. G. Basov (USSR)		S. van der Meer (Neth)
	P. Curie (Fr)	1937	C. Davisson (USA)		A. M. Prokhorov (USSR)	1985	K. von Klitzing (Ger)
	M. Curie (Fr)		Sir G. P. Thomson (UK)	1965	J. S. Schwinger (USA)	1986	E. Ruska (Ger)
1904	Lord Rayleigh (UK)	1938	E. Fermi (It)		R. P. Feynman (USA)		G. Binnig (Ger)
1905	P. Lenard (Ger)	1939	E. Lawrence (USA)		S. Tomonaga (Jap)		H. Rohrer (Switz)
1906	Sir J. J. Thomson (UK)	1940	no award	1966	A. Kastler (Fr)	1987	A. Müller (Switz)
1907	A. A. Michelson (USA)	1941	no award	1967	H. A. Bethe (USA)		G. Bednorz (Ger)
1908	G. Lippmann (Fr)	1942	no award	1968	L. W. Alvarez (USA)	1988	L. M. Lederman (USA)
1909	G. Marconi (It)	1943	O. Stern (USA)	1969	M. Gell-Mann (USA)		M. Schwartz (USA)
	K. Braun (Ger)	1944	I. Rabi (USA)	1970	H. Alvén (Swed)		J. Steinberger (Ger)
1910	J. Van der Waals (Neth)	1945	W. Pauli (Austria)		L. Néel (Fr)	1989	H. Dehmelt (USA)
1911	W. Wien (Ger)	1946	P. Bridgman (USA)	1971	D. Gabor (UK)		W. Paulm (Ger)
1912	N. G. Dalen (Swed)	1947	Sir E. Appleton (UK)	1972	J. Bardeen (USA)		N. Ramsey (USA)
1913	H. Kamerlingh Onnes (Neth)	1948	P. Blackett (UK)		L. N. Cooper (USA)	1990	J. Friedman (USA)
		1949	H. Yukawa (Jap)		J. R. Schrieffer (USA)		H. Kendall (USA)
1914	M. von Laue (Ger)	1950	C. Powell (UK)	1973	L. Esaki (Jap)		R. Taylor (Can)
1915	Sir W. Bragg (UK)	1951	Sir J. Cockcroft (UK)		I. Giaever (USA)	1991	P. De Gennes (Fr)
	Sir L. Bragg (UK)		E. Walton (Ire)		B. Josephson (UK)	1992	G. Charpak
1916	no award	1952	F. Bloch (USA)	1974	Sir M. Ryle (UK)	1993	R. Hulse (USA)
1917	C. Barkla (UK)		E. Purcell (USA)		A. Hewish (UK)		J. Taylor (USA)
1918	M. Planck (Ger)	1953	F. Zernike (Neth)	1975	J. Rainwater (USA)	1994	B. Brockhouse (Can)
1919	J. Stark (Ger)	1954	M. Born (UK)		A. Bohr (Den)		C. Shull (USA)
1920	C. Guillaume (Swtz)		W. Bothe (Ger)		B. Mottelson (Den)	1995	M. Perl (USA)
1921	A. Einstein (Switz)	1955	W. Lamb, Jr. (USA)	1976	B. Richter (USA)		F. Reines (USA)
1922	N. Bohr (Den)		P. Kusch (USA)		S. Ting (USA)	1996	D. M. Lee (USA)
1923	R. Millikan (USA)	1956	W. Shockley (USA)	1977	P. W. Anderson (USA)		D. D. Oscherof (USA)
1924	K. Siegbahn (Swed)		J. Bardeen (USA)		Sir N. F. Mott (UK)		R. C. Richardson (USA)
1925	J. Franck (Ger)		W. Brattain (USA)		J. H. van Vleck (USA)	1997	S. Chu (USA)
	G. Hertz (Ger)	1957	T.-D. Lee (China)	1978	P. L. Kapitsa (USSR)	1998	R. B. Laughlin (USA)
1926	J. Perrin (Fr)		C. N. Yang (China)		A. A. Penzias (USA)		H. L. Störmer (Ger)
1927	A. H. Compton (USA)	1958	P. A. Cherenkov (USSR)		R. W. Wilson (USA)		D. C. Tsui (USA)
	C. Wilson (UK)		I. M. Frank (USSR)	1979	S. L. Glashow (USA)	1999	G. 't Hooft (Neth)
1928	Sir O. Richardson (UK)		I. Y. Tamm (USSR)		A. Salam (Pak)		M. J. G. Veltman (Neth)
1929	Prince L. de Broglie (Fr)	1959	E. Segrè (USA)		S. Weinberg (USA)	2000	Z. I. Alferov (Russia)
1930	Sir C. Raman (India)		O. Chamberlain (USA)	1980	J. Cronin (USA)		H. Kroemer(USA)
1931	no award	1960	D. Glaser (USA)		V. Fitch (USA)		J. S. Kilby (USA)
1932	W. Heisenberg (Ger)	1961	R. Hofstadter (USA)	1981	K. Siegbahn (Swed)	2001	E. A. Cornell (USA)
1933	P. A. M. Dirac (UK)		R. Mössbauer (Ger)		N. Bloembergen (USA)		C. E. Wieman (USA)
	E. Schrödinger (Austria)	1962	L. D. Landau (USSR)		A. Schawlow (USA)		W Ketterle (Ger/USA)
		1963	J. H. D. Jensen (Ger)	1982	K. G. Wilson (USA)		

Chemistry

1901	J. V. Hoff (Neth)	1934	H. Urey (USA)	1962	J. C. Kendrew (UK)	1985	H. Hauptman (USA)
1902	E. Fischer (Ger)	1935	F. Joliot-Curie (Fr)		M. F. Perutz (UK)		J. Karle (USA)
1903	S. Arrhenius (Swed)		I. Joliot-Curie (Fr)	1963	G. Natta (It)	1986	D. Herschbach (USA)
1904	Sir W. Ramsay (UK)	1936	P. Debye (Neth)		K. Ziegler (Ger)		Y. Tseh Lee (USA)
1905	A. von Baeyer (Ger)	1937	Sir W. Haworth (UK)	1964	D. M. C. Hodgkin (UK)		J. Polanyi (Can)
1906	H. Moissan (Fr)		P. Karrer (Switz)	1965	R. B. Woodward (USA)	1987	D. Cram (USA)
1907	E. Buchner (Ger)	1938	R. Kuhn (Ger)	1966	R. S. Mulliken (USA)		J. Lehn (Fr)
1908	Lord Rutherford (UK)	1939	A. Butenandt (Ger)	1967	M. Eigen (Ger)		C. Pedersen (USA)
1909	W. Ostwald (Ger)		L. Ruzicka (Switz)		R. G. W. Norrish (UK)	1988	J. Diesenhofer (Ger)
1910	O. Wallach (Ger)	1940	no award		G. Porter (UK)		R. Huber (Ger)
1911	M. Curie (Fr)	1941	no award	1968	L. Onsager (USA)		H. Michel (Ger)
1912	V. Grignard (Fr)	1942	no award	1969	D. H. R. Barton (UK)	1989	S. Altman (USA)
	P. Sabatier (Fr)	1943	G. de Hevesy (Hung)		O. Hassel (Nor)		T. Cech (USA)
1913	A. Werner (Switz)	1944	O. Hahn (Ger)	1970	L. F. Leloir (Arg)	1990	E. Cory (USA)
1914	T. Richards (USA)	1945	A. Virtanen (Fin)	1971	G. Herzberg (Can)	1991	R. Ernst (Switz)
1915	R. Willstätter (Ger)	1946	J. Sumner (USA)	1972	C. B. Anfinsen (USA)	1992	R. Marcus (Can)
1916	no award		J. Northrop (USA)		S. Moore (USA)	1993	K. Mullis (USA)
1917	no award		W. Stanley (USA)		W. H. Stein (USA)		M. Smith (USA)
1918	F. Haber (Ger)	1947	Sir R. Robinson (UK)	1973	E. Fischer (Ger)	1994	G. Olah (USA)
1919	no award	1948	A. Tiselius (Swed)		G. Wilkinson (UK)	1995	P. Crutzen (Neth)
1920	W. Nernst (Ger)	1949	W. Giauque (USA)	1974	P. J. Flory (USA)		M. Molina (Mex)
1921	F. Soddy (UK)	1950	O. Diels (Ger)	1975	J. W. Cornforth (Austral)		F. Rowland (USA)
1922	F. Aston (UK)		K. Alder (Ger)			1996	Sir H. Kroto (UK)
1923	F. Pregl (Austria)	1951	E. McMillan (USA)		V. Prelog (Switz)		R. Curl (USA)
1924	no award		G. Seaborg (USA)	1976	W. M. Lipscomb (USA)		R. Smalley (USA)
1925	R. Zsigmondy (Austria)	1952	A. Martin (UK)	1977	I. Prigogine (Belg)	1997	P. D. Boyer (USA)
1926	T. Svedberg (Swed)		R. Synge (UK)	1978	P. Mitchell (UK)		J. C. Skou (Den)
1927	H. Wieland (Ger)	1953	H. Staudinger (Ger)	1979	H. C. Brown (USA)		J. E. Walker (UK)
1928	A. Windaus (Ger)	1954	L. C. Pauling (USA)		G. Wittig (Ger)	1998	W. Kohn (USA)
1929	Sir A. Harden (UK)	1955	V. du Vigneaud (USA)	1980	P. Berg (USA)		J. A. Pope (UK)
	H. von Euler-Chelpin (Swed)	1956	N. Semyonov (USSR)		W. Gilbert (USA)	1999	A. H. Zewail (Egypt\USA)
			Sir C. Hinshelwood (UK)		F. Sanger (UK)	2000	A. J. Heeger (USA)
1930	H. Fischer (Ger)	1957	Sir A. Todd (UK)	1981	K. Fukui (Jap)		A. G. MacDiarmid (USA)
1931	K. Bosch (Ger)	1958	F. Sanger (UK)		R. Hoffmann (Pol)		Hideki Shirakawa (Japan)
	F. Bergius (Ger)	1959	J. Heyrovsky (Czech)	1982	A. Klug (UK)	2001	W. S. Knowles (USA)
1932	I. Langmuir (USA)	1960	W. Libby (USA)	1983	H. Taube (USA)		Ryoji Noyori (Jap)
1933	no award	1961	M. Calvin (USA)	1984	R. B. Merrifield (USA)		K. B. Sharpless (USA)

Physiology or Medicine

1901	E. von Behring (Ger)	1938	C. Heymans (Belg)	1963	Sir J. C. Eccles (Aus-tral)	1981	R. Sperry (USA)
1902	Sir R. Ross (UK)	1939	G. Domagk (Ger)		A. L. Hodgkin (UK)		D. Hubel (USA)
1903	N. R. Finsen (Den)	1940	no award		A. F. Huxley (UK)		T. Wiesel (Swed)
1904	I. Pavlov (Russia)	1941	no award	1964	K. Bloch (USA)	1982	S. K. Bergstrom (Swed)
1905	R. Koch (Ger)	1942	no award		F. Lynen (Ger)		B. I. Samuelson (Swed)
1906	C. Golgi (It)	1943	H. Dam (Den)	1965	F. Jacob (Fr)		J. R. Vane (UK)
	S. Ramón y Cajal (Sp)		E. A. Doisy (USA)		A. Lwoff (Fr)	1983	B. McClintock (USA)
1907	A. Laveran (Fr)	1944	J. Erlanger (USA)		J. Monod (Fr)	1984	N. K. Jerne (Den)
1908	P. Ehrlich (Ger)		H. S. Gasser (USA)	1966	C. B. Huggins (USA)		G. J. F. Köhler (Ger)
	I. Metchnikov (Russia)	1945	Sir A. Fleming (UK)		F. P. Rous (USA)		C. Milstein (UK)
1909	E. Kocher (Switz)		E. B. Chain (UK)	1967	H. K. Hartline (USA)	1985	J. Goldstein (USA)
1910	A. Kossel (Ger)		Lord Florey		G. Wald (USA)		M. Brown (USA)
1911	A. Gullstrand (Swed)		(Austral)		R. A. Granit (Swed)	1986	S. Cohen (USA)
1912	A. Carrel (Fr)	1946	H. J. Muller (USA)	1968	R. W. Holley (USA)		R. Levi-Montalcini (It)
1913	C. Richet (Fr)	1947	C. F. Cori (USA)		H. G. Khorana (USA)	1987	S. Tonegawa (Jap)
1914	R. Bárány (Austria)		G. T. Cori (USA)		M. W. Nirenberg (USA)	1988	J. W. Black (UK)
1915	no award		B. Houssay (Arg)	1969	M. Delbrück (USA)		G. B. Elion (USA)
1916	no award	1948	P. Müller (Switz)		A. D. Hershey (USA)		G. H. Hitchings (USA)
1917	no award	1949	W. R. Hess (Switz)		S. E. Luria (USA)	1989	M. Bishop (USA)
1918	no award		A. E. Moniz (Port)	1970	J. Axelrod (USA)		H. Varmus (USA)
1919	J. Bordet (Belg)	1950	P. S. Hench (USA)		Sir B. Katz (UK)	1990	J. Murray (USA)
1920	A. Krogh (Den)		E. C. Kendall (USA)		U. von Euler (Swed)		E. Thomas (USA)
1921	no award		T. Reichstein (Switz)	1971	E. W. Sutherland, Jr. (USA)	1991	E. Neher (Ger)
1922	A. V. Hill (UK)	1951	M. Theiler (S Af)	1972	G. M. Edelman (USA)		B. Sakmann (Ger)
	O. Meyerhof (Ger)	1952	S. A. Waksman (USA)		R. R. Porter (UK)	1992	E. Fischer (USA)
1923	Sir F. G. Banting (Can)	1953	F. A. Lipmann (USA)	1973	K. von Frisch (Ger)		E. Krebs (USA)
	J. J. R. Macleod (UK)		Sir H. A. Krebs (UK)		K. Lorenz (Ger)	1993	R. Roberts (USA)
1924	W. Einthoven (Neth)	1954	J. F. Enders (USA)		N. Tinbergen (Neth)		P. Sharp (USA)
1925	no award		T. H. Weller (USA)	1974	A. Claude (USA)	1994	A. Gilman (USA)
1926	J. Fibiger (Den)		F. Robbins (USA)		C. de Duve (Belg)		M. Rodbell (USA)
1927	J. Wagner von Jauregg	1955	A. H. Theorell (Swed)		G. E. Palade (Belg)	1995	E. Lewis (USA)
	(Austria)	1956	W. Forssmann (Ger)	1975	D. Baltimore (USA)		C. Nüsslein-Volhard
1928	C. Nicolle (Fr)		D. Richards (USA)		R. Dulbecco (USA)		(Ger)
1929	C. Eijkman (Neth)		A. F. Cournand (USA)		H. M. Temin (USA)		E. Wieschaus (USA)
	Sir F. Hopkins (UK)	1957	D. Bovet (It)	1976	B. S. Blumberg (USA)	1996	P. Doherty (Austral)
1930	K. Landsteiner (USA)	1958	G. W. Beadle (USA)		D. G. Gajdusek (USA)		R. Zinkernagel (Switz)
1931	O. Warburg (Ger)		E. L. Tatum (USA)	1977	R. S. Yalow (USA)	1997	S. B. Prusiner (USA)
1932	E. D. Adrian (UK)		J. Lederberg (USA)		R. Guillemin (USA)	1998	R. F. Furchgott (USA)
	Sir C. Sherrington (UK)	1959	S. Ochoa (USA)		A. V. Schally (USA)		L. J. Ignarro (USA)
1933	T. H. Morgan (USA)		A. Kornberg (USA)	1978	W. Arber (Switz)		F. Murad (USA)
1934	G. R. Minot (USA)	1960	Sir F. M. Burnet		D. Nathans (USA)	1999	G. Blobel (USA)
	W. P. Murphy (USA)		(Austral)		H. Smith (USA)	2000	A. Carlsson (Sweden)
	G. H. Whipple (USA)		P. B. Medawar (UK)	1979	A. M. Cormack (USA)		P. Greengard (USA)
1935	H. Spemann (Ger)	1961	G. von Békésy (USA)		G. N. Hounsfield (UK)		E. Kandel (USA)
1936	Sir H. H. Dale (UK)	1962	F. H. C. Crick (UK)	1980	G. Snell (USA)	2001	L. H. Hartwell (USA)
1936	O. Loewi (Ger)		J. D. Watson (USA)		J. Dausset (Fr)		P. M. Nurse (UK)
1937	A. Szent-Györgyi (Hung)	1962	M. Wilkins (UK)		B. Benacerraf (USA)		R. T. Hunt (UK)

Literature

1901	S. Prudhomme (Fr)	1924	W. S. Reymont (Pol)	1952	F. Mauriac (Fr)	1976	S. Bellow (USA)
1902	T. Mommsen (Ger)	1925	G. B. Shaw (Ire)	1953	Sir W. S. Churchill (UK)	1977	V. Aleixandre (Sp)
1903	B. Bjørnson (Nor)	1926	G. Deledda (It)	1954	E. Hemingway (USA)	1978	I. B. Singer (USA)
1904	F. Mistral (Fr)	1927	H. Bergson (Fr)	1955	H. K. Laxness (Ice)	1979	O. Elytis (Greece)
	J. Echegaray y	1928	S. Undset (Nor)	1956	J. R. Jiménez (Sp)	1980	C. Miłosz (USA)
	Eizaguirre (Sp)	1929	T. Mann (Ger)	1957	A. Camus (Fr)	1981	E. Canetti (Bulg)
1905	H. Sienkiewicz (Pol)	1930	S. Lewis (USA)	1958	B. L. Pasternak (declined	1982	G. García Márquez (Colombia)
1906	G. Carducci (It)	1931	E. A. Karlfeldt (Swed)		award) (USSR)	1983	W. Golding (UK)
1907	R. Kipling (UK)	1932	J. Galsworthy (UK)	1959	S. Quasimodo (It)	1984	J. Seifert (Czech)
1908	R. Eucken (Ger)	1933	I. Bunin (USSR)	1960	S-J. Perse (Fr)	1985	C. Simon (Fr)
1909	S. Lagerlöf (Swed)	1934	L. Pirandello (It)	1961	I. Andrić (Yugos)	1986	W. Soyinka (Nigeria)
1910	P. von Heyse (Ger)	1935	no award	1962	J. Steinbeck (USA)	1987	J. Brodsky (USA)
1911	M. Maeterlinck (Belg)	1936	E. O'Neill (USA)	1963	G. Seferis (Greece)	1988	N. Mahfouz (Egypt)
1912	G. Hauptmann (Ger)	1937	R. M. du Gard (Fr)	1964	J. P. Sartre (declined	1989	C. J. Cela (Sp)
1913	Sir R. Tagore (India)	1938	P. Buck (USA)		award) (Fr)	1990	O. Paz (Mex)
1914	no award	1939	F. E. Sillanpää (Fin)	1965	M. Sholokhov (USSR)	1991	N. Gordimer (S Af)
1915	R. Rolland (Fr)	1940	no award	1966	S. Y. Agnon (Isr)	1992	D. Walcott (St Lucia)
1916	V. von Heidenstam	1941	no award		N. Sachs (Swed)	1993	T. Morrison (USA)
	(Swed)	1942	no award	1967	M. A. Asturias (Guat)	1994	K. Oë (Jap)
1917	K. Gjellerup (Den)	1943	no award	1968	K. Yasunari (Jap)	1995	S. Heaney (Ire)
	H. Pontoppidan (Den)	1944	J. V. Jensen (Den)	1969	S. Beckett (Ire)	1996	W. Szymborska (Pol)
1918	no award	1945	G. Mistral (Chile)	1970	A. I. Solzhenitsyn (USSR)	1997	D. Fo (It)
1919	C. Spitteler (Switz)	1946	H. Hesse (Switz)	1971	P. Neruda (Chile)	1998	J. Saramago (Port)
1920	K. Hamsun (Nor)	1947	A. Gide (Fr)	1972	H. Böll (Ger)	1999	G. Grass (Ger)
1921	A. France (Fr)	1948	T. S. Eliot (UK)	1973	P. White (Austral)	2000	Gao Xingjian (China)
1922	J. Benavente y Martinez	1949	W. Faulkner (USA)	1974	E. Johnson (Swed)	2001	V. S. Naipaul (UK/born
	(Sp)	1950	B. Russell (UK)		H. Martinson (Swed)		Trinidad)
1923	W. B. Yeats (Ire)	1951	P. F. Lagerkvist (Swed)	1975	E. Montale (It)		

Peace

1901	J. H. Dunant (Switz)	1928	no award	1957	L. B. Pearson (Can)	1984	Bishop D. Tutu (S Af)
	F. Passy (Fr)	1929	F. B. Kellogg (USA)	1958	D. G. Pire (Belg)	1985	International Physicians
1902	E. Ducommun (Switz)	1930	N. Söderblom (Swed)	1959	P. J. Noel-Baker (UK)		for the Prevention of
	C. A. Gobat (Switz)	1931	J. Addams (USA)	1960	A. J. Luthuli (S Af)		Nuclear War
1903	Sir W. Cremer (UK)		N. M. Butler (USA)	1961	D. Hammarskjöld (Swed)	1986	E. Wiesel (USA)
1904	Institute of International	1932	no award	1962	L. C. Pauling (USA)	1987	O. Arias Sánchez
	Law	1933	Sir N. Angell (UK)	1963	International Red Cross		(Costa Rica)
1905	Baroness Von Suttner	1934	A. Henderson (UK)		Committee	1988	The United Nations
	(Austria)	1935	C. von Ossietzky (Ger)		League of Red Cross		peacekeeping forces
1906	T. Roosevelt (USA)	1936	C. S. Lamas (Arg)		Societies (Geneva)	1989	Dalai Lama (Tibet)
1907	E. Teodoro Moneta (It)	1937	Viscount Cecil of	1964	M. L. King, Jr. (USA)	1990	M. S. Gorbachov (Russia)
	L. Renault (Fr)		Chelwood (UK)	1965	United Nations	1991	A. San Suu Kyi (Burma)
1908	K. P. Arnoldson (Swed)	1938	Nansen International		Children's Fund	1992	R. Menchu (Guat)
1909	Baron d'Estournelles de		Office for Refugees	1966	no award	1993	F. W. de Klerk (S Af)
	Constant (Fr)	1939	no award	1967	no award		N. Mandela (S Af)
	A. Beernaert (Belg)	1940	no award	1968	R. Cassin (Fr)	1994	Y. Arafat (Palestine)
1910	International Peace	1941	no award	1969	International Labour		S. Peres (Isr)
	Bureau	1942	no award		Organization		Y. Rabin (Isr)
1911	T. Asser (Neth)	1943	no award	1970	N. E. Borlaug (USA)	1995	J. Rotblat (UK)
	A. Fried (Austria)	1944	International Red Cross	1971	W. Brandt (Ger)	1996	J. Ramos-Horta (E Timor)
1912	E. Root (USA)		Committee	1972	no award		C. Belo (E Timor)
1913	H. Lafontaine (Belg)	1945	C. Hull (USA)	1973	H. Kissinger (USA)	1997	The International
1914	no award	1946	E. G. Balch (USA)		Le Duc Tho (declined		Campaign to Ban
1915	no award		J. R. Mott (USA)		award) (N Viet)		Landmines (headed by
1916	no award	1947	American Friends'	1974	S. MacBride (Ire)		J. Williams, a co-
1917	International Red Cross		Service Committee		E. Sato (Jap)		recipient of the prize)
	Committee		(USA)	1975	A. S. Sakharov (USSR)	1998	J. Hume (N Ire)
1918	no award		Friends' Service Council	1976	B. Williams (N Ire)		D. Trimble (N Ire)
1919	W. Wilson (USA)		(London)		M. Corrigan (N Ire)	1999	Médicins sans Frontières
1920	L. Bourgeois (Fr)	1948	no award	1977	Amnesty International	2000	Kim Dae Jung (S Korea)
1921	K. Branting (Swed)	1949	Lord Boyd-Orr (UK)	1978	A. Sadat (Egypt)	2001	United Nations and
	C. L. Lange (Nor)	1950	R. Bunche (USA)		M. Begin (Isr)		Kofi Annan (Ghana)
1922	F. Nansen (Nor)	1951	L. Jouhaux (Fr)	1979	Mother Teresa (Yugos)		
1923	no award	1952	A. Schweitzer (Fr)	1980	A. P. Esquivel (Arg)		
1924	no award	1953	G. C. Marshall (USA)	1981	Office of the United		
1925	Sir A. Chamberlain (UK)	1954	Office of the United		Nations High		
	C. G. Dawes (USA)		Nations High		Commission for		
1926	A. Briand (Fr)		Commission for		Refugees		
1926	G. Stresemann (Ger)		Refugees	1982	A. Garcia Robles (Mex)		
1927	F. Buisson (Fr)	1955	no award		A. Myrdal (Swed)		
	L. Quidde (Ger)	1956	no award	1983	L. Wałęsa (Pol)		

Economics

1969	R. Frisch (Nor)	1978	H. A. Simon (USA)	1990	H. Markowitz (USA)	1997	R. C. Merton (USA)
	J. Tinbergen (Neth)	1979	T. W. Schultz (USA)		W. F. Sharpe (USA)		M. S. Scholes (USA)
1970	P. A. Samuelson (USA)		A. Lewis (UK)		M. Miller (USA)	1998	A. Sen (India)
1971	S. Kuznets (USA)	1980	L. R. Klein (USA)	1991	R. H. Coase (UK)	1999	R. A. Mundell (Can)
1972	R. Hicks (UK)	1981	J. Tobin (USA)	1992	G. S. Becker (USA)	2000	J. J. Heckman (USA)
	K. J. Arrow (USA)	1982	G. J. Stigler (USA)	1993	R. Fogel (USA)		D. L. McFadden (USA)
1973	W. Leontief (USA)	1983	G. Debreu (USA)	1993	D. North (USA)	2001	G. A. Akerlof (USA)
1974	G. Myrdal (Swed)	1984	R. Stone (UK)	1994	J. Harsanyi (USA)		A. M. Spence (USA)
	F. A. von Hayek (UK)	1985	F. Modigliani (USA)		J. Nash (USA)		J. E. Stiglitz (USA)
1975	L. Kantorovich (USSR)	1986	J. M. Buchanan, Jr. (USA)		R. Selton (Ger)		
	T. C. Koopmans (USA)	1987	R. M. Solow (USA)	1995	R. Lucas (USA)		
1976	M. Friedman (USA)	1988	M. Allais (Fr)	1996	J. Mirrlees (UK)		
1977	B. Ohlin (Swed)	1989	T. Haavelmo (Nor)		W. Vickrey (Can)		
	J. E. Meade (UK)						

Units of Measurement

SI units (Système International d'Unités) are now widely used throughout the world, especially for scientific purposes. SI units are metric units, based on the metre, kilogram, and second.

The base units are:

physical quantity	SI unit	symbol
length	metre	m
mass	kilogram	kg
time	second	s
electric current	ampere	A
thermodynamic temperature	kelvin	K
luminous intensity	candela	cd
amount of substance	mole	mol
plane angle (supplementary unit)	radian	rad
solid angle (supplementary unit)	steradian	sr

The derived units with special names are:

physical quantity	SI unit	symbol
frequency	hertz	Hz
energy	joule	J
force	newton	N
power	watt	W
pressure	pascal	Pa
electric charge	coulomb	C
electric potential difference	volt	V
electric resistance	ohm	W
electric conductance	siemens	S
electric capacitance	farad	F
magnetic flux	weber	Wb
inductance	henry	H
magnetic flux density (magnetic induction)	tesla	T
luminous flux	lumen	lm
illuminance	lux	lx
absorbed dose	gray	Gy
activity	becquerel	Bq
dose equivalent	sievert	Sv

SI units are used in decimal mutliples, e.g. 1 km = 1000 metres, often written $10^3 = (1 \times 10^3 = 10 \times 10 \times 10 = 1000)$; 1 cm = 1/100 of a metre, often written 10^{-2} m $(1 \times 10^{-2} = 1 \div (10 \times 10) = 1/100)$. The following prefixes are used:

submultiple	prefix	symbol	multiple	prefix	symbol
10^{-1}	deci-	d	10	deca-	da
10^{-2}	cent-	c	10^2	hecto-	h
10^{-3}	milli-	m	10^3	kilo-	k
10^{-6}	micro-	m	10^6	mega-	M
10^{-9}	nano-	n	10^9	giga-	G
10^{-12}	pico-	p	10^{12}	tera-	T
10^{-15}	femto-	f	10^{15}	peta-	P
10^{-18}	atto-	a	10^{18}	exa-	E
10^{-21}	zepto-	z	10^{21}	zetta-	Z
10^{-24}	yocto-	y	10^{24}	yotta-	Y

These prefixes are used with all SI units.

length
SI base unit: metre
Imperial units: inch, foot, yard, mile

1 cm = 0.3937 in	1 in = 2.54 cm
1 m = 3.2808 ft = 1.09361 yds	1 ft = 0.3048 m
1 km = 0.62137 mile	1 mile = 1.60934 km

Examples
The radius of an electron is about 3 femtometres $(3 \times 10^{-15}$ m).
The distance between the sun and its nearest neighbour (Proxima Centauri) is about 40 petametres $(4 \times 10^{16}$ m).

mass
SI base unit: kilogram
Imperial units: ounce, pound, ton

1 g = 0.03527 oz	1 oz = 28.3495 g
1 kg = 2.20462 lb	1 lb = 0.45359 kg
1 tonne = (1000 kg) = 0.9842 ton	1 ton = 1.01605 tonnes

Examples
The mass of a carbon atom is about 2 hundredths of a zeptogram (2×10^{-23}).
The mass of the earth is about six thousand yottagrams $(6 \times 10^{27}$ g).

time
SI base unit: second
Other units: minute, hour, day, year

Examples
The time between collisions of oxygen molecules at 0°C (760mmHg) is about 0.2 nanosecond $(2 \times 10^{-10}$ s).
The earth is about 145 petasecond $(1.45 \times 10^{17}$ s) old.

temperature
SI base unit: kelvin
Other units: degree Celsius (centigrade), degree Fahrenheit
    1 kelvin = 1°C
    1 kelvin = 1.8°F

Examples
Absolute zero is a temperature of 0 kelvin.
The temperature inside the hottest stars is about 1 gigakelvin $(10^9$ K).

energy
SI unit: joule (J)
Other units: calorie, British thermal unit

1 joule = 0.2388 cal	1 cal = 4.1868 joules
1000 joules = 0.9478 Btu	1 Btu = 1055.06 joules

Examples
The energy released by a single disintegrating uranium atom is 40 picojoules $(4 \times 10^{-11}$ J).
The Hiroshima atom bomb released 84 terajoules $(8.4 \times 10^{13}$ J).

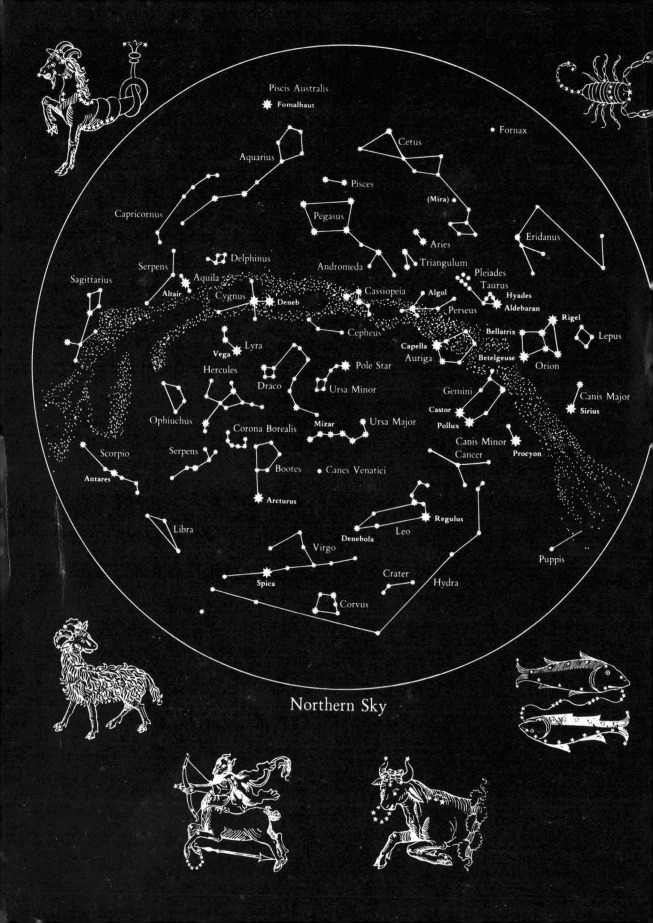

Piscis Australis
★ Fomalhaut

Cetus

Fornax

Aquarius

Pisces

Capricornus

Pegasus

(Mira) ✴

Aries

Eridanus

Serpens

Delphinus

Andromeda

Triangulum

Sagittarius

Aquila

Altair

Cygnus

Deneb

Cassiopeia

Cepheus

Algol

Perseus

Pleiades
Taurus

Hyades
Aldebaran

Rigel

Lepus

Bellatrix

Capella
Auriga

Betelgeuse

Orion

Lyra

Vega

Pole Star

Gemini

Canis Major

Sirius

Hercules

Draco

Ursa Minor

Castor

Pollux

Ophiuchus

Corona Borealis

Mizar

Ursa Major

Canis Minor
Cancer

Procyon

Scorpio

Serpens

Bootes

Canes Venatici

Antares

Arcturus

Regulus

Libra

Leo

Virgo

Denebola

Puppis

Spica

Crater

Hydra

Corvus

Northern Sky